Fashn	fashion	时装
Fin	finance	金融
Fishg	fishing	渔业
Games	games	游戏
Geog	geography	地理
Geol	geology	地质
Geom	geometry	几何
Herald	heraldry	纹章
Hist	history	历史
Horse racing	horse racing	赛马
Hort	horticulture	园艺
Hunt	hunting	狩猎
Ind	industry, manufacturing	工业、制造业
Insur	insurance	保险
Journ	journalism	新闻
Jur	law	法律
Ling	linguistics	语言学
Literat	literature	文学
Math	mathematics	数学
Meas	measurement, unit of	度量衡
Metall	metallurgy	冶金
Mech	mechanics	机械
Med	medicine	医学
Meteorol	meteorology	气象
Mgmt	management	管理
Mil	military	军事
Miner	mineralogy	矿物学
Mining	mining	矿业
Motor racing	motor racing	赛车
Mus	music	音乐
Mythol	mythology	神话
Naut	nautical	航海
Nucl	nuclear physics	核物理
Optics	optics	光学
Pharm	pharmacology	药理学
Philos	philosophy	哲学
Phon	phonetics	语音学
Phot	photography	摄影
Phys	physics	物理
Physiol	physiology	生理
Pol	politics	政治
Police	police	警务用语
Post	postal services	邮政
Print	printing	印刷
Psych	psychology	心理学
Publg	publishing	出版
Radio	radio	无线电
Rail	railways	铁路
Relig	religion	宗教
Sch	school	学校
Sci	science	科学
Sewing	sewing	缝纫
Soc Admin	social security, welfare	社会保障
Sociol	sociology	社会学
Sport	sport	体育
Stat	statistics	统计
Tax	taxation	税务
Tech	technology, technical	科技
Telecom	telecommunications	电信
Tex	textiles	纺织
Theat	theatre	戏剧
Tourism	tourism	旅游
Transp	transport	交通
TV	television	电视
Univ	university	大学
Vet	veterinary medicine	兽医
Video	video	录像
Wine	wine-making, -tasting etc.	酒业
Zool	zoology	动物学

Register labels 语体标签

archaic	archaic	古词或古义
child lang	child language	儿语
colloq	colloquial	口语
dial	dialect	方言
dated	dated	旧词
euph	euphemistic	委婉语
fig	figurative	比喻或比喻义
formal	formal	正式用语
hum	humorous	诙谐语
iron	ironical	反语
lit	literal	本义
liter	literary	书面语
offensive	offensive	冒犯语
pej	pejorative	贬义
Prov	proverb	谚语
sl	slang	俚语
taboo sl	taboo slang	忌讳语

* **Proprietary** [illegible] which are, or are asse[illegible] eir inclusion does not in[illegible] non-proprietary [illegible] ent implied concerning [illegible] e some evidence tha[illegible] mark this is indicated [illegible] the legal status of suc[illegible]

* **专有名称** 本[illegible]词汇中有一些是专有或据称为专有的商标名。这些名称的收录并不表明其已在法律意义上获得非专有或通用意义，也不暗示对其法律地位的其他任何裁断。编辑人员有证据认定某词汇作为专有商标使用时，以符号 ® 标示，但不表示对其法律地位作出判断或暗示。

e Oxford Chinese Dictionary
牛津英汉汉英词典

The Oxford Chinese Dictionary

English-Chinese • Chinese-English

Chief Editors

Julie Kleeman • Harry Yu

外语教学与研究出版社

FOREIGN LANGUAGE TEACHING AND RESEARCH PRESS

牛津英汉汉英词典

英汉・汉英

主 编

Julie Kleeman・于海江

外语教学与研究出版社
FOREIGN LANGUAGE TEACHING AND RESEARCH PRESS

OXFORD
UNIVERSITY PRESS

Great Clarendon Street, Oxford OX2 6DP

Oxford University Press is a department of the University of Oxford.
It furthers the University's objective of excellence in research, scholarship,
and education by publishing worldwide in

Oxford New York

Auckland Cape Town Dar es Salaam Hong Kong Karachi
Kuala Lumpur Madrid Melbourne Mexico City Nairobi
New Delhi Shanghai Taipei Toronto

With offices in

Argentina Austria Brazil Chile Czech Republic France Greece
Guatemala Hungary Italy Japan Poland Portugal Singapore
South Korea Switzerland Thailand Turkey Ukraine Vietnam

Published in the United States
by Oxford University Press Inc., New York

First published 2010

The Chinese-English source text is adapted from
the New Century Chinese-English Dictionary,
published by Foreign Language Teaching and Research Press

British Library Cataloguing in Publication Data
Data available

Library of Congress Cataloging in Publication Data
Data available

Typeset by Oxford University Press (China) Ltd.
Printed in China by C&C Offset Printing Co., Ltd.

ISBN 978-0-19-920761-9

10 9 8 7 6 5 4 3 2 1

Contents
目录

List of contributors
编写人员名单

Chief Editors 主编

Julie Kleeman
Harry Yu 于海江

Project Management 项目管理

Michael Clark
Lau Yung Keung 刘勇强
Yao Hong 姚虹

Senior Editors 高级编辑

Benny Chan 陈文浩
Shen Wei 申葳

Project Administrator 项目统筹

Patience Zhou 周颖

Revising Editors 审校

Li Yun 李云
Tang Hui 唐辉
Xia Tian 夏天
Windy Wong 黄雪孟
Cathy Wang 汪纯子
Jason Chu 朱绩崧
Hommy Zhang 张浩渺
Dawn Chow 周晓彤
Natalie Lui 吕寡人
Elisabeth Hallett
Diana Kingsbury
David Tugwell
Roy Russell

Finalizers 定稿

Yao Xiaoping 姚小平
Chen Dezhang 陈德彰
Li Ming 李明
Zhao Cuilian 赵翠莲

Editors 编纂人员

Sheng Jiuchou 盛九畴
Shirley Xie 谢曦
Zeng Yan 曾艳
Zhao Genzong 赵根宗
Ma Lanmei 马兰梅
Zou Xiaoling 邹晓玲
Su Bo 苏擘
Zhang Ligang 张立刚
Wang Yuzhang 王玉章
Christopher Allen
Susan Wilkin
Joanna Rubery
Aventurina King
Anne McConnell
Lesley Brown
Donald Watt
Susan Chan
Bernadette Mohan
Louise Manners
Yuen Chan
Jennifer Eagleton
Rachel Silberstein
John Steinhardt

Translators 翻译

Hua Suyang 华苏扬
Yan Hongmei 闫红梅
Zhang Yibei 张轶蓓
Ma Hongqi 马红旗
Zhao Weitao 赵伟韬
Hu Yang 胡阳
Zhou Wen 周汶
Li Anxing 李安兴
Zhou Honghong 周红红

Keyboarders 录入

Candy Xu 许春春
Andrew Lam 林耀辉

Supplementary Materials 附录编写

Wu Yicheng 吴义诚
Hu Longbiao 胡龙彪
Sarah Waldram

Database Managers 数据库管理

Mark Baillie
Tetyana Bogdan

Thanks go to Franky Lau, Zhuang Xinglai, Zhou Yixing, Shen Zhongfeng, Li Xin, Xu Lixin, Xu Xiaoyin, Zheng Xuchu, Lilly Zhang, Christine Shi, and Ken Moore for their contribution at various stages of the project.

感谢刘浩贤、庄星来、周懿行、沈中锋、李欣、徐立新、徐笑音、郑旭初、张娱、施谛文以及 Ken Moore 等人在项目不同阶段的参与。

Academic Advisory Panel 学术顾问小组

Prof. Lu Gusun 陆谷孙教授
Prof. Shen Jiaxuan 沈家煊教授
Prof. Yao Xiaoping 姚小平教授
Prof. Benjamin K T'sou 邹嘉彦教授
Dr Katharine Carruthers
Prof. Glen Dudbridge
Prof. Howard Goldblatt
Prof. David Pollard

The editors would like to thank the members of the Academic Advisory Panel for their valuable comments and suggestions on the text during the preparation of the *Oxford Chinese Dictionary*.

谨此感谢学术顾问小组在《牛津英汉汉英词典》编纂过程中提出的宝贵意见和建议。

The LIVAC Corpus LIVAC 语料库

The editors would like to thank the ChiLinStar (Zhuhai) and its parent organization, the Language Information Sciences Research Centre of the City University of Hong Kong, for providing data from the LIVAC Synchronous Corpus.

特别鸣谢麒麟星信息技术有限公司(珠海)及其上属机构——香港城市大学语言资讯科学研究中心为我们提供 LIVAC 共时语料库中的数据。

Preface
序 言

The *Oxford Chinese Dictionary* is a unique and ground-breaking project in every way. This landmark publication is the result of six years' cooperation between two of the world's foremost reference publishers: Oxford University Press (OUP) in the UK, US, and Hong Kong, and Foreign Language Teaching and Research Press (FLTRP) in Beijing.

It is the largest one-volume English-Chinese/Chinese-English dictionary, and the first and only dictionary of its size to have been created by English and Chinese publishers working together. OUP is one of the world's leading publishers of bilingual dictionaries; OUP China has published English-Chinese dictionaries for over 25 years from its base in Hong Kong; and FLTRP is one of the biggest and most respected dictionary publishers in China. Together, OUP and FLTRP represent the state of the art in bilingual dictionary publishing.

The dictionary is also exceptional in that it is based on corpus research, which means that it draws on real evidence about the way that words are used in English and in Chinese. The English side of the dictionary is based on the two billion-word Oxford English Corpus, which provides evidence for English meanings and usage, while the choice of new words added to the Chinese-English side of the dictionary is based on the Linguistic Variations in Chinese Speech Communities (LIVAC) Corpus from the City University of Hong Kong.

The dictionary was compiled by translators and editors – working simultaneously in the UK, the US, and China – who could see and edit each other's work as the dictionary developed. This was made possible by a pioneering web-based electronic dictionary compilation system, which allowed native speaker experts from each country, immersed in contemporary English and Chinese, to provide the most up-to-date and accurate translations possible. As a result, the dictionary provides modern idiomatic coverage of general Chinese and English, with thousands of new words from fields such as computing, business, the media and the arts – words which have never appeared in a Chinese/English dictionary before – as well as thousands of colloquial expressions, and tens of thousands of real-language example sentences that illustrate key points of construction and usage. A wide range of literary vocabulary has also been included, together with vocabulary from specialized fields including science, technology and medicine – an inclusion that reflects the enormous volume of cultural interchange between modern China and the English-speaking world.

The *Oxford Chinese Dictionary* provides translators, students at all levels, teachers, and business people with a reference work that is without rival in authority, currency, and accuracy.

The Publishers

无论从何种角度看，《牛津英汉汉英词典》都是一项不同寻常且极富开拓性的工程。它的出版具有里程碑意义，因为这是位居世界工具书出版前沿的牛津大学出版社（英国总部及美国和香港分社）和外语教学与研究出版社（北京）精诚合作六载的不凡成果。

本词典是目前规模最大的单卷本英汉/汉英词典，也是同等规模中首部，并且是唯一一部由中英两国出版社合作编写的词典。牛津大学出版社是世界上首屈一指的双语词典出版机构，总部位于香港的牛津大学出版社中国有限公司已有25年的英汉词典出版历史，而外语教学与研究出版社也是中国词典出版领域规模最大、最具影响力的出版社之一。两社携手合作，代表了双语词典出版的最高水准。

本词典的另一独特之处在于它是基于语料库研究编纂而成的，本词典采用的中英文均为源自真实语境中的地道用语。英汉部分基于包含20亿词的牛津英语语料库，该语料库为英语词条的含义和用法提供了充足的佐证；汉英部分的新词添加则借助了香港城市大学的LIVAC共时语料库。

本词典由来自英国、美国和中国的编者和译者同步合作完成。在编纂过程中，编者和译者可以随时查看并修改彼此的工作，这得益于网络的开创性电子词典编纂系统。该系统对来自各方专注于现代英语和汉语研究的本族语专家们颇有助益，使他们能给出最新、最精确的翻译。因此，本词典包含了地道的现代通用汉语和英语，此外还收录了数千条同类词典中从未收录的计算机、商务、媒体和艺术等领域的新词。与此同时，本词典还收录了数千条口语表达法以及数万条源于真实语境的例句，用于讲解关键结构和用法。本词典广泛收录语文性词汇，同时收录科技、医药等领域的专业词汇，充分反映了当今中国和英语国家之间大量的文化交流。

《牛津英汉汉英词典》是译者、各级学生、教师和商务人士最好的参考书，它在权威性、实用性、准确性方面均无与伦比。

出版者

Introduction

Users of this dictionary will find that it contains a whole range of effective tools for tackling practical linguistic tasks. In designing this dictionary the editors have ensured that every entry provides as much information as possible for each of the following users and tasks:

- the native English speaker trying to understand Chinese
- the native English speaker trying to write or speak Chinese
- the native Chinese speaker trying to understand English
- the native Chinese speaker trying to write or speak English

Users have different levels of skills and knowledge. For the advanced user, we provide thorough coverage of up-to-date language. We include a wide range of vocabulary in specialist but nonetheless highly topical areas such as business, politics, sport, information technology, and the environment. New developments in popular culture and contemporary lifestyles are also reflected in this dictionary.

For intermediate users, we have designed the dictionary to enable them to work with the foreign language, using it correctly and well. Particular care has been taken in the selection of the translations. Our electronic corpora give us a wealth of examples of words in use in real, everyday circumstances. When one good translation has been identified and checked in many contexts, it will be given as the only general translation for one sense of the headword. It has been our general policy throughout to give two or more translations only in those rare cases where they are consistently interchangeable, and to avoid adding less safe alternatives when one equivalent is adequate. Where appropriate, other equivalents, which have been found to work in more restricted contexts, will be shown in the examples.

Where nuances of meaning within a sense of the headword are translated in different ways, these nuances are pinpointed by means of semantic indicators and/or typical collocates. For a step-by-step guide to using this type of information to arrive at the most suitable translation, see the section *Using this dictionary* on p. xii.

Translations given in isolation are, however, not enough to enable someone to work in a foreign language: grammatical constructions are also needed if the translation is to be used correctly. For these reasons, one of the editors' principal concerns has been to include these constructions wherever they are required. This is a significant feature of our dictionary.

On the English-Chinese side of the dictionary, headwords, compounds, and phrasal verbs stand out clearly on the page. English compounds are found in their proper place within the overall alphabetical order of headwords. Phrasal verbs are given a very full and explicit presentation which avoids ambiguous meta-language and, for the Chinese user, shows very clearly the positioning of the noun object.

This dictionary has a wide coverage of North American as well as British English, and exclusively British or North American English is marked. Where appropriate, American variants are given in translations of Chinese words and phrases in the Chinese-English side of the dictionary, and marked accordingly.

The needs of users extend beyond the bounds of individual dictionary entries. To make it an effective aid for somebody working in a language that is not their own, the dictionary offers access to the language in several different ways. The user thumbing through this dictionary will find lexical usage notes, cultural notes, features on particularly difficult aspects of the Chinese language such as kinship terms and measure words, a list of irregular English verbs, model letters and CVs, and sections on electronic text messaging and using email and the Internet.

Lexical usage notes

These are boxed notes which appear within the dictionary text. They give the user facts about certain types of words that behave alike, for example names of countries, languages, colour terms, and days of the week, and provide ways of discussing topics such as age, date, time, and measurement. A full index to these notes is given on p. xxix.

The purpose of these notes is to make generalizations across lexical items, by summarizing syntactic facts that are common to most members of the set. This supplements the coverage of individual entries: in a one-volume dictionary it is not possible to give all the facts at each headword. Cross-references to the notes are given at all relevant entries, normally immediately after the pronunciation of the headword. The reference is to the page in the dictionary on which the usage note appears.

These notes are intended for specific users: people seeking to express themselves in a language not their own. Thus, the usage notes which appear in the English-Chinese half of the dictionary are written in English and present facts about expression in Chinese, and vice versa in the Chinese-English section. Since they are designed to help translation into a foreign language, they do not represent a systematic analysis of linguistic facts, nor do they set out to give a comprehensive survey of all possible translations. Containing helpful additional information about Chinese and English to enable the user to see how the building blocks of the language fit together, their overarching purpose is to allow the user to say and write specific things accurately and naturally in the target language.

Many of the lexical usage notes represent a functional approach to language use, grouping the basic structures and expressions necessary in order to write or talk about a specific topic. Thus, as well as being readily usable reference aids for the individual user, they will also serve as valuable vocabulary-teaching material for teachers of Chinese and English.

Cultural notes

This dictionary incorporates a wide variety of cultural notes covering aspects of Chinese, British and American society, institutions, and culture. These are conveniently located at the relevant alphabetical position in the word list to provide additional information on a term where a translation is impossible or cannot convey enough information on its own. Cultural notes containing information on aspects of Chinese culture include those on *Confucianism*, *the Temple of Heaven*, *dough sticks*, *hutongs*, *the Yellow Emperor* and *dragon boat racing*. These notes are intended for specific users: people seeking to gain a deeper understanding of a culture that is not their own. Thus, the cultural notes which appear in the Chinese-English half of the dictionary are written in English, and vice versa on the English-Chinese side. There are over three hundred cultural notes in total.

History and culture

There are very few overlaps between British and American traditions and those of the Chinese. There are also striking differences in history, governance, and administration. In order to address this in more detail, the dictionary contains separate sections that include brief chronologies of Chinese, British, and American history; UK counties and US states; sections on the various Chinese, British, and American holidays and festivals; and a list of the different Chinese ethnic groups. These sections can be found in the middle of the dictionary.

Model letters

A rich and varied set of model letters is to be found in a special section in the centre of the dictionary. Once again, these are designed for people seeking to write in a language not their own. Thus, the model letters for the English-speakers are written in Chinese but introduced in English, and vice versa. Chinese and English letters are grouped according to broad themes covering personal and social correspondence, travel, and employment. The letters in the two languages are shown on facing pages for ease of comparison but are not direct translations. Each spread of letters provides a typically idiomatic treatment of a similar theme in order to highlight the differences in letter-writing conventions between English and Chinese.

Using the telephone

This section offers practical advice on the language of calling procedures.

SMS (text message) abbreviations

In order to reflect the prominence of electronic text messaging in contemporary society, the basic vocabulary of text messaging and SMS abbreviations are presented.

Using email and the Internet

This section introduces the basic vocabulary of email and the Internet. It features model email messages and presents the vocabulary used in standard web pages, allowing ease of navigation in the target language.

简介

在处理实际语言问题时，本词典将成为读者的有效工具，其编排设计确保以下各类读者从词条中均可获取最大量的信息：

- 尝试理解汉语的英语母语者
- 尝试表达汉语的英语母语者
- 尝试理解英语的汉语母语者
- 尝试表达英语的汉语母语者

读者的语言技巧及知识水平各不相同。针对语言水平较高者，本词典收录了当今英语和汉语中的众多词语，也广泛收录了专业词汇，这些专业领域，如商务、政治、体育、信息技术、环境等，频现于日常会话中。流行文化和现代生活方式的最新时尚在本词典中亦有体现。

外语水平中等的读者可借助本词典正确恰当地使用外语。词目的释义、例证的翻译均经斟酌而定。大量例证遴选自计算机语料库，以展现外语使用的日常语境。若某一释义可同时适用于多个语境，它即成为词目义项的唯一释义。本词典关于词目对应词的原则为：某一对应词若足以应对不同语境，则将其作为该义项的唯一释义；仅当两个或以上对应词可完全互换时，才同时予以列出，此类状况在本词典中并不多见。若其他对应词适用于更为具体的语境，则列为例证。

词目的同一义项有多个不同对应词时，各释义分列在不同指示词后，或与不同搭配词并置，由指示词或搭配词凸显其细微差别。利用此信息作出恰当翻译的具体步骤请参见“使用说明”(第 xxi 页)。

单独出现的释义并不足以帮助读者正确使用外语，语法结构也必不可少。因此本词典的关注点之一即是囊括必需的语言结构，此亦为本词典的特色。

本词典英汉部分的词目、复合词及短语动词均以黑体字排印。复合词依字母顺序与词目一并列出。短语动词的编排清晰全面，避免了元语言语义不清，汉语母语者可对名词宾语在短语动词中的位置一目了然。

本词典涵盖了北美英语和英国英语，对于仅限于英国或北美英语其一而不能通用的词语均予以标示。汉英部分的某些词目释义也列出了美国英语的变体。

仅用词典的词条难以满足读者多样的外语使用需求。为使读者更好地使用外语，本词典提供了另外几种更为有效的途径：特别收录的语用信息框、文化知识框、汉语中亲属称谓和量词等难点、英语不规则动词表、信函、简历等范文，以及短信息、电子邮件和互联网应用专题。

语用信息框

本词典正文内设有语用信息框，对用法相似的词汇，如国名、语言、颜色、星期等进行分类例解，以及提供谈论年龄、日期、时间、度量等话题的多种表达方式。“英语·汉语语用信息框一览表”见第 xxix 页。

词典因篇幅所限，无法于每一词条给出详尽释义。语用信息框旨在作超越词汇层面的概括，总结出语义相关的整套词汇所共同的句法特性，以补充词条信息。与语用信息框相关的词条均在词目的音标后标有参见符号，指向所参语用信息框所在的页码。

语用信息框的设立旨在帮助尝试用外语表达的读者。英汉部分的语用信息框以英语描述了汉语语境中的多种表达方式，汉英部分反之。由于以将母语译为外语为目的，本词典并未对语料做系统性分析，亦未试图列出所有可行的译文。这些有关英汉两种语言的补充材料有助于读者弄清语言的各个成分如何相互结合，构建成句子，其最终目的是让读者能够用外语准确自然地表达具体事物。

语用信息框将表达具体话题所必需的结构与措辞归纳分类，从功能方面阐释语言的应用。读者可套用这些表达方式，对于外语教师这也是极有价值的词汇教学材料。

文化知识框

本词典融合了大量关于中国、英国、美国的社会、习俗、文化背景知识，按字母顺序列在相关词条下，是对词条信息的有力补充。英美文化背景知识包括迪士尼乐园（Disneyland®）、唐宁街（Downing Street）、联邦调查局（the FBI）、敲门问答笑话（knock-knock joke）、超级碗橄榄球赛（the Super Bowl）等英美文化的方方面面。这些信息旨在帮助读者深入理解别国文化。中国文化背景知识以英语介绍，英美部分用汉语写成。本词典总计收录文化知识三百余条。

历史与文化

英美与中国的文化传统共通之处甚少，历史、国体、行政管理等方面也有巨大差异。本词典特在全卷中部辟专章列出中、英、美的历史、文化年表、节假日、民族，以彰显诸多不同之处。

信函范例

本词典在全卷中部特辟专章提供各种类型信件文书范例，这也是专为尝试用外语书写的读者而设。英语母语者可借鉴英文说明的汉语信件文书范例，汉语母语者反之。信件类型涵盖私人、社交、旅行、应聘，相同类型信件文书的典型处理编排在同一对开页上以便对比两语书写习惯的差异，但二者并非简单互译。

打电话

本节列举打电话时的常用语言。

短信息中的缩略语

针对当代社会短信息使用频增的现象，本词典罗列了短信息的基本词汇和常用缩写。

电子邮件和互联网

本节介绍了使用电子邮件和互联网的基本词汇，展示了电子邮件范例，罗列了一般网页的常用词汇，使浏览外语网页更为轻松。

Using this dictionary

English-Chinese dictionary

Order of entries

All entries (with the exception of phrasal verbs) are entered in strict alphabetical order, ignoring hyphens, apostrophes, and spaces. Headwords spelt the same, but with unrelated meanings (homographs) are entered separately, with a raised number following each. Compound words are entered in their alphabetical place in the dictionary, either as separate entries or, where several fall together in the alphabet, grouped together under the first element.

> **back end**
> **A** *n* 1 (part) 后端; (of vehicle) 尾部; **to look like the ~ of a bus** Brit colloq 十分邋遢 2 Brit (period) 后期; **the ~ of the year** 年尾 3 Comput 后端
> **B back-end** *adj* Comput 后端的
> **backer** /ˈbækə(r)/ *n* 1 Fin (of project, event, business) 赞助者 2 (supporter) 支持者 3 Games 下注者

> **back: ~fire** *vi* 1 Aut «*vehicle, engine*» 逆火; 2 (have opposite effect) «*plan, scheme*» 事与愿违; **to ~fire on sb.** 对某人产生适得其反的效果; **~ flip** *n* 后空翻; **~ formation** *n* 1 [c] (word) 逆构词; 2 [u] (process) 逆构法; **~gammon** ▸p. 307 *n* [u] 十五子棋

Structure of entries

Each entry on the English-Chinese side of the dictionary is organized hierarchically, by grammatical category, then sense category. Grammatical categories and senses are ordered according to frequency of use, the most commonly-used coming first. Phrasal verbs always appear at the end of the entry.

> **bash** /bæʃ/ colloq
> **A** *n* 1 (blow) 猛击 2 (dent) 凹痕; **my car has a ~ on the door** 我那辆车的车门撞瘪了一块 3 (attempt) 尝试; **to have a ~ at sth., to give sth. a ~** 尝试做某事 4 (party) 盛大聚会; **a birthday ~** 生日庆典
> **B** *vt* 1 (hit or punch hard) 猛击 2 (collide with) 猛撞 ‹*vehicle, person, wall*› 3 (criticize) 无端地指责 ‹*race, political opponent, trade union*›
> **C** *vi* 猛烈撞击; **to ~ into sb./sth.** 猛地撞上某人/某物
> Phrasal verbs
> • **bash about, bash around** *vt* [**~ sb. about** *or* **around**] colloq 殴打
> • **bash in, bash down** *vt* [**~ sth. in, ~ in sth.**] colloq 不断猛击 [使之毁坏]; **to ~ the door in** 砸倒房门; **~ those cardboard boxes in** 砸瘪那些纸盒
> • **bash on** *vi* colloq 坚持; **to ~ on (with sth.)** 坚持（做某事）

Within sense categories, distinctions between alternative translations are shown by sense indicators in round brackets and/or collocates in angle brackets (showing words with which the translation typically occurs). Field labels and style labels further assist the user to recognize restrictions in a word's context or register.

> **massive** /ˈmæsɪv/ *adj* 1 (large and solid or heavy) 厚实的 ‹*building, walls*›; 粗大的 ‹*tree*› 2 (very large) 巨大的 ‹*victory*›; 大量的 ‹*increase, crowd*›; 大规模的 ‹*shift, attack*›; 大额的 ‹*bill*› 3 (very serious) 非常严重的 ‹*heart attack*›; **a ~ haemorrhage/stroke** 大出血/严重中风 4 colloq (successful) 极为成功的; **the band are going to be ~** 该乐队会大获成功

> **back end**
> **A** *n* 1 (part) 后端; (of vehicle) 尾部; **to look like the ~ of a bus** Brit colloq 十分邋遢 2 Brit (period) 后期; **the ~ of the year** 年尾 3 Comput 后端

Where two translations are given with no indicators or collocates to distinguish them, they are synonymous and interchangeable. Occasionally, there is no equivalent translation. Sometimes an explanation will be given in its place: this is shown in square brackets.

> **in** /ɪn/ ▸**p. 487**
> **A** *prep* 1 (within enclosed space) 在…里; (within flat
> …
> 五分之一的机会; **a tax of 22 pence ~ the pound** 每英镑 22 便士的税率 20 Brit (approximately within) [表示约数]; **~ the** *or* **their hundreds/thousands** 数以百计/千计

Sometimes a phrase or example will be given instead: this implies that the headword cannot be used outside of the example or phrase context.

> **in** /ɪn/ ▸**p. 487**
> …
> **G ins** *npl* colloq **the ~s and outs (of sth.)** （某事的）详情; **to know the ~s and outs of a job** 了解工作的全部细节

General translations of headwords are often followed by phrases in which the general translation is most commonly used, as well as those in which it may not be used. Examples always appear at the end of the entry or sense and include typical usages, fixed phrases, idioms, and proverbs. All examples are printed in bold type. A swung dash is used to represent the headword. Note that synonymous forms of expression in English are indicated through the use of the word 'or', which appears in italics.

> **pandemonium** /ˌpændɪˈməʊnɪəm/ *n* [u] 混乱; **it's sheer** *or* **absolute ~** 简直是一片混乱

Translating into Chinese

To translate *to experience extreme difficulties*, you would go through the steps shown on the right. The section that follows gives other examples of how to get the best out of the English-Chinese side of the dictionary for various translation tasks.

Translating into Chinese

Goal 1 Translate *to experience extreme difficulty*

Process

1 Identify the problem words or phrases.

experience and *extreme*

2 Look up *experience* and choose the appropriate grammatical category.

B *vt*

> **experience** /ɪks'pɪərɪəns/
> **A** *n* **1** [u] (knowledge, skill) 经验; **to have ~ of sth./doing sth.** 有某事物/做某事的经验; **to** …
> **B** *vt* **1** (undergo) 经历 ‹*problems, change*›; **to ~ sth. at first hand** *or* **personally** 亲身经历某事; **to ~ difficulty doing sth.** 做某事遇到困难 **2** (feel) 体验 ‹*pain, fear*›; 体会 ‹*emotion*›; **to ~ pleasure** 感受愉悦; **to ~ profound relief** 感到极大的宽慰

3 Choose the appropriate sense category.

1 (undergo)

> **B** *vt* **1** (undergo) 经历 ‹*problems, change*›; **to ~ sth. at first hand** *or* **personally** 亲身经历某事; **to ~ difficulty doing sth.** 做某事遇到困难 **2** (feel) 体验 ‹*pain, fear*›; 体会 ‹*emotion*›; **to ~ pleasure** 感受愉悦; **to ~ profound relief** 感到极大的宽慰

4 Choose the most appropriate phrase or collocate in the sense. Note the translation.

经历 ‹*problems, change*›

to ~ difficulty doing sth. 做某事遇到困难

> **B** *vt* **1** (undergo) 经历 ‹*problems, change*›; **to ~ sth. at first hand** *or* **personally** 亲身经历某事; **to ~ difficulty doing sth.** 做某事遇到困难 **2** (feel) 体验 ‹*pain, fear*›; 体会 ‹*emotion*›; **to ~ pleasure** 感受愉悦; **to ~ profound relief** 感到极大的宽慰

5 Look up *extreme* and choose the appropriate grammatical and sense categories in the same way that you have done for *experience*. Choose the most appropriate phrase or collocate included in the sense. Note the translation.

> **extreme** /ɪk'stri:m/
> **A** *adj* **1** (very great) 极度的; **~ poverty** 赤贫; **~ caution/pleasure/urgency** 极度的谨慎/快乐/紧迫 **2** (unusual) 极端的; **~ weather conditions** 极端恶劣的天气条件; **to go to ~ lengths to do sth.** 不遗余力地做某事; **to an ~ degree** 极端地 **3** (extremist) 偏激的 ‹*political view*›; **the ~ right/left** 极右/左派

6 If necessary, look up *difficulty* in the same way.

> **difficulty** /'dɪfɪkəltɪ/ *n* **1** [u] (of task, activity) 困难; **the ~ of doing sth.** 做某事的难处; **to have ~ (in) doing sth.** 做某事有困难; **to have ~ with sth.** 在某事上有问题; **to have ~ with one's eyesight** 视力有问题; **to be under some ~** 在困难的条件下 **2** [u] (complexity) 难度; **the level of ~ of sth.** 某事的难办程度 **3** [u and c] (trouble) 麻烦; (obstacle) 障碍; **in ~** 处于麻烦中; **to create** *or* **make difficulties** 制造麻烦; **to meet difficulties** 遇到麻烦; **to run into difficulties** 碰到难题; **to have difficulties with sth.** 在某事上碰到麻烦

Result The translation 经历极度的困难

Goal 2	Translate	*a posh nightclub*
Process	**1** Look up *nightclub*. English compounds appear in alphabetical order in the word list. **~club**	**night:** ~ **bird** *n* 1 Zool 夜间活动的鸟; 2 ~**bird** colloq 夜猫子; ~**-blind** *adj* 夜盲的; ~ **blindness** *n* [u] 夜盲; ~**cap** *n* 1 (drink) 夜酒; **to have a ~cap** 睡前喝些酒; 2 (hat) 睡帽; ~**clothes** *npl* 睡衣; ~**club** *n* 夜总会; **a ~club hostess/singer** 夜总会女招待/歌手; ~**clubbing** *n* [u] 泡夜总会; **to go ~clubbing** 去泡夜总会; ~**dress** *n* （女式）睡衣; ~ **editor** *n* 夜
	2 Note the translation. 夜总会	~**club** *n* 夜总会; **a ~club hostess/singer** 夜总会女招待/歌手; ~**clubbing** *n* [u] 泡
	3 Look up *posh* and choose the appropriate grammatical category. **A** *adj*	**posh** /pɒʃ/ **A** *adj* 1 colloq (elegant) 雅致的 ‹*clothes*›; (stylishly luxurious) 豪华的 ‹*restaurant, area, wedding*› 2 Brit (upper class) 上流社会的 ‹*person, voice*› **B** *adv* Brit 以上流社会腔调; **to talk ~** 谈吐优雅 Phrasal verb · **posh up** *vt* [~ **sb./sth. up,** ~ **up sb./sth**] Brit colloq 使…变得漂亮 ‹*house, clothes, oneself*›; **to be all ~ed up** 打扮得漂漂亮亮
	4 Select the most appropriate numbered sense category. 1 (stylishly luxurious)	**A** *adj* 1 colloq (elegant) 雅致的 ‹*clothes*›; **(stylishly luxurious)** 豪华的 ‹*restaurant, area, wedding*› 2 Brit (upper class) 上流社会的 ‹*person, voice*›
	5 Look for the noun collocate, in angle brackets, which is closest to your context. *restaurant*	**A** *adj* 1 colloq (elegant) 雅致的 ‹*clothes*›; (stylishly luxurious) 豪华的 ‹***restaurant***, *area, wedding*› 2 Brit (upper class) 上流社会的 ‹*person, voice*›
	6 Note the translation. 豪华的	**A** *adj* 1 colloq (elegant) 雅致的 ‹*clothes*›; (stylishly luxurious) **豪华的** ‹*restaurant, area, wedding*› 2 Brit (upper class) 上流社会的 ‹*person, voice*›
Result	The translation	一个豪华的夜总会

Goal 3 Translate *it's natural for her to want to stay a little longer*

Process

1 Look up *natural* and choose the appropriate grammatical category.

A *adj*

> **natural** /ˈnætʃrəl/
> **A** *adj* **1▸** (usual, normal) 正常的 ‹*reaction, consequence*›; **it is ~ (for sb.) to do sth.** （某人）做某事是很正常的; **it is ~ that ...** …是很正常的; **it is ~ that he should want to see his daughter** 他想见女儿是很自然的; **the ~ thing to do would be to protest** 抗议是理所当然的; **it's only ~** 这很正常 **2▸** (in accordance with nature) 本能的 ‹*urge, behaviour, aversion*›; (innate) 天生的 ‹*ability, orator, linguist*›; **it is ~ (for sb./sth.) to do sth.** （某人/某物）天生会做某事; **it's not ~!** 这有悖天性！; **sb.'s ~ inclinations** 某人与生俱来的爱好; **a ~ gift for singing** 歌唱的天赋 **3▸** (unaffected) 自然的; **to be ~ with sb.** 与某人在一起时轻松自如; **try and look more ~** 尽量表现得再自然一些 **4▸** (not man-
> ...

2 Choose the most appropriate numbered sense category.

1▸ (usual, normal)

> **A** *adj* **1▸** **(usual, normal)** 正常的 ‹*reaction, consequence*›; **it is ~ (for sb.) to do sth.** （某人）做某事是很正常的; **it is ~ that ...** …是很正常的; **it is ~ that he should want to see his daughter** 他想见女儿是很自然的; **the ~ thing to do would be to protest** 抗议是理所当然的; **it's only ~** 这很正常 **2▸** (in accordance with nature) 本能的 ‹*urge, behaviour, aversion*›; (innate) 天生的 ‹*ability, orator, linguist*›; **it is ~ (for sb./sth.) to do sth.** （某人/某物）天生会做某事; **it's not ~!** 这有悖天性！; **sb.'s ~ inclinations** 某人与生俱来的爱好; **a ~ gift for singing** 歌唱的天赋 **3▸** (unaffected) 自然的; **to be ~ with sb.** 与某人在一起时轻松自如; **try and look more ~** 尽量表现得再自然一些 **4▸** (not man-

3 Look for the basic structure you need.

it is ~ (for sb.) to do sth.

> **A** *adj* **1▸** (usual, normal) 正常的 ‹*reaction, consequence*›; **it is ~ (for sb.) to do sth.** （某人）做某事是很正常的; **it is ~ that ...** …是很正常的; **it is ~ that he should want to see his daughter** 他想见女儿是很自然的; **the ~ thing to do would be to protest** 抗议是理所当然的; **it's only ~** 这很正常

4 Note the translation.

（某人）做某事是很正常的

> **A** *adj* **1▸** (usual, normal) 正常的 ‹*reaction, consequence*›; **it is ~ (for sb.) to do sth.** **（某人）做某事是很正常的**; **it is ~ that ...** …是很正常的; **it is ~ that he should want to see his daughter** 他想见女儿是很自然的; **the ~ thing to do would be to protest** 抗议是理所当然的; **it's only ~** 这很正常

5 Use the translation of the basic structure to translate your sentence.

Result The translation 她想多待一会儿是很正常的

Goal 4 Translate *the police have sealed off the area*

Process

1 *Seal off* is a phrasal verb, so go to the end of the entry *seal* where you will find the phrasal verbs listed in alphabetical order, each verb clearly signalled by a round bullet.

· seal off

> Phrasal verbs
> · **seal in** *vt* [~ **sth. in,** ~ **in sth.**] 密封住 ‹*smell, flavour*›
> · **seal off** *vt* [~ **sth. off,** ~ **off sth.**]
> 1 (make separate from) 隔开 ‹*section of building*›
> 2 (prevent access to) 封锁 ‹*building, street, area*›
> · **seal up** *vt* [~ **sth. up,** ~ **up sth.**] 封死 ‹*door, window*›

2 Select the appropriate sense category of the phrasal verb pattern.

2 (prevent access to)

> · **seal off** *vt* [~ **sth. off,** ~ **off sth.**]
> 1 (make separate from) 隔开 ‹*section of building*›
> **2** **(prevent access to)** 封锁 ‹*building, street, area*›

3 Select the appropriate collocate showing context for the translation, in this case typical objects of the verb translations.

area

> · **seal off** *vt* [~ **sth. off,** ~ **off sth.**]
> 1 (make separate from) 隔开 ‹*section of building*›
> 2 (prevent access to) 封锁 ‹*building, street,* ***area***›

4 Identify the appropriate translation.

封锁

> · **seal off** *vt* [~ **sth. off,** ~ **off sth.**]
> 1 (make separate from) 隔开 ‹*section of building*›
> 2 (prevent access to) **封锁** ‹*building, street, area*›

5 If necessary, look up *area* and select the appropriate translation.

地区

> **area** /ˈeərɪə/ *n* 1 (measurement) 面积 2 Geog **地区**; **a mountain/desert** ~ 山区/沙漠地区; **residential/port** ~ 住宅区/港区 3 (part of building) 场地; **the reception/waiting** ~ 接待处/等候区 4 Anat 区; **the** ~ **of the brain controlling speech** 大脑的言语控制区 5 (sphere of knowledge) 领域; (part of activity, business, economy) 方面; **that's not my** ~ 那不是我的专长; ~ **of interest/responsibility** 兴趣/责任范围

6 Now construct the translation of the sentence.

Result The translation 警察把这个地区封锁了

Chinese-English dictionary

Order of entries

Entries on the Chinese-English side of the dictionary are organized according to the traditional method, first by single-character entry, then with multiple-character entries beginning with the same character listed below them.

柄 bǐng
柄权 bǐngquán

饼 (餅) bǐng
饼铛 bǐngchēng
饼肥 bǐngféi
饼干 bǐnggān
饼子 bǐngzi

炳 bǐng

屏 bǐng
屏除 bǐngchú
屏迹 bǐngjì
屏绝 bǐngjué
...

Single-character entries are ordered according to their Pinyin pronunciation, alphabetically, and then by tone. Chinese has four tones and a neutral tone. The four tones are marked above the relevant vowel in the Pinyin. The neutral tone is not marked.

妈 mā
麻 má
马 mǎ
骂 mà
吗 ma

Characters with the same Pinyin and tone are ordered by the number of strokes in the character. The character with the smallest number of strokes is listed first.

陂 bēi
杯 bēi
卑 bēi
背 bēi
悲 bēi
碑 bēi
鹎 bēi

Characters with the same Pinyin, tone, and stroke number are ordered by the first stroke in the character. These strokes are listed according to the following sequence: — (horizontal line), | (vertical line), ノ (left slash), ㇏ (dot), ㇕ (straight stroke with a bending tip, or with an extended bending stroke such as 亅㇄㇛).

Multiple-character entries listed below single-character entries are similarly ordered by Pinyin, tone, and then the number of strokes.

Characters with more than one pronunciation contain cross-references to the alternative Pinyin. These are marked with a ▶. For example:

答 dā = 答 dá [only used in phrases like 答理, 答应, etc.]
▶dá

If you do not know the pronunciation for the Chinese character you are searching for, you can refer to the Chinese radical index. See p. R58 for further information.

Structure of entries

Each entry on the Chinese-English side is organized hierarchically, by grammatical category, then sense category. Grammatical categories and senses are ordered according to frequency of use, the most commonly-used coming first. Note that idioms, including chengyu (成语) are not accorded a part of speech. This is because they are often phrasal.

Sense categories are also ordered according to frequency of use. Literal senses will always appear before figurative senses.

Within sense categories, distinctions between alternative translations are shown through the use of sense indicators in round brackets. Sense indicators include the following:

- synonyms indicating difference in sense:

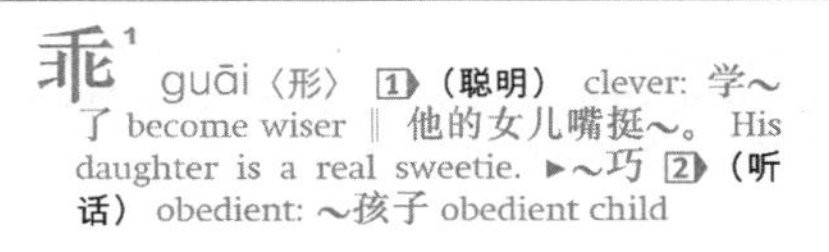
乖[1] guāi 〈形〉 1 (聪明) clever: 学~了 become wiser ‖ 他的女儿嘴挺~。 His daughter is a real sweetie. ▶~巧 2 (听话) obedient: ~孩子 obedient child

- information indicating a typical context for the headword:

【挂号】 guàhào 〈动〉 1 (指在医院) register: ~请排队。 Please queue up to register. 2 (指邮寄) send by registered post: 这封信要~吗? Do you want to have the letter sent registered?

- information defining or restricting the headword:

广[2] (廣) Guǎng 〈名〉 1 (指省) Guangdong Province 2 (指市) Guangzhou City
▶ān

Field labels (in square brackets) and style labels (in angle brackets) further assist the user to recognize restrictions in a word's context or register:

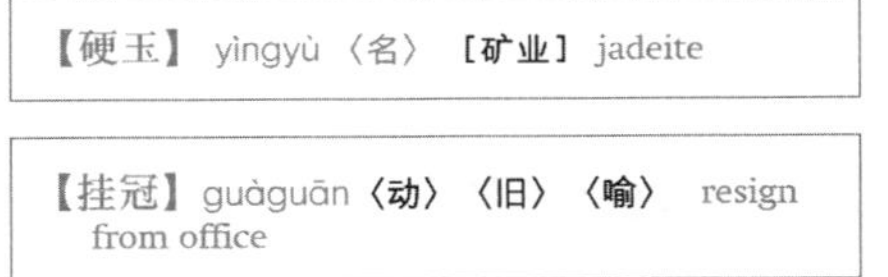
【硬玉】 yìngyù 〈名〉 [矿业] jadeite

【挂冠】 guàguān 〈动〉 〈旧〉 〈喻〉 resign from office

Entries may contain cross-references to multi-character entries, which contain further exemplification of the sense. The marker ▶ is used:

黎 lí 〈形〉 〈书〉 1 (众多) numerous: ▶~民, ~庶 2 (黑) black: ▶~黑

Some head characters may only be used in conjunction with other characters, and in combinations in which this character appears after the other character in question. In these cases, the user is directed to the predominant character combination. The marker ▶ is used:

蚧 jiè ▶蛤蚧 géjiè

When two dictionary entries share an identical translation, the translation for one will often be directly cross-referenced to the other. The user will be directed to the target entry or sense with an equals sign = , as below:

【暗房】ànfáng = **暗室** ànshì 1

案[2] àn
A 〈名〉 1 （案件） case: 强奸/诈骗～ rape/fraud case ‖ 该～即将由法院审理。 The case will go to trial. ▶～件, 惨～, 破～
2 （文书） record: ▶～卷, 备～, 有～可查
3 （文件） plan: ▶草～, 教～, 提～
B = **按**[2] àn A

Occasionally, two translations may be provided with no indicators to distinguish them: these may be considered synonymous and interchangeable.

【八开】bākāi 〈名〉 ［印刷］ octavo, 8vo

Sometimes there is no equivalent translation. In these cases an explanation will be given instead: this is shown in square brackets.

笔（筆） bǐ
...
C 〈量〉 1 （用于款项） [for sums of money]: 一～钱 a sum of money ‖ 一～生意 a business deal ‖ 一～债 a debt 2 （用于书画） [for writing or drawing]: 写一～好字 write well 3 （用于笔画） [for strokes]: "凸"字有 5 ～。 The character 凸 has five strokes.

Where British and American English yield different translations, the variants are both provided, and marked accordingly.

【电影】diànyǐng 〈名〉 **film** 〈英〉; **movie** 〈美〉: 放映～ show a film ‖ 拍（摄）～ shoot a film ▶立体～

General translations of headwords are often followed by phrases in which the general translation is most commonly used, as well as those in which it may not be used. Examples always appear at the end of the entry or sense and include typical usages, fixed phrases, idioms, and proverbs. All examples are printed in bold type. A swung dash is used to represent the headword.

瓣 bàn
A 〈名〉 1 （指花） petal: ▶花～ 2 （指蒜） clove; （指水果） segment: **蒜～儿 cloves of garlic** ‖ **橘子～儿 orange segments** 3 （指物品） piece: **碗摔成了好几～。** The bowl broke into several pieces. 4 （瓣膜） lamella: ▶三尖～
B 〈量〉 section: **一～橘子 a slice of orange** ‖ **一～蒜 a clove of garlic**
【瓣膜】bànmó 〈名〉 ［生理］ valve: **她的心脏～有毛病。** She has problems with a heart valve.

Translating into English

To translate 危险的运动 in the phrase 攀岩是项很危险的运动, you would go through the steps shown on the right. The section that follows gives another example of how to get the best out of the Chinese-English side of the dictionary for various translation tasks.

Translating into English

Goal 1 Translate 危险的运动 in the phrase 攀岩是项很危险的运动

Process

1 Look up 运动. Multi-character Chinese words appear in Pinyin order under single-character entries.

> 运（運）yùn
> A〈动〉1（运动）move: ▶~动, ~行, ~转 2（运送）carry: ~货 transport goods ‖ ~煤专线 new railway lines for the specific purpose of transporting coal ▶~输, 空~ 3（使用）utilize: ~针 manipulate an acupuncture needle ▶~笔, ~思, ~用
> ...
> 【运动】yùndòng〈名〉1［物理］motion: 加速~ accelerated motion ‖ 圆周~ circular motion 2［哲学］motion: ~是物质存在的形式。Motion is the physical manifestation of matter. 3 ▶p. 909［体育］sports: 爱好体育~ enjoy physical exercise ‖ 球类~ ball games ‖ 全身~ full body exercise 4（社会政治）movement: 工人~ labour movement ‖ 群众~ mass campaign ‖ 1919年的"五四"~ the 'May 4th' Movement of 1919

2 Select the most appropriate numbered sense category.
3［体育］

> 【运动】yùndòng〈名〉1［物理］motion: 加速~ accelerated motion ‖ 圆周~ circular motion 2［哲学］motion: ~是物质存在的形式。Motion is the physical manifestation of matter. 3 ▶p. 909 **［体育］** sports: 爱好体育~ enjoy physical exercise ‖ 球类~ ball games ‖ 全身~ full body exercise 4（社会政治）movement: 工人~ labour movement ‖ 群众~ mass campaign ‖ 1919年的"五四"~ the 'May 4th' Movement of 1919

3 Note the translation.
sports

> 【运动】yùndòng〈名〉1［物理］motion: 加速~ accelerated motion ‖ 圆周~ circular motion 2［哲学］motion: ~是物质存在的形式。Motion is the physical manifestation of matter. 3 ▶p. 909［体育］**sports**: 爱好体育~ enjoy physical exercise ‖ 球类~ ball games ‖ 全身~ full body exercise 4（社会政治）movement: 工人~ labour movement ‖ 群众~ mass campaign ‖ 1919年的"五四"~ the 'May 4th' Movement of 1919

4 Look up 危险 under the single-character entry 危.

> 危 wēi
> A〈形〉1〈书〉（高耸）precipitous: ~峰 towering peak ‖ ~崖 precipitous cliff 2〈书〉（端正）proper: ▶正襟~坐
> ...
> 【危险】wēixiǎn〈形〉dangerous: ~地带 danger zone ‖ ~人物 dangerous person ‖ ~因素 hazards ‖ 她的处境非常~。She is in great peril. ‖ 他有生命~。His life is in danger.

5 Note the translation.
dangerous

> 【危险】wēixiǎn〈形〉**dangerous**: ~地带 danger zone ‖ ~人物 dangerous person ‖ ~因素 hazards ‖ 她的处境非常~。She is in great peril. ‖ 他有生命~。His life is in danger.

Result The translation of the whole sentence *rock climbing is a very dangerous sport*

Goal 2		Translate	塞翁失马，焉知非福
Process	1	Look up all the words you do not know and find a literal translation. If this does not make sense in your context, ask yourself whether the phrase could be an idiom, saying, or proverb. The answer is yes, because you can see immediately that the 'old frontiersman losing a horse' has no relation to the wider context.	
	2	Search for the head character and check to see whether the phrase may be listed at the headword level below it. ▶ ~翁失马, 焉知非福	塞 sài 〈名〉 stronghold: ▶**~翁失马，焉知非福**, 边~, 要~
	3	Note the label 〈成〉 which indicates that the expression is an idiom in Chinese. The translation in English is also idiomatic.	**【塞翁失马，焉知非福】** sàiwēng shī mǎ, yān zhī fēi fú **〈成〉** 〈喻〉 a blessing in disguise
Result		The translation	*a blessing in disguise*

使用说明

本词典共有2,000余页，其中附录等约100页。读者对象是以英语或汉语为母语，且其作为外语的汉语或英语水平已达中高级程度的学习者和使用者。本词典设计的创新性在于，它既可用于作解码（即对所学外语的理解），又可用于编码（即对所学外语的使用）。以下分别讲解英汉及汉英部分的体例及使用方法。

《英汉词典》

本部分收录的既有现代英语中的核心词汇、一般词汇，也包括常见的专科术语、世界各个国家和地区以及主要城市的名称等。

译文方面，在注重语言简洁准确的同时，也注意文体风格，力求做到“以口译口，以古译古”。翻译例句时，在不违反现代汉语表达方式的原则下，尽量体现英文原句的句式。

条目安排

所收词条均按英文字母顺序排列，连字号、撇号、空格等不计。拼写相同但意义没有关联的词目（即同形异义者）会分列，并用上标数字以作区分。复合词也按英文字母顺序排列，可作独立词条列出，或置于一组复合词内，如下例的back end，因为有两个词类，所以作为单独词条列出，而~flip、~formation、~gammon等一组复合词则在同一段落内接排：

> **back end**
> **A** *n* **1** (part) 后端; (of vehicle) 尾部; **to look like the ~ of a bus** Brit colloq 十分邋遢 **2** Brit (period) 后期; **the ~ of the year** 年尾 **3** Comput 后端
> **B back-end** *adj* Comput 后端的
> **backer** /ˈbækə(r)/ *n* **1** Fin (of project, event, business) 赞助者 **2** (supporter) 支持者 **3** Games 下注者

> **back: ~fire** *vi* **1** Aut «*vehicle, engine*» 逆火; **2** (have opposite effect) «*plan, scheme*» 事与愿违; **to ~fire on sb.** 对某人产生适得其反的效果; **~ flip** *n* 后空翻; **~ formation** *n* **1** [c] (word) 逆构词; **2** [u] (process) 逆构法; **~gammon** ▸**p. 307** *n* [u] 十五子棋

词条结构

《英汉词典》的词条中，词类及各个义项的次序按使用频率排列，最常用的在前。短语动词集中排在所属动词词条的最后。

> **bash** /bæʃ/ colloq
> **A** *n* **1** (blow) 猛击 **2** (dent) 凹痕; **my car has a ~ on the door** 我那辆车的车门撞瘪了一块 **3** (attempt) 尝试; **to have a ~ at sth., to give sth. a ~** 尝试做某事 **4** (party) 盛大聚会; **a birthday ~** 生日庆典
> **B** *vt* **1** (hit or punch hard) 猛击 **2** (collide with) 猛撞 ‹*vehicle, person, wall*› **3** (criticize) 无端地指责 ‹*race, political opponent, trade union*›
> **C** *vi* 猛烈撞击; **to ~ into sb./sth.** 猛地撞上某人/某物
> Phrasal verbs
> • **bash about, bash around** *vt* [**~ sb. about** *or* **around**] colloq 殴打
> • **bash in, bash down** *vt* [**~ sth. in, ~ in sth.**] colloq 不断猛击 [使之毁坏]; **to ~ the door in** 砸倒房门; **~ those cardboard boxes in** 砸瘪那些纸盒

词条结构的详情请参看“《英汉词典》的词条结构”（第xxiv页）；标签及缩写，请参看封面内页的一览表。

注音

《英汉词典》的注音采用国际音标（IPA）。除少量复合词及派生词外，基本上是每个词目均有注音。若其在美式英语中有不同的发音时，美式发音用Amer引出，且只标出与英式发音不同的部分，如：

> **abomination** /əˌbɒmɪˈneɪʃn, Amer -məˈn-/ *n*

所有注音符号的读法，请参看“英语音标及其读音”（第xxvi页）。

释义

本词典采用多种手段区分不同义项或不同使用领域中，英文词语的不同中文译法，每个义项一般只给一个最常用的对应词。如有不同译法，则用指示语（请参下文“指示语”一节）、搭配词（请参下文“搭配词”一节）、学科及使用领域标签（请参封面内页的“学科及使用领域标签”一览表）等加以区分。如：

> **elaborately** /ɪˈlæbərətli/ *adv* **1** (in great detail) 周详充分地 ‹*devised, constructed*›; (with careful attention to detail) 精心地 ‹*plan, conceive*› **2** (extravagantly) 精美地 ‹*patterned, ornamented*› **3** (in a complicated way) 复杂地 ‹*ritualized*›

在没有对应的中文翻译时，则以解释性文字代替或添加辅助说明，以方括号标示，如：

> **do**[1] /duː/
> …
> **~ be careful!** 一定要小心！; **don't you tell me what to ~!** 用不着你来告诉我该怎么做！ **5** (in tag questions, responses) [用于附加疑问句和回答]; **he knows her, does he?** 他认识她，是吗？; **shall I tell him? — no, don't**

> **assignation** /ˌæsɪgˈneɪʃn/ *n* formal or hum [尤指男女间的] 约会; **a secret ~** 幽会

> **CIF** *abbr* **= cost, insurance, and freight** 到岸价格 [成本、保险费加运费]

有些词目只会在某一特定短语中出现，这时只解释这一短语：

> **pikestaff** /ˈpaɪkstɑːf, Amer -stæf/ *n* **as plain as a ~** 显而易见的

指示语

指示语置于圆括号内，用于区分不同义项。如下例中的 action 和 exit point:

> **egress** /ˈiːgres/ *n formal* 1 [u] (action) 外出 2 [c] (exit point) 出口

通常每个指示语下只给一个对应词，除非两个（或以上的）对应词在意义、用法及通用程度上完全可以互换。

搭配词

本词典提供部分词语或例证的常用搭配词语及相应的中文翻译，包括动词的主语和宾语，与形容词搭配的名词，与副词搭配的动词和形容词，等等。其中可搭配的主语置于双尖括号《 》内，排在中文翻译之前；其他搭配词置于尖括号〈 〉内，排在中文翻译之后。如:

> • **lock on to** *vt* [～ **on to sth.**] 《*radar, bomb*》 锁定 〈*target, building*〉

> **leniently** /ˈliːnɪəntli/ *adv* 仁慈地 〈*govern, judge*〉; 宽大地 〈*treat*〉; 宽松地 〈*mark*〉

参见项

参见符号包括 ▶ 和 =。= 用于副词条与主词条意义相同时，如:

> **absolute pitch** *n* [u] = **perfect pitch**

▶ 用于副词条需要参考主词条或与其相关的信息框时，如:

> **lake: L～ Baikal** /ˌleɪk baɪˈkɑːl/ ▶**p. 424** *pr n* 贝加尔湖; ～ **dweller** *n* 湖上居民;

《汉英词典》

《汉英词典》的收词以现代汉语的语文词目为主，兼及常见的百科性词语。对方言词语、古旧词语、词语变体及不规范用法等从严收录。

条目安排

单字条目一律按汉语拼音字母顺序排列。同音异调字按声调顺序排列（轻声字排在去声之后）。同音异形字按笔画排列：笔画少的在前，多的在后；笔画数相同的按起笔笔形横、直、撇、点、折的顺序排列；起笔笔形相同的按第二笔笔形顺序排列，依此类推。《汉英词典》之前设有“音节表”和“部首检字表”，以帮助读者检索。

单字词目有繁体或异体的，加括号附于简体字之后，如:

> 乐（樂） lè

多字词目置于实心鱼尾号【】中，随其第一个字排列于所属单字条目之后。同一单字条目下的多字条目遵照上述单字排序办法按第二个字的汉语拼音顺序、笔画数及笔形顺序排列；第二个字相同时，按第三个字排序，依此类推。如:

> 【寄予】jìyǔ
>
> 【寄语】jìyǔ
>
> 【寄寓】jìyù

以西文字母开头的词如【T恤衫】、【X光】等，一律收录在词典正文之后的“常见字母词”中。含有西文字母的其他词语，仍排在其第一个汉字之下，其中的英语字母按其读音排列，如【阿Q】ākiū 等。

注音

所有词目均加注汉语拼音。声调一般只注原调，不注变调。儿化音只在原词拼音后加 r，如:

> 【离格儿】lígér = 离谱 lípǔ
>
> 【零活儿】línghuór 〈名〉 odd job: 做～ do odd jobs

“常用字母词”中所收词语不注音，不标词性，如:

> 【A股】 A-share: ～市场 A-share market

> 【APEC】 Asia-Pacific Economic Cooperation [亚太经济合作组织]

释义

词典释义以现代汉语用法为主。如果一个对应词能用于多数情况，只给一个对应词即可。如果各对应词意义相同，且可互相替代，才给两个或以上。同一义项有两个以上对应词的，用逗号隔开，如:

> 【八开】bākāi 〈名〉［印刷］ octavo, 8vo

但如果意思有所区别，需加指示语、文体及语用标签区分，此时各义项间应用分号隔开。指示语置于圆括号内，用于区分不同义项，如:

> 操 cāo
>
> A 〈动〉 1 （拿） hold; （掌握） grasp: ～生杀大权 have absolute power ‖

英文释义所用的词语仅限于英式或美式英语中使用的，在该词语后面加标签〈英〉或〈美〉。

某些词语既有字面义，又有比喻义的，且两者均常用时，分为两个义项分别解释，如:

> 【按兵不动】 ànbīng-bùdòng 〈成〉 1 〈本〉 hold one's troops where they are 2 〈喻〉 take no action: 大家都在复习迎考，你怎么还～呢？ Everyone is preparing for the exams. How come you still haven't got yourself in gear?

释义中，对译文加以限定，或提供补充或解释性信息等，置于方括号，如:

> 【鼻韵母】bíyùnmǔ 〈名〉 [in Chinese pronunciation] vowel followed by a nasal consonant [eg an, en, in, un, ang, ing etc.]

> 【案发】ànfā 〈动〉 [of a crime] take place:

> 【老旦】lǎodàn 〈名〉 *laodan* [an old female role in traditional Chinese opera]

> 【八宝】bābǎo 〈名〉 eight treasures [assorted ingredients for certain special dishes]:

视为释义一部分或注明替换词用圆括号，如：

【鞍部】ānbù〈名〉 saddle **(of a mountain)**

【别家】biéjiā〈名〉 other households **(enterprises, shops, etc.)**: 除了我们，～商店都关门了。 All shops are closed except ours.

【臂纱】bìshā〈名〉 **(black)** armband: 戴～

有些单字条目的义项以词典中收录的多字条目为例证，用 ▶ 引出该多字条目，两个以上的多字条目间用逗号连接，如：

黎 lí〈形〉〈书〉 1（众多） numerous: ▶～民，～庶 2（黑） black: ▶～黑

本词典所用的标签及缩写，请参封底内封的一览表。

参见项

单字条目字形相同而音或调不同的分别立条，在条目后用箭头 ▶ 引出其他读音，相互参见，如：

喝[2] hē = 嗬 hē
▶hè

喝 hè〈动〉 shout loudly: 大～一声 shout loudly ▶～彩，～令，吆～
▶hē

音形相同而意义上需要分别处理的单字条目予以分立，如：

诞[1]（誕） dàn〈形〉 absurd: ▶怪～，荒～

诞[2]（誕） dàn
A〈动〉 be born: ▶～辰，～生
B〈名〉 birthday: ▶华～，圣～，寿～

形同而音不同的多字条目，分立条目，用 ▶ 引出其他读音，如：

【同行】tónghάng A〈动〉 engage in the same trade: 他俩～，都是学医的。 Both of them are in the same profession — medicine. B〈名〉 people of the same trade: ～是冤家。 People of the same trade can never agree. ‖ 他们是～。 They are in the same profession.
▶tóngxíng

【同行】tóngxíng〈动〉 travel together: ～伙伴 travel companion ‖ 与他～的还有两位同学。 Two of his classmates travelled with him.
▶tónghάng

用相关条目作例证时，以 ▶ 引出参见条目，如：

安[1] ān
A〈形〉 1（平安） safe: ～抵目的地 reach a destination safely ▶～全，～然无恙，平～

两个词目意思相同时，可在一处作解释，另一处用等号 = 参见到此词目或此词目下的相关义项，如：

【暗房】ànfáng = **暗室** ànshì 1

（表示“暗房”义同“暗室”第一义。）

案[2] àn
A〈名〉 1（案件） case: 强奸/诈骗～ rape /fraud case ‖ 该～即将由法院审理。 The case will go to trial. ▶～件，惨～，破～
2（文书） record: ▶～卷，备～，有～可查
3（文件） plan: ▶草～，教～，提～
B = **按[2]** àn A

只能用作构词成分不能单独使用的汉字，用 ▶ 参见至相关词条，如：

蚧 jiè ▶**蛤蚧** géjiè

附录及注释

附录共有 17 个（见目录页），为读者及学习者提供文化上及语言上的各种实用参考知识。例如，“信函范例”胪列了一些中英语言环境中常用的书信例子，读者可以加以参考，遇到类似的情况时可与他人以书面形式进行沟通。又如，“汉语量词”可加深以英语为母语的学习者的认识，从而更准确地运用汉语量词。

本词典的个别地方会附加文化知识框，对一些词语加以补充。如对 ABC 的注释（紧接词条 ABC）。

另外，对个别用语及语言范畴亦附有语用信息框（见“英语 • 汉语语用信息框一览表”），如 Adverbs（紧接词条 adverb）。

The structure of English-Chinese entries
《英汉词典》的词条结构

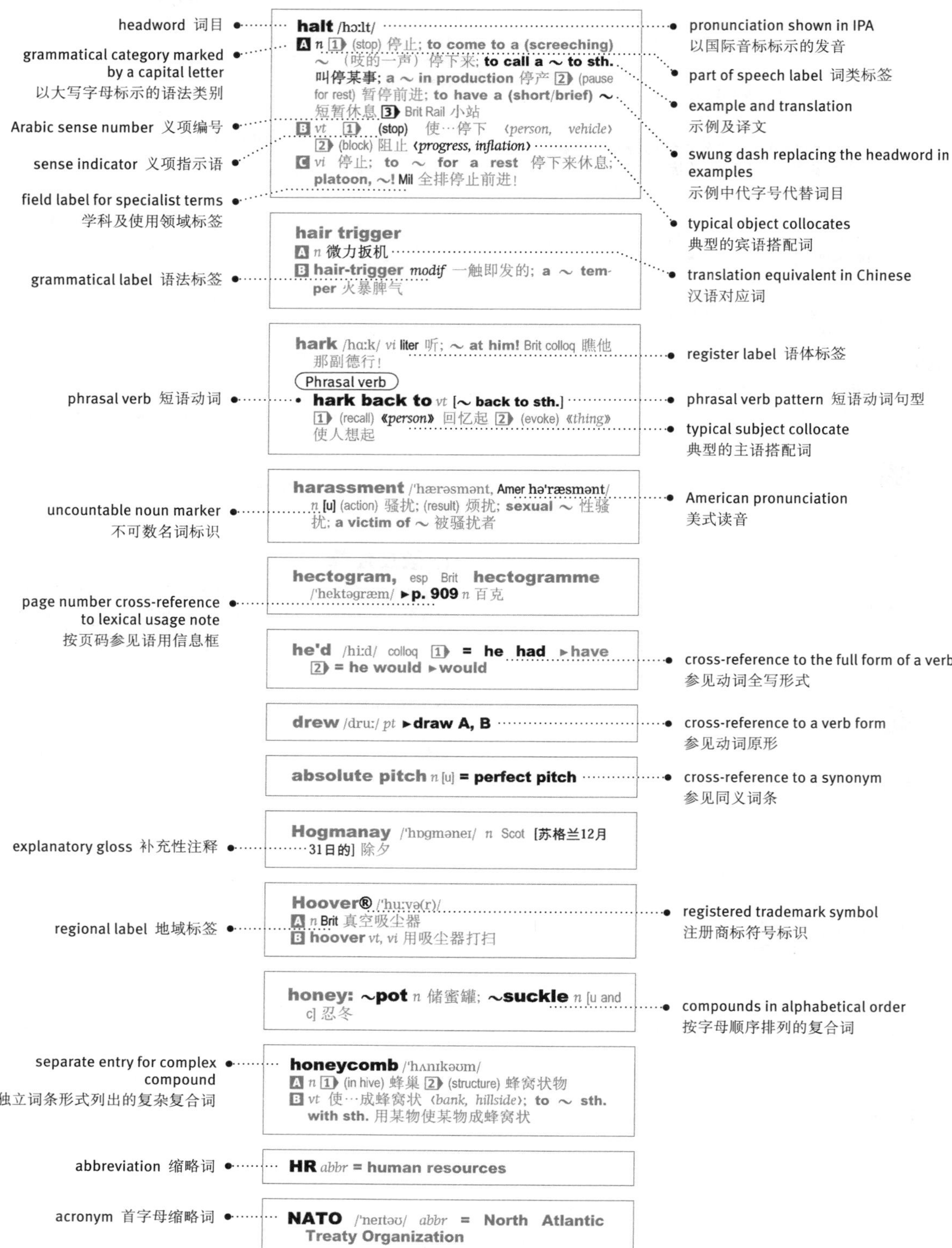

headword 词目
halt /hɔːlt/
pronunciation shown in IPA
以国际音标标示的发音
grammatical category marked by a capital letter
以大写字母标示的语法类别
A n 1 (stop) 停止; to come to a (screeching) ～ (吱的一声) 停下来; to call a ～ to sth. 叫停某事; a ～ in production 停产 2 (pause for rest) 暂停前进; to have a (short/brief) ～ 短暂休息 3 Brit Rail 小站
part of speech label 词类标签
example and translation
示例及译文
Arabic sense number 义项编号
B vt 1 (stop) 使…停下 ‹person, vehicle› 2 (block) 阻止 ‹progress, inflation›
sense indicator 义项指示语
swung dash replacing the headword in examples
示例中代字号代替词目
C vi 停止; to ～ for a rest 停下来休息; platoon, ～! Mil 全排停止前进!
field label for specialist terms
学科及使用领域标签
typical object collocates
典型的宾语搭配词
hair trigger
A n 微力扳机
B hair-trigger modif 一触即发的; a ～ temper 火暴脾气
translation equivalent in Chinese
汉语对应词
grammatical label 语法标签
hark /hɑːk/ vi liter 听; ～ at him! Brit colloq 瞧他那副德行!
register label 语体标签
Phrasal verb
phrasal verb 短语动词
• hark back to vt [～ back to sth.]
phrasal verb pattern 短语动词句型
1 (recall) «person» 回忆起 2 (evoke) «thing» 使人想起
typical subject collocate
典型的主语搭配词
harassment /ˈhærəsmənt, Amer həˈræsmənt/ n [u] (action) 骚扰; (result) 烦扰; sexual ～ 性骚扰; a victim of ～ 被骚扰者
American pronunciation
美式读音
uncountable noun marker
不可数名词标识
hectogram, esp Brit hectogramme /ˈhektəgræm/ ▸p. 909 n 百克
page number cross-reference to lexical usage note
按页码参见语用信息框
he'd /hiːd/ colloq 1 = he had ▸have 2 = he would ▸would
cross-reference to the full form of a verb
参见动词全写形式
drew /druː/ pt ▸draw A, B
cross-reference to a verb form
参见动词原形
absolute pitch n [u] = perfect pitch
cross-reference to a synonym
参见同义词条
Hogmanay /ˈhɒgməneɪ/ n Scot [苏格兰12月31日的] 除夕
explanatory gloss 补充性注释
Hoover® /ˈhuːvə(r)/
A n Brit 真空吸尘器
B hoover vt, vi 用吸尘器打扫
registered trademark symbol
注册商标符号标识
regional label 地域标签
honey: ～pot n 储蜜罐; ～suckle n [u and c] 忍冬
compounds in alphabetical order
按字母顺序排列的复合词
separate entry for complex compound
以独立词条形式列出的复杂复合词
honeycomb /ˈhʌnɪkəʊm/
A n 1 (in hive) 蜂巢 2 (structure) 蜂窝状物
B vt 使…成蜂窝状 ‹bank, hillside›; to ～ sth. with sth. 用某物使某物成蜂窝状
abbreviation 缩略词
HR abbr = human resources
acronym 首字母缩略词
NATO /ˈneɪtəʊ/ abbr = North Atlantic Treaty Organization

The structure of Chinese-English entries
《汉英词典》的词条结构

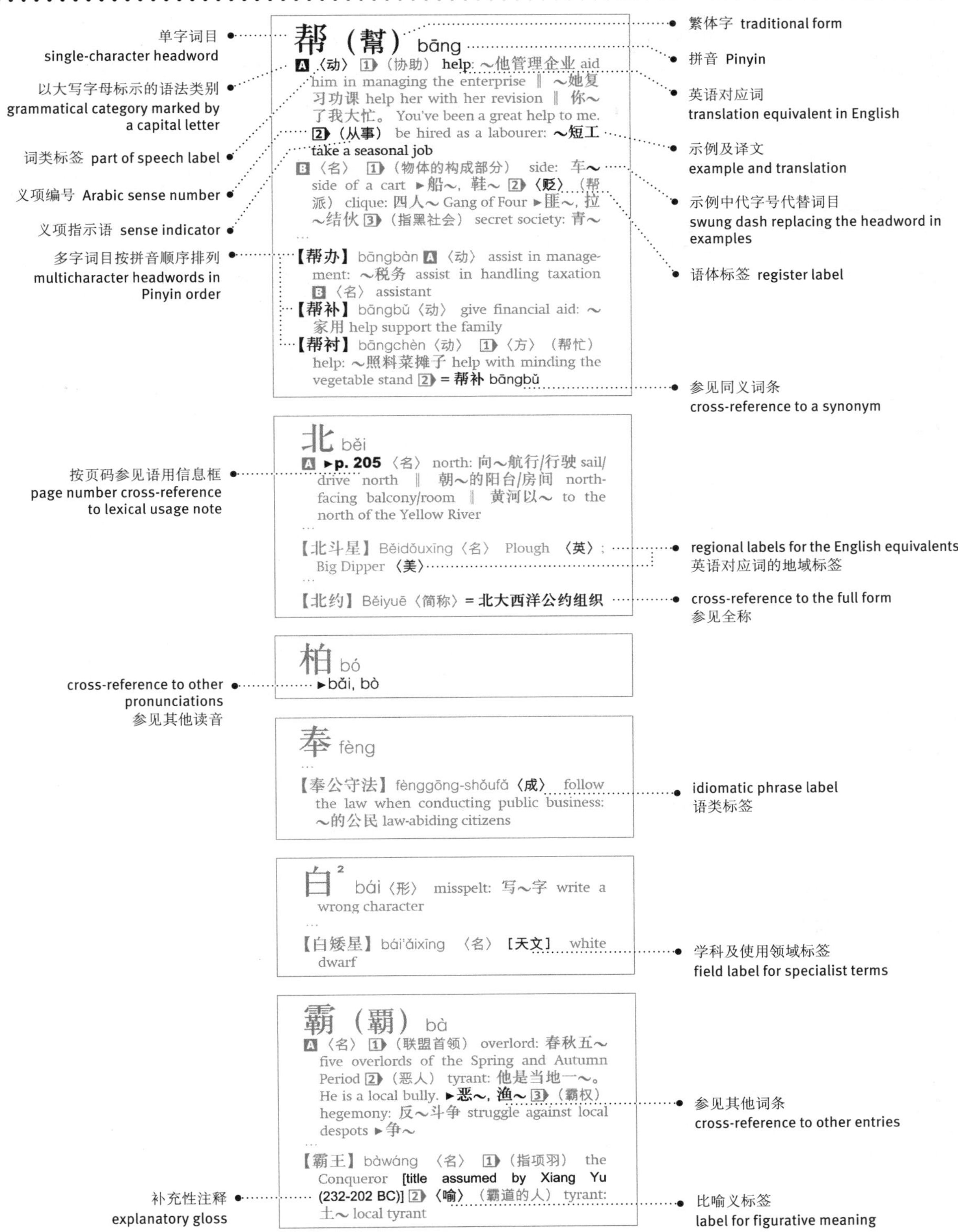

单字词目
single-character headword
以大写字母标示的语法类别
grammatical category marked by a capital letter
词类标签 part of speech label
义项编号 Arabic sense number
义项指示语 sense indicator
多字词目按拼音顺序排列
multicharacter headwords in Pinyin order
繁体字 traditional form
拼音 Pinyin
英语对应词
translation equivalent in English
示例及译文
example and translation
示例中代字号代替词目
swung dash replacing the headword in examples
语体标签 register label
帮（幫）bāng
A〈动〉1（协助）help: ～他管理企业 aid him in managing the enterprise ‖ ～她复习功课 help her with her revision ‖ 你～了我大忙。You've been a great help to me. 2（从事）be hired as a labourer: ～短工 take a seasonal job
B〈名〉1（物体的构成部分）side: 车～ side of a cart ▸船～，鞋～ 2〈贬〉（帮派）clique: 四人～ Gang of Four ▸匪～，拉～结伙 3（指黑社会）secret society: 青～
…
【帮办】bāngbàn A〈动〉assist in management: ～税务 assist in handling taxation B〈名〉assistant
【帮补】bāngbǔ〈动〉give financial aid: ～家用 help support the family
【帮衬】bāngchèn〈动〉1〈方〉（帮忙）help: ～照料菜摊子 help with minding the vegetable stand 2 = 帮补 bāngbǔ
参见同义词条
cross-reference to a synonym
按页码参见语用信息框
page number cross-reference to lexical usage note
北 běi
A ▸p. 205〈名〉north: 向～航行/行驶 sail/drive north ‖ 朝～的阳台/房间 north-facing balcony/room ‖ 黄河以～ to the north of the Yellow River
…
【北斗星】Běidǒuxīng〈名〉Plough〈英〉; Big Dipper〈美〉
…
【北约】Běiyuē〈简称〉= 北大西洋公约组织
regional labels for the English equivalents
英语对应词的地域标签
cross-reference to the full form
参见全称
cross-reference to other pronunciations
参见其他读音
柏 bó
▸bǎi, bò
奉 fèng
…
【奉公守法】fènggōng-shǒufǎ〈成〉follow the law when conducting public business: ～的公民 law-abiding citizens
idiomatic phrase label
语类标签
白² bái〈形〉misspelt: 写～字 write a wrong character
…
【白矮星】bái'ǎixīng〈名〉［天文］white dwarf
学科及使用领域标签
field label for specialist terms
霸（覇）bà
A〈名〉1（联盟首领）overlord: 春秋五～ five overlords of the Spring and Autumn Period 2（恶人）tyrant: 他是当地一～。He is a local bully. ▸恶～，渔～ 3（霸权）hegemony: 反～斗争 struggle against local despots ▸争～
…
【霸王】bàwáng〈名〉1（指项羽）the Conqueror [title assumed by Xiang Yu (232-202 BC)] 2〈喻〉（霸道的人）tyrant: 土～ local tyrant
参见其他词条
cross-reference to other entries
补充性注释
explanatory gloss
比喻义标签
label for figurative meaning

Guide to English pronunciation
英语音标及其读音

本词典标出的英式读音为较年轻的人使用的英式读音。标出的美式读音也是尽可能通用的，而非某个特定地区的读音。如果某个词语的英式读音和美式读音有差异，会先给出英式读音，再给出美式读音，美式读音前用 Amer 标示。

辅音

p	pen	/ pen /
b	bad	/ bæd /
t	tea	/ tiː /
d	did	/ dɪd /
k	cat	/ kæt /
g	get	/ get /
tʃ	chain	/ tʃeɪn /
dʒ	jam	/ dʒæm /
f	fall	/ fɔːl /
v	van	/ væn /
θ	thin	/ θɪn /
ð	this	/ ðɪs /
s	see	/ siː /
z	zoo	/ zuː /
ʃ	shoe	/ ʃuː /
ʒ	vision	/ ˈvɪʒn /
h	hat	/ hæt /
m	man	/ mæn /
n	now	/ naʊ /
ŋ	sing	/ sɪŋ /
l	leg	/ leg /
r	red	/ red /
j	yes	/ jes /
w	wet	/ wet /
x	loch	/ lɒx /

符号 (r) 表示 /r/ 这个音在英式读音中，只有当后面紧接的词以元音开头时才发音，如 wear away，否则 /r/ 就省略不读。在美式英语中，所有的 /r/ 音都应读出。

元音和双元音

iː	see	/ siː /
i	happy	/ ˈhæpi /
ɪ	sit	/ sɪt /
e	ten	/ ten /
æ	cat	/ kæt /
ɑː	father	/ ˈfɑːðə(r) /
ɒ	got	/gɒt /
ɔː	saw	/ sɔː /
ʊ	put	/ pʊt /
uː	too	/ tuː /
ʌ	cup	/ kʌp /
ɜː	fur	/ fɜː(r) /
ə	about	/ əˈbaʊt /
eɪ	say	/ seɪ /
əʊ	go	/ gəʊ /
aɪ	my	/ maɪ /
ɔɪ	boy	/ bɔɪ /
aʊ	now	/ naʊ /
ɪə	near	/ nɪə(r) /
eə	hair	/ heə(r) /
ʊə	pure	/ pjʊə(r) /

英式发音常用 /ɔː/ 代替双元音 /ʊə/，尤其在一些常见词汇中，如 sure 的发音就成了 /ʃɔː(r)/。

在美式英语中没有 /ɒ/ 音。英式读音中的 /ɒ/ 音在美式读音中以 /ɑː/ 或 /ɔː/ 取代，如 got 在英式英语中读作 /gɒt/，在美式英语中则读作 /gɑːt/；而 fog 在英式英语中读作 /fɒg/，在美式英语中则读作/fɔːg/。

音节辅音

/l/ 和 /n/ 音常可成音节，即没有元音也可构成一个音节。在 middle 惯常的读音 /ˈmɪdl/ 中 /l/ 构成一个音节，在 sudden 惯常的读音 /ˈsʌdn/ 中 /n/ 也构成一个音节。

弱元音 /i/

/iː/ 和 /ɪ/ 音一定要区分清楚，如要区分 heat /hiːt/ 和 hit /hɪt/。/i/ 这个元音读音像 /iː/，但是发得较短，如 happy /hæpi/ 一词中的 /i/。/i/ 后接 /ə/ 时亦可读为 /jə/，因此 dubious 一词可读作 /ˈdjuːbiəs/ 或 /ˈdjuːbjəs/。

弱读式与强读式

某些常用词有强读和弱读两种读音，如 at、and、for、can。要强调时就必须用强读音。词位于句末时一般也要强读。不强调时就用弱读音。如:

► *I'll help if I can* /kæn/.（强读）

► *Can* /kən/ *you help?*（弱读）

重音

符号 /ˈ/ 标示一个词的主重音位置，如 able /ˈeɪbl/ 重音在第一音节，ability /əˈbɪləti/ 重音在第二音节。

较长的词可能有一个或多个次重音，以 /ˌ/ 标示，如 abbreviation /əˌbriːviˈeɪʃn/ 和 agricultural /ˌægrɪˈkʌltʃərəl/。

两个单词同在一个短语中时，第一个单词的主重音可能会变为次重音，以避免两个相邻的重音节冲突。如 ˌafterˈnoon 的主重音在 noon，但在短语 ˌafternoon ˈtea 中，noon 的重音就消失了。ˌwell ˈknown 的主重音在 known，但在短语 ˌwell-known ˈactor 中，known 的重音消失了。

声门闭塞音

在英式英语和美式英语中，单词或音节中的 /t/ 音常可用声门闭塞音 /ʔ/（短暂屏息产生的停顿）代替。不过，若 /t/ 后是元音或成音节 /l/，就不可以代替。因此，football 可读作 /ˈfʊʔbɔːl/ 而不读 /ˈfʊtbɔːl/，button 可读作 /ˈbʌʔn/ 而不读 /ˈbʌtn/，但 bottle 或 better 的 /t/ 音不能用声门闭塞音代替，因为 /t/ 后面分别是成音节 /l/ 和元音。

Guide to Chinese pronunciation
汉语拼音及其发音方法

Chinese is not a phonetic language. This means that from looking at a Chinese character alone, it is impossible to be sure of its pronunciation. Over the years scholars have come up with various systems for phoneticizing Chinese. The dominant system in use today is Hanyu Pinyin, or simply Pinyin, the official romanization system of the People's Republic of China, and the system most commonly used in the global media. It is also the system that this dictionary uses.

The pronunciation of letters in Pinyin is not based on any one language. Although many letters in Pinyin share similar pronunciations with their counterparts in English, other letters are pronounced completely differently. In addition to learning the new pronunciation, learners of Chinese must master the four tones. As Chinese is a tonal language, the pitch at which a word is pronounced is vital in distinguishing it from other similar words. Below is a brief guide to Pinyin pronunciation, and to the tones.

The pronunciation rules below apply to Standard Chinese. There are considerable variations in pronunciation and even in tones in different parts of the People's Republic of China. Although the differences between dialects can be so great that they sound like completely different languages, today Standard Chinese is widely spoken or understood by most Chinese people, especially those living in urban areas.

Initials and Finals

Each Chinese character is pronounced as a single syllable. Most syllables are made up of two parts: an 'initial' and a 'final'. The initial is the consonant sound that makes up the first part of the syllable. The final is the sound that follows. Only certain combinations of initials and finals are allowed. The chart below shows the initials down the left side, the finals along the top, and all possible combinations in between.

There are a few points to note here. Firstly, it is possible for finals to stand alone, with no initial consonant sound. So some characters are pronounced, for example, as **ai** or **en**. Secondly, when a final beginning with the letter **u**, **ü** or **i** stands alone, it is given the initial **w** or **y**. For example, **u** becomes **wu**, **uang** becomes **wang**, **i** becomes **yi** and **ü** becomes **yu**. **w** and **y** are not considered true initials because they are not pronounced as strongly as the other initials. **yi**, for example, is pronounced somewhat like the 'ee' in 'see', similar to the 'i' in French 'si'.

Learning Chinese may seem like a daunting task, but it is possible to take comfort from the fact that once you have mastered the pronunciations of the combinations below, you will be able to pronounce every single word in the Chinese language.

Pronunciation

Initials

The initials **b**, **p**, **m**, **f**, **d**, **t**, **n**, **l**, **g**, **k**, **h**, **s**, **sh**, **ch** and **j** are pronounced much as a native English speaker would expect. The remaining initials are not hard to pronounce, but as the letters do not correspond to their equivalents in English, the individual pronunciations have to be learnt:

c- is similar to 'ts' in 'bits'

z- is similar to 'ds' in 'beds'

zh- is similar to 'dg' in 'fudge'

r- is similar to 's' in 'measure', but with slightly more of an English 'r' sound

q- is similar to 'ch' in 'cheat'

x- is halfway between 'sh' in 'sheet' and 's' in 'seat'

Finals

Most of the finals are not difficult for native speakers of English to pronounce. The endings **n** and **ng** are pronounced much as they are in English. Pronunciation points to note are listed below:

-a is similar to the exclamation 'ah'

-o and **-uo** are similar to 'or' without the 'r' pronounced

-e is similar to the 'ur' in 'fur' without the 'r' pronounced

-ai is pronounced as 'eye'

-ei is pronounced as the 'ay' in 'hay'

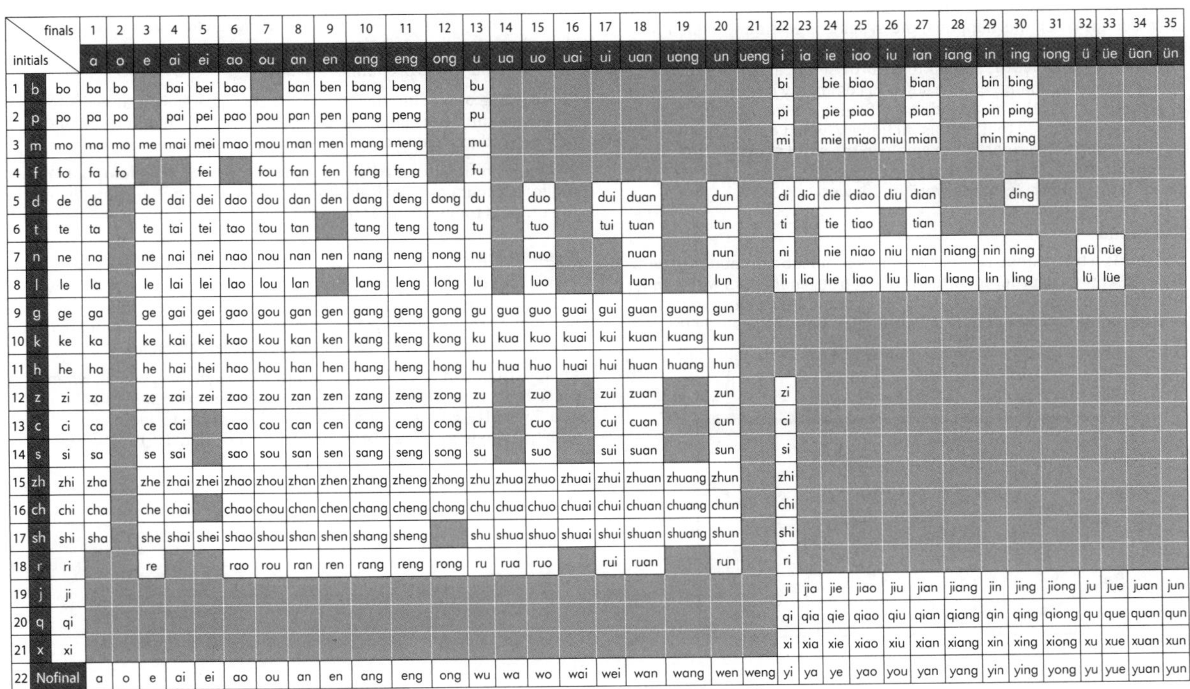

initials \ finals			1	2	3	4	5	6	7	8	9	10	11	12	13	14	15	16	17	18	19	20	21	22	23	24	25	26	27	28	29	30	31	32	33	34	35
			a	o	e	ai	ei	ao	ou	an	en	ang	eng	ong	u	ua	uo	uai	ui	uan	uang	un	ueng	i	ia	ie	iao	iu	ian	iang	in	ing	iong	ü	üe	üan	ün
1	b	bo	ba	bo		bai	bei	bao		ban	ben	bang	beng		bu									bi		bie	biao		bian		bin	bing					
2	p	po	pa	po		pai	pei	pao	pou	pan	pen	pang	peng		pu									pi		pie	piao		pian		pin	ping					
3	m	mo	ma	mo	me	mai	mei	mao	mou	man	men	mang	meng		mu									mi		mie	miao	miu	mian		min	ming					
4	f	fo	fa	fo			fei		fou	fan	fen	fang	feng		fu																						
5	d	de	da		de	dai	dei	dao	dou	dan	den	dang	deng	dong	du		duo		dui	duan		dun		di	dia	die	diao	diu	dian			ding					
6	t	te	ta		te	tai	tei	tao	tou	tan		tang	teng	tong	tu		tuo		tui	tuan		tun		ti		tie	tiao		tian								
7	n	ne	na		ne	nai	nei	nao	nou	nan	nen	nang	neng	nong	nu		nuo			nuan		nun		ni		nie	niao	niu	nian	niang	nin	ning		nü	nüe		
8	l	le	la		le	lai	lei	lao	lou	lan		lang	leng	long	lu		luo			luan		lun		li	lia	lie	liao	liu	lian	liang	lin	ling		lü	lüe		
9	g	ge	ga		ge	gai	gei	gao	gou	gan	gen	gang	geng	gong	gu	gua	guo	guai	gui	guan	guang	gun															
10	k	ke	ka		ke	kai	kei	kao	kou	kan	ken	kang	keng	kong	ku	kua	kuo	kuai	kui	kuan	kuang	kun															
11	h	he	ha		he	hai	hei	hao	hou	han	hen	hang	heng	hong	hu	hua	huo	huai	hui	huan	huang	hun															
12	z	zi	za		ze	zai	zei	zao	zou	zan	zen	zang	zeng	zong	zu		zuo		zui	zuan		zun		zi													
13	c	ci	ca		ce	cai		cao	cou	can	cen	cang	ceng	cong	cu		cuo		cui	cuan		cun		ci													
14	s	si	sa		se	sai		sao	sou	san	sen	sang	seng	song	su		suo		sui	suan		sun		si													
15	zh	zhi	zha		zhe	zhai	zhei	zhao	zhou	zhan	zhen	zhang	zheng	zhong	zhu	zhua	zhuo	zhuai	zhui	zhuan	zhuang	zhun		zhi													
16	ch	chi	cha		che	chai		chao	chou	chan	chen	chang	cheng	chong	chu	chua	chuo	chuai	chui	chuan	chuang	chun		chi													
17	sh	shi	sha		she	shai	shei	shao	shou	shan	shen	shang	sheng		shu	shua	shuo	shuai	shui	shuan	shuang	shun		shi													
18	r	ri			re			rao	rou	ran	ren	rang	reng	rong	ru	rua	ruo		rui	ruan		run		ri													
19	j	ji																						ji	jia	jie	jiao	jiu	jian	jiang	jin	jing	jiong	ju	jue	juan	jun
20	q	qi																						qi	qia	qie	qiao	qiu	qian	qiang	qin	qing	qiong	qu	que	quan	qun
21	x	xi																						xi	xia	xie	xiao	xiu	xian	xiang	xin	xing	xiong	xu	xue	xuan	xun
22	Nofinal		a	o	e	ai	ei	ao	ou	an	en	ang	eng	ong	wu	wa	wo	wai	wei	wan	wang	wen	weng	yi	ya	ye	yao	you	yan	yang	yin	ying	yong	yu	yue	yuan	yun

-ao is pronounced as the 'ow' in 'cow'

-ou is pronounced as the 'ow' in 'snow'

-an is similar to the 'un' in 'bun', but a little longer

-u is usually pronounced like the 'oo' in 'food'. However, when preceded by **j**, **q** or **x**, it is pronounced as **ü**.

-ua is pronounced like the **a** above, preceded by a 'w' sound

-uai is similar to 'why'

-ui is similar to 'way'

-uan is usually pronounced like **an** above preceded by a 'w' sound. However, when preceded by **j**, **q**, **x** or **y**, -uan is pronounced as **ü** closely followed by an 'en', as at the end of the English 'when'.

-un The 'u' in **un** is usually pronounced as **u** above. However, when preceded by **j**, **q** or **x**, the 'u' is pronounced **ü**.

-i is usually pronounced somewhat like the 'ee' in 'see', similar to the 'i' in French 'si'. However, when preceded by **c**, **ch**, **s**, **sh**, **z**, **zh** or **r**, its pronunciation changes. To make the right sound, try making a prolonged 'zzzzz' sound. The 'i' should be pronounced in a similar way to the vowel sound that results.

-ia is pronounced as 'ya' in the colloquial English 'see ya'

-ie is pronounced 'yeah'

-iao is pronounced like the **ao** above preceded by a 'y' sound

-iu is pronounced like the 'yo' in 'yolk'

-ian is pronounced 'yen'

-iang is pronounced 'yang'

-iong is pronounced 'oong', with the 'oo' as in 'book', preceded by a 'y' sound

-ü is pronounced like a German ü. This can be achieved by making a continuous 'ee' sound, rounding your lips into the position to make an 'oo' sound as you do so.

-ue is a **ü** followed by an **e** merged into a single syllable

There is one syllable which is not mentioned in the table of initials and finals: **er** (儿). It is pronounced like the word 'are' in North American English, with a heavy 'r' sound. This sound can stand alone as a syllable in its own right, for example in the word **értóng** (儿童), which means child. But **er** can also function as a suffix which changes the pronunciation of the whole syllable to which it is attached. Syllables that have no **n** or **ng** ending are then pronounced with a heavy 'r' sound at the end. Words that end in **n** or **ng** have their endings replaced with an 'r' sound. When this happens, the syllable is written with an 'r' on the end. For example, the word **wán** (玩), which means 'to play', is often pronounced **wánr**, similar to a North American 'are' with a 'w' sound at the beginning. **er** as a suffix is commonly heard in the speech of people from north China, and in the Beijing dialect, in particular. It should also be noted that, in this dictionary, when **er** stands alone as a syllable in its own right, for example in the word **értóng**, 儿童, it is written large, as 儿. But when **er** functions as a suffix, it is written as a small 儿, as in **huār**, 花儿, the word for 'flower'.

The Tones

Chinese is a tonal language. Each character must be pronounced with the correct tone in order to differentiate it from characters with similar initials and finals. There are four tones in Standard Chinese, plus a neutral, or light tone, which is not generally considered a true tone.

The chart below gives a graphical representation of the four main tones:

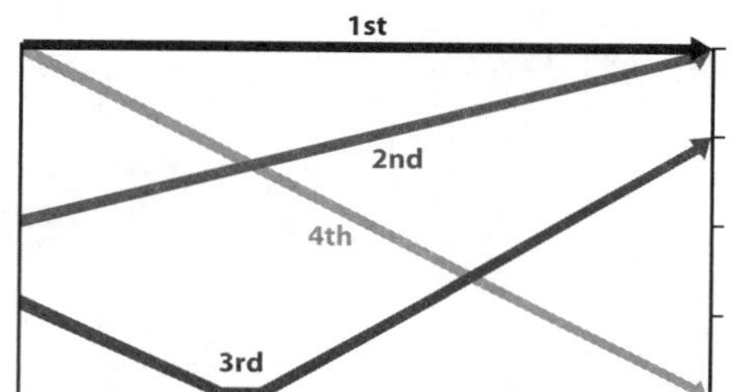

In Pinyin, the tones are represented by markers positioned above the letters.

The first tone

The first tone is a high-pitched even tone, represented by a flat line, eg mā. The pitch must stay the same throughout the whole of the syllable.

The second tone

The second tone is a rising tone, represented by a line rising from left to right, eg má. English-speakers use this tone when asking a one-word question such as "who?".

The third tone

The third tone is a falling-rising tone, shown using a v-shaped marker, eg mǎ. Starting from a mid-range pitch, the pitch should fall and then rise again. Beginners sometimes find that it helps to lower and then raise the chin when making this sound, as if tracking the tone's shape.

The fourth tone

The fourth tone is a sharp, falling tone, represented by a line falling from left to right, eg mà. English speakers use this tone when issuing an expletive or a command. Imagine ordering a disobedient dog to 'sit'.

The neutral tone

Characters pronounced with a neutral tone are pronounced lightly, with no emphasis. This is represented by the absence of a tone marker, eg ma.

Tonal Changes

Two common characters change their tone according to the characters that follow them. These are 一 (**yī**) meaning 'one' and 不 (**bù**) meaning 'not'.

不 is pronounced in the fourth tone (**bù**). However, when followed by another fourth tone character, 不 becomes second tone (**bú**). For example, 不是 meaning 'is not' is pronounced **bú shì**.

一 is pronounced in the first tone (**yī**) when pronounced on its own. However, it changes its tone depending on the tone of the following character.

一 is pronounced in the fourth tone (**yì**) when followed by a first tone, second tone or third tone character. For example:

一张 (one sheet) is pronounced **yì zhāng**
一瓶 (one bottle) is pronounced **yì píng**
一点儿 (a little) is pronounced **yì diǎnr**

一 is pronounced in the second tone (**yí**) when followed by a fourth tone character. For example:

一束 (a bunch) is pronounced **yí shù**

There is one other situation in which a character may change its tone. When two third-tone characters appear next to each other, the first is pronounced as second tone. For example:

你 (you) is pronounced **nǐ** and 好 (good) is pronounced **hǎo**, but 你好 (hello) is pronounced **ní hǎo**. Note that in this dictionary usually only the original tones are indicated, not the tonal changes.

General Tips

Remember that it is important to pronounce each character as only a single syllable. So 'dian' is pronounced not as 'di-en' but 'dyen' and 'liang' not as 'lee-ang' but as 'lyang'. Similarly, 'Tian'anmen' is pronounced not as 'Ti-en-an-men', but as 'Tyen-an-men'.

An apostrophe may be used to separate two syllables which, when placed together, look like a single syllable. For example, 'pi'ao' (皮袄) and 'Xi'an' (西安) are separated by an apostrophe to avoid confusion with the single syllable words 'piao' (票) and 'xian' (线).

Index of English and Chinese lexical usage notes
英语·汉语语用信息框一览表

Aa

A, a /eɪ/ *n* (*pl* **As** *or* **A's**) 1▸ (letter) [英语字母表的第1个字母]; **from A to Z** 从头至尾; **the A to Z of cooking** 烹饪大全 2▸ (first of two or more points or possibilities) 第一（个）; **a) ... b) ...** 第一… 第二… 3▸ **A** Mus A音, A调 4▸ **a** (in house or flat number) A座 5▸ Sch, Univ (grade) 优 [指学业成绩第一等]; **he got an A for his essay** 他的文章得了优 6▸ **A** (place) 某地; **how to get from A to B** 如何从甲地到乙地 7▸ **A** Brit Transp A级公路 [英国次于高速公路的主干公路]; **we only drove on A roads — we didn't go on the motorways at all** 我们只是在主干公路上开的车—根本没上高速公路

a /eɪ, ə/; *before a vowel or silent 'h'* **an** /æn, ən/ ▸**p. 2, p. 162** *det* 1▸ (before countable or singular nouns) 一（个）; **~ horse** 一匹马; **an aunt/egg** 一位姑母/一个鸡蛋; **~ man came out of the room** 一名男子从屋里走出来; **I'll have ~ think about it** 我要想一想这事 2▸ (before uncountable nouns with adjective) [用于带修饰语的不可数名词之前]; **~ good knowledge of French** 对法语的精通; **~ sadness that won't go away** 挥之不去的悲伤 3▸ (any) 任何一个; **I haven't got ~ thing to wear** 我没衣服可穿; **she didn't say ~ word** 她一言不发 4▸ (each of a species) 每一个; **~ lion is a dangerous animal** 狮子是危险的动物 5▸ (indicating membership of a group) [表示某一类中的一员]; **is that ~ Monet?** 那是一幅莫奈的画吗? 6▸ (before two nouns forming a unit) [用于构成一个单位的两个名词之前]; **~ knife and fork** 一副刀叉 7▸ (with numbers) **~ hundred** 一百; **~ quarter of an hour** 一刻钟; **half ~ cup/spoonful** 半杯/半勺 8▸ (per) 每; **twice ~ day** 每天两次 9▸ (someone like) 类似…的一个; **you're no better than ~ Hitler** 你简直和希特勒一样坏 10▸ (a certain) 某个; **~ Mr Smith telephoned** 有位史密斯先生来过电话 11▸ (with days) [表示星期中的某一天]; **he died on ~ Monday** 他是在一个星期一去世的

A1 *adj* colloq 很棒的; **guitar for sale: ~ condition** 吉他出售: 品相上佳

A2 level *n* Brit (course) 第二学年高级考试科目; (exam) 第二学年高级证书考试

AA *abbr* Brit = **Automobile Association** 汽车协会

AAA *abbr* 1▸ Amer = **American Automobile Association** 美国汽车协会 2▸ Brit = **Amateur Athletics Association** 业余体育协会

A&E *abbr* Brit = **Accident and Emergency**

AB *abbr* 1▸ Naut = **able seaman** 2▸ Amer Univ = **BA**

aback /ə'bæk/ *adv* **to take sb. ~** 使某人震惊; **to be taken ~ (by sth./sb.)** （因某事物/某人）大吃一惊; **I was taken ~ by his reply/retort** 他的回答/反驳把我吓了一大跳

abacus /'æbəkəs/ *n* (*pl* **~es**) 算盘

abalone /ˌæbə'ləʊni/ *n* 鲍鱼

abandon /ə'bændən/

A *vt* 1▸ (desert) 抛弃 ‹*person*›; 离弃 ‹*place, building*›; **to ~ sb. to his/her fate** 抛弃某人让其听天由命; **to ~ one's post** 擅离职守; **to ~ ship** 弃船 2▸ (stop, give up) 放弃 ‹*hope, plan*›; 中止 ‹*match, project, search*›; 戒除 ‹*habit*›

B *v refl* **to ~ oneself to sth.** 沉湎于; **to ~ oneself to a life of pleasure** 恣意享乐; **to ~ oneself to despair** 陷入绝望

C *n* [u] 放纵; **with gay** *or* **wild ~** 放纵地

abandoned /ə'bændənd/ *adj* 1▸ (deserted) 被遗弃的; **~ children** 弃儿; **an ~ car** 被丢弃的车 2▸ (wild) 无拘束的 ‹*movements, gestures*›; 奔放的 ‹*dancing*› 3▸ (licentious) 放荡的 ‹*behaviour*›

abandonment /ə'bændənmənt/ *n* 1▸ (desertion) 离弃; **the earthquake led to the ~ of whole villages** 地震使得整村的村民背井离乡 2▸ (giving up) (of hope, plan) 放弃; (of match, project, search) 中止

abase /ə'beɪs/ *v refl* **to ~ oneself before sb.** 在某人面前低声下气

abashed /ə'bæʃt/ *adj* 羞愧的

abate /ə'beɪt/

A *vi* «*flood, temperature*» 减退; «*epidemic, pain, anger*» 减轻; «*feeling, terror, noise*» 减少; **the wind had ~d from force 10 to force 8** 风力已从10级降到8级; **her fever ~d a little** 她的烧退了一点

B *vt* 1▸ (gen) 减少 ‹*tax, noise, pollution*› 2▸ Jur (end) 消除; **to ~ a nuisance** 消除妨害

abatement /ə'beɪtmənt/ *n* (of storm, wind) 减弱; (of fever) 减退; (of feeling, terror, noise) 减轻

abattoir /'æbətwɑː(r), Amer ˌæbə'twɑːr/ *n* 屠宰场

abbess /'æbes/ *n* 女修道院院长

abbey /'æbi/ *n* (monastery, convent) 修道院; (church) 教堂

abbot /'æbət/ *n* 男修道院院长

abbreviate /ə'briːvieɪt/ *vt* 缩写 ‹*word, sentence, name*›; 压缩 ‹*passage, speech*›; **'Mister' is usually ~d to 'Mr'** Mister通常缩写成Mr

abbreviation /əˌbriːvi'eɪʃn/ *n* 1▸ [c] (short form) 缩略形式; **the article has an excessive number of ~s** 这篇文章的缩略语太多 2▸ [u] (process) 缩写

> **ABC**
>
> 美国广播公司，全称 American Broadcasting Company。和全国广播公司（▸**NBC**）及哥伦比亚广播公司（▸**CBS**）同为美国的三大全国性广播电视公司。总部位于纽约，前身为NBC的蓝网。NBC本来拥有两个广播网，一个称红网（Red Network），一个称蓝网（Blue Network）。因美国联邦通信委员会规定一家公司不得拥有两个以上广播网，NBC在1943年将蓝网出售，后由爱德华·约翰·诺布尔（Edward John Noble）购得，并命名为 American Broadcasting System，翌年改称为 American Broadcasting Company。自1996年起，ABC被迪士尼公司（The Walt Disney Company）收购为子公司。

ABC

A *n* 1▸ (alphabet) 字母表; **to be as easy/simple as ~** 非常容易/简单 2▸ (alphabetical guide) 指南; **the London ~** 伦敦指南 3▸ (basics) 基础知识; **the ~ of cookery** 烹饪入门

B *abbr* = **American Broadcasting Company** 美国广播公司

abdicate /'æbdɪkeɪt/

A *vt* 1▸ (renounce) 退出; **to ~ the throne** «*monarch*» 退位 2▸ (fail to fulfil) 放弃 ‹*duty, responsibility*›

B *vi* «*monarch*» 退位

abdication /ˌæbdɪ'keɪʃn/ *n* (royal) 退位; (of responsibility) 放弃; **~ of duty** 弃责

abdomen /'æbdəmən/ *n* 腹部

abdominal /æb'dɒmɪnl/ *adj* 腹部的; **~ muscles/pains** 腹肌/腹痛

abduct /əb'dʌkt/ *vt* 绑架

abduction /əb'dʌkʃn/ *n* 绑架; **cases of child ~** 诱拐儿童案件

abductor /əb'dʌktə(r)/ *n* 1▸ (kidnapper) 绑架者 2▸ Anat **~ (muscle)** 外展肌

aberrant /ə'berənt/ *adj* 反常的 ‹*behaviour, ideas*›; 异常的 ‹*results, conclusions*›; **~ forms of religious belief** 宗教信仰的畸态

aberration /ˌæbə'reɪʃn/ *n* 1▸ (deviation) 反常 2▸ (lapse) 偏离; **in a moment of ~** 一时糊涂

abet /ə'bet/ *vt* (*pres p etc.* **-tt-**) 怂恿 ‹*person*›; 唆使 ‹*crime, accomplice*›; **to aid and ~ sb. in doing sth.** 伙同某人做某事

abeyance /ə'beɪəns/ *n* [u] **in ~** 被搁置; **the law is currently in ~** 这项法律目前尚未实施; **to fall into ~** «*law, agreement*» 中止

abhor /əb'hɔː(r)/ *vt* (*pres p etc.* **-rr-**) 憎恶; **they ~ having to write reports** 他们讨厌要写报告; **nature ~s a vacuum** 自然界里不存在真空

abhorrence /əb'hɒrəns, Amer -'hɔːr-/ *n* [u] 憎恶; **to have an ~ of sth., to hold sth. in ~** 憎恶某事物

abhorrent /əb'hɒrənt, Amer -'hɔːr-/ *adj* 令人憎恶的; **to be ~ to sb.** 令某人憎恶

abide /ə'baɪd/

A *vt* 忍受; **I can't ~ that/doing that** 我不能容忍那事/做那事

B *vi* **to ~ by** 服从 ‹*decree, judgement*›; 遵守 ‹*rule, promise, agreement*›

abiding /ə'baɪdɪŋ/ *adj attrib* 持久的 ‹*friendship, interest, memory*›; 难以消除的 ‹*hatred, mistrust*›; 坚定的 ‹*faith*›

ability /ə'bɪləti/

A *n* [u] 1▸ (capability) 能力; **(the) ~ to pay** 支付能力; **to the best of one's ~** 竭尽所能; **within the limits of one's ~** 在自己的能力范围内 2▸ (talent) 才智; **someone of proven ~** 有才实干的人

B **abilities** *npl* 技能; **mental abilities** 智力; **musical abilities** 音乐才能

ability: ~ level *n* 能力水平; **~ range** *n* 能力范围

abject /'æbdʒekt/ *adj* 1▸ (miserable) 悲惨的 ‹*condition*›; **~ poverty** 赤贫; **~ misery** 凄惨 2▸ (servile) 卑贱的 ‹*coward, slave*›; 卑躬屈节的 ‹*flattery, surrender*›; 低声下气的 ‹*apology*›

abjectly /'æbdʒektli/ *adv* 1▸ (miserably) 悲惨地 ‹*live, subsist*› 2▸ (servilely) 卑躬屈膝地 ‹*behave, surrender*›; 低声下气地 ‹*apologize*›

abjure /əbˈdʒʊə(r)/ vt formal 声明放弃 ‹right, title, religion›; 发誓戒除 ‹vice›

ablaze /əˈbleɪz/ adj pred 1 (alight) 燃烧的; **to set sth. ~** 焚烧某物 2 (lit up) 明亮的; **to be ~ with candles/lights/fireworks** 被烛光/灯光/烟花照亮 3 fig 热烈的; **eyes ~ with rage** 喷射怒火的眼睛

able /ˈeɪbl/ adj 1 (having power, means, skill, opportunity) 有…能力的; **to be ~ to do sth.** 能做某事; **he wasn't ~ to read it** 他读不懂这个; **she was ~ to play chess when she was three** 她三岁时就会下象棋; ▸**ready C1** 2 (skilled) 能干的; **a very ~ lawyer** 很有才干的律师; **the dancers were technically very ~** 这些舞蹈演员舞技高超; **the ~st student in the class** 班上最有才华的学生

able-bodied adj 体格健全的; **the only ~ man on the farm** 农场里唯一的壮劳力

able seaman n Brit 一等水兵

ablutions /əˈbluːʃnz/ npl 1 formal or hum (washing) 沐浴; **to perform one's ~** 沐浴 2 Brit hum (building) 澡堂

ably /ˈeɪbli/ adv 出色地 ‹demonstrated, translated›; 有力地 ‹supported›; 巧妙地 ‹guided›; **~ assisted by his colleagues** 在他同事的得力帮助下; **he performs ~ on the piano** 他钢琴弹得很出色

ABM abbr = **anti-ballistic missile** 反弹道导弹

abnegate /ˈæbnɪgeɪt/ vt formal 放弃 ‹pleasures, privileges, rights, religion›; 交出 ‹powers›; **to ~ personal responsibility** 规避个人责任

abnegation /ˌæbnɪˈgeɪʃn/ n [u] formal 1 (of pleasures, privileges, rights, religion) 放弃 2 (self-denial) 自我克制; **to live a life of total ~** 过严格自律的生活

ℹ A / an, one, and the

■ 'A', 'an', or 'one' can sometimes be translated as 一, though often they are not exactly equivalent to 一.

A / an

■ When 'a/an' means 'one', it can be translated as 一:

a/one hundred
= 一百

a/one thousand
= 一千

a/one third
= 三分之一

There are three bananas and one orange on the table
= 桌子上有三根香蕉和一个橘子

■ When 'a/an' means 'per', it is translated as 每:

I go to the gym once a week
= 我每周去次健身房

The pills must be taken three times a day
= 这药片要每天吃 3 次

She earns about £20,000 a year
= 她每年大概挣 20,000 英镑

The lawyer normally charges £120 an hour
= 律师一般每小时收费 120 英镑

The lunch costs £15 a person
= 午餐每人 15 镑

The apples are £2 a kilo
= 苹果每公斤两镑

■ When 'a/an' refers to a person or thing not previously mentioned or does not refer to a particular person or thing, it can be translated as 一 followed by a measure word such as 个, 位, 张, etc. In such cases 一 may be omitted:

She bought a shirt. It looks so nice on her
= 她买了（一）件衬衫，穿上去很好看

I have a pet cat. She is called Dora
= 我有（一）只宠物猫，她叫多拉

My mother bought me a book
= 母亲给我买了（一）本书

She's got a husband
= 她有（一）个丈夫

■ When 'a/an' is used to refer to a person or thing in a particular category, no article is required in Chinese:

She can ride a motorbike
= 她会骑摩托车

I'd love a beer
= 我想喝啤酒

■ When 'a/an' refers to an occupation, no article is required in Chinese:

She is a teacher
= 她是老师

He is a doctor
= 他是医生

■ When 'a/an' is used before a name to refer to someone not known, it may be translated into Chinese as 某个, 一个 or 一位:

There was a call from a Miss Davis
= 有一个戴维斯小姐打过电话来

A Mr. Lincoln is waiting for you
= 一位姓林肯的先生在等你

One

■ 'One', meaning the number '1', can be translated as 一 or 一 followed by a measure word such as 个, 位, 张, 岁, 年, etc.:

one per cent
= 百分之一

one hundred tables
= 一百张桌子

She has three apples, and I have only one
= 她有三个苹果，我只有一个

The baby is just one year old
= 宝宝刚满一岁

Ten letters came today, but only one was for Dennis
= 今天到了十封信，但只有一封是丹尼斯的

■ 'One' referring to a member of a group may be translated as …之一, 有一个… or …的一个…:

One of my sons is working abroad
= 我有一个儿子在国外工作

One of her sisters is married
= 她的一个姐姐已经结了婚

Princes Street is one of the busiest streets in Edinburgh
= 王子大街是爱丁堡最繁忙的街道之一

Hong Kong Airport is one of the biggest airports in the world
= 香港机场是世界上最大的机场之一

The

■ There are many cases in Chinese where the definite article 'the' is not translated, as in the following examples:

■ When the object(s) is/are considered to be unique:

the Earth
= 地球

the sky
= 天空

■ When 'the + singular noun' represents a class of things or people:

The primary school teacher is highly respected in this country
= 在这个国家里小学老师很受尊敬

■ When 'the + adjective' represents a class of people:

the rich
= 富人

the sick
= 病人

■ When 'the + the plural surname' refers to the family:

the Duncans
= 邓肯一家

■ When 'the' is used before certain proper nouns, including names of oceans, seas, rivers, archipelagos, mountains, countries, deserts, regions, etc.:

the Pacific Ocean
= 太平洋

the Yellow River
= 黄河

the Solomon Islands
= 索罗门群岛

the Himalayas
= 喜马拉雅山脉

the United States
= 美国

the Sahara
= 撒哈拉大沙漠

the Middle East
= 中东

■ When 'the' is used before certain nouns and proper names:

the National Gallery
= 国家美术馆

the Tower of London
= 伦敦塔

the Beatles
= 披头士乐队

the Guardian
= 卫报

the first month
= 第一个月

the most popular singer
= 最受欢迎的歌星

the only way
= 唯一的办法

abnormal /æb'nɔːml/ *adj* 反常的 ‹*behaviour, weather*›; 不正常的 ‹*person, circumstances, interest*›; 异常的 ‹*specimen*›; **physically/mentally ~** 身体异常的/精神失常的; **sexually ~** 性变态的

abnormality /ˌæbnɔː'mæləti/ *n* **1** [u] (state) 反常; **sexual/social/physical/psychological ~** 性行为/社会行为/身体/心理异常 **2** [c] (feature) 异常特征; **a congenital ~** 先天畸形

abnormally /æb'nɔːməli/ *adv* 异常地 ‹*high, expensive, hot, low, easy*›; 反常地 ‹*behave, react, develop*›

Abo, abo /'æbəʊ/ *n* Austral colloq offensive 土著居民

aboard /ə'bɔːd/
A *adv* 在船上/车上/飞机上; **to come** *or* **go** *or* **step ~** 上船/上车/登机
B *prep* 在…上 ‹*aircraft, train, bus, ship*›; **all ~!** 请上船/上车/登机!

abode /ə'bəʊd/ *n* **1** [c] formal or liter (home) 住所; **my humble ~** hum 寒舍; **sb. with** *or* **of no fixed ~** 居无定所的人 **2** [u] Jur (residence) 居住; **the right of ~** 居住权

abolish /ə'bɒlɪʃ/ *vt* 废除 ‹*law, right, tax, penalty, custom, system, slavery*›; 取消 ‹*subsidy, service, allowance*›; **they argued that divorce should be ~ed** 他们主张应当禁止离婚

abolition /ˌæbə'lɪʃn/ *n* [u] (of law, right, tax, penalty, custom, system, slavery) 废除; (of subsidy, service, allowance) 取消; **a petition for the ~ of animal experiments** 禁止动物实验的请愿书

abolitionist /ˌæbə'lɪʃənɪst/ *n* (opposed to slavery) 废奴主义者; (opposed to the death penalty) 主张废除死刑者

abominable /ə'bɒmɪnəbl, Amer -mən-/ *adj* 恶劣的 ‹*conditions, weather*›; 恶毒的 ‹*accusation*›; 令人讨厌的 ‹*behaviour*›; 糟糕的 ‹*music, handwriting, food*›; 少得可怜的 ‹*wages*›

Abominable Snowman *n* **the ~** 雪人 [据传生活在喜马拉雅山雪域、似人或熊的巨大长毛动物]

abominably /ə'bɒmɪnəbli, Amer -mən-/ *adv* **1** (terribly) 糟糕地 ‹*act, treat*›; **the pianist played ~** 这个弹钢琴的人弹得很差劲 **2** (as intensifier) 极其 ‹*hot, bad, rude*›

abominate /ə'bɒmɪneɪt, Amer -mən-/ *vt* formal 憎恶

abomination /əˌbɒmɪ'neɪʃn, Amer -mə'n-/ *n* **1** [u] (loathing) 憎恶; **to hold sb./sth. in ~** 憎恶某人/某事物 **2** [c] (loathsome thing) 令人憎恶的事物; **what an ~!** 真恶心!

aboriginal /ˌæbə'rɪdʒənl/
A *adj attrib* 土著的 ‹*inhabitant, settlement, tribe*›; 本地的 ‹*plant, species, animal*›
B *n* **1** (original inhabitant, animal, or plant) 土著 **2** **Aboriginal = aborigine 2**

aborigine /ˌæbə'rɪdʒəni/ *n* **1** (original people) 土著居民 **2** **Aborigine** (original people living in Australia) (澳大利亚) 土著

abort /ə'bɔːt/
A *vt* **1** (terminate) 使…流产 ‹*baby, embryo*›; 终止 ‹*pregnancy*› **2** (abandon) 取消 ‹*mission, attack, project, process, deal*› **3** Comput 中止 ‹*program, operation*›
B *vi* **1** (miscarry) «*baby, embryo, mother*» 流产 **2** Comput «*program, operation*» 中止

abortifacient /əˌbɔːtɪ'feɪʃənt/
A *adj* 堕胎的 ‹*drug*›; **to have ~ properties** 会导致流产
B *n* 堕胎药

abortion /ə'bɔːʃn/ *n* 流产; **to perform** *or* **carry out an ~ on sb.** 给某人做人工流产手术; **a spontaneous/an induced ~** 自然/人工流产; **a backstreet ~** 非法堕胎

abortionist /ə'bɔːʃənɪst/ *n* [尤指非法] 施行堕胎手术者; **a backstreet ~** 非法施行堕胎手术者

abortive /ə'bɔːtɪv/ *adj attrib* 失败的

abound /ə'baʊnd/ *vi* «*fish, food, drink*» 大量存在; fig «*ideas*» 丰富; «*energy*» 充沛; **rumours ~ed** 传言四起; **to ~ in sth.** 充满某物; **this career ~s in opportunities** 这个职业充满机遇

about /ə'baʊt/ ▸**p. 487**
A *prep* **1** (concerning, regarding) 关于; **a book/film ~ sth.** 有关某内容的书/电影; **I'm ringing ~ my results** 我打电话来问一下我的检查结果; **what was all that ~?** 这到底是怎么回事? **2** (bound up with) 为了; **business is ~ making profits** 做生意就是为了赢利 **3** (in the nature of) 在…的特征中; **what I like ~ her is her frankness** 我喜欢她的地方是她的直率; **there's something odd ~ him** 他这人有点怪; **there's something ~ the place that intrigues me** 这地方总有什么东西让我着迷 **4** (occupied with) 从事于; **to know what one is ~** 明白自己在做什么; **while you're ~ it** 趁着你干这件事的时候; **(and) be quick ~ it!** 快点干完! **5** esp Brit (in many directions within, in many parts of) 在…各处; **we wandered ~ the town all afternoon** 我们整个下午都在城里四处游逛; **he looked anxiously ~ the room** 他在房间里焦急地四下察看 **6** (in invitations, suggestions, when soliciting opinions) [用于邀请、建议、询问]; **what/how ~ sb./sth.?** 某人/某事物怎么样/如何?; **how ~ a drink?** 来一杯怎么样?; **what ~ going into town?** 进城去好吗?; **how ~ you?** 你呢? **7** (with) 在…身上; **he said he had no money ~ him** 他说他没带钱; **to have drugs/weapons ~ one's person** 身上藏有毒品/武器 **8** Brit (surrounding) 围绕着; (on either side of) 在…两侧; **there were trees ~ the house** 屋子四周绿树环绕
B *adv* **1** ▸**p. 32** (approximately) 大约; **at ~ 6 p.m.** 下午 6 点左右; **(and) ~ time too!** 再说正是时候呢!; **that's ~ it** (that's all) 就是这些; (that's the situation) 就是这样; **as far as I know, that's ~ it** 据我所知, 就这么回事 **2** (almost) 几乎; **we're ~ ready** 我们差不多准备好了; **I've had just ~ enough** 我差不多吃饱了 **3** esp Brit (within area) 在四周; **I had difficulty finding my way ~** 我不知该怎么走; **there was no one ~** 附近没有人 **4** esp Brit (in circulation) 存在着; **there was a lot of flu ~** 那时流感正在肆虐 **5** esp Brit (indicating reverse position) 向相反方向; **it's the wrong way ~** 方向搞反了
C *adj* **1** (expressing future intention) 刚要…的; **we're (just) ~ to start** 我们正要开始 **2** (awake and out of bed) 活动中的; **to be up and ~** [睡醒或病愈后] 起来四处走动; **you were up and ~ early this morning** 你今天早晨起来得很早嘛 **3** (rejecting course of action) 愿意; **I'm not ~ to tell him** 我不想告诉他

about-face esp Amer, **about-turn** Brit *ns* **1** esp Mil 向后转 **2** fig 彻底转变; **the government has done an ~** 政府的态度来了个 180 度的大转变

above /ə'bʌv/
A *prep* **1** (in/at a higher place than) 在…上面; **2,000 feet ~ sea level** 海拔 2,000 英尺; **the water came ~ my knees** 水没过了我的膝盖; **you are ~ me on the list** 名单上你排在我前面 **2** (north of) 在…以北 **3** (upstream of) 在…的上游 **4** (morally) 不屑于; **he's not ~ bending the rules** 他不在乎随意改变规则 **5** (in preference to) 优先于; **to admire sth. ~ all others** 独好某事物; **to value happiness ~ wealth** 珍视幸福甚于财富 **6** (higher than, superior in status to) 高于; **the E ~ middle C** 高于中央 C 音的 E 音; **she married ~ her** 她嫁给了地位比自己高的人; **to be/get ~ oneself** 自高自大/变得自高自大 **7** (greater in quantity than) 大于; **children ~ the age of 3** 3 岁以上的儿童; **to rise ~** 上升至…以上 ‹*amount, average*› **8** (beyond) 超脱于; **to be ~ suspicion** 无可置疑 **9** (too difficult for) 超出…能力所及; **the book was ~ most readers** 那书多数读者读不懂
B *adv* **1** (in/at a higher place) 在上面; **the room ~** 上面的屋子; **the view from ~** 高处看到的景致 **2** (superior in status) 在上级; **an order from ~** 上级的命令 **3** (earlier in text) 在上文; **see ~** 见前文; **as stated ~** 如前所述 **4** (in the sky) 在空中; **the stars ~** 天上的星星; **in Heaven ~** 在天上
C *adj attrib* 上述的
D **the above** *pron* formal (person) 上文提到的人; (thing) 上文提到的事物; **I agree with the ~** 我同意上文所述
E **above all** *adv phr* (most importantly) 最重要的是; (especially) 尤其; **he is concerned ~ all with facts** 他最在意的是事实; **~ all else he's a businessman** 他说到底是个商人

above board
A *adj pred* 光明正大的; **certain transactions were not totally ~** 某些交易并非完全光明正大
B *adv* 合法公正地; **to make money ~** 通过合法手段赚钱
C **above-board** *adj attrib* 光明正大的

above: ~-mentioned *adj attrib* 上述的; **~-named** *adj attrib* 上文提及的

abracadabra /ˌæbrəkə'dæbrə/ *excl* 阿布拉卡达布拉 [魔术师表演魔术时所念的模拟咒语]

abrasion /ə'breɪʒn/ *n* **1** [c] (on skin) 擦伤处; (on surface) 磨损处 **2** [u] (process) 磨损

abrasive /ə'breɪsɪv/
A *adj* **1** (for grinding) 有研磨作用的 ‹*substance*›; 擦洗的 ‹*cleaner*›; **emery paper is less ~ than sandpaper** 金刚砂纸比砂纸细 **2** (harsh) 粗鲁的 ‹*criticism, remark, tone, personality, manner*›
B *n* 磨料; **a harsh/light ~** 粗/细磨料

abrasiveness /ə'breɪsɪvnɪs/ *n* [u] **1** (of material, substance) 磨耗性 **2** (of criticism, remark, tone, personality, manner) 粗鲁

abreast /ə'brest/ *adv* **1** (side by side) 并排; **to cycle three ~** 三辆自行车并排而行; **to be/come ~ of** 与/上来与…并排 ‹*vehicle, person*› **2** (in touch with) **~ of** 与…齐头并进; **to keep ~ of the times/new developments** 与时俱进/跟上新发展

abridge /ə'brɪdʒ/ *vt* 删节; **an ~d version** 节本

abridgement, abridgment /ə'brɪdʒmənt/ *n* **1** [c] (version) 节本 **2** [u] (process) 删节

abroad /ə'brɔːd/ *adv* **1** (in other countries) 在国外; (to other countries) 到国外; **imported from ~** 从国外进口的; **news from home and ~** 国内外新闻 **2** (in circulation) 在流传中; **there is a rumour ~ that ...** 纷纷谣传…; **there is a feeling ~ that ...** 人们普遍感到…

abrogate /'æbrəgeɪt/ *vt* 废除 ‹*law, treaty*›; 取消 ‹*privilege*›

abrogation /ˌæbrə'geɪʃn/ *n* [u] 废除

abrupt /ə'brʌpt/ *adj* **1** (sudden) 突然的 ‹*departure, arrival, change*›; 意外的 ‹*dismissal*›; **to come to an ~ end** 骤然停止 **2** (curt) 粗鲁的 ‹*manner, person*›; 生硬的 ‹*tone*› **3** (disjointed) 不连贯的 ‹*speech, style*›; **short, ~ sentences** 突兀的短句 **4** (steep) 陡峭的 ‹*slope*›; (sharp) 急转的; **an ~ turn in the road** 公路的急转弯

abruptly /ə'brʌptli/ *adv* **1** (suddenly) 突然地 ‹*leave, arrive, change*› **2** (curtly) 唐突地 ‹*speak, behave*›; 不客气地 ‹*dismiss*› **3** (steeply) 陡峭地 ‹*drop (away), rise (up), climb*›; **to turn ~ left** 向左急转

abruptness /ə'brʌptnɪs/ *n* [u] **1** (suddenness) 突然 **2** (brusqueness) 唐突

abscess /'æbses/ *n* 脓肿

abscond /əb'skɒnd/ *vi* 逃走; **to ~ from somewhere** 逃离某处; **to ~ with the funds** 携卷资金潜逃

absconder /əb'skɒndə(r)/ *n* (escapee) 潜逃者; (prisoner) 逃犯

abseil /'æbseɪl/
A *vi* 绕绳下降; **to ~ down a rock** 沿岩石绕绳下降
B *n* 绕绳下降

abseiling /'æbseɪlɪŋ/ *n* [u] 绕绳下降; **~ device** 绳降装置; **~ technique** 绳降技巧; **to go ~** 绕绳下降

absence /'æbsəns/ *n* [u] **1** (being away) 缺席; **in** *or* **during sb.'s ~** 某人不在时; **~ with pay** 带薪休假; **leave of ~** 休假; **to be conspicuous by one's ~** 因缺席而引人注目; **~ of mind** 心不在焉; **~ makes the heart grow fonder** Prov 别久情更深 **2** (lack) 缺乏; **in the ~ of** 在缺乏…的情况下 ‹*alternative, cooperation, evidence, assurances*›; **notable** *or* **conspicuous by** *or* **for its/their ~** 因缺失而引人注目

absent
A /'æbsənt/ *adj* **1** (not present) 缺席的; **to be ~ from work** 缺勤; **to be ~ from school** 缺课; **she was conspicuously ~** 她的缺席很显眼; **(to) ~ friends!** (as toast) 为不在场的朋友们干杯!; **to be/go ~ without leave** Mil 擅离职守 **2** (preoccupied) 心不在焉的 ‹*person, expression, manner*› **3** *pred* (lacking, missing) «*emotions, features*» 缺乏的
B /əb'sent/ *v refl* **to ~ oneself** 不到场

absentee /ˌæbsən'tiː/ *n* 缺席者

absentee ballot *n* Amer [在外公民的] 邮寄式投票

absenteeism /ˌæbsən'tiːɪzəm/ *n* [u] (from work) 缺勤; (from school) 缺课

absentee: ~ landlord *n* 在外业主; **~ rate** *n* (of workers) 缺勤率; (of students) 缺课率; **~ voter** *n* 邮寄式投票者

absently /'æbsəntli/ *adv* 心不在焉地

absent: ~-minded *adj* 心不在焉的; **to become ~-minded with age** 因上了年纪而健忘; **~-mindedly** *adv* 心不在焉地; **~-mindedness** *n* [u] 心不在焉

absinthe /'æbsɪnθ/ *n* [u] 苦艾酒

absolute /'æbsəluːt/
A *adj* **1** (complete) 绝对的 ‹*truth, freedom, trust, secrecy, devotion*›; 断然的 ‹*refusal*›; 确凿的 ‹*proof*›; 专断的 ‹*monarch, power*›; **an ~ majority** Pol 绝对多数; **an ~ beginner** 不折不扣的新手 **2** (emphatic) 十足的 ‹*fool, mess, scandal*› **3** Phys, Chem 绝对的; **~ temperature** 绝对温度; **~ value** 绝对值; **~ scale** 绝对温标; **~ humidity** 绝对湿度; **~ alcohol** 纯酒精 **4** Brit Jur 绝对的 ‹*order, rule*›; **decree ~** 绝对判决 [离婚诉讼中解除婚姻关系的最终判决]
B *n* 绝对事物; **rigid ~s** 僵化的绝对准则; **the ~** Philos 绝对

absolute discharge *n* 无条件释放

absolutely /'æbsəluːtli/ *adv* **1** (totally) 绝对地 ‹*agree, believe, right, opposed to*›; 断然地 ‹*refuse*›; 极其 ‹*fascinating*›; **you ~ must come and see us soon!** 你无论如何得早日到我们这儿来啊!; **I ~ adore opera!** 我对歌剧十分着迷! **2** (certainly) 当然; **~ not!** 当然不!

absolute pitch *n* [u] = **perfect pitch**

absolution /ˌæbsə'luːʃn/ *n* [u] 赦罪; **to give sb. ~ from their sins** 赦免某人的罪孽

absolutism /'æbsəluːtɪzəm/ *n* [u] **1** Pol 专制政体 **2** Philos 绝对主义

absolutist /'æbsəluːtɪst/
A *n* **1** Pol (practising absolutism) 专制者; (advocating absolutism) 支持专制政体者 **2** Philos 绝对主义者
B *adj* **1** Pol (practising absolute government) 专制的; (advocating absolute government) 专制主义的 **2** Philos 持绝对主义观点的 ‹*person, position*›; **~ beliefs/principles** 绝对信仰/原则

absolve /əb'zɒlv/ *vt* **1** (clear) 使免除; **to ~ sb. from** *or* **of sth.** 使某人免于某事; **to ~ him from a crime** 赦免他的罪行 **2** Relig (forgive) 赦免…的罪 ‹*sinner, guilty person*›; **to ~ sb. from sin** 赦免某人的罪孽

absorb /əb'zɔːb/ *vt* **1** lit 吸收 ‹*water, drug, oxygen, heat*› **2** fig 掌握 ‹*knowledge, facts*›; 吸引 ‹*attention*› **3** (take control of) 吞并 ‹*business, village*› **4** (withstand) 消减 ‹*shocks, sound*›; 承受 ‹*blows, punishment, impact, pressure*›; **to ~ immigrants/refugees** 吸纳移民/难民

absorbable /əb'zɔːbəbl/ *adj* 可吸收的 ‹*material*›; **~ suture** *or* **stitches** 可吸收手术缝合线

absorbed /əb'zɔːbd/ *adj* 全神贯注的; **~ in a book/one's work** 专心读书/工作; **to get** *or* **become ~ in sth.** 对某事物着迷

absorbency /əb'zɔːbənsi/ *n* [u] 吸收性; **a high-~ material** 高吸收性材料

absorbent /əb'zɔːbənt/ *adj* 易吸收液体的 ‹*material, cloth*›; **~ cotton wool** 脱脂棉

absorbent cotton *n* Amer 卫生棉

absorbing /əb'zɔːbɪŋ/ *adj* 吸引人的 ‹*work, activity, book, programme*›; **a totally ~ film** 扣人心弦的影片

absorption /əb'zɔːpʃn/ *n* [u] **1** (of substance) 吸收 **2** fig (integration) (of people) 融合; (of business) 合并; **the slow ~ of immigrants into a new land** 移民融入新国家的缓慢过程 **3** (of shock, impact) 消减; **shock ~** 消震; **sound ~** 声吸收 **4** (in activity, book) 专注

abstain /əb'steɪn/ *vi* **1** also Relig 戒除; **to ~ from sth./doing sth.** 刻意回避/不做某事; **to ~ from alcohol** *or* **drinking** 戒酒; **to ~ from sex** 禁欲 **2** Pol 弃权; **to ~ from voting** 投票时弃权

abstainer /əb'steɪnə(r)/ *n* **1** (teetotaller) 滴酒不沾的人 **2** (in vote) 弃权者

abstemious /æb'stiːmɪəs/ *adj* 有节制的 ‹*person*›; 简朴的 ‹*meal, diet, habit*›; **you're being very ~!** 你可真够抠的!

abstemiously /æb'stiːmɪəsli/ *adv* 节俭地 ‹*live*›; 有节制地 ‹*eat, drink*›

abstemiousness /æb'stiːmɪəsnɪs/ *n* [u] 节制

abstention /əb'stenʃn/ *n* **1** [u and c] (from vote) 弃权; **his ~ from voting** 他弃权不投票 **2** [u] = **abstinence**

abstinence /'æbstɪnəns/ *n* [u] 节制; **many religions practice ~** 许多宗教都有斋戒习俗; **~ from sth.** 对某事物的刻意回避

abstinent /'æbstɪnənt/ *adj* 节制的; **to be totally ~ from alcohol** 滴酒不沾

abstract
A /'æbstrækt/ *adj* **1** (theoretical) 抽象的 ‹*idea, theory, entity, symbol*›; 理论上的 ‹*argument, speculation, problem*› **2** Art 抽象(派)的 **3** Ling 抽象的 ‹*noun, adjective, verb*›
B /'æbstrækt/ *n* **1** [u] (theoretical) 抽象; **in the ~** 在抽象意义上 **2** [c] (summary) 摘要 **3** [c] Art 抽象派作品
C /əb'strækt/ *vt* **1** (summarize) 写…的摘要 ‹*information, book*› **2** formal (remove) 提取; **~ facts from a mound of periodicals** 从一大堆期刊中摘取事实
D /əb'strækt/ *v refl* **to ~ oneself from sth.** 使自己脱离某事物

abstracted /əb'stræktɪd/ *adj* 出神的 ‹*look, stare, air, expression*›; **he seemed rather ~** 他看上去心不在焉

abstraction /əb'strækʃn/ *n* **1** [u] (absent-mindedness) 出神; **an air of ~** 出神的样子 **2** [c] (idea) 抽象概念; **to talk in ~s** 讲话时用上很多抽象概念

abstruse /əb'struːs/ *adj* 深奥的 ‹*remark, information, calculations*›; 费解的 ‹*details, explanation*›

abstruseness /əb'struːsnɪs/ *n* [u] 深奥

absurd /əb'sɜːd/
A *adj* 荒唐的 ‹*behaviour, question, suggestion, idea*›; 怪诞的 ‹*look*›; **to be ~ (of sb.) to do sth.** (某人)做某事很荒唐; **it is ~ that ...** …真是荒唐可笑
B *n* **the ~** 荒诞

absurdity /əb'sɜːdəti/ *n* **1** [u] 荒谬; **the height of ~** 绝伦的荒谬; **to the point of ~** 达到荒唐的地步 **2** [c] (absurd concept) 荒唐的想法; (absurd event) 怪诞事

absurdly /əb'sɜːdli/ *adv* **1** (extremely) 极其 ‹*high, rich, expensive, cheap, stupid*› **2** (stupidly) 荒唐地 ‹*act, behave*›; **he was driving ~ fast** 他开车快得离谱

ABTA /'æbtə/ *abbr* Brit = **Association of British Travel Agents** 英国旅行社协会

Abu Dhabi /ˌæbuː 'dɑːbi/ *pr n* (state) [阿联酋的] 阿布扎比酋长国; (capital) 阿布扎比

Abuja /ə'buːdʒə/ *pr n* 阿布贾

abundance /ə'bʌndəns/ *n* [u] **1** (profusion) 大量; **the island has water in ~** 岛上淡水充沛; **an ~ of wildlife** 众多的野生生物 **2** (prosperity) 富足; **to live a life of ~** 过富裕的生活

abundant /ə'bʌndənt/ *adj* 大量的; **an area ~ in red roses** 盛产红玫瑰的地区; **a country ~ in natural resources** 自然资源丰富的国家

abundantly /ə'bʌndəntli/ *adv* **1** (in large quantities) 大量地 ‹*supplied, available, yield*›; 茂盛地 ‹*grow*› **2** (very) 极其; **to make sth. ~ clear (to sb.)** (对某人)彻底讲清楚某事

abuse
A /ə'bjuːz/ *vt* **1** (mistreat) 虐待; (sexually) 对…进行性虐待 **2** (misuse) 滥用 ‹*power, position, drugs*›; **to ~ sb.'s confidence** 辜负某人的信任; **to ~ the hostess's hospitality** 利用女主人的好客 **3** (insult) 辱骂 ‹*person*›
B /ə'bjuːs/ *n* **1** [u] (maltreatment) 虐待; (sexual) 性虐待 **2** [u and c] (misuse) 滥用; **~s of the judicial system** 践踏司法体制的行为; **alcohol ~** 酗酒 **3** [u] (insult) 辱骂; **a stream** *or* **shower of ~** 一通谩骂; **a term of ~** 骂人话; **to hurl ~ at sb.** 破口大骂某人

abuser /ə'bjuːzə(r)/ *n* **1** (maltreater) (of people) 虐待者; (sexual) 性虐待者 **2** **substance ~** (of drugs) 嗜毒者; (of alcohol) 酗酒者

abusive /ə'bjuːsɪv/ *adj* **1** (rude) 粗鲁的 ‹*person*› **2** (insulting) 辱骂的 ‹*remarks*› **3** (violent) 虐待的 **4** (improper) 被滥用的 ‹*influence, position*›; 腐败的 ‹*practices*›

abusively /ə'bjuːsɪvli/ *adv* 侮辱性地

abut /ə'bʌt/ (*pres p etc.* **-tt-**)
A *vt* 与…邻接; **our land ~s theirs** 我们的土地和他们的挨着
B *vi* 邻接; **the garden ~s on the playing fields** 花园紧挨着运动场; **to ~ against sth.** 靠着某物

abutment /ə'bʌtmənt/ *n* (of building) 拱座; (on bridge) 桥台

abuzz /ə'bʌz/ *adj, adv* 嗡嗡响的(地); **to be ~ with** *or* **about** *or* **over sth.** 因某事物而嘈杂; **the whole village was ~ with rumours/the news** 全村谣言四起/对这消息议论纷纷

abysmal /ə'bɪzml/ *adj* 糟透的; **to work in ~ conditions/for ~ wages** 在极恶劣的条件下/为赚取微薄的工资工作

abysmally /ə'bɪzməli/ *adv* 极其 ‹*bad, ignorant, poor*›; 极糟糕地 ‹*act, behave*›; **to fail ~** 惨败

abyss /ə'bɪs/ *n* lit, fig 深渊; **two ideologies divided by an ~** 截然不同的两种意识形态

AC *abbr* = **alternating current**

a/c *abbr* = **account A1**

acacia /ə'keɪʃə/ *n* 金合欢树

academe /'ækədiːm/ *n* [u] 学术界; **the halls** *or* **groves of ~** 学府

academia /ˌækə'diːmɪə/ *n* [u] 学术界

academic /ˌækə'demɪk/
A *adj* 1 (of universities, colleges) 大学的 ‹*study, course, system*›; 学业的 ‹*progress, adviser*›; 学术的 ‹*freedom, standards*›; **~ qualifications** 学历; **an ~ rank** 学衔; **an ~ year** 学年; **an ~ gown** 学位服 2 (scholarly) 学业优秀的 ‹*person*›; 学术性的 ‹*institution, style, approach*›; **she's not very ~** 她学习不太好; **~ subjects** 学科 3 (theoretical) 纯理论的 ‹*debate, question*›; **a matter of ~ interest** 纯理论的问题
B *n* (teacher) 高校教师; (researcher) 高校科研人员; (scholar) 学者

academically /ˌækə'demɪkli/ *adv* (educationally) 学业上; (intellectually) 学术上 ‹*sound, respectable, gifted*›; **to be well-qualified ~** 在学术方面完全符合资格; **~-minded** 有学术头脑的

academicals /ˌækə'demɪklz/ *npl* = **academic dress**

academic dress *n* [u] 学位服

academician /əˌkædə'mɪʃn, Amer ˌækə-/ *n* 1 (member of learned society) 学会会员 2 Amer (academic, teacher) 高校教师; (researcher) 高校科研人员; (scholar) 学者

academy /ə'kædəmi/ *n* 1 (learned society) 研究院 2 (training school) 专科院校; **~ of music** 音乐学院; **~ of art** 艺术学校 3 Amer, Scot (secondary school) 中等学校

Academy Award *n* 学院奖

> **Academy Award**
>
> 学院奖，即奥斯卡金像奖，是 1927 年成立的美国电影艺术与科学学院（Academy of Motion Picture Arts and Sciences）创立的电影奖项。正式名称为“学院成就奖”（Academy Award of Merit）。自 1929 年起，每年颁发一次。奖品为高 13.5 英寸、重 8.5 磅的镀金铜像，是一个手持宝剑站立在电影胶片卷轴上的骑士，由美国著名雕塑家乔治·斯坦利（George Stanley）设计制作。卷轴上的五根辐条代表电影艺术与科学学院最初的五类成员：演员、导演、制片、编剧与技术人员。有关“奥斯卡”这一名称的由来，较为流行的说法是学院的图书管理员玛格丽特·赫里克（Margaret Herrick）认为铜像像她的叔叔奥斯卡（Oscar）。1939 年，“奥斯卡”的别名被正式采用。

ACAS /'eɪkæs/ *abbr* Brit = **Advisory Conciliation and Arbitration Service** 咨询调解与仲裁局

accede /ək'siːd/ *vi* **to ~ to sth.** 1 (give in to) 答应 ‹*request, demand*›; 满足 ‹*wish*› 2 (assume) 就任 ‹*post*›; **to ~ to the throne** 即位 3 Pol 加入 ‹*treaty, agreement*›

accelerate /ək'seləreɪt/
A *vi* 1 Aut 加速; **to ~ away** 加速离开; **to ~ from 0 to 60 mph** 从每小时 0 英里加速到 60 英里 2 fig 加快; **the fall in unemployment has ~d** 失业率加速下降
B *vt* also Phys 加快; **the new machinery ~d the work rate** 新机器提高了工作效率

accelerated learning *n* [u] 1 (intensive study) 速成学习 2 (educational system) 速成体制 [允许优秀学生跳级的教育体制]

acceleration /əkˌselə'reɪʃn/ *n* [u] 1 Aut 加速; **the new car has much better ~** 新车的加速性能良好得多; **~ time** 加速时间 2 (increase) 加快; **the recent ~ in the growth of drug-related crimes** 最近涉毒犯罪活动的急遽增长 3 Phys 加速度

accelerator /ək'seləreɪtə(r)/ *n* 1 Aut 油门; **to tread** *or* **step on the ~** 踩油门; **to ease up on the ~** 松开油门 2 Phys 粒子加速器

accelerator: ~ key *n* 快捷键; **~ pedal** *n* 油门踏板

accent
A /'æksent, -sənt/ *n* 1 (gen) 口音; **in** *or* **with a French ~** 带法国口音 2 Ling, Mus (stress) 重音; Ling (mark) 重音符号; **to put the ~ on sth.** (stress) 将重音放在某音节上; (mark) 给某词加重音符号; fig 强调某事; **with the ~ on quality** 对质量的强调; **the ~ is on participation** 重在参与
B /æk'sent/ *vt* 1 Ling 重读; Mus 以重音演奏 2 fig (make prominent) 强调

accented /'æksentɪd/ *adj* 1 (with an accent) 有口音的; **he speaks a heavily ~ English** 他说英语带有浓重的口音 2 (stressed) 重读的 ‹*syllable*›

accentuate /æk'sentʃʊeɪt/ *vt* 1 (gen) 重读 ‹*speech*›; 使…更明显 ‹*feature, feelings*› 2 Mus 加重音符号于

accentuation /ækˌsentʃʊ'eɪʃn/ *n* 1 (gen) 强调 2 Mus 重音

accept /ək'sept/ *vt* 1 (take, receive) 接受 2 (take as suitable) 采用 3 (take in) 吸收; (take on) 聘用 ‹*applicant*› 4 (recognize as true) 相信; **it is generally ~ed that ...** 普遍认为… 5 (resign oneself to) 忍受 6 (tolerate) 容忍 ‹*behaviour*› 7 (take upon oneself) 承担 ‹*blame*›

acceptability /əkˌseptə'bɪləti/ *n* [u] 可接受性; **to gain ~ in the market** 在市场上获得认可

acceptable /ək'septəbl/ *adj* 1 (satisfactory) 可接受的; **to propose a compromise ~ to both parties** 提出一个双方都能接受的折中方案 2 (allowable) 可容忍的; **within ~ limits** 在可忍受的限度之内; **to be ~ to do sth.** 做某事是可以容忍的 3 dated (welcome) 受欢迎的; **oh, a cup of tea would be most ~!** 噢，来杯茶再好不过了!

acceptably /ək'septəbli/ *adv* 1 (in an acceptable manner) 可接受地; **he behaved quite ~ despite our disagreements** 尽管我们持不同意见，但他的表现还能让人接受 2 (satisfactorily) 令人满意地; **he found the hotel rooms ~ comfortable** 他觉得酒店房间相当舒适

acceptance /ək'septəns/ *n* 1 [u and c] (of offer) 接受; **a letter of ~** 接受函 2 [u] (of plan, proposal) 赞成; **to meet with** *or* **find ~** 得到认同; **to gain ~** 受欢迎 3 [u] (resignation) 忍受; **the numb ~ of one's fate** 对命运的麻木忍受 4 [u and c] Fin, Insur (of bill, policy) 承兑; Comm (of goods) 验收; **to present a bill for ~** 递交承兑汇票; **~ of goods/delivery** 收货/交货验收

acceptance trials *npl* 验收试航

accepted /ək'septɪd/ *adj* 公认的; **it's a generally ~ fact that ...** 公认的事实是…; **the ~ sense of the word/term** 该词/术语的通用意义

acceptor /ək'septə(r)/ *n* 承兑人

access /'ækses/
A *n* [u] 1 (means of entry) 入口; **~ to the centre is from the street** 中心的入口在大街上; **'no ~'** “禁止入内”; **to obtain** *or* **get** *or* **gain ~ to sth.** 获得进入某处的机会; **an ~ door** 通道门 2 (ability to obtain, use) 享用机会; **to have ~ to information/education** 有获得信息/接受教育的机会 3 Jur (right to visit) 探视权; **to have/grant/deny right of ~** 拥有/给予/拒绝给予探视权 4 Comput 存取
B *vt* 1 (approach, enter) 进入; **the island can be ~ed by road at low tide** 退潮时可从陆路登上该岛 2 Comput 存取 ‹*data*›; 访问 ‹*website*›

accessary *n* = **accessory**

access: ~ code *n* (of computer network) 访问码, 存取码; (of building) 密码; **~ course** *n* Brit 大学入学补习课程

accessibility /əkˌsesə'bɪləti/ *n* [u] 1 (ease of reaching) 容易到达 2 (understandability) 可理解; **the limited ~ of modern music** 现代音乐的不易理解 3 (affordability) 可负担

accessible /ək'sesəbl/ *adj* 1 (easy to reach) 容易到达的; **a park easily ~ to the public** 公众往来方便的公园 2 (easy to obtain or use) 易获得的 3 (easy to understand) 易理解的 4 (affordable) 负担得起的; **to make foreign travel ~ to the general public** 让普通民众负担得起出国旅游

accession /æk'seʃn, ək-/ *n* 1 [u] (to treaty, organization) 正式加入; **the country's ~ to the treaty/organization** 这个国家的正式加入该条约/组织 2 [u] (to power, title) 就职; (to throne) 即位 3 [c] (new item) 新增物品; **~s to the library** 图书馆的新增藏书

accession: ~ country *n* 欧盟候补成员国; **~ language** *n* 欧盟候补成员国语言

accessory /ək'sesəri/
A *n* 1 (piece of equipment) 附件; **a home computer with all the accessories** 一台配件齐全的家用电脑 2 Fashn 装饰品 3 Jur 从犯; **an ~ to murder** 谋杀案从犯; **~ before/after the fact** 事前/事后从犯
B *modif* 附加的 ‹*item, device*›

access: ~ point 1 (to river, hiking trail etc.) 入口; 2 Comput 存取点; **~ port** *n* 存取端口; **~ provider** *n* 互联网接入服务供应商; **~ road** *n* (to building, site) 通道; (to motorway) 支路; **~ television** *n* [u] 向公众开放的电视时间; **~ television programme** 公众电视节目; **~ time** *n* 存取时间

accident /'æksɪdənt/ *n* 1 (mishap) 事故; **to meet with/have an ~** 碰上/出事故; **a slight/serious/fatal ~** 轻微/严重/致命的事故; **~ and emergency service** 急诊服务; **I had an ~ with the teapot** 我不小心把茶壶打翻了; **~s will happen!** 出意外是难免的!; **the baby's had a little ~** euph 婴儿拉到裤子里了; **a chapter of ~s** 接二连三的事故 2 (chance) 偶然的事; **it is no ~ that ...** …绝非偶然; **by ~** 意外地; **he is rich by an ~ of birth** 他碰巧生来就富有

accidental /ˌæksɪ'dentl/
A *adj* 1 (by mishap) 意外的 ‹*death, injury, killing*› 2 (by chance) 偶然的 ‹*meeting, event*›; **an ~ meeting** 不期而遇 3 (incidental) 附带的 ‹*benefit, effect*›; 次要的 ‹*element, feature*›
B *n* Mus 临时记号

accidentally /ˌæksɪ'dentəli/ *adv* (by accident) 意外地 ‹*happen, drop, break*›; (by chance) 偶然地 ‹*meet*›; **to do sth. ~ on purpose** iron 看似无心实则有意地做某事

accident: A~ and Emergency *n* [u] 急诊室; **~ and Emergency Department** *n* 急诊部; **~ and Emergency Unit** *n* 急诊室; **~ blackspot** *n* Brit 交通事故多发区; **~ insurance** *n* [u] 意外伤害保险; **~ prevention** *n* [u] 事故预防; **~-prone** *adj* 易出事故的; **don't let him go skiing, he's so ~-prone** 别让他去滑雪了，他动不动就出事; **~ victim** *n* 事故受害者

acclaim /ə'kleɪm/
A *vt* 1 (praise) 称赞 2 fig (cheer) 为…喝彩; **the new system was ~ed as a technological breakthrough** 这个新系统被誉为技术上的一大突破 3 (proclaim) 拥立; **to ~ sb. king** 拥立某人为国王
B *n* [u] 1 (praise) 赞扬; **to win ~** 赢得赞扬 2 (cheering) 欢呼; **roars of ~** 阵阵欢呼声

acclaimed /ə'kleɪmd/ *adj* 受到赞扬的; **her much ~ exploits** 她那些广受称颂的功绩

acclamation /ˌæklə'meɪʃn/ *n* [u] 1 (loud and enthusiastic approval) 喝彩; **he received great ~ wherever he spoke** 他不论在哪里演讲都受到热烈欢迎 2 (vocal approval without ballot) **elected** *or* **chosen by ~** 经口头表决当选

acclimate /'æklɪmeɪt, Amer ə'klaɪ-/ = **acclimatize**

acclimation /ˌæklaɪ'meɪʃn/ *n* [u] Amer = **acclimatization**

acclimatization /əˌklaɪmətaɪ'zeɪʃn, Amer -tɪ'z-/ *n* [u] 适应环境

acclimatize /ə'klaɪmətaɪz/
A *vt* 使适应; **to ~ sb./oneself/sth. to sth.** 使某人/自己/某物适应某一环境; **eventually**

a

she became ~d to the novel surroundings 最后她习惯了新环境
B *vi* 适应; **yes, it's very cold, but I'll ~ in a week or two** 是的，天很冷，但过一两个星期我就会习惯的

accolade /ˈækəleɪd, ˌækəˈleɪd/ *n* 1 (specific honour) 荣誉; **to confer** *or* **bestow an ~ on sb.** 将一项荣誉授予某人 2 (praise) 赞扬; **to receive** *or* **win ~s from all sides** 赢得各方的赞誉 3 (on being knighted) 骑士称号的授予仪式 [君主将剑搭在受册封者肩上]

accommodate /əˈkɒmədeɪt/
A *vt* 1 (provide space for) 为…提供住宿 ‹*guests*›; 容纳 ‹*passengers*›; **how many cars will the car park ~?** 这个停车场能停多少辆车?; **the site can ~ 10 factories** 这个地方能建 10 座工厂 2 (adapt to) 适应 3 formal (meet request of) 为…提供便利 ‹*client*›; 关照 ‹*interests*›; **I think I can ~ you** 我想我可以为你提供方便
B *v refl* **to ~ oneself to sb./sth.** 使自己适应某人/某事物; **it took a long time for me to ~ myself to the notion** 我花了很长时间才接受了这个观念

accommodating /əˈkɒmədeɪtɪŋ/ *adj* 与人方便的; **she was very ~ in allowing us to use her phone** 她很乐于助人，允许我们使用她的电话; **he showed himself ~** 他显得通情达理

accommodation /əˌkɒməˈdeɪʃn/ *n* 1 (*also* **~s** Amer) (living quarters) 住所; **'~ to let'** Brit "房屋出租"; **1st class/de luxe ~** 最高档的/豪华客房; **the office block had ~ for thousands of clerks** 办公大楼可容纳数千职员 2 (agreement) 和解; **to come to** *or* **reach an ~ on** *or* **over sth. with sb.** 与某人就某事达成和解

accommodation: ~ address *n* Brit 临时通信地址; **~ bureau** Brit, **~s bureau** Amer *n* 住宿联络处 [为游客提供短租信息]; **~ ladder** *n* 舷梯; **~ officer** Brit, **~s officer** Amer ▸**p. 409** *n* 住宿协调员

accompaniment /əˈkʌmpənɪmənt/ *n* 1 Mus 伴奏; **as an ~ to ...** 作为对…的伴奏; **with piano ~** 以钢琴伴奏; **to the ~ of soft music** 在轻柔音乐的伴奏下 2 Culin 佐餐食物; **red wine is an excellent ~ to cheese** 红酒是奶酪最佳的搭配食物

accompanist /əˈkʌmpənɪst/ *n* 伴奏者

accompany /əˈkʌmpəni/
A *vt* 1 (go with) 陪同; **to be accompanied by sb.** 由某人陪伴; **to ~ sb. (to) somewhere** 陪某人去某地 2 Mus 为…伴奏; **to ~ sb. (at** *or* **on an instrument)** (用乐器) 为某人伴奏 3 fig (occur with, provide alongside) 伴随; **poverty and illness usually ~ one another** 贫穷往往与疾病相伴; **diagrams ~ing the text** 附在正文里的多张图表
B *vi* Mus 伴奏

accomplice /əˈkʌmplɪs, Amer əˈkɒm-/ *n* 共犯; **an ~ to** *or* **in (a) crime** 同案犯

accomplish /əˈkʌmplɪʃ, Amer əˈkɒm-/ *vt* 完成 ‹*task, job, mission*›; 达到 ‹*goal*›; 结束 ‹*journey*›; **he ~ed a lot in a long career** 他在漫长的职业生涯中成就颇丰

accomplished /əˈkʌmplɪʃt, Amer əˈkɒm-/ *adj* 技艺娴熟的 ‹*dancer, cook, performance*›; 有造诣的 ‹*poet*›; **a most ~ dress designer** 技艺纯熟的服装设计师; **to be ~ at sth./doing sth.** 在某事/做某事方面技艺高超

accomplishment /əˈkʌmplɪʃmənt, Amer əˈkɒm-/ *n* 1 [u] (act of accomplishing) 实现; **the ~ of a task** 任务的完成 2 [c] (thing accomplished) 成就; **that's no mean** *or* **small ~!** 那可是了不起的成绩! 3 **accomplishments** *pl* 技艺; **a young person of many and varied ~s** 一个多才多艺的年轻人

accord /əˈkɔːd/
A *n* 1 [u] (harmony) 一致; **we are all in ~ with one another on this issue** 在这个问题上我们全体意见一致; **with one ~** 一致地; **of my own ~** 自愿地 2 [c] (treaty, agreement) 协议; **to reach an ~** 达成协议
B *vt* 给予 ‹*favour*›; **these facts weren't ~ed much space or importance in the report** 报告没有给这些事实以足够的篇幅和重视
C *vi* **to ~ with sth.** 与某事物相符; **I'm glad your plans ~ with ours** 很高兴，你们的计划与我们的一致; **his statement did not ~ with the evidence** 他的陈述与证据不符

accordance /əˈkɔːdəns/ **in accordance with** *prep phr* 1 (in line with) 依照; **in ~ with custom** 遵照习俗; **in ~ with rules/regulations** 按照规则/规定 2 (proportional to) 与…相称; **taxes levied in ~ with the individual's ability to pay** 依个人支付能力征收的税赋

according /əˈkɔːdɪŋ/
A according to *prep phr* 1 (in agreement with) 根据，按照; **~ to plan/regulations** 按照计划/规定; **salary will be fixed ~ to age and experience** 薪水将视年龄和资历而定 2 (by reference to) 取决于; **you get a different answer ~ to who you ask** 你问的人不同，就会得到不同的答案
B according as *conj phr* formal 取决于; **I'll act ~ as things turn out** 我将见机行事

accordingly /əˈkɔːdɪŋli/ *adv* 1 (consequently) 因此; **they withdrew support and ~ I cancelled the project** 他们终止了援助，所以我也就取消了这个项目 2 (appropriately) 相应地; **whatever I decide, I expect you to act ~** 不管我作出什么决定，我希望你都能采取相应的行动

accordion /əˈkɔːdiən/ ▸**p. 395** *n* 手风琴

accordionist /əˈkɔːdiənɪst/ ▸**p. 395, p. 409** *n* 手风琴演奏者

accost /əˈkɒst/ *vt* (confront) 上前与…搭话; (solicit for sexual purpose) 勾搭; **reporters ~ed him in the street** 记者们在街上上前去和他搭讪

account /əˈkaʊnt/
A *n* 1 (money held at bank) 账户; **to pay money into an ~** 把钱存入账户; **to withdraw money from an ~** 从账户中取钱; **to have an ~ with** *or* **at a bank** 在银行开有账户; **to open/close an ~** 开户/销户 2 (credit agreement) (with shop, supplier etc.) 赊购账; (with utility or credit-card company) 账单; **to charge sth. to** *or* **put sth. on sb.'s ~** 将某物记在某人账上; **to settle one's ~** 结账; **to settle an ~** *or* **~s with sb.** fig 找某人算账 3 Advertg (client) 广告业务 4 (financial record) 账目; **to keep an ~** 记账 5 Brit (on stock exchange) 交易账期 6 **on ~** (on credit) 以赊账方式; (as part payment) 作为部分账款 7 (description) (gen) 描述; (in newspaper) 报道; **he gave the police a full ~ of what he had seen** 他向警方详述了他看见的情况; **by** *or* **from all ~s** 据大家所述 8 **to call** *or* **bring** *or* **hold sb. to ~ (for sth./for doing sth.)** (bring to book) (为某事/做某事) 责问某人; **one day you'll be called to ~ for your carelessness** 总有一天你会因为自己的粗心大意而受到诘责 9 (impression) 印象; **to give a good/bad ~ of oneself** 表现出色/不佳 10 (grounds) 理由; **on ~ of sb./sth.** 由于某人/某事物; **on this/that ~** 由于这个/那个缘故; **there had been a threat of terrorist attack, and the visit was cancelled on that ~** 有人威胁要发动恐怖袭击，访问因此被取消; **on no ~, not on any ~** 决不; **don't cancel your outing on my ~** 你们别因为我而取消出游 11 (benefit) 利益; **on sb.'s/one's own ~** 为某人/自己; **there's no need to cook a meal on my ~** 没有必要专门为我做一顿饭; **to set up in business on one's own ~** 独力创业 12 (advantage) **to turn** *or* **put sth. to (good) ~** (充分) 利用某事物 13 (importance) 重要性; **to be of little/no/some** *etc.* **~ (to sb.)** (对于某人) 无足轻重/无关紧要/有些重要等; **she was a woman of some ~** 这女人有点来头 14 (consideration) 考虑; **to take ~ of sth., to take sth. into ~** 把某事物考虑在内
B accounts *npl* (records) 会计账目; **to keep the ~s** 记账; **to balance the ~s** 使收支平衡
C accounts *n* [u] (department) 会计部门
D accounts *modif* 会计的 ‹*staff, assistant, office*›
E *vt* formal 认为; **her father was ~ed a genius in his day** 她父亲当年被视为天才; **she was ~ed lucky to escape** 她能逃脱，算得上是幸运了

Phrasal verb

• **account for** *vt* [**~ for sth.**]
1 (clarify reason for) 解释…的原因 ‹*event, fact, behaviour*›; (be the reason for) 是…的原因 ‹*event, fact, behaviour*›; **how do you ~ for the disappearance of the letter?** 信不见了，你作何解释?; **the accident cannot be ~ed for** 事故原因不明; **oh, that ~s for it** 噢，原来是这么一回事 2 (provide reckoning of) 说明…的下落 ‹*missing vehicle, money*›; **all the children have now been ~ed for** 现在所有的孩子都已经找到下落; **two of the aircraft were never ~ed for** 其中两架飞机一直下落不明 3 (represent, make up) 占 ‹*proportion, percentage*›; **exports ~ for 70% of their trade** 出口占他们贸易量的70% 4 (destroy, kill) 摧毁 ‹*vehicle*›; 杀死 ‹*soldier, attacker*›; **the Germans ~ed for a number of our aircraft** 德国人击落我方多架飞机 5 Sport 使…出局 ‹*batsman, opponent*›

accountability /əˌkaʊntəˈbɪləti/ *n* [u] (responsibility) 负有责任; (answerability) 问责性; **there should be clear lines of ~ for all decisions made** 所有决策都应该有分明的责任界限

accountable /əˈkaʊntəbl/ *adj* (answerable) 应作解释的; (responsible) 负有责任的; **the government should be ~ to the people** 政府应该向人民作出解释; **to hold sb. ~ for sth.** 要某人对某事负责

accountancy /əˈkaʊntənsi/ *n* [u] 1 (profession) 会计工作; **to go into ~** 做会计; **~ qualification** 会计资格 2 (studies) 会计学

accountant /əˈkaʊntənt/ ▸**p. 409** *n* 会计师，会计; **a trainee/qualified/chartered ~** 实习/注册/特许会计师

account: ~ book *n* 账本; **~ day** *n* 结算日; **~ executive** *n* 客户经理; **~ holder** *n* (with bank, building society, credit company) 开户人; (with shop, business) 客户

accounting /əˈkaʊntɪŋ/ *n* [u] (process, work) 会计; (studies) 会计学

account: ~ manager *n* 客户经理; **~ number** *n* 账号; **~s department** *n* 会计部门; **~s payable** *n* 应付账款; **~s receivable** *n* 应收账款

accoutrements /əˈkuːtrəmənts/ esp Brit, **accouterments** /əˈkuːtərmənts/ Amer *npl* 装备

Accra /əˈkrɑː/ *pr n* 阿克拉

accredit /əˈkredɪt/ *vt* 1 (appoint) 任命; **to ~ sb. to** *or* **as sth.** 委任某人担任某职务 2 (approve) 认可; **the exam board refused to ~ the course** 考试委员会不认可这门课程 3 (credit) 把…归于; **he was ~ed with turning the airline into a commercial success** 大家认为这家航空公司取得商业成功都是他的功劳

accreditation /əˌkredɪˈteɪʃn/ *n* 1 (of officials) 委派; **the envoy's ~ to the Vatican** 出使梵蒂冈的委派 2 (of institution, qualification) 鉴定合格; **~ by the ministry is necessary for all nursing homes** 所有疗养院都必须取得政府部门的资格认证

accredited /əˈkredɪtɪd/ *adj* 正式认可的 ‹*representative, envoy*›; 鉴定合格的 ‹*course, institution*›

accretion /ə'kriːʃn/ *n* **1** [u] (process) 渐增 **2** [c] (substance) (soot, dirt) 堆积物; Geol (deposits, lava) 冲积层

accrual /ə'kruːəl/ *n* 累积; **~ of interest** 利息的累积; **last year's ~** 去年的结余

accrue /ə'kruː/ *vi* 累积; **the interest accruing to my account** 我账户内的累积利息

accrued /ə'kruːd/ *adj* 累积的 ‹*interest, dividend, charges*›

acculturate /ə'kʌltʃəreɪt/
A *vi* 适应新文化; **those who have ~d to the United States** 那些适应了美国文化的人
B *vt* 使适应新文化

acculturation /əˌkʌltʃə'reɪʃn/ *n* [u] 对新文化的适应

accumulate /ə'kjuːmjʊleɪt/
A *vt* 积累 ‹*interest, worries, evidence*›
B *vi* «*dirt, rubbish*» 积聚; «*interest, worries, evidence*» 累积; **a pile of dust had ~d in the fireplace** 壁炉里积了一堆灰

accumulation /əˌkjuːmjʊ'leɪʃn/ *n* (process, quantity) 积累; (of rubbish) 聚积物; **the ~ of dust** 灰尘的积聚; **the ~ of knowledge is its own reward** 知识的积累本身就是一种回报

accumulative /ə'kjuːmjʊlətɪv, Amer -leɪtɪv/ *adj* 累积的 ‹*experience, effect, result, evidence*›; **their ~ experience** 他们积累的经验

accumulator /ə'kjuːmjʊleɪtə(r)/ *n* **1** Elec 蓄电池 **2** Sport (bet) 累计赌注 **3** Comput 累加器

accuracy /'ækjərəsi/ *n* [u] 精确; **I doubt the ~ of the reports** 我对报告的准确性表示怀疑; **they bombarded the fort with great ~** 他们非常精准地轰炸了那座要塞

accurate /'ækjərət/ *adj* 精确的; **is your watch ~?** 你的表准吗？; **would it be ~ to say that you forgot?** 确切地说，是你忘了，对吗？

accurately /'ækjərətli/ *adv* 精确地 ‹*calculate*›; 清楚地 ‹*remember*›; **if I remember ~, it was ten years ago** 我没记错的话，那是10年前的事了

accursed /ə'kɜːsɪd/ *adj* **1** (under a curse) 被诅咒的 **2** dated (despicable) 卑劣的; **oh, all these ~ bills!** 唉，这些可恶的账单！

accusation /ˌækjuː'zeɪʃn/, **accusal** /ə'kjuːzəl/ *n* **1** [c] (charge, claim) 指控; **to make** *or* **bring** *or* **level an ~** 提起指控 **2** [u] (act of accusing) 提起指控; **to prevent the ~ of an innocent man** 防止无辜男子受到控告

accusative /ə'kjuːzətɪv/
A *adj* 宾格的 ‹*case, form*›
B *n* [u] 宾格

accusatory /ə'kjuːzətəri, Amer -tɔːri/ *adj* 指责的

accuse /ə'kjuːz/ *vt* **1** (gen) 指责 **2** Jur 指控; **she ~d him of theft/murder** 她指控他盗窃/谋杀; **he ~d me of stealing his pen** 他告我偷他的笔

accused /ə'kjuːzd/ *n* **the ~** 被告

accuser /ə'kjuːzə(r)/ *n* 指控者; also Jur 原告

accusing /ə'kjuːzɪŋ/ *adj* 指责的 ‹*voice, tone, manner, speech*›; **to point an ~ finger at sb.** 指责某人

accusingly /ə'kjuːzɪŋli/ *adv* 指责地; **to speak ~ of sth.** 以指责的口气说起某事物

accustom /ə'kʌstəm/
A *vt* **to ~ sb. to sth./to doing sth.** 使某人习惯于某事/做某事
B *v refl* **to ~ oneself to sth.** 使自己习惯于某事; **she gradually ~ed herself to the strange life** 她逐渐习惯了这种陌生的生活

accustomed /ə'kʌstəmd/ *adj* **1** **to be ~ to sth./to doing sth.** 习惯于某事/做某事; **to get** *or* **become** *or* **grow ~ to sth./to doing sth.** 渐渐习惯于某事/做某事 **2** *attrib* (usual) 惯常的 ‹*manner, way, tone, seat, greeting*›

AC/DC
A *abbr* = **alternating current/direct current**
B *adj* colloq 双性恋的

ace /eɪs/
A *n* **1** (in cards) A纸牌, 爱司; **the ~ of hearts** 红心A **2** fig (trump) 王牌; **to play one's ~** 使出绝招; **to have** *or* **keep an ~ up one's sleeve** *or* Amer **in the hole** 有应对的良策; **to hold all the ~s** 稳操胜券; **to be** *or* **come within an ~ of sth.** 差一点做成某事 **3** (in tennis) 爱司球 [发球得分] **4** colloq (expert) 能手; **a flying ~** 王牌飞行员; **to be an ~ at sth./at doing sth.** 在某事上/做某事方面是佼佼者
B *adj* colloq 第一流的; **ace! we've done it!** 好极了！我们成功了！

acerbic /ə'sɜːbɪk/ *adj* 尖刻的

acerbity /ə'sɜːbəti/ *n* [u] 尖刻

acetate /'æsɪteɪt/ *n* 醋酸盐; **sodium ~** 醋酸钠

acetic acid /əˌsiːtɪk 'æsɪd/ *n* [u] 乙酸, 醋酸

acetone /'æsɪtəʊn/ *n* [u] 丙酮

acetylene /ə'setɪliːn/ *n* [u] 乙炔, 电石气

acetylene: ~ burner *n* 乙炔焊枪; **~ lamp** *n* 乙炔灯; **~ torch** *n* 乙炔焊炬; **~ welding** *n* [u] (process) 乙炔焊接; (joint) 乙炔焊点

ache /eɪk/
A *n* **1** (physical) 疼痛; **I've got a dull ~ in my left arm** 我的左胳膊隐隐作痛 **2** (emotional) 痛苦; **the ~ in my heart did not diminish with time** 我内心的痛苦并没有随着时间流逝而减轻
B *vi* **1** (suffer physically) 疼痛; **to ~ all over** 浑身疼痛 **2** liter (suffer emotionally) 感到痛苦; **to ~ with ...** 因…而痛苦 ‹*humiliation, despair*›; **my heart ~s for the refugees** 我非常同情那些难民 **3** (yearn) **to ~ for sth.** 渴望某事物; **he just ~d to see her again** 他就是渴望再见到她

achieve /ə'tʃiːv/ *vt* 达到 ‹*standard*›; 实现 ‹*ambition*›; 取得 ‹*success, victory*›; 获得 ‹*fame, peace of mind*›; **I've ~d what I set out to do** 我完成了既定任务; **to ~ something in life** 人生中事业有成; **to ~ nothing** 一事无成

achievement /ə'tʃiːvmənt/ *n* **1** [c] (feat) 成就; **a university noted for its scientific ~s** 一所以科学成就闻名的大学 **2** [u] Sch, Univ 成绩; **to recognize sb. for his/her ~** 因其学习成绩而认可某人 **3** [u] (attainment) 实现; **a sense of ~** 成就感; **the ~ of all his dreams** 他所有梦想的实现

achievement test *n* 学业测试

achiever /ə'tʃiːvə(r)/ *n* **(high) ~** 成功人士; **low ~** 成绩平庸的人

Achilles /ə'kɪliːz/ *pr n* 阿喀琉斯 [希腊神话中的英雄，因出生后被母亲提着脚跟在冥河中浸过，故除脚跟外全身刀枪不入]

Achilles: ~ heel *n* 致命弱点; **~ tendon** *n* 跟腱

aching /'eɪkɪŋ/ *adj* **1** (suffering physically) 疼痛的; **to have ~ feet** 脚痛 **2** fig 痛苦的 ‹*heart*›; **an ~ void** 痛苦的空虚感

acid /'æsɪd/
A *n* **1** [c] Chem 酸; **strong/weak ~** 强酸/弱酸; **an ~ solution** 酸溶液 **2** [u] colloq (drug) 迷幻药 [即LSD]
B *adj* **1** (sour) 酸的 ‹*taste*›; 酸味的 ‹*fruit*›; 酸性的 ‹*soil*› **2** fig 尖酸的 ‹*tone*›

acid: ~ drop *n* 酸味糖果; **~-free** *adj* 无酸的; **~-free paper/board** 无酸纸/板

acid green
A *n* 鲜绿色
B **acid-green** *adj* 鲜绿色的

acidic /ə'sɪdɪk/ *adj* **1** (containing acid) 酸性的 ‹*soil, compound*› **2** (sharp-tasting) 浓烈的 ‹*wine*›; 极酸的 ‹*fruit*› **3** (cutting) 尖酸的 ‹*remark, tone, retort, humour*›; **to make an ~ comment** 作尖刻的评论

acidification /əˌsɪdɪfɪ'keɪʃn/ *n* [u] 酸化

acidify /ə'sɪdɪfaɪ/
A *vt* 使酸化; **to ~ the soil** 使土壤酸化
B *vi* 酸化

acidity /ə'sɪdəti/ *n* [u] **1** Chem 酸性 **2** fig (of tone, remark) 尖刻

acid: ~ radical *n* 酸基, 酸根; **~ rain** *n* 酸雨; **~ rock** *n* [u] 迷幻摇滚乐; **~ snow** *n* [u] 酸雪; **~ stomach** *n* 胃酸过多; **~ test** *n* fig 严峻的考验

ack-ack /ˌæk'æk/ *n* [u] **1** (gun) 高射炮 **2** (weapon fire) 高射炮火

acknowledge /ək'nɒlɪdʒ/ *vt* **1** (admit) 承认 ‹*mistake, fact, debt*›; **I ~ myself to be in error** 我承认自己错了; **to ~ doing sth.** 承认做过某事 **2** (accept legitimacy of, recognize) 认可; **to ~ an illegitimate child** 承认私生子; **to be ~d to be an excellent lawyer/doctor** 被公认为是优秀的律师/医生; **she ~d him as her heir** 她认他为继承人 **3** (express thanks for) 感谢; **to ~ one's sources** (in book) 注明引文出处并致谢 **4** (confirm receipt of) 告知收悉; **we will of course ~ all letters** 来信必复 **5** (show recognition of) 向…致意; **he ~d them with a wave** 他挥手向他们致意

acknowledged /ək'nɒlɪdʒd/ *adj* 公认的 ‹*expert, fact*›

acknowledgement, acknowledgment /ək'nɒlɪdʒmənt/
A *n* **1** (admission of error, guilt, problem, etc.) 承认; **in ~ that ...** 确认…; **they refused to make any ~ of their guilt** 他们拒不认罪 **2** (confirmation of receipt) 确认通知; **a signed ~ of receipt of the documents** 文件签收单; **I write in ~ of your letter** 来信收到，特此回信告知 **3** (gratitude) 答谢的表示; **in ~ of sth.** 作为对某事的答谢 **4** (recognition of presence) 示意看到; **a slight nod was the only ~ of my presence** 只是轻轻点头以示看到了我 **5** (recognition of legitimacy, validity) 认可; **his belated ~ of his illegitimate children** 他对其私生子女们迟来的承认; **their ~ of him as their leader** 他们对他作为领导的认可
B **acknowledgements** *npl* 鸣谢; **a list of ~s in the preface to the book** 该书前言中的致谢名录

acme /'ækmi/ *n* [u] 顶点; **to reach** *or* **attain the ~ of success** 达到成功的顶峰

acne /'ækni/ ▸**p. 377** *n* [u] 痤疮; **to suffer from ~** 长粉刺

acolyte /'ækəlaɪt/ *n* **1** Relig 侍祭 **2** fig (follower, assistant) 追随者

aconite /'ækənaɪt/ *n* 乌头 [野生植物]

acorn /'eɪkɔːn/ *n* 橡子; **oaks from little ~s grow** Prov 参天大树，生于毫末

acoustic /ə'kuːstɪk/ *adj* 音响的 ‹*effects*›; 听觉的 ‹*range*›; 原声的 ‹*instrument, performance*›

acoustically /ə'kuːstɪkli/ *adv* 在声学上; **an ~ dead environment** 完全无声的环境

acoustic guitar *n* ▸**p. 395** 原声吉他

acoustics /ə'kuːstɪks/ *npl* **1** + *v sing* (science) 声学 **2** + *v pl* (properties) 音响效果

acquaint /ə'kweɪnt/
A *vt* 使了解; **to ~ sb. with sth.** 使某人了解某事物; **to be** *or* **get** *or* **become ~ed with sb.** 认识/结识某人; **how did you two become ~ed?** 你们两个是怎样认识的？
B *v refl* **to ~ oneself with sth.** 使自己了解某事物

acquaintance /ə'kweɪntəns/ *n* **1** (friend) 相识的人; **an ~ of mine** 我的一个熟人; **to have a wide circle of ~s** 交游很广 **2** (relationship) 结识; **to make sb.'s ~** 结识某人; **to strike up an ~ with sb.** 开始与某人相识; **on closer** *or* **further ~** 进一步熟悉之后; **to**

have a nodding/casual ~ with sb. 与某人是点头/泛泛之交 **3** (knowledge) 了解; **to have a nodding** *or* **passing ~ with sth.** 对某事物略知一二

acquaintance rape *n* 熟人强奸

acquaintanceship /ə'kweɪntənsʃɪp/ *n* [u and c] **1** (relationship) 相识; **our ~ has been brief** 我们才认识不久; **to strike up/keep up an ~ with sb.** 结识某人/与某人保持交往 **2** (knowledge) 了解; **an ~ with sth.** 对某事物的了解

acquiesce /,ækwɪ'es/ *vi* **1** (concede, accept) 默许; **to ~ in a proposal** 默认一项提议 **2** (collude) 勾结; **to ~ in** *or* **to a plan/scheme** 勾结起来施行计划/阴谋

acquiescence /,ækwɪ'esns/ *n* [u] **1** (agreement) 默许; **her proposals met with ready ~** 她的提议立刻得到了默许; **sb.'s ~ in sth.** 某人对某事物的默认 **2** (collusion) 勾结; **sb.'s ~ in sth.** 某人在某事上的串通

acquiescent /,ækwɪ'esnt/ *adj* **1** (in agreement) 默认的; **they were ~** 他们持默认态度 **2** (unassertive) 顺从的

acquire /ə'kwaɪə(r)/ *vt* **1** (obtain) 获得 ‹*possession, money*›; 购得 ‹*car, house*›; fig hum 得到 ‹*husband, wife*› **2** (learn, develop) 习得 ‹*knowledge, experience, language*›; **to ~ a taste for sth.** 养成对某事物的喜好; **he has ~d a reputation as a Casanova** 他有好色之名

acquired /ə'kwaɪəd/ *adj* 习得的 ‹*characteristic*›; **an ~ taste** 后天养成的喜好

acquisition /,ækwɪ'zɪʃn/ *n* **1** [u] (obtaining) 获得; **he was dedicated to the ~ of wealth** 他一心想发财 **2** [u] (learning, developing) 习得; **the ~ of knowledge can be a pursuit in itself** 求知本身就可以是一种追求 **3** [c] (thing acquired) 获得物; (company) 收购; **the latest ~s have to be catalogued first** 最近添置的物品得先编目

acquisitive /ə'kwɪzətɪv/ *adj* 贪婪的

acquit /ə'kwɪt/ (*pres p etc.* **-tt-**)

A *vt* Jur 宣判…无罪; **to be ~ted of murder/of murdering sb.** 被判谋杀/谋杀某人的罪名不成立

B *v refl* 表现; **she ~ted herself well in the competition** 她在比赛中表现得很好

acquittal /ə'kwɪtl/ *n* 宣判无罪; **to plead for an ~** 作无罪辩护

acre /'eɪkə(r)/

A *n* 英亩; **300 ~s of good farmland** 300 英亩良田

B acres *npl* colloq 大量; **~s (and ~s) of room** 巨大的空间; **~s of empty beer cans** 一大堆空啤酒罐

acreage /'eɪkərɪdʒ/ *n* 英亩数; **farms with an ~ of over 50 acres** 总面积超过 50 英亩的农场

acrid /'ækrɪd/ *adj* 刺鼻的

acridine /'ækrɪdiːn/ *n* [u] 吖啶 [一种无色固体化合物]

acriflavine /'ækrɪfleɪvɪn/ *n* [u] 吖啶黄 [用作防腐剂]

acrimonious /,ækrɪ'məʊnɪəs/ *adj* 讥讽的 ‹*tone, manner*›; 激烈的 ‹*atmosphere, dispute, discussion*›; **the divorce was ~** 离婚闹得不可开交

acrimony /'ækrɪməni/ *n* [u] 尖刻

acrobat /'ækrəbæt/ ▸**p. 409** *n* 杂技演员

acrobatic /,ækrə'bætɪk/ *adj* 杂技的; **an ~ dive** 特技跳水

acrobatics /,ækrə'bætɪks/ *npl* **1** + *v sing* (art) 杂技 **2** + *v pl* (movements) 技巧; **mental ~** 脑筋急转弯

acronym /'ækrənɪm/ *n* 首字母缩略词; **NATO is an ~ for 'North Atlantic Treaty Organization'** NATO是"北大西洋公约组织"的首字母缩略词

across /ə'krɒs/

A *prep* **1** (from one side to the other) 横穿过; **to build a bridge ~ the river** 在河上建一座桥; **to walk ~ the room** 走过房间; **we travelled ~ country** 我们穿过田间旅行 **2** (on the other side of) 在…对面 ‹*street*›; 在…对岸 ‹*river*›; **she shouted ~ the room to them** 她在房间另一头向他们喊叫 **3** (all over, throughout) 遍及; **newspapers were scattered ~ the floor** 报纸落了一地板; **the company has branches ~ the world** 公司在世界各地都设有分支机构

B *adv* **1** (from one side to the other) 从一边到另一边; **the lake is two miles ~ at the widest point** 湖面最宽的地方有两英里 **2** (to the other side) 到对面; **we could just swim ~** 我们游过去好了

across-the-board

A *adj* 全面的 ‹*increase, cut, approach*›; **there will be an ~ salary increase this April** 今年四月将普涨薪水

B across the board *adv* 全面地

acrostic /ə'krɒstɪk/ *n* [u] 离合诗 [每行的某些字母组合起来能构成词的一种诗体]

acrylic /ə'krɪlɪk/ *n* **1** Tex 丙烯酸纤维 **2** Art **~ (paint)** 丙烯酸涂料

ACT *abbr* = **American College Test** 美国高等院校入学考试

act /ækt/

A *n* **1** (action, deed) 行为; **to commit** *or* **carry out an ~ of cruelty** 做出残忍的行为; **to be in the ~ of doing sth.** 正在做某事 **2** (*also* **Act**) Jur, Pol 法案; **drug trafficking ~** 反贩毒法; **an Act of Parliament/Congress** 议会/国会法案 **3** Theat 一幕; **a comedy/tragedy in three ~s** 一部三幕喜剧/悲剧 **4** (performance, routine) 表演; **to put on an ~** fig 假装; **it's all an ~** fig 这就是一场戏; **to get** *or* **be in on the ~** colloq 插一手; **to get one's ~ together** colloq 使行动有条理; **to do a song and dance ~** esp Brit colloq 小题大做

B *vt* 扮演 ‹*role, part*›; **to ~ the fool** 装傻; **to ~ the stern father** 拿出严父的样子

C *vi* **1** (take action) 行动; **I'm not empowered to ~ in such matters** 我无权在此类事情上采取行动; **to ~ for** *or* **on behalf of sb.** 代表某人行事; **to ~ on insufficient evidence** 证据不足就行事; **to ~ for the best/out of fear** 出于好意/恐惧 **2** (behave) 表现 **3** Theat 表演; fig (pretend) 假装 **4** (serve) 担当; **to ~ as sth./sb./in a role** 充当某物/某人/某角色; **the grand piano also ~s as a drinks table** 这架大钢琴也兼作吧台; **she ~ed as the interpreter** 她担任口译 **5** (take effect) 有作用; **this drug ~s very fast** 这种药见效很快; **alcohol ~s on the brain** 酒精对大脑有影响

Phrasal verbs

- **act out** *vt* [**~ sth. out, ~ out sth.**] 将…表演出来 ‹*part, scene*›; 流露 ‹*feelings*›; 充当 ‹*role*›; **to ~ out one's sexual fantasies** 实现自己的性幻想
- **act up** *vi* (misbehave) 捣蛋; (malfunction) 出毛病; **my rheumatic joints are ~ing up in this cold!** 天太冷，我的风湿性关节炎又犯了！

acting /'æktɪŋ/

A *n* (performance) 表演; (occupation) 演艺业; **have you done any ~?** 你演过戏吗？; **her ~ was criticized in the press** 她的演技受到了媒体批评; **the ~ profession** 演艺职业

B *adj* 代理的 ‹*manager, director, position, responsibilities*›

actinium /æk'tɪnɪəm/ *n* [u] 锕

action /'ækʃn/

A *n* **1** [u and c] (process of doing something, deed) 行动; **to take ~ (against sb./sth.)** (针对某人/某事物) 采取行动; **a man/woman of ~** 实干的男人/女人; **to be pushed into ~ against sb./sth.** 被迫对某人/某事采取措施; **to put** *or* **translate a plan/an idea into ~** 将计划/想法付诸实施; **to want a piece** *or* **share of the ~** colloq 想分一杯羹; **to judge sb. by his/her ~s** 通过某人的表现来评判某人; **to suit the ~ to the word** 言行一致; **~s speak louder than words** Prov 事实胜于雄辩 **2** [u and c] Mil 作战; **to see (some) ~** 经历战斗; **to be killed in ~** 阵亡; **to be in** *or* **go into ~** 投入战斗; fig **he's laid up and out of ~** 他因伤卧床，不能参战 **3** [u and c] Theat, Cin 情节; **the ~ of the drama takes place in antiquity** 剧中的故事发生在古代; **~!** (director's instruction) 开拍！ **4** [c] Jur 诉讼; **to institute** *or* **bring an ~ against sb.** 起诉某人 **5** [c] Mech 机械装置; **the piano had a very stiff ~** 那架钢琴的琴键很紧 **6** [c] Sport (of cricketing bowler or tennis player) 动作 **7** [c] Chem 作用; **the ~ of salt on ice causes it to melt** 盐作用于冰使其融化

B *vt* 实施 ‹*procedure*›; 采取 ‹*measure*›; 处理 ‹*request*›

actionable /'ækʃənəbl/ *adj* 可以起诉的 ‹*conduct, remark*›

action: **~ committee** *n* 行动委员会; **~ film** *n* 动作片; **~ group** *n* 行动小组; **the Child Poverty A~ Group** 消除儿童贫困行动小组; **~ movie** *n* esp Amer = **~ film**; **~-packed** *adj* 充满刺激的 ‹*film, holiday*›; **~ painting** *n* 动作绘画 [在画布上随意泼洒颜料的抽象派绘画]; **~ plan** *n* 行动计划; **~ point** *n* 行动方案; **~ replay** *n* **1** TV 即时慢镜头重放; **to show an ~ replay of a goal** 重放进球的慢镜头; **2** colloq (exact repetition) 重演; **an ~ replay of the accident** 事故的再次发生; **~ shot** *n* 动态照片; **~ stations** *npl* 战位; **~ stations!** 各就各位！

activate /'æktɪveɪt/ *vt* **1** (gen) 启动 ‹*machine, procedure, system*›; 触发 ‹*alarm*›; **a rise in inflation ~s increases in pensions** 通货膨胀率的上升会引发养老金的增加 **2** Chem 使活化

activated carbon *n* [u] 活性碳

activation /,æktɪ'veɪʃn/ *n* [u] **1** (gen) 激活; (of machine, system, procedure) 启动; (of alarm) 触发 **2** Chem 活化

active /'æktɪv/ *adj* **1** (gen) 积极的 ‹*person, life, consideration, resistance*›; 活跃的 ‹*mind, imagination*›; **to be ~ in** 积极参加 ‹*organization*›; **to be ~ in doing sth.** 积极做某事; **to play an ~ role** *or* **part in sth.** 在某事中起积极作用; **to take an ~ interest in sth.** 对某事怀有浓厚的兴趣; **an ~ volcano** 活火山; **sexually ~** 性行为活跃的 **2** Mil **to be on ~ service** 服现役 **3** Ling 主动的 ‹*voice, construction*› **4** Jur 正在审理的 ‹*case, file*›

active: **~ duty** *n* [u] 现役; **~ ingredient** *n* 活性成分; **~ list** *n* 现役军官名单; **an officer on the ~ list** 现役军官

actively /'æktɪvli/ *adv* 积极地; **to be ~ considering doing sth.** 积极考虑做某事

active service *n* [u] = **active duty**

activism /'æktɪvɪzəm/ *n* [u] 激进主义

activist /'æktɪvɪst/ *n* 激进分子; **an animal rights ~** 动物权益保护激进人士

activity /æk'tɪvəti/ *n* **1** [u] 活跃; **to hum with ~** 忙忙碌碌; **the town centre was a scene of great ~** 镇中心非常热闹 **2** **activities** *pl* 活动; **to resume/break off one's activities** 重新开始/中断活动

activity holiday *n* Brit 活力假日 [以某项活动为中心，与"懒散假日"相对]

act: **~ of faith** *n* 信仰行为; **~ of God** *n* 不可抗力; **~ of war** *n* 战争行为

actor /'æktə(r)/ *n* **1** ▸**p. 409** Cin, Theat 演员; **don't believe the tears, she's just a good ~!** 别相信这些眼泪，她只是演得很逼真而已！ **2** (participant) 参与者; **employers are key ~s in industrial relations** 雇主在劳资关系中扮演着关键角色

actress /'æktrɪs/ ▸**p. 409** *n* 女演员

actual /'æktʃʊəl/ *adj* **1** (real, specific) 实际的; **I don't remember the ~ words/figures**

我没有记住确切的话/数字; **in ~ fact** 事实上 **2** (genuine) 真实的; **this is the ~ room that Shakespeare worked in** 这就是莎士比亚原来工作过的那间屋子 **3** (as such) 严格意义上的; **he didn't give me an ~ cheque** 他给我的不是一张真正的支票

actual bodily harm *n* Brit 实际身体伤害

actuality /ˌæktʃʊ'æləti/

A *n* [u] 真实; **to pass from possibility into ~** 由可能转化为现实

B actualities *npl* 真实情况

actualize /'æktʃʊəlaɪz/ *vt* **1** (make real) 使…成为现实 ‹*possibilities, projects*› **2** (represent realistically) 真实地表现 ‹*situation, idea*›

actually /'æktʃʊəli/ *adv* **1** (in reality) 的确; **yes, it ~ happened!** 是的, 确有此事! ; **they didn't ~ complain** 他们其实并没有真的抱怨 **2** (exactly) 确切地; **what ~ happened?** 到底发生了什么? **3** (expressing surprise, indignation) 竟然; **she ~ thanked me!** 没想到她还谢我! ; **she ~ accused me of lying!** 她居然说我撒谎! **4** (contrary to expectation) 实际上; **~, I'm not at all surprised** 其实我一点也不惊奇; **their profits have ~ risen** 他们的利润实际上是增加了

actuarial /ˌæktʃʊ'eəriəl/ *adj* 精算师的 ‹*exam, report*›; 精算的 ‹*firm, calculation*›

actuary /'æktʃʊəri, Amer -tʃʊeri/ ▸**p. 409** *n* 精算师

actuate /'æktʃʊeɪt/ *vt* **1** Tech 开动 ‹*machine*› **2** (motivate) 激励

acuity /ə'kju:əti/ *n* [u] formal 敏度; **visual ~** 视敏度

acumen /'ækjʊmən, ə'kju:mən/ *n* [u] 精明; **business ~** 生意上的精明果断

acupressure /'ækjʊpreʃə(r)/ *n* [u] 指压按摩; **an ~ point** 指压点

acupuncture /'ækjʊpʌŋktʃə(r)/ *n* [u] 针疗; **to do** *or* **perform ~ on sb.** 对某人进行针疗; **to have ~** 接受针疗

acupuncturist /'ækjʊpʌŋkʃərɪst/ ▸**p. 409** *n* 针疗医师

acute /ə'kju:t/ *adj* **1** (intense) 极度的; **~ pain** 剧痛; **to cause sb. ~ embarrassment** 使某人极为尴尬 **2** Med 急性的 ‹*disease, condition*›; **an ~ patient** 急性病人 **3** (keen) 敏锐的 ‹*mind, observer, sense*› **4** Math 锐角的; **an ~ angle** 锐角; **an ~ triangle** 锐角三角形 **5** Ling 尖音的 ‹*accent*›

acute-angled *adj* 锐角的; **an ~ triangle** 锐角三角形

acutely /ə'kju:tli/ *adv* **1** (intensely) 深切地 ‹*feel, suffer*›; 极其 ‹*anxious, lacking*›; 严重地 ‹*ill*›; **I am ~ aware of these problems** 我深切地意识到这些问题; **here the need for more funding is felt most ~** 这里看来急需更多的资金 **2** (shrewdly) 敏锐地

AD ▸**p. 181** *abbr* = **Anno Domini** 公元; **49 ~** 公元 49 年

ad /æd/ *n* colloq = **advertisement**

A/D *abbr* = **analogue-digital** 模拟－数字的

adage /'ædɪdʒ/ *n* 格言

adagio /ə'dɑ:dʒɪəʊ/

A *adv* 缓慢地 ‹*play*›

B *adj* 慢板的; **~ movement/finale** 慢板乐章/慢板终曲

C *n* 慢板

Adam /'ædəm/ *pr n* (first man) 亚当 [《圣经》故事中人类的始祖]; (anyone bearing that name) 亚当; **not to know sb. from ~** 根本不认识某人

adamant /'ædəmənt/ *adj* 坚决的 ‹*attitude, refusal*›; 坚定的 ‹*stance, position*›; **to be ~ about sth./that ...** 坚持某事/认为…

adamantly /'ædəməntli/ *adv* 坚决地

Adam's apple *n* 喉结

adapt /ə'dæpt/

A *vt* 调整…以适用 ‹*policy*›; 改编 ‹*novel, film*›; **to ~ the old machines for new purposes** 改造旧机器以适应新用途

B *vi* 适应

C *v refl* **to ~ oneself to sth.** 使自己适应某事物

adaptability /əˌdæptə'bɪləti/ *n* [u] **1** (of person, system, machine) 适应性; **ready ~ to new situations** 迅速适应新环境的能力 **2** (of book, film) 可改编性

adaptable /ə'dæptəbl/ *adj* **1** (capable of adjusting) 有适应能力的 ‹*person*›; 适用的 ‹*machine, tool, system*›; **to be ~ to sth.** 能适应某事物 **2** (suitable for adapting) 可改编的; **to be ~ for television/the big screen** 可改编成电视/电影

adaptation /ˌædæp'teɪʃn/ *n* **1** [u and c] (adjustment) 适应 **2** [c] Cin, TV 改编

adapter, adaptor /ə'dæptə(r)/ *n* **1** Elec, Mech (for joining) 适配器; (socket) 多功能插头 **2** (of novel, play, etc.) 改编者

add /æd/ *vt* **1** (gen) 补充; **to ~ that ...** 补充说… **2** Math 把…加起来; **to add three and four** 把三和四加起来

Phrasal verbs

- **add in** *vt* [**~ sth. in, ~ in sth.**] 把…包括在内
- **add on** *vt* [**~ sth. on, ~ on sth.**] 附加; **to ~ on the expenses** 把费用也算在内
- **add to** *vt* [**~ to sth.**] 增加 ‹*difficulty, danger*›; 扩充 ‹*property*›; **their house has been ~ed to** 他们的房子已经扩建了
- **add together** *vt* = **add up A**
- **add up**

A *vt* [**~ sth. up, ~ up sth.**] **1** (total) 把…加起来 ‹*figures*› **2** (consider together) 综合考虑 ‹*advantages and disadvantages*›

B *vi* 得到应有的总数; **it doesn't ~ up** fig colloq 这说不通; **it all ~s up** lit 数字加起来完全吻合; fig 说得通; **to ~ up to** 合计达 ‹*total, amount*›; **his achievements ~ up to very little** 他的成就微不足道

added /'ædɪd/ *adj* 额外的 ‹*benefit, disappointment*›; 附加的 ‹*features*›; **it's expensive, ~ to which it's ugly!** 这东西又贵又难看!

addendum /ə'dendəm/ *n* (*pl* **addenda** /ə'dendə/) 补遗

adder /'ædə(r)/ *n* **1** (snake) 蝰蛇 **2** Comput 加法器

addict /'ædɪkt/ *n* **1** (drug user) 有瘾的人; **a coffee ~** 喝咖啡上瘾的人 **2** fig (enthusiast) 入迷的人; **a telly ~** colloq 电视迷

addicted /ə'dɪktɪd/ *adj* 上瘾的; **to be** *or* **become ~ to sth.** lit 对某物上瘾; fig (enthusiastically devoted) 对某事物着迷; **he's ~ to computers** 他迷上了电脑

addiction /ə'dɪkʃn/ *n* **1** (dependency) 瘾; **her ~ to heroin** 她的海洛因瘾 **2** fig (enthusiastic devotion) 嗜好; **his ~ to football** 他对足球的痴迷

addictive /ə'dɪktɪv/ *adj* **1** lit (causing dependency) 使人上瘾的 ‹*drug, habit, effect*›; (susceptible to addiction) 易上瘾的 ‹*behaviour*› **2** fig (irresistible, compelling) 使人着迷的 ‹*personality*›

add-in *n* 插件

adding machine /'ædɪŋ məˌʃi:n/ *n* 加法器

Addis Ababa /ˌædɪs 'æbəbə/ *pr n* 亚的斯亚贝巴

addition /ə'dɪʃn/

A *n* **1** [u] Math 加法 **2** [c] (person) 新增人员; (thing) 添加物

B in addition *adv phr* 另外

C in addition to *prep phr* 除…之外

additional /ə'dɪʃənl/ *adj* 额外的; **~ charge** 附加费用

additionally /ə'dɪʃənəli/ *adv* 另外

additive /'ædɪtɪv/ *n* 添加剂

addled /'ædld/ *adj* 变质的 ‹*egg*›; fig, esp hum 糊涂的 ‹*brain*›

add-on *n* **1** (gen) 附加物; **an ~ device/feature** 附加装置/特色 **2** Comput 附件

address /ə'dres, Amer 'ædres/

A *n* **1** (place of residence) 地址; **not known at this ~** 查无此人 **2** (speech) 演说; **to give** *or* **deliver an ~** 发表演说 **3** (as etiquette) 称呼; **form** *or* **manner of ~ (for sb.)** (对某人的) 称呼 **4** Comput 地址

B *vt* **1** (write address on) 在…上写姓名地址; **to ~ sth. to sb.** 把某物写上姓名地址寄给某人; **to be wrongly ~ed** 写错姓名地址 **2** (speak to) 向…发表演说; **Mr X will now ~ the meeting** 现在由 X 先生向大会致辞 **3** (aim) 使…有针对性 ‹*remark*›; **to ~ sth. to sb.** 向某人述说某事; **any complaints should be ~ed to the manager** 任何意见都应当向经理提出 **4** (tackle) 处理 ‹*task, problem*› **5** (use title of) 称呼; **to ~ sb. as sth.** 用某称呼叫某人

C *v refl* **to ~ oneself to sth.** 致力于某事; **we'll have to ~ ourselves seriously to the task** 我们将不得不认真对待这一任务

address book *n* 通讯簿

addressee /ˌædre'si:/ *n* 收件人

adduce /ə'dju:s, Amer ə'du:s/ *vt* formal 举出 ‹*proof, reason*›; 援引 ‹*fact*›

adenoids /'ædɪnɔɪdz, Amer -dən-/ *npl* 增殖腺

adept

A /ə'dept/ *adj* 熟练的; **to be ~ at sth./doing sth.** 擅长某事/做某事

B /'ædept/ *n* 能手; **an ~ in** *or* **at sth.** 某方面的行家

adequacy /'ædɪkwəsi/ *n* [u] **1** (sufficiency of amount) 足够 **2** (satisfactoriness of description, explanation, theory) 恰当 **3** (competence, aptitude) 胜任

adequate /'ædɪkwət/ *adj* **1** (sufficient, enough) 足够的 ‹*amount*›; **an ~ range of options** 足够大的选择范围 **2** (satisfactory) 适当的 ‹*description, explanation*› **3** (competent) 能胜任的 ‹*person*›; **to be ~ to the task** 胜任这一任务 **4** (acceptable but mediocre) 过得去的; **to be better than ~** 还算好

adequately /'ædɪkwətli/ *adv* **1** (sufficiently) 充分地 ‹*prepared, equipped*›; 足够地 ‹*insured*› **2** (well enough, satisfactorily) 合适地 ‹*paid, rewarded*›; **this ~ meets our needs** 这很好地满足了我们的需求

adhere /əd'hɪə(r)/ *vi* **1** lit 黏附; **the paint ~s to any surface** 这种油漆可附着于各种表面 **2** fig (follow) 遵守; **to ~ to a principle** 坚持原则; **to ~ to a treaty/schedule/rule** 遵守协议/工作计划/规则; **to ~ to a promise** 信守诺言

adherence /əd'hɪərəns/ *n* [u] (to belief, ideology) 信奉; (to rule, deadline) 遵守; (to plan, method, policy) 遵循; (to commitment) 信守

adherent /əd'hɪərənt/ *n* (of party, plan, policy) 拥护者; (of cult, religion) 信徒; (of doctrine) 追随者

adhesion /əd'hi:ʒn/ *n* [u] **1** lit (sticking together) 粘连 **2** fig (attachment to belief, religion, ideal) 信奉 **3** (grip, traction) 附着力

adhesive /əd'hi:sɪv/

A *adj* 黏合的; **~ tape** 胶带; **~ envelope** 胶口信封

B *n* 黏合剂

ad hoc /ˌæd 'hɒk/

A *adj* 临时的 ‹*decision*›; 特别的 ‹*committee, body*›; **on an ~ basis** 临时性地

B *adv* 临时地

adieu /ə'dju:, Amer ə'du:/ dated

A *n* (*pl* **~s**) 告辞; **to bid sb. ~** 向某人道别

B *excl* 再见

ad infinitum /ˌæd ˌɪnfɪ'naɪtəm/ *adv* 永远地

adipose /'ædɪpəʊs/ *adj* 含脂肪的; **~ fin** 脂鳍

adjacent /ə'dʒeɪsnt/ *adj* **1** (touching) 毗连的; **~ to sth.** 与某物毗连的 **2** (nearby) 附近的 **3** Math 相邻的; **~ angles** 邻角

adjectival /ˌædʒɪk'taɪvl/ *adj* 形容词的

adjectivally /ˌædʒɪkˈtaɪvəli/ *adv* 作为形容词地

adjective /ˈædʒɪktɪv/ *n* 形容词

adjoin /əˈdʒɔɪn/
A *vt* 与…毗连
B *vi* «*buildings, land*» 毗邻; «*rooms*» 紧挨着

adjoining /əˈdʒɔɪnɪŋ/ *adj attrib* 毗邻的

adjourn /əˈdʒɜːn/
A *vt* 将…延期 ‹*session, trial*›; 使…休会 ‹*parliament*›; **I hereby ~ the meeting for two days** 我在此宣布休会两天
B *vi* **1** Jur (suspend proceedings) 休庭 **2** (close session) 休会; **Parliament/the House ~ed** (for break) 议会/议院休会; (at end of debate) 议会/议院辩论结束; **we ~ed for the summer break** 我们休会过暑假 **3** esp hum (move on) 换地方; **suppose we ~ to my place?** 咱们换个地方到我家去怎么样?

adjournment /əˈdʒɜːnmənt/
A *n* (of trial) 休庭; (of session, parliament) 休会; (of debate) 暂停辩论
B *modif* Brit Pol 休会前的 ‹*debate, motion*›

adjournment: ~ debate *n* Brit 休会辩论; **~ motion** *n* Brit 休会动议

adjudge /əˈdʒʌdʒ/ *vt* esp Jur 宣判; **the court ~d him (to be) guilty** 法庭宣判他有罪; **to be ~d as ...** 被判定为…

adjudicate /əˈdʒuːdɪkeɪt/
A *vt* 裁决 ‹*competition, claim, matter*›
B *vi* 裁决; **to ~ on sth.** 裁决某事

adjudication /əˌdʒuːdɪˈkeɪʃn/ *n* **1** [u] (of competition) 裁判 **2** [u and c] Jur 裁决; **under ~** 在审理中

adjudicator /əˈdʒuːdɪkeɪtə(r)/ *n* **1** (of game, contest) 裁判 **2** Jur 法官

adjunct /ˈædʒʌŋkt/
A *n* **1** (addition) 附属物 **2** (person) 助手 **3** Ling 修饰成分
B *adj* Amer Univ (temporary) 兼职的; (assistant) 副的; **an ~ professor** 副教授

adjust /əˈdʒʌst/
A *vt* **1** also Tech 调整 ‹*machine, equipment*›; 整理 ‹*clothing*›; 调节 ‹*volume*›; **to ~ the terms to the revised contracts** 根据修订的合同调整条款; **to ~ sth. upwards/downwards** 把…上调/下调 **2** Insur 理算…的金额 ‹*claim*›
B *vi* **1** (adapt) «*person*» 适应; **to ~ to sth.** 适应某事物 **2** (be alterable) «*controls, seat, harness*» 可调节; **to ~ to sth.** 可按某物进行调节

adjustable /əˈdʒʌstəbl/ *adj* 可调的

adjustable spanner, adjustable wrench *n* 活络扳手

adjuster /əˈdʒʌstə(r)/ *n* 理算员

adjustment /əˈdʒʌstmənt/ *n* **1** Fin, Tech (modification) 调整; **to make ~s to** 调整 ‹*machine, strategy, system*› **2** (mental, physical) 适应; **to make the ~ to** 努力适应 ‹*culture, lifestyle*›

adjutant /ˈædʒʊtənt/ *n* 副官

ad-lib /ˌæd ˈlɪb/
A *n* (on stage) 即兴的台词; (witticism) 俏皮话
B *adj* 即兴的 ‹*remarks, speech, performance*›
C **ad lib** *adv* 即兴地
D **ad lib** *vt* (*pres p etc.* **-bb-**) 临时插入 ‹*lines*›; 当场进行 ‹*performance*›
E *vi* (*pres p etc.* **-bb-**) 即兴插入台词

adman /ˈædmæn/ *n* (*pl* **admen** /ˈædmen/) colloq 广告商

admin /ˈædmɪn/
A *n* [u] esp Brit colloq 管理
B *adj* 管理的

administer /ədˈmɪnɪstə(r)/ *vt* **1** (manage) 管理 ‹*affairs, organization, funds*›; 治理 ‹*country, region*› **2** (deal out) 执行 ‹*justice*›; 实行 ‹*rewards, punishments*›; 主持…的仪式 ‹*rites*›; 发放 ‹*relief*›; **to ~ an oath to a witness** 请证人宣誓; **to ~ the law** 执法 **3** Med (dispense) 施用 ‹*medicine*›; **to ~ an injection** 注射针剂

administrate /ədˈmɪnɪstreɪt/ *vt* = **administer 1**

administration /ədˌmɪnɪˈstreɪʃn/ *n* **1** [u] (management of affairs, organization, funds) 管理; **~ costs** 行政费用 **2** [u] Jur (of company) 司法监管; **to go into ~** 处于司法监管之下 **3** [u] (handing out) 执行 **4** [c] esp Amer (government) 政府; Amer (government department) 政府部门 **5** [u] (paperwork) 行政工作

administrative /ədˈmɪnɪstrətɪv, Amer -streɪtɪv/ *adj* 行政的

administratively /ədˈmɪnɪstrətɪvli, Amer -streɪtɪv-/ *adv* 行政上

administrator /ədˈmɪnɪstreɪtə(r)/ ▸**p. 409** *n* **1** Comm, Mgmt 管理者 **2** (of hospital, school, theatre) 行政人员 **3** Jur 遗产管理人; Fin 破产监护人

admirable /ˈædmərəbl/ *adj* 令人敬佩的

admirably /ˈædmərəbli/ *adv* 令人敬佩地

admiral /ˈædmərəl/ *n* 海军上将; **A~ of the Fleet** Brit 海军元帅

Admiralty /ˈædmərəlti/ *n* Brit (administration) 英国海军部; (building) 英国海军大楼

admiration /ˌædməˈreɪʃn/ *n* [u] 敬佩; **to look at sb./sth. with** *or* **in ~** 仰慕某人/赞赏某事物; **to command ~** 令人仰慕; **to be the ~ of sb.** 是某人所钦佩的人

admire /ədˈmaɪə(r)/ *vt* 羡慕 ‹*person*›; 赞赏 ‹*thing, success, behaviour*›; 欣赏 ‹*work of art*›; **to ~ sb. for doing sth.** 因某人做了某事而对其表示赞赏

admirer /ədˈmaɪərə(r)/ *n* **1** (person who admires) 崇拜者; **an ~ of Keats** 济慈的崇拜者 **2** (suitor) [女子的] 追求者

admiring /ədˈmaɪərɪŋ/ *adj* 赞赏的 ‹*look, glance, words*›; 仰慕的 ‹*fans*›

admiringly /ədˈmaɪərɪŋli/ *adv* 赞赏地

admissibility /ədˌmɪsəˈbɪləti/ *n* [u] esp Jur 可采纳性

admissible /ədˈmɪsəbl/ *adj* **1** esp Jur 可采纳的 ‹*evidence*› **2** (allowed to be admitted) 可进入的; **to be ~ to sth.** 可进入某处

admission /ədˈmɪʃn/
A *n* **1** [u] (entry) 准许进入; **~ to a country/an organization** 入境/加入组织; **to gain ~ (to)** 获准入内; **~ by ticket only** 凭票入场 **2** [u] (fee charged) 入场费; **~ free** 免费入场 **3** [c] (confession) 承认; **by sb.'s own ~** 按某人自己所供认; **an ~ of guilt/error** *etc.* 认罪/认错等
B **admissions** *npl* **1** Univ 录取人数 **2** Med 住院人数; **hospital ~s** 住院人数 **3** (to cinema, concert) 观众人数

admission: ~ fee *n* 入场费; **~(s) office** *n* 招生办公室; **~(s) officer** ▸**p. 409** *n* 招生工作人员; **~(s) procedure** *n* 招生程序; **~(s) tutor** ▸**p. 409** *n* 招生负责人

admit /ədˈmɪt/ (*pres p etc.* **-tt-**)
A *vt* **1** (accept, concede) 承认; **it is generally ~ted that ...** 普遍认为…; **to ~ defeat** 认输 **2** (confess) 供认 **3** (allow to enter) «*person, ticket*» 准许…进入; **to be ~ted to hospital** 被收治入院 **4** (allow to become a member) 允许…加入; **to be ~ted to the university** 被大学录取
B *vi* 容许; **to ~ of sth.** 容许某事; **the situation ~s of no delay** 这种情况刻不容缓

admittance /ədˈmɪtns/ *n* [u] 准许进入; **to gain ~** 获准进入; **to refuse** *or* **deny sb. ~** 不许某人进入; **no ~!** 不得入内!

admittedly /ədˈmɪtɪdli/ *adv* 诚然; **~, he did lie, but ...** 他的确撒谎了，但是…

admonish /ədˈmɒnɪʃ/ *vt* **1** (reprimand) 责备; **to ~ sb. for sth./for doing sth.** 就某事告诫某人/告诫某人不要做某事 **2** (advise, warn) 力劝; **to ~ sb. against sth./doing sth.** 力劝某人避免某事物/不要做某事

admonition /ˌædməˈnɪʃn/ *n* **1** (reprimand) 告诫 **2** (advice, warning) 劝告; **she left him with ~s to take care of his health** 她离开时嘱咐他要注意身体

ad nauseam /ˌæd ˈnɔːziæm/ *adv* 令人厌烦地 ‹*discuss, repeat*›

ado /əˈduː/ *n* [u] 忙乱; **without more** *or* **further ~** 立即; **this is all much ~ about nothing** 这纯粹是无事生非

adobe /əˈdəʊbi/ *n* [u] 黏土; **an ~ house** 黏土坯房

adolescence /ˌædəˈlesns/ *n* [u] 青春期

adolescent /ˌædəˈlesnt/
A *n* 青少年
B *adj* **1** (teenage) 青春期的 ‹*problems, behaviour*›; **an ~ boy/girl** 少男/少女 **2** (childish) 幼稚的 ‹*remark, behaviour*›

adopt /əˈdɒpt/
A *vt* **1** (legally bring up) 领养; **to have one's baby ~ed** 把自己的小孩送人收养 **2** Pol 提名; **to ~ sb. as candidate** 推举某人为候选人 **3** (take as one's own, choose) 选用 ‹*name*›; 移居 ‹*country*› **4** (assume, take up) 采用 ‹*style of dress, plan, policy*›; 采取 ‹*attitude*›; **why did he ~ such an aggressive tone of voice?** 他的语气为什么如此咄咄逼人? **5** (accept, approve) 正式通过
B *vi* 领养孩子

adopted /əˈdɒptɪd/ *adj* **1** (having been adopted) 收养的; **an ~ son/daughter** 养子/养女 **2** (chosen as one's own, assumed) 移居的 ‹*country*›; **under an ~ name** 用化名

adoption /əˈdɒpʃn/ *n* [u] **1** (of child) 收养 **2** (of idea, method, style, plan, etc.) 采用 **3** (of candidate) 推举 **4** (of name) 选用; (of country) 移居; **to be French by ~** 移居入法国籍

adoption agency *n* 收养机构

adoptive /əˈdɒptɪv/ *adj* **1** (related by adoption) 收养的; **her ~ parents** 她的养父母 **2** (taken as one's own) 移居的 ‹*country, city*›

adorable /əˈdɔːrəbl/ *adj* 可爱的 ‹*person, animal*›; 漂亮的 ‹*dress, house, garden*›

adoration /ˌædəˈreɪʃn/ *n* [u] 敬爱; **his ~ for his mother** 他对母亲的敬爱; **in ~** 爱慕地

adore /əˈdɔː(r)/ *vt* **1** (love) 敬爱 ‹*person*›; 宠爱 ‹*animal*› **2** colloq (like very much) 喜爱

adoring /əˈdɔːrɪŋ/ *adj* 爱慕的; **an ~ fan** 崇拜者

adoringly /əˈdɔːrɪŋli/ *adv* 爱慕地

adorn /əˈdɔːn/ liter
A *vt* 装饰
B *v refl* **to ~ oneself with sth.** 用某物装扮自己

adornment /əˈdɔːnmənt/ *n* **1** [c] (decoration, ornament) 饰物 **2** [u] (decorating) 装饰

adrenal gland /əˈdriːnl glænd/ *n* 肾上腺

adrenalin, adrenaline /əˈdrenəlɪn/ *n* [u] 肾上腺素; **a rush** *or* **surge of ~** 突然的一阵兴奋; **to get the ~ flowing** 使人热血沸腾

Adriatic /ˌeɪdrɪˈætɪk/
A *adj* 亚得里亚的; **the ~ Sea** 亚得里亚海
B *pr n* **the ~** 亚得里亚

adrift /əˈdrɪft/ *adj, adv* **1** (floating free) 漂流着的（地）; **to set** *or* **cast ~** 使漂流; **to be ~** 漂流着 **2** fig (aimless) 漫无目标的（地） **3** fig colloq (loose) 脱开的（地）; **to come ~** 脱落 **4** Brit Sport colloq 落后的（地）; **two goals ~ of their rivals** 落后他们的对手两个球

adroit /əˈdrɔɪt/ *adj* 灵巧的 ‹*movement*›; 精明的 ‹*person*›; 机敏的 ‹*response, mind*›; **to be ~ at doing sth.** 擅长做某事

adroitly /əˈdrɔɪtli/ *adv* 敏捷地 ‹*move*›; 巧妙地 ‹*handle, respond*›

ADSL *abbr* = **asymmetric digital subscriber line** [利用电话线上网的] 非对称数字用户线路

adspeak /ˈædspiːk/ *n* [u] 广告行话

aduki /æˈduːki/ *n* ~ **(bean)** 赤豆

adulation /ˌædjʊˈleɪʃn, Amer ˌædʒʊ-/ *n* [u] 吹捧; **in** ~ 谄媚地

adult /ˈædʌlt, əˈdʌlt/
A *n* 成年人; **~s only** 仅限成年人
B *adj* **1** (fully grown) 成年的 **2** (relating to or for adults) 成人的 ‹*life, education, classes*›; **the ~ population** 成年人口 **3** (mature) 成熟的 ‹*behaviour, response*› **4** euph (pornographic) 色情的; **~ films** 成人电影

adulterate /əˈdʌltəreɪt/ *vt* 在…中掺假; **~d milk/wine** 掺水牛奶/葡萄酒

adulteration /əˌdʌltəˈreɪʃn/ *n* [u] 掺假

adulterer /əˈdʌltərə(r)/ *n* 奸夫

adulteress /əˈdʌltərɪs/ *n* 奸妇

adulterous /əˈdʌltərəs/ *adj* 通奸的; **an ~ affair** 奸情

adultery /əˈdʌltəri/ *n* [u] 通奸; **to commit ~** 通奸

adulthood /ˈædʌlthʊd/ *n* [u] 成年; **to survive into/reach ~** 活到/到了成年

adult literacy *n* [u] Brit 成人读写能力; **~ class** 成人扫盲班

advance /ədˈvɑːns, Amer -ˈvæns/
A *vi* **1** also Mil (move forward) 前进 **2** (progress) «*person, civilization*» 进步; «*work*» 取得进展; **to ~ in one's career** 在事业上取得进步 **3** (increase) «*price, value, shares*» 上涨 **4** formal (be promoted) 得到晋升
B *vt* **1** (move forward) 使…向前移动 ‹*tape, film, cursor*›; 把…拨快 ‹*hands (of clock), date (on watch)*› **2** (move to earlier date) 提前 ‹*time, date*› **3** (improve) 增进 ‹*understanding, knowledge*› **4** Mil 推进 **5** (in chess) 向前移动 ‹*piece*› **6** (promote) 提高 ‹*interests*›; 促进 ‹*cause*› **7** (put forward) 提出 ‹*idea, theory*› **8** (lend, pay up front) 预支; **to ~ sb. sth.** 给某人预支某款额 **9** formal (increase) 提高 ‹*price, interest rates*›
C *n* **1** also Mil (forward movement) 推进; **with the ~ of old age** 随着年岁渐老 **2** (improvement) 发展; **a great ~ for democracy** 民主的一大进步; **recent ~s in medicine** 医学的新进展 **3** (sum of money) 预付款; **to ask for an ~ on one's salary** 要求预支薪金 **4** (increase) 增加; **any ~ on £100?** (at auction etc.) 100 英镑还有加价的吗?
D **advances** *npl* (overtures) 主动姿态; (sexual) 求爱; **to make ~s to sb.** 勾引某人
E **in advance** *adv phr* 预先; **a month in ~** 提前一个月; **here's £30 in ~** 这是 30 英镑预付款
F **in advance of** *adv phr* 比…提前; **she arrived half an hour in ~ of the others** 她比其他人早到半个小时; **a thinker in ~ of his time** 一个超越其时代的思想家
G *adj attrib* **1** (given or done beforehand) 预先的 ‹*payment, deposit*›; **an ~ warning system** 预警系统 **2** Mil (sent on ahead) 先遣的

advance: ~ booking *n* 预订; **~ booking office** *n* 预订处; **~ copy** *n* 新书样本

advanced /ədˈvɑːnst, Amer -ˈvænst/ *adj* **1** 高级的 ‹*research*›; 高阶的 ‹*students*›; **~ mathematics/physics** 高等数学/物理 **2** (innovative, groundbreaking) 超前的 ‹*ideas, views*› **3** (highly developed, sophisticated) 先进的 **4** (at a late stage) 晚期的 ‹*illness*›; **be ~ in years** 年事已高; **an ~ stage** 晚期 **5** *pred* (having progressed in time) 进入后半期的; **the day was not ~ enough for it to be really hot** 当时天色尚早，还不到真正热的时候

advanced: ~ gas-cooled reactor *n* 改进型气冷反应堆; **~ level** *n* Brit = **A level**; **~ supplementary level** *n* Brit = **AS level**

advance: ~ guard *n* 先遣部队; **~ man** *n* Amer 先遣人员

advancement /ədˈvɑːnsmənt, Amer -ˈvæns-/ *n* **1** [c] (of knowledge, cause, science) 发展 **2** [u] formal (promotion) 晋升

advance: ~ notice *n* 预先通知; **~ party** *n* also Mil 先遣队; **~ payment** *n* 预付款; **~ warning** *n* 预先警告; **we were given no ~ warning** 我们事先没有收到任何警告

advantage /ədˈvɑːntɪdʒ, Amer -ˈvæn-/ *n* **1** [c] (asset) 有利条件; **to have the ~ of a good education** 具有受过良好教育的有利条件; **'computing experience an ~'** (in job advertisement) "有计算机工作经验者优先" **2** [u and c] (favourable position) 有利地位; **to be at an** *or* **in a position of ~** 处于有利地位; **the other team had the ~ of numbers** 另一个队有人多的优势; **to have an** *or* **the ~ over sb.** 胜过某人 **3** [u] (beneficial aspect) 好处; **there is little ~ in having a car if you can't drive!** 不会开车要汽车有什么用!; **if you had your own car, it would give you the ~ of being more mobile** 自己有车的话，出行会更方便 **4** [u] (profit, interest) 利益; **to use sth. to one's ~** 利用某物; **to turn sth. to one's (own) ~** 使某事变得对自己有利; **it would be to your ~ to wait a while** 等一会儿对你会有好处的 **5** [u] (use) 用处; **to take ~ of sth.** 利用某事物; **to take ~ of sb.** (exploit) 占某人的便宜 **6** [u] (best effect) 最佳效果; **to the best ~** 效果最佳地; **the skirt showed off her legs to ~** 这条裙子突出了她双腿的优美线条 **7** [u] (in tennis) [局末平分后的] 优势分; **'~ Federer'** "费德勒占先"

advantaged /ədˈvɑːntɪdʒd, Amer -ˈvæn-/ *adj* 处境优越的

advantageous /ˌædvənˈteɪdʒəs/ *adj* 有利的; **to be ~ to sb.** 有利于某人; **to be ~ to do sth.** 做某事有好处

advantageously /ˌædvənˈteɪdʒəsli/ *adv* 有利地; **to work out ~ for sb.** 结果对某人有利

Advent /ˈædvent/ *pr n* [u] 基督降临节 [圣诞节前的四个星期]

advent /ˈædvent/ *n* [u] (of technique, product) 出现; (of person) 到来; **the ~ of a new era** 新时代的到来

Advent calendar *n* Brit 基督降临历 [一种日历，12月25日之前每天可打开卡片上的一扇小窗或小门]

Adventist /ˈædventɪst/ *n* 基督复临论者

adventitious /ˌædvenˈtɪʃəs/ *adj* formal 偶然的

adventure /ədˈventʃə(r)/ *n* **1** [c] (exciting experience, trip) 冒险活动; **to have an ~** 经历一次历险; **~ stories/films** 惊险故事/电影 **2** [u] (excitement) 冒险的刺激; **a sense/spirit of ~** 冒险意识/精神

adventure: ~ holiday *n* Brit 探险假期; **~ park** *n* 探险乐园; **~ playground** *n* Brit 探险游乐场 [提供绳子、滑道等，让孩子们进行创造性游戏活动]

adventurer /ədˈventʃərə(r)/ *n* **1** (daring person) 冒险家 **2** pej (schemer) 投机分子

adventurous /ədˈventʃərəs/ *adj* **1** (daring, enterprising) 富于冒险精神的 ‹*person, policy, tastes*›; 新奇的 ‹*repertoire*›; **the company is beginning to get a bit more ~** 这家公司开始更加锐意进取些了 **2** (exciting) 惊险刺激的 ‹*experience, holiday*›

adverb /ˈædvɜːb/ ▸**p. 12** *n* (single word) 副词; (phrase) 状语词组

adverbial /ədˈvɜːbɪəl/
A *adj* 副词的
B *n* 状语

adverbially /ədˈvɜːbɪəli/ *adv* 作为状语

adversarial /ˌædvəˈseərɪəl/ *adj* **1** (gen) 敌对的 ‹*nature, manner*› **2** Jur 对抗的; **the ~ system of justice** 审判对抗制

adversary /ˈædvəsəri, Amer -seri/ *n* 对手

adverse /ˈædvɜːs/ *adj* 不利的 ‹*effect, criticism*›; **~ weather conditions** 恶劣的天气; **~ circumstances/winds** 逆境/逆风

adversely /ˈædvɜːsli/ *adv* 不利地; **to affect** *or* **influence sb./sth. ~** 对某人/某事物有负面影响

adversity /ədˈvɜːsəti/ *n* **1** [u] 逆境; **in ~** 在逆境中; **to overcome ~** 克服困境 **2** [c] (instance of misfortune) 灾难

advert /ˈædvɜːt/ *n* Brit colloq = **advertisement**

advertise /ˈædvətaɪz/
A *vt* **1** (for publicity) 公布 **2** (for sale) 为…做广告 ‹*product, film*› **3** (for applications) 为…公开征聘 ‹*job, vacancy*› **4** (make known) 显示 ‹*arrival*›; **to ~ (the fact) that ...** 张扬…(的事实); **to ~ one's presence** 让人注意到自己的存在; **we would like to ~ our willingness to ...** 我们想对…表示愿意
B *vi* 刊登招聘广告; **to ~ in the newspaper for an accountant** 在报纸上登广告招聘一名会计

advertisement /ədˈvɜːtɪsmənt, Amer ˌædvərˈtaɪzmənt/ *n* **1** (for company, product, house, etc.) 广告; **a good/bad ~ for sth.** fig 对某事物好的/不好的宣传; **unhappy clients are not a good ~ for the firm** 客户不满意，会影响公司口碑的 **2** (for event, concert) 公告 **3** **(job) ~** 招聘广告

advertiser /ˈædvətaɪzə(r)/ *n* 广告商

advertising /ˈædvətaɪzɪŋ/ *n* [u] **1** (advertisements) 广告 **2** (profession) 广告业; (activity) 广告活动

advertising: ~ agency *n* 广告公司; **~ agent** ▸**p. 409** *n* 广告代理人; **~ campaign** *n* 广告宣传活动; **~ executive** ▸**p. 409** *n* 广告主管; **~ industry** *n* 广告业; **~ revenue** *n* 广告收入; **A~ Standards Authority** *n* Brit **the A~ Standards Authority** 广告标准局

advertorial /ˌædvɜːˈtɔːrɪəl/ *n* 社论式广告 [社论或客观新闻报道形式的软性广告]

advice /ədˈvaɪs/ *n* **1** [u] (counsel) 劝告; **my ~ (to you) is that you should ...** 我(给你)的建议是你应该…; **a word** *or* **piece of ~** 一句劝告; **to give sb. ~** 劝告某人; **to take** *or* **follow sb.'s ~** 听从某人的劝告; **sound** *or* **good ~** 忠告 **2** [u] (professional guidance) 意见; **to follow medical ~** 遵从医嘱 **3** [c] Comm 通知; **~ of delivery** 发货通知

advice: ~ column *n* 答读者问专栏; **~ columnist** *n* 答读者问专栏作者; **~ note** *n* 通知单

advisability /ədˌvaɪzəˈbɪləti/ *n* [u] 可取; **to have doubts about the ~ of doing sth.** 怀疑做某事是否明智

advisable /ədˈvaɪzəbl/ *adj* 可取的; **it is ~ to ...** …是明智的

advise /ədˈvaɪz/
A *vt* **1** (give advice to) 劝告; **what would you ~?** 有何高见?; **to ~ sb. to do sth./against doing sth.** 劝某人做/不要做某事; **you are ~d to ...** 你最好… **2** (recommend) 建议 ‹*course of action, approach, holiday, caution*›; **the doctor has ~d a complete rest** 医生嘱咐要静养 **3** (act as adviser to) 给…当顾问 ‹*government, organization*›; **to ~ sb. on sth.** 就某事给某人出主意 **4** formal (inform) 通知; **to ~ sb. of sth./that ...** 告知某人某事物/…
B *vi* 提出建议; **to ~ on sth.** (give advice) 就某事提出建议; (inform) 告知某事; **he has been appointed to ~ on monetary matters** 他被任命为金融顾问; **to ~ on doing sth.** 在做某事方面提出建议

advisedly /əd'vaɪzɪdli/ *adv* 经周密考虑; **I've used the term 'old'** ～ 我用"老"这个词是经过反复考虑的

adviser, advisor /əd'vaɪzə(r)/ *n* (in official capacity) 顾问; (unofficially) 提供意见者

advisory /əd'vaɪzəri/ *adj* **1** (recommendatory) 顾问的 ‹*committee, board, council*› **2** (consultative) 咨询的 ‹*work, role*›; **to act/do sth. in an ～ capacity** 担任顾问/以顾问身份做某事 **3** (recommended) 建议性的; **an ～ figure** 建议数字

advisory: ～ **group** *n* 顾问小组; ～ **service** *n* 咨询服务

advocaat /'ædvəkɑ:/ *n* [u] 荷兰蛋酒

advocacy /'ædvəkəsi/ *n* [u] **1** (gen) 拥护; **the ～ of sth. by sb.** 某人对某事物的拥护 **2** Jur 出庭辩护

advocate
A /'ædvəkeɪt/ *vt* 支持 ‹*reform, policy*›; **to ～ abolishing the law** 主张废除法律
B /'ædvəkət/ *n* **1** (supporter) 拥护者 **2** ▸**p. 409** Jur 辩护人

advt *abbr* = **advertisement**

adware /'ædweə(r)/ *n* [u] 广告软件

adze, Amer **adz** /ædz/ *n* 锛子

adzuki /əd'zu:ki/ *n* = **aduki**

AEA *abbr* Brit = **Atomic Energy Authority**

Aegean /i:'dʒi:ən, ɪ-/
A *adj* 爱琴海的; **the ～ Sea** 爱琴海
B *pr n* **the ～** 爱琴海

Aegean Islands /i:'dʒi:ən ˌaɪləndz/ *pr npl* **the ～** 爱琴群岛

aegis /'i:dʒɪs/ *n* **under the ～ of** (with the support of) 在…的支持下; (with the protection of) 在…的保护下

aeon /'i:ən/ *n* 极漫长的时期; **through (the) ～s of time** 经过亿万年的时间; **～s ago** colloq hum 老早以前

aerate /'eəreɪt/ *vt* 使…透气 ‹*soil*›; 向…中充气 ‹*liquid*›; 向…中充氧 ‹*blood*›; **to ～ the lawn** 给草坪松土

aerial /'eərɪəl/
A *adj* **1** (by aircraft) 空中的 ‹*attack, photography, survey*› **2** (suspended) 架空的 ‹*railway, walkway*›; ～ **roots** 气根
B *n* 天线; **TV/radio/satellite ～** 电视/收音机/卫星天线

aerial: ～ **camera** *n* 航空摄影机; ～ **ladder** *n* Amer [消防车上的] 云梯; ～ **warfare** *n* [u] 空战

aerie /'eəri/ *n* Amer = **eyrie**

aerobatic /ˌeərə'bætɪk/ *adj* 特技飞行的

aerobatics /ˌeərə'bætɪks/ *npl* **1** + *v sing* (show) 特技飞行表演 **2** + *v pl* (manoeuvres) 飞行特技

aerobic /eə'rəʊbɪk/ *adj* **1** Biol 需氧的 ‹*respiration, organism*› **2** (relating to exercise) 有氧健身的; **an ～ exercise** 有氧运动; **～ gymnastics** 有氧操

aerobics /eə'rəʊbɪks/ ▸**p. 307** *npl* + *v sing* 有氧运动

aerodrome /'eərədrəʊm/ *n* Brit 小型飞机场

aerodynamic /ˌeərəʊdaɪ'næmɪk/ *adj* **1** (in form, shape) 流线型的 **2** (relating to aerodynamics) 空气动力学的

aerodynamics /ˌeərəʊdaɪ'næmɪks/ *npl* **1** + *v sing* (science) 空气动力学 **2** + *v sing* (styling) 流线型 **3** + *v pl* (forces) 空气动力特性

aeroengine /'eərəʊendʒɪn/ *n* 航空发动机

aerofoil /'eərəʊfɔɪl/ *n* Brit 翼型

aerogenerator /'eərəʊdʒenəreɪtə(r)/ *n* 风力发电机

aerogramme, Amer **aerogram** /'eərəɡræm/ *n* 航空邮笺

aeromodelling Brit, **aeromodeling** Amer /'eərəʊmɒdəlɪŋ/ *n* [u] 航模爱好

aeronautical /ˌeərə'nɔ:tɪkl/, **aeronautic** /ˌeərə'nɔ:tɪk/ *adj* (referring to study) 航空学的; (referring to practice) 航空的

aeronautical: ～ **engineer** ▸**p. 409** *n* 航空工程师; ～ **engineering** *n* [u] 航空工程

ℹ Adverbs

■ In Chinese, the words or phrases which act as adverbial adjuncts are usually placed before and sometimes also after the word (eg verb predicate) they modify. Many kinds of Chinese words or phrases can act as adverbial adjuncts. These include adverbs (刚, 经常, etc.), nouns of time and locality (明天, 外边, etc.), and adjectives (高兴, 慢, etc.).

Adverbs of manner

■ In Chinese, an adverb of manner usually consists of either a two-syllable adjective or repeated adjectives followed by 地:

He examined the list quickly
= 他很快地查看了一下清单

I briefly considered the problem
= 我粗略地考虑了这个问题

The weather gradually got colder
= 天气渐渐地变冷了

She quietly left
= 她静静地离开了

He sat there idly
= 他懒洋洋地坐在那儿

■ 地 is generally omitted in imperatives, where single-syllable adjectives are either repeated or extended by words such as 点儿 or 些:

Walk properly!
= 好好走!

Run fast!
= 快点儿跑!

Get up early!
= 早些起来!

Adverbs of place

■ In Chinese, various words or phrases can function as adverbs of place. These include prepositional phrases (从这边, 在房间, etc.), nouns (外边, 到处, etc.), and location phrases (花园里, 办公室里, etc.):

She lives abroad
= 她在国外生活

I saw her in the cinema
= 我在电影院看到了她

He looked for his sister everywhere
= 他到处找他妹妹

Can we discuss it in the office, please?
= 我们办公室里谈, 好吗?

■ Phrases with 'here' and 'there':

Here's David
= 戴维来了

There's John
= 约翰在那儿

Here comes the bus
= 公共汽车开来了

There goes the train
= 火车开走了

■ In Chinese, when there is more than one adverb of place in a sentence, the largest entity comes first, as in the following examples:

I used to work in Manchester, England
= 我曾在英格兰曼彻斯特工作

He was born in a small village near Edinburgh, Scotland
= 他出生在苏格兰爱丁堡附近的一个小村庄里

Adverbs of time

■ In Chinese, various words or phrases can function as adverbs of time. These include adverbs (曾经, 刚刚, etc.), nouns (后年, 星期三, etc.), location phrases (8 天以后, 两点以前, etc.) and numeral-measure word phrases (3 天, 8 点, etc.):

We often go to the library
= 我们经常去图书馆

Tomorrow I'll be 40
= 我明天就 40 岁了

I'll be there before 3
= 我 3 点以前到那儿

I'll be able to finish reading the book in 5 days
= 我能在 5 天内读完这本书

■ In Chinese, if there is more than one adverb of time in a sentence, the larger unit comes first:

I'll set out at 8 am tomorrow
= 我明天早上 8 点出发

She was born at 9 am on 16th April 2000
= 她于 2000 年 4 月 16 日上午 9 点出生

Order of complex adverbial adjuncts

■ A sentence may contain several adverbial adjuncts which are made up of adverbs and/or adverbial phrases. In Chinese, the order is time, place and manner:

I work happily anywhere
= 我在哪儿都开开心心地工作

We talked about it briefly before
= 我们以前简单地谈过这件事

I will wait for you in the museum at 2 o'clock
= 我两点钟在博物馆等你

She queues patiently at the bus stop every day
= 她每天都在公共汽车站耐心地排队等车

aeronautics /ˌeərəˈnɔːtɪks/ *n + v sing* (subject) 航空学; (practice) 航空术

aeroplane /ˈeərəpleɪn/ *n* esp Brit 飞机

aerosol /ˈeərəsɒl, Amer -sɔːl/ *n* **1** (spray can) 喷雾器; **~ spray/can** 气雾喷雾器/气溶胶罐 **2** (substance) 气雾剂

aerospace /ˈeərəʊspeɪs/ *n* [u] 航空航天工业

aesthete /ˈiːsθiːt, ˈes-/ *n* 审美家

aesthetic /iːsˈθetɪk, es-/ *adj* **1** (relating to aesthetics) 审美的 〈*standards, values*〉; **an ~ sense** 美感 **2** (pleasing) 美观的 〈*design, arrangement, architecture*〉

aesthetically /iːsˈθetɪkli, es-/ *adv* 美观地; **~ appealing** 优美动人的

aestheticism /iːsˈθetɪˌsɪzəm, es-/ *n* [u] 唯美主义

aesthetics /iːsˈθetɪks, es-/ *n + v sing* **1** Philos 美学 **2** (set of principles) 美学理论

af *abbr* = **audio frequency**

afar /əˈfɑː(r)/ *adv* liter (at a distance) 在远处; (to a distance) 向远处; **news from ~** 来自远方的消息

affability /ˌæfəˈbɪləti/ *n* [u] 和蔼可亲

affable /ˈæfəbl/ *adj* 和蔼可亲的; **lunch was an ~ affair** 吃午饭是一件轻松愉快的事

affably /ˈæfəbli/ *adv* 和蔼可亲地

affair /əˈfeə(r)/

A *n* **1** (event, incident) 事件; (thing) 东西; **the wedding was a grand ~** 这场婚礼盛大隆重; **the dress/cake was an extraordinary ~** 这件连衣裙/这块蛋糕很特别 **2** (matter) 事情; **state of ~s** 形势; **it's a sad state of ~s** 情况令人伤心 **3** (relationship) 恋爱; (casual) 风流韵事; **a passionate ~** 热恋 **4** (concern) 个人的事; **it's my ~** 这是我自己的事

B affairs *npl* **1** Pol, Journ 公共事务; **~s of state** 国务; **Egypt's (internal) ~s** 埃及的(内部)事务; **he deals with consumer ~s** 他负责处理消费者权益事务 **2** (private situation) 私人事务; **to put one's ~s in order** 安排好自己的事务; **financial ~s** 财务

affect /əˈfekt/ *vt* **1** (influence) 影响 〈*decision, event, result, person, career*〉 **2** (emotionally disturb) 打动; **the pictures of the disaster ~ed her badly** 有关那场灾难的图片令她唏嘘不已 **3** Med (afflict) «*medical condition*» 侵袭; «*habit*» 损害; **a high percentage of people are ~ed by cancer** 大部分人患有癌症; **the disease often ~s people's sight** 这种病常会损害人的视力 **4** formal (feign) 假装 〈*ignorance, astonishment, mannerism*〉; **to ~ to do sth.** 假装做某事 **5** formal (like to wear) 喜欢穿 〈*clothing, style of dress*〉

affectation /ˌæfekˈteɪʃn/ *n* **1** [u and c] (behaviour) 矫揉造作 **2** [c] (studied display) 假装; **~s of interest/sympathy** 装作有兴趣/同情

affected /əˈfektɪd/ *adj* pej **1** (mannered) 做作的 〈*behaviour, speech*〉; 不自然的 〈*dress*〉 **2** (feigned) 假装的 〈*politeness, indifference*〉

affectedly /əˈfektɪdli/ *adv* 做作地

affecting /əˈfektɪŋ/ *adj* 令人感动的

affection /əˈfekʃn/ *n* **1** [u] (fondness) 喜爱; **to show ~ for sb.** 喜欢某人 **2** [c] (romantic feeling) 爱情; **to transfer one's ~s to sb.** 移情别恋爱上某人

affectionate /əˈfekʃənət/ *adj* 有爱心的 〈*person*〉; 亲昵的 〈*gesture, action*〉; 充满深情的 〈*memory, letter, account*〉; **her parents are very ~ towards each other** 她的父母十分恩爱

affectionately /əˈfekʃənətli/ *adv* 深情地; **yours ~** (ending letter) 你的亲爱的; **~ known as ...** 被亲昵地称为…

affidavit /ˌæfɪˈdeɪvɪt/ *n* 宣誓书; **to swear an ~ (that ...)** (对…) 立下宣誓书

affiliate

A /əˈfɪlieɪt/ *vt* 使隶属; **to be ~d to** or **with sb./sth.** «*organization, society*» 隶属于某人/某组织; **the union decided it would not ~ itself with any political party** 该工会决定不加入任何政党

B /əˈfɪlieɪt/ *vi* «*society*» 并入; «*members*» 加入

C /əˈfɪliət/ *n* 附属机构; **an ~ member** 成员; **an ~ professor** 加盟教授

affiliated /əˈfɪlieɪtɪd/ *adj* 附属的; **an ~ company** 分公司

affiliation /əˌfɪlɪˈeɪʃn/ *n* **1** [u] (process, state) 隶属 **2** [c] (link) 隶属关系; **what is his political ~?** 他属于哪个政治党派?

affinity /əˈfɪnəti/ *n* **1** (resemblance) 类同; **to have an ~ with sb./sth.** 与某人/某事物相似 **2** (liking, attraction) 喜爱; **to have** or **feel an ~ with** or **for ...** 深受…的吸引 **3** (relationship) 密切关系; **there is (a) close ~ between the two languages** 这两种语言关系密切

affinity: ~ card, ~ credit card *ns* 爱心信用卡 [银行把持卡消费额的一部分捐赠给慈善机构等]; **~ group** *n* Amer 亲和团体 [有共同兴趣或目标的团体]

affirm /əˈfɜːm/ *vt* **1** (state positively) 断言; **I can ~ that no one will lose their job** 我可以肯定, 没人会丢掉工作 **2** (state belief in) 申明 〈*policy, belief, right*〉

affirmation /ˌæfəˈmeɪʃn/ *n* [u] 肯定; **an ~ of the power of love** 对爱情力量的歌颂

affirmative /əˈfɜːmətɪv/

A *adj* 肯定的 〈*answer, statement, response*〉; **to give an ~ nod** 点头表示赞同

B *n* 肯定的话; **to reply in the ~** 作肯定的答复

C *excl* Amer 是的

affirmative action *n* [u] 反歧视行动 [旨在维护弱势群体的权益]

affirmatively /əˈfɜːmətɪvli/ *adv* 肯定地; **to vote ~** 投票赞成

affix

A /əˈfɪks/ *vt* **1** (stick) 粘上 〈*stamp, label, poster*〉; (attach) 固定 **2** (append, add) 签 〈*signature*〉; 盖 〈*seal*〉

B /ˈæfɪks/ *n* Ling 词缀

afflict /əˈflɪkt/ *vt* 使痛苦; **to be ~ed by** or **with** 蒙受 〈*disaster, poverty*〉; 患 〈*disease*〉

affliction /əˈflɪkʃn/ *n* **1** [c] (illness) 疾病; (hardship) 苦事 **2** [u] (suffering) 痛苦; **in ~** 受苦的

affluence /ˈæfluəns/ *n* [u] 富裕

affluent /ˈæfluənt/

A *adj* 富裕的

B *n + v pl* **the ~** 富人

afford /əˈfɔːd/ *vt* **1** (have money for) 支付得起; **to be able to ~ sth.** 买得起某物; **to be able to ~ to do sth.** 有钱做某事; **please give what you can ~** 请慷慨解囊 **2** (spare) 能抽出 〈*time, energy*〉; **we can't ~ the space to include all these examples** 我们没有足够篇幅把这些例子都加进去 **3** (risk) 承受得起 〈*scandal, job losses*〉; **the government can't ~ the risk/to lose** 政府担不起这样的风险/输不起; **he can ~/can ill ~ to wait** 他等得及/等不及 **4** formal (give) 提供 〈*protection, information, opportunity*〉; **the window ~ed a magnificent view of the gardens** 从这个窗户可以看到花园的美景

affordable /əˈfɔːdəbl/ *adj* 买得起的 〈*home*〉; 付得起的 〈*rent, price*〉; **~ for all** 人人都能负担得起的

affordable housing *n* [u] 廉价住房

afforest /əˈfɒrɪst, Amer əˈfɔːr-/ *vt* 造林于

afforestation /əˌfɒrɪˈsteɪʃn, Amer əˌfɔːr-/ *n* [u] 植树造林

affray /əˈfreɪ/ *n* Jur 斗殴

affricate /ˈæfrɪkət/ *n* 塞擦音

affront /əˈfrʌnt/

A *n* 侮辱

B *vt usu passive* 侮辱

Afghan /ˈæfgæn/ ▸**p. 503, p. 426**

A *adj* (of Afghanistan) 阿富汗的; (of the people) 阿富汗人的; (of the language) 阿富汗语的

B *n* **1** [c] (person) 阿富汗人 **2** [u] (language) 阿富汗语

Afghan: ~ coat *n* 阿富汗外套 [一种翻羊皮毛边外套]; **~ hound** *n* 阿富汗猎犬

Afghanistan /æfˈgænɪstɑːn, -stæn/ *pr n* 阿富汗

aficionado /əˌfɪsjəˈnɑːdəʊ, əˌfɪʃjə-/ *n* (*pl* **~s**) 狂热爱好者; **a jazz ~** 爵士乐迷

afield /əˈfiːld/ *adv* **far afield** (at a distance) 在远处; (to a distance) 向远处; **to look/go further ~** 看/走得更远; **from as far ~ as China and India** 远自中国和印度

afire /əˈfaɪə(r)/ liter

A *adj pred* **1** (on fire) 燃烧着的 **2** (full of emotion) 激动的; **to be ~ with enthusiasm** 激情燃烧

B *adv* 燃烧着; **to set sth. ~** 点燃某物

aflame /əˈfleɪm/ liter

A *adj pred* **1** (on fire) 燃烧着的 **2** (red) **to be ~** «*sky, trees*» 火红的; **her cheeks were ~** 她两颊飞红 **3** (excited) 激动的; **he was ~ with desire** 他欲火如焚

B *adv* 燃烧着; **to set sth. ~** 点燃某物

AFL-CIO *abbr* = **American Federation of Labor and Congress of Industrial Organizations** 劳联–产联 [美国的劳工联合会–产业工会联合会]

afloat /əˈfləʊt/ *adj, adv* **1** (in water) 漂浮的(地); **to stay** or **remain ~** 漂浮在水上; **to get a boat ~** 使船航行 **2** (at sea, on the water) 在海上的; 在海上; **a day/week ~** 在海上航行的一天/一周 **3** (financially) (经济上)能应付的; 能应付; **to remain** or **stay ~** 无债务困扰; **to keep the economy ~** 维持经济的运转

afoot /əˈfʊt/ *adj pred* «*plan*» 进行中的; **there is something ~** 有点不对劲; **there is mischief ~** 有人在捣鬼

aforementioned /əˌfɔːˈmenʃənd/ *adj* 上述的; **the ~ Fred Jones** 前面提到的弗雷德·琼斯

aforesaid /əˈfɔːsed/ *adj* = **aforementioned**

aforethought /əˈfɔːθɔːt/ *adj* Jur 蓄意的; **with malice ~** 蓄意犯罪地

afoul /əˈfaʊl/ *adv* Amer **to run ~ of ...** 与…发生冲突

afraid /əˈfreɪd/ *adj pred* **1** (frightened) 畏惧的; **she's ~ of you/the dark** 她怕你/怕黑; **to be ~ of doing sth.** 害怕做某事 **2** (anxious) 担忧的; **I'm ~ it might rain** 恐怕会下雨; **to be ~ for sb./sth.** 为某人/为某事物担忧; **to be ~ of (hard) work** 不乐意干 (辛苦) 活 **3** (in expressions of regret) [表示遗憾]; **I'm ~ I can't come** 可惜我不能来; **did they win? — I'm ~ not** 他们赢了吗? ——很遗憾, 没有; **(I'm) ~ so** 恐怕是这样 **4** (as polite formula) [礼貌用语]; **I'm ~ the house is in a mess** 不好意思, 屋子里乱七八糟; **I'm ~ I don't agree** 很抱歉, 我不同意

afresh /əˈfreʃ/ *adv* 重新 〈*look, do*〉; **to start ~ in life** 开始新生活

Africa /ˈæfrɪkə/ *pr n* 非洲

African /ˈæfrɪkən/

A *adj* (of Africa) 非洲的; (of the people) 非洲人的; (of the languages) 非洲语言的

B *n* 非洲人

African American

A *adj* 非洲裔美国人的

B *n* 非洲裔美国人

African: ~ elephant *n* 非洲象; **~ National Congress** *n* 非洲人国民大会

Afrikaans /ˌæfrɪˈkɑːns/ ▸**p. 426** *n* 南非荷兰语

Afrikaner /ˌæfrɪˈkɑːnə(r)/ ▸**p. 503**

A *adj* 南非荷兰人的

B *n* 南非荷兰人

a

African American

非洲裔美国人，即美国黑人。他们大多为 19 世纪非洲黑人奴隶的后代。20 世纪 60 年代后期，因对不同族裔人群的划分转向侧重地理、文化和历史的来源，而不再提及肤色，African American、Asian American（亚裔美国人，▸**Asian American**）等词开始广为流行，而且被认为政治上更为正确。

Afro /ˈæfrəʊ/ *n* ~ **(haircut)** 非洲式发型［短而卷曲的发型］

Afro-American *adj, n* = **African American**

Afro-Caribbean
A *adj* 非洲裔加勒比人的
B *n* 非洲裔加勒比人

Afro-Caribbean

（英国）非洲裔加勒比人。19 世纪废除奴隶贸易之前，许多非洲人被卖到加勒比海地区的英国种植园。第二次世界大战以后，英国劳动力短缺，雇主开始从加勒比地区招募劳工。1948 年，英国通过《英国国籍法》（*British Nationality Act*），授予所有英联邦成员国公民英国公民身份，并允许他们来英国定居。早期的非洲裔加勒比移民多住在伦敦诺丁山（Notting Hill）和布里克斯顿（Brixton）地区。因为种族歧视等原因，加勒比移民在融入英国社会时遇到困难。经过数十年的时间，加勒比裔居民已经形成独特的文化。20 世纪 60 年代开始的诺丁山狂欢节（Notting Hill Carnival）现在每年吸引全世界数百万人参加。

aft /ɑːft, Amer æft/
A *adv* **1** Naut 向船尾 ‹go›; 在船尾 ‹*stand, stow*› **2** Aviat 向机尾 ‹go›; 在机尾 ‹*stand, stow*›
B *adj* **1** Naut 船尾的 **2** Aviat 机尾的

after /ˈɑːftə(r), Amer ˈæftər/
A *conj* **1** (in sequence of events) 在…以后; ~ **we left, we realized we had forgotten to say thank you** 我们离开后才意识到忘了道谢 **2** (as a result of the fact that, given that) 鉴于; **why did he do that ~ we'd warned him?** 我们警告过他，可他为什么还要那样做？; ~ **you explained the situation, they didn't call the police** 由于你解释了这个情况，他们才没有报警
B *prep* **1** (later in time than) 在…以后; **the day ~ tomorrow** 后天; **the week ~ next** 下下周; **shortly ~ 10 p.m.** 晚上 10 点钟后不久 **2** (behind) 在…后面; **to run ~ sb./sth.** 追赶某人/某物; **please shut the gate ~ you** 请随手关上大门 **3** (given) 由于; **I'll never forgive him ~ what he said** 他竟然这样说，为此我永远也不会原谅他 **4** (in spite of) 尽管; ~ **what she's been through, she's still interested?** 经历了这些之后，她仍然有兴趣吗？ **5** (in contrast to) 与…对照; **it's boring here ~ Paris** 与巴黎相比，这里很乏味 **6** (following in sequence, rank, precedence) 次于; ~ **you!** 您先请！; ~ **you with the paper** 报纸你看完后给我看; **he's the tallest ~ Richard** 他的个头仅次于理查德 **7** (in the direction of) 向着…的背影; **'don't forget!' Mary called ~ her** "别忘了！" 玛丽在她背后喊道 **8** (in the wake of) 紧随…之后; **I'm not tidying up ~ you!** 别让我跟在你屁股后面收拾！ **9** (trying to find, catch, or obtain) 在追寻; **the police are ~ him** 警方正在追捕他; **it's me he's ~** (to settle score) 他要报复的人是我; **I wonder what she's ~?** 不知道她要得到什么？; **I think he's ~ my job** colloq 我看他在觊觎我的工作; **to be ~ sb.** (sexually) 追求某人 **10** (at the farther side of) 在…的那边; (to the farther side of) 去…的那边; **about 400 metres ~ the crossroads** 十字路口过去约 400 米 **11** (stressing continuity, repetitiveness) ［表示连续不断］; **day ~ day** 日复一日; **generation ~ generation** 一代又一代; **time ~ time** 一再; **it was one disaster ~ another** 灾难接二连三 **12** (about) 关于; **to ask ~ sb.** 问候某人 **13** (in honour or memory of) 以…的名字 ‹*monument, person*›; **to name a child ~ sb.** 以某人的名字给孩子取名 **14** (in the manner of) 以…为模仿对象; **it's a painting ~ Klee** 这是一幅模仿克利的画 **15** Amer (when telling time) 晚于; **it's twenty ~ eleven** 现在是 11 点 20 分
C *adv* **1** (following specific time) 之后; **the week/year ~** 下一周/年; **we left the day ~** 我们于翌日离开 **2** (following time or event) 以后; **for weeks ~** 后来几个星期; **right ~** 紧接着
D **afters** *npl* Brit colloq 餐后甜食; **there's fruit salad for ~s** 甜点是水果色拉
E **after all** *adv phr* **1** (when reinforcing point) 要知道; ~ **all, nobody forced you to leave** 别忘了，没人强迫你离开; **he should have paid: he suggested it ~ all** 该付款的是他：本来就是他的提议 **2** (when reassessing) 终究; **he decided not to stay ~ all** 他毕竟还是决定不留下

after: **~birth** *n* [u and c] 胞衣; **~burner** *n* Aviat 加力燃烧室; **~care** *n* [u] **1** Med 出院后的护理; **2** (on release from prison) 出狱后的安置; **3** (after purchase) 售后服务; **~-dinner drink** *n* (gen) 正餐后饮料; (alcoholic) 餐后酒; **~-dinner speaker** *n* 宴会后演说者; **~-dinner speech** *n* 宴会后的演说; **~-effect** *n* **1** Med 后效; **2** fig 后果; **~glow** *n* [u] **1** (light in the sky) 夕照; **2** (feelings) 美好的回忆; **~-hours drinking** *n* [u] Brit 打烊后酒品交易; **~life** *n* 来生

aftermath /ˈɑːftəmæθ, -mɑːθ, Amer ˈæf-/ *n* 后果; **in the ~ of ...** 在…结束后的一段时间里

afternoon /ˌɑːftəˈnuːn, Amer ˌæf-/ ▸**p. 831**
A *n* **1** (part of day) 下午; **in the ~** 在下午; **in the early/late ~** 午后不久/快到傍晚时; **on a cold January ~** 在1月份一个寒冷的下午; **~ nap** 午觉; **to work ~s** 每天下午工作 **2** liter (later period) 后期; **in the ~ of (one's) life** 在（自己的）后半生
B ▸**p. 333** *excl* colloq **~!** 下午好!
C **afternoons** *adv* colloq 每天下午

afternoon: **~ performance** *n* 下午场演出; **~ tea** *n* [u] (snack) 午后茶点; (drink) 下午茶

after: **~pains** *npl* 产后痛; **~-sales service** *n* [u] 售后服务; **~-school** *adj attrib* 课外的 ‹*activity*›; 课外活动的 ‹*club, programme*›; **~shave** *n* [u and c] 须后水; **~shock** *n* **1** Geol 余震; **2** fig 余悸; **~-sun** *n* [u] 晒后修复霜; **~taste** *n* [u and c] **1** lit 余味; **2** fig 回味; **~thought** *n* (thought of later) 事后想法; (added later) 事后添加的东西; **almost as an ~thought** 事后才想起来似的; **~word** *n* 跋

afterwards /ˈɑːftəwədz, Amer ˈæf-/ esp Brit, **afterward** /ˈɑːftəwəd, Amer ˈæf-/ Amer *adv* (after) 以后; (later) 后来; **we saw a film, went to the restaurant, and then went home ~** 我们看了场电影，吃了顿饭，然后就回家了; **immediately** *or* **directly ~** 紧接着; **straight ~** Brit 紧接着; **for years ~** 在过后的很多年里; **I regretted it ~** 我随后就后悔了

afterword /ˈɑːftəwɜːd/ *n* 跋

Aga® /ˈɑːgə/ *n* 雅家炉［高级炊具，用于持续保温］

again /əˈgeɪn, əˈgen/ *adv* **1** (one more time) 再一次; **when will I see you ~?** 我什么时候能再见到你？; **not ~!** 怎么又是这样！; **never ~!** 绝对没有第二次！; **~ and ~** 一再 **2** (as previously) ［回到原处或先前的状态］; **he was glad to be home ~** 他很高兴又回到家了; **now she's well ~** 她现在康复了 **3** (in addition) ［加上］; **half as much ~** 增加一半; **the same ~** 再来一份同样的 **4** (further) 而且; **~, there are striking differences** 再说了，差异十分显著; **~, you may think that more could have been done** 此外，你可能认为本来可以做得更多 **5** (on the other hand) 另一方面; **then** *or* **there ~** 不过

against /əˈgeɪnst, əˈgenst/
A *prep* **1** (in contact with) 紧靠着 **2** (in collision with) 碰着; **waves crashed ~ the rocks** 浪头拍打着岩石; **frustration made him bang his head ~ the wall** 他懊恼得用头撞墙 **3** (objecting to) 反对; (in opposition to) 对抗; **protests ~ the war** 反战抗议; **a warning ~ drug abuse** 对滥用毒品的警告; **I've got nothing ~ him personally** 我个人对他没有什么意见; **Smith ~ Jones** 史密斯诉琼斯案; **to be ~ the law** 违法; **she was forced to marry ~ her will** 她被迫违心结了婚 **4** (unfavourable to) 对…不利; **to discriminate ~ women** 歧视妇女; **she's prejudiced ~ me** 她对我有成见 **5** (in opposite direction to) 逆向 **6** (as protection or a defence) 预防; **vaccination ~ cholera** 霍乱疫苗的接种; **insurance ~ fire** 火险; **precautions ~ burglary** 防盗措施; **he turned up his collar ~ the wind** 他竖起领子挡风 **7** (compared with) 相对于; **the pound rose/fell ~ the dollar** 英镑对美元升值/贬值了; **the rate of exchange ~ the euro** 对欧元的汇率 **8** (having as a background) 以…为背景; (having as a contrast) 在…的衬托下; **to stand out ~ ...** 在…的映衬下显得醒目 ‹*sky, sunset*›; **dark trees stood out ~ the snow** 黑压压的树木在白雪的映衬下夺目显眼 **9** formal (in preparation for) 为…作准备; **she is saving ~ her retirement** 她在为退休存钱; **preparations were being made ~ his return** 人们正在为他的归来作准备 **10** (in exchange for) 以…作为交换; **payment will be ~ presentation of the bill of lading** 货款将在出示提单后支付
B *adv* 反对; **did you vote for or ~?** 你投了赞成票还是反对票?

agape /əˈgeɪp/
A *adj pred* 大张着嘴的
B *adv* 大张着嘴地; **he stood there ~** 他目瞪口呆地站在那里

Aga saga *n* Brit 雅家炉世家小说［以中产阶级人物生活的半农村地区为背景］

agate /ˈægət/ *n* [u] 玛瑙

agave /əˈgeɪvi/ *n* 龙舌兰

age /eɪdʒ/
A *n* **1** (length of existence) 年龄; **to be/reach x years of ~** 是/到 X 岁; **the building is of (a) great ~** 这建筑物历史悠久; **to live to a great** *or* **ripe old ~** 活到高龄; **at the ~ of 17** 17 岁时; **act** *or* **be your ~!** 成熟点吧！; **to look one's ~** 容貌与年龄相当; **to feel one's ~** 感到自己上了年纪; **at a tender ~** 在幼年; **to come of ~** 达到法定年龄; **to be under ~** 未到法定年龄; **the ~ of consent** 同意年龄［可与之发生性关系的法定年龄］ **2** (latter part of life) (of people) 老年; (of mature wine, cheese etc.) 陈年; **the wine will improve with ~** 葡萄酒年久味更醇 **3** (era) 时代; **to be of** *or* **at an ~ when ...** 在…的时代; **the ~ of space travel** 太空旅行时代; **through** *or* **throughout the ~s** 从古到今 **4** colloq (long time) 长时间; **it's ~s since I've played tennis** 我很久很久没打网球了
B *vi* «*person*» 变老; «*building*» 变旧; «*wine*» 变陈; **to ~ beyond one's years** 显得比实际年龄老; **he's ~ing very well** 他不显老; **it is a good vintage and ~s well** 这酒酿制得好，且年久弥醇
C *vt* **1** (cause to grow, feel, or appear older) 使显老; **to ~ sb. ten years** 使某人苍老 10 岁 **2** (allow to mature) 使…变陈 ‹*wine, whisky*›

age bracket *n* = **age range**

aged
A *adj* **1** /eɪdʒd/ (of an age) …岁的; **~ between 20 and 25** 20 到 25 岁之间的; **a boy ~ 12** 12 岁的男孩 **2** /ˈeɪdʒɪd/ (old) 年迈的
B /ˈeɪdʒɪd/ *n + v pl* **the ~** 老人; **a home for the ~** 养老院

age: **~ difference** *n* [u and c] 年龄差距; **~ discrimination** *n* [u] 年龄歧视; **~ group** *n* = **~ range**

ageing /ˈeɪdʒɪŋ/
A *adj* 变老的 ‹*person*›; 变陈旧的 ‹*system, technology, computer, car*›; **that hairstyle is really ~** 那种发型真老气
B *n* [u] (of person) 变老; (of wine, cheese) 变陈; **the wine improves through ~** 葡萄酒年久味更醇

ageism /ˈeɪdʒɪzəm/ *n* [u] 对老年人的歧视

ageist /ˈeɪdʒɪst/
A *adj* (against people on grounds of age) 有年龄歧视的; (against older people) 歧视老年人的
B *n* (against people on grounds of age) 有年龄歧视的人; (against older people) 歧视老年人的人

ageless /ˈeɪdʒlɪs/ *adj* **1** (not appearing to age) 青春永驻的; (of indeterminate age) 看不出年龄的 **2** (timeless) 永恒的 ‹*quality, mystery*›

age limit *n* 年龄限制; **an upper/lower ~** 年龄上限/下限

agency /ˈeɪdʒənsi/ *n* **1** [c] (organization, office) 代理机构; **to get sb. through an ~** 通过中介找到某人; (in advertisement) **'no agencies'** "谢绝中介" **2** [c] Brit (representing firm) 代理; **to have the sole ~ for** 是…的独家代理 ‹*company, product*› **3** [c] (department, body) 专门机构 **4** [u] (influence) 介入; **by** *or* **through the ~ of sb.** 通过某人从中斡旋 **5** [u] Phys, Geol 作用; **by the ~ of erosion** 在侵蚀的作用下

agency: A~ for International Development *n* 美国国际开发署; **~ nurse** *n* 中介介绍的护士; **~ staff** *n* 中介介绍的员工

agenda /əˈdʒendə/ *n* **1** Admin 议事日程; **to be on the ~** 列入日程表 **2** fig (list of priorities) 工作事项; **a hidden** *or* **secret ~** 秘密事项; **unemployment is high on the political ~** 失业是重要的政治议题

agent /ˈeɪdʒənt/ *n* **1** (acting for customer, artist, firm) 代理人; **to go through an ~** 通过代理人 **2** (spy) 特工 **3** (cause, means) 动因; **wind is the ~ of plant pollination** 风是帮助植物传粉的媒介 **4** (chemical substance) 剂; **cleansing ~** 清洁剂 **5** Ling 施事者

agent noun *n* 施事名词

agent provocateur *n* (*pl* **agents provocateurs** /ˌæʒɒ̃ prəˌvɒkəˈtɜː(r)/) [受雇滋事的]密探

age: ~-old *adj* 由来已久的 ‹*custom, remedy, ceremony*›; **an ~-old joke** 老掉牙的笑话; **~ range** *n* 年龄组; **people in the 25-30 ~ range** 25 到 30 岁年龄段的人

agglomerate
A /əˈɡlɒmərət/ *n* **1** Comm 集团公司 **2** Geol 集块岩
B /əˈɡlɒməreɪt/ *vt* **1** Comm 合并 **2** Geol 使结块
C /əˈɡlɒməreɪt/ *vi* **1** Comm 合并 **2** Geol 结块

agglomeration /əˌɡlɒməˈreɪʃn/ *n* **1** [u] also Comm 合并 **2** [u] Geol 凝结 **3** [c] (group) 堆; **an ~ of buildings** 密集的建筑物群; **large ~s of capital** 大批量的资金

agglutinating language /əˈɡluːtɪneɪtɪŋ ˌlæŋɡwɪdʒ/ *n* 黏着语

agglutinative /əˈɡluːtɪnətɪv, Amer -təneɪtɪv/ *adj* 黏着性的

aggrandizement /əˈɡrændɪzmənt/ *n* [u] formal 增长

aggravate /ˈæɡrəveɪt/ *vt* **1** (make worse) 使恶化 **2** colloq (annoy) 惹恼

aggravated /ˈæɡrəveɪtɪd/ *adj attrib* Jur 严重的 ‹*offence*›; **~ burglary** 入室盗窃重罪

aggravating /ˈæɡrəveɪtɪŋ/ *adj* colloq (irritating) 使人恼火的

aggravation /ˌæɡrəˈveɪʃn/ *n* **1** [u] colloq (problems, irritations) 麻烦 **2** [u] (worsening) 恶化 **3** [c] (annoyance) 烦心事

aggregate
A /ˈæɡrɪɡət/ *n* **1** [c] (total amount) 总数; **the ~ of unemployment figures** 失业总人数; **an ~ of five years** 总共 5 年; **in (the) ~** (added together) 总共; (considered as a group) 作为总体;

ℹ Age

Asking about age

■ In Chinese, there are various ways of asking a person's age, depending on their age and status:

What age are you?
= 你几岁/多大了? (when asking a child)
or 你/您多大岁数了? (denotes respect when asking an elderly person)

How old are you?
= 你多大了? (when asking anyone's age)

Could you tell me your age, please?
= 能告诉我你的年龄吗? (formal)

Indicating exact age

■ 岁 (year), 月(month), and 天 (day) are used to express an exact age. 岁 can be omitted in most cases. 岁 is normally used for ages of ten years and under:

She is 37
or ***She is 37 years old***
or ***She is 37 years of age***
= 她 37
or 她 37 岁

I am 10
= 我 10 岁

The baby is 10 days old
= 宝宝 10 天了

Mary is 11 months old
= 玛丽 11 个月大了

■ Note the use of 有, 穿, 用, and 年 for expressing the age of things:

The church is a hundred years old
= 这所教堂有 100 年了

The shirt is 5 years old
= 这件衬衫穿了 5 年了

The table is 3 years old
= 这张桌子用了 3 年了

■ Generally speaking, 岁 should not be omitted when it is used before a noun as a modifier:

a man aged 50
= 50 岁的男人

a boy of 6
= 6 岁的男孩

■ Note the different ways of expressing compound adjectives and compound nouns in Chinese:

a ten-month-old baby
= 10 个月大的婴儿

a twenty-three-year-old student
= 23 岁的学生

a five-year-old car
= 用了 5 年的车
or 开了 5 年的车

a twenty-year-old wine
= 20 年陈酒

twelve-year-olds
= 12 岁的儿童

a fifty-year-old
= 50 岁的人

Indicating approximate age

■ In Chinese, approximate age is expressed in the following ways:

They are in their thirties
= 他们三十几岁

I am in my early forties
= 我 40 出头

He is in his mid-twenties
= 他二十五六岁

She is in her late forties
= 她四十八九岁

My mum is over fifty
= 我妈妈五十多岁了

The students are above the age of 20
= 这些学生在 20 岁以上

My brother is under 15
= 我弟弟不到 15
or 我弟弟不满 15

They are below the age of 30
= 他们在 30 岁以下
or 他们不到 30 岁

I am nearly 30
= 我差不多 30 了

The cat is about 9 years old
= 这猫大概 9 岁了
or 这猫大约 9 岁了

The coat is at least 5 years old
= 这件外套至少有 5 年了
or 这件外套至少穿 5 年了

toys for under-fives
= 适合 5 岁以下儿童的玩具

clubs for over-sixties
= 60 岁以上老人俱乐部

■ Note the use of 大 and 小 in Chinese to express similarity or difference in age:

children of Jane's age
= 像简一样大的孩子

She is the same age as you
or ***She is as old as you***
= 她和你一样大
or 她和你同岁

They are the same age
= 他们一样大
or 他们同龄
or 他们同岁

She is older than you
= 她比你大

She is younger than you
= 她比你小
or 她比你年轻

She is 5 years older than you
= 她比你大 5 岁

She is 3 years younger than you
= 她比你小 3 岁

a

to win/lose on ～ 总体上赢/输 **2** [u] Geol, Miner 聚合体 **3** [u] Constr 集料
B /ˈæɡrɪɡət/ *adj attrib* 总的 ‹*value, profit*›
C /ˈæɡrɪɡeɪt/ *vt* 合计 ‹*figures, totals*›

aggression /əˈɡreʃn/ *n* [u] **1** (aggressive feelings) 敌对情绪 **2** (aggressive behaviour) 侵犯; **military ～** 军事侵略

aggressive /əˈɡresɪv/ *adj* **1** (provoking conflict) 好斗的 ‹*person*›; 凶猛的 ‹*animal*›; 侵略成性的 ‹*nation*›; 挑衅的 ‹*behaviour, language, tactics*›; 暴躁的 ‹*mood*› **2** Comm, Pol (tough) 积极强硬的 ‹*management, policy*›; 激烈的 ‹*competition*›; 进取的 ‹*attitude*›

aggressive accounting *n* [u] 激进会计法 [做假账以取悦投资者并抬高股价]

aggressively /əˈɡresɪvli/ *adv* **1** (in an aggressive manner) 挑衅地 ‹*act, glare, shout*›; 激烈地 ‹*argue*› **2** Comm, Fin 竭力地 ‹*promote*›; 激烈地 ‹*compete*›

aggressiveness /əˈɡresɪvnɪs/ *n* [u] **1** (gen) 挑衅行为 **2** (in business) 激烈竞争; **the ～ of their campaign** 他们推销活动的凶猛势头

aggressor /əˈɡresə(r)/ *n* 侵略者; **the ～ nation** 侵略国

aggrieved /əˈɡriːvd/
A *adj* **1** (resentful) 怨愤的; **to be ～ at sth./doing sth.** 因某事/做某事而愤愤不平 **2** Jur (wronged) 受害的
B *n* Jur **the ～** 受害方

aggro /ˈæɡrəʊ/ *n* [u] Brit colloq **1** (aggressive behaviour) 闹事 **2** (hassles) 麻烦

aghast /əˈɡɑːst, Amer əˈɡæst/ *adj pred* 惊恐的; **to be ～ at sth.** 被某事物惊呆

agile /ˈædʒaɪl, Amer ˈædʒl/ *adj* **1** (lithe) 敏捷的 ‹*person, animal, movement*›; (fit) 灵活的 ‹*body*› **2** *attrib* (mentally acute) 机敏的 ‹*mind, intellect*›

agility /əˈdʒɪləti/ *n* [u] (physical) 敏捷; (mental) 机敏

aging /ˈeɪdʒɪŋ/ *adj, n* = **ageing**

agism /ˈeɪdʒɪzəm/ *n* [u] = **ageism**

agist /ˈeɪdʒɪst/ *adj, n* = **ageist**

agitate /ˈædʒɪteɪt/
A *vt* **1** (cause anxiety to) 使焦虑 **2** (shake) 搅动 ‹*mixture*›
B *vi* 鼓动; **to ～ for/against sth.** 鼓动支持/煽动反对某事

agitated /ˈædʒɪteɪtɪd/ *adj* 焦虑的 ‹*person, voice*›; 令人不安的 ‹*message*›

agitatedly /ˈædʒɪteɪtɪdli/ *adv* 焦虑不安地

agitation /ˌædʒɪˈteɪʃn/ *n* [u] **1** (anxiety) 焦虑; **to be in a state of ～** 处于焦虑不安的状态 **2** (political turmoil) 鼓动 **3** (stirring of liquid) 搅动

agitator /ˈædʒɪteɪtə(r)/ *n* **1** (person) 鼓动者 **2** (machine) 搅拌器

agitprop /ˈædʒɪtprɒp/ *n* [u] [尤指文艺方面的] 政治宣传; **an ～ documentary** 宣传纪录片

aglow /əˈɡləʊ/ *adj pred* **to be ～** «*sky*» 泛红光; «*hills*» 光照融融; **to set sth. ～** 照亮某物; **she was ～ with pleasure** 她高兴得满面红光

AGM *abbr* = **Annual General Meeting**

agnostic /æɡˈnɒstɪk/
A *adj* 持不可知论的
B *n* 不可知论者

agnosticism /æɡˈnɒstɪsɪzəm/ *n* [u] 不可知论

ago /əˈɡəʊ/ *adv* 以前; **a few minutes/two years ～** 几分钟/两年前; **long ～** 很久以前; **as long ～ as 1986** 早在1986年

agog /əˈɡɒɡ/ *adj pred* (excited) 兴奋期待的; (eager) 渴望的; **to be ～ at sth.** 为某事物感到兴奋; **to be (all) ～ for sth./to do sth.** 渴望得到某物/做某事; **to be ～ with excitement** 兴奋地期待

agonize /ˈæɡənaɪz/ *vi* 焦虑不已; **to ～ over** *or* **about sth.** 为某事物犯愁

agonized /ˈæɡənaɪzd/ *adj* 极度痛苦的 ‹*scream, look*›

agonizing /ˈæɡənaɪzɪŋ/ *adj* 使人极度痛苦的

agony /ˈæɡəni/ *n* [u and c] 极度痛苦; **to prolong the ～** 延长痛苦; **it was ～!** fig hum 真是凄惨！; **to pile on the ～** Brit 故意夸大痛苦; **to suffer agonies of remorse** 因懊悔而痛苦不堪

agony: ～ aunt *n* Brit 答读者问专栏女作者; **～ column** *n* Brit 答读者问专栏; **～ uncle** *n* Brit 答读者问专栏男作者

agoraphobia /ˌæɡərəˈfəʊbɪə/ *n* [u] 广场恐惧症

agoraphobic /ˌæɡərəˈfəʊbɪk/
A *adj* 患广场恐惧症的 ‹*person*›; 产生广场恐惧的 ‹*situation*›
B *n* 广场恐惧症患者

AGR *abbr* Brit = **advanced gas-cooled reactor**

agrammatical /ˌeɪɡrəˈmætɪkl/ *adj* 不符合语法的

agrarian /əˈɡreərɪən/ *adj* 农业的 ‹*society, economy*›; 土地的 ‹*reform, laws, revolution*›

agree /əˈɡriː/
A *vi* **1** (hold same opinion) 同意; **to ～ with sb.** 同意某人; **to ～ about** *or* **on sth.** 就某事达成一致; **to ～ to** *or* **with sth.** 同意某事; **to ～ to sb.('s) doing sth.** 允许某人做某事 **2** (hold with, approve) **to ～ with** 赞成 ‹*belief, idea, practice*› **3** (come to joint decision) 取得一致意见; **they failed to ～** 他们未能达成共识; **the jury ～d in finding him guilty** 陪审团一致裁定他有罪; **to ～ about sth./doing sth.** 商定某事/做某事 **4** (tally) 相符; **her account doesn't ～ with yours** 她的叙述与你的不符; **the two theories ～ (with each other)** 这两种看法一致 **5** Ling [在数和人称等方面] 一致 **6** (suit) **to ～ with sb.** 适合某人 **7** (be easily digested) 易消化; **I like cheese, but it doesn't ～ with me** 我喜欢奶酪，但吃了会不适
B *vt* **1** (concur) 认同; **he ～d (that) he'd made a mistake** 他承认犯了一个错误 **2** (consent) **to ～ to do sth.** 同意做某事 **3** (settle on, arrange) 商定 ‹*time, venue, route, policy*›; 谈妥 ‹*terms, price*›; **we can't ～ where to go for our summer holidays** 关于到哪里过暑假，我们各执己见; **as ～d** 按照约定 **4** (approve) 核准 ‹*figures*›; 批准 ‹*pay rise, plan, candidate*›; **don't forget to ～ the menu with the embassy** 别忘了与大使馆核定菜单

agreeable /əˈɡriːəbl/ *adj* **1** (likeable) 亲切友善的 ‹*person, character, company*›; **to be ～ to sb.** 对某人和蔼可亲 **2** (enjoyable) 宜人的 ‹*weather*›; 愉快的 ‹*trip, sensation*› **3** *pred* formal (willing) **to be ～ to sth./to doing sth.** 欣然同意某事物/做某事 **4** formal (acceptable) 可接受的 ‹*plan, terms*›; **is this ～ to you?** 你觉得这样可以吗?

agreeably /əˈɡriːəbli/ *adv* **1** (pleasantly) 令人愉快地; **to be ～ surprised** 又惊又喜; **an ～ dry wine** 适口的干葡萄酒 **2** (amicably) 友善地

agreed /əˈɡriːd/ *adj* **1** (predetermined) 商定的 ‹*price, budget*›; 约定的 ‹*date, place, signal*›; **but you've got to do it! it's all ～!** 但你必须做这事！都说好了的！ **2** *pred* (in agreement) 意见一致的; **are we all ～?** 大家都同意了吗？; **to be ～ about** *or* **on sth.** 同意某事物 **3** (acceptable) 同意的; (as a question) **we'll go tomorrow: ～?** 我们明天走，可以吗？; (as an exclamation) **I suggest we ignore it — ～!** 我建议我们不睬它——同意！

agreement /əˈɡriːmənt/ *n* **1** [u] (consensus) 意见一致; **to be in ～ (with sb.) about** *or* **on sth.** 在某方面（与某人）意见一致; **there is little ～ as to what should be done about the problem** 对于解决问题的方法，意见分歧不小; **there is general ～ that ...** 大家一致认为… **2** [u] (consent) 同意; **to nod in ～** 点头表示同意; **tacit ～** 默许; **～ to sth.** 对于…的同意 ‹*plan, suggestion*›; **her ～ to pay for the petrol helped a great deal** 她答应付汽油钱，真是帮了大忙 **3** [c] (decision, arrangement, contract) 协议; **an ～ on disarmament** 裁军协议; **to draw up/sign an ～** 起草/签订协议; **to reach (an) ～ (with sb.)** （与某人）达成协议; **by ～ with sb.** 根据与某人的协议 **4** [u] Ling [在人称、数等方面的] 一致

agribusiness /ˈæɡrɪbɪznɪs/ *n* **1** [u] (large-scale agriculture) 企业化农业 **2** [c] (business, company) 农业企业 **3** [u] (businesses collectively) 农业企业界

agricultural /ˌæɡrɪˈkʌltʃərəl/ *adj* 农业的 ‹*land, worker*›; 农用的 ‹*machinery, implements*›; **～ college/produce** 农学院/农产品

agriculturalist /ˌæɡrɪˈkʌltʃərəlɪst/ Brit, **agriculturist** /ˌæɡrɪˈkʌltʃərɪst/ Amer ▸**p. 409** *n* (farmer) 农场主; (person working in agriculture) 农艺师

agricultural show *n* 农业博览会

agriculture /ˈæɡrɪkʌltʃə(r)/ *n* [u] (practice) 农业; (methods) 农艺; (science) 农学

agriproduct /ˈæɡrɪprɒdʌkt/ *n* 农产品

agriscience /ˈæɡrɪsaɪəns/ *n* [u] 农业科学

agritourism /ˈæɡrɪtʊərɪzəm/ *n* [u] 农家乐旅游

agrochemical /ˌæɡrəʊˈkemɪkəl/
A *n* 农用化学品
B *adj* 农用化学品的

agro-industry /ˈæɡrəʊɪndəstri/ *n* **1** [u and c] (agrochemical industry) 农用化工业 **2** [u] (industrial agriculture) 产业化农业

agronomist /əˈɡrɒnəmɪst/ ▸**p. 409** *n* 农学家

agronomy /əˈɡrɒnəmi/ *n* [u] 农学

agroterrorism /ˈæɡrəʊterərɪzəm/ *n* [u] 农业恐怖主义 [指故意传入植物病害或动物疾病以破坏农业生产的行为]

aground /əˈɡraʊnd/
A *adv* 搁浅地; **to go** *or* **run ～** 搁浅
B *adj pred* 搁浅的; **a cargo ship ～** 搁浅的货船

ah /ɑː/ *excl* 啊 [表示惊讶、同情、喜悦等]; **～ well!** (resignedly) 唉，算啦！

aha /ɑːˈhɑː, əˈhɑː/ *excl* 啊哈 [表示满意、胜利、惊讶、同意等]

ahead /əˈhed/
A *adv* **1** (spatially) 向前; **I'll run ～ and warn them** 我要跑上前头去警告他们; **we've sent Joe on ～** 我们已经派乔到前面去了; **to send one's luggage on ～** 提前把行李送走; **full speed ～!** Naut 全速前进！ **2** (in time) 今后; **the months ～** 以后几个月; **to apply at least a year ～** 至少提前一年提出申请; **we've got a lot of hard work ～** 我们往后还有很多艰苦工作要做 **3** fig (in a better position) 领先; (towards a better position) 向领先地位; **he was slightly ～ on points** 他点数上略占先; **another goal put them ～** 又进一球使他们领先; **to be 10 points ～** 领先 10 分 **4** fig (more advanced) 先进; **to be ～ in physics** 在物理学方面领先
B **ahead of** *prep phr* **1** (spatially) 在…的前面 ‹*person, vehicle*› **2** (earlier than) 早于; **to be three seconds ～ of the next competitor** 比下一名选手快了三秒; **our rivals are one year ～ of us** 我们的对手比我们早了一年; **～ of schedule/time** 提前 **3** (in store for) 等待着; **they had a long drive ～ of them** 他们还要开很长时间的车; **there are difficult times ～ of us** 我们面临着困难时期 **4** fig (more advanced than) «*student, business*» 领先于; **she was always well ～ of the rest of the class** 她总是遥遥领先班上其他同学; **to be ～ of one's time** 超越时代; **their model was years ～ of its time** 他们的型号比那个时代先进许多年

ahoy /əˈhɔɪ/ *excl* Naut 啊嗬 [用以引起注意]; **ship ～!** 喂，那条船呀！

AI *abbr* **1** = **artificial intelligence** **2** = **artificial insemination** **3** = **Amnesty International**

AID *abbr* **1** = **Artificial Insemination by Donor** 供体人工授精 **2** = **Agency for International Development**

aid /eɪd/

A *n* [u] **1** (help) 帮助; **with sb.'s ～** 靠某人的帮助; **with the ～ of sb./sth.** 靠某人/某事物的帮助; **a collection in ～ of cancer charities** 资助癌症慈善事业的募捐; **what's all this shouting in ～ of?** Brit colloq hum 这样大喊大叫究竟是为什么? **2** (charitable or financial support) 救助; **an ～ scheme** 救助计划 **3** (device, technique) 辅助物

B *vt* 帮助 ‹*person*›; 有助于 ‹*digestion, recovery, development*›

C *vi* **1** (help) 帮助; **to ～ in sth./doing sth.** 在某事上提供帮助/帮助做某事; **women were ～ed in childbirth by midwives** 妇女在分娩时得到助产士的帮助 **2** Jur **to ～ and abet sb.** 伙同某人作案

aid agency *n* 非政府援助机构

aide /eɪd/ *n* 助手

aide: aide-de-camp /ˌeɪddəˈkɒm, Amer -ˈkæmp/ *n* (*pl* **～s-de-camp**) 副官; **～-memoire** /ˌeɪdmemˈwɑː(r)/ *n* (*pl* **～s-memoires** *or* **～s-memoire** /ˌeɪdmemˈwɑː(r)/) (document, book) 备忘录; (reminder) 帮助记忆的东西

aid: ～ package 一揽子援助计划; **～ plan** 援助计划; **～ programme** *n* **1** (for country) 援助计划; **2** Amer (for person) 助学金计划

Aids, AIDS /eɪdz/ ▸p. 377 *abbr* = **Acquired Immune Deficiency Syndrome** 艾滋病, 获得性免疫缺陷综合征

Aids: ～ awareness *n* [u] 艾滋病意识; **～ baby** *n* 艾滋婴儿; **～ education** *n* [u] 艾滋病教育

Aids-related *adj* 与艾滋病相关的 ‹*illness*›; 艾滋病引起的 ‹*complications, death*›

Aids-related complex *n* [u] 艾滋病相关症

aid station *n* 救助站

Aids test *n* 艾滋病检查

aid worker *n* 援助人员

ail /eɪl/ *vt* **1** (trouble) 给…带来麻烦 ‹*society, economy*› **2** archaic (afflict) (physically) 使受病痛; (mentally) 使苦恼

aileron /ˈeɪlərɒn/ *n* [飞机的] 副翼

ailing /ˈeɪlɪŋ/ *adj* **1** (ill) 生病的 **2** fig (failing) 境况不佳的 ‹*company, region*›; **an ～ economy** 不景气的经济

ailment /ˈeɪlmənt/ *n* 小病

AIM *abbr* = **Alternative Investment Market**

aim /eɪm/

A *vt* **1** (direct) 把…对准 ‹*stone, ball, kick*›; **the gun/blow was ～ed at my head** 枪指着/那一拳对准了我的脑袋; **well-～ed** 正中目标的 ‹*blow, kick*› **2** (target) 使…针对 ‹*remark, product, insult*›; **to ～ sth. at sb./sth.** 使某事物针对某人/某事物; **an anti-smoking campaign ～ed at young people** 针对年轻人的反吸烟运动 **3** (strive to achieve) 想完成; **to be ～ed at sth./doing sth.** «*action, effort*» 针对某事/旨在做某事

B *vi* **1** (direct with weapon etc.) 瞄准; **to ～ at** *or* **for sth.** 瞄准某物 **2** (direct efforts) 致力于; **to ～ at/for sth.** 目的在于/致力于某事; **to ～ at doing sth.** 尝试做某事; **to ～ to do sth.** 打算做某事; **to ～ high** fig 胸怀大志

C *n* **1** (purpose) 目的; **with the ～ of doing sth.** 以做某事为目的 **2** (target) 瞄准; **to take ～ at sth./sb.** 瞄准某物/某人

aimless /ˈeɪmlɪs/ *adj* 无目的的

aimlessly /ˈeɪmlɪsli/ *adv* 无目的地

ain't /eɪnt/ colloq **1** = **am not, is not, are not** ▸**be** **2** = **has not, have not** ▸**have**

air /eə(r)/

A *n* **1** [u] (substance) 空气; **warm ～ rises** 暖气流上升; **the sound of children's voices filled the ～** 到处都是孩子们说话的声音; **I need some ～** 我要透透气; **in the open ～** 在户外; **to come up for ～** 浮出水面吸气; **the ～ temperature was 16° below zero** 气温是零下16度 **2** [u] (atmosphere, sky) 天空; **the birds of the ～** 飞禽; **the heron took to the ～** 那只苍鹭飞上了天空; **he threw the ball up into the ～** 他把球抛到空中; **the battle was fought on the ground and in the ～** 战斗在地面和空中进行; **～ attacks/transport** 空袭/空运; **to travel by ～** 乘飞机旅行; **most of the mail goes by ～** 大多数邮件都是航空邮寄; **there's something in the ～** fig 似乎要出事; **to be up in the ～** fig 悬而未决; **to be walking** *or* **treading** *or* **floating on ～** fig 得意扬扬 **3** [u] Radio, TV **to be** *or* **come** *or* **go on the ～** 播放; **the series will be back on the ～ in January** 该系列节目将在1月份重新开播; **the minister went on (the) ～ to reassure the public** 部长发表了广播讲话, 以打消公众的疑虑; **to be** *or* **go off the ～** 停止播放; **to take off the ～** 停播…的节目 ‹*broadcaster, interviewee*›; 停播 ‹*programme*› **4** [c] (impression) 样子; **with a knowing ～** 以心照不宣的神态; **phrases like these have a quaint, old-fashioned ～** 像这样的短语显得古朴有趣; **with an ～ of indifference/innocence** 显示出漠不关心/天真的样子; **an ～ of mystery surrounds the project** 这个项目充满了神秘感; **she has a certain ～ about her** 她有某种魅力 **5** [c] Mus dated 曲调; **Bach's 'A～ on a G String'** 巴赫的《G弦上的咏叹调》

B **airs** *npl* 矫揉造作; **to give oneself ～s** 摆架子; **～s and graces** 装腔作势

C *vt* **1** (make dry) 晾干 ‹*clothes, sheets*› **2** (make fresh) 使…通风 ‹*room, house*›; **fold back the duvet to ～ the bed** 叠起羽绒被让床透气 **3** (express) 表达 ‹*opinions, feelings*›; 诉说 ‹*grievances*›; 卖弄 ‹*knowledge*› **4** Radio, TV (broadcast) 播放

D *vi* **1** (become dry) «*clothes, sheets*» 晾干; **she put the sheets in front of the fire to ～** 她将被单放在火炉前烘干 **2** (become fresh) «*room, building*» 通风 **3** (be broadcast) 播出

air: ～ ambulance *n* 救护直升机; **～ bag** *n* Aut 安全气囊; **～ base** *n* 空军基地; **～ bed** *n* Brit 充气床垫; **～ bladder** *n* **1** Bot, Zool (air-filled sac) 气囊; **2** (swim bladder) 鳔; **～borne** *adj* **1** (carried through the air) 空气传播的 ‹*seeds, bacteria, dust*›; **2** *attrib* Mil 空降的 ‹*troops, division*›; **3** *usu pred* (in flight) «*plane, missile*» 飞行中的; **4** (transported by aircraft) 空运的 ‹*cargo, passenger*›; **5** *attrib* (done using aircraft) 使用飞机的; **～borne attack** 空袭; **～ brake** *n* **1** Aut, Rail 气闸; **2** Aviat 减速板; **～ brick** *n* Brit 空心砖; **～ bridge** *n* Brit 空运线

airbrush /ˈeəbrʌʃ/

A *n* [喷颜料的] 气笔

B *vt* **1** Art 用气笔喷绘 ‹*picture, design*› **2** Phot 用气笔修 ‹*photograph, face*›

air: ～ bubble *n* (in liquid, glass, wallpaper) 气泡; **～burst** *n* 空中爆炸; **～bus** *n* 空中客车; **～ chief marshal** *n* [u and c] Brit 空军上将; **～ commodore** *n* [u and c] Brit 空军准将; **～ con** *n* [u] colloq 空调; **～-condition** *vt* 给…安装空调; **～-conditioned** *adj* 装有空调的; **～-conditioner** *n* 空调; **～-conditioning** *n* [u] 空调; **～-cooled** *adj* 气冷的 ‹*engine*›; **～ corridor** *n* 空中走廊; **～ cover** *n* [u] 空中掩护

aircraft /ˈeəkrɑːft, Amer -kræft/ *n* (*pl* **aircraft**) 飞行器

aircraft: ～ carrier *n* 航空母舰; **～man** /-mən/ *n* Brit 空军士兵; **～woman** *n* Brit 空军女兵

air: ～ crash *n* 飞机坠毁; **～crew** *n* 空勤人员; **～ cushion** *n* 气垫; **～-cushion vehicle** *n* (for use on land) 气垫车; (for use on water) 气垫船; **～ cylinder** *n* 压缩空气瓶; **～ disaster** *n* 空难; **～ display** *n* 飞行表演; **～drome** *n* Amer = **aerodrome**

airdrop /ˈeədrɒp/

A *n* 空投

B *vt* (*pres p etc.* **-pp-**) 空投

air-dry

A *vt* 风干 ‹*meat, flower, foliage*›

B *vi* «*meat, flower, foliage*» 被风干

air duct *n* 通气管道

Airedale /ˈeədeɪl/ *n* **～ (terrier)** 艾尔谷狗

airer /ˈeərər/ *n* 晾衣架

air: ～ exclusion zone *n* 禁飞区; **～fare** *n* 飞机票价; **～field** *n* 飞机场; **～ filter** *n* 空气过滤器; **～flow** *n* **1** (past stationary object) 空气的流动; **2** (past moving object) 气流; **～foil** *n* Amer = **aerofoil**

air force *n* 空军

air force blue *n* [u] 空军蓝

airframe /ˈeəfreɪm/ *n* 机身

airfreight /ˈeəfreɪt/ *n* [u] **1** (method of transport) 空运 **2** (goods) 空运的货物 **3** (charge) 航空运费

airfreight terminal *n* 空运货站

air: ～-freshener /eə(r)ˈfreʃnə(r)/ *n* 空气清新剂; **～ gap** *n* 空气隙; **～ guitar** *n* [u] colloq 隐形吉他 [指模仿吉他手弹拨的想象中的吉他]; **to play ～ guitar** 弹隐形吉他; **～ gun** *n* 气枪; **～head** *n* colloq pej 傻瓜; **～ hole** *n* **1** (in container) 通气孔; **2** (in ice) 冰窟窿; **～ hostess** ▸p. 409 *n* Brit dated 空姐

airily /ˈeərɪli/ *adv* 漫不经心地

airiness /ˈeərɪnɪs/ *n* [u] **1** (of room, house, place) 通风 **2** pej (of manner, attitude, gesture) 漫不经心 **3** pej (of promise) 轻率; (of idea, theory) 不切实际

airing /ˈeərɪŋ/ *n* **1** (drying) (of linen etc.) 晾 **2** (freshening) (of room) 通风 **3** fig (voicing) 公开; **to give sth. an ～** 把某事物公诸于众 **4** Radio, TV 广播

airing cupboard *n* 烘柜

air: ～ kiss *n* 嘟嘴示吻; **to give** *or* **blow sb. an ～ kiss** 向某人嘟嘴示吻; **～ lane** *n* 航线

airless /ˈeəlɪs/ *adj* **1** (stuffy) 不通风的 ‹*room*› **2** (without wind) 无风的 ‹*weather, evening*›; **it's so ～: I can't sleep** 天气太闷了, 我睡不着

air letter *n* 航空邮笺

airlift /ˈeəlɪft/

A *n* 空运

B *vt* 空运 ‹*people, supplies*›

air: ～line *n* **1** (company) 航空公司; **2** (tube carrying air, source of air) 空气输送管; **3** (for diver) 通气管; **～liner** *n* 大型客机; **～lock** *n* **1** (in pipe, pump) 气塞; **2** (chamber) 气密过渡舱

airmail /ˈeəmeɪl/

A *n* **1** (postal system) 航空邮政; **to send sth. (by) ～** 航空邮寄某物 **2** (item of mail) 航空邮件

B *vt* 航空邮寄

airmail: ～ envelope *n* 航空信封; **～ label** *n* 航空邮寄标签; **～ letter** *n* 航空信; **～ paper** *n* [u] 航空信纸

air: ～man /-mən/ *n* **1** (pilot) 男飞行员; (aircrew member) 男空乘人员; **2** (in RAF or USAF) 空军士兵; **～ marshal** *n* Brit 空军中将; **～ mass** *n* 气团; **～ mattress** *n* 充气床垫; **Air Miles®** *npl* 航程积分; **～ miss** *n* Brit 险些发生的撞机事故; **～plane** *n* Amer = **aeroplane**; **～play** *n* [u] 播送; **～**

a

pocket *n* 1 (in enclosed space) 气窝; 2 Aviat 气阱; ~ **pollution** *n* [u] 空气污染
airport /'eəpɔːt/ *n* 机场
airport: ~ **fiction** *n* [u] 机场小说 [指在机场出售的通俗小说]; ~ **tax** *n* 机场税
air: ~ **power** *n* [u] 空军实力; ~ **pressure** *n* [u] 大气压力; ~ **pump** *n* 气泵; ~ **purifier** *n* 空气净化器; ~ **quality** *n* [u] 空气质量; ~ **rage** *n* [u] 空怒 [指飞机乘客在航途中的狂暴行为]; ~ **raid** *n* 空袭; ~**-raid precautions** *npl* 防空措施; ~**-raid shelter** *n* 防空掩蔽所; ~**-raid siren** *n* 空袭警报器; ~**-raid warden** *n* 空袭警报哨; ~**-raid warning** *n* 空袭警报; ~ **rifle** *n* 气步枪; ~**screw** *n* Brit 飞机螺旋桨; ~**-sea rescue** *n* esp Brit 1 [u] (method) 海空搜索救援; 2 [c] (rescue attempt) 海空搜索救援行动; 3 [u] (organization) 海空搜索救援队; ~ **shaft** *n* 通风井; ~**ship** *n* 飞艇; ~ **show** *n* (flying show) 飞行特技表演; (trade exhibition) 航空展; ~ **shuttle** *n* 穿梭航班; ~**sick** *adj* 晕机的; ~**sickness** *n* [u] 晕机
airside /'eəsaɪd/
A *n* [u] 机场限制区
B *adv* 在机场限制区
air: ~ **sock** *n* 风向袋; ~ **space** *n* [u] 领空
airspeed /'eəspiːd/ *n* 空速
airspeed indicator *n* 空速表
air: ~**stream** *n* 气流; ~ **strike** *n* 空中打击; ~**strip** *n* 简易机场; ~ **support** *n* [u] 空中支援; ~ **suspension** *n* [u] 空气悬架法; ~ **terminal** *n* 1 (at airport) 航空站; 2 Brit (in town) 城市中心民航班车站; ~ **ticket** *n* 机票; ~**tight** *adj* 1 (tightly sealed) 密封的; 2 fig (unassailable) 无懈可击的; ~**time** *n* [u] Radio, TV 广播时间; ~**-to-~** *adj* 空对空的 ‹*missile*›; 空中的 ‹*refuelling*›; ~**-to-surface** *adj* 空对面的 ‹*missile*›; ~ **travel** *n* [u] 航空旅行; ~ **traveller** *n* 航空旅行者; ~ **valve** *n* 空气阀; ~ **vent** *n* 通气孔; ~ **vice-marshal** *n* Brit 空军少将; ~ **war** *n* 1 [c] (individual war) 空中战斗; 2 [u] (warfare) 空中战争; ~**waves** *npl* 无线电波; **on the ~waves** 在广播中; ~**way** *n* 1 Aviat (route) 航线; 2 Anat 气道; ~**woman** *n* 1 (pilot) 女飞行员; (aircrew member) 女空乘人员; 2 (in RAF or USAF) 空军女兵; ~**worthiness** *n* [u] 适航性; ~**worthy** *adj* 适航的
air traffic *n* [u] 空中交通
air traffic: ~ **control** *n* [u] (activity) 空中交通管制; (organization) 空管部门; ~ **controller** ▸p. 409 *n* 航空调度员
airy /'eəri/ *adj* 1 (spacious) 通风的 ‹*building*› 2 (casual) 漫不经心的 ‹*manner, behaviour*›; **an ~ disregard for the law** 对法律的满不在乎 3 pej (not serious) 轻率的 ‹*promise*›; (not practical) 不切实际的 ‹*idea, theory*›
airy-fairy /ˌeərɪ'feəri/ *adj* esp Brit colloq pej 不切实际的
aisle /aɪl/ *n* 走道; **to have sb. rolling in the ~s** 逗得某人捧腹大笑; **to lead sb. up the ~** hum 与某人结婚
aisle seat *n* 靠走道的座位
aitch /eɪtʃ/ *n* (*pl* ~**es**) 字母H; **to drop one's ~es** 不发词首的h音
ajar /ə'dʒɑː(r)/
A *adj pred* **to be ~** ‹*door, window*› 微开着的
B *adv* 微开着
AK *abbr* Amer = **Alaska**
aka *abbr* = **also known as** 又称
akimbo /ə'kɪmbəʊ/ *adj* **(with) arms ~** 双手叉腰
akin /ə'kɪn/ *adj* 类似的; **to be ~ to sth.** 与某事物相似; **to be ~ to sth./to doing sth.** 等于某事物/做某事
AL *abbr* Amer = **Alabama**
Alabama /ˌælə'bæmə/ *pr n* 亚拉巴马州
alabaster /'æləbɑːstə(r), Amer -bæs-/
A *n* 雪花石膏
B *modif* (made of alabaster) 雪花石膏制的; (resembling alabaster) 光洁雪白的 ‹*skin*›
alacrity /ə'lækrəti/ *n* [u] formal 乐意; **with ~** 欣然
Aladdin's cave /əˌlædɪnz 'keɪv/ *n* fig (阿拉丁) 宝库
alarm /ə'lɑːm/
A *n* 1 [u] (concern) 担忧; (fear, deep anxiety) 惊慌; **in ~** 惊慌地 2 [c] (warning signal) 警报; (warning device) 警报装置; **to activate** *or* **set off an ~** 触发警报; **to raise the ~** lit 发出警报; fig 引起警觉 3 = **alarm clock**
B *vt* 1 (worry) 使担忧; (frighten) 使惊慌 2 (fit system to) 给…安装警报装置
alarm: ~ **bell** *n* 警铃; ~ **bells are ringing** fig 感到担心; **to set the ~ bells ringing** fig 引起警觉; ~ **call** *n* 1 (warning) 惊叫; **the piercing ~ call of the seagulls** 海鸥的刺耳惊叫; 2 Telecom 叫早电话; ~ **clock** *n* 闹钟
alarmed /ə'lɑːmd/ *adj* (worried) 担忧的; (afraid) 惊慌的
alarming /ə'lɑːmɪŋ/ *adj* (worrying) 令人担忧的; (causing fear) 使人惊慌的
alarmingly /ə'lɑːmɪŋli/ *adv* (worryingly) 令人担忧地; (in a way that causes fear) 惊人地 ‹*increase, deteriorate, act*›
alarmist /ə'lɑːmɪst/
A *n* 危言耸听的人
B *adj* 危言耸听的
alarm: ~ **signal** *n* 警报信号; ~ **system** *n* 警报系统
alas /ə'læs/ *excl* 哎呀
Alaska /ə'læskə/ *pr n* 阿拉斯加州
Alaskan /ə'læskən/
A *adj* (of Alaska) 阿拉斯加州的; (of the people) 阿拉斯加州人的
B *n* 阿拉斯加州人
Albania /æl'beɪnɪə/ *pr n* 阿尔巴尼亚
Albanian /æl'beɪnɪən/ ▸p. 503, p. 426
A *adj* (of Albania) 阿尔巴尼亚的; (of the people) 阿尔巴尼亚人的; (of the language) 阿尔巴尼亚语的
B *n* 1 [c] (person) 阿尔巴尼亚人 2 [u] (language) 阿尔巴尼亚语
albatross /'ælbətrɒs, Amer -trɔːs/ *n* (*pl* ~**es**) 1 Zool 信天翁; **an ~ around sb.'s neck** fig 某人无法摆脱的苦恼 2 (in golf) 双鹰 [比标准杆低三杆]
albedo /æl'biːdəʊ/ *n* [u and c] (*pl* ~**s**) 反照率
albeit /ˌɔːl'biːɪt/ *conj* formal 尽管; **I tried, ~ unsuccessfully, to phone her** 我给她打过电话，但没有打通
Alberta /æl'bɜːtə/ *pr n* 艾伯塔省
albino /æl'biːnəʊ/ *n* (person) 患白化病的人; (animal) 患白化病的动物
album /'ælbəm/ *n* 1 (book) 册子; **photo/stamp ~** 相册/集邮簿 2 Mus 歌曲专辑
albumen /'ælbjʊmɪn, Amer æl'bjuːmən/ *n* [u] (part of egg) 蛋白; (protein contained) 白蛋白
albumin /'ælbjʊmɪn, Amer æl'bjuːmɪn/ *n* [u] Biol 白蛋白
alchemist /'ælkəmɪst/ *n* 炼金术士
alchemy /'ælkəmi/ *n* [u] 1 Chem, Hist 炼金术 2 fig (power, ability) 魔力
alcohol /'ælkəhɒl, Amer -hɔːl/ *n* [u] 1 (liquid) 酒精 2 (intoxicating drinks) 酒; **he never touches ~** 他滴酒不沾
alcohol-free *adj* 无酒精的 ‹*drink*›; 不饮酒的 ‹*person*›; 禁酒的 ‹*place*›
alcoholic /ˌælkə'hɒlɪk, Amer -hɔːl-/
A *n* 嗜酒者
B *adj* 1 (containing alcohol) 含酒精的 ‹*drink, ingredient*› 2 (caused by drinking alcohol) 喝酒引起的; **be in an ~ stupor** 醉得不省人事
Alcoholics Anonymous *pr n* 嗜酒者互诫协会
alcoholism /'ælkəhɒlɪzəm, Amer -hɔːl-/ *n* [u] 酗酒
alcopop /'ælkəʊpɒp/ *n* Brit colloq 波普甜酒
alcove /'ælkəʊv/ *n* 凹处
alder /'ɔːldə(r)/ *n* 桤木
alderman /'ɔːldəmən/ *n* (*pl* **aldermen**) 1 Brit esp Hist 高级市政官 2 Amer, Austral 市政委员会委员
ale /eɪl/ *n* 艾尔啤酒 [指黑啤酒或贮藏啤酒之外的任何啤酒]
alec, aleck /'ælɪk/ ▸**smart alec**
alert /ə'lɜːt/
A *adj* 1 (attentive) 警惕的 ‹*guard*›; 留心的 ‹*reader, listener*›; **to be ~ to** 对…保持警惕 ‹*danger, fact, possibility*› 2 (lively) 机灵的 ‹*child*›; 机敏的 ‹*old person*›
B *n* 1 [u] (state of being watchful) 警戒; **to be on the ~ for** 对…保持警惕 ‹*danger*›; **to be on full ~** Mil 处于全面戒备状态 2 [c] (warning) 警报; **to give** *or* **sound the ~** 发出警报
C *vt* 1 (make aware of sth.) 提醒…注意; **to ~ sb. to sth.** 提醒某人注意某事 2 (warn about a dangerous situation) 向…报警
alertness /ə'lɜːtnɪs/ *n* [u] 1 (attentiveness) 警惕 2 (liveliness of mind) 机敏
Aleutian Islands /ə'luːʃɪən ˌaɪləndz/ *pr n* **the ~** 阿留申群岛
A level *n* Brit [中学普通教育文凭] 高级考试; **~ maths/English** 数学/英语高级证书考试
alexandrine /ˌælɪg'zændraɪn/ *n* 亚历山大格式的诗行 [每行含6个抑扬格音步]
alfalfa /æl'fælfə/ *n* 苜蓿
alfresco /æl'freskəʊ/
A *adj* 在户外的
B *adv* 在户外
algae /'ældʒiː, 'ælgaɪ/ *npl* 水藻
algal /'ælgəl/ *adj* 水藻的
algal bloom *n* [u and c] 赤潮
algebra /'ældʒɪbrə/ *n* [u] 代数
algebraic /ˌældʒɪ'breɪɪk/ *adj* 代数的
Algeria /æl'dʒɪərɪə/ *pr n* 阿尔及利亚
Algerian /æl'dʒɪərɪən/ ▸p. 503
A *adj* (of Algeria) 阿尔及利亚的; (of the people) 阿尔及利亚人的
B *n* 阿尔及利亚人
algicide /'ældʒɪsaɪd, 'ælgɪ-/ *n* 杀藻剂
Algiers /æl'dʒɪəz/ *pr n* 阿尔及尔
algorithm /'ælgərɪðəm/ *n* 算法
algorithmic /ˌælgə'rɪðmɪk/ *adj* 算法的
alias /'eɪlɪəs/
A *n* (*pl* ~**es**) 1 (assumed name) 化名 2 Comput 同义名
B *adv* 又名; **George Orwell, ~ Eric Blair** 乔治·奥威尔，又名埃里克·布莱尔
alibi /'ælɪbaɪ/ *n* (*pl* ~**s**) 1 Jur 不在犯罪现场的证据 2 colloq (excuse) 借口
Alice band /'ælɪs bænd/ *n* 发圈
alien /'eɪlɪən/
A *n* 1 Jur (foreigner) 外侨 2 (being from space) 外星人
B *adj* 1 Jur 外国的 ‹*powers, land*› 2 (unfamiliar) 陌生的 ‹*environment, concept*› 3 (atypical) 不相容的; **to be ~ to sb./sth.** ‹*feeling, practices, custom*› 与某人/与某事物格格不入 4 (from space) 外星人的
alienate /'eɪlɪəneɪt/ *vt* 1 (estrange) 使疏远 2 (separate) 使脱离; **to be ~d from society** 与社会脱节
alienation /ˌeɪlɪə'neɪʃn/ *n* [u] 1 (process) 疏远 2 (state) 隔绝; **feelings of despair and ~** 绝望和孤立的感觉
alight¹ /ə'laɪt/ *adj* 1 (burning) 燃烧着的; **to set sth. ~** 把某物点着 2 fig 闪亮的; **her eyes were ~ with curiosity** 她的眼里透着

好奇; **his face was ~ with happiness** 他满脸幸福的神情

alight² *vi* 1 (get out of) «*passenger*» 下来; **~ from the train** 下火车 2 (settle) 飞落; **to ~ on sth.** «*bird, butterfly*» 飞落到某物上 3 fig (happen upon) 偶然发现; **to ~ on sth.** «*glance*» 偶然发现某物; «*thoughts*» 偶然想起某事物

align /ə'laɪn/
A *vt* 使…成一直线 ‹*line*›; 校准 ‹*weapon, wheels*›; **~ the ruler with the edge of the paper** 把尺和纸的边缘对齐
B *v refl* Pol **to ~ oneself with sb./sth.** 与某人/某团体结盟

alignment /ə'laɪnmənt/ *n* 1 [u] (position) 成一直线; **to be in/out of ~ with sb./sth.** 与某人/某物成/不成一直线; **the wheels are out of ~** 轮子没有校准 2 [c] (alliance) 结盟

alike /ə'laɪk/
A *adj* (identical) 相同的; (similar) 相似的
B *adv* 1 (similarly) 相似地 ‹*think, dress*›; **we treat them ~** 我们对他们一视同仁 2 (both) 同样地; **young and old ~** 老少都一样; **share and share ~!** 平均分担!

alimentary canal /ˌæliˌmentəri kə'næl/ *n* 消化道

alimony /'ælɪməni, Amer -məʊni/ *n* Jur 赡养费

alive /ə'laɪv/ *adj pred* 1 (living) 活着的; **to stay ~** 活着; **to be taken** *or* **captured ~** 被活捉; **~ and well** 好端端活着的; **~ and kicking** fig 活蹦乱跳的 2 (lively) 有活力的; **to bring ~** 使…活灵活现 ‹*story*›; **to come ~** 活跃起来 3 (in existence) 存在的; **to keep hopes ~** 保持希望 4 (teeming) **to be ~ with sth.** 充满着某物; **the countryside was ~ with insects and butterflies** 乡下到处是昆虫和蝴蝶 5 (aware) **to be ~ to sth.** 意识到某事物

alkali /'ælkəlaɪ/ *n* (*pl* **~s**) 碱

alkaline /'ælkəlaɪn/ *adj* (containing an alkali) 含碱的; (having the properties of an alkali) 碱性的; **~ soil** 碱性土壤

alkalinity /ˌælkə'lɪnəti/ *n* 碱度

alkaloid /'ælkəlɔɪd/ *n* 生物碱

alky /'ælki/ *n* colloq 酒鬼

all /ɔːl/
A *pron* 1 (everything, the whole amount) 全部; **that's ~** 就这些了; **to risk ~** 孤注一掷; **~ or nothing** 要么全有, 要么全无; **when ~ is said and done** 说到底; **~ in good time!** 不用急!; **we're doing ~ (that) we can** 我们正尽力而为; **it's not ~ (that) it should be** «*performance, service, efficiency*» 不尽人意; **~'s well that ends well** 结果好就一切都好; **I ate it ~** 我全吃光了 2 (the only thing) 唯一; **that's ~ I want** 那是我唯一想要的; **~ I know is (that) ...** 我只知道…; **that's ~ we need!** iron 我们才不要呢! 3 (everyone) 人人; (emphasizing unanimity or entirety) 全体; **~ but a few were released** 除了少数几个, 其他人都被释放了; **one and ~** 所有人; **thank you, one and ~** 谢谢大家
B *det* 1 (each one of) 一切的; (the whole of) 全部的; **~ kinds of people** 各种各样的人; **it wasn't bad, ~ things considered** 总的来看, 这事还不坏; **~ day/evening/year** 整天/整晚/一年到头; **alcohol, drugs, and ~ that sort of thing** 酒精、毒品以及诸如此类的东西; **~ London wondered what would happen next** 全伦敦的人都想知道接下来会发生什么事 2 (total) 完全的; **with ~ possible speed** 以尽可能快的速度; **in ~ innocence/seriousness** 十分天真/一本正经地 3 (any) 任何的; **beyond ~ expectations** 完全出乎意料; **beyond ~ doubt** 毫无疑问
C *adv* 1 (completely) 完全地; **~ alone, ~ on one's own** 独自一人; **to be ~ wet** 湿透; **~ in one piece** 安然无恙; **he's forgotten ~ about us!** 他把我们忘得一干二净!; **it's ~ one** *or* **the same to me** 对我来说都一样; **if it's ~ the same to you, I'd prefer coffee** 如果你无所谓, 我想要咖啡; **~ there** colloq 神志正常; **he's not ~ there** 他呆呆的; **to be ~ go** Brit colloq 忙得要命; **that's ~ very well, that's ~ well and good** 那好倒是好; **it's ~ very well for him to talk** 他说说当然容易 2 (nothing but) 只有; **to be ~ legs** 腿很长; **to be ~ smiles** 满面笑容; **to be ~ thumbs** 笨手笨脚; **to be ~ ears** 全神贯注地听; **he was ~ sympathy** 他充满同情 3 Sport 每一方; **(they are) six ~** (他们的比分是) 六平
D *n* 一切; **to give one's ~ for sb./sth.** 为某人/某事物献出一切
E **all along** *adv phr* 一直; **it was in my pocket ~ along** 它一直在我口袋里
F **all at once** *adv phr* 1 (simultaneously) 同时; **don't eat it ~ at once!** 别把它一下子吃光! 2 (suddenly) 突然; **~ at once a bell rang** 突然响起了铃声
G **all but** *adv phr* 几乎; **the party was ~ but over when we arrived** 我们到的时候, 聚会已经快要结束了
H **all for** *prep phr* 完全赞成; **I'm ~ for women joining the army** 我完全支持妇女参军
I **all in all** *adv phr* 总的来说
J **all of** *adv phr* 足足 [常作反语, 用于说话者认为很小的量]; **it cost ~ of £70** 它花了整整70英镑呢
K **all round** *adv phr* 1 (in every respect) 在各方面 2 (to or for everyone) 对在场的每个人; **congratulations ~ round!** 祝贺各位!
L **all that** *adv phr* 非常; **she's not ~ that happy** 她不太高兴; **it's not as far as ~ that** 没那么远
M **all the more** *adv phr* 更加; **to laugh ~ the more** 笑得更厉害; **~ the more difficult** 更加困难
N **all the same** *adv phr* (even so) 即便如此; (anyway) 无论如何; **we had to go ~ the same** 我们不得已还是去了; **thanks ~ the same, but I've something else on tonight** 我照样要多谢你, 但今晚我有些事情要办
O **all too** *adv phr* 过于 ‹*accurate, easy, widespread*›; **~ too soon we realized the awful truth** 很快我们就意识到了这个可怕的真相
P **and all** *adv phr* 1 (included) 包括在内; **he jumped into the river clothes and ~** 他连衣服也没脱就跳进河中 2 Brit colloq (as well) 也; **I'm freezing! — yeah, me and ~!** 我都快冻僵了! ——对, 我也是!
Q **at all** *adv phr* [表示完全]; **not at ~** (acknowledging thanks) 别客气; (answering query) 一点也不; **I don't agree at ~** 我完全不同意; **if he goes at ~** 万一他真要走的话; **seldom if at ~** 非常难得
R **for all** *prep phr* 1 (despite) 尽管; **for ~ its clarity of style, the book is not easy reading** 这本书尽管行文清晰, 却不容易读懂 2 (as far as) [表示对某人不重要或无所谓]; **for ~ sb. knows** 说不定与某人所知相反; **for ~ sb. cares** 与某人无关; **you can do what you like for ~ I care** 你可以随心所欲, 我才不管呢
S **in all** *adv phr* 总共
T **of all** *prep phr* 1 (in rank) 在所有…之中; **the last question was the easiest of ~** 最后那道题是最容易的; **first of ~, let's say hello to Sarah** 首先让我们向萨拉问好 2 (emphatic) 在所有的…当中偏偏; **I didn't think you, of ~ people, would become a vegetarian!** 我真没想到众人之中偏偏你会成为素食者!; **I've locked myself out! of ~ the stupid things to do!** 我把自己锁在门外了! 居然做出这等蠢事!

Allah /'ælə/ *pr n* 安拉 [伊斯兰教信奉的真主的名称]

all: ~-American *adj* 1 (characteristically American) 具有典型美国人特点的 ‹*quality, appearance*›; **an ~-American boy** 典型的美国男孩; 2 (only American) 全由美国人组成的 ‹*team, competition*›; **~-around** *adj* Amer **= ~-round**

allay /ə'leɪ/ *vt* 减轻 ‹*fears, doubts, worries*›; **to ~ hunger** 解饿

all: ~-clear *n* 1 Mil 空袭警报解除信号; **to ~ sb./sth. the ~-clear** 向某人/某物发出解除警报信号; 2 fig 平安信号; **~-consuming** *adj* 强烈的 ‹*passion, desire*›; 剧烈的 ‹*pain*›; **~-day** *adj* 全天的

allegation /ˌælɪ'geɪʃn/ *n* (gen) 指责; Jur 指控; **to make an ~ (against sb.)** (对某人) 提出指控

allege /ə'ledʒ/ *vt* 声称; **X ~d that Y had phoned him** X声称Y给他打过电话; **the documents were ~d to be fakes** 这些文件据说是伪造的

alleged /ə'ledʒd/ *adj attrib* 声称的 ‹*author, reason*›; 被控的 ‹*crime, fraud*›; **the ~ culprit** 被指控的疑犯

allegedly /ə'ledʒɪdli/ *adv* 据宣称; **the papers are ~ false** 这些文件据说是假的

allegiance /ə'liːdʒəns/ *n* 忠诚; **to swear ~ to sb./sth.** 宣誓效忠某人/某组织

allegorical /ˌælɪ'gɒrɪkl, Amer -'gɔːr-/ *adj* 寓言的

allegory /'ælɪgəri, Amer -gɔːri/ *n* 1 [c] (story) 寓言 2 [u] (style) 讽喻法

allegro /ə'legrəʊ/
A *adv* 急速地 ‹*play*›
B *adj* 快板的; **~ movement/finale** 快板乐章/快板终曲
C *n* 快板

alleluia /ˌælɪ'luːjə/ *excl* **= hallelujah**

all-embracing *adj* 包罗万象的

Allen key® /'ælən kiː/ *n* 内六角扳手

Allen screw® /'ælən skruː/ *n* 六角固定螺丝

allergen /'ælədʒən/ *n* 过敏原

allergic /ə'lɜːdʒɪk/ *adj* 1 Med (caused by an allergy) 过敏性的; **to be ~ to sth.** 对某物过敏; **to have** *or* **suffer from an ~ reaction** 产生/有过敏反应 2 fig **to be ~ to sth.** colloq (dislike) 对某事物极其反感

allergist /'ælədʒɪst/ ▸p. 409 *n* 过敏症专科医生

allergy /'ælədʒi/ *n* 过敏; **to have an ~ to sth.** 对某物过敏

allergy clinic *n* 过敏病科

alleviate /ə'liːvieɪt/ *vt* 减轻 ‹*suffering, pain*›; 缓解 ‹*overcrowding, stress, unemployment*›; **~ boredom** 解闷

alleviation /əˌliːvɪ'eɪʃn/ *n* [u] (of suffering, pain) 减轻; (of overcrowding, stress, unemployment) 缓解

alley /'æli/ *n* 1 (for pedestrians or vehicles) 小巷; **it's right up my ~** colloq 那正合我的胃口 2 Sport (in bowling etc.) 球道 3 Amer (on tennis court) [单打边线与双打边线之间的] 狭长地带

alley: ~ cat *n* 流浪猫; **~way** *n* **= alley 1**

all: All Fools' Day *n* [u] Brit **= April Fools' Day**; **~-found** *adj* 食宿全包的 ‹*accommodation*›

alliance /ə'laɪəns/ *n* (agreement) 结盟; (pact) 盟约; **in ~ with ...** 与…结盟的; **to form an ~** 结盟

> **the Alliance Party**
>
> 联盟党, 全称北爱尔兰联盟党 (the Alliance Party of Northern Ireland), 缩写为APNI。成立于1970年4月。占北爱尔兰人口多数的新教徒大多是统一主义者 (Unionist), 不希望北爱尔兰脱离英国。而天主教徒则更多为民族主义者和共和主义者, 希望成立统一的共和政体的爱尔兰国。同盟党反对天主教和新教两派中的极端观点, 争取通过联合两派的温和势力解决北爱尔兰问题, 主要代表中产阶级的利益。

allied /'ælaɪd/ *adj* 1 (joined) 结盟的 ‹*country, party, army*›; 联军的 ‹*attack*›; **the ~ nations** 盟国; **to be ~ to sb./sth.** 与某人/某组织结盟 2 (linked) 有关联的; (similar) 类似的; **be ~**

to sth. 与某事物有关 3 **Allied** Pol (in the First World War and after) 协约国的; (in the Second World War and after) 同盟国的

alligator /'ælɪgeɪtə(r)/
A *n* 短吻鳄
B *modif* 短吻鳄皮革制的; **～ shoes** 鳄鱼皮皮鞋

alligator clip *n* esp Amer **= crocodile clip**

all-important *adj* 至关重要的

all in
A *adj pred* Brit colloq 精疲力竭的
B *adv* 费用全包地
C **all-in** *adj* Brit 全包的 ‹*price, cost*›

all-inclusive *adj* 全包的 ‹*price, holiday*›

all-in-one
A *n* 连体服
B *adj* 多合一的; **an ～ cooker** 多功能炊具

all-in wrestling *n* [u] 自由式摔跤

alliteration /ə,lɪtə'reɪʃn/ *n* [u and c] 头韵

alliterative /ə'lɪtərətɪv, Amer ə'lɪtəreɪtɪv/ *adj* 头韵的 ‹*style, effect, poem*›

all-night *adj* 通宵的 ‹*event, party*›; 通宵服务的 ‹*bar, bus service*›

allocate /'æləkeɪt/ *vt* 分配; **to ～ the tasks** 分派任务; **to ～ more funds to the health service** 增加对公共医疗卫生服务的拨款; **to ～ money for repair work** 拨款作维修用

allocation /,ælə'keɪʃn/ *n* 1 [c] (amount) 分配额; **they've already spent their ～ for this year!** 他们已经把今年拨给他们的经费花光了! 2 [u] (process) 分配

allophone /'æləfəʊn/ *n* 音位变体

all-or-nothing *adj* 成败在此一举的 ‹*approach, decision, attitude*›

allot /ə'lɒt/ *vt* (*pres p etc.* **-tt-**) 分配 ‹*money, time*›; 分派 ‹*duties, job*›; **within the ～ted time** 在规定的时间内; **before the end of one's ～ted lifespan** 在有生之年

allotment /ə'lɒtmənt/ *n* 1 [c] Brit (garden) [租来种菜的] 地块 2 [c] (allocation) 分配物 3 [u] (allotting) 分配

all-out
A *adj* 全面的 ‹*ban*›; 全力以赴的 ‹*effort, bid*›; **to make an ～ effort** 全力以赴; **～ war was inevitable now** 全面战争已不可避免
B **all out** *adv* 竭尽全力地; **to go all out to do sth./for sth.** 为做某事/为某事物全力以赴

all over
A *adj* 全部结束的; **it's ～ between us** 我们之间到此为止
B *adv* 1 (everywhere) 到处; **to be trembling ～** 浑身发抖 2 (typically) 典型地; **that's Mary ～!** 玛丽就是这个样子!
C *prep* 1 (in every part of) 在…的各处; **～ China** 中国各地; **I have spots ～ my arms** 我的两只胳膊上到处都是丘疹; ▸**place A1** 2 (known throughout) **to be ～** «*news, secret*» 传遍 ‹*village, office*› 3 colloq (fawning over) 谄媚; **to be ～ sb.** 向某人献殷勤

all-over *adj* 遍布表面的 ‹*pattern, design*›; 全身的 ‹*tan*›

allow /ə'laʊ/ *vt* 1 (permit) 允许; (authorize) 准许; **passengers are not ～ed to talk to the driver** 乘客不得与司机交谈; **we're not ～ed visitors** 我们不可以会客; **the government has ～ed the situation to get worse** 政府听任局势恶化; **I'm going to ～ myself two more chocolates!** 我让自己多吃两块巧克力! ; **～ me!** 让我来! ; **if you will ～ me to continue!** 请让我把话说完! 2 (admit) «*organization*» 允许…进入; **the club's rules do not ～ male members** 俱乐部规定不接收男会员; **pets are not ～ed** 宠物不得入内 3 (accept, concede) 认可; **I'll ～ that this isn't always the case** 我承认情况并不总是这样的; **the referee ～ed the goal** 裁判判得分有效; **the insurance company ～ed the claim** 保险公司同意理赔 4 (enable) 使成为可能; **increased funding would ～ the company to be more adventurous in its productions** 投资增加将使该公司能够大胆地扩大生产; **the improved rail service ～s easier connections to the main line to London** 铁路服务得到了改进，经由干线往伦敦更方便了 5 (allocate) 分配; (set aside) 留出; **you ought to ～ more material for long sleeves** 长袖子得预备更多的布料; **to ～ sb. a discount of £50** 给某人优惠 50 英镑; **to ～ a margin for error** 留出误差余地

Phrasal verbs
- **allow for** *vt* [**～ for sth.**] 将…考虑在内 ‹*delay, mistake, cost*›; **have you ～ed for shrinkage?** 你考虑到缩水了吗?
- **allow of** *vt* [**～ of sth.**] formal 容许…的发生

allowable /ə'laʊəbl/ *adj* 允许的 ‹*expenses, behaviour*›

allowance /ə'laʊəns/ *n* 1 (money for outgoings) 补贴; **an ～ of £20 per day** 每天 20 英镑的补贴; **a daily/weekly/monthly ～** 日/周/月津贴 2 (pocket money) 零花钱 3 (entitlement) 限量; **an ～ of 20 kg for your luggage** 20 公斤的行李限重 4 (discount, rebate) [尤指旧车、旧家具等的] 折价; **old car ～** 旧车折价 5 Tax 免税额; **personal/single person's/married couple's ～** 个人所得/单身人士/已婚夫妇免税额 6 (concession) **to make ～s for** 考虑到 ‹*inflation, growth, variations*›; **to make ～s for sb.** 体谅某人

alloy
A /'ælɔɪ/ *n* 合金
B /ə'lɔɪ/ *vt* 将…铸成合金; **lead is ～ed with tin to make solder** 铅和锡合在一起制成焊锡

alloy: ～ steel *n* [u] 合金钢; **～ wheel** *n* 合金轮毂

all: ～-party *adj attrib* 包括所有政党的 ‹*talks, support*›; **～-pervasive** *adj* 遍及各方面的; **the free market was not ～-pervasive as it is today** 过去，自由市场的影响不像今天这样无孔不入; **～ points bulletin** *n* Amer 全境通报; **～-powerful** *adj* 万能的 ‹*God, idea*›; **on the medieval battlefield the longbow had been ～-powerful** 在中世纪的战场上，长弓是最强大的武器; **～-purpose** *adj* 多用途的 ‹*tool, food*›

all right
A *adj* 1 (satisfactory) 合意的; **is the coffee ～?** 这咖啡还行吗? ; **she's ～** (agreeable) 她招人喜欢; (attractive) 她有魅力; **you look ～** 你气色不错; **would you like some more wine? — I'm ～ for the moment, thanks** 再来点葡萄酒好吗? ——我暂时不要了，谢谢; **it's ～ by me if it's ～ by you** 如果你不反对，我也没意见; **it's an ～ sort of place** 那个地方还凑合 2 *pred* (safe) 安好的; **how are you? — ～, thanks** 你怎么样? ——没事，谢谢; **will the children be ～ on their own?** 孩子们独自待着会平安无事吗? 3 (well) 健康的; **she had flu, but she's ～ now** 她患了流感，但现在康复了 4 (acceptable) 适宜的; **that's (quite) ～!** (accepting thanks) 别客气! ; (accepting apology) 不要紧! ; **is that ～ with you?** 那对你来说合适吗? ; **it's ～ (for sb.) to do sth.** (某人) 做某事没问题; **it's ～ for some, isn't it?** 有些人就是运气好，是不是? 5 *pred* (able to manage) 能对付的; **don't worry: we're ～** 别担心，我们维持得下去; **to be ～ for** 有足够的 ‹*money, time, work*›; **if we won this competition, we'd be ～ for life, wouldn't we?** 如果我们赢了这场竞赛，一辈子的花销就有了，对不对?
B *adv* 1 (satisfactorily) 合意地; **to get along** *or* **on ～** 进展顺利; **their business is doing ～** 他们的生意做得不错 2 (without a doubt) 确实; **he's an idiot, ～!** 他是个十足的白痴! ; **that's the man, ～** 就是那个人，没错
C *particle* 1 (giving agreement) [表示同意]; **would you like to help? — ～** 你愿意帮忙吗? ——可以 2 (conceding a point) [表示让步承认]; **～, I know it wasn't the most diplomatic approach** 当然了，我知道这不是最有策略的方法; **～, ～, I'm sorry I suggested it!** 算啦，很抱歉我提出了这个建议! 3 (seeking consensus) [表示寻求共识]; **I want you to complete these two pages, ～?** 请填写这两页，好吗? 4 (seeking information) [表示问讯，也稍有挑战或威胁意]; **～, what's going on here?** 喂，这里是怎么回事? ; **～, what's the joke?** 哎，乱开什么玩笑? 5 (introducing topic) [用于引出话题]; **～, the next thing to do is to take a vote** 就这样吧，下面该进行表决了
D *n* [u] Brit colloq **she's a bit of ～** 她蛮性感的

all: ～-risk *adj* 综合险的 ‹*insurance, policy, cover*›; **～-round** *adj* 1 Brit (versatile) 多才多艺的 ‹*person*›; 多用途的 ‹*tool*›; 2 (general) 多方面的; **to have ～-round talent** 多才多艺; 3 (involving all sides) 全方位的; **～-rounder** *n* Brit (person) 多面手; (thing) 有多种用途之物; **～-round vision** *n* [u] 全域视觉; **All Saints' Day** *n* [u] (基督教) 诸圣日 [11月1日]; **～-seater stadium** *n* 全坐席体育场; **All Souls' Day** *n* [u] (天主教) 万灵节 [11月2日]; **～spice** *n* [u] 多香果; **～ square** *adj* 1 (even) **to be ～ square** «*game, players*» 两不相欠; 2 Sport **to be ～ square** 打平; **～-star** *adj* 全明星的 ‹*cast, team*›; **～-terrain bike** *n* 山地自行车; **～-terrain vehicle** *n* 全地形车; **～-ticket** *adj* 全部凭票入场的; **～-time** *adj* 创纪录的 ‹*best seller, inflation*›; **this film is one of the ～-time greats** 这部电影是有史以来最杰出的作品之一; **to reach an ～-time high** 创历史最高纪录; **～ told** *adv* 1 (in total) 总共; **that makes 32, ～ told** 总共 32 个; 2 (all in all) 总的说来

allude /ə'lu:d/ *vi* **to ～ to sth./sb.** 间接提及某事物/某人

all-up weight *n* esp Brit [包括乘客、货物、燃料等的] 飞机总重量

allure /ə'lʊə(r)/
A *n* 诱惑力; **the ～ of the stage** 舞台的魅力
B *vt* 诱惑

alluring /ə'lʊərɪŋ/ *adj* 迷人的

allusion /ə'lu:ʒn/ *n* [u and c] 间接提及; **an ～ to the situation at the time** 对当时形势的影射; **a classical ～** 典故

allusive /ə'lu:sɪv/ *adj* 多用典故的 ‹*style, work*›; **a highly ～ poet** 一个好用典故的诗人

alluvial /ə'lu:vɪəl/ *adj* 冲积层的; **～ soil/plains** 冲积土/平原

alluvium /ə'lu:vɪəm/ *n* (*pl* **～s** *or* **alluvia** /-vɪə/) 冲积层

all: ～-weather *adj* 全天候的 ‹*pitch, playing field*›; **～-wheel drive** *n* [u] esp Amer 四轮驱动

ally
A /'ælaɪ/ *n* (*pl* **allies**) 1 (country) 同盟国; (person) 同盟者 2 **the Allies** Mil, Hist (during World War I) 协约国; (during World War II) 同盟国
B /ə'laɪ/ *v refl* **to ～ oneself with sb./sth.** 与某人/某机构结盟

all-year-round *adj* 全年的

alma mater /,ælmə 'mɑ:tə(r), 'meɪtə(r)/ *n* 母校

almanac, almanack /'ɔ:lmənæk, Amer also 'æl-/ *n* 历书

almighty /ɔ:l'maɪtɪ/
A *adj* 1 colloq (huge) 极大的 ‹*row, noise*› 2 **Almighty** Relig 全能的; **God A～** 全能的上帝
B **the Almighty** *n* Relig 上帝

almond /'ɑ:mənd/ *n* 1 (nut) 杏仁; **～ cake** 杏仁饼 2 **～ (tree)** 扁桃树

almond: ～-eyed *adj* 杏眼的; **～ paste** *n* **= marzipan**

almost /'ɔ:lməʊst/ *adv* 1 (practically) 几乎; **we're ～ ready** 我们快准备好了; **the soup was ～ cold** 汤差不多凉了; **it's ～ dark**

天就要黑了 **2** (implying narrow escape) 差点儿; **she ~ fell** 她差点摔倒

alms /ɑːmz/ *npl* dated (money) 施舍金; (clothes, food, etc.) 施舍物; **to give ~** 施舍; **to beg/ask for ~** 乞求/请求施舍

alms: ~ box *n* dated 施舍箱; **~house** *n* archaic 救济院

aloft /əˈlɒft, Amer əˈlɔːft/ *adj, adv* **1** (gen) 在空中的; 在空中 ‹*hold, soar*›; 在高处的; 在高处 ‹*be seated, be perched*›; **flags flying ~** 高高飘扬的旗帜 **2** Naut 在帆索上的; 在帆索上

alone /əˈləʊn/

A *adj attrib* **1** (on one's own) 独自的; **all ~** 独自一人; **to leave sb. ~** lit 让某人独自待着; (in peace) 不打扰某人; **leave that bike ~!** 别动那辆自行车! **2** (isolated) 单独的; **she ~ believed him** 只有她一个人相信他; **not to be ~ in sth./in doing sth.** 在某事上不单一个人/不单一个人做某事; **to stand ~** fig 独一无二

B *adv* **1** (on one's own) 单独地; **to live ~** 独居 **2** (on one's own) 独自地; **to go it ~** 独自干; **I can manage ~** 我自己一个人就能应付 **3** (exclusively) 仅仅; **for this reason ~** 仅仅因为这个原因; **man does not live by bread ~** Prov 人不能只靠面包活着

along /əˈlɒŋ, Amer əˈlɔːŋ/

A *adv* **1** (forward on route, in time or progress) 向前; **to push/pull sth. ~** 向前推/拉某物; **our house is two doors ~** 往前过去两个门就是我们的房子; **the project was already quite far ~** 该项目已取得相当大的进展; **the message was passed ~** 消息传开了; **to drag ~** 拖拖拉拉 **2** (with company) 一起; **to ask/invite sb. ~** 叫/邀请某人一起去; **to take sth. ~** 带上某物 **3** (arrived in a place) 到某处; (present in a place) 在某处; **she'll be ~ shortly** 她一会儿就到; **there'll be another bus ~ in half an hour** 过半个小时还会来一辆公共汽车

B *prep* (extending or moving on) 沿着; (at point on) 沿着…的某处; **cottages ~ the riverbank** 河岸上的小屋; **to walk ~ the beach** 沿海滩散步; **there were chairs ~ the wall** 沿墙边摆放着椅子; **~ here/there** 沿这边/那边; **taxis can't park ~ there** 那边不能停靠出租车; **halfway ~ the path/the corridor** 在小路半途中/走廊中间; **somewhere ~ the way** 沿途某处; **somewhere ~ the way he had become hard and cynical** 他从某个时候起变得不近人情、愤世嫉俗

C **along with** *prep phr* **1** (accompanied by) 与…一起; **the President boarded the helicopter ~ with two bodyguards** 总统与两名保镖一起登上了直升机 **2** (at same time as) 与…同时; **he was convicted ~ with two others** 他和另外两人被同时定罪

alongside /əˈlɒŋsaɪd, Amer əˌlɔːŋˈsaɪd/

A *prep* **1** (next to) 在…旁边 **2** (together with) 和…在一起; **to learn to live ~ each other** 学会共同生活

B *adv* **1** (gen) 在旁边 **2** Naut 靠拢着; **to come ~** 靠上来

aloof /əˈluːf/ *adj* **1** (remote) 冷漠的; **to remain** *or* **stand ~** 漠不关心 **2** (uninvolved) 超然的; **to remain** *or* **stand ~ from ...** 不参与…

aloud /əˈlaʊd/ *adv* **1** (audibly) 出声地; **to read ~** 朗读; **to think ~** 自言自语 **2** (loudly) 大声地; **to call ~ for help** 大声呼救

alpaca /ælˈpækə/ *n* (*pl* **~** *or* **~s**) (animal) 羊驼; (wool) 羊驼毛

alpenhorn /ˈælpənhɔːn/ *n* 木制长号角

alpha /ˈælfə/

A *n* **1** (letter) 阿尔法 [α, 希腊语字母表的第1个字母]; **the ~ and omega of sth.** 事物的始与终 **2** Brit dated (grade) 优等

B *modif* Phys α 粒子的, 阿尔法粒子的

alphabet /ˈælfəbet/ *n* 字母表

alphabetical /ˌælfəˈbetɪkl/, **alphabetic** /ˌælfəˈbetɪk/ *adj* 按字母顺序的 ‹*list*›; **in ~ order** 按字母顺序

alphabetically /ˌælfəˈbetɪkli/ *adv* 按字母顺序

alphabetize /ˈælfəbətaɪz/ *vt* 按字母顺序排列

alpha male *n* (animal) 领头雄性动物; (person) 领头男子

alphameric /ˌælfəˈmerɪk/ *adj* = **alphanumeric**

alphanumeric /ˌælfənjuːˈmerɪk, Amer -nuː-/ *adj* 字母数字组成的

alpha: ~ particle *n* α 粒子, 阿尔法粒子; **~ radiation** *n* [u] α 辐射, 阿尔法辐射; **~ ray** *n* α 射线, 阿尔法射线; **~ test** *n* esp Comput α 测试, 初版测试

alpine /ˈælpaɪn/

A *adj* **1** (*also* **Alpine**) (gen) 高山上的 ‹*village, plants, troops*› **2** Sport 高山的 ‹*race, club, skiing*›

B *n* Bot 高山植物

Alps /ælps/ *pr npl* **the ~** 阿尔卑斯山脉

Al-Qaeda /ˌælkæˈiːdə/ *pr n* 基地组织 [伊斯兰极端恐怖组织]; **an ~ terrorist/network** 基地组织的恐怖分子/网络

already /ɔːlˈredi/ *adv* **1** (before particular time) 已经; **he's ~ left** 他已经离开了; **the children were ~ in bed** 孩子们已经睡了 **2** (earlier than expected) [表示惊奇]; **is it ten o'clock ~?** 都十点钟了?; **I can't believe it's June ~!** 我无法相信已到六月份了! **3** (as it is) [强调情况或问题早已存在]; **you've got too many clothes ~** 你本来衣服就已经够多了 **4** Amer colloq (expressing irritation) [表示恼火]; **so come on ~** 得了吧; **(that's) enough ~!** 这就够了!

alright /ɔːlˈraɪt/ *adj, adv, particle, n* = **all right**

Alsatian /ælˈseɪʃn/ *n* Brit 阿尔萨斯狼狗

also /ˈɔːlsəʊ/ *adv* **1** (too, as well) 也; **he ~ likes golf** 他也喜欢打高尔夫球; **rubella, ~ known as German measles** 风疹, 亦称德国麻疹 **2** (furthermore) 此外; **~, there wasn't enough to eat** 再说, 也没有足够的东西吃

altar /ˈɔːltə(r)/ *n* **1** (in church) [基督教堂内的] 圣餐台; **to lead sb. to the ~** dated hum 娶某人为妻 **2** (for offerings, sacrifices) 祭坛; **to be sacrificed on the ~ of sth.** fig 为某事物作出牺牲

altar: ~ boy *n* 祭坛助手; **~ piece** *n* 圣坛装饰画; **~ rail** *n* 圣坛围栏

alter /ˈɔːltə(r)/

A *vi* 改变; **to ~ for the better/worse** 好转/恶化

B *vt* 改变 ‹*opinion, person, policy, habit*›; 更改 ‹*will, document*›; 改 ‹*garment*›; **to ~ course** 改道

alterable /ˈɔːltərəbl/ *adj* 可改变的

alteration /ˌɔːltəˈreɪʃn/

A *n* (of building) 改建; (of will, document; also result) 更改; (of timetable, route, circumstances) 改变; (of garment) 改动; **an ~ in the interest rate** 利率的调整

B **alterations** *npl* Constr 改建

altercation /ˌɔːltəˈkeɪʃn/ *n* formal 争吵

alter ego /ˌæltər ˈegəʊ, Amer ˈiːgəʊ/ *n* **1** Psych 第二自我 **2** (close friend) 挚友

alternate

A /ɔːlˈtɜːnət/ *adj* **1** (successive) 交替的 ‹*actions, states*›; **~ circles and squares** 圆形与方形相间 **2** (every other) 间隔的; **to count ~ lines** 隔行数; **on ~ days/Mondays** 每隔一天/一周的周一 **3** Amer = **alternative A**

B /ˈɔːltəneɪt/ *vi* **1** (swap) «*people*» 轮流; «*actions, states, objects*» 交替; **to ~ with sb.** 与某人轮流; **to ~ between hope and despair/laughing and crying** 时而充满希望, 时而感到绝望/时笑时哭 **2** Elec 交流

C /ˈɔːltəneɪt/ *vt* 使交替; **he ~d persuasion with threats** 他时而劝说, 时而威胁; **to ~ crops** 轮作; **she ~d men and women round the dinner table** 她安排男女围着餐桌相间而坐

alternate angles *npl* 错角

alternately /ɔːlˈtɜːnətli/ *adv* 交替地; **they criticize and praise him ~** 他们对他时而表扬, 时而批评

alternating current /ˌɔːltəneɪtɪŋ ˈkʌrənt/ *n* 交流电

alternation /ˌɔːltəˈneɪʃn/ *n* 交替; **the ~ of day and night** 日夜的更替; **the ~ of black and white stripes** 黑白条纹的相间

alternative /ɔːlˈtɜːnətɪv/

A *adj* **1** *attrib* (other) 可供替代的 ‹*plan, route, method, suggestion*› **2** (unconventional) 非传统的 ‹*art form, lifestyle*›; **~ sources of energy** 非传统能源; **an ~ culture** 另类文化

B *n* **1** (specified option) 选择; **the ~ is to wait and see** 要么就是等着看事态的发展; **you have the ~ of marrying or remaining a bachelor** 你要么结婚, 要么继续做单身汉 **2** (possible option) 可能的选择; **there are several ~s to surgery** 除外科手术之外还有其他几种选择; **to choose between two ~s** 在两者中作出选择; **to have no ~ but to do sth.** 除了做某事之外别无选择

alternative: ~ comedian *n* 另类喜剧演员; **~ comedy** *n* [u] 另类喜剧; **~ energy** *n* [u] 替代能源; **~ fuel** *n* 替代燃料; **A~ Investment Market** *n* 另类投资市场

alternatively /ɔːlˈtɜːnətɪvli/ *adv* 或; **or ~ we could go home** 要不, 我们也可以回家

alternative: ~ medicine *n* **1** [u] (science) 另类医学; **2** [c] (particular therapy) 另类疗法; **~ school** *n* esp Amer 另类学校; **~ society** *n* 他择性社会; **~ technology** *n* [u and c] 非传统技术

alternator /ˈɔːltəneɪtə(r)/ *n* 交流发电机

although /ɔːlˈðəʊ/ *conj* **1** (in spite of the fact that) 虽然; **they're generous, ~ poor** 他们虽然贫穷, 但很大方; **~ the sun was shining, it wasn't very warm** 尽管太阳高照, 却不是很暖和; **~ small, the kitchen is well designed** 厨房虽小, 但设计得很好 **2** (but) 不过; **I felt he was wrong, ~ I didn't say so at the time** 我觉得他错了, 不过我当时没说

altimeter /ˈæltɪmiːtə(r), Amer ælˈtɪmətər/ *n* 测高仪

altitude /ˈæltɪtjuːd, Amer -tuːd/ *n* **1** (above sea level) 海拔; **at an ~ of 20,000 ft** 在海拔 2 万英尺的高度 **2** (high place) 高海拔地区; **at these ~s** 在这些海拔高的地区; **at ~** 在海拔高的地方 **3** Astron 地平纬度

altitude sickness *n* [u] 高空病

Alt key /ˈɔːlt kiː/ *n* 交替键

alto /ˈæltəʊ/ *n* (*pl* **~s**) **1** (singer) (female) 女低音歌手; (male) 男声最高音歌手 **2** (part) (female) 女低音; (male) 男声最高音 **3** (instrument) 中音乐器

alto clef *n* 中音谱表

altocumulus /ˌæltəʊˈkjuːmjʊləs/ *n* (*pl* **altocumuli** /ˌæltəʊˈkjuːmjʊli/) 高积云

altogether /ˌɔːltəˈgeðə(r)/

A *adv* **1** (completely) 完全; **he gave up ~** 他彻底放弃了; **I don't ~ agree with you** 我不完全同意你的意见; **that's an ~ different question** 那完全是另外一个问题 **2** (in total) 总共; **that'll be £27.50 ~** 一共 27.5 英镑 **3** (all things considered) 总之; **~, it was a mistake** 总之, 那是个错误

B *n* [u] dated colloq hum **in the ~** 赤身裸体

altostratus /ˌæltəʊˈstrɑːtəs/ *n* [u] 高层云

altruism /ˈæltruːɪzəm/ *n* [u] 利他主义; **an act of ~** 无私的行为

altruistic /ˌæltruːˈɪstɪk/ *adj* 无私的

alum /ˈæləm/ *n* [u] 明矾

aluminium /ˌæljʊˈmɪnɪəm/ Brit, **aluminum** /əˈluːmɪnəm/ Amer *n* [u] 铝; **an ~ alloy** 铝合金

aluminium foil *n* 铝箔

alumna /əˈlʌmnə/ *n* (*pl* **alumnae** /əˈlʌmniː/) 女校友

alumnus /əˈlʌmnəs/ *n* (*pl* **alumni** /əˈlʌmniː, -naɪ/) 男校友

alveolar /ˌælˈvɪələ(r), ˌælvɪˈəʊlə(r)/
A *adj* 齿龈音的
B *n* 齿龈音

always /ˈɔːlweɪz/ *adv* [1] (at all times, in all cases) 总是; **there's ~ somebody at home in the evenings** 晚上总有人在家; **if you have any problems, my door is ~ open** 你若有困难，我的大门永远为你敞开 [2] (every time) 每次都; **he's nearly ~ right** 他几乎每次都正确; **as ~, she was late** 她像平时一样，又迟到了 [3] (for a long time already) 一直; (for all future time) 永远; **Pat has ~ loved gardening** 帕特一直喜爱园艺; **I'll ~ love him/remember it** 我将永远爱他/记住它; **for ~** 永远 [4] (expressing annoyance) 老是; **that phone's ~ ringing** 电话老是响个不停 [5] (as a last resort) 至少还能; **you could ~ refuse** 你总还可以拒绝嘛

alyssum /ˈælɪsəm/ *n* 香雪球

Alzheimer's disease /ˈæltshaɪməz dɪˌziːz/ ▸**p. 377** *n* [u] 阿耳茨海默氏病 [即早老性痴呆症]

AM *abbr* [1] Radio **= amplitude modulation** [2] Amer Univ **= Master of Arts**

am /æm/ ▸**be**

a.m. ▸**p. 831** *abbr* **= ante meridiem** 上午; **three ~** 凌晨 3 点

AMA *abbr* **= American Medical Association** 美国医学协会

amalgam /əˈmælgəm/ *n* [1] [u] (alloy) 汞合金; **dental ~** 牙科汞合金 [2] [c] (blend) 混合物

amalgamate /əˈmælgəmeɪt/
A *vi* «*companies, clubs*» 合并; **to ~ with sb./sth.** 与某人/某物合并
B *vt* 将…合并 ‹*posts, organizations*›; **~ several companies into one large enterprise** 把几家公司合并成一家大企业

amalgamation /əˌmælgəˈmeɪʃn/ *n* [u and c] (of companies, clubs) 合并; (of styles, traditions) 混合

amanuensis /əˌmænjʊˈensɪs/ *n* (*pl* **amanuenses** /əˌmænjʊˈensiːz/) formal 文书助手

amass /əˈmæs/ *vt* 积聚 ‹*wealth*›; 收集 ‹*evidence, objects*›; **to ~ a fortune** 积累财富

amateur /ˈæmətə(r)/ *n* [1] (gen) 业余爱好者; **~ dramatics** 业余戏剧表演 [2] Sport 业余运动员 [3] pej (dabbler) 外行

amateurish /ˈæmətərɪʃ/ *adj* pej 外行的 ‹*work, efforts*›; **to do sth. in an ~ way** 不熟练地做某事

amateurism /ˈæmətərɪzəm/ *n* [u] [1] (non-professional status) 业余身份 [2] pej (ineptness) 不熟练

amaze /əˈmeɪz/ *vt* 使大为惊奇; **to be ~d by sth.** 对某事物大为惊奇; **to be ~d to hear sth.** 听到某事大为惊奇

amazed /əˈmeɪzd/ *adj* 十分惊奇的; **I'm ~ (that) ...** 使我大为惊奇的是…

amazement /əˈmeɪzmənt/ *n* [u] 惊奇; **in** *or* **with ~** 惊奇地; **to everyone's ~, ...** 使大家惊奇的是…

amazing /əˈmeɪzɪŋ/ *adj* 使人十分惊奇的; **it's ~ that so many people come** 有这么多人来真是令人惊奇

amazingly /əˈmeɪzɪŋli/ *adv* 令人惊奇地; **~ (enough), he didn't show up** 令人惊奇的是，他居然没到场

Amazon[1] /ˈæməzən, Amer -zɒn/ ▸**p. 663** *pr n* **the ~** 亚马孙河

Amazon[2] *n* (*also* **amazon**) liter 健硕的女子

Amazonia /ˌæməˈzəʊnɪə/ *pr n* [1] (around the Amazon) 亚马孙地区 [2] (national park) 亚马孙尼亚国家公园

Amazonian /ˌæməˈzəʊnɪən/ *adj* 亚马孙河流域的

ambassador /æmˈbæsədə(r)/ *n* [1] (diplomat) 大使; fig 使者; **the British A~ to Greece** 英国驻希腊大使; **to be a good ~ for one's country** 是自己国家很好的形象大使 [2] (representative) 特使

ambassador-at-large *n* (*pl* **ambassadors-at-large**) Amer 巡回大使

ambassadorial /æmˌbæsəˈdɔːrɪəl/ *adj* 大使的 ‹*post, residence*›

ambassadress /æmˈbæsədrɪs/ *n* [1] dated (diplomat) 女大使; fig 女形象大使 [2] (ambassador's wife) 大使夫人

amber /ˈæmbə(r)/ ▸**p. 134**
A *n* [u] [1] (resin) 琥珀 [2] Brit Aut (traffic signal) 黄色交通信号灯 [3] (colour) 琥珀色
B *adj* 琥珀色的 ‹*dress, wine, light*›

amber: ~-coloured *adj* 琥珀色的; **~ fluid** *n* [u] **= amber liquid**

ambergris /ˈæmbəgriːs, Amer -grɪs/ *n* [u] 龙涎香

amber liquid, amber nectar *ns* [u] esp Austral hum 啤酒

ambidextrous /ˌæmbɪˈdekstrəs/ *adj* 两手都善用的; **an ~ tennis player** 左右开弓的网球手

ambience /ˈæmbɪəns/ *n* [u] [1] (of place) 氛围 [2] (of sound recording) 环境音效

ambient /ˈæmbɪənt/ *adj* [1] (surrounding) 周围的 ‹*noise, temperature*› [2] Mus 环境音乐的 ‹*album, band*›

ambient music *n* [u] 环境音乐

ambiguity /ˌæmbɪˈgjuːəti/ *n* [1] [u] (of speech, reasoning, humour) 歧义 [2] [u] (of position, stance, or situation) 模棱两可 [3] [c] (in speech, reasoning) 有歧义的词句 [4] [c] (in position, stance, or situation) 不明确之处

ambiguous /æmˈbɪgjʊəs/ *adj* [1] (having more than one possible meaning) 有歧义的 ‹*argument, speech, humour*› [2] (uncertain in meaning or intention) 意义含糊的 ‹*nod, look, gesture, smile*› [3] (involving contradictions) 不明确的 ‹*position, stance, situation*›

ambiguously /æmˈbɪgjʊəsli/ *adv* [1] (so as to have more than one possible meaning) 有歧义地 ‹*word, state, argue*›; **an ~ worded statement** 措词有歧义的声明 [2] (so as to be uncertain in meaning or intention) 意义含糊地 ‹*nod, look*›; **she smiled ~** 她微微一笑，令人捉摸不透

ambit /ˈæmbɪt/ *n* [u] formal 范围; **to fall** *or* **lie within the ~ of sth.** 属于…的范围之内 ‹*power, authority*›

ambition /æmˈbɪʃn/ *n* [1] [c] (aim) 追求的目标; **a lifelong ~** 毕生的夙愿 [2] [u] (quality) 志向; **to have ~** 有志向; **to be filled with ~ (to become/do sth.)** 胸怀大志（要成为某人/做某事）

ambitious /æmˈbɪʃəs/ *adj* [1] (full of ambition) 有志向的; **to be ~ to succeed** 立志要有所成就; **to be ~ for one's children** 望子成龙 [2] (difficult to achieve) 耗时费力的

ambitiously /æmˈbɪʃəsli/ *adv* 雄心勃勃地

ambivalence /æmˈbɪvələns/ *n* [u] 矛盾心态; **~ about** *or* **to** *or* **towards sth./sb.** 对某事物/某人的矛盾心理

ambivalent /æmˈbɪvələnt/ *adj* 有矛盾心态的 ‹*person*›; 矛盾的 ‹*attitude*›

amble /ˈæmbl/
A *vi* [1] (stroll) 漫步; **to ~ around the garden** 在花园里四处闲逛 [2] (move) «*vehicle*» 缓慢行驶 [3] Equit 缓行
B *n* [1] [c] (stroll) 漫步 [2] [u] (pace) 从容的步态; **walk at an ~** 徐行 [3] [u] Equit 缓行步态

ambrosia /æmˈbrəʊzɪə, Amer -ˈbrəʊʒə/ *n* [u] [1] Mythol 仙馐 [希腊神话中有长生不老功效的食物] [2] fig 珍馐美味

ambulance /ˈæmbjʊləns/ *n* 救护车

ambulance: ~ chaser *n* esp Amer pej 怂恿事故受伤者起诉的律师; **~ chasing** *n* [u] esp Amer pej 怂恿事故受伤者起诉; **~ driver** ▸**p. 409** *n* 救护车司机; **~man** /-mən/ ▸**p. 409** *n* (driver) 救护车司机; (paramedic) 救护员; **~ service** *n* 救护服务; **~ station** *n* 救护中心; **~woman** ▸**p. 409** *n* (driver) 救护车女司机; (paramedic) 女救护员

ambulatory /ˈæmbjʊlətəri, Amer -tɔːri/ *adj* [1] Med 能走动的; **~ patient** 门诊病人 [2] (walking) 步行的; **~ aid** 步行辅助装置

ambulatory care *n* [u] 非卧床护理

ambush /ˈæmbʊʃ/
A *n* [u and c] [1] (attack) 伏击; **to lie in ~** 打埋伏; **to walk** *or* **fall into an ~** 中埋伏 [2] (people) 伏击者 [3] (place) 伏击点
B *vt* 伏击; **to be ~ed** 遭到伏击

ameba /əˈmiːbə/ *n* Amer **= amoeba**

amebic /əˈmiːbɪk/ *adj* Amer **= amoebic**

ameliorate /əˈmiːlɪəreɪt/ formal
A *vt* 改善; **to ~ living standards** 提高生活水平
B *vi* 改善

amelioration /əˌmiːlɪəˈreɪʃn/ *n* [u] formal 改善; **~ in living standards** 生活水平的提高

amen /ɑːˈmen, eɪ-/ *excl* [1] Relig 阿门 [用于祈祷结束时，表示诚心所愿] [2] (gen) (expressing agreement) 赞同; **~ to that!** 我同意!

amenable /əˈmiːnəbl/ *adj* [1] (obliging) 顺从的; **a person ~ to advice** 听从劝告的人 [2] (answerable) 有服从义务的; **to be ~ to the law** 须服从法律 [3] (testable) 经得起检验的; **~ to proof/demonstration** «*case, theory*» 经得起验证/论证的

amend /əˈmend/ *vt* [1] Jur, Pol (alter) 修改 ‹*law, treaty*› [2] (correct) 纠正 [3] (improve) 改进 ‹*habits, behaviour*›

amendment /əˈmendmənt/ *n* [1] [c] Jur, Pol (alteration to law, contract) 修正案 [2] [u] Jur, Pol (altering) 修改 [3] [u] formal (improvement) 改进

amends /əˈmendz/ *npl* **to make ~** (make up for) (with apology, deed) 赔罪; (with money) 赔偿

amenity /əˈmiːnəti, -ˈmen-/
A **amenities** *npl* (facilities) 便利设施; **public amenities** 公共福利设施
B *n* [u] formal (pleasantness) 宜人

amenity bed *n* Brit 特殊病床 [指须另付费用、环境清静的病床]

amenorrhoea /eɪˌmenəˈrɪə/ *n* [u] 闭经

Amerasian /ˌæməˈreɪʃn, -ˈreɪʒn/
A *adj* 美亚混血的
B *n* 美亚混血儿

America /əˈmerɪkə/ ▸**USA** *pr n* [1] (USA) 美国 [2] (continent) 美洲

American /əˈmerɪkən/ ▸**p. 503, p. 426**
A *adj* [1] (of USA) 美国的 [2] (of continent) 美洲的
B *n* [1] [c] (person) (from USA) 美国人; (from continent) 美洲人 [2] [u] (language) 美国英语

Americana /əˌmerɪˈkɑːnə/ *npl* 美国文物

American: ~ Civil War *pr n* 美国内战（1861-1865）; **~ College Test** *n* 美国大学入学考试; **~ dream** *n* [u] 美国梦; **~ eagle** *n* [1] Zool 秃鹰; [2] (emblem) [作为美国象征的] 秃鹰标志; **~ English** *n* [u] 美国英语; **~ football** *n* [u] 美式橄榄球

American Indian ▸**p. 503** *n, adj* **= Native American**

Americanism /əˈmerɪkənɪzəm/ *n* 美式词语

Americanize /əˈmerɪkənaɪz/ *vt* 使美国化; **to become ~d** 变得美国化

American: ~ Legion *pr n* 美国军团 [美国全国性退伍军人组织]; **~ National Standards Institute** *pr n* 美国国家标准学会; **~ plan** *n* [u] 美国式收费制

[包括膳宿及一应服务费在内的旅馆收费制度]; ～ **Revolution** *pr n* Hist 美国革命

the American Civil War

美国内战，又称南北战争。1861-1865 年发生在北方联邦政府（Union）和南方 11 个州之间的战争。1776 年美国独立以后，南部各州继续保留以黑人奴隶为主要劳动力的种植园经济。北方的工业州因需要大批的自由劳动力，越来越多的人主张废除奴隶制。北方和南方在各个问题上矛盾日趋尖锐。1860 年，反对奴隶制的共和党候选人亚伯拉罕·林肯（Abraham Lincoln）当选为总统。其后不久，南方11个州先后宣布脱离联邦政府，于 1861 年 2 月成立南部邦联（Confederacy），推举杰斐逊·戴维斯（Jefferson Davis）为总统。1861 年 4 月 12 日，南方军队挑起内战，史称“南北战争”。1862 年，林肯颁布《解放宣言》（*Emancipation Proclamation*），废除叛乱各州的奴隶制，允许奴隶作为自由人参加北方军队。1863 年 7 月，北方军队取得葛底斯堡（Gettysburg）战役的胜利，开始反攻。林肯在葛底斯堡发表著名演说，承诺建立“民有、民治、民享”（of the people, by the people, for the people）的政府。1865 年 4 月 9 日，南方军队总司令罗伯特·李（Robert Lee）率部队投降，内战结束。4 月 14 日晚，林肯遭不甘心南方失败的约翰·威尔克斯·布思（John Wilkes Booth）开枪行刺，翌日逝世。

the American dream

美国梦。dream首字母常大写。指相信在美国不必依靠出身，只要通过个人的不懈努力就可以致富并获得成功。也指相信美国的社会、政治和经济制度能提供平等的机会，让所有人发挥自己的潜能。美国梦是美国社会的传统信念，几乎贯穿整个美国历史。American dream 作为短语，最早见于 1931 年詹姆斯·特拉斯洛·亚当斯（James Truslow Adams）的小说《美国史诗》（*The Epic of America*）。时至今日，美国梦有时会用于讽刺，意指脱离社会现实。

the American Revolution

美国革命。英国称为美国独立战争（War of American Independence），指 1775-1783 年北美 13 个殖民地反对英国殖民统治、争取民族独立的战争。18 世纪后半期，英国对北美殖民地实行掠夺和高压政策，与殖民地之间的矛盾日趋尖锐。1775 年 5 月 10 日，殖民地代表在费城（Philadelphia）召开第二次大陆会议（Second Continental Congress），决定建立大陆军（Continental Army），并任命乔治·华盛顿（George Washington）为总司令，独立战争全面打响。1776 年 7 月 4 日，第二届大陆会议发表《独立宣言》（▸**the Declaration of Independence**），宣告北美 13 个殖民地脱离英国独立。1777 年，美军取得萨拉托加（Saratoga）大捷，促使法国和西班牙先后向英国宣战。1781 年 10 月，美、法联军攻下英军最后据点约克镇（Yorktown）。1783 年 9 月，英国和美国在巴黎签订和约，英国承认美国独立。

Amerindian /ˌæməˈrɪndɪən/ ▸**p. 503** Amer
A *adj* 美洲印第安人的
B *n* 美洲印第安人

amethyst /ˈæməθɪst/ *n* **1** [u and c] (mineral) 紫晶 **2** [u and c] (gem) 紫蓝色宝石; ～ **jewellery** 紫晶宝石首饰 **3** [u] ▸**p. 134** (colour) 紫色

Amex /ˈeɪmeks/ *abbr* = **American Stock Exchange** 美国证券交易所

amiability /ˌeɪmɪəˈbɪləti/ *n* [u] 亲切友好

amiable /ˈeɪmɪəbl/ *adj* 亲切友好的; **in an ～ mood** 心情好的

amiably /ˈeɪmɪəbli/ *adv* 亲切友好地

amicable /ˈæmɪkəbl/ *adj* 友好的 ‹*relationship*›; **an ～ settlement** *or* **solution** 和解

amicably /ˈæmɪkəbli/ *adv* 友好地

amid /əˈmɪd/ *prep* **1** (against a background of) 在…中 ‹*laughter, applause, criticism, reports*›; **the firm collapsed ～ allegations of fraud** 这家公司因受到欺诈指控而倒闭了 **2** (surrounded by) 环绕在…中 ‹*fields, wreckage*›; **a chalet ～ the trees** 林中小屋

amidships /əˈmɪdʃɪps/ *adv* 在船体中部

amidst /əˈmɪdst/ *prep* = **amid**

amino acid /əˌmiːnəʊ ˈæsɪd/ *n* 氨基酸

Amish /ˈæmɪʃ, ˈɑː-, ˈeɪ-/
A *pr n* **the ～** 阿曼门诺派 [基督教派]
B *adj* 阿曼门诺派的

amiss /əˈmɪs/
A *adj* 出差错的; **there is something ～ with him** 他有点儿不对头; **nothing is ～** 一切正常
B *adv* 出差错地; **to go** *or* **come ～** 出错

Amman /əˈmɑːn/ *pr n* 安曼

ammeter /ˈæmɪtə(r)/ *n* 安培计

ammo /ˈæməʊ/ *n* [u] colloq = **ammunition**

ammonia /əˈməʊnɪə/ *n* [u] **1** (gas) 氨 **2** (liquid) 氨水

ammonite /ˈæmənaɪt/ *n* 菊石

ammonium /əˈməʊnɪəm/ *n* [u] 铵

ammunition /ˌæmjʊˈnɪʃn/ *n* [u] **1** lit 弹药 **2** fig 证据材料; ～ **against sb.** 对某人不利的证据

ammunition: ～ **belt** *n* 子弹带; ～ **depot** *n* 弹药库; ～ **dump** *n* 弹药储藏所

amnesia /æmˈniːzɪə, Amer -ˈniːʒə/ *n* [u] 遗忘症

amnesiac /æmˈniːzɪæk, Amer -ˈniːʒɪæk/
A *n* 遗忘症患者
B *adj* 遗忘症的

amnesty /ˈæmnəsti/
A *n* **1** (pardon) 赦免; **to grant an ～ to sb.** 赦免某人 **2** (period) 赦免期
B *vt* 赦免

Amnesty International *pr n* 大赦国际 [总部设于英国的国际组织，专事争取释放因信仰问题被关押者，并提倡取消刑讯、废除死刑]

amniocentesis /ˌæmnɪəʊsenˈtiːsɪs/ *n* [u and c] 羊膜穿刺

amniotic /ˌæmnɪˈɒtɪk/: ～ **fluid** *n* [u] 羊水; ～ **sac** *n* 羊膜囊

amoeba /əˈmiːbə/ *n* (*pl* ～**s** *or* **amoebae** /əˈmiːbiː/) 阿米巴，变形虫

amoebic /əˈmiːbɪk/ *adj* (of amoebae) 阿米巴的; (caused by amoebae) 由阿米巴引起的

amoebic dysentery *n* [u] 阿米巴痢疾

amok /əˈmɒk/ *adv* **to run ～** «*person, animal*» 横冲直撞; «*imagination*» 极为活跃; «*prices*» 失去控制

among /əˈmʌŋ/, **amongst** /əˈmʌŋst/ *prep* **1** (amid) 在…中; **to be ～ friends** 和朋友在一起; ～ **those present was the ambassador** 出席的人中有那位大使; **George, ～ others, objects strongly** 乔治等人强烈反对; **discontent ～ the masses is growing** 群众的不满情绪在增长 **2** (one of) …之一; **she was ～ those who survived** 她是幸存者之一; **I count him ～ my closest friends** 我把他当作我最要好的朋友之一 **3** (between) 在…之间; **they discussed it quietly ～ themselves** 他们内部之间悄悄地讨论了这事; **cooperation ～ several European countries** 几个欧洲国家之间的合作; **one bottle ～ 5 isn't enough** 五人分一瓶不够

amoral /ˌeɪˈmɒrəl, Amer ˌeɪˈmɔːrəl/ *adj* (lacking morals) 无道德感的; (without moral distinction) 不分是非的

amorality /ˌeɪməˈrælɪti/ *n* [u] (lacking morals) 无道德感; (without moral distinction) 是非不分

amorous /ˈæmərəs/ *adj* 多情的 ‹*person*›; 含情脉脉的 ‹*look*›; **an ～ affair** 风流韵事; ～ **poetry** 情诗; **an ～ letter** 情书

amorously /ˈæmərəsli/ *adv* 情意绵绵地

amorphous /əˈmɔːfəs/ *adj* **1** (shapeless) 无固定形状的 ‹*mass*›; **an ～ shape** 不定的形状 **2** (confused) 杂乱的 ‹*ideas, style*› **3** Chem, Geol 非晶态的

amortization /əˌmɔːtɪˈzeɪʃn, Amer ˌæmərtɪ-/ *n* [u] 分期偿还

amortize /əˈmɔːtaɪz, Amer ˈæmərtaɪz/ *vt* 分期偿还

amount /əˈmaʊnt/ *n* **1** (quantity) （数）量; **large ～s of cash** 大量现金; **a small ～ of onlookers** 少数旁观者; **a considerable** *or* **fair ～ of …** 相当多的…; **quite an ～** 不小的数目; **an enormous ～ of harm** 极大的危害; **a certain ～ of respect/imagination** 一定的尊重/想象力; **no ～ of persuasion would make him come** 无论怎么劝，他都不肯来 **2** (total) 金额; **can you afford this ～?** 你付得起这笔钱吗？; **debts to the ～ of £20,000** 总额达 2 万英镑的债务; **the outstanding ～, the ～ outstanding** 未付金额; **the ～ of turnover** 营业额

Phrasal verb

- **amount to** *vt* [～ **to sth.**]
1 (add up to) 总计; **a cargo ～ing to 2,000 tons** 共计 2,000 吨的货物 **2** (be equivalent to) 相当于; **it ～s to blackmail** 这等于勒索; **it ～s to the same thing (to sb.)** （对某人而言）都是一回事; **the rain didn't ～ to much** 雨并没有下大; **he'll never ～ to much** 他绝不会有多大出息的

amp /æmp/ *n* = **ampere**

amperage /ˈæmpərɪdʒ/ *n* [u] 安培数

ampere /ˈæmpeə(r), Amer ˈæmpɪə(r)/ *n* 安培

ampere-hour *n* 安时

ampersand /ˈæmpəsænd/ *n* &符号

amphetamine /æmˈfetəmiːn/ *n* [u and c] 安非他明

amphibian /æmˈfɪbɪən/
A *n* **1** Zool 两栖动物 **2** Aviat 水陆两用飞机 **3** Aut 水陆两用车
B *adj* = **amphibious**

amphibious /æmˈfɪbɪəs/ *adj* **1** Zool 两栖的 **2** Aut 水陆两用的 **3** Mil 两栖作战的; **an ～ assault** 两栖攻击; **an ～ landing** 两栖登陆

amphitheatre Brit, **amphitheater** Amer /ˈæmfɪθɪətə(r)/ *n* **1** (outdoor arena) 圆形露天剧场 **2** (room) 阶梯教室 **3** Brit (in theatre) 阶梯式楼座 **4** Geol 圆形凹地

amphora /ˈæmfərə/ *n* (*pl* **amphorae** /ˈæmfəriː/ *or* ～**s**) 两耳细颈罐

ample /ˈæmpl/ *adj* **1** (enough) 足够的 ‹*time, money, space*› **2** (plenty) 大量的 ‹*supplies*›; 充分的 ‹*reasons*›; **an ～ salary** 高薪; **to have ～ means** 很富有 **3** (large) 宽大的 ‹*garment*›; 粗壮的 ‹*waist*›; 丰满的 ‹*bosom*›; **to have an ～ stomach** 大腹便便; **an ～ helping** 一大份; **a man of ～ proportions** hum 大块头男人

amplification /ˌæmplɪfɪˈkeɪʃn/ *n* **1** [u] Audio 放大 **2** [u] Elec 增强 **3** [u] (of idea, writing) 扩展 **4** [c] (added detail) 补充的细节

amplifier /ˈæmplɪfaɪə(r)/ *n* 放大器

amplify /ˈæmplɪfaɪ/ *vt* **1** Audio 放大 ‹*sound*› **2** Elec 增强 ‹*current, signal*› **3** (expand on) 扩展 ‹*statement, idea*›; **notions that need ～ing** 需要进一步阐释的概念

amplitude /ˈæmplɪtjuːd, Amer -tuːd/ *n* [u] **1** formal (abundance) 丰富 **2** hum (largeness) 巨大

amplitude modulation *n* [u] 调幅

amply /ˈæmpli/ *adv* 充分地; **to be ～ rewarded** 得到充分回报

ampoule Brit, **ampule** Amer /ˈæmpuːl/ *n* 安瓿

amputate /ˈæmpjʊteɪt/
A *vt* 截除 ‹*limb*›
B *vi* 截肢

amputation /ˌæmpjʊˈteɪʃn/ *n* [u and c] 截肢

amputee /ˌæmpjʊˈtiː/ *n* 被截肢者

Amsterdam /ˈæmstədæm/ *pr n* 阿姆斯特丹

Amtrak /ˈæmtræk/ *pr n* Amer 美铁 [美国全国铁路客运公司的简称]

amuck /əˈmʌk/ *adv* = **amok**

amulet /ˈæmjʊlɪt/ *n* 护身符

amuse /əˈmjuːz/ *vt* **1** (cause laughter) 逗…笑; **to be ~d at** *or* **by sth.** 被某事物逗乐; **I'm not ~d!** hum 我不觉得好笑! **2** (entertain) 给…提供消遣; **we ~d ourselves by playing chess** 我们下棋自娱

amusement /əˈmjuːzmənt/ *n* **1** [u] (mirth) 欢乐; **to my great ~** 令我觉得十分有趣的是; **to do sth. for sb.'s ~** 做某事使人发笑; **a look of ~** 饶有兴味的神情; **to hide one's ~** 忍俊 **2** [c] (pastime) 消遣 **3** [c] *usu pl* (device, ride) 娱乐器械

amusement: ~ arcade *n* Brit 游戏机厅; **~ park** *n* 游乐园

amusing /əˈmjuːzɪŋ/ *adj* 有趣的; **to be highly ~** 引人入胜; **I don't find that ~** 我觉得那并不好笑

amusingly /əˈmjuːzɪŋli/ *adv* 有趣地; **an ~ worded letter** 一封措词风趣的信

an /ən, *stressed* æn/ *det* [用于元音前]; ▸ **a**

anabolic steroid /ˌænəˌbɒlɪk ˈstɪərɔɪd, ˈster-/ *n* 促蛋白合成类固醇

anachronism /əˈnækrənɪzəm/ *n* **1** (thing in wrong historical period) 时代错误 **2** (person) 落伍的人; (custom) 过时的风俗

anachronistic /əˌnækrəˈnɪstɪk/ *adj* **1** (in wrong historical period) 时代错误的 **2** (out of date) 过时的

anaconda /ˌænəˈkɒndə/ *n* 森蚺

anaemia /əˈniːmɪə/ ▸ **p. 377** *n* [u] Brit 贫血

anaemic /əˈniːmɪk/ *adj* Brit **1** Med 患贫血症的 ‹*condition*›; 贫血的 ‹*symptom*› **2** fig pej 缺少活力的 ‹*performance*›; 虚弱的 ‹*person*›

anaerobic /ˌæneəˈrəʊbɪk/ *adj* **1** Biol 厌氧的 **2** (relating to exercise) 无氧的 ‹*training, endurance*›

anaesthesia /ˌænɪsˈθiːzɪə/ *n* [u] Brit 麻醉; **general/local ~** 全身/局部麻醉

anaesthetic /ˌænɪsˈθetɪk/ Brit
A *n* **1** [c] (substance) 麻醉剂 **2** [u] (process) 麻醉; **to be under ~** 处于麻醉状态
B *adj* 麻醉的 ‹*effect*›; **~ drug** 麻药

anaesthetist /əˈniːsθətɪst/ ▸ **p. 409** *n* Brit 麻醉师

anaesthetize /əˈniːsθətaɪz/ *vt* Brit **1** (administer drug to) 对…施行麻醉 **2** (make numb) 使麻木

anagram /ˈænəgræm/ *n* 同字母异序词 [词的字母顺序变换后组成的新词]

anal /ˈeɪnl/ *adj* **1** Anat 肛门的; **the ~ region** 肛门区 **2** Psych 肛欲的 **3** fig colloq 极度刻板的

analgesia /ˌænælˈdʒiːzɪə, Amer -ʒə/ *n* [u] 痛觉缺失

analgesic /ˌænælˈdʒiːsɪk/
A *adj* 止痛的
B *n* 止痛剂

analog /ˈænəlɔːg/ *adj, n* Amer = **analogue**

analogous /əˈnæləgəs/ *adj* 类似的 ‹*situation, relationship*›; **to be ~ to** *or* **with sth.** 与某事物类似

analogue /ˈænəlɒg/ Brit
A *adj* 模拟的 ‹*data, signal*›
B *n* (thing) 类似物; (person) 类似的人

analogue: ~ clock *n* 指针式钟; **~ computer** *n* 模拟计算机; **~-digital converter** *n* 模数转换器; **~ television** *n* **1** [u] (system) 模拟电视; **2** [c] (TV set) 模拟电视机; **~ watch** *n* 指针式手表

analogy /əˈnælədʒi/ *n* **1** [c] (similarity) 类似; **to draw an ~ between sth. and sth.** 把某事物与某事物作类比 **2** [u] (reasoning) 类推

anal retentive Psych
A *adj* 极度刻板的
B *n* 极度刻板的人

analyse /ˈænəlaɪz/ *vt* Brit **1** (gen) 分析 ‹*data, language, sample*›; 解读 ‹*reason, painting*›; **to ~ sth. in depth** 深入分析某事物 **2** Psych 给…作心理分析

analysis /əˈnælɪsɪs/ *n* (*pl* **analyses** /əˈnælɪsiːz/) **1** [u and c] 分析; **in the final** *or* **last ~** 归根结底 **2** [u and c] (statement) 分析报告 **3** [u] Psych = **psychoanalysis**

analyst /ˈænəlɪst/ ▸ **p. 409** *n* **1** (person) 分析员 **2** Psych = **psychoanalyst**

analytic /ˌænəˈlɪtɪk/, **analytical** /ˌænəˈlɪtɪkl/ *adj* 分析的 ‹*method*›; **she has a very ~ mind** 她很善于分析

analytical: ~ language *n* 分析型语言; **~ psychology** *n* [u] 分析心理学

analyze /ˈænəlaɪz/ *vt* Amer = **analyse**

anaphora /əˈnæfərə/ *n* [u] [语法中的] 前指代

anaphylactic /ˌænəfɪˈlæktɪk/ *adj* 过敏的; **~ shock** 过敏性休克; **~ reaction** 过敏反应

anarchic /əˈnɑːkɪk/, **anarchical** /əˈnɑːkɪkl/ *adj* 无政府的; fig 胡闹的 ‹*comedy*›

anarchism /ˈænəkɪzəm/ *n* [u] 无政府主义

anarchist /ˈænəkɪst/
A *n* 无政府主义者
B *adj* 无政府主义的 ‹*view, movement, group*›

anarchy /ˈænəki/ *n* [u] **1** Pol 无政府状态 **2** (disorder) 混乱

anathema /əˈnæθəmə/ *n* (person) 令人厌恶的人; (thing) 令人厌恶的东西; **racism is (an) ~ to him** 他对种族主义深恶痛绝

anatomical /ˌænəˈtɒmɪkl/ *adj* 解剖学的 ‹*study*›; 解剖的 ‹*structure*›

anatomist /əˈnætəmɪst/ *n* 解剖学家

anatomy /əˈnætəmi/ *n* **1** [u] Med (study) 解剖学 **2** [c] Biol (structure) [动植物的] 结构 **3** [c] hum (body) 人体 **4** [c] fig (analysis) 剖析

ANC *abbr* = **African National Congress**

ancestor /ˈænsestə(r)/ *n* **1** (person) 祖先 **2** fig (version) 原型

ancestral /ænˈsestrəl/ *adj* 祖先的 ‹*village*›; 祖传的 ‹*lands, rights*›; **the ~ home** 祖居

ancestry /ˈænsestri/ *n* **1** (lineage) 世系; **to come from a distinguished ~** 出身名门 **2** (ancestors) 祖先 **3** fig (origin) 起源

anchor /ˈæŋkə(r)/
A *n* **1** Naut 锚; **to drop/slip/raise (the) ~** 下锚/弃锚/起锚; **to ride at ~** 抛锚停泊 **2** fig (source of stability) 精神支柱 **3** = **anchorman, anchorwoman**
B *vi* 抛锚; **we ~ed in the harbour** 我们停泊在港内
C *vt* **1** (moor) 用锚把…固定住 **2** (secure) 使固定; **to ~ sth. to sth.** 把某物固定在某物上

Phrasal verb
• **anchor down** *vt* [**~ down sth., ~ sth. down**] 把…固定住

anchorage /ˈæŋkərɪdʒ/ *n* **1** [c] Naut (place) 锚地 **2** [u] Naut (fee) 停泊税 **3** [c] Tech 固定物; **an ~ point** 固定点

anchorite /ˈæŋkəraɪt/ *n* Hist 隐居修道者

anchor: ~man /-mæn/ ▸ **p. 409** *n* 男主持人; **~woman** ▸ **p. 409** *n* 女主持人

anchovy /ˈæntʃəvi, Amer ˈæntʃəʊvi/ *n* 鳀

ancient /ˈeɪnʃənt/
A *adj* **1** (dating from BC) 古代的; (dating from long ago) 古老的 ‹*custom, rocks*›; **in ~ times** 在古代; **~ Rome** 古罗马 **2** colloq (very old) 年老的 ‹*person, animal*›; 陈旧的 ‹*thing*›; **to feel ~** 觉得自己老了; **~-looking** 古色古香的
B **the ancients** *n* Hist 古人

ancient: A~ Greek *n* [u] 古希腊语; **~ history** *n* **1** lit 古代史; **2** fig colloq 旧闻; **~ monument** *n* 古迹; **~ world** *n* **the ~ world** 古代世界

ancillary /ænˈsɪləri, Amer ˈænsəleri/
A *adj* 辅助的 ‹*staff, roads*›; 附加的 ‹*costs*›; **to be ~ to ...** (complementary) 是对…的补充; (subordinate) 从属于…; **~ duties** 辅助职责
B *n* (thing) 附属物; (office) 分公司; (person) 助手

and /ənd, *stressed* ænd/ *conj* **1** (joining words or clauses) 和; **ham ~ eggs** 火腿蛋; **a knife ~ fork** 一副刀叉; **she shouted ~ screamed** 她大喊大叫; **we were hungry ~ thirsty** 我们又饥又渴; **~ all that** colloq 等等; **education ~ all that** 教育之类的事; **~ so on** *or* **forth** 等等; **~ that** Brit colloq 等等; **did you miss me? — ~ how!** 你想我了吗？——当然啦！; **~/or** 和/或; **she goes swimming in the sea summer ~ winter** 她不论冬夏都到海里游泳 **2** (indicating one person or thing) [连接双重身份]; **my friend ~ colleague Joe Brown** 我的朋友兼同事乔·布朗 **3** (used in numbers) [连接数字]; **four hundred ~ sixty-two** 四百六十二; **five ~ a quarter** 五又四分之一 **4** (plus) 加; **2 ~ 2 is** *or* **makes 4** 2 加 2 等于 4 **5** (then) 然后; **I got up ~ opened the door** 我起来开了门 **6** (as a result) 因此; **tell the truth ~ I'll believe you** 你说实话我就相信你 **7** (but) 但是; **you like classical music ~ I like rock** 你喜欢古典音乐，而我喜欢摇滚乐 **8** (with comparatives) [表示程度加强]; **it got worse ~ worse** 越来越糟了 **9** (expressing continuation) [表示持续的动作]; **I waited ~ waited** 我等了又等 **10** (expressing contrast) [表示对比]; **there are cities ~ cities** 城市各有不同 **11** (for emphasis) [表示强调]; **we got there nice ~ early** 我们早早地到了那里 **12** (in order to) 为了; **to come/go ~ do sth.** 来/去做某事 **13** (express surprise or annoyance) [用于go之后，表示惊讶或恼怒]; **to go ~ do sth.** 居然做某事; **he went ~ lost my pen** 他竟然把我的钢笔弄丢了 **14** (or) 或; **I haven't got pen ~ paper** 我没有纸笔 **15** (introducing comment) 而且 [引出附加评论或感叹语]; **~ he didn't even say thank you!** 而且他竟然没说声谢谢! **16** (introducing question) 那么 [引出与前文相关的提问]; **I found the letter in her bag — ~ did you open it?** 我在她的包里找到了这封信——那么你拆开了吗？; **I'm the new teacher — ~?** 我是新来的老师——然后呢？ **17** (introducing new topic) [表示转入新话题]; **~ now the main point on the agenda** 下面谈谈议程的要点

Andalucia, Andalusia /ˌændəluːˈsɪə/ *pr n* 安达卢西亚

Andalucian, Andalusian /ˌændəluːˈsɪən/
A *adj* (of Andalucia) 安达卢西亚的; (of the people) 安达卢西亚人的
B *n* 安达卢西亚人

andante /ænˈdænteɪ/
A *adv* 徐缓地 ‹*play*›
B *adj* 行板的; **~ movement/finale** 行板乐章/行板终曲
C *n* 行板乐曲

Andean /ænˈdiːən/ *adj* 安第斯山脉的

Andes /ˈændiːz/ *pr npl* **the ~** 安第斯山脉

Andorra /ænˈdɔːrə/ *pr n* 安道尔

androgynous /ænˈdrɒdʒɪnəs/ *adj* **1** (of indeterminate sex) 中性化的 ‹*person, look*› **2** Biol 雌雄同序的 ‹*flower*›; 雌雄同体的 ‹*organism*›

android /ˈændrɔɪd/ *n* 机器人

anecdotal /ˌænɪkˈdəʊtl/ *adj* 轶事的; **~ memoirs** 包含许多轶事的回忆录; **on the basis of ~ evidence** 基于道听途说

anecdote /ˈænɪkdəʊt/ *n* 轶事

anemia /əˈniːmiə/ *n* Amer = **anaemia**

ℹ And

■ The conjunction 'and' may be translated into Chinese as 和, 跟, 同, 与, or 及. However, these words are not identical in meaning to 'and'. They each also have variations in meaning.

■ 和 links nouns, pronouns, nominal phrases, verbs, adjectives and verbal phrases. 跟, 同, and 与 link nouns, pronouns, and nominal phrases. 及 is used only in written Chinese to link nouns and nominal phrases:

Simon and Victor
= 西蒙和 / 跟 / 同 / 与 / 及维克托

tables and chairs
= 桌子和 / 跟 / 同 / 与 / 及椅子

English newspapers and Chinese books
= 英文报和 / 跟 / 同 / 与 / 及汉语书

you and me
= 你和 / 跟 / 同 / 与我

healthy and happy
= 健康和快乐

read and write
= 读和写

review the new words and write an article
= 复习生词和写文章

■ When 'and' links two adjectives, it is normally omitted in Chinese, and a slight-pause mark '、' is used instead:

She is tall and graceful
= 她身材高挑、举止优雅

Glasgow is a modern and exciting city
= 格拉斯哥是个现代化的、令人兴奋的城市

■ 和 is used both in spoken and written Chinese. 跟 is commonly used in spoken Chinese. 同, 与, and 及 are used mainly in written Chinese:

I have been to France, Spain, and Britain
= 我去过法国、西班牙和英国

My husband and I are lawyers
= 我和我丈夫都是律师

David and I have been friends for many years
= 戴维跟我是多年的朋友了

The manager and I participated in the Edinburgh International Book Festival
= 我同经理参加了爱丁堡国际图书节

'War and Peace'
=《战争与和平》

Teachers, pupils, and parents attended the school-opening ceremony
= 老师、学生及家长都出席了开学典礼

■ 和, 跟, 同, 与, and 及 are used to link only words or expressions, not clauses:

He likes apples, and I like oranges
= 他喜欢苹果，我喜欢橘子

Zoe is American, and Vera is British
= 佐耶是美国人，薇拉是英国人

anemic /ə'ni:mɪk/ *adj* Amer **= anaemic**

anemometer /ˌænɪ'mɒmɪtə(r)/ *n* 风速计

anemone /ə'neməni/ *n* 银莲花

aneroid barometer /ˌænərɔɪd bə'rɒmɪtə(r)/ *n* 膜盒气压计

anesthesia /ˌænəs'θi:ʒə/ *n* [u] Amer **= anaesthesia**

anesthetic /ˌænəs'θetɪk/ *n, adj* Amer **= anaesthetic**

anesthetist /ə'ni:sθətɪst/ ▸**p. 409** *n* Amer **= anaesthetist**

anesthetize /ə'ni:sθətaɪz/ *vt* Amer **= anaesthetize**

aneurysm, aneurism /'ænjʊrɪzəm, Amer -nʊ-/ *n* 动脉瘤

anew /ə'nju:, Amer ə'nu:/ *adv* **1** (once more) 再一次 **2** (in a new way) 重新; **to begin ~** 重新开始

angel /'eɪndʒl/ *n* **1** lit 天使; **to rush in where ~s fear to tread** 鲁莽行事; **to be on the side of the ~s** 站在道义一方 **2** fig (person) 天使 [指美丽、纯真或善良的人]; **to sing like an ~** 唱得婉转动听; **be an ~ and answer the phone!** 乖，去接电话！; **don't be deceived! she's no ~!** 当心受骗！她可不是善茬！

angel cake *n* 天使蛋糕

Angeleno /ˌændʒə'li:nəʊ/ *n* Amer 洛杉矶人

angel: ~fish *n* 神仙鱼; **~ food cake** *n* Amer **= angel cake**

angelic /æn'dʒelɪk/ *adj* (of an angel) 天使的; (like an angel) 天使般的

angelica /æn'dʒelɪkə/ *n* [u] 当归蜜饯

Angelino /ˌændʒə'li:nəʊ/ *n* Amer **= Angeleno**

angelus /'ændʒələs/ *n* [u] **1** Relig [天主教于早、午、晚诵念的] 奉告祈祷 **2** (ringing of bells) 奉告祈祷钟

anger /'æŋgə(r)/
A *n* [u] 愤怒; **in ~** 怒气冲冲地; **in a fit of ~** 一怒之下; **to be filled with ~** 满腔怒火; **more in sorrow than in ~** 出于悲哀多于愤怒
B *vt* 使发怒; **she was ~ed by his comment** 她被他的评论激怒了; **to be easily ~ed** 动辄发怒

angina (pectoris) /ænˌdʒaɪnə ('pektərɪs)/ ▸**p. 377** *n* [u] 心绞痛

angle¹ /'æŋgl/
A *n* **1** (space) 角; **a right/an acute/an obtuse ~** 直角/锐角/钝角; **at an ~** 倾斜地; **at an ~ of 45°** 以 45°角; **at an ~ to ...** 与…不平行; **to make** *or* **form an ~ with sth.** 与某物成一个角度 **2** (position from which to take photograph, fire gun etc.) 角度 **3** (perspective, point of view) 视角; **what's your ~ on the current situation?** 你对时局的看法是什么？; **to see sb./sth. from sb.'s ~** 从某人的角度看某人/某事物; **from all/various/different ~s** 从所有/各种/不同的视角; **the news ~** 媒体角度 **4** (corner of building, object, etc.) 拐角
B *vt* **1** (move) 斜移; (place) 斜置; **to ~ the camera** 使相机倾斜; **~d at 45° (to sth.)** (与某物) 成 45°角; **to ~ sth. upwards/downwards/obliquely** 使某物上倾/下倾/倾斜; **his kick was ~d out to the wing** 他把球斜传给边锋 **2** (present) 面向; **to ~ sth. at** *or* **to** *or* **towards sb./sth.** 使某事物偏向于某人/某事物; **the programme is ~d at young viewers** 这个节目面向年轻观众

angle² *vi* **1** (fish) 垂钓; **to ~ for salmon** 钓三文鱼 **2** **to ~ for sth.** fig colloq 谋取某事物; **to ~ for compliments** 博取恭维

angle: ~ bracket *n* **1** (in text) 尖括号; **2** (support) 角形托座; **~ grinder** *n* 角磨器; **~ of incidence** *n* 入射角; **~ of reflection** *n* 反射角; **~ of refraction** *n* 折射角; **~ plate** *n* 角板

Anglepoise® /'æŋglpɔɪz/ *pr n* 曲臂台灯

angler /'æŋglə(r)/ *n* 垂钓者

angler fish *n* [u] 鮟鱇

Anglesey /'æŋgəlsi/ *pr n* (island) [英国威尔士西北部的] 安格尔西岛; (county) 安格尔西郡

Anglican /'æŋglɪkən/
A *adj* 英国国教的
B *n* 英国国教信徒

Anglicanism /'æŋglɪkənɪzəm/ *n* [u] 英国国教的教义

anglicism /'æŋglɪsɪzəm/ *n* (way of saying sth.) 典型的英国说法; (word or phrase) [说另一语言的人所使用的] 英语词语

Anglicist /'æŋglɪsɪst/ *n* (expert) 英国语言文学专家; (student) 英国语言文学研究者

anglicize /'æŋglɪsaɪz/ *vt* (make like England) 使英国化; (make like English) 使英语化; **an ~d form of a French word** 拼法英语化了的法语单词

angling /'æŋglɪŋ/ ▸**p. 307** *n* [u] 垂钓; **an ~ competition** 钓鱼比赛

Anglo /'æŋgləʊ/ *n* **1** Amer [非西班牙或墨西哥裔的] 美国白人 **2** Can 操英语的加拿大人

Anglo-American ▸**p. 503**
A *adj* 英美的
B *n* 英裔美国人

Anglo-French ▸**p. 503, p. 426** *adj* 英法的

Anglo-Indian ▸**p. 503**
A *adj* **1** (of England and India) 英国和印度的 **2** (of mixed parentage) 英印混血的
B *n* 英印混血儿

Anglo-Irish ▸**p. 503**
A *adj* 英格兰和爱尔兰的
B *npl* **the ~** 英裔爱尔兰人

Anglophile /'æŋgləʊfaɪl/ *n* 崇英者

Anglophobe /'æŋgləʊfəʊb/ *n* (hating England) 仇英者; (fearing England) 恐英者

Anglophobia /ˌæŋgləʊ'fəʊbɪə/ *n* [u] (hatred of England) 仇英; (fear of England) 恐英

Anglophone /'æŋgləʊfəʊn/
A *adj* 操英语的
B *n* 操英语的人

Anglo-Saxon /ˌæŋgləʊ'sæksn/ ▸**p. 503, p. 426**
A *adj* **1** Hist 盎格鲁－撒克逊人的 **2** Ling 古英语的
B *n* **1** [c] Hist (person) 盎格鲁－撒克逊人 **2** [c] (person of English descent) 英裔人 **3** [u] Ling 古英语

Angola /æŋ'gəʊlə/ *pr n* 安哥拉

Angolan /æŋ'gəʊlən/ ▸**p. 503**
A *adj* (of Angola) 安哥拉的; (of the people) 安哥拉人的
B *n* 安哥拉人

angora /æŋ'gɔ:rə/ *n* **1** [c] (cat) 安哥拉猫; (goat) 安哥拉山羊; (rabbit) 安哥拉兔 **2** [u] (yarn) 安哥拉毛纱; (fabric) 安哥拉毛呢

angrily /'æŋgrɪli/ *adv* 愤怒地

angry /'æŋgri/ *adj* **1** (very cross) 发怒的; **to be ~ at** *or* **with sb.** 生某人的气; **to be ~ at** *or* **about sth./doing sth.** 为某事/做某事而生气; **to get** *or* **grow ~** 恼怒起来 **2** fig (stormy) 狂暴的; **the sea looks ~** 海涛汹涌; **the sky looks ~** 乌云滚滚 **3** (expressing anger) 表示愤怒的; **~ words** 气话 **4** (inflamed) 肿痛发炎的 ‹*wound, rash*›

angry-looking *adj* **1** (appearing annoyed) 表情愤怒的 **2** (stormy) 乌云滚滚的 ‹*sky*›; 波涛汹涌的 ‹*sea*›; **~ clouds** 乱云 **3** (inflamed) 红肿发炎的 ‹*wound, rash*›

angstrom /'æŋstrəm/ *n* 埃 [用于衡量波长及原子间距离的长度单位，等于10^{-10}米]

a

anguish /ˈæŋgwɪʃ/ *n* [u] 极度痛苦; **to be in ~** 痛苦万分

anguished /ˈæŋgwɪʃt/ *adj* 极度痛苦的

angular /ˈæŋgjʊlə(r)/ *adj* [1] (having angles or sharp corners) 有尖角的 ‹*structure, building*› [2] (bony) 瘦骨嶙峋的 ‹*body, features*› [3] (awkward) 笨拙的 ‹*posture, gait*›

Anhui /ænˈhweɪ/ ▸**p. 604** *pr n* **~ (Province)** 安徽（省）

anhydrous /ænˈhaɪdrəs/ *adj* 无水的

aniline /ˈænɪliːn, Amer ˈænəlaɪn/ *n* 苯胺; **~ dye** 苯胺染料

animal /ˈænɪml/ *n* [1] (creature, genus) 动物; **domestic ~s** 家畜; **wild ~s** 野兽; **~ instincts** 动物本能; **~ desires** 兽欲 [2] (brutish person) 残暴的人; **to behave like ~s** 行为如畜生一般; **to bring out the ~ in sb.** 激起某人的兽欲; **to treat sb. like an ~** 不把某人当人对待 [3] fig (type of person) 一类人; (type of thing) 一类物; **man is a political ~** 人是政治动物; **there's no such ~** colloq 那东西根本不存在

animal: ~ activism *n* [u] 极端动物保护主义; **~ activist** *n* 极端动物保护主义者; **~ crackers** *npl* Amer 动物饼干; **~ experiment** *n* 动物实验; **~ hospital** *n* 动物医院; **~ husbandry** *n* [u] 畜牧业; **~ kingdom** *n* 动物界; **~ liberation** *n* [u] 动物解放; **~ lover** *n* 爱动物的人; **~ magnetism** *n* [u] [尤指对异性的] 魅力; **~ product** *n* 畜产品; **~ rights** *npl* 动物权益; **~ rights campaigner** *n* 动物权益倡导者; **~ sanctuary** *n* 动物保护区; **~ testing** *n* [u] 动物试验

animate
[A] /ˈænɪmət/ *adj* 有生命的; **~ beings** 生物
[B] /ˈænɪmeɪt/ *vt* [1] (enliven) 使…有生气 ‹*person, face, conversation*› [2] (motivate) 激励; **to ~ sb. with sth.** 用某事物激励某人 [3] Cin 把…摄制成动画片

animated /ˈænɪmeɪtɪd/ *adj* [1] (lively) 活跃的; **an ~ discussion** 热烈的讨论; **an ~ smile** 欢乐的微笑 [2] Cin 动画的; **an ~ film** 动画片

animatedly /ˈænɪmeɪtɪdli/ *adv* 活跃地

animation /ˌænɪˈmeɪʃn/ *n* [1] [u] (liveliness) 生气; **her face radiated ~ and happiness** 她的脸上洋溢着活力与幸福 [2] [u] Cin 动画片制作技术 [3] [c] (film) 动画片

animator /ˈænɪmeɪtə(r)/ ▸**p. 409** *n* 动画片制作者

animatronic /ˌænɪməˈtrɒnɪk/ *adj* 电子动画的

animatronics /ˌænɪməˈtrɒnɪks/ *npl* [1] + *v sing* (technique) 电子动画技术 [2] + *v pl* (effects) 电子动画效果

animism /ˈænɪmɪzəm/ *n* [u] 泛灵论

animist /ˈænɪmɪst/ *n* 泛灵论者

animosity /ˌænɪˈmɒsəti/ *n* [u] 敌意; **to feel ~ towards sb.** 对某人怀有敌意

anise /ˈænɪs/ *n* 茴芹

aniseed /ˈænɪsiːd/ *n* [u] 茴香籽

Ankara /ˈæŋkərə/ *pr n* 安卡拉

ankle /ˈæŋkl/ ▸**p. 71** *n* [1] (joint) 踝关节; **to sprain** *or* **twist one's ~** 扭伤脚踝 [2] (part of leg) 脚踝

ankle: ~bone *n* 距骨; **~ chain** *n* 脚链; **~-deep** *adj* 齐脚踝深的; **we were ~-deep in water** 水没到了我们的脚踝处; **~-length** *adj* 长至脚踝处的 ‹*dress*›; **~ sock** *n* 短袜

anklet /ˈæŋklɪt/ *n* [1] (jewellery) 脚镯 [2] Amer (sock) 短袜

annalist /ˈænəlɪst/ *n*

annals /ˈænlz/ *npl* [1] (chronicle of events) 编年史 [2] (historical records) 历史记载; **to go down in the ~ (of history)** 被载入史册

anneal /əˈniːl/ *vt* 使退火

annex
[A] /ˈæneks/ *n* (*also* **annexe** Brit) [1] (building) 附属建筑物; **an ~ to the hotel** 旅馆的附楼 [2] esp Jur (appendix) 附件; **an ~ to the will** 遗嘱的附件
[B] /əˈneks/ *vt* 吞并 ‹*country, territory*›

annexation /ˌænɪkˈseɪʃn/ *n* [u and c] 吞并

annihilate /əˈnaɪəleɪt/ *vt* [1] (destroy) 歼灭 ‹*enemy*›; 摧毁 ‹*city, building*› [2] fig (defeat) 彻底击败

annihilation /əˌnaɪəˈleɪʃn/ *n* [u] [1] (destruction) 毁灭 [2] fig (defeat) 惨败

anniversary /ˌænɪˈvɜːsəri/ *n* 周年纪念日; **a wedding ~** 结婚周年纪念日

Anno Domini /ˌænəʊ ˈdɒmɪnaɪ/ *adv* 公元; **1620 ~** 公元 1620 年

annotate /ˈænəteɪt/ *vt* 给…作注释; **an ~d edition** 注释版

annotation /ˌænəˈteɪʃn/ *n* [u and c] 注释

announce /əˈnaʊns/ *vt* [1] (declare publicly) 宣布; **we are pleased to ~ that ...** 我们很高兴地宣布… [2] (inform of arrival) 通报…的到来 ‹*train, guests*›; **dark clouds ~d the imminent storm** 乌云预示着暴风雨即将到来 [3] (introduce) 介绍 ‹*celebrity, performer*›

announcement /əˈnaʊnsmənt/ *n* 通告; **to make an ~** 发布通告; **to put an ~ in the newspapers** 在报纸上登一则启事

announcer /əˈnaʊnsə(r)/ *n* (on radio or TV) 播音员; (at rail station) 广播员

annoy /əˈnɔɪ/ *vt* [1] (irritate) 惹恼 [2] (harass) 打搅; **the mosquitoes ~ed me so much I couldn't sleep** 几只蚊子闹得我无法入睡

annoyance /əˈnɔɪəns/ *n* [1] [u] (irritation) 恼怒; **much to my ~ the train arrived an hour late** 火车晚点一个小时，我非常恼火 [2] [c] (nuisance) 讨厌的东西; **a petty** *or* **trifling ~** 小麻烦

annoyed /əˈnɔɪd/ *adj* 恼怒的; **she was ~ with him for being late** 他迟到了，她很生气

annoying /əˈnɔɪɪŋ/ *adj* 恼人的; **the ~ thing is that ...** 令人烦恼的是…; **how ~!** 真讨厌！

annoyingly /əˈnɔɪɪŋli/ *adv* 恼人地; **~, the train was late** 让人恼火的是，火车晚点了

annual /ˈænjʊəl/
[A] *adj* [1] (occurring yearly) 一年一次的 ‹*event, meeting*› [2] (calculated yearly) 年度的; **~ rent** 年租金; **~ rainfall** 年降雨量; **~ income** 年收入 [3] (of one year's duration) 持续一年的 ‹*course*›; **~ budget** 年度预算; **~ subscription** 全年订阅
[B] *n* [1] (book) 年刊 [2] (plant) 一年生植物

Annual General Meeting *n* (meeting of shareholders) 年度股东大会; (meeting of members) 年度会员大会

annually /ˈænjʊəli/ *adv* 每年

annual: ~ percentage rate *n* 年度成本百分率; **~ report** *n* 年度报告; **~ ring** *n* 年轮

annuity /əˈnjuːəti, Amer -ˈnuː-/ *n* [1] (fixed sum) 年金; **life** *or* **lifetime ~** 终身年金 [2] Insur 年金保险

annul /əˈnʌl/ *vt* (*pres p etc.* **-ll-**) 宣告…无效 ‹*marriage, contract*›; 废除 ‹*law*›

annular /ˈænjʊlə(r)/ *adj* 环状的; **an ~ eclipse** 日环食

annulment /əˈnʌlmənt/ *n* (of marriage, contract) 宣告无效; (of law) 废除

Annunciation /əˌnʌnsɪˈeɪʃn/ *n* [1] Relig **the ~** 天使传报 [2] (festival) 圣母领报节 [3月25日]

anode /ˈænəʊd/ *n* 阳极

anodyne /ˈænədaɪn/ *adj* [1] (inoffensive) 无锋芒的 [2] pej (bland) 平淡乏味的

anoint /əˈnɔɪnt/ *vt* [1] Relig 涂油于 [2] (appoint to high office) 施涂油礼以示…已就高职; **to be sb.'s ~ed heir** 成为某人的选定继承人

anomalous /əˈnɒmələs/ *adj* 反常的

anomaly /əˈnɒməli/ *n* (situation, law, fact) 反常的事物; (person) 与众不同的人

anon /əˈnɒn/ *adv* dated hum 不久; **see you ~** 再见; **more of that ~** 此事容日后再谈

anon. /əˈnɒn/ *abbr* = **anonymous 2**

anonymity /ˌænəˈnɪməti/ *n* [u] [1] (being unknown) 匿名; **to preserve one's ~** 不透露真实姓名 [2] (uniformity) 无个性特征; **the ~ of much 20th century architecture** 许多 20 世纪建筑设计风格的千篇一律

anonymous /əˈnɒnɪməs/ *adj* [1] (not made public) 名字不公开的 [2] (not identified by name) 匿名的; **to wish to remain ~** 不希望披露姓名; **an ~ gift** 匿名赠送的礼物 [3] (unremarkable) 无个性特征的; **an ~ little town** 普普通通的小镇

anonymously /əˈnɒnɪməsli/ *adv* 匿名地; **to donate money ~** 匿名捐款

anorak /ˈænəræk/ *n* [1] (jacket) 带风帽厚夹克 [2] Brit colloq pej 怪僻的呆子

anorexia (nervosa) /ˌænəˈreksɪə (nɜːˈvəʊsə)/ *n* [u] 神经性厌食症

anorexic /ˌænəˈreksɪk/
[A] *adj* 患神经性厌食症的
[B] *n* 神经性厌食症患者

another /əˈnʌðə(r)/
[A] *det* [1] (an additional) 再一的; **would you like ~ drink?** 想再喝一杯吗？; **they want to have ~ child** 他们想再要个孩子; **in ~ five months** 再过 5 个月; **we have received yet ~ letter/complaint** 我们又收到一封信/一起投诉 [2] (a different) 另一的; **~ time** 下次; **he has ~ job/girlfriend now** 他现在有新工作/新女友了; **that's quite ~ matter** 那完全是另一回事; **to put it ~ way** 换言之 [3] (a new) 一个类似的; **she'll be ~ Garbo** 她将成为又一个嘉宝
[B] *pron* [1] (an additional) 再一; **can I have ~?** 我能再来一份吗？; **it's a bill — oh, not ~!** 这是账单——啾，别又来一张！ [2] (a different one) 另一; **to go from one house to ~** 挨家挨户地去; **she loves ~** liter 她另有所爱; **~ of the witnesses said that ...** 另一位证人说…; **one after ~** 一个接一个地; **she tried on one hat after ~** 她试了一顶又一顶帽子; **for one reason or ~** 由于某种原因; **of one kind** *or* **sort** *or* **type or ~** 各种不同的; **in one way or ~** 以某种方式; **ignorance is one thing, vulgarity is quite ~** 无知是一回事，庸俗则完全是另一回事 [3] (a new one) (person) 类似的人; (thing) 类似的事物; **there'll never be ~ like him** 不会再有像他那样的人了

ANSI *abbr* = **American National Standards Institute**

answer /ˈɑːnsə(r), Amer ˈænsər/
[A] *n* [1] (reply) 回答; **to give an ~** 作出答复; **she's too cheeky; she always has an ~!** 她脸皮太厚，总有说辞！; **there was no ~** (on phone) 没人接; (at door) 没人应门; **a written ~, an ~ in writing** 书面回复; **a ready ~** 不假思索的回答; **I won't take no for an ~!** 不许拒绝！; **there's no ~ to that!** 对此无话可说！ [2] (solution) 解决办法; **this could be the ~ to all our problems** 这可能会是解决我们所有问题的办法; **the right/wrong ~** 正确/错误的答案; **to have** *or* **know all the ~s** （自以为）什么都知道 [3] Jur 答辩; **an ~ to a charge** 对指控的辩解
[B] *vt* [1] (reply to) 回答 ‹*person, question*›; 回应 ‹*attack, criticism*›; **he must ~ the invitation** 他必须回复请帖; **to ~ that ...** 回答说…; **to ~ the door** *or* **bell** 应门; **to ~ the telephone** 接电话 [2] Jur 答辩; **to ~ a charge** 对指控进行辩解; **his lawyer claimed there was no case to ~** 他的律师宣称无须答辩 [3] (satisfy) 满足 ‹*needs*›; 符合 ‹*purpose*›
[C] *vi* [1] (respond) 回应; **to ~ to the name of ...** 名叫… [2] (be suitable) 符合; **to ~ to the**

description (of sb./sth.) 符合（对某人/某物的）描述

Phrasal verbs

• **answer back**
A *vi* **1** (defend oneself) 辩解 **2** (respond cheekily) 顶嘴
B *vt* [~ **sb. back**] 和…顶嘴

• **answer for** *vt* [~ **for sth.**]
1 (be responsible for) 对…负责; **he will have to ~ for his crimes one day** 总有一天，他得为自己的罪行负责 **2** (speak for) 代表…讲话; (speak in support of) 证明; **I can ~ for the truth of what she says** 我可以证明她的话属实

• **answer to** *vt* [~ **to sb.**] 向…负责; **all the sales assistants ~ directly to the store manager** 所有售货员都向商店经理直接负责

answerable /ˈɑːnsərəbl, Amer ˈæns-/ *adj* **1** (accountable) 有责任的; **to be ~ for sth.** 应对…负责 ‹*decision, actions*›; **to be ~ to sb.** 向某人负责 **2** (able to be answered) 可答复的 ‹*question*›; 可反驳的 ‹*argument*›

answering: ~ machine *n* 电话答录机; **~ service** *n* 代接电话服务

answerphone /ˈɑːnsəfəʊn, Amer ˈæns-/ *n* 电话答录机

ant /ænt/ *n* 蚂蚁; **to have ~s in one's pants** colloq 焦躁不安

antacid /æntˈæsɪd/
A *n* 解酸剂
B *adj* 解酸的

antagonism /ænˈtæɡənɪzəm/ *n* [u and c] 敌意; **to feel ~ against** *or* **to** *or* **towards sb./sth.** 对某人/某事物怀有敌对情绪; **the old ~s** 宿怨

antagonist /ænˈtæɡənɪst/ *n* 对手

antagonistic /ænˌtæɡəˈnɪstɪk/ *adj* **1** (hostile) 敌对的; **to be ~ to** *or* **towards sb./sth.** 对某人/某事物持敌对态度 **2** (mutually opposed) 相对抗的; **the two ideas are mutually ~** 这两个观点截然相反

antagonize /ænˈtæɡənaɪz/ *vt* (annoy) 引起…的反感; (arouse hostility) 引起…的敌意; **I don't want to ~ him** 我不想惹恼他

Antarctic /ænˈtɑːktɪk/
A *pr n* **the ~** 南极地区
B *adj* (*also* **antarctic**) 南极地区的

Antarctica /ænˈtɑːktɪkə/ *pr n* 南极洲

Antarctic: ~ Circle *n* 南极圈; **~ Ocean** *n* 南大洋

ante /ˈænti/
A *n* [u] 赌注; **to up the ~** lit 加大赌注; fig 提高要求
B *vt* 投入

anteater /ˈæntiːtə(r)/ *n* 食蚁动物

antecedent /ˌæntɪˈsiːdnt/
A *n* **1** (preceding thing) 前事; (preceding circumstance) 前情; **the ~s of our modern political institutions** 现代政治建制的前身 **2** (ancestor) 祖先
B *adj* 先前的

antechamber /ˈæntɪtʃeɪmbə(r)/ *n* = **anteroom**

antedate /ˌæntɪˈdeɪt/ *vt* **1** (put earlier date on) 在…上填写更早的日期; **the document had been ~d by three days** 该文件的日期填早了3天 **2** (predate) 先于; **to ~ sth. by several centuries** 早于某事物几个世纪

antediluvian /ˌæntɪdɪˈluːvɪən/ *adj* 陈旧的

antelope /ˈæntɪləʊp/ *n* (*pl* **~** *or* **~s**) 羚羊

antenatal /ˌæntɪˈneɪtl/
A *adj* 产前的
B *n* [u] 产前检查

antenatal: ~ class *n* 产前学习班; **~ clinic** *n* 产前检查诊所; **~ complications** *npl* 产前并发症; **~ ward** *n* 产前病房

antenna /ænˈtenə/ *n* **1** (*pl* **antennae** /ænˈteniː/) Zool 触角 **2** (*pl* **antennae** *or* **~s**) esp Amer (aerial) 天线

antepenultimate /ˌæntɪpəˈnʌltɪmət/ *adj* 倒数第三的

ante-post *adj* Brit 赛马号码公布前下注的

anterior /ænˈtɪərɪə(r)/ *adj* **1** esp Anat, Biol (in position) 前部的 **2** formal (in time) 先前的

anteroom /ˈæntɪruːm, -rʊm/ *n* (room leading to a larger one) 前厅; (waiting room) 候见室

antheap /ˈænthiːp/ *n* = **anthill**

anthem /ˈænθəm/ *n* 颂歌

anther /ˈænθə(r)/ *n* 花药

anthill /ˈænthɪl/ *n* 蚁冢

anthology /ænˈθɒlədʒɪ/ *n* 选集

anthracite /ˈænθrəsaɪt/ *n* [u] 无烟煤

anthrax /ˈænθræks/ ▸**p. 377** *n* [u] 炭疽

anthropoid /ˈænθrəpɔɪd/
A *adj* 类人的
B *n* 类人猿

anthropological /ˌænθrəpəˈlɒdʒɪkl/ *adj* 人类学的

anthropologist /ˌænθrəˈpɒlədʒɪst/ ▸**p. 409** *n* 人类学家

anthropology /ˌænθrəˈpɒlədʒɪ/ *n* [u] 人类学

anthropomorphic /ˌænθrəpəˈmɔːfɪk/ *adj* **1** (of or relating to anthropomorphism) 拟人化的 **2** (human-like) 人格化的

anthropomorphism /ˌænθrəpəˈmɔːfɪzəm/ *n* [u] 拟人化

anthroposophy /ˌænθrəˈpɒsəfɪ/ *n* [u] 人智学

anti /ˈænti/ *prep* 反对; **to be ~ sth.** 反对某事物

antiabortion /ˌæntɪəˈbɔːʃn/ *adj attrib* 反对堕胎的

antiabortionist /ˌæntɪəˈbɔːʃənɪst/ *n* 反堕胎者

anti-aircraft *adj attrib* 防空的; **an ~ gun** 高射炮

anti-apartheid *adj* 反种族隔离的

antiauthoritarian /ˌæntɪɔːθɒrɪˈteərɪən/ *adj* 反权威的

antibacterial /ˌæntɪbækˈtɪərɪəl/ *adj* 抗菌的

antiballistic /ˌæntɪbəˈlɪstɪk/ *adj* 反弹道导弹的 ‹*warfare, satellite*›; **an ~ missile** 反弹道导弹

antibiotic /ˌæntɪbaɪˈɒtɪk/
A *n* 抗生素
B *adj* 抗生的

antibody /ˈæntɪbɒdi/ *n* 抗体

Antichrist /ˈæntɪkraɪst/ *n* **1** **the ~** 敌基督 **2** (opponent of Christ) 反对基督者; (opponent of the Christian church) 反对基督教者

anticipate /ænˈtɪsɪpeɪt/ *vt* **1** (expect) 预料; **as ~d** 正如所料; **I didn't ~ him doing that** 我没料到他会那样做; **to ~ trouble/difficulty** 往坏处/难处想 **2** (guess in advance) 预见…并作准备; **she ~s all her mother's needs** 她能预知并满足母亲的所有需求 **3** (look forward to) 期望 **4** (prefigure) 是…的先驱; **these early sketches ~ her later work** 这些早期的素描是她后来作品的铺垫

anticipation /ænˌtɪsɪˈpeɪʃn/ *n* **1** (expectation) 预料; **in ~ of sth.** 预计到某事物; **thanking you in ~** (in letter) 预致谢意 **2** (eagerness) 期望; **in ~ of sth.** 期待着某事物; **in ~** 期待地

anticipatory /ænˌtɪsɪˈpeɪtəri/ *adj* formal 预先的 ‹*precautions, action*›; 期望的 ‹*delight, pleasure*›; **to take ~ measures** 采取预先措施

anticlerical /ˌæntɪˈklerɪkl/ *adj* 反教权主义的

anticlericalism /ˌæntɪˈklerɪkəlɪzəm/ *n* [u] 反教权主义

anticlimax /ˌæntɪˈklaɪmæks/ *n* 令人扫兴的结尾; **there was a sense of ~** 有一种虎头蛇尾的感觉

anticline /ˈæntɪklaɪn/ *n* 背斜（层）

anticlockwise /ˌæntɪˈklɒkwaɪz/ *adj, adv* Brit 逆时针的（地）

anticoagulant /ˌæntɪkəʊˈæɡjʊlənt/
A *adj* 抗凝血的
B *n* 抗凝血剂

anticorrosive /ˌæntɪkəˈrəʊsɪv/ *adj* 防腐蚀的

antics /ˈæntɪks/ *npl* 滑稽的举止

anticyclone /ˌæntɪˈsaɪkləʊn/ *n* 反气旋

antidandruff /ˌæntɪˈdændrʌf/ *adj attrib* 去头屑的

antidepressant /ˌæntɪdɪˈpresənt/
A *adj* 抗抑郁的
B *n* 抗抑郁药

antidote /ˈæntɪdəʊt/ *n* **1** Med 解毒药 **2** fig 对抗手段; **laughter is a good ~ for** *or* **to stress** 笑是解压的灵药

anti-establishment *adj* 反正统的

anti-European *adj* 反对欧洲联合的

antifreeze /ˈæntɪfriːz/ *n* 防冻剂

antigen /ˈæntɪdʒən/ *n* 抗原

anti-glare *adj* 防眩光的

anti-globalization *n* [u] 反全球化; **the ~ movement** 反全球化运动

Antigua and Barbuda /ænˌtiːɡwə ənd bɑːˈbuːdə/ *pr n* 安提瓜和巴布达

anti-hero *n* [小说、戏剧中缺乏英雄品格的] 反主角

antihistamine /ˌæntɪˈhɪstəmɪn/ *n* 抗组胺药

anti-inflammatory
A *adj* 消炎的
B *n* 消炎药

anti-inflation *adj attrib* 遏制通货膨胀的

anti-inflationary *adj* 遏制通货膨胀的

antiknock /ˈæntɪnɒk/ *n* 抗爆剂

Antilles /ænˈtɪliːz/ *pr npl* **the ~** 安的列斯群岛

anti-lock *adj attrib* 防抱死制动的

antilogarithm /ˌæntɪˈlɒɡərɪðəm, Amer -ˈlɔːɡ-/ *n* 反对数

antimacassar /ˌæntɪməˈkæsə(r)/ *n* (for back of chair) 靠背套; (for arms of chair) 扶手套

antimagnetic /ˌæntɪmæɡˈnetɪk/ *adj* 防磁的

anti-marketeer *n* Brit 反对英国加入欧盟的人

antimatter /ˈæntɪmætə(r)/ *n* [u] 反物质

antimissile /ˈæntɪmɪsaɪl, Amer -mɪsl/ *adj* 反导弹的

antimony /ˈæntɪməni, Amer -məʊni/ *n* [u] 锑

antinuclear /ˌæntɪˈnjuːklɪə(r), Amer -ˈnuː-/ *adj* 反对使用核武器的

antinuke /ˌæntɪˈnjuːk, Amer -ˈnuːk/ *adj* colloq = **antinuclear**

antiparticle /ˈæntɪˌpɑːtɪkl/ *n* 反粒子

antipathetic /ˌæntɪpəˈθetɪk/ *adj* 感到厌恶的; **to be ~ to** *or* **towards sb./sth.** 对某人/某事物感到厌恶

antipathy /ænˈtɪpəθɪ/ *n* 强烈的厌恶; **~ to** *or* **towards** *or* **against sb./sth.** 对某人/某事物的强烈厌恶; **~ between sb. and sb.** 某人和某人之间的嫌隙

antipersonnel /ˌæntɪˌpɜːsəˈnel/ *adj attrib* 杀伤性的

antiperspirant /ˌæntɪˈpɜːspɪrənt/
A *n* 止汗剂
B *adj* 止汗的

Antipodean /ænˌtɪpəˈdiːən/
A *adj* **1** (of Australia) 澳大利亚的 **2** (of New Zealand) 新西兰的
B *n* **1** (Australian) 澳大利亚人 **2** (New Zealander) 新西兰人

a

Antipodes /æn'tɪpədiːz/ *npl* **the ～** 澳大利亚和新西兰

antiquarian /ˌæntɪ'kweərɪən/ ▸**p. 409**
A *adj* 古文物研究的
B *n* (dealer) 古董商; (scholar) 古文物研究者; (collector) 古文物收藏家

antiquarian: ～ bookseller *n* 古籍商; **～ bookshop** *n* 古籍书店

antiquark /'æntɪkwɑːk/ *n* 反夸克

antiquated /'æntɪkweɪtɪd/ *adj* 陈旧的

antique /æn'tiːk/
A *n* 古董
B *adj* **1** (historical) 古时的 ‹*furniture, weapons*› **2** (old-style) 古式的 ‹*oak, mirror*›

antique: ～ dealer ▸**p. 409** *n* 古董商; **～ fair, ～s fair** *ns* 古董市场; **～ shop** *n* 古董商店

antiquity /æn'tɪkwəti/ *n* **1** [u] (ancient times) 古代 **2** [u] (great age) 古老; **of great ～** 非常古老的 **3** [c] (object) 古物; (architecture) 古迹

anti-racism *n* [u] 反种族歧视

antiracist /ˌæntɪ'reɪsɪst/
A *adj* 反种族主义的
B *n* 反种族主义者

antireligious /ˌæntɪrɪ'lɪdʒəs/ *adj* 反宗教的

anti-riot *adj attrib* 防暴的; **the ～ squad** 防暴队

anti-roll bar *n* 角位移横向平衡杆

antirrhinum /ˌæntɪ'raɪnəm/ *n* 金鱼草

anti-rust *adj attrib* 防锈的

anti-segregationist
A *adj* 反种族隔离的
B *n* 反对种族隔离的人

anti-Semite *n* 反犹分子

anti-Semitic *adj* 反犹的

anti-Semitism /ˌæntɪ'semɪtɪzəm/ *n* [u] 反犹主义

antiseptic /ˌæntɪ'septɪk/
A *n* 抗菌剂
B *adj* **1** (preventing sepsis) 防腐的 ‹*lotion*› **2** (sterile) 无菌的; **an ～ bandage** 消毒绷带

anti-skid *adj attrib* 防滑的

anti-slavery *adj* 反奴隶制的

anti-smoking *adj* 反对吸烟的

antisocial /ˌæntɪ'səʊʃl/ *adj* **1** (annoying) 令人讨厌的 **2** (reclusive) 不爱社交的 **3** (inhibiting social life) 妨碍社交的 ‹*work, shift, timetable*›; **extra payment for working ～ hours** 休息时间加班的额外报酬

antisocial behaviour order *n* 反社会行为令 [用以约束行为对公众造成危害的人的指令]

anti-spam *adj attrib* 反垃圾邮件的

anti-submarine *adj attrib* 反潜的

anti-tank *adj attrib* 反坦克的

anti-terrorist *adj attrib* 反恐怖主义的; **～ forces** 反恐部队

anti-theft *adj attrib* 防盗的

antithesis /æn'tɪθəsɪs/ *n* (*pl* **antitheses** /-siːz/) **1** (opposite) 对立物; **his behaviour was the ～ of good manners** 他的行为很不礼貌 **2** (contrast) 对照; **her views are in complete ～ to his** 她的想法和他完全相反

antithetical /ˌæntɪ'θetɪkl/, **antithetic** /ˌæntɪ'θetɪk/ *adj attrib* 对立的; **to be ～ to sth.** 与某事物相对立

antitoxic /ˌæntɪ'tɒksɪk/ *adj* 抗毒的

antitoxin /ˌæntɪ'tɒksɪn/ *n* 抗毒素

antitrust /ˌæntɪ'trʌst/ *adj attrib* Amer 反托拉斯的

antiviral /ˌæntɪ'vaɪərəl/
A *adj* **1** Med 抗病毒的 **2** Comput 防病毒的
B *n* Med 抗病毒药物

antivirus software /ˌæntɪ'vaɪərəs ˌsɒftweə(r), Amer ˌsɔːft-/ *n* [u] 防病毒软件

anti-vivisection *adj* 反对动物活体解剖的

anti-vivisectionist *n* 反对动物活体解剖的人

anti-war *adj* 反战的

antler /'æntlə(r)/ *n* 鹿角

antonym /'æntənɪm/ *n* 反义词

Antrim /'æntrɪm/ *pr n* 安特里姆郡

antsy /'æntsi/ *adj* Amer colloq 烦躁的; **to feel ～** 感到坐立不安

anus /'eɪnəs/ *n* (*pl* **～es**) 肛门

anvil /'ænvɪl/ *n* 铁砧

anxiety /æŋ'zaɪəti/ *n* **1** (apprehension) 焦虑; **to feel great ～ about sth.** 对某事物感到焦虑不已; **～ for sb./sth.** 对某人/某事物的担心; **～ neurosis** 焦虑性神经症 **2** (source of worry) 令人焦虑的事; **the child's illness is a great ～ to her** 孩子的病让她焦虑万分 **3** (eagerness) 渴望; **a great ～ to please** 急于讨好的心情

anxiety attack *n* 焦虑的发作

anxious /'æŋkʃəs/ *adj* **1** (worried) 焦虑的; **to be ～ about doing sth.** 为做某事而发愁; **to be ～ about sb./sth.** 为某人/某事物担心 **2** (causing worry) 令人焦虑的 ‹*moment, time*› **3** (eager) 渴望的; **I am ～ for him to know** *or* **that he should know** 我急于让他知道; **she is most ～ to meet you** 她急于同你会面

anxiously /'æŋkʃəsli/ *adv* 焦虑地

anxiousness /'æŋkʃəsnɪs/ *n* **= anxiety 1, 3**

any /'eni/
A *det* **1** (in questions and conditional sentences) 一些; (with negative or implied negative) 丝毫的; **is there ～ tea/bread?** 有茶/面包吗? ; **if I can help in ～ way** 如果我能帮上忙的话; **he hasn't got ～ money/food** 他一点儿钱/吃的也没有; **we want to avoid ～ trouble** 我们根本不想惹麻烦; **he managed it without ～ difficulty** 他毫不费力地完成了这件事 **2** (in positive sentences) 任何的; **～ hat/pen will do** 什么帽子/笔都行; **he might return at ～ time** 他随时都可能回来; **～ one** 任何一个的; **～ number** *or* **quantity** *or* **amount of ...** 大量的…; **there are ～ number of reasons to be sceptical about it** 有很多理由怀疑它 **3** (ordinary) 一般的; **not just ～ ...** 不寻常的…; **it isn't just ～ day: it's my birthday** 今天不是一般的日子: 是我的生日
B *pron* **1** (with negative or implied negative) 丝毫; **he hasn't got ～** 他一点儿也没有; **she doesn't like ～ of them** 她不喜欢他们中的任何一个; **I've spent hardly ～ of the money** 这钱我几乎一点儿也没花; **he returned without ～ of the others** 就他一个人回来了; **sb. isn't having ～ of it** (is not interested) 某人对此毫无兴趣; (does not agree) 某人不同意这点 **2** (in questions and conditional sentences) 一些; **did ～ of you see it?** 你们有人见过它吗? ; **I'd like some tea, if you have ～** 如果你有茶的话，我想喝一口; **very few, if ～, knew the truth** 几乎没人知道真相 **3** (in positive sentences) 任何一个; **take ～ you like** 你喜欢哪个就拿哪个; **～ of ...** …中的任何一个; **～ of those pens will do** 那些笔随便哪一支都行
C *adv* 丝毫; **is he feeling ～ better?** 他身体好些了吗? ; **I can't leave ～ later than 6 o'clock** 我绝对不能晚于 6 点离开; **I don't like him ～ more than you do** 我和你一样不喜欢他; **you don't love me ～ more** *or* **longer** 你不再爱我了; **if you don't say anything, no one will be ～ the wiser** 如果你什么都不说，谁也不会知道; **that doesn't help me ～** esp Amer colloq 那对我没用; **it didn't bother him ～** esp Amer colloq 他根本不在乎

anybody /'enɪbɒdi/ *pron* **1** (with negative or implied negative) 任何人; **without ～ hearing her/knowing** 没有任何人听见她说的话/知道; **is ～ there?** 那儿有人吗? ; **if ～ asks, say he's ill** 如果有人问起，就说他病了; **hardly ～ came** 几乎没人来; **I don't like him, and neither does ～ else** 我不喜欢他，别人也都不喜欢; **I haven't met ～ new** 我还没见到过新来的人 **2** (in positive sentences) 随便哪个人; **～ can make a mistake** 谁都会犯错; **～ but Anne** 除安妮以外的任何人; **～ with any intelligence would realize that ...** 稍微有点头脑的人都会意识到…; **～ else would have screamed** 换了谁都会大叫的 **3** (somebody important) 重要人物; **he is not just ～** 他不只是个大人物; **～ who was ～ was at the party** 所有头面人物都参加了聚会

anyhow /'enɪhaʊ/ *adv* **1** **= anyway 1** **2** (in a careless, untidy way) 随便地; (not in any order) 杂乱无章地; **there were clothes scattered around the room ～** 屋子里衣服扔得到处都是; **they splashed the paint on ～** 他们胡乱泼了些油漆

anyone /'enɪwʌn/ *pron* **= anybody**

anyplace /'enɪpleɪs/ *adv* Amer colloq **= anywhere**

anything /'enɪθɪŋ/ *pron* **1** (with negative, in questions, conditional sentences) 任何事物; **I didn't say/do ～** 我什么也没说/没做; **if ～ happens to him ...** 如果他有个三长两短…; **is there ～ in what he says?** 他说的是实话吗? ; **not for ～** 决不; **not to think ～ of sth./doing sth.** 认为某事物/做某事很平常; **～ like/near sth.** 多少有点像某事物; **or ～** colloq 或类似的事情; **I hope she isn't ill or ～** 我希望她没有生病什么的; **if ～** 真要说起来; **if ～, he was quite pleased** 其实他是蛮高兴的 **2** (in positive sentences) 无论什么; **～ is possible** 一切皆有可能; **it could cost ～ between £50 and £100** 它的价格可能在 50 到 100 英镑之间; **as ... as ～** colloq 极其…; **as boring/easy as ～** 非常乏味/容易; **～ but** 丝毫不; **he was ～ but happy/a liar** 他一点也不高兴/根本不是骗子; **was it fun? — ～ but!** colloq 好玩吗? ——一点儿都不! ; **～ goes** colloq 随便什么都行; **like ～** colloq 非常迅猛地; **to run/work like ～** 拼命奔跑/工作

anytime /'enɪtaɪm/ *adv* (*also* **any time**) esp Amer 在任何时候; **come ～ you like** 你什么时候来都行; **will she be back ～ soon?** 她很快就会回来吗?

anyway /'enɪweɪ/ *adv* **1** (in any case, besides) 无论如何; **I don't want to go, and ～ I have to wait for Debbie** 我不想去，反正我还得等黛比; **～, we arrived at the station** 不管怎样，我们到达了火车站 **2** (nevertheless) 不过; **I don't really like hats, but I'll try it on ～** 我不太喜欢戴帽子，不过还是会试一试这顶; **thanks ～** 不过还是谢谢你 **3** (at least, at any rate) 至少; **we can't go out, not yet ～** 我们不能出去，至少现在不能; **that's what he said ～** 至少他是这么说的 **4** (well) [用作句子副词，无明确意义]; **～, let's forget about that for a moment** 好吧，咱们暂时别再提这件事了

anywhere /'enɪweə(r)/
A *adv* **1** (in any place) 在任何地方; (to any place) 去任何地方; **we didn't go ～ special/interesting** 我们没去什么特别/有趣的地方; **I'll go ～ where there's sun** 只要有阳光的地方我都想去; **have you seen Andrew ～?** 你在什么地方见过安德鲁吗? ; **I didn't come ～** (in contests) 我没有取得名次; **we're going to Spain, if ～** 我们要去就去西班牙; **she's not ～ near ready/as clever** 她远没有准备好/那么聪明 **2** (within a range) 介于…之间; **～ between 50 and 100 people** 介于 50 到 100 人之间
B *pron* 任何地方; **I don't have ～ to stay** 我没有地方可待

Anzac /'ænzæk/ *abbr* Hist **= Australia-New Zealand Army Corps** 澳新军团士兵

Anzac Day *pr n* 澳新军团节

AOB *abbr* Brit **= any other business** 任何其他事项

AOD *abbr* **= audio on demand** 音频点播

aorist /'eərɪst/ *n* 不定过去时

aorta /eɪ'ɔːtə/ *n* 主动脉

aortic /eɪ'ɔːtɪk/ *adj* 主动脉的

AP *abbr* **= Associated Press**

apace /ə'peɪs/ *adv* liter **1** (quickly) 迅速地 **2** (abreast) 齐头并进地; **to keep ～ with sth.** 与某事物并驾齐驱

Apache /ə'pætʃi/ ▸**p. 503, p. 426** *n* 阿帕切人

apart /ə'pɑːt/
A *adv* **1** (at a distance in time or space) 相隔; **the trees were planted 10 metres ～** 这些树每隔 10 米种一棵; **stand with one's feet** *or* **legs ～** 叉开腿站着; **be born 3 years ～** 相差 3 年出生 **2** (living or staying separately from each other) 分开地; (aloof) 疏远地; **they need to be kept ～** 得让他们分开生活; **she keeps herself ～ from other people** 她与其他人保持距离 **3** (to or on one side) 在一边; **he took me ～ for a quiet talk** 他把我带到一边私下谈话 **4** (leaving aside) 除外; **dogs ～, I don't like animals** 除了狗，我不喜欢动物 **5** (expressing uniqueness) 与众不同地; **a race/world ～** 独特的种族/世界; **his work is in a class ～** 他的作品别具一格 **6** (different) 有分歧地; **to be worlds ～ from ...** 与…截然不同; **we are very far ～ on the subject of immigration** 我们对移民问题的看法大相径庭 **7** (in pieces) 零碎地; **he had the TV ～ on the floor** 他把电视机放在地板上拆散了
B **apart from** *prep phr* **1** (except for) 除了…外（别无）; **the car was empty ～ from the dog** 车上空空的，只有这条狗 **2** (in addition to) 除了…外（还有）; **～ from being illegal, it's also dangerous** 这事不但违法，还有危险

apartheid /ə'pɑːteɪt, -aɪt/ *n* [u] [南非的] 种族隔离

apartment /ə'pɑːtmənt/
A *n* esp Amer 公寓套间
B **apartments** *npl* [宫殿或豪华住宅的] 套间

apartment: ～ block *n* 公寓大楼; **～ hotel** *n* 公寓式酒店; **～ house** *n* 公寓楼

apathetic /ˌæpə'θetɪk/ *adj* 冷淡的; **he is very ～ towards his family** 他对家人非常冷漠

apathy /'æpəθi/ *n* [u] 冷淡; **public ～ to politics** 公众对政治的淡漠

APB *abbr* **= all points bulletin**

ape /eɪp/
A *n* **1** Zool 猿 **2** fig pej (person) 粗笨的大汉 **3** **to go ～ over** *or* **about sb./sth.** Amer colloq 为某人/某事物如痴如狂
B *vt* pej 模仿; **to ～ the ways of sb.** 学某人的样子

APEC *abbr* **= Asia-Pacific Economic Cooperation** 亚太经济合作组织

aperitif /ə'perətɪf, Amer əˌperə'tiːf/ *n* 开胃酒

aperture /'æpətʃʊə(r)/ *n* **1** (small gap) 隙缝; (in wall, door) 孔 **2** (in telescope, camera) 孔径

apeshit /'eɪpʃɪt/ *adj* taboo sl **to go ～ (over sth.)** （为某事物）勃然大怒

APEX /'eɪpeks/ *abbr* **= Advance Purchase Excursion** 优惠票预订

apex /'eɪpeks/ *n* (*pl* **～es** *or* **apices** /'eɪpɪsiːz/) **1** (highest point) 顶; fig 顶峰; **the ～ of the mountain** 山顶; **to reach the ～ of one's career** 达到事业的顶峰 **2** Math 顶点

aphelion /ap'hiːlɪən/ *n* (*pl* **aphelia** /-lɪə/) 远日点

aphid /'eɪfɪd/ *n* 蚜虫

aphorism /'æfərɪzəm/ *n* 格言

aphrodisiac /ˌæfrə'dɪziæk/
A *n* 催欲剂
B *adj* 激发性欲的

API *abbr* **1** **= application programming interface** **2** **= air pollution index** 空气污染指数

apiarist /'eɪpɪərɪst/ ▸**p. 409** *n* 养蜂人

apiary /'eɪpɪəri, Amer -ɪeri/ *n* 养蜂场

apiece /ə'piːs/ *adv* (person) 每人; (thing) 每个; **an apple ～** 每人一个苹果; **one dollar ～** 每个一美元

aplenty /ə'plenti/ *adj postpos* 丰富的; **there are apples ～ for all of you** 苹果很多，足够你们每个人吃的

aplomb /ə'plɒm/ *n* [u] 沉着; **with great ～** 泰然自若地

apocalypse /ə'pɒkəlɪps/ *n* **1** Relig 世界末日 **2** (violent event) 大灾变; **a stock market ～** 股票市场的崩盘

apocalyptic /əˌpɒkə'lɪptɪk/ *adj* 预示大灾变的

apocryphal /ə'pɒkrɪfl/ *adj* 真实性可疑的; **an ～ story** 杜撰的故事

apogee /'æpədʒiː/ *n* **1** Astron 远地点 **2** fig 最高点; **the ～ of one's career** 事业的顶峰

apolitical /ˌeɪpə'lɪtɪkl/ *adj* (uninterested) 不关心政治的; (unbiased) 无政治倾向的

apologetic /əˌpɒlə'dʒetɪk/ *adj* 表示歉意的; **an ～ letter** 道歉信; **to be ～ about sth.** 为某事物感到惭愧

apologetically /əˌpɒlə'dʒetɪkli/ *adv* 表示歉意地; **the child nodded ～** 那孩子点头认错了

apologia /ˌæpə'ləʊdʒɪə/ *n* formal 书面辩护

apologist /ə'pɒlədʒɪst/ *n* 辩护者; **an ～ for sth./sb.** 为某事/某人辩护的人

apologize /ə'pɒlədʒaɪz/ *vi* 道歉; **to ～ for sb./sth.** 为某人/某事道歉

apology /ə'pɒlədʒi/ *n* **1** (excuse) 道歉; **to make an ～ for sth.** 为某事道歉; **to send one's apologies** 为不能出席而致歉; **to publish an ～** 公开发表道歉信 **2** (poor substitute) 勉强的替代物; **he's an ～ for a husband!** 他当丈夫不够格! **3** (justification) 辩护

apoplectic /ˌæpə'plektɪk/ *adj* **1** (furious) 大怒的; **to be ～ (with rage)** 勃然大怒 **2** Med dated 中风的; **an ～ fit** 中风的发作

apoplexy /'æpəpleksi/ *n* [u] **1** (rage) 暴怒 **2** Med dated 中风

apostasy /ə'pɒstəsi/ *n* [u] 叛教; fig 变节

apostate /ə'pɒsteɪt/ formal
A *n* (defector) 叛教者; fig 变节者
B *adj* (traitorous) 叛教的; fig 变节的

a posteriori /ˌeɪ ˌpɒsterɪ'ɔːraɪ/ *adj, adv* formal 归纳的（地）

apostle /ə'pɒsl/ *n* **1** **Apostle** Relig 使徒; **the A～s' Creed** 使徒信经 **2** (follower) 鼓吹者

apostolic /ˌæpə'stɒlɪk/ *adj* (of the Apostles) 使徒的; (of the Pope) 教皇的

apostrophe /ə'pɒstrəfi/ *n* 撇号

ℹ Apologizing

■ In fairly formal contexts, the following constructions and phrases may be used to express apology:

I must apologize for what I have done
= 我必须为我做的事道歉

I apologize unreservedly for what I said
= 我为我说的话深表歉意

I must make an apology for the mess I made
= 我把事情弄糟了，我必须为此道歉

I owe you an apology, and take back all I said
= 我要向你道歉，并收回我说的话

I very much regret that I have had to cancel the appointment
= 我不得不取消约会，非常抱歉

I am sorry to inform you that I have to cancel the meeting
= 很抱歉通知你，我不得不取消会议

I must ask you to excuse my stupidity
= 请您原谅我的愚蠢

I hope you will pardon me for my carelessness
= 希望您能原谅我的粗心

Please forgive me for not having kept my promise
= 我失信了，请原谅

■ In less formal situations, the following phrases and expressions can be used:

Sorry!
or ***Excuse me!***
= 对不起！
or 不好意思！

Sorry about this
= 对不起了

Sorry I'm late
or ***Sorry for being late***
= 对不起，我迟到了

Sorry to bother you
or ***Sorry to disturb you***
= 对不起，打扰你了

Sorry to interrupt
= 对不起，打断一下

I'm very sorry, but I have to go
= 真对不起，我得走了

I'm sorry I can't go to the cinema with you
= 对不起，我不能和你一起去看电影

I'm sorry. I didn't mean that
= 对不起，我不是那意思

It was all my fault
= 都是我的错
or 都是我不好

I really feel bad about that
= 对那件事，我真的很难过

I'm terribly sorry for getting your name wrong
= 把你名字搞错了，实在对不起

Sorry to trouble you, but can I use your telephone?
= 打扰一下，我能用一下你的电话吗？

Excuse me, do you mind if I open the window?
= 不好意思，我把窗打开好吗？

Excuse me for a second
or ***Excuse me for a moment***
= 对不起，我要离开一会儿

a

apothecary /əˈpɒθəkəri, Amer -keri/ *n archaic* 药剂师

apotheosis /əˌpɒθɪˈəʊsɪs/ *n* (*pl* **apotheoses** /-siːz/) formal 完美的典型; **this piece of music is the ～ of classical style** 这首乐曲是古典风格的巅峰之作

app /æp/ *abbr* = **application 5**

appal /əˈpɔːl/ *vt* (*pres p etc.* **-ll-**) Brit 使惊骇; **to be ～led at** *or* **by sth.** 被某事物吓得魂不附体; **he was ～led to hear that ...** 他听到…后，惊恐万分

Appalachian /ˌæpəˈleɪtʃɪən/ *adj* 阿巴拉契亚山脉的; **the ～ Mountains** 阿巴拉契亚山脉

Appalachians /ˌæpəˈleɪtʃɪənz/ *pr npl* **the ～** 阿巴拉契亚山脉

appall /əˈpɔːl/ *vt* Amer = **appal**

appalling /əˈpɔːlɪŋ/ *adj* [1] (shocking) 骇人听闻的 ‹*crime, sight, damage*›; **an ～ waste of resources** 惊人的资源浪费 [2] (very bad) 极恶劣的 ‹*behaviour, manners*›; **an ～ smell** 极难闻的气味

appallingly /əˈpɔːlɪŋli/ *adv* [1] (shockingly) 骇人听闻地; **unemployment figures are high** 失业数字大得惊人 [2] (extremely) 非常; **an ～ difficult problem** 极难回答的问题

apparatchik /ˌæpəˈrɑːtʃɪk/ *n* hum pej 党政官僚; **a party ～** 党棍

apparatus /ˌæpəˈreɪtəs, Amer -ˈrætəs/ *n* (*pl* **～es**) [1] [u] (set of equipment) （成套）设备; **laboratory ～** 实验室设备; **photographic ～** 摄影器材; **heating ～** 取暖器 [2] [c] (piece of equipment) （一件）设备 [3] [c] (organization) 机构; **the ～ of government** 政府机构 [4] [u] Physiol 器官; **digestive ～** 消化器官 [5] [u] Literat 文学评论资料

apparel /əˈpærəl/ *n* [u] formal 衣服; **sports ～** 运动服; **women's ～** 女装; **bathing ～** 游泳衣

apparent /əˈpærənt/ *adj* [1] (clear) 明显的; **for no ～ reason** 无缘无故地 [2] (seeming) 表面上的; **her reluctance to sing was more ～ than real** 她表面上不想唱歌，其实不然

apparently /əˈpærəntli/ *adv* 明显地

apparition /ˌæpəˈrɪʃn/ *n* 幻影

appeal /əˈpiːl/

A *vi* [1] (call, request) 呼吁; **to ～ for sth.** 呼吁某事; **the manager ～ed for calm** 经理呼吁保持冷静; **to ～ to sb. for/to do sth.** 恳请某人给予某物/做某事; **he ～ed to the court for mercy** 他恳求法庭宽恕 [2] Jur 上诉; **to ～ to a higher court** 向上级法院申诉; **to ～ against sth.** 不服某事提出上诉 [3] Sport 诉诸裁判 [4] (attract, interest) 有吸引力; **does this colour ～ to you?** 这种颜色你喜欢吗？

B *n* [1] (call, request) 呼吁; **an ～ for sth.** 对某事的呼吁; **an ～ to sb.** 向某人发出的呼吁; **he made an ～ to the citizens for tolerance** 他恳请公民要宽容 [2] Jur 上诉; **to make** *or* **lodge an ～ against sth.** 不服某事提出上诉 [3] Sport 诉诸裁判 [4] (attraction, interest) 吸引力

appeal: ～ court = ~s court; **～ fund** *n* 救助金

appealing /əˈpiːlɪŋ/ *adj* [1] (attractive) 有吸引力的 [2] (beseeching) 恳求的

appealingly /əˈpiːlɪŋli/ *adv* [1] (attractively) 迷人地 ‹*smile*›; 有感染力地 ‹*speak*› [2] (beseechingly) 恳求地

appeal: ～ judge *n* 上诉法官; **～s court** *n* 上诉法庭

appear /əˈpɪə(r)/ *vi* [1] (become visible) 出现; **the ghost ～s on the stairs** 幽灵在楼梯上现身了 [2] (turn up) （突然）来到; **where did you ～ from?** 你从哪里冒出来的？ [3] (seem) 显得; **you ～ rather sad** 你好像很难过; **to ～ to be/do sth.** 似乎是某事物/在做某事; **to ～ (to sb.) that ...** （在某人）看来…; **it ～ed to me that we were in a dangerous position** 当时我觉得我们处境危险; **so it ～s, so it would ～** 看来如此 [4] Publg «*newspaper, magazine, journal, book*» 出版; «*article*» 发表; «*photograph*» 刊登 [5] Jur 出庭; **to ～ before the court** 出庭; **to ～ as a witness against/for the accused man** 作为证人出庭指证被告/为被告作证 [6] Theat (act) 演出; **to ～ as King Lear** 扮演李尔王 [7] (be present) 到场; **～ in person** 亲自到场

appearance /əˈpɪərəns/ *n* [1] (arrival) 到来; (becoming visible) 出现; **the ～ of the snowdrops heralds the start of spring** 雪花莲开花宣告春天的开始 [2] (look) 外表; **for the sake of ～s, for ～s' sake** 为了装点门面; **you shouldn't go by** *or* **judge by ～s** 你不应单从外表判断; **to all ～s** 从一切迹象来看; **to keep up ～s** 若无其事 [3] Publg (of newspaper, magazine, journal, book) 出版; (of article) 发表; (of photograph) 刊登 [4] Jur 出庭; **he has already had several court ～s** 他已经出庭好几次了 [5] (on stage, screen) 演出; (presence at function) 到场; **to put in** *or* **to make an ～** 露一下面; **a guest ～** 客串出演; **in order of ～** 按出场顺序

appease /əˈpiːz/ *vt* 抚慰 ‹*person*›; 平息 ‹*anger*›; 缓解 ‹*hunger*›

appeasement /əˈpiːzmənt/ *n* [1] (gen) 安抚 [2] Pol 绥靖; **a policy of ～** 绥靖政策

appellation /ˌæpəˈleɪʃn/ *n* formal 名称

append /əˈpend/ *vt* 附加; **will you ～ your signature?** 请附上您的签名好吗？

appendage /əˈpendɪdʒ/ *n* [1] Biol 附器 [2] (attachment) 附属物

appendectomy /ˌæpenˈdektəmi/, **appendicectomy** /əˌpendɪˈsektəmi/ *n* Brit 阑尾切除术

appendices /əˈpendɪsiːz/ *pl* ▸ **appendix**

appendicitis /əˌpendɪˈsaɪtɪs/ ▸ **p. 377** *n* [u] 阑尾炎

appendix /əˈpendɪks/ *n* (*pl* **～es** *or* **appendices**) [1] Anat 阑尾 [2] (of book, document) 附录

appertain /ˌæpəˈteɪn/ *vi* formal [1] (relate) 有关联; **to ～ to sb./sth.** 涉及某人/某事物 [2] (be applicable) 适用

appetite /ˈæpɪtaɪt/ *n* [1] lit 食欲; **he has a good/poor ～** 他食欲旺盛/不振; **to work up an ～** 激起食欲; **it'll spoil** *or* **take away your ～** 那会让你倒胃口 [2] fig 欲望; **he has no ～ for that sort of work** 他对那样的工作没兴趣

appetite suppressant *n* 食欲抑制剂

appetizer /ˈæpɪtaɪzə(r)/ *n* (food) 开胃菜; (drink) 开胃饮料

appetizing /ˈæpɪtaɪzɪŋ/ *adj* 引起食欲的

applaud /əˈplɔːd/

A *vi* 鼓掌

B *vt* [1] (clap) 向…鼓掌喝彩 [2] (approve of) 称赞

applause /əˈplɔːz/ *n* [u] 鼓掌

apple /ˈæpl/ *n* (fruit) 苹果; (tree) 苹果树; **the ～ of sb.'s eye** fig 掌上明珠; **there's a bad ～ in every bunch** 哪儿都有害群之马; **to upset the ～ cart** 打乱计划; **an ～ a day keeps the doctor away** Prov 天天吃苹果，医生远离我

apple: ～ blossom *n* 苹果花; **～ brandy** *n* 苹果白兰地（酒）; **～ core** *n* 苹果核

apple green ▸ **p. 134**

A *n* [u] 苹果绿

B *adj* 苹果绿的

applejack /ˈæpldʒæk/ *n* Amer 苹果酒

apple juice *n* 苹果汁

apple pie

A *n* [1] [c] Culin 苹果派 [2] [u] Amer (homeliness) 家庭的温馨

B *adj* Amer (characteristic of US values) **(as) American as ～** 地道美国式的

apple pie: ～ bed *n* 苹果派式床 [在对折的被单中夹藏怪异物品的恶作剧]; **～ order** *n* 整齐条理; **in ～ order** 井然有序

applet /ˈæplɪt/ *n* 小应用程序

apple tree *n* 苹果树

appliance /əˈplaɪəns/ *n* [1] [c] (device, piece of equipment) 器具; **an electrical ～** 电器 [2] [u] Brit (applying) 应用

applicability /ˌæplɪkəˈbɪləti, əˌplɪk-/ *n* [u] 适用性

applicable /ˈæplɪkəbl, əˈplɪk-/ *adj* (appropriate) 适当的; (able to be applied) 可应用的; **discounts where ～ are shown on the bill** 如有折扣，账单上会标明; **to be ～ to sb./sth.** 适用于某人/某事物

applicant /ˈæplɪkənt/ *n* 申请人; **a job/visa ～** 求职者/申请签证的人

application /ˌæplɪˈkeɪʃn/ *n* [1] [c] (request) 申请; **to make an ～ for sth.** 申请某事物; **to make a job ～** 提出求职申请; **～ for shares** 股票的申购; **to fill out a job/passport ～** 填写求职/护照申请表; **a letter of ～** 申请书 [2] [u] (use) (of law, penalty, rule) 实施; (of logic, theory, training) 应用; (of equipment) 用途; **the ～ of common sense might resolve the problem** 或许凭常识就能解决这个问题 [3] [c and u] (spreading) 敷用; **for external ～ only** 仅供外用 [4] [u] (diligence) 勤奋 [5] [c] Comput 应用程序

application: ～ form *n* 申请表; **～ programming interface** *n* 应用程序接口

applicator /ˈæplɪkeɪtə(r)/ *n* 涂抹器

applied /əˈplaɪd/ *adj* 应用的; **～ linguistics/mathematics/psychology** 应用语言学/数学/心理学; **a course in ～ arts** 应用工艺美术课

apply /əˈplaɪ/

A *vi* [1] (make request) 申请; **to ～ (to sb.) for sth./to do sth.** （向某人）申请某事物/做某事; **to ～ to college/university** 向学院/大学申请 [2] (be valid) «*rule, definition*» 适用; **that theory cannot ～ in this case** 那个理论不适用于这种情况; **to ～ to sb./sth.** 适用于某人/某事物; **that description doesn't ～ to him** 他不是描述的那个样子

B *vt* [1] (use) 应用; **to ～ the brake** 踩刹车; **he applied a slight pressure to the catch** 他轻轻按下门闩; **to ～ the theory to the practice** 将理论付诸实践 [2] (spread) 涂 ‹*cream, glue, paint*›

C *v refl* **to ～ oneself to sth.** (work hard at) 致力于某事物; (concentrate on) 专注于某事物

appoint /əˈpɔɪnt/ *vt* [1] (name) 任命; **he has been ～ed director** 他被任命为主任; **to ～ sb. as sth.** 任命某人担任某职务; **to ～ sb. to do sth.** 委派某人做某事 [2] (specify) 确定 ‹*time, place*› [3] (equip) 装设; **well ～ed** 陈设齐全的

appointee /əˌpɔɪnˈtiː/ *n* 被任命的人

appointment /əˈpɔɪntmənt/ *n* [1] [c] (meeting) 约会; **by ～** 根据约定; **to make an ～** 预约; **to break an ～** 失约 [2] [u] (selection for job) 任命 [3] [c] (job) 职位; **'～s'** (newspaper section) 招聘广告; **to take up an ～ (as sth.)** 就任（某职位）

apportion /əˈpɔːʃn/ *vt* 分配; **to ～ sth. among/between ...** 在…之间分配某物; **to ～ sth. to sb.** 把某物分给某人

apposite /ˈæpəzɪt/ *adj* 恰当的

apposition /ˌæpəˈzɪʃn/ *n* 同位; **in ～ to ...** 与…同位

appraisal /əˈpreɪzl/ *n* 评价; **to make an ～ of sth.** (estimation) 评价某事物; **to give an ～ of sth.** (statement of value) 给某物估价

appraise /əˈpreɪz/ *vt* [1] (examine critically) 评价 [2] (evaluate) 评估

appreciable /əˈpriːʃəbl/ *adj* 明显的

appreciably /əˈpriːʃəbli/ *adv* 明显地

appreciate /əˈpriːʃɪeɪt/
A *vt* **1▸** (be grateful for) 感谢; **an early reply would be ～d** 如蒙早复，不胜感激; **I ～ being consulted** 我很高兴能征求我的意见 **2▸** (understand) 意识到; **you don't ～ how hard he has worked** 你不了解他工作有多努力 **3▸** (enjoy) 欣赏
B *vi* Fin 升值

appreciation /əˌpriːʃɪˈeɪʃn/ *n* **1▸** [u] (gratitude) 感谢; **as a mark of (sb.'s) ～** 以表（某人的）谢意; **to show one's ～** 表示感谢 **2▸** [u] (understanding) 理解; **to have some/no ～ of ...** 对…有所认识/没有意识到 ‹*difficulty, importance*› **3▸** [u] (enjoyment) 欣赏; **her ～ of family life** 她对家庭生活的重视 **4▸** [u] Fin 增值 **5▸** [c] (commentary) 评论

appreciative /əˈpriːʃətɪv/ *adj* **1▸** (grateful) 感激的; **to be ～ of sth.** 对某事物表示感谢 **2▸** (admiring) 赞赏的; **he shot an ～ glance at his wife** 他对妻子投以赞许的目光

appreciatively /əˈpriːʃətɪvli/ *adv* **1▸** (gratefully) 感激地 **2▸** (admiringly) 赞赏地

apprehend /ˌæprɪˈhend/ *vt* **1▸** (arrest) 逮捕 **2▸** formal (comprehend) 意识到 ‹*seriousness, difficulty*›

apprehension /ˌæprɪˈhenʃn/ *n* **1▸** (anxiety) 忧虑; **～ about sth.** 对某事的担心; **I picked up the phone with ～** 我忐忑不安地拿起电话 **2▸** (arrest) 逮捕 **3▸** (understanding) 看法; **he is under the ～ that ...** 他认为…

apprehensive /ˌæprɪˈhensɪv/ *adj* 担心的

apprehensively /ˌæprɪˈhensɪvli/ *adv* 担心地

apprentice /əˈprentɪs/
A *n* 学徒; **an ～ hairdresser/mechanic** 理发/技工学徒; **to be an ～ to** *or* **with sb./sth.** 做某人/某行业的学徒
B *vt* **to be ～d to sb.** 给某人当学徒

apprenticeship /əˈprentɪsʃɪp/ *n* (period) 学徒期; (job) 学徒工作; **to serve/complete one's ～** 做学徒/学徒期满; **to take an ～ with a firm** 在一家公司做学徒

apprise /əˈpraɪz/ *vt* formal 通知; **to ～ sb. of sth.** 把某事通知某人

appro /ˈæprəʊ/ *abbr* Brit Comm **= approval**

approach /əˈprəʊtʃ/
A *vi* «*person, animal, vehicle*» 接近; «*event, season, date*» 临近; **night is ～ing** 夜幕即将降临; **the ～ing wedding** 即将举行的婚礼
B *vt* **1▸** (advance towards) 接近 ‹*person, place, number, record*› **2▸** (make overtures to) 与…接洽; **he ～ed us about the problem** 他找我们谈了这个问题; **to ～ sb. to do sth.** 为做某事与某人接洽; **easy/difficult to ～** 容易/难以接近的 **3▸** (tackle) 处理 ‹*problem, task*›; **he ～es every new job with enthusiasm** 他对待每项新工作都很热情
C *n* **1▸** [c] (access route) 通道; **all ～es to the city have been sealed off** 通往这座城市的所有道路都已封闭 **2▸** [u] (drawing near) 靠近; **the ～ of footsteps** 脚步声的临近; **the ～ of autumn/old age** 秋天/老年的来临 **3▸** [c] (method) 方法 **4▸** [c] (overture, proposal) 提议; **we have received an ～ from a rival company** 我们公司已经收到一家竞争对手公司的接管出价 **5▸** [c] (approximation) 近似的事物; **this was the nearest ～ to a solution** 这是最接近的答案
D **approaches** *npl* (overture) 接近的表示; (sexual) 挑逗; **to make ～es to sb./sth.** 主动与某人/某机构接洽

approachable /əˈprəʊtʃəbl/ *adj* **1▸** (friendly) 和蔼可亲的 **2▸** (reachable) 可通达的

approaching /əˈprəʊtʃɪŋ/ *adv* 将近

approach: ～ lights *npl* 进场灯; **～ path** *n* 进场航线; **～ road** *n* Brit 引道; **～ shot** *n* 打上球穴区的一杆

approbation /ˌæprəˈbeɪʃn/ *n* formal 赞同; **with the ～ of ...** 经…批准

appropriate
A /əˈprəʊprɪət/ *adj* **1▸** (suitable) 合适的; **to be ～ for** *or* **to sb./sth.** 适合某人/某事物; **to be ～ for sb. to do sth.** 某人做某事很合适 **2▸** (relevant) 有关的 ‹*department, authority*›
B /əˈprəʊprɪeɪt/ *vt* **1▸** (gen) 占用 **2▸** esp Jur 拨发 ‹*funds, assets*›

appropriately /əˈprəʊprɪətli/ *adv* 合适地

appropriate technology *n* 适用技术

approval /əˈpruːvl/ *n* **1▸** (favourable opinion) 赞同; **she nodded/smiled her ～** 她点头/微笑表示赞同 **2▸** (authorization) 批准; **to subject to sb.'s ～** 需某人批准; **to give (one's) ～ to ...** 批准…; **on ～** 包退包换

approvals procedure *n* 审批程序

approve /əˈpruːv/
A *vt* 批准; **the motion was ～d by 20 to 3** 动议以 20 票对 3 票获得通过
B *vi* 赞成; **to ～ of sb./sth.** 赞成某人/某事

approving /əˈpruːvɪŋ/ *adj* 赞成的

approvingly /əˈpruːvɪŋli/ *adv* 赞成地

approx /əˈprɒks/ *abbr* **= approximately**

approximate
A /əˈprɒksɪmət/ ▸**p. 32** *adj* 大约的; **the ～ value/date** 近似值/大概日期; **an ～ idea** 大致的想法
B /əˈprɒksɪmeɪt/ *vi* 接近; **to ～ to sth.** 接近某事物; **his story ～s to the one given by his accomplice** 他的供述与同犯所讲的基本相符

approximately /əˈprɒksɪmətli/ ▸**p. 32** *adv* 大约; **it holds ～ 10 litres** 它能装 10 升左右; **at ～ four o'clock** 大约在 4 点钟

approximation /əˌprɒksɪˈmeɪʃn/ ▸**p. 32** *n* **1▸** (idea) 近似; **a rough ～** 粗略近似物; **the nearest ～ to it is ...** 与它最接近的是… **2▸** (rough calculation) 近似值

appurtenances /əˈpɜːtɪnənsɪz/ *npl* **1▸** formal (trappings) 附属物 **2▸** Jur (of house) 附属建筑

APR *abbr* **= annual percentage rate**

Apr *abbr* **= April**

après-ski /ˌæpreɪˈskiː/
A *n* 滑雪后的社交活动
B *adj attrib* 滑雪后的

apricot /ˈeɪprɪkɒt/ ▸**p. 134**
A *n* **1▸** (fruit) 杏子; **～ stone** 杏核 **2▸** (tree) 杏树 **3▸** (colour) 杏黄色
B *adj* (colour) 杏黄色的

April /ˈeɪprɪl/ ▸**p. 490** *n* 四月; **last/this/next ～** 上个/本年/下个四月份; **in early/late ～** 四月上旬/下旬; **～ weather/morning** 四月的天气/早晨

April: ～ Fool *n* 愚人节被耍的人; **～ Fools' Day** *n* 愚人节; **～ Fools' trick** *n* 愚人节恶作剧

a priori /ˌeɪ praɪˈɔːraɪ/ formal
A *adj* 演绎的; **an ～ assumption** 推理假设
B *adv* 经演绎

apron /ˈeɪprən/ *n* **1▸** (garment) 围裙; **to be tied to sb.'s ～ strings** fig 过分依恋某人 **2▸** (for vehicles) 回车场; (for planes) 停机坪 **3▸** Theat 台口

apron stage *n* 台口

apropos /ˌæprəˈpəʊ/
A *prep* 关于; **～ of nothing** 莫明其妙地
B *adj* 恰当的; **an ～ remark** 中肯的话

apse /æps/ *n* 半圆壁龛

apt /æpt/ *adj* **1▸** (inclined) **to be ～ to do sth.** 易于做某事; **this is ～ to happen** 这事很容易发生 **2▸** (suitable) 恰当的 **3▸** (clever) 聪明的; **to be ～ at doing sth.** 善于做某事

aptitude /ˈæptɪtjuːd, Amer -tuːd/ *n* 天资; **he has no ～ for this work** 他根本没有能力做这件工作; **to show an ～ for sth.** 显示出做某事的天赋; **to have an ～ for maths** 有数学天赋

aptitude test *n* 能力倾向测验

aptly /ˈæptli/ *adv* 恰当地

aquaculture /ˈækwəkʌltʃə(r)/ *n* [u] 水产养殖

aqualung /ˈækwəlʌŋ/ *n* 水肺

aquamarine /ˌækwəməˈriːn/ ▸**p. 134**
A *n* **1▸** [c] (gemstone) 海蓝宝石 **2▸** [u] (colour) 浅蓝色
B *adj* 浅蓝色的

aquaplane /ˈækwəpleɪn/
A *vi* **1▸** Sport 乘滑水板滑行 **2▸** Aut 打滑
B *n* Sport 滑水板

Aquarian /əˈkweərɪən/ *n* 属宝瓶座的人

aquarium /əˈkweərɪəm/ *n* (*pl* **～s, aquaria** /-rɪə/) 水族池

Aquarius /əˈkweərɪəs/ *n* **1▸** [u] Astron 宝瓶（星）座 **2▸** [u] Astrol (sign) 宝瓶宫［黄道第十一宫］ **3▸** [c] *sing* Astrol (person) 属宝瓶（星）座的人

aquarobics /ˌækwəˈrɒbɪks/ ▸**p. 307** *npl* + *v sing* 水中有氧操

aquatic /əˈkwætɪk/ *adj* **1▸** (growing or living in or near water) 水生的 ‹*plant, animal*› **2▸** (taking place on or in water) 水上的 ‹*environment, sport*›

aqueduct /ˈækwɪdʌkt/ *n* 沟渠

aqueous /ˈeɪkwɪəs/ *adj* **1▸** (watery) 水的 **2▸** (like water) 水状的

aquiline /ˈækwɪlaɪn/ *adj* 似鹰的; **an ～ nose** 鹰钩鼻

AR *abbr* Amer **= Arkansas**

Arab /ˈærəb/ ▸**p. 503**
A *n* 阿拉伯人
B *adj* 阿拉伯的; **the ～ world** 阿拉伯世界; **the ～ League** 阿拉伯联盟

arabesque /ˌærəˈbesk/ *n* **1▸** Art (curvy design) 阿拉伯式花饰 **2▸** (ballet pose) 阿拉贝斯克舞姿

Arabia /əˈreɪbɪə/ *pr n* 阿拉伯半岛

Arabian /əˈreɪbɪən/ *adj* 阿拉伯的; **the ～ Sea** 阿拉伯海

Arabic /ˈærəbɪk/ ▸**p. 426**
A *adj* (of Arabs) 阿拉伯的; (of the people) 阿拉伯人的; (of the language) 阿拉伯语的
B *n* [u] 阿拉伯语

Arab-Israeli *adj attrib* 阿拉伯—以色列间的

Arabist /ˈærəbɪst/ *n* **1▸** (scholar) (of culture) 阿拉伯文化专家; (of language) 阿拉伯语学者 **2▸** Pol 阿拉伯民族主义者

arable /ˈærəbl/ *adj* 可耕的; **～ land** 耕地; **an ～ farm** 农场

arachnid /əˈræknɪd/ *n* 蛛形纲动物

Aramaic /ˌærəˈmeɪɪk/ ▸**p. 426**
A *adj* 阿拉姆语的
B *n* [u] 阿拉姆语

arbiter /ˈɑːbɪtə(r)/ *n* **1▸** (trendsetter) 权威人士; **an ～ of taste** 品位的引领者; **～s of fashion** 时装权威 **2▸** (person settling a dispute) 仲裁人; (person making decision) 做决定的人

arbitrage /ˈɑːbɪtrɪdʒ, ɑːbɪˈtrɑːʒ/ *n* [u] 套利

arbitrarily /ˈɑːbɪtrərəli, Amer -tre-/ *adv* 武断地

arbitrary /ˈɑːbɪtrəri, Amer -tre-/ *adj* 武断的; **our choice was purely ～** 我们的选择完全是随意的

arbitrate /ˈɑːbɪtreɪt/
A *vt* 裁决
B *vi* 进行仲裁; **to ～ between the litigants** 在诉讼当事人之间作出仲裁

arbitration /ˌɑːbɪˈtreɪʃn/ *n* [u] 仲裁; **to go to ～** 诉诸仲裁; **to refer a case to ～** 将案件提请仲裁

arbitration: ～ award *n* 仲裁裁定; **A～ Tribunal** *n* Brit 劳资仲裁委员会

arbitrator /ˈɑːbɪtreɪtə(r)/ *n* 仲裁人

arbor /ˈɑːrbər/ *n* Amer **= arbour**

Arbor Day /ˈɑːrbər deɪ/ *n* Amer 植树节

arboreal /ɑːˈbɔːrɪəl/ *adj* 树栖的

arboretum /ˌɑːbəˈriːtəm/ *n* (*pl* **～s, arboreta** /-riːtə/) 植物园

a

arboriculture /ˈɑːbərɪkʌltʃə(r)/ *n* [u] 树木栽培

arbour /ˈɑːbə(r)/ *n* Brit 凉棚

ARC *abbr* = **Aids-related complex**

arc /ɑːk/
A *n* **1** Geom 弧 **2** (curve) 弧形 **3** Elec 电弧
B *vi* **1** (move) 做弧形运动 **2** Elec 形成电弧

arcade /ɑːˈkeɪd/ *n* 拱廊

arcane /ɑːˈkeɪn/ *adj* **1** (mysterious) 神秘的 **2** (incomprehensible) 晦涩难解的

arch¹ /ɑːtʃ/
A *n* **1** Archit 拱; **a Norman/Gothic ～** 诺曼式半圆拱/哥特式尖拱; **a triumphal ～** 凯旋门 **2** (of foot) 足弓; (of eyebrows) 眉弓; **to have fallen ～es** 足弓下陷
B *vi* 呈弓形
C *vt* 使成弓形; **to ～ one's back** 拱起背

arch² *adj* pej (mischievous) 调皮的; (cunning) 狡黠的

arch- *combining form* 最主要的; **～enemy** 主要敌人; **～rival** 主要竞争对手

archaeological /ˌɑːkɪəˈlɒdʒɪkl/ *adj* Brit 考古学的

archaeologist /ˌɑːkɪˈɒlədʒɪst/ ▸**p. 409** *n* Brit 考古学家

archaeology /ˌɑːkɪˈɒlədʒi/ *n* [u] Brit 考古学

archaic /ɑːˈkeɪɪk/ *adj* **1** (not in current use) 古体的 **2** (ancient) 古代的 **3** (old-fashioned) 过时的

archaism /ˈɑːkeɪɪzəm/ *n* **1** [c] (old word) 古词 **2** [u] (use of old words) 拟古

archangel /ˈɑːkeɪndʒl/ *n* 天使长

archbishop /ˌɑːtʃˈbɪʃəp/ *n* 大主教

archdeacon /ˌɑːtʃˈdiːkən/ *n* 会吏总 [地位仅次于主教的牧师]

ℹ Approximation

■ The most common Chinese expressions of approximation using nouns require measure words.

Several or a few

■ 几 or 两 (several or a few) occur before measure words (like 张 and 本) or nouns (like 天 and 年) if the number is under ten. Although 两 has the literal meaning of 'two', it functions in a similar way to 几 when indicating approximation:

I have several stamps
= 我有几张邮票

I'll see you in a few days
= 我过两天见你
or 我过几天见你

■ 几 (several or a few) may be used before 十, 百, 千, 万, 亿, etc. When used with nouns, measure words are generally required:

dozens of cars
= 几十辆车

a few dozen people
= 几十个人
or 几十人

a few hundred books
= 几百册书籍

a few million trees
= 几百万棵树

■ Note that 几 can also indicate 'odd' when it is placed after 十 (ten) or its multiples from twenty to ninety:

a dozen odd types of fragrance
= 十几种香水

fifty odd tables
= 五十几张桌子

■ Note the difference between 十几 and 几十 :

a dozen or so magazines
= 十几本杂志

but

a few dozen magazines
= 几十本杂志

More than / less than

■ 多 (more than) must be placed after 十 (ten) and multiples of 十, 百, 千, 万, 亿, etc. when indicating a number bigger than the given one:

over 10 pupils
= 十多个小学生
or 十几个小学生

above 40 teachers
= 四十多个老师
or 四十几个老师

more than a thousand apples
= 一千多只苹果

■ Note that 多 must be put after the measure word or noun when the number is not 十 or its multiples. This normally applies to expressions related to age, height, distance, weight, etc.:

over 9 years old
= 9 岁多

more than 22 kilograms
= 22 公斤多

above 108 kilograms
= 108 公斤多

■ 以上 (more than) is placed after 'numeral + measure + noun' or 'numeral + measure':

more than 5 guests
= 5 位客人以上

over 10 days
= 10 天以上

■ 以下 (less than) is placed after 'numeral + measure + noun' or 'numeral + measure':

less than 100 people
= 100 个人以下

below 3 years
or ***under 3 years***
= 3 年以下

More or less

■ 来, 大约, 左右, 上下 or 前后 (about or around) are used to indicate a number close to the given one.

■ 来 is mostly used in spoken Chinese after 十, 百, 千, 万, etc. It requires a measure word when used with nouns:

about ten new words
= 十来个生词

around two hundred new faces
= 两百来张新面孔

■ 大约 is placed before the numeral. It can also be used together with 来 in informal contexts:

about 20 tickets
= 大约 20 张票

approximately 100 visitors
= 大约一百来个访问者

■ 左右 or 上下 is placed after 'numeral + measure + noun' or 'numeral + measure'. 左右 can be used with any forms of approximation. 上下 is normally limited to approximations of age, weight, height, etc.:

roughly 300 children
= 300 个儿童左右

around three o'clock
= 3 点钟左右

about 60 kilograms
= 60 公斤上下

18 years or so
= 18 岁上下 / 左右

■ 前后 (or so) can only be used to indicate approximation about a specific moment of time or a certain day/date, and not a period of time. It is placed after the time:

around Christmas
= 圣诞前后

11 o'clock or so
= 11 点前后

12th June or so
= 6 月 12 日前后

but

about three days
= 3 天左右

Two adjacent numbers

■ Measure words must be used with nouns when two consecutive numerals appear in ascending order. Note that the word 或 (or) is not required in Chinese:

seven or eight girls
= 七八个女孩儿

five or six years
= 五六年

three or four thousand posters
= 三四千张海报

■ In Chinese, only the non-adjacent numerals 三五 are used together to indicate approximation:

three to five days
= 三五天

three to five hundred days
= 三五百天

■ In Chinese, both 两三个 and 三两个 are permissible, but 三两个 emphasizes the smaller number:

two or three apples
= 两三个苹果

I will see you in two or three days
= 我过两三天见你。
or 我过三两天就见你了。(very soon)

archdiocese /ˌɑːtʃ'daɪəsɪs/ *n* 大主教管辖区

archduke /ˌɑːtʃ'djuːk, Amer -'duːk/ *n* 大公

arched /'ɑːtʃd/ *adj* 弓形的; ~ **door/brows** 拱门/弯月眉

archeological /ˌɑːkɪə'lɒdʒɪkl/ *adj* Amer = **archaeological**

archeologist /ˌɑːkɪ'ɒlədʒɪst/ *n* Amer = **archaeologist**

archeology /ˌɑːkɪ'ɒlədʒi/ *n* [u] Amer = **archaeology**

Archeozoic /ˌɑːkɪə'zəʊɪk/
A *adj* (of the period) 太古代的; (of the rock system) 太古界的
B *n* **the** ~ (period) 太古代; (rock system) 太古界

archer /'ɑːtʃə(r)/ *n* [1] Mil, Hist 弓箭手 [2] Sport 射箭运动员 [3] **Archer** Astron 人马（星）座; Astrol 人马宫

archery /'ɑːtʃəri/ *n* [u] 射箭; ~ **contest** 射箭比赛

archetypal /ˌɑːkɪ'taɪpl/ *adj* 原型的

archetype /'ɑːkɪtaɪp/ *n* 原型

Archimedean screw /ɑːkɪˌmiːdɪən 'skruː/ *n* 阿基米德螺旋泵

Archimedes /ˌɑːkɪ'miːdiːz/**:** ~ **Principle** *n* 阿基米德原理; ~ **screw** *n* = **Archimedean screw**

archipelago /ˌɑːkɪ'peləgəʊ/ *n* [1] (island group) 群岛 [2] (sea with islands) 多岛屿的海

architect /'ɑːkɪtekt/ ▸**p. 409** *n* [1] (designer of buildings) 建筑设计师 [2] fig (deviser) 设计师

architectural /ˌɑːkɪ'tektʃərəl/ *adj* [1] (relating to a building) 建筑的 [2] (relating to the subject) 建筑学的

architecturally /ˌɑːkɪ'tektʃərəli/ *adv* 在建筑学上

architecture /'ɑːkɪtektʃə(r)/ *n* [1] [u] (designing of buildings) 建筑学 [2] [u] (style of a building) 建筑风格 [3] [c] (structure) 结构 [4] [c] Comput 体系结构

architrave /'ɑːkɪtreɪv/ *n* [1] (modern) [门、窗等的] 头线条板 [2] (classical) 柱顶过梁

archive /'ɑːkaɪv/
A *n* [1] (collection) 档案; **film** ~**s** 电影档案 [2] (place of storage) 档案馆
B *vt* also Comput 把…存档

archive file *n* 存档文件

archivist /'ɑːkɪvɪst/ *n* 档案保管员

archpriest /ˌɑːtʃ'priːst/ *n* 大祭司

arc lamp, arc light *ns* 弧光灯

Arctic /'ɑːktɪk/
A *pr n* **the** ~ 北极
B *adj* [1] Geog 北极的 [2] (suitable for the Arctic) 适用于北极的 [3] **arctic** colloq (very cold) 极冷的; fig (icy) 冷淡的

Arctic: ~ **Circle** *pr n* **the** ~ **Circle** 北极圈; ~ **Ocean** *pr n* **the** ~ **Ocean** 北冰洋

arc: ~ **welder** *n* [1] (equipment) 弧焊机; [2] (person) 弧焊工; ~ **welding** *n* [u] 弧焊

ardent /'ɑːdnt/ *adj* 热烈的 ‹*love, praise*›; 热切的 ‹*eyes, gaze*›; **she was an** ~ **follower of the cause** 她是这项事业的热烈追随者; **she made an** ~ **defence of free speech** 她为言论自由进行了激烈的辩护

ardently /'ɑːdntli/ *adv* 热切地

ardour, Amer **ardor** /'ɑːdə(r)/ *n* [u] Brit 激情; **with** ~ 充满激情地; **to cool sb.'s** ~ 给某人的热情降温

arduous /'ɑːdjʊəs, Amer -dʒʊ-/ *adj* [1] (requiring great effort) 艰苦的; **an** ~ **task/climb** 艰巨的任务/艰难的攀登 [2] (hard to tolerate) 难以忍受的 ‹*climate, winter*›

arduously /'ɑːdjʊəsli, Amer -dʒʊ-/ *adv* 拼命地

are /ɑː(r)/ ▸**be**

area /'eərɪə/ *n* [1] (measurement) 面积 [2] Geog 地区; **a mountain/desert** ~ 山区/沙漠地区; **residential/port** ~ 住宅区/港区 [3] (part of building) 场地; **the reception/waiting** ~ 接待处/等候区 [4] Anat 区; **the** ~ **of the brain controlling speech** 大脑的言语控制区 [5] (sphere of knowledge) 领域; (part of activity, business, economy) 方面; **that's not my** ~ 那不是我的专长; ~ **of interest/responsibility** 兴趣/责任范围

area: ~ **code** *n* Amer 电话区号; ~ **manager** *n* 地区经理; **A**~ **of Outstanding Natural Beauty** *n* Brit 自然美景保护区

arena /ə'riːnə/ *n* [1] (space for entertainments or sports) 圆形运动场; **a circus** ~ 马戏场 [2] fig (place of combat) 斗争场所; **the political** ~ 政治舞台

aren't /ɑːnt/ colloq **= are not** ▸**be**

Argentina /ˌɑːdʒən'tiːnə/ *pr n* 阿根廷

Argentine /'ɑːdʒəntaɪn/
A *adj* (of Argentina) 阿根廷的; (of the people) 阿根廷人的
B *pr n* [1] (country) **the** ~ 阿根廷 [2] (person) 阿根廷人

Argentinian /ˌɑːdʒən'tɪnɪən/
A *adj* **= Argentine A**
B *n* 阿根廷人

argon /'ɑːgɒn/ *n* [u] 氩

arguable /'ɑːgjʊəbl/ *adj* [1] (able to be argued or asserted) 可论证的 [2] (open to disagreement) 可疑的; **it is** ~ **whether or not they were in the right** 他们当时是对是错还是个问题

arguably /'ɑːgjʊəbli/ *adv* 可论证地; **he was** ~ **the best** 他可以说是最好的

argue /'ɑːgjuː/
A *vi* [1] (quarrel) 争论; **to** ~ **over** *or* **about sth.** 为某事争辩; **we** ~**d over who should pay** 我们为了该谁付账而争吵; **don't** ~ **with me!** 别跟我争吵! [2] (debate) 辩论; **to** ~ **about sth.** 对某事进行辩论; **to** ~ **against/for sth.** 据理反对/力争某事 [3] (be evidence) 提供证明; **to** ~ **against sb.** ‹*person, fact, action*› 提供对某人不利的证明; **to** ~ **favourably/well for sb.** 为某人提供有利/有力的证明
B *vt* [1] (maintain, assert) 主张; (offer proof for) 提出理由证明; **she** ~**d that they should all go** 她主张他们都应该去 [2] (suggest) 表明 ‹*feeling, motive, quality*›; **it** ~**d the rightness of our cause** 它说明了我们的事业是正义的 [3] (persuade) 说服; **to** ~ **sb. into/out of doing sth.** 说服某人做/不做某事 [4] (discuss, achieve by debate) 辩论; **to** ~ **the point** 讨论这个问题; **to** ~ **one's way into sth./doing sth.** 据理力争得到某物/得以做某事; **to** ~ **one's way out of sth./doing sth.** 据理力争得以从某事中脱身/不做某事; **to** ~ **the toss (about sth.)** colloq（为某事物）无谓地争吵

argument /'ɑːgjʊmənt/ *n* [1] [u and c] (quarrel) 争吵; **to have/get into an** ~ **with sb.** 与某人吵架; **without** ~ 不加争辩地 [2] [u and c] (discussion) 辩论; **to have a reasoned** ~ 据理力争; **there is a lot of** ~ **about this at the moment** 目前对此存在许多争议; **to be beyond** ~ 无可争辩; **sb. is open to** ~ 某人乐意听取不同意见; **sth. is open to** ~ 某事有待商榷; **one side of the** ~ 一面之词; **both sides of the** ~ 辩论双方的观点; **for the sake of** ~, **for** ~**'s sake** 为了便于讨论; **to win/lose an** ~ 辩胜/辩输 [3] [c] (reason) 理由; **to advance** *or* **put forward an** ~ 提出理由; ~**(s) for sth./doing sth.** 赞成某事/做某事的理由; ~**(s) against sth./doing sth.** 反对某事/做某事的理由; **he made the** ~ **for surrender** 他主张投降; **I can't follow his** ~ 我不能理解他的论点 [4] [c] (main theme) 主题

argumentation /ˌɑːgjʊmen'teɪʃn/ *n* [u] 论证

argumentative /ˌɑːgjʊ'mentətɪv/ *adj* 好争论的

argy-bargy /ˌɑːdʒɪ'bɑːdʒi/ *n* [u and c] colloq 争吵

aria /'ɑːrɪə/ *n* (*pl* ~**s**) 咏叹调

arid /'ærɪd/ *adj* [1] (barren) 干旱的 [2] fig (lacking interest) 枯燥的

aridity /ə'rɪdəti/ *n* [u] [1] (barrenness) 干旱 [2] (lack of interest) 枯燥

Aries /'eəriːz/ *n* [1] [u] Astron 白羊（星）座 [2] [u] Astrol (sign) 白羊宫［黄道第一宫］[3] [c] *sing* Astrol (person) 属白羊（星）座的人

aright /ə'raɪt/ *adv* formal 正确地; **to set** *or* **put sth.** ~ 把某事物弄对头

arise /ə'raɪz/ *vi* (*pt* **arose**; *pp* **arisen** /ə'rɪzən/) [1] (occur) 产生; **to** ~ **from sth.** 源于某事物; **if the question** ~**s, should the question** ~ 如果出现问题; **if the need** ~**s** 如有需要 [2] (be the result) 被引出; **matters arising** [议程中] 尚待解决的事项 [3] liter or fomal (rise) «*person*» 起身; «*sun, moon*» 升起

aristocracy /ˌærɪ'stɒkrəsi/ *n* (people) 贵族; (class) 贵族阶层

aristocrat /'ærɪstəkræt, Amer ə'rɪst-/ *n* 贵族

aristocratic /ˌærɪstə'krætɪk, Amer əˈrɪst-/ *adj* [1] (belonging to the aristocracy) 贵族的 ‹*family, privilege*› [2] (like an aristocrat) 有贵族气派的 ‹*features, demeanour*›

Aristotelian /ˌærɪstə'tiːlɪən/ *adj* 亚里士多德的

arithmetic
A /ə'rɪθmətɪk/ *n* [u] 算术; **mental** ~ 心算
B /ˌærɪθ'metɪk/ *adj* 算术的

arithmetical /ˌærɪθ'metɪkl/ *adj* 算术的

arithmetician /əˌrɪθmə'tɪʃn/ *n* 算术家

arithmetic: ~ **mean** *n* 算术平均值; ~ **progression** *n* 算术级数

Arizona /ˌærɪ'zəʊnə/ *pr n* 亚利桑那州

ark /ɑːk/ *n* **Noah's Ark** 挪亚方舟; **to be out of the** ~ colloq 老掉牙

Arkansas /'ɑːkənsɔː/ *pr n* 阿肯色州

arm[1] /ɑːm/ *n* [1] ▸**p. 71** Anat 臂; ~ **in** ~ 臂挽臂地; **in sb.'s** ~**s, in the** ~**s of sb.** (in embrace) 在某人怀里; (being carried) 被某人抱着; **to fall into sb.'s** ~**s** 投入某人的怀抱; **to take sb. in** *or* **into one's** ~**s** 将某人拥入怀中; **on sb.'s** ~ 挽着某人的手臂; **over one's** ~ 搭在胳膊上; **under one's** ~ 在腋下; **to put one's** ~**(s) around** *or* **round sb./sb.'s shoulders** 搂住某人/某人的肩膀; **(with)** ~**s (wide) apart** 张开双臂地; **in** *or* **within** ~**'s reach** lit 在手边; fig 在附近; **to cost an** ~ **and a leg** colloq 耗费一大笔钱; **to have a long** ~ fig 势力很大; **the long** *or* **strong** ~ **of the law** 恢恢法网; **to keep sb. at** ~**'s length** fig 与某人保持一定距离; **with open** ~**s** 热烈地; **to chance one's** ~ Brit colloq 冒险; **to twist sb.'s** ~ fig 向某人施压; **to give one's right** ~ **for sth./to do sth.** fig 为某事/做某事不惜代价 [2] (sleeve) 袖子 [3] (thing resembling an arm) 臂状物; **the eight** ~**s of an octopus** 章鱼的八条腕足; **the** ~ **of a robot/crane/windmill** 机器人手臂/吊车吊臂/风车叶片; **the** ~**s of a pair of spectacles** 眼镜腿; **the** ~ **of a chair** 椅子扶手 [4] fig (subsidiary branch) 附属部分; **an** ~ **of the sea/a river** 海湾/河湾; **the company's publishing** ~ 该公司的出版部 [5] Mil 军种; **naval** ~ 海军

arm[2]
A *vt* [1] (provide with weapons) 武装; **to** ~ **sb. with sth.** 用某物武装某人; **I** ~**ed myself with a poker** 我带上一根拨火棒当武器 [2] (make ready to explode) 解除…的保险 ‹*missile, grenade*›; **to** ~ **a bomb** 打开炸弹的保险 [3] fig (provide with equipment) 给…配备; **they arrived** ~**ed with mops and buckets** 他们带着拖把和水桶来了; **she** ~**ed herself with all the necessary information** 她准备好了所有必要的信息
B *vi* 备战

Armada /ɑː'mɑːdə/ *n* [1] Hist (fleet sent against England) **the** ~ 无敌舰队 [2] **armada** (any fleet) 舰队; **an** ~ **of small vessels** 一大批小船

a

armadillo /ˌɑːməˈdɪləʊ/ *n* (*pl* **~s**) 犰狳

Armageddon /ˌɑːməˈgedn/
A *pr n* Bible (battle before the Last Judgement) 善恶大决战; (place) 哈米吉多顿 [世界末日善恶大决战的战场]
B *n fig* 大决战

Armagh /ɑːˈmɑː/ *pr n* 阿马郡

armament /ˈɑːməmənt/
A *n* 1 [c] (weapons system) 武器 2 [u] (process of arming) 战备
B **armaments** *npl* 军备; **the ~s industry** 军火工业

armature /ˈɑːmətʃʊə(r)/ *n* 电枢

arm: **~band** *n* 1 (for buoyancy) 手臂浮圈; 2 (for mourner) 黑纱; 3 (for identification) 臂章; **~ candy** *n* [u] colloq 挽臂甜心 [指在社交场所陪伴名人等的性感女子]

armchair /ˈɑːmtʃeə(r)/
A *n* 扶手椅
B *modif* 无实际经验的; **an ~ general** 纸上谈兵的将军; **an ~ traveller** 坐而神游的旅行者

armed /ɑːmd/ *adj* 1 (carrying arms) 武装的; **~ police** 武警; **to be ~ to the teeth** 全副武装 2 (ready to explode) [炮弹等] 解除保险的 3 fig (equipped) 准备充分的; **~ with sth.** 准备好某物的

-armed *combining form* 手臂…的; **long/hairy~** 手臂长的/汗毛浓密的

armed forces, armed services *npl* 武装部队; **to be in the ~** 在部队服役

Armenia /ɑːˈmiːnɪə/ *pr n* 亚美尼亚

Armenian /ɑːˈmiːnɪən/ ▸**p. 503, p. 426**
A *adj* (of Armenia) 亚美尼亚的; (of the people) 亚美尼亚人的; (of the language) 亚美尼亚语的
B *n* 1 [c] (person) 亚美尼亚人 2 [u] (language) 亚美尼亚语

armful /ˈɑːmfʊl/ *n* (*pl* **~s**) 一抱之量; **by the ~** 成抱地; **in ~s** 一抱一抱的

armhole /ˈɑːmhəʊl, Amer -hoʊl/ *n* 袖孔

armistice /ˈɑːmɪstɪs/ *n* 休战

Armistice Day *n* (actual day) 第一次世界大战停战日 [1918年11月11日]; (anniversary) 第一次世界大战停战纪念日

armlet /ˈɑːmlɪt/ *n* 臂钏

armor /ˈɑːrmər/ *n* Amer = **armour**

armored /ˈɑːrmərd/ *adj* Amer = **armoured**

armorer /ˈɑːrmərər/ *n* Amer = **armourer**

armorial /ɑːˈmɔːrɪəl/ *adj* 有纹章的

armorial bearings *npl* 纹章

armory /ˈɑːməri/ *n* Amer 1 = **armoury** 2 (arms factory) 兵工厂

armour /ˈɑːmə(r)/ *n* Brit 1 (clothing) 盔甲; **a suit of ~** 一副盔甲; **a knight in shining ~** lit 盔甲铮亮的骑士; fig 白马王子 2 (protective covering on tank, ship etc.) 装甲 3 (military vehicles) + *v sing or pl* 装甲部队

armour-clad *adj* 装甲的

armoured /ˈɑːməd/ *adj* Brit 装甲的; **the 7th A~ Brigade** 第七装甲旅

armoured: **~ car** *n* 装甲车; **~ personnel carrier** *n* 装甲运兵车

armourer /ˈɑːmərə(r)/ *n* Brit (repairer of firearms) 军械师; (manufacturer) 军械制造商; (supplier) 军械供应商

armour: **~-piercing** *adj* 穿甲的; **~ plate** *n* [u and c] 装甲板; **~-plated** *adj* 装甲的; **~ plating** *n* [u] = **~ plate**

armoury /ˈɑːməri/ *n* Brit 1 (arms store) 军械库 2 (arms supply) 武器装备 3 fig (available resources) 宝库; **she has more than just determination in her ~** 她的长处不只是果断

arm: **~pit** *n* 腋窝; **~rest** *n* [座椅的] 扶手

arms /ɑːmz/ *npl* 1 (weapons) 武器; **~ race/manufacture** 军备竞赛/军火生产 2 Herald 纹章

arms: **~ control** *n* [u] 军备控制; **~ control treaty/talks** 军控条约/谈判; **~ dealer** *n* 军火商; **~ dump** *n* 废旧军火库; **~ embargo** *n* 武器禁运

arm's-length *adj* 1 Comm 关系正常的; **an ~ transaction** 正常交易 2 (distanced) 保持距离的; **an ~ relationship** 不即不离的关系

arms: **~ limitation** *n* [u] 军备限制; **~ reduction** *n* [u] 武器削减; **~ trade** *n* [u] 军火贸易

arm: **~-twisting** *n* [u] 强迫; **~ wrestle** *vi* 掰腕子; **~ wrestling** ▸**p. 307** *n* [u] 掰腕子

army /ˈɑːmi/ *n* 1 Mil 陆军; **in the ~** 在陆军服役; **to go into** *or* **join the ~** 参军 2 fig 大群; **the ~ of the unemployed** 失业大军

army: **~ officer** *n* 陆军军官; **~ surplus** *n* [u] 剩余军用物资; **~ surplus store** *n* [面向大众的] 额外军需品商店; **~ uniform** *n* 军装

aroma /əˈrəʊmə/ *n* 芳香

aroma: **~therapist** *n* 香薰治疗师; **~therapy** *n* [u] 香薰疗法

aromatic /ˌærəˈmætɪk/
A *adj* 芳香的
B *n* 芳香料

arose /əˈrəʊz/ *pt* ▸**arise**

around /əˈraʊnd/
A *adv* 1 ▸**p. 32** (approximately) 大约; **~ £200** 大约 200 英镑; **at ~ 3 p.m.** 在下午三点钟左右 2 (in the vicinity) 在附近; **to be (somewhere) ~** 在附近（某处）; **there's nobody ~** 附近没有人 3 (in circulation) «*product, technology*» 面市; **I wish I'd been ~ 50 years ago** 我希望自己 50 年前就在这世上了; **one of the most gifted musicians ~** 当今最具才华的音乐家之一; **she's been ~** fig colloq 她是过来人; **be ~ again** «*fashion, style*» 再度流行 4 (in all directions) 在四处; **all ~** 到处; **to travel ~** 到各地旅行; **for miles ~** 周围数英里内 5 (in a circle) 环绕着; **the mill wheel moved ~ slowly** 水车轮缓慢转动着; **the wall goes all the way ~** 围墙环绕四周; **what goes ~ comes ~** 善恶皆有报 6 (in circumference) 以周长计; **the tree trunk is three metres ~** 树围长三米 7 (in different direction) 朝不同方向; (in opposite direction) 朝相反方向; **to go the long way ~** 绕远道; **to do sth. the other way ~** fig 以相反方式做某事; **the right/wrong way ~** 正过来/反过来; **to put one's skirt on the wrong way ~** 把裙子前后穿反; **you're Ben and you're Tom: is that the right way ~?** 你是本，而你是汤姆，这回对了吧？ 8 (in place) 在某处; (to place) 至某地; (in home) 在家里; (to home) 到家里; **I'll be ~ in a minute** 我马上就过来; **to ask** *or* **invite sb. ~** 邀请某人来家里
B *prep* 1 (in a circle, on all sides of) 围绕; **the villages ~ Dublin** 都柏林周围的村庄; **she had a scarf ~ her head** 她的头上裹着一条围巾; **she put her arm ~ his shoulders** 她搂着他的肩膀; **the first person to fly ~ the world** 环球飞行第一人 2 (throughout) 在…各处; **there were clothes scattered ~ the room** 屋子里衣服扔得到处都是; **(from) (all) ~ the world** （从）世界各地 3 (in the vicinity of, near) 在…附近; **somewhere ~ the house/Paris** 在房子/巴黎周围的某个地方; **she's not from ~ here** 她不是本地人 4 ▸**p. 32** (approximately at) 在…前后; **~ midnight/1990** 大约在午夜/1990 年 5 (to the other side of, so as to avoid) 绕过; **there's a way ~ the problem** 有一种方法可避开这个问题; **to go ~ the corner/a bend** 绕过拐角/转弯处 6 (on the basis of) 以…为基础; (having a centre in) 以…为中心; **a society built ~ Christian ethics** 建立在基督教伦理基础之上的社会; **she had built her life ~ her children** 她的生活以她的孩子们为中心 7 when measuring 绕…一周; **he's 90 cm ~ the chest** 他的胸围是 90 厘米

arousal /əˈraʊzl/ *n* [u] 1 (excitation) 激动; **sexual ~** 性冲动 2 (awakening) 醒来

arouse /əˈraʊz/ *vt* 1 (cause) 引起; **the picture ~d a feeling of disgust in me** 那幅画让我感到恶心 2 (excite) 激起…的性欲 3 (waken) 唤醒; **to ~ sb. from sleep** 把某人从睡梦中唤醒; **to ~ sb. to sth./to do sth.** 唤起某人做某事

arpeggio /ɑːˈpedʒɪəʊ/ *n* 琶音

arraign /əˈreɪn/ *vt* 1 Jur 传讯; **to ~ sb. before the court** 传讯某人到庭; **to be ~ed on a charge of murder** 因谋杀罪被传讯 2 fig (censure) 指责

arraignment /əˈreɪnmənt/ *n* [u] 1 Jur 传讯 2 fig (censure) 指责

arrange /əˈreɪndʒ/
A *vt* 1 (put in place) 整理 ‹*ornaments, hair, garment*›; 布置 ‹*furniture, room*›; 排列 ‹*entries, cards*›; **~ the chairs in a circle** 将椅子摆成一圈; **to ~ flowers** 插花 2 (plan) 安排; **we are arranging a celebration** 我们正在筹备庆祝会; **to ~ a marriage** 包办婚姻; **to ~ sth. with sb.** 与某人商定某事 3 (settle) 达成 ‹*deal, terms*› 4 Mus 改编
B *vi* 作安排; **to ~ for sth./sth. to take place** 为某事/某事的发生作好安排; **to ~ to do sth.** 安排好做某事; **I have ~d for the goods to be delivered** 我已经安排好送货了

arranged marriage *n* 包办婚姻

arrangement /əˈreɪndʒmənt/ *n* 1 (putting in order) 整理; **she paid great attention to the ~ of her hair** 她非常注意梳理头发; **the ~ of the chairs** 椅子的摆放; **seating ~s** 座次安排; **the ~ of ideas** 思路的梳理 2 (plan) 安排; **to make ~s to do sth.** 安排做某事 3 (agreement) 约定; **to make** *or* **reach** *or* **arrive at** *or* **come to an ~** 达成协议; **by ~ with ...** 根据与…的约定 4 Mus (act of composing) 改编; (composition) 改编曲

arrant /ˈærənt/ *adj* liter 十足的; **it's ~ nonsense!** 一派胡言！

array /əˈreɪ/
A *n* 1 (arrangement) (of people, goods, products, weaponry) 大批; (of problems, factors) 系列; (of troops) 队列; **battle ~** 战斗队形 2 Comput, Math (of numbers) 数组 3 liter (clothes) 服装; **in all their ~** 身着盛装的
B *vt* 1 (set in order) 排列 ‹*goods, produce*›; 部署 ‹*troops*› 2 liter (deck out) 打扮

arrears /əˈrɪəz/ *npl* 逾期欠款; **to be in** *or* **to fall into ~ with sth.** 在某事上拖欠; **to be paid in ~** (at the end of a term) 后付; (overdue) 被逾期支付; **my payments are in ~, I am in ~ with my payments** 我的欠款逾期未付

arrest /əˈrest/
A *vt* 1 (seize legally) 逮捕; **to ~ sb. on a charge/on suspicion of sth.** 以某罪名/因涉嫌某事逮捕某人 2 (halt) 阻止; **~ed growth/development** 生长/发育停滞 3 (attract) 吸引
B *n* Jur 逮捕; **to be under ~** 被捕; **to put sb. under ~** 逮捕某人

arrestable /əˈrestəbl/ *adj* 可逮捕的; **an ~ offence** 可逮捕罪行

arresting /əˈrestɪŋ/ *adj* 引人注意的

arrest warrant *n* 逮捕证

arrhythmia /əˈrɪðmɪə/ *n* [u and c] 心律失常

arrival /əˈraɪvl/
A *n* 1 [u] (of transport, person, package) 到达; **on sb.'s/sth.'s ~** 当某人/某物到达时; **dead on ~** 到医院已死亡的 2 [u] (of baby) 出生 3 [u] (of new character or phenomenon) 出现; **her ~ on the scene** 她的出现 4 [c] (person arriving) 到达者; (baby) 新生儿; **late/new ~s** 迟来的/新来的人们 5 [c] (newly emerged phenomenon) 新兴事物

B **arrivals** *npl + v sing* 到港区; **international ~s** 国际航班到达厅

arrival: ~(s) hall *n* 到达大厅; **~(s) lounge** *n* 下机旅客休息室; **~ platform** *n* 下客站台; **~s board** *n* 到达班次通告板; **~ time** *n* 到达时间

arrive /əˈraɪv/ *vi* **1** (reach destination) 到达; **to ~ on the scene** lit (of actor) 出场; fig 到场 **2** (appear) «*time*» 来临; «*product*» 问世 **3** **to ~ at** (reach) 达成 ‹*agreement, settlement*›; 作出 ‹*decision*›; 得出 ‹*conclusion*› **4** (be born) 出生 **5** fig colloq (be successful) 成功

arrogance /ˈærəgəns/ *n* [u] 傲慢

arrogant /ˈærəgənt/ *adj* 傲慢的

arrogantly /ˈærəgəntli/ *adv* 傲慢地

arrow /ˈærəʊ/

A *n* **1** (missile) 箭; **to fire an ~ at the target** 对准靶子射箭 **2** (symbol) 箭头; **marked with an ~** 用箭头标示的

B *vt* 以箭头标示

arrowhead /ˈærəʊhed/ *n* 箭头

arse /ɑːs/ *n* Brit taboo sl 屁股; **get off your ~!** 滚开!; **he doesn't know** *or* **can't tell his ~ from his elbow** 他屁都不懂

Phrasal verb

• **arse about, arse around** *vi* Brit sl 鬼混

arse: ~hole *n* taboo sl **1** (anus) 屁眼; **2** (stupid person) 笨蛋; (irritating person) 讨厌鬼; **~licker** /ˈɑːslɪkə(r)/ *n* taboo sl 马屁精 pej

arsenal /ˈɑːsənl/ *n* **1** (weapons collection) 武器储备 **2** (store) 军火库; (factory) 兵工厂 **3** fig (array of resources) 资源库

arsenic /ˈɑːsnɪk/ *n* [u] 砷; **~ poisoning** 砷中毒

arson /ˈɑːsn/ *n* [u] 纵火; **to commit ~** 犯纵火罪

arsonist /ˈɑːsənɪst/ *n* 纵火犯

art /ɑːt/

A *n* **1** [u] (production of works) 美术; (work produced) 美术作品; **work/works of ~** 艺术品 **2** [u and c] (skill) 技能; **the ~ of listening/survival** 倾听/生存的技能

B **arts** *npl* **1** (culture) **the ~s** 艺术 **2** Univ 文科; **an ~s** *or* **Arts degree/course** 文科学位/课程

art: ~ collection *n* (of paintings only) 绘画收藏品; (of other artworks) 艺术收藏品; **~ collector** *n* (of paintings only) 绘画作品收藏家; (of other artworks) 艺术品收藏家; **~ college** *n* 美术学院; **~ dealer** ▸**p. 409** *n* (of paintings only) 绘画作品经销商; (of other artworks) 艺术品经销商

art deco /ˌɑːt ˈdekəʊ/

A *n* [u] 装饰派艺术

B *adj* 装饰派艺术的

artefact /ˈɑːtɪfækt/ *n* Brit 人工制品

arterial /ɑːˈtɪərɪəl/ *adj* **1** Anat 动脉的 **2** Transp 主干的; **an ~ road/line** 干线公路/干线

arteriosclerosis /ɑːˌtɪərɪəʊskləˈrəʊsɪs/ ▸**p. 377** *n* [u] 动脉硬化

artery /ˈɑːtəri/ *n* **1** Anat 动脉 **2** Transp (road, railway) 干线

artesian well /ɑːˌtiːzɪən ˈwel, Amer ɑːrˌtiːʒn/ *n* 自流井

art: ~ exhibition *n* 艺术作品展; **~ form** *n* **1** (category of art) 艺术形式; **2** (medium of expression) 表现形式

artful /ˈɑːtfl/ *adj* **1** (cunning) 狡猾的 **2** (tasteful) 巧妙的; **an ~ choice of language** 妙语

artfully /ˈɑːtfəli/ *adv* **1** (skilfully) 巧妙地 **2** (cunningly) 狡猾地

art: ~ gallery *n* (museum) 美术馆; (commercial) 画廊; **~ house** *n* 艺术影院; **~-house film** *n* (artistic) 艺术电影; (experimental) 实验电影

arthritic /ɑːˈθrɪtɪk/

A *adj* (concerning arthritis) 关节炎的; (suffering from arthritis) 患关节炎的

B *n* 关节炎患者

arthritis /ɑːˈθraɪtɪs/ ▸**p. 377** *n* [u] 关节炎

artic /ɑːˈtɪk/ *n* Brit colloq = **articulated lorry**

artichoke /ˈɑːtɪtʃəʊk/ *n* **1** (globe) **~** (edible flower head) 洋蓟 **2** Brit (edible tuber) 菊芋

article /ˈɑːtɪkl/ *n* **1** (item) 物件; **an ~ of clothing/jewellery** 一件衣物/珠宝首饰 **2** Journ 文章; **the leading ~ in yesterday's paper** 昨天报纸上的社论 **3** Admin, Jur (clause) 条款; **in** *or* **under A~ 12** 根据第 12 条; **it is an ~ of faith that ...** …无庸置疑 **4** ▸**p. 2** Ling 冠词; **definite/indefinite/partitive ~** 定冠词/不定冠词/部分冠词

articled clerk *n* 见习律师

articulate

A /ɑːˈtɪkjʊlət/ *adj* 善于表达的 ‹*person*›; 表达清楚的 ‹*idea, writing*›

B /ɑːˈtɪkjʊleɪt/ *vt* **1** (pronounce) 清晰地发; **to ~ one's words clearly** 口齿清晰 **2** (express) 明确地表达

C /ɑːˈtɪkjʊleɪt/ *vi* 清晰地发音

articulated lorry *n* Brit 铰接式卡车

articulately /ɑːˈtɪkjʊlətli/ *adv* 表达清楚地

articulation /ɑːˌtɪkjʊˈleɪʃn/ *n* [u] **1** (expression) 表达 **2** Phon 发音

artifact /ˈɑːtɪfækt/ *n* Amer = **artefact**

artifice /ˈɑːtɪfɪs/ *n* **1** [c] (trick) 诡计 **2** [u] (cunning) 灵巧

artificial /ˌɑːtɪˈfɪʃl/ *adj* **1** (man-made) 人造的; **~ eye/hair** 义眼/假发 **2** fig (invalid) 人为的; **the dialogue sounded ~** 对话听起来很假 **3** (insincere) 假装的; **with an ~ smile** 假笑着

artificial: ~ aid *n* 人工辅助器材; **~ insemination** *n* [u] 人工授精; **~ intelligence** *n* [u] 人工智能

artificiality /ˌɑːtɪfɪʃɪˈæləti/ *n* [u] (of person, manner, emotion) 做作; (of situation) 人为状态

artificial limb *n* 义肢, 假肢

artificially /ˌɑːtɪˈfɪʃəli/ *adv* 人工地 ‹*dyed, coloured*›; 做作地 ‹*act*›; **~ coloured hair** 染了色的头发

artificial respiration *n* [u] 人工呼吸; **to give sb. ~, to perform ~ on sb.** 给某人做人工呼吸

artillery /ɑːˈtɪləri/ *n* **1** [u] (guns) 大炮 **2** [c] (part of an army) **the ~** 炮兵部队

artisan /ˌɑːtɪˈzæn, Amer ˈɑːrtɪzn/ *n* 工匠

artist /ˈɑːtɪst/ ▸**p. 409** *n* **1** (gen) 艺术家; (painter) 画家 **2** colloq (skilled person) 能手

artiste /ɑːˈtiːst/ *n* 艺人

artistic /ɑːˈtɪstɪk/ *adj* **1** (relating to art) 艺术的 **2** (good at art) 有艺术天赋的; **to have an ~ temperament** 有艺术家气质 **3** (pleasing) 精美的

artistically /ɑːˈtɪstɪkli/ *adv* **1** (in terms of art) 艺术上 **2** (tastefully) 精美地

artistic director ▸**p. 409** *n* 艺术总监

artistry /ˈɑːtɪstri/ *n* [u] **1** (talent) 艺术才能 **2** (workmanship) 艺术技巧

artless /ˈɑːtlɪs/ *adj* **1** (guileless) 天真的 **2** (natural and simple) 质朴的 **3** (lacking skill) 缺乏艺术性的

art: ~ paper *n* [u] Brit 铜板纸; **~ room** *n* 艺术工作室; **~s and crafts** *npl* 手工艺; **~ school** *n* 美术学院; **~s funding** *n* [u] (by state) 艺术资助; (by sponsors) 艺术赞助; **~ student** *n* 美术专业学生; **~work** *n* **1** [u] (non-textual material) 插图; **2** [u and c] (paintings, drawings etc.) 艺术品

arty /ˈɑːti/ *adj* colloq pej 附庸风雅的

arty: ~-crafty /ˌɑːtiˈkrɑːfti/ esp Brit, **artsy-craftsy** /ˌɑːtsiˈkrɑːftsi/ esp Amer *adj* colloq pej 附庸风雅的; **~-farty** /ˌɑːtiˈfɑːti/ esp Brit, **artsy-fartsy** /ˌɑːtsiˈfɑːtsi/ esp Amer *adj* colloq pej 附庸风雅的

Aryan /ˈeərɪən/

A *adj* **1** (of Indo-European racial stock) 雅利安人的 **2** Hist (in Nazi ideology) 非犹太民族的白种人的

B *n* **1** (of Indo-European racial stock) 雅利安人 **2** Hist (in Nazi ideology) 非犹太民族的白种人

as /æz, əz/

A *prep* **1** (specifying function or status) 作为; **he works ~ a pilot/an engineer** 他的职业是飞行员/工程师; **my rights ~ a parent** 我作为家长的权力; **to be treated ~ an equal** 受到平等待遇; **it came ~ a shock to learn that ...** 得知…, 令人震惊; **he was quoted ~ saying that ...** 用他的话来说…; **with Lauren Bacall ~ Vivien** 由劳伦·芭考尔饰演维维恩 **2** (in order to appear to be) 如同; **to be dressed ~ a sailor** 打扮得像个水手; **to be disguised ~ a clown** 装扮成小丑; **in the book he is portrayed ~ a victim** 在那本书中, 他被描写成了受害者 **3** (expressing start of period) **~ from** *or* **of ...** 自…起; **~ from** *or* **of April** 从四月份起; **~ of yet** 迄今为止 **4** **as to** (about, concerning) 关于; **this gave them no clue ~ to his motives** 他们并未因此获得任何有关他动机的线索 **5** **as for** (in the case of) 至于; **~ for him, he can go to hell** colloq 他嘛, 让他见鬼去吧 **6** **as against** (in comparison) 和…相比; **the figure was 75% this year, ~ against 35% last year** 与去年的35%相比, 今年的数字为75%

B *conj* **1** (in the manner that) 以…方式; **he likes reading, ~ I do** 他像我一样, 喜欢阅读; **~ you know** 正如你所知; **~ a matter of principle, he should apologize** 原则上, 他应该道歉; **~ I see/understand it** 依我看/据我理解; **~ he lived, so did he die** 他生如斯, 死亦如斯; **leave it ~ it is** 别管它了; **we're in enough trouble ~ it is** 我们目前的麻烦够多的了; **two is to four ~ four is to eight** 2比4等于4比8; **~ you were!** Mil 还原! **2** (when, while) 当…时; **~ she grew older, she grew richer** 她越老越富有; **~ a student, I had strong left-wing views** 我当学生的时候有强烈的左派观点 **3** (because, since) 因为; **~ it's Sunday, the smaller shops are shut** 由于是星期天, 小店铺都关门了; **~ she is sick, she cannot go out** 她病了, 所以不能外出 **4** (though) 尽管; **clever ~ he is, he is still inexperienced** 他虽然聪明, 但还缺乏经验; **be that ~ it may** 尽管如此; **try ~ he might, he could not forget it** 他努力去忘记却还是忘不了这件事 **5** (expressing similarity) 如同; **the same ... ~** 同…一样…; **the same man ~ I saw last week** 我上周见到的那个人; **the same ~ always** 一如既往 **6** (expressing purpose) 为了; **so ~ to do sth.** 以便做某事; **so ~ not to wake him** 以免把他吵醒

C *adv* **1** ▸**p. 140** (expressing degree, extent) **~ ... ~ ...** 与…同样地…; **he is not ~** *or* **so intelligent ~ you** 他不如你聪明; **she can play the piano ~ well ~ her sister** 她钢琴弹得和她姐妹一样好; **run ~ fast ~ you can** 能跑多快就跑多快; **~ many ~ 10,000 people** 多达1万人; **~ strong ~ an ox** 壮得像头牛; **~ long ago ~ 1849** 早在 1849 年; **they have a house in Nice ~ well ~ an apartment in Paris** 他们除了在巴黎有一套公寓, 在尼斯还有一幢房子; **~ well ~ being a poet, he is a novelist** 他不只是诗人, 也是小说家; **only half ~ expensive ~ ...** 只有…的一半贵; **their profits are down by ~ much ~ 30%** 他们的利润减少了 30% 之多 **2** (expressing similarity) 像…一样; **they tried to carry on ~ before** 他们试图像往常一样继续下去; **I thought ~ much!** 我原本也这么想!; **V ~ in Victor** 如 Victor 中的 V

D **as and when** *conj phr* 当…时; **~ and when the need arises** 一旦有需要; **drop in ~ and when you want** 你随时可以过来坐坐

a

E **as if** *conj phr* 似乎; **it seems ～ if she was right all along** 好像她一直都是对的; **it looks ～ if we've lost/won** 我们看上去输了/赢了; **～ if by magic** 神奇地; **～ if I cared!** 我才不在乎呢!

ASA *abbr* = **American Standards Association** 美国标准协会

asap *abbr* = **as soon as possible** 尽快

asbestos /æz'bestɒs, æs-/ *n* [u] 石棉; **～ dust** 石棉尘; **～ fibre** 石棉纤维

asbestosis /ˌæzbe'stəʊsɪs, ˌæs-/ ▸**p. 377** *n* [u] 石棉沉着病

asbestos mat *n* 石棉垫 [用于隔热]

ASBO, Asbo /'æzbəʊ/ *abbr* (*pl* **ASBOs, Asbos**) Brit = **antisocial behaviour order**

ascend /ə'send/ formal
A *vt* 攀登; **to ～ the throne** 登基
B *vi* «*aircraft, spirit*» 升高; «*person*» 登高; **in ～ing order** 按升序排列的; **to ～ to the throne** 登基

ascendancy /ə'sendənsi/ *n* [u] 优势; **to be in the ～** 占优势; **to have/gain the ～ over sb.** 拥有/获得对某人的优势

ascendant /ə'sendənt/
A *n* **1** [c] Astrol 星位; **to be in the ～** 交好运 **2** [u] formal (powerful position) 优势; **in the ～** 占优势的
B *adj* formal (rising) 上升的; (in a powerful position) 占优势的

Ascension /ə'senʃn/ *n* [u] **the ～** 耶稣升天

ascent /ə'sent/ *n* **1** (upward physical movement) (into the air) 上升; (climbing) 登高 **2** (upward slope) 上坡路 **3** formal (advancement) 提高

ascertain /ˌæsə'teɪn/ *vt* 查明; **it has not yet been ～ed who she was talking to** 还没弄清楚当时她在和谁谈话

ascertainable /ˌæsə'teɪnəbl/ *adj* 可查明的

ascetic /ə'setɪk/
A *adj* 苦行的
B *n* 苦行者

asceticism /ə'setɪsɪzəm/ *n* [u] 苦行主义

ASCII /'æski/ *abbr* = **American Standard Code for Information Interchange** 美国信息互换标准代码

ascorbic acid /əˌskɔːbɪk 'æsɪd/ *n* [u] 抗坏血酸

ascribable /ə'skraɪbəbl/ *adj* **～ to sth./sb.** (belonging) 可归属于某事物/某人的; (causing) 可归因于某事物/某人的

ascribe /ə'skraɪb/ *vt* (regard as due to) 把…归因于; (regard as belonging to) 把…归属于; **the accident can be ～d to human error** 这次事故可以归因于人为失误

ascription /ə'skrɪpʃn/ *n* (of sth. to a cause) 归因; (of text, etc. to a person or period) 归属; **the ～ of the poem to Shakespeare is contested** 这首诗系莎士比亚所作的说法受到质疑

ASEAN /'æsɪən/ *abbr* = **Association of South East Asian Nations** 东南亚国家联盟

aseptic /ˌeɪ'septɪk, Amer ə'sep-/ *adj* 无菌的

asexual /ˌeɪ'sekʃʊəl/ *adj* **1** Biol 无性的; **sexual and ～ reproduction** 有性和无性生殖 **2** fig (sexless) 性冷淡的

asexually /ˌeɪ'sekʃʊəli/ *adv* 无性繁殖地

ASH /æʃ/ *abbr* Brit = **Action on Smoking and Health** 禁烟与保健行动

ash¹ /æʃ/
A *n* (burnt residue) 灰烬
B **ashes** *npl* (remains) 灰烬; (of body after cremation) 骨灰; **to reduce/burn sth. to ～es** 把某物化为/烧成灰烬

ash² *n* **1** [c] (tree) 梣 **2** [u] (wood) 梣木

ashamed /ə'ʃeɪmd/ *adj* 惭愧的; **to be ～ of** *or* **about sth./doing sth.** 因某事物/做某事而感到惭愧; **she was ～ to be seen with him** 她不好意思让别人看到自己和他在一起; **it's nothing to be ～ of** 这没有什么难为情的; **to be ～ for sb.** 替某人感到羞愧

ash: ～bin *n* **1** Amer (dustbin) 垃圾箱; **2** (bin for ashes) 炉灰箱; **～can** *n* Amer 垃圾箱

ash blond
A *adj* 银灰色的
B *n* 头发是银灰色的人

ashen /'æʃn/ *adj* 灰白色的

ashen-faced *adj* 脸色苍白的

Ashgabat /'æʃgəbæt/ *pr n* 阿什哈巴德

ashlar /'æʃlə(r)/ *n* 琢石

ashore /ə'ʃɔː(r)/ *adv* **1** (towards shore) 向岸 **2** (arriving on shore) 上岸; **to come/go ～** 离船上岸来/去 **3** (on land) 在陆地上; **to spend a week ～** 在陆上过一周

ash pan *n* 贮灰盘

ashram /'æʃrəm/ *n* 静修处

ashtray /'æʃtreɪ/ *n* 烟灰缸

Ash Wednesday *n* 圣灰星期三 [大斋节的第一天]

Asia /'eɪʃə, 'eɪʒə/ *pr n* 亚洲

Asia Minor /ˌeɪʃə'maɪnə(r), ˌeɪʒə-/ *pr n* 小亚细亚

Asian /'eɪʃn, 'eɪʒn/
A *adj* (of Asia) 亚洲的; (of the people) 亚洲人的
B *n* 亚洲人

Asian American
A *adj* 亚裔美国人的
B *n* 亚裔美国人

> **Asian American**
>
> 亚裔美国人，多指父母双方都是亚洲人、但在美国出生或归化入籍的美国公民。该词在 20 世纪 60 年代后期首次出现，和非洲裔美国人（▸**African American**）相似，体现了美国少数族裔对平等的追求。要注意区别 Asian American 和 Amerasian。Amerasian 由 American 和Asian 缩合而成，意为美亚混血儿，亦出现于 20 世纪 60 年代，主要指美国军人在亚洲服役时和亚洲女性所生的后代。

Asian: ～ Briton *n* 亚裔英国人; **～ flu** ▸**p. 377** *n* [u] 亚洲型流感

Asiatic /ˌeɪʃɪ'ætɪk, ˌeɪʒɪ-/ *adj* 亚洲的

aside /ə'saɪd/
A *adv* 向旁边; **to put money ～** 存钱; **will you put these goods ～ for me?** 你帮我把这些货留着好吗？; **put your cares ～** 抛开你的烦恼; **to stand/step ～ (for ...)** fig (给…) 让位; **to take sb. ～** 把某人拉到一旁; **to turn ～ from sth./sb.** (turn one's back on) 转身背对某物/某人; (ignore) 无视某事物/某人; **money worries ～, things are going well** 除了钱的问题令人发愁外，事情进展顺利; **joking ～** 玩笑归玩笑; **～ from ...** 除了…之外
B *n* Cin,Theat 旁白; **to say sth. as** *or* **in an ～** 在旁白中说某事

asinine /'æsɪnaɪn/ *adj* pej 愚蠢的

ask /ɑːsk, Amer æsk/
A *vt* **1** (inquire) 问 ‹*time, way, question, person*›; **to ～ sb. if** *or* **whether ...** 问某人是否…; **I ～ you, as if I would be able to find that sort of money!** Brit colloq 真是的，好像我能找到那种钱似的！; **don't ～ me** colloq 别来问我 **2** (request) 请求 ‹*person, permission*›; 索要 ‹*price*›; **he's ～ing £5,000 for the car** 这辆汽车他要价 5,000 英镑; **to ～ sb. to do sth.** 请某人做某事; **to ～ sth. of** *or* **from sb.** 向某人要求某物; **to ～ the impossible** 要求明知不可能的事; **to be there for the ～ing** 只需要求，便可得到 **3** (invite) 邀请; **to ～ sb. along** 叫上某人; **to ～ sb. back/home** 请某人再来/来家里; **to ～ sb. out** 约某人外出; **to ～ sb. round** 请某人来家里
B *vi* **1** (request) 要求; **you only have to ～** 你尽管开口 **2** (make enquiries) 询问; **to ～ about** 询问; **to ～ around** 四处打听

Phrasal verbs

- **ask after** *vt* [**～ after sb.**] 问候
- **ask for** *vt* [**～ for sb./sth.**]
  1 (request) 要求; **to be ～ing for it** *or* **trouble** 自找麻烦 **2** (ask to see) 求见; (want to go to) 说要去; **when you get on the bus, ～ for the second-last stop** 你上了公交车之后，就说你要在倒数第二站下车

askance /ə'skæns/ *adv* 怀疑地; **to look ～ at sb./sth.** 怀疑地看待某人/某事物

askew /ə'skjuː/
A *adv* 歪斜地
B *adj pred* 歪斜的

asking price *n* 要价

asleep /ə'sliːp/ *adj pred* **1** (sleeping) 睡着的; **to fall ～** 入睡; **to be half ～** (not yet awake) 睡眼惺忪; (falling asleep) 昏昏欲睡; **to be sound** *or* **fast ～** 熟睡; **to be ～ on one's feet** 睡得很警醒 **2** (numb) 麻木的

AS level *n* Brit 准高级水平考试; **～ subject/results** 准高级水平考试科目/成绩

Asmara /æs'mɑːrə/ *pr n* 阿斯马拉

asocial /eɪ'səʊʃl/ *adj* **1** (avoiding social interaction) 不合群的 **2** (inconsiderate) 不关心他人的

asp /æsp/ *n* 角蝰

asparagus /ə'spærəgəs/ *n* **1** [u] Culin 芦笋; **a bunch/bundle of ～** 一束/一捆芦笋; **～ soup/sauce** 芦笋汤/芦笋汁 **2** [c] (plant) 石刁柏; **～ root/shoot** 石刁柏根/石刁柏芽

asparagus tip *n* 芦笋尖

ASPCA *abbr* = **American Society for the Prevention of Cruelty to Animals** 美国防止虐待动物协会

aspect /'æspekt/ *n* **1** (feature, part) 部分 **2** (angle) 方面; **seen from this ～** 从这一角度看; **to examine every ～ of sth.** 研究某事物的各个方面 **3** (orientation) 朝向; **a house with a westerly ～** 面朝西的房子 **4** liter (view) 景色; **a pleasant ～** 宜人的景色 **5** liter (appearance) 外表; **a man of repulsive ～** 面目狰狞的男子 **6** Ling (of verb) 体

aspen /'æspən/ *n* (in North America) 颤杨; (in Europe) 山杨

Asperger's syndrome /'æspɜːdʒəz ˌsɪndrəʊm/ ▸**p. 377** *n* 阿斯波哥尔综合征

asperity /ə'sperəti/ *n* [u] formal 严厉

aspersions /ə'spɜːʃnz, Amer -ʒnz/ *npl* formal 诽谤; **to cast ～ on sb./sth.** 诽谤某人/某事物; **are you casting ～?** 你在造谣吗？

asphalt /'æsfælt, Amer -fɔːlt/
A *n* [u] 沥青; **an ～ road/playground** 沥青公路/操场
B *vt* 铺沥青于

asphyxia /əs'fɪksɪə, Amer æs'f-/ *n* [u] 窒息

asphyxiate /əs'fɪksɪeɪt, Amer æs'f-/
A *vt* 使窒息; **they were ～d by the smoke** 他们被烟熏得窒息了
B *vi* 窒息

asphyxiation /əsˌfɪksɪ'eɪʃn/ *n* [u] 窒息; **to die of** *or* **from ～** 窒息而死; **to cause death by** *or* **through ～** 引起窒息死亡

aspic /'æspɪk/ *n* [u] 肉冻; **salmon in ～** 三文鱼冻; **to preserve sth. in ～** fig 使某物保持原貌

aspidistra /ˌæspɪ'dɪstrə/ *n* 蜘蛛抱蛋 [一种绿叶植物]

aspirant /ə'spaɪərənt/
A *n* 有抱负的人; **to be an ～ to** *or* **for sth.** 有志于追求某事物的人
B *adj* 渴望的; **these ～ actors/managers** 这些渴望当演员/经理的人

aspirate
A /'æspɪreɪt/ *vt* **1** Phon 发 h 音读出 **2** Med 从…中抽吸体液 ‹*organ, joint*›; 吸出 ‹*fluid*›
B /'æspərət/ *n* Phon 送气音

aspiration /ˌæspɪ'reɪʃn/ *n* **1** [c] (desire) 志向; **to have ～s to/to do sth.** 有志于某事物/做

某事; **to have ~s of sth./doing sth.** 渴望某事物/做某事; **to have ~s for sth.** 渴望得到某物 **2** [u and c] Phon 送气 **3** [u] Med 吸引术

aspire /ə'spaɪə(r)/ *vi* 渴望; **to ~ to sth./to do sth.** 渴望某事物/做某事; **to ~ after sth.** 追求某事物

aspirin /'æsprɪn/ *n* [u and c] 阿司匹林; **two ~(s)** 两片阿司匹林

aspiring /ə'spaɪərɪŋ/ *adj attrib* (wanting to be successful) 有抱负的; (wanting to start a career) 渴望从事…的; **an ~ author/journalist** 有抱负的作家/记者

ass /æs/ *n* **1** also colloq (donkey) 驴 **2** colloq (fool) 傻瓜; **to make an ~ of oneself** 出洋相; **the law is an ~** Brit 这条法律很荒唐 **3** Amer taboo sl (buttocks) 屁股; (anus) 屁眼; **my ~!** 狗屁! ; **he can stick the parking ticket up his ~** 去他妈的违章停车传票

assail /ə'seɪl/ *vt* formal **1** (attack) 攻击; **a terrible noise ~ed my ears** 我听到一种十分刺耳的噪声 **2** (harass) 困扰; **to be ~ed by worries/doubts** 为焦虑/疑虑所困扰

assailant /ə'seɪlənt/ *n* 攻击者

assassin /ə'sæsɪn, Amer -sn/ *n* 暗杀者

assassinate /ə'sæsɪneɪt, Amer -sən-/ *vt* 暗杀

assassination /əˌsæsɪ'neɪʃn, -sə'neɪʃn/ *n* 暗杀

assault /ə'sɔːlt/

A *vt* **1** Jur 袭击; **to be indecently ~ed** 遭到猥亵 **2** fig (criticize) 抨击 **3** (affect unpleasantly) 刺激 ‹*ears, senses*›

B *n* **1** [c] (physical attack) 袭击; **~s on prisoners were frequent** 虐待囚犯的情况很常见 **2** [u] Jur (on person) 人身侵犯; (sexual) 强奸 **3** [c] Mil 攻击; **to launch an ~ on the enemy** 对敌人发动进攻; **to be under ~** 遭到攻击 **4** [c] (forceful effort) 冲击; **they made an ~ on the summit ridge** 他们开始攀登顶峰 **5** [c] fig (criticism) 抨击 **6** [c] fig (on ears, senses) 刺激

assault: ~ and battery *n* [u] 暴力殴打; **~ charge** *n* 人身侵犯指控; **~ course** *n* 野战训练场; **~ craft** *n* 突击艇; **~ rifle** *n* 突击步枪

assay /ə'seɪ, 'æseɪ/ *n, vt* 检验

ass-backwards Amer taboo sl

A *adj* 违反常规的

B *adv* 违反常规地; **he does everything ~** 他做啥事都不按常理

assemblage /ə'semblɪdʒ/ *n* formal **1** [u] (of people, animals, objects, ideas) 聚集; **an ~ of distinguished writers** 一批著名作家 **2** [c] (object) 组装件 **3** [u] (assembling) 组装

assemble /ə'sembl/

A *vt* **1** (gather) 召集 ‹*people*›; 收集 ‹*objects, evidence, ideas*› **2** Ind, Tech (construct) 装配

B *vi* 集合

assembly /ə'sembli/ *n* **1** [u] (of people) 人群 **2** [c] Admin, Pol (institution) 立法机构; **legislative/National ~** 立法会议/国民议会 **3** [c] Sch [全校师生的] 晨会 **4** [u] Pol (congregating) 集会; **freedom of ~** 集会自由 **5** [u] Ind, Tech (fitting together) 装配 **6** [c] (collection) 聚集

assembly hall *n* 礼堂

assembly line *n* 装配线

assembly-line worker *n* 装配工

assembly: ~man /-mən/ *n* Amer 男议员; **~ plant** *n* 装配厂; **~ point** *n* 集合点; **~ room** *n* Brit 礼堂; **~woman** *n* Amer 女议员

assent /ə'sent/

A *n* 同意; **to give one's ~ to sth.** 对某事物表示同意; **by common ~** 经一致同意

B *vi* 同意; **to ~ to sth.** 同意某事

assert /ə'sɜːt/

A *vt* **1** (state) 断言; **to ~ one's innocence/that ...** 坚称自己无辜/坚称… **2** (cause to be recognized) 主张; **to ~ one's authority/strength** 维护自己的权威/势力

B *v refl* **to ~ oneself** 坚持自己的主张

assertion /ə'sɜːʃn/ *n* **1** [c] (statement) 断言 **2** [u and c] (asserting) 主张; **it was an ~ of her authority** 这是在维护她的权威

assertive /ə'sɜːtɪv/ *adj* 坚定自信的; **his personality is rather too ~** 他的个性过于自信

assertiveness /ə'sɜːtɪvnɪs/ *n* [u] 自信

assertiveness training *n* [u] 自信心确立训练

assess /ə'ses/ *vt* **1** (gen) 估算 ‹*value, damage*› **2** Fin, Insur, Jur 核定…的金额; **to ~ sth. at £5,000** 确定某物的价值为 5,000 英镑 **3** (evaluate) 评价 ‹*student, candidate, work, idea, aptitude*›

assessment /ə'sesmənt/ *n* **1** [c] (estimate) 估价; **to make an ~ of the cost** 估算费用 **2** [u and c] (evaluation) 评价; **~ of pupils** 小学生评估 **3** [u and c] Fin,Tax 核定的付款额; **my tax ~ is too high** 我的应缴税款太高了

assessor /ə'sesə(r)/ ▸**p. 409** *n* **1** Fin, Tax 估税员; Insur 估价员 **2** Jur 特别顾问

asset /'æset/ *n* **1** Fin, Comm, Jur 资产 **2** fig (advantage, quality, skill) 优势; **good health and good looks are great ~s** 健康和美貌是莫大的财富 **3** (person) 有价值的人; **she is an ~ to the company** 她是公司的骨干

asset: ~ stripper *n* 资产倒卖者; **~ stripping** *n* [u] 资产倒卖

asshole /'æshəʊl/ *n* Amer taboo sl = **arsehole**

assiduous /ə'sɪdjʊəs, Amer -dʒʊəs/ *adj* (diligent, hard-working) 刻苦的; (persistent) 坚持不懈的

assiduously /ə'sɪdjʊəsli, Amer -dʒʊəsli/ *adv* (diligently) 刻苦地; (persistently) 坚持不懈地

assign /ə'saɪn/ *vt* **1** (allocate) 分配 ‹*room, task*›; **to ~ sth. to sb., to ~ sb. sth.** 把某事物分配给某人; **I have ~ed a difficult project to my students** 我布置给学生们一个很难的课题 **2** (delegate) 指派; **to ~ sb. to do sth.** 派某人去做某事; **the newspaper ~ed 18 reporters to the case** 报社派出了 18 位记者去报道这一事件 **3** (attribute) 把…归于 ‹*title, motive*›; **to ~ a motive to sb./a crime** 确定某人/罪案的动机 **4** (fix) 确定 ‹*date*›; **the date ~ed for the conference is 13 March** 会议定于 3 月 13 日召开; **would you care to ~ a date to this piece of pottery?** 请您确定这件陶器的年代好吗?

assignation /ˌæsɪg'neɪʃn/ *n* formal or hum [尤指男女间的] 约会; **a secret ~** 幽会

assignment /ə'saɪnmənt/ *n* **1** [c] (task, piece of work) 任务 **2** [c] Sch, Univ (project, essay) 作业; **a written ~** 书面作业 **3** [u] (allocation) 分配; **the ~ of sth. to sb.** 分配某物给某人; **the ~ of sb. to sth.** 指派某人做某事

assimilate /ə'sɪmɪleɪt/

A *vt* **1** (absorb) 吸收 ‹*idea, food*›; **other artists ~d his influence** 其他艺术家受到了他的影响 **2** (integrate) 同化 ‹*person, community*›

B *vi* ‹*person, community*› 被同化; **to ~ into sth.** 被某事物同化; **we hope the refugees will ~ into the local community** 我们希望难民们能够融入当地的社区

assimilation /əˌsɪmɪ'leɪʃn/ *n* [u] **1** (absorption) 吸收; **the ~ of facts** 事实的接受; **~ of food/nutrients** 食物/营养的吸收 **2** (integration) 同化; **the ~ of immigrants** 移民的同化; **racial/social/cultural ~** 种族/社会/文化融合

assist /ə'sɪst/

A *vt* 帮助; **to ~ one another** *or* **each other** 互相帮助; **to ~ sb. in/out/down** 扶某人进来/出去/下来; **to ~ sb. to his/her feet** 扶某人站起来; **a man is ~ing police with their inquiries** euph 一名男子正在协助警方调查

B *vi* **1** (help) 帮助; **to ~ in sth./doing sth.** 在某事中帮忙/帮助做某事 **2** (be present) 列席; **they ~ed at the ceremony** 他们列席了典礼

assistance /ə'sɪstəns/ *n* [u] 帮助; **to come to sb.'s ~, to come to the ~ of sb.** 来帮助某人; **with the ~ of ...** 在…的帮助下; **to be of ~ (to sb.)** (对某人) 有帮助; **to provide/render ~** 提供/给予帮助; **financial/medical/technical ~** 财政/医疗/技术援助

assistant /ə'sɪstənt/ ▸**p. 409** *n* **1** (helper) 助手; (in bureaucratic hierarchy) 助理; **an ~ engineer/manager** 助理工程师/副经理 **2** Brit Sch, Univ 助教

assistant professor ▸**p. 409** *n* Amer 助理教授

assistantship /ə'sɪstəntʃɪp/ *n* [u] Amer [研究生半工半读的] 助理研究工作

assisted: ~ reproduction *n* [u] 人工辅助生殖; **~ suicide** *n* [u and c] 辅助性自杀

assizes /ə'saɪzɪz/ *npl* Brit 巡回审判

ass-kisser /'æskɪsə(r)/ *n* Amer taboo sl 马屁精 pej

associate

A /ə'səʊʃɪeɪt, -sɪeɪt/ *vt* **1** (connect in thought or imagination) 把…联系起来; **these symptoms are ~d with old age** 这些是年老的症状 **2** (be involved in) 与…有关系; **I don't want to be ~d with this** 我不想卷入这件事; **to ~ oneself with sth.** 表示赞成某事

B /ə'səʊʃɪeɪt, -sɪeɪt/ *vi* 交往; **to ~ with sb.** 与某人交往

C /ə'səʊʃɪət, -sɪət/ *n* **1** (colleague, partner) 伙伴; **an ~ in crime** 同案犯; **Brown and A~s** Comm 布朗及合伙人事务所 **2** (subordinate member of society, academic body) 准会员

D /ə'səʊʃɪət, -sɪət/ *modif* 副的 ‹*director, editor, dean*›; 非正式的 ‹*member*›; 陪审的 ‹*judge*›

associate company *n* 联营公司

Associated Press *pr n* 美联社

associate: ~ justice *n* Amer (not the chief justice) 陪审法官; (of a higher state court) 大法官; **~ professor** *n* Amer 副教授

association /əˌsəʊsɪ'eɪʃn/ *n* **1** (club, society) 协会; **to form/join an ~** 成立/加入一个协会 **2** (cooperation) 联合; **a close ~ between ...** …之间的密切合作; **in ~ with ...** 和…联合 **3** (friendship) 友谊; (relationship) 恋爱关系; **his ~ with the lady** 他同那位女士的交往 **4** (link) 关联; **to have ~s with sth.** 和某事有关联 **5** (mental evocation) 联想; **to have good/bad ~s for sb.** 使某人产生美好/不好的联想

association football *n* [u] 英式足球

assonance /'æsənəns/ *n* [u] 半谐音

assorted /ə'sɔːtɪd/ *adj usu attrib* 各种各样的; **a tin of ~ biscuits** 一听什锦饼干

assortment /ə'sɔːtmənt/ *n* 各种各样; **in an ~ of colours/sizes** 以各种颜色/尺寸

Asst. *abbr* = **assistant**

assuage /æ'sweɪdʒ/ *vt* liter 缓解; **to ~ one's thirst/hunger/pain** 解渴/充饥/镇痛

assume /ə'sjuːm, Amer ə'suːm/ *vt* **1** (suppose) 假定; **I ~d him to be French** 我把他当成了法国人; **tomorrow, I ~** 我想是明天; **they just ~ (that) he can't do it** 他们只是想当然地认为他干不了这个; **to ~ the worst** 作最坏的打算; **to be ~d innocent/guilty** 被假定为无罪/有罪 **2** (take on) 获得 ‹*power*›; 承担 ‹*responsibility*›; 担任 ‹*role*›; **to ~ office** 就职 **3** (adopt falsely) 装出; **~d innocence/indifference** 假装的清白无辜/满不在乎 **4** (develop) 呈现 ‹*importance*›; 露出 ‹*expression*› **5** (change to) 换用 ‹*name, identity*›

assumed name *n* 化名; **under an ~** 隐姓埋名地

Assumption /ə'sʌmpʃn/ *n* Relig (reception of the Virgin Mary into heaven) 圣母升天; (feast) 圣母升天节 [8月15日]

assumption /ə'sʌmpʃn/ *n* **1** [c] (belief, supposition) 假定; **on the ~ that ...** 根据…这一假定; **to make an ~** 作出假定; **a wrong** *or* mistaken ～ 错误的假定 2 [u] (of power) 获得; (of duty, role) 承担

assurance /ə'ʃɔ:rəns, Amer ə'ʃʊərəns/ *n* 1 [c] (declaration) 保证; **to give sb. an/every ～ that ...** 向某人保证/百分百地保证…; **you have my ～ that ...** 我向你保证… 2 [u] (self-confidence) 自信; **with ～** 自信地 3 [u] Brit Insur, Fin 保险; **life ～** 人寿保险

assure /ə'ʃɔ:(r), Amer ə'ʃʊər/ *vt* 1 (tell positively) 向…保证; **to ～ sb. of sth./that ...** 向某人保证某事/…; **to be ～d of sth.** 得到某事物上的保证; **rest ～d that ...** 放心… 2 (make certain) 弄清; **to ～ oneself that ...** 弄清… 3 (ensure) 确保; **this ～s her a place in the team** 这确保她在队里有一席之地 4 Brit Insur, Fin 给…保险

assured /ə'ʃɔ:d, Amer ə'ʃʊərd/
A *adj* 自信的
B *n* [u] **the ～** + *vpl* Brit Insur 被保险人; **the money on the deaths of the ～** 被保险人死亡赔付金

assuredly /ə'ʃɔ:rɪdli, Amer -'ʃʊər-/ *adv* formal, liter 确实地; **the account is ～ true** 描述的确属实

AST *abbr* = **Atlantic Standard Time**

Astana /ə'stɑ:nə/ *pr n* 阿斯塔纳

astatine /'æstəti:n/ *n* [u] 砹

aster /'æstə(r)/ *n* 紫菀

asterisk /'æstərɪsk/
A *n* 星号; **marked with an ～** 用星号标注的
B *vt* 标注星号于

astern /ə'stɜ:n/ *adv* Naut 1 (behind the rear) 在船尾; (towards the rear) 向船尾; **to stand ～** 站在船尾; **to go ～** 去船尾 2 (backwards) 向后; **full speed ～!** 全速后退!

asteroid /'æstərɔɪd/ *n* 小行星

asthma /'æsmə, Amer 'æzmə/ ▸**p. 377** *n* 哮喘; **to suffer from/have ～** 患有哮喘; **～ sufferer** 哮喘患者

asthmatic /æs'mætɪk/
A *adj* 哮喘的 ‹*chest*›; 哮喘引起的 ‹*pain*›; 患哮喘的 ‹*person*›
B *n* 哮喘患者

astigmatism /ə'stɪgmətɪzəm/ *n* [u] 散光

astonish /ə'stɒnɪʃ/ *vt* 使大为惊奇; **it ～es me that ...** 我真没料到…; **you ～ me!** lit 真想不到!; iron 一点都不奇怪!

astonished /ə'stɒnɪʃt/ *adj* 大为惊奇的; **to be ～ by** *or* **at sb./sth.** 对某人/某事物大为惊奇

astonishing /ə'stɒnɪʃɪŋ/ *adj* 令人大为惊奇的; **it is ～ that ..., the ～ thing is that ...** 难以置信的是, …

astonishingly /ə'stɒnɪʃɪŋli/ *adv* 令人大为惊奇地; **～ (enough), they won!** 难以置信的是, 他们竟然赢了!

astonishment /ə'stɒnɪʃmənt/ *n* [u] 惊讶; **in** *or* **with ～** 惊奇地; **to sb.'s ～, to the ～ of sb.** 令某人惊奇的是

astound /ə'staʊnd/ *vt* 使震惊; **to be ～ed by sth.** 对某事物感到震惊; **you never fail to ～ me!** hum 你总能让我大跌眼镜!

astounded /ə'staʊndɪd/ *adj* 感到震惊的; **to be ～ to see/hear/learn sth.** 看到/听到/得知某事感到震惊; **to be ～ at** *or* **by sb./sth.** 对某人/某事物感到震惊

astounding /ə'staʊndɪŋ/ *adj* 令人震惊的

astrakhan /,æstrə'kæn, Amer 'æstrəkən/ *n* 1 (fleece) 阿斯特拉罕羔羊毛 2 (fabric) 仿阿斯特拉罕羔羊毛织物; **an ～ coat/collar** 仿阿斯特拉罕羔羊毛外套/衣领

astray /ə'streɪ/ *adv* 1 **to go ～** (in direction, route) 迷路; (go missing) 被丢失 2 (in course of action) 方向错误地; fig (in behaviour) 误入歧途地; **to lead sb. ～** 把某人引入邪路

astride /ə'straɪd/
A *adv* 1 (with one leg either side) 跨着 2 (with legs wide apart) 叉开腿地
B *prep* 1 (seated) 跨在…上 2 (standing) 叉开腿站在…上

astringent /ə'strɪndʒənt/
A *adj* 1 Cosmet, Med 收敛性的 2 fig 尖刻的 ‹*comment, criticism*›
B *n* 收敛剂

astrologer /ə'strɒlədʒə(r)/ ▸**p. 409** *n* 占星家

astrological /,æstrə'lɒdʒɪkl/ *adj* 占星术的

astrologist /ə'strɒlədʒɪst/ *n* = **astrologer**

astrology /ə'strɒlədʒi/ *n* [u] 占星术

astronaut /'æstrənɔ:t/ ▸**p. 409** *n* 宇航员

astronautical /,æstrə'nɔ:tɪkl/ *adj* (relating to astronautics) 航天的; (relating to astronauts) 宇航员的

astronautics /,æstrə'nɔ:tɪks/ *npl* + *v sing* 航天学

astronomer /ə'strɒnəmə(r)/ ▸**p. 409** *n* (expert) 天文学家; (student) 天文学学生

astronomical /,æstrə'nɒmɪkl/, **astronomic** /,æstrə'nɒmɪk/ *adj* 1 Astron 天文学的; **an ～ telescope/object** 天文望远镜/天体 2 fig (large in degree, amount) 巨大的

astronomically /,æstrə'nɒmɪkəli/ *adv* colloq 极其地; **to be ～ high/expensive** 极高/极贵

astronomical unit *n* 天文单位

astronomy /ə'strɒnəmi/ *n* [u] 天文学

astrophysicist /,æstrəʊ'fɪzɪsɪst/ ▸**p. 409** *n* 天体物理学家

astrophysics /,æstrəʊ'fɪzɪks/ *npl* + *v sing* 天体物理学

AstroTurf® /'æstrəʊtɜ:f/ *n* [u] 阿斯特罗特草皮

astute /ə'stju:t, Amer ə'stu:t/ *adj* 精明的

astutely /ə'stju:tli, Amer -'stu:t-/ *adv* 精明地

astuteness /ə'stju:tnɪs, Amer -'stu:t-/ *n* [u] 精明

Asunción /ə,sʊnsɪ'ɒn/ *pr n* 亚松森

asunder /ə'sʌndə(r)/ *adv* liter or archaic 撕碎地; **a country ripped ～ by civil war** 因内战而分崩离析的国家

asylee /ə,saɪ'li:/ *n* Amer, Austral 获准政治避难者

asylum /ə'saɪləm/ *n* 1 [u] (protection) 避难; **to grant/seek ～** 准予/寻求避难; **political ～** 政治避难 2 [c] dated (institution) 精神病院

asylum-seeker *n* 寻求政治避难者

asymmetric /,eɪsɪ'metrɪk/, **asymmetrical** /,eɪsɪ'metrɪkl/ *adj* 不对称的

asymmetric bars *npl* 高低杠

asymmetry /eɪ'sɪmɪtri/ *n* [u and c] 不对称

asynchronous /eɪ'sɪŋkrənəs/ *adj* 异步的

AT *abbr* = **alternative technology**

at /æt, ət/ ▸**p. 487** *prep* 1 (indicating location) 在; **～ the corner** 在拐角处; **be ～ church/the concert** 在教堂做礼拜/在听音乐会; **～ work/school** 在上班/上学 2 (indicating time) 在 [某时间或时刻]; **～ 2 o'clock/the weekend** *etc.* 在两点钟/在周末等; **～ the time of doing sth.** 在做某事的时候; **～ this stage in the game** Brit 在比赛的这个阶段 3 (indicating age) 在…岁时; **she got married ～ 25** 她 25 岁结的婚 4 (indicating distance) 从相隔…远的地方; **I held it ～ arm's length** 我伸直胳膊握着它; **～ fifty metres** 在 50 米远处 5 (in the direction of) 向; **somebody threw paint ～ the prime minister** 有人朝首相泼油漆; **he clutched wildly ～ the rope** 他拼命想抓住绳子 6 (indicating state or situation) 处于…状态; **be ～ war** 正在交战; **be ～ a disadvantage** 处于不利地位; **he's ～ lunch** colloq 他正在吃午饭; **I've been (hard) ～ it all day** colloq 我整天都在 (拼命) 干; **they're ～ it again!** colloq 他们又干起来了!; **～ that** 而且还; **he managed to buy a car after all — and a nice one ～ that** 他还是设法买了一辆汽车——而且还挺不错的; **where sb. is ～** colloq 某人的处境; **where it's ～** dated, colloq 热门活动/场所; **while sb. is ～ it** colloq 某人在做某事的同时 7 (followed by superlative) [处于最佳或最差等状态]; **～ sb.'s/sth.'s best/worst** *etc.* 处于某人/某事物的最佳/最差状态等; **the garden's ～ its most beautiful in June** 六月的花园最美丽; **she was ～ her best ～ 50** 她 50 岁时达到了事业的巅峰 8 (indicating rate or speed) 以; **to drive ～ 70 mph** 以每小时 70 英里的速度驾驶; **～ two-minute intervals** 每隔两分钟; **～ £2.50 (each)** 以 (每件) 2.5 英镑的价格; **three ～ a time** 每次三个 9 (with respect to) 在…方面; **she's hopeless ～ managing people/teaching** 她对人事管理/教学一窍不通 10 (because of) 因为; **be impatient/delighted ～ sth.** 对某事物不耐烦/感到高兴 11 formal (in response to) 应; **～ the chairman's invitation** 应这位主席的邀请; **I did it ～ his insistence** 我是在他的坚持下做这件事的 12 colloq (harassing) 缠着; **he's been (on) ～ me to buy a new car** 他一直缠着要我买辆新汽车

atavism /'ætəvɪzəm/ *n* lit 返祖现象; fig 复古

atavistic /,ætə'vɪstɪk/ *adj* (relating to sth. ancestral) 返祖性的; (relating to sth. ancient) 原始的

ate /eɪt/ *pt* ▸**eat**

atheism /'eɪθɪɪzəm/ *n* [u] 无神论

atheist /'eɪθɪɪst/ *n* 无神论者

atheistic /,eɪθɪ'ɪstɪk/ *adj* 无神论的

Athens /'æθɪnz/ *pr n* 雅典

athlete /'æθli:t/ *n* 1 (trained sportsperson) 运动员 2 (sporty person) 擅长体育运动的人

athlete's foot ▸**p. 377** *n* 足癣

athletic /æθ'letɪk/ *adj* 1 (of athletics) 运动的; (of athletes) 运动员的 2 (fit, active) 健壮的

athletics /æθ'letɪks/ ▸**p. 307** *npl* + *v sing* esp Brit 田径运动; **an ～ meeting/club** 田径运动会/俱乐部

athletic support Brit, **athletic supporter** Amer *ns* 下体弹力护身

atishoo /ə'tɪʃu:/ *excl* 阿嚏 [指喷嚏声]

Atlantic /ət'læntɪk/
A *pr n* **the ～** 大西洋
B *adj* 大西洋的

Atlantic: ～ Ocean *n* **the ～ Ocean** 大西洋; **～ Standard Time** *n* Amer 大西洋标准时间

atlas /'ætləs/ *n* (*pl* **～es**) 地图册

ATM *abbr* = **automated teller machine**

atmosphere /'ætməsfɪə(r)/ *n* 1 (layer of gases) (around the Earth) 大气; (around other planets) 气体; **the Earth's ～** 地球大气层 2 (air) 空气 3 (mood) 气氛; **the film is full of ～** 这部电影很有感染力; **there was a bit of an ～** colloq 气氛有些紧张

atmospheric /,ætməs'ferɪk/ *adj* 1 Meteorol, Phys 大气的 2 (evocative) 有氛围的

atoll /'ætɒl/ *n* 环状珊瑚岛

atom /'ætəm/ *n* 1 Phys 原子 2 fig (tiny amount) 微量; (tiny thing) 微粒; **to be smashed/blown to ～s** 被摔得/打得粉碎

atom bomb *n* 原子弹

atomic /ə'tɒmɪk/ *adj* 原子的

atomic: ～ clock *n* 原子钟; **A～ Energy Authority** *n* Brit 原子能管理局; **～ mass** *n* 原子质量; **～ number** *n* 原子序数; **～ particle** *n* 原子粒子; **～ physics** *npl* + *v sing* 原子物理学; **～ power station** *n* 原子能发电站; **～ reactor** *n* 原子反应堆; **～ theory** *n* [u] 原子理论

atomize /'ætəmaɪz/ *vt* 1 Phys 使分裂成原子 2 (into spray) 使雾化; (into particles) 使成为微粒 3 (destroy) 用原子武器毁灭

atomizer /'ætəmaɪzə(r)/ *n* 雾化器

atonal /eɪ'təʊnl/ *adj* 无调性的

atone /ə'təʊn/ *vi* formal [对罪错等] 弥补; **to ～ for a sin** *or* **crime** 赎罪

atonement /əˈtəʊnmənt/ *n* formal 赎罪; **to make ~ for sth.** 弥补某事物

atop /əˈtɒp/ esp Amer liter
A *adv* 在顶上
B *prep* 在…顶上

atria /ˈeɪtrɪə/ *pl* ▸**atrium**

at-risk *adj* 处于危险中的

atrium /ˈeɪtrɪəm/ *n* (*pl* **atria** *or* **~s**) **1** Archit (entrance hall) 门廊; (central court) 天井 **2** Anat 心房

atrocious /əˈtrəʊʃəs/ *adj* **1** (horrifyingly cruel) 骇人听闻的 **2** (bad) 糟透的

atrociously /əˈtrəʊʃəsli/ *adv* **1** (horrifyingly cruelly) 凶残地 **2** (badly) 糟糕地

atrocity /əˈtrɒsəti/ *n* **1** [c] (action) 残暴行为 **2** [u] (state) 残暴

atrophy /ˈætrəfi/
A *n* [u] **1** Med 萎缩 **2** fig (degeneration) 衰退
B *vi* **1** Med 萎缩 **2** fig (degenerate) 衰退

at sign *n* @符号

attaboy /ˈætəbɔɪ/ *excl* Amer 好样的

attach /əˈtætʃ/
A *vt* **1** (fasten) 固定; (to letter) 附上; **to ~ a label to the suitcase** 把标签贴在手提箱上 **2** (connect to) 使附属; **to be ~ed to a government department** 隶属于政府部门 **3** (attribute) 把…归于; **to ~ blame to sb. for sth.** 把某事的责任归于某人; **to ~ importance to the rumours** 重视这些谣言
B *vi* formal 归属; **to ~ to sb./sth.** 与某人/某事物有关
C *v refl* **to ~ oneself to sb.** 缠上某人

attaché /əˈtæʃeɪ, Amer ˌætəˈʃeɪ/ *n* **1** (person at embassy) 专员; **a cultural/military ~** 文化参赞/武官 **2** Amer = **attaché case**

attaché case *n* 公文包

attached /əˈtætʃt/ *adj* **1** (fond) 喜爱的; **to be ~ to sb./sth.** 喜欢某人/某事物; **to become** *or* **grow ~ to sb./sth.** 喜欢上某人/某事物 **2** (adjoined) 附属的; **the ~ form/document** 附表/附件 **3** (adjacent) 附联式的; **a house with ~ garage, a house with garage ~** 与车库相连的房屋

attachment /əˈtætʃmənt/ *n* **1** [c] (affection) 爱慕; (devotion) 忠诚; **to form an ~ to** *or* **with sb.** 对某人产生爱慕之情 **2** [c] (device) 附加装置 **3** [c] (in email) 附件 **4** [u] Brit (placement) 临时隶属; **to be on ~ to sb./sth.** 暂时在某人手下/某处工作

attack /əˈtæk/
A *vt* **1** also Mil 攻击; Sport 进攻; (criminally) 袭击 **2** fig (criticize) 抨击 **3** (tackle) 着力解决 ‹*problem*›; 猛吃 ‹*food*›; 彻底清理 ‹*room*› **4** (damage) 损害 ‹*nervous system*›; 腐蚀 ‹*metal*›; 蛀 ‹*wood*›
B *vi* also Mil 攻击; Sport 进攻
C *n* **1** [u and c] also Mil 攻击; Sport 进攻; (unprovoked, criminal) 袭击; **an ~ on** *or* **against ...** 对…的进攻; **to come under ~ from sb./sth.** 遭到某人/某物的攻击; **on the ~** 采取攻势地 **2** [u and c] (criticism) 抨击; **open to ~** 易受抨击的 **3** [c] (attempt to tackle) 着手处理; **to launch an ~ on the living room** 对起居室进行大扫除 **4** [c] Med (bout) 突然发作; **to have an ~ of flu** 患流感; **to have an ~ of hiccups/giggles** 突然打嗝/发出一阵咯咯傻笑 **5** [u] Sport (offensive players) 进攻队员; (the process of attacking) 进攻

attack: ~ aircraft *n* 强击机; **~ alarm** *n* 遭袭报警器

attacker /əˈtækə(r)/ *n* **1** (gen) 袭击者 **2** Mil 攻击者; Sport 进攻队员

attack helicopter *n* 武装直升机

attain /əˈteɪn/ *vt* **1** (achieve) 实现 ‹*goal*›; 获得 ‹*knowledge, position, happiness*› **2** (reach) 达到 ‹*age, level*›

attainable /əˈteɪnəbl/ *adj* 可实现的 ‹*goal*›; 可获得的 ‹*knowledge, position, happiness*›

attainment /əˈteɪnmənt/ *n* **1** [u] (achieving) (of goal) 实现; (of knowledge, position, happiness) 获得 **2** [c] (success) 成就

attainment target *n* 学业目标

attempt /əˈtempt/
A *vt* 企图; **to ~ to do sth.** 试图做某事; **to ~ suicide** 企图自杀; **~ed robbery/murder** 抢劫/谋杀未遂
B *n* **1** (try) 企图; **to make an ~ to do** *or* **at doing sth.** 试图做某事; **in an ~ to ...** 为了…; **on his first ~** 在他第一次尝试时; **to make an ~ on a record** 尝试打破纪录; **good ~!** 做得好！; **he made an ~ at a smile** 他努力想微笑一下 **2** (attack) 杀人企图; **to make an ~ on sb.'s life** 企图杀害某人

attend /əˈtend/
A *vt* **1** (be present at) 参加; (go to) 去; **the event was well/poorly ~ed** 参加活动的人很多/很少; **to ~ school/church** 上学/去教堂做礼拜; **to ~ a course** 上课 **2** formal (accompany) 伴随; **the risks that ~ experiments of this kind** 与这种试验相伴的风险 **3** (take care of) 照料; **to ~ a patient at home** 在家中护理病人
B *vi* **1** (be present) 出席 **2** (pay attention) 注意; **to ~ to sb./sth.** 专心听某人说话/注意某事物

Phrasal verb

- **attend to** *vt* [**~ to sb./sth.**] **1** (deal with) 处理; **that lock needs ~ing to** 那把锁需要修理 **2** (serve, assist) 接待 ‹*customer, client*›; 护理 ‹*patient*›; 满足 ‹*needs*›; **are you being ~ed to?, is someone ~ing to you?** 有人接待您吗？

attendance /əˈtendəns/ *n* **1** (number of people present) 出席人数 **2** (presence) (at event, meeting, course) 出席; (at clinic) 就诊; **school ~** 学生出勤率; **to take ~** Amer Sch 点名; **to be in ~** 到场; **in ~ on sb.** 护卫某人的

attendance: ~ allowance *n* Brit 护理津贴; **~ centre** *n* Brit 少年犯教育中心; **~ officer** ▸**p. 409** *n* 出席率督察员; **~ record** *n* **1** Brit also Sch (record of sb.'s presence) 考勤记录; **2** (highest number of people attending) 出席人数最高纪录; **~ register** *n* Brit 考勤簿

attendant /əˈtendənt/
A *n* **1** ▸**p. 409** (gen) 服务员; (in cinema) 引座员 **2** (for bride etc.) 陪伴者; **the queen and her ~s** 女王和她的侍从
B *adj* formal **1** (associated) 伴随的; **the ~ problems/diseases** 随之而来的问题/并发症 **2** (attending) 侍奉的; **~ nurses/aides** 专责护士/随行助理

attendee /əˈtendiː/ *n* 出席者

attention /əˈtenʃn/
A *n* [u] **1** (notice, interest) 注意; **to get/have/hold sb.'s ~** 引起/得到/攫住某人的注意; **to give sb. one's full ~** 全神贯注在某人身上; **to pay ~ (to sb./sth.)** 注意（某人/某事物）; **pay ~ please!** 请注意！; **to bring sth. to sb.'s ~** 提请某人注意某事物; **I acted as soon as this matter came to my ~** 我一获悉此事就采取了行动 **2** (care) 关心; **the centre of ~** 关注的中心; **to give some ~ to sb./sth.** 给予某人/某事物一些关注; **I shall give the matter my earliest ~** 我将在第一时间处理此事; **this handle needs ~, it's coming loose** 把手松了，需要修理 **3** Mil 立正; **to come** *or* **stand to ~** 立正; **to stand at** *or* **to ~** (be standing) 立正
B *excl* Mil 立正

attention deficit disorder, attention deficit hyperactivity disorder *ns* [u] 注意力缺乏（多动）症 [简称多动症]

attention-seeking
A *n* [u] 寻求注意行为
B *adj* 寻求注意的

attention span *n* 注意力持久度

attentive /əˈtentɪv/ *adj* **1** (alert) 专心的 **2** (solicitous) 关心的; **to be ~ to sb./sth.** 关心某人/某事物

attentively /əˈtentɪvli/ *adv* **1** (alertly) 专心地 **2** (solicitously) 关心地

attenuate /əˈtenjʊeɪt/ *vt* 减弱 ‹*signal, strength*›

attenuated /əˈtenjʊeɪtɪd/ *adj* 减弱的

attenuation /əˌtenjʊˈeɪʃn/ *n* 减弱

attest /əˈtest/ formal
A *vt* **1** (prove) 证实; (declare) 为…作证; **an ~ed fact** 得到证明的事实; **to ~ that ...** 证明… **2** Jur (authenticate) 连署以证明…真实 ‹*signature*›
B *vi* 证明; **to ~ to sth.** 证明某事物; **as the figures will ~** 正如这些数字将要说明的那样

attic /ˈætɪk/ *n* 阁楼

Attila /əˈtɪlə, ˈætɪlə/ *pr n* **~ the Hun** 匈奴王阿提拉

attire /əˈtaɪə(r)/ formal
A *n* 服装; **in formal ~** 着正装
B *vt* **to be ~d in ...** 穿着…衣服

attitude /ˈætɪtjuːd, Amer -tuːd/ *n* **1** (way of behaving or thinking) 态度; **her ~ to life/the world** 她的人生观/世界观; **a change in ~** 态度的转变; **to have** *or* **take the ~ that ...** 持…态度 **2** (physical position) 姿势; **they sat around in ~s of dejection** 他们垂头丧气地坐在那里; **to strike an ~** 摆姿势

attitudinize /ˌætɪˈtjuːdɪnaɪz, Amer -ˈtuːdən-/ *vi* pej 装腔作势

attorney /əˈtɜːni/ *n* **1** (legally appointed person) 代理人; **power of ~** 代理权; **a letter of ~** 授权书 **2** ▸**p. 409** esp Amer (lawyer) 出庭律师

attorney: ~-at-law ▸**p. 409** *n* (*pl* **~s-at-law**) Amer 出庭律师; **A~ General** *n* (*pl* **A~s General**) Amer 司法部长; Brit, Austral 检察总长

attract /əˈtrækt/ *vt* **1** (draw, appeal) 吸引; **to be ~ed to sb./sth.** 受到某人/某事物的吸引; **a magnet will not ~ aluminium** 磁石不吸铝 **2** (be cause of attraction) 引起…的好感; **his sense of humour ~ed me to him** 他的幽默感使我对他产生好感 **3** (evoke) 引起; **to ~ attention/criticism** 引起注意/招致批评

attraction /əˈtrækʃn/ *n* **1** [u] (appealing quality) 吸引力; **an irresistible ~ to sth.** 某事物不可抗拒的吸引力; **~ between two people** 两人之间的爱慕 **2** [c] (favourable feature) 优点; **I can't see the ~ of ...** 我看不出…有什么好处 **3** [c] (entertainment, sight) 有吸引力的地方; **a great tourist ~** 旅游胜地 **4** [u] Phys 引力; **gravitational/magnetic ~** 重力/磁力

attractive /əˈtræktɪv/ *adj* **1** (pleasing) 漂亮的 ‹*flower, face, arrangement*›; 动听的 ‹*music*›; 诱人的 ‹*food*› **2** (appealing) 有吸引力的; (beneficial) 有益的

attractively /əˈtræktɪvli/ *adv* **1** (nicely, pleasantly) 漂亮地 **2** (interestingly) 吸引人地; (suitably) 得体地; **~ priced/worded** 价格诱人的/用词得体的

attractiveness /əˈtræktɪvnɪs/ *n* [u] 吸引力

attributable /əˈtrɪbjʊtəbl/ *adj* **to be ~ to sb./sth.** «*event*» 可归因于某人/某事物; «*origin, authorship*» 可归属于某人/某事物

attribute
A /əˈtrɪbjuːt/ *vt* **1** (state cause, reason) **to ~ sth. to sb./sth.** 把某事物归因于某人/某事物 **2** (state origin, authorship) **to ~ sth. to sb.** 认为某事物出自某人 **3** (associate) **to ~ sth. to sb./sth.** 把…归咎于某人/某事物 ‹*guilt, blame*›; 认为某人/某事物具有 ‹*motive, emotion*›
B /ˈætrɪbjuːt/ *n* **1** (property, quality) 属性; **the ~s of patience and kindness** 耐心和善良的品质 **2** (material symbol) 标志; **the sceptre is an ~ of kingly power** 节杖是王权的象征

attribution /ˌætrɪˈbjuːʃn/ *n* (to cause, reason) 归因; (to origin, author) 归属

attributive /əˈtrɪbjʊtɪv/ *adj* 用作定语的; **an ~ adjective** 定语形容词

attributively /əˈtrɪbjʊtɪvli/ *adv* 作为定语

attrition /əˈtrɪʃn/ *n* [u] **1** (gradual weakening) 消耗; **a war of ~** 消耗战 **2** (friction, abrasion) 磨损 **3** Amer **= natural wastage**

attune /əˈtjuːn, Amer əˈtuːn/ *vt* 使适应; **to be/become ~d to sth.** 适应/开始适应某事物; **to ~ oneself to sth.** 使自己适应某事物

ATV *abbr* **= all-terrain vehicle**

atypical /ˌeɪˈtɪpɪkl/ *adj* 非典型的 ‹*feature, colour*›; 反常的 ‹*behaviour*›

AU *abbr* **= astronomical unit**

aubergine /ˈəʊbəʒiːn/ *n* **1** [c] esp Brit (vegetable) 茄子 **2** [u] (colour) 深紫色

auburn /ˈɔːbən/ ▸**p. 134** *adj* 红褐色的 ‹*hair*›

auction /ˈɔːkʃn, ˈɒkʃn/

A *n* 拍卖; **at ~** 在拍卖会上; **to sell/for sale by ~** 拍卖/供拍卖; **to be up for ~** 交付拍卖; **to put sth. in** *or* **into an ~** 把某物拿去拍卖

B *vt* 拍卖

Phrasal verb

- **auction off** *vt* [**~ sth. off, ~ off sth.**] 拍卖掉; **to ~ off old furniture/damaged warehouse stock** 拍卖掉旧家具/破损的库存商品

auctioneer /ˌɔːkʃəˈnɪə(r)/ ▸**p. 409** *n* 拍卖商

auction: ~ house *n* 拍卖行; **~ room** *n* 拍卖大厅; **~ sale** *n* 拍卖

AUD *abbr* **= Australian dollar** 澳元

audacious /ɔːˈdeɪʃəs/ *adj* **1** (bold) 大胆的 **2** (impudent) 放肆的

audaciously /ɔːˈdeɪʃəsli/ *adv* (boldly) 大胆地; (impudently) 放肆地

audacity /ɔːˈdæsəti/ *n* (boldness) 大胆; (impudence) 放肆; **to have the ~ to do/say sth.** 胆大妄为地做某事/说某话

audibility /ˌɔːdəˈbɪləti/ *n* [声音的] 清晰度; **just above/below the threshold of ~** 刚好超过/低于听阈

audible /ˈɔːdəbl/ *adj* 听得见的

audibly /ˈɔːdəbli/ *adv* 以听得见的响度

audience /ˈɔːdɪəns/ *n* **1** (for show, performance, TV programme) 观众; Radio 听众; **to hold an ~** 吸引观众 **2** (for books) 读者; (for ideas) 受众; **to reach a wider ~** 拥有更多的受众 **3** formal (meeting) 会见; **to grant an ~ to sb.** 准许某人谒见; **an ~ with the Pope** 教皇的接见

audience: ~ participation *n* Radio 听众的参与; TV 观众的参与; **~ ratings** *npl* Radio 收听率; TV 收视率; **~ research** *n* [u] Radio 听众调查; TV 观众调查

audio /ˈɔːdɪəʊ/ *adj* 声音的

audio: ~book *n* 有声读物; **~ cassette** *n* 盒式录音磁带; **~ frequency** *n* 音频; **~ tape** *n* **1** [u] (material) 磁带; **2** [c] (cassette) 盒式录音带; **~ typist** *n* 听音打字员; **~visual** *adj* 视听的

audit /ˈɔːdɪt/

A *n* 审计; **to carry out** *or* **do an ~** 进行审计

B *vt* **1** (conduct financial inspection of) 审查 ‹*accounts, company*› **2** Amer Univ 旁听 ‹*class*›

audition /ɔːˈdɪʃn/

A *n* (for acting role) 试演; (for singing role) 试唱; (as musician) 试奏

B *vi* **to ~ for sth.** «*actor*» 试演某角色; «*singer*» 试唱某曲目; «*musician*» 试奏某曲目

C *vt* 对…进行面试; **to be ~ed for sth.** 为某事接受面试

auditor /ˈɔːdɪtə(r)/ ▸**p. 409** *n* **1** Fin 审计员; **an internal/external ~** 内部/外部审计员 **2** Amer Univ 旁听生

auditorium /ˌɔːdɪˈtɔːrɪəm/ *n* (*pl* **~s** *or* **auditoria** /ˌɔːdɪˈtɔːrɪə/) **1** (in theatre) 观众席; (in concert hall) 听众席 **2** Amer (for meetings) 礼堂

auditor's report *n* 审计报告

auditory /ˈɔːdɪtri, Amer -tɔːri/ *adj* 听觉的 ‹*nerve, stimulation*›; 听到的 ‹*information*›

audit trail *n* 审核跟踪

Aug *abbr* **= August**

auger /ˈɔːgə(r)/ *n* (for wood) 木螺钻; (for ground) 土螺钻

augment /ɔːgˈment/ *vt* 增加; **to ~ sth. with sth./by doing sth.** 以某事物/通过做某事增加某事物

augmentation /ˌɔːgmenˈteɪʃn/ *n* 增加; **breast ~** 隆胸

augur /ˈɔːgə(r)/ *vi* 预兆; **to ~ well/badly for ...** 对…来说是个好/坏兆头

augury /ˈɔːgjʊri/ *n* liter 预兆

August /ˈɔːgəst/ ▸**p. 490** *n* 八月; **last/this/next ~** 上个/本年/下个八月份; **in early/late ~** 八月上旬/下旬; **~ weather/morning** 八月的天气/早晨

august /ɔːˈgʌst/ *adj* formal 威严的 ‹*body of people, presence*›; 雄伟的 ‹*building*›; 高贵的 ‹*lineage*›

aunt /ɑːnt, Amer ænt/ ▸**p. 419** *n* (father's sister) 姑姑; (mother's sister) 姨母; (wife of father's older brother) 伯母; (wife of father's younger brother) 婶婶; (wife of mother's brother) 舅母; (close family friend) 阿姨; **A~ Dodie** 多迪姨妈

auntie, aunty /ˈɑːnti, Amer ˈænti/ *n* colloq **= aunt**

au pair /ˌəʊ ˈpeə(r)/ *n* "互裨"生 [寄住国外家庭、以服务换取食宿并学习语言]

aura /ˈɔːrə/ *n* (*pl* **~s** *or* **aurae** /ˈɔːriː/) (of place) 氛围; (of person) 气质

aural /ˈɔːrəl, ˈaʊrəl/

A *n* **1** Sch 听力练习 **2** Mus 辨音测验

B *adj* **1** (gen) 听觉的 **2** Med 耳的; **~ surgeon** 耳外科医生 **3** Sch 听力的

aurora /ɔːˈrɔːrə/ *n* (*pl* **~s** *or* **aurorae** /ɔːˈrɔːriː/) 极光

aurora: ~ australis /ɔːˌrɔːrə ɒˈstrɑːlɪs/ *n* 南极光; **~ borealis** /ɔːˌrɔːrə ˌbɒrɪˈeɪlɪs/ *n* 北极光

auspices /ˈɔːspɪsɪz/ *npl* 支持; **under the ~ of ...** 在…的支持下

auspicious /ɔːˈspɪʃəs/ *adj* 吉利的; **an ~ start to one's career** 事业上的开门红

auspiciously /ɔːˈspɪʃəsli/ *adv* 吉利地

Aussie /ˈɒzi/ colloq

A *n* (Australian person) 澳大利亚人; (Australia) 澳大利亚

B *adj* 澳大利亚的

austere /ɒˈstɪə(r), ɔːˈstɪə(r)/ *adj* **1** (plain) 朴素的 ‹*style*›; 简陋的 ‹*room*› **2** (strict) 严厉的 ‹*person*›; 严肃的 ‹*expression, attitude*›; 厉行节俭的 ‹*life*›

austerely /ɒˈstɪəli, ɔːˈstɪəli/ *adv* **1** (plainly) 朴素地 **2** (strictly) 严厉地

austerity /ɒˈsterəti, ɔːˈsterəti/ *n* **1** [u] (plainness) 朴素; (severity) 严厉; **years of ~ during the war** 艰苦的战争岁月 **2** **austerities** 艰苦条件

Australasia /ˌɒstrəˈleɪʒɪə, ˌɔːs-/ *pr n* 澳大拉西亚

Australasian /ˌɒstrəˈleɪʒn, ˌɔːs-/

A *adj* 澳大拉西亚的

B *n* 澳大拉西亚人

Australia /ɒˈstreɪlɪə, ɔːˈstr-/ *pr n* (country) 澳大利亚; (continent) 澳大利亚洲

Australian /ɒˈstreɪlɪən, ɔːˈstr-/ ▸**p. 503**

A *adj* (of Australia) 澳大利亚的; (of the people) 澳大利亚人的

B *n* **1** [c] (person) 澳大利亚人 **2** [u] Ling 澳大利亚英语

Australian Rules, Australian Rules Football *ns* [u] 澳大利亚式橄榄球

Austria /ˈɒstrɪə, ˈɔːs-/ *pr n* 奥地利

Austrian /ˈɒstrɪən, ˈɔːs-/ ▸**p. 503**

A *adj* (of Austria) 奥地利的; (of the people) 奥地利人的

B *n* 奥地利人

AUT *abbr* Brit **= Association of University Teachers** 大学教师协会

authentic /ɔːˈθentɪk/ *adj* **1** (genuine) 真品的; **an ~ Van Gogh** 凡·高的真迹 **2** (reliable) 真实可信的; **~ account/data** 真实的描述/数据

authenticate /ɔːˈθentɪkeɪt/ *vt* 证明…是真的

authentication /ɔːˌθentɪˈkeɪʃn/ *n* 验证

authenticity /ˌɔːθenˈtɪsəti/ *n* [u] **1** (genuineness) 真实性 **2** (reliability) 可靠性

author /ˈɔːθə(r)/ ▸**p. 409** *n* **1** (of book, play, report) 作者 **2** (by profession) 作家 **3** (of plan, scheme) 发起人

authoress /ˈɔːθərɪs/ ▸**p. 409** *n* dated 女作家

authoring /ˈɔːθərɪŋ/ *n* [u] 制作

authoritarian /ɔːˌθɒrɪˈteərɪən/

A *adj* 专制的; **an ~ government** 专制政体

B *n* 专制主义者

authoritarianism /ɔːˌθɒrɪˈteərɪənɪzəm/ *n* [u] 专制主义

authoritative /ɔːˈθɒrətətɪv, Amer -teɪtɪv/ *adj* **1** (forceful) 专断的; **the ~ tone in her voice** 她那命令式的口气 **2** (reliable) 权威性的; **an ~ report** 一份具有权威性的报告

authority /ɔːˈθɒrəti/

A *n* **1** [u] (power) 权力; **to have (the) ~ to do sth.** 有权做某事; **to exercise one's ~** 行使权力; **who's in ~ here?** 这里谁当权? ; **to do sth. on sb.'s ~** 根据某人的指示做某事; **to be** *or* **act under sb.'s ~** 受某人支配; **he has recently assumed ~ for our transport division** 他最近接管了我们的运输部门 **2** [u] (forcefulness, confidence) 威信; **a person of ~** 有威信的人; **to speak with ~** 用权威的口吻讲话; **to lack ~** 缺少威信 **3** [u] (permission) 授权; **to give sb. ~ to do sth., to give ~ for sb. to do sth.** 批准某人做某事 **4** [c] (expert) 专家; (book, film) 权威; **an ~ on sth.** 某方面的权威 **5** [c] (source) 来源; **what is your ~ for these figures?** 你的这些数字出自何处? ; **I have it on good ~ that ...** 我有充分根据说…

B **the authorities** *npl* (organization) 当局; **to report sth. to the authorities** 向官方报告某事

authorization /ˌɔːθəraɪˈzeɪʃn/ *n* **1** [u] (authority) 授权; (permission) 批准; **to give** *or* **grant ~ (to do sth.)** 授权 (做某事); **~ to do/for sth.** 做某事/某事物的许可 **2** [c] (document) 授权书

authorize /ˈɔːθəraɪz/ *vt* 批准; **to ~ sb. to do sth.** 授权某人做某事

authorized /ˈɔːθəraɪzd/ *adj* 经授权的; **an ~ dealer** 指定经销商

authorship /ˈɔːθəʃɪp/ *n* [u] **1** (of book, poem) 作者身份; **a book of unknown ~** 作者不详的书 **2** (profession) 作家职业

autism /ˈɔːtɪzəm/ ▸**p. 377** *n* [u] 自闭症

autistic /ɔːˈtɪstɪk/ *adj* 患自闭症的

auto /ˈɔːtəʊ/ *n* esp Amer 汽车; **the ~ industry** 汽车业; **an ~ accident** 车祸

autobiographical /ˌɔːtəʊbaɪəˈgræfɪkl/, **autobiographic** /ˌɔːtəʊbaɪəˈgræfɪk/ *adj* 自传 (体) 的

autobiography /ˌɔːtəʊbaɪˈɒgrəfi/ *n* **1** [c] (book) 自传 **2** [u] (genre) 自传体

autoclave /ˈɔːtəʊkleɪv/ *n* 高压灭菌器

autocracy /ɔːˈtɒkrəsi/ *n* **1** [u] (system of government) 独裁政体 **2** [c] (country) 独裁国家 **3** [u] (style of management) 独裁

a

autocrat /ˈɔːtəkræt/ *n* 1 (ruler) 独裁者 2 (domineering person) 独断专行的人

autocratic /ˌɔːtəˈkrætɪk/ *adj* 1 (of ruler) 独裁的 2 (domineering) 独断专行的

autocrime /ˈɔːtəʊkraɪm/ *n* [u and c] 汽车犯罪 [指盗、抢汽车等]

autocross /ˈɔːtəʊkrɒs/ *n* [u] 1 Brit 汽车越野赛 2 Amer 汽车竞技比赛

autocue /ˈɔːtəʊkjuː/ *n* esp Brit 自动提词机

autodidact /ˈɔːtəʊdaɪdækt/ *n* formal 自学者

auto-erotic /ˌɔːtəʊɪˈrɒtɪk/ *adj* 自体性行为的

autofocus /ˈɔːtəʊfəʊkəs/ *n* [u] 自动对焦

autograph /ˈɔːtəgrɑːf, Amer -græf/
A *n* 亲笔签名; **an ～ hunter** 热衷于求人签名留念的人
B *vt* 在…上签名

autoimmune /ˌɔːtəʊɪˈmjuːn/ *adj* 自体免疫的 ‹*disease*›; 自身免疫的 ‹*system*›

automata /ɔːˈtɒmətə/ *pl* ▸**automaton**

automate /ˈɔːtəmeɪt/ *vt* 使自动化; **fully ～d** 全自动的

automated teller machine *n* 自动柜员机

automatic /ˌɔːtəˈmætɪk/
A *adj* 1 (of machine, car) 自动的 2 (spontaneous) 无意识的 ‹*gesture, movement*›; 不假思索的 ‹*response, decision*› 3 (as a matter of course) 必然的
B *n* 1 (car) 自动换挡汽车 2 (pistol) 自动手枪; (rifle) 自动步枪 3 (washing machine) 自动洗衣机 4 (setting) 自动挡; **to be on ～** «*machine, heating*» 处于自动挡上; **to be in ～** 机械性地运转

automatically /ˌɔːtəˈmætɪkli/ *adv* 1 (mechanically) 自动地 2 (spontaneously) 不假思索地 3 (as a matter of course) 必然地

automatic: ～ pilot *n* (device) 自动驾驶仪; (system) 自动驾驶系统; **to be on ～ pilot** lit 由自动驾驶仪驾驶; fig 机械性地做; **～ teller machine** *n* 自动柜员机

automation /ˌɔːtəˈmeɪʃn/ *n* [u] 自动化; **office ～** 办公自动化

automaton /ɔːˈtɒmətən, Amer -tɒn/ *n* (*pl* **～s, automata**) 1 (robot) 小机器人 2 pej (person) 做事机械的人

automobile /ˈɔːtəməbiːl, ˌɔːtəməˈbiːl/ *n* esp Amer 汽车

automotive /ˌɔːtəˈməʊtɪv/ *adj* 汽车的

autonomous /ɔːˈtɒnəməs/ *adj* 1 (self-governing) 自治的 2 (acting independently) 自主的

autonomous region *n* 自治区

autonomy /ɔːˈtɒnəmi/ *n* [u] (self-government) 自治; (independence) 自主

autopilot /ˈɔːtəʊpaɪlət/ *n* = **automatic pilot**

autopsy /ˈɔːtɒpsi/ *n* 验尸; **to do** *or* **perform** *or* **carry out an ～ on a corpse** 进行尸检

autosave /ˈɔːtəʊseɪv/ Comput
A *n* [u] 自动保存
B *vt* 自动保存

autosuggestion /ˌɔːtəʊsəˈdʒestʃən/ *n* [u] 自我暗示

autoteller /ˌɔːtəʊˈtelə(r)/ *n* 自动柜员机

autotimer /ˈɔːtəʊtaɪmə(r)/ *n* 自动定时器

autowind /ˈɔːtəʊwaɪnd/ *n* [u] (gen) 自动卷绕; (on camera) 自动卷片

autozoom /ˈɔːtəʊzuːm/ *n* [u] 自动变焦

autumn /ˈɔːtəm/ ▸**p. 692** *n* esp Brit 秋季; **in (the) ～** 在秋天; **in the ～ of her years** 在她的暮年; **～ leaves** 秋叶; **～ colours/fashions** 秋天的色彩/流行式样

autumnal /ɔːˈtʌmnəl/ *adj* 秋天的

auxiliary /ɔːgˈzɪlɪəri/
A *adj* 辅助的; **an ～ generator** 备用发电机
B *n* 1 (person) 辅助者; (thing) 辅助物; **a medical ～** 医疗辅助员 2 Ling 助动词 3 Hist (soldier) 外国援军

auxiliary: ～ nurse ▸**p. 409** *n* 助理护士; **～ verb** *n* 助动词

AV *abbr* = **audiovisual**

avail /əˈveɪl/ formal
A *n* **to be of no/little ～** 没有用/没什么用; **to no/little ～** 结果无效/没什么效果
B *v refl* **to ～ oneself of sth.** 利用某事物

availability /əˌveɪləˈbɪləti/ *n* [u] (of option, strategy, service) 可利用性; (of drugs, oil) 可获得性; **～ of credit** 获得信贷的可能性; **demand exceeds ～** 供不应求

available /əˈveɪləbl/ *adj* 1 (able to be used or obtained) 可获得的; **to make sth. ～ to sb.** 使某人能够得到某物; **to be ～ from ...** 可从…获得; **by every ～ means** 用一切可能的办法; **this model is no longer ～** 这种型号下市了 2 (free) 有空的; **to make oneself ～** 抽空; **she is not ～ for comment** 没法找她置评 3 (for relationship, sex) 单身的

avalanche /ˈævəlɑːnʃ, Amer -læntʃ/ *n* 1 (fall of snow, ice) 雪崩; (fall of rock) 山崩 2 fig (huge quantity) 大批

avalanche shelter *n* 雪崩掩体

avant-garde /ˌævɒŋˈgɑːd/
A *adj* 前卫派的
B *n* **the ～** 前卫派

avarice /ˈævərɪs/ *n* [u] 贪婪

avaricious /ˌævəˈrɪʃəs/ *adj* 贪婪的

avatar /ˈævətɑː(r)/ *n* 1 Relig lit (person) 下凡化作人形; (animal) 下凡化作兽形; fig 化身 2 Comput [代表人的] 可移动图标

Ave *abbr* = **avenue 1**

avenge /əˈvendʒ/
A *vt* 报…之仇 ‹*wrong, death*›; 替…报仇 ‹*person*›
B *v refl* **to ～ oneself on sb.** 向某人寻仇

avenging /əˈvendʒɪŋ/ *adj* 报仇的; **an ～ angel** 复仇天使

avenue /ˈævənjuː, Amer -nuː/ *n* 1 (street) 大街; **35 Acacia A～** 刺槐大道35号 2 (driveway) 车道 3 (path) 林荫道 4 fig (possibility) 途径

aver /əˈvɜː(r)/ *vt* (*pres p etc.* **-rr-**) formal 断言; **he ～red his innocence, he ～red that he was innocent** 他坚称自己是清白的

average /ˈævərɪdʒ/
A *n* 1 Math 平均数; **at an ～ of ...** 以…的平均值; **to take an ～** 取平均值 2 (standard amount, level) 一般水平; **the national ～** 全国平均水平; **on ～** 以平均数论; **the law of ～s** 平均律
B *adj* 1 Math 平均的 2 (usual, ordinary) 普通的; **we have above ～ inflation in this country** 我国的通货膨胀率偏高; **it was a pretty ～ sort of film** 这部电影很一般
C *vt* 平均达到; **I ～ seven hours' work a day** 我平均一天工作7小时

Phrasal verb

• **average out**
A *vi* **to ～ out to** *or* **at ...** 平均为…; **their working day ～s out at 7-8 hours** 他们每个工作日平均为7到8小时; **I pay the mortgage and he pays the bills: it seems to ～ out okay** 我付按揭还款，他付日常开支：看来两者持平
B *vt* [**～ sth. out, ～ out sth.**] 算出…的平均值

averse /əˈvɜːs/ *adj* 嫌恶的; **to be ～ to sth./doing sth.** 不喜欢某事/做某事

aversion /əˈvɜːʃn, Amer əˈvɜːrʒn/ *n* 厌恶; **to have an ～ to sb./to sth./to doing sth.** 厌恶某人/某物/做某事

aversion therapy *n* [u] 厌恶疗法

avert /əˈvɜːt/ *vt* 1 (avoid, prevent) 防止 2 (turn away) 将…移开; **to ～ one's eyes** *or* **gaze from sth.** 不再看某物; **to ～ one's mind from sth.** 不再想某事

avian flu /ˌeɪvɪən ˈfluː/ ▸**p. 377** *n* [u] 禽流感

aviary /ˈeɪvɪəri, Amer -vieri/ *n* 大型鸟舍

aviation /ˌeɪvɪˈeɪʃn/ *n* [u] 航空

aviation: ～ fuel *n* [u] 航空燃料; **～ industry** *n* 航空业

aviator /ˈeɪvɪeɪtə(r)/ ▸**p. 409** *n* dated (pilot) 飞行员; (crew member) 机组人员

avid /ˈævɪd/ *adj* 1 *attrib* 热衷的; **an ～ reader/supporter** 酷爱阅读的人/积极拥护的人 2 *pred* 渴望的; **to be ～ for sth.** 渴望得到某物

avidly /ˈævɪdli/ *adv* 热衷地; **he reads science fiction novels ～** 他酷爱科幻小说

avionics /ˌeɪvɪˈɒnɪks/ *npl* 1 + *v sing* (subject) 航空电子学 2 + *v pl* (electronic equipment) 航空电子设备; **～ systems/equipment** 航空电子系统/设备

avo /ˈɑːvəʊ/ ▸**p. 174** *n* 分 [澳门辅币名]

avocado /ˌævəˈkɑːdəʊ/ *n* 1 [u and c] (fruit) 鳄梨; **～ salad** 鳄梨色拉 2 [c] (tree) 鳄梨树 3 [u] (colour) 鳄梨色

avocet /ˈævəset/ *n* 反嘴鹬

avoid /əˈvɔɪd/ *vt* 1 (prevent) 避免; **to ～ doing sth.** 避免做某事 2 (keep away from) 避开; **to ～ sb./sth. like the plague** 像躲瘟疫一样避开某人/某事物; **to ～ sb./sb.'s gaze** 避开某人/某人的目光

avoidable /əˈvɔɪdəbl/ *adj* 可避免的

avoidance /əˈvɔɪdəns/ *n* [u] (of responsibility) 逃避; (of issue, subject, problem, emotion) 回避; (of person) 躲避; ▸**tax avoidance**

avoirdupois /ˌævədəˈpɔɪz/ *n* [u] 常衡

avow /əˈvaʊ/ *vt* formal 1 (admit) **to ～ oneself to be sth.** 公开承认自己是某身份 2 (declare) 公开宣称

avowal /əˈvaʊəl/ *n* formal 1 (confession) 公开承认 2 (declaration) 公开宣称

avowed /əˈvaʊd/ *adj* 1 (confessed) 公开承认的 2 (declared) 公开宣称的

avuncular /əˈvʌŋkjʊlə(r)/ *adj* 慈爱的

AWACS /ˈeɪwæks/ *abbr* = **Airborne Warning and Control System** 机载警报与控制系统; **～ aircraft** 预警飞机

await /əˈweɪt/ *vt* 1 (wait for) 等候; **long-～ed** 期待已久的; **in prison ～ing trial** 在狱中等候审判 2 (to be in store) 将降临到…身上; **a warm welcome ～s you** 你将受到热烈欢迎

awake /əˈweɪk/
A *adj* 1 (not asleep) 醒着的; **half ～** 半睡半醒的; **to lie ～** 毫无睡意地躺着; **to shake sb. ～** 把某人摇醒; **to be wide ～** 毫无睡意 2 (aware) 意识到的; **to be ～ to the dangers** 意识到各种危险
B *vt* (*pt* **awoke**, *pp* **awoken**) 1 (from sleep) 唤醒 2 fig 唤起; **the incident awoke old memories** 这件事勾起了对往事的回忆
C *vi* (*pt* **awoke**, *pp* **awoken**) 1 (from sleep) 醒来 2 (become aware) 察觉; **to ～ to sth.** 意识到某事物

awaken /əˈweɪkən/
A *vt* 1 (from sleep) 唤醒 2 (generate) 唤起; **to ～ a love of classical music** 激发对古典音乐的喜爱 3 (make aware) 使意识到; **to ～ sb. to dangers/problems** 使某人意识到危险/问题
B *vi* 1 (from sleep) 醒来; **to ～ to sth.** 醒来发现某事物 2 (become aware) 意识到; **to ～ to sth.** 意识到某事物

awakening /əˈweɪkənɪŋ/
A *n* 1 lit (from sleep) 醒 2 fig (of emotion, interest) 唤醒; (of awareness) 觉醒; **the ～ of love** 爱情的萌动; **rude ～** lit 突然的醒来; fig 猛然的意识
B *adj* lit 正在醒来的; fig 正在产生的; **his ～ desire** 他那萌动的欲望

award /əˈwɔːd/
A *n* 1 (prize) 奖; (medal) 奖章; (certificate) 奖状; **an ～ for bravery** 英勇奖; **the ～ for the best actor** 最佳男演员奖; **to win/present an ～** 获奖/颁奖 2 (grant) 奖学金 3 (decision to give) (of prize, grant) 授予; Jur 赔偿裁定额; **an ～ of damages** 对损害赔偿金的裁定

a

B *vt* **1** (bestow) 授予; **to ~ a prize for sth.** 为某事而授奖; **to ~ a prize to sb., to ~ sb. a prize** 给某人授奖 **2** Jur, Sport 判给; **to ~ damages of £200,000** 判给20万英镑的损害赔偿金; **to ~ a penalty** 处以罚球 **3** (grant) 给予

award: ~ ceremony *n* 颁奖仪式; **~ winner** *n* 获奖者; **~-winning** *adj* 获奖的

aware /ə'weə(r)/ *adj* **1** (conscious) 意识到的; (informed) 知道的; **to be ~ of** (realize) 意识到; (know that) 知道; **to become ~ that ...** 觉察到…; **to make sb. ~ that ...** 使某人意识到…; **I'm well ~ of that** 对那一点我很清楚 **2** (well-informed) 有知识的; (interested) 感兴趣的; **to be politically/environmentally ~** 有政治觉悟/环境意识

awareness /ə'weənɪs/ *n* [u] 意识; **public ~ of this problem has increased** 公众对这个问题的意识增强了; **political ~** 政治觉悟

awareness campaign *n* 意识培养

awash /ə'wɒʃ/ *adj pred* **1** (flooded) 被淹没的; (washed over) 被漫过的 **2** fig (having too much, too many) 充斥的; **the resort is ~ with tourists** 这处旅游胜地客满为患

away /ə'weɪ/

A *adv* **1** (not present, gone) 不在; **I have to be ~ by 10** 我 10 点钟之前一定要走; **to be ~** (from work) 缺勤; (from school) 缺课; **to be ~ on holiday/business** 外出休假/出差 **2** (distant in space) 在…距离处; (distant in time) 间隔…的时间; **50m ~** 50 米之外; **stand ~ from the edge** 远离边沿; **the exam is only days ~** 没几天就要考试了; **we live 3 hours ~ from London** 我们住在离伦敦有 3 个小时行程的地方; **~ with you!** (go away) 滚开!; (nonsense) 胡说! **3** (from here/there) 向别处; **to crawl ~** 爬走; **to drive ~** 驾车离开; **the shift ~ from traditional values** 对传统价值观的偏离; **to move ~ from party orthodoxy** 偏离党派的正统观念 **4** (for emphasis) [用于强调]; **~ over on the other side of the lake** 远在湖对面; **~ back in 1920/in the old days** 早在 1920 年/在很久以前 **5** Sport 在客场 ‹*play, win*›

B *adj* **1** *attrib* Sport 在客场的 ‹*goal, match*›; **the ~ team** 客队 **2** *pred* Brit colloq (drunk) 醉酒的; **to be well ~** 酩酊大醉

awe /ɔ:/

A *n* [u] 敬畏; **to watch/listen in ~** 敬畏地看/听; **to stand** *or* **be in ~ of sb./sth.** 对某人/某事物感到敬畏

B *vt* 使敬畏; **to be ~d by sth.** 敬畏某事物

awe-inspiring *adj* 令人敬畏的 ‹*person*›; 令人惊叹的 ‹*sight*›

awesome /'ɔ:səm/ *adj* **1** (impressive) 令人惊叹的; (frightening) 使人惊惧的; (difficult) 很困难的; **a problem of ~ complexity** 十分复杂的问题 **2** colloq (stunningly good) 呱呱叫的

awe-struck *adj* 令人顿生敬畏的

awful /'ɔ:fl/ *adj* **1** (bad) 坏的; **that ~ woman!** 那个坏女人!; **you are ~!** hum 你太不像话了!; **it was ~ to have to sit there doing nothing** 不得不无所事事地坐着真是太难受了 **2** (horrifying, tragic) 可怕的 **3** (unwell) 生病的; **to feel/look ~** 感到不舒服/面带病容 **4** (guilty) 难过的 **5** colloq (emphasizing) 极其; **an ~ lot (of)** 很多很多(的); **to be in an ~ hurry** 急急忙忙; **an ~ cheek** *or* **nerve** 厚脸皮

awfully /'ɔ:fli/ *adv* **1** colloq (very) 非常; **he's ~ late/early** 他太晚/早了; **I'm not ~ sure** 我不是很肯定; **thanks ~** 万分感谢 **2** (terribly) 糟糕地

awfulness /'ɔ:fəlnɪs/ *n* [u] (of situation, place, object) 糟糕; (of person) 极坏

awhile /ə'waɪl/ *adv* liter 片刻; **not yet ~** 一时还不

awkward /'ɔ:kwəd/ *adj* **1** (difficult to use) 使用不便的; (difficult to deal with) 难对付的; **the room has ~ proportions** 房间的比例不协调; **to be sitting in an ~ position** 坐姿不舒服 **2** (complicated, inconvenient) 不方便的; **to make life ~ for sb.** 给某人找麻烦 **3** (embarrassing) 令人尴尬的; **you've put me in a very ~ position!** 你把我弄得很狼狈! **4** (uncooperative) 难相处的; **he's being ~ about the whole thing** 他在整件事情中都不肯合作; **the ~ age** 尴尬年龄 [指青春期] **5** (clumsy) 笨拙的; **an ~ style of writing** 冗赘的写作风格 **6** (embarrassed) 局促不安的; **to feel ~ about sth./doing sth.** 对某事/做某事感到局促不安

awkwardly /'ɔ:kwədli/ *adv* **1** (inconveniently) 不方便地; **~ placed/designed** 放置/设计得不方便的 **2** (with embarrassment) 尴尬地 **3** (clumsily) 笨拙地

awkwardness /'ɔ:kwədnɪs/ *n* [u] **1** (delicacy of situation) 棘手 **2** (inconvenience) 不方便 **3** (embarrassment) 尴尬 **4** (clumsiness) 笨拙 **5** (shyness) 羞怯

awl /ɔ:l/ *n* (for leather) 尖锥; (for wood etc.) 钻子

awning /'ɔ:nɪŋ/ *n* (to keep from sunlight) 凉篷; (to keep from rain) 雨篷

awoke /ə'wəʊk/ *pt* ▸**awake B, C**

awoken /ə'wəʊkən/ *pp* ▸**awake B, C**

AWOL /'eɪwɒl/ *abbr* **= absent without (official) leave** 擅离职守的; **to be** *or* **go ~** Mil 擅离职守; hum 开小差

awry /ə'raɪ/

A *adj* 歪斜的; **with one's clothing ~** 衣冠不整地

B *adv* 出错; **to go ~** 出岔子; **to put sth. ~** 使某事物出岔子

axe, Amer **ax** /æks/

A *n* **1** (tool) 斧; **to have an ~ to grind** fig 另有所图 **2** fig 裁减; **the ~ has fallen** 裁员开始了; **to face the ~** 面临解雇; **to get the ~** colloq (lose one's job) 被解雇; (be cancelled) 被取消

B *vt* 大量削减

axiom /'æksɪəm/ *n* 公理

axiomatic /ˌæksɪə'mætɪk/ *adj* **1** Ling, Math, Philos 公理的 **2** (self-evident) 不证自明的; **it is ~ that ...** …是不言自明的

axis /'æksɪs/ *n* (*pl* **axes** /'æksi:z/) **1** (gen) 轴; **~ of rotation** 旋转轴 **2** Math 坐标轴; **on the x/y ~** 在X/Y轴上 **3** Pol, Hist (alliance) 轴心; **the A~ Powers** 轴心国

axle /'æksl/ *n* 车轴; **the front/rear ~** 前/后车轴

axle grease *n* [u] 轮轴润滑油

ayatollah /ˌaɪə'tɒlə/ *n* 阿亚图拉 [对伊朗什叶派领导人的尊称]

aye /aɪ/

A *excl* **1** dial (yes) 是 **2** Naut **~, ~, sir** 遵命, 长官

B **the ~s** *n* (vote) 赞成票; (person) 投赞成票者; **the ~s have it!** 投赞成票者占多数!

AYH *abbr* **= American Youth Hostels (Association)** 美国青年招待所（协会）

AZ *abbr* Amer **= Arizona**

azalea /ə'zeɪlɪə/ *n* 杜鹃花

Azerbaijan /ˌæzəbaɪ'dʒɑ:n/ *pr n* 阿塞拜疆

Azerbaijani /ˌæzəbaɪ'dʒɑ:ni/ **▸p. 503, p. 426**

A *adj* (of Azerbaijan) 阿塞拜疆的; (of the people) 阿塞拜疆人的; (of the language) 阿塞拜疆语的

B *n* **1** [c] (person) 阿塞拜疆人 **2** [u] (language) 阿塞拜疆语

azimuth /'æzɪməθ/ *n* **1** Astron 地平经度 **2** (of compass bearing) 方位角

azine /'eɪzi:n/ *n* [u] 吖嗪

Azores /ə'zɔ:z/ *pr npl* **the ~** 亚速尔群岛

Aztec /'æztek/ **▸p. 503, p. 426** Hist

A *adj* (of the people) 阿兹特克人的; (of the language) 阿兹特克语的

B *n* **1** [c] (person) 阿兹特克人 **2** [u] (language) 阿兹特克语

azure /'æʒə(r), -zjə(r)/ **▸p. 134**

A *adj* 蔚蓝色的

B *n* [u] 蔚蓝色

Bb

B, b /biː/
A *n* (*pl* **Bs** *or* **B's**) [1] (letter) [英语字母表的第2个字母] [2] (second of two or more points or possibilities) 第二（个）; **a) ... b) ...** 第一… 第二… [3] **B** Mus B 音, B 调 [4] **B** Sch, Univ (grade) 良 [指学业成绩第二等]; **he got a B in English at A level** 他在高级证书考试中英语得了良 [5] (house or flat number) B 座 [门牌号]; **he lives at flat 2b, Park Road** 他住在公园路 2b 号 [6] **B** (road number) B 级公路 [道路编号]; **the B3107** B3107 号公路
B *abbr* **b = born** 出生; **Neil Smith, b 25 April 1942** 尼尔·史密斯, 生于 1942 年 4 月 25 日

BA *abbr* = **Bachelor of Arts** 文学士; **to have/do a ~** 持有/攻读文学士学位

baa /bɑː/
A *n* 咩
B *vi* (*pres* **~s**; *pt, pp* **~ed**) «*sheep, lamb*» 发咩声

babble /ˈbæbl/
A *vi* [1] (talk rapidly, incoherently) 含糊不清地说 [2] «*baby*» 咿呀学语 [3] (make bubbling sound) «*stream*» 潺潺作响; **a babbling brook** 潺潺的小溪
B *n* 含糊不清的话; **a ~ of voices** 人声的嘈杂
C *vt* 含糊不清地说; **'yes, yes,' he ~d** "是的, 是的," 他含混不清地应着

Phrasal verb

- **babble on** *vi* pej 喋喋不休

babe /beɪb/ *n* [1] liter 婴儿; **a ~ in arms** lit 襁褓中的婴儿; fig 生手 [2] colloq (addressing woman) 宝贝儿

babel /ˈbeɪbl/ *n* 嘈杂声

baboon /bəˈbuːn/ *n* 狒狒

baby /ˈbeɪbi/
A *n* [1] (child) 婴儿; **she's going to have a ~** 她马上要生孩子了; **don't be such a ~!** colloq 别这么孩子气!; **to be left holding the ~** fig 被迫做苦差事; **to throw the ~ out with the bathwater** fig 把婴儿和洗澡水一起倒掉; **smooth as a ~'s bottom** 十分光滑 [2] (youngest member) 最年幼的成员 [3] colloq (pet project) 钟爱的项目; **the show/project is his ~** 这个展览/项目是他的得意之作 [4] esp Amer colloq (girlfriend) 女友; (boyfriend) 男友; (as address) 宝贝儿
B *modif* [1] (young) 幼小的; **a ~ daughter/son** 小女儿/儿子; **a ~ bird** 幼鸟 [2] (for a baby) 婴儿用的; **~ clothes** 婴儿服装
C *vt* colloq pej 百般呵护

baby blue ▸ **p. 134**
A *adj* 婴儿蓝的
B *n* [u] 婴儿蓝

baby: ~ blues *npl* colloq 产后抑郁症; **to get hit with the ~ blues** 患产后抑郁症; **~ boom** *n* colloq 生育高峰; **~ boomer** *n* colloq 生育高峰儿 [指20世纪50年代生育高峰期出生的人]; **~ bouncer** *n* 幼儿体操架; **~ buggy** *n* Brit 婴儿车; **~ carriage** *n* Amer 婴儿车; **~ carrier** *n* 婴儿背带; **~ doll pyjamas** *npl* 娃娃装睡衣裤; **~-faced** *adj* 长着娃娃脸的; **~ grand** ▸ **p. 395** *n* 小型卧式钢琴

> **the baby boom**
>
> 生育高峰。指 1945 年第二次世界大战结束至1964年导致人口急剧增长的生育高峰期。20 世纪 30 年代的经济萧条及第二次世界大战导致英美等国人口出生率大幅度下降。随着二战结束后经济的发展, 这些国家的人口出生率急速上升。在此期间出生的婴儿称为 baby boomer, 美国英语中简称 boomer。现在也泛指任何生育高峰期。

Babygro® /ˈbeɪbɪgrəʊ/ *n* 婴儿连身衣

babyhood /ˈbeɪbɪhʊd/ *n* [u] 婴儿期; **in** *or* **during ~** 在婴儿期

babyish /ˈbeɪbɪɪʃ/ *adj* [1] (of a baby) 婴儿的 ‹*toy, book*› [2] pej (like a baby) 稚气的 ‹*behaviour, child*›; **these stories are too ~ for her now** 这些故事现在对她来说太幼稚了

baby: ~ minder *n* Brit 临时保姆; **~ monitor** *n* 婴儿监听器; **~ oil** *n* [u] 婴儿润肤油

baby-sit
A *vt* (*pres p* **-tt-**; *pt, pp* **baby-sat**) 临时照看 ‹*children*›
B *vi* 当临时保姆

baby: ~-sitter *n* 临时保姆; **~-sitting** *n* [u] 当临时保姆; **to go** *or* **do ~-sitting** 代人临时照看小孩; **~ sling** *n* 娃娃背带; **~ snatcher** *n* 偷婴儿的人; **~ talk** *n* [u] (used by babies) 儿语; (used by adults) 模仿儿语; **~ tooth** *n* colloq 乳牙; **~ walker** *n* 学步车; **~wear** *n* [u] 婴儿服装; **~ wipe** *n* 婴儿湿巾

baccalaureate /ˌbækəˈlɔːrɪət/ *n* [1] Sch 中学毕业会考; **European/International B~** 欧洲/国际中学毕业会考 [2] Univ (diploma) 学士学位

baccarat /ˈbækərɑː/ *n* [u] 巴卡拉纸牌戏

bacchanalian /ˌbækəˈneɪlɪən/ *adj* 狂欢闹饮的

baccy /ˈbæki/ *n* [u] Brit colloq 烟草

bachelor /ˈbætʃələ(r)/ *n* [1] (unmarried man) 单身男子; **a confirmed ~** 抱独身主义的男子; **an eligible ~** 合意的单身男子; **to remain a ~** 保持独身; **a ~'s life** 单身汉的生活 [2] **Bachelor** Univ (degree) 学士; **B~ of Arts/Law** 文学士/法学士; **a B~'s degree** 学士学位

bachelor apartment Amer, **bachelor flat** Brit *ns* 单身公寓

bachelorette party /ˌbætʃələˈret ˌpɑːti/ *n* Amer [女子结婚前夕的] 告别单身聚会

bachelor girl *n* dated 单身女子

bachelorhood /ˈbætʃələhʊd/ *n* [u] [男子的] 单身时期

bachelor: ~ pad *n* colloq = **bachelor apartment**; **~ party** *n* Amer [男子结婚前夕的] 告别单身聚会

bacillus /bəˈsɪləs/ *n* (*pl* **bacilli** /bəˈsɪliː/) (disease-causing bacterium) 病菌; (rod-shaped bacterium) 杆菌

back /bæk/
A *n* [1] (part of body) 背部; **he was lying on his ~** 他仰面而卧; **to travel on the ~ of a donkey** 骑驴旅行; **to be at the ~ of sth.** 策划 ‹*conspiracy, proposal*›; **to do sth. behind sb.'s ~** 背着某人做某事; **to break the ~ of sth.** 完成某事的主要部分; **we've broken the ~ of the problem** 我们攻克了问题的难点; **to be (flat) on one's ~** lit 仰卧; fig colloq 卧病; **to be at sb.'s ~** 支持某人; **to be glad to see the ~ of sb./sth.** colloq 庆幸终于摆脱某人/某事物; **to have one's ~ to sb./sth.** 背对着某人/某物; **to live off sb.'s ~** 靠剥削某人生活; **to put one's ~ into sth.** colloq 全力以赴做某事; **to put** *or* **get sb.'s ~ up** colloq 惹恼某人; **to get off sb.'s ~** colloq 不再烦扰某人; **to be on sb.'s ~ (to do sth.)** colloq 纠缠某人（去做某事）; **to succeed on the ~ of sth.** 由于某事物获得成功; **to turn one's ~ on sb./sth.** lit 转身背对某人/某物; fig 背弃某人/某事物 [2] (human spine) 脊梁骨; **to put one's ~ out** 闪腰 [3] (spine of book) 书脊 [4] (reverse side) 背面; (of head) 后脑勺; **the ~ of the knife/hand** 刀背/手背; **to hang one's coat on the ~ of the door** 把外套挂在门后; **the ~ of the fridge/house/shelves** 冰箱背面/房子后墙/架子后挡板 [5] (rear part) 尾部; ▸ **lorry** [6] (area behind building) 屋后; **to be out** *or* Brit **round the ~** 在屋后; **to be in the ~** *or* **in ~ of the house** Amer (in the garden) 在后花园; (in the yard) 在后院 [7] (furthest reaches of cupboard, drawer, fridge) 深处; (of stage) 后部; **at the ~ of the audience** 在观众席的后排; **at the very ~** 在最后; **to sit at** *or* **in the ~ of the bus** 坐在公共汽车的后部; **the ~ of the throat/mouth** 咽喉深处/口腔后部 [8] (supporting part of chair, sofa) 靠背 [9] Sport 后卫 [10] (final pages of book, newspaper etc.) 最后几页; **at the ~ of the book/file** 在书/文件的最后几页
B *adj attrib* [1] (rear) 后面的; **~ garden** Brit 后花园; **the ~ pages of a book** 书的最后几页 [2] (remote, minor) 偏僻的 ‹*alley*›; (subsidiary) 辅助的 [3] (backwards) 向后的; **a ~ pass to the goalkeeper** 给守门员的回传球
C *adv* [1] (indicating return after absence) 返回; **to be ~ (from school/work)** （放学/下班）回来; **they arrived ~ from holiday** 他们度完假回来了; **it's good to be ~ home** 回到家真好 [2] (fashionable again) 再次流行; **roller-skates are ~ (in fashion)** 滑旱冰又流行起来了 [3] (in return) 回报; (in reply) 回答; **to punch sb. ~** 用拳头回击某人; **he didn't email me ~** 他没有给我回复电子邮件; **'OK,' he shouted ~** "可以," 他大声回答道 [4] (backwards, in a reverse direction) 向后; **to glance/look ~** 向后扫视/看 [5] (away) 有距离; **~ from sb./sth.** 离开某人/某物; **~!** 退后!; **he moved ~ from the edge of the cliff** 他从悬崖边向后退 [6] (ago) 以前; (a long time ago) 久远地; **a week/five minutes ~** 一周/五分钟以前; **~ in the days when ...** 早在…的时候; **way ~ in the winter** 远在冬天的时候; **as far ~ as last year/1985** 早在去年/1985 年 [7] (once again) 回到原状; **she's ~ in power** 她再次掌权; **Paul is ~ at the wheel** 保罗又开起车来了 [8] (earlier in book *or* journey) 在前面; **several pages/ten lines ~** 前几页/十行; **we overtook him 20 km ~** 在前面 20 公里处我们就超过了他 [9] (indicating

return to sb.'s possession) 归还; **I have my books ~ now** 我那些书还回来了; **I want my money ~** 我想要回我的钱 10 (indicating return to proper position) 回原处; (expressing return to a former location) 回原地; **is everything ~ where it belongs?** 所有的东西都放回原处了吗？; **the journey to Madrid and ~** 往返马德里的旅程 11 (in a different location) 在别处; (at earlier location) 在原处; **~ in the studio, recording had begun** 而在录音室，录制工作已经开始; **the folks ~ home are counting on him** 老家的父母都指望着他; **I'll see you ~ at the house/in the office** 我还在那幢房子/那间办公室见你

D **back and forth** *adv phr* 反复往返; **to go** *or* **travel ~ and forth (between ...)** 往返（于…之间）; **to swing ~ and forth** «*pendulum*» 来回摆动; **the film cuts** *or* **moves ~ and forth between New York and Paris** 电影画面在纽约和巴黎两地之间切换

E *vt* 1 (support) 支持; **the strike is ~ed by the union** 罢工得到了工会的支持 2 (finance) 资助 ‹*project, enterprise, undertaking*› 3 (substantiate) 证实; **to ~ an argument/a claim with ...** 通过…证实论点/说法 4 (reverse) 使倒退; **to ~ the car into the garage** 把汽车倒进车库; **to ~ sb. into/against sth.** 使某人退入某处/退到某物前; **she ~ed him into the corner** 她把他逼进了角落 5 (bet on) 下赌注于 ‹*horse, favourite team*›; **to ~ the wrong horse** lit 赛马中下错赌注; fig 支持失败的一方; **to ~ a loser/winner** «*racegoer*» 赌错/赌对了马; «*investor*» 投资失误/成功; «*supporter*» 支持失败者/成功者 6 (stiffen) 在…背后加固; (line) 为…加衬里; **to ~ sth. with sth.** (reinforce for strength) 用某物给…加背衬 ‹*book, fabric*›; 用某物裱糊 ‹*map, painting*› 7 (accompany with music) 为…伴奏; (sing in accompaniment) 为…伴唱 8 Brit (have sth. to the rear) 位于…的后面; **to be ~ed by sth.** 后面是某物; **the house is ~ed by fields** 房屋的后面是田野

F *vi* 1 (reverse) 倒退 2 Naut «*wind*» 逆时针转向

Phrasal verbs

- **back away** *vi* 1 (move backwards) 退后; **to ~ away from sb./sth.** 退避 2 (steer clear) 退缩; **to ~ away from sth.** 回避 ‹*problem, confrontation*›
- **back down**

A *vi* 放弃; **to ~ down from sth.** 放弃 ‹*fight*›; **to ~ down on** *or* **over sth.** 取消 ‹*sanctions, allegations*›

B *vt* [~ down sth.]
1 (go down backwards) 沿…退下 ‹*slope*› 2 (go along backwards) 沿…返回 ‹*road, drive*›

- **back in**

A *vi* (go in backwards) 退进; **the car ~ed in** 汽车倒了进来

B *vt* [~ sth. in, ~ in sth.] (put in backwards) 把…倒进来 ‹*car*›; 使…退进来 ‹*horse*›

- **back off** *vi* 1 (move away) 走开 2 (give way) 放弃; **to ~ off over sth.** 在…上让步 ‹*issue, matter*›; **to ~ off from a reform** 放弃改革
- **back on to** *vt* [~ on to sth.] «*house*» 背向 ‹*fields, railway*›
- **back out**

A *vi* 1 (go out backwards) 退出; **to ~ out of** «*person, horse*» 从…中退出 ‹*room*›; «*driver, car*» 从…中倒出 ‹*parking space*› 2 (withdraw) «*competitor, team*» 退出; **to ~ out of** 退出 ‹*event, deal*›

B *vt* [~ sth. out, ~ out sth.] «*driver*» 把…倒出 ‹*car*›; «*rider*» 使…退出 ‹*horse*›; **to ~ sth. out of sth.** 使某物从某处中退出

- **back up**

A *vi* 1 (go backwards) «*person, horse*» 后退; «*driver*» 倒车; «*car*» 向后倒; **to ~ up a few yards** 后退几码 2 Comput 备份 3 (accumulate) «*water*» 聚集 4 (become blocked) «*drains*» 堵塞 5 (tail back) «*traffic*» 拥塞

B [~sth. up, ~ up sth.] *vt*
1 (support) «*facts, evidence*» 证实 ‹*claim, case, theory*›; **to ~ sth. up with sth.** 通过某事物来支持某事物; **to ~ up demands with threats** 威胁着要满足要求 2 (make go backwards) «*driver*» 倒 ‹*car*›; «*rider*» 使…后退 ‹*horse*› 3 Comput 备份 ‹*data, file*› 4 (cause to tail back) 阻塞 ‹*traffic*›

C [~ sb. up, ~ up sb.] *vt* 支持 ‹*person*›

back: ~ache *n* [c and u] 背痛; **to have ~ache** Brit, **to have a ~ache** Amer 腰背酸痛; **~ alley** *n* 陋巷; **~ bacon** *n* [u] 猪背熏肉; **~beat** *n* 基调强节奏

backbench /ˌbæk'bentʃ/ *n* Brit 1 **the ~es** (area of the House of Commons) 后座议员席; (MPs) 后座议员; **support from the ~es** 后座议员的支持 2 *modif* 后座议员的 ‹*committee, discussion, revolt*›; **a ~ MP** 下院普通议员

back: ~bencher *n* Brit 后座议员; **~biting** *n* [u] 背后诽谤; **~board** *n* 篮板; **~ boiler** *n* 家用热水炉; **~bone** *n* 1 [c] (spine) (of person, animal) 脊柱; (of fish) 脊骨; 2 [c] (central ridge) 主山脊; 3 [c] Amer (of book) 书脊; 4 [c] fig (strong feature) 支柱; **to be the ~bone of ...** 是…的中坚/基础; 5 [u] fig (courage) 胆量; (perseverance) 毅力; **to have the ~bone to do sth.** 有胆量做某事; 6 [c] Comput 网络中枢; **~-breaking** *adj* 艰苦繁重的 ‹*work, day*›; **~ burner** *n* **to put sth. on the ~ burner** 暂时搁置某事; **~chat** *n* [u] Brit colloq 顶撞; **~cloth** *n* 1 Theat 背景幕; 2 fig (setting) 背景; **against a ~cloth of sth.** 在某背景下; **~comb** *vt* 反梳…使之蓬起 ‹*hair*›; **~ copy** *n* 过刊; **~ country** *n* [u] esp Amer (rural area) 边远地区; (mountains) 山区; **~ court** *n* 1 (area) 后场; 2 (basketball players) 后卫; **~ cover** *n* 封底; **~date** *vt* 1 (write earlier date on) 在…上写下比实际早的日期 ‹*cheque, letter*›; **to be ~dated to 1 April** 被填上过去了的4月1日; 2 (make retrospectively valid) 使…在较早的日期开始生效 ‹*payment, pension*›; **a payrise** Brit *or* Amer **raise ~dated to 1 January** 追溯到1月1日起算的加薪

back door

A *n* 后门; **by** *or* **through the ~** fig 走后门

B **back-door** *adj* 偷偷摸摸的 ‹*attempt, tax increase*›

backdrop /'bækdrɒp/ *n* 1 Theat 背景幕 2 fig 背景; **to be a ~ to** *or* **for sth.** 是某事物的背景; **to take place against a ~ of war** 发生在战争年代

-backed /bækt/ *combining form* 1 Anat …脊背的; **a black~ gull** 黑脊鸥 2 (of furniture) …靠背的; **a high/low~ chair** 一张高/低靠背椅 3 (of clothing) …后背的; **a low~ dress** 低开背连衣裙 4 (of book) …封面的; **a leather~ photograph album** 皮面的相册; **a soft~ book** 简装书 5 (lined, stiffened) …背衬的; **foam/fleecy~** 背面为泡沫材料的/羊毛衬里的 6 (supported) 由…支持的; **a French~ mission** 由法国援助的行动 7 (financed) 由…投资的; **government~ loans** 政府资助的贷款

back end

A *n* 1 (part) 后端; (of vehicle) 尾部; **to look like the ~ of a bus** Brit colloq 十分邋遢 2 Brit (period) 后期; **the ~ of the year** 年尾 3 Comput 后端

B **back-end** *adj* Comput 后端的

backer /'bækə(r)/ *n* 1 Fin (of project, event, business) 赞助者 2 (supporter) 支持者 3 Games 下注者

backfill /'bækfɪl/

A *vt* 回填; **to ~ a hole to street level** 把洞回填到与街面齐平

B *vi* 回填

C *n* [u] 回填物

back: ~fire *vi* 1 Aut «*vehicle, engine*» 逆火; 2 (have opposite effect) «*plan, scheme*» 事与愿违; **to ~fire on sb.** 对某人产生适得其反的效果; **~ flip** *n* 后空翻; **~ formation** *n* 1 [c] (word) 逆构词; 2 [u] (process) 逆构法; **~gammon** ▸p. 307 *n* [u] 十五子棋

background /'bækɡraʊnd/ *n* 1 (of painting, photo, scene) 背景; **in the ~** 在背景中; **against a ~ of trees** 以树丛为背景; **on a ~ of dark green** 在暗绿色的底子上 2 (inconspicuous place) 不显著的位置; **to keep oneself/sb. in the ~** 使自己/某人不引人注目; **to push sb. into the ~** 逼迫某人退到幕后; **to remain** *or* **stay in the ~** 待在幕后 3 (sound, music) 声音背景; **piano music coming from somewhere in the ~** 从某处传来的钢琴曲; **to talk against a ~ of constant noise** 在持续不断的嘈杂背景中交谈 4 (context, circumstances) 背景; **~ information/research** 背景资料/调查; **to give sb. (some of) the ~ (to sth.)** 给某人提供（某事物的）（一些）背景资料; **against a ~ of increasing unemployment** 在失业不断增多的情况下 5 (upbringing, circumstances) 出身背景; (experience) 经历; **to have the right ~ for the job** 拥有胜任这项工作的资历; **people from poor ~s** 出身贫寒的人

background: ~ lighting *n* [u] 背景灯光; **~ music** *n* [u] 背景音乐; **~ noise** *n* [u] 背景噪声; **~ radiation** *n* [u] 本底辐射; **~ reading** *n* [u] 背景资料的阅读

backhand /'bækhænd/

A *n* 反手击球

B *adj attrib* 反手的 ‹*volley, drive*›

backhanded /ˌbæk'hændɪd/ *adj* 拐弯抹角的 ‹*tribute, testimony*›; **a ~ compliment** 隐含讥刺的恭维

backhander /'bækhændə(r)/ *n* 1 (blow) 反手一击 2 Sport colloq 反手击球 3 Brit colloq (bribe) 贿赂

backhoe /'bækhəʊ/ *n* 反铲挖土机

backing /'bækɪŋ/ *n* 1 [u and c] (layer) (for support) 背衬 2 [u] Fin 资助 3 [u] (support) 支持 4 [u] Mus (instrumental) 伴奏; (vocal) 伴唱; **~ music** 伴奏音乐; **~ singer** 伴唱歌手

backing: ~ store *n* 后备存储器; **~ track** *n* 伴奏录音

back: ~ issue *n* 过刊; **~ kitchen** *n* 1 (at rear) 屋后的厨房; 2 (side room) 厨房旁的餐具室; **~ lane** *n* 后巷

backlash /'bæklæʃ/ *n* 1 [c] (reaction) 强烈反对; **a ~ against sth.** 对某事物的强烈反对 2 [u] Tech 后冲

backless /'bæklɪs/ *adj* 露背的 ‹*dress*›

back: ~ line *n* 1 (in tennis) 底线; 2 (in rugby) 后卫线; **~list** *n* 重版书目录; **~ lit** *adj* 从后面照亮的; **~log** *n* 积压; **to clear one's ~log** 处理自己积压待办之事; **~lot** *n* 外景地; **~ marker** *n* Brit 落在最后的参赛者; **~ matter** *n* [u] 正文后附补充; **~ number** *n* 1 Publg (periodical) 过刊; (newspaper) 过期报纸; 2 colloq (outdated person) 过时的人; (outdated thing) 过时的事物; **~ office** *n* 后台管理部门; **~-of-the-envelope** *adj* 粗略的 ‹*calculation, reasoning*›; **~ order** *n* (item) 缺货; (order) 缺货订单

back-order

A *adj* 缺货的 ‹*item, list*›

B *vt* 预订

backpack /'bækpæk/

A *n* 背包

B *vi* 背包旅行

backpacker /'bækpækə(r)/ *n* 背包客

backpacking /'bækpækɪŋ/ *n* [u] 背包旅行; **to go ~** 去背包旅行

back: ~ pain ▸p. 377 *n* [u] 背痛; **~ passage** *n* Brit colloq euph 直肠; **~ pay** *n* [u] 欠薪; **~-pedal** *vi* (*pres p etc.* **-ll-** Brit, **-l-** Amer) 1 lit 倒踩自行车的脚蹬; 2 (on foot) 倒退; 3 fig 撤回; **to ~-pedal on plans to change the law** 撤回修改法律的计划; **~-pedalling** *n* [u] 1 lit 倒踩自行车; 2 (on foot) 倒退; 3 fig 撤回; **no more ~-pedalling!** 别再变卦了！; **~ pocket** *n* 后面的口袋; **~**

projection *n* 1 [u] (technique) 背投技术; 2 [c] (image) 背投的图像; ～ **rent** *n* [u] 欠租; ～ **rest** *n* 靠背

back room
A *n* 1 (at the back) 后室 2 (for secret work) 密室
B **backroom** *modif* 幕后的; **backroom staff** 幕后工作人员

backroom boys *npl* 无名功臣

back: ～ **row** *n* [u] (in rugby) 第三排前锋; ～**scratcher** *n* 背挠; ～ **seat** *n* 后座; **to take a** ～ **seat** fig 居于人下; ～**seat driver** *n* 对驾驶员指手画脚的乘客; fig 多管闲事的人; ～**shift** *n* Brit (shift) 中班; (workers) 上中班的工人; ～**side** *n* colloq 屁股; ～**sight** *n* 1 Mil 表尺缺口; 2 (in surveying) 后视; ～**slang** *n* [u] Brit 倒拼暗语; ～**slapping** *n* [u] 拍背祝贺; ～**slash** *n* 反斜线; ～**slider** *n* 故态复萌的人; ～**sliding** *n* [u] 故态复萌

backspace /ˈbækspeɪs/
A *n* 退格键
B *vi* 退格

backspace key *n* 退格键

back: ～**spin** *n* [u] 下旋; **to put** ～**spin on a ball** 使球下旋; ～**-stabbing** *n* [u] 暗箭伤人; **a** ～**-stabbing opportunist** 暗箭伤人的政治投机分子

backstage /ˈbæksteɪdʒ/
A *adv* 1 Theat (location) 在后台 ‹*work*›; (direction) 往后台 ‹*go*› 2 (in secret) 秘密地
B *adj* 1 Theat 后台的 ‹*staff, pass*› 2 (secret) 秘密的 ‹*manoeuvre, role*›

backstairs /ˈbæksteəz/
A *npl* 后楼梯
B **backstair** *adj attrib* 1 (of servants) 仆人的 ‹*life, work*› 2 fig (secret) 幕后的
C *adv* 在仆人区

backstitch /ˈbækstɪtʃ/
A *n* [u] 回式针迹
B *vi* 用回式针迹缝
C *vt* 用回式针迹缝 ‹*edge*›

back: ～**stop** *n* 1 Sport (player) 捕手; (screen) 挡网; 2 fig (precaution) 后盾; ～ **straight** *n* Brit 非终点直道

backstreet /ˈbækstriːt/
A *n* 偏僻街道
B *modif* 非法的 ‹*abortion*›

back: ～**stroke** *n* [u] 1 (style) 仰泳; 2 (race) 仰泳比赛; ～**swept** *adj* 1 (brushed backwards) 向后梳的 ‹*hair*›; 2 Aviat 后掠的 ‹*wing*›; ～**talk** *n* [u] Amer colloq = ～**chat**; ～ **tax** *n* [u and c] 欠税

back-to-back
A *adj* 1 (consecutive) 连续的 2 Brit 连排式的 ‹*houses, cottages*›
B **back to back** *adv* 1 (with backs touching) 背靠背地 2 (consecutively) 连续地; **to watch two episodes back to back** 连看两集
C *n* Brit 连排式房屋

back to front
A *adj* 前后颠倒的; fig 弄错的
B *adv* 前后颠倒地

back: ～ **tooth** *n* 后牙; ～**track** *vi* 1 (retrace one's steps) 原路返回; 2 fig 出尔反尔; **to** ～**track on a promise** 背弃诺言; ～ **translation** *n* [c and u] 回译

backup /ˈbækʌp/ *n* 1 [u] (support) 支持; Mil 增援; **a** ～ **team** 增援队伍 2 [c] (replacement) 备用物品; (person) 后备人员; **a** ～ **plan** 备用计划; **to keep a battery as a** ～ 留一节电池备用 3 [c and u] Comput (copy) 备份; **a** ～ **file** 备份文件

backup light *n* Amer 倒车灯

back vowel *n* 后元音

backward /ˈbækwəd/
A *adj attrib* 1 (towards the rear) 向后的; **a** ～ **glance** 向后的一瞥; **a** ～ **somersault** 后空翻 2 (retrograde) 倒退的; **a** ～ **step** 退步 3 (primitive) 落后的; **to be technologically** ～ 技术上落后 4 (hesitant) 犹豫的; **not to be** ～ **in** *or* **about doing sth.** 毫不犹豫地做某事; **she isn't** ～ **in coming forward** Brit colloq 她一点都不腼腆 5 Psych, Sch 迟钝的 ‹*child, pupil*›
B *adv* esp Amer = **backwards**

backward-looking *adj* 守旧的

backwardness /ˈbækwədnɪs/ *n* [u] 1 (of culture, economy) 落后 2 Psych, Sch 迟钝 3 (shyness) 害羞 4 (reticence) 迟疑; ～ **in** *or* **about doing sth.** 在做某事方面的犹豫不决

backwards /ˈbækwədz/ *adv* esp Brit 1 (in a reverse direction) 向后; **to face** ～ 面向后方; **to move/slope** ～ 向后移动/倾斜; ～ **and forwards** 来来回回; **to bend** *or* **fall** *or* **lean over** ～ **(to do sth.)** colloq 竭力(做某事) 2 (starting from the end) 倒着 ‹*play, say*›; **to count** ～ 倒数 3 (the wrong way round) 前后颠倒; **to put a dress on** ～ 前后穿反连衣裙; **to get sth.** ～ 误解 ‹*message, instructions*›; **you've got it all** ～ 你完全理解错了 4 (into past) 向以前; **to look** ～ 回顾; **a journey** ～ **through time** 逆时光旅行 5 (into worse state) 倒退地; **a step** ～ 退步 6 (thoroughly) 彻底地; **to know sth.** ～ 对某事了如指掌

backwards-compatible *adj* 向后兼容的

back: ～**wash** *n* [u] 1 Naut 尾流; 2 (of waves) 退浪; 3 fig (effects) 不良后果; **the** ～**wash from sth.** 某事造成的恶果; ～**water** *n* 1 (of river) 死水; 2 fig (isolated area) 荒僻处; 3 pej (backward area) 落后地区; (situation) 落后状态; **to live in a cultural** ～**water** 生活在文化落后地区; ～**woods** *npl* esp Amer 1 (remote forest) 边远林区; 2 (backward area) 边远落后地区; ～**woodsman** /-mən/ *n* 1 esp Amer (rustic) 边远落后地区的居民; 2 Brit Pol colloq "蛮荒"议员 [指难得出席会议的上议院议员]; ～**yard** *n* 1 Brit (courtyard) 后院; **in one's (own)** ～**yard** fig 在自己的"后院"; 2 Amer (garden) 屋后场院

bacon /ˈbeɪkən/ *n* [u] 熏猪肉; ～ **rind** 熏猪肉皮; **to bring home the** ～ fig 养家糊口; **to save sb.'s** ～ fig 解救某人

bacon slicer *n* 熏猪肉切片机

bacteria /bækˈtɪərɪə/ *npl* (*sing* **bacterium**) 细菌

bacterial /bækˈtɪərɪəl/ *adj* (of bacteria) 细菌的 ‹*species*›; (caused by bacteria) 细菌引起的 ‹*disease*›

bacteriological /bækˌtɪərɪəˈlɒdʒɪkl/ *adj* 细菌学的

bacteriologist /bækˌtɪərɪˈɒlədʒɪst/ ▸ **p. 409** *n* 细菌学家

bacteriology /bækˌtɪərɪˈɒlədʒi/ *n* [u] 细菌学

bacterium /bækˈtɪərɪəm/ *n sing* ▸ **bacteria**

Bactrian camel /ˈbæktrɪən ˌkæml/ *n* 双峰驼

bad /bæd/
A *adj* (*comp* **worse,** *superl* **worst**) 1 (unpleasant, unfavourable, negative) 不愉快的 ‹*holiday*›; 不好的 ‹*weather, news, sign, result, reaction*›; 艰难的 ‹*time*›; **a** ～ **dream** 噩梦; **the patient had a** ～ **night** 病人难受了一个晚上; **he's had a** ～ **day** 他今天很倒霉; **not** ～ **(at all)** (相当)不错; **that's** ～! 真遗憾!; **it has its good points and its** ～ **points** 它有利有弊; **it's been a** ～ **year for apples** 今年苹果歉收; **it looks** ～ 看来情况不妙; ▸ **taste A, job A8** 2 (of low standard or quality, incompetent, unacceptable) 劣质的 ‹*book, performance*›; 不好的 ‹*advice, harvest, school*›; 不正确的 ‹*decision, pronunciation, spelling*›; 贫瘠的 ‹*soil, land*›; 昏暗的 ‹*light*›; **problems due to** ～ **workmanship** 粗制滥造引起的问题; **the shoes are a** ～ **fit** 鞋不合脚; **the portrait is not a** ～ **likeness** 这幅肖像画跟本人还是蛮像的; **she's a** ～ **singer** 她歌唱得难听; **you're a** ～ **liar** 你说的谎不高明; **to be** ～ **at sth./doing sth.** 不擅长某事/做某事; **that's not so** ～: **it could have been worse** 还不算太糟: 本来可能更糟; **too** ～ (sympathetic) 太可惜了; (unsympathetic, impatient) 太倒霉了; (angry) 太不像话了; **a** ～ **business** 不幸的事; ▸ **riddance** 3 (rotten) 腐坏的 ‹*food*›; **a** ～ **tooth** 蛀牙; **a smell of** ～ **eggs** 臭鸡蛋的气味; **to go** ～ 腐烂 4 (ill) (with a weakness) 生病的; (with injury) 受伤的; **to have a** ～ **heart** 有心脏病; **ouch! that's my** ～ **finger!** 哎唷! 我那根手指有伤!; **how are you? — not so** ～ (in health) 你感觉怎么样?——还可以吧; (in reply to greeting) 你好吗?——还行; **to feel** ～ 感觉不舒服; **to be in a** ～ **way** colloq (in health) 生病; (in general situation) 境况不佳 5 (wicked) 不道德的; **to lead a** ～ **life** 过放荡的生活; **it is** ～ **(of sb.) to do sth.** (某人)做某事是不对的 6 (naughty) 淘气的 ‹*child, conduct*›; 不听话的 ‹*animal*› 7 (offensive) 无礼的 ‹*word*›; 坏的 ‹*habit*›; ～ **language** 脏话 8 (sorry, guilty) 愧疚的; **to feel** ～ **about sth./doing sth.** 对某事/做某事感到歉疚 9 (harmful) 有害的; **to be** ～ **for sb./sth.** «*alcohol, worrying, weather*» 对某人/某事物有害 10 (inappropriate) 不适合的 ‹*weather, place, example*›; **you picked a** ～ **moment to ask him** 你问他问得不是时候 11 (severe, serious) 严重的 ‹*mistake, damage*›; 拥挤的 ‹*traffic*›; 强烈的 ‹*shock, storm*›; **to have** ～ **toothache** 牙痛得厉害; **a** ～ **cold** 重感冒; **to look** ～ 看上去很严重 12 (counterfeit or invalid) 伪造的 ‹*note, money*›; 无效的 ‹*loan, insurance claim*› 13 (insufficient) 少的 ‹*pay, salary*›; 低的 ‹*price, rate of interest*›; **the kitchen is not a** ～ **size** 厨房不算小
B *n* 1 [u] (evil, wickedness) 邪恶; **the conflict between good and** ～ 善恶之间的斗争; **to go to the** ～ dated 堕落 2 [u] (unpleasantness, unfavourableness) 不幸; **to take the** ～ **with the good** 经历人生的顺逆; **to be to the** ～ (disadvantageous) 处于不利地位; (in deficit) 亏损 3 + *v pl* **the** ～ (wicked people) 坏人
C *adv* esp Amer colloq 非常 ‹*want, need*›; 严重地 ‹*hurt*›; **he beat her up real** ～ 他狠狠地揍了她一顿; **to have got it** ～ (enthusiastic) 走火入魔; (in love) 坠入爱河

bad apple *n* colloq 害群之马

bad ass Amer sl
A *n* 坏家伙
B *adj* 1 (tough) 胡作非为的 2 (great) 极好的

bad: ～ **blood** *n* [u] 敌意; **there is** ～ **blood between them** 他们俩之间有仇; ～ **boy** *n* 坏小子; ～ **breath** *n* [u] 口臭; ～ **cheque** *n* 空头支票; ～ **debt** *n* [u and c] 坏账

baddy, baddie /ˈbædi/ *n* Brit colloq 坏人

bade /beɪd, bæd/ *pt* ▸ **bid²**

badge /bædʒ/ *n* 1 lit 徽章; **a school** ～ 校徽 2 fig (symbol) 象征

badger /ˈbædʒə(r)/
A *n* 獾; ～ **hunting** 猎獾
B *vt* 纠缠; **to** ～ **sb. to do sth.** 缠着某人做某事

bad: ～ **guy** *n* esp Amer colloq 坏蛋; ～ **hair day** *n* 1 lit colloq 头发梳理不顺的一天; 2 fig hum 凡事都不顺的一天; ～**lands** /-ləndz/ *npl* 1 (eroded, uncultivable land) 不毛之地; 2 **Badlands** (in US) 崎岖地区 [主要位于南北达科他州和内布拉斯加州境内]

badly /ˈbædli/ *adv* (*comp* **worse,** *superl* **worst**) 1 (unsatisfactorily, unacceptably, inadequately) 差; **to fit** ～ 大小不合适; **not get on too** ～ **with sb.** 与某人相处得不算太坏; **a** ～ **managed business** 经营不善的企业; **he behaved** ～ **at school** 他在学校里很调皮; **to take sth.** ～ 对某事感到难过; **try not to think** ～ **of me** 别把我想得太坏; **a** ～ **lit street** 光线昏暗的街道 2 (unsuccessfully) 失败地; **to come off** ～ **in sth.** 在…中失利 ‹*fight, argument, bargain*›; **to go** ～ «*exam, meeting, business*» 进展不顺利; **to do** ～ «*candidate, company*» 表现不佳; **to do** ～ **out of sb./sth.** 从某人处/某事物中几乎一无所获 3 (unfairly, cruelly) 恶

b

b

劣地; **treat sb.** ~ 虐待某人; **to be/feel/look ~ done by** 受到/感觉受到/看上去受到…的不公平对待 4 (seriously, severely) 严重地; **her father's death affected her** ~ 她父亲的死对她打击很大; **to be ~ beaten** (physically) 遭到痛打; (in contest) 遭到惨败; **to be ~ mistaken** 大错特错; **to have got it** ~ colloq (enthusiastic) 走火入魔; (in love) 坠入爱河 5 (very much) 非常 ‹*need*›; **to be ~ in need of** 急需 ‹*help, cleaning*› 6 (guiltily) **to feel ~ about sth.** 对某事感到歉疚

badly-behaved *adj* 表现不好的 ‹*child, dog*›

badly off *adj* 1 (poor) 贫穷的 2 *pred* (in bad situation) 处境不好的 3 *pred* Brit (lacking) 缺少的; **to be ~ for sth.** 缺少某物

bad: ~man /-mæn/ *n* Amer (gunman) 受雇的枪手; (outlaw) 亡命匪徒; **~-mannered** *adj* 没有礼貌的; **it is ~-mannered to do sth.** 做某事是不礼貌的

badminton /ˈbædmɪntn/ ►**p. 307** *n* [u] 羽毛球运动; **they play ~ once a week** 他们每周打一次羽毛球

badmouth /ˈbædmaʊð/ *vt* colloq 说…的坏话 ‹*person*›

badness /ˈbædnɪs/ *n* [u] 1 (of person, deed) 邪恶; (of behaviour) 放荡 2 (of book, film, performance, workmanship, etc.) 糟糕 3 (of weather) 恶劣

bad-tempered *adj* 1 (temporarily) 发脾气的 ‹*person, look*› 2 (habitually) 易怒的 ‹*person, nature*›

baffle /ˈbæfl/

A *vt* 1 (perplex) 使困惑; **police were ~d by the case** 案子把警方难住了 2 (restrain, regulate) 阻隔 ‹*noise, gas*›

B *n* ~ **(board** *or* **plate)** (for sound) 隔板; (for fluid) 挡板

baffled /ˈbæfld/ *adj* 感到困惑的

bafflement /ˈbæflmənt/ *n* [u] 困惑

baffling /ˈbæflɪŋ/ *adj* 令人困惑的

> **BAFTA**
>
> 英国电影和电视艺术学院，全称 British Academy of Film and Television Arts。前身为英国电影电视艺术学会（Society of Film and Television Arts）。1976 年改为现名，总部设在伦敦皮卡迪利（Piccadilly）。学院每年颁奖一次，分为电影奖、电视奖（包括电视制作奖）、儿童电影电视奖和视频游戏奖。奖杯是一个面具，由美国女雕塑家米茨·坎利夫（Mitzi Cunliffe）设计。自 1989 年起，洛杉矶分部开始独立颁发奖项，称为不列颠奖（Britannia Awards）。

bag /bæg/

A *n* 1 (container) 袋; **(it's) in the ~** 十拿九稳; **a mixed ~** 良莠不齐; **she's (just) a ~ of bones** 她骨瘦如柴; **~ and baggage** 所有财物; **to have ~s under one's eyes** 有眼袋; ►**cat 1** 2 (contents) 一袋; **he ate the whole ~!** 他把一整袋全吃光了! 3 Hunt 猎获物; **to get a good ~** 猎获甚丰 4 sl pej (woman) 泼妇

B bags *npl* 1 (baggage) 行李; **to pack one's ~s** 打点行装; fig 永远离开 2 Brit colloq (lots) 大量; **~s of ...** 很多 ‹*money, time*›

C *vt* (*pres p etc.* **-gg-**) 1 (pack) = **bag up** 2 Brit colloq (get) 占有 ‹*seat, food*›; **to ~ sth. for sb., to ~ sb. sth.** 为某人抢占某物; **~s I do/have sth.** 就该让我做某事/拥有某物; **~s I go first!** 我要第一个去! 3 colloq (catch) 捕获 ‹*animal, fish*›

Phrasal verb

- **bag up** *vt* [~ **sth. up,** ~ **up sth.**] 把…装进袋子

bagatelle /ˌbægəˈtel/ *n* 1 [u] (game) 巴格代拉桌球戏 2 [c] (trifle) 琐事; (cinch) 容易的事; **a mere ~** 小事一桩

bagel /ˈbeɪgl/ *n* 硬面包圈

bagful /ˈbægfʊl/ *n* 满满一袋; **four ~s of leaves** 满满四袋的叶子

baggage /ˈbægɪdʒ/ *n* [u] 1 esp Amer lit 行李 2 fig (beliefs) 既有观念; **emotional ~** 感情包袱

baggage: ~ allowance *n* 行李限重; **5 kilos over the ~ allowance** 行李超重 5 公斤; **~ car** *n* Amer 行李车; **~ carousel** *n* 行李传送带; **~ check, ~ check-room** *ns* Amer 行李寄存处; **~ check-in** *n* 1 [u] (process) 行李托运; 2 [c] (desk) 行李托运处; **~ hall** *n* = **~ reclaim**; **~ handler** ►**p. 409** *n* 行李搬运员; **~ handling** *n* [u] 行李搬运; **~ locker** *n* Amer 行李存放柜; **~ reclaim** *n* [u] 行李领取处; **~ room** *n* Amer 行李寄存处

bagger /ˈbægə(r)/ *n* 1 Amer (worker) 装袋工 2 (machine) 装袋机

baggies /ˈbægɪz/ *npl* colloq 宽松裤

baggy /ˈbægi/ *adj* 宽松的 ‹*clothes*›; **a ~ T-shirt** 宽松的T恤衫

Baghdad /ˌbægˈdæd/ *pr n* 巴格达

bag: ~ lady *n* colloq 流浪女人; **~man** /-mən/ *n* Amer, Austral colloq 马仔 [指代人收取或分发非法收入的人]; **~pipes** ►**p. 395** *npl* 风笛; **~ snatcher** *n* 抢包贼

baguette /bæˈget/ *n* 法式长条面包

Bahamas /bəˈhɑːməz/ *pr n* **the ~** 巴哈马群岛

Bahrain, Bahrein /bɑːˈreɪn/ *pr n* 巴林

bail[1] /beɪl/ Jur

A *n* [u] 1 (money) 保释金; **to remand sb. on ~** 准某人交保候审; **to be (out) on ~** 具保候审; **to stand ~ for sb.** 做某人的保释人 2 (temporary release) 保释; **to jump/skip ~** 弃保潜逃

B *vt* 保释; **he was ~ed to appear in court tomorrow** 他获得保释，定于明天到庭

Phrasal verb

- **bail out** *vt* [~ **out sb.,** ~ **sb. out**] 1 Jur 保释 2 colloq (help) 帮助…脱离困境 ‹*person, industry*›

bail[2]

A *vt* Naut 往外舀 ‹*water*›

B *vi* 往外舀水

Phrasal verb

- **bail out**

A *vt* [~ **out sth.,** ~ **sth. out**] 往外舀 ‹*water*›; 从…里往外舀水 ‹*boat*›

B *vi* 1 Naut 往外舀水 2 Aviat «*pilot*» 跳伞

bail[3] *n* (in cricket) 三柱门上的横木

bail bond *n* 保释保证书

bailey /ˈbeɪli/ *n* 1 (wall) 郭 2 (court) 堡场

Bailey bridge /ˈbeɪli brɪdʒ/ *n* 活动便桥

bailiff /ˈbeɪlɪf/ ►**p. 409** *n* 1 Jur (law officer) 执达官 2 Amer Jur (usher) 法警 3 Brit (steward) 管家

bailout /ˈbeɪlaʊt/ *n* colloq 紧急财政援助

bairn /beən/ *n* esp Scot 小孩

bait /beɪt/

A *n* [u] 饵; fig 诱饵; **to rise to** *or* **swallow the ~** lit 吞饵; fig 上钩

B *vt* 1 Fishg, Hunt 在…上放诱饵 ‹*hook*›; **they ~ed the trap with her son** 他们用她的儿子当诱饵来设圈套 2 (taunt) 激怒 3 (set dogs on) 纵犬袭击

baize /beɪz/ *n* [u] 台面呢

bake /beɪk/

A *vt* 1 Culin 烘，烤 2 (in sun) 晒干 ‹*earth*›; **~d hard by the sun** 被太阳晒得硬邦邦的 3 (in kiln) 烧硬 ‹*brick*›

B *vi* 1 (make bread) 烘面包; (make pastry) 烘糕点 2 (cook) «*bread*» 在烤炉里烘烤 3 fig «*earth*» 被晒干; «*brick*» 被烧硬

C *n* [u] 烘烤食品; **fish/vegetable ~** 烤鱼/烘烤的蔬菜

baked /beɪkt/ *adj* 烘烤的

baked: ~ Alaska *n* [c and u] 火烧冰淇淋; **~ beans** *npl* 烘豆; **~ potato** *n* 烤土豆

baker /ˈbeɪkə(r)/ ►**p. 409** *n* (of bread) 面包师傅; (of bread and cakes) 面包糕点师傅; **~'s (shop)** 面包店

baker's dozen *n* 十三

bakery /ˈbeɪkəri/ *n* 面包店

bake sale *n* Amer 家制糕点义卖

Bakewell tart /ˌbeɪkwel ˈtɑːt/ *n* Brit [c and u] 杏味果酱馅饼

baking /ˈbeɪkɪŋ/

A *n* [u] 烤制; **a ~ dish** 烤盘

B *adj* colloq 酷热的; **it's ~ today!** 今天热得要命!

baking: ~ powder *n* [u] 发酵粉; **~ sheet** *n* [u] 烤板; **~ soda** *n* [u] 小苏打; **~ tray** *n* esp Brit 烤盘

Baku /ˈbækuː/ *pr n* 巴库

balaclava /ˌbæləˈklɑːvə/ *n* ~ **(helmet)** 巴拉克拉瓦盔式帽

balalaika /ˌbæləˈlaɪkə/ ►**p. 395** *n* 巴拉莱卡琴

balance /ˈbæləns/

A *n* 1 [u] (of body) 平衡; **to lose/keep one's ~** 失去/保持平衡; **to throw sb. off ~** lit 使某人失去平衡; fig 使某人不知所措 2 [u and c] (between different elements) 均衡; **political ~** 政治上的均势; **the right ~ of sweetness and spiciness** 甜与辣的恰当搭配; **to achieve/keep a ~ (between sth. and sth.)** （在两事物之间）取得/保持平衡; **to strike a ~ (between sth. and sth.)** （在两事物之间）找到折中办法 3 [u] (mental stability) 镇定 4 [u] (of sound) 协调 5 [c] (scales) 天平; **the ~ may still swing in our favour** fig 胜利的天平可能还会朝我们这边倾斜; **to be** *or* **hang in the ~** 悬而未决; **on ~** 总的说来 6 [c] (in clock, watch) 平衡轮 7 [u] (preponderance) 大部分; **the ~ of opinion was ...** 多数人认为… 8 [c] Fin, Comm (in account) 余额; **~ brought forward** 余额承前; **~ carried forward** 余额结转下期; **~ in hand** 现有余额 9 [c] Fin, Comm (money still owed) 结欠款; (money still remaining) 余款 10 [c] (remaining amount or part) 剩余部分; **the ~ of sb.'s annual leave** 某人未休的年假

B *vt* 1 (perch) 使保持平衡; **he ~d the bottle on top of the heap of stones** 他把瓶子在石堆顶上放稳 2 (weigh same as) 和…重量相等 3 (create symmetry with) 与…对称; **you need something to ~ the vase on that side** 你得找样东西来照应那边的花瓶 4 ~ **(out)** (compensate for) 和…相抵; **his lack of experience was ~d by his willingness to learn** 他的好学弥补了经验的不足 5 (adjust) 使…均衡 ‹*composition, diet, timetable*›; **to ~ work and family life** 兼顾工作与家庭 6 (weigh up, compare) 权衡 ‹*plans, suggestions, solutions*›; **to ~ sth. against sth.** 比较两事物 7 Fin, Comm 使…收支平衡 ‹*expenses, budget, economy*›; **to ~ the books** 结平账目 8 Aut 使…平衡 ‹*wheels*› 9 Math 使…平衡 ‹*equation*›

C *vi* 1 (be perched) 保持平衡; **to ~ on sth.** 在某物上保持平衡; **to ~ on one leg** 单腿站立 2 (weigh the same) 重量相等; **the scales ~** 天平两边的秤盘平衡 3 ~ **(out)** (be compensated for) 相抵消; **the advantages and disadvantages ~ out** 利弊相抵 4 Fin «*accounts, figures, budget*» 收支平衡; **to make sth. ~, to get sth. to ~** 使…收支平衡 5 Math «*equation, sides*» 平衡

balanced /ˈbælənst/ *adj* 1 (stable) 心平气和的 ‹*person, attitude*› 2 (objective) 客观公正的 ‹*report, judgement*› 3 (well-structured) 均衡的 ‹*diet*›; 安排合理的 ‹*schedule*› 4 (in proportion) 匀称的 ‹*design, composition*› 5 Fin 收支平衡的 ‹*budget, economy*›

balance: ~ of nature *n* [u] 生态平衡; **~ of payments** *n* [u] 国际收支差额; **the ~ of payments surplus/deficit** 国际收支顺差/逆差; **~ of power** *n* [u] 1 (parity) 均势; 2 (determining force) 举足轻重的力量; **to hold**

the ～ of power 处于举足轻重的地位; **～ of terror** *n* [u] 恐怖均势; **～ of trade** *n* [u] 国际贸易差额; **～ sheet** *n* 资产负债表; **～ wheel** *n* 平衡轮

balancing act /ˈbælənsɪŋ ˌækt/ *n* **1** (in circus) 走钢丝表演 **2** fig 斡旋; **to do/perform a ～** 进行调停

balcony /ˈbælkəni/ *n* **1** (on building) 阳台 **2** Theat 楼厅; **～ tickets** 楼座票

bald /bɔːld/ *adj* **1** (lacking hair) 秃头的; **to go ～** 变秃; **～ as a coot** 头顶全秃的; **he has a ～ spot** *or* **patch on his head** 他的头秃了一块 **2** (lacking growth, covering) 光秃的 ‹*mountain, terrain, lawn*›; 磨光的 ‹*carpet*› **3** Aut 磨平的 ‹*tyre*› **4** (blunt) 不加掩饰的 ‹*statement, question*›

bald eagle *n* **= American eagle**

balderdash /ˈbɔːldədæʃ/ colloq dated
A *n* [u] 胡言乱语
B *excl* 胡说八道

bald-headed /ˌbɔːldˈhedɪd/ *adj* 秃顶的; **a ～ man** 秃顶男子

balding /ˈbɔːldɪŋ/ *adj* 变秃的; **a ～ man** 正在秃顶的男子; **he's slightly ～** 他有点谢顶了

baldly /ˈbɔːldli/ *adv* 不加掩饰地 ‹*say*›

baldness /ˈbɔːldnɪs/ *n* [u] **1** (of person) 秃顶 **2** (of mountain, terrain, lawn) 光秃; (of carpet) 磨光 **3** (of tyre) 磨平 **4** (of statement) 不加掩饰; (of style) 单调

baldy /ˈbɔːldi/ *n* colloq 秃子

bale /beɪl/
A *n* 大捆; **a hay ～** 一捆干草; **～s of old newspaper** 数捆旧报纸
B *vt* **1** (bind) 把…扎成大捆 ‹*hay, cotton, wool*› **2** Brit **= bail² A**

Phrasal verb
- **bale out** *vt* Brit **= bail out**

Balearic Islands /ˌbælɪˈærɪk ˌaɪləndz/, **Balearics** /ˌbælɪˈærɪks/ *pr nspl* **the ～** 巴利阿里群岛

baleful /ˈbeɪlfl/ *adj* liter 有害的 ‹*influence*›; 凶恶的 ‹*look, presence*›

balefully /ˈbeɪlfəli/ *adv* liter 凶恶地 ‹*look*›

balk /bɔːlk, bɔːk/ *n, vi, vt* esp Amer **= baulk**

Balkan /ˈbɔːlkən/
A *adj* 巴尔干半岛各国的 ‹*people, languages, culture*›; 巴尔干半岛的 ‹*States*›
B **Balkans** *pr npl* **the ～s** 巴尔干半岛各国

balkanization, Balkanization /ˌbɔːlkənaɪˈzeɪʃn, Amer -nɪˈz-/ *n* [u] 巴尔干化

ball¹ /bɔːl/
A *n* **1** Sport 球 **2** (rounded object) 团; **a ～ of clay/string** 泥团/细绳团; **a ～ of fire** 火球; **to knead dough into a ～** 把面揉成团; **to curl up into a ～** «*person, cat*» 蜷曲成一团 **3** Sport (single kick or throw) 开球; (other movement) 传球; **there are six ～s in an over** (in cricket) 每一轮有六次投球 **4** Anat 球状部位; **the ～s of one's feet/thumbs** 脚趾球/拇指球 **5** fig (in phrases) **to play ～ (with sb.)** (与某人) 合作; **to set the ～ rolling** 开始活动; **to keep the ～ rolling** 使活动持续进行; **to be on the ～** (alert) 保持警觉; (very able) 非常能干; **the ～ is in your court** 下一步就看你的了; **to keep one's eye on the ～/take one's eye off the ～** 保持警觉/放松警觉; **that's the way the ～ bounces** Amer 这是没办法的事
B **balls** *npl* taboo sl **1** lit (testicles) 睾丸; **to have sb. by the ～s** fig 抓住某人的小辫子; **to break one's ～s to do sth.** fig 拼命干某事 **2** fig (nonsense) 胡说八道; **that's a lot** *or* **load of ～s** 那完全是瞎说 **3** fig (courage) 胆量; **she's got ～s** 她胆子很大; **to have the ～s to do sth.** 有胆量做某事
C **balls** *excl* taboo sl 胡说
D *vt* **1** (clench) 把…捏成球状 ‹*fist, napkin*›; (wind) 把…绕成团 ‹*wool, string*› **2** Amer taboo sl (have sex with) 和…交媾
E *vi* **1** (clench) «*fist*» 攥成球状 **2** Amer taboo sl (have sex) 交媾

Phrasal verb
- **balls up** Brit, **ball up** Amer *vt* taboo sl [～ **up sth.**, ～ **sth. up**] 把…搞得一团糟 ‹*plan, job*›

ball² *n* (dance) 舞会; **a college ～** 学院舞会; **to have a ～** fig 玩得很痛快

ballad /ˈbæləd/ *n* **1** (narrative poem or song) 民谣 **2** (popular song) 情歌

ball: ～ and chain *n* lit 球镣; fig 累赘; **～-and-socket joint** *n* **1** Anat 球窝关节; **2** Tech 球窝接头

ballast /ˈbæləst/ *n* [u] **1** (in ship) 压舱物; (in balloon) 镇重物; **a ship in ～** 装载了压舱物的船 **2** (on rail track, road) 道砟

ball: ～ bearing *n* **1** (bearing) 滚珠轴承; **2** (ball) 滚珠; **～boy** *n* (in tennis) 球童; **～cock** *n* 浮球阀; **～ control** *n* [u] 控球; **～ dress** *n* 舞裙

ballerina /ˌbæləˈriːnə/ ▸**p. 409** *n* 芭蕾舞女演员

ballet /ˈbæleɪ/ *n* **1** [u] (art form) 芭蕾舞; **classical ～** 古典芭蕾舞; **～ shoes/dress** 芭蕾舞鞋/服装 **2** [c] (performance) 芭蕾舞剧; **to go to the ～** 去看芭蕾舞剧 **3** [c] (troupe) 芭蕾舞团; **the Kirov B～** 基洛夫芭蕾舞团

ballet: ～ dancer ▸**p. 409** *n* 芭蕾舞演员; **～ dancing** *n* [u] 芭蕾舞

balletic /bəˈletɪk/ *adj* **1** (of ballet) 芭蕾舞的 **2** (elegant) 优雅的

ball: ～ game *n* **1** (game) 球类运动; **the children played ～ games all day** 孩子们整天都在打球; **2** Amer 篮球比赛; **3** fig (situation) 局面; **that's a whole new/completely different ～ game** 那是全新的局面/完全不同的情况; **～ girl** *n* 女球童; **～ gown** *n* 舞裙

ballistic /bəˈlɪstɪk/ *adj* 弹道学的 ‹*principles*›; 弹道的 ‹*flight, weapon*›; **to go ～** colloq 勃然大怒

ballistic missile *n* 弹道导弹

ballistics /bəˈlɪstɪks/ *npl* + *v sing* 弹道学

ball lightning *n* [u] 球状闪电

balloon /bəˈluːn/
A *n* **1** (toy) 气球; **to blow up a ～** 吹气球 **2** Aviat 热气球; **to go down** Brit *or* **go over** Amer **like a lead ～** hum 非常不受欢迎; **when the ～ goes up** fig 出乱子时 **3** (for cartoon speech) 气球框 [漫画中圈出人物对白的气球形圆圈]
B *vi* **1** (travel) **to go ～ing** 乘热气球飞行 **2** (swell) «*garment, sail, curtain*» 鼓起 **3** (increase quickly) «*price*» 暴涨; «*debt*» 剧增

balloon: ～ catheter *n* 气囊导管; **～ glass** *n* 矮脚球形大酒杯

ballooning /bəˈluːnɪŋ/ ▸**p. 307** *n* [u] 乘热气球飞行; **a ～ adventure** 乘热气球探险

balloonist /bəˈluːnɪst/ *n* 乘热气球飞行的人

balloon tyre *n* 低压轮胎

ballot /ˈbælət/
A *n* **1** (process) 投票表决; **the election was held by secret ～** 选举采用了无记名投票的方式 **2** (single vote) 投票; (total number of votes cast) 投票总数; **the first/second ～** 第一轮/第二轮投票; **a strike ～** 决定是否罢工的投票; **a postal ～** Brit 邮寄投票; **to take a ～** 进行投票 **3** (form, slip) 选票 **4** Amer (list of candidates) 候选人名单
B *vt* (*pres p etc.* **-tt-**) 要求…对某事物投票; **we will have to ～ our members on this matter** 我们将不得不要求成员就这一事项投票
C *vi* (*pres p etc.* **-tt-**) 投票; **the workers ～ed for a strike** 工人们投票决定罢工

ballot: ～ box *n* **1** lit 投票箱; **2** fig (system) 投票选举制; **～-box stuffing** *n* [u] Amer 偷塞假选票

balloting /ˈbælətɪŋ/ *n* [u] 投票表决

ballot paper *n* 选票

ball: ～park *n* Amer 棒球场; **to be/not to be in the right ～park** fig 大致正确/不着边际; **～park figure** *n* 大致正确的数字; **～point (pen)** *n* 圆珠笔; **～ pond, ～ pool** *ns* [供幼儿玩耍嬉戏的] 彩球池; **～room** *n* 舞厅; **～room dancing** *n* [u] 交际舞; **～-shaped** *adj* 球形的 ‹*object*›; **～s-up** Brit, **～-up** Amer *ns* taboo sl 一团糟; **he makes a ～s-up of everything he does** 他每样事情都做得一塌糊涂

ballsy /ˈbɔːlzi/ *adj* sl 有胆量的

ball valve *n* **1** (one-way valve) 球阀 **2** Brit **= ball cock**

ballyhoo /ˌbælɪˈhuː, Amer ˈbælɪhuː/ *n* [u] colloq dated **1** (fulsome praise) 大吹大擂 **2** (fuss) 喧闹

balm /bɑːm/ *n* **1** [c] (ointment) 香膏 **2** [u] (natural substance) 香脂油 **3** [u] fig liter (calming or soothing influence) 安慰物; **it was ～ to my soul** 它是我灵魂的慰藉 **4** [u] Bot 香脂草

balmy /ˈbɑːmi/ *adj* 温暖惬意的 ‹*weather, evening, air*›

baloney /bəˈləʊni/ Amer colloq
A *n* [u] 胡说
B *excl* 胡扯

balsa /ˈbɔːlsə/ *n* [u] **～ (wood)** 轻木

balsam /ˈbɔːlsəm/ *n* **1** [u] (substance) 香脂 **2** [c] (ointment) 香膏

balsamic vinegar /bɔːlˌsæmɪk ˈvɪnɪgə(r), bɒl-/ *n* [u and c] 香脂醋

Baltic /ˈbɔːltɪk/
A *adj* 波罗的海国家的; **～ shipping/trade** 波罗的海航运/贸易
B *pr n* **the ～** 波罗的海

Baltic Sea *pr n* **the ～** 波罗的海

Baltic States *pr n* **the ～** 波罗的海诸国

baluster /ˈbæləstə(r)/ *n* 栏杆柱

balustrade /ˌbæləˈstreɪd/ *n* 栏杆

bamboo /bæmˈbuː/ *n* [u] 竹子; **made of ～** 竹制的; **～ fence** 竹篱

bamboo: ～ curtain *n* Pol (*also* **B～ Curtain**) **the ～ curtain** 竹幕; **～ shoot** *n* 竹笋

bamboozle /bæmˈbuːzl/ *vt* colloq **1** (trick) 欺骗; **to ～ sb. into doing sth.** 哄骗某人做某事; **to ～ sb. out of** 从某人处骗得 ‹*money*› **2** (mystify) 使迷惑

ban /bæn/
A *vt* (*pres p etc.* **-nn-**) 明令禁止 ‹*activity, publication, film, drug*›; **to ～ sb. from doing sth.** 禁止某人做某事; **traffic is ～ned from the city centre** 市中心禁止车辆通行
B *n* 禁令; **a smoking ～** 禁烟令; **to impose/lift a ～ on sth.** 颁布/解除对某事物的禁令

banal /bəˈnɑːl, Amer ˈbeɪnl/ *adj* 平庸的 ‹*person, film, book*›; **～ topics** 乏味的话题; **what a ～ remark!** 真是陈词滥调!

banality /bəˈnæləti/ *n* **1** [u] (quality) 平庸; **the ～ of the situation** 情形的单调乏味 **2** [c] (remark) 陈词滥调

banana /bəˈnɑːnə/ *n* **1** (fruit) 香蕉; **a bunch of ～s** 一串香蕉 **2** (tree) 香蕉树 **3** **to go ～s** colloq (go mad or crazy) 发疯; (become angry) 发怒

banana: ～ republic *n* pej 香蕉共和国 [政府无能、依赖外援的贫穷国家]; **～ skin** *n* lit 香蕉皮; fig 尴尬事; **the tax reform was a bit of a ～ skin for the government** 税制改革使政府陷入尴尬; **～ split** *n* 香蕉圣代

bancassurance /ˈbæŋkəˌʃʊərəns/ *n* [u] Brit 银行保险业

band /bænd/
A *n* **1** Mus 乐队 **2** + *v sing or pl* (group of people) 一帮人; **a small ～ of troublemakers** 一小撮捣乱分子 **3** Radio 波段 **4** (of light, colour, land) 带状物; **a ～ of sunlight** 一束阳光; **a ～ of trees** 一片树林 **5** Brit Sch, Tax (category) 年龄段; **he was in the under-16 age ～** 他属

b

于 16 岁以下年龄段 6 (strip of material) 细带; **a hair/hat/waist ~** 发带/帽带/腰带; **an arm/a head ~** 臂箍/头箍 7 Brit Sch (level) 级 8 (of machine) 传送带 9 Amer (ring) 戒指; **a wedding ~** 婚戒

B *vt* 1 (categorize) 将…分类; Brit Sch 把…按能力分班 2 (bind, decorate) 给…装上箍; **the doors are ~ed with iron to make them stronger** 在门上装了铁箍使其更牢固

Phrasal verb

• **band together** *vi* 联合起来

bandage /'bændɪdʒ/

A *n* 绷带

B *vt* 用绷带包扎; **to have one's foot ~d** 用绷带把脚包扎起来

Phrasal verb

• **bandage up** *vt* [**~ sb./sth. up, ~ up sb./sth.**] 用绷带包扎; **he was (all) ~d up** 他全身缠满了绷带

Band-Aid® *n* 邦迪牌创可贴; **a ~ solution** fig pej 权宜之计

bandanna /bæn'dænə/ *n* 印花围巾

B & B /ˌbiː ən 'biː/ *abbr* Brit **= bed and breakfast**

banding /'bændɪŋ/ *n* [u] Brit 1 Tax (division) 分类 2 Sch 按能力分班; **some schools do not have a policy of ~** 有些学校没有按能力给学生分班的政策 3 (stripes) 条纹

bandit /'bændɪt/ *n* 土匪

bandit country *n* [u] 土匪横行的地区

banditry /'bændɪtri/ *n* [u] 土匪行为

band: ~ leader *n* 领队; **~master** *n* (of military band) 军乐队指挥; (of brass band) 管乐队指挥

bandolier, bandoleer /ˌbændə'lɪə(r)/ *n* 子弹带

band: ~ saw *n* 钢带锯; **~sman** /-mən/ *n* (of military band) 军乐队成员; (of brass band) 管乐队成员; **~stand** *n* 演奏台; **~wagon** *n* **to jump** *or* **climb on the ~wagon** 随大流; **~width** *n* 1 Electron (for transmitting a signal) 频率范围; 2 Electron (over which a system can operate) 频带宽度; 3 Comput 带宽

bandy /'bændi/

A *adj* 向外弯的; **to have ~ legs** 有罗圈腿

B *vt* 来回互致; **to ~ words/blows with sb.** dated 跟某人斗嘴/打架

Phrasal verb

• **bandy about, bandy around** *vt* [**~ sth. about** *or* **around**] 随口提及 ‹*statistics, name*›

bandy-legged /ˌbændɪ'legd, -'legɪd/ *adj* 罗圈腿的

bane /beɪn/ *n* 祸根; **she/it is the ~ of my life** *or* **existence!** 是她/它毁了我一生!

baneful /'beɪnfəl/ *adj* liter 邪恶的 ‹*effect, ideas*›

bang /bæŋ/

A *n* 1 (noise) 突然的巨响; **to shut the door with a ~** 砰的一声关上门; **to go with a ~** 很成功; **~ go my chances of promotion** 我晋升的机会告吹了 2 (knock, blow) 猛击; **a ~ on the head** 头部受到的撞击

B *adv* (exactly) 正好; (absolutely) 完全地; **to be ~ up to date** 是最先进的

C *excl* (imitating gun, explosion) 砰

D *vt* 1 (place sth. noisily) 砰地一摔 ‹*stick, book*›; **to ~ sth. down on sth.** 砰地把某物扔在某物上 2 (strike) 猛撞; **to ~ one's fist on the table** 用拳头猛捶桌子; **to ~ one's head against a brick wall** fig 徒劳无益 3 (make noise by hitting) 猛敲 ‹*drum, pulpit*› 4 (slam) 砰地关上 ‹*door*› 5 taboo sl (have sex with) 和…性交 ‹*woman*›

E *vi* 1 (strike) **to ~ on sth.** 猛击某物; **to ~ on the table with one's fist** 用拳头猛捶桌子 2 (make noise) 发出砰的一声; **to ~ shut** 砰地关上

Phrasal verbs

• **bang about, bang around**

A *vi* 乒乓作响地闹腾

B *vt* [**~ sth. about**] 乒乓作响地四处扔; **stop ~ing your toys about** 不要把你的玩具扔来丢去

• **bang down** *vt* [**~ sth. down, ~ down sth.**] 砰地放下 ‹*window*›; 砰地扔下 ‹*book, telephone receiver*›; 砰地捶下 ‹*fist*›

• **bang into** *vt* [**~ into sth.**] «*person, car*» 猛地撞上

• **bang on** *vi* colloq **to ~ on about sth.** 唠叨某事

• **bang out** *vt* [**~ out sth., ~ sth. out**] 响亮地奏出 ‹*tune*›

• **bang up** *vt* [**~ sb. up, ~ up sb.**] sl 把…关进监狱; **to be ~ed up for five years** 坐了 5 年牢

banger /'bæŋə(r)/ *n* colloq 1 (firework) 奇响爆竹; **to let off a ~** 放一个奇响爆竹 2 (car) 破车 3 Brit (sausage) 香肠; **~s and mash** 香肠和土豆泥

Bangkok /ˌbæŋ'kɒk/ *pr n* 曼谷

Bangladesh /ˌbæŋglə'deʃ/ *pr n* 孟加拉国

Bangladeshi /ˌbæŋglə'deʃi/ ▸ **p. 503**

A *adj* (of Bangladesh) 孟加拉国的; (of the people) 孟加拉国人的

B *n* 孟加拉国人

bangle /'bæŋgl/ *n* (around arm) 手镯; (around ankle) 脚镯

bang-on *adj* Brit colloq 完全正确的

bangs /bæŋz/ *npl* esp Amer **= fringe A1**

bang-up *adj* Amer colloq 很棒的; **for a novice, he did a ~ job** 作为一个新手, 他干得很棒

banish /'bænɪʃ/ *vt* 1 formal (expel) 驱逐; **the government ~ed him from the country** 政府把他驱逐出境 2 liter, often hum (drive away) 驱走 ‹*person, animal, idea*›; **to ~ dogs from the house** 把狗从房子里赶出去; **to ~ all thoughts of winter** 打消所有关于冬天的想法

banishment /'bænɪʃmənt/ *n* [u] formal 驱逐

banister /'bænɪstə(r)/ *n* Brit **~(s** *pl***)** 栏杆; **leaning on the ~(s)** 靠在栏杆上; **to slide down the ~(s)** 顺着楼梯的扶手滑下

banjax /'bændʒæks/ *vt* colloq 损坏; **the television is ~ed** 电视坏了

banjaxed /'bændʒækst/ *adj* colloq 疲惫不堪的; **I'm absolutely ~** 我累得不行了

banjo /'bændʒəʊ/ ▸ **p. 395** *n* (*pl* **~s** *or* **~es**) 班卓琴

Banjul /bæn'dʒuːl/ *pr n* 班珠尔

bank[1] /bæŋk/

A *n* 1 [c] (of river, lake) 岸 2 [c] (mound, pile) 堆; **a ~ of snow** 一堆雪 3 [c] (slope) (of hill etc.) 斜坡; (of road or racetrack) 边坡 4 [c] (section of sea bed) 浅滩; **a sand ~** 沙洲 5 [c] (mass) 大量; **a ~ of thick cloud** 厚厚的云层 6 [c] (embankment) 路堤 7 [u] Aviat (拐弯时的) 向内侧倾斜 8 [c] (of switches, electrical equipment etc.) 组

B *vt* 1 (pile up) **~ (up)** 堆积 ‹*snow, mud*› 2 (border) **to be ~ed by sth.** «*road, river*» 被某物像堤岸般围住; **the canal is ~ed on one side by high buildings** 运河的一边高楼林立 3 Aviat 使…转弯时倾斜飞行 ‹*aeroplane*› 4 (slope) **~ (up)** 使…的转弯处向内侧倾斜 ‹*road, racetrack*› 5 (dam) **~ (up)** 在…上筑堤 ‹*river*› 6 (on a fire) 封; **to ~ (up) the fire** 压火

C *vi* 1 (pile up) **to ~ (up)** «*snow, mud*» 堆积 2 Aviat 转弯时倾斜飞行

bank[2]

A *n* 1 Fin (establishment, building) 银行; **the B~ of England/China** 英格兰/中国银行 2 (stock, repository) 库 3 (in gambling) 赌本; **to break the ~** lit 使庄家输光钱; fig 倾家荡产

B *vt* 把…存入银行 ‹*cheque, cash*›

C *vi* **to ~ with ...** 在…银行开账户

Phrasal verb

• **bank on** *vt* [**~ on sth.**] 指望; **to ~ on sb.'s support** 依赖某人的支持

bankable /'bæŋkəbl/ *adj* 1 Fin 银行可承兑的 ‹*cheque, asset, banknote*› 2 fig (certain to bring profit or success) 有票房号召力的; **a ~ star** 卖座明星 3 (reliable) 可靠的; **a ~ promise** 可信的承诺

bankable asset *n* 银行可承兑资产

bank: ~ acceptance *n* 银行承兑汇票; **~ account** *n* 银行账户; **I have a ~ account with HSBC** 我在汇丰银行有一个账户

bankassurance /'bæŋkəˌʃɔːrəns, Amer -əˌʃʊərəns/ *n* **= bancassurance**

bank: ~ balance *n* 银行存款余额; **she's only interested in your ~ balance!** 她只对你的银行存款感兴趣!; **~ bill** *n* Amer 钞票; **~book** *n* 银行存折; **~ card** *n* **= cheque card**; **~ charges** *npl* 银行收费; **~ clerk** ▸ **p. 409** *n* 银行职员; **~ draft** *n* 银行汇票

banker /'bæŋkə(r)/ ▸ **p. 409** *n* 1 Fin (owner) 银行家; (executive) 银行高级职员 2 Games 庄家

banker: ~'s card *n* **= cheque card**; **~'s draft** *n* **= bank draft**; **~'s order** *n* Brit **= standing order**; **~'s reference** *n* 银行资信证明书

bank: B~ for International Settlements *pr n* 国际清算银行; **B~ Giro Credit** *n* Brit 银行转账信贷; **~ holiday** *n* Brit 银行假; Amer 银行休业日

> **bank holiday**
>
> 1. (英国) 银行假。英国法定假日 (不包括星期六和星期日)。1871 年首次施行。银行假期间, 除市政、消防、急救、警察等公共基础服务部门外, 银行和多数商店、工厂等都会放假。银行假每年的日期并不固定, 以英格兰为例, 依次为元旦 (New Year's Day)、耶稣受难日 (Good Friday)、复活节星期一 (Easter Monday)、五朔节 (May Day, 5 月的第一个星期一)、春假 (Spring Holiday, 5 月的最后一个星期一)、夏假 (Late Summer Bank Holiday, 8 月的最后一个星期一)、圣诞节 (Christmas)、节礼日 (Boxing Day, 圣诞节后的第一个工作日)。银行假和周末重叠时, 日期相应顺延。
>
> 2. (美国) 银行休业日。银行根据政府指令在此期间停止营业, 避免出现金融问题。

banking /'bæŋkɪŋ/ *n* [u] 1 (business) 银行业务 2 (profession) 银行业; **to study ~** 学习银行专业

banking hours *npl* 银行营业时间

bank: ~ lending *n* [u] 银行借贷; **~ loan** *n* 银行贷款; **to take out a ~ loan** 获得一笔银行贷款; **~ manager** ▸ **p. 409** *n* 银行分行经理; **~note** *n* 钞票; **£50,000 in used ~notes** 5 万英镑的旧钞票; **~ raid** *n* 银行抢劫; **~ rate** *n* Brit **= base rate**; **~ robber** *n* 银行抢劫犯; **~ robbery** *n* 银行抢劫案

bankroll /'bæŋkrəʊl/

A *n* Amer 一卷钞票

B *vt* esp Amer colloq 资助; **to ~ an election campaign** 为竞选提供资金

bankrupt /'bæŋkrʌpt/

A *adj* 1 (financially ruined) 破产的 ‹*person, company, business*›; **to be declared/made ~** 被宣布/被逼破产; **to go ~** 破产; **~ stock** 破产拍卖品 2 (lacking) 完全缺乏的; **to be morally ~** 道德沦丧; **to be ~ of sth.** 毫无 ‹*ideas, principles*›

B *vt* 使…破产 ‹*person, organization*›

C *n* 破产者; **he's a ~** 他破产了

bankruptcy /'bæŋkrʌptsi/ *n* [u and c] 1 lit (financial) 破产 2 fig 彻底丧失; **the moral ~ of terrorism** 恐怖主义的道德沦丧

bankruptcy proceedings *npl* 破产程序

bank: ~ statement *n* 银行结单; **~ transfer** *n* 银行转账

banner /'bænə(r)/

A *n* 1 (at protest, festival) 横幅 2 (slogan) 口号; **under the ~ of sth.** 声称支持某事物 3 Hist (flag) 旗帜 4 Comput = **banner advertisement**

B *adj* 特别好的 ⟨*day*⟩

banner: ~ advertisement, ~ ad colloq, **~ advert** Brit colloq *ns* 网页广告条; **~ headline** *n* 通栏大字标题

bannister /'bænɪstə(r)/ *n* Brit = **banister**

banns /bænz/ *npl* 结婚预告; **to read the ~** 宣读结婚预告

banoffi pie /bə,nɒfi 'paɪ/ *n* 香蕉太妃派

banquet /'bæŋkwɪt/

A *n* 宴会; **to hold a ~ in honour of sb.** 宴请某人; **a wedding ~** 婚宴

B *vi* 赴宴

banquet hall, banqueting hall *ns* 宴会厅

banshee /bæn'ʃi:, Amer 'bænʃi:/ *n* [爱尔兰传说中预报死讯的] 女妖; **to howl/wail like a ~** 尖厉地嚎叫/号哭

bantam /'bæntəm/ *n* 矮脚鸡

bantamweight /'bæntəmweɪt/ *n* 最轻量级拳击运动员; **~ champion** 最轻量级拳击冠军

banter /'bæntə(r)/

A *n* [u] 打趣

B *vi* 打趣; **to ~ with sb.** 跟某人开玩笑

bantering /'bæntərɪŋ/ *adj* 开玩笑的 ⟨*tone, remark*⟩

baptism /'bæptɪzəm/ *n* 1 [u] (rite) 洗礼 2 [c] (ceremony) 洗礼仪式 3 [c] fig (initiation) 初次的考验; **a ~ of fire** 严峻的考验

baptismal /bæp'tɪzməl/ *adj* 洗礼的; **~ name** 教名

Baptist /'bæptɪst/

A *n* 浸礼会教友

B *adj attrib* 浸礼会的 ⟨*group, church*⟩

baptistery, baptistry /'bæptɪstri/ *n* 洗礼堂

baptize /bæp'taɪz/ *vt* 1 Relig 给…施洗礼; **to be ~d a Catholic** 受洗成为天主教徒 2 (name) 给…取教名

bar /bɑ:(r)/

A *n* 1 (strip of wood, metal) 长条; **the gate had a ~ across it** 大门上着门闩; **behind ~s** 在狱中 2 (block) (of soap, chocolate etc.) 块; **a ~ of gold** 一根金条 3 (place for drinking) 酒吧 4 (counter) 吧台 5 (obstacle) 障碍; **a ~ on people coming here to live** 人们来这里居住的障碍 6 Jur (in court) **the ~** 围栏; **the prisoner at the ~** 受审讯的刑事被告 7 **the Bar** Jur (profession) 大律师职业; **to be called to the Bar** 获得大律师资格 8 Brit Sport (crossbar) 球门横梁 9 Mus 小节 10 Brit (in electric fire) 供热电阻丝 11 (of light, colour) 带; **~s of sunlight** 一道道阳光; **a ~ of red across the sky** 横贯天空的一抹红

B *vt* (*pres p etc.* **-rr-**) 1 (fasten) 闩上 ⟨*door*⟩ 2 (block) 阻挡 ⟨*way*⟩; **the police ~red the entrance** 警察封锁了入口 3 (exclude) 禁止; **to ~ sb. from doing sth.** 禁止某人做某事; **a no holds ~red contest** 激烈的竞争

C *prep* 除…外; **they all turned up to the party ~ one** 除一人缺席外, 他们都出席了晚会; **~ none** 没有例外地

barb /bɑ:b/ *n* 1 (on hook, arrow) 倒钩 2 fig (remark) 尖刻的话

Barbados /bɑ:'beɪdɒs/ *pr n* 巴巴多斯

barbarian /bɑ:'beərɪən/

A *n* 1 Hist 未开化的人 2 fig 没教养的人

B *adj* 1 (primitive) 原始的 ⟨*person, customs*⟩ 2 (uncultured, brutish) 粗野的 ⟨*behaviour, manners*⟩

barbaric /bɑ:'bærɪk/ *adj* 1 (brutal, primitive) 粗野的 ⟨*person, habit, action*⟩ 2 (violent, brutal) 残暴的 ⟨*person, terrorist act, behaviour*⟩

barbarically /bɑ:'bærɪkli/ *adv* 野蛮地 ⟨*act, behave*⟩

barbarism /'bɑ:bərɪzəm/ *n* [u] 1 (absence of culture) 未开化状态 2 (brutal actions) 残暴行为

barbarity /bɑ:'bærəti/ *n* 1 [u] (brutality, primitiveness) 野蛮 2 [c] (brutal act) 残暴行为

barbarous /'bɑ:bərəs/ *adj* 1 (uncivilized) 粗野的 ⟨*behaviour, manners*⟩ 2 (brutal) 残暴的 ⟨*atrocities, acts of terrorism*⟩

barbecue /'bɑ:bɪkju:/

A *n* 1 (party) 户外烧烤 2 (grill) 烤架 3 (food) 烧烤

B *vt* 烧烤

barbecue sauce *n* [u] 烧烤酱

barbed /'bɑ:bd/ *adj* 1 (having a short sharp point or hook) 有倒钩的 ⟨*arrow, hook*⟩ 2 *attrib* (hurtful) 尖刻的 ⟨*remark, criticism*⟩

barbed wire *n* [u] 带刺铁丝

barbel /'bɑ:bl/ *n* 1 (fish) 鲃 2 (filament) 触须

barbell /'bɑ:bel/ *n* 杠铃

barber /'bɑ:bə(r)/ ▸**p. 409** *n* 理发师; **to go to the ~'s** 去理发店

barber: ~shop *n* Amer 1 [c] (shop) 理发店; 2 [u] Mus 无伴奏男声四重唱; **~shop quartet** *n* [u] 无伴奏男声四重唱; **~'s pole** Brit, **~ pole** Amer *ns* 理发店旋转彩柱; **~'s shop** Brit *n* 理发店

barbie /'bɑ:bi/ *n* colloq 1 (grill) 烤架 2 (party) 烧烤野餐

Barbie doll® *n* 1 芭比娃娃 2 colloq 花瓶女

barbiturate /bɑ:'bɪtjʊrət/ *n* 巴比妥酸盐

barbwire /'bɑ:rbwaɪər/ *n* [u] Amer = **barbed wire**

Barcelona /,bɑ:sə'ləʊnə/ *pr n* 巴塞罗那

bar: ~ chart *n* 条形图; **~ code** *n* 条形码; **~-coded** *adj* 有条形码的; **~-code reader** *n* 条形码阅读器

bard /bɑ:d/ *n* 1 (poet) 诗人; **the B~ of Avon** 埃文河畔的游吟诗人 [即莎士比亚] 2 archaic (minstrel) 游吟诗人

bare /beə(r)/

A *adj* 1 (naked) 裸露的 ⟨*body, blade*⟩; **to walk with ~ feet** 赤脚走路; **to sit in the sun with one's head ~** 不戴帽坐在太阳底下; **~ to the waist** 赤膊的; **with one's ~ hands** 赤手空拳地 2 (exposed) 无遮盖的; **to strip sth. down to the ~ bones** 去除某事物的枝节; **~ walls** 没有装饰的墙壁; **he laid ~ their evil plan** 他揭露了他们的恶毒计划; **to lay one's soul** *or* **heart ~** 袒露心扉 3 (empty) 空的 ⟨*cupboard, room*⟩; **the burglars stripped the house ~** 窃贼将房子洗劫一空 4 (stark) 光秃秃的 ⟨*mountain, tree*⟩; **a barren landscape which was ~ of almost every sign of life** 几乎毫无生命迹象的不毛之地 5 (mere) 仅仅的; **a ~ 3%/20 dollars** 仅仅 3%/区区 20 美元; **to last a ~ 30 seconds** 持续了只不过 30 秒钟 6 (just sufficient) 刚够的; **the ~ minimum** 最低限度; **the ~ essentials** *or* **necessities** 最低限度的必需品 7 (unembellished) 不加掩饰的 ⟨*facts*⟩

B *vt* 裸露 ⟨*part of body*⟩; 袒露 ⟨*heart, soul*⟩; **to ~ one's teeth** 龇牙咧嘴; **to ~ one's head** 脱帽致敬; **to ~ all** 袒胸露体; **to ~ one's heart** *or* **soul to sb.** 向某人袒露心扉

bare: ~-ass, ~-assed *adjs* Amer taboo sl 一丝不挂的; **~back** *adv* 不用鞍地; **he rode ~back** 他骑光背马; **~back rider** *n* 不用马鞍的骑手; **~-bones** *adj* 最基本的; **we quickly came up with a ~-bones plan of action** 我们很快拿出了一个行动计划纲要

barefaced /'beəfeɪst/ *adj attrib* 厚颜无耻的; **a ~ lie** 无耻的谎言; **~ cheek** 厚颜无耻

barefoot /'beəfʊt/

A *adj* 赤脚的; **to be ~** 打赤脚

B *adv* 赤着脚 ⟨*walk*⟩

bareheaded /,beə'hedɪd/ *adj* 头上不戴东西的

bare-legged /,beə'legd, -'legɪd/

A *adj* 光腿的

B *adv* 光着腿

barely /'beəli/ *adv* 1 (only just) 仅仅; (almost not) 几乎不; **she had ~ finished when ...** 她刚刚完成就…; **~ 12 hours later** 仅仅 12 个小时后; **to be ~ able to walk** 勉强能走路 2 (meagrely) 贫乏地; **a ~ furnished room** 陈设简陋的房间

bareness /'beənɪs/ *n* [u] 1 (lack of covering) 无遮盖; (of floorboards) 无地毯; (of walls) 无装饰 2 (sparseness) 光秃秃 3 (emptiness) 空无一物; **what struck me was the ~ of the room** 使我吃惊的是房间里空无一物

Barents Sea /,bærənts 'si:/ *pr n* **the ~** 巴伦支海

bar exams *npl* Brit 律师资格考试

barfly /'bɑ:flaɪ/ *n* Amer colloq 酒吧常客

bargain /'bɑ:gɪn/

A *n* 1 (deal) 协议; **to make** *or* **strike a ~** 达成协议; **to keep one's side of the ~** 遵守自己的诺言; **to drive a hard ~** 极力讨价还价 2 (good buy) 便宜货; **what a ~!** 真便宜啊!; **to get a ~** 买到便宜货

B *vi* 1 (for deal) 讲条件; **to ~ with sb. (over** *or* **for sth.)** (就某事物) 与某人商谈 2 (over price) 讨价还价; **to ~ for a lower price** 砍价; **to ~ with sb. (over** *or* **for sth.)** (就某事物) 与某人讨价还价 3 (expect) **to ~ for** *or* **on sth.** 预料到某事物; **we got more than we ~ed for** 我们得到的超过了我们的预期; **I didn't really ~ on this happening** 我真的没料到会发生这事

bargain: ~ basement *n* 减价商品部; **~ hunter** *n* 淘便宜货的人

bargaining /'bɑ:gɪnɪŋ/ *n* [u] 谈判

bargaining: ~ chip *n* 讨价还价的筹码; **~ position** *n* 谈判地位; **~ power** *n* [u] 谈判实力; **~ rights** *npl* 谈判权利

bargain: ~ offer *n* 特价出售; **~ price** *n* 特价

barge /bɑ:dʒ/

A *n* 1 (boat) 大型平底船; (for cargo only) 驳船 2 (for ceremony, pageant) 结彩大游艇 3 (in navy) 舰载艇

B *vt* 闯出; **she ~d her way to the front of the queue** 她硬闯到队伍前面去了

C *vi* 冲撞; **to ~ past sb.** 横冲直撞地挤过某人身边

Phrasal verbs

- **barge in** *vi* (enter noisily) 闯进; (interrupt) 打扰; **sorry to ~ in** 抱歉, 打扰了; **to ~ in on sb.** 打扰/打断某人; **to ~ in on a meeting** 闯入会议
- **barge into** *vt* [**~ into sth.**] (enter noisily) 闯进; (interrupt) 打扰

bargee /bɑ:'dʒi:/ ▸**p. 409** *n* esp Brit (in charge of a barge) 驳船船长; (working on a barge) 驳船船员

bargepole /'bɑ:dʒpəʊl/ *n* 撑篙; **I wouldn't touch it/her with a ~** colloq 我压根儿不愿和它/她牵扯到一起

bar graph *n* esp Amer = **bar chart**

barista /bɑ:'rɪstə/ *n* 咖啡馆服务生

baritone /'bærɪtəʊn/ *n* 1 [u] (voice) 男中音; **to sing ~** 唱男中音 2 [c] (singer) 男中音歌手 3 [c] (instrument) 上低音乐器; **a ~ part** 上低音声部

barium /'beərɪəm/ *n* [u] 钡

barium meal *n* 钡餐

b

bark[1] /bɑːk/
A *n* 1 (of dog, seal) 吠叫; (of other animal) 叫声; **his ~ is worse than his bite** 他嘴上凶，但心不坏 2 (of human) 咆哮; **a short ~ of laughter** 短促响亮的笑声
B *vt* (shout) 厉声说出; **'shut up!', ~ed the teacher** "闭嘴！"老师呵斥道; **the officer ~ed (out) orders at the soldiers** 军官厉声向士兵下达命令
C *vi* 《*dog*》吠; 《*other animal*》叫; 《*person*》咆哮; **to ~ at sth./sb.** 对着某物/某人咆哮; **to be ~ing up the wrong tree** fig colloq 弄错目标

Phrasal verb
• **bark out** *vt* [**~ out sth.**] 厉声说出

bark[2]
A *n* [u] (of tree) 树皮
B *vt* 1 (strip) 剥去…的皮 2 (graze skin from) 擦破…的皮

barkeeper /ˈbɑːkiːpə(r)/ ►**p. 409** *n* 1 (owner of bar) 酒吧老板 2 (server at bar) 酒吧招待

barker /ˈbɑːkə(r)/ *n* 大声招徕顾客的人

barking /ˈbɑːkɪŋ/ Brit colloq
A *adj* 彻底发疯的
B *adv* **~ mad** 完全疯了

barley /ˈbɑːli/ *n* [u] 大麦

barley: ~corn *n* [u] 大麦粒; **~ field** *n* 大麦田; **~ sugar** *n* [u] 麦芽糖; **~ water** *n* [u] 大麦茶; **~ wine** *n* [u] Brit 麦芽啤酒

bar: ~maid ►**p. 409** *n* 1 Brit (woman serving in bar) 吧台女招待; 2 Amer (waitress) 酒吧女招待; **~man** /-mən/ ►**p. 409** *n* esp Brit 酒保; **~ manager** ►**p. 409** *n* 酒吧经理

barmy /ˈbɑːmi/ *adj* Brit colloq 傻乎乎的 ‹*person*›; 疯疯癫癫的 ‹*idea, plan*›; **to go ~** 发疯

barn /bɑːn/ *n* 1 (for crops) 谷仓; (for cattle) 牛栏; (for horses) 马厩 2 colloq (large uninviting building) 空落落的建筑物; **a great ~ of a place** 一座空荡荡的大房子

barnacle /ˈbɑːnəkl/ *n* 1 (crustacean) 藤壶 2 pej (person) 缠住不放的人; **lovers clinging on to one another like ~s** 彼此形影不离的恋人

barnacle goose *n* 黑雁

barn: ~ dance *n* 谷仓舞; **~ door** *n* 谷仓大门; **as big as a ~ door** 宽大如门板的; **built like a ~ door** colloq 身材高大的

barney /ˈbɑːni/ *n* Brit colloq 争吵; **to have a ~ with sb.** 和某人争吵

barn owl *n* 仓鸮

barnstorm /ˈbɑːnstɔːm/ Amer
A *vi* 乡下巡回演出
B *vt* 在…作巡回竞选演说

barnstormer /ˈbɑːnstɔːmə(r)/ *n* Amer (performer) 下乡巡回演出的人; (politician) 作巡回竞选演说的人

barnstorming /ˈbɑːnstɔːmɪŋ/ *adj* 活力四射的 ‹*performance, performer*›

barnyard /ˈbɑːnjɑːd/ *n* 仓院

barograph /ˈbærəgrɑːf, Amer -græf/ *n* 自记气压计

barometer /bəˈrɒmɪtə(r)/ *n* 1 Meteorol 气压计 2 fig (indicator) 变化的标志; **to be a ~ of sth.** 是某事物的晴雨表; **opinion polls are a good ~ of public opinion** 民意测验可以很好地反映舆论

barometric /ˌbærəˈmetrɪk/ *n* 气压的 ‹*change, tendency*›; 气压计的 ‹*error, data*›; **~ pressure** 大气压

baron /ˈbærən/ *n* 1 (British noble) 男爵 2 (tycoon) 大亨; **an oil/industrial ~** 石油/工业界巨头; **a drug ~** 大毒枭 3 Hist 分封贵族

baroness /ˈbærənɪs/ *n* 1 (British noble) 女男爵 2 (title) 男爵夫人

baronet /ˈbærənɪt/ *n* 准男爵

baronial /bəˈrəʊnɪəl/ *adj* 1 (of a baron) 男爵的; **a ~ hall** 男爵的乡村宅第 2 fig (splendid) 富丽堂皇的; **the ~ splendour of the entrance hall** 大堂的豪华

baroque /bəˈrɒk, Amer bəˈrəʊk/
A *n* [u] **the B~** 巴罗克风格
B *adj* 1 Archit, Art, Mus 巴罗克风格的 2 (highly ornate) 绮靡的

barque /bɑːk/ *n* 三桅帆船

barrack /ˈbærək/
A *vt* Brit, Austral, NZ 向…喝倒彩
B *vi* Austral, NZ 喝彩

barracking /ˈbærəkɪŋ/ *n* [u] Brit, Austral, NZ 哄叫

barrack room
A *n* 营房
B *modif* pej 粗鲁下流的; **a ~ joke** 下流的笑话

barracks /ˈbærəks/ *n + v sing or pl* 1 (soldier's quarters) 营房 2 pej (large, ugly building) 简陋的大房子

barrack square *n* 营区练兵场

barracuda /ˌbærəˈkuːdə/ *n* (*pl* **~** *or* **~s**) 魣

barrage /ˈbærɑːʒ, Amer bəˈrɑːʒ/ *n* [u] 1 Civ Eng 堰 2 (heavy gunfire) 火力网 3 (of questions, criticism, complaints, publicity) 一连串; **a ~ of questions from the press** 记者提出的一连串问题

barrage balloon *n* 阻拦气球

barrel /ˈbærəl/
A *n* 1 (for wine, beer) 桶; **to have sb. over a ~** fig 使某人听从摆布; **to scrape the bottom of the ~** fig 退而求其次; **a ~ of laughs/fun** colloq 十分开心/有趣 2 Meas 一桶 3 (of cannon) 炮管; (of firearm) 枪管; **to give sb. both ~s** lit 用双管猎枪向某人射击; fig 猛烈抨击某人; **lock, stock, and ~** 全部; **they had to move house lock, stock, and ~** 他们得把房子里的东西全都搬走 4 (of fountain pen) 笔杆 5 (of watch, clock) 发条盒 6 (of lock) 锁芯
B *vt* (*pres p etc.* **-ll-**, **-l-**) 把…装桶 ‹*wine, oil*›
C *vi* (*pres p etc.* **-ll-**, **-l-**) **to ~ along** Amer colloq 高速行驶

barrel: ~-chested *adj* 胸部厚实的 ‹*man, animal*›; **~house** *n* 1 [c] Amer (saloon) 低级酒店; 2 [u] Mus 低级酒店爵士乐; **~ organ** *n* 手摇风琴

barren /ˈbærən/ *adj* 贫瘠的 ‹*land, soil*›; 不结果实的 ‹*plant*›

barrette /bəˈret/ *n* Amer 条状发夹

barricade /ˌbærɪˈkeɪd/
A *n* 路障; **to man the ~s** lit, fig 竖起路障; **to form a human ~** 筑起一道人墙
B *vt* 堵住 ‹*door, street*›
C *v refl* **to ~ oneself in sth.** 躲在某物里

barrier /ˈbærɪə(r)/ *n* 1 (obstacle) 障碍物 2 fig 障碍; **to break down** *or* **remove emotional/cultural/political ~s** 消除情绪/文化/政治隔阂; **trade/language ~s** 贸易壁垒/语言障碍

barrier: ~ cream *n* 护肤脂; **~ method** *n* 屏障避孕法; **~ reef** *n* 堡礁

barring /ˈbɑːrɪŋ/ *prep* 除…以外; **~ accidents** 除非有意外; **nobody ~ a madman would start a nuclear war** 只有疯子才会发动核战争

barrio /ˈbɑːrɪəʊ/ *n* Amer 说西班牙语的移民区

barrister /ˈbærɪstə(r)/ ►**p. 409** *n* Brit **~(-at-law)** 出庭律师

barroom /ˈbɑːruːm/ *n* esp Amer 酒吧间; **a ~ brawl** 酒吧间里的斗殴

barrow[1] /ˈbærəʊ/ *n* Brit (cart) 手推车

barrow[2] *n* Archaeol 古坟

barrow boy *n* ►**p. 409** Brit 街头推车小贩

bar: ~ stool *n* 酒吧间高脚凳; **~tender** *n* Amer **= ~man**

barter /ˈbɑːtə(r)/
A *n* [u] 易货贸易
B *vt* 以…作易货贸易; **to ~ sth. for sth.** 以某物换某物
C *vi* (by exchange) 以货易货; (haggle) 讨价还价

basalt /ˈbæsɔːlt, Amer ˈbeɪ-, bəˈsɔːlt/ *n* [u] 玄武岩

bascule bridge /ˈbæskjuːl brɪdʒ/ *n* 竖旋桥

base[1] /beɪs/
A *n* 1 (lowest part) (gen) 底部; (of sculpture, statue) 底座; **at the ~ of the cliff** 在悬崖脚下; **a lamp ~** 灯座 2 (headquarters) 总部 3 (underside of object) 底面 4 (centre of operations) (gen) 大本营; Mil 基地; **air ~** 空军基地 5 (basis) 根据; **the ~ on which income tax is calculated** 计算所得税的依据 6 Comm, Pol 基础; **a strong industrial ~** 坚实的工业基础 7 (basic ingredient) 基本成分; (basic layer) 底层 8 Math 基数 9 Geom (of figure) 底边 10 Chem 盐基 11 (in baseball) 垒 12 Amer fig colloq **to be off ~** 完全错误; **to catch sb. off ~** 使某人措手不及; **to steal a ~ on sb.** 超越某人; **to touch ~ (with sb.) (about sth.)** （为某事物）（和某人）联系
B *vt* 1 (take as foundation) 把…建立在基础上; **to ~ sth. on sth.** 把某事物建立在某事物上; **our relationship is ~d on trust** 我们的关系建立在信任的基础上; **a film ~d on a novel by Henry James** 一部根据亨利·詹姆斯的小说改编的电影 2 (have as centre of operations) 以…为基地; **the company is ~d in Hong Kong** 公司总部设在香港; **I am currently ~d in New York** 我现在驻纽约工作

base[2] *adj* 1 liter (ignoble) 卑鄙的 ‹*person, conduct, reason*› 2 (not made of precious metal) 伪造的 ‹*coin*›

baseball /ˈbeɪsbɔːl/ ►**p. 307** *n* 1 [u] (game) 棒球运动 2 [c] (ball) 棒球

baseball: ~ bat *n* 棒球球棒; **~ cap** *n* 棒球帽

base: ~board *n* Amer **= skirting board**; **~ camp** *n* 登山大本营; **~ coat** *n* 底漆

-based /beɪsd/ *combining form* 1 (indicating location) 基地在…的; **a Manchester~ sales executive** 驻曼彻斯特的销售主管; **a Yorkshire~ company** 总部设在约克郡的公司 2 (indicating main activity) 以…为主的; **an export~ company** 主营出口业务的公司

base: ~ form *n* 基本形式; **~ jump** *n* 高处跳伞; **~ jumper** *n* 高处跳伞者; **~ jumping** ►**p. 307** *n* [u] 高处跳伞运动; **~ lending rate** *n* **= ~ rate**

baseless /ˈbeɪslɪs/ *adj* 无根据的 ‹*accusation, criticism*›

baseline /ˈbeɪslaɪn/ *n* 1 Sport 底线 2 (starting point) 起点

basement /ˈbeɪsmənt/ *n* 地下室; **a ~ kitchen** 位于地下室的厨房

base: ~ metal *n* 贱金属; **~ rate** *n* 1 (of central bank) 基准利率; 2 (of any bank) 基本利率; **~ station** *n* Telecom 基站

bash /bæʃ/ colloq
A *n* 1 (blow) 猛击 2 (dent) 凹痕; **my car has a ~ on the door** 我那辆车的车门撞瘪了一块 3 (attempt) 尝试; **to have a ~ at sth., to give sth. a ~** 尝试做某事 4 (party) 盛大聚会; **a birthday ~** 生日庆典
B *vt* 1 (hit or punch hard) 猛击 2 (collide with) 猛撞 ‹*vehicle, person, wall*› 3 (criticize) 无端地指责 ‹*race, political opponent, trade union*›
C *vi* 猛烈撞击; **to ~ into sb./sth.** 猛地撞上某人/某物

Phrasal verbs
• **bash about, bash around** *vt* [**~ sb. about** *or* **around**] colloq 殴打
• **bash in, bash down** *vt* [**~ sth. in, ~ in sth.**] colloq 不断猛击 [使之毁坏]; **to ~ the door in** 砸倒房门; **~ those cardboard boxes in** 砸瘪那些纸盒
• **bash on** *vi* colloq 坚持; **to ~ on (with sth.)** 坚持（做某事）
• **bash out** *vt* [**~ out sth., ~ sth. out**] colloq 大量粗制滥造
• **bash up** *vt* [**~ sb./sth. up, ~ up sb./sth.**] colloq 猛击

bashful /ˈbæʃfl/ *adj* 羞怯的; **to be ~ about doing sth.** 为做某事感到难为情

bashfully /ˈbæʃfəli/ *adv* 羞怯地

bashfulness /ˈbæʃflnɪs/ *n* [u] 羞怯

bashing /ˈbæʃɪŋ/ *n* 1 (beating) 痛打; **to give sb. a ~** 殴打某人 2 colloq (defeat) 失败; **to give sb. a ~** 击败某人; **to take a ~** (defeat) 失败; (damage) 损毁

basic /ˈbeɪsɪk/

A *adj* 1 *attrib* (fundamental, central) 基本的 ‹*principle, problem, necessity*›; 核心的 ‹*aim*›; **honesty is ~ to a good relationship** 诚实是友好关系的基础 2 (elementary) 初步的; (initial level) 初级的 3 (rudimentary) 简陋的; **the accommodation was rather ~** pej 膳宿相当简朴 4 *attrib* (before additions) 不包括附加部分的 ‹*working hours, arrangements, sketch, dress*›; **your ~ salary is £200 per week, before overtime** 你的基本工资是每周 200 英镑，不包括加班费

B basics *npl* 1 (of knowledge, study) 基本原理; **to get down to (the) ~s** 从基本问题着手; **to go back to (the) ~s** 回归本原 2 (food) 基本食物

basically /ˈbeɪsɪkli/ *adv* (fundamentally) 根本地; (for emphasis) 从根本上来说; **a ~ capitalist society** 本质上实行资本主义的社会; **~, I don't like him very much** 总的来说，我不太喜欢他

basic: B~ Law *n* 基本法; **~ rate** *n* 1 (of pay) 基本工资; 2 Tax 基本税率; **~ training** *n* [u] 新兵基本训练

basil /ˈbæzl/ *n* [u] 罗勒 [一种芳香植物，多用于烹调]

basilica /bəˈzɪlɪkə/ *n* Archit 长方形廊柱大厅; (religious building) 长方形廊柱大厅式基督教堂

basilisk /ˈbæzɪlɪsk/ *n* 1 Mythol 蛇怪 [传说其目光或气息可致命] 2 (reptile) 鬣蜥

basin /ˈbeɪsn/ *n* 1 Culin 调菜盆 2 (for washing) 洗涤槽 3 Geog (area lower than the surrounding area) 盆地 4 Geog (region) 流域; **the Amazon ~** 亚马孙河流域 5 (body of water) 内湾 6 (of port) 船坞; (of canal) 内港

basis /ˈbeɪsɪs/ *n* (*pl* **bases** /ˈbeɪsiːz/) 1 (set of principles) 基础; (of discussion) 出发点; **on the ~ of/that ...** 基于…; **to be** *or* **form the ~ for sth.** 是/构成某事物的基础; **on a part-time/full-time/temporary ~** 以兼职/全职/临时的方式; **on a first-name ~** 以直呼其名的方式 2 (for belief, argument, claim) 根据; **that argument has no factual ~** 那个论点没有事实依据

basis point /ˈbeɪsɪs pɔɪnt/ *n* 基点 [等于0.01%]

bask /bɑːsk, Amer bæsk/ *vi* 1 (lie in sun) «*person, animal, landscape*» 沐浴在阳光下; **to ~ in the sun** 晒太阳 2 fig (luxuriate) 感到舒适温馨; **he ~ed in the warmth of his father's approval** 他沉浸在父亲的赞许中，感到很温馨; **to ~ in sb.'s reflected glory** 沾某人的光

basket /ˈbɑːskɪt, Amer ˈbæskɪt/ *n* 1 (with or without handles) 篮; (carried on back) 篓; (on donkey) 筐 2 (contents) 一篮; **she brought a ~ of strawberries** 她带来了一篮草莓 3 Fin 一组; **a ~ of currencies** 一揽子货币 4 (in basketball) 篮; **to make** *or* **score a ~** 投篮得分

basketball /ˈbɑːskɪtbɔːl, Amer ˈbæsk-/ ▸p. 307 *n* 1 [u] (game) 篮球运动 2 [c] (ball) 篮球

basket: ~ case *n* 1 colloq (person) 神经质的人; **she's a ~ case** 她是个神经病; 2 (country) 濒于瘫痪的国家; (economy) 萧条的经济; **~ chair** *n* 藤椅

basketful /ˈbɑːskɪtfʊl, Amer ˈbæsk-/ *n* 一满篮; **a ~ of vegetables** 一篮蔬菜

basket: ~ maker ▸p. 409 *n* 编篮人; **~-making** *n* [u] 编制篮筐; **~work** *n* [u] (objects) 藤编制品; (craft) 藤编技艺

basking shark /ˈbɑːskɪŋ, Amer ˈbæsk-/ *n* 姥鲛

basmati rice /bæzˌmæti ˈraɪs/ *n* [u] 印度香米

Basque /bæsk, bɑːsk/ ▸p. 503, p. 426

A *adj* (of the Basque Country) 巴斯克地区的; (of the people) 巴斯克人的; (of the language) 巴斯克语的

B *n* 1 [c] (person) 巴斯克人 2 [u] (language) 巴斯克语

Basque Country *pr n* **the ~** 巴斯克地区

bas-relief /ˈbæsrɪliːf, ˈbɑːrɪliːf/

A *n* 浅浮雕

B *adj* 浅浮雕的

bass¹ /beɪs/ *n* 1 (lowest tone) 低音 2 (low male voice) 男低音 3 (musical part) 男低音部; **to sing (the) ~** 唱男低音部 4 ▸p. 395 (instrument) (electric guitar) 低音电吉他; (double bass) 低音提琴 5 Audio 低音

bass² /bæs/ *n* (fish) 鲈鱼

bass /beɪs/: **~-baritone** *n* 低男中音; **~ clef** *n* 低音谱号; **~ drum** ▸p. 395 *n* 大鼓

basset /ˈbæsɪt/ *n* **~ (hound)** 短腿猎犬

bass guitar /ˌbeɪs ɡɪrˈtɑː(r)/ *n* 低音电吉他

bassist /ˈbeɪsɪst/ ▸p. 395 *n* 1 (bass guitar player) 低音电吉他手 2 (double bass player) 低音提琴手

bassoon /bəˈsuːn/ ▸p. 395 *n* 巴松管

bastard /ˈbɑːstəd, Amer ˈbæs-/

A *n* 1 sl (term of abuse) 杂种 offensive; **you rotten ~!** 你这下流坯! 2 sl (used humorously) 家伙; **poor ~!** 可怜的家伙!; **the silly ~!** 那个笨蛋!; **you lucky ~!** 你太幸运了! 3 sl (difficult problem, task) 麻烦事; **that was a ~ of a question!** 那个问题真伤脑筋! 4 dated pej (illegitimate child) 私生子

B *adj attrib* 1 dated pej (illegitimate) 私生的 ‹*child*› 2 fig (debased) 不纯的 ‹*form, dialect*›

bastardized /ˈbɑːstədaɪzd, Amer ˈbæs-/ *adj* 不实的 ‹*account*›; 不规范的 ‹*language*›

baste /beɪst/ *vt* 1 Culin 在…上浇油汁 2 (in sewing) 粗缝

bastion /ˈbæstɪən/ *n* 1 Archit 棱堡 2 fig (stronghold) 堡垒; (defence) 捍卫者; **love is a ~ against loneliness** 爱情让人不孤独

bat¹ /bæt/

A *n* 1 (in cricket, table tennis) 球板; (in baseball) 球棒; **to do sth. off one's own ~** 主动做某事; **off the ~** Amer 毫不犹豫地 2 Brit colloq (speed) 速度; **he disappeared at a tremendous ~** 他飞快地消失了 3 (cudgel) 短棍

B *vt* (*pres p etc.* **-tt-**) 1 **to ~ one's eyelids** *or* **eyes** 眨眼; **without ~ting an eyelid** *or* **eye** fig 连眼睛都不眨一下 2 (hit) 击打

C *vi* (*pres p etc.* **-tt-**) 用球板击球; **to go to ~ for sb.** fig esp Amer colloq 支持某人

Phrasal verb

- **bat around** *vt* [**~ sth. around, ~ around sth.**] 详细讨论 ‹*idea, proposal*›

bat² *n* 1 (mammal) 蝙蝠; **as blind as a ~** 视力很差的; **like a ~ out of hell** colloq 一溜烟地; **to have ~s in the belfry** colloq 疯疯癫癫 2 colloq pej (woman) 丑老太婆

batch /bætʃ/

A *n* 1 (quantity) 一批; **we produce 400 ~es of tins daily** 我们每天生产 400 批罐头; **I have a huge ~ of letters to answer** 我有一大批信要回复; **in ~es** 分批 2 Comput 批处理

B *vt* 分批处理 ‹*newspapers, orders*›

batch: ~ file *n* 批处理文件; **~ mode** *n* [u] 批处理模式; **~ processing** *n* [u] 批处理

bated /ˈbeɪtɪd/ *adj attrib* **with ~ breath** 屏息以待地

bath /bɑːθ, Amer bæθ/

A *n* 1 (wash) 洗澡; (washing water) 洗澡水; **to have** *or* **take a ~** 洗一个澡; **to run a ~** 把浴缸放满水; **to give sb. a ~** 给某人洗澡 2 Brit (tub) 浴缸 3 Chem, Phot 浴器

B baths *npl* 1 (for swimming) 公共游泳池 2 (in spa) 矿泉疗养浴场 3 Brit (public) 公共浴室

C *vt* Brit 给…洗澡

D *vi* Brit 洗澡

bath: B~ bun *n* Brit 巴思圆面包; **~ cube** *n* 洗浴香精块

bathe /beɪð/

A *vt* 1 (cleanse) 浸洗; **to ~ one's wounds** 清洗自己的几处伤口 2 liter (flow along) 沿着…流淌; **the Mediterranean ~s the shores of Italy** 地中海拍打着意大利的海岸 3 lit, fig (drench) 使沉浸; **the athlete was ~d in sweat** 那位运动员汗流浃背; **the valley was ~d in sunlight** 山谷沐浴着阳光

B *vi* 1 Brit (swim) 游泳; **to go bathing** 去游泳 2 Amer (take bath) 洗澡

C *n* Brit formal 游泳

bather /ˈbeɪðə(r)/ *n* 游泳者

bathhouse /ˈbɑːθhaʊs/ *n* 1 (for bathing) 公共浴室 2 (spa) 矿泉疗养浴场

bathing /ˈbeɪðɪŋ/ *n* [u] 游泳

bathing: ~ cap *n* 游泳帽; **~ costume** *n* 游泳衣; **~ hut** *n* 更衣房; **~ machine** *n* Hist 更衣车; **~ suit** *n* dated **= ~ costume**; **~ trunks** *npl* dated **= swimming trunks**

bath: ~ mat *n* 浴室脚垫; **~ oil** *n* [u] 沐浴润肤油

bathos /ˈbeɪθɒs/ *n* [u] 突降法 [由庄严崇高突然降至平庸可笑的修辞方法]

bathrobe /ˈbɑːθrəʊb/ *n* 浴衣

bathroom /ˈbɑːθruːm, -rʊm/ *n* 1 (for washing) 浴室 2 Amer (toilet) 洗手间; **to go to the ~** 上厕所

bathroom: ~ cabinet *n* 卫生间镜箱; **~ fittings** *npl* 卫生间器具; **~ scales** *npl* 体重秤

bath: ~ salts *npl* 浴盐; **~ soap** *n* [u] 浴皂; **~ towel** *n* 浴巾; **~tub** *n* (portable) 澡盆; (fixed) 浴缸; **~water** *n* [u] 洗澡水; ▸baby A1

bathysphere /ˈbæθɪsfɪə(r)/ *n* 探海球

batik /bəˈtiːk, bæˈtiːk/ *n* 1 [u] (method) 蜡防印花法 2 [c] (item) 蜡防印花布制品

batman /ˈbætmən/ *n* Brit dated 勤务兵

baton /ˈbætn, ˈbætɒn, Amer bəˈtɒn/ *n* 1 Mus 指挥棒; **under the ~ of sb.** 在某人的指挥下 2 Brit (of policeman) 警棍 3 (in parade) 指挥杖 4 (in relay race) 接力棒; **to pass (on) the ~** fig 移交权力 5 Mil 节杖

baton: ~ charge *n* Brit 持警棍驱散行动; **~ round** *n* Brit 防暴弹; **~ twirler** *n* Amer 行进乐队领队

batsman /ˈbætsmən/ *n* (*pl* **batsmen**) 击球手

battalion /bəˈtælɪən/ *n* 1 Mil 营 2 fig (large group) 大群

batten /ˈbætn/

A *n* 板条

B *vt* 1 用板条固定 2 Naut 封住; **to ~ down the hatches** fig 做好应对危机的准备

Phrasal verb

- **batten on** *vt* [**~ on sb.**] pej 享…的福

batter¹ /ˈbætə(r)/

A *vt* 1 (hit violently) 殴打; **to ~ sb. to death** 殴打某人致死 2 (strike violently) 重击

B *vi* (strike repeatedly) 连续猛击; **the rain ~s against the windows** 雨点砰砰地打在窗户上

Phrasal verb

- **batter down** *vt* [**~ sth. down, ~ down sth.**] 砸倒 ‹*door*›

batter² *n* [u] Culin 面糊; **pancake ~** 烤薄饼用的面糊; **fish in ~** 蘸了面糊的鱼

batter³ *n* Sport 击球员

battered /ˈbætəd/ *adj* 1 (damaged) 受损的; fig (emotionally) 受伤害的 2 (physically) 受虐待的 3 Culin 裹面糊的

battered baby syndrome *n* [u] 受虐儿童综合征

b

b

battering /ˈbætərɪŋ/ *n* 1 (beating, damage) 击打; **to take** *or* **get a ~** «*army, team*» 遭到重创; «*object, building*» 受损; **this car has taken a ~ over the years** 这辆车多年来被弄得破破烂烂 2 (from critics) 抨击; **to take a ~** 受到抨击

battering ram *n* 攻城槌

battery /ˈbætəri/ *n* 1 [c] Elec, Aut 电池; **to recharge one's batteries** fig 恢复体力 2 [c] Mil 排炮 3 [c] Agric (for hens) 层架式鸡笼 4 [c] fig (large number) 一系列; (of questions) 一连串 5 [u] Jur 殴打

battery: ~ acid *n* 蓄电池酸液; **~ charger** *n* 电池充电器; **~ chicken** *n* 层架式养鸡笼养的鸡; **~-controlled** *adj* 遥控的; **~ farming** *n* [u] 密集式饲养; **~ hen** *n* 层架式养鸡笼养的母鸡; **~ operated, ~ powered** *adjs* 电池驱动的; **~ shaver** *n* 电动剃须刀

battle /ˈbætl/

A *n* 1 [c] (fight) Mil 战斗; **to win/lose a ~** 战胜/战败; **the field of ~** 战场; **they are fighting a ~ against the invading army** 他们正在和侵略军作战 2 [u and c] fig (struggle) 斗争; **to do ~ against** *or* **with sb./sth.** 与某人/某事物进行斗争; **to fight a losing ~ against sth.** 与某事物进行毫无胜算的斗争; **to be half the ~** 是成功的关键 3 [c] (contest) 较量; **a ~ of wits/words** 一场智斗/舌战

B *vi* 1 (fight) 战斗; **to ~ for sth.** 为某事物而战 2 fig (struggle) 斗争; **to ~ for sth.** 为某事物而斗争; **to ~ to do sth.** 奋力做某事物

Phrasal verbs

- **battle on** *vi* 坚持奋斗
- **battle out** *vt* [**~ sth. out, ~ out sth.**] 决一胜负; **let's leave them to ~ it out between them** 就让他们俩去决一雌雄吧

battle: ~axe *n* 1 Mil, Hist 战斧; 2 colloq (formidably aggressive woman) 悍妇; **~ cruiser** *n* 战列巡洋舰; **~ cry** *n* 1 Mil 喊杀声; 2 fig (slogan) 口号; **~dress** *n* [u] 作战服; **~ drill** *n* 实战演习; **~ fatigue** *n* [u] 战斗疲劳症; **~field** *n* lit, fig 战场; **~field missile** *n* 战术导弹; **~ formation** *n* 战斗编队; **~ground** *n* = **~field**; **~ honour** *n* Amer 战功; **~ line** *n* 战线

battlements /ˈbætlmənts/ *npl* 城垛

battle: ~ royal (*pl* **~s royal** *or* **~ royals**) *n* 1 (fight) 殊死战; 2 (heated argument) 激烈争论; **~-scarred** *adj* 1 (disfigured by battle) 有战伤的; 2 fig (physically, emotionally) 身心俱伤的; **~ scene** *n* 战斗场面; **~ship** *n* 战列舰; **~ stations** *npl* 战斗岗位; **~ zone** *n* (on land) 交战区; (at sea) 交战水域

batty /ˈbæti/ *adj* colloq 古怪的; **to go ~** 变得疯疯癫癫

bauble /ˈbɔːbl/ *n* 1 (ornament) 装饰球 2 pej (item of jewellery) 廉价首饰

baud /bɔːd/ *n* 波特 [资料传输速度单位]

baud rate *n* 波特率

bauhinia /bɑʊˈhɪnɪə/ *n* 紫荆花

baulk /bɔːlk, bɔːk/

A *n* 1 Constr 大梁 2 (ridge) 埂

B *vi* 1 (be unwilling) 畏缩; **to ~ at ...** 不肯直面…; **the government ~ed at the idea** 政府回避了这个意见; **the very thought of it makes me ~** 一想到这个我就要退缩 2 (stop) 止步不前

C *vt* 阻碍 ‹*plan, scheme*›; **to ~ sb. of ...** 阻止某人得到…; **he ~ed me of the chance to see Sue** 他不让我有机会见苏

bauxite /ˈbɔːksaɪt/ *n* [u] 铝土岩

Bavaria /bəˈveərɪə/ *pr n* 巴伐利亚州

Bavarian /bəˈveərɪən/

A *adj* 巴伐利亚的

B *n* 巴伐利亚人

bawdiness /ˈbɔːdɪnɪs/ *n* [u] (humorously indecent) 淫乐; (of person) 下流

bawdy /ˈbɔːdi/ *adj* 淫秽的 ‹*joke, language*›

bawl /bɔːl/

A *vt* 大声叫出; **the major ~s orders down the telephone** 少校对着电话大声发布命令

B *vi* 1 (cry loudly) 放声痛哭 2 (shout) 大叫; **to ~ at sb.** 冲着某人大叫

Phrasal verb

- **bawl out** *vt* 1 [**~ sb. out, ~ out sb.**] colloq 大声训斥 ‹*troops, student*› 2 [**~ out sth.**] 大声叫出

bay¹ /beɪ/ *n* 1 Geog 湾; **the Bay of Bengal** 孟加拉湾 2 (parking area) 停车区 3 Archit (section of building) 分隔间; (recess) 壁凹; (window) 凸窗

bay² *n* Bot **~ (tree)** 月桂

bay³

A *vi* «*dog, wolf*» 连续吠叫; **to ~ at the moon** 对月长嗥; **to ~ for sb.'s blood** fig 要对某人施暴

B *n* [u] Hunt **to be at ~** 被困住; **to hold** *or* **keep at ~** fig 不让…逼近 ‹*attacker, opponent*›; **to bring to ~** 把…围困住 ‹*fox, stag*›

bay⁴

A *adj* 枣红色的 ‹*horse*›

B *n* 枣红马

bay leaf *n* 干月桂叶

bayonet

A /ˈbeɪənɪt/ *n* 刺刀; **to fix ~s** 上刺刀; **at ~ point** 在刺刀尖下

B /ˈbeɪənɪt, ˌbeɪəˈnet/ *vt* (*pres p etc.* **-t-** *or* **-tt-**) 用刺刀刺

bayonet: ~ charge *n* 持刺刀的冲锋; **~ fitting** *n* 卡口式组装件; **~ practice** *n* [u] 拼刺刀操练; **~ socket** *n* 卡口插座

bayou /ˈbaɪuː/ *n* Amer 支流

bay window *n* 凸窗

bazaar /bəˈzɑː(r)/ *n* 1 (Middle Eastern) 集市 2 (sale of work) 义卖 3 (shop) 杂货店

bazooka /bəˈzuːkə/ *n* 火箭筒

BBC *abbr* = **British Broadcasting Corporation**

> **the BBC**
>
> 英国广播公司，全称 British Broadcasting Corporation。英国最早和最大的广播电视机构。成立于 1922 年，始称 British Broadcasting Company，是一家私营公司。1927 年获得皇家特许状（Royal Charter），开始接受政府资助，成为公共广播机构，始用现名。1936 年 11 月开始定时电视广播。BBC 在广播、电视领域曾长期保持垄断地位。目前拥有 8 个交互式电视频道、10 个广播网络及 50 余家地方电视台和广播电台。BBC 对议会负责，但在运营上保持独立。

> **BBC English**
>
> BBC 英语。指 BBC 新闻播音员和主持人的口音。语言学上称为标准发音（Received Pronunciation，简称 RP）。也有学者认为标准发音的说法已经过时，应以 BBC 英语取代。标准发音源于英格兰南部受过良好教育者的口音，为英国的公学和牛津、剑桥大学采用，代表操该口音者具有较高的社会地位。BBC 一度大力推行标准英语发音，但在 20 世纪 50 年代开始使用非标准发音的播音员。这种趋势目前在 BBC 地方台节目中尤为明显。标准发音在英语作为外语的教学中依然占主导地位。

BB gun *n* Amer BB型气枪

BBQ *abbr* = **barbecue**

BBS *abbr* = **bulletin board system** 电子布告栏

BC ▸p. 181 *abbr* = **Before Christ** 公元前; **33 ~** 公元前 33 年

bcc *abbr* = **blind carbon copy**

BCE ▸p. 181 *abbr* = **before the Common Era** 公元前; **800 ~** 公元前 800 年

BCG *abbr* = **Bacillus Calmette-Guérin** 卡介苗

BD *abbr* = **Bachelor of Divinity** 神学学士

be /biː/ (*pres* **I am, he/she/it is, you/we/they are**; *pt* **I/he/she/it was, you/we/they were**; *pres p* **being**; *pp* **been**)

A *copula* 1 (indicating quality or attribute) [表明属性]; **I'm married** 我结婚了; **he is ~ing nice to them** 他现在对他们很好; **she is an Italian** 她是意大利人; **he'll ~ a big boy by now** 他现在该是个大小伙子了 2 (indicating state, conditions, circumstances) [表明状态]; **to ~ ill** 生病; **the weather was freezing** 天气极冷; **it was still light outside** 外面还很亮 3 (identifying the subject) [表明主题]; **he is the person I was speaking about** 他就是我提到的那个人; **is this Manchester?** 这里是曼彻斯特吗？; **this book is your uncle's** 这本书是你叔叔的 4 (indicating occupation, status) (pursue a profession) 从事…职业; (pursue a pastime) 有…消遣; (have a role in organization, society) 担任…职位; (have a title) 拥有…头衔; **to ~ a teacher** 当老师; **he is Primate of All Ireland** 他是全爱尔兰首席大主教; **they were both keen tennis players** 他们两个都爱打网球 5 (play the role of) 扮演; **I was Juliet in the school play** 在校园剧中，我扮演了朱丽叶 6 (giving more information) [提供信息]; **the fact is that I'm too old** 事实是我太老了; **the snag was, the tide was out** 问题是，退潮了 7 (giving time, date, age) [表示时间、年龄]; **it's six o'clock** 现在 6 点钟; **it was midnight before we got home** 午夜过后我们才到家; **our house is over 100 years old** 我们的房子有 100 多年了 8 (giving cost) 值; (giving weight, measurement) 有; **how much are those eggs?** 这些鸡蛋多少钱？; **how tall is she?** 她有多高？; **it was three degrees below zero** 那时气温为零下 3 度 9 Math (equal) «*unit, measurement*» 等于; (represent) «*variable, symbol*» 表示; **two times three is six** 二乘三等于六; **let x ~ 3** 设 x 为 3 10 (comprise) «*place, structure*» 由…组成; **London is not England** 伦敦不是英格兰的全部 11 (mean) 意味着; **he was everything to her** 对她而言，他就是一切; **£500,000 is nothing to him** 50 万英镑对他毫无意义 12 (in tag questions, short answers) [用于附加疑问成分及简短回答]; **their house is lovely, isn't it?** 他们的房子很漂亮，对吧？; **are you a doctor? — no, I'm not** 你是医生吗？——不，我不是; **you're not going out tonight? — yes, I am** 你今晚不出去吧？——不，我要出去的

B *vi* 1 (exist) 存在; **can such things ~?** 会有这样的事情吗？; **I think, therefore I am** 我思故我在; **to ~ or not to ~** 生存还是死亡; **Miss Jones as was** (before marrying) 婚前名琼斯小姐; (before a change in name) 曾用名琼斯小姐 2 (remain in the same state) 保持原状; (remain in the same place) 留在原地; **let it ~** 随它去; **let the poor dog ~!** 别招惹这条可怜的狗！ 3 (indicating time taken) 持续; **how long has he been here?** 他在这儿待了多长时间了？; **how long will dinner ~?** 晚饭什么时候才会好啊？; **I shan't ~ a moment** 我一会儿就好 4 (indicating place) 在; **he's upstairs** 他在楼上; **Hungary is in the heart of Europe** 匈牙利位于欧洲的中心; **who's in the movie?** 谁出演这部电影？ 5 (happen, take place) 发生; **the concert is tomorrow** 音乐会明天举行; **they made plans to marry, but it was not to ~** 他们本来计划要结婚的，但却不了了之 6 (go) 去; (come) 来; **~ off with you!** 滚一边儿去！; **I'm off home** 我要回家了; **is this the bus for London?** 这是去伦敦的公交车吗？; **you've really been (and gone) and done it now!** Brit colloq 你居然真的做了这事！ 7 (on visit etc.) 造访; **have you ever been to London?** 你去过伦敦吗？; **has anyone been?** (called at house etc.) 有人来过吗？ 8 (in phrases) **so ~ it** 那就这样吧; **as it is/was** 像原来一样

C *v aux* 1 (forming passive) [构成被动语态]; **the child was found (by the search party)** 孩子（被搜索队）找到了 2 (forming continuous tenses) [构成进行时]; (active) **the train was departing when I got there** 我到达的时候，列车正要开出; (passive) **the house is ~ing built** 房子正在建造 3 (forming future) [构成将来时]; **the plane is leaving tomorrow at midday** 飞机明天中午起飞; **when are you seeing her?** 你什么时候见她?

D **to ~ to** 1 (expressing obligation) [表明责任]; **I am to inform you that ...** formal 我特此通知你…; **you are to report to the police** 你必须向警方报到; **I am not to ~ disturbed** 不许打扰我 2 (expressing future or arrangement) [表示将来计划]; **the Queen is to arrive at 3 p.m.** 女王定于下午3点到达; **he was to arrive** *or* **have arrived last Monday** 他上周一就该到了 3 (expressing possibility) [表示可能性]; **what are we to do?** 我们能做什么呢?; **he wasn't to know** 他不可能知道; **if reports are to ~ believed, he's going to resign** 如果报道可信的话，那么他将会辞职 4 (expressing destiny) [表示必然性]; **they were never to meet again** 他们注定再也无法见面了; **the empire was to collapse a century later** 帝国在一个世纪之后还是瓦解了

E **-to-be** *combining form* 未来的; **her husband-to-~** 她的未婚夫; **a mother-to-~** 准妈妈

beach /biːtʃ/

A *n* (at the edge of sea) 海滩; (on river) 河滩; (on lake) 湖滨

B *vt* (haul a boat ashore) 把…拖上岸; (run a boat ashore) 使搁浅; **a ~ed whale** lit 搁浅的鲸鱼; fig (building, object) 横卧着的庞然大物; (person) 横卧着的大个子

beach: **~ ball** *n* 沙滩球; **~ buggy** *n* 沙滩车; **~ bum** *n* colloq 海滩游民; **~comber** /ˈbiːtʃkəʊmə(r)/ *n* 1 (person) 海滩拾荒者; 2 (wave) 拍岸浪; **~head** *n* 滩头堡; **~ hut** *n* 海滨小屋; **~robe** *n* 沙滩袍; **~ umbrella** *n* 沙滩遮阳伞; **~ volleyball** ▸p. 307 *n* [u] 沙滩排球; **~wear** *n* [u] 海滩装

beacon /ˈbiːkən/ *n* 1 Naut (lighthouse) 灯塔; (lantern) 导航灯; (signalling buoy) 信号浮标; fig 指路明灯; **to shine like a ~** fig 像灯塔般照耀; **to act as a ~ to sb.** fig 做某人的指路明灯 2 (on ambulance, police car) 警示灯 3 Aviat 灯标 4 (transmitter) 无线电信标 5 Hist (on hill etc.) 烽火 6 Brit (hill) 烽火山

bead /biːd/ *n* 1 (jewellery) 珠子; **a string of ~s** 一串珠子 2 Relig (rosary) 念珠; **to say** *or* **tell one's ~s** dated 数着念珠祈祷 3 (drop of sweat or dew) 小滴; **~s of perspiration had formed on his forehead** 他前额上渗出点点汗珠 4 (on gun) 圆形准星; **to draw a ~ on sth./sb.** 瞄准某物/某人

bead curtain *n* 珠帘

beaded /ˈbiːdɪd/ *adj* 1 (covered in decorative beads) 饰有小珠的 ‹*garment*› 2 (covered in drops of moisture) 带有小水珠的 ‹*brow, grass*›

beading /ˈbiːdɪŋ/ *n* [u] 1 (on furniture, stonework etc.) 串珠缘饰 2 (on dress) 小珠饰

beady /ˈbiːdi/ *adj* 亮晶晶的; **~ eyes** 亮晶晶的小眼睛; **I've got my ~ eye on you** Brit hum 我一直睁大眼睛盯着你

beady-eyed *adj* 1 (having small, gleaming eyes) 眼睛亮晶晶的 ‹*person, animal*› 2 (observant) 目光锐利的 ‹*person, look*›

beagle /ˈbiːgl/ *n* 比格犬

beak /biːk/ *n* (of bird) 喙; (of turtle) 喙状嘴

beaker /ˈbiːkə(r)/ *n* 1 (cup) 细高杯子 2 Chem 烧杯

be-all *n* 最重要的事情; **the ~ and end-all (of sth.)** （某事物）一切的一切

beam /biːm/

A *n* 1 (of light) 光柱; **the car headlights are on full ~** 汽车的前灯大开着 2 Phys 束 3 Constr 梁 4 (in gymnastics) 平衡木; **to score top marks on the ~** 在平衡木项目上得了最高分 5 (of weighing scales) 杠杆 6 Aviat, Naut (radio or radar course) 射束指示的航道; **to be off ~** fig 不对头 7 Naut (cross-member) 船舷; (greatest width) 船宽; **on the port/starboard ~** 在左/右舷正横方向; **to be broad in the ~** fig hum 臀部肥大 8 (smile) 笑容

B *vt* 1 Radio, TV, Telecom 定向传送 ‹*signal, information*›; **the concert was ~ed all over the world** 音乐会向全世界转播 2 fig (smile) 以微笑表示; **his father ~ed his congratulations** 他父亲微笑着表示祝贺

C *vi* 1 (emit light, heat) «*sun, moon*» 照耀 2 (smile) 笑容满面; **to ~ with pleasure** 高兴得笑容满面

beam end *n* 横梁末端; **to be on its ~s** «*vessel*» 几乎倾覆; **to be on one's ~s** Brit fig colloq 十分拮据

beaming /ˈbiːmɪŋ/ *adj* 1 *attrib* (with light) 发光的 ‹*sun*› 2 (with happiness) 欣喜的 ‹*smile, face*›

bean /biːn/

A *n* 1 (seed, pod) 豆; **green** *or* **French ~** 青刀豆; **coffee ~** 咖啡豆; **soya ~** 大豆; **to spill the ~s** fig 泄漏秘密; **to be full of ~s** Brit fig 精力充沛 2 **old ~** Brit colloq dated 老兄 3 fig (small amount) 一丁点; **to not have a ~** 身无分文; **to not be worth a ~** 毫无价值; **to not know a ~ about sth.** 对某事物一窍不通

B *vt* esp Amer colloq 击打…的头部

bean: **~bag** *n* 1 (seat) 豆袋坐垫; 2 (for throwing) 豆子袋; **~burger** *n* 菜豆蔬菜汉堡; **~ counter** *n* colloq pej 精于计算的人; **~ curd** *n* [u] = **tofu**; **~feast** *n* colloq 盛宴

beanie /ˈbiːni/ *n* **~ (cap** *or* **hat)** 无檐小便帽

beano /ˈbiːnəʊ/ *n* (*pl* **~s**) Brit colloq 欢庆

bean: **~pole** *n* 1 (cane) 支竿; 2 fig (thin person) 瘦高个子; **~ shoot, ~ sprout** *ns* 豆芽

bear[1] /beə(r)/ (*pt* **bore**, *pp* **borne**)

A *vt* 1 (carry) 承载; **he bore a tray of food into the room** 他托着一盘食物进了房间; **the seeds are borne on the wind** 种子随风飘散 2 (bring) 携带 ‹*flowers, food, message*› 3 (be marked with) 带有…的印记; **to ~ one's signature** 有某人的签名; **he still ~s the scars** (physical) 他身上还留有伤疤; (mental) 他仍留有痛苦的回忆 4 (have) 具有; **to ~ a resemblance to sb./sth.** 与某人/某事物相似; **to ~ no relation to sb./sth.** 与某人/某事物不相干; **to ~ no comparison with sb./sth.** 比不上某人/某事物 5 (be called by) 拥有 ‹*title*›; **the machine ~s his name** 那种机器以他的名字命名 6 (support) 承受 ‹*load, weight*›; 承受…的重量 ‹*person*› 7 (accept) 承担 ‹*cost, blame*›; **to ~ one's responsibilities lightly** 举重若轻 8 (endure, tolerate) 忍受 ‹*pain, hardship*›; **to be more than sb. can ~** 令某人难以容忍; **she can't ~ the smell of paint/to see them suffer** 她受不了油漆味儿/不忍心看到他们受苦 9 (stand up to) 经得起 ‹*scrutiny, inspection*›; **to not ~ close examination** 经不起推敲; **the jokes don't ~ repetition** 这些笑话说第二遍就没意思了; **the consequences don't ~ thinking about** 后果不堪设想 10 (yield) 结 ‹*fruit*›; 开 ‹*blossom*›; 长出 ‹*crops*› 11 (generate) «*account, investment*» 产生 ‹*interest*›; «*effort, attempt*» 取得 ‹*result*›; **an account that ~s no interest** 无息账户 12 (feel) 心怀; **to ~ no hatred towards sb.** 不恨某人; **to ~ sb. ill will** 对某人有恶意 13 formal (give birth to) 生 ‹*young*›; **to ~ sb. a child** 为某人生孩子; ▸**born A**

B *vi* 1 (move) «*person, vehicle*» 行进; «*road, track*» 延伸; **~ (to the) left** 向左拐 2 (be directed) **to bring sth. to ~ (on sb./sth.)** lit 把某物对准（某人/某物）; fig 把某物用于（某人/某事物）; **to bring all one's energies to ~ on sth.** 全力以赴做某事

C *v refl* **to ~ oneself proudly/with dignity** 昂首阔步/举止庄重

Phrasal verbs

- **bear along** *vt* [**~ sb./sth. along, ~ along sb./sth.**]
  1 (carry) 运送; **to be borne along by the tide** 随潮水漂走 2 fig (excite) 刺激; **to be borne along by one's enthusiasm** 被激情冲昏头脑
- **bear away**
  A *vt* [**~ sb./sth. away, ~ away sb./sth.**] 带走
  B *vi* Naut 改变航向顺风行驶
- **bear down** *vi* 1 (press) «*person, load*» 向下压; **to ~ down on sb./sth.** 压住某人/某物 2 (in childbirth) «*woman*» 用力
- **bear down on, bear down upon** *vt* [**~ down on** *or* **upon sb./sth.**] 冲向; **the hounds bore down on the helpless fox** 猎犬扑向无助的狐狸
- **bear in on, bear in upon** *vt* **to be borne in on** *or* **upon sb.** 被某人认识到; **the truth was gradually borne in on** *or* **upon them** 他们逐渐了解到真相
- **bear off** [**~ sb./sth. off, ~off sb./sth.**] *vt* 1 (transport away) 带走 2 Naut 驶离
- **bear on** *vt* [**~ on sb./sth.**]
  1 (be relevant to) «*fact, decision, story*» 和…有关; **factors ~ing directly on the outcome** 直接影响结果的那些因素 2 (be burden on) **to ~ hard** *or* **heavily on sb./sth.** «*law, price increase*» 给某人/某机构带来沉重负担; **to ~ heavily on sb.'s conscience** 使某人倍感愧疚
- **bear out** *vt* [**~ sb./sth. out, ~ out sb./sth.**] 为…作证; **I think you will ~ me out on this** 我想在这一点上你会为我作证
- **bear up** *vi* 1 (cope) 保持振作; **to ~ up under** *or* **against sth.** 经受得住 ‹*shock, misfortune*› 2 (support weight) «*bridge, branch*» 支撑住; **will the ice ~ up under our weight?** 冰能承受得住我们的重量吗?
- **bear upon** *vt* = **bear on**
- **bear with** *vt* [**~ with sb./sth.**] 耐心对待; **please ~ with me for a minute** 请耐心听我说两句; **if you ~ with it, ...** 如果你有耐心的话，…

bear[2] *n* 1 Zool 熊; **the ~ family** 熊科; ▸**sore A1** 2 (toy) **(teddy) ~** 玩具熊 3 **the Bear** Astron (Great Bear) 大熊星座; (Little Bear) 小熊星座 4 colloq (large man) 体态笨重的人 5 Fin 空头

bearable /ˈbeərəbl/ *adj* 可忍受的

bear: **~-baiting** *n* [u] 纵狗斗熊; **~ cub** *n* 幼熊

beard /bɪəd/

A *n* 1 (on man) 胡须; **a bushy ~** 浓密的胡须; **to grow/wear a ~** 蓄须; **a full ~** 络腮胡子 2 (tuft, barbel) (on animal) 颌毛; (on fish) 触须; (on bird) 须状羽毛 3 (on wheat, barley) 芒

B *vt* 公然反对; **to ~ the lion in his den** Prov 大胆妄为

bearded /ˈbɪədɪd/ *adj* 有胡须的; **a ~ youth** 有胡须的男青年

bearer /ˈbeərə(r)/ *n* 1 (of news, gift) 递送人 2 (of note, cheque, passport) 持有人 3 (of name) 姓名的拥有者 4 (at funeral) 抬棺人 5 (on expedition, safari) 脚夫

bearer: **~ bond** *n* 无记名债券; **~ cheque** *n* 无记名支票

bear: **~ garden** *n* 1 fig (unruly place) 嘈杂混乱的场所; 2 Hist (place for bear-baiting) 纵狗斗熊场; **~ hug** *n* 紧紧的拥抱; **to give sb. a ~ hug** 紧紧拥抱某人

bearing /ˈbeərɪŋ/

A *n* 1 [u] (posture) 姿态; **of soldierly ~** 具有军人风度的; **regal ~** 王室的气度 2 [u] (behaviour) 行为; **his dignified ~** 他的庄重举止 3 [u] (relevance) 关系; **to have no/little ~ on sth.** 与某事物无关/几乎无关 4 [u] (endurance) 忍耐; **to be past/beyond (all) ~** 令人难以忍受 5 [c] Naut 方位; **the ~ is 137°** 方位是137度; **to take a (compass) ~ (on sth.)** （用罗盘）测（某物的）方位; **to take the**

b

ship's ~s 测定船的方位 6 [c] Aut, Mech 轴承 7 [c] Herald 图案

B bearings *npl* 方向感; **to get** *or* **find one's ~s** 熟悉环境; **to lose one's ~s** lit, fig 迷失方向; **to take one's ~s** 确定自己的位置

bearish /ˈbeərɪʃ/ *adj* 1 pej (like a bear) 粗鲁的 ‹*person, behaviour*› 2 Fin (characterized by falling share prices) 行情下跌的; **a ~ market** 熊市

bear: ~ market *n* 熊市; **~ pit** *n* 熊坑

bearskin /ˈbeəskɪn/ *n* 1 [u and c] (pelt) 熊皮; **~ rug** 熊皮地毯 2 [c] Mil (hat) 熊皮高帽

beast /biːst/ *n* 1 (animal) 兽; **the king of the ~s** 百兽之王 2 **the Beast** Bible 反基督者 3 colloq pej (annoying person) 讨厌的人; (brutal person) 畜生; **he's a selfish ~!** 他是个自私的讨厌鬼!; **to bring out the ~ in sb.** (make angry) 激怒某人; (make lustful, brutal) 使某人兽性大发 4 colloq pej (task, problem) 讨厌的事情; **it's a ~ of a job!** 这份工作真是糟透了!

beastly /ˈbiːstli/ colloq dated

A *adj* 讨厌的 ‹*person, behaviour, event, illness, weather*›; **what a ~ thing to do!** 这事真烦人!

B *adv* Brit 非常; **it's ~ hot today** 今天热得要命

beast: ~ of burden *n* 役畜; **~ of prey** *n* 猛兽

beat /biːt/

A *vt* (*pt* **beat**, *pp* **beaten**) 1 (strike) 击打 ‹*person, animal*›; **to ~ sb./sth. to death** 打死某人/某动物; **to ~ sb. into submission** 打得某人屈服; **to ~ sb. black and blue** 把某人打得鼻青脸肿; **to ~ a bit of respect into sb.** 迫使某人学会对人尊重一点; **to ~ grammar into sb.'s head** 给某人灌输语法知识 2 (strike with tool, part of body) 锤打 ‹*metal*›; 拍打 ‹*carpet*›; 敲打 ‹*door*›; «*bird, animal*» 拍打 ‹*air, ground*›; **to ~ sth. into shape** 把某物打造成型 3 (cause to strike) 用…打; **he ~ his fists against the door** 他用拳头砸门 4 Mus (produce sound on) 敲 ‹*drum, gong*› 5 Mus (indicate rhythm) 打 ‹*rhythm*›; **to ~ time (with sth.)** (用某物) 打拍子 6 Mil «*drummer*» 敲奏出 ‹*tattoo, signal*›; ▸**retreat A1, A2** 7 (mix vigorously) 快速搅拌 ‹*cream, mixture*›; **~ the eggs** 打蛋; **to ~ sth. into sth.** 将某物搅拌入某物 8 Hunt [为惊起猎物而] 拍打 ‹*undergrowth*› 9 (create route by walking) 踏出 ‹*path*›; ▸**path 1** 10 (make way by removing obstacles) 辟出; **to ~ a path through the jungle** 在丛林中开出一条路; **to ~ one's way through the onlookers** 从旁观的人群中挤过去 11 **to ~ it** colloq (leave quickly) 走开; **we decided to ~ it** 我们决定溜之大吉 12 (flap) 拍打; **the bird/insect ~ its wings** 鸟/昆虫拍动翅膀 13 (defeat) 打败 ‹*opponent, team, army*›; **to be beaten at sth.** 输掉某事; **if you can't ~ 'em, join 'em** Prov hum 打不赢, 就投靠 14 (overcome) 解决…问题 ‹*unemployment, child abuse, inflation*›; 战胜 ‹*illness*›; **to ~ heroin addiction** 戒掉海洛因毒瘾 15 (do or be better than) 超过 ‹*target, score*›; **to ~ the record** 打破纪录; **~ that (if you can)!** 有本事你来试试!; **that ~s everything!** 真是绝无仅有!; **you can't ~ Italian shoes** 意大利的皮鞋无与伦比 16 (baffle) «*problem, puzzle*» 难倒 ‹*person*›; **a mystery that ~s even the experts** 连专家都解不开的谜; **to have sb. ~** colloq *or* **beaten** 难住某人; **why did he leave? — ~s me** colloq 他为什么离开了? ——我说不上来 17 Amer colloq (be acquitted of) 逃避 ‹*rap, charge*› 18 (arrive before) 抢先; **he ~ me to the door** 他抢在我之前到了门口; **to ~ sb. to the altar** 比某人早结婚; **to ~ sb. to it** 比某人抢先一步 19 (avoid) 避免; **to ~ the rush hour** 避开交通高峰时段

B *vi* (*pt* **beat**, *pp* **beaten**) 1 (collide) **to ~ against/on sth.** «*waves*» 拍打 ‹*shore, cliff*›; «*rain*» 击打 ‹*window, face*› 2 (strike repeatedly) **to ~ at** *or* **on sth.** 接连击打 ‹*door*›; 接连扑打 ‹*flames*› 3 Physiol «*heart, pulse*» 跳动 4 (make sound) «*drum*» 敲响; **drums ~ing in the distance** 远处的鼓声 5 (flap) «*wings*» 扑扇 6 Hunt [为惊起猎物而] 拍打树丛等 7 Naut «*person, boat*» 以"之"字形抢风航行; **to ~ to windward** 抢上风航行

C *n* 1 (hitting sound) 敲击声; **the ~ of the drums** 鼓声 2 Mus (rhythm) 节奏; (in bar) 节拍; **to follow** *or* **keep to the ~** 跟上节奏 3 (in poetry) 强音 4 (of heart, pulse) 跳动; **sb.'s heart misses** *or* **skips a ~** 某人的心里咯噔一下 5 Phys 拍音 6 (in policing) (area) 辖区; (route) 巡逻路线; **a policeman on the ~** 巡警 7 (area or route worked) 负责区域; **the journalist's ~** 记者的采访区域 8 (field of interest) 专长; **to be off sb.'s ~** 非某人本行

D *adj pred* colloq 筋疲力尽的; **I'm (dead) ~** 我累垮了

Phrasal verbs

- **beat back** *vt* [**~ sb./sth. back, ~ back sb./sth.**] 击退 ‹*person*›; 压住 ‹*flames*›
- **beat down**

A *vi* 1 (fall) «*rain*» 倾泻; «*hail*» 猛地砸落 2 (shine) **to ~ down on sb./sth.** «*sun*» 强烈照射某人/某物

B [**~ sth. down, ~ down sth.**] *vt* 1 (flatten) «*wind*» 吹倒 ‹*crops, grass*›; «*rain*» 冲倒 ‹*crops, grass*› 2 (knock down) 砸开 ‹*door*›

C [**~ sb./sth. down, ~ down sb./sth.**] *vt* (force to reduce price) «*buyer*» 使…降价 ‹*seller*›; «*buyer*» 压低 ‹*price*›

- **beat in** *vt* [**~ sth. in, ~ in sth.**] 砸破 ‹*head, door, box*›
- **beat off** *vt* [**~ off sb./sth., ~ sb./sth. off**] 击退 ‹*attacker, attack*›; 赶走 ‹*insect*›
- **beat out**

A *vt* [**~ sth. out, ~ out sth.**] 1 (flatten) 锤平 ‹*metal*›; **the gold was beaten out into thin sheets** 金子被锤打成金箔 2 (remove) 敲平 ‹*dent, lump*›; 拍落 ‹*dust, dirt*›; **to ~ sth. out of sth.** 把某物从某物上拍落下来; **to ~ the shit** taboo sl *or* **crap** taboo sl *or* **hell** colloq **out of sb.** 痛打某人; ▸**daylight B** 3 (put stop to) 遏止 ‹*behaviour*›; 消除 ‹*habit, attitude*› 4 (extinguish) 扑灭 ‹*flames*› 5 (produce) «*person, drum*» 敲奏出 ‹*rhythm, tune*›

B *vt* **to ~ sth. out of sb.** (extract) 逼迫某人说出 ‹*truth, confession*›

- **beat up** *vt* colloq 1 [**~ sb. up, ~ up sb.**] (assault) 痛打 2 esp Amer (blame) **to ~ oneself up about** *or* **over sth.** 因某事而自责

beaten /ˈbiːtn/

A *pp* ▸**beat A, B**

B *adj* 1 (defeated) 被打败的 ‹*team, opponent, army*› 2 (flattened) 锤薄的 ‹*metal*›; 踏硬的 ‹*earth*›; **off the ~ track** 偏僻的; **to go off the ~ track** 到人迹罕至的地方去 3 Culin 搅成糊状的 ‹*egg, cream*›

beaten-up *adj* colloq 破旧的 ‹*car, hat*›

beater /ˈbiːtə(r)/ *n* 1 Hunt 驱出猎物者 2 (for carpet) 掸子 3 Culin 搅拌器 4 Amer colloq (car) 破旧的汽车

beatification /bɪˌætɪfɪˈkeɪʃn/ *n* [u] 宣福 [天主教会发布的某人已升入天堂的教令]

beatify /bɪˈætɪfaɪ/ *vt* 为…宣福

beating /ˈbiːtɪŋ/ *n* 1 [u and c] (punishment) 打; **to get a ~** 挨打; **to give sb. a ~** 打某人 2 [u and c] (defeat) 失败; **to take** *or* **get a ~** 遭到失败; **to give sb. a ~** 击败某人; **to take some** *or* **a lot of ~** (be hard to surpass) 难以超越; (be better than most others) 难以匹敌 3 [c] (criticism) 批评; **to take** *or* **get a ~** 受到批评 4 [c] (rough treatment) **to take** *or* **get a ~** 经受磨砺; **the toys are designed to take a good ~** 这些玩具设计得经久耐用; **to give sth. a ~** 不爱惜某物 5 [u] (flattening of metal) 锤打 6 [u and c] (cleaning of carpet) 拍打 7 [u] Mus (striking) 敲击; (sound made) 敲击声; **the ~ of the drums** 鼓声 8 [u] (of rain, hail, waves etc.) 击打 9 [u] (of heart, pulse) 跳动 10 [u] (of wings) 扑扇 11 [u] Hunt [为惊起猎物的] 拍打灌木丛

beating up *n* colloq 毒打; **to get a ~** colloq 遭毒打; **to give sb. a ~** 毒打某人

beatnik /ˈbiːtnɪk/ *n* "垮掉的一代"的一员

beat-up *adj* colloq 破旧的 ‹*vehicle, instrument, furniture*›

Beaufort scale /ˈbəʊfət skeɪl/ *n* 蒲福风级

beaut /bjuːt/ esp Austral, NZ colloq

A *n* 1 (fine specimen) 出众的东西; **the idea was a ~** 这个主意真棒 2 (beautiful person) 美人

B *adj* (good) 很棒的; (beautiful) 很美的; **a ~ view** 美景

beautician /bjuːˈtɪʃn/ ▸**p. 409** *n* 美容师

beautiful /ˈbjuːtɪfl/ *adj* 1 (attractive) 美丽的; **she is the most ~ woman I know** 她是我认识的女人中最漂亮的; **a ~ Beethoven sonata** 一首优美的贝多芬奏鸣曲 2 (wonderful) 令人愉悦的 ‹*weather, holiday, feeling*› 3 (skilful) 出色的; **he's a ~ writer** 他写得一手好文章 4 (superb) 完美的 ‹*specimen*›; **a ~ example of sth.** 某事物的完美体现

beautifully /ˈbjuːtɪfəli/ *adv* 1 (attractively) 美丽地; **~ dressed** 穿着漂亮的 2 (skilfully) 出色地; **he drives ~** 他开车很熟练; **the essay was so ~ written that it deserved full marks** 文章写得非常漂亮, 应得满分 3 (emphatic) 非常; **a ~ clean room** 非常干净的房间

beautiful people *npl* **the ~** 名流

beautify /ˈbjuːtɪfaɪ/

A *vt* 美化

B *v refl* **to ~ oneself** 打扮

beauty /ˈbjuːti/ *n* 1 [u] (quality) 美; **to spoil** *or* **mar the ~ of ...** 破坏…的美; **~ is only skin-deep** 美丽只是外表; ▸**beholder** 2 [c] (woman) 美女; **B~ and the Beast** 美女与野兽 [民间传说] 3 [c] (beautiful feature) 优美之处; **the beauties of nature** 大自然的胜景 4 [c] (advantage) 优点; **the ~ of the system is that ...** 这一系统的好处是…; **that's the ~ of it** 妙处就在这里 5 [c] (perfect example) 典型的例子; **a ~ of a goal/car** 精妙的射门/无可挑剔的汽车; **that's a real ~** hum 那可真绝了啊

beauty: ~ competition, ~ contest *ns* 选美比赛; **~ cream** *n* [c and u] 美容霜; **~ editor** ▸**p. 409** *n* 美容专栏主笔; **~ hint** *n* 美容秘诀; **~ parlour** *n* dated = **~ salon**; **~ preparation, ~ product** *ns* 美容产品; **~ queen** *n* 选美比赛冠军; **~ salon** *n* 美容院; **~ sleep** *n* [u] hum 美容觉; **to need one's ~ sleep** 需要睡美容觉; **~ specialist** ▸**p. 409** *n* 美容师; **~ spot** *n* 1 (place with beautiful scenery) 风景名胜; 2 (natural mark on skin) 美人痣; (fake mark on skin) 美人斑; **~ tip** *n* = **~ hint**; **~ treatment** *n* 美容护理

beaver /ˈbiːvə(r)/ *n* (*pl* **~** *or* **~s**) (animal) 河狸; (fur) 河狸毛皮; **an eager ~** fig 勤奋做事的人; **to work like a ~** 兢兢业业地工作

Phrasal verb

- **beaver away** *vi* Brit 勤奋工作; **to ~ (away) at sth.** 努力做某事

becalmed /bɪˈkɑːmd/ *adj* 因无风而停泊的

became /bɪˈkeɪm/ *pt* ▸**become**

because /bɪˈkɒz, Amer *also* -kɔːz/

A *conj* 因为; **they must be at home, ~ the light's on** 他们一定在家, 因为灯亮着; **don't do it just ~ you can** 不要仅仅因为你能做就去做

B **because of** *prep phr* 因为; **~ of the rain** 因为下雨; **we're late, and it's all ~ of you!** 我们迟到了, 都是因为你!

beck[1] /bek/ *n* (gesture) [以点头或手势表示的] 召唤; **to be at sb.'s ~ and call** 唯某人之命是从; **to have sb. at one's ~ and call** 随心所欲地使唤某人

beck[2] *n* N Eng (stream) 溪流

beckon /ˈbekən/ *vt, vi* 1 lit (with gesture) 向…示意; **to ~ sb. in** 示意某人进去; **to ~ to**

sb. to do sth. 示意某人做某事 2 fig (entice, lure) 吸引; a bright future ～s you 光明的前途召唤着你; adventure ～ed 冒险令人神往

become /bɪˈkʌm/ (*pt* **became**, *pp* **become**)
A *vi* 1 (grow to be) 变成; (begin to be) 开始变得; (achieve position of) 成为; **to ～ an adult** 长大成人; **to ～ thin/fat** 变瘦/长胖; **to ～ known in the art world** 在艺术界成名; **she is becoming very hard of hearing** 她耳朵越来越背了; **to ～ king/a doctor/a father** 成为国王/医生/父亲 2 (happen to) 发生; **what became of the photographs?** 那些照片放哪儿了?; **what will ～ of her?** 她的命运将会怎样?
B *vt* (be appropriate for) 适合; **to ～ sb.** «*garment, colour, hairstyle*» 使某人显得漂亮; «*manner, attitude, utterance*» 与某人的身份相称; **modesty ～s a young person** 年轻人应该谦虚; **to ill ～ sb.** 不适合某人

becoming /bɪˈkʌmɪŋ/ *adj* 1 (appropriate) 合适的 ‹*behaviour, costume*› 2 (flattering) 好看的 ‹*clothes, hairstyle*›

becquerel /ˈbekərəl/ *n* 贝可勒尔 [放射性活度单位]

BEd /ˌbiːˈed/ *abbr* = **Bachelor of Education** 教育学士

bed /bed/
A *n* 1 [u and c] (item of furniture) 床; **to get into/out of ～** 就寝/起床; **to go** *or* **retire to ～** 上床睡觉; **to get sb. out of ～** 叫某人起床; **to be in ～** 躺在床上; **to take to one's ～** (go to bed) 上床睡觉; (because of illness) 卧病在床; **to make the ～** 整理床铺; **to give sb. a ～ for the night** 留某人过夜; **to be confined to ～** 卧床不起; **a 20-～ hotel** 一家有 20 个床位的旅馆; **life's not all a ～ of roses** fig 人生未必尽如意; **a ～ of nails** fig 极其艰难的境况; **to get out of ～ on the wrong side** fig 起床后一整天都心情不好; **you've made your ～, now you must lie in it** Prov 自作自受 2 [u] (with reference to sex) 房事; **to go to** *or* **to share one's ～ with sb.** 跟某人上床; **to get in ～ with sb./sth.** fig 与某人/某机构建立合作关系 3 [c] (for growing seedlings) 苗床; (for growing flowers) 花坛 4 [c] Geol 地层 5 [c] (of machine tool) 底座 6 [c] Constr (of road) 路基; (of building) 地基 7 [c] (of sea) 海底; (of river) 河床
B *vt* 1 Hort 把…栽于苗床 ‹*plants, seedlings*›; 把…栽于花圃 ‹*plants*› 2 (put in place) 埋置 ‹*post, foundations*› 3 dated (have sex with) 和…性交

Phrasal verbs

- **bed down**
A *vi* 临时睡下
B *vt* [**～ sb./sth. down, ～ down sb./sth.**] 给…铺草窝 ‹*animals*›; 为…安顿床铺 ‹*children*›
- **bed in** *vt* [**～ sth. in, ～ in sth.**] 埋置 ‹*post*›; 嵌入 ‹*beam*›
- **bed out** *vt* [**～ sth. out, ～ out sth.**] 移栽 ‹*plant, seedling*›

bed and board *n* [u] 食宿

bed and breakfast *n* 1 [u] (accommodation) 住宿加早餐; **to offer ～** 提供住宿加早餐 2 [c] (building) 提供住宿加早餐的旅馆

bed: **～bug** *n* 臭虫; **～clothes** *npl* 床上用品

bedcover /ˈbedkʌvə(r)/
A *n* = **bedspread**
B **bedcovers** *npl* = **bedclothes**

bedding /ˈbedɪŋ/ *n* [u] 1 (for humans) 寝具 2 (for animals) 垫草

bedding plant *n* 花坛植物

bedeck /bɪˈdek/ *vt* liter 装饰; **to ～ (sth.) with sth.** 用某物装饰 (某物)

bedevil /bɪˈdevl/ *vt* (*pres p etc.* **-ll-** Brit, **-l-** Amer) 1 (cause trouble to) «*problem, misfortune*» 困扰 ‹*person, activity*›; **a project ～led by a lack of funds** 受资金缺乏困扰的项目 2 (torment) «*doubt, ill luck*» 折磨 ‹*person*›

bedfellow /ˈbedfeləʊ/ *n* 1 fig (ally) 伙伴; **they make strange ～s** 他们同床异梦; **commerce and art have always been uneasy ～s** 商业和艺术总是格格不入 2 lit dated 同床之人

Bedfordshire /ˈbedfədʃə(r)/ *pr n* 贝德福德郡

bed head *n* Brit 床挡头

bedlam /ˈbedləm/ *n* [u] 混乱喧闹的场面; **it's ～ in here!** 这里闹成了一团!

bed linen *n* [u] 床单和枕套

Bedouin /ˈbedʊɪn/
A *adj* 贝都因人的 ‹*people, culture*›
B *n* 贝都因人

bed: **～ pan** *n* 床上便盆; **～ post** *n* 床柱

bedraggled /bɪˈdrægld/ *adj* 1 (wet) 湿漉漉的 ‹*clothes, person*› 2 (untidy) 乱蓬蓬的 ‹*hair*› 3 (dirty) 脏兮兮的 ‹*appearance*›

bed: **～ rest** *n* [u] 卧床休息; **～ridden** *adj* 卧床不起的; **～rock** *n* [u] 1 Geol 基岩; 2 fig (basis) 基础; **～roll** *n* esp Amer 铺盖

bedroom /ˈbedruːm, -rʊm/
A *n* 卧室
B *modif* 1 (for a bedroom) 卧室的; **～ slippers** 在家穿的拖鞋 2 (sexual) 性爱的; **a ～ scene** 床上戏

bedroom suburb *n* Amer 城郊住宅区

Beds. *abbr* Brit = **Bedfordshire**

bed-settee *n* 沙发床

bedside /ˈbedsaɪd/ *n* 床旁; **a ～ lamp** 床头灯; **a ～ book** 床头消遣读物; **they were at his ～ when he died** 他死的时候，他们在他床边

bedside manner *n* 医疗服务态度; **the doctor has a good ～** 大夫对病人的态度很好

bed: **～sit, ～sitter, ～sitting room** *ns* Brit 卧室兼起居室; **～sock** *n* 睡袜; **～sore** *n* 褥疮; **～spread** *n* 床罩; **～spring** *n* 床垫弹簧; **～stead** *n* 床架; **～time** *n* [u] 就寝时间; **it's ～time** 该睡觉了; **11 o'clock is my ～time** 我在 11 点上床睡觉; **a ～time story** 睡前讲的故事

bedwetting /ˈbedwetɪŋ/ *n* [u] 尿床

bee /biː/ *n* 1 Zool (insect) 蜜蜂; **to have a ～ in one's bonnet about sth.** fig 痴迷于某事; **the ～'s knees** colloq (person) 最了不起的人; (object) 出类拔萃之物 2 Amer (meeting) 聚会; **spelling ～s are very popular in the USA** 拼单词比赛在美国很流行

Beeb /biːb/ *n* Brit colloq hum **the ～** 英国广播公司

beech /biːtʃ/ *n* 1 [c] (tree) 山毛榉 2 [u] (wood) 山毛榉木材

beech nut *n* 山毛榉果

beef /biːf/
A *n* 1 [u] Culin 牛肉 2 [u] colloq (muscle) 肌肉; **put a bit of ～ into it!** 加把劲儿! 3 [c] (*pl* **beeves**) Agric 菜牛 4 [c] colloq (grievance) 牢骚; **what's your ～?** 你在抱怨什么?; **I've got no ～ with you** 我对你没有什么不满的
B *vi* colloq 发牢骚; **to ～ (on) about sth.** 抱怨某事

Phrasal verb

- **beef up** *vt* [**～ up sth., sth. up**] 增加 ‹*resources, budget, control*›

beef: **～burger** *n* 牛肉汉堡; **～cake** *n* [u] colloq 健美男子; **～ cattle** *npl* 菜牛; **～eater** *n* 伦敦塔卫兵; **～steak** *n* [c and u] 牛排; **～steak tomato** *n* 大番茄; **～ tea** *n* [u] 牛肉汤

beefy /ˈbiːfi/ *adj* 1 colloq (muscular) 粗壮的 2 (in flavour) 牛肉味的

beehive /ˈbiːhaɪv/ *n* 蜂窝; **a ～ hairstyle** 蜂窝式发型

bee: **～keeper** ▸p. 409 *n* 养蜂人; **～-keeping** *n* [u] 养蜂; **～line** *n* 直线; **to make a ～line for sb./sth.** 直奔某人/某物而去

been /biːn, Amer bɪn/ *pp* ▸**be**

beep /biːp/
A *n* 嘟嘟声
B *vt* 传呼
C *vi* 嘟嘟响

beeper /ˈbiːpə(r)/ *n* 传呼机

beer /bɪə(r)/ *n* 1 [u and c] (alcoholic drink) 啤酒 2 [c] (glass etc. of beer) 一份啤酒

beer: **～ belly** *n* colloq 啤酒肚; **～ bottle** *n* 啤酒瓶; **～ can** *n* 啤酒罐; **～ engine** *n* Brit 啤酒泵; **～ festival** *n* 啤酒节; **～ garden** *n* 露天啤酒店; **～ gut** *n* colloq = **～ belly**; **～ mat** *n* 酒杯垫; **～swilling** *adj attrib* pej 灌饱啤酒的; **～ tent** *n* 出售啤酒的帐篷

beery /ˈbɪəri/ *adj* 1 (smelling of beer) 有啤酒味的 ‹*atmosphere, breath*› 2 (affected by beer) 灌饱啤酒的 ‹*person*›; 畅饮啤酒的 ‹*party*›

bee sting *n* 蜂蜇的肿块

beeswax /ˈbiːzwæks/
A *n* [u] 1 (from honeycomb) 蜂蜡 2 (polish) 蜂蜡上光剂
B *vt* 用蜂蜡给…上光

beet /biːt/ *n* 甜菜

beetle /ˈbiːtl/ *n* 甲虫

beetle-browed *adj* 眉毛浓密的

beetroot /ˈbiːtruːt/ *n* [u and c] Brit 红甜菜根; **to turn as red as a ～** 满脸通红

beet sugar *n* [u] 甜菜糖

befall /bɪˈfɔːl/ (*pt* **befell** /bɪˈfel/, *pp* **befallen** /bɪˈfɔːlən/) liter
A *vt* «*fate*» 降临于; **I hope no harm will ever ～ him** 但愿他永远平安
B *vi* «*fate, event*» 降临; **whatever may ～, I shall never forget our meeting** 不管发生什么，我永远不会忘记我们的会面

befit /bɪˈfɪt/ *v impers* (*pres p etc.* **-tt-**) formal «*language, behaviour*» 适合于 ‹*person, occasion*›; **as ～s sth./sb.** 与某事物/某人相称; **it ill ～s him to do that** 他不该做那事

befitting /bɪˈfɪtɪŋ/ *adj* formal 适当的 ‹*attire, manner*›; **in a style ～ a managing director** 以适合总经理的方式

before /bɪˈfɔː(r)/
A *prep* 1 (earlier than) 在…以前; **～ now** 此前; **she got there ～ us** 她比我们早到那里; **the day ～ yesterday** 前天; **I was there the week ～ last** 我上上周在那儿; **～ leaving, he phoned** 他在离开前打了个电话; **he became a doctor, like his father ～ him** 他承继父业，当了一名医生; **～ long** 不久; **～ long it will be winter** 冬天很快就要到来了 2 (in position, order, hierarchy) 在…前面; **G comes ～ H in the alphabet** 字母表中G在H之前; **your name comes ～ mine on the list** 名单上你的名字排在我前面; **turn left a mile ～ the crossroads** 在十字路口前一英里处左拐; **～ sb.'s (very) eyes** 当着某人的面; **to play ～ the home crowd** 在主场观众面前比赛; **to bring a bill ～ parliament** 向国会提交议案 3 (in importance, priority) 优先于; **to put quality ～ quantity** 优先考虑质量而非数量; **～ all else** *or* **everything** 先于一切; **for him, work comes ～ everything else** 对他而言，工作重于一切 4 Amer (in telling time) [表示差几分到整点]; **it's ten ～ six** 6 点差 10 分 5 formal (in reaction to, in the face of, for the consideration of) [表示面对某人、某事物时的反应或应考虑的事宜]; **they retreated ～ the enemy** 面对敌人，他们撤退了; **these are the alternatives ～ us** 这些就是我们可以考虑的变通方法 6 (awaiting) [表示临近]; **the whole summer lay ～ me** 整个夏季正等待着我
B *adv* 1 (earlier) 以前; (already) 已经; **long ～** 很久以前; **it's never happened ～** 这事以前

b

从未发生过; have you been to India ~? 你去过印度吗？; I'll try to talk to her ~ 我会尽量在之前和她谈一谈; as ~ 一如既往 2 (preceding) 在前面; that page and the one ~ 这一页和前面的一页 3 archaic (ahead) 提前; to ride ~ 在前面骑马

C *conj* 1 (prior to) 在…以前; ~ I go, I would like to say that ... 我走以前想说…; ~ you can say Jack Robinson dated 说时迟，那时快; ~ you know where you are ... 突然…; oh, ~ I forget, did you remember to post that letter? 噢，差点忘了，你记得把那封信寄出去了吗？ 2 (until) 到…时; it will be years ~ I earn that much money! 我得到猴年马月才能挣到那么多钱！ 3 (in threats or warnings) 不然; get out of here ~ I call the police! 走开，不然我叫警察了！ 4 (as necessary condition) 以便; (in order to prevent) 以免; you have to show your ticket ~ they'll let you in 你得凭票入内; do it ~ you forget 尽早动手，免得忘了 5 (rather than) 不愿; I'd die ~ I apologize 我宁死也不道歉; he would die ~ admitting he was wrong 他死也不肯认错

beforehand /bɪˈfɔːhænd/ *adv* (ahead of time) 提前; (earlier) 事先; let me know ~ 提前告诉我; a year/one hour ~ 提前一年/一小时; journalists knew ~ 记者们事先已经知道了; we had seen them shortly ~ 不久前我们见过他们

befriend /bɪˈfrend/ *vt* (make friends with) 和…交朋友; (look after) 帮助 [朋友]

befuddle /bɪˈfʌdl/ *vt* 使…糊涂 ‹*person, mind*›; be ~d by drink 喝得醉醺醺的

beg /beg/ (*pres p etc.* -gg-)

A *vi* 1 (solicit) 乞讨; to ~ for sth. 讨要某物; to be going ~ging colloq 没人要 2 (plead, entreat) 恳求; to ~ for mercy/help 恳求怜悯/帮助

B *vt* 1 (solicit) 乞讨 ‹*money, food*›; can I ~ a light from you? 可以跟您借个火吗？ 2 formal (request) 请求 ‹*favour*›; I ~ your pardon 请原谅; to ~ sb.'s forgiveness 请某人宽恕; to ~ leave *or* permission to do sth. 请求允许做某事; to ~ to differ (with sb.) 恕不赞同（某人） 3 (plead, entreat) 恳求; to ~ sb. to do sth. 恳求某人做某事 4 (leave unresolved) 回避 ‹*issue*›; to ~ the question 回避问题

Phrasal verb

• **beg off** *vi* colloq 推辞; to ~ off at the last minute 在最后时刻反悔

began /bɪˈgæn/ *pt* ▸begin

beget /bɪˈget/ *vt* (*pres p* begetting, *pt* begot /bɪˈgɒt/ *or* archaic begat /bɪˈgæt/; *pp* begotten /bɪˈgɒtn/) 1 archaic (father) 成为…之父; they hoped that the king might ~ an heir by his new queen 他们希望国王新娶的王后可以为他生一位继承人 2 liter (bring about) 引起; violence ~s more violence 暴力招致暴力

beggar /ˈbegə(r)/

A *n* 1 (pauper) 乞丐; ~s can't be choosers Prov 要饭的就不能挑肥拣瘦 2 Brit colloq (person) 家伙; a lucky ~ 幸运的家伙; a poor ~ 可怜虫

B *vt* 1 (impoverish) 使贫穷; to ~ description «*appearance, dress, sunset, poverty*» 难以形容; to ~ belief 令人难以置信 2 (reduce to ruin) 摧毁; industry has been ~ed by government policy 工业因政府的政策而衰败了

beggarly /ˈbegəli/ *adj* 1 (poor, meagre) 贫穷的 ‹*existence*› 2 (inadequate) 少得可怜的 ‹*amount, wage, meal*›

beggar-my-neighbour ▸p. 307

A *n* [u] "吃光"牌戏

B *modif* 损人利己的; ~ tactics 损人利己的策略

begging: ~ **bowl** *n* lit 讨饭碗; fig 求助; ~ **letter** *n* 借钱的求助信

begin /bɪˈgɪn/ (*pt* began, *pp* begun)

A *vt* 1 (start doing, start out on) 开始 ‹*career, meeting, game*›; to ~ to do sth., to ~ doing sth. 开始做某事; ~ a new paragraph 另起一段; to ~ a journey 起程; they began their married life in a bedsitter 他们结婚时住在起居兼卧室两用的租间里; she began life as a grocer's daughter 她出生于食品杂货商家庭; to ~ sth. by doing sth./with sth. 以做某事/以某事物作为某事的开端 2 (start using) 开启 ‹*bottle*›; 开始吃 ‹*loaf*›; 开始用 ‹*page, notebook*› 3 (say as first words) «*letter*» 开始写道; «*story*» 开始讲道; 'once upon a time,' she began "从前啊，"她开始说道 4 (have slightest success) 一点也; I can't ~ to tell you how grateful I am 我对你的感激之情难以言表; I didn't ~ to understand 我完全不明白 5 (initiate) 发起 ‹*campaign*›; 创建 ‹*dynasty*›; 引起 ‹*debate, dispute, trend*›; 散布 ‹*rumour*› 6 (come first in) 在…中居首位 ‹*series, collection, festival*›; A ~s the alphabet A是字母表中的第一个字母

B *vi* 1 (start doing sth., do first stage) 开始做; it's very complicated: I don't know where to ~ 这事很复杂，我不知从何处下手; to ~ by doing sth./with sth. 先做某事/从某事物着手; she began as a sales assistant 她先是担任销售助理 2 (have first stage, start happening) «*play, meeting, disease, problem, storm*» 开始; a name ~ning with C 以C开头的名字; to ~ as sth. 起初是某事物; ~ning from July 1st, ... 从7月1日起，…; the pain began when I tried to move my leg 我那时腿一动就疼 3 (have starting point) «*country, road*» 起始; «*river*» 发源

C **to begin with** *adv phr* 1 (at first) 起初 2 (firstly) 首先 3 (originally) 本来; was it like that to ~ with? 它原本就是那样吗？ 4 (at all) 根本; I wish I'd never bought the house to ~ with 真希望我压根就没有买那幢房子

Phrasal verbs

• **begin at** *vt* [~ at sth.] «*goods*» 底价为; «*prices*» 从…起

• **begin on** *vt* [~ on sth.] 着手做

beginner /bɪˈgɪnə(r)/ *n* 初学者; Spanish for ~s 西班牙语入门; ~'s luck 新手的好运气

beginning /bɪˈgɪnɪŋ/

A *n* 1 (point where sth. starts) 起点; since the ~ of time 自古以来; the ~ of the legend 传说的起源; to start at *or* from the ~ 从头开始; to go back to the ~ 回到起点; from ~ to end 自始至终 2 (first part) 开始; in the ~ 起初; at the ~ (of sth.) 在（某事物）开始时; at the ~ of May 在5月初; a good/bad ~ 良好/不好的开端; the ~ of the end (for sb./sth.) （某人/某事物）结局的开始

B **beginnings** *npl* (origins) 起源; (earliest stages) 初始阶段; to have its ~s (in sth.) 起源（于某事物）; to start *or* grow from small ~s «*company*» 从小生意起步; the ~s of a headache 头痛的先兆

begonia /bɪˈgəʊnɪə/ *n* 秋海棠

begot /bɪˈgɒt/ *pt* ▸beget

begotten /bɪˈgɒtn/ *pp* ▸beget

begrudge /bɪˈgrʌdʒ/ *vt* 1 (give resentfully) 吝惜 ‹*money, time, assistance*›; to ~ doing sth. 不愿做某事 2 (envy, resent) 忌妒; to ~ sb. sth. 嫉妒某人拥有某物

beguile /bɪˈgaɪl/ *vt* 1 (entice, trick) 诱骗; to ~ sb. into doing sth. 诱骗某人去做某事 2 (charm) 使着迷 3 (pass pleasantly) 愉快地度过; an interesting book to ~ the long hours 能使人轻松消磨漫长时光的有趣的书

beguiling /bɪˈgaɪlɪŋ/ *adj* 诱人的 ‹*voice, manner, prospect*›; she had the most ~ smile 她的微笑最迷人

begun /bɪˈgʌn/ *pp* ▸begin

behalf /bɪˈhɑːf, Amer -ˈhæf/ (on ~ of Brit, in ~ of Amer) *prep phr* 1 (as representative of) 代表; on my own ~ 以我个人的名义 2 (in the interest of) 为了…的利益; don't be uneasy on my ~ 不要为我担心

behave /bɪˈheɪv/

A *vi* 1 (act in specified manner) 表现; the supporters ~d well/badly 支持者们表现得很好/差; he ~d badly towards her 他对她不礼貌; what a way to ~! 这成什么样子！; how does this metal ~ under pressure? 这种金属在压力下有何反应？ 2 (function) «*device, machine*» 运转

B *v refl* to ~ oneself 表现良好; ~ yourself! 放规矩点！; is the computer behaving itself? hum 这台电脑现在行吗？

behaviour, Amer **behavior** /bɪˈheɪvjə(r)/ *n* [u] 1 (conduct) 行为; good/bad ~ 良好/恶劣行为; patterns of ~ 行为模式; to be on one's best ~ 举止得体 2 (of substance, chemical) 反应; the ~ of mercury at different temperatures 汞在不同温度下的性能 3 (of device, machine) 运转情况

behavioural, Amer **behavioral** /bɪˈheɪvjərəl/ *adj* 行为的 ‹*changes, problems, characteristics*›; 行为科学的 ‹*theory, studies*›

behavioural science *n* [u and c] 行为科学

behaviourism, Amer **behaviorism** /bɪˈheɪvjərɪzəm/ *n* [u] 行为主义

behaviourist, Amer **behaviorist** /bɪˈheɪvjərɪst/

A *adj* 行为主义的 ‹*doctrine, approach*›

B *n* 采用行为疗法的精神病医生

behead /bɪˈhed/ *vt* 砍掉…的头

beheld /bɪˈheld/ *pt, pp* ▸behold

behemoth /bɪˈhiːmɒθ/ *n* 1 fig (building, organization, vehicle, project) 庞然大物; a ~ of a project 庞大的工程 2 (beast) 巨兽

behest /bɪˈhest/ *n* formal or liter 命令; at the ~ of sb., at sb.'s ~ 按某人的吩咐

behind /bɪˈhaɪnd/ ▸p. 487

A *adv* 1 (at the rear of sb./sth.) 在背后; (towards the back of sb./sth.) 向后 ‹*look, glance*›; from ~ 从后面; he grabbed her from ~ 他从背后抓住了她 2 (remaining after departure) 留在原处; to stay *or* remain ~ 留下来; to keep sb. ~ 把某人留下 3 (further back) 在后面; the car ~ 后面的汽车; winter is not far ~ 冬天即将到来 4 (in competition) 落后; two goals ~ 落后两个球; to be far *or* a long way ~ 远远落后 5 (late) 滞后; to be weeks/years ~ 滞后好几周/好几年; to be ~ with *or* in sth. 积压 ‹*work, studies*› 6 (in arrears) 拖欠; to be ~ with sth. 拖欠 ‹*rent, payments*›

B *prep* 1 (at the rear of) 在…的后面; (towards the back of) 向…的后面; look ~ you 回头看看你背后; the mountains ~ the town 城镇后面的山峦; the sun came out from ~ a cloud 太阳拨云而出; they were miles ~ us 他们落在我们后面好几英里; she shut the gate ~ her 她随手关上大门 2 (underlying) 隐藏在…后面; the hatred ~ his apparent friendliness 藏在他友善外表下面的仇恨; the real story ~ the news 新闻背后的实情 3 (responsible for) 作为…的原因; the man ~ the plan 制定计划的人; what is ~ his actions? 他的动机是什么？; who is ~ this proposal? 谁提出的这个议案？ 4 (in support of) 支持; (giving guidance) 指引; to be (solidly) ~ sb. （坚决）支持某人; he has no family ~ him 他没有家人的支持 5 (less advanced than) 落后于; to be ~ the others «*pupil*» 落后于其他人; we're 3 points ~ the other team 我们比另一支队伍落后了3分 6 (in one's past) 成为…的过去; those days are ~ me now 对我来说，那些日子已经过去了; he has three years' experience ~ him 他已经有3年的经验了; to put sth. ~ one 忘掉某事

C *n* colloq 屁股; he needs a kick in the ~ 他需要鞭策

behindhand /bɪˈhaɪndhænd/ *adj pred* 拖欠的; to be *or* get ~ with ... 拖延着的 ‹*work, studies*›

behind-the-scenes
A *adj attrib* **1** Theat 幕后的 ‹*work, worker*› **2** (hidden) 秘密的 ‹*activity*›; **I suspected the politicians of having some ~ deal going** 我怀疑那些政客在做什么私下交易
B **behind the scenes** *adv* **1** Theat 在幕后 ‹*work, happen*› **2** (out of sight) 秘密地; **behind the scenes, the princess was an avid reader** 公主在私底下是个酷爱读书的人; **diplomatic manoeuvres going on behind the scenes** 秘密实施的外交策略

behold /bɪ'həʊld/ *vt* (*pt, pp* **beheld**) archaic *or* liter 看见; **it was a wonder to ~** 那真是个奇观

beholden /bɪ'həʊldən/ *adj* formal 负有义务的; **to be ~ to sb.** 对某人负有义务

beholder /bɪ'həʊldə(r)/ *n* archaic *or* liter 观看者; **beauty is** *or* **lies in the eye of the ~** Prov 情人眼里出西施

behove Brit /bɪ'həʊv/, **behoove** Amer /bɪ'hu:v/ *v impers* formal 理应; **it ~s sb. to do sth.** 某人理应做某事; **it ill ~s her to ...** 她不应当…

beige /beɪʒ/ ▸**p. 134**
A *adj* 米色的
B *n* [u and c] 米色

Beijing /beɪ'dʒɪŋ/ ▸**p. 604** *pr n* 北京; **~ (Municipality)** 北京（市）

being /'bi:ɪŋ/ *n* **1** [c] (living creature, entity) 生物; **man is a rational ~** 人是有理性的动物; **~s from another planet** 外星生物 **2** [c] (essence) 身心; **with one's whole ~** 全身心地 **3** [u] (existence) 存在; **the union came into ~ in 1965** 该工会成立于1965年; **to bring sth. into ~** 使某物出现

Beirut /beɪ'ru:t/ *pr n* 贝鲁特

bejewelled Brit, **bejeweled** Amer /bɪ'dʒu:əld/ *adj* 珠宝点缀的

belabour Brit, **belabor** Amer /bɪ'leɪbə(r)/ *vt* **1** lit (attack physically) 痛打; **he ~ed the donkey with blows** 他猛揍那头驴子 **2** fig (attack verbally) 责骂

Belarus /ˌbjelə'ru:s/ *pr n* 白俄罗斯

belated /bɪ'leɪtɪd/ *adj* 迟来的 ‹*apology, greetings, measures, response*›; **blame the train company for my ~ arrival!** 我的迟到要归咎于火车运营公司！

belatedly /bɪ'leɪtɪdli/ *adv* 迟来地; **he acknowledged ~ that he had been wrong all along** 他很晚才承认自己一直都是错的

belay /bɪ'leɪ/
A *vt* **1** Naut 系绕 **2** (in climbing) 把…固定在岩石上
B *vi* **1** Naut 系绕缆绳 **2** (in climbing) 拴牢保护绳
C *n* (in climbing) 保护绳固定点

belch /beltʃ/
A *vi* **1** (burp) 打嗝 **2** (emerge) «*smoke, flames*» 喷出
B *vt* 喷出 ‹*smoke, flames*›
C *n* (action) 打嗝; (sound) 打嗝声

Phrasal verb
- **belch out**
A *vi* 喷出
B *vt* [**~ sth. out, ~ out sth.**] 喷出 ‹*smoke, flames*›

beleaguered /bɪ'li:gəd/ *adj* **1** lit (besieged) 被包围的 ‹*troops, city*› **2** fig (experiencing difficulties) 处于困境的; (experiencing criticism) 饱受指责的

Belfast /bel'fɑ:st, 'belfɑ:st/ *pr n* 贝尔法斯特

belfry /'belfri/ *n* **1** (part of a tower) 钟室 **2** (tower or steeple) 钟塔

Belgian /'beldʒən/ ▸**p. 503**
A *adj* (of Belgium) 比利时的; (of the people) 比利时人的
B *n* 比利时人

Belgium /'beldʒəm/ *pr n* 比利时

Belgrade /bel'greɪd/ *pr n* 贝尔格莱德

belie /bɪ'laɪ/ *vt* **1** (show to be false) 证明…是错误的 ‹*rumour, assurances, fears*› **2** (fail to fulfil) 使…落空 ‹*hopes, forecasts, expectations*› **3** (disguise) 掩饰; **his smile ~d his despair** 他微笑的外表下是绝望

belief /bɪ'li:f/ ▸**p. 325** *n* **1** [u and c] (sth. accepted as true) (gen) 信念; Relig 信仰; **a political/religious ~** 政治/宗教信仰; **to go against sb.'s ~s** 违背某人的信仰; **a popular/traditional ~** 普遍/传统看法; **past** *or* **beyond ~** 难以置信的 **2** [u and c] (conviction) 相信; **it's my (firm) ~ that ...** 我坚信…; **in the ~ that ...** 相信…; **to the best of my ~** 据我所知; **my ~ in Father Christmas** 我对圣诞老人的深信不疑 **3** [u] (confidence) **~ in sb./sth.** 对某人的信任/对某事物的信心; **to shake/reinforce sb.'s ~** 动摇/增强某人的信心 **4** [u] Relig 宗教信条

believable /bɪ'li:vəbl/ *adj* 可信的

believe /bɪ'li:v/
A *vt* **1** (take as true) 相信; **~ it or not** 信不信由你; **if he's to be ~d** 如果可以信任他的话; **I can't ~ it of him** 我不相信他会做出那种事; **to let sb. ~** *or* **lead sb. to ~ that ...** 使某人相信…; **~ you me** 相信我吧; **I'll ~ you, thousands wouldn't** colloq 我可以相信你，但大家不会; **I couldn't ~ my eyes/ears** 我简直不相信自己的眼睛/耳朵 **2** (think) 认为; **he is ~d to be dead** 据信他已经死了; **has he arrived? — I ~ so/not** 他来了吗？——我想是的/还没有; **to have reason (not) to ~ that ...** 有理由（不）认为…; **Dr Wang, I ~?** 您是王博士，对吧？; **I don't ~ she intends to return to England** 我认为她不打算回到英格兰
B *vi* **1** (take as true) 相信; **to ~ in sth.** 相信某事物的存在; **seeing is believing** 眼见为实 **2** (have confidence) 相信; **to ~ in sth./doing sth.** 相信某事/做某事有用; **to ~ in sb./oneself** 相信某人/自己; **he ~s in self-discipline** 他信奉自律 **3** Relig 信教; **do you ~ in God?** 你信上帝吗？

believer /bɪ'li:və(r)/ *n* **1** (gen) 相信…的人; **to be a ~ in doing sth.** 是主张做某事的人; **she's not a ~ in ghosts/miracles** 她不相信有鬼/奇迹; **he's a great ~ in exercise** 他极力推崇健身 **2** Relig 信徒

Belisha beacon /bəˌli:ʃə 'bi:kən/ *n* Brit 贝利沙人行横道指示灯

belittle /bɪ'lɪtl/ *vt* **1** (disparage) 贬低 **2** (dismiss as unimportant) 轻视; **to feel ~d** 感觉受到轻视

belittling /bɪ'lɪtlɪŋ/ *adj* **1** (disparaging) 贬低的 **2** (demeaning) 轻视的

Belize /be'li:z/ *pr n* 伯利兹

bell /bel/ *n* **1** (on bicycle, for servant, in school etc.) 铃; (in church) 钟; (on cow, toy, cat) 铃铛; **to ring the ~s** 摇铃; **as clear as a ~** fig 如铃声般清脆; **as sound as a ~** fig 身体棒极了; **to ring a ~** fig colloq 听起来耳熟 **2** (buzzer) 蜂鸣器 **3** (warning device) 警铃 **4** Brit colloq (phone call) **to give sb. a ~** 给某人打个电话 **5** Naut 船钟 [每隔半小时鸣钟一次]; **to ring eight ~s** 敲响八击钟 **6** (in boxing) 铃声

bell: ~-bottomed, ~-bottom *adj* 喇叭形的; **~-bottoms** *npl* 喇叭裤; **~boy** ▸**p. 409** *n* Amer 行李生

belle /bel/ *n* 美女; **the ~ of the ball** 舞会皇后

bellhop /'belhɒp/ *n* Amer = **bellboy**

bellicose /'belɪkəʊs/ *adj* formal 好斗的 ‹*person*›; 好战的 ‹*state*›

bellicosity /ˌbelɪ'kɒsəti/ *n* [u] formal (of people) 好斗性; (of country) 好战性

belligerence /bɪ'lɪdʒərəns/ *n* [u] (of person) 好斗性; (of country) 好战性

belligerent /bɪ'lɪdʒərənt/
A *adj* **1** (person) 好斗的; (country) 好战的 **2** Pol (at war) 交战中的
B *n* Pol 交战国

bell jar *n* 钟形玻璃罩

bellow /'beləʊ/
A *vi* 吼叫
B *vt* 大声说出
C *n* 吼叫声

Phrasal verb
- **bellow out** *vt* [**~ out sth.**] 大声唱 ‹*song*›; 大声发出 ‹*command*›

bellows /'beləʊz/ *npl* 风箱; **a pair** *or* **set of ~** 手压吹风机

bell: ~-pull *n* (handle) 拉铃索手柄; (rope) 拉铃索; **~-push** *n* Brit 电铃按钮; **~-ringer** *n* 敲钟人; **~-ringing** *n* [u] 鸣钟; **the ancient art of ~-ringing** 古老的鸣钟艺术; **~ rope** *n* (in church) 钟绳; (in house) 拉铃索; **~-shaped** *adj* 钟形的; **~ tent** *n* 钟形帐篷; **~ tower** *n* 钟塔; **~wether** *n* **1** (sheep) 系铃领头羊; **2** fig (trendsetter) 楷模

belly /'beli/
A *n* **1** (stomach) 胃; **sb.'s eyes are bigger than their ~** colloq 某人眼大肚子小 **2** (abdomen) 腹部; **to go ~ up** fig colloq 完蛋 **3** (curved part) 凸起部分; **the ~ of a ship/plane/sail** 船腹/机腹/帆腹; **the ~ of a jar** 罐腹 **4** (of violin, cello) 面板
B *vt* «*wind, draught*» 使…鼓起 ‹*sail, flag, curtain*›
C *vi* «*sail, flag, curtain*» 鼓起

bellyache /'belɪeɪk/
A *n* [u and c] 肚子痛
B *vi* (*pres p* **bellyaching**) colloq 发牢骚

belly: ~aching *n* [u] colloq 牢骚; **stop your ~aching!** 别抱怨了！; **~ button** *n* colloq 肚脐; **~ dance** *n* 肚皮舞; **~ dancer** *n* 跳肚皮舞者; **~ dancing** *n* [u] 跳肚皮舞

bellyflop /'belɪflɒp/
A *n* colloq 肚子先着水的跳水动作
B *vi* **1** (dive badly) 肚子先着水地跳水 **2** fig (fail) 惨败 **3** Aviat 以机腹着陆

bellyful /'belɪfʊl/ *n* colloq 一肚子; **to have a** *or* **one's ~ (of sth.)** fig 受够了（某事物）

belly: ~ landing *n* 机腹着陆; **to make a ~ landing** 以机腹着陆; **~ laugh** *n* 捧腹大笑

belong /bɪ'lɒŋ, Amer -lɔ:ŋ/ *vi* **1** (be property of) **to ~ to sb./sth.** 属于某人/某物; **it ~s to me** 那是我的; **those bones ~ to a prehistoric animal** 那些骨头是一种史前动物留下的; **the Athens Olympics ~ed to Kelly Holmes** 雅典奥运会上，凯莉·霍姆斯独领风骚 **2** (be member of) **to ~ to sth.** 是某组织的成员; **do you ~ to a trade union?** 你是工会会员吗？; **this cup ~s to the set** 这个杯子是这套茶具里的; **he ~s with us** 他是我们中的一员 **3** (have exact place) «*object*» 应被放置（在…处）; **put it back where it ~s** 把它放回老地方 **4** (fit) 合得来; **we ~ together** 我们俩情投意合; **a sense of ~ing** 归属感

belongings /bɪ'lɒŋɪŋz, Amer -'lɔ:ŋ-/ *npl* 财物; **personal ~** 个人物品

Belorussia /ˌbeləʊ'rʊʃə/ *pr n* = **Belarus**

beloved
A *adj* **1** /bɪ'lʌvɪd/; *attrib* (dearly loved) 钟爱的 **2** /bɪ'lʌvd/; *pred* (much liked, very popular) **to be ~ by** *or* **of sb.** 深受某人喜爱
B /bɪ'lʌvɪd/ *n* 心爱的人

below /bɪ'ləʊ/
A *prep* **1** (lower than) 在…下面; (extending underneath) 到…下面; **~ the knee/waist** 在膝盖/腰部以下; **~ (the) ground** 在地面以下; **your name comes just ~ mine** 你的名字就列在我的下面; **cables run ~ the floorboards** 线缆布在地板下面 **2** (less than) 少于; (in pitch) 在…以下; **~ average/10%** 低于平均水平/10%; **~ the age of 7** 不满7岁; **10° ~ zero** 零下10度; **his performance was ~ his usual standard** 他没有发挥出通常的水平 **3** (inferior in rank to) 低于; **to be ~ sb. in rank** 级别低于某人; **the teams ~ them**

b

in the table 积分榜上排名低于他们的队伍 **4** (downstream from) 在…的下游 **5** (south of) 在…以南; ~ **Liverpool** 利物浦以南 **6** (unworthy of) 有失…的身份; **to be ~ sb. to do sth.** 做某事有失某人的身份
B *adv* **1** (beneath surface) 在下面; (underneath) 在底下; **100 metres ~** 下面 100 米; **miners working ~** 在地下作业的矿工; **there were voices coming from ~** 有声音从下面传来 **2** (on page) 在一页的末端; **see ~** 见本页末; **your name comes just ~** 你的名字就列在下面 **3** (in amount) 少于…的数量; (of standard, rank) 在…级以下; **a mark of 39% or ~** 39%或以下的水平; **20° ~** 零下 20 度; **at departmental level and ~** 在部门及以下各级 **4** Naut (on lower deck) 在下层甲板; (to lower deck) 到下层甲板

below: ~-the-line *adj attrib* 线下的; **~-the-line costs/items** 线下成本/项目; **~-the-line-advertising** *n* [u] 线下广告

belt /belt/
A *n* **1** (for clothes) 腰带; Aut, Aviat 安全带; Mil, Sport 弹药带; **to tighten one's ~** fig 省吃俭用; **to have sth. under one's ~** fig 有过某种经历; **~ and braces** Brit fig 稳妥可靠的 ‹*approach, job*›; **below the ~** fig 不公正; **her remark was below the ~** 她的话有失公允 **2** (section) (of land) 地带; (of weather) 气候带; (in space) 星带; **the stockbroker ~** 股票经纪人聚居区 **3** (machine part) 传送带 **4** Sport (symbol of rank) 段级标识带; **heavyweight ~** (in boxing) 重量级拳王金腰带 **5** colloq (hit) 重击; **to give sb. a ~** 猛击某人; **to give the ball a good ~** 用力击球
B *vt* **1** (fasten) 用带子系紧 **2** (punish) 用皮带抽 **3** colloq (hit) 猛击; **he ~ed six more runs** 他又打出了 6 次跑垒得分
C *vi* colloq «*person*» 飞奔; «*vehicle*» 疾驰; **the boy ~ed home** 男孩飞奔回家

Phrasal verbs
- **belt out** *vt* [**~ sth. out, ~ out sth.**] colloq «*person*» 放声高唱; «*radio*» 大声播放
- **belt up** *vi* **1** (fasten seat belt) 系上安全带 **2** Brit colloq (be quiet) 闭嘴; **just ~ up, will you!** 你给我安静点行不行!

belter /'beltə(r)/ *n* colloq **1** (outstanding example) 极好的榜样 **2** (singer) 嗓音嘹亮的歌手 **3** (song) 嘹亮的歌

belt: ~-tightening *n* [u] 紧缩开支; **~way** *n* Amer 环路

belvedere /'belvɪdɪə(r)/ *n* 观景楼

bemoan /bɪ'məʊn/ *vt* formal 哀叹

bemuse /bɪ'mju:z/ *vt* 使困惑

bemused /bɪ'mju:zd/ *adj* 困惑的

bemusement /bɪ'mju:zmənt/ *n* [u] 困惑

bench /bentʃ/ *n* **1** (seat) 长凳; Sport 替补队员席; **to be on the (substitute's) ~** 等候上场 **2** Brit Pol 议员席; **to be on the opposition ~es** 在反对党议员席 **3** (workbench) 工作台; (in lab) 实验台 **4** (*also* **Bench**) Jur 法官; **~ and bar** 法官和律师; **to be** *or* **sit on the ~** 出任法官; **to be on the ~ for a case** 裁决案件

benchmark /'bentʃmɑ:k/
A *n* **1** also Civ Eng, Comput 基准 **2** (price) 标准价
B *vt* 用标准衡量

benchmark job *n* 基准职位

bench: ~ press *n* 杠铃推举练习; **~ seat** *n* 统座; **~ test** *n* 运行测试

bend /bend/
A *vt* (*pt, pp* **bent**) **1** (curve) 使弯曲; **to ~ one's elbows/knees/back** 屈肘/曲膝/弓背; **she bent her head in shame** 她羞愧地低下了头; **to be bent out of shape** 已弯曲变形; **to ~ one's elbow** Amer fig colloq 喝酒; **to ~ sb.'s ear** fig 向某人唠叨诉说; **to ~ sb. to one's will/wishes** 强迫某人顺从自己的意愿/愿望 **2** (direct) 使…朝向 ‹*attention, gaze*›; **she kept her eyes bent on her book** 她目不转睛地盯着书看; **to be bent on sth./doing sth.** 专心于某事/做某事; **to ~ one's steps in the direction of home** liter 转身往家走 **3** (distort) 对…作变通 ‹*rules, the law*›; **I never lend money, but I'll ~ my principle this once** 我从不借钱给别人，但这次破一回例
B *vi* (*pt, pp* **bent**) **1** (form curve) 弯曲 **2** (incline) «*back*» 弯下; «*head*» 低下; **to ~ forward/backwards** 前倾/后仰; **to ~ over one's books** 埋头读书 **3** (submit) **to ~ before** *or* **to sth.** 顺从 ‹*will, wishes*›; 服从 ‹*authority*›
C *n* **1** (in road, river) 弯道; **to take** *or* **turn a ~** 转弯; **a sharp/sudden ~** 急弯; **round** *or* **around the ~** Brit fig colloq 发疯的 **2** (angled part) 弯曲; **the ~ of one's elbow/hips** 胳膊肘/髋关节
D **the bends** *npl* 减压病

Phrasal verbs
- **bend back**
A *vt* [**~ sth. back, ~ back sth.**] **1** (to original position) 把…扳回; **to ~ sth. back into shape** 把某物扳回原来的形状 **2** (away from natural position) 把…向后扳; **to ~ one's fingers back** 把手指向后扳
B *vi* «*path, person*» 折回; **the road ~s back on itself at several points** 这条路七拐八拐的
- **bend down**
A *vi* «*person*» 俯身; «*branch*» 弯曲
B *vt* [**~ sth. down, ~ down sth.**] 使向下弯曲
- **bend over**
A *vi* 俯身; **to ~ over backwards** lit 后仰; fig 竭尽全力
B *vt* [**~ sth. over, ~ over sth.**] 折弯

bender /'bendə(r)/ *n* colloq 狂饮; **to go on a ~** 饮酒作乐

bend sinister *n* [盾形纹章上从左上方到右下方的] 对角条纹

bendy /'bendi/ *adj* colloq **1** (flexible) 易弯曲的 ‹*straw, plastic*› **2** (twisty) 多弯道的 ‹*route*›; **a ~ road** 弯弯曲曲的路

bendy bus *n* Brit colloq 铰接式公共汽车

beneath /bɪ'ni:θ/
A *prep* **1** (lower than, underneath) 在…下方; (to a lower position than) 到…下方; **~ the table** 在桌子底下; **her name was ~ mine on the list** 名单上她的名字排在我的下面; **deep ~ the earth** 地下深处 **2** (concealed by) 在…的掩盖下; **he hid his disappointment ~ a polite smile** 他礼貌地微笑着以掩饰失望 **3** (inferior in rank to) 低于; **the men ~ him** 比他级别低的人 **4** (unworthy of) 有失…的身份; **to be ~ sb. to do sth.** 做某事有失某人的身份
B *adv* **1** (lower down, underneath) 在下面; **the valley/river ~** 下面的山谷/河流; **the apartment ~** 楼下的公寓单元 **2** (concealed) 掩藏着; **the smile revealed the evil ~** 微笑中透出内心的邪恶

Benedictine
A *n* **1** /ˌbenɪ'dɪktɪn/ [c] Relig 本笃会修士 **2** **Benedictine®** /ˌbenɪ'dɪkti:n/ [u] (liqueur) 本尼迪克甜酒
B /ˌbenɪ'dɪktɪn/ *adj* 本笃会的

benediction /ˌbenɪ'dɪkʃn/ *n* **1** [c and u] (blessing) 祝福; **in ~** 作为祈祷 **2** [c] (service) 赐福祈祷

benefaction /ˌbenɪ'fækʃn/ *n* formal 捐赠

benefactor /'benəˌfæktə(r)/ *n* 赞助人; **an unknown/anonymous ~** 不知名的/匿名的捐助者

benefice /'benɪfɪs/ *n* 有俸圣职

beneficial /ˌbenɪ'fɪʃl/ *adj* **1** (advantageous) 有益的 ‹*influence, treatment*›; 有利的 ‹*outcome*›; **to be ~ to sth./for sb.** 对某事物/某人有利 **2** Jur 受益的; **~ interest/owner** 受益权/人

beneficially /ˌbenɪ'fɪʃəli/ *adv* 有益地

beneficiary /ˌbenɪ'fɪʃəri, Amer -'fɪʃɪeri/ *n* **1** (recipient) 受惠者 **2** Jur 受益人

benefit /'benɪfɪt/
A *n* **1** [u and c] (advantage) 益处; (good) 好处; **social ~s** 社会效益; **to be of ~ to sb./sth.** 有益于某人/某事物; **to be to sb.'s ~ to do sth.** 做某事有利于某人; **for the ~ of humankind** 为了造福人类; **I'm doing this for your ~** 我这样做是为你好; **he's crying for your ~** iron 他只是在哭给你看; **with the ~ of hindsight/experience** 借助后见之明/经验; **to give sb. the ~ of the doubt** 把某人往好处想; **the ~s outweigh the disadvantages** 利大于弊 **2** [c] (fundraiser) 募捐活动; **a ~ match/performance** 一场义赛/义演 **3** [u and c] Soc Admin (allowance) 救济金; **housing/maternity ~s** 住房/生育补助金; **to be on ~(s)** 靠领取救济金生活 **4** [c] (perk) 额外待遇; **tax-free ~s** 免税优惠; **~s in kind** 实物津贴
B *vt* (*pres p etc.* **-t-** *or* **-tt-**) 有益于; **to ~ sb./sth.** 对某人/某事物有益
C *vi* (*pres p etc.* **-t-** *or* **-tt-**) 获益; **to stand to ~ (from sth.)** 可能会（从某事物中）获益

benefit: ~ association *n* Amer 互济会; **~ concert** *n* 慈善募捐音乐会; **~ payment** *n* 社会福利金; **~s package** *n* 福利套餐; **~ tourist** *n* Brit colloq 福利游客

Benelux /'benɪlʌks/ *pr n* 比荷卢经济联盟; **~ countries** 比荷卢经济联盟国

benevolence /bɪ'nevələns/ *n* [u] **1** (kindness) 仁慈 **2** (charity) 善行

benevolent /bɪ'nevələnt/ *adj* **1** (kindly) 仁慈的 ‹*person, government*›; 善意的 ‹*gesture*›; 和蔼的 ‹*smile*› **2** (charitable) 慈善的 ‹*organization, fund*›

benevolently /bɪ'nevələntli/ *adv* 仁慈地

BEng *abbr* = **Bachelor of Engineering** 工学士

Bengal /beŋ'gɔ:l/ *pr n* 孟加拉

Bengali /beŋ'gɔ:li/ ▸**p. 503, p. 426**
A *adj* (of Bengal) 孟加拉的; (of the people) 孟加拉人的; (of the language) 孟加拉语的
B *n* **1** [c] (person) 孟加拉人 **2** [u] (language) 孟加拉语

Bengal tiger *n* 孟加拉虎

benighted /bɪ'naɪtɪd/ *adj* **1** (ignorant) 愚昧无知的 **2** liter (overtaken by night) 陷入黑暗的

benign /bɪ'naɪn/ *adj* **1** (mild, genial) 和善的 ‹*person, expression*›; 宜人的 ‹*climate*› **2** (beneficial) 有益的 **3** Med 良性的 ‹*tumour*›; 不危及生命的 ‹*medical condition*›

Benin /be'ni:n/ *pr n* 贝宁

bent /bent/
A *pt, pp* ▸**bend A, B**
B *adj* **1** (curved) 弯曲的 ‹*nail, wire*›; 驼背的 ‹*person*› **2** *pred* (determined) 决意的; **to be ~ on doing sth./on sth.** 一心想做某事/想着某事物 **3** Brit colloq (corrupt) 贪赃枉法的 **4** Brit colloq offensive (homosexual) 同性恋的; **he's ~** 他是同性恋
C *n* (talent, flair) 天赋; (liking) 爱好; **to have a ~ for maths** 有数学天赋; **to be of a studious ~** 生性好学

benumb /bɪ'nʌm/ *vt* 使麻木

benumbed /bɪ'nʌmd/ *adj* 麻木的

Benzedrine® /'benzədri:n/ *n* [u and c] 苯齐巨林

benzene /'benzi:n/ *n* [u] 苯

benzene ring *n* 苯环

benzine /'benzi:n/ *n* [u] 轻质汽油

benzol, benzole /'benzəʊl/ *n* [u] 工业苯

bequeath /bɪ'kwi:ð/ *vt* **1** lit (leave in will) 遗赠 ‹*property, land*› **2** fig (hand on) 把…传下去 ‹*custom, legislation, concept*›

bequest /bɪ'kwest/ *n* **1** [c] (legacy) 遗产 **2** [u] (bequeathing) 遗赠; **by ~** 通过遗赠

berate /bɪ'reɪt/ *vt* 斥责

Berber /'bɜ:bə(r)/ ▸**p. 426**
A *adj* (of the people) 柏柏尔人的; (of the language) 柏柏尔语的
B *n* **1** [c] (person) 柏柏尔人 **2** [u] (language) 柏柏尔语

bereave /bɪ'riːv/ *vt* 1 (*pt, pp* ~**d**) (by death) 使…丧失 ‹*family*›; **to ~ sb. of a loving father** 使某人失去慈父 2 (*pt, pp* **bereft**) liter (deprive) 使失去; **to ~ sb. of sth.** «*event, fate*» 使某人失去某物

bereaved /bɪ'riːvd/
A *adj* 丧失亲人的 ‹*person, family*›
B *npl* **the ~** 死者的亲友

bereavement /bɪ'riːvmənt/ *n* [u and c] 丧失亲友

bereavement: ~ counselling *n* [u] 善别辅导; **~ counsellor** ▸**p. 409** *n* 善别辅导员

bereft /bɪ'reft/
A *pt, pp* ▸**bereave 2**
B *adj* liter 1 (utterly deprived) 完全丧失的; **~ of ideas/hope** 无计可施/绝望 2 (forlorn) 孤寂的

beret /'bereɪ, Amer bə'reɪ/ *n* 贝雷帽

bergamot /'bɜːgəmɒt/ *n* 1 [u] (extract) 香柠檬油 2 [u and c] (fruit) 香柠檬 3 [c] (tree) 香柠檬树 4 [u and c] (herb) 薄荷 5 [c] (pear) 王子梨

beriberi /ˌberɪ'berɪ/ ▸**p. 377** *n* [u] 脚气病

Bering Sea /ˌbeərɪŋ 'siː/ *pr n* **the ~** 白令海

Bering Strait /ˌbeərɪŋ 'streɪt/ *pr n* **the ~** 白令海峡

berk /bɜːk/ *n* Brit colloq 傻瓜

Berks. *abbr* Brit = **Berkshire**

Berkshire /'bɑːkʃɪə(r)/ *pr n* 伯克郡

Berlin /bɜː'lɪn/ *pr n* 柏林; **the ~ Wall** 柏林墙

berm /bɜːm/ *n* esp Amer (of river, canal) 护堤; (of railway) 月台; (of road) 路肩

Bermuda /bə'mjuːdə/ *pr n* 百慕大群岛

Bermudas[1] /bə'mjuːdəz/ *pr npl* **the ~** 百慕大群岛

Bermudas[2] /bə'mjuːdəz/ *npl* = **Bermuda shorts**

Bermuda: ~ shorts *npl* 百慕大短裤; **~ Triangle** *pr n* **the ~** 百慕大三角

Berne /bern/ *pr n* 伯尔尼

berry /'berɪ/ *n* 浆果; **to be as brown as a ~** 皮肤黑黝黝的

berserk /bə'sɜːk/ *adj* 狂怒的; **to go ~** 勃然大怒

berth /bɜːθ/
A *n* 1 (bed) 卧铺; **upper/lower/middle ~** 上铺/下铺/中铺 2 Naut (for ship) 泊位; **a safe ~** 一处安全的锚地; **at ~** 停泊; **to give sth./sb. a safe ~** fig 避开某事物/某人 3 colloq (job, position) 职位
B *vi* Naut (dock) 停泊; (drop anchor) 抛锚
C *vt* 使停泊; **to be ~ed in** *or* **at number 4 dock** 停泊在 4 号码头

beryl /'berəl/ *n* [u] 绿柱石

beryllium /bə'rɪlɪəm/ *n* [u] 铍

beseech /bɪ'siːtʃ/ *vt* (*pt, pp* **besought** *or* ~**ed**) liter 恳求 ‹*permission, forgiveness*›; **to ~ sb. to do sth.** 哀求某人做某事

beseeching /bɪ'siːtʃɪŋ/ *adj attrib* 哀求的

beset /bɪ'set/ *vt* (*pt, pp* **beset**) 1 (trouble) 困扰; **a project ~ with problems/difficulties** 问题成堆/困难重重的项目; **a country ~ by strikes** 受罢工困扰的国家 2 (surround) 围攻

besetting /bɪ'setɪŋ/ *adj attrib* 摆脱不开的 ‹*fear, problem*›; **his ~ sin** 他那无法摆脱的恶习

beside /bɪ'saɪd/ *prep* 1 ▸**p. 487** (next to) 在…旁边; **~ the sea/the road** 在海边/在路边; **to be ~ oneself with rage/happiness** 勃然大怒/无比幸福 2 (in collaboration with) 与…协作; **they fought ~ American troops** 他们和美军并肩作战 3 (in comparison with) 与…相比; **my problems seem rather insignificant ~ yours** 与你相比，我的困难显得微不足道 4 (apart from) = **besides B**

besides /bɪ'saɪdz/
A *adv* 1 (moreover) 而且; **it's too expensive, and ~, we don't need it** 它太贵了，而且我们也不需要它 2 (in addition, as well) 此外; **he has a car, and a bicycle ~** 他有一辆汽车，还有一辆自行车
B *prep* 除…以外; **they need other things ~ money** 除了钱，他们还需要其他东西; **~ having a headache, I've got a temperature** 我不仅头疼，还发烧了; **~ which he was late** 此外，他还迟到了

besiege /bɪ'siːdʒ/ *vt* 1 Mil «*army*» 围攻 ‹*city, garrison*› 2 fig (surround and harass) 团团围住 ‹*person, place*› 3 fig (pester) 纠缠; **to ~ sb. with complaints/requests** 没完没了地向某人抱怨/提要求

besmirch /bɪ'smɜːtʃ/ *vt* liter 玷污 ‹*person*›; 败坏 ‹*reputation*›

besotted /bɪ'sɒtɪd/ *adj* 痴迷的; **to be ~ with** *or* **by sb./sth.** 对某人/某事物痴迷

besought /bɪ'sɔːt/ *pt, pp* ▸**beseech**

bespatter /bɪ'spætə(r)/ *vt* 溅污; **to ~ sb. with dirty water** 溅某人一身脏水

bespeak /bɪ'spiːk/ *vt* (*pt* **bespoke,** *pp* **bespoken**) formal 1 (be evidence of) 证明 2 (order in advance) 预订 ‹*goods, room, seat*›

bespectacled /bɪ'spektəkld/ *adj* 戴眼镜的

bespoke /bɪ'spəʊk/
A *pt* ▸**bespeak**
B *adj* Brit 定做的 ‹*suit*›; 定制的 ‹*software*›; **a ~ tailor** 定做裁缝

bespoken /bɪ'spəʊkən/ *pp* ▸**bespeak**

best /best/
A *adj* 1 (of the highest quality, standard) 最好的; **the ~ book I've ever read** 我读过的最棒的书; **the ~ thing about sth./doing sth.** 某事物/做某事的最大好处; **her ~ dress** 她最漂亮的连衣裙; **in your ~ handwriting** 用你最工整的笔迹; **she speaks the ~ French** 她的法语说得最流利; **~ before (end) May 2010** 保质期至 2010 年 5 月（底）; **the ~ things in life are free** Prov 人生最美好的东西都是免费的; ▸**foot A1** 2 (most appealing) 最有吸引力的; **to look ~** 看上去最漂亮; **this wine is ~ served chilled** 这种葡萄酒冰镇饮用时口感最佳 3 (most competent) 最有才能的; **the award for ~ actor** 最佳演员奖; **which of you is the ~ swimmer?** 你们谁游泳最棒？; **to be ~ at sth./doing sth.** 最擅长于某事/做某事 4 (most appropriate or suitable) 最合适的; (most beneficial or advantageous) 最有裨益的; **the ~ idea/advice/decision** 最好的主意/建议/决定; **the ~ time to plant tomatoes** 播种西红柿的最佳时节; **this is not the ~ place to run out of petrol!** 在这个地方用完了汽油真是糟糕!; **to be ~ for sb./sth./doing sth.** 最适合某人/某事/做某事; **the ~ person for the job** 这项工作的最佳人选; **it's ~ if** *or* **that you go now** 你最好现在就走; **to think it ~ (to do sth.)** 认为最好（做某事）; **to be ~ for sb.** «*exercise, food*» 对某人最有好处; ▸**job A8, next best, honesty, sliced bread** 5 (most accurate) 最准确的 ‹*account*›; **which photograph is the ~ likeness?** 哪张照片最像？; **to keep the ~ time** «*clock*» 走时很准 6 (largest in amount) 最大的 ‹*range*›; 最高的 ‹*price, salary*›; **the ~ selection of used cars** 二手汽车的首选
B *adv* 1 (to highest standard) 最出色地; (to highest degree) 最高程度地; **to behave/sleep ~** 表现最好/睡得最香; **I can manage ~ on my own** 我自己能够应付裕如; **the ~ educated/mannered** 最有教养的/礼貌的; **the best dressed/written** 穿得/写得最好的; **to like sth. ~ (of all)** 最喜欢某物; **the ~ laid plans/schemes (often go astray)** 最周详的计划（也会经常出错）; **to do ~** 取得最大成功; **as ~ one can/could** 尽可能; **~ of all** 尤其可取的是; **~ of all, it's tax-deductible!** 最值得一提的是，它是可以抵税的! 2 (most appropriately) 最适合地; **long skirts suit her ~** 她最适合穿长裙; **to be ~ qualified to do sth.** 最有资格做某事; **to do ~ to do sth.** 最好做某事; **such advice is ~ ignored/followed** 这样的建议最好不理会/听取; **you'd ~ close the gate** 你最好把大门关上; **she thought she knew ~!** 她以为她什么都懂呢!; **do as you think ~** 你觉得怎么最合适就怎么做
C *n* 1 (sth. of the highest quality, standard) 最好的事物; **the ~ of its type** *or* **kind** 同类中最好的东西; **the ~ of the weather will be in the north** 北方将出现极佳的天气; **my mother-in-law and I are the ~ of friends** 我和婆婆相处和睦; **the ~ of a bad bunch** *or* **lot** 矮子中的将军 2 (best clothes) 最好的服装; **one's (Sunday) ~** 某人最好的衣服; **to keep sth. for ~** 留着某件衣服仅在特殊场合穿 3 (most appealing) 最吸引人的事物; **to look one's/its ~** 显得极好看; **this necklace looks the ~ with that dress** 这条项链和那件连衣裙搭配最好看 4 (most competent person) 最能干的人; **to be the ~ of all** 是佼佼者; **to be the ~ at sth./doing sth.** 最擅长于某事/做某事; **to do sth. with the ~ of them** 做某事不亚于任何人; **it happens to the ~ of us** (mishap, failure) 这种事谁都会遇上 5 (peak, height) 最佳状态; **to be at its ~** «*wine, cheese*» 口感最佳; «*city, view*» 最美; **an example of modern architecture at its ~** 现代建筑的最佳典范; **to be at one's ~** 处于最佳状态; **this is Eliot at her ~** 这是艾略特的巅峰之作; **to feel at one's ~** 感觉状态极佳; **to be past one's/its ~** 过了巅峰期; **in the ~ of health** 身体处于最佳状态 6 (greatest personal effort) 最大努力; (highest standard) 最高水平; **to do** *or* **try one's (level** *or* **very) ~ to do sth.** 竭尽全力做某事; **she seemed to be doing her ~ to cause trouble** 她似乎在想方设法制造麻烦; **to get the ~ out of ...** 使…尽其所能 ‹*pupil, worker*›; 充分利用 ‹*gadget*›; **to give of one's ~** formal 尽力而为; **to the ~ of one's knowledge/recollection/belief** 据某人所知/回忆/了解; **they did the job to the ~ of their ability** 他们在这项工作上尽了全力 7 (virtues, qualities) 优秀品质; **to bring out the ~ in sb.** «*crisis, suffering*» 激发出某人的优秀品质; **(with) the ~ of intentions** *or* **motives** （出于）好意 8 (most advantageous or pleasing part) 最大优点; **the ~ of sth./doing sth. is ...** 某事/做某事的最大好处是…; **the ~ of it is ...** (best thing) 最大优点是…; (most amusing) 最有趣的是…; **to have/get the ~ of sth.** 在…中占上风 ‹*deal, bargain*›; 在…中占优势 ‹*arrangement*›; **to make the ~ of sth./it/things** 尽力而为 9 (most appropriate, desirable, or valid one) 最合适的事物; **it's not the ~ of times to do sth.** 现在不是做某事的最佳时机; **it's for the ~** (recommending course of action) 最好这么做; (referring to something done) 这样最好; **I don't want you to leave, but perhaps it's for the ~** 我并不想让你走，但也许还是走为好; **to do/mean sth. for the ~** 出于好意做/想做某事 10 (most favourable thing) 最有利的情况; (highest amount) 最大数量; **£50 is the ~ I can offer you** 我最多出 50 英镑; **at ~** 充其量; **you'll sell 500 copies at ~** 你最多能卖出 500 册; **(even) at the ~ of times** （即使）在最好的情况下; **he found it difficult at the ~ of times to remember names** 连最简单的名字他都觉得很难记住 11 (good wishes) 美好祝愿; **give my ~ to your mother** 代我向你母亲问好; **all the ~** 万事如意 12 (winning majority) 决胜局数; **(to play) the ~ of three/five** （玩）三局两胜/五局三胜 13 (record) 最高记录; **a personal ~** 个人最好成绩
D *vt* 胜过; **to be ~ed in an argument** 在辩论中被驳倒

best: ~-before date *n* Brit 保质期; **~ boy** *n* 灯光助手; **~ end (of neck)** *n* [u and c] Brit [羔羊等靠近肋条的] 颈根; **~ friend** *n* 1 lit (closest friend) 密友; 2 fig (reliable person)

可依赖的人; (sth. of greatest value) 最有价值的东西; **man's ~ friend** 人类最亲密的朋友

bestial /ˈbestɪəl, Amer ˈbestʃəl/ *adj* 凶残的

bestiality /ˌbestɪˈæləti, Amer ˌbestʃɪ-/ *n* **1** [u] (sex with an animal) 兽奸 **2** [u] (inhuman behaviour) 兽性 **3** [c] (bestial act) 兽行

b

bestir /bɪˈstɜː(r)/ *v refl* (*pres p etc.* **-rr-**) formal **to ~ oneself** 发奋

best: ~-known *adj* 大名鼎鼎的; **~ man** *n* 男傧相

bestow /bɪˈstəʊ/ *vt* formal 授予 ‹*honour, title*›; 给予 ‹*benefit, praise, attention*›; **to ~ sth. on** *or* **upon sb.** 把某物授予某人

bestowal /bɪˈstəʊəl/ *n* formal 赠与

bestseller /ˌbestˈselə(r)/ *n* **1** (product) 畅销商品; (book) 畅销书 **2** (writer) 畅销书作者

best-selling *adj* 畅销的 ‹*product, book*›; 作品畅销的 ‹*author*›; **the ~ novelist of 2009** 2009 年最畅销长篇小说的作者

bet /bet/

A *vt* (*pres p* **-tt-**; *pt, pp* **bet**) **1** (gamble) 赌 ‹*money*›; 用…打赌 ‹*object*›; (in casino) 用…下注 ‹*cash, chips*› **2** (be sure) 敢说; **you can ~ your life** *or* **your bottom dollar** *or* **your boots that ...** fig colloq 有绝对把握…; **you can ~ your life on it** 绝对错不了; **~ you can/can't!** colloq 你保证做得到/做不到!

B *vi* (*pres p* **-tt-**; *pt, pp* **bet**) **1** (gamble) 赌博; **to ~ on horses** 赌马 **2** (be sure) 确信; **you want to ~ on it?** 你敢肯定吗?; **don't ~ on it!** 我看不一定!; **it really hurt — I ~ it did!** 真的很痛——这我相信!; **you ~!** colloq 当然!; **I** *or* **I'll ~** colloq (in disbelief) 我才不信呢; (with sympathy) 我能理解

C *n* **1** (gamble) 打赌; **to win/lose a ~** 赌赢/赌输; **to have a ~ on sth.** 对某事物打赌 **2** (stake) 赌注; **'place your ~s'** (in roulette) "请下注"; **to place/lay a ~ (on a horse/race)** 押赌注 (在一匹马/一场比赛上) **3** (alternative) 选择; **your best ~** 最好的办法 **4** (guess) 推测; **it's a good/safe ~ that ...** 很有可能…

beta /ˈbiːtə, Amer ˈbeɪtə/

A *n* **1** (letter) 贝塔 [β, 希腊语字母表的第2个字母] **2** Brit dated (grade) 良好

B *modif* Phys β粒子的, 贝塔粒子的

beta: ~-blocker *n* β-受体阻滞药; **~ particle** *n* β粒子, 贝塔粒子; **~ radiation** *n* [u] β辐射, 贝塔辐射; **~ ray** β射线, 贝塔射线

beta test

A *n* β测试, 最后测试 [尤指由不相关的人或机构进行的最后测试]

B **beta-test** *vt* 对…进行β测试, 对…进行最后测试

beta: ~ tester *n* β测试者, 最后测试者; **~ version** *n* β测试版, 最后测试版

betcha /ˈbetʃə/ sl

A *vi* **you ~!** 当然啦!

B *vt* **1** (when making bet) 我和你打赌; **~ ten pounds they'll lose** 我和你赌 10 英镑他们会输 **2** (expressing certainty) 我敢打赌你…; **~ can't hold your breath for five minutes** 我敢打赌你憋不了 5 分钟的气

betel /ˈbiːtl/ *n* **1** [u] (stimulant) 槟榔叶 **2** [u and c] Bot 蒌子

betel nut *n* 槟榔果

betide /bɪˈtaɪd/ liter

A *vt* 降临于

B *vi* 发生

betoken /bɪˈtəʊkən/ *vt* formal **1** (signify) 表示 **2** (portend) 预示

betray /bɪˈtreɪ/ *vt* **1** (be disloyal to) 背叛 ‹*country, person, interests*›; **to feel ~ed** 感到被出卖了 **2** (reveal treacherously) 泄露 ‹*secret*› **3** (reveal inadvertently) 暴露 ‹*ignorance, intentions, feelings*› **4** (violate) 辜负 ‹*trust*›; 违背 ‹*vow, principle*›

betrayal /bɪˈtreɪəl/ *n* [u and c] 背叛; **a ~ of trust** 对信任的辜负; **a sense of ~** 被出卖的感觉

betrayer /bɪˈtreɪə(r)/ *n* 背叛者

betroth /bɪˈtrəʊð/ *vt* formal or dated 许配; **to be ~ to sb.** 许配给某人

betrothal /bɪˈtrəʊðl/ *n* formal 订婚

betrothed /bɪˈtrəʊðd/ formal or dated

A *adj* 已订婚的; **to be ~** 订婚; **the ~ couple** 未婚夫妻

B *n* (*pl* **betrothed**) (fiancé) 未婚夫; (fiancée) 未婚妻

better¹ /ˈbetə(r)/ ▸**p. 140**

A *adj* **1** (more pleasing, superior) 更好的; (more appealing) 更吸引人的; (happier) 更愉快的; **nothing could be ~!** 再好不过了!; **the weather's no ~** 天气根本没有好转; **playing is ~ than watching** 参与运动比观看更有意思; **to be (all) the ~ for sth.** 从某事中获益; **to taste all the ~ for a dash of cream** 加少许奶油味道会好得多; **to feel ~ for sth./doing sth.** 某事物过后/做某事后感觉好一些; **little/no ~ than sth.** (almost or just the same as) 同某事物差不多; (almost or just as bad as) 比某事物好不到哪里去; **to be a ~ man/woman than sb.** 比某人更完美 **2** (with reference to illness) 《*person, body part*》好转的; (affecting sb. less) 缓解的; (not affecting sb. at all) 痊愈的; **to be/get ~** 康复/正在康复; **to make sb./sth. ~** 治好某人/某种疾病; **the doctor will make you ~** 医生会治好你的病 **3** (more competent) 更能干的; **to be a ~ swimmer than sb.** 比某人更会游泳; **to be a ~ actor than a dancer** 更擅长演戏而不是跳舞; **to be ~ at sth./doing sth.** 更擅长于某事/做某事; **to be ~ with words/children** 更擅长于文字表达/带孩子 **4** (more appropriate, suitable) 更合适的; **have you got a ~ suggestion?** 你有更高明的建议吗?; **to be ~ for sth./doing sth.** 更适合某事/做某事; **to be ~ (for sb.) to do sth.** (某人) 做某事更可取; **it's ~ that she should live with her parents** 她和父母住在一起更好; **to be ~ doing sth.** 做某事更好些; **shall I make some coffee? — haven't you got anything ~ to do?** 我来弄点咖啡吧?——你就没有更好的事可做了吗?; **~ than nothing** 聊胜于无; **the less said about sb./sth. the ~** 最好别提某人/某事物; **who/where ~ to do sth. (than ...)?** (除了…) 还有谁/什么地方更适合做某事?; ▸**devil 2, prevention, safe A6, never A1** **5** (more beneficial, advantageous) 更有益的; **to be ~ for sb./sth.** 《*food, exercise*》对某人/某事物更有益; **swimming is ~ for you than jogging** 对你来说, 游泳比慢跑更好 **6** (more accurate) 更准确的; **to be a ~ likeness/match** 更像/更相配; **to keep ~ time** 走时更准 **7** (larger in amount) 更多的 ‹*selection*›; 更大的 ‹*size, range*›; 更高的 ‹*price, salary*›; ▸**discretion**

B *adv* **1** (to higher standard/degree, more favourably) 更好地; **to fit/behave ~ than ...** 比…更合适/更有礼貌; **to be ~ tempered/mannered** 脾气更好/更有礼貌; **the ~ to do sth.** formal 以便更好地做某事; **I leant forward the ~ to hear him** 我俯身向前以便听清楚他说话; **to do ~** (in career, life) 更成功; (in exam, essay) 有进步; (in health) 病情好转; **'could do ~'** (in school report) "有待提高"; **to go ~** 更加出色; **to go one ~ (than sb.)** colloq (比某人) 更胜一筹; **it could not have been ~ received** 它非常受欢迎 **2** (more appropriately) 更恰当地; **you would be ~ advised to leave now** 你最好现在离开; **he is ~ left alone** 还是别打扰他; **you'd ~ do sth.** (advising, warning, threatening) 你最好做某事; **will she come? — she'd ~!** colloq 她会来吗?——她得来!; **more cake? — I'd ~ not** 还要蛋糕吗?——我还是不要了; **turn that radio down or, ~ still, turn it off altogether!** 把收音机开小点声, 关掉更好!

C *n* **1** (sth. preferable, more excellent) **the ~** 较好者; **much** *or* **by far the ~ of the two** 二者中的佼佼者 **2** (more desirable state of affairs) 更好的状况; **to deserve/expect/hope for ~** 应该/期望/希望更好; **a change** *or* **turn for the ~** 好转; **to change** *or* **take a turn for the ~** 好转; **for ~ or (for) worse** 无论怎样; **for ~ for worse, for richer for poorer** (in wedding vow) 不论祸福贫富; **so much the ~, all the ~** 那就更好了 **3** (superiority) 优越地位; **to get the ~ of sb./sth.** 占某人/某事物的上风; **curiosity/the problem got the ~ of her** 她抑制不住好奇心/这个问题把她难倒了; **to have the ~ of sb.** formal 比某人占优势

D **betters** *npl* dated or hum **one's ~s** (in rank, status) 上司; (in experience, ability, etc.) 更高明的人

E *vt* **1** (surpass) 超越 ‹*achievement*›; 超过 ‹*result, score*›; 打破 ‹*record*›; **to ~ one's rival's performance/offer** 表现/出价超过对手 **2** (improve) 改善 ‹*condition*›; 提高 ‹*quality, standard, status*›

F *v refl* **to ~ oneself** 自我提高

better² *n* (person placing bet) 打赌的人

betterment /ˈbetəmənt/ *n* [u] **1** formal (improvement) 改进 **2** Jur (increased value) 增值

better off

A *adj* **1** (more wealthy) 更富裕的; **their ~ neighbours** 比他们富裕的邻居; **I was ~ then** 我当时比较有钱 **2** (having more) 有更多的; **to be ~ for ...** 有更多的 ‹*space, books*› **3** (in a better situation) 处境更好的; **you'd have been ~ apologizing** 你如果道歉会更好的

B *npl* **the better-off** 富裕的人

betting /ˈbetɪŋ/

A *n* [u] **1** (gambling) 打赌 **2** (odds) 投注赔率 **3** Brit colloq (likelihood) 可能性; **what's the ~ they've forgotten?** 他们有可能忘了吗?

B *modif* 赌博的; **a ~ man** 赌徒

betting: ~ shop *n* Brit 彩票销售点; **~ slip** *n* 彩票; **~ tax** *n* 博彩税

bettor /ˈbetə(r)/ *n* esp Amer 打赌者

between /bɪˈtwiːn/

A *prep* **1** (in space or time, indicating connection, contrast) 在…之间; **there is a wall ~ the two gardens** 两个花园之间有一堵墙; **~ the ages of 12 and 18** 在12岁和18岁之间; **the link ~ smoking and cancer** 吸烟与癌症之间的联系; **nothing stands ~ us and success** 没有什么能阻止我们获得成功; **you must settle it ~ yourselves** 你们必须自己解决这件事; **I don't want to come ~ them** 我不想破坏他们之间的关系 **2** (on a scale or range) 介于…之间; **it's ~ 50 and 60 kilometres away** 它距离这里有 50 到 60 公里; **something ~ a novel and an autobiography** 介于小说和自传之间的作品 **3** (to and from) 往返于…之间; **flights ~ Beijing and London** 往返于北京和伦敦之间的航班 **4** (indicating sharing, division, combination) 由…分享; **they had only one suitcase ~ (the three of) them** 他们 (三人) 只有一个手提箱; **~ (the two of) them they had drunk the whole bottle of wine** 他们 (两个) 喝了一整瓶酒; **this is just ~ ourselves** *or* **~ you and me** 这事只限我们两人知道; **they wrote the article ~ them** 他们合写了这篇文章

B *adv* **(in) ~** (in space, scale, range) 在中间; **Oxford Street, the Euston Road, and the area (in) ~** 牛津街、尤斯顿路以及这之间的区域; **she spent four years at university and two years training, with a year off (in) ~** 她上了四年大学, 接受了两年培训, 其间休息一年; **neither red nor orange but somewhere (in) ~** 既非红色亦非橙色, 而是介于两者之间的某种颜色; ▸**few A1**

betwixt and between /bɪˈtwɪkst/ *adv* colloq dated 模棱两可地

bevel /ˈbevl/

A *n* **1** (slope) 斜面; (angle) 斜角 **2** (tool) 斜角规

B *vt* (*pres p etc.* **-ll-** Brit, **-l-** Amer) 把…切成斜面 ‹*edge, mirror*›

bevel: ~ edge *n* 斜边; **~ gear** *n* 锥齿轮

beverage /ˈbevərɪdʒ/ *n* formal 饮料

bevvy /ˈbevi/ *n* Brit colloq 一杯酒; **we had a few bevvies at the pub** 我们在酒馆喝了几杯

bevy /ˈbevi/ *n* **1** (of people or things) 一群 **2** (of game birds) 一窝

bewail /bɪˈweɪl/ *vt* 为…而悲伤 ‹*lack, loss*›

beware /bɪˈweə(r)/

A *excl* 当心

B *vi* 小心; **you must ~ of losing your wallet** 你得提防丢钱包; **'~ of pickpockets'** "当心扒手"

C *vt* 谨防; **~ doing sth./that ...** 提防做某事/提防…; **~ taking your parents for granted** 别把你的父母不当回事

bewilder /bɪˈwɪldə(r)/ *vt* 使迷惑

bewildered /bɪˈwɪldəd/ *adj* 困惑的

bewildering /bɪˈwɪldərɪŋ/ *adj* 令人困惑的; **a ~ array of goods** 令人眼花缭乱的商品陈设

bewilderingly /bɪˈwɪldərɪŋli/ *adv* 令人困惑地; **~ complex/imprecise** 复杂/不准确到难以捉摸的地步的

bewilderment /bɪˈwɪldəmənt/ *n* [u] 困惑; **to her ~** 令她困惑的是

bewitch /bɪˈwɪtʃ/ *vt* **1** (put spell on) 施魔法于 **2** (fascinate) 使着迷; **he was completely ~ed by her beauty** 他完全被她的美貌迷住了

bewitching /bɪˈwɪtʃɪŋ/ *adj* 迷人的

bewitchingly /bɪˈwɪtʃɪŋli/ *adv* 迷人地; **~ beautiful** 妖艳的

beyond /bɪˈjɒnd/

A *prep* **1** (on the further side of) 在…的那一边; (to the further side of) 向…的那一边; **~ the city walls** 在城墙的那一边; **the countries ~ the Atlantic** 大西洋彼岸的国家 **2** (after point in time) 迟于; **~ 2009/the age of 15** 2009 年/15 岁以后; **to go ~ a deadline** 超过最后期限 **3** (too far or too much for, further than) 超出; **to be ~ sb.'s reach** 某人够不着; **to be ~ sb.'s abilities** 超出某人的能力; **the authority of the inspectors goes ~ ordinary police powers** 巡官的权力高于普通警察; **to be wise ~ one's years** 少年老成; **it won't go ~ these four walls** 这件事不会有其他人知道; **it is ~ belief that ...** …, 这真是令人难以置信; **to be ~ sb.** ‹*activity*› 使某人无法想象; ‹*task*› 使某人无法完成; **it's not ~ him to make the dinner!** iron 他又不是做不了这顿饭! **4** (other than) 除…以外; **he gets nothing ~ the basic salary** 除了基本工资以外, 他没有什么收入; **~ doing sth.** 除了做某事以外

B *adv* **1** (on the further side) 在更远处; (to the further side) 向更远处; **in the room ~** 在那边的房间里; **~, there was a garden** 在更远处有一座花园 **2** (further on in time) 以后; **up to the year 2009 and ~** 至 2009 年及以后; **healthcare during pregnancy and ~** 孕期及产后的卫生保健 **3** (extending further) 更进一步; **and ~** 并且更进一步地; **they are pushing the laws to their limits and ~** 他们把这些法规推行得过了头 **4** (higher) 更多地; **he can count up to ten now, and ~** 他现在能够数到十以上了 **5** (in addition) 除外; **they provide the essentials but nothing ~** 他们只提供必需品

C *n* **the ~** 未知事物; (life after death) 来世; **the back of ~** colloq 穷乡僻壤

bezel /ˈbezl/ *n* **1** (of tool) 刃角 **2** (mount for gem) [镶嵌宝石的] 底座

b.f. *abbr* **= brought forward** 转下页

B film *n* B级影片

BFPO *abbr* Brit **= British Forces Post Office** 英军邮政

BGC *abbr* **= Bank Giro Credit**

Bhutan /buːˈtɑːn/ *pr n* 不丹

biannual /baɪˈænjuəl/ *adj* 一年两次的

bias /ˈbaɪəs/

A *n* (*pl* **~es**) **1** [u and c] (inclination) 倾向; **a female ~** 对女性的偏爱; **a left-wing ~** 左翼倾向 **2** [u and c] (prejudice) 偏见; **to display ~** 表现出偏见; **political/media ~** 政治/媒体偏见 **3** [u and c] (active discrimination) 歧视; **racial/sexual ~** 种族/性别歧视 **4** [u and c] Sewing 斜纹; **to cut sth. on the ~** 斜裁某物 **5** [u and c] Stat 偏差

B *vt* (*pres p etc.* **-s-** *or* **-ss-**) 使有偏见; **to ~ sb. against/in favour of ...** 使某人对…产生偏见/使某人偏向…

biased, biassed /ˈbaɪəst/ *adj* 有偏见的; **this report is ~** 这篇报道有倾向性; **he's politically ~** 他有政治偏见; **to be ~ against/in favour of ...** 对…有偏见/偏向…

biathlete /baɪˈæθliːt/ *n* 冬季两项赛选手

biathlon /baɪˈæθlɒn/ *n* 冬季两项 [包括越野滑雪和步枪射击]

bib /bɪb/ *n* **1** (baby's) 围嘴 **2** (of apron) 围裙的上部; (of dungarees) 工装裤的上身

Bible /ˈbaɪbl/ *n* **1** Relig (scriptures) **the ~** 《圣经》 **2** fig (authoritative book) 权威著作

Bible: ~ basher *n* colloq pej (expounder) 《圣经》的狂热宣讲者; (follower) 《圣经》的狂热信徒; **~ Belt** *n* 《圣经》地带 [指美国南部和中西部以及加拿大西部地区, 此处许多人信奉新教教义]; **~ puncher, ~ thumper** *ns* colloq pej **= ~ basher**

biblical /ˈbɪblɪkl/ *adj* **1** Relig 《圣经》的 **2** fig (very great) 非常大的 ‹*proportion, scale*›

bibliographer /ˌbɪbliˈɒɡrəfə(r)/ ▸ **p. 409** *n* 书志学家

bibliographical /ˌbɪbliəˈɡræfɪkl/, **bibliographic** /ˌbɪbliəˈɡræfɪk/ *adj* 书目的

bibliography /ˌbɪbliˈɒɡrəfi/ *n* **1** (list of specific books) 书目 **2** (list of sources) 参考文献

bibliophile /ˈbɪbliəfaɪl/ *n* (lover of books) 书籍爱好者; (collector of books) 藏书者

bibulous /ˈbɪbjʊləs/ *adj* formal or hum **1** (fond of alcohol) 嗜酒的 ‹*person*› **2** (involving alcohol) 饮酒的 ‹*party, evening*›

bicarbonate /ˌbaɪˈkɑːbənət/ *n* **1** [c] Chem 碳酸氢盐 **2** [u] **~ (of soda)** 碳酸氢钠

bicentenary /ˌbaɪsenˈtiːnəri, Amer -ˈsentəneri/, **bicentennial** /ˌbaɪsenˈteniəl/

A *ns* 200 周年纪念日

B *adjs attrib* 200 周年的

biceps /ˈbaɪseps/ *n* (*pl* **biceps**) 二头肌

bicker /ˈbɪkə(r)/ *vi* **1** (squabble) 争吵 **2** liter (flicker) ‹*candle, lamp*› 闪烁; ‹*flame*› 跳动 **3** liter (patter) ‹*water, stream*› 发潺潺声; ‹*rain*› 滴答作响

bickering /ˈbɪkərɪŋ/ *n* [u] 争吵

bicky /ˈbɪkiː/ *n* colloq 饼干

bicycle /ˈbaɪsɪkl/

A *n* 自行车; **to go to school by ~** 骑自行车上学; **to ride a ~** 骑自行车; **to fall off a ~** 从自行车上摔下来; **to get on/off a ~** 跨上/跨下自行车; **a ~ shop/wheel** 自行车行/车轮

B *vi* 骑自行车

bicycle: ~ chain *n* 自行车链条; **~ clip** *n* 裤管夹; **~ lane** *n* 自行车道; **~ messenger** *n* 自行车信使; **~ pump** *n* 自行车打气筒; **~ race** *n* 自行车赛; **~ rack** *n* 自行车停车架; **~ rickshaw** *n* 三轮人力车; **~ shed** *n* 自行车棚; **~ track** *n* 自行车道

bid¹ /bɪd/

A *n* **1** (at auction, for property or company) 出价; (for contract) 投标; **to make a ~ (for sth.)** 出价竞买 (某物); **to put in a ~** 投标 **2** (attempt) 争取; **a ~ for power** 夺权的企图; **to make a ~ for sth.** 企图得到某物; **an Olympic ~** 奥运会的申办 **3** (in card games) 叫牌; **to make a ~** 叫牌; **'no ~'** "不叫牌"; **is it my ~?** 轮到我叫牌了吗?

B *vt* (*pres p* **-dd-**; *pt, pp* **bid**) **1** Comm, Fin 出价 **2** (in card games) 叫; **to ~ four spades/six clubs** 叫 4 黑桃/6 梅花

C *vi* (*pres p* **-dd-**; *pt, pp* **bid**) **1** Comm (make offer) ‹*buyer*› 出价竞买; ‹*contractor*› 投标争取; **to ~ against sb.** 与某人竞价 **2** (in card games) 叫牌

Phrasal verb

- **bid up** *vt* **1** [**~ sth. up, ~ up sth.**] (increase) 抬高 ‹*price, rent*› **2** [**~ sb. up, ~ up sb.**] (force to pay more) 迫使对…出高价

bid² *vt* (*pt* **bid** *or* **bade**, *pp* **bid** *or* **bidden**) **1** (say in greeting) 表达; **to ~ sb. farewell/good morning/welcome** 向某人道别/问早安/表示欢迎 **2** archaic or liter (command) 命令; **to ~ sb. (to) do sth.** 吩咐某人做某事

biddable /ˈbɪdəbl/ *adj* **1** (obedient) 听话的 **2** (in card games) 可叫牌的 ‹*hand, suit*› **3** Comm 可出价的

bidden /ˈbɪdn/ *pp* ▸**bid²**

bidder /ˈbɪdə(r)/ *n* **1** (at auction) 出价者; **to go to the highest ~** 卖给出价最高的人 **2** (for contract, land, property) 投标者; **~s for the company** 那家公司的投标商 **3** (in card games) 叫牌人

bidding /ˈbɪdɪŋ/ *n* [u] **1** Comm (at auction, for property, company, contract) 出价; **the ~ opened at £1 million** 起拍价为 100 万英镑; **the ~ closed at £50,000** 落槌价为 5 万英镑 **2** (command) 命令; **he did my ~** 他听命于我; **he did it at my ~** 他是按我命令做的; **she needed no second ~** 她闻令即行 **3** (in card games) 叫牌

bidding war *n* 竞标大战

biddy /ˈbɪdi/ *n* colloq 婆娘

bide /baɪd/

A *vt* **to ~ one's time** 等待时机

B *vi* archaic 等待

bidet /ˈbiːdeɪ, Amer biːˈdeɪ/ *n* 坐浴盆

bidirectional /ˌbaɪdəˈrekʃənl, -dɪ-/ *adj* 双向的

bid price *n* 买入价

biennial /baɪˈeniəl/

A *adj* 两年生的 ‹*plant*›; 两年一次的 ‹*event*›

B *n* **1** (plant) 两年生植物 **2** (event) 两年一次的活动

bier /bɪə(r)/ *n* (stand for coffin) 棺材架; (stand for body) 停尸架

biff /bɪf/ colloq

A *vt* 猛击

B *n* 猛击

bifocal /baɪˈfəʊkl/

A *adj* 双焦的 ‹*lens*›; 双光的 ‹*spectacles*›

B **bifocals** *npl* 双光眼镜

big /bɪɡ/

A *adj* **1** (in size, quantity, degree, intensity) 大的; **a ~ book** (thick) 厚书; (large-format) 大开本的书; **a ~ bowl of soup** 一大碗汤; **this car has a ~ger engine** 这辆车的发动机更大; **I had a ~ lunch** 我午饭吃得很饱; **a ~ thank you to everyone** 向大家深表谢意; **he gave me a ~ smile** 他冲我咧嘴一笑; **give granny a ~ kiss** 使劲亲奶奶一下; **to do sth. in a ~ way** 大张旗鼓地做某事; **he fell for her in a ~ way** 他深深地爱上了她; **to have a ~ mouth** colloq (talk too much) 喋喋不休; (reveal secret) 口风不紧; ▸**boot¹ A1** **2** (in build) 高个的; (fat) 胖的; (plump) 丰满的; (pregnant) 大肚子的; **to get ~** (tall) 长 (得更) 高; (fat) 变 (得更) 胖 **3** fig (grown-up) 长大了的; **she's a ~ girl** 她是个大姑娘了 **4** *attrib* colloq (elder) 年龄较大的; **my ~ sister/brother** 我姐姐/哥哥 **5** *attrib* colloq (capital) 大写的 ‹*letter*› **6** (in scope) 宏大的 ‹*plans*›; 大规模的 ‹*operation*›; **to have ~ ideas** 雄心勃勃; **what's the ~ idea?** 你这是什么意思? **7** *attrib* colloq (to great degree) 十足的; **I'm your ~gest fan** 我是你最狂热的追随者; **I'm not a ~ reader** 我不怎么看书 **8** (important) 重要的; **the ~ three** 三巨头; **China is one of**

b

b

the ~ five 中国是五大国之一; **a/the ~ day/match** 关键的一天/一场比赛; **something ~** 大事; **he's ~ in the music business** colloq 他在音乐界颇具影响力; **to look ~** colloq 显得了不起 9 colloq (popular) 大受欢迎的 ‹*band, activity*›; **miniskirts were ~ in the sixties** 迷你裙在 60 年代风靡一时 10 colloq (enthusiastic) 热心的; **to be ~ on sb./sth.** 热衷于某人/某事物 11 (generous) usu iron 大方的; **that's ~ of you!** colloq iron 你还挺大方啊!
B *adv* colloq **to talk ~** 说大话; **to think ~** 想干一番大事; **to go over** *or* **down ~ (with sb.)** 大受 (某人) 欢迎; **to make it ~** 取得成功; **she's finally made it ~** 她最终干出了点名堂

bigamist /ˈbɪɡəmɪst/ *n* 重婚者

bigamous /ˈbɪɡəməs/ *adj* 重婚的

bigamy /ˈbɪɡəmi/ *n* [u] 重婚罪

big: Big Apple *n* colloq **the Big Apple** 大苹果城 [纽约市的别称]; **~ band** *n* 大乐队 [指流行于20世纪30至50年代的大型爵士乐队或伴舞乐队]; **~ bang** *n* 1 Astron (宇宙) 大爆炸; 2 **the Big Bang** Brit [1986年伦敦证券交易所实施的] "大爆炸"改革; **Big Ben** *n* 大本钟; **~-boned** *adj* 大块头的 ‹*person*›; **~ boys** *npl* colloq (people) 大人物; (organization) 势力雄厚的组织; **Big Brother** *n* 老大哥 [指独裁者或独裁政府]; **Big Brother is watching you** 老大哥正在看着你呢 [源自奥威尔的小说《一九八四》]; **~ business** *n* 1 [c] (companies) 大企业; 2 [u] (activity) 大生意; **~ cat** *n* 大型猫科动物; **~ cheese** *n* colloq 大亨; **~ city** *n* 大都市; **~ crunch** *n* Astron 大坍缩; **~ dipper** *n* 1 Brit dated 过山车; 2 **the Big Dipper** Amer Astron 北斗七星; **~ end** *n* Brit Aut [连杆的] 大端; **~ fish** *n* fig colloq 大人物; **a ~ fish in a small pond** 小地方的大人物; **~ game** *n* 大猎物; **~ game hunter** *n* 大猎物猎手; **~ game hunting** *n* [u] 大猎物狩猎; **~ government** *n* [u] esp Amer 大政府 [过多干涉公民生活]; **~ gun** *n* 1 Mil 大炮; 2 colloq (important person) 大人物; **~ hand** *n* 分针; **~-head** *n* colloq pej 自负的人; **~-headed** *adj* colloq pej 自负的; **~-headedness** *n* [u] colloq pej 自负; **~-hearted** *adj* 仁慈慷慨的; **~ hitter** *n* colloq 大人物

> **Big Ben**
>
> 大本钟。指英国议会大厦钟楼内的大钟。最初指大钟的钟铃，正式名称为 Great Bell。大钟的设计者是埃德蒙·贝克特·丹尼森 (Edmund Beckett Denison)，大钟有 4 个钟面，直径长 7 米。钟铃重 13.5 吨、直径 2.7 米。1859 年，大钟第一次敲响。大本钟这一称呼的由来，通常认为与当年负责监制该钟的政府专员本杰明·霍尔爵士 (Sir Benjamin Hall) 有关，因为他名字的昵称是 Ben，且体态丰硕，故被议员们称为 Big Ben。1859 年议会在讨论钟铃的名称时，有人建议以 Big Ben 命名，自此流传开来。也有人认为该名称源自当时的一位重量级拳击冠军本杰明·康特 (Benjamin Caunt)。自 1924 年以来，大本钟一直为 BBC 报时，现已成为伦敦的标志性景观。

bight /baɪt/ *n* 海湾; **the Great Australian B~** 大澳大利亚湾

big: ~ money *n* [u] colloq 大笔的钱; **to make ~ money** 挣大钱; **~mouth** *n* 1 colloq pej (indiscreet person) 多嘴的人; 2 (boastful person) 爱吹牛的人; **~-mouthed** *adj* 1 colloq pej (indiscreet) 多嘴的; 2 (boastful) 爱吹牛的; **~ name** *n* (person) 名人; (organization) 知名机构; **to be a ~ name (in sth.)** (在某方面) 有名; **~ noise** *n* colloq 要人

bigot /ˈbɪɡət/ *n* pej [政治、宗教、种族等问题上的] 偏执者

bigoted /ˈbɪɡətɪd/ *adj* pej 偏执的

bigotry /ˈbɪɡətri/ *n* [u] pej 偏执

big: ~ screen *n* **the ~ screen** 大银幕 [指电影]; **~ shot** *n* colloq 有权势的人; **Big Smoke** *n* Brit hum **the Big Smoke** 大城市 [尤指伦敦]; **~ stick** *n* colloq 大棒 [指军事、经济、政治等方面的威胁]; **to carry** *or* **wield a ~ stick** 实行大棒政策; **~ talk** *n* [u] colloq 大话; **to be full of ~ talk** 夸夸其谈; **~-ticket** *adj attrib* 昂贵的; **~-ticket items** 昂贵的项目

big time
A *n* [u] colloq **the ~** 最高水平
B **big-time** *modif* 第一流的; **big-time gambler** 赌场圣手

big: ~ toe *n* 大脚趾; **~ top** *n* 1 lit (tent) 马戏场大帐篷; 2 fig (circus) 马戏表演; **~ wheel** *n* 1 Brit (at funfair) 摩天轮; 2 colloq (important person) 大人物; **~wig** *n* colloq 大亨; **~ word** *n* 大词

bijou /ˈbiːʒuː/ *adj* esp Brit 小巧玲珑的 ‹*residence*›

bike /baɪk/ colloq
A *n* 1 (cycle) 自行车; **to ride a ~** 骑自行车; **a ~ race** 自行车赛 2 (motorbike) 摩托车
B *vi* 1 (cycle) 骑自行车; **she ~s to work every day** 她每天骑自行车上班 2 (motorbike) 骑摩托车

biker /ˈbaɪkə(r)/ *n* colloq 1 (motorcyclist) 骑摩托车的人 2 (cyclist) 骑自行车的人

bike: ~ rack *n* = **bicycle rack**; **~ shed** *n* = **bicycle shed**

bikini /bɪˈkiːni/ *n* 比基尼泳装

bilateral /ˌbaɪˈlætərəl/ *adj* 1 (undertaken by or affecting both parties) 双边的 2 (on both sides of an axis) 在两侧的

bilaterally /ˌbaɪˈlætərəli/ *adv* 1 (by both parties) 双边地 2 (on both sides) 在两侧

bilberry /ˈbɪlbəri, Amer -beri/ *n* 欧洲越橘

bile /baɪl/ *n* [u] 1 Physiol 胆汁 2 dated or formal (anger) 愤怒

bile duct *n* 胆管

bi-level /ˈbaɪlevl/
A *adj* 1 (on two levels) 双层的 2 Amer (with a semi-basement) 半层入口的 ‹*house*›
B *n* Amer 半层入口房屋 [指一种二层房屋，底层有一半低于地面，入口在半层处]

bilge /bɪldʒ/ *n* 1 [c] Naut (interior of ship's hull) 底舱; (outer area of ship's hull) 船舭 2 [u] colloq dated (nonsense) 废话

bilge: ~ pump *n* 舱底水泵; **~ water** *n* [u] 舱底污水

bilharzia /bɪlˈhɑːtsɪə/ ▸**p. 377** *n* [u] 血吸虫病

bilingual /ˌbaɪˈlɪŋɡwəl/ *adj* 双语的; **she's ~ in Chinese and English** 她能讲汉语和英语两种语言

bilingualism /ˌbaɪˈlɪŋɡwəlɪzəm/ *n* [u] (ability) 熟练双语能力; (condition) 双语制

bilious /ˈbɪlɪəs/ *adj* 1 Med (nauseous) 恶心的 2 fig (distasteful) 难看的

bilk /bɪlk/ *vt* 1 (cheat) 欺骗; **to ~ sb. of** *or* **out of sth.** 从某人处骗取某物 2 (thwart) 挫败

bill[1] /bɪl/
A *n* 1 Comm (for services, utilities) 账单; **to pay** *or* **settle a ~** 结账; **add it to** *or* **put it on the ~** 把它记在账上; **to fit** *or* **fill the ~** fig colloq 符合要求 2 Jur, Pol 议案 3 Brit (printed advertisement) 海报 4 Theat, Cin 节目单; **to head** *or* **top the ~** 领衔主演 5 ▸**p. 174** Amer (banknote) 钞票 6 (certificate) 证明书; **to have a clean ~ of health** «*person*» 有健康证书; fig «*company*» 有清白证明
B *vt* 1 Comm (for payment) 给…开账单 ‹*person, company*›; **to ~ sb. (for sth.)** 给某人开具 (某物的) 账单 2 Theat (advertise) 宣布; **the show is ~ed as a comedy** 这出戏被宣传为喜剧

bill[2] Zool
A *n* 喙
B *vi* «*birds*» 接喙; **to ~ and coo** colloq 卿卿我我

billboard /ˈbɪlbɔːd/ *n* 广告牌

billet /ˈbɪlɪt/
A *n* 临时宿营地
B *vt* 安排…临时住宿

bill: ~fold *n* Amer 皮夹子; **~ hook** *n* 钩镰

billiard /ˈbɪlɪəd/: **~ ball** *n* 台球; **~ cue** *n* 台球杆

billiards /ˈbɪlɪədz/ ▸**p. 307**
A *npl* + *v sing* 台球
B **billiard** *modif* 台球的 ‹*player, match, cue*›

billiard table *n* 台球桌

billing /ˈbɪlɪŋ/ *n* [u] 1 Comm 开具发票; **itemized ~** 明细账单的开具; **~ address** 发票地址 2 Theat 演员表名次; **to get top ~** 领衔主演 3 Zool (birds' rubbing of bills) 接喙

billion /ˈbɪljən/ ▸**p. 521**
A *n* 十亿
B **billions** *npl* colloq 大量
C *adj* 1 (a thousand million) 十亿的; **two ~ dollars** 二十亿美元 2 colloq (lots of) 大量的; **a ~ people** 无数人

billionaire /ˌbɪljəˈneə(r)/ *n* 亿万富翁

billionth /ˈbɪljənθ/
A *adj attrib* 1 (as occurrence) 第十亿的 2 (as fraction) 十亿分之一的
B *n* 1 (fraction) 十亿分之一 2 (occurrence) 第十亿

bill: ~ of exchange *n* 汇票; **~ of fare** *n* 菜单; **~ of lading** /ˈleɪdɪŋ/ *n* 提货单; **~ of rights** *n* 权利法案; **the B~ of Rights** Amer Hist 《人权法案》; **~ of sale** *n* 转让契据

billow /ˈbɪləʊ/
A *n* 1 (of smoke) 滚滚浓烟; (of steam) 升腾的蒸汽; (of clouds) 滚滚乌云 2 **the ~s** liter (sea) 大海
B *vi* «*sails*» 鼓起; «*clouds*» 翻滚; «*smoke*» 喷涌

Phrasal verb
- **billow out** *vi* 1 (swell outwards) «*clothing*» 鼓起 2 (escape in billows) «*steam*» 升腾

billposter /ˈbɪlpəʊstə(r)/, **billsticker** /ˈbɪlstɪkə(r)/ ▸**p. 409** *ns* 广告张贴者

billy /ˈbɪli/ *n* 1 Brit, Austral (cooking pot) **~ (can)** (tin) 带盖金属罐; (enamel) 带盖搪瓷罐 2 Amer (truncheon) 木棒

billy goat *n* 公山羊

billy-o, billy-oh /ˈbɪlɪəʊ/ *n* [u] colloq dated **to run like ~** 拼命跑

biltong /ˈbɪltɒŋ/ *n* [u] esp S Afr 干肉条

bimbo /ˈbɪmbəʊ/ *n* colloq pej 傻靓妞儿

bimetallic strip /ˌbaɪmɪˌtælɪk ˈstrɪp/ *n* 双金属条

bimonthly /ˌbaɪˈmʌnθli/
A *adj* 1 (two-monthly) 两月一次的 2 (twice-monthly) 一月两次的
B *adv* 1 (every two months) 两月一次地 2 (twice a month) 一月两次地

BIN *abbr* = **Bank Identification Number** 银行标识号

bin /bɪn/
A *n* 1 Brit (for rubbish) 垃圾箱; **put** *or* **throw it in the ~** 把它扔到垃圾箱里去 2 (for storage) 容器; (for grain) 仓; (for wine) 酒瓶架
B *vt* (*pres p etc.* **-nn-**) colloq 把…扔进垃圾箱

binary /ˈbaɪnəri/ *adj* 1 (involving a pair) 由两部分组成的 2 Math, Comput 二进制的

binary: ~ code *n* [u] 二进制码; **~ digit** *n* 二进制位; **~ number** *n* 二进制数; **~ star** *n* 双星; **~ system** *n* 1 Math, Comput 二进制; 2 (two-part system) 双轨制; **~ weapon** *n* 合成化学武器

binaural /bɪˈnɔːrəl, baɪ-/ *adj* 1 (involving both ears) 双耳的 2 Elec, Mus 两路立体声的

bind /baɪnd/
A *vt* (*pt, pp* **bound**) 1 (tie up) 捆 ‹*item, person*›; 束 ‹*hair*›; 包扎 ‹*wound*›; **to ~ sth. into bundles** 把某物扎成一捆一捆的; **bound and gagged** 被捆住手脚塞住嘴 2 (unite) 使结合; **to ~ together** 使…关系密切 ‹*people,*

nations›; **to ~ sb. to sb.** «*act, feeling*» 使某人与某人结合在一起 **3** (hold) 束缚; **to ~ sb. to sth.** «*promise, law*» 使…受某事物的约束 ‹*person, group*›; **to ~ sb. to secrecy** 使某人保证不泄密; **to ~ oneself (to do sth.)** 保证（做某事） **4** (hold together) «*ice*» 冻结 ‹*soil*›; 黏合 ‹*ingredients*›; **~ the mixture with an egg** 加一个鸡蛋让混合料黏合在一起 **5** Sewing 给…镶边; **the blanket is bound with satin** 毛毯以缎子包边 **6** Publg 装订 ‹*book*›

B *vi* (*pt, pp* **bound**) **1** (cohere) «*soil*» 冻结; «*ingredients*» 黏合 **2** Chem **to ~ to sth.** 与某物化合 **3** (stick) 锁死; **when the brakes are applied, the wheels ~** 刹车时车轮会抱死

C *n* colloq **1** (bother) 麻烦事; **to be a ~** 是个麻烦; **housework is a real ~** 做家务真讨厌 **2** (difficulty) 困境; **to be in a ~** 陷入困境

Phrasal verbs

- **bind over** *vt* [**~ sb. over, ~ over sb.**] Jur «*judge*» 令…具结保证; **he was bound over to keep the peace** 他被责令具保不再闹事
- **bind up** *vt* **1** [**~ sth. up, ~ up sth.**] 把…扎起来; **the nurse will ~ up your wounds** 护士会为你包扎伤口 **2** **to be bound up in ...** fig colloq (involved with) 忙于…; **he's too bound up in his work to have time for his children** 他工作太忙，没时间和孩子们在一起; **to be bound up with ...** 与…紧密相连; **my life became closely bound up with hers** 我的生活和她的密不可分

binder /ˈbaɪndə(r)/ *n* **1** (for papers) 活页夹 **2** Agric 割捆机 **3** Constr, Ind 黏合剂 **4** = **bookbinder**

binder twine *n* [u] 捆扎绳

bindery /ˈbaɪndəri/ *n* 装订工场

binding /ˈbaɪndɪŋ/

A *n* **1** [c] (book cover) 封皮 **2** [u and c] Sewing 镶边 **3** [c] (on ski) 皮靴固定装置

B *adj* 有约束力的 ‹*agreement, commitment*›; **to be ~ on sb.** 对某人有约束力

bindweed /ˈbaɪndwiːd/ *n* [u] 旋花属植物

bin end *n* 清仓处理的酒

binge /bɪndʒ/ colloq

A *n* 大吃大喝; **to go on a ~** 饮酒行乐; **to have a ~** 饮食无度 [尤指进食障碍]

B *vi* (*pres p* **~ing** *or* **binging**; *pt, pp* **~d**) 尽情享用; **to ~ on chocolate** 大嚼巧克力

binge: ~ drinker *n* colloq 酒徒; **~ drinking** *n* [u] colloq 狂饮; **~ eating** *n* [u] colloq 暴饮暴食

bingo /ˈbɪŋɡəʊ/ ▸**p. 307**

A *n* [u] 宾果游戏; **~ hall** 宾果游戏厅

B *excl* (in bingo) 赢了; (in any success) 好

bingo: ~ caller *n* 宾果游戏报数员; **~ card** *n* 宾果游戏数字卡

bin: ~liner *n* Brit 垃圾桶袋; **~man** /-mæn/ *n* Brit colloq 垃圾工

binnacle /ˈbɪnəkl/ *n* 罗经柜

binocular /bɪˈnɒkjʊlə(r)/ *adj* 双目的

binoculars /bɪˈnɒkjʊləz/ *npl* 双筒望远镜

binomial /baɪˈnəʊmɪəl/

A *n* 二项式

B *adj* 二项式的

bint /bɪnt/ *n* Brit sl pej 娘儿们 sl pej

bioactive /ˌbaɪəʊˈæktɪv/ *adj* 生物活性的

biochemical /ˌbaɪəʊˈkemɪkl/ *adj* 生物化学的

biochemist /ˌbaɪəʊˈkemɪst/ ▸**p. 409** *n* 生化学家

biochemistry /ˌbaɪəʊˈkemɪstri/ *n* **1** [u] Sci 生物化学; **~ laboratory** 生物化学实验室 **2** [c] (chemical structure) 生化结构; (chemical behaviour) 生化特性

biocidal /ˌbaɪəʊˈsaɪdl/ *adj* 危害生命的; **to be highly ~ for** *or* **to a range of micro-organisms** 危害一系列微生物

bioclimate /ˈbaɪəʊklaɪmɪt/ *n* 生物气候

biocompatible /ˌbaɪəʊkəmˈpætəbl/ *adj* 生物适合的

biocomputer /ˈbaɪəʊkəmˌpjuːtə(r)/ *n* 生物计算机

biocomputing /ˌbaɪəʊkəmˈpjuːtɪŋ/ *n* [u] 生物计算

biocontrol /ˈbaɪəʊkəntrəʊl/ *n* = **biological control**

biodegradable /ˌbaɪəʊdɪˈɡreɪdəbl/ *adj* 可生物降解的

biodegrade /ˌbaɪəʊdɪˈɡreɪd/ *vi* 生物降解

biodiesel /ˈbaɪəʊˌdiːzl/ *n* [u] 生物柴油

biodiversity /ˌbaɪəʊdɪˈvɜːsəti, -daɪ-/ *n* [u] 生物多样性

bioenergy /ˈbaɪəʊenədʒi/ *n* [u] 生物能

bioengineering /ˌbaɪəʊˌendʒɪˈnɪərɪŋ/ *n* [u] 生物工程

bioethics /ˌbaɪəʊˈeθɪks/ *npl* + *v sing* 生物伦理学

biofeedback /ˌbaɪəʊˈfiːdbæk/ *n* [u] 生物反馈

biofilm /ˈbaɪəʊfɪlm/ *n* 生物膜

biofuel /ˈbaɪəʊfjʊəl/ *n* [u and c] 生物燃料

biographer /baɪˈɒɡrəfə(r)/ ▸**p. 409** *n* 传记作者

biographical /ˌbaɪəˈɡræfɪkl/ *adj* 传记的

biography /baɪˈɒɡrəfi/ *n* [c and u] 传记; **~ is a popular branch of literature** 传记是一种通俗文学

biohazard /ˈbaɪəʊˌhæzəd/ *n* 生物危害

bioinformatics /ˌbaɪəʊˌɪnfəˈmætɪks/ *npl* + *v sing* 生物信息学

biological /ˌbaɪəˈlɒdʒɪkl/ *adj* **1** (relating to living organisms) 生物的 **2** (using enzymes) 加酶的

biological: ~ clock *n* 生物钟; **~ control** *n* **1** [u] (method) 生物防治; **2** [c] (agent) 生物天敌

biologically /ˌbaɪəˈlɒdʒɪkli/ *adv* 在生物方面

biological: ~ parent *n* 生身父母; **~ shield** *n* 生物屏蔽 [在反应器或放射源周围设置的辐射吸收体]; **~ warfare** *n* [u] 生物战; **~ washing powder** *n* [u and c] 生物洗衣粉; **~ waste** *n* [u] 生物废弃物; **~ weapon** *n* 生物武器

biologist /baɪˈɒlədʒɪst/ *n* ▸**p. 409** 生物学家

biology /baɪˈɒlədʒi/ *n* **1** [u] (branch of science) 生物学; **a ~ department** 生物系 **2** [c] (organism's nature) 生理

bioluminescence /ˌbaɪəʊˌluːmɪˈnesns/ *n* [u] **1** (emitting light) 生物发光 **2** (light) 生物发的光

biomarker /ˈbaɪəʊˌmɑːkə(r)/ *n* 生物标记

biomass /ˈbaɪəʊmæs/ *n* [u] **1** Biol 生物量 **2** (used as fuel) 有机燃料

biomathematics /ˌbaɪəʊmæθˈmætɪks/ *npl* + *v sing* 生物数学

biome /ˈbaɪəʊm/ *n* 生物群落区

biomechanics /ˌbaɪəʊmɪˈkænɪks/ *npl* + *v sing* **1** (subject) 生物力学 **2** (practice) 生物力学上的运作

biomedical /ˌbaɪəʊˈmedɪkl/ *adj* 生物医学的

biometrics /ˌbaɪəʊˈmetrɪks/ *npl* + *v sing* 生物统计学

bionic /baɪˈɒnɪk/ *adj* 仿生学的

bionics /baɪˈɒnɪks/ *npl* + *v sing* 仿生学

biophysical /ˌbaɪəʊˈfɪzɪkl/ *adj* **1** (relating to biophysics) 生物物理学的 **2** (biological and physical) 生物与物理的

biophysicist /ˌbaɪəʊˈfɪzɪsɪst/ ▸**p. 409** *n* 生物物理学家

biophysics /ˌbaɪəʊˈfɪzɪks/ *npl* + *v sing* 生物物理学

biopic /ˈbaɪəʊpɪk/ *n* colloq 传记片

biopsy /ˈbaɪɒpsi/ *n* 活组织检查

bioregion /ˈbaɪəʊˌriːdʒən/ *n* 生物区

biorhythm /ˈbaɪəʊˌrɪðəm/ *n* 生物节律

BIOS /ˈbaɪɒs/ *abbr* = **basic input-output system** 基本输入输出系统

biosafety /ˌbaɪəʊˈseɪfti/ *n* [u] 生物安全性

biosecurity /ˌbaɪəʊsɪˈkjʊərəti/ *n* [u] 生物安全保障

biosensor /ˌbaɪəʊˈsensə(r)/ *n* 生物传感器

biosphere /ˈbaɪəʊsfɪə(r)/ *n* 生物圈

biosphere reserve *n* 生物圈保护区

biosynthesis /ˌbaɪəʊˈsɪnθəsɪs/ *n* [u] 生物合成

biosynthetic /ˌbaɪəʊsɪnˈθetɪk/ *adj* 生物合成的

biota /baɪˈəʊtə/ *npl* 生物区

biotech /ˈbaɪəʊtek/ *n* [u] = **biotechnology**

biotechnologist /ˌbaɪəʊtekˈnɒlədʒɪst/ ▸**p. 409** *n* 生物工艺学家

biotechnology /ˌbaɪəʊtekˈnɒlədʒi/ *n* [u] 生物工艺学; **a ~ company** 生物科技公司

bioterrorism /ˌbaɪəʊˈterərɪzəm/ *n* [u] 生物恐怖主义

bioterrorist /ˌbaɪəʊˈterərɪst/ *n* 生物恐怖分子

biotope /ˈbaɪətəʊp/ *n* 生物小区

biowarfare /ˌbaɪəʊˈwɔːfeə(r)/ *n* [u] = **biological warfare**

bipartisan /ˌbaɪpɑːtɪˈzæn, Amer baɪˈpɑːtɪzn/ *adj* **1** (involving the agreement of two) 为两党所拥护的 **2** (made up of two) 由两党构成的

bipartite /baɪˈpɑːtaɪt/ *adj* **1** (between two parties) 有两方面参加的; **a ~ treaty** 双边条约 **2** (having two parts) 有两个部分的; **a ~ leaf** 二深裂叶

biped /ˈbaɪped/ *n* 二足动物

bipedal /baɪˈpiːdl/ *adj* 双足行走的 ‹*animal, species*›; 用两足的 ‹*gait*›

biplane /ˈbaɪpleɪn/ *n* 双翼飞机

bipolar /baɪˈpəʊlə(r)/ *adj* **1** ▸**p. 377** Psych 躁郁的; **~ disorder** 躁狂抑郁性精神病 **2** (having two poles) 有两极的 ‹*planet, transistor*›

birch /bɜːtʃ/

A *n* **1** [c] (tree) 白桦树 **2** [u] (wood) 桦木 **3** [c] **~ (rod)** Hist 桦条鞭; **to get the ~** 受到惩罚

B *vt* Hist 用桦条鞭打

birch tree *n* 桦树

birchwood /ˈbɜːtʃwʊd/ *n* [u] 桦木; **~ floor/furniture** 桦木地板/家具

bird /bɜːd/ *n* **1** Zool 鸟; **a ~ in the hand is worth two in the bush** Prov 双鸟在林不如一鸟在手; **a little ~ told me** colloq 是一位消息灵通人士告诉我的; **~s of a feather flock together** Prov 物以类聚; **(strictly) for the ~s** colloq 毫无用处; **the ~s and the bees** colloq 基本的性知识 **2** Brit colloq (girl) 姑娘; **to pull the ~s** 吸引女孩子 **3** colloq (person) 家伙; **a funny** *or* **queer old ~** 古怪的老家伙

bird: ~ bath *n* 鸟澡盆; **~-brain** *n* colloq 傻瓜; **~cage** *n* 鸟笼; **~ call** *n* **1** (bird's sound) 鸟叫声; **2** (instrument) 鸟叫声模仿器

birder /ˈbɜːdə(r)/ *n* = **birdwatcher**

bird: ~ fancier *n* 养鸟爱好者; **~ feeder** *n* 鸟食槽; **~ flu** ▸**p. 377** *n* [u] 禽流感

birdie /ˈbɜːdi/ *n* **1** colloq (bird) 小鸟 **2** (in golf) 小鸟球

birding /ˈbɜːdɪŋ/ *n* [u] = **birdwatching**

bird: ~ life *n* [u] 鸟类; **~-like** *adj* 小鸟似的; **~lime** *n* [u] 粘鸟胶; **~ of paradise** *n* 天堂鸟; **~ of prey** *n* 猛禽; **~ sanctuary** *n* 鸟类保护区; **~ scarer** *n* **1** (device) 惊鸟器; **2** (person) 赶鸟的雇工; **~seed** *n* [u] 鸟食; **~'s-eye view** *n* 鸟瞰; **~'s nest** *n* 鸟巢; **~'s nest soup** *n* [u] 燕窝汤; **~song** *n* [u and c] 鸟鸣; **~ species** *n* 鸟的种类; **~ table** *n* 鸟食台; **~watcher** *n* 观鸟者; **~watching** *n* [u] 观鸟

b

biro® /ˈbaɪərəʊ/ *n* (*pl* **~s**) Brit 伯罗圆珠笔; **to write in ~** 用伯罗圆珠笔书写

birth /bɜːθ/ *n* [1] [u] (start of life) 出生; **at ~** 出生时; **he is Swiss by ~** 他是瑞士血统; **of high/low ~** 出身高贵/低微的; **blind from ~** 天生失明的 [2] [u and c] (process of giving birth) 分娩; **to give ~ to** 生 ‹*animal, young*›; **a difficult/easy ~** 难产/顺产 [3] [c] fig (beginning) 创始; **the ~ of a new era** 新时代的开始

birth certificate *n* 出生证明

birth control
[A] *n* [u] 节育; **to practise ~** 实行计划生育
[B] *modif* (in society) 计划生育的; (by couple) 避孕的

birthday /ˈbɜːθdeɪ/ *n* 生日; **to wish sb. (a) happy ~** 祝某人生日快乐; **on my ~** 在我生日那天

birthday: ~ boy *n* (man) 寿星; (boy) 小寿星; **~ cake** *n* 生日蛋糕; **~ card** *n* 生日贺卡; **~ girl** *n* (woman) 女寿星; (girl) 小女寿星; **~ honours** *npl* Brit 寿辰勋誉; **~ party** *n* 生日聚会; **~ present** *n* 生日礼物; **~ suit** *n* **in one's ~ suit** colloq hum 光着身子

birth: ~ defect *n* 先天缺陷; **~mark** *n* 胎记; **~ pangs** *npl* [1] Med 分娩时的阵痛; [2] fig 初期的艰难; **~ pill** *n* = **contraceptive A**; **~place** *n* [1] lit 出生地; [2] fig 发源地; **~rate** *n* 出生率; **~right** *n* (gen) 与生俱来的权利; (of first-born) 长子的特权; **~s column** *n* 出生公告专栏; **~ sign** *n* 出生时的星座; **~stone** *n* 诞生石; **~ weight** *n* 出生时的体重

biscuit /ˈbɪskɪt/
[A] *n* [1] [c] Brit (thin crisp cake) 饼干; **plain/sweet ~s** 淡/甜饼干; **to take the ~** Brit colloq (be most surprising) 极为惊人; (be most annoying) 极其讨厌 [2] [c] Amer (soft bread) 小松饼 [3] [u] (colour) 淡褐色
[B] ▸**p. 134** *adj* 淡褐色的

biscuit: ~ barrel *n* 饼干桶; **~ factory** *n* 饼干厂; **~ tin** *n* 饼干罐

bisect /baɪˈsekt/ *vt* [1] (divide into two) 把…分为两部分 [2] Math 把…二等分

bisection /baɪˈsekʃn/ *n* [1] [u and c] (division into two) 一分为二 [2] [u] Math 二等分

bisector /baɪˈsektə(r)/ *n* (line) 平分线; (plane) 平分面

bisexual /baɪˈsekʃʊəl/
[A] *adj* [1] (attracted to both sexes) 双性恋的 [2] (having characteristics of both sexes) 两性的
[B] *n* 双性恋者

Bishkek /biːʃˈkek/ *pr n* 比什凯克

bishop /ˈbɪʃəp/ *n* [1] Relig 主教 [2] (in chess) 象

bishopric /ˈbɪʃəprɪk/ *n* [1] (position) 主教职位 [2] (diocese) 主教辖区

bismuth /ˈbɪzməθ/ *n* [u] 铋

bison /ˈbaɪsn/ *n* (*pl* **bison**) 野牛

bisque /bɪsk/
[A] *n* [u and c] [1] Culin 贝类浓汤; **lobster ~** 龙虾浓汤 [2] (earthenware) 素瓷 [3] (colour) 淡褐色
[B] *adj* 淡褐色的

Bissau /bɪˈsaʊ/ *pr n* 比绍

bistro /ˈbiːstrəʊ/ *n* 小餐馆

bit[1] /bɪt/
[A] *n* [1] (piece) 一小块; **a ~ of paper/string/wood/coal** 一小片纸/一小段绳/一小片木头/一小块煤块; **a little ~ of garden** 一座小小的花园; **to be in/fall to ~s** 变成碎片; **the ~s of an appliance** 器械的配件; **blown to ~s** 被炸得粉碎; **~s and bobs** *or* **pieces** colloq 零碎的东西; **thrilled to ~s** colloq 激动不已; **to love sb./sth. to ~s** colloq 深爱某人/某事物 [2] (small amount) (of time) **a ~** 一会儿; (of distance) 一小段; (of news) 一些; (of sun, rain, luck, trouble) 少许; (of silence) 片刻; **to have/get into a ~ of difficulty** 有点/遇到一点困难; **a ~ of rain** 零星小雨; **let me have a ~ of peace** 让我清静一会儿; **there's a ~ of his father in him** 他有点像他父亲; **I've got a ~ of a cold** 我有点感冒了; **she's a ~ of a fool** 她有点傻; **a ~ of skiing/walking** 滑一会儿雪/走一会儿路; **to do one's ~** colloq 干分内的事; **~ by ~** 渐渐地 [3] **quite a ~ of ..., a good** *or* **nice ~ of ...** colloq (a lot) 相当多的…; **not a ~ (of it)** colloq (none) 一点也不; **not a ~ of good/use** 一点用都没有; **every ~ of sth.** 整个儿; **every ~ of her wanted to go** 她一心想要去 [4] Brit (of text, film) 一部分; **the end ~** 结尾部分 [5] **~ on the side** Brit sl 第三者 [6] Amer dated colloq (coin) 12.5 美分 [仅用于偶倍数]; **not worth two ~s** 一文不值
[B] *adv* esp Brit [1] **a ~** (slightly) 有点; **he looked a ~ confused** 他看上去有些困惑; **a ~ too ...** 有点太…; **wait a ~ longer** 稍微再等一会儿; **a ~ like ...** 有几分像… [2] **a good ~, quite a ~** (considerably) 相当; **a ~ much** 太过分; **every ~ as good/clever (as ...)** (和…)一样好/聪明; **the secretary is every ~ as powerful as the treasurer** 秘书的权力完全不亚于财务主管; **he's every ~ a lawyer** 他是个十足的律师 [3] **a ~** (a little) 稍微; **wait a ~!** 等一下! ; **move up a ~** 往前走一点; **I don't care for him one ~!** 我一点都不在乎他!

bit[2] *n* [1] Equit 嚼子; **to champ** *or* **chafe at the ~** «*horse*» 使性子大咬嚼子; fig «*person*» 烦躁不安地急欲挣脱束缚; **to have** *or* **take the ~ between one's teeth** fig 果断行事 [2] (of drill, brace) 钻头; (of soldering iron) 烙铁头

bit[3] *n* Comput 比特, 位元

bit[4] *pt* ▸**bite A, B**

bitch /bɪtʃ/
[A] *n* [1] (dog) 母狗; (wolf) 母狼; (fox) 母狐; (otter) 母獭 [2] colloq pej (malicious woman) 坏女人; **you son of a ~!** 你这狗娘养的! [3] colloq (aggravation) 棘手的事; **life's a ~** 活着真受罪
[B] *vi* [1] colloq (gossip spitefully) 说人坏话 [2] Amer (complain) 抱怨

bitchy /ˈbɪtʃi/ *adj* colloq 恶毒的 ‹*person, remark*›; **to be ~ about sb.** 对某人非常狠毒

bite /baɪt/
[A] *vt* (*pt* **bit**, *pp* **bitten**) [1] (cut into with teeth) 咬; **to ~ sth. in two** 把某物咬成两段; **to ~ one's nails** 咬指甲; **to ~ the dust** fig colloq 死; **to ~ the hand that feeds one** fig 恩将仇报; **once bitten, twice shy** Prov 一次被咬, 下次胆小 [2] (wound) 咬伤; **to be bitten by the dancing bug** fig colloq 迷上跳舞
[B] *vi* (*pt* **bit**, *pp* **bitten**) [1] (inflict wounds) «*snake*» 咬; «*insect*» 叮; **go and speak to him, he won't ~** fig 去和他说吧, 他不会吃了你 [2] (take effect) «*process, policy, reality*» 产生影响 [3] Fishg 吞饵
[C] *n* [1] [c] (act of biting) 咬; (mouthful) 咬下的一口; **to have** *or* **take a ~ of sth.** 咬某物一口; **to take a ~ out of sth.** fig 削减某物; **a ~ of the cherry** Brit, **a ~ of the apple** Amer fig 做某事的机会 [2] [c] colloq (snack) 少量食物; **to have** *or* **grab a quick ~ (to eat)** 匆匆吃点东西 [3] [u] fig (impact, keen edge) (of wind, cold) 刺骨; (of food) 辛辣; (of argument, style) 尖锐; **his speech has ~** 他讲话锋芒毕露 [4] [c] (from insect) 叮咬; (from dog, snake) 咬伤; **sb.'s bark is worse than their ~** fig 某人是刀子嘴豆腐心 [5] [c] Fishg 吞饵; **to have a ~** 咬钩; **the house is up for sale, but we haven't had any ~s yet** 房子已经上市, 但是我们还没有招徕到任何买主

Phrasal verbs

- **bite back**
[A] *vt* [**~ back sth., ~ sth. back**] 把…咽下去 ‹*remark*›
[B] *vi* 反击
- **bite into** *vt* [**~ into sth.**]
[1] lit (use teeth on) 咬进 [2] (corrode) 腐蚀 [3] (affect) 对…产生影响
- **bite off** *vt* [**~ off sth., ~ sth. off**] 咬掉; **to ~ sb.'s head off** fig colloq 痛骂某人; **to ~ off more than one can chew** fig 不自量力
- **bite on** *vt* [**~ on sth.**] 咬住
- **bite through** *vt* [**~ through sth.**] 咬穿; **the wind bit through my thin jacket** fig 风吹透了我的薄夹克衫

bite mark *n* (by animal) 咬痕; (by insect) 叮痕

biter /ˈbaɪtə(r)/ *n* (person) 下口咬的人; (animal) 下口咬的动物; **the ~ bit** fig 害人者害己

bite-sized *adj* [1] (mouth-sized) 一口能吃下的; **~ chunks of chicken** 小块鸡肉 [2] (very short) 很短的 ‹*section, text*›

biting /ˈbaɪtɪŋ/ *adj* [1] (chilling) 刺骨的 ‹*wind, cold*› [2] (incisive) 辛辣的 ‹*irony, comment*› [3] *attrib* (stinging) 叮咬的 ‹*insect*›

bitingly /ˈbaɪtɪŋli/ *adv* [1] (chillingly) 刺骨地 [2] (incisively) 辛辣地

bit: ~map *n* 位图; **~ part** *n* 小角色; **~ player** *n* 龙套演员; **~ rate** *n* 比特速率

bitten /ˈbɪtn/ *pp* ▸**bite A, B**

bitter /ˈbɪtə(r)/
[A] *adj* [1] (sour) 味苦的 [2] (resentful) 愤恨的 [3] (fierce) 激烈的 ‹*rivalry*›; 强烈的 ‹*hatred*›; **~ enemies** 势不两立的敌人 [4] (cold) 严寒的 [5] (difficult to accept or endure) 艰难的; **a ~ blow** 沉重的打击; **to learn from ~ experience** 从惨痛的经历中得到教训; **a ~ pill to swallow** fig 难以下咽的苦果
[B] *n* [u and c] Brit (beer) 苦啤酒
[C] **bitters** *npl* (flavoured liquor) 苦味药酒

bitter: ~ aloes /ˈæləʊz/ *npl* + *v sing* 苦芦荟汁; **~ lemon** *n* [u and c] 苦柠檬汽水

bitterly /ˈbɪtəli/ *adv* [1] (resentfully) 愤恨地 [2] (intensely) 极其; **a ~ divided party** 内部分歧很大的党派; **it's ~ cold** 天气很冷

bittern /ˈbɪtən/ *n* 麻鳽

bitterness /ˈbɪtənɪs/ *n* [u] [1] (sour flavour) 苦味 [2] (resentfulness) 愤恨 [3] (fierceness) (of criticism) 激烈; (of hatred) 强烈 [4] (cold) 严寒

bitter orange *n* [u and c] 酸橙

bitter-sweet /ˌbɪtəˈswiːt/ *adj* lit 又苦又甜的; fig 苦乐参半的 ‹*memory, feeling, experience*›

bitty /ˈbɪti/ *adj* [1] esp Brit (scrappy) 零碎的 ‹*information, account*› [2] colloq (tiny) **(little) ~** 小小的

bitumen /ˈbɪtjʊmɪn, Amer bəˈtuːmən/ *n* [u] 沥青

bituminous /bɪˈtjuːmɪnəs, Amer -ˈtuː-/ *adj* 含沥青的

bivalve /ˈbaɪvælv/ *n* 双壳类动物

bivouac /ˈbɪvʊæk/
[A] *n* 露营地
[B] *vi* (*pres p etc.* **-ck-**) 露营

biweekly /ˌbaɪˈwiːkli/
[A] *adj* [1] (twice a week) 一周两次的 [2] (two-weekly) 两周一次的
[B] *adv* [1] (twice weekly) 一周两次地 [2] (every two weeks) 两周一次地
[C] *n* (twice-weekly publication) 半周刊; (two-weekly publication) 双周刊

biz /bɪz/ *n* [u] colloq 生意; **to be just the ~** 很合时宜

bizarre /bɪˈzɑː(r)/ *adj* 古怪的; **~ clothes** 奇装异服

bizarrely /bɪˈzɑːli/ *adv* 古怪地

blab /blæb/ (*pres p etc.* **-bb-**) colloq
[A] *vi* [1] (reveal indiscreetly) 泄密 [2] (chatter) 瞎扯
[B] *vt* = **blab out**

Phrasal verbs

- **blab on** *vi* colloq 喋喋不休
- **blab out** *vt* [**~ out sth., ~ sth. out**] colloq 泄漏

blabber /ˈblæbər/ colloq
[A] *vi* (talk nonsense) 胡扯; (talk excessively) 喋喋不休; **to ~ (on) about sth.** 喋喋不休地谈论某事
[B] *n* [u] (nonsense) 胡言乱语; (excessive talk) 喋喋不休

blabbermouth /ˈblæbəmaʊθ/ *n* colloq 碎嘴子

black /blæk/ ▸**p. 134**
[A] *adj* [1] (colour) 黑色的; **to go** *or* **turn ~** 变黑; **to paint sth. ~** 把某物漆成黑色; **pitch/jet**

～乌黑的 **2** **Black** (of African, Australian Aboriginal ancestry) 黑人的; **a predominantly B～ suburb** 以黑人为主要居民的郊区 **3** (without milk) 不加牛奶的; **he drinks his tea ～** 他喝清茶 **4** (without light) 昏暗的; **a ～, starless night** 一个没有星星的黑夜; **a big ～ cloud** 一大片乌云; **(as) ～ as ink/pitch** 漆黑 **5** (dirty) 脏的; **my hands were ～ after reading the paper** 读完报纸后，我的手上黑乎乎的; ▸**pot¹ A1** **6** (gloomy) 暗淡的 ‹*day, future, year*›; **she painted a very ～ picture of the situation** 她把情况描述得很糟糕 **7** (angry) 愤怒的 ‹*look*›; **his face was as ～ as thunder** 他满面怒容 **8** (evil) 邪恶的 ‹*deed, heart*› **9** (macabre) ～ **humour/comedy** 黑色幽默/喜剧 **10** Brit dated (boycotted) 受工会抵制的 ‹*goods, work*›

B *n* **1** [u] (colour) 黑色 **2** [u] (in mourning) 丧服 **3** [u] (paint, dye) 黑颜料; (polish) (for footwear) 黑鞋油; (for metal) 黑色上光剂 **4** **Black** [c] (person) 黑人 **5** [u] Fin **to be in the ～** 有盈余 **6** **Black** [u] Games (player) 执黑棋方; (pieces) 黑棋; (in roulette) [轮盘赌赌具上的] 黑槽 **7** [c] (snooker ball) 黑球 **8** [u] liter (darkness) **the ～** 黑暗; **the ～ of (the) night** 夜幕

C *vt* **1** (make black) 使…变黑 ‹*face*› **2** (polish) 在…上涂黑色鞋油 ‹*shoes*› **3** Brit (bruise) **to ～ sb.'s eye** 把某人的眼睛打青 **4** Brit dated (boycott) «*union, striker*» 抵制 ‹*goods, factory*›

Phrasal verb

• **black out**

A *vi* 昏厥

B *vt* [～ **out sth.**, ～ **sth. out**]

1 (hide lights of) 对…实行灯火管制 ‹*building, town*›; **a house with ～ed-out windows** 窗户被遮住而透不出光亮的房子 **2** (cut power to) 使…停电 ‹*building, area*›; **a power failure ～ed out the city** 停电使整个城市陷入一片漆黑 **3** Theat 熄灭…上的灯光 ‹*stage*› **4** (darken) «*curtain*» 遮住…使房间内一片黑暗 ‹*windows*›; **the room must be ～ed out** 这房间不得有光亮 **5** Radio, TV 阻止…播出 ‹*broadcast*›; 阻止…播节目 ‹*station*› **6** (suppress) 封锁 ‹*news, information*› **7** (obliterate) 涂掉 ‹*writing*›

black Africa *pr n* 黑非洲 [通常指撒哈拉沙漠以南、黑人为主要人口的非洲地区]

black American

A *adj* 美国黑人的

B *n* 美国黑人

black and blue *adj* 遍体鳞伤的

black and white ▸**p. 134**

A *adj* **1** Cin, Phot, TV 黑白的 **2** (clear-cut) 黑白分明的 ‹*case*›; 明确的 ‹*decision*›

B *n* [u] **1** Cin 黑白电影; Phot 黑白照片 **2** (in writing) 书面; **here it is in ～** 它用白纸黑字写在这里 **3** (opposites) 黑白分明; **he sees everything in ～** 他认为凡事都是绝对的，非好即坏

black: ～ arts *npl* 巫术; **～ball** *vt* **1** (refuse membership to) 投反对票阻止…加入; **2** (ostracize) 排斥; **～ bear** *n* (American) 美洲黑熊; (Asian) 亚洲黑熊; **～ beetle** *n* 蟑螂; **～ belt** *n* **1** (rank) 黑带级; **2** (person) 黑带级选手

blackberry /ˈblækbəri, -beri/ *n* 黑莓; **a ～ bush** 黑莓丛

blackberrying /ˈblækbərɪŋ, -ber-/ *n* [u] 摘黑莓; **to go ～** 去摘黑莓

black: ～bird *n* (European) 乌鸫; (American) 黑鹂; **～board** *n* 黑板; **～board duster** *n* 黑板擦; **～board jungle** *n* Brit colloq 学生无组织无纪律的学校; **～ book** *n* fig 黑名册; **to be in sb.'s ～ book** *or* **～ books** 失去某人的宠爱; **to get into sb.'s ～ book** *or* **～ books** 引起某人的厌恶; **～ box** *n* **1** Aviat 黑匣子; **2** Comput 未知框; **～ bread** *n* [u] 黑面包; **～ cab** *n* Brit 黑色出租车; **～cap** *n* **1** Zool 黑顶山雀; **2** **black cap** Brit Jur, Hist 黑色法官帽; **B～ Country** *pr n* Brit **the B～ Country** 黑区 [英格兰西米德兰兹郡工业区]

blackcurrant /ˌblækˈkʌrənt/ *n* 黑加仑子

black: B～ Death *n* Hist **the B～ Death** 黑死病; **～ economy** *n* Brit 黑市经营

blacken /ˈblækən/

A *vt* **1** (make black) 使变黑; **the ～ed remains of a car** 汽车烧黑的残骸 **2** (with dirt) 弄脏 **3** fig (diminish) 败坏 ‹*name*›

B *vi* 变黑

black: B～ English *n* [u] 黑人英语; **～ eye** *n* 青肿的眼眶; **to give sb. a ～ eye** 打得某人眼眶青肿; **～fly** *n* (*pl* **～fly** *or* **～flies**) **1** [c] (aphid) 黑蝇; **2** [u] (infestation) 黑蝇虫害; **B～ Forest** *pr n* **the B～ Forest** 黑森林; **B～ Forest gateau** Brit, **B～ Forest cake** Amer *ns* [u and c] 黑森林蛋糕; **～ gold** *n* [u] colloq 黑金子 [指石油]; **～head** *n* 黑头粉刺; **～-headed gull** *n* 黑头海鸥; **～-hearted** *adj* liter 黑心肠的; **～ hole** *n* Astron 黑洞; **a financial ～ hole** colloq 经济上的无底洞; **B～ Hole of Calcutta** *n* fig colloq 黑暗闷热的狭小地方; **～ ice** *n* [u] 黑冰

blacking /ˈblækɪŋ/ *n* [u] **1** (polish) (for stoves, fireplaces) 黑色涂料; (for shoes, boots) 黑鞋油 **2** Brit dated (boycotting) 抵制行动

blackish /ˈblækɪʃ/ ▸**p. 134** *adj* 发黑的

blackjack /ˈblækdʒæk/ *n* esp Amer **1** ▸**p. 307** [u] Games 21 点纸牌游戏 **2** [c] (weapon) 包革铁棍

blacklead /ˈblækled/

A *n* [u] **1** (in pencil) 笔铅 **2** (for stove) 石墨

B *vt* 给…涂石墨 ‹*stove*›

blackleg /ˈblækleg/ Brit pej

A *n* 破坏罢工者

B *vi* (*pres p etc.* **-gg-**) 破坏罢工

blacklist /ˈblæklɪst/

A *n* 黑名单; **to put sb./sth. on a ～** 把某人/某事物列入黑名单

B *vt* 把…列入黑名单

black magic *n* [u] 巫术

blackmail /ˈblækmeɪl/

A *n* [u] **1** Jur 敲诈 **2** (pressure) 胁迫; **emotional ～** 情感上的胁迫 **3** (money demanded) 敲诈所得的钱财

B *vt* **1** (extort money from) 敲诈 **2** (pressurize) 胁迫; **to ～ sb. into doing sth.** 胁迫某人做某事

black: ～mailer *n* 敲诈者; **B～ Maria** *n* Brit colloq dated 囚车; **～ mark** *n* fig 污点

black market

A *n* 黑市; **on the ～** 在黑市上

B **black-market** *modif* 黑市的; **～ trade** 黑市交易

black: ～ marketeer *n* 黑市商人; **～ mass** *n* 戏拟弥撒; **B～ Muslim** *pr n* 黑人穆斯林; **B～ nationalism** *n* [u] 黑人民族主义

blackness /ˈblæknɪs/ *n* [u] **1** (colour) 黑色 **2** (of night) 夜色 **3** (dirtiness) 肮脏 **4** (gloominess) 暗淡 **5** (angriness) 怒气 **6** (evilness) 邪恶

blackout /ˈblækaʊt/ *n* **1** (in wartime) 灯火管制 **2** (power cut) 停电 **3** Radio, TV 禁止播放 **4** (news suppression) 封锁 **5** Theat 舞台灯光熄灭 **6** (memory loss) 暂时性失忆 **7** (faint) 暂时性晕厥

blackout curtain *n* 不透光窗帘

black: B～ Panther *pr n* Amer 黑豹党人; **the B～ Panthers** 黑豹党; **～ pepper** *n* [u] 黑胡椒; **B～ Power (movement)** *n* [u] Amer 黑人权力（运动）; **～ pudding** *n* [u and c] Brit 黑香肠; **B～ Rod** *n* Brit Pol 黑杖侍卫; **B～ Sea** ▸**p. 424** *pr n* **the B～ Sea** 黑海; **～ sheep** *n* fig 害群之马; **the ～ sheep of the family** 家族败类; **～smith** ▸**p. 409** *n* 铁匠; **～spot** *n* Brit (for accidents) 事故多发地段; fig 问题成堆的地方; **an unemployment/accident ～ spot** 失业率高的地区/事故多发区; **B～ Studies** *npl* 美国黑人文化研究; **～ taxi** *n* Brit 黑色出租车; **～thorn** *n* [u and c] 黑刺李

black tie

A *n* **1** [c] (tie) 黑领结 **2** [u] (formal suit) 晚礼服

B **black-tie** *modif* 需穿晚礼服的 ‹*function, dinner*›

black: ～ velvet *n* [u and c] 黑丝绒鸡尾酒 [烈性黑啤酒和香槟酒混合饮料]; **～ widow** *n* **～ widow (spider)** 黑寡妇球腹蛛

bladder /ˈblædə(r)/ *n* **1** Anat 膀胱 **2** (in ball) 球胆 **3** Bot 膨胀的果皮

blade /bleɪd/ *n* **1** (of sharp tool) 锋刃 **2** (of propeller, turbine, oar) 桨叶; (of fan) 叶片 **3** (of ice skate) 冰刀 **4** (of windscreen wiper) 刮水片 **5** (of grass) 叶片 **6** (of the tongue) 舌面

blah /blɑː/ colloq

A *n* [u] **1** (nonsense) 废话 **2** (as substitute for real words) ～ ～ ～ 等等,等等

B *adj pred* Amer 乏味的

C *npl* **to have the ～s** Amer 感觉乏味

Blairite /ˈbleəraɪt/ Brit

A *n* 布莱尔的支持者

B *adj* 支持布莱尔的

blamable /ˈbleɪməbl/ *adj* Amer = **blameable**

blame /bleɪm/

A *vt* 责怪; **to ～ sb./sth. (for sth.)** （把某事）归咎于某人/某事物; **don't ～ me** 别怪我; **who's to ～ for the broken vase?** 花瓶打破了应该怪谁？; **you have only yourself to ～** 只能怪你自己

B *v refl* **to ～ oneself for sth.** 因某事而自责

C *n* [u] **1** (censure) 责备; **to get the ～ (for sth.)** （因某事）受到责备 **2** (responsibility) 过错责任; **to lay** *or* **place** *or* **put the ～ on sb./sth.** 归咎于某人/某事; **to take** *or* **bear the ～ (for sth.)** （为某事物）承担责任; **the government is not without ～** 政府并非没有责任

blameable /ˈbleɪməbl/ *adj* 应受责备的

blameless /ˈbleɪmlɪs/ *adj* 无可责备的 ‹*person*›; **a ～ life** 无瑕的一生; **he is not entirely ～** 他并非完全没有过错

blamelessly /ˈbleɪmlɪsli/ *adv* 无可责备地 ‹*act, live*›

blameworthy /ˈbleɪmwɜːði/ *adj* **1** (responsible) 负有责任的 **2** (reprehensible) 应受谴责的

blanch /blɑːntʃ, Amer blæntʃ/

A *vt* **1** (bleach) «*sun*» 使…变白 ‹*hair, surface*› **2** Culin 焯 **3** Hort 遮荫种植

B *vi* **1** (turn white) 变白; **she ～ed with terror** 她吓得脸色发白 **2** (fade) 褪色

blancmange /bləˈmɒnʒ/ *n* [u and c] 牛奶冻

bland /blænd/ *adj* **1** (lacking taste) 淡而无味的 ‹*food, texture*›; 清淡的 ‹*flavour*› **2** (lacking interest) 乏味的 ‹*person, artwork, statement, assurance*› **3** (lacking emotion) 无动于衷的 ‹*reaction*›; **～ smile** 木然的微笑

blandishment /ˈblændɪʃmənt/ *n* dated 奉承

blandly /ˈblændli/ *adv* **1** (uninterestingly) 乏味地 **2** (showing little emotion) 无动于衷地

blandness /ˈblændnɪs/ *n* [u] **1** (lack of taste) 清淡 **2** (lack of interest) 乏味 **3** (lack of emotion) 无动于衷

blank /blæŋk/

A *adj* **1** (empty) 空白的 ‹*paper, space, CD*›; **the ～ expanse of the sea** 空旷的大海; **fill in the ～ form** 填写空白表格 **2** fig colloq (expressionless) 无表情的; **he had a ～ expression on his face** 他面无表情 **3** (uncomprehending) 困惑的; **to look ～** 面露困惑之色; **don't give me such a ～ look** 不要呆呆地看着我; **to stare at sth. in ～ amazement** 目瞪口呆地看着某物 **4** colloq (not remembering) 已遗忘的; **I tried to remember, but my mind went ～** 我试着回忆，但是脑子里一片空白 **5** *attrib* (absolute) 完全的; **his ～ refusal** *or* **rejection of me** 他对我的断然拒绝

B *n* **1** (space to fill in) 空白处; (clean form) 空白表格; **to fill in the ～s** 填空 **2** (empty space) 空白; **to draw a ～** 落空; **the search drew a ～** 搜寻一无所获 **3** (dummy bullet) 空包弹; **to**

b

fire ~s lit 发射空包弹; fig [指男性] 不能生育 4 (semifinished product) 坯件 5 (domino) 空白骨牌

(Phrasal verb)

- **blank out**

A *vt* [~ **sth. out,** ~ **out sth.**]
1 (make undecipherable) 删去 ‹*text*›; 使…无效 ‹*signal*› 2 fig colloq (erase from memory) 抹去

B *vi* fig colloq (suddenly become empty) «*mind, person*» 突然空白; **the screen suddenly ~ed out** 屏幕突然变成一片空白

blank: ~ **cartridge** *n* 空包弹; ~ **cheque** *n* 1 Fin 空白支票; 2 fig 自由行动权; **have a ~ cheque to handle affairs** 有全权处理事务

blanket /ˈblæŋkɪt/

A *n* 1 (for bed) 毯子; **an electric ~** 电热毯 2 fig (layer) 覆盖层; **to escape under the ~ of night** 在夜幕的掩护下逃跑

B *modif* 1 (global) 全面的; **a ~ ban on smoking** 全民禁烟 2 (indiscriminate) 不加区分的; **the ~ use of antibiotics** 抗生素的滥用

C *vt* 1 (cover) 覆盖; **to be ~ed in fog** 被笼罩在雾霭之中 2 (obscure) 使…模糊不清 ‹*view, sound*›

(Phrasal verb)

- **blanket out** *vt* [~ **sth. out,** ~ **out sth.**] 完全覆盖

blanket: ~ **cover** *n* [u] Insur 全保保障; ~ **coverage** *n* [u] 全程报道; ~ **finish** *n* 几乎同时到达终点; ~ **insurance** *n* [u] 全保保险; ~ **rate** *n* 统括率

blankety-blank /ˌblæŋkətɪˈblæŋk/ hum colloq

A *adj* 该死的

B *n* [u] 笨蛋

blankly /ˈblæŋkli/ *adv* 1 (uncomprehendingly) 困惑地 2 (without expression) 茫然地

blankness /ˈblæŋknɪs/ *n* [u] 1 (lack of comprehension) 困惑 2 (lack of expression) 茫然 3 (lack of content) 空洞 4 colloq (lack of memory) 遗忘

blank verse *n* [u] 无韵诗

blare /bleə(r)/

A *vt* 刺耳地鸣响 ‹*siren, horn*›; 刺耳地发出 ‹*sound*›

B *vi* = **blare out A**

C *n* 刺耳的响声

(Phrasal verb)

- **blare out**

A *vi* 大声响起; **music ~d out from his room** 他的房间音乐声大作

B *vt* [~ **sth. out,** ~ **out sth.**] 大声播放

blarney /ˈblɑːni/ *n* [u] Ir colloq 1 (flattery) 奉承话 2 (nonsense) 胡扯

blarney stone *n* **the ~** 巧言石

blasé /ˈblɑːzeɪ, Amer blɑːˈzeɪ/ *adj* 无动于衷的; **to be ~ about sth.** 认为某事物司空见惯

blaspheme /blæsˈfiːm/ *vi* 亵渎

blasphemer /blæsˈfiːmə(r)/ *n* 亵渎神灵者

blasphemous /ˈblæsfəməs/ *adj* 亵渎神灵的

blasphemously /ˈblæsfəməsli/ *adv* 亵渎神灵地

blasphemy /ˈblæsfəmi/ *n* [u and c] 亵渎神灵; **it is ~ to say that ...** 说…是对神灵的亵渎

blast /blɑːst, Amer blæst/

A *n* 1 [u] (explosion) 爆炸; ~ **effect** 爆炸后果 2 [c] (gust) 一阵; ~**s of hot air** 阵阵热浪 3 [c] (from explosion) 冲击波 4 [c] (burst of sound) 突然发出的响声; **to give a ~ on the trumpet** 吹号; **a ~ of the ship's siren** 轮船的汽笛声; **he gave a quick ~ on the horn** 他短促地按了按喇叭; **a ~ from the past** colloq 勾起回忆的东西 5 [u] (power) 功率; **the music is at full ~** 音乐正以最大音量播放; **the machine is operating at full ~** 机器在全速运转 6 [c] (criticism) 严厉的批评 7 [c] colloq (enjoyable experience) 狂欢

B *vt* 1 (blow up) 炸 ‹*building, vehicle*›; **to be ~ed into oblivion** 被炸得无影无踪 2 (open by explosion) 炸出 ‹*tunnel, hole*› 3 (blow at with force) «*wind*» 向…猛吹 ‹*building*›; **the gale ~ed the trees** 大风冲击着树木 4 colloq (criticize) 痛斥; **his manager ~ed him** 经理严厉批评了他 5 Sport (strike) «*soccer player*» 猛踢; «*golfer, cricketer*» 用力击打

C *vi* 1 (blare) 突然鸣响; **trumpets ~ed, horns sounded** 喇叭高奏,号角齐鸣 2 colloq (speed) 疾驰

D *excl* Brit colloq 该死

(Phrasal verbs)

- **blast away** *vi* 连续射击
- **blast off** *vi* «*spacecraft*» 点火发射
- **blast out**

A *vi* «*music, loudspeaker*» 大声播放

B *vt* [~ **sth. out,** ~ **out sth.**] «*loudspeaker*» 大声播放 ‹*speech, music*›; «*musician, instrument*» 大声演奏出 ‹*music*›

blasted /ˈblɑːstɪd, Amer ˈblæst-/ *adj attrib* colloq 该死的; **this ~ weather!** 这鬼天气!

blast furnace *n* 高炉

blast-off /ˈblɑːstɒf, Amer ˈblæst-/ *n* [u and c] 发射; **three, two, one, ~!** 三, 二, 一, 发射!

blatant /ˈbleɪtnt/ *adj* 明显的 ‹*example*›; 露骨的 ‹*lie*›; 公然的 ‹*abuse, disregard, copy*›; **to be ~ about ...** 对…毫不忌讳

blatantly /ˈbleɪtntli/ *adv* 公然地 ‹*abuse, disregard, copy*›; 露骨地 ‹*lie*›; **to be ~ obvious** 赤裸裸

blather /ˈblæðə(r)/ colloq

A *vi* 胡说; **to ~ on about sth.** 喋喋不休地胡说某件事情

B *n* [u] 废话

blaze[1] /bleɪz/

A *n* [u] 1 (fire) 大火; (accidental) 火灾; (in a hearth) 火焰; **in full ~** 熊熊燃烧 2 (bright display) 光辉; **a ~ of light/fire** 一道亮光/火光; **the gardens are a ~ of colour** 几座花园五光十色 3 fig (sudden appearance) 迸发; **a ~ of glory/anger/publicity** 荣耀的闪现/勃然大怒/大力宣传

B *vi* 1 (burn fiercely) «*fire*» 熊熊燃烧 2 (shine) 发亮光; **candles were blazing brightly** 烛光通明; **the sun ~d overhead** 烈日当头 3 (shoot) 射击; **(with) all guns blazing** 枪炮齐鸣; fig 大张旗鼓

C **blazes** *npl* fig colloq **go to ~s!** 去死吧!; **what the ~s are you doing?** 你究竟在干什么?; **to run like ~s** 拼命跑

(Phrasal verbs)

- **blaze away** *vi* 1 (burn) 熊熊燃烧 2 (shoot) 连续射击
- **blaze down** *vi* 火辣辣地照射; **the sun ~d down on us** 太阳火辣辣地照在我们身上
- **blaze up** *vi* «*fire, oil*» 突然熊熊燃烧起来; fig «*feeling*» 爆发; **his anger ~d up suddenly** 他勃然大怒; **enthusiasm ~d up in him** 他迸发出满腔热情

blaze[2]

A *vt* **to ~ a trail** 做开路先锋

B *n* [动物面部的] 白斑

blazer /ˈbleɪzə(r)/ *n* 1 (bright, lightweight jacket) 轻便夹克 2 (formal jacket) 正装夹克 3 (as part of uniform) 制服夹克; **school ~** 校服; **team ~** 队服

blazing /ˈbleɪzɪŋ/ *adj attrib* 1 (on fire) 熊熊燃烧的 2 (bright) 鲜艳的 3 (hot) 炽热的 4 colloq (angry) 极其愤怒的

blazon /ˈbleɪzn/

A *n* 纹章的绘制

B *vt* 1 Herald 绘制 ‹*coat of arms*› 2 (gen) **to ~ (forth** *or* **out)** 宣布

bleach /bliːtʃ/

A *n* [u and c] 1 **(household) ~** 漂白剂 2 (for hair) 染白剂

B *vt* 1 (whiten) 漂白 ‹*linen*›; 染白 ‹*hair*› 2 (clean) 用漂白剂清洁 ‹*sink, surface*›

(Phrasal verb)

- **bleach out** *vt* [~ **out sth.,** ~ **sth. out**] 1 (whiten) 使…变白 ‹*colour, mark*› 2 (clean) 用漂白剂清洁

bleachers /ˈbliːtʃəz/ *npl* Amer [体育场馆的] 廉价露天座位

bleaching: ~ **agent** *n* [c and u] 漂白剂; ~ **powder** *n* [u and c] 漂白粉

bleak /bliːk/ *adj* 1 (desolate) 荒凉的 2 (cold) 阴冷的 3 (miserable, depressing, discouraging) 凄凉的 ‹*surroundings*›; 凄惨的 ‹*story*›; 暗淡的 ‹*outlook, future*›; **to paint a ~ picture of ...** 把…描述得很暗淡

bleakly /ˈbliːkli/ *adv* 1 (coldly) 阴冷地 2 (hopelessly, depressingly) 黯然地 ‹*stare, end*›; ~ **desolate** 满目荒凉

bleakness /ˈbliːknɪs/ *n* [u] 1 (of weather, land) 阴冷 2 (of outlook, future) 暗淡

bleary /ˈblɪəri/ *adj* 视线模糊的; **to feel ~** 感觉两眼昏花

bleary-eyed *adj* 视线模糊的

bleat /bliːt/

A *vi* 1 lit «*sheep, calf*» 咩咩叫 2 fig pej (complain) 抱怨; **to ~ on (about sth.)** 絮絮叨叨地抱怨 (某事物)

B *vt* pej 抱怨说

C *n* 1 (of sheep) 咩咩声 2 pej (of person) 抱怨

bleed /bliːd/

A (*pt, pp* **bled** /bled/) *vi* 1 (lose blood) 流血; **to ~ to death** 失血而死 2 fig (feel sympathy for another) 悲伤; **my heart ~s for the victims** 我由衷地同情那些罹难者; **you have to go to Italy? my heart ~s for you!** iron 你一定要去意大利? 你真可怜! 3 (lose colour) 褪色 4 Print 印成出血版

B (*pt, pp* **bled** /bled/) *vt* 1 Med, esp Hist 给…放血 2 fig (drain money from) 榨取…的钱财; **to ~ sb. white** *or* **dry** 榨干某人的钱财 3 Tech (draw liquid from) 抽干…中的液体; (draw air from) 抽干…中的气体 4 Print 把…印成出血版

C *n* Med 出血

bleeder /ˈbliːdə(r)/ *n* 1 Brit pej (despised person) 浑蛋 2 Brit sl dated (pitied person) 家伙; **poor/silly ~** 可怜虫/蠢蛋 3 colloq (hemophiliac) 血友病患者

bleeding /ˈbliːdɪŋ/

A *n* [u] 1 Med 出血; **to stop the ~** 止血 2 (drawing blood) 抽血

B *adj attrib* 1 (losing blood) 出血的 ‹*arm, cut, person*› 2 Brit sl (damned) 该死的; **this ~ car!** 这辆破车!; ~ **idiot!** 该死的傻瓜!

C *adv* Brit sl (damned) 非常; ~ **awful weather** 糟透了的天气

bleep /bliːp/

A *n* 1 TV, Radio (signal) 哔哔声 2 Brit = **bleeper**

B *vt* 1 TV, Radio 用哔哔声覆盖 ‹*word, swearing*› 2 Brit (summon) 用传呼机呼叫 ‹*person*›

C *vi* «*alarm*» 发出哔哔声

(Phrasal verb)

- **bleep out** *vt* [~ **sth. out,** ~ **out sth.**] 用哔哔声覆盖

bleeper /ˈbliːpə(r)/ *n* Brit 传呼机

blemish /ˈblemɪʃ/

A *n* 1 (mark) 瑕疵; (on fruit) 疤; (on skin) 粉刺 2 fig (on beauty) 白璧微瑕; (on record, reputation) 污点

B *vt* 1 (mar) «*scar, mark*» 损毁 ‹*surface, beauty*› 2 fig «*moral flaw*» 玷污 ‹*character*›; «*failure*» 破坏…的完美 ‹*record*›

blench /blentʃ/ *vi* 1 (flinch) 退缩 2 (pale) 变苍白

blend /blend/

A *vt* 1 (mix) 混合 ‹*ingredients*›; **to ~ A and B (together)** 把A和B混合起来 2 fig (use together) 掺合使用 ‹*colours*›; 使…融合 ‹*sounds, ideas*›

B *vi* 1 (mix) «*ingredients*» 混合 2 (go together) «*styles, colours, voices*» 协调; **to ~ (well)**

together 相协调 3 (merge) 融合; **to ~ together** 交融; **to ~ with sth.** 与某物相融合; **to ~ into sth.** 融入某物

C *n* 1 (fusion) 混合 2 Culin 混合物 3 (pleasing mix) 融合 4 Tex 合成面料

Phrasal verb

• **blend in**

A *vi* 交融; **to ~ in with sth.** 和某物融和在一起

B *vt* [~ **in sth.**, ~ **sth. in**] 把…混合在一起

blended whisky *n* [u and c] 混成威士忌

blender /ˈblendə(r)/ *n* 1 Culin 搅拌器 2 Comm (person, company) 调配师; **tea/coffee/whisky ~** 茶艺师/咖啡师/调酒师

bless /bles/

A *vt* 1 Relig 祈神保佑 ‹*person, marriage, building*›; 祈神赐予 ‹*food, harvest*›; **God ~ America/the Queen** 神佑美国/女王; **God ~ you** 上帝保佑你 2 colloq (affectionately) **~ her!** 愿上帝保佑她! ; **~ you!** (after sneeze) 保重! 3 dated colloq (in surprise) **~ me!, ~ my soul!** 天啊! 4 (favour) 赋予; **to be ~ed with** 拥有 ‹*skill, beauty*›; **we are truly ~ed** 我们真的很有福气; **we were never ~ed with children** 我们从来就没有生儿育女的福分 5 (be grateful to) 感激; **~ you for coming** 谢谢你的光临; **you paid the bill? ~ you!** 你付了账单? 谢谢!

B *v refl* **to ~ oneself** 在胸口划十字

blessed /ˈblesɪd/

A *adj* 1 Relig (holy) 神圣的; **the B~ Sacrament/Virgin** 圣餐/圣母; **our B~ Lord** 神圣的主 2 *attrib* Relig (favoured by God) 受上帝赐福的; **~ are the poor** 贫者有福 3 *attrib* (beatified) 真福; **the B~ Teresa** 真福特蕾莎修女 4 *attrib* (welcome) 令人幸福的 ‹*time, quiet*› 5 *attrib* colloq dated (damned) 该死的; **the whole ~ day** 该死的一整天

B *npl* **the ~** 受教皇宣福礼的死者

blessedly /ˈblesɪdli/ *adv* 幸运地; **~ warm/quiet** 温暖/宁静惬意

blessing /ˈblesɪŋ/ *n* 1 [c] (benefit) 福气; **a ~ in disguise** 因祸得福之事; **count your ~s!** 谢天谢地! 2 [c] (relief) 幸事; **it is a ~ that he came** 所幸的是他来了 3 [c] (approval) 同意; **to give one's ~ (to sth.)** 允许 (某事); **with the ~ of sb., with sb.'s ~** 经某人同意 4 [u and c] Relig 祈神赐福; **to say a ~ over sth./sb.** 为某事物/某人祈祷; **to ask God's ~ on sth.** 祈求上帝赐福于某事物

blether /ˈbleðə(r)/ *vi, n* esp Scot = **blather**

blew /bluː/ *pt* ▸**blow A, B**

blight /blaɪt/

A *n* [u and c] 1 Bot 枯萎病 2 fig (on society) 毁坏; **to cast a ~ on sth.** 给某事物蒙上阴影; **urban ~** 有损市容的地方; **planning ~** 计划病

B *vt* fig 毁掉 ‹*future, hopes, life*›; 破坏 ‹*environment, city*›

blighter /ˈblaɪtə(r)/ *n* Brit dated colloq 1 (person) 家伙; **you lucky ~!** 你真是个幸运儿! 2 (annoying person) 讨厌鬼; (annoying thing) 讨厌的事

Blighty /ˈblaɪti/ *pr n* Brit dated sl 英国老家

blimey /ˈblaɪmi/ *excl* Brit colloq 哎呀

blimp /blɪmp/ *n* colloq 1 Aviat 软式飞艇 2 Brit pej **(Colonel) B~** 顽固自大的保守分子 3 Amer pej (fat person) 大胖子

blimpish /ˈblɪmpɪʃ/ *adj* Brit colloq pej 顽固自大且保守的

blind /blaɪnd/

A *adj* 1 (unable to see) 失明的; **a ~ man/woman** 一位盲人; **to go ~** 失明; **to turn a ~ eye (to sth.)** fig (对某事物) 视而不见 2 (having bad eyes) 视力差的; **as ~ as a bat** hum 像瞎子一样 3 (overwhelmed) 不知所措的; **to be ~ with sth.** 因…而失去理智 ‹*rage, pain*› 4 (unquestioning) 盲目的 ‹*faith*›; **love is ~** 爱情是盲目的 5 *attrib* (uncontrollable) 不能自制的 ‹*fury, panic*› 6 *attrib* (not ruled by purpose) 无理性的; **~ chance** 盲目的偶然性; **~ force** 无法抵挡的力量 7 *pred* (unaware) 未察觉的; **to be ~ to sth.** 对…视而不见 ‹*fault, danger*›; **are you ~?** 你难道看不见吗? 8 (without looking) 不凭视觉的 ‹*taste, test*› 9 Aviat 仅凭仪表操纵的 ‹*landing*› 10 *attrib* (hidden) 隐蔽的 ‹*entrance, alley*›; (unable to be seen around) 看不见的 ‹*corner, turning*› 11 (blank) 无门窗的 ‹*wall, facade*› 12 Brit colloq (slightest) 一丁点儿的; **this book's not a ~ bit of use** 这本书一点用都没有

B *n* 1 **the ~** *pl* (people) 盲人; **the ~ leading the ~** fig 盲人给瞎子引路 2 esp Brit (for window) 窗帘 3 (front) 掩饰; **his job was only a ~ for his real profession of spying** 他真正的职业是间谍, 而他的工作只是个掩人耳目的幌子 4 Amer Hunt 埋伏处

C *vt* 1 (deprive of sight) «*disease, injury*» 使…失明 ‹*person, eye*› 2 (dazzle) «*light*» 使目眩; **she was ~ed by the sun** 她被阳光照得头昏眼花 3 (overwhelm) «*emotion*» 使失去判断力; **to be ~ed by ...** 因…而失去理智 ‹*emotion, love*›; **to ~ sb. to sth.** 使某人看不清某事物; **to ~ sb. with science** 用深奥的语言使某人困惑

D *adv* 1 (without looking) 不凭视觉地 ‹*taste*› 2 Aviat 仅凭仪表操纵地 ‹*fly*›

blind: ~ alley *n* 死胡同; fig 绝境; **to lead sb. up a ~ alley** 把某人带向死胡同; **~ carbon copy** *n* 无信头复写副本; **~ date** *n* 1 (meeting) 男女间的初次约会; 2 (man) 初次约会的男方; (woman) 初次约会的女方; **~ drunk** *adj* colloq 烂醉的

blinder /ˈblaɪndə(r)/

A *n* Brit Sport colloq 出色的表现

B **blinders** *npl* Amer (for horse) 马眼罩

blindfold /ˈblaɪndfəʊld/

A *n* 眼罩

B *vt* 蒙住…的眼睛

C **blindfolded** *adj* 蒙住眼睛的

D **blindfolded** *adv* 1 (with eyes covered) 蒙住眼睛地 2 fig (with ease) 轻易地

blinding /ˈblaɪndɪŋ/ *adj* 1 (dazzling) 刺眼的 ‹*light, glare*› 2 (intense) 剧烈的 ‹*pain*›; 强烈的 ‹*rage*› 3 fig (sudden) 突如其来的 4 *attrib* Brit colloq (exceptional) 极棒的

blindingly /ˈblaɪndɪŋli/ *adv* 1 (dazzlingly) 刺眼地 ‹*shine*› 2 (extremely) 极其 ‹*clear, obvious*›

blindly /ˈblaɪndli/ *adv* 1 (without being able to see) 摸黑地 2 (unthinkingly) 不假思索地; **to ~ accept what he says** 盲目听信他的话

blind man's buff ▸**p. 307** *n* [u] 捉迷藏

blindness /ˈblaɪndnɪs/ *n* [u] 1 Med 失明 2 fig 视而不见

blind: ~ spot *n* 1 (in car, on hill) 视线盲区; 2 (in eye) 盲点; 3 fig (ignored thing) 忽视的事物; **to have a ~ spot about money** 对钱财一窍不通; **~ test** *n* 盲测; **~worm** *n* = **slowworm**

bling /blɪŋ/, **bling bling** /ˈblɪŋ blɪŋ/ *ns* [u] colloq 珠光宝气的穿戴

blink /blɪŋk/

A *vi* 1 (close and open eyes) 眨眼; **without ~ing** lit 不眨眼地; fig 毫不犹豫地 2 (flash) «*light, signal*» 闪烁

B *vt* 眨 ‹*eye*›

C *n* 1 (of eye) 眨眼; **in a** *or* **the ~ of an eye** fig 一眨眼功夫; **on the ~** colloq 出毛病 2 (flash) 闪烁

Phrasal verbs

• **blink at** *vt* [~ **at sth.**] 1 (ignore) 漠视 2 (be taken aback by) 对…感到吃惊

• **blink away** *vt* [~ **sth. away**, ~ **away sth.**] 眨眼挤掉 ‹*tears, dust*›

• **blink back** *vt* [~ **sth. back**, ~ **back sth.**] 眨眼控制 ‹*tears*›

blinker /ˈblɪŋkə(r)/

A *n* (flashing light) 闪光信号灯; Aut 闪光交通灯

B **blinkers** *npl* Brit Equit 马眼罩; **to wear ~s** lit 戴眼罩; fig (be uninformed) 故意视而不见; (be prejudiced) 有偏见

C *vt* 1 Equit 给…戴上眼罩 ‹*horse*› 2 fig (limit) 蒙蔽

blinkered /ˈblɪŋkəd/ *adj* 1 Equit 戴眼罩的 ‹*horse*› 2 fig (narrow) 狭隘的; (prejudiced) 有偏见的

blinking /ˈblɪŋkɪŋ/

A *adj attrib* 1 (flashing) 闪烁的 ‹*light*›; 一眨一眨的 ‹*eye*› 2 Brit colloq (for emphasis) 该死的; **a ~ idiot** 十足的白痴

B *adv* Brit colloq **~ well do it!** 该死的快去干! ; **I ~ well won't!** 我偏不!

blip /blɪp/ *n* 1 (on screen) 光点; (on graph) 尖峰 2 (sound) 哔哔声 3 (hitch) 暂时的问题 4 Econ, Fin (drop) 回落

bliss /blɪs/ *n* [u] 1 (happiness) 极乐; **wedded ~** 婚后的幸福; **ignorance is ~** Prov 无知是福 2 Relig 天堂

Phrasal verb

• **bliss out** *vi* Amer colloq 欣喜若狂

blissful /ˈblɪsfl/ *adj* 1 (contented) 满足的 2 (happy) 极乐的 3 Relig 天堂般的

blissfully /ˈblɪsfəli/ *adv* 1 (contentedly) 十分满足地 2 (happily) 极乐地; **~ happy** 极其幸福; **to be ~ ignorant/unaware of/that ...** 对…乐得无知/不知情

blister /ˈblɪstə(r)/

A *n* (on skin) 水疱; (in paint, glass) 气泡; (on metal) 泡疤

B *vt* 使…起水疱 ‹*skin*›; 使…起泡 ‹*metal*›; **~ed glass/paint** 有气泡的玻璃/油漆涂层

C *vi* «*skin*» 起水疱; «*paint*» 起泡

blistering /ˈblɪstərɪŋ/

A *n* [u] (of skin) 起水疱; (of paint) 起泡

B *adj* 1 (hot) 炎热的; **~ heat/day** 酷热/大热天 2 fig (cruel) 尖酸的 ‹*tongue*›; 激烈的 ‹*attack*› 3 (fast) 极快的; **at a ~ pace** 步伐极快地

blisteringly /ˈblɪstərɪŋli/ *adv* 非常; **~ hot** 酷热的; **~ sarcastic/fast** 极其尖刻的/极快的

blister: ~ pack *n* 吸塑包装; **~ packed** *adj* 吸塑包装的

blithe /blaɪð/ *adj* 1 (nonchalant) 漫不经心的 ‹*assume, remark*›; **with a ~ disregard for ...** 全然不顾… 2 liter (cheerful) 快乐的

blithely /ˈblaɪðli/ *adv* 1 (nonchalantly) 漫不经心地 ‹*assume, remark*›; **to be ~ ignorant/unaware of sth.** 对某事物浑然不知/毫无察觉 2 liter (cheerfully) 快乐地

blithering /ˈblɪðərɪŋ/ *adj attrib* colloq 十足的 ‹*idiot*›

blitz /blɪts/

A *n* 1 Mil 闪电战; **the B~** Brit Hist 伦敦大轰炸 [1940-1941年德国对英国的空袭] 2 fig (campaign) 闪电式行动; **advertising/media ~** 广告战/媒体宣传战 3 fig (concentrated effort) 突击; **to have a ~ on sth.** 突击做某事

B *vt* 对…发动闪电战; fig 突袭; **to ~ sb. with questions** 连珠炮般地向某人发问

blizzard /ˈblɪzəd/ *n* 1 lit 暴风雪 2 fig 突然出现的一大批; **a ~ of paper/publicity** 突如其来的一大堆文件/大量宣传

bloat /bləʊt/ *vt* 使…饱胀 ‹*stomach*›; 使…浮肿 ‹*face, body*›; 使…臃肿 ‹*bureaucracy, organization, workforce*›

bloated /ˈbləʊtɪd/ *adj* 1 lit 浮肿的 ‹*face, body*›; 饱胀的 ‹*stomach*›; **to feel ~** 感觉胃胀 2 fig (too large) 臃肿的 ‹*bureaucracy, organization, workforce*› 3 fig (overblown) 夸张的 ‹*estimate, style*›; 夸大的 ‹*statistics*›

bloater /ˈbləʊtə(r)/ *n* 腌熏鲱鱼

blob /blɒb/

A *n* 1 (of paint) 一滴; (of cream) 少量; **a ~ of pink/light** 粉红色斑点/光斑 2 (indistinct shape) 一团

B *vt* (*pres p etc.* **-bb-**) 涂抹

bloc /blɒk/ *n* 阵营; ▸**en bloc**

block /blɒk/
A *n* **1** (slab) 大块; (rectangular portion) 方块; **a ~ of marble/ice cream** 一方大理石/一块冰激凌; **a ~ of paper** esp Brit 一沓纸 **2** (for chopping meat) 肉案; (for executions) 垫头木; **to put** *or* **lay one's head on the ~** fig 冒着名誉受损的危险; **to go on the ~** 被拿去拍卖 **3** Sport = **starting block** **4** Brit (building) 大楼; **~ of flats** 公寓楼; **office/residential ~** 办公楼/住宅楼 **5** (group of buildings) 街区; **he lives three ~s away/south** Amer 他住在三个街区以外/以南; **to have been around the ~ a few times** colloq 很有经验 **6** (group) (of seats, tickets) 一批; (of stamps) 一套; (of shares) 大宗; **a ~ of three lessons** 连续三节课 **7** (obstruction) 阻碍; **to be a ~ to progress** 妨碍发展; **to put a ~ on the price** 阻止涨价; **to have a (mental) ~ (about sth.)** (对某事物) 有心理障碍 **8** Print 印板 **9** Tech (housing for pulleys) 滑轮组 **10** colloq (head) 脑袋; **I'll knock your ~ off** 小心我敲掉你的脑袋 **11** (flat area) (of colour, ground, sky) 一片
B *vt* **1** (obstruct) 阻塞 ‹*pipe, exit, traffic*›; **to ~ sb.'s way** *or* **path** 挡住某人的路; **to have a ~ed nose** 鼻子不通气 **2** (impede) 阻碍 ‹*movement, advance*›; 阻止…通过 ‹*bill*›; **you're ~ing my light/view** 你挡住了我的光/视线 **3** Sport 拦截 ‹*ball, opponent*›

Phrasal verbs
- **block in** *vt* [**~ sb./sth. in**] **1** (when parking) 堵住 ‹*driver, vehicle*› **2** Art (outline) 画出…的草图; (add) 给草图填充 ‹*colour*›
- **block off** *vt* [**~ sth. off, ~ off sth.**] 封锁
- **block out** *vt* [**~ out sth., ~ sth. out**] **1** (hide) 挡住 ‹*light, view*›; 屏蔽 ‹*noise*› **2** fig (suppress) 忘掉 ‹*idea*›; 抹去 ‹*memory*› **3** (outline) 画出…的草图; fig 大致描述
- **block up**
A *vt* [**~ up sth., ~ sth. up**] 堵塞 ‹*passage, hole*›
B *vi* «*passage, hole*» 被堵塞

blockade /blɒˈkeɪd/
A *n* **1** Mil 封锁 **2** (barrier) 障碍物
B *vt* **1** Mil 封锁 ‹*port*› **2** (block up) 阻塞

blockage /ˈblɒkɪdʒ/ *n* **1** [c] (obstruction) 阻塞物 **2** [u] (being blocked) 阻塞

block: ~ and tackle *n* 滑轮组; **~board** *n* [u] Brit 芯块胶合板; **~-booking** *n* [u and c] 大宗订购

blockbuster /ˈblɒkbʌstə(r)/ colloq
A **1** (book) 畅销巨著 **2** (film) 流行大片 **3** Mil 重磅炸弹
B *modif* 轰动的

block: ~busting *adj attrib* colloq 非常成功的; **~ capital** *n* 大写字母; **in ~ capitals** 用大写字母; **~ diagram** *n* 方框图; **~ grant** *n* Brit 政府的大宗拨款; **~head** *n* colloq pej 傻瓜; **~house** *n* **1** Mil 碉堡; **2** Amer Hist (fort) 木堡; **3** Aerosp 发射管制台

blocking software *n* [u] 拦截软件

block: ~ letter *n* = **~ capital**; **~ release** *n* [u] Brit 定期脱产进修; **~ release course** 脱产进修课程; **~ vote** *n* Brit **1** (voting system) 集团投票制; **2** (vote) 一个集团所投的票; **~ voting** *n* [u] **1** Brit (use of block vote) 集团投票法; **2** (voting the same way) 统一投票; **3** (voting for multiple candidates) 连记投票

blog /blɒg/ *n* 博客
blogger /ˈblɒgə(r)/ *n* 博客维护者
blogging /ˈblɒgɪŋ/ *n* [u] 博客维护
blogosphere /ˈblɒgəsfɪə(r)/ *n* [u] colloq **the ~** 博客世界
bloke /bləʊk/ *n* Brit colloq 家伙
blokeish, blokish /ˈbləʊkɪʃ/ *adj* Brit colloq 爷们儿气的
blonde, blond /blɒnd/ ▸ **p. 134**
A *adj* **1** (pale gold) 金黄色的 **2** (fair-haired) 头发金黄的
B *n* 头发金黄的人 [多指女人]; **a stunning ~** 绝色金发美女

blood /blʌd/
A *n* [u] **1** Physiol 血; **the ~ rushed to his cheeks** 他的脸颊一下子涨得通红; **out for sb.'s ~, after sb.'s ~** fig 决心报复某人; **to sweat ~** fig 拼命工作; **like getting ~ out of a stone** 像水中捞月一样不可能; **to have (sb.'s) ~ on one's hands** fig 对 (某人的) 伤亡罪责难逃; **both sides have ~ on their hands** 双方都血债累累; **to draw first ~** fig 先拔头筹 **2** (lineage) 血统; **they are related by ~** 他们是血亲; **to run** *or* **be in sb.'s ~** fig 是某人与生俱来的; **~ is thicker than water** Prov 血浓于水; **of the ~ (royal)** liter 王室的 **3** fig (feeling of anger, resentment, etc.) 脾气; **to make sb.'s ~ boil** 使某人怒不可遏; **her ~ is up** 她发火了; **his ~ curdles/freezes/runs cold** 他不寒而栗; **to freeze** *or* **chill the/sb.'s ~** 使人/使某人毛骨悚然; **bad ~** 仇恨; **to have bad ~ between two families** 两家之间有仇 **4** fig (energy) 活力; **fresh** *or* **new ~** 新鲜血液
B *vt* 使获得初次经验; **troops already ~ed in battle** 经过战火初次洗礼的部队

blood: ~-and-thunder *n* [u] (bloodshed and violence) 血腥暴力; (melodramatic work) 情节耸人听闻的作品; **a ~-and-thunder novel/film** 惊悚小说/电影; **~ bank** *n* 血库; **~bath** *n* 大屠杀; **~ blister** *n* 血疱; **~ brother** *n* 结义兄弟; **~ cell** *n* 血细胞; **~-cholesterol** *n* [u] 血液胆固醇; **~-cholesterol level** 血液胆固醇水平; **~ clot** *n* 血栓; **~ clotting agent** *n* 凝血剂; **~ corpuscle** *n* 血细胞; **~ count** *n* 血细胞计数; **~curdling** *adj* 使人毛骨悚然的; **a ~curdling scream** 令人不寒而栗的尖叫; **~ donor** *n* 献血者; **~ feud** *n* 血仇; **~ flow** *n* 血流; **~ group** *n* 血型; **~ heat** *n* [u] 人体血液的正常温度; **~hound** *n* 寻血犬

bloodless /ˈblʌdlɪs/ *adj* **1** (peaceful) 不流血的 ‹*revolution, coup*› **2** (pale) 苍白的 **3** fig (lacking vigour) 无生气的

blood: ~letting *n* [u] **1** Med, esp Hist 放血疗法; **2** (killing) 杀戮; **3** fig (quarrelling) 激烈的争吵; **~line** *n* 血统; **~ lust** *n* [u] 杀戮欲; **~mobile** /ˈblʌdmə,biːl/ *n* Amer 流动采血车; **~ money** *n* [u] **1** (payment for murder) 付给杀手的酬劳; **2** (compensation) 付给被杀者亲属的补偿金; **~ orange** *n* 血橙; **~ plasma** *n* [u] 血浆; **~ poisoning** *n* [u] 败血症; **~ pressure** *n* [u] 血压; **low/high ~ pressure** 低/高血压; **my ~ pressure rose/fell** 我的血压升高了/下降了; **~ product** *n* 血制品; **~ pudding** *n* [u] 血香肠

blood-red ▸ **p. 134**
A *adj* 血红色的
B *n* [u] 血红色

blood: ~ relation, ~ relative *ns* 血亲; **~ sausage** *n* [u] Amer = **~ pudding**; **~ serum** *n* [u] 血清; **~shed** *n* [u] 流血事件; **~shot** *adj* 布满血丝的 ‹*eyes*›; **~-soaked** *adj* 染血的; **~ sport** *n* 猎杀运动; **~stain** *n* 血迹; **~stained** *adj* 有血迹的; **~stock** *n + v sing or pl* 纯种马; **~stream** *n* 体内循环的血液; **~sucker** *n* 吸血虫; fig 吸血鬼; **~ sugar** *n* [u and c] 血糖; **~ sugar level** 血糖水平; **~ test** *n* 验血; **~thirsty** *adj* 嗜杀成性的 ‹*person*›; 描写暴力的 ‹*film, story*›; **~ ties** *npl* 血缘关系; **~ transfusion** *n* 输血; **~ type** *n* 血型; **~ vessel** *n* 血管

bloody /ˈblʌdi/
A *adj* **1** (covered in blood) 流血的 ‹*finger, face*›; 沾满血的 ‹*dagger, bandages*›; **have a ~ nose** 流鼻血 **2** (violent) 血腥的 ‹*battle*› **3** (cruel) 残暴的 ‹*dictator, regime*› **4** *attrib* Brit sl 非常的; pej 该死的; **it's a ~ nuisance/miracle** 真讨厌/真是个奇迹; **you've got a ~ cheek/nerve** 你脸皮真厚/好大胆子; **~ hell!** 真该死!
B *adv* Brit sl 非常; **(it was) ~ awful** (这件事) 糟透了; **~ well** [尤用于命令, 表示气愤或恼怒]; **you ~ (well) do it!** 你非做不可!
C *vt* 使沾上血; **bloodied but unbowed** 百折不挠的

bloody: B~ Mary *n* 血玛丽鸡尾酒; **~-minded** *adj* Brit 存心刁难的; **he's just being ~-minded** 他是在存心找茬儿

bloom /bluːm/
A *n* **1** [c] (flower) 花 **2** [u] (flowering) **in (full) ~** 盛开; **to come into ~** 开花 **3** [u] (on skin, fruit) 粉霜 **4** [u] fig 风华正茂; **to be in the ~ of youth** 正值豆蔻年华; **to take the ~ off sth.** 使某物陈旧
B *vi* **1** (be in/come into flower) 开花 **2** (flourish) 处于繁盛时期; «*person*» 容光焕发; «*confidence*» 大大增加; «*friendship*» 迅速发展

bloomer[1] /ˈbluːmə(r)/ *n* Brit colloq dated (mistake) 愚蠢的错误

bloomer[2] *n* (plant) 开花植物; **late/early ~** lit 花期晚/早的植物; fig 成材晚/早的人

bloomers /ˈbluːməz/ *npl* **1** dated (knickers) 女式短灯笼衬裤 **2** Hist (trousers) 女式短灯笼裤

blooming /ˈbluːmɪŋ/ Brit colloq
A *adj* (for emphasis) 十足的; **~ idiot!** 大傻瓜!
B *adv* 极其; **it ~ well isn't!** 绝对不是!

blooper /ˈbluːpə(r)/ *n* Amer colloq 洋相

blossom /ˈblɒsəm/
A *n* **1** [u] (flowers) 全部花朵; **in full ~** 鲜花盛开; **to come into ~** 开花; **~ time** 花期 **2** [c] (flower) 花
B *vi* **1** (flower) 开花 **2** fig 发展; **she is ~ing into a lovely woman** 她正长成一个楚楚动人的女子

blot /blɒt/
A *n* (mark) 污渍; (of ink) 墨水渍; fig 污点; **a ~ on her character** 她品格上的污点; **a ~ on the landscape** 大煞风景的东西
B *vt* (*pres p etc.* **-tt-**) **1** (dry) 擦干; **to ~ one's lipstick** 擦掉多余的口红 **2** (stain) 弄脏; fig 玷污 ‹*reputation*›

Phrasal verbs
- **blot out** *vt* [**~ out sth., ~ sth. out**] **1** (obscure, make invisible) «*mist, smoke*» 遮蔽; fig 涂掉 ‹*mark, signature*›; 忘却 ‹*thought, memory*› **2** (destroy) 毁灭
- **blot up** *vt* [**~ up sth., ~ sth. up**] 擦干

blotch /blɒtʃ/
A *n* **1** (on skin) 红斑 **2** (of ink, colour) 污渍
B *vt* 弄脏 ‹*paper, face*›
C *vi* 留下污渍

blotchy /ˈblɒtʃi/ *adj* 有斑点的 ‹*skin, complexion*›; 有污渍的 ‹*drawing, page*›

blotter /ˈblɒtə(r)/ *n* **1** (for ink) (paper) 吸墨纸; (pad) 吸墨板 **2** Amer (recording book) 临时记录册

blotting paper /ˈblɒtɪŋ/ *n* [u] 吸墨纸

blotto /ˈblɒtəʊ/ *adj pred* Brit colloq 烂醉的

blouse /blaʊz, Amer blaʊs/ *n* **1** (woman's) 女衬衫 **2** Mil 军装上衣

blow /bləʊ/
A *vi* (*pt* **blew**, *pp* **blown**) **1** (move with air current) «*wind*» 吹; **to see which way the wind is ~ing** fig 看清形势 **2** (be moved by wind) «*leaves, curtain*» 被风吹动 **3** (expel air) 吹气; **she blew on her hot coffee** 她吹着热咖啡 **4** (sound) «*foghorn, whistle*» 吹响 **5** (pant) 喘气; **to puff and ~** 气喘吁吁 **6** Zool «*whale*» 喷水 **7** Elec (burn out) «*fuse*» 熔断 **8** Aut (burst) «*tyre*» 爆裂 **9** Amer colloq (leave quickly) 匆匆离开; ▸ **hot 1**
B *vt* (*pt* **blew**, *pp* **blown**) **1** (propel with air) «*person, wind*» 吹; **to ~ (sb.) a kiss** (向某人) 送飞吻; **to ~ smoke rings** 吐烟圈; **to ~ glass** 吹玻璃; **to be blown off course** 被风吹得偏离航线; **it's ~ing a gale/hurricane** 在刮大风/飓风 **2** (clear) 擤 ‹*nose*› **3** (cause to sound) 吹奏 ‹*musical instrument*›; 吹 ‹*horn*› **4** (explode apart) «*explosion, bomb*» 炸飞; (explode open) 炸开 ‹*safe*›; **to be blown to pieces** 被炸成碎片; **to ~ sb.'s mind** fig colloq

使某人十分诧异 5 Elec (burn out) 熔断 ‹*fuse*›; **to ~ a fuse** *or* **a gasket** *or* **one's lid** *or* **one's top** fig colloq 气炸了 6 Aut (burst) 使…爆裂 ‹*tyre*› 7 colloq (squander) 挥霍 ‹*money*› 8 colloq (mess up) 把…搞砸; **to ~ one's chances** 错失机会; **to ~ one's lines** 念错台词 9 colloq (reveal) 泄露; **to ~ sb.'s cover** 暴露某人的身份 10 (*pp* **~ed**) Brit dated colloq (damn) [表示生气、吃惊或不在意] **~ it!** 该死!; **well, ~ me (down)!** 唉呀, 天哪!; **let's take a taxi, and ~ the expense** 我们坐出租车吧, 管它多少钱

C *n* 1 [c] (stroke) 重击; **to fell sb. with a ~** 一下子将某人打倒; **he was killed by a ~ to the head** 他被击中脑部而死; **to exchange ~s** 互殴; **to come to ~s (over sb./sth.)** (因某人/某事物而) 动武; **to strike a ~ against/for sth.** fig 反对/拥护 ‹*freedom, justice*› 2 [c] fig (shock) 打击; **to deal sb./sth. a ~, to deal a ~ to sb./sth.** 给某人/某物以打击 3 [c] (of nose) **to give one's nose a ~** 擤鼻子 4 [c] Mus 吹奏 5 [u] Brit sl (marijuana) 大麻

Phrasal verbs

• **blow away**

A *vi* «*hat, tent*» 被吹走

B [**~ sth. away, ~ away sth.**] *vt*
1 (with air current) 把…吹走; **to ~ the dust away** 吹去灰尘 2 (with explosives) «*blast*» 把…炸毁

C [**~ sb. away, ~ away sb.**] *vt*
1 colloq (kill with gun) 把…毙了 2 fig colloq (defeat easily) 轻松击败 3 fig colloq (impress) 使感动

• **blow down**

A *vi* «*tree*» 被刮倒

B *vt* [**~ sth. down, ~ down sth.**] «*wind*» 刮倒 ‹*tree*›

• **blow in**

A *vi* 1 (enter) «*rain*» 被吹进来 2 (from blast) «*door, window*» 被向内炸开 3 colloq (arrive) 突然到来

B *vt* [**~ sth. in, ~ in sth.**]
1 (cause to enter) «*wind*» 把…吹进来 ‹*rain*›
2 (by blast) «*bomb*» 向内炸开 ‹*door, window*›

• **blow off**

A *vi* 1 (be removed by the wind) «*hat*» 被吹走 2 (escape) «*gas*» 泄漏 3 Brit colloq (break wind) 放屁

B [**~ sth. off, ~ off sth.**] *vt*
1 (with air current) 把…吹掉 ‹*hat, dust*› 2 (in explosion) «*blast*» 把…炸掉 ‹*limb*› 3 (with one's breath) 把…吹去 ‹*ash, dust*› 4 Amer fig colloq (not attend) 缺席; **to ~ off class** 逃课 5 Amer colloq (ignore) 不理睬 ‹*offer*›

C [**~ sb. off, ~ off sb.**] *vt* Amer colloq 1 (not meet) 放…鸽子 ‹*person*› 2 (end relationship with) 甩掉 ‹*person*›

• **blow out**

A *vi* 1 (be extinguished) «*flame*» 被吹灭 2 (erupt) «*oil well*» 喷发 3 Aut «*tyre*» 爆裂 4 (from blast) «*door, window*» 被向外炸开 5 Amer colloq (be injured) «*knee*» 受重伤

B *vt* [**~ sth. out, ~ out sth.**]
1 (extinguish) 吹灭 ‹*flame*› 2 Aut 使…爆裂 ‹*tyre*› 3 (inflate) 鼓起 ‹*cheeks*› 4 (in explosion) «*blast*» 向外炸开 ‹*door, window*› 5 Amer colloq (injure) 使…受重伤 ‹*knee*› 6 **to ~ itself out** (lose force) «*gale*» 平息

• **blow over**

A *vi* 1 (lose force) «*storm, dispute*» 平息 2 (fall) «*tree*» 被吹倒

B *vt* [**~ sth. over, ~ over sth.**] «*wind*» 吹倒 ‹*tree*›

• **blow up**

A *vi* 1 (explode) «*bomb, building, vehicle*» 爆炸; **to ~ up in sb.'s face** fig «*plan, affair, issue*» 砸锅 2 (gather force) 加剧; **a storm was ~ing up** 狂风大作 3 (start) «*trouble*» 突然发生; «*affair*» 突然曝光 4 colloq (lose temper) 大发雷霆 5 (be inflated) 充气

B [**~ sth. up, ~ up sth.**] *vt*
1 (cause to explode) 引爆 ‹*bomb*›; «*bomb, person*» 炸毁 ‹*building, vehicle*› 2 (inflate) 给…充气 ‹*balloon, tyre*› 3 Phot (enlarge) 放大 ‹*image, photograph*› 4 fig (exaggerate) 夸大 ‹*story*›

C [**~ sb. up, ~ up sb.**] *vt*
1 (with bomb) 炸死 2 colloq dated (reprimand) 训斥

blow-by-blow *adj attrib* 极为详细的

blow-dry

A *n* 吹干; **a cut and ~** 一次剪吹

B *vt* 吹干 ‹*hair*›

blow-dryer, blow-drier *n* 电吹风器

blower /ˈbləʊə(r)/ *n* 1 Brit colloq (telephone) 电话; **to get on the ~ (to sb.)** (给某人) 打电话 2 (machine that blows) 鼓风机

blow: ~fly *n* 丽蝇; **~gun** *n* = **~pipe 1**; **~hole** *n* 1 (of whale) 鼻孔; 2 (in ice) 冰孔; **~ job** *n* taboo sl 口交; **to give sb. a ~ job** 给某人口交; **~lamp** *n* Brit = **blow torch**

blown /bləʊn/ *pp* ▸**blow A, B**

blow: ~out *n* 1 Elec 保险丝熔断; 2 (of tyre) 爆胎; 3 (in oil or gas well) 井喷; 4 colloq (large meal) 大餐; **~pipe** *n* 1 (weapon) 吹矢枪; 2 (of blowtorch) 吹火管; 3 (in glassmaking) 吹管

blowsy /ˈblaʊzi/ *adj* pej 肥硕邋遢的 ‹*woman*›

blow torch *n* 喷灯

blow-up

A *n* 1 Phot 放大的照片 2 colloq (outburst) 大发雷霆

B *adj attrib* 充气的

blowy /ˈbləʊi/ *adj* colloq 刮风的

blowzy /ˈblaʊzi/ *adj* = **blowsy**

blub /blʌb/ *vi* colloq 号啕大哭

blubber /ˈblʌbə(r)/

A *n* 1 [u] (of whale) 鲸脂 2 [u] colloq pej (of person) 赘肉 3 [c] colloq hum (cry) 号啕大哭; **to have a ~** 大哭一场

B *vi* colloq 号啕大哭

blubbery /ˈblʌbəri/ *adj* pej 肥厚的; **to have ~ lips** 嘴唇厚

bludge /blʌdʒ/ Austral, NZ colloq

A *vi* 1 (scrounge) 榨取; **she was bludging off her parents** 她在揩她父母的油 2 (loaf about) 游手好闲

B *n* 轻活儿

bludgeon /ˈblʌdʒən/

A *n* 大头短棒

B *vt* 1 (beat) 用重器击打; **to ~ sb. to death** 重击某人致死 2 fig (to coerce) 逼迫; **to ~ sb. into doing sth.** 强迫某人做某事

bludger /ˈblʌdʒə(r)/ *n* Austral, NZ colloq = **scrounger**

blue /bluː/ ▸**p. 134**

A *adj* 1 (in colour) 蓝色的; **out of the clear ~ sky** colloq 突然; **once in a ~ moon** fig 千载难逢; **to be ~ with** *or* **from cold** 冻得发紫; **black and ~** 青一块紫一块; **to do sth. until one is ~ in the face** colloq 竭尽所能却徒劳无功; **to shout until one is ~ in the face** colloq 喊破喉咙也没用 2 *pred* colloq (depressed) 忧郁的; **to be** *or* **feel ~** 感到忧郁 3 (obscene) 色情的 ‹*movie*› 4 Brit Pol colloq 保守党的; **a true ~ Tory** 真正的英国保守党人

B *n* 1 [u and c] (colour) 蓝色; **he wore ~** 他穿着蓝衣服; **the boys in ~** colloq 警察 2 [u] liter **the ~** (sky) 碧空; (sea) 碧海; fig (faraway place) 遥不可及的地方; **to happen out of the ~** 突然发生; **to vanish into the ~** 消失得无影无踪 3 [c] Brit Univ, Sport (team member) 校队队员 [代表牛津或剑桥大学参加两校之间比赛的运动员]; (award) 蓝色荣誉 [授予参加牛津和剑桥大学之间比赛的运动员的荣誉] 4 [c] Austral, NZ colloq (mistake) 错误 5 [c] Austral, NZ colloq (fight) 打斗

blue: ~ baby *n* 青紫婴儿; **~ baby syndrome** *n* [u] 青紫婴儿综合征; **~bell** *n* (wood hyacinth) 风信子; Scot (harebell) 圆叶风铃草; **B~ Berets** *npl* = **Blue Helmets**; **~berry** *n* 蓝莓; **~bird** *n* 蓝鸲

blue-black ▸**p. 134**

A *adj* 深蓝色的

B *n* [u] 深蓝色

blue: ~ blood *n* 1 [u] (noble lineage) 贵族出身; 2 [c] (person) 出身贵族的人; **~-blooded** *adj* 贵族出身的; **~ book** *n* 1 Brit Pol 蓝皮书; 2 Amer Sch 笔试用蓝皮簿; 3 Amer (society listing) 社会名人录; **~bottle** *n* 青蝇; **~ cheese** *n* [u] 蓝纹奶酪; **~ cheese dressing, ~ cheese sauce** *ns* [u and c] 蓝纹奶酪色拉酱; **~-chip** *adj* 1 Fin 稳妥可靠的; **~-chip shares** 蓝筹股票; 2 (top-quality) 一流的 ‹*product, institution*›; **~-collar** *adj* esp Amer 蓝领的 ‹*worker, union, job*›; **~-eyed** *adj* 蓝眼睛的; **~-eyed boy** *n* Brit fig colloq 宠儿; **~ flag** *n* 1 (award) [欧洲颁发给洁净安全的海滩的] "蓝旗" 奖; 2 Motor racing 蓝旗 [用以示意车手有人试图超车]; **~grass** *n* 1 [u and c] Amer Bot 六月禾; 2 [u] Mus 蓝草音乐

blue-green ▸**p. 134**

A *adj* 青色的

B *n* [u] 青色

blue: B~ Helmets *npl* **the B~ Helmets** 蓝盔战士 [指联合国维和部队成员]; **~ jeans** *npl* 蓝布牛仔裤; **~ law** *n* Amer 蓝色法规 [禁止星期日购物等活动]

Blue Nile ▸**p. 663** *pr n* **the ~** 青尼罗河

blue pencil

A *n* [修改文稿用的] 蓝铅笔; **to go through sth. with a ~** 用蓝铅笔修改某文稿

B **blue-pencil** *vt* (*pres p etc.* Brit, **-l-, -ll-** Amer) 修改 ‹*manuscript, film*›; 删除 ‹*words, section*›

Blue Peter *n* [蓝底正中有白方格的] 开船旗

blueprint /ˈbluːprɪnt/ *n* 1 Archit, Tech 蓝图 2 fig (plan) 规划; **it's a ~ for success** 这是成功的蓝图

blue riband /bluː ˈrɪbənd/, **blue ribbon**

A *ns* 1 (first prize) 蓝绶带 2 (top event) 重大事件; (highest achievement) 最高成就

B **blue-riband, blue-ribbon** *adjs attrib* 一流的

blue: ~ rinse *n* 蓝染发剂; **~ rinse brigade** *n* Brit hum pej 染发大军 [由保守的中老年妇女组成]; **~-sky** *adj* colloq 不切实际的 ‹*thinking*›; 不能实施的 ‹*project*›; **~stocking** *n* pej 才女

blues /bluːz/ *npl* + *v sing or pl* 1 Mus **(the) ~** 布鲁斯音乐, 蓝调; **~ music** 蓝调音乐 2 colloq (feeling of melancholy) **the ~** 忧郁; **to have the ~** 感到忧郁

bluesy /ˈbluːzi/ *adj* 布鲁斯音乐的, 蓝调的

blue: ~ tit *n* 青山雀; **~tongue** *n* [u] 蓝舌病; **~ whale** *n* 蓝鲸

bluff[1]

A *n* (attempt to deceive) 虚张声势; **to call sb.'s ~** 要某人摊牌

B *vi* 虚张声势

C *vt* 靠吹牛哄骗; **to ~ sb. (into doing sth.)** 靠吹牛骗某人 (做某事); **to ~ it out** 蒙混过关

bluff[2] /blʌf/ *adj* (frank, genial) 坦率的

bluff[3]

A *n* (bank) 陡岸; (cliff) 峭壁

B *adj* (steep and broad) 陡峭的

bluffer /ˈblʌfə(r)/ *n* 虚张声势者

bluish /ˈbluːɪʃ/ ▸**p. 134** *adj* 带蓝色的; **~-green/-grey** 绿/灰中带蓝的

blunder /ˈblʌndə(r)/

A *n* 大错

B *vi* 1 (make mistake) 犯大错; **~ badly** 犯大错 2 (move clumsily) 跌跌撞撞地走; **he ~ed into the table** 他跟跟跄跄撞上了桌子

C *vt* 笨嘴拙舌地说

Phrasal verbs

• **blunder about, blunder around**

b

vi 跌跌撞撞; **she ~ed about in the dark** 她摸黑四处瞎撞

• **blunder on, blunder upon** *vt* [**~ on** *or* **upon sth.**] 偶然碰上

blunderbuss /ˈblʌndəbʌs/ *n* 1 Hist (gun) 老式大口径枪 2 fig colloq (clumsy person) 笨拙的人

blunderer /ˈblʌndərə(r)/ *n* 犯大错的人

blundering /ˈblʌndərɪŋ/

A *adj attrib* 笨拙的; **~ idiot!** 白痴!

B *n* 犯大错

blunt /blʌnt/

A *adj* 1 (not sharp) 钝的 ‹*knife*›; 不尖的 ‹*pencil, needle*›; **a ~ instrument** 钝器 2 (frank) 率直的 ‹*person, manner, reply*›; **to be ~ with you** 坦率地说

B *vt* 1 (make less sharp) 使…变钝 ‹*knife, scissors*› 2 fig 减弱; **to ~ one's appetite/enthusiasm** 破坏胃口/冲淡热情

bluntly /ˈblʌntli/ *adv* 直言不讳地; **to put it ~** 坦白地说

bluntness /ˈblʌntnɪs/ *n* [u] 1 (of blade) 钝 2 fig (of person, manner, reply) 直率

blur /blɜː(r)/

A *n* 1 (indistinct shape, events) 模糊形状; **the writing was just a ~ to me** 那笔迹我根本看不清楚; **her memories are just a ~** 她的记忆模糊不清 2 (smudge, mark) 污渍

B *vt* (*pres p etc.* **-rr-**) 使模糊不清; **to ~ the distinction between X and Y** 混淆X和Y之间的区别

C *vi* (*pres p etc.* **-rr-**) «*eyes, boundaries, memories, judgement*» 变模糊

blurb /blɜːb/ *n* (on book cover) 简介; (in advertisement) 产品推介

blurred /blɜːd/ *adj* 模糊不清的; **to have ~ vision** 视线模糊; **a ~ memory of sth.** 对某事物的模糊记忆; **to become ~** «*eyes*» 变模糊

blurry /ˈblɜːri/ *adj* 模糊不清的

blurt /blɜːt/ *vt* = **blurt out**

Phrasal verb

• **blurt out** *vt* [**~ sth. out, ~ out sth.**] 脱口说出; **he ~ed everything out** 他不假思索地说出了一切

blush /blʌʃ/

A *vi* 1 (redden) 脸红; **to ~ at the idea** 因这种想法而脸红 2 (be ashamed) 羞愧; **to ~ for sb.** 为某人感到羞愧; **I ~ to admit it** 我不好意思承认这事

B *n* 1 (flush) 脸红; **without a ~** 不知羞耻地; **to spare sb.'s ~es** 给某人留面子; **to hide one's ~es** 掩饰窘态 2 (rosy tint) 红色; (rosy glow) 红光; **at the first ~ of dawn** 破晓的红霞; **at first ~** liter 据初步印象

blusher /ˈblʌʃə(r)/ *n* [u] 胭脂

blushing /ˈblʌʃɪŋ/ *adj attrib* 脸红的

bluster /ˈblʌstə(r)/

A *vi* 1 (aggressively) 盛气凌人地说话; (indignantly) 气呼呼地说话; **to ~ at sb.** 对某人咆哮 2 (boastfully) 夸口

B *n* [u] 1 (threatening talk) 咄咄逼人的话 2 (empty boasts) 夸口

blustering /ˈblʌstərɪŋ/ *n* [u] 咆哮

blustery /ˈblʌstəri/ *adj* 狂风大作的; **a ~ wind/day** 狂风/大风天

BM *abbr* = **Bachelor of Medicine** 医学士; **to have/do a ~** 持有/攻读医学士学位

BMA *abbr* = **British Medical Association** 英国医学会

BMI *abbr* = **body mass index**

B movie *n* B级电影

BMus *abbr* = **Bachelor of Music** 音乐学士

BNP *abbr* = **British National Party**

BO *abbr* colloq = **body odour**

boa /ˈbəʊə/ *n* 1 Zool 蟒蛇 2 (stole) 长围巾; **a feather ~** 羽毛披肩

boa constrictor /ˈbəʊə kənˌstrɪktə(r)/ *n* 巨蚺

boar /bɔː(r)/ *n* (*pl* **~** *or* **~s**) 1 [c] (wild) 野猪 2 [u] Culin 猪肉 3 [c] (uncastrated male pig) [未阉的] 公猪

board /bɔːd/

A *n* 1 [c] (plank) 木板 2 [c] (for notices) 公告牌 3 [c] Games 棋盘 4 [u] (meals) 膳食; **room and ~** 食宿; **full/half ~** 伙食全包/半包 5 [c] + *v sing or pl* (of organization) 委员会; (of company) 董事会; **to be on the ~** (of organization) 担任委员; (of company) 担任董事; **the ~ of trustees** 理事会; **a ~ meeting** 董事会会议 6 [u] Naut **to go on ~** 上船; **to be on ~** 在船上; **to take sth. on ~** lit 把…装上船 ‹*cargo*›; 让…上船 ‹*passengers*›; fig (accept and understand) 接受; **to take on ~ new ideas** 接纳新观点

B **boards** *npl* Theat colloq **to tread** *or* **walk the ~s** 当演员

C *vt* 1 (get on) 上 ‹*vehicle, ship, aircraft*› 2 Naut (to inspect, to plunder) «*official, pirates*» 强行登上 ‹*ship*› 3 (cover with boards) 用木板覆盖; **to ~ over the floor** 铺地板; **to ~ up the windows** 用木板封窗 4 (accommodate) 收费为…提供食宿 ‹*person*›; 饲养 ‹*animal*›

D *vi* 1 (lodge and have meals) 得到食宿; **to ~ at sb.'s house** 在某人家寄宿 2 (be ready for passengers to get on) «*aircraft*» 请乘客登机; **flight 723 is now ~ing** 723 号航班现在开始登机

boarder /ˈbɔːdə(r)/ *n* 1 (lodger) 寄膳宿者 2 Sch 寄宿生

board game ▸ p. 307 *n* 棋盘游戏

boarding /ˈbɔːdɪŋ/ *n* [u] 1 Aviat 登机; Naut 登船 2 Naut (by customs officer) 检查 3 (boards) (collectively) 木板; (fence) 木栅栏; (floor) 木地板

boarding: ~ card *n* Aviat 登机牌; Naut 登船牌; **~ house** *n* 1 (lodgings) 供膳宿的私人住宅; 2 (school) 寄宿楼; **~ kennel** *n*, **~ kennels** *npl* Brit [狗的] 临时寄养所; **~ party** *n* 登舰部队; **~ pass** *n* = **~ card**; **~ school** *n* 寄宿学校

boardroom /ˈbɔːdruːm, -rʊm/ *n* 1 (room) 董事会会议室 2 fig (people) 董事会; **everyone from shopfloor to ~** 从工人到董事每一个人

board: ~sailing ▸ p. 307 *n* [u] 风帆冲浪运动; **~walk** *n* Amer 木板人行道

boast /bəʊst/

A *vi* 自夸; **to ~ of** *or* **about sth./doing sth.** 自吹某事物/做某事; **nothing to ~ about** 没什么可夸耀的

B *vt* 自豪地拥有; **the town ~s a beautiful church** 小镇上有一座漂亮的教堂

C *n* 夸耀; **it is his ~ that he is never late** 他自吹说从不迟到

boaster /ˈbəʊstə(r)/ *n* 自吹自擂的人

boastful /ˈbəʊstfl/ *adj* 自吹自擂的; **without being ~** 不带吹嘘地; **to make ~ remarks** 自夸

boastfully /ˈbəʊstfəli/ *adv* 自吹自擂地

boastfulness /ˈbəʊstflnɪs/ *n* [u] 自吹自擂

boasting /ˈbəʊstɪŋ/ *n* [u] 吹嘘

boat /bəʊt/

A *n* 1 (small vessel) 小船; **to be in the same ~** fig 处于同样的困境; **to burn one's ~s** Brit fig colloq 破釜沉舟; **to miss the ~** fig colloq 坐失良机; **to push the ~ out** Brit fig colloq 尽情欢庆; **to rock the ~** fig colloq 捣乱 2 (small passenger ship) 渡船; **by ~** 乘船

B *modif* 船的 ‹*shape*›; 乘船的 ‹*trip*›

C *vi* 乘船

boat deck *n* 救生艇甲板

boater /ˈbəʊtə(r)/ *n* 1 (hat) 平顶硬草帽 2 (person) 划船游玩者

boatful /ˈbəʊtfʊl/ *n* (people) 一船人; (cargo) 一船货物

boat: ~hook *n* 撑篙; **~house** *n* 船库

boating /ˈbəʊtɪŋ/ *n* [u] 划船

boat: ~ lift *n* 起船台; **~load** *n* 1 (boatful) 一船; **~loads of tourists** 一船船的游客; 2 fig colloq (large quantity) 大量; **~man** /-mən/ *n* (on ferry) 船夫; (hiring out) 船主; **~ people** *npl* 船民 [指乘船出逃的难民]

boatswain /ˈbəʊsn/ *n* 水手长

boatswain's chair *n* (of a boat) 船侧悬挂作业坐板; (of a building) 高空作业坐板

boat: ~ train *n* 港口联运火车; **~yard** *n* 船坞

bob[1] /bɒb/

A *vi* (*pres p etc.* **-bb-**) 1 (move) 上下快速移动; **to ~ up and down** 颠簸 2 Games 试咬住悬挂物; **to ~ for apples** 咬苹果 3 (curtsy) 行屈膝礼

B *vt* (*pres p etc.* **-bb-**) 1 (nod) 点 ‹*head*›; **to ~ one's head** 点头 2 (curtsy) **to ~ a curtsy (to sb.)** (向某人) 行屈膝礼

C *n* 1 (nod) 点头 2 (curtsy) 屈膝礼 3 (weight) (on plumb line) 铅垂; (on pendulum) 摆锤; (on fishing line) 浮子

bob[2]

A *vt* 剪短 ‹*hair, tail*›

B *n* 1 (hairstyle) 短发 2 (tail) 剪短的马尾

bob[3] *n* (*pl* **bob**) Brit colloq 先令; **I bet that costs a ~ or two** 我敢说那得花不少钱; **he's not short of a ~ or two** 他很有钱

bob[4] *n* Sport (sledge) 大雪橇

bobbin /ˈbɒbɪn/ *n* 线轴

bobble /ˈbɒbl/

A *n* 1 (on hat etc.) 小绒球 2 Amer Sport (fumble) 接球失误

B *vi* 上下跳动

C *vt* Amer Sport 接…失误 ‹*ball*›

bobble hat *n* 绒球羊毛帽

bobby /ˈbɒbi/ *n* Brit dated colloq 警察

bobby: ~-dazzler *n* Brit dated colloq (person) 顶呱呱的人; (thing) 顶呱呱的东西; **~ pin** *n* Amer 发夹; **~ socks, ~ sox** *nspl* Amer 短袜

bobcat /ˈbɒbkæt/ *n* 红猫

bobsleigh Brit /ˈbɒbsleɪ/, **bobsled** Amer /ˈbɒbsled/ ▸ p. 307

A *ns* 大雪橇

B *vi* 乘大雪橇

bobtail /ˈbɒbteɪl/ *n* 1 (tail) 截短的尾巴 2 (dog) 尾巴截短的狗; (horse) 尾巴截短的马

bod /bɒd/ *n* Brit colloq 家伙

bode /bəʊd/ liter

A *vi* 预示; **to ~ well/ill (for sth./sb.)** (对某事物/某人) 是吉兆/凶兆

B *vt* 为…的兆头; **the 12 per cent interest rate ~s difficult times ahead for retailers** 12% 的利率对于零售商来说预示着前景艰难

bodge /bɒdʒ/ Brit colloq

A *vt* 拙劣地修补

B *n* 临时性的修补

bodhran /ˈbaʊrɑːn/ *n* [爱尔兰的] 宝兰鼓

bodice /ˈbɒdɪs/ *n* 1 (of dress) 连衣裙的上身 2 (undergarment) 女式紧身胸衣

bodice ripper *n* hum (novel) 历史色情暴力小说; (film) 历史色情暴力电影

bodily /ˈbɒdɪli/

A *adv* 全部地; **to throw sb. out ~** 把某人整个扔出去

B *adj attrib* 身体的 ‹*function, need*›; **~ fluids** 体液

bodkin /ˈbɒdkɪn/ *n* 大针眼缝针

body /ˈbɒdi/ *n* 1 [c] (of living being) 身体; **~ and soul** fig 全身心地; **to keep ~ and soul together** 勉强糊口; **~ lotion** 润肤露; **~ paint** 人体彩绘 2 [c] (corpse) 尸体 3 [c] (main part) 主体; (of text) 正文; (of car) 车身; (of plane, camera) 机身; (of ship) 船体; (of church) 中殿; (of violin, guitar) 共鸣箱 4 [c] (large quantity) 大量; **a ~ of water** 一片水域; **a large ~ of evidence** 大量证据; **a ~ of support** 众多支持 5 [c] (group) 群体; **the main ~ of the army**

部队的主力; **the student ～** 全体学生; **in a ～** 一起 **6** [c] (organization) 机构; **an advisory ～** 咨询机构 **7** [c] Phys 物体; **heavenly bodies** 天体 **8** [u] (fullness, richness) (of food) 稠度; (of wine) 醇度; (of hair) 浓密度

body: ～ **armour** *n* [u and c] 防弹衣; ～ **art** *n* [u] 人体艺术; ～ **bag** *n* 运尸袋; ～ **belt** *n* **1** Ind, Sport [将保护绳系在上面的] 腰间安全带; **2** (for valuables) 腰包; ～ **blow** *n* **1** lit (punch) 对上体的重击; **2** fig (setback, disappointment) 重挫; **to deal sb./sth. a ～ blow, to deal a ～ blow to sb./sth.** 让某人/某事受重挫; **～board** *n* 卧式冲浪板; **～boarder** *n* 卧式冲浪者; **～boarding** *n* [u] 卧式冲浪运动; **～builder** *n* 健身运动者; **～building** ▸**p. 307** *n* [u] Sport 健身; **～building exercise** 健身运动; **～building food** 健身食品

body-check

A *n* 身体阻截

B *vt* 用身体阻截 ‹*player, opponent*›

body: ～ **clock** *n* 人体钟; ～ **count** *n* 死亡人数统计; **carry out a ～ count** 统计死亡人数; ～ **double** *n* 替身; ～ **fat** *n* [u] 脂肪组织; ～ **filler** *n* [u and c] 车身填充物; ～ **fluids** *npl* 体液; **～guard** *n* **1** (individual) 保镖; **2** (group) 警卫队; ～ **hair** *n* [u] 体毛; ～ **heat** *n* [u] 体温; ～ **image** *n* [u and c] 身体意象; ～ **language** *n* [u] 身势语; ～ **mass index** *n* 体重指数; ～ **mike** *n* colloq 佩戴式话筒; ～ **odour** *n* [u] 体臭; ～ **part** *n* 身体部位; ～ **piercing** *n* [u and c] 人体穿刺 [在人体上刺孔悬挂饰物的行为]; ～ **politic** *n* **the ～ politic** 全体人民; ～ **scan** *n* (examination) 人体扫描检查; (image) 人体扫描图; **～-scanner** *n* 人体扫描机

body search

A *n* 搜身

B **body-search** *vt* 对…搜身

body: ～ **shell** *n* 车架; ～ **shop** *n* esp Amer (for repairs) 车身修理厂; (for manufacture) 车身制造厂; **～snatcher** /-snætʃə(r)/ *n* [昔时盗尸供解剖之用的] 掘墓盗尸人; ～ **stocking** *n* 连裤紧身内衣; **～suit** *n* [运动或跳舞时穿的] 紧身衣; **～surfing** *n* [u] 人体冲浪; ～ **type** *n* 体型; ～ **warmer** *n* 棉背心; ～ **weight** *n* [u and c] 体重; **～work** *n* [u] 车身

Boer /bɔː(r)/ Hist

A *n* 布尔人

B *adj* 布尔人的; **the ～ Wars** 布尔战争

boffin /ˈbɒfɪn/ *n* Brit colloq hum 科研工作者; **a computer ～** 计算机研发人员

bog /bɒg/ *n* [u and c] **1** (marshy ground) 泥塘; **a peat ～** 泥炭沼 **2** Brit sl (toilet) 厕所

Phrasal verb

- **bog down** *vt* **to be/get ～ged down (in sth.)** «*vehicle*» 下陷/开始下陷（进某物中）; **you must not get ～ged down in detail** 千万别拘泥于细节

bogey /ˈbəʊgi/ *n* **1** (evil spirit) 鬼怪 **2** (imagined fear) 使人害怕的事物; **the ～ of recession** 对经济萧条的恐惧 **3** (in golf) 超一击 [超过标准杆数的一击]; **to make** *or* **take a ～** 打出超一击 **4** Brit sl (from nose) 干鼻屎

bogeyman /ˈbəʊgɪmæn/ *n* **1** (evil spirit) 鬼怪; **here comes the ～!** 妖怪来了! **2** (person) 可怕的人; (thing) 可怕的事物

boggle /ˈbɒgl/ colloq

A *vi* **1** (be amazed) 吃惊; **the mind ～s!** 难以置信! ; **the mind** *or* **imagination ～s at the idea** 这个想法真荒唐 **2** (hesitate) 迟疑; **to ～ at sth./doing sth.** 对某事/做某事犹疑不决

B *vt* 使吃惊; **it ～s the mind** 这事难以置信

boggy /ˈbɒgi/ *adj* 湿软的 ‹*ground, patch*›

bogie /ˈbəʊgi/ *n* Brit 转向架

BOGOF /ˈbɒgɒf/ *abbr* = **buy one get one free** 买一送一

Bogotá /ˌbɒgəˈtɑː/ *pr n* 波哥大

bog: ～ **paper** *n* [u] Brit sl 卫生纸; ～ **roll** *n* [u and c] Brit sl 一卷手纸; **～-standard** *adj* Brit colloq (ordinary) 普通的; (basic) 基本的

bogus /ˈbəʊgəs/ *adj* 假的 ‹*claim, qualifications*›; 假冒的 ‹*official*›

bogus caller *n* Brit 假称官员的来访者

Bohemia /bəʊˈhiːmɪə/ *pr n* 波希米亚

Bohemian /bəʊˈhiːmɪən/ ▸**p. 503**

A *adj* **1** (of Bohemia) 波希米亚的 **2** **bohemian** (unconventional) 放荡不羁的 ‹*lifestyle*›; 反世俗陈规的 ‹*mores, quarter*›; **a bohemian style of dress** 另类的穿着风格

B *n* **1** (person from Bohemia) 波希米亚人 **2** **bohemian** (unconventional person) 放荡不羁的人

boil[1] /bɔɪl/

A *vi* **1** Culin «*liquid*» 沸腾; «*pot*» 开; **to ～ dry** 烧干 **2** fig (be turbulent) «*sea*» 翻腾; (be angry) 发怒; **she was ～ing with rage** 她气得火冒三丈

B *vt* **1** (heat) 烧开 ‹*liquid*› **2** Culin (cook) 煮 **3** (wash) 煮沸洗涤 ‹*laundry*›

C *n* [u] **(to be) on the ～** Brit lit 沸腾; fig «*project*» (进行得) 如火如荼; **to go off the ～** Brit lit 停止沸腾; fig «*project*» 进度放慢; «*romance*» 降温; «*person*» 势头减弱; **to bring sth. to the ～** lit 将某物煮沸; fig 使某事紧张进行; **to come to the ～** lit 开始沸腾; **the situation came to the ～** 局势达到白热化

Phrasal verbs

- **boil away** *vi* **1** (keep boiling) 持续沸腾 **2** (evaporate) (become less) 煮浓; (disappear) 煮干
- **boil down**

  A *vi* **1** Culin (be reduced) 熬浓 **2** **to ～ down to sth.** fig (be the essence of) 归结为某事物

  B *vt* [**～ sth. down**] **1** Culin 熬浓 **2** fig (make shorter) 压缩 ‹*report*›; **to ～ the speech down to ten minutes** 将演讲压缩到 10 分钟
- **boil over** *vi* **1** lit (overflow) 溢出 **2** fig (erupt) «*person, situation*» 失控; **to ～ over into open conflict** 失控而演变为公开冲突

ℹ The human body

Describing people

■ Describing hair:

She has long hair
= 她留着长发

Her hair is very long
= 她的头发很长

a lady with long hair
or ***a long-haired lady***
= 一位长发女子

■ Describing eyes:

He has blue eyes
= 他有双蓝眼睛

He is blue-eyed
or ***His eyes are blue***
= 他蓝眼睛

a blue-eyed gentleman
or ***a gentleman with blue eyes***
= 一位蓝眼睛的绅士

■ Describing other features:

His nose is big
or ***He has a big nose***
= 他的鼻子大
or 他有个大鼻子

He has high cheekbones
= 他的颧骨高高的

She is rosy-cheeked
or ***She has rosy cheeks***
= 她的脸颊红扑扑的

She has a pretty face
= 她有一张漂亮的脸蛋儿
or 她长得很漂亮

She has an oval face
= 她是鹅蛋脸

He has a round face
= 他的脸圆圆的
or 他有张圆脸

She has a small mouth
= 她嘴巴小小的

He has a big/wide mouth
= 他嘴巴大大的

Use of the possessive adjective

■ Unlike in English, Chinese does not use a possessive adjective when the subject and recipient of the action are the same person:

The boy raised his hand
= 那男孩举起了手

Close your eyes
= 闭上眼睛

Open your mouth wide, please
= 请把嘴张大

I broke my arm
= 我弄断了胳膊

She was holding her face in her hands
= 她用手捂着脸

He held me in his arms
= 他抱住了我

He rubbed his eyes sleepily
= 他困倦地揉了揉眼

I put my hands in my pockets
= 我把手放进口袋

■ In Chinese, as in English, in a sentence where the subject and recipient of the action are different, the possessive must be included before the recipient:

My mother put her hand on my forehead
= 母亲把手放在我的额头上

The little girl stroked the cat's head with her fingers
= 小姑娘轻轻地用手指抚摸猫的头

She held her husband's hand
= 她握住了丈夫的手

■ Note the difference in the Chinese translation of the two examples below. A possessive adjective must be used in the second example because the person whose body it is does not perform the action:

She broke her toes
= 她弄断了脚趾

The glass bowl broke her toes
= 玻璃碗弄断了她的脚趾

b

• **boil up**
A *vi* **1** lit (come to the boil) «*liquid*» 沸腾 **2** fig (surge up) 即将爆发
B *vt* [**~ up sth., ~ sth. up**] Brit 把…煮沸

boil² *n* Med 疖

boiled /bɔɪld/ *adj* 煮沸的 ‹*liquid*›; 煮熟的 ‹*vegetables, meat*›; **~ water** 开水; **a ~ sweet** Brit 硬糖

boiler /ˈbɔɪlə(r)/ *n* (in heating system, locomotive) 锅炉; (for storing hot water) 盛热水器

boiler: ~ house *n* 锅炉房; **~maker** ▸**p. 409** *n* (manufacturing) 锅炉制造工; (repairing) 锅炉修理工; (for assemblage) 锅炉装配工; **~ room** *n* **1** lit 锅炉间; **2** Comm 电话推销室 [以硬性或欺骗性手段向投资者推销产品]; **~ suit** *n* Brit 连裤工作服

boiling /ˈbɔɪlɪŋ/
A *adj* **1** *attrib* (at boiling point) 达到沸点的 ‹*liquid*›; **~ water kills the bacteria** 沸水能杀菌 **2** *pred* fig colloq (hot) «*weather*» 炎热的; «*temperature*» 极高的; **it's ~ in here!** 这里热极了!; **I'm ~!** 我热死了! **3** *pred* fig colloq (enraged) 很恼火的; **to be ~ with rage** 怒不可遏
B *adv* 非常; **a ~ hot day** 酷热的一天; **the water was ~ hot** 水很烫
C *n* [u] (act of boiling) 沸腾; (point of boiling) 沸点

boiling point *n* [u and c] lit 沸点; fig 爆发点; **to reach ~** 达到沸点; **he/his temper was close to ~** 他那时快要发火了

boil-in-the-bag meal *n* 袋装方便餐

boisterous /ˈbɔɪstərəs/ *adj* 活泼好动的 ‹*person*›; 热闹的 ‹*game*›

boisterously /ˈbɔɪstərəsli/ *adv* 热闹地

bok choy /bɒk ˈtʃɔɪ/ *n* [u] Amer **= pak choi**

bold /bəʊld/
A *adj* **1** (daring) 大胆的; (courageous) 勇敢的; **it was a ~ step to take** 迈出这一步很勇敢; **put on** *or* **up a ~ front** 表现出勇气 **2** (forward, impudent) 冒失的; **if I may make so ~ as to suggest that ...** formal 恕我冒昧提议…; **as ~ as brass** colloq 厚颜无耻 **3** (strong, clear) 醒目的 ‹*colour, pattern, underlining*›; **paint with ~ strokes of the brush** 笔法遒劲地绘画 **4** Print 黑体的; **~ type/letters** 黑体/黑体字
B *n* Print **~(face)** 黑体; **in ~** 用黑体

boldly /ˈbəʊldli/ *adv* **1** (daringly) 大胆地 **2** (impudently) 冒失地 **3** (strongly, clearly) 清晰地 ‹*stand out, draw*›; **~ coloured** 色彩鲜艳的

boldness /ˈbəʊldnɪs/ *n* [u] **1** (intrepidity) 勇敢 **2** (impudence) 冒失 **3** (of design, colour) 鲜明

bole /bəʊl/ *n* 树干

Bolivia /bəˈlɪvɪə/ *pr n* 玻利维亚

Bolivian /bəˈlɪvɪən/ ▸**p. 503**
A *adj* (of Bolivia) 玻利维亚的; (of the people) 玻利维亚人的
B *n* 玻利维亚人

boll /bəʊl/ *n* 棉铃

bollard /ˈbɒlɑːd/ *n* **1** (on quay, ship) 系缆柱 **2** Brit (on road etc.) 护柱

bollocking /ˈbɒləkɪŋ/ *n* Brit taboo sl 臭骂; **to give sb. a ~** 把某人臭骂一通; **to get a ~** 挨一通臭骂

bollocks /ˈbɒləks/ Brit taboo sl
A *n* (rubbish) 废话; **it's a load of ~!** 一派胡言!
B *excl* 胡说
C *npl* (testicles) 睾丸

Phrasal verb

• **bollocks up** *vt* [**~ sth. up, ~ up sth.**] Brit taboo sl 把…搞糟

Bollywood /ˈbɒlɪwʊd/ *pr n* 宝莱坞 [印度电影业]; **a ~ film** 宝莱坞影业

Bologna /bəˈləʊnjə/
A *pr n* Geog 波伦亚
B **bologna** *n* Amer Culin 波伦亚大红肠

Bolognese /ˌbɒləˈneɪz/ *adj* 番茄牛肉末的; **~ sauce** 番茄牛肉酱; **spaghetti ~** 意大利番茄牛肉面

boloney /bəˈləʊni/ *n* **1** **= baloney** **2** Amer **= Bologna B**

Bolshevik /ˈbɒlʃəvɪk, Amer ˈbəʊl-/ Hist
A *n* **1** (party member) 布尔什维克; (supporter) 布尔什维克支持者 **2** pej (revolutionary) 极端分子
B *adj* 布尔什维克的; **~ party/revolution** 布尔什维克党/革命

Bolshevism /ˈbɒlʃəvɪzəm, Amer *also* ˈbəʊl-/ *n* [u] Hist 布尔什维克主义

Bolshevist /ˈbɒlʃəvɪst, Amer *also* ˈbəʊl-/ Hist
A *n* (party member) 布尔什维克; (supporter) 布尔什维克支持者
B *adj* 布尔什维克的; **~ party/revolution** 布尔什维克党/革命

bolshie, bolshy /ˈbɒlʃi/ *adj* Brit colloq 难缠的 ‹*person*›; 抵触的 ‹*attitude, mood*›; **to get ~** 变得不合作

bolster /ˈbəʊlstə(r)/
A *n* 长枕
B *vt* **1** (boost) 鼓舞 ‹*morale*›; 增强 ‹*confidence*›; **to ~ sb.'s ego** 增强某人的自尊心 **2** (support, shore up) 支持 ‹*economy, argument*› **3** (pad) 给…加衬垫 ‹*seat*›

bolt¹ /bəʊlt/
A *n* **1** (lock) 插销; **to shoot a ~** (lock) 插上插销; (unlock) 拔下插销 **2** Tech (screw) 螺栓 **3** **a ~ of lightning** 闪电; **a ~ from the** *or* **out of the blue** fig (sth. good) 意外惊喜; (sth. bad) 飞来横祸 **4** (for crossbow) 弩箭; **to have shot one's ~** colloq 已竭尽全力 **5** (of rifle) 枪栓
B *vt* **1** (lock) 用插销闩上 ‹*window, door*›; **to be ~ed shut** 被闩住 **2** Constr 用螺栓固定 ‹*plate, section*›
C *adv* **~ upright** 笔直地

bolt²
A *vi* **1** (flee) «*person*» 逃跑; «*horse*» 脱缰; **to ~ in/out/off** 逃进/逃出/逃离 **2** (run) 猛跑; **he ~ed in, grabbed his briefcase, and ~ed out again** 他冲进来抓起公文包又冲了出去 **3** Hort «*plant*» 过早结实
B *vt* **~ (down)** (swallow) 匆匆吞下 ‹*food*›
C *n* (dash) 猛冲; **to make a ~ for it** 迅速逃跑; **to make a ~ for the door/the garden** 突然冲向门口/花园

bolt-hole *n* Brit **1** (burrow) 地洞 **2** fig (refuge) 藏身处

bomb /bɒm/
A *n* **1** (explosive device) 炸弹; **the B~** 核武器; **this room looks like a ~'s hit it** colloq 这间屋子里乱七八糟的; **to go like a ~** Brit colloq «*vehicle*» 飞驰; **to go down a ~** Brit colloq 大获成功 **2** Brit colloq (large sum) 大笔钱; **to cost/spend a ~** colloq 花一大笔钱
B *vt* 轰炸
C *vi* colloq **1** Brit (move fast) «*car, train*» 疾驰; «*person*» 飞奔; **to ~ up/down the road** 沿路飞驰而来/去 **2** Theat (fail) «*show, play, film*» 惨败

Phrasal verb

• **bomb out** *vt* [**~ sb./sth. out, ~ out sb./sth.**] 炸毁 ‹*building*›; 把…炸得无家可归 ‹*person, family*›

bomb: ~ aimer *n* 轰炸机瞄准手; **~ alert** *n* Brit 炸弹警告

bombard /bɒmˈbɑːd/ *vt* **1** Mil 轰炸 **2** fig (overwhelm) 使应接不暇; **to be ~ed with questions/criticisms** 受到连珠炮般的提问/遭到大肆抨击 **3** Phys 轰击; **to ~ sth. with sth.** 用某物轰击

bombardier /ˌbɒmbəˈdɪə(r)/ *n* **1** Brit Aviat, Mil 炮兵下士 **2** Amer (in US air force) 投弹手

bombardment /bɒmˈbɑːdmənt/ *n* **1** [u and c] Mil 轰炸 **2** [c] fig (barrage) 一连串; **a ~ of electronic messages** 接二连三的电子邮件 **3** [u and c] Phys 轰击

bombast /ˈbɒmbæst/ *n* [u] 大话

bombastic /ˌbɒmˈbæstɪk/ *adj* 华而不实的 ‹*speech, style*›

bombastically /ˌbɒmˈbæstɪkli/ *adv* 浮夸地 ‹*speak, write*›

bomb: ~ attack *n* 炸弹袭击; **suicide ~ attacks** 自杀式炸弹袭击; **~ bay** *n* 炸弹舱; **~ blast** *n* (explosion) 炸弹爆炸; (blast wave) 冲击波; **~ crater** *n* 弹坑

bomb disposal *n* [u] 炸弹处理

bomb disposal: ~ expert ▸**p. 409** *n* 炸弹处理专家; **~ squad, ~ unit** *ns* 炸弹处理小组

bombed /bɒmd/ *adj* Amer colloq (intoxicated) (by drink) 烂醉的; (by drugs) 晕乎乎的

bomber /ˈbɒmə(r)/ *n* **1** Aviat, Mil 轰炸机; **a ~ squadron/pilot** 轰炸机中队/飞行员 **2** (terrorist) (planting) 安放炸弹者; (throwing) 投掷炸弹者

bomber jacket *n* 紧腰短夹克

bombing /ˈbɒmɪŋ/ *n* **1** [u] Mil 轰炸; **a ~ mission** 轰炸任务 **2** [c] (terrorist act) 炸弹袭击; **a ~ target** 炸弹袭击的目标

bombing: ~ campaign *n* **1** (by air force) 系列空袭; **2** (by terrorists) 系列爆炸行动; **~ raid** *n* 空袭; **~ run** *n* 轰炸航路

bomblet /ˈbɒmlɪt/ *n* 小炸弹

bomb: ~load *n* 载弹量; **~proof** *adj* 防弹的 ‹*shelter, window*›; **~ scare** *n* 炸弹恐吓; **~shell** *n* **1** fig (shock) 令人震惊的事物; **to drop a ~shell** 宣布惊人的消息; **2** colloq (woman) 性感美女; **a blonde ~shell** 金发美女; **~ shelter** *n* 防空洞; **~sight** *n* 轰炸瞄准器; **~site** *n* 轰炸后的废墟; **the flat looked like a ~site when I got home** 我回家后发现公寓中一片狼藉; **~ squad** *n* + *v sing or pl* 反爆组

bona fide /ˌbəʊnə ˈfaɪdi/ *adj* 真正的 ‹*tourist, member*›; 真诚的 ‹*offer, agreement*›

bona fides /ˌbəʊnə ˈfaɪdiːz/ *n* + *v sing or pl* formal 诚意

bonanza /bəˈnænzə/
A *n* 发财机遇
B *modif* 获利丰厚的 ‹*year, period*›

bond /bɒnd/
A *n* **1** (link) 纽带; **to feel a strong ~ with sb.** 感到和某人关系密切; **the experience forged a ~ between them** 那次经历把他们联系在了一起 **2** (fetter) 镣铐; fig liter 枷锁; **to break the ~s of routine** 打破常规的束缚 **3** Fin 债券 **4** (adhesion) 黏合剂 **5** Chem 键 **6** Jur (deposit, guarantee) 契约; **my word is my ~** 我一定会履行诺言 **7** Constr 砌合 **8** (at customs) 关栈保税 [指把货物放在海关的堆栈中, 待完税后取出]; **in ~** 在关栈中
B *vt* **1** (stick) **~ (together)** «*adhesive*» 黏合 ‹*surfaces, materials*› **2** (at customs) 把…存入关栈 ‹*goods*›
C *vi* **1** esp Psych 建立密切关系; **the mother and baby ~ed quickly** 母亲和婴儿很快建立了感情 **2** (adhere) «*material, surface*» 黏合

bondage /ˈbɒndɪdʒ/ *n* [u] **1** liter (slavery) 奴役; fig 束缚; **be in ~ to sb./sth.** 成为某人/某事物的奴隶 **2** (sexual practice) 捆绑式性交

bonded warehouse *n* 关栈, 保税仓库

bondholder /ˈbɒndˌhəʊldə(r)/ *n* 债券持有人

bonding /ˈbɒndɪŋ/ *n* [u] esp Psych (establishment of bond) 亲密关系的形成; (bonds) 情谊; **male ~** 男性情谊; **~ time/period** 亲密关系形成时期

bone /bəʊn/
A *n* **1** [c] (of human, animal) 骨头; **a fish ~** 一根鱼刺; **to break a ~** 骨折; **no ~s broken** 没有伤筋动骨; **a ~ of contention** (cause) 争端的起因; (subject) 争议点; **close** *or* **near to the ~** (accurate) 说话太直率的; (risqué) 下流的; **to cut close to the ~** 一针见血; **to cut sth. to the ~** 尽量削减某物; **to have a ~ to pick with sb. (about sth.)** colloq (因某事物) 对某人有怨言; **I've got a ~ to pick with you**

about this report 我对你这份报告不满意 **2** [u] (calcified material) 骨质; **a ～ handle/button/ornament** 骨质把手/纽扣/饰物 **3** [c] (in corset etc.) 鲸骨

B **bones** *npl* (human remains) 尸骨; (animal skeleton) 骨骼; **I need somewhere to rest my old ～s** hum 我这把老骨头得找个地方休息一下了; **(he's just) a bag of ～s** colloq (他)骨瘦如柴; **to feel sth. in one's ～s** 凭直觉感觉到某事物; **to make no ～s about sth.** 对某事直言不讳; ▸**bare A2**

C *vt* 剔去…的骨头 ‹*joint, piece of meat*›; 剔去…的刺 ‹*fish*›

Phrasal verb

- **bone up on** *vt* [**～ up on sth.**] colloq 温习 ‹*subject*›

bone: ～ china *n* [u] 骨灰瓷; **～-crunching** *adj* colloq 凶猛的 ‹*tackle, force*›

boned /bəʊnd/ *adj* **1** Culin 去骨的 ‹*joint, fillet*› **2** Clothg 用鲸骨撑起的 ‹*corset, etc.*›

-boned /bəʊnd/ *combining form* 有…骨骼的; **fine/strong～** 骨骼纤细的/强壮的

bone: ～ dry *adj* 干透的; **～head** *n* colloq 傻瓜; **～headed** *adj* colloq 愚蠢的 ‹*person, remark*›; **～ idle** *adj* Brit colloq 很懒散的

boneless /ˈbəʊnlɪs/ *adj* **1** lit 去骨的 ‹*meat, fish*› **2** fig (feeble) 软弱的

bone: ～ marrow *n* [u] 骨髓; **～-marrow transplant** *n* 骨髓移植; **～meal** *n* [u] 骨粉

boner /ˈbəʊnə(r)/ *n* Amer **1** colloq (mistake) 愚蠢的错误; **to pull a ～** 犯愚蠢的错误 **2** taboo sl (erection) 阴茎勃起

bone: ～ shaker *n* Brit colloq **1** (old vehicle) 破旧的车辆; **2** (bicycle) 无橡胶轮胎的老式自行车; **～ structure** *n* **1** (facial) 脸盘; **2** (skeleton) 骨架; **～yard** *n* Amer colloq 墓地

bonfire /ˈbɒnfaɪə(r)/ *n* (of rubbish) 火堆; (for celebration) 篝火; **to have a ～** 燃起篝火

Bonfire Night *n* 篝火之夜

> **Bonfire Night**
>
> 篝火之夜，亦称盖伊·福克斯之夜（Guy Fawkes Night）。1605年，一批天主教教徒不满信奉新教的英国王室统治，暗中策划火药阴谋（Gunpowder Plot），企图在11月5日国会开幕典礼的时候炸死国王詹姆斯一世（James I）、炸毁国会大楼。但在11月5日的前一天晚上，负责点燃火药的盖伊·福克斯在国会大楼附近一处地下室被抓，火药被发现，阴谋败露。11月5日晚，英国民众点燃篝火，庆祝阴谋失败。后来就成了每年一度的传统。

bongo /ˈbɒŋɡəʊ/ ▸**p. 395** *n* (*pl* **～s** *or* **～es**) **a ～ (drum)** 邦戈手鼓

bonhomie /ˌbɒnəˈmiː/ *n* [u] 和蔼; **false ～** 伪善

bonk /bɒŋk/

A *vt* **1** colloq (hit) 撞击 ‹*person, part of body*›; **to ～ one's head against sth.** 头部撞到某物 **2** Brit taboo sl hum (have sex with) 与…性交

B *vi* Brit taboo sl hum 性交

C *n* **1** colloq (blow) 敲击; **give it a ～ with the hammer** 用锤子敲它一下 **2** Brit taboo sl hum (sexual intercourse) 性交; **to have a ～** 性交 **3** (sound) 嘭声; **there was a ～ as if something had fallen over** 嘭的一声像是有东西倒了

D *adv* colloq 在轻微的撞击下 ‹*come down, fall down*›; **it fell over ～ on its side** 它被撞了一下就侧着倒下了

bonkers /ˈbɒŋkəz/ *adj* Brit colloq 疯狂的; **you must be ～ to turn down a job like that!** 你拒绝了那样一份工作简直愚蠢透顶!; **this puzzle is driving me ～!** 这个谜快把我逼疯了!

bonnet /ˈbɒnɪt/ *n* **1** (hat) (baby's) 童帽; (woman's) 系带女帽; Scot 无边呢帽 **2** Brit Aut 引擎罩

bonny /ˈbɒni/ *adj* Scot **1** (attractive, fine) 漂亮的 ‹*lass, lad, house*› **2** (plump) 胖嘟嘟的 ‹*baby*›

bonsai /ˈbɒnsaɪ/ *n* **1** [u] (art) 盆栽艺术 **2** [c] (*pl* **bonsai**) (plant) 盆景; **a ～ garden** 盆景花园

bonus /ˈbəʊnəs/ *n* (*pl* **～es**) **1** Comm (paid to employee) 奖金; (paid to shareholder) 红利 **2** Brit (insurance) 分红; **the company is paying a ～ of 5% on dividends**; 公司将支付5%的红利 **3** (advantage) 额外的好处

bonus: ～ issue *n* Brit 红股发行; **～ point** *n* 奖励分; **～ scheme** *n* 奖金方案; **～ share** *n* 红股

bony /ˈbəʊni/ *adj* **1** (thin) 瘦削的 ‹*person, finger, face*› **2** (with many bones) 多骨的; **～ fish** 硬骨鱼 **3** (of bone) 骨质的; (like bone) 似骨的 ‹*material*›

bonzer /ˈbɒnzə(r)/ *n* Austral, NZ colloq 极好的; **it was a ～ weekend** 那是个美妙的周末

boo /buː/

A *excl* (surprising sb.) 嗨; (jeer) 嘘; **he/she wouldn't say ～ to a goose** 他/她非常羞怯; **～! ～! send him off, ref!** 嘘! 嘘! 让他下去，裁判!

B *n* 嘘声

C *vt* (*3rd pers sing pres* **～s**; *pt, pp* **～ed**) 向…发嘘声; **be ～ed off the stage** 在一片倒彩声中下台

D *vi* (*3rd pers sing pres* **～s**; *pt, pp* **～ed**) 发嘘声

boob /buːb/ colloq

A *n* **1** Brit (mistake) 愚蠢的错误 **2** (woman's breast) 乳房 **3** Amer colloq (idiot) 傻瓜

B *vi* Brit 犯愚蠢的错误

boo-boo /ˈbuːbuː/ *n* Amer colloq 愚蠢的错误; **to make a ～** 犯愚蠢的错误

boob tube *n* colloq **1** Brit Clothg 紧身无带胸衣 **2** Amer (television) 电视机

booby /ˈbuːbi/ *n* **1** colloq dated (silly person) 傻瓜 **2** Zool (gannet) 鲣鸟 **3** esp Amer colloq = **boob A3**

booby prize *n* 末名奖 [作为玩笑颁发]

booby trap

A *n* **1** Mil 饵雷 **2** (joke) 恶作剧

B **booby-trap** *vt* (*pres p etc.* **-pp-**) 在…中放置饵雷 ‹*car, building*›

boogie /ˈbuːɡi/

A *n* [u] 布吉乐

B *vi* colloq 随流行乐起舞

boogie: ～ board *n* 冲浪趴板; **～-woogie** *n* = **boogie A**

boogy board *n* = **boogie board**

boohoo /ˌbuːˈhuː/ *excl* usu hum 呜呜

booing /ˈbuːɪŋ/ *n* [u] 喝倒彩

book /bʊk/

A *n* **1** (printed work) 书; **a ～ of quotations/poems/proverbs** 引语集/诗集/谚语集; **a ～ about** *or* **on sb./sth.** 关于某人/某事物的书; **a ～ by sb.** 某人写的书; **the first ～ of the trilogy** 三部曲之第一部; **Carlton B～s** 卡尔顿图书公司; **to read sb. like a ～** 对某人了如指掌; **to be a closed ～ to sb.** 令某人无法理解; **～ trade/publishing** 图书贸易/出版; **a ～ review** 书评 **2** (part of printed work) 卷; **Paradise Lost is an epic poem in twelve ～s** 《失乐园》是一部12卷的史诗 **3** Fin (for recording deposits, withdrawals) 账簿 **4** Sch (exercise book) 练习本; **in sb.'s ～** 依某人看; **to be in sb.'s good/bad ～s** 令某人喜欢/厌烦; **one for the ～** colloq 值得注意的事 **5** Sport (of referee) 犯规登记本 **6** (set of items) 板; **a ～ of tickets/stamps/matches** 一本票券/一封邮票/一纸板火柴 **7** (in betting) 赌注登录; **to open** *or* **start a ～ on sb./sth.** 对某人/某事物下赌注; **to keep** *or* **make a ～** *or* Amer **make ～ on sb./sth.** 拿某人/某物打赌 **8** colloq (telephone directory) **the ～** 电话簿 **9** (rule book) 规章手册; **by the ～** 严格遵守规章; **we must go by the ～** 我们必须照章办事; **to throw the ～ at sb.** (reprimand) 痛斥某人; (accuse) 拼命给某人加罪名; (punish) 严惩某人; (sentence) 重判某人; **to bring sb. to ～ (for sth./doing sth.)** esp Brit (make them explain) (因某事物/做某事)要求某人做出解释; (punish) (因某事/做某事)惩罚某人 **10** (libretto of opera) 唱词; (libretto of musical) 歌词; (script of play) 剧本

B **books** *npl* **1** Comm 账目; **to do/keep the ～s** 查账/记账; **to close the ～s** 结平账目 **2** Admin (records) 记录; **to be on sb.'s/sth.'s ～s** 已在某人处/某机构登记入册; **to take sb./sth. off the ～s** 将某人/某物除名; **she is on the ～s of the tennis and golf clubs** 她是网球和高尔夫俱乐部的注册会员; **to be on the ～s** ‹*law*› 是现行法律; **as long as repressive laws remain on the ～s ...** 只要压迫性法律仍然存在…

C *vt* **1** (reserve) 预订; (secure services or time of) 预约; (secure a period of time for) 提前安排 ‹*appointment, holiday, time*›; **to ～ sth. for sb., to ～ sb. sth.** 为某人预订某物; **to ～ sb. into a hotel** 为某人预订酒店; **to ～ oneself into a hotel** 为自己预订酒店; **～ sb. on a plane/train/bus/ship (arrange for sb. to travel on)** 为…预订飞机/火车/公车/船; **2** Jur 将…记录在案 ‹*person*›; **to ～ sb. for sth.** 因某事物将某人记录在案 **3** Brit Sport ‹*referee*› 记名警告 ‹*player*›; **to ～ sb. for sth./doing sth.** 因某事物/做某事记名警告某人

D *vi* 预订; **～ now to avoid disappointment** 现在预订，以免落空

Phrasal verbs

- **book in** Brit

A *vt* [**～ sb./sth. in, ～ in sb./sth.**] **1** (make reservation for) 为…预订; **to ～ the car in for its service** 为小轿车预定保养服务; **to ～ oneself in** 为自己预订房间 **2** (register arrival of) 为…办理入住手续 ‹*passenger*›; **to ～ oneself in** 为自己办理入住手续

B *vi* 办理入住手续

- **book into** *vt* [**～ into sth.**] (arrange to stay at) 办理手续入住 ‹*hotel*›; **I ～ed straight into a hotel** 我径直登记住进了旅馆
- **book on, book on to** *vt* [**～ on sth.**] (arrange to travel on) 预订 ‹*plane, train, bus, ship*›
- **book up** *vt* **1** [**～ sth. up, ～ up sth.**] (reserve) 把…预订一空 ‹*hotel, restaurant, plane*› **2** **to be ～ed up** (be busy, have no time or space) 已排满

bookable /ˈbʊkəbl/ *adj* 可预订的 ‹*flight, ticket*›

book: ～binder ▸**p. 409** *n* 装订工; **～binding** *n* [u] 装订; **～case** *n* 书架; **～ club** *n* **1** (organization selling books) 读者俱乐部; **2** (reading group) 书友会; **～-club edition** *n* 读者俱乐部专卖版; **～end** *n* 书挡; **～ fair** *n* 书市

> **the Booker Prize**
>
> 布克奖，亦称曼-布克奖（Man Booker Prize），简称the Booker。英国著名小说奖，始创于1968年，每年秋天颁奖，颁奖对象定为由英联邦成员国及爱尔兰共和国作家创作的、当年出版的英语小说。获奖者的奖金最初由英国的布克-麦康内尔（Booker-McConnell）公司提供。2002年，布克奖基金会成立，曼集团公司（Man Group）取得奖金的赞助权，将其改为曼-布克奖。2005年开始设国际奖（Man Booker International Prize），每两年颁发一次，对象为其他国家作家的英语作品或译著。

bookie /ˈbʊki/ *n* colloq **1** (person) 赌注登记经纪人 **2** **bookie's** (shop) 赌注登记处

booking /ˈbʊkɪŋ/ *n* **1** [u and c] Brit (reservation) 预订; **to make/accept a ～** 预订/接受预订 **2** [c] (engagement for performance) 演出约定 **3** [c] Brit Sport (from referee) 记名警告; **to get a ～** 受到记名警告

b

booking: ~ clerk ▸p. 409 *n* Brit 售票员; **~ fee** *n* (for room, seat) 预订费; (for ticket) 订票费; **~ form** *n* Brit 预订表; **~ office** *n* Brit 售票处

bookish /ˈbʊkɪʃ/ *adj* [1] (studious) 学究气的 ‹*person, appearance*› [2] (literary) 书面的; 书卷气的 ‹*style*›; **~ language** 书面语

bookishness /ˈbʊkɪʃnɪs/ *n* [u] [1] (studiousness) 学究气 [2] (literariness) 书卷气

book: ~ jacket *n* 护封; **~keeper** ▸p. 409 *n* 簿记员; **~keeping** *n* [u] 簿记; **~-learning** *n* [u] 书本知识

booklet /ˈbʊklɪt/ *n* 小册子

book: ~list *n* 书单; **~ lover** *n* 喜欢书籍的人; **~maker** ▸p. 409 *n* [1] (person) 赌注登记经纪人; [2] **bookmaker's** (shop) 赌注登记处; **~making** *n* [u] 赌注登记

bookmark /ˈbʊkmɑːk/

A *n* [1] (for books) 书签 [2] Comput 电子书签, 收藏夹

B *vt* Comput 为…做电子书签, 把…添加到收藏夹 ‹*site, page*›

book: ~mobile /ˈbʊkməˌbiːl/ *n* Amer [设在汽车上的] 流动图书馆; **~plate** *n* 藏书票; **~rest** *n* Brit 看书架; **~seller** ▸p. 409 *n* [1] (person) 书商; [2] **bookseller's** (shop) 书店; **~selling** *n* [u] 书籍销售; **~shelf** *n* 书架; **~shop** *n* esp Brit 书店; **~stall** *n* [1] (at fair, market) 书摊; [2] Brit (at airport, station) 书报亭; **~store** *n* esp Amer 书店; **~ token** *n* Brit [作为礼物的] 购书礼券; **I sent her a ~ token for Christmas** 我送给她一张购书券作为圣诞礼物; **~ value** *n* 账面价值; **~worm** *n* 书虫; **he's a real ~worm** 他真是个书呆子

Boolean /ˈbuːlɪən/ *adj* 布尔数学体系的

boom[1] /buːm/

A *n* [1] [c] (of artillery, thunder, sea, waves) 隆隆声; (of wind) 呼呼声; (of organ, voices) 嗡嗡声 [2] [u and c] Comm, Econ (increase) 繁荣; (in prices) 暴涨; (period of prosperity) 繁荣期; **a population ~** 人口激增; **a ~ year** 兴盛的一年

B *vi* [1] (thunder, reverberate) «*organ, voice, person*» 发出嗡嗡声; «*wind*» 呼呼作响; «*guns, sea, thunder*» 发出隆隆声 [2] Comm, Econ «*economy, trade*» 繁荣; «*prices*» 暴涨; «*exports, sales*» 激增; **business is ~ing** 生意兴隆; **tennis is ~ing as a sport** 网球作为一项运动正迅速发展

C *vt* 低沉有力地说; **'welcome to our humble abode', he ~ed** 他瓮声瓮气地说: "欢迎光临寒舍。"

Phrasal verb

- **boom out**

A *vi* «*cannon*» 发出隆隆声; «*voice*» 低沉有力地发出

B *vt* [**~ sth. out, ~ out sth.**] 低沉有力地传达 ‹*order*›; 轰鸣地奏响 ‹*music*›; **the loudspeaker ~ed out an announcement/a list of names** 喇叭嗡嗡地广播了一则公告/一份名单

boom[2] *n* [1] Naut (barrier) 水栅 [2] Naut (spar on mast) 帆桁 [3] TV, Cin (话筒) 吊杆; **a ~ microphone** 吊杆麦克风

boom: ~-and-bust *adj* = **~-bust**; **~ baby** *n* 生育高峰儿 [指20世纪50年代生育高峰期出生的人]; **~-bust** *adj* 经济大起大落的 ‹*cycle, market*›

boomerang /ˈbuːməræŋ/

A *n* 回飞镖

B *vi* «*plan, words, action*» 使人自作自受; **to ~ on sb.** 让某人自食其果

booming /ˈbuːmɪŋ/ *adj* [1] (loud, deep) 隆隆作响的 ‹*sound*›; 洪亮的 ‹*laugh*› [2] (flourishing) 繁荣的 ‹*economy*›; 激增的 ‹*exports*›

boom town *n* 繁荣的城市

boon /buːn/ *n* [1] (advantage) 好处; (invaluable asset) 非常有用的东西; **the route will be a ~ to many travellers** 这条路线将使很多旅行者受益无穷 [2] archaic (request) 请求; (favour) 恩泽

boon companion *n* 一起寻欢作乐的密友

boondocks /ˈbuːndɒks/ *npl* Amer colloq (rural area) **the ~** 穷乡僻壤; (rough country) 荒野; **out in the ~** 在偏远地区

boondoggle /ˈbuːndɒɡl/ *n* Amer colloq (wasteful project) 浪费时间金钱的事情; (unnecessary project) 瞎忙; (fraudulent project) 虚假的事情

boonies /ˈbuːniːz/ *npl* colloq = **boondocks**

boor /ˈbʊə(r), bɔː(r)/ *n* (person) 粗鲁的人; (man) 莽汉

boorish /ˈbʊərɪʃ, ˈbɔː-/ *adj* 粗鲁的 ‹*person, remark, manner*›

boorishly /ˈbʊərɪʃli, ˈbɔː-/ *adv* 粗鲁地 ‹*behave, remark*›

boorishness /ˈbʊərɪʃnɪs, ˈbɔː-/ *n* [u] 粗鲁

boost /buːst/

A *n* [1] (stimulus) 促进; (encouragement) 激励; **to give sth./sb. a ~** 推动某事/给某人以鼓舞 [2] (increase, improvement) 增长; **a ~ in exports** 出口量的增长 [3] (publicity) 宣传; **to give sth. a ~** 宣传某事物

B *vt* [1] (increase) 增加 ‹*production, exports*›; **to ~ sb.'s confidence** 增强某人的自信心; **to ~ morale** 鼓舞士气 [2] Amer Advertg (promote) 宣传 [3] Electron, Telecom (amplify) 放大 [4] Elec 升高 ‹*voltage*› [5] Aerosp 推送 ‹*space vehicle*›

booster /ˈbuːstə(r)/ *n* [1] Radio, Telecom 信号放大器 [2] Elec 升压器 [3] Med (vaccine) 强化注射剂量; **a ~ injection** 强化注射 [4] Aerosp 助推器 [5] Amer colloq (fan) 热心支持者; **a ~ club** 支持者俱乐部

booster: ~ cushion *n* 儿童坐垫; **~ rocket** *n* 助推器; **~ seat** *n* 儿童加高座位; **~ station** *n* 中继电台

boot[1] /buːt/

A *n* [1] (footwear) 靴子; **a sports ~** 运动靴; **the ~ is on the other foot** Brit fig 情况正好相反; **to put the ~ in** Brit colloq 猛踢; fig 落井下石; **to lick sb.'s ~s** fig 拍某人的马屁; **to be too big for one's ~s** 变得自以为是 [2] colloq (dismissal) 解雇; **to get the ~** (be dismissed from job) 被解雇; (be deserted) 被抛弃; **to give sb. the ~** (dismiss from job) 解雇某人; (end relationship with) 抛弃某人 [3] Brit Aut 行李箱

B *vt* [1] colloq (kick) 猛踢 ‹*person, ball*› [2] Comput 启动 ‹*operating system, program*›

C *vi* Comput 启动

Phrasal verbs

- **boot out** *vt* [**~ sb./sth. out, ~ out sb./sth.**] colloq 赶走; **to ~ sb. out of sth.** 把某人赶出某地; **she was ~ed out of Yale for cheating in an exam** 她因为考试作弊被耶鲁大学开除
- **boot up** *vt* [**~ sth. up, ~ up sth.**] 启动 ‹*computer*›

boot[2] *n* **to ~** 此外; **all this and a diamond ring to ~, you are a lucky girl!** 这一切外加一枚钻戒, 你真是个幸运的女孩!

bootable /ˈbuːtəbl/ *adj* 可启动计算机的; **~ CD** 启动光盘

boot: ~ camp *n* Amer [1] Mil, Naut (training camp) 新兵训练营; [2] (prison) 少年犯劳教营; **~ device** *n* 启动装置; **~ disk** *n* 启动盘; **~ drive** *n* 启动器

bootee /buːˈtiː/ *n* [1] (knitted shoe) 婴儿毛绒鞋; (sock) 婴儿毛绒袜 [2] (lined boot) 短筒女靴

booth /buːð, Amer buːθ/ *n* (for telephone) 电话亭; (for voting) 投票间; (in restaurant, language lab) 小隔间; (at fairground) 售货棚

bootlace /ˈbuːtleɪs/ *n* 靴带

bootleg /ˈbuːtleɡ/

A *adj* (produced illegally) 非法生产的; (sold illegally) 非法销售的

B *vt* (produce illegally) 非法生产; (sell illegally) 非法销售

C *n* Mus [尤指音乐会上录制的] 非法音乐唱片

boot: ~legger /ˈbuːtleɡə(r)/ *n* (of alcoholic drink) 非法制贩酒者; (of recording, software) 盗版者; **~licker** /ˈbuːtlɪkə(r)/ *n* colloq 马屁精; **~ polish** *n* [u and c] 皮鞋上光剂; **~ sale** *n* Brit 行李箱旧物销售; **~ scraper** *n* 蹭鞋垫; **~strap** *n* [1] (on boot) 拔靴带; **pull** *or* **drag oneself up by one's (own) ~straps** 自力更生; [2] Comput 引导

booty /ˈbuːti/ *n* [u] (for thieves) 赃物; (for army) 战利品

booze /buːz/ colloq

A *n* [u] 酒; **to be on the ~** 嗜酒; **he's off the ~** 他戒酒了

B *vi* 狂饮

booze cruise *n* colloq [1] (drunken cruise) 乘船饮酒游 [2] Brit (trip to buy cheap alcohol) 乘船沽酒游 [指到欧洲大陆买便宜的酒]

boozed /buːzd/ *adj* colloq 喝醉的

boozer /ˈbuːzə(r)/ *n* colloq [1] (person) 酒鬼 [2] Brit (pub) 酒吧

booze-up *n* Brit colloq 狂饮聚会

boozy /ˈbuːzi/ *adj* colloq 暴饮的 ‹*party, person*›; 醉醺醺的 ‹*chorus, laughter*›; **we had a ~ evening/weekend** 我们晚上/周末大喝了一场; **his ~ uncle** 他的酒鬼叔叔

bop[1] /bɒp/

A *n* colloq (dance) 博普舞; (party) 博普舞会; **to go for a ~** 去跳博普舞

B *vi* (*pres p etc.* **-pp-**) 跳博普舞

bop[2] colloq

A *n* (blow) 轻拍

B *vt* (*pres p etc.* **-pp-**) 快击

borax /ˈbɔːræks/ *n* [u] 硼砂

bordello /bɔːˈdeləʊ/ *n* esp Amer 妓院

border /ˈbɔːdə(r)/

A *n* [1] (frontier) 边界; fig (dividing line) 界线; **France's ~ with Spain** 法国与西班牙的国界线; **on the Swiss ~** 在瑞士边境; **a ~ town** 位于边境的城镇; **~ guards** 边防警卫; **to have ~s with six countries** 与六国接壤; **to cross the ~** 穿越边界; **just on the ~ between pass and fail** 就在成败的一线之间 [2] (edge of forest, lake, field) 边缘 [3] (decorative edge on crockery, paper, picture) 边饰 [4] Hort [草坪、小路边的] 狭长花坛

B Borders *pr npl* **the B~s (Region)** [英格兰和苏格兰的] 交界地区

C *vt* [1] (have a frontier with) 与…接壤; **France ~s Italy** 法国与意大利接壤; **to be ~ed by ...** 与…毗邻 [2] (surround, form edge) 环绕; **to be ~ed on three sides by trees** 三面树木环绕; **to be ~ed with lace** 镶有花边

Phrasal verb

- **border on** *vt* [**~ on sth.**] [1] (have a frontier with) «*country*» 与…接壤; «*garden*» 挨着 [2] fig (verge on) 接近; **the accusation ~s on the absurd** 指控近乎荒唐

border: ~ agency *n* 边境署; **B~ collie** *n* 边境牧羊犬; **~ dispute** *n* 边境争端; **~ guard** *n* 边防警卫; **~ incident** *n* 边境冲突; **~land** /-lænd/ *n* [1] Geog 边境; [2] fig (overlap) 边缘; **the ~land between sleeping and waking** 半梦半醒之间

borderline /ˈbɔdəlaɪn, Amer ˈbɔrdər-/

A *n* [1] Geog 边界线; **on the ~** 在边界线上 [2] (division, line) 分界线; **the ~ between success and failure** 成功与失败的分界线

B *modif* 边缘的; **he's a ~ schizophrenic** 他是个边缘型精神分裂症患者; **to be a ~ fail/pass** 刚刚不及格/及格

border: ~ police *n + v pl* 边防警察; **~ post** *n* 边防检查站; **~ raid** *n* 越境袭击

bore[1] /bɔː(r)/

A *vt* [1] (drill) 钻; (dig) 挖 [2] (hollow out) 在…上钻孔 ‹*rock, wood*›

B *vi* «*drill*» 钻孔; «*machine*» 镗孔; «*insect*» 钻进去; **to ~ into/through sth.** 钻进/穿透某物; **her eyes ~d into me** fig 她盯着我看

C *n* 1 (diameter of gun barrel, pipe) 口径 2 = **borehole**

bore²
A *n* (person) 讨厌的人; (situation) 烦人的事; **he's such a ～** 他真烦人; **it's an awful ～ having to wait** 不得不等待真是烦人
B *vt* 使厌倦; **to ～ sb. stiff** *or* **to death** *or* **to tears** colloq 使某人极其厌倦

bore³ *n* (wave) 激潮

bore⁴ *pt* ▸**bear¹ A, B, C**

boreal /ˈbɔːrɪəl/ *adj* 北方的

bored /bɔːd/ *adj* 厌倦的; **to get/be ～** 感到厌倦; **to look ～** 显得厌倦

boredom /ˈbɔːdəm/ *n* [u] 1 (feeling) 厌倦 2 (of activity, job, lifestyle) 乏味

borehole /ˈbɔːhəʊl/ *n* 钻孔

borer /ˈbɔːrə(r)/ *n* 1 (tool) 钻; **a tunnel ～** 隧道掘进机 2 Zool 钻蛀虫

boric acid /ˌbɔːrɪk ˈæsɪd/ *n* [u] 硼酸

boring /ˈbɔːrɪŋ/ *adj* 1 (tedious) 令人厌倦的 ‹*person, meeting*›; 无聊的 ‹*job*› 2 (dull, unimaginative) 乏味的 ‹*landscape, design*›; 暗淡的 ‹*colour*›

boringly /ˈbɔːrɪŋli/ *adv* 无聊地; **the film ends ～** 影片结尾很乏味

born /bɔːn/
A *adj* 出生的; **to be ～** 出生于; **she was ～ into a Jewish family** 她出生于一个犹太家庭; **to be ～ deaf/blind** 先天失聪/失明; **to be a ～ leader** 天生是个领导; **a Londoner ～ and bred** 土生土长的伦敦人; **in all my ～ days** colloq 在我的一生中; **to be ～ (out) of sth.** fig «*idea, group*» 来源于…; **I wasn't ～ yesterday** 我不是三岁小孩子; **there's one ～ every minute!** colloq 那种傻瓜屡见不鲜!
B **-born** /bɔːn/ *combining form* …出生的; **London/Irish～** 伦敦/爱尔兰出生的

born-again *adj* 1 Relig 再生的; **a ～ Christian** 皈依基督教的人 2 fig hum 转而积极参与的 ‹*environmentalist, non-smoker*›

borne /bɔːn/ *pp* ▸**bear¹ A, B, C**

Borneo /ˈbɔːnɪəʊ/ *pr n* 婆罗洲

boron /ˈbɔːrɒn/ *n* [u] 硼

borough /ˈbʌrə, Amer ˈbʌrəʊ/ *n* (in UK) 自治镇; (in London, New York) 行政区

borough council *n* Brit 自治镇政务会

borrow /ˈbɒrəʊ/
A *vt* 1 (take temporarily) 借; **to ～ sth. from sb./sth.** 向某人/从某处借某物; **to be living on ～ed time** lit 来日无多; fig 好景不长; **to ～ trouble** Amer 自寻烦恼 2 (copy) 引用 ‹*word, motif*›; **ideas ～ed from earlier writers** 借用自早期作家的观点
B *vi* 借钱; **to ～ against ...** 以…为借贷担保 ‹*income*›

borrower /ˈbɒrəʊə(r)/ *n* 1 (from person, bank) 借方 2 (from library) 借书人

borrowing /ˈbɒrəʊɪŋ/ *n* 1 [u] Fin 借款; **an increase in ～** 借贷数额的增加; **～ costs** 贷款费用 2 [c] Ling 借词; Literat 借用

borrowing: ～ requirement *n* 借贷需求; **～ rights** *npl* (at library) 借阅权

bosh /bɒʃ/ *n* [u] colloq 胡说

bos'n /ˈbəʊsn/ *n* = **boatswain**

Bosnia-Herzegovina /ˌbɒznɪə ˌhɜːtsəɡəʊˈviːnə/ *pr n* 波斯尼亚－黑塞哥维那

Bosnian /ˈbɒznɪən/ ▸**p. 503**
A *adj* (of Bosnia) 波斯尼亚的; (of the people) 波斯尼亚人的
B *n* 波斯尼亚人

Bosnian: ～ Muslim *n* 波斯尼亚穆斯林; **～ Serb** *n* 波斯尼亚塞尔维亚人

bosom /ˈbʊzəm/ *n* 1 [u and c] (breasts) 乳房 2 [c] (chest) 胸部; **to hug sb. to one's ～** 把某人抱在怀里 3 [c] fig (heart, soul) 胸怀; **to be in the ～ of one's family/of the community** 在家庭/社区的温暖怀抱中; **to take sb. to one's ～** 与某人推心置腹 4 [c] Clothg 胸襟

bosom: ～ buddy *n* Amer colloq 知己; **～ friend** *n* 知己

Bosphorus, Bosporus /ˈbɒspərəs/ *pr n* 博斯普鲁斯海峡

boss¹ /bɒs/
A *n* (person in charge) 老板; **go ahead, you're the ～** iron 说吧, 你是头儿嘛; **she's the ～ in the house** colloq 家里她做主; **we'll show them who's ～** 我们会让他们知道谁是老大
B *adj* Amer colloq 极好的; **this work is ～** 这活儿真棒

Phrasal verb
- **boss about, boss around** *vt* colloq [**～ sb. about** *or* **around**] 对…发号施令

boss² *n* (on shield) 饰钉; (on ceiling) 凸饰; (on wheel, propeller) 轮毂

boss-eyed *adj* Brit colloq 斜视眼的; **to be ～** 长有一双斗鸡眼

bossiness /ˈbɒsɪnɪs/ *n* [u] colloq 专横

bossy /ˈbɒsɪ/ *adj* colloq 爱发号施令的

bosun /ˈbəʊsn/ *n* = **boatswain**

botanical /bəˈtænɪkl/ *adj* 植物学的

botanical gardens, botanic gardens /bəˌtænɪk ˈɡɑːdnz/ *nspl* 植物园

botanist /ˈbɒtənɪst/ ▸**p. 409** *n* 植物学家

botany /ˈbɒtəni/ *n* [u] 植物学

botch /bɒtʃ/
A *vt* **to ～ (up)** 笨拙地弄糟; **a ～ed job** 干得很糟糕的活儿
B *n* (*also* **botch-up**) 拙劣的工作; **to make a ～ of sth.** 把某事物弄得一团糟; **it was a real ～** 那实在是糟透了

botched /bɒtʃt/ *adj* 拙劣的

both /bəʊθ/
A *adj* 两个; **～ his eyes/parents** 他的双眼/双亲; **～ children came** 两个孩子都来了; **～ sides of the road** 路的两边
B *adv* **～ ... and ...** 不仅…而且…; **to show ～ firmness and tact** 表现得既坚定又策略; **～ you and I saw him** 你和我都看见他了; **to act ～ wisely and swiftly** 明智且迅速地行动
C *pron + v pl* 两个都; **they speak English or French or ～** 他们说英语或法语或两种语言都说; **which do you want? — ～** 你想要哪一个? ——两个都要
D **both of** *pron phr + v pl* …两个都; **let's take ～ of them** 我们把两个都带上吧; **～ of you are wrong** 你们俩都错了

bother /ˈbɒðə(r)/
A *vt* 1 (disturb, inconvenience) 打扰; **to ～ sb. with sth.** 以某事物打扰某人; **if I could ～ you for just one minute** 打扰一下; **to be ～ed** 费心; **they could come but they just can't be ～ed** 他们本可以过来, 只是懒得来 2 (annoy) 使烦恼; **you can smoke if you like, it doesn't ～ me** 你想吸烟就吸吧, 没关系 3 (worry, concern) 使…不安 ‹*person*›; **to be ～ed about/that ...** 担心…; **I'm not ～ed** 我不在乎; **it ～s me that ...** 让我感到不安的是…; **to ～ oneself** *or* **one's head about sth.** 为某事操心 4 (hurt) «*wound, injury*» 使…疼痛 ‹*person, animal*› 5 dated (ignore, forget) 不在乎; **～ the effort/waste of time!** 去他的努力/浪费时间吧!; **～ the neighbours! let's make as much noise as we like** 管他什么邻居呢! 我们想多大声就多大声 6 (expressing annoyance) …真烦人; **～ the woman, she's put sugar in my tea again** 那个女人真讨厌, 她又在我的茶里放糖了
B *vi* 1 (take trouble) 费事; **to ～ to do sth., to ～ about doing sth.** 费心做某事; **to ～ with sth./sb.** 为某事物/某人费心; **she never even ～ed to reply** 她甚至懒得答复; **I won't ～ with a hat, it's not that cold** 我懒得戴帽子, 没那么冷 2 (worry) 担心; **to ～ about sth./sb.** 担心某事物/某人
C *n* 1 [u] (trouble, effort) 麻烦; **to go to the ～ of doing sth.** 费心做某事; **to put sb. to the ～ of doing sth.** 麻烦某人做某事; **to go to much ～** 费事; **don't go to any ～** 不用费心; **a spot** *or* **bit of ～** Brit 一点小麻烦; **it's no ～** 没关系 2 [c] Brit (person) 令人烦恼的人; (thing) 麻烦事
D *excl* Brit 真讨厌; **oh ～! I forgot to phone Andrew** 唉呀糟糕! 我忘了给安德鲁打电话了

botheration /ˌbɒðəˈreɪʃn/ *excl* dated 讨厌

bothersome /ˈbɒðəsəm/ *adj* 讨厌的

Botox® /ˈbəʊtɒks/ *n* [u] 保妥适 [用于除皱纹的化妆品]

Botswana /bɒtˈswɑːnə/ *pr n* 博茨瓦纳

bottle /ˈbɒtl/
A *n* 1 [c] (for drinks, perfume, medicine) 瓶; (for baby) 奶瓶; **a ～ of wine** 一瓶葡萄酒 2 [u] fig colloq (alcohol) **to hit** *or* **take to the ～** 开始酗酒; **to be on the ～** 酗酒 3 [c] (gas cylinder) 钢瓶; **oxygen/gas ～** 氧气瓶/煤气瓶 4 [u] Brit colloq (courage) 勇气; **to lose one's ～** 丧失勇气
B *vt* 1 (put in bottles) 把…装入瓶中 ‹*milk, wine, water*› 2 Brit (preserve) 把…装瓶腌制 ‹*fruit, vegetables*›

Phrasal verbs
- **bottle out** *vi* Brit colloq 因惧怕而放弃
- **bottle up** *vt* [**～ sth. up, ～ up sth.**] 1 (suppress) 抑制 ‹*emotion*›; **you shouldn't ～ things** *or* **your feelings up** 你不应该压抑情感 2 (confine) 限制; **the blockade kept the navy ～d up in the harbour** 海军被封锁在港口内

bottle: ～ bank *n* (container) 旧瓶回收箱; (collection point) 旧瓶回收点; **～brush** *n* 洗瓶刷; **～-fed** *adj* 用奶瓶喂养的; **～-feed** *vt* 用奶瓶喂养 ‹*baby*›; **～ feeding** *n* [u] 奶瓶喂养; **～ glass** *n* [u] 瓶玻璃

bottle green ▸**p. 134**
A *n* [u] 深绿色
B **bottle-green** *adj* 深绿色的

bottle: ～neck *n* 1 (traffic jam, narrow part of road) 瓶颈路段; 2 fig (hold-up) 瓶颈; **～-opener** *n* 开瓶器; **～ party** *n* 自带瓶酒的酒会; **～ rack** *n* 酒瓶架; **～ top** *n* 瓶盖; **～ warmer** *n* 热奶器; **～washer** *n* (person) 洗瓶工人; (machine) 洗瓶机; **chief cook and ～washer** hum 家务总管

bottom /ˈbɒtəm/
A *n* 1 (lowest part) 底部; (of hill, mountain) 山脚; **your name is at the ～ of the list** 你的名字列在名单末尾; **from the ～ of one's heart** fig 衷心地 2 (deepest part, underside of container) 底; **they let the rope down to the ～ of the well** 他们把绳子放到井底; **～ up** 底朝上; **～s up!** Brit colloq 干杯!; **the ～ drops** *or* **falls out of sth.** fig 某物行情暴跌; **the ～ has fallen** *or* **dropped out of the housing market** 楼市出现了暴跌; **the ～ fell** *or* **dropped out of her world** 她的生活崩溃了 3 (lowest rank, position) (of job, career) 最低职位; (of class, league) 末位; **to start at the ～** 从最基层干起; **they're at the ～ of the league** 他们联赛排名垫底 4 fig (root cause) 根源; **to get to the ～ of sth.** 找出某事的起因; **to be at the ～ of sth.** 是某事的根源; **she's at the ～ of all these rumours** 这些流言都是她散布的; **at ～, science is exploration** 从本质上讲, 科学就是探索 5 (bed of sea, lake, river) 水底; **to go to the ～** 沉入水底 6 (furthest point of street, garden) 尽头; **there's a chemist's at the ～ of the street** 街尽头有一家药店 7 esp Brit (buttocks) 屁股; ▸**baby A 1** 8 Clothg [套装的] 下半身; **a bikini ～** 比基尼泳裤; **pyjama/tracksuit ～s** 睡裤/运动裤 9 Aut 最低挡; **in ～** 挂一挡
B *adj* 1 *attrib* (lowest) 最下面的 ‹*shelf*›; **the ～ layer/part** 底层/底部; **the ～ half of the list** 名单后半部分 2 (last) 排名最后的 ‹*person, place*›; **to come ～** 垫底

Phrasal verb
- **bottom out** *vi* «*prices, inflation*» 降到最低点; «*recession*» 触底

b

bottom: ~ drawer *n* Brit dated 嫁衣箱; **~ end** *n* 1 lit (far end) 末端; **there's a stream at the ~ end of the garden** 花园的尽头有条小溪; 2 (base) 底端; 3 fig (of league, division) 末位; (of market) 低端; **~ feeder** *n* 1 (fish) 水底鱼; 2 Amer colloq pej (person) 在底层谋生的人; **~ gear** *n* 低速排挡; **~less** *adj* 1 (deep) 极深的; 2 (having no limit) 无穷无尽的 ‹*reserves, funds*›; **a ~less pit** lit 无底深渊; fig (endless supply) 取之不尽的储备; (money drain) 花不完的钱; **~ line** *n* 1 Comm 账本底线; 2 (decisive factor) 关键; **the ~ line is that ...** 底线是…; **that's the ~ line** 那是问题的关键; **~most** *adj* 最低的; **~-up** *adj attrib* 自下而上的; **~-up programming** 自下而上的程序设计

botulism /ˈbɒtjʊlɪzəm/ ▸**p. 377** *n* [u] 肉毒中毒

boudoir /ˈbuːdwɑː(r)/ *n* dated or hum 闺房

bouffant /ˈbuːfɑːn/ *adj* 蓬松的 ‹*hairstyle, hair*›

bougainvillea /ˌbuːɡənˈvɪlɪə/ *n* 叶子花

bough /baʊ/ *n* 粗树枝

bought /bɔːt/ *pt, pp* ▸**buy A**

bouillon /ˈbuːjɒn/ *n* [u] 清汤

boulder /ˈbəʊldə(r)/ *n* 巨砾

boulevard /ˈbuːləvɑːd, Amer ˈbʊl-/ *n* 林荫大道; (in street names) 大道

bounce /baʊns/
A *vi* 1 (rebound) «*ball*» 反弹; «*light, sound, signal*» 反射 2 (move up and down repeatedly) «*ball*» 弹跳; «*vehicle*» 颠簸; (jump) «*person*» 蹦跳; **to ~ up and down on sth.** 在某物上弹跳; **the car ~d along the track** 小轿车在小道上颠簸行进 3 fig (move energetically) 蹦蹦跳跳 4 Fin colloq «*cheque*» 被退回
B *vt* 1 (cause to rebound) 使反弹; (reflect) 反射 ‹*radio waves, signal*›; **he ~d the ball off the neighbour's gate** 他把球掷到邻居家大门上弹了回来 2 (repeatedly) 使跳动; **to ~ a baby on one's knee** 把婴儿放在膝上颠着玩 3 Fin colloq (refuse to honour) 拒付 ‹*cheque*›; (return) 退回 ‹*cheque*›
C *n* 1 [c] (rebound of ball) 反弹 2 [u] (of mattress, ball, hair) 弹性 3 [u and c] fig (vigour) 活力

Phrasal verb
- **bounce back** *vi* 重整旗鼓

bouncer /ˈbaʊnsə(r)/ *n* 门卫

bouncing /ˈbaʊnsɪŋ/ *adj attrib* 健壮的 ‹*baby*›

bouncy /ˈbaʊnsɪ/ *adj* 1 (able to bounce) 有弹性的 ‹*ball, mattress, hair*› 2 fig (lively) 充满活力的 ‹*person*›

bouncy castle *n* 充气欢乐堡

bound¹ /baʊnd/
A *pt, pp* ▸**bind A, B**
B *adj* 1 *pred* (certain) 一定的; **to be ~ to do sth.** 一定会做某事; **she's ~ to know** 她肯定知道 2 *pred* (obliged) 有义务的; **to be ~ (by sth.) to do sth.** (受某事物约束)有义务做某事; **to be ~ by custom/tradition to take part in the ceremony** 按照风俗/传统必须参加典礼; **you no longer need to feel ~ by the promise you made** 你不必再受自己许诺的约束; **I'll be ~** Brit 我敢肯定 3 Publg 有封皮的 ‹*book, volume*›

bound² *adj pred* (going towards) 正在前往…的; (ready to go towards) 准备前往…的; **to be ~ for ...** 准备前往…

bound³
A *n* 跳越
B *vi* 跳越着跑; **the horse ~ed away from the start** 那匹马从起点冲了出去

bound⁴ *vt* 1 (border) 形成…的边界; **the farm is ~ed on three sides by marsh** 农场三面都是沼泽地 2 fig (restrict) 限制; **freedom of action is ~ed by law** 行动自由受法律的约束

-bound /baʊnd/ *combining form* 1 (headed for) 前往…的 2 (confined to) 限制在…的 3 (immobilized by) 因…受阻的 4 Publg 用…封皮的

boundary /ˈbaʊndri/
A *n* 1 (frontier) 边界 2 fig (dividing line, limit) 界限; **the boundaries of human knowledge** 人类知识的极限 3 (in cricket) 击球过边界线得分
B *modif* 作为边界的; **a ~ marker/stone** 界标/界石

boundary: B~ Commission *n* Brit 选区界定委员会; **~ line** *n* 1 lit (marking boundary) 分界线; (between countries) 边界; 2 fig (distinction, limit) 界限

bounder /ˈbaʊndə(r)/ *n* Brit colloq dated 无赖

boundless /ˈbaʊndlɪs/ *adj* 广阔无垠的 ‹*area*›; 无限的 ‹*generosity, admiration, energy*›

bounds /baʊndz/ *npl* 界限; **in ~** lit 在界内; Sport 在界内; **out of ~** lit 在界外; Sport 出界; fig 令人无法接受; **within/beyond the ~ of ...** 在…范围内/范围外; **their joy/anger knew no ~** 他们特别高兴/生气

bountiful /ˈbaʊntɪfl/ *adj* 1 (ample) 丰富的 ‹*supply*› 2 (generous) 慷慨的 ‹*person*›

bounty /ˈbaʊnti/ *n* 1 [c] (reward) 赏金 2 [u] liter (generosity) 慷慨; **food from Nature's ~** 大自然慷慨赐予的食物

bounty hunter *n* 赏金猎人 [指为获得赏金而追捕罪犯的人]

bouquet /bʊˈkeɪ/ *n* 1 (of flowers) 花束; fig (compliment) 赞扬 2 (scent of wine, perfume) 芳香

bourbon /ˈbɜːbən/ *n* [u and c] Amer 波旁威士忌酒

bourgeois /ˈbɔːʒwɑː, Amer ˌbʊəˈʒwɑː/
A *adj* 中产阶级的
B *n* 中产人士

bourgeoisie /ˌbɔːʒwɑːˈziː, Amer ˌbʊəʒwɑːˈziː/ *n* + *v sing or pl* 中产阶级

bout /baʊt/ *n* 1 (attack, episode) 一次; (period of activity) 一阵; **a ~ of insomnia** 一次失眠; **a ~ of coughing** 一阵咳嗽; **to go on a drinking ~** 狂饮一番 2 Sport (boxing, wrestling) 比赛

boutique /buːˈtiːk/ *n* 1 (shop) 时装店 2 (department) 时装部

bovine /ˈbəʊvaɪn/ *adj* 1 (of cattle) 牛的 2 fig (sluggish, stupid) 愚笨的

bovine spongiform encephalopathy /ˈbəʊvaɪn ˈspʌndʒɪfɔːm enˌsefəˈlɒpəθɪ, -ˌkef-/ *n* [u] 牛海绵状脑病

bovver /ˈbɒvə(r)/ *n* [u] Brit sl 暴力行为

bovver: ~ boots *npl* Brit colloq 街斗钉靴; **~ boy** *n* Brit colloq 混混儿

bow¹ /bəʊ/
A *n* 1 Sport, Hist 弓; **he drew his ~ and shot the arrow** 他拉弓射箭; **to have many strings to one's ~** Brit fig 有多种应对方案; **to have/add another string to one's ~** Brit fig 另有准备 2 Mus 琴弓 3 (knot) 蝴蝶结; (decorative ribbon) 蝶形丝带
B *vt* 用琴弓拉 ‹*cello, passage, notes*›

bow² /baʊ/
A *vi* 1 lit (bend forward) 鞠躬; **to ~ to sb./sth.** 向某人/某物鞠躬; **to ~ and scrape** 奴颜婢膝 2 fig (give in, defer) 让步; **to ~ to** *or* **before sth.** 屈从于某事; **we must ~ to their wishes** 我们必须顺从他们的愿望; **to ~ to the inevitable** 听天由命 3 (bend) «*plank, branch*» 弯曲
B *vt* 1 (bend) 低下 ‹*head*›; 使…弯曲 ‹*branch, plank*›; **age had ~ed his back** 他年老背驼; **to ~ the knee (to sth.)** fig (对某事物)卑躬屈膝 2 (show by bowing) 鞠躬表示; **the chairman ~ed his consent/agreement** 主席点头表示同意; **he ~ed his acknowledgement of the applause** 他鞠躬感谢人们的掌声
C *n* (with the head) 点头致意; (with the body) 鞠躬; **to make a ~** 鞠躬; **to make one's ~** fig 首次公开露面; **to take a ~** Theat 谢幕

Phrasal verbs
- **bow down**
A *vi* 1 (make a bow) 鞠躬 2 fig (submit) 屈服
B *vt* [**~ sb./sth. down, ~ down sb./sth.**] 1 (bend) «*weight*» 压弯 ‹*sapling, person*› 2 fig (weigh down, defeat) 压垮; **a nation ~ed down by the burden of debt** 为债务所累的国家
- **bow out**
A *vi* 1 (withdraw) 退出; **to ~ out of sth.** 退出某事 2 (retire) 退休 3 (resign) 辞职
B *vt* [**~ sb. out, ~ out sb.**] 鞠躬送…出门

bow³ /baʊ/ *n* Naut **bow(s)** 船头; **on the port/starboard ~** 在左舷/右舷船头

bowdlerize /ˈbaʊdləraɪz/ *vt* 删剪

bow doors /baʊ ˈdɔːz/ *npl* 船头大门

bowel /ˈbaʊəl/ *n* 1 Anat 肠; **~ cancer** 肠癌; **to have upset ~s** 肚子不舒服; **to move one's ~s, to have a ~ movement** 排便 2 **bowels** fig (inner depths) 内部最深处

bower /ˈbaʊə(r)/ *n* liter 1 (arbour) 树荫处 2 (chamber) 闺房

bowing /ˈbəʊɪŋ/ *n* [u] Mus 弓法

bowl¹ /bəʊl/ *n* 1 (dish) (for food) 碗; (large) (for soup) 汤盆; (for washing) 洗碗盆; **a ~ of milk** 一碗奶 2 (hollow part) (of pipe) 斗; (of spoon) 匙头; (of lavatory) 桶身; (of lamp) 球形灯罩

bowl²
A *n* (in bowls) 木球; (in ten-pin bowling) 保龄球
B *vt* 1 (roll) 使滚动; **she ~ed the ball along the ground** 她让球在地面上滚动 2 (throw) 把…投给击球手 ‹*ball*› 3 Brit (in cricket) **= bowl out**
C *vi* 1 Sport 投球 2 **~ along/off** (move fast) «*person*» 飞奔; «*vehicle*» 疾驰

Phrasal verbs
- **bowl out** *vt* [**~ sb. out**] (in cricket) «*bowler*» 击中三柱门把…杀出局 ‹*batsman*›
- **bowl over** *vt* [**~ sb. over**] 1 (knock down) 撞倒 ‹*skittles, person*› 2 fig (impress) 使印象深刻; (surprise) 使惊讶; **she was totally ~ed over** 她惊呆了

bow /bəʊ/**: ~-legged** /-ˈleɡɪd/ *adj* 罗圈腿的; **he is ~-legged** 他是罗圈腿; **~ legs** *npl* 罗圈腿

bowler¹ /ˈbəʊlə(r)/ *n* (in cricket) 投球手; (in bowls) 玩木球游戏的人; (in ten-pin bowling) 玩保龄球的人

bowler² *n* esp Brit **~ (hat)** 常礼帽

bowl game *n* Amer 橄榄球季后赛

bowline /ˈbəʊlɪn/ *n* 单套结

bowling /ˈbəʊlɪŋ/ ▸**p. 307** *n* [u] Sport 1 (ten-pin) 保龄球运动 2 (on grass) 草地滚木球戏 3 (in cricket) 投球

bowling: ~ alley *n* 1 (building) 保龄球球场; 2 (track) 保龄球球道; **~ green** *n* 草地滚木球场

bowls /bəʊlz/ ▸**p. 307** *npl* + *v sing* 草地滚木球戏; **a ~ club/match** 草地木滚球俱乐部/比赛

bow: ~man /ˈbəʊmən/ *n* 弓箭手; **~sprit** /ˈbəʊsprɪt/ *n* 船首斜桁; **~string** /ˈbəʊ-/ *n* 弓弦; **~ tie** /ˈbəʊ/ *n* 蝶形领结; **~ wave** /ˈbaʊ/ *n* 船头波; **~ window** /ˈbəʊ/ *n* 圆肚窗

bow-wow /ˈbaʊwaʊ/
A *n* child lang or hum 狗狗
B *excl* 汪汪; **the dog went '~!'** 狗"汪汪!"地叫了起来

box¹ /bɒks/
A *n* 1 (large container) 箱; (small container) 盒; (small case, casket) 匣; **a shoe/hat/jewellery ~** 鞋盒/帽盒/首饰盒; **a ~ of matches/chocolates** 一盒火柴/巧克力; **they'll have to carry me out of here in a wooden ~** colloq hum (coffin) 他们得用棺材把我从这里抬出去 2 (square or rectangular area) 方框; **put a tick in the ~** 在方框内打钩; **the ~** (penalty box) 罚球区; (batting area in baseball) 击球区 3 Brit Aut (at junction) 交

叉路口黄格区 4 Theat 包厢; **the royal ～** 王室包厢 5 (stall for horse) 分隔厩 6 Brit colloq (television) **the ～** 电视机 7 Journ [报社内所设的] 应征来函信箱

B *vt* 1 (pack) 把…装箱 ‹*gift*› 2 Naut **to ～ the compass** 依次说出罗盘方位

Phrasal verbs

- **box in** *vt* [**～ sb./sth. in, ～ in sb./sth.**] 1 (enclose) 把…包起来 ‹*basin, bath*›; **～ed in by tall buildings** 被高楼包围的 2 (restrict movement of) 封堵 ‹*runner, racehorse, car*›; **I was ～ed in between two big lorries and couldn't overtake** 我被两辆大卡车夹在中间，超不了车
- **box up** *vt* [**～ sth. up, ～ up sth.**] 1 (pack) 把…装箱 ‹*goods, belongings*› 2 (confine) 禁闭; **she felt very ～ed up in the apartment** 她觉得困在公寓里十分憋闷

box²
A *vi* Sport 参加拳击比赛; **to ～ clever** Brit colloq fig 做事精明
B *vt* 1 Sport 与…进行拳击比赛 ‹*person*› 2 (hit) 击打; **to ～ sb.'s ears** 扇某人耳光
C *n* 击打; **he gave her a ～ on the ear** 他打了她一记耳光

box³ *n* **～ (tree)** 黄杨

box: ～ camera *n* 方镜箱照相机; **～car** *n* Amer 货车车厢

boxer /'bɒksə(r)/ ►**p. 409** *n* 1 Sport 拳击手 2 (dog) 拳师犬

boxer shorts *npl* 男式宽松短内裤

box file *n* 文件盒

boxful /'bɒksfʊl/ *n* 一箱

box girder *n* 箱形梁

boxing /'bɒksɪŋ/ ►**p. 307** *n* [u] 拳击; **to take up ～** 参加拳击运动; **a ～ champion/match** 拳王/拳击比赛

boxing: B～ Day *n* [u] Brit 节礼日 [圣诞节的次日]; **～ glove** *n* 拳击手套; **～ ring** *n* 拳击台

box: ～ junction *n* Brit 交叉路口黄格区; **～ kite** *n* 箱形风筝; **～ number** *n* 信箱号码

box office
A *n* 1 [c] (ticket office) 售票处 2 [u and c] fig (commercial success) 票房收入; **to do well/badly at the ～** 卖座/不卖座; **to be good ～** «*show*» 票房高
B *modif* 票房的; **to be a ～ attraction/success** 有票房吸引力/卖座

box room *n* Brit (for storage) 储藏室; (bedroom) 小卧室

boxwood /'bɒkswʊd/ *n* [u] 黄杨木

boy /bɔɪ/ *n* 1 (young male) 男孩; **from a ～** 从小以来; **that's my ～!** 好样的! ; **～s will be ～s** 男孩子总归是男孩子; **he seems (like) a nice ～** 他看上去真是个不错的小伙子; **come here, ～!** dated [教师用语] 过来，小子! ; **the little ～'s room** euph hum 男洗手间; **a ～ genius/hero** 少年天才/英雄; **a ～ soprano** 童声高音 2 (son) 儿子 3 **the boys** colloq (social group) 一帮男伙伴; **let's leave the ～s to talk business** 我们让男人们谈正事吧; **to be one of the ～s** 是弟兄们中的一员; **the ～s in blue** Brit 警察 4 (talking to dog) [对雄性狗的称呼]; **down ～!** 趴下!

boy band *n* 男孩乐队

boycott /'bɔɪkɒt/
A *n* 抵制; **a trade/cultural ～** 贸易/文化抵制
B *vt* 抵制 ‹*goods, person*›; **American athletes ～ed the games** 美国运动员抵制了运动会

boyfriend /'bɔɪfrend/ *n* 男朋友

boyhood /'bɔɪhʊd/
A *n* 男子的童年
B *modif* 男子童年的 ‹*friend, experience, dream*›

boyish /'bɔɪɪʃ/ *adj* 1 (youthful) 像男孩的 ‹*good looks, ambition, prank*›; **her ～ figure/looks** 她那男孩子般的身材/容貌 2 (childlike) 男孩子气的

boy: ～-meets-girl *adj attrib* 言情的 ‹*film*›; **～ racer** *n* colloq 飞车族成员; **Boy Scout** *n* dated 童子军

bozo /'bəʊzəʊ/ *n* Amer colloq 笨蛋

BPR *abbr* **= business process re-engineering**

bps *abbr* **= bits per second** 位/秒

bra /brɑː/ *n* 胸罩

brace /breɪs/
A *n* 1 Constr 支架 2 (tool) **～ and bit** 手摇曲柄钻 3 (for teeth) 牙箍; **to wear a ～** 戴牙箍 4 Med (support) 梏具 5 (pair of birds, animals, pistols) 一对 6 Print 大括弧; Mus 连谱号
B *vt* 1 (press against) 用…顶住; **to ～ one's legs/feet against sth.** 用腿/脚抵住某物 2 Constr 加固 ‹*wall, structure*› 3 fig (prepare) 使有所准备; **to ～ oneself for sth.** 为某事物做好准备
C *vi* 俯身抱头 [飞机事故时采用以减轻伤害]

Phrasal verb

- **brace up** *vi* Amer 打起精神

bracelet /'breɪslɪt/ *n* 1 (jewellery) 手镯 2 (watchstrap) 表链

brace position *n* 俯身抱头姿势; **to take up** *or* **adopt the ～** 俯身抱头

bracer /'breɪsə(r)/ *n* colloq 烈性饮料

braces /'breɪsɪz/ *npl* Brit 吊裤带

bracing /'breɪsɪŋ/ *adj* 令人神清气爽的 ‹*climate, air*›

bracken /'brækən/ *n* [u] 欧洲蕨

bracket /'brækɪt/
A *n* 1 Print (round) 圆括号; (square) 方括号; **in ～s** 在括号中 2 (support) (for shelf) 托架; (for lamp) 壁灯座 3 Archit 支架 4 (category) 等级; **age/income ～** 年龄段/收入等级
B *vt* 1 Print (put in brackets) 把…放入括号; (group together in brackets) 用括号把…括在一起 2 (categorize) **to ～ (together)** 把…归为一类; **to ～ sb./sth. with ...** 把某人/某事物与…相提并论

brackish /'brækɪʃ/ *adj* 微咸的

bract /brækt/ *n* 苞片

brad /bræd/ *n* 角钉

bradawl /'brædɔːl/ *n* 打眼钻

brae /breɪ/ *n* Scot 陡坡

brag /bræg/
A *vi* (*pres p etc.* **-gg-**) 吹嘘; **nothing to ～ about** 没什么可炫耀的
B *vt* (*pres p etc.* **-gg-**) 夸耀; **to ～ that ...** 吹嘘说…
C *n* 1 [c] (boast) 大话 2 [u] (card game) 勃莱格纸牌戏

braggart /'brægət/ *n* 吹牛大王

bragging /'brægɪŋ/ *n* [u] 吹牛

Brahman /'brɑːmən/, **Brahmin** /'brɑːmɪn/ *n* 婆罗门

braid /breɪd/
A *n* 1 [c] Amer (plait) 辫子; **she wears her hair in a long ～** 她梳着长辫子 2 [u] (trimming) 穗带; **gold ～** 金穗带
B *vt* 1 Amer (plait) 把…编成辫子 ‹*hair, strands*› 2 (trim) 用穗带镶缀 ‹*cuff, jacket, cushion*›

Braille /breɪl/ *n* [u] 布莱叶盲文; **a ～ book** 盲文写成的书

brain /breɪn/
A *n* 1 Anat 脑; **～ tissue/cell** 脑组织/脑细胞; **to blow sb.'s ～s out** colloq 把某人的脑袋打开花 2 (mind) 智力; **to have a good ～** 脑子聪明; **to have football on the ～** colloq 对足球着迷
B **brains** *npl* 1 + *v pl* (intelligence) 智慧; **to have ～s** 聪明; **to use one's ～s** 动脑筋 2 + *v sing* colloq (intelligent person) 聪明人; **she was the ～s behind the operation** 她是这次行动的策划者
C *vt* colloq 猛击…的头部

brain: ～box *n* Brit colloq 极其聪明的人; **～child** *n* colloq (idea) 主意; (invention) 发明; **～ damage** *n* [u] 脑损伤; **～-damaged** *adj* 脑损伤的; **～-dead** *adj* 1 Med 脑死亡的; 2 fig colloq pej 极其愚蠢的; **～ death** *n* [u] 脑死亡; **～ drain** *n* colloq 人才流失; **～ fever** *n* [u] dated 脑炎

brainiac /'breɪnɪæk/ *n* esp Amer sl 超天才

brainless /'breɪnlɪs/ *adj* 愚蠢的

brain: ～ pan *n* esp Amer colloq 脑壳; **～ scan** *n* (process) 脑部扫描; (picture) 脑部扫描 X 光片; **～ scanner** *n* 脑部扫描装置

brainstorm /'breɪnstɔːm/
A *n* 1 Brit colloq 突然神志不清; **to have a ～** 一时糊涂 2 (group discussion) 头脑风暴 [指集体自由讨论] 3 colloq (brainwave) 奇思妙想
B *vi* 进行头脑风暴

brain: ～storming *n* [u] 头脑风暴 [指集体自由讨论]; **～s trust** *n* Brit 智囊团; **～ surgeon** *n* ►**p. 409** 脑外科医生; **～ surgery** *n* [u] 脑外科手术; **it isn't ～ surgery** colloq 没什么大不了的; **～-teaser** *n* colloq 趣味智力题; **～ trust** *n* Amer [政府或政治家委任的] 顾问班子; **～wash** *vt* 给…洗脑; **they were ～washed into thinking that ...** 他们被洗了脑，认为…; **～washing** *n* [u] 洗脑; **～wave** *n* 1 colloq (inspiration) 奇思妙想; **to have a ～wave** 灵机一动; 2 Med 脑电波; **～work** *n* [u] 脑力劳动

brainy /'breɪnɪ/ *adj* colloq 聪明的

braise /breɪz/ *vt* 煨

brake /breɪk/
A *n* 1 Aut 刹车; **to apply** *or* **put on the ～(s)** 踩刹车 2 fig (curb) 约束; **to put a ～ on price rises** 控制价格上涨
B *vi* «*driver, vehicle*» 刹车

brake: ～ block *n* 刹车片; **～ disc** *n* 制动盘; **～ drum** *n* 制动鼓; **～ fluid** *n* 制动液; **～ horsepower** *n* [u] 制动马力; **～ lever** *n* 制动手柄; **～ light** *n* 制动信号灯; **～ lining** *n* 制动衬片; **～man** /-mən/ *n* Amer Rail [火车上的] 制动手; **～ pad** *n* 刹车片; **～ pedal** *n* 制动踏板; **～ shoe** *n* 制动瓦

braking /'breɪkɪŋ/ *n* [u] 刹车

braking: ～ distance *n* 制动距离; **～ power** *n* [u] 制动功率; **～ system** *n* 制动系统

bramble /'bræmbl/ *n* 1 (plant) 黑莓灌木 2 Brit (fruit) 黑莓

bran /bræn/ *n* [u] 糠

branch /brɑːntʃ, Amer bræntʃ/
A *n* 1 (bough) 树枝 2 fig (smaller or less important part) (gen) 分支; (of road, pipe) 支路; (of river) 支流; (of study) 分科 3 (division) (of shop) 分店; (of bank) 支行; (of company) 分公司; (of organization) 分部; (of library) 分馆; **main ～** (of company) 总部 4 Comput 分支指令
B *vi* 1 «*plant*» 出枝桠 2 «*road, river*» 分叉

Phrasal verbs

- **branch off** *vi* **to ～ off (from sth.)** «*road*» (从某处) 分岔; fig 偏离 (某主题)
- **branch out** *vi* **to ～ out (into sth.)** 将活动范围扩大 (到某处); **to ～ out on one's own** 独立创业

branch: ～ line *n* 支线; **～ manager** *n* (of shop) 分店经理; (of company) 分公司经理; (of bank) 支行经理; **～ office** *n* 分部

brand /brænd/
A *n* 1 Comm (make) 品牌; **a well-known ～** 名牌 2 (type, kind) 类型 3 (on hide, skin) 烙印; fig (stigma) 污名 4 liter (burning wood) 燃烧的木块
B *vt* 1 (mark) 给…打上烙印 ‹*cattle*›; fig 使刻骨铭心; **the image was ～ed on my memory** 这一形象铭刻在我的记忆中 2 fig (label) 加污名于; **to ～ sb. (as) sth.** 给某人加上…的污名; **to be ～ed as sth.** 被丑化为…

brand: ～ acceptance *n* [u] 品牌接受度; **～-aware** *adj* 了解品牌的; **～ awareness** *n* [u] 品牌认知

branded /'brændɪd/ *adj attrib* 有品牌的 ‹*goods*›

b

b

brand image *n* [c and u] 品牌形象
branding /ˈbrændɪŋ/ *n* [u] Comm 品牌创建
branding iron *n* 烙铁
brandish /ˈbrændɪʃ/ *vt* 气势汹汹地挥舞 ‹*weapon*›; 挥动 ‹*paper, sign*›
brand: ~ **leader** *n* 领导品牌; ~ **loyalty** *n* [u] 品牌忠诚; ~ **management** *n* [u] 品牌经营; ~ **manager** *n* 品牌经营者; ~ **name** *n* 商标; ~**-new** *adj* 崭新的; ~ **piracy** *n* [u] 品牌盗用; ~ **recognition** *n* [u] 品牌知名度; ~ **switching** *n* [u] 换品牌
brandy /ˈbrændi/ *n* **1** [u and c] (drink) 白兰地 **2** [c] (serving) 一杯白兰地
brandy: ~ **glass** *n* 白兰地酒杯; ~ **snap** *n* 姜味薄脆饼
bran tub *n* Brit [装满麸皮的] 摸彩桶
brash /bræʃ/ *adj* **1** (overbearingly or cheekily self-assertive) 自以为是的 **2** (garish) 俗艳的
brashly /ˈbræʃli/ *adv* (cockily) 自以为是地; (breezily) 轻率地
brashness /ˈbræʃnɪs/ *n* [u] 自以为是
Brasilia /brəˈzɪljə/ *pr n* 巴西利亚
brass /brɑːs, Amer bræs/ *n* **1** [u] (metal) 黄铜 **2** [u] (fittings) 黄铜饰 **3** [u] Mus 铜管乐器部分 **4** [c] (memorial) 黄铜纪念牌 **5** [u] colloq (nerve) 厚脸皮; **to be (as) bold as** ~ 厚颜无耻 **6** [u] Brit colloq (money) 钱
brass: ~ **band** *n* 铜管乐队; ~ **farthing** *n* 不值钱的东西; **it's not worth a** ~ **farthing** colloq 它一文不值; ~ **foundry** *n* 黄铜铸造厂; ~ **hat** *n* Mil colloq 高级将领
brassière /ˈbræzɪə(r), Amer brəˈzɪər/ *n* 胸罩
brass: ~ **instrument** ▸**p. 395** *n* 铜管乐器; ~ **knuckles** *npl* Amer 指节铜套; ~ **monkey** *n* colloq **it's** ~ **monkeys outside** 外面冷极了; ~ **neck** *n* [u] Brit colloq 厚脸皮; ~**-necked** *adj* Brit colloq 厚脸皮的; ~ **plate** *n* 黄铜门牌; ~ **rubbing** *n* **1** [u] (action) 拓印; **2** [c] (image) 拓片; ~ **tacks** *npl* colloq **to get down to** ~ **tacks** 开始考虑实质性问题; ~**ware** *n* [u] 黄铜器皿; ~**work** *n* [u] **1** (parts) 黄铜部件; **2** (activity) 黄铜器皿制造
brassy /ˈbrɑːsi, Amer ˈbræsi/ *adj* **1** ▸**p. 134** (in colour) 黄铜色的 **2** (loud, harsh) 刺耳的 ‹*tone, note*› **3** pej (showy) 花哨的 ‹*woman, appearance*›
bra strap *n* 胸罩吊带
brat /bræt/ *n* pej colloq 顽童; **you little** ~**!** 你这个小淘气鬼!
Bratislava /ˈbrætɪˈslɑːvə/ *pr n* 布拉迪斯拉发
brat pack *n* colloq 新鼠党 [指闹哄哄的一群青年明星]
brattish /ˈbrætɪʃ/ *adj* 没规矩的
bravado /brəˈvɑːdəʊ/ *n* [u] 虚张声势; **an act of (sheer)** ~ (纯粹的) 逞能
brave /breɪv/
A *adj* **1** (courageous) 勇敢的; **to be** ~ **about sth./doing sth.** 在某事/做某事上很勇敢; **to put on a** ~ **face/front** 硬着头皮 **2** liter (fine) 美好的 ‹*show, sight*›; **a** ~ **new world** iron 美丽新世界 [含讽刺意味]
B *n* **1** dated (Indian) 美洲印第安武士 **2** + *v pl* **the** ~ (people) 勇敢的人
C *vt* 勇敢面对 ‹*danger, storm*›
Phrasal verb
• **brave out** *vt* [~ **sth. out**] 勇敢地挺过
bravely /ˈbreɪvli/ *adv* 勇敢地
bravery /ˈbreɪvəri/ *n* [u] 勇敢
bravery award *n* 勇敢奖
bravo /brɑːˈvəʊ/
A *excl* 好啊
B *n* 喝彩声
bravura /brəˈvʊərə/ *n* [u] 出色表现; **a** ~ **performance** 出色的表演
brawl /brɔːl/
A *n* (fight) 斗殴; (quarrel) 争吵; **a drunken** ~ 酒后斗殴
B *vi* (fight) 打斗; (quarrel) 争吵; **to** ~ **with sb.** 与某人打斗
brawn /brɔːn/ *n* [u] **1** (strength) 体力; **(he's) all** ~**, no brains** (他) 四肢发达, 头脑简单 **2** Brit Culin 碎猪肉冻
brawny /ˈbrɔːni/ *adj* 强壮的 ‹*man*›; 肌肉发达的 ‹*arms*›
bray /breɪ/
A *vi* **1** «*donkey*» 嘶叫 **2** pej (speak) 刺耳地大声说; (laugh) 刺耳地大笑
B *n* **1** (of donkey) 驴叫声 **2** pej (of person) 刺耳的声音
braze /breɪz/ *vt* (form) 用黄铜铸造; (solder) 用黄铜焊接
brazen /ˈbreɪzn/ *adj* 厚颜无耻的; **a** ~ **hussy** 不知羞耻的荡妇
brazenly /ˈbreɪznli/ *adv* 厚颜无耻地
brazier /ˈbreɪzɪə(r)/ *n* 火盆
Brazil /brəˈzɪl/ *pr n* 巴西
Brazilian /brəˈzɪljən/ ▸**p. 503**
A *adj* (of Brazil) 巴西的; (of the people) 巴西人的
B *n* 巴西人
Brazil nut *n* 巴西坚果
Brazzaville /ˈbrɑːzəvɪl/ *pr n* 布拉柴维尔
breach /briːtʃ/
A *n* **1** [u and c] (infringement) 违反; ~ **of copyright/contract/promise** 侵犯版权/违背合同/违背诺言; ~ **of trust/secrecy** 背信/泄密; **a** ~ **of good manners** 失礼; **to be in** ~ **of** 违犯 ‹*law*›; ~ **of the peace** Jur 扰乱治安 **2** [c] (break in relations) 破裂 **3** [c] (gap) 缺口; **to step into the** ~ [尤指在最后时刻] 站出来接替
B *vt* **1** (infringe) 违反 ‹*law, contract*› **2** (break through) 在…上打开缺口 ‹*wall, defences*›
bread /bred/ *n* [u] **1** Culin 面包; **to be on** ~ **and water** 吃粗茶淡饭; **to know which side one's** ~ **is buttered** colloq 知道自己的利益所在; **to break** ~ **(with sb.)** dated (与某人) 共餐; **to cast one's** ~ **upon the waters** fig 真心行善不图报; ~ **and wine** Relig 圣餐 **2** colloq (money) 钱 **3** (livelihood) 生计; **to earn one's (daily)** ~ 谋生; **to take the** ~ **out of sb.'s mouth** 砸某人的饭碗; **to put** ~ **on the table** 挣钱糊口
bread and butter
A *n* [u] fig 生计
B **bread-and-butter** *adj attrib* 基本的; **the bread-and-butter issues** 根本问题
bread: ~**-and-butter pudding** *n* [u and c] 黄油面包布丁; ~**basket** *n* **1** lit 面包篮; **2** fig (region) 盛产粮食的地方; (barn) 粮仓; **3** colloq (belly) 肚子; ~**bin** *n* Brit 面包箱; ~**board** *n* 切面包板; ~**box** *n* Amer 面包箱; ~**crumb** *n usu pl* 面包屑; ~**fruit** *n* (tree) 面包果树; (fruit) 面包果; ~**knife** *n* 切面包刀; ~**line** *n* **1** [u] Brit **the** ~**line** 贫困线; **to be on the** ~**line** 很贫穷; **above/below the** ~**line** 高于/低于贫困线; **2** [c] Amer 等候领施舍食物的队伍; ~ **pudding** *n* [u and c] 面包布丁; ~ **roll** *n* 小圆面包; ~ **sauce** *n* [u] 面包调味汁; ~**stick** *n* 棒形面包
breadth /bredθ/ ▸**p. 436** *n* **1** [u and c] Meas 宽度; **the length and** ~ **of sth.** fig 某地的各处 **2** [u] (scope) 广度; ~ **of experience** 阅历的丰富; ~ **of knowledge** 知识的渊博
breadwinner /ˈbredwɪnə(r)/ *n* 挣钱养家的人
break /breɪk/
A *vt* (*pt* **broke,** *pp* **broken**) **1** (separate into pieces) 打破 ‹*window, table*›; 弄断 ‹*stick, chain*›; **to** ~ **sth. open, to** ~ **open sth.** 把某物砸开; **to** ~ **sth. in half** *or* **two** 把某物一分为二; **she broke the chocolate into eight pieces** 她把巧克力掰成了八块; **he broke the brick with a hammer** 他用锤子敲碎了砖; **the bird** ~**s the shell with its beak** 鸟用喙啄破了贝壳; **to** ~ **an egg/a nut/the ice** 打蛋/砸开坚果/破冰 **2** Anat 折断 ‹*bone, arm, wing*›; **to** ~ **one's neck** 折断脖子 **3** (split open) 划破 ‹*skin*›; **the dog bit me, but it didn't** ~ **the skin** 狗咬了我, 但没咬破皮; **to** ~ **surface** «*submarine, diver*» 浮出水面 **4** (split apart) 拆开 ‹*set, seal*›; 拆分 ‹*line, text*› **5** (make inoperative) 弄坏 ‹*radio, watch, torch, camera, etc.*› **6** (contravene) 违反 ‹*law, promise*›; 破坏 ‹*embargo, strike*›; **to** ~ **every rule in the book** 违反书中的所有规定; **the president broke his word** 总裁食言了; **to** ~ **an appointment** 爽约 **7** (exceed, surpass) 冲破 ‹*sound barrier, class barrier*›; **to** ~ **the record/speed limit** 打破记录/超速 **8** (interrupt visually) «*object*» 破坏…的连续性 ‹*line*›; **a group of hills broke the horizon in the distance** 远处的群山矗立在地平线上 **9** (end) 打破 ‹*spell, monotony*›; 打乱 ‹*sequence*›; 打断 ‹*train of thought, concentration, continuity*›; 中断 ‹*link, contact*›; **to** ~ **one's silence** 打破缄默 **10** esp Brit (make pause in) 在…中稍停; **to** ~ **one's journey** 在旅途中停留 **11** Elec 切断 ‹*current, circuit, contact*› **12** (lessen impact of) 减缓…的势头; **the hedge helps to** ~ **the wind** 树篱可挡风; **a small tree broke her fall** 她摔落时被一棵小树挡了一下 **13** (ruin financially) 使…破产 ‹*person, organization*› **14** (crush, overcome power of) 使…垮掉 ‹*person, health*›; 瓦解 ‹*organization, resistance*›; **to** ~ **sb.'s/sth.'s hold over sb./sth.** 打破某人/某事物对某人/某事物的控制; **to** ~ **sb.'s spirit/resolve** 瓦解某人的精神/决心; **the death of his wife broke him completely** 妻子的去世使他悲痛欲绝 **15** (resolve successfully) 冲破 ‹*siege, blockade, deadlock*›; 镇压 ‹*rebellion*›; 中止 ‹*strike*› **16** (in tennis) 接…得分 ‹*service*›; 接…的发球得分 ‹*opponent*› **17** (give up) 戒除 ‹*habit*›; **to** ~ **sb./oneself of a habit** 使某人改掉/改掉习惯 **18** (announce) 透露; **to** ~ **the news to sb.** 向某人透露消息; **to** ~ **it to sb. gently** 婉转地告知某人此事 **19** (decipher) 破译 ‹*code, cipher*› **20** (leave) **to** ~ **camp** 拔营; **to** ~ **jail** 越狱 **21** (change for coins) 兑开 ‹*bill, note*›
B *vi* (*pt* **broke,** *pp* **broken**) **1** (separate into pieces) «*table, ice, box*» 破裂; (shatter) «*window, egg*» 破碎; (snap) «*pencil, bone, neck, wing*» 折断; (be pulled apart) «*shoelace, rope, wool*» 拉断; **to** ~ **in half** *or* **two** 断成两半 **2** (cease to be operational) «*radio, watch, torch*» 损坏 **3** (disperse) «*clouds*» 消散 **4** (stop for a rest) 休息; **let's** ~ **for ten minutes** 我们休息10分钟吧; **to** ~ **for tea/coffee** 休息用茶/咖啡 **5** Sport «*boxers, wrestlers*» 分开 **6** (change) «*weather*» 突变; **the heatwave has broken at last** 热浪终于过去了 **7** (begin) «*dawn*» 开始; **we'll leave as soon as day** ~**s** 天一亮我们就动身 **8** (begin violently) 爆发; **the storm broke as they were halfway home** 他们回家走到半路时风雨大作 **9** (dissolve) «*waves, sea*» 迸溅; **to** ~ **against/on/over sth.** 拍打在某物上溅开 **10** (become known) «*news, scandal, story*» 突然传开; ~**ing news** 突发新闻 **11** (get away) «*person, animal*» 挣脱; «*boat*» 脱缆; **to** ~ **from sth.** 挣脱某事物 **12** Med (in pregnancy) «*waters*» 破 **13** (weaken) «*health*» 垮掉; «*spirit, resistance*» 瓦解; «*strength*» 削弱; **to** ~ **under sth.** 在…之下垮掉 ‹*questioning, torture, strain*›; **we'll keep going until we** ~ 我们要走到筋疲力尽为止 **14** (falter) «*voice*» 变调; (in adolescence) «*boy's voice*» 变粗; **to** ~ **with sth.** 因…而语不成声 ‹*emotion, grief, anger*› **15** Sport (in billiards, pool, snooker) «*player*» 开球
C *n* **1** (fracture) (instance) 折断; (point) 破裂处; **a** ~ **in an arm/a leg** 手臂/腿骨折 **2** (crack, split) 裂缝; (gap, space) 空隙; **a** ~ **in sth.** 某物上的缝隙 **3** (interruption of sequence or process) 中断; **a** ~ **in sth.** 某过程的间断; **a** ~ **in a child's education** 孩子教育的中断; **without a** ~ 不停地 **4** (pause) (in TV, radio programme) 间隙; (in game, match, performance) 休息; **a** ~ **for**

advertisements *or* **commercials** 插播广告的间歇; **to take a ~** 休息一下 [插播广告时的用语] **5** (rest) 休息; **a ~ from sth.** 停下某事休息; **to have** *or* **take a ~ (from sth./doing sth.)** （停下某事/做某事）休息一下; **to give sb. a ~ (from sth./doing sth.)** 让某人（停下某事/做某事）去休息; **give me a ~!** colloq (stop annoying me) 别烦我了！; (stop lying) 别瞎扯了！; **morning/afternoon ~** Brit Sch 上午/下午课间休息 **6** Ling (in word) 移行处; (in line) 停顿; (in sentence) 省略号; (in paragraph) 断纸 [指段落之间的空白处] **7** Elec, Phys (interruption) (in transmission) 断开; (in electrical circuit) 断路 **8** (holiday) 短假; **a ~ from sth.** 离开某处的休假; **a weekend ~ in Amsterdam** 在阿姆斯特丹的周末度假 **9** (decisive change) 决裂; **a ~ with sb./sth.** 与某人/某事物的决裂; **a ~ in sth.** 在某方面的决裂; **to make a** *or* **the ~ with ...** (from family) 与…断绝关系; (from job) 坚决放弃… **10** Meteorol 突变; **a ~ in the weather** 天气的突变 **11** (change of tone) 音调突变; **a ~ in sb.'s voice** 某人声音的突变 **12** colloq (escape bid) 逃跑; **a prison ~** 越狱; **to make a ~ for sth./it** 向某处逃去/逃跑 **13** colloq (opportunity) 机会; **to give sb. a ~** (help in career) 给某人一次机会; (make allowances) 谅解某人; **to give sb. an even ~** 给某人以平等的机会 **14** (in tennis) 接发球得分; **service ~, ~ of serve** 破发球 **15** (in billiards, pool, snooker) (series of shots) 接连击中; (first shot) 开球; **to make a 50 point ~** 连得 50 分 **16** (in jazz or popular music) 华彩段

Phrasal verbs

• **break away**

A *vi* **1** (become detached, move away) 脱离; **to ~ away from sb./sth.** 脱离某人/某事物; **the young elephant broke away from the herd** 小象离群了 **2** (escape) «*person, animal, boat, kite*» 挣脱; **to ~ away from sb./sth.** 摆脱某人/某事物逃走 **3** Sport «*runner, cyclist*» 领先; **to ~ away from sb./sth.** 甩开某人/某群

B *vt* [**~ sth. away, ~ away sth.**] 使脱离; **to ~ the shell away from the egg** 剥去蛋壳; **part of the cliff had been broken away** 悬崖的一部分已经崩落

• **break down**

A *vi* **1** (stop functioning) «*machine, system*» 发生故障 **2** (fail) «*negotiations*» 失败; «*relations*» 破裂; «*discipline, agreement*» 失效; «*moral values, system, coalition*» 崩溃 **3** (collapse mentally or physically) «*person, health*» 垮掉; **to ~ down under interrogation/torture** 经不起质问/折磨而垮掉 **4** (weep) «*person*» 失声痛哭 **5** (be classified) «*results, data*» 分类 **6** Chem, Biol «*compound, substance, food*» 分解; **to ~ down into sth.** 分解成某物

B *vt* [**~ down sth., ~ sth. down**]
1 (knock down) 撞倒 ‹*door, barrier*› **2** (overcome) 克服 ‹*shyness, obstacle, attitude*›; 瓦解 ‹*resistance, opposition*› **3** Chem, Biol (cause to separate into parts) 分解 ‹*compound, substance, food*›; **to ~ sth. down into sth.** 把某物分解成某物

• **break in**

A *vi* **1** (enter forcibly) «*thief, fire brigade*» 破门而入 **2** (interrupt) «*noise, action*» 打断; **to ~ in on sb./sth.** 打断某人/某事; **don't keep ~ing in!** 不要总插嘴!

B [**~ sth. in, ~ in sth.**] *vt*
1 (knock in) 砸破…进入 ‹*box*›; **the police broke the door in** 警察破门而入 **2** (wear, use) 把…穿得合脚 ‹*shoes*›; 使…合用 ‹*false teeth, tennis racket*› **3** Equit 驯 ‹*horse*›

C [**~ sb. in, ~ in sb.**] *vt* 训练 ‹*recruit, novice*›; **to ~ sb. in gently** colloq hum 逐渐驯化某人

• **break into** *vt* [**~ into sth.**]
1 (enter by force) 闯入 ‹*house, bank*›; **firefighters broke into the burning building** 消防员冲进燃烧的大楼 **2** (open by force) 砸开 ‹*safe, money box, car*› **3** (start to use) 开启 ‹*new box, new bottle*›; (resort to using) 动用 ‹*emergency supplies, savings*› **4** (pay with) 兑开 ‹*note*› **5** (encroach on) 占用 ‹*leisure time*›; **he doesn't want to ~ into his evening** 他不想占用晚上的时间 **6** (begin to do) 突然发出 ‹*laughter, cheers*›; (change pace to) 突然加速 ‹*run, trot*›; **she broke into song** 她突然唱起歌来; **the horse broke into a gallop** 那匹马突然飞奔起来 **7** (make headway in) 打入 ‹*market, show business*›

• **break off**

A *vi* **1** (snap off) «*tip, twig*» 折断 **2** (stop doing sth.) 突然停止; **to ~ off from sth./doing sth.** 停止某事/做某事; **he broke off as his wife came into the room** (stopped speaking) 妻子一进屋他便不讲话了

B [**~ off sth.**] *vt* (be snapped off) «*end, handle, mast, twig*» 从…处折断

C [**~ sth. off, ~ off sth.**] *vt*
1 (snap off) 折断 ‹*handle, twig, mast, part*›; **to ~ sth. off sth.** 把某物从某处折断; **he broke off a piece of chocolate and gave it to me** 他掰下一块巧克力给了我; **~ a bit off the end** 从末端折下一点 **2** (stop) 中断 ‹*activity, meeting*›; (terminate) 终止 ‹*negotiations*›; 断绝 ‹*connection, relations*›; **to ~ off doing sth.** 暂停做某事; **to ~ off sth. with sb.** 与某人断绝某种关系; **they've broken off their engagement** 他们取消了婚约

• **break out**

A *vi* **1** (start) «*war, argument, plague*» 爆发; **fire broke out on the third floor** 大火是从三楼烧起来的 **2** (appear) «*spots, pimples*» 突然冒出; **to ~ out over/on sth.** 突然布满某处; **sweat broke out all over his body** 他突然冒出一身汗 **3** (escape) 逃脱; **to ~ out of sth.** 逃出 ‹*cage, trap*›; 摆脱 ‹*routine, rut, depression*›; **to ~ out of prison** 越狱

B *vt* [**~ sth. out, ~ out sth.**] 打开…使用; **shall we ~ out the champagne?** 我们开了这瓶香槟酒吧?

• **break out in** *vt* [**~ out in sth.**] 布满 ‹*spots, pimples*›; **I broke out in a cold sweat** 我冒出一身冷汗

• **break through**

A *vi* **1** (force way through) «*person, animal, vehicle*» 冲过; **the army broke through** 部队突围了 **2** (succeed) 取得突破; **to ~ through in the fight against cancer** 在抗癌方面取得突破 **3** (appear) «*moon, sun*» 露出

B *vt* [**~ through sth.**]
1 (force way through) 冲破 ‹*door, obstacle*›; 穿透 ‹*floor, ground*›; 突破 ‹*defence*›; **the deer broke through the undergrowth** 那只鹿穿过了矮树丛 **2** (overcome) 克服; **to ~ through sb.'s reserve** 消除某人的矜持 **3** (emerge from) «*sun, moon*» 从…后露出 ‹*clouds, fog*›

• **break up**

A [**~ sth. up, ~ up sth.**] *vt*
1 (reduce to pieces) 把…弄碎 ‹*ice, table, chocolate*›; 拆散 ‹*machine, jigsaw puzzle*›; **frost had broken up the surface of the road** 严寒把路面冻裂了; **to ~ sth. up into sth.** 把某物拆分成某物 **2** (divide) 分 ‹*estate, job, paragraph*›; **to ~ up sth. into sth.** 把某物分成某物; **the academic year is broken up into three terms** 一学年分为三个学期 **3** (make more interesting) 使…更有趣 ‹*evening, journey, routine*›; **to ~ up sth. with sth.** 用某事物调剂某事物; **making food helps to ~ up the day** 做饭可以使日子不至于太单调 **4** (disperse) 解散 ‹*party, meeting*›; 驱散 ‹*protest, crowd*›; 制止 ‹*fight*›; **the troops used tear gas to ~ up the riot** 军队使用催泪弹驱散了骚乱的人群; **~ it up!** (stop fighting) 别打了!; (disperse) 散开!; hum (stop kissing) 别亲了! **5** (end) 使…解体 ‹*empire, coalition*›; 使…破裂 ‹*marriage, relationship*›; 拆散 ‹*family*›; **to ~ up a successful team** 解散一支成功的球队; **this diplomatic incident broke up the alliance between the two countries** 这一外交事件导致了两国联盟的解体

B [**~ sb. up.**] *vt* esp Amer colloq (cause to laugh) 使大笑

C *vi* **1** (be reduced to pieces) «*ice, rock, cake*» 破碎; «*clouds*» 散开; **to ~ up into sth.** 碎裂成某物; **the ship broke up on the rocks** 船触礁解体了 **2** (be divided) «*empire, party*» 分裂; **to ~ up into sth.** 分裂成某物 **3** (disperse) «*meeting, demonstration, people*» 解散 **4** Brit Sch «*school, students*» 期末放假 **5** (come to an end) «*coalition*» 解体; «*marriage, relationship*» 破裂 **6** (end relationship) «*couple*» 分手; **to ~ up with sb.** 与某人分手; **the band broke up in 2002** 该乐队于2002年解散 **7** Radio, Telecom 被干扰; **I can't hear you; you're ~ing up** 我听不到你说话；你的信号被干扰了 **8** esp Amer colloq (laugh) 大笑

• **break with** *vt* **1** [**~ with sb./sth.**] (end relationship with) 与…断绝关系 ‹*friend, family, church*› **2** [**~ with sth.**] (no longer follow) 摒弃 ‹*tradition, old habits*›; **to ~ with the past** 彻底告别过去

breakable /ˈbreɪkəbl/

A *adj* **1** (fragile) 易碎的 **2** (decipherable) 可破译的 ‹*code*›

B **breakables** *npl* 易碎物品

breakage /ˈbreɪkɪdʒ/ *n* **1** [u and c] (act) 损坏; **accidental ~** 意外的破损 **2** [c] (object) 破碎物品; **'~s must be paid for'** “物品损毁，必须赔偿”

breakaway /ˈbreɪkəweɪ/

A *n* **1** (from person, group) 脱离; **a ~ from sb./sth.** 与某人的分手/从某组织的脱离 **2** (change) 彻底改变; **a ~ from sth.** 对某事物的改变 **3** Sport (in race) 甩开; (in football) 转守为攻; **to make a ~** 甩开他人

B *adj attrib* Pol 获得独立的 ‹*country*›; 另立门户的 ‹*group*›

break dance

A *n* [u and c] 霹雳舞

B *vi* 跳霹雳舞

break: ~ dancer *n* 跳霹雳舞的人; **~ dancing** *n* [u] 霹雳舞; **~down** *n* **1** [u and c] Aut, Mech 故障; *modif* 抢修的 ‹*service*›; **~down truck** Brit 拖车; **2** [u and c] (collapse) (of economy, health) 崩溃; (of order) 瘫痪; (of alliance) 破裂; (of plan) 失败; **a ~down in communications/discipline** 通信的中断/纪律的涣散; **3** [c] Med 精神崩溃; **to have a (nervous) ~down** 精神失常; **to be on the verge of a ~down** 几近崩溃; **4** [c] (account) (of figures) 分析; (by profile) 分类; **a ~down according to age** 按年龄的分类; **5** [u] Biol, Chem 分解

breaker /ˈbreɪkə(r)/ *n* **1** (wave) 大浪 **2** ▸ **p. 409** Brit (dismantler) 废品回收商 **3** (on CB radio) 民用波段使用者 **4** = **circuit breaker**

breaker's yard *n* Brit 废品回收场

break: ~-even *n* [u] 收支相抵; **~-even point** 收支相抵点, 盈亏平衡点; **~-even price** *n* 保本价格

breakfast /ˈbrekfəst/

A *n* 早饭; **to have** *or* **eat ~** 吃早饭; **to have** *or* **eat sb. for ~** colloq 对付某人是小菜一碟

B *vi* 吃早饭; **to ~ on sth.** 早餐吃某物

breakfast: ~ bar *n* (counter) 早餐台; (buffet) 自助早餐; **~ bowl** *n* 粥碗; **~ cereal** *n* 早餐麦片; **~ meeting** *n* 早餐工作会议; **~ room** *n* 早餐厅; **~ television** *n* [u] 早间电视节目; **~ time** *n* 早餐时间; **~ TV** *n* [u] = **~ television**

break-in *n* 非法闯入

breaking: ~ and entering *n* [u] 入室盗窃罪; **~ point** *n* **1** [u and c] Tech 断裂点; **2** [u] fig (collapse) 顶点; **to be at ~ point** 达到极限; **to be close to ~ point** 濒于崩溃; **my patience had reached ~ point** 我的耐心已经到了极点; **~ strength** *n* [u] 抗断强度

break: ~neck *adj attrib* 极快而危险的 ‹*speed*›; **~ of day** *n* [u] 黎明; **he left at/before ~ of day** 他在黎明时分/黎明前离开; **~out** *n* 越狱; **~ point** *n* (in tennis) 破发点; **~point** *n* Comput 断点; **~through** *n*

1 (discovery, development) 突破; **2** Mil 突围; **~-up** *n* [u and c] **1** (end of relationship, alliance) 破裂; **2** (of empire, union) 解体; **~water** *n* 防波堤

bream /briːm/ *n* (*pl* **bream**) 欧鳊

breast /brest/
A *n* **1** [c] Anat (woman's) 乳房 **2** [c] liter (chest) 胸部; **to make a clean ~ of sth.** 坦陈某事; **to beat one's ~** 捶胸 **3** [c] (of bird) 胸脯 **4** [u and c] Culin (of poultry, lamb) 胸脯肉 **5** [c] fig liter (heart) 心窝 **6** [c] (of jacket, shirt) 前胸
B *vt* **1** Sport **to ~ the tape** «*runner*» 冲线 **2** (walk through) 挺胸穿过 ‹*waves, crowd*› **3** esp Brit (reach top of) 登上…的顶部 ‹*hill*›

breast: ~-beating *n* [u] 捶胸; **~ bone** *n* 胸骨; **~ cancer** ▸**p. 377** *n* [u] 乳腺癌; **~fed** *adj* 母乳喂养的

breastfeed (*pt, pp* **breastfed**)
A *vt* 用母乳喂养
B *vi* «*mother*» 哺乳

breast: ~feeding *n* [u] 母乳喂养; **~ milk** *n* [u] 母乳; **~-plate** *n* 胸铠; **~ pocket** *n* 胸部口袋; **~ stroke** *n* [u] 蛙泳; **~work** *n* 矮防护墙

breath /breθ/ *n* **1** [u] (air taken in or expelled from lungs) 气息; **to smell sth. on sb.'s ~** 从某人呼出的气中闻到某气味; **(to have) bad ~** （有）口臭; **under one's ~** 低声地; **to be the ~ of life (to sb.)** 是（某人）生命中不可或缺的东西 **2** [u] (breathing) 吸入的空气; **to stop/pause for ~** 停下来/暂停下来喘气; **to draw ~** lit 吸气; fig liter 活着; **as kind a man as ever drew ~** 天底下最善良的人; **(to be) out of ~** 上气不接下气; **(to be) short of ~** 呼吸困难; **to get one's ~ back** Brit 喘过气来; **I hardly had time to get my ~ back between meetings** 我的会一个接一个，几乎没时间喘口气; **to hold one's ~** 屏住呼吸; **don't hold your ~!** colloq (no need for immediate action, excitement) 别急！; **to catch one's ~** 歇口气; **to take sb.'s ~ away** fig 使某人惊叹; **to save one's ~** colloq 不费口舌; **to waste one's breath (doing sth.)** 白费口舌（做某事） **3** [c] (inhalation) 吸气; **to take a deep ~** lit 深吸一口气; fig 注意听着; **a ~ of fresh air** lit (clean air) 新鲜空气; fig (refreshing change) 新鲜的刺激; **to go outside for a ~ of (fresh) air** 出去透透气; **to count to 50 in a single ~** 一口气数到 50; **in the same ~** 同时; **with one's last** *or* **dying ~** 在弥留之际; **to draw one's last ~** liter 死去 **4** [c] *sing* (air, movement) 轻拂; **a ~ of air** *or* **wind** 一丝微风; **the first ~ of spring** 第一股春天的气息 **5** [c] *sing* fig (hint, suggestion) 迹象; **a ~ of sth.** 某事的迹象; **a ~ of scandal** 丑闻的蛛丝马迹

breathable /ˈbriːðəbl/ *adj* **1** (fit to breathe) 适合吸入的 ‹*air*› **2** Tex 透气的 ‹*fabric, clothing, footwear*›

breathalyse Brit, **breathalyze** Amer /ˈbreθəlaɪz/ *vt* 对…作呼气测醉检测 ‹*driver*›

breathalyser Brit, **Breathalyzer®** Amer /ˈbreθəlaɪzə(r)/ *n* 呼气测醉器

breathe /briːð/
A *vi* **1** (respire) 呼吸; **to ~ hard/heavily** 喘粗气; **the singer marks on the score where she is going to ~** 歌手把要换气的地方标在乐谱上; **he's still breathing** 他还活着; **now we can ~ (easily** *or* **freely) again!** fig 现在我们又可以松一口气了！ **2** (exhale) 呼气; **to ~ on/into sth.** 对某物呼气; **to ~ down sb.'s neck** colloq (follow closely) 紧紧跟在某人后面; (watch closely) 密切监视某人 **3** (expose to the air) «*wine*» 通气透香
B *vt* **1** (inhale) 吸入 ‹*air, dust*›; **to ~ one's last (breath)** liter 辞世 **2** (exhale) 呼出 ‹*air*›; 喷出 ‹*fire*›; **to ~ sth. into sth.** 把某物吹入某物; **to ~ air into a balloon** 吹气球; **to ~ smoke in sb.'s face** 把烟喷到某人脸上; **to ~ fire** 大怒 **3** (say quietly) 低声说; **to ~ sth. to sb.** 轻轻地对某人说某事; **don't ~ a word of this to anybody** 不要对任何人透露这件事; **to ~ loving words in sb.'s ear** 在某人耳边说情话 **4** (exude) 流露 ‹*optimism, defiance*›; **the team was breathing confidence** 球队信心十足 **5** fig (inspire with) 激发; **to ~ sth. into sb./sth.** 使某人/某事物产生 ‹*confidence, motivation*›; **to ~ hope into sb.** 激起某人的希望; **to ~ new** *or* **fresh life into sb./sth.** 赋予某人/某事物新的活力 **6** fig (be enthusiastic about) 专注于; **he lives and ~s football** 他狂迷足球

Phrasal verbs

• **breathe in**
A *vi* 吸气
B *vt* [**~ in sth., ~ sth. in**] 吸入 ‹*air, dust*›

• **breathe out**
A *vi* 呼气
B *vt* [**~ sth. out, ~ out sth.**] 呼出 ‹*air*›

breather /ˈbriːðə(r)/ *n* colloq **1** (rest) 短暂休息; **to have** *or* **take a ~** 喘口气 **2** (breath of fresh air) 透气; **he went outside for a ~** 他出去透透气

breath freshener *n* (tablet) 口气清新含片; (spray) 口气清新喷剂

breathing /ˈbriːðɪŋ/ *n* [u] 呼吸

breathing: ~ apparatus *n* [u and c] 呼吸面罩; **~ space** *n* [c and u] 喘息时机; **to give sb./oneself a** *or* **some ~ space** 给某人/自己一个喘息的机会

breathless /ˈbreθlɪs/ *adj* **1** (winded) 气喘吁吁的; **to make** *or* **leave sb. ~** 使某人上气不接下气; **to be ~ from sth./doing sth.** 因某事物/做某事而喘不过气来 **2** (fast) 极快的 ‹*speed*›; **with ~ haste** 仓促地; **at a ~ pace** 以疾速的步伐 **3** fig (excited) 屏住呼吸的; **to be left ~** 屏息; **to be ~ with wonder/joy** 惊叹不已/无比兴奋 **4** *attrib* fig (with anticipation, apprehension) 扣人心弦的 **5** *attrib* (still) 令人窒息的 ‹*calm, air*›

breathlessly /ˈbreθlɪsli/ *adv* **1** (panting) 气喘吁吁地; fig (excitedly) 激动得上气不接下气地 ‹*exclaim*› **2** fig (with anticipation, apprehension) 焦急地 ‹*wait, watch*›

breathlessness /ˈbreθlɪsnɪs/ *n* [u] 气喘吁吁

breathtaking /ˈbreθteɪkɪŋ/ *adj* 惊人的 ‹*speed, feat, audacity*›; 壮观的 ‹*view*›

breathtakingly /ˈbreθteɪkɪŋli/ *adv* 惊人地 ‹*beautiful, spectacular, audacious*›

breathtest /ˈbreθtest/
A *n* 呼气酒精测试
B *vt* 对…作呼气测醉检测 ‹*driver*›

breath testing *n* [u] 呼气测醉检测

breathy /ˈbreθi/ *adj* 伴着呼吸声的 ‹*voice*›

bred /bred/ *vi pt, pp* ▸**breed A, B**

breech /briːtʃ/ *n* [c] [枪炮的] 后膛

breech: ~ birth *n* 臀位分娩; **~block** *n* (of gun) 枪闩; (of cannon) 炮闩; **~ delivery** *n* 臀位分娩

breeches /ˈbrɪtʃɪz/ *npl* **1** (trousers) **(knee) ~** 七分裤 **2** Equit **(riding) ~** 马裤

breeches buoy /ˈbriːtʃɪz bɔɪ/ *n* 裤形救生圈

breed /briːd/
A *vt* (*pt, pp* **bred**) **1** Agric 培育; Zool 饲养 **2** fig (engender) 孕育; **lack of information ~s false rumours** 信息的缺乏会滋生谣言; **success ~s complacency** 成功导致自满
B *vi* (*pt, pp* **bred**) 繁殖
C *n* **1** Agric, Zool 品种 **2** (type) 类型; **a new ~ of politician(s)/computer** 新一代政治家/新型计算机

breeder /ˈbriːdə(r)/ *n* **1** (of animals) 饲养员; (of plants) 栽培者 **2** Nucl **~ (reactor)** 增殖反应堆

breeding /ˈbriːdɪŋ/ *n* [u] **1** Agric, Hort 繁殖 **2** Zool 饲养 **3** (good manners) 教养; **a man of ~** 有教养的男子

breeding: ~ ground *n* **1** Zool 繁殖地; **2** fig (hotbed) 滋生地; **a ~ ground for** *or* **of sth.** 某事物的滋生地; **~ period, ~ season** *ns* 繁殖季节; **~ site** *n* 繁殖地

breeze /briːz/
A *n* **1** (wind) 微风; Meteorol 2 级到 6 级的风; **in the ~** 在微风中; **a stiff/light ~** 6 级/2 级风 **2** colloq (easy task) 轻而易举的事; **it's a ~** 这事易如反掌
B *vi* colloq **1** (move lightheartedly) 飘然而行; **to ~ in/out** 一阵风似地飘然进来/出去 **2** (do easily) **to ~ through sth.** 轻松完成某事; **to ~ through life** 无忧无虑地生活

breeze block *n* Brit 煤渣砌块; **a ~ building** 煤渣块砌成的建筑

breezeway /ˈbriːzweɪ/ *n* Amer [房屋间的] 有顶过道

breezily /ˈbriːzɪli/ *adv* (casually) 随意地; (cheerfully) 欢快地; (confidently) 轻松自信地

breezy /ˈbriːzi/ *adj* **1** Meteorol 有微风的 ‹*weather*›; **a ~ morning** 微风吹拂的早晨 **2** (open to breezes) 通风的 ‹*place*› **3** colloq (casual) 随意的; (cheerful) 欢快的; (confident) 轻松自信的; **bright and ~** 充满活力的

brekkie, brekky /ˈbreki/ *n* [u] Brit colloq 早饭

Brent crude /ˈbrent kruːd/ *n* [u] 布伦特原油

brent goose /ˈbrent guːs/ *n* (*pl* **brent geese**) 黑雁

brethren /ˈbreðrən/ *npl* **1** Relig (monks) 弟兄们 [教友间的称呼] **2** hum (members of particular group) 同仁

Breton /ˈbretən/ ▸**p. 426**
A *adj* (of Brittany) 布列塔尼的; (of the people) 布列塔尼人的; (of the language) 布列塔尼凯尔特语的
B *n* **1** [c] (person) 布列塔尼人 **2** [u] (language) 布列塔尼凯尔特语

breve /briːv/ *n* 二全音符

breviary /ˈbriːvɪəri, Amer -ieri/ *n* 祈祷书

brevity /ˈbrevəti/ *n* [u] **1** (conciseness) 简洁; **~ is the soul of wit** Prov 言贵简洁 **2** (of time) 短暂

brew /bruː/
A *vt* **1** (make) 酿制; **home ~ed beer** 家酿啤酒 **2** (infuse) 沏 ‹*tea*›; 冲泡 ‹*coffee*› **3** fig (plot) 图谋 ‹*mischief*›; **to ~ trouble** 制造麻烦 **4** (concoct) 调制 ‹*potion, poison*›
B *vi* **1** (infuse) 泡; **let the tea ~ a while** 让茶泡上一会儿; **coffee is ~ing** 咖啡正泡着呢 **2** (make beer) 酿啤酒 **3** (ferment) «*beer*» 酿 **4** fig (develop) «*storm, crisis*» 酝酿; **something's ~ing** 要出事了; **there's trouble ~ing** 要有麻烦了
C *n* **1** (beer) 啤酒 **2** (infusion) 冲泡饮料; **a weak/strong ~ (of sth.)** 冲泡得淡的/浓的（某种）饮料 **3** (concoction) 调配液体; **a ~ of sth.** 某物的调配液体 **4** fig (mixture) 交融

Phrasal verb

• **brew up**
A *vi* Brit colloq 泡茶
B *vt* [**~ up sth., ~ sth. up**] 调制

brewer /ˈbruːə(r)/ ▸**p. 409** *n* 啤酒酿造者

brewer: ~'s droop *n* [u] Brit colloq hum 醉酒后的阳萎; **~'s yeast** *n* [u] (for beer) 啤酒酵母; (vitamin) 干酵母粉

brewery /ˈbruːəri/ *n* 啤酒厂; **he smells like a ~** colloq 他酒气熏天

brewhouse /ˈbruːhaʊs/ *n* 小啤酒厂

brewing /ˈbruːɪŋ/ *n* [u] (industry) 啤酒酿造业; (process) 啤酒酿造过程; **~ industry** 酿制啤酒业; **~ method** 酿制啤酒法

brew: ~pub *n* esp Amer 自酿啤酒的啤酒吧; **~-up** *n* Brit colloq 泡茶; **to have a ~-up** 泡茶

briar /ˈbraɪə(r)/ *n* **~ (rose)** 野蔷薇丛

bribe /braɪb/
A *n* 贿赂; **to offer sb. a ~ to do sth.** 贿赂某人做某事; **to give sb. a ~** 向某人行贿; **to offer/accept a ~** 行贿/受贿

B *vt* (on large scale) 向…行贿; (on small scale) 哄骗; **to ~ sb. with sth.** 用某物贿赂某人; **the children have to be ~d with sweets** 孩子得用糖果哄; **to ~ sb. to do sth.** 贿赂某人做某事

bribery /ˈbraɪbəri/ *n* [u] 贿赂; **~ and corruption** 贿赂和腐败

bric-a-brac /ˈbrɪkəbræk/ *n* [u] 小摆设; **a ~ stall** 小饰品摊位

brick /brɪk/
A *n* 1 [c and u] Constr 砖; ▸**cat 1; made of ~** 砖砌的 2 [c] (block) 砖块状物; **a ~ of ice cream** 一方冰激凌 3 [c] Brit (toy) 积木 4 [c] Brit colloq dated (reliable person) 可靠的朋友
B *modif* 砖砌的; **to bang one's head against a ~ wall** colloq 屡屡碰壁; **to come** *or* **run up against** *or* **hit a ~ wall** colloq 碰钉子; **I might as well be talking to a ~ wall** colloq 我还不如对着一堵砖墙讲呢
C *vt* Brit sl (be afraid) 害怕; (be worried) 担心; **to be ~ing it** 担心得要命

Phrasal verb
- **brick up** *vt* [**~ sth. up, ~ up sth.**] 用砖堵住 ‹*hole, window*›

brick: ~bat *n* 1 fig colloq (criticism) 尖锐的批评; 2 (missile) 投掷用砖块; **~-built** *adj* 砖结构的 ‹*house*›

brickie /ˈbrɪki/ ▸**p. 409** *n* Brit colloq 砌砖工

brick: ~ kiln *n* 砖窑; **~layer** ▸**p. 409** *n* 砌砖工; **~laying** *n* [u] 砌砖

brick red ▸**p. 134**
A *n* [u] 砖红色
B **brick-red** *adj* 砖红色的

brick: ~work *n* [u] 1 (bricks) 砖结构; 2 (building) 砌砖; **~works** *npl* + *v sing* Brit 砖厂; **~yard** *n* 砖厂

bridal /ˈbraɪdl/ *adj* (of bride) 新娘的; (of wedding) 婚礼的; **a ~ veil** 新娘的面纱; **a ~ limousine** 婚车; **~ chamber** 洞房

bridal: ~ gown *n* 婚纱; **~ party** *n* + *v sing or pl* 新娘一方; **~ registry** *n* esp Amer 新婚贺礼登记服务; **~ suite** *n* [酒店的] 新婚套房; **~ wear** *n* [u] 新婚服饰

bride /braɪd/ *n* (on wedding day) 新娘; (bride-to-be) 准新娘; **the ~ and (~)groom** 新娘新郎

bridegroom /ˈbraɪdgruːm, -grʊm/ *n* (on wedding day) 新郎; (to be married) 准新郎

bridesmaid /ˈbraɪdzmeɪd/ *n* 伴娘; **always the ~, never the bride** fig 总当陪衬

bride-to-be *n* 准新娘

bridge /brɪdʒ/
A *n* 1 [c] Constr 桥梁; **a ~ over** *or* **across sth.** 架在…上方的桥; **to be water under the ~** fig 事情都过去了; **a lot of water has flowed under the ~ since then** fig 自那以后已然物是人非; **we'll cross that ~ when we come to it** fig 我们暂且把那个问题放一放 2 [c] fig (link) 纽带; **to act as a/build a ~ between sth. and sth.** 作为/建立一事与另一事之间的联系 3 [c] (intermediate stage) 过渡; **a ~ to a new career** 通向新职业的踏板 4 [c] Naut 舰桥 5 [c] (of nose) 鼻梁 6 [c] (of glasses) 鼻梁架 7 [c] Mus 琴马 8 [c] Dent 齿桥 9 ▸**p. 307** [u] Games 桥牌
B *vt* 1 Constr 在…上架桥 ‹*river*› 2 fig (reduce) 消除; **to ~ the gap between two countries/levels** 消除两国之间的隔阂/两个层次之间的差距 3 fig (fill in) 弥补; **to ~ a gap in the conversation** 打破冷场局面 4 (span) 跨越 ‹*period, centuries, eras*›

bridge: ~-builder *n* 1 lit 造桥的人; 2 fig 调解人; **~-building** *n* [u] 1 lit 造桥; 2 fig 调解; **~head** *n* Mil 桥头堡; **~ loan** *n* Amer = **bridging loan**; **~ roll** *n* Brit 小面包卷

Bridgetown /ˈbrɪdʒtaʊn/ *pr n* 布里奇顿

bridgework *n* [u] (treatment) 齿桥植入; (dental bridge(s)) 齿桥

bridging: ~ course *n* Brit 预备课程; **~ loan** *n* Brit 过渡性贷款

bridle /ˈbraɪdl/
A *n* 1 [c] Equit 马笼头 2 [u] fig 约束; **to put a ~ on sth.** 限制 ‹*power*›; 控制 ‹*emotions*›
B *vt* 1 Equit 给…套笼头 ‹*horse*› 2 (curb) 控制 ‹*emotions, temper*›; **to ~ one's tongue** 出言谨慎
C *vi* 动怒; **to ~ at sth.** 对某事怒不可遏

bridle path, bridle track, bridleway *ns* 马道

brief /briːf/
A *adj* 1 (lasting a short time) 短暂的 ‹*visit, period, life, career*›; **for a** *or* **one ~ moment** 一瞬间; **a few ~ hours** 短短几小时 2 (concise) 简洁的; **the news in ~** 简要新闻 3 (curt) 唐突无礼的; **to be ~ with sb.** 对某人不耐烦 4 (scanty) 暴露的 ‹*nightdress, bikini*›; **~ skirt** 超短裙
B **in brief** *adv phr* 简言之
C *n* Brit 1 (role, responsibility) 职责; **it is your ~ to ..., your ~ is to ...** 你的任务是…; **to fall within/to exceed sb.'s ~** 属于/超出某人的职权范围 2 (instructions) 任务介绍; **designer's ~** 设计师细则; **to stick to a ~** 做分内事 3 Jur (summary) 案情摘要; (case) 辩护委托; **to hold a ~ for sb.** (as counsel) 当某人的辩护律师; (as advocate) 支持某人; **to hold no ~ for sb./sth.** 不支持某人/某事物
D **briefs** *npl* 短内裤
E *vt* 1 (inform) 向…通报情况 ‹*journalists*›; Mil 向…布置基本任务 ‹*troops, crew*›; **to be well ~ed** 完全掌握情况 2 Jur 向…提供案情摘要 ‹*lawyer*›; **to ~ sb. to do sth.** 向某人提供案情摘要以便做某事

briefcase /ˈbriːfkeɪs/ *n* 公文包

briefing /ˈbriːfɪŋ/ *n* 1 (meeting) 情况通报会; **~ session/documents** 情况通报会/文件; **~ officer** 情况发布官 2 (information) 情况介绍; Mil 简要指示; **to give sb. a ~ on sth.** 向某人通报某事

briefly /ˈbriːfli/ *adv* 1 (for a short time) 短暂地 2 (concisely) 简洁地 3 (curtly) 唐突无礼地 4 (in short) 简言之; **~, this is what he said ...** 简言之，他是这么说的…

briefness /ˈbriːfnɪs/ *n* [u] = **brevity**

brier /ˈbraɪə(r)/ *n* = **briar**

brig /brɪg/ *n* 1 (ship) 横帆双桅船 2 colloq (prison) [尤指军舰上的] 禁闭室

brigade /brɪˈgeɪd/ *n* 1 + *v sing or pl* Mil (subdivision) 旅; **infantry/cavalry/artillery ~** 步兵旅/骑兵旅/炮兵旅 2 + *v sing or pl* colloq (group) 一伙人; **the anti-smoking ~** pej 反吸烟大军; **he is one of the old ~** hum 他是个老夫子 3 (service) 队; **the fire/ambulance ~** 消防队/救护队

brigadier /ˌbrɪgəˈdɪə(r)/ *n* Brit 陆军准将

brigand /ˈbrɪgənd/ *n* liter or archaic 强盗

bright /braɪt/
A *adj* 1 ▸**p. 134** (vivid) 鲜艳的 ‹*colour, clothes*›; **he went ~ red** 他脸涨得通红 2 (luminous, light, shiny) 明亮的 ‹*room, star, eyes*› 3 (clear) 晴朗的 ‹*weather, period*›; **a ~ spell** 一段晴朗的日子 4 (clever, original) 聪明的; **it is ~ of sb. (to do sth.)** 某人（做某事）是明智的; **a ~ idea** 好主意 5 (cheerful, optimistic) 快活的 ‹*person, expression*› 6 (promising) 光明的 ‹*future*›; **in ~er days** 在更有希望的日子里; **to look on the ~ side** 持乐观态度
B *adv* esp liter 明亮地 ‹*shine, burn*›
C **bright and early** *adv phr* 大清早; **you're up ~ and early this morning** 你今天起得可真早啊

brighten /ˈbraɪtn/
A *vi* 1 (become brighter) «*sunshine, moonlight, star*» 变亮 2 (become clearer) «*weather*» 放晴 3 (become cheerful) «*face, expression*» 快活起来; **his eyes ~ed at the prospect of making lots of money** 想到要赚大钱，他的眼睛亮了起来 4 (light up) «*eyes*» 发亮 5 (improve) «*situation*» 改善; «*prospects*» 变得光明
B *vt* 1 (illuminate) 照亮 ‹*dark place, sky, room*› 2 (improve) 使…变得光明 ‹*prospects, outlook*› 3 (make brighter) 使…更亮 ‹*light, colour, TV picture*›

Phrasal verb
- **brighten up**
A *vi* 1 (cheer up) «*person*» 高兴起来; «*face*» 露出喜色; «*eyes*» 发亮 2 (become clearer) 放晴 3 (improve) «*situation*» 好转
B *vt* [**~ up sth., ~ sth. up**] 1 (make brighter) «*decorations*» 使…生色 ‹*room, garden*› 2 (uplift, invigorate) 使…活跃起来 ‹*occasion, conversation*› 3 (make bright, shiny) 使…发亮 ‹*surface*›

bright: ~-eyed *adj* 眼睛明亮的; **~ lights** *npl* fig 灯红酒绿的都市生活; **the lure of the ~ lights** 五光十色的都市生活的诱惑

brightly /ˈbraɪtli/ *adv* 1 (vividly) 鲜艳地 ‹*coloured*› 2 (luminously) 熊熊地 ‹*burn*›; 明亮地 ‹*polished, glitter*›; **the sun was shining ~** 阳光明媚 3 (intensely) 强烈地; **a ~ lit studio** 灯光明亮的工作室 4 (cheerfully) 欢快地 ‹*smile, say*›

brightness /ˈbraɪtnɪs/ *n* [u] 1 (of light, star, sky, eyes, place) 明亮; (of colour) 鲜艳 2 (intelligence) 聪明 3 (lustre of metal) 光亮 4 (cheerfulness) 快活 5 TV 亮度; **to adjust the ~** 调节亮度

bright: ~ spark *n* Brit colloq 机灵鬼; **some ~ spark has parked in the entrance to the fire station** iron 有个家伙把车停在了消防站门口，可真"机灵"; **~ young thing** *n* Brit 渴望飞黄腾达的年轻人

brill /brɪl/ Brit colloq
A *adj* 顶呱呱的
B *excl* **~!** 太棒了!

brilliance /ˈbrɪlɪəns/ *n* [u] 1 (luminosity of light, colour, star) 光辉 2 (cleverness) 才华横溢 3 (great skill of person, work, performance) 才华; **a pianist of astonishing ~** 才华横溢的钢琴家

brilliant /ˈbrɪlɪənt/ *adj* 1 (shining) 明亮的 ‹*sunshine, diamond*› 2 (vivid) 鲜艳的 ‹*colours*›; **a ~ blue sky** 湛蓝的天空 3 (clever) 才华横溢的 ‹*person, mind*›; 绝妙的 ‹*idea*›; 杰出的 ‹*invention*› 4 (successful) 一帆风顺的 ‹*career*›; 美好的 ‹*future, prospects*› 5 (impressive, spectacular) 精彩的 ‹*performance*›; 高明的 ‹*wit*›; 漂亮的 ‹*style*› 6 Brit colloq (excellent) 极好的; **we had a ~ time** 我们玩得很痛快

brilliantly /ˈbrɪlɪəntli/ *adv* 1 (very brightly) 明亮地 2 (vividly) 鲜艳地 ‹*coloured*› 3 (cleverly, skilfully) 巧妙地 ‹*original*›; 出色地 ‹*perform*› 4 (successfully) 成功地 ‹*work, executed*›

Brillo pad® /ˈbrɪləʊ pæd/ *n* 布瑞罗钢丝刷碗垫

brim /brɪm/
A *n* 边缘; **a hat with a wide ~** 宽檐帽; **to fill sth. to the ~** 把某容器装得满满的; **filled to the ~ with water** 盛满水的
B *vi* (*pres p etc.* **-mm-**) 1 (with liquid) «*glass, jug*» 盛满; **to ~ with sth.** 装满某物; **his eyes ~med with tears** 他的眼里噙满泪水 2 (with other substance, objects) 装满; **to ~ with sth.** «*bag*» 塞满某物; «*bus, city*» 挤满某物; **~ming with impatience/confidence** 非常没耐心/充满信心

Phrasal verb
- **brim over** *vi* 1 lit «*container, liquid*» 满溢 2 fig 充满; **he was ~ming over with emotion/indignation** 他激动万分/义愤填膺

brimful /ˈbrɪmfʊl/ *adj pred* 1 (of liquid) 满的; **the cup was ~ of coffee** 杯子里盛满了咖啡 2 fig 充满的; **the children were ~ of energy** 孩子们精力充沛

brimstone /ˈbrɪmstəʊn/ *n* 1 [u] archaic 硫磺; **fire and ~** 地狱之火; **she's breathing fire and ~** fig 她暴跳如雷 2 [c] Zool (butterfly) 黄粉蝶

brindled /ˈbrɪndld/ *adj* 棕色带斑纹的

brine /braɪn/ *n* [u] **1** Culin 腌制盐水 **2** (sea water) 海水

bring /brɪŋ/ (*pt, pp* **brought**) *vt* **1** (carry, convey, arrive with) 带来; **to ~ sth./sb. to a place** 把某物/某人带到某处; **to ~ sth./sb. into a room** 把某物/某人带入房间; **to ~ sth./sb. with one** 携带某物/带着某人; **to ~ sb. sth., to ~ sth. for sb.** 为某人带来某物; **to ~ sb. home** (transport home) 送某人回家; (to meet family) 带某人见家人; **to ~ sb. to ...** 带某人去… ‹*wedding, party, office*› **2** (move, cause to go) «*appeal, call*» 使移动; **to ~ sb./sth. to a place** 把某人/某物引到某处; **the judge brought his hammer down on the table** 法官用木槌敲桌子; **I brought him to the ground** 我把他打翻在地; **what ~s you here?** 什么风把你吹来了?; **his cries for help brought the police to his hiding place** 他求救的喊声把警察引到了他的藏身处 **3** (be conduit for) 输送 ‹*water, oil, electricity*› **4** (be route for) «*road*» 引导 ‹*person, vehicle*›; **this track should ~ us to the edge of the forest** 沿这条小路可以走到森林的边缘 **5** (receive) «*television, station, program*» 播送 ‹*programme, event, news*›; «*magazine, newspaper*» 刊载 ‹*news, feature*›; **television pictures brought to you from the other side of the world** 从世界的另一边传送过来的电视画面; **the concert will be brought to us live from Sydney** 音乐会将从悉尼向我们现场直播 **6** (cause to move on to) 使想到; **to ~ sb. to ...** 使某人想到 ‹*subject*› **7** (be a time of, the cause of) 带来 ‹*weather, fortune, income, happiness*›; 招致 ‹*destruction, shame*›; **wait and see what tomorrow ~s** 等着看明天会发生什么事情吧; **to ~ sth. to** *or* **on sb./sth.** 给某人/某事物带来某事物; **he has brought disgrace on his family** 他使家庭蒙羞; **to ~ sb. happiness** 给某人带来幸福; **to ~ sth. on** *or* **upon oneself** 给自己招来某事; **clouds do not always ~ rain** 有云未必会有雨; **her performance brought praise from the critics** 她的表演受到了评论家的好评 **8** (make available) 提供; **to ~ experience/knowledge to sth.** 把经验/知识应用于…; **to ~ one's talent(s) to sth.** 把聪明才智应用于某方面; **the new manager ~s ten years' experience to the job** 新经理到任时已有 10 年的工作经验 **9** (cause to be in particular state) 使处于某状态; **to ~ sb./sth. under control** 控制住某人/某事物; **to ~ sb. into contact with sb./sth.** 使某人接触某人/某事; **she brought the car to a halt** 她把车停了下来; **to ~ the kettle to the boil** 把壶烧开; **his plans for the company brought him into conflict with the other directors** 他对公司的规划使他与其他董事产生了冲突 **10** (elicit) 使…显现 ‹*smile, frown*›; **to ~ a blush to sb.'s cheeks** 令某人脸红; **to ~ a tear to sb.'s eye** 使某人流泪 **11** (cause to amount to) 使达到; **to ~ sth. to sth.** 使某事达到某程度; **that ~s the total to £120** 这使总数达到 120 英镑 **12** (force) 促使; **to ~ sb./oneself to do sth.** 促使某人/自己做某事; **she couldn't ~ herself to tell him the bad news** 她不忍心告诉他这个坏消息 **13** Jur (initiate) 提起 ‹*action*›; Admin, Jur (present for judgement, decision) 把…提交裁决; **to ~ sth. against sb.** 对某人提起… ‹*charge, accusation*›; **to ~ sb./sth. before a judge/committee** 把某人/某事交由法官/委员会裁决; **to ~ sb./sth. before the court** 将某人/某事提交法庭裁决; **to ~ a bill before parliament** 把议案提交议会表决

Phrasal verbs

• **bring about** *vt* **1** [**~ about sth., ~ sth. about**] (cause) 导致 ‹*war, death, event, situation*›; **the mediators managed to ~ about a settlement** 那些调停人促成了和解 **2** [**~ sb./sth. about**] Naut 使…掉头 ‹*boat*›; **the helmsman brought us about** 舵手把我们的船头掉转过来

• **bring along** *vt* [**~ along sth./sb., ~ sth./sb. along**] 带来; **to ~ sth./sb. along with one** 带来某物/某人

• **bring around** *vt* Amer = **bring round**

• **bring back**

A [**~ sth. back, ~ back sth.**] *vt*
1 (return) 把…带回来 ‹*pen, memory, person*›; **to ~ sth. back from sth.** 从某处带回某物; **to ~ sth./sb. back with one** 带回某物/某人; **the path brought us back to where we had started from** 我们顺着这条路回到了出发地; **the boat brought them safely back to shore** 船把他们安全送回岸上; **she brought back a rather unfavourable impression of the city** 她回来时对这座城市印象很差; **he forgot to ~ back the book he had borrowed** 他忘了归还借的书 **2** (restore) 恢复 ‹*discipline, health, democracy*›; **a walk in the country will ~ the colour back to your cheeks** 到乡间走一走会使你的面色恢复红润; **we must try to ~ her temperature back to normal** 我们必须设法让她的体温恢复正常 **3** (revive memory of) «*smell, event*» 使人想起 ‹*experience, day*›; **to ~ back memories (of sth.)** 令人回忆（起某事物）

B [**~ sb. back, ~ back sb.**] *vt* (resurrect) 使…起死回生 ‹*person*›; (save life of) 使…苏醒 ‹*person*›; **to ~ sb. back to consciousness/life** 使某人恢复知觉/复活

• **bring down**

A [**~ sb./sth. down, ~ down sb./sth.**] *vt*
1 (carry from higher place) 把…拿下来; **to ~ sth. down with one** 随身把某物拿下来; **to ~ sb. down sth., to ~ sth. down for sb.** 为某人把某物拿下来; **will you ~ me down a drink?** 给我拿杯饮料下来好吗? **2** (cause to crash) 击落 ‹*aircraft, pilot*›; **he was brought down over France** 他在法国上空被击落了 **3** (cause to land) 使…着陆 ‹*aircraft*›; **the pilot brought us down safely** 飞行员让我们安全着陆 **4** (shoot) 打落 ‹*bird*›; 撂倒 ‹*animal, person*›; (cause to fall) 使…跌倒 ‹*person*›; 使…坍塌 ‹*building*› **5** (overthrow) 推翻 ‹*leadership, leader*›; **the scandal brought the government down** 这起丑闻使政府倒了台

B [**~ sth. down, ~ down sth.**] *vt*
1 (move downwards) 用…抽 ‹*whip*›; **he brought the cane down on the child's hand** 他用笞杖打孩子的手 **2** (reduce) 降低 ‹*price, unemployment, temperature*›; **a cold compress will ~ down the swelling** 冷敷可以消肿 **3** liter or hum (provoke) 招致 ‹*anger*›; **to ~ down sth. on sb.** 使某事降临到某人的头上; **you don't want to ~ down his wrath** 你可别惹他发火 **4** Math 把…移入下栏 ‹*number, digit*›

C [**~ sb. down**] *vt* colloq (depress) 使消沉

• **bring forth** *vt* [**~ forth sth., ~ sth. forth**]
1 formal (provoke) 招致 ‹*reaction, complaint*›
2 archaic (produce) 生产 ‹*crops*›; 结 ‹*fruit*›
3 archaic (give birth to) 生 ‹*child*›

• **bring forward**

A [**~ sth. forward, ~ forward sth.**] *vt*
1 (make sooner) 把…提前 ‹*meeting, wedding*›
2 (propose) 提出 ‹*suggestion, question*›; **I intend to ~ this matter forward at the next meeting** 我打算在下次会议上提出这

ℹ Bring and take, come and go

■ Generally speaking, 'bring' is translated as 带, a phrase with 带, or 拿 with 来, 给, etc. 'Take' is translated as 拿, a phrase with 拿, or 带 with 去, 走, etc.

■ 带, 带来, 带给, 带到, 拿来, 拿给, etc. are used to describe movement towards the speaker or listener:

Can I bring my girlfriend to your party?
= 我能带女朋友去你的聚会吗?

She will bring new ideas to the company
= 她会给公司带来新想法

He brought us some cakes
= 他给我们带来了一些蛋糕

Please bring your French text books to school
= 请把法语课本带到学校

Bring me a glass of water, please
= 请给我拿一杯水
or 请给我拿杯水（来）

Can you please bring me an English dictionary?
= 你能给我拿一本英语词典吗?

■ 拿, 拿走, 拿到, 带走, 带去, 带上, etc. are used to describe movement away from the speaker or listener:

It's David who took it
= 是戴维拿了

The table was taken away by someone
= 桌子被人拿走了

The exam papers were taken to the exam room
= 考卷拿到了考场

Please take an umbrella with you
= 请拿把雨伞
or 请带上雨伞

Do take your father a bunch of flowers when visiting him
= 你看望父亲时务必带上一束鲜花

Can you take the cat to the vet?
= 你能带猫去看兽医吗?

Come and go

■ 来 (come) is used to describe movement towards the speaker or listener:

The teachers haven't come yet
= 老师们还没来

Can you come to my house?
= 你能来我家吗?

They came here from London to teach English
= 他们从伦敦来这儿教英语

■ 去 or 走 (go) is used to describe movement away from the speaker or listener. It can also mean 'leaving one place to reach another':

I have to go now
= 我得走了

They went to the zoo yesterday
= 他们昨天去了动物园

Are you going there by bus?
= 你要乘公共汽车去那儿吗?

However, note the use of 开 in the following example:

What time does the bus go?
= 公共汽车几点开?

件事情来讨论 3 (move forwards) 往前移动 ‹*chair*›; 往前梳 ‹*hair*› 4 Fin 把…转入下一栏 ‹*figure, balance*›

B [**~ sb. forward, ~ forward sb.**] *vt* (present) 把…带上来 ‹*witness*›

- **bring in**

A [**~ sth. in, ~ in sth.**] *vt*

1 (carry in) 把…带进来 ‹*box, book*›; **shall I ~ in the dessert now?** 现在可以上甜点了吗? 2 (introduce) 提出 ‹*subject*›; Pol (present for debate) 将…提交讨论 ‹*bill, reform*›; **at this point the author ~s in a new character** 故事发展到这一情节时, 作者引入了一个新人物 3 (start to use) 引入 ‹*system, scheme*› 4 Comm (generate) 挣 ‹*money*›; **to ~ sb. in sth., ~ in sth. for sb.** 为某人赚取某物; **our export business brought in £5 million last year** 我们的出口业务去年赢利 500 万镑 5 Jur «*jury*» 宣布 ‹*verdict*› 6 (harvest) 收获 ‹*crop, fruit*›; **we brought in a good harvest last year** 我们去年收成很好

B [**~ sb. in, ~ in sb.**] *vt*

1 (attract) «*shop, town, person*» 吸引 ‹*person, customer*› 2 (to police station) 押…到警察局 ‹*suspect*›; **to ~ sb. in for questioning** 带某人到警察局讯问 3 (involve) 让…参与 ‹*adviser, expert*›; **to ~ sb. in on sth./to do sth.** 使某人参与某事/做某事; **they have brought in a public relations adviser** 他们聘请了一位公关顾问; **to be angry at not being brought in on the new housing proposal** 因为新住房提案没有征求其意见而生气 4 (call in for help) 调来 ‹*rescue workers, police*›

- **bring into** *vt* 1 **to ~ sb. into sth.** (involve) 使参与某事; **don't ~ me into this!** 别把我扯进去! 2 **~ sth. into sth.** (introduce) 把…引入 ‹*subject*›; **he always manages to ~ politics into the conversation** 他谈话时总能扯上政治

- **bring off** *vt* 1 [**~ off sb., ~ sb. off**] (rescue) «*person, lifeboat, helicopter*» 救出 ‹*person, crew, passengers*›; **to ~ sb. off sth.** 把某人从某处救出 2 [**~ off sth., ~ sth. off**] (achieve) 实现 ‹*ambition, plan*›; 达成 ‹*deal*›; 完成 ‹*task*›; **the goalkeeper brought off a superb save** 守门员作出了精彩的扑救

- **bring on**

A [**~ sth. on, ~ on sth.**] *vt*

1 (cause to happen) «*weather, noise*» 引起 ‹*rheumatism, nervous breakdown*›; **a heart attack brought on by lack of exercise** 缺乏锻炼引发的心脏病; **to ~ on labour** 引产 2 (help to grow) 促进…生长 ‹*crops, flowers, plants*›

B [**~ sb./sth. on, ~ on sb./sth.**] *vt* (cause to appear) 引…上场 ‹*dancer, player*›; 把…搬上场 ‹*piano*›; **to ~ on the next contestant** 让下一名选手出场; **to ~ on a substitute** 换上替补队员

C [**~ sb. on, ~ on sb.**] *vt* (help to develop) 帮助…进步 ‹*student, athlete, player*›; **they ~ the children on too quickly at that school** 那个学校对学生的培养操之过急了

- **bring out**

A [**~ out sth., ~ sth. out**] *vt*

1 (remove from within) 取出; **to ~ sth. out of sth.** 从某处取出某物 2 (carry out) 带…出来; **to ~ sb./sth. out of sth.** 把某人/某物从某处带出来; **to ~ sth. out with one** 把某物带出来; **did you ~ your umbrella out with you?** 你出来时带雨伞了吗? ; **to ~ sb. out sth., to ~ sth. out for sb.** 为某人拿出某物 3 Comm (publish, launch) 出版 ‹*book, magazine, record*›; 推出 ‹*product, film*›; **it's about time they brought out a new edition** 他们该出新版本了 4 (cause to grow) «*sunshine, weather*» 使…开放 ‹*flower*› 5 (cause to be displayed) 激发出 ‹*quality, tendency, spirit*›; **to ~ out the best/worst in sb.** 使某人表现出最佳/最差的一面; **disasters like these often ~ out the best in people** 在这样的灾难中人们往往会表现出最优秀的品质; **their pompous attitude ~s out the worst in me** 他们自负的态度把我惹火了 6 (accentuate) 突出 ‹*detail, colour, sound*›; **the carpet ~s out the red in the curtains** 地毯衬托出窗帘的红色; **to ~ out the flavour of the vegetables** 使蔬菜出味 7 (reveal) 揭示 ‹*meaning, truth*›; **his remarks brought out the gravity of the situation** 他的话说明了情况的严重性

B [**~ out sb., ~ sb. out**] *vt*

1 (cause to go on strike) 发动…罢工 ‹*workers*›; **to ~ sb. out on strike** 发动某人罢工 2 (make more confident) «*experience, activity*» 使…自信 ‹*person*›; **to ~ sb. out of himself/herself** 使某人克服羞怯心理; **he's very shy; we're trying to ~ him out** 他很腼腆, 我们正努力使他放开一点

C *vt* **to ~ sb. out in sth.** (cause to be covered in) «*food, heat, excitement*» 使某人皮肤上布满某物; **chocolate ~s me out in spots** 我吃巧克力皮肤上会长斑; **the shock brought him out in a cold sweat** 他惊出一身冷汗

- **bring round** Brit

A [**~ sth./sb. round, ~ round sth./sb.**] *vt* (carry, escort from one place to another) 把…带来; **to ~ sth./sb. round with one** 带来某物/某人

B [**~ sb. round, ~ round sb.**] *vt*

1 (convince) 说服; **to ~ sb. round to sth.** 说服某人赞成某事; **she brought me round to the idea** 她说服我同意了这个想法 2 (revive) «*brandy*» 使苏醒

C [**~ sth. round, ~ round sth.**] *vt*

1 (cause to move to other side) 把…移到另一边 ‹*object*›; **~ the car round to the front of the house** 把车开到房前 2 (manoeuvre) **to ~ the conversation round to sth.** 把话题转到某事物上; **she always manages to ~ the discussion round to politics** 她总能把讨论内容引到政治上

- **bring to** *vt* 1 [**~ sb. to**] (revive) 使苏醒; **to ~ sb. to himself/herself** 使某人苏醒 2 [**~ sth. to**] Naut 停下 ‹*boat*›

- **bring together** *vt* 1 (cause to touch) 连接 ‹*ends, pieces*›; **when the glue is almost dry, ~ the two surfaces together** 胶水快干时, 把两个表面压到一起 2 (cause people to gather) 把人召集起来; (create bond between people) 使团结; **to ~ the two sides together** 促使双方进行商谈; **our mother's illness brought us closer together** 母亲生病使我们更加亲密无间了; **their love of sailing brought them together** 对帆船运动的热爱使他们走到了一起

- **bring up**

A [**~ sb. up, ~ up sb.**] *vt*

1 (rear) 抚养 ‹*child*›; **well/badly brought up** 有/没教养; **to ~ sb. up to do sth.** 从小教育某人做某事; **I was brought up on a farm** 我是在农场长大的; **my parents brought me up very strictly** 我父母对我管教很严 2 (escort from lower place) 带上来 3 (cause to stop) 使急停; **his remark brought her up short** 他的话把她噎了回去; **the sight of the gun brought us up sharply** 我们一看到枪就停下脚步 4 Jur (present for judgement) 传讯; **to ~ sb. up before the judge** 传讯某人到法官面前; **he was brought up on a charge of drunken driving** 他因被控酒醉驾驶受到传讯

B [**~ sth. up, ~ up sth.**] *vt*

1 (carry from lower place) 把…拿上来; **to ~ sth. up with one** 随身把某物拿上来; **to ~ sb. up sth., to ~ sth. up for sb.** 把某物给某人拿上去; **can you ~ me up a glass?** 给我拿个杯子上来好吗? 2 (improve) 改进 ‹*work*›; 提高 ‹*standard, salary*›; **to ~ sth. up to standard** 使某事物达标 3 (vomit) 呕出 ‹*food, meal*› 4 (mention) 提出 ‹*question, subject*›; **I'm sorry, I won't ~ it up again** 对不起, 我不会再提这件事了 5 Comput (cause to appear) 调出 ‹*menu*›

bring and buy sale *n* Brit 义卖会

brink /brɪŋk/ *n* 1 lit (edge) 边缘; **the ~ of sth.** 某物的边缘 2 fig (on the point of) 紧要关头; **to be on the ~ of doing sth.** 正要做某事; **to pull (sb.) back from the ~** (使某人) 悬崖勒马; **to push sb. to/over the ~** 使某人几乎难以忍受/无法忍受; **on the ~ of disaster/success** 濒于灾难/几近成功; **his incompetence has brought us to the ~ of ruin** 他的无能几乎毁掉了我们

brinkmanship /ˈbrɪŋkmənʃɪp/ *n* [u] 边缘政策 [不断将外交形势推至战争边缘, 以试探对手国的忍耐极限, 以获取最大利益]

briny /ˈbraɪnɪ/ *adj* liter 咸的 ‹*water, taste, smell*›

briquette, briquet /brɪˈket/ *n* 煤砖

brisk /brɪsk/ *adj* 1 (energetic) 轻快的 ‹*exercise, movements*›; **to go for a ~ walk** 去快步走 2 (efficient) 干练的 ‹*person, manner, tone*› 3 (good) 兴隆的 ‹*business*›; **~ trading on the stock exchange** 股票交易所活跃的交投 4 (cold and dry) 干冷的 ‹*wind, climate*›; 清新的 ‹*morning air*›; **a ~ March morning** 一个空气清冷的三月早晨 5 (brusque) 唐突的 ‹*person, manner*›

brisket /ˈbrɪskɪt/ *n* [u] 胸脯肉

briskly /ˈbrɪsklɪ/ *adv* 1 (efficiently) 麻利地; **she moved ~ on to the next point** 她很快转入下一点; **to deal ~ with a problem** 利索地处理问题 2 (quickly) 轻快地 3 (well) 兴隆地; **the half-price shoes sold ~** 打对折的鞋子卖得很快 4 (brusquely) 唐突地

briskness /ˈbrɪsknɪs/ *n* [u] 1 (efficient manner) 麻利 2 (speed) 轻快 3 (of trading, selling etc.) 兴隆 4 (brusqueness) 唐突

bristle /ˈbrɪsl/

A *n* 1 [c] *usu pl* (on pig) 猪鬃; (on animal) 刚毛; (on plant) 刺毛; (on man) 胡茬 2 [u] (material) 刷子毛

B *vi* 1 lit «*hairs, fur*» 竖立; **the cat ~d at the sight of the dog** 猫一看见那条狗, 毛就竖起来了 2 fig (react angrily) 发怒; **to ~ with sth.** 因某事物而怒发冲冠; **to ~ at sth.** 对某事物大发光火

Phrasal verb

- **bristle with** *vt* [**~ with sth.**]

1 (be covered with) 插满; **porcupines/cacti bristling with spines** 长满刚毛的豪猪/长满刺的仙人掌 2 (abound in) 充满; **the problem ~s with difficulties** 这个问题困难重重; **he was bristling with energy** 他精力充沛

bristly /ˈbrɪslɪ/ *adj* 1 (covered with bristles) 长满硬毛的 ‹*skin*›; 长满胡茬的 ‹*chin, face*›; 长满刺的 ‹*leaves, plant*› 2 (stiff and prickly) 短而硬的 ‹*hair, beard*›

Brit /brɪt/ *n* colloq 英国人

Britain /ˈbrɪtn/ *pr n* 英国

Britannia /brɪˈtænjə/ *pr n* 不列颠尼亚

> **Britannia**
>
> 不列颠尼亚。古罗马人称不列颠为 Britannia, 并将其形象化为女神, 后来成为英国的象征。从 17 世纪开始, 英国的许多硬币上都有 Britannia 的形象, 为女武士, 常呈坐姿, 戴头盔, 手持三叉戟。

Britannic /brɪˈtænɪk/ *adj* formal 英国的; **Her/His ~ Majesty** 女王/英王陛下

britches /ˈbrɪtʃɪz/ *npl* Amer colloq = **breeches**

Briticism /ˈbrɪtɪsɪzəm/ *n* 英国英语的特用词

British /ˈbrɪtɪʃ/ ▸ **p. 503**

A *adj* (from Great Britain) 英国的; (typical of Great Britain) 英国典型的; **the ~ embassy/ambassador** 英国大使馆/大使; **the best of ~ (luck) (to sb.)** colloq (祝某人) 走好运 [常用作反语]

B *npl* **the ~** 英国人

British: ~ Airports Authority *pr n* **the ~ Airports Authority** 英国机场管理局; **~ Antarctic Territory** *pr n* **the ~ Antarctic Territory** 南极英国领地; **~ Broadcasting Corporation** *pr n* **the ~ Broadcasting Corporation** 英国广播公司; **~ Columbia** *pr n* [加拿大] 不列颠哥伦比亚省

British English
A *n* [u] 英国英语
B *adj* 英国英语的

Britisher /ˈbrɪtɪʃə(r)/ *n* Amer colloq 英国佬 colloq

British: ~ **Isles** *pr npl* **the** ~ **Isles** 不列颠群岛; ~ **Legion** *n* + *v sing or pl* **the** ~ **Legion** 英国退伍军人协会; ~ **Library** *pr n* **the** ~ **Library** 大英图书馆; ~ **Museum** *pr n* **the** ~ **Museum** 英国博物馆; ~ **National Party** *n* **the** ~ **National Party** 英国民族党

Britishness /ˈbrɪtɪʃnɪs/ *n* [u] 英国性质; **to confirm sb.'s** ~ 证实某人是英国人

British: ~ **Summer Time** *n* [u] 英国夏时制 [比格林尼治时间提前 1 小时]; ~ **thermal unit** *n* 英制热单位

Briton /ˈbrɪtn/ *n* 1 esp Journ (from the UK) 英国人 2 Hist 布立吞人

Brittany /ˈbrɪtəni/ *pr n* 布列塔尼

brittle /ˈbrɪtl/
A *adj* 1 lit (delicate and easily broken) 易碎的 ‹*object*›; **to suffer from** ~ **bones** 患骨质疏松症 2 fig (insecure) 脆弱的 ‹*nerves, economy, relationship, peace*›; 敏感的 ‹*temper*›; 短暂的 ‹*popularity, glamour*› 3 (deceptively confident) 外强中干的 ‹*person, personality*›
B *n* [u] 果仁薄脆糖

bro /brəʊ/ *abbr* colloq = **brother A1**

broach /brəʊtʃ/ *vt* 1 (raise for discussion) 引入 ‹*subject*›; **to** ~ **sth. with sb.** 开始与某人讨论某事物 2 (make hole in) 钻孔开启 ‹*barrel*› 3 (start using) 启用 ‹*supply*›; (start using contents of) 启用…中的物品 ‹*box*›

broad /brɔːd/
A *adj* 1 (wide) 宽阔的 ‹*street, river*›; 体宽的 ‹*person*›; 宽的 ‹*chest, face, shoulders*›; **she's** ~ **in the hips** 她臀部宽大; **his mouth widened into a** ~ **grin** 他咧嘴笑了; **to grow** ~**er** 身体长得更魁梧; **to make sth.** ~**er** 拓宽某物; **to have a** ~ **back** fig 勇挑重担; **it's as** ~ **as it's long** Brit 两种选择都一样 2 *attrib* (extensive) 辽阔的 ‹*area*› 3 (wide-ranging, far-reaching) 广泛的 ‹*choice, interests, usage, support*›; **in the** ~**est sense (of the term/word)** 从（这个术语/词）最广义的角度讲 4 (general) 概括的 ‹*description, introduction*›; 宽泛的 ‹*principle*›; **to reach** ~ **agreement** 大体达成一致 5 (unsubtle) 直白的 ‹*hint*› 6 *usu attrib* Ling 乡音重的 ‹*accent, dialect*›; **poems written in** ~ **Scots** 用苏格兰方言写的诗; **a** ~ **Yorkshire accent** 很重的约克郡口音 7 *attrib* (complete) **in** ~ **daylight** 光天化日之下 8 (liberal) 开明的 ‹*mind, ideas*›
B *n* 1 Amer colloq pej (woman) 娘们儿 colloq pej 2 Anat **the** ~ **of the** *or* **one's back** 肩膀

B road *n* Brit B级公路

broadband /ˈbrɔːdbænd/ *n* [u] 宽带; ~ **Internet technology** 宽带互联网技术

broadband: ~ **connection** *n* 宽带连接; ~ **modem** *n* 宽带调制解调器

broad: ~**-based** *adj* = **broadly-based**; ~ **bean** *n* 蚕豆; ~**brush** *adj attrib* 粗略的 ‹*approach, analysis, survey*›

broadcast /ˈbrɔːdkɑːst, Amer -kæst/
A *n* 广播; **a TV/radio/news** ~ 电视/电台/新闻广播; **a live** ~ 现场直播; **the** ~ **of sth.** 某事的播出; **sb.'s** ~ **to the nation** 某人对全国的广播讲话
B *vt* (*pt, pp* ~ *or* ~**ed**) 1 TV, Radio (transmit) 播送 ‹*programme, news*›; 播出 ‹*sporting event, concert*› 2 (tell) pej 散布 ‹*news, rumour*›; **there's no need to** ~ **it!** 没有必要大肆宣扬此事! 3 Agric 撒播 ‹*seeds*›
C *vi* (*pt, pp* ~ *or* ~**ed**) 1 (transmit) «*TV, radio station*» 播放 2 (present) «*person*» 广播节目; **to** ~ **on ...** 在…广播节目 ‹*TV, radio*›

broadcaster /ˈbrɔːdkɑːstə(r), Amer -kæst-/ ▸**p. 409** *n* 播音员; **a** ~ **on opera** 歌剧节目主持人

broadcasting /ˈbrɔːdkɑːstɪŋ, Amer -kæst-/ *n* [u] 1 (field) 广播业; **to work in** ~ 从事广播工作 2 (programmes) 广播（节目）; **a** ~ **satellite** 广播卫星

broadcasting: ~ **ban** *n* 禁播令; ~ **station** *n* TV 电视台; Radio 广播电台

broadcast media *npl* 广播媒体

broad: **B**~ **Church** *n* Relig 广教会派; ~ **church** *n* (organization) 广泛包容的机构; (movement) 广泛包容的运动; **the women's movement is a** ~ **church** 妇女运动阵势庞大

broaden /ˈbrɔːdn/
A *vt* 扩大 ‹*scope, social circle*›; 增加 ‹*support*›; 开拓 ‹*horizon*›; **travel** ~**s the mind** 旅行使人眼界开阔
B *vi* 1 (expand) «*range, horizon, social circle*» 扩大; «*support*» 增加 2 (widen) «*road, river*» 变宽; **his smile** ~**ed** 他笑逐颜开

Phrasal verb

- **broaden out** *vi* 1 lit (become wider) «*road, skirt*» 变宽; **to** ~ **out into ...** «*river*» 逐渐变宽成为… 2 fig (become more general) «*conversation*» 变得更宽泛

broad: ~ **jump** *n* Amer 跳远; ~**-leaved,** ~**leaf** *adjs* 阔叶的 ‹*tree, species*›; ~ **left, B**~ **Left** *n* + *v sing or pl* Brit Pol 广泛左翼联盟; **a** ~**-left candidate** 广泛左翼联盟候选人

broadly /ˈbrɔːdli/ *adv* 1 (in general) 大体上; ~ **speaking** 总体上说 2 (widely) 咧开嘴地 ‹*smile, grin*›

broadly-based *adj* 有广泛基础的 ‹*campaign, membership*›

broad-minded *adj* 宽宏大量的 ‹*person, attitude, outlook*›

broadness /ˈbrɔːdnɪs/ *n* [u] 1 (great width) 宽阔; **the** ~ **of her mind** 她心胸的广阔 2 (of accent) 乡音重

broad: ~**sheet** *n* 1 (newspaper) 大幅报纸; 2 (advertisement) 大幅广告; ~**-shouldered** *adj* 宽肩膀的; ~**side** *n* 1 fig (criticism) 猛烈抨击; **to aim** *or* **deliver a** ~**side at ...** 对…进行猛烈抨击; 2 Naut (salvo) 舷炮齐射; **to deliver a** ~**side** 舷炮齐射; ~**-spectrum** *adj attrib* 广谱的; **a** ~**-spectrum antibiotic** 广谱抗生素; ~**sword** *n* 大砍刀

Broadway /ˈbrɔːdweɪ/ *pr n* 百老汇; **on** ~ 在百老汇

> **Broadway**
>
> 百老汇。纽约的著名商业街。起初由荷兰人建于 17 世纪初期，今长约 27 公里。百老汇的中段是美国商业性戏剧娱乐中心，19 世纪 50 年代起成为美国戏剧的代名词，20 世纪 20 年代达到鼎盛。百老汇剧院的中心地带位于时代广场（Times Square）附近，在 44 号大街和 45 号大街之间。因剧场众多，夜间灯火辉煌，自 19 世纪末起称为白色大道（Great White Way）。百老汇的演出以场面宏大的音乐剧为主。为保证票房收入，现在大多重演以前的成功剧目，趣味上趋向传统。这种主流戏剧称为内百老汇（on Broadway）。第二次世界大战以后，成本较低的实验性戏剧作为外百老汇（off-Broadway）上演。20 世纪 60 年代末，外百老汇逐渐商业化，其后由制作成本更低、更为前卫的外外百老汇（off-off-Broadway）替代。

brocade /brəˈkeɪd/
A *n* [u and c] 织锦; **gold** ~ 金黄色锦缎; **a** ~ **curtain** 织锦窗帘
B *vt* 在…上织出凸花纹; **to** ~ **sth. with sth.** 在某物上织出某种凸花纹

broccoli /ˈbrɒkəli/ *n* [u] 西兰花

brochure /ˈbrəʊʃə(r), Amer brəʊˈʃʊər/ *n* (gen) 小册子; Comm, Tourism 指南

brogue /brəʊg/ *n* 1 (accent) 土腔; **a thick** ~ 浓重的口音 2 (shoe) 拷花皮鞋

broil /brɔɪl/
A *vt* 1 Amer (grill) 烤 ‹*meat, fish*› 2 fig «*sun*» 灼烤 ‹*person*›
B *vi* 1 Amer (grill) «*meat, fish*» 被烤 2 fig «*person*» 受灼热; **we sat** ~**ing in the sunshine** 我们坐在太阳下暴晒

broiler /ˈbrɔɪlə(r)/ *n* 1 ~ **(chicken)** 适于烤焙的嫩鸡 2 Amer (grill) 烤架

broiler house *n* 烤焙用鸡饲养房

broiling /ˈbrɔɪlɪŋ/ *adj* esp Amer 酷热的

broke /brəʊk/
A *pt* ▸**break A, B**
B *adj* colloq (insolvent) 不名一文的 ‹*person*›; 破产的 ‹*company*›; **to go** ~ «*company*» 破产; **to go for** ~ 孤注一掷; **flat** *or* **stony** ~ 不名一文的

broken /ˈbrəʊkən/
A *pp* ▸**break A, B**
B *adj* 1 (damaged, in pieces) 破碎的 ‹*glass, biscuits*›; 折断的 ‹*stick, fingernail*›; (fractured) 骨折的 ‹*leg, neck*› 2 (non-functional) 损坏的 ‹*machine, device, furniture*› 3 (interrupted) 间断的 ‹*curve*›; 断断续续的 ‹*journey, sleep, voice*›; 时有时无的 ‹*sunshine*›; ~ **cloud/line** 碎云/虚线 4 (irregular) 崎岖不平的 ‹*surface, road*›; 波浪滔滔的 ‹*sea*› 5 (defeated and despairing) 沮丧的 ‹*person, spirit*› 6 (not honoured) 未履行的 ‹*promise, contract*› 7 *attrib* (flawed) 蹩脚的 ‹*English, sentence*› 8 (ruined) 名誉扫地的 ‹*man, woman*›; 毁了的 ‹*reputation*›

broken: ~**-down** *adj attrib* 1 (non-functional) 坏掉的 ‹*vehicle, machine*›; 2 (damaged) 破烂的 ‹*building, state*›; 3 (worn out) 破旧的 ‹*old car*›; 衰弱的 ‹*person, horse*›; ~ **heart** *n* fig 破碎的心; **she has a** ~ **heart** 她伤心欲绝; **to die of a** ~ **heart** 悲伤至死; ~**-hearted** *adj* fig 极其伤心的; **to be** ~**-hearted** 悲痛欲绝; ~ **home** *n* 破裂的家庭; ~ **marriage** *n* 破裂的婚姻

broker /ˈbrəʊkə(r)/ ▸**p. 409** *n* 1 Fin (middleman, agent) 代理人 2 (on stock exchange) 股票经纪人 3 Comm (dealer) 掮客; **a wine/fine art/commodity** ~ 酒商/美术品商/货商; **a ticket** ~ 票贩子; **a foreign exchange** ~ 外汇交易经纪人; **a real-estate** ~ Amer 不动产经纪人

brokerage /ˈbrəʊkərɪdʒ/ *n* 1 [u] (business) 经纪业务 2 [u] (fee) 经纪人佣金 3 [c] (company) 经纪行

broking /ˈbrəʊkɪŋ/ *n* [u] Brit 经纪业

brolly /ˈbrɒli/ *n* Brit colloq 雨伞

bromide /ˈbrəʊmaɪd/ *n* [u and c] 溴化物

bromine /ˈbrəʊmiːn/ *n* [u] 溴

bronchial /ˈbrɒŋkɪəl/ *adj* 支气管的; ~ **pneumonia** 支气管肺炎

bronchitis /brɒŋˈkaɪtɪs/ ▸**p. 377** *n* [u] 支气管炎; **to have** ~ 患支气管炎; **an attack of** ~ 支气管炎发作; **a** ~ **sufferer** 支气管炎患者

bronco /ˈbrɒŋkəʊ/ *n* (*pl* ~**s**) 布朗科野马

broncobuster /ˈbrɒŋkəʊbʌstə(r)/ *n* colloq 驯野马师

Bronx cheer /ˌbrɒŋks ˈtʃɪə(r)/ *n* Amer colloq 咂舌声 [表示蔑视或嘲笑]; **to give sb. a** *or* **the** ~ 对某人发出嘘声

bronze /brɒnz/
A *n* 1 [u] (metal) 青铜 2 [c] (statue) 青铜像 3 [u] (colour) 古铜色 4 [c] = **bronze medal**
B *adj* 古铜色的
C *vt* «*sun*» 使…呈古铜色 ‹*skin, body*›
D *vi* «*skin, body*» 呈古铜色

Bronze Age *n* **the** ~ 青铜器时代; ~ **tools** 青铜器时代的工具

bronzed /brɒnzd/ *adj* 晒成古铜色的 ‹*person, skin*›

bronze medal *n* 铜牌

bronzer /ˈbrɒnzə(r)/ *n* 古铜色化妆品

brooch /brəʊtʃ/ *n* 饰针

brood /bruːd/

A *n + v sing or pl* 1 (of birds, small mammals) 一窝 2 colloq hum (of children) 一大家孩子

B *vi* 1 (think) 忧思; **to ~ about** *or* **on** *or* **over ...** 为…而焦虑 ‹*problem, event*›; 因…而闷闷不乐 ‹*disappointment*›; **there's no point (in) ~ing about things** 担忧也无济于事 2 Zool «*bird*» 孵蛋 3 liter (loom) **to ~ over sth.** «*cliffs, castle*» 森然矗立于某物上方; «*darkness, dark clouds*» 笼罩某物

brooding /ˈbruːdɪŋ/ *adj attrib* 忧思的 ‹*look*›; 阴森的 ‹*atmosphere*›; 凶险的 ‹*threat*›

broody /ˈbruːdi/ *adj* 1 Agric 要抱窝的; **a ~ hen** 抱窝鸡 2 Brit colloq (wanting a baby) 很想要孩子的 ‹*woman*› 3 (thoughtful and unhappy) 闷闷不乐的

brook¹ /brʊk/ *n* 溪流; **a babbling ~** 潺潺小溪

brook² *vt* formal 允许 ‹*delay, half-measures*›; **I will not ~ anyone interfering in my affairs** 我不允许任何人干涉我的事

broom /bruːm, brʊm/ *n* 1 [c] (brush) 扫帚; **a new ~** fig 刚上任的新官; **a new ~ sweeps clean** Prov 新官上任三把火 2 [u] Bot 金雀花

broom: ~ cupboard *n* Brit 存放清扫工具的壁橱; **~ handle** *n* 扫帚柄; **~stick** *n* 扫帚柄

Bros. /brɒs/ *abbr* = **Brothers** 兄弟公司 [用于公司名称]

broth /brɒθ, Amer brɔːθ/ *n* [u and c] (stock) 高汤; (soup) 炖汤 [常加入蔬菜、大麦或大米]

brothel /ˈbrɒθl/ *n* 妓院

brother /ˈbrʌðə(r)/

A *n* 1 ▸p. 419 (younger sibling) 弟弟; (older sibling) 哥哥; (male sibling) 兄弟; **my eldest ~** 我大哥 2 (fellow man) 弟兄; **~s in arms** 战友; **a ~ officer/worker** 军官同僚/工友 3 (trade unionist) 工会会友 4 (*pl* **~s** *or* **brethren** /ˈbreðrən/) Relig 教友; **B~ Luke** 卢克修士 5 Amer colloq (term of address) 老兄 6 esp Amer colloq (fellow black person) 黑人兄弟

B *excl* colloq 啊呀; **oh ~!** 天哪!

brotherhood /ˈbrʌðəhʊd/ *n* 1 [u] (feeling of kinship) 同志情谊; **(the) ~ of man** 人类的友爱 2 [c] + *v sing or pl* (organization) 兄弟会 3 [c] + *v sing or pl* (of monks) 修士会; **a Christian ~** 基督教修士会 4 [u] (being brothers) 兄弟关系

brother-in-law ▸p. 419 *n* (*pl* **brothers-in-law**) (elder brother of husband) 大伯子; (younger brother of husband) 小叔子; (elder brother of wife) 内兄; (younger brother of wife) 内弟; (husband of elder sister) 姐夫; (husband of younger sister) 妹夫; (husband of wife's sister) 连襟; (husband of husband's elder sister) 丈夫的姐夫; (husband of husband's younger sister) 丈夫的妹夫

brotherly /ˈbrʌðəli/ *adj* (characteristic of brothers) 兄弟般的; (between brothers) 兄弟间的; **~ love** 兄弟间的爱

brought /brɔːt/ *pt, pp* ▸**bring**

brouhaha /ˈbruːhɑːhɑː, Amer bruːˈhɑːhɑː/ *n* [u] 1 (commotion) 喧闹 2 (publicity) 哄动

brow /braʊ/ *n* 1 (forehead) 额头 2 liter (eyebrow) 眉毛; **to knit** *or* **furrow one's ~s** 紧锁眉头 3 (of hill) 山脊

browbeat /ˈbraʊbiːt/ *vt* (*pt* **browbeat**, *pp* **browbeaten**); **to ~ sb. into doing sth.** 威逼某人做某事; **to ~ sb. into submission/silence** 逼迫某人屈服/保持沉默

brown /braʊn/ ▸p. 134

A *adj* 1 (in colour) 棕色的; **to go** *or* **turn ~** 变成棕色; **to paint/dye sth. ~** 把某物漆成/染成棕色; **dark** *or* **deep ~** 深褐色的; **light** *or* **pale ~** 浅棕色的 2 (tanned) 晒黑的 ‹*person, face, skin*›; **to be very ~** 被晒得黝黑; **to go ~** 被晒黑 3 (as racial feature) 棕色人种的 ‹*skin*›

B *n* 1 [u and c] (colour) 棕色; **in ~** 穿棕色衣服; **a deep ~** 深褐色 2 [c] (snooker ball) 棕色球

C *vt* 使…呈褐色 ‹*meat, potatoes*›; **to ~ sth. under the grill** 用烤架把某物烤成褐色

D *vi* «*meat, potatoes*» 变成褐色

brown: ~ ale *n* [u and c] Brit 黑啤酒; **~ bear** *n* 棕熊; **~ bread** *n* [u] 黑面包; **~ coal** *n* = **lignite**; **~ dwarf** *n* 棕矮星

browned-off *adj* Brit colloq (fed up) 厌烦的; (depressed) 沮丧的; **to be ~ with sb.** 对某人感到厌倦

brown: ~ envelope *n* 牛皮纸信封; **~ fat** *n* [u] 肩胛间腺

brownfield site /ˈbraʊnfiːld/ *n* 棕色地带 [城镇中拆迁后要重建的地带]

brown goods *npl* 棕色家电 [指电视、音响设备等家用电器]

Brownian motion /ˈbraʊnɪən ˈməʊʃn/, **Brownian movement** /ˈbraʊnɪən ˈmuːvmənt/ *ns* [u] 布朗运动 [流体中悬浮颗粒所作的不规则运动]

brownie /ˈbraʊni/ *n* 1 Amer (cake) 果仁巧克力蛋糕 2 (elf) 棕仙 3 **Brownie** Brit 幼女童军

brownie point *n* colloq hum (credit, commendation) 讨好上级所得的信任; **to gain** *or* **earn** *or* **win a ~/~s (for doing sth.)** (因做某事而) 得到嘉许

browning /ˈbraʊnɪŋ/ *n* [u] Brit 深色调色料 [用以给肉汁调色]

brownish /ˈbraʊnɪʃ/ *adj* 近棕色的

brown-nose Amer colloq

A *n* 马屁精

B *vt* 拍…的马屁

brown: ~out *n* Amer 部分灯火管制; **~ owl** *n* Brit = **tawny owl**; **~ paper** *n* [u] 浅棕色包装纸; **~ paper bag** *n* 棕色购物纸袋; **~ rice** *n* [u] 糙米; **~-skinned** *adj* 棕色皮肤的 ‹*person, race*›; **~stone** *n* [u] 1 (sandstone) 褐砂石; 2 Amer (house) 褐砂石房屋; **~ study** *n* [u] dated **to be in a ~ study** 想得出神; **~ sugar** *n* [u] 红糖

browny /ˈbraʊni/ *adj* 近棕色的

browse /braʊz/

A *vi* 1 (read) 浏览; **to ~ through a catalogue/archives** 浏览目录/档案 2 (look at objects in shop) 随意逛商店; **can I help you? — no, I'm just browsing** 需要帮忙吗? ——不用, 我只是随便看看 3 (graze) «*deer, cattle*» 吃嫩枝叶

B *vt* 1 Comput 浏览 ‹*websites, pages*› 2 (feed) «*deer, cattle*» 吃 ‹*plants, foliage*›

C *n* 浏览; **to have a ~ in a bookshop** 逛书店; **to have a ~ through a book** 翻阅一本书

browser /ˈbraʊzə(r)/ *n* 浏览器; **a web ~** 网络浏览器

bruise /bruːz/

A *n* 1 (on skin) 青肿; **covered in ~s** 浑身青肿的; **to suffer cuts and ~s** 受轻伤 2 (on fruit) 碰伤

B *vt* 1 (inflict injury on) 使…出现伤痕 ‹*arm, person*›; **she fell and ~d herself** 她摔了一跤, 碰伤了 2 (damage) 碰伤 ‹*fruit*› 3 fig (emotionally) 伤害 ‹*person, heart*›; 挫伤 ‹*ego*›

C *vi* 1 lit (physically) 出现青肿 2 (be damaged) «*fruit*» 被碰伤 3 fig (emotionally) 受到伤害

bruised /bruːzd/ *adj* 1 lit (physically) 青肿的; **he was badly ~** 他瘀伤得很严重 2 (damaged) 碰伤的 ‹*fruit*› 3 fig (emotionally) 受伤害的 ‹*heart, spirit*›

bruiser /ˈbruːzə(r)/ *n* colloq 好斗的彪形大汉

bruising /ˈbruːzɪŋ/

A *adj* 1 lit (physically) 激烈的 ‹*encounter, struggle*› 2 fig (emotionally) 令人受到伤害的 ‹*experience, criticism, divorce*›

B *n* [u] Med 青肿

brunch /brʌntʃ/ *n* [u and c] 早午餐

Brunei /bruːˈnaɪ/ *pr n* 文莱

brunette /bruːˈnet/ ▸p. 134

A *n* 深褐发年轻白人女子

B *modif* 深褐色的 ‹*hair*›

brunt /brʌnt/ *n* (worst part) 最糟糕的部分; (main impact) 主要的影响; **to bear** *or* **take the ~ of** 在…中首当其冲 ‹*disaster, unemployment*›

brush /brʌʃ/

A *n* 1 [c] (implement) 刷子; (for painting) 画笔 2 [c] (act of brushing) 刷; **to give sth. a ~** 刷一下某物 3 [c] (light touch) 轻拂; **I felt the ~ of the bird's wing against my cheek** 我感到这只鸟的翅膀拂过我的脸颊 4 [c] (encounter) 小冲突; **to have a ~ with sb.** 与某人闹别扭; **to have a ~ with sth.** 撞上某事物; **to have a ~ with death** 与死神擦肩而过 5 [u] esp Amer, Austral (undergrowth) 灌木丛 6 [u] (twigs) 断落的树枝 7 [c] Zool (tail) 狐狸尾巴 8 [c] Elec 电刷

B *vt* 1 (sweep, clean) 刷 ‹*clothes, shoes, teeth*›; **to wear one's hair ~ed back** 梳着背头 2 (remove with brush) 刷掉; **to ~ sth. off (sth.)** 把某物 (从某处) 刷掉; **to ~ sth. into sth.** 把某物刷进某处; **to ~ sth. away (from sth.)** 把某物 (从某处) 刷去; **all the snow has been ~ed off the steps/into the gutter** 台阶上的雪都已经扫除了/扫进了排水沟里 3 (touch lightly) 拂过; **her skirt ~es the ground as she walks** 她走路时裙子拂过地面

C *vi* 拂过; **to ~ against sb./sth.** 拂过某人/某物

Phrasal verbs

- **brush aside** *vt* 1 [**~ sth./sb. aside, ~ aside sth./sb.**] (dismiss) 不理会 ‹*idea, feeling, objection, person*› 2 [**~ sb. aside, ~ aside sb.**] (beat) 轻松击败 ‹*opponent*› 3 [**~ sth. aside, ~ aside sth.**] (move away) 把…移开 ‹*object*›; **she ~ed aside the curtain** *or* **~ed the curtain aside** 她撩开帘子
- **brush down** *vt* [**~ down sth., ~ sth. down**] (remove dirt from) 刷干净; (remove creases from) 抹平; **to ~ oneself down** 把自己掸干净; **he stood up and ~ed himself down** (after a fall) 他站起来把身上拍干净
- **brush off**

A *vt* [**~ off sb./sth., ~ sb./sth. off**] colloq 不理会 ‹*question, person, criticism, threat*›; **to ~ sth. off as sth.** 把某事物当作某事物打发掉; **he's very keen on her, but she keeps ~ing him off** 他很迷恋她, 但她总是不搭理他; **to ~ off failure** 漠视失败

B *vi* «*dirt*» 被刷掉; **mud ~es off easily when it's dry** 泥干后容易刷掉

- **brush up**

A *vt* [**~ up sth., ~ sth. up**] 1 (clear up) 刷除 2 colloq (improve) 温习 ‹*knowledge, skills*›

B *vi* **to ~ up on sth.** colloq (improve) 温习 ‹*French, piano playing*›

brushed /brʌʃt/ *adj attrib* 起绒的; **~ cotton** 绒布; **~ denim** 磨毛劳动布; **~ nylon** 拉绒尼龙

brushfire /ˈbrʌʃfaɪə(r)/ *n* 灌丛火

brush: ~-off *n* colloq 拒绝; **to give sb. the ~-off** 不理睬某人; **to get the ~-off** 碰一鼻子灰; **~stroke** *n* 画笔的一笔; **~up** *n* Brit 1 (of appearance) 打扮; **to have a (wash and) ~up** (梳洗) 打扮一下; 2 (of skills) 温习; **to give one's French/piano-playing a ~up** 温习一下法语/重练一下钢琴; **~wood** *n* [u] 柴火枝; **~work** *n* [u] 笔法

brusque /bruːsk, Amer brʌsk/ *adj* 唐突的 ‹*person, manner, reply*›; **to be ~ with sb.** 对某人简慢

brusquely /ˈbruːskli, Amer ˈbrʌ-/ *adv* 唐突地 ‹*say, dismiss, apologize*›

Brussels /ˈbrʌslz/ *pr n* 布鲁塞尔

Brussels sprout, Brussel sprout *n* 抱子甘蓝

brutal /ˈbruːtl/ *adj* 1 (cruel, violent) 残酷的 ‹*person, regime*›; 野蛮的 ‹*attack, treatment*›; 残

b

忍的 ‹murderer› **2** (direct) 不留情面的 ‹reply, accuracy, honesty› **3** (harsh) 粗暴的 ‹intervention, refusal›

brutality /bruːˈtæləti/ *n* **1** [u] (violence) 残酷; **the ~ of the murder** 凶杀的残酷 **2** [c] (violent incident) 暴行

brutalize /ˈbruːtəlaɪz/ *vt* **1** (make brutal) «*experience, environment*» 使变得残酷 **2** (treat brutally) 残酷对待

brutally /ˈbruːtəli/ *adv* **1** (cruelly) 残酷地 ‹torture, treat› **2** (in an unpleasant way) 不留情面地 ‹reply, accurate›; **he is ~ honest about his dislike of foreigners** 他毫不掩饰地表示讨厌外国人

brute /bruːt/

A *n* **1** (man) 粗野的人; **an ugly/clumsy ~** 丑陋/笨拙的粗人 **2** (animal) 野兽; **war brings out the ~ in man** 战争激发出人的兽性 **3** fig (difficult thing) 麻烦; **this lock's a ~; it just won't open** 这把锁真烦人，就是打不开

B *adj* **1** *attrib* (physical) 身体的 ‹strength›; **by (sheer) ~ force** 用蛮劲 **2** pej (animal-like) 野兽般的 ‹passion, cunning, stupidity› **3** (simple) 最基本的 ‹fact›; **~ matter** 非生物; **out of ~ necessity** 纯粹出于必要

brutish /ˈbruːtɪʃ/ *adj* 粗野的 ‹person, behaviour, manners›; 野兽般的 ‹instinct›; 残酷的 ‹war›

BS *abbr* **1** Brit Ind = **British Standard** 英国标准 **2** Amer Univ = **Bachelor of Science** 理学士

BSc *abbr* Brit = **Bachelor of Science** 理学士; **to have/do a ~ degree** 持有/攻读理学士学位

BSE *abbr* = **Bovine Spongiform Encephalopathy**

BSI *abbr* Brit = **British Standards Institution** 英国标准协会

B side *n* dated (of disc) B面

BST *abbr* = **British Summer Time**

BTEC /ˈbiːtek/ *abbr* = **Business and Technician Education Council** 商业与技术教育委员会

Btu, BTU *abbr* = **British thermal unit**

bubble /ˈbʌbl/

A *n* **1** (in air, liquid, paintwork) 气泡; **to blow ~s** 吹泡泡; **she was up to her elbows in ~s** 她忙着洗餐具; **the ~ has burst** fig 成为泡影 **2** Comm, Fin (inflated price) 泡沫; **the house price ~** 房价泡沫 **3** (sound of bubbling) 汩汩声 **4** Med (germ-free chamber) 无菌室

B *vi* **1** (form bubbles) «*liquid*» 起泡; **to ~ beneath the surface** fig 潜涌 **2** (be lively, happy) 生气勃勃; **to ~ with** 充满着 ‹confidence, enthusiasm, ideas› **3** (make bubbling sound) 发汩汩声

Phrasal verbs

- **bubble over** *vi* **1** (be full of) 洋溢; **she was bubbling over with suggestions** 她滔滔不绝地提建议 **2** (overflow) «*liquid, stew*» 沸溢
- **bubble up** *vi* «*liquid, gas*» 冒泡

bubble: ~ and squeak *n* [u] Brit 洋白菜煎土豆; **~ bath** *n* **1** [u] (cosmetic) 泡泡剂; **2** [c] (act of bathing) 泡泡浴; **to have a ~ bath** 洗泡泡浴; **~ car** *n* Brit 有透明圆罩的微型汽车; **~ chamber** *n* 气泡室; **~gum** *n* [u] 泡泡糖; **~jet printer** *n* 喷墨打印机; **~ pack** *n* [c] Brit 气泡袋; **~-wrap, B~ Wrap®** *n* [u] Amer 气泡塑料包装材料; **~-wrapped** *adj* 用气泡塑料包装的

bubbling /ˈbʌblɪŋ/

A *n* [u] 汩汩声

B *adj* **1** *attrib* (forming bubbles) 冒泡的 ‹liquid›; **glasses of ~ champagne** 一杯杯冒着泡沫的香槟酒 **2** (gurgling) 汩汩作响的

bubbly /ˈbʌbli/

A *adj* **1** (fizzy) 充满泡沫的 ‹liquid, drink› **2** (vivacious) 活泼的 ‹personality›

B *n* [u] colloq 汽酒

bubonic plague /bjuːˌbɒnɪk ˈpleɪɡ/ ▸p. 377 *n* [u] 腺鼠疫; **a ~ victim** 腺鼠疫患者

buccaneer /ˌbʌkəˈnɪə(r)/ *n* **1** Hist (pirate) 海盗 **2** fig (unscrupulous businessman) 冒险家

buccaneering /ˌbʌkəˈnɪərɪŋ/ *adj attrib* fig 冒险的 ‹businessman, venture, exploits›

Bucharest /ˌbjuːkəˈrest/ *pr n* 布加勒斯特

buck[1] /bʌk/

A *n* **1** (male animal) 雄兽 [尤指鹿、羊、兔]; **a ~ rabbit** 公兔; **a ~ deer** 雄鹿 **2** (responsibility) 责任; **to pass the ~** colloq 推卸责任 **3** colloq (man) 男人; **a young ~** 一个小伙子

B *vi* «*horse*» 弓背跃起

C *vt* **1** (throw) 使摔下; **the horse ~ed the rider off** 马把骑手甩了下来 **2** (oppose) 抵抗 ‹trend, market›; **to ~ the system** 反抗体制

D *adj* Amer Mil 最低一级的

Phrasal verb

- **buck up** colloq

A *vi* **1** (cheer up) 振作; **~ up, things aren't as bad as you think** 高兴点儿，事情没你想的那么糟 **2** (hurry up) 赶快

B *vt* [**~ sb./sth. up, ~ up sb./sth.**] 振作 ‹spirits›; **the good news ~ed us all up** 好消息使我们振奋

buck[2] *n* colloq **1** esp Amer, Austral (dollar) 元 **2** (money) 钱; **to make a fast** *or* **quick ~** 迅速捞一笔钱; **to make a few ~s** 赚几个钱

bucket /ˈbʌkɪt/

A *n* **1** (container) 桶; **to kick the ~** colloq 翘辫子 **2** Tech (of pump) 活塞; (of scoop, dredger) 挖斗

B **buckets** *npl* colloq (large amount) 大量; **to cry ~s** 泪如泉涌

C *vi* Brit colloq **to ~ (down)** «*rain*» 倾盆而下

bucket: ~ dredge, ~ dredger *ns* 斗式挖掘机; **~ elevator** *n* 斗式提升机

bucketful /ˈbʌkɪtfʊl/ *n* 一桶

bucket: ~ seat *n* 斗式单人座椅; **~ shop** *n* **1** Brit Tourism 廉价机票店; **2** Fin 空壳证券经纪公司

buckeye /ˈbʌkaɪ/ *n* **1** (tree) 七叶树 **2** (fruit) 娑罗子

bucking bronco /ˌbʌkɪŋ ˈbrɒŋkəʊ/ *n* [美国西部的] 野马

> **Buckingham Palace**
>
> 白金汉宫。英国君主在伦敦的王宫，位于威斯敏斯特市（City of Westminster），重要王室典礼和国事活动也常在这里举行。1703 年由白金汉公爵（Duke of Buckingham）兴建，始称白金汉府（Buckingham House），现在俗称为 Buck House。1761 年由英王乔治三世（King George III）购得，供王后居住，称王后宫殿（Queen's House）。1825 年，英王乔治四世（King George IV）开始加以扩建，准备用作王宫。1837 年维多利亚女王登基后正式成为王宫。君主在宫中时，宫殿上方会悬挂王室旗帜，外出时则悬挂英国国旗。白金汉宫前有著名的近卫军换岗仪式（Changing the Guard）。

Buckinghamshire /ˈbʌkɪŋəmʃə(r)/ *pr n* 白金汉郡

buckle /ˈbʌkl/

A *n* **1** (clasp) 搭扣 **2** (dent) (in metal) 凹痕; (in wheel) 凹槽

B *vt* **1** (fasten) 扣上 ‹belt, shoe›; **he ~d the child into the seat** 他把孩子用安全带固定在座椅上 **2** (damage) 使变形; **the crash ~d the front of my car** 我的汽车前部被撞瘪了

C *vi* **1** (give way) «*limbs*» 撑不住; **I could feel my legs buckling under me** 我觉得腿都软了 **2** (fasten) «*shoe, strap*» 扣上 **3** (bend) «*metal*» 弯曲变形; «*surface*» 凹陷 **4** fig (emotionally) 垮掉

Phrasal verbs

- **buckle down** *vi* **to ~ down to sth.** 下决心认真干某事
- **buckle on** *vt* [**~ on sth., ~ sth. on**] 扣上 ‹holster, weapon›
- **buckle up** *vi* 系好安全带

buck: ~ naked *adj* Amer colloq 赤条条的; **~-passing** *n* [u] 推卸责任

Bucks. *abbr* Brit = **Buckinghamshire**

buck's fizz *n* [u and c] Brit 橙汁香槟酒

buckshee /bʌkˈʃiː/ *adj, adv* Brit colloq 免费的（地）

buck: ~shot *n* [u] 大号铅弹; **~skin** *n* [u and c] 鹿皮; **~ teeth** *npl* 龅牙; **~-toothed** *adj* 长有龅牙的 ‹person, rabbit›; **~wheat** *n* [u] 荞麦

bucolic /bjuːˈkɒlɪk/ *adj* 乡村的 ‹setting, pursuits›; **a ~ painting** 以乡村生活为题材的画作; **the ~ tranquillity of the Hudson Valley** 哈得孙谷宁静的田园风光

bud[1] /bʌd/

A *n* Bot (of leaf) 芽; (of flower) 花蕾; **in ~** 在发芽; **to nip sth. in the ~** fig 把某事物消灭在萌芽状态

B *vi* (*pres p etc.* **-dd-**) Bot **1** (develop leaf buds) 发芽; (develop flower buds) 长出花蕾 **2** (appear as buds) «*leaves*» 成芽; «*flowers*» 形成花苞

bud[2] *n* Amer colloq (term of address) 老兄

Budapest /ˌbjuːdəˈpest/ *pr n* 布达佩斯

Buddha /ˈbʊdə/

A *pr n* (god) 佛陀

B *n* (representation) 佛像

Buddhism /ˈbʊdɪzəm/ *n* [u] 佛教

Buddhist /ˈbʊdɪst/

A *n* 佛教徒

B *adj* 佛教的 ‹art›; 信奉佛教的 ‹person, country›; **a ~ monk** 和尚; **a ~ temple** 禅寺

budding /ˈbʌdɪŋ/ *adj attrib* **1** Bot (into leaf) 正在发芽的; (into flower) 含苞待放的 **2** fig (promising) 崭露头角的 ‹artist, athlete, genius› **3** fig (beginning) 萌芽中的 ‹romance, interest›

buddleia /ˈbʌdlɪə/ *n* 醉鱼草

buddy /ˈbʌdɪ/ colloq

A *n* **1** esp Amer (friend) 哥儿们 **2** (in Aids care) 志愿关爱者

B *vi* Amer **to ~ up to sb.** 成为某人的哥儿们

buddy: ~ movie *n* esp Amer 哥们儿影片 [描写两名亲密无间的男主角的电影]; **~ system** *n* 伙伴制 [两人结对互助的安排]

budge /bʌdʒ/

A *vt* **1** lit 挪动; **the removal men couldn't ~ the piano** 搬运工移不动那架钢琴 **2** fig 使改变想法; **you can never ~ him from his opinion** 你永远也不可能让他改变主张

B *vi* **1** lit 挪动 **2** fig 让步; **she will not ~ an inch on this issue** 她在这个问题上寸步不让; **he won't ~ from his position** 他不会改变立场

Phrasal verb

- **budge over, budge up** *vi* colloq 向座位一边挪动 [以便别人坐下]; **~ over and make room for me** 挪过去一点，给我腾个位置

budgerigar /ˈbʌdʒərɪɡɑː(r)/ *n* 虎皮鹦鹉

budget /ˈbʌdʒɪt/

A *n* **1** [u and c] (personal, commercial) 预算; **to go over/stay within ~** 超出/未超出预算; **to be on a tight ~** 预算很紧; **my ~ doesn't run to expensive wines** 我手上的钱买不起昂贵的酒 **2** Brit Pol (*also* **Budget**) 预算案; **to beat the B~** 预算案公布前抢先交易

B *modif* **1** Econ, Pol 预算的 ‹cuts, surplus› **2** Advertg (cheap) 便宜的 ‹hotel›; 低廉的 ‹price›; 花钱少的 ‹holiday›

C *vt* 把…编入预算 ‹(sum of) money›; **I've ~ed £400 for next year's holiday** 我准备明年花 400 英镑度假

D *vi* «*company, institution*» 做预算安排; **firms that do not ～ properly** 预算做得不好的公司; **we're ～ing for next year's holiday** 我们在计划明年的度假费用

budget account *n* Brit 预算账户 [用于支付水电费等]

budgetary /ˈbʌdʒɪtəri, Amer -teri/ *adj* 预算的 ‹*concerns, restrictions, policy*›

budget: ～ day, B～ day *n* Brit 预算案发表日; **～ debate** *n* 预算案辩论

budgeting /ˈbʌdʒɪtɪŋ/ *n* [u] 预算编制

Budget speech *n* Brit 预算案演讲

budgie /ˈbʌdʒi/ *n* colloq **= budgerigar**

Buenos Aires /ˌbwenəs ˈeərɪz/ *pr n* 布宜诺斯艾利斯

buff /bʌf/

A *n* **1** [c] colloq (enthusiast) 爱好者; **an opera/a film/computer ～** 歌剧迷/电影迷/电脑迷; **art lovers and culture ～s** 热爱文化艺术的人 **2** [u] (colour) 米色 **3** [u] esp Brit colloq hum (nakedness) **in the ～** 一丝不挂; **strip down to the ～** 脱得精光

B *adj* 浅黄褐色的

C *vt* [用软布等] 擦亮 ‹*shoes, metal, fingernails*›

buffalo /ˈbʌfələʊ/ *n* (*pl* **～** *or* **～es**) Amer (bison) 野牛; (of Asia) 水牛

buffer[1] /ˈbʌfə(r)/ *n* **1** fig (protection) (thing) 缓冲物; (person) 缓冲人; **his sense of humour was a useful ～ when times were bad** 在艰苦时期他的幽默感是一种有用的调剂; **gold is the best ～ against inflation** 黄金是抵御通货膨胀的最有效屏障 **2** Rail (on line, train) 减震器; **to run into the ～s** fig 突遭挫败 **3** Comput **～ (memory)** 缓冲存储器; **printer/screen/file ～** 打印机/屏幕/文件缓冲存储器 **4** (for polishing) 抛光器

buffer[2] *n* Brit colloq (elderly, old-fashioned man) 老顽固; **the old ～s in the House of Lords** 上议院中的老顽固

buffer: ～ state *n* 缓冲国; **～ store** *n* 缓冲存储器; **～ zone** *n* 缓冲地带

buffet[1] /ˈbʊfeɪ, ˈbʌfeɪ, Amer bəˈfeɪ/ *n* **1** Rail (in station) 快餐部; (on rail carriage) 餐车 **2** Culin 自助餐; **a ～ supper** 自助晚餐

buffet[2] /ˈbʌfɪt/

A *vt* **1** lit «*wind*» 连续吹打; «*waves*» 连续冲击; «*rain*» 连续抽打; **to ～ sth. about** 从四面八方猛击某物 **2** fig «*fate*» 打击 ‹*person*›; **they were ～ed by a major recession** 他们受到经济大衰退的重创

B *vi* «*wind*» 连续吹打; «*waves*» 连续拍打; «*rain*» 连续抽打; **to ～ against sth.** 连续猛击某物

buffet car /ˈbʊfeɪ ˌkɑː(r), ˈbʌfeɪ-, Amer bəˈfeɪ-/ *n* Brit 餐车

buffeting /ˈbʌfɪtɪŋ/

A *n* **1** (of wind) 吹打; (of waves) 拍打; (of rain) 抽打 **2** (series of blows) 连续的击打

B *adj attrib* 肆虐的 ‹*wind, waves, rain*›

buffoon /bəˈfuːn/ *n* **1** (ridiculous or amusing person) 活宝 **2** (clown) 小丑

buffoonery /bəˈfuːnəri/ *n* [u] **1** (silly but amusing behaviour) 插科打诨 **2** (clowning) 扮小丑

bug /bʌg/

A *n* **1** colloq (any insect) 虫子 **▸rug 1** **2** (bedbug) 臭虫 **3** colloq (illness) 小病 **4** colloq (germ) 病菌 **5** (fault) (gen) 故障; Comput 程序错误 **6** (hidden microphone) 窃听器 **7** colloq (craze) 着迷; **to be bitten by the golf ～** 对高尔夫球运动着迷 **8** Amer colloq (enthusiast) 爱好者; **a jogging ～** 慢跑迷

B *vt* (*pres p etc.* **-gg-**) **1** (hide microphones in) 在…里装窃听器 ‹*room, telephone*›; (record) 窃听 ‹*conversation, person*› **2** colloq (annoy) 烦扰 ‹*person*›

Phrasal verbs

- **bug off** *vi* Amer colloq 滚开
- **bug out** *vi* Amer colloq 突出

bugaboo /ˈbʌgəbuː/ *n* (*pl* **～s**) esp Amer **= bogey 1, 2**

bug: ～bear *n* 烦恼的根由; **late payment is a constant ～bear for freelance translators** 付酬逾期是自由译者经常遇到的头痛事; **～-eyed** *adj* 眼珠凸出的

bugger /ˈbʌgə(r)/ esp Brit sl

A *n* **1** pej (person) 浑蛋 offensive; hum (said sympathetically) 家伙; **the poor little ～s** 这些可怜的小家伙; **to play silly ～s** 做蠢事; **you stupid ～!** 你这个蠢货! **2** (difficult or annoying thing) 难题; **what a ～!** 真他妈的麻烦!; **this screw is a ～!** 这个螺丝真难拧! **3** also Jur (sodomite) 鸡奸者

B *excl* 妈的; **～ (it)!** 该死!

C *vt* **1** (expressing surprise) [表示惊奇]; (dismissing sth.) [表示不重要]; **～ me!** 哎呀!; **I'll be ～ed!** 我真该死!; **～ that!** 管他呢!; **I'm ～ed if I know!** 我发誓我不知道! **2** (have anal sex with) 鸡奸 ‹*person*›; 兽奸 ‹*animal*›

Phrasal verbs

- **bugger about, bugger around** esp Brit sl

A *vi* 闲混; **to ～ about with sth.** 用某事消磨时间

B *vt* [**～ sb. about**] 难为

- **bugger off** *vi* esp Brit sl 走开
- **bugger up** *vt* [**～ sth. up, ～ up sth.**] esp Brit sl 搞砸 ‹*job, task, exam*›; 破坏 ‹*chances*›

bugger all Brit sl

A *pron* 啥也没有; **there's ～ to do in the evenings** 晚上没什么屁事可做 sl

B *adj attrib* 啥都没有的; **he's got ～ qualifications** 他有个屁资格 sl

buggered /ˈbʌgəd/ *adj pred* Brit sl **1** (broken) 破烂不堪的 **2** (tired) 精疲力竭的; **you look ～** 你看上去累坏了

buggery /ˈbʌgəri/ *n* [u] Jur 鸡奸; (bestiality) 兽奸

bugging /ˈbʌgɪŋ/ *n* [u] 安装窃听器; **a ～ device** 窃听器

buggy /ˈbʌgi/ *n* **1** Brit (pushchair) 折叠式童车 **2** Amer (pram) 婴儿车 **3** Hist (carriage) 轻便马车 **4** Aut (small car) 专用小车

bughouse /ˈbʌghaʊs/ *n* Amer colloq 精神病院

bugle /ˈbjuːgl/ **▸p. 395** *n* 军号

bugler /ˈbjuːglə(r)/ *n* 号手

build /bɪld/

A *vt* (*pt, pp* **built**) **1** (construct) 建造 ‹*house, ship*›; 筑 ‹*road, dyke*›; **to ～ sb. sth., to ～ sth. for sb.** 为某人建造某物; **to ～ sth. out of/from sth.** 用某物建造某物; **to ～ sth. on (to sth.)** (给某物) 扩建某物; **birds ～ their nests out of twigs** 鸟用细树枝筑巢 **2** fig (develop) 培养 ‹*character*›; 树立 ‹*reputation*›; 创立 ‹*theory, career, business*›; 建设 ‹*future, society*› **3** fig (establish) 创建; **to ～ sth. on** *or* **upon sth.** «*person, organization*» 将…建立在某基础上 ‹*society, policy, career*›; **the government is ～ing its hopes on an upturn in the economy** 政府寄希望于经济复苏 **4** (make stronger) 增强 ‹*strength*›; 使…发达 ‹*muscles*› **5** Games (form) 组成 ‹*words, sequences*›

B *vi* (*pt, pp* **built**) **1** fig (use as foundation) 发展; **to ～ on sth.** 在…的基础上继续发展 ‹*achievement, success, result*› **2** (increase in intensity) «*pressure*» 加强; «*piece of music, protests*» 渐渐变强; **to ～ to a climax/crescendo** 渐渐向高潮发展 **3** Constr 盖房子; **to ～ on sth.** 在某处盖房子

C *n* [u] 体形; **a man of powerful/average ～** 体格强壮/中等身材的男子; **she is slender in ～** 她身材苗条

Phrasal verbs

- **build in** *vt* [**～ in sth., ～sth. in**] **1** (construct) 嵌入建造; **we're having new wardrobes/bookcases built in** 我们正在嵌造新壁橱/书架 **2** fig (incorporate) 包括 ‹*provision, feature*›; **they say they'll sign the contract if we ～ in extra safeguards** 他们说如果我们把额外保证条款写进合同中, 他们就会签字

- **build up**

A *vi* **1** (increase in amount) 逐渐增加; **the traffic is ～ing up on roads into the city** 通往市区公路上的车辆越来越多 **2** (become more intense) «*excitement*» 加强; **tension built up as the crisis approached** 随着危机的临近, 气氛变得越来越紧张

B *vt* [**～ up sth., ～sth. up**]

1 (accumulate) 积聚 ‹*wealth*›; 集结 ‹*troops*› **2** (boost) 鼓舞 ‹*morale*›; 增强 ‹*confidence*›; 提高 ‹*output, production*›; 使…更强烈 ‹*excitement, tension*› **3** (establish) 树立 ‹*reputation*›; 逐步建立 ‹*database, organization*›; **a relationship of trust needs to be built up between the police and the public** 警民之间需要建立起互信关系 **4** *usu passive* (cover with buildings) 在…上造满房子 ‹*land*› **5** colloq (promote) 吹捧 ‹*person, event*›; **to ～ sth./sb. up as sth.** *or* **to be sth.** 把某事物/某人吹嘘为某事物 **6** (improve physically) 增强 ‹*strength*›; **to ～ oneself up** 增强体质; **regular exercise will ～ up your muscles** 经常锻炼可以使肌肉变得强壮

builder /ˈbɪldə(r)/ **▸p. 409** *n* **1** (contractor) 建筑商; (worker) 建筑工人 **2** (manufacturer) 生产商; **the biggest ～ of cars in the country** 国内最大的汽车制造商

builder: ～'s labourer ▸p. 409 *n* 建筑小工; **～'s merchant ▸p. 409** *n* 建材供应商; **～'s yard** *n* 建材仓库

building /ˈbɪldɪŋ/ *n* **1** [c] (structure) 建筑物; **apartment/office/residential ～s** 公寓楼/写字楼/住宅楼; **farm/school ～s** 农场/学校建筑 **2** [u] (industry) 建筑业 **3** [u] (action) 建造; **the ～ of new homes** 新住房的建造

building: ～ and loan association *n* Amer 建房互助和储蓄借贷协会; **～ block** *n* **1** (child's toy) 积木; **2** fig (basic element) 基础成分; **the basic ～ blocks of matter** 物质的构成要素; **～ contractor ▸p. 409** *n* 建筑承包商; **～ costs** *npl* 建筑成本; **～ industry** *n* 建筑业; **～ land** *n* [u] 建筑用地; **～ materials** *npl* 建筑材料; **～ permit** *n* 建筑许可证; **～ plot** *n* 建筑地块; **～ regulations** *npl* 建筑规范; **～ site** *n* 建筑工地; fig 未完工的乱糟糟的地方; **～ society** *n* Brit 建房互助协会; **～ surveyor ▸p. 409** *n* 建筑测量师; **～ trade** *n* **the ～ trade** 建筑行业; **～ work** *n* [u] **1** (activity of building) 建筑作业; **2** (work that needs doing) 建筑工程; **～ worker ▸p. 409** *n* Brit 建筑工人; **～ works** *npl* 建筑施工

building societies and savings and loan associations

建房互助协会和储蓄借贷协会。建房互助协会是英国的一种金融机构。已知最早的建房互助协会是 1775 年在伯明翰成立的。早期互助协会的会员定期向协会缴纳一笔钱款，通过这种集资方式逐一帮助每个会员建房或买房。在所有会员都拥有住房之后，协会即自行解散。自 1845 年起，英国成立了许多永久性的互助协会。互助协会提供存款服务，但核心业务是提供住房抵押贷款（mortgage）。和银行不同，建房互助协会不是公司，而是一个互利性机构（mutual organization）。1986 年，英国通过《建房互助协会法案》（*Building Societies Act*），允许这些协会从事抵押贷款之外的多种金融服务，从而直接和银行产生竞争。英国的建房互助协会的模式后来传到其他国家，美国的类似机构称为储蓄借贷协会（Savings and Loan Association，亦作 S & Ls 或 thrift）。1831 年，费城（Philadelphia）的牛津节俭建房协会（Oxford Provident Building Association of Philadelphia）开始营业，成为美国的第一个储蓄借贷协会。起初，这些储蓄借贷协会也属于互利性机构，主要提供抵押贷款和存款业务，和银行属于不同的体系。到 20 世纪 80 年代，协会开始提供和银行业务相似的服务。

b

build: ~ quality *n* [u] 工艺质量; **~-up** *n* [1] (increase) (in tartar, deposits, traffic, weapons, stocks) 积聚; (in tension, excitement) 增强; **a military ~-up** 军备增长; **a ~-up of pressures within the government** 政府内部压力的增大; [2] (publicity) 造势; **the ~-up to sth.** 对某事物的宣扬; **to give sth./sb. a good/huge ~-up** 为某事物/某人大造声势; [3] (preparations) 准备期; **the whole ~-up to the competition** 赛前的全部准备

built /bɪlt/
A *pt, pp* ▸**build A, B**
B *adj* [1] (made) (referring to building) 由…建成的; (referring to person) 有…体形的; **to be ~ (out) of sth.** «*house, vehicle*» 用某物建成; **a house ~ (out) of stone/bricks** 石头/砖头砌的房子; **he's powerfully/slightly ~** 他身材魁梧/瘦小; **he's ~ for hard work** 他有干重活的体格 [2] (designed) 有…构造的; **to be ~ for sth./to do sth.** 为了某事/做某事而建的

-built /bɪlt/ *combining form* …造的; **a stone~ house** 石头房子

built environment *n* **the ~** 建筑环境

built-in *adj* [1] lit (made as part of) 嵌入式的 ‹*mirror*›; 内置的 ‹*microphone, clock*›; **a ~ wardrobe** 壁橱 [2] fig (incorporated into) 固有的 ‹*feature, difficulty*›; 内在的 ‹*safeguard*›; **the system has a ~ resistance to change** 这个制度本身排斥变革; **a pay deal with ~ guarantees of employment** 一份包含就业保障的工资协议

built-up *adj* [1] (covered by buildings) 建筑物密集的; **the centre of the town has become very ~** 市中心已挤满了建筑; **a ~ area** 建筑物密集区 [2] (increased in height) 加高的; **~ shoes** 后跟垫高的鞋子

bulb /bʌlb/ *n* [1] Elec 电灯泡; **a 60-watt ~** 60 瓦的灯泡 [2] Bot 球茎; **daffodil/tulip ~s** 水仙/郁金香鳞茎 [3] (of thermometer, test tube) 球部

bulbous /ˈbʌlbəs/ *adj* [1] (round and fat) 圆鼓鼓的 ‹*growth*›; **his nose was red and ~** 他长了个红红的蒜头鼻 [2] Bot 球茎状的

Bulgaria /bʌlˈɡeərɪə/ *pr n* 保加利亚

Bulgarian /bʌlˈɡeərɪən/ ▸**p. 503, p. 426**
A *adj* (of Bulgaria) 保加利亚的; (of the people) 保加利亚人的; (of the language) 保加利亚语的
B *n* [1] [c] (person) 保加利亚人 [2] [u] (language) 保加利亚语

bulge /bʌldʒ/
A *n* [1] (swelling) 鼓起; **the ~ of his stomach** 他的肚腩 [2] Stat 快速增长; **a demographic/statistical ~** 人口/统计上的快速增长 [3] (increase) 激增; **a ~ in the birth/unemployment rate** 出生率/失业率的激增 [4] Mil 突出部 [5] Amer Sport colloq (advantage) 优势
B *vi* [1] (protrude) «*surface, cheeks, pipe*» 鼓起; **his eyes were bulging out of their sockets** 他的两只眼睛从眼窝里鼓出来了 [2] (be full) «*container, vehicle*» 塞满; **to be bulging with sth.** 鼓鼓囊囊地装满某物; **the train was bulging with passengers** 火车上挤满了乘客

bulging /ˈbʌldʒɪŋ/ *adj* [1] (protruding) 鼓起的 ‹*eyes, wall, surface, cheeks, muscles*›; **her ~ tummy** 她那发胖的肚子 [2] (very full) 塞满的 ‹*pocket, bag*›; **his ~ wallet** 他鼓鼓囊囊的钱包

bulimia (nervosa) /bjuːˌlɪmɪə (nɜːˈvəʊsə)/ *n* [u] 贪食症

bulimic /bjuːˈlɪmɪk/
A *adj* 患贪食症的 ‹*person, disorder*›
B *n* 贪食症患者

bulk /bʌlk/
A *n* [1] [u] (large quantity) 大量; **to buy/sell sth. in ~** 大批购买/出售某物 [2] [u] (majority) 大部分 [3] [u] (large size) 大块; **the dark ~ of the manor house** 阴森高大的庄园主宅第 [4] [c] (large body) 肥硕的身躯 [5] [u] (dietary fibre) 粗纤维食品
B *modif* 大宗的 ‹*order, supplies*›; **~ raw materials** 大批原材料; **~ discounts are available** 量大可打折
C *vi* **to ~ large** «*idea, theme, memory*» 显得重要; **these matters ~ large in his eyes** 这些事情在他眼里很重要

bulk: ~-buy *vt, vi* 批量购买; **~-buying** *n* [u] 大宗购买; **~ carrier** *n* 散装货船; **~head** *n* Naut 舱壁; Aviat 隔板

bulkiness /ˈbʌlkɪnɪs/ *n* [u] [1] (of object) 庞大笨重 [2] (of person) 高大肥胖

bulk: ~ mail *n* [u] esp Amer 大宗邮件; **~ purchase** *n* 大宗购买

bulky /ˈbʌlki/ *adj* [1] (large and unwieldy) 笨重的 ‹*package, equipment*›; **a ~ paperback** 一本大部头的平装书 [2] (heavily built) 高大肥胖的 ‹*person, animal*›

bull¹ /bʊl/
A *n* [1] [c] (male bovine animal) 公牛; **to take** *or* **grab** *or* **seize the ~ by the horns** fig 不畏艰险 [2] [c] (large man) 彪形大汉 [3] [u] Astrol **the B~** 金牛座 [4] [c] Fin 多头户 [5] [u] colloq (nonsense) 胡扯 [6] [c] Brit **= bullseye 1** [7] [c] (male elephant) 雄象; (male whale) 雄鲸
B *modif* Fin 行情看涨的; **a ~ market** 牛市
C *vt* sl **= bullshit B**
D *vi* sl **= bullshit C**

bull² *n* Relig 教皇诏书

bull bar *n* 保险杠

bulldog /ˈbʊldɒɡ/
A *n* 斗牛犬
B *modif* fig 顽强的 ‹*spirit, determination, tenacity*›; **the ~ breed** 强悍的一类

bulldog clip *n* 长尾夹

bulldoze /ˈbʊldəʊz/ *vt* [1] (knock down) 推倒 ‹*building, wall, village*›; (clear, move) 铲平 ‹*area, rubble*›; **the village was ~d to the ground** 村庄被推土机夷为平地 [2] fig (force) 强行通过; **to ~ one's way into/through sth.** «*person*» 强行进入/穿过某处 [3] fig colloq (forcibly persuade) 胁迫; **to ~ sb. into doing sth.** 胁迫某人做某事 [4] fig colloq (push through) 强行使…被接受 ‹*idea, plan*›; **the government is trying to ~ the bill through parliament** 政府正试图强行让国会通过这个法案 [5] fig colloq (push away) 推开; **to ~ sb./sth. away/aside/out** 猛地把某人/某物推开/推到一边/推出去

bulldozer /ˈbʊldəʊzə(r)/ *n* 推土机

bullet /ˈbʊlɪt/ *n* 子弹; **a ~ wound** 枪伤; **a ~ hole** 弹孔; **to put a ~ in sb./in sb.'s head** colloq 给某人吃枪子; **to bite (on) the ~** fig 硬着头皮接受

bullet-headed *adj* 圆头的 ‹*man*›; **~ Nazis** 纳粹光头党党员

bulletin /ˈbʊlətɪn/ *n* [1] (news broadcast) 简要新闻 [2] (public statement) 公告; **a health ~** 健康状况报告 [3] (newsletter) 简报; **a monthly ~** 每月简报

bulletin board *n* [1] Amer (noticeboard) 布告牌 [2] Comput 公告板

bullet point *n* [1] (mark on paper) 点句引导号 [2] (item) 点句

bulletproof /ˈbʊlɪtpruːf/
A *adj* 防弹的 ‹*vest, glass, car*›
B *vt* 使能防弹

bullet train *n* 子弹头列车 [尤指日本“新干线”高速列车]

bull: ~fight *n* 斗牛; **~fighter** ▸**p. 409** *n* 斗牛士; **~fighting** *n* [u] 斗牛; **~finch** *n* 红腹灰雀; **~frog** *n* 牛蛙; **~horn** *n* Amer 扩音器

bullion /ˈbʊlɪən/ *n* [u] [1] (gold in bulk) 金块; (gold in bars) 金条 [2] (silver in bulk) 银块; (silver in bars) 银条

bullish /ˈbʊlɪʃ/ *adj* [1] Fin 看涨的 [2] (very confident) 非常自信的 ‹*mood*›; 乐观的 ‹*forecast*›

bull: ~ neck *n* 短而粗的头颈; **~-necked** *adj* 头颈短而粗的

bullock /ˈbʊlək/ *n* (young bull) 阉小公牛; (mature bull) 阉牛

bullock cart *n* 牛车

bull: ~ring *n* 斗牛场; **~ session** *n* Amer colloq [尤指男人之间的] 闲聊

bullseye /ˈbʊlzaɪ/ *n* [1] (centre of a target) 靶心 [2] **to hit the ~** fig 正中要害 [3] (sweet) 球形薄荷硬糖

bullshit /ˈbʊlʃɪt/
A *n* [u] taboo sl 胡说; **to talk ~** 胡说八道
B *vt* (*pres p etc.* **-tt-**) 哄骗; **to ~ one's way out of a tricky situation** 靠忽悠脱离微妙局势; **don't ~ me!** 别哄我了!
C *vi* (*pres p etc.* **-tt-**) 哄骗; **stop ~ting and tell me the truth!** 别忽悠了, 告诉我实情!

bull: ~shitter /ˈbʊlʃɪtə/ *n* taboo sl 大忽悠 pej; **~ terrier** *n* 斗牛㹴

bully /ˈbʊli/
A *n* (*pl* **bullies**) (child) 小霸王; (adult) 恶霸; **the class ~** 班里的小恶霸
B *vt* (frighten) 威吓; (hurt) 伤害; **to ~ sb. into doing sth.** 胁迫某人做某事; **I won't be bullied!** 我不会被吓倒的!
C *vi* 横行霸道
D *excl* **~ for you/him!** colloq iron 你/他做得真不错!

bully boy *n* colloq pej 流氓; **his ~ style** 他的流氓作风

bullying /ˈbʊlɪɪŋ/
A *n* [u] 霸道
B *adj attrib* 霸道的

bulrush, bullrush /ˈbʊlrʌʃ/ *n* 宽叶香蒲

bulwark /ˈbʊlwək/ *n* [1] (defence) 保障 [2] **bulwarks** *pl* Naut 舷墙

bum /bʌm/ colloq
A *n* [1] Brit (buttocks) 腚 [2] esp Amer (vagrant) 流浪汉; **to be on the ~** 流浪 [3] (lazy person) 懒汉
B *adj attrib* Amer (bad) 蹩脚的; (defective) 有缺陷的; (useless) 没用的; **to get a ~ deal** 上当受骗; **to give sb. a ~ steer** colloq 向某人提供虚假信息
C *vt* (*pres p etc.* **-mm-**) 乞求; **to ~ sth. off** *or* **from sb.** 向某人索要某物; **can I ~ a cigarette off you?** 给我根烟好吗?

Phrasal verb

- **bum around** *vi* colloq [1] (travel aimlessly) 浪游 [2] (be lazy) 闲混; **~ming around doing nothing** 无所事事

bumbag /ˈbʌmbæɡ/ *n* colloq 腰包

bumble /ˈbʌmbl/ *vi* [1] (move clumsily) 踉跄; **to ~ about/along** 到处/一路跌跌撞撞 [2] (mumble) **to ~ (on)** 东拉西扯; **to ~ (on) about sth.** 瞎扯某事

bumblebee /ˈbʌmblbiː/ *n* 熊蜂

bumbler /ˈbʌmblə(r)/ *n* 糊涂虫

bumbling /ˈbʌmblɪŋ/ *adj* [1] (incompetent) 笨手笨脚的 ‹*person, idiot*›; (disorganized) 无条理的 ‹*behaviour, manner*› [2] (mumbling) 口齿不清的 ‹*old man, speaker*›; (incoherent) 语无伦次的 ‹*apology, speech*›

bumf /bʌmf/ *n* [u] Brit colloq 无用的书面材料

bumfluff /ˈbʌmflʌf/ *n* [u] Brit colloq 刚长出的胡子

bummer /ˈbʌmə(r)/ *n* colloq (useless thing) 无用的东西; (annoying thing) 令人讨厌的东西

bump /bʌmp/
A *vi* [1] (knock) 撞; **to ~ into sth./sb.** 撞上某物/某人; **to ~ against sth.** 撞上某物 [2] (move jerkily) 颠簸行进; **to ~ along/over sth.** 沿/在某处颠簸行进
B *vt* [1] (knock) 使碰撞; **to ~ sth. against** *or* **on sth.** 使…碰上某物 ‹*part of the body, object*›; **to ~ one's head on sth.** 头撞到某物上 [2] (collide with) 撞上; **the two cars/boats ~ed each other** 两辆车/两艘船相撞了
C *n* [1] (jolt) 碰撞; **a violent ~** 猛烈的撞击 [2] (sound of fall) 碰撞声; **the book fell to the**

ground with a ～ 书咚的一声掉在地上 3 (lump on body) 肿块; **～s on one's head** 头上起的包 4 (lump on road surface) 隆起; **a road with a lot of ～s in it** 凹凸不平的路

D *adv* 呼的一声; **to go ～** 呼的一声碰撞; **the car went ～ into the tree** 汽车呼的一声撞在树上; **things that go ～ in the night** 夜间稀奇古怪的响声

Phrasal verbs

- **bump into** *vt* [**～ into sb.**] colloq 碰见
- **bump off** *vt* [**～ sb. off, ～ off sb.**] colloq 结束…的性命
- **bump up** *vt* [**～ up sth., ～ sth. up**] 1 colloq (increase) 使…猛增 ‹*salaries, prices*›; **to ～ sth. up (from ...) to ...** 使某物(从…)猛增到… 2 colloq (exaggerate) 夸大 ‹*statistics, sales*›

bumper /'bʌmpə(r)/

A *n* Aut 保险杠

B *adj attrib* (successful) 丰收的 ‹*season, harvest*›; (enormous) 特大的 ‹*issue, book, sales*›; **a ～ crop** 丰收

bumper: ～ car *n* 碰碰车; **～ sticker** *n* 保险杠小标语; **～-to-～** *adj* 一辆紧接一辆的

bumph /bʌmf/ *n* [u] Brit colloq **= bumf**

bumpkin /'bʌmpkɪn/ *n* colloq pej 乡巴佬; **a bit of a country ～** 有点儿老土

bumptious /'bʌmpʃəs/ *adj* pej 狂妄的

bumpy /'bʌmpi/ *adj* 1 (uneven) 凹凸不平的 2 (with sudden jumps and jerks) 颠簸的; **to be in for a ～ ride** fig 即将进入困难时期

bum: ～ rap *n* 1 Amer colloq (false charge) 诬告; 2 (unfair judgement) 不公正的训斥; **～'s rush** *n* [u] esp Amer colloq **to get the ～'s rush** 被赶走

bun /bʌn/ *n* 1 (bread roll) 圆面包; (small cake) 小圆蛋糕; **to have a ～ in the oven** colloq hum 有喜 2 (hairstyle) 圆发髻

bunch /bʌntʃ/

A *n* 1 (of flowers) 束; (of vegetables) 捆; (of fruit, bananas) 串; **a ～ of feathers** 一簇羽毛; **a ～ of keys** 一串钥匙 2 colloq (group of people) 一群人; **a ～ of friends** 一群朋友; **a great ～** colloq 一群好人; **the best** *or* **pick of the ～** (person) 精英; (thing) 精品 3 (of hair) [扎在头两侧的] 发辫; **to wear one's hair in ～es** 梳着两条辫子 4 Sport (in running, cycling, etc.) 运动员群

B *vt* 把…扎成捆

Phrasal verbs

- **bunch together** *vi* «*runners, riders*» 聚拢
- **bunch up**

A *vi* **= bunch together**

B *vt* [**～ up sth., ～ sth. up**] 使…打褶 ‹*garment, bedclothes*›

bundle /'bʌndl/

A *n* 1 (collection) 捆; **a ～ of sticks** 一捆木棍; **to go a ～ on sb./sth.** colloq 十分喜爱某人/某事物; **a ～ of joy** (baby) 闹腾的婴儿; **a ～ of nerves** 神经极度紧张的人; **the child/kitten was a ～ of mischief** 那小孩/小猫经常搞恶作剧 2 colloq (large amount of money) 一大笔钱; **to make a ～** 赚大钱

B *vt* 1 colloq (push, carry) 推搡; **to ～ sb. through/into/out of sth.** 把某人推过/推进/推出某处 2 **= bundle up 1** 3 Comput 捆绑销售

C *vi* colloq **to ～ into/out of sth.** 向/从某处匆忙地走

Phrasal verbs

- **bundle off**

A *vt* 1 [**～ sb. off**] (send) 匆忙送走; **to ～ sb. off somewhere** 把某人匆忙送往某处; **to ～ sb. off to school/to sb.'s house** 把某人匆忙送到学校/家 2 [**～ off sth.**] (get off) 匆忙离开; **the children ～d off the bus** 孩子们从公共汽车上一拥而下

B *vi* 匆忙下去

- **bundle up** *vt* 1 [**～ sth. up, ～ up sth.**] (make into a bundle) 捆扎 2 [**～ sb. up**] (wrap up) 使穿得暖和; **to ～ oneself up (in sth.)** (用某物) 把自己裹得严严实实

bundled software *n* [u] 捆绑式软件

bung /bʌŋ/

A *n* 1 (plug) 塞子 2 colloq (bribe) 贿赂

B *vt* 1 (plug up) 用塞子塞住 2 Brit colloq (put or throw) 扔; **to ～ sth. somewhere** 把…扔到某处 ‹*object*›

Phrasal verbs

- **bung in** *vt* [**～ sth. in, ～ in sth.**] Brit colloq «*shopkeeper*» 把…作为添头 ‹*article, extras*›
- **bung out** *vt* [**～ sth. out, ～ out sth.**] Brit colloq 扔掉
- **bung up** *vt* [**～ sth. up, ～ up sth.**] 堵住 ‹*nose, drain*›

bungalow /'bʌŋgələʊ/ *n* 1 (one-storey house) 平房 2 (in India) 孟加拉式平房

bungee /'bʌndʒi/

A *n* (for bungee jumping) 蹦极索; (for luggage) 弹力绳

B *vi* 进行蹦极跳

bungee: ～ jump *n* 蹦级跳; **～ jumper** *n* 玩蹦级跳的人; **～ jumping** ▸p. 307 *n* [u] 蹦极跳

bungle /'bʌŋgl/

A *vt* 把…搞砸 ‹*attempt*›; 错失 ‹*opportunity*›; **the whole job was ～d** 整个工作都搞砸了

B *vi* 把工作搞砸

C *n* 1 (mistake) 失误 2 (sth. badly done) 拙劣的工作

bungler /'bʌŋglə(r)/ *n* 草包

bungling /'bʌŋglɪŋ/

A *n* [u] 无能

B *adj attrib* (clumsy) 笨拙的 ‹*person*›; 拙劣的 ‹*attempt, speech*›; **you ～ idiot!** 你这个白痴!

bunion /'bʌnjən/ *n* 拇囊肿

bunk[1] /bʌŋk/

A *n* (bed) 床铺; (whole unit) 双层床; **the top/lower ～** 上铺/下铺

B *vi* colloq **to ～ (down)** 睡觉; **to ～ at ...** 在…住宿; **to ～ with sb.** 和某人同宿

bunk[2] *n* **to do a ～** Brit colloq (depart hastily) 溜走

Phrasal verb

- **bunk off** Brit colloq

A *vi* 离开

B *vt* **to ～ off school** 逃学

bunk[3] *n* [u] colloq **= bunkum**

bunk bed *n* 双层床

bunker /'bʌŋkə(r)/

A *n* 1 Mil (shelter) 掩体; (beneath building) 地堡; **a command ～** 指挥部掩体 2 (in golf) 沙坑 3 (fuel container) 煤舱

B *vt* (in golf) 把…击入沙坑; **he ～ed his first shot** 他第一杆就把球打进了沙坑

bunker mentality *n* 地堡心态 [指自我防御意识过强]

bunkhouse /'bʌŋkhaʊs/ *n* Amer 工棚

bunkum /'bʌŋkəm/ *n* [u] colloq 胡说; **to talk ～** 瞎扯; **that's absolute ～!** 真是一派胡言!

bunk-up *n* Brit colloq 托起; **to give sb. a ～** 托某人一把

bunny /'bʌni/ *n* 1 child lang (rabbit) **～ (rabbit)** 兔子 2 (nightclub hostess) **～ girl** 兔女郎招待 3 colloq (person) 人; **a happy ～** 快乐的人

Bunsen burner /ˌbʌnsn 'bɜːnə(r)/ *n* 本生灯 [实验室用的煤气灯]

bunting[1] /'bʌntɪŋ/ *n* [u] (small flags) 彩旗

bunting[2] *n* Zool 鹀

buoy /bɔɪ/

A *n* 浮标

B *vt* 1 (make cheerful) **to ～ (up)** 使振作 2 Fin **to ～ (up)** 使…上涨 ‹*stock market, currency*› 3 (keep afloat) **to ～ (up)** 使…漂浮 ‹*vessel*› 4 Naut (mark out) 用浮标标出

buoyancy /'bɔɪənsi/ *n* [u] 1 lit (of floating object, supporting medium) 浮力 2 fig (cheerfulness) 乐观的性格 3 Fin (of stock market) (tendency to rise) 看涨; (tendency to stay high) 高价的持稳

buoyancy aid *n* 救生浮具

buoyant /'bɔɪənt/ *adj* 1 (able to float) 能浮起的 2 (able to keep something floating) 有浮力的; **sea water is more ～ than fresh water** 海水比淡水浮力大 3 (optimistic) 乐观的 ‹*person, mood*› 4 Fin 看涨的 ‹*stock market*›; 繁荣的 ‹*economy*›

bur /bɜː(r)/ *n* **= burr 3, 4**

burble /'bɜːbl/

A *n* [u] **= burbling A**

B *vi* 1 (babble) «*baby*» 咿呀学语; «*senile person*» 嘟嘟囔囔 2 pej (ramble on) **to ～ (on)** 唠叨; **to ～ (on) about sth.** 喋喋不休地谈论某事物 3 (murmur) «*liquid, stream*» 发汩汩声; **the stream ～d through the woods** 小溪潺潺流过树林

burbling /'bɜːblɪŋ/

A *n* [u] 1 (rambling talk) 唠叨 2 (of stream) 汩汩声

B *adj* 1 (rambling) 前言不搭后语的 ‹*politician, idiot*› 2 (making murmuring sound) 汩汩作响的 ‹*stream, fountain*›; 咿呀学语的 ‹*baby*›

burden /'bɜːdn/

A *n* 1 (load) 重负 2 (duty, responsibility) 重担; (misfortune) 负担; **to ease the ～ on sb.** 减轻某人的负担; **the ～ of proof** Jur 举证责任; **to bear** *or* **carry a heavy ～** 承担重任 3 (central theme) 要旨; **the ～ of her speech** 她演讲的主题; **the ～ of his complaint** 他抱怨的主要内容

B *vt* 1 (load heavily) 加负荷于; **to ～ sb. (down) with sth.** 让某人携带某重负; **refugees ～ed (down) with all their possessions** 带着所有家产的难民们 2 fig (cause worry or difficulty to) 烦扰; **to ～ oneself/sb. (down) with sth.** 让自己/某人担负某事; **industry is heavily ～ed with taxation** 工业纳税负担很重

burdensome /'bɜːdnsəm/ *adj* 1 (onerous) 沉重的 2 (worrying, distressing) 烦人的

burdock /'bɜːdɒk/ *n* [u] 牛蒡

bureau /'bjʊərəʊ/ *n* (*pl* **～s** *or* **bureaux** /'bjʊərəʊz/) 1 (agency) 社; (local office) 办事处; **an information ～** 问讯处; **the Tokyo ～ of an American news agency** 一家美国新闻机构的东京分社 2 esp Amer (government department) 局; **immigration/census ～** 移民局/统计局 3 Brit (writing desk) 写字台 4 Amer (chest of drawers) 五斗橱

bureaucracy /bjʊə'rɒkrəsi/ *n* usu pej 1 [u] (procedure, rules) 官僚主义 2 [c] (system of government) 官僚体制 3 [c] (officials) 政府官员; **the prison/trade union ～** 监狱/工会的官僚

bureaucrat /'bjʊərəkræt/ *n* usu pej 官僚

bureaucratic /ˌbjʊərə'krætɪk/ *adj* usu pej 1 (rule-bound) 官僚主义的 2 (relating to a bureaucracy) 官僚体制的

bureaucratically /ˌbjʊərə'krætɪkli/ *adv* usu pej 官僚地

burette /bjʊə'ret/ *n* 滴定管

burgeon /'bɜːdʒən/ *vi* 1 (grow, multiply) «*population, debt*» 激增 2 (flourish) «*talent, economy, organization*» 迅速发展; «*confidence*» 迅速增强

burgeoning /'bɜːdʒənɪŋ/ *adj attrib* 1 (growing, multiplying) 急剧增长的 ‹*population, debt*› 2 (flourishing) 迅速发展的 ‹*talent, economy, organization*›

burger /'bɜːgə(r)/ *n* 汉堡包

burger: ～ bar *n* (counter) 汉堡包柜台; (shop) 汉堡包店; (stall) 汉堡包摊; **～ bun** *n* 汉堡包面包

burglar /'bɜːglə(r)/ *n* 入室盗贼

burglar alarm *n* 防盗铃

burglarize /'bɜːgləraɪz/ *vt* Amer **= burgle**

burglar-proof *adj* 防盗的; **a ～ safe** 保险柜

b

burglary /ˈbɜːgləri/ *n* **1** [u] (housebreaking) 入室盗窃罪 **2** [c] (break-in) 入室盗窃

burgle /ˈbɜːgl/ *vt* 入室盗窃; **we've been ~d** 我们家失窃了

Burgundy /ˈbɜːgəndi/ ▸**p. 134**
A *pr n* Geog 勃艮第
B **burgundy** *n* [u and c] **1** (wine) 勃艮第葡萄酒 **2** (purplish red) 紫红色
C **burgundy** *adj* 紫红色的

burial /ˈberɪəl/ *n* **1** [u] (burying of body) 埋葬; **a ~ place** 埋葬地 **2** [c and u] (funeral, ceremony) 葬礼; **a ~ service** 殡葬机构; **~ at sea** 海葬; **to be present at the ~** 参加葬礼 **3** [u] (burying) 掩埋

burial: ~ chamber *n* 墓室; **~ ground** *n* 墓地; **~ mound** *n* 墓冢; **~ vault** *n* (under church) 教堂地下墓室; (in cemetery) 墓穴

burin /ˈbjʊərɪn/ *n* 雕刻刀

burka, burkha /ˈbəːkə, ˈbʊrkɑ/ *n* 布尔卡 [伊斯兰国家妇女在公共场所穿的遮盖全身的长袍]

Burkina Faso /ˌbɜːkɪnə ˈfæsəʊ/ *pr n* 布基纳法索

burlap /ˈbɜːlæp/ *n* [u] 粗麻布

burlesque /bɜːˈlesk/
A *n* **1** [u] Literat, Theat 诙谐模仿 **2** [c] Amer dated (comedy show) 滑稽歌舞杂剧
B *adj attrib* 滑稽歌舞杂剧的
C *vt* 模仿嘲弄

burly /ˈbɜːli/ *adj* 魁梧的

Burma /ˈbɜːmə/ *pr n* 缅甸

Burmese /bɜːˈmiːz/ ▸**p. 503, p. 426**
A *adj* (of Burma) 缅甸的; (of the people) 缅甸人的; (of the language) 缅甸语的
B *n* **1** [c] (person) 缅甸人; **the ~** *pl* 缅甸人 **2** [u] (language) 缅甸语

burn¹ /bɜːn/
A *vt* (*pt, pp* **~ed** *or* esp Brit **burnt**) **1** (damage by heat or fire) 烧毁; **to ~ sth. to ashes/to a cinder** *or* **crisp** 把某物烧成灰/烧焦; **to ~ sb. alive** 把某人活活烧死; **to ~ sb. to death** 把某人烧死 **2** (use) 烧 ‹*fuel*›; **the system ~s too much oil** 这个系统太费油 **3** (damage accidentally) 烧坏 ‹*possessions, clothes*›; 烧出 ‹*hole*›; «*fire*» 烧伤 ‹*part of body*›; «*heat*» 烫伤 ‹*part of body*›; **he ~ed his mouth on the hot soup** 他喝热汤烫伤了嘴; **their skin was burnt by the sun** 他们的皮肤被阳光灼伤了; **to ~ one's fingers, to get one's fingers burnt** fig 因考虑不周而蒙受损失; **to ~ one's boats** *or* **bridges** fig 自断后路; **burnt into one's memory** 铭刻在记忆中的; **the experience ~ed itself into my memory** 这一经历在我的记忆中打下了烙印; ▸**candle** **4** (spoil, overcook) 烧糊 ‹*milk*›; 烤焦 ‹*cake, meat*› **5** Comput (put information on) 刻录 ‹*CD*›
B *vi* (*pt, pp* **~ed** *or* esp Brit **burnt**) **1** (be consumed by fire) 烧毁; **their house burnt to the ground** 他们的房子被大火夷为平地; **to fiddle while Rome ~s** Prov 大难临头仍歌舞升平 **2** (produce flames and heat) «*wood, fire*» 燃烧; **coal ~s well in this stove** 这炉子烧煤很好; **the fire ~ed (down) low** 火势减弱了 **3** (be switched on) 发光; **a light was ~ing in the hall** 大厅里亮着一盏灯 **4** (be overcooked, spoiled) «*food, dinner*» 烧糊 **5** (be painful, sore) «*part of body, wound*» 火辣辣地痛 **6** (be sunburnt) «*person, part of body*» 晒伤 **7** fig (be aroused) 渴望; **to ~ with desire (for sb./sth.)** 渴望（得到某人/某事物）; **to ~ with impatience** 急不可待; **to ~ for revenge** 渴望复仇 **8** (eat into) «*acid*» 腐蚀
C *n* **1** (injury, mark) (from fire) 烧伤; (from heat) 烫伤; (from sun) 晒伤; **severe/superficial/slight ~s** 严重/表面/轻微烧伤; **cigarette ~s** 烟头烫伤; **rope ~s** 绳子勒痕; **there were ~s all over the furniture** 家具上满是烧灼的痕迹 **2** (consumption of fuel) 燃料消耗

Phrasal verbs

- **burn away**
A *vi* **1** (continue to burn) «*fire, flame*» 持续燃烧 **2** (be consumed by fire) «*log, candle*» 烧掉
B *vt* [**~ sth. away, ~ away sth.**] 烧掉 ‹*wood, paint, skin*›

- **burn down**
A *vi* **1** (be destroyed) «*house*» 烧毁 **2** (have lower flame) «*stick*» 烧短; «*fire*» 减弱; **the candle had almost ~ed right down** 蜡烛几乎烧没了
B *vt* [**~ sth. down, ~ down sth.**] 烧毁 ‹*structure, house*›

- **burn off**
A *vi* «*substance*» 烧尽
B *vt* [**~ sth. off, ~ off sth.**] 烧掉 ‹*paint, vegetation*›

- **burn out**
A *vi* **1** (stop burning) «*fire, candle*» 熄灭 **2** (stop working) «*fuse, motor, light bulb*» 烧坏
B *vt* **1** [**~ sth. out, ~ out sth.**] (make unserviceable) 烧坏 ‹*clutch, engine, motor*› **2** [**~ sth. out, ~ out sth.**] (destroy) 烧毁 ‹*car, building*› **3** [**~ sb. out, ~ out sb.**] (force out) «*person*» 放火驱出; «*fire*» 烧毁…的家; **we burnt the enemy troops out of their shelter** 我们放火把敌军逼出了掩体; **burnt out of house and home** 因火灾而不得不离家的
C *v refl* **to ~ oneself out** (become exhausted) 筋疲力尽

- **burn up**
A *vi* **1** (burn more strongly) «*flame, fire*» 烧得更旺 **2** (be destroyed) «*rocket, satellite, meteorite*» 烧毁
B *vt* **1** [**~ up sth., ~ sth. up**] (destroy) 烧掉 **2** [**~ up sb., ~ sb. up**] Amer colloq (make angry) «*behaviour, attitude*» 激怒; **not getting the promotion burnt her up** 她因未能升职而怒气冲冲

burn² *n* Scot 溪流

burned-out *adj* = **burnt-out**

burner /ˈbɜːnə(r)/ *n* **1** (on gas cooker) 煤气头; (of lamp) 灯头; **to turn the ~ up/down** 把煤气开大/关小 **2** (stove) 炉子; (lamp) 灯; **a gas/oil ~** 煤气炉/油炉

burning /ˈbɜːnɪŋ/
A *adj* **1** (aflame, alight) 燃烧的; fig (very hot) 炽热的; **a ~ sensation** 烧灼的感觉 **2** fig (intense) 强烈的; **a ~ question** *or* **issue** 当务之急
B *n* [u] **1** (being on fire) 燃烧; **I can smell ~!** 我闻到有东西烧着了! **2** (setting on fire) 纵火

burnish /ˈbɜːnɪʃ/ *vt* **1** (polish by hand) 擦亮; **~ed steel** 擦得锃亮的钢 **2** (polish with machine) 磨光

burnout /ˈbɜːnaʊt/ *n* [u] **1** (mental, physical exhaustion) 精疲力竭 **2** (failure of electronic device) 烧坏

burns unit *n* 烧伤科

burnt /bɜːnt/
A *pt, pp* ▸**burn¹ A, B**
B *adj* **1** (damaged by fire) 烧伤的 ‹*person, flesh*›; **a ~ sacrifice** 燔祭品 **2** hum 烧糊的; **~ toast** 烤焦的面包片 **3** *attrib* (associated with burning) 焦糊的 ‹*smell, taste*›

burnt: ~ offering *n* hum 烧焦的食物; **~ orange** ▸**p. 134** *n* [u] 橙红色; **~-out** *adj* **1** (gutted by fire) 烧毁的; **2** (unserviceable) 烧坏的; **3** fig (exhausted) 精疲力竭的

burnt sienna ▸**p. 134**
A *n* [u] **1** (pigment) 煅黄土 **2** (colour) 赭褐色
B *adj* 赭褐色的

burnt umber ▸**p. 134**
A *n* [u] **1** (pigment) 烧棕土 **2** (colour) 深赭色
B *adj* 深赭色的

burp /bɜːp/
A *vi* 打嗝
B *vt* 使…打嗝 ‹*baby*›
C *n* 打嗝

burr /bɜː(r)/ *n* **1** (sound of phone, car) 呼呼声 **2** (accent) 地方口音; **a soft Scottish ~** 轻柔苏格兰口音 **3** (tool) 圆头锉 **4** Bot (seed case) 刺果; (flower head) 带刺头状花序; **to stick** *or* **cling to sb. like a ~** fig (follow closely) 黏着某人

burrito /bʊˈriːtəʊ/ *n* (*pl* **~s**) 玉米粉卷饼

burrow /ˈbʌrəʊ/
A *n* 地洞; **to make a ~** 挖洞
B *vt* **1** (tunnel) 挖掘; **to ~ one's way into sth.** 掘洞钻进某处 **2** (dig out) 挖出 ‹*hole, tunnel*› **3** fig (press closely) 使偎依; **to ~ one's face into sth.** 把脸埋在某物里
C *vi* **1** (make a hole) 挖洞; **to ~ into sth.** 掘洞钻进某物; **to ~ under sth.** 在某物下掘洞 **2** fig (nestle into) 偎依; **to ~ under sth.** 钻到某物下面 **3** fig (investigate) **to ~ into sth.** 调查某事物

bursar /ˈbɜːsə(r)/ ▸**p. 409** *n* esp Brit 财务主管

bursary /ˈbɜːsəri/ *n* **1** Educ (grant) 奖学金; **to award/receive/win a ~** 授予/获得/赢得一笔奖学金 **2** (office) 财务办公室

burst /bɜːst/
A *vt* (*pt, pp* **burst**) **1** (puncture, rupture) 使破裂; **to ~ a balloon** 扎破气球; **the car ~ a tyre** 汽车爆胎了; **they ~ the door open and rushed in** 他们破门而入; **to ~ one's sides (with laughter)** 笑破肚皮; **to ~ a blood vessel** Med 使血管破裂 **2** (break through) 冲破 ‹*dam, barrier, crowd*›; **the river ~ its banks** 河决堤了
B *vi* (*pt, pp* **burst**) **1** (explode) «*bomb*» 爆炸 **2** (split) «*dam*» 溃决; «*bag*» 胀破; «*tyre, pipe*» 爆裂 **3** (be full to overflowing) «*room, bag, container*» 挤满; «*person*» 吃撑; **to be full** *or* **filled to ~ing** 装得满满的; **to be fit** *or* **ready to ~** colloq 吃得肚皮都要胀破了 **4** **to be ~ing with sth.** (be full of) 充满某事物; **to be ~ing with happiness/pride** 洋溢着幸福/自豪 **5** **to be ~ing to do sth.** fig (be very keen) 迫不及待地要做某事; **to be ~ing (for the toilet)** colloq 内急 **6** (emerge suddenly) 突然出现; **to ~ into the room** 闯入这房间; **to ~ in on sb./sth.** 闯入打断某人/某事; **to ~ open** 猛然打开; **to ~ on** *or* **on to sth.** 突然在某处出现; **the sun ~ through the clouds** 太阳破云而出 **7** (begin suddenly) 爆发; **to ~ into sth.** 突然开始做某事; **to ~ into tears** 突然大哭起来; **the trees ~ into bud** 树木发芽
C *n* **1** (series of shots) 连发射击; **to fire a ~ at sth./sb.** 向某物/某人连续射击; **~s of gunfire** 阵阵炮火; **bomb ~s** 炮弹的发射 **2** (rupturing of pipe) 爆裂; (hole, split in pipe) 裂口 **3** (spurt, outbreak) 爆发; **a ~ of speed** 猛然的加速; **~s of laughter/applause/rage** 阵阵笑声/掌声/怒火

Phrasal verb

- **burst out** *vi* **1** (exclaim) 突然大喊 **2** (begin suddenly) 突然开始; **to ~ out laughing/crying/singing** 突然大笑/大哭/高歌起来 **3** (exit suddenly and noisily) 冲出; **to ~ out of the room** 冲出房间

burster /ˈbɜːstə(r)/ *n* Comput, Print 分页器

burton /ˈbɜːtn/ *n* **to go for a ~** Brit colloq dated 被毁坏

Burundi /bəˈrʊndi/ *pr n* 布隆迪

bury /ˈberi/ *vt* **1** (after death) 埋葬 ‹*person, animal*›; **to ~ sb. at sea** 把某人海葬; **to ~ sb. alive** 活埋某人; **dead and buried** 被埋葬了的 **2** (cover) «*rocks, snow*» 掩埋 ‹*person, place*› **3** (hide in ground) «*person, animal*» 埋藏 ‹*precious object, nuts*›; **to ~ one's head in the sand** fig (ignore realities) 逃避现实; (ignore problems) 回避问题 **4** fig (forget) 抛开 ‹*differences, hatred*›; **to ~ the hatchet** *or* Amer **tomahawk** 消除隔阂 **5** (conceal) 掩藏 ‹*oneself, part of body*›; **she buried her face in her hands** 她双手掩面 **6** (hide away) 隐藏; **a tiny hamlet buried deep in the country** 隐没在乡野的小村子 **7** (involve deeply) **to ~ oneself in sth.** 自己沉浸于某事物; **to be buried in a book** 埋头读书; **to be buried in thought** 沉思

8 (sink) 把…插入; **the leopard buried its teeth into my leg** 豹子狠狠地咬了我的腿; **she buried her hands in her pockets** 她把手插在兜里

bus /bʌs/
A *n* (*pl* **~es**; Amer also **~ses**) **1** (passenger vehicle) 公共汽车; **by ~** 乘公共汽车; **on the ~** 在公共汽车上; **to get on/off a ~** 上/下公共汽车; **to catch** *or* **take a ~ (to somewhere)** 搭乘公共汽车（去某地）; **to miss the ~** fig 错过机会 **2** colloq dated (old vehicle) 老爷车 **3** Comput 总线
B *vt* (*pres p etc.* **-ss-** *or* **-s-**) Brit (transport by bus) 用公共汽车运送; Amer (transport to school) 用校车送; **we were ~sed from the airport to our hotel** 公共汽车把我们从机场拉到了旅馆
C *vi* (*pres p etc.* **-ss-** *or* **-s-**) **1** colloq (travel by bus) 乘公共汽车旅行; **to ~ back/to work** 乘公共汽车回去/上班 **2** Amer (clear tables in restaurant) 收盘子

bus: ~bar *n* 母线; **~boy** *n* Amer 餐厅勤杂工

busby /ˈbʌzbi/ *n* 毛皮高顶帽

bus: ~ conductor ▸**p. 409** *n* 公共汽车售票员; **~ conductress** ▸**p. 409** *n* 公共汽车女售票员; **~ depot** *n* 公共汽车维修总厂; **~ driver** ▸**p. 409** *n* 公共汽车司机; **~ garage** *n* 公共汽车维修厂

bush¹ /bʊʃ/ *n* **1** [c] (shrub) 灌木; **a ~ of hair** 浓密的头发; **to beat about the ~** fig 旁敲侧击; ▸**bird 1** **2** [u] **the ~** (wild or uncultivated country) 荒野

bush² *n* **1** (metal lining) 衬套 **2** (protective sleeve) 绝缘套管

bush: ~ baby *n* 丛猴; **~craft** *n* [u] 野外生存知识与技能

bushed /bʊʃt/ *adj pred* Amer colloq 疲惫不堪的

bushel /ˈbʊʃl/ *n* (capacity measure) 蒲式耳; **~s of** Amer colloq 很多; **to hide one's light under a ~** fig 不露锋芒

bush: ~fighter *n* 丛林游击队员; **~fighting** *n* [u] 丛林战; **~fire** *n* 林区大火; **~ jacket** *n* 丛林夹克衫

bush league Amer colloq pej
A *n* 二流棒球队
B **bush-league** *adj* 次等的

bush: ~ leaguer /ˈbʊʃ ˌliːɡə(r)/ *n* **1** Amer colloq pej (minor baseball league player) 二流棒球队队员; **2** fig (useless person) 草包; **B~man** /-mən/ *n* 布须曼人; **~ranger** *n* **1** Amer (backwoodsman) 偏远地区居民; **2** Austral, NZ (outlaw) 藏匿在山林中的逃犯; **~ telegraph** *n* **1** lit (method of communication) 丛林信息传播方法; **2** fig hum (informal network) 小道消息的口头传播

bushwhack /ˈbʊʃwæk/ Amer, Austral, NZ
A *vi* **1** (beat path) 在丛林中开路 **2** (live in the bush) 在丛林中生活
B *vt* 伏击 ‹*person*›; **they'll get ~ed** 他们会遭到伏击

bushwhacker /ˈbʊʃwækə(r)/ *n* **1** Amer, Austral, NZ (inhabitant of the bush) 丛林居民; (traveller in the bush) 丛林游历者 **2** Amer, Austral (outlaw) 丛林强盗

bushy /ˈbʊʃi/ *adj* **1** (covered with bushes) 灌木丛生的 **2** (bush-shaped) 茂密的 ‹*shrub, tree*› **3** (growing thickly) 浓密的 ‹*beard, hair*›; 毛茸茸的 ‹*tail*›

busily /ˈbɪzɪli/ *adv* **1** (actively) 忙碌地; **~ working/writing** 忙着工作/写 **2** pej (nosily) 起劲地; **~ meddling in other people's affairs** 瞎起劲地插手别人的事

business /ˈbɪznɪs/ *n* **1** [u] (commerce, trade) 商业; **to go into ~ (for oneself), to set up in ~ (for oneself)** （独立）开业; **to set up in ~ as sb.** 开业担当某角色; **(to go) out of ~** 停止经商; **to put sb./sth. out of business** 使某人/某企业停业; **to do ~ with sb.** 与某人做生意; **to be in ~** lit 经商; fig colloq 开始工作; **all we need is a car, and we'll be in ~** 我们只需要有一辆车就可以动手了; **she's away on ~** 她出差了; **big ~** (large companies) 大企业; (important business) 大生意; **to mix ~ with pleasure** 工作与玩乐兼顾; **~ is ~** 公事公办; **one's line of ~** 行业; **to be good/bad ~** 生意好/不好 **2** [u] (trade) 营业额; **to drum up ~** 努力提高营业额; **~ is usually brisk in the summer** 夏季通常是营业旺季 **3** [u] (custom) 惠顾; **I'm taking my ~ elsewhere** 我要去别处买东西了 **4** [c] (company) 公司; **to launch a ~** 开办公司; **to manage/operate/run a ~** 管理/运作/经营一家公司 **5** [u] (responsibility) 职责; **to make it one's ~ to do sth.** 负责办某事; **to go about one's ~** 履行职责; **to send sb. about his/her ~** dated 打发某人走 **6** [u] (important matters) 事务; **what's your ~ with Jim?** 你找吉姆有什么事? **7** [u] (concern) 所关心的事; **that's none of your ~!** 这不干你的事! ; **you've no ~ doing that!** 你无权那样做! ; **mind your own ~!** 少管闲事! **8** [c] colloq (nuisance) 难事; **it was quite a ~** 那真是件麻烦事; **to make a (great) ~ of sth.** 重视某事物; **there's some funny ~ going on!** 事情有点不对劲! **9** [u] euph (defecation) 大便; **to do one's ~** 解大手

business: ~ account *n* 企业账户; **~ accounting** *n* [u] 企业会计; **~ activity** *n* [u] 业务活动; **~ address** *n* 单位地址; **~ administration** *n* [u] 企业管理; **~ angel** *n* 投资天使 [投资于高风险、高收益的新兴企业的人]; **~ associate** *n* 商业合作者; **~ call** *n* (visit) 公务拜访; (phone call) 公务电话; **~ card** *n* 名片; **~ centre** *n* 商业中心; **~ class** *n* Aviat 商务舱; **to travel ~ class** 乘商务舱旅行; **~ college** *n* 商学院; **~ consultant** ▸**p. 409** *n* 商业顾问; **~ contact** *n* 业务联系电话号码; **~ cycle** *n* 商业周期; **~ deal** *n* 生意; **~ development** *n* [u] 业务发展; **~ development manager** 业务发展部经理; **~ end** *n* [u] hum 使用的一头; **the ~ end of a gun/knife** 枪口/刀口; **~ ethics** *npl* **1** + *v sing* (branch of study) 商业伦理学; **2** + *v pl* (moral principles) 商业道德; **~ expenses** *npl* 业务支出; **~ failure** *n* 经营亏损; **~ hours** *npl* (of office) 办公时间; (of shop) 营业时间; **~ language** *n* [u] 商务语言; **~ language courses** 商务语言课程; **~like** *adj* (professional) 效率高的; (appearance) 干练的; (method) 有条不紊的; **brisk and ~like** 干脆利落的; **~ lunch** *n* 商务午餐; **~ machine** *n* 办公设备; **~man** /-mən/ ▸**p. 409** *n* 商人; **~ manager** ▸**p. 409** *n* 业务经理; **~ meeting** *n* 商务会议; **~ model** *n* 商业模式; **~ park** *n* 商业园区; **~ person** *n* (*pl* **~ people**) 商人; **~ plan** *n* 商业规划; **~ premises** *npl* 商务楼; **~ process re-engineering** *n* [u] 企业流程再造; **~ proposition** *n* 商务提议; **~ rate** *n* Brit 地税; **~ reply envelope** *n* 商业回函信封; **~ reply service** *n* 商业回函服务; **~ school** *n* 商学院; **~ sense** *n* [u] 商业头脑; **this decision makes good ~ sense** 这个决定很有商业意识; **~ software** *n* [u] 商务软件; **~ studies** *npl* 企业管理研究; **~ suit** *n* 日常西装; **~-to-~** *adj* 商家对商家的; **~ tourism** *n* [u] 商务旅游; **~ trip** *n* 商务旅行; **~ unit** *n* 业务部门; **~woman** *n* 女商人

busing /ˈbʌsɪŋ/ *n* [u] Amer = **bussing**

busk /bʌsk/ *vi* 街头卖艺

busker /ˈbʌskə(r)/ *n* 街头艺人

bus: ~ lane *n* 公共汽车车道; **~load** *n* 公共汽车的载客数量; **a ~load of tourists** 一公共汽车的游客; **students were arriving by the ~load** 学生一车一车地到了; **~man** /-mən/ *n* 公共汽车司乘人员; **a ~man's holiday** 照常工作的假日; **~ pass** *n* 公共汽车乘车证; **~ route** *n* 公共汽车运行线路; **~ service** *n* 公共汽车服务; **~ shelter** *n* 公共汽车候车亭

bussing /ˈbʌsɪŋ/ *n* [u] Amer 用校车接送

bus: ~ station *n* 公共汽车站; **~ stop** *n* 公共汽车停靠站

bust¹ /bʌst/ colloq
A *vt* (*pt, pp* **~** *or* **~ed**) **1** (break) 弄坏; **to ~ a gut doing sth./to do sth.** 竭尽全力做某事; **to ~ one's ass** 拼命 **2** (break up) 摧毁; **the police ~ed the drugs ring** 警方粉碎了这个贩毒团伙 **3** Amer (raid) 突击搜查 **4** (arrest) 逮捕 **5** Amer colloq (demote) 把…降职 **6** esp Amer (hit) 重击; **to ~ sb. on the nose/in the mouth** 猛击某人的鼻子/嘴
B *vi* (*pt, pp* **~** *or* **~ed**) 爆裂; **Brighton or ~!** 一定要去布赖顿! ; **fit to ~** 用力; **to laugh fit to ~** 放声大笑
C *adj* **1** (not working) 坏了的 ‹*machine, device, car*› **2** (bankrupt) 破产的; **to be/go ~** 破产
D *n* **1** Amer (police raid) 突击搜查 **2** Amer (failure) 失败

Phrasal verb

• **bust up**
A *vi* colloq **to ~ up (with sb.)** （和某人）分手
B *vt* [**~ sth. up, ~ up sth.**] 解散 ‹*meeting*›; 驱散 ‹*gathering*›; 使…破裂 ‹*relationship, friendship*›

bust² *n* **1** (woman's bosom) 女子胸部; **~ size/measurement** 胸围 **2** Art (sculpture) 半身雕像

bustard /ˈbʌstəd/ *n* 鸨

buster /ˈbʌstə(r)/ *n* Amer colloq pej 小子

bus: ~ terminus *n* esp Brit 公共汽车终点站; **~ ticket** *n* 公共汽车车票

bustier /ˈbʌstɪeɪ/ *n* 紧身无带胸衣

bustle /ˈbʌsl/
A *vi* **1** (hurry) 匆忙走动; **to ~ in/out** 匆忙进来/出去 **2** (to be full of activity) 奔忙; **to ~** *or* **be bustling with activity** 忙碌; **to ~ about** *or* **around** 忙得团团转
B *vt* 催促; **she ~d the children off to school** 她催孩子们去上学
C *n* [u] 忙乱; **hustle and ~** 繁忙喧闹

bustling /ˈbʌslɪŋ/ *adj* 熙熙攘攘的

bust-up *n* colloq **1** (quarrel) 激烈争吵; **to have a ~ with sb.** 和某人大吵一场 **2** (break-up) 破裂; **the ~ of their marriage** 他们婚姻的破裂

busty /ˈbʌsti/ *adj* colloq 胸部丰满的

busy /ˈbɪzi/
A *adj* **1** (occupied) 无暇的; (full of activity) 热闹的 ‹*street, shops*›; 忙碌的 ‹*time, life*›; **to be ~ doing sth.** 忙着做某事; **to keep sb./sth. ~** 使某人/某物忙个不停; **to be ~ with sb./sth.** 忙着应对某人/某事物; **to get ~** 开始工作; **to be too ~ to do sth.** 忙得没时间做某事; **to be at one's busiest** 忙得不可开交; **to look ~** (appear busy) 显得很忙; (hurry up) 抓紧做; **to be as ~ as a bee** 忙得不可开交; **the town's always ~ on a Saturday** 周六小镇上总是熙熙攘攘 **2** pej (too elaborate) 花色繁复的 ‹*painting, carpet*› **3** Amer (occupied, engaged) 被占用的 ‹*room, photocopier*›; **the line's ~** 电话占线
B *v refl* **to ~ oneself (with sth./doing sth.)** 忙于（某事物/做某事）; **I busied myself addressing envelopes** 我忙着往信封上写地址

busy: ~ bee *n* colloq 勤奋的人; **~body** *n* colloq pej 爱管闲事的人; **he's a real ~body** 他真爱管闲事; **~ Lizzie** *n* 凤仙花; **~ signal** *n* Amer 忙音

but /bʌt, bət/
A *conj* **1** (expressing contrast, contradiction) 而 [表示相反]; **it's not an asset ~ a disadvantage** 这不是优点而是劣势; **I'll do it, ~ not yet** 我会做的，但不是现在; **I agree, ~ I may be wrong** 我同意，但是也许我错了 **2** (and yet) 然而; **he's about your height ~ fatter** 他身高和你差不多，但更胖些; **cheap ~ nourishing** 便宜但却富有营养 **3** (expressing

b

reluctance, protest, surprise) 但是; ～ **that's ridiculous/wonderful!** 但那很荒谬/很精彩！; ～ **we can't afford it!** 可我们负担不起啊! **4** (except) 除非; **I had no choice ～ to sign the contract** 我别无选择，只好签了合同 **5** (without it being the case that) [强调一贯真实]; **never a day goes by ～ she telephones** 她没有一天不打电话; **there's no doubt ～ he'll come** 他一定会来的 **6** (in apologies) 不过; **I'm sorry ～ I can't stay any longer** 抱歉我不能再呆下去了; **I may be old-fashioned, ～ ...** 我也许保守，不过… **7** (for emphasis) [表示强调]; **nothing, ～ nothing would make him change his mind** 没有什么，绝对没有什么能使他改变主意 **8** (adding to the discussion) [用于引出新话题]; ～ **to continue ...** 而接下来…; ～ **first, let's consider the advantages** 但首先，我们来考虑一下有利条件

B *adv* 仅仅; **these are ～ two of the possibilities** 这只是其中的两种可能; **he's ～ a child** 他只是个孩子; **to name ～ a few** 仅列举几个

C *prep* 除…以外; **everybody ～ Paul will be there** 除了保罗，大家都会到场; **there's nothing for it ～ to leave** 除了离开别无办法; **it's nothing ～ an insult** 这绝对是侮辱; **the last day ～ one** 倒数第二天; **the next road ～ two** 第三条马路

D **but for** *prep phr* **1** (if not for) 如果没有; **we would have married ～ for the war** 如果没有这场战争，我们都已结婚了; **I'd have won ～ for him** 要不是他，我就赢了 **2** (except for) 除…以外; **the square was empty ～ for a couple of cabs** 除了几辆出租车，广场上空空如也

E **but then (again)** *conj phr* **1** (on the other hand) 然而; **he might agree, ～ then again he might have a completely different opinion** 他可能同意，但他也可能持完全相反的意见 **2** (giving explanation) 那是因为; **she speaks very good Italian, ～ then she did live in Rome for a year** 她的意大利语讲得很流利，不过她毕竟在罗马生活过一年

F *n* 借口; **no ～s: just get out of here** 别找借口，马上滚出去

butane /ˈbjuːteɪn/ *n* [u] 丁烷

butch /bʊtʃ/ *adj* **1** colloq (mannish) 男性化的 ‹*lesbian, woman*› **2** (masculine) 阳刚的 ‹*man*›

butcher /ˈbʊtʃə(r)/ ▸**p. 409**

A *n* **1** (meat seller) 肉贩; **a ～'s (shop)** 肉店; **a ～'s boy** 肉店伙计; **to have/take a ～'s at sb./sth.** Brit colloq 看某人/某物一眼 **2** (murderer) fig 刽子手; **a ～ of innocent civilians** 滥杀无辜者 **3** (bungler) 笨拙的人; **not a skilled carpenter but a ～** 不是技艺精湛的木匠，而是笨手笨脚的拙匠

B *vt* **1** (slaughter) 屠宰 ‹*animal*›; (cut up) 切开 ‹*meat, carcass*› **2** fig (murder) 屠杀 ‹*person, victim*› **3** (bungle) 弄砸; **the players really ～ed that sonata** 演奏者们把那首奏鸣曲给糟蹋了

butchery /ˈbʊtʃəri/ *n* [u] **1** (savage killing) 大屠杀 **2** (preparing meat to be sold) 屠宰工作; (trade) 屠宰行业

butler /ˈbʌtlə(r)/ ▸**p. 409** *n* 男管家

butt¹ /bʌt/

A *vt* (hit, push) «*person*» 用头撞; «*animal*» 用角顶; **to ～ one's way through sth.** 从某处挤出来; **to ～ sb. in the stomach/belly** 用角猛撞某人的肚子; **to ～ one's head/horns into/against sth.** 用头/用角顶某物

B *n* (blow) 顶撞

Phrasal verb

- **butt in** *vi* **1** (on conversation) 插嘴; **he kept ～ing in on our conversation** 我们谈话时他老插嘴; **there's no need for you to ～ in** 你没必要插嘴; **sorry to ～ in but ...** 对不起，打断一下… **2** (meddle) 干涉; **there's no need for you to ～ in!** 不用你插手！; **to ～ in on sth./sb.** 干涉某事/某人

butt² *n* (target of criticism, ridicule) 对象; **to be the ～ of sth.** 成为某事的对象; **to be a ～ for ridicule** 受到嘲弄

butt³

A *n* **1** (end of rifle) 枪托 **2** (end of cigarette) ～ **(end)** 烟头 **3** Amer colloq (buttocks) 屁股; **get off your ～!** 起来!

B *vt* Constr 使对头连接

butt⁴ *n* (barrel) 大桶; **water/beer ～** 水桶/啤酒桶

butter /ˈbʌtə(r)/

A *n* [u] 黄油; **to go through sth. like a knife through ～** 轻而易举地通过某处; **to look as if ～ wouldn't melt in one's mouth** fig colloq 假装一副老实相

B *vt* 在…上涂黄油

Phrasal verb

- **butter up** *vt* [**～ sb. up, ～ up sb.**] colloq 奉承; **he ～ed her up good and proper** 他真会拍她的马屁

butter: ～ball *n* **1** Culin 黄油球; **2** Amer colloq pej (fat person) 胖子; **～ bean** *n* 利马豆; **～cup** *n* 毛茛; **～ dish** *n* 盛黄油的碟子; **～fat** *n* [u] 乳脂; **～fingered** *adj* colloq 常掉落东西的; 常丢球的 ‹*player*›; **～fingers** *n* colloq 常掉落东西的人

butterfly /ˈbʌtəflaɪ/ *n* **1** [c] (insect) 蝴蝶; **to have/get butterflies (in the** *or* **one's stomach)** fig 紧张得犯恶心 **2** [c] (showy or frivolous person) 花枝招展的人; **she's a bit of a social ～** 她有点像交际花 **3** [u] Sport = **butterfly stroke**

butterfly: ～ effect *n* 蝴蝶效应 [指一个复杂系统中的微小变化可能导致别处的巨大变化]; **～ net** *n* 捕蝴蝶网; **～ nut** *n* 蝶形螺帽; **～ stroke** *n* 蝶泳

butter: ～ knife *n* 涂黄油刀; **～milk** *n* [u] 脱脂乳; **～nut squash** *n* 冬南瓜; **～scotch** *n* [u] 黄油硬糖

buttery /ˈbʌtəri/

A *adj* **1** (substance, taste) 黄油般的 **2** (covered with butter) 涂黄油的

B *n* Brit 饮食服务部

buttock /ˈbʌtək/ *n* (of person) 半边臀部; (of animal) 臀尾部

button /ˈbʌtn/

A *n* **1** (on garment) 纽扣; **to do up/to undo a ～** 系上/解开扣子; **to be not worth a ～** colloq 不值钱 **2** (switch, knob) 按钮; **(right) on the ～** colloq (exactly right) 准确; (punctual) 准时 **3** Amer (badge) 圆形小徽章; **party ～** 党徽 **4** (button-shaped thing) 纽扣状物; **a chocolate ～** 小块巧克力

B *vt* **to ～ (up) sth., to ～ sth. (up)** 系上某物的纽扣; **you've ～ed your jacket (up) wrong** 你把夹克衫的扣子扣错了; **to ～ one's lip** colloq (stop talking) 住口; (refrain from talking) 不吭声

C *vi* 扣上纽扣; **this blouse ～s (up) at the back** 这衬衫是从后背系扣的

button: ～ bar *n* 按钮条; **～ battery** *n* 纽扣电池; **～-down** *adj* 领尖有纽扣的 ‹*shirt, collar*›

buttoned-up *adj* 沉默寡言的

buttonhole /ˈbʌtnhəʊl/

A *n* **1** (in garment) 扣眼 **2** (lapel flower) 别在扣眼上的花

B *vt* colloq 强留…谈话; **I ～d her and insisted she listen to me** 我硬拉住她听我讲

buttonhole stitch *n* 圈针迹

button: ～ mushroom *n* 小蘑菇; **～-through** *adj* 从上到下都扣纽扣的

buttress /ˈbʌtrɪs/

A *n* 扶壁

B *vt* **1** (support) 以扶壁加固 ‹*building, wall*› **2** fig 支持 ‹*position, argument*›

butty /ˈbʌti/ *n* esp N Eng colloq 三明治

butyl rubber /ˌbjuːtɪl ˈrʌbə(r)/ *n* [u] 丁基橡胶

buxom /ˈbʌksəm/ *adj* 丰满的

buy /baɪ/

A *vt* (*pt, pp* **bought**) **1** (purchase) 买; **to ～ sth. from** *or* **off sb.** 从某人手中买某物; **to ～ sth. for sb., to ～ sb. sth.** 给某人买某物; **to ～ in bulk** 大宗购买; **to ～ sth. cheap/retail/wholesale/at a price** 以低价/零售价/批发价/高价购买某物 **2** fig (obtain) 赢得 ‹*time, freedom, health*›; **money can't ～ you love/happiness** 钱不能够换来爱情/幸福 **3** (bribe) 收买 ‹*person*›; **he/she can't be bought** 他/她是不可能买通的; **to ～ sb.'s loyalty/silence** 出钱换取某人的忠诚/沉默 **4** colloq (believe) 相信 ‹*story, excuse*› **5** **to ～ it** Brit colloq (die) 被杀死; **he bought it when he was shot down** 他中弹身亡

B *n* 买的东西; **a good/bad ～** 买得合算/不合算的东西

Phrasal verbs

- **buy in** *vt* [**～ sth. in, ～ in sth.**] Brit 买进 ‹*goods, stock*›
- **buy into** *vt* [**～ into sth.**] **1** Comm (buy shares in) 购买某公司的股份 **2** colloq (believe) 相信某事
- **buy off** *vt* [**～ sb. off, ～ off sb.**] 收买
- **buy out** *vt* [**～ sb. out, ～ out sb.**] 买断…的股份
- **buy up** *vt* [**～ sth. up, ～ up sth.**] 全部买下 ‹*supplies, shares, land, property*›

buy-back *n* **1** (repurchase) 回买 **2** (repurchase agreement) 回购; **～ agreement** 回购协议

buyer /ˈbaɪə(r)/ *n* ▸**p. 409** **1** (purchaser) 买主; **a ～'s market** 买方市场 **2** (profession) 采购员

buying /ˈbaɪɪŋ/ *n* [u] 购买; **impulse ～** 冲动购物

buying power *n* [u] 购买力

buy: ～out *n* 控股权收购; **～-to-let** *n* **1** [u] (practice) 买房出租; **2** [c] (property) 买来供出租的房产

buzz /bʌz/

A *n* **1** (of insect, device) 嗡嗡声 **2** hum (noise) 唧唧喳喳; **the proposals were greeted with a ～ of approval** 大家七嘴八舌地对提议表示赞成 **3** colloq (rumour) 谣言; **what's the ～?** 大家都在嚼什么舌呢? **4** colloq (phone call) 打电话; **to give sb. a ～** 给某人打电话 **5** colloq (thrill, pleasure) 愉悦; **to get a ～ out of/from sth.** 因某事感到兴奋

B *vi* **1** (make humming sound) «*insect, machine*» 发出嗡嗡声; **three huge flies were ～ing round the kitchen** 3只大苍蝇在厨房里嗡嗡地飞; **all the talk made my ears ～** 这些话让我的耳朵嗡嗡作响 **2** fig (be full of activity) «*place*» 充满活动; **to ～ with sth.** 充满某活动; **her head was ～ing with thoughts/ideas** 她满脑袋各种各样的想法/念头 **3** (sound a buzzer) 按响蜂鸣器; **to ～ for sth./sb.** 按蜂鸣器要某物/找某人

C *vt* **1** (call) 用蜂鸣器呼叫 ‹*person*›; **to ～ sb. for service/attention** 按蜂鸣器要求某人提供服务/来处理 **2** colloq (phone) 给…打电话 **3** Aviat colloq 低飞掠过 ‹*town, troops*›; 逼近 ‹*plane*›

Phrasal verb

- **buzz off** *vi* Brit colloq 走开

buzzard /ˈbʌzəd/ *n* 秃鹫

buzzer /ˈbʌzə(r)/ *n* 蜂鸣器

buzzing /ˈbʌzɪŋ/ *n* [u] 嗡嗡声; **to have a ～ in one's ears** 耳鸣

buzz: ～ saw *n* Amer 电动圆锯; **～word** *n* colloq 时髦词语

by /baɪ/

A *prep* **1** (indicating agent of passive verb, after noun denoting action) 被; **a building destroyed ～ fire** 烧毁的大楼; **I was startled ～ her reaction** 她的反应令我大吃一惊; **some remarks ～ Mrs White** 怀特夫人说的一些话 **2** (identifying author) 由…创作; **a novel ～ Virginia Woolf** 弗吉尼娅·伍尔夫写的一部小说; **who's it ～?** 这是谁创作的?

3 (indicating means) 用; **you can reach me ~ phone** 你可以打电话找我; **to pay ~ cheque** 用支票付账; **to travel ~ bus/train** 乘坐公共汽车/火车旅行; **to make sth. ~ hand/machine** 手工/用机器制造某物; **to begin ~ saying that ...** 开头说道… 4 (via, passing through) 经由; **we entered ~ the back door** 我们从后门进入; **we'll get there quicker if we go ~ Birmingham** 如果从伯明翰走的话，我们会更快到达那里; **~ the left/right, quick march!** Mil 从左翼/右翼，齐步走！ 5 (near, beside) 在…旁边; **~ the bed/the window** 在床边/窗边; **come and sit ~ me** 过来坐在我边上 6 (past) 经过; **she walked ~ me** 她从我身边走过; **a car sped ~ our house** 一辆汽车从我们家前面飞驰而过 7 (before, not later than) 在…之前; **it must be done ~ next Thursday** 这件事必须在下周四前完成; **they should have been here ~ now** 他们现在本应该到这儿了; **but ~ then it was too late** 然而那时已经太晚了; **~ the time she had got downstairs, he was gone** 等她到了楼下的时候，他已经走了 8 (during) 在…期间; **to travel ~ day** 白天旅行; **~ day as well as ~ night** 日以继夜 9 (to the extent or degree of) 达; **prices have risen ~ 20%** 价格上升了 20%; **he's taller than me ~ two centimetres** 他比我高两厘米 10 (in measurements) **a room 20 metres ~ 10 metres** 20 米长 10 米宽的房子 11 (in multiplication, division) 以; **10 multiplied ~ 5 is 50** 10 乘以 5 等于 50 12 (showing rate, quantity) 按; **to pay ~ the hour** 按小时付酬; **to sell sth. ~ the dozen/the kilo** 按打/按公斤出售某物 13 (in successive degrees, units) 接着; **day ~ day** 日复一日地; **one ~ one** 一个接着一个地; **it was getting worse ~ the minute** 情况时时刻刻都在恶化 14 (indicating parentage) 由…所生; **he has two children ~ his first wife** 他和第一任妻子有两个孩子 15 (indicating circumstances) 由于; **~ accident/mistake** 偶然地/无意地; **~ candlelight/moonlight** 借着烛光/月光 16 (according to, from evidence of) 根据; **~ the rules/~ law** 依据规则/法律; **what time is it ~ your watch?** 你的表现在几点了?; **it's all right ~ me** 我觉得可以; **I knew her ~ her laugh** 听到笑声我就知道是她 17 (with respect to) 关于; **she had done her duty ~ him** 她对他已经尽到责任了; **~ birth/nature** 生来/天生地 18 Naut (in compass directions) 偏; **north ~ north west** 西北偏北 19 (in promises, oaths) 以…的名义; **I swear ~ Almighty God** 我以全能上帝之名发誓

B *adv* 1 (past) 经过; **the car roared ~** 汽车呼啸而过; **she walked on ~ without stopping** 她走过去，没有停留 2 (near) 在附近; **he lives close ~** 他就住在附近 3 (in reserve) 保留着; **I have some money ~** 我存了些钱 4 (at sb.'s home) 短暂来访; **did you have anyone ~ tonight?** 今晚有人来过你家吗?

C **by and by** *adv phr* dated (before long) 不久; (eventually) 终于; **~ and ~ she met an old man with a beard** 不久她见到了一位留胡子的老人

D **by and large** *adv phr* 大体上; **~ and large, I enjoyed my time at school** 总体而言，我上学时很愉快

E **(all) by oneself** *adv phr* 独自地; **she was sitting ~ herself** 她一个人坐着; **he did it all ~ himself** 他全凭自己完成了这事

F **by the by** *or* **bye** *adv phr* 1 (incidentally) 顺便; **where's John, ~ the ~?** 顺便问一下，约翰在哪儿? 2 (without importance) 无关紧要; **but that's ~ the ~** 但那无关紧要

bye¹ /baɪ/ *excl* colloq 再见; **~ for now!** 再见了!

bye² *n* Brit Sport 轮空; **to have** *or* **get a ~** 轮空

bye-bye

A *excl* colloq 再见

B **bye-byes** *npl* child lang or colloq 睡觉; **to go ~** 去睡觉

bye-election *n* = **by-election**

byelaw /ˈbaɪlɔː/ *n* = **by-law**

by-election *n* 补缺选举

Byelorussia /ˌbjeləʊˈrʊʃə/ *pr n* = **Belarus**

bygone /ˈbaɪɡɒn/

A *adj attrib* 很久以前的

B **bygones** *npl* 过去的事情; **let ~s be ~s** 过去的事就让它过去吧

by-law *n* 1 (of local authority) 地方法规 2 (of company or society) 内部章程

by-line *n* 1 Journ 署名行 2 Sport 球门线

BYOB *abbr* = **bring your own bottle** 请自带酒水

bypass /ˈbaɪpɑːs/

A *n* 1 (road) 旁路 2 Med 心脏搭桥手术

B *vt* 1 (avoid) 为…加设旁路 2 (not consult) 越过; **he ~ed his supervisor and gave the report to the manager** 他越过主管直接把报告给了经理 3 (circumvent) 避开; **the security measures could be easily ~ed** 安全措施很容易被钻空子 4 (travel round) 绕过; **they ~ed the hotel and headed for the nearby bar** 他们绕过旅馆去了附近的酒吧 5 Med 用旁通管取代; **surgery to ~ an artery** 用旁通管取代动脉的手术

bypass: ~ operation *n* 心脏搭桥手术; **~ surgery** *n* [u] 心脏搭桥手术

by: ~play *n* [u] 戏剧中的穿插情节; **~-product** *n* 1 Ind, Biol 副产品; 2 (secondary result) 附带结果; **a ~-product of unemployment** 失业的附带后果

byre /ˈbaɪə(r)/ *n* Brit 牛棚

byroad /ˈbaɪrəʊd/ *n* 小路

bystander /ˈbaɪstændə(r)/ *n* 旁观者

byte /baɪt/ *n* 字节

byway /ˈbaɪweɪ/ *n* 1 (small road) 偏僻小路 2 (little known area) 冷僻领域

byword /ˈbaɪwɜːd/ *n* 1 (typical example) 典范; **to be/become a ~ for sth.** 成为某事的典范; **a ~ for elegance** 优雅的代名词 2 (motto) 格言; **caution is his ~** 谨慎是他的座右铭

by-your-leave *n* **without so much as a ~** 毫无歉意地

Byzantine /baɪˈzæntaɪn, ˈbɪzəntaɪn/ *adj* 1 (relating to Byzantium) 拜占庭的 2 (relating to the Eastern Orthodox Church) 东正教的 3 fig (complex) 错综复杂的; **~ insurance regulations** 复杂的保险条例

Byzantium /bɪˈzæntɪəm, baɪ-/ *pr n* 拜占庭

Cc

C, c /siː/

A *n* (*pl* **Cs** *or* **C's**) **1** (letter) [英语字母表的第3个字母] **2** (third of three or more points or possibilities) 第三（个）; **a) ... b) ... c) ...** 第一… 第二… 第三… **3** Mus C音, C调 **4** **C** Sch, Univ (grade) 中 [指学业成绩第三等] **5** (house or flat number) C座 [门牌号] **6** (Roman numeral) [罗马数字的] 100; **CXXI** 121

B *abbr* **1** **c = century/centuries** 世纪; **19thC, 19C** 19世纪 **2** **C** ►p. 814 **= Celsius, centigrade** **3** **c** Amer **= cent(s)** 分; **4** **C** Pol **= Conservative** ►**conservative A4**

c. /'sɜːkə/ *abbr* **= circa; c. 1890** 1890年左右

CA *abbr* **1** Amer **= California** **2** **= Central America** **3** Brit **= chartered accountant** ►**chartered**

ca *abbr* **= circa**

CAA *abbr* Brit **= Civil Aviation Authority**

CAAC *abbr* **= Civil Aviation Administration of China** 中国民航

cab /kæb/ *n* **1** (taxi) 出租车; **to get** *or* **call a ～** 叫出租车; **to hail a ～** 招手叫出租车; **to go by ～** 乘出租车去 **2** (driver's compartment) 驾驶室 **3** dated (horse-drawn) 出租马车

cabal /kə'bæl/ *n* **1** (clique, faction) 阴谋小集团 **2** (plot) 阴谋

cabana /kə'bɑːnə/ *n* Amer [海滩上或游泳池边的] 小屋

cabaret /'kæbəreɪ, Amer ˌkæbə'reɪ/ *n* **1** [c] (show) 卡巴莱歌舞表演 **2** [c] (nightclub) 卡巴莱夜总会; (restaurant) 卡巴莱餐馆 **3** [u] (genre) 卡巴莱歌舞

cabbage /'kæbɪdʒ/ *n* **1** (vegetable) 卷心菜 **2** Brit colloq pej (brain-damaged person) 植物人 **3** Brit colloq (dull person) 木讷的人

cabbage white *n* 菜粉蝶

cabby, cabbie /'kæbi/ *n* colloq 出租车司机

cab driver *n* 出租车司机

> **the Cabinet**
>
> 内阁。内阁作为政府机构始于英国。起初是英国国王的最高咨询机关枢密院（Privy Council）的一部分，因开会地点在王宫内室（cabinet），故称内阁。内阁是集体决策机构。议会大选后，英国君主（国家元首）召见在选举中获得多数席位的政党领袖，任命其为首相，并授权组阁。首相提名约20名议员进入内阁，由君主任命。内阁在首相的领导下，决定并执行国家内外政策，集体对议会全权负责。内阁成员通常负责财政、外交、国防、内政等重要部门。内阁会议的内容保密，作出的决定一旦通过，阁员必须公开支持，否则就必须辞职。
>
> 和英国不同，美国的内阁仅是总统的顾问团，不是集体决策机构。总统可自行决定是否召开内阁会议并决定是否采纳内阁的建议。内阁成员由总统任命，通常由联邦政府的15位部长组成，对总统负责。美国的内阁开始于第一任总统乔治·华盛顿（George Washington）。1789年，华盛顿召集高级官员举行非正式会议，称为内阁会议。1791年以后，定期召开内阁会议成为惯例。

caber /'keɪbə(r)/ *n* 长木柱 [在苏格兰用于掷远比赛]

cabin /'kæbɪn/ *n* **1** (hut in holiday camp etc.) 小木屋 **2** Naut 房舱; **a first class/tourist class ～** 头等舱/二等舱 **3** Aviat 座舱

cabin: ～ boy *n* 轮船服务生; **～ class** *n* [u] 二等舱; **～ crew** *n + v sing or pl* (attending to passengers) 客舱乘务员; (attending to cargo) 货舱服务员; **～ cruiser** *n* 舱式游艇

cabinet /'kæbɪnɪt/ *n* **1** (cupboard) 储藏柜; (decorative, on legs) 陈列柜; **a drinks ～** 饮料柜 **2** **Cabinet** (government ministers) 内阁; **to be appointed to the C～** 被任命为内阁阁员 **3** **Cabinet** Amer (advisers) 总统顾问团

Cabinet: c～maker ►**p. 409** *n* 家具木工; **c～making** *n* [u] (trade) 家具制造; (craft) 家具制作技艺; **～ meeting** *n* Brit 内阁会议; **～ minister** *n* Brit 内阁成员; **～ Office** *n* Brit **the ～ Office** 内阁办公室; **～ reshuffle** *n* Brit 内阁改组

cable /'keɪbl/

A *n* **1** (electric for TV, telephone) 电缆; **to lay a ～** 铺设电缆 **2** (as support for bridge etc.) 缆绳 **3** dated (message) 电报

B *vt* **1** (provide with power lines) 给…接电缆; (provide with cable television) 给…装有线电视 **2** dated (send a message to) 给…发电报; (send by telegraph) 用电报发 ‹*message*›; **to ～ sth. to sb.** 电告某人某事; **to ～ sb. with sth.** 电告某人某事

cable: ～-access *adj attrib* 有线电视的 ‹*programme*›; **～-access television/TV station** 有线电视/电视台; **～ car** *n* 缆车; **～ channel** *n* 有线电视频道; **～ company** *n* 有线电视公司; **～ network** *n* **1** TV 有线电视网; **2** Elec 电网; **～ railway** *n* 缆索铁路; **～-ready** *adj attrib* 能接收有线电视的 ‹*computer, television, device*›; **～ release** *n* 快门线; **～ stitch** *n* 缆绳状编织花样; **～ television, ～ TV** *ns* [u] 有线电视; **a ～ television company** 有线电视公司

caboodle /kə'buːdl/ *n* colloq **the whole ～** 全部; **I want everything moved, the whole ～!** 我希望把东西一股脑儿全部搬走!

caboose /kə'buːs/ *n* Amer 守车 [通常挂在列车末尾，供列车员工使用]

cab rank /'kæbræŋk/, **cabstand** /'kæbstænd/ *ns* 候租出租车停车站

cacao /kə'kɑːəʊ, kə'keɪəʊ/ *n* **1** [u] (seeds) 可可豆 **2** [c] (*pl* **～s**) (plant) 可可树

cache /kæʃ/

A *n* **1** (hoard) 贮藏物; **an arms ～** 藏匿的军火 **2** (place) 贮藏处

B *vt* 贮藏 ‹*food, weapon, treasure*›

cache memory *n* 高速缓冲存储器

cachet /'kæʃeɪ, Amer kæ'ʃeɪ/ *n* 威望; **to have a certain ～** 有某种不凡的气度

cack-handed /ˌkæk'hændɪd/ *adj* Brit colloq 笨拙的 ‹*person, way*›; **you're completely ～!** 你真是笨到家了!

cackle /'kækl/

A *vi* **1** «*hen, goose*» 咯咯叫 **2** «*person*» 嘎嘎笑; **to ～ with laughter** 嘎嘎大笑

B *n* **1** (of hen) 咯咯的叫声 **2** (of person) 嘎嘎的笑声; **cut the ～!** colloq 废话少说!

cackling /'kæklɪŋ/ *n* [u] **1** (of hen) (act) 咯咯叫; (noise) 咯咯的叫声 **2** pej (laughter) 嘎嘎的笑声

cacophonous /kə'kɒfənəs/ *adj* 刺耳的

cacophony /kə'kɒfəni/ *n* 刺耳的声音; **a ～ of animal noises** 刺耳的动物叫声

cactus /'kæktəs/ *n* (*pl* **cacti** /'kæktaɪ/ *or* **～es**) 仙人掌

CAD *abbr* **= computer-aided design**

cad /kæd/ *n* Brit dated or hum 无赖

cadaver /kə'dɑːvə(r), -'deɪv-, Amer -'dævər/ *n* formal 尸体

cadaverous /kə'dævərəs/ *adj* 憔悴惨白的 ‹*face*›; 形容枯槁的 ‹*figure*›

CADCAM /'kædkæm/ *abbr* **= computer-aided design and computer-aided manufacture** 计算机辅助设计和制造

caddie /'kædi/

A *n* 球童

B *vi* 当球童; **to ～ for sb.** 为某人当球童

caddy /'kædi/ *n* **1** Brit (for tea) 茶叶罐 **2** Sport **= caddie**

cadence /'keɪdns/ *n* **1** (intonation) 抑扬顿挫 **2** Mus 终止

cadence braking *n* [u] 点刹

cadenza /kə'denzə/ *n* 华彩乐段

cadet /kə'det/ *n* **1** (young trainee) 军校学员; **an air/a police ～** 空军/警校学员 **2** (at school, college) 接受军训的学生

cadet corps, cadet force *ns* 军训队

cadge /kædʒ/ colloq

A *vt* 乞讨; **to ～ a meal** 蹭饭; **to ～ a lift off sb.** 搭某人的便车

B *n* [u] **to be on the ～** 伺机占便宜; **to be on the ～ for cigarettes** 讨烟抽

cadger /'kædʒə(r)/ *n* colloq pej (of money) 讨钱的人; (of meals) 蹭饭的人

cadmium /'kædmɪəm/ *n* [u] 镉

cadmium: ～ cell *n* 镉电池; **～ yellow** *n* [u] 镉黄 [含硫化镉的黄色颜料]

cadre /'kɑːdə(r), Amer 'kædri/ *n* **1** (group) 骨干队伍 **2** (person) 干部

Caesarean /sɪ'zeərɪən/ Brit

A *adj* 剖宫产的; **a ～ birth/delivery** 剖腹产

B *n* 剖宫产; **to have a ～** 接受剖宫产手术

Caesarean section *n* 剖宫产

Caesar salad /ˌsiːzə 'sæləd/ *n* 凯撒色拉 [用生菜、油炸小面包块加色拉油和柠檬汁等调料制成]

caesium /'siːzɪəm/ Brit *n* [u] 铯

caesium clock *n* 铯钟

cafe /'kæfeɪ, Amer kæ'feɪ/ *n* **1** (small restaurant) 小餐馆 **2** Amer (bar) 酒吧; (nightclub) 夜总会

cafe society *n* [u] 咖啡馆社交界 [指经常出入咖啡馆、夜总会的时髦人士]

cafeteria /ˌkæfə'tɪərɪə/ *n* (self-service restaurant) 自助餐厅; (in school, workplace, etc.) 自助食堂

cafetière /ˌkæfə'tjeə(r)/ *n* 法式咖啡壶

caff /kæf/ *n* Brit colloq 小餐馆

caffeine /'kæfiːn/ *n* [u] 咖啡因

caffeine-free *adj* 不含咖啡因的
caftan /ˈkæftæn/ *n* = **kaftan**
cage /keɪdʒ/
A *n* **1** (for bird, animal) 笼子 **2** (of lift) 电梯梯厢; (in mine) 升降车
B *vt* 把…关进笼子 ‹*bird, animal*›
Phrasal verbs
- **cage in** *vt* [~ **sb. in,** ~ **in sb.**] 囚禁
- **cage up** *vt* [~ **sb./sth. up,** ~ **up sb./sth.**] 把…关进笼子 ‹*animal, bird*›; 囚禁 ‹*person*›

cage: ~**bird** /ˈkeɪdʒbɜːd/ *n* 观赏鸟; ~**fighting** *n* [u] 笼斗
cagey /ˈkeɪdʒi/ *adj* colloq **1** (secretive) 守口如瓶的; **to be** ~ **about sth.** 对做某事物三缄其口 **2** (wary) 谨小慎微的; **to be** ~ **about doing sth.** 对做某事很谨慎
cagily /ˈkeɪdʒɪli/ *adv* colloq **1** (secretively) 守口如瓶地 **2** (warily) 谨小慎微地
cagoule /kəˈguːl/ *n* 连帽轻便长雨衣
cagy /ˈkeɪdʒi/ *adj* colloq = **cagey**
cahoots /kəˈhuːts/ *npl* colloq **in** ~ **with sb.** 与某人同谋; **the drug barons and the police are in** ~ **with one another** 毒枭与警察串通一气
caiman /ˈkeɪmən/ *n* = **cayman**
Cain /keɪn/ *pr n* **to raise** ~ colloq (make trouble) 闹事; (create a commotion) 大吵大闹; **the boss raised** ~ 老板大发雷霆
cairn /keən/ *n* **1** (of stones) [作路标或纪念用的]堆石标 **2** (burial mound) [史前的]石墓堆
Cairngorms /ˈkeəngɔːmz/ *pr npl* **the** ~ 凯恩戈姆山脉
Cairo /ˈkaɪrəʊ/ *pr n* 开罗
caisson /ˈkeɪsn/ *n* **1** (chamber) [水下作业用的]沉箱 **2** (floating structure) [打捞沉船用的] 充气浮筒
cajole /kəˈdʒəʊl/
A *vt* 劝诱; **to** ~ **sth. from** *or* **out of sb.** 从某人处骗取某物; **to** ~ **sb. into/out of doing sth.** 劝诱某人做/不做某事
B *vi* 劝诱
cajolery /kəˈdʒəʊləri/ *n* [u] 劝诱
Cajun /ˈkeɪdʒən/ ▸p. 426
A *adj* (of the people) 卡津人的; (of the language) 卡津方言的
B *n* **1** [c] (person) 卡津人 [法裔路易斯安那州人] **2** [u] (language) 卡津方言 [法裔路易斯安那州人讲的法语]

> **Cajun**
> 卡津人。主要居住于美国路易斯安那州（Louisiana）的少数族裔。祖先为法国裔的加拿大阿卡迪亚人（Arcadian），居住在阿卡迪亚地区（Arcadia）。1755 年，阿卡迪亚人被英国人驱逐，一部分人南迁至路易斯安那，逐渐形成相对封闭的小型社区。卡津人操卡津法语，吸收了英语、西班牙语、德语、黑人语言等多种语言成分。在文化上，卡津人以活泼的音乐和辣味食品著称。Cajun 是 Arcadian 的变体。

cake /keɪk/
A *n* **1** [u and c] Culin 蛋糕; **to bake a** ~ 烤蛋糕; **help yourself to some more** ~**!** 再吃点蛋糕！; **you can't have your** ~ **and eat it (too)** 鱼和熊掌不可兼得; **to sell** *or* **go like hot** ~**s** 畅销; **to be the icing on the** ~ 锦上添花; **to take the** ~ esp Amer 空前惊人; **to want/demand a (larger) slice** *or* **share of the** ~ 想要/要求得到（更多的）利益; **to be a piece of** ~ colloq 十分容易 **2** [c] (of soap, wax) 块状物; **a** ~ **of soap** 一块肥皂 **3** [c] (of fish, potato) 饼状食物; **fish** ~**s** 鱼糜饼
B *vt* «*blood, salt*» 在…上结块 ‹*face, hair, shoes*›; **to be** ~**d with blood** 粘着血块
cake: ~ **decoration** *n* **1** [u] (activity) 蛋糕裱花; **2** [c] (small item) 蛋糕装饰品; ~ **flour** *n* [u and c] Amer = **plain flour**; ~ **mix** *n* 混合好的蛋糕粉; ~ **pan** *n* Amer = ~ **tin**; ~ **shop** *n* 糕饼店; ~ **stand** *n* 糕饼架; ~ **tin** *n* **1** (for baking) 烤模; **2** (for storing) 糕饼罐; ~**walk** *n* colloq 易如反掌的事
CAL *abbr* = **computer-aided learning**
Cal *abbr* Amer = **California**
calabash /ˈkæləbæʃ/ *n* **1** (fruit) 加拉巴果 **2** (tree) 加拉巴木 **3** (container) 葫芦制容器; (percussion instrument) 葫芦制打击乐器
calaboose /ˌkæləˈbuːs/ *n* Amer colloq 监狱
calabrese /ˈkæləbriːs, ˌkæləˈbreɪzi/ *n* [u] 花茎甘蓝
calamine /ˈkæləmaɪn/ *n* [u] 炉甘石
calamine lotion *n* [u] 炉甘石洗剂
calamitous /kəˈlæmɪtəs/ *adj* 灾难性的 ‹*decision, result*›
calamity /kəˈlæməti/ *n* 灾难
calcium /ˈkælsɪəm/ *n* [u] 钙
calcium carbonate *n* [u] 碳酸钙
calculable /ˈkælkjʊləbl/ *adj* 可计算的 ‹*amount*›; 可估计的 ‹*effect, risk*›
calculate /ˈkælkjʊleɪt/ *vt* **1** (work out) 计算 ‹*distance, number, cost*› **2** (estimate) 估计 ‹*probability, risk, consequence*› **3** (intend) 计划; **to be** ~**d to do sth.** 计划做某事; **the government's measures were** ~**d to raise more revenue** 政府采取这些措施是为了增加财政收入
Phrasal verb
- **calculate on** *vt* [~ **on sth.**] 指望 ‹*event, weather, result*›; **to** ~ **on doing sth.** 指望做某事; **to** ~ **on sb./sth. doing sth.** 指望某人/某物做某事

calculated /ˈkælkjʊleɪtɪd/ *adj* **1** (carefully planned) 深思熟虑的; **to take a** ~ **risk** *or* **gamble** 甘冒风险 **2** (deliberate) 故意的 ‹*insult, act of violence, use of force*›
calculating /ˈkælkjʊleɪtɪŋ/ *adj* 工于心计的; **a** ~ **killer** 诡诈的凶手; **cold and** ~ 冷酷又有心计的
calculating machine *n* 计算器
calculation /ˌkælkjʊˈleɪʃn/ *n* **1** [u and c] (operation) 计算; **to make** *or* **do** ~**s** 进行计算; **by my** ~**s** 根据我的计算 **2** [u] (by evaluation) 估计; **after much** ~ 经过慎重考虑 **3** [u] (scheming) 算计
calculator /ˈkælkjʊleɪtə(r)/ *n* 计算器
calculus /ˈkælkjʊləs/ *n* [u] 微积分
calendar /ˈkælɪndə(r)/ *n* **1** (divisions of year) 历法 **2** (chart) 日历 **3** (timetable) 日程表; **what's on your** ~ **this week?** 你本周有什么安排？
calendar: ~ **month** *n* 历月; ~ **year** *n* 历年
calf /kɑːf, Amer kæf/ *n* (*pl* **calves**) **1** [c] (of cow) 牛犊; **to be in** ~ 怀了小牛; **to kill the fatted** ~ fig 大宴宾客 **2** [c] (of other animal) 幼兽 **3** [u] (leather) 小牛皮 **4** [c] (of leg) 腿肚子
calf: ~**-length** *adj* 齐腿肚的; ~**skin** *n* 小牛皮; ~**skin gloves** 小牛皮手套
caliber /ˈkælɪbə(r)/ *n* Amer = **calibre**
calibrate /ˈkælɪbreɪt/ *vt* **1** (mark) 标定 ‹*thermometer, scale*› **2** (adjust) 校准 ‹*instrument, gun, gauge*›
calibration /ˌkælɪˈbreɪʃn/ *n* **1** [u] (marking) 标定; (of instrument, gun, gauge) 校准; **accurate** ~ **of all gauges is essential** 所有仪表的精确校准极其重要 **2** [c] (marks) 刻度
calibre /ˈkælɪbə(r)/ *n* Brit **1** (of person, character) 素质; (level of ability) 能力 **2** (standard) 水准 **3** (of gun barrel) 口径
calico /ˈkælɪkəʊ/ *n* Brit 白棉布; **a** ~ **dress** 白棉布连衣裙
Calif. /ˈkælɪf/ *abbr* Amer = **California**
California /ˌkælɪˈfɔːnɪə/ *pr n* 加利福尼亚州
Californian /ˌkælɪˈfɔːnɪən/
A *adj* 加利福尼亚州的
B *n* 加利福尼亚人
caliper /ˈkælɪpə(r)/
A *n* Med (splint) 双脚规形夹
B **calipers** *npl* (for measuring) 双脚规
caliper brake *n* [自行车的] 夹式刹车器
calisthenics /ˌkælɪsˈθenɪks/ *npl* + *v sing* Amer = **callisthenics**
calk /kɔːk/ *n, vt* Amer = **caulk**
call /kɔːl/
A *vt* **1** (give name to) 给…取名; (address or refer to by name) 称呼; **a boy** ~**ed David** 一个名叫戴维的男孩; **her name is Elizabeth, but everybody** ~**s her Liz** 她的名字是伊丽莎白，但大家都叫她莉兹; **the pupils** ~ **the teachers by their first names** 学生对老师直呼其名 **2** (describe as) 认为…是; **how dare you** ~ **me fat/a cheat!** 你竟敢说我胖/是骗子！; **it's not what you'd** ~ **an exciting book, but it's very readable** 这算不上一本激动人心的书，但可读性很强; **he hasn't a place to** ~ **his own** 他无处安身; **parapsychology or whatever they** *or* **you** ~ **it** 超心理学或者什么来着; ~ **it what you will** 随便叫什么都一样 **3** colloq (agree on) 把…算作; **that'll be £25.04: let's** ~ **it £25** 共计 25.04 英镑，就算作 25 英镑吧 **4** (say loudly) 大声说出; **didn't you hear me** ~ **your name?** 你没听到我叫你的名字吗？; **to** ~ **the register** *or* **roll** 点名; **'come here at once!' she** ~**ed** 她喊道："马上过来！"; **has our flight been** ~**ed yet?** 广播通知我们的航班登机了吗？; **I** ~**ed heads, but it was tails** 我猜的是硬币正面，但结果是反面 **5** (summon by shouting) 呼唤; **please** ~ **the manager** 请叫经理来; ~ **the next witness** 传下一个证人 **6** (telephone) 给…打电话 ‹*person, number, organization*›; **don't** ~ **us, we'll** ~ **you** hum 别给我们打电话，我们会打给你的 [常暗示说话者不接受对方] **7** (summon by telephone) 打电话叫 ‹*doctor, fire brigade, ambulance*›; **to** ~ **the police** 打电话报警; **I've** ~**ed you a taxi** 我已经为你打电话叫了辆出租车 **8** (waken) 叫醒 **9** (summon by letter) 写信请…前来 ‹*person*›; **she has been** ~**ed for a second interview** 她接到通知去参加第二次面试; **I've been** ~**ed as a witness** 我被传唤作证 **10** (to vocation) «*God, destiny*» 感召; **something was** ~**ing me to join the army** 冥冥中有什么在召唤我参军 **11** (arrange) 召开 ‹*meeting*›; 举行 ‹*election, rehearsal, strike*› **12** Games (nominate) 指定 ‹*trumps*›; 指定…为王牌 ‹*hearts, clubs, diamonds, spades*›; (ask to show hand) 叫…摊牌; (make bid) 叫（牌）; **I** ~**ed two diamonds** 我叫了两个方块 **13** Sport 判定; **the linesman** ~**ed the ball out** 司线员判该球出界 **14** Comput 调用 ‹*file, program, subroutine*›
B *vi* **1** (cry out) 喊叫; **I** ~**ed to my friends and asked them to help** 我朝朋友们呼喊，要他们来帮忙 **2** Zool «*bird*» 鸣叫; «*animal*» 叫 **3** (telephone) 打电话; **can I speak to Mr Smith, please — who's** ~**ing?** 我能和史密斯先生通话吗？——您是哪位？ **4** Radio 呼叫; **(this is) London** ~**ing** （这是）伦敦呼叫 **5** (visit) 拜访; **Martin** ~**ed while you were out** 你不在家时马丁来过; **he** ~**ed at the library to return his books** 他去图书馆还了书 **6** Games (nominate trumps) 指定王牌; (make bid) 叫牌 **7** Sport (when tossing a coin, racket) 猜正反面
C *v refl* **to** ~ **oneself sth.** (give name to) 给自己取某名字; (claim to be) 自称某身份; **she** ~**s herself Madame Mimi** Theat 她给自己取名米米夫人; **he** ~**s himself a writer, but he's never had anything published** 他自称作家，但从未发表过任何作品; **I was ashamed to** ~ **myself his daughter** 我羞于说自己是他的女儿
D *n* **1** [c] (loud cry) 喊叫; (of bird, animal) 叫声; **a** ~

C

C

for help 呼救声; within ～ 在附近; they told us to remain within ～ 他们叫我们不要走远 2 [c] Telecom 电话; to have or get or receive a ～ (from sb./sth.) 接到（某人/某处的）电话; to make a ～ (to sb./sth.)（给某人/某处）打电话; to put a ～ through to sb. 接通给某人的电话; to return sb.'s ～ 给某人回电话; there's a ～ for you 有你的电话 3 [c] (to wake sb.) 叫醒; to give sb. a ～ 叫醒某人 4 [c] (summons by voice) 召唤; the last ～ Aviat 最后一次登机提示; this is your ten-minute ～ Theat 十分钟后该你上场了; to put out a ～ for sb. (over public address or radio) 广播呼叫某人 5 [c] (signal from trumpet, bugle) 号声 6 [u] (duty) 随叫随到; to be on ～ «doctor, engineer, police officer» 随叫随到; Dr Brown is on ～ tonight 布朗医生今晚值班 7 [c] (vocation) 感召; he felt the ～ of the priesthood 他感到神意要他成为神父; a ～ to do sth. 做某事的使命感 8 [c] (allure) 吸引力; the ～ of the sea 大海的魅力 9 [c] (visit) 短暂的拜访; the doctor is out on a ～ 医生在外出诊; my next ～ was at the butcher's 我接下来去了肉店; to make a ～ 拜访; to pay a ～ (on sb.) dated 拜访（某人） 10 [c] (request) 要求; the president made a ～ for national unity 总统号召全国上下团结一致 11 [c] (claim) 需求; a ～ on sth. 对某事物的需求; she has many ～s on her time 有很多事情等着她去办; to have first ～ on sb./sth. 享有对某人/某事物的优先权; the children always have first ～ on her time 她的时间总是先花在孩子们身上 12 [u] (demand) 需要; (need) 必要; there's little ～ for black-and-white televisions these days 如今对黑白电视机几乎没有需求了; there was no ～ for him to react that way 他没必要有那样的反应 13 [c] (bid in card games) 叫牌; it's your ～ 该你叫牌了 14 [c] Sport (when tossing a coin, racket) 猜正反面的权利; it's your ～ 由你来猜正反面 15 [c] Sport (shout by official) [裁判的] 判决 16 [c] colloq (decision) 决定; it's your ～ 由你来决定 17 [u and c] Fin 催还; on or at ～ 即期支付的

Phrasal verbs

- **call at** vt [～ at sth.] esp Brit «vehicle» 在…停留; the trains ～ing at Oxford 在牛津停留的列车; the ship ～s at a number of ports 这艘船在很多港口停靠
- **call away** vt [～ sb. away] 把…叫走; the doctor had been ～ed away to an urgent case 医生被叫去看急诊了
- **call back**

A [～ sb. back] vt
1 (summon by shouting) 叫…回来 2 (telephone again) 再给…打电话 3 (telephone in return) 给…回电话

B [～ sb. back, ～ back sb.] vt 召回 ‹representative, diplomat, minister›

C vi 1 (telephone again) 再打电话 2 (telephone in return) 回电话 3 (visit again) 再次拜访; sorry, they haven't come in yet: ～ back next week 抱歉，还没到货，下周再来吧

- **call by** vi 顺便拜访; I'll ～ by some time and pick them up 我会找个时候顺便去一趟把它们取走
- **call down**

A vt 1 [～ sb. down] (summon from above) 叫…下来 2 [～ down sth., ～ sth. down] liter (invoke) 激起 ‹anger›; 祈求 ‹wrath, vengeance›; he ～ed down curses on his enemies 他诅咒敌人

B vi (shout from above) 朝下面喊叫

- **call for**

A [～ for sb./sth.] vt
1 (summon by shouting) 叫…来 ‹person›; 叫人拿来 ‹object›; the queen ～ed for her advisers 女王宣召了顾问大臣; to ～ for help/assistance 大声呼救/喊人帮忙 2 (go/come to collect) 去接/来接 ‹person›; 去取/来取 ‹object›

B [～ for sth.] vt
1 (demand) 要求; they are ～ing for talks to be extended 他们要求延长会谈 2 (require) 需要; this ～s for a celebration! 这该庆祝一下！; that was not ～ed for! 多此一举！

- **call forth** vt [～ forth sth., ～ sth. forth] liter «situation, action, speech» 引起 ‹response, emotion›
- **call in**

A vt 1 [～ sb./sth. in, ～ in sb./sth.] (summon inside) 叫…进来 2 [～ in sb., ～ sb. in] (send for) 召来; to ～ in a doctor/the police 叫医生/警察来 3 [～ in sth., ～ sth. in] (recall) «government, bank, library, company» 要求收回 ‹currency, library book, product›; the manufacturers have ～ed in all cars of this model 生产商已经把这一型号的车全部召回了 4 Fin 要求还清 ‹loan›

B vi 1 (pay visit) 拜访; to ～ in at the baker's 去面包店; he ～ed in on his friend on the way home 他在回家路上顺便去看望了朋友 2 (telephone) 打电话来; to ～ in sick «employee» 打电话请病假

- **call off**

A [～ sth. off, ～ off sth.] vt
1 (cancel) 取消 ‹event› 2 (halt) 停止 ‹search, investigation, strike›; 解除 ‹engagement, arrangement, deal›

B [～ sb./sth. off, ～ off sb./sth.] vt (order to stop attacking) 命令…停止攻击; ～ your men off 叫你的人住手; ～ the dog off 把狗叫开

- **call on**

A [～ on sb.] vt (visit) 拜访; I ～ed on her yesterday 我昨天去看望了她

B [～ on sb./sth.] vt = call upon

- **call out**

A [～ sth. out, ～ out sth.] vt (say loudly) 大声说出; 'what do you want?' I ～ed out "你想要什么？" 我喊道

B [～ sb. out, ～ out sb.] vt
1 (summon outside, away) 把…叫出来 2 (send for) 召来 ‹specialist, emergency services, troops›; if the storm continues, we'll have to ～ out the lifeboat 如果暴风雨不停，我们就必须呼叫救生船 3 (on strike) 下令…罢工; the shop steward ～ed the union members out on strike 工会谈判代表下令工会会员罢工

C vi 大声呼喊; to ～ out to sb. 对某人大喊; to ～ out for sb./sth. 喊着要某人/某事物

- **call over** vt 1 [～ sb. over, ～ over sb.] (summon by shouting) 叫…过来 2 [～ sb. over] (invite) 请来
- **call round** vi Brit 来访; do ～ round when you have the time 你有时间一定要来看我; I'll ～ round this afternoon and pick it up 我今天下午去一趟，把它取走
- **call up**

A [～ up sb./sth., ～ sb./sth. up] vt
1 (telephone) 给…打电话 ‹person, organization, number› 2 (supernaturally) 用魔法召唤 ‹spirit›; the medium ～ed up the ghost of my grandmother 灵媒让我的祖母显灵了 3 Mil (conscript) 征召…入伍 4 Mil (summon) 召集 ‹reinforcements, troops› 5 Sport 选拔 ‹player, reserve› 6 (evoke) 使人想起; the church ～ed up memories of our wedding day 教堂勾起了我们婚礼那天的回忆 7 Comput 打开 ‹program, data›

B vi 1 (telephone) 打电话 2 (shout from below) 朝上面喊叫

- **call upon**

A [～ upon sb.] vt
1 (invite) 邀请; I'd now like to ～ upon our next speaker 现在有请下一位发言人; to ～ upon sb. to do sth. 请某人做某事 2 (urge) 要求; to ～ upon sb. to do sth. 要求某人做某事; I feel ～ed upon to warn you that ... 我觉得我应该警告你…; they delivered a petition ～ing upon the government to ban vivisection 他们递交了一份请愿书，呼吁政府禁止活体解剖 3 (appeal to) 求助于; to ～ upon sb. for sth. 恳求某人给予 ‹help, support›

B [～ upon sth.] vt (make use of) 利用; we may need to ～ upon your services 我们可能有用到你的地方; you will have to ～ upon all your patience and courage 你得拿出全部耐心和勇气

callback /ˈkɔːlbæk/ n 1 [c] (returning phone call) 回电话 2 [c and u] (ringing back) 回叫 3 [c and u] Comput 身份验证 4 [c] esp Amer (for audition, interview) 再次面试 5 [c] (recall) 召回

callback facility n 回叫装置

call: ～ **barring** n [u] 呼叫限制; ～ **box** n 1 Brit (phone booth) 公用电话亭; 2 Amer (emergency phone) 应急报警电话; ～ **button** n 1 (on phone) 呼叫键; 2 (summoning sb.) 呼叫按钮; ～ **centre** Brit n 呼叫中心 [大型公司的客户服务部门]; ～ **charge** n 话费; ～ **diversion** n [u] 呼叫转移

caller /ˈkɔːlə(r)/ n 1 Telecom 打电话者 2 (visitor) 来访者 3 (for dancers) 舞步指挥

caller display n [u] 来电显示

call: ～ **forwarding** n [u] 呼叫转移; ～ **girl** n 电话应召妓女

calligrapher /kəˈlɪɡrəfə(r)/, **calligraphist** /kəˈlɪɡrəfɪst/ ▸ p. 409 ns 书法家

calligraphy /kəˈlɪɡrəfi/ n [u] 书法

call-in n Amer 听众来电直播节目; a ～ programme/guest 热线直播节目/嘉宾

calling /ˈkɔːlɪŋ/ n 1 (vocation) 使命感; (divine command) 感召; he believes it is his ～ to become a priest 他认为当神父是自己的使命 2 (profession) 职业

calling card n esp Amer 名片

calliper /ˈkælɪpə(r)/ n = caliper

callisthenics /ˌkælɪsˈθenɪks/ npl + v sing Brit 健美操

call: ～ **letters** npl Amer [电台、电视台的] 呼号; ～ **option** n 认购期权

callosity /kəˈlɒsəti/ n 老茧

callous /ˈkæləs/

A adj 冷酷无情的 ‹person, behaviour, speech›; to be ～ to sth. 对某事物无动于衷

B n = callus

calloused /ˈkæləst/ adj = callused

callously /ˈkæləsli/ adv 冷酷无情地 ‹behave, speak›

callousness /ˈkæləsnɪs/ n [u] 冷酷无情

call-out n 上门维修; he charges £50 for a ～ 叫他上门维修需付 50 英镑; ～ charge/service 上门维修费/服务

callow /ˈkæləʊ/ adj 稚嫩无经验的; a ～ youth 乳臭未干的年轻男子

call: ～ **queuing** n [u] 呼叫排队; ～ **return** n [u] 来电回拨; ～ **return service** 来电回拨服务; ～ **screening** n [u] 来电筛选; ～ **screening device/service** 来电筛选装置/服务; ～ **sign** n 呼叫信号; **～-up** n 1 [u] Mil 征召; 2 [c] Sport (of player, reserve) [尤指国家队运动员的] 选拔; **～-up papers** npl 征召令

callus /ˈkæləs/ n 老茧

callused /ˈkæləst/ adj 生老茧的 ‹hands, feet›

call waiting n [u] 呼叫等待

calm /kɑːm, Amer also kɑːlm/

A adj 1 (still) 平静的 ‹sea, surface›; 无风的 ‹day, weather› 2 (not excited or nervous) 镇静的; keep ～! 保持镇定！ 3 (peaceful) 宁静的

B n 1 (of place, atmosphere) 宁静; the ～ before/after the storm 暴风雨来临前/过后的平静 2 (of person) 镇静; to keep one's ～ 保持镇定

C vt 使…平静 ‹person›; 稳定 ‹situation›; 平息 ‹fear, anger›

Phrasal verb

- **calm down**

A vi 平静下来

B vt [～ sb./sth. down] 使…平静 ‹person›; 稳定 ‹situation›

calming /ˈkɑːmɪŋ, Amer *also* ˈkɑːlm-/ *adj* 使人平静的 ‹*influence, effect*›

calmly /ˈkɑːmli, Amer *also* ˈkɑːlm-/ *adv* **1** (quietly) 平静地 ‹*speak, react*› **2** (brazenly) 厚颜无耻地

calmness /ˈkɑːmnɪs, Amer also ˈkɑːlm-/ *n* [u] **1** (stillness) (of water, weather) 平静; (of day, night) 无风 **2** (composure of person) 镇静; (in adversity) 沉着; **the ~ of sb.'s voice** 嗓音的平静 **3** (tranquillity of place) 宁静; **an atmosphere of ~** 宁静的气氛

Calor gas® /ˈkælə gæs/ *n* [u] Brit 罐装液化气

caloric /ˈkælərɪk/ *adj* esp Amer 热的; **~ energy** 热能

calorie /ˈkæləri/ *n* 大卡

calorie-conscious *adj* 关注饮食热量的

calorific /ˌkæləˈrɪfɪk/ *adj* 热卡的; **chocolate is highly ~** 巧克力热量很高

calorific value *n* 发热值

calque /kælk/ *n* 仿造词语

calumny /ˈkæləmni/ *n* [c and u] formal 诽谤; **to heap ~ on sb.** 大肆诬蔑某人

calve /kɑːv, Amer kæv/ *vi* «*cow*» 产犊; «*other mammal*» 产崽

calves /kɑːvz, Amer kævz/ *pl* ▸ **calf**

Calvinism /ˈkælvɪnɪzəm/ *n* [u] 加尔文主义

Calvinist /ˈkælvɪnɪst/
A *n* 加尔文主义信徒
B *adj* = **Calvinistic**

Calvinistic /ˌkælvɪˈnɪstɪk/ *adj* 加尔文主义的 ‹*idea*›; 加尔文宗的 ‹*church*›

calypso /kəˈlɪpsəʊ/ *n* 卡利普索小调 [西印度群岛地区的一种即兴讽刺歌]

calyx /ˈkeɪlɪks/ *n* (*pl* **~es** *or* **calyces** /ˈkeɪlɪsiːz/) 花萼

CAM *abbr* = **computer-aided manufacturing**

cam /kæm/ *n* 凸轮

camaraderie /ˌkæməˈrɑːdəri, -ˈræd-/ *n* [u] 同志情谊

camber /ˈkæmbə(r)/
A *n* 拱曲; **this road has a pronounced ~** 这条路中间有处很明显的拱曲
B *vt* 使…成拱形 ‹*beam, deck, bridge*›; **a steeply ~ed road** 中间高高拱起的路

Cambodia /kæmˈbəʊdɪə/ *pr n* 柬埔寨

Cambodian /kæmˈbəʊdɪən/ ▸ **p. 503**
A *adj* (of Cambodia) 柬埔寨的; (of the people) 柬埔寨人的; (of the language) 柬埔寨语的
B *n* **1** [c] (person) 柬埔寨人 **2** [u] (language) 柬埔寨语

Cambrian /ˈkæmbrɪən/
A *adj* (of the period) 寒武纪的; (of the rock system) 寒武系的
B *n* **the ~** (period) 寒武纪; (rock system) 寒武系

cambric /ˈkæmbrɪk/ *n* [u] (linen) 麻纱; (cotton) 细棉布

Cambridgeshire /ˈkeɪmbrɪdʒʃə(r)/ *pr n* 剑桥郡

Cambs. *abbr* Brit = **Cambridgeshire**

camcorder /ˈkæmkɔːdə(r)/ *n* 便携式摄像机

came /keɪm/ *pt* ▸ **come A, B**

camel /ˈkæml/ *n* 骆驼; **the straw that broke the ~'s back** fig 最终将人压垮的事物

camel hair *n* [u] 驼毛; **a ~ coat** 驼毛大衣

camellia /kəˈmiːlɪə/ *n* (shrub) 山茶树; (flower) 山茶花

camembert /ˈkæməmbeə(r)/ *n* [u] 卡门贝干酪

cameo /ˈkæmɪəʊ/ *n* **1** (piece of jewellery) 多彩浮雕宝石; **a ~ brooch/ring** 多彩浮雕宝石胸针/戒指 **2** Theat, Cin 名演员出演的小角色; **a ~ role** 客串的配角 **3** (piece of writing) 小品文

cameo appearance *n* 客串 [指名演员出演小角色]

camera /ˈkæmərə/ *n* **1** (for photographs) 照相机; Cin 摄影机; TV 摄像机; **on/off ~** 在/不在摄制中; **to face the ~(s)** 面对镜头 **2** Jur **in ~** 在法官的私室里; **the case will be heard in ~** 该案件将不公开审理

camera: ~ angle *n* 镜头角度; **~ bag** *n* 相机包; **~ case** *n* 相机套; **~ crew** *n* [u] + *v sing or pl* 摄制组; **~man** /-mæn/ ▸ **p. 409** *n* 摄影师; **~ obscura** /ˌkæmərə əbˈskjʊərə/ *n* 暗箱式房屋 [顶部装有反光镜可使人欣赏外景的圆形小建筑]; **~ phone** *n* 可拍照手机; **~ range** *n* [u] 相机视距范围; **~-ready copy** *n* [可立即制版的] 正稿; **~ shake** *n* [u] 相机抖动; **~-shy** *adj* 怯镜头的; **she's ~-shy** 她不愿意照相; **~work** *n* [u] 摄影作品

Cameroon /ˌkæməˈruːn/ *pr n* 喀麦隆

camiknickers /ˈkæmɪnɪkəz/ *npl* Brit 女式连裤紧身内衣

camisole /ˈkæmɪsəʊl/ *n* 背心式女内衣

camomile /ˈkæməmaɪl/ *n* [u] 黄春菊

camomile tea *n* [u and c] 黄春菊花茶

camouflage /ˈkæməflɑːʒ/
A *n* [u] **1** Mil 伪装 **2** (colouring) 保护色; (covering) 伪装物 **3** fig (cover-up) 伪装手段; **his property business is ~ for a money-laundering operation** 他做地产生意是为了掩盖洗钱勾当
B *vt* **1** (disguise) 伪装 **2** (conceal) 掩饰

camp¹ /kæmp/
A *n* **1** (of tent, building) 营地; **to make** *or* **pitch ~** 扎营; **to break** *or* **strike ~** 拔营 **2** (holiday centre) 度假营 **3** fig (group) 阵营; **to have a foot in both ~s** 脚踩两只船
B *vi* **1** (in tent) 露营; **to go ~ing** 去露营 **2** (live temporarily) 暂住

Phrasal verbs

- **camp on** *vi* 呼叫等待; **to ~ on to sth.** 等待接通某电话
- **camp out** *vi* **1** (in tent) 露营 **2** (live temporarily) 暂住

camp²
A *adj* **1** (exaggerated) 做作的 ‹*person, manner, performance*› **2** (effeminate) 娘娘腔的
B *n* [u] (affected style) 做作; (effeminate manners) 娘娘腔

Phrasal verb

- **camp up** *vt* **to ~ it/things up** 装腔作势

campaign /kæmˈpeɪn/
A *n* **1** Mil 战役; **to mount** *or* **launch a ~** 发起一场战役 **2** (course of action) 运动; **to launch** *or* **mount** *or* **wage a ~ for/against sth.** 发起一场支持/反对某事物的运动 **3** (underhand action) 秘密的破坏活动; **a smear ~** 造谣中伤
B *vi* **1** Mil 作战; **after ten years of ~ing** 交战10年后 **2** (promote cause) 发起运动; **I'm ~ing hard to get the policy changed** 为了改变这项政策，我四处奔走游说

campaigner /kæmˈpeɪnə(r)/ *n* **1** (gen) 运动参加者; **an animal rights ~** 动物权利保护者 **2** Mil 参战人员; **an old ~** 老兵

campaign: ~ headquarters *npl* + *v sing or pl* Brit **1** (place) 竞选总部; **2** (people) 竞选总部的全体工作人员; **~ literature** *n* [u] [尤指用于竞选等的] 政治运动宣传材料; **~ medal** *n* 战役勋章; **~ trail** *n* 竞选旅行; **to be on the ~ trail** 在竞选旅行途中; **~ worker** *n* Brit 竞选工作人员

camp: ~ bed *n* Brit 行军床; **~ chair** *n* 轻便折椅; **~craft** *n* [u] (knowledge) 野营知识; (skill) 野营技能

camper /ˈkæmpə(r)/ *n* **1** (person) 野营者 **2** Brit **~ (van)** 野营车

camp: ~fire *n* 营火; **~ follower** *n* **1** Mil 随军杂役; **2** (hanger-on) 追随者; **he's not really committed to world peace, he's just a ~ follower** 他并非真的致力于世界和平，不过是随声附和罢了

camphor /ˈkæmfə(r)/ *n* [u] 樟脑

camphorated oil /ˌkæmfəreɪtɪd ˈɔɪl/ *n* [u] 樟脑油

camping /ˈkæmpɪŋ/ *n* [u] 野营; **to go ~** 去野营

camping: ~ equipment *n* [u] 野营装备; **~ gas** *n* [u] 野营罐装燃气; **~ ground** *n* = **campsite**; **~ holiday** *n* 野营假; **~ stool** *n* 轻便折凳; **~ stove** *n* 野营炉

camp: ~ meeting *n* Amer Relig 野营布道会; **~site** *n* 野营地; **~ stool** *n* = **comping stool**

campus /ˈkæmpəs/ (*pl* **~es**) *n* 校园; **to live on/off ~** 住在校内/校外

campus: ~ life *n* [u] 大学生活; **~ police** *n* [u] 校园警察; **~ university** *n* 校园大学 [校园不在市中心的大学]

CAMRA /ˈkæmrə/ *abbr* Brit = **Campaign for Real Ale** 争取散装鲜啤酒运动

camshaft /ˈkæmʃɑːft, Amer -ʃæft/ *n* 凸轮轴

can¹ /kæn, kən/ *modal aux* (*negative pres* **cannot** *or* colloq **can't**; *pt* **could**; *negative pt* **could not** *or* colloq **couldn't**) **1** (be possible) 可能; **he can't be more than 10 years old** 他不会超过10岁; **nothing could be simpler** 没有比这更简单的了; **as happy/excited as ~** *or* **could be** 高兴/兴奋得不得了; **could be** colloq 也许吧; **no ~ do** colloq 我不干; **to do all/what one ~** 尽力而为 **2** (be permitted to) 可以; (making offer, request) 能; **anyone ~ enrol** 人人均可参加; **we can't wear jeans** 我们不准穿牛仔裤; **~ I help you?** 要我帮忙吗? ; **can't you leave me alone?** 你就不能让我清静点吗?; **could I interrupt?** 能打断一下吗? **3** (be capable of) 会; (be in a position to) 能; **~ he type/speak Chinese?** 他会打汉字/说中文吗? ; **I could drive a car before I left school** 我中学没毕业就会开车了; **I couldn't possibly accept the money** 我不可能收下这笔钱 **4** (be able to, using senses) [凭感官能力] 能够; **I ~ smell/see the ocean** 我闻到了大海的气息/看到了大海; **I can't hear/see (it)** 我听不到/看不见（它）; **she ~ feel a lump in her breast** 她摸到自己的乳房里有一个肿块 **5** (indicating tendency) 有时会; **he ~ be quite abrupt** 他有时很鲁莽; **Italy ~ be hot in summer** 意大利夏天有时很热 **6** (be willing to) 愿意; **I couldn't leave the children** 我不愿离开这些孩子; **I cannot give up work** 我不会放弃工作 **7** (expressing emphasis) [表示强调] 究竟会; **what ~ she possibly want?** 她究竟想要什么呢? ; **you can't be serious!** 你不是当真吧! ; **you can't have forgotten!** 你怎么会忘了呢! ; **they couldn't have been nicer** 他们实在太好了; **I couldn't agree more!** 我非常赞同! **8** (expressing reproach) 应该 [表示责备]; **they could have warned us** 他们本该提醒我们的; **you could at least say sorry!** 你至少应该道个歉! ; **how could you!** 你怎么能这样! ; **you ~ get lost!** 你给我滚! ; **if he doesn't like it, he ~ lump it** 他就算不喜欢也得忍着 **9** (expressing exasperation) 真想; **I could murder him!** 我真想杀了他! **10** (used to avoid repetition of verb) [用以避免动词重复]; **leave as soon as you ~** 你得尽快离开; **can anyone give me a lift home? — we ~** 谁能让我搭车回家? ——我们可以

can² /kæn/
A *n* **1** (cylindrical container) 金属罐; **a petrol ~** 汽油桶; **an aerosol ~** 喷雾罐; **to carry the ~** fig colloq 代人受过; **in the ~** colloq 已经录制好的 **2** (for food, drink) 罐头; **a ~ of peaches** 一罐桃; **a ~ of worms** fig 复杂棘手的事物; **to open up a huge ~ of worms** 引起一场大乱 **3** **the ~** Amer colloq (lavatory) 厕所 **4** **the ~** Amer colloq (prison) 监牢
B *vt* (*pres p etc.* **-nn-**) **1** (preserve) 把…装罐保存 **2** **~ it!** colloq (be quiet) 安静! ; **can't you ~**

C

that noise? 别嚷嚷了行不行？ **3** Amer colloq (dismiss) 解雇

Canada /ˈkænədə/ *pr n* 加拿大

Canada goose *n* (*pl* **Canada geese**) 黑额黑雁

Canadian /kəˈneɪdɪən/ ▸**p. 503**
A *adj* (of Canada) 加拿大的; (of the people) 加拿大人的
B *n* 加拿大人

canal /kəˈnæl/ *n* **1** (waterway) 运河; (for irrigation) 灌溉渠 **2** Anat 道; **the alimentary ~** 消化道

canal: ~ barge *n* 运河驳船; **~ boat** *n* 运河船; **~ holiday** *n* 乘船游览运河的假日

canalization /ˌkænəlaɪˈzeɪʃn, Amer -lɪˈz-/ *n* [u] 运河开凿

canalize /ˈkænəlaɪz/ *vt* **1** (convert into canal) 把…改建成运河 ‹*river*›; (provide with canals) 在…开凿运河 ‹*region*› **2** fig (give direction, purpose) 引导; **to ~ sth. into sth.** 把…引导到某事物上去 ‹*opinion, emotion*›; **to ~ young people's energies into constructive projects** 引导年轻人把精力放到建设性的项目上

canalside /kəˈnælsaɪd/ *n* 运河河堤; *modif* 运河边的

canapé /ˈkænəpeɪ, Amer ˌkænəˈpeɪ/ *n* (bread, toast) [涂有作料的] 面包片; (cocktail biscuit) [涂有作料的] 开胃饼干

Canaries /kəˈneərɪz/ *pr npl* = **Canary Islands**

canary /kəˈneəri/ *n* **1** [c] (bird) 金丝雀 **2** [u] (colour) = **canary yellow**

Canary Islands *pr npl* **the ~** 加那利群岛

canary yellow ▸**p. 134**
A *n* [u] 淡黄色
B *adj* 淡黄色的

can bank *n* 易拉罐回收箱

Canberra /ˈkænbərə/ *pr n* 堪培拉

cancan /ˈkænkæn/ *n* 康康舞 [一种由穿宽松裙子的女子把腿高高踢起的快节奏舞蹈]

cancel /ˈkænsl/ (*pres p etc.* **-ll-** Brit, **-l-** Amer)
A *vt* **1** (call off, withdraw from service) 取消 ‹*meeting, match, train, flight*›; (annul) 使…无效 ‹*debt, agreement, cheque*›; (rescind) 撤销 ‹*decree, message*›; **if we ~ our order, we lose our deposit** 如果我们撤销订单，就会损失定金; **to ~ a contract** 取消合同 **2** (punch, stamp) 盖销 ‹*ticket, permit*› **3** Math 约去 ‹*figures, sums*› **4** Comput 撤销 ‹*command, instruction, process*›
B *vi* 取消

Phrasal verb
• **cancel out**
A *vt* [**~ out sth.**, **~ sth. out**]
1 Math 约去 ‹*figures, sum*› **2** fig 抵消 ‹*effect, factor, argument*›; **the opposing forces ~led each other out** 两种对立的力量相互抵消了
B *vi* **1** Math 约去 **2** (counterbalance each other) ‹*factors, forces, arguments*› 相互抵消

cancellation Brit, **cancelation** Amer /ˌkænsəˈleɪʃn/ *n* **1** (of event, order, booking, train, flight) 取消 **2** (of sth. resellable, rebookable) 被取消之物; **we have three ~s** 我们有 3 张退票

cancellation charge, cancellation fee *ns* 退订费; **~s for rail tickets** 火车票退票费

Cancer /ˈkænsə(r)/ *n* **1** [u] Astron 巨蟹（星）座 **2** [u] Astrol (sign) 巨蟹宫 [黄道第四宫] **3** [c] (*pl* **~s**) Astrol (person) 属巨蟹（星）座的人 **4** Geog ▸**tropic A**

cancer /ˈkænsə(r)/ ▸**p. 377** *n* **1** [u and c] (disease) 癌症; **to have lung ~** 患肺癌 **2** [c] (tumour) 恶性肿瘤 **3** [c] fig (evil influence) 弊端; **a ~ in society** 社会毒瘤

cancer: ~-causing *adj* 致癌的; **~ hospital** *n* 肿瘤医院

cancerous /ˈkænsərəs/ *adj* **1** lit 癌的 ‹*growth*›; 生癌的 ‹*tissue*›; **~ cells** 癌细胞 **2** fig (pervasive and evil) 如癌般扩散的

cancer: ~ patient *n* 癌症病人; **~ research** *n* [u] 癌症研究; **~ screening** *n* [u] 癌症筛查; **~ specialist** ▸**p. 409** *n* 癌症专家; **~ stick, ~ tube** *ns* Brit colloq 香烟; **~ ward** *n* 癌症病房

candelabra /ˌkændɪˈlɑːbrə/ *n* (*pl* **~** *or* **~s**) (for candles) 大枝形烛台; (for lamps) 大枝形吊灯

candelabrum /ˌkændɪˈlɑːbrəm/ *n* (*pl* **candelabra** *or* **~s**) = **candelabra**

candid /ˈkændɪd/ *adj* 率直的; **a ~ biography** 一部秉笔直书的传记; **to be ~ with sb.** 对某人开诚布公

candidacy /ˈkændɪdəsi/ *n* 候选人身份; **to announce one's ~** 宣布自己为候选人

candidate /ˈkændɪdət, Amer -deɪt/ *n* **1** Pol 候选人; **a ~ for the presidency** 总统候选人; **to stand** *or* **run as a ~ (in an election)** 作为（选举的）候选人参加竞选; **to adopt/select/endorse sb. as ~** 提名/推举/支持某人为候选人 **2** (for job) 求职者; **to be a likely ~ for the job** 有可能获得工作职位 **3** (in exam) 应试的人或事物 **4** fig 可能有某种结局者; **the sector is a ~ for restructuring** 这个部门早晚要改组

candidature /ˈkændɪdətʃə(r)/ *n* Brit = **candidacy**

candidly /ˈkændɪdli/ *adv* 率直地; **quite ~, I think you are making a big mistake** 说实话，我认为你在犯大错误

candidness /ˈkændɪdnɪs/ *n* [u] 率直; **with perfect ~** 十分坦率地

candied /ˈkændɪd/ *adj* 糖制的; **~ fruits** 果脯

candle /ˈkændl/ *n* 蜡烛; **to burn the ~ at both ends** fig 起早贪黑地劳作; **it** *or* **the game is not worth the ~** fig 这件事不值得做; **to be unable to hold a ~ to sb.** fig 远远比不上某人

candle: ~ holder *n* 烛台; **~light** *n* [u] 烛光; **to work by ~light** 秉烛工作; **a ~light dinner** 烛光晚餐

candlelit dinner /ˌkændllɪt ˈdɪnə(r)/ *n* 烛光晚餐

candle: ~power *n* 旧烛光 [发光强度单位]; **~stick** *n* 烛台; **~ wax** *n* [u] 烛蜡; **~wick** *n* [u] 烛芯纱

can-do *adj* colloq 积极进取的 ‹*attitude, approach*›

candour Brit, **candor** Amer /ˈkændə(r)/ *n* [u] = **candidness**

C&W *abbr* = **country and western**

candy /ˈkændi/
A *n* [u and c] Amer 糖果; **a (piece of) ~** 一颗糖; **it's like taking ~ from a baby** 这等于从娃娃手里抢糖吃 [指欺骗某人很容易]
B *vt* 把…制成蜜饯

candy: ~-ass *n* Amer colloq 胆小鬼; **~-assed** *adj* Amer colloq 胆小的; **~ bar** *n* Amer 巧克力条; **~ floss** *n* [u] Brit 棉花糖; **~ store** *n* Amer 糖果店; **~ striped** *adj* 有条纹的 ‹*fabric, dress*›

cane /keɪn/
A *n* **1** [c] (stem of sugar, bamboo) 茎 **2** [u] (rattan) 藤条; (bamboo) 竹竿; (sugar cane) 甘蔗 **3** [c] (of raspberry, blackberry) 主茎 **4** [c] (for walking) 手杖; (for riding) 马鞭 **5** [u and c] Brit (for punishment) 笞条; **to get the ~** 遭受鞭笞; **to give sb. the ~** 鞭笞某人
B *vt* **1** Brit (punish) 用笞条打 **2** colloq (defeat) 打败

cane: ~brake *n* Amer (of sugar cane) 甘蔗丛; (of bamboo) 竹丛; (of rattan) 藤丛; **~ sugar** *n* [u] 蔗糖

canine /ˈkeɪnaɪn/
A *adj* **1** (of a dog) 犬的; (resembling a dog) 似犬的 **2** Dent 犬齿的
B *n* **1** (dog specifically) 犬; (member of canine species) 犬科动物 **2** Dent 犬齿

caning /ˈkeɪnɪŋ/ *n* Brit **1** [u and c] (punishment) 鞭笞 **2** [c] colloq (defeat) 大败; **to give sb. a ~** 使某人遭受惨败; **to get a ~** 惨败

canister /ˈkænɪstə(r)/ *n* **1** (for storage) 小罐 **2** (of gas) 霰弹筒; **a ~ of tear gas** 催泪弹

canker /ˈkæŋkə(r)/ *n* **1** [u] Bot 溃疡病 **2** [u] Med 溃疡; (of horses) 马蹄疮 **3** [c] fig (malign influence) 祸患

cannabis /ˈkænəbɪs/ *n* [u] 大麻

cannabis resin *n* [u] 大麻脂

canned /kænd/ *adj* **1** (preserved) 罐装的 ‹*food, soup*› **2** colloq (pre-recorded) 预录的 ‹*music, laughter*› **3** colloq (drunk) 喝醉了的

cannelloni /ˌkænɪˈləʊni/
A *npl* 面卷
B *n* [u and c] 塞馅粗通心粉

cannery /ˈkænəri/ *n* 罐头食品厂

cannibal /ˈkænɪbl/ *n* (person) 食人肉者; (animal) 同类相食的动物

cannibalism /ˈkænɪbəlɪzəm/ *n* [u] 同类相食

cannibalization /ˌkænɪbəlaɪˈzeɪʃn, Amer -lɪˈz-/ *n* [u] **1** (using for spare parts) [机器零部件的] 拆用 **2** Comm 同类相残 [有竞争力产品的推出造成的同类产品销售量下降]

cannibalize /ˈkænɪbəlaɪz/ *vt* **1** (use for spare parts) 拆用…的零部件 ‹*machine, vehicle*›; **to ~ a vehicle** 拆取一辆车的可用零件 **2** Comm [因推出同类产品而] 减少…的销量 ‹*product*›

canning /ˈkænɪŋ/ *n* [u] 罐头食品制造

canning factory *n* 罐头食品厂

cannon /ˈkænən/
A *n* (*pl* **~** *or* **~s**) 大炮
B *vi* 相撞; **to ~ into** *or* **against sth./sb.** 与某物/某人相撞

cannon: ~ball *n* 炮弹; **~ fodder** *n* [u] 炮灰

cannot /ˈkænɒt/ *negative pres* ▸**can¹**

canny /ˈkæni/ *adj* 精明谨慎的 ‹*person, answer, bargain*›

canoe /kəˈnuː/
A *n* 独木舟; **to paddle one's own ~** fig 自力更生
B *vi* 划独木舟

canoeing /kəˈnuːɪŋ/ ▸**p. 307** *n* [u] (activity) 划独木舟; (sporting event) 皮划艇运动; **to go ~** 去划独木舟

canoeist /kəˈnuːɪst/ *n* **1** (gen) 划独木舟的人 **2** Sport 皮划艇运动员

canon¹ /ˈkænən/ *n* **1** (rule) 准则; **to establish/lay down a ~** 制定准则 **2** Relig (law) 教规 **3** Literat (complete works) 真作全集 **4** Mus 卡农曲

canon² *n* Relig (priest) 大教堂教士

canonical /kəˈnɒnɪkl/
A *adj* **1** (authoritative) 权威性的 ‹*rule, opinion, principle*› **2** Mus 卡农曲的 **3** Relig (of a cathedral chapter) 大教堂全体教士的; (of a member of it) 大教堂教士的
B **canonicals** *npl* 礼服

canonical form *n* 基本形式

canonization /ˌkænənaɪˈzeɪʃn, Amer -nɪˈz-/ *n* 封圣

canonize /ˈkænənaɪz/ *vt* 封…为圣 ‹*martyr, missionary*›

canoodle /kəˈnuːdl/ *vi* colloq 卿卿我我

can-opener *n* 开罐器

canopy /ˈkænəpi/ *n* **1** (cloth covering) 罩; (for throne, altar, procession) 华盖; **a bed ~** 床罩 **2** Archit 天棚 **3** (of parachute) 伞衣 **4** (of cockpit) 座舱盖 **5** (of forest) 树冠层

cant¹ /kænt/ *n* [u] **1** (false words) 虚伪言辞 **2** (of prisoners, thieves) 黑话

cant²
A *n* (sloping surface) 斜面

B *vt* 使…倾斜
C *vi* «*surface, roof, floor*» 倾斜

can't /kɑ:nt/ colloq **= cannot ▸can¹**

cantaloupe /ˈkæntəlu:p/ *n* **~ (melon)** 罗马甜瓜

cantankerous /kænˈtæŋkərəs/ *adj* 脾气坏的

cantata /kænˈtɑ:tə/ *n* 康塔塔 [多乐章的大型声乐套曲]

canteen /kænˈti:n/ *n* **1** Brit (dining room) 食堂 **2** (flask) 水壶 **3** Brit (of cutlery) 餐具柜; **a ~ of silver** 银餐具柜

canter /ˈkæntə(r)/
A *vi* «*horse*» 慢跑; «*rider*» 策马慢跑
B *vt* 使…慢跑 ‹*horse*›
C *n* 慢跑; **to go at a ~** 慢跑; **to go for a ~** 去骑马; **to win at** *or* **in a ~** fig 轻易取胜

cantilever /ˈkæntɪli:və(r)/ *n* 悬臂

cantilever: **~ beam** *n* 悬臂梁; **~ brake** *n* 悬臂式刹车器; **~ bridge** *n* 悬臂桥

cantilevered /ˈkæntɪli:vəd/ *adj* 悬臂支撑的 ‹*roof, bridge, balcony*›

canto /ˈkæntəʊ/ *n* 诗章

Canton /kænˈtɒn/ *pr n* 广州

canton /ˈkæntɒn/ *n* **1** (of country) 行政区 **2** (in Switzerland) 州

Cantonese /ˌkæntəˈni:z/ **▸p. 503, p. 426**
A *adj* (of Canton) 广州的; (of the people) 广州人的; (of the language) 粤语的
B *n* **1** [c] (person) 广州人 **2** [u] (language) 粤语

Cantopop /ˈkæntəʊpɒp/ *n* [u] 粤语流行音乐

canvas /ˈkænvəs/ *n* **1** [u] (cloth) 帆布; **under ~** (in a tent) 在帐篷里; (under sail) 扬着帆 **2** [u and c] (for art) 油画布 **3** [c] (oil painting) 油画 **4** [u] (in boxing) **the ~** 地板; **to put one's opponent on the ~** 将对手击倒在地

canvass /ˈkænvəs/
A *vt* **1** Pol 向…拉选票 ‹*electorate*›; **to ~ voters for their votes** 向选民拉选票; **to ~ an area for** *or* **on behalf of sb./sth.** 为某人/某组织在一个地区拉选票 **2** (in survey) 向…征求意见 ‹*member, shareholder*›; 征求 ‹*view, opinion*› **3** Comm 向…兜售 ‹*people, customer*›; 在…兜售 ‹*district*›; 兜售 ‹*product*›; **to ~ people/an area for** *or* **to get custom** 向人们/在一个地区兜售产品
B *vi* **1** Pol 拉选票; **to ~ for sb./a party** 为某人/某党派拉选票 **2** Comm 兜售; **to ~ for a product/service** 兜售产品/服务
C *n* **1** (for votes) 拉选票 **2** (of opinion) 征求 **3** Comm 兜售

canvasser /ˈkænvəsə(r)/ *n* **1** Pol 拉选票者 **2** Comm 推销员

canvassing /ˈkænvəsɪŋ/ *n* [u] **1** Pol 拉选票 **2** Comm 兜售 **3** (of opinion) 征求

canyon /ˈkænjən/ *n* 峡谷

canyoning /ˈkænjənɪŋ/ **▸p. 307** *n* [u] 溪降运动

CAP *abbr* **= Common Agricultural Policy**

cap /kæp/
A *n* **1** (hat) 便帽 **2** (part of uniform) 制服帽; **~ and gown** [包括方顶帽和长袍的] 学位服; **to go/come to sb. ~ in hand** (asking for a favour) 谦恭地去/来求某人帮忙; (apologizing) 谦恭地向某人道歉; **to put one's thinking ~ on** 动脑筋 **3** (lid) 盖子; **the ~ of a pen** 笔帽; **plastic bottle ~s** 塑料瓶盖 **4** Sport (cap itself) 队员帽 [作为入选国家队或其他运动队的标志]; (player) 入选运动员; **he's got his Scottish ~** 他入选了苏格兰代表队; **he's an England ~** 他是英格兰队队员 **5** (upper limit) 上限; **wage ~** 工资上限 **6** (for toy gun) 火药帽 **7** Dent 齿冠 **8** (contraceptive) 子宫帽 **9** (of mushroom) 菌盖
B *vt* (*pres p etc.* **-pp-**) **1** (cover) 覆盖; **cloud-~ped mountains** 云雾笼罩的群山 **2** Brit Sport 授予…队员帽; **to be ~ped for Wales** 入选威尔士队 **3** Dent 给…镶上齿冠 **4** (outdo) 胜过; **to ~ a tale** 讲一个更好的故事; **to ~ it all** 更有甚者; **to ~ it all, it cost less than £10 a head** 更让人高兴的是, 每人才花了不到 10 英镑 **5** (impose limit on) 对…封顶 ‹*rates, tax, spending*›

capability /ˌkeɪpəˈbɪləti/ *n* **1** [u] (capacity) 能力; (aptitude) 才能; **the ~ of doing** *or* **to do sth.** 做某事的能力; **within/outside my capabilities** 在我的能力范围之内/外; **to have ~ as a cricketer** 具有成为板球手的素质 **2** [u] Mil (potential strength) 军事力量; **nuclear ~** 核能力 **3** [c] (of machine, system) 性能; **to have a ~ for doing sth.** 具有做某事的功能

capable /ˈkeɪpəbl/ *adj* **1** (competent) 能干的; **she's such a ~ woman** 她是个很能干的女性; **a ~ driver** 熟练的驾驶员; **to be in sb.'s ~ hands** 由能干的某人掌管 **2** **to be ~ of doing sth.** (able to do sth.) 有能力做某事 **3** (having potential to) 有…可能的; **to be ~ of a better result** 有可能取得更好的结果; **she's so angry, she's ~ of murder** 她气得想杀人 **4** (be in danger of) 有…危险的; **a bomb ~ of exploding at any moment** 随时会爆炸的炸弹

capably /ˈkeɪpəbli/ *adv* (in a capable manner) 能干地; (with skill) 熟练地

capacious /kəˈpeɪʃəs/ *adj* 容量大的 ‹*car, boot*›; 宽敞的 ‹*room*›; **a coat with ~ pockets** 有大口袋的外套

capacitance /kəˈpæsɪtəns/ *n* [u] 电容

capacitor /kəˈpæsɪtə(r)/ *n* 电容器

capacity /kəˈpæsəti/
A *n* **1** [u and c] (ability to hold) 容纳的能力; **a bucket with a ~ of 4 gallons** 一只容量为 4 加仑的桶; **the bus has a seating ~ of 72** 这辆公共汽车有 72 个座位; **to double the ~ of British roads** 使英国道路的运力翻一番; **the theatre was full to ~** 剧院里座无虚席 **2** [u and c] (ability to produce) 产能; **the production line has a ~ of 300 cars a week** 这条生产线一周能生产 300 辆汽车; **the factory was at full ~** 这家工厂已满负荷生产; **the plant is stretched to ~** 这家工厂正开足马力生产 **3** [u and c] (mental ability) 能力; **intellectual ~** 智力; **a ~ for sth./for doing sth./to do sth.** 做某事的能力; **she has a great ~ for laughter** 她特别爱笑; **winning this race is well within your ~** 赢得这场比赛对你而言易如反掌 **4** [c] (role) 职位; **in a private ~** 以私人身份; **she was employed in the ~ of manager** 她被聘为经理; **in one's ~ as sth.** 以…的身份 ‹*manager, doctor*› **5** [u and c] Aut (of a vehicle's engine) 功率 **6** [u and c] Comput (of disk, storage system) 存储量
B *modif* 达到最大限度的; **~ attendance was recorded at the AGM** 本次年会座无虚席

capacity: **~ audience** *n + v sing or pl* 满座; **~ crowd** *n + v sing or pl* 满座; **stadiums are expecting ~ crowds** 各体育场馆将会爆满

cape¹ /keɪp/ *n* (garment) 披肩; **a waterproof ~** 雨披; **a short black ~** 黑色短披肩

cape² *n* Geog 海角

Cape: **~ Coloured** *n* 开普省有色人; **~ Horn** *pr n* 合恩角; **~ of Good Hope** *pr n* 好望角

caper¹ /ˈkeɪpə(r)/
A *n* **1** (playful leap) 雀跃; **to cut a ~** 蹦蹦跳跳 **2** colloq (dishonest scheme) 不法行为; **what's your little ~?** 你搞什么名堂? **3** (escapade) 胡闹; **what a ~!** colloq 简直一团糟!
B *vi* 雀跃

caper² *n* **1** Bot 刺山柑 **2** Culin 腌刺山柑

Cape Verde Islands /keɪp ˈvɜ:d ˌaɪləndz/ *pr npl* **the ~** 佛得角 (群岛)

capful /ˈkæpfʊl/ *n* 一盖子

cap gun *n* 玩具火药枪

capillary /kəˈpɪləri, Amer ˈkæ-/
A *n* **1** Anat 毛细血管 **2** (tube) **~ (tube)** 毛细管
B *adj attrib* **1** Anat 毛细血管的 ‹*blood, system*› **2** Phys 毛细的 ‹*pressure*›

capillary action *n* [u] 毛细作用

capital¹ /ˈkæpɪtl/
A *n* **1** [c] (letter) 大写字母; **with a ~ (A, B** *etc.***)** fig 确确实实; **she's crazy with a ~ C** 她确实发疯了 **2** [c] (of country) 首都; (of state) 首府; (of province) 省会 **3** [c] (leader) 重要都市; **the fashion ~ of the world** 世界时装之都 **4** [u and c] (money, wealth) 资本; **a starting ~ of £50,000** 5 万英镑的启动资金 **5** [u] (capitalist interests) 资方; **~ and labour** 劳资双方 **6** [u] (profit, advantage) 好处; **to make ~ out of sth.** 利用某事物谋私利; **to make political ~ out of sth.** 从某事物中捞取政治资本
B *adj* **1** Jur 可处死刑的; **a ~ crime** *or* **offence** 死罪; **to carry a ~ sentence** 可判处死刑 **2** (essential) 主要的; **to be of ~ importance** 至关重要

capital² *n* Archit 柱顶

capital: **~ allowances** *npl* 资本免税额; **~ assets** *npl* 资本资产; **~ budget** *n* 资本预算; **~ charges** *npl* 资本费用; **~ city** *n* 首都; **~ cost** *n* 资本成本; **~ expenditure** *n* 资本支出; **~ gain** *n* 资本收益; **~ gains tax** *n* 资本收益税; **~ goods** *npl* 资本货物; **~-intensive** *adj* 资本密集的; **~ investment** *n* **1** [u] (process) 基建投资; **2** [c] (item) 基建投资项目

capitalism /ˈkæpɪtəlɪzəm/ *n* [u] 资本主义

capitalist /ˈkæpɪtəlɪst/
A *n* **1** (investor) 资本家 **2** (supporter of capitalism) 资本主义者
B *adj* **1** (having capital) 拥有资本的; **the ~ class** 资产阶级 **2** (supporting capitalism) 资本主义的

capitalistic /ˌkæpɪtəˈlɪstɪk/ *adj* **= capitalist B2**

capitalization /ˌkæpɪtəlaɪˈzeɪʃn, Amer -lɪˈz-/ *n* **1** Ling 字母大写 **2** (par value) 资本总额 **3** (market value) 市值

capitalize /ˈkæpɪtəlaɪz/
A *vt* **1** Ling 用大写字母写 **2** Fin (convert into capital) 使资本化; (realize value of) 使变现
B *vi* **to ~ on sth.** 利用某事物

capital: **~ market** *n* 资本市场; **~ outlay** *n* **= ~ expenditure**; **~ punishment** *n* [u] 死刑; **~ reserves** *npl* 资本储备; **~ spending** *n* [u] 资本支出; **~ structure** *n* 资本结构; **~ sum** *n* esp Insur [付给被保险人的] 一次给付金

capitation /ˌkæpɪˈteɪʃn/
A *n* 按人付费
B *modif* 按人计算的 ‹*allowance, fee*›

Capitol /ˈkæpɪtl/
A *pr n* **the ~** 国会大厦
B **capitol** *n* Amer 州议会大厦

Capitol Hill *pr n* **1** (district) 国会山 **2** (US congress) 国会

capitulate /kəˈpɪtʃʊleɪt/ *vi* 投降; **to ~ to sb./sth.** 向某人/某事物投降; **to ~ to sb.'s pressure** 屈服于某人的压力

capitulation /kəˌpɪtʃʊˈleɪʃn/ *n* 投降

caplet, Caplet® /ˈkæplɪt/ *n* 囊片

capo /ˈkæpəʊ/ *n* 弦枕

capon /ˈkeɪpən, -pɒn/ *n* 阉鸡

cappuccino /ˌkæpʊˈtʃi:nəʊ/ *n* 卡布其诺咖啡

caprice /kəˈpri:s/ *n* **1** [c] (sudden change) 变化无常; **the ~s of the weather** 天气的变幻莫测 **2** [c] (whim) 突发奇想; **buying this scarf was just a ~ of mine** 买下这条围巾完全出于我一时心血来潮 **3** [u] (tendency to change one's mind) 多变的倾向; **a creature of ~** 任性的人 **4** [c] Mus 随想曲

capricious /kəˈprɪʃəs/ *adj* **1** (changeable) 变化无常的 ‹*weather, destiny*›; 任性的 ‹*person*› **2** (unpredictable) 突发奇想的 ‹*whim, fancy*›; **it was a wholly ~ decision** 这完全是个心血来潮的决定

capriciously /kəˈprɪʃəsli/ *adv* ‹*act, behave*› 变化无常地; ‹*decide*› 突发奇想地

Capricorn /ˈkæprɪkɔːn/ *n* **1** [u] Astron 摩羯（星）座 **2** [u] Astrol (sign) 摩羯宫 [黄道第十宫] **3** [c] Astrol (person) 属摩羯（星）座的人 **4** Geog ▸**tropic A**

caps /kæps/ *abbr* = **capital letters** 大写字母

capsicum /ˈkæpsɪkəm/ *n* **1** (plant) 辣椒 **2** (fruit) 辣椒荚

capsize /kæpˈsaɪz, Amer ˈkæpsaɪz/
A *vi* «*vessel*» 倾覆
B *vt* 使…倾覆 ‹*vessel*›

caps lock *n* 大写锁定键

capstan /ˈkæpstən/ *n* **1** Naut 绞盘 **2** Tech [录音机的] 主动轮

capsule /ˈkæpsjuːl, Amer ˈkæpsl/ *n* **1** Med 胶囊 **2** Aerosp 航天舱 **3** (covering of bottle cork) 瓶封

Capt *abbr* = **captain A**

captain /ˈkæptɪn/
A *n* **1** Naut 船长; Aviat 机长 **2** Mil (in British army) 陆军上尉; (in US and Canadian air forces) 空军上尉 **3** (of team) 队长
B *vt* **1** 担任…的船长 ‹*ship*› **2** 担任…的队长 ‹*team*›

captaincy /ˈkæptɪnsi/ *n* **1** Mil 上尉职位; Naut 船长职位 **2** Sport (position) 队长职位; (period) 队长任期

captain of industry *n* (*pl* **captains of industry**) 实业巨头

caption /ˈkæpʃn/
A *n* **1** (title) 标题; (explanation) 说明文字 **2** (subtitle) 字幕
B *vt* **1** (provide with title) 给…加标题; (provide with explanation) 给…加说明文字 **2** (provide with subtitle) 为…配字幕

captious /ˈkæpʃəs/ *adj* formal 吹毛求疵的 ‹*remark, comment*›

captivate /ˈkæptɪveɪt/ *vt* 使入迷; **he was ~d by her** 他被她迷住了

captivating /ˈkæptɪveɪtɪŋ/ *adj* 迷人的 ‹*person*›; 动人的 ‹*story*›; 可爱的 ‹*child*›

captive /ˈkæptɪv/
A *n* (person) 俘虏; (animal) 捕获物
B *adj* **1** (confined) 被俘虏的 ‹*person*›; 被关起来的 ‹*animal*›; **~ birds in cages** 笼中鸟; **to take sb. ~** 俘虏某人; **to hold sb. ~** 关押某人 **2** (controlled) 受控制的; **a ~ market** 垄断市场; **a ~ audience** (having no choice) 别无选择的听众; (captivated) 入迷的听众

captivity /kæpˈtɪvəti/ *n* 囚禁; **to be held** *or* **kept in ~** 被囚禁; **animals in ~** 被关起来的动物

captor /ˈkæptə(r)/ *n* (of person) 俘获他人者; (of animal) 捕获猎物者

capture /ˈkæptʃə(r)/
A *vt* **1** (take by force) 俘获 ‹*person*›; 捕获 ‹*animal*›; 占领 ‹*place*›; **to ~ the market** 占有市场 **2** (in game, contest) 吃 ‹*chess piece*›; 夺取 ‹*fortress*› **3** fig (record) 刻画; **to ~ sth. on film** 用胶片拍下某物; **to ~ a/sb.'s likeness** 画像/给某人画像
B *n* (of person) 俘获; (of animal) 捕获; (of place) 占领

car /kɑː(r)/ *n* **1** Aut 汽车 **2** Rail 车厢 **3** (of lift) 轿厢; (of cable car) 缆车车厢; (of hot-air balloon) 吊舱

Caracas /kəˈrækəs/ *pr n* 加拉加斯

car accident *n* 交通事故

carafe /kəˈræf/ *n* **1** (vessel) 卡拉夫瓶 [盛酒或水的喇叭形玻璃瓶] **2** (quantity) 一卡拉夫瓶

car: ~ alarm *n* 汽车警报器; **~ allowance** *n* 汽车补贴

caramel /ˈkærəmel/ *n* **1** [u] (burnt sugar) 焦糖 **2** [c] (toffee) 卡拉梅尔糖

caramelize /ˈkærəməlaɪz/
A *vt* 使变成焦糖
B *vi* 变成焦糖

carapace /ˈkærəpeɪs/ *n* [龟、蟹等的] 背甲

carat /ˈkærət/ *n* **1** (measure of purity) 开; **a necklace in 24 ~ gold** 24 开的金项链 **2** (unit of weight) 克拉

caravan /ˈkærəvæn/ *n* **1** Brit (for touring, holidays) 活动房车 **2** (horse-drawn) 大篷车 **3** (group of traders or travellers) 沙漠旅行队

caravanette /ˌkærəvæˈnet/ *n* Brit 旅游房车

caravanner /ˈkærəvænə(r)/ *n* Brit 乘活动房车度假者

caravanning /ˈkærəvænɪŋ/ *n* [u] Brit 乘活动房车度假

caravan site *n* Brit 活动房车停车场

caraway /ˈkærəweɪ/ *n* [u] **1** (seeds) 葛缕子籽 **2** (plant) 葛缕子

car badge *n* **1** Aut 汽车车标 **2** Admin 许可标牌; **~ badges for disabled parking** 残疾人停车许可标牌

carbine /ˈkɑːbaɪn/ *n* 卡宾枪

carbohydrate /ˌkɑːbəˈhaɪdreɪt/ *n* **1** (compound) 碳水化合物 **2** (food containing carbohydrates) 淀粉质食物

carbolic /kɑːˈbɒlɪk/**: ~ acid** *n* [u] 石炭酸; **~ soap** *n* [u] 石炭酸皂

car bomb *n* 汽车炸弹

carbon /ˈkɑːbən/ *n* [u] 碳

carbonate /ˈkɑːbəneɪt/
A *n* (salt) 碳酸盐; (ester) 碳酸酯
B *vt* 给…充二氧化碳; **a bottle of ~d water** 一瓶汽水

carbonation /ˌkɑːbəˈneɪʃn/ *n* [u] 充二氧化碳

carbon: ~ brakes *npl* 碳纤维刹车; **~ capture and storage** *n* [u] 碳捕获与存储; **~ copy** *n* **1** Print 复写本; **2** fig (person) 一模一样的人; (thing) 一模一样的事物; **~ credits** *npl* 碳信用额; **~ cycle** *n* 碳循环; **~-date** *vt* 用碳定年法测定…的年代; **~ dating** *n* [u] 碳定年法; **~ dioxide** *n* [u] 二氧化碳; **~ emissions** *npl* 碳排放; **~ fibre** *n* 碳纤维; **~ filter** *n* 活性碳过滤器; **~ fixation** *n* [u] 碳固定; **~ footprint** *n* 碳足迹 [指个人或团体活动的碳排放量]

carbonic acid /kɑːˌbɒnɪk ˈæsɪd/ *n* [u] 碳酸

carboniferous /ˌkɑːbəˈnɪfərəs/
A *adj* **1** (carbon-producing) 产碳的 **2** **Carboniferous** (of the period) 石炭纪的; (of the rock system) 石炭系的
B *n* **the C~** (period) 石炭纪; (rock system) 石炭系

carbonize /ˈkɑːbənaɪz/ *vt* 使碳化

carbon: ~ monoxide *n* [u] 一氧化碳; **~-neutral** *adj* 碳中性的 ‹*energy, process*›; **~ offsetting** *n* [u] 碳抵消; **~ paper** *n* [u] 复写纸; **~ sink** *n* 碳汇; **~ steel** *n* [u] 碳素钢; **~ tax** *n* 碳税; **~ tetrachloride** /ˌkɑːbən tetrəˈklɔːraɪd/ *n* [u] 四氯化碳; **~ trading** *n* [u] 碳交易

car boot sale *n* Brit 行李箱旧货销售

carborundum /ˌkɑːbəˈrʌndəm/ *n* [u] 金刚砂

carboy /ˈkɑːbɔɪ/ *n* 细颈大玻璃瓶

carbuncle /ˈkɑːbʌŋkl/ *n* **1** Med 痈 **2** (gem) 红玉

carburation /ˌkɑːbjʊˈreɪʃn/ *n* [u] 燃料汽化

carburettor /ˌkɑːbəˈretə(r)/ Brit, **carburetor** /ˈkɑːrbəreɪtər/ Amer *n* 汽化器

carcass /ˈkɑːkəs/ *n* **1** (of animal) 胴体 **2** pej (of human) (dead) 尸体; (alive) 身体; **move your ~** hum 挪一挪你的身子 **3** (of building, ship, etc.) 残骸

car chase *n* 汽车追逐

carcinogen /kɑːˈsɪnədʒən/ *n* 致癌物

carcinogenic /ˌkɑːsɪnəˈdʒenɪk/ *adj* 致癌的

carcinoma /ˌkɑːsɪˈnəʊmə/ *n* 癌

card /kɑːd/ *n* **1** [u] (material) 卡片纸 **2** [c] (postcard) 明信片; (scorecard) 记分卡; (for filing) 档案卡片; (for indexing) 索引卡片; **to get** *or* **be given one's ~s** fig 被解雇 **3** ▸**p. 307** [c] Games 纸牌; **to play ~s** 打牌; **a pack of ~s** 一副纸牌; **sb.'s last ~** fig 某人的最后一招; **sb.'s strongest ~** fig 某人的王牌; **to have a ~ up one's sleeve** fig 留有一手; **on the ~s** Brit, **in the ~s** Amer 很可能的; **to have (all the) ~s stacked in one's favour/against one** fig 处于有利/不利的地位; **to hold all the ~s** fig 掌握全局; **to lay** *or* **put one's ~s on the table** fig 摊牌; **to play one's best/last ~** fig 打出王牌/使出最后一招; **to play one's ~s right** fig 办事高明; **to play the ... ~** fig 使出…的一招; **to play the law and order ~** 打出法治这张牌 **4** [c] (for greetings) 贺卡; (for condolences) 慰问卡; **a Christmas/birthday ~** 圣诞/生日贺卡 **5** [c] (for business) 名片 **6** [c] Horse racing 赛事日程表 **7** [c] (for membership) 会员证 **8** [c] (for payment) (credit card) 信用卡; (debit card) 借记卡 **9** [c] Comput 扩展卡 **10** [c] Brit dated (witty person) 引人发笑的人; (eccentric person) 怪人

cardamom, cardamum /ˈkɑːdəməm/ *n* [u] **1** (seeds) 豆蔻干籽 **2** (plant) 豆蔻

cardboard /ˈkɑːdbɔːd/
A *n* 硬纸板
B *modif* fig 呆板的 ‹*character*›; 硬纸板制的; **a ~ box** 硬纸箱

cardboard: ~ city *n* 纸板街区 [为无家可归者提供用纸板箱搭建的临时住所的城市街区]; **~ cut-out** *n* **1** (shape) 硬纸板图样; **2** fig (person) 呆板的人

card: ~-carrying *adj attrib* 持证的; **a ~-carrying member** 正式会员; **~ catalogue** *n* 卡片目录; **~ file** *n* = **card index**; **~ game** *n* 纸牌戏; **~holder** *n* 持卡人

car deck *n* [渡轮上的] 汽车甲板

cardiac /ˈkɑːdɪæk/ *adj* (relating to the heart) 心脏的; (relating to heart disease) 心脏病的

cardiac: ~ arrest *n* [u and c] 心搏停止; **~ failure** *n* [u and c] = **heart failure**

cardie /ˈkɑːdi/ *n* Brit colloq = **cardigan**

Cardiff /ˈkɑːdɪf/ *pr n* 加的夫

cardigan /ˈkɑːdɪgən/ *n* 开襟毛衣

cardinal /ˈkɑːdɪnl/
A *n* **1** Relig 红衣主教 **2** (colour) **~ (red)** 鲜红
B *adj attrib* **of ~ importance** 极其重要的

cardinal: ~ number *n* 基数; **~ point** *n* 方位基点; **~ virtue** *n* 基本德性 [指传统定义的四德——审慎、公正、节制、坚毅——中的任何一种，现常指任何重要的道德品质]

card index *n* 卡片索引

cardiogram /ˈkɑːdɪəʊgræm/ *n* 心电图

cardiograph /ˈkɑːdɪəʊgrɑːf, Amer -græf/ *n* 心电图仪

cardiography /ˌkɑːdɪˈɒgrəfi/ *n* [u] 心动描记法

cardiologist /ˌkɑːdɪˈɒlədʒɪst/ ▸**p. 409** *n* (specialist) 心脏病学家; (doctor) 心脏病医生

cardiology /ˌkɑːdɪˈɒlədʒi/ *n* [u] 心脏病学

cardiovascular /ˌkɑːdɪəʊˈvæskjʊlə(r)/ *adj* 心血管的

card: ~ key *n* 钥匙卡; **~phone** *n* 磁卡电话; **~ reader** *n* **1** (for memory card) 读卡器; **2** (for plastic card) 刷卡机

car driver *n* 汽车司机

card: ~ sharp, ~ sharper *ns* 赌牌作弊的人; **~ swipe** *n* **1** (reader) 刷卡机; **2** (act) 刷卡; **~ table** *n* 牌桌; **~ trick** *n* 纸牌戏法; **~ vote** *n* Brit 凭卡投票法 [投票者代表其组织的所有成员投票]

cardy /ˈkɑːdi/ *n* Brit colloq = **cardigan**

care /keə(r)/
A *n* **1** [u] (attention) 小心; **take ~!** (be careful) 当心！; (expression of farewell) 保重！; **you**

should take more ~ over your work 你应该更加用心工作; **~ should be taken to avoid spelling mistakes** 注意避免拼写错误; **handle with ~** Post 小心轻放 **2** [u] (looking after person, animal) 照顾; **to take ~ of sb./sth.** 照顾某人/某动物; **in sb.'s ~, in the ~ of sb.** 由某人照料; **a mother's ~ for her children** 母亲对孩子的呵护; **to take ~ of oneself** (attend to oneself) 照顾自己; (cope) 自己应付; (defend oneself) 保护自己; **you should take more ~ of yourself** 你自己要多当心; **~ of ...** Post 由…转交 [用于信件、包裹等上, 常简写为c/o] **3** [u] (maintenance) (of house, plants) 照管; (of car, clothes) 保养 **4** [u] Med, Psych 护理; **medical ~** 医疗; **to be in/under the ~ of sb.** 接受某人的治疗 **5** [u] Brit (protective custody) 收养; **to be in ~** 由收养所收养; **to take** *or* **put sb. into ~** «*social worker, parent, guardian*» 把…送入收养所 ‹*child*› **6** [u] **to take ~ of sth.** (deal with) 处理某事; **I've just got one or two things to take ~ of** 我手头刚好有一两件事情要处理; **the bill has been taken ~ of** 账单已经付过了; **Tom will take ~ of the spider** 汤姆会收拾这只蜘蛛的 **7** [u and c] (feeling of worry) 忧虑; (cause of worry) 令人忧虑的事; **he was full of ~** 他忧心忡忡; **not to have a ~ in the world** 无忧无虑

B *vt* formal 想要; **to ~ to do sth.** 想要做某事; **would you ~ to sit down?** 要不要坐下?; **I've been working here for more years than I ~ to remember** 我一直在这儿工作, 都记不清有多少个年头了; **he has a good brain, when he ~s to use it** hum 他愿意动脑子的时候, 脑子倒很灵光

C *vi* **1** (love) 喜欢; **to ~ about** *or* **for sb.** 在乎某人; **show him that you ~** 向他表明你在乎他; **I didn't know you ~d!** 才发现你喜欢过我! **2** (feel concern) 关心; **what do you want for lunch? — I don't ~** 你午饭想吃什么?——随便; **he didn't seem to ~ about failing the exam** 他好像并不在乎考试不及格; **sb. couldn't ~ less (about sth.)** 某人(对某事物)根本不在乎; **he couldn't ~ less who wins** 他毫不在乎谁会赢; **for all sb. ~s** 某人根本不在乎; **she can go and sleep in the park, for all I ~** 她可以去公园里睡觉, 我才不管呢; **sb. doesn't ~ a damn/tuppence/two hoots** *etc.* colloq 某人根本就不在乎; **as if I/he ~d!** 好像我/他很在乎似的!

care assistant, care attendant ▸**p. 409** *ns* Brit **= care worker**

career /kə'rɪə(r)/
A *n* **1** (occupation) 职业; **a ~ as a journalist** 记者职业; **to abandon one's/a ~** 放弃自己的/一项事业; **to follow a ~** 从事一种职业 **2** (progress) 生涯; **a political/musical ~** 政治/音乐生涯
B *vi* 猛冲; **to ~ off the road** 冲出道路

career: ~ break *n* 离职期; **~ change** *n* 职业改换; **~ development** *n* [u] 职业发展; **~ girl** *n* 职场女郎

careerism /kə'rɪərɪzəm/ *n* [u] 事业至上

careerist /kə'rɪərɪst/ *n* 事业狂

career: ~ ladder *n* 职业阶梯; **~ move** *n* [影响职业发展的] 职业变动; **~ prospects** *npl* 职业前景; **~s adviser** ▸**p. 409** *n* 就业顾问; **~s guidance** *n* [u] 就业指导; **~s library** *n* 就业信息资料室; **~s master** ▸**p. 409** *n* Brit 男就业指导员; **~s mistress** ▸**p. 409** *n* Brit 女就业指导员; **~s office** *n* 就业指导办公室; **~s officer** *n* Brit **= ~s adviser**; **~s service** *n* Brit 就业指导服务; **~s teacher** ▸**p. 409** *n* 就业指导教师; **~ structure** *n* 职位结构; **~ woman** *n* 职业女性

care: ~ facility *n* (giving health care) 护理中心; (giving child care) 托儿所; **~free** *adj* 无忧无虑的

careful /'keəfl/ *adj* **1** (prudent) 谨慎的; (gentle) 小心的; **to be ~ to do** *or* **about doing sth.** 小心谨慎地做某事; **~ of that nail!** 当心那枚钉子!; **be ~ with that knife!** 用那把刀时要小心!; **these glasses require ~ handling** 这些玻璃杯要小心轻放; **~ driving** 谨慎的驾驶; **you can't be too ~!** 你越小心越好! **2** (meticulous) 一丝不苟的; **~ preparations** 精心的准备; **his work is not ~ enough** 他的工作还不够细致 **3** *pred* (thrifty) 节俭的; **to be ~ with money** 花钱精打细算

carefully /'keəfəli/ *adv* **1** (cautiously) 小心地; (thoughtfully) 谨慎地 ‹*reply, write, say*›; **go ~!** 慢走!; **go ~: he's easily upset** 当心点, 他很容易生气 **2** (meticulously) 一丝不苟地; **listen/think ~!** 仔细听/思考!; **the temperature is ~ controlled** 温度得到精确控制

care: ~giver *n* **= carer**; **~ home** *n* (for children) 保育院; (for the elderly) 养老院; (for the sick, disabled) 护理院; **~ label** *n* "使用须知"标签

careless /'keəlɪs/ *adj* **1** (negligent) 粗心的; **a ~ mistake** 粗心造成的错误; **it was ~ of her to leave the book on the bus** 她太粗心, 把书忘在了公交车上; **to be ~ about one's appearance** 不在意自己的外貌 **2** (carefree) 不担忧的; (nonchalant) 不关心的; **to do sth. ~ of the risks** 做某事不计风险; **she dresses with a ~ elegance** 她的穿着透出一种不事雕琢的雅致

carelessly /'keəlɪsli/ *adv* **1** (negligently) 粗心地 **2** (casually) 随便地; (nonchalantly) 漠不关心地

carelessness /'keəlɪsnɪs/ *n* [u] **1** (negligence) 粗心 **2** (carefree attitude) 随便

care: ~ manager ▸**p. 409** *n* (in social services) 护理管理人员; (in hospital) 护士长; (in care home) 护理员; **~ order** *n* Jur 儿童监护令

carer /'keərə(r)/ ▸**p. 409** *n* 私人看护

caress /kə'res/
A *n* 爱抚
B *vt* 爱抚; **the wind ~ed my face** 风儿轻拂我的面颊

caret /'kærət/ *n* **~ (sign)** 脱字号 [即"^"]

caretaker /'keəteɪkə(r)/ ▸**p. 409**
A *n* **1** Brit (maintenance person) 看门人 **2** esp Amer (for owner) 看管人 **3** esp Amer (looking after people) 照顾者
B *modif* 临时代理的; **a ~ government** 看守政府; **a ~ manager** 代理主教练

care: ~ worker ▸**p. 409** *n* Brit 护理人员; **~worn** *adj* 忧心忡忡的; **to look ~worn** 看上去忧心忡忡; **a ~worn face** 愁云密布的脸

car: ~fare *n* Amer 车费; **~ ferry** *n* 汽车渡轮; **~-free** *adj* 无车的 ‹*zone, living*›

cargo /'kɑːgəʊ/ *n* (*pl* **~es**) 货物

cargo: ~ plane *n* 货机; **~ ship** *n* 货船

car: ~ hire *n* [u] 汽车租赁; **~-hire company** *n* 汽车租赁公司; **~hop** ▸**p. 409** *n* Amer "免下车"餐馆服务员

Caribbean /ˌkærɪ'biːən, kə'rɪbɪən/
A *adj* 加勒比地区的
B *n* **the ~** 加勒比地区

Caribbean Sea *pr n* **the ~** 加勒比海

caribou /'kærɪbuː/ *n* (*pl* **caribou**) Amer **= reindeer**

caricature /'kærɪkətʃʊə(r)/
A *n* **1** [c] (intentional distortion) (pictorial) 漫画; (written) 夸张的描述; (acted) 夸张的模仿 **2** [u] (art form) (pictorial) 漫画艺术; (acted) 夸张的模仿艺术 **3** [c] (unintentional distortion) 拙劣的模仿; **a ~ of a manager** 一个蹩脚的经理
B *vt* (with a picture) 用漫画表现; (in words) 夸张地描述; (in acting) 夸张地模仿

caricaturist /'kærɪkətʃʊərɪst/ ▸**p. 409** *n* 漫画家

caries /'keəriːz/ *n* [u] 龋; **dental ~** 龋齿

car industry *n* 汽车业

caring /'keərɪŋ/ *adj* **1** (loving) 关爱的; **~ parents** 慈爱的父母; **a ~ environment** 充满关爱的环境 **2** (compassionate) 为他人着想的; **a ~ society** 爱心社会 **3** *attrib* (specializing in health care) 护理的; (specializing in social care) 社会福利的; **charities and other ~ organizations** 慈善团体和其他社会福利机构; **the ~ professions** (health care) 护理职业; (social care) 社会福利职业

car: ~ insurance *n* [u] **1** (cover) 汽车保险; **2** (premium) 汽车保险费; **~jacking** *n* [u and c] esp Amer 汽车抢劫; **~ journey** *n* 汽车旅行; **~ key** *n* 车钥匙; **~ licence** *n* 汽车牌照; **~load** *n* 一汽车; **a ~load of people** 满满一车的人; **by the ~load** 大量地; **~ maintenance** *n* [u] 汽车保养; **~-maker** *n* 汽车制造商

Carmarthenshire /kə'mɑːðənʃɪə(r)/ *pr n* 卡马森郡

carnage /'kɑːnɪdʒ/ *n* [u] **1** (slaughter) 大屠杀 **2** fig (heavy defeat) 彻底击败; (being defeated heavily) 惨败

carnal /'kɑːnl/ *adj* (physical) 肉体的; (sexual) 性欲的; **to have ~ knowledge of sb.** dated 与某人发生性关系; **~ desires** 肉欲

carnation /kɑː'neɪʃn/ *n* 康乃馨

carnet /'kɑːneɪ/ *n* **1** (vehicle permit) 过境驾驶执照 **2** (camping permit) 宿营许可证

carnival /'kɑːnɪvl/ *n* **1** (festival) 狂欢节; **a charity ~** 慈善嘉年华 **2** Amer (funfair) 游艺团

carnivore /'kɑːnɪvɔː(r)/ *n* **1** (animal) 食肉动物 **2** (plant) 食虫植物

carnivorous /kɑː'nɪvərəs/ *adj* 食肉的 ‹*animal*›; 食虫的 ‹*plant*›

carob /'kærəb/ *n* **1** (pod) 角豆荚 **2** (tree) 角豆树

carol /'kærəl/
A *n* 圣诞颂歌
B *vi* (*pres p etc.* **-ll-** Brit, **-l-** Amer) 欢唱

carol: ~ service *n* 唱圣诞颂歌的仪式; **~-singer** *n* 唱圣诞颂歌者

carotene /'kærətiːn/ *n* [u] 胡萝卜素

carotid /kə'rɒtɪd/
A *n* 颈动脉
B *adj* 颈动脉的

carouse /kə'raʊz/ *vi* 狂饮作乐

carousel /ˌkærə'sel/ *n* **1** esp Amer (merry-go-round) 旋转木马 **2** (for luggage) 行李传送带 **3** (in slide projector) 旋转式幻灯放映机

carp[1] /kɑːp/ *n* **1** [c] (fish) 鲤科鱼 **2** [u] (as food) 鲤鱼

carp[2] *vi* 挑剔; **to ~ (on) at sb. (about sth.)** (因某事物)找某人的茬儿; **she's always ~ing on about the noise the children make!** 她一直不停地抱怨孩子们吵闹!

carpal /'kɑːpl/
A *n* 腕骨
B *adj attrib* 腕的 ‹*ligament, tunnel*›

carpal tunnel syndrome *n* [u] 腕管综合征

car park *n* esp Brit 停车场

Carpathian Mountains /kɑː'peɪθɪən/ *pr npl* **the ~** 喀尔巴阡山脉

Carpathians /kɑː'peɪθɪənz/ *pr npl* **the ~ = Carpathian Mountains**

carpel /'kɑːpl/ *n* 心皮

carpenter /'kɑːpəntə(r)/ ▸**p. 409** *n* 木匠

carpentry /'kɑːpəntri/ *n* [u] **1** (technique) 木工手艺 **2** (products) 木器

carpet /'kɑːpɪt/
A *n* **1** [u and c] (floor covering) 地毯; **to sweep** *or* **brush** *or* **push sth. under the ~** fig 掩盖某事; **to be on the ~** fig colloq 被训斥 **2** [c] fig (covering) 厚厚的一层; **a ~ of flowers/snow** 满地的花/一层厚厚的雪
B *vt* **1** (cover with carpet) 在…上铺地毯 **2** fig 覆

C

盖; **the island was ～ed with flowers** 岛上满布鲜花 3 colloq (reprimand) 训斥

carpet: ～ bag *n* 旅行包; **～bagger** *n* 1 Amer Hist 提包客［指美国内战后重建时期到南方去投机的北方人］; 2 esp Amer Pol 外来政客; **～-bomb** *vt* 对…进行地毯式轰炸; **～ bombing** *n* [u] 地毯式轰炸; **～ fitter** ▸**p. 409** *n* 铺地毯工

carpeting /ˈkɑːpɪtɪŋ/ *n* 1 [u] (carpet material) 地毯织料; (carpets in general) 地毯 2 [c and u] colloq (reprimand) 训斥

carpet: ～ layer *n* = **～ fitter**; **～ slipper** *n* 室内拖鞋; **～ square** *n* = **～ tile**; **～ sweeper** *n* 地毯清扫器; **～ tile** *n* 方形地毯片

car phone *n* 车载电话

carping /ˈkɑːpɪŋ/ *n* [u] 挑剔

car: ～ pool *n* esp Amer 1 (arrangement) 拼车; 2 (group) 拼车族; **～port** *n* 汽车棚; **～ radio** *n* 汽车收音机; **～ rental** *n* [u] = **～ hire**

carriage /ˈkærɪdʒ/ *n* 1 [c] (vehicle) 四轮马车 2 [c] Brit (of train) 客车厢 3 [u] Brit (conveying) 运输; (charge made) 运费 4 [c] (of machine) 滑动承载架; **a typewriter ～** 打字机滑架 5 [c] (deportment) 仪态

carriage: ～ bolt *n* Amer = **coach bolt**; **～ clock** *n* 旅行钟; **～ paid** *adv* 运费已付; **～ return** *n* 1 **～ return (key)** (on typewriter, computer keyboard) 回车（键）; 2 Comput 回车符; (line break) 换行符; **～way** *n* Brit 车道

carrier /ˈkærɪə(r)/ *n* 1 (transport company) 运输公司; **to send sth. by ～** 由承运商发送某物 2 (of disease) 带菌者; **mosquitoes are ～s of malaria** 蚊子传播疟疾 3 (vehicle, vessel) 运输工具 4 Brit colloq (bag) 购物袋; **a plastic ～** 塑料购物袋

carrier: ～ bag *n* Brit 购物袋; **～ pigeon** *n* 信鸽

carrion /ˈkærɪən/ *n* [u] 腐肉

carrion crow *n* 小嘴乌鸦

carrot /ˈkærət/ *n* 1 (vegetable) 胡萝卜; **～ juice** 胡萝卜汁 2 fig (incentive) 诱饵; **to offer sb. sth. as a ～** 以某事物利诱某人

carrot: ～-and-stick *adj* 软硬兼施的; **～ cake** *n* 胡萝卜蛋糕; **～ top** *n* hum (head of red hair) 红头发; (person) 红头发的人

carroty /ˈkærəti/ *adj* 橘红色的

carry /ˈkæri/

A *vt* 1 (support and take) 抱〈*child*〉; 拿〈*suitcase, umbrella*〉; 搬〈*box, chair*〉; «*more than two people*» 抬; **she carried the baby in her arms** 她把孩子抱在怀里; **they carried the injured man away on a stretcher** 他们用担架把伤员抬走了; **will you ～ the tray out, please** 请你把托盘端出去好吗; ▸**coal 2** 2 (take in vehicle) 运送; **the minibus carries 12 people** 这辆中巴可载 12 人 3 (transport on air or water) 带走; **his hat was carried away by a gust of wind** 他的帽子被一阵风吹走了; **the tide carried the boat back towards the shore** 潮水把船冲回岸边 4 (act as conduit for) «*pipe*» 输送〈*water, oil, gas*〉; «*line, wire*» 传导〈*sound, signal, electricity*〉; **the veins ～ blood back to the heart** 静脉将血液输送回心脏 5 (take to place, position) 推进; **to ～ sth. too far** 把某事做得太过分; **she carries modesty to extremes** 她谦虚得过了头; **her abilities carried her to the top of her profession** 她的才能使她在本行业出类拔萃; **the war was carried into enemy territory** 战事推进到了敌方境内 6 (have with one) 带有; **I don't usually ～ much cash with me** 我通常不多带现金; **he will ～ the memory with him for the rest of his life** 他将一生铭记这一切; **to ～ sth. in one's head** *or* **mind** 牢记某事物 7 (publish) «*newspaper, magazine, poster*» 刊登〈*news, information*〉; (broadcast) «*programme*» 播出〈*news, information*〉 8 (be marked by) «*object*» 附有〈*label, symbol*〉; **the notepaper carries the company logo** 信纸上印有公司的标识 9 (have as quality, feature) 具有〈*conviction, authority*〉; (have as a result) «*job, venture, plan, crime*» 带来〈*risk, boredom, excitement, penalty*〉; **the offence carries a maximum fine of £50** 这种违法行为最高可处 50 英镑罚款; **the new post carries increased responsibility** 这一新职位的责任更大; **the video recorder carries a 12-month guarantee** 这部录像机保修 12 个月; **to ～ weight** 有影响力 10 (be pregnant with) 怀; **she is ～ing twins** 她怀了双胞胎; **the elephant carries its young for 22 months** 大象孕期有 22 个月 11 Med (be infected with) 携带〈*germ, virus*〉; 传染〈*disease, condition*〉 12 Comm (stock, sell) «*shop, trader*» 出售〈*goods, brand*〉 13 (support weight of) «*pillars*» 支撑〈*weight*〉; «*road, bridge, table*» 承载〈*load*〉 14 (take responsibility for) 承担; **he is ～ing the entire department** 他主持着整个部门的工作; **we can't afford to ～ passengers** 我们养不起闲人; **to ～ a (heavy) burden** *or* **load** 肩负重担 15 (win) 在…中获胜〈*battle, argument, match*〉; 攻占〈*fortress, town*〉; 打败〈*enemy, opponent*〉; **to ～ the day** 获胜; **to ～ all** *or* **everything before one** 大获全胜 16 (approve) 使…获得通过〈*amendment, bill, proposal*〉; **the motion was carried by 25 votes to 13** 这一动议以 25 票对 13 票获得通过 17 (gain in election) «*candidate, party*» 在…获得多数票〈*state, district*〉 18 (persuade) «*person, speech*» 打动〈*audience, voters*〉; **he carried the congregation with him** 他打动了教堂会众 19 Math 使…进位〈*number*〉

B *vi* 1 (be audible) «*sound, voice*» 传到远处; **the noise of the explosion carried several miles** 爆炸声传到了几英里外 2 (go) «*missile*» 射出一定距离; **the ball carried over the boundary** 球出界了

C *v refl* **to ～ oneself** (move, behave) 保持姿态; **she carried herself like a model** 她举手投足像个模特; **he carried himself with dignity** 他举止庄重

D *n* colloq (in sb.'s arms) 抱; (on sb.'s back) 背; (transporting in a vehicle) 送; **to give sb. a ～** 送某人一程

(Phrasal verbs)

• **carry away** *vt* [**～ sb. away**] 使失去自制力; **he was carried away by the splendour of the palace** 他被壮观的宫殿完全吸引住了; **sorry I'm late: I was trying out my new computer and I got carried away** 对不起，我来晚了；我在试用新电脑，结果忘了时间

• **carry back** *vt* [**～ sb. back**] 使回想起过去; **to ～ sb. back to sth.** 使某人回想起某事物; **the smell of the sea air carried her back to childhood holidays** 大海的气息使她回想起儿时度假的情景

• **carry forward** *vt* [**～ sth. forward, ～ forward sth.**] 1 (transfer to new page or account) 结转〈*balance, figure, total*〉 2 (keep to use or deal with later) «*person, company*» 冲转〈*sum, loss*〉

• **carry off** *vt* 1 [**～ sb./sth. off, ～ off sb./sth.**] (take by force) 强行带走; **she was carried off by the terrorists** 她被恐怖分子抓走了; **the burglars carried off the family silver** 窃贼们盗走了家里的银器 2 [**～ off sth.**] (win) 赢得〈*prize, honour*〉 3 [**～ sth. off, ～ off sth.**] (succeed with) 成功处理; **to ～ it off** 轻松应付过去; **she carried the speech off brilliantly** 她十分出色地完成了演讲; **he was unable to ～ off the deception** 他的诡计没能得逞 4 [**～ sb. off, ～ off sb.**] (kill) «*disease*» 导致…死亡; **she was carried off by cancer** 她被癌症夺去了生命

• **carry on**

A *vi* 1 (continue, resume activity) 继续; **if it carries on raining, we'll have to cancel the match** 如果雨下个不停的话，我们将不得不取消比赛; **I'll ～ on with this work after lunch** 午饭后我会继续做这个工作 2 esp Brit (continue in same direction) 继续行进; **to ～ on down** *or* **along the road** (in car) 沿路一直开下去; (on foot) 沿路一直走下去 3 colloq (behave) 有某种举止; **that's no way to ～ on** 绝不可以有那样的行为 4 colloq (make fuss) 不断抱怨; **to ～ on about sb./sth.** 不停抱怨某人/某事物 5 colloq dated (have love affair) 有暧昧关系; **to ～ on with sb.** 与某人关系暧昧

B [**～ on sth.**] *vt* 1 (conduct) 经营〈*business*〉; 从事〈*work, trade*〉; 进行〈*negotiations, conversation, research*〉; **they carried on a correspondence for several years** 他们保持了好几年通信联系 2 (continue) 继续保持〈*tradition*〉; 继续经营〈*family business*〉; 继续进行〈*conversation, activity*〉

• **carry out** *vt* [**～ out sth., ～ sth. out**] 1 (go through with) 实行〈*plan, policy, reform*〉; 执行〈*order, instruction, mission*〉; 履行〈*duty, promise*〉; **do you think she will ～ out her threat?** 你认为她会把威胁付诸行动吗？ 2 (conduct) 进行〈*research, repair*〉; 实施〈*attack*〉

• **carry over**

A *vt* [**～ over sth., ～ sth. over**] 1 (transfer) 使继续下去; **she carried her business problems over into her private life** 她把工作上的问题带到了自己的私人生活中; **this custom has been carried over from the 19th century** 这一习俗从 19 世纪保持至今 2 (postpone) 推迟〈*event*〉; **this debate has been carried over from the last meeting** 这一争议是上次会议遗留下来的 3 Fin = **carry forward**

B *vi* 继续存在; **these attitudes have carried over from childhood** 童年时期形成的这些观念一直保持至今

• **carry through** *vt* 1 [**～ through sth., ～ sth. through**] (accomplish) 顺利完成; **to ～ through the reforms** 把改革进行到底 2 [**to ～ sb. through**] (help to survive) «*courage, sense of humour*» 帮助…渡过难关; **his determination carried him through the ordeal** 他靠坚定的信心熬过了这场磨难

carry: ～all *n* Amer 大手提包; **～cot** *n* Brit 手提式婴儿床

carrying-on colloq *n* (*pl* **carryings-on**) 1 (noisy behaviour) 吵闹 2 (questionable behaviour) 轻率的举动

carry-on colloq *n* 1 Brit (fuss) 大惊小怪 2 Amer (bag) ［可随身带上飞机的］小箱包; **～ baggage** 随身携带的行李

carryout /ˈkærɪaʊt/

A *n* 1 Amer, Scot (food) 外卖食品 2 Amer, Scot (shop) 外卖餐馆 3 Scot (alcohol) 外卖酒

B *modif* Amer, Scot 外卖的〈*food, restaurant*〉

car: ～ seat *n* (fixed) 汽车座位; (portable, for child) 婴儿安全座椅; **～ sharing** *n* [u] 合伙用车; **～sick** ▸**p. 377** *adj* 晕车的; **～ sickness** ▸**p. 377** *n* [u] 晕车; **～ stereo** *n* 汽车音响

cart /kɑːt/

A *n* 1 (for hay, goods) 大车; **to put the ～ before the horse** fig 本末倒置; **to be in the ～** Brit colloq fig 陷入困境 2 (for passengers) 两轮轻便敞篷马车 3 (for small loads) 手推车 4 Amer **(shopping) ～** 购物推车

B *vt* 1 (move by cart) 用大车运送 2 colloq (carry) 携带; (transport generally) 运送; **to ～ sth. up/down the stairs** 把某物搬上楼/搬下楼; **I've been ～ing this heavy briefcase around all day** 我提着这个沉重的公文包都一整天了 3 colloq (remove by force) 费力运走; **to ～ sth. away** 费大力气把某物运走

(Phrasal verb)

• **cart off** *vt* [**～ sb. off**] colloq 强行带走; **the police ～ed her off to the police station** 警察把她押到警察局

carte blanche /ˌkɑːt ˈblɑːnʃ/ *n* [u] 全权; **to have/be given ～ (to do sth.)** 具有/被授予全权（做某事）

cartel /kɑːˈtel/ *n* 卡特尔 [操纵价格或商品供应的企业集团]; **a price/drug(s) ~** 价格卡特尔/贩毒团伙

Cartesian /kɑːˈtiːzɪən/
A *adj* 笛卡尔的
B *n* 笛卡尔主义者

cartful /ˈkɑːtfʊl/ *n* 一车; **a ~ of hay/manure** 一车干草/肥料

carthorse /ˈkɑːthɔːs/ *n* Brit 挽马

cartilage /ˈkɑːtɪlɪdʒ/ *n* [u] 软骨

cartload /ˈkɑːtləʊd/ *n* **1** (quantity) 满满一车 **2** colloq (of people, things) 大量

cartographer /kɑːˈtɒgrəfə(r)/ ▸p. 409 *n* 地图绘制员

cartography /kɑːˈtɒgrəfi/ *n* [u] (science) 制图学; (practice) 地图绘制

carton /ˈkɑːtn/ *n* (made of cardboard) 纸板盒; (made of plastic) 塑料盒; **a ~ of milk** 一盒牛奶; **a ~ of cigarettes** Amer 一条香烟

cartoon /kɑːˈtuːn/ *n* **1** Cin 动画片 **2** (drawing) 漫画 **3** (picture story) 连环漫画 **4** Art (sketch) 草图

cartoonist /kɑːˈtuːnɪst/ ▸p. 409 *n* **1** Cin 动漫师 **2** (in print) 漫画家

cartoon strip *n* = **comic strip**

car transporter *n* 车辆运输车

cartridge /ˈkɑːtrɪdʒ/ *n* **1** (for gun) 弹壳 **2** (for pen) 笔芯 **3** (for tape) 磁带盒 **4** (for record player) 拾音头

cartridge: ~ belt *n* 子弹带; **~ clip** *n* 弹夹; **~ drive** *n* (for tape) 磁带驱动器; (for disk) 磁盘驱动器; **~ paper** *n* [u] [画画或制信封用的] 粗面纸; **~ pen** *n* 芯式笔

cart: ~-track *n* 马车道; **~wheel** *n* **1** (of cart) 大车车轮; **2** (in gymnastics) 侧手翻

car valeting *n* [u] 洗车行业

carve /kɑːv/
A *vt* **1** (sculpt) 雕刻; **to ~ sth. in stone/wood** 在石头/木头上雕刻某物; **to ~ sth. out of** *or* **from sth.** 用某物雕刻某物 **2** (engrave, inscribe) 刻; **to ~ patterns** 刻图案; **to ~ sth. into stone** 在石头上刻某物; **to ~ an inscription on a gravestone** 在墓碑上刻碑文 **3** Culin 切开 ‹*meat*›; **to ~ a slice** 切下一片
B *vi* 切肉

Phrasal verbs
- **carve out** *vt* [**~ out sth., ~ sth. out**] **1** (cut) 雕刻出 ‹*statue*› **2** (erode) «*river*» 冲刷出 ‹*valley*› **3** fig (create) 开创出; **to ~ out a niche (for oneself)** （为自己）谋得合适的位置; **to ~ out a career (for oneself)** （为自己）创出一番事业
- **carve up** *vt* **1** [**~ up sth., ~ sth. up**] colloq (divide) 划分; **to ~ up the market** 瓜分市场 **2** [**~ up sb./sth., ~ sb./sth. up**] Aut colloq 超车抢…的道

carvers /ˈkɑːvəz/ *npl* Brit 切肉刀叉

carvery /ˈkɑːvəri/ *n* Brit 烤肉馆

carve-up /ˈkɑːvʌp/ *n* Brit pej colloq 瓜分

carving /ˈkɑːvɪŋ/ *n* **1** [c] (sculpture) 雕刻品 **2** [u] (technique) 雕刻技术 **3** [u] Culin 切肉

carving knife *n* 切肉刀

car: ~ wash *n* (area) 洗车场; (machine) 自动洗车设备; **~ worker** ▸p. 409 *n* 汽车工

cascade /kæˈskeɪd/
A *n* **1** (of water) 小瀑布 **2** fig (of hair, flowers) 瀑布状物
B *vi* **1** «*water*» 倾泻 **2** fig «*hair, ribbons*» 如瀑布般垂下
C *vt* **1** 传递 ‹*information*› **2** Comput 层叠 ‹*windows, menu*›

cascade effect *n* **1** (of water) 瀑布效果 **2** fig (of events) 级联效应 [指一系列事件之间的连锁反应]

cascading /kæˈskeɪdɪŋ/ *adj attrib* Comput 层叠式的 ‹*window, menu*›

case[1] /keɪs/
A **1** [c] (instance) 事例; **on a ~ by ~ basis** 逐一地; **in 7 out of 10 ~s** 十之七八; **it's a classic ~ of bad planning** 这是典型的计划不周; **a ~ in point** 恰当的例子 **2** [c] (state of affairs, situation) 情况; **in some ~s** 在某些情况下; **in that ~** 如果那样的话; **if that's the ~, we need more staff** 如果真是那样，我们就需要更多的员工了; **as** *or* **whatever the ~ may be** 视具体情况而定; **such** *or* **this being the ~** 既然如此 **3** [c] (relating to individual) 个案; **in your ~, we are prepared to be lenient** 根据你的情况，我们准备从宽处理; **I cannot make an exception in your ~** 我不能对你破例 **4** [c] (argument) 论据; **to have a ~** 有足够的证据打赢官司; **to put the ~ for the defence** 为被告辩护; **to state one's ~** 陈述自己的观点; **to make (out) a good** *or* **strong ~ for/against sth./doing sth.** 提出充分的理由支持/反对某事物/做某事 **5** [c] Jur (trial) 诉讼; **a criminal/civil ~** 刑事/民事诉讼; **to win/lose one's ~** 胜诉/败诉; **to hear a ~** 审案; **to bring a ~ against sb./sth.** 起诉某人/某机构 **6** [c] Jur (criminal investigation) 案件; **to work** *or* **be on a ~** 办案; **a murder ~** 谋杀案; **a ~ of theft** 偷窃案 **7** [c] Med (instance of disease) 病例; (patient with disease) 病人; (patient with injury) 伤员; **a severe ~ of typhoid** 严重的伤寒病例; **a psychiatric ~** 精神病患者 **8** [c] Soc Admin (instance of problem) 需要救助的情况; (client) 需要救助的对象; **the local social services discussed her ~** 当地的社会福利部门讨论了她的救助问题; **he's a problem ~** 他是个困难户 **9** [c] colloq (pitiable person) 可怜的人; (person without hope) 无可救药的人 **10** [u and c] Ling 格; **the nominative ~** 主格
B **in any case** *adv phr* **1** (besides, anyway) 无论如何 **2** (at any rate) 至少
C **in case** ▸p. 147 *conj phr* **1** (because of possibility) 以防; **you'd better take the keys in ~ I'm out** 你最好带上钥匙，以防我不在家; **take the street map just in ~** 带上街道地图，以防万一 **2** (if) 假使; **in ~ you haven't figured it out, let me explain** 假如你还没弄明白，就让我来解释吧
D **in case of** ▸p. 147 *prep phr* 如果发生; **in ~ of fire, ring the alarm bell** 如遇火警，即按警铃

case[2]
A *n* **1** (protective container) 容器 [盒、箱、套、鞘等]; (of piano, clock) 外壳; (of book) 书壳; **a cigarette/display ~** 烟盒/陈列柜 **2** Brit (suitcase) 手提箱 **3** (of wine, beer) 箱; **to buy wine by the ~** 成箱地买葡萄酒 **4** (husk) 外皮
B colloq *vt* **1** (enclose) 包裹; **to be ~d in sth.** 用某物包裹住 **2** colloq (reconnoitre) 预先探察; **to ~ the joint** «*thief*» 踩点

case: ~book *n* **1** (doctor's record) 病例记录; (investigator's record) 个案记录; **2** Jur 案例记录; **3** Amer (compilation) 专题资料汇编; **~ conference** *n* 个案讨论会; **~ file** *n* 案件档案; **~ grammar** *n* [u] 格语法; **~-harden** *vt* 使…表面渗碳硬化 ‹*steel*›; **~ history** *n* **1** Med 病历; Soc Admin 个案史; **2** (exemplary study) = **~ study 2**; **~ law** *n* [u] 判例法; **~load** *n* [医生、律师、社会工作者等的] 工作量; **~ management** *n* [u] 个案管理

casement /ˈkeɪsmənt/ *n* 竖铰链窗

casement window *n* 竖铰链窗

case: ~ notes *npl* **1** Med 病例记录; **2** Jur, Soc Admin 案例记录; **~-sensitive** *adj* 区分大小写的; **~ study** *n* **1** (research) 跟踪研究; **2** (exemplary study) 个案研究; **~ system** *n* **1** Jur 判例教学法; **2** Ling 格系统; **~work** *n* [u] 社会工作; **~worker** ▸p. 409 *n* 社会工作者

cash /kæʃ/ ▸p. 174
A *n* [u] **1** (bills, coins) 现金; **to pay in ~** 用现金支付; **£50 ~ in hand, ~ down** 以现金支付 50 英镑 **2** (money in general) 钱; **to be short of ~** 缺钱
B *modif* 现金的 ‹*advance*›; 需要付现金的 ‹*transaction*›
C *vt* «*person, bank*» 兑现 ‹*bonds, tokens, cheque*›

Phrasal verbs
- **cash in** *vt* [**~ in sth., ~ sth. in**] 把…兑成现金 ‹*bonds, tokens, cheques*›
- **cash in on** *vt* [**~ in on sth.**] colloq 从…中获利; **she ~ed in on her popularity** 她利用自己的名气牟利
- **cash up** *vi* «*cashier, bank*» 结算账款

cashable /ˈkæʃəbl/ *adj* 可兑换成现金的 ‹*cheque, token*›

cash: ~-and-carry *n* 现款取货商店; **~ assets** *npl* 现金资产; **~back** *n* [u] **1** (withdrawal) 消费提现服务 [消费者购物时利用借记卡提取现金]; **2** (refund) 现金返还; **~ box** *n* 钱箱; **~ buyer** *n* 现金购买者; **~ call** *n* 筹现金通知; **~ card** *n* 现金卡; **~ contribution** *n* 出资; **~ cow** *n* fig colloq 现金母牛 [指能带来稳定收入或利润的企业或投资]; **~ crop** *n* 经济作物; **~ deficit** *n* 现金赤字; **~ desk** *n* 付款处; **~ dispenser** *n* Brit = **~ machine**

cashew /ˈkæʃuː/ *n* **1** **~ (nut)** 腰果 **2** (tree) 腰果树

cash flow *n* 现金流转

cashier[1] /kæˈʃɪə(r)/ ▸p. 409 *n* 出纳员

cashier[2] *vt* 开除…的军职

cash: ~-in *n* colloq 渔利; **~ inflow** *n* 现金流入; **~ injection** *n* 现金注入

cashless /ˈkæʃlɪs/ *adj* 不用现金的 ‹*transaction, society*›

cash: ~ limit *n* (on spending) 现金支出限额; (on withdrawal) 取款限额; **~ machine** *n* 自动取款机

cashmere /ˈkæʃmɪə(r)/ *n* [u] **1** (wool) 羊绒 **2** (cloth) 羊绒织物; **a ~ sweater** 羊绒毛衣

cash: ~ offer *n* 现金出价; **~ on delivery** *n* 货到付款; **~ outflow** *n* 现金流出; **~point®** *n* Brit = **automated teller machine**; **~point card** *n* Brit = **~ card**; **~ ratio** *n* **1** (in firm) 现金比率; **2** (in bank) 现金准备率; **~ register** *n* 现金出纳机; **~ reserves** *npl* 现金储备; **~-rich** *adj* 有钱的; **~ squeeze** *n* 银根收缩; **~-strapped** *adj* colloq 缺钱的; **~ value** *n* 现金价值

cash with order
A *n* 订货付现
B *adv* 以订货付现方式 ‹*pay, buy*›

casing /ˈkeɪsɪŋ/ *n* **1** (case) 外壳; Mil (of shell) 炮弹壳; Aut (of gear mechanism) 齿轮箱; (of cylinder) 汽缸 **2** (of tyre) 外胎 **3** (of sausage) 肠衣

casino /kəˈsiːnəʊ/ *n* 赌场

cask /kɑːsk, Amer kæsk/ *n* **1** (barrel) 酒桶 **2** (quantity) 一桶

cask-conditioned *adj* 桶内二次发酵的 ‹*beer*›

casket /ˈkɑːskɪt, Amer ˈkæskɪt/ *n* **1** (box) 小盒; **a jewel ~** 珠宝盒 **2** Brit (for ashes) 骨灰盒 **3** Amer (coffin) 棺材

Caspian Sea /ˌkæspɪən ˈsiː/ *pr n* **the ~** 里海

cassava /kəˈsɑːvə/ *n* **1** [u] Culin (root) 木薯根; (starch) 木薯粉 **2** [c] Bot 木薯

casserole /ˈkæsərəʊl/
A *n* **1** (food) 炖锅菜 **2** (vessel) 炖锅
B *vt* Brit 用炖锅煮

cassette /kəˈset/ *n* **1** Audio 盒式磁带 **2** Video 盒式录像带 **3** Phot 盒式胶片

cassette: ~ deck *n* 盒式磁带录音座; **~ player** *n* 盒式磁带放音机; **~ recorder** *n* 盒式磁带录音机; **~ recording** *n* 盒式磁带录音; **~ tape** *n* **1** Audio 盒式录音带; **2** Video 盒式录像带

cassock /ˈkæsək/ *n* [某些神职人员穿的] 长袍

cast /kɑːst, Amer kæst/

A vt (pt, pp **cast**) 1 Cin, Theat (select for role) 选派…扮演角色; **to ~ sb. as sth.** 选派某人扮演某角色; **she was ~ in the part** or **role of Ophelia** 她给选中扮演奥菲莉亚这个角色 2 Cin, Theat (assign parts in) 为…选派演员; **it's a very difficult play to ~** 这部戏的演员很难选 3 (describe) 描述 ‹person›; **he ~ himself as the innocent victim** 他把自己说成是无辜的受害者; **somebody is always ~ in the role of scapegoat** 总是有人会当替罪羊的 4 Art, Tech (shape material in mould) 浇铸 ‹metal, cement, plaster› 5 Art, Tech (make by casting) 铸造; **a statue ~ in bronze** 青铜铸像 6 (throw) 扔; Naut 抛 ‹anchor, sounding line›; **to ~ a net/fishing line** 撒网/抛钓线; **he was ~ into jail** 他被投入了监狱 7 Zool «snake» 蜕 ‹skin›; «deer» 脱 ‹antlers› 8 (lose) «horse» 掉落 ‹shoe› 9 (cause to appear) 投射; **the setting sun ~ an orange glow over the mountains** 群山笼罩在夕阳的橘黄色光辉中; **the houses ~ long shadows** 房子投下长长的影子 10 (cause to affect) 把…加于 ‹uncertainty, disparagement›; **to ~ doubt on** or **upon sth.** 使人对某事物生疑; **to ~ (a) new light on sth.** 使人对某事物有新的认识 11 (direct) 投射; **to ~ an eye over sth.** 粗略地看一下某事物; **she ~ a welcoming smile in his direction** 她朝他微笑以示欢迎; **she ~ him a desperate glance** 她绝望地瞥了他一眼; **to ~ one's mind back (to/over sth.)** 回忆（某事） 12 (cause to take effect) **to ~ a spell (on** or **over sb.)** lit （对某人）施魔法; fig 迷住（某人） 13 (present) 表述; **a statement ~ in carefully diplomatic tones** 一份用外交口吻措词谨慎的声明; **the work was ~ in the form of a novella** 该作品是一部中篇小说 14 (in election) «voter» 投 ‹vote› 15 Astrol «astrologer» 占卜; **to ~ sb.'s horoscope** 给某人占星算命

B vi (pt, pp **cast**) 抛钓线

C n 1 + v sing or pl (performers) 全体演员; **members of the ~** 剧组成员; **the film has an all-star ~** 这部电影拥有全明星阵容; **the supporting ~** (actors) 全体配角; **a ~ of characters** (in novel) 全部人物 2 Tech (object moulded out of plaster, plastic) 模件; (object moulded out of iron, bronze, steel) 铸件; (mould of metal, sand, plaster) 模子 3 Med (plaster cast) 石膏绷带; **her leg's in a ~** 她一条腿打上了石膏 4 (type) 类型; **she was of a philosophical ~ of mind** 她头脑冷静沉着 5 (throw) 扔; (of dice) 掷; (of net) 撒; (of fishing line) 抛 6 (produced by worm) 排泄物

Phrasal verbs

• **cast about for, cast around for** vt [~ **about** or **around for sth.**] 努力寻找 ‹solution, excuse, method, inspiration›

• **cast aside** vt [~ **aside sb./sth.,** ~ **sb./sth. aside**]
1 (throw aside) 把…扔到一边; **he ~ her aside roughly and ran out** 他粗鲁地推开她，跑了出去 2 (reject) 抛弃 ‹inhibitions, caution, person›; 消除 ‹anxieties, doubts›; **he ~ aside this suggestion** 他对这个建议置之不理

• **cast away**
A [~ **sb. away**] vt Naut 使…离船流落; **to be ~ away on a desert island** 流落荒岛
B [~ **away sth.,** ~ **sth. away**] vt liter 1 (throw away) 扔掉 2 (reject) 抛弃 ‹cares, inhibitions›; **she ~ away the unwelcome thought** 她打消了那个令人不快的念头

• **cast down** vt [~ **down sb./sth.,** ~ **sb./sth. down**]
1 liter (throw down) 扔下 2 (direct downwards) 垂下 ‹eyes, gaze› 3 **to be ~ down** liter (be depressed) 沮丧

• **cast off**
A vi 1 Naut 解船缆 2 (in knitting) 收针
B [~ **off sb./sth.,** ~ **sb./sth. off**] vt
1 (discard, get rid of) 摆脱 ‹oppression›; 抛弃 ‹person›; **the town is still trying to ~ off its dull image** 这座城镇仍在努力改变其单调的形象 2 (remove) 迅速脱下 ‹garment› 3 (in knitting) 收 ‹stitch›; 给…收针 ‹row, sleeve›

• **cast on**
A [~ **on sth.**] vt 起 ‹stitch›; 给…起针 ‹row, sleeve›
B vi 起针

• **cast out** vt [~ **out sb./sth.,** ~ **sb./sth. out**] liter 1 (force to leave) 赶走; **he claimed to have the power to ~ out demons** 他声称有驱魔的法力 2 (get rid of) 去除 ‹emotion, evil›

• **cast up** vt [~ **up sth.,** ~ **sth. up**]
1 (wash ashore) «tide, sea, flood» 把…冲上岸 ‹body, dead fish, seaweed› 2 (direct upwards) 抬高 ‹eyes, gaze›

castanets /ˌkæstəˈnets/ ▸**p. 395** npl 响板

castaway /ˈkɑːstəweɪ, Amer ˈkæst-/ n (person shipwrecked) 遭遇船难者; (person abandoned) 被遗弃的人

caste /kɑːst/ n 1 [u] (system) [印度社会的] 种姓制度 2 [c] (class) 种姓; **~ system** 种姓制度 3 [u] (status) 种姓地位; **to lose ~** fig 失去社会地位

castellated /ˈkæstəleɪtɪd/ adj 像城堡的 ‹building›; 有雉堞的 ‹wall›

caster /ˈkɑːstə(r), Amer ˈkæstər/ n = **castor**

caster sugar n [u] Brit 精白砂糖

castigate /ˈkæstɪgeɪt/ vt formal 严厉批评; **to ~ sb. (for sth./for doing sth.)** «teacher, report» （因某事物/因做某事）严厉批评 ‹pupil, group›

castigation /ˌkæstɪˈgeɪʃn/ n [u and c] formal 严厉的批评

casting /ˈkɑːstɪŋ, Amer ˈkæst-/ n 1 [u] Ind (process) 浇铸 2 [c] Ind (object) 铸件 3 [u] Theat 演员挑选

casting: ~ agent ▸**p. 409** n 演员经纪人; **~ couch** n colloq **the ~ couch** [以出卖肉体换取角色的] 选角潜规则; **~ director** ▸**p. 409** n 选角导演; **~ vote** n 决定票; **to have a** or **the ~ vote** 拥有决定性一票

cast iron
A n [u] 铸铁
B **cast-iron** modif 1 lit 铸铁制的 2 fig 确定无疑的; **a cast-iron alibi** 不在犯罪现场的铁证

castle /ˈkɑːsl, Amer ˈkæsl/ n 1 lit 城堡; **an Englishman's home is his ~** 英国人的家就是他们的城堡 [意在强调个人隐私的重要性] 2 fig **~s in the air/in Spain** 空中楼阁

cast list n 演员名单

cast-off
A **cast-offs** npl 1 (garment) 扔掉的旧衣服 2 (person) 被抛弃的人; (thing) 丢弃物; **society's ~s** 被社会抛弃的人
B adj attrib 1 (no longer worn) 不再穿的; **~ clothes** 不穿的旧衣服 2 (discarded) 被抛弃的 ‹lover, object›

castor /ˈkɑːstə(r), Amer ˈkæs-/ n 1 (wheel) 小脚轮 2 (jar) 筛眼调味品瓶

castor oil n [u] 蓖麻油

castrate /kæˈstreɪt, Amer ˈkæstreɪt/ vt 阉割

castration /kæˈstreɪʃn/ n 阉割

casual /ˈkæʒʊəl/
A adj attrib 1 (chance) 偶然的; **a ~ encounter** 邂逅; **a ~ remark** 随口说出的话; **a ~ call** 顺便来访; **~ customers** 偶然光顾的客人 2 (in informal dress) 随意的; (in attitude) 不拘礼节的; **a ~ conversation** 闲聊 3 (superficial) 漫不经心的; **a ~ inspection** 粗略的检查; **a ~ reader** 马虎的读者; **~ sex** 一夜情 4 (relaxed) 轻松的 ‹atmosphere› 5 (offhand) 不负责任的 ‹attitude, approach› 6 (nonchalant) 漠不关心的 ‹tone› 7 (temporary) 临时的 ‹labour, job›
B n (temporary worker) 临时工
C **casuals** npl (clothes) 便装; (shoes) 便鞋

casually /ˈkæʒʊəli/ adv 1 (informally) 随意地 ‹dress, converse, stroll› 2 (by chance) 偶然地 ‹encounter, remark, call› 3 (superficially) 漫不经心地 ‹inspect, read› 4 (offhandedly) 不负责任地 ‹behave, treat› 5 (nonchalantly) 漠不关心地 ‹talk›

casualness /ˈkæʒʊəlnɪs/ n [u] 1 (nonchalance) 漠不关心 2 (carelessness) 漫不经心; **the ~ of the details** 细节的马虎 3 Fashn 休闲

casualty /ˈkæʒʊəlti/ n 1 [c] (person) 伤亡人员; **to suffer heavy casualties** 伤亡惨重 2 [c] fig (victim) 受害者; **to be a ~ of sth.** 是某事物的受害者 3 [u] Brit (emergency room) 急诊室

casualwear /ˈkæʒʊəlweə(r)/ n [u] 便装

casuistry /ˈkæzjʊɪstri/ n [u] 1 formal (sophistry) 诡辩 2 Philos 决疑论

cat /kæt/ n 1 (domestic) 猫; **a ~ basket** 养猫的篮子; **the ~'s whiskers** or **pyjamas** Brit or **pajamas** Amer colloq (person) 最棒的人; (thing) 最棒的事物; **he thinks he's the ~'s whiskers** colloq 他自命不凡; **enough to make a ~ laugh** colloq 让人笑掉大牙的; **to fight like ~ and dog** 激烈地打斗; **to grin like a Cheshire ~** 咧嘴傻笑; **the ~'s out of the bag** colloq 秘密泄露了; **like a ~ on a hot tin roof** esp Amer or **on hot bricks** Brit colloq 如坐针毡的; **like a scalded ~** colloq 非常迅速地; **like a ~ that's got the cream** esp Brit, **like the ~ that got** or **ate the canary** Amer 得意扬扬的; **to look like something the ~ brought** or **dragged in** colloq «person» 看上去邋遢不堪; **no room to swing a ~** colloq 非常狭小; **not to have** or **stand a ~ in hell's chance (of doing sth.)** colloq 毫无机会（做某事）; **to play (a game of) ~ and mouse (with sb.), to play a ~-and-mouse game (with sb.)** 耍弄（某人）; **to rain ~s and dogs** colloq 下倾盆大雨; **to (wait and) see which way the ~ jumps** colloq [作决定前] 观望形势; **to set** or **put the ~ among the pigeons** Brit 招惹是非; **curiosity killed the ~** Prov 好奇心害死猫 [指人不要太爱管闲事]; **a ~ may look at a king/queen** Prov 猫也有权看国王/女王 [指小人物也该有些权利]; **there is more than one way to skin a ~** Prov hum 有的是办法; **when** or **while the ~'s away, the mice will play** Prov 猫儿不在，老鼠欢快 2 (feline) 猫科动物; **lions are members of the ~ family** 狮子是猫科动物 3 colloq pej (woman) 恶毒的女人 4 esp Amer colloq dated (man) 爵士乐爱好者

cataclysm /ˈkætəklɪzəm/ formal n 1 (violent natural event) 大灾变 2 fig (upheaval) 大动乱

cataclysmic /ˌkætəˈklɪzmɪk/ adj formal 灾难性的

catacombs /ˈkætəkuːmz, Amer -kəʊmz/ npl 地下墓穴

catafalque /ˈkætəfælk/ n 灵柩台

Catalan /ˈkætəlæn/ ▸**p. 503, p. 426**
A adj (of Catalonia) 加泰罗尼亚的; (of the people) 加泰罗尼亚人的; (of the language) 加泰罗尼亚语的
B n 1 [c] (person) 加泰罗尼亚人 2 [u] (language) 加泰罗尼亚语

catalogue, Amer **catalog** /ˈkætəlɒg, Amer -lɔːg/
A n 1 (of goods) 目录; **a ~ number** 产品目录编号; **a ~ price** 商品目录价格 2 (in library) 图书目录; (in gallery) 展品目录 3 fig (series) 一系列; **a ~ of complaints** 一连串的抱怨 4 Amer Univ 课程概览
B vt 将…编入目录

Catalonia /ˌkætəˈləʊnɪə/ pr n 加泰罗尼亚

catalysis /kəˈtæləsɪs/ n [u] 催化作用

catalyst /ˈkætəlɪst/ n 1 Chem 催化剂 2 fig (impetus) 促进因素; **to be/act as a ~ (for sth.)** 是/作为（某事物的）促进因素

catalytic /ˌkætəˈlɪtɪk/ adj 催化的 ‹reaction, process›

catalytic: ~ **converter** *n* 催化式排气净化器; ~ **cracker** *n* 催化裂化器

catamaran /ˌkætəməˈræn/ *n* 双体船

catapult /ˈkætəpʌlt/

A *n* **1** (for stones) 弹弓; **to use a** ~ 打弹弓 **2** Aviat **a** ~ **(launcher)** 弹射器 **3** Mil 弩炮

B *vt* **1** (propel) 猛掷; **the explosion** ~**ed the car into a tree** 爆炸把车腾空弹起撞在树上 **2** fig (launch) 使跃起; **to be** ~**ed to success** 一跃成功; **to** ~ **sb. to fame** 使某人一举成名

cataract /ˈkætərækt/ *n* **1** (waterfall) 大瀑布 **2** (deluge) 急流; (downpour) 倾盆大雨 **3** Med 白内障

catarrh /kəˈtɑː(r)/ *n* [u] 鼻喉部黏膜炎

catastrophe /kəˈtæstrəfi/ *n* **1** (natural disaster) 灾难 **2** fig (major setback or problem) 劫难

catastrophe theory *n* [u] 突变理论

catastrophic /ˌkætəˈstrɒfɪk/ *adj* 灾难性的 ‹*loss, event, mistake*›

catastrophically /ˌkætəˈstrɒfɪkli/ *adv* 灾难性地 ‹*happen, fail*›

catatonic /ˌkætəˈtɒnɪk/

A *adj* **1** Med 紧张症的 ‹*patient*› **2** colloq (numb) 呆住的

B *n* 紧张症患者

cat burglar *n* 飞贼

catcall /ˈkætkɔːl/

A *n* **1** (to girl) 口哨声 **2** (of derision) 嘘声

B *vi* **1** (to girl) 吹口哨 **2** (with derision) 发嘘声

catch /kætʃ/

A *vt* (*pt, pp* **caught**) **1** (stop and hold) 接住 ‹*ball*› **2** (capture) 捕获; **how many fish did you** ~**?** 你捕到多少鱼? ; **they have caught the burglars** 他们捉住了几个窃贼 **3** (seize) 抓住; **he caught my arm/caught me by the arm** 他抓住了我的胳膊; **to** ~ **sb. by the throat** 掐住某人的脖子 **4** (act as recipient for) «*person, container*» 接 ‹*drips, liquid, dust*› **5** (engage) 引起 ‹*attention, interest, imagination*›; **to** ~ **sb.'s eye** 引起某人的注意 **6** (discover) 当场发现; **to** ~ **sb. doing sth.** 撞见某人在做某事; **to get caught** 被当场发现; **to** ~ **oneself doing sth.** 意识到自己在做某事; **she caught herself wishing that her ex-husband was there** 她意识到自己盼望前夫在场; **to** ~ **sb. red-handed** 当场抓住某人; **to** ~ **sb. at it** *or* **in the act** colloq 当场发现某人在干坏事 **7** (take by surprise) 使意外; **you've caught me at an awkward moment** 你现在来找我可不是时候; **to** ~ **sb. napping** 乘某人不备; **they caught the enemy napping** 他们打了敌人一个措手不及; **to** ~ **sb. with his/her trousers** Brit *or* **pants** Amer **down** colloq 乘某人措手不及; **to be** *or* **get caught in the rain/in a blizzard** 被雨淋着了/遭遇暴风雪 **8** (succeed in finding and speaking to) 逮住…说几句; **I caught her just before she left** 我在她就要离开时截住她说了几句 **9** (be in time for) 赶上 ‹*bus, plane, train*›; **to** ~ **the post** Brit 赶上邮局的一班收信时刻 **10** Cin, Theat, TV, Radio colloq (manage to see, hear) 赶上看 ‹*play, film*›; 赶上听 ‹*broadcast, concert*› **11** Amer (attend) 观看 ‹*show, play, movie*› **12** (manage to hear) 听见; **we couldn't quite** ~ **what they were saying** 我们听不大清他们在说什么 **13** (manage to understand) 理解; **do you** ~ **my meaning?** 你明白我的意思吗? **14** (manage to get) 设法获得; **did you manage to** ~ **any sleep?** 你有没有抽空睡一会儿? **15** (perceive) 察觉; **I caught a whiff of tobacco/the sound of bells** 我闻到了一股烟草味/听到了钟声; **he caught sight of her leaving the shop** 他瞥见她离开了商店 **16** Med 传染上 ‹*disease, virus*› **17** (get stuck) 绊住; **she caught her sleeve/got her sleeve caught on the nail** 她的袖子被钉子挂住了; **I caught my foot in a pothole** 我一只脚陷进了凹坑里; **the child got his head caught between the railings** 那个男孩的头夹在了栏杆之间 **18** (hit) 击中; **the stone caught the child on the head** 石子打中了孩子的头; **she caught my glass with her elbow** 她的胳膊肘撞到了我的杯子; **I caught him a blow in the stomach** 我一拳打在他的肚子上 **19** (reproduce) 精确再现; **the article has caught the atmosphere at the concert** 该文逼真地再现了音乐会上的气氛 **20** (in cricket) «*fielder*» 把…接杀出局 ‹*batsman*› **21** (deceive) 欺骗; **you can't** ~ **me with that old trick** 你那套老把戏骗不了我 **22** (strike) «*light*» 照射到 ‹*shiny object*›; «*current, wave*» 拍打 ‹*boat*›; «*gust, wind*» 吹动 ‹*paper*›; **the sunlight caught the drops of rain on the web** 蛛网上的雨滴在阳光照射下闪闪发亮 **23** (be struck by) **to** ~ **fire** 着火; **to** ~ **the sun** «*person, part of the body*» 晒黑; **to** ~ **the light** «*jewel*» 在光照下闪闪发亮 **24** (draw in) 屏住; **to** ~ **one's breath** 屏息 **25** colloq **to** ~ **it** (get scolding) 挨骂; (get other punishment) 受罚; **she really caught it that time!** 那次她可被骂惨了!

B *vi* (*pt, pp* **caught**) **1** (become stuck) 被绊住; **to** ~ **on sth.** «*dress, sleeve*» 被…挂住 ‹*nail, branch*›; **the wheel is** ~**ing on the frame** 轮胎不停地蹭擦着轮框 **2** (start to burn) 开始燃烧; **we couldn't get the fire to** ~ 我们生不着火; **the logs have caught** 木头着火了 **3** (become fastened) «*hook*» 扣住; «*lock*» 锁住

C *n* **1** [c] (fastening) (on purse, brooch, etc.) 搭扣; (on window) 窗钩; (on door) 门闩 **2** [c] (drawback) 暗藏的不利因素; **what's the** ~**?** 这里面有什么鬼名堂? **3** [c] Fishg (haul) 渔获量; (one fish) 渔获物; **to have a huge/good** ~ **(of fish)** 捕获大量/相当数量的鱼 **4** [c] esp Sport 接住; **to take a** ~ Brit, **to make a** ~ Amer 接球 **5** [u] (child's game) 传接球游戏 **6** [c] (break in voice) 哽咽

Phrasal verbs

- **catch at** *vt* [~ **at sth.**] 试图抓住; **he caught at my sleeve and begged me to stay** 他一把抓住我的袖子, 求我留下来
- **catch on** *vi* **1** (become fashionable) 流行起来; **to** ~ **on with sb.** 受到某人的欢迎 **2** colloq (start to understand) 开始理解; **to** ~ **on to sth.** 开始理解某事物
- **catch out** *vt* [~ **sb. out**] Brit **1** (trick into making mistake) 诱使…犯错误; **she tried to** ~ **him out with a trick question** 她试图用一个刁钻的问题难住他; **he was caught out by their disguise** 他被他们的伪装欺骗了 **2** (take by surprise) 使突陷困境; **they were caught out by the sudden rise in interest rates** 利率骤升让他们措手不及
- **catch up**

A *vi* **1** (reach by going faster, attain same level) 赶上; **to** ~ **up with sb.** 赶上某人; **to** ~ **up with** *or* **on sb./sth.** colloq 赶上 ‹*person, vehicle*› **2** (making up for neglect) 补做; **he's got a lot of work to** ~ **up on** 他有很多工作要补上; **you must** ~ **up on your sleep** 你一定要补觉 **3** (get up to date) 了解情况; **to** ~ **up on** *or* **with sth.** 了解 ‹*news, gossip*›

B *vt* **1** [~ **sb./sth. up**] (reach by going faster than, attain same level as) 赶上 ‹*person, vehicle*› **2** [~ **sb./sth. up,** ~ **up sb./sth.**] (pick up) 一把抓起 ‹*object, baby*›; **he caught up his briefcase and rushed out of the office** 他一把抓起公文包冲出了办公室 **3** [~ **sth. up**] (get stuck) 把…绊住; **the fly got caught up in the web** 苍蝇被蜘蛛网黏住了; **I caught my skirt** *or* **got my skirt caught up in the thorns** 我的裙子被荆棘钩住了

- **catch up in** *vt* **to be** *or* **get caught up in sth.** 被卷入; **we were caught up in their excitement** 我们被他们的兴奋情绪感染
- **catch up with** *vt* [~ **up with sb.**] **1** (find) 找到; **death eventually** ~**es up with all of us** 人人都难逃一死 **2** (start to affect) 开始困扰; **she was terrified that one day her past problems would** ~ **up with her** 她十分害怕过去的问题总有一天又会来困扰她; **all these late nights are finally** ~**ing up with him** 他多日熬夜, 现在终于开始尝到苦果了

catch-22 *n* [u and c] 进退两难的境地

> **catch-22**
>
> 第22条军规。源自美国作家约瑟夫·海勒(Joseph Heller) 1961 年出版的同名小说。故事以第二次世界大战期间美国空军基地的一个医院为背景。空军上尉约翰·尤赛林 (John Yossarian) 对战争和军队腐败的官僚体制感到幻灭, 试图通过装疯扮癫以停止执行轰炸任务。根据第 22 条军规的规定, 疯癫之后可以停飞, 但需要申请。然而如果一个人感到有危险而提出停飞, 即说明申请人神志正常, 因此必须继续执行飞行任务。尤赛林无论如何也不可能达到停飞的目的, 最后只能开小差逃往中立国瑞典。该词现用来比喻无法逃脱的两难境地。

C

catch: ~**-all** *n* **1** (word) 笼统的话; **a** ~ **phrase/list** 笼统的词语/清单; **2** Amer (container) 杂物容器; ~ **crop** *n* (between seasons) 填闲作物; (in same season) 间种作物

catcher /ˈkætʃə(r)/ *n* 接球手

catching /ˈkætʃɪŋ/ *adj pred* **1** Med 传染性的 **2** fig «*enthusiasm, fear*» 有感染力的

catchline /ˈkætʃlaɪn/ *n* **1** (slogan) 醒目的广告语 **2** (headline) 醒目的标题

catchment /ˈkætʃmənt/ *n* 集水

catchment area *n* **1** (of water) 汇水面积 **2** (of school) 招生区; (of hospital) 服务区

catch: ~**phrase** *n* 流行语; ~ **question** *n* 怪题

catchup /ˈkætʃʌp/ *n* = **ketchup**

catch-up /ˈkætʃʌp/ *n* [u] **to play** ~ 赶超

catchword /ˈkætʃwɜːd/ *n* 流行语

catchy /ˈkætʃi/ *adj* 易记的 ‹*tune, slogan*›

catechism /ˈkætəkɪzəm/ *n* [基督教的] 教理问答

categorical /ˌkætəˈɡɒrɪkl, Amer -ˈɡɔːr-/, **categoric** /ˌkætəˈɡɒrɪk, Amer -ˈɡɔːr-/ *adj* 绝对的 ‹*assurance*›; 明确的 ‹*denial, statement*›

categorically /ˌkætəˈɡɒrɪkli, Amer -ˈɡɔːr-/ *adv* 绝对地 ‹*wrong, true*›; 明确地 ‹*deny, state*›

categorize /ˈkætəɡəraɪz/ *vt* 将…分类; **to** ~ **sth. into four groups** 把某事物分四类; **to** ~ **people according to age** 按年龄分组

category /ˈkætəɡəri, Amer -ɡɔːri/ *n* 种类; **to fall into three main categories** 分三大类

cater /ˈkeɪtə(r)/

A *vi* **1** (provide food) **to** ~ **for sb./sth.** 为某人/某事物提供饮食; **they** ~ **for wedding receptions** 他们承办婚宴 **2** (provide) **to** ~ **for sb./sth.** 满足某人/某事物的需要; **to** ~ **for the needs/tastes of ...** 满足…的需要/迎合…的口味 **3** (consider) **to** ~ **for sb./sth.** 考虑到某人/某事物 **4** (satisfy demands) **to** ~ **to sb./sth.** 迎合某人/某事物

B *vt* 为…提供饮食; **he** ~**ed a lunch for 25** 他为 25 个人准备午餐

cater-cornered Amer, **cater-corner**

A *adj* (diagonal) 对角线的; (diagonally opposite) 斜置的; **a** ~ **walk crosses the park** 一条斜穿公园的便道

B *adv* 斜对地

caterer /ˈkeɪtərə(r)/ ▸**p. 409** *n* (for parties, receptions) 酒席承办者; (for businesses) 饮食提供者

catering /ˈkeɪtərɪŋ/ *n* [u] **1** (career) 餐饮业 **2** (service) 酒席承办; ~ **staff/industry** 餐饮服务人员/餐饮业

caterpillar /ˈkætəpɪlə(r)/ *n* **1** Zool 毛虫 **2** (vehicle) 履带式车辆 **3** **Caterpillar**® (on tank) ~ **(track)** 履带

caterwaul /ˈkætəwɔːl/

A *vi* **1** «*cat*» 号叫 **2** «*person*» 尖叫

B *n* 尖叫

caterwauling /ˈkætəwɔːlɪŋ/ *n* [u and c] (by cat) 号叫; (by person) 尖叫

cat: ~ fight *n* colloq 女人吵架; **~fish** *n* (*pl* **~fish** *or* **~fishes**) 鲶鱼; **~flap** *n* 猫洞; **~ food** *n* [u and c] 猫粮; **~gut** *n* [u] 肠线

catharsis /kəˈθɑːsɪs/ *n* [u] 情感宣泄

cathartic /kəˈθɑːtɪk/ *adj* ① (purging) 有宣泄作用的 ‹*experience*› ② Psych 宣泄式的 ‹*analysis, effect*›

Cathay /kæˈθeɪ/ *pr n* liter or archaic 中国

cathedral /kəˈθiːdrəl/ *n* 教区总教堂; **St Paul's C~** 圣保罗大教堂; **~ architecture/clergy** 大教堂建筑设计/总教堂教士

cathedral: ~ choir *n* 教区总教堂唱诗班; **~ city** *n* 教区总教堂所在城市; **~ school** *n* 教区总教堂附属学校

Catherine wheel /ˈkæθrɪn wiːl, Amer -hwiːl/ *n* 凯瑟琳车轮式焰火

catheter /ˈkæθɪtə(r)/ *n* 导管

cathode /ˈkæθəʊd/ *n* ① (negative) 阴极 ② (positive) 阳极

cathode: ~ ray *n* 阴极射线; **~-ray tube** *n* 阴极射线管

catholic /ˈkæθəlɪk/

A *adj* ① **Catholic** Relig 天主教的 ② (eclectic) 广泛的 ‹*tastes, interests*›; 兼收并蓄的 ‹*person, view*›; 包罗万象的 ‹*selection*›

B **Catholic** *n* 天主教教徒

Catholicism /kəˈθɒlɪsɪzəm/ *n* [u] ① (doctrine) 天主教教义 ② (belief) 天主教信仰 ③ (organization) 天主教组织

cathouse /ˈkæthaʊs/ *n* Amer colloq 妓院

cation /ˈkætaɪən/ *n* 阳离子

catkin /ˈkætkɪn/ *n* 柔荑花序

catlick /ˈkætlɪk/ *n* Brit 马虎的一洗

catlike /ˈkætlaɪk/ *adj* 像猫一样的; **with stealth** 偷偷摸摸地; **with ~ tread** 蹑手蹑脚地

cat: ~ litter *n* [u] 猫砂; **~mint** *n* [u] Brit 假荆芥

catnap /ˈkætnæp/

A *n* 盹儿

B *vi* (*pres p etc.* **-pp-**) 打盹儿

cat: ~nip *n* [u] Amer = **~mint**; **~-o'-nine-tails** *n* Hist 九尾鞭 [旧时用于鞭打犯人]; **~'s cradle** *n* [u] 挑绷子; **~'s-eye** *n* ① (gem) 猫眼石; ② **catseye®** Brit (on road) 反光路标; **~suit** *n* 女式紧身连衣裤

catsup /ˈkætsəp/ *n* Amer = **ketchup**

cattery /ˈkætəri/ *n* 猫代养所

cattle /ˈkætl/ *n* + *v pl* 牛; **a herd of ~** 一群牛

cattle: ~ grid Brit, **~ guard** Amer *ns* 拦畜沟栅; **~man** /-mən/ ▸ **p. 409** ① Brit (herdsman) 牧牛人; ② Amer (breeder) 养牛人; **~ market** *n* 牛市; **~ prod** *n* 赶牛尖头棒; **~ ranch** *n* 大牧牛场; **~ shed** *n* 牛棚; **~ truck** *n* 运牛卡车

catty /ˈkæti/ *adj* ① (spiteful) 恶毒的 ‹*person, remark*› ② (of cats) 猫的; (catlike) 像猫的

catty-corner, catty-cornered *adj, adv* Amer colloq = **cater-cornered**

catwalk /ˈkætwɔːk/ *n* ① (narrow walkway) 狭窄通道 ② (at fashion show) T型台

Caucasian /kɔːˈkeɪʒn, -ˈkeɪzɪən/

A *adj* ① (referring to racial division) 高加索人的 ② (pale-skinned) 白种人的 ③ (of the Caucasus) 高加索的

B *n* ① (pale-skinned person) 白种人 ② (native of the Caucasus) 高加索人

Caucasus /ˈkɔːkəsəs/ *pr n* **the ~** 高加索

caucus /ˈkɔːkəs/ *n* (*pl* **~es**) ① Amer, NZ (meeting) 政党决策会 ② Brit (faction) 派别

caught /kɔːt/ *pt, pp* ▸ **catch A, B**

cauldron /ˈkɔːldrən/ *n* ① (pot) 大锅 ② fig (unstable situation) 波动的情绪; **a ~ of anger** 群情激愤

cauliflower /ˈkɒlɪflaʊə(r), Amer ˈkɔːlɪ-/ *n* ① [c] Bot 花椰菜 ② [u] Culin 花菜

cauliflower: ~ cheese *n* [u] 奶酪花菜; **~ ear** *n* 菜花耳 [被反复击打而肿胀变形的耳朵]

caulk /kɔːk/

A *n* [u] 填料

B *vt* ① (seal) 填嵌; **to ~ sth. with sth.** 以某物填嵌 ‹*pipe, joint*› ② Naut 捻…的缝; **to ~ sth. with sth.** 用某物捻…的缝 ‹*ship, deck*›

causal /ˈkɔːzl/ *adj* ① (of cause) 原因的; (acting as a cause) 构成原因的; **the ~ relationship between poverty and disease** 贫穷和疾病之间的因果关系 ② Ling 表示原因的; **a ~ conjunction** 原因连词

causality /kɔːˈzæləti/ *n* [u] ① (relationship) 因果关系 ② (principle) 因果性

causation /kɔːˈzeɪʃn/ *n* [u] ① (causality) 因果关系 ② (causing) 起因

causative /ˈkɔːzətɪv/

A *adj* ① (as cause) 成为原因的 ‹*agent, effect, relationship*›; **a ~ link between X and Y** X和Y之间的因果关系 ② Ling 使役的; **a ~ verb** 使役动词

B *n* 使役动词

cause /kɔːz/

A *n* ① [u and c] (person, thing making sth. happen) 原因; **to die of** *or* **from natural ~s** 自然死亡; **the ~ of the accident** 事故的起因; **the root ~ of a problem** 问题的根源 ② [u] (reason) 理由; **there is no ~ for alarm** 不必惊慌; **you have no ~ for complaint** 你没理由抱怨; **to give ~ for concern** 令人担忧; **to have ~ to do sth.** 有理由做某事; **with/without good ~** 理由充分地/无缘无故地 ③ [u and c] (principle, aim) 事业; **to be (all) in** *or* **for a good ~** 有好的初衷; **a lost ~** 注定失败的事业; **to make common ~ with sb./sth.** 与某人/某团体联合起来 ④ [u and c] Jur (grounds) 诉讼理由; **a ~ of action** 起诉的理由; **to show ~** 陈述理由 ⑤ [c] Jur (claim, dispute) 诉讼案; **to plead sb.'s ~** 为某人辩护

B *vt* 引起; **to ~ sb. to do sth.** 使某人做某事; **to ~ trouble** 惹麻烦; **to ~ sb. problems/anxiety** 给某人带来问题/使某人感到焦虑; **the heavy rains ~d widespread flooding** 大雨造成了大面积的洪涝

cause célèbre /ˌkɔːz seɪˈlebrə/ (*pl* **causes célèbres** /ˌkɔːz seɪˈlebrə/) *n* 轰动事件

causeway /ˈkɔːzweɪ/ *n* 堤道

caustic /ˈkɔːstɪk/ *adj* ① fig (sarcastic) 尖刻的 ‹*words, satire*› ② Chem 腐蚀性的 ‹*substance*›

caustic soda *n* [u] = **sodium hydroxide**

cauterization /ˌkɔːtəraɪˈzeɪʃn/ *n* [u and c] 烧灼

cauterize /ˈkɔːtəraɪz/ *vt* 烧灼 ‹*wound, skin*›

caution /ˈkɔːʃn/

A *n* ① [u] (care, wariness) 小心; **to drive with ~** 谨慎驾驶; **to exercise ~** 多加小心; **for the sake of ~** 为谨慎起见; **to err on the side of ~** 宁可谨慎; **to throw** *or* **cast** *or* **fling ~ to the winds** 冒险行事 ② [u and c] (warning) 警告; **to sound a note of ~** 发出警告提示 ③ [u] Brit Jur (verbal) [对犯罪嫌疑人的] 法律权利告知; **to be under ~** 被告知法律权利 ④ [c] Brit Jur (as punishment) 警告判决; **to get off** *or* **be let off with a ~** 只受到警告了事 ⑤ [c] colloq dated (amusing person) 可笑的人; (surprising person) 令人惊奇的人

B *vt* ① (warn) 警告; **to ~ sb. against doing sth.** 警告某人不要做某事; **to ~ sb. against** *or* **about sth.** 警告某人防范 ‹*danger, risk, problem*›; **the doctor ~ed the patient against over-exertion** 医生告诫病人不要过度劳累; **the Chancellor ~ed that economic uncertainties remained** 总理警告说经济形势仍不明朗 ② Brit Jur «*policeman*» 警诫 ‹*suspect*› ③ Brit Jur, Sport (warn officially) «*policeman, referee*» 对…作出警告判决 ‹*suspect, player*›; **to ~ sb. for sth./doing sth.** 因某事物/做某事对某人给予警告; **to be ~ed for speeding** 因超速而受到警告

C *vi* **to ~ against** *or* **about sth.** 警告防范 ‹*danger, risk, problem*›; **to ~ against doing sth.** 警告不要做某事; **I would ~ against getting too involved** 我想奉劝一句，不要陷得太深

cautionary /ˈkɔːʃənəri, Amer -neri/ *adj* 警告的; **a ~ word** *or* **comment** 告诫; **to strike a ~ note** 敲警钟; **a ~ tale** 警世故事

caution money *n* [u] Brit 保证金

cautious /ˈkɔːʃəs/ *adj* 小心谨慎的 ‹*person, attitude, reaction*›; **to be ~ about spending money** 用钱仔细

cautiously /ˈkɔːʃəsli/ *adv* 小心谨慎地; **to be ~ optimistic** 持谨慎乐观的态度

cautiousness /ˈkɔːʃəsnɪs/ *n* [u] 小心谨慎

cavalcade /ˌkævlˈkeɪd/ *n* ① (on horseback) 骑马队列 ② (motorized) 车队 ③ (on foot) 游行队伍

cavalier /ˌkævəˈlɪə(r)/

A **Cavalier** *pr n* Brit Hist 保王党成员

B *adj* (offhand) 漫不经心的; (haughty) 傲慢的; **to treat sb. in a ~ manner** 慢待某人

cavalierly /ˌkævəˈlɪəli/ *adv* (in an offhand manner) 漫不经心地; (haughtily) 傲慢地

cavalry /ˈkævlri/ *n* ① Hist 骑兵 ② (troops in armoured vehicles) 装甲兵

cavalryman /ˈkævlrimən/ *n* 骑兵

cave /keɪv/

A *n* 洞穴

B *vi* 探察洞穴; **to go caving** 去探察洞穴

Phrasal verb

- **cave in** *vi* ① lit (subside, collapse) 倒塌; **after the explosion the tunnel ~d in** 爆炸过后隧道塌了 ② fig (capitulate, submit) «*opposition, victim*» 屈服; **she'll ~ in under the strain** 她会承受不住压力垮下来的

caveat /ˈkæviæt, Amer ˈkeɪviæt/ *n* ① (warning) 警告 ② Jur 预告

cave: ~ dweller *n* 穴居者; **~-in** *n* 坍塌; **~man** /-mæn/ *n* ① Archaeol 穴居野人; ② colloq hum (boor) 粗野的人; **~ painting** *n* 洞穴壁画

caver /ˈkeɪvə(r)/ *n* 洞穴探察者

cavern /ˈkævən/ *n* 大洞穴

cavernous /ˈkævənəs/ *adj* ① (empty, hollow) 大而深的; **a bleak, ~ house** 阴冷空落的房子; **the ~ depths of the cellar** 黑洞洞的地窖深处 ② fig (dark, deep) 深陷的 ‹*mouth, eyes*›; **he opened his mouth wide in a ~ yawn** 他张大嘴，深深地打了个呵欠

caviar, caviare /ˈkæviɑː(r), ˌkæviˈɑː(r)/ *n* [u] 鱼子酱; **to be ~ to the general** fig 过于高雅

cavil /ˈkævl/

A *vi* (*pres p etc.* **-ll-** Brit, **-l-** Amer) 吹毛求疵; **to ~ about** *or* **at sth.** 对某事物吹毛求疵

B *n* 吹毛求疵

caving /ˈkeɪvɪŋ/ *n* [u] 洞穴探察

cavity /ˈkævəti/ *n* ① (in solid body or material) 孔 ② (in human body) 腔; **the chest ~** 胸腔 ③ (in tooth) 龋洞

cavity: ~ block *n* 空心砌块; **~ brick** *n* 空心砖; **~ wall** *n* 空心墙; **~ wall insulation** *n* [u] ① (process) 空心墙隔热材料填充; ② (material) 空心墙隔热材料

cavort /kəˈvɔːt/ *vi* ① **~ (about** *or* **around)** (jump around) 欢跃; **boys ~ing in the corridor** 在走廊里欢蹦乱跳的男孩们 ② colloq (indulge in pleasurable pursuits) 寻欢作乐

cavy /ˈkeɪvi/ *n* 豚鼠

caw /kɔː/

A *vi* 呱呱地叫

B *n* [乌鸦等的] 呱呱的叫声

cawing /ˈkɔːɪŋ/ *n* [u] 呱呱的叫声

cay /keɪ/ *n* = **key²**

cayenne /keɪˈen/ *n* [u] **~ (pepper)** 辣椒粉

cayman /ˈkeɪmən/ *n* 宽吻鳄

CB *abbr* = **Citizen's Band**

CBE *abbr* Brit **= Commander of the Order of the British Empire** 英国国高级勋位; **to be made/awarded a ～** 被授予英帝国高级勋位

CBE

英帝国高级勋位，全称 Commander of the Order of the British Empire。为英王乔治五世（King George V）1917 年设立的英帝国勋位（Order of the British Empire）的第三等（▸**the honours system**），故亦译作英帝国三等勋章。主要授予负责地区事务的高级官员或在各自领域有杰出贡献的人士，如较大地方政府的行政长官、大型志愿机构人士、在业界地位举足轻重的公司董事长或总裁。获此勋位者可在名字后加 CBE。

CBI *abbr* Brit **= Confederation of British Industry** 英国工业联合会

CBS

哥伦比亚广播公司，全称 Columbia Broadcasting System。美国三大全国性商业广播电视网之一，总部设在纽约。业务几乎涉及传媒和娱乐的所有方面，并向美国多家电视台提供新闻、娱乐和体育节目。1927 年成立，始称独立广播电台联合公司（United Independent Broadcasters），后改为现名。20 世纪 40 年代进入电视领域。收视率长期占据三大广播公司首位。公司的电视新闻节目颇具特色，1968 年首播的《60 分钟》（*60 Minutes*）堪称美国电视的王牌节目，曾经五次登上收视率榜首，也是获得美国电视最高奖——艾美奖（Emmy Awards）次数最多的节目。其台标是一只眼睛。

cc *abbr* **1** **= cubic centimetre(s)** 立方厘米; **a 500 ～ motorbike** 一辆排量为 500cc 的摩托车 **2** **= carbon copy**

CCTV *abbr* **= closed-circuit television**

CD *abbr* **= compact disc**

CD burner *n* 光盘刻录机

CD-I *abbr* **= compact disc interactive**

CDMA *abbr* **= code division multiple access** 码分多址; **a CDMA mobile phone** ～手机

CD player *n* 光盘播放机

Cdr *abbr* **= Commander** (in navy, airforce) 指挥官

CD-ROM /ˌsiːdiːˈrɒm/ *n* **= compact disc read-only memory** 只读光盘存储器; **～ drive** 只读光盘驱动器

CD-RW *abbr* **= compact disc rewritable** 可擦写光盘

CD system *n* **= CD player**

CDT *abbr* **1** Amer **= Central Daylight Time** **2** Brit **= craft, design, and technology** 工艺、设计和技术课程

CD writer *n* **= CD burner**

CE *abbr* **= Church of England**

cease /siːs/

A *vi* (stop) 停止; (let up, ease off) «*activity, noise*» 终止; **without ceasing** 不停地; **the rain ～d** 雨停了

B *vt* 停止; **to ～ to do sth., to ～ doing sth.** 停止做某事; **to ～ from sth./doing sth.** 停止某事/做某事; **to ～ to be important** 不再重要; **you never ～ to amaze me!** 你总是让我吃惊! ; **to ～ fire** 停止射击

C *n* 停止; **without ～** 不停地

ceasefire /ˈsiːsfaɪə(r)/ *n* **1** [u] (order) 停火命令; (signal) 停火信号 **2** [c] (truce) 停火; **～ agreement/negotiations** 停火协议/谈判

ceaseless /ˈsiːslɪs/ *adj* 不停的; **the ～ flow of traffic** 络绎不绝的车流

ceaselessly /ˈsiːslɪsli/ *adv* 不停地

cedar /ˈsiːdə(r)/ *n* **1** [c] **～ (tree)** 雪松 **2** [u] **～ (wood)** 雪松木; **～ furniture** 雪松木制家具

cede /siːd/ *vt* 放弃 ‹*right, entitlement, point*›; «*government, country*» 割让 ‹*land, territory*›; **to ～ control of sth.** 放弃对某事物的控制

cedilla /sɪˈdɪlə/ *n* 下加符

Ceefax® /ˈsiːfæks/ *n* [u] Brit [英国广播公司提供的] 图文电视

ceilidh /ˈkeɪli/ *n* 同乐会 [有音乐、歌舞或讲故事等的非正式集会]

ceiling /ˈsiːlɪŋ/ *n* **1** (in room) 天花板; **a high-～ed room** 天花板很高的房间; **to hit the ～** fig 勃然大怒 **2** fig (upper limit) 上限; **to put** *or* **set a ～ on sth.** 对某事物规定最高限度 **3** Aviat 绝对升限; **this aircraft has a ～ of 32,000 ft** 这种飞机的升限为 32,000 英尺

ceiling: ～ joist *n* 平顶搁栅; **～ light** *n* 顶灯; **～ price** *n* 最高限价; **～ rose** *n* 天花板接线盒

celeb /sɪˈleb/ *n* colloq 名人

celebrate /ˈselɪbreɪt/

A *vt* **1** (mark occasion) 庆祝 ‹*victory, festival, anniversary*› **2** Relig «*priest*» 主持 ‹*mass*› **3** (pay tribute to) «*person, song, ceremony*» 颂扬 ‹*person, event, emotion*›; **to ～ life** 赞美生活

B *vi* 庆祝

celebrated /ˈselɪbreɪtɪd/ *adj* 著名的

celebration /ˌselɪˈbreɪʃn/ *n* **1** [u] (action of celebrating) 庆祝; **a day of ～** 庆祝日; **in ～ of sb./sth.** 纪念某人/某事物; **～ banquet/parade** 庆祝宴会/游行 **2** [c] (occasion) 庆祝活动; **birthday ～s** 生日庆祝会 **3** [c] Relig 宗教仪式的举行

celebratory /ˌselɪˈbreɪtəri, Amer -tɔːri/ *adj* 庆祝的 ‹*event, song*›; **to have a ～ drink** 喝庆功酒

celebrity /sɪˈlebrəti/ *n* **1** [c] (person) 名人 **2** [u] (fame) 名声; **to gain ～** 成名; **～ guest/chef** 名人嘉宾/名厨师

celeriac /sɪˈleriæk/ *n* [u] **1** Culin 块根芹根 **2** Bot 块根芹

celery /ˈseləri/ *n* [u] 芹菜; **a stick/head of ～** 一根/棵芹菜

celestial /sɪˈlestiəl/ *adj* **1** (heavenly) 天国的; **a ～ angel** 天使 **2** (of the sky) 天空的; **a ～ body** *or* **object** 天体; **a ～ globe** 天球仪 **3** (supremely good) 精妙的; **the ～ beauty of music** 音乐的美妙动听

celibacy /ˈselɪbəsi/ *n* [u] **1** (abstaining from sex) 禁欲 **2** (being unmarried) 独身; **a vow of ～** 独身誓言

celibate /ˈselɪbət/ *adj* **1** (abstaining from sex) 禁欲的 **2** (unmarried) 独身的

cell /sel/ *n* **1** (for prisoner) 单人牢房; (for monk) [修道院中的] 小间 **2** Biol, Bot 细胞 **3** Pol fig (small group) 秘密小组; **terrorist ～s** 恐怖团伙 **4** Telecom 基站信号覆盖区 **5** Elec, Chem 电池

cellar /ˈselə(r)/ *n* **1** (under house) 地窖 **2** (stock of wine) 藏酒; **to keep a (good) ～** 藏有大量优质酒

cell: ～ biologist ▸p. 409 *n* 细胞生物学家; **～ biology** *n* [u] 细胞生物学; **～ block** *n* 牢房; **～ culture** *n* [u and c] 细胞培养; **～ division** *n* [u and c] 细胞分裂; **～ formation** *n* **1** [u and c] (forming) 细胞形成; **2** [c] (arrangement) 细胞排列

cellist /ˈtʃelɪst/ ▸p. 395, p. 409 *n* 大提琴手

cellmate /ˈselmeɪt/ *n* 狱友

cello /ˈtʃeləʊ/ ▸p. 395 *n* (*pl* **～s**) 大提琴; **to play the ～** 拉大提琴

Cellophane® /ˈseləʊfeɪn/ *n* [u] 玻璃纸

cellphone /ˈselfəʊn/ *n* **= mobile phone**

cellular /ˈseljʊlə(r)/ *adj* **1** Biol (of cells) 细胞的; (consisting of cells) 由细胞组成的 **2** Telecom 蜂窝式的 ‹*phone, system*›

cellular: ～ blanket *n* 网眼毯; **～ phone, ～ telephone** *ns* esp Amer **= mobile phone**

cellulite /ˈseljʊlaɪt/ *n* [u] 皮下脂肪团

cellulitis /ˌseljʊˈlaɪtɪs/ ▸p. 377 *n* [u] 蜂窝织炎

celluloid® /ˈseljʊlɔɪd/ *n* [u] **1** (material) 赛璐珞 **2** Cin 电影

cellulose /ˈseljʊləʊs/ *n* [u] 纤维素

cell wall *n* 细胞壁

Celsius /ˈselsɪəs/ ▸p. 814

A *adj* 摄氏的; **at 100° ～** 在 100 摄氏度

B *n* 摄氏温标

Celt /kelt, Amer selt/ *n* 凯尔特人

Celtic /ˈkeltɪk, Amer ˈseltɪk/ *adj* (of the Celts) 凯尔特人的; (of the culture) 凯尔特文化的; (of the language) 凯尔特语的; **a ～ cross** 凯尔特式十字架

Celtic: ～ fringe *n* **the ～ fringe** 凯尔特外缘 [指来自苏格兰高地、爱尔兰、威尔士以及康沃尔的凯尔特人后裔]; **～ Tiger** *n* **1** (boom) **the ～ Tiger** 凯尔特虎奇迹 [指自20世纪90年代以来爱尔兰的经济繁荣]; **2** (Ireland) **the ～ Tiger** 凯尔特虎 [指20世纪90年代经济繁荣时期的爱尔兰]

cement /sɪˈment/

A *n* **1** Constr 水泥 **2** Dent 黏固粉 **3** Anat 牙骨质 **4** (for fixing tiles) 胶合剂 **5** Geol 碎屑岩的基质

B *vt* **1** Constr 用水泥黏结 ‹*bricks, tiles*› **2** Dent 用黏固粉黏结 ‹*teeth*› **3** fig (settle, establish) 巩固 ‹*alliance, treaty, relationship*›; **their common grief ～ed their friendship** 共同的不幸加深了他们的友谊

cement mixer *n* 混凝土搅拌机

cemetery /ˈsemətri, Amer -teri/ *n* 墓地

cenotaph /ˈsenətɑːf, Amer -tæf/ *n* [尤指阵亡将士的] 纪念碑

Cenozoic /ˌsiːnəˈzəʊɪk/

A *adj* (of the period) 新生代的; (of the rock system) 新生界的

B *n* **the ～** (period) 新生代; (rock system) 新生界

censor /ˈsensə(r)/

A *n* **1** (examiner) 审查者; **the film was banned by the ～** 这部电影被审查部门禁映 **2** (in ancient Rome) [负责人口调查并监督公众道德行为的] 监察官

B *vt* 删改 ‹*publication, film, broadcast*›

censorious /senˈsɔːrɪəs/ *adj* formal 吹毛求疵的; **to be ～ of** *or* **about sb./sth.** 挑剔某人/某事物

censorship /ˈsensəʃɪp/ *n* [u] (instance) 审查; (system) 审查制度; **to exercise/lift ～** 实行/撤销审查

censorware /ˈsensəweə(r)/ *n* [u] 信息过滤软件

censure /ˈsenʃə(r)/

A *vt* 谴责; **to ～ sb. for sth.** 为某事物谴责某人

B *n* [u] formal 谴责; **a vote of ～** 谴责投票; **to lay oneself open to public ～** 使自己遭受公众的谴责

census /ˈsensəs/ *n* (*pl* **～es**) (survey of population) 人口普查; (survey of class of things) 统计调查; **to take/conduct a ～** 进行人口调查

cent /sent/ ▸p. 174 *n* **1** (monetary unit) 分 **2** (coin) 一分硬币 **3** colloq (small sum) 一点点钱; **I haven't got a ～** 我身无分文; **to be not worth a ～** 一钱不值; **I'm not giving her a ～** 我一个子儿也不会给她

centaur /ˈsentɔː(r)/ *n* 半人马

centenarian /ˌsentɪˈneərɪən/

A *n* 百岁老人

B *adj attrib* 百岁的 ‹*population, person*›

centenary /senˈtiːnəri/ esp Brit

A *n* 一百周年纪念

B *adj* 一百周年纪念的 ‹*celebration, concert*›

C

C

centennial /sen'tenɪəl/ esp Amer
A *n* 一百周年纪念
B *adj* 一百周年纪念的〈*celebration, concert*〉

center /'sentə(r)/ *n, vt* Amer = **centre**

centigrade /'sentɪgreɪd/ ▸**p. 814**
A *adj* 摄氏的; **at 100° ~** 在100摄氏度; **in degrees ~** 以摄氏度
B *n* 摄氏温标

centigram, Brit also **centigramme** /'sentɪgræm/ ▸**p. 909** *n* 厘克

centilitre Brit, **centiliter** Amer /'sentɪli:tə(r)/ *n* 厘升

centimetre Brit, **centimeter** Amer /'sentɪmi:tə(r)/ ▸**p. 436** *n* 厘米

centipede /'sentɪpi:d/ *n* 蜈蚣

central /'sentrəl/ *adj* **1** (in the middle) 位于中心的; **to live in ~ London** 住在伦敦市中心; **our house is very ~** 我们的房子就在市中心 **2** (in the town centre) 容易到达的; **the supermarket is in a very ~ location** 该超市位于交通便利的中心区 **3** (key) 最重要的〈*argument, role, message*〉; **to be ~ to sth.** 是某事物的核心部分; **the ~ character** 中心人物 **4** (having overall power) 中央的〈*government, committee, planning*〉

Central: ~ African Republic *pr n* **the C~ African Republic** 中非共和国; **~ America** *pr n* 中美洲

Central American
A *adj* 中美洲的
B *n* (native) 中美洲人; (country) 中美洲国家

central: C~ Asia *pr n* 中亚; **~ bank** *n* 中央银行; **~ city** *n* Amer [大都市区的] 中心城市; **C~ Committee** *n + v sing or pl* 中央委员会; **C~ Daylight Time** *n* [u] Amer 中部夏令时间; **C~ Europe** *pr n* 中欧

Central European
A *adj* **1** (of Central Europe) 中欧的 **2** (of people) 中欧人的
B *n* 中欧人

central: C~ European Time *n* [u] 欧洲中部时间; **~ government** *n* **1** [u and c] + *v sing or pl* (institution) 中央政府; **2** [u] (governing) 中央统治; **~ heating** *n* [u] 集中供暖系统; **C~ Intelligence Agency** *n* Amer **the ~ Intelligence Agency** 中央情报局

centralism /'sentrəlɪzəm/ *n* [u] 中央集权

centralist /'sentrəlɪst/
A *adj* 中央集权（主义）的〈*government, policy*〉
B *n* 中央集权主义者

centralization /,sentrəlaɪ'zeɪʃn, Amer -lɪ'z-/ *n* [u] 集权化

centralize /'sentrəlaɪz/ *vt* 对…实行中央集权〈*country, society*〉; 集中〈*power*〉

central locking *n* [u] 中央控制门锁

centrally /'sentrəli/ *adv* (at or near the centre) 位于中心; (controlled from central point or by central power) 集中地; **a ~ heated house** 集中供暖的房子; **a ~ planned economy** 中央计划经济

central: ~ nervous system *n* 中枢神经系统; **~ office** *n* **1** (place) 总部; **2** + *v sing or pl* (people) 总部工作人员; **~ processing unit, ~ processor** *ns* 中央处理器; **~ reservation** *n* Brit 中央分车带; **C~ Standard Time** *n* [u] Amer 中央标准时间 [比格林尼治时间晚6小时]

centre /'sentə(r)/ Brit
A *n* **1** (middle) 正中; **the ~ of the circle** 圆心; ▸**left² C 2** esp Brit (of town, city) 中心区; **the city ~** 市中心 **3** (focus, hub) 中心; **the ~ of controversy** 争论的焦点; **to be the ~ of attention** 引人注目; **an industrial/cultural ~** 工业/文化中心; **a ~ of population** 人口密集区 **4** Admin (seat) 行政中心; **a ~ of government** 政府所在地; **a ~ of power** 权力的核心 **5** (designated building or area) 活动中心; **a leisure/sports ~** 休闲/体育中心 **6** Pol **the ~** 中间派; **a party of the ~** 中间党派; **to be left of ~** 持中间偏左立场 **7** Sport (player) 中锋 **8** Sport (kick, hit in football, rugby, hockey) 传中 **9** Culin 夹心; **chocolates with a hard ~** 硬心巧克力糖
B *modif* **1** (in the middle) 中间的〈*lane, section*〉; **~ seats** 当中的座位; **he had a ~ parting in his hair** 他头路中分 **2** Pol 中间派的〈*party, politician*〉
C *vt* **1** (put in middle) 把…放在中央 **2** Sport (kick, hit) 把…传中〈*ball*〉
D *vi* 传中

Phrasal verbs

- **centre around** *vt* [~ **around sb./sth.**] **1** (have as main focus)《*thoughts, emotion, activity*》集中于〈*person, place, topic*〉; **state occasions always ~d around the king** 国事活动总以国王为中心 **2** (cause to be main focus) 使集中于; **their demands are ~d around pay and conditions at work** 他们提出的要求主要集中在薪酬和工作条件上
- **centre in** *vt* **to be ~d in sth.**《*activity, event*》集中于〈*place*〉; **most of the fighting was ~d in the north of the capital** 战斗大多发生在首都北部
- **centre on** *vt* [~ **on sb./sth.**] **1** (have as focus)《*thoughts, emotion, activity*》集中于〈*person, topic*〉; **public interest ~s on the outcome of next week's elections** 公众的注意力集中在下周的选举结果上 **2** (cause to be focus) 使集中于; **discussions were ~d on developments in eastern Europe** 讨论围绕着东欧的发展而展开
- **centre round** *vt* = **centre around**
- **centre upon** *vt* = **centre on**

centre: ~board *n* 中插板; **~ console** *n* 中控台; **~-fold** *n* **1** (pages) 中间插页; **2** (illustration) 中间插页上的图画; **~ forward** *n* 中锋; **~ ground** *n* 中间地带; **to capture/occupy the ~ ground** 夺取/占领中间地带; **~ line** *n* 中线; **~ of gravity** *n* 重心; **~-piece** *n* **1** (of table) 中心装饰品; **2** (focus of attention) 最引人注目的事物; **~ punch** *n* 中心冲头; **~ spread** *n* 中间跨页

centre stage
A *n* **1** Theat 舞台中心 **2** fig (prime position) 首要位置; **to take/occupy ~** 占据首要位置
B *adv* **1** (in theatre) 在舞台中心 **2** (in prominent position) 处于首要位置

centrifugal /,sentrɪ'fju:gl, sen'trɪfjʊgl/ *adj* 离心的

centrifugal force *n* 离心力

centrifuge /'sentrɪfju:dʒ/
A *n* 离心机
B *vt* 使受离心作用

centripetal /,sentrɪ'pi:tl, sen'trɪpɪtl/ *adj* 向心的

centrism /'sentrɪzəm/ *n* [u] 中间路线

centrist /'sentrɪst/
A *adj* 中间路线的
B *n* 执行中间路线的人

centurion /sen'tjʊərɪən, Amer -tʊər-/ *n* Hist [古罗马军团的] 百人队队长

century /'sentʃəri/ ▸**p. 181** *n* **1** (100 years) 一百年 **2** (from birth of Christ) 世纪; **in the 20th ~** 在20世纪; **at the turn of the ~** 在世纪之交 **3** (in cricket) [击球手一局中得的] 一百分; **to make** *or* **score** *or* **get a ~** 得百分

CEO *abbr* = **chief executive officer**

cephalopod /'sefələpɒd/ *n* 头足动物

ceramic /sə'ræmɪk/
A *adj* 陶瓷的; **the ~ arts** 陶瓷艺术; **~ processing** 陶瓷加工工艺
B **ceramics** *npl* **1** + *v sing* (art) 制陶艺术 **2** (objects) 陶瓷器
C *n* [u] (material) 陶瓷

ceramic hob *n* [电磁炉的] 陶瓷面板

cereal /'sɪərɪəl/ *n* **1** (grain) 谷物 **2** (grass) 谷类植物 **3** (food) 谷类食物

cerebra /se'rɪbrə/ *pl* ▸**cerebrum**

cerebral /'serɪbrəl, Amer sə'ri:brəl/ *adj* **1** Anat 大脑的 **2** (intellectual) 理智的; **his poetry is highly ~** 他的诗富于理性; **the ~ reader** 理智型读者

cerebral palsy /,serɪbrəl 'pɔ:lzi, Amer sə'ri:brəl/ ▸**p. 377** *n* [u] 大脑性麻痹

cerebrum /'serɪbrəm/ *n* (*pl* **cerebra**) 大脑

Ceredigion /,kerə'dɪgɪən/ *pr n* 锡尔迪吉恩郡

ceremonial /,serɪ'məʊnɪəl/
A *adj* (of ceremony) 礼仪的; (used for ceremony) 用于礼仪的; (involving a ceremony) 拘于礼仪的; **a ~ robe** 礼袍; **a ~ occasion** 正式场合
B *n* [u] 礼仪; **with due ~** 按照应有的礼仪

ceremonially /,serɪ'məʊnɪəli/ *adv* 合乎礼仪地〈*dressed*〉; 按照仪式地〈*display, perform*〉

ceremonious /,serɪ'məʊnɪəs/ *adj* 隆重的〈*function, ritual, occasion*〉; 彬彬有礼的〈*greeting, manners*〉

ceremoniously /,serɪ'məʊnɪəsli/ *adv* 彬彬有礼地〈*greet, behave*〉

ceremony /'serɪməni, Amer -məʊni/ *n* **1** [c] (act) 仪式; **a marriage** *or* **wedding ~** 婚礼; **the coronation ~** 加冕典礼 **2** [u] (behaviour) 礼节; **to stand on ~** 讲客套; **with due ~** 以应有的礼节; **without ~** 不拘礼节地

cerise /sə'ri:z, -'ri:s/
A *adj* 鲜红色的
B *n* [u] 鲜红色

cerium /'sɪərɪəm/ *n* [u] 铈

CERN /sɜ:n/ *abbr* = **European Organization for Nuclear Research** 欧洲核研究组织

cert /sɜ:t/ *n* Brit colloq **1** (event) 必然的事; **it was a ~ that she'd cry if she won** 她赢了肯定会哭 **2** (horse) 有把握赢的赛马; **a dead ~** 铁定能赢的赛马 **3** (person) 必定做某事的人; **he's a ~ to win an Oscar** 他肯定能获得奥斯卡奖

certain /'sɜ:tn/
A *adj* **1** (definitely going to happen) 确定的; **they face ~ death** 他们必死无疑; **to make ~ (of sth.)** (establish as true) 弄清楚（某事物）; (make sure) 确保（某事物）; **phone her and remind her, just to make ~** 为保险起见，打电话提醒她一下; **to make ~ of doing sth./to do sth.** 确保能做某事; **for ~** 肯定地; **I can't say for ~ when he will arrive** 我说不准他什么时候会到; **to be** *or* **make ~ of a seat** 确保有座 **2** (sure) 确信的; **I'm ~ that he refused** 我肯定他拒绝了; **he feels ~ of success** 他确信会获得成功; **I let him do it in the ~ knowledge that he would fail** 虽然明知他会失败，我仍然让他做这件事 **3** (specific) 某; **on a ~ day** 在某一天; **for ~ reasons** 由于某些原因 **4** formal (named, but not known) 某位; **a ~ Mr Brown phoned** 有个叫布朗的先生来过电话 **5** (slight) 轻微的; **there was a ~ coldness in her attitude to me** 她对我的态度有点儿冷淡; **to a ~ extent** 在一定程度上
B *pron* formal 某些; **~ of those present** 有些出席的人

certainly /'sɜ:tnli/ *adv* **1** (without doubt) 无疑地; **we shall ~ attend the meeting** 我们一定会参加会议 **2** (indicating assent) 当然; **~ not!** 当然不是！; **may I borrow your pen? — ~** 我可以借你的钢笔用吗?——当然可以

certainty /'sɜ:tnti/ *n* **1** [c] (sure thing) 必然的事; **moral certainties** 道德上确定无疑的事; **this candidate is a ~ for election** 这位候选人当选已成定局; **that horse is a ~!** 那匹马赢定了！ **2** [u] (guarantee) 确定; **with ~** 确定无疑地; **we have no ~ of success** 我们没有成功的把握

CertEd /,sɜ:t'ed/ *abbr* Brit = **Certificate in Education**

certifiable /ˌsɜːtɪˈfaɪəbl/ *adj* 1 (verifiable) 可证明的 2 (mentally ill) 确诊患有精神病的; **he's obviously ～** colloq hum 他真是疯了

certificate
A /səˈtɪfɪkət/ *n* 1 (academic) 结业证书; **a degree ～** 学位证书 2 (of safety, esp of public transport) 合格证; **a ～ of airworthiness** 适航合格证 3 (of birth, death, marriage) 证明文书; Comm (of authenticity, quality) 凭证 4 Cin 审查分级; **an 18-～ film** 限 18 岁以上成年人观看的电影
B /səˈtɪfɪkeɪt/ *vt* 用证书证明

certificated /səˈtɪfɪkeɪtɪd/ *adj* (awarded a certificate) 持有证书的; (qualified) 合格的

Certificate in Education Brit *n* 教育学证书

certification /ˌsɜːtɪfɪˈkeɪʃn/ *n* [u] 鉴定; **the film is awaiting ～** 这部电影正等待分级审查

certified /ˈsɜːtɪfaɪd/ *adj* 证明合格的

certified: ～ accountant *n* 注册会计师; **～ cheque** *n* 保付支票; **～ mail** *n* [u] Amer = **recorded delivery**; **～ public accountant** *n* Amer 执业会计师

certify /ˈsɜːtɪfaɪ/ *vt* 1 证明 ‹*statement, fact*›; **to ～ sb./sth. (as) ...** 证明某人/某事物是…; **the painting has been certified as being genuine** 这幅画被鉴定为真迹; **to ～ a cheque** 签署保付支票 2 Psych 正式确诊…患有精神病; **you ought to be certified!** colloq 你简直是个疯子!

certitude /ˈsɜːtɪtjuːd, Amer -tuːd/ *n* [u] formal 1 (certainty) 确定 2 (conviction) 确信

cervical /ˈsɜːvɪkl/ *adj* 1 (of cervix) 子宫颈的 2 (of neck) 颈的 ‹*vertebra, artery*›

cervical: ～ cancer ▸p. 377 *n* [u] 子宫颈癌; **～ screening** *n* [u] Brit 子宫颈癌检查; **～ smear** *n* Brit 子宫颈刮片

cervix /ˈsɜːvɪks/ (*pl* **cervices** /ˈsɜːvɪsiːz/ *or* **～es**) *n* 1 (of uterus) 子宫颈 2 (neck) 颈

Cesarean, Cesarian /sɪˈzeərɪən/ *adj, n* Amer = **Caesarean**

cesium /ˈsiːzɪəm/ *n* Amer = **caesium**

cessation /seˈseɪʃn/ *n* [u] formal 停止; **a ～ of hostilities** 停战; **without ～** 无休止地

cession /ˈseʃn/ *n* [u] (ceding territory) 割让; (ceding rights) 转让

cesspit /ˈsespɪt/ *n* 1 (of sewage) 污水坑; (from toilet) 粪池 2 fig (filthy place) 污秽之处; (corrupt place) 腐败之处

cesspool /ˈsespuːl/ *n* 1 (for sewage) 地下污水池; (from toilet) 粪池 2 fig (filthy place) 污秽之处

CET *abbr* 1 = **Central European Time** 2 = **College English Test** 大学英语考试

cetacean /sɪˈteɪʃn/
A *n* 鲸目动物
B *adj* 鲸目动物的

cf. *abbr* = **compare with** 参看; **～ page 76** 参见第 76 页

CFC *abbr* = **chlorofluorocarbon**

CFC-free *adj* 不含氯氟烃的 ‹*propellant, inhaler*›; **～, energy-efficient refrigerators** 无氟节能冰箱

CFE *abbr* Brit = **college of further education**

CFO *abbr* esp Amer = **chief financial officer** 首席财务官

cg *abbr* = **centigram**

ch. *abbr* 1 = **chapter 1** 2 = **church**

cha-cha /ˈtʃɑː tʃɑː/
A *n* 1 (dance) 恰恰舞 2 (music) 恰恰舞音乐
B *vi* 跳恰恰舞

Chad /tʃæd/ *pr n* 乍得; **Lake ～** 乍得湖

chad /tʃæd/ *n* 孔屑

chador /ˈtʃʌdə(r)/ *n* 黑袍 [常指穆斯林妇女所穿的只露出脸部的深色罩袍]

chafe /tʃeɪf/
A *vt* 1 (rub) «*clothes, rope*» 擦伤 ‹*skin*› 2 (warm) 擦热
B *vi* 1 (rub) «*clothes, rope*» 摩擦; **to ～ on** *or* **against sth.** 在某物上摩擦 2 (feel irritated) 恼怒; **to ～ at** *or* **under sth.** 对某事物恼火; **to ～ at the bit** 迫不及待

chaff[1] /tʃɑːf, tʃæf, Amer tʃæf/ *n* [u] 1 (husks) 糠 2 (fodder) 草料 3 fig **to separate** *or* **sort the wheat from the ～** 分清好坏 4 Aviat [干扰雷达用的] 金属箔片; **to drop ～** 投放金属碎箔

chaff[2] *vt* 取笑; **to ～ sb. about sth.** 因某事物取笑某人

chaffinch /ˈtʃæfɪntʃ/ *n* 苍头燕雀

chagrin /ˈʃægrɪn, Amer ʃəˈgriːn/
A *n* [u] 失望; **(much) to his ～** 使他 (大为) 懊恼的是
B *vt* 使受屈辱

chagrined /ˈʃægrɪnd, Amer ʃəˈgriːnd/ *adj* (annoyed) 懊恼的; (humiliated) 受到屈辱的

chain /tʃeɪn/
A *n* 1 [u and c] (metal links) 链条; **a length of ～** 一截链条; **to put** *or* **keep sb. in ～s** 给某人戴上镣铐; **the mayor was not wearing his ～** (of office) 市长没有佩戴链徽; **to pull the (lavatory) ～** 冲马桶; **a bicycle ～** 自行车链; **a door ～** (for security) 防盗门链 2 [c] fig liter (restriction) 束缚; **the ～s of poverty** 贫穷的枷锁 3 [c] (connected elements) 一系列; (line of people, things) 一连串; **a ～ of events** 一系列事件; **they formed a human ～** 他们排成了一条长龙 4 [c] (of mountains) 山链; (of islands) 岛链 5 [c] Chem 链 6 [c] Comm 联号; **a supermarket ～** 连锁超市 7 [c] Meas 测链 [用于丈量土地, 长度为66英尺或20.12米]
B *vt* 用链条拴住; **the prisoners were ～ed to the wall** 囚犯被链条锁在墙上; **to be ～ed to one's desk** fig 离不开办公桌

Phrasal verbs
- **chain down** *vt* [**～ down sb./sth., ～ sb./sth. down**] 用链条拴住 ‹*person, animal*›
- **chain up** *vt* [**～ up sb./sth., ～ sb./sth. up**] 用链条拴牢 ‹*person, animal, bicycle*›

chain: ～ bridge *n* 链索桥; **～ drive** *n* 链传动系统; **～ gang** *n* 用铁链拴在一起的囚犯; **～ guard** *n* 链罩; **～ letter** *n* 连锁信; **～-link** *adj* 钢丝网眼的; **a ～-link fence** 钢丝网眼栅栏; **～ mail** *n* [u] 锁子甲; **～ of command** *n* Admin 行政管理系统; Mil 指挥系统; **～ of office** *n* (*pl* **～s of office**) 官职佩链; **～ reaction** *n* 1 Chem 链式反应; 2 (events) 连锁反应; **～ saw** *n* 链锯; **～-smoke** *vt, vi* **to ～-smoke (cigarettes)** 一支接一支地抽 (烟); **～-smoker** *n* 老烟枪; **～ stitch** *n* (embroidery) 链状绣; (crochet) 链式针迹; **～ store** *n* 1 (shop) 连锁店; 2 (retail group) 连锁集团

chair /tʃeə(r)/
A *n* 1 (seat) (with no arms and unupholstered) 椅子; (with arms and upholstered) 单人沙发; **to sit on/in a ～** 坐在椅子上/单人沙发里; **a dentist's ～** 牙医诊疗椅; **to have** *or* **take a ～** 坐下 2 (chairperson) 主席; **to take** *or* **be in the ～** 担任主席 3 Univ 教授职位; **to hold the ～** 担任教授 4 **the ～** Amer colloq (electric chair) 电椅; **to go to the ～** 坐上电椅被处死; **to be sent to the ～** 被送上电椅处死
B *vt* 1 (preside over) 主持 ‹*meeting*› 2 Brit (carry) 把…以坐姿高高抬起 ‹*winner, captain*›

chairbound /ˈtʃeəbaʊnd/ *adj* 坐轮椅的

chair lift *n* 登山吊椅

chairman /ˈtʃeəmən/ *n* 1 (of meeting) 主席; **Mr/Madam C～** 主席先生/女士 2 (of organization) 会长; (of company) 董事长; (at parliament) 议长 3 **Chairman** (in China) 主席; **～ Mao** 毛主席

chairmanship /ˈtʃeəmənʃɪp/ *n* 1 [c] (position) 主席职位 2 [u] (leadership) 主席身份; **under the ～ of sb.** 在某主席的领导下

chair: ～person *n* (of meeting) 主席; (of organization) 会长; (of company) 董事长; (at parliament) 议长; **～woman** *n* (of meeting) 女主席; (of organization) 女会长; (of company) 女董事长; (at parliament) 女议长

chaise longue /ˌʃeɪz ˈlɒŋ, Amer ˈlɔːŋ/ *n* (*pl* **chaise(s) longues**) 躺椅

chalet /ˈʃæleɪ/ *n* 1 (alpine house) 小木屋 2 Brit (cabin) 小屋

chalet style *n* 小木屋式风格; **～ architecture** 小木屋式建筑

chalice /ˈtʃælɪs/ *n* (large cup) 大酒杯; (at Eucharist) 圣餐杯

chalk /tʃɔːk/
A *n* 1 [u] (rock) 白垩; **(not) by a long ～** colloq 差得远; **as different as ～ and cheese** 截然不同的 2 [u and c] (for writing) 粉笔; **a stick** *or* **piece of ～** 一支粉笔; **coloured ～(s)** 彩色粉笔
B *modif* 1 **～ (mark)** Art, Sewing 粉笔线 2 Geol 白垩岩的 ‹*cliff*›; 白垩系的 ‹*layer*›
C *vt* 1 (write) 用粉笔写; (draw) 用粉笔画 2 (whiten) 用白垩粉使变白 3 (in snooker, billiards, pool) 用白垩粉擦 ‹*cue (tip)*›

Phrasal verbs
- **chalk out** *vt* [**～ sth. out, ～ out sth.**] 1 (write) 用粉笔写出; (draw) 用粉笔画出 2 fig (outline) 勾画出 ‹*plan, project*›
- **chalk up** *vt* [**～ up sth., ～ sth. up**] 1 (write) 用粉笔写; (draw) 用粉笔画; fig (mark) 记下; **～ them up to me** fig colloq 把它们记到我账上 2 fig colloq (achieve) 达到; (win) 赢得 ‹*victory*› 3 fig (ascribe) 把…归因于; **to ～ it up to experience** 把它归因于经验

chalk: ～ and talk *n* [u] Brit 灌输式教学法; **～board** *n* Amer, Can 黑板; **～face** *n* [u] Brit 教学工作; **at the ～face** 在上课; **～face experience** 教学经验

chalky /ˈtʃɔːki/ *adj* 1 (made of chalk) 白垩的; (chalk-like) 似白垩的 2 (covered in chalk) 布满粉笔灰的 ‹*hand, clothes*› 3 (pale) 苍白的 ‹*face*›

challenge /ˈtʃælɪndʒ/
A *n* 1 (invitation) 比赛邀请; **to put out** *or* **throw down** *or* **issue a ～** 发出比赛邀请; **to take up** *or* **respond to a ～** 接受比赛邀请 2 (dispute) 质问; **a ～ to sth.** 对某事物的质疑 3 (difficult task, difficult situation) 挑战; **to present/face a ～** 提出/面对挑战; **to rise to** *or* **meet the ～** 成功应对难题; **unemployment is a ～** 失业对人是一种考验 4 Jur 反对 5 Mil [为验明身份而作的] 口令盘问
B *vt* 1 (invite to compete) 向…挑战; **to ～ sb. to a duel** 要求与某人决斗 2 (invite to justify) 要求…证明; (dispute) 质疑 ‹*claim, belief*›; **to ～ sb.'s authority** 质疑某人的权威 3 (test ability of) 激发 ‹*ability, skill*›; 激励 ‹*person*› 4 Jur 宣布反对 ‹*juror*›; 对…表示怀疑 ‹*witness*› 5 Mil «*guard*» 向…盘问口令

challenged /ˈtʃælɪndʒd/
A *adj* 1 (disabled) 有残疾的 2 hum 有缺陷的; **I'm just vertically ～** 我只是个子不高罢了; **attention-～ adolescents** 注意力不集中的青少年
B *npl* **the physically ～** 残疾者; **the mentally ～** 智障者

challenger /ˈtʃælɪndʒə(r)/ *n* 挑战者; **a ～ to the reigning champion** 卫冕冠军的挑战者

challenging /ˈtʃælɪndʒɪŋ/ *adj* (stimulating) 挑战性的 ‹*problem, book*›; (testing ability) 考验能力的 ‹*job, undertaking*›

chamber /ˈtʃeɪmbə(r)/
A *n* 1 archaic or liter (room) 私室; (bedroom) 卧室 2 (large room) 大厅 3 Brit Pol 议院; **the upper/lower ～** 上/下议院 4 Anat 腔; **the ～s of the heart** 心室; **the ～s of the eye** 眼房 5 (cave) 洞穴 6 Mech 舱; (of gun) 弹膛;

the ~ of a rifle 步枪弹膛; a combustion ~ 燃烧室

B **chambers** *npl* [1] Jur 法官室 [2] (set of rooms) 事务所

chamberlain /ˈtʃeɪmbəlɪn/ *n* Hist (of monarch) 内臣; (of noble) 管家

chamber: ~maid ▸**p. 409** *n* [打扫房间的] 女服务员; **~ music** *n* [u] 室内乐; **C~ of Commerce** *n* 商会; **~ of horrors** *n* [展示恐怖物像或情景的] 恐怖屋; **C~ of Trade** *n* 全国总商会; **~ orchestra** *n* 室内乐队; **~ pot** *n* 夜壶

chameleon /kəˈmiːlɪən/ *n* [1] Zool 变色龙 [2] fig (person) 见风使舵的人

chamfer /ˈtʃæmfə(r)/
A *vt* 把…切成斜面; **a ~ed joint** 斜接
B *n* 斜面

chamois /ˈʃæmwɑː, Amer ˈʃæmi/
A *n* (*pl* **chamois**) [1] Zool 岩羚羊 [2] (cloth) [用羊皮、鹿皮等制成的] 擦拭用软皮
B *vt* 用软皮擦

chamois leather *n* [u and c] [用羊皮、鹿皮等制成的] 柔软皮革

chamomile /ˈkæməmaɪl/ *n* = **camomile**

champ¹ /tʃæmp/
A *vt* (horse) 咔嚓咔嚓地咀嚼 ‹*hay*›; 咯咯地咬 ‹*bit*›
B *vi* [1] (chew) 大声地咀嚼 [2] fig colloq (be impatient) 急不可耐; **to be ~ing to do sth.** 迫不及待地想做某事; **to ~ at the bit** 迫不及待

champ² *n* colloq 冠军

champagne /ʃæmˈpeɪn/ ▸**p. 134**
A *n* [1] [c] Wine 香槟酒 [2] [u] (colour) 香槟色 [指淡米黄色或浅黄色]
B *adj* 香槟色的

champagne: ~ cocktail *n* 香槟鸡尾酒; **~ glass** *n* 香槟酒杯; **~ socialist** *n* Brit pej 香槟酒社会主义者 [指怀有社会主义理想但生活奢侈的人]

champers /ˈʃæmpəz/ *n* [u] Brit colloq 香槟酒

champion /ˈtʃæmpɪən/
A *n* [1] (winner) 冠军; **a ~ boxer, a boxing ~** 拳击冠军 [2] (defender) 捍卫者; (advocate) 提倡者; **a ~ of free speech** 言论自由的卫士; **a ~ of human rights** 人权捍卫者
B *modif* 优胜的 ‹*team*›; **the ~ pumpkin** 最佳南瓜; **they own a ~ racehorse** 他们拥有一匹冠军赛马
C *vt* 支持

championship /ˈtʃæmpɪənʃɪp/ *n* [1] [c] Sport 锦标赛; **a ~ medal** 锦标赛奖牌 [2] [c] (position of champion) 冠军地位 [3] [u] (support) 拥护

chance /tʃɑːns, Amer tʃæns/
A *n* [1] [c] (opportunity) 机会; **a ~ to do sth.** *or* **of doing sth.** 做某事的机会; **now's your ~!** 你的机会来了!; **to give sb./sth. half a ~** 给某人/某事物一点机会; **if you give me half a ~, I'll tell you what happened** 如果你让我插句话，我会告诉你发生了什么; **to take one's ~** 充分利用自己的机会; **the tablets aren't working — you haven't given them a ~ yet** 药片还没什么效果——你还得再等一等 [2] [u and c] (likelihood) 可能性; **there's a ~ (that) ...** 有可能…; **the ~s are that he'll resign** 他可能会辞职; **what are our ~s of success?** 我们成功的希望有多大?; **any ~ of a cup of coffee?** colloq 能来杯咖啡吗?; **not a ~, no ~!** colloq 没门儿!; **to be (still) in with a ~** colloq (还) 有成功的可能; **he doesn't stand a ~ of persuading them** 他不可能说服他们; **do you have his address by any ~?** 也许你有他的地址吧?; ▸**cat 1** [3] [u] (luck) 运气; **by ~** 偶然; **to leave nothing to ~** 不存任何侥幸之心; **to leave sth. to ~** 某事靠碰运气; **as ~ would have it** 碰巧; **it was ~ that brought us together** 机缘把我们聚在了一起 [4] [c] (coincidence) 巧合; **by a happy ~, a policeman was passing at the time** 幸好当时有个警察路过 [5] [c] (risk) 冒险; **to take a ~ (on sth./doing sth.)** (在某事物/做某事上) 冒险; **to take ~s (with sth.)** (拿某事物去) 冒险; **he was willing to take a ~ on losing the contract** 他甘冒失去合同的风险
B *modif* 偶然的; **a ~ encounter** 邂逅; **a ~ acquaintance** 偶然结识的人
C *vt* [1] (risk) 冒…的险; **to ~ doing sth.** 冒做某事的风险; **to ~ one's luck** colloq 冒险一试; **to ~ it** 冒险一试 [2] formal (happen to) 碰巧; **to ~ to do sth.** 碰巧做某事; **it ~d that they had sold the last one that morning** 不巧他们那天上午卖出了最后一件

Phrasal verb

• **chance on, chance upon** *vt* [1] [**~ on sth.**] (find) 偶然找到 ‹*object*› [2] [**~ on sb.**] (meet) 偶然遇到

chancel /ˈtʃɑːnsl, Amer ˈtʃænsl/ *n* [教堂内的] 祭坛; **a ~ screen** 祭坛屏风

chancellery /ˈtʃɑːnsələri, Amer ˈtʃæns-/ *n* [1] (office) [大臣、大法官等的] 官署 [2] (residence) [大臣、大法官等的] 官邸 [3] esp Amer (embassy office) 大使馆办公处; (consulate office) 领事馆办公处

chancellor /ˈtʃɑːnsələ(r), Amer ˈtʃæns-/ *n* [1] **Chancellor** Brit = **Chancellor of the Exchequer** [2] Brit Univ 名誉校长 [3] Amer Univ 校长 [4] Jur (state official) 大臣; (law official) 大法官; **the Lord C~** [英国上议院的] 大法官 [5] (state leader) 总理

Chancellor of the Exchequer *n* Brit 财政大臣

chancer /ˈtʃɑːnsə(r)/ *n* Brit colloq 唯利是图者

chancery /ˈtʃɑːnsəri, Amer ˈtʃæns-/ *n* [1] Brit Jur 大法官法庭; **a ward in ~** 受大法官监护的未成年人 [2] Amer Jur 衡平法院

chancy /ˈtʃɑːnsi, Amer ˈtʃænsi/ *adj* colloq [1] (risky) 冒险的; **a ~ investment scheme** 有风险的投资计划 [2] (unpredictable) 不确定的 ‹*matter*›; 无把握的 ‹*method*›

chandelier /ˌʃændəˈlɪə(r)/ *n* 枝形吊灯

chandler /ˈtʃɑːndlə(r), Amer ˈtʃæn-/ ▸**p. 409** *n* 船具商

change /tʃeɪndʒ/ ▸**p. 174**
A *vt* [1] (alter by modifying) 改变; **to ~ sb.'s mind** 使某人改变主意; **to ~ one's ways** 换一种生活方式; **the road has been ~d into a dual carriageway** 这条路改成了双向车道 [2] (alter by replacement) 替换; (exchange, swap) 交换; **the water in the goldfish bowl should be ~d regularly** 金鱼缸里的水应当定期更换; **the comma had been ~d to a full stop** 那个逗号改成了句号; **they've ~d their car for a smaller one** 他们换了辆小点的车; **to ~ (one's) clothes** 换衣服; **to ~ places (with sb.)** (与某人) 交换位置; **she ~d places with her boss for a day** 她和老板互换工作一天; **to ~ ends** Sport 交换场地 [3] (put clean nappy on) 给…换尿布 ‹*baby*› [4] (accept or take back for exchange) «*customer, shop, shopkeeper*» 退换 ‹*bought item*›; **can I ~ this for a size 12, please?** 请问，我能把这个换成 12 号的吗?; **if it's too big, we'll ~ it for you** 要是太大，我们会为您调换的 [5] Fin 兑换 ‹*note, foreign currency, traveller's cheque*›; **to ~ dollars into euros** 把美元换成欧元; **can you ~ a £20 note?** 你能换开一张 20 英镑的钞票吗?; **can you ~ this £20 note for two tens, please?** 你能把这张 20 英镑的钞票换成两张 10 英镑的吗? [6] (move from one to another) 更换 ‹*job, address, seat, TV channel*›; 换乘 ‹*train, plane*›; 转变 ‹*side*›; «*vehicle, wind, river*» 改变 ‹*course*›; **the wind has ~d direction** 风向变了; **she ~d the bag from her left hand to her right hand** 她把袋子从左手换到右手; **to ~ hands** fig 转手; **jewels that have ~d hands several times** 几易其主的珠宝首饰 [7] (get services of sb. different) 另找 ‹*lawyer, supplier, agent*›; **to ~ one's doctor** 另找一位医生看病; **he has ~d publishers again** 他又换了出版商 [8] (transform) «*person, magic spell, process*» 使…转变 ‹*person, animal, substance*›; **the witch ~d him from a prince into a frog** 巫婆把他从王子变成了青蛙; **the sugar is ~d into alcohol** 糖被制成酒精
B *vi* [1] (become different) 改变; **the price of petrol hasn't ~d much** 汽油价格变化不大; **spring ~s into summer** 春去夏来; **the colour of the leaves ~d from green to brown** 叶子的颜色由绿转褐 [2] (to control traffic flow) «*traffic lights, signal*» 变换; **the traffic lights ~d from green to amber** 交通灯从绿灯变成了黄灯 [3] (into different clothes) 换衣服; **to ~ for dinner** 赴宴前更衣; **he ~d into a clean shirt** 他换了一件干净的衬衣; **you'd better ~ out of those wet clothes** 你最好把那些湿衣服都换掉 [4] Transp 换乘; **you have to ~ at Crewe** 你得在克鲁换车; **we ~d from a train to a bus** 我们下火车换乘公共汽车; **all ~!** 全体换车! [5] Aut (go into different gear) 换挡; **to ~ into reverse** 换成倒挡 [6] (alter direction) «*wind*» 变向 [7] (be transformed) **to ~ (from sth.) into sth.** «*person, animal, substance*» (从某物) 变成某物
C *n* [1] [u and c] (alteration) 改变; **a ~ in the weather** 天气的变化; **a time of great social ~** 社会大变革时期; **I've made a few minor ~s to the wording of the letter** 我对这封信的措词作了几处小改动; **a ~ of heart (over sth.)** (对某事物) 态度的改变; **a change for the better/worse** 变好/坏 [2] [c] (replacement) 更换; **a ~ of government** 政府的更迭; **please note my ~ of address** 请注意我变更了地址; **a tyre ~** 轮胎的更换 [3] [c] (new experience) 变化; **to need a ~ of scene/air** 需要换个环境; **it's a ~ from staying at home** 这是对居家生活的一种调剂; **spending the weekend at home together will make a refreshing ~** 全家人一起在家度周末会让大家感到新鲜; **for a ~** (for variety) 为了改变一下; (as improvement) 作为改进; **I think I'll have steak for a ~** 我想来份牛排，换换口味; **why don't you try being polite to people for a ~?** 你为什么就不能对人有礼貌呢? [4] [c] (clothes) 替换物; **a ~ of clothes/socks** 一套换洗的衣服/一双换洗的袜子 [5] [c] Transp 换乘; **I had to make a ~ at Birmingham** 我得在伯明翰换车 [6] [u] (money given back after paying) 找头; **she gave me 68p ~** 她找给我68便士; **'no ~ given'** (on machine) “不找零”; **keep the ~!** 零头不用找了!; **to get no ~ out of sb.** Brit colloq (receive no help) 从某人那里得不到帮助; (receive no information) 从某人那里打听不到消息; (be unable to exploit sb.) 从某人那里占不到便宜 [7] [u] (coins) 硬币; **have you any small ~?** 你有没有小额硬币? [8] [u] (money to exchange for larger units) 零钱; **have you got ~ for a £10 note?** 你有没有零钱换开一张 10 英镑的钞票? [9] [u] colloq (menopause) **the ~** 绝经期; **she's going through the ~** 她正处于更年期 [10] [c] (in bell-ringing) **to ring the ~s** lit 敲奏钟乐; fig 变换花样; **a wide range of styles and colours with which to ring the ~s** 可以用不同方式搭配的各种样式和颜色

Phrasal verbs

• **change around**
A [**~ around sb./sth., ~ sb./sth. around**] *vt* [1] (to different positions) 变换…的位置 ‹*people, thing*› [2] (to different roles) 将…对调职位 ‹*people*›
B *vi* «*people*» 交换位置

• **change down** *vi* Brit 换低一挡

• **change over**
A *vi* [1] (adopt new system) **to ~ over (from sth.) (to sth.)** «*person, organization*» (从某事物) 改变 (成某事物); **the company is changing over from car manufacture to aircraft manufacture** 这家公司正从生产汽车转而生产飞机; **more and more people are changing over to unleaded petrol** 越来越多的人改用无铅汽油 [2] (swap roles) «*people, drivers*» 交换位置; **we shared the driving,**

changing over at lunchtime 我们轮流驾驶，午饭时换了班
B *vt* [~ **over sth.**, ~ **sth. over**] 将…对调位置 ‹*two things*›
• **change round** *vt* Brit = **change around**
• **change up** *vi* Brit 换高一挡

changeability /ˌtʃeɪndʒəˈbɪləti/ *n* [u] **1** (unpredictability) 易变性 **2** (alterability) 可变性

changeable /ˈtʃeɪndʒəbl/ *adj* **1** (unpredictable) 易变的 ‹*weather, person, situation*›; ~ **moods** 变化无常的情绪 **2** (liable to change) 可改变的 ‹*price, rule, appearance*› **3** (that can be changed) 可更换的 ‹*bulb, tyre*›

changed /tʃeɪndʒd/ *adj attrib* 变得截然不同的; **he's a ~ man** 他已判若两人

changeless /ˈtʃeɪndʒlɪs/ *adj* 不变的 ‹*beauty, routine*›

changeling /ˈtʃeɪndʒlɪŋ/ *n* [神话传说中] 被仙女偷换后留下的孩子

change: ~ **machine** *n* 硬币兑换机; ~ **management** *n* [u] 变革管理; ~ **of address** *n* 地址变更; **a ~ of address notification** 地址变更通知; ~ **of life** *n* 更年期; **~over** *n* **1** (transition) 转变; **the ~over from the imperial to the metric system** 从英制向公制的转变; **2** (replacement) (of leaders, employees) 更换; (of guards) 换防; **3** Sport (of sides) 交换场地; (in relay) 交棒; ~ **purse** *n* Amer 零钱包; **~-ringing** *n* [u] (of church bells) 编钟敲奏; (of handbells) 手铃演奏

changing /ˈtʃeɪndʒɪŋ/
A *adj attrib* 变化的 ‹*world, prices, weather*›; 转变的 ‹*opinions, attitudes*›; 变更的 ‹*seasons*›; 改变的 ‹*principles*›
B *n* [u] 变化; **the ~ of the seasons** 季节的变换

changing: ~ **mat** *n* 换尿布的垫子; ~ **room** *n* **1** Sport 更衣室; **2** Amer (in shop) 试衣间

Chang Jiang /tʃæŋ ˈdʒæŋ/ *pr n* ▸p. 663 长江

Channel /ˈtʃænl/ *pr n* **the ~** 英吉利海峡; *modif* 英吉利海峡的 ‹*crossing, port*›

channel /ˈtʃænl/
A *n* **1** TV 电视台; **a programme on ~ 4** 第4台的一个节目; **to change** *or* **switch ~s** 换台 **2** Radio 频道 **3** fig (for communication) 途径; **to do sth. through the proper ~s** 通过正当途径做某事; **secret ~s of information** 消息的秘密来源; **to open ~s of communication** 开辟沟通的渠道 **4** fig (for expression) 表达方式; **music is a great ~ for releasing your emotions** 音乐是释放情感的好方法 **5** (passage for water) 水渠; **an irrigation ~** 灌溉渠 **6** Geog (navigable stretch of water) 航道 **7** Geog (joining two areas of water) 海峡 **8** Comput 通道 **9** Tech (groove) 槽
B *vt* (*pres p etc.* **-ll-**, Amer **-l-**) **1** (cut) 使形成沟槽; **deep grooves had been ~led in the rock by the action of water** 岩石表面在水的作用下形成了许多深槽 **2** (carry) 经沟槽输送; **water is ~led to the fields through a series of irrigation canals** 水通过一系列灌溉渠引到田里 **3** fig (direct) 引导; **we must ~ all our resources into the project** 我们必须把全部资源都投入到这个项目中来; **all our efforts must be ~led into/towards finding an antidote** 我们必须尽一切努力找到解毒剂

Phrasal verb
• **channel off** *vt* [~ **off sth.**, ~ **sth. off**] **1** (carry away) 排出 ‹*water, liquid*› **2** fig (direct away) 拨出 ‹*energy, resources*›; **the government has ~led off substantial funds to deal with the emergency** 政府已调拨了大量资金应急

channel: ~ **capacity** *n* [u] 通路容量; ~ **changer** *n* 电视遥控器; **C~ crossing** *n* 横渡英吉利海峡; **C~ ferry** *n* 英吉利海峡渡轮; **~-hop** *vi* (*pres p etc.* **-pp-**) **1** TV 不断转换电视频道; **2** Transp 频繁往返于英吉利海峡两岸; **~-hopping** *n* [u] **1** TV 不断转换电视频道; **2** Transp 频繁往返于英吉利海峡两岸; **C~ Islander** *n* 海峡群岛人; **C~ Islands** *pr npl* **the C~ Islands** 海峡群岛

channelize /ˈtʃænəlaɪz/ *vt* 为…挖掘通道 ‹*stream, water*›

channel: ~ **selector** *n* 频道选择器; **~-surfing** *n* [u] = **~-hopping 1**; **C~ Tunnel** *pr n* **the C~ Tunnel** 英吉利海峡隧道

chant /tʃɑːnt, Amer tʃænt/
A *vt* **1** Relig ‹‹*choir*›› 吟唱 ‹*psalm*›; ‹‹*priest*›› 念诵 ‹*prayer*› **2** (shout) 反复喊 ‹*slogan*› **3** (sing) 重复唱 ‹*word*›
B *vi* **1** Relig ‹‹*choir*›› 吟唱; ‹‹*priest*›› 念诵 **2** (shout) 反复呼喊 **3** (sing) 重复唱歌
C *n* **1** Mus, Relig 吟诵; **Gregorian ~** 格列高利圣咏 **2** (slogan) 反复呼喊的口号 **3** (song) 吟唱

chaos /ˈkeɪɒs/ *n* [u] **1** (disorder) 混乱; **to cause ~** 引起混乱; **in a state of ~** 处于杂乱状态; **economic ~** 经济混乱 **2** Phys 混沌

chaos theory *n* [u] 混沌理论

chaotic /keɪˈɒtɪk/ *adj* **1** (gen) 混乱的 ‹*state, situation*›; 杂乱的 ‹*lifestyle*›; **absolutely ~** colloq 一片混乱的 **2** Phys 混沌的 ‹*system, state*›

chap[1] /tʃæp/ (*pres p etc.* **-pp-**)
A *vt* ‹‹*wind, cold*›› 使…皲裂 ‹*skin*›; **~ped lips** 皲裂的嘴唇
B *vi* ‹‹*skin, lips*›› 皲裂

chap[2] *n* Brit colloq (boy) 小家伙; (young man) 小伙子; **an old ~** 老兄

chap. *abbr* = **chapter 1**

chaparral /ˌʃæpəˈræl/ *n* [u] Amer 荆棘丛

chapatti, chapati /tʃəˈpɑːti/ *n* [印度的] 薄煎饼

chapel /ˈtʃæpl/ *n* **1** Relig (building) 小教堂 **2** (in church for small services) 附属小礼拜堂; (in church for private prayer) 私人祈祷室 **3** Brit (Nonconformist) 非国教徒的教堂 **4** Journ 工会会员

chapel of rest *n* Brit 殡仪馆停尸室

chaperone /ˈʃæpərəʊn/
A *n* **1** (to child) 监护人; **to be a ~ to sb.** 是某人的监护人 **2** dated (to woman) 年长女伴
B *vt* 当…的监护人 ‹*child*›; 做…的年长女伴 ‹*young lady*›; **to be ~d by sb.** 由某人陪伴

chaplain /ˈtʃæplɪn/ *n* 牧师; **a school/prison ~** 学校/监狱牧师

chaplaincy /ˈtʃæplɪnsi/ *n* [u] **1** (position) 牧师职位 **2** (term) 牧师任期 **3** (office) 牧师办公处

chaplet /ˈtʃæplɪt/ *n* **1** dated (garland) 花冠 **2** Relig (beads) 小串念珠

chappie, chappy /ˈtʃæpi/ *n* Brit colloq = **chap**[2]

chaps /tʃæps, ʃæps/ *npl* Amer [牛仔穿的] 皮护腿套裤

chapter /ˈtʃæptə(r)/ *n* **1** (in book) 章; **in ~ three** 在第三章; **to give** *or* **quote ~ and verse** 给出确切出处 **2** fig (period) 重要时期; **a new ~ in** *or* **of life/history** 生活/历史的新篇章; **that ~ is closed** 那件事情到此为止; **a ~ of accidents** 接二连三的不幸 **3** (branch) 地方分会 **4** (of church) 全体教士大会; (of monastery) 全体修士大会

chapter house *n* **1** (building) 宗教团体议事堂 **2** Amer Univ 大学生联谊会会所

char[1] /tʃɑː(r)/ (*pres p etc.* **-rr-**)
A *vt* 把…烧焦 ‹*wood*›; **~red remains** 烧焦的残骸
B *vi* (scorch) 烧焦

char[2] Brit colloq dated
A *n* (cleaner) 女清洁工
B *vi* (*pres p etc.* **-rr-**) (clean) 当清洁女工

char[3] *n* Brit colloq dated (tea) 茶

character /ˈkærəktə(r)/ *n* **1** [u] (personality) 性格; **not in** *or* **out of ~ (for sb.)** 不符合（某人）自身的性格 **2** [u] (reputation) 名誉; **a person of good/bad ~** 口碑好/不好的人 **3** [u] (personal strength) 骨气; **strength of ~** 刚毅; **~-building** 磨炼意志的 **4** [u] (nature) 特性; (individuality) 个性; **a house with ~** 有特色的房子 **5** [c] (features) 特征; **to take on the ~ of sth.** 具有某种特征 **6** [c] (individual) 有个性的人; **to be quite a ~** colloq 相当有个性; **a local ~** 当地的名人 **7** [c] pej (odd person) 怪人; **a suspicious ~** 可疑的人 **8** [c] Literat, Theat 人物; **the ~s in the novels of Dickens** 狄更斯小说中的人物; **to play the ~ of sb.** 扮演某角色 **9** [c] Print (letter) 字; (mark) 符号

character: ~ **actor** ▸p. 409 *n* 性格男演员; ~ **actress** ▸p. 409 *n* 性格女演员; ~ **assassination** *n* [u] 诽谤; ~ **code**

Characters and words

■ 字 (character) in Chinese normally represents a single syllable of sound. For example, 的 in 我的 and 阿 in 阿哥 are 字. 字 without context is sometimes meaningless by itself and must be combined with other 字 or 词 to make up 词 (words). 词 is the smallest unit in Chinese which can be used independently and also has a meaning in itself. 词 can be represented by a single syllable (我 or 哥), two syllables (电脑 or 花儿) or three or more syllables (摩托车 or 环保主义者).

■ In written Chinese, a character (字) is usually represented by a single syllable. In English, a 'character' can mean a letter, a number, a sign used in writing, or the space one of these takes. Due to the different concepts between 'character' and 字, the translation of 'character' can either be 字 or 字符 depending on the context (字符 means both syllables and signs in Chinese):

The title of the book is written in Chinese characters
= 这本书的标题是汉字

My computer screen is 88 characters wide
= 我电脑的屏幕有 88 个字符宽

■ 'Word' is not exactly equivalent to 词 and therefore will have different translations according to context. Note the different translations of 'word' in the following examples:

The Chinese word for 'tablecloth' is 台布
= tablecloth 这个词在汉语里是"台布"

The word was spelt correctly
= 这个词拼对了

I didn't say a word about it
= 关于这件事我一句话都没说

I couldn't put my feelings into words
= 我无法用言语表达我的感情

The article should be about three thousand words long
= 这篇文章要写 3,000 字左右

n 字符代码; **~-forming** *adj* 形成性格的 ‹*experience, period*›

characteristic /ˌkærəktəˈrɪstɪk/
A *adj* 典型的 ‹*feature*›; 独特的 ‹*behaviour, appearance, quality*›; **to be ~ of sb./sth.** 是某人/某事物的特点; **steep roofs ~ of Alpine houses** 阿尔卑斯山区房屋特有的陡峭屋顶
B *n* 1 (trait) (of person) 特征; (of place, work) 特性; **a family ~** 家族特征 2 Math [对数的] 首数

characteristically /ˌkærəktəˈrɪstɪkli/ *adv* 典型地 ‹*calm, selfish*›; **~, he said nothing** 一如平常，他什么也没说

characterization /ˌkærəktəraɪˈzeɪʃn/ *n* 1 (by writer, dramatist) 角色刻画; (by actor) 人物塑造 2 (depiction) 性格描写

characterize /ˈkærəktəraɪz/ *vt* 1 (portray character of) 描绘 ‹*person, place, era*›; **to ~ sb./sth. as ...** 将某人/某事物描绘成… 2 (typify) 《*feature, quality*》 是…的特征 ‹*person, place, era*›; **to be ~d by sth.** 具有某种特点; **this civilization was ~d by its materialism** 这一文明的特点曾是物质主义 3 (describe features of) 《*writer, portrait*》 刻画

characterless /ˈkærəktəlɪs/ *adj* 无个性的 ‹*person*›; 无特色的 ‹*place*›

character: ~ part *n* 性格角色; **~ recognition** *n* [u] 字符识别; **~ reference** *n* 品德证明信; **~ set** *n* 字符集; **~ witness** *n* 品德见证人

charade /ʃəˈrɑːd, Amer ʃəˈreɪd/ *n* 1 pej (pretence) 装模作样; **their marriage had turned into a pathetic ~** 他们的婚姻变成了一场装模作样的可怜把戏 2 **charades** + *v sing* (game) 字谜游戏; **to play ~s** 玩字谜游戏

charbroil /ˈtʃɑːbrɔɪl/ *vt* Amer 用炭火烤 ‹*meat*›; **~ed food may contain carcinogens** 炭烧烤食物可能含有致癌物

charcoal /ˈtʃɑːkəʊl/ ▸p. 134
A *n* [u] 1 (fuel) 木炭; **a ~ fire** 炭火 2 Art 炭笔; **a stick of ~** 一支炭笔 3 (colour) 深灰色
B *adj* 深灰色的

charcoal: ~ burner *n* 1 (stove) 炭炉; 2 ▸p. 409 (person) 烧炭工; **~ filter** *n* 炭滤器; **~ grey** *n* 深灰色; **~-grey** *adj* 深灰色的

charge /tʃɑːdʒ/
A *vt* 1 (ask for as payment) 收取 ‹*amount, sum, interest, commission*›; (ask as payment from) 向…收费 ‹*customer, client*›; **she ~d me £3 for cleaning the windows** 她擦窗户要了我3英镑; **we ~ postage to the customer** *or* **the customer for postage** 我们向顾客收取邮资 2 (pay on account) 把…记在账上; **I never carry cash: I ~ everything** 我从不带现金，一切都记账 3 Amer (pay for with credit card) 用信用卡支付; **don't worry: I'll ~ it** 别担心，我会用信用卡付款的 4 (make accusation against) 指责; Jur (officially accuse of crime) 指控; **they ~d her with murder/driving in excess of the speed limit** 他们指控她谋杀/超速驾车; **they ~d him with hypocrisy/neglecting his duty** 他们指责他虚伪/玩忽职守 5 Jur (instruct) 《*judge*》 向…发出指示 ‹*jury*› 6 (attack) 《*troops*》 进攻 ‹*enemy lines*›; 《*person, animal*》 冲向 ‹*person, fence*› 7 formal (fill) 把…装满 ‹*container*›; **please ~ your glasses and drink a toast to the bride and groom!** 请各位斟满酒，为新娘和新郎干杯! 8 formal (load) 为…装弹药 ‹*firearm, shell*› 9 (pervade) 使充满; **her voice was ~d with anxiety** 她的声音饱含焦虑 10 Elec **to ~ (up)** 给…充电 ‹*battery, accumulator, capacitor*› 11 formal (give responsibility to) 赋予…职责; **she was ~d with organizing the reception** 她负责组织招待会; **they have ~d me with an important mission** 他们交给我一项重要的使命
B *vi* 1 (ask for payment) 收费; **to ~ for delivery** 收取送货费 2 (attack) 《*troops*》 进攻; 《*person, animal*》 猛冲; **~!** Mil 冲啊! ; **the police ~d towards the demonstrators** 警察冲向示威者; **the bull ~d into the tree** 公牛一头撞在树上 3 (rush) 冲; **he ~d upstairs to answer the phone** 他冲上楼去接电话 4 Elec 《*battery*》 充电
C *n* 1 [u and c] (fee) 费用; **free of ~** 免费; **delivery ~** 送货费 2 [u] (control) 主管; **who's in ~ here?** 这里谁负责? ; **to take ~** 接管; **to take ~ of sb./sth.** 负责照管某人/负责某事物; **to be in/have ~ of sb./sth./of doing sth.** 负责照管某人/负责某事物/负责做某事; **in** *or* **under sb.'s ~, in** *or* **under the ~ of sb.** 由某人负责; **to leave/put sb. in ~ (of sth./doing sth.)** 让某人负责（某事物/做某事） 3 [c] (attack) 进攻; (onrush) 猛冲; **to mount a ~ against sb./sth.** 对某人/某物发起进攻; **a bayonet ~** 白刃战; **the bull lowered its head and made a ~ towards** *or* **at the fence** 公牛低头冲向围栏 4 [c] (accusation) 指责; Jur (against accused) 指控; **to make a ~ against sb.** 指责某人; **to drop the ~s** 撤销指控; **to bring** *or* **press** *or* **prefer ~s (against sb.)** 起诉（某人）; **to arrest sb. on a ~ of murder** 以谋杀罪拘捕某人 5 [c] Jur (instruction) 指示; **a ~ to sb.** 给…的指示 ‹*jury*› 6 [c] formal (sb. in sb.'s care) 被照管的人; (sth. in sb.'s care) 被照管的物品; **the ~s of a teacher** 老师分管的学生 7 [c] formal (task) 任务; (duty) 职责 8 [c] (explosive) 炸药量 9 [u and c] Amer colloq (credit account) 赊购账; **is it cash or ~?** 是付现金还是记账? 10 [u and c] Phys 电荷; **a positive/negative ~** 正/负电荷 11 [u] Elec (amount of electricity) 电量; **is there any ~ left in the battery?** 电池还有电吗? ; **a unit of electric ~** 电量单位 12 [u and c] Elec (act of filling with electricity) 充电; **on ~** 在充电 13 [c] dated (burden) 负担

chargeable /ˈtʃɑːdʒəbl/ *adj* 1 (payable) 应支付的; **a fee of 20 dollars is ~** 应支付20美元的费用; **tax is ~ at 25%** 应付税率为25% 2 Fin (to company, account) 应入账的 ‹*interest*›; **~ expenses** 可报账的支出; **~ assets** 应纳税的资产 3 Jur 可被指控的 ‹*offence*›

charge: ~ account *n* 赊欠账户; **~ card** *n* 签账卡; **~-coupled device** *n* 电荷耦合器件

charged /tʃɑːdʒd/ *adj* 1 Phys 带电的 ‹*matter*›; **a negatively ~ particle** 带负电的粒子 2 (intense) 紧张的 ‹*atmosphere*›; **a highly ~ meeting** 气氛高度紧张的会议; **an emotionally ~ scene** 震撼人心的一幕; **a voice ~ with anxiety** 充满了焦虑的嗓音

chargé d'affaires /ˌʃɑːʒeɪ dæˈfeə(r)/ *n* (*pl* **chargés d'affaires**) 1 (in major country) (job) 临时代办职位; (person) 临时代办 2 (in minor country) (job) 代办职位; (person) 代办

charge: ~ hand ▸p. 409 *n* Brit 工头; **~ nurse** ▸p. 409 *n* Brit 护士长

charger /ˈtʃɑːdʒə(r)/ *n* 充电器

charge sheet *n* Brit 嫌犯案情记录

chargrill /ˈtʃɑːgrɪl/ *vt* 炭烤 ‹*meat, fish, vegetable*›

charily /ˈtʃeərɪli/ *adv* 谨慎地 ‹*open, approach*›

chariot /ˈtʃærɪət/ *n* (for battle) 双轮战车; (for racing) 双轮比赛马车

charioteer /ˌtʃærɪəˈtɪə(r)/ *n* 双轮战车驾驭者

charisma /kəˈrɪzmə/ *n* [u] 非凡的个人魅力; **she has a distinct lack of ~** 她显然缺乏个人魅力

charismatic /ˌkærɪzˈmætɪk/
A *adj* 1 (compelling) 有非凡个人魅力的 2 Relig 蒙受神恩的
B *n* 信奉神恩运动的人

charitable /ˈtʃærɪtəbl/ *adj* 1 (giving) 乐善好施的 ‹*person, group*›; **to be ~ to** *or* **towards sb.** 对某人慷慨 2 (of a charity) 慈善的 ‹*body, donation*›; **a ~ trust** 慈善信托基金

charitably /ˈtʃærɪtəbli/ *adv* 宽厚地 ‹*speak*›; 仁爱地 ‹*act*›; 慈善地 ‹*give*›

charity /ˈtʃærəti/ *n* 1 [c] (organization) 慈善机构 2 [u] (gifts) 施舍物; **to live on** *or* **off ~** 靠赈济过活; **to accept/refuse ~** 接受/拒绝施舍 3 [u] (generosity) 慈善; **to do sth. out of ~** 出于仁慈之心做某事; **to give to/collect money for ~** 捐赠给慈善事业/为慈善事业募捐; **a ~ sale** 慈善义卖 4 [u] (tolerance) 宽容 5 [u] (kindness) 慈爱; **~ begins at home** 慈爱始于家人

charity: ~ box *n* 捐赠箱; **C~ Commission** *n* Brit 慈善事业委员会; **C~ Commissioners** *npl* Brit 慈善事业委员会成员; **~ school** *n* 慈善学校; **~ shop** *n* Brit 慈善商店; **~ work** *n* [u] 慈善工作; **~ worker** ▸p. 409 *n* 慈善工作者

charlady /ˈtʃɑːleɪdi/ ▸p. 409 *n* Brit dated = **charwoman**

charlatan /ˈʃɑːlətən/ *n* 假内行; **he's not a doctor at all, he's just a ~** 他根本不是医生，只是个冒牌货

charleston /ˈtʃɑːlstən/ *n* 查尔斯顿舞

charley horse /ˈtʃɑːli hɔːs/ *n* Amer colloq 肌肉痉挛

Charlie /ˈtʃɑːli/ colloq *n* 1 [c] Brit (fool) 傻瓜 2 [u] (cocaine) 可卡因

charlotte /ˈʃɑːlɒt/ *n* 水果布丁

charm /tʃɑːm/
A *n* 1 [u] (attractiveness) 魅力; **a lady of great ~** 魅力十足的女士; **to turn on the ~** 开始放电 2 [c] (pleasing quality) 迷人之处; **a woman's ~s** 女人的妩媚; **the hidden ~s of the city** 城市蕴含的魅力 3 [c] (trinket) 小挂件 4 [c] (for luck) 护身符 5 [c] (magic words) 咒语; (act) 魔法; **to work like a ~** 立见功效
B *vt* 1 (attract) 吸引; (fascinate) 使陶醉 2 (influence) 诱使; **he ~ed her into going to the cinema** 他把她哄去看电影了 3 (by magic) 以魔力控制

charm bracelet *n* 吊坠手链

charmed /tʃɑːmd/ *adj* 如有神佑的; **he leads a ~ life** 他过着一帆风顺的生活

charmer /ˈtʃɑːmə(r)/ *n* 有魅力的人

charming /ˈtʃɑːmɪŋ/ *adj* 1 迷人的; **a man with ~ manners** 风度翩翩的男子 2 iron **~!** 真是了不起啊! [表示评价不高]

charmingly /ˈtʃɑːmɪŋli/ *adv* 迷人地 ‹*sing, act, speak, write*›; **~ simple** 朴素而又不失妩媚的

charm: ~ offensive *n* 魅力攻势; **~ school** *n* 礼仪学校

charnel house /ˈtʃɑːnl haʊs/ *n* 存骸所

chart /tʃɑːt/
A *n* 1 (graph) 图表; (table) 表格; (diagram) 图解 2 Naut, Aviat 地图; **a weather ~** 天气图; **to navigate a ship by means of ~s** 用海图为船导航; **to fly with the help of a ~** 依靠航图飞行 3 Astrol 星象盘; **a birth** *or* **natal ~** 出生图 4 **the ~s** Mus 每周排行榜; **to be number one in the ~s** 位居流行歌曲每周排行榜首位
B *vt* 1 (map) 绘制…的地图 ‹*land*›; 绘制…的海图 ‹*coast*› 2 (plot) 《*navigator, analyst*》 标示 ‹*route, sales*›
C *vi* 进入每周排行榜; **the record will ~ at about no. 34** 这张唱片将在每周排行榜上排名第34位左右

charter /ˈtʃɑːtə(r)/
A *n* 1 (grant) 特许状; **to be granted a ~** 获准取得执照; **a bank ~** 银行特许权 2 (constitution) 宪章 3 (table of rights) 章程 4 (hire transport) 包租; **on ~ to ...** 被包租给…
B *vt* 1 (hire) 包租; **a ~ed plane** 包机 2 (grant charter to) 给…颁发执照

charter aircraft *n* 包机

chartered /ˈtʃɑːtəd/ *adj attrib* 持有特许状的; **a ~ accountant/bank/engineer** 特许会计师/银行/工程师

charter: ~ flight *n* Brit 包机航班; **C~ Mark** *n* Brit 1 [c] (award) 优秀公益宪章奖;

2 [u] (scheme) 优秀公益宪章奖计划; ~ **plane** *n* Brit 包机; ~ **school** *n* Amer 特许公立学校

chart: ~ **plotter** *n* 电子海图仪; ~ **recorder** *n* 图表记录器

chartreuse /ʃɑːˈtrəːz/ *n* [u] 1 (liqueur) 查特酒 2 (light yellow) 浅黄色; (green) 浅绿色

chart: ~ **table** *n* 海图桌; **~-topper** *n* colloq 排行榜冠军歌曲

charwoman /ˈtʃɑːwʊmən/ ▸**p. 409** *n* Brit dated 女清洁工

chary /ˈtʃeəri/ *adj* (wary) 谨慎的 ‹*attitude*›; 仔细的 ‹*person*›; (suspicious) 多疑的; **to be ~ of sth./doing sth.** 对某事物/做某事小心谨慎

chase /tʃeɪs/

A *vt* 1 (pursue) 追赶; **my dog likes chasing rabbits** 我的狗喜欢追逐兔子; **police ~d the stolen car through the city** 警方全城追赶那辆被盗的汽车; **go and ~ yourself!** colloq 走开, 别来捣乱! 2 (drive in particular direction) 驱赶; **to ~ the boys out of the room** 把男孩们赶出房间 3 colloq (make sexual advances to) 向…求爱; **he's always chasing girls!** 他总是在追女孩子! 4 (try to win) 追逐 ‹*money, job, success, title*› 5 colloq (remind) 催促; **I need to ~ him about organizing the meeting** 关于筹办会议这件事, 我得催催他

B *vi* 追赶; **they kept chasing, but couldn't catch him** 他们一直在追, 但就是抓不到他

C *n* 1 (pursuit) 追赶; **to give ~ (to sb.)** 开始追赶（某人）; **a police ~** 警方的追捕 2 fig (attempt to win) 追逐; **the ~ for the prize** 该奖项的角逐 3 (hunting) **the ~** 打猎 4 Brit (area of land) 狩猎地; **the royal ~** 皇家猎场 5 Equit = **steeplechase 1**

Phrasal verbs

- **chase about** *vi* Brit = **chase around**
- **chase after** *vt* 1 [~ **after sb./sth.**] (pursue) 追赶 2 [~ **after sb.**] colloq (make sexual advances to) 向…求爱; **he's been chasing after her for months** 他已经追求她几个月了 3 [~ **after sth.**] (try to reach or obtain) 追求 ‹*target, title, money, job, success*›
- **chase around**

A *vi* 到处奔走; **the children were chasing around in the garden** 孩子们在花园里跑来跑去

B *vt* [~ **around sth.**] 在…奔走; **I've been chasing around town all morning looking for a suitable present for her** 为了送给她一件合适的礼物, 我一上午都在全镇奔走寻找

- **chase away** *vt* [~ **sb./sth. away,** ~ **away sb./sth.**]

1 (force to run away) 赶走 ‹*person, animal*› 2 (dispel) 消除 ‹*anxiety, fear*›

- **chase down** *vt* Amer = **chase up**
- **chase off** *vt* [~ **sb./sth. off,** ~ **off sb./sth.**] 赶走
- **chase up**

A [~ **sb. up,** ~ **up sb.**] *vt* colloq (remind) 催促; **to ~ sb. up for sth.** 向某人催讨某物; **to ~ sb. up about sth.** 就某事催促某人

B [~ **sth. up,** ~ **up sth.**] *vt*

1 Brit colloq (investigate) 查找 ‹*details, statistics*› 2 (make sth. happen more quickly) 催办

chaser /ˈtʃeɪsə(r)/ *n* colloq [喝淡酒后饮用的]烈酒

chasm /ˈkæzəm/ *n* 1 (abyss) 深坑 2 fig (wide gap) 鸿沟; **the ~ between rich and poor** 巨大的贫富差距

chassis /ˈʃæsi/ *n* (*pl* **chassis** /ˈʃæsiz/) 底盘; **she's got quite a ~** Amer fig colloq 她体形很棒

chassis number *n* 底盘编号

chaste /tʃeɪst/ *adj* 1 (celibate) 禁欲的; (abstaining from sex) 贞洁的; (abstaining from extramarital sex) 忠贞的 2 (non-sexual) 纯洁的 ‹*relationship, kiss*›

chastely /ˈtʃeɪstli/ *adv* 贞洁地 ‹*live, behave*›; 朴实无华地 ‹*write, decorate*›

chasten /ˈtʃeɪsn/ *vt* 使愧疚

chastened /ˈtʃeɪsnd/ *adj* 感到愧疚的

chastening /ˈtʃeɪstnɪŋ/ *adj* 使人愧疚的 ‹*experience, event, thought*›; **to have a ~ effect on sb.** 有使某人愧疚的效果

chastise /tʃæˈstaɪz/ *vt* 1 (reprimand) 责备; **to ~ sb. for sth./doing sth.** 因为某事物/做某事而斥责某人 2 dated (punish) 体罚

chastisement /tʃæˈstaɪzmənt/ *n* 1 (reprimand) 责备 2 dated (physical punishment) 体罚

chastity /ˈtʃæstəti/ *n* [u] 贞洁

chastity belt *n* 贞操带

chat /tʃæt/

A *n* 1 [c] (conversation) 聊天; **we had a ~ on the phone** 我们在电话里闲聊了一会儿; **I must have a ~ with her** 我必须和她谈一谈 2 [u] (talking) 谈话

B *vi* (*pres p etc.* **-tt-**) 聊天; **to ~ to** *or* **with sb.** 和某人闲聊; **she spends hours ~ting online** 她花好几个小时上网聊天

Phrasal verb

- **chat up** *vt* [~ **up sb.,** ~ **sb. up**] Brit colloq 与…调情

chat: **~line** *n* 聊天热线; **~room** *n* 聊天室; ~ **show** *n* 访谈节目

chattel /ˈtʃætl/ *n* 1 (possession) 私人财产; **goods and ~s** 私人财产 2 Jur 动产

chattel mortgage *n* Amer 动产抵押

chatter /ˈtʃætə(r)/

A *n* [u] 1 (talk) (of person) 唠叨; (of crowd, audience) 喋喋不休 2 (noises) (of birds) 啁啾声; (of monkeys) 唧唧声; (of machine) 哒哒声; (of teeth) 打战声

B *vi* 1 (talk) 唠叨 2 (make noises) «*bird*» 啁啾; «*monkey*» 唧唧叫; «*machinery*» 发出哒哒声 3 «*teeth*» 打战; **his teeth were ~ing with the cold** 他冷得牙齿直打战

chatterbox /ˈtʃætəbɒks/ *n* colloq 话匣子 [尤指小孩]

chattering /ˈtʃætərɪŋ/ *n* [u and c] 1 (of people) (action) 唠叨; (noise) 唠叨声 2 (of animals) (action) 鸣叫; (noise) 唧唧声 3 (of machine) 哒哒声 4 (sound of teeth) 打战声

chattering classes *npl* Brit pej **the ~** 喋喋不休的阶层 [指好发表自由言论的知识界或艺术界人士]

chatty /ˈtʃæti/ *adj* esp Brit colloq 1 (talkative) 爱闲聊的 2 (in tone) 聊天式的 ‹*letter, style*›

chat-up line *n* Brit colloq 搭讪调情的开场白

chauffeur /ˈʃəʊfə(r), Amer ʃəʊˈfɜːr/ ▸**p. 409**

A *n* [受雇的] 汽车司机; **a ~-driven car** 由专职司机驾驶的汽车

B *vt* 专职为…开车

chauvinism /ˈʃəʊvɪnɪzəm/ *n* [u] 1 (aggressive patriotism) 沙文主义 2 = **male chauvinism**

chauvinist /ˈʃəʊvɪnɪst/

A *n* 1 (aggressively patriotic person) 沙文主义者 2 = **male chauvinist A**

B *adj* 1 (aggressively patriotic) 沙文主义的 2 = **male chauvinist B**

chauvinistic /ˌʃəʊvɪˈnɪstɪk/ *adj* = **chauvinist B**

chav /tʃæv/ Brit colloq pej

A *n* 品位低俗的年轻人

B *adj* 品位低俗的 ‹*person, lifestyle*›

cheap /tʃiːp/

A *adj* 1 (low in price) 便宜的; **it's ~ to produce** 这生产起来造价不高; **it works out ~er to take the train** 算下来坐火车更便宜; **the ~ seats** 廉价座位; **~ and cheerful** 物美价廉; **life is ~** 人命不值钱; **on the ~** 便宜地 2 (good value) 合算的; **it's ~ at the price** 以这个价购买, 物超所值; **this shirt is very ~ at £15.00** 这件衬衫价格 15 英镑很划算 3 (shoddy) 劣质的 ‹*furniture, wine*›; **it's ~ and nasty** 这东西质劣价低 4 (insincere) 浅薄的 ‹*flattery, compliment*›; (worthless) 无价值的 5 (easy) 不费力的; **a ~ thrill** 唾手可得的刺激; **talk is ~** 说空话不费力 6 (mean) 粗鄙的 ‹*joke, remark, trick*›; 卑鄙的 ‹*behaviour*›; **a ~ shot** 恶意的中伤; **to feel ~** 感到低三下四

B *adv* colloq 便宜地; **they're going ~** 他们在降价销售

cheapen /ˈtʃiːpən/ *vt* 1 (make less expensive) 使…下降 ‹*cost, price, value*› 2 fig (degrade) 贬低

cheapie /ˈtʃiːpi/ *n* 1 Brit colloq (inexpensive item) 便宜货 2 Amer (mean person) 小气鬼

cheapjack /ˈtʃiːpdʒæk/ *adj* 劣质的; ~ **goods** 劣质商品

cheap labour *n* [u] 廉价劳动力

cheaply /ˈtʃiːpli/ *adv* 便宜地; **I was able to buy the shares ~** 我低价买到了这些股票; **to get off ~** 获从轻发落

cheapness /ˈtʃiːpnɪs/ *n* [u] 1 (of article) 便宜 2 fig (of joke, remark, trick) 粗鄙

cheapo /ˈtʃiːpəʊ/ *adj attrib* colloq 便宜的 ‹*flight, ticket, holiday, product*›

cheap rate *n* 低费率

cheapskate /ˈtʃiːpskeɪt/ *n* colloq 小气鬼

cheat /tʃiːt/

A *vi* 欺骗; **to ~ in sth.** 在某事上作弊; **to ~ at cards** 打牌作弊; **to ~ on sb.** colloq 对某人不忠

B *vt* 1 (trick, deceive) 欺骗; **to feel ~ed** 感觉被骗; **to ~ sb. (out) of sth.** 骗取某人的某物 2 fig (escape) 侥幸逃脱; **to ~ death** 幸免于难

C *n* 1 (person) 骗子; **~s never prosper** 骗子不聚财 2 (action, trick) 欺骗

cheating /ˈtʃiːtɪŋ/

A *n* [u] 欺骗; **to accuse sb. of ~** 控告某人欺诈

B *adj attrib* 欺骗的

cheat sheet *n* colloq [作弊用的] 夹带

Chechen /ˈtʃetʃen/ ▸**p. 503, p. 426**

A *adj* (of Chechnya) 车臣的; (of the people) 车臣人的; (of the language) 车臣语的

B *n* 1 [c] (*pl* ~ *or* **~s**) (person) 车臣人 2 [u] (language) 车臣语

Chechen Republic *pr n* 车臣共和国

Chechnya /ˌtʃetʃˈnjɑː/ *pr n* 车臣共和国

check¹ /tʃek/

A *vt* 1 (ensure) 查明; **to ~ that/whether the shelf is level** 查看一下搁板是否平整; **to ~ the availability of the product before ordering** 下订单前先确认是否有货; **~ what he wants for breakfast** 问清楚他早饭想吃什么; **have you ~ed with Tom that we can use the conference room?** 你跟汤姆确认过我们可以使用会议室吗? 2 (inspect, examine) 检查; **she ~ed the signature** 她查验了签名; **we'd better ~ the contents against the inventory** 我们最好参照存货清单查点货物; **the nurse ~ed his temperature every few hours** 护士每隔几小时就为他量一次体温; **he's not in the lounge — ~ the kitchen** 他不在起居室——到厨房去看看 3 (stop from developing) 制止; (cause sth. to develop more slowly) 控制; **to ~ the enemy's advance** 阻止敌人向前推进; **to apply pressure to the wound to ~ the flow of blood** 给伤口加压止血; **to ~ the growth of public spending** 控制公共开支的增长 4 (stop from moving) 使…停下 ‹*person, animal*›; **she ~ed her horse** 她把马带住 5 (restrain, keep in) 抑制 ‹*emotions, laughter*›; **to ~ one's anger/tears** 忍住怒火/眼泪; **he ~ed an impulse to run away** 他克制住想逃走的冲动 6 (in chess) 将 ‹*king*›; 将…的军 ‹*person*› 7 (in ice hockey) 阻截 8 Amer (leave for safekeeping) 寄放 9 Amer (consign for loading on plane, train) 托运 ‹*bag, luggage*› 10 esp Amer (tick) 在…上打钩 ‹*box, item*›

C

C

B *vi* 1 (ensure) 查明; **have you locked the door? — I think so, but you'd better ~** 你锁门了吗? ——锁了, 但你最好再查看一下; **I'll ~ with an expert to see if it's possible** 我会找专家核实这是否可能 2 (inspect) 检查; **to ~ for a gas leak** 检查煤气是否泄漏 3 (stop) «*person, animal*» 突然停下 4 (tally) «*facts, statements, figures*» 相符; **to ~ with sth.** 与某事物相符

C *n* 1 [c] (inspection) 检查; **the police are making random** *or* **spot ~s on cars** 警方正在对汽车进行抽查; **this is a useful ~ for accuracy** 这是一种检验准确性的有用方法; **she gave the bill a quick ~** 她很快核对了一下账单 2 [c] (monitoring) 监视; **to keep a ~ on sb./sth.** 监视 ‹*person, sb.'s movements*›; 监控 ‹*expenditure*›; 监测 ‹*temperature*› 3 [u and c] (sth. halting progress) 制止物; (sth. retarding progress) 抑制物; (restraint) 控制; **to put** *or* **place a ~ on sth.** 控制 ‹*immigration, production, growth, spending*›; **the presence of the headmistress served as a ~ on their behaviour** 女校长在场, 他们不敢乱来; **to hold oneself in ~** 控制住自己; **the enemy was held in ~ by the floodwaters** 敌人被洪水挡住了 4 [u] (in chess) 将军; **to put the king in ~** 使王被将军; **you're in ~!** 将你一军! 5 [c] Amer (ticket) 存物牌 6 [c] Amer (bill) 账单; **to pay the ~** 付账; **to pick up the ~** 做东请客 7 Amer = **tick¹ A3**

D *v refl* 1 (restrain) **to ~ oneself** 克制自己 2 (inspect) **to ~ oneself in the mirror** 照镜子

E *excl* 1 (in chess) **~!** 将 (军)! 2 esp Amer colloq (expressing agreement) [用以表示同意或已办好某项事务]; **do you have your tickets? — ~ — passport? — ~** 你拿上票了吗? ——拿了——护照呢? ——带了

Phrasal verbs

- **check in**

A *vi* 办理登记手续; **you'd better ~ in at your hotel first** 你最好先到宾馆办理住宿登记; **do we have to show our passports when we ~ in?** 我们办理登记手续时要出示护照吗?

B [**~ sb. in, ~ in sb.**] *vt* (as hotel guest, passenger) 为…办理登记手续; **his job is to ~ the passengers in** 他负责为乘客办理登机手续

C [**~ sth. in, ~ in sth.**] *vt* 1 (register as baggage) «*clerk, passenger*» 托运 ‹*bag, luggage*› 2 Amer (leave for safekeeping) «*attendant, customer, passenger*» 寄放 ‹*clothing, baggage*›

- **check into** *vt* [**~ into sth.**] 在…登记住宿 ‹*hotel, guesthouse*›
- **check off** *vt* [**~ off sth., ~ sth. off**] Amer 打钩核对 ‹*item, entry, number*›
- **check on** *vt* [**~ on sb./sth.**]

1 (monitor) 监控; **will you ~ on the baby when you go upstairs, please?** 你上楼时看一眼宝宝, 好吗?; **she kept coming in to ~ on our progress** 她老是进来查看我们的进展 2 (investigate) 核查; **I ~ed on all the details before I wrote the article** 我写这篇文章之前核实过所有细节; **will you go and ~ on what the children are doing, please?** 你去看看孩子们在做什么, 好吗?

- **check out**

A *vi* 1 (leave) 办理退房手续; **to ~ out of sth.** 退房离开 ‹*hotel, guesthouse*› 2 (be correct) «*statement, credentials*» 对得上; **do the figures ~ out?** 这些数字对得上吗?

B [**~ sth. out, ~ out sth.**] *vt*
1 (inspect) 检查 ‹*place, package*› 2 Amer (retrieve from safekeeping) «*customer, passenger*» 从寄放处领取 ‹*clothing, baggage*› 3 Amer (at supermarket) «*customer*» 为…付款 ‹*goods*› 4 (from a library) «*borrower*» 借出 ‹*book*› 5 colloq (try) 尝试 ‹*restaurant, shop, food*›; **this new website is worth ~ing out** 这个新网站值得一试

C [**~ sb./sth. out, ~ out sb./sth.**] *vt*
1 (investigate) 调查; **to ~ out sb.'s references** 查证某人的推荐材料; **I've had him ~ed out** 我已经让人调查过他了 2 colloq (look at) 瞧; **~ that man out!** 瞧瞧那个人!

D [**~ sb. out, ~ out sb.**] *vt* (from hotel) «*receptionist*» 为…办理退房手续 ‹*guest*›

- **check over** *vt* 1 [**~ sth. over**] (inspect) 检查; **to ~ the bill over** 核对账单 2 [**~ sb. over**] Med «*doctor, paramedic*» 为…检查身体 ‹*patient, accident victim*›
- **check through** *vt* [**~ sth. through, ~ through sth.**]

1 (examine carefully) 仔细检查 ‹*figures, letter, manuscript*› 2 Amer (when travelling by air) 托运 ‹*baggage*›

- **check up**

A *vi* 查明

B [**~ up sth., ~ sth. up**] *vt* 核查; **to ~ up that all is well** 看看是否一切顺利

- **check up on** *vt* 1 [**~ up on sb.**] (investigate) 调查 2 [**~ up on sth.**] (verify) 核实 ‹*story, details*›; **they are ~ing up on the reliability of the system** 他们正在查验系统的可靠性

check² *n* 1 (pattern) 格子图案; (square in pattern) 方格; **a broken ~** 犬牙格; **cotton fabric with a pink ~** 有粉红色格子图案的棉织物 2 Tex (fabric, garment) 格子织物; **a fine black-and-white ~** 黑白细格子花织物; **a green-and-white ~ tablecloth** 绿白格子的桌布

check³ *n* Amer = **cheque**

check: ~book *n* Amer = **chequebook**; **~box** *n* 复选框

checked /tʃek/ *adj* 有方格图案的

checker /ˈtʃekə(r)/ ▸**p. 409** *n* 1 (verifier) 审核员; (examiner) 检验员; **a ticket ~** 检票员 2 (device, machine) 检查装置 3 Amer (cashier) 收银员 4 Amer (draughts piece) 西洋跳棋棋子

checkerboard /ˈtʃekəbɔːd/ *n* Amer 西洋跳棋棋盘

checkered /ˈtʃekəd/ *adj* Amer = **chequered**

checkers /ˈtʃekəz/ *n* Amer = **chequers**

check-in

A *n* 1 [c] (place) **~ (desk)** 登机手续办理处 2 [u] (procedure) 办理登机手续

B *modif* 办理登机手续的 ‹*procedure, time*›

checking account *n* Amer 活期账户

checklist /ˈtʃeklɪst/ *n* 核对清单

checkmate /ˈtʃekmeɪt/

A *n* 1 (chess position) 将死 2 [u] fig (deadlock) 僵局; (defeat) 败北

B *vt* 1 (in chess) 将死 2 fig (frustrate) 挫败; (defeat) 使彻底失败 3 (exclamation) **~!** 将军!

checkout /ˈtʃekaʊt/ *n* 1 [c] (in supermarket) **~ (counter)** 收银台 2 [u] (from hotel) 结账; **~ time** 退房时间

checkout assistant, checkout operator ▸**p. 409** *ns* 收银员

check: ~point *n* 1 (for security) 检查站; 2 (in race) 检查点; **~room** *n* Amer 1 (cloakroom) 衣帽间; 2 (left luggage office) 行李寄存处; **~s and balances** *npl* 制衡制度; **~-up** *n* 1 Med 体格检查; **to go for/have a ~-up** 去做体检/做体检; 2 Dent 定期牙科检查

cheddar /ˈtʃedə(r)/ *n* 切达干酪

cheek /tʃiːk/

A ▸**p. 71** *n* 1 [c] (of face) 面颊; **to dance ~ to ~** 跳贴面舞; **~ by jowl** 紧挨着; **to turn the other ~** fig 甘心容忍 2 [c] (in mouth) 内颊 3 [c] colloq (buttock) 半边屁股 4 [u] colloq (impudence) 厚颜无耻; **to have the ~ to do sth.** 竟有脸做某事; **what a ~!** 真不要脸!; **she's got a (bit of a) ~** 她真是 (有点) 无耻

B *vt* Brit colloq 无礼地对…讲话

cheekbone /ˈtʃiːkbəʊn/ ▸**p. 71** *n* 颧骨

cheekily /ˈtʃiːkɪli/ *adv* 放肆地

cheekiness /ˈtʃiːkɪnɪs/ *n* [u] 厚颜无耻

cheeky /ˈtʃiːki/ *adj* 放肆的; **a ~ chappie** 大大咧咧的家伙

cheep /tʃiːp/

A *n* [u] 吱吱叫

B *vi* 吱吱地叫

cheer /tʃɪə(r)/

A *vt* 1 (applaud) 向…欢呼; **to be loudly ~ed** 博得热烈的喝彩 2 (comfort) 使振奋; (gladden) 使高兴

B *vi* «*audience*» 欢呼; **to ~ for ...** 为…喝彩

C *n* 1 [c] (shout of joy, praise) 欢呼声; **to give a ~** 发出一阵欢呼; **to get a big ~** 博得一阵热烈的欢呼声; **to give three ~s for ...** 为…欢呼三声 2 [u] dated (happiness) 高兴; (optimism) 振奋; **be of good ~!** 振作起来!

D **cheers** *excl* 1 (toast) 干杯 2 Brit colloq (thanks) 谢谢 3 Brit colloq (goodbye) 再会

Phrasal verbs

- **cheer on** *vt* [**~ on sb., ~ sb. on**] 为…加油 ‹*player, team*›
- **cheer up**

A *vi* 振作起来; **~ up!** 振作起来!

B *vt* [**~ up sb., ~ sb. up**] 使振作起来

cheerful /ˈtʃɪəfl/ *adj* 1 (happy) 高兴的 ‹*smile, disposition, mood*›; **to be ~ about sth.** 为某事物高兴 2 (pleasant) 令人愉快的 ‹*news, nature*› 3 (bright) 明亮的 ‹*colour, room*› 4 (willing) 诚心的 ‹*worker, dedication*›

cheerfully /ˈtʃɪəfəli/ *adv* 1 (happily) 兴高采烈地 2 (inspiring good spirits) 令人愉快地 3 (willingly) 乐意地

cheerfulness /ˈtʃɪəflnɪs/ *n* [u] 兴高采烈

cheerily /ˈtʃɪərɪlɪ/ *adv* 兴高采烈地

cheering /ˈtʃɪərɪŋ/

A *adj* (encouraging) 令人振作的; (gladdening) 令人高兴的 ‹*words*›

B *n* [u] 欢呼声

cheerio /ˌtʃɪərɪˈəʊ/ *excl* Brit colloq 再见

cheerleader /ˈtʃɪəliːdə(r)/ *n* esp Amer 拉拉队队员

cheerless /ˈtʃɪəlɪs/ *adj* 阴郁的 ‹*day*›; 阴暗的 ‹*room*›; 暗淡的 ‹*prospect*›

cheery /ˈtʃɪəri/ *adj* 兴高采烈的 ‹*smile, greeting*›

cheese /tʃiːz/ *n* [c and u] 奶酪; **hard ~!** Brit colloq 真不走运!; **say ~** 说"茄子"; **a big ~** colloq 要人

Phrasal verb

- **cheese off** *vt* [**~ sb. off, ~ off sb.**] colloq 使感到厌倦; **to be ~d off with ...** 对…感到厌烦

cheese: ~board *n* 1 (board) 干酪切板; 2 (selection) 奶酪拼盘; **~burger** *n* 奶酪汉堡包; **~cake** *n* 1 [u and c] Culin 干酪饼; 2 [u] colloq dated (pin-ups) 性感女人像; **~cloth** *n* [u] 薄纱棉布; **~ counter** *n* 奶酪柜台

cheese-paring

A *adj* 小气的

B *n* [u] 小气

cheese: ~ spread *n* 奶酪酱; **~ straw** *n* 干酪酥条; **~ wire** *n* 钢丝干酪切割器

cheesy /ˈtʃiːzi/ *adj* 1 (cheese-like) 似干酪的 2 colloq (tacky) 粗俗的; (cheap, fake) 劣质的

cheetah /ˈtʃiːtə/ *n* 猎豹

chef /ʃef/ ▸**p. 409** *n* (professional cook) 厨师; (chief cook) 主厨

Chelsea bun /ˌtʃelsi ˈbʌn/ *n* Brit 切尔西葡萄干圆面包

chemical /ˈkemɪkl/

A *n* 化学制品

B *adj* 1 (relating to chemistry) 化学的 2 (produced by or using chemicals) 用化学品制造的; **~ fertilizers** 化肥

chemical: ~ agent *n* 1 (chemical preparation) 化学试剂; 2 Mil 化学毒剂; **~ engineer** ▸**p. 409** *n* 化学工程师; **~ engineering** *n* [u] 化学工程

chemically /ˈkemɪkli/ *adv* **1** (by the use of chemicals) 通过化学品; **the soil has to be ~ fertilized** 这种土壤必须施化肥 **2** (with respect to chemistry) 在化学上; **~ different substances** 化学性质不同的物质

chemical: ~ reaction *n* 化学反应; **~ toilet** *n* 可移动化学除臭马桶; **~ warfare** *n* [u] 化学战; **~ waste** *n* 化学废料; **~ weapon** *n* [u] 化学武器

chemise /ʃəˈmiːz/ *n* 宽松内衣

chemist /ˈkemɪst/ ▸**p. 409** *n* **1** Brit (pharmacist) 药剂师; (seller) 药商; **~'s (shop)** 药店 **2** (scientist) 化学家

chemistry /ˈkemɪstri/ *n* **1** [u] (science, subject) 化学; **a ~ laboratory** 化学实验室 **2** [c] (structure) 化学结构; (properties) 化学特性 **3** [c] (composition) 化学成分 **4** [u] fig (complex process or phenomenon) 神秘 **5** [u] fig (rapport) 默契; **sexual ~** 两性间的强烈吸引

chemistry set *n* 化学实验套件

chemoprevention /ˌkiːməʊprɪˈvenʃn/ *n* [u] 化学预防

chemoreceptor /ˈkiːməʊrɪseptə(r)/ *n* 化学受体

chemotherapy /ˌkiːməʊˈθerəpi/ *n* [u] 化学疗法; **a course of ~** 一个疗程的化疗

chenille /ʃəˈniːl/ *n* [u] **1** (cord, yarn) 绳绒线 **2** (fabric) 绳绒线织物

cheongsam /ˈtʃɪɒŋsæm/ *n* 旗袍

cheque /tʃek/ ▸**p. 174** *n* Brit 支票; **to pay by ~** 用支票支付; **to make out** *or* **write a ~ for £20** 填写一张 20 英镑的支票; **to cash a ~** 兑现支票; **to stop a ~** 止付一张支票; **a blank ~** lit 空白支票; fig 自由处理权

cheque: ~book *n* Brit 支票簿; **~book journalism** pej 有偿新闻; **~ card** *n* 支票保付限额卡

chequer /ˈtʃekə(r)/ Brit
A *n* **1** Games 中国跳棋棋子 **2** (pattern or design) 方格图案; **a blue and green ~ pattern** 蓝绿相间的方格图案
B *vt* 使具有方格图案; **a lawn ~ed with sunlight and shade** 光影交错的草坪

chequered /ˈtʃekəd/ *adj* Brit **1** (marked) 有方格图案的 **2** fig 盛衰无常的 ‹*history, career*›

chequered flag *n* 黑白格子旗

chequers /ˈtʃekəz/ ▸**p. 307** *n* [u] Brit 西洋跳棋

cheque stub *n* 支票存根

cherish /ˈtʃerɪʃ/ *vt* **1** (nurture) 珍爱 ‹*possession, pet*›; **her most ~ed ambition** 她最大的夙愿 **2** (love) 爱护 **3** (keep in mind) 怀有 ‹*memory, idea*› **4** (value) 珍视 ‹*right, freedom*›

cheroot /ʃəˈruːt/ *n* 方头雪茄烟

cherry /ˈtʃeri/ *n* **1** [u] (fruit) 樱桃; **a bowl of cherries** 乐事; **a bite at the ~** colloq (opportunity) 一次机会; (attempt) 一次尝试; **the ~ on the cake** fig 锦上添花; **to lose one's ~** colloq 失身; **to pop sb.'s ~** colloq 使某人的处女膜破裂 **2** [c] (tree) 樱桃树 **3** [u] (wood) 樱桃木 **4** [u] (colour) 鲜红色

cherry: ~ blossom *n* [u] 樱花; **~ brandy** *n* 樱桃白兰地; **~ orchard** *n* 樱桃园; **~-pick** *vt* 精选; **~ picker** *n* **1** (machine) 移动升降台; **2** ▸**p. 409** (person) 精挑细选的人; **~ stone** *n* 樱桃核; **~ tomato** *n* 樱桃番茄; **~ tree** *n* 樱桃树

cherub /ˈtʃerəb/ *n* **1** Relig (*pl* **cherubim** *or* **~s**) 二级天使 [九级天使中的第二级] **2** (in art) 小天使 **3** (pretty child) 可爱的小孩

cherubic /tʃɪˈruːbɪk/ *adj* 天使般的 ‹*child*›; 胖乎乎的 ‹*face*›

cherubim /ˈtʃerəbɪm/ *pl* ▸**cherub**

Ches. *abbr* Brit = **Cheshire**

Cheshire /ˈtʃeʃə(r)/ *pr n* 柴郡

chess /tʃes/ ▸**p. 307** *n* [u] 国际象棋; **a game of ~** 一盘国际象棋

chess: ~board *n* (for chess) 国际象棋棋盘; (for draughts) 西洋跳棋棋盘; **~piece, ~man** /-mæn/ *ns* 国际象棋棋子; **~player** *n* 棋手; **~ set** *n* 一副国际象棋

chest /tʃest/
A *n* **1** Anat 胸膛; **to get sth. off one's ~** fig 倾吐心中的烦恼; **to keep** *or* **play one's cards close to one's ~** fig 把事情藏在心间; **~ pains** 胸部疼痛 **2** (container) 大箱子; (furniture) 柜子; (for packing) 包装箱 **3** Brit (treasury) 金库; (fund) 资金
B *vt* 《*footballer*》用胸部停住 ‹*ball*›

chest cold ▸**p. 377** *n* 影响到胸腔的感冒

chesterfield /ˈtʃestəfiːld/ *n* 坐卧两用长沙发

chest: ~ expander *n* 拉力器; **~ freezer** *n* 卧式冰柜; **~ infection** *n* 胸部感染; **~ measurement** *n* 胸围

chestnut /ˈtʃesnʌt/
A *n* **1** [c] (tree) **~ (tree)** 七叶树; (sweet) 栗树 **2** [u] (wood) 栗木 **3** [c] (edible nut) 栗子; (conker) 七叶树果实 **4** [u] (colour) 红棕色 **5** [c] sl fig (joke) 老掉牙的笑话; (story) 老掉牙的故事
B *adj* 红棕色的 ‹*horse*›

chest of drawers *n* esp Brit 五斗橱

chesty /ˈtʃesti/ *adj* colloq **1** Brit (having catarrh in the lungs) 胸部有炎症的 **2** (having large or prominent breasts) 乳房突出的

chevron /ˈʃevrən/ *n* **1** (line, stripe) V 形臂章 **2** Herald 人字形图记

chew /tʃuː/
A *vt* **1** (break down) 咀嚼; **~ your food well before you swallow it** 吃东西要细嚼慢咽 **2** (gnaw persistently) 不停地啃; **she was anxiously ~ing her nails** 她焦急地啃着指甲; **to ~ one's lip** 咬嘴唇; **to ~ the fat** *or* **rag** fig colloq 吵吵嚷嚷; **to bite off more than one can ~** colloq 不自量力
B *vi* 咀嚼
C *n* **1** (act) 咀嚼 **2** (chewable object) 咀嚼物 **3** (sweet) 耐嚼糖果

Phrasal verbs

- **chew on** *vt* [**~ on sth.**] **1** lit 反复啃咬 **2** fig colloq 仔细考虑 ‹*problem*›
- **chew over** *vt* [**~ over sth., ~ sth. over**] colloq 仔细考虑
- **chew up** *vt* **1** [**~ up sth., ~ sth. up**] (chew thoroughly) 嚼碎 **2** [**~ sb. up**] colloq (reprimand) 痛斥

chewing gum *n* [u] 口香糖

chewy /ˈtʃuːi/ *adj* 需要多嚼的; **a ~ toffee** 耐嚼的太妃糖

chic /ʃiːk/
A *adj* (elegant) 雅致的; (stylish) 时髦的
B *n* [u] (elegance) 雅致; (style) 时髦

Chicana /tʃɪˈkɑːnə/ *n* Amer 女奇卡诺人 [指墨西哥裔美国人]

chicane /ʃɪˈkeɪn/ *n* [赛车道上的] 双急转弯

chicanery /ʃɪˈkeɪnəri/ *n* **1** [u] (trickery) 欺骗 **2** [c] (trick) 诡计

Chicano /tʃɪˈkɑːnəʊ/ *n* Amer 奇卡诺人 [指墨西哥裔美国人]

chichi /ˈʃiːʃiː/ *adj* colloq (affectedly pretty) 故作风雅的; (affectedly stylish) 时髦而做作的

chick /tʃɪk/ *n* **1** (young bird) 雏鸟; (of fowl) 小鸡 **2** colloq (young woman) 少妇; (girl) 小妞

chickadee /ˈtʃɪkədiː/ *n* Amer 山雀

chicken /ˈtʃɪkɪn/
A *n* **1** [c] (fowl) 鸡; **to keep ~s** 养鸡; **to count one's ~s before they are hatched** fig 过早乐观; **a ~ and egg situation** 因果难定的情况; **to be no (spring) ~** colloq 年纪不小了; ▸**roost B** **2** [u] (meat) 鸡肉 **3** [c] colloq (coward) 胆小鬼 **4** [u] (game) 比试胆量的游戏; **to play ~** 玩"胆小鬼"游戏
B *adj pred* colloq 胆小的

Phrasal verb

- **chicken out** *vi* colloq 临阵退缩; **he ~ed out of his dental appointment** 他因害怕没敢按预约去看牙医

chicken: ~ breast *n* 鸡胸肉; **~ casserole** *n* 砂锅炖鸡; **~ coop** *n* 家禽笼; **~ curry** *n* 咖喱鸡; **~ drumstick** *n* 鸡腿; **~ farmer** ▸**p. 409** *n* 养鸡户; **~ farming** *n* [u] 养鸡业; **~ feed** *n* [u] **1** lit 鸡饲料; **2** fig colloq 微不足道的款项; **~-hearted** *adj* fig colloq 胆小的; **~ pox** ▸**p. 377** *n* [u] 水痘; **~ run** *n* 养鸡场; **~ wire** *n* [u] 细铁丝网; **a ~ wire fence** 细铁丝网围栏

chick: ~ flick *n* colloq [迎合年轻女子口味的] 年轻女性电影; **~ lit** *n* [u] colloq [迎合年轻女子口味的] 年轻女性文学; **~pea** *n* **1** (seed) 鹰嘴豆种实; **2** (plant) 鹰嘴豆

chicory /ˈtʃɪkəri/ *n* [u] **1** (vegetable) 菊苣菜 **2** (coffee substitute) 菊苣根

chide /tʃaɪd/ *vt* dated (rebuke) 指责; (scold) 斥责

chief /tʃiːf/
A *n* **1** (leader of a tribe or clan) 部落首领; **too many ~s and not enough Indians** 将多兵少 **2** (high-ranking person) 领袖; **a party ~** 党魁; **defence ~s** 国防部高官 **3** colloq (boss) 老板
B *adj* **1** (primary) 首要的; (main) 主要的 **2** *attrib* (highest in rank) 最高级别的; **the ~ adviser** 首席顾问
C **in chief** *adv phr* 主要地
D **-in-chief** *combining form* 为首的; **commander-in-~** 总司令

chief: ~ accountant *n* 总会计师; **~ administrator** *n* 行政主管; **~ assistant** *n* 首席助理; **~ constable** *n* Brit 地区警察局长; **~ education officer** *n* Brit 教育局长; **~ engineer** *n* **1** (of project) 总工程师; **2** (of ship) 轮机长

chief executive *n* **1** (of organization) 最高行政长官 **2** = **chief executive officer** **3** Amer Pol 总统

chief executive officer *n* 首席执行官

chief: ~ inspector *n* Brit 总督察; **~ justice** *n* Amer 最高法院首席法官; Brit 首席法官

chiefly /ˈtʃiːfli/ *adv* **1** (primarily) 首要地 **2** (mostly) 大部分地; (mainly) 主要地

chief: ~ of police *n* 警察局长; **C~ of Staff** *n* **1** Mil 参谋长; **2** (of White House) 办公厅主任; **~ petty officer** *n* 上士; **C~ Rabbi** *n* 首席拉比; **~ superintendent** *n* Brit 警务长

chieftain /ˈtʃiːftən/ *n* (of a tribe) 酋长; (of a clan) 族长

chief whip *n* Brit 首席党鞭 [督促党内议员执行党纪等的政党高级要员]

chiffon /ˈʃɪfɒn, Amer ʃɪˈfɒn/ *n* [u] 雪纺绸

chignon /ˈʃiːnjɒn/ *n* 发髻

chihuahua /tʃɪˈwɑːwɑː/ *n* 吉娃娃狗

chilblain /ˈtʃɪlbleɪn/ *n* 冻疮

child /tʃaɪld/ *n* (*pl* **children**) **1** (non-adult) 儿童, 小孩; **when I was a ~** 我小时候; **a ~ of six** 6 岁的小孩; **a ~ star/prodigy** 童星/神童; **to be ~'s play** 是轻而易举的事; **spare the rod and spoil the ~** Prov 孩子不打不成器; **the ~ is father to the man** Prov 三岁看到老; **to be with ~** archaic 怀孕 **2** 子女 [可指儿子或女儿]; **her mother's ~** 有其母必有其女 **3** (immature person) 孩子气的人; **don't be such a ~!** 别孩子气啦! **4** (inexperienced person) 幼稚的人 **5** fig (product) 产物; **a ~ of the 60s/of nature** 60 年代的人/大自然之子 **6** **children** (descendants) 后代

child: ~ abuse *n* [u] 儿童虐待; **~ abuser** *n* 虐童者; **~bearing** *n* [u] 生育; **constant ~bearing** 没完没了的生孩子; **women of ~bearing age** 育龄妇女; **~ benefit** *n* [u] Brit 儿童补助金 [由政府定期发给一定年龄以下儿童的父母]; **~birth** *n* [u] 分

娩; **to die in ~birth** 死于难产; **~ bride** *n* 童养媳; **~care** *n* [u] (bringing up children) 儿童保育; (in nursery etc.) 儿童照管; **~care facilities** *npl* (places) 儿童照管场所; (resources) 儿童照管设施; **~ guidance** *n* [u] 儿童心理指导; **~hood** *n* [u] 童年; **in one's second ~hood** 在某人的老小孩时期; **in early/late ~hood** 在童年早期/晚期; **~hood games/friends/memories** 童年的游戏/朋友/记忆

childish /ˈtʃaɪldɪʃ/ *adj* **1** (of a child) 孩子的; (appropriate to a child) 适合孩子的; **~ games** 儿童游戏 **2** pej (immature) 幼稚的 ‹*behaviour, attitude*›; (silly) 傻气的 ‹*behaviour, manners, attitude, speech*›

C

childishly /ˈtʃaɪldɪʃli/ *adv* pej (immaturely) 幼稚地 ‹*behave, act*›; (in a silly way) 傻气地 ‹*behave, act, speak*›

childishness /ˈtʃaɪldɪʃnɪs/ *n* [u] (immaturity) 幼稚; (silliness) 傻气

child: ~ labour *n* [u] 童工雇用; **~ language** *n* [u] 儿童用语

childless /ˈtʃaɪldlɪs/ *adj* 无子女的 ‹*couple, marriage*›

childlike /ˈtʃaɪldlaɪk/ *adj* 孩子般的; **a ~ innocence/pleasure** 孩子般的天真/快乐

child: ~ lock *n* [防止儿童开启的] 儿童锁; **~minder** ▸p. 409 *n* Brit 受雇照看孩子者; **~ molester** *n* 对儿童进行性侵犯者; **~ pornography** *n* [u] 儿童色情作品; **~-proof** *adj* 对儿童安全的 ‹*lock*›; 防止儿童开启的 ‹*container, top*›; **~ protection register** *n* Brit 儿童保护登记册; **~ psychiatrist** ▸p. 409 *n* 儿童精神病医师; **~ psychiatry** *n* [u] (study) 儿童精神病学; (treatment) 儿童精神病治疗; **~ psychology** *n* [u] 儿童心理学

children /ˈtʃɪldrən/ *pl* ▸**child**

children's home *n* [收留无人照管儿童的] 儿童之家

child: ~ seat *n* 儿童安全座椅; **C~ Support Agency** *n* Brit 儿童援助局; **~ Tax Credit** *n* [u and c] Brit 孩童抵税额

Chile /ˈtʃɪli/ *pr n* 智利

Chilean /ˈtʃɪlɪən/ ▸**p. 503**
A *adj* (of Chile) 智利的; (of the people) 智利人的
B *n* 智利人

chili /ˈtʃɪli/ *n* (*pl* **~es**) Amer = **chilli**

chill /tʃɪl/
A *n* **1** [u] (coldness) 寒冷; **there is a ~ in the air** 空气中透着几分寒意 **2** [c] (illness) 风寒; **to catch a ~** 着凉 **3** [c] fig (feeling of fear) 害怕; **to send a ~ through sb.** *or* **down sb.'s spine** 令某人毛骨悚然; **to cast a ~ over sth.** 使某事物蒙上一层阴影
B *vt* **1** (make cold) 使…感到冷 ‹*person*›; 使…变冷 ‹*air*›; fig 使…变得扫兴 ‹*atmosphere*›; **to ~ sb. to the bone** *or* **marrow** 使某人感到寒气刺骨 **2** fig (cause to fear) 惊吓; **to ~ sb.'s** *or* **the blood** 令某人不寒而栗 **3** Culin (refrigerate) 使…冷却 ‹*drink*›; (keep cool) 冷藏 ‹*food, melon*›
C *vi* **1** Culin 冷却 **2** colloq (relax) 放松
D *adj* **1** (cold) 寒冷的 ‹*wind, weather*› **2** fig (causing fear) 令人恐惧的 ‹*warning*›; (grim) 令人寒心的 ‹*reminder*›

Phrasal verb
- **chill out** *vi* colloq 放松一下

chill cabinet *n* Brit 冷藏柜

chilled /tʃɪld/ *adj* (cool) 冷却了的; (refrigerated) 冷藏起来的

chiller /ˈtʃɪlə(r)/ *n* colloq **1** (machine) 冷却器 **2** (book, film) = **spine-chiller**

chill factor *n* 风寒指数

chilli /ˈtʃɪli/ *n* (*pl* **~es**) **1** [c] (pod) 辣椒 **2** [u] (powder) 辣椒粉 **3** [u] = **chilli con carne**

chilli con carne /ˌtʃɪli kɒn ˈkɑːni/ *n* [u] 辣味牛肉末

chilliness *n* [u] **1** (coldness) 寒冷 **2** fig (unfriendliness) 冷淡

chilling /ˈtʃɪlɪŋ/ *adj* 令人恐惧的 ‹*words, sound, look*›

chillingly /ˈtʃɪlɪŋli/ *adv* 令人恐惧地

chilli: ~ pepper *n* 辣椒; **~ powder** *n* [u] 辣椒粉; **~ sauce** *n* [u and c] 辣酱

chilly /ˈtʃɪli/ *adj* **1** (cold) 冷飕飕的 ‹*day, room, wind*›; **it's ~ today** 今天真冷啊 **2** fig (unfriendly) 冷漠的 ‹*stare, manner*›; 冷淡的 ‹*reception, welcome*›

chime /tʃaɪm/
A *n* **1** (of clock) 报时装置; (of church bell) 敲钟装置; (set of bells) 排钟; **the ~s of the clock** 时钟的报时装置 **2** (sound) 钟声
B **chimes** *npl* (doorbell) 门铃
C *vi* **1** (strike, indicate time) 钟鸣; **the clock ~d three** 钟敲3点 **2** (play tune) 奏出和谐的乐声
D *vt* **1** (ring) 敲响 ‹*bell*› **2** (show time) 用钟声报 ‹*8 o'clock midnight*›

Phrasal verb
- **chime in** *vi* **1** (interrupt) 插话; **he kept chiming in with his own opinions** 他不停地插嘴讲自己的看法 **2** (agree) 与…一致; **to ~ in with sth.** 和某事物一致

chimera /kaɪˈmɪərə/ *n* **1** liter (beast) 喀迈拉 [狮头羊身蛇尾的吐火女怪] **2** fig (impossible idea) 妄想 **3** Biol 嵌合体

chimney /ˈtʃɪmni/ *n* (*pl* **~s**) **1** (for smoke, gas) 烟囱 **2** (glass tube) 玻璃灯罩 **3** (in mountaineering) [岩石间的] 狭窄裂口

chimney: ~ breast *n* 壁炉腔; **~ corner** *n* 壁炉角; **~ fire** *n* 烟囱火; **~piece** *n* Brit 壁炉台; **~pot** *n* 烟囱管帽; **~stack** *n* 烟囱体; **~ sweep** ▸**p. 409** *n* 烟囱清扫工

chimp /tʃɪmp/ *n* colloq = **chimpanzee**

chimpanzee /ˌtʃɪmpənˈziː, ˌtʃɪmpænˈziː/ *n* 黑猩猩

chin /tʃɪn/ *n* 下巴; **a double ~** 双下巴; **~ up!** 振作起来!; **to keep one's ~ up** fig 不气馁; **to take it on the ~** fig 无怨无悔地承受

China /ˈtʃaɪnə/ *pr n* 中国

china /ˈtʃaɪnə/ *n* [u] **1** (ceramic material) 瓷; **a ~ vase** 瓷花瓶 **2** (objects) 瓷器; **a piece of rare ~** 一件珍稀瓷器; **(like) a bull in a ~ shop** fig 笨手笨脚动辄闯祸的

china: ~ cabinet *n* 瓷器柜; **~ clay** *n* [u] = **kaolin**; **~ cupboard** *n* 瓷器柜

China: ~ Sea *pr n* **the ~ Sea** 中国海; **~ tea** *n* 中国茶; **~town** *n* 唐人街

chinchilla /tʃɪnˈtʃɪlə/ *n* **1** [c] (rodent) 绒鼠 **2** [c] (cat) [有银灰色长毛的] 家猫; (rabbit) 丝毛兔 **3** [u] (fur of chinchilla) 绒鼠毛皮; (fur of chinchilla rabbit) 丝毛兔毛皮; **a ~ (coat)** 一件绒鼠毛皮大衣

Chinese /tʃaɪˈniːz/ ▸**p. 503, p. 426**
A *adj* **1** (of China) 中国的; **~ art/culture/history** 中国艺术/文化/历史; **a ~ meal** 中餐; **the ~ language** 中文 **2** (of the people) 中国人的 **3** (of the language) 中文的
B *n* **1** [c] (native of China) 中国人; (of Chinese origin) 华裔; **an American ~** 美籍华人; **an overseas ~** 华侨; **the ~** *pl* 中国人民 **2** [u] (language) 汉语; **to speak ~** 说中文; **in ~** 用中文; **to translate into ~** 译成中文 **3** [c] Brit colloq (meal) 中餐; **fancy going out for a ~?** 想出去吃顿中餐吗?

Chinese: ~ lantern *n* [可折叠的] 纸灯笼; **~ New Year** *n* 中国农历新年; **~ puzzle** *n* **1** lit (game) 中国智力玩具 [七巧板、九连环等]; **2** fig (complex problem) 复杂难懂的事物; (mystery) 难解之谜; **~ wall** *n* (desirable) 铜墙铁壁; (undesirable) 难以逾越的障碍; **~ whispers** *npl + v sing* [内容越传越走样的] 悄声传口信游戏

Chink /tʃɪŋk/ *n* colloq offensive 中国佬

chink[1] /tʃɪŋk/ *n* **1** (slit in wall) 裂缝; (in door, curtain) 缝隙; **a ~ in sb.'s armour** fig 某人的弱点 **2** (of light) [透过缝隙的] 一线光

chink[2]
A *vt* 使…叮当作响 ‹*coins*›; **we ~ed our glasses together** 我们互相碰杯
B *vi* «*glasses, metallic objects*» 叮当作响; **the coins ~ed together in his pocket** 硬币在他口袋里叮当作响
C *n* (sound) 叮当声

chinless /ˈtʃɪnlɪs/ *adj* **1** (weak-chinned) 无下巴的 **2** Brit fig colloq (weak) 懦弱的; **a ~ wonder** 懦弱的上等人

chinoiserie /ʃiːnˈwɑːzəri/ *n* [u] **1** (style) [尤指18世纪欧洲艺术品、家具、建筑等所模仿的] 中国式装饰风格 **2** (objects) 具有中国式装饰风格的物品

chinstrap /ˈtʃɪnstræp/ *n* [固定头盔等用的] 颏带

chintz /tʃɪnts/ *n* [u] [作窗帘或家具罩等用的] 印花棉布; **~ curtains** 印花棉布窗帘

chin-up *n* esp Amer 引体向上; **to do ~s** 做引体向上

chinwag /ˈtʃɪnwæg/ Brit colloq
A *n* 闲聊; **to have a ~** 聊一会儿天
B *vi* (*pres p etc.* **-gg-**) 闲聊

chip /tʃɪp/
A *n* **1** (fragment) 碎片; **~s of wood** 木屑; **a ~ off the old block** colloq 酷似父亲的人 [尤指男孩]; **to have a ~ on one's shoulder** colloq 心怀怨恨; **he's got a ~ on his shoulder about not having gone to university** 他因为没有上过大学而愤愤不平 **2** (mark, flaw) 缺损处; **the mug has a ~ in it** 那只马克杯上有个豁口 **3** Culin Brit 炸薯条; Amer 炸薯片 **4** (in gambling) 筹码; **to cash in one's ~s** lit 兑现筹码; fig colloq 完蛋; **when the ~s are down** colloq 在关键时刻; **to have had one's ~s** Brit colloq 完蛋 **5** Comput 芯片 **6** Sport (in golf, cricket) 切削击球; (in football) 撮球
B *vt* (*pres p etc.* **-pp-**) **1** (break) 把…碰出缺口; **he ~ped my best glass** 他把我最好的玻璃杯碰了个缺口; **to ~ a tooth** 崩坏一颗牙 **2** (carve) 凿刻 ‹*wood, stone*› **3** Brit Culin 把…切成条 **4** Sport (in golf, cricket) 切削击 ‹*ball*›; (in football) 撮 ‹*ball*›
C *vi* (*pres p etc.* **-pp-**) **1** (become damaged) «*china, glass, gemstone*» 碰出缺口; «*paint, veneer*» 剥落; «*tooth*» 崩坏 **2** Sport (in golf, cricket) 切削击球; (in football) 撮球

Phrasal verbs
- **chip away**
A *vt* [**~ away sth., ~ sth. away**] 小块小块地弄掉 ‹*veneer, paint, plaster*›
B *vi* «*veneer, paint, plaster*» 不断剥落
- **chip away at** *vt* [**~ away at sth.**]
1 (carve) 不停凿去; **the sculptor ~ped away at the stone** 雕刻家不停地雕琢那块石头 **2** fig (reduce, weaken) 逐步削弱 ‹*power, authority, confidence*›
- **chip in** *vi* Brit colloq **1** (interrupt) 插话; **she ~ped in with some pertinent remarks** 她插的几句话蛮切题的 **2** (contribute) 凑钱; **he ~ped in with £5** 他凑了5英镑
- **chip off**
A *vt* [**~ off sth., ~ sth. off**]
1 (remove from surface) 使剥落; **we ~ped off the plaster from the wall** 我们从墙上铲下灰泥 **2** (break off) 碰掉 ‹*lump, fragment*›; **he ~ped off a piece of his tooth** 他崩掉了一块牙
B *vi* 小块剥落; **to ~ off** «*veneer, paint, plaster*» 一片片剥落

chip: C~ and PIN, ~ and pin *n* [u] 密码刷卡支付系统; **~-based** *adj* 基于微型芯片的 ‹*system, network, credit card*›; **~board** *n* [u] 刨花板

chipmunk /ˈtʃɪpmʌŋk/ *n* 金花鼠

chipolata /ˌtʃɪpəˈlɑːtə/ *n* Brit 契普拉特小香肠

chip pan *n* [用于炸薯条、内有滤油网架的] 深平底锅

chipped potatoes *npl* 炸薯条

chipper /ˈtʃɪpə(r)/ *adj* colloq dated 1 (cheerful) 兴高采烈的 2 (lively) 活泼的

chippings /ˈtʃɪpɪŋz/ *npl* 铺路碎石; **danger! loose ~!** 危险！小心碎石！

chippy /ˈtʃɪpi/ *n* Brit colloq 炸鱼薯条店

chip: ~set *n* 芯片组; **~ shop** *n* Brit = **fish and chip shop**

chiropodist /kɪˈrɒpədɪst/ ▸**p. 409** *n* 足病诊疗师

chiropody /kɪˈrɒpədi/ *n* [u] 足病治疗

chiropractic /ˌkaɪərəʊˈpræktɪk/ *n* [u] 脊骨按摩治疗

chiropractor /ˈkaɪərəʊpræktə(r)/ ▸**p. 409** *n* 脊骨按摩治疗师

chirp /tʃɜːp/

A *vi* 1 lit «*bird*» 啁啾; «*grasshopper, cricket*» 唧唧叫 2 fig «*person*» 欢快地说话

B *n* (of bird) 啁啾声; (of grasshopper, cricket) 唧唧声

chirpily /ˈtʃɜːpɪli/ *adv* 欢快地 ‹*sing, whistle, say*›

chirpy /ˈtʃɜːpi/ *adj* colloq 欢快的 ‹*song, voice, person*›

chirrup /ˈtʃɪrəp/

A *vi* 叽叽喳喳地叫

B *n* 叽叽喳喳声

chisel /ˈtʃɪzl/

A *n* 凿子

B *vt* (*pres p etc.* **-ll-**, Amer **-l-**) 1 (cut, shape) «*carpenter*» 凿 ‹*wood*›; «*sculptor*» 雕刻 ‹*stone, metal*›; **to ~ sth. into sth.** 把某物雕刻成某物; **to ~ a figure out of a piece of wood** 把一块木头雕刻成人像 2 colloq (swindle) 诈骗; **to ~ sb. out of sth.** 骗取某人的某物

chiseler /ˈtʃɪzələ(r)/ *n* Amer colloq = **chiseller**

chiselled /ˈtʃɪzəld/ *adj* 1 lit 凿刻成的 2 fig 轮廓鲜明的; **finely ~ features** 清秀端正的容貌

chiseller /ˈtʃɪzələ(r)/ *n* colloq 骗子

Chisinau /ˌkɪʃɪˈnaʊ/ *pr n* 基希纳乌

chit¹ /tʃɪt/ *n* colloq pej (immature young woman) 幼稚的人; (impudent young woman) 冒失鬼; **a ~ of a girl** 莽撞的黄毛丫头

chit² *n* Brit (voucher) 凭单; (bill) 欠条; (note) 便条

chitchat /ˈtʃɪttʃæt/ *n* [u] colloq 聊天; **to spend one's time in idle ~** 把时间花在闲聊上

chivalrous /ˈʃɪvəlrəs/ *adj* 1 (heroic) 有骑士风范的 ‹*champion, conduct*› 2 (courteous towards women) 彬彬有礼的 ‹*man, behaviour*›

chivalrously /ˈʃɪvəlrəsli/ *adv* 彬彬有礼地; **to act** *or* **behave ~ towards sb.** 对某人彬彬有礼

chivalry /ˈʃɪvəlri/ *n* [u] 1 (knightly system of the Middle Ages) 骑士制度 2 (knightly qualities of the Middle Ages) 骑士品质 3 (courtesy towards women) 彬彬有礼

chives /tʃaɪvz/ *npl* 细香葱

chivvy, chivy /ˈtʃɪvi/ *vt* 催促; **to ~ sb. into sth./doing sth.** 因某事物催促某人/催促某人做某事

chlamydia /kləˈmɪdɪə/ *n* (*pl* ~ *or* **chlamydiae** /kləˈmɪdɪiː/) 衣原体

chlorate /ˈklɔːreɪt/ *n* 氯酸盐

chloride /ˈklɔːraɪd/ *n* 氯化物

chlorinate /ˈklɔːrɪneɪt/ *vt* 1 (treat) 用氯处理; **~d water** 加氯水 2 Chem 使氯化

chlorination /ˌklɔːrɪˈneɪʃn/ *n* [u] 1 (treatment) 加氯处理 2 Chem 氯化

chlorine /ˈklɔːriːn/ *n* [u] 氯

chlorofluorocarbon /ˌklɔːrəˌflʊərəʊˈkɑːbən/ *n* 含氯氟烃

chloroform /ˈklɒrəfɔːm, Amer ˈklɔːr-/

A *n* [u] 氯仿

B *vt* 用氯仿麻醉

chlorophyll /ˈklɒrəfɪl/ *n* [u] 叶绿素

choc /tʃɒk/ *n* Brit colloq 巧克力

chocaholic /ˌtʃɒkəˈhɒlɪk/ *n* colloq = **chocoholic**

choc ice /ˈtʃɔkaɪs/ *n* Brit 巧克力脆皮冰激凌

chock /tʃɒk/

A *n* 1 (for boat, plane, vehicle) 垫块 [用于防止滑动]; **to put a ~ under sth.** 在某物下面放一个垫块; **~s away!** 把垫块挪走！ 2 (support) 定盘 [用于甲板上安置小艇等]; **to put sth. on ~s** 把某物放置在定盘上

B *vt* 1 (wedge) 用垫块垫住 ‹*wheel, door, barrel*› 2 Brit Naut 把…置于定盘上 ‹*boat, cask*›

chock-a-block /ˌtʃɒkəˈblɒk/ *adj pred* colloq (completely full) 挤满的; (tightly packed) 塞满的; **the town centre was ~ with traffic** 市中心车水马龙

chock-full /ˌtʃɒkˈfʊl/ *adj pred* 塞满的; **~ of people/cars** 挤满了人/车的

chocoholic /ˌtʃɒkəˈhɒlɪk/ *n* colloq 贪吃巧克力的人

chocolate /ˈtʃɒklət/ ▸**p. 134** *n* 1 [u] (substance) 巧克力; **a bar of ~** 一块巧克力; **~ biscuits/cake/ice cream** 巧克力饼干/蛋糕/冰激凌 2 [c] (sweet) 巧克力糖 3 [u] (drink) 巧克力饮料 4 [u] (colour) 巧克力色

chocolate box

A *n* 巧克力盒

B *adj attrib* 温馨的 ‹*view, picture*›

chocolate: ~ chip cookie *n* 巧克力豆饼干; **~-coated, ~-covered** *adjs* 涂巧克力的 ‹*confectionery, biscuit*›; **~ drop** *n* 圆形巧克力糖; **~ eclair** *n* 巧克力长形泡夫

chocolatey, chocolaty /ˈtʃɒkləti/ *adj* 1 (made with or tasting of chocolate) 巧克力制的 ‹*biscuit, cake, sauce, icing, ice cream*›; 巧克力的 ‹*taste, smell*› 2 (dirty) 沾满巧克力的 ‹*finger, mouth, cheek*›

choice /tʃɔɪs/

A *n* 1 [c] (selection) 选择; **to make a ~** 作出选择 2 [u] (right to choose) 选择权; **to have the ~** 拥有选择权; **to have a free ~** 有自由选择的权力 3 [c] (option) 可选物; **you have a ~ of three colours** 你可以在三种颜色中选择; **to have no ~ but to ...** 除了…外别无选择 4 [u] (range of options) 选择范围; **a wide/narrow ~** 广泛的/有限的选择范围; **to be spoilt for ~** 选择太多而拿不定主意 5 [c] (preference) 选中的对象; **a car of my ~** 我自己相中的汽车; **out of** *or* **from ~** 自愿地; **my first ~ would be a Rolls Royce** 我的首选是劳斯莱斯汽车; **you pays your money and you takes your ~** colloq 你自己看着办吧

B *adj* 1 (quality) 上等的 ‹*food, drink*›; 优质的 ‹*goods*› 2 (well-chosen) 仔细推敲过的 ‹*word, phrase*›; **~ language** euph 尖酸刻薄的语言

choir /ˈkwaɪə(r)/ *n* 1 (of church) 唱诗班; (of school, village, festival) 合唱团 2 Archit 唱诗席 3 (group) [同类乐器的] 合奏

choir: ~boy *n* 唱诗班男童; **~ festival** *n* 合唱节; **~girl** *n* 唱诗班女童; **~master** *n* 唱诗班指挥; **~mistress** *n* 唱诗班女指挥; **~ organ** *n* 唱诗风琴; **~ practice** *n* [u and c] 合唱练习; **~ school** *n* Brit 唱诗班学校; **~stall** *n* 唱诗班座位

choke /tʃəʊk/

A *vt* 1 (throttle) 掐住…的脖子; **to ~ sb. to death** 掐死某人 2 (impede breathing) «*smoke*» 使窒息 3 (render speechless) 使说不出话; **she was ~d with emotion** 她激动得声音哽塞; **a voice ~d with sobs** 抽泣声 4 (block) «*weeds, leaves*» 堆满 ‹*garden*›; 塞住 ‹*pipe, tube*›; «*traffic*» 堵塞 ‹*road*›; **the drain is ~d (up) with dead leaves** 下水道塞满了枯叶

B *vi* 1 (be unable to breathe) 窒息; (because of food) 噎住; (because of liquid) 呛; **to ~ on a fish bone/on a drink** 被鱼刺鲠住/被饮料呛了一口; **to ~ to death** 窒息而死 2 (become speechless) 说不出话来; **he was choking with anger** 他气得说不出话 3 Amer Sport colloq (tense up) [因紧张而] 失败

C *n* 1 (action) 窒息; (sound) 呛住的声音 2 (of emotion) 哽咽; **with a ~ in one's voice** 声音哽咽地 3 Aut 阻气门; **to pull out/use the ~** 拔出/使用阻气门

Phrasal verbs

- **choke back** *vt* [**~ back sth.**] 强忍住 ‹*tears*›; 克制住 ‹*feelings*›; **to ~ back one's anger** 强压怒火
- **choke down** *vt* [**~ sth. down, ~ down sth.**] 硬吞下
- **choke off** *vt* [**~ off sth.**] 制止
- **choke up** *vt* [**~ sth. up, ~ up sth.**] 堵塞住; **the street was ~d up with traffic** 街上交通拥堵

choked /tʃəʊkt/ *adj pred* colloq (angry) 生气的; (upset) 沮丧的; **to be ~ about sth.** 因某事物而心烦意乱

choke point *n* Amer 阻塞点

choker /ˈtʃəʊkə(r)/ *n* (necklace) 贴颈项链; (band of material) 项圈; **a pearl ~** 一串珍珠贴颈项链

choking /ˈtʃəʊkɪŋ/ *n* [u] 窒息

cholera /ˈkɒlərə/ ▸**p. 377** *n* [u] 霍乱

cholesterol /kəˈlestərɒl/ *n* [u] 胆固醇

cholesterol: ~ count, ~ level *ns* 胆固醇含量; **~ test** *n* 胆固醇检测

chomp /tʃɒmp/ *vt, vi* = **champ¹ B1**

Chongqing /ˌtʃʊŋˈtʃɪŋ/ *pr n* **~ (Municipality)** 重庆（市）

choo-choo /ˈtʃuːtʃuː/ *n* child lang 呜呜 [模仿火车或火车头的声音]

choose /tʃuːz/ (*pt* **chose**, *pp* **chosen**)

A *vt* 1 (select) 选择; **we chose him from a shortlist of five candidates** 我们从入围的5名候选人中选择了他; **we chose him as our representative** 我们选他作为我们的代表 2 (decide) 决定; **to ~ (not) to do sth.** 决定（不）做某事; **to ~ when/how/whether ...** 决定何时/如何/是否…

B *vi* 1 (select) 选择; **there's nothing to ~ between X and Y** X与Y相差无几; **there are many models to ~ from** 有许多型号可供挑选 2 (prefer) 宁愿; **whenever you ~** 你愿意什么时候就什么时候; **do as you ~** 随你便; **to ~ to do sth.** 情愿做某事; **if you (so) ~** 如果你愿意（这样）的话

chooser /ˈtʃuːzə/ *n* **beggars can't be ~s** 叫花子不能挑肥拣瘦

choosy /ˈtʃuːzi/ *adj* colloq (careful in choosing) 精挑细选的; (fussy) 挑剔的; **I can't afford to be ~** 我没资格挑三拣四

chop¹ /tʃɒp/

A *vt* (*pres p etc.* **-pp-**) 1 (cut up) 劈开 ‹*wood*›; 切碎 ‹*vegetables*›; 剁碎 ‹*meat*›; **to ~ sth. into cubes** 把某物切成丁; **to ~ sth. to pieces** *or* **bits** 把某物切碎; **to ~ sth. finely** 把某物剁得细碎 2 (hit) 砍 3 fig (stop, reduce) «*person, government*» 砍掉 ‹*service, expenditure, project*› 4 Sport (give chopping blow to) 掌劈; (in table tennis) 削 ‹*ball*›

B *n* 1 (with tool) 砍; (with hand) 掌劈; **to cut sth. off with one ~** 一下子砍掉某物; **a karate ~** 空手道的掌劈 2 (meat) 排骨; **a pork ~** 猪排 3 **the ~** Brit colloq (dismissal) 解雇; (cancellation) 砍掉; **to be for the ~** 可能会丢饭碗; **the ferry service got the ~ in 1963** 轮渡服务于1963年被砍掉了 4 (in table tennis) 削球

Phrasal verbs

- **chop down** *vt* [**~ down sth., ~ sth. down**] 砍倒
- **chop off** *vt* [**~ off sth., ~ sth. off**] 砍下
- **chop through** *vt* [**~ through sth.**] 劈开; **to ~ one's way through the undergrowth** 从矮树丛中劈出一条路来
- **chop up** *vt* [**~ up sth., ~ sth. up**] 切碎; **to ~ the meat up into small cubes** 把肉切成丁

chop² *vi* **to ~ and change** 变化无常

chop-chop colloq
A *adv* 赶快
B *excl* 快; **~! hurry up!** 快点! 赶紧!

chopper /ˈtʃɒpə(r)/
A *n* **1** (axe) 斧头; (cleaver) 砍刀 **2** colloq (helicopter) 直升机
B **choppers** *npl* sl (teeth) 假牙; **a set of ~s** 一副假牙

chopping: ~ block, ~ board *ns* 砧板; **~ knife** *n* 菜刀

choppy /ˈtʃɒpi/ *adj* 波浪起伏的 ‹*sea, water*›

chops /tʃɒps/ *n* colloq **1** (jaws, mouth) 嘴 **2** (cheeks) 腮帮子

chopstick /ˈtʃɒpstɪk/ *n* 筷子; **a pair of ~s** 一双筷子

chop suey /ˌtʃɒp ˈsuːi/ *n* [u] 炒杂碎

choral /ˈkɔːrəl/ *adj* (of a choir) 唱诗班的; (of a chorus) 合唱团的; (sung by a choir or chorus) 合唱的 ‹*music*›

chorale /kəˈrɑːl/ *n* **1** (music) 众赞歌 **2** Amer (choir) 唱诗班; (group of singers) 合唱团

choral: ~ society *n* 合唱团; **~ symphony** *n* 合唱交响曲

chord /kɔːd/ *n* **1** Mus 和弦 **2** fig (emotional response) 心弦; **to strike a ~ (with sb.)** 触动(某人的)心弦; **it struck a ~ in** *or* **with him** 这引起了他的共鸣 **3** Math 弦

chore /tʃɔː(r)/ *n* **1** (routine task) 例行工作; (around the house) 家务活; **to do the ~s** 做家务 **2** pej (unpleasant task) 讨厌的工作; **shopping is such a ~!** 购物真是件苦差事!

choreograph /ˈkɒrɪəɡrɑːf, Amer -ɡræf/ *vt* **1** lit 为…设计舞蹈动作; **he ~ed a new ballet** 他编了一套新的芭蕾舞 **2** fig (plan, control) 安排; **the meeting was meticulously ~ed** 会议得到了精心组织

choreographer /ˌkɒrɪˈɒɡrəfə(r)/ ▸**p. 409** *n* 舞蹈编导

choreographic /ˌkɒrɪəˈɡræfɪk/ *adj* 舞蹈的 ‹*style, talent*›; 编舞的 ‹*principle*›

choreography /ˌkɒrɪˈɒɡrəfi/ *n* 编舞

chorister /ˈkɒrɪstə(r), Amer ˈkɔːr-/ *n* (choirboy) 唱诗班男童; (choirgirl) 唱诗班女童; (member of choir) 合唱团成员

chortle /ˈtʃɔːtl/
A *vi* (laugh heartily) 哈哈大笑; (chuckle) 咯咯笑; **to ~ at** *or* **about** *or* **over sth.** (laugh heartily) 因某事物而哈哈大笑; (chuckle) 因某事物而咯咯笑; **to ~ with pleasure** 高兴地哈哈大笑
B *n* (hearty laughter) 哈哈笑; (chuckle) 咯咯笑

chortling /ˈtʃɔːtlɪŋ/ *n* [u] 哈哈大笑

chorus /ˈkɔːrəs/
A *n* (*pl* **~es**) **1** (supporting singers) 合唱队; (dancers, actors, etc.) 歌舞队 **2** (piece of music) 合唱曲 **3** (in opera, oratorio) 合唱部分 **4** (refrain) 副歌; **to join in the ~** «*one person*» 跟着唱副歌; «*several people*» 齐唱副歌 **5** (simultaneous utterance) 异口同声; **the usual ~ of protest** 惯常的一片抗议声; **in ~** 一齐 **6** + *v sing* Theat [古希腊戏剧中解释剧情的] 歌队
B *vt* 齐声说; **the crowd ~ed their discontent** 人群齐声表示不满

chorus: ~ girl *n* (singer) 合唱团女成员; (dancer) 歌舞队女演员; **~ line** *n* + *v sing or pl* 歌舞编队

chose /tʃəʊz/ *pt* ▸**choose**

chosen /ˈtʃəʊzn/ *pp* ▸**choose**

chosen few *n* 享有特权的少数人

chough /tʃʌf/ *n* 红嘴山鸦

choux pastry /ˌʃuː ˈpeɪstri/ *n* [u] 鸡蛋松软面团

chow[1] /tʃaʊ/, **chow chow** *ns* (dog) 狮子狗

chow[2] *n* [u] esp Amer colloq (food) 食物

chowder /ˈtʃaʊdə(r)/ *n* [u] 海鲜杂烩浓汤

chow mein /ˌtʃaʊ ˈmeɪn/ *n* [u] 炒面

Christ /kraɪst/
A *pr n* 基督
B *excl* sl 天哪

Christ child *n* **the ~** 幼年基督

christen /ˈkrɪsn/ *vt* **1** Relig (baptize) 为…施洗礼 ‹*person, baby*›; (name) 给…取教名 ‹*person, baby*›; **I was ~ed John** 我受洗时取名为约翰 **2** (name) 为…命名 ‹*ship, building*›; (give nickname to) 给…取绰号; **they ~ed the dog Max** 他们管那条狗叫马克斯

Christendom /ˈkrɪsndəm/ *n* [u] dated **1** (Christians) 基督教徒 **2** (Christian world) 基督教世界

christening /ˈkrɪsnɪŋ/ *n* 洗礼; **~ ceremony** 洗礼仪式

Christian /ˈkrɪstʃən/
A *adj* **1** 基督教的 ‹*church, faith, doctrine*›; 信仰基督的 ‹*community, country*› **2** (charitable and humane) 表现基督精神的; **jealousy is not a ~ virtue** 妒忌不是基督徒的美德; **it wasn't very ~ of him to refuse to make a donation** 他拒不捐赠, 这不太符合基督精神
B *n* 基督徒

Christian era *n* **the ~** 基督纪元; **the early part of the ~** 公元纪元早期

Christianity /ˌkrɪstɪˈænəti/ *n* [u] **1** (religion) 基督教 **2** (quality, character) 基督教精神

Christianize /ˈkrɪstʃənaɪz/ *vt* 使皈依基督教

Christian: ~ name *n* 教名; **~ Science** *n* [u] 基督教科学派 [创始于1879年的教派, 主张靠信仰治愈疾病]; **~ Scientist** *n* 基督教科学派成员

Christlike /ˈkraɪstlaɪk/ *adj* 似基督的 ‹*forgiveness, otherworldliness*›

Christmas /ˈkrɪsməs/ *n* **1** (day) 圣诞节; **Merry ~!, Happy ~!** 圣诞节快乐! **2** (period) 圣诞节节期; **over ~** 在圣诞节期间; **to spend ~ at home/away** 在家/在外度圣诞节假期

Christmas: ~ bonus *n* 圣诞节奖金; **~ box** *n* Brit [尤指给雇员及邮差等的] 圣诞礼包; **~ cactus** *n* 蟹爪仙人掌; **~ cake** *n* [覆有杏仁蛋白糊和糖霜的] 圣诞蛋糕; **~ card** *n* 圣诞贺卡; **~ carol** *n* 圣诞颂歌; **~ cracker** *n* Brit 圣诞彩包爆竹 [内装小礼品等的纸彩筒, 两边一拉即噼啪作响]; **~ Day** *n* 圣诞节; **~ dinner** *n* 圣诞正餐; **~ Eve** *n* 圣诞前夜; **~ present** *n* 圣诞节礼物; **~ pudding** *n* Brit 圣诞布丁; **~ stocking** *n* 圣诞袜 [圣诞夜供圣诞老人放礼物用的袜子]

Christmassy /ˈkrɪsməsi/ *adj* colloq 有圣诞节特征的 ‹*music, mood, atmosphere*›; **I'm not feeling very ~** 我没感受到多少圣诞节的气氛

Christmas: ~ time *n* [u] 圣诞节节期; **~ tree** *n* 圣诞树

chromatic /krəʊˈmætɪk/ *adj* **1** Mus 半音的 ‹*key, melody, keyboard*› **2** Art 色彩的 ‹*contrast, stimulus*›

chromatic scale *n* 半音阶

chromatogram /krəˈmætəɡræm/ *n* 色谱

chromatography /ˌkrəʊməˈtɒɡrəfi/ *n* [u] 色谱法

chrome /krəʊm/
A *n* [u] **1** (chromium plate) 镀铬层 **2** (colour) **~ (yellow)** 铬黄
B *modif* **1** 镀铬的 ‹*handle, cutlery*› **2** **~ (yellow)** 鲜黄色的

chrome steel *n* [u] 铬钢

chromium /ˈkrəʊmɪəm/ *n* [u] 铬

chromium: ~-plated *adj* 镀铬的 ‹*metal, cutlery*›; **~ plating** *n* [u] **1** (process) 镀铬; **2** (coating) 铬镀层

chromosome /ˈkrəʊməsəʊm/ *n* 染色体

chromosome map *n* 染色体图

chronic /ˈkrɒnɪk/ *adj* **1** (long-lasting) 慢性的 ‹*illness, bronchitis, arthritis*›; 久病的 ‹*patient*›; 长期的 ‹*alcoholism, unemployment*› **2** fig (habitual) 积习难改的 ‹*liar*› **3** Brit colloq (bad) 糟透的 ‹*performance, performer*›

chronically /ˈkrɒnɪkli/ *adv* **1** 长期地 ‹*sick, depressed, disabled, affected*›; **to be ~ ill** 患慢性病 **2** fig (severely) 严重地; **the country is ~ short of ...** 该国严重缺乏…

chronicle /ˈkrɒnɪkl/
A *n* **1** (historical account) 编年史; **a ~ of the French Revolution** 一部法国革命史 **2** (tale) 述事; **a ~ of misfortunes/misunderstandings** 对不幸遭遇/误解的记述
B *vt* «*historian*» 把…载入编年史 ‹*events*›; «*diary, history book, eyewitness*» 记述 ‹*daily life, events*›; **to ~ the growth of feminism/the life of Marx** 记录女权主义的发展史/马克思的一生

chronicler /ˈkrɒnɪklə(r)/ ▸**p. 409** *n* 编年史家

chronological /ˌkrɒnəˈlɒdʒɪkl/ *adj* 按时间先后顺序排列的 ‹*list, table, method*›; **in ~ order** 按时间先后顺序

chronologically /ˌkrɒnəˈlɒdʒɪkli/ *adv* 按时间先后顺序

chronology /krəˈnɒlədʒi/ *n* **1** [c] (record) 年表 **2** [u] (recording of events) [历史事件的] 年代顺序编排; (dating) 年代确定

chronometer /krəˈnɒmɪtə(r)/ *n* 精密计时器

chrysalis /ˈkrɪsəlɪs/ *n* (*pl* **~es**) 蝶蛹

chrysanth /krɪˈsænθ/ *n* colloq **= chrysanthemum**

chrysanthemum /krɪˈsænθəməm/ *n* 菊花

chubby /ˈtʃʌbi/ *adj* 胖乎乎的 ‹*child, face, finger*›

chubby-cheeked, chubby-faced *adjs* 脸蛋胖胖的 ‹*child, baby*›

chuck[1] /tʃʌk/
A *vt* **1** colloq (throw) 扔; **to ~ sb. sth., to ~ sth. to sb.** 把某物扔给某人; **to ~ sth. somewhere** 把某物扔到某处; **it's ~ing it down** colloq (raining heavily) 现在正下着倾盆大雨 **2** colloq (end relationship with) 甩掉 ‹*boyfriend, girlfriend*›; (give up) 放弃 ‹*job, evening class*› **3** (stroke) 轻抚 ‹*pet*›; (touch) 轻拍 ‹*child, loved one*›; **to ~ sb. under the chin** 轻抚某人的下巴
B *n* **1** (stroke) 轻抚 **2** **the ~** Brit (rejection) 抛弃; (dismissal) 辞退; **to get the ~** 被解雇; **he's been given the ~ by his girlfriend** 他被女友甩了

Phrasal verbs

- **chuck away** *vt* colloq [**~ sth. away, ~ away sth.**]
 1 (throw away) 扔掉 ‹*rotting food, old newspapers*› **2** (squander) 浪费 ‹*money, chance, life*›; **to ~ away sth. on sth./sb.** 将某事物浪费在某事物上/某人身上
- **chuck in** *vt* colloq [**~ sth. in, ~ in sth.**] 放弃 ‹*job, research, marriage*›
- **chuck out** *vt* colloq **1** [**~ sth. out, ~ out sth.**] (throw away) 扔掉 ‹*old furniture, clothes*› **2** [**~ sb. out, ~ out sb.**] (eject) 赶走 ‹*troublemaker*›; **to be ~ed out of** 被撵出 ‹*college, club*›
- **chuck up** sl
 A *vi* 呕吐
 B *vt* [**~ sth. up, ~ up sth.**] 吐出; **he ~ed up his dinner** 他把晚饭吃的东西都吐了出来

chuck[2] *n* (on lathe) 卡盘; (on drill) 夹盘

chuck[3] *n* (cut of beef) **~ (steak)** 牛肩胛肉

chucker-out *n* (*pl* **chuckers-out**) Brit colloq [酒吧等处的] 护场人员

chucking-out time *n* Brit colloq [酒吧等的] 关门时间

chuck key *n* 夹头扳手

chuckle /ˈtʃʌkl/
A *n* 轻声的笑
B *vi* 低声轻笑; **to ~ at** *or* **about** *or* **over sth.** 对某事物低声轻笑; **to ~ to oneself** 暗自发笑

chuck wagon *n* Amer [大农场等的] 流动炊事车

chuffed /tʃʌft/ *adj* Brit colloq (pleased) 开心的; (proud) 骄傲的; **to be ~ about** *or* **at sth./doing sth.** 对某事物/做某事感到很开心; **I was dead ~ about winning the prize** 我因为得了奖，心里非常骄傲

chug /tʃʌg/
A *vi* (*pres p etc.* **-gg-**) 发出突突声; **the train ~ged into/out of the station** 火车咔嚓咔嚓驶入/驶出车站
B *n* 突突声

Phrasal verb
• **chug along** *vi* **1** (move) «*train, old car*» 突突地行驶 **2** colloq (progress) «*life, work*» 按部就班地进行; **the project is ~ging along nicely** 工程进展顺利

chum /tʃʌm/ *n* colloq **1** (close friend) 好友 **2** (form of address) 老兄; **watch it, ~!** 小心点，老兄!

Phrasal verb
• **chum up** *vi* colloq 交朋友

chummy /ˈtʃʌmi/ *adj* colloq 很友好的 ‹*person, greeting*›; **to be ~ with sb.** 与某人关系亲密; **they're very ~** 他们关系很铁; **she's got very ~ with the boss** pej 她和老板关系很密切

chump /tʃʌmp/ *n* colloq **1** (foolish person) 傻瓜 **2** **to be off one's ~** Brit (crazy) 发疯

chunder /ˈtʃʌndə(r)/ colloq
A *vi* 呕吐
B *n* 呕吐物

chunk /tʃʌŋk/ *n* **1** (piece of meat, fruit, bread, etc.) 大块; **a ~ of plaster** 一块厚厚的灰泥 **2** colloq (large amount) 相当大的量; **a fair ~ of the essay** 文章的大部分

chunky /ˈtʃʌŋki/ *adj* **1** (containing chunks) 满是大块的 ‹*stew, dog food*› **2** (thick and heavy) 厚实的 ‹*sweater*›; 粗重的 ‹*jewellery*›; **a ~ gold bracelet** 沉甸甸的金手镯 **3** (stocky) 壮实的 ‹*boxer, body*›

Chunnel /ˈtʃʌnl/ *n* **the ~** Brit colloq 英吉利海峡隧道

church /tʃɜːtʃ/
A *n* **1** [c] (building) 教堂 **2** [u] (service) 礼拜; **to go to ~** (service) 去做礼拜; (Catholic) 去做弥撒; **in/at ~** 在做礼拜 **3** [c] (*also* **Church**) + *v sing or pl* (denomination) 基督教教派; **the Anglican/Catholic/Russian Orthodox ~** 英国国教/天主教/俄罗斯东正教; **the ~** (body of people) 全体基督徒; (political or social force) 教会组织; **to go into** *or* **enter the ~** 成为神职人员
B *modif* 教堂的 ‹*bell*›; 教会的 ‹*land, festival*›; 在教堂举行的 ‹*wedding*›

church: C~ Commissioners *npl* Brit **the C~ Commissioners** 英国国教会财务委员会; **~goer** *n* 去教堂做礼拜的人

churchgoing /ˈtʃɜːtʃgəʊɪŋ/
A *adj* 经常去教堂的 ‹*person*›; **they're good ~ folk** 他们是常去教堂的好人
B *n* [u] 去教堂; **~ is not as popular as it used to be** 现在去教堂做礼拜不像以前那么普遍了

church: ~ hall *n* 教堂副厅; **~ leader** *n* 教会领袖; **~man** /-mən/ *n* 牧师; **C~ of England** *n* **the C~ of England** 英国国教会; **~ school** *n* 教会学校; **~ service** *n* 教堂礼拜; **~warden** *n* 堂会理事; **~woman** *n* 女神职人员

churchy /ˈtʃɜːtʃi/ *adj* colloq pej 恪守教会信条的 ‹*person, family*›; 使人联想到教会的 ‹*activity, music*›

churchyard /ˈtʃɜːtʃjɑːd/ *n* (yard) 教堂庭院; (graveyard) 教堂墓地

churlish /ˈtʃɜːlɪʃ/ *adj* (surly) 粗暴的; (rude) 无礼的 ‹*remark*›; (bad-tempered) 脾气坏的; (mean-spirited) 气量小的

> **the Church of England**
>
> 英格兰国教会。英格兰官方的基督教新教教会，原本隶属于罗马天主教。16 世纪时，英国国王亨利八世（King Henry VIII）宣布脱离罗马教廷，成立独立的新教教会。1534 年，亨利八世指使议会通过《至尊法案》（*Act of Supremacy*），规定英格兰教会为国教，国王取代罗马教皇成为英格兰教会的最高领袖。1553 年，亨利八世女儿玛丽即位，天主教短暂复辟，新教人士遭到残酷镇压，历史上称玛丽女王为“血腥玛丽”（Bloody Mary）。1558 年伊丽莎白女王（Queen Elizabeth I）即位后重新确立了英格兰教会的国教地位。
>
> 英格兰国教会保留了天主教的主教制度，国教会由坎特伯雷大主教（Archbishop of Canterbury）领导。主教（bishop）、神职人员（clergy）和平信徒（laity）组成英国国教总会（General Synod），是国教会的决策机构。国教会分坎特伯雷和约克两个教省（province），由大主教（archbishop）负责。教省下设主教辖区（diocese），由主教负责。大主教和主教经首相推荐，由英国君主任命。主教辖区下设堂区（parish），堂区负责人称作教区长（rector 或 vicar）。
>
> 国教会最重要的仪式为领圣餐（Holy Communion，简称 Communion）。领圣餐者吃面饼，喝葡萄酒，以纪念耶稣为人类做出的牺牲。人们通常在婴儿时期举行洗礼（baptism 或 christening），成为教徒。长大后理解并接受教会的教义，举行坚振礼（confirmation），之后就可以开始领圣餐。

churlishly /ˈtʃɜːlɪʃli/ *adv* (surlily) 粗暴地 ‹*refuse, criticize*›; (rudely) 无礼地 ‹*behave, remark*›; (meanly) 小气地 ‹*begrudge*›

churlishness /ˈtʃɜːlɪʃnɪs/ *n* [u] (surliness) 粗暴; (rudeness) 无礼; (mean-spiritedness) 小气

churn /tʃɜːn/
A *n* **1** (machine) 搅乳器 **2** (container) 奶桶
B *vt* **1** (stir, agitate) 搅 ‹*milk, cream*›; (produce by churning) 搅制; **freshly ~ed butter** 刚搅好的黄油 **2** fig **= churn up 2**
C *vi* **1** (be upset) 反胃; **my stomach was ~ing** (with nausea) 我感到恶心; (with nerves) 我紧张得想吐 **2** (be disturbed) «*water*» 翻腾; **the seas ~ed** 海浪翻滚

Phrasal verbs
• **churn out** *vt* [**~ sth. out, ~ out sth.**] pej «*company*» 粗制滥造 ‹*products*›; «*author*» 大量炮制 ‹*novels*›
• **churn up** *vt* **1** [**~ sth. up, ~ up sth.**] (stir) «*vehicle*» 翻搅 ‹*ground*›; «*storm*» 使…翻腾 ‹*water*›; **the earth had been ~ed up by (the wheels of) the tractor** 泥土被拖拉机（车轮）卷起 **2** [**~ sb. up**] (upset) 使心神不安

churn rate *n* 用户流失率

chute /ʃuːt/ *n* **1** (into swimming pool) 滑梯; (from plane) [逃生用的] 滑道 **2** (for rubbish) 倾卸槽; (for coal) 溜道 **3** colloq (parachute) 降落伞

chutney /ˈtʃʌtni/ *n* [u and c] 酸辣酱; **tomato ~** 番茄味酸辣酱

chutzpah /ˈhʊtspə/ *n* [u] colloq (self-confidence) 无所顾忌; (nerve) 胆量

CI *abbr* **= Channel Islands**

CIA *abbr* Amer **= Central Intelligence Agency**

cicada /sɪˈkɑːdə, Amer -ˈkeɪdə/ *n* 蝉

CID *abbr* Brit **= Criminal Investigation Department**

cider /ˈsaɪdə(r)/ *n* **1** [u] (alcoholic drink) 苹果酒 **2** [c] (glass) 一杯苹果酒

cider: ~ apple *n* 酿苹果酒的苹果; **~ press** *n* 苹果榨汁器; **~ vinegar** *n* [u] 苹果醋

CIF *abbr* **= cost, insurance, and freight** 到岸价格 [成本、保险费加运费]

cigar /sɪˈgɑː(r)/ *n* 雪茄烟; **a ~ box/case** 雪茄烟盒; **close, but no ~** Amer colloq 功亏一篑

cigarette /ˌsɪgəˈret, Amer ˈsɪgəret/ *n* 香烟; **a packet** *or* Amer **pack of ~s** 一包香烟

cigarette: ~ ash *n* [u] 烟灰; **~ butt** *n* 烟头; **~ card** *n* Brit 烟卡 [装在香烟包内可收集的画片]; **~ case** *n* 烟盒; **~ end** *n* 烟头; **~ holder** *n* 香烟烟嘴; **~ lighter** *n* (portable) 打火机; (in car) 点烟器; **~ machine** *n* 自动售烟机; **~ packet** Brit, **~ pack** Amer *ns* 香烟壳; **~ paper** *n* 卷烟纸; **~ smoke** *n* [u] 香烟烟雾; **~ tobacco** *n* [u] 烟丝

cigar: ~ holder *n* 雪茄烟嘴; **~-shaped** *adj* 雪茄状的

ciggie, ciggy /ˈsɪgi/ *n* colloq 香烟

cilantro /sɪˈlæntrəʊ/ *n* [u] esp Amer 芫荽叶

C-in-C /ˌsiː ɪn ˈsiː/ *abbr* **= commander-in-chief**

cinch /sɪntʃ/ *n* colloq **1** (easy task) 容易的事 **2** (certainty) 必然的事; **that horse is a ~ to win** 那匹马肯定会赢

cinder /ˈsɪndə(r)/ *n* (glowing) 余烬; (ash) 灰烬; (in volcano) 火山渣; **to burn sth. to a ~** 把某物烤焦; **~s** (in fireplace) 木炭灰; (in furnace) 煤灰

cinder block *n* Amer 煤渣砖

Cinderella /ˌsɪndəˈrelə/ *pr n* **1** (fairy tale character) 灰姑娘 **2** **cinderella** (sth. undervalued) 被忽视的事物; (sb. neglected) 被忽视的人; **pistol shooting is something of a c~ among Olympic Sports** 手枪射击是奥运会上不太受重视的运动项目

cinder track *n* 煤渣跑道

cine: ~ camera *n* 电影摄影机; **~ film** *n* Brit **1** [u] (material) 电影胶片; **2** [c] (recording) 电影节目

cinema /ˈsɪnəmɑː, ˈsɪnəmə/ *n* **1** [c] esp Brit (building) 电影院; **to go to the ~** 去看电影 **2** [u] (film-making) 电影制片术; (art form) 电影艺术; (entertainment industry) 电影业; **a wonderful piece of ~** 一部精彩的影片

cinema: ~ complex *n* 多厅电影院; **~goer** *n* 电影院常客

cinemagoing /ˈsɪnəmɑːgəʊɪŋ/
A *adj attrib* **the ~ public** 去电影院看电影的观众
B *n* [u] 去电影院看电影

cinematic /ˌsɪnəˈmætɪk/ *adj* **1** (relating to cinema) 电影的 ‹*techniques, genius*› **2** (characteristic of films) 适宜于拍电影的 ‹*subject*›; 具有电影特征的 ‹*scene, beauty*›; **the novel is not particularly ~** 这部小说不太适合拍成电影

cinematographer /ˌsɪnəməˈtɒgrəfə(r)/ ▸**p. 409** *n* esp Amer **1** (cameraman) 电影摄影师 **2** (projectionist) 电影放映员

cinematography /ˌsɪnəməˈtɒgrəfi/ *n* [u] (process) 电影摄制; (art) 电影摄制艺术

cinema-vérité /ˌsɪnəməˈveriteɪ/ *n* [u] (art) 实录电影艺术; (technique) 实录电影制片术

cineplex /ˈsɪnɪpleks/ *n* esp Amer 多厅电影院

cine projector *n* 电影放映机

cinnamon /ˈsɪnəmən/ ▸**p. 134**
A *n* **1** [u] (spice) 桂皮 **2** [c] (tree) 肉桂树 **3** [u] (colour) 浅黄褐色
B *adj* **1** (containing cinnamon) 含桂皮的 ‹*cakes, biscuits*› **2** (yellowish-brown) 浅黄褐色的

cipher /ˈsaɪfə(r)/ *n* **1** (code) 密码; **to write a message in ~** 写密码信 **2** pej (nonentity) 无足轻重的人 **3** (monogram) [字母交错组成的] 花押字

circa /ˈsɜːkə/ *prep* 大约; **a population of ~ five million** 大约 500 万人口

circadian rhythm /sɜːˌkeɪdɪən ˈrɪðəm/ *n* 昼夜节律

circle /ˈsɜːkl/
A *n* **1** (geometrical shape) 圆; **to square the ~** 作与圆面积相等的正方形; fig 做不可能的事 **2** (sth. with circular outline) 环状物; **a ~ of**

stones 一圈石头; **to stand in a ～** 站成一圈; **a ～ of mountain peaks could be seen above the clouds** 可以看到山峰环绕，高耸入云 **3** (round flat object) 圆形物; **to cut out two ～s of paper** 剪出两个圆纸片 **4** (circular movement) 环形运动; **to move/fly in a ～** 转圈/盘旋; **to go round** *or* **around in ～s** 在原地兜圈子; fig 徒劳无功; **to come full ～** «*person, situation*» 兜了个圈子回到原处 **5** **circles** *pl* (under eyes) 黑眼圈 **6** Brit Cin, Theat 弧形楼座 **7** (group) 圈子; **have a large ～ of friends** 交游甚广; **in theatrical ～s** 在戏剧界; **to move in fashionable ～s** 出入时尚界

B *vt* **1** (move around) 环绕…转圈; **the moon ～s the earth every 28 days** 月球每 28 天绕地球一周; **the plane ～d the airport before landing** 飞机降落前在机场上空盘旋 **2** (completely surround) 围绕; **a town ～d by hills** 群山环绕的城镇 **3** (draw ring around) 围绕…画圈; **the spelling mistakes are ～d in red ink** 拼写错误用红笔圈出

C *vi* «*bird, plane*» 盘旋; «*vehicle, rider, animal*» 转圈; **to ～ around** *or* **about sb./sth.** 绕某人/某物转圈; **to ～ over** *or* **above sb./sth.** 在某人/某物上空盘旋

circuit /ˈsɜːkɪt/ *n* **1** Elec 电路; **to complete/break the ～** 接通/断开电路 **2** (lap) 环行; **to do 15 ～s of the track** 绕跑道 15 圈 **3** (for motor racing, horse racing) [田径场的] 跑道; (for athletics) 环道 **4** (round trip) 巡游 **5** (regular round) 巡回活动; (of shows) 巡回表演; (of sports events) 巡回比赛; **to earn one's living on the lecture ～** 靠巡回讲学谋生; **the cabaret/tennis ～** 卡巴莱歌舞巡回演出/网球巡回赛 **6** Jur (journey) 巡回审判; **to be on the ～** 在进行巡回审判 **7** Jur (district) 巡回审判区

circuit: ～ board *n* (board) 电路板; (printed circuit) 印刷电路; **～ breaker** *n* 断路器; **～ court** *n* 巡回法院; **～ diagram** *n* 电路图; **～ judge** ▸p. 409 *n* Jur 巡回法官

circuitous /sɜːˈkjuːɪtəs/ *adj* **1** (indirect) 迂回的 ‹*route*›; 绕行的 ‹*one-way system*› **2** fig (roundabout) 拐弯抹角的 ‹*argument, explanation, reply*›; 间接的 ‹*means, method*›

circuitously /sɜːˈkjuːɪtəsli/ *adv* **1** (indirectly) 迂回地 ‹*proceed*›; 绕行地 ‹*climb, navigate*› **2** (in a roundabout manner) 拐弯抹角地 ‹*argue, explain, reply*›

circuitry /ˈsɜːkɪtri/ *n* [u] (circuits) 电路系统; (components) 电路元件

circuit training *n* [u] [轮番进行不同项目锻炼的] 循环训练

circular /ˈsɜːkjʊlə(r)/

A *adj* **1** (round) 圆的 ‹*shape, coin*› **2** (moving in a circle) 环行的 ‹*route, tour*› **3** Philos 循环论证的 ‹*logic, reasoning*›; **your argument is ～!** 你这是循环论证!

B *n* (newsletter) 通知; (advertisement) 传单

circular breathing *n* [u] [吹奏乐器时用的] 循环呼吸

circularity /ˌsɜːkjʊˈlærəti/ *n* [u] 循环论证

circularize /ˈsɜːkjʊləraɪz/ *vt* «*company, local authority*» 将传单发给 ‹*clients, members, public*›

circular: ～ letter *n* 传单; **～ saw** *n* 电动圆锯

circulate /ˈsɜːkjʊleɪt/

A *vi* **1** (flow) «*blood*» 循环; «*air*» 流通; «*liquid*» 环流 **2** (spread) «*news, information*» 传播; «*rumour*» 流传; «*newspaper*» 发行; «*goods*» 易手 **3** (mingle) «*host, guest*» 四处应酬

B *vt* **1** (spread) 散布 ‹*rumour*›; 传播 ‹*news, information*›; (publish) 发行 ‹*newspaper*›; (distribute) 行销 ‹*goods*›; **to ～ sth. among …** 在…中间散布某消息; **to ～ sth. somewhere** 把某消息传送到某处 **2** (send out) 散发 ‹*documents*›; (send copies to) 向…分发 ‹*members, branches*›; **the report was ～d to the members** 报告分发给了各位成员 **3** (pass around) 传看 ‹*photograph*›; 传递 ‹*bottle*›; 传送 ‹*correspondence*›

circulation /ˌsɜːkjʊˈleɪʃn/ *n* **1** [u] (flow) (of blood) 循环; (of air) 流通; **to have good/bad ～** 血液循环良好/不好 **2** [u] (dissemination) (of news, information) 传播; (of document) 传阅; (of rumours) 流传; **for ～ to …** (on document) 供…传阅 **3** [u] (of money, goods) 流通; **in ～** 在流通; **to take sth. out of** *or* **withdraw sth. from ～** 停止流通某物 **4** [u] **to be back in ～** (socially active again) 重回社交界 **5** [u and c] (readership) 发行量

circulation: ～ area *n* 发行区域; **～ department** *n* 发行部; **～ figures** *npl* 发行量; **～ manager** ▸p. 409 *n* 发行部经理

circulatory /ˌsɜːkjʊˈleɪtəri, Amer ˈsɜːkjələtɔːri/ *adj* 血液循环的; **the ～ system** 血液循环系统

circumcise /ˈsɜːkəmsaɪz/ *vt* **1** (cut off foreskin of) 环切…的包皮 ‹*boy, penis*› **2** (cut off clitoris from) 切除…的阴蒂 ‹*girl*›

circumcision /ˌsɜːkəmˈsɪʒn/ *n* [u and c] (of boy) 包皮环切; (of girl) 阴蒂切除

circumference /səˈkʌmfərəns/ *n* (line) 圆周; (distance round) 圆周长; **to be 4 km in ～** 周长为 4 公里

circumflex /ˈsɜːkəmfleks/ *n* **～ (accent)** 音调符号 [加在元音字母上表示音调的符号(^)]

circumlocution /ˌsɜːkəmləˈkjuːʃn/ *n* [u and c] formal 迂回的说法

circumnavigate /ˌsɜːkəmˈnævɪgeɪt/ *vt* 环绕…航行

circumnavigation /ˌsɜːkəmˌnævɪˈgeɪʃn/ *n* [u and c] formal 环球航行

circumscribe /ˈsɜːkəmskraɪb/ *vt* **1** formal (limit) 限制 ‹*freedom*›; 限定 ‹*role*›; 约束 ‹*powers*›; **a life ～d by poverty** 受制于贫困的生活 **2** Math 画…的外接图形; **to ～ an ellipse around a rhombus** 画菱形的外接椭圆

circumspect /ˈsɜːkəmspekt/ *adj* formal 小心谨慎的 ‹*person*›; 深思熟虑的 ‹*guess*›; 仔细的 ‹*glance*›; **to be ～ about** 慎重考虑 ‹*likelihood, chance*›; **to be ～ about predicting/making a commitment** 对于作出预测/承诺持谨慎态度

circumspection /ˌsɜːkəmˈspekʃn/ *n* [u] formal 小心谨慎

circumspectly /ˈsɜːkəmspektli/ *adv* formal 小心谨慎地 ‹*behave*›; 深思熟虑地 ‹*proceed*›; 仔细地 ‹*look*›

circumstance /ˈsɜːkəmstəns/

A *n* [c and u] (event(s), fact(s)) 状况; **a strange ～** 一个奇怪的情况; **a victim of ～** 客观环境的牺牲品

B **circumstances** *npl* **1** (situation) 形势; **～s forced us to change our plans** 形势迫使我们改变计划; **in** *or* **under the ～s** 在目前情况下; **in** *or* **under no ～s** 无论如何不; **due to ～s beyond our control** 由于我们不能控制的情况 **2** (conditions of life) 境况; (financial affairs) 经济状况; **in easy/poor ～s** 经济宽裕/拮据

circumstantial /ˌsɜːkəmˈstænʃl/ *adj* 间接推测的 ‹*evidence, case*›

circumvent /ˌsɜːkəmˈvent/ *vt* formal **1** (avoid) 规避 ‹*law, rule*›; 避开 ‹*official, middleman*› **2** (frustrate) 智胜 ‹*adversary*›; 挫败 ‹*blackmail attempt, coup*› **3** (go around) 绕过

circus /ˈsɜːkəs/ *n* (*pl* **～es**) **1** (show) 马戏; **to go to the ～** 去看马戏; **～ clowns/animals** 马戏团的小丑/动物 **2** colloq pej (commotion) 喧闹的场面

cirrhosis /sɪˈrəʊsɪs/ ▸p. 377 *n* [u] **～ (of the liver)** 肝硬化

cirrus /ˈsɪrəs/ *n* [u] 卷云

CIS *abbr* = **Commonwealth of Independent States**

cissy /ˈsɪsi/ *n, adj* colloq = **sissy**

Cistercian /sɪˈstɜːʃn/

A *adj* 西多会的 ‹*monk, nun, monastery*›

B *n* (male) 西多会修士; (female) 西多会修女

cistern /ˈsɪstən/ *n* **1** (of lavatory) 水箱 **2** (in loft) 蓄水箱; (underground) 储水罐

citadel /ˈsɪtədəl/ *n* 城堡

citation /saɪˈteɪʃn/ *n* **1** (quotation) 引述; (words, sentence etc. cited) 引文 **2** Mil (official commendation) 嘉奖; (document) 嘉奖令; **a ～ for bravery** 因英勇而受到的嘉奖 **3** Amer Jur (order) 传唤; (summons) 传票

cite /saɪt/ *vt* **1** (quote) 引用 ‹*word, sentence*›; 引述 ‹*book, author*› **2** (give as reason) 援引 ‹*example, fact, name*› **3** (mention) 例举 **4** Mil (commend) 嘉奖 ‹*member of the armed forces*›; **to ～ sb. for sth.** 因某事物嘉奖某人 **5** Jur 传唤 ‹*witness*›; **to be ～d in divorce proceedings** 在离婚诉讼中受到传唤

citizen /ˈsɪtɪzn/ *n* **1** (of state) 公民 **2** (of town, city) 居民

citizenry /ˈsɪtɪznri/ *n* [u] + *v sing or pl* formal 全体市民

citizen: C～'s Advice Bureau *n* Brit 公民咨询局; **～'s arrest** *n* 公民拘捕 [普通公民不持逮捕证抓捕他人的行为]; **C～'s Band** *n* [u] 民用波段

citizenship /ˈsɪtɪznʃɪp/ *n* [u] 公民身份; **to apply for/be granted British ～** 申请/获得英国国籍

citizenship test *n* 公民入籍测试

citric acid /ˌsɪtrɪk ˈæsɪd/ *n* 柠檬酸

citrus /ˈsɪtrəs/: **～ fruit** *n* 柑橘; **～ tree** *n* 柑橘树

city /ˈsɪti/ *n* **1** (large town) 城市; **～ streets/people** 城市的街道/居民; **～ life** 城市生活 **2** (inhabitants) 全市居民 **3** **the City** Brit (London as financial centre) 伦敦城 [指伦敦金融中心]

> **the City**
>
> 伦敦（金融）城，全称the City of London。伦敦市的商业和金融中心。位于伦敦中心、泰晤士河北岸。伦敦金融城比作为英国首都的伦敦小得多，面积只有 1.1 平方英里（约 2.6 平方公里），因此有 Square Mile（平方英里）的别称。现在的伦敦基本上是以它为基础发展而来。伦敦金融城和伦敦其他 32 个自治市（borough）组成首都伦敦，即大伦敦（Greater London）。伦敦金融城的地位和纽约的华尔街相似，城内设有英格兰银行（Bank of England）、伦敦证券交易中心（London Stock Exchange）和劳埃德保险社（Lloyd's of London）等许多著名金融机构。现在 the City 常指金融城内的金融从业人员。

city: C～ and Guilds certificate *n* 城市同业公会协会证书; **C～ and Guilds Institute** *n* 城市同业公会协会 [英国颁发技术和手艺证书的机构]; **～ centre** *n* 市中心; **～ council** *n* 市议会; **～ councillor** *n* Brit 市议会议员; **～ councilman** /-mən/ *n* Amer 市议会议员; **～ councilwoman** *n* Amer 市议会女议员; **～ desk** *n* **1** Brit (for financial news) 财经新闻部; **2** Amer (for local news) 本地新闻部; **～-dweller** *n* 城市居民; **～ editor** ▸p. 409 *n* **1** Brit (of financial news) 财经新闻编辑; **2** Amer (of local news) 本地新闻编辑; **～ fathers** *npl* 城市要人; **～ hall** *n* Amer **1** (municipal offices) 市政厅; **2** (municipal officers) 市政官员; **～ limits** *npl* Amer 城市范围; **～ manager** ▸p. 409 *n* Amer 城市经理; **～ news** *n* Brit 伦敦城财经新闻; **～ planner** ▸p. 409 *n* Amer 城市规划师; **～ planning** *n* [u] Amer 城市规划; **～scape** *n* (appearance) 都市风光; (landscape) 城市风景; **～ slicker** *n* colloq pej 油头滑脑的城里人; **～ state** *n* 城邦; **C～ Technology College** *n* Brit 城市职业技校

civet /ˈsɪvɪt/ *n* ～ (cat) 麝猫

civic /ˈsɪvɪk/ *adj* **1** (municipal) 市政的 ‹*officials, administration*›; (of a city) 城市的 ‹*function, ceremony, occasion*› **2** (of a community) 市民的 ‹*pride, duties*›

civic centre *n* **1** Brit (municipal offices) 市府大厦 **2** (community centre) 市民活动中心

civics /ˈsɪvɪks/ *npl* + *v sing* 市政学

civies /ˈsɪviːz/ *npl* Amer colloq = **civvies**

civil /ˈsɪvl/ *adj* **1** (of citizens) 公民的 ‹*affairs*›; 文职的 ‹*administration, authorities, government*› **2** (between citizens) 公民间的 ‹*disorder, strife*› **3** (civic) 民用的; (non-religious) 世俗的 ‹*marriage, ceremony*› **4** (polite) 有礼貌的 ‹*person, reply, manner*›; **to keep a ～ tongue in one's head** 谈吐文雅 **5** Jur 民事的; **a ～ court/case/offence** 民事法庭/案件/犯罪

civil: C～ Aviation Authority *n* Brit **the C～ Aviation Authority** 民航管理局; **～ defence** *n* [u] 民防; **～ disobedience** *n* [u] 非暴力反抗; **～ engineer** ▸**p. 409** *n* 土木工程师; **～ engineering** *n* [u] 土木工程

civilian /sɪˈvɪlɪən/

A *n* 平民

B *adj* 平民的 ‹*life, clothes*›; 文职的 ‹*government*›

civility /sɪˈvɪləti/

A *n* [u] 礼貌; **you should show more ～ to** *or* **towards your host** 你应该对主人更礼貌些

B civilities *npl* 客套; **the usual civilities** 日常的客套

civilization /ˌsɪvəlaɪˈzeɪʃn, Amer -vəlɪˈz-/ *n* **1** [u] (human development) 文明; **the history of (human) ～** (人类) 文明史 **2** [u] (cultivation) 开化过程 **3** [u and c] (society) 文明社会; **western ～** 西方文明社会 **4** [u] (all people and societies) 文明世界; **environmental damage threatens the whole of ～** 环境破坏威胁到整个文明世界 **5** [u] hum (comforts of modern life) 现代文明生活; **they live far from ～** 他们的生活远离现代文明

civilize /ˈsɪvəlaɪz/ *vt* **1** (improve and educate) 使…开化 ‹*nation, tribe*› **2** (refine) 使…有教养 ‹*manners, behaviour, child*›; (improve manners or behaviour of) 使…文雅 ‹*child, boor*›

civilized /ˈsɪvəlaɪzd/ *adj* **1** (advanced, developed) 文明的 ‹*country, society, people*›; **to become ～** 变得文明 **2** (polite) 有礼貌的 ‹*conversation*›; (good-mannered) 文雅的

civilizing /ˈsɪvəlaɪzɪŋ/ *adj* 使人开化的 ‹*mission*›; 使人文雅的 ‹*effect*›; **she is a ～ influence on him** 她的影响令他变得文雅

civil: ～ law *n* [u] 民法; **～ liberty** *n* 公民自由; **C～ List** *n* **the C～ List** (allowance) 王室年俸; (list) 王室年俸名单

civilly /ˈsɪvəli/ *adv* 有礼貌地 ‹*behave, reply, cooperate*›

> **the civil rights movement**
>
> 民权运动。一般指 20 世纪五六十年代美国黑人反对种族隔离与歧视、争取民主权利的运动。美国内战虽然废除了南方的奴隶制度，但直到二战以后，美国的黑人社会地位依然很低，种族隔离现象仍根深蒂固。在青年黑人牧师马丁·路德·金（Martin Luther King）的领导下，黑人及白人支持者采取抵制、静坐等非暴力抗议手段争取黑人的平等权利。1963 年 8 月，约 25 万人向华盛顿进发，马丁·路德·金在林肯纪念堂前作了著名的演讲《我有一个梦》（I Have a Dream），呼吁建立平等的社会。黑人运动的巨大影响迫使约翰逊政府于 1964 年 7 月通过了《民权法案》（*Civil Rights Act*），禁止出于种族、肤色、宗教、性别等原因的任何歧视。1965 年 8 月，《选举权利法》（*Voting Rights Act*）获得通过，从而废除了种种剥夺黑人选举权的制度。

civil: ～ marriage *n* [u and c] 世俗婚姻; **～ partnership** *n* [u and c] 同性民事伴侣关系; **～ rights** *npl* 公民权; **the ～ rights movement** 民权运动; **～ servant** ▸**p. 409** *n* 公务员

civil service *n* + *v sing or pl* (government departments) 行政部门; (government employees) 公务员

Civil Service Commission *n* + *v sing or pl* 公务员制度委员会

civil service examination *n* 公务员考试

> **the civil service**
>
> 公务员制度。现代公务员制度起源于19世纪中叶的英国。英国的公务员（civil servant）起初被称为君主的仆役（servant of the Crown），这种称呼至今仍然可用。英国的各个部下设大臣（Minister或Secretary of State）、次官（junior minister），次官以下即是各个级别的公务员。职务最高的公务员称常务次官（permanent secretary）。公务员部门受内阁办公室（Cabinet Office）和财政部（Treasury）领导。英国的首相和各部大臣、次官会因选举而轮替，不属于公务员。公务员队伍不受政党更迭影响。英国的公务员制度比较重要的原则包括：第一、政治中立；第二、择优录用和提拔；第三、长期任职。
>
> 美国的公务员是政府雇员。要成为公务员需要参加公务员考试（Civil Service Examination），择优录用。和英国相似，美国的公务员也必须保持政治中立，不能支持任何政党，同时也不受政党轮替的影响。但英国的公务员通常只限于中央政府的文职人员，而美国的公务员则包括联邦政府和地方政府的文职人员。

civil: ～ society *n* [u and c] 公民社会; **～ war** *n* [u and c] 内战; **～ wedding** *n* 世俗婚礼

civvies /ˈsɪvɪz/ *npl* colloq 便装; **to be (dressed) in ～** 身穿便服

Civvy Street /ˈsɪvi striːt/ *n* [u] colloq 平民生活; **to be on ～** 过平民百姓的生活

CJD *n* = **Creutzfeldt-Jakob disease**

cl *abbr* = **centilitre(s)** 厘升

clack /klæk/

A *n* (of castanets) 噼啪声; (of knitting needles) 啪嗒声; (of typewriter) 哒哒声

B *vi* **1** (make sound) «*castanets*» 噼啪作响; «*knitting needles*» 发出啪嗒声; «*typewriter*» 哒哒作响 **2** pej (chatter loudly) 喋喋不休; **tongues were ～ing** 人们在喋喋不休地说着话

clad /klæd/

A *adj* formal or hum 穿…衣服的; **motorcyclists ～ in leather** 身穿皮衣的摩托车手; **scantily ～ dancers** 衣着暴露的舞蹈演员

B -clad *combining form* **1** (clothed) 穿…衣服的; **black～** 身着黑衣的; **armour～ warriors** 身披盔甲的战士 **2** formal (covered) 被…覆盖的; **an ivy～ tower** 爬满常春藤的塔

cladding /ˈklædɪŋ/ *n* [u] 覆面; **timber/plastic/metal ～** 木料/塑料/金属覆面

claim /kleɪm/

A *vt* **1** (assert right to) 要求…的所有权 ‹*land, property, throne*›; 认领 ‹*lost property*›; **she ～ed ownership of the land** 她要求得到这块土地的所有权; **each student ～ed a desk in the new classroom** 在新教室里每个学生拥有一张课桌 **2** (assert) 声称; **both sides are ～ing victory** 双方均宣称获胜; **I can ～ some credit for the success of the project** 我可以说这个项目的成功有我一份贡献; **she ～s (that) she is related to the Queen** 她声称跟女王沾亲带故; **some amazing things have been ～ed for this new drug** 这种新药据称有奇效 **3** Insur «*policyholder*» 凭保险单索取 ‹*compensation*› **4** Admin 向政府申请 ‹*allowance, benefi*› **5** (in industrial relations) «*workers, trade union*» 向资方要求 ‹*pay rise*›; **the workers are ～ing a 10% pay increase** 工人们要求 10% 的加薪 **6** (request refund of) 申请报销 ‹*expenses*› **7** (require) 要求 ‹*energies, attention*›; **most of my free time is ～ed by the community work** 我的大部分空闲时间都花在社区工作上了; **the causes ～ing one's sympathies** 值得支持的事业 **8** (win) 获得 ‹*victory*›; **she has finally ～ed a place on the team** 她终于成了该队的一员 **9** (cause death of) «*disaster, war*» 造成…的死亡 ‹*victims*›; **the hurricane has ～ed hundreds of lives** 飓风夺去了数百人的生命

B *vi* **1** Insur 索赔; **to ～ for damages** «*policyholder*» 索取损害赔偿金 **2** Admin 向政府申请救济; **to ～ for sb./sth.** 为某人/某事物申请救济

C *n* **1** [u and c] (right) 所有权; **a ～ on sth.** 对…的要求 ‹*time, funds, attention*›; **to lay ～ to sth.** 提出对…的所有权 ‹*land, property, throne, title*›; **a ～ to fame** 出名的事由; **to assert/renounce one's ～ to the throne** 坚持/放弃获得王位的权利; **you have no ～ on** *or* **to my sympathy** 你没法博得我的同情 **2** [c] (assertion) 声称; **to make a ～** 作出断言; **to make ～s for sb./sth.** 渲染某人/某事物; **nobody believed his ～ to be innocent** 他自称清白，可谁也不相信; **I lay no ～ to being an expert** 我不以专家自居 **3** [c] Insur 索赔; **to make** *or* **lodge** *or* **put in a ～ (for sth.)** （对…）提出索赔 ‹*damages*› **4** [c] Admin 政府救济申请; **a ～ for sth.** 对…的申请 ‹*allowance, benefit*›; **to make** *or* **put in a ～** 提出救济申请 **5** [c] (in industrial relations) [对资方提出的] 要求; **to make a wage ～** 提出加薪的要求; **the workers have put in a ～ for union recognition** 工人们要求资方承认工会

Phrasal verb

- **claim back** *vt* [**～ sth. back, ～ back sth.**] 要求退还 ‹*expenses, tax*›; **you can ～ your money back if the goods are damaged** 如货物受损，可要求退款; **to ～ sth. back on the insurance** 根据保险合同要求赔偿某物

claimant /ˈkleɪmənt/ *n* **1** Brit (of state benefit) 社会保障金申领人 **2** Jur (to title, estate) 继承人; (for compensation) 索赔人

claim form *n* **1** Insur 理赔单 **2** Admin 申请表

claims: ～ adjuster *n* 理赔理算员; **～ department** *n* 理赔部

clairvoyance /kleəˈvɔɪəns/ *n* [u] 洞察力

clairvoyant /kleəˈvɔɪənt/

A *n* 先知

B *adj* 洞悉未来的 ‹*gypsy, powers*›

clam /klæm/

A *n* **1** Zool 蛤蜊 **2** Culin 蛤肉

B *vi* (*pres p etc.* **-mm-**) esp Amer (dig for clams) 挖蛤; (collect clams) 拾蛤

Phrasal verb

- **clam up** *vi* colloq (become silent) 变得沉默; (refuse to speak) 拒绝开口; **to ～ up on sb.** 对某人保持缄默

clambake /ˈklæmbeɪk/ *n* Amer 海滨烤蛤野餐会

clamber /ˈklæmbə(r)/

A *vi* 攀爬; **to ～ over/up/across ...** 翻爬过/爬上/爬行穿过…; **to ～ down the cliff** 爬下悬崖

B *n* 攀爬; **a ～ up the cliff path** 顺着悬崖小径向上的攀爬

clam chowder *n* [u and c] Amer 蛤肉羹

clammy /ˈklæmi/ *adj* **1** (moist) 湿腻的 ‹*hands, face, fish*› **2** (humid) 闷湿的 ‹*weather*›

clamor /ˈklæmə(r)/ *n, vi* = **clamour**

clamorous /ˈklæmərəs/ *adj* **1** (noisy) 喧闹的 ‹*crowd, voices*› **2** (demanding) 大声疾呼的 ‹*protests, demands*›

clamour /ˈklæmə(r)/ Brit

A *n* [u] **1** (loud shouting) 喧闹声 **2** (demand) 大声疾呼; **a ～ for revenge** 复仇的呼声

B *vi* **1** (shout loudly) «*crowd, protesters*» 高喊;

C

to ～ about or over sth. 为某事物叫喊 2 (demand) «public, crowd» 大声疾呼; to ～ for sb. to do sth. 大声疾呼要某人做某事; to ～ for/against sth./sb. 大声疾呼支持/反对某事物/某人

clamp¹ /klæmp/
A n 1 (for fastening, holding) 夹具; a surgical/dental ～ 手术钳/拔牙钳 2 Aut 车轮夹锁 3 fig (restriction) 钳制; to put a ～ on public spending 限制公共开支
B vt 1 (fasten, hold) [用夹具] 夹住; to ～ A and B together 将A和B夹在一起; to ～ A to B 将A夹到B上 2 Aut «traffic warden» 给…上夹锁 ‹vehicle, wheel› 3 (fix tightly) «hands» 紧紧抓住 ‹gun›; «handcuffs» 紧紧铐住 ‹wrists›; to ～ a hand over sth. 一只手紧紧抓住某物; his jaws were ～ed shut 他牙关紧咬 4 esp Amer (impose) «authorities, government» 强行实施 ‹curfew, restrictions›; to ～ sth. on sth./sb. 强制某机构/某人接受某事物

Phrasal verb
• **clamp down** vi to ～ down on sb./sth. 严厉打击 ‹crime, drug peddlers, football hooligans, tax evasion›; 严禁 ‹smoking, speeding›; 压制 ‹media›; 严格限制 ‹public spending›

clamp² n Brit Agric [贮藏在土或干草中的] 块根作物堆

clampdown /'klæmpdaʊn/ n (on crime, drug peddlers, football hooligans, tax evasion) 严厉打击; (on smoking, speeding) 严禁; (on the media) 压制; (on public spending) 严格限制

clamshell /'klæmʃel/ n 蛤壳

clamshell phone n 翻盖手机

clan /klæn/ n 1 (Scottish family) 宗族 2 (close-knit family) 大家族

clandestine /klæn'destɪn/ adj 秘密的 ‹meeting, organization, marriage›; 偷偷摸摸的 ‹activities›

clang /klæŋ/
A vi «bell» 当当作响; «gong» 铿锵作响; the iron gate ～ed shut 铁门咣当一声关了
B vt 当当敲响 ‹bell›; 铿锵击响 ‹gong›
C n (of bell) 当当声; (of gong) 铿锵声

clanger /'klæŋə(r)/ n Brit colloq (mistake) 令人难堪的大错; (gaffe) 失态; to drop a ～ 出言不慎

clanging /'klæŋɪŋ/ n [u] 铿锵声

clangour Brit, **clangor** Amer /'klæŋgə(r)/ n liter 当当声

clank /klæŋk/
A vi «chains, armour» 发当啷声; to ～ along 当啷当啷地向前走
B vt 使…发当啷声 ‹chains›
C n 当啷声

clanking /'klæŋkɪŋ/ n [u] 当啷声

clannish /'klænɪʃ/ adj pej 排他的 ‹profession, behaviour, mentality›

clansman /'klænzmən/ n (pl **clansmen**) 苏格兰宗族男成员

clap¹ /klæp/
A vi (pres p etc. -pp-) 鼓掌; to ～ to sth. 随着某节奏鼓掌
B vt (pres p etc. -pp-) 1 (strike together) 拍 ‹hands›; (applaud) 为…鼓掌 ‹performer, performance› 2 (slap) 轻拍 ‹person›; to ～ sb. on the back 轻拍某人的背部 3 (place) 迅速放置; to ～ one's hands over one's ears/mouth 突然用手捂住耳朵/嘴巴; to ～ sb. in irons/in jail 突然把某人锁上镣铐/投进监狱; to ～ hold of sth./sb. colloq 一把抓住某物/某人 4 = clap on 2
C n 1 (round of applause) 鼓掌; (handclap) 拍手; (sound of handclapping) 拍手声; to get a ～ 赢得一阵掌声; to give sb. a ～ 为某人鼓掌 2 (friendly slap on the back) 轻拍 3 (of thunder) 霹雳声; a ～ of thunder 一声霹雳

Phrasal verb
• **clap on** vt [～ sth. on, ～ on sth.] 1 (put on) 扣上 ‹hat›; (slam on) 猛踩 ‹brakes› 2 (impose) to ～ sth. on sth. 将…强加于某事物 ‹surcharge, tax, duty›; the airline has ～ped an extra 25 per cent on fares 航空公司硬是将票价提高了 25%

clap² n [u] colloq the ～ 花柳病 [尤指淋病]; he caught a dose of the ～ 他得了淋病

clapboard /'klæpbɔːd, 'klæbəd/ n Amer [建筑物外墙的] 护墙板

clapped-out adj colloq 破旧的 ‹machinery, vehicle›; 精疲力竭的 ‹horse, politician›; 陈旧的 ‹ideas›; 一蹶不振的 ‹economy›

clapper /'klæpə(r)/ n 钟锤; to run/work like the ～s Brit colloq 飞奔/拼命工作

clapperboard /'klæpəbɔːd/ n Brit [拍摄电影时用的] 场记板

clapping /'klæpɪŋ/ n [u] (sound) 鼓掌声; (action) 鼓掌

claptrap /'klæptræp/ n [u] colloq (talk) 蠢话; (ideas) 荒唐的想法

claque /klæk/ n 1 (followers) 一帮马屁精 2 (paid applauders) 受雇捧场的一群人; (paid hecklers) 受雇喝倒彩的一群人

claret /'klærət/ ▸ p. 134
A n 1 [u and c] (wine) [法国波尔多产的] 红葡萄酒 2 [u] (colour) 深红色
B adj 深红色的

clarification /ˌklærɪfɪ'keɪʃn/ n [u] 1 (explanation) 澄清 2 Culin 净化

clarify /'klærɪfaɪ/ vt 1 (explain) 澄清 ‹problem, situation›; a ～ing statement 起澄清作用的声明; to become clarified 变得明晰 2 Culin 净化; clarified butter 已净化的黄油

clarinet /ˌklærə'net/ ▸ p. 395 n 单簧管

clarinettist /ˌklærə'netɪst/ ▸ p. 395, p. 409 n 单簧管演奏者

clarion call /'klærɪən kɔːl/ n 号召; a ～ to sth./to do sth. 某事物/做某事的号召; a ～ to sb. 对某人的号召

clarity /'klærəti/ n [u] 1 (of sound, vision) 清楚 2 (of thought, expression) 清晰 3 (certainty) 明确性

clash /klæʃ/
A vi 1 (meet and fight, coincide inconveniently) 冲突; police ～ed with demonstrators 警察与示威者发生了冲突; your party ～es with my sister's wedding 你的聚会和我姐姐的婚礼在时间上有冲突 2 fig (disagree, be in conflict) 有分歧; to ～ (with sb.) on or over sth. (与某人) 在某事物上有分歧; to ～ with sth. 与某事物相抵触 3 (not match) «colours, designs, dresses» 不协调; to ～ with sth. 与某物不相配 4 (strike together) «swords» 撞击发出刺耳响声; «cymbals» 哐当擦响
B vt 使撞击发出刺耳响声 ‹swords›; 哐当擦响 ‹cymbals›
C n 1 (confrontation) (inconvenient coincidence) 冲突; a ～ between A and B A和B之间的冲突; there's a ～ of meetings 几次会议在时间上有冲突 2 (disagreement) 争论; a ～ with sb. (on or over sth.) (在某事物上) 与某人的分歧 3 (incompatibility) 差异; a ～ of beliefs/cultures 信仰/文化的冲突; a personality ～ 个性冲突 4 (mismatch) 不协调; a ～ of colours 色彩的不搭配 5 (noise) 撞击声; a ～ of cymbals 铙钹的哐当声

clasp /klɑːsp, Amer klæsp/
A vt 1 (hold tightly) 握紧 ‹knife›; 攥紧 ‹money›; he ～ed her hand 他紧紧握住她的手; to ～ sth. to one's breast 将某物紧紧抓在胸前 2 (embrace) 抱紧 ‹baby, bag›; to ～ sb. to one's breast 紧紧拥抱某人
B n 1 (fastening) 搭扣 2 (grip) 紧握 3 (embrace) 紧抱

clasp knife n 折叠刀

class /klɑːs, Amer klæs/
A n 1 [c] (category) 类别; (grade) 等级; to be in a ～ of one's own 出类拔萃; to be in a different ～ from ... 和…不属于同一类; he's not in the same ～ as the other players 他比其他运动员逊色多了 2 [c and u] Sociol (group) 阶级; (system) 等级制度; the upper/middle/working ～(es) 上层/中产/工人阶级 3 [c] Sch, Univ (group of students) 班级; (lesson) 课; in ～ 在课堂上 4 [c] Amer Sch, Univ (year group) 同届毕业生; the ～ of 72 72 届毕业生 5 [u] colloq (elegance) 优雅; to add a touch of ～ to sth. 给某事物增添几分雅致 6 [c] Transp 等级; to travel first/second ～ 乘头等舱/二等舱旅行 7 [c] Brit Univ (of degree) 学位等级; a first-/second-～ degree 一级/二级优等学位 8 [c] Biol 纲
B vt 将…归类 ‹person, specimen, book›; to ～ sth./sb. as/among/with sth. 将某事物/某人归入某类别
C adj colloq (excellent) 出类拔萃的 ‹athlete, horse›; she's a real ～ act 她真是魅力非凡

class: ～ **action** n Amer 集体诉讼; ～ **conscious** adj 1 usu pej (aware of one's class) 有阶级意识的; 2 (gen) (in Marxist discourse) 有阶级斗争意识的; ～ **consciousness** n [u] 1 usu pej (awareness of one's class) 阶级意识; 2 (in Marxist discourse) 阶级斗争意识; ～ **distinction** n 阶级差别; ～ **divisions** npl (disagreements between classes) 阶级对立; (differences between classes) 阶级差异

classic /'klæsɪk/
A adj 1 (definitive, standard) 经典的 ‹novel, film›; 一流的 ‹performance› 2 (typical) 典型的 ‹example, case, symptoms› 3 (traditional) 传统的 ‹design, style›
B n 1 (work of art or literature) 经典作品; ▸ classics 2 (outstanding example) 优秀典范 3 colloq (hilarious example) 荒唐的事; (joke) 令人捧腹的笑话

classical /'klæsɪkl/ adj 1 (relating to ancient Greek and Roman civilization) 古典的 ‹literature, architecture, ballet›; a ～ scholar 研究希腊文和拉丁文古典著作的学者; a ～ composer 古典音乐作曲家 2 (traditional) 传统的 ‹design›; 古典的 ‹economics›

classical education n 古典文化教育

classically /'klæsɪkli/ adv 以古典方式; ～ elegant 典雅的; a ～ proportioned fashion model 身形具古典美的时装模特; ～ trained 受过古典艺术训练的

classical: ～ **music** n [u] 古典音乐; ～ **studies** npl [研究古希腊与古罗马文化的] 古典学研究

classicism /'klæsɪsɪzəm/ n [u] 古典主义

classicist /'klæsɪsɪst/ n (student) 古典学学生; (teacher) 古典学教师; (scholar) 古典学者

classics /'klæsɪks/ n 1 + v pl (classical works) (of writers) 古典文学作品; (of philosophers) 古典哲学作品 2 **Classics** + v sing (classical studies) 古典学课程

classifiable /'klæsɪfaɪəbl/ adj 可分类的; to be ～ as sth. 可归入某类事物

classification /ˌklæsɪfɪ'keɪʃn/ n 1 [u] (categorization) 分类; he objected to his ～ as an illegal alien 他反对自己被归入非法外侨; ～ (of sth.) under sth. (将某事物) 归入某类事物的分类 2 [c] (category) 类别; books of different ～s 不同门类的书

classified /'klæsɪfaɪd/ adj 1 (categorized) 分类的 ‹statistics, catalogue› 2 (secret) 机密的 ‹document, information›

classified advertisement, colloq **classified ad** ns 分类广告

classifieds /'klæsɪfaɪdz/ npl 分类广告

classified section n 分类广告栏

classify /'klæsɪfaɪ/ vt 1 (categorize) 将…分类 ‹documents, chemicals, data›; (assign to a class) 将…归类 ‹specimen, object, person›; to ～ sth. under 'personal' 将某事物归入"私人"类 2 (declare secret) 将…定为机密 ‹document, information›

classless /'klɑːslɪs, Amer 'klæs-/ adj 1 Sociol 无阶级的 ‹society, utopia› 2 (with no obvious class) 不属于任何阶级的 ‹person, accent›

class: ~ list *n* **1** Brit Univ 毕业生学位等级名单; **2** Sch (list of pupils) 班级学生名单; **~ mark** *n* 分类号; **~mate** *n* 同班同学; **~ number** *n* **=** **~ mark**; **~ president** *n* Amer 班长; **~ rank** *n* Amer 同届毕业生成绩排名; **~-ridden** *adj* pej 受阶级影响的 ‹*attitude*›; 等级森严的 ‹*society*›; **~room** *n* 教室; **~ society** *n* 阶级社会; **~ structure** *n* 阶级结构; **~ struggle** *n* 阶级斗争; **~ system** *n* 阶级制度; **~ teacher** *n* Brit 班主任; **~ trip** *n* 班级旅行; **~ war** *n* [c and u] 阶级战争; **~ warfare** *n* [u] 阶级战争

classy /ˈklɑːsi, Amer ˈklæsi/ *adj* colloq 时髦的 ‹*clothes, actress*›; 豪华的 ‹*car, hotel, furniture*›; **she's really ~** 她真的很时尚

clatter /ˈklætə(r)/
A *vi* «*cutlery*» 叮当响; «*horse's hoofs*» 嗒嗒响; **to ~ in/out/down** 嗒嗒地进去/出去/下去
B *vt* 使叮当作响; **stop ~ing those dishes!** 别把那些碟子碰得叮当响!
C *n* 叮当声; **a ~ of dishes** 碟子碰撞的叮当声

clause /klɔːz/ *n* **1** Ling 分句; **a main/subordinate/relative ~** 主句/从句/关系从句 **2** Jur, Pol (in will, contract etc.) 条款

claustrophobia /ˌklɔːstrəˈfəʊbɪə/ *n* [u] 幽闭恐怖症

claustrophobic /ˌklɔːstrəˈfəʊbɪk/
A *adj* **1** Psych 患幽闭恐怖症的 ‹*person*›; 幽闭恐怖的 ‹*feeling, sensation*›; **to get ~** 感到幽闭恐怖 **2** (inducing claustrophobia) 引起幽闭恐怖的 ‹*room, atmosphere, conditions*›; **it's ~ in here** 这里让人觉得幽闭恐怖
B *n* 幽闭恐怖症患者

clavicle /ˈklævɪkl/ *n* 锁骨

claw /klɔː/
A *n* **1** (of animal, bird) 爪子; (of crab, lobster) 螯 **2** **claws** *pl* fig colloq pej (hand) 手; **get your ~s off those cakes!** 别碰那些蛋糕! ; **to get one's ~s into sb.** «*woman*» 死死缠住某男人 **3** (on hammer) 起钉爪; (on crane) 爪斗
B *vt* **1** (scratch) «*cat, bird of prey*» 用爪子抓; «*desperate person*» 用指甲抓 **2** (tear) 撕扯 **3** fig 拼命努力; **he ~ed his way to the top** 他千辛万苦做到了高层
C *vi* (scratch at) 抓; **to ~ at sth./sb.** 向某物/某人抓去; **the cat was ~ing at the chair leg** 那只猫在抓挠椅子腿

Phrasal verb

- **claw back** *vt* [**~ sth. back, ~ back sth.**]
  1 Brit Fin, Tax «*government, tax authorities*» 收回 ‹*money, benefits*›; **to ~ sth. back from sb.** 向某人收回某物 **2** Comm, Sport 夺回 ‹*position*›

clawback /ˈklɔːbæk/ *n* Brit 已付钱款的收回; **the ~ represents 2% of the excess income** 回收款占额外收入的 2%

claw hammer *n* 起钉锤

clay /kleɪ/ *n* [u] **1** (for sculpture) 陶土; **to have feet of ~** 性格有缺陷 **2** (soil) 黏土 **3** (in tennis) 红土网球场

clay court *n* 红土网球场

clayey /ˈkleɪi/ *adj* 黏土质的 ‹*soil*›; 黏土状的 ‹*mass*›

clay: ~ pigeon *n* 泥鸽; **~ pigeon shooting** ▸**p. 307** *n* [u] 泥鸽飞靶射击运动; **~ pipe** *n* 黏土烟斗

clean /kliːn/
A *adj* **1** (not dirty) 干净的; **~ air** 清洁的空气; **a ~ wound** 未感染的伤口; **to lick one's plate ~** lit 把盘子舔干净; fig 吃光盘中的食物; **my hands are ~** lit 我的手很干净; fig 我是清白的 **2** (attentive to hygiene) 爱干净的; **it's not very ~ to drink out of somebody else's glass** 用别人的杯子喝不太卫生 **3** Ecol 无污染的 ‹*energy*›; **a ~ fuel** 清洁燃料 **4** (not marked) 空白的 ‹*sheet of paper, blackboard*› **5** (not obscene) 不下流的 ‹*joke, comedian, act*›; **the evening was all good ~ fun** 这台晚会文明有趣 **6** (unsullied) 清白的; **a ~ driving licence** 无违章记录的驾照; **I've checked him out: he's ~** colloq 我已经查过他了，他没有前科 **7** sl (without illicit property) 没有违禁品的; **I've searched him, and he's ~** 我搜了他的身，他没有携带违禁品 **8** sl (no longer addicted) 不再吸毒的 **9** Sport (following rules) 守规则的; **a ~ tackle** 正当的阻截 **10** (done smoothly and skilfully) 干净利落的 ‹*hit, blow, movement*› **11** (with smooth edge) 边缘平整的 ‹*cut, fracture*›; **a ~ break** Med 整齐的骨折; fig 彻底的决裂 **12** (elegant, neat) 流畅匀称的 ‹*curves, shape, profile*›; **the car's ~ lines** 那辆车流畅的线条
B *n* 清扫; **to give sth. a ~** 清扫某物; **to give the room a ~** 打扫房间
C *adv* 完全地; **to come ~ (with sb.) (about sth.)** （向某人）和盘托出（某事）; **I've got to come ~ with you: I was the one who told him** 我得跟你说实话：是我告诉他的; **the thief got ~ away** colloq 小偷跑得没影了; **I'd ~ forgotten about her birthday** colloq 我把她的生日忘得一干二净
D *vt* **1** (remove dirt from) 把…弄干净; **to ~ the room** 打扫房间; **to ~ the blackboard** 擦黑板; **to ~ oneself** 把身体洗干净; **she ~ed the dirt from her fingernails** 她除掉了指甲里的污垢; **to have a suit (dry-)~ed** 把西服拿去（干）洗 **2** Culin «*cook*» 清除…的内脏 ‹*chicken, fish*›
E *vi* **1** (do housework) 打扫 **2** (become clean) 变干净; **these brass handles don't ~ very easily** 这些黄铜把手不容易弄干净

Phrasal verbs

- **clean down** *vt* [**~ sth. down, ~ down sth.**] 把…清扫干净; **to ~ down the walls** 把墙壁擦洗干净
- **clean off**
  A *vt* [**~ sth. off, ~ off sth.**] 清除 ‹*writing, marks, graffiti*›; **I've got to ~ the mud off the car** 我得把车上的泥撵掉
  B *vi* «*stain*» 被除掉; **this mark won't ~ off** 这块污渍擦不掉
- **clean out** *vt* **1** [**~ sth. out, ~ out sth.**] (cleanse thoroughly) 把…的内部清扫干净 ‹*oven, toilet*›; **you need to ~ out your ears!** 你该掏一下耳朵了! **2** [**~ sb. out, ~ out sb.**] colloq (leave penniless) 把…的钱花光 ‹*person*›; **the new car's ~ed me out of all my savings** 这辆新车花光了我的全部积蓄 **3** [**~ sb./sth. out, ~ out sb./sth.**] colloq (rob) «*thief, swindler*» 把…洗劫一空 ‹*person, house*›; **the burglars ~ed her out of all her jewellery** 窃贼把她的珠宝洗劫一空
- **clean up**
  A [**~ sth. up, ~ up sth.**] *vt*
  1 (get rid of) 清除 ‹*mess, remains*›; **to ~ the rubbish up off** *or* **from the floor** 把地板上的垃圾清走 **2** (remove crime, corruption from) 清理整顿 ‹*city, streets, local government*› **3** colloq (make less obscene, violent) 使…变得纯洁 ‹*TV, programme*›; **to ~ up one's act** lit «*comedian*» 使表演文雅; fig «*person*» 洁身自好
  B [**~ sb./sth. up, ~ up sb./sth.**] *vt* (remove dirt from) 把…弄干净; **to ~ up the kitchen** 把厨房打扫干净; **to ~ oneself up** 把身体洗干净
  C *vi* **1** (remove dirt) 打扫干净 **2** (tidy up) 整理; **to ~ up after sb.** 跟在某人后面收拾 **3** (wash oneself) 把身体洗干净 **4** colloq (make profit) «*entrepreneur, gambler, film*» 赚大钱; **to ~ up on sth.** 因…赚大钱 ‹*deal, sale*›

clean: C~ Air Act *n* 洁净空气法令 [美国于1970年通过的改善空气质量的法律]; **~ and jerk** *n* [u] [举重中的] 挺举; **~-cut** *adj* 整洁体面的 ‹*student, appearance*›; 轮廓分明的 ‹*features, outline*›

cleaner /ˈkliːnə(r)/ ▸**p. 409** *n* **1** (person) 清洁工 **2** (machine) 清洁机; **a carpet ~** 地毯清洁机 **3** (shop) **~('s)** 干洗店; **to take sb. to the ~'s** (cheat sb. of all their money) 骗光某人的钱财; (inflict crushing defeat) 彻底打败某人 **4** (detergent) 清洁剂

clean fuel *n* 清洁燃料

cleaning /ˈkliːnɪŋ/ *n* [u] (domestic) 打扫; (commercial) 清洁; **to do the ~** 打扫卫生

cleaning: ~ cloth *n* 抹布; **~ lady** ▸**p. 409** *n* 清洁女工; **~ product** *n* 清洁用品

cleanliness /ˈklenlɪnɪs/ *n* [u] 清洁; **~ is next to godliness** 清洁的重要性仅次于虔诚

clean-living *adj* 安分守己的 ‹*person, lifestyle*›

cleanly /ˈkliːnli/ *adv* **1** (smoothly, easily) 利索地 ‹*catch*›; 干净利落地 ‹*cut*›; **to break off ~** 整齐地折断; **she hits the notes ~** 她音符唱得很圆润 **2** (without pollution) 无污染地

clean-out *n* colloq 大扫除

clean room *n* **1** Ind 洁净室 **2** Med 无菌室

cleanse /klenz/ *vt* **1** lit 清洁 ‹*skin*›; 清洗 ‹*wound*› **2** fig liter 净化; **she felt ~d of her sins** 她感觉免除了罪过; **to ~ one's mind of impure thoughts** 驱除杂念

cleanser /ˈklenzə(r)/ *n* [c and u] **1** Cosmet 洁肤品 **2** (household) 清洁剂

clean: ~-shaven *adj* 胡子刮干净的 ‹*man, chin*›; **~ sheet** *n* **1** (record) 清白历史; **to have kept a ~** 历史清白; **2** (in football) 零失球

cleansing /ˈklenzɪŋ/
A *adj attrib* Cosmet 洁肤的; **~ cream/lotion/tissue** 洁肤霜/乳液/纸巾
B *n* [u] 清洁

cleansing department *n* Brit 环卫部门

clean sweep *n* **1** (removal) 彻底清除 **2** Sport 大获全胜; **to make a ~ of all the medals** 囊括所有奖牌

cleanup /ˈkliːnʌp/ *n* **1** (gen) 清扫; **to give sth. a ~** 把某处打扫一下 **2** (ending of immorality, crime, corruption) 肃清

cleanup campaign *n* **1** (to remove dirt, litter) 清洁运动 **2** (to reduce crime, corruption) 打击犯罪运动

clear /klɪə(r)/
A *adj* **1** (transparent) 透明的 ‹*glass, plastic, varnish*›; 清澈的 ‹*water, river, lake*› **2** (free from cloud, mist, rain) 晴朗的 ‹*sky, night, day*› **3** (pure) 清脆的 ‹*sound, tone, voice*› **4** (easy to understand) 清楚的 ‹*explanation, signal, style*›; **she gave the police a ~ account of what happened** 她向警察清楚地讲述了发生的事情; **is that ~?** 明白吗? ; **to get sth. ~** 明确某事物; **to make oneself ~** 把自己的意思表达清楚; **to make sth. ~ (to sb.)** （向某人）讲清楚某事物 **5** (not confused) 清晰的 ‹*reasoning, thought, idea*›; 清醒的 ‹*mind*›; 思维清晰的 ‹*person, thinker*›; **to have a ~ picture in one's mind of sth.** 对某事物了如指掌; **to keep a ~ head** 保持头脑清醒; **he's ~ about what the job entails** 他明白这份工作意味着什么 **6** (pure, intense) 纯净的 ‹*colour*›; **~ green** 纯绿色 **7** (distinct) 清晰的 ‹*photograph, sound, print, reflection*›; 声音清晰的 ‹*speaker*›; **I didn't get a ~ look at the car** 我没有看清楚那辆车 **8** (obvious) 明显的; **it's a ~ case of fraud** 这是一起明显的诈骗案; **it's ~ that they don't want to come** 显然他们不想来; **it is quite ~ to me that she is in pain** 我很清楚地感觉到她身处痛苦中 **9** (free of obstructions) 无遮挡的 ‹*view*›; 畅通无阻的 ‹*road, pipe*›; 收拾干净的 ‹*surface*›; **the path is ~ of snow** 这条小路上没有积雪; **we're keeping this space ~ for the new bookcase** 我们留着这个地方放新书柜 **10** (unblemished) 光洁的 ‹*skin, complexion*› **11** Culin 稀薄的; **~ soup** 清汤 **12** Med **to be ~** «*X-ray, scan*» 未见异常 **13** (free of sth. undesirable) 免除的; **~ of sth.** 摆脱某事物的; **they were ~ of debt at last** 他们终于还清了债务; **you are now ~ of all suspicion** 你

现在已经排除所有嫌疑了; **in the ~** (free from danger) 无危险的; (free from suspicion) 无嫌疑的; (free to do sth.) 无阻碍的; **she was very ill for a few days, but she's in the ~ now** 她有几天病得很厉害，但现在已经脱离危险了; **they've dropped the case: you're in the ~** 他们已经撤诉了，你现在没嫌疑了 [14] (free from engagements) 空闲的 ‹*day, week, calendar*›; **my diary for June is completely ~** 我整个6月份都有空; **I'm keeping next Saturday ~ for my Christmas shopping** 我留出下周六来为圣诞节购物 [15] (whole) 完整的 ‹*day, month*›; **that gives them a ~ week to carry out the repairs** 这让他们有整整一周时间来维修 [16] Fin (net) 净的; **a ~ profit/amount** 净利/净值 [17] *pred* Fin (paid off) **to be ~** «*account*» 未透支 [18] (not touching) 不接触的; **keep going: you're well ~** 继续走，不会碰到的; **park the car about 25 cm ~ of the kerb** 把车停在离路缘大约25厘米的地方; **they were ~ of London** 他们离开了伦敦

B *adv* [1] 离开; **stand ~ (of the doors)!** 站开（别站在门口）!; **to jump** *or* **leap ~ (of sth.)** (jump out (of)) 跳离（某物）; (take avoiding action (from)) 避开（某事物）; **she leapt ~ of the burning car** 她从燃烧的汽车中跳了出来; **to steer** *or* **keep** *or* **stay ~ of sb./sth.** 避开某人/某物; **her doctor advised her to steer ~ of fattening foods** 医生建议她不要吃使人发胖的食物; **I prefer to stay ~ of the town centre during the rush hour** 我不愿意在交通高峰期去市中心; **to get ~ of sth.** 摆脱 ‹*traffic jam, exams*› [2] (completely) 完全; **he got ~ away** 他逃得无影无踪

C *vt* [1] (remove) 清除; **she ~ed the leaves from the path** 她清扫掉小路上的树叶; **can you ~ the papers off the desk?** 你能把桌上的文件都拿走吗?; **to ~ sth. out of the way** (from surface) 把某物拿开; **the rainforest is being ~ed at an alarming rate** 砍伐雨林的速度惊人; **his confident reply ~ed all the doubts from her mind** 他自信的回答消除了她心中所有的疑虑 [2] (free from obstruction, blemishes) 清理; **to ~ the drains** 疏通下水道; **to ~ the road of snow** 清扫路上积雪; **to ~ the way (for sb./sth.)** lit, fig（为某人/某事物）扫清道路; **~ the way: we need to get through!** 让开，我们要过去!; **the police went ahead to ~ the way for the ambulance** 警察在前面为救护车开道; **to ~ one's throat** 清嗓子; **this cream will ~ your complexion** 这种乳霜可以使你面部光洁; **the aim is to ~ your mind of painful memories** 目的是让你忘掉那些痛苦的记忆 [3] (create) 清理出 ‹*space*›; **she ~ed a path through the undergrowth** 她在灌木丛中开出一条小路来; **she ~ed her way through the crowd of onlookers** 她从围观的人群中挤了过去 [4] (cause to leave a place) 使离开; **the troops were called in to ~ the crowds** 军队被调来驱散人群; **the rain ~ed the sunbathers from the beach** 这场雨把海滩上晒日光浴的人都淋跑了 [5] (cause people to leave) 遣散…的人员; **the fire alarm ~ed the building** 听到火警后，人们都撤离了大楼; **the police ~ed the stadium of spectators** 警察疏散了体育馆里的观众 [6] (achieve mental clarity) 使变清醒; **to ~ one's head** *or* **mind** 使头脑清醒 [7] Comput 删除…中的数据 ‹*memory, computer, disk*›; 删除 ‹*data, figures, picture*› [8] (pay off) 清偿 ‹*debt, loan*›; 结清 ‹*account*› [9] (deal with) 处理 ‹*work, goods, stock*›; **we were faced with a huge backlog of work to ~** 我们有一大堆积压的工作要处理; **to be reduced to ~** 清仓甩卖 [10] (free from blame) 使无罪; **you have been ~ed of all charges** 对你的所有指控都已撤销; **to be ~ed of suspicion** 被排除嫌疑; **to ~ sb.'s name** *or* **reputation** 恢复某人的清白名誉 [11] (authorize) 批准…做机密工作 ‹*person*›; **she's been ~ed to consult these classified documents** 她已经获准查阅这些机密文件 [12] (approve, give permission for) 批准; (gain approval, get permission for) 使获得批准; **the report has to be ~ed by the censors** 这篇报道必须经审查员审批; **the plane has been ~ed for take-off** 飞机已得到起飞许可; **the project has been ~ed with head office** 项目已经获得总部批准; **have you ~ed these goods for export?** 你这些货物已经获准出口了吗? [13] (satisfy requirements of) 合乎…要求; **to ~ customs** «*person, goods, baggage*» 通关 [14] (freshen) 使面目一新; **to ~ the air** «*storm*» 使空气清新; fig (improve a difficult situation) 改善困境; (improve a tense situation) 缓解紧张局势 [15] (disperse) 驱散 ‹*mist, smoke, gas, smell*› [16] (clarify) 澄清 ‹*wine, beer*› [17] (pass without touching) 越过 ‹*fence, wall, hurdle*›; 通过 ‹*gate, bridge, doorway*›; 通过时不接触 ‹*bottom, ceiling, rock*›; **the winner ~ed two metres** 获胜选手跳过了2米; **the van only just ~ed the gatepost** 那辆货车险些撞上门柱 [18] Sport (in football, rugby) 大脚踢开…解围 ‹*ball*›; (in hockey) 把…击出己方球门区 ‹*ball*› [19] Fin (pass through clearing house) 结算 ‹*cheque*› [20] (make) 净赚 ‹*amount, profit*›; **he's ~ing more than £20,000 a year** 他一年净赚2万多英镑

D *vi* [1] (become transparent) «*window, mirror*» 变透明; «*water, solution, wine*» 变清澈 [2] (become free from cloud, mist, rain) «*sky, weather*» 转晴 [3] (become free from smoke, pollution, smell) «*air*» 变清新; «*room*» 变得空气清新 [4] (disperse) «*mist, gas, smoke, smell*» 消散 [5] (become free from spots, rash) «*skin, face*» 变光洁 [6] (disappear from skin) «*spots, acne, rash*» 消失 [7] (look happier) 变明朗; **his face/brow ~ed when I told him the good news** 我告诉他这个好消息时，他面露喜色/眉头舒展开来 [8] Fin «*cheque*» 结算

E *n* **in ~** (without cryptographic protection) 用普通文字

Phrasal verbs

- **clear away**

A *vt* [**~ sth. away, ~ away sth.**]
[1] (remove) 清除; **~ your toys away** 把你的玩具收走; **we ~ed the snow away from the doorstep** 我们扫掉了门口台阶上的积雪 [2] (disperse) 驱散 ‹*mist, smoke, gas, smell*›

B *vi* (after meal) 收拾餐桌

- **clear off**

A *vi* colloq (go away) 走开; **~ off! can't you see I'm busy?** 走开! 你没看见我正忙着吗?; **they ~ed off without paying** 他们没付钱就溜掉了

B *vt* [**~ off sth.**]
[1] colloq (get off) 从…走开 ‹*land, property*›
[2] Amer (remove dishes from) 收拾 ‹*table*›

- **clear out**

A *vt* [**~ sth. out, ~ out sth.**]
[1] (tidy) 整理 ‹*cupboard, drawer, room*›
[2] (empty) 清空 ‹*cupboard, drawer, room*›
[3] (throw away) 清理掉 ‹*rubbish, old clothes, toys*›

B *vi* colloq (get out) 离开; **he ~ed out before the police arrived** 他在警察到来前溜掉了; **~ out of here!** 从这儿滚出去!

- **clear up**

A *vt* [1] (get rid of, tidy away) 清理掉 ‹*rubbish, books, dishes*› [2] (make tidy) 清理 ‹*desk, room, street, beach*› [3] (solve) 解开 ‹*mystery, puzzle*› [4] (resolve) 解决 ‹*problem, issue*›; 消除 ‹*misunderstanding, disagreement*›; 解释 ‹*point, subject*› [5] (cure) «*treatment, substance, medicine*» 治愈 ‹*spots, infection, illness*›

B *vi* [1] (tidy up) 收拾; **to ~ up after sb.** 跟在某人后面收拾; **they always ~ up after themselves** 他们总是随时收拾 [2] (improve) «*weather*» 转晴 [3] (be cured) «*spots*» 消失; «*infection, illness*» 治愈; **the cold will ~ up in a few days** 感冒过几天就会好的

clearance /ˈklɪərəns/ *n* [1] [u and c] (removal) 清除 [2] [u and c] (freeing of road, water course) 疏通; (freeing of land) 清理 [3] [u and c] (emptying of room, building) 清空 [4] [u and c] (evacuation of people) 清场 [5] [u and c] (selling of goods) 清仓销售; **a stock ~** 清仓大甩卖 [6] [u] (handling of work, backlog) 处理 [7] [u and c] (of debt, loan, mortgage, etc.) 清偿; (of account) 结清 [8] [u and c] (authorization, permission) 批准; **to have ~ to do sth.** 获准做某事; **to have ~ for take-off** «*aircraft*» 获准起飞; **to send the report to the security department for ~** 把报告呈交安全部门审批 [9] [c] (customs certificate) 结关证; **~ inwards/outwards** 入/出境结关证 [10] [u and c] Fin (of cheque) 结算 [11] [u and c] Constr (below bridge, barrier) 净空; (between two objects) 间隙; **the bridge has a 4 metre ~** 桥下净空为4米; **there was a ~ of less than a metre between the boat and the rocks** 船与礁石之间的间隙不足1米 [12] [c] (in football, rugby) 解围; (in hockey) 击球出球门区 [13] [c] (in snooker, pool) 一杆清台 [将台面上剩下的球全部击入袋中]

clearance sale *n* [1] (of superfluous stock) 清仓贱卖 [2] (closing-down sale) 歇业甩卖

clear-cut *adj* [1] 明确的 ‹*plan, idea*›; 明显的 ‹*difference, problem*›; **the matter is not so ~** 这件事不是很清楚 [2] (sharp) 清晰的 ‹*outline, shape*›; **~ features** 轮廓分明的容貌

clear: ~felling *n* [u] 皆伐 [指将某伐区内的林木全部伐除]; **~-headed** *adj* 头脑清醒的 ‹*person*›; 思路清晰的 ‹*decision, action*›; **~-headedly** *adv* 头脑清醒地

clearing /ˈklɪərɪŋ/ *n* [1] [c] (glade) 林中空地 [2] [u] Brit (filling of university places) 本科生补招制度; **to get in/apply through ~** 通过补招入学/申请补招入学

clearing: ~ bank *n* Brit 清算银行; **~ house** *n* [1] Fin 清算中心; [2] Admin 信息交换中心

clearing-up *n* [u] 清扫; **I've got some ~ to do** 我要打扫卫生

clearly /ˈklɪəli/ *adv* [1] (distinctly) 清楚地; **the footprints could be ~ seen** 脚印清晰可见 [2] (intelligibly) 易懂地; **you should have explained more ~** 你本应解释得更明白些 [3] (logically, correctly) 清晰地 ‹*think, reason*›; 清楚地 ‹*remember*› [4] (obviously) 显然地; **~, we must take action as soon as possible** 很显然，我们必须尽快采取行动

clearness /ˈklɪənɪs/ *n* [u] [1] (of glass, plastic, varnish) 透明; (of water, river, lake) 清澈 [2] (of sky, day) 晴朗 [3] (of colour) 纯净 [4] (purity, melodiousness of sound) 清脆 [5] (distinctness of sound, print, memory) 清晰 [6] (intelligibility) 易懂 [7] (of thinking, idea) 清楚; (of head, mind) 清醒

clear-out *n* esp Brit colloq 清理; **to have a ~** 进行清理; **to give sth. a ~** 清理某物

clear: ~ round *n* [马术障碍赛中的] 满分圈; **~-sighted** *adj* 有眼光的 ‹*person*›; 有远见的 ‹*decision, judgement*›; **~-sightedness** *n* [u] 有远见; **~way** *n* Brit 禁停公路

cleat /kliːt/

A *n* [1] esp Naut (wooden) 小木桩; (metal) 金属桩 [2] (on sole) 防滑钉

B **cleats** *npl* Amer 防滑运动鞋

cleavage /ˈkliːvɪdʒ/ *n* [1] [c and u] (of breasts) 乳沟 [2] [c] (of opinion) 分歧; **a ~ between the two wings** 两个派别之间的一处分歧

cleave[1] /kliːv/

A *vt* (*pt* **clove** *or* **~d**, *pp* **cleft** *or* **~d**) liter 劈开 ‹*block of wood, rock*›; 切开 ‹*piece of meat*›; 砍下 ‹*head*›; **to ~ sth. in two** 将某物劈成两半

B *vi* (*pt, pp* **~d**) liter [1] (split) «*wood, rock, skull*» 裂开 [2] (cut, slice) «*axe, sword*» 劈; **to ~ through sth.** 劈开某物; **a ship cleaving through the water** fig 破浪前进的船

cleave[2] *vi* (*pt, pp* **~d**) [1] lit **to ~ to sth.** (stick fast to) 紧贴某物 [2] fig (adhere to) **to ~ to a belief/principle/tradition** 坚守信仰/原则/传统

cleaver /ˈkliːvə(r)/ *n* 砍肉刀

C

clef /klef/ *n* 谱号; **in the treble/bass ~** 用高音/低音谱号

cleft[1] /kleft/
A *n* 裂缝
B *pp* ▸**cleave**[1] **A**
C *adj* 有裂缝的 ‹*bone*›; 开裂的 ‹*stick*›

cleft[2] *pp* ▸**cleave**[1] **A**

cleft: ~ palate *n* 腭裂; **~ stick** *n* **(to be) (caught) in a ~ stick** 进退维谷

clematis /ˈklemətɪs, kləˈmeɪtɪs/ *n* [c and u] 铁线莲

clemency /ˈklemənsi/ *n* [u] liter or formal 仁慈; **to show ~ towards sb.** 对某人仁慈

clement /ˈklemənt/ *adj* liter or formal 1 (mild) 和煦的 ‹*weather, climate*› 2 (merciful) 仁慈的; **to be ~ towards sb.** 对某人仁慈

clementine /ˈkleməntiːn/ *n* 小柑橘

clench /klentʃ/ *vt* 1 (close tightly) 捏紧 ‹*fingers*›; 咬紧 ‹*jaws*›; **to ~ one's fist** 攥紧拳头; **to say sth. between ~ed teeth** 咬牙切齿地说… 2 (hold tightly) 握紧 ‹*money, sb.'s hand*›; **to ~ sth. between one's teeth** 紧紧咬住某物

clerestory /ˈklɪəstɔːri/ *n* 嵌有高窗的墙

clergy /ˈklɜːdʒi/ *n* + *v pl* 神职人员

clergy: ~man /-mən/ ▸**p. 409** *n* 男神职人员; **~woman** ▸**p. 409** *n* 女神职人员

cleric /ˈklerɪk/ *n* (priest) 神职人员; (religious leader) 宗教领袖

clerical /ˈklerɪkl/ *adj attrib* 1 Comm, Admin 办公室工作的; **she has a ~ post** 她从事文书工作 2 Relig 神职人员的

clerical: ~ assistant ▸**p. 409** *n* 文书助理; **~ collar** *n* 牧师领; **~ error** *n* 笔误; **~ student** *n* 神学院学生; **~ work** *n* [u] 文书工作; **~ worker** ▸**p. 409** *n* 办公室工作人员

clerihew /ˈklerɪhjuː/ *n* 四行打油诗

clerk /klɑːk, Amer klɜːrk/ ▸**p. 409**
A *n* 1 Comm (in office, bank etc.) 职员; **a counter ~** 银行出纳 2 Brit (Parliament) 书记员; (to lawyer) 律师助理; **the ~ of the court** 法庭书记员 3 Constr (in UK) **~ of (the) works** 建筑工程现场监理 4 Amer (in hotel) 前台接待员 5 Amer (in shop) 店员
B *vi* Amer 1 Jur 当书记员; **to ~ for a judge** 给法官当书记员 2 (in shop) 当店员

clerkship /ˈklɜːkʃɪp, Amer ˈklɜːrk-/ *n* Amer (position) 职员职位; (job) 职员工作

clever /ˈklevə(r)/ *adj* 1 (intelligent) 聪明的; **to be ~ at sth./at doing sth.** 擅长某事物/做某事; **that wasn't very ~!** 那可不太明智! 2 (ingenious, skilful) 机敏的 ‹*idea, solution*›; 构思巧妙的 ‹*gadget*›; **how ~ of you to find the solution** 你找到了解决办法, 真是太聪明了 3 (shrewd) 巧妙的 ‹*plot, excuse*›; (cunning) 狡猾的; **too ~ by half** 过于精明; **the lawyer was too ~ for us** 那个律师对我们来说真是太精明了; **she was too ~ for me** 对我来说, 她太滑头了 4 (dextrous) 灵巧的; **he's ~ with his hands** 他的手很灵巧 5 usu pej (cheeky) 油腔滑调的 ‹*remark, answer*› 6 *only with negative* Brit colloq (well, healthy) 健康的; **I don't feel too ~** 我感觉不太舒服

clever: ~-clever *adj* pej 卖弄小聪明的 ‹*person, remark*›; **~ clogs, ~ Dick** *ns* Brit colloq 自以为是的人

cleverly /ˈklevəli/ *adv* (intelligently) 聪明地; (shrewdly, cunningly) 精明地; (dextrously) 灵巧地

cleverness /ˈklevənɪs/ *n* [u] (intelligence) 聪明; (ingenuity) 巧妙; (quick-wittedness) 机敏; (dexterity) 灵巧; **~ with numbers/at languages** 在数字/语言方面的擅长; **the ~ of his replies** 他的回答所表现出的机敏

cliché /ˈkliːʃeɪ, Amer kliːˈʃeɪ/ *n* 1 [c] (over-used phrase) 陈词滥调; **a ~-ridden style** 充满陈词滥调的风格 2 [c] (over-used idea) 陈腐的想法; (over-used technique) 陈旧方法; **the car chase is a cinema ~** 追车戏是电影中的老一套 3 [u] (use of clichés) 使用陈词滥调

clichéd /ˈkliːʃeɪd, Amer kliːˈʃeɪd/ *adj* 陈腐的 ‹*saying, view*›

click /klɪk/
A *vi* 1 (make sound) 发出咔嗒声; **the photographers were ~ing away** 摄影师们咔嚓咔嚓拍个不停 2 colloq (become clear) 变清楚; **suddenly something ~ed** 突然顿悟 3 colloq (strike a rapport) 成为朋友; (as friends) 我们一见如故; (sexually) 我们一见钟情 **we just ~ed** 4 colloq (work well together) 合作良好; **the team don't seem to have ~ed yet** 这个团队似乎还没磨合好 5 (work out perfectly) 进展顺利; **everything ~ed for them** colloq 他们一切顺利 6 Comput 点击; **to ~ on sth.** 点击某处
B *vt* (make sound with) 使发出咔嗒声; **to ~ one's fingers** 打响指; **to ~ one's tongue** 咂舌; **to ~ one's heels** 啪地立正; **to ~ sth. open/shut** 咔嗒一声打开/合上某物
C *n* 1 (sound) 咔嗒声; (of tongues) 咂舌声; **with a ~ of her fingers** 随着她的一声响指 2 Comput 点击

clickable /ˈklɪkəbl/ *adj* 可点击的 ‹*text, image*›

clickety-click /ˌklɪkətɪˈklɪk/ *n* 咔嗒咔嗒声; **to go ~** ‹*machine*› 咔嗒咔嗒地响

click: ~s and mortar *adj* 鼠标加灰泥的 [指互联网和传统商业模式结合的] ‹*company*›; **~through** *n* 网络广告点击量; **high ~ rates** 很高的网络广告点击率

client /ˈklaɪənt/ *n* 1 (of lawyer, accountant) 委托人, 当事人; (customer, user) 客户; (of social worker) 救济对象; (of psychotherapist) 病人; (of prostitute) 嫖客; **a lawyer with many famous ~s** 为众多有名气的委托人提供服务的律师 2 Comput 客户机

client base *n* 客户群; **he has a very loyal ~** 他有一群非常忠实的客户

clientele /ˌkliːənˈtel, Amer ˌklaɪənˈtel/ *n* 1 (clients) 委托人 2 (customers) 顾客

client: ~-server *adj* 主从式网络的 ‹*technology, network*›; **~ state** *n* 附庸国

cliff /klɪf/ *n* 悬崖

cliff: ~ face *n* 崖壁; **~hanger** *n* 1 (exciting ending) 悬念式结尾; 2 (film) 扣人心弦的电影; (story) 惊险故事; (situation) 紧张情形; (moment) 紧张时刻; **the match was a real ~hanger** 这场比赛真是紧张激烈; **~hanging** *adj attrib* 有悬念的 ‹*ending, contest, election*›; **~side** *n* 悬崖侧壁; **~top** *n* 悬崖顶部

climactic /klaɪˈmæktɪk/ *adj* 高潮的 ‹*moment, ending*›

climate /ˈklaɪmɪt/ *n* 1 [c and u] Meteorol 气候 2 [c] fig (surroundings) 氛围; **the current ~ of opinion** 当前的舆论倾向; **the present political/economic ~** 当前的政治气候/经济环境

climate: ~ change *n* [u] 气候变化; **~ control** *n* [u] 空气调节; **~-controlled** *adj* 有空调的 ‹*building, car*›

climatic /klaɪˈmætɪk/ *adj* 气候的; **~ conditions/changes/factors** 气候条件/变化/因素

climatologist /ˌklaɪməˈtɒlədʒɪst/ ▸**p. 409** *n* 气候学家

climatology /ˌklaɪməˈtɒlədʒi/ *n* [u] 气候学

climax /ˈklaɪmæks/
A *n* 1 (culmination, end) (of war, speech, play) 高潮; (of career) 巅峰; **to come to** *or* **reach a ~** 达到高潮; **the exciting ~ of the tournament** 联赛激动人心的高潮 2 (orgasm) 性高潮; **to have** *or* **experience a ~** 达到性高潮
B *vi* 1 (reach a high point) 达到高潮; **to ~ in** *or* **with sth.** ‹*events, novel*› 以某事物达到高潮 2 (sexually) 达到性高潮

climb /klaɪm/
A *vi* 1 (move upwards) 攀登; **to ~ up sth.** 爬上 ‹*ladder, tree, steps*›; **to ~ (up) to the summit** 登上顶峰 2 (scale a mountain) 登山 3 (clamber) 费力爬; **to ~ over the fence** 费力翻过篱笆; **to ~ into bed** 费力爬上床 4 (go higher in sky) ‹*plane, rocket*› 爬升; ‹*sun*› 升起; **to ~ to 10,000 metres** 上升到1万米的高度 5 (slope upwards) ‹*road*› 向上斜升; (grow upwards) ‹*plant*› 向上攀缘; **there were roses ~ing up the walls** 有几株玫瑰爬上了墙 6 (increase) ‹*currency*› 升值; ‹*price*› 上涨; ‹*profits*› 增加; ‹*temperature, birth rate*› 上升 7 (improve position, status) 晋升; **in a few years he had ~ed to the top of his profession** 他在几年内攀升到了职业生涯的顶峰; **the team has now ~ed to fourth in the league** 该队现已上升到联赛第四名
B *vt* 攀登 ‹*mountain, stairs, ladder*›; **the car slowly ~ed the hill** 汽车慢慢爬上了山
C *n* 1 (ascent) 攀登; **it's an hour's ~ to the summit** 登顶需一小时 2 (mountain) 攀登的山; **the most difficult ~ in the Alps** 阿尔卑斯山脉中最难攀登的山峰 3 (slope) 上坡 4 Aviat 爬升 5 (increase) 上升; **a ~ in prices** 价格的上涨; **the dollar's ~ against the euro** 美元对欧元汇率的上升 6 (improvement in position, status) 晋升; **the book recounts her ~ (from obscurity) to stardom** 这本书讲述了她（从默默无闻到）成为明星的经历

Phrasal verb

- **climb down** *vi* (admit a mistake) 认错; (withdraw) 退让; **to ~ down from sth.** 放弃 ‹*accusation, threat, demand*›; **to ~ down over sth.** 在…上让步 ‹*issue, plan*›

climbdown *n* (admission of mistake) 认错; (withdrawal) 退让

climber /ˈklaɪmə(r)/ *n* 1 (mountaineer) 登山者; (rock climber) 攀岩者; (animal) 攀爬的动物 2 (plant) 攀缘植物

climbing /ˈklaɪmɪŋ/ ▸**p. 307**
A *n* [u] 登山运动
B *adj* 1 Bot 攀缘的; **a ~ plant/vine** 攀缘植物/藤蔓 2 Zool 善于攀爬的 ‹*monkey, insect*›

climbing: ~ boot *n* 登山靴; **~ expedition** *n* 登山探险; **~ frame** *n* Brit 儿童攀爬架; **~ shoe** *n* 登山鞋; **~ speed** *n* 爬升速度; **~ wall** *n* 攀岩墙

clime /klaɪm/ *n* liter 气候带; **in sunnier ~s** 在日照更多的地带

clinch /klɪntʃ/
A *vt* 1 (secure) 成功取得; **to ~ an agreement/a deal** 达成协议/成交 2 (resolve) 解决 ‹*matter*›; **this point ~ed the argument for me** 这个论点让我信服 3 Sport 赢得 ‹*victory, championship*›
B *vi* 1 Sport ‹*boxers*› 扭抱 2 (embrace) 拥抱
C *n* 1 (in boxing) 扭抱 2 (embrace) 拥抱; **to be in a ~** 拥抱着

clincher /ˈklɪntʃə(r)/ *n* (act) 决定性举动; (remark) 起决定作用的话; (argument) 决定性的论点; **as a ~ they offered him a company car** 最终说服他的是, 他们为他提供了公司用车

cling /klɪŋ/ *vi* (*pt, pp* **clung**) 1 (physically) 抓紧; **to ~ to sth./sb.** 紧紧抓住某物/某人; **to ~ together** 紧紧抱在一起; **to ~ on to sth. for dear life** 死命地抓住某物 2 **to ~ to sth.** fig (refuse to give up) 不愿放弃某事物; **to ~ to the hope that ...** 抱着…的希望 3 (emotionally) 依恋; **he ~s to me all the time** 他老是缠着我; **she ~s to people for support** 她贴近人民以赢得支持 4 (adhere) 紧贴; **a dress that ~s to the body** 紧身连衣裙 5 (stay close) 紧靠; **the road clung to the mountain** 路紧挨着山

Phrasal verb

- **cling on** *vi* 1 (hold on) 紧紧抓住; **to ~ on to sth.** 紧紧抓住某物 2 **to ~ on to sth.** (refuse to give up) 不愿放弃某事物; **she clung**

on to life for two more years 她顽强地又活了两年

cling film *n* [u] Brit 保鲜膜

clinging /'klɪŋɪŋ/ *adj* **1** (close-fitting) 紧身的; **a ～ dress/swimsuit** 紧身连衣裙/泳装 **2** (that sticks) 攀附的 ‹*plant, ivy*›; 难去除的 ‹*smell*› **3** fig pej (emotionally dependent) 依赖性强的 ‹*person*›; 缠人的 ‹*child*›

clingy /'klɪŋi/ *adj* **1** (liable to cling) 易贴在身上的 ‹*dress*› **2** (emotionally dependent) 有依赖性的 ‹*child*›

clinic /'klɪnɪk/ *n* **1** (treatment centre) 诊所; **an outpatients' ～** 门诊部 **2** (advice session) 门诊时间; (teaching session) 临床教学

clinical /'klɪnɪkl/ *adj* **1** Med 临床的; **～ medicine/training** 临床医学/培训 **2** fig (unemotional) 冷漠的; (objective) 客观的; **with ～ detachment** 无动于衷地 **3** fig (functional) 简朴的 ‹*room, building*› **4** fig (precise, efficient) 准确有效的 ‹*approach*›; **his punches landed with ～ accuracy** 他打出的拳落点精准

clinically /'klɪnɪkli/ *adv* **1** (medically) 以临床方式 ‹*tested, observed, trained*›; **～ dead** 临床死亡的; **～ depressed** 临床诊断为抑郁症的 **2** fig (unemotionally) 冷漠地; (objectively) 客观地 **3** fig (precisely, efficiently) 准确有效地

clinical: **～ psychologist** ▸**p. 409** *n* 临床心理学家; **～ psychology** *n* [u] 临床心理学; **～ thermometer** *n* 体温计; **～ trial** *n* 临床实验

clinician /klɪ'nɪʃn/ ▸**p. 409** *n* 临床医生

clink[1] /klɪŋk/

A *vi* 发出叮当声

B *vt* 使发出叮当声; **to ～ glasses (with sb.)** （与某人）碰杯

C *n* 叮当声

clink[2] *n* [u] colloq (prison) 牢房; **to be in (the) ～** 坐牢

clinker /'klɪŋkə(r)/ *n* **1** [u] (burnt coal) 煤渣; (inside furnace) 炉渣 **2** [c] Amer colloq (wrong note) 错误音符; **the singer hit a ～** 歌手唱错了一个音符

clinometer /klaɪ'nɒmɪtə(r)/ *n* 测斜仪

clip[1] /klɪp/

A *n* **1** (for gripping) 夹子 **2** Elec 线夹 **3** (on badge) 别针

B *vt* (*pres p etc.* **-pp-**) **1** (fasten) 夹住 ‹*papers, tie*›; **to ～ sth. to/on sth.** 将某物夹到某物上; **to ～ papers together** 将文件夹在一起; **a bill ～ped to the letter** 夹在信上的账单 **2** Amer colloq (swindle) 诈骗; **the tourists were being ～ped for up to 200 dollars** 游客被骗金额多达 200 美元

Phrasal verb

• **clip on**

A [**～ sth. on, ～ on sth.**] *vt* (by fastening) 夹戴 ‹*earring*›; 夹上 ‹*cheque*›; (by hooking) 别上 ‹*brooch*›

B *vi* (by fastening) «*earrings*» 能夹戴; (by hooking) «*brooch*» 能别上; **to ～ on to sth.** 夹到某物上

clip[2]

A *vt* (*pres p etc.* **-pp-**) **1** (trim) 修剪 ‹*hedge, nails*›; 剪 ‹*wool*›; **to ～ the wings of ...** lit 修剪…的翅膀; fig 限制…的自由 **2** (cut out) 剪下 ‹*article*›; **to ～ sth. out of the paper** 从报纸上剪下某物 **3** Brit (punch) «*conductor*» 剪 ‹*ticket*› **4** (hit) 击打 ‹*jaw*›; (glancingly) 碰擦 ‹*corner*›; **to ～ sb. round the ear** 扇了某人一记耳光 **5** (speak tersely) 简短地说; **to ～ one's speech** 发言简短 **6** Comput 截取; **to ～ an image/photograph** 截取图像/照片

B *n* **1** Cin, Radio (excerpt) 片段 **2** (smart blow) 击打; (glancing blow) 抽打; **(to give sb.) a ～ around the ear** （给某人）一记耳光 **3** (trim) 修剪; **to give sth. a ～** 修剪某物 **4** colloq (speed) 速度; **at a fair/good ～** 以较快/很快的速度 **5** **at a ～** Amer colloq (at a time) 一次; **eight hours at a ～** 每次 8 小时

clip: **～ art** *n* [u] 剪贴画; **～board** *n* **1** (for writing) 写字夹板; **2** Comput 剪贴板; **～-clop** *n* 得得声; **～ frame** *n* 画夹; **～ joint** *n* colloq pej (bar) 宰客酒吧; (nightclub) 收费极高的夜总会

clip-on

A *adj* 用别针别住的 ‹*bow tie*›; **～ earrings/sunglasses** 夹式耳环/太阳镜

B **clip-ons** *npl* (earrings) 夹式耳环; (sunglasses) 夹式太阳镜

clipped /klɪpt/ *adj* 短促的 ‹*accent, pronunciation*›; 简短的 ‹*speech, style*›

clipper /'klɪpə(r)/

A *n* Naut 快速帆船

B **clippers** *npl* (for nails) 指甲刀; (for hair) 理发推子; (for hedge) 大剪刀

clipping /'klɪpɪŋ/

A *n* (from newspaper) 剪报

B **clippings** *npl* 剪下物

clippings library *n* 剪报馆

clippity-clop /ˌklɪpətɪ'klɒp/ *n* colloq = **clip-clop**

clique /kli:k/ *n + v sing or pl* pej 小集团; **a small ～ of intellectuals** 知识分子的小圈子

cliquey /'kli:ki/, **cliquish** /'kli:kɪʃ/ *adjs* pej (exclusive) 排外的; (divided) 结成小集团的; **the office is very ～** 这间办公室里拉帮结派的气氛浓重

clitoris /'klɪtərɪs/ *n* (*pl* **clitorides** /klɪ'tɒrɪdi:z/) 阴蒂

Cllr *abbr* Brit = **councillor; ～ (John/Jane) Smith** 委员（约翰·/简·）史密斯

cloak /kləʊk/

A *n* **1** (garment) 披风 **2** fig (front) 掩饰; **to be a ～ for sth.** 是某事物的伪装; **to lift the ～ of secrecy** 揭开秘密面纱; **under the ～ of darkness** 在黑暗的掩护下

B *vt* **1** (cover) 给…披上披风; fig «*snow*» 覆盖 ‹*land*›; «*darkness*» 笼罩 ‹*land*›; **to be ～ed in fog** 被笼罩在雾中; **to ～ sb. in sth.** 将某人裹在某事物里 **2** (hide) 遮掩 ‹*activities, intentions*›; **negotiations were ～ed in secrecy** 谈判笼罩在秘密的气氛中

cloak-and-dagger *adj* (involving espionage) 间谍的; (involving intrigue) 阴谋的; **～ activities** 间谍活动

cloakroom /'kləʊkrʊm/ *n* **1** (for coats) 衣帽间 **2** Brit (toilet) 厕所; **the ladies' ～(s)** 女洗手间

cloakroom: **～ attendant** ▸**p. 409** *n* **1** (for coats) 衣帽间侍者; **2** Brit (at toilets) 洗手间侍者; **～ ticket** *n* 衣帽间寄存票

cloaks cupboard *n* Brit dated 衣橱

clobber /'klɒbə(r)/ colloq

A *vt* **1** (hit) 狠揍; **to ～ sb. with sth.** 用某物狠狠地打某人 **2** (penalize) 严厉惩罚 **3** (defeat) 彻底击败 ‹*opponent, team*›; **to get ～ed** 遭到惨败 **4** (criticize) 痛斥

B *n* [u] Brit colloq (gear) 装备; (belongings) 个人物品; (clothes) 衣服

cloche /klɒʃ/ *n* **1** Hort 保护罩 **2** **～ (hat)** 钟形女帽

clock /klɒk/

A *n* **1** ▸**p. 831** (timepiece) 钟; **to put the ～(s) forward/back** 把时钟拨快/拨回; **around the ～** 夜以继日; **to beat the ～** 提前完成任务; **against the ～** (timed) 计时地; (to deadline) 争分夺秒地; **a race against the ～** 和时间赛跑; **the referee has stopped the ～** 裁判已经停止记时; **to turn** *or* **set the ～ back** pej 倒退 **2** colloq (milometer) 计程器; **a car with 20,000 kilometres on the ～** 计程器上显示已行驶 2 万公里的汽车 **3** colloq (in taxi) 计价器; **to only pay what's on the ～** 只付计价器显示的金额 **4** Comput 时钟脉冲发生器 **5** (in workplace) 记时钟; **to punch the ～** (starting work) 打卡记录上班时间; (stopping work) 打卡记录下班时间

B *vt* **1** (reach) «*athlete*» 达到 ‹*time, speed*›; **he ～ed 9.6 seconds in the 100 metres** 他的 100 米跑了 9.6 秒 **2** (measure) 测量…的速度 ‹*person*›; 测量 ‹*speed*›; **wind speeds of up to 150 kilometres per hour have been ～ed** 测到的风速高达每小时 150 公里; **the police ～ed her doing over 100 miles per hour** 警察测出她车速超过了每小时 100 英里 **3** esp Brit colloq (hit) 打; **to ～ sb. one** 打某人一下 **4** Brit colloq (notice) 注意到; **he didn't even ～ that anything was wrong** 他甚至没有注意到有什么不对劲的地方 **5** Brit Aut colloq 动手脚拨少…的里程数 ‹*vehicle*›

Phrasal verbs

• **clock in** *vi* 打卡记录上班时间; **I ～ in at 8.30** 我 8 点 30 分打卡上班

• **clock off** *vi* 打卡记录下班时间; **I ～ off at 5.30** 我 5 点 30 分打卡下班

• **clock on** *vi* = **clock in**

• **clock out** *vi* = **clock off**

• **clock up** *vt* [**～ sth. up, ～ up sth.**] 达到…数值; **this car has ～ed up 70,000 kilometres** 这辆汽车已经行驶了 7 万公里; **I ～ed up nine hours' work yesterday** 我昨天工作了 9 个小时

clock face *n* 钟面

clocking-in *n* [u] 上班打卡; **～ time** 上班打卡时间

clock: **～maker** ▸**p. 409** *n* 钟表匠; **～ patience** ▸**p. 307** *n* [u] 单人纸牌游戏; **～ radio** *n* 闹钟收音机; **～ speed** *n* 时钟频率; **～ tower** *n* 钟楼; **～-watch** *vi* pej 老是看钟等下班; **～-watcher** *n* pej 老是看钟等下班的人; **～-watching** *n* [u] pej 老是看钟等下班

clockwise /'klɒkwaɪz/

A *adj* 顺时针的; **in a ～ direction** 按顺时针方向

B *adv* 顺时针方向地 ‹*move, rotate*›

clockwork /'klɒkwɜ:k/

A *n* [u] (in clock) 钟表机械; (in toy) 发条装置; **the music box runs on ～** 这个八音盒靠上发条运行; **as regular as ～** fig 极有规律地; **like ～** fig 十分顺利地

B *adj* **1** (driven by ～) 有齿轮发条的 ‹*toy, train*› **2** (smooth) 顺利的; **with ～ precision** 极精确地 **3** (repetitive) 有规律的

clockwork radio *n* 发条收音机

clod /klɒd/ *n* **1** (of dirt) 土块 **2** colloq (fool) 笨蛋

clodhopper /'klɒdhɒpə(r)/ *n* **1** pej (person) 笨蛋 **2** colloq (shoe) 笨重的鞋子

clog[1] /klɒg/ (*pres p etc.* **-gg-**)

A *vt* 堵塞 ‹*drain, pores, arteries*›; 阻塞 ‹*road*›; **to be ～ged with dirt** 被污垢堵塞

B *vi* «*drain, pores, arteries*» 被堵塞; «*road*» 被阻塞

Phrasal verb

• **clog up**

A *vt* [**～ up sth., ～ sth. up**] 堵塞 ‹*drain, pores, arteries*›; 阻塞 ‹*road*›

B *vi* «*drain, pores, arteries*» 被堵塞; «*road*» 被阻塞

clog[2] *n* 木屐

cloisonné /'klwɑ:zɒneɪ, -'zɒneɪ/ *n* [u] 景泰蓝; **～ ware** 景泰蓝瓷器

cloister /'klɔɪstə(r)/

A *n* [教堂、修道院等的] 回廊

B *vt* 使与世隔绝; **to be ～ed away (from sb./sth.)** （与某人/某事物）隔绝; **to ～ oneself away in books** 埋头读书; **to lead a ～ed existence** 过与世隔绝的生活

clomp /klɒmp/

A *vi* 脚步沉重地走路

B *n* 沉重的脚步声

clone /kləʊn/

A *n* **1** Biol 克隆 **2** Comput 克隆机 **3** fig pej (person resembling sb. else) 一味仿效的人

B *vt* 克隆 ‹*cell, organism*›

cloning /'kləʊnɪŋ/ *n* [u] 克隆

clonk /klɒŋk/ *n, vt* ▸**clunk A1, A2, C**

close[1] /kləʊs/

A *adj* **1** (near in space, time) 近的; **to be ~ to sb./sth.** 离某人/某事物近; **to be ~ by sb./sth.** 在某人/某事物旁边; **the ambulance is ~ by** 救护车就在一旁; **the time is ~ when ...** …的时刻近了; **at ~ quarters** (gen) 逼近地; Mil 短兵相接; **at ~ range** 在近距离 **2** (near in degree) 接近的; **to have ~ links with sb./sth.** 与…有密切关系 ‹*country, group*›; **to bear a ~ resemblance to sb./sth.** 与某人/某事物极其相似; **in ~ harmony** 以密集和声; **to be ~ to doing sth.** 几乎要做某事; **he was ~ to tears** 他几乎要掉眼泪了 **3** (in friendship) 亲密的 ‹*friend, colleague*›; **she and her brother are very ~** 她和弟弟很亲; **to be ~ to sb.** 与某人亲近; **they have a ~ friendship** 他们有深厚的友谊 **4** (in family relationship) 亲属关系近的; **a ~ relative** 近亲 **5** (similar) 近似的; **that's ~ enough** (acceptable as answer) 差不多了; **it's a ~ match** (in colour etc.) 这很相配; **~ on a century ago** colloq 近一个世纪前 **6** (faithful) 准确的; **a ~ translation of the original** 紧扣原文的翻译 **7** *attrib* (careful, rigorous) 严密的; **keep him under ~ supervision** 严格监督他; **to pay ~ attention to sb./sth.** 密切注意某人/某事物; **to keep a ~ watch** *or* **eye on sb./sth.** 严密监视某人/某事物 **8** *attrib* (tightly guarded) 严守的; **the donor's identity is a ~ secret** 捐赠人的身份严格保密 **9** *pred* (secretive) 嘴紧的; **he was ~ about his past** 他对自己的过去守口如瓶 **10** (stuffy) 闷热的 ‹*weather*› **11** (compactly aligned) 细密的 ‹*texture, grain*›; 密密麻麻的 ‹*handwriting, print*›; **in ~ formation** *or* **order** 以密集编队 **12** (evenly contested) 势均力敌的; **the vote was ~** 投票结果很接近; **the candidates are very ~** 各候选人实力相近

B *adv* **1** (near in space) 靠近地; **don't come too ~!** 别靠太近！; **to hold sb./sth. ~** 紧抱某人/某物; **to follow ~ behind sb./sth.** 紧紧跟在某人/某物后面; **(from) ~ up** （从）近处看; **to live/work ~ by** 在附近居住/工作; **~ by sb./sth.** 紧靠某人/某物 **2** (near in time) 临近地; **Christmas is getting ~** 圣诞节就快到了 **3** (near in degree) 接近地; **to come ~ to** 非常接近 ‹*ideal, conception*›; **to come ~ to doing sth.** 几乎要做某事

C *n* Brit **1** (road) 死路 **2** (area around cathedral) 教堂围地

close[2] /kləʊz/

A *vt* **1** (move so as to cover opening) 盖上 ‹*container*›; 关上 ‹*door, window*›; **she ~d the gate behind her** 她随手关上了大门 **2** (move parts of sth. together) 合上 ‹*book, umbrella*›; 闭上 ‹*eyes, mouth*›; 握起 ‹*fist*›; **to ~ a wound with stitches** 缝合伤口; **to ~ one's mind to sth.** 拒不考虑某事物 **3** (prevent access to) 关闭 ‹*airport*›; 封闭 ‹*road*›; 封锁 ‹*area of town*›; **the country has ~d its borders** 这个国家已经关闭了边境 **4** (seal, block) 封上 ‹*grave*›; 堵住 ‹*hole, pipe*› **5** (stop operating temporarily) 暂时关闭 ‹*shop, office, factory, station, airport, hospital*›; **the museum has been ~d for renovation** 博物馆已经暂时闭馆进行翻新 **6** (stop operating permanently) 永久关闭 ‹*shop, office, factory, station, airport, hospital*›; **the club was ~d by the police** 这家俱乐部被警方查封了 **7** (bring to an end) 结束 ‹*meeting, discussion, investigation*›; 结清 ‹*account*›; **to ~ a case** 结案 **8** (reduce) 使缩小; **to ~ the gap (between ...)** fig 缩小（…之间的）差距; **to ~ the gap on sb./sth.** lit, fig 赶上某人/某事物; **to ~ the gaps (in sth.)** (improve shortcomings) 弥补（某事物的）缺陷 **9** (agree) 商定; **to ~ a deal with ...** 与…做成一笔交易 **10** Elec 闭合 ‹*circuit*›

B *vi* **1** (move so as to cover opening) «*window*» 关上; «*container, lid*» 合上; **the doors open and ~ automatically** 这几扇门都是自动开关的 **2** (move together) «*eyes, mouth*» 闭上; «*fist*» 握紧; «*wound*» 愈合; **to ~ around/on sb./sth.** 围住/盖住某人/某物; **her arms ~d round the child** 她搂住了孩子; **its jaws ~d on the rabbit** 它的嘴紧紧咬住了野兔 **3** (stop operating temporarily) «*shop, office, factory*» 关门; «*station, airport, polls*» 关闭; **the museum has ~d** 博物馆已经闭馆了 **4** (stop operating permanently) «*hospital, business*» 倒闭; «*station*» 关闭; «*play, show*» 停演 **5** (come to an end) «*meeting, investigation, play*» 结束; **the offer ~s at the end of the week** 报价截止到本周末; **to ~ with sth.** 以…结束 ‹*event, song*› **6** (get nearer) 赶上; **the police car was closing fast** 警车快速追了上来; **to ~ on sb./sth.** 渐渐逼近某人/某物 **7** (get smaller) 变小; **the gap is closing between ...** lit, fig …之间的差距在缩小 **8** Fin «*currency, index, shares*» 收盘; **the market ~d down/up** 市场收跌/收涨; **the pound ~d up against the euro** 英镑对欧元收涨

C *n* **1** (end of period) 结束; **at the ~ of the 19th century** 在19世纪末; **to come** *or* **draw to a ~** 结束; **to bring sth. to a ~** 结束某事物 **2** Fin **the ~** 收盘

Phrasal verbs

- **close down**

A *vi* **1** (stop operating permanently) «*hospital, business*» 倒闭; «*shop, office, factory*» 关闭 **2** Brit Radio, TV 停播

B *vt* [**~ down sth., ~ sth. down**] 关闭 ‹*shop, office, factory*›

- **close in** *vi* **1** (get nearer) «*pursuers, enemy*» 逼近 **2** (get worse) «*weather*» 变坏; «*fog*» 变浓 **3** (get shorter) «*days*» 变短 **4** (get darker) «*darkness*» 加深; **night was closing in** 夜色渐深 **5** (get denser) 变浓密; **the jungle ~d in around them** 他们周围的丛林越来越密

- **close off** *vt* [**~ off sth., ~ sth. off**] 封锁 ‹*road, district*›; **they've ~d off parts of the castle** 他们关闭了城堡的几个部分

- **close out** *vt* [**~ out sth., ~ sth. out**] Amer **1** Comm (sell off) 抛售 ‹*goods, stock*› **2** (end) 结束

- **close up**

A *vi* **1** (move together) 合拢; **the cut was starting to ~ up** 伤口开始愈合了 **2** (come closer together) 靠拢; **cars were closing up behind each other** 汽车一辆紧接着一辆 **3** (shut and lock premises) 关门 **4** (become emotionless) 不流露感情; **she ~d up when I asked about her family** 我问及她的家庭情况时，她闭口不谈了 **5** (become blocked, narrower) «*hole, entrance, pipe*» 堵塞; **his throat ~d up with fear** 他吓得说不出话来

B *vt* [**~ up sth., ~ sth. up**] **1** (shut and lock) 关闭 ‹*shop, office, factory*› **2** (block, make narrower) 堵塞 ‹*hole, pipe*›; **they ~d up the entrance to the tunnel** 他们堵住了通往隧道的入口

- **close with** *vt* [**~ with sb.**] «*troops*» 与…短兵相接 ‹*enemy*›

close: ~ call, ~ shave *ns* colloq 幸免于难; **~ combat** *n* [u] 近距离作战; **~-cropped** *adj* 剪得很短的 ‹*hair, grass*›

closed /kləʊzd/ *adj* **1** (shut) 关闭的 ‹*window, drawer*›; 闭着的 ‹*eyes, mouth*›; **that door is now ~ to me** fig 现在我永远失去了那个机会; **behind ~ doors** fig 秘密地 **2** (not open) 不开放的; **to be ~ to cars/the public** 不允许汽车通行/不对公众开放; **~ for repairs/the winter** 因维修/过冬而关闭 **3** (shut down) 停业的 ‹*shop, factory*› **4** (finished) 结束的; **the case is ~** 本案已结 **5** (insular) 封闭的 ‹*economy, society*› **6** (restricted) 秘密的 ‹*meeting, organization*›; **a ~ session (of congress)** （国会的）秘密会议 **7** fig pej (blinkered) 守旧的 ‹*mind*›; **to be ~ to sth.** 不愿接受某事物

closed: ~ book *n* colloq 不了解的对象; **he was a ~ book to her** 她对他一无所知; **~-circuit television** *n* [u] 闭路电视

closedown /ˈkləʊzdaʊn/ *n* **1** [c] Comm, Ind 停业 **2** [u] Brit Radio, TV 停止播放

closed: ~ primary *n* Amer 闭门预选; **~ season** *n* esp Amer = **close season**; **~ set** *n* 闭集; **~ shop** *n* 只雇用工会会员的制度

close-fitting *adj* 紧身的 ‹*clothes*›

close-hauled

A *adj* 顶风航行的 ‹*ship*›

B *adv* 顶风航行地

close: ~-knit *adj* fig 紧密结合的 ‹*community, family*›; 密切的 ‹*relationship*›; **~-lipped** *adj* 嘴紧的

closely /ˈkləʊsli/ *adv* **1** (near in space) 紧紧地 ‹*follow, hold*›; 仔细地 ‹*look*›; **a ~ written manuscript** 一份写得密密麻麻的手稿; **to be ~ packed** 塞得满满当当 **2** (near in time) 紧接着; **his resignation was ~ followed by that of the minister** 那位大臣紧跟在他之后辞职了 **3** (near in degree) 接近地; **the two events are ~ connected** 这两起事件联系密切; **she resembled her mother ~** 她长得非常像她母亲; **to work ~ together** 密切协作; **to be ~ related (to sb./sth.)** （与某人/某生物）是近亲 **4** (rigorously, in detail) 仔细地 ‹*observe, listen, study, question*›; 严密地 ‹*monitor*›; **a ~ guarded secret** 严守的秘密 **5** (evenly) 均衡地; **to be ~ contested** *or* **fought** 势均力敌; **to be ~ matched** 不相上下 **6** (near to skin, body) 贴近地; **to fit ~** «*garment*» 贴身

close-mouthed *adj* = **close-lipped**

closeness /ˈkləʊsnɪs/ *n* [u] **1** (proximity) 接近; **the ~ of the pursuers** 追赶者的迫近 **2** (intimacy) 亲密; (rapport) 密切关系; **~ to nature** 与自然的密切关系 **3** (stuffiness) 湿闷 **4** (exactness) 精确; **the ~ of a resemblance** 酷似; **the ~ of the translation** 翻译的准确 **5** (rigour) 严格; (thoroughness) 严密 **6** (density of texture, weave) 致密

closeout /ˈkləʊzaʊt/ *n* Amer **~ (sale)** 清仓甩卖

close: ~-run *adj* 势均力敌的 ‹*race, election*›; **~-set** *adj* 紧靠着的; **~-set eyes/houses** 距离很近的眼睛/紧挨着的房屋; **~ season** /ˈkləʊz ˌsiːzən/ *n* Brit **1** (for fishing) 禁渔期; (for killing game) 禁猎期; **2** Sport 比赛淡季; **~ thing** *n* colloq (escape) 幸免于难; **~-up lens** *n* 特写镜头

closet /ˈklɒzɪt/

A *n* **1** esp Amer (cupboard) 壁橱; (for clothes) 衣橱 **2** (room) 储藏室 **3** dated (lavatory) 盥洗室 **4** fig colloq **the ~** 隐秘; **to come out of the ~** 公开自己的同性恋身份; **to bring sth./sb. out of the ~** 公开讨论某事物/某人

B *adj attrib* 隐秘的; **a ~ fascist/homosexual** 潜伏的法西斯分子/不公开的同性恋

C *vt* fig **to be ~ed with sb.** 与某人关门密谈; **to be ~ed in the boardroom/with one's advisers** 在董事会会议室/和顾问们密谈; **a ~ed world** 封闭的世界

close-up *n* [u and c] 特写; **in ~** 在特写镜头中; **~ pictures** 特写照片

closing /ˈkləʊzɪŋ/

A *n* [u] **1** 关闭; **a ~ of ranks** fig 队列的聚拢 **2** (of shop) 停业; **Sunday ~** 周日停业

B *adj attrib* 最后的 ‹*scene, years*›; **~ remarks** 结束语; **the ~ speech** 闭幕词

closing: ~ balance *n* 期终余额; **~ date** *n* 截止日期; **~-down sale** *n* Brit 歇业甩卖; **~ entry** *n* 结账分录; **~-out sale** *n* Amer = **~-down sale**; **~ price** *n* 收盘价; **~ time** *n* 打烊时间

closure /ˈkləʊʒə(r)/ *n* **1** [u and c] (temporary) 关闭; (permanent) 倒闭 **2** [c] (lid) 盖子; (tie) 金属捆扎绳 **3** [u] fig (from traumatic event) 解脱; **to get ~** 得到解脱; **a sense of ~** 释怀感 **4** [u] Pol 终止辩论提付表决

clot /klɒt/

A *n* **1** also Physiol 凝块; (lump) 结块; (mass) 团; **a ~ in a blood vessel/on the brain** 血管/大脑里的血块 **2** Brit colloq pej (idiot) 傻瓜

B *vi* (*pres p etc.* **-tt-**) «*blood*» 凝结成块

C

C *vt* (*pres p etc.* **-tt-**) «*drug*» 使…凝结成块 ‹*blood*›

cloth /klɒθ, Amer klɔ:θ/ *n* **1** [u] (fabric) 布料; **to cut one's coat according to one's ~** fig 量入为出 **2** [c] (piece of fabric) 一块布 **3** [c] (piece of fabric for cleaning) 一块抹布; **a damp ~** 湿抹布 **4** [u] Publg 布面; **bound in ~** 布面装订的

cloth: ~ binding *n* [u and c] 布面装订; **~-bound** *adj* 布面装订的 ‹*book*›

cloth cap
A *n* Brit lit 羊毛软帽
B **cloth-cap** *modif* fig 工人阶级的

clothe /kləʊð/ *vt* **1** (dress) 给…穿衣服; **to be ~d/to ~ oneself in sth.** 穿着某种衣服; **fully ~d** 衣着完整的 **2** (provide for) 为…提供衣物; **to feed and ~ …** 为…提供衣食 **3** fig (cover) 覆盖; **to ~ sth. in sth.** 用某物盖住某物; **a landscape ~d in mist** 笼罩在薄雾中的风景

cloth: ~-eared *adj* Brit colloq pej 耳背的; **~-ears** *n + v sing* Brit colloq pej 耳背的人

clothes /kləʊðz, Amer kləʊz/ *npl* 衣服; **with one's ~ on/off** 穿着衣服/光着身子; **without any ~ on** 一丝不挂; **with only the ~ one stood up in** 一无所有; **to steal sb.'s ~** fig pej 剽窃某人的点子

clothes: ~ airer *n* 晾衣架; **~ basket** *n* = **laundry basket**; **~ brush** *n* 衣刷; **~ drier** *n* **1** (machine) 干衣机; **2** (airer) 晾衣架; **~ hamper** *n* 洗衣筐; **~hanger** *n* 衣架; **~ horse** *n* 晾衣架; **~ line** *n* 晾衣绳; **~ moth** *n* 衣蛾; **~ peg** Brit, **~pin** Amer *ns* 晾衣夹子; **~ prop** *n* 晾衣绳支撑杆; **~ rack** *n* 晾衣架; **~ shop** *n* 服装店; **~ tree** *n* Amer 立柱式衣帽架

clothier /'kləʊðɪə(r)/ ▸**p. 409** *n* formal (seller) 服装商; (shop) 服装店; (company) 服装公司

clothing /'kləʊðɪŋ/ *n* [u] 衣服; **an item** *or* **article of ~** 一件衣服; **protective/waterproof ~** 防护服/防水服; ▸**wolf 1**

clothing: ~ allowance *n* 制服津贴; **~ industry, ~ trade** *ns* 服装业

clotted cream *n* [u] Brit 凝脂奶油

cloture /'kləʊtʃə(r)/ *n* [u] Amer = **closure 4**

cloud /klaʊd/
A *n* **1** [u and c] Meteorol 云; **some patches of ~** 几片云; **to have one's head in the ~s** 抱有幻想; **every ~ has a silver lining** Prov 黑暗中总有一线光明; **(to be) on ~ nine** colloq 乐不可支 **2** [c] (mass of particles) 云状物; (of insects, birds) 一群; **a ~ of smoke/dust** 一片烟雾/尘雾; **a ~ of starlings** 一群椋鸟 **3** [c] (in liquid) 混浊团; (in gem) 云纹; (on glass) 雾气 **4** [c] fig (dark spot) 阴影; **a ~ of gloom/suspicion** 一片忧虑/一团疑云; **to cast a ~ over sth.** 给某事物蒙上一层阴影; **to leave/be under a ~ (of suspicion)** 留下疑团/受到怀疑
B *vt* **1** (blur) 使…模糊 ‹*sky, vision*›; **eyes ~ed with tears** 泪水模糊的眼睛 **2** fig (confuse) 使…迷惑 ‹*mind*›; 使…混乱 ‹*memory*› **3** fig (blight) 破坏 ‹*future, atmosphere*›

Phrasal verb
- **cloud over** *vi* **1** lit «*sky*» 阴云密布 **2** fig «*expression, face*» 阴沉下来

cloud: ~burst *n* 大暴雨; **~ chamber** *n* 云室; **~ computing** *n* [u] 云计算; **~ cover** *n* [u] 云覆盖; **~-cuckoo land** *n* colloq 脱离现实的幻境

clouded /'klaʊdɪd/ *adj* **1** lit 阴云密布的 ‹*sky*› **2** fig 阴沉的 ‹*expression, face*›

cloudiness /'klaʊdɪnɪs/ *n* [u] **1** (having a lot of clouds) 多云; (being overcast) 阴天 **2** (of water, glass) 混浊

cloudless /'klaʊdlɪs/ *adj* **1** (clear) 晴朗的 ‹*sky*› **2** fig (untroubled) 一片光明的 ‹*future*›

cloudy /'klaʊdi/ *adj* **1** Meteorol (having a lot of clouds) 多云的; (overcast) 阴天的 **2** (murky) 混浊的 ‹*liquid*›

clout /klaʊt/ colloq
A *n* **1** [c] (blow) 重击; **a ~ across the back of the head** 后脑勺上挨的一巴掌 **2** [u] fig (power) 势力; (influence) 影响力; **to have** *or* **carry** *or* **wield a great deal of ~** 有巨大影响力
B *vt* 重击 ‹*person, ball*›; **she ~ed him across the mouth** 她狠狠地扇了他一个嘴巴

clove[1] /kləʊv/ *n* **1** (spice) 丁香 **2** (bulb) 鳞茎; **a ~ of garlic** 一瓣蒜

clove[2] *pt* ▸**cleave**[1] **A**

clove hitch *n* 卷结

cloven /'kləʊvn/ *pp* ▸**cleave**[1] **A**

cloven: ~ foot *n* = **~ hoof**; **~-footed** *adj* = **~-hoofed**; **~ hoof** *n* 偶蹄; **~-hoofed** *adj* 偶蹄的; **a ~-hoofed animal** 偶蹄动物

clover /'kləʊvə(r)/ *n* [u] 三叶草; **to be/live in ~** colloq 过舒适奢侈的生活

cloverleaf /'kləʊvəli:f/ *n* Amer 三叶草式立交桥

clown /klaʊn/
A *n* **1** (in circus) 小丑; (comic) 喜剧演员 **2** pej (fool) 蠢货
B *vi* **1** = **clown around 2** (perform) 扮演小丑

Phrasal verb
- **clown around, clown about** *vi* 扮滑稽相

clowning /'klaʊnɪŋ/ *n* [u] **1** (as job) 扮演小丑 **2** colloq pej (fooling) 胡闹; **his ~ (about** *or* **around) got on my nerves** 他的故作滑稽让我觉得很烦

cloy /klɔɪ/
A *vi* **1** (sicken) «*food*» 倒胃口 **2** fig (disgust) «*fame, pleasure*» 使人腻烦
B *vt* «*sweetness, smell*» 使…腻烦 ‹*person, senses*›

cloying /'klɔɪɪŋ/ *adj* **1** (sickly) 甜腻的 ‹*smell*› **2** fig pej (sentimental) 令人腻烦的 ‹*words, manner*›

club[1] /klʌb/
A *n* ▸**p. 307** **1** *+ v sing or pl* (group) 俱乐部; **to join a chess/film/working-men's ~** 加入国际象棋/电影/工人俱乐部; **a football ~** Sport 足球俱乐部; **join the ~!** colloq 我们处境都一样!; **in the (pudding) ~** Brit colloq 怀孕 **2** (nightclub) 夜总会; **the ~ scene** 夜总会活动 **3** (gentleman's) 绅士俱乐部 **4** Comm [采用邮购手段销售商品、让利会员的] 销售俱乐部; **a book ~** 书友会
B *vi* (*pres p etc.* **-bb-**) 去夜总会; **to go ~bing** colloq 去泡夜总会

Phrasal verb
- **club together** *vi* 分摊费用

club[2]
A *n* **1** (stick) 棍棒 **2** (for golf) 球杆 **3** (in cards) 梅花; **the ace/five/king of ~s** 梅花 A/五/老 K; **to play a ~** 出一张梅花
B *vt* (*pres p etc.* **-bb-**) 用棍棒击打; **to ~ sb. with sth.** 用某物打某人; **to ~ sb. to death** 用棍棒打死某人

clubber /'klʌbə(r)/ *n* 夜总会常客

clubbing /'klʌbɪŋ/ *n* [u] 泡夜总会

club: ~ car *n* Amer 休息车厢; **~ chair** *n* Amer 低背安乐椅

club class Brit
A *n* [u] 商务舱
B *adv* 乘商务舱 ‹*travel, fly*›

club: ~ foot *n* 足内翻; **to have a ~ foot** 患足内翻; **~-footed** *adj* 患足内翻的; **~goer** *n* = **clubber**; **~house** *n* 俱乐部会所; **~land** /-lænd/ *n* [u] Brit **1** (area) 俱乐部区; **2** (milieu) 夜总会天地; **~room** *n* 俱乐部聚会室; **~ sandwich** *n* 总会三明治; **~ soda®** *n* Amer 苏打水; **~ steak** *n* Amer 小牛排

cluck /klʌk/
A *vi* **1** lit «*hen*» 咯咯叫 **2** fig (fuss) 啧啧地表示关心; **to ~ over sb.** 啧啧地关心某人; **to ~ with sympathy** 啧啧地表示同情 **3** (express disapproval) 啧啧地表示不赞成
B *vt* **to ~ one's tongue** 用舌发啧啧声
C *n* **1** (of hen) 咯咯声 **2** (of annoyance) 不耐烦的啧啧声

clucking /'klʌkɪŋ/ *n* [u] 咯咯声

clue /klu:/ *n* **1** (sign) 线索 **2** (idea) 想法; **to not have a ~ (about sth.)** (对某事物)一无所知; **she doesn't have a ~ about cooking** 她对烹调一窍不通; **he doesn't have a ~!** 他笨得很! **3** (hint) 提示; (in game) 提示语; **give me a ~** 给我点提示吧

Phrasal verb
- **clue in** *vt* [**~ sb. in**] 给…提供最新信息; **to ~ sb. in about** *or* **on sth.** colloq 为某人提供某事物的最新消息; **to ~ sb. in on recent events** 让某人了解最近发生的事; **he's been ~d in** 他已知情

clued-up *adj* Brit colloq 熟悉情况的; **to be ~ about** *or* **on sth.** 了解某事物

clueless /'klu:lɪs/ *adj* colloq pej 一无所知的; **to be ~ (about sth.)** (对某事物)一窍不通

clump[1] /klʌmp/
A *n* **1** (of plants) 丛; **~s of flowers** 一簇簇花朵; **a ~ of bushes** 灌木丛 **2** (of buildings, people) 群; **a ~ of houses** 住宅群; **~s of fans** 成群的追随者 **3** (of earth) 块; **a large ~ of earth** 一大块土 **4** (of hair) 绺
B *vt* **to ~ (together)** 使聚拢; **to ~ plants/objects together** 将植株/物件聚在一起
C *vi* 聚集; **to ~ together** 聚在一起

clump[2]
A *vi* **1** (walk heavily) 迈着沉重的步子走路; **to ~ along/about** *or* **around** 步履沉重地走 **2** (fall heavily) 砰然落下; **to ~ (down) on to sth.** «*heavy object*» 重重落在某物上
B *vt* 砰的一声扔掉; **he ~ed the heavy suitcase down on the floor** 他把沉重的手提箱砰的一声摔在地板上
C *n* 沉重的脚步声

clumsily /'klʌmzɪli/ *adv* **1** (awkwardly) 笨拙地 **2** (ungracefully) 不雅地 **3** (inelegantly) 不得体地; **the essay was ~ written** 这篇短文写得很拙劣 **4** (tactlessly) 无技巧地

clumsiness /'klʌmzɪnɪs/ *n* [u] **1** (awkwardness) 笨拙 **2** (carelessness) 疏忽 **3** (ungainliness) 不雅观; (inelegance of style, writing) 不得体 **4** (unwieldiness) 设计欠佳 **5** (tactlessness) 不得体

clumsy /'klʌmzi/ *adj* **1** (awkward) 笨拙的; **to be ~ with one's hands** 双手笨拙; **to be ~ with a knife** 用起刀来笨手笨脚 **2** (careless) 不优美的 ‹*gesture, dance*›; 难看的 ‹*figure, design*›; 欠考虑的 ‹*attempt*› **3** (unrefined) 粗劣的 ‹*style, workmanship*›; 制作粗糙的 ‹*table, chair*› **4** (unwieldy) 设计欠佳的 ‹*tool, machine*› **5** (unskilful) 不娴熟的 ‹*writer, craftsman*› **6** (tactless) 无技巧的 ‹*remark*›

clung /klʌŋ/ *pt, pp* ▸**cling**

clunk /klʌŋk/
A *n* **1** (sound) 哐啷声; **the ~ of wood on** *or* **against stone** 木头撞击石头的嗵嗵声; **to go ~** 砰砰作响 **2** colloq (blow) 敲打; **to give sb. a ~ on the head** 敲某人的头 **3** Amer colloq (idiot) 白痴
B *vi* «*machine*» 哐啷作响
C *vt* colloq 敲打; **to ~ sb. on the head** 敲某人的头

clunky /'klʌŋki/ *adj* colloq **1** (clumsy) 笨重的 **2** (old-fashioned) 过时的; (awkward to use) 难用的 **3** (making a clunking sound) 哐啷作响的

cluster /'klʌstə(r)/
A *n* **1** (of people, houses, islands, trees) 群; (of grapes, gems) 串; (of flowers, bombs) 束; (of ideas) 组 **2** Astron 星团 **3** Stat 数据组 **4** Ling (of vowels) 元音丛; (of consonants) 辅音丛
B *vi* «*people, animals*» 聚集; «*plants*» 丛生; **to ~ round** *or* **around sth.** 聚在某事物周围; **to ~ together** 聚在一起
C *vt* 使聚集; **to be ~ed round** *or* **around sth.**

聚在某事物周围; **the jewels were ～ed together** 珠宝集中镶嵌在一起

cluster bomb *n* 集束炸弹

clutch /klʌtʃ/

A *vt* 抓紧; **to ～ sth. in one's hand** 手里紧紧抓住某物; **to ～ sb./sth. to one's chest/body** 紧拥/抱紧某人/某物

B *n* **1** (grip) 抓紧 **2** (grab) 抢夺; **to make a ～ at sth.** 突然抢夺某物 **3** Aut (device) 离合器; (pedal) 离合器踏板; **to disengage/engage the ～** 松开/踩下离合器 **4** (of eggs, chicks) 一窝; (of stories) 一系列; (of awards, homes) 一批; (of people) 一群 **5** Amer fig (jam) 紧急关头

C clutches *npl* 控制; **to be in/fall into sb.'s ～es** 处于/落入某人的掌控之中; **to escape from the ～es of ...** 摆脱…的控制; **to have sb. in one's ～es** 控制某人

Phrasal verb

- **clutch at** *vt* [～ at sth.] 拼命想抓住 ‹*arm, rope*›; fig 拼命想利用 ‹*excuse, chance*›; **to ～ at any pretext for divorce** 拼命抓住任何借口离婚

clutch: ～ bag *n* 小手包; **～ cable** *n* 离合器电缆; **～ disc** *n* **= ～ plate**; **～ pedal** *n* 离合器踏板; **～ plate** 离合器片

clutter /ˈklʌtə(r)/

A *n* [u] **1** (things) 杂乱的东西; **a room full of ～** 堆满杂物的房间 **2** (mess) 杂乱; **in a ～** 凌乱不堪; **what a ～!** 真是一团糟!

B *vt* **= clutter up**

Phrasal verb

- **clutter up** *vt* [～ sth. up, ～ up sth.] **1** (make untidy by filling) 把…弄得乱七八糟 ‹*room, garden, desk*› **2** (make too full) 乱哄哄地挤满 ‹*space, street*›; 杂乱无序地填满 ‹*book*›; fig 使…混乱 ‹*brain*›

cluttered /ˈklʌtəd/ *adj* 乱七八糟的 ‹*room, garden, desk*›

cm *abbr* **= centimetre(s)** 厘米

Cmdr *abbr* **= commander**

CND *abbr* **= Campaign for Nuclear Disarmament** 核裁军运动

CNG *abbr* **= compressed natural gas** 压缩天然气

CNN *abbr* **= Cable News Network** [美国] 有线电视新闻网

> **CNN**
>
> 有线电视新闻网，全称 Cable News Network。全球第一个 24 小时播出新闻的电视频道。总部设于亚特兰大（Atlanta）。1980 年由特德·特纳（Ted Turner）创办。1991 年因对海湾战争的报道声名鹊起。1996 年被时代华纳（Time Warner）收购。CNN 的特色是全方位的现场直播。这种新闻报道现在对公众舆论、新闻事件的进程和结果、甚至政府决策等都会产生重要影响，称为“CNN 效应”（CNN effect）。

CNY *abbr* **= Chinese yuan** 人民币

CO *abbr* **1 = commanding officer** **2** Amer **= Colorado** **3 = conscientious objector**

Co. *abbr* **1 = company 1** **2 and co.** colloq 以及类似种种; **Mark and ～** 马克那几个人 **3 = county**

c/o *abbr* **= care of** 由…转交; **J ～ P** 由 P 转交 J

coach /kəʊtʃ/

A *n* **1** (bus) 长途汽车 **2** Rail (carriage) 火车车厢 **3** Sport 教练 **4** Theat, Mus 指导 **5** (tutor) 辅导教师 **6** (horse-drawn) 四轮马车; **to drive a ～ and horses through sth.** Brit fig 使某事物无效 **7** Amer Aviat, Rail **～ (class)** 经济舱

B *vt* **1** Sport 训练; **to ～ sb. for sth.** 为某事物训练某人 **2** (teach) 辅导; **to ～ sb. in/for sth.** 在某方面/为某事物辅导某人

C *vi* 当教练; **to ～ for a living** 以当教练为生

coach: ～ bolt *n* Brit 圆头大螺栓; **～builder** ▸p. 409 *n* Brit (person) 汽车车身制造工; (firm) 汽车车身制造厂; **～building** *n* [u] Brit 汽车车身制造; **～ driver** ▸p. 409 *n* Brit 长途汽车司机

coaching /ˈkəʊtʃɪŋ/ *n* [u] **1** Sport 训练 **2** (lessons) 辅导

coaching inn *n* Brit Hist 驿车旅馆

coach: ～load *n* Brit [乘同一辆车的] 长途汽车团体旅客; **～man** /-mən/ *n* 马车夫; **～ operator** *n* Brit 长途汽车营运商; **～ park** *n* Brit 长途汽车停车场; **～ party** *n* + *v sing or pl* Brit [乘同一辆车的] 长途汽车旅行团; **～ station** *n* Brit 长途汽车总站; **～ terminus** *n* Brit 长途汽车终点站; **～ trip** *n* Brit 乘长途汽车的旅行; **to go on a ～ trip** 乘长途汽车旅行; **～work** *n* [u] Brit Aut 汽车车身制造; Rail 火车车厢制造

coagulant /kəʊˈægjʊlənt/ *n* 凝结剂

coagulate /kəʊˈægjʊleɪt/

A *vt* 使…凝固 ‹*liquid, blood, milk*›

B *vi* «*liquid, blood, milk*» 凝固

coagulation /ˌkəʊægjʊˈleɪʃn/ *n* [u] 凝固

coal /kəʊl/ *n* **1** [u] 煤; **a piece** *or* **lump of ～** 一块煤 **2** [c] (piece of) 煤块; **hot** *or* **live ～s** 燃烧着的煤块; **to carry ～s to Newcastle** fig 多此一举; **to drag** *or* **haul** *or* **rake sb. over the ～s** fig 申斥某人

coal: ～-based *adj* 煤基的; **～-based fuels** 煤基燃料; **～-based products** 煤炭产品; **～-black** *adj* 乌黑的 ‹*hair, face*›; 漆黑的 ‹*night*›; **～ box** *n* 煤箱; **～ bunker** *n* 煤舱; **～-burning** *adj attrib* 烧煤的 ‹*stove*›; **～ cutter** *n* **1** (man) 截煤工; **2** (machine) 截煤机; **～ deposits** *npl* 煤矿床; **～ depot** *n* 贮煤场; **～ dust** *n* [u] 煤尘

coalesce /ˌkəʊəˈles/ *vi* formal «*substances, groups*» 合并

coalescence /ˌkəʊəˈlesns/ *n* [u] formal 合并

coal: ～face *n* 采煤工作面; **at the ～face** lit 在采煤工作面上; Brit fig 在工作第一线; **～field** *n* 煤田; **～ fire** *n* 煤火; **～-fired** *adj* 烧煤的 ‹*boiler*›; 燃煤的 ‹*power station*›; **～ gas** *n* [u] 煤气; **～-hole** *n* Brit dated 储煤间; **～ industry** *n* 煤炭工业

coalition /ˌkəʊəˈlɪʃn/ *n* esp Pol 联盟; **to form/dissolve a ～** 形成/解散联盟; **a ～ between ...** …之间的联盟; **a ～ of two parties** 两党联盟

coalition government *n* 联合政府; **to form a ～** 组成联合政府

coal: ～ man, ～ merchant ▸p. 409 *ns* **1** (seller) 煤商; **2** (deliverer) 运煤工; **～ mine** *n* 煤矿; **～ miner** ▸p. 409 *n* 煤矿工人; **～ mining** *n* [u] 采煤; **the ～-mining industry** 采煤业; **～ pit** *n* 煤矿; **～ reserves** *npl* 煤矿藏; **～ scuttle** *n* 煤斗; **～ seam** *n* 煤层; **～ strike** *n* 煤矿工人罢工; **～ tar** *n* [u] 煤焦油; **～ tit** *n* 煤山雀; **～ yard** *n* 煤场

coaming /ˈkəʊmɪŋ/ *n* 舱口围板

coarse /kɔːs/ *adj* **1** (grainy) 粗的; **～ sand/salt** 粗沙/粗盐 **2** (rough) 粗糙的 ‹*material, skin, wood*›; **a ～ fabric/weave** 粗布/粗纺 **3** (ill-bred, vulgar) 粗鲁的 ‹*manners, accent, remark*›

coarse: ～ fish *n* (*pl* **～ fish**) Brit 淡水杂鱼 [不包括鲑鳟鱼和鲑]; **～ fishing** *n* [u] Brit 捕淡水杂鱼; **～-grained** *adj* **1** (not fine) 质地粗的; **～-grained salt/sand** 粗盐/粗沙; **2** (rough) 粗糙的 ‹*material, skin, wood*›

coarsely /ˈkɔːsli/ *adv* **1** (chunkily) 大块地 ‹*cut*› **2** Tex 粗糙地; **～ woven cloth/fabric** 粗纺布/粗纺织物 **3** (vulgarly) 粗鲁地 ‹*behave*›

coarsen /ˈkɔːsn/ *vt* **1** (make coarse) 使…变粗 ‹*fabric, texture*›; **to ～ the fibre with wool** 掺入羊毛使纤维变粗 **2** (roughen) 使…变粗糙 ‹*skin, hands*›

coarseness /ˈkɔːsnɪs/ *n* **1** (of sand, salt) 粗 **2** (of cloth, skin) 粗糙 **3** (of person, behaviour, manners) 粗鲁

coast /kəʊst/

A *n* **1** (part of land beside sea) 海岸; **off the ～** 在近海岸的海上; **from ～ to ～** 在整个大陆; **the ～ is clear** fig 四下无人 **2** (region) 沿海地区; **the Atlantic ～** 大西洋沿岸地区 **3** (seaside) 海边 **4** (glide) 滑行

B *vi* **1** (freewheel) 靠惯性滑行; **to ～ along at 50 mph** 以每小时 50 英里的速度滑行 **2** (glide) 平稳行进; fig 不费力地前进; **to ～ along** (glide) 平稳前行; fig 顺利进展; **to ～ through an exam** 顺利通过考试; **to ～ to victory** 轻松取胜

coastal /ˈkəʊstl/ *adj* 近海的 ‹*waters, navigation*›; 海滨的 ‹*town*›; 沿海的 ‹*population*›

coaster /ˈkəʊstə(r)/ *n* **1** (for cup) 杯子垫 **2** Naut 沿岸货船

coaster brake *n* 脚刹车

coastguard /ˈkəʊstgɑːd/ ▸p. 409 *n* **1** + *v sing or pl* (group) 海岸警卫队 **2** (person) 海岸警卫队员

coastguard: ～ station *n* 海岸警卫瞭望所; **～ vessel** *n* 海岸警卫船

coast: ～line *n* 海岸线; **～ path** *n* 海边步行道; **～ road** *n* 沿海公路; **～-to-～** *adj attrib* 横穿大陆的 ‹*road, walk*›

coat /kəʊt/

A *n* **1** (garment) 外套; **to put on/take off one's ～** 穿上/脱下外套; ▸cloth 1 **2** (of woman's two piece suit) 上衣; **a matching ～ and skirt** 裙服套装 **3** (of animal) 皮毛; **the dog is losing its ～** 那条狗正在脱毛 **4** (layer) 层; **to apply a ～ of sth.** 覆盖一层某物; **give it a/another ～ (of paint)** 给/再给它刷一层（涂料）

B *vt* **1** (cover) 覆盖; **to ～ sth. with** 给某物涂一层 ‹*paint, glue*›; **to ～ biscuits in** *or* **with chocolate** 在饼干上涂一层巧克力 **2** Ind 电镀 ‹*metal*›

coat: ～ check *n* Amer **= cloakroom 1**; **～ dress** *n* 外套式连衣裙

coated /ˈkəʊtɪd/ *adj* **1** (covered) 有覆盖层的; **a ～ pill** 糖衣药片 **2** Phot, Optics 有镀膜的 ‹*glass*›; **a ～ lens** 镀膜镜片 **3** Med 有舌苔的 ‹*tongue*›

coat hanger *n* 衣架

coating /ˈkəʊtɪŋ/ *n* **1** [c] (covering) 覆盖层; **a light ～ of dust/snow** 薄薄的一层灰尘/雪; **a protective plastic ～** 塑料膜防护层 **2** [u] Culin 涂层; **a chocolate/honey/egg ～** 巧克力/蜂蜜/蛋液涂层; **with a ～ of sth.** 裹了一层某物

coat: ～ of arms *n* 盾形徽章; **～ of mail** *n* 锁子铠甲; **～ rack** *n* 衣帽架; **～room** *n* Amer **= cloakroom 1**; **～ stand** *n* 衣帽架; **～-tails** *npl* (style) 燕尾服; (tails) 燕尾; **to be hanging on to sb.'s ～-tails** fig 缠着某人; **to ride on sb.'s ～-tails** fig 依仗某人提携; **～ tree** *n* Amer 立柱式衣帽架

co-author

A *n* 合著者

B *vt* 合著 ‹*book*›; 合编 ‹*play*›; **he ～ed the book with a colleague** 他与一位同事合写了这本书

coax /kəʊks/ *vt* **1** (persuade) 哄劝; **to ～ sb. to do** *or* **into doing sth.** 哄某人做某事; **to ～ sb. out of a bad mood** 耐心开导某人摆脱坏心情 **2** (obtain) 诱得 ‹*money, gifts*›; **she managed to ～ £100 out of her father** 她哄着父亲给了她 100 英镑 **3** (lure) 引诱; **to ～ sb. into the room** 将某人诱入房间; **to ～ sb. away from sth.** 引诱某人离开某处; **she ～ed him towards the door** 她诱使他朝门走去 **4** fig (urge) 耐心摆弄; **to ～ a fire back to life** 小心翼翼地把火再弄旺; **to ～ hair into ringlets** 耐心把头发做成卷

coaxial /kəʊˈæksɪəl/ *adj* **1** (on one axis) 同轴的; **a set of ～ circles** 一组共轴圆 **2** Electron 同轴传输的; **～ cable** 同轴电缆

coaxing /ˈkəʊksɪŋ/

A *n* [u] **1** (persuasion) 劝诱 **2** (urging) 耐心摆弄;

C

the car needs a great deal of ~ to start 发动这辆车得十分耐心
B *adj* 劝诱的 ‹*manner, tone*›; **a few ~ words** 几句甜言蜜语

cob /kɒb/ *n* **1** (of maize) **= corncob** **2** (nut) **= cobnut** **3** (horse) 矮脚壮马 **4** (swan) 雄天鹅 **5** Brit (loaf) 圆面包

cobalt /ˈkəʊbɔːlt/ *n* [u] **1** Chem 钴 **2** (colour) **~ (blue)** 钴蓝

cobber /ˈkɒbə(r)/ *n* Austral, NZ colloq 老兄

cobble¹ /ˈkɒbl/
A **cobbles** *npl* 鹅卵石
B *vt* 用鹅卵石铺 ‹*street*›

cobble² *vt* dated (make) 手工缝制 ‹*shoes*›; (mend) 手工修补 ‹*shoes*›

Phrasal verb

- **cobble together** *vt* [**~ sth. together, ~ together sth.**] pej 草率制订 ‹*plans*›; 胡乱拼凑 ‹*report*›

cobbled /ˈkɒbld/ *adj* 铺鹅卵石的 ‹*street*›

cobbler /ˈkɒblə(r)/ *n* **1** ▸**p. 409** [c] (shoemaker) 鞋匠 **2** [u and c] (pie) 脆皮水果馅饼 **3** [c] esp Amer (drink) 酒味果汁冷饮

cobblers /ˈkɒbləz/ *n* Brit colloq 废话; **a load/a lot of ~** 一派胡言

cobblestones /ˈkɒblstəʊnz/ *npl* 鹅卵石

cobnut /ˈkɒbnʌt/ *n* 欧洲榛子

cobra /ˈkəʊbrə/ *n* 眼镜蛇; **a king ~** 眼镜王蛇

cobweb /ˈkɒbweb/ *n* 蜘蛛网; **to blow** *or* **sweep** *or* **clear away the ~s** fig 使头脑清醒

cobwebbed /ˈkɒbwebd/, **cobwebby** /ˈkɒbwebi/ *adjs* 布满蛛网的 ‹*room*›

coca /ˈkəʊkə/ *n* **1** [u] (leaves) 干古柯叶 **2** [c] (bush) 古柯

Coca-Cola® /ˌkəʊkəˈkəʊlə/ **1** [u] 可口可乐 **2** [c] (glass) 一杯可口可乐; (can) 一听可口可乐

cocaine /kəʊˈkeɪn/ *n* 可卡因; **to snort ~** 吸可卡因粉; **a shot of ~** 一针可卡因; **~ addiction** 可卡因瘾

co-chair
A *n* 联合主席
B *vt* 担任…的联合主席

co-chairman *n* (*pl* **co-chairmen**) 联合主席

cochineal /ˌkɒtʃɪˈniːl/ *n* [u] **1** Culin 胭脂虫红色素 **2** (colour) 胭脂虫红色 **3** (dye) 胭脂虫红染料

cochlea /ˈkɒklɪə/ *n* (*pl* **cochleae** /ˈkɒklɪiː/) 耳蜗

cock /kɒk/
A *n* **1** [c] (rooster) 公鸡; **to be ~ of the walk** 称王称霸 **2** [c] Zool (male bird) 雄禽; **a ~ pheasant/sparrow** 雄野鸡/雄麻雀 **3** [c] taboo sl (penis) 鸡巴 offensive **4** [u] Brit colloq (nonsense) 胡言乱语; **a load/lot of ~** 一通胡说八道 **5** [c] Brit dated sl (term of address) 伙计 **6** [u and c] (of firearm) 击铁; **at full/half ~** 处于全/半击发状态; **to go off at half ~** Brit colloq 匆忙行事; **you always go off at half ~** 你总是操之过急
B *vt* **1** (raise) «*animal*» 立起; **the dog ~ed its ears** 这只狗竖起耳朵; **to ~ an eyebrow** 扬起眉毛 **2** (tilt) 侧转; **the bird ~ed its head on** *or* **to one side** 鸟把头转向一侧; **to ~ an ear** 侧耳倾听; **to keep an ear/eye ~ed** 留心听/看 **3** (make ready for firing) 扳起…的击铁 ‹*firearm*›

Phrasal verb

- **cock up** *vt* [**~ sth. up, ~ up sth.**] Brit colloq 把…搞糟; **how did you manage to ~ up the arrangements?** 你怎么会安排得一塌糊涂?

cockade /kɒˈkeɪd/ *n* [缎带或羽毛结的] 帽子花结

cock-a-doodle-doo /ˌkɒkəˌduːdlˈduː/ *n* [u and c] 喔喔喔; **to go ~** 喔喔叫

cock-a-hoop /ˌkɒkəˈhuːp/ *adj pred* colloq 扬扬得意的; **to be (all) ~ (about** *or* **at sth.)** (为某事物) 感到得意扬扬

cock a leekie soup /ˌkɒkəliːki ˈsuːp/ *n* [u] Brit 鸡肉韭葱汤

cockamamie, cockamamy /ˌkɒkəˈmæmi/ *adj* Amer colloq 荒谬可笑的; **a ~ theory** 荒唐的理论

cock-and-bull story *n* colloq 荒唐的说法

cockatoo /ˌkɒkəˈtuː/ *n* 葵花鹦鹉

cockchafer /ˈkɒktʃeɪfə(r)/ *n* 金龟子

cocked hat *n* (with two points) 卷檐帽; (with three points) 无沿三角帽

cockerel /ˈkɒkərəl/ *n* 小公鸡

cocker spaniel /ˌkɒkə ˈspænjəl/ *n* 可卡犬

cockeyed /kɒkˈaɪd/ *adj* colloq **1** (crooked) 歪向一边的 ‹*picture, hat*› **2** (absurd) 荒谬的 ‹*idea*›

cock: **~fight** *n* 斗鸡; **~fighting** *n* [u] 斗鸡

cockily /ˈkɒkɪli/ *adv* pej colloq 狂妄自大地 ‹*say, act*›

cockiness /ˈkɒkɪnɪs/ *n* [u] pej colloq 狂妄自大

cockle /ˈkɒkl/ *n* **1** Zool 鸟蛤 **2** fig **to warm the ~s of one's heart** 深感欣慰

cockleshell /ˈkɒklʃel/ *n* 鸟蛤壳

cockney /ˈkɒkni/
A *n* **1** [c] (person) 伦敦东区人 **2** [u] (dialect) 伦敦东区方言
B *adj* 伦敦东区人的 ‹*humour, accent*›

> **cockney**
>
> 1\. 伦敦东区人，以性格活泼、幽默著称。cockney 传统上指在出生地能听到博钟（Bow Bells）钟声的人——博钟位于伦敦金融城（City of London）圣玛丽・勒・博（St. Mary-le-Bow）教堂内。伦敦东区以前是贫民窟，因此 cockney 常常也指伦敦的工人阶层，泛指带伦敦口音的人。cockney 含轻蔑或戏谑意味。19 世纪英国诗人约翰・济慈（John Keats）和他的朋友利・亨特（Leigh Hunt）等就曾被轻蔑地称为 Cockney School（伦敦佬派）。
>
> 2\. 伦敦东区方言或口音。发音时常略去 h 音。亦以同韵俚语（▸**rhyming slang**）著称。
>
> 由 cockney 还衍生出一个新的单词 mockney。它是 mock（模仿、嘲弄）和 cockney 的缩合词，指对伦敦东区方言做作的模仿，或者指模仿这种方言的人。

cockpit /ˈkɒkpɪt/ *n* **1** Aviat 驾驶舱 **2** Aut 驾驶座 **3** Naut 舵手座

cockroach /ˈkɒkrəʊtʃ/ *n* 蟑螂

cockscomb /ˈkɒkskəʊm/ *n* 鸡冠

cocksure /ˌkɒkˈʃɔː(r), Amer ˌkɒkˈʃʊər/ *adj* pej 自以为是的 ‹*way, words*›; **to be ~ about sth.** 对某事物过分自信

cocktail /ˈkɒkteɪl/ *n* **1** [c] (drink) 鸡尾酒; **to mix a ~** 调制鸡尾酒 **2** [u and c] Culin 冷盘; **a fruit/shrimp ~** 水果拼盘/大虾冷盘 **3** [u] fig (mix) 混合物; **he was killed by a ~ of drink and drugs** 他因服用了混合了药物的酒而死亡

cocktail: **~ bar** *n* 酒吧间; **~ biscuit** *n* 开胃饼干; **~ cabinet** *n* 酒柜; **~ dress** *n* 女式晚礼服; **~ hour** *n* 鸡尾酒时间; **~ lounge** *n* 酒吧间; **~ party** *n* 鸡尾酒会; **~ sausage** *n* 开胃香肠; **~ shaker** *n* 鸡尾酒摇壶; **~ stick** *n* 取食签; **~ table** *n* Amer 矮茶几; **~ waitress** ▸**p. 409** *n* 鸡尾酒女招待

cock-teaser, cock-tease *ns* taboo sl 狐狸精 pej

cock-up *n* Brit sl 一团糟; **to make a ~ of sth.** 把某事物弄得一团糟

cocky /ˈkɒki/ *adj* colloq pej 狂妄自大的 ‹*person, remark*›; 傲慢的 ‹*attitude, gesture*›; **to be ~ about sth.** 在某事上自以为是

cocoa /ˈkəʊkəʊ/ *n* **1** [u] (powder) 可可粉 **2** [u and c] (drink) 可可茶; **two ~s, please!** 请来两杯可可茶!

cocoa butter *n* [u] 可可油

coconut /ˈkəʊkənʌt/ *n* **1** [c] (seed) 椰子; **~ milk** 椰子汁 **2** [u] (flesh) 椰子肉; **~ oil** 椰油 **3** [c] (tree) 椰子树

coconut: **~ ice** *n* [u] Brit 椰子蜜饯; **~ matting** *n* [u] 椰棕垫; **~ shy** *n* Brit 打椰子游戏

cocoon /kəˈkuːn/
A *n* **1** Zool 茧; **to spin a ~** 结茧; **~ stage** 结茧期 **2** (nest) 安乐窝; **wrapped in a ~ of blankets** 裹在舒适的毯子里 **3** fig 呵护; **a ~ of love** 爱的呵护
B *vt* **1** (wrap) 小心地包裹 ‹*child, object*›; **to ~ a baby in blankets** 小心翼翼地把婴儿裹在毯子里 **2** fig (protect) 保护; **to be ~ed from the world** 与世隔绝; **a ~ed existence** 蚕茧式的生活

COD *abbr* **1** Brit **= cash on delivery** **2** Amer **= collect on delivery** 货到收款

cod /kɒd/ *n* (*pl* **cod**) **1** [c] Zool 鳕鱼 **2** [u] Culin 鳕鱼肉

coda /ˈkəʊdə/ *n* **1** Mus 结尾乐段 **2** Literat 尾声

coddle /ˈkɒdl/ *vt* **1** (pamper) 娇惯 ‹*child*›; 悉心照顾 ‹*patient*› **2** Culin 用文火煮 ‹*eggs*›

code /kəʊd/
A *n* **1** [u and c] (cipher) 密码; **to be in ~** 用密码编写; **to break** *or* **crack the ~** 破译密码; **to speak in ~** fig 说晦涩难懂的行话 **2** [c] (set of rules or laws) 法规 **3** [c] (of behaviour) 规范; **to break the ~** 违反规则; **an unwritten ~** 不成文的准则; **a ~ of practice** 行业规则; **a ~ of ethics** 道德规范 **4** [c] Telecom 区号; **area/country ~** 区号/国家代码 **5** [u] Comput 编码; **assembly/machine ~** 汇编码/机器码
B *vt* 将…编码 ‹*message*›

code book *n* 密码簿

coded /ˈkəʊdɪd/ *adj attrib* **1** Comput 编码的 ‹*message*› **2** fig 间接的 ‹*criticism*›

code dating *n* [u] 代码日期标注

co-defendant *n* 共同被告

codeine /ˈkəʊdiːn/ *n* [u] 可待因 [鸦片提取物，用于镇痛或催眠]

code letter *n* 代码字母

code name
A *n* 代号
B **code-name** *vt* 用代号命名 ‹*operation, spy*›

code: **~ number** *n* 税籍编号; **~ of conduct** *n* 行为规范; **~-sharing** *n* [u] [航空公司之间的] 代码共享; **~-switching** *n* [u] 语码转换; **~word** *n* 暗语

codger /ˈkɒdʒə(r)/ *n* colloq 老家伙; **an old ~** 老头儿

codicil /ˈkəʊdɪsɪl, Amer ˈkɒdəsl/ *n* 遗嘱修改附录

codify /ˈkəʊdɪfaɪ, Amer ˈkɒd-/ *vt* 把…编成法规

coding /ˈkəʊdɪŋ/ *n* **1** [u] Comput 编码 **2** [u] (converting to code) 编成密码 **3** [u] (assigning code) 分配编码 **4** [c] (code) 编号

co-director *n* **1** Theat, Cin 副导演 **2** (of company) 合伙经营者 **3** (of institute) 联执主任

cod-liver oil *n* [u] 鱼肝油

co-driver *n* 副驾驶员

codswallop /ˈkɒdzwɒləp/ *n* [u] Brit colloq pej 胡说八道; **a load of (old) ~** 一派胡言

coed /ˌkəʊˈed/
A *adj* **= coeducational; to go ~** 上男女同校的学校
B *n* Amer dated [在男女同校的学校就读的] 女生

co-edit *vt* 合作编辑

co-editor *n* 合编者

coeducation /ˌkəʊedʒuːˈkeɪʃn/ *n* [u] 男女同校教育

coeducational /ˌkəʊedʒuːˈkeɪʃənl/ *adj* 男女同校的 ‹*school, system*›

coefficient /ˌkəʊɪˈfɪʃnt/ *n* 系数

coerce /kəʊˈɜːs/ *vt* 胁迫; **to ~ sb. into doing sth.** 强迫某人做某事

coercion /kəʊˈɜːʃn, Amer -ʒn/ *n* [u] 胁迫

coercive /kəʊˈɜːsɪv/ *adj* 强制的 ‹*methods, tactics*›

coexist /ˌkəʊɪgˈzɪst/ *vi* **1** (exist together) «*species, illness*» 共存; **to ~ with sth.** 与某事物共存 **2** (get along) «*nations, peoples*» 和平共处

coexistence /ˌkəʊɪgˈzɪstəns/ *n* [u] **1** (existing together) 共存 **2** (getting along) 和平共处

coexistent /ˌkəʊɪgˈzɪstənt/ *adj* **1** (existing together) 共存的 ‹*values, concepts*› **2** (in mutual tolerance) 和平共处的 ‹*nations, peoples*›

C of E *abbr* **= Church of England**

coffee /ˈkɒfi, Amer ˈkɔːfi/
A *n* **1** [u] (drink) 咖啡 **2** [c] (cup) 一杯咖啡; **three ~s, please** 请来三杯咖啡; **black/white ~** 清咖/奶咖 **3** [u] (beans) 咖啡豆; (ground) 研磨咖啡; (powder) 咖啡粉 **4** [u] (shrub) 咖啡树
B *modif* 咖啡色的 ‹*cloth, dress*›

coffee: ~ bag *n* 咖啡袋; **~ bar** *n* 咖啡馆; **~ bean** *n* 咖啡豆; **~ break** *n* 工间休息时间; **~ cake** *n* **1** [u] Brit 咖啡味蛋糕; **2** [c] Amer 咖啡伴侣甜点; **~-coloured** *adj* 咖啡色的; **~ cup** *n* 咖啡杯; **~ filter** *n* 咖啡滤纸; **~ grinder** *n* 咖啡豆研磨机; **~ grounds** *npl* 咖啡渣; **~ house** *n* 咖啡馆; **~ klatch** /ˈkɒfi klætʃ/ *n* Amer 咖啡聚会; **~ machine** *n* **1** (coffee maker) 咖啡机; **2** (vending machine) 自动咖啡售卖机; **~ maker** *n* (electric) 咖啡机; (on stove) 咖啡壶; **~ mill** *n* **= ~ grinder**; **~ morning** *n* Brit [为慈善募捐等而举办的] 咖啡早茶会; **~ percolator** *n* **= percolator**; **~ pot** *n* 咖啡壶; **~ service, ~ set** *ns* 一套咖啡具; **~ shop** *n* **1** (café) 咖啡馆; **2** (shop) 咖啡店; **~ spoon** *n* 咖啡匙; **~ table** *n* 矮茶几; **~-table book** *n* 茶几书籍 [指装帧精美的大开本画册]; **~ whitener** *n* 咖啡代脂粉

coffer /ˈkɒfə(r)/
A *n* (box) 保险柜
B coffers *npl* 金库; **the ~s of the state** 国库

cofferdam /ˈkɒfədæm/ *n* 水下作业箱

coffin /ˈkɒfɪn/ *n* 棺材

cog /kɒg/ *n* **1** lit (tooth) 轮齿; (wheel) 齿轮 **2** fig 不可缺少的小人物; **a ~ in the machine** 大机构中的小成员

cogency /ˈkəʊdʒənsi/ *n* [u] 说服力

cogent /ˈkəʊdʒənt/ *adj* **1** (clear) 中肯的 ‹*logic, reasoning*› **2** (convincing) 有说服力的 ‹*example, defence*›

cogently /ˈkəʊdʒəntli/ *adv* 中肯地 ‹*argue, express*›

cogitate /ˈkɒdʒɪteɪt/ *vi* formal 深思; **to ~ on** *or* **about sth.** 慎重考虑某事物

cogitation /ˌkɒdʒɪˈteɪʃn/ *n* [u] formal 深思

cognac /ˈkɒnjæk/ *n* **1** [u and c] 科尼亚克白兰地 **2** [c] (serving) 一杯科尼亚克白兰地

cognate /ˈkɒgneɪt/
A *adj* **1** formal (related) 同类的 ‹*studies, forms*› **2** Ling 同源的 ‹*words, languages*›; **to be ~ with sth.** 与某词语同源
B *n* 同源词

cognition /kɒgˈnɪʃn/ *n* [u] **1** Psych 认知 **2** Philos 认识

cognitive /ˈkɒgnɪtɪv/ *adj* 认知的; **~ theory/science** 认知理论/科学

cognizance /ˈkɒgnɪzəns/ *n* [u] formal **to take ~ of sth.** 认识到某事物

cognizant /ˈkɒgnɪzənt/ *adj* formal **to be ~ of sth.** 认识到某事物

cognoscenti /ˌkɒgnəˈʃenti/ *npl* 行家

cog: ~ railway *n* 齿轨铁路; **~wheel** *n* 齿轮

cohabit /kəʊˈhæbɪt/ *vi* 同居

cohabitation /ˌkəʊhæbɪˈteɪʃn/ *n* [u] 同居

cohere /kəʊˈhɪə(r)/ *vi* **1** (stick together) «*substance*» 黏合 **2** fig (be consistent) «*ideas*» 连贯

coherence /kəʊˈhɪərəns/ *n* [u] **1** (logical consistency) 连贯性; **to give ~ to sth.** 使某事物有条理 **2** (unity of group) 协调一致

coherent /kəʊˈhɪərənt/ *adj* **1** (logical) 连贯一致的 ‹*policy, thought, behaviour, analysis*› **2** (lucid) 条理清楚的 ‹*account, person*›; **to be barely ~** 几乎语无伦次

coherently /kəʊˈhɪərəntli/ *adv* **1** (logically) 连贯一致地 ‹*speak, think*› **2** (lucidly) 条理清楚地 ‹*talk*›

cohesion /kəʊˈhiːʒn/ *n* [u] **1** (social unity) 团结 **2** (unity of ideas) 一致性; **to lack ~** 前后不一致 **3** (artistic unity) 完整性; **a sense of ~** 整体感 **4** Phys 内聚力

cohesive /kəʊˈhiːsɪv/ *adj* **1** (united) 团结的 ‹*group*› **2** (unifying) 使结合的; **a ~ force** 内聚力

cohort /ˈkəʊhɔːt/ *n* **1** Hist [古罗马的] 步兵队 **2** fig (group) 一伙人

COI *abbr* Brit **= Central Office of Information** 中央新闻署

coiffure /kwɑːˈfʊə(r)/ *n* formal or hum 发型

coil /kɔɪl/
A *vt* 把…盘起 ‹*rope, hair*›; 蜷缩 ‹*body*›; **to be ~ed into a ring** 被绕成一个环
B *vi* «*rope, hair*» 盘起; «*road*» 蜿蜒; «*parade*» 蜿蜒行进; «*person, animal, body*» 蜷缩; **to ~ upwards** «*smoke*» 袅袅升起; **the river ~ed into the distance** 这条河蜿蜒流向远方
C *n* **1** (loops of rope) 卷; (of cables) 盘 **2** (one loop) (of rope, cable) 一圈; (of hair) 一卷; (of snake) 一盘; **smoke rose in ~s** 烟袅袅上升 **3** Elec 线圈 **4** Aut 点火线圈 **5** (contraceptive) 避孕环

Phrasal verb

- **coil up**

A *vi* «*person, animal, body*» 蜷缩
B *vt* [**~ sth. up, ~ up sth.**] 把…盘起 ‹*rope, hair*›; **to ~ up a hose** 盘起软管

coil spring *n* 螺旋弹簧

coin /kɔɪn/
A ▸**p. 174** *n* **1** [u and c] (piece of money) 硬币; **two sides of the same ~** fig 问题的两方面; **the other side of the ~** fig 事情的反面 **2** [u] (money) 金属货币; **to pay sb. back in their own ~** fig 以其人之道还治其人之身
B *vt* **1** (make) 铸造; **a new fifty piece is being ~ed** 新版5角硬币正在铸造中; **to be ~ing it in** Brit colloq 发大财 **2** fig (invent) 创造 ‹*word*›; **to ~ a phrase** iron 套用一句老话

coinage /ˈkɔɪnɪdʒ/ *n* **1** [u] (coins) 硬币; (currency) 货币制度 **2** [c] fig (new word) 新创词语 **3** [u and c] fig (creation of new word) 新词语的创造

coin box *n* **1** (gen) 投币盒 **2** Brit (pay phone) 投币电话

coincide /ˌkəʊɪnˈsaɪd/ *vi* **1** (occur together) «*events, dates*» 同时发生; **our visits will not ~** 我们不能同时去参观了 **2** (meet) «*borders*» 相接 **3** (tally) «*accounts, views*» 相符

coincidence /kəʊˈɪnsɪdəns/ *n* **1** [u and c] (chance) 巧合; **it is a ~ that ...** 碰巧…; **by sheer ~** 纯属巧合; **what a ~!** 真巧啊! **2** [u] formal (concurrence) 同时发生 **3** [u and c] formal (agreement) 相符; **a ~ of views** 观点的一致

coincidental /kəʊˌɪnsɪˈdentl/ *adj* 巧合的

coincidentally /kəʊˌɪnsɪˈdentəli/ *adv* 巧合地

coin: ~-op *n* 投币自助洗衣店; **~-operated** *adj* 投币式的; **a ~-operated game** 投币玩的游戏

coir /ˈkɔɪə(r)/ *n* [u] 椰棕纤维; **~ rope** 椰棕绳

coitus /ˈkəʊɪtəs/ *n* formal 性交; **~ interruptus** 体外射精

Coke® /kəʊk/ *n* [u and c] 可口可乐; **two ~s, please** 请来两份可乐

coke[1] /kəʊk/ *n* [u] (fuel) 焦炭

coke[2] *n* [u] colloq (cocaine) 可卡因

Col. *abbr* **= colonel**

cola /ˈkəʊlə/ *n* [u and c] 可乐

colander /ˈkʌləndə(r)/ *n* 滤盆

cold /kəʊld/ ▸**p. 814**
A *adj* **1** (chilly) 寒冷的 ‹*day, climate, weather, house*›; 冷的 ‹*meal*›; 冰凉的 ‹*metal, floor, hands*›; **~ water** 冷水; **a ~ shower** 冷水浴; **it's going to be a ~ day** 今天天气会很冷; **the soup should be served ~** 汤要凉了再上; **to feel ~** «*person, room, object*» 感觉冷; **the glass felt ~ to the touch** 玻璃摸上去很凉; **to get ~** «*weather, person, food*» 变冷; **your dinner's getting ~** 你的饭都快凉了; **don't let the baby get ~** 别让婴儿着凉; **to keep sth. ~** 冷藏 ‹*food*›; **to be as ~ as ice** «*person, body part, room*» 冰冷; **in ~ blood** 残忍地; **to pour** *or* **throw ~ water on sth.** fig 给…泼冷水 ‹*plan, suggestion*›; **to have** *or* **get ~ feet** fig 打退堂鼓 **2** (creating impression of low temperature) 给人冷感的; **blue is a ~ colour** 蓝色是冷色; **the light is too ~** 这种光线给人的感觉太冷了; **in the ~ light of day** (after a night's sleep) 在大清早 (思维清晰时); (rationally) 冷静后 (再看); **let's wait and see how it looks in the ~ light of day** 我们等冷静下来了再看看情况到底如何 **3** (unemotional, unfriendly) 冷酷的 ‹*person, heart, smile*›; 冷漠的 ‹*expression, look*›; 冷冰冰的 ‹*atmosphere, manner, voice*›; **to be ~ to** *or* **towards sb.** 对某人冷淡; **to leave sb. ~** 激不起某人的兴趣; **football leaves me ~** 我对足球没兴趣 **4** (dispassionate) 冷静的 ‹*reasoning, judgement*› **5** (not recent) 过时的 ‹*news*›; 已变淡的 ‹*scent*›; **the trail has gone ~** 踪迹已变淡 **6** *pred* (in guessing) 猜得离谱的; (in hunting) 远离目标的; **you're getting ~er!** 你越猜越离谱! **7** *pred* colloq (unconscious) **to be out ~** 昏迷不醒; **to knock sb. (out) ~** 打昏某人 **8** *pred* (dead) 尸体变凉的; **she was already ~ when they found her** 当他们找到她时, 她的尸体已经凉了
B *n* **1** [u] (chilliness) 寒冷; **the ~ of winter** 冬天的严寒; **this plant doesn't like the ~** 这种植物不耐寒; **to feel the ~** 对寒冷敏感; **he was shivering with ~** 他冷得直发抖; **to be out in the ~** 待在外面的严寒中; **to come in from** *or* **out of the ~** 进来避寒; fig (return to favour) 重新得宠; (be included) 不再被冷落; **to leave sb. out in the ~** fig 将某人排除在外 **2** [c] Med 感冒; **to have** *or* **get** *or* **catch a ~** 患感冒
C *adv* **1** colloq (without preparation) 无准备地 ‹*speak, perform*›; **they tried to play the piece ~** 他们尝试不排练就演奏这支曲子 **2** Amer 完全地; **his final request stopped her ~** 他最后的请求让她不知所措

cold: ~-blooded *adj* **1** lit 冷血的 ‹*animal*›; **2** fig 冷酷无情的 ‹*murderer, tyrant*›; 残忍的 ‹*act, attack*›; **they were quite ~-blooded about the redundancies** 他们对裁员无动于衷; **~-bloodedly** *adv* 冷酷无情地; **~ call** *n* (visit) 上门推销; (phone call) 电话推销; **~ calling** *n* [u] (visiting) 上门推销; (by phone) 电话推销; **~ chisel** *n* 冷凿; **~ comfort** *n* [u] 不起作用的安慰; **~ cream** *n* [u and c] 冷霜; **~ cuts** *npl* 冷盘肉片; **~ frame** *n* 冷床; **~ front** *n* 冷锋; **~ fusion** *n* [u] 冷核聚变; **~-hearted** *adj* 冷酷无情的 ‹*person, act*›; **~-heartedly** *adv* 冷酷无情地

coldly /ˈkəʊldli/ *adv* **1** (unfeelingly) 冷漠地 ‹*speak, smile*›; **~ polite** 礼貌而冷淡的 **2** (unemotionally) 冷静客观地 ‹*judge, reason*›

coldness /ˈkəʊldnɪs/ *n* [u] **1** (chilliness) (of day, weather, house) 寒冷; (of water, hands) 冰冷 **2** (of

C

colour, light) 寒意; **the ～ of the blue of the walls** 墙壁的蓝色给人的寒意 **3** (lack of emotion, unfriendliness) 冷漠 **4** (dispassionateness) 冷静

cold: ～-pressed *adj* 冷榨的 ‹*oil*›; **～ remedy** *n* 感冒药; **～ room** *n* 冷藏室; **～-shoulder** *vt* 冷落; **～ shoulder** *n* **to give sb. the ～ shoulder** 冷落某人; **～ snap** *n* 寒汛期; **～ sore** *n* 唇疱疹; **～ start** *n* [计算机的] 冷启动; **～ steel** *n* [u] 利器; **～ storage** *n* [u] 冷藏; **to put sth. into ～ storage** lit 冷藏某物; fig 搁置某事物; **～ store** *n* (building) 冷藏库; (room) 冷藏室; **～ sweat** *n* 冷汗; **to be in a ～ sweat about sth.** 由于某事而冒冷汗; **to bring sb. out in a ～ sweat** 把某人吓出一身冷汗; **～ tap** *n* 冷水龙头; **～ turkey** *n* [u] colloq **1** (treatment) 突然戒毒疗法; **to go ～ turkey** 接受突然戒毒治疗; **2** (reaction) 突然戒毒反应; **～ war, C～ War** *n* 冷战; **～ wave** *n* 寒潮

C

coleslaw /'kəʊlslɔː/ *n* [u] 蛋黄酱凉拌菜

colic /'kɒlɪk/ *n* 腹绞痛

colicky /'kɒlɪki/ *adj* 患腹绞痛的

collaborate /kə'læbəreɪt/ *vi* **1** (work or cooperate) 合作; **to ～ with sb. in doing sth.** 与某人合作做某事; **to ～ with sb. (over** *or* **on sth.)** (在某事物上) 与某人合作 **2** pej (cooperate traitorously) 通敌

collaboration /kə,læbə'reɪʃn/ *n* **1** [u and c] (joint work) 合作 **2** [c] (end result) 合作成果 **3** [u] pej (traitorous cooperation) 通敌

collaborative /kə'læbərətɪv/ *adj* 合作的

collaborator /kə'læbəreɪtə(r)/ *n* **1** (gen) 合作者 **2** pej (traitor) 通敌者

collage /'kɒlɑːʒ, Amer kə'lɑːʒ/ *n* **1** [u and c] Art (picture) 拼贴画; (technique) 拼贴艺术 **2** [c] (composition) 大杂烩; **the film is a ～ of various special effects** 这部电影拼凑了各种特技效果

collagen /'kɒlədʒən/ *n* [u] 胶原蛋白

collapse /kə'læps/

A *vi* **1** (give way) «*building, wall*» 倒塌; **the chair ～d under his weight** 椅子被他坐塌了 **2** (fall to ground, faint) 晕倒; (lose control) 支撑不住; **he ～d from loss of blood** 他因失血而虚脱; **to ～ with laughter** 笑得直不起腰 **3** colloq (sit or lie down heavily) 累得倒下; **to ～ into/on to sth.** 累得倒在某物里面/上面 **4** (fail) «*regime, health, system, economy*» 垮掉; «*bank, company, newspaper*» 倒闭; «*deal, talks, relationship*» 破裂; «*case, plan, trial*» 失败; «*hopes*» 破灭; «*government*» 垮台; **to ～ into chaos** 乱成一团 **5** (to drop in value) «*shares, prices, market*» 暴跌 **6** (deflate) «*lung*» 萎陷; «*balloon, cake*» 瘪掉 **7** (fold) «*furniture, equipment, umbrella*» 折叠起来

B *vt* **1** (fold) 折叠 ‹*furniture, equipment, umbrella*› **2** (combine) 合并 ‹*ideas, paragraphs*›

C *n* [u and c] **1** (giving way) 倒塌; **the ～ of the roof** 屋顶的坍塌 **2** (physical or mental breakdown) (illness) 病倒; (falling ill) 晕倒; **she suffered a complete ～** 她彻底崩溃了; **to be in a state of nervous/emotional ～** 处于精神崩溃/情绪失控状态 **3** (failure) (of regime, health, system, economy) 崩溃; (of bank, company, newspaper) 倒闭; (of deal, talks, relationship) 破裂; (of case, plan, trial) 失败; (of hope) 破灭; (of government) 垮台; **to be in a state of total ～** 土崩瓦解 **4** (drop in value) 暴跌 **5** (deflation) (of lung) 萎陷; (of balloon, cake) 瘪掉

collapsible /kə'læpsəbl/ *adj* 可折叠的; **a ～ bed/bike/umbrella** 折叠床/折叠自行车/折叠伞

collar /'kɒlə(r)/

A *n* **1** (on garment) 领子; **to get hot under the ～** fig 发怒; **to have one's ～ felt** fig 被逮住 **2** (for animal) 项圈 **3** Tech (ring) 套管; (bearing seat) 轴承座

B *vt* colloq **1** (capture) 逮住 **2** (waylay) 拦住 **3** (take) 擅自拿走

collarbone /'kɒləbəʊn/ *n* 锁骨

collared /'kɒləd/ *adj* **1** Cloth 带衣领的 ‹*garment*› **2** Zool 戴颈圈的 ‹*animal, bird*›

collar: ～-length *adj* 长及衣领的 ‹*hair*›; **～ size** *n* 衣领尺寸; **～ stud** *n* 领扣

collate /kə'leɪt/ *vt* **1** (compare and combine) 核对 ‹*evidence, information*›; 校勘 ‹*manuscripts, books, reports, editions*›; **to ～ sth. with sth.** 对比某物和某物 **2** Print 检点 ‹*pages*›

collateral /kə'lætərəl/

A *adj* **1** (subordinate) 附带的 ‹*evidence, aim*› **2** Fin 有担保的; **a ～ loan/security** 抵押贷款/抵押品

B *n* [u] 抵押物; **to put up ～ for a loan** 进行抵押贷款

collateral damage *n* [u] [军事行动的] 附带性破坏

collation /kə'leɪʃn/ *n* [u and c] (of evidence, information) 核对; (of manuscripts, books, reports, editions) 校勘

colleague /'kɒliːg/ *n* 同事

collect /kə'lekt/

A *vt* **1** (gather) 收集 ‹*glasses, information, evidence*›; «*animal*» 采集 ‹*leaves, nuts*› **2** (as hobby) 收藏 ‹*stamps, works of art, rare books*› **3** (get control of) 使镇定; **to ～ one's thoughts** 冷静下来; **to ～ one's wits** 镇定思绪 **4** (muster) 积聚起; **to ～ one's courage** 鼓起勇气; **to ～ one's strength** 奋力 **5** (receive) «*surface, container*» 接收 ‹*liquid, powder, gas*›; **I put out a bucket to ～ some rainwater** 我把一个水桶放在外面接些雨水; **a substance that ～s moisture from the air** 一种吸收空气中水分的物质 **6** (accumulate) «*surface*» 积聚 ‹*liquid, dust*›; **this skirt always ～s dog hairs** 这条裙子老是粘狗毛 **7** (get money owed) 收取 ‹*money, debt, tax*›; **the landlord ～s the rent on Fridays** 房东逢周五收房租 **8** (be awarded) 获取 ‹*prize, award, degree*›; **she went up to ～ her prize** 她走上前去领奖; **when will she be able to start ～ing her pension?** 她什么时候能开始领退休金?; **the winner collects £2,000** 优胜者获得 2,000 英镑 **9** (for cause, charity) 募集 ‹*money, donation*› **10** (take away) 收 ‹*empty bottles, rubbish*›; 领取 ‹*goods, parcel*›; **'buyer ～s'** (in small ad) "买家自提"; **to ～ the mail** *or* **post** 取邮件 **11** (pick up) «*person, car*» 接 ‹*person*›; 取 ‹*keys, book*›

B *vi* **1** (come together) 聚集; **by the time the police arrived, a small crowd had ～ed** 警察赶到时, 已经聚集起了一小群人 **2** (accumulate) «*dust, water, gas*» 聚积 **3** (for cause, charity) **to ～ for sb./sth.** 为某人/某事物募捐 **4** colloq (make money) 获得大笔款项

C *v refl* **to ～ oneself** 镇静下来

D *adv* Amer 由接收人付款; **to call (sb.) ～** (给某人) 打由受话人付费的电话

Phrasal verbs

- **collect together** *vt* [**～ sth. together, ～ together sth.**] 收拾
- **collect up** *vt* [**～ sth. up, ～ up sth.**] 把…收放好

collectable /kə'lektəbl/ *adj* **1** (worth collecting) 值得收藏的 ‹*doll, porcelain, prints*› **2** (able to be collected) 可领取的

collectables /kə'lektəblz/ *npl* 收藏品

collect call *n* Amer 受话人付费电话

collected /kə'lektɪd/ *adj* **1** *attrib* (in one edition) 收成全集的; **the ～ works of Charles Dickens** 查尔斯·狄更斯全集 **2** *pred* (calm) 镇静的; **cool, calm, and ～** 冷静镇定, 处之泰然

collecting: ～ box *n* 募捐箱; **～ tin** *n* 募捐罐

collection /kə'lekʃn/ *n* **1** [u] (gathering) 收集; **the ～ of data/solar energy** 数据/太阳能的收集 **2** [c] (assemblage) (of objects) 一批; (of people) 一群; **a large ～ of dictionaries** 许多词典; **an odd ～ of people** 没有共同点的一群人; **a rambling ～ of houses** 杂乱无章的住宅群 **3** [c] (of paintings, stamps etc.) 收藏物; **a ～ of stamps/paintings** 一批邮票/绘画藏品 **4** [c] Fashn 时装系列 **5** [u] (of tax, rent, debts etc.) 收取; **the ～ of taxes** 收税 **6** [c] (of donations) (act of collecting) 募捐; (sum collected) 募集款; **to have** *or* **make a ～ (for sb./sth.)** (为某人/某事物) 募捐; **we had a ～ for Sarah's wedding present** 我们凑份子给萨拉买了结婚礼物; **the ～ raised £650** 募捐筹集到 650 英镑 **7** [c] (in church) 捐施 **8** [u and c] (picking up, fetching) 取走; **you have to pay for ～** (of rubbish) 你得交垃圾清运费; (of mail) 你得交邮件收取费; **the car is ready for ～** 汽车可以提货了

collection: ～ charge *n* 托收手续费; **～ plate** *n* 募捐盘; **～ point** *n* **1** (for parcels, goods) 领取点; **2** (for donations) 募集点; **3** (for recycling) 收运点

collective /kə'lektɪv/

A *adj* **1** (as a group) 集体的 ‹*leadership, decision, action*›; 共同的 ‹*responsibility, effort*› **2** Ling 集合的; **a ～ name** 统称

B *n* **1** (cooperative enterprise) 集体企业 **2** Ling 集合名词

collective: ～ agreement *n* [劳资双方的] 集体协议; **～ bargaining** *n* [u] [劳方组织的] 集体谈判; **～ farm** *n* 集体农庄

collectively /kə'lektɪvli/ *adv* 集体地; **～ owned** 集体所有的; **to be known ～ as ...** 统称为…

collective: ～ noun *n* 集合名词; **～ ownership** *n* [u] 集体所有; **～ security** *n* [u] 集体安全; **～ unconscious** *n* [u] 集体无意识

collectivism /kə'lektɪvɪzəm/ *n* [u] 集体主义

collectivist /kə'lektɪvɪst/

A *adj* 集体主义的 ‹*theory, principle, approach*›; 集体主义制度的 ‹*state, society*›

B *n* 集体主义者

collectivization /kə'lektɪvaɪzeɪʃn/ *n* [u] 集体化

collectivize /kə'lektɪvaɪz/ *vt* 使…集体化 ‹*agriculture, enterprise, land*›

collector /kə'lektə(r)/ *n* **1** (hobbyist) 收藏者; **a stamp ～** 集邮者 **2** (of taxes, rates) 征收者; (of rent, debts, funds) 收款者; **a tax/ticket/rent ～** 收税员/查票员/收租人

collector's item *n* 收藏品

colleen /'kɒliːn/ *n* Ir dated 姑娘

college /'kɒlɪdʒ/ *n* **1** (institution, part of university) 学院 **2** Amer (university) 大学; **to go to ～** 上大学 **3** (vocational training establishment) 职业学校 **4** (professional body) (of doctors, surgeons) 协会; (of midwives, nurses) 社团; **the ～ of cardinals** 枢机团 **5** Brit (private secondary school) 公学; **Winchester/Eton ～** 温切斯特/伊顿公学

college: ～-bound *adj* Amer (studying) 上大学的; (about to go to) 准备上大学的; **～ education** *n* 大学教育; **to have a ～ education** 接受大学教育; **～ of agriculture** *n* 农学院; **～ of education** *n* 教育学院; **～ of further education** *n* Brit 继续教育学院; **～ student** *n* Brit 学院学生; Amer 大学生

collegiate /kə'liːdʒət/ *adj* **1** Brit formal (relating to a college) 大学的 ‹*life, structure*› **2** (having colleges) 设有书院的; **～ system** 书院制; **Oxford is a ～ university** 牛津大学下设若干书院

collide /kə'laɪd/ *vi* **1** (crash together) 碰撞; **I ～d with a tree** 我撞到了一棵树上 **2** (disagree) 冲突; **to ～ over tax cuts** 在减税方面意见不一致

collider /kə'laɪdə(r)/ *n* 粒子加速对撞机

collie /'kɒli/ *n* 柯利牧羊犬

collier /'kɒlɪə(r)/ ▸p. 409 *n* esp Brit dated **1** (miner) 煤矿工人 **2** (ship) 运煤船

colliery /ˈkɒlɪəri/ *n* esp Brit 煤矿 [包括建筑物、设备及工人]

collision /kəˈlɪʒn/ *n* **1** (crash) 碰撞; **a head-on ~ between two trains** 两列火车的迎头相撞; **to come into ~ with ...** 与…发生碰撞 **2** (conflict) 冲突; **her approach will bring her into ~ with the authorities** 她的方式会导致与当局的冲突

collision: ~ course *n* **1** Naut, Aviat 碰撞航向; **the planes were on a ~ course** 两架飞机朝着可能会碰撞的方向航行; **2** fig 导致冲突的轨迹; **to be on a ~ course with sth.** 沿着与某机构有冲突的轨迹; **the government is on a ~ course with the unions** 政府的行事方向可能会与工会发生冲突; **~ damage waiver** *n* [u] 碰撞损失免除险

collocate

A /ˈkɒləkət/ *n* 搭配词; **'left' and 'right' are ~s of 'hand'** left 和 right 可以与 hand 搭配

B /ˈkɒləkeɪt/ *vi* 搭配; **'dry' and 'wet' ~ with 'towel'** dry 和 wet 可以与 towel 搭配

collocation /ˌkɒləˈkeɪʃn/ *n* **1** [u] (combining) 搭配 **2** [c] (phrase) 词组

colloquia /kəˈləʊkwɪə/ *pl* = **colloquium**

colloquial /kəˈləʊkwɪəl/ *adj* 口语的; **he writes in an easy, ~ style** 他用一种轻松的口语体写作

colloquialism /kəˈləʊkwɪəlɪzəm/ *n* 口语用词

colloquially /kəˈləʊkwɪəli/ *adv* **1** (in a conversational manner) 用口语体 ‹*speak, write*› **2** (informally) 非正式地 ‹*call, term*›

colloquium /kəˈləʊkwɪəm/ *n* (*pl* **~s** *or* **colloquia**) 学术研讨会

collude /kəˈluːd/ *vi* 共谋; **to ~ with sb./sth. (in doing sth.)** 与某人/某机构密谋（做某事）

collusion /kəˈluːʒn/ *n* [u] 共谋; **to act in ~ with sb. to do sth.** 与某人密谋做某事

collywobbles /ˈkɒlɪwɒblz/ *npl* colloq hum **1** (nerves) 紧张; **to have** *or* **get the ~** 感到紧张 **2** (indigestion) 肚子疼

Colombia /kəˈlɒmbɪə/ *pr n* 哥伦比亚

Colombian /kəˈlɒmbɪən/ ▸ **p. 503**

A *adj* (of Colombia) 哥伦比亚的; (of the people) 哥伦比亚人的

B *n* (person) 哥伦比亚人

colon¹ /ˈkəʊlən, -lɒn/ *n* Anat 结肠

colon² *n* Ling 冒号

colonel /ˈkɜːnl/ *n* 上校

colonial /kəˈləʊnɪəl/ *adj* 殖民地的; **in the 19th century Britain was a great ~ power** 19 世纪时英国是个殖民大国

colonialism /kəˈləʊnɪəlɪzəm/ *n* [u] 殖民主义

colonialist /kəˈləʊnɪəlɪst/

A *n* 殖民主义者

B *adj* 殖民主义的

colonic /kəˈlɒnɪk/ *adj* 结肠的; **(a course of) ~ irrigation** 灌肠（疗程）

colonist /ˈkɒlənɪst/ *n* 殖民地定居者

colonization /ˌkɒlənaɪˈzeɪʃn, Amer -nɪˈz-/ *n* [u] 殖民化

colonize /ˈkɒlənaɪz/ *vt* **1** (establish colony in) 将…建成殖民地 ‹*country, area*› **2** (appropriate) 将…据为己用; **the retail market has yet to be ~d by the mail-order business** 零售市场尚未被邮购业占领 **3** Biol «*animals*» 在…聚居; «*plants*» 在…大批生长

colonizer /ˈkɒlənaɪzə(r)/ *n* 殖民地开拓者

colonnade /ˌkɒləˈneɪd/ *n* 列柱

colonnaded /ˌkɒləˈneɪdɪd/ *adj* 带列柱的

colony /ˈkɒləni/ *n* **1** (settlement, territory) 殖民地; (inhabitants) 殖民地居民 **2** (group of people) 有相同特点的人群; **a leper ~** 聚居的麻风病患者; **a ~ of sun-worshippers** 一群爱晒太阳的人 **3** (community) 聚居的侨民; **the Italian ~ in New York** 聚居纽约的意大利侨民 **4** Biol 群体; **a vast ~ of ants/seals** 一大群蚂蚁/海豹

color /ˈkʌlər/ *n, vt, vi* Amer = **colour**

Colorado /ˌkɒləˈrɑːdəʊ/ *pr n* 科罗拉多州

Colorado beetle *n* 科罗拉多甲虫

colorant /ˈkʌlərənt/ *n* Amer = **colourant**

coloration /ˌkʌləˈreɪʃn/ *n* [u] [生物天然的] 色彩; **the ~ of the marble/tropical fish** 大理石的花纹/热带鱼的色彩

coloratura /ˌkɒlərəˈtʊərə/ *n* [u] 花腔

colored /ˈkʌləd/ *adj, n* Amer = **coloured**

colorful /ˈkʌləfl/ *adj* Amer = **colourful**

color line *n* Amer = **colour bar**

colossal /kəˈlɒsl/ *adj* **1** (large) 巨大的; **he eats a ~ amount** 他胃口极大 **2** (large-scale) 大规模的 ‹*task, undertaking*›; 巨大的 ‹*problem, mistake*›; 宏大的 ‹*ambition*›

colossus /kəˈlɒsəs/ *n* (*pl* **colossi** /kəˈlɒsaɪ/ *or* **~es**) **1** fig (large person) 巨人; (important person) 大人物; (big thing) 巨物; **a ~ in English 19th century poetry** 一位英国 19 世纪的诗歌巨匠 **2** (statue) 巨型雕像

colostomy /kəˈlɒstəmi/ *n* 结肠造口术; **a ~ bag** 结肠瘘袋

colostrum /kəˈlɒstrəm/ *n* [u] 初乳

colour /ˈkʌlə(r)/ ▸ **p. 134** Brit

A *n* **1** [u and c] (hue) 颜色; **a bright/dark/pale/warm/cold ~** 亮色/深色/浅色/暖色/冷色; **to take the ~ out of sth.** 使某物褪色; **to change ~** 变色; **wait until you've seen the ~ of his money** 等先弄清他是不是真的有钱再说 **2** [u] (not black-and-white) 彩色; **in ~** 彩色的; **a ~ TV/picture** 彩色电视/照片 **3** [u] (vividness) 生动; **the last movement is full of ~** 最后一个乐章非常生动; **to give** *or* **lend ~ to sth.** (authenticity) 使某事物显得可信; (vividness) 使某事物更加生动 **4** [u and c] (paint, cosmetic) 颜料; (dye) 染料; (additive) 色素; **I hope the ~ won't run** 我希望这种颜料不渗色; **hair ~** 染发液; **cheek/eye/lip ~** 腮红/眼影/口红; **to paint sth. in glowing ~s** fig 把某事物描绘得很美好 **5** [u] (complexion) 脸色; **to change ~** (go pale) 面色变苍白; (go red) 脸红; **to bring ~ to sb.'s cheeks, to put ~ into sb.'s cheeks** 使某人脸色红润; **to get one's ~ back** 恢复气色 **6** [u and c] (racial pigmentation) 肤色; **~ prejudice** 肤色歧视

B **colours** *npl* **1** (clothing) (of sports team) 队服; **to show one's true ~s** 露出真面目 **2** Sch, Univ (badge, cap) 校体育运动队队标; **to get ~s, to win one's ~s** 入选运动队 **3** esp Brit (flag) (of a country) 国旗; (of a regiment) 团旗; (of a ship) 船旗; **they saluted the ~s** 他们向国旗敬礼; ▸ **nail B1**

C *vt* **1** (put colour on) 给…着色 ‹*picture, food*›; **to ~ sth. blue** 把某物染成蓝色; **to ~ one's hair** 染发 **2** pej (prejudice) 影响 ‹*opinion, judgement, attitude*› **3** pej (enhance) (by exaggeration) 渲染 ‹*account, excuse*›; (by distortion) 歪曲 ‹*account*›; **she ~ed her story with an exaggerated description of the attack** 她夸大其词地描述那次袭击，从而使她的故事更加生动

D *vi* **1** (change colour) 变色 **2** (go red) **to ~ (up)** 脸红; **to ~ (up) at sth.** 听到…脸红 ‹*laughter, applause*›; **to ~ (up) with sth.** 因…而脸红 ‹*anger, embarrassment*›

Phrasal verb

- **colour in** *vt* [**~ sth. in, ~ in sth.**] 给…上色

colourant /ˈkʌlərənt/ *n* Brit 染色剂

colour: ~ bar *n* 种族歧视; **~-blind** *adj* 色盲的; **~ blindness** *n* [u] 色盲

colour code

A *n* 色码

B **colour-code** *vt* 给…标色码

colour-coded *adj* 标有色码的

coloured /ˈkʌləd/ Brit

A *adj* **1** lit 彩色的; **a brightly ~ shirt** 色彩鲜艳的衬衣 **2** fig (exaggerated, emotive) 夸张的; **a highly ~ account** 过分夸张的陈述 **3** **Coloured** dated offensive (non-white) 有色人种的 **4** **Coloured** S Afr 混血种的

B **Coloured** *n* **1** dated offensive 有色人种的人 **2** S Afr 混血人

C **coloureds** *npl* (laundry) 有色织物

D **-coloured** *combining form* 有…色的; **copper ~ leaves** 红棕色的叶子

colour: ~-fast *adj* 不褪色的; **~ filter** *n* 彩色滤光片

colourful /ˈkʌləfl/ *adj* Brit **1** lit 色彩鲜艳的 ‹*fabric, clothes*›; 五彩缤纷的 ‹*garden, picture*›; 绚丽的 ‹*scene*› **2** fig (vivid, lively) 丰富多彩的 ‹*life, career*›; 引人入胜的 ‹*story, account*› **3** fig (interesting, amusing) 有趣的 ‹*person, character*›

colourfully /ˈkʌləfəli/ *adv* Brit 色彩鲜艳地

colouring /ˈkʌlərɪŋ/ *n* Brit **1** [u] (gen) 色调; (of plant, animal, pattern) 色彩 **2** [u] (complexion) 脸色; (of hair) 发色; (of skin) 肤色 **3** [u] (colouring in) 着色 **4** [u and c] (dye) (for hair) 染剂; (for food) 色素

colouring book *n* 涂色图册

colourless /ˈkʌləlɪs/ *adj* Brit **1** lit 无色的 ‹*liquid, gas, substance*› **2** (pale) 苍白的 ‹*face, cheeks, lips*›; (dull) 暗淡的 ‹*drink, clothes*› **3** fig (uninteresting) 乏味的 ‹*story, account*›; 无聊的 ‹*life, person*›

colour: ~ magazine *n* 彩色杂志; **~ scheme** *n* 色彩设计; **~ sense** *n* 色彩感; **~ sergeant** *n* 掌旗军士; **~ set** *n* 彩色电视机; **~ supplement** *n* Brit 彩色增刊; **~ television** *n* 彩色电视机; **~way** *n* 配色

colt /kəʊlt/ *n* **1** (horse) 雄马驹 **2** (boy) 新手 **3** Brit Sport 年轻队员 **4** **Colt®** (pistol) 科尔特左轮手枪

coltish /ˈkəʊltɪʃ/ *adj* 无拘无束的 ‹*behaviour, nature*›

columbine /ˈkɒləmbaɪn/ *n* 耧斗菜

Columbus Day /kəˈlʌmbəs deɪ/ *n* Amer 哥伦布纪念日

column /ˈkɒləm/ *n* **1** Archit 柱子 **2** (moving line) 纵队; **we walked in a ~** 我们排成纵队行进; **a long ~ of cars** 一长列车 **3** (vertical mass of air, smoke, steam) 柱状物; **a ~ of smoke** 烟柱 **4** (vertical arrangement) 列; **to borrow one from the tens ~** 从十位数借一 **5** Journ 专栏; **letters ~** 读者来信栏

column inch *n* 栏英寸 [报刊上横占一栏纵占一英寸的篇幅]

columnist /ˈkɒləmnɪst/ *n* 专栏作家

coma /ˈkəʊmə/ *n* **1** Med 昏迷; **to be in/go into a ~** 处于/陷入昏迷状态; **to come out of a ~** 从昏迷中醒来 **2** fig (sleepy state) 昏昏欲睡; **to be in a drunken ~** 醉得不省人事

comatose /ˈkəʊmətəʊs/ *adj* **1** Med 昏迷的 **2** fig 昏昏欲睡的

comb /kəʊm/

A *n* **1** (for combing hair) 梳子; (for fixing in hair) 压发梳; **a fine-toothed/wide-toothed ~** 细齿/宽齿梳子 **2** (act) 梳头; **to give one's hair a ~** 梳一下头发 **3** (honeycomb) 蜂巢 **4** (cock's crest) 鸡冠

B *vt* **1** 梳理 ‹*hair, wool*› **2** (search) 彻底搜查 ‹*area, territory*›

Phrasal verbs

- **comb out** *vt* [**~ out sth., ~ sth. out**] 梳通 ‹*hair, knot*›; 梳掉 ‹*lice, fleas*›
- **comb through** *vt* [**~ through sth.**] 彻底搜查

combat /ˈkɒmbæt/

A *n* [u and c] 战斗; **in ~** 在战斗中

B *vt* (*pres p etc.* **-tt-**) (struggle against) 与…战斗; (prevent or control) 对付; **measures to ~ crime/inflation/disease** 防止犯罪/通货膨胀/疾病的措施

combat aircraft *n* 战斗机

C

combatant /'kɒmbətənt/
A *n* 参战者
B *adj* 参战的

combat: ~ **duty** *n* [u] 战时服役; **to be on ~ duty** 参加战斗; ~ **fatigue** *n* [u] 战斗疲劳症; ~ **fatigues** *npl* 迷彩服

combative /'kɒmbətɪv/ *adj* 好斗的; **to be in a ~ mood** 斗志昂扬

combat: ~ **jacket** *n* 作战服; ~ **mission** *n* 战斗任务; ~ **troops** *npl* 作战部队; ~ **zone** *n* 战区

combe /ku:m/ *n* Brit = **coomb**

combination /,kɒmbɪ'neɪʃn/ *n* **1** [c] (two or more things together, mixture) 混合体; **the weather was a ~ of bitter cold and sun** 那天天气既有阳光又很寒冷; **for a ~ of reasons** 由于种种原因 **2** [u] (linking, mixing) 混合; **in ~ with ...** 与…结合地; **the producer, in ~ with the designer, has achieved a miracle** 生产商与设计师联手创造了奇迹 **3** [c] (sequence) 组合; **the canvasses may be arranged in any number of ~s** 这些船帆可以进行多种组合 **4** [c] Sport 组合动作; **a good uppercut/hook ~** 漂亮的上钩拳/勾拳连击 **5** [c] (for lock) 密码组合 **6** [c] (motorcycle and sidecar) 跨斗摩托车

combination lock *n* 密码锁

combine
A /kəm'baɪn/ *vt* **1** (pair up, link) 使结合; (mix) 使合并; (cooperate) 使合作; **to ~ sth. with** *or* **and sth.** 将某事物与某事物结合在一起; **to ~ business with pleasure** 寓工作于娱乐; **to ~ forces to do sth.** lit 协同作战; fig 合力做某事 **2** Culin 混合 ‹*ingredients*› **3** Chem 使化合
B /kəm'baɪn/ *vi* **1** (go together) «*people, group(s)*» 联合; «*styles, factors*» 结合; «*colour(s)*» 搭配; **her black top ~s well with her red skirt** 她的黑上衣与红裙子很搭配; **they ~d to buy her a present** 他们凑份子给她买了件礼物 **2** Chem «*chemical substance(s)*» 化合; **oxygen ~s with haemoglobin** 氧能与血红蛋白结合
C /'kɒmbaɪn/ *n* **1** Comm 联合企业 **2** Agric = **combine harvester**

combined /kəm'baɪnd/ *adj* **1** (joint) 联合的; **a ~ operation** Mil 联合作战; fig 联合行动; **a ~ effort** 协力 **2** (in one) 多功能组合的; **a ~ washer and dryer** 洗衣干衣机 **3** (total) 合计的; **two men whose ~ age is 150** 两个加在一起 150 岁的男人 **4** (put together) 合在一起的; **the ~ effects/forces of ...** …的共同作用/力量

combined: ~**-cycle** *adj* 联合循环的; ~ **drug therapy** *n* [u] 复合药物疗法; ~ **honours** *npl* + *v sing or pl* (degree) 联合荣誉学位; (degree course) 联合荣誉学位课程; ~ **pill** *n* 复合避孕片; **to be on the ~ pill** 服用复合避孕片

combine harvester *n* 联合收割机

combining form *n* 构词成分

combo /'kɒmbəʊ/ *n* colloq **1** Mus 小型乐队 **2** Amer (food combination) 套餐; **a steak and chicken ~ platter** 牛排鸡肉套餐

combust /kəm'bʌst/
A *vi* 烧掉
B *vt* 烧 ‹*waste, fuel*›

combustible /kəm'bʌstəbl/ *adj* **1** (able to burn) 可燃的 **2** fig (fiery) 易激动的 ‹*temperament*›

combustion /kəm'bʌstʃn/ *n* [u] 燃烧; ~ **point/plant** 燃点/燃烧装置

come /kʌm/ ▸**p. 82**
A *vi* (*pt* **came**, *pp* **come**) **1** (move towards) 来; **(I'm) coming!** (我) 来了! ; **to ~ home** 回家; **to ~ to sb.** 来到某人跟前; **to ~ to the door/phone** 过来开门/接电话; **to ~ by sth.** «*letter*» 通过…寄来 ‹*airmail, special delivery*›; **to ~ down/up sth.** «*person*» 下/上 ‹*stairs*›; «*person, vehicle*» 沿…下来/上来 ‹*street*›; **he fell coming down the ladder** 他从梯子上跌了下来; **a bus came up the hill** 一辆公交车开上了山坡; **to ~ into sth.** 进入 ‹*house, garden*›; **a train's coming into the station** 火车正在进站; **to ~ past** «*procession, car*» 经过; **to ~ from school/work** 从学校/上班的地方过来; **a ball came over the fence** 一个球越过栅栏飞来; **to ~ through sth.**

Colours

■ In Chinese, in some cases 色 (colour) may follow the colour word, but sometimes it may be omitted:

What colour is it? — It's red
= 是什么色的? —— 红的 / 红色
or 是什么颜色的? —— 红色

I painted the table brown
= 我把桌子漆成了棕色

She dyed her hair red
= 她把头发染成了红色

a white jacket
= 白夹克
or 白色的夹克

black trousers
= 黑裤子
or 黑色的裤子

blue sky
= 蓝天

yellow signs
= 黄色标志

■ In English, colour words can act as nouns as well as adjectives (see the examples above). In Chinese, colour words are always adjectives and have different meanings when used as nouns. For example, 蓝 used as a noun means 'indigo plant' (and not 'blue'):

I like pink
= 我喜欢粉红色

Black suits her
= 黑色很适合她

He is dressed in white
= 他穿着白衣服

The girl in purple is my classmate
= 穿紫色衣服的女孩是我同班同学

■ In English, some colour words (eg black, yellow, grey) can also function as verbs. Other colour nouns are transformed into verbs by adding the suffix -en (eg blacken, whiten, redden). In Chinese, according to context, colour nouns can be combined with the verbs like 变, 发, 涂, 熏, 刷, etc.:

The photo has yellowed
= 照片已变黄了
or 照片已发黄了

He blacked his face
= 他把脸涂黑了
or 他把脸抹黑了

The furniture was blackened with soot
= 家具被煤烟熏黑了

I whitened my trainers
= 我把运动鞋刷白了

■ Some English colour words have their exact equivalent in Chinese. However in certain contexts these English words are translated completely differently into Chinese:

a grey coat
= 灰色大衣

Her hair has greyed a lot
= 她的头发已花白

brown hair
= 棕色头发

brown sugar
= 红糖

black hair
= 黑头发

black tea
= 红茶

blue flags
= 蓝色旗子

blue movies
= 黄色电影 (黄色 suggests something pornographic or obscene in Chinese)

white shirts
= 白衬衫

white coffee
= 牛奶咖啡

Shades of colour

■ Degrees of colour intensity such as 'pale', 'light', 'dark' and 'bright' are expressed in Chinese as in the following examples:

light green
= 浅绿
or 淡绿
or 嫩绿

dark green
= 深绿
or 暗绿
or 墨绿

bright green
= 亮绿
or 明绿
or 鲜绿

■ In Chinese, 色 or a colour word can be added to nouns like 'chocolate', 'strawberry', etc. to describe a particular colour, for example, 苹果色, 枣红, 葡萄紫, etc. Hyphens are never used in Chinese:

apple-green tablecloths
= 苹果绿桌布
or 苹果色桌布

a sky-blue shirt
= 天蓝色衬衫

chocolate-brown-coloured trousers
= 巧克力色裤子

■ In English, the suffix '-ish' is used to indicate approximation to a certain colour. There is no exact equivalent in Chinese. However, 略带 or 发 (eg 略带紫色 and 发紫) can be used before the colour word to suggest this meaning:

The pearl necklace is a greenish colour
= 这条珍珠项链略带绿色
or 这条珍珠项链有点发绿

穿越…过来 ‹*town, tunnel*›; 穿过…进来 ‹*window, letterbox*›; **the rain is coming through my coat** 雨水浸透了我的外衣; **tears came to his eyes** 泪水涌上了他的双眼; **to ~ together** 到一起; **to ~ limping down the stairs** 一瘸一拐地走下楼梯; **to ~ streaming through sth.** «*light*» 从…泻入 ‹*glass, door*›; **to not know whether one is coming or going** 不知所措 **2** (approach) 来做; **to ~ for/about sth.** 为某事物而来; **I've ~ about the ad** 我是为广告的事来的; **to ~ and do sth.** 来做某事; **~ and help me move the bed** 过来帮我搬一下床; **to ~ for sb.** 来找某人; **the police came for him** 警察来抓他; **she came to me for advice/sympathy/money** 她来征求我的意见/寻求我的同情/找我借钱; **to ~ to sb.'s assistance** *or* **aid** 来帮助某人; **to ~ close** *or* **near** 接近; **to ~ close to doing sth.** 差点做某事; **he came close to a breakdown** 他快要精神崩溃了; **that doesn't ~ anywhere near what I asked for** 这离我想要的差远了 **3** (arrive) 来到; **to ~ to sth.** 来到 ‹*place*›; **have any letters ~?** 有信吗?; **winter has ~ early** 冬天来得早; **wisdom ~s with age** 年长智慧增; **opportunities that ~ your way** 到你跟前的机会; **happier days to ~** 未来的幸福日子; **it came as a shock/surprise** 这事令人震惊/惊讶; **to ~ as sth.** (to a party) 打扮成某种样子出现; **to ~ and go** (be intermittent) 断断续续; (be transitory) 转瞬即逝 **4** (be due) 应到来; **to take what's coming to one** 认命; **to get what's coming to one** 遭到报应; **he had it coming (to him)** 他遭报应了; **your turn will ~** 总会轮到你的; **he has a lot of money coming to him** 他将继承一大笔钱 **5** colloq (happen) 发生; **how ~?** 怎么会呢?; **how ~ you never married?** 你怎么一直没结婚呢?; **~ what may** 不管怎样; **~ to think of it ...** 现在看来… **6** (attend) 来参加; **to ~ to sth.** 来参加 ‹*event*›; **~ to tea on Friday** 星期五来喝茶; **thank you for coming** formal 谢谢光临; **~ as you are** 你可以穿便装出席 **7** (accompany sb.) 一起去; **to ~ and do sth. with sb.** 和某人一起去做某事; **~ skating with us** 和我们一起去溜冰吧 **8** (travel) 行进; **we've ~ 200 miles** 我们已经走了 200 英里; **have you ~ far?** 你走了很远吗? **9** (reach) **to ~ to sth.** 到达某处; **the dress came to her ankles** 连衣裙长及她的脚踝 **10** (be available) 可提供; **to ~ in different styles/colours** 提供各种样式/颜色; **the T-shirt ~s in three sizes** 这种 T 恤有 3 个尺码出售; **to ~ complete with sth.** 配以某物出售; **new cars don't ~ cheap** 新车都不便宜 **11** (end up) 达到 [某程度]; **to ~ to like/dislike sth.** 渐渐开始喜欢/讨厌某事物; **to ~ to be known as ...** 后来被称为… **12** (start) 开始; **when I came to open the window, I found it was jammed** 我要开窗的时候发现它被卡住了; **when you ~ to think of it, it's not so surprising** 仔细想一想，其实不足为奇 **13** (become) 变得; **my shoelaces have ~ undone** 我的鞋带松开了; **it'll all ~ right in the end** 最后一切都会好起来的 **14** (be) **to ~ easily to sb.** 对某人来说很轻松; **I did what came naturally** 我自自然然便这么做了; **he's as clever as they ~** colloq 他聪明极了; **as it ~s** 随便 **15** (be situated) **to ~ first/second** (in ranking) 名列第一/第二; (in importance) 最重要/居其次; **I came top in maths** colloq 我数学考了第一; **to ~ a close second** 屈居第二; **family ~s first; work ~s second** 家庭放在首位，工作其次; **to ~ in the first act/chapter** 出现在第一幕/章 **16** colloq (have orgasm) 达到性高潮; (ejaculate) 射精 **17** **~ again?** colloq (asking for repetition) 再说一遍?

B *vt* (*pt* **came**, *pp* **come**) Brit pej colloq (act) 假装; **she came the helpless female** 她装得像个无助的女人; **don't ~ the innocent with me!** 别在我面前扮无辜!

C *n* [u] colloq (semen) 精液

D *prep* colloq 到…时; **it'll be a year ~ June** 到六月份就有一年了

E *excl* **1** (disapprovingly) **~ now, you know that's not true** 得了吧，你知道那不是真的 **2** (reassuringly) **~ now, don't be afraid** 好啦，别怕

Phrasal verbs

- **come about** *vi* **1** (happen) 发生; **how did the discovery ~ about?** 这一发现是如何产生的? **2** Naut 转向
- **come across**

A *vi* **1** (be conveyed) «*idea, feeling*» 得以传达; **his meaning didn't ~ across** 他的意思没说清楚; **her love of animals came across** 她表现出了对动物的关爱 **2** (give impression) 留下印象; **he came across badly/well** 他给人留下了很坏/很好的印象; **she came across as honest/an expert** 她给人的印象很诚实/是个行家

B *vt* [**~ across sb./sth.**] **1** (encounter) 遇见 ‹*person*›; 遇到 ‹*story, problem*› **2** (by chance) 碰到 ‹*old friend*›; 偶然发现 ‹*lost object*›

- **come after**

A *vt* [**~ after sb./sth.**] **1** 追赶; **he came after me with a gun** 他拿着枪来追我 **2** (be situated) 位于…之后; (in importance) 不如…重要

B *vi* **1** (follow) 在…之后进行 **2** (succeed) 是继承人

- **come along** *vi* **1** (arrive) 到达 **2** (attend) **to ~ along to** 来参加 ‹*event*›; **~ along if you're free** 你有空的话一定要来 **3** **~ along!** (hurry) 快点!; (come here) 过来!; (keep going) 加油! **4** **~ along with ...** (accompany) 与…一起来 **5** (turn up) «*person, fame*» 出现; **if the chance ~s along** 一旦有机会; **to wait for success to ~ along** 等待成功的到来 **6** (make progress) «*student, skill*» 进步; «*injury, invalid*» 好起来; «*plant, garden*» 生长; «*project*» 进展; **how's the dinner/thesis coming along?** 晚饭吃得/论文写得怎么样了?; **my new play isn't coming along very well** 我的新剧本写得不太顺利
- **come apart** *vi* **1** (fall apart) «*toy, device*» 破碎; «*shoes, clothes*» 裂开; «*bundle*» 散开; **the camera came apart in my hands** 照相机在我手中散架了 **2** (be designed to be dismantled) «*toy, machine*» 可拆卸; **the bed ~s apart** 这张床可以拆卸 **3** (be separable) «*pages, components*» 可分开
- **come around** *vi* esp Amer = **come round**
- **come at** *vt* [**~ at sb./sth.**] **1** (rush towards) «*attacker*» 向…扑来 **2** fig (be directed at) «*questions, facts*» 向…涌来; «*abuse, complaints*» 向…袭来 **3** (approach) 考虑
- **come away** *vi* **1** (leave) 离开 **2** (move away) 走开; **~ away from the window!** 离开窗口! **3** (end up) **to ~ away disappointed/with a feeling of guilt** 失望/内疚地离开 **4** (become detached) «*knob, wallpaper*» 脱落; «*meat on bone*» 分离; **the shelf has ~ away from the wall** 架子从墙上掉下来了
- **come back** *vi* **1** (return) 回来; **~ back soon!** 早点回来!; **to ~ back home** 回家; **to ~ back to sb.** 回到某人身边 **2** (turn back) «*letter, person*» 返回 **3** (visit again) 再来 **4** (recur) «*feeling*» 再次出现; «*rash, fever*» 复发; **the colour is coming back to her cheeks** 她的脸上又有了血色; **warm weather should ~ back next week** 下周天气又将回暖 **5** (recover) «*person, team*» 扳回; **to ~ back from a losing position** 扭转不利局面 **6** (be recalled) «*event*» 被回想起来; «*memory, skill, language*» 恢复 **7** (reply) 回应; (in writing) 回复; **to ~ back with a better offer** 以更优厚的报价答复; **to ~ back with a sharp reply** 给予尖锐反驳 **8** (be popular again) «*fashion*» 再度流行; **miniskirts have ~ back** 超短裙又开始流行了 **9** (be restored) «*system, law*» 恢复; «*regime*» 复辟; **capital punishment will never ~ back** 死刑将永不恢复 **10** (after death) 复活; **to ~ back as sth.** 来生做某物
- **come back to** *vt* [**~ back to sth.**] 回到; **to keep coming back to the same topic** 总是回到同一个话题; **to ~ back to what you were saying, ...** 回到你刚才所说的问题，…
- **come before** *vt* [**~ before sb./sth.**] (be presented for discussion or decision) «*question, case*» 交由…讨论 ‹*panel, board*›; **to ~ before the court/judge** 提交法庭/法官审理
- **come between** *vt* [**~ between sb. and sb.**] **1** (divide) «*person, belief*» 使失和; **don't let this ~ between us** 别因此伤了我们的和气 **2** (prevent from achieving, pursuing) 妨碍; **to let a problem ~ between sb. and sth.** 因一个问题而妨碍某人做某事; **nothing ~s between me and my football!** 没什么能阻碍我对足球的喜爱!
- **come by**

A *vi* **1** colloq (visit) 串门; **to ~ by for a chat** 来这里聊聊天; **you must ~ by with the baby** 你一定要带着宝宝来坐坐 **2** (get past) «*vehicle, person*» 过去; **do you want to ~ by?** 你想过去吗?; **let the car ~ by** 让车先过去

B *vt* [**~ by sth.**] **1** (call at) 来…一趟; **can you ~ by the office on your way home?** 你回家时能顺便来办公室一趟吗? **2** (get) 获得 ‹*fame, success*›; 得到 ‹*money, wealth, property*›; **to ~ by an injury** 受伤; **hard to ~ by** 很难找到

- **come down** *vi* **1** (move lower) «*person, blind, cable car*» 下来; **to ~ down from sth.** 从某处下来; **what goes up must ~ down** 怎么来的还得怎么去 **2** Theat «*curtain*» 落下 **3** Meteorol «*rain, mist*» 降下; **to ~ down in torrents** 大雨滂沱; **the fog came down** 起雾了 **4** Aviat (land) «*pilot, plane*» 着陆; (crash) 坠落 **5** (fall) «*tree*» 倒下; «*house*» 倒塌; «*hem*» 垂下; **to ~ down in a storm** 在暴风雨中倒塌 **6** (be demolished) 被推倒 **7** (be removed) «*picture, curtains*» 被摘下; **it's time the picture came down** 该把那幅画拿下来了 **8** (from north) 南下; (from larger place) 下来; **to ~ down for a few days** 过来住几天; **to ~ down from London** 从伦敦过来 **9** **to ~ down to sth.** (reach) «*hair, dress*» 垂及; **his trousers barely came down to his ankles** 他的裤脚刚及脚踝 **10** (decrease) «*temperature, pressure, demand*» 下降; «*price*» 下跌; **to ~ down from 5% to 1%** 从 5% 降到 1% **11** (be passed on) «*tradition, property*» 传下来; **to ~ down to sb.** 传给某人; **sth. that has ~ down through the ages** 世代流传的某事物; **to ~ down from the Middle Ages** 从中世纪流传下来 **12** Admin (decide) 决定; **to ~ down against sb.** 宣布反对某人 **13** Brit Univ dated [尤指从牛津或剑桥大学] 毕业
- **come down on** *vt* [**~ down on sb./sth.**] (rebuke) 斥责; (criticize) 指责; (penalize) 处罚; (punish) 惩罚; ▸**ton 1**
- **come down to** *vt* [**~ down to sth.**] 可归结为; **it ~s down to ...** 实质上是…; **what it came down to was that ...** 归结起来就是…
- **come down with** *vt* [**~ down with sth.**] 生…病
- **come forward** *vi* **1** (move to front) 走上前来; (towards speaker) 过来 **2** (step up) **to ~ forward as** 主动来当 ‹*witness, volunteer*›; **to ~ forward to join sth.** 前来参加某事; **to ~ forward with** 主动提供 ‹*information, offer*›; **to ~ forward to give evidence** 站出来作证
- **come from** *vt* [**~ from sth.**] **1** (be obtained from) «*substance*» 由…制成; (be produced in) «*product*» 产自; **to ~ from far and wide** 来自四面八方; **wine ~s from grapes** 葡萄酒是用葡萄酿制的; **the fabric ~s from China** 这种布料产自中国 **2** (be derived from) «*word*» 源于 ‹*language*›; **to ~**

C

from Old English 源自古英语 [3] (originate from or in) «*song, quotation*» 出自 ‹*book, musical, collection*›; «*person, object*» 来自 ‹*place*›; «*noise, smell*» 从…传来 ‹*place*›; «*attitude, style*» 源于 ‹*experience, era*›; **coming from him, that's quite a compliment!** 从他嘴里说出来，那可是相当高的赞誉呢！; **where do you ~ from?** 你是哪里人？ [4] (be descended from) 出身于 [5] **I see where you're coming from** colloq 我明白你的意思了

- **come in** *vi* [1] (enter) 进来; **~ in!** 请进! [2] (penetrate) «*water*» 渗入; «*wind, air*» 进入; **rain came in through a hole** 雨水从洞里漏进来了 [3] (towards land) «*tide*» 上涨; «*flotsam, smell*» 上岸; **a cool wind coming in from the sea** 海上吹来的一阵凉风 [4] (arrive) «*train, plane, ship*» 到达; **has the Glasgow train ~ in yet?** 从格拉斯哥来的列车到站了没有? [5] (finish in race) 取得…名次; **she came in third** 她获得第三名 [6] (be earned) 被挣得; **money coming in from investments** 投资所得的收入 [7] (be received) «*letter, report*» 送达; **the telephone bill hasn't ~ in yet** 电话账单还没收到; **letters came in from all over the country** 信从全国各地寄来 [8] (return) 回来; (go home) 回家 [9] Sport «*batsman*» 开球 [10] Pol «*candidate*» 当选; «*party*» 开始执政 [11] (become popular) «*fashion*» 流行; **to ~ in in the 1960s** 流行于20世纪60年代 [12] (come into use) 开始被采用 [13] (be available) 到货; (be in season) 上市; **winter clothes ~ in as early as August** 冬装早在八月就已到货; **strawberries don't ~ in until June** 草莓要到六月才上市 [14] (start off) 开始 [15] (interject) 插话; **let me ~ in here ...** 说到这儿我来插句话吧… [16] Telecom (reply) 回答; **~ in, please** 请回答 [17] (participate) 参加; **to ~ in on sth.** 参与 ‹*deal, venture*›; **to ~ in on a project** 加入某项目 [18] colloq (serve a purpose) 起作用; **where does Sue ~ in?** 苏与此有何关系？; **we need A, B, and C — where does C ~ in?** 我们需要A、B和C——要C干嘛？ [19] (prove to be) **to ~ in handy** *or* **useful** «*item, skill*» 会有用; **to ~ in handy** *or* **useful as sth.** «*item, skill*» 可派上某用场
- **come in for** *vt* [~ in for sth.] 受到 ‹*criticism, praise*›
- **come into** *vt* [~ into sth.]
  [1] (inherit) 继承; **to ~ into a fortune** 继承一笔财产 [2] (be relevant) **to ~ into it** «*skill, age, quality*» 重要; **good health also ~s into it** 身体健康也很重要
- **come of** *vt* [~ of sth.] 是…的结果; **no good will ~ of this** 这不会有好结果的; **this is what ~s of being soft-hearted** 这就是心软的下场
- **come off**

A *vi* [1] (fall off) «*hat, button, cover*» 掉下; «*rider*» 摔下 [2] (become detached) «*knob, wheel*» 脱落; «*paint, wallpaper*» 剥落; **the label won't ~ off** 标签撕不下来; **to ~ off on sth.** «*lipstick*» 印到…上 ‹*collar*› [3] (be removed) «*clothes*» 被脱掉; «*lid, hood, glasses*» 被取下; **my ring won't ~ off** 我的戒指脱不下来了 [4] (wash off) «*stain, writing*» 被去掉; **to ~ off with a damp cloth** «*mark*» 被用湿布擦去; **indelible ink doesn't ~ off** 不褪色墨水是擦不掉的 [5] (on exit road) 驶离公路; **to ~ off at junction 2** 在2号岔口驶下高速公路 [6] Sport 被换下场 [7] (take place) «*event*» 举行; «*show*» 举办; «*deal, merger*» 发生; **did your trip to France ever ~ off?** 你的法国之旅成行了吗？ [8] colloq (fare) **to ~ off worst/best** 彻底失败/大获全胜; **to ~ off the winner/loser** 成为赢家/输家; **we came off quite well in that deal** 我们那笔生意谈得不错 [9] colloq (succeed) «*attempt, trick*» 成功 [10] Theat, TV (stop) 停演; **to ~ off after two weeks** «*show*» 两周后停演

B *vt* [~ off sth.]
[1] (fall off) «*cover*» 从…上掉下 ‹*bed*›; «*button*» 从…上掉落 ‹*device, appliance*›; «*rider*» 摔下 ‹*horse, cycle, motor cycle*› [2] (leave) 驶离 ‹*road*›; **to ~ off the motorway at ...** 在…处驶离高速公路 [3] (become detached from) «*knob, label*» 从…上脱落 ‹*door, clothes*›; «*paint, wallpaper*» 从…上剥落 ‹*wall*› [4] (be detachable from) «*top, hood*» 可从…卸下; **do the legs ~ off the table?** 桌子腿可以卸下来吗？; **the lid won't ~ off the jar** 坛子盖打不开 [5] (be washed from) «*mark, writing*» 从…上被除去 ‹*clothes, paper*›; **the stains came off his shirt** 他衬衣上的污渍洗掉了 [6] (be deducted from) «*amount, money*» 从…中被减去 ‹*price, wages*›; **3% has ~ off interest rates** 利率已下降了3% [7] (stop work on) 停下 ‹*project*›; **to ~ off the case** 停下手头的案子 [8] colloq (stop using) **to ~ off drugs/alcohol** 戒毒/戒酒 [9] **~ off it!** colloq (expressing disagreement) 别胡说！

- **come on**

A *vi* [1] Theat, Mus «*band, actor*» 登台; Sport «*player*» 上场; **to ~ on for** *or* **in place of sb.** 顶替某人上场 [2] (follow) 跟随; **you'd better go: I'll ~ on later** 你快动身吧，我随后就到 [3] **~ on!** (urging) 加油！; (hurrying) 快点！; (expressing disbelief) 得了吧！; (as challenge) 来！; **~ on, this way!** 来呀，往这儿走！; **~ on, it's safe!** 没事的，很安全！; **~ on: tell me what happened!** 快点，告诉我发生了什么事！; **~ on, you're okay** 喂，你行的; **~ on in/out/down/up!** 快进来/快出来/快下来/快上来吧！; **~ on, we're late!** 快点，我们要迟到了！; **~ on! hit me!** 来呀！打我啊！ [4] (make progress) «*student, skill*» 进步; «*patient, injury*» 恢复; «*plant, garden*» 生长; «*work, book*» 进展; **how are the new recruits coming on?** 新兵的情况怎么样？; **how's your arm? — it's coming on** 你的手臂怎么样了？——正在恢复; **her piano playing is really coming on** 她的钢琴弹得真是越来越好听了 [5] (begin) «*illness*» 开始; «*darkness, season*» 到来; **I've got a cold coming on** 我要感冒了; **winter is coming on** 冬天来了; **before night came on** 在天黑前 [6] (be turned on) «*electricity, water*» 开始供应; «*appliance, heating*» 开始运行; **the power came back on** 恢复供电了 [7] Theat 上演; TV 播出; **the show's coming on!** 演出就要开始了！

B *vt* = **come upon**

- **come on to** *vt* [1] [~ on to sth.] (deal with) 开始谈论; **to ~ on to the question later** 以后再讨论那个问题 [2] [~ on to sb.] colloq (flirt with) 与…调情; **he came on to her in the bar** 他在酒吧里和她调情
- **come out** *vi* [1] (leave place) «*person, vehicle*» 出来; **to ~ out of hospital** 出院; **to ~ out from behind/under** *etc.* **sth.** 从某物后面/下面等出来 [2] Brit (strike) 罢工; **to ~ out on strike** 举行罢工 [3] (openly acknowledge one's homosexuality) 出柜 [即公开自己的同性恋身份] [4] (fall out) «*nail, lens*» 脱落; «*hair, tooth*» 掉落 [5] (be sociable) 变得外向 [6] (be removable) «*drawer*» 可拉出; «*cork, plug*» 可拔出 [7] (be emitted) «*fluid, air*» 喷出; **smoke came out of the chimney** 烟囱里冒着烟 [8] (be removed) «*dirt*» 去掉; «*colour*» 褪色; «*wrinkles*» 消失 [9] (be deleted) «*word*» 被删去; **that paragraph can ~ out** 那一段可以删去 [10] (be produced) «*model, product*» 上市; «*book*» 出版; «*film, CD*» 发行 [11] (rise) «*stars, sun*» 升起; (emerge) «*sun*» 露出; **the sun came out** 太阳出来了 [12] (come into bloom) 开花; **the daffodils came out early** 水仙花开得早 [13] (erupt) «*rash*» 出现 [14] (become known) «*truth, secret*» 被获知; **the results came out** 结果出来了; **it's all coming out now!** 一切真相大白了！ [15] (be shown) «*quality, feelings*» 显露出来; **his true feelings ~ out in his attitude** 他的态度流露出真实感情; **the meaning doesn't ~ out in this translation** 这篇译文没有表达出这层意思 [16] Phot, Print (be processed) «*photo*» 冲洗出来; «*copy*» 复制出来; (be reproduced) «*detail, object*» 复制效果…; **to ~ out well in a photo** 照片冲洗效果好; **to ~ out clearly** 印得清晰; **red won't ~ out on the photocopy** 红色复印不出来 [17] (end up) 结果是; (be placed) 位居; **to ~ out all right** 一切顺利; **to ~ out of sth. a loser/winner** 做某事以失败告终/最终取得胜利; **to ~ out on top** 结果名列前茅; **to ~ out first/bottom in the exam** 在考试中名列第一/垫底 [18] (state one's position) **to ~ out against/in favour of sb./sth.** 公开反对/支持某人/某事物; **to ~ out in support of sb./sth.** 公开表明对某人/某事物的支持 [19] (be said) «*remark, words*» 被说出; **that didn't ~ out as I intended** 我说这话是有口无心
- **come out at** *vt* [~ out at sth.] «*price, total*» 共计 ‹*amount*›; **to ~ out at a rate of 3%** 总计费率为3%
- **come out in** *vt* [~ out in sth.] [皮肤上] 出 ‹*rash*›; **to ~ out in spots** 起丘疹; **to ~ out in a cold sweat** 冒出一身冷汗
- **come out of** *vt* [~ out of sth.]
  [1] (originate in) «*person, thing*» 来自; **one of the songs that have ~ out of Ireland** 源于爱尔兰歌谣中的一首 [2] (result from) 由…产生; **something good came out of the disaster** 这场灾难也产生了一些积极的东西
- **come out with** *vt* [~ out with sth.] 说出; **to ~ out with extraordinary/rude remarks** 语出惊人/说话粗鲁; **just ~ straight out with it!** 直说吧！
- **come over**

A *vi* [1] (travel) [尤指越过海洋] 过来 [2] (approach) 走近; **she came over to my desk** 她走到我的桌子旁 [3] (drop in) 造访; **~ over and see us** 来看望我们 [4] (change sides) 改变立场; **to ~ over to sth.** 转而加入某一方; **to ~ over to our side** 转而加入我们这一边 [5] (be conveyed) «*message, feeling*» 得以传达; **her love of animals came over** 她表现出了对动物的关爱 [6] (give impression) 留下印象; **to ~ over badly/well** 给人的印象差/好 [7] Brit colloq (start to be) 开始变得; (start to feel) 突然感觉; **to ~ over all misty-eyed** 突然眼泪汪汪

B *vt* [~ over sb.] «*attack, fit, sense*» 突然影响; **a feeling of relief came over me** 我顿时感到松了一口气; **I don't know what came over me** 我不知道我是怎么了

- **come round** *vi* esp Brit [1] (make detour) 绕道; **we had to ~ round the other way** 我们不得不绕道过来 [2] (circulate) «*waiter*» 走来走去 [3] (visit) 拜访; **do ~ round and see us** 一定要来看望我们; **to ~ round for dinner** 来家里吃晚饭吧 [4] (occur) «*holiday, season*» (再次) 来临; **to ~ round more quickly every year** 一年比一年来得快; **to wait until sth. ~s round** 一直等到某事物到来 [5] (awake from unconscious state) 苏醒; (from trance) 回过神; (from sleep) 醒来 [6] (change mind) 改变看法; **she finally came round to our way of thinking** 她终于转而认同了我们的想法
- **come through**

A *vi* [1] (penetrate) «*light*» 穿过; **the heat is coming through** 热气透进来了 [2] (be received) «*news, signal*» 传来; **the call hasn't ~ through** 电话还没来; **there's a call coming through** 有一个电话打进来 [3] (arrive) «*results, orders*» 到来; **to wait for sth. to ~ through** 等待某事物获准 [4] (survive) 挺过; **he was very ill, but he came through** 虽然病得很厉害，但他还是熬过来了; **he came through without a scratch** 他毫发无损地幸存了下来 [5] (be evident) «*quality, devotion*» 显露出来; **her personality ~s through in her art** 她的个性表现在艺术作品中

B *vt* [~ through sth.]
[1] (penetrate) «*light*» 透过 ‹*cloth*›; «*ink*» 浸透 ‹*paper*›; **the sweat came through his shirt** 汗水浸透了他的衬衫 [2] (survive) 挺过 ‹*crisis, war*›; 经历…后活下来 ‹*operation, illness*›; 熬过 ‹*recession*›

- **come to**
A *vi* **1** (awake from unconscious state) 苏醒; (from trance) 回过神; (from sleep) 醒来; **she's coming to** 她开始苏醒了 **2** Naut «*ship*» 停住
B [**~ to sth.**] *vt*
1 (amount to) «*total, expenses*» 共计 ‹*amount*›; **what did the bill ~ to?** 账单总共多少钱？
2 (result in) 得到结果; **will it ~ to a fight?** 会打起来吗？; **to ~ to nothing** 没有结果; **all her efforts came to nothing** 她的一切努力均付诸东流; **his plans never came to anything** 他的计划均毫无成效; **to not ~ to much** 不很成功; **I didn't think it would ~ to this!** 我没想到事情会发展到这一步！; **when it ~s to it** 在关键时刻 **3** (pertain to) 涉及; **when it ~s to sth.** 说到某事物; **when it ~s to work, he's useless** 说到工作，他一无是处; **~ to that ...** Brit (when adding remark) 说到这一点…
C [**~ to sb.**] *vt* (be recalled or realized) 被…想到; **it'll ~ to me soon** 我很快就会想起来的; **it suddenly came to her that ...** 她突然意识到…
- **come under** *vt* [**~ under sth.**]
1 (be subjected to) 受到 ‹*influence, criticism, pressure*›; 遭到 ‹*attack*›; **the document came under close scrutiny** 这份文件已经仔细审查过了 **2** (be classified under) 属于; **to ~ under different headings** 分属不同的题目; **hawks ~ under 'birds of prey'** 鹰属于"猛禽类"
- **come up** *vi* **1** (ascend) 上来; «*diver*» 浮上来; (climb stairs) 上楼; **~ up to the attic** 上阁楼来 **2** (emerge) «*plant*» 破土发芽 **3** (rise) «*sun*» 升起 **4** (be vomited) «*food*» 被吐出; **her lunch came up** 她把午饭吐了 **5** (reach) «*water, plant*» 达到; **the tide came up to the road** 潮水漫到了路上; **the boots ~ up to my knees** 靴子长及我的膝部 **6** (approach) 靠近; **a van came up and ...** 一辆货车开过来，然后…; **he came up to me** 他走到我跟前 **7** (occur) «*job, opportunity*» 出现; **chances like this don't ~ up very often** 这样的机会不常有; **did something ~ up?** 发生了什么事吗？ **8** (happening soon) «*event*» 即将发生; **the show is coming up** 很快就要开始演出了; **he's coming up to retirement** 他快退休了; **coming up next: ...** 接下来是…; **... coming up!** …马上就好！ **9** (be mentioned) 被提起; **I was afraid that might ~ up** 我担心会提到那件事 **10** (from south) 北上; (from smaller place) 上到; **she often ~s up to London** 她经常上伦敦来 **11** (be handled) 被处理; **her case ~s up next week** 她的案子将于下周审理; **she came up before the board** 她被交由董事会处置 **12** Brit Univ dated 上大学 [尤指上牛津或剑桥大学]; **she came up to Oxford to study law** 她进了牛津大学攻读法律 **13** (be drawn in lottery) 中奖
- **come up against** *vt* [**~ up against sb./sth.**] 面对 ‹*obstacle, challenge*›; 遭遇 ‹*rival, champion*›
- **come up for** *vt* [**~ up for sth.**]
1 (be candidate for) 成为…的候选人; **he's coming up for promotion** 他是此次晋升的候选人 **2** (be about to undergo) 即将经受; **to ~ up for auction/sale** 即将被拍卖/降价出售
- **come upon** *vt* [**~ upon sb./sth.**]
1 (meet) 碰见 **2** (find) 意外发现 ‹*missing item*›; **if you ~ upon a better idea, ...** 如果你碰巧想到了一个更好的主意，… **3** (attack) 袭击 ‹*person, animal*› **4** (affect) 影响; **the feeling/realization gradually came upon me that ...** 我慢慢感觉到/意识到…
- **come up to** *vt* [**~ up to sth.**] 达到 ‹*standard*›; **the performance didn't ~ up to our expectations** 演出没有我们预想的那么好
- **come up with** *vt* [**~ up with sth.**]
1 (think of) 想到 ‹*idea, plan*›; **what excuse did she ~ up with?** 她找了个什么借口？ **2** esp pej (produce) 拿出; (find) 找到; **what brainwave has he ~ up with now?** 他又想出了什么妙计？; **is this the best room you can ~ up with?** 这是你们能找到的最好的房间了？

comeback /ˈkʌmbæk/ *n* **1** [c] (bid for success) 复出; **to make** *or* **stage a ~** 东山再起 **2** [c] (return to fashion) 重新流行; **do you think flared trousers will ever make a ~?** 你觉得喇叭裤还会再流行吗？ **3** [c] (retort) 反驳; **to make a ~** 进行反驳 **4** [u] (redress) 补偿; **to have no ~** 无法获得赔偿

comedian /kəˈmiːdɪən/ ▸p. 409 *n* **1** (actor, entertainer) 喜剧演员 **2** (joker) 逗乐的人; **Lizzie was the ~ of the family** 莉齐是家里的开心果

comedown /ˈkʌmdaʊn/ *n* colloq **1** (decline in status) 落泊; **it's quite a ~ for her to have to do her own housework** 她不得不自己做家务，实在是屈尊 **2** (disappointment) 失望

comedy /ˈkɒmədi/ *n* **1** [c] (comic piece) 喜剧作品 **2** [u] (genre) 喜剧; **slapstick/satirical ~** 打闹剧/讽刺剧; **a ~ of manners** 风尚喜剧 **3** [u] (funny aspect) 滑稽; **moments of high ~** 很滑稽的时刻

come-hither *adj attrib* colloq 勾引的; **to give sb. a ~ look** 挑逗地看某人一眼

comely /ˈkʌmli/ *adj* archaic or hum 秀丽的

come-on *n* colloq **1** (sexual) 勾引; **to give sb. the ~** 勾引某人 **2** (inducement) 引诱; **bargain offers and other ~s** 提供便宜货及其他促销手段

comer /ˈkʌmə(r)/ *n* **1** open to all **~s** 所有人均可参加 **2** Amer colloq (potential success) (person) 可能成功的人; (thing) 可能成功的事物; **many in the party see tax relief as a ~** 党内很多人都认为减免税收有望实现

comet /ˈkɒmɪt/ *n* 彗星; **the tail of a ~** 彗尾

comeuppance /kʌmˈʌpəns/ *n usu sing* colloq 报应; **to get one's ~** 得到应有的惩罚

comfort /ˈkʌmfət/
A *n* **1** [u] (physical well-being) 舒适; **she did all she could for our ~** 她竭尽所能让我们舒适些 **2** [u] (prosperity) 富足; **to live in ~** 过优裕的生活; **a life of ~ and security** 安逸的生活 **3** [c] (amenity) 使生活舒适之物 **4** [u and c] (consolation, source of consolation) 安慰; **to bring** *or* **give ~ to sb.** 给某人安慰; **to take** *or* **derive ~ from sth.** 从某事物中得到安慰; **we can take ~ from the fact that ...** 令我们感到安慰的是…; **we did catch the train, but it was too close for ~** 我们确实赶上了火车，但是太悬了，让人心有余悸; **spiritual ~** 精神慰藉; **to be a ~ to sb.** «*person, knowledge, belief*» 对某人是个安慰
B *vt* «*person, words, gift*» 安慰; **the little girl ran to her mother to be ~ed** 小女孩跑到妈妈那里寻求安慰; **to be ~ed by the thought that ...** 因想到…而感到安慰

comfortable /ˈkʌmftəbl, Amer -fərt-/ *adj* **1** (promoting well-being) 舒适的 ‹*house, clothes, temperature*›; **the patient had a ~ night** 病人晚上未受病痛折磨 **2** (relaxed) 舒服的; **to make oneself ~** (in chair) 坐得舒服; (at ease) 不拘束 **3** (reassuring) 给人以安慰的 ‹*idea, belief*›; 容易相处的 ‹*person*›; 轻松愉快的 ‹*job, lifestyle, routine*› **4** (considerable) 相当大的 ‹*majority, victory, margin*›; **their lead in the polls is still ~** 他们在民意调查中仍处于明显的领先地位; **a ~ winner** 以较大优势获胜的选手 **5** (well-off) 宽裕的; **she's not rich, but she's quite ~** 她不算富有，但还是相当宽裕 **6** (happy) 内心舒坦的; **I don't feel ~ doing that** 我觉得做那事心里不踏实; **I would feel more ~ about leaving if ...** 如果…，我离开会觉得更心安理得 **7** (confident) 自信的; **he is more ~ with computers than with people** 比起与人相处，他和电脑打交道时更能应付自如

comfortably /ˈkʌmftəbli, Amer -fərt-/ *adv* **1** (physically) 舒适地 **2** (socially) 随和地; **to smile ~** 随和地微笑 **3** (financially) 宽裕地 **4** (easily) 容易地; **they are ~ ahead in the opinion polls** 他们在民意调查中遥遥领先

comfort: ~ break *n* esp Amer euph 上厕所时间; **we stopped for a ~ break and refreshments** 我们停下来上个厕所，吃点东西; **~ eating** *n* [u] 安慰性进食

comforter /ˈkʌmfətə(r)/ *n* **1** (person) 安慰者 **2** Brit (dummy) 奶嘴 **3** Amer (quilt) 厚被子

comfort food *n* [u and c] 家常美食

comforting /ˈkʌmfətɪŋ/ *adj* **1** (pleasant) 令人舒适的 **2** (reassuring) 令人安慰的; **it is ~ to know that ...** 得知…令人欣慰

comfortless /ˈkʌmfətlɪs/ *adj* 没有舒适设施的 ‹*premises*›; **a chilly and ~ room** 冷冰冰的简陋房间

comfort: ~ station *n* Amer euph 公厕; **~ zone** *n* [让人觉得安全、轻松的] 舒适区

comfy /ˈkʌmfi/ *adj* colloq 舒服的

comic /ˈkɒmɪk/ ▸p. 409
A *adj* **1** (funny) 滑稽的 ‹*event, performance*› **2** *attrib* (relating to comedy) 喜剧的; **a ~ writer/actor** 喜剧作家/演员
B *n* **1** (entertainer) 喜剧演员 **2** (funny person) 滑稽的人 **3** (magazine) 连环漫画杂志
C **comics** *npl* Amer 连环漫画栏

comical /ˈkɒmɪkl/ *adj* 滑稽的

comically /ˈkɒmɪkli/ *adj* 滑稽地

comic: ~ book *n* 连环漫画书; **~ opera** *n* [u and c] 喜歌剧; **~ relief** *n* [u] 喜剧性调剂; **~ strip** *n* 连环漫画

coming /ˈkʌmɪŋ/
A *n* **1** (arrival) 到来; **~s and goings** 来来往往 **2** (approach of winter, old age, new era, event) 来临
B *adj attrib* **1** (imminent) 即将来临的; **I leave this ~ Monday** 我下周一离开 **2** (likely to succeed) 可能成功的; **he's a ~ man/politician** 他是个有前途的人/政治家; **the ~ thing** 正变得热门的事物

coming of age
A *n sing* 成年 [即21岁或18岁]
B **coming-of-age** *modif* 成年的 ‹*party, day*›

coming-out *n* [u] **1** (of homosexual) 公开同性恋身份 **2** dated (of debutante) 初入社交界; **a ~ party/ball** 初入社交界的聚会/舞会

comma /ˈkɒmə/ *n* **1** Ling 逗号 **2** **~ (butterfly)** 银纹多角蛱蝶

command /kəˈmɑːnd, Amer -ˈmænd/
A *n* **1** [u and c] (order) 命令; **at sb.'s ~** 听从某人的命令; **on ~** 按照命令; **by royal ~** 奉谕旨 **2** [u] Mil (authority) 控制权; (people) 指挥权; **to be in ~ (of** *or* **over sb./sth.)** 指挥（某人/某事物）; **to be under the ~ of sb., to be under sb.'s ~** 受某人指挥 **3** [u] (control) 控制; **in ~ of oneself/the situation** 能控制自己/局面 **4** [u] (mastery of skill, language, etc.) 掌握; **he had an excellent ~ of Russian** 他精通俄语; **she had a good ~ of computing skills** 她电脑操作技能娴熟; **to have sth. at one's ~** 精通某事物 **5** [c] Comput 指令 **6** [c] + *v sing or pl* Mil (group of soldiers) 所辖部队 **7** [c] Mil (district) 防区
B *vt* **1** (order) «*person*» 命令采取 ‹*behaviour, measures*›; **he ~ed us to enter** 他命令我们进去; **she ~ed silence** 她命令保持安静; **'put it down', he ~ed** "把它放下来"，他命令道 **2** Mil (be in charge of) 指挥 ‹*regiment, operation*›; 控制 ‹*territory, air, sea*› **3** (have available) 拥有 ‹*funds, resources*›; **the power and finances ~ed by the police** 警方拥有的权力和财力; **the party was no longer able to ~ a majority in Parliament** 该党在议会中不再占多数了 **4** (deserve and get) «*person*» 赢得 ‹*respect, support*›; «*action*» 值得 ‹*attention, sympathy*›; **to ~ a good price** 值高价 **5** (dominate) «*fortress*» 对…呈控制之势 ‹*valley*›; (overlook) «*building*» 俯临 ‹*view*›; **their encampment ~ed the only approach road** 他们的营地扼住了唯一的通路
C *vi* **1** (order) 命令 **2** Mil (be in charge) 当指挥官

commandant /ˈkɒməndænt/ *n* 指挥官

C

C

command: ~ centre *n* 指挥中心; **~-driven** *adj* 受指令驱动的 ‹*program, computer*›; **~ economy** *n* 计划经济

commandeer /ˌkɒmənˈdɪə(r)/ *vt* 征用

commander /kəˈmɑːndə(r), Amer -mæn-/ *n* **1** (gen) 指挥官; **the ~ of a parachute regiment** 空降团指挥官 **2** Naut 海军中校

commander-in-chief *n* 总司令

commanding /kəˈmɑːndɪŋ, Amer -ˈmæn-/ *adj* **1** (authoritative) 威严的 ‹*look, voice*›; **she has a ~ manner and dignified bearing** 她举止威严，仪态高雅 **2** (dominant) 占明显优势的; **to have a ~ lead in the polls** 在民意调查中遥遥领先; **a ~ 13-6 lead** 13 比 6 的压倒性优势 **3** (elevated) 居高临下的; **the house has a ~ view over the lake** 从这所房子可以俯瞰湖上风光

commanding officer *n* 指挥官

command line *n* 指令行

commandment /kəˈmɑːndmənt, Amer -ˈmæn/ *n* **1** Relig 戒条; **the Ten Commandments** 十诫; **to keep the ~s** 遵守戒律 **2** liter or hum (order) 命令

command module *n* 指挥舱

commando /kəˈmɑːndəʊ, Amer -ˈmæn-/ *n* (*pl* **~s**) **1** [c] Mil (soldier) 突击队员 **2** [c] Mil (unit) 突击队 **3** [u] **to go ~** colloq hum 不穿内裤

command: ~ performance *n* 御前演出; **~ post** *n* 指挥所; **~ structure** *n* 指挥结构

commemorate /kəˈmeməreɪt/ *vt* **1** (recall) «*monument, work of art*» 作为对…的纪念; **this stone ~s the battle of Waterloo** 这块石头是滑铁卢之战的纪念 **2** (mark) «*ceremony*» 纪念

commemoration /kəˌmeməˈreɪʃn/ *n* **1** [u] (commemorating) 纪念; **in ~ of ...** 为纪念… **2** [c] (ceremony) 纪念仪式

commemorative /kəˈmemərətɪv, Amer -ˈmeməreɪt-/ *adj* 纪念性的; **to issue ~ stamps** 发行纪念邮票

commence /kəˈmens/ formal

A *vi* 开始; **to ~ with a song** 以一首歌开始

B *vt* 开始; **to ~ doing sth.** 开始做某事; **to ~ proceedings (against sb.)** (对某人) 提起诉讼

commencement /kəˈmensmənt/ *n* **1** [u] formal (start) 开始 **2** [u and c] Amer Univ (ceremony) 学位授予典礼; (day) 学位授予日

commend /kəˈmend/

A *vt* **1** (praise) 称赞; **she was ~ed for bravery** 她因勇敢而受到表扬 **2** formal (recommend) 推荐; **to have much to ~ it** 优点很多; **to have little** *or* **almost nothing to ~ it** 乏善可陈 **3** formal (entrust) 委托; **to ~ one's soul to God** 将灵魂托付给上帝

B *v refl* **to ~ oneself/itself to sb.** 受到某人的欣赏; **his work had ~ed itself to his superiors** 他的工作受到上级的赏识

commendable /kəˈmendəbl/ *adj* 值得称赞的

commendably /kəˈmendəbli/ *adv* 值得称赞地; **~ quick/restrained** 令人赞赏地快的/克制的

commendation /ˌkɒmenˈdeɪʃn/ *n* **1** [u] (praise) 称赞; **with the ~ of ...** 带着…的赞誉; **to receive ~ for sth./doing sth.** 由于某事物/做某事而受到表扬 **2** [c] Mil (medal) 奖章; (citation) 嘉奖令

commensurate /kəˈmenʃərət/ *adj* formal **1** (proportionate) 相称的 ‹*extent, amount, size*›; **to be ~ with sth.** 和某事物相称 **2** (appropriate) 适当的 ‹*feeling, action, attitude*›

comment /ˈkɒment/

A *n* **1** [c and u] (remark(s)) 评论; **to make ~s (about sth.)** (对某事物) 作评论; **no ~** 无可奉告; **without ~** 不加评论地; **a ~ on** *or* **about sth.** 对某事物的意见 **2** [c] Literat 注解; **edited by J. Jones with ~s by S. Smith** 由 J. 琼斯编辑并由 S. 史密斯注释的 **3** [c] (unfavourable reflection) 批评; **to be a ~ on sth.** 是对某事物的指责 **4** [u] (response) 意见; **the plans were sent to the council for ~** 计划已呈送委员会征求意见; **to evoke ~** 引发议论

B *vt* 评论; **to ~ that ...** 评论说…

C *vi* **1** (make remark) 评论; **to ~ on sth./sb.** 对某事物/某人发表意见 **2** Literat «*scholar, text*» 作评注; **to ~ on sth.** 对某事物作评注

commentary /ˈkɒməntri, Amer -teri/ *n* **1** [c] Radio, TV 实况报道; **to do** *or* **give a ~ on sth.** 对某事物进行实况报道; **a running ~** 实况追踪报道; **a race/football/tennis ~** 赛跑/足球/网球实况报道; **~ position** 现场报道席 **2** [u and c] Journ (analysis) 评论; **a ~ on sth.** 关于某事物的评论 **3** [c] Literat 评注

commentary box *n* 现场解说室

commentate /ˈkɒmənteɪt/ *vi* 作实况报道; **to ~ on sth.** 对…作现场解说 ‹*sporting event, performance, public ceremony*›

commentator /ˈkɒmənteɪtə(r)/ ▸ p. 409 *n* **1** Radio, TV (on sports event, performance, public ceremony) 实况解说员 **2** Journ (on current affairs) 评论员; **a political/financial ~** 政治/财经评论员

comment card *n* 留言卡

commerce /ˈkɒmɜːs/ *n* **1** [u] (trade) 贸易; **to be** *or* **work in ~** 从事商贸; **to go into ~** 开始从事商贸; **Secretary/Department of C~** Amer 商务部长/商务部 **2** [c] liter (instance of trade) 交易; **a ~ in sth.** 某方面的交易

commercial /kəˈmɜːʃl/

A *adj* **1** (relating to commerce) 商业的 ‹*interests, establishment, training*›; 商务的 ‹*dealings, journal*›; **the ~ world** 商界; **a ~ building** 商用楼; **a ~ college** 商学院; **the ~ heart of the city** 城市的商业中心 **2** (profitable) 营利性的; **a ~ product/enterprise** 营利性产品/企业; **a ~ success/failure** 商业上的成功/失败; **his paintings are brilliant, but not ~** 他的画很出色，但卖不出去 **3** (large-scale, industrial) 大型的 ‹*machine*›; 工业用的 ‹*chemical*› **4** (funded from advertisements) 靠商业广告赞助的; **~ TV/radio** 商业电视/电台

B *n* Radio, TV 广告

commercial: ~ art *n* [u] 商业美术; **~ artist** *n* 商业艺术家; **~ bank** *n* 商业银行; **~ break** *n* 插播广告时段

commercialism /kəˈmɜːʃəlɪzəm/ *n* [u] **1** (principles of commerce) 商业精神 **2** pej (profit-seeking) 营利主义

commercialization /kəˌmɜːʃəlaɪˈzeɪʃn, Amer -lɪˈz-/ *n* [u] 商业化

commercialize /kəˈmɜːʃəlaɪz/ *vt* 使…商业化 ‹*organization, activity, place*›; 使…商品化 ‹*art, music*›

commercialized /kəˈmɜːʃəlaɪzd/ *adj* 商业化的

commercial law *n* [u] 商法

commercially /kəˈmɜːʃəli/ *adv* **1** (as regards profit) 营利性地; **~ viable** 可营利的; **~, I have no interest in it** 从赚钱角度讲，我对它没兴趣 **2** (as regards business) 商业性地; **the new model will be ~ available next year** 新款将于明年上市

commercial: ~ traveller ▸ p. 409 *n* Brit dated 销售代表; **~ value** *n* [u] 商业价值; **~ vehicle** *n* 商用车辆

Commie /ˈkɒmi/ colloq pej

A *n* 共产党员

B *adj attrib* 共产党员的

comminuted /ˈkɒmɪnjuːtɪd/ *adj* 粉碎的; **a ~ fracture** 粉碎性骨折

commiserate /kəˈmɪzəreɪt/

A *vi* **1** (express sympathy) 表示慰问; **to ~ with sb. about sth.** 就某事物对某人表示慰问 **2** (feel sympathy) 同情; **to ~ with sb.** 同情某人

B *vt* 同情地说; **'how awful for you,' she ~d** "你太倒霉了，" 她同情地说

commiseration /kəˌmɪzəˈreɪʃn/

A *n* [u] 同情

B **commiserations** *npl* (expressions of sympathy) 同情的话语; **to accept sb.'s ~s** 接受某人的安慰; **congratulations to the winners, and ~s to the losers** 对赢家表示祝贺，对输家表示同情

commissar /ˈkɒmɪsɑː(r)/ *n* Hist 人民委员

commissariat /ˌkɒmɪˈseərɪət/ *n* 军需处

commissary /ˈkɒmɪsəri/ *n* Amer **1** (store) 军营杂货店 **2** (canteen) 员工餐厅

commission /kəˈmɪʃn/

A *n* **1** [c] (committee) 委员会; **a ~ on human rights** 人权委员会 **2** [u and c] (payment for goods sold) 佣金; **to work (for sb.) on ~** *or* **on a ~ basis** 以拿佣金的方式 (为某人) 工作 **3** [c] (professional fee) 手续费 **4** [c] (order, instruction) 委托; (piece of work) 受委托创作的作品; **to have a ~ to do sth.** 受委托做某事; **to get a ~ from sb.** 得到某人的委托 **5** [c] Mil 委任状; **to resign one's ~** 辞去委任的军职 **6** [u] formal (perpetration) (of crime, sin) **the ~ of a crime** 犯罪 **7** [u] (operation) **to be in ~** «*vehicle, equipment, system*» 在使用中; **the new submarine will be in ~ in June** 新潜艇将在 6 月投入服役; **to be out of ~** «*vehicle, equipment, system*» 不能使用; «*person*» 不能工作; **to put the boat out of ~** 弃用那条船; **he'll be out of ~ for the World Cup** 他将不能征战世界杯

B *vt* **1** (order) 委托创作 ‹*work of art, music, painting*›; 委托写 ‹*book, report*›; 委托做 ‹*investigation*›; **to ~ an author to write a novel** 约作者写小说 **2** Mil 授予…委任状; **a ~ed officer** 军官; **he was ~ed as an officer in 1972** 他于 1972 年被任命为军官 **3** (prepare for service) 将…投入使用 ‹*vehicle, equipment, system*›; **the power station will be ~ed next March** 电站将于明年 3 月投入使用

commission agent ▸ p. 409 *n* Brit 代理商

commissionaire /kəˌmɪʃəˈneə(r)/ ▸ p. 409 *n* Brit 门口侍应

commissioner /kəˈmɪʃənə(r)/ *n* **1** Admin 长官; **a fire/water ~** 消防/水利局长; **a European C~** 欧盟委员会委员 **2** Brit (police chief) 警察局长 **3** Amer Sport [体育协会的] 总干事

commissioner for oaths *n* Brit 监誓官 [经授权主持宣誓的律师]

Commission for Racial Equality *n* Brit 种族平等委员会

commissioning editor ▸ p. 409 *n* 组稿编辑

commission sale *n* 委托销售

commit /kəˈmɪt/ (*pres p etc.* **-tt-**)

A *vt* **1** (perpetrate) 犯 ‹*crime, mistake*›; **to ~ adultery/manslaughter/murder/perjury** 犯通奸罪/过失杀人罪/谋杀罪/伪证罪; **to ~ suicide** 自杀 **2** (bind) 使承诺; **to ~ sb. to doing sth./to sth.** 使某人承诺做某事/承诺某事物; **to be ~ted to doing sth.** 承诺做某事; **to be ~ted to sth./sb.** 忠于某事物/某人; **no, I'm sorry, I'm ~ted all Thursday** 不行，我很抱歉，我周四一整天都有事 **3** (assign) 耗费 ‹*money, resources*›; **are you willing to ~ an hour a day to this work?** 你愿意每天花一个小时做这项工作吗？ **4** (transfer, record) 记下; **to ~ sth. to paper/writing** 将某事记在纸上/写下来; **to ~ sth. to memory** 记住某事物 **5** Jur 关押; **to ~ sb. for trial** 将某人关押起来候审; **to have sb. ~ted** 把某人关进精神病院

B *v refl* **1** (undertake to do sth.) **to ~ oneself to doing sth.** 承诺做某事; **to ~ oneself to sb.** 承诺忠于某人 **2** (be explicit) **to ~ oneself as to** *or* **with regard to ...** 对…表态; **he could not ~ himself as to the size of the award** 他无法对奖品的丰厚程度明确表态

C *vi* 承诺; **why are so many men scared to ～?** 为什么这么多男人都害怕作出承诺?

commitment /kə'mɪtmənt/ *n* **1** [c] (undertaking, obligation) 承诺; **a ～ to sth./to doing sth.** *or* **to do sth.** 对某事物/做某事的承诺; **to take on a ～ to sb.** 对某人作出承诺; **to give a firm ～ that ...** 坚决保证…; **absent due to family ～s** 由于家庭事务而缺席的 **2** [u and c] (sense of duty) 责任感; **a sense of ～ (to sth.)** (对某事物的) 责任感; **to have a strong ～ to doing sth./to sth.** 有做某事/对某事物的强烈责任感 **3** [u and c] (allocation of money, time, resources) 花费; **a financial ～** 资金投入

committal /kə'mɪtl/ *n* [u and c] (to prison) 关押; (to psychiatric hospital) 禁闭; (to court) 提付审议; **a ～ order** 提付审议的指令

committal proceedings *npl* 提付审议的程序

committed /kə'mɪtɪd/ *adj attrib* 尽心尽责的 ‹*carer, teacher*›; 忠诚的 ‹*supporter*›; 坚定的 ‹*Christian, Communist*›

committee /kə'mɪti/ *n* **1** [c] + *v sing or pl* (group) 委员会; **to be on** *or* **sit on** *or* **serve on a ～** 担任委员会委员; **to appoint** *or* **set up** *or* **form a ～** 设立委员会; **a ～ on sth.** 关于某事务的委员会 **2** [u] (sitting as a committee) **in ～** 由委员会审议中

committee: ～man /-mən, -mæn/ *n* Amer 地方政党领导人; **～ meeting** *n* 委员会会议; **～ member** *n* 委员会委员; **～woman** *n* Amer 地方政党女领导人

commode /kə'məʊd/ *n* 座椅式马桶

commodities /kə'mɒdətiːz/**: ～ broker** ▸p. 409 *n* 商品交易经纪人; **～ market** *n* **1** (sector) 商品交易区; **2** (place) 商品市场

commodity /kə'mɒdəti/ *n* **1** Comm 商品; **～ prices/markets/trading** 商品价格/市场/贸易 **2** (useful thing) 有用的东西; **household/staple/daily commodities** 家居/基本/日常用品 **3** fig (valuable attribute) 可贵品质; **candour is a rare ～ in business** 坦诚是商界稀缺的品质

commodore /'kɒmədɔː(r)/ *n* 海军准将

common /'kɒmən/

A *adj* **1** (often encountered) 常见的; **in ～ use** 常用的; **it is ～ (for sb.) to do sth.** (某人) 常做某事; **to be ～ as muck** colloq 司空见惯 **2** (shared) 共同的 ‹*purpose, interest, language*›; 共有的 ‹*wall, land*›; **to be ～ knowledge** 人所共知; **by ～ consent/agreement** 经一致同意; **the two countries share a ～ frontier** 这两个国家有一条共同边界 **3** *attrib* (ordinary) 普通的; **the ～ man/people** 普通人; **to be in/out of the ～ run (of things)** 平常/不寻常; **the ～ touch** 平易近人的特点 **4** *attrib* (minimum expected) 起码的; **it would just be ～ courtesy to apologize** 道歉只是起码的礼貌 **5** pej (vulgar) 粗俗的; **her dress and accent were ～** 她的衣着和口音都很俗气 **6** Math 公共的; **a ～ factor** 公因子

B *n* [u and c] 公地

C **in common** *adv phr* 共同地; **we have a lot/nothing/very little in ～** 我们有很多/没有任何/几乎没有共同之处; **to hold sth. in ～** 共同拥有 ‹*property, estate*›; **in ～ with many people, they decided not to vote** 与很多人一样, 他们决定不投票

common: C～ Agricultural Policy *n* 共同农业政策; **～ assault** *n* [u and c] 普通人身侵犯行为; **～ carrier** *n* **1** Transp 公共运输商; **2** Amer Telecom 公共电信公司; **～ cold** ▸p. 377 *n* 感冒; **～ core** *n* 基础课程; *modif* **～ core curriculum** 必修课程; **～ currency** *n* **1** [c] Fin 共同货币; **2** [u] (sth. widespread) 普遍存在的事物; **violence against journalists is ～ currency** 针对记者的暴力事件很普遍; **the word is in ～ currency** 这个词很常见; **～ denominator** *n* 公分母; **C～ Entrance** *n* Brit [英国13岁儿童参加的] 统一入学考试

commoner /'kɒmənə(r)/ *n* 平民

common: ～ fraction *n* = **vulgar fraction**; **～ ground** *n* [u] 共同基础; **to search** *or* **look for/find ～ ground (with sb.)** 寻求/找到 (与某人的) 共同点

common law *n* [u] Brit 普通法

common-law: ～ husband *n* 事实婚姻的男方; **～ marriage** *n* [u and c] 事实婚姻; **～ wife** *n* 事实婚姻的女方

commonly /'kɒmənli/ *adv* **1** (usually) 通常 **2** pej (vulgarly) 粗俗地 ‹*speak, dress, behave*›

common market *n* **1** Econ 共同市场 **2** (of Europe) **the Common Market** dated 欧洲共同市场

commonness /'kɒmənnɪs/ *n* [u] **1** (frequency) 普遍 **2** (vulgarity) 粗俗

common: ～ noun *n* 普通名词; **～-or-garden** *adj attrib* Brit 常见的 ‹*activity, variety, animal, plant*›

commonplace /'kɒmənpleɪs/

A *adj* **1** (widespread) 普遍的 **2** (banal) 平淡无奇的

B *n* **1** (usual thing) 寻常的事物 **2** (platitude) 陈词滥调

common room *n* esp Brit **1** (room) 公共休息室; **a senior/junior/middle ～** 教师/本科生/研究生交谊厅 **2** + *v sing or pl* (people) 公共休息室里的师生

Commons /'kɒmənz/ *npl* Brit **the ～** 下议院; **a ～ debate** 下议院的辩论

common: ～ salt *n* [u] 食盐; **～ sense** *n* [u] 常识; **to have/show (some) ～ sense** 有/表现出 (一点) 常识; **use your ～ sense!** 凭常识想想! ; **a ～-sense approach** 按照常理的方法; **～ stock** *n*, **～ stocks** *npl* Amer 普通股; **～ time** *n* [u] 四分之四拍

Commonwealth /'kɒmənwelθ/ *n* **the ～ (of Nations)** 英联邦; **～ member/summit** 英联邦成员/峰会; **～ head of state** 英联邦国家首脑; **the ～ of Australia** 澳大利亚联邦; **the ～ of Kentucky/Virginia** 肯塔基州/弗吉尼亚州

Commonwealth: ～ Day *n* [u] 英联邦日 [三月的第二个星期一]; **～ Games** *npl* **the ～ Games** 英联邦国家运动会; **～ of Independent States** *pr n* **the ～ of Independent States** 独立国家联合体

commotion /kə'məʊʃn/ *n* [u and c] **1** (noise) 喧闹声; **to make a ～** 喧闹 **2** (upheaval, disturbance) 骚乱; **to cause/create a ～** 引起/制造骚乱

communal /'kɒmjʊnl, kə'mjuːnl/ *adj* **1** (shared in common) 公共的 ‹*property, area*›; 共同的 ‹*well-being, effort, ownership*›; 公用的 ‹*telephone, kitchen*›; **～ living, the ～ life** 集体生活 **2** (within a community) 各团体之间的 ‹*rivalry, relationships*›

communally /'kɒmjʊnəli, kə'mjuːnəli/ *adv* **1** (shared by community) 共同地 ‹*own, run*› **2** (as community) 集体地 ‹*act, live*›

commune

A /'kɒmjuːn/ *n* **1** (group of people) 群体; **a women's/hippy ～** 女性/嬉皮士群体 **2** (communal settlement in a communist country) 公社; **a Soviet ～** 苏维埃公社 **3** Admin (in France, Italy, Belgium, Spain) (territory) 市镇; (people) 全镇居民; **the mayor and ～** 镇长与全镇居民

B /kə'mjuːn/ *vi* **1** **to ～ with sb./sth.** (share thoughts with) 《*person, soul*》 与…默默沟通 ‹*person, soul, God*› **2** **to ～ with sth.** (feel close to) 与…融为一体 ‹*nature, natural features*›

communicable /kə'mjuːnɪkəbl/ *adj* **1** formal (able to be communicated) 可传达的 **2** Med 可传染的; **a ～ disease/virus** 传染病/传染性病毒

communicant /kə'mjuːnɪkənt/ *n* 领圣餐者; **a ～ member of the Church of England** 英国国教会中受领圣餐的教友

communicate /kə'mjuːnɪkeɪt/

A *vt* **1** (convey) 《*person*》 传达 ‹*news, order*›; 《*work of art, gesture, expression*》 表达 ‹*idea, emotion*› **2** Med (transmit) 传染 ‹*disease, virus*›

B *v refl* **to ～ itself** 《*feeling*》 显露; **her anxiety ～s itself to others** 她表现得焦虑不安

C *vi* **1** (share information) 交流; **to ～ with sb.** 与某人交流; **to ～ by phone/radio** 用电话/无线电交流; **to ～ through dance/by gestures** 通过舞蹈/手势交流 **2** (express oneself) 表达想法; **to ～ well/badly** 表达力强/差 **3** (connect) 相连; **to ～ with sth.** 与…相通 ‹*room, apartment*›

communicating door *n* 连通门

communication /kə,mjuːnɪ'keɪʃn/

A *n* **1** [u] (exchange) 交流; (imparting) (of information) 传达; (of ideas, feelings) 表达; **to be in ～ (with sb.)** (与某人) 联络; **to get into ～ with sb.** 与某人进行交流; **a means/system/channel of ～** 传播方式/体系/渠道; **non-verbal ～** 非言语交流; **～ skills** 交际能力 **2** [c] formal (message) 信息; **a ～ from previous employers/the police** 来自你过去的雇主/警方的信息 **3** [u] Med (of disease, virus) 传染

B **communications** *npl* **1** Telecom 通信; **～s technology** 通信技术; **a breakdown in ～s** 通信中断 **2** Transp (infrastructure) 交通联系; **to have good ～s with sth.** 与…保持畅通的交通联络 ‹*port, city*› **3** + *v sing* (field of study) 传播学; **～s studies** 传播学研究

communication: ～ cord *n* Brit [火车车厢里的] 紧急制动索; **～ gap** *n* 交流沟; **～ interface** *n* 通信接口; **～ line** *n* 通信线路; **～s centre** *n* 通信中心; **～ science** *n* [u] 传播学; **～s director** ▸p. 409 *n* 联络总监; **～s industry** *n* 通信业; **～s link** *n* 通信线路; **～s network** *n* 通信网络; **～s satellite** *n* 通信卫星; **～ theory** *n* [u] 传播理论

communicative /kə'mjuːnɪkətɪv, Amer -keɪtɪv/ *adj* **1** (talkative) 健谈的 ‹*person*›; (willing to provide information) 乐意提供信息的 ‹*institution*›; **to be ～ about sth.** 关于某事物很健谈 **2** (involving communication) 交际的; **the ～ approach to language teaching** 语言交际教学法

communicator /kə'mjuːnɪkeɪtə(r)/ *n* 交流者

communion /kə'mjuːnɪən/ *n* **1** [u and c] formal 交流; **a ～ of hearts and souls** 心灵的交融 **2** **Communion** [u] Relig (bread and wine) **(Holy) C～** 圣餐; **to take/receive (Holy) C～** 领受圣餐 **3** **Communion** [u] Relig (service) **(Holy) C～** 圣餐仪式

Communion: ～ cup *n* 圣餐杯; **～ rail** *n* 领圣餐围栏; **～ service** *n* 圣餐仪式; **～ table** *n* 圣餐台; **～ wine** *n* [u and c] 圣餐酒

communiqué /kə'mjuːnɪkeɪ, Amer kə,mjuːnə'keɪ/ *n* 公报; **to issue a ～ to the press** 向媒体发表公报

communism /'kɒmjʊnɪzəm/ *n* [u] 共产主义

communist /'kɒmjʊnɪst/

A *adj* 共产主义的 ‹*ideal, principle, ideology, society*›; **his sympathies were ～** 他赞成共产主义

B *n* 共产主义者

Communist Party *n* 共产党

community /kə'mjuːnəti/

A *n* **1** [c] (social, cultural grouping) 团体; **ethnic communities** 种族团体; **the academic/business/scientific ～** 学术界/商业界/科学界; **the gay/student ～** 同性恋/学生团体; **a virtual ～** 虚拟社团 **2** [c] (geographical grouping) (at local level) 社区; (at national level) 社会; **the village had a close-knit ～** 这个村子的村民关系很密切; **the international ～** 国际社会; **the local ～ was** *or* **were shocked** 当地社会感到震惊 **3** [u and c] (sharing) 共享; **a sense of ～** 团体意识; **a ～ of interest** 利益的一致 **4** [c] (of plants, animals) 群落

C

B *modif* (locally funded) 地方出资的 ‹*library, park, health service*›

community: ~ **care** *n* [u] Brit 社区护理服务; ~ **centre** *n* 社区活动中心; ~ **charge** *n* Brit Hist 社区收费; ~ **chest** *n* Amer 社区福利基金; ~ **college** *n* **1** Amer 社区学院; **2** Brit 社区中学; ~ **education** *n* [u] 社区教育; ~ **education programme** 社区教育计划; ~ **health centre** *n* 社区护理服务中心; ~ **home** *n* 青少年犯教养所; ~ **hospital** *n* 社区医院; ~ **leader** *n* 社区领导人; ~ **life** *n* [u] 社区生活; ~ **medicine** *n* [u] 大众医疗; ~ **policeman** ▸p. 409 *n* 社区警官; ~ **policing** *n* [u] 社区治安; ~ **property** *n* [u] Amer 夫妻共有财产; ~ **school** *n* = ~ **college 2**; ~ **service** *n* [u] **1** Brit (punishment) [惩罚性质的] 社区服务; ~ **service order** 社区服务指令; **2** (voluntary work) 社区志愿者工作; ~ **singing** *n* [u] 全场大合唱; ~ **spirit** *n* [u] 社区精神; ~ **worker** ▸p. 409 *n* 社区工作者

commutable /kə'mju:təbl/ *adj* **1** (convenient for commuting) 上下班方便的 ‹*journey, distance*› **2** Jur 可减轻的; **the prison sentence is ~ into a fine** 入狱判决可减轻为罚款 **3** Fin 可折偿的 ‹*pension, annuity*›; **to be ~ into sth.** 可以某物代偿

commutation /ˌkɒmju:'teɪʃn/ *n* [u] **1** (punishment, sentence) 减刑 **2** Fin 折合偿付 **3** Amer Transp 上下班交通

commutation ticket *n* Amer = **season ticket**

commute /kə'mju:t/

A *vi* 通勤; **to ~ between Oxford and London** 上下班往返于牛津和伦敦之间

B *vt* **1** Jur 减轻 ‹*sentence, penalty*›; **to ~ sth. into** *or* **to sth.** 将某刑罚减为较轻的某刑罚 **2** Fin 把…折偿 ‹*pension, annuity*›; **to ~ sth. for** *or* **into sth.** 将某物折算成某物

C *n* 上下班路程; **I have a long ~ to work** 我上班的路程很长

commuter /kə'mju:tə(r)/ *n* 通勤者 [远距离上下班往返的人]

commuter: ~ **belt** *n* Brit 通勤带; ~ **train** *n* 通勤列车

commuting /kə'mju:tɪŋ/ *n* [u] 通勤; **I live within ~ distance of Dublin** 我住在离都柏林上下班可乘车往返的地方

> **commuting**
>
> 通勤。指长途上下班。通勤者称为commuter。如今，通勤者可以乘坐火车、轻轨（light rail）或者自己开车去城里上班。也有人在家利用互联网进行工作，称电子通勤（telecommuting）。城市周围通勤者集中的地区称为通勤带（commuter belt）。伦敦的通勤带有一部分称为股票经纪人带（stockbroker belt），因为住在那里的都是富有的商人。
>
> 所有人同时上下班会加剧城区的交通拥堵（traffic jam）问题。为了减小市区的交通流量，许多城市建立了停车转乘体系（park and ride），通勤者开车进入转乘停车场存车，然后转乘公共交通工具到市中心上班。政府还鼓励通勤者拼车（car pooling，英国称 car sharing），即多个人合开一辆车上班。

Comoros /'kɒmərəʊz/ *pr n* 科摩罗

compact

A /kəm'pækt/ *adj* **1** (compressed) 坚实的 ‹*substance, soil*›; **a ~ cluster of houses** 一片密集的房屋 **2** (small and neatly constructed) 小巧紧凑的 ‹*kitchen, piece of equipment*›; **on journeys he took a ~ chess set** 旅行时，他带了一副袖珍国际象棋 **3** (sturdy) 结实的; **a man/woman of ~ build** 体格健壮的男人/女人 **4** fig (concise) 简洁的 ‹*style, text*›

B /'kɒmpækt/ *n* **1** (agreement) 协议; **to make a ~** 达成协议; **a ~ between sb. and sb.** 某人与某人之间的契约 **2** Cosmet 带镜粉盒 **3** Amer Aut ~ **(car)** 小型汽车

C /kəm'pækt/ *vt* 压实 ‹*substance, object*›; 压缩 ‹*data*›

compact camera *n* 袖珍照相机

compact disc *n* **1** (gen) 光盘 **2** Mus 激光唱片

compact: ~ **disc interactive** *n* 交互式光盘; ~ **disc player** *n* 光盘播放机; ~ **fluorescent light** *n* 节能灯

compactly /kəm'pæktli/ *adv* 紧凑地

compactness /kəm'pæktnɪs/ *n* [u] 紧凑

compact newspaper *n* Brit 缩微报纸

compactor /kəm'pæktə(r)/ *n* (for compacting rubbish, scrap metal) 压实机; (for compacting ground) 夯土机

Companies /'kʌmpənɪz/: ~ **Act** *n* Brit **the ~ Act** 公司法案; ~ **House** *n* Brit 公司注册登记局

companion /kəm'pænɪən/ *n* **1** (friend) 朋友; **travelling ~s** 旅伴; **hunger and thirst were his constant ~s** 他常常忍饥挨渴; **a ~ in arms** 战友 **2** (sb. one meets) 伙伴; **a dinner ~** 同桌进餐者; **a drinking ~** 酒友 **3** (item of matching pair) 成对物品之一; ~ **volume** 姊妹卷 **4** (book) 指南; **a C~ to Florence** 佛罗伦萨旅游指南 **5** (fellow sufferer) 有同样遭遇的人; **we became ~s in adversity** *or* **misfortune** 我们成了患难之交

companionable /kəm'pænɪənəbl/ *adj* 友善的 ‹*person, silence*›; 气氛友好的 ‹*talk, meal*›

ℹ Comparison

■ In Chinese, there are no comparative forms of adjectives and adverbs. Comparison in Chinese is expressed by using such words and phrases as 比, 跟, 像, and 越来越.

The comparative and 'than'

■ In Chinese, 比 is used when comparing the difference in property or degree of two persons or things:

I am taller than her
= 我比她高

Ruth can sing better than Sally
= 露丝比萨莉歌唱得好

My sister can run faster than me
= 我妹妹比我跑得快

This suitcase is slightly lighter than the other one
= 这个手提箱比另外一个稍微轻点儿

His skin colour is much darker than mine
= 他的肤色比我的黑得多

■ The adverbs 更 and 还 can be used before the predicate to denote a further degree:

She is even more beautiful than Sara
= 她比萨拉还漂亮

Tomorrow will be even hotter than today
= 明天会比今天更热

■ The negative form of the 比 pattern is to add 不 before 比. 不 is never placed before the predicate:

She is not taller than you
= 她不比你高

He can not walk faster than me
= 他不比我走得快
or 他走得不比我快

■ In Chinese, when comparing the ages of two people, 大 (old) or 小 (young) is used as the predicate. When specifying a difference in age, 岁 is used instead of 年:

He is older than me
= 他比我大

I am younger than him
= 我比他小

My brother is 4 years younger than me
= 我弟弟比我小 4 岁

Equivalence or similarity

■ In Chinese, equivalence is conveyed by using 跟…一样…. 跟, 和 and 同 are used interchangeably. The negative form of the pattern is …不如 / 没有…（那么）…:

This photo is as beautiful as the other one
= 这张照片跟另外一张一样好看

He can do crosswords as quickly as I can
= 他做纵横字谜同我一样快

This box is not as big as the other one
= 这个箱子不如另外一个大
or 这个箱子没有另外一个大

She can't run as fast as you
= 她不如你跑得快
or 她没有你跑得快

■ In Chinese, similarity is conveyed by using 像 with 一样 or 像 with 这么 or 那么. The negative form places 不 in front of 像:

He is as clever as his big brother
= 他像他哥哥一样聪明

This house is as beautiful as a palace
= 这所房子像宫殿一样美

Today is not as hot as yesterday
= 今天不像昨天那么热

Parallel comparisons

■ In Chinese, 越…越… is used to express parallel increase:

Are you looking for a flat? — Yes, the cheaper the better
= 你在找公寓吗？—— 是的，越便宜越好

The more I am with him, the less I like him
= 我和他在一起越多，就越不喜欢他

■ 越来越… is used to express gradual increase or decrease in sentences where two comparatives are joined by 'and':

The weather is becoming warmer and warmer
= 天气变得越来越暖和

More and more people are visiting the botanic garden
= 参观植物园的人越来越多

My husband is less and less interested in pubs
= 我丈夫对酒吧越来越不感兴趣了

companion: ~ **hatch** *n* 舱室升降口; ~ **ladder** *n* 舱室升降梯

companionship /kəmˈpænɪənʃɪp/ *n* [u] 友谊

companionway /kəmˈpænɪənweɪ/ *n* 升降口扶梯

company /ˈkʌmpəni/ *n* 1 [c] (firm) 公司 2 [c] (group of performers) 剧团 3 [u] (companionship, companions) 陪伴; (society) 交往; **to enjoy sb.'s ~** 喜欢和某人在一起; **in sb.'s ~** 与某人在一起; **in mixed ~** 在男女混杂的场合; **to keep sb. ~** 陪伴某人; **to keep bad ~** 与坏人混在一起; **a man is known by the ~ he keeps** Prov 观其友则知其人; **to part ~ (with sb.)** (leave) (与某人) 分手; fig (disagree) (与某人) 意见不合; **to part ~ (with sth.)** (与某事物) 分离; **two's ~(, three's a crowd)** Prov 两人为伴 (, 三人添乱); **to be in good ~** fig 很多人也有过同样的尴尬; **in ~ with most teachers, she was underpaid** 与大多数教师一样, 她工资很低; ▸**present**[1] **A1** 4 [u] (visitors) 客人; **to have (got) ~** 有客人 5 [c] + *v sing or pl* formal (gathering) 一群; **a large ~ of young people** 一大群年轻人; **the assembled ~** 聚在一起的一群人 6 [c] + *v sing or pl* Mil 连 7 [c] + *v sing or pl* Naut **(ship's) ~** 全体船员

company: ~ **car** *n* 公司配车; ~ **commander** *n* 连长; ~ **director** ▸**p. 409** *n* 公司董事; ~ **doctor** ▸**p. 409** *n* 公司医生; ~ **headquarters** *npl* + *v sing or pl* 公司总部; ~ **law** *n* [u] 公司法; ~ **lawyer** ▸**p. 409** *n* 1 (specialist in company law) 公司法专家; 2 (lawyer working for company) 公司律师; ~ **man** *n* 处处以公司为重的员工; ~ **meeting** *n* 公司会议; ~ **name** *n* 公司名称

company pension *n* 公司养老金

company pension scheme *n* 公司养老金方案

company: ~ **policy** *n* [u and c] 公司政策; ~ **secretary** ▸**p. 409** *n* 公司秘书; ~ **tax** *n* [u] 公司税; ~ **union** *n* Amer 公司工会

comparable /ˈkɒmpərəbl/ *adj* 1 (equivalent) 比得上的; **to be ~ with** *or* **to sb.** 比得上某人 2 (similar) 相似的; **to be ~ with** *or* **to sth.** 与某事物类似

comparative /kəmˈpærətɪv/

A *adj* 1 (relative) 相对的; **in ~ terms** 相对而言; **he's a ~ stranger** 我不怎么认识他 2 (based on comparison) 比较的 ‹*method*›; **a ~ study** 比较研究 3 Ling 比较级的; **a ~ form/adjective/adverb** 比较级形式/形容词/副词

B *n* 1 (degree of comparison) **the ~** 比较级; **in the ~** 以比较级形式 2 (word) 比较级形式的词

comparative literature *n* [u] 比较文学

comparatively /kəmˈpærətɪvli/ *adv* 1 (fairly) 相当 ‹*easy, difficult, famous, successful*› 2 (for comparison) 相比较地; **~ speaking** 相比较而言

compare /kəmˈpeə(r)/

A *vt* 1 (contrast) 比较; **to ~ A and** *or* **with** *or* **to B** 比较A与B; **to ~ like with like** 比较两种相似的事物; **to ~ notes with sb.** fig 与某人交换意见 2 (liken) 把…比作 ‹*oneself, thing, activity*›; **to ~ A and** *or* **with** *or* **to B** 把A比作B

B *vi* 相比; **to ~ with sb./sth.** 与某人/某事物相比较; **the two televisions ~ well for price** 这两台电视的价格都还行; **to ~ favourably/unfavourably with sth.** 比某事物好/差

C *n* [u] liter 比较; **to be beyond** *or* **past** *or* **without ~** 无与伦比; **a beauty/leader beyond ~** 绝世美人/无人能比的领导者

comparison /kəmˈpærɪsn/ *n* 1 [u] (comparing) 比较; **the two cities invite ~** 这两个城市很类似; **here's a bigger size for ~** 这里有大点的尺码供比较; **to bear** *or* **stand ~ with sb./sth.** 比得上某人/某事物; **Cherubini cannot stand ~ with Mozart** 凯鲁比尼比不上莫扎特; **by** *or* **in ~ with ...** 与…相比较; **I'm small/tall by** *or* **in ~ with my father** 我比父亲个头小/个子高 2 [c] (act of comparing) 对比; **a ~ of the rail systems in England and Germany** 英格兰和德国铁路系统的比较; **to make a ~ of sth. with sth.** 将某事物与某事物进行对比; **to draw a ~ between ... and ...** 在…与…之间相比较; **~s are odious** 无谓的攀比令人厌恶 3 [u] (equivalence) 类似; **there is** *or* **can be no ~** 那没法比; **beyond ~** 无与伦比 4 [c] (analogy) 类比; **he had a taste for elaborate ~s** 他事事喜欢打比方 5 [u] Ling 比较

comparison: ~ **site** *n* 对比网站; ~ **test** *n* 比较测试

compartment /kəmˈpɑːtmənt/ *n* 1 Rail 车厢; **a sleeping/first-class ~** 卧铺/头等车厢 2 (section) (of box) 隔间; (of wallet, desk, refrigerator) 隔层; (of ship) 舱; **the briefcase has a secret ~** 这只手提箱有一个暗层; **he kept his life in separate ~s: home, office, and the football club** 他把生活分成几部分: 家庭、办公室以及足球俱乐部

compartmentalize /ˌkɒmpɑːtˈmentəlaɪz/ *vt* 划分 ‹*institution, life*›; **since the college became so ~d, I hardly speak to him** 自从学院这样划分以后, 我几乎跟他说不上话了

compass /ˈkʌmpəs/ ▸**p. 142**

A *n* 1 [c] (gen) 指南针; Naut 罗盘; **a magnetic ~** 磁罗经; **a radio/mariner's/pocket ~** 无线电/航海/袖珍罗盘; **the points of the ~** 罗盘方位点; **to take a ~ reading** 读取罗盘度数 2 [u] formal (extent) 范围; **within/beyond/outside the ~ of sth.** 在某事物范围之内/超出某事物范围/在某事物范围之外

B **compasses** *npl* Math 圆规; **a pair of ~es** 一副圆规

compass: ~ **bearing** *n* 罗盘方位; **to take a ~ bearing on sth.** 测量某物的罗盘方位; ~ **card** *n* 罗经刻度盘; ~ **course** *n* 罗盘航向

compassion /kəmˈpæʃn/ *n* [u] 同情; **to feel/show ~ for sb.** 同情/表示同情某人; **to take ~ on sb.** 同情某人

compassionate /kəmˈpæʃənət/ *adj* 1 (showing compassion) 有同情心的 ‹*person, act, account*› 2 (based on compassion) 基于同情的; **on ~ grounds** 出于同情

compassionate leave *n* [u] Brit 恩假; **to be/go on ~** 在/去休恩假

compassionately /kəmˈpæʃənətli/ *adv* 有同情心地

compassion fatigue *n* [u] 同情心淡漠

compass: ~ **point** *n* 罗经点; ~ **rose** *n* 罗经花

compatibility /kəmˌpætəˈbɪləti/ *n* [u] 1 (well-suitedness) 和睦相处 2 (absence of conflict) (in religion, aim, activity) 一致性; (of living organisms) 共存性; (in medicine) 配伍性 3 Comput 兼容性 4 (fitting together) 相容; **the ~ of motherhood and a demanding job** 做母亲与高强度工作之间的协调

compatible /kəmˈpætəbl/ *adj* 1 (well suited) 和睦相处的; **to be ~ with sb.** 与某人和睦相处 2 (not in conflict) 一致的 ‹*religions, aims, methods*›; 可配伍的 ‹*medicines*› 3 (consistent) 相符的 ‹*behaviour, activity*›; **you must learn to work at a speed ~ with efficiency** 你必须学会工作中兼顾速度与效率; **the symptoms are ~ with rheumatoid arthritis** 这些症状符合类风湿性关节炎的特征 4 Comput 兼容的 ‹*computer, software, system*›; **to be ~ with sth.** 与某物兼容; **X-~** 兼容X的

compatriot /kəmˈpætrɪət, Amer -ˈpeɪt-/ *n* 同胞

compel /kəmˈpel/ *vt* (*pres p etc.* **-ll-**) 1 (force) 强迫 ‹*person*›; **to ~ sb. to do sth.** 强迫某人做某事; **to feel ~led to do sth.** 觉得必须做某事 2 (enforce) 强求 ‹*action, change*›; «*law*» 规定 ‹*attendance, participation*›; «*person, quality*» 博得 ‹*admiration*›; **ill health ~led his retirement** 他因身体不好被迫退休; **to ~ respect/attention from sb.** 使某人肃然起敬/不得不注意

compelling /kəmˈpelɪŋ/ *adj* 1 (powerful, irresistible) 引人入胜的 ‹*work of art*›; 难以抗拒的 ‹*personality, desire*›; **his eyes were strangely ~** 他的目光有一种奇异的魅力 2 (convincing) 令人信服的 ‹*argument, evidence*›

compellingly /kəmˈpelɪŋli/ *adv* 1 (powerfully) 引人入胜地 ‹*play*›; 魅力十足地 ‹*smile*›; 扣人心弦地 ‹*act, write*› 2 (convincingly) 令人信服地 ‹*speak, argue*›

compendium /kəmˈpendɪəm/ *n* (*pl* **~s** *or* **compendia** /kəmˈpendɪə/) 1 (handbook) 手册 2 (small encyclopedia) 简明百科全书 3 Brit (box of games) 游戏拼盒

compensate /ˈkɒmpenseɪt/

A *vt* 赔偿; **to ~ sb. for sth./doing sth.** 为某事物/做某事赔偿某人

B *vi* 补偿; **to ~ for sth.** 为…进行补偿 ‹*loss, difficulty*›; **to go a long way to ~** *or* **towards compensating for ...** 费一番周折来弥补…

compensation /ˌkɒmpenˈseɪʃn/ *n* 1 [u] (recompense) 补偿; **in** *or* **as** *or* **by way of ~ (for sth.)** 作为 (对某事物的) 补偿; **to award/claim/pay/receive/seek ~** 给予/索取/支付/得到/寻求补偿; **he was awarded £3,000 ~ for his injuries** 他得到了3,000英镑的受伤赔偿; **a ~ claim** 索赔 2 [u and c] (counterbalance) 弥补; **the rise in salary was no ~ for the long hours** 加薪弥补不了长时间工作; **getting older has its ~s** 上年纪有上年纪的好处

compensatory /ˌkɒmpenˈseɪtəri, Amer kəmˈpensətɔːri/ *adj* 1 (financial) 赔偿的 ‹*sum of money*›; **~ damages** 损失赔偿金 2 (non-financial) 补偿的 ‹*action*›

compère /ˈkɒmpeə(r)/ Brit

A *n* 主持人; **to act as ~ (for ...)** 当 (…的) 主持人

B *vt* 主持 ‹*show, TV/radio game*›

compete /kəmˈpiːt/ *vi* 1 (strive for success) 竞争; **to ~ against** *or* **with sb. for sth.** 与某人竞争以获取某物; **Mozart's music cannot ~ with Bach's** 莫扎特的音乐不能与巴赫的音乐相媲美 2 Comm 竞争; **to ~ for ...** 为…竞争 ‹*profits, custom, contract, market share*›; **to ~ against** *or* **with ...** 与…竞争 3 esp Sport 比赛; **to ~ in sth.** 参加某比赛; **to ~ against** *or* **with sth./sb.** 与某队伍/某人比赛; **to ~ for a place/medal/prize** 为赢得资格/奖牌/奖品而参赛 4 fig (conflict) «*tastes*» 串味; «*sounds*» 混杂; **the smell of fish ~d with petrol and cigarette smoke** 鱼的味道里掺杂着汽油和香烟味

competence /ˈkɒmpɪtəns/, **competency** /ˈkɒmpɪtənsi/ *n* 1 [u] (ability) 能力; **to have the ~ to do sth.** 有做某事的能力 2 [c] (particular skill) 技能 3 [u] Jur 权限; **a decision within/beyond the judge's ~** 法官权限之内/之外的判决 4 [u] Ling 语言能力; **language** *or* **linguistic ~** 语言能力

competent /ˈkɒmpɪtənt/ *adj* 1 (capable, efficient) 有能力的; **to be ~ to do sth.** 有能力做某事; **to be ~ at** *or* **in sth.** 能胜任某事 2 (adequate) 足够的 ‹*knowledge*›; 符合要求的 ‹*person, performance*›; **she spoke only ~ French** 她的法语只能满足一般交流 3 Jur 有决定权的 ‹*court, judge, authority*›

competently /ˈkɒmpɪtəntli/ *adv* 1 (capably) 有能力地; **a ~ organized display/report** 组织有序的展示/结构清晰的报告 2 (adequately) 足够地; **she sings ~, but without passion** 她唱得还不错, 但是没有激情

C

competition /ˌkɒmpəˈtɪʃn/ *n* 1 [u] also Comm 竞争; **unfair/keen ~** 不公平的/激烈的竞争; **to be in ~ with sth./sb.** 与某机构/某人竞争; **to be in ~ for/to do sth.** 为某事物/做某事竞争; **to be in ~ for top place** 竞争第一名; **all the boys were in ~ to invite her out first** 男孩子们争着第一个约她出来 2 [c] (contest) 比赛; **to enter/go in for a ~** 参加比赛; **to hold** *or* **stage** *or* **put on a ~** 举行一场比赛 3 + *v sing or pl* **the ~** (competitors) 竞争者; **I was delighted to get the job: the ~ was** *or* **were very strong** 我很高兴得到这份工作: 竞争对手都很强

competition: C~ Commission *n* Brit 竞争委员会; **~ commissioner** *n* 欧盟竞争委员会专员; **~ watchdog** *n* (person) 竞争监察人; (organization) 竞争监察机构

competitive /kəmˈpetɪtɪv/ *adj* 1 (enjoying rivalry) 好竞争的 ‹*spirit*›; **she has a ~ streak** 她有争强好胜的天性 2 (involving competition) 取决于竞争的 ‹*entry*›; 竞技性的 ‹*sport*›; 竞争的 ‹*market, environment, advantage*›; **~ bidding** 竞争性投标; **by ~ examination** 按以考试成绩择优录取的方式 3 Comm 有竞争力的 ‹*goods, prices, performance*›; **a ~ edge** 竞争优势; **to be ~ with sth.** 相对某物有竞争力

competitively /kəmˈpetɪtɪvli/ *adv* 1 (in spirit of rivalry) 好竞争地 2 (in competitions) 竞争性地 3 Comm 有竞争力地; **~ priced** 定价有竞争力的

competitiveness /kəmˈpetɪtɪvnɪs/ *n* [u] 1 (desire to compete) 竞争意识 2 Comm 竞争力

competitive tendering *n* [u] 竞争性招标

competitor /kəmˈpetɪtə(r)/ *n* 1 (in sport) 参赛者; (for job) 竞争者 2 Comm 竞争对手

compilation /ˌkɒmpɪˈleɪʃn/ *n* 1 [u] (act of compiling) (of radio/TV programme, video, album, entry) 编辑; (of reference book) 编写; (of report) 撰写; (of dossier, list, index, catalogue, record) 编制; **great care has been taken in the ~ of this dictionary** 这本词典编纂得很严谨 2 [c] (collection of information or items) 汇编; **a ~ album** (唱片) 专辑

compile /kəmˈpaɪl/ *vt* 1 (accumulate, draw up) 编制 ‹*dossier, list, index, catalogue, record*› 2 (produce from information) 编写 ‹*reference book*›; 撰写 ‹*report*›; 编辑 ‹*radio/TV programme, video, album, entry*›; **to ~ a dictionary** 编纂一部词典 3 Comput 编译 ‹*program, instructions*›

compiler /kəmˈpaɪlə(r)/ *n* 1 (person) 编纂者 2 Comput 编译程序

complacency /kəmˈpleɪsnsi/ *n* [u] 自满; **to have (no) cause** *or* **grounds for ~** (没)有理由自鸣得意; **there is no room for ~ (about sth.)** (对某事物) 不容自满

complacent /kəmˈpleɪsnt/ *adj* 1 (self-satisfied) 自满的 ‹*person*›; 自鸣得意的 ‹*manner, voice*›; **to be ~ about sth.** 为…感到沾沾自喜 ‹*success, future*› 2 (uncritical) 安于现状的 ‹*institution, attitude*›; **to grow ~ about ...** 对…变得满不在乎 ‹*danger, threat*›

complacently /kəmˈpleɪsntli/ *adv* 1 (in a self-satisfied way) 自满地 ‹*speak, gesture*› 2 (uncritically) 安于现状地; **the government say ~ that infant mortality is down to 1%** 政府满不在乎地声称婴儿死亡率已降至 1%

complain /kəmˈpleɪn/
A *vi* (gen) 抱怨; (officially) 抗议; **to ~ to sb. (about sth.)** (gen) 向某人抱怨 (某事物); (officially) «*person, institution*» (就某事物) 向某人提出抗议; **how's life? — I can't ~** colloq 最近怎么样? ——挺好; **to ~ to the police** 向警方投诉; **to ~ of sth.** «*patient*» 诉说 ‹*pain, headache*›
B *vt* 抱怨; **to ~ (to sb.) that ...** (向某人) 抱怨…

complaint /kəmˈpleɪnt/ *n* 1 [u and c] (gen) 抱怨; (official) 抗议; **without a word of ~** 毫无怨言; **tiredness is a common ~** 人们常常抱怨疲劳; **a ~ about sb./sth.** 关于某人/某事物的牢骚; **a ~ that ...** …的抱怨; **no ~s** colloq 还挺好; **to have cause** *or* **grounds for ~** 有理由投诉; **to make** *or* **submit a ~ (to sb.)** (向某人) 投诉; **a letter of ~** 投诉信; **to lay** *or* **lodge** *or* **file a ~ against sb.** 控诉某人 2 [c] Med 疾病; **common ~s** 常见病

complaints: ~ department *n* (place) 顾客投诉部; (people) 投诉部工作人员; **~ procedure** *n* 投诉受理程序

complement /ˈkɒmplɪmənt/
A *n* 1 (improving addition) 补充的东西; **to be a ~ to sth./sb.** 是某事物/某人的补充 2 (quota) 足额; **with a full ~ of staff** 工作人员满员地 3 Ling 补语 4 Math 余角
B *vt* 补充 ‹*colour, flavour*›; 使更具吸引力 ‹*person*›; **to ~ one another** 互补; **wine ~s cheese** 乳酪佐以葡萄酒, 味道很好

complementary /ˌkɒmplɪˈmentri/ *adj* 互补的 ‹*quality, function, flavour, style*›; 配套的 ‹*institution, clothes*›; 辅助性的 ‹*role, person*›; **to be ~ to ...** 与…相辅相成

complementary: ~ angle *n* 余角; **~ colour** *n* 互补色; **~ medicine** *n* [u and c] Brit 辅助性医疗; **acupuncture and osteopathy are ~ medicines** 针灸和整骨术是辅助疗法

complete /kəmˈpliːt/
A *adj* 1 (entire) 全部的 ‹*staff*›; 完整的 ‹*edition, record*›; (comprehensive) 全面的 ‹*report, understanding, annihilation*›; **a ~ set** 整套; **~ works/collection** 全集/全套藏品; **the machine came ~ with tool kit** 这台机器配备了一套工具; **the party won't be ~ without you** 这个聚会没有你就会有缺憾; **to make his happiness ~** 让他的幸福到完满的程度 2 *attrib* (total) 十分的 ‹*surprise, chaos*›; 圆满

ℹ Points of the compass

■ The points of the compass:

north	北
south	南
east	东
west	西

■ Note that in Chinese the order of the points of the compass is not the same as in English: 东, 西, 南, 北. The combination of points is also different:

north-east	东北
north-west	西北
south-east	东南
south-west	西南

Compass point words used with in, to, etc.

■ 'West' can be translated as 西, 西边, 西方, or 西部, depending on context. Other points of the compass may be treated in the same way. 西 indicates direction. 西边 and 西方 refer to a place inside or outside a specific region. 西部 usually refers to a place within a specific region:

He drove off in a westward direction
= 他朝西开走了

They walked towards the north
= 他们向北走去

Germany lies to the west of Poland
= 德国在波兰的西边 / 西面

France is located in the west of Europe
= 法国位于欧洲的西部

I live in the west of China
= 我住在中国西部

■ If it is clear from the context where north, south, etc. is, it is possible to say:

She comes from the north
= 她来自北方 / 北部

Edward was born in the south
= 爱德华出生在南方 / 南部

However, it is conventional to use 部 and not 方, as in the examples below:

He comes from the west
= 他来自西部

William was born in the east
= 威廉出生在东部

Tomorrow there will be strong winds in the southwest
= 明天西南部将有强风

Compass point words used as modifiers

■ Chinese compass point words are nouns and can be used to modify other nouns:

the North Pole
= 北极

South America
= 南美洲

the west coast of Britain
= 英国西部海岸

the east exit
= 东门

a north-west wind
= 西北风

eastern countries
= 东方国家

Sanya is the most southerly seaside city in China
= 三亚是中国最南部的海滨城市

Other phrases

a west-facing house
= 朝西的房子

a westbound train
= 西行的火车

to go west
or ***to go westwards***
or ***to go towards the west***
= 朝西去

The garden faces east
= 花园朝东

The Royal Observatory is situated a few miles south of the river
= 皇家天文台位于河以南几英里处

The castle is about three miles to the north of here
= 城堡在这里向北大约 3 英里处

的 ‹*success, ending*›; 彻底的 ‹*failure, freedom, change, paralysis*›; 十足的 ‹*idiot, stranger*›; **the ~ opposite** 截然相反; **with ~ accuracy/confidence** 绝对精确/信心十足地; **~ and utter** 完完全全的; **~ and utter rubbish** 一堆废话 **3** *pred* (finished) 完成的 ‹*work*›; 结束的 ‹*activity*›; **far from/not yet ~** 远未/尚未完成的 **4** (consummate) 真正意义上的 ‹*gentleman, scholar*›; 技艺高超的 ‹*artist, sportsman*›

B *vt* **1** (make whole) 使…完整 ‹*quote*›; 使…成套 ‹*outfit*›; 使…圆满 ‹*victory, happiness*›; **I need one more card to ~ the set** 我只差一张卡片就配成全套了; **the arrival of my sister ~d our little group** 我姐姐来后，我们小组人就齐了; **to ~ sth. with sth.** 用某物配齐某物; **just to ~ things, we ran out of petrol** 最糟糕的是，我们没有汽油了 **2** (finish) 完成 ‹*task, journey*›; **to ~ a job** 完工; **to ~ a jail sentence** 服完刑期 **3** (fill in) 填写 ‹*form, crossword*›

completely /kəm'pliːtli/ *adv* (totally) 彻底地 ‹*dry, clean*›; 完全地 ‹*forget, satisfy, destroy*›; **~ different** 迥然不同的; **to be ~ full** «*container*» 非常满; «*person*» 非常饱; **to be ~ and utterly broke** colloq 彻底破产; **to ~ lose one's temper** 勃然大怒

completeness /kəm'pliːtnɪs/ *n* [u] 完整; **the ~ of your information** 你信息的完整性

completion /kəm'pliːʃn/ *n* [u] **1** (act, process) 完成; **~ of the course** 结业; **due for ~** 到完工期 **2** (state) (of work) 结束; (of building) 竣工 **3** Brit Comm, Jur (of contract) 签约完成; (of property sale) 交易完成; **payment on ~ of contract** 合同签署完毕时付款

completion date *n* (for works, project) 完工日; (for contract, sale, order) 签约日; (for house purchase) 交易完成日

complex

A /'kɒmpleks, Amer kəm'pleks/ *adj* **1** (intricate) 复杂的 ‹*structure, life*›; **~ number/quantity** Math 复数/复合量 **2** (complicated) 难懂的 ‹*theory, person, situation*›

B /'kɒmpleks, Amer 'kɑːmpleks/ *n* **1** (buildings) 建筑群; **an industrial/a sports ~** 大型工业中心/综合体育场; **a leisure/show/housing ~** 休闲/展览/住宅中心 **2** Psych 情结; **guilt/Electra ~** 不正常的负罪感/恋父情结 **3** (network) 综合体系; **round the missile base there was a ~ of access roads** 在导弹基地周围路网错综复杂

complexion /kəm'plekʃn/ *n* **1** (skin colouring) 肤色; **to have a clear/bad/fair/dark ~** 肤色光洁/差/白皙/黝黑; **to have a spotty ~** 皮肤有雀斑 **2** fig (nature of event, state of affairs, problem) 性质; **to put a (whole) new ~ on sth.** 赋予某事物（全）新的面貌

complexity /kəm'pleksəti/ *n* **1** [u] (intricacy) 错综复杂 **2** [u] (complicatedness of problem, theory, argument, person) 复杂难懂 **3** [c] (complicated aspect of system, network, arrangement) 复杂方面; **the complexities of family life** 家庭生活的各种难题

compliance /kəm'plaɪəns/ *n* [u] **1** (acceptance of suggestion, order, plan) 接受; **in ~ with sth.** 接受某事物 **2** (conformity with ruling, regulation, standard) 服从; **to bring sth. into ~ with ...** 使某事物符合…; **to do sth. in ~ with procedure/the law** 遵照程序/法律办某事 **3** (yielding disposition) 顺从; **~ with sth.** 对某事物的顺从

compliance costs *npl* 合规成本

compliant /kəm'plaɪənt/ *adj* **1** (willing to agree) 顺从的; **to be ~ with** *or* **to sth.** 依从某事物 **2** (conforming with rules, standards) 符合的; **to be ~ with sth.** 符合某事 **3** (yielding) 屈从的; **you cannot afford to be ~; this is a matter of principle** 你不能唯唯诺诺，这可是原则问题

complicate /'kɒmplɪkeɪt/ *vt* 使复杂化; **to ~ matters/life** 使事态/生活变得复杂

complicated /'kɒmplɪkeɪtɪd/ *adj* **1** (intricate) 复杂的 ‹*wiring, machinery, diagram, music*› **2** (difficult) 难懂的 ‹*explanation, relationship*›; 难对付的 ‹*person*›; 棘手的 ‹*situation*›

complication /ˌkɒmplɪ'keɪʃn/ *n* **1** [c] (problem) 难题; **to make ~s** «*person*» 制造难题 **2** [c] Med 并发症; **to develop ~s** 患上并发症; **~s set in, and a week later he was dead** 他出现了并发症，一周后便死了 **3** [u] (intricacy) 错综复杂 **4** [c] (difficulty) 困难

complicit /kəm'plɪsɪt/ *adj* 串通的; **to be ~ (with sb.) in sth.** 在某事上（和某人）串通一气

complicity /kəm'plɪsəti/ *n* [u] 串通; **~ in sth.** 在某事上的串通; **~ in a cover-up** 受到隐瞒包庇的同谋

compliment /'kɒmplɪmənt/

A *n* **1** (remark) 赞扬; **to pay sb. a ~ on sth.** 在某事物上称赞某人; **to return the ~** 回应他人的称赞; fig iron 照样回敬; **to take sth. as a ~** 把某话当成赞美之词 **2** (act) 致意; **it's a ~ to the bride to dress up on her special day** 在新娘大喜的日子里穿上盛装是对她的祝贺

B **compliments** *npl* **1** (expressions of praise) 称赞之词; **to give sb. one's ~s** 给某人以赞美; **to angle** *or* **fish for ~s** 故意寻求别人的恭维 **2** formal (in greetings) 问候; **to give sb. one's ~s** 问候某人; **with the ~s of the season** (on Christmas cards) 致以节日的问候; **my ~s to your wife** 请向尊夫人致意; **with ~s** (on transmission slip) 谨此致意; **the champagne comes with the ~s of the management** 香槟酒是管理层赠送的

C *vt* 称赞; **to ~ sb. on sth.** 为某事物称赞某人

complimentary /ˌkɒmplɪ'mentri/ *adj* **1** (flattering) 赞美的 ‹*comment, remark, letter*›; 恭维的 ‹*person*›; **~ reviews** 好评; **he wasn't very ~ about my poems** 他并不十分欣赏我的诗 **2** (free) 赠送的; **~ drink/food** 免费饮料/食物

complimentary: ~ copy *n* 赠书; **~ ticket** *n* 赠券

compliments slip *n* Brit 礼帖

comply /kəm'plaɪ/ *vi* **1** (obey) 服从; **to ~ with** 遵从 ‹*wish, request*› **2** (with criteria, regulation, etc.) 遵守; **to ~ with sth.** «*person*» 遵守某规则; «*practice, product, machine*» 按照某标准

component /kəm'pəʊnənt/

A *n* **1** (of machine, vehicle, piece of equipment) 零件; **car/bicycle ~s** 汽车/自行车零部件; **electronic ~s** 电子元件 **2** fig (factor) 要素 **3** Mech, Phys (vector) 分力 **4** Chem 组分

B *adj attrib* 组成的 ‹*element*›

componential analysis /ˌkɒmpə'nenʃl ə'næləsɪs/ *n* [u] 成分分析

component: ~ part *n* 组成部分; **~s factory** *n* 零部件生产厂

comport /kəm'pɔːt/ *v refl* formal **to ~ oneself** 举止; **to ~ oneself with great dignity** 举止庄重

comportment /kəm'pɔːtmənt/ *n* [u] formal 举止; **she won admiration for her ~ during the trial** 她在审判过程中的表现受到了赞赏

compose /kəm'pəʊz/

A *vt* **1** (constitute) 组成 ‹*whole, compound, proportion, part*›; **to be ~d of ...** 由…组成 **2** Literat, Mus 创作 ‹*music, literary work*› **3** (write carefully) 撰写 ‹*letter, speech*›; **the first sentence is so hard to ~** 第一个句子很难下笔 **4** (create) 构思 ‹*picture, photograph*› **5** (order) 整理 ‹*thoughts, elements of work*›; **it was a shock, but she ~d her features and restrained her tears** 那件事令人震惊，但是她调整好表情，忍住了泪水 **6** Print 给…排版 ‹*text, book*›

B *vi* Mus 创作

C *v refl* **to ~ oneself** 平静下来

composed /kəm'pəʊzd/ *adj* 镇静的

composer /kəm'pəʊzə(r)/ ▸p. 409 *n* 作曲家

composite /'kɒmpəzɪt/

A *adj* (compound) 复合的 ‹*construction material*›; 拼合的 ‹*text, photo*›; **a ~ picture/word** 拼图/合成词

B *n* 合成物; **to be a ~ of sth. and sth.** 是某事物与某事物的综合

composition /ˌkɒmpə'zɪʃn/ *n* **1** [u and c] (make-up) 构成; **metallic/similar in ~** 金属成分的/成分相似的 **2** [u] Mus, Literat (act or art of composing) 创作; **to study ~** 学习作曲; **of my/her own ~** 由我/她自己创作的 **3** [c] Mus, Literat (work) 作品 **4** [u] Sch (writing of essay) 写作 **5** [c] Sch (essay) 作文 **6** [u] Print 排版; **~ techniques** 排版技术

compositor /kəm'pɒzɪtə(r)/ ▸p. 409 *n* 排版人员

compos mentis /ˌkɒmpəs 'mentɪs/ *adj pred* formal *or* hum 心神健全的; **I am never fully ~ till 11.00 a.m.** 我上午 11 点前从不会完全清醒

compost /'kɒmpɒst/

A *n* **1** [u] (decayed material) 堆肥 **2** [u and c] (commercial product) 混合肥料

B *vt* **1** (make into compost) 将…制成堆肥 ‹*organic material*› **2** (put compost on) 给…施堆肥 ‹*soil*›

compostable /'kɒmpəstəbl/

A *adj* 可制成堆肥的 ‹*material, waste*›

B **compostables** *npl* 可制成堆肥的物质; **kitchen ~s** 可制成堆肥的厨房垃圾

compost: ~ bin *n* 堆肥箱; **~ heap** *n* 堆肥堆

composure /kəm'pəʊʒə(r)/ *n* [u] 镇静; **to lose/regain one's ~** 失去/恢复镇静

compote /'kɒmpəʊt, -pɒt/ *n* [u and c] 蜜饯

compound

A /'kɒmpaʊnd/ *n* **1** (enclosure with buildings) 有围墙的建筑群; **a diplomatic/industrial/military/prison ~** 外交人员公寓/工业园/军方基地/监狱场地 **2** S Afr (living area) 矿工院 **3** Chem 化合物; **carbon ~s** 碳化合物 **4** Ling 复合词; **an adjective ~** 复合形容词 **5** (mixture) 混合物; **his policy is a ~ of caution and imagination** 他的政策既谨慎又富有想象力

B /'kɒmpaʊnd/ *adj attrib* **1** Biol, Bot 复的; **a ~ eye/leaf** 复眼/复叶 **2** Ling 复合的; **a ~ word/adjective/tense/sentence** 复合词/形容词/时态/句

C /kəm'paʊnd/ *vt* **1** fig (exacerbate) 使…加剧 ‹*difficulty, anxiety*›; **to ~ misfortune with error** 出错而使不幸加剧 **2** **to be ~ed of** *or* **from sth.** formal (be formed) «*whole, policy, theory, language*» 由某物构成; **his character was ~ed of wisdom and generosity** 他的性格兼具智慧和大度 **3** Chem, Pharm (mix) 混合 ‹*ingredient(s), chemicals*›; **to ~ sth. with sth.** 将某物与某物混合

compound: ~ fracture *n* 复合骨折; **~ interest** *n* [u] 复利; **to lend money at ~ interest** 按复利放贷; **~ microscope** *n* 复显微镜; **~ noun** *n* 复合名词

comprehend /ˌkɒmprɪ'hend/ *vt* **1** (understand) 理解 ‹*idea, scope, extent, explanation*›; **the generals failed to ~ the gravity of the situation** 将军们不清楚情况的严重性; **I simply cannot ~ what has happened/how it could have happened** 我就是弄不明白发生了什么事/这事怎么会发生 **2** formal (include) 包括; **the study/report ~s all aspects of the proposals** 该研究/报告囊括了这些提议的方方面面

comprehensible /ˌkɒmprɪ'hensəbl/ *adj* 可理解的 ‹*words, emotion, act*›; **it is scarcely** *or* **hardly ~ that they refused him a visa** 他们拒绝给他签证，这几乎叫人无法理解

comprehension /ˌkɒmprɪ'henʃn/ *n* **1** [u] (understanding) 理解; **that is beyond** *or* **above/within my ~** 那事让我无法理解/我能理解

C

2 [u and c] Sch, Univ 理解练习; **a listening/reading/written ～** 听力/阅读/书面理解练习; **a ～ paper/test** 理解测试卷/测试

comprehensive /ˌkɒmprɪˈhensɪv/
A *adj* **1** (all-embracing) 全面的 ‹*survey, knowledge, planning, exposition, study*›; **a ～ motor insurance policy** 汽车全险保单 **2** Brit Sch 综合性的 ‹*school, system*›; 在综合学校就读的 ‹*pupil*›; **to go ～** 办成综合学校 **3** (outright) 绝对的 ‹*victory, defeat*›
B *n* 综合中学; **to go to a ～** 上综合中学

compress
A /kəmˈpres/ *vt* **1** (condense) 压缩 ‹*object, material, substance*›; **to ～ one's lips** 抿紧双唇; **～ed gas** 压缩气体 **2** fig (shorten) 缩短 ‹*text, account, time*›; 简化 ‹*style*›; 剪辑 ‹*film*›; **to ～ sth. into sth.** 将某事物压缩成某事物 **3** Comput 压缩 ‹*data, document, file*›
B /kəmˈpres/ *vi* 压缩; **will the two volumes ～ into one?** 两卷将会压缩成一卷吗？; **her lips ～ed into a thin line** 她双唇抿成了一道缝
C /ˈkɒmpres/ *n* 敷布; **to apply a (hot/cold) ～** 敷上一块（热/冷）敷布

compressed air *n* [u] 压缩空气

compression /kəmˈpreʃn/ *n* [u] **1** (of air, gas, substance, object) 压缩; **the material is resistant to ～** 这种材料耐压 **2** fig (of books, chapters) 缩写 **3** Comput 压缩; **data ～** 数据压缩 **4** Aut [燃料的] 压缩

compression ratio *n* 压缩比

compressor /kəmˈpresə(r)/ *n* 压缩机

comprise /kəmˈpraɪz/ *vt* **1** (consist of) «*complex whole, collection*» 由…构成 ‹*parts, elements*›; **the house ～s seven bedrooms** 这所房子有 7 间卧室 **2** (constitute) «*parts, elements*» 组成 ‹*whole*›; **to be ～d of ...** 由…组成

compromise /ˈkɒmprəmaɪz/
A *n* **1** [c] (settlement) 妥协; **to make** *or* **reach** *or* **come to a ～** 达成妥协; **to agree to a ～** 同意达成妥协; **he was the ～ candidate, not anybody's first choice** 他是个折中的候选人，并不是任何人的首选; **a ～ plan/proposal** 折中计划/提议 **2** [u] (willingness to settle) 妥协态度
B *vi* 妥协; **to ～ on sth.** 在某事上作出让步
C *vt* **1** (threaten) 危及; **she was much ～d by the gossip surrounding her divorce** 关于她离婚的闲言碎语令她声誉受到很大损害 **2** (weaken) «*person*» 减少 ‹*chances, hope*›; «*person*» 在…上让步 ‹*principles*›; «*event*» 损害 ‹*reputation*›; **to ～ success** 减少成功的机会
D *v refl* **to ～ oneself** 使自己受到损害

compromising /ˈkɒmprəmaɪzɪŋ/ *adj* 有失体面的 ‹*information, evidence*›; **to be caught in a ～ situation** 陷入有损声誉的情形

comptroller /kənˈtrəʊlə(r)/ ▸**p. 409** *n* 主管会计

compulsion /kəmˈpʌlʃn/ *n* **1** [u] (force) 强迫; **a ～ on sb. to do sth.** 强迫某人做某事; **there is no ～ on students to attend classes** 没有强求学生上课; **to act under ～** 被迫行动 **2** [c] (urge) 冲动; **to feel a ～ to do sth.** 感觉有做某事的冲动 **3** [u and c] Psych 强迫; **the patient suffers from a ～ to injure himself** 这个病人患有自残强迫症

compulsive /kəmˈpʌlsɪv/ *adj* **1** (inveterate) 难以控制的; **a ～ gambler/liar** 嗜赌/说谎成性的人; **a ～ eater/smoker/drinker** 吃东西/吸烟/饮酒无节制的人 **2** (fascinating) 吸引人的; **to be** *or* **make (for) ～ viewing** 看着叫人欲罢不能

compulsively /kəmˈpʌlsɪvli/ *adv* **1** (obsessively) 强迫性地 **2** (fascinatingly) 吸引人地; **to be ～ readable/watchable** 读/看起来引人入胜

compulsorily /kəmˈpʌlsərɪli/ *adv* 强制地; **the colonel was ～ retired by the army at 62** 这位上校在 62 岁时被强制退役

compulsory /kəmˈpʌlsəri/ *adj* 必修的 ‹*subject*›; 必须做的 ‹*sport, games*›; **～ education/military service** 义务教育/兵役; **attendance at Church is ～ on Sundays** 礼拜天去教堂做礼拜是必须去的; **～ liquidation** 强制清算

compulsory purchase order *n* Brit 强制征购令

compunction /kəmˈpʌŋkʃn/ *n* [u] 内疚; **to have no ～ in** *or* **about doing sth.** 对做某事没有内疚; **without the slightest ～** 丝毫不内疚地

computation /ˌkɒmpjuːˈteɪʃn/ *n* [u and c] 计算; **statistical ～s** 统计计算; **at the highest/lowest ～** 按最高/最低标准计算

computational /ˌkɒmpjuːˈteɪʃənl/ *adj* **1** Math, Stat 计算的; **～ analysis/approach/studies** 计算分析/方法/研究 **2** Comput 计算机的

computational linguistics *npl + v sing* 计算语言学

compute /kəmˈpjuːt/ *vt* 计算; **the hire charge is ～d on a daily basis** 租费按日计算; **to ～ a solution** 盘算解决方案

computer /kəmˈpjuːtə(r)/ *n* 计算机; **to do sth. by ～** *or* **on a ～** 用计算机做某事; **to have/put sth. on ～** 将某资料存入计算机; **the ～ is up/down** 这台计算机在运行/无法运行; **a personal/home/laptop ～** 个人/家用/笔记本电脑; **to be** *or* **work in ～s** 在计算机行业工作

computer age *n* **the ～** 计算机时代

computer-aided, computer-assisted *adjs* 计算机辅助的 ‹*engineering, forecast, research*›; 计算机辅助设计的 ‹*picture*›

computer-aided, computer-assisted: ～ design *n* [u] 计算机辅助设计; **～ design program/system/techniques** 计算机辅助设计程序/系统/技术; **～ language learning** *n* [u] 计算机辅助语言学习; **～ learning** *n* [u] 计算机辅助学习; **～ manufacturing** *n* [u] 计算机辅助制造

computer animation *n* [u and c] 电脑动画

computerate /kəmˈpjuːtərət/ *adj* colloq 具备计算机知识的 ‹*person*›

computer: ～ breakdown *n* [u and c] 计算机故障; **～ buff** *n* colloq (expert) 计算机行家; (enthusiast) 计算机迷; **～ chip** *n* 计算机芯片; **= microchip**; **～ code** *n* [u and c] 计算机编码; **～-controlled** *adj* 计算机控制的 ‹*process, system, machine*›; **～ crash** *n* 计算机崩溃

computer dating *n* [u] 电脑婚介

computer dating service *n* 电脑婚介服务

computer: ～ engineer ▸**p. 409** *n* 计算机工程师; **～ error** *n* 计算机错误

computerese /kəmˌpjuːtəˈriːz/ *n* [u] colloq 计算机行话

computer: ～ failure *n* [u and c] (malfunction) 计算机故障; (total collapse) 计算机崩溃; **～ fraud** *n* [u] 计算机诈骗; **～ game** *n* 电脑游戏; **～ graphics** *npl* **1** + *v sing* (function) 计算机制图; **2** + *v pl* (images) 计算机图画; **～ hacker** *n* colloq 电脑黑客; **～ hacking** *n* [u] colloq 电脑黑客入侵; **～ hardware** *n* [u] 硬件

computerization /kəmˌpjuːtəraɪˈzeɪʃn, Amer -rɪˈz-/ *n* [u] **1** (of records, accounts) 计算机存储 **2** (of work, workplace, system) 计算机化; **the ～ of the checkout system in a supermarket** 超市结账系统的计算机化

computerize /kəmˈpjuːtəraɪz/ *vt* **1** (store) 将…存入计算机 ‹*information, records*› **2** (produce on computer) 将…制成电子文本 ‹*account, bank of statement*›; **the electricity company sent me a ～d account** 电力公司给我发了一份电子账目 **3** (convert to computer operation) 使…计算机化 ‹*process*›; **management intend to ～ every office** 管理部门打算给每间办公室都配备计算机

computer: ～ keyboard *n* 计算机键盘; **～ keyboarder** ▸**p. 409** *n* 计算机录入员; **～ language** *n* 计算机语言; **～ literacy** *n* [u] 使用计算机的能力; **～-literate** *adj* 懂计算机的; **to be ～-literate** 会操作计算机; **～-mad** *adj* 沉迷于计算机的; **～ model** *n* 计算机模拟; **～ operator** ▸**p. 409** *n* 计算机操作员; **～ printout** *n* 计算机打印件; **～ program** *n* 计算机程序; **～ programmer** ▸**p. 409** *n* 计算机程序设计员; **～ programming** *n* [u] 计算机程序设计; **～ publishing** *n* [u] 计算机辅助出版; **～ room** *n* 计算机房; **～ science** *n* [u] 计算机科学; **～ scientist** ▸**p. 409** *n* 计算机科学家; **～ screen** *n* 计算机屏幕; **～ simulation** *n* **= ～ model**; **～ software** *n* [u] 电脑软件; **～ studies** *npl + v sing or pl* 计算机研究; **～ typesetting** *n* [u] 计算机排版; **～ virus** *n* 计算机病毒

computing /kəmˈpjuːtɪŋ/
A *n* [u] (study) 计算机学; (technique) 计算机操作
B *modif* 计算机的 ‹*facilities, services, skills*›; **he's on a ～ course** 他在修一门计算机课程

comrade /ˈkɒmreɪd, Amer -ræd/ *n* **1** dated (friend) 朋友; **the two boys were close ～s** 这两个男孩是亲密的伙伴 **2** Pol (communist, socialist, trades unionist) 同志

comrade-in-arms *n* (*pl* **comrades-in-arms**) 战友; fig 患难之交

comradeship /ˈkɒmreɪdʃɪp, Amer -ræd-/ *n* [u] 同志情谊

con[1] /kɒn/ colloq
A *vt* (*pres p etc.* **-nn-**) 欺骗; **to ～ sb. into doing sth.** 哄骗某人做某事; **to ～ sb. out of sth.** 从某人处骗得某物; **the salesman ～ned me out of £5** 那个推销员骗了我 5 英镑
B *n* (deception) 诈骗; **it was all a ～** 那完全是个骗局

con[2] *n* (disadvantage) 不利条件; **to weigh up the pros and ～s of sth.** 权衡某事物的利弊

con[3] *n* colloq (convict) 囚犯; **he's an ex-～** 他以前坐过牢

con[4] *vt* (*pres p etc.* **-nn-**) Naut 指挥…的航向 ‹*ship*›

Conakry /ˈkɒnəkri/ *pr n* 科纳克里

con artist *n* colloq 骗子

concatenate /kənˈkætɪneɪt/ *vt* **1** formal 把…联系起来 ‹*thoughts, ideas, principles, events, factors, circumstances*› **2** Comput 串联 ‹*data*›

concatenation /kənˌkætɪˈneɪʃn/ *n* **1** [c] (of ideas, events) 一连串事物; **a ～ of events/ideas** 一系列事件/想法 **2** [u] (linking of thoughts, ideas, principles, events, factors, circumstances) 联系 **3** [c and u] (of computer data) 串联

concave /ˈkɒŋkeɪv/ *adj* 凹的 ‹*surface, mirror*›; **～ lens** 凹透镜; **his cheeks were hollow, almost ～** 他的双颊没有肉，几乎是凹进去的

concavity /kɒnˈkævəti/ *n* **1** [u] (state) 凹陷 **2** [c] (surface) 坑

conceal /kənˈsiːl/ *vt* **1** (obscure from view) 隐藏 ‹*person, natural feature*›; **the house was ～ed by trees** 那所房子被树木遮住了 **2** (keep secret) 隐瞒 ‹*evidence, information*› **3** (not show) 掩饰 ‹*emotion*›

concealed /kənˈsiːld/ *adj* **1** (obscured from view) 隐藏的 ‹*entrance, road*›; **～ lighting** 隐蔽照明 **2** (not shown) 掩饰的

concealment /kənˈsiːlmənt/ *n* [u] **1** (concealing from view) 隐藏; (keeping secret) 隐瞒 **2** (state) 躲避; **he sought ～ in the attic** 他躲在阁楼上

concede /kənˈsiːd/
A *vt* **1** (admit) [不情愿地] 承认 ‹*defeat, victory, argument*›; **to ～ that ...** 不情愿地承认…;

to ~ sb. sth. 向某人承认某事; **I'll ~ you that ...** 我向你承认…… **2** (surrender) 让与 ‹*territory, possession, privilege*›; **Italy ~d two goals to Holland in the second half** 意大利队在下半场输给荷兰队两球 **3** Sport (admit defeat in) 承认……失败 ‹*match*›
B *vi* 退让; **to ~ to sth.** 对某事作出让步

conceit /kən'siːt/ *n* **1** [u] (vanity) 自负 **2** [c] Literat (elaborate image) 别出心裁的形象; (poem) 短而精巧的诗 **3** [c] (artistic device) 艺术手法

conceited /kən'siːtɪd/ *adj* 自负的; **she is so ~ about her personal appearance** 她对自己的外貌甚为得意

conceitedly /kən'siːtɪdli/ *adv* 自负地 ‹*speak, write, behave*›

conceivable /kən'siːvəbl/ *adj* 可想到的 ‹*characteristic, place, date, reason*›; **it is ~ that ...** 能想见的是……; **I can think of no ~ circumstances in which that could happen** 我想不出什么情况下会发生那样的事

conceivably /kən'siːvəbli/ *adv* 可以想象地; **I suppose it might just ~ cost more than £100, but ...** 我想它可能要花 100 多英镑, 可是……; **~, I might arrive before 10 am** 我可能上午 10 点前到达; **women (and ~ men) can be selected** 女性 (也有可能是男性) 会被选中

conceive /kən'siːv/
A *vt* **1** (imagine, originate) 想出 ‹*idea*›; 构思 ‹*project, work of art*›; **I cannot ~ that he would simply take the money** 我无法想象他会就那么把钱拿走了 **2** fig liter (develop) 怀有 ‹*feeling*›; **to ~ a hatred for sb./sth.** 对某人/某事物怀恨 **3** 怀 ‹*child, embryo*›; **I was ~d in Italy** 我是在意大利被怀上的 (become pregnant with)
B *vi* **1** (become pregnant) 怀孕 **2** (think, imagine) **to ~ of sth.** 想出 ‹*idea*›; **to ~ of doing sth.** 想象做某事

concentrate /'kɒnsntreɪt/
A *vi* **1** (pay attention) «*person*» 全神贯注; «*mind*» 集中; **~! you're not paying attention!** 专心点! 你走神了!; **to ~ on sth./sb./doing sth.** 专注于某事物/某人/做某事 **2** (focus) «*book, film, journalist*» 聚焦; **to ~ on sth.** 集中讲述某事物 **3** (congregate) «*people, animals*» 聚集; **troops are concentrating north of the city** 部队正在城市北部集结
B *vt* **1** (focus) 集中 ‹*attention, hope(s), thoughts*›; **to ~ one's gaze on sth.** 聚精会神看某物; **I ~d all my efforts on finding somewhere to live** 我尽力在找住处; **fear/pain/the prospect of death ~s the mind** 脑子里充斥着恐惧感/疼痛的感觉/可能会死的念头 **2** (gather together) 聚集 ‹*people, supplies, resources*›; Mil 集中; **the division ~d its attack on the bridge** 该师集中进攻那座桥; **to ~ fire** 集中火力; **to be ~d in sth.** «*ownership, power, population, activity*» 集中于某事物 **3** Chem, Culin 使……浓缩 ‹*liquid, solution*›; **to ~ the stock by boiling fast** 通过快速煮沸收汁
C *n* [c and u] Chem, Culin 浓缩物; **a tin of tomato/orange ~** 一听浓缩番茄汁/橙汁

concentrated /'kɒnsntreɪtɪd/ *adj* **1** Chem, Culin 浓缩的 ‹*extract, solution, food*›; **~ sulphuric acid** 浓硫酸 **2** fig (intense) 集中的; **~ efforts** 专心致志的努力; **it was a ~ attack** 那是一场集中突袭

concentration /ˌkɒnsn'treɪʃn/ *n* **1** [u] (attention) 专注; **to lose one's ~** 注意力涣散; **with great ~** 聚精会神地; **~ on sales/on electrical goods** 专门从事销售/专营电器 **2** [c] (accumulation) 聚集; **a ~ of troops/power** 部队的集结/权力的集中 **3** [u and c] Chem 浓度

concentration camp *n* 集中营

concentric /kən'sentrɪk/ *adj* 同心的 ‹*geometric shapes, spheres*›

concept /'kɒnsept/ *n* 概念; **a philosophical ~** 哲学概念

concept car *n* 概念车

conception /kən'sepʃn/ *n* **1** [c] (idea) 概念; **to have no ~ of sth.** 不明白某事物; **Marx's ~ of social justice** 马克思对社会公平这一概念的理解 **2** [u] (origination) (idea, work of art) 构思; (product, plan) 构想 **3** [u and c] Med 受孕; **measures to prevent ~** 避孕措施

conceptual /kən'septʃʊəl/ *adj* 概念的 ‹*understanding, attitude, method*›; **a ~ framework/work of art** 概念框架/艺术品

conceptual: ~ art *n* [u] 概念艺术; **~ artist** *n* 概念艺术家

conceptualism /kən'septʃʊəlɪzəm/ *n* [u] **1** Philos 概念论 **2** = **conceptual art**

conceptualize /kən'septʃʊəlaɪz/ *vt* 将……概念化 ‹*idea, product, art work*›; **to ~ sth. as sth.** 将某事物概念化成某事物; **to ~ sth. in terms of sth.** 从某方面来构思某事物; **the way people ~ the world** 人们认识世界的方式

conceptually /kən'septʃʊəli/ *adv* 概念上; **the ability to think ~** 理性思维的能力; **to be ~ possible/impossible** 概念上可能/不可能; **~, these are distinct issues** 从概念上讲, 这些是截然不同的问题

concern /kən'sɜːn/
A *n* **1** [u] (worry) 担心; **to have ~ for sb./sth.** 担心某人/某事物; **to give rise to ~** 引起担忧; **an expression** *or* **a look of ~** 一副忧虑的表情; **there is growing ~ about crime** 人们日益担忧犯罪问题; **a matter of/cause for ~** 令人关切的事/引起关切的原因 **2** [u and c] (preoccupation) 令人关切的事物; **environmental/petty ~s** 环境问题/微不足道的事物; **to be of ~ to sb.** 是某人关注的事物; **to have ~ for sb./sth.** 关心某人/某事物 **3** [u] (personal business) 私事; **that's no ~ of sb.'s** *or* **none of sb.'s ~** 那不关某人的事 **4** [c] Comm 公司; **a going/paying ~** 生意兴隆/赚钱的公司
B *vt* **1** (affect, interest) 与……有关; **to whom it may ~** formal 敬启者; **as far as sb. is ~ed** 就某人而言; **the matter doesn't ~ you** 这件事不关你的事; **all (those) ~ed** 所有 (那些) 相关人员; **as ~s sb./sth.** 关于某人/某事物; **where sb./sth. is ~ed** 有关某人/某事物之处 **2** (worry) 担忧; **the doctor was ~ed by the new symptoms** 医生对出现的新症状很担忧 **3** (involve) 牵涉; **to be ~ed with sth./sb.** «*person, government, institution*» 关注 ‹*state of affairs, security, publicity, person*›; **to be ~ed in** «*person, government, institution*» 牵涉进 ‹*scandal, event, plan*›; **was he ~ed in the affair?** 他卷进了那件事吗?; **to be ~ed to do sth.** 认为有必要做某事 **4** (be about) «*text, speech, radio/TV programme*» 关于; **to be ~ed with sth./sb.** 讲述某事物/某人
C *v refl* **1** (take an interest) **to ~ oneself with doing sth.** 对做某事物感兴趣; **to ~ oneself with sth./sb.** 对某事物/某人感兴趣; **to ~ oneself about sth.** 对某事物感兴趣 **2** (worry) **to ~ oneself about sth.** 担心某事物; **don't ~ yourself, my lips are sealed** 别担心, 我的嘴很严 **3** (be about) **to ~ itself with sth./sb.** «*text, speech, radio/TV programme*» 讲述某事物/某人

concerned /kən'sɜːnd/ *adj* (anxious) 不安的; **to be ~ for sb.** 为某人担忧; **I was ~ by** *or* **at the decision** 我对该决定表示担忧; **to be ~ at the news/to hear that ...** 听到这一消息/听说……后感到不安; **to be ~ that sb. may** *or* **might do sth.** 担心某人会做某事

concerning /kən'sɜːnɪŋ/ *prep* 关于

concert /'kɒnsət/ *n* **1** [c] Mus 音乐会; **to give a ~** 举办一场音乐会; **in ~** 在举行音乐会; **a ~ pianist** 钢琴演奏家 **2** [u] formal (harmony, agreement) 合作; **to act/sing in ~** 一起行动/齐唱

concerted /kən'sɜːtɪd/ *adj* 齐心协力的 ‹*action, campaign*›; **to make a ~ effort to do sth.** 合力做某事; **a ~ attack** 联合攻击

concert: ~goer *n* 常去听音乐会的人; **~ grand** ▸**p. 395** *n* 大钢琴; **~ hall** *n* 音乐厅

concerti /kɒn'tʃeəti, -'tʃɜːt-/ *pl* ▸**concerto**

concertina /ˌkɒnsə'tiːnə/
A ▸**p. 395** *n* 六角手风琴
B *vi* (*pt, pp* **~ed** *or* **~'d**) Brit «*vehicle*» 挤在一起; **three carriages had ~ed (together)** 三节车厢挤压在了一起

concertmaster /'kɒnsətmɑːstə(r)/ *n* Amer 乐队首席

concerto /kən'tʃeətəʊ, -'tʃɜːt-/ *n* Mus (*pl* **~s** *or* **concerti**) **1** (with soloist) 协奏曲; **double/triple ~s** 二/三重奏曲 **2** (without soloist) 巴洛克式合奏乐

concert: ~ party *n* **1** Mus, Theat 歌舞表演团; **a touring ~ party** 巡回歌舞表演团; **2** Fin 协同控股人; **~ performance** *n* **1** (in hall) 音乐会表演; **2** Brit (of concert version) [歌剧或芭蕾舞剧的] 演奏会形式的演出; **~ pitch** *n* [u] 国际音高; **at ~ pitch** 以国际音高; **~ tour** *n* 巡回音乐会; **~ version** *n* 音乐会版本 [指未上演的歌剧、芭蕾舞剧或戏剧音乐]

concession /kən'seʃn/ *n* **1** [c] (compromise) 让步; **to make a ~ to sth.** 对某事作出让步; **she made no ~s to his age** 她丝毫不体谅他的年龄; **to make ~s to sb.** 向某人让步; **to win a ~ from sb.** 赢得某人的让步 **2** [u] (yielding) 让与; **the ~ of their rights to the colonists** 他们的权利向殖民者的让与 **3** [c] Brit (discount) 折扣; **a tax/travel ~** 税收/旅行优惠 **4** [c] (property rights) 特许权; **an oil ~** 石油开采特许权 **5** [c] (sales area) 销售场地; **to run a perfume ~** 经营一家香水店 **6** [c] (marketing rights) 特许经营权

concessionaire /kənˌseʃə'neə(r)/ *n* Brit 特许经销商

concessional /kən'seʃənl/ *adj attrib* 优惠的 ‹*allowance, funding*›; **on ~ terms** 以优惠条件; **lending at a ~ interest rate** 按优惠利率提供贷款

concessionary /kən'seʃənəri/ *adj usu attrib* Brit 优惠的 ‹*rate, fare, travel*›

concessive /kən'sesɪv/
A *adj* 表示让步的 ‹*preposition, construction*›; **'although' is a ~ conjunction** "although" 是一个让步连词
B *n* 表示让步的形式; **'despite' is a ~** "despite" 是一个让步词

conch /kɒŋk, kɒntʃ/ *n* (*pl* **~s** *or* **~es**) **1** (shell) 海螺壳 **2** (mollusc) 海螺

conciliate /kən'sɪlɪeɪt/
A *vt* «*government*» 安抚; «*person*» 抚慰 ‹*person, group*›
B *vi* 调解; **to ~ between management and strikers** 在资方和罢工者之间进行调解

conciliation /kənˌsɪlɪ'eɪʃn/
A *n* [u and c] 和解
B *modif* 调解的 ‹*meeting, service*›; **a ~ board** 调解委员会

conciliator /kən'sɪlɪeɪtə(r)/ *n* 调解人; **she is the ~ in the family** 她是家中的和事老

conciliatory /kən'sɪlɪətəri, Amer -tɔːri/ *adj* 调解的 ‹*approach, procedure*›; 安抚的 ‹*gesture, remark*›; 和解的 ‹*spirit*›; **his tone was hardly ~** 他的语气几乎没有缓和

concise /kən'saɪs/ *adj* **1** (succinct) 简洁的 ‹*analysis, instructions*› **2** *attrib* Publg 简略的; **A C~ History of Celtic Art** 《凯尔特艺术简史》

concisely /kən'saɪsli/ *adv* 简洁地 ‹*speak, write*›

conciseness /kən'saɪsnɪs/, **concision** /kən'sɪʒn/ *ns* [u] 简洁

conclave /'kɒŋkleɪv/ *n* [u and c] **1** (private meeting) 秘密会议; **to be in/go into ~** 参加秘密会议 **2** Relig [选举教皇的] 红衣主教密会

conclude /kən'klu:d/
A *vt* **1** (end) 结束〈*agenda*〉; 完成〈*book*〉; **to be ~d** TV 下集播完; Journ 下期登完; **'finally,' he ~d, 'my thanks to you all'** "最后," 他最后说,"谢谢大家" **2** (deduce) 推断; **to ~ that sb. is innocent** Jur 判定某人无罪 **3** (decide) 决定; **to ~ that ...** 决定… **4** (settle) 达成; **to ~ a treaty/an alliance** 缔结条约/结成联盟
B *vi* 结束; **to ~ with sth./by doing sth.** 以某事/做某事告终; **she ~d by saying that she was leaving the firm** 她最后说她要离开公司

C

concluding /kən'klu:dɪŋ/ *adj attrib* 最后的〈*moment, episode, musical note*〉; **~ remarks** 结束语

conclusion /kən'klu:ʒn/ *n* **1** [c] (end) 结尾; **in ~** 最后; **to bring sth. to a ~** 结束某事; **the ~ of the event/book/performance** 事件/书/演出的结尾 **2** [c] (judgement, decision) 结论; **to come to** *or* **reach a ~** 得出结论; **to draw a ~ from sth.** 从某事物中得出结论; **to lead sb. to a ~** «*event, factor, consideration*» 使某人得出结论; **to jump** *or* **leap to ~s** 匆忙下结论; **the result of the inquiry is a foregone ~** 调查结果不出意料; **to take an argument to its logical ~** 把论点归结到合乎其逻辑的结论 **3** [u] (settlement) 缔结; **the ~ of a free-trade accord** 一份自由贸易协定的签订

conclusive /kən'klu:sɪv/ *adj* 确定的〈*findings, evidence*〉; **~ proof** 确凿的证据; **your argument is strong but not ~** 你的论点很有力, 但不足为信

conclusively /kən'klu:sɪvli/ *adv* 不容置疑地〈*argue, prove*〉

concoct /kən'kɒkt/ *vt* **1** Culin 调制〈*drink*〉; 配制〈*soup*〉; 烹制〈*dish*〉 **2** fig pej (invent) 编造; **to ~ an excuse/a plot** 编造理由/虚构情节

concoction /kən'kɒkʃn/ *n* **1** [c] Culin (drink) 调制; (dish) 烹制 **2** [u and c] Culin (preparation) 调制品; **she fed me a delicious ~ of cream and oysters** 她给我吃了一道由奶油与牡蛎制成的美味菜肴 **3** [c] fig (mixture of styles, effects) 混合物; **what's that ~ you're wearing on your head?** 你头上戴的是什么乱七八糟的玩意儿? **4** [c] fig (invention) 编造; **her story is an improbable ~** 她的故事多半为杜撰

concomitant /kən'kɒmɪtənt/ formal
A *adj* 伴随的〈*circumstance, characteristic*〉; **to be ~ with sth.** 伴随着某事物; **the undertaking had its ~ risks** 这项事业有其相应的风险
B *n* 伴随出现的事物; **some people see pain and illness as ~s of the stresses of life** 有些人认为病痛是随生活压力而来的

concord /'kɒŋkɔ:d/ *n* **1** [u] formal (harmony) 和谐; **to live in ~ with neighbouring states** 与邻邦和睦相处 **2** [c] formal (treaty) 协定; **an unspoken ~** 不言可喻的协定 **3** [u] Ling 一致; **grammatical ~** 语法上的一致

concordance /kən'kɔ:dəns/ *n* **1** [u] formal (agreement) 一致; **to be in ~ with ...** 与…一致 **2** [c] (index) 词语索引; **a ~ to the New Testament/Shakespeare** 《圣经·新约》/莎士比亚作品词语索引

concordancing program *n* 检索程序

concordant /kən'kɔ:dənt/ *adj* formal 一致的〈*practice, feature, belief*〉; **to be ~ with sth.** 与某事物一致

concordat /kən'kɔ:dæt/ *n* 政教协定

Concorde /'kɒŋkɔ:d/ *pr n* 协和式飞机

concourse /'kɒŋkɔ:s/ *n* (interior area) 大厅; (open space) 广场; **a station ~** 车站大厅

concrete /'kɒŋkri:t/
A *n* [u] 混凝土; **prestressed/reinforced ~** 预应力/钢筋混凝土
B *adj* **1** Constr 混凝土制的; **a ~ building/slab/floor/path** 混凝土建筑物/预制板/地板/小路 **2** (specific) 具体的〈*answer, proposal*〉; **in ~ terms** 具体来说; **~ evidence** 确凿的证据 **3** (physical) 有形的〈*object*〉 **4** Ling 实的; **a ~ noun** 具体名词 **5** Literat 具体派诗歌的; **~ poetry/poets** 具体派诗歌/具体派诗人

Phrasal verbs

- **concrete in** *vt* [**~ in sth., ~ sth. in**] 把…铸在混凝土中
- **concrete over** *vt* [**~ over sth.**] 用混凝土覆盖〈*ground*〉; **to ~ over a lawn** 用混凝土铺草坪

concrete: ~ jungle *n* pej 混凝土丛林; **~ mixer** *n* = **cement mixer**

concubine /'kɒŋkjʊbaɪn/ *n* esp Hist (of emperor) 妃子; (of commoner) 妾

concur /kən'kɜ:(r)/ (*pres p etc.* **-rr-**)
A *vt* **1** (agree) 同意; **all ~red that it had been a success** 大家一致认为那是成功的 **2** (in speech) 赞同说; **'that's right,' he ~red** "没错," 他赞同说
B *vi* **1** (agree) 同意; **to ~ with sb. in sth./doing sth.** 在某事/做某事上与某人意见一致; **to ~ with sth.** 同意某事 **2** (tally) «*opinions, features*» 一致

concurrence /kən'kʌrəns/ *n* formal **1** [u] (agreement) 同意; **in ~ with ...** 与…意见一致; **these proposals met with her full ~** 这些提议得到了她的完全赞同 **2** [u and c] (combination) 同时发生

concurrent /kən'kʌrənt/ *adj* **1** (simultaneous) 同时发生的; **to be given two ~ sentences of six months** 被判处两项 6 个月刑期, 同期执行 **2** formal (in agreement) 一致的〈*opinions, results*〉; **the magistrate's views were ~ with those of the police** 地方执法官的看法与警方一致

concurrently /kən'kʌrəntli/ *adv* 同时〈*happen*〉; **he ordered that the sentences be served ~** 他命令合并执行这些判决

concuss /kən'kʌs/ *vt* 使脑震荡; **to be ~ed** 患脑震荡

concussion /kən'kʌʃn/ *n* [u and c] 脑震荡

condemn /kən'dem/ *vt* **1** (censure) 谴责; **to ~ sb. for sth./doing sth.** 因某事/做某事谴责某人; **to ~ sth. as pointless/provocative** 指责某事物毫无意义/有挑衅性; **to ~ sb. as an opportunist** 谴责某人是机会主义者 **2** Jur 判处; fig 证明…有罪; **to ~ sb. to death/life imprisonment** 判处某人死刑/终生监禁; **she was ~ed by her refusal to speak/out of her own mouth** 她拒绝开口/她说的话证明了她自己有罪 **3** fig (doom) 迫使…接受困境; **to be ~ed to do sth.** 被迫做某事; **to ~ sb. to sth.** «*circumstances, characteristic*» 迫使…接受某状况〈*person*〉; **the stroke has ~ed her to a wheelchair for life** 她中风后只能在轮椅上度过余生 **4** (declare unsafe) 宣告…不安全〈*building, food*〉; **the pool has been ~ed as a health hazard** 那个游泳池被宣布为健康隐患

condemnation /ˌkɒndem'neɪʃn/ *n* [u and c] **1** (censure) 谴责; **in a tone of ~** 以谴责的口吻 **2** (indictment) (that sb./sth. is guilty) 宣告有罪; (that sb./sth. is unsatisfactory) 宣告不完善; **to be a ~ of sth.** 宣告某事物不完善; **it's no ~ to say that he is particular about appearances** 说他过于注重外表并不是批评他

condemned /kən'demd/ *adj attrib* **1** Jur (sentenced) 被判处死刑的 **2** (unsafe) 不适合居住的〈*building*〉; 不适合使用的〈*facility*〉

condemned cell *n* Brit 死囚牢房

condensation /ˌkɒnden'seɪʃn/ *n* **1** [u] (droplets) 凝结的水珠; **he rubbed the ~ off his glasses** 他擦去凝结在镜片上的水汽 **2** [u] Chem (process) 凝结 **3** [u] (of a gas) 冷凝 **4** [c] fig (abridged version) 缩写本 **5** [u] fig (abridgement) 简缩; **the ~ of ten years' research into one book** 10 年调查研究浓缩成的一本书

condense /kən'dens/
A *vt* **1** Chem 使…凝结〈*gas, vapour*〉; **to ~ sth. into sth.** 使某物凝结成某物 **2** Culin, Ind 使…浓缩〈*liquid*〉; **to ~ the sauce by fast boiling** 通过迅速煮沸的方法使沙司变浓 **3** fig (abridge) 简缩; **the information was ~d into just three pages** 信息被压缩到区区 3 页
B *vi* **1** Chem «*gas, vapour*» 冷凝; **to ~ into sth.** 凝结成某物 **2** Culin, Ind «*liquid*» 变浓

condensed /kən'denst/ *adj attrib* **1** Culin, Ind 浓缩的; **to add water to the ~ soup** 往浓缩汤汁中加水 **2** fig (abridged) 缩写的; **a ~ version of War and Peace** 《战争与和平》的缩写本

condensed milk *n* [u] 炼乳

condenser /kən'densə(r)/ *n* **1** Chem 冷凝器 **2** Phys 聚光器 **3** Elec = **capacitor**

condescend /ˌkɒndɪ'send/ *vi* **1** (deign) 屈尊; **to ~ to do sth.** 屈尊做某事; **she actually ~ed to send me a Christmas card!** iron 她居然放下架子给我寄了一张圣诞贺卡! **2** (patronize) 表现出优越感; **to ~ to sb.** 对某人表现得高人一等

condescending /ˌkɒndɪ'sendɪŋ/ *adj* 有优越感的〈*manner, remark*〉; **I can't stand her: she's so arrogant and ~!** 我受不了她, 她太傲慢, 目中无人!

condescendingly /ˌkɒndɪ'sendɪŋli/ *adv* 有优越感地〈*speak, behave*〉

condescension /ˌkɒndɪ'senʃn/ *n* [u] 优越感; **her smile was a mixture of pity and ~** 她的笑中带有怜悯和傲慢

condiment /'kɒndɪmənt/ *n* **1** Brit (seasoning) 调味品 [指盐、胡椒和芥末等] **2** Amer (sauce) 调味汁; **served with a ~** 带调味汁上桌的

condition /kən'dɪʃn/
A *n* **1** [u] (neutral state) 状况; (negative state) 处境; **to be in good/bad ~** 状况良好/很差; **to keep sth. in good ~** 使某物保持良好状况; **the human ~** 人类的生存状态; **the ~ of the urban poor** 城市贫民的处境; **you're not going out in shoes in that ~!** 你不能穿那么烂的鞋出门! **2** [c] (stipulation) 条件; (in contract, will) 条款; **to make ~s** 制定条件; **to fulfil** *or* **meet** *or* **satisfy the ~s** 满足条件; **on ~ that ...** 在…的条件下; **on one ~** 在一个条件下; **on no ~** 决不; **terms and ~s of employment** 雇用条款 **3** [u] (state of health) 健康状况; **his mental/physical ~** 他的精神/身体状态; **to be in good ~** 身体健康; **to be out of ~** 身体健康; **to be in no ~ to do sth.** 身体状况不适合做某事 **4** [c] (disease) 疾病; **a medical ~** 内科疾病; **a heart/skin ~** 心脏病/皮肤病; **a fatal/an incurable ~** 致命的疾病/不治之症; **her ~ is serious** 她病情危重; **to be in a stable/critical ~** 病情稳定/危重
B **conditions** *npl* 条件; **under difficult/favourable** *etc.* **~s** 在困难的/有利的等条件下; **working/living/housing ~s** 工作/生活/居住条件; **icy/humid ~s** 冰冷的/潮湿的环境; **weather ~s** 天气情况
C *vt* **1** (train) 训练; (accustom) 使适应; **to ~ sb./sth. to do sth.** 训练…做某事〈*animal, person*〉; **to be ~ed into doing sth.** 习惯于做某事; **a ~ed reflex** *or* **response** 条件反射; **to ~ oneself/sb. for sth.** 使自己/某人适应某事物 **2** (determine) «*event, system*» 决定〈*development, choices*〉 **3** (treat) 护理〈*hair, skin*〉 **4** (prepare) 处理〈*leather, fabric*〉

conditional /kən'dɪʃənl/
A *adj* **1** (subject to conditions) 附有条件的〈*agreement, promise, offer*〉; **to be ~ on** *or* **upon sth.** 以某事物为条件; **to make sth. ~ on** *or* **upon sth.** 使某事物以某事物为条件 **2** Ling 条件的; **a ~ clause/conjunction** 条件从句/连词; **in the ~ tense** 用条件时
B *n* **1** [u] (tense) 条件时; **in the ~** 用条件式 **2** [c] (clause, conjunction, statement) 条件式

conditional discharge *n* 有条件释放; **to get** *or* **be given a ～** 被判处有条件释放

conditionally /kən'dɪʃənəli/ *adv* 有条件地 ‹*agree, offer*›; **to be ～ discharged** 被有条件释放

conditioner /kən'dɪʃənə(r)/ *n* [u and c] (for hair) 护发素; (for skin) 护肤剂; (for laundry) 柔顺剂; (for leather) 护革剂; (for lawn) 草坪改良剂; **a lip ～** 润唇膏

conditioning /kən'dɪʃənɪŋ/ *n* [u] 条件作用; **social ～** 社会熏陶; **is personality the result of ～ from parents and society?** 性格是父母和社会熏陶的结果吗?

condo /'kɒndəʊ/ *n* Amer colloq = **condominium**

condolence /kən'dəʊləns/

A *n* [u] (sympathy on bereavement or loss) 慰唁; **a letter of ～** 吊唁信

B condolences *npl* (expressions of sympathy on bereavement, loss) 慰问的话语; **to express one's ～s** 表示慰唁; **please accept my heartfelt ～s on your father's death** 请接受我对你父亲去世的真诚哀悼

condom /'kɒndɒm/ *n* (as contraceptive) 避孕套; (to prevent infection) 安全套; **a ～ machine** *or* **dispenser** 避孕套发放机

condominium /,kɒndə'mɪnɪəm/ *n* Amer **1** (complex) 分套购置的公寓楼 **2** (apartment) **a ～ (unit)** 产权公寓

condone /kən'dəʊn/ *vt* **1** (tolerate) 容忍 ‹*terrorism, crime, fault*›; **the government can never ～ violence** 政府决不能姑息暴力 **2** (sanction) 勉强批准 ‹*act, event*›

condor /'kɒndɔː(r)/ *n* 秃鹫

conducive /kən'djuːsɪv, Amer -'duː-/ *adj* **to be ～ to** 有助于 ‹*action, situation, attitude*›

conduct

A /'kɒndʌkt/ *n* [u] **1** (behaviour) 行为; **code of ～** 行为规范; **disorderly ～** 目无法纪的行为; **a medal for good ～** 优良表现勋章 **2** (handling) 处理; (of campaign, survey) 实施; (of business) 经营

B /kən'dʌkt/ *vt* **1** (lead) 为…做向导 ‹*visitor*›; **she ～ed us around the house** 她领我们在房子里转了转 **2** (manage) 处理 ‹*affairs*›; 安排 ‹*life*›; 经营 ‹*business*›; 进行 ‹*negotiations, survey, campaign*›; **to ～ an inquiry** 进行调查; **to ～ a case/defence** 处理案件/进行辩护 **3** Mus 指挥 ‹*choir, concert*›; **she regularly ～s Mozart** 她经常指挥演奏莫扎特作品 **4** Elec, Phys 传导 ‹*energy, electricity*›; **does water ～ heat well?** 水的导热性好吗?

C /kən'dʌkt/ *vi* 指挥; **he ～ed from the piano** 他通过钢琴来指挥; **he went on a ～ing course** 他上了指挥课

D /kən'dʌkt/ *v refl* **to ～ oneself** 表现; **the government has ～ed itself in the most shameful way** 该政府的表现令人不齿; **the little girl ～ed herself like a perfect lady** 这个小姑娘的举止像一位淑女

conductance /kən'dʌktəns/ *n* [u and c] 电导率

conducted /kən'dʌktɪd/ *adj attrib* 有导游陪同的 ‹*tour, visit*›

conduction /kən'dʌkʃn/ *n* [u] 传导

conductive /kən'dʌktɪv/ *adj* **1** (conducting heat, electricity) 有传导性的 ‹*material, surface*› **2** (relating to conduction) 传导的 ‹*property, path*›; **～ heating/cooling** 传导加热/制冷

conductivity /,kɒndʌk'tɪvəti/ *n* [u and c] 传导性; **electrical ～** 电传导

conductor /kən'dʌktə(r)/ ▸**p. 409** *n* **1** Mus 指挥 **2** (on bus, tram) 售票员 **3** Amer (on train) 列车长 **4** (guide) 向导 **5** Elec, Phys 导体

conduct report *n* 在校行为报告

conductress /kən'dʌktrɪs/ ▸**p. 409** *n* Brit dated 女售票员

conduit /'kɒndɪt, 'kɒndjuːɪt, Amer 'kɒndwɪt/ *n* **1** (pipe) 管道 **2** Elec 导线管 **3** fig (person, organization) 渠道

cone /kəʊn/ *n* **1** (shape) 圆锥体; **a paper ～ full of popcorn** 盛满爆米花的锥形纸筒 **2** Bot 锥形球果 **3** (for ice cream) 冰激凌蛋筒 **4** (on road) 锥形路标 **5** Geol 火山锥 **6** Anat 视锥

Phrasal verb

- **cone off** *vt* [**～ sth. off, ～ off sth.**] «*workers, police*» 用锥形路标关闭 ‹*lane, junction*›

cone-shaped *adj* 锥形的

confab /'kɒnfæb/ colloq *n* **1** (conversation) 闲谈; **to have a ～ about sth.** 聊某事物 **2** Amer (meeting) 会议

confection /kən'fekʃn/ *n* **1** Culin (cake) 糕饼; (sweetmeat) 蜜饯; (dessert) 甜点 **2** (elaborate garment, hat, building) 精工制作的物品; **the mosque was a ～ of domes and minarets** 这座清真寺由拱顶和光塔组成，工艺复杂精美

confectioner /kən'fekʃənə(r)/ ▸**p. 409** *n* 甜品商

confectioner's sugar *n* Amer = **icing sugar**

confectionery /kən'fekʃənəri, Amer -ʃəneri/ *n* [u and c] 甜食

confederacy /kən'fedərəsi/ *n* **1** Pol 联盟 **2 Confederacy** Amer Hist 邦联; **the (Southern) C～** (南部) 邦联

confederate

A /kən'fedərət/ *n* **1** (accomplice) 同伙; **she was his ～ in the kidnapping** 在绑架案中，她是他的同伙 **2 Confederate** Amer Hist 南部邦联支持者

B /kən'fedərət/ *adj attrib* **1** (allied) 联盟的 ‹*body, state*›; **all ～ members of the association** 所有加盟该协会的成员 **2 Confederate** Amer Hist 南部邦联的; **the C～ States (of America)** (美国) 南部邦联

C /kən'fedəreɪt/ *vt* 使…结盟 ‹*nations, businesses, industries*›; **the new ～d Europe** 结成同盟的新欧洲

confederation /kən,fedə'reɪʃn/ *n* 联盟

C

Conditionals

■ Chinese conjunctions indicating supposition include 如果, 假如, 假使, 倘若, 如 or 若. Like 'if' in English, these conjunctions are used in the subordinate clause (the first clause in Chinese). 那么 or 就 are used in the main clause (the second clause in Chinese).

■ 那么 can be used only between two clauses. 就 can be placed only before the predicate of the main clause. 那么…就… can also be used together in the main clause.

■ 如果, 假如, 假使, 倘若, and 如 are used at the beginning of the subordinate clause or after the subject of the subordinate clause. This is different from the English 'if' which is placed only at the beginning of the subordinate clause:

If you send the letter by air, they will receive it in two days
= 如果你寄航空信，他们两天后就能收到
or 你如果寄航空信，(那么) 他们两天后能收到
or 如果你寄航空信，(那么) 他们两天后就能收到
or 你如果寄航空信，(那么) 他们两天后就能收到

I'll do it for you if you want
= 假如你愿意，(那么) 我来为你做
or 你假如愿意，我就来为你做
or 假如你愿意，(那么) 我就来为你做
or 你假如愿意，(那么) 我就来为你做

■ 如果, 假如, etc. can be used on their own in the first clause without 就 or 那么 being necessary in the second clause:

I'll go there myself if you have no time
= 如果你没时间，我自己去那儿

If it is fine tomorrow, then we can go downtown
= 假如明天天好，我们可以进城

■ 如果, 假如, 假使, 倘若 (excluding 如 and 若 found in written Chinese) can be omitted in the first clause, with 就 being used on its own in the main clause to indicate the result that may be produced from the supposed condition:

You don't have to come if you are not free
= 你没有时间就不必来了

If nobody drives, we can't get to the train station on time
= 没人开车我们就不能按时赶到火车站

■ 如果 is often used in spoken Chinese. 假如 and 假使 can be used both in written and spoken Chinese. 倘若, 若, and 如 are mostly used in written Chinese:

We can have a snowball fight if there is enough snow tomorrow
= 如果明天雪大的话，我们可以打雪仗

If everyone agrees, then we can start tomorrow
= 假使大家都同意，我们明天开始

I'd like to cancel the appointment, if you don't mind
= 倘若您不介意，我想取消预约

Break glass in case of fire
= 如遇火灾，请击碎玻璃
or 若遇火灾，请击碎玻璃

■ In Chinese conditional sentences, the subjunctive mood is conveyed by context rather than by verb tense:

If I were in your shoes, I would speak to the line manager
= 如果我处于你的境地，我会和部门经理谈谈

Should you require more assistance, please ring this number
= 若需更多帮助，请拨打此号码

I would have picked you up if I had known you were arriving today
= 假如知道你今天到，我就去接你了

Had the ambulance come earlier, my brother's life would have been saved
= 倘若救护车早到一些的话，我弟弟的命就会保住了

confer /kənˈfɜː(r)/ (*pres p etc.* **-rr-**)
A *vt* «*person, institution*» 授予 ‹*title, academic degree, right, honour*›; «*person, institution, quality*» 赋予 ‹*benefit, status*›; **to ~ sth. on sb.** 将某事物授予某人; **the body has the right to ~ degrees** 这个团体有学位授予权; **health ~s happiness** 健康带来快乐
B *vi* «*person*» 商量; «*jury, council*» 协商; **to ~ with sb. about sth.** 就某事物与某人协商

conference /ˈkɒnfərəns/ *n* **1** [u and c] (meeting) 会议; **to be in ~ (with ...)** 在（与…）开会; **to hold/call/host a ~ on ...** 举行/召开/主办关于…的会议; **to go into ~** 进行会议讨论 **2** [c] (symposium) 研讨会 **3** [u and c] + *v sing or pl* (people) 与会者; **~ voted to reject the motion** 与会者投票否决了这一动议 **4** [c] Amer Sport 体育联合会

conference: ~ call *n* 电话会议; **to make a ~ call** 召开电话会议; **~ centre** *n* 会议中心; **~ committee** *n* Amer 会议协调委员会［审议消除两院通过的同类议案中的文字差异的临时委员会］; **~ hall** *n* 会议厅; **~ room** *n* 会议室; **~ table** *n* lit, fig 会议桌; **to get together round the ~ table** 一起坐下来进行协商

conferment /kənˈfɜːmənt/ *n* [u] (of title, academic degree, right, honour) 授予; (of benefit, status) 赋予; **the vice chancellor performed the ~ of degrees** 副校长颁发了学位证书

confess /kənˈfes/
A *vi* **1** (plead guilty) 认罪; **~!** 坦白吧！; **to ~ to sth.** 坦白 ‹*specific crime, neglect, sins*›; **to ~ to doing sth.** 供认做过某事 **2** (acknowledge reluctantly) 承认; **to ~ to a liking for sth.** 承认喜好某事物 **3** Relig «*penitent*» 忏悔
B *vt* **1** (admit responsibility for, acknowledge reluctantly) 承认 ‹*mistake, desire, inability*›; 供认 ‹*guilt*›; 忏悔 ‹*sins*›; **to ~ that ...** 承认…; **'I damaged your car,' she ~ed** "我弄坏了你的车，" 她坦白说; **he was reluctant to ~ his ignorance** 他不愿承认自己无知; **a (self-)~ed failure** （自己）认输 **2** Relig (acknowledge belief in) 宣称信奉 ‹*belief*› **3** Relig (hear confession of) «*priest*» 聆听…的忏悔 ‹*parishioner, penitent*›
C *v refl* formal **to ~ oneself to be sth.** 承认某事; **she ~ed herself to be reluctant to move** 她承认不愿意搬家

confession /kənˈfeʃn/ *n* **1** [c] Jur 供认; **to make a (full) ~** （全面）供认; **a written ~** 供认状; **a ~ of rape/murder/burglary** 对强奸/谋杀/入室盗窃罪的招供 **2** [c] (reluctant acknowledgement) 承认; **I've a ~ to make — I lied about my age** 我要承认错误——我谎报了年龄; **a ~ of failure** 认输 **3** [u and c] Relig (admission of sins) 忏悔; **to go to ~** 去忏悔; **to make one's ~** 忏悔

confessional /kənˈfeʃənl/
A *n* 告解室
B *adj* **1** Relig 忏悔的 ‹*prayer, psalm*› **2** (personally revealing) 自白的; **his ~ outpourings** 他自白式的倾诉

confetti /kənˈfeti/ *n* [u]［婚庆场合使用的］五彩纸屑

confidant /ˌkɒnfɪˈdænt/ *n* 知己; **sb.'s friend and ~** 某人的密友; **a close/trusted ~** 亲密的/可信赖的知心好友

confidante /ˌkɒnfɪˈdænt/ *n* 女性知己; **a close/trusted ~** 亲密的/可信赖的知心姐妹

confide /kənˈfaɪd/
A *vt* 吐露 ‹*secret, trouble*›; **to ~ to sb. that ...** 向某人吐露…; **'I'm frightened to go,' he ~d** "我害怕去，" 他承认道
B *vi* 吐露秘密; **to ~ in sb.** 向某人透露秘密; **she ~d in her sister about her fears for the future** 她向姐姐诉说了自己对未来的恐惧

confidence /ˈkɒnfɪdəns/ *n* **1** [u] (faith) 信任; **to have (every) ~ in sb./sth.** （完全）信任某人/某事物; **to enjoy/gain sb.'s ~** 为某人所信任/得到某人的信任; **to put one's ~ in sb.** 信任某人; **to pass a vote of ~** 通过信任投票 **2** [u] (self-assurance) 自信; **to be full of/bursting with ~** 充满/满怀自信; **to lack/lose ~** 缺乏/失去自信 **3** [u] (certainty) 把握; **in the full ~ that ...** 对…非常有把握; **I have every ~ that she will succeed** 我确信她会成功 **4** [u] (confidentiality) 信赖; **to take sb. into one's ~** 将某人当作知己; **to tell/write sb. sth. in (strict) ~** （很）信赖地告诉/写信告知某人某事; **a breach of ~** 泄密 **5** [c] (secret) 秘密; **to betray a ~** 泄密

confidence: ~-booster *n* (person) 增强信心的人; (thing, event) 增强信心的事物; **the win was a huge ~-booster for the team** 这次胜利极大地增强了队伍的信心; **~ game** *n* Amer **= ~ trick**; **~ level** *n* **1** Stat 置信度; **2** (feeling) 自信度; **~ trick** *n* Brit 骗局; **~ trickster** *n* Brit 骗子

confident /ˈkɒnfɪdənt/ *adj* **1** (self-assured) 自信的 ‹*speech, manner*› **2** (sure) 确信的; **to be ~ that ...** 确信…; **to be ~ of sth./doing sth.** 对某事物/做某事有把握; **she felt ~ about the future** 她对未来很有把握

confidential /ˌkɒnfɪˈdenʃl/ *adj* 机密的 ‹*information*›; 秘密的 ‹*service*›; **strictly ~** 绝密的; **a ~ secretary** 机要秘书

confidentiality /ˌkɒnfɪdenʃɪˈæləti/ *n* [u] 机密性; **to respect the ~ of sth.** 对某事保密; **a ~ agreement** 保密协议

confidentially /ˌkɒnfɪˈdenʃəli/ *adv* 秘密地; **~ speaking, ...** 私下里说说, …

confidently /ˈkɒnfɪdəntli/ *adv* **1** (with self-assurance) 自信地 ‹*behave, write*› **2** (with certainty) 有把握地 ‹*speak, expect*›

confiding /kɒnˈfaɪdɪŋ/ *adj* 轻信他人的 ‹*person, nature*›; 信任的 ‹*smile, air*›

configuration /kənˌfɪɡəˈreɪʃn, Amer -ˌfɪɡjə-/ *n* **1** (arrangement) 结构; **the ~ of the solar system** 太阳系的构成; **the broad ~ of the economy** 经济的大框架 **2** Comput 配置

configure /kənˈfɪɡə(r), Amer -ˈfɪɡjər/ *vt* **1** (arrange) 装配 ‹*machine*›; 设定 ‹*template*›; 安排 ‹*space*›; 编排 ‹*team*›; **to ~ sth. as sth.** 把某物设定为某物; **to ~ sth. for/to do sth.** 为某事物/做某事设定某物 **2** Comput 配置 ‹*computer, system*›; **to ~ sth. as sth.** 把某物配置成某物; **to ~ sth. for/to do sth.** 为某事物/做某事配置某物

confine
A /kənˈfaɪn/ *vt* **1** (in room) 禁闭 ‹*person*›; 关起 ‹*animal*›; (in cell, prison) 监禁; (in institution) 关押; **to be ~d to bed/the house/a wheelchair** 卧病在床/被困在家里/离不开轮椅; **to be ~d to barracks** 被禁闭在营房内 **2** (limit) 限制; **to ~ sth. to sth.** 将某事物限制在某范围内; **please ~ your comments to the matter in hand** 请就眼下的问题发表评论; **to be ~d to sth.** «*problem, activity*» 局限于 ‹*topic, area*›; **the problem is not ~d to old people** 这个问题并不限于老年人
B /kənˈfaɪn/ *v refl* **to ~ oneself to sth./doing sth.** 将自己局限于某事/做某事; **please ~ yourself to the facts** 请你不要脱离实际情况
C **confines** /ˈkɒnfaɪnz/ *npl* **1** (borders) 界限; **within/beyond the ~s of ...** 在…的界限内/超越了…的界限 **2** fig (constraints) 限制; **within the ~s of morality/the law** 在道德/法律允许的范围内

confined /kənˈfaɪnd/ *adj attrib* 狭窄的 ‹*space*›; 受约束的 ‹*atmosphere*›

confinement /kənˈfaɪnmənt/ *n* **1** [u] (restriction, imprisonment) (in room) 禁闭; (in cell, prison) 监禁; (in institution) 关押; **during my ~ to bed/to the house** 在我卧病在床/被困在家期间; **~ to barracks/quarters/base** 禁闭在营房/住所/基地; **he was kept in ~ during investigations** 他在调查期间受到监禁 **2** [u and c] dated (in childbirth) 分娩

confirm /kənˈfɜːm/ *vt* **1** (state as true) 证实 ‹*theory, news, suspicion*›; **to ~ that ...** 证实…; **two people were ~ed dead** 两人被证实死亡; **to ~ receipt of** 确认收到 ‹*cheque, goods*›; **'yes, it's Tuesday,' he ~ed** "对，今天是星期二，" 他肯定说 **2** (make definite) 确认 ‹*appointment, reservation*›; 批准 ‹*treaty*›; **to ~ sb. as director** 批准某人担任负责人; **to ~ sb. in office** 批准某人上任 **3** (justify) 巩固 ‹*authority, position*›; 加强 ‹*opinion, resolve, emotion, doubt*›; **her letter ~ed my resolve to go to Africa** 她的信更坚定了我去非洲的决心; **to ~ sb. in their dislike of .../reluctance to ...** 使某些人更确信自己不喜欢/不愿意… **4** Relig 给…施坚信礼 ‹*person*›

confirmation /ˌkɒnfəˈmeɪʃn/ *n* **1** [u] (statement of truth) 证实 **2** [u] (of appointment, reservation) 确认; (of treaty) 批准; **I should like written ~ of the reservation** 我想要预订的书面确认 **3** [u and c] (justification) (of authority, position) 巩固; (of opinion, resolve, emotion, doubt) 加强 **4** [u and c] Relig 坚信礼; **~ service** 坚信礼

confirmed /kənˈfɜːmd/ *adj attrib* **1** (unlikely to change) 坚定的 ‹*non-smoker*›; 成习惯的 ‹*drunkard, liar*›; **a ~ bachelor** 抱定终身不娶信念的单身汉 **2** (unshakeable) 根深蒂固的 ‹*habit, belief*›

confiscate /ˈkɒnfɪskeɪt/ *vt* 没收 ‹*property*›

confiscation /ˌkɒnfɪˈskeɪʃn/ *n* [u] 没收

conflagration /ˌkɒnfləˈɡreɪʃn/ *n* formal 大火

conflate /kənˈfleɪt/ *vt* 把…合并 ‹*categories, texts*›; 把…混淆 ‹*information, issues*›; **to ~ A and** *or* **with B** 合并A和B

conflation /kənˈfleɪʃən/ *n* **1** [u] (action) 合并 **2** [c] (result) 合并物; **the text is a ~ of earlier sources** 这个文本是先前资料的综合

conflict
A /ˈkɒnflɪkt/ *n* [u and c] **1** Mil 战斗; **armed ~** 武装冲突 **2** (dispute) 争端; **to be in/come into ~ (with ...)** （与…）有分歧/发生争执; **to bring sb. into ~ with sb./sth.** 使某人与某人/某机构发生争执; **his views brought him into ~ with the establishment** 他的观点使他与当权派发生争执 **3** (dilemma) 冲突; **a ~ of interests/loyalties** 利益/效忠冲突
B /kənˈflɪkt/ *vi* **1** (contradict) **to ~ with sth.** «*statement, judgement*» 与某事物矛盾 **2** (clash) 冲突; **to ~ with sth.** «*TV/radio programme, event*» 与某事物冲突

conflicting /kənˈflɪktɪŋ/ *adj* **1** (incompatible) 矛盾的 ‹*views, interests*› **2** *attrib* (coinciding) 时间上冲突的 ‹*TV/radio programmes, events*›

confluence /ˈkɒnfluəns/ *n* **1** (of rivers) 汇流处 **2** fig formal (of people, ideas, factors) 汇集; **a major ~ of the world's financial markets** 世界各金融市场的一次大融合

conform /kənˈfɔːm/ *vi* **1** (behave as expected or in accordance with convention) 遵从; **she has always ~ed** 她总是循规蹈矩的; **to ~ with sth.** 遵从某事; **you must try to ~ with acceptable behaviour** 你必须努力使自己的行为举止符合规范 **2** (correspond) 符合; **to ~ to** *or* **with sth.** 符合某事物; **to ~ to type** 符合标准; **he tried to make his lifestyle ~ to hers** 他试图使自己的生活方式和她的相一致 **3** (obey) 遵守; **to ~ to sth.** «*person, product, practice*» 遵照 ‹*regulation, specification*› **4** formal (fit) 相一致; **to ~ to sth.** 与某事物相一致; **a shoe that ~s to the foot** 一只合脚的鞋子

conformist /kənˈfɔːmɪst/ pej
A *adj* 墨守成规的 ‹*person, attitude, behaviour*›; **the school has a ~ approach to teaching** 这所学校的教学方法因循守旧
B *n* 遵奉者

conformity /kənˈfɔːməti/ *n* [u] **1** (compliance with law, regulation, standard, specification) 遵守; **~ to** *or* **with sth.** 对某事物的遵守 **2** (agreement, correspondence) 符合; **to be in ~ with sth.** 与某事物一致 **3** pej (being like others) 从众; **strict ~** 绝对盲从

C

confound /kən'faʊnd/
A *vt* 1 (perplex) 使困惑; **the entire team was ~ed by his betrayal** 全队都对他的背叛大惑不解 2 (prove wrong) 证明…有误 ‹*prediction, suspicion*›; **she ~ed the critics by winning first prize** 她赢得了一等奖，从而让批评家大失脸面 3 (mix up) 混淆 ‹*concepts*›; **to ~ A and** *or* **with B** 混淆A和B
B *excl* colloq dated 该死; **~ him!** 去他的!

confounded /kən'faʊndɪd/ *adj attrib* colloq dated 讨厌的; **what a ~ nuisance!** 真讨厌!

confront /kən'frʌnt/ *vt* 1 (face) 面对; **to ~ the truth** 面对事实; **the cases that ~ lawyers** 律师们面临的案子 2 fig (challenge) 与…对证 ‹*person*›; **in the witness box, the pathologist ~ed her with his findings** 证人席上的病理学家用他的发现向她发出质询 3 fig (present itself to) «*challenge, danger*» 临到…头上 ‹*person*›; **to be ~ed by** *or* **with sth.** 面临某事 4 (face up to) 大胆面对; **you must learn to ~ difficult situations** 你必须学会勇敢地面对困难处境

confrontation /ˌkɒnfrʌn'teɪʃn/ *n* [u and c] 1 (battle) 对抗; **a classic ~ between two top runners** 两位顶尖赛跑运动员之间的经典较量 2 (dispute) 冲突; **we had a ~ with our manager** 我们和经理发生了冲突

confrontational /ˌkɒnfrən'teɪʃənl/ *adj* 对抗的 ‹*manner, relationship*›; 咄咄逼人的 ‹*person, style*›

Confucian /kən'fjuːʃn/
A *adj* 1 (relating to Confucius) 孔子的 2 (relating to Confucianism) 儒家的 ‹*tradition, philosopher*›
B *n* 儒学信徒

Confucianism /kən'fjuːʃənɪzəm/ *n* [u] 儒学

Confucius /kən'fjuːʃəs/ *pr n* 孔子; **the sayings of ~** 孔子语录

confuse /kən'fjuːz/ *vt* 1 (bewilder) 使迷惑; **to ~ sb. by doing sth.** 做某事迷惑某人 2 (fail to distinguish) 混淆; **to ~ A and** *or* **with B** 混淆A和B 3 (complicate) 使…含混不清 ‹*argument, reasoning*›; **she ~d the issue by quoting opposing theories** 她引用的理论互相矛盾，把问题弄复杂了

confused /kən'fjuːzd/ *adj* 1 (bewildered) 困惑的 ‹*mind, expression*›; **he was ~ about the instructions** 操作指南把他给搞糊涂了; **the ~ elderly** 糊涂的老年人 2 (muddled) 混乱的 ‹*account*› 3 (hard to distinguish) 分辨不清的 ‹*sounds, voices*›; **~ memories of childhood** 模糊的童年记忆

confusedly /kən'fjuːzɪdli/ *adv* 1 (in bewilderment) 困惑地 2 (unclearly) 不清楚地; **he spoke ~ of his plans** 他颠三倒四地谈了自己的各项计划

confusing /kən'fjuːzɪŋ/ *adj* 1 (perplexing) 令人困惑的 ‹*experience*› 2 (complicated) 复杂难懂的 ‹*instructions*›; **a very ~ email** 一封极其令人费解的电子邮件

confusion /kən'fjuːʒn/ *n* 1 [u] (bewilderment) 困惑; **in (a state of total) ~** （极度）困惑地 2 [u and c] (lack of clarity) 混淆; **to avoid ~** 避免混淆 3 [u] (chaos) 混乱; **to throw sb./sth. into ~** 使某人/某事物陷入混乱 4 [u] (embarrassment) 窘迫; **to sb.'s ~** 使某人尴尬的是; **to her great ~, he asked her to marry him** 让她大为尴尬的是，他向她求婚了; **in sb.'s ~** 在某人很窘迫的情况下; **in my ~ and delight, I quite forgot to thank her** 我既局促又高兴，居然忘了感谢她 5 [u] (uncertainty) 不确定; **there was some ~ about what to do next** 下面该怎么做还不明确

conga /'kɒŋɡə/ *n* 1 (dance) 康茄舞 2 Mus 康茄鼓; **she beat/played a ~** 她击打/演奏了一曲康茄鼓

con game *n* Amer colloq **= confidence trick**

congeal /kən'dʒiːl/
A *vi* 凝结
B *vt* 使…凝结 ‹*blood, milk, paint*›

congenial /kən'dʒiːnɪəl/ *adj* 1 (suitable, pleasant) 令人愉快的 ‹*surroundings, work*› 2 (likeable) 意气相投的 ‹*company*›; **he found few people ~ to him** 他发现没有什么人同自己意气相投

congenital /kən'dʒenɪtl/ *adj* 1 Med 先天的 ‹*disease, defect*›; **a ~ sufferer from sth.** 天生有某疾病的人 2 *attrib* fig (inveterate) 天生的 ‹*inability, fear, emotion*›; **a ~ liar** 生性好撒谎的人

congenitally /kən'dʒenɪtəli/ *adv* 先天地; **~ blind/deaf/malformed** 先天失明/失聪/畸形

conger /'kɒŋɡə(r)/ *n* **~ (eel)** 康吉鳗

congested /kən'dʒestɪd/ *adj* 1 (crowded) (with people) 拥挤的; (with vehicles) 拥堵的; **to be ~ with ...** 挤满… 2 Med (blocked) (with blood) 充血的 ‹*lung*›; (with mucus) 黏液阻塞的 ‹*nose*›; **his arteries were ~** 他患了动脉梗阻

congestion /kən'dʒestʃn/ *n* [u] 1 (overcrowding) (with people) 拥挤; (with vehicles) 拥堵 2 Med (being blocked) (with blood) 充血; (with mucus) 黏液阻塞; **for nasal ~, try this new spray** 试试这种新喷剂，可治疗鼻塞

congestion charge *n* Brit 交通拥堵费; **~ area** 收取交通拥堵费的地段

conglomerate
A /kən'ɡlɒmərət/ *n* 1 [c] Comm 集团公司 2 [u and c] Geol 砾岩
B /kən'ɡlɒmərət/ *adj* 1 Comm 大型联合的 ‹*company*› 2 (composed of several elements) 不同成分组成的 ‹*substance*› 3 Geol 砾岩的
C /kən'ɡlɒməreɪt/ *vt* (bring together) 使…聚集 ‹*particles, elements*›
D /kən'ɡlɒməreɪt/ *vi* 1 (come together) «*particles, elements*» 聚集; **to ~ into sth.** 聚集成某事物 2 Comm «*companies*» 组成集团公司

conglomeration /kənˌɡlɒmə'reɪʃn/ *n* 1 [u] (coming or bringing together) 合并 2 [c] (mixture) 聚集物; **a ~ of little houses outside the village proper** 村外簇拥在一起的小房子

Congo /'kɒŋɡəʊ/ ▸**p. 663** *pr n* 1 **Democratic Republic of the ~** 刚果民主共和国 2 **(Republic of) the ~** 刚果共和国 3 **the ~** (river) 刚果河

Congolese /ˌkɒŋɡə'liːz/ ▸**p. 503**
A *adj* (of the Republic of the Congo) 刚果的; (of the Democratic Republic of the Congo) 刚果的; (of the people of the Republic of the Congo) 刚果人的; (of the languages of the Republic of the Congo) 刚果语的
B *n* 1 [c] (person of the Republic of the Congo) 刚果人 2 [u] (languages of the Republic of the Congo) 刚果语

congratulate /kən'ɡrætʃʊleɪt/
A *vt* 向…祝贺 ‹*person, institution*›; **to ~ sb. on their success/engagement** 祝贺某人的成功/订婚
B *v refl* **to ~ oneself on sth.** 为某事物感到自豪

congratulation /kənˌɡrætʃʊ'leɪʃn/
A *n* [u] 祝贺; **in ~, I would like to say that ...** 为表示祝贺，我想说…
B **congratulations** *npl* 贺词; **~s!** 祝贺你!; **~s on your success/the birth of your new baby** 祝贺你取得成功/恭喜你的宝宝出生; **to offer one's warmest** *or* **heartiest ~s to sb.** 向某人表示最热烈/最衷心的祝贺

congratulatory /kən'ɡrætʃʊlətəri, Amer -tɔːri/ *adj* 祝贺的 ‹*speech, manner*›; **a ~ card** 贺卡

congregate /'kɒŋɡrɪɡeɪt/ *vi* 聚集

congregation /ˌkɒŋɡrɪ'ɡeɪʃn/ *n + v sing or pl* (in church) 礼拜会众; (in parish) 教区全体教徒

congress /'kɒŋɡres, Amer 'kɒŋɡrəs/ *n* 1 [c] (conference) 代表大会; **to convene/hold a ~ on sth.** 召开/举行关于某事的代表大会 2 **Congress** [u] Amer Pol 国会; **a session of C~** 一届国会会期 3 **Congress** [u] Pol (in India) 国民大会党; **C~ candidates** 国大党候选人

> **Congress**
>
> 国会。根据1789年宪法，美国联邦政府实行立法、行政和司法机构三权分立。国会是美国的最高立法机关，实行两院制（bicameral），分上下两院。上院为参议院（▸**the Senate**），共有100名参议员（Senator），每州两名，任期六年，每两年改选三分之一，可连任。下院为众议院（House of Representatives），共有435名众议员（Representative），按每州人口比例选出，任期两年，可连任。议员不得担任其他政府职务。国会最主要的职责是起草并通过议案（bill）。议案经上下两院通过，送交总统批准后即成为正式法律。除立法外，国会还有权弹劾并罢免总统，并拥有征税、铸币、规范贸易和宣战等权力。国会的办公大楼称the Capitol，位于华盛顿特区的国会山（Capitol Hill）。

congressional /kən'ɡreʃənl/ *adj attrib* 1 (relating to conference) 代表大会的 ‹*proceedings, findings, participant*› 2 **Congressional** Amer Pol 国会的 ‹*hearing, bill, election*›

Congressional District *n* Amer 国会选区

congress: ~man /-mən/ *n* Amer 国会议员; **~person** *n* (*pl* **~people**) Amer 国会议员; **~woman** *n* Amer 女国会议员

congruent /'kɒŋɡrʊənt/ *adj* 1 formal (in agreement) 一致的 ‹*objective, theory*›; 合适的 ‹*measure*›; **to be ~ with ...** 与…一致; **a ~ punishment with such an offence** 适用于这种罪行的处罚 2 Math 全等的; **~ triangles** 全等三角形

conical /'kɒnɪkl/ *adj* 圆锥形的

conifer /'kɒnɪfə(r), 'kəʊn-/ *n* 针叶树

coniferous /kə'nɪfərəs, Amer kəʊ'n-/ *adj* Bot 1 (having cones) 结球果的 ‹*tree*› 2 (composed of conifers) 针叶树的; **a ~ forest** 针叶林

conjectural /kən'dʒektʃərəl/ *adj* 凭推测的 ‹*theory, evidence*›

conjecture /kən'dʒektʃə(r)/
A *n* 1 [u] (guessing) 推测; **to be open to ~** 尚不确定; **that's pure** *or* **mere ~** 那纯属猜测; **a matter for ~** 需要推测的事 2 [c] (guess) 猜测结果; **to make a ~** 作猜测
B *vt* 推测; **he ~d that she might have taken a later train** 他推测她可能已经乘坐了晚一些的火车
C *vi* 猜测; **to ~ about sth.** 对某事物作推测

conjoined twins /kən'dʒɔɪnd ˌtwɪnz/ *npl* **= Siamese twins**

conjugal /'kɒndʒʊɡl/ *adj* 婚姻的 ‹*life*›; 夫妻之间的 ‹*affection, loyalty*›; **~ bliss** 婚姻幸福; **~ rights/property** 夫妻同房权/共同财产

conjugate /'kɒndʒʊɡeɪt/
A *vt* 列举…的变化形式 ‹*verb, tense*›; **to ~ the verb 'to have'** 列举动词"to have"的变化形式
B *vi* 词形变化

conjugation /ˌkɒndʒʊ'ɡeɪʃn/ *n* 1 [u and c] (conjugating, verb forms) 动词变化形式 2 [c] (verb class) 词形变化相同的一类动词

conjunction /kən'dʒʌŋkʃn/ *n* 1 [u and c] formal (combination) 结合; **in ~ with sb./sth.** 与某人/某事物一起; **a happy ~ of circumstances** 幸好几件事情同时发生 2 [u] Astrol, Astron 合; **to come into ~ with ...** 开始与…相合; **the ~ of Mars and Venus** 火星和金星的相合 3 [c] Ling 连接词; **a coordinating/subordinating ~** 并列/从属连词

conjunctive /kən'dʒʌŋktɪv/ *adj* 连接的; **'therefore' as a ~ adverb** 作为连接副词的"therefore"

conjunctivitis /kənˌdʒʌŋktɪ'vaɪtɪs/ ▸**p. 377** *n* [u] 结膜炎

conjure /ˈkʌndʒə(r)/
A *vt* (summon by magic) 用魔术变出 ‹*object*›; 念咒召唤 ‹*spirit, devil*›; **he ~d a dinner out of thin air** fig 他变魔术般地做出了一顿饭
B *vi* 变魔术; **a name to ~ with** fig 有影响力的人物

Phrasal verbs
- **conjure away** *vt* [**~ away sth., ~ sth. away**] 把…变走
- **conjure up** *vt* [**~ up sth., ~ sth. up**] **1** «*person, story, picture*» 使…呈现于脑际 ‹*memory, feeling*›; **to ~ up an image of sth.** 在脑海中浮现出某事物的形象 **2** (summon) 用魔法召唤 ‹*spirit, ghost*› **3** (produce) 令人惊讶地造出 ‹*food*›; 如用魔法般地说出 ‹*joke*›

C

conjurer /ˈkʌndʒərə(r)/ *n* **= conjuror**
conjuring /ˈkʌndʒərɪŋ/ *n* [u] 魔术
conjuring trick *n* 魔术
conjuror /ˈkʌndʒərə(r)/ *n* 魔术师
conk /kɒŋk/ *n* Brit colloq 鼻子

Phrasal verb
- **conk out** *vi* colloq «*machine, appliance*» 出故障; **the boiler has ~ed out, and we've no hot water** 锅炉坏了，所以我们没有热水

conker /ˈkɒŋkə(r)/ *n* Brit colloq **1** (nut) 七叶树果 **2** **conkers** + *v sing* (game) 康克戏 [一种儿童游戏]; **to play ~s** 玩康克戏
con man *n* colloq 骗子
connect /kəˈnekt/
A *vt* **1** (join) 连接 ‹*object, place*›; Rail 加挂 ‹*carriage*›; **to ~ sth. to sth.** 将某物与某物连接起来; **to be ~ed to the mainland by bridge** 通过桥梁与大陆相连 **2** (associate, link) 联系 ‹*person, topic*›; **to ~ sb./sth. with sb./sth.** 将某人/某事物与某人/某事物联系起来; **I always ~ Oxford with rain** 我总是一下雨就想到牛津 **3** (to mains) 接通 ‹*utilities*›; 为…接通 ‹*household, area*›; (attach) 使连接 ‹*wires*›; **to ~ sth. to the mains** 给某物接通电源; **to ~ sb. to the gas supply/phone network** 给某人接通煤气/电话; Telecom 给…接通电话 ‹*caller*›; **to ~ sb. with sb./sth.** 为某人接通某人/某处的电话; **to ~ sb. to sth.** 使某人与…保持电话联系 ‹*reception, department*›
B *vi* **1** Transp «*bus, plane, service*» 联运; **to ~ with the Oxford service** 与牛津的车次联运 **2** (provide access) «*rooms*» 连通; **to ~ with sth.** «*road, corridor*» 与某处相连 **3** Comput 联网; **to ~ to sth.** 与某处联网; **to ~ to the Internet** 连接到因特网 **4** colloq (hit target) «*fist, racket*» 击中; **to ~ with sb./sth.** (deliberately) 打中某人/某物; (accidentally) 无意间砸中某人/某物 **5** fig colloq (form relationship) 沟通; **to ~ with sb.** 与某人建立良好关系

Phrasal verb
- **connect up** *vt* [**~ sb./sth. up, ~ up sb./sth.**] 将…接通 ‹*wires, appliance*›; **to ~ sb./sth. up to sth.** 将某人/某物与某物接通; **to be ~ed up to a heart monitor** 被接上心率监视器

connected /kəˈnektɪd/ *adj* **1** (related) 相关的 ‹*topic, matter, comment, person*›; **to be ~ with** *or* **to sb./sth.** 与某人/某事物有关; **how are you ~ to the organization?** 你和这个组织有什么关系？; **to be closely ~** 紧密相关 **2** (in family) 有血统关系的 ‹*person, family*›; **his family is well ~** 他的家庭血统高贵; **to be ~ by marriage** 联姻 **3** (linked by channel, network) 相连的; **to be ~ to** *or* **with ...** 与…相连 **4** (ordered) 连贯的 ‹*language, story*›; **he was too excited for ~ thought** 他太兴奋了，无法理清思路
Connecticut /kəˈnetɪkət/ *pr n* 康涅狄格州
connecting /kəˈnektɪŋ/ *adj attrib* **1** Transp 联运的 ‹*flight, train, bus*› **2** (adjoining) 相连的 ‹*room*› **3** (communicating) 连通的 ‹*door*›
connection, Brit **connexion** /kəˈnekʃn/ *n* **1** [u and c] (logical link) 联系; **a direct/close/strong ~ (with sb./sth.)** (与某人/某事物)直接的/密切的/牢固的联系; **a ~ between sb./sth. and sb./sth.** …与…之间的联系; **to make a/the ~ (between sb./sth. and sb./sth.)** 看出 (…与…之间的) 关系; **in ~ with sb./sth.** 与某人/某事物有关; **in ~ with a theft** 与失窃案有关; **in this/that ~** 在这/那方面 **2** [u and c] (joining of wires, pipes, etc.) 连接; (to mains, network) 接通; **~ to the Internet** 因特网连接; **~ to the gas supply was delayed for three days** 拖延了 3 天才接通煤气 **3** [c] Telecom 接通电话; **a wrong/bad ~** 接错的/信号不好的电话 **4** [c] (point of joining) 连接点; **a loose ~** 接触不良 **5** [u and c] (personal tie) 人际关系; (of love) 情爱关系; **a ~ between sb./sth. and sb./sth.** …与…之间的关系; **a ~ with sb./sth.** 与某人/某群体的关系; **to have close ~s with** 与…关系密切 ‹*family, institution*› **6** [c] (contact) (gen) 熟人; (in business) 往来客户; **to have ~s in the building trade** 在建筑业有往来客户 **7** [c] (train) 联运火车; (bus) 联运公交车; (plane) 联运飞机; (ferry) 联运轮渡; (arrangement) 联运; **to miss/make one's ~** 错过/赶上联运车 **8** [c] colloq esp Amer (drug deal) 毒品交易; (supplier) 毒品贩子
connection charge *n* (网络) 接入费
connective /kəˈnektɪv/
A *adj* Anat 连接的 ‹*structure*›; **~ tissue** 结缔组织
B *n* **= conjunction 3**
connectivity /ˌkɒnekˈtɪvəti/ *n* [u] (connected state, capacity for interconnection) 连接; **global ~** 全球连通; **wireless/broadband ~** 无线/宽带连接
connector /kəˈnektə(r)/ *n* **1** (link) 接头; **a pipe/power ~** 管箍/电源连接器 **2** Elec 连接管
conning tower /ˈkɒnɪŋ taʊə(r)/ *n* [潜艇的] 指挥塔
conniption /kəˈnɪpʃn/ *n* Amer colloq 歇斯底里; **to go into ~s** 变得抓狂
connivance /kəˈnaɪvəns/ *n* [u] pej 纵容; **with the ~ of sb., in ~ with sb.** 在某人的纵容下
connive /kəˈnaɪv/ *vi* pej **1** (be implicated) 纵容; **to ~ at** *or* **in sth.** 纵容 ‹*crime, betrayal*› **2** (conspire) 合谋; **to ~ with sb. to do sth.** *or* **in doing sth.** 与某人合谋做某事
conniving /kəˈnaɪvɪŋ/ *adj attrib* pej (conspiratorial, devious) 暗算他人的; (willing to allow sth. illegal) 纵容的; **a ~ look/act** 不怀好意的神态/行为
connoisseur /ˌkɒnəˈsɜː(r)/ *n* 鉴赏家
connotation /ˌkɒnəˈteɪʃn/ *n* 含义; **derogatory ~s** 贬义
connote /kəˈnəʊt/ *vt* **1** Ling 有…的含义 **2** (summon up) 使人想到; **the Lake District ~s peace and beauty** 英国的湖区给人以祥和美丽之感
connubial /kəˈnjuːbɪəl, Amer -ˈnuː-/ *adj* liter 婚姻的; **~ bliss** 婚姻的幸福; **the ~ bed** 婚床
conquer /ˈkɒŋkə(r)/ *vt* **1** Mil 占领 ‹*lands, nation*›; **~ed territories** 被占领土; **they've ~ed new markets in Japan** 他们在日本开拓了新市场 **2** fig (master) 克服 ‹*weakness, obstacle, jealousy*›; 解决 ‹*unemployment, deficit*›; 戒除 ‹*habit*›; 攻克 ‹*technology*›; **we are doing all we can to ~ Aids** 我们正竭尽全力攻克艾滋病 **3** fig (defeat) 战胜 ‹*rival, competitor*› **4** fig (climb) 成功攀登; **many expeditions have now ~ed Mount Everest** 已有多支探险队成功登上了珠穆朗玛峰
conquering /ˈkɒŋkərɪŋ/ *adj attrib* 获胜的 ‹*army, nation*›
conqueror /ˈkɒŋkərə(r)/ *n* (in battle, sport) 获胜者; (in exploration, mountaineering) 征服者; **William the C~** 征服者威廉; **the ~ of my heart** 俘虏了我的心的人; **a ~ of space/nature** 太空/大自然的征服者
conquest /ˈkɒŋkwest/ *n* **1** [u] (of territory) 征服; **man's ~ of space** 人类对太空的征服; **the ~ of Mount Everest** 珠峰的登顶 **2** [u] (mastery over sth. undesirable) 控制; **the ~ of inflation** 对通货膨胀的控制 **3** [c] fig hum (person) 被俘虏的人; **her latest ~** 她最近俘获的男人
conscience /ˈkɒnʃəns/ *n* **1** [u and c] (moral sense) 良心; **to have no ~** 没良心; **to have a guilty** *or* **bad ~** 问心有愧; **to have a clear ~** 问心无愧 **2** [u and c] (sense of guilt) 内疚; **to have to live with one's ~** 不得不怀着内疚度日; **to have sth./sb. on one's ~** 对某事/某人感到愧疚 **3** [u] formal (fairness) **in all/good ~** 公平地
conscience-stricken *adj* 受良心谴责的
conscientious /ˌkɒnʃɪˈenʃəs/ *adj* 勤勉认真的 ‹*person, attitude*›; 煞费苦心的 ‹*work, effort*›
conscientiously /ˌkɒnʃɪˈenʃəsli/ *adv* 勤勉认真地 ‹*work, train, practise*›
conscientiousness /ˌkɒnʃɪˈenʃəsnɪs/ *n* [u] 责任心
conscientious: ~ objection *n* [u] 出于良心的抗拒 [通常指拒绝服兵役或堕胎等]; **~ objector** *n* 出于良心而拒服兵役者
conscious /ˈkɒnʃəs/
A *adj* **1** Med 神志清醒的 ‹*patient, moment*›; **to be fully ~** 完全清醒 **2** Psych 有意识的 ‹*mind, memory*› **3** (aware) 意识到的; **to be ~ of sth.** 意识到某事物; **to be environmentally/socially ~** 有环境/社会意识; **health-/status-~** 有健康/地位意识的 **4** (deliberate) 故意的 ‹*motive, effort*›
B *n* Psych **the ~** 意识
consciously /ˈkɒnʃəsli/ *adv* **1** (with awareness) 有意识地 **2** (deliberately) 故意地
consciousness /ˈkɒnʃəsnɪs/ *n* [u] **1** Med 知觉; **to lose/regain ~** 丧失/恢复知觉 **2** (awareness) 意识; **~ that ...** …的意识; **safety ~** 安全意识; **the public/collective/political ~** 公众/集体/政治观念
consciousness raising *n* [u] (political) 觉悟提高; (social) 意识加强
conscript
A /ˈkɒnskrɪpt/ *n* 应征入伍者; **a ~ army** 应征入伍者组成的部队
B /kənˈskrɪpt/ *vt* 征募 ‹*soldier*›; 征用 ‹*worker, helper*›; **they were ~ed into the army** 他们应征入伍
conscription /kənˈskrɪpʃn/ *n* [u] 征兵
consecrate /ˈkɒnsɪkreɪt/ *vt* (declare sacred) 给…祝圣; (dedicate to the service of God) 使圣化; 使…就任圣职 ‹*priest*›; **~d ground** 圣地; **a day ~d to their memory** 他们记忆中神圣的一天; **to be ~d (as) bishop** 被祝圣为主教
consecration /ˌkɒnsɪˈkreɪʃn/ *n* (of church, building, religious object) 祝圣; (of bishop) 圣职授任; **a ~ service** 祝圣礼
consecutive /kənˈsekjʊtɪv/ *adj* 连续的 ‹*days, weeks, words, events*›; **for three ~ weeks** 连续 3 周; **five ~ events** 接连发生的 5 起事件
consecutively /kənˈsekjʊtɪvli/ *adv* 连续地; **the sentences to run** *or* **be served ~** 连续执行的判决/需连续服的刑期
consensual /kənˈsensjʊəl, -ˈsenʃʊəl/ *adj* (of more than two parties) 一致同意的 ‹*behaviour, decision*›; (of two parties) 两厢情愿的 ‹*relationship, sex*›
consensus /kənˈsensəs/ *n* [u and c] 一致意见; **the ~ is that ...** 人们一致同意…; **a broad ~ for** *or* **in favour of sth.** 支持某事物的广泛共识; **a ~ of opinion** 一致看法
consensus politics *npl* + *v sing* 共识政治
consent /kənˈsent/
A *vi* (agree) 同意; **to ~ to sth./to do sth.** 同意某事/做某事; **to ~ to sb. doing sth.** 允许某人做某事; **between ~ing adults** 在你情我愿的成人之间 [指在同意发生同性性关系的成年人之间]

B *n* [u] (agreement) 同意; (permission by person in authority) 准许; **by common/mutual ~** 经一致/双方同意; **informed ~** 知情同意 [尤指患者在了解医疗风险后表示的同意]; **silence means ~** 沉默即准许; **without the owner's ~** 未经所有者许可; **the age of ~** (for marriage) 法定最低结婚年龄; (for sex) 法定最低性行为年龄

consent form *n* Brit 同意书 [要求父母填写是否同意学校带孩子外出游览的表格]

consequence /ˈkɒnsɪkwəns, Amer -kwens/ *n* 1 [u and c] (result) 结果; **as a ~ of ...** 作为…的结果; **in ~** formal 因此; **to suffer/take/face the ~s** 遭受/承受/面对后果 2 [u] formal (importance) 重要性; **a matter of some ~** 较重要的事; **a man of no ~** 无足轻重的人; **a man of ~** 举足轻重的人

consequent /ˈkɒnsɪkwənt, Amer -kwent/ *adj* (resulting) 作为结果的; (following) 随之发生的; **the strike, and the ~ disruption** 罢工以及由此引发的混乱; **~ on** *or* **upon sth.** 作为某事结果的; **the firm's closure was ~ on its heavy losses** 公司的倒闭是由其严重亏损导致的

consequential /ˌkɒnsɪˈkwenʃl/ *adj* 1 (resultant) 作为结果的; **the ~ loss** 随之产生的损失 2 (influential) 有影响力的 〈*person*〉; (important) 重大的 〈*issue*〉

consequently /ˈkɒnsɪkwəntli, Amer -kwentli/ *adv* 因此; **she was the youngest child and ~ spoilt** 她是最小的孩子，因此被宠坏了

conservancy /kənˈsɜːvənsi/ *n* 1 **Conservancy** [c] + *v sing or pl* (body) 自然资源管理机构; **Texas Nature C~** 得克萨斯州自然资源管理委员会 2 [u] **= conservation**

conservation /ˌkɒnsəˈveɪʃn/ *n* [u] 1 also Ecol (preservation) 保护; **the ~ of our heritage** 对我们遗产的保护; **~ treatment** 保护性处理; **wildlife ~** 野生动植物保护 2 (economical use of resources) 节约; **energy/water/fuel ~** 节能/节水/节约燃料 3 Phys 守恒; **~ of energy** 能量守恒

conservation area *n* Brit 保护区

conservationist /ˌkɒnsəˈveɪʃənɪst/ *n* 自然环境保护主义者; **a ~ group** 自然环境保护主义团体

conservation: ~ officer ▸p. 409 *n* Brit 1 (for natural environment) 自然环境保护官员; 2 (for buildings) 历史建筑保护官员; **~ site** *n* 1 (protected area) 自然环境保护区; 2 Comput 自然环境保护网站

conservatism /kənˈsɜːvətɪzəm/ *n* [u] 1 (resistance to change) 守旧 2 Pol (theory) 保守主义 3 **Conservatism** Pol （英国）保守党的政策原则

> **the Conservative Party**
>
> 保守党，全称保守统一党（Conservative and Unionist Party），亦称 the Conservatives，是英国最古老的政党。前身为 17、18 世纪的托利党（Tory Party）。保守党的名称始见于 1830 年，1834 年被罗伯特·皮尔（Robert Peel）正式采用，但 the Tories 或 Tory Party 作为别称一直沿用至今。1912 年和自由统一党（Liberal Unionist Party）合并，改称保守统一党。第一次世界大战结束以前一直和自由党（Liberal Party）轮流执政。一战后自由党衰落，工党（▸**the Labour Party**）兴起，又和工党轮流执政。保守党是右翼政党，党员主要来自土地所有者和中产阶级。意识形态上强调传统，反对急剧的社会变革。同时强调资本主义自由竞争的企业制度，反对政府干预经济。保守党的标志已由蓝色的自由火炬（Torch of Freedom）改为绿色橡树（Oak）。

conservative /kənˈsɜːvətɪv/
A *adj* 1 (opposed to change) 保守的 2 (purposely low) 谨慎的; **at a ~ estimate** 据保守估计 3 (conventional) 传统的 〈*style, taste*〉 4 **Conservative** Brit Pol 保守党的
B *n* 1 (person resistant to change) 保守者 2 **Conservative** Brit Pol (member) 保守党人; (supporter) 保守党支持者

Conservative Party *n* Brit **the ~** 保守党

conservatoire /kənˈsɜːvətwɑː(r)/ *n* Brit 古典音乐戏剧学院

conservator /ˈkɒnsəveɪtə(r)/ ▸p. 409 *n* 文物管理员

conservatory /kənˈsɜːvətri, Amer -tɔːri/ *n* 1 (for plants) 暖房 2 Amer Mus **= conservatoire**

conserve /kənˈsɜːv/
A *vt* 1 (save up) 节省 〈*resources, supplies*〉; 保存 〈*strength*〉 2 Fin (save) 存储 〈*cash, stocks*〉 3 (preserve) 保护 〈*heritage, environment, wildlife*〉
B *n* [u and c] 什锦果酱

consider /kənˈsɪdə(r)/
A *vt* 1 (give thought to) 考虑; **to ~ doing sth.** 考虑做某事; **to ~ sb. for/as sth.** 考虑让某人做某事/担任某角色; **to ~ sb./sth. favourably** 作出对某人/某事物有利的考虑 2 (bear in mind) 考虑到 〈*risk, cost*〉; (show care for) 顾及 〈*person, feelings, wishes*〉; **when you ~ that ...** 当你考虑到…; **all things ~ed** 总体来看 3 (regard) 认为; **to ~ sb./sth. (to be) sth.** 认为某人/某事是某情况; **I ~ him responsible** 我认为他负有责任; **to ~ oneself sth./to be sth.** 自认为是某情况; **to ~ it one's duty to do sth.** 自认为有义务做某事; **to ~ sth. a compliment** 视…为赞美; **to be ~ed successful/a poet** 被认为很成功/是诗人; **~ it done** 这事包在我身上; **~ it forgotten** 我早把它忘了; **~ it a deal!** 成交！; **~ yourself lucky!** 算你走运！ 4 formal (look at) 凝视 〈*person, painting*〉
B *vi* 考虑; **give me time to ~** 我需要些时间考虑

considerable /kənˈsɪdərəbl/ *adj* 1 (substantial) 相当大的 〈*quantity, proportions, building*〉; **~ expense** 相当可观的费用; **to a ~ extent** *or* **degree** 很大程度上; **the damage was ~** 毁坏相当严重 2 (important) 重大的 〈*victory, achievement*〉; 著名的 〈*person*〉

considerably /kənˈsɪdərəbli/ *adv* 相当多地; **to be ~ better/worse** 好/坏得多; **the weather is ~ improved** 天气明显转好了

considerate /kənˈsɪdərət/ *adj* 体贴的 〈*person*〉; 考虑周到的 〈*action, decision*〉; **to be ~ towards sb./of sb.'s feelings** 体谅某人/某人的感情; **how ~ of her!** iron 她真会体贴人！

considerately /kənˈsɪdərətli/ *adv* (caringly) 体贴地; (thoughtfully) 考虑周到地

consideration /kənˌsɪdəˈreɪʃn/ *n* 1 [c and u] (deliberation) 考虑; **to deserve/require ~** 值得/需要考虑; **to give (careful/serious) ~ to sth.** (仔细/认真)考虑某事; **on ~ of sth.** 经过对某事的考虑; **to take sth. into ~** 考虑某事; **to be under ~** 在考虑中; **she's under ~ for the job** 正在考虑让她做这份工作; **(to submit sth.) for sb.'s ~** （提交某物）供某人考虑; **in ~ of sth.** 考虑到某事物; **~ is being given to ...** 正在考虑… 2 [u] (care) 关心; **~ for sb./sth.** 对某人/某事物的关心; **to show ~ (for sb./sth.)** 体谅（某人/某事）; **to do sth. out of ~ (for sb./sth.)** 出于（对某人/某事物的）考虑做某事 3 [c] (factor) 要考虑的因素; **commercial/political ~s** 需要考虑的商业/政治因素 4 [c] formal (fee) 报酬; **for a ~** 收取报酬地; **in ~ of sth.** 作为对…的酬报

considered /kənˈsɪdəd/ *adj* 经仔细考虑的 〈*reply, view*〉; **it is my ~ opinion that ...** 我经过慎重考虑认为…

considering /kənˈsɪdərɪŋ/
A *prep* 考虑到; **~ the circumstances** 考虑到这种情况
B *conj* 考虑到; **~ that ...** 考虑到…
C *adv* colloq (in view of adverse circumstances) 考虑到不利条件; (taking everything into consideration) 总的来说

consign /kənˈsaɪn/ *vt* formal 1 (in order to get rid of) 打发; **to ~ sth. to the flames** 将某物付之一炬; **a writer ~ed to oblivion** 一位湮没无闻的作家 2 (entrust) 托付; **to ~ sb./sth. to sb.** 将某人/某事物托付给某人; **to ~ sth. to sb.'s care** *or* **to the care of sb.** 将某物托付某人照管

consignment /kənˈsaɪnmənt/ *n* 1 [c] (goods) 交运的货物 2 [u] (delivery) 递送; **for ~** 供发送; **to ship/sell goods on ~** 以寄售方式装运/出售货物

consignment note *n* 发货通知单

consist /kənˈsɪst/ *vi* 1 **to ~ of sth.** (be made up of) 由某事物组成; **the committee ~s of five members** 委员会由 5 名成员组成 2 **to ~ in sth.** (to be essentially) 存在于某事物; **the beauty of the city ~s in its magnificent buildings** 这个城市的美在于它宏伟的建筑

consistency /kənˈsɪstənsi/ *n* 1 [u] (of view, policy) 统一性; (of achievement) 连贯性; **she played with great ~ all season** 她整个赛季表现相当稳定 2 [u and c] (texture) 黏稠度

consistent /kənˈsɪstənt/ *adj* 1 (constant) 一贯的 〈*behaviour, kindness*〉; (unwavering) 始终如一的 〈*criticism, support*〉 2 (repeated) 持续的 〈*growth, demands, attempts*〉 3 (uniform) 不变的 〈*level, quality*〉; **to be of a ~ standard** 前后标准统一 4 (logical) 连贯一致的 〈*argument, performance, method*〉; **to be ~ with sth.** 与某事物相符; **it is ~ that he pay no attention to the rules** 他一贯都无视规定

consistently /kənˈsɪstəntli/ *adv* 1 (constantly) 一贯地 〈*behave*〉; (invariably) 始终如一地 〈*criticize, support*〉 2 (repeatedly) 不断地 〈*complain, argue*〉 3 (uniformly) 始终 〈*good, bad*〉 4 (logically) 连贯一致地 〈*argue, think*〉

consolation /ˌkɒnsəˈleɪʃn/ *n* 1 [u] (comfort) 安慰; **to be of (no)~ to sb.** 对某人（不）是安慰; **it's no ~ that the car is intact** 汽车完好无损并不能让人感到宽慰; **a letter of ~** 慰问信; **to be small ~** 几乎起不到安慰作用 2 [c] (source of comfort) (person) 令人安慰的人; (thing) 令人慰藉的事; **it's a ~ to know that ...** 得知…令人安慰; **she was a great ~ to him when his wife died** 他妻子去世后，她就成了他莫大的安慰

consolation prize *n* 安慰奖

consolatory /kənˈsɒlətəri, Amer -tɔːri/ *adj* 安慰的 〈*words, gesture, offer*〉

console[1] /kənˈsəʊl/
A *vt* 安慰; **to ~ sb. on** *or* **for sth.** 就某事安慰某人; **to ~ sb. with sth./by doing sth.** 以某物/通过做某事安慰某人
B *v refl* **to ~ oneself with sth.** 以某事物安慰自己; **to ~ oneself that ...** 安慰自己说…

console[2] /ˈkɒnsəʊl/ *n* 1 (control panel) 控制面板; (control system) 控制台; **a computer/lighting ~** 电脑/灯光控制台 2 (cabinet) [放置电视、音响设备等的] 落地柜 3 Comput 游戏机 4 (of organ) 风琴演奏台

consolidate /kənˈsɒlɪdeɪt/
A *vt* 1 (strengthen) 加固 〈*structure*〉; fig 巩固 〈*knowledge, position*〉 2 (unite) 整合 〈*operations, resources*〉; 统一 〈*territories*〉 3 (merge) 使…合并 〈*funds, companies*〉 4 esp Brit Jur 合并 〈*pieces of legislation*〉
B *vi* (unite) 《*businesses, banks*》 合并

consolidated school *n* Amer 联合公立学校

consolidation /kənˌsɒlɪˈdeɪʃn/ *n* [u and c] 1 (strengthening) 巩固; **the ~ of power/skills** 权力/技能的巩固 2 (merging) 合并; **a ~ of Japanese banks/two political parties** 几家日本银行/两个政党的合并

consoling /kənˈsəʊlɪŋ/ *adj* 安慰的 〈*thought, words, gesture, fact*〉

C

C

consommé /kən'sɒmeɪ/ *n* [u and c] 清炖肉汤

consonance /'kɒnsənəns/ *n* [u] formal 辅音韵

consonant /'kɒnsənənt/ *n* [1] (letter) 辅音字母 [2] Phon 辅音; **voiced/unvoiced ~s** 浊/清辅音

consonantal /ˌkɒnsə'næntl/ *adj* 辅音的 ‹*ending, shift, system*›

consort

A /kən'sɔːt/ *vi* formal 厮混; **to ~ with sb.** 与某人厮混

B /'kɒnsɔːt/ *n* [1] (of monarch) [君主的] 配偶; **the prince ~** 亲王 [2] (of musicians) 合奏乐队; (of instruments) 一组乐器

consortium /kən'sɔːtɪəm/ *n* (*pl* **consortia** /kən'sɔːtɪə/ *or* **~s**) 财团

conspectus /kən'spektəs/ *n* (*pl* **~es**) formal 概要

conspicuous /kən'spɪkjʊəs/ *adj* [1] (visible) 显眼的 ‹*person, feature, place, object*›; (noticeable) 引人注意的 ‹*quality, fact*›; **to make oneself ~** 使自己引人注目; **to be ~ for sth./doing sth.** 由于某事物/做某事而引人注目; **to be ~ in sth.** 在某方面引人注目; **he showed ~ bravery** 他表现得极其勇敢; **to be/to make oneself ~ by one's absence** iron 由于缺席而引人注意 [2] (noteworthy) 显著的; (showy) 炫耀的; **a ~ lack of sth.** 某物的明显缺乏; **a ~ success/failure** 巨大的成功/失败; **~ consumption/expenditure** 炫耀性消费/花费

conspicuously /kən'spɪkjʊəsli/ *adv* [1] (visibly) 显眼地 ‹*dressed, placed*›; **~ loud** 极其喧闹 [2] (noticeably) 引人注意地 ‹*act, think*›; (unusually) 非同寻常地 ‹*brave, kind, decent*› [3] (notably) 炫耀地 ‹*spend*›; 显著地 ‹*change*›; **a ~ successful career** 极为成功的事业

conspiracy /kən'spɪrəsi/ *n* [1] [c] Jur (illegal plot) 阴谋活动; **to enter into/hatch/crush a ~ against sb.** 参与/策划/粉碎针对某人的阴谋活动 [2] [u] Jur (illegal conspiring) 密谋罪; **~ to do sth.** 做某事的阴谋 [3] [c] (harmful plot) 共谋; **a ~ of silence** 保持缄默的密约

conspiracy theory *n* 阴谋论

conspirator /kən'spɪrətə(r)/ *n* [1] Jur 密谋者 [2] (plotter) 策划阴谋者

conspiratorial /kənˌspɪrə'tɔːrɪəl/ *adj* [1] (suggestive of conspiracy) 会意的 ‹*gesture, manner*› [2] Jur 密谋的 ‹*group, activities*›

conspire /kən'spaɪə(r)/ *vi* [1] (plot) 密谋; **to ~ against sb./sth.** 阴谋反对某人/某事物; **to ~ to do sth.** 密谋做某事 [2] (combine) «*circumstances*» 共同起作用; **to ~ to do sth.** 共同导致某事; **everything ~d to make his life a misery** 他命运多舛; **to ~ against sb./sth.** 共同与某人/某事物作对

constable /'kʌnstəbl, Amer 'kɒn-/ *n* Brit 警察; **C~ Jones** 琼斯警官

constabulary /kən'stæbjʊləri, Amer -leri/ *n* Brit 警察部队

constant /'kɒnstənt/

A *adj* [1] (unceasing) 持续的 ‹*supply, stress, use*›; 不断的 ‹*questions, interruptions*›; 反复的 ‹*visits, attempts*› [2] (unchanging) 不变的 ‹*factor, level, condition*›; 恒定的 ‹*growth, speed, temperature*› [3] liter (faithful) 忠实的 ‹*person*›

B *n* [1] Math 常数 [2] Phys 恒量 [3] (unchanging thing) 不变的事物; **his love has always remained a ~** 他的爱始终如一

constantly /'kɒnstəntli/ *adv* [1] (continually) 不断地 [2] (invariably) 始终地 [3] (faithfully) 忠诚地

constellation /ˌkɒnstə'leɪʃn/ *n* [1] Astron 星座 [2] fig liter (collection) (of people) 一群; (of reasons, characteristics) 一系列; **a ~ of famous names** 一群名人

consternation /ˌkɒnstə'neɪʃn/ *n* [u] 惊愕; **in ~** 惊愕地; **to sb.'s ~** 令某人震惊地

constipated /'kɒnstɪpeɪtɪd/ *adj* 便秘的

constipation /ˌkɒnstɪ'peɪʃn/ ▸**p. 377** *n* [u] 便秘

constituency /kən'stɪtjʊənsi/ *n* [1] esp Brit (district) 选区 [2] (voters) 选区的选民; **~ opinion** 选区选民的意见

constituency party *n* 选区政党

constituent /kən'stɪtjʊənt/

A *n* [1] (of mixture, substance) 成分; (of event, work of art) 部分 [2] Pol 选民

B *adj* [1] (component) 组成的 ‹*part, ingredient*›; **the ~ gases of air** 构成空气的各种气体 [2] Pol 有选举权的; **a ~ assembly** 立宪会议

constitute /'kɒnstɪtjuːt/ *vt* [1] (represent) «*act, words*» 形成 ‹*violation, admission*›; **their action ~d a threat to national security** 他们的行为是对国家安全的威胁 [2] (form) 成为; **they ~d the majority of the group** 他们占这个集体的多数 [3] (compose) 构成 ‹*part, whole*›; **oxygen ~s one of the elements of water** 氧是构成水的元素之一 [4] formal (set up) 成立 ‹*organization, body*›

constitution /ˌkɒnstɪ'tjuːʃn, Amer -'tuːʃn/ *n* [1] [c] (of country) 宪法; (or club, society, organization) 章程; **a written/unwritten ~** 成文/不成文宪法 [2] [c] (physical state) 体质; **an iron ~** 钢铁般强壮的体格 [3] [c] (composition) 构造 [4] [u] formal (setting up of organization) 成立

constitutional /ˌkɒnstɪ'tjuːʃənl, Amer -'tuː-/

A *adj* [1] (of a state's constitution) 宪法的 ‹*reform, crisis, change*›; (approved by a state's constitution) 符合宪法的 ‹*action, right, monarchy*›; (approved by an organization's constitution) 符合章程的 ‹*action, right*› [2] (physical) 体质的 ‹*weakness*›; (innate) 生来的 ‹*insecurity*›

B *n* dated hum 健身散步; **to go for a ~** 去散步健身

constitutionally /ˌkɒnstɪ'tjuːʃənəli, Amer -'tuː-/ *adv* [1] (in accordance with a constitution) (of state) 按照宪法; (of organization) 按照章程 [2] (physically) 体质上; **~ weak/strong** 体质虚弱/强壮的 [3] (innately) 本质上; **he is ~ incapable of saying no** 他生性不会说不

constitutive /'kɒnstɪtjuːtɪv, Amer -tuː-/ *adj* formal [1] (constituent) 组成的 ‹*part, element, ingredient*› [2] (executive) 有制定权的

constrain /kən'streɪn/ *vt* [1] (limit) 限制 ‹*person, freedom, creativity*›; **to ~ sb. from doing sth.** 限制某人做某事 [2] (compel) 强迫; **to ~ sb. to do sth.** 迫使某人做某事; **I am ~ed to ask you to ...** 我迫不得已，要请你…

constraint /kən'streɪnt/ *n* [1] [u and c] (limit) 限制; **to impose/put a ~ on sb.** 对某人加以限制; **without ~** 无拘无束地 [2] [u] (compulsion) 强迫; **to do sth. under ~** 被迫做某事

constrict /kən'strɪkt/

A *vt* [1] (make narrower) 收缩 ‹*blood vessel, throat, chest*›; 缩小 ‹*flow, opening*›; 减弱 ‹*breathing*› [2] fig «*rule, convention, conditions*» 束缚 ‹*person*› [3] Zool «*snake*» 绞缠 ‹*prey*›

B *vi* «*throat, chest*» 收缩

constricted /kən'strɪktɪd/ *adj* 收缩的 ‹*throat, chest*›; 缩小的 ‹*opening, flow*›; 压抑的 ‹*voice*›

constricting /kən'strɪktɪŋ/ *adj* [1] (too tight) 过紧的 ‹*garment*›; 挤脚的 ‹*shoe*› [2] (limiting) 约束的 ‹*concept, lifestyle, relationship*›

constriction /kən'strɪkʃn/ *n* [1] [c] (constraint) 约束; **~ on sth.** 对某事物的约束 [2] [c and u] Med (in chest) 压迫感; (in throat) 紧缩感 [3] [u] (narrowing) 紧缩; **a feeling of ~** 束缚感 [4] [u] (by snake) 绞缠

construct

A /kən'strʌkt/ *vt* [1] 建造 ‹*building, bridge*›; 构建 ‹*model*›; 制造 ‹*machine, vehicle*›; **to ~ sth. of** *or* **out of** *or* **from ...** 用…建造某物; **the house was ~ed in stone** 这栋房子是用石头建的 [2] (form) 创立 ‹*theory*›; 构思 ‹*work of art*› [3] Ling 构造; **to ~ a sentence** 造句 [4] Math 绘制 ‹*geometric figure*›

B /'kɒnstrʌkt/ *n* [1] (concept, idea) 构想 [2] Psych 构念 [3] Ling 结构体 [4] (made object) 建造物

construction /kən'strʌkʃn/ *n* [1] [u] (act of building) 建造; **to be under ~** 正在建造; **a house of poor ~** 造得很差的房子; **the ~ industry** 建筑业 [2] [u] Ind 建筑业; **to work in ~** 从事建筑业 [3] [u] (assembly of car, machine) 装配 [4] [c] (of abstract entity) 构思; **the ~ of a hypothesis** 假设的构想 [5] [c] (structure) 建筑物 [6] [c] (interpretation) 解释; **to put a ~ on** *or* **upon sth.** 对某事物作解释说明 [7] Ling [u] (syntax) 结构; [c] (syntactic unit) 结构体

constructional /kən'strʌkʃənl/ *adj* [1] (relating to building) 建筑的 [2] Ling 语法结构的

construction: ~ engineer ▸**p. 409** *n* 建筑工程师; **~ site** *n* 建筑工地; **~ worker** ▸**p. 409** *n* 建筑工人

constructive /kən'strʌktɪv/ *adj* 建设性的 ‹*criticism, advice*›; 有助益的 ‹*person*›

constructive dismissal *n* [u and c] 间接解雇 [即通过变换雇员的工作或工作条件迫使其辞职]

constructively /kən'strʌktɪvli/ *adv* 建设性地 ‹*criticize, suggest*›; **to work ~ together** 积极地携手工作

constructor /kən'strʌktə(r)/ ▸**p. 409** *n* 建造者

construe /kən'struː/ *vt* (interpret) 解释 ‹*words, speech, article*›; **to be wrongly ~d** 被误解; **to ~ sth. as sth.** 将某事物理解成某事物; **his question was ~d to be** *or* **as an insult** 他的问题被认为是一种侮辱

consul /'kɒnsl/ *n* 领事; **the French ~** 法国领事

consular /'kɒnsjʊlə(r), Amer -səl-/ *adj* 领事的; **~ service/officials** 领事服务/领事

consulate /'kɒnsjʊlət, Amer -səl-/ *n* 领事馆; **a ~ general** 总领事馆

consult /kən'sʌlt/

A *vt* [1] (ask) 咨询; **to ~ sb. about sth.** 就某事物请教某人 [2] (refer to) 查阅 ‹*book*›; 查看 ‹*watch, stars*›

B *vi* 商量; **to ~ with sb. about sth.** 与某人商讨某事物; **to ~ together** 一起商量

consultancy /kən'sʌltənsi/

A *n* [1] [c] (company) **a ~ (firm)** 咨询公司 [2] [u] (advice) [咨询公司的] 咨询意见

B *modif* 咨询的 ‹*firm, fee, time*›

consultant /kən'sʌltənt/ ▸**p. 409** *n* [1] (expert) 顾问; **a beauty/careers ~** 美容/职业顾问; **a ~ accountant** 顾问会计师; **to be a ~ on sth.** 是某方面的顾问; **to be a ~ to sb.** 担任某人的顾问 [2] Brit (doctor) 会诊医师; **a ~ cardiologist** 心脏病会诊医师; **to be a ~ in sth.** 是某领域的会诊医师

consultation /ˌkɒnsl'teɪʃn/ *n* [1] [c] (meeting) (for discussion) 商讨会; (for advice) 咨询会; **to have** *or* **hold a ~** *or* **~s with sb.** 与某人开会协商; **a ~ about** *or* **on sth.** 关于某事物的商讨会 [2] [u] (process) 商讨; **after ~ with sb.** 征求某人意见后 [3] [u] (reference) 查阅; **for ~** 以备查阅

consultative /kən'sʌltətɪv/ *adj* (advisory) 顾问的; (providing information, suggestions) 咨询的; (negotiating) 磋商的; **a ~ body/committee** 顾问机构/委员会; **a ~ document** 咨询文件

consulting: ~ engineer ▸**p. 409** *n* 顾问工程师; **~ hours** *npl* Brit 门诊时间; **~ room** *n* Brit 诊疗室

consumables /kən'sjuːməblz, Amer -'suːm-/ *npl* 消耗品

consume /kən'sjuːm, Amer -'suːm-/ *vt* [1] (eat) 吃; (drink) 喝 [2] (use up) 耗尽 ‹*resources, money, time*› [3] (destroy) «*fire*» 烧毁; «*illness*» 毁灭 [4] (overwhelm) «*emotion*» 充满; **to be ~d by** *or* **with envy** 妒火中烧

consumer /kən'sjuːmə(r), Amer -'suːm-/ *n* [1] (of goods, services) 消费者; **~ culture/rights** 消费文化/消费者权益 [2] (of a supply)

消耗者; **this engine is a terrible ～ of petrol** 这种引擎特别耗油

consumer: ～ advice *n* [u] 消费者咨询; **～ advice centre** *n* 消费者咨询中心; **～ choice** *n* [u] 消费者的选择; **～ confidence** *n* [u] 消费者信心; **～ credit** *n* [u] 消费信贷; **～ demand** *n* [u] 消费需求; **～ durables** *npl* 耐用消费品; **～ electronics** *npl* 1 + *v pl* (goods) 家电产业; 2 + *v sing* (production and sale) 家电产销; **～ goods** *npl* 消费品; **～ group** *n* (generally) 消费者群体; (as pressure group) 消费者团体

consumerism /kən'sjuːmərɪzəm, Amer -'suːm-/ *n* [u] 1 (consumer protection) 消费者权益保护 2 pej (preoccupation with acquisition) 消费沉迷

consumerist /kən'sjuːmərɪst, Amer -'suːm-/ *adj* 消费主义的 ‹*society, economics*›

consumer: ～ price index *n* 消费价格指数; **～ products** *npl* 消费品; **～ protection** *n* [u] 消费者权益保护; **～ research** *n* [u] 消费者调查; **～ society** *n* [u] 消费社会; **～ spending** *n* [u] 消费性开支; **～ survey** *n* 消费者调查; **～ unit** *n* 总配电箱

consuming /kən'sjuːmɪŋ, Amer -suːm-/ *adj* 强烈的 ‹*urge, ambition, passion*›

consummate
A /'kɒnsəmeɪt/ *vt* formal 通过圆房完成; **to ～ the marriage** 完婚
B /kən'sʌmət/ *adj* 完美的 ‹*ability, grace*›; 技艺精湛的 ‹*artist*›; **a ～ liar** 撒谎高手

consummation /ˌkɒnsə'meɪʃn/ *n* [u] formal 圆房; **the ～ of the marriage** 完婚

consumption /kən'sʌmpʃn/ *n* [u] 1 (consuming of food, drink) 消耗; (amount consumed) 消耗量 2 (purchasing) 消费 3 (reception) 接受; **for public ～** 让公众了解 4 ▸**p. 377** Med dated 痨病

consumptive /kən'sʌmptɪv/ dated
A *adj* 患肺痨的
B *n* 肺痨病人

cont. *abbr* **= continued** 继续的; **to be ～** 待续

contact
A /'kɒntækt/ *n* 1 [u] (touch) 接触; **to come in** or **into/get in** or **into/make ～ with ...** 接触到…; **to maintain/lose ～** 保持/脱离接触; **to explode on ～ (with ...)** (与…)一触即爆 2 [u] (communication) 联系; **to make/maintain ～** 建立/保持联系; **to break off/lose ～** 中断/失去联系; **to come in** or **into ～ with ...** 开始接触; **to bring sb. in** or **into ～ with ...** 使某人接触… 3 [u] (by radar, radio) 通讯; **to be in ～** 处于通讯联系状态 4 [c] (acquaintance) 熟人 5 [c] (meeting, acquaintanceship) 交往; **business/social ～s** 商业往来/社会关系 6 [c] Elec (connection) 接触; (device) 接触器 7 [c] colloq **= contact lens**
B /kən'tækt, 'kɒntækt/ *vt* 联系; **he could not be ～ed by phone** 无法通过电话联系到他

contactable /kən'tæktəbl, 'kɒn-/ *adj* 可联系到的; **she is not ～ by phone at the moment** 这会儿电话联系不上她

contact: ～ adhesive *n* [c and u] 接触型黏合剂; **～ breaker** *n* **= circuit breaker**; **～ lens** *n* 隐形眼镜片; **～ print** *n* 接触印相照片; **～ sport** *n* 接触性运动

contagion /kən'teɪdʒən/ *n* 1 [u] Med 接触传染 2 [c] fig 蔓延

contagious /kən'teɪdʒəs/ *adj* 1 Med 接触传染的 ‹*disease*›; 有接触传染病的 ‹*person*› 2 fig 有感染力的 ‹*laughter*›; 蔓延的 ‹*pessimism, optimism, enthusiasm*›

contain /kən'teɪn/ *vt* 1 (hold) 容纳 2 (have as a component) 含有 ‹*ingredient*›; 包括 ‹*subcategory*›; (include) 包含 ‹*idea, image*› 3 (curb) 抑制 ‹*growth, problem*›; 阻止 ‹*strike*› 4 (keep within physical boundaries) 遏制 ‹*natural disaster, terrorism, epidemic*› 5 (control) 克制 ‹*excitement, anger*›; **he managed to/couldn't ～ himself** 他设法克制住了/无法克制自己

container /kən'teɪnə(r)/ *n* 1 (receptacle) 容器; **a plastic/glass ～** 塑料/玻璃容器; **a water ～** 盛水的容器 2 Transp (large metal box) 集装箱

container: ～ depot *n* 集装箱仓库; **～ gardening** *n* [u] 盆栽园艺; **～-grown** *adj* 盆栽的 ‹*plant*›

containerization /kənˌteɪnəraɪ'zeɪʃn/ *n* [u] 集装箱装运

containerize /kən'teɪnəraɪz/ *vt* 用集装箱装运 ‹*goods, exports*›

container: ～ lorry *n* Brit **= ～ truck**; **～ port** *n* 集装箱货港; **～ ship** *n* 集装箱船; **～ terminal** *n* 集装箱装卸区; **～ transport** *n* [u] 集装箱运输; **～ truck** *n* 集装箱卡车

containment /kən'teɪnmənt/ *n* [u] 1 (keeping under control) 控制 2 Pol 遏制; **a policy of ～** 遏制政策

contaminate /kən'tæmɪneɪt/ *vt* 1 (pollute) 污染 ‹*substance, water, food*›; fig 毒害 ‹*mind*› 2 (irradiate) 对…造成放射性污染 ‹*area, plant, animal, people, soil*›

contaminated /kən'tæmɪneɪtɪd/ *adj* 1 (polluted) 受到污染的 ‹*substance, water, food*› 2 (irradiated) 受到放射性污染的 ‹*area, plant, animal, people, soil*›

contamination /kənˌtæmɪ'neɪʃn/ *n* [u] 1 lit, fig 污染; **the ～ of Chinese with English** 汉语中夹杂英文 2 (irradiation) 放射性污染

contd *abbr* **= cont.**

contemplate /'kɒntəmpleɪt/
A *vt* 1 (consider deeply) 深入思考 ‹*idea, future, situation*› 2 (envisage) 设想 ‹*course of action*›; **to ～ doing sth.** 打算做某事; **it's too awful to ～** 这事太可怕了, 真不敢去想 3 (look at) 凝视; **to ～ one's navel** fig 陷入冥想
B *vi* 沉思

contemplation /ˌkɒntem'pleɪʃn/ *n* 1 [u and c] (deep thought) 沉思 2 [u] (looking) 凝视

contemplative /kən'templətɪv, 'kɒntempleɪtɪv/ *adj* 1 (meditative) 好沉思的 ‹*person, personality*›; 严肃深沉的 ‹*work of art*› 2 (religious) 敛心默祷的; **the ～ life** 宗教上的默观生活

contemporaneous /kənˌtempə'reɪnɪəs/ *adj* formal 同时发生的 ‹*events*›; 同时存在的 ‹*situations*›; **a ～ publication** 同期出版物

contemporaneously /kənˌtempə'reɪnɪəsli/ *adv* formal 同时 ‹*occur, exist*›

contemporary /kən'temprəri, Amer -pəreri/
A *adj* 1 (of same period) 同时代的 2 (present-day) 当代的 3 (up-to-date) 最现代的 ‹*design, fashions*›
B *n* (of same period) 同时代的人; (of same age) 同龄人; **he was a ～ of mine at university** 他是我大学时的同届; **our contemporaries** 我们的同龄人

contempt /kən'tempt/ *n* [u] 1 (disdain) 蔑视; **to hold sb./sth. in ～** 鄙视某人/某事物; **to show** or **demonstrate ～ (for sb./sth.)** (对某人/某事物)不屑一顾; **to feel ～ for sb.** 蔑视某人; **lies and deceit are beneath ～** 说谎和欺骗为人不齿 2 (disregard) 藐视; **～ for sth.** 不顾某事物 3 Jur 藐视法庭罪

contemptible /kən'temptəbl/ *adj* 可鄙的 ‹*deed, person*›

contempt of court *n* 1 [u] 藐视法庭罪 2 [c] (*pl* **contempts of court**) (instance) 藐视法庭行为

contemptuous /kən'temptjʊəs/ *adj* 轻蔑的 ‹*look, attitude, comment*›; **to be ～ of sb.** 鄙视某人

contemptuously /kən'temptjʊəsli/ *adv* 轻蔑地

contend /kən'tend/
A *vi* 1 (struggle) 斗争; **to ～ with** or **against sth.** 应付某问题 2 (compete) «*candidate, rivals*» 竞争; **she was ～ing with him for first place** 她和他争夺第一名
B *vt* (argue) 主张; **to ～ that ...** 认为…

contender /kən'tendə(r)/ *n* also Sport 竞争者; **the top/main ～** 领先的/主要的角逐者; **to be a ～ for sth.** 是…的争夺者

contending /kən'tendɪŋ/ *adj attrib* 参与竞争的; **the ～ candidates/horses/armies** 竞选人/参赛马匹/交战部队

content¹ /'kɒntent/
A *n* [u] 1 (relative quantity) 含量; **the fat/vitamin ～** 脂肪/维生素含量; **to have a low/high lead ～** 铅含量低/高 2 (meaning) 内容; **debates about form and ～** 有关形式与内容的争论 3 (subject matter) 主题 4 (of web site) 网站内容
B **contents** *npl* 1 (of jar, bag) 容纳的东西; **she sold the flat and its ～s** 她把公寓和里面的东西都卖了 2 (of book, magazine) **(list** or **table of) ～s** 目录 3 (subject matter of book etc.) 内容

content² /kən'tent/
A *adj* 1 (satisfied) 满意的; (willing) 愿意的; **to be ～ with sth.** 对某事物满意; **to be ～ to do sth.** 愿意做某事; **not ～ with doing ...** 不愿意做… 2 (peacefully happy) 心满意足的
B *vt* (please) 使满意; **to ～ sb. with sth.** 用某事物来满足某人; **to be easily ～ed** 容易满足
C *v refl* **to ～ oneself** 满足; **to ～ oneself with sth.** 使自己满足于某事物
D *n* [u] 满足; **a feeling of ～** 满足感

contented /kən'tentɪd/ *adj* 满足的; **a ～ smile/feeling** 惬意的微笑/满足感

contentedly /kən'tentɪdli/ *adv* 满足地

contention /kən'tenʃn/ *n* formal 1 [c] (assertion) 论点; **it is my ～ that ...** 我认为… 2 [u] (disagreement) 争论; **a matter** or **point of ～** 争论点; **a bone of ～** 争执所在 3 [u] (competition) 竞争; Sport 竞赛; **to be in/out of ～ for sth.** 有/没有机会赢得某比赛; **to be in ～ to win the election** 有机会赢得竞选

contentious /kən'tenʃəs/ *adj* 1 (controversial) 有争议的 ‹*issue, matter*›; **to hold ～ views on sth.** 对某事物有争议 2 (argumentative) 好争论的

contentment /kən'tentmənt/ *n* [u] 满足; **with ～** 心满意足地; **a look of ～** 心满意足的样子

content provider *n* 1 (web site) 信息网站 2 (business) 内容提供商

contest
A /'kɒntest/ *n* 1 (competition) 比赛; **to enter/hold a ～** 参加/举行比赛 2 (struggle) 争夺; (in election) 竞争; **a leadership ～** 领导权的争夺; **the presidential ～** 总统竞选
B /kən'test/ *vt* 1 (object to) 辩驳 ‹*position*›; 质疑 ‹*decision, result*›; **to ～ a will** 对遗嘱提出质疑 2 (compete for) 争取赢得 ‹*victory, game*›; **a strongly ～ed seat** 激烈争夺的席位; **to ～ an election** 竞选

contestant /kən'testənt/ *n* 1 (competitor) 参赛者 2 Sport (adversary) 对手 3 (candidate) 竞争者

context /'kɒntekst/ *n* [c and u] 1 (setting) 环境; **in the historical ～** 在历史背景下; **when you put the violence into ～** 当你了解这一暴力事件的来龙去脉 2 (surrounding text) 上下文; **to examine/quote sth. out of ～** 脱离上下文检查/断章取义地引用某段话

context-sensitive *adj* 1 Ling 语境制约的 ‹*grammar, language, rules*› 2 Comput 上下文关联的 ‹*interface, menu*›

context-sensitive help *n* [u] 上下文关联帮助

contextual /kən'tekstʃʊəl/ *adj* (in text) 上下文的; (in surroundings) 与环境相关的; **～ criticism** 背景批评

contextualize /kən'tekstʃʊəlaɪz/ *vt* (in text) 将…置于上下文中; (in surroundings) 将…置于环境中; **to ~ sb.'s behaviour and experiences** 从所处环境考虑某人的行为和经历

contiguous /kən'tɪgjʊəs/ *adj* formal 毗邻的 ‹*area, property*›; **to be ~ to** *or* **with sth.** 与某物相邻

continent /'kɒntɪnənt/ *n* [1] (land mass) 大陆; **the Asian ~** 亚洲大陆 [2] Brit (mainland Europe) **the ~** *or* **C~** 欧洲大陆

continental /,kɒntɪ'nentl/
A *adj* [1] Geog 大陆的; **a ~ climate** 大陆性气候 [2] (*also* **Continental**) Brit (of mainland Europe) 欧洲大陆的
B *n* colloq 欧洲大陆人

continental: ~ breakfast *n* 欧陆式早餐 [以咖啡、面包卷、黄油和果酱为主]; **~ drift** *n* [u] 大陆漂移; **C~ Europe** *pr n* 欧洲大陆; **~ quilt** *n* Brit = **duvet**; **~ shelf** *n* 大陆架; **~ system** *n* 大陆封锁政策 [指拿破仑对英国实行的贸易封锁]

contingency /kən'tɪndʒənsi/ *n* [1] [c] (gen) 偶发事件; **to provide for** *or* **be prepared for contingencies** 为各种不测事件作好准备 [2] [c and u] (provision) 应急措施

contingency: ~ fund *n* 应急基金; **~ plan** *n* 应急计划; **~ planning** *n* [u] 应急计划制定; **~ reserve** *n* 应急储备金

contingent /kən'tɪndʒənt/
A *n* [1] (group) 一组; **a ~ of tourists** 一群游客 [2] Mil 分遣队; **an air ~** 一支空军小分队
B *adj* 依情况而定的; **to be ~ on** *or* **upon sth.** 取决于某事物

continual /kən'tɪnjʊəl/ *adj* [1] (continuous) 持续的 ‹*pain, stress*› [2] (repeated) 反复的 ‹*noise, complaint*›

continually /kən'tɪnjʊəli/ *adv* [1] (continuously) 连续地 [2] (repeatedly) 反复地

continuance /kən'tɪnjʊəns/ *n* [u] formal [1] (continuation) 持续 [2] Amer Jur 延期

continuation /kən,tɪnjʊ'eɪʃn/ *n* [1] [u] (carrying on) (of activity, weather) 持续; (of relationship, salary, studies, enquiry, journey) 继续 [2] [u] (resumption) (of campaign, work, conversation, screening) 重新开始; **the/a ~ of sth.** …的继续 ‹*situation, process*›; **the ~ of a conversation/search** 谈话/搜查的继续 [3] [u] (extension) (of road) 延伸; (of time) 延续; **~ of the route** 道路的延伸; **~ of a loan** 贷款的延期 [4] [c] (sequel) 续篇

continuation school *n* Amer 就业补习学校

continue /kən'tɪnju:/
A *vi* [1] (keep happening) «*noise, weather, trial*» 持续; (carry on into future) 持续下去; (persist) «*symptoms, problems, difficulties, bombing*» 持续不断; **rain ~d falling** *or* **to fall** 雨下个不停 [2] (keep doing) 继续; **to ~ doing** *or* **to do sth.** 持续做某事; **to ~ with sth.** 继续做 ‹*task*›; 继续进行 ‹*treatment*›; **he ~d to act strangely** 他的举止一直很古怪 [3] (keep going) 继续走; **to ~ over/through/across sth.** 一直走过/穿过/越过某处; **to ~ down the road** 一直沿着马路走; **to ~ on one's way** 继续走下去; **to ~ in the belief that ...** 一直认为… [4] (extend) 延伸; **to ~ across the desert/to the sea/into the distance** «*road*» 穿过沙漠/延伸到海边/延伸到远方 [5] (resume) «*noise, conversation*» 重新开始; «*story, TV series*» 继续; (resume speaking) 继续说; **she ~d by saying ...** 她接着说道… [6] (remain) **to ~ as sth.** 继续担任 ‹*manager, CEO*›; **to ~ in sth.** 继续做 ‹*job*›; 继续担任 ‹*role*›; **to ~ at one's post** 留任原职; **to ~ at school** 留校
B *vt* [1] (keep on with) 继续 ‹*relationship, salary, studies, enquiry, journey*› [2] (resume) 再开始 ‹*campaign, work*›; (中断后) 继续 ‹*conversation, screening*›; **'to be ~d'** "待续"; **'~d overleaf/on page 8'** "接下页/第8页" [3] (resume saying) 继续说; **'as I was explaining,' he ~d** "我正在解释时，" 他继续说 [4] (retain) 保持 ‹*tradition, lifestyle, skills*›; 保留 ‹*measures, standards, culture*›; **to ~ a way of life** 保持一种生活方式

continuity /,kɒntɪ'nju:ɪti/ *n* [u] [1] (consistent existence or operation) 连续性; **to provide ~ of services** 提供连续服务 [2] Cin, TV (consistency of action and detail) 衔接 [3] TV (linking of items) 节目串联

continuity: ~ announcer ▸p. 409 *n* 节目串联播音员; **~ girl** ▸p. 409 *n* [1] Cin 女场记员; [2] TV, Radio 节目串联女播音员; **~ man** ▸p. 409 *n* 节目串联男播音员

continuo /kən'tɪnjʊəʊ/ *n* [u and c] (*pl* **~s**) 数字低音

continuous /kən'tɪnjʊəs/ *adj* [1] (uninterrupted) 连续的 ‹*line, surface*›; (without gaps or spaces) 不间断的 ‹*growth, decline*›; **a ~ performance** Cin 连续放映 [2] (constant, lasting) 持久的 ‹*love, affection*›; 不松懈的 ‹*vigilance*› [3] Ling 进行的; **the present ~ tense** 现在进行时

continuous assessment *n* [u] Brit 连续评估 [即根据整个课程的学习而不是考试进行的评定]

continuously /kən'tɪnjʊəsli/ *adv* 连续地

continuum /kən'tɪnjʊəm/ *n* (*pl* **~s** *or* **continua** /kən'tɪnjʊə/) 连续体; **the space-time ~** 时空连续体

contort /kən'tɔ:t/
A *vt* [1] (twist) 使…扭曲 ‹*body, face*›; **his features were ~ed with rage** 他愤怒得脸都扭曲了 [2] fig (distort) 歪曲 ‹*truth, account*›
B *vi* «*features, body, steel bar*» 扭曲

contortion /kən'tɔ:ʃn/ *n* [1] (involuntary) 扭曲 [2] (voluntary) 扭曲的动作 [3] fig 歪曲; **intellectual ~s** 费脑筋的歪曲

contortionist /kən'tɔ:ʃənɪst/ *n* 柔体杂技演员

contour /'kɒntʊə(r)/ *n* [1] (outline) 轮廓 [2] Geog = **contour line**

contour: ~ line *n* 等高线; **~ map** *n* 等高线地图

contraband /'kɒntrəbænd/ *n* [u] 走私货; **~ goods** 走私货物

contraception /,kɒntrə'sepʃn/ *n* [u] 避孕; **to practise ~** 采取避孕措施

contraceptive /,kɒntrə'septɪv/
A *n* (pill) 避孕药物; (device) 避孕用具
B *adj* 避孕的 ‹*technique, device*›

contraceptive pill *n* 避孕药丸

contract
A /'kɒntrækt/ *n* [1] (agreement) 合同; **to enter into a ~ with sb. for sth.** 就某事物与某人签订合约; **sold subject to ~** 按合同出售; **to be under ~ with** *or* **to sb./sth.** 签约为某人/某组织工作 [2] Comm (for goods/services) 承包合同; **to award** *or* **assign a ~ to sb.** 将合同承包给某人; **to win a ~** 中标; **to put work out to ~** 签约将工作外包 [3] sl (for killing) 暗杀协议; **to put out a ~ on sb.** 雇凶谋杀某人
B /kən'trækt/ *vt* [1] Med (develop) 感染 ‹*disease*› [2] formal (enter into) 约定建立…关系 ‹*marriage, alliance*›; **he ~ed a marriage/an alliance with her** 他和她订了婚/结了盟 [3] (tighten) 收缩 ‹*muscle*› [4] (make shorter) 缩约 ‹*word, phrase*›
C /kən'trækt/ *vi* [1] (in size) «*metal*» 收缩; «*territory*» 缩小; (decrease) «*supplies, support*» 减少 [2] Physiol «*muscle*» 收缩 [4] Comm, Jur (undertake) «*firm, person, government*» 订立合同; **to ~ into sth.** 订约加入某事; **to ~ with sb. to ...** 与某人就…签约

Phrasal verbs

- **contract in** *vi* Brit 订约参与
- **contract out**

A *vt* [**~ out sth., ~ sth. out**] 订约将…外包 ‹*work, building*›; **to ~ sth. out to sb.** 将某工作订约外包给某人
B *vi* Brit 订约退出; **to ~ out of sth.** 退出关于某事的合约

contract: ~ bridge ▸p. 307 *n* [u] 定约桥牌; **~ cleaners** *npl* 清洁服务承包公司

contractile /kən'træktaɪl, Amer -tl/ *adj* 可收缩的 ‹*tissue, muscle*›

contraction /kən'trækʃn/ *n* [1] [u] (of metal) 收缩; (of industry, market, sector) 缩小; (of supplies, support) 减少 [2] [c] (muscular) 收缩; (in childbirth) 宫缩; **intervals between ~s** 宫缩间隙 [3] [c] Ling 缩约形式

contract: ~ killer *n* 雇佣杀手; **~ killing** *n* [u and c] 雇凶谋杀

contractor /kən'træktə(r)/ ▸p. 409 *n* (person) 承包商; (firm) 承包公司; **an electrical ~** 电器承包商

contractual /kən'træktʃʊəl/ *adj* 合同的; **~ agreement/obligations** 契约/合同规定的义务

contractually /kən'træktʃʊəli/ *adv* 按照合同; **to be ~ obliged** *or* **required to do sth.** 按照合同必须/要求做某事

contract: ~ work *n* [u] 承包工作; **~ worker** *n* 合同工

contradict /,kɒntrə'dɪkt/
A *vt* [1] (conflict with) 与…相矛盾; **all the reports ~ each other** 所有的报告都相互矛盾 [2] (dispute) 反驳 ‹*person, statement*›
B *vi* 反驳; **don't ~!** 不要顶嘴!

contradiction /,kɒntrə'dɪkʃn/ *n* [1] (lack of agreement) 矛盾; **to be in ~ with sth.** 与某事物相互矛盾; **it's a ~ in terms!** 那是个自相矛盾的说法! [2] (saying the opposite) 反驳

contradictory /,kɒntrə'dɪktəri/ *adj* 矛盾的 ‹*ideas, statements*›; **to be ~ to sth.** 与某事物相矛盾

contraflow /'kɒntrəfləʊ/ Brit *n* 单车道双向行驶; **~ lane/system/traffic** 双向行车线/系统/车流

contraindication /,kɒntrəɪndɪ'keɪʃn/ *n* 禁忌

contralto /kən'træltəʊ/ *n* (*pl* **~s**) [1] (voice) 女低音; **a lovely ~ voice** 优美的女低音嗓音 [2] (singer) 女低音歌手

contraption /kən'træpʃn/ *n* hum 新奇装置

contrarily /kən'treərɪli, Amer -trer-/ *adv* 乖张地 ‹*behave, act*›

contrariness /kən'treərɪnɪs, Amer -trer-/ *n* [u] 乖张; **out of pure** *or* **sheer ~** 完全出于逆反心理

contrariwise /kən'treərɪwaɪz, Amer -trer-/ *adv* [1] (conversely) 相反地 [2] (in the opposite direction) 逆向地

contrary[1] /'kɒntrəri, Amer also -treri/
A *adj* [1] (opposing) 相反的 ‹*points of view, ideas*›; **to be ~ to the general belief** 与一般的看法相反 [2] (opposite) 逆向的; **to travel in ~ directions** 逆向行驶; **to be ~ to sth.** 与某物逆向 [3] **~ to sth.** (despite) 尽管…; **~ to popular belief** 不管大家怎么想
B *n* 相反情况; **quite the ~, on the ~** 恰恰相反; **claims/evidence to the ~** 相反的说法/证据

contrary[2] /'kɒntreəri, Amer also -treri/ (perverse) 执拗的 ‹*person, character*›

contrast
A /'kɒntrɑ:st, Amer -træst/ *n* [1] [u and c] (difference) 差异; **by** *or* **in ~** 相比之下; **a ~ with sb./sth.** 与某人/某事物的对照; **the ~ between sb./sth. and sb./sth.** …与…之间的差异 [2] [c] (unlike thing) 明显不同的事物; (unlike person) 明显不同的人; **to be a ~ with** *or* **to sb./sth.** 与某人/某事物截然不同 [3] [u] (opposition) 反面; **in ~ to sb./sth.** 与某人/某事物相反地 [4] [u] Art, Phot (of colour) 反差; (of light) 明暗对比; TV 对比度
B /kən'trɑ:st, Amer -'træst/ *vi* 形成对比; **to ~**

with sb./sth. 与某人/某事物形成对比; **to ～ in style** 在风格上形成对比; **to ～ sharply** 形成鲜明对照

C /kən'trɑːst, Amer -'træst/ *vt* 对比; **to ～ sb./sth. with sb./sth.** 将…与…作对比

contrasting /kən'trɑːstɪŋ/ *adj* 截然不同的 〈*opinions, styles, tastes*〉; 完全不同的 〈*colours*〉

contrastive /kən'trɑːstɪv, -'træst-/ *adj* 对比的; **～ analysis/study** 对比分析/研究

contravene /ˌkɒntrə'viːn/ *vt* formal **1** (offend against) «*person*» 违犯 〈*law, code*〉 **2** (infringe) «*action*» 侵犯 〈*right*〉; (conflict with) 与…相抵触 〈*principle*〉

contravention /ˌkɒntrə'venʃn/ *n* **1** [c] (offence against law) 违法行为; (against ruling) 违规行为; **to be in ～ of** 违反 〈*rule, law*〉 **2** [u] (infringement) 侵犯

contribute /kən'trɪbjuːt/

A *vt* **1** (give) 捐献 〈*money, aid, goods*〉; **to ～ money to** *or* **towards sth.** 为某事物捐款 **2** (offer) 提出 〈*suggestion, views, ideas, advice*〉 **3** Journ, Publg 把…投稿 〈*article, poem*〉

B *vi* **1** **to ～ to ...** (be a factor in) 是…的原因之一; **unemployment ～s to a high crime rate** 失业是犯罪率高的原因之一 **2** (give money on regular basis) 定期缴款; **she ～s to a pension fund every month** 她每月都要缴纳养老基金 **3** (give to charity, campaign) 捐助 **4** Journ (give one's views) 发表意见; (write articles) 撰稿; **to ～ to a magazine** 向一本杂志投稿

contribution /ˌkɒntrɪ'bjuːʃn/ *n* **1** (role played) 作用; (to achieving a goal) 贡献; **her outstanding ～ to politics** 她在政治上的突出贡献; **a pathetic ～** 小得可怜的作用; **a small ～ to saving the earth's atmosphere** 帮助拯救地球大气层的小小贡献 **2** (to charity, campaign) 捐助; **to make a ～** 捐款; **all ～s gratefully received** 捐款均已收到，谨此深表谢意 **3** (to tax, pension) 缴费 **4** Insur 保险金分担 **5** (to discussion) 发表意见

contributor /kən'trɪbjʊtə(r)/ *n* **1** (donor) 捐赠人 **2** (participant) 发表意见者 **3** (writer) 投稿人 **4** (factor) 促成因素

contributory /kən'trɪbjʊtəri, Amer -tɔːri/ *adj* **1** (playing a part) 促成的; **to be ～ to sth.** 促成某事; **this event was ～ to his downfall** 这一事件导致了他的倒台; **a ～ cause of the disease** 这种病的一个诱因; **～ negligence** 共同过失 **2** (involving donations to a fund) 需要定期缴费的 〈*fund, health insurance*〉; **a ～ pension scheme** Brit *or* Amer **plan** 分担养老金计划

con trick *n* Brit colloq **= confidence trick**

contrite /'kɒntraɪt, kən'traɪt/ *adj* 懊悔的 〈*person, expression, tone*〉; **to be ～ about the accident** 对这次事故感到后悔

contritely /kən'traɪtli/ *adv* 懊悔地 〈*apologize, confess*〉

contrition /kən'trɪʃn/ *n* [u] formal 懊悔

contrivance /kən'traɪvəns/ *n* **1** [u] (artificiality) 矫揉造作 **2** [c] (clever or complicated device or tool) 精巧复杂的装置 **3** [c] (artistic device) 雕琢

contrive /kən'traɪv/ *vt* **1** (succeed in doing or creating) 设法促成 〈*event, situation*〉; **to ～ to do sth.** 设法做成某事 **2** hum (inadvertently succeed) 出乎意料地做到; **she ～d to spill the can of paint** 她竟然弄得整罐油漆都洒了

contrived /kən'traɪvd/ *adj* pej **1** (deliberately arranged) 人为的 〈*meeting, incident*〉 **2** (artificial) 矫揉造作的 〈*story, film plot*〉

control /kən'trəʊl/

A *n* **1** [u] (gen) 控制; (of investigation, operation, project) 管理; (of traffic) 管制; **Labour gained ～ of the council** 工党获得了议会的控制权; **to have ～ of** *or* **over** 控制 〈*territory, town*〉; 掌控 〈*fate, life*〉; **to take ～ of** 管理 〈*organization*〉; 控制 〈*situation, territory*〉; **she's too inexperienced to take ～ of the project** 她太缺乏经验，接不了这个项目; **in ～ of** 控制着 〈*situation, territory, town*〉; 管理着 〈*organization, operation*〉; **the person in ～ of the helicopter** 驾驶直升机的人; **to be under sb.'s ～, to be under the ～ of sb.** 处于某人的控制之下; **beyond/outside sb.'s ～** 超出某人的控制范围; **due to circumstances beyond our ～** 由于出现了我们无法控制的情况; **to keep/lose ～ (of sb./sth.)** （对某人/某事物）控制得住/失去控制; **to have ～ over sb./sth., to have sb./sth. under ～** 控制住 〈*animals, crowd, children*〉; **to get or bring sth. under ～** 控制住某事物; **to be/get out of ～** 失控; **to be under ～** 受到控制; **is the situation under ～?** 局势得到控制了吗？; **this spray will keep your hair under ～** 这种喷发胶可以保持你的发型 **2** [u] (self restraint) 克制; **to exercise considerable ～** 作出相当大的克制; **to have no ～ over one's emotions** 克制不住感情; **to lose ～ of oneself** 失去自制 **3** [c] (control apparatus) 控制装置; **to be at the ～s (of the spaceship)** 负责操纵（宇宙飞船）; **a ～ panel/knob/button** 控制面板/旋钮/按钮; **a ～ lever** 操纵杆 **4** [u and c] (regulation) (of trade, wages, speed) 管制; (of spending, volume, temperature) 控制; **to be subject to ～s** «*experimentation*» 受控制; «*immigration*» 受管制; **～s on military expenditure** 对军费开支的控制; **to go out of ～** «*prices, circumstances*» 失控 **5** [u and c] (verification of quality) 检验 **6** [c and u] (place) (where orders are made) 指挥部; (where checks are made) 检查站 **7** [c] Sci (experiment) 对照实验; (person for comparison) 对照人; (thing for comparison) 对照物 **8** [u] Comput 控制键

B *vt* **1** 控制 〈*situation*〉; 管理 〈*operation, investigation, organization*〉; 管制 〈*traffic*〉; **some teachers just can't ～ their pupils** 有些老师就是管不住学生; **he can't ～ his bodily functions** 他大小便失禁; **he could ～ his tears no longer** 他再也忍不住眼泪了; **to ～ the ball** 控球 **2** (keep neat) «*product*» 使…定型 〈*hair*〉 **3** (hold in check) 克制 〈*emotions, temper, impulse*〉; **to ～ oneself** 自我克制; **～ yourself: it's not as bad as it seems** 镇定点，事情并不像看上去的那么糟 **4** (regulate) 管制 〈*immigration, trade*〉 **5** (verify) 检查 〈*quality, accounts*〉

control: ～ character *n* 控制符; **～ column** *n* 操纵杆; **～ experiment** *n* 对照实验; **～ freak** *n* colloq 爱控制一切的人; **～ group** *n* 对照组; **～ key** *n* 控制键

controllable /kən'trəʊləbl/ *adj* 可控制的 〈*disease, situation, emotions*〉; 可驾驭的 〈*person, animal*〉; 可控制在一定值的 〈*rate, volume, expenditure*〉

controlled /kən'trəʊld/ *adj* **1** (calm) 冷静的 〈*voice, expression*〉; 克制的 〈*emotion*〉 **2** (performed carefully and safely) 受控制的 〈*emergency landing, explosion*〉; **manually/electronically ～** 手动/电子控制的; **under ～ conditions** 在受控制的条件下

controlled: ～ drug *n* 管制药品; **～ economy** *n* **= command economy**; **～ substance** *n* 毒品

controller /kən'trəʊlə(r)/ *n* **1** (gen) 管理者 **2** Radio, TV 主管 **3** Comm, Fin 财务总管; **a financial ～** 财务主管

controlling /kən'trəʊlɪŋ/ *adj* **1** (being in charge) 管理的 〈*group, organization*〉; **～ power** 控制权; **the ～ body** 管理机构 **2** (decisive) 决定性的 〈*factor*〉; **to acquire a ～ share/stake (in sth.)** Fin 获得控股权

controlling interest *n* 控股权益

control: ～ menu *n* 控制菜单; **～ panel** *n* 控制面板; **～ point** *n* 检查点; **～ rod** *n* 控制棒; **～ room** *n* 控制室; **～ tower** *n* 指挥塔台

controversial /ˌkɒntrə'vɜːʃl/ *adj* 有争议的 〈*proposition, issue, politician, book*〉

controversially /ˌkɒntrə'vɜːʃəli/ *adv* 有争议地

controversy /'kɒntrəvɜːsi, kən'trɒvəsi/ *n* [u and c] 争论; **to arouse** *or* **cause bitter ～** 引起激烈争论; **to be the subject of much ～** 是很有争议的话题

contusion /kən'tjuːʒn, Amer -'tuː-/ *n* 挫伤

conundrum /kə'nʌndrəm/ *n* **1** (problem, enigma) 复杂难解的问题 **2** (word puzzle) 字谜; **to set a ～** 出一道字谜

conurbation /ˌkɒnɜː'beɪʃn/ *n* 都市圈

convalesce /ˌkɒnvə'les/ *vi* «*patient*» 康复

convalescence /ˌkɒnvə'lesns/ *n* [u] **1** (recovery) 康复 **2** (period) 康复期

convalescent /ˌkɒnvə'lesnt/

A *adj* **1** (relating to convalescence) 康复的 〈*leave, break*〉; **a ～ sanatorium** 康复疗养院 **2** (recovering) 正在康复的 〈*patient*〉

B *n* 康复期病人

convection /kən'vekʃn/ *n* [u] 对流; **a ～ current** 对流气流

convection heater *n* **= convector**

convector /kən'vektə(r)/ *n* **a ～ (heater)** 对流加热器

convene /kən'viːn/

A *vt* 召开 〈*meeting, conference*〉

B *vi* 开会

convener /kən'viːnə(r)/ *n* **1** (organizer) 会议召集人; (chairperson) 会议主持人 **2** Brit (trade union official) 工会官员

convenience /kən'viːniəns/ *n* **1** [u] (advantage) 方便; **for ～, for ～'s sake, for the sake of ～** 为方便起见 **2** [u] (suitable time) 方便的时间; **at your ～** 在你方便时; **at your earliest ～** 请尽快 **3** [c] (practical feature, device) 便利设施; (way of doing things) 便利措施; **modern ～s** 各种现代化设备 **4** [c] Brit formal (toilet) 公厕

convenience: ～ food *n* 方便食品; **～ store** *n* esp Amer 便利店

convenient /kən'viːniənt/ *adj* **1** (suitable) 方便的; **to be ～ for sb. (to do sth.)** （做某事）对某人来说很方便 **2** (accessible) 近便的 〈*place*〉; **to be ～ for sth.** 离某处近 **3** (practical) 省时省力的 〈*device, gadget*〉; **a ～ way to do** *or* **of doing sth.** 做某事的便捷方法

conveniently /kən'viːniəntli/ *adv* 方便地 〈*arranged, located*〉; **the conference was ～ timed to coincide with ...** 会议安排与…正好同时; **rather ～, the will could not be found!** iron 也真巧，遗嘱找不到了！

convenor /kən'viːnə(r)/ *n* **= convener**

convent /'kɒnvənt, Amer -vent/ *n* **1** (Christian community) 女修道院; **to retire to a ～** 退隐当修女 **2** **a ～ (school)** 女修会学校

convention /kən'venʃn/ *n* **1** [c] (meeting, conference) 大会; **to hold an annual ～** 召开年会 **2** [u and c] (social norm) 习俗; **according to ～** 按习俗; **to flout** *or* **defy ～** 无视习俗; **a slave to ～** 循规蹈矩的人 **3** [c] (accepted practice) 惯例; **a theatrical ～** 戏剧的传统手法 **4** [c] (agreement) 公约; **the Geneva C～** 日内瓦公约

conventional /kən'venʃənl/ *adj* **1** (conformist) 符合习俗的 〈*behaviour, remarks, beliefs*〉; 墨守成规的 〈*person*〉; **to be ～ in sth.** 在某方面守旧 **2** (traditionally accepted) 传统的 〈*method, design*〉 **3** (non-nuclear) 常规的; **～ warfare/weapons** 常规战争/武器

conventionality /ˌkənvenʃə'næləti/ *n* [u] 恪守常规

conventionally /kən'venʃənəli/ *adv* 按照常规; **～ dressed** 穿着保守的; **a ～ armed missile** 常规装备导弹

convention centre *n* **= conference centre**

conventioneer /kənˌvenʃə'nɪə(r)/ *n* Amer 与会者

C

converge /kən'vɜːdʒ/ *vi* 1 (come together) «*lines, roads*» 相交; «*moving objects, people*» 汇聚; **to ~ on** *or* **upon sb./sth.** 与某人会合/在某地汇聚 2 fig (become similar) «*views, theories, tendencies*» 趋于一致

convergence /kən'vɜːdʒəns/ *n* [u] (of lines) 相交; (of ideas) 趋同; (of people, objects) 汇聚; **the point of ~** 相交点

convergent /kən'vɜːdʒənt/ *adj* 相交的 ‹*lines, roads*›; 趋于一致的 ‹*views, tendencies, theories*›

conversant /kən'vɜːsnt/ *adj* **to be ~ with sth.** 熟悉某事物

conversation /ˌkɒnvə'seɪʃn/ *n* 1 [c] (chat) 谈话; **to have** *or* **hold a ~ with sb.** 与某人谈话; **to strike up/break off** *or* **interrupt a ~** 开始/中断谈话; **a ~ about sb.** 关于某人的谈话 2 [u] (talking) 交谈; **to make ~** 找话说; **to be (deep) in ~** 在（深入）交谈中

conversational /ˌkɒnvə'seɪʃənl/ *adj* 1 (of conversation) 交谈的 ‹*powers, ability*›; **~ talent** 口才 2 (informal) 谈话式的 ‹*tone, voice*›; **a pleasant ~ manner** 亲切随和的态度

conversationalist /ˌkɒnvə'seɪʃənəlɪst/ *n* 健谈的人

conversation: ~ piece *n* 1 (object of talk) 谈资; 2 (painting) 人物风俗画; **~ stopper** *n* colloq 使人语塞的话

converse[1] /kən'vɜːs/ *vi* (talk) 交谈; **to ~ with sb. about sth.** 与某人谈论某事物

converse[2] /'kɒnvɜːs/

A *n* 1 (opposite) 相反之物; (of situation) 相反情况; (of statement) 相反说法 2 Math, Philos 逆命题

B *adj* 相反的 ‹*statement, situation*›

conversely /'kɒnvɜːsli/ *adv* 相反地; **you can add the fluid to the powder or, ~, the powder to the fluid** 可以把液体加入粉末，或反过来把粉末加入液体

conversion /kən'vɜːʃn, Amer -'vɜːrʒn/ *n* 1 [u and c] (of vehicle, appliance, raw material) 转变; **the ~ of sth. to** *or* **into sth.** 从某物到某物的转变; **the ~ of light into electricity** 光电转化 2 [u and c] (of measurement, weight) 换算; (of currency) 兑换 3 [u] (of building) 改建 4 [c] Brit (building) 改建的房屋 5 [u and c] Relig, Pol 皈依; **to undergo a ~ to Buddhism** 转而皈依佛教 6 [c] Sport 附加得分

conversion: ~ course *n* 专业转换课程; **~ kit** *n* 改装工具包; **~ rate** *n* 汇率; **~ table** *n* 换算表

convert

A /kən'vɜːt/ *vt* 1 (change into sth. else) 转变; **to ~ the country from a primitive society to a near-industrial one** 使这个国家从原始社会转变成接近工业化的社会 2 (modify) 改装 ‹*vehicle, appliance*› 3 Math 换算 ‹*measurement, weight, currency*›; Comput 转换; Fin 兑换 ‹*currency*› 4 Archit 改建 ‹*building*› 5 Relig, Pol 使改变信仰; **to ~ sb. to sth.** 使某人皈依某信仰 6 Sport 赢得…的附加分; **to ~ a touchdown** 触地得分后赢得附加分; **to ~ a try** 把球踢过球门赢得附加分

B /kən'vɜːt/ *vi* 1 (change) «*person, country, matter*» 转变; **Britain ~ed to decimal currency in 1971** 英国于1971年改用十进位制货币 2 (be convertible) (in use) 可改变用途; (in form) 可改变形式; **to ~ to** *or* **into sth.** 可改变成某物; **this sofa does not ~** 这个长沙发不能改作睡床 3 Relig, Pol 改变信仰; **he ~ed from atheism to Zen Buddhism** 他从信仰无神论转为皈依禅宗 4 Sport 赢得附加分

C /'kɒnvɜːt/ *n* 1 Relig 皈依者 2 Pol 改变信仰者

converter /kən'vɜːtə(r)/ *n* 1 Elec 变流器 2 Ind 转炉

convertibility /kənˌvɜːtə'bɪləti/ *n* [u] (gen) 可转化性; (of currency) 可兑换性; **the ~ of sth. to** *or* **into sth.** 某物向某物的可转换性

convertible /kən'vɜːtəbl/

A *adj* 1 (able to be converted) 可转化的 ‹*energy*›; 可改变用途的 ‹*room, appliance*›; **the sofa is ~** 这只沙发是两用的 2 Fin 可兑换的 ‹*bond, currency*›

B *n* 折篷汽车

convertor /kən'vɜːtə(r)/ *n* **= converter**

convex /'kɒnveks/ *adj* 凸面的 ‹*mirror, surface*›; **a ~ lens** 凸透镜

convexity /kɒn'veksəti/ *n* [u] 凸出

convey /kən'veɪ/ *vt* 1 (communicate) 表达 ‹*feelings, ideas*›; 传达 ‹*order, information*›; **to ~ (to sb.) that ...** （向某人）传达…; **this ~s nothing to me!** 这没有向我传递任何信息！; **to ~ one's thanks to sb.** 向某人表示谢意 2 (transport) 运送 ‹*passengers, cargo*›; 传送 ‹*sound waves*›; 递送 ‹*letter*›; **to ~ sb./sth. to sb./sth.** 将…送给某人/送到某处; **to ~ sth. from A to B** 将某物从A处送到B处

conveyance /kən'veɪəns/ *n* 1 [u] (of goods) 运输; (passengers) 运送; **a means of ~** 运输方式 2 [c] formal *or* hum (vehicle) 交通工具; **a public ~** 公共交通工具 3 [u] Jur (transfer of property, title) 产权转让 4 [c] Jur (document) 产权转让证书

conveyancing /kən'veɪənsɪŋ/ *n* [u] 1 (branch of law) 产权转让事务 2 (document preparation) 产权转让证书制作

conveyor /kən'veɪə(r)/ *n* 1 (in factory, for luggage) **a ~ (belt)** 传送带 2 (service provider) 运输商; (thing that conveys) 运输工具; **a ~ of goods by road** 公路运货车

convict

A /kən'vɪkt/ *vt* «*judge, jury, court*» 判决…有罪; **to ~ sb. of sth.** 判决某人犯有某罪; **to be ~ed on a charge of ...** 被判犯…罪; **a ~ed drug dealer** (in prison) 已定罪、正服刑的毒贩; (released) 曾获罪服刑的毒贩

B /kən'vɪkt/ *vi* 判决

C /'kɒnvɪkt/ *n* 囚犯

conviction /kən'vɪkʃn/ *n* 1 [c] Jur 定罪; **a ~ for drug trafficking** 贩毒罪; **to obtain/quash** *or* **overturn/uphold a ~** 获得/撤销/维持判决 2 [u and c] (belief) 坚定信念; (certitude) 确信; **a deep ~ of sth.** 对某事物的深信不疑; **to have/lack the courage of one's ~s** 有/没有勇气做自己认为对的事; **with/without ~** 坚定地/不坚定地; **he is, by ~, a socialist** 他是一个坚定的社会主义者

conviction: ~ politician *n* 有信念的政治家; **~ politics** *npl* + *v sing* 基于个人信念的政治

convince /kən'vɪns/ *vt* 1 (persuade) 说服; **to ~ sb. to do sth.** 说服某人做某事 2 (gain credibility of) 使…信服 ‹*jury, reader, listener*›; **to ~ sb. of** *or* **about sth.** 使某人相信某事

convinced /kən'vɪnst/ *adj* 1 (certain) 确信的; **to be ~ of sth.** 确信某事; **to be ~ that ...** 确信… 2 *attrib* (staunch) 坚定的 ‹*communist, vegetarian, pacifist, atheist*›; 虔诚的 ‹*Christian*›; **a ~ enemy of male chauvinism** 大男子主义的死敌

convincing /kən'vɪnsɪŋ/ *adj* 有说服力的 ‹*speaker, speech, argument*›; **a ~ victory** 毫无争议的胜利

convincingly /kən'vɪnsɪŋli/ *adv* 令人信服地 ‹*present, win*›; **a ~ argued statement** 令人信服的陈述

convivial /kən'vɪvɪəl/ *adj* 1 (sociable) 欢快友好的 ‹*person*› 2 (enjoyable) 欢乐的 ‹*evening, atmosphere*›

conviviality /kənˌvɪvɪ'æləti/ *n* [u] 1 (of person) 欢快友好 2 (of atmosphere) 欢乐

convocation /ˌkɒnvə'keɪʃn/ *n* 1 [c] + *v sing or pl* Brit Relig 主教大会 2 [c] + *v sing or pl* Brit Univ 毕业生校务评议会; Amer Univ 学位授予典礼 3 [u] formal (calling together) 召集

convoke /kən'vəʊk/ *vt* formal 召集…开会 ‹*persons*›; 召开 ‹*meeting*›; **to ~ Parliament** 召开国会

convoluted /'kɒnvəluːtɪd/ *adj* 1 (complicated) 错综复杂的 ‹*argument, style, ideas*› 2 formal (coiled) 盘绕的; (twisted) 弯曲的

convolution /ˌkɒnvə'luːʃn/ *n* formal 1 (coil) 盘绕; (twist) 弯曲 2 fig 错综复杂

convoy /'kɒnvɔɪ/

A *n* (of road vehicles) [受护送的] 车队; (of ships) [受护送的] 船队; **in ~** 受护送/结队

B *vt* 结队护送; **to ~ sth. across/to sth.** 结队护送某物通过/到某处

convulsant /kən'vʌlsənt/

A *adj* 引起惊厥的 ‹*drug*›

B *n* 引厥剂

convulse /kən'vʌls/ *vt* 1 使痉挛; **to be ~d with pain/laughter** 疼得抽搐/笑弯了腰 2 fig «*riots, unrest*» 震撼 ‹*country*›

convulsion /kən'vʌlʃn/ *n* 1 Med 痉挛; **to go into ~s** 抽搐起来; **to be in/go into ~s** (with laughter) 在/开始狂笑; **to have sb. in ~s** 让某人笑得前仰后合 2 fig (disturbance) 动乱; **political ~s** 政治动乱

convulsive /kən'vʌlsɪv/ *adj* 1 痉挛的 ‹*spasm, grasp*›; **waves of ~ laughter** 阵阵大笑 2 fig 狂暴的 ‹*upheaval, riot*›

coo[1] /kuː/

A *vi* 1 (murmur) «*woman*» 柔声低语; «*baby*» 咿咿呀呀; **to ~ over a baby** 对婴儿柔声细语 2 «*dove, pigeon*» 咕咕叫

B *vt* 柔声地说

C *n* (of dove, pigeon) 咕咕声

coo[2] *excl* Brit colloq dated 唔 [表示惊讶、羡慕等]

cooing /'kuːɪŋ/ *n* [u] 咕咕声

cook /kʊk/

A *vt* 1 Culin 做 ‹*meal*›; 烹制 ‹*food*›; **to ~ sb. sth., to ~ sth. for sb.** 为某人烹调某食品; **I'll ~ some eggs for breakfast** 早餐我要做几个鸡蛋; **to ~ sb.'s goose** fig colloq 坏某人的事儿 2 colloq (falsify) 篡改 ‹*accounts, statistics*›; **to ~ the books** 做假账

B *vi* 1 (make food) 做饭 2 (be heated) «*food*» 被烹制; **lunch is ~ing** 正在做午餐 3 fig colloq (happen) 发生; **what's ~ing?** 在搞什么把戏？

C *n* ▸**p. 409** (person who cooks) 做饭的人; (as profession) 厨师; **to be a good/poor ~** 善于/不善于做饭; **too many ~s spoil the broth** Prov 厨子多了烧坏汤

Phrasal verb

- **cook up** *vt* [**~ up sth., ~ sth. up**] 1 Culin 做 ‹*meal*›; 烹制 ‹*food*› 2 colloq (invent) 编造 ‹*excuse, story*›

cook: ~book *n* 烹饪书; **~-chill** *adj* Brit（预煮）速冻的; **~-chill food/processes**（预煮）速冻食品/工序

cooked /kʊkt/ *adj* 烧熟的 ‹*food, meal*›

cooked meats *npl* 冷餐肉

cooker /'kʊkə(r)/ *n* 1 Brit (appliance) 炉灶; **a gas/an electric ~** 燃气厨灶/电灶 2 colloq (apple) 煮食苹果

cooker hood *n* 吸油烟机

cookery /'kʊkəri/ *n* [u] 烹饪; **a ~ course** 烹饪课程

cookery book *n* esp Brit 烹饪书

cookhouse /'kʊkhaʊs/ *n* Mil (place for cooking) 伙房; (camp kitchen) 野营厨房

cookie /'kʊki/ *n* 1 Amer (biscuit) 曲奇饼; **that's the way the ~ crumbles** colloq 事已至此，无法挽回 2 colloq (person) [某种类型的] 人; **a tough ~** 坚强的人; **a smart ~** 机灵鬼 3 Comput 网上信息块

cookie: ~ jar *n* Amer 饼干罐; **to get caught** *or* **found with one's hand in the ~ jar** fig 被当场抓住; **~ sheet** *n* Amer **= baking sheet**

cooking /'kʊkɪŋ/ *n* [u] 1 (activity) 烹饪; **to do the ~** 做饭; **to be good at ~** 长于庖厨 2 (cooked food) 饭菜; **Chinese ~** 中国菜; **home/plain ~** 家常菜/简单的饭菜

cooking: ~ **apple** *n* 煮食苹果；~ **chocolate** *n* [u] 烹调用巧克力；~ **film** *n* [u] 食品保鲜膜；~ **foil** *n* [u] 烹调用铝箔；~ **oil** *n* [u] 食用油；~ **salt** *n* [u] 食盐

cook: ~**out** *n* Amer 露天烧烤餐；~**top** *n* Amer 灶台；~**ware** *n* [u] 烹调用具

cool /kuːl/

[A] *adj* [1] (moderately cold) 凉的〈*water, wind, skin*〉；凉快的〈*place, day, dress*〉；(refreshing) 凉爽的〈*breeze, weather*〉；**to feel/look/keep** ~ 感觉/看上去/保持清凉；**to keep an engine** ~ 使发动机保持冷却；**'keep** *or* **store in a** ~ **place'** "贮存于阴凉处" [2] (calm) 镇静的〈*person*〉；冷静的〈*judgement*〉；**to stay** *or* **keep** ~ 保持镇静；**to keep a** ~ **head** 保持头脑冷静；**a** ~ **customer** colloq 冷静的人；**to play it** ~ (stay calm) 不露声色；(be indifferent) 无动于衷；▸**collected 2** [3] (aloof) 冷淡的〈*person, manner*〉；**to be** ~ **with** *or* **towards sb.** 对某人冷淡；**to be** ~ **about sth.** 对某事物冷漠 [4] colloq (casually confident) 潇洒自信的〈*person, manner*〉；[5] (of colours) 使人感到凉爽的〈*blue, green*〉；**a** ~ **colour/shade** 冷色/冷色调 [6] colloq (for emphasis) 整整的；**a** ~ **million dollars** 整整100万美元 [7] colloq (fashionable) 很酷的〈*person, clothes*〉；(great) 很棒的；**it's not** ~ **to smoke** 抽烟并不酷

[B] *vt* [1] (make cool) 使变凉；**to** ~ **the building/sb.'s brow** 给这栋楼/某人的前额降温；**to** ~ **the pan/engine** 使锅/发动机冷却 [2] (calm) 使…平静下来〈*emotions, excitement*〉；使…冷静下来〈*person*〉；平息〈*anger*〉；**to** ~ **sb.'s ardour/passion/enthusiasm** 给某人的热情降温；~ **it!** colloq (be calm) 冷静点！；(stop it) 住手！

[C] *vi* [1] (become cool)《*air, tea, building*》变凉；《*pan, engine*》冷却；**the metal contracts as it** ~**s** 金属遇冷收缩 [2] (calm)《*passion*》平静下来；《*love*》冷淡下来；《*anger*》平息；**tempers have** ~**ed a bit** 大家的气消了一点

[D] *n* [u] [1] (coolness) **the** ~ 凉快处；(cool air) 凉气；**the** ~ **of the water/cave** 水/山洞的凉爽；**the** ~ **of the evening** 夜晚的凉爽 [2] colloq (calm) **to keep one's** ~ 保持冷静；**to lose one's** ~ (get excited) 激动起来；(get angry) 发火；(get frantic) 惊慌失措

Phrasal verbs

- **cool down**

[A] *vt* [~ **sb./sth. down,** ~ **down sb./sth.**] [1] (make cool)《*breeze*》使…感到凉快〈*person*〉；使…变凉〈*air, building, tea*〉；冷却〈*pan, engine*〉[2] (calm) 使…平静下来〈*person*〉；平息〈*situation*〉

[B] *vi* [1] (become cool)《*air, building, tea*》变凉；《*pan, engine*》冷却；**to do sth. to** ~ **down**《*person*》做某事凉快凉快 [2] (become calmer)《*person, situation*》平静下来；《*tensions*》缓和；~ **down!** 镇静点！

- **cool off**

[A] *vt* [~ **sb./sth. off,** ~ **off sb./sth.**] [1] (make cool)《*breeze*》使…感到凉快〈*person*〉；使…变凉〈*air, building, tea*〉；冷却〈*pan, engine*〉；**to do sth. to** ~ **oneself off** 做某事使自己凉快 [2] (make calmer) 使…平静下来〈*person*〉；平息〈*situation*〉

[B] *vi* [1] (become cool) 变凉；**to do sth. to** ~ **off**《*person*》做某事凉快凉快 [2] (become calmer)《*person, situation*》平静下来；**to** ~ **off towards sb.** 对某人冷淡下来

coolant /ˈkuːlənt/ *n* [c and u] 冷却剂

cool: ~ **bag** *n* Brit 冰袋；~ **box** *n* Brit 冰盒

cooler /ˈkuːlə(r)/ *n* [1] (container) 冷却器；**a wine/beer** ~ 葡萄酒/啤酒冷却器 [2] Amer (refrigerator) 冰箱 [3] esp Amer (long drink) 大杯清凉饮料 [4] colloq (prison) **the** ~ 牢房

cool-headed *adj* 头脑冷静的〈*person*〉；镇定的〈*manner, response*〉

coolie /ˈkuːli/ *n* dated pej [旧时中国、印度等亚洲国家的] 苦力

cooling /ˈkuːlɪŋ/ *adj* 冷却的；**a** ~ **agent** 冷却剂；**a** ~ **breeze** 凉风

cooling: ~**-off period** *n* [1] (in industrial relations) 冷静期；[2] Comm, Insur 可变更期；~ **rack** *n* 冷却架；~ **system** *n* 冷却系统；~ **tower** *n* 冷却塔

coolly /ˈkuːlli/ *adv* [1] (lightly) 凉爽地〈*dressed*〉[2] (calmly) 冷静地〈*say, reply, respond, approach*〉[3] (in an emotionless manner) 客观地〈*consider, react, judge*〉[4] (without warmth) 冷淡地〈*smile, say, respond, treat*〉[5] (with casual confidence) 潇洒自信地〈*march, demand*〉

coolness /ˈkuːlnɪs/ *n* [u] [1] (moderate coldness) 凉；(feeling) 凉快；(of clothing, room) 凉爽 [2] (calmness) 冷静 [3] (aloofness) 冷淡 [4] colloq (impudence) 厚脸皮 [5] colloq (fashionableness) 酷 [6] (of colour) 冷色系

coomb /kuːm/ *n* Brit 冲沟

coon /kuːn/ *n* [1] Amer colloq = **raccoon** [2] sl offensive (black person) 黑鬼 offensive

coop /kuːp/ *n* 家禽笼；**to fly the** ~ colloq 逃跑

Phrasal verb

- **coop up** *vt* [~ **sb./sth. up**] 关起；**to** ~ **sb./sth. up in sth.** 将某人/某物拘禁在某处

co-op /ˈkəʊɒp/ *n* [1] colloq = **cooperative (society)** [2] **the Co-op** Brit 高品公司 [出售廉价货物并与买主分摊利润的大型连锁商店]

cooper /ˈkuːpə(r)/ ▸**p. 409** *n* 箍桶匠

cooperate /kəʊˈɒpəreɪt/ *vi* [1] (work together) 合作；**to** ~ **with sb. (on/in sth.)** 与某人（在某事上）进行合作；**to** ~ **in doing** *or* **to do sth.** 合作做某事 [2] (comply with requests)《*person*》配合；《*official*》协助

cooperation /kəʊˌɒpəˈreɪʃn/ *n* [u] [1] (collaboration) 合作；**in (close)** ~ 在（紧密）合作下；~ **in doing sth./on sth.** 在做某事/在某事上合作；~ **between A and B** A和B之间的合作；**the** ~ **of sb./sth.** 某人/某组织的合作 [2] (compliance) 配合；(helpfulness) 协助；**he gave us his full** ~ 他全力协助我们

cooperative /kəʊˈɒpərətɪv/

[A] *adj* [1] (joint) 合作的；**a** ~ **action** 联合行动；**a** ~ **venture/enterprise** 合资企业 [2] (helpful) 配合的〈*person, attitude*〉；**to organize sth. along** ~ **lines** 按照合作的思路组织某事 [3] Comm, Pol 合作性质的；**a** ~ **movement** 合作社运动

[B] *n* (organization) 合作机构；(enterprise) 合作企业

cooperative: ~ **bank** *n* Amer 合作银行；~ **farm** *n* 集体农场

cooperatively /kəʊˈɒpərətɪvli/ *adv* 合作地；**to act** ~ 联合行动

cooperative society *n* 合作社

co-opt *vt* [1] (on to committee) 增选；**to be** ~**ed on to the committee** 被增选为委员 [2] (commandeer) 指定；**to** ~ **sb. as sth./to do sth.** 指定某人任某职/做某事

co-option *n* 增补；**there have been several** ~**s on the committee** 增补了几次新委员

coordinate

[A] /kəʊˈɔːdɪnət/ *n* (on graph, map) 坐标；**the x and y** ~**s on a graph** 图上的 x 坐标和 y 坐标

[B] **coordinates** *npl* Fashn 套装

[C] /kəʊˈɔːdɪneɪt/ *vt* 协调〈*limbs, movements, efforts, response, strategy, plan, attempt*〉；**we must** ~ **our action with that of our allies** 我们的行动必须和盟友协调

coordinate clause /kəʊˌɔːdɪnət ˈklɔːz/ *n* 并列从句

coordinated /kəʊˈɔːdɪneɪtɪd/ *adj* [1] (well organized) 组织有序的〈*movements, efforts, response, strategy, plan, attempt*〉；动作协调的〈*person*〉；**to be well/badly** ~ 协调性好/差 [2] (matching) 互相搭配的〈*clothes, furnishings*〉

coordinate geometry /kəʊˌɔːdɪnət dʒɪˈɒmətri/ *n* [u] 解析几何

coordinating conjunction *n* 并列连词

coordination /kəʊˌɔːdɪˈneɪʃn/ *n* [u] [1] (action) 协调；**in** ~ 协调地 [2] (physical) 协调性

coordinator /kəʊˈɔːdɪneɪtə(r)/ *n* 协调人

coot /kuːt/ *n* [1] Zool 白骨顶 [一种水鸟]；**as bald as a** ~ Brit colloq 头顶光秃秃的 [2] **old** ~ colloq [尤指年老的] 傻瓜

co-owner *n* 共有人

cop[1] /kɒp/ *n* colloq 警察；**to play** ~**s and robbers** 玩"警察抓小偷"游戏

cop[2]

[A] *vt* (*pres p etc.* **-pp-**) [1] colloq (receive) 遭到〈*blow, punishment*〉；遭受〈*damage*〉；遭遇〈*trouble, bad weather*〉[2] colloq (catch) 抓住；**to** ~ **hold of sth.** 抓住某物；**the teacher** ~**ped him cheating in the exam** 老师抓到他考试作弊 [3] colloq (arrest) 逮捕；**to get** ~**ped doing sth.** 做某事被当场逮住 [4] Brit colloq **to** ~ **it** (be punished) 受罚；(be killed) 丢掉性命 [5] Amer Jur (plead guilty) **to** ~ **a plea** 避重就轻地认罪

[B] *n* [1] colloq Brit (arrest) 逮捕；**it's a fair** ~**!** 我有罪！ [2] **to be not much** ~ Brit colloq (not much good) 不怎么样

Phrasal verb

- **cop out** *vi* colloq 逃避；**to** ~ **out of doing sth.** 逃避做某事

co-parenting *n* [u] [分居或离婚者的] 共同抚育子女

copartner /kəʊˈpɑːtnə(r)/ *n* 合伙人

copartnership /kəʊˈpɑːtnəʃɪp/ *n* [1] [u] (co-ownership) 合伙 [2] [c] (partnership) 合作团体

cope /kəʊp/ *vi* [1] (manage practically or financially) 应付；**to learn to** ~ **alone** 学会独自应付；**how do you** ~ **with all those kids?** 你怎么应付那么多孩子啊？；**to** ~ **in Cantonese** 用粤语交流；**to** ~ **on £60 a week** 靠每周 60 英镑收入度日 [2] (manage emotionally) 承受；**she struggled to** ~ **with the death of her father** 她尽力承受父亲去世这一事实

copeck /ˈkəʊpek/ *n* = **kopek**

Copenhagen /ˌkəʊpənˈheɪgən/ *pr n* 哥本哈根

Copernican /kəˈpɜːnɪkən/ *adj* 哥白尼的〈*principle, revolution*〉；**the** ~ **system/theory** 哥白尼体系/日心说

copier /ˈkɒpɪə(r)/ *n* [1] (photocopier) 复印机 [2] (imitator) 模仿者

co-pilot *n* [飞机的] 副驾驶员

coping saw /ˈkəʊpɪŋ ˌsɔː/ *n* 手弓锯

copious /ˈkəʊpɪəs/ *adj* (plentiful) 大量的〈*tears, harvest, data*〉；巨大的〈*amount*〉；详尽的〈*notes*〉；**a** ~ **supply of food and drink** 充足的食物和饮料储备

copiously /ˈkəʊpɪəsli/ *adv* 大量地〈*supplied, grow*〉；详尽地〈*documented*〉；**to weep** ~ 大哭

cop-out *n* colloq (avoiding commitment) 失信；(avoiding responsibility) 逃避责任

copper[1] /ˈkɒpə(r)/ *n* [1] [u] Chem 铜；~ **pipe/alloy** 铜管/铜合金 [2] [c] Brit colloq (coin) 铜币；**it only costs a few** ~**s** 这东西花不了几个钱 [3] [c] Brit Hist (for washing) 大铜锅

copper[2] *n* Brit colloq (police officer) 警察

copper: ~ **beech** *n* 紫叶山毛榉；~**-bottomed** *adj* Brit fig 稳妥可靠的〈*guarantee, deal, investment*〉；~**-coloured** ▸**p. 134** *adj* 紫铜色的；~**plate** *n* [u] 铜版；~ **plate (handwriting)** 铜版体；~**-rich** *adj* 富含铜的〈*alloy, ore, substance*〉；~**smith** ▸**p. 409** *n* 铜匠；~**'s nark** *n* Brit colloq dated 警方线人；~ **sulphate** *n* [u] 硫酸铜；~**ware** *n* [u] 铜器

coppery /ˈkɒpəri/ ▸**p. 134** *adj* 似铜的〈*colour, taste, smell*〉

coppice /ˈkɒpɪs/

[A] *n* 矮林

[B] *vt* 修剪〈*trees, woodland*〉

C

copra /ˈkɒprə/ *n* [u] 干椰肉

co-president *n* 共同主管人; **he is ～ of an international company** 他是一家跨国公司的共同总裁

copse /kɒps/ *n* 矮林

cop shop *n* Brit colloq 局子 [指警察局]

copula /ˈkɒpjʊlə/ *n* (*pl* **～s**) （联）系词

copulate /ˈkɒpjʊleɪt/ *vi* formal 《*person*》 性交; 《*animal*》 交配; **the male ～s with the female** 雄性与雌性交配

copulation /ˌkɒpjʊˈleɪʃn/ *n* [u] formal (of person) 性交; (of animal) 交配

copy /ˈkɒpi/

A *n* **1** [c] (reproduction) 复制品; (imitation) 仿制品; **to run off a ～** 复印一份材料; **a master/true/fair/rough ～** 底本/正本/誊清本/草稿本 **2** [c] (issue, edition) 一册; (of newspaper, record, report) 一份; (of book) 一本 **3** [u] (journalist's, advertiser's text) 稿件; **to be** *or* **make good ～** 是新闻报道的好材料; **to file (one's) ～** 把稿件归档

B *vt* **1** (write out by hand) 抄写; **to ～ sth. from sth.** 从某处抄写某文字; **the children copied the passage from the board** 孩子们从黑板上抄下了这个段落 **2** (duplicate) 复制; **to ～ sth. from sth.** 用某物复制某物; **to ～ sth. on to paper/a disk** 把某物复制到纸上/光盘上 **3** (imitate) 模仿

C *vi* 《*exam candidate, schoolchild*》 抄袭

Phrasal verbs

- **copy down** *vt* [**～ down sth., ～ sth. down**] 把…抄下来
- **copy in** *vt* [**～ sb. in, ～ in sb.**] 抄送; **can you ～ me in on your report?** 你的报告能抄送给我一份吗?
- **copy out** *vt* [**～ out sth., ～ sth. out**] 把…抄下来

copybook /ˈkɒpɪbʊk/

A *n* 习字簿; **to blot one's ～** 自毁声誉

B *modif* 标准规范的 ⟨*operation, landing*⟩

copycat /ˈkɒpɪkæt/

A *n* colloq pej 学别人样的人

B *adj attrib* 模仿的 ⟨*killing, crime*⟩

copy: ～-edit *vt* 对…进行文字编辑; **～ editor** ▸**p. 409** *n* 文字编辑; **～holder** *n* 原稿架; **～-protected** *adj* 防拷贝的 ⟨*software, CD, content*⟩; **～read** *vt* 校对 ⟨*text, manuscript*⟩; **～reader** ▸**p. 409** *n* 校对员

copyright /ˈkɒpɪraɪt/

A *n* [u and c] 版权; **to have** *or* **hold** *or* **own the ～ of** *or* **on sth.** 拥有某物的版权; **to be under/out of ～** 受/不再受版权保护; **～ reserved** 版权所有

B *vt* 获得…的版权 ⟨*book, piece of music, invention*⟩

C *adj* 受版权保护的 ⟨*material*⟩

copyright library *n* Brit 版本图书馆 [可免费获得英国出版的每一版本的图书]

copy: ～ typist ▸**p. 409** *n* 稿件打字员; **～writer** ▸**p. 409** *n* 广告文字撰稿人

coquetry /ˈkɒkɪtri/ *n* [u and c] 卖弄风情

coquette /kɒˈket/ *n* 卖弄风情的女人

coquettish /kɒˈketɪʃ/ *adj* 卖弄风情的 ⟨*woman, manner, look*⟩

cor /kɔː(r)/ *excl* Brit colloq 哎呀; **～ blimey!** 天哪!

coracle /ˈkɒrəkl/ *n* 科拉科尔小圆舟

coral /ˈkɒrəl, Amer ˈkɔːrəl/

A *n* **1** [u] (substance) 珊瑚 **2** [c] (animal) 珊瑚虫

B ▸**p. 134** *adj* (colour) 珊瑚色的

C *modif* 珊瑚制的; **a ～ necklace/earring** 珊瑚项链/耳环

coral: ～ atoll *n* = **atoll**; **～ island** *n* 珊瑚岛

coral pink ▸**p. 134**

A *n* [u] 浅珊瑚红

B *adj* 浅珊瑚红的

coral reef *n* 珊瑚礁

cord /kɔːd/

A *n* **1** (of pyjamas, light switch, curtains, etc.) 线绳 **2** Elec 花线 **3** (of phone) 软线

B **cords** *npl* colloq 灯芯绒裤

corded /ˈkɔːdɪd/ *adj* **1** (ribbed) 有凸纹的 ⟨*fabric, cloth*⟩ **2** (equipped with a cord) 配有软线的 ⟨*telephone*⟩; 带电源线的 ⟨*kettle, drill*⟩

cordial /ˈkɔːdɪəl, Amer ˈkɔːrdʒəl/

A *adj* **1** (friendly) 热情友好的 ⟨*atmosphere, smile, handshake*⟩; **to be ～ to** *or* **towards sb.** 对某人热诚 **2** (strongly felt) 强烈的 ⟨*dislike*⟩

B *n* [u and c] **1** (fruit drink) 甜果汁饮料 **2** Amer (liqueur) 烈性甜酒

cordiality /ˌkɔːdɪˈæləti, Amer ˌkɔːrdʒɪ-/ *n* **1** [u] 热情友好 **2** **cordialities** *pl* 热情友好的话语

cordially /ˈkɔːdɪəli, Amer -dʒəli/ *adv* **1** (in a friendly manner) 热情友好地 **2** (strongly) 强烈地 ⟨*dislike*⟩

cordite /ˈkɔːdaɪt/ *n* [u] 无烟线状火药

cordless /ˈkɔːdlɪs/ *adj* 无绳的 ⟨*telephone*⟩; 不带电源线的 ⟨*kettle, drill*⟩

cordon /ˈkɔːdn/

A *n* 警戒线; **to throw a ～ around sth.** 在某物周围设置警戒线

B *vt* = **cordon off**

Phrasal verb

- **cordon off** *vt* [**～ off sth., ～ sth. off**] 封锁

cordon: ～ bleu /ˌkɔːdɒn ˈblɜː/ *adj* 一流佳肴的; **a ～ bleu cook** 烹饪大师; **～ sanitaire** /ˌkɔːdɒn ˌsænɪˈteə(r)/ *n* **1** (guarded line) 防疫线; **2** Pol 缓冲地带

corduroy /ˈkɔːdərɔɪ/ *n* **1** [u] (fabric) 灯芯绒 **2** **corduroys** *pl* 灯芯绒裤子; **a pair of brown ～s** 一条棕色灯芯绒裤子

corduroy road *n* Amer [在沼泽地带用圆木铺就的] 木排路

core /kɔː(r)/

A *n* **1** (of apple, pear) 核 **2** fig (of problem, issue) 核心; **to the ～** 彻底地; **he's rotten to the ～** 他坏透了 **3** (of planet) 核; (of the Earth) 地核 **4** Phys, Nucl 活性区 **5** (of magnet) 磁芯 **6** (of cable) 芯线

B *vt* 挖去…的核 ⟨*apple, pear*⟩

core: ～ curriculum *n* 基础课程; **～ inflation** *n* [u] 核心通货膨胀; **～ sample** *n* 岩心样品; **～ skill** *n* 基本技艺

co-respondent /ˌkəʊrɪˈspɒndənt/ *n* [通奸引起的离婚诉讼中的] 共同被告

core: ～ subject *n* 基础科目; **～ time** *n* [弹性工作时间制中的] 基本上班时间

corgi /ˈkɔːgi/ *n* (*pl* **～s**) 柯基犬 [头似狐狸的矮脚犬]

coriander /ˌkɒrɪˈændə(r), Amer ˌkɔːr-/ *n* [u] 芫荽

cork /kɔːk/

A *n* **1** [u] (substance) 软木 **2** [c] (of bottle) 软木塞

B *modif* 软木制的; **a set of ～ table mats** 一套软木餐具垫

C *vt* 用软木塞塞住 ⟨*bottle, barrel*⟩

Phrasal verb

- **cork up** *vt* [**～ sth. up, ～ up sth.**] 塞住 ⟨*bottle, barrel*⟩

corkage /ˈkɔːkɪdʒ/ *n* [u] 开瓶费; **this restaurant doesn't charge ～** 这个饭店不收开瓶费

corker /ˈkɔːkə(r)/ *n* Brit colloq dated (story) 惊人的事; (remark) 惊人的话; (person) 出众的人; (stroke, shot) 漂亮的击球; **she's a real ～!** 她真是个大美人啊!

corkscrew /ˈkɔːkskruː/

A *n* 开塞钻

B *modif* 螺旋形的; **～ curls** 螺旋卷

C *vi* 《*airplane*》 盘旋

corm /kɔːm/ *n* 球茎

cormorant /ˈkɔːmərənt/ *n* 鸬鹚

corn¹ /kɔːn/ *n* [u] **1** Brit (wheat) 小麦; **an ear of ～** 一穗麦 **2** Amer, Austral (maize) 玉米 **3** (seed) 谷粒 **4** colloq pej (in book, film, etc.) (hackneyed) 老掉牙的东西; (sentimental) 令人伤感的东西

corn² *n* (on foot) 鸡眼; **to tread on sb.'s ～s** fig colloq 惹恼某人

cornball /ˈkɔːnbɔːl/ Amer colloq

A *adj* (trite) 陈腐的; (sentimental) 伤感的

B *n* (person with trite ideas) 思想陈腐的人; (person with sentimental ideas) 伤感的人

corn: C～ Belt *n* Amer **the C～ Belt** 玉米地带 [指美国中部盛产谷物的平原地区]; **～ bread** *n* [u and c] Amer 玉米面包; **～cob** *n* 玉米棒子芯; **～crake** *n* 长脚秧鸡; **～ dog** *n* Amer 玉米热狗; **～ dolly** *n* Brit 稻草人

cornea /ˈkɔːnɪə/ *n* (*pl* **～s**) 角膜

corneal /ˈkɔːnɪəl/ *adj* 角膜的; **a ～ graft** *or* **transplant** 角膜移植

corned beef /ˌkɔːnd ˈbiːf/ *n* [u] 咸牛肉

corner /ˈkɔːnə(r)/

A *n* **1** (of page, table, field, mouth, eye) 角; (of room, box, garden) 角落; **a ～ table/seat** 角落的桌子/座位; **to fold sth. (from) ～ to ～** 把某物对角折叠; **to watch/see sb./sth. out of the ～ of one's eye** 用眼角余光观察/瞟见某人/某事物 **2** (of street) 街角; (bend in road) 拐角; **a ～ house** 街角的房屋; **the store at** *or* **on the ～** 街角的商店; **(just) round** *or* **around the ～** lit (around the bend) （就）在街角附近; (nearby) （就）在附近; fig 即将来临; **to turn the ～** lit 拐过街角; fig 好转; **to take a ～ at 50 mph** 以每小时 50 英里的速度拐弯; **to cut (off) a/the ～** 抄近路; **to cut ～s** fig 图省事 **3** (remote place) 偏远地区; **the four ～s of the earth/world** 世界各地; **in a remote ～ of India** 在印度的一个偏远地区; **a quiet ～** 僻静的地方; **in the dark ～s of his mind** 在他隐秘的思想深处 **4** (difficult situation) 困境; **to be in a ～** 陷入困境; **to back** *or* **force** *or* **drive sb. into a ～** 把某人逼进困境; **to paint** *or* **box oneself into a ～** 使自己陷入困境 **5** Sport (kick, shot) 角球 **6** Sport (of boxing ring) 场角 **7** Comm (monopoly) 垄断; **a ～ on sth.** 对某物品的囤积居奇; **to have a ～ on iron ore** 垄断铁矿石

B *vt* **1** (trap) 使…落入圈套 ⟨*person*⟩; 使…落入陷阱 ⟨*animal*⟩; fig 使…陷入困境 ⟨*person*⟩; **to be ～ed (in sth.)** （在某处）被逼得走投无路; **a ～ed animal** 困兽 **2** Comm (monopolize) 垄断 ⟨*commodity*⟩; **to ～ the market in sth.** 垄断某商品的市场

C *vi* 《*driver, vehicle*》 转弯

corner: ～ cupboard *n* 角柜; **～ flag** *n* 角旗

cornering /ˈkɔːnərɪŋ/ *n* [u] 转弯性能

corner: ～ shop *n* 街头小店; **～stone** *n* 奠基石; fig 基础

cornet /ˈkɔːnɪt/ ▸**p. 395** *n* **1** Mus 短号 **2** Brit (for ice cream) 冰激凌蛋筒

cornetist, cornettist /kɔːˈnetɪst/ ▸**p. 395, p. 409** *n* 短号手

corn: ～-fed *adj* 谷饲的; (on maize) 玉米饲养的; **～field** *n* **1** Brit 麦田; **2** Amer (maize field) 玉米田; **～flakes** *npl* 脆玉米片; **～flour** *n* [u] Brit 玉米粉; **～flower** *n* 矢车菊

cornice /ˈkɔːnɪs/ *n* **1** Archit (plaster moulding) 楣; (on outside wall) 飞檐 **2** (of snow) 雪檐 [指冻结在悬崖边缘的冰雪块]

Cornish /ˈkɔːnɪʃ/ ▸**p. 426**

A *adj* (of Cornwall) 康沃尔郡的; (of the people) 康沃尔郡人的; (of the language) 康沃尔郡古凯尔特语的

B *n* **1** [c] (person) 康沃尔郡人 **2** [u] (language) 康沃尔郡古凯尔特语

C *npl* **the ～** 康沃尔郡人

Cornish: ～ cream *n* [u] = **clotted cream**; **～ pasty** *n* 半月形菜肉烘饼

corn: ～meal *n* [u] **1** Amer (from maize flour) 玉米粉; **2** Scot (from oat flour) 燕麦粉; **～ oil** *n* [u] 玉米油; **～ on the cob** *n* [u] 玉米棒; **～ plaster** *n* 鸡眼膏; **～ pone** *n* [u]

Amer (baked) 玉米面包; (fried) 煎玉米饼; ~ **starch** n [u] Amer = **~flour**; ~ **syrup** n [u] Amer 玉米糖浆

cornucopia /ˌkɔːnjʊˈkəʊpɪə/ n formal 丰盛; **a ~ of vegetables/information** 大量的蔬菜/信息

Cornwall /ˈkɔːnwɔːl/ pr n 康沃尔郡

corn whisky, corn whiskey n [u] 玉米威士忌酒

corny /ˈkɔːni/ adj colloq pej 老掉牙的 ‹joke›; 哆声哆气的 ‹song›

corolla /kəˈrɒlə/ n 花冠

corollary /kəˈrɒləri, Amer ˈkɒrəleri/ n 必然结果; **the ~ of** *or* **to sth.** 某事的必然结果

corona /kəˈrəʊnə/ n (pl **coronae** /kəˈrəʊniː/) 日冕

coronary /ˈkɒrənri, Amer ˈkɔːrəneri/

A adj 冠状动脉的; **a ~ artery** 冠状动脉

B n 冠状动脉血栓形成; **to have a ~** 患有冠状动脉血栓症

coronary: ~ care unit n 冠心病监护室; ~ **thrombosis** n [u and c] (pl ~ **thromboses**) 冠状动脉血栓形成

coronation /ˌkɒrəˈneɪʃn, Amer ˌkɔːr-/ n (ceremony) 加冕典礼; (act) 加冕; **a ~ ceremony** 加冕典礼; ~ **day/robe** 加冕日/加冕礼袍

coroner /ˈkɒrənə(r), Amer ˈkɔːr-/ n 验尸官

coroner's inquest n 验尸

coronet /ˈkɒrənet, Amer ˈkɔːr-/ n 小冠冕

Corp. /kɔːp/ abbr Amer = **corporation 1**

corpora /ˈkɔːpərə/ pl ▸**corpus**

corporal /ˈkɔːpərəl/ n 下士

corporal punishment n [u] 体罚

corporate /ˈkɔːpərət/

A adj **1** (collective) 全体的 ‹action, decision›; 共同的 ‹ownership, responsibility› **2** Comm, Fin 公司的 ‹policy, assets, profits› **3** (united) 联合的 ‹body, institution›

B n 企业集团; **smaller companies are being forced out by the ~s** 规模较小的公司逐渐被大型企业集团淘汰出局

corporate: ~ advertising n [u] 企业广告; ~ **body** n 法人团体; ~ **culture** n 企业文化; ~ **governance** n [u] 公司治理; ~ **hospitality** n [u] 公司款待 [尤指在运动比赛或其他社交场合招待客户以进行促销]; ~ **identity,** ~ **image** ns [u and c] 公司形象; ~ **law** n [u] Amer 公司法; ~ **lawyer** n ▸**p. 409** Amer 公司法律顾问; ~ **name** n Amer 公司名称; ~ **planning** n [u] 公司规划; ~ **raider** n 蓄意收购公司者; ~ **state** n **1** (state with corporatism) 集团国 [指由大型利益集团控制的国家]; **2** (state controlled by business) 公司国 [指由公司或公司对政府决策有重大影响的国家]; ~ **tax** n 公司所得税

corporation /ˌkɔːpəˈreɪʃn/ n **1** Comm 大公司 **2** Brit (town council) 市政委员会 **3** Brit colloq hum (paunch) 大肚腩

corporation tax n Brit 公司所得税

corporatism /ˈkɔːpərətɪzəm/ n [u] 集团主义

corporeal /kɔːˈpɔːrɪəl/ adj formal **1** (bodily) 肉体的 **2** (not spiritual) 物质的

corps /kɔː(r)/ n + v sing or pl **1** Mil 军 **2** (technical branch) 技术部门; **the Intelligence ~** 情报处 **3** (specialist group) 团队; **the press ~** 记者团

corps de ballet /ˌkɔː də bæˈleɪ/ n + v sing or pl 芭蕾舞群舞演员

corpse /kɔːps/ n 尸体

corpulence /ˈkɔːpjʊləns/ n [u] formal 发福

corpulent /ˈkɔːpjʊlənt/ adj formal 发福的

corpus /ˈkɔːpəs/ n (pl **corpora** or **~es**) **1** Literat 全集; **the Darwinian ~** 达尔文全集 **2** Ling 语料库

corpuscle /ˈkɔːpʌsl/ n 血球; **red/white (blood) ~** 红/白血球

corral /kəˈrɑːl, Amer -ˈræl/

A n Amer (enclosure) 畜栏

B vt esp Amer **1** (put in a corral) 把…赶进畜栏 ‹cattle› **2** (surround) 包围 ‹demonstrators, football fans›

correct /kəˈrekt/

A adj **1** (right) 正确的; **to be ~ in every detail** 每个细节都正确; **would I be ~ in thinking that you are going to help us?** 您会帮我们吗? **2** (appropriate) 合乎规范的 ‹dress, language, procedure›; (proper) 得体的 ‹manners, behaviour›

B vt **1** (put right) 纠正 ‹spelling, mistake, pronunciation› **2** (mark errors in) 批改 ‹essay, papers›; 审订 ‹proof, text› **3** (point out mistakes of) 指出…的错误 ‹person›; **I was wrong: I stand ~ed** 我错了, 承蒙指正 **4** (rectify) 矫正 ‹eyesight›; 调整 ‹imbalance› **5** (adjust) 调节 ‹headlights›; **to ~ course** Naut, Aviat 校正航向

correcting fluid n [u and c] = **correction fluid**

correction /kəˈrekʃn/

A n **1** [u] (action of correcting) 改正; (of papers, schoolwork) 批改; (of scripts, proofs, error) 订正 **2** [c] (alteration, mark) 更正; **to make a ~** 作出一项更正; **a course ~** Naut, Aviat 航向校正 **3** [u] Amer formal (punishment) 惩罚

B excl 更正一下; **six, ~, five** 6, 不, 是 5

correctional /kəˈrekʃənl/ adj esp Amer 改造的; **a ~ centre/officer** 劳改中心/劳教官

correction fluid n [u and c] 修正液

corrective /kəˈrektɪv/

A adj **1** (gen) 改正的; ~ **training** 纠正训练; ~ **measures** 纠偏措施 **2** Med 矫正的; **a ~ surgery** 矫正手术

B n 起纠正作用的东西; **this is a ~ to the idea that ...** 这是对…想法的纠正

correctly /kəˈrektli/ adv **1** (without making mistakes) 正确地 ‹answer, estimate, pronounce› **2** (in an appropriate manner) 得体地 ‹behave, dress, speak›

correctness /kəˈrektnɪs/ n [u] 正确性

correlate /ˈkɒrəleɪt, Amer ˈkɔːr-/

A vi «facts, data» 相关联; **to ~ with sth.** 与某事物相关

B vt 显示…的关联 ‹facts, data›; **to ~ sth. with sth.** 显示某物与某事物相关; **to ~ sth. and sth.** 显示某物和某事物的相关性

correlation /ˌkɒrəˈleɪʃn/ n [u and c] 相关; **a high/poor ~** 高/低相关性

correspond /ˌkɒrɪˈspɒnd, Amer ˌkɔːr-/ vi **1** (match up) «account, set of figures» 相符; **to ~ with sth.** 与某事物相符; **to ~ with one's needs** 符合需要; **to ~ to sample** Comm 符合样本标准 **2** (be equivalent) «institutions, tasks» 相当; **they roughly ~** 它们大致相似; **to ~ to sth.** 相当于某事物 **3** (exchange letters) «persons» 通信; **to ~ about sth.** 就某事通信; **to ~ with sb.** 与某人通信

correspondence /ˌkɒrɪˈspɒndəns, Amer ˌkɔːr-/ n **1** [u and c] (similarity) 相似; **a ~ with sth.** 与某事物的相似之处; **a ~ between sth. and sth.** 某事物与某事物的相似之处 **2** [u] (exchange of letters) 通信; (letters) 信件; **to be in ~ with sb. about sth.** 与某人就某事有书信往来; **to enter into ~** 开始通信

correspondence: ~ college n 函授大学; ~ **column** n 读者来信栏; ~ **course** n 函授课程; ~ **school** n 函授学校

correspondent /ˌkɒrɪˈspɒndənt, Amer ˌkɔːr-/ ▸**p. 409** n **1** (journalist) 记者; **a special/Europe/sports ~** 特派/驻欧洲/体育记者 **2** (letter writer) 通信者; **a good/bad ~** 勤于/懒于写信的人

corresponding /ˌkɒrɪˈspɒndɪŋ, Amer ˌkɔːr-/ adj attrib **1** (matching) 相关的; ~ **increases in costs** 成本的相应增长 **2** (similar) 相似的; ~ **to sth.** 与某事物相似; **in the ~ month last year** 在去年同月

correspondingly /ˌkɒrɪˈspɒndɪŋli, Amer ˌkɔːr-/ adv **1** (consequently) 因此; **they will adjust the plan ~** 他们将对计划作相应调整 **2** (proportionately) 相应地; **high profits and ~ greater risks** 高利润与相应的更高风险

corridor /ˈkɒrɪdɔː(r), Amer ˈkɔːr-/ n **1** (in building, train) 走廊; **the ~s of power** fig 权力走廊 [指左右决策的权力中心] **2** Geog, Pol 走廊 [指狭长地带]

corridor train n Brit 软卧列车

corrigendum /ˌkɒrɪˈdʒendəm, Amer ˌkɔːr-/ n (pl **corrigenda** /ˌkɒrɪˈdʒendə, Amer ˌkɔːr-/) 勘误表

corroborate /kəˈrɒbəreɪt/ vt 确证 ‹theory, explanation, innocence›

corroboration /kəˌrɒbəˈreɪʃn/ n [u] 确证; **in ~ of sth.** 为确证某事; **the witness provided ~ of his statement** 证人为其证词提供了确证

corroborative /kəˈrɒbərətɪv, Amer -reɪtɪv/ adj 起确证作用的 ‹evidence, figures›

corrode /kəˈrəʊd/

A vi «metal, frame, bodywork» 受腐蚀; **to ~ away** 腐蚀掉

B vt «acid» 腐蚀; «rust» 锈蚀; «water» 侵蚀; **jealousy ~s friendship** 嫉妒破坏友谊

corrosion /kəˈrəʊʒn/ n **1** (by acid) 腐蚀; (by rust) 锈蚀; (by water) 侵蚀 **2** (corroded part) 腐蚀部位

corrosive /kəˈrəʊsɪv/

A adj 腐蚀性的 ‹acid›; **a ~ remark** 恶语

B n 腐蚀剂

corrugated /ˈkɒrəgeɪtɪd, Amer ˈkɔːr-/ adj 有褶皱的 ‹surface›; **a ~ conduit/roof** 波纹套管/屋顶

corrugated: ~ cardboard n [u] 瓦楞纸板; ~ **iron** n [u] 波纹铁; ~ **paper** n [u] 瓦楞纸

corrupt /kəˈrʌpt/

A adj **1** (immoral) 腐败的 ‹society›; 腐化堕落的 ‹life› **2** (willing to accept bribes) 受贿的 ‹official›; ~ **practices** 贪污腐败 **3** (containing errors) 有错误的 ‹text, files›; Comput 有乱码的 ‹file, data›

B vt **1** (pervert) 使…腐化堕落 ‹person›; 败坏 ‹morals› **2** (through bribery) 贿赂 ‹official› **3** (introduce errors into) 使…出错 ‹text, language›; **the data/file has become ~ed** 数据/文件被破坏了

C vi 使人腐化堕落

corruptible /kəˈrʌptəbl/ adj 易腐化堕落的 ‹young people›; 易贪污腐败的 ‹politician›

corruption /kəˈrʌpʃn/ n **1** [u] (immorality) 腐化堕落; ~ **of a minor** Jur 未成年人的堕落 **2** [u] (by bribery) 贪污贿赂 **3** [c] (of text, data) 出错; (altered data) 出错数据; **4** [c] (altered word) 讹误文字

corruptness /kəˈrʌptnɪs/ n [u] **1** (immorality) 腐化堕落; **the ~ of the nation's morals** 国民道德的沦丧 **2** (willingness to take bribes) 贪污腐败 **3** (of text, data) 出错

corset /ˈkɔːsɪt/ n 紧身胸衣; Med [为治疗目的穿的] 胸衣

cortège /kɔːˈteɪʒ/ n 送葬队伍

cortex /ˈkɔːteks/ n (pl **cortices** /ˈkɔːtɪsiːz/) **1** (of brain) 脑皮层 **2** (of other organ) 皮层

cortisone /ˈkɔːtɪzəʊn/ n [u] 可的松

corundum /kəˈrʌndəm/ n [u] 刚玉

corvette /kɔːˈvet/ n 小型护卫舰

cos[1]**, 'cos** /kɒz/ conj colloq = **because**

cos[2] /kɒz, kɒs/ abbr = **cosine**

cosec /ˈkəʊsek/ abbr = **cosecant**

cosecant /kəʊˈsiːkənt/ n 余割

cosh /kɒʃ/ Brit colloq

A n [包橡胶的] 金属棒

B vt 用短棒打

C

C

co-sign /ˌkəʊ'saɪn/
A *vt* 联名签署
B *vi* 当联署人; **to ~ for sb.** 当某人的联署人

co-signatory /ˌkəʊ'sɪgnətəri, Amer -tɔːri/ *n* 联署人; **to be a ~ of** *or* **to sb.** 当某人的联署人

cosily /'kəʊzɪli/ *adv* 舒适地

cosine /'kəʊsaɪn/ *n* 余弦

cosiness /'kəʊzɪnɪs/ *n* [u] **1** (comfort) 舒适 **2** (intimacy) 亲密

cosmeceutical /ˌkɒzmə'sjuːtɪkl/ *n* 药用化妆品

cosmetic /kɒz'metɪk/
A *n* 化妆品; **to use/put on/apply ~s** 使用化妆品
B *adj* **1** lit 化妆用的 **2** fig pej 装点门面的 ‹*measures, reforms*›

cosmetically /kɒz'metɪkli/ *adv* 表面上地

cosmetician /ˌkɒzme'tɪʃn/ ▸**p. 409** *n* Amer (seller) 化妆品经销商; (adviser) 化妆师

cosmetic surgery *n* [u] 整容外科手术

cosmic /'kɒzmɪk/ *adj* 宇宙的 ‹*laws, radiation*›; **a disaster of ~ proportions** fig 天大的灾难

cosmic: ~ dust *n* [u] 宇宙尘; **~ rays** *npl* 宇宙射线

cosmography /kɒz'mɒgrəfi/ *n* [u] 宇宙结构学

cosmological /ˌkɒzmə'lɒdʒɪkl/ *adj* 关于宇宙的

cosmologist /kɒz'mɒlədʒɪst/ ▸**p. 409** *n* 宇宙学家

cosmology /kɒz'mɒlədʒi/ *n* [u] 宇宙学

cosmonaut /'kɒzmənɔːt/ ▸**p. 409** *n* [俄罗斯的] 宇航员

cosmopolitan /ˌkɒzmə'pɒlɪtn/ *adj* **1** (international) 国际性的 ‹*city, club*› **2** (worldly) 见多识广的 ‹*person*›; 具有世界眼光的 ‹*attitude*›

cosmos /'kɒzmɒs/ *n* [u] **the ~** 宇宙

Cossack /'kɒsæk/
A *n* 哥萨克人
B *adj* 哥萨克人的

cosset /'kɒsɪt/ *vt* 溺爱 ‹*child*›; «*government*» 过度保护 ‹*group, industry*›

cossie /'kɒzi/ *n* colloq 游泳衣

cost /kɒst, Amer kɔːst/ ▸**p. 174**
A *vt* (*pt, pp* **cost**) **1** (be priced at) 价钱为 ‹*amount*›; **to ~ sb. sth.** 花费某人某数量的费用; **to ~ sth. to do sth.** 花费某数量的费用做某事; **the necklace will ~ £50 to repair** 修这条项链要花 50 英镑; **it ~ me £32 to get my hair cut** 我理发花了 32 英镑; **to ~ money** (not free) 要花钱; (expensive) 价钱不菲; **it'll ~ you** colloq 这东西贵得很; **to ~ an arm and a leg** colloq 要花一大笔钱; ▸**pretty A** **2** (cause loss of) 使失去 ‹*life, job, love*›; 使输掉 ‹*match, election*›; 花费 ‹*time, effort*›; **to ~ sb. sth.** 使某人失去某物; **politeness ~s nothing** 礼貌待人不会错; **whatever it ~s** 无论付出多大代价; **reckless driving could ~ you your life** 鲁莽驾驶会要了你的命; **this mistake ~ him his career** 这个错误毁了他的事业; **to ~ (sb.) sth. to do sth.** (使某人) 付出某代价做某事 **3** (*pt, pp* **~ed**) Comm, Fin 估算…的成本 ‹*product*›; **the project was ~ed at £100,000** 这项工程的估算成本是 10 万英镑
B *n* [u and c] **1** (price) 价钱; **to estimate the ~ at £30** 估价为 30 英镑; **the high ~ of property** 高昂的房价 **2** (expense) 费用; fig 代价; **the ~ of sth./doing sth.** lit 某事物/做某事的花费; fig 某事物/做某事的代价; **the ~ of repairs/insurance** 维修费/保险费; **at great ~ to his parents** 由他的父母承担高昂的费用; **(to do sth.) at one's own ~** 自己出钱 (做某事); **(to do sth.) at no extra ~** 免除额外费用地 (做某事); **to count the ~ of sth./doing sth.** lit 考虑某事/做某事的费用; fig (suffer consequences) 尝到某事/做某事的苦头; (assess advisability) 考虑某事/做某事的风险; **to know sth./find sth. out to one's ~** 吃了苦头之后才知道/发现某情况; **he's a ruthless businessman, as I know to my ~** 我吃了苦头后才知道他是个无情的商人; **the ~ in sth.** 在某方面的代价; **the ~ in human lives was great** 付出的生命代价巨大; **at great/little ~ (to sb./sth.)** 以 (对某人/某事物) 极大/微不足道的代价; **at any ~** 不惜一切代价地; **at all ~s** 不论如何 **3** Comm, Fin 成本; **at ~** 按成本价; **to sell sth. at ~** 以成本价销售某产品; **~ analysis/control** 成本分析/控制
C **costs** *npl* **1** Jur **(legal) ~s** 诉讼费用 **2** Comm, Fin 成本; **to cut ~s** 削减成本; **to cover one's ~s** 保本

cost: ~ accountant ▸**p. 409** *n* 成本会计师; **~-accounting** *n* [u] 成本会计; **~ and freight** *n* [u] 货价加运价

co-star
A *n* 联合主演明星
B *vi* (*pres p etc.* **-rr-**) 联合主演; **to ~ with sb. (in sth.)** (在某项演出中) 与某人联合主演
C *vt* (*pres p etc.* **-rr-**) «*film, play*» 由…联袂主演 ‹*actors*›; **the new TV show ~s a young British actress** 一位年轻英国女演员在这部新电视剧中是主演之一

Costa Rica /ˌkɒstə'riːkə/ *pr n* 哥斯达黎加

Costa Rican /ˌkɒstə'riːkən/ ▸**p. 503**
A *adj* (of Costa Rica) 哥斯达黎加的; (of the people) 哥斯达黎加人的
B *n* 哥斯达黎加人

cost: ~-benefit analysis *n* 成本效益分析; **~ centre** *n* 成本中心; **~-cutting** *n* [u] 成本削减; *modif* 削减成本的 ‹*package, plan*›; **~-effective** *adj* 有成本效益的; **~-effectiveness** *n* [u] 有成本效益

costing /'kɒstɪŋ, Amer 'kɔːstɪŋ/ *n* **1** [u] (process) 成本计算 **2** [c] (estimated costs) 预计成本

costliness /'kɒstlɪnɪs, Amer 'kɔːst-/ *n* [u] 昂贵; **the ~ of their mistake/failure** 他们错误/失败的高昂代价

costly /'kɒstli, Amer 'kɔːstli/ *adj* **1** (expensive) 昂贵的 ‹*jewels, clothes*›; 奢侈的 ‹*habits, tastes*› **2** fig 代价高昂的 ‹*mistake, failure*›

cost: ~ of living *n* [u] 生活费用; **~ of living allowance** *n* 生活费用补贴; **~ of living index** *n* **= retail price index**; **~ of money** *n* [u] (of borrowing money) 借款成本; (of using money) 用钱成本; **~ overrun** *n* **1** [u and c] (exceeding of costs) 成本超支; **2** [c] (amount) 成本超支额 **~-plus** *n* 成本加成; **a ~-plus contract** 成本加成合同 **~ price** *n* 成本价; **at ~ price** 按成本价

costume /'kɒstjuːm, Amer -tuːm/ *n* **1** [u and c] Fashn 服装; **national/period ~** 民族/某一时期的服装 **2** [u and c] Theat 戏装; **to be in ~** 穿着戏装 **3** [c] Brit **(swimming) ~** 游泳衣 **4** [c] dated (woman's suit) 女式套装

costume: ~ ball *n* [c] 化装舞会; **~ drama** *n* [u and c] 古装戏; **~ jewellery** *n* [u] 人造珠宝; **~ play** *n* 古装剧

costumier /kɒ'stjuːmɪə(r), Amer -'stuː-/ esp Brit, **costumer** /kɒ'stjuːmə(r)/ Amer ▸**p. 409** *n* (maker) 戏服制造商; (renter) 戏服租售商

cosy /'kəʊzi/ Brit
A *adj* **1** (comfortable) 舒适的 ‹*room, chair*› **2** (intimate) 亲密的 ‹*chat, atmosphere*›; (pleasant) 轻松愉快的 ‹*get-together, evening*› **3** fig (unchallenging, complacent) 惬意的 ‹*life*›; 自我满足的 ‹*belief, assumption*›; **to have it ~** 过得悠然自得; **a ~ deal** 大有油水的交易 [多指有欺诈目的]
B *n* (for teapot, boiled egg) 保暖罩

Phrasal verb
- **cosy up** *vi* Brit colloq 依偎; **to ~ up to sth./sb.** 依偎某物/和某人套近乎

cot /kɒt/ *n* **1** Brit (for baby) 幼儿床 **2** Amer (camp bed) 行军床; **a folding ~** 折叠床

cotangent /kəʊ'tændʒənt/ *n* 余切

cot death *n* Brit 婴儿猝死

coterie /'kəʊtəri/ *n* 小集团

cottage /'kɒtɪdʒ/ *n* (small house) 小屋; (in country) 村舍

cottage: ~ cheese *n* [u] 农家干酪; **~ hospital** *n* Brit 乡间诊疗所; **~ industry** *n* 家庭手工业; **~ loaf** *n* Brit 双层面包; **~ pie** *n* [u and c] Brit 土豆泥肉馅饼

cottager /'kɒtɪdʒə(r)/ *n* 农舍居民

cottaging /'kɒtɪdʒɪŋ/ *n* [u] Brit colloq 泡公厕 [为寻找男同性恋者伴侣而常跑公厕的行为]

cotter pin /'kɒtə pɪn/ *n* 开口销

cotton /'kɒtn/ *n* **1** [u] (plant fibre) 棉花; **~ gauze** 棉纱 **2** [u] Bot (plant) 棉株; **a ~ field** 棉田 **3** [u and c] (cloth) 棉布 **4** [u] (thread) 棉线

Phrasal verbs
- **cotton on** *vi* colloq 开始明白; **to ~ on to sth.** 意识到某事
- **cotton to** *vt* Amer colloq **1** [**~ to sb./sth.**] (take a liking to) 喜欢上 **2** [**~ to sth.**] (approve) 赞同

cotton: ~ batting *n* [u] Amer **= ~ wool**; **C~ Belt** *n* Amer **the C~ Belt** 棉花带 [指美国东南部产棉区]; **~ bud** *n* Brit 棉签; **~ candy** *n* [u] Amer 棉花糖; **~ grass** *n* [u] 羊胡子草; **~ mill** *n* 棉纺厂; **~ picker** ▸**p. 409** *n* **1** (person) 采棉人; **2** (machine) 摘棉机

cotton-picking
A *n* [u] 采棉花
B *adj* Amer colloq 糟糕的; **you ~ layabout!** 你这个没出息的小混混!

cotton: ~ reel *n* 棉线轴; **~seed** *n* 棉籽; **~ waste** *n* [u] [尤用于擦机器的] 废棉; **~ wool** *n* [u] Brit 卫生棉; **to wrap sb. in ~ wool** fig 百般呵护某人; **~ worker** ▸**p. 409** *n* 棉纺工人

cotyledon /ˌkɒtɪ'liːdn/ *n* 子叶

couch[1] /kaʊtʃ/
A *n* **1** (sofa) 长沙发 **2** (doctor's, psychoanalyst's) 诊疗床; **to be on the ~** 接受心理治疗
B *vt* 表达 ‹*thought, feelings*›; **a reply ~ed in conciliatory terms** 意在和解的回复

couch[2] /kaʊtʃ, kuːtʃ/ *n* [u] **= couch grass**

couchette /kuː'ʃet/ *n* [列车上的] 折叠式卧铺

couch: ~ grass *n* [u] 匍匐冰草; **~ potato** *n* colloq 电视迷

cougar /'kuːgə(r)/ *n* Amer 美洲狮

cough /kɒf, Amer kɔːf/
A *n* (act) 咳嗽; (sound) 咳嗽声; (illness) 咳嗽病; **to give a ~** 咳嗽一声; **a dry ~** 干咳; **she has a bad ~** 她咳得厉害
B *vi* «*person*» 咳嗽; «*engine*» 喀喀地响; **to ~ away** 咳嗽不止

Phrasal verb
- **cough up** *vt* [**~ up sth., ~ sth. up**] **1** lit 咳出 ‹*blood, phlegm*› **2** fig colloq 勉强提供 ‹*money, information*›

cough drop *n* **= cough sweet**

coughing /'kɒfɪŋ, Amer 'kɔːfɪŋ/ *n* [u] 咳嗽; **a ~ fit** 一阵咳嗽

cough: ~ mixture *n* [u] 止咳药水; **~ sweet** *n* 止咳糖; **~ syrup** *n* [u] 止咳糖浆; **= ~ mixture**

could /kʊd, kəd/ ▸**can**[1]

couldn't /'kʊdnt/ colloq **= could not** ▸**can**[1]

could've /'kʊdəv/ *abbr* colloq **= could have** ▸**can**[1]

coulee /'kʊliː/ *n* Amer 深峡谷

coulomb /'kuːlɒm/ *n* 库仑 [电量单位]

council /'kaʊnsl/
A *n* + *v sing or pl* **1** (of a state) 议会; (of an organization) 理事会; **the C~ of Europe** 欧洲理事会 **2** (of town, city, parish, county) 地方议会 **3** (meeting) 协商会议
B *modif* Brit 地方议会的 ‹*elections*›; 市政住房的 ‹*services*›

council: ~ chamber *n* 议事厅；**~ estate** *n* Brit 市政住宅群；**~ flat** *n* Brit 市政公寓套间；**~ house** *n* Brit 市政楼房；**~ housing** *n* [u] Brit 市政住房

councillor, Amer **councilor** /ˈkaʊnsələ(r)/ *n* 政务委员会委员

council: ~man /-mən/ *n* Amer 地方议会议员；**~ tax** *n* [u] Brit 市政税；**~ tenant** *n* Brit 市政住房租住者；**~woman** *n* Amer 地方议会女议员

counsel /ˈkaʊnsl/

A *n* 1 [u] formal (advice) 劝告；**to follow sb.'s ~** 听从某人的劝告；**to keep one's own ~** 不透露自己的意见；**a ~ of perfection** 完美而不切实际的建议；**to take ~ together** 共同磋商；**to hold** *or* **take ~ with sb.** 与某人商讨 2 [c] (*pl* **counsel**) Jur 律师；**~ for the defence/prosecution** 辩护/公诉律师

B *vt* 1 (give professional advice to) 向…提供专业咨询 ‹*patient, student*›；**to ~ sb. about** *or* **on sth.** 就某事物向某人提供咨询 2 formal (recommend) 建议；(advise) 劝告；**to ~ sb. to do ...** 建议某人做…；**I would ~ caution/delay** 我建议谨慎行事/推迟；**to ~ sb. against sth.** 劝告某人不要做某事

counselling Brit, **counseling** Amer /ˈkaʊnsəlɪŋ/ *n* [u] 1 (practical or psychological advice) 咨询 2 Sch 辅导

counselling service *n* 咨询机构

counsellor Brit, **counselor** Amer /ˈkaʊnsələ(r)/ ▸**p. 409** *n* 1 (adviser) 咨询顾问；Psych 心理咨询师 2 Sch 辅导员 3 **~(-at-law)** Amer, Ir 律师

count¹ /kaʊnt/

A *vi* 1 (recite numbers) 数数；**to ~ (up) to sth.** 数到某个数；**to ~ from 1 to 5** 从1数到5；**to ~ backwards** 倒数；**to ~ in fives/tens** 5个/10个一数；**to ~ on one's fingers** 扳着手指数 2 (calculate) 计算；**to ~ from sth.** 从某物算起；**the fourth seat, ~ing from the right** 右起第4个座位；**I've had six drinks, but who's ~ing?** 我喝了6杯了，管它呢！ 3 fig (be relevant) 被算入；**children over the age of 14 don't ~** 14岁以上的孩子不算；**to ~ towards sth.** 被计入某事物；**work that ~s towards the final assessment** 计入最终考核的作业 4 fig (be important) 重要；(be of value) 有价值；**he's only a servant: he doesn't ~** 他只是个仆人，无足轻重；**she's an expert: her opinion ~s** 她是专家，她的意见很有价值；**every second ~s!** 每秒钟都很重要！；**it's the thought that ~s** 贵在心意；**to ~ for sth.** «*effort, experience*» 有某价值；**friendship ~s for a lot** 友谊很重要 5 Mus 数拍子 6 (be considered) 算作；**to ~ as sth.** 算作某情况；**children over 15 ~ as adults** 15岁以上的孩子算是成人；**handbags don't ~ as luggage** 手提包不算行李

B *vt* 1 (add up) 数 ‹*objects, people, times*›；**to ~ how many people/books there are** 数一数有多少个人/多少本书；**to ~ heads/votes/cash** 清点人数/选票/现金；**a program that ~s words** 统计词数的程序；**to ~ the pennies** fig 精打细算；**to ~ the minutes/hours** 一分钟一分钟/一小时一小时地盼着；**she was ~ing the days until Christmas** 她一天一天盼着圣诞节到来；**to ~ sheep** 数羊[以求入睡]；**to stand up and be ~ed** 公开表示支持；▸**chicken A1** 2 Mus 数 ‹*beats*› 3 (include) 把…算入；**I didn't ~ the money I spent on bus fares** 我没有把公共汽车费算在内；**55 people, not ~ing the children** 不包括孩子在内，共55人 4 (consider) 认为；**to ~ sb./sth. (as) sth.** 认为某人/某事物是某状况；**to ~ oneself lucky/fortunate** 觉得自己运气好/幸运；**~ yourself lucky that you only got a fine** 你只被罚款，算是幸运了

C *n* 1 (calculation of total) 清点；(total) 总数；**to do** *or* **make** *or* **take a ~ (of sb./sth.)** 清点（某人/某事物的）数目；**by sb.'s ~** 根据某人的清点；**at the last ~** 最后一次清点时；**to keep/lose ~ (of sb./sth.)** 知道/不知道（某人/某物的）确切数目；**that's your fifth cake — I didn't know you were keeping ~** 那是你吃的第五块蛋糕了——我不知道你在数着呢；**I've lost ~ of the number of times I've warned him** 我不知警告过他多少次了；**the ~ stands at 476** 总数为476 2 (level) 计数；**bacteria/cholesterol ~** 细菌/胆固醇计数 3 (recital of numbers) 数数；(in boxing, wrestling) 数十 [指倒地后须在10秒内站起，否则判输]；**a ~ of sth.** 数到某数；**on a ~ of three: one, two, three, go!** 数三下开始：一、二、三，开始！；**he was down for a ~ of seven** 他被击倒在地，直至数到七才站起来；**to be out for the ~** Brit *or* Amer **down for the ~** Sport [被击倒后数到十] 无法站立起来；fig (unconscious) 不省人事；(asleep) 熟睡；(exhausted) 精疲力竭 4 Jur 罪状；**she was found guilty on both ~s** 她被判两项罪名都成立 5 (point) 方面；**they were satisfied on all ~s** 他们对一切都感到满意

Phrasal verbs

- **count against** *vt* 1 [**~ against sb.**] (be held against) «*age, background, fault*» 对…不利；**his criminal record is bound to ~ against him in job applications** 他有前科势必对他找工作不利 2 **to ~ sth. against sb.** (hold sth. against) 认为…对某人不利 ‹*criminal record, clumsiness, youth*›；**you should not ~ her inexperience against her** 你不应该因为她缺乏经验就小看她
- **count among** *vt* 1 [**~ sb./sth. among sb./sth.**] (include as) 把…归入…之列 2 [**~ among sb./sth.**] (be included as) 被归入…之列
- **count down** *vi* 倒计时；**to ~ down to sth.** 对某事作倒计时
- **count in** *vt* 1 [**~ sb. in**] (include) 把…算入 ‹*person*›；**don't ~ Michael in; he's very busy at the moment** 别把迈克尔算上，他此刻非常忙 2 [**~ sb. in, ~ in sb.**] Mus 为…报节拍 ‹*person, instrument*›；**I'll ~ you in** 我会提醒你节拍的
- **count on** *vt* [**~ on sb./sth.**] 指望 ‹*person, event*›；**we're ~ing on you** 我们就靠你了；**you may get a pay rise this year, but don't ~ on it!** 今年你可能会加薪，不过这可没准儿！；**to ~ on sb./sth. doing** *or* **to do sth.** 指望某人/某物做某事；**she was ~ing on the train being late** 她指望着火车晚点；**to ~ on sb./sth. for sth.** 依靠某人/某事物得到某事物；**he ~s on his parents for advice** 他指望父母拿主意；**I knew I could ~ on you to make a stupid remark** 我就知道你准会冒出句傻话来
- **count out**

A [**~ out sth., ~ sth. out**] *vt* (dispense) 逐一数出 ‹*money, stamps, cards*›；**he ~ed out 20 £10 notes** 他数出了20张10英镑的钞票

B [**~ sb. out, ~ out sb.**] *vt* 1 (in boxing, wrestling) 数十后判…输掉比赛 ‹*boxer, wrestler*› 2 (exclude) 不把…算在内；**~ me out: I'm not interested in opera** 别把我算上，我对歌剧不感兴趣；**to ~ sb. out as sth.** 不把某人算作某角色；**to ~ sb. out of sth.** 不把某人纳入 ‹*plans, calculations*›

- **count up** *vt* [**~ up sth., ~ sth. up**] 合计 ‹*people, words, money*›；**they're still ~ing up the votes** 他们还在清点选票；**~ up how many hours you spend on the work** 算一下干这活儿你总共花了多少小时
- **count upon** *vt* = **count on**

count² *n* (nobleman) [除英国以外的欧洲国家中的] 伯爵

countability /ˌkaʊntəˈbɪləti/ ▸**p. 162** *n* [u] 可数性

countable /ˈkaʊntəbl/ *adj* 可数的 ‹*use*›；**a ~ noun** 可数名词

countdown /ˈkaʊntdaʊn/ *n* lit 倒计时；fig 最后的准备

countenance /ˈkaʊntənəns/

A *n* liter (face) 面容；(expression) 表情；**to keep one's ~** 不动声色

B *vt* formal (tolerate) 容许；(accept) 接受；**to ~ sb. doing sth.** 同意某人做某事

counter¹ /ˈkaʊntə(r)/ *n* 1 (surface) 柜台；**to pay at the ~** 在柜台付款；**this medicine is available over the ~** 这种药可以不用处方在店里买到；**to do a deal under the ~** 私下交易 2 (section of a shop) 专柜；**the perfume ~** 香水专柜 3 (token) 筹码 4 (counting device) 计数器

counter²

A **counter to** *adv phr* 逆向地；**to run ~ to sth.** 与某事物相违背；**he acted ~ to our wishes** 他违背我们的意愿行事

B *vt* 反驳 ‹*criticism, claim, accusation*›；反击 ‹*enemy, terrorism*›

C *vi* 1 (answer back) 反驳；**they ~ed with a different proposal** 他们以一个不同的提议来反驳 2 (fight back) 反击；**the police ~ed with tear gas** 警方以催泪瓦斯反击 3 (in boxing, fencing, etc.) 还击

counteract /ˌkaʊntəˈrækt/ *vt* 抵抗 ‹*threat*›；抵制 ‹*extremism*›；抵消 ‹*effect*›；**to ~ global warming/a fever** 应对全球变暖/退热

counter-argument *n* 相反论点；**a ~ to** *or* **against sth.** 与某观点相反的论点

counter-attack *n, vi* 反击

counter-attraction *n* 反引力

counterbalance /ˈkaʊntəbæləns/

A *vt* lit 对…起平衡作用；fig 抵消

B *n* (weight) 平衡重物；(force) 抗衡力；**to be a ~ to sth.** lit 与某物重量平衡；fig 是对某事物的抗衡

counter-bid *n, vi* 还价

counterblast /ˈkaʊntəblɑːst, Amer -blæst/ *n* 有力反驳

counter-charge

A *n* 1 Jur 反诉 2 Mil 反攻

B *vt* Jur 对…提出反诉

counter: ~-claim *n* Jur 反诉；**to bring a ~-claim** 提出反诉；**~ clerk** ▸**p. 409** *n* Amer 柜员；**~-clockwise** *adj, adv* Amer = **anticlockwise**；**~culture** *n* [c and u] 反主流文化；**~-espionage** *n* [u] 反间谍活动；**a ~ network/agent** 反间谍网络/探员；**~ activities** 反间谍活动

counterfeit /ˈkaʊntəfɪt/

A *adj* 伪造的 ‹*banknote, document*›；假冒的 ‹*signature*›

B *n* 伪造物

C *vt* 伪造

counterfeiter /ˈkaʊntəfɪtə(r)/ *n* 伪造者

counterfoil /ˈkaʊntəfɔɪl/ *n* (of cheque) 存根；(of ticket) 票根

counter: ~-inflationary *adj* 反通货膨胀的 ‹*measure, policy*›；**~-insurgency** *n* [u] 反叛乱；**~-intelligence** *n* [u] 反情报行动；**a ~ network/expert** 反情报网络/专家；**~ activities** 反情报活动；**~-intuitive** *adj* 反直觉的

countermand /ˌkaʊntəˈmɑːnd, Amer -ˈmænd/ *vt* 撤销

counter: ~measure *n* 对策；**~move** *n* 对抗行动；**~offensive** *n* 反攻；**to launch a ~offensive against sb./sth.** 对某人/某事物发起反击；**~-offer** *n* 还价；**~part** *n* (of person) 相当的人；(of object) 对应物；(of document) 副本；**a ~part to** *or* **of sb.** 与某人职位相当的人；**the US president and his French ~part** 美国总统与法国总统；**~point** *n* 1 [u] (technique) 对位法；2 [c] (melody) 复调；**~-productive** *adj* 适得其反的；**~-productiveness** *n* [u] 适得其反；**~-proposal** *n* 反提议

counterpunch /ˈkaʊntəpʌntʃ/ *vi, n* 回拳

counter-revolution *n* [u and c] 反革命

counter-revolutionary
A *adj* 反革命的
B *n* 反革命分子

countersign /ˈkaʊntəsaɪn/ *vi, vt* 副署

countersink /ˈkaʊntəsɪŋk/
A *vt* (*pt, pp* **countersunk**) 把…扩钻成埋头孔 ‹*hole*›; 把…装入埋头孔 ‹*screw*›
B *n* 埋头钻

counter staff *n + v sing or pl* 全体柜员

countersunk /ˈkaʊntəˌsʌŋk/ *pt, pp* ▸**countersink A**

counter: ~-tenor *n* (person) 男声最高音歌手; (voice) 男声最高音部; **~terrorism** *n* [u] 反恐

counter-terrorist
A *adj attrib* 反恐的; **~ operation/training** 反恐行动/训练
B *n* 反恐怖主义者

countervailing /ˈkaʊntəvaɪlɪŋ/ *adj attrib formal* 补偿的 ‹*advantage*›; 抗衡的 ‹*force, factor*›; **~ duty** 反补贴税

counterweight /ˈkaʊntəweɪt/ *n* **1** lit 平衡重 **2** fig 平衡; **the new bill serves as a ~ to previous proposals** 新法案对先前的提案起到了平衡作用

countess /ˈkaʊntɪs/ *n* **1** (wife, widow of count) 伯爵夫人 **2** (noblewoman) 女伯爵

counting /ˈkaʊntɪŋ/
A *n* [u] 计数
B *modif* 学习计数的 ‹*game, rhyme*›; 计数用的 ‹*device, apparatus*›; **an abacus is a ~ frame** 算盘是一种计数用的框架结构工具
C *prep* 包括; **there are four of us, ~ me** 算上我, 我们共有四人

countless /ˈkaʊntlɪs/ *adj* 无数的; **on ~ occasions he felt out of place** 他无数次感到格格不入

count noun *n* 可数名词

countrified /ˈkʌntrɪfaɪd/ *adj* **1** (rural) 乡村的 **2** pej 土气的 ‹*person*›; 粗俗的 ‹*life, view, outlook*›; **sb. with ~ ways** 土里土气的某人

country /ˈkʌntri/ *n* **1** [c] (state) 国家; **to die for one's ~** 为国捐躯; **one's line of ~** 擅长的领域; **up ~** (away from the coast) 向内陆; (away from the capital) 向首府以外 **2** [u] (nation, people) **the ~** 全国人民; **to go** *or* **appeal to the ~** Brit Pol 解散议会举行大选 **3** [c] (native land) 家乡; **the old ~** 英伦老家 **4** [u] (districts outside town) 乡下; **to travel across ~** 穿越乡间; **deep in the** *or* **in the heart of the ~** 在偏僻的乡间; **a place in the ~** 一处村居 **5** [u] (region) 地带; **fishing/walking ~** 钓鱼/步行区域; **open ~** 空旷地带 **6** [u] **~ (music)** 乡村与西部音乐; **a ~ singer** 乡村与西部音乐歌手

country: ~ and western *n* [u] 乡村与西部音乐; **~-bred** *adj* 农村长大的; **~ bumpkin** *n* pej 乡巴佬 pej; **~ club** *n* 乡村俱乐部; **~ code** *n* 国家代码; **~ cousin** *n* pej 乡巴佬 pej; **~ dance** *n* esp Brit 乡村舞; **~ dancer** *n* esp Brit 乡村舞演员; **~ dancing** *n* [u] esp Brit 跳乡村舞; **to go ~ dancing** 去跳乡村舞; **~ gentleman** *n* 乡绅; **~ house** *n* 乡间邸宅; **~man** /-mən/ *n* **1** (from the same country) (fellow) **~** 同胞; **2** (living in the countryside) 乡下人; **~ mile** *n* colloq 远程; **it's a ~ mile!** 那里老远了! ; **~ music** *n* [u] 乡村与西部音乐; **~ park** *n* Brit 乡村公园; **~ rock** *n* [u] 乡村摇滚乐; **~ seat** *n* 乡间邸宅

countryside /ˈkʌntrɪsaɪd/ *n* [u] 乡下; **in the ~** 在乡下

countryside: ~ code *n* Brit 乡村游览行为规则; **C~ Commission** *n + v sing or pl* **the C~ Commission** Brit 英国乡村保护委员会

countrywide /ˈkʌntrɪwaɪd/ *adj, adv* 遍及全国的 (地)

Countability

■ Chinese nouns have no separate singular or plural forms apart from the plural suffix 们 added to nouns referring to people. Whether a Chinese noun is singular or plural is usually determined by context or by the addition of numbers or words expressing the plural.

Countable and uncountable nouns

■ Chinese common nouns are countable, and require the use of measure words as well as numbers. Common nouns referring to people add the plural suffix 们:

one novel
= 1 部小说

three apples
= 3 个苹果

some coins
= 一些硬币
or 几枚硬币

two painters
= 两位画家

friends
= 朋友们

■ 们 cannot be used together with a number or words expressing the plural:

nine students
= 9 个学生
but not
9 个学生们

some doctors
= 一些医生
but not
一些医生们

■ Uncountable nouns must also take measure words as in the following examples:

two pieces of information
= 两条信息

a piece of cloth
= 1 块布

five items of furniture
= 5 件家具

a loaf of bread
= 1 条面包

a round of applause
= 一阵掌声

a grain of rice
= 1 粒米

three glasses of water
= 3 杯水

four packets of cereal
= 4 包麦片

a set of textbooks
= 1 套课本

a pair of shoes
= 1 双鞋

Nouns that are both countable and uncountable

■ In English, some nouns can be both countable and uncountable, often with a difference in meaning. The countable noun is specific, while the uncountable noun is more general. When translated into Chinese, both numbers and measure words are normally used to express the specific meaning:

I don't like sport
= 我不喜欢运动

Table tennis is a sport
= 乒乓球是一项运动

Translation is an art
= 翻译是一门艺术

The word 'letter' has several different Chinese translations
= letter 一词有几种不同的汉语翻译

I don't drink coffee or tea
= 我不喝咖啡, 也不喝茶

Two coffees and three teas, please
= 请来两杯咖啡、三杯茶

Nouns of time

■ With time nouns, 个 is usually omitted before monosyllabic time nouns such as 周, 年, etc. With disyllabic time nouns, 个 is sometimes present, and sometimes must be omitted (due to language convention):

two years
= 两年
but not
两个年

three days
= 3 天
but not
3 个天

five mornings
= 5 个上午
but not
5 上午

four weeks
= 4 周
or 4 个周
or 4 个星期

eight minutes
= 8 分钟
but not
8 个分钟

six hours
= 6 小时
or 6 个小时

■ The measure word 个 is usually present before 月 (month) to avoid ambiguity:

one month
= 1 个月
but not
1 月 (= January)

three months
= 3 个月
but not
3 月 (= March)

countrywoman /'kʌntrɪwʊmən/ *n* (*pl* **countrywomen**) **1** (from the same country) **(fellow)** ～ 女同胞 **2** (living in the countryside) 乡下女人

county /'kaʊnti/ *n* (in Britain) 郡; (in USA) 县; ～ **boundaries** 郡分界线

county: ～ **agent** ▸p. 409 *n* Amer 县农业和家政顾问; ～ **council** *n* Brit 郡政务委员会; ～ **councillor** *n* Brit 郡政务委员; ～ **court** *n* **1** Brit 郡法院; **2** Amer 县法院; ～ **seat** *n* Amer = ～ **town**; ～ **town** *n* Brit 郡首府; Amer 县城

coup /kuː/ *n* **1** (seizure of power) 政变; **to stage a** ～ 发动政变 **2** (successful move) 突然的成功之举; **to pull off/score a** ～ 大获成功

coup: ～ **de grâce** /ˌkuː də 'græs/ *n* (*pl* ～**s de grâce** /ˌkuː də 'græs/) 最后一击; ～ **d'état** /ˌkuː deɪ'tɑː/ *n* (*pl* ～**s d'état** /ˌkuː deɪ'tɑː/) 政变

coupé /'kuːpeɪ/ *n* 双门斜背轿车

couple /'kʌpl/

A *n* **1** (married) 夫妻; (romantic) 情侣 **2** (two objects or people) 两个; **a** ～ **of girls** 两个女孩 **3** (a few) 几个; **a** ～ **of times** 几次

B *vt* **1** lit 连接; **the restaurant car was** ～**d (on) to the last coach** 餐车挂在最后一节车厢上 **2** fig 把…联系起来 ‹*people, things, ideas*›; **to** ～ **(the name of) Bill Gates with Microsoft** 把比尔·盖茨（的名字）和微软联系起来

couplet /'kʌplɪt/ *n* 对句

coupling /'kʌplɪŋ/ *n* **1** [u] lit 连接 **2** [u] fig 联系; **the** ～ **of soaring costs with higher unemployment** 成本飞涨与失业率走高之间的联系 **3** [c] Rail 耦接头

coupon /'kuːpɒn/ *n* **1** (for rations, esp during wartime) 配给券; **a petrol** ～ 汽油票 **2** (money-off voucher) 优惠券 **3** (form for competition) 参赛表 **4** (form for ordering goods) 订货单

courage /'kʌrɪdʒ/ *n* [u] 勇气; **to pluck up the** ～ **to do sth.** 鼓起勇气做某事; **it takes** ～ **to …** …需要勇气; **to screw up one's** ～, **to take one's** ～ **in both hands** 鼓起勇气

courageous /kə'reɪdʒəs/ *adj* 勇敢的; ～ **words** 豪言壮语

courageously /kə'reɪdʒəsli/ *adv* 勇敢地

courageousness /kə'reɪdʒəsnɪs/ *n* [u] 勇敢

courgette /kɔː'ʒet/ *n* Brit 密生西葫芦

courier /'kʊrɪə(r)/ ▸p. 409 *n* **1** (company) 快递公司; (employee) 快递员; **to send sth. by** ～ 用快递送某物 **2** (messenger) 情报员 **3** (guide) **(travel)** ～ 导游

courier company *n* 快递公司

course /kɔːs/

A *n* **1** [c] (progression) 进程; **the** ～ **of nature/history/justice** 自然规律/历史进程/司法程序; **in the** ～ **of sth./doing sth.** 在…/做某事的过程中; **in the** ～ **of an hour** 在1小时内; **in the normal/ordinary** ～ **of events/things** 按通常情况; **in the** ～ **of time** 总有一天; **a building in** ～ **of construction** 正在建造的大楼; **to run** *or* **take** *or* **follow its** ～ 任其发展; **his grief had run its** ～ 他的悲痛过去了; **let fate take its** ～ 听天由命; **the law must take its** ～ 必须按法律行事 **2** [c and u] (direction of ship, aircraft) 航向; (route) (of aircraft, ship) 航线; (of river) 水道; (of road) 路线; (direction of star, planet) 方位; fig 行动方向; **to be on a** ～ 保持某一航向; **on** ～ 在正确的方向上; **the economy is back on** ～ 经济重新走上了正轨; **to be on** ～ **for sth.** lit 在去某地的路上; fig 很可能做成某事; **the company is on** ～ **for bankruptcy** 公司很可能破产; **off** ～ 偏离方向地; **to go off** ～ 偏离方向; **to steer/hold a** ～ 保持航向; **to plot a** ～ 标绘航线; **to change (one's)** ～ lit 改变（自己的）方向; fig 改变（自己的）方针; **the river has changed its** ～ **many times** 这条河已多次改道; **to set (a)** ～ **for sth.** 确定去某地的路线 **3** [c] (procedure) 行动方式; **to take a** ～ **of action** 采取一种办法 **4** [c] (series of lessons) 课程; **a French/art/degree** ～ 法文/艺术/学位课程; **the college offers a wide range of** ～**s** 学院开设课程范围广泛; **a** ～ **of sth.** 某种课程; **a** ～ **of study** Sch, Univ 学习课程; **she gave a** ～ **of lectures on Mozart** 她开设了一个关于莫扎特的讲座; **to take a** ～ **in linguistics** 修一门语言学课程; **the college runs** ～**s in a variety of subjects** 这所学院开设有各种科目的课程; **to be/go on a** ～ 在/去修一门课程; **to send sb. on a** ～ 派某人去修一门课程 **5** [c] Med, Vet 疗程; **a** ～ **of** 一个…的疗程 ‹*drugs, injections*›; **the doctor prescribed a** ～ **of antibiotics** 医生开了一个疗程的抗生素 **6** [c] (for golf) 高尔夫球场 **7** [c] (for racing) 赛道; (for runners) 跑道; **to stay the** ～ 坚持到比赛结束; fig 坚持到底 **8** [c] (part of meal) 一道菜; **the first/second/third** ～ 头/第二/第三道菜; **the soup/fish** ～ 一道汤/鱼; **a three/four/five-**～ **meal** 有三/四/五道菜的饭食 **9** [c] Constr [墙砖、屋顶瓦等的] 层

B *vi* liter «*river, blood, tears*» 迅速流动; **to** ～ **through sth.** 迅速地流过某物; **to** ～ **down sth.** 沿某物流下来; **the tears** ～**d down her cheeks** 泪珠沿着她的脸颊滚落下来; **to** ～ **in sth.** 在某物里迅速流动

C **of course** *adv phr* 当然; **of** ～ **not!** 当然不！; **I may of** ～ **be wrong** 当然，我可能是错的; **of** ～**! I remember now** 当然啦！我现在记起来了; **I did all I could to help — of** ～ **you did** 我已尽全力帮忙了——的确如此; **may I borrow your pen — of** ～**!** 我可以借用你的钢笔吗？——当然可以！

course: ～**book** *n* Brit 教科书; ～ **material** *n* [u], ～ **materials** *npl* 课程资料; ～**ware** *n* [u] 课件; ～**work** *n* [u] 课程作业

coursing /'kɔːsɪŋ/ *n* [u] 追踪狩猎

court /kɔːt/

A *n* **1** [c and u] Jur 法庭; **to appear in** ～ 出庭; **a** ～ **appearance** 出庭; **to bring sth./sb. to** ～ 把某物/某人带上法庭; **to take sb. to** ～ 起诉某人; **to go to** ～ **over sth.** 为某事打官司; **to put/rule sth. out of** ～ 摒弃某事; **to laugh sth. out of** ～ 对某事一笑了之; **to settle sth. out of** ～ 庭外解决某事; **in open/closed** ～ 公开/不公开审理 **2** [u] (people present in court) 出庭人员; **to address the** ～ 当庭发言 **3** [c and u] (of sovereign) 宫廷; **to be presented at** ～ 朝见君主; **to hold** ～ lit 主持御前会议; fig (entertain admirers) 接待仰慕者; (entertain visitors) 接待来宾 **4** [c] Sport 球场; **to be on** ～ 在场上; **the ball is in sb.'s** ～ fig 轮到某人作出反应了 **5** = **courtyard**

B *vt* **1** (woo) «*man*» 向…求爱 ‹*woman*›; «*male animal*» 向…求偶 ‹*female animal*› **2** (seek favour with) 巴结 ‹*director, leader*› **3** (try hard to win) 力图获得 ‹*applause, favour*› **4** (risk incurring) 招致 ‹*defeat, disaster*›

C *vi* 恋爱; **a** ～**ing couple** 恋爱中的情侣; **in our** ～**ing days** 在我们恋爱的日子里

court: ～ **card** *n* Brit 花牌 [指纸牌中的 K、Q 和 J]; ～ **circular** *n* 宫廷活动公报

courteous /'kɜːtɪəs/ *adj* 礼貌的; ～ **words** 谦词; **to be** ～ **to** *or* **towards sb.** 对某人彬彬有礼

courteously /'kɜːtɪəsli/ *adv* 有礼貌地

courtesan /ˌkɔːtɪ'zæn, 'kɔːtɪzn/ *n* 高级妓女

courtesy /'kɜːtəsi/ *n* **1** [u] 礼貌; **to have the** ～ **to …** 懂得…的礼数; **it is only common** ～ **to …** …只是起码的礼貌; **(by)** ～ **of** (with permission from) 蒙…允许 ‹*rightful owner*› **2** [c] (action) 礼貌的举止; (remark) 客气话; **please do me the** ～ **of hearing me out** 请耐心听我把话说完; **to exchange courtesies** 相互寒暄

courtesy: ～ **call** *n* 礼节性拜访; **to make a** ～ **call (on sb.)** 礼节性拜访（某人）; ～ **car** *n* 免费用车; ～ **coach** *n* 免费班车; ～ **light** *n* 门控车内照明灯; ～ **title** *n* Brit 尊称; ～ **visit** *n* = ～ **call**

courthouse /'kɔːthaʊs/ *n* **1** Brit Jur 法院大楼 **2** Amer Admin 县政府大楼

courtier /'kɔːtɪə(r)/ *n* 侍臣

courtly /'kɔːtli/ *adj* 彬彬有礼的

courtly love *n* [u] 典雅爱情 [指欧洲12至14世纪期间骑士和贵妇之间的精神恋爱]

court-martial

A *n* (*pl* **courts-martial** *or* **court-martials**) 军事法庭

B *vt* (*pres p etc.* **-ll-**) 依军法审判

court: **C**～ **of Appeal** Brit, **C**～ **of Appeals** Amer *n* 上诉法院; **C**～ **of Auditors** *n* EU 审计院; ～ **of first instance** *n* 初审法院; ～ **of inquiry** *n* **1** esp Amer Mil 军事调查法庭; **2** Brit (into accident, disaster) 调查法庭; ～ **of law** *n* 法庭; **C**～ **of Session** *n* Scot 最高民事法院; ～ **order** *n* 法院指令; ～ **reporter** ▸p. 409 *n* 书记员; ～**room** *n* 审判室

courtship /'kɔːtʃɪp/ *n* [u and c] **1** (period of courting) 求爱期 **2** (act of courting) 求爱; **a** ～ **ritual** 求偶仪式

court: ～ **shoe** *n* 半高跟浅帮鞋; ～**yard** *n* 庭院

cousin /'kʌzn/ ▸p. 419 *n* **1** (older male on paternal side) 堂兄; (younger male on paternal side) 堂弟; (older female on paternal side) 堂姐; (younger female on paternal side) 堂妹 **2** (older male on maternal side) 表兄; (younger male on maternal side) 表弟; (older female on maternal side) 表姐; (younger female on maternal side) 表妹

cove /kəʊv/ *n* 小海湾

coven /'kʌvn/ *n* (group) 女巫帮; (meeting) 女巫聚会

covenant /'kʌvənənt/

A *n* **1** (agreement) 契约; **a deed of** ～ 契据 **2** (clause) 契约条款

B *vt* 立约承诺; **he's** ～**ed £60 a year to his favourite charity** 他立约承诺每年向他中意的慈善团体捐款 60 英镑; **I've** ～**ed £100 a year to them** 我立约保证每年给他们 100 英镑; **to** ～ **to do sth.** 立约保证做某事

Coventry /'kɒvəntri/ *pr n* 考文垂; **to send sb. to** ～ fig 排斥某人

cover /'kʌvə(r)/

A *vt* **1** (put sth. over) 遮盖 ‹*table, legs*›; 遮挡 ‹*window*›; 捂住 ‹*ears, face*›; 包 ‹*wound*›; 盖住 ‹*hole*›; **to** ～ **sb./sth. with sth.** 用某物盖上某人/某物; ～ **your mouth when you yawn** 打哈欠时要捂住嘴; **a skirt that** ～**s the knees** 长过膝盖的裙子; **to** ～ **the pot** 盖上锅盖 **2** (use to decorate) 给…加套子 ‹*sofa, chair*›; 给…加封皮 ‹*book*›; (form outer layer of) «*fur, skin, bark*» 包裹 ‹*animal, tree*›; **to** ～ **sth. with** *or* **in sth.** 用某物把某物包起来; **to be** ～**ed with** *or* **in sth.** 被某物裹着; **fish are** ～**ed in scales** 鱼全身是鳞; **birds' eggs are** ～**ed with a hard shell** 禽蛋有一层硬壳 **3** (spread over) 涂; (lay over) 铺; (be spread over) «*mud, leaves*» 覆盖 ‹*ground, person, animal*›; «*mist, sand, dust*» 蒙上; (be in many parts of) «*litter, marks, blossom*» 遍布 ‹*ground*›; **to** ～ **sb./sth. with** *or* **in sth.** 用某物涂 ‹*hands, face, cake*›; **a gust of wind** ～**ed everything with sand** 一阵风吹过，让一切都蒙上了一层沙; **a van** ～**ed her with muddy water** 一辆货车溅了她一身泥水; **the floor had been** ～**ed with concrete** 地面铺了混凝土; **to be** ～**ed with** *or* **in sth.** 覆盖着某物; **flood water** ～**ed the fields** 洪水淹没了田地; **clouds** ～**ed the sky** 天上阴云密布; **her face was** ～**ed in blood** 她满脸是血; **she** ～**ed the walls of her bedroom with photos** 她在卧室的墙壁上贴满了照片; **the bushes were** ～**ed with fruit** 矮树丛结满了果实 **4** (extend over) «*property, town*» 占 ‹*site, area*›; **the estate** ～**s 24 acres** 这处房产占地 24 英亩; **the damage caused by the earthquake** ～**ed a wide area** 地震造成了大范围的损失 **5** (travel over) 走过

C

C

‹*ground, distance*›; **we ~ed a lot of ground during our holiday** 我们休假期间走了很多地方; **to ~ 50 miles a day** 一天走 50 英里 **6** (deal with, treat) 处理; **the issue of taxation was inadequately ~ed in the minister's speech** 部长的演讲对税收问题论述不够充分; **research that ~s a wide field** 涉及范围很广的研究; **we'll ~ intransitive verbs in the next lesson** 我们将在下一堂课讲不及物动词; **to ~ the entire syllabus** 涵盖课程大纲上的所有教学内容; **do the instructions ~ how to dismantle the motor?** 使用说明里写了如何拆卸发动机吗? **7** (include) 包括; **that price ~s everything** 那个价格包括了所有费用; **the bill ~s all the work done so far** 本账单记录了到目前为止已完成的所有工作的花费; **all mechanical parts are ~ed by the guarantee** 所有的机械部件都在保修之列 **8** (be responsible for) 负责 ‹*area, activity, people*›; **the sales department ~s advertising** 销售部负责广告事务 **9** (report on) 报道 ‹*news, event*›; **Peter will ~ the human angle** 彼得将从人性角度进行报道; **the wedding will be ~ed live on Channel 4** 第 4 频道将对婚礼进行直播 **10** (relate to) «*rule, act*» 适用于 ‹*situation, organization, person*› **11** (pay for) 支付 ‹*outgoings, loss*›; **they gave us £50 to ~ our travelling expenses** 他们给了我们 50 英镑支付旅费; **how much do you need? — £20 should ~ it** 你需要多少钱? —— 20 英镑应该够了; **to ~ one's costs** 支付费用 **12** Insur (protect) «*insurance, policy, company*» 为…保险 ‹*person, property*›; (provide insurance against) 保…险 ‹*loss, accident, damage*›; **the camera is ~ed under my household insurance** 这部照相机属于我的家庭财产保险的承保项目; **to ~ sb./sth. for** *or* **against sth./doing sth.** 为…保某方面的险/做某事保险; **are you ~ed for fire and theft?** 你投保火险和盗险了吗? ; **the insurance doesn't ~ wear and tear** 日常磨损不在保险范围之内 **13** (protect with gunfire) 火力掩护 ‹*person, advance, retreat*›; **to ~ oneself** fig «*person, organization*» 自我保护; **to ~ oneself against sth.** 对某事留后手; **to ~ oneself by doing sth.** 通过做某事来保护自己; **to ~ one's back** *or* esp Amer **ass** fig colloq 留后手 **14** (threaten with gun) 用枪瞄准 ‹*person*›; **to keep/have got sb. ~ed** 用枪瞄准某人 **15** Sport (mark) 盯防 ‹*opponent*›; (take care of) 防守 ‹*area*›; (assist, guard) 掩护 ‹*player*› **16** (conceal or disguise) 掩饰 ‹*emotions, ignorance, embarrassment, guilt*›; 掩盖 ‹*facts, noise*›; **have a mint: it'll ~ the smell of alcohol on your breath** 来一颗薄荷糖: 它会去掉你嘴里的酒味 **17** (cause to affect) «*action, circumstance*» 给…带来影响 ‹*person, organization*›; **to ~ sb./oneself with** *or* **in sth.** 使某人/自己蒙受某事; **he returned ~ed with glory** 他载誉归来; **we were ~ed with shame** 我们蒙受了耻辱 **18** Mus (make version of) 翻唱 ‹*song, tune*› **19** Zool (mate with) «*male*» 与…交配 ‹*female*›

B *vi* 顶替; **can you get someone to ~ (for me) while I'm on holiday?** 我休假时你能找人顶替(我)一下吗?

C *n* **1** [c] (sth. laid over) 覆盖物; (sth. fitting over) 套子; (for duvet) 被套; (for CD) 封套; (lid) 盖子; **a protective ~** 护套 **2** [c] (of book, magazine) 封皮; **the front/back ~** 封面/封底; **to make the ~ of Time** 上《时代》杂志的封面; **to read sth. from ~ to ~** 从头至尾阅读某物; **~ design** 封面设计 **3** [u] (shelter) 躲避处; **to give sb. ~** 给某人提供庇护所; **to take ~** 躲避; **to be/get under ~** 在掩蔽下/找到掩护; **under ~ of sth.** 在某物的掩护下; **to leave under ~ of darkness** 在黑暗的掩护下离开; **to break ~** 冲出隐蔽处 **4** [c and u] (front) 掩护; (false identity) 掩护身份; **a ~ for sth.** 某事物的掩护; **under ~ of sth.** 打着某事的幌子; **to blow sb.'s ~** colloq (discover) 揭穿某人的伪装; (reveal) 暴露某人的身份; **to work under ~** 做秘密工作; **a ~ occupation/operation** 掩护身份的职业/掩护行动; **a ~ name/identity** 假名/掩护身份 **5** [u] Mil 火力掩护; **to provide air ~** 提供空中掩护; **to give (sb.) ~** 给予(某人)掩护 **6** [u] (substitute) 代班人员; (substitution) 代替工作; **emergency ~** 急救替班 **7** [u] Brit Insur 保险; (sum of money) 保额; **to give** *or* **provide ~ for** *or* **against sth.** 提供某事故的保险; **fire/accident ~** 火灾险/事故险; **full ~** 全险 **8** [c] (table setting) 全套餐具 **9** [c] = **cover version**

D **covers** *npl* (quilt) 被子; (bedspread) 床罩; (blankets) 毯子

Phrasal verbs

- **cover for** *vt* [~ **for sb.**] 顶替 ‹*person*›
- **cover in** *vt* [~ **in sth.**, ~ **sth. in**] 给…装顶棚 ‹*area, passage*›
- **cover over** *vt* [~ **sth. over**, ~ **over sth.**] (for concealment, protection) 盖住 ‹*table, body, hole*›; 覆盖 ‹*picture, word*›; **to ~ sth. over with sth., to ~ over sth. with sth.** 用某物盖住某物; **she ~ed the mistake over with Tippex** 她用修改液涂掉了错字
- **cover up**

A [~ **sb./sth. up**, ~ **up sb./sth.**] *vt* (for concealment, warmth) 盖住 ‹*mark, corpse, person, animal*›; (spread over) «*snow*» 覆盖 ‹*footprints*›; **to ~ sb./sth. up with sth., to ~ up sb./sth. with sth.** 用某物盖住某人/某物; **he ~ed up the answer with his hand** 他用手遮住了答案; **she ~ed up the sleeping child with a blanket** 她给熟睡的孩子盖上了毛毯; **to ~ oneself up (with sth.)** (用某物)裹住自己; **we'd better ~ ourselves up: it's cold outside** 我们最好裹严实点儿, 外面很冷

B [~ **up sth.**, ~ **sth. up**] *vt* (keep secret) 掩盖 ‹*mistake, scandal, crime, truth*›; (disguise) 掩饰 ‹*emotions, ignorance, guilt*›; **there's nothing to ~ up** 没什么可掩盖的; **he laughed to ~ up his embarrassment** 他哈哈大笑, 掩饰自己的尴尬

C *vi* **1** (put clothes on) 穿上衣服; **it's advisable to ~ up during the hottest part of the day** 在一天最热的时候最好裹住身体 **2** (conceal truth) «*person, government*» 掩盖真相; **to ~ up for sb./sth.** 替某人/某事物掩饰; **he's always ~ing up for his younger brother** 他对弟弟总是很护短

coverage /ˈkʌvərɪdʒ/ *n* [u] **1** (in media) 新闻报道; **television/newspaper ~** 电视/报纸新闻报道; **not to give** *or* **have much ~ of foreign news** 对国外新闻报道得不多; **there will be live ~ of the elections** 将对选举作现场报道 **2** (in book, dictionary, programme) 覆盖; **the dictionary's ~ of technical terms is good** 这部词典收录的专业术语很全面 **3** Amer Insur = **cover C7** **4** (scope of company) 覆盖面 **5** (of paint, varnish, etc.) 遮盖面

cover: ~alls *npl* Amer 连裤工作服; **~ charge** *n* 服务费

covered /ˈkʌvəd/ *adj* **1** (having a roof) 有顶棚的 ‹*veranda, swimming pool*› **2** (having a lid) 有盖的 ‹*pan*›; (having a lid in place) 盖好盖的 ‹*dish*›

covered: ~ market *n* 有顶棚的集市; **~ wagon** *n* 大篷车

cover girl *n* 封面女郎

covering /ˈkʌvərɪŋ/ *n* **1** (for wall, floor) 覆盖物; (wrapping) 包装纸; **a ~ for the head** 盖在头上的东西; **remove the protective ~** 去掉防护层 **2** (layer) 一层; **a ~ of dust** 一层灰

covering: ~ fire *n* [u] 掩护火力; **~ letter** *n* 附信

coverlet /ˈkʌvəlɪt/ *n* 床罩

cover: ~ letter *n* Amer = **covering letter**; **~ note** *n* Brit 暂保单; **~ sheet** *n* (for fax) 封面; **~ story** *n* **1** Journ 封面故事; **2** (excuse) 借口

covert /ˈkʌvət, Amer ˈkəʊvɜːrt/ *adj* 隐蔽的 ‹*threat, surveillance, activity*›; **a ~ military operation** 秘密军事行动; **he stole a ~ glance at her** 他偷偷瞥了她一眼

covertly /ˈkʌvətli, Amer ˈkəʊvɜːrtli/ *adv* 暗中 ‹*observe, threaten*›

cover: ~-up *n* 掩盖; **~ version** *n* 翻唱版

covet /ˈkʌvɪt/ *vt* 贪求; **I gave up a ~ed job** 我放弃了一份别人梦寐以求的工作

covetous /ˈkʌvɪtəs/ *adj* 贪求的; **to be ~ of sth.** 对某事物分外眼热

covetousness /ˈkʌvɪtəsnɪs/ *n* [u] 贪求

covey /ˈkʌvi/ *n* (*pl* **~s**) (of birds) 一窝; fig (of people) 一小群

cow¹ /kaʊ/ *n* **1** (female ox) 母牛; **a dairy ~** 奶牛; **till the ~s come home** fig colloq 长时间地 **2** (female of other species) 母兽; **a ~ elephant** 母象 **3** colloq pej (woman) 婆娘

cow² *vt* 恐吓; **a ~ed look** 畏惧的神色; **they had been ~ed into silence** 他们吓得不敢吭声了

coward /ˈkaʊəd/ *n* 胆小鬼

cowardice /ˈkaʊədɪs/ *n* [u] 怯懦; **a streak of ~** 一丝胆怯

cowardliness /ˈkaʊədlɪnɪs/ *n* [u] = **cowardice**

cowardly /ˈkaʊədli/ *adj* 胆小的 ‹*person*›; 可鄙的 ‹*lie*›; 懦夫的 ‹*act*›

cowbell *n* **1** Agric 牛颈铃 **2** Mus 牛铃

cowboy /ˈkaʊbɔɪ/ *n* **1** ▸**p. 409** (in US) 牛仔 **2** Brit pej (incompetent worker) 半吊子; **a ~ builder** 半吊子建筑工

cowcatcher /ˈkaʊkætʃə(r)/ *n* Amer 排障器

cower /ˈkaʊə(r)/ *vi* 畏缩; **to ~ away from sb./sth.** 在某人/某事物面前退缩

cow: ~girl ▸**p. 409** *n* 牧牛女工; **~hand** ▸**p. 409** *n* 牧牛工; **~herd** ▸**p. 409** *n* 牧牛人; **~hide** *n* [u] 母牛皮

cowl /kaʊl/ *n* **1** (hood) 大风帽; (on monk's gown) 蒙头斗篷; **~ neck** *or* **neckline** 垂领 **2** (on chimney) 烟囱帽

cowlick /ˈkaʊlɪk/ *n* Amer [额前的] 小簇竖发

cowling /ˈkaʊlɪŋ/ *n* [尤指飞机的] 整流罩

cowman /ˈkaʊmæn/ ▸**p. 409** *n* 牧牛人

co-worker *n* 同事

cow: ~ parsley *n* [u] 峨参 [一种欧洲常见的树篱植物]; **~pat** *n* Brit 牛屎; **~poke** *n* Amer colloq = **cowboy 1**; **~pox** *n* [u] 牛痘; **~puncher** *n* Amer colloq = **cowboy 1**

cowrie /ˈkaʊri/ *n* 宝贝 [一种海生软体动物, 其贝壳旧时在亚非部分地区用作货币]

co-write *vt* (*pt* **co-wrote**, *pp* **co-written**) 合著; **she co-wrote the script with the director** 她和导演合写了剧本

co-writer *n* 合著者

cowry /ˈkaʊriː/ *n* = **cowrie**

cow: ~shed *n* 牛棚; **~slip** *n* 黄花九轮草

cox /kɒks/

A *n* 舵手

B *vt* 担任…的舵手; **~ed pairs/fours** 有舵手双人艇/四人艇

C *vi* 担任舵手

coxswain /ˈkɒksn/ *n* 舵手

coy /kɔɪ/ *adj* **1** (bashful) 扭怩作态的; **to look ~** 看上去忸忸怩怩的 **2** (reticent) 不愿直说的; **to be ~ about sth.** 对某事吞吞吐吐

coyly /ˈkɔɪli/ *adv* **1** (shyly) 故作腼腆地 **2** (reticently) 含糊其辞地

coyote /kɔɪˈəʊti, Amer ˈkaɪəʊt/ (*pl* **~** *or* **~s**) *n* **1** (dog) 丛林狼 **2** Amer colloq (people smuggler) 蛇头 [组织从拉丁美洲偷渡去美国的人]

coypu /ˈkɔɪpuː/ *n* (*pl* **~s**) 河狸鼠

cozy *adj* /ˈkəʊzi/ Amer colloq = **cosy A**

Phrasal verb

- **cozy up** *vi* Amer colloq = **cosy up**

cozzie /ˈkɒzi:/ *n* colloq = **cossie**

CP *abbr* = **Communist Party**

cp *abbr* = **compare**

CPA Amer = **certified public accountant**

CPI *abbr* = **consumer price index**

Cpl *abbr* = **corporal**

CPS *abbr* Brit = **Crown Prosecution Service**

cps *abbr* 1 Phys = **cycles per second** 每秒周数 2 Comput = **characters per second** 每秒字符数

CPU *abbr* = **central processing unit**

crab¹ /kræb/

A *n* 1 [c] Zool 蟹; **to catch a ~** fig 失一桨 [指桨划空或划得过深] 2 [u] Culin 蟹肉; **dressed ~** 调好味的蟹肉

B crabs *npl* colloq (lice) 阴虱寄生病

crab² *vi* (*pres p etc.* **-bb-**) colloq pej (complain, grumble) 发牢骚

crab apple *n* (tree) 花红树; (fruit) 花红

crabbed /ˈkræbɪd/ *adj* 1 (difficult to read) 细小难辨认的 «*writing*»; **in a ~ hand** 笔迹潦草 2 (difficult to understand) 晦涩的 ‹*style, language*› 3 (ill-humoured) 易怒的

crabby /ˈkræbi/ *adj* colloq 脾气坏的

crack /kræk/

A *n* 1 [c] (fissure) 裂缝; (in skin) 裂口; (narrow opening) 缝隙; **a ~ in sth.** 某物上的裂缝; **~s over sth.** 某物上的多处裂纹; **a hairline ~** 细缝; **to look/peep through a ~** 透过缝隙看/窥视; **to open the door/leave the door open a ~** 把门开/给门留一条缝 2 [c] fig (in relationship) 裂痕; (in policy) 漏洞; **to fall through** *or* **slip between the ~s** 被遗漏; **to paper** *or* **paste over the ~s (in sth.)** 掩盖（某事物上的）问题; **the ~ of dawn** *or* **day** 大清早; **to leave at the ~ of dawn** 一大早离开; **the ~ of doom** 世界末日 3 [c] (noise) (of whip, gun) 噼啪声; (of twig, bone) 咔嚓声; **a ~ of thunder** 一声霹雳; **a ~ of the bat** (in baseball, cricket) 击球声; **a fair ~ of the whip** fig colloq 均等的机会 4 [c] (blow) 猛击; **to get a ~ on the head/jaw** 头部/下巴受到猛击 5 [c] colloq (jibe) 俏皮话; **a ~ about sb./sth.** 对某人/某事物的挖苦; **to make** *or* **have a ~ (about** *or* **at sb./sth.)** 嘲笑（某人/某事物） 6 [c] colloq (attempt) 尝试; **to have a ~ at sth./doing sth.** 尝试某事物/做某事 7 [u] colloq (drug) 强效纯可卡因

B *vt* 1 (make fracture(s) in) 使…裂开 ‹*glass, ice, wall, bone, rib, wrist*› 2 (break open) 砸开 ‹*nut, safe*›; 敲开 ‹*egg*›; **to ~ sth. open** 砸开某物; **to ~ one's head open** 撞破头 3 (hit) 猛击 ‹*head, person*›; **to ~ sb. over the head** 猛击某人头部; **to ~ one's elbow against** *or* **on a shelf** 胳膊肘撞到架子上 4 (make sound with) 使…噼啪作响 ‹*twig*›; **to ~ the whip** lit 甩响鞭; fig 鞭策; **to ~ one's knuckles** 使指关节噼啪作响 5 (overcome) 瓦解 ‹*defence, opposition, system*› 6 colloq (solve) 破解 ‹*problem*›; **to ~ a case/code** 破案/破译密码 7 colloq (open) 开; **to ~ (open) a bottle of champagne** 开香槟酒 8 colloq (tell) **to ~ a joke** 开玩笑 9 Chem 使…裂化 ‹*oil*›; **to ~ crude oil** 裂化原油

C *vi* 1 (develop crack(s)) «*skin, wall, paint*» 裂开; **to ~ into a smile** «*face*» 绽放出笑容 2 (make sound) «*whip, knuckles, twig*» 噼啪响; «*firearm*» 发出爆裂声; **to get ~ing (with** *or* **on sth.)** colloq (hurry up) 动手（干某事） 3 fig (break down) «*resistance, person*» 垮掉; **to ~ under pressure** 在压力之下垮掉; **to ~ under interrogation** 在审问之下招认; **something inside him ~ed** 他的内心崩溃了; **his composure/confidence began to ~** 他开始不安/失去信心 4 (change) «*voice*» (at puberty) 变粗; (with emotion) 变沙哑

D *adj attrib* 技艺高超的 ‹*sportsperson*›; 精锐的 ‹*troops, regiment*›; **he's a ~ shot** 他是个神枪手; **a team of ~ players** 由顶尖选手组成的队伍

Phrasal verbs

- **crack down** *vi* «*government, police*» 镇压; «*parents, school*» 严格管理; **to ~ down on sb./sth.** (with force) 严厉打击某人/某事物; (with rules) 竭力管制某人/某事物
- **crack on** *vi* Brit colloq 拼命干; **to ~ on with sth.** 拼命做某事
- **crack up**

A *vi* colloq 1 (have breakdown) 垮掉 2 (laugh) 大笑起来

B *vt* **to ~ sb./sth. up to be sb./sth.** colloq 把…吹捧成…; **to be ~ed up to be sth.** 被吹捧成某事物

crack: ~ baby *n* colloq 毒瘾婴儿 [吸毒者所产下的婴儿]; **~-brained** *adj* colloq (foolish) 愚蠢的; (crazy) 疯狂的; **~ cocaine** *n* [u] 强效纯可卡因; **~down** *n* 镇压; **the police ~down on drug-dealing** 警方对毒品交易的严厉打击

cracked /krækt/ *adj* 1 (damaged) 有裂纹的 ‹*mug*›; 干裂的 ‹*lips*›; **he suffered ~ ribs** 他断了几根肋骨 2 (strained) 粗哑的; **in a ~ voice** 用沙哑的声音 3 colloq (insane) 发疯的

cracked wheat *n* [u] 碎麦粒

cracker /ˈkrækə(r)/ *n* 1 (biscuit) 薄脆饼干 2 (firework) 爆竹 3 (for Christmas) 彩包爆竹 4 Brit colloq (attractive person) 有魅力的人 [一般指女性]; **what a ~!** 真是个大美人! 5 Brit colloq (excellent example) 好东西; **don't miss this ~ of a CD** 别错过了这张极品CD 6 Comput colloq 黑客

cracker-barrel *adj* Amer *attrib* 朴素的

crackerjack /ˈkrækədʒæk/ esp Amer

A *adj* 出色的

B *n* (person) 出色的人; (thing) 优质的东西

crackers /ˈkrækəz/ *adj* Brit colloq 1 (mad) 发疯的; **to drive sb. ~** 把人逼疯; **to go ~** 发疯 2 (angry) 极为恼火的; **to go ~** 大发雷霆

crack: ~head *n* colloq 强效可卡因吸食者; **~ house** *n* colloq 可卡因馆 [吸食、买卖强效纯可卡因的场所]

cracking /ˈkrækɪŋ/

A *adj* 1 Brit colloq (outstanding) 出色的 2 (fast, exciting) 生气勃勃的; **at a ~ pace** 步履轻捷地

B *adv* 极其; **a ~ good shot** 极精彩的一击

C *n* [u] 1 (damage) 开裂 2 (noise) 爆裂声; **the ~ of thunder** 霹雳声

crackle /ˈkrækl/

A *vi* 1 (make cracking noise) 发噼啪声 2 fig (be lively or tense) 充满活力; **the atmosphere in the room ~d with tension** 室内气氛十分紧张

B *n* [u] (sound) 噼啪声

crackling /ˈkræklɪŋ/ *n* [u] 1 (sound) 劈啪声 2 (on pork) 脆皮

cracknel /ˈkræknl/ *n* 1 [c] (biscuit) 脆饼 2 [u and c] (sweet) 脆糖

crackpot /ˈkrækpɒt/ colloq

A *n* (eccentric person) 怪人; (fool) 笨蛋

B *adj attrib* (impractical) 不切实际的; (eccentric) 古怪的

crack-up *n* colloq 精神崩溃

cradle /ˈkreɪdl/

A *n* 1 (for baby) 摇篮; **from the ~ to the grave** 一生; **the ~** fig 婴儿时期; **the hand that rocks the ~ rules the world** 晃动摇篮之手掌握未来世界 [指母亲对孩子的成长影响巨大] 2 fig (origin) 发源地; **the ~ of sth.** 某事物的发源地; **the ~ of civilization** 文明的发祥地 3 (framework) Naut [修造船只用的] 托架; Med [使床单不碰到受伤肢体的] 支架 4 (telephone rest) 听筒架 5 (platform) [空中作业时用的] 吊篮

B *vt* 轻轻抱着; **to ~ sb./sth. in one's arms** 把某人/某物抱在怀里

cradlesnatcher /ˈkreɪdlsnætʃə(r)/ *n* colloq pej 抢劫摇篮者 [指与远比自己年轻的异性结婚或有性关系的人]

craft /krɑːft, Amer kræft/

A *n* 1 [c] (art-related skill) 工艺; (job-related skill) 手艺; (occupation) 行业; **the potter's ~** 陶艺; **to master a ~** 掌握一门手艺; **arts and ~s** 手工艺; **a ~ guild** 行会 2 [u] (cunning) 骗术 3 [c] (boat) 船 4 [c] (aircraft, spaceship) 航空器

B *vt* 熟练地制作; **a beautifully ~ed silver goblet** 一只制作精美的银酒杯

craft: ~ centre *n* 手工艺品中心; **~ fair** *n* 手工艺品展销会

craftily /ˈkrɑːftɪli, Amer ˈkræft-/ *adv* (cunningly) 狡猾地; (cleverly) 巧妙地; **a ~ constructed argument** 立论巧妙的论点

craftiness /ˈkrɑːftɪnɪs, Amer ˈkræft-/ *n* [u] (cunning) 狡猾; (cleverness) 巧妙

craftsman /ˈkrɑːftsmən/ *n* 手艺人

craftsmanship /ˈkrɑːftsmənʃɪp/ *n* [u] (workmanship) 做工; (skill) 技艺

craftswoman /ˈkrɑːftswʊmən/ *n* 女手艺人

craft: ~ union *n* 行业工会; **~work** *n* [u] (activity) 手工艺; (object) 手工艺品

crafty /ˈkrɑːfti, Amer ˈkræfti/ *adj* 1 (cunning) 狡猾的; **a ~ (old) fox** 狡猾的（老）狐狸 2 colloq (clever) 灵巧的; **what a ~ gadget!** 这个小玩意儿真精巧!

crag /kræɡ/ *n* 悬崖

craggy /ˈkræɡi/ *adj* 1 (rocky) 峻峭的 ‹*mountain, hillside*› 2 (rugged) 轮廓分明的 ‹*face, features*›

cram /kræm/ (*pres p etc.* **-mm-**)

A *vt* 1 (pack) 把…塞进; **to ~ sth. in** *or* **into** 把某物塞入 ‹*container, bag*›; **to ~ sth. into one's mouth** 把某物塞进嘴里; **to ~ a lot into one day** 把许多事情都挤在一天做 2 (fill to capacity) 把…塞满; **to ~ sth. with sth.** 用某物塞满 ‹*container, drawer*›; **to ~ one's mouth with food** 往嘴里塞满食物; **to be ~med full of furniture** 放满家具; **tourists ~med the streets** 街道上挤满了游客

B *vi* 1 (pack) 挤; **they all ~med into the car** 他们全都挤进了那辆车 2 (study) 恶补; **to ~ for sth.** 为了某个考试恶补功课

cram-full *adj pred* 塞满的; **to be ~** 塞得满满的; **to be ~ of sth.** 塞满某物

crammer /ˈkræmə(r)/ *n* Brit (school) 强化补习学校; (person) 强化补习教师

cramp¹ /kræmp/

A *n* [u and c] Med 痉挛; **a ~ in one's foot/leg** 脚/腿抽筋

B *vt* 限制; **to ~ sb.'s style** 使某人不能放开手脚

cramp²

A *n* 1 (clamp) 钳子 2 Constr **a ~ (iron)** 铁夹钳

B *vt* 用铁夹钳夹紧 ‹*beam, wall*›

cramped /kræmpt/ *adj* 1 (confined) 狭小的 ‹*seating, office*›; **~ working conditions** 拥挤的工作环境; **to be ~ for space** 空间小得无法自如活动 2 (difficult to read) 细密难辨的 ‹*handwriting*›

crampon /ˈkræmpən/ *n* 带钉铁鞋底

cranberry /ˈkrænbəri, Amer -beri/ *n* 1 (berry) 越橘果实 2 (shrub) 越橘

cranberry: ~ jelly *n* [u] 越橘果冻; **~ sauce** *n* [u] 越橘果酱

crane¹ /kreɪn/

A *n* Constr 起重机

B *vt* 伸长; **to ~ one's neck** 伸长脖子

Phrasal verb

- **crane forward** *vi* 探头往前

crane² *n* Zool 鹤

crane: ~ driver ▸p. 409 *n* 起重机驾驶员; **~ fly** *n* 大蚊; **~ operator** ▸p. 409 *n* = **~ driver**

crania /ˈkreɪnɪə/ *pl* ▸**cranium**

cranial /ˈkreɪnɪəl/ *adj* 颅的; **damage to the ~ nerves** 颅神经损伤

cranium /ˈkreɪnɪəm/ *n* (*pl* **~s** *or* **crania**) 颅; **surgery on the ~** 开颅手术

crank¹ /kræŋk/ *n* colloq pej (eccentric person) 怪人; **a health-food ～** 只吃保健食品的怪人

crank²
A *n* (handle) 曲柄
B *vt* 用曲柄启动 ‹*engine, car*›

Phrasal verbs
- **crank out** *vt* colloq [**～ out sth., ～ sth. out**] 机械地完成 ‹*work, articles*›
- **crank up** *vt* [**～ up sth., ～ sth. up**] colloq **1** lit 用曲柄启动 ‹*car, machine*› **2** fig 调高 ‹*volume, production*›

crank: ～case *n* 曲轴箱; **～shaft** *n* 曲轴

cranky /'kræŋki/ *adj* colloq **1** esp Amer (grumpy) 脾气坏的 **2** Brit (eccentric) 古怪的

cranny /'kræni/ *n* 缝隙; ▸**nook 2**

crap /kræp/ taboo sl
A *n* **1** [u] (nonsense) 胡扯; **to talk a load of ～** 胡扯一通; **he's full of ～** 他满口胡言 **2** [u] (rubbish) 蹩脚货; **this film is ～!** 这是一部烂电影! **3** [u] (worthless thing) 废物 **4** [u] (faeces) 屎 **5** [c] (defecation) 拉屎; **to have a ～** 拉屎
B *adj* 非常糟糕的; **to be ～ at chemistry** 化学很糟糕
C *vi* (*pres p etc.* **-pp-**) 拉屎

crape /kreɪp/ *n* = **crêpe 2**

crappy /'kræpi/ *adj* taboo sl 蹩脚的

craps /kræps/ *n* [u] 双骰子赌博戏; **to shoot ～** 掷双骰子赌博

crash /kræʃ/
A *vi* **1** (make noise) «*cymbals*» 锵锵作响; «*thunder, explosive*» 发出轰鸣声 **2** (fall) «*tree*» 哗啦一声倒下; «*dishes*» 哗啦一声破碎; **to come ～ing down on** *or* **upon sb.** «*ceiling*» 哗啦一声砸到某人; fig «*life*» 使某人崩溃 **3** (collide) «*cars*» 碰撞; «*planes*» 坠毁; **to ～ into sth.** 撞到某物上; **to ～ into each other** 相撞 **4** (move loudly) 声响很大地猛冲; **to ～ into a room** 动静很大地闯进房间 **5** Fin «*market*» 暴跌; «*firm*» 倒闭 **6** Comput «*computer, system, program*» 死机
B *vt* **1** (involve in accident) 使…坠毁 ‹*aircraft*›; 使…碰撞 ‹*vehicle*› **2** Aut 使…发出嘎吱声 ‹*gears*› **3** colloq (gatecrash) 擅自闯入 ‹*party, event*›
C *n* **1** (noise) 碰撞声; **the ～ of thunder** 霹雳声 **2** (collision) 碰撞; **a car/train ～** 汽车/火车撞车事故; **a plane ～** 飞机失事; **to have a ～** «*car, train*» 发生碰撞; «*aircraft*» 失事 **3** Fin «*market*» 暴跌; «*firm*» 倒闭 **4** Comput 崩溃
D *adv* 哗啦一声; **～ went the bolt** 霹雳炸响了; **～, bang, wallop** colloq 噼里啪啦一阵巨响

Phrasal verb
- **crash out** *vi* colloq **1** (sleep) 入睡 **2** (pass out) **to be ～ed out** [尤指因醉酒或吸毒后] 昏睡过去

crash: ～ barrier *n* Brit 防撞护栏; **～ course** *n* 强化速成课; **～ diet** *n* 快速减肥饮食

crash-dive
A *n* (of submarine) 紧急下潜; (of aircraft) 俯冲坠毁
B *vi* «*submarine*» 紧急下潜; «*aircraft*» 俯冲坠毁

crash helmet *n* 安全帽

crash-land
A *vi* «*pilot, aircraft*» 摔机着陆
B *vt* 使…摔机着陆 ‹*aircraft*›

crash: ～ landing *n* 摔机着陆; **～ pad** *n* colloq 临时借宿处; **～ programme** *n* 强化速成研发计划; **～-test** *vt* 对…进行碰撞试验 ‹*vehicle, aircraft*›; **～-test dummy** *n* 碰撞试验假人

crass /kræs/ *adj* **1** (stupid) 愚钝的; (insensitive) 迟钝的 **2** (utter) 极度的 ‹*ignorance*›

crassly /'kræsli/ *adv* (stupidly) 愚钝地; (insensitively) 迟钝地

crate /kreɪt/
A *n* **1** (wooden container) 木箱; **a ～ of bananas** 一箱香蕉 **2** (for bottles) 分隔箱 **3** colloq (car) 破旧汽车; (aircraft) 老旧飞机
B *vt* 把…装箱 ‹*bottles, goods*›

crater /'kreɪtə(r)/ *n* **1** (on planet's surface) 陨石坑 **2** (of volcano) 火山口 **3** (caused by explosion) [爆炸等形成的] 坑

cravat /krə'væt/ *n* [男用] 阔领带

crave /kreɪv/ *vt* **1** (desire) 渴望得到 **2** archaic (beg for) 恳求; **to ～ sb.'s forgiveness** 恳求某人的原谅; **to ～ sb.'s permission to do sth.** 请求某人允许做某事

Phrasal verb
- **crave for** *vt* [**～ for sth.**] 渴望获得

craven /'kreɪvn/ *adj* formal 怯懦的

craving /'kreɪvɪŋ/ *n* 渴望; **a ～ for sth.** 对某事物的渴望

craw /krɔː/ *n* dated [鸟或昆虫的] 嗉囊; **to stick in sb.'s ～** fig 令某人难以接受

crawl /krɔːl/
A *vi* **1** (move) «*person, insect*» 爬; **to ～ in/out** 爬进/爬出; **to ～ out from under sth.** 从某物下面爬出来; **to ～ into bed** 爬上床; **to make sb.'s skin** *or* **flesh ～** 使某人起鸡皮疙瘩 **2** (move slowly) «*person*» 缓慢行进; **to ～ along** 缓缓前行 **3** (be crowded) **to be ～ing with sth.** 挤满了某物 **4** colloq (flatter, behave obsequiously) 巴结; **to ～ to sb.** 对某人低三下四
B *n* **1** (swimming stroke) 自由泳; **to do** *or* **swim the ～** 游自由泳 **2** (slow pace) 慢行; **at a ～** 缓慢行进地; **to slow** *or* **be reduced to a ～** 减速慢行

crawler /'krɔːlə(r)/ *n* **1** (slow vehicle) 慢行车辆 **2** Brit colloq (flatterer, obsequious person) 马屁精 **3** Comput 爬虫程序 [一种互联网搜索程序]

crawler lane *n* 重型车辆通道

crayfish /'kreɪfɪʃ/ *n* 小龙虾

crayon /'kreɪən/
A *n* **1** (**wax**) **～** 蜡笔 **2** (**pencil**) **～** 彩色铅笔
B *vt* 用彩笔画; **to ～ sth. in** 用彩笔给某物勾边
C *vi* 用彩笔画

craze /kreɪz/
A *n* **1** (enthusiasm) [一时的] 狂热; **a ～ for sth.** 对某事物的狂热 **2** (fad) 风靡一时的事物
B *vi* **～ (over)** «*china, glaze, glass*» 产生纹裂

crazed /kreɪzd/ *adj* 发疯的; **power-～** 权迷心窍的

crazily /'kreɪzɪli/ *adv* **1** (madly) 疯狂地; **～ escalating prices** 疯狂上涨的价格 **2** (at an angle) 摇摇欲坠地 ‹*tilt, lean*›

crazy /'kreɪzi/ colloq
A *adj* **1** (insane) 发疯的; **to go ～** 发疯; **he would be ～ to …** 他要是…就真是疯啦; **～ with …** 因…发疯的 ‹*grief, worry*›; **to drive sb. ～** 把某人逼疯 **2** (stupid) 愚蠢的 ‹*idea, behaviour*›; **to be ～ to do sth.** 做某事是愚蠢的 **3** (enthusiastic) 狂热的; (infatuated) 神魂颠倒的; **to be ～ about sth.** 对某事物很着迷; **to be ～ about sb.** 为某人神魂颠倒 **4** (angry) 非常气愤的; **to go ～** 发火 **5** (startling) 惊人的 ‹*prices, height, speed*›
B *n* esp Amer 疯子

crazy: ～ bone *n* Amer = **funny bone**; **～ golf** ▸**p. 307** *n* [u] Brit = **miniature golf**; **～ paving** *n* [u] Brit 形状不规则的铺路石

CRC *abbr* = **camera-ready copy**

creak /kriːk/
A *n* 嘎吱声
B *vi* 嘎吱作响; **the door ～ed open** 门嘎吱一声开了

creaky /'kriːki/ *adj* **1** (creaking) 嘎吱作响的 ‹*hinge, wheel, gate*› **2** fig (unsound) 站不住脚的 ‹*argument, policy*›; 摇摇欲坠的 ‹*position*› **3** fig (decrepit) 老朽的; **our ～ electric power system** 我们陈旧的电力系统; **I'm feeling a bit ～ today** 我如今感觉自己有点过时

cream /kriːm/ ▸**p. 134**
A *n* **1** [u] (dairy product) 奶油 **2** [u] Cosmet 护肤霜; (polish) 膏状物; (medication) 乳膏; **shoe ～** 鞋油 **3** [c] (sweet) 奶油糖 **4** [c] (biscuit) 奶油夹心饼干; **orange ～** 橘味奶油夹心饼干 **5** [u] (soup) **～ of tomato/mushroom (soup)** 奶油番茄/蘑菇汤 **6** [u] fig (best) **the ～** 精华; **the ～ of the students** 尖子学生; **the ～ of society** 社会精英 **7** [u] (colour) 米黄色
B *adj* (colour) 米黄色的
C *vt* **1** Culin (mash) 在…中拌入奶油; **～ed potatoes** 奶油拌土豆 **2** Culin (form into a paste) 把…搅成糊状; **～ the butter and sugar** 把黄油和糖搅拌成糊状 **3** Amer colloq (defeat heavily) 彻底打败

Phrasal verb
- **cream off** *vt* [**～ off sth., ～ sth. off**] 提取; **the best pupils are being ～ed off** 最好的学生正在被挖走

cream: ～ cake *n* 奶油蛋糕; **～ cheese** *n* [u] 奶油干酪; **～ cleaner** *n* [u and c] (household) 去污膏; (cosmetic) 洁面乳; **～ cracker** *n* Brit 奶油饼干

creamer /'kriːmə(r)/ *n* **1** [c] Amer (jug) 奶盅 **2** [u] (coffee whitener) 咖啡伴侣

creamery /'kriːməri/ *n* **1** (factory) 乳品厂 **2** (shop) 乳品店

cream: ～ jug *n* Brit 奶盅; **～ of tartar** *n* [u] 酒石 [用作发酵粉]; **～ puff** *n* **1** (cake) 奶油泡芙; **2** colloq pej (weakling) 软弱无能的人; **～ soda** *n* [u and c] esp Amer 奶油苏打水; **～ tea** *n* Brit 奶油茶点

creamy /'kriːmi/ *adj* **1** (containing cream) 含奶油的 **2** (resembling cream) 光滑细腻的 ‹*texture*› **3** (cream-coloured) 浅黄色的

crease /kriːs/
A *n* **1** (untidy line or ridge) 褶痕 **2** (deliberate fold) 褶缝; **to put a ～ in a pair of trousers** 给裤子熨出裤缝 **3** (wrinkle) 皱纹
B *vt* **1** (crumple) 弄皱; **to get ～d** 被弄皱 **2** (iron a crease into) 给…烫出褶缝 ‹*trousers, shirt*›; **perfectly ～d trousers** 裤缝笔直的裤子
C *vi* **1** (become crumpled) «*cloth*» 起皱 **2** (wrinkle) «*face*» 皱起; **her face ～d into a smile** 她的脸上露出了微笑

Phrasal verb
- **crease up** Brit colloq
A *vi* 大笑起来; **I ～d up laughing** 我大笑起来
B *vt* [**～ sb. up**] 使大笑起来

creased /kriːst/ *adj* 皱巴巴的

crease-resistant *adj* 抗皱的 ‹*fabric*›

create /kriː'eɪt/
A *vt* **1** (make) 创造 ‹*new product, jobs, recipe*›; 设计 ‹*hairstyle, programme*›; 创建 ‹*institution, rule*›; 开创 ‹*precedent*›; 创作 ‹*art*› **2** (cause) 引起 ‹*problem, fuss, noise*›; **to ～ a good impression** 留下好的印象 **3** (appoint) 册封 ‹*peer, viscount*›
B *vi* Brit colloq 发脾气; **to ～ about the loss of time** 为浪费时间而发脾气

creation /kriː'eɪʃn/ *n* **1** [u] (making) 创造; **the ～ of the universe** 宇宙的诞生; **job ～** 就业机会的创造; **the ～ of a new party** 新政党的创建; **the problem is of your own ～** 这个麻烦是你自己惹出来的 **2** [c] (work) 作品; **her latest ～** 她最新的作品; **what's that weird ～ she's wearing?** 她穿的那是什么怪衣服啊? **3** **Creation** [u] Relig **the C～** 上帝的创造天地 **4** **Creation** [u] (all things) 天地万物; **the greatest fool in (all) C～** 世界上最愚蠢的人

creationism /kriː'eɪʃənɪzəm/ *n* [u] 神创论

creationist /kriː'eɪʃnɪst/
A *n* 神创论者
B *adj* 神创论的

creative /kriː'eɪtɪv/ *adj* **1** (inventive) 有创造力的 ‹*imagination*›; **she's very ～** 她很有创造力; **a ～ solution to a problem** 问题的创

造性解决方案 **2** (productive) 创造性的 ‹*act, energy, process*›

creative accountancy, creative accounting *ns* [u] 创造性做账 [指利用法规漏洞来获利或提供虚假会计信息的做法]

creatively /kriːˈeɪtɪvli/ *adv* **1** (in creative way) 创造性地 **2** (regarding creativity) 在创造性上

creative writing *n* [u] 文学创作

creativity /ˌkriːeɪˈtɪvəti/ *n* [u] 创造性

creator /kriːˈeɪtə(r)/ *n* **1** (originator) 创造者; **the ~ of the role** 这个角色的塑造者 **2** **Creator** (God) **the C~** 造物主

creature /ˈkriːtʃə(r)/ *n* **1** (animal) 动物; **a sea/water ~** 海洋/水生动物 **2** (person) [某种类型的] 人; **a charming ~** 迷人的人; **(the) poor ~!** 可怜的人儿! ; **I'm a ~ of habit** 我是个按规矩做事的人 **3** pej (puppet) 工具; **the ~ of one's employer** 受雇主支配的人

creature comforts *npl* 物质享受

crèche /kreʃ, kreɪʃ/ *n* **1** Brit (nursery) 日间托儿所; **~ facilities** 托儿所设施 **2** Amer (nativity scene) 基督诞生塑像

credence /ˈkriːdns/ *n* [u] formal (plausibility) 可信性; (belief or acceptance) 相信; **to attach** *or* **give ~ to sth.** 相信某事物; **to lend ~ to sth.** 使某事物可信; **to gain ~** 获得认可

credentials /krɪˈdenʃlz/ *npl* **1** (qualifications) 资格; **to establish one's ~ as a writer** 确立作家资格 **2** (of ambassador) 国书; **to present one's ~** 呈递国书

credibility /ˌkredəˈbɪləti/ *n* [u] **1** (trustworthiness) 可靠性; **the party has maintained/lost ~ with electors** 该党一直为选民所信赖/失去了选民的信赖 **2** (believability) 可信性; **the ~ of the story** 那种说法的可信度

credibility gap *n* 言行不一

credible /ˈkredəbl/ *adj* **1** (believable) 可信的 ‹*witness, report*› **2** (likely) 可行的 ‹*alternative*›; **a ~ threat** 实质性的威胁

credit /ˈkredɪt/

A *n* **1** [u] Fin (system) 信贷; (ability to borrow and pay back) 信用; (professional repute) 声誉; **her ~ is good** 她的信用很好; **to live on ~** 靠借贷为生; **unlimited ~** 无限制的信用额度; **to be refused ~** 被拒绝贷款; **cheap ~** 低息贷款; **to give a customer ~** 允许顾客赊账; **to buy/sell sth. on ~** 赊购/赊销某商品 **2** [u] (recognition) 赞扬; (honour) 荣誉; **to get the ~ for sth./doing sth.** 因某事物/做某事得到称赞; **to give sb. (the) ~ for sth./doing sth.** (reluctantly) 因某事物/做某事认可某人; (in praise) 因某事物/做某事称赞某人; **she's not given ~ for her ability** 人们并不认可她的能力; **to take ~ for sth./doing sth.** 因某事物/做某事而居功; **to take the ~ away from sb.** 抢某人的功劳; **~ where ~ is due** 该表扬的就要表扬; **to do** *or* **bring ~ to sb./sth.** 为某人/某机构争光; **to be to sb.'s ~** «*achievements*» 属于某人; «*behaviour*» 使某人值得赞扬; **she has two operas to her ~** 她出演了两部歌剧; **to her ~, she refused** 她拒绝了, 这值得赞扬 **3** [c] (source of) (person) 添荣誉的人; (thing) 添荣誉的事物; **to be a ~ to sb./sth.** «*person*» 是某人/某机构的光荣 **4** [u and c] Fin (positive balance) 贷方余额; (order to pay) 付款凭证; Accts (payment in) 存入金额; (balance sheet entry) 贷记; **to be in ~** «*account, person*» 有结余; **to have £200 to one's ~** 账上有 200 英镑的存款; **on the ~ side of an account** 在账户的贷记栏里 **5** [c] Univ (unit of study) 学分

B **credits** *npl* Cin, TV 演职人员字幕

C *vt* **1** (attribute) 归于; **to ~ sb. with sth./doing sth.** 把某事物/做某事归功于某人; **she is ~ed with the discovery/with discovering sth.** 人们认为这一发现/发现某物是她的功劳; **to ~ sth. to sb.** 把某事物算到某人头上; **the screenplay is ~ed to an American writer** 这个电影剧本是一位美国作家写的 **2** Accts 把…记入贷方 ‹*money*›

3 Brit (believe) 相信; **would you ~ it!** 真是不可思议!

creditable /ˈkredɪtəbl/ *adj* **1** (praiseworthy) 值得称赞的 ‹*effort, performance*› **2** (morally good) 可尊敬的 ‹*action, history*›

creditably /ˈkredɪtəbli/ *adv* (respectably) 值得称道地; (tolerably) 尚可地

credit: ~ account *n* Brit **= charge account**; **~ agency** *n* 信用调查机构; **~ arrangement** *n* 信贷安排; **~ balance** *n* 贷方余额; **~ broker** ▸**p. 409** *n* 信贷机构; **~ bureau** *n* Amer **= ~ reference agency**; **~ card** *n* 信用卡; **~ charges** *npl* 贷款手续费; **~ control** *n* [u and c] 信贷控制; **~ crunch** *n* 信贷紧缩; **~ default swap** *n* 信用违约互换; **~ entry** *n* 贷方分录; **~ facilities** *npl* 信贷手段; **~ freeze** *n* 信贷冻结; **~ history** *n* 信用记录; **~ hour** *n* Amer 学分时; **~ limit** *n* 信用额度; **~ line** *n* **1** Cin, TV 致谢名单; **2** Fin **= line of credit**; **~ note** *n* 保值凭单 [退货后商家开具的凭证, 消费者可用来购买等值的商品]

creditor /ˈkredɪtə(r)/ *n* 债权人

credit: ~ rating *n* 信用等级; **~ reference agency** *n* 信用调查机构; **~ risk** *n* 信贷风险; **~ sale** *n* 赊销; **~ side** *n* **1** Accts 贷方; **2** fig 积极的一面; **on the ~ side** 就优点而言; **~ squeeze** *n* 信用紧缩; **~ standing, ~ status** *ns* 信用状况; **~ terms** *npl* 信贷条件; **~ titles** *npl* 摄制人员名单; **~ transfer** *n* [u and c] Brit 银行转账; **~ union** *n* 信用合作社

creditworthiness /ˈkredɪtwɜːðɪnɪs/ *n* [u] 信誉度

creditworthy /ˈkredɪtwɜːði/ *adj* 信用可靠的

credo /ˈkriːdəʊ, ˈkreɪ-/ *n* 信条

credulity /krɪˈdjuːləti, Amer -ˈduː-/ *n* [u] 轻信; **to strain** *or* **stretch sb.'s ~** 使某人很难相信

credulous /ˈkredjʊləs, Amer -dʒə-/ *adj* 轻信的; **a ~ consumer** 容易上当的顾客

credulously /ˈkredjʊləsli, Amer -dʒə-/ *adv* 轻信地

creed /kriːd/ *n* **1** (set of beliefs) 信念; **political ~** 政治信念 **2** (faith) 信仰 **3** **Creed** Relig **the C~** 信经; **the Apostles' C~** 使徒信经

creek /kriːk/ *n* **1** Brit (inlet) (of sea, river) 小湾; **to be up the ~ (without a paddle)** fig colloq 陷入困境 **2** Amer, Austral (stream) 小溪

creel /kriːl/ *n* 鱼篓

creep /kriːp/

A *vi* (*pt, pp* **crept**) **1** (furtively) 悄悄行进; **he crept down the stairs** 他蹑手蹑脚地下了楼 **2** (slowly) 缓慢行进; **the train crept into the station** 火车缓缓驶进了车站 **3** Bot, Hort «*plant*» 蔓生 **4** fig (progress) 逐渐发展; **the months crept by** 几个月慢慢过去了; **a blush crept over her face** 她的脸渐渐红了起来

B *n* colloq **1** (weirdo) 讨厌鬼; **he's a ~** 他真讨厌 **2** Brit (flatterer) 马屁精 **3** **to give sb. the ~s** (frighten or revolt sb.) 使某人心里发毛

Phrasal verbs

- **creep in** *vi* «*errors, changes, feelings*» 不知不觉中产生
- **creep into** *vt* [**~ into sth.**] «*errors, changes*» 不知不觉在…中产生; **to let personal feelings ~ into sth.** 把个人感情带入某事
- **creep over** *vt* [**~ over sb.**] 逐渐影响; **tiredness crept over me** 我渐渐感到累了
- **creep up** *vi* 缓慢增长; **house prices are ~ing up again** 房价又在慢慢上涨
- **creep up on** *vt* [**~ up on sb.**] **1** (approach) 悄悄走近; **don't ~ up on me like that!** 别那么一声不响地靠近我! **2** fig (in time) «*event*» 渐渐临近 **3** (begin to affect) «*fatigue, age*» 不知不觉开始影响; **old age tends to ~ up on us** 年老往往不期而至

creeper /ˈkriːpə(r)/ *n* 蔓生植物

creeping /ˈkriːpɪŋ/ *adj* **1** (insidious) 不知不觉发生的 ‹*change, inflation*› **2** Bot, Hort 蔓生的 ‹*plant*›

creepy /ˈkriːpi/ *adj* colloq 使人心里发毛的; **the film was a bit ~** 那部电影有点吓人

creepy-crawly /ˌkriːpɪˈkrɔːli/ *n* colloq 爬虫

cremate /krɪˈmeɪt/ *vt* 火化

cremation /krɪˈmeɪʃn/ *n* **1** [c] (ceremony) 火葬仪式 **2** [u] (practice) 火化

crematorium /ˌkreməˈtɔːrɪəm/ (*pl* **crematoria** /ˌkreməˈtɔːrɪə/ *or* **~s**), Amer **crematory** /ˈkremətəri, Amer -tɔːri/ *ns* 火葬场

crème de la crème /ˌkrem də læ ˈkrem/ *n* (person) 精英; (thing) 精华; **this school takes only the ~** 这所学校只招收高材生; **the ~ of British universities** 英国的顶尖大学

Creole /ˈkriːəʊl/ ▸**p. 426**

A *adj* **1** (of the people) 克里奥尔人的; (of the language) 克里奥尔语的 **2** Culin 克里奥尔式的 ‹*dish*›

B *n* **1** [c] (person) 克里奥尔人 **2** [u] (language) 克里奥尔语

creosote /ˈkriːəsəʊt/

A *n* 杂酚油

B *vt* 用杂酚油处理 ‹*wood, fence, shed*›

crêpe, crepe /kreɪp/ *n* **1** [c] Culin 薄饼 **2** [u] Tex 绉织物 **3** [c] (for shoes) **~ (rubber)** 绉胶

crêpe: ~ bandage *n* 弹力绷带; **~ paper** *n* [u] 绉纸

crept /krept/ *pt, pp* ▸**creep A**

crescendo /krɪˈʃendəʊ/

A *n* **1** (*pl* **~s** *or* **crescendi** /krɪˈʃendi/) Mus 渐强 **2** (*pl* **~s**) fig (climax) 高潮; (of noise) 顶点; **the shouting reached a ~** 叫喊声达到了最大

B *adj* 渐强的

C *adv* 渐强地

crescent /ˈkresnt/ *n* **1** (shape) 新月形 **2** Brit (street) 新月形街道; **I live at 7 Beech C~** 我住在比奇新月街7号

crescent moon *n* 新月

cress /kres/ *n* [u] 水田芥

crest /krest/

A *n* **1** (of wave) 波峰; **on the ~ of a wave** fig 处于巅峰时期 **2** (of hill, mountain) 顶峰 **3** Zool (of fur) 肉冠; (of feathers) 羽冠; (spines) 颈脊 **4** (plume on helmet) 羽饰 **5** Herald (emblem) 饰章; (coat of arms) 盾形徽章

B *vt* 到达…的顶点 ‹*hill, wave*›

crested /ˈkrestɪd/ *adj* **1** Zool 有羽冠的 ‹*bird*›; 有颈脊的 ‹*animal*› **2** (with coat of arms) 有纹章的 ‹*stationery*›

crestfallen /ˈkrestfɔːlən/ *adj* 垂头丧气的 ‹*look*›

Cretaceous /krɪˈteɪʃəs/

A *adj* (of the period) 白垩纪的; (of the rock system) 白垩系的

B *n* **the ~** (period) 白垩纪; (rock system) 白垩系

Crete /kriːt/ *pr n* 克里特岛; **in** *or* **on ~** 在克里特岛上

cretin /ˈkretɪn, Amer ˈkriːtn/ *n* **1** pej (idiot) 蠢货 **2** Med dated 呆小病患者

cretinous /ˈkretɪnəs, Amer ˈkriːt-/ *adj* pej 非常愚蠢的

Creutzfeldt-Jakob disease /ˌkrɔɪtsfeldˈjækɒb dɪˌziːz/ ▸**p. 377** *n* [u] 克－雅氏病

crevasse /krɪˈvæs/ *n* [尤指冰川中的] 裂隙

crevice /ˈkrevɪs/ *n* 裂缝

crew[1] /kruː/

A *n* + *v sing or pl* **1** Naut 全体船员; Aviat 全体机务人员 **2** Radio 全体工作人员 **3** Cin, TV 全体剧组人员 **4** colloq pej (gang) 一帮人

B *vi* 当工作人员; **to ~ for sb.** 给某人当工作人员

C *vt* 在…上当工作人员; **the vessel was ~ed mainly by Filipinos** 那条船上的船员大部分是菲律宾人

crew[2] *pt* ▸**crow**[2]

crew: ~cut *n* 平头; **~man** /-mən/ *n* (on ship) 船员; (on aircraft) 乘务员; **~ neck** *n* (neckline) 水手领; (sweater) 水手领衫; **~-neck sweater** *n* 水手领衫

crib /krɪb/

A *n* 1 [c] (manger) 饲料槽 2 [c] Amer (for baby) 童床 3 [c] Brit (nativity scene) 基督诞生塑像 4 [c] colloq (copy) 剽窃的东西 5 [c] Sch colloq (illicit aid) [考试作弊用的] 夹带 6 [c] colloq (translation) 对照译文 7 [u] colloq = **cribbage**

B *vi* (*pres p etc.* **-bb-**) colloq 抄袭; **to ~ from sb.** 从某人处抄袭; **to be caught ~bing in the test** 考试作弊被抓

C *vt* (*pres p etc.* **-bb-**) colloq 抄袭; **to ~ the plot from a film** 从电影中抄袭情节

cribbage /ˈkrɪbɪdʒ/ *n* [u] 克里比奇牌戏

cribbage board *n* 克里比奇牌戏记分板

crib death *n* Amer = **cot death**

crick /krɪk/

A *n* 扭伤; **a ~ in one's back/neck** 背部/颈部扭伤

B *vt* 扭伤 ‹*back, neck*›

cricket[1] /ˈkrɪkɪt/ *n* (insect) 蟋蟀

cricket[2] ▸**p. 307** *n* [u] Sport 板球; **to play ~** 打板球; **a ~ stump/ball** 板球门柱/板球; **it's (just) not ~** Brit colloq 这不公平

cricketer /ˈkrɪkɪtə(r)/ *n* 板球运动员

crikey /ˈkraɪki/ *excl* Brit colloq dated 哎呀

crime /kraɪm/ *n* 1 [c] (offence) 罪; **to commit a ~** 犯罪; **~s against humanity** 反人类罪 2 [u] (criminal acts) 犯罪活动; **the fight against ~** 与犯罪活动的斗争 3 [c] (immoral act) 罪过; **it's a ~ the way you waste food** 你这样浪费食物，真是罪过

crime: ~ buster *n* colloq = **~ fighter**; **~-busting** *adj attrib* colloq 打击犯罪的 ‹*organization, unit, measure, strategy*›; **~ correspondent** ▸**p. 409** *n* 法制记者; **~ desk** *n* 1 Police 警察局新闻处; 2 Journ 法制部; **~ fiction** *n* [u] 侦探小说; **~ fighter** *n* 打击犯罪的斗士; **~-fighting** *n* [u] 打击犯罪; **a ~-fighting organization/measure** 打击犯罪组织/措施; **~ figures** *npl* 犯罪数字; **~ novel** *n* 侦探小说; **~ of passion** *n* (*pl* **~s of passion**) 激情犯罪; **~ prevention** *n* [u] 犯罪预防; **~ prevention officer** ▸**p. 409** *n* 预防犯罪警官; **~ squad** *n* 重案组; **~ wave** *n* 犯罪高潮; **~ writer** ▸**p. 409** *n* 侦探小说作家; **~ writing** *n* [u] 1 (fiction) 侦探小说; 2 (activity) 侦探小说创作

criminal /ˈkrɪmɪnl/

A *n* 罪犯

B *adj* 1 (relating to crime) 犯罪的; (concerning criminal law) 刑事的; **the ~ elements in society** 社会上的少数犯罪分子 2 fig 可耻的; **it would be ~ to miss this chance** 如果错过这次机会，就太不应该了

criminal: ~ act *n* [u] 犯罪行为; **~ assault** *n* [u] 刑事暴行; **~ case** *n* 刑事案件; **~ charges** *npl* 刑事诉讼; **to press/drop ~ charges (against sb.)** 提起/撤回（对某人的）刑事诉讼; **~ code** *n* 刑法典; **~ conspiracy** *n* [u and c] 犯罪共谋; **~ conviction** *n* 刑事定罪; **~ court** *n* 刑事法庭; **~ damage** *n* [u] 刑事毁坏; **~ injuries compensation** *n* [u] Brit 刑事伤害赔偿; **~ inquiry** *n* 刑事调查; **~ intent** *n* [u] 犯罪意图; **~ investigation** *n* = **~ inquiry**; **C~ Investigation Department** *n* Brit [伦敦警察局的] 刑事侦察处

criminality /ˌkrɪmɪˈnæləti/ *n* [u] 犯罪

criminalization /ˌkrɪmɪnəlaɪˈzeɪʃn, Amer -lɪˈz-/ *n* [u] 1 (making illegal) 非法化 2 (making into a criminal) 罪犯化; **these new byelaws effectively result in the ~ of the homeless** 这些新的地方法规事实上把无家可归者视为罪犯

criminalize /ˈkrɪmɪnəlaɪz/ *vt* 1 (make illegal) 使不合法 2 (make into a criminal) 把…当罪犯对待 ‹*person, group*›

criminal: ~ justice *n* [u] 刑事司法; **~ justice system** *n* 刑事司法制度; **~ law** *n* [u] 刑法; **~ lawyer** ▸**p. 409** *n* 刑事案件律师; **~ liability** *n* [u] 刑事责任; **~ libel** *n* [u and c] 诽谤罪

criminally /ˈkrɪmɪnəli/ *adv* 1 Jur 刑事上; **a ~ motivated act** 有犯罪动机的行为; **to be ~ negligent** 犯罪过失 2 (shamefully) 可耻地; **standards are ~ low** 标准低得太不像话

criminally insane

A *adj* 因精神错乱犯罪的 ‹*person, act*›; **to be ~** 因精神错乱而犯罪

B *npl* **the ~** 精神病罪犯

criminal: ~ negligence *n* [u] 犯罪过失; **~ offence** *n* 刑事罪; **~ procedure** *n* 刑事诉讼程序; **~ proceedings** *npl* 刑事诉讼; **~ record** *n* 前科

criminologist /ˌkrɪmɪˈnɒlədʒɪst/ ▸**p. 409** *n* 犯罪学家

criminology /ˌkrɪmɪˈnɒlədʒi/ *n* [u] 犯罪学

crimp /krɪmp/

A *vt* 1 (make wavy) 把…烫成卷发 2 (bend) 把…压出折边 ‹*metal*›; (connect) 压接 ‹*wire*› 3 (put folds in) 给…打褶子 ‹*pastry, fabric*› 4 Amer colloq (restrict) 束缚

B *n* 1 (folded edge of pastry) 褶子; (of metal) 折边 2 Amer colloq (restriction) 束缚; **the ~ on pay** 工资限制

Crimplene® /ˈkrɪmpliːn/ *n* [u] 克林普纶 [一种抗皱合成纤维]

crimson /ˈkrɪmzn/ ▸**p. 134**

A *adj* 深红色的 ‹*lips, rose*›; **to go** *or* **blush ~** 脸涨得通红

B *n* [u] 深红色

cringe /krɪndʒ/ *vi* 1 (in fear) 畏缩; **to ~ away from sth.** 吓得躲开某物 2 (in embarrassment) 感到难堪; **to ~ to think of sth., to ~ at the thought of sth.** 想到某事物就局促不安 3 (in servility) 奴颜婢膝; **to ~ before sb.** 对某人卑躬屈膝

cringe-making *adj* colloq 令人尴尬的 ‹*speech, act*›

cringing /ˈkrɪndʒɪŋ/ *adj attrib* 1 (fearful) 胆怯的 2 (servile) 逢迎的 ‹*smile*›

crinkle /ˈkrɪŋkl/

A *vt* **to ~ (up)** 使…起皱 ‹*fabric, paper*›; **he ~d up his face** 他的脸皱了起来

B *vi* **to ~ (up)** «*paper*» 起皱; «*face*» 起皱纹

C *n* (in fabric, paper) 折皱

crinkle-cut /ˈkrɪŋklkʌt/ *adj* 切成瓦楞状的 ‹*chips*›

crinkly /ˈkrɪŋkli/ *adj* 卷曲的 ‹*hair*›; 起皱的 ‹*fabric, paper*›; 多皱纹的 ‹*eyes*›

cripple /ˈkrɪpl/

A *n* 1 offensive (disabled person) 跛子 offensive 2 fig pej 有缺陷的人; **an emotional ~** 情感不健全的人

B *vt* 1 (disable) «*accident, bullet*» 使成跛子; **to be ~d for life** 终身跛足 2 fig 严重破坏 ‹*nation, vehicle*›; «*debt, poverty*» 把…压垮 ‹*person, economy*›

crippled /ˈkrɪpld/ *adj* 1 (disabled) 跛腿的; **to be ~ with arthritis** 因患关节炎而瘸腿 2 fig 严重受损的 ‹*engine, vehicle*›; **to become ~d emotionally** 遭受严重的感情创伤; **a country with a ~ economy** 经济瘫痪的国家; **families ~ by heavy debt repayments** 被沉重债务压垮的家庭

crippling /ˈkrɪplɪŋ/ *adj* 1 lit 致残的 ‹*disease*›; **the ~ effects of arthritis** 关节炎的致残后果 2 fig 造成严重损害的 ‹*problems, debts*›

crisis /ˈkraɪsɪs/ *n* [u and c] (*pl* **crises** /ˈkraɪsiːz/) 危机; **to be in ~** 处于危机之中; **to reach a ~** 发展到危急关头; **a personal/an emotional ~** 个人/感情危机

crisis: ~ centre *n* 紧急救援中心; **~ intervention** *n* [u] 危机干预; **~ management** *n* [u] 危机管理; **~ point** *n* 危机关头; **to reach ~ point** 到了紧要关头

crisp /krɪsp/

A *adj* 1 (brittle) 松脆的 ‹*biscuit*›; **~ snow** 踩上去咯吱作响的雪 2 (crunchy) 鲜脆的 ‹*apple, carrot*› 3 (uncreased) 挺括的 ‹*shirt, bank note*› 4 (bracing) 清新的 ‹*air*›; **a ~ morning/day** 怡人的早上/一天 5 (concise) 简明扼要的 ‹*comment, presentation, letter*› 6 (terse) 生硬的 ‹*rebuke, refusal*›

B *n* 1 Brit **(potato) ~** 炸薯片 2 **to burn sth. to a ~** 把某物烧焦

C *vt* **to ~ (up)** 把…烤脆 ‹*bread, pitta*›

crispbread /ˈkrɪspbred/ *n* [u and c] 薄脆饼干

crisper /ˈkrɪspə(r)/ *n* [冰箱的] 保鲜储藏格

crisply /ˈkrɪspli/ *adv* 1 (neatly) 平整地 ‹*ironed*› 2 (concisely) 简明扼要地 3 (tersely) 生硬地; **a ~ worded reply** 措词生硬的回复

crispness /ˈkrɪspnɪs/ *n* [u] 1 (of biscuits) 松脆; (of fruit) 鲜脆 2 (of air) 清新 3 (of fabric) 挺括 4 (conciseness) 简明扼要 5 (terseness) 生硬

crispy /ˈkrɪspi/ *adj* 松脆的 ‹*fried food*›; 鲜脆的 ‹*fruit, vegetables*›; **~ noodles** 干脆面

criss-cross

A *adj* 十字形的 ‹*pattern, lines*›

B *adv* 十字交叉地; **the streets run ~** 街道纵横交错

C *n* 十字形

D *vt* 在…上构成十字形; **the whole country is ~ed by a rail network** 全国有纵横交错的铁路网

E *vi* «*wires*» 纵横交错

criterion /kraɪˈtɪərɪən/ *n* (*pl* **criteria** /kraɪˈtɪərɪə/) 标准; **to meet a ~** 符合标准

critic /ˈkrɪtɪk/ ▸**p. 409** *n* 1 (reviewer) 评论家; **an art ~** 艺术评论家 2 (opponent) 批评者

critical /ˈkrɪtɪkl/ *adj* 1 (criticizing) 批评性的 ‹*comment*›; 挑剔的 ‹*person*›; **to be ~ of sb./sth.** 批评某人/某事物; **don't be so ~ with your children** 别对你的孩子那么挑剔 2 (crucial) 关键的 ‹*situation*›; **to be ~ to ...** 对…至关重要 ‹*future, success*›; **to be of ~ importance** 极为重要 3 Med 危重的 ‹*condition, patient*› 4 Literat 异文校勘的 ‹*edition*› 5 (of reviewers) 评论家的 ‹*acclaim*›; **to be a ~ success** 博得评论界好评 6 (discriminating) 有鉴别力的 ‹*reader*›; 审慎的 ‹*attitude*›; **to take a ~ look at sth.** 谨慎地看待某事物

critical: ~ angle *n* 临界角; **~ care** *n* [u] 病危护理; **~ care unit** 危重症监护病房

critically /ˈkrɪtɪkli/ *adv* 1 (disapprovingly) 批判性地; **she viewed the failure very ~** 她对这次失败颇有微词 2 (crucially) 极其 ‹*important*› 3 Med 危重地; **he's ~ ill in hospital** 他病情危重，正在住院治疗 4 (with judgement) 审慎地 ‹*consider*›

critical: ~ mass *n* [u and c] 临界质量; **~ path** *n* 关键路径; **~ path analysis** *n* [u and c] 关键路径分析法

criticism /ˈkrɪtɪsɪzəm/ *n* 1 [u] (analysis) 评论; **literary ~** 文艺评论 2 [u and c] (censure) 批评; **he received a lot of ~** 他受到了很多批评

criticize /ˈkrɪtɪsaɪz/ *vt* 1 (find fault with) 批评; **to ~ sb. for sth.** 因某事物指责某人 2 (analyse) 评论 ‹*performance, book*›

critique /krɪˈtiːk/

A *n* 评论

B *vt* esp Amer 评论 ‹*work of art*›

critter /ˈkrɪtə(r)/ *n* Amer colloq 1 (animal) 动物; **wild ~s** 野生动物 2 (person) [某种] 人

croak /krəʊk/

A *vi* 1 «*animal*» 呱呱叫; «*person*» 声音沙哑地说话 2 sl (die) 咽气

B *vt* 声音沙哑地说; **to ~ a reply** 声音沙哑地回答

C *n* (of animal) 呱呱叫声; (of person) 沙哑的说话声

Croat /ˈkrəʊæt/ ▸**p. 503, p. 426**
A *adj* (of Croatia) 克罗地亚的; (of the people) 克罗地亚人的; (of the language) 克罗地亚语的
B *pr n* **1** [c] (person) 克罗地亚人 **2** [u] (language) 克罗地亚语

Croatia /krəʊˈeɪʃə/ *pr n* 克罗地亚

Croatian /krəʊˈeɪʃn/ ▸**p. 503, p. 426** *n, adj* = **Croat**

crochet /ˈkrəʊʃeɪ, Amer krəʊˈʃeɪ/
A *n* [u] (art) 钩针编织; (work) 钩针编织品
B *vi, vt* 用钩针编织

crochet hook *n* 钩针

crock¹ /krɒk/ Brit colloq
A *n* **(old)** ~ (car) 破车; (person) 老朽的人
B *vt* 使受伤

crock² *n* **1** (pot) 瓦罐 **2** (shard) 碎瓦片 **3** dated (plate, cup) 陶器; **the ~s** 待洗餐具

crockery /ˈkrɒkəri/ *n* [u] 陶器

crocodile /ˈkrɒkədaɪl/ *n* **1** [c] (reptile) 鳄鱼; **to cry** *or* **shed ~ tears** 流鳄鱼眼泪 **2** [u] (leather) 鳄鱼皮; **a ~ wallet** 鳄鱼皮钱夹 **3** [c] Brit (line) 成对行进的小学生

crocodile clip *n* esp Brit 鳄嘴夹

crocus /ˈkrəʊkəs/ *n* (*pl* **~es** *or* **croci** /ˈkrəʊkaɪ/) 番红花

croft /krɒft, Amer krɔːft/ *n* Brit [苏格兰的] 小农场

crofter /ˈkrɒftə(r), Amer ˈkrɔːft-/ *n* Brit [苏格兰的] 佃农

croissant /ˈkrwɑːsɒŋ/ *n* 羊角面包

cromlech /ˈkrɒmlek/ *n* 凯尔特石圈

crone /krəʊn/ *n* pej 丑老太婆

crony /ˈkrəʊni/ *n* pej 密友

cronyism /ˈkrəʊnɪɪzəm/ *n* [u] pej 任人唯亲

crook /krʊk/
A *n* **1** (rogue) 坏蛋; (criminal) 骗子 **2** (of arm) **(in) the ~ of one's arm** *or* **elbow** （在）臂弯里 **3** (staff) 曲柄杖
B *vt* 使…弯曲〈*finger*〉
C *adj* Austral colloq (hurt) 受伤的; (sick) 有病的

crooked /ˈkrʊkɪd/ *adj* **1** (bent, twisted) 弯曲的〈*path, back*〉; 歪斜的〈*teeth*〉; 弯腰驼背的〈*person*〉; **a ~ smile** 不自然的微笑 **2** fig colloq (dishonest) 不诚实的〈*lawyer*〉; (illegal) 不正当的〈*plan*〉; **a ~ share deal** 内幕股票交易

crookedly /ˈkrʊkɪdli/ *adv* 歪歪扭扭地〈*hang, grow*〉; 不自然地〈*smile*〉

croon /kruːn/
A *vi* **1** (sing softly) 哼唱 **2** Mus《*singer*》柔情地唱歌
B *vt* **1** (sing softly) 哼唱〈*lullaby*〉 **2** (say) 柔情地说 **3** Mus《*singer*》柔情地唱〈*ballad*〉

crooner /ˈkruːnə(r)/ *n* 情歌手

crop /krɒp/
A *n* **1** Agric 作物; (in field) 庄稼; **an export ~** 出口作物; **the rotation of ~s** 农作物轮种 **2** (harvest) 收成; (of animal) 一季的产量; **a bumper ~** 丰收; **to harvest** *or* **get in the ~** 收获庄稼; **a second ~ of carrots** 第二茬胡萝卜收成 **3** fig (batch) **a ~ of applicants/letters** 一批申请人/信件; **the cream of the ~** 精英 **4** fig (abundance) 浓密的头发; **a ~ of startling red hair** 一头浓密鲜艳的红头发 **5** (haircut) 平头 **6** Equit (whip) 短马鞭; (whip handle) 鞭把 **7** Zool 嗉囊
B *vt* (*pres p etc.* **-pp-**) **1** (cut) 剪短〈*hair, animal's ears*〉; **to ~ the hedge/lawn** 修剪树篱/草坪 **2** (eat)《*animal*》啃吃〈*grass*〉 **3** Agric (harvest) 收获〈*vegetables, fruit*〉; 收割〈*cereal*〉; 采摘〈*cotton*〉 **4** Agric (grow crop(s) on) 在…上播种〈*land*〉 **5** Phot 裁切〈*photo*〉
C *vi* (*pres p etc.* **-pp-**) 有收成; **to ~ well** *or* **heavily**《*field, plant*》丰收; **to ~ early/late** 早熟/晚熟

Phrasal verbs
- **crop out** *vi*《*rock formation*》露出地面
- **crop up** *vi*《*problem, opportunity*》出现;《*name, subject*》被提及; **if anything ~s up ...** 如果有突发事件…; **her name is always ~ping up in the papers** 报纸上总是提到她的名字

crop: ~ circle *n* 麦田怪圈 [指庄稼倒伏所形成的圆圈等图案]; **~ duster** *n* = **~ sprayer**; **~ dusting** *n* [u] = **~ spraying**

cropped /krɒpt/ *adj* **1** (short) 剪短的〈*hair*〉; 齐根修剪的〈*grass*〉 **2** Fashn 短款的〈*jacket, trousers*〉; 露脐的〈*top*〉 **3** Phot 裁了边的〈*photo*〉 **4** Agric 播种过的〈*field*〉

cropper /ˈkrɒpə(r)/ *n* **1** (crop) 作物; **a heavy/late ~** 高产/晚产作物 **2** Brit colloq **to come a ~** (fall) 重重地摔倒; (do badly) 栽大跟头

crop: ~ rotation *n* [u] 轮作; **~ spray** *n* (pesticide) 杀虫喷剂; (fertilizer) 化肥喷剂; **~ sprayer** *n* **1** (machine) 喷雾器; **2** (aircraft) 作物喷洒飞机; **~ spraying** *n* [u] 作物喷洒; **~-spraying aircraft** *n* 作物喷洒飞机; **~ top** *n* 露脐装

croquet /ˈkrəʊkeɪ, Amer krəʊˈkeɪ/ ▸**p. 307** *n* [u] 槌球游戏; **a ~ match** 槌球比赛

croquette /krəˈket/ *n* 炸丸子; **fish/potato ~s** 炸鱼丸/炸土豆泥丸

cross /krɒs, Amer krɔːs/
A *n* **1** (x shape) 叉形; Sch (marking as wrong) 叉; (+ shape) 十字形; **to make one's ~** 画押 **2** Relig (as jewellery, at altar) 十字架; (as monument) 十字形纪念碑; (as marker) 十字标; **the C~** [钉死耶稣基督的] 十字架; **to make (sign of) the C~** 用手画十字 **3** fig (sth. to be endured) 磨难; **to take up one's ~** 承受磨难; **we all have our ~ to bear** 每人都有自己的苦难要承担 **4** Bot, Hort, Zool 杂交种; fig (mixture) 混合物; **a ~ between sth. and sth.** 某物与某物杂交的产物; **a ~ between sth./sb. and sth./sb.** …与…的混合体 **5** **the C~** Astron 十字星座 **6** Sewing **on the ~** 沿对角 **7** Sport (in football) 横传; (in boxing) 钩拳; **a right ~** 右手钩拳
B *adj* **1** (bad-tempered) 坏脾气的〈*person*〉; (annoyed) 生气的〈*look, person*〉; **to be ~ with sb.** 生某人的气; **to be ~ about sth./doing sth.** 因某事物/做某事生气; **to get ~ (with sb.)** （对某人）发脾气; **we've never had a ~ word** 我们从来没吵过架 **2** *attrib* (transverse) 横向的〈*timbers*〉 **3** *attrib* Sport 斜线的〈*shot, volley*〉
C *vt* **1** (go across) 穿过〈*land, road, bridge*〉; 渡过〈*water, sea*〉; 越过〈*border, mountains*〉;《*competitor*》冲过〈*finish line*〉;《*aircraft*》飞越〈*sky*〉;《*meteor*》划过〈*sky*〉; **to ~ the stage** 从舞台的一端走到另一端; **to ~ the floor (of the House)** Brit Pol 改变立场加入对手政党; **to ~ sb.'s palm (with money)** 付钱请某人做事 **2** (be across)《*road, cable*》横穿〈*land, ceiling*〉;《*bridge*》横跨〈*sea*〉; **a line ~ed the page** 这一页上划了一条横线 **3** fig (go across) 超越〈*generation gap*〉;《*look, thought*》掠过〈*face, mind*〉; **it ~ed my mind that ...** 我突然想到… **4** (intersect)《*line, road*》与…相交〈*line, road, border*〉; (place crosswise) 使…交叉〈*feet, wires*〉; **to ~ each other** 相交; **to ~ paths**《*people*》相遇; **to ~ one's arms on** *or* **over one's chest** 双臂交叉于胸前; **to ~ one's legs** 跷起二郎腿; **to ~ one's eyes** 做斗鸡眼; **to ~ one's fingers** lit 交叉食指与中指; fig 祈求交好运 **5** (mark) 在…上打叉〈*choice, box*〉 **6** (draw line across) 画横线于〈*letter t*〉; **to ~ a cheque** Brit 在支票上画线 [表示只能经银行账户兑现] **7** Relig 用手画十字于〈*oneself, thing*〉; **I ~ my heart (and hope to die)** fig 我发誓（，否则不得好死） **8** (obstruct) 阻挠〈*person*〉; **to ~ sb. in sth.** 在某事上反对某人; **to be ~ed in love** 恋爱受挫 **9** Bio, Hort, Zool 使杂交; **to ~ sth. with** *or* **and sth.** 使…与某物杂交 **10** Sport《*player*》横传〈*ball*〉
D *vi* **1** (go across)《*person, vehicle*》穿过;《*boat*》渡过;《*bird, aircraft*》飞过;《*meteor*》划过; **to ~ from ... (to ...)** (on land, in room) 穿过…（到…）; (over or through water) 渡过…（到…）; **to ~ the river on a ferry** 乘渡船过河; **to ~ into Italy** 越过边界进入意大利 **2** (intersect)《*road, legs, beams*》交叉; **our paths ~ frequently** 我们经常相遇 **3** (pass in opposite directions)《*vehicles, bullets*》迎面而过; Post《*parcels, orders*》错过; **we ~ed in the hall** 我们在大厅里擦肩而过; **to ~ with sth.** 与某物交错而过; **to ~ in the post** 在邮寄过程中相互错过 **4** Sport《*footballer*》传中

Phrasal verbs
- **cross off** *vt* [**~ sth. off, ~ off sth.**] 把…画掉〈*name, item*〉; **to ~ sth./sb. off sth.** 把某物/某人从某处画掉
- **cross out** *vt* [**~ sth. out, ~ out sth.**] 把…画掉〈*text, letter, name*〉
- **cross over**
A *vi* **1** (go across)《*pedestrian*》过马路; **to ~ over to** fig 转变立场投靠〈*political party*〉 **2** (intersect)《*railway tracks*》相交;《*ideas*》融合
B *vt* [**~ over sth.**] 穿过
- **cross through** *vt* [**~ sth. through, ~ through sth.**] 在…上画线〈*text, name*〉

cross: ~bar *n* **1** (of bike) 车架横梁; **2** esp Sport 横木; **~beam** *n* 横梁; **~ bench** *n* usu pl Brit 中立议员席; **~-bencher** *n* Brit 中立议员; **~bones** *npl* 交叉股骨图形 [用于海盗旗帜或警示标记]; ▸**skull and crossbones**; **~-border** *adj* 跨国的〈*trade, attack*〉; **~bow** /-bəʊ/ *n* 弩; **~-bred** *adj* 杂交的〈*animal, plant*〉

crossbreed /ˈkrɒsbriːd, Amer ˈkrɔːs-/
A *vt* (*pt, pp* **crossbred** /ˈkrɒsbred, Amer ˈkrɔːs-/) 使杂交; **to ~ a lion with** *or* **and a tiger** 使狮虎杂交
B *vi* (*pt, pp* **crossbred**)《*animal, plant*》杂交繁育
C *n* 杂交品种; **a ~ dog** 杂种狗

cross: ~breeding *n* [u] 杂交繁育; **~-Channel** *adj attrib* 跨英吉利海峡的〈*ferry, trip*〉

cross-check *vt, vi, n* 反复核实

cross-country
A *adj* **1** (across country) 横穿全国的〈*road, train*〉 **2** esp Sport 越野的〈*event, runner, trip*〉
B *adv* 越野地〈*ride, ski*〉; **to cycle 10 miles ~** 越野骑车 10 英里
C *n* Sport **1** [u] (running) 越野赛跑; (skiing) 越野滑雪 **2** [c] (race) 越野比赛

cross: ~-court *adj* 斜线的〈*shot*〉; **~-cultural** *adj* 跨文化的; **~-cultural study/communication** 跨文化研究/交际; **~-current** *n* lit 逆流; fig 对立的观点; **~-curricular** *adj* 跨课程的〈*activity, teaching*〉; **~-cut** *adj* 横切的〈*incision, tool*〉; **~-cut saw** *n* 横锯; **~-disciplinary** *adj* 跨学科的〈*study*〉; **~-dress** *vi* 穿异性服装; **~-dresser** *n* 穿异性服装者; **~-dressing** *n* [u] 穿异性服装

crossed /krɒst/ *adj* 交扰的; **to have a ~ line** 电话串线; **we got our wires ~** fig 我们电话串线了; fig 我们误会了对方

cross: ~-examination *n* [u and c] **1** Jur 反诘问; **2** (gen) 盘问; **~-examine** *vt* **1** Jur 反诘问〈*witness*〉; **2** (gen) 盘问; **to ~-examine sb. about sth.** 就某事物盘问某人; **~-examiner** *n* 诘问者; **~-eyed** *adj* **1** lit 内斜视的; **2** fig colloq 斗鸡眼的; **to go ~-eyed** 变成斗鸡眼; **~-fertilization** *n* [u] **1** Bot 异花授粉; **2** fig 丰富思想的交流

cross-fertilize
A *vt* **1** Bot 使…异花授粉〈*plants*〉 **2** fig 使…通过交流变得丰富〈*ideas*〉
B *vi*《*plants*》异花授粉

cross: ~fire *n* [u] **1** Mil 交叉火力; **2** fig 激烈交锋; **to be** *or* **get caught in the ~fire of questions/criticism** 遭到来自四面八方的质问/批评; **~ hairs** *npl* [望远镜、瞄准器上用于确定位置、瞄准或测量的] 十字准线; **~-hatch** *vt* 用网格线描画〈*area*〉; **~-hatching** *n* [u] **1** (act) 用网格线描画; **2** (pattern) 交叉平行线图案

crossing /ˈkrɒsɪŋ, Amer ˈkrɔːsɪŋ/ *n* **1** [c] (over water) 横渡; **my first single-handed Channel ~** 我的首次单独横渡英吉利海峡 **2** [c] (on street) 人行横道; **a school ~ patrol** 学生过街护送员 **3** [c] Rail 道口 **4** [c] (intersection) 十字路口; (junction) 交叉点 **5** [c] (border crossing) 过境处 **6** [u and c] (of border, road) 穿越 **7** [u] Biol, Bot, Zool 杂交

crossing-out *n* (*pl* **crossings-out**) 画掉之处; **the letter was full of crossings-out** 这封信里有多处文字的勾画删改

cross-legged /ˌkrɒsˈlegɪd, Amer ˌkrɔːs-/
A *adj* 盘腿的 ‹*position*›
B *adv* 以盘腿姿势; **to sit ~ on the floor** 盘腿坐在地板上

crossly /ˈkrɒsli, Amer ˈkrɔːsli/ *adv* 生气地

crossover /ˈkrɒsəʊvə(r), Amer ˈkrɔːs-/
A *n* **1** [c] (crossing) 穿越; (crossing place) 穿越处 **2** [c] (intersection) 交叉点 **3** [c] Rail 中转站 **4** [u] Mus 交叉风格; **a jazz-classical ~ CD** 一张结合了爵士乐和古典音乐两种风格的激光唱片
B *adj attrib* 交叉的 ‹*straps, bodice, front, back*›

cross: ~-ownership *n* [u] 交叉所有权; **~-party** *adj* 跨党的 ‹*cooperation, campaign, group*›; **~patch** colloq *n* 脾气暴躁的人; **~piece** *n* 横杆

cross-ply Brit
A *n* 斜交轮胎
B *adj* 有交叉帘布层的; **a ~ tyre** 斜交轮胎

cross-pollinate
A *vt* «*bee, wind*» 使…异花传粉 ‹*plants, flowers*›
B *vi* 异花传粉; **to ~ with sth.** «*plants, flowers*» 与某植物异花传粉

cross: ~-pollination *n* [u] 异花传粉; **~-purposes** *npl* **to be at ~-purposes (with sb.)** (misunderstand) (和某人) 相互误解; (disagree) (与某人) 各执一词; **to talk at ~-purposes** 各说各的; **~-question** *vt* 盘问; **to ~-question sb. about sth.** 就某事物追问某人

cross-refer
A *vt* 指引…参见; **to ~ sth. to sth.** 指引读者从…参见某物 ‹*article, word*›; **to ~ sb. to sth.** 指引某人参见某物
B *vi* 作参见指引; **to ~ to sth.** 参见至某物

cross-reference
A *n* 参见项; **a ~ from sth. to sth.** 从书的某处到某处的参见条; **a ~ to sth.** 至某处的参见条
B *vt* 为…提供参阅资料 ‹*book, word*›

cross: ~roads *n* (*pl* **~roads**) **1** lit 十字路口; **2** fig 关键时刻; **she had reached a ~roads in her career** 她的事业发展到了紧要关头; **~-section** *n* **1** (transverse view) 横断面; (illustration) 剖面图; **in ~-section** 以剖面图显示的; **2** (thin slice) 切片; **3** fig (representative sample) 典型代表; **a broad ~-section of the public** 公众中具有广泛代表性的各类人物; **a ~-section of ideas/views/beliefs** 具代表性的想法/观点/信念; **~-selling** *n* [u] 交叉销售 [指向已购买公司产品的人推销其他产品的行为]

cross-stitch /ˈkrɒsstɪtʃ, Amer ˈkrɔːs-/
A *n* **1** [c] (stitch) 十字形针迹 **2** [u] (cross-stitching) 十字形绣
B *vt* 用十字针迹缝制 ‹*design, cloth*›
C *vi* 做十字绣

cross: ~ street *n* Amer 十字街; **~talk** *n* [u] **1** Radio, Telecom 串话干扰; **2** Brit (repartee) 相声; **~tie** *n* Amer 轨枕; **~-town** *adj attrib* Amer 穿越市区的 ‹*bus, road*›; **~trees** *npl* 桅顶横杆; **~-voting** *n* [u] (for more than one party) 给一个以上党派投票; (not for one's party) 跨党投票; **~walk** *n* Amer, Austral 人行横道; **~way** *n* Amer 交叉路

crossways /ˈkrɒsweɪz/ *adj, adv* = **crosswise**

crosswind /ˈkrɒswɪnd/ *n* 侧风

crosswise /ˈkrɒswaɪz, Amer ˈkrɔːs-/
A *adj* **1** (diagonal) 斜穿的 ‹*strut, stripe*› **2** (transverse) 横穿的 ‹*beam, band, step*› **3** (cross-shaped) 十字形的 ‹*structure*›
B *adv* **1** (diagonally) 斜着 ‹*move, go*› **2** (transversely) 横向地 ‹*lay, cut, fold*› **3** (in the form of a cross) 交叉地; **their arms were held out ~** 他们的胳膊交叉着伸出来

crossword /ˈkrɒswɜːd, Amer ˈkrɔːs-/ *n* **a ~ (puzzle)** 填字游戏; **to do a ~** 做填字谜游戏

> **crossword**
>
> 填字游戏，亦称纵横字谜游戏（crossword puzzle）。现代的填字游戏最早见于1913年12月21日美国《纽约世界报》（*New York World*）的星期日副刊。填字游戏可分为两部分。一部分为谜面，分为含编号的横向（across）和纵向（down）两组填字线索。另一部分是纵横交叉的方格图形，在填字开始的方格内含有编号，和填字线索的编号相对应。方格通常分为黑白两种。白色方格用于填入字母，每个方格填一个字母。黑色方格则用于分开单词。根据线索的不同，填字游戏可以分为两种基本类型：快速填字（quick crossword）和隐性填字（cryptic crossword）。快速填字的线索一般是谜底的直接定义，在美国比较常见。隐性填字发源于英国，其线索本身就是一个字谜，谜面设置方式多种多样。

crotch /krɒtʃ/ *n* **1** Anat 胯部 **2** (in trousers) 裤裆

crotchet /ˈkrɒtʃɪt/ *n* Brit 四分音符

crotchety /ˈkrɒtʃɪti/ *adj* 脾气坏的

crotchless /ˈkrɒtʃlɪs/ *adj* 开裆的 ‹*garment*›

crouch /kraʊtʃ/
A *vi* **1** (squat) «*person, animal*» 蹲伏; **to ~ down** 蹲下 **2** (hunch forward) 俯身
B *n* 蹲伏

croup /kruːp/ *n* [u] 哮吼 [儿童罹患的一种喉部和气管炎症，伴有病毒感染和呼吸困难]

croupier /ˈkruːpɪə(r)/ ▸p. 409 *n* 赌台管理员

crouton /ˈkruːtɒn/ *n* 油炸面包丁

crow[1] /krəʊ/ *n* (bird) 乌鸦; **as the ~ flies** 沿直线; **to eat ~** Amer colloq (accept sth. unwanted) 忍气吞声; (retract a boast) 收回大话

crow[2] *vi* (*pt* **~ed** *or* **crew**) **1** (call) «*cock*» 啼叫 **2** (gloat) «*person*» 自鸣得意; **to ~ over** *or* **about sth.** 对某事沾沾自喜

crowbar /ˈkrəʊbɑː(r)/ *n* 撬棍

crowd /kraʊd/
A *n + v sing or pl* **1** (throng, group of people) 人群; (group of things) 一堆; **~s of people** 成群结队的人; **to attract** *or* **draw a large ~** 吸引一大群人; ▸company 3 **2** Cin, Theat 观众; Radio 听众 **3** (the masses) **the ~** 群众; **to go/move with** *or* **follow the ~** 随大溜; **as a teacher, she stands out from the ~** 作为一名教师，她出类拔萃 **4** colloq (gang) 一帮人; **the ~ from the office** 一帮同事
B *vi* (press forward or close) 挤; **to ~ in/on** 挤进/挤上; **to ~ into/on to sth.** 挤进/挤上某处; **to ~ through (sth.)** 挤过（某处）; **to come ~ing in** fig «*worries, memories*» 涌上心头; **to ~ (up) against ...** 挤向…; **to ~ together** 聚拢在一起; **to ~ round** *or* **around (sb./sth.)** 挤在（某人/某物）周围
C *vt* **1** (cram) «*people, cars*» 挤满 ‹*hall, road*›; (push) 挤; **to be ~ed with sth.** «*room*» 塞满某物; «*mind*» 充满某事; «*time*» 安排满某事; **to ~ sb. off the pavement** 把某人挤出人行道; **stop ~ing me!** 别挤我！ **2** (squash in) 塞进; **to ~ in** 把…塞进 ‹*people, vehicles, activities*›; **to ~ people/animals into sth.** 把人/动物塞进某处; **to ~ people/animals on (to sth.)** 把人/动物塞到（某物）上面; **to ~ people/animals together** 使人/动物挤在一起 **3** fig colloq (pressure) 催促; **to ~ sb. (into doing sth.)** 催促某人（做某事）

Phrasal verbs

• **crowd in on**
A [**~ in on sb./sth.**] *vt* (approach) 挤近 ‹*person, place*›
B [**~ in on sb.**] *vt*
1 (surround) «*walls, trees*» 从周围向…压过来
2 fig (overwhelm) «*thoughts, memories*» 涌上…的心头

• **crowd out** *vt* [**~ sth./sb. out, ~ out sth./sb.**] 把…排挤出去 ‹*person, business, plant*›; **to ~ sb./sth. out of sth.** 将某人/某事物从某处挤走; **dreams of fame and glory ~ed out my fears** 对名声和荣誉的渴望使我不再恐惧

crowd: ~ control *n* [u] 人群控制; **~ control barrier** *n* 人群隔离栏

crowded /ˈkraʊdɪd/ *adj* **1** (full of people) 拥挤的 ‹*place*›; 人满为患的 ‹*earth, profession*›; **to be ~ with tourists** 挤满游客 **2** (cluttered) 塞得满满的 ‹*car park, display, head*›; **a room ~ with furniture** 塞满家具的房间; **my mind is ~ with useless facts** 我的脑子里塞满了无用的事实 **3** (busy, full) 排满的 ‹*schedule*›; 忙碌的 ‹*life, day*›

crowd: ~-pleaser *n* (person) 吸引众人的人; (thing) 吸引众人的东西; **~-puller** *n* colloq (person) 吸引大批观众的人; (event) 吸引众人的事件; **~-pulling** *adj* 吸引大批观众的 ‹*event, performer, performance*›; **~ safety** *n* [u] 人群安全; **~ scene** *n* 群众场面; **~ trouble** *n* [u] 群殴

crown /kraʊn/
A *n* **1** (of monarch) 王冠; (wreath) 花冠; **a ~ of thorns** Bible 荆棘冠冕 **2** **the C~** (monarchy) 王位; (reigning monarch) 君主; **C~ property/estate** 王室不动产 **3** Brit Jur (prosecuting authority) **the C~** 公诉方; **a C~ witness** 公诉证人 **4** Sport (award, distinction) 桂冠; **to fight for the world heavyweight ~** 争夺世界重量级拳击冠军 **5** (top of hill, mountain, hat, head) 顶; **the ~ of the road** 路拱 **6** (of bend) 最弯处 **7** Dent (part of tooth) 齿冠; (artificial tooth) 假齿冠
B *vt* **1** (invest as monarch) 为…加冕 ‹*king, queen*›; **to ~ sb. king/queen/emperor** 立某人为国王/王后/皇帝 **2** esp Sport 使…封冠 ‹*victor*›; **she was ~ed Wimbledon champion** 她被宣布为温布尔登网球公开赛冠军 **3** (cover, form top of) «*trees, battlements*» 覆盖在…的顶部 ‹*hill, tower*›; **to be ~ed with sth.** 顶部覆盖着某物; **beautiful fair hair ~s her head** 她长了一头美丽的金发; **the Christmas tree was ~ed with a gold star** 圣诞树顶有一颗金色的星星 **4** **to be ~ed with sth.** (culminate in) 以某事物完美收场; **the prize ~ed her career** 这个奖项使她的事业达到了顶峰; **her efforts were ~ed by success** 她的努力获得圆满成功; **to ~ it all, I won** colloq 最令人高兴的是，我赢了; **to ~ it all, I lost my key** iron 最糟糕的是，我把钥匙丢了 **5** colloq (hit on the head) «*person, object*» 打…的头; **he nearly ~ed himself when he stood up** 他站起来时，差点儿碰着头 **6** Dent «*dentist*» 为…镶假齿冠 ‹*tooth*›

crown: ~ cap *n* 冠形瓶盖; **~ colony** *n* 英国直辖殖民地; **C~ court** *n* Brit [英格兰和威尔士的] 刑事法庭

crowned heads *npl* 君主; **the ~ of Europe** 欧洲的君主

crowning /ˈkraʊnɪŋ/ *adj attrib* 登峰造极的 ‹*moment, achievement, success*›

crown: C~ jewels *npl* 御宝; **~ land** *n* Brit 王室土地; **C~ prince** *n* 王储; **C~ princess** *n* **1** (female heir) 女王储; **2** (wife of Crown prince) 王储妃; **C~ Prosecution Service** *n + v sing or pl* [英格兰和威尔士的] 皇家检控署; **C~ prosecutor** *n* [英格兰、威尔士和加拿大的] 皇家检察官

crow: ~'s feet *npl* 鱼尾纹; **~'s nest** *n* 桅杆瞭望台

cruces /ˈkruːsiːz/ *pl* ▸ **crux**

crucial /ˈkruːʃl/ *adj* 至关重要的 ‹*decision, issue*›; **to be ~ to** *or* **for sth.** 对某事极其重要

crucially /ˈkruːʃəli/ *adv* 至关重要地; **~ important** 极端重要的; **~, he was there** 关键是，他在那儿

crucible /ˈkruːsɪbl/ *n* **1** Chem 坩埚 **2** fig (place of severe trial) 严峻考验; **the ~ of sth.** 某事物的严峻考验

crucifix /ˈkruːsɪfɪks/ *n* 耶稣十字架受难像

crucifixion /ˌkruːsɪˈfɪkʃn/ *n* [u and c] 钉死在十字架上; **the C~** 耶稣之十字架受难

crucify /ˈkruːsɪfaɪ/ *vt* **1** (execute) 把…钉死在十字架上 **2** fig colloq (criticize severely) 严厉批评; **to ~ sb. for sth./doing sth.** 为某事物/为做某事痛斥某人

crud /krʌd/ *n* [u] colloq 污垢

crude /kruːd/ *adj* **1** (vulgar, rude) 粗鲁的 ‹*person, remark, insult, behaviour*› **2** (unsubtle) 不加掩饰的 **3** (rough, approximate) 粗略的 ‹*sketch, method, guess*›; **~ statistical data** 未经处理的统计数据 **4** (rudimentary, makeshift) 粗糙的 ‹*furniture, dwelling, weapons*› **5** (unrefined) 未加工的 ‹*sugar, ore*›; **~ oil** 原油

crudely /ˈkruːdli/ *adv* **1** (vulgarly) 粗鲁地 ‹*behave, insult, leer*› **2** (simply, bluntly) 直白地 ‹*explain*›; 直截了当地 ‹*dismiss*›; **~ speaking, ...** 坦率地说…; **to put it ~ ...** 简而言之，… **3** (without skill) 粗糙地 ‹*built, fashioned, drawn*›

crudity /ˈkruːdɪti/, **crudeness** /ˈkruːdnɪs/ *ns* [u] **1** (vulgarity) 粗俗 **2** (of method, manufacture) 简陋; **despite the ~ of their weapons** 尽管他们的武器很简陋

cruel /ˈkrʊəl/ *adj* **1** (brutal, callous) 残忍的 ‹*person, deed*›; 刻毒的 ‹*words*›; **to be ~ to sb.** 残忍地对待某人; **to be ~ to be kind** 让人痛苦却是出于好意 **2** (harsh) 残酷的; **a ~ blow** 惨痛的打击; **life has been ~ to her** 她的生活一直很悲惨

cruelly /ˈkrʊəli/ *adv* **1** (brutally, callously) 残忍地 ‹*treat, punish*› **2** (harshly) 残酷地; **a ~ unfair decision** 极不公平的决定

cruelty /ˈkrʊəlti/ *n* **1** [u] (cruel behaviour) 残忍; **~ to sb.** 对某人的虐待; **emotional ~** 感情虐待; **the Theatre of C~** 残酷戏剧 **2** [c] (cruel action) 暴行 **3** [u] (harshness of fate, life, decision) 残酷性

cruelty-free *adj* **1** (made without cruelty to animals) 以不虐待动物的方式制造的 ‹*cosmetic, product, food*› **2** (relating to cruelty-free products) 不涉及虐待动物产品的 ‹*standard, shopping*›

cruet /ˈkruːɪt/ *n* **a ~ (stand** *or* **set)** 调味瓶架

cruise /kruːz/

A *vi* **1** (sail for pleasure) 乘船游览 **2** (travel slowly) 平稳行驶; **to ~ at 10,000 metres/at 500 km/h** 在 1 万米高空/以每小时 500 公里的速度巡航 **3** esp Sport colloq (do easily) 轻松获取; **to ~ to victory/into first place** 轻松获得胜利/第一名; **to ~ through an exam** 轻而易举通过考试 **4** (travel around unhurriedly) 巡行; (travel around looking for sth.) 徘徊寻觅; **a police car ~d past us** 一辆巡逻警车从我们身边驶过; **taxis ~d about, hoping to pick up fares** 出租汽车四处寻觅乘客 **5** colloq «*homosexual*» 寻觅性伙伴

B *vt* **1** (sail for pleasure) 乘船游览 **2** (travel slowly) 平稳行驶于 ‹*sea, oceans, skies*›; **to ~ a sea/river** 在海/河上平稳航行 **3** (travel around unhurriedly) «*person*» 徘徊于; «*car*» 巡行于; **the teenagers were aimlessly cruising the mall** 这些少年漫无目的地在购物中心闲逛; **a police car was cruising the streets** 一辆警车在街上巡逻 **4** (travel around looking for sth.) «*police car, vigilantes, teenagers in cars, taxi*» 在…徘徊寻觅 ‹*streets, city, area*› **5** colloq (homosexual) 在…寻觅性伙伴 ‹*bars, area*›

C *n* 乘船游览; **to be/go on a ~** 在/去乘船游览

cruise: ~ control *n* [u and c] 巡行车速控制器; **~ liner** *n* 大型游船; **~ missile** *n* 巡航导弹

cruiser /ˈkruːzə(r)/ *n* 巡洋舰

cruiserweight /ˈkruːzəweɪt/ *n* esp Brit **= light-heavyweight**

cruise ship *n* **= cruise liner**

cruising: ~ altitude *n* [c and u] 巡航高度; **~ range** *n* 续航距离; **~ speed** *n* [c and u] 巡行速度

crumb /krʌm/ *n* **1** (fragment of bread, cake) 食物碎屑 **2** fig (small amount) 少许; **~(s) of sth.** 少量的某物; **a ~ of comfort** 些许安慰 **3** esp Amer colloq pej (person) 可鄙的人

crumble /ˈkrʌmbl/

A *vi* **1** (break) 成碎屑; (disintegrate, decay) 碎裂; **to ~ into** *or* **to sth.** 碎裂成某物; **this bread/cake ~s easily** 这种面包/蛋糕容易碎裂; **those mountains will eventually ~ into the sea** 那些山脉最终将崩裂垮坍，沉入海底 **2** fig (diminish, fail) «*empire, self-confidence, resistance*» 崩溃; «*marriage*» 破裂; **their hopes had ~d to dust** 他们的希望成了泡影

B *vt* **~ (up)** 使…成碎屑 ‹*bread*›; 使…碎裂 ‹*soil*›; **to ~ sth. into** *or* **to sth.** 使某物碎成某物

C *n* **1** [u and c] Brit (pudding) 酥皮水果布丁 **2** [u] (topping) [水果食品的] 酥皮

crumbling /ˈkrʌmblɪŋ/ *adj* **1** (falling to pieces) 逐渐碎裂的 ‹*building, cliff, plaster, concrete*› **2** fig (disintegrating) 衰败的 ‹*civilization, empire, economy*›; 正在破裂的 ‹*relationship, unity*›

crumbly /ˈkrʌmbli/ *adj* 易碎的 ‹*bread, soil*›

crumbs /krʌmz/ *excl* Brit colloq dated 哎哟; **she earns £100,000 a year — ~!** 她年薪 10 万英镑——哎哟!

crummy /ˈkrʌmi/ *adj* colloq pej 微薄的 ‹*pay*›; 破旧的 ‹*hotel*›; 糟糕的 ‹*neighbourhood, job*›

crumpet /ˈkrʌmpɪt/ *n* **1** [c] Culin 烤面饼 **2** [u] Brit colloq hum (sexually attractive women) 性感女子

crumple /ˈkrʌmpl/

A *vt* 弄皱; **to ~ sth. (up) into a ball** 把某物揉成一个球; **he collapsed into a ~d heap** 他瘫作一团

B *vi* **1** (be creased, crushed) «*paper, material*» 起皱; «*metal, bumper*» 压瘪; fig «*face, features*» 显得委靡 **2** fig (collapse) «*resistance, self-confidence*» 崩溃; **he ~d on to the floor** 他瘫倒在地板上

crumpled /ˈkrʌmpld/ *adj* **1** (wrinkled) 皱巴巴的 ‹*garment, paper*›; fig 扭曲的 ‹*face*› **2** (bent) 压瘪的 ‹*car, bumper*› **3** (doubled up) 瘫倒的

crumple zone *n* [机动车前后的] 防撞缓冲区

crunch /krʌntʃ/

A *vt* **1** (eat noisily) 嘎吱嘎吱地嚼 ‹*crisps, bone*›; **don't ~ your food!** 吃东西别那么大声! **2** (make noise) «*feet, wheels*» 使…发出碎裂声 ‹*broken glass, gravel, snow*›; **to ~ the gears** colloq 嘎吱嘎吱地换挡

B *vi* **1** (make noise) «*snow, gears*» 发出嘎吱声; **his shoes ~ed on the gravel** 他的鞋踩得碎石嘎吱作响 **2** (eat noisily, munch) 嘎吱嘎吱地咀嚼

C *n* **1** (sound) 嘎吱声 **2** colloq (decisive moment) 关键时刻; **when/if it comes to the ~ ...** 等到了紧要关头…

Phrasal verb

- **crunch up** *vt* [**~ up sth., ~ sth. up**] 嘎吱嘎吱地把…弄碎; **to ~ sth. up into sth.** 嘎吱嘎吱地把…弄碎成某物 ‹*eggshells, scrap metal, stones*›

crunchy /ˈkrʌntʃi/ *adj* 松脆的 ‹*biscuits*›; 嘎吱作响的 ‹*snow*›; 脆生生的 ‹*apple*›; **these vegetables are a bit ~** 这些蔬菜有点儿松脆

crusade /kruːˈseɪd/

A *n* **1** (*also* **Crusade**) Hist 圣战; **the C~s** 十字军东征; **to go/be on a ~** 参加圣战/正在进行圣战 **2** (campaign) 运动; **a ~ against/for sth.** 反对/支持某事物的运动; **on a ~** 投入运动的

B *vi* (campaign) 投身运动; **to ~ against/for sth.** 参加运动反对/支持某事物

crusader /kruːˈseɪdə(r)/ *n* **1** (*also* **Crusader**) Hist 十字军战士 **2** (campaigner) 运动参加者; **moral ~s** 提倡道德运动的志士; **a ~ against/for sth.** 反对/支持某事的斗士

crusading /kruːˈseɪdɪŋ/ *adj attrib* 富有斗争精神的 ‹*campaigner, organization*›

crush /krʌʃ/

A *vt* **1** (squash) 压坏 ‹*person, bones*›; **to be ~ed against the railings** 被挤压在栏杆上; **to ~ sb. to death** 把某人压死 **2** (pulverize) 压碎 ‹*nuts, rocks*›; (press) 榨 ‹*grapes, seeds*›; 捣 ‹*garlic*›; **to ~ sth. to pieces/a powder** 把某物压碎/碾成粉末 **3** (crease) 弄皱 ‹*clothes, paper*› **4** fig (destroy) 镇压 ‹*enemy, protest*›; «*news*» 使…破灭 ‹*hopes*›; (defeat) «*competitor*» 击败 ‹*opponent*›; (through argument) 驳倒 **5** fig (sadden) «*event*» 使…悲伤 ‹*person*› **6** fig (humiliate) «*remark*» 羞辱 ‹*person*›

B *vi* **1** (crowd) 挤; **to ~ into a car** 挤进汽车 **2** (crease) «*clothes, paper*» 起皱

C *n* **1** [c] (crowd) 拥挤的人群; **it was a bit of a ~ in the car** 车里有点儿拥挤 **2** [c] colloq (infatuation) 热恋; **to have a ~ on sb.** 迷恋某人 **3** [u and c] Brit (drink) 果汁饮料; **lemon ~** 柠檬汁

Phrasal verbs

- **crush out** *vt* [**~ sth. out, ~ out sth.**] 榨出 ‹*juice, oil*›; 熄灭 ‹*cigarette*›; 耗尽 ‹*spirit*›; **to ~ sth. out of sth.** 从某物中榨出某物; **to ~ sth. out of sb.** fig 使某人耗尽某物; **the job pretty much ~ed the life out of me** 这工作快把我累死了
- **crush up** *vt* [**~ sth. up, ~ up sth.**] 碾碎; **to ~ sth. up into small pieces** 将某物碾成细小碎片

crush: ~ bar *n* Brit [剧院里的] 小酒吧; **~ barrier** *n* Brit 防挤栏杆

crushing /ˈkrʌʃɪŋ/ *adj* **1** (overwhelming) 压倒性的 ‹*defeat, victory*› **2** (devastating) 毁灭性的 ‹*blow*› **3** (humiliating) 使人受不了的 ‹*remark, look, criticism*›

crushproof /ˈkrʌʃpruːf/ *adj* 抗皱的 ‹*garment, fabric, packing*›

crust /krʌst/ *n* **1** (outer part of loaf) 面包皮; (end slice of loaf) [长面包两头的] 面包片; (of pie) 馅饼皮; **he'd share his last ~** 他连最后一块食物都愿与人分享 **2** Brit colloq (living, livelihood) **to earn one's ~** 谋生 **3** (layer) 硬层; **a ~ of mud/frozen snow** 一层硬泥/冻雪; **the earth's ~** 地壳

crustacean /krʌˈsteɪʃn/ *n* 甲壳纲动物

crusty /ˈkrʌsti/ *adj* **1** (with a thick crust) 有硬皮的 ‹*bread, pie*› **2** colloq (irritable) 易怒的 ‹*old man, professor*›; 粗暴的 ‹*reply*›

crutch /krʌtʃ/ *n* **1** Med 腋杖; **to walk** *or* **be on ~es** 拄着腋杖走路 **2** (stay, support) 支撑物 **3** fig (prop) 依靠; **religion is a ~ for** *or* **to her** 宗教是她的精神支柱 **4** Brit (crotch) 胯部; (in trousers) 裤裆

crux /krʌks/ *n* (*pl* **~es** *or* **cruces**) (the most difficult point) 难点; (the vital point) 关键; **the ~ of the matter** 事情的症结

cry /kraɪ/

A *vi* **1** (weep) 哭; (shed tears) 流泪; **to ~ about** *or* **over sth.** 为某事物而哭泣; **to ~ for sth./sb.** (because of) 因为某事物/某人而哭泣; (calling for) 哭着要某物/某人; **to ~ with pain/hunger** 疼/饿得直哭; **to ~ with laughter** 笑出眼泪; **to ~ for joy** 喜极而泣; **to ~ over spilt milk** fig 为无法挽回的事忧伤 **2** (call out) **= cry out A** **3** Zool «*bird*» 鸣; «*animal*» 嗥叫

B *vt* **1** (weep) 流出; **to ~ tears of joy** 喜极而泣 **2** (shout) 大声表示 ‹*approval, dismay*›; 大声发出 ‹*warning*›; «*vendor*» 叫卖 ‹*wares*›; **'look out!' he cried** "小心!" 他喊道

C *v refl* **to ~ oneself to sleep** 哭到睡着

D *n* **1** (call) 叫喊; (of vendor) 叫卖声; (in protest) 呐喊; **to utter a ~** 发出一声叫喊; **a ~ for help** 呼救声; **to be a ~ for help/attention** fig 迫切需要帮助/注意; **to be a far ~ from sth.** 与某事物大相径庭 **2** Zool 叫声; (huntsman) 吠声; **to be in full ~** lit 吠叫着紧追不舍; fig 大声疾呼; **to be in full ~ against sb.** «*crowd*» 激情呐喊反对某人 **3** (demand) 呼声; (slogan) 口号; **a ~ for/against sth.** 支持/反对某事物的呼声 **4** (weeping) 哭; (fit of weeping) 一阵哭泣; **to have a good ~** 大哭一场; **to have a ~ over sth.** 因某事物而哭泣

Phrasal verbs

- **cry down** *vt* [**~ sth. down, ~ down sth.**] dated 贬低 ‹*efforts, success*›
- **cry off** *vi* Brit colloq 打退堂鼓; **to ~ off from doing sth.** 变卦不做某事
- **cry out**

A *vi* (call out) 呼喊; (yell) 叫喊; **to ~ out to sb.** 朝某人叫喊; **to ~ out for sth./sb.** lit 呼喊着要求得到某物/某人; fig 迫切需要某物/某人; **to ~ out for help** 大声呼救; **for ~ing out loud!** colloq 我的天哪!; **to ~ out in pain/ecstasy** 痛得/狂喜得大叫

B *vt* **to ~ one's eyes/heart out** 痛哭流涕

crybaby /'kraɪbeɪbi/ *n* colloq pej 爱哭的人

crying /'kraɪɪŋ/

A *n* [u] 哭泣

B *adj attrib* **1** (very bad) 糟透的 ‹*injustice, waste, neglect*›; **it's a ~ shame, the way they treat their children** 他们这样对待孩子实在不像话 **2** (great, desperate) 极度的 ‹*urgency, shortage*›; **a ~ need for more nurses** 增加护士的迫切需要

cryobiology /ˌkraɪəʊbaɪ'ɒlədʒi/ *n* [u] 低温生物学

cryogenics /ˌkraɪə'dʒenɪks/ *npl + v sing* **1** Phys 低温学 **2** = **cryonics**

cryonics /kraɪ'ɒnɪks/ *npl + v sing* 人体冷冻学 [将病人躯体冷冻留待将来有治疗方法可使其痊愈的科学]

cryosurgery /ˌkraɪəʊ'sɜːdʒəri/ *n* [u] 冷冻手术

cryotherapy /ˌkraɪə'θerəpi/ *n* [u] 低温疗法

crypt /krɪpt/ *n* 教堂地下室

cryptanalysis /ˌkrɪptə'nælɪsɪs/ *n* [u] (process) 密码破译; (art) 密码破译法

cryptic /'krɪptɪk/ *adj* 隐秘的 ‹*allusion, remark*›; 神秘的 ‹*smile*›; 难解的 ‹*code, message, puzzle*›; 扑朔迷离的 ‹*crossword, clue*›

cryptically /'krɪptɪkli/ *adv* 隐晦地 ‹*remark, allude*›; 神秘地 ‹*smile*›; **~ worded** 措词隐晦的

crypto- /'krɪptəʊ/ *combining form* 隐蔽的; **~communist** 地下共产党员

cryptogram /'krɪptəgræm/ *n* (encoded message) 密文; (with pictures or symbols) 密码图

cryptographer /ˌkrɪp'tɒgrəfə(r)/ ▸**p. 409** *n* 密码专家

cryptography /ˌkrɪp'tɒgrəfi/ *n* [u] 密码学

crystal /'krɪstl/

A *n* **1** [c] Chem 结晶体 **2** [u and c] Miner 水晶 **3** [u] (glass) 晶质玻璃; **a ~ vase/chandelier** 晶质玻璃花瓶/枝形吊灯 **4** [u] (articles) 晶质玻璃制品

B *adj* liter 清澈的 ‹*waters, fountain*›; 水晶般的 ‹*purity, clarity*›

crystal: ~ ball 水晶球 [用于占卜预测未来]; **~ clear** *adj* **1** (transparent, unclouded) 清澈的 ‹*water*›; 清晰的 ‹*TV picture, sound*›; **2** (easily understood) 显而易见的 ‹*idea, explanation*›; **it is now ~ clear what happened** 发生了什么现在已经一清二楚; **~-gazing** *n* [u] **1** (divination) 水晶球占卜; **2** (prediction) 预测未来

crystalline /'krɪstəlaɪn/ *adj* 晶体的 ‹*structure*›; 结晶的 ‹*mineral, sulphur*›

crystallize /'krɪstəlaɪz/

A *vi* **1** Chem, Miner «*salt, liquid, mineral*» 结晶 **2** fig (become clear) «*plans, thoughts*» 成形; **to ~ into sth.** 形成具体的某事物

B *vt* **1** Chem, Miner «*chemical process, reagent*» 使…结晶 ‹*chemical solution, rock*› **2** fig (make clear) «*experience, discussion*» 使…具体化 ‹*plans, thoughts*›; **to ~ sth. into sth.** 使某事物成为具体的某事物

crystallized /'krɪstəlaɪzd/ *adj* 蜜饯的; **~ fruit** 蜜饯果品

crystallography /ˌkrɪstə'lɒgrəfi/ *n* [u] 晶体学

CSC *abbr* = **Civil Service Commission**

CSE *abbr* Brit Hist = **Certificate of Secondary Education** 中等教育证书

CS gas *n* [u] 催泪性毒气

CST *abbr* amer = **Central Standard Time**

CT *abbr* **1** = **computerized** *or* **computed tomography** 计算机断层照相术 **2** Amer = **Connecticut**

ct *abbr* = **carat**

CTC *abbr* Brit = **City Technology College**

cub /kʌb/ *n* **1** Zool 幼兽; **a lion/tiger ~** 幼狮/幼虎 **2** **Cub (Scout)** 幼童军 [指少年童子军]

Cuba /'kjuːbə/ *pr n* 古巴

Cuban /'kjuːbən/ ▸**p. 503**

A *adj* (of Cuba) 古巴的; (of the people) 古巴人的

B *n* 古巴人

Cuban heel *n* 半高跟

cubbyhole /'kʌbɪhəʊl/ *n* colloq **1** (cramped space) 窄小空间 **2** (snug room) 舒适小房间 **3** (storage space) 小储藏间

cube /kjuːb/

A *n* **1** (small block) 小方块 **2** Math (geometry) 立方体 **3** Math (multiplication of number) 三次幂

B *vt* **1** Math 求…的立方 ‹*number*› **2** Culin 把…切成小方块 ‹*meat, potato*›

cube: ~ farm *n* esp Amer hum 方格农庄 [指分成若干小隔间的大办公室]; **~ root** *n* 立方根

cubic /'kjuːbɪk/ *adj* **1** (cube-shaped) 立方形的 ‹*structure, container, molecule*› **2** (in measurements) 立方的; **two ~ metres** 两立方米 **3** Math 三次的; **a ~ equation/function** 三次方程/函数

cubic capacity *n* (of container) 容量; (of engine) 容积

cubicle /'kjuːbɪkl/ *n* 小隔间

cubic measure *n* 立方单位制

cubism /'kjuːbɪzəm/ *n* [u] 立体派

cubist /'kjuːbɪst/

A *adj* 立体派的 ‹*painting, painter, style*›

B *n* 立体派画家

cub reporter ▸**p. 409** *n* colloq 初出茅庐的记者

cuckoo /'kʊkuː/

A *n* Zool 杜鹃; **the ~ in the nest** fig pej 不速之客

B *adj* colloq 疯狂的 ‹*person, idea, behaviour*›; **to go ~** 发疯

cuckoo clock *n* 布谷鸟自鸣钟

cucumber /'kjuːkʌmbə(r)/ *n* 黄瓜; **as cool as a ~** 非常镇静的

cud /kʌd/ *n* [u] 反刍的食物; **to chew the ~** lit 反刍; fig 反复考虑

cuddle /'kʌdl/

A *vt* 搂住 ‹*person, teddy bear*›; **she ~d the baby in her arms** 她把宝宝搂在怀里

B *vi* «*lovers*» 卿卿我我

C *n* 搂抱; **to have a ~** 拥抱一下; **to give sb. a ~** 给某人一个拥抱

Phrasal verb

- **cuddle up**

A *vi* **to ~ up to** *or* **against sb./sth.** 偎依着某人/某物; **to ~ up for warmth** 偎依着取暖

B *vt* **to be ~d up to** *or* **against sb./sth.** 偎依着某人/某物; **to be ~d up (together)** 依偎在一起

cuddly /'kʌdli/ *adj* **1** (soft) 毛茸茸的 ‹*teddy bear, small animal*› **2** (affectionate) 和蔼可亲的 ‹*person*›

cuddly toy *n* 动物毛绒玩具

cudgel /'kʌdʒl/

A *n* 短棍; **to take up the ~s for** *or* **on behalf of sb./sth.** (support) 毅然支持某人/某事物; (defend) 奋起保卫某人/某事物

B *vt* (*pres p etc.* **-ll-** Brit, **-l-** Amer) 用短棍打; **to ~ sb. with sth.** 用某物打某人; **to ~ one's brain(s)** fig 冥思苦想

cue[1] /kjuː/

A *n* **1** (signal) 暗示; Theat, TV, Radio, Cin (signal to start performing) 提示; (prompt) 提白; Mus 提示音; **the ~ for sth./to do sth.** 某事/做某事的信号; **your ~ is 'here comes the king'** 你一听到"国王驾到"就上场; **to come in on ~** 听到提示音就进来; **to give sb. the ~ to enter** 提示某人上场; **as if on ~** iron 似乎接到信号一样; **(right** *or* **bang) on ~** 恰好在这个时候 **2** fig (example) 榜样; **to take one's ~ from sb.** 照某人的样子做

B *vt* 提示…开始表演 ‹*actor*›; 在表演中切入 ‹*speech, entrance, lights*›; **~ camera one!** 切入一号摄影机!

cue[2] Snooker, Billiards, Pool

A *n* 球杆

B *vt* 用球杆击

C *vi* [使用球杆] 击球

cue: ~ ball *n* 主球; **~ card** *n* [为播音员提词的] 提示卡

cuff[1] /kʌf/ *n* **1** (end part of sleeve) 袖口; **off the ~** (unprepared) 未经准备地; (casually) 随意地; **to speak off the ~** 即兴说几句 **2** Amer (on trousers) 翻边 **3** **cuffs** *pl* colloq (handcuff) 手铐; **put the ~s on him** 给他戴上手铐

cuff[2]

A *vt* (hit, slap) 拍打; **she ~ed him playfully on the ear** 她闹着玩地打了他一耳光

B *n* (hit, slap) 拍打

cufflink /'kʌflɪŋk/ *n* [衬衫的] 袖口链扣; **a pair of ~s** 一对袖口链扣

cuisine /kwɪ'ziːn/ *n* [u and c] (style of cooking) 烹饪; (food cooked) 饭菜; **French/Italian ~** 法国/意大利菜式

cul-de-sac /'kʌldəsæk/ *n* 死胡同; **they found themselves in a political ~** 他们发现自己在政治上陷入僵局

culinary /'kʌlmərі, -neri/ *adj* 烹饪的; **the ~ art(s)** 烹饪技术

cull /kʌl/

A *vt* **1** (slaughter) 限量捕杀 ‹*seals, elephants, herd*› **2** (select) 挑出 ‹*information, quotations*›

B *n* **1** (slaughter) 限量捕杀 **2** (animals killed) 限量捕杀的动物

culminate /'kʌlmɪneɪt/ *vi* 告终; **to ~ in sb.** *or* **sb.'s doing sth.** «*efforts, career, process*» 以某人做某事告终; **a long struggle that ~d in success** 以胜利告终的长期斗争

culmination /ˌkʌlmɪ'neɪʃn/ *n* **1** [c] (outcome) 结果 **2** [u] (high point of work, career) 巅峰 **3** [u] (process of culminating) 告终

culottes /kjuː'lɒts/ *npl* 裙裤; **a pair of ~** 一条裙裤

culpable /'kʌlpəbl/ *adj* formal 应受责备的; **to be ~ for sth.** 因某事而应受责备

culpable: ~ homicide *n* [u] 过失杀人; **~ negligence** *n* [u] 重大疏忽

culpably /'kʌlpəbli/ *adv* formal 应受责备地

culprit /'kʌlprɪt/ *n* **1** (guilty person) 犯错的人; (criminal) 罪犯 **2** (cause of problem) 问题的根源

cult /kʌlt/
A *n* **1** (religious group) 异教团体 **2** (religious practice) 宗教信仰; **the ～ of ancestor worship** 供奉祖先的习俗 **3** (excessive admiration) 狂热崇拜; **the ～ of sth./sb.** 对某事物/某人的狂热崇拜 **4** esp pej (craze) 狂热; **the current healthy-eating ～** 当前的健康饮食时尚
B *modif* 受追捧的 ‹*band, TV series, writer, film*›

cultivar /ˈkʌltɪvɑː(r)/ *n* 栽培品种

cultivate /ˈkʌltɪveɪt/ *vt* **1** (prepare and use) 耕作 ‹*land, soil*› **2** (raise, grow) 种植 ‹*crops, plants*›; 栽培 ‹*flowers*› **3** (improve, educate) 培养 ‹*interests, tastes*›; 陶冶 ‹*mind*› **4** (develop) 逐渐形成 ‹*sense of responsibility*›; 建立 ‹*friendship, relationship*› **5** (win friendship of) 结交 ‹*person*›

cultivated /ˈkʌltɪveɪtɪd/ *adj* **1** Agric 耕作的 ‹*land*›; 栽培的 ‹*crops*› **2** (educated, refined) 有修养的 ‹*person, manners*›; 高雅的 ‹*tastes*›

cultivation /ˌkʌltɪˈveɪʃn/ *n* [u] **1** Agric 耕种; **under ～** 正在耕种的; **to be out of ～** 处于休耕期 **2** (development) (of skill, quality) 培养; (of relationship) 建立 **3** (refinement) 教养; **a veneer of ～** 彬彬有礼的伪装

cultivator /ˈkʌltɪveɪtə(r)/ ▸**p. 409** *n* **1** (machine) 耕耘机 **2** (person) 耕种者; **the ～ of several new varieties of roses** 培育了几个玫瑰新品种的人

cultural /ˈkʌltʃərəl/ *adj* **1** (aesthetic) 文化艺术的; **a ～ festival** 文化艺术节; **his interests are mainly ～** 他主要对文化艺术方面的东西感兴趣 **2** Sociol 文化的 ‹*background, differences*›; **the origins of racism are ～** 种族主义的根源是文化方面的; **the ～ diversity of British society** 英国社会的文化多样性

cultural attaché ▸**p. 409** *n* 文化参赞

culturally /ˈkʌltʃərəli/ *adv* **1** (aesthetically, intellectually) 在文化艺术方面 ‹*sophisticated*›; **a politically troubled but ～ refined epoch** 一个政治动荡但文化艺术卓有成就的时代 **2** Sociol 在文化方面 ‹*deprived, ingrained*›; **a ～ diverse country** 文化多样化的国家; **～ speaking** 从文化上说; **to be ～ determined** 由文化决定

Cultural Revolution *n* Hist **the ～** [中国的]文化大革命

culture /ˈkʌltʃə(r)/ *n* **1** [u] (the arts, intellectual achievement) 文化; **Greek ～** 希腊文明; **to bring ～ to the masses** 普及文化艺术 **2** [u and c] Sociol (of particular group) 文化群体; (way of life) 文化方式; **the junk food/mass media ～** 垃圾食品/大众传媒文化; **US popular ～** 美国大众文化 **3** [u] Agric (of plants) 种植 **4** [c] Biol 培养菌; **a ～ of cholera germs** 培养的霍乱菌

culture-bound *adj* **= culture-specific**

cultured /ˈkʌltʃəd/ *adj* 高雅的 ‹*person, tastes*›

culture dish *n* 培养皿

cultured pearl *n* 人工养殖珍珠

culture: ～-fair *adj* Amer 文化公平的 ‹*test, assessment, approach*›; **～ gap** *n* 文化差距; **～ medium** *n* 培养基; **～ shock** *n* [u] 文化冲击; **～-specific** *adj* 某种文化特有的 ‹*belief, term, disease*›; 受文化局限的 ‹*test*›; **～ vulture** *n* colloq hum 文化迷

culvert /ˈkʌlvət/ *n* (pipe) 涵洞管道; (tunnel) 涵洞

-cum- /kʌm/ *combining form* 兼; **a garage ～workshop** 车库兼车间; **a gardener ～handyman** 园艺师兼巧手工匠

cumbersome /ˈkʌmbəsəm/ *adj* **1** (unwieldy) 笨重的 ‹*box, machine*› **2** (slow, complicated) 笨拙的 ‹*method*›; 累赘的 ‹*grammatical construction*›

Cumbria /ˈkʌmbrɪə/ *pr n* 坎布里亚郡

cumin /ˈkʌmɪn/ *n* [u] 莳萝籽

cum laude /ˌkʌm ˈlɔːdi, ˌkʊm ˈlaʊdeɪ/ *adv* Amer 以优等成绩

cumulative /ˈkjuːmjʊlətɪv, Amer -leɪtɪv/ *adj* 累积的 ‹*effect, stress*›

cumulatively /ˈkjuːmjʊlətɪvli, Amer -leɪtɪvli/ *adv* 累积地 ‹*affect, build up*›

cumulative voting *n* [u] 累积投票制 [投票人可将与候选人人数相等的选票全部投给一个或分投几个候选人]

cumulonimbus /ˌkjuːmjʊləʊˈnɪmbəs/ *n* [u and c] (**cumulonimbi** /ˌkjuːmjʊləʊˈnɪmbi/) 积雨云

cumulus /ˈkjuːmjʊləs/ *n* [u and c] (*pl* **cumuli** /ˈkjuːmjʊli/) 积云; **a ～ cloud** 一块积云

cunnilingus /ˌkʌnɪˈlɪŋgəs/ *n* [u] 舔阴; **to perform ～ on sb.** 为某女子舔阴

cunning /ˈkʌnɪŋ/
A *adj* **1** (crafty) 狡猾的 ‹*person, trap, wink*›; **to be ～ at sth./doing sth.** 在某事/做某事上很狡猾; **he's a ～ old fox** 他是只老狐狸 **2** (clever, ingenious) 精巧的 ‹*gadget*›; 巧妙的 ‹*argument*›; **to be ～ at sth./doing sth.** 在某事/在做某事方面很灵巧
B *n* [u] **1** pej (craftiness) 狡猾; **he had a reputation for ～** 他是出了名的狡猾 **2** (cleverness, ingenuity) 灵巧

cunningly /ˈkʌnɪŋli/ *adv* **1** (craftily) 狡猾地 ‹*deceive*› **2** (cleverly) 巧妙地 ‹*solve*›

cunt /kʌnt/ *n* taboo sl **1** (female genitals) 屄 taboo sl **2** (person) 傻屄 taboo sl

cup /kʌp/
A *n* **1** (container) 杯子 **2** (cupful) 一杯; **a ～ of tea** 一杯茶; **(not) sb.'s ～ of tea** fig （并非）某人的喜好 **3** Sport (competition) 优胜杯赛; (trophy itself) 奖杯; **to win a ～ for swimming** 赢得游泳奖杯; **in the ～** 在优胜杯赛中; **a good ～ run** 在杯赛中良好的势头 **4** (of bra) 罩杯 **5** (of flower, acorn) 萼 **6** Relig (chalice) 圣餐杯
B *vt* (*pres p etc.* **-pp-**) **1** 使成杯状; **to ～ one's hands (around sth.)** 把双手合成杯状（捧住某物）; **to ～ one's hands around one's mouth** 双手在嘴上做成喇叭状 **2** (hold) 捧起; **to ～ sth. (in** *or* **with one's hands)** （用双手）捧起 ‹*chin, breast, ball*›

cupboard /ˈkʌbəd/ *n* 橱柜; **a kitchen ～** 厨房用橱柜; **the ～ is bare** fig 没什么钱了

cupboard: ～ love *n* [u] Brit 有所企图的亲热; **～ space** *n* [u] 橱柜储存空间

cupcake /ˈkʌpkeɪk/ *n* 纸杯蛋糕

Cup Final *n* Brit 优胜杯决赛

cupful /ˈkʌpfʊl/ *n* 一杯

Cupid /ˈkjuːpɪd/ *pr n* 丘比特; **to play ～** 做媒人

cupola /ˈkjuːpələ/ *n* 穹顶

cuppa /ˈkʌpə/ *n* Brit colloq 一杯茶

cupro-nickel /ˌkjuːprəʊˈnɪkl/ *n* [u] 铜镍合金

cup tie *n* 优胜杯比赛

cur /kɜː(r)/ *n* pej **1** (dog) 恶狗 **2** dated pej (person) 卑鄙小人

curable /ˈkjʊərəbl/ *adj* 可治愈的

curacao /ˌkjʊərəˈsəʊ, Amer -ˈsaʊ/ *n* [u and c] 库拉索酒 [一种用橘子皮酿制的利口酒]

curate /ˈkjʊərət/ *n* 助理牧师

curate's egg *n* Brit 好坏参半之物

curative /ˈkjʊərətɪv/ *adj* 能治病的 ‹*drug, treatment, power, properties*›

curator /ˌkjʊəˈreɪtə(r), Amer *also* ˈkjʊərətər/ ▸**p. 409** *n* [博物馆等收藏机构的] 馆长

curb /kɜːb/
A *vt* (control) 控制 ‹*feelings, inflation*›; 限制 ‹*police powers, public spending*›; **to ～ one's temper** 克制脾气
B *n* **1** (control) 控制; **a ～ on sth.** 对某事物的控制 **2** Amer **= kerb**

curb: ～ cut *n* Amer **= dropped kerb**; **～side** *adj* Amer **= kerbside**; **～stone** *n* Amer **= kerbstone**; **～ weight** *n* Amer **= kerb weight**

curd /kɜːd/ *n* [u], **curds** /kɜːdz/ *npl* 凝乳; **～s and whey** 酥酪

curd cheese *n* [u] 凝乳干酪

curdle /ˈkɜːdl/
A *vi* 凝结; **to make sb.'s blood ～** 把人吓得浑身冰凉
B *vt* 使凝结; **to ～ the blood** 令人惊恐万分

cure /kjʊə(r)/
A *vt* **1** Med 治愈 ‹*disease*›; **to ～ sb. of sth.** 治好某人的某种病 **2** fig (resolve) 解决 ‹*problem, shortage, unemployment*›; 戒除 ‹*bad habit, jealousy*›; 消除 ‹*misery, poverty*›; **to ～ sb./sth. of sth.** 解决某人/某事物的某问题 **3** Culin (dry) 晒干 ‹*meat, fish, animal skin*›; (salt) 腌制 ‹*meat, fish*›; (smoke) 熏制 ‹*meat, fish*›; (roast) 烤制 ‹*tobacco*›
B *n* **1** [c] (remedy) 疗法; (drug) 药物; **a ～ for sth.** 某种病的治疗方法 **2** [u] (recovery) 治愈; **to effect** *or* **work a ～** 治愈; **beyond** *or* **past ～** 无药可治的; ▸**prevention** **3** [u and c] (solution) 解决方法; **a ～ for sth.** 解决某事的方法; **the situation is beyond ～** 这种局面已无可救药了

cure-all *n* lit, fig 万应灵药

curfew /ˈkɜːfjuː/ *n* [c and u] (regulation) 宵禁令; (time) 宵禁时间; **to impose/lift a ～** 实施/撤销宵禁; **after ～** 开始宵禁后; **under ～** 在宵禁中

curie /ˈkjʊəri/ *n* 居里 [放射性强度单位]

curio /ˈkjʊərɪəʊ/ *n* (*pl* **～s**) 珍稀物品

curiosity /ˌkjʊərɪˈɒsəti/ *n* **1** [u] (desire to know) 好奇; **to arouse/satisfy sb.'s ～** 引起/满足某人的好奇心; **out of ～** 出于好奇; **～ about sth.** 对某事物的好奇; **～ killed the cat** Prov 过分好奇惹是非 **2** [c] (object) 珍稀物; **a collection of 18th-century curiosities** 18世纪古玩藏品 **3** [c] (person) 怪人

curious /ˈkjʊərɪəs/ *adj* **1** (interested) 好奇的; **to be ～ about sth.** 对某事物好奇; **I'm just ～!** 我只是好奇! **2** (odd) 稀奇古怪的 ‹*object, incident, remark*›

curiously /ˈkjʊərɪəsli/ *adv* **1** (oddly) 古怪地 ‹*behave, designed*›; 奇怪地 ‹*unconcerned, silent*›; **～ enough, ...** 说来也怪，… **2** (out of curiosity) 好奇地 ‹*ask, peer*›

curl /kɜːl/
A *vt* **1** (make curly) 弄卷 ‹*hair*› **2** (coil) 卷曲 ‹*object, edge*›; 弯曲 ‹*body*›; **to ～ sth. round** *or* **around sth.** 用某物缠绕某物; **she ～ed her body around the pole** 她将身体缠绕在柱子上; **to ～ itself round sth.** «*snake*» 盘绕某物; **she ～ herself into a ball** 她蜷成一团; **to ～ one's fingers/toes round sth.** 用手指捏住/脚趾夹住某物; **to ～ one's legs under oneself** 盘腿坐下
B *vi* **1** (be curly) «*hair*» 变卷; **it's enough to make your hair ～** fig colloq 这够让你毛骨悚然的了 **2** (coil) «*object, edge*» 打卷; «*plant*» 盘绕; **smoke ～ed upwards** 烟袅袅上升; **his finger ～ed around the trigger** 他的手指扣住扳机; **his lip ～ed** 他撇了撇嘴; **to make sb.'s toes ～** fig colloq 使某人厌恶
C *n* **1** (of hair) 卷发; **her ～s are natural** 她的头发是自来卷 **2** (object) 卷状物; (shape or movement) 卷曲; (wave) 浪卷; **a ～ of smoke** 一缕青烟; **'of course,' he said, with a ～ of his lip** “当然，”他撇撇嘴说道

Phrasal verb

• **curl up**
A *vi* **1** (sit or lie in curved position) «*person*» 蜷曲; **to ～ up (in bed) with a good book** （在床上）蜷起身子看一本好书; **to ～ up into a ball** 蜷成一团; **to ～ up laughing** *or* **with laughter** 笑得直不起腰来; **to ～ up with embarrassment** 十分窘迫; **to ～ up and die** fig 羞得无地自容 **2** (curve or turn up) «*leaf, piece of paper, edge*» 卷起; **his lip ～ed up in scorn** 他轻蔑地撇了撇嘴
B *vt* **1** **to be ～ed up** (sit or lie in curved position) «*person, animal*» 蜷成一团 **2** [**～ sth. up, ～**

up sth.] (curve or turn up) 卷起 ‹object›; 撅起 ‹lip›; **to be ~ed up** 起卷; **to ~ oneself up into a ball** 将身体蜷成一团

C *v refl* **to ~ oneself** (sit) 蜷曲着坐; (lie) 蜷曲着躺; **she ~ed herself up on the sofa** 她蜷卧在长沙发上

curler /'kɜːlə(r)/ *n* 卷发夹; **to put one's ~s in** 戴上卷发夹; **to take one's ~s out** 取下卷发夹

curlew /'kɜːljuː/ *n* (*pl* ~ *or* ~**s**) 鹬

curlicue /'kɜːlɪkjuː/ *n* (in calligraphy) 花体; (in design) 花饰

curling /'kɜːlɪŋ/ ▸ **p. 307** *n* [u] 冰壶运动

curling tongs *npl* 烫发钳

curly /'kɜːli/ *adj* 卷曲的

curly-haired, curly-headed *adjs* 头发打卷儿的

curmudgeon /kəː'mʌdʒ(ə)n/ *n* 脾气坏的人

curmudgeonly /kɜː'mʌdʒənli/ *adj* 脾气坏的 ‹*person*›; 粗暴的 ‹*attitude, refusal*›

currant /'kʌrənt/ *n* **1** (dried fruit) 无核小葡萄干 **2** (shrub, berry) 茶藨子

currant: ~ bun *n* 葡萄干小圆面包; **~ loaf** *n* 葡萄干面包

currency /'kʌrənsi/ *n* **1** [c] Fin 货币 **2** [u] (of word, term) 通行; **to gain ~** 开始流行; **to give** *or* **lend ~ to sth.** 散布某事

currency: ~ converter *n* 货币换算工具; **~ devaluation** *n* [c and u] 货币贬值; **~ market** *n* 货币市场; **~ unit** *n* 货币单位

current /'kʌrənt/

A *adj* **1** (present) 当前的 ‹*situation, price*›; 现在的 ‹*boy/girlfriend, leader*›; **the ~ year/month/week** 本年度/本月/本周; **the ~ concern about pollution** 当前对污染的关注; **the ~ issue of a magazine** 杂志的最近一期 **2** (generally used or accepted) 流行的 ‹*opinions, beliefs, term*›; **in ~ use** 通用中

B *n* **1** (flow) (of electricity) 电流; (of water) 水流; (of air) 气流 **2** fig (tendency) 趋势; **to go** *or* **drift with the ~** 随大溜; **to go against the ~** 逆潮流而动; **a ~ of opinion** 意见倾向

current: ~ account *n* Brit 活期账户; **~ account deficit** *n* 经常项目赤字; **~ account surplus** *n* 经常项目盈余; **~ affairs** *npl* 时事; **~ assets** *npl* 流动资产; **~ liabilities** *npl* 短期债务

currently /'kʌrəntli/ *adv* 当前; **are you ~ employed?** 你目前有工作吗？; **~ held opinions** 时下的观点

curriculum /kə'rɪkjʊləm/ *n* (*pl* ~**s** *or* **curricula** /kə'rɪkjʊlə/) 课程; **to be on the ~** 列入课程

curriculum: ~ development *n* [u] 课程改革; **~ vitae** /kəˌrɪkjʊləm 'viːtaɪ/ *n* (*pl* **curricula vitae**) 简历

curry[1] /'kʌri/

A *n* [c and u] 咖喱菜肴; **(a) chicken ~** 咖喱鸡; **a hot/mild ~** 浓味/淡味咖喱菜

B *vt* 用咖喱粉烧 ‹*meat, vegetables*›; **curried chicken** 咖喱烧鸡

curry[2] *vt* **to ~ favour with sb.** 讨好某人

curry powder *n* [u] 咖喱粉

curse /kɜːs/

A *n* **1** (spell) 咒语; **to put a ~ on ...** 对…下咒; **to be** *or* **live under a ~** 受诅咒 **2** (swear word) 骂人话 **3** (affliction) 祸害; **the ~ of poverty** 贫困这个祸患之源; **to be a ~ to sb.** 对某人来说是个祸害

Currencies and money

■ Chinese money:

	Currency	Abbreviation	Standard Symbol	
Chinese Mainland	Renminbi Yuan (人民币元)	RMB¥	CNY	1 CNY (圆 or 元) = 10 jiao (角) 1 jiao (角) = 10 fen (分)
Hong Kong	Hong Kong Dollar (港币 or 港元)	HK$	HKD	1 HKD (圆 or 元) = 100 cents (分)
Macao	Macao Pataca (澳门元 or 澳元)	Pat or P	MOP	1 MOP (圆 or 元) = 100 avos (分)
Taiwan	New Taiwan Dollar (新台币)	NT$	NWD	1 NWD (圆 or 元) = 10 jiao (角) 1 jiao (角) = 100 fen (分)

■ There are no abbreviations for 'jiao' or 'fen'. The colloquial term for 'yuan' is 'kuai' (块) and for 'jiao' is 'mao' (毛):

Written	Spoken
RMB¥0.10	一角 / 一毛
RMB¥0.20	两角 / 两毛
RMB¥0.35	三角五分 or 三毛五分 or 三毛五
RMB¥1.00	一元
RMB¥2.00	两元
RMB¥3.55	三元五角五分 or 三块五毛五分 or 三块五毛五
RMB¥ 200	两百元 or 二百元
RMB¥180	一百八十元
RMB¥100.23	一百零二角三分 or 一百元二角三分
RMB¥100.04	一百元零四分 or 一百零四分
RMB¥1000	一千元
RMB¥1600	一千六百元
RMB¥1,050.60	一千零五十元零六角 or 一千零五十元六角
RMB¥1,050.06	一千零五十元零六分
RMB¥10,000.00	一万元
RMB¥100,000.00	十万元
RMB¥1,000,000.00	一百万元

■ British money:

Written	Spoken
1p	一便士
60p	六十便士
£1	一镑
£1.50	一镑五十便士
£10 sterling	十英镑
a ten-pound note	十英镑纸币
a two-pound coin	两英镑硬币
a 2p piece	两便士硬币

■ USA money:

Written	Spoken
1c	一美分
50c	五十美分
$1	一美元
$3.60	三美元六十美分
a twenty-dollar bill	二十美元的纸币
a one-dollar coin	一美元硬币
a 5c piece	五美分硬币

■ How much?

How much is it? — It's £20
= 多少钱？—— 20 英镑

How much does the printer cost?
— It costs £100
= 打印机多少钱？—— 100 英镑

What is the price of this TV?
— It is ¥3,500
It is over/more than ¥3,500
It is under/less than ¥3,500
= 电视机价格是多少？
—— 3,500 元
超过 3,500 元 / 3,500 元以上
不到 3,500 元

■ Handling money:

a 30-pence stamp
= 面值 30 便士的邮票

a £15 ticket
= 一张 15 英镑的票

a £1,000 cheque
= 1,000 英镑的支票

£5 in change
= 5 英镑零钱

£500 in travellers' cheques
= 500 英镑的旅行支票

a twenty-thousand-pound scholarship
= 20,000 英镑奖学金

¥100 in cash
= 100 元人民币现金

a cheque for ¥20,000
= 20,000 元人民币支票

Could you change a £50 note for five tens, please?
= 你能把 50 英镑的纸币换成 5 张 10 英镑的吗？

Could you change a £5 note for small change, please?
= 你能把 5 英镑纸币换成零钱吗？

Can you change my pounds into yuan?
= 你能把我的英镑换成人民币吗？

How would you like to pay?
— I'd like to pay by cheque/cash/card
= 你想怎么付款？
—— 我想用支票 / 现金 / 银行卡付

In what currency would you like to pay?
— I'd like to pay in Hong Kong dollars
= 你想用什么货币来付？—— 我想用港元

What is the exchange rate from Pounds Sterling to Yuan Renminbi?
— It is 1 pound to 12.8 yuan
= 英镑对人民币的汇率是多少？
—— 1 英镑兑换 12.8 元

B *vt* [1] (put curse on) 对…下咒; **to be ~d** «*person, place, enterprise*» 被施了魔咒; **to be ~d with sth.** 受某事物的折磨 [2] (express anger about) 咒骂; **to ~ sb./sth. for sth.** 因某事物而咒骂某人/某事物; **I ~ the day that he was born!** 他一出娘胎我就诅咒他!

C *vi* 诅咒; **to ~ and swear** 谩骂; **to ~ at sb./sth.** 诅咒某人/某事物

cursive /'kɜːsɪv/ *adj* 草书的; **in ~ script** 用草体字

cursor /'kɜːsə(r)/ *n* 光标

cursorily /'kɜːsərəli/ *adv* 草草地 ‹*inspect, read*›; **to glance ~ at ...** 向…匆匆瞥一眼

cursor key *n* 光标键

cursory /'kɜːsəri/ *adj* 草草的 ‹*inspection, reading*›; **to give sth. a ~ glance** 匆匆地瞥一眼某物

curt /kɜːt/ *adj* 唐突无礼的 ‹*greeting, manner*›; **to be ~ with sb.** 对某人唐突无礼

curtail /kɜː'teɪl/ *vt* [1] (restrict) 限制 ‹*rights, freedoms, activities*› [2] (cut back) 减少 ‹*spending, service*› [3] (cut short) 缩短 ‹*speech, holidays*›; **a promising political career ~ed by scandal** 被丑闻断送前途的政治生涯

curtailment /kɜː'teɪlmənt/ *n* [c and u] [1] (of rights, freedom) 限制 [2] (of expenditure, service) 缩减 [3] (of holiday, career) 中断

curtain /'kɜːtn/

A *n* [1] (for window) 窗帘; (for door) 门帘; **a pair of ~s** 一副窗帘; **to open/draw the ~s** 拉开/拉上窗帘 [2] fig (screen, cover) 幕状物; **a ~ of rain** 雨幕; **a ~ of silence** 以沉默编织的帷幕 [3] Theat 帷幕; **after the final ~** 最后一幕之后; **to raise/lower the ~** 启幕/落幕; **the ~ has fallen on ...** …结束了 ‹*career, era*›; **the ~ rose on the new millennium** 新千年开始了 [4] **to be ~s (for sb.)** colloq (某人) 该完蛋了

B *vt* 给…装上帘子 ‹*window, room*›

Phrasal verb

- **curtain off** *vt* [~ **sth. off**, ~ **off sth.**] 用帘子隔开; **to ~ sth. off from sth.** 把…和某物用帘子隔开 ‹*hospital bed, cubicle, alcove*›; **to be ~ed off from the rest of the room** 被帘子和房间的其他部分隔开

curtain: ~ **call** *n* 谢幕; **to take a ~ call** 上台谢幕; ~ **pole** *n* 窗帘杆; ~ **raiser** *n* [1] (entertainment) 开场小戏; [2] fig (precursor) 序曲; ~ **ring** *n* 窗帘挂环; **~-up** *n* [u] 幕启

curtly /'kɜːtli/ *adv* 唐突无礼地

curtness /'kɜːtnɪs/ *n* [u] 唐突无礼

curtsy, curtsey /'kɜːtsi/

A *vi* (*pt, pp* **curtsied** *or* **~ed**) 行屈膝礼; **to ~ to sb.** 向某人行屈膝礼

B *n* (*pl* **curtsies** *or* **~s**) 屈膝礼; **to make** *or* **drop a ~** 行屈膝礼

curvaceous /kɜː'veɪʃəs/ *adj* 有曲线美的

curvature /'kɜːvətʃə(r), Amer -tʃʊər/ *n* (fact of being curved) 弯曲; (degree to which sth. is curved) 曲度; ~ **of the spine** 脊柱弯曲度; **the ~ of the earth's surface** 地球表面的曲率

curve /kɜːv/

A *n* (in line, on graph) 曲线; (in road) 弯曲处; (of landscape, cheek, hips) 弯曲部分; **~s** [女性的] 曲线轮廓; **in a ~** 以弧线; **on an upward/downward ~** 呈上升/下降趋势; **to be behind/ahead of the ~** fig «*businessman, politician, business, government*» 落后/领先于现时趋势; **the broadcaster has been behind the ~ in launching digital services** 这家广播公司在推出数字服务方面一直都跟不上形势

B *vi* [1] (form a curve) «*path, line*» 弯曲; **to ~ inwards/outwards** 向内/外弯曲; **the road ~s down to the sea** 这条路向下弯弯曲曲通向大海 [2] (move in curve) «*projectile, arm*» 沿曲线运动; «*mouth*» 咧开

C *vt* 使…弯曲 ‹*edge, beam, surface*›; **age has ~d her spine** 岁月压弯了她的脊背

curved /kɜːvd/ *adj* 弯曲的 ‹*arch, road, line, surface*›; 弧形的 ‹*blade, wall*›

curvy /'kɜːvi/ *adj* 有曲线美的

cushion /'kʊʃn/

A *n* [1] (soft furnishing) 垫子; **a seat/chair ~** 坐垫/椅垫 [2] (protection, support) 缓冲物; **a ~ of air** 气垫; **a ~ between carpet and floor** 地毯和地板之间的保护层; **a good ~ against inflation** 对抗通货膨胀的有效手段 [3] (in snooker, billiards, pool) [台球桌内侧边缘的] 弹性衬垫; **to play off the ~** 打反弹球

B *vt* [1] (soften impact of) 缓和…的冲击 ‹*fall, blow*› [2] (protect, support) 使免遭损害; **to ~ sb./sth. against** *or* **from sth.** 使某人/某物免遭某物的伤害

cushion cover *n* 垫子套

cushy /'kʊʃi/ *adj* colloq 舒适的 ‹*life, job*›; **a ~ number** Brit 轻松的工作

cusp /kʌsp/ *n* [1] Dent 牙尖 [2] Astrol (of sign) 黄道记号尖端; (of house) 天宫入口; **she's on the ~ between Sagittarius and Capricorn** 她出生于人马宫和摩羯宫会切的时段 [3] (point of transition) 转折点; **he operates on the ~ between genius and insanity** 他的行为介于天才和疯癫之间

cuss /kʌs/ colloq

A *n* [1] (person) 讨厌的家伙; **a queer old ~** 老怪物 [2] (oath) 诅咒

B *vi* 诅咒

cussed /'kʌsɪd/ *adj* colloq 倔强的

cussedness /'kʌsɪdnɪs/ *n* [u] colloq 倔强

cuss word /'kʌswɜːd/ *n* colloq 骂人话

custard /'kʌstəd/ *n* [u] (sauce) 蛋奶沙司; (dessert) 蛋奶糕

custard: ~ **cream** *n* 奶油夹心饼干; ~ **pie** *n* [c and u] 蛋奶馅饼; (also in slapstick) [滑稽剧中逗乐用的] 蛋奶馅饼; ~ **powder** *n* [u] 蛋奶沙司粉; ~ **tart** *n* [c and u] 蛋挞

custodial /kʌ'stəʊdɪəl/ *adj* [1] Jur 监禁的; **a ~ sentence** 监禁判决 [2] (caring, protecting) 监护的 ‹*duty, care*› [3] (in museum etc.) 看管的 ‹*staff*›

custodian /kʌ'stəʊdɪən/ ▸p. 409 *n* [1] (of collection) 保管人; (of building) 看管者 [2] (of morals, tradition etc.) 卫士

custody /'kʌstədi/ *n* [u] [1] (detention) 拘留; (imprisonment) 监禁; **in ~** 被拘留; **to take sb. into ~** 拘留某人; **to be remanded in ~** 还押候审; **to escape from ~** 逃离羁押 [2] Jur (of minor) 监护; **in the ~ of ...** 由…监护 [3] formal (keeping) 保管; **in the ~ of ...** 由…保管; **in safe ~** 被妥善保管

custom /'kʌstəm/ *n* [1] [c] (convention) 习俗; **it is the ~ to ...** 做…是风俗习惯 [2] [c] (personal habit) 习惯; **it is her ~ to ...** 她的习惯是…; **as is his ~** 按他的习惯 [3] [u] (patronage) 惠顾; **they've lost a lot of ~** 他们失掉了很多顾客; **I shall take my ~ elsewhere** 我将在其他地方买东西; **we would like to have your ~** 欢迎光顾本店

customary /'kʌstəməri, Amer -meri/ *adj* 惯常的 ‹*method, greeting*›; 遵照习俗的 ‹*celebrations*›; **it is ~ for sb. to do sth.** 某人惯常做某事; **as is ~** 按惯例; **his ~ smile** 他惯有的微笑

custom: **~-built**, **~-made** *adjs* 定制的; **~-built for sb./sth.** 为某人/某事定做的; ~ **car** *n* 定制汽车; **~-designed** *adj* 定做的

customer /'kʌstəmə(r)/ *n* [1] (client) 顾客; **the ~ is always right** 顾客永远是对的 [2] colloq (person) 家伙; **she's a difficult ~** 她这个人很难对付; **he's an odd ~** 他是个怪人

customer: ~ **care** *n* [u] 客户服务; **the ~ care department** 客户服务部; ~ **care line** *n* 客服热线; ~ **service department** *n* 客户服务部; ~ **services** *npl* 客户服务部

customize /'kʌstəmaɪz/ *vt* (make) 定做; (adapt) [按顾客要求] 改造

custom-made /ˌkʌstəm'meɪd/ *adj* 定做的

customs /'kʌstəmz/ *npl* 海关; **at ~** 在海关; **to go through ~** 通过海关

customs: **C~ and Excise** *n* Brit (英国) 海关; ~ **clearance** *n* [u] 结关; ~ **declaration** *n* 报关单; ~ **duties** *npl* 关税; ~ **hall** *n* 海关大厅; ~ **house** *n* 海关; ~ **inspection** *n* [u and c] 海关检查; ~ **officer** ▸p. 409 *n* 海关关员; ~ **post** *n* 海关检查站; ~ **service** *n* 海关; ~ **shed** *n* 海关货棚; ~ **union** *n* 关税同盟

cut /kʌt/

A *vt* (*pres p* **-tt-**; *pt, pp* **cut**) [1] (slice) «*knife*» 切 ‹*bread*›; «*scissors*» 剪 ‹*paper*›; «*mower*» 割 ‹*grass*›; «*axe*» 砍; «*saw*» 锯; **to ~ sth. open, to ~ open sth.** 剪开 ‹*bag*›; 锯开 ‹*box*›; **to ~ sth. from sth.** 从某物上切下某物; **to ~ sth. into pieces/slices** 把某物切成小块/小片; **to ~ sth. to shreds** lit 把某物切成碎片; fig 彻底摧毁某物; **the boat was ~ in half** *or* **two by the tanker** 小船被油轮撞成了两截; **to ~ one's ties** *or* **links with sb./sth.** 断绝与某人/某事物的联系 [2] (carve out) 挖出 ‹*tunnel*›; «*scissors*» 剪出 ‹*hole*›; «*axe*» 砍出 ‹*opening*›; 刻出 ‹*inscription*›; **to ~ one's way through the jungle** 在丛林中开辟出一条路来 [3] (accidentally wound) 划破; (deliberately wound) 割破; fig «*wind, remark*» 刺痛 ‹*person*›; **ouch! I've ~ myself** 哎哟! 我把自己割伤了; **to ~ oneself/sb. on sth.** 被某物划伤/某人被某物划伤; **to ~ one's finger/leg open on a branch** 手指/腿被树枝划出很深的口子; **to ~ sb./sth. open** Med 切开 ‹*person, part of body*› [4] (trim) 理 ‹*hair*›; 修剪 ‹*nails, hedge*› [5] (shape) 雕刻 ‹*statue, wood*›; 雕琢 ‹*jewel, glass*›; 裁剪 ‹*paper, pattern, clothes*›; 配 ‹*key*›; **to ~ sth. from sth.** (using scissors) 从某物上剪下某物; (using knife) 在某物中雕出某物; **to ~ sth. into sth.** (using scissors) 把某物剪成某物; (using knife) 把某物雕成某物; **to ~ sth. to shape/size** (using scissors) 把某物剪成形/剪成合适的大小; (using knife) 把某物雕成形/雕成合适的大小 [6] **to ~ sth./sb. free** *or* **loose (from sth.)** (liberate) 使某物/某人 (摆脱某物) 获得自由; **to ~ sb. (free) from the wreckage** 从废墟中把某人解救出来 [7] (reduce) (gen) 减少; Comm, Econ 削减; **to ~ sth. by sth.** 将某物减少某数量; **to ~ prices/taxes** 减价/减税; **to ~ expenditure** 削减开支 [8] (abridge) 删节 ‹*book, film*›; (remove) 删除 ‹*scene, programme*›; **to ~ sth. from sth.** 从某物中删除某物 [9] (edit) 剪辑 ‹*film*› [10] (record) 录制 ‹*disc, album*› [11] (interrupt, sever) 中断 ‹*transmission, programme*›; 切断 ‹*route, supplies*›; **to ~ sth. short, to ~ short sth.** 中断 ‹*activity, career*›; **to ~ a long story short** 长话短说; **to ~ sb. short** 打断某人 [12] colloq (turn off) 关掉 ‹*light, power, engine*› [13] Comput 剪切 ‹*text*›; **to ~ and paste** 剪贴 [14] (divide) 分割; **the wall ~ the city in two** *or* **half** 城墙把这座城一分为二 [15] (mine) 挖 ‹*coal*› [16] (intersect) «*line, road*» 与…相交 ‹*line, road*› [17] colloq (stop) 停止; **to ~ the formalities** 免掉礼节; **~ the chatter**/taboo sl **crap!** 别唠叨了/废话少说! [18] colloq (skip) 逃避 ‹*lecture*›; **to ~ class** 旷课 [19] Brit colloq dated (ignore) 不理睬; **to ~ sb. dead** 对某人视而不见 [20] Games 切 ‹*deck, cards*› [21] (grow) 出 ‹*tooth*›; **to ~ one's teeth on sth.** fig 获得某方面的最初经验 [22] (dilute) 冲淡 ‹*wine, drug*›; **the heroin had been ~ with chalk dust** 海洛因已用粉笔灰稀释了

B *vi* (*pres p* **-tt-**; *pt, pp* **cut**) [1] (slice) «*knife*» 切; «*scissors*» 剪; «*machine, laser*» 切割; «*mower, razor*» 修剪; «*axe*» 砍; **this knife won't ~** 这把刀不快; **this saw doesn't ~ straight** 这把锯子锯不直; **to ~ along/around sth.** 沿着/绕着某处切; **to ~ across sth.** 横切某物; **to ~ both** *or* **two/several ways** fig «*argument*» 两方面/几方面都说得通; «*outcome*» 有

C

利也有弊 [2] (be able to be cut) «*paper, rope, fabric*» 可剪切; «*wood*» 可砍削; «*metal, stone*» 可切割; «*cheese, meat*» 可切; «*grass, hay*» 可割; **this bread ~s well** 这种面包很容易切 [3] (wound) «*criticism, attitude*» 伤人 [4] (move) 移动; (take direct route) 抄近路; **to ~ to the left/right** 拐到左边/右边; **to ~ in front of sb.** (in queue) 插到某人前面; (in car) 抢道超某人的车; **to ~ through/across sth.** 抄近路穿过/越过某处 [5] colloq **to ~ and run** (flee) 撒腿就跑; **to ~ loose** Amer (blurt out) 破口大骂; (revel) 狂欢作乐 [6] Cin, TV (stop filming) 停拍; **~!** 停! [导演指示停止拍摄] [7] Cin, TV (change scene) 切换镜头; **the film scene ~s from the living room to the garden** 电影场景由起居室切换至花园 [8] Games 切牌; **to ~ for sth.** 切牌决定某事

C *n* [1] (stroke, blow) 切 [2] (trim) **to give sb.'s hair a ~** 给某人理发; **to give sb.'s nails a ~** 为某人修剪 (finger) 指甲/ (toe) 趾甲; **to give the grass/hedge a ~** 给草坪/树篱修剪一下 [3] (opening) 切口; (wound) 伤口; **to make a ~ (in sth.)** (在某物上) 开一个切口; **to be a ~ above (sth./sb.)** fig (比某物/某人) 略胜一筹 [4] Culin (of meat) 切下来的一块肉; **a large ~ of meat** 一大块肉 [5] colloq (share) 分成; **what's my ~?** 我分多少? ; **to get** *or* **take a ~ of the profits** 取得一份利润 [6] (hairstyle) 发型 [7] Sewing 款式; **the ~ of the dress** 连衣裙的款式 [8] (reduction) 削减; **tax/pay/wage ~s** 减税/减酬/减薪; **a ~ in sth.** 某事物的减少; **to make a ~ (in sth.)** (对某物) 进行削减 [9] (interruption) 中断; **a power ~** 停电 [10] Publg, Cin (editing) 删节; **to make a ~ (in sth.)** (对某物) 进行删节 [11] Cin (version) 版本 [12] Cin, TV (change of shot) 切换; **a ~ (from sth.) to sth.** (从某镜头) 到某镜头的切换 [13] Games 切牌

D *adj* [1] (divided into pieces) 切开的 ‹*bread, fruit*›; 剪开的 ‹*paper, fabric*›; 劈开的 ‹*trees*›; **fine-~ tobacco** 细烟丝 [2] (detached) 切下的 ‹*piece, slice*›; 割下的 ‹*crop, hay*›; **~ flowers** 鲜切花 [3] (injured) 割破的 ‹*part of body*› [4] (trimmed) 修剪好的 ‹*hair, nails, grass*› [5] (ground) 经雕琢的 ‹*diamond*›; **~ glass** 雕花玻璃 [6] (shortened) 经删节的 ‹*film, version*›; (censored) 删去的 ‹*scene, sentence*›

Phrasal verbs

• **cut across** *vt* [**~ across sth.**]
[1] (take direct route through) 抄近路穿过 ‹*field*›; **to ~ across sb.'s path** (in haste) 突然插到某人前面 [2] fig (transcend) «*ideas, action*» 超越 ‹*barrier, lines*› [3] fig (contradict) «*action, event*» 与…相抵触 ‹*policy, status quo*›

• **cut at** *vt* [**~ at sth.**] 猛砍 ‹*wood, stone, person*›; 狂剪 ‹*hair*›

• **cut away**
A *vt* [**~ sth. away, ~ away sth.**] 切除 ‹*rotten part, excess*›; 剪掉 ‹*border*›; 砍掉 ‹*dead wood*›
B *vi* 反复切削; **to ~ away at sth.** 反复切削某物

• **cut back**
A *vt* [**~ sth. back, ~ back sth.**]
[1] Hort 修剪 ‹*plant*›; 砍掉 ‹*dead wood*›
[2] (reduce) 削减 ‹*production, workforce, spending*›
B *vi* 削减; **to ~ back on staff/production** 裁员/减产

• **cut down**
A *vt* [**~ down sth./sb., ~ sth./sb. down**]
[1] (chop) 砍倒 ‹*tree*›; 割 ‹*long grass*› [2] (trim) 把…改短 ‹*clothes*›; 截短 ‹*carpet, rope, wood*›; **to ~ sb. down to size** fig 让某人有自知之明 [3] (kill) 杀死; (injure) 使受伤; **to be ~ down in the prime of (one's) life** 英年早逝 [4] (reduce) 削减 ‹*amount, time*›; **to ~ sth. down by sth.** 将某物减少某数量; **they aim to ~ public spending down from £30 million to £20 million** 他们打算把公共开支由 3,000 万英镑削减至 2,000 万英镑 [5] (abridge) 删节 ‹*text, film*›; **to ~ sth. down (from sth.) to sth.** 把某物 (从某物) 删成某物; **~ the article down from 3,000 to 2,000 words** 把文章由 3,000 字删减到 2,000 字
B *vi* 削减; **to ~ down on sth.** 减少某物

• **cut in**
A *vi* [1] (interrupt) 打断; **to ~ in on sth./sb.** 打断某事/某人; **to ~ in on a discussion** 在讨论时插话 [2] Aut «*driver, vehicle*» 超车抢道; **to ~ in on sb.** 抢道超某人的车
B *vt* [**~ sb. in**] colloq 让…加入 ‹*person*›; **to ~ sb. in on sth.** 让某人加入某事; **~ me in next time!** 下次把我算上!

• **cut into** *vt* [**~ into sth.**]
[1] (penetrate) 切入 ‹*flesh, metal*›; «*rope, chain*» 勒进 ‹*part of body*›; «*acid*» 腐蚀 ‹*metal*› [2] (begin to cut) 动手切 [3] fig (interrupt) 打断 ‹*conversation, programme*› [4] fig (impinge on) 占用 ‹*time, working day*›

• **cut off** *vt* [**~ sth./sb. off, ~ off sth./sb.**]
[1] (remove) 切掉 ‹*part, length*›; 减少 ‹*quantity*›; 砍掉 ‹*head*›; 割掉 ‹*ear*›; 剪掉 ‹*flower, hair*›; **to ~ sth. off sth.** 从某物上切下某物; **he had his arm ~ off by the machine** 他的手臂给机器切掉了 [2] (reduce) 减掉; **to ~ sth. off sth.** 从某物中减掉 ‹*percentage, amount*›; **they've ~ 10% off all their prices** 他们已把所有价格降低了一成 [3] (stop) 中断 ‹*supply, service*›; **the phone/electricity has been ~ off** 电话/供电被切断了 [4] (block) 阻挡 ‹*view*›; 切断 ‹*path, escape route*›; 阻截 ‹*army*› [5] (disinherit) 剥夺…的继承权 ‹*person*›; **to ~ sb. off without a penny** 不给某人留一分钱遗产 [6] (interrupt) 中断 ‹*broadcast, call*›; 打断 ‹*person, speech*› [7] (seal off, isolate) 隔绝 ‹*person*›; **to be ~ off (from sth.)** «*area*» 被 (与某处) 隔断; **to be ~ off by snow/flooding** 被大雪/被洪水围困; **to ~ sb./sth. off from sth./sb.** 使…与…隔绝; **his deafness ~ him off from society** 耳聋使他与社会隔绝; **regions/nations that are ~ off from civilization** 与文明社会隔绝的地区/民族; **to feel ~ off (from sth./sb.)** 感到被 (与某处/某人) 隔绝; **to ~ oneself off from sth./sb.** 断绝与某处/某人的联系

• **cut out**
A *vt* [**~ sth. out, ~ out sth.**]
[1] (make, fashion) 剪下 ‹*article*›; 剪出 ‹*shape*›; 裁剪出 ‹*dress*›; **to ~ sth. out of sth.** 用某物剪出某物; **to ~ sth. out of wood** 拿木头刻出某物; **to be ~ out for sth./doing sth.** fig colloq 适合某事物/做某事; **to be ~ out for sb.** colloq 与某人很般配; **they are ~ out for each other** 他们是天造地设的一对; **to be ~ out to be sth.** colloq 是做某事的料; **he's not ~ out to be a chef** 他不是当厨师的料; **to have one's work ~ out (doing sth.** *or* **to do sth.)** colloq (做某事) 着实不容易 [2] (carve out) 挖出 ‹*opening, tunnel*› [3] (remove) 切除 ‹*core, tumour*›; 删节 ‹*text, scene*›; **to ~ sth. out of sth.** 从某物中除去某物 [4] colloq (stop, abstain from) 停止; (quit) 戒 ‹*smoking*›; 不再吃 ‹*food item*›; 停用 ‹*luxury*›; **~ it out!** 打住! ; **to ~ sth. out of one's diet** 忌吃某食物 [5] (exclude) 把…排除在外 ‹*person*›; **to ~ sb. out of sth.** 不让某人参与某事; **to ~ sb. out of one's will** 不让某人继承遗产 [6] (block) 挡住 ‹*light, noise*›
B *vi* Mech (fail, switch itself off) «*engine, heater, machine*» 停止运转

• **cut through** *vt* [**~ through sth.**]
[1] (sever) 切割开 «*metal, stone*»; 锯开 ‹*wood*›; **to ~ through red tape** 免掉繁文缛节 [2] (penetrate) 溶解 ‹*grease*›; fig «*wind*» 吹透 ‹*coat*›; «*sound*» 打破 ‹*silence*› [3] (move through) 穿行于 ‹*water, air*›; **to ~ through the waves** «*boat*» 破浪而行

• **cut up**
A [**~ sth. up, ~ up sth.**] *vt*
[1] (into pieces) 剪碎 ‹*paper*›; 切碎 ‹*food, body*›; 劈 ‹*firewood*›; 解剖 ‹*animal, person, body part*›; **to ~ sth. up into pieces/slices** 把某物切碎/切成片 [2] Aut colloq 抢道超越 ‹*driver, vehicle*›
B [**~ sb. up**] *vt usu passive* colloq (upset) 使伤心; **to be/seem ~ up (about/by sth.)** (对某事物/因某事物) 感到/似乎感到伤心
C *vi* [1] (be able to be cut up) **to ~ up easily/into pieces** «*vegetables, animal*» 易切/切成块; «*paper*» 易剪裁/剪成片; «*wood*» 易劈开/劈成块 [2] Amer colloq (misbehave) 胡闹

cut and dried *adj* 已成定局的; **I like everything to be ~** 我喜欢一切都安排妥帖

cut and paste
A *vt, vi* 剪贴
B *n* [u] 剪贴法

cut: ~ and thrust *n* [u] 激烈交锋; **the ~ and thrust of debate** 辩论中的针锋相对; **the ~ and thrust of professional sport** 职业体育的白热化竞争; **~away** *n* [1] (drawing) 剖面图; (model) 剖面模型; [2] Cin [画面的] 切出; **~back** *n* 削减; **~back(s) in ...** 开支…的削减 ‹*defence, health, education*›; **~-down** *adj attrib* 缩减过的

cute /kjuːt/ *adj* [1] (endearing) 可爱的 ‹*baby, kitten, dimples*›; 小巧玲珑的 ‹*cottage, village*› [2] esp Amer colloq (good-looking) 可人的; **she's one ~ honey!** 她真是个迷人的小甜心! [3] (clever) 机敏的 ‹*remark*›; 精明的 ‹*person*›; 聪明伶俐的 ‹*kid*›; **to get ~** pej 装出很内行的样子; **to get ~ with sb.** 对某人耍手腕

cutely /ˈkjuːtli/ *adv* (sweetly) 可爱地 ‹*smile, behave*›; 别致地 ‹*arranged, named*›

cutesy /ˈkjuːtsi/ *adj* colloq 矫揉造作的

cut glass
A *n* [u] 刻花玻璃
B **cut-glass** *modif* 刻花玻璃的 ‹*goblet, vase*›; fig 发音清晰的 ‹*voice, accent*›

cuticle /ˈkjuːtɪkl/ *n* [指甲周围的] 皮质

cuticle remover *n* 皮质软化剂

cutie /ˈkjuːti/ *n* colloq 可人儿

cutlass /ˈkʌtləs/ *n* 短弯刀

cutlery /ˈkʌtləri/ *n* [u] 餐具; **a set of ~** 一套餐具

cutlet /ˈkʌtlɪt/ *n* [1] (meat) 肉排; **a lamb ~** 小羊排 [2] (croquette) 炸饼

cut-off *n* [1] (point, level) 界限; **the ~ for applications** 申请的截止日期; **~ level** 限定水平; **there is a distinct ~ between the middle and upper classes** 中产阶级和上流阶层之间界限分明 [2] (device) (for shutting off power) 断开器; (for water flow) 截止阀; **a ~ device** 断开装置

cut: ~-off date *n* 截止日期; **~-off point** *n* 截止点

cut-out
A *n* [1] (shape) 剪下的图样 [2] (device) 断开器
B *adj attrib* 剪下的 ‹*coupon, figure*›

cutover /ˈkʌtəʊvə(r)/ *n* 快速转换; **the ~ from the old system to the new** 由旧系统到新系统的迅速过渡

cut-price
A *adj attrib* [1] Brit 减价的 ‹*goods*› [2] (selling goods at a reduced price) 出售减价货的 ‹*retailer, store*›
B *adv* 打折地; **she buys all her clothes ~** 她所有衣服都是减价买的

cut-rate *adj* Amer = **cut-price A1**

cutter /ˈkʌtə(r)/ *n* [1] (sharp tool) 切割工具; **a multipurpose ~** 多用途切割机; **a pair of (wire) ~s** 一把 (电线) 钳子; **a cigar/biscuit ~** 雪茄/饼干切刀 [2] (person) 切割者; **a skilled diamond ~** 熟练的钻石切割技工; **he works as a ~ in a tailoring firm** 他在制衣厂做剪裁工 [3] Naut 独桅纵帆船

cut-throat *adj* 严酷无情的; **a ~ business** 竞争残酷的生意

cut-throat razor *n* Brit 直柄剃刀

cutting /ˈkʌtɪŋ/
A *n* [1] Brit (from newspaper, magazine) 剪报 [2] Hort 插条; **to take a ~** 截取一根插条 [3] (for road, railway etc.) 路堑 [4] (piece cut off) 切割下的东西; **grass ~s** 割下来的草

B *adj* **1** *attrib* (used to cut) 切割的 ‹*machine, tool*›; 锋利的 ‹*edge*› **2** fig (sharp) 刺骨的 ‹*wind, pain*›; **to deal sb. a ~ blow** lit 给某人狠狠一击; fig 猛烈抨击某人 **3** (hurtful) 尖刻的 ‹*remark*›; **she has a ~ tongue** 她说话刻薄

cutting: ~ board *n* (for food) 砧板; (for sewing, crafts) 裁剪板; **~ disc** *n* 切割圆盘

cutting edge
A *n* **1** (of blade) 刀刃 **2** fig (latest stage) 前沿; **to be at the ~ of …** 处于…的前沿 ‹*technology, fashion*›
B **cutting-edge** *adj* 最前沿的; **cutting-edge technology** 尖端技术

cutting: ~ equipment *n* [u] 切割工具; **~ room** *n* 剪辑室; **~s library** *n* Brit 剪报汇编; **~ table** *n* 裁剪台

cuttlebone /'kʌtlbəʊn/ *n* [c and u] 乌贼骨

cuttlefish /'kʌtlfɪʃ/ *n* [c and u] 乌贼

cut: ~ up *adj pred* colloq 痛苦的; **~water** *n* **1** Naut 艏柱分水处; **2** Civ Eng 桥墩分水角

CV *abbr* **= curriculum vitae**

cwt *abbr* **= hundredweight**

cyan /'saɪæn/ *n* [u] 青色

cyanide /'saɪənaɪd/ *n* [u] 氰化物

cyber /'saɪbə(r)/**: ~art** *n* [u] (on the Internet) 网络艺术; (by digital technology) 数字艺术; **~café** *n* 网吧; **~citizen** *n* 网民; **~crime** *n* [u and c] 网络犯罪; **~criminal** *n* 网络罪犯; **~culture** *n* [u] 网络文化; **~investing** *n* [u] 网络投资

cybernaut /'saɪbənɔːt/ *n* **1** (Internet user) 网络用户 **2** (in virtual reality) 虚拟现实体验者

cybernetics /ˌsaɪbə'netɪks/ *npl + v sing* 控制论

cyber: ~police *npl* 网络警察; **~punk** *n* [u] 电脑科幻小说 [描述由电脑技术控制的、没有法制的社会]; **~sex** *n* [u] 网上性行为; **~space** *n* [u] 网络空间; **~squatter** *n* 抢注域名者; **~squatting** *n* [u] 域名抢注; **~stalker** *n* 网络骚扰者; **~terrorism** *n* [u] 网络恐怖主义; **~terrorist** *n* 网络恐怖分子; **~world** *n* **the ~ = ~space**

cyborg /'saɪbɔːg/ *n* 电子人

cyclamen /'sɪkləmən, Amer 'saɪk-/ *n* 仙客来

cycle /'saɪkl/
A *n* **1** also Phys, Tech (movement, series) 循环; **the ~ of the seasons** 季节的循环更替; **a frequency of 800 ~s per second** 每秒 800 周的频率 **2** (bicycle) 自行车; (tricycle) 三轮车; (unicycle) 独轮车; **a ~ bell/pump/wheel** 自行车铃/打气筒/轮子 **3** Literat, Mus (of songs) 组歌; (of plays) 组剧; **a Schubert song ~** 舒伯特的组歌
B *vi* 骑自行车; **to go cycling** 去骑自行车

cycle: ~ clip *n* [骑车时用的] 裤腿夹; **~ computer** *n* 自行车车载电脑; **~ lane** *n* 自行车道; **~ race** *n* 自行车赛; **~ rack** *n* 自行车停放架; **~ rickshaw** *n* 人力三轮车; **~ ride** *n* 骑自行车出行; **~ shed** *n* 自行车车棚; **~ shop** *n* 自行车商店; **~ track** *n* 自行车道

cyclic /'saɪklɪk, 'sɪk-/, **cyclical** /'saɪklɪkl, 'sɪk-/ *adj* 循环的 ‹*rhythm, pattern*›; 首尾循环的 ‹*novel*›; **in a ~ manner** 以循环方式; **the ~ nature of economic activity** 经济活动的周期性

cycling /'saɪklɪŋ/ ▸**p. 307** *n* [u] (activity) 骑自行车; (sport) 自行车运动

cycling: ~ holiday *n* Brit 骑自行车度假; **C~ Proficiency Test** *n* Brit 骑自行车能力考试; **~ shorts** *npl* 自行车运动短裤; **~ tour** *n* 骑自行车旅行; **~ track** *n* 自行车赛道; **~ vacation** *n* Amer **= ~ holiday**

cyclist /'saɪklɪst/ *n* 骑自行车的人; (sportsperson) 自行车运动员

cyclo-cross /'saɪkləʊkrɒs/ ▸**p. 307** *n* [u] 自行车越野赛

cyclone /'saɪkləʊn/ *n* **1** (weather system) 气旋 **2** (storm) 龙卷风

cyclonic /saɪ'klɒnɪk/ *adj* 旋风的 ‹*conditions*›; 气旋的 ‹*weather system*›

cyclotron /'saɪklətrɒn/ *n* 回旋加速器

cygnet /'sɪgnɪt/ *n* 幼天鹅

cylinder /'sɪlɪndə(r)/ *n* **1** Math 圆柱体 **2** Aut 汽缸; **a four-~ engine** 四缸发动机; **to be firing** *or* **working on all ~s** fig 全力以赴 **3** (container) 圆筒容器 **4** (cylindrical-shaped object) 圆柱状物

cylinder: ~ block *n* 汽缸体; **~ head** *n* 汽缸盖

cylindrical /sɪ'lɪndrɪkl/ *adj* 圆柱形的

cymbal /'sɪmbl/ ▸**p. 395** *n* 钹; **to play the ~s** 击钹

cynic /'sɪnɪk/ *n* 愤世嫉俗者

cynical /'sɪnɪkl/ *adj* **1** (seeing bad rather than good) 愤世嫉俗的; **to be ~ about sth.** 对某事物持怀疑态度 **2** (selfish) 冷漠自私的 ‹*action, person*›; **a ~ disregard for the employees' safety** 对员工安全的冷血漠视

cynically /'sɪnɪkli/ *adv* 冷嘲热讽地 ‹*remark*›; 无所顾忌地 ‹*act, deceive*›

cynicism /'sɪnɪsɪzəm/ *n* [u] 愤世嫉俗

cypher /'saɪfə(r)/ *n, vt* **= cipher**

cypress /'saɪprəs/ *n* **a ~ (tree)** 柏树

Cypriot /'sɪprɪət/ ▸**p. 503**
A *adj* (of Cyprus) 塞浦路斯的; (of the people) 塞浦路斯人的
B *n* 塞浦路斯人

C

Cyprus /'saɪprəs/ *pr n* 塞浦路斯

Cyrillic /sɪ'rɪlɪk/
A *adj* 西里尔字母的
B *n* [u] 西里尔字母

cyst /sɪst/ *n* 囊胞

cystic fibrosis /ˌsɪstɪk faɪ'brəʊsɪs/ ▸**p. 377** *n* [u] 囊肿性纤维化

cystitis /sɪ'staɪtɪs/ ▸**p. 377** *n* [u] 膀胱炎

cytogenetics /ˌsaɪtəʊdʒə'netɪks/ *npl + v sing* 细胞遗传学

cytologist /saɪ'tɒlədʒɪst/ *n* ▸**p. 409** 细胞学家

cytology /saɪ'tɒlədʒi/ *n* [u] 细胞学

czar /zɑː(r)/ *n* **= tsar**

czarina /zɑː'riːnə/ *n* **= tsarina**

czarist /'zɑːrɪst/ *n, adj* **= tsarist**

Czech /tʃek/ ▸**p. 503, p. 426**
A *adj* (of the Czech Republic) 捷克的; (of the people) 捷克人的; (of the language) 捷克语的
B *n* **1** [c] (person) 捷克人 **2** [u] (language) 捷克语

Czechia /'tʃekɪə/ *pr n* 捷克共和国

Czechoslovak /ˌtʃekə'sləʊvæk/ ▸**p. 503** Hist
A *adj* 捷克斯洛伐克的
B *n* 捷克斯洛伐克人

Czechoslovakia /ˌtʃekəsləʊ'vækɪə/ *pr n* Hist 捷克斯洛伐克

Czechoslovakian /ˌtʃekəsləʊ'vækɪən/ *adj, n* Hist **= Czechoslovak**

Czech Republic *pr n* **the ~** 捷克共和国

Dd

D, d /diː/

A *n* (*pl* **Ds or D's**) **1** (letter) [英语字母表的第4个字母] **2** **D** Mus D音，D调 **3** **D** Sch, Univ (grade) [学业成绩] 第四等

B *abbr* **1** **D = dimension A1; 3-D** 立体; **a 3-D photo/movie** 立体照片/电影 **2** **d = died** 死亡的 **3** **D** Amer (Democrat) 民主党人; (Democratic) 民主党的; **Senator Hart (D)** 参议员哈特（民主党） **4** **d** Brit Hist **= penny 2**

DA *abbr* Amer **= district attorney**

dab /dæb/

A *vt* **1** (pat) 轻触; **to ~ sth. with sth.** 用某物轻擦 **2** (apply) 轻涂 ‹*ointment, paint*›; **to ~ antiseptic on a wound** 往伤口上擦抗菌剂; **to ~ a stain off** 把污迹擦掉

B *n* **1** (small bit) 少量; **a ~ of glue/powder** 一点点胶水/粉末 **2** (application) 轻触; **to apply ointment with light ~s** 轻轻抹上药膏

C **dabs** *npl* Brit colloq 指纹; **to take sb.'s ~s** 取某人的指纹

Phrasal verbs

- **dab at** *vt* [**~ at sth.**] 轻拭; **to ~ at one's eyes (with sth.)** （用某物）轻轻擦眼睛
- **dab off** *vt* [**~ off sth., ~ sth. off**] 轻轻擦去; **to ~ sth. off with sth.** 用某物将某物轻轻擦去
- **dab on** *vt* [**~ on sth., ~ sth. on**] 轻轻涂抹; **to ~ sth. on with sth.** 用某物轻轻涂某物

dabble /ˈdæbl/

A *vt* 用…嬉水 ‹*hands, feet*›; **to ~ one's fingers in the fountain** 把手指放在喷水池里玩水

B *vi* ‹*bird*› [用喙在浅水中] 来回啄食; **to ~ for food** 用喙在浅水里来回觅食

Phrasal verb

- **dabble in** *vt* [**~ in sth.**] 涉猎; **to ~ in the stock market** 涉足证券市场; **painting? I just ~ in it** 绘画？我只是略会一点

dabbler /ˈdæblə(r)/ *n* 浅尝者; **to be a ~ in sth.** 涉足某事

dabchick /ˈdæbtʃɪk/ *n* 小䴙䴘

dab hand *n* Brit colloq 高手; **to be a ~ at sth./doing sth.** 是某事/做某事的高手

dace /deɪs/ *n* (*pl* **dace**) 雅罗鱼

dachshund /ˈdækshʊnd/ *n* 腊肠犬

dactyl /ˈdæktɪl/ *n* [韵律学中的] 扬抑抑格

dad /dæd/ *n* colloq child lang 爸爸; hum (to adult) 老头

Dada /ˈdɑːdɑː/ *n* [u] **= Dadaism**

Dadaism /ˈdɑːdɑːɪzəm/ *n* [u] 达达主义

Dadaist /ˈdɑːdɑːɪst/

A *adj* 达达主义的 ‹*art, movement*›

B *n* 达达主义艺术家

daddy /ˈdædi/ *n* colloq 爸爸

daddy-long-legs *n* (*pl* **daddy-long-legs**) Brit 长腿大蚊; Amer 盲蛛

dado /ˈdeɪdəʊ/ *n* (*pl* **~es**) 护墙板; **~ rail** 护墙板饰条

daemon /ˈdiːmən/ *n* 后台驻留程序

daff /dæf/ *n* Brit colloq **= daffodil**

daffodil /ˈdæfədɪl/ *n* 黄水仙

daffy /ˈdæfi/ *adj* colloq 古怪的 ‹*person, voice*›; 愚蠢的 ‹*idea*›

daft /dɑːft, Amer dæft/ *adj* esp Brit **1** (silly) 愚蠢的 ‹*person, idea*›; **(as) ~ as a brush** 愚蠢透顶 **2** (infatuated with) 狂热的; **to be ~ about sb./sth.** 对某人/某事物入迷

Dagestan /ˌdægɪˈstɑːn/ *pr n* 达吉斯坦

dagger /ˈdægə(r)/ *n* **1** (weapon) 匕首; **to stab sb. with a ~** 用匕首刺某人; **to be at ~s drawn (with sb.)** fig （与某人）势不两立; **to look ~s at sb.** 对某人怒目而视 **2** Print 剑号

daggy /dægi/ *adj* esp Austral, NZ colloq pej 邋遢的

dago /ˈdeɪgəʊ/ *n* (*pl* **~s** *or* **~es**) colloq offensive 拉丁佬

dahlia /ˈdeɪlɪə, Amer ˈdælɪə/ *n* 大丽花

daily /ˈdeɪli/

A *adj attrib* **1** (every day) 每日的 ‹*visit*›; **a ~ paper** *or* **newspaper** 日报; **the ~ grind/routine** 日常琐事/事务; **to earn one's ~ bread** 挣钱糊口 **2** (day by day) 按日的; **~ rate (of pay)** 日工资; **~ production/earnings** 日产量/日收入; **on a ~ basis** 按日

B *adv* 每日 ‹*earn, visit*›; **to take sth. twice ~** 每天吃某物两次; **to worry/suffer ~** 天天担忧/受苦

C *n* (*pl* **dailies**) **1** (newspaper) 日报 **2** **~ (help)** Brit colloq dated 日间女佣

> **the Daily Telegraph**
>
> 《每日电讯报》。英国全国性日报，和《泰晤士报》（▶**the Times**）及《卫报》（▶**The Guardian**）并称为英国的三大严肃报纸。1855年创刊于伦敦。始称《每日电讯信使报》（*Daily Telegraph and Courier*），售价2便士。不久由约瑟夫·摩西·利维（Joseph Moses Levy）购得，改名《每日电讯报》，售价1便士，是英国第一份便士报。1888年，《每日电讯报》发行量达30万份，远远超过《泰晤士报》（6万份），是当时世界上发行量最大的报纸。
>
> 《每日电讯报》在创刊初期政治观点比较激进，但现在代表保守党和中产阶级的观点。报纸信息量较大，尤擅长体育报道。1961年，姊妹报《星期日电讯报》（*Sunday Telegraph*）创刊。

daintily /ˈdeɪntɪli/ *adv* 文雅地 ‹*curtsy, eat*›; 优雅地 ‹*dance*›; 精巧地 ‹*carved*›

daintiness /ˈdeɪntɪnɪs/ *n* (of movement) 优雅; (of figure) 娇小; (of object) 小巧玲珑; **the ~ of sb.'s figure** 某人身材的优美

dainty /ˈdeɪnti/

A *adj* **1** (delicate) 娇小可爱的 ‹*feet, shoes*›; 小巧玲珑的 ‹*porcelain, carving*›; **a ~ pose/figure** 娇美的姿势/娇小的身材 **2** dated (delicious) 美味的; **a ~ morsel** 一小口美食

B *n* 美味佳肴

daiquiri /ˈdækəri, ˈdaɪk-/ *n* 代基里鸡尾酒

dairy /ˈdeəri/

A *n* **1** (on farm) 乳品场 **2** Comm (company) 乳品公司; (shop) 乳品店

B *adj attrib* **1** Agric 乳品的; **~ cattle** 乳牛; **a ~ farm** 奶牛场 **2** Comm 奶制的; **~ cream/product** 奶油/乳制品

dairy: **~ butter** *n* 乳制黄油; **~ cattle** *npl* 乳牛; **~ cow** *n* 奶牛; **~ cream** *n* [u] 乳制奶油; **~ farm** *n* 乳牛场; **~ farming** *n* [u] 乳牛养殖业; **~ ice cream** *n* [u] 牛奶冰激凌; **~maid** *n* dated 乳牛场女工; **~man** /-mən/ *n* (in shop) 乳品店店员; (on farm) 乳牛场工人

dais /ˈdeɪɪs/ *n* 讲台

daisy /ˈdeɪzi/ *n* 雏菊; **(as) fresh as a ~** colloq 精神饱满的; **to be pushing up (the) daisies** fig colloq 已安葬

daisy chain *n* 雏菊花环

Dakar /ˈdækɑː(r)/ *pr n* 达喀尔

daks /dæks/ *npl* Austral, NZ colloq 裤子

dale /deɪl/ *n* 山谷; **up hill and down ~, over hill and ~** 翻山越谷

dalliance /ˈdælɪəns/ *n* **1** (relationship) 调情; **~s with sb.** 与某人的调情 **2** fig (association) 随意涉猎; **his political ~s** 他对政治的随便涉足

dally /ˈdæli/ *vi* **1** (flirt) 戏弄; **to ~ with sb./sb.'s affections** 玩弄某人/某人的感情; **to ~ with a political party** 随便涉足一个政党 **2** fig (consider casually) **to ~ with** 漫不经心地考虑 ‹*idea, project*› **3** (linger) 磨蹭; **to ~ over sth.** 慢腾腾地干某事

Dalmatian /dælˈmeɪʃn/ *n* 达尔马提亚狗

dam[1] /dæm/

A *n* **1** (barrier) 水坝; **the Three Gorges Dam** 三峡大坝 **2** (reservoir) 水库 **3** (built by beaver) 堤堰

B *vt* (*pres p etc.* **-mm-**) 在…中筑坝 ‹*river, valley*›

Phrasal verb

- **dam up** *vt* [**~ up sth., ~ sth. up**] 筑坝拦住 ‹*river, gorge*›; **to ~ a lake/valley up (with sth.)** （用某物）在湖中/峡谷中筑坝

dam[2] *n* Zool 母兽

damage /ˈdæmɪdʒ/

A *n* [u] (to building, machine, vehicle) 损坏; (to crops, health, economy, reputation, relationship, organization) 损害; (to environment) 破坏; (to person, self-esteem) 伤害; **to do** *or* **cause ~ (to sth.)** （对某物）造成损坏; **~ to property** 财产损失; **to repair the ~ caused to sth. by sb.** 弥补某人对某事物造成的损害; **the divorce did a great deal of ~ to her self-confidence** 离婚极大地伤害了她的自信心; **what's the ~?** hum 多少钱？

B **damages** *npl* Jur 损害赔偿金; **to be liable for ~s** 对损失负有赔偿责任; **to claim for ~s** 提出索赔

C *vt* 损坏 ‹*building, machine, vehicle*›; 损害 ‹*crops, health, economy, reputation, relationship, organization*›; 破坏 ‹*environment*›; 伤害 ‹*person, self-esteem*›; **~d fruit/clothes** 破损的水果/衣服; **'slightly ~d'** "略有瑕疵"; **it could ~ the whole police operation** 这有可能破坏警方的整个行动

damaged goods *npl* **1** (merchandise) 受损商品 **2** fig pej (person) 次品 [指某方面有欠缺的人]

damage limitation *n* [u] 损害控制 [指为限制或减轻事故或失误的不良影响而采取的行动]

damaging /ˈdæmɪdʒɪŋ/ *adj* (to person, country) 有害的; (to environment) 破坏性的; **to be ~ to sth./sb.** 对某事物/某人有害; **to be ~ to sb.'s health** «*drugs, alcohol*» 有损某人的健康; **to deal a ~ blow to the economy** 对经济造成严重损害

Damascus /dəˈmæskəs/ *pr n* 大马士革

damask /ˈdæməsk/

A *n* [u] 锦缎

B *adj attrib* **1** (made of damask) 锦缎的 ‹*tablecloth*› **2** (colour) 粉红色的

damask rose *n* 大马士革蔷薇

dame /deɪm/ *n* **1** **Dame** Brit 女爵士 **2** Amer colloq 女人 **3** Brit Theat [通常由男子扮演的] 滑稽老太婆

dammit /ˈdæmɪt/ *excl* colloq 该死; **as near as ~** 几乎

damn /dæm/

A *excl* colloq 该死; **~! I've forgotten my keys!** 真该死! 我忘了带钥匙! ; **~ (and blast)! we've missed the last bus!** 倒霉! 我们错过了最后一班公交车!

B *vt* **1** colloq (curse) 诅咒; **he ~ed his ill luck** 他咒骂自己运气差; **~ this radio!** 这该死的收音机! ; **~ it! I've run out of money** 该死! 我把钱花光了; **homework be ~ed, I'm going out tonight!** 让作业见鬼去吧, 我今天晚上要出去玩! ; **(let's enjoy ourselves and) ~ the consequences/expense!** (咱们只管玩个痛快,) 去他妈的后果/花费吧! ; **well I'll be ~ed: she won after all!** 天哪, 她居然还是赢了! ; **where is he? — at the pub, I'll be ~ed** 他在哪儿? ——在酒馆, 我绝对肯定; **(I'm/I'll be) ~ed if ...** 要是…才怪呢; **I'll be ~ed if it isn't Joe Smith!** 这不是乔·史密斯才怪呢! ; **where is he? — ~ed if I know** 他在哪儿? ——我怎么知道 **2** (condemn) 使注定失败; **this project was ~ed from the start** 这个项目一开始就注定要失败; **he ~ed himself out of his own mouth** 他自己的话证明了他有罪 **3** (criticize) 严厉指责 ‹*person, actions*›; **to ~ sb. for sth./doing sth.** 因某事/做某事斥责某人; **to ~ sb./sth. with faint praise** 对某人/某事物明褒暗贬 **4** Relig «*God*» 罚…入地狱 ‹*sinner, heretic, soul*›

C *n* colloq 丝毫; **to not care** *or* **give a ~ about sb./sth.** 对某人/某事物毫不在乎; **his promise isn't worth a ~ to me** 他的承诺对我而言一文不值

D *adj attrib* colloq 该死的; **it's none of your ~ business!** 不关你的事! ; **what a ~ nuisance!** 真讨厌!

E *adv* colloq 非常; **that restaurant was ~ cheap!** 那家餐馆便宜得要命! ; **you ~ near caused a serious accident!** 你差点造成严重的事故! ; **I know ~ all about computers/cars** 我对电脑/汽车一窍不通

damnable /ˈdæmnəbl/ *adj* **1** (disgraceful) 可憎的; **~ behaviour/crime** 可耻的行为/可恶的罪行 **2** dated (awful) 糟糕的 ‹*weather*›

damnably /ˈdæmnəbli/ *adv* **1** (disgracefully) 可憎地; **to behave ~ towards sb.** 对某人态度恶劣 **2** dated (extremely) 极其; **~ hot** 热得要命

damnation /dæmˈneɪʃn/

A *n* [u] 罚入地狱; **to suffer eternal ~** 遭受永罚

B *excl* colloq 该死

damned /dæmd/

A *adj* **1** Relig 罚入地狱的 ‹*sinner, soul*› **2** *attrib* colloq (used for emphasis) 该死的; **it's none of your ~ business!** 不关你的事!

B *adv* colloq 非常; **~ good/stupid** 棒极了/愚蠢透顶

C *npl* **the ~** 罚入地狱的灵魂

damnedest /ˈdæmdɪst/ colloq

A *n* 最大努力; **to do** *or* **try one's ~ (to do sth./for sb.)** 竭尽全力 (做某事/为某人)

B *adj* 最惊人的; **the ~ thing** 最见鬼的事

damning /ˈdæmɪŋ/ *adj* 谴责性的 ‹*criticism*›; 可定罪的 ‹*evidence*›; 诅咒的 ‹*remark*›

Damocles /ˈdæməkliːz/ *pr n* **the sword of ~** lit, fig 达摩克利斯之剑 [喻指随时可能降临的危险]

damp /dæmp/

A *adj* 潮湿的 ‹*surface, weather, house*›

B *n* [u] 潮湿

C *vt* **1** = **dampen 1** **2** = **damp down** **3** Mus 抑制…的音 ‹*string, note*›

Phrasal verb

- **damp down** *vt* [**~ sth. down, ~ down sth.**] **1** (reduce) 使…减弱 ‹*fire, furnace*› **2** (extinguish) 使…熄灭 ‹*fire, furnace*›

damp course *n* = **damp-proof course**

dampen /ˈdæmpən/ *vt* **1** lit «*person, water*» 使…潮湿 ‹*cloth, walls*› **2** fig 抑制; **to ~ sb.'s spirits/enthusiasm** 扫某人的兴/给某人的热情泼冷水

dampener *n* = **damper 1**

damper /ˈdæmpə(r)/ *n* **1** (subduing effect) 抑制物; **to put a ~ on sth.** 使某事情变得令人扫兴; **to put a ~ on the party** 使聚会扫兴 **2** (in flue) 调节风门 **3** Mus 减音器

dampness /ˈdæmpnɪs/ *n* [u] 潮湿; **the ~ of the grass** 青草的湿润

damp: ~-proof *adj* 防潮的 ‹*wall, brick*›; **~-proof course** *n* Brit 防潮层; **~ squib** *n* Brit 令人扫兴的事

damsel /ˈdæmzl/ *n* liter 姑娘; **a ~ in distress** hum 落难女子

damselfly /ˈdæmzlflaɪ/ *n* 豆娘 [一种昆虫]

damson /ˈdæmzn/ *n* **1** (fruit) 西洋李子; **~ jam** 西洋李子果酱 **2** (tree) 西洋李子树

dan /dæn/ *n* 段 [柔道、空手道等的等级]; **a 12th-~ judo expert** 一位12段柔道高手

dance /dɑːns, Amer dæns/

A *vi* **1** lit 跳舞; **to ~ to music** 跟着音乐跳舞; **to ~ with sb.** 和某人一起跳舞 **2** fig «*person, flames*» 跃动; **to ~ on/in/along ...** 在…上面/在…里面/沿着…跃动; **the little boat was dancing on the waves** 小船随着波浪摇荡颠簸; **to ~ up and down with joy/rage** 高兴得手舞足蹈/气得双脚跳

B *vt* **1** (perform) 跳 ‹*ballet, dance*›; **to ~ the night away** 通宵达旦跳舞 **2** (move in a lively way) 使轻快移动; **to ~ a child around** 拉着孩子蹦蹦跳跳; **to ~ attendance on sb.** 讨好某人

C *n* **1** [c] (act of dancing) 跳舞; **to ask sb. for a ~** 请某人跳舞; **to lead sb. a (merry) ~** fig 给某人造成极大麻烦 **2** [c] (music) 舞曲; **to sit out the next ~** 坐在一旁等下一支舞曲结束; **~ music/a tune** 舞曲 **3** [u] (art, study of) 舞蹈; **modern ~** 现代舞; **a ~ critic/company** 舞蹈评论家/舞蹈团 **4** [c] (party) 舞会; **to give** *or* **hold a ~** 举行舞会

Phrasal verb

- **dance about** *vi* 四处蹦跳

dance: ~ band *n* 舞曲乐队; **~ floor** *n* 舞池; **~ hall** *n* 舞厅; **~ notation** *n* 舞谱

dancer /ˈdɑːnsə(r), Amer ˈdænsər/ *n* **1** (professional) 舞蹈演员 **2** (amateur) 跳舞者

dance step *n* 舞步

dancing /ˈdɑːnsɪŋ, Amer ˈdæn-/ ▸**p. 307** *n* [u] 舞蹈; **ballroom/disco ~** 交际舞/迪斯科舞; **a ~ school/teacher** 舞蹈学校/教师

dancing: ~ girl *n* 女舞蹈演员; **~ partner** *n* 舞伴

dandelion /ˈdændɪlaɪən/ *n* 蒲公英

dandle /ˈdændl/ *vt* 摇晃逗弄; **to ~ a baby on one's knee** 把婴儿放在膝上颠着玩

dandruff /ˈdændrʌf/ *n* [u] 头屑; **to have/get rid of ~** 有/去头皮屑

dandy[1] /ˈdændi/ *n* 花花公子; **a rich ~** 富家公子哥

dandy[2] *adj* esp Amer colloq 绝妙的 ‹*idea*›; 很棒的 ‹*dress, outfit*›; **fine and ~** 好极了

Dane /deɪn/ ▸**p. 503** *n* **1** Geog 丹麦人 **2** (Viking) 维京人

dang /dæŋ/ *excl, adj, adv* Amer = **damn A, D, E**

danger /ˈdeɪndʒə(r)/ *n* **1** [u] (risk) 危险; **to be in ~ (of sth.)** 处于 (某事的) 危险之中; **to be out of ~** 脱离危险; **to put sb./sth. in ~** 置某人/某物于危险之中; **there is (no) ~ in doing sth./that ...** 做某事/… (没) 有危险; **the ~ is that ...** 危险在于… **2** [c] (hazard) (person) 危险之人; (thing) 危险事物; **a ~ to sb./sth.** 对某人/某事物的威胁

danger: ~ area *n* 危险地带; **~ list** *n* 重危病人名单; **to be on the ~ list** 病危; **~ money** *n* [u] 危险工作津贴

dangerous /ˈdeɪndʒərəs/ *adj* 危险的 ‹*substance, animal, idea, precedent*›; **to be ~ for** *or* **to sb.** 对某人有危险; **to be ~ to do sth.** 做某事是危险的; **to be in a ~ situation** 情势危急; **to be ~ for the economy** 对经济有威胁

dangerous driving *n* [u] 危险驾驶

dangerously /ˈdeɪndʒərəsli/ *adv* **1** (perilously) 危险地 ‹*drive, burn*›; **to live ~** 冒险地生活; **~ high voltages/toxic fumes** 危险的高电压/有毒烟雾 **2** (very) 极其 ‹*misleading, naive*›; **to be ~ close to bankruptcy/the truth** 濒临破产/非常接近真相

danger: ~ point *n* 危险点; **to be at ~ point** 处于危险关头; **to reach ~ point** 达到危险地步; **~ signal** *n* lit, fig 危险信号; **~ zone** *n* = **~ area**

dangle /ˈdæŋgl/

A *vi* «*rope, arm*» 悬荡; **to ~ from sth.** 悬吊在某物上; **with legs dangling** 两腿晃荡着; **to keep sb. dangling** fig colloq 使某人的心悬着

B *vt* **1** (hang loosely) 使…悬荡 ‹*key, arm*›; **to ~ one's legs in the water** 把双腿悬垂在水中 **2** fig (offer) 用…诱惑 ‹*reward, promotion*›; **to ~ sth. in front of** *or* **before sb./sb.'s eyes** 用某事物诱惑某人

Danish /ˈdeɪnɪʃ/ ▸**p. 503, p. 426**

A *adj* (of Denmark) 丹麦的; (of the people) 丹麦人的; (of the language) 丹麦语的

B *n* [u] (language) 丹麦语

C *npl* **the ~** (people) 丹麦人

Danish pastry *n* 丹麦酥皮饼

dank /dæŋk/ *adj* 阴湿的 ‹*cellar, cave*›; 湿冷的 ‹*weather, air*›

Danube /ˈdænjuːb/ ▸**p. 663** *pr n* **the ~** 多瑙河; **the Blue ~** Mus 《蓝色多瑙河》

Dao /daʊ/ *n* [u] = **Tao**

Daoism /ˈdaʊɪzm/ *n* [u] = **Taoism**

Daoist /ˈdaʊɪst/ *adj* = **Taoist**

daphnia /ˈdæfnɪə/ *n* (*pl* **daphnia**) 水蚤

dapper /ˈdæpə(r)/ *adj* 精干利落的; **a ~ little man** 矮小精干的男子

dapple /ˈdæpl/

A *n* **1** (marking) 斑点 **2** (animal) 花斑动物

B *vt* 使…有斑点 ‹*surface, face*›; **to ~ the ground** «*sunlight*» 斑斑点点洒在地上

dappled /ˈdæpld/ *adj* 有斑点的 ‹*animal*›; 斑驳的 ‹*colours, sky*›; **to be ~ with moonlight/freckles** 洒满斑斑点点的月光/有点点雀斑

dapple-grey

A *adj* 菊花青色的 ‹*horse*›

B *n* [u] 菊花青马

Darby and Joan /ˌdɑːbi ən ˈdʒəʊn/ *n* esp Brit 幸福的老夫妇; **~ club** 老年俱乐部

Dardanelles /ˌdɑːdəˈnelz/ *pr npl* **the ~** 达达尼尔海峡

dare /deə(r)/

A *vt* 激; **to ~ sb. to do sth.** 激某人做某事; **somebody ~d me to jump off the bridge** 有人激我从桥上跳下去; **I ~ you to ask her (to dance)** 我谅你不敢邀请她 (跳舞)

d

d

B *modal aux* **1** (have the courage) 敢; **to ~ (to) do sth.** 敢做某事; **she ~(s) not** *or* **daren't** *or* **doesn't ~ leave the baby alone** 她不敢让宝宝独自待着; **I ~ say, ...** 也许, …; **she says it wasn't her fault — I ~ say!** 她说那不是她的错——可能吧！; **~ I say it, ...** 我斗胆说一句, … **2** (expressing anger, indignation) 竟敢; **don't you ~!** 你敢！; **don't you ~ (ever) speak to me like that again!** 看你敢再这样对我讲话！; **how ~ you!** 你好大的胆子！; **how ~ you take my bicycle without my permission!** 你竟敢未经我允许就骑走我的自行车!

C *n* 激将; **to do sth. for a ~** 受到激将做某事; **why did you climb on to the roof? — it was a ~** 你怎么爬到房顶上了？——有人激我呢

daredevil /ˈdeədevl/
A *n* 鲁莽大胆的人
B *adj attrib* 鲁莽大胆的

daren't /ˈdeənt/ colloq **= dare not ▸dare B**

daring /ˈdeərɪŋ/
A *adj* **1** (bold) 胆大的 ‹*person*›; (shocking) 大胆的 ‹*action, attempt, style, dress*›; **a ~ new art form** 惊世骇俗的新艺术形式 **2** (innovative) 标新立异的 ‹*idea, new model*›
B *n* [u] 胆量

daringly /ˈdeərɪŋli/ *adv* **1** (boldly) 勇敢地 ‹*attack, dive*› **2** (shockingly) 大胆地 ‹*suggest, reveal*›

dark /dɑːk/
A **▸p. 134** *adj* **1** (lacking in light) 黑暗的 ‹*night, sky, room*›; **it is getting ~** 天就要黑了; **the ~ side of the moon** 月球背面; **~est Africa** dated 非洲最偏僻的地区 **2** (in colour) 深的 ‹*colour*›; 深色的 ‹*clothes, paint, liquid*›; 黑色的 ‹*eyes, hair*› **3** *usu pred* (having ~ hair) **to be ~** «*person*» 是黑发 **4** (not pale) 黝黑的 ‹*skin, complexion*›; **he's very ~** 他皮肤很黑 **5** (gloomy) 暗淡的 ‹*future*›; 悲观的 ‹*prediction, mood*›; **to look on the ~ side (of things)** 看（事物）阴暗的一面; **the ~est days of the war** 战争中最惨淡的日子 **6** (mysterious) 隐秘的 ‹*thought, hint, purpose, motivation*›; **the ~est recesses of the unconscious mind** 潜意识中最隐秘的角落; **to keep sth. ~ (from sb.)** （对某人）隐瞒某事物 **7** (sinister) 恶毒的 ‹*threat, warning*›; (evil) 邪恶的 ‹*power, force*›; **a ~ reputation** 昭彰恶名; **there was a ~er side to his nature** 他本性中有更为邪恶的一面 **8** (angry) 愤怒的; **to give sb. a ~ look** 愤怒地瞪某人一眼 **9** Theat 关门停演的 ‹*theatre*› **10** Ling 暗的 ‹*'l'*›
B *n* [u] **1** (absence of light) 黑暗; **in the ~** 在黑暗中; **before/after ~** 天黑以前/以后; **until ~** 直到天黑; **patterns of light and ~** 明暗交织的图案 **2** **to be in the ~ (about** *or* **as to sth.)** （对某事）全然不知; **to keep** *or* **leave sb. in the ~ (about** *or* **as to sth.)** （关于某事）将某人蒙在鼓里; **a shot/stab in the ~** 瞎猜

dark: **~ ages** *npl* **1** **the D~ Ages** Hist 黑暗时代 [指欧洲中世纪]; **2** **the ~ ages** fig (the past) 未开化时期; **~ chocolate** *n* [u] 黑巧克力

darken /ˈdɑːkən/
A *vt* **1** (reduce light in) «*clouds, person*» 使…变暗 ‹*sky, room*›; **to ~ sb.'s door** fig 擅自踏进某人家门 **2** (make dark) 使…变深 ‹*colour, paint*›; **~ed glass** 深色玻璃 **3** fig (make gloomy) «*worry, news*» 使…蒙上阴影 ‹*mood, thought*›; **to ~ one's wedding day/the atmosphere** 给婚礼带来不快/使气氛变得沉重
B *vi* **1** (lose light) «*sky, room*» 变暗 **2** (become less pale) «*skin*» 变黑; «*liquid*» 颜色变深 **3** fig (become gloomy) «*mood, atmosphere*» 变得阴沉; **his brow/face ~ed (at the thought of sth.)** 他（一想起某事就）沉下脸来

dark: **~-eyed** *adj* 黑眼睛的; **a ~-eyed man** 一个黑眼睛男人; **~ glasses** *npl* 墨镜; **~ horse** *n* **1** Sport 黑马; **2** fig colloq (enigmatic person) 深藏不露的人; **you're a bit of a ~ horse!** 你是真人不露相啊!

darkly /ˈdɑːkli/ *adv* **1** (grimly) 阴森森地 ‹*warn, threaten*› **2** (sombrely) 郁闷地 ‹*ponder*›; (gloomily) 悲观地 ‹*predict*›; **~ humorous** 黑色幽默的 **3** (crossly) 生气地; **to look ~ at sb.** 阴沉着脸看某人 **4** (in colour) 阴暗地; **~ coloured/tanned** 深色的/晒得黝黑的; **to stand out ~ against the sky** 黑漆漆地映衬在天空中

dark matter *n* [u] 暗物质

darkness /ˈdɑːknɪs/ *n* [u] **1** (blackness) 黑暗; **to be in/be plunged into (the) ~** 在/陷入黑暗之中; **as ~ fell** 当天黑下来时 **2** (of colour) 深色; **the ~ of sb.'s skin** 某人肤色的黝黑 **3** fig (evil) 邪恶; **the forces of ~** 邪恶势力 **4** fig (gloom) 忧郁; **in moments of ~** 在郁闷的时刻

darkroom /ˈdɑːkruːm, -rʊm/ *n* 暗室

darling /ˈdɑːlɪŋ/
A *n* **1** (term of address) 亲爱的; **my little ~** 我的小宝贝 **2** (lovable person) 可爱的人; **her father is a ~** 她爸爸挺有趣的 **3** (parent's favourite) 宠儿; (media or party favourite) 红人
B *adj attrib* **1** (term of endearment) 心爱的 ‹*person*›; **my ~ husband/wife** 我亲爱的丈夫/妻子 **2** (cute) 可爱的 ‹*dress, baby*›; **a ~ little house** 漂亮的小房子

darn¹ /dɑːn/
A *vt* 织补 ‹*sock, hole*›
B *n* 织补处

darn² *excl, vt, adj* esp Amer **= damn A, B, D**

darning /ˈdɑːnɪŋ/ *n* [u] **1** (activity) 织补; **~ needle** 织补针 **2** (articles) 织补物

darning wool *n* [u] 织补毛线

dart /dɑːt/
A *n* **1** **▸p. 307** Sport 飞镖; **(a game of) ~s** 掷镖游戏; **to play ~s** 玩飞镖 **2** (arrow) 镖状物; **poisoned/tranquillizer ~s** 毒箭/麻醉枪 **3** (dash) 猛冲; **to make a ~ for** *or* **at sth.** 朝某物冲去 **4** Sewing 缝褶; **to put a ~/~s in sth.** 给某物加缝褶; **a jacket with ~s in it** 带缝褶的夹克
B *vi* 猛冲; **to ~ in/out/away/across ...** 冲进/出/离/过…
C *vt* 投射; **to ~ a look/glance at sb.** 猛地朝某人看/瞥一眼; **to ~ a paw/tongue at ...** 向…伸出爪子/吐舌头

dartboard /ˈdɑːtbɔːd/ *n* 镖靶

Darwinian /dɑːˈwɪnɪən/ *adj* 达尔文的 ‹*theory*›; 进化论的 ‹*classification*›

Darwinism /ˈdɑːwɪnɪzəm/ *n* [u] 达尔文主义

dash /dæʃ/
A *vi* **1** (go quickly) «*person, vehicle*» 猛冲; **the children ~ed into/out of the room** 孩子们冲进/出房间; **the ambulance ~ed to the scene of the accident** 救护车飞驰到事故现场; **I must ~** colloq 我得赶紧走 **2** (strike forcibly) «*waves*» 冲击; **to ~ against sth.** 撞击某物
B *vt* **1** (fling, force) «*person*» 猛砸 ‹*glass*›; «*wave*» 猛击 ‹*boat*›; «*wind*» 激起 ‹*waves*›; **to ~ sth. against sth.** 将某物猛砸在某物上; **to ~ sth. to the ground** 把某物砸到地上; **to ~ sth. to pieces** 把某物砸得粉碎; **a passing car ~ed mud all over us** 一辆汽车飞驰而过, 溅了我们一身泥 **2** fig (destroy, frustrate) 使…破灭 ‹*hopes, expectations, prospects*›; 使…受挫 ‹*morale, optimism*› **3** colloq dated (damn) **~ it (all)!** 糟糕!
C *n* **1** (rush) 猛冲; **to make a ~ for sth.** 冲向某物; **to make a ~ for it** 赶紧跑 **2** (punctuation mark) 破折号 **3** (in Morse code) 长画; **dot, dot, ~** 点、点、画 **4** (small amount) 少量; **a ~ of eye-shadow** 一点眼影; **bitter with a ~ of lemonade** Brit 加少许柠檬水的苦啤酒 **5** (flair) 才干; (vigour, energy) 活力; (elegance) 雅致; (charm) 魅力; **to cut a ~** 神气活现 **6** Aut **= dashboard**
D *excl* colloq dated 糟糕; **~ (it)! I've forgotten my keys** 糟糕！我忘带钥匙了

Phrasal verb
• **dash off**
A *vt* [**~ off sth., ~ sth. off**] 匆匆地写 ‹*note, essay*›; 匆匆地画 ‹*sketch*›
B *vi* 飞奔; **he ~ed off without saying goodbye** 他"再见"都没说就匆匆离开了

dashboard /ˈdæʃbɔːd/ *n* 仪表板

dashing /ˈdæʃɪŋ/ *adj* 风度翩翩的 ‹*person*›; 华丽的 ‹*uniform*›; 潇洒的 ‹*manner*›; 迷人的 ‹*smile*›

dastardly /ˈdæstədli/ *adj* dated or hum 邪恶的 ‹*villain, trick*›; 残忍的 ‹*deed*›

DAT /dæt/ *n* **= digital audio tape**

data /ˈdeɪtə/ *npl* [u] 数据

data: **~ analysis** *n* 数据分析; **~ analyst** **▸p. 409** *n* 数据分析员; **~back** *n* 数据机背; **~ bank, ~base** *ns* 数据库; **~base management system** *n* 数据库管理系统; **~ capture** *n* [u] 数据捕捉; **~ carrier** *n* 数据载体; **~ collection** *n* [u] 数据采集; **~ communications** *npl* 数据通信; **~ corruption** *n* [u] 数据损坏; **~ dictionary** *n* 数据字典; **~ directory** *n* 数据目录; **~ encryption** *n* [u] 数据加密; **~ entry** *n* [u] 数据录入; **~ file** *n* 数据文件; **~ handling** *n* [u] 数据处理; **a ~ handling tool/system** 数据处理工具/系统; **~ highway** *n* 数据信息通路; **~ input** *n* [u] 数据输入; **~ item** *n* 数据项; **~ link** *n* 数据链路; **~ management** *n* [u] 数据管理; **~ mining** *n* [u] 数据挖掘; **~ preparation** *n* [u] 数据准备

data processing *n* [u] 数据处理

data processing manager **▸p. 409** *n* 数据处理师

data: **~ processor** *n* **1** (machine) 数据处理器; **2** (worker) 数据处理员; **~ protection** *n* [u] Brit 数据保护; **the D~ Protection Act** 数据保护法案; **~ recovery** *n* [u] 数据恢复; **~ retrieval** *n* [u] 数据检索; **~ security** *n* [u] 数据安全; **~ set** *n* 数据集

data storage *n* [u] **1** (process) 数据存储 **2** (medium) 数据存储器

data storage device *n* 数据储存装置

data: **~ structure** *n* 数据结构; **~ terminal** *n* 数据终端; **~ theft** *n* [u and c] 数据盗窃; **~ transmission** *n* [u] 数据传输; **~ type** *n* 数据类型; **~ warehouse** *n* 数据仓库; **~ warehousing** *n* [u] 数据仓储

date¹ /deɪt/
A *n* **1** (day of the month) 日期; **what's the ~ today?** 今天几号？; **~ of birth** 出生日期; **~ of expiry** 到期日; **at a later ~** 日后; **at a** *or* **some future ~** 将来某一天; **to ~** 到目前为止 **2** (year of event) 年份; **the ~ of the Battle of Hastings** 黑斯廷斯战役的年份; **Shakespeare's ~s are 1564-1616** 莎士比亚的生卒年份是1564-1616年 **3** (romantic meeting) 约会; **to go (out) on a ~ (with sb.)** （与某人）约会; **to have a ~ with sb.** 与某人约会; **on their first ~** 他们第一次约会时 **4** Brit (appointment to meet) 约见; **a lunch ~** 午餐会晤; **to make a ~** 约好见面时间 **5** esp Amer (boyfriend/girlfriend) 约会对象
B *vt* **1** (mark with date) 给…注明日期 ‹*cheque, document, work of art*›; **in reply to your letter ~d May 12th** 兹答复你方5月12日来信 **2** (identify age of) 确定…的年代 ‹*fossil, artefact*›; **experts have ~d the skeleton to** *or* **at 300 BC** 专家们确定这具骷髅的年代在公元前300年 **3** (reveal age of) «*clothes, hairstyle, tastes*» 使…显老 ‹*person*›; **that ~s me, doesn't it?** 这使我显老了, 对吧？ **4** esp Amer (have romantic association with) 与…约会; **she is dating my brother** 她正在和我哥哥谈恋爱

C *vi* **1** (originate) 追溯; **to ～ from** *or* **back to** 追溯到 ‹*point in time, event*›; **the college ～s back to the 14th century** 这所学院始建于14世纪; **her fear of fire ～s from** *or* **back to a childhood accident** 她怕火，这一点始于她小时候发生的一起事故 **2** (become dated) «*fashion, movie*» 过时; **this style of shoe will never ～** 这种款式的鞋子永远都不会过时

date² *n* **1** (fruit) 海枣 **2** (tree) **～ (palm)** 海枣树

datebook /'deɪtbʊk/ *n* Amer 约会簿

dated /'deɪtɪd/ *adj* 过时的

Date Line *n* Geog **the (International) ～** 国际日期变更线

date line *n* Journ 日期栏

date rape *n* [u and c] 约会强奸

date stamp
A *n* **1** (tool) 邮戳 **2** (mark) 邮戳印
B **date-stamp** *vt* 在…上盖邮戳 ‹*envelope, receipt*›

dating agency *n* 婚姻介绍所

dative /'deɪtɪv/
A *adj* 与格的
B *n* **1** (word, form) 与格词 **2** **the ～** (case) 与格; **in the ～ (case)** 用与格

daub /dɔːb/
A *vt* **1** (smear) 涂抹; (cover) 涂覆; **to ～ sth. over** *or* **on sth.** 把…涂在某物上 ‹*paint, mud, cream*›; **to ～ sth. with sth.** 用某物涂盖 ‹*wall, face*› **2** (write, draw) 涂画; **to ～ graffiti on** *or* **over the wall** 在墙上涂鸦
B *n* **1** (smear) 污迹 **2** colloq pej (picture) 拙劣的画

daughter /'dɔːtə(r)/ ▸**p. 419** *n* **1** lit 女儿 **2** fig 产物 [指某个人、某种环境等的女性后代或阴性产物]; **a ～ of the Church** 基督教之女

daughter: ～board *n* 子板; **～-in-law** ▸**p. 419** *n* (*pl* **～s-in-law**) 儿媳妇

daunt /dɔːnt/ *vt* 使畏惧; **(not) to be ～ed by sth.** (不) 被某事物吓倒; **nothing ～ed** 毫不畏惧

daunting /'dɔːntɪŋ/ *adj* 令人却步的 ‹*task, obstacle*›; **it is ～ to think/read that ...** 想起/读到…就感到气馁

dauntless /'dɔːntlɪs/ *adj* 无所畏惧的 ‹*spirit, character, determination, fighter*›

davenport /'dævnpɔːt/ *n* **1** Brit (desk) 小书桌 **2** Amer (sofa) 坐卧两用长沙发

davit /'dævɪt/ *n* 吊艇柱

Davy Jones's Locker /ˌdeɪvi ˌdʒəʊnzɪz 'lɒkə(r)/ *n* hum 海底; **to go to ～** 葬身海底

Davy lamp /'deɪvi læmp/ *n* 戴维安全灯

dawdle /'dɔːdl/ *vi* **1** (waste time) 拖延; **to ～ over sth.** 磨磨蹭蹭地做某事 **2** (amble) 游荡; **to ～ along** *or* **around the streets** 在街上闲逛

dawdler /'dɔːdlə(r)/ *n* 拖拖拉拉的人; **you're such a ～!** 你真是太磨蹭了!

dawn /dɔːn/
A *n* **1** lit (time of day) 黎明; **from ～ to** *or* **till dusk** 从早到晚; **～ broke** 天亮了; **do sth. until ～** 彻夜做某事; **at ～** 黎明时; **at the crack of ～** 一大早 **2** fig (beginning of sth. new) 开端; **the ～ of civilization/a new era** 文明/新纪元的开端; **since the ～ of time** 自开辟鸿蒙以来

d

Dates

■ When saying or writing dates in Chinese, the order is: year, month, day.

■ In Chinese, cardinal numbers (written either as Arabic numerals or Chinese characters) and not ordinal numbers are used for saying or writing dates.

■ The general patterns in Chinese for expressing dates in writing are:

2008 年 6 月 30 日 / 号

Note that 日 is more formal than 号. This pattern is the one most commonly used in Chinese.

This pattern is used in formal contexts:

二〇〇八年六月三十日

This pattern is used in informal contexts:

2008.6.30

■ If the day of the week is included, it must be put after the date. The generally accepted way of expressing days of the week in Chinese is 星期一 (Monday), 星期五 (Friday), etc. However, Sunday is 星期日 or 星期天:

Tuesday 12 August 2008
= 2008 年 8 月 12 日星期二

Saturday 5th July
= 7 月 5 日星期六

Saying and writing dates

■ Asking what the date is:

What's the date today?
— It's the thirteenth
= 今天几号? —— 13 号

What was the date yesterday?
— It was 11 August
= 昨天几号? —— 8 月 11 号

■ Saying and writing dates:

1 June
Spoken: 六月一号
Written: 六月一日
or 六月一号
or 6.1

31 July 2008
Spoken: 二〇〇八年七月三十一号
Written: 2008 年 7 月 31 日
or 二〇〇八年七月三十一日
or 2008.07.31

08.1966
Spoken: 一九六六年八月
Written: 1966 年 8 月
or 一九六六年八月
or 1966.08

31.07.97
Spoken: 九七年七月三十一号
Written: 97.07.31

AD 400
Spoken: 公元四百年
Written: 公元 400 年
or 公元四百年

2000 BC
Spoken: 公元前两千年
Written: 公元前 2000 年
or 公元前两千年

Expressing 'when'

■ While English uses 'on' or 'in' with dates, in Chinese such prepositions are not commonly used, although sometimes 在 or 于 are included:

I went there on 23 September 2005
= 我 2005 年 9 月 23 号去过那儿

I was born on 11 February 1971
= 我 1971 年 2 月 11 日出生
or 我是 1971 年 2 月 11 日出生的 (colloquial)
or 我生于 1971 年 2 月 11 日 (formal)
or 我于 1971 年 2 月 11 日出生 (formal)

I will see you on the 14th November
= 我 11 月 14 号见你

She will arrive on the 16th
= 她 16 号到
or 她将在 16 日到达 (formal)

I pay the bill on the 1st of every month
= 我每月 1 号付账单

I went to university in September 1987
= 我是 1987 年 9 月上的大学

That happened in May
= 那事发生在 5 月

Other phrases

at the beginning of December
= 12 月初

in the middle of December
= 12 月中旬

at the end of December
= 12 月末

in early March
= 在 3 月上旬

in the middle of May
or ***in mid-May***
= 在 5 月中旬

in late April
= 在 4 月下旬

from November 22
= 从 11 月 22 号起
or 从十一月二十二日起

from the 14th to 26th July
= 从 7 月 14 号到 26 号

by the 30th April
= 在 4 月 30 号前

around October 11th
= 在 10 月 11 日前后 / 左右

I won't come back until 10th March
= 我到 3 月 10 号才回来

I will stay till the end of this month
= 我会一直待到月底

in the 1890s
= 在 19 世纪 90 年代
or 在十九世纪 九十年代

in the twentieth century
= 在 20 世纪
or 在二十世纪

in the early 17th century
= 在 17 世纪早期

in the late 17th century
= 在 17 世纪晚期

in the middle of the 15th century
= 在 15 世纪中叶

in the first half of the 15th century
= 在 15 世纪上半叶

in the latter/second half of the 15th century
= 在 15 世纪下半叶

B *vi* **1** (become light) «*day*» 破晓; **the day ~ed sunny and warm** 天亮了，阳光明媚，温暖宜人; **the day will ~ when ...** fig …的那一天会来的 **2** fig (begin to develop) 开始; **a new era has ~ed in China** 中国进入了一个新纪元; **hope ~ed on the horizon** 希望出现了 **3** **to ~ on** *or* **upon sb.** «*truth*» 被某人认识到; «*idea*» 被某人想到; **it ~ed on me/him that ...** 我/他突然明白…; **inspiration/the answer ~ed on him** 他突然来了灵感/想出了答案

dawn chorus *n* **the ~** 破晓时的鸟鸣声

dawning /ˈdɔːnɪŋ/ *n* **1** liter (dawn) 黎明 **2** fig (beginning) 开端; **the ~ of civilization/the digital age** 文明的曙光/数码时代的开始

dawn raid *n* 凌晨突袭

day /deɪ/ *n* **1** (24-hour period) 一天; **every ~** 每天; **a ~ visit/excursion** 为期一天的拜访/一日游; **what ~ is it today?** 今天星期几？; **~ in, ~ out** 日复一日; **~ by ~** 一天天; **~ after ~** 一天又一天; **the ~ before yesterday** *or* **last** 前天; **the ~ after tomorrow** *or* **next** 后天; **the ~ before, the previous ~** 前一天; **the ~ after, the following ~** 次日; **one ~** (past) 某一天; (future) 有一天; **one of these ~s** 日内; **to take one ~ at a time** 按部就班地处理问题; **to this ~** 直到现在; **from that ~ on** *or* **onwards** 从那天起; **to change from ~ to ~** *or* **from one ~ to the next** 一天一个样; **from ~ one** 从第一天; **(on) the ~ (when/that) ...** 在…的那天; **it's 15 years to the ~ since we first met** 从我们第一次见面到现在已整整 15 年; **I can't tell you to a ~** 我说不出准确日子; **that'll be the ~!** 怎么可能！; **35? she's 40 if she's a ~!** 35 岁？她起码 40 岁了！; **why did it have to rain today of all ~s!** 为什么偏偏今天要下雨呢！; **how long will it take? — ~s** 这要多久？——很长时间; **in (a matter of) ~s** 在几天内; **many a long ~** 很久 **2** (as opposed to night) 白天; **all ~** 整天; **to be** *or* **take all ~ (doing** *or* **to do** *or* **about sth.)** 花一整天时间（做某事）; **it's been a long ~** 今天忙了一整天; **as soon as ~ breaks** 等天一亮; **it is already ~** 天已经亮了; **the ~s are closing in** *or* **drawing in** *or* **getting shorter** 白昼在变短; **the ~s are drawing out** *or* **getting longer** 白昼在变长; **all ~ and every ~** 天天从早到晚; **to make a ~ of it** 痛快地玩一整天; **to make sb.'s ~** 使某人很开心; **as clear as ~** 一清二楚; **to see the light of ~** 被公开; **to pass the time of ~ (with sb.)** （与某人）寒暄; **to give sb. the time of ~** 和某人打招呼; **it's not every ~ you pass your driving test!** 通过驾驶考试没那么容易！ **3** (until evening) 日常活动日; **a working/school ~** 工作/上学日; **a ~ student/worker** 走读生/零工; **she works a three-~ week** 她一周工作 3 天; **to be paid by the ~** 按日取酬; **£10 a** *or* **per ~** 每天10英镑; **to work ~s, to be on ~s** 上日班; **a ~ off** 休息日; **to ask for a ~ off** 请一天假; **to be all in a ~'s work (for sb.)** 是（某人）日常工作的一部分; **to call it a ~** 结束; **to carry** *or* **win the ~** 获胜; **to lose the ~** 失败 **4** (specific day) [特定的] 日子; **International No-Smoking Day** 国际禁烟日; **my shopping ~** 我的购物日; **it's decision ~ for the government** 今天政府必须作出决策; **I forgot my lines on the ~** 我在正式演出那天忘了词儿; **to her dying ~** 直到她去世的那天; **the ~ of judgement** 世界末日; **it's not sb.'s ~** colloq 某人今天真倒霉; **one of those ~s** 特别不顺的日子 **5** (particular period) 时期; **the ~s of rationing** 配给制时期; **in the ~s to come** 在来日; **the rest of his ~s** 他的余生; **these ~s** 如今; **in ~s gone by** 在过去的岁月里; **in ~s of old** 在古代; **in the old ~s** 在过去; **in the ~s of sb., in sb.'s ~** 在某人的时代; **sb.'s fighting/dancing ~s** 某人的拳击/舞蹈生涯; **in those ~s** 那时; **those were the ~s!** 那时候多美好啊！; **to have seen better ~s** 风光不再; **(to live) to see the ~ (when ...)** （活到）能看到（…的）那一天 **6** (time of success) 鼎盛时期; **to have had one's/its ~** 已过全盛时期; **she had her ~ in the 1960s** 她在 20 世纪 60 年代曾经风光过; **the ~s of sth./sb. are over** *or* **have passed** 某物/某人的时代已经过去了; **sb.'s ~ will come** 某人将会时来运转

day: **~ bed** *n* **1** (for daytime) 日间睡床; **2** Amer (couch) 坐卧两用长沙发; **~ book** *n* 日记账; **~ boy** *n* Brit [寄宿学校的] 走读男生; **~break** *n* 破晓; **~care** *n* **1** [u] (for the elderly) 日间护理; (for children) 日托; **2** [c] Amer (centre) 日间托儿所; **~ centre, ~-care centre** *ns* 日间护理站

daydream /ˈdeɪdriːm/

A *n* 白日梦; **to be lost in a ~** 沉浸在幻想之中

B *vi* 做白日梦; **to ~ about sth.** 幻想某事; **I was ~ing** 我走神了

ℹ Days of the week

■ Days of the week are expressed in Chinese in a number of ways:

English	Chinese
Monday	星期一 / 周一 / 礼拜一
Tuesday	星期二 / 周二 / 礼拜二
Wednesday	星期三 / 周三 / 礼拜三
Thursday	星期四 / 周四 / 礼拜四
Friday	星期五 / 周五 / 礼拜五
Saturday	星期六 / 周六 / 礼拜六
Sunday	星期天 / 周日 / 礼拜天
week	星期 / 周 / 礼拜
weekday	工作日
weekend	周末

In China the week begins on Monday. 星期 and 周 are more commonly used than 礼拜.

What day is it?

What day is it (today)? — It's Tuesday
= 今天星期几？—— 星期二
or 今天礼拜几？—— 礼拜二
or 今天周几？—— 周二

Omitting prepositions

■ Where English uses 'on' or 'at', no such prepositions are normally used in Chinese, although the preposition 在 is used occasionally:

She is arriving on Saturday
= 她星期六到
or 她将星期六到
or 她将在星期六到

She is arriving on Saturday evening
= 她星期六晚上到

I visit my mother on Saturday evenings
= 我每周六的晚上去看我母亲

My dancing class is on a Tuesday
= 我的舞蹈课在星期二
or 我的舞蹈课是在星期二

We meet on the first Monday in the month
= 我们每月的第一个星期一见面

We are going to the theatre at the weekend
= 我们周末去看戏

He goes to the gym on weekdays
= 他工作日去健身房
or 他在工作日去健身房

He never drinks on weekdays/during the week
= 他工作日期间从不喝酒
or 他在工作日期间从不喝酒

a week on Saturday
= 一周后的星期六

a week last Saturday
= 一周前的星期六

early on Monday
= 礼拜一一大早

late on Monday
= 礼拜一晚点儿的时候

from Sunday onwards
= 从星期天起

Other expressions

one Wednesday afternoon
= 一个星期三下午

that Thursday evening
= 那个星期四晚上

this Thursday evening
= 这个星期四晚上

last Friday
= 上个星期五

this Friday
= 这个星期五

next Friday
= 下个星期五

every/each Saturday
= 每星期六

every other Saturday
= 隔周星期六

most Saturdays
= 大部分星期六

some Saturdays
= 某些星期六

every week
= 每周

every other week
= 每两周
or 每隔一周

every third week
= 每三周
or 每隔两周

Relating to a specific day

Monday evening
= 星期一晚上 (a specific Monday evening)

Monday evenings
= 每星期一的晚上 (every Monday evening)

the Sunday papers
= 星期日报

the British Sunday papers
= 英国的星期日报

day: ~dreamer *n* 爱空想的人; **~ girl** *n* Brit [寄宿学校的] 走读女生; **~ job** *n* [白天的] 正职; **don't give up the ~ job** colloq 别放弃老本行; **so you want to be a TV comedian? — my advice is don't give up the ~ job** 这么说你想当一名电视喜剧演员? ——我劝你别误了正事儿; **~ labourer** *n* 临时工; **~ nursery** *n* 日间托儿所; **~ patient** *n* Brit 门诊病人

daylight /'deɪlaɪt/
A *n* **1** (light) 日光; **in (the) ~** (by day) 在白天; (in natural light) 在日光下; **to see (the) ~** fig 弄明白; *modif* **~ hours** 白天时间 **2** (dawn) 天明; **before ~** 天亮前
B *npl* fig colloq **to beat** *or* **knock the living ~s out of sb.** 狠揍某人一顿

daylight: ~ robbery *n* [u] Brit colloq 漫天要价; **it's ~ robbery!** 这简直是敲竹杠!; **~ saving time** *n* esp Amer 夏令时

daylight saving time

夏令时，简称 DST，亦称 summer time（夏时制）。北半球的夏令时通常是在每年的 3 月或 4 月将时间拨快一小时，到 10 月或 11 月再拨回标准时间。夏令时期间，人们早起早睡，可以减少照明时间，节约能源。1784 年，本杰明・富兰克林（Benjamin Franklin）首次提出夏时制的设想。一战和二战期间，夏令时为不少国家采用。在实施过程中，各国对夏令时的起止时间有所调整。目前，英国的夏令时为 3 月的最后一个星期日到 10 月的最后一个星期日。自 2007 年起，美国和加拿大大部分地区的夏令时从 3 月的第二个星期日开始，到 11 月的第一个星期日结束。

day: ~-long *adj attrib* 整天的 ‹*activity, meeting*›; **~ patient** *n* 日间留院病人

day release Brit
A *n* [u] 脱产学习; **on ~** 在脱产学习
B **day-release** *modif* **day-release course** 脱产学习课程

day: ~ return *n* Brit **~ return (ticket)** [打折的] 当日往返车票; **~ room** *n* 日间娱乐室; **~ school** *n* **1** (school) 走读学校; **2** (course) 专题短训; **~ shift** *n* **1** (time period) 白班; **to be on (the) ~ shift** 上白班; **2** + *v sing or pl* (workers) 白班工人; **~ surgery** *n* [u] Brit 门诊手术; **~ trader** *n* 当日交易者; **~ trading** *n* [u] 当日交易; **~ trip** *n* 一日游; **~ tripper** *n* 一日游游客; **~wear** *n* [u] 日常便装

daytime /'deɪtaɪm/ *n* [u] 白天; **during** *or* **in the ~** 在白天; **~ services/television** 日间业务/电视节目

day-to-day /ˌdeɪtə'deɪ/
A *adj* **1** *attrib* (daily) 日常的 ‹*routine, event*› **2** (short-term) 每天的; **(to do sth.) on a ~ basis** 按日（做某事）; **to live ~** 过一天算一天
B *adv* 按日

daze /deɪz/
A *n* **in a ~** 茫然; **to be in a complete ~** 茫然不知所措
B *vt* 使茫然; **to be ~d by sth.** 因某事物而茫然

dazed /deɪzd/ *adj* 茫然的; **he looks a bit ~** 他看上去有点恍惚; **to wear** *or* **have a ~ expression** 一脸茫然

dazzle /'dæzl/
A *vt* **1** lit «*light, sun*» 使目眩; **my eyes were** *or* **I was ~d by the sun** 阳光照得我睁不开眼 **2** fig «*beauty, brilliance*» 使倾倒; **to ~ sb. with sth.** 因某事物使某人赞叹不已; **to be ~d by sb.'s knowledge** 为某人的学识所折服
B *n* 耀眼

dazzler /'dæzlə(r)/ *n* (person) 令人倾倒的人; (thing) 令人倾倒的事物

dazzling /'dæzlɪŋ/ *adj* **1** lit 耀眼的 ‹*light, sun*› **2** fig 非凡的 ‹*skill, achievements*›; 令人赞叹的 ‹*performance, beauty*›

dB *abbr* = **decibel**

DBMS *abbr* = **database management system**

DC *abbr* **1** = **direct current** **2** Amer = **District of Columbia**

DD *abbr* = **Doctor of Divinity**

D-day *n* **1** Mil, Hist (in World War II) 诺曼底登陆日 [即1944年6月6日] **2** (important day) 重大事件开始日

D-day

诺曼底登陆日，即 1944 年 6 月 6 日。1944 年，为开辟欧洲第二战场，配合东线苏联对法西斯德国的作战，在德怀特・D・艾森豪威尔将军（General Dwight D. Eisenhower）的指挥下，以美国和英国为主导的盟军（the Allies）准备从英国横渡英吉利海峡（English Channel），在法国北部的诺曼底（Normandy）登陆。这次战略性登陆代号为"霸王"（Overlord）。诺曼底登陆的胜利使盟军成功建立滩头堡，为解放法国、最终击败法西斯德国创造了条件。D 是 Day 的首字母，D-Day 原为美军常用军事术语，后来也指重大事件发生的日子。

DDT *abbr* = **dichlorodiphenyltrichloroethane** 滴滴涕 [杀虫剂]

DE *abbr* Amer = **Delaware**

deacon /'di:kən/ *n* (Roman Catholic) 执事; (Orthodox) 辅祭; (Anglican) 会吏

dead /ded/
A *adj* **1** (no longer living) 死的 ‹*human, animal, plant*›; 凋谢的 ‹*flower*›; 枯萎的 ‹*leaf, grass*›; **to sweep up the ~ leaves** 把枯叶扫在一起; **~ skin** 死皮; **a ~ body** 尸体; **to drop (down) ~** 猝死; **drop ~!** sl 去死吧!; **to leave sb. for ~** 撇下某人让其等死; **to shoot sb. ~** 开枪打死某人; **~ and buried** lit 已死的; fig 结束的; **~ on arrival** 到医院时已经死亡的; **more ~ than alive** 奄奄一息的; **wanted, ~ or alive** 通缉嫌犯，死活不论; **they've been working all day; they must be absolutely ~** colloq 他们忙了一整天，肯定累死了; **over my ~ body!** colloq 绝对不行!; **(as) ~ as a doornail** *or* **as mutton** colloq 死僵了的; **to be ~ from the neck up** colloq 非常笨; **to be ~ to the world** colloq 酣睡; **sb. wouldn't be seen ~ doing sth./with sb.** colloq 某人死也不愿意做某事/和某人在一起; **to step into ~ men's shoes** 补缺; **~ men tell no tales** Prov 死人不会告密 **2** (inanimate) 无生命的 ‹*matter, rock, statue, planet*›; (barren) 寸草不生的 ‹*soil, land, planet*› **3** (without feeling) 麻木的 ‹*part of body, gums, nerves*›; **to go ~** «*feet, legs*» 发麻 **4** (impervious) **to be ~ to sth.** 对某事物无动于衷; **he is ~ to shame** 他恬不知耻 **5** (expressionless) 冷漠的 ‹*voice, eye*› **6** (no longer in use or valid) 过时的 ‹*issue, subject*›; 失效的 ‹*law*›; 不复存在的 ‹*organization, custom, tradition*›; **a ~ language** 死语言; **the peace plan is not yet ~** 和平计划尚未成为泡影; **the campaign is as ~ as a dodo** colloq 这场运动已完全成了过去时了 **7** (no longer functioning) 没电的 ‹*battery*›; 失灵的 ‹*engine*›; 熄灭的 ‹*fire*›; **~ coals** 煤烬; **a ~ match/cigarette** 划过的火柴/抽过的烟; **the hard disk is ~** 硬盘坏了; **are all these glasses ~?** colloq 这些杯子还有人用吗?; **to go ~** «*phone, line*» 没声音 **8** (dull, not lively) 乏味的 ‹*party, acting*›; 冷清的 ‹*town, season*›; **to go ~** 沉寂 **9** (absolute, complete) 绝对的 ‹*certainty, level*›; **~ calm** 死寂; **in a ~ sleep** 在沉睡; **in ~ earnest** 极其认真地; **to be a ~ shot** colloq 是神射手; **to come to a ~ stop** 完全停止; **the ~ centre of the target** 靶心 **10** Sport 界外的; **the manager had to wait until the ball was ~ before making the substitution** 球队教练只好等到出现死球时才换人
B *adv* 绝对地; **to be ~ against sth.** 坚决反对某事; **to be ~ on time** 十分准时; **to be ~ drunk** 烂醉; **I was ~ tired** 我累死了; **~ ahead** 在正前方; **~ straight** 笔直的; **to stop ~** 死死地停住; **'~ slow'** "慢速行驶"; **I'm ~ scared** colloq 吓死我了; **you're ~ right!** colloq 你完全正确!
C *n* **1** + *v pl* (people) **the ~** 死者; **a monument to the ~** 死难者纪念碑 **2** (death) **to rise from the ~** 死而复生; **to be raised from the ~** 被救活 **3** fig (depths) **at ~ of night, in the ~ of night** 夜深人静时; **in the ~ of winter** 在隆冬

dead: ~-and-alive *adj attrib* Brit pej 死气沉沉的 ‹*town, place*›; **~ ball** *n* 死球; **a ~-ball situation** 定位球情况

deadbeat colloq
A /ˌded'bi:t/ *adj pred* 筋疲力尽的
B /'dedbi:t/ *n* pej 游手好闲者

dead: ~bolt *n* 插销锁; **~ cert** *n* colloq **1** (person) 必胜之人; (animal) 必胜的参赛动物; **2** **it's a ~ cert that ...** …是确定无疑的; **~ duck** *n* Brit colloq (person) 注定要完蛋的人; (thing) 注定要完蛋的事物

deaden /'dedn/ *vt* **1** (reduce intensity) 缓和 ‹*pain, shock*›; 抑制 ‹*feeling, passion*›; 减弱 ‹*sound, pang*› **2** (numb) «*drug, alcohol*» 使…麻木 ‹*nerve, senses*›; **to ~ sb. to sth.** 使某人对某事物麻木

dead end
A *n* **1** lit (of road) 尽头 **2** fig (situation) 绝境; **to come to/be at a ~** 陷入僵局
B **dead-end** *adj* 没有前途的 ‹*job*›

deadening /'dednɪŋ/ *adj* 麻痹的; **a ~ effect on the sound** 消声作用; **a ~ routine** 呆板的例行公事

dead hand *n* pej 不散的阴魂; **the ~ of sth.** 某物的流毒; **the ~ of bureaucracy/the past** 官僚主义/过去的阴影

deadhead /'dedhed/
A *n* **1** (flower) 枯花 **2** Brit pej (stupid person) 笨蛋 **3** Amer (person with free ticket) 持免费乘车证的人
B *vt* 摘去…的枯花 ‹*plant*›

dead: ~ heat *n* 同时到达终点; **to end in a ~ heat** 结果不分胜负; **~ letter** *n* **1** Jur 形同虚设的法律; **to become a ~ letter** 成了一纸空文; **2** Post (unclaimed, undelivered item of mail) 死信; **~ letter box, ~ letter drop** *ns* 信件的约定存取点; **the spy used a ~ letter box to pass on confidential documents** 间谍在约定地点传送机密文件; **~line** *n* 最后期限; **to meet/miss/set/extend a ~line** 正赶上/超过/设立/延长最后期限; **to work to a ~line** 按规定期限完成工作; **I have a 10 o'clock ~line for this article** 这篇文章我10点钟必须交

deadlock /'dedlɒk/
A *n* **1** [u] (impasse) 僵局; **to reach/end in ~** 陷入/最终陷入僵局; **to be at ~** 处于僵持阶段; **to break a ~** 打破僵局 **2** [c] Brit (lock) 插销锁
B *vt* **to be ~ed** 陷入僵局

dead loss *n* colloq **1** (person) 无用之人; (object) 无用之物 **2** (venture, situation) 注定失败的状况; **the film was a ~** 这部电影票房惨败

deadly /'dedli/
A *adj* **1** fig (lethal) 致命的 ‹*disease, weapon, blow*›; **the cold was ~** 冷得要死 **2** (intense) 极度的 ‹*fear, hatred*›; **in ~ earnest** 非常认真地; **with ~ accuracy** 极其精确地 **3** (effective) 有效的; **his aim is ~** 他弹无虚发; **she uses wit with ~ effect** 她把自己的机智诙谐发挥得淋漓尽致 **4** colloq (dull, boring) 乏味的 ‹*concert, lecture, party*›
B *adv* **1** (extremely) 极其 ‹*serious, earnest, boring*› **2** (suggestive of death) 死一般地; **to be ~ quiet/pale** 死一般地寂静/苍白

deadly: ~ nightshade /ˌdedlɪ 'naɪtʃeɪd/ *n* 颠茄; **~ sin** *n* 罪源 [即骄傲、贪婪、嫉妒、

贪食、愤怒、淫邪和懒惰之一]; **the seven ～ sins** 七宗罪

dead: ～ man's handle, ～ man's pedal *ns* 安全手柄; **～ march** *n* 丧礼进行曲

deadpan /ˈdedpæn/
A *adj* 假装正经的 ‹*face, look, voice, expression*›; 不带感情色彩的 ‹*style*›; **～ humour** 冷面幽默
B *adv* 面无表情地 ‹*look, say*›

dead: ～ reckoning *n* [u] 航位推算; **by ～ reckoning** 通过航位推算; **～ ringer** *n* (person) 酷似的人; (thing) 一模一样的东西; **to be a ～ ringer for sb.** 和某人长得一模一样; **D～ Sea** *pr n* **the D～ Sea** 死海; **the D～ Sea Scrolls** 死海古卷

dead set
A *adj pred* 坚定不移的; **to be ～ on doing sth.** 坚决要做某事
B *adv* 完全彻底地; **to be ～ against sth.** 坚决反对某事
C *n* Brit 坚定不移的努力; **to make a ～ at sth./sb.** 对某事物/某人志在必得

dead: ～ weight *n* **1** lit (load) 沉重的重量; **2** fig (burden) 重负; **3** Naut 载重量; **～ wood** *n* [u] **1** lit 枯木; **2** Brit fig (person who is no longer useful) 冗员; (thing that is no longer useful) 废物

deaf /def/
A *adj* **1** (unable to hear) 聋的; **to go ～** 变聋; **to be ～ in one ear** 一只耳朵聋; **as ～ as a post** 聋得什么也听不到; **there are none so ～ as those who will not hear** Prov 拒听之人耳最不聪 **2** fig (not willing to listen) 不愿听的; **to be ～ to sb./sth.** 对某人/某事充耳不闻; **to turn a ～ ear to sb./sth.** 对某人/某事置之不理; **to fall on ～ ears** «*request, advice, plea*» 被当成耳旁风
B *npl* **the ～** 聋子; **the ～ and hard of hearing** 耳聋和耳背的人们

deaf aid *n* Brit 助听器

deaf-and-dumb
A *adj* 聋哑的
B *npl* **the ～** 聋哑人

deaf-blind *adj* 聋盲的

deafen /ˈdefn/ *vt* **1** (cause hearing loss) 使变聋; **they were ～ed by the explosion** 爆炸声把他们的耳朵震聋了 **2** (with noise) 淹没; **the roar of the water ～ed them** 水的咆哮声压倒了他们的声音 **3** (make unaware) 使听不见; **to ～ sb. to ...** 使某人听不见…; **the engine noise ～ed him to the telephone** 发动机吵得他没听见电话铃声

deafening /ˈdefnɪŋ/ *adj* 震耳欲聋的 ‹*noise, crash, roar*›

deafeningly /ˈdefnɪŋli/ *adv* 震耳欲聋地

deaf-mute dated
A *n* 聋哑人
B *adj* 聋哑的

deafness /ˈdefnɪs/ *n* [u] 聋

deal[1] /diːl/
A *n* **1** Comm 交易; **a business/property/arms ～** 商业/房地产/军火交易; **a cash/credit ～** 现金/信用交易; **a fair/square/crooked/shady ～** 公平/公正/非法/不正当交易; **the ～'s off!** 交易告吹!; **to do/negotiate a ～** 做/洽谈一笔交易; **to pull off a ～** colloq 完成一笔交易; **to close** *or* **finalize** *or* **strike a ～** 达成交易 **2** (arrangement) 协议; **to make a ～** 订立协议; **to get the best/worst of a ～** 从协议中获益/受损最大; **a pay ～** 工资协议; **it's a ～!** colloq 就这样定了!; **what's the ～?** colloq 情况怎么样? **3** (treatment) 待遇; **to have/get a good/bad ～** 受到好/差的待遇; **to give sb. a fair ～** 给某人公平的待遇; **he got a raw** *or* **lousy** *or* **rotten ～ in life** colloq 他一生都受到不公正的待遇 **4** Pol 特定政策; **a new ～** 新政 **5** **a big ～** colloq (fuss) 大事; **to make a big ～ (out) of sth.** 把某事搞大; **he always has to make a big ～ of everything** 他总要小题大做; **it's no big ～, it's not (such) a big ～** 小事一桩; **big ～!** iron 真了不起! **6** (amount) 数量; **a good** *or* **great ～** 很多; **a good** *or* **great ～ of ...** 大量…; **he's a great ～ older than me** 他比我大多了; **he travels a great ～** 他游历颇多; **they don't have a great ～ in common** 他们没有多少共同之处; **that's saying a good ～** 那只是说说而已 **7** (in cards) 发牌; **it's Anne's ～** 该安妮发牌
B *vt* (*pt, pp* **dealt**) **1** (in cards) 发; **you've dealt me a good/lousy hand!** 你给我发了一手好/烂牌!; **to ～ sb. in** 给某人发牌让其加入牌局 **2** (inflict) **to ～ sb./sth. a blow, to ～ a blow to sb./sth.** «*death, fate, person*» 给某人/某事物以打击
C *vi* (*pt, pp* **dealt**) **1** Comm 交易; **to ～ in sth.** 经营某物 **2** (in cards) 发牌

Phrasal verbs

- **deal out** *vt* [**～ out sth., ～ sth. out**] **1** (distribute) 分发 ‹*cards, money, gifts*› **2** (mete out) 给予 ‹*punishment*›; 处以 ‹*fine*›
- **deal with** *vt* **1** [**～ with sb./sth.**] (handle) 处理 ‹*matter, mail, complaint, crisis*›; 接待 ‹*patient, customer*›; 惩处 ‹*culprit*›; **I'll ～ with you later!** 我以后收拾你!; **she's a difficult person to ～ with** 她可不好对付; **he did not ～ fairly with us** 他对我们不公 **2** [**～ with sb./sth.**] Comm 与…做生意 ‹*person, company*› **3** [**～ with sth.**] (take as subject) «*book, film, play*» 讲述 ‹*topic, issue*›; «*speaker, teacher*» 讲解 ‹*topic, issue*›

deal[2] *n* [u] (fir wood) 冷杉木板; (pine wood) 松木板; **a ～ table** 松木桌

dealer /ˈdiːlə(r)/ ▸p. 409 *n* **1** (in goods) 经销商; **to be a ～ in sth.** 经销某物; **an antiques ～** 古董商 **2** (in stocks) 证券交易人 **3** (in card games) 发牌者

dealership /ˈdiːləʃɪp/ *n* 专卖店; **car ～** 汽车经销店

dealing /ˈdiːlɪŋ/ *n* [u and c] 交易; **foreign exchange ～** 外汇交易; **～ on the Stock Exchange** 证券市场交易; **arms/drugs ～** 军火/毒品交易

dealing room *n* 股票交易室

dealings /ˈdiːlɪŋz/ *npl* **1** (in business) 商业往来; **to have ～ with sb.** 与某人有业务往来; **～ in stocks and shares** 股票交易 **2** (with people) 交往; **one's ～ with sb.** 与某人的交往

dealmaker /ˈdiːlmeɪkə(r)/ *n* 交易人

dealt /delt/ *pt, pp* ▸**deal**[1] **B, C**

dean /diːn/ *n* **1** Brit Univ (head of faculty) 院长; (head of department) 系主任; (fellow) [尤指剑桥、牛津大学的] 学监 **2** (of cathedral) 座堂主任牧师 **3** Brit (member of clergy) 乡村主任牧师

dear /dɪə(r)/
A *adj* **1** (expressing attachment) 珍爱的; **to be ～ to sb.** 为某人所珍视; **to hold sb./sth. very ～** 十分看重某人/某物; **to be ～ to sb.'s heart** 为某人所心爱; **one's ～est wish is to do ...** 做…是某人由衷的希望; **～ old Simon** 亲爱的老西蒙 **2** (expressing admiration) 可爱的; **a ～ old lady** 受人爱戴的老妇人; **she's a ～ child** (in appearance) 她是个漂亮的孩子; (in behaviour) 她是个讨人喜欢的孩子 **3** (in letter) 亲爱的; **D～ Sir/Madam** 亲爱的先生/夫人; **My ～ Catherine** 我亲爱的凯瑟琳 **4** (expensive) 昂贵的
B *n* **1** (term of address) 亲爱的; **you poor ～** (to child) 你这可怜的小乖乖; (to adult) 你这可怜的人; **thank you, ～** 谢谢你，亲爱的 **2** (sweet person) 可爱的人儿; **there's a ～** 这才乖呢; **be a ～ and answer the phone** 劳驾接一下电话
C *adv* **1** lit (costly) 昂贵地 **2** fig (with much effort and sacrifice) 高代价地; **buy cheap and sell ～** 贱买贵卖; **to cost sb. ～** 让某人花大钱; **she bought her freedom ～** 她的自由得来不易
D *excl* 哎呀; **oh ～!** (dismay, surprise) 天哪!; (less serious) 哎呀!; **～ me!** 哎呀; **～, ～!** 哎呀呀!

dearie /ˈdɪəri/
A *n* Brit colloq 亲爱的; **what's the matter, ～?** 怎么啦，亲爱的?
B *excl* 哎呀; **～ me!** 哎呀!

Dear John letter *n* [由女性写给男友的] 绝情信

dearly /ˈdɪəli/ *adv* **1** (very much) 非常; **to ～ love to do sth.** 很想做某事; **our ～ beloved son** formal 我们深爱的儿子 **2** fig (at great cost) 代价极大地; **to pay ～ for sth.** 为某事付出高昂代价; **you will pay ～ for this insult** 你会为这次的无礼付出惨重的代价

dearth /dɜːθ/ *n* 缺乏; **a ～ of sth.** 某物的匮乏

death /deθ/ *n* **1** [u] (dying, being killed) 死亡; **the cause of ～** 死因; **to meet one's ～** 丧命; **～ by hanging/drowning** 绞死/淹死; **～ from starvation/suffocation** 饿死/窒息死亡; **to be burnt to ～** 被烧死; **to starve/freeze to ～** 饿死/冻死; **they work them-selves/their employees to ～** fig colloq 他们简直要把自己/员工累死; **I'm sick to ～ of his rudeness** colloq 我对他的粗野行为厌恶得要死; **they frightened us to ～** fig colloq 他们吓死我们了; **they fought to the ～** 他们战斗到死; **to put sb. to ～** 处死某人; **to sentence sb. to ～** 判处某人死刑; **that motorbike will be the ～ of her** 那辆摩托车会要了她的命; **those kids will be the ～ of me!** fig colloq 那些孩子会折腾死我的!; **to be at ～'s door** 奄奄一息; **to look like ～ warmed up** colloq 看上去像害了场大病似的; **I feel like ～ (warmed up)** colloq 我快累死了; **to do sth. to ～** colloq 把某事做腻; **you've done that joke to ～** 你那笑话都说得人烦了 **2** [c] (instance of dying or being killed) 死亡; **two ～s in the family** 两个家庭成员的死亡; **to die a violent ～** 横死 **3** [u] fig (of hopes, dreams) 破灭; (of plans) 终止; (of capitalism, democracy) 灭亡; (of civilization) 毁灭; (of business) 倒闭

deathbed /ˈdeθbed/ *n* 临终床; **to be on one's ～** 生命垂危; **to make a ～ conversion/repentance** 临终时皈依/忏悔

death: ～ benefit *n* 死亡保险金; **～ blow** *n* (impact, stroke) 致命的一击; fig (destructive action, event) 导致毁灭的事情; **to deal sb./sth. a ～ blow** 给某人/某事物致命的打击; **the accident dealt a ～ blow to her sporting career** 这次事故毁了她的运动生涯; **～ camp** *n* 死亡集中营; **～ cell** *n* 死囚牢房; **～ certificate** *n* 死亡证书; **～ duty** *n* 遗产税; **～ knell** *n* (bell) 丧钟; fig (herald of end, destruction) 毁灭的预兆; **to sound** *or* **toll the ～ knell for** *or* **of ...** 敲响…的丧钟

deathless /ˈdeθlɪs/ *adj* liter 不朽的 ‹*glory, verse*›

death list *n* 处决人员名单

deathly /ˈdeθli/
A *adj* 死一般的 ‹*pallor, stillness*›
B *adv* 死一般地 ‹*pale, quiet*›

death: ～ mask *n* 死人面部模型; **～ penalty** *n* 死刑; **～ rate** *n* 死亡率; **～ rattle** *n* 临终喉鸣; **～ ray** *n* 死光 [科幻小说中用作武器]; **～ row** *n* esp Amer 死囚区; **to be on ～ row** 是死囚; **～ sentence** *n* 死刑; **to pass a ～ sentence on sb.** 宣判某人死刑; **～'s head** *n* 骷髅头; **～ squad** *n* 暗杀小队; **～ tax** *n* Amer = **inheritance tax**; **～ threat** *n* 死亡威胁; **～ throes** *npl* **1** (dying) 临终疼痛; **in one's ～ throes** 在临终疼痛阶段; **2** fig (final stages) 最终衰败阶段; **the company is in its ～ throes** 公司行将倒闭; **～ toll** *n* 死亡人数; **～ trap** *n* 死亡陷阱; **to be a ～ trap** 是安全隐患; **this car is a real ～ trap** 这辆车确实不安全; **～ warrant** *n* **1** (official document) 死刑执行令; **to sign a ～ warrant** 签署死刑执行令; **2** fig (cause of destruction, failure) 致命打击; **to sign one's own ～ warrant** 自取灭亡

death-watch beetle *n* 红毛窃蠹 [专蛀旧木，发出类似表的滴答声的小甲虫]

death wish *n* 死亡愿望; **anyone who drives so fast must have a ～** 把车开得如此快的人一定想找死

deb /deb/ *n* colloq **= debutante**

debacle /deɪ'bɑːkl/ *n* 溃败; **what a ～!** 真是一败涂地!

debar /dɪ'bɑː(r)/ (*pres p etc.* **-rr-**) *vt* 把…排除在外 ‹*person*›; **to ～ sb. from doing sth.** 禁止某人参与做某事; **to be ～red from voting** 被禁止投票

debase /dɪ'beɪs/
A *vt* **1** (lower quality of) 贬低; **to ～ the reputation/value of ...** 败坏…的名誉/贬低…的价值 **2** (degrade) 降低…的道德品质; **war ～s people** 战争使人们的道德水准下降 **3** Hist 使…贬值 ‹*coin*›; 降低…的成色 ‹*metal*›
B *v refl* **to ～ oneself (by doing sth.)** (因做某事而) 自我羞辱

debatable /dɪ'beɪtəbl/ *adj* 有争议的 ‹*point, issue*›; **it is ～ whether the project is feasible** 这个项目是否可行有待商榷

debate /dɪ'beɪt/
A *n* **1** (formal discussion) 辩论; **to hold a ～ on** *or* **about sth.** 就某事物进行辩论 **2** (argument) 讨论; **to be under ～** 在讨论中; **to be open to ～** 有待讨论; **a ～ on** *or* **about sth.** 有关某事物的争论
B *vt* **1** (discuss formally) «*government, committee*» 辩论 ‹*policy, proposal*› **2** (discuss informally) 讨论; **to ～ the pros and cons of a situation** 讨论某情况的利弊
C *vi* 考虑; **to ～ about sth./whether to do sth.** 盘算某事/是否做某事

debater /dɪ'beɪtə(r)/ *n* 辩论者; **a good ～** 优秀辩手

debating: ～ **point** *n* [辩论时用以取得优势的] 非实质性论点; ～ **society** *n* 辩论社团

debauched /dɪ'bɔːtʃt/ *adj* 骄奢淫逸的 ‹*lifestyle*›; 道德败坏的 ‹*practices, behaviour*›

debauchery /dɪ'bɔːtʃəri/ *n* [u] 骄奢淫逸; **to lead a life of ～** 过着放荡的生活

debenture /dɪ'bentʃə(r)/ *n* Brit 公司债券

debenture: ～ **bond** *n* Amer 无担保债券; ～ **holder** *n* 债券持有人; ～ **stock** *n* 借款股份

debilitate /dɪ'bɪlɪteɪt/ *vt* **1** (enfeeble) «*illness, climate*» 使虚弱; **we were ～d by the sultry weather** 闷热的天气使我们感到乏力 **2** fig (hinder) «*action, decision*» 削弱…的力量 ‹*government, economy*›; **the country's ～d iron and steel industry** 这个国家衰落的钢铁业

debilitating /dɪ'bɪlɪteɪtɪŋ/ *adj* **1** (physically hindering) 使人虚弱的 ‹*disease, weather, effect*› **2** fig (hindering) 削弱性的 ‹*action, legislation, reform*›; **the ～ effects of underinvestment** 投资不足的掣肘

debility /dɪ'bɪləti/ *n* [u] 虚弱; **nervous ～** 神经衰弱

debit /'debɪt/
A *n* **1** (entry) 借记; **the account records a ～ of £50** 账目上记录着50镑的借款; **on the ～ side** lit 在借记方; fig 处于不利地位 **2** (sum) 借项
B *vt* «*bank, financial organization*» 把…记入账户的借方 ‹*money, amount*›; **to ～ a sum against** *or* **to sb.'s account, to ～ sb.** *or* **sb.'s account with a sum** 把一笔钱记入某人账户的借方

debit card *n* 借记卡

debonair /ˌdebə'neə(r)/ *adj* 温文尔雅的 ‹*manner, attitude*›; 潇洒的 ‹*man*›

debrief /ˌdiː'briːf/ *vt* 盘问; **to be ～ed on sth.** 被要求汇报某事

debriefing /ˌdiː'briːfɪŋ/ *n* **1** [u] (of person) (giving account) 布置任务; (questioning) 盘问; **the soldiers will remain here for ～** 士兵们将在这里待命 **2** [c] (report) [执行任务的] 口头汇报

debris /'deɪbriː, 'de-, Amer də'briː/ *n* [u] **1** (remains of plane) 残骸; (remains of building) 瓦砾; **to clear (up** *or* **away) the ～** 清理残骸 **2** hum (remnants, leftovers of meal) 残羹剩饭 **3** (rubbish) 垃圾 **4** Geol 岩屑

debt /det/ *n* **1** [c] (amount) 欠款; **to run up a ～** 积欠债务; **to cancel** *or* **write off a ～** 勾销一笔欠款; **to recover a ～** 追回欠款; **to pay off one's ～s** 付清欠款; **a bad ～** 坏账 **2** [u] (state) 负债; **to be in ～ to sb.** 欠某人的钱; **to get into/out of ～** 背上/清偿债务; **to be out of ～** 不负债; **she is $2,000 in ～** 她欠了 2,000 元的债 **3** [c] fig (obligation, gratitude) 人情债; **to be in sb.'s ～** 受某人的恩惠; **a ～ of honour** 信用债; **to pay one's ～ to society** 报答社会; **to acknowledge one's ～ to sb.** 向某人表达感激之情; **I'm forever in your ～** 我永远都感激你

debt: ～ **burden** *n* 债务负担; ～ **collector** *n* 收债人; ～ **counselling** *n* [u] 债务咨询; ～ **counsellor** *n* 债务顾问; ～ **financing** *n* [u] 债务融资; **～-laden** *adj* 负债累累的

debtor /'detə(r)/ *n* 债务人

debt relief *n* [u] 债务减免

debug /ˌdiː'bʌɡ/ *vt* (*pres p etc.* **-gg-**) **1** Comput 排除…的错误 ‹*program, system*› **2** (remove microphones from) 拆除…的窃听器 ‹*room, building*› **3** Amer (remove insects from) 给…除虫 ‹*room, bed, clothes*›

debugger /ˌdiː'bʌɡə(r)/ *n* 排错程序

debunk /ˌdiː'bʌŋk/ *vt* **1** colloq (expose) 揭穿…的真相 ‹*belief, legend, myth*› **2** colloq 驳斥 ‹*evidence, theory*›; 批判 ‹*doctrine, institution*› **3** (ridicule) «*person, reason*» 嘲弄…的虚假 ‹*claim, reputation, image*›; **comedy takes delight in ～ing heroes** 喜剧喜欢嘲弄英雄的名不副实

debut /'deɪbjuː, Amer deɪ'bjuː/ *n* **1** Cin, Theat 首次亮相; **a ～ performance** 首次登台演出; **a ～ album** 首张专辑; **to make one's screen ～** 首次在银幕上亮相; **to make one's ～ as ...** 作为…初次登台 **2** (social) 初次进入社交界

debutante /'debjuːtɑːnt/ *n* dated 首次进入社交界的上流社会年轻女子

Dec *abbr* **= December**

decade /'dekeɪd, dɪ'keɪd, Amer dɪ'keɪd/ *n* 十年; **a ～ ago** 十年前; **2010 — the beginning of a new ～** 2010 年——一个新十年的开始

decadence /'dekədəns/ *n* [u] **1** (moral decline) 堕落; (cultural decline) 衰落; **Western ～** 西方的堕落 **2** (decadent behaviour) 堕落行为 **3** (self-indulgence) 放纵

decadent /'dekədənt/ *adj* **1** (morally, culturally) 堕落的 ‹*person, lifestyle*›; 颓废的 ‹*society*›; 衰落的 ‹*civilization*› **2** (self-indulgent) 放纵的 ‹*behaviour, habits*›

decaf /'diːkæf/ *n* colloq **= decaffeinated coffee** 脱咖啡因咖啡

decaffeinate /ˌdiː'kæfɪneɪt/ *vt* 脱去…的咖啡因 ‹*coffee*›

decaffeinated /ˌdiː'kæfɪneɪtɪd/ *adj* 脱咖啡因的 ‹*coffee*›

decalitre Brit, **decaliter** Amer /'dekəliːtə(r)/ *n* 十升

decametre Brit, **decameter** Amer /'dekəmiːtə(r)/ ▸p. 436 *n* 十米

decamp /dɪ'kæmp/ *vi* 潜逃; **to ～ with sth.** 带着某物逃走; **to ～ from/to somewhere** 逃离/逃往某地

decant /dɪ'kænt/ *vt* 倒入 ‹*liquid, wine*›; **to ～ sth. into sth.** 把某物注入某物

decanter /dɪ'kæntə(r)/ *n* 玻璃酒瓶; **ship's ～** 喇叭底醒酒壶

decapitate /dɪ'kæpɪteɪt/ *vt* 砍掉…的头; **to ～ sb. with sth.** 用某物砍掉某人的头

decapitation /dɪˌkæpɪ'teɪʃn/ *n* 斩首

decathlete /dɪ'kæθliːt/ *n* 十项全能运动员

decathlon /dɪ'kæθlɒn/ *n* 十项全能运动

decay /dɪ'keɪ/
A *vi* **1** (rot) «*wood, leaf, bone, body*» 腐烂 **2** (collapse, crumble) «*building*» 破损; «*stone, wall*» 坍塌 **3** fig (decline, fade) «*strength, hope, talent*» 衰退; «*civilization, society*» 衰落; **her beauty has not ～ed with age** 她虽然上了年纪，但风采依旧 **4** Phys «*radioactive substance*» 衰减; «*particle*» 衰变
B *vt* **1** (cause to rot) «*bacteria, chemicals, exposure*» 使腐烂 **2** Dent 蛀蚀 ‹*teeth*›
C *n* [u] **1** (rotting, decomposition) 腐朽; **the stench of ～** 腐臭气 **2** (of building, wall, structure) 破损; **to fall into ～** 破烂不堪; **a state of ～** 破损状态 **3** Dent 蛀蚀; **to have ～** 有龋齿; **to prevent tooth** *or* **dental ～** 预防蛀牙 **4** fig (of society, culture, nation, civilization) 衰落; (of economy, institution, industry, health, strength) 衰退; **political/moral/physical ～** 政治衰败/道德败坏/健康衰退 **5** Phys 衰减

decayed /dɪ'keɪd/ *adj* **1** (rotted) 腐烂的 ‹*wood, leaf, flesh, bone*› **2** (collapsed, crumbled) 破烂不堪的 ‹*building, ruins*›; 破败的 ‹*town*› **3** Dent 蛀蚀的; **～ teeth** 龋齿 **4** Phys 衰减的

decaying /dɪ'keɪɪŋ/ *adj* **1** (rotting) 正在腐烂的 ‹*wood, leaf, flesh, bone*› **2** Dent 正在蛀蚀的 ‹*teeth*› **3** (collapsing, crumbling) 摇摇欲坠的 ‹*church, building*›; 日渐破败的 ‹*town*›

decease /dɪ'siːs/ *n* formal 亡故

deceased /dɪ'siːst/ formal
A *adj* 亡故的
B *n* **the ～** 死者

deceit /dɪ'siːt/ *n* **1** [u] (deceiving) 欺诈; **to get sth. by ～** 骗得某物 **2** [c] (instance) 欺骗行为

deceitful /dɪ'siːtfl/ *adj* **1** (duplicitous) 欺诈的 ‹*person*›; **you ～ child!** 你这个骗人的孩子! **2** (misleading, dishonest) 不诚实的 ‹*words, behaviour*›

deceitfully /dɪ'siːtfəli/ *adv* 欺骗地

deceitfulness /dɪ'siːtflnɪs/ *n* [u] 欺骗

deceive /dɪ'siːv/
A *vt* **1** (lie to and mislead) 欺骗; **to ～ sb. into doing sth.** 哄某人做某事; **to be ～d** 受骗; **don't be ～d by his mildness/good humour** 别被他的随和/好脾气蒙骗了; **do my eyes ～ me?** colloq 我看错了吗? **2** (be unfaithful to) 对…不忠实; **to ～ sb. with sb.** 背叛某人与某人私通
B *vi* 使人误信; **with intent to ～** 想误导地; **appearances often ～** 外表往往有欺骗性
C *v refl* **to ～ oneself** 自我欺骗

decelerate /ˌdiː'seləreɪt/
A *vi* **1** Aut, Mech «*vehicle, machine*» 减速 **2** fig «*inflation, economic growth*» 减缓; «*disease*» 缓解
B *vt* **1** Aut, Mech 使…减速 ‹*vehicle, machine*› **2** fig 使…减缓 ‹*inflation, economic growth*›; 使…缓解 ‹*disease*›

deceleration /ˌdiːselə'reɪʃn/ *n* [u] **1** (slowing down) (of vehicle, machine) 减速; **they measured the car's ～ (rate)** 他们测了汽车的减速度 **2** fig (decrease) 减缓

December /dɪ'sembə(r)/ ▸p. 490 *n* 十二月; **last/this/next ～** 上个/本年/下个十二月份; **in early/late ～** 十二月上旬/下旬; **～ weather/morning** 十二月的天气/早晨

decency /'diːsnsi/ *n* **1** [u] (good manners) 得体; **to have the ～ to do sth.** 得体地做某事; **they might have had the ～ to thank us** 他们其实应该谢谢我们; **you can't in all ～ ask him to pay** 最起码你不能让他付钱; **you can't do that! where's your sense of ～?** 你不能那么做! 你懂礼貌吗? **2** [u] (morality) 正派; **he hasn't an ounce of ～** 他的品行一点都不端正 **3** [u and c] (propriety) 礼仪; **for the sake of ～** 为合乎礼仪; **to observe the decencies** formal 遵守规矩;

d

common ~ demands you pay your taxes 纳税是每个人的基本行为准则

decent /ˈdiːsnt/ *adj* 1 (respectable) 正派的 ‹*person, family, company*› 2 (proper) 得体的; **to give sb. a ~ burial** 给某人举行体面的葬礼; **he decided to do the ~ thing** 他决定做体面的事 3 (of an acceptable standard) 合宜的 ‹*language*›; 得体的 ‹*clothes*›; 符合礼仪的 ‹*behaviour*›; **are you ~?** 你穿好衣服了吗? 4 (adequate, acceptable) 像样的; **to make a ~ living** 过相当不错的生活; **I've nothing ~ to wear** 我没一件像样的衣服穿; **you need a ~ night's sleep** 你需要好好睡一晚上; **they do a ~ fish soup here** 这里的鱼汤不错 5 colloq (kind, pleasant) 善良的 ‹*person*›; **a ~ sort of woman** 好女人; **it was ~ of them to help** 他们来帮忙真是很热心

decently /ˈdiːsntli/ *adv* 1 (respectably) 体面地; **she was ~ brought up** 她很有教养; **we saw to it that he was ~ buried** 我们把他体面地安葬了 2 (properly) 得体地 ‹*behave, dressed*›; 合宜地 ‹*treat*›; **they left as soon as was ~ possible** 他们在不失礼的前提下尽快走了; **we couldn't ~ refuse** 我们若拒绝就显得失礼 3 (acceptably) 适当地; **I'm not yet ~ dressed** 我还没穿好衣服呢 4 (adequately) 像样地 ‹*paid, fed, housed*›

decentralization /diːˌsentrəlaɪˈzeɪʃn, Amer -lɪˈz-/ *n* [u] 1 (of power, authority) 权力下放 2 (of department, organization) 权力分散

decentralize /ˌdiːˈsentrəlaɪz/
A *vt* 下放 ‹*power, authority*›; 分散…的权力 ‹*department, organization*›; 疏散…的分布 ‹*industry*›; 疏散 ‹*population*›
B *vi* 分权

deception /dɪˈsepʃn/ *n* 1 [u] (act of deceiving) 欺骗; **to obtain sth. by ~** 骗得某物 2 [c] (trick) 骗术; **I saw through her ~** 我看穿了她的小伎俩

deceptive /dɪˈseptɪv/ *adj* 欺骗性的; **appearances can be ~** 外表往往靠不住; **the depth of the water may be ~** 水深难测; **he writes with a ~ simplicity** 他的文笔貌似简单

deceptively /dɪˈseptɪvli/ *adv* 有欺骗性地; **~ easy/calm** 貌似简单/镇定的; **~ spacious** 看上去宽敞的

decibel /ˈdesɪbel/ *n* 1 (unit) 分贝 2 (degree of loudness) 响度; **his voice went up several ~s** 他提高了嗓门

decide /dɪˈsaɪd/
A *vt* 1 (reach a decision about) 决定; **to ~ to do sth.** 决定做某事; **I ~d that I would leave** 我决定离开; **it has been ~d that ...** 已经决定…; **to ~ whether/when/how/which ...** 决定是否/何时/如何/哪个… 2 (settle) 解决 ‹*question, matter, dispute, issue*›; 裁决 ‹*competition, contest*›; **to ~ a case** ‹*jury, judge*› 断案 3 (persuade) 使决定; **to ~ sb. to do sth.** 使某人决定做某事; **to ~ sb. against sth./doing sth.** 使某人决定不做某事; **the barrister's speech ~d the jury** 律师的发言使陪审团下了决断 4 (decisively influence) 决定…的结果; **this point could ~ (the outcome of) the match** 这 1 分可能决定比赛的胜负; **her father's death ~d her future/fate** 她父亲的去世决定了她的未来/命运
B *vi* 1 (make up one's mind) 决定; **I can't ~** 我拿不定主意; **to ~ between A and B** 在 A 和 B 之间选择; **to ~ against sth./doing sth.** 决定不做某事; **to ~ in favour of sth./doing sth.** 作出有利于某事物/做某事的决定 2 (make judgement) 裁决; **to ~ against sb./sth.** 作出对某人/某事物不利的裁决; **to ~ in favour of sb./sth.** 作出对某人/某事物有利的裁决; **to ~ for sb.** Jur 作出对某人有利的判决

Phrasal verb

• **decide on** *vt* [**~ on sth.**] 选定; **she ~d on a career in medicine** 她决定从医; **what made you ~ on this candidate?** 你为什么选定了这位候选人?; **they are expected to ~ on closing the school** 大家期望他们会决定关闭学校

decided /dɪˈsaɪdɪd/ *adj attrib* 明确无误的 ‹*improvement, difference, change, increase*›; **I have very ~ views on the subject** 我对这个问题的观点很明确

decidedly /dɪˈsaɪdɪdli/ *adv* 确实地; **~ happier** 明显更加高兴了

decider /dɪˈsaɪdə(r)/ *n* 1 Brit (game, match, set, race) 决胜局; (point) 决胜分; (goal) 决胜球 2 (deciding factor) 决定因素

deciding /dɪˈsaɪdɪŋ/ *adj* 决定性的 ‹*factor*›; 决胜的 ‹*point, goal, game*›

deciduous /dɪˈsɪdjʊəs, dɪˈsɪdʒʊəs/ *adj* 每年落叶的 ‹*tree, shrub, forest*›

decigram, decigramme /ˈdesɪɡræm/ ▸ p. 909 *n* 分克

decilitre Brit, **deciliter** Amer /ˈdesɪliːtə(r)/ *n* 分升

decimal /ˈdesɪml/ ▸ p. 521
A *n* [c] (fraction) **~ (fraction)** 小数; **convert 4/5 to a ~** 把 4/5 化为小数
B *adj* (in tenths or tens) 小数的; 十进制的 ‹*currency, measures*›; **~ number/system** 小数/十进制; **to go ~** 采用十进制

decimalization /ˌdesɪməlaɪˈzeɪʃn, Amer -lɪˈz-/ *n* [u] 1 Math 化小数 2 (of currency, measure) 采用十进制

decimalize /ˈdesɪməlaɪz/ *vt* 把…改为十进位 ‹*number*›; 把…化为小数 ‹*fraction*›; 把…改为十进制 ‹*currency, coinage, system*›

decimal: ~ place *n* 小数位; **to calculate sth. to two ~ places** 计算某数到小数点后两位; **~ point** *n* 小数点

decimate /ˈdesɪmeɪt/ *vt* 1 (kill, destroy) 大批毁灭 ‹*population, species*›; 大批杀死 ‹*people, animals*› 2 (drastically reduce) 大大削弱 ‹*transport, industry*›

decimation /ˌdesɪˈmeɪʃn/ *n* [u] 1 (killing, destruction) 毁灭; **the ~ of a tribe** 对一个部落的大批杀戮 2 (drastic reduction) 大幅度削弱

decimetre Brit, **decimeter** Amer /ˈdesɪmiːtə(r)/ ▸ p. 436 *n* 分米

decipher /dɪˈsaɪfə(r)/ *vt* 1 (decode) 破译 ‹*code, symbols, inscription, message*› 2 (make out) 辨认 ‹*handwriting*›; 理解 ‹*word, letters*›

decipherable /dɪˈsaɪfrəbl/ *adj* 可破译的 ‹*code, symbols, inscription, message*›

decision /dɪˈsɪʒn/ *n* 1 [c] (choice) 决定; **a ~ about sth./to do sth.** 关于某事/做某事的决定; **to make or take a ~** 作决定; **to come to or reach a ~** 作出决定; **the final ~ is yours** 最终的决定权在你手里 2 [c] (conclusion, judgement) 判决; **a ~ on sth.** 对某事的判决; **the referee's ~ is final** 裁判的判决不可更改 3 [u] (making up one's mind) 作决定; **the moment/burden of ~** 作决定的时刻/重任 4 [u] (decisiveness) 果断; **to do sth. with ~** 果断地做某事

decision-making *n* [u] 决策; **to be good at ~** 善于作决定; **~ process** 决策过程

decision theory *n* [u] 决策论

decisive /dɪˈsaɪsɪv/ *adj* 1 (able to decide quickly) 果断的 2 (conclusive) 决定性的 ‹*battle, victory, moment, influence*›

decisively /dɪˈsaɪsɪvli/ *adv* 果断地

decisiveness /dɪˈsaɪsɪvnɪs/ *n* [u] 1 (of person) 果断 2 (of approach) 决定性 3 (of answer, gesture) 确定无疑

deck /dek/
A *n* 1 Naut 甲板; **to be on ~** 在甲板上; **to go (up/out) on ~** 到甲板上去; **on/below ~** 在甲板上面/下面; **upper/car ~** 上层/车辆甲板 2 (on bus, plane) 层面; **upper/lower ~** 上层/下层; **the flight ~** 飞机驾驶舱 3 Audio (for records) 转盘支托面; (for cassettes) 走带机构 4 Amer (of cards) **a ~ of cards** 一副纸牌
B *vt* 1 (decorate) 装饰; **to ~ sth. with sth.** 用某物装饰 ‹*room, building, Christmas tree*› 2 (dress up) 盛装打扮; **to ~ sb. with sth.** 用…打扮某人 ‹*jewellery, clothes*›

Phrasal verb

• **deck out** *vt* 1 [**~ sth. out, ~ out sth**] (decorate) 装饰 2 [**~ sb. out**] (dress) 打扮; **to ~ oneself out in or with sth.** 用某物打扮自己

deck: ~chair *n* [户外用的] 帆布折椅; **~hand** *n* 普通水手; **~house** *n* 甲板室

decking /ˈdekɪŋ/ *n* [u] 甲板铺板

deck: ~ passenger *n* 统舱旅客; **~ quoits** *npl + v sing* Brit 甲板套环游戏

declaim /dɪˈkleɪm/
A *vt* 朗诵 ‹*poem, lines*›; 慷慨激昂地发表 ‹*views, speech*›
B *vi* 1 (speak aloud) 激昂陈词; **a preacher ~ing from the pulpit** 在讲坛上慷慨陈词的传道者 2 (protest) 激辩; **to ~ against sth.** (in speech, writing) 激烈抨击某事物

declamatory /dɪˈklæmətəri, Amer -tɔːri/ *adj* 慷慨激昂的 ‹*words, speech, style*›; 词藻华丽的 ‹*lines*›

declarable /dɪˈkleərəbl/ *adj* 应申报的 ‹*income, option*›

declaration /ˌdekləˈreɪʃn/ *n* 1 (proclamation) 宣布; **a ~ of war** 宣战; **the D~ of Independence/Human Rights** 《独立宣言》/《人权宣言》 2 (formal statement) 申报; **a ~ of income** 收益申报表; **a customs ~** 报关单 3 (assertion) 宣称; **a ~ of love** 爱的表白 4 (in cricket) 宣布结束赛局; **the ~ came just before tea** 比赛在喝茶时间快到时结束 5 Brit (in election) 宣布投票结果; **the ~ is expected within the next half hour** 预计半小时内将宣布投票结果

> **the Declaration of Independence**
>
> 《独立宣言》。北美洲的 13 个殖民地宣布脱离英国殖民统治而独立的文件。主要由后来成为美国第三任总统的托马斯·杰斐逊（Thomas Jefferson）起草。1776 年 7 月 4 日经第二次大陆会议（Second Continental Congress）通过，并由大部分代表于 8 月 2 日签署。7 月 4 日后来成为美国的独立纪念日（Independence Day）。宣言大体可分为三个部分。第一部分阐述独立的理论依据，“人人生而平等”（all men are created equal）的名言即出自该部分内容。第二部分历数英王在北美殖民地的暴政。第三部分正式宣布独立。《独立宣言》影响深远，对后来法国大革命的《人权宣言》更是产生了重要影响。有各州代表签名的《独立宣言》原稿现在保存在华盛顿特区的国家档案馆（National Archives）内。

declare /dɪˈkleə(r)/
A *vt* 1 (announce) 宣告; **to ~ war on sb.** 向某人宣战; **to ~ a state of emergency** 宣布进入紧急状态; **to ~ sb. guilty/the winner** 宣布某人有罪/获胜; **I ~ the meeting closed** 我宣布会议结束 2 (state firmly) 断言; (proclaim) 宣布; **to ~ that ...** 宣称…; **'this has never happened before,' I ~d** “这事以前从没发生过，”我断然地说; **a ~d atheist** 公开表态的无神论者 3 Fin, Jur, Tax 申报 ‹*goods, income*›; **nothing to ~** 没有什么要申报; **to ~ one's interest in a company** 申报在公司的股份
B *vi* 1 (make choice) 表态; **to ~ for/against sb./sth.** 声明支持/反对某人/某事 2 Amer Pol 宣布竞选总统; **the Governor of California is expected to ~ tomorrow** 加利福尼亚州州长可能于明天宣布竞选总统 3 (in cricket) [在所有击球手出局前] 宣布结束赛局; **Hampshire ~d at 420 for 6** 汉普郡队以 420 比 6 主动结束该局比赛
C *v refl* **to ~ oneself to be sb./sth.** 宣称自己是某人/某情况

declassify /ˌdiːˈklæsɪfaɪ/ *vt* «*government, authority*» 将…解密 ‹*document, paper, file*›

declension /dɪˈklenʃn/ *n* **1** [u] (variation of part of speech) [名词、代词、形容词的] 词形变化 **2** [c] (class of part of speech) [名词、代词、形容词的] 词形变化类别

declinable /dɪˈklaɪnəbl/ *adj* 可变格的 ‹*noun, adjective, pronoun*›

declination /ˌdeklɪˈneɪʃn/ *n* **1** Geog 磁偏角 **2** Astron 赤纬

decline /dɪˈklaɪn/

A *vi* **1** (become smaller) «*rate, sales*» 下降; «*quantity, demand, number*» 减少 **2** (wane) «*health*» 恶化; «*business*» 衰退; «*power, strength*» 衰弱; «*empire*» 衰落; «*influence, support, confidence*» 减退; «*status*» 下降 **3** (refuse) 婉拒 **4** Ling «*word*» 变格

B *vt* **1** 婉拒 ‹*offer, honour, promotion*›; **to ~ to do sth.** 婉拒做某事 **2** Ling 使…变格 ‹*word*›

C *n* **1** [u] (decrease) 下降; **a (small/steep) ~ in sth.** 某物的（小幅/急剧）下降; **to be on the** *or* **in ~** 在下降; **a 5% ~ to 175** 下降 5% 至 175 **2** [u and c] (waning) 衰退; **to be on the** *or* **in ~** 在衰退; **a ~ in sth.** 某事的衰退; **to go** *or* **fall into (a) ~** 陷入衰退; **his ~ into madness** 他发疯的过程

declining /dɪˈklaɪnɪŋ/ *adj* **1** (getting fewer, less) 逐渐减少的 ‹*numbers, rate, size, quantity*› **2** (waning) 日渐衰弱的 ‹*health*›; 衰落的 ‹*power*›; 下降的 ‹*interest*›

declining years *npl* 晚年; **the ~ of the empire** 帝国日渐没落的时期

decode /ˌdiːˈkəʊd/ *vt* **1** (convert code into plain text) 破译 **2** Comput 译解 **3** (analyse, interpret) 解读

décolletage /ˌdeɪkɒləˈtɑːʒ/ *n* = **décolleté B**

décolleté /deɪˈkɒlteɪ/

A *adj* 低胸的

B *n* 低胸

decolonize /ˌdiːˈkɒlənaɪz/ *vt* 使非殖民地化

decompose /ˌdiːkəmˈpəʊz/

A *vi* **1** (rot, decay) «*body, flesh, leaves, wood*» 腐烂 **2** Phys, Chem «*substance, chemical, light, organism*» 分解; **to ~ into sth.** 分解成某物

B *vt* **1** (cause to decay) «*bacteria, fungus, chemical*» 使…腐烂 ‹*body, flesh, leaf, wood*› **2** Phys, Chem «*process, device*» 分解 ‹*substance*›

decomposition /ˌdiːkɒmpəˈzɪʃn/ *n* [u] **1** (rot, decay) 腐烂 **2** Phys, Chem 分解

decompress /ˌdiːkəmˈpres/ *vt* **1** Comput 使解压缩 **2** (after dive) 使…减压 ‹*diver*›

decompression /ˌdiːkəmˈpreʃn/ *n* **1** (loss of air pressure) 失压 **2** (of diver) 减压 **3** Comput 解压缩

decompression: ~ chamber *n* 减压室; **~ sickness** *n* [u] 减压病

decongestant /ˌdiːkənˈdʒestənt/

A *n* 减充血剂

B *adj* 减轻充血的

deconsecrate /ˌdiːˈkɒnsɪkreɪt/ *vt* 把…改作俗用 ‹*church*›

decontaminate /ˌdiːkənˈtæmɪneɪt/ *vt* 给…消毒 ‹*person, room, bedding*›; 消除…的污染 ‹*area, building*›

decontamination /ˌdiːkənˌtæmɪˈneɪʃn/ *n* [u] (person, room, bedding) 消毒; (area, building) 消除污染

decontrol /ˌdiːkənˈtrəʊl/ *vt* (*pres p etc.* **-ll-**) 解除对…的控制 ‹*prices, trade, commodity*›

decor /ˈdeɪkɔː(r), Amer deɪˈkɔːr/ *n* [u] **1** (of house) 装饰布局 **2** Theat 舞台布景

decorate /ˈdekəreɪt/

A *vt* **1** (adorn) 装饰 ‹*cake, Christmas tree*›; **to ~ sth. with sth.** 用某物装饰某物 **2** (with paint and wallpaper) 粉刷装潢 **3** Mil 颁授; **to be ~d with** 获授予 ‹*medal*›; **the soldier was ~d for bravery** 这名士兵因表现英勇获得勋章

B *vi* (in house) 粉刷装潢

decorating /ˈdekəreɪtɪŋ/ *n* [u] 粉刷装潢; **a painting and ~ business** 油漆和粉刷装潢业务

decoration /ˌdekəˈreɪʃn/ *n* **1** [c] (ornament) 装饰品; **to put up/take down ~s** 挂起/取下装饰品 **2** [u] (act and state of decorating) 装饰; **sth. is only for ~** 某物只是摆设 **3** [u] (painting) 粉刷; (wallpapering) 裱糊墙纸 **4** [u] (quality, style) 装饰风格 **5** [c] Mil 勋章; **to be awarded a ~ for sth.** 因某事被授予勋章

decorative /ˈdekərətɪv, Amer ˈdekəreɪtɪv/ *adj* 装饰性的

decoratively /ˈdekərətɪvli/ *adv* 装饰性地

decorator /ˈdekəreɪtə(r)/ *n* esp Brit 室内装潢工

decorous /ˈdekərəs/ *adj* 端庄稳重的 ‹*action, gesture, manners*›; 礼貌得体的 ‹*behaviour, language, speech*›

decorously /ˈdekərəsli/ *adv* 端庄稳重地

decorum /dɪˈkɔːrəm/ *n* [u] 端庄稳重; **with ~** 端庄礼貌地; **a sense of ~** 懂礼节

decoy

A /ˈdiːkɔɪ/ *n* **1** (lure) 诱饵 **2** (false) 假物品; **a ~ gun** 仿真枪 **3** Hunt (bird) 假鸟; (animal) 假兽; **a ~ duck** 诱饵鸭子

B /dɪˈkɔɪ/ *vt* **1** Mil 诱骗; **to ~ sb. into sth.** 引诱某人进入某处; **to ~ sb. away from sth.** 把某人从某处引开 **2** Hunt 引诱; **to ~ animals into the trap** 把动物诱入陷阱

decrease

A /dɪˈkriːs/ *vi* «*number, amount, sales, population*» 减少; «*size, volume, strength, power*» 减小; «*price, value, speed, temperature*» 降低; «*enthusiasm*» 减退; **to ~ in size/number/value** 尺寸减小/数量减少/价值降低

B /dɪˈkriːs/ *vt* 减少 ‹*number, amount, sales, population*›; 减小 ‹*size, volume, strength, power*›; 降低 ‹*price, value, speed, temperature*›

C /ˈdiːkriːs/ *n* 减少; **a ~ in** *or* **of sth.** 某物的减少; **to be on the ~** 在下降

decreasing /dɪˈkriːsɪŋ/ *adj* 逐渐减少的

decreasingly /dɪˈkriːsɪŋli/ *adv* 逐渐减少地

decree /dɪˈkriː/

A *n* **1** [c and u] (order and issue of an order) 法令; **by government/royal ~** 根据政府/皇家法令; **to issue a ~** 颁布政令 **2** [c] (judgement) 裁定; **~ absolute/nisi** 最终/暂准判决

B *vt* **1** (order, announce) «*ruler, president, pope*» 颁布; «*head teacher*» 规定; **it was ~d that ...** 据裁定… **2** Jur 裁决

decrepit /dɪˈkrepɪt/ *adj* **1** (old and infirm) 老弱的; **a ~ old man** 龙钟老翁 **2** (ruined) 破旧的 ‹*building*›

decriminalize /ˌdiːˈkrɪmɪnəlaɪz/ *vt* 使合法化

decry /dɪˈkraɪ/ *vt* 公开谴责

decrypt /diːˈkrɪpt/ *vt* 破译

decryption /diːˈkrɪpʃn/ *n* 破译密码

dedicate /ˈdedɪkeɪt/

A *vt* **1** (devote) 献出; **to ~ sb./sth. to sth.** 把…奉献给某事物 ‹*time, energy*›; **she ~d her life to ...** 她毕生致力于…; **to be ~d to sb./sth.** 对某人一心一意/致力于某事物 **2** (cite) 在…上题献词; **to ~ sth. to sb.** 把…献给某人 ‹*book, record, performance, film*› **3** Relig 为…举行奉献典礼 ‹*church, chapel, temple*›; 为…举行落成仪式 ‹*monument*›

B *v refl* **to ~ oneself to sth.** 献身于某事

dedicated /ˈdedɪkeɪtɪd/ *adj* **1** (devoted) 献身的 ‹*person*›; **to be ~ to sth./doing sth.** 专心致志于某事/做某事; **she's a ~ shopper!** 她真是个购物狂! **2** (assigned to a person, restricted to a purpose) 专用的; **a ~ telephone line** 专用电话线; **a ~ leisure area** 专门的休闲区

dedication /ˌdedɪˈkeɪʃn/ *n* **1** [u] (devoted attitude) 奉献精神; **~ to sb./sth.** 对某人/某事物的奉献精神 **2** [c] (in a book, work) 献词; **a ~ to sb.** 给某人的献词 **3** [u] Relig 奉献典礼;

the ~ of the church/temple/mosque 奉献教堂/寺院/清真寺的典礼

deduce /dɪˈdjuːs, Amer -ˈdus/ *vt* 推断; **to ~ sth. from sth.** 根据某事物推断某事; **to ~ that ...** 推断出…; **to ~ what/where/who/why ...** 推断出什么/哪里/谁/为什么…

deducible /dɪˈdjuːsəbl, Amer -ˈduːs-/ *adj* 可推论的; **to be ~ from sth.** 可根据某事物推断

deduct /dɪˈdʌkt/ *vt* 扣除; **to ~ sth. from sth.** 把某数量从某数量中减去; **income tax is ~ed at source** 所得税在源头征收

deductible /dɪˈdʌktəbl/

A *adj* 可扣除的 ‹*costs, sum*›; 可减免的 ‹*expenses*›

B *n* Amer Insur 免赔额

deduction /dɪˈdʌkʃn/ *n* **1** [u] (act of deducting) 扣除 **2** [c] (deducted amount) 扣除额; **after ~s** 扣税后 **3** [c] (conclusion) 推论; **to make a ~ (from sth.)** （从某事物）得出推论; **a ~ about/from sth.** 有关某事物/从某事物得出的推论 **4** [u] (reasoning) 推理; **by ~** 通过推理

deductive /dɪˈdʌktɪv/ *adj* 演绎的; **~ reasoning** 演绎推理

deed /diːd/ *n* **1** (action) 行为; **to do one's good ~ for the day** 做善事; **in ~ if not in name** 事实上而不是名义上; **in word and ~** 言行上 **2** liter (heroic feat) 英勇事迹 **3** Jur (esp of property) 契约; **the ~s to the house** 房契; **my name wasn't on the ~s** 我的名字不在契据上; **~ box** 契据文书保险箱

deed: ~ of covenant *n* Brit 付款契据; **~ poll** *n* Brit 单务契约; **to change one's name by ~ poll** 依单务契约改名

deejay /ˈdiːdʒeɪ/ *n* colloq = **disc jockey**

deem /diːm/ *vt* 认为; **to ~ sb./sth. to be sth.** 认为某人怎么样/某事是某事; **to be ~ed to be/do sth.** 被认为怎么样/干某事; **your essay was ~ed the best** 你的短文评价最高; **it was ~ed necessary/advisable to ...** 大家认为…有必要/是明智的

deep /diːp/

A ▸**p. 436** *adj* **1** (vertically) 深的; **a hole 10 metres ~, a 10-metre-~ hole** 10 米深的洞; **ankle-/waist-~** 齐踝/腰深的; **a ~-pile carpet** 厚绒地毯; **to be in ~ water** fig 处于困境 **2** (horizontally) 纵深的; **the cupboard isn't ~ enough** 碗橱进深不够; **that plot of land is 50 metres ~** 那块地纵深有 50 米; **a 30-centimetre-~ shelf** 一个进深 30 厘米的架子; **the people stood six ~** 人们站成 6 排 **3** (low in pitch) 低沉的 ‹*note, sound, tone, voice*› **4** ▸**p. 134** (intense in tone) [色调] 深的; **~ darkness** 漆黑; **a ~ tan** 晒得黝黑的肤色 **5** (strongly felt, profound) 深切的 ‹*emotion, impression*›; 浓厚的 ‹*interest*›; 由衷的 ‹*admiration*›; 极度的 ‹*outrage, trouble*›; **~ love** 挚爱; **~ faith** 坚定的信仰; **~ depression** 深深的沮丧; **you have my ~est sympathy** 我对你深表同情; **it is with ~est regret that we announce the death of ...** 我们非常遗憾地宣告…去世了; **in ~ disgrace** 极不光彩地 **6** (impenetrable) 茂密的 ‹*jungle, forest, undergrowth*›; **they live in ~est Wales** hum 他们生活在威尔士极偏远的地区 **7** (impossible to understand) 捉摸不透的 ‹*person, secret, mystery*› **8** (intellectually profound) 深奥的 ‹*book*›; 深刻的 ‹*thinker, thought, insight*›; 深入的 ‹*discussion*›; 渊博的 ‹*knowledge*›; 造诣精深的 ‹*writer, person*›; **at a ~er level** 在更深的层面上; **you're a ~ one!** hum 你是真人不露相啊! **9** (from which it is hard to wake) 深度的 ‹*sleep, coma, trance*› **10** *pred* (involved, absorbed) 深深陷入的; **she was ~ in thought** 她陷入深思; **he's ~ in a book** 他在专心看书; **we are ~ in debt** 我们债台高筑 **11** Sport 靠近对方端线的 ‹*shot, pass, serve*› **12** (slow and steady) [呼吸] 深的; **she gave a ~ sigh of relief** 她深深松了一口气; **~ breathing** 深呼吸

B *adv* **1** (a long way down) 深深地 ‹*dig, bury, cut*›; **~ beneath the earth's surface** 地表下深处; **she plunged the knife ~ into his body**

d

她把刀深深地捅进了他的身体 **2** (a long way in) 深入地 ‹*venture, penetrate*›; **to go ~ into enemy territory** 深入敌境; **our house is ~ in the (heart of the) countryside** 我们的房子远在农村（腹地）; **to read/work/talk/dance ~ into the night** 看书/工作/谈话/跳舞到深夜; **to gaze** *or* **look ~ into sb.'s eyes** 深深地凝视某人; **in ~** colloq 深陷其中 **3** fig (emotionally) 强烈地; **to go ~** «*loyalty, faith, instinct, emotion*» 变得强烈; **her problems go ~er than just temporary depression** 她的问题不止是一时的沮丧; **~ in my heart** 在我内心深处; **~ down (inside)** 在内心深处; **their prejudices run ~** 他们的偏见根深蒂固 **4** Sport 靠近对方端线 ‹*kick, serve, hit*›

C *n* liter **the ~** 大海

deepen /'di:pən/

A *vt* **1** (make deeper or darker) 使…变深 ‹*hollow, river, colour*› **2** (lower in pitch) 使…低沉 ‹*note, sound, tone, voice*› **3** (intensify) 使…变强烈 ‹*emotion, interest*› **4** (make more profound) 加深 ‹*understanding, awareness*›; 增长 ‹*knowledge*›

B *vi* **1** «*water, wrinkle, colour*» 变深; «*snow, mud*» 变厚; **his frown ~ed** 他皱紧了眉头; **his tan ~ed** 他晒得更黑了 **2** (lower in pitch) «*note, sound, tone, voice*» 变低沉 **3** (become more intense) «*emotion, interest*» 变强烈; «*friendship*» 变深厚; «*trouble, crisis*» 恶化 **4** (become more profound) «*knowledge, understanding, awareness*» 加深 **5** (become more impenetrable) «*night*» 变黑; «*mystery*» 变深奥; **the darkness ~ed** 天更黑了

deep end *n* [游泳池的] 深水区; **to go off (at) the ~** fig colloq 立刻变得非常激动; **to jump** *or* **be thrown in at the ~** fig colloq 陷入未能料到的艰难处境

deepening /'di:pənɪŋ, 'di:pnɪŋ/ *adj attrib* **1** (increasing in depth, becoming darker in colour) 越来越深的 ‹*water, wrinkle, colour*›; 越来越厚的 ‹*snow, mud*› **2** (becoming lower in pitch) 越来越低沉的 ‹*note, sound, tone, voice*› **3** (becoming more intense) 越来越强烈的 ‹*emotion, interest*›; 逐渐加深的 ‹*friendship*›; 日益严重的 ‹*trouble, crisis*› **4** (becoming more profound) 越来越深刻的 ‹*knowledge, understanding, awareness*› **5** (becoming more impenetrable) 越来越深的 ‹*darkness, night*›; 越来越难解的 ‹*mystery*›

deep: ~-fat-fryer *n* 油炸锅; **~-felt** *adj* 深切的; **to express one's ~-felt thanks** 表达自己深深的感谢

deep-freeze

A *n* 冰柜

B *vt* (*pt* **deep-froze,** *pp* **deep-frozen**) 冷冻

deep: ~-fried *adj* 油炸的; **~-fry** *vt* 油炸; **~ fryer** *n* 油炸锅

deeply /'di:pli/ *adv* **1** (intensely) 强烈地; **the ~ held convictions** 坚定的信念 **2** (analytically) 深刻地 ‹*think, analyse*›; 深入地 ‹*study, discuss*›; **to go ~ into sth.** 深入探讨某事; **~ meaningful** 意义深刻的 **3** (to a great depth) 深层地; **to be ~ divided about sth.** 在某事上分歧很大; **to be ~ wounded by sth.** 被某事深深地伤害; 深深地 ‹*breathe, sigh*›; **to sleep ~** 酣睡

deep: ~-rooted *adj* **1** fig 根深蒂固的; **~-rooted prejudice/belief/custom/affection** 难以消除的偏见/坚定不移的信仰/根深蒂固的习惯/强烈的爱; **2** Bot 根深的 ‹*plant*›; **~-sea** *adj attrib* 深海的; **~-sea diver** ▸p. 409 *n* 深海潜水员; **~-sea diving** *n* [u] 深海潜水; **~-sea fisherman** ▸p. 409 *n* 深海渔民; **~-sea fishing** *n* [u] 深海捕鱼; **~-seated** *adj* **1** = **~-rooted 1**; **2** Med 深位的 ‹*disease, infection*›; **~-set** *adj* 深陷的; **D~ South** *n* Amer **the D~ South** 南方腹地; **~ space** *n* [u] = **outer space**; **~-vein thrombosis** ▸p. 377 *n* [u] 深静脉血栓形成

deer /dɪə(r)/ *n* (*pl* **deer**) **1** (species) 鹿 **2** (female) 母鹿

> **the Deep South**
>
> 南方腹地，亦称 Lower South。美国东南部的几个州，通常认为包括亚拉巴马（Alabama）、佐治亚（Georgia）、密西西比（Mississippi）和南卡罗来纳（South Carolina），有时也包括得克萨斯东部（East Texas）。这些州在历史上都是蓄奴州，在1861-1865 年的美国内战中曾脱离联邦；现代美国民权运动亦发源于这一地区。同时，这一地区被视作美国南方传统文化的腹地，政治和宗教立场多偏于保守。

deer: ~skin *n* [u] 鹿皮; **~stalker** *n* 猎鹿帽

de-escalate /ˌdi:'eskəleɪt/

A *vt* 使降级; **to ~ tension/strike/violence** 逐步缓和紧张局势/使罢工降级/减少暴力行为

B *vi* 降级

deface /dɪ'feɪs/ *vt* **1** (damage) 污损…的外观 ‹*picture, monument, town*›; **to ~ a wall with graffiti** 在墙壁上涂鸦 **2** (make illegible) 涂掉 ‹*inscription, notice, signature*›

de facto /ˌdeɪ 'fæktəʊ/

A *adj* 事实上的; **a ~ one-party system** 事实上的一党制

B *adv* 事实上

defamation /ˌdefə'meɪʃn/ *n* [u] 诬蔑; **~ of character** 人格诽谤

defamatory /dɪ'fæmətri, Amer -tɔ:ri/ *adj* 诽谤性的

defame /dɪ'feɪm/ *vt* 诽谤

default /dɪ'fɔ:lt/

A *n* **1** (failure to pay) 未履行债务; **to be in ~ of payment** 拖欠付款; **the company is in ~** 这个公司未履行债务 **2** Comput 默认; **the ~ settings** 系统预设值

B *vi* **1** (fail to pay) 拖欠; **to ~ on payments/a loan/a fine** 拖欠付款/借款/罚款; **to ~ on one's obligations/promise** 未履行职责/违背诺言 **2** Comput 默认; **to ~ to sth.** 预设为… **3** (fail to appear in court) 未到庭

C **by default** *adv phr* (due to lack of opposition) 因对手缺席; (due to lack of conscious choice) 因没有主动选择; **to win by ~** 因对手不到场而获胜; **she was held responsible by ~** 她因为没有采取措施而负有责任; **he became an actor by ~** 他当上演员并非刻意所为

D **in default of** *prep phr* 由于缺乏

defaulter /dɪ'fɔ:ltə(r)/ *n* 未履行债务者

defeat /dɪ'fi:t/

A *n* **1** [u and c] Mil, Pol, Sport (loss) 失败; (victory (over)) 击败; **to meet with** *or* **suffer a ~** 遭到失败; **to concede** *or* **admit ~** 认输; **to stare ~ in the face** 眼看就要失败; **the ~ of fascism** 战胜法西斯主义 **2** [u] (of proposal, bill) 否决 **3** [u] (of hope, plan) 落空; **to give up in ~** 无功而返

B *vt* **1** Mil, Pol, Sport (vanquish) 击败; **Labour ~ed the Conservatives by nearly 2,000 votes** 工党以高出近 2,000 张选票的优势击败了保守党 **2** Pol (achieve rejection of) 否决 ‹*proposal, bill, motion, amendment*› **3** (overcome in argument) 驳倒 ‹*speaker, argument*› **4** (thwart) 使…落空 ‹*hope, plan, ambition*›; **to be ~ed in one's attempts/efforts (to do sth.)** （做某事的）企图/努力受挫; **don't be ~ed!** 别气馁！; **to ~ one's own purpose** *or* **ends** 违背初衷 **5** (baffle) «*problem, task, concept*» 难倒 ‹*person*›; **the instruction manual completely ~ed me** 说明书完全把我搞晕了

defeated /dɪ'fi:tɪd/ *adj* **1** (beaten) 被击败的; **the ~ army/proposal** 败军/被否决的提议 **2** (demoralized) 泄气的; **to look ~** 看上去消沉

defeatism /dɪ'fi:tɪzəm/ *n* [u] 失败主义

defeatist /dɪ'fi:tɪst/

A *n* 失败主义者; **don't be such a ~!** 别那么没斗志！

B *adj* 失败主义者的

defecate /'defəkeɪt/ *vi* formal 排便

defecation /ˌdefə'keɪʃn/ *n* [u] formal 排便

defect

A /'di:fekt/ *n* (flaw) 瑕疵; (disability) 缺陷; **a character ~** 性格缺陷; **a visual/hearing/speech ~** 视觉/听觉/言语缺陷; **a congenital ~ of the spine** 脊椎的先天畸形

B /dɪ'fekt/ *vi* 叛变; **to ~ from sth./somewhere** 背叛某机构/叛离某地; **to ~ to sth./somewhere** 叛逃到某机构/某地

defection /dɪ'fekʃn/ *n* 背叛; **a ~ from/to sth.** 背叛/叛逃到某机构

defective /dɪ'fektɪv/ *adj* **1** (faulty) 有缺点的; (referring to body part) 有缺陷的 ‹*vision, hearing, speech, gene*›; **~ workmanship** 工艺缺陷; **structurally ~** 结构上有缺陷的; **a ~ notion of the truth** 对事实的曲解 **2** Ling 不完全变化的

defector /dɪ'fektə(r)/ *n* 背叛者

defence /dɪ'fens/ Brit *n* **1** [u] (act of protecting) 保卫; **to come** *or* **go to sb.'s ~** 保护某人; **to put up a brave ~** 勇敢自卫; **to die in ~ of one's country** 为保卫祖国而牺牲; **Ministry/Minister of D~** Brit 国防部/国防大臣; **~ expenditure/budget** 国防开支/预算 **2** [c] (means of protection) 防御物; **a line of ~** 防线; **a ~ against invaders** 防御侵略者的屏障; **sea ~s** 海防工事 **3** [u and c] (support) 辩解; **to come** *or* **go to sb.'s ~** 为某人辩解; **in ~ of sb./sth.** 为某人/某事辩解; **I want to say in my ~ that ...** 我想为自己辩解的是…; **he leapt to her ~** 他挺身为她辩解; **to put up a ~** 进行辩解 **4** [u and c] Jur (case) 辩护; **to conduct sb.'s/one's own ~** 为某人/自己进行辩护; **a witness for the ~** 辩方证人; **a ~ lawyer/witness** 辩方律师/证人 **5** [u] Sport (defending) 防守; **his main role is (in) ~** 他的主要任务是防守 **6** [c] Sport (team members) 防守队员; **to play in** *or* **for the ~** 打防守 **7** [u] Sport (protection of title) 卫冕; **Barcelona's ~ of the European Cup** 巴塞罗纳队对欧洲冠军杯的成功卫冕

Defence Department *n* Brit 国防部

defenceless Brit /dɪ'fensləs/ *adj* **1** (vulnerable) 不能自卫的; **a ~ old woman** 没有自卫能力的老妇人; **~ civilians** 手无寸铁的民众 **2** (without defence) 无防御的 ‹*town, country*›

defencelessness /dɪ'fensləsnəs/ *n* Brit (of person, animal) 无自卫能力; (of town, country) 无防御

defence: ~ mechanism *n* Brit **1** (of the body) 防御机理; **2** Psych 防御机制; **D~ Minister** *n* Brit 国防部长

defend /dɪ'fend/

A *vt* **1** (protect, guard) «*armed forces*» 保卫 ‹*country, territory*›; «*person, animal*» 保护 ‹*person, young*›; **to ~ against** *or* **from sth.** 抵御某事物 **2** (support) 捍卫 ‹*freedom, interests, rights*›; 为…辩解 ‹*action, decision*› **3** Jur «*lawyer*» 为…辩护 ‹*client*› **4** Sport (protect) «*player, goalkeeper*» 防守 ‹*goal*› **5** (in contest) 保住 ‹*championship, record*›; **to successfully ~ one's title** 成功卫冕; **the government is fighting to ~ its majority** 内阁力争保住自己多数党的地位

B *vi* Sport 防守

C *v refl* **1** (protect oneself) **to ~ oneself (against** *or* **from sb./sth.)** 保护自己（免遭某人/某物的侵害） **2** (protect against criticism) **to ~ oneself (against sth.)** （针对某事）为自己辩解

defendant /dɪ'fendənt/ *n* 被告

defender /dɪ'fendə(r)/ *n* **1** (protector) 捍卫者; **D~ of the Faith** 护教者 **2** Sport 防守队员

defending /dɪ'fendɪŋ/ *adj attrib* **1** Sport 卫冕的; **the ~ champion** 卫冕冠军 **2** Jur 辩护的; **a ~ counsel** 辩护律师

defense /dɪ'fens/ *n* Amer = **defence**

Defense Department *n* Amer 国防部

defenseless /dɪ'fensləs/ *n* Amer = **defenceless**

Defense Secretary *n* Amer 国防部长

defensible /dɪˈfensɪbl/ *adj* 1 (justifiable) 有正当理由的; **a morally ~ penal system** 合乎道德的刑罚制度; **~ behaviour** 合乎情理的行为 2 (capable of being protected) 可防卫的; **a fort with a ~ yard** 有护院的城堡; **territory with ~ boundaries** 边界可防御的领土

defensive /dɪˈfensɪv/
A *adj* 1 (intended to defend) 防御的; **~ barriers** 防御屏障; **to take ~ action** 采取防御措施 2 (anxious to defend) 有戒心的 ‹*attitude*›; 辩护的 ‹*speech, article*›; **to be very ~ about sth.** 竭力维护某事物 3 *attrib* Sport 守势的; **a slick ~ move** 巧妙的防守动作
B *n* [u] 1 (gen) 戒备状态; **to put sb. on the ~** 使某人警觉起来 2 Sport 守势; **to be on the ~** 处于守势

defer[1] /dɪˈfɜː(r)/ *vt* (*pres p etc.* **-rr-**) 推迟; **to ~ making a decision** 推迟作决定; **to ~ sentence** Jur 延期判刑; **to ~ sb.'s military service** 使某人缓期服役; **~red payment** 延期支付; **a ~red loan/share** 递延的贷款费/延期派息股

defer[2] *vi* (*pres p etc.* **-rr-**) **to ~ to sb./sth.** 听从某人/遵从某事物

deference /ˈdefərəns/ *n* [u] 遵从; **in ~ to sb./sth.** 尊重某人/遵从某事物地; **out of ~ to sb./sth.** 出于对某人/某事物的尊重; **to show ~ to sb.** 对某人表示敬意

deferential /ˌdefəˈrenʃl/ *adj* 恭敬的; **to be ~ to sb.** 对某人毕恭毕敬

deferentially /ˌdefəˈrenʃəli/ *adv* 恭敬地

deferment /dɪˈfɜːmənt/, **deferral** /dɪˈfɜːrəl/ *ns* [c and u] 推迟; **~ of a debt/the sentence** 延期还债/判决

deferred annuity *n* 延期年金

defiance /dɪˈfaɪəns/ *n* 违抗; **to do sth. in ~** 一意孤行做某事; **in ~ of sth./sb.** 公然违抗某事/某人地; **a gesture/an act of ~** 反抗的表示/行为; **~ of danger/orders** 对危险的藐视/对命令的违抗

defiant /dɪˈfaɪənt/ *adj* 违抗的 ‹*person*›; 藐视的 ‹*manner, tone*›; **to be ~ of sb./sth.** 反抗某人/某事

defiantly /dɪˈfaɪəntli/ *adv* 反抗地

defibrillation /ˌdiːfɪbrɪˈleɪʃn/ *n* 去心脏纤颤

defibrillator /ˌdiːˈfɪbrɪleɪtə(r)/ *n* 去纤颤器

deficiency /dɪˈfɪʃənsi/ *n* 1 (shortage) 缺乏; **a ~ of funds** 资金不足 2 (inadequacy) 缺点; **his deficiencies as a poet** 他作为诗人的不足之处 3 (mental or physical defect) 缺陷; **a hearing ~** 听力缺陷

deficiency disease *n* 营养缺乏病

deficient /dɪˈfɪʃnt/ *adj* 1 (lacking) 缺乏的; **to be ~ in sth.** 缺少某物 2 (faulty) 有缺点的; **a ~ service** 不完善的服务

deficit /ˈdefɪsɪt/ *n* 赤字; **a ~ of £50,000** 5万英镑的亏空; **to be in ~** 出现亏空; **a budget ~** 预算赤字

deficit: ~ financing *n* [u] 赤字财政; **~ spending** *n* [u] 赤字开支

defile[1] /dɪˈfaɪl/ *vt* 1 (pollute) 污染 ‹*water, land, countryside*›; fig 玷污 ‹*purity, nobility, reputation*› 2 Relig 亵渎 ‹*church, temple, altar, tomb*›

defile[2] /ˈdiːfaɪl/ *n* 峡道

defilement /dɪˈfaɪlmənt/ *n* [u] 1 (pollution) (of water, land, countryside) 污染; fig (of purity, nobility, reputation) 玷污 2 Relig (of church, temple, altar, tomb) 亵渎

definable /dɪˈfaɪnəbl/ *adj* 可定义的; **my feelings are not easily ~** 我的感情不容易说清楚

define /dɪˈfaɪn/ *vt* 1 (give definition of) 给…下定义 ‹*word, term, phrase, idiom*›; **to ~ sth. as sth.** 把某物定义为某物 2 (express clearly) 阐明 ‹*feeling, change, problem, quality*›; **I can't ~ how I feel about him** 我无法说清对他的感觉 3 (specify limits of) 界定 ‹*duty, jurisdiction, function, role*›; **clearly ~d responsibilities** 明确规定的责任 4 (delineate) 描出…的外形; **to be ~d against sth.** «*tree, building, profile*» 在某物的映衬下显出轮廓

defined /dɪˈfaɪnd/ *adj* 1 (described) 确定的 ‹*limits, power, terms*› 2 (marked out) 清晰的 ‹*outline, shape*›

defined: ~ benefit pension plan *n* 固定收益养老金计划; **~ contribution pension plan** *n* 固定缴费养老金计划

definite /ˈdefɪnɪt/ *adj* 1 (clear and precise) 明确的 ‹*answer, result, opinion*›; **~ evidence** 确凿的证据 2 (fixed) 不能更改的 ‹*decision, plan, arrangement*›; **there's nothing ~ yet, nothing is ~ yet** 什么都没定下来呢; **it is ~ that ...** …是肯定的; **to give sb. a ~ refusal** 断然拒绝某人 3 *attrib* (noticeable) 明显的 ‹*change, improvement, increase, mark*› 4 *pred* (certain, clear) **to be ~ about sth.** «*person*» 对某事物有把握 5 *attrib* (confident, assertive) 自信的 ‹*manner, tone of voice*›

definite article *n* 定冠词

definitely /ˈdefɪnɪtli/ *adv* 1 (certainly) 确实地; **this one is ~ the best/cheapest** *etc.* 这个肯定是最好的/最便宜的等; **he's ~ not my type** 他的确不是我喜欢的那种人 2 (perceptibly) 明显地; **it is ~ colder today** 今天显然冷多了 3 (categorically) 明确地; **she stated her opinion very ~** 她非常明确地表明了观点

definition /ˌdefɪˈnɪʃn/ *n* 1 [c] (of word, term, phrase, idiom) 释义; (of feeling, change, problem, quality) 描述; (of duties, jurisdiction, function, role) 限定; **by ~** 根据定义 2 [u] (clarity) 清楚; **his ideas lack ~** 他的看法不明确 3 [u] TV, Comput, Phot 清晰度; **a photo with good/bad ~** 清晰度高/低的照片

definitive /dɪˈfɪnətɪv/ *adj* 1 (conclusive) 最终的 ‹*result, decision, solution*› 2 (authoritative) 最权威的 ‹*book, research, interpretation*›; **a ~ performance** 最佳表演

definitively /dɪˈfɪnətɪvli/ *adv* 1 (conclusively) 决定性地; **to determine ~ the cause of the accident** 最终确定事故的原因 2 (authoritatively) 最权威地; **I can't speak ~ on the matter** 关于这件事我的说法并非是最权威的

deflate /dɪˈfleɪt/
A *vt* 1 (let air out of) 放掉…的气 ‹*tyre, balloon, ball*› 2 fig 使泄气; **her harsh words ~d his pride** 她尖刻的话挫损了他的自尊; **to be ~d by someone's criticism/lack of enthusiasm** 因某人的批评/缺乏热情而失去信心 3 Econ 紧缩; **to ~ the economy** 紧缩经济
B *vi* «*tyre, balloon, ball*» 瘪掉

deflated /ˌdiːˈfleɪtɪd/ *adj* 1 (emptied of air) 瘪的 ‹*ball, balloon, tyre*› 2 (less confident or proud) 泄气的 ‹*person*›; 受挫的 ‹*ego, confidence, pride*›; 受损的 ‹*reputation, image*›

deflation /dɪˈfleɪʃn/ *n* [u] 1 Econ 通货紧缩 2 (of tyre, balloon etc.) (act) 放气; (state) 瘪 3 (of person, confidence etc.) 泄气; **a feeling of ~** 灰心丧气的感觉

deflationary /ˌdiːˈfleɪʃənəri, Amer -neri/ *adj* 通货紧缩的 ‹*measures, policy*›

deflect /dɪˈflekt/
A *vt* 1 (from direction, course) 使…偏斜 ‹*bullet*›; 使…转向 ‹*air, water*›; **the ball was ~ed into the goal** 球反弹进了球门; **the missile was ~ed from its course** 导弹偏离了轨道 2 fig 转移 ‹*attention, criticism, accusation*›; **to ~ sth. from sth.** 把某事从某事移开 3 (dissuade) 劝阻; **to ~ sb. from their purpose/action** 使某些人放弃自己的意图/停止自己的行动
B *vi* «*missile, ball, bullet*» 偏斜; «*air, water*» 转向

deflection /dɪˈflekʃn/ *n* [u and c] (of missile) 偏离; (of indicator needle) 偏度

deflower /ˌdiːˈflaʊə(r)/ *vt* dated or liter 夺去…的贞操

defog /ˌdiːˈfɒg/ *vt* Amer = **demist**

defogger /ˌdiːˈfɒgə(r)/ *n* esp Amer = **demister**

defoliant /ˌdiːˈfəʊlɪənt/ *n* 脱叶剂

defoliate /ˌdiːˈfəʊlɪeɪt/ *vt* 除去…的叶

defoliation /ˌdiːfəʊlɪˈeɪʃn/ *n* [u] (act) 除叶; (state) 落叶

deforest /ˌdiːˈfɒrɪst/ *vt* 砍伐…的森林

deforestation /ˌdiːfɒrɪˈsteɪʃn/ *n* [u] 砍伐森林

deform /dɪˈfɔːm/
A *vt* 1 (distort) 使…成畸形 ‹*limb, skull, organ*›; **a disease that ~s the spine** 使脊柱畸变的疾病 2 (alter shape of) 使…变形 ‹*structure, outline, metal, plastic*›
B *vi* «*limb, skull, organ*» 畸变; «*structure, outline, metal, plastic*» 变形

deformation /ˌdiːfɔːˈmeɪʃn/ *n* 1 [c] Med (act or process) 畸变; (state) 畸形; **~ of the fingers** 手指的畸形 2 [u] (of structure, outline, metal, plastic) 变形; **rock undergoing slow ~** 形状发生缓慢变化的岩石

deformed /dɪˈfɔːmd/ *adj* 畸形的 ‹*person, limb*›; 变形的 ‹*object*›

deformity /dɪˈfɔːməti/ *n* 1 [c] (instance) 畸形; **a ~ of sth.** 某物的畸形 2 [u] (state or condition) 畸变; **spinal ~** 脊柱畸变

DEFRA /ˈdefrə/ *abbr* Brit = **Department for Environment, Food, and Rural Affairs**

defrag /ˌdiːˈfræg/ *vt* 去除…的碎片 ‹*disk*›

defraud /dɪˈfrɔːd/ *vt* 骗取; **to ~ sb. of sth.** 诈取某人某物

defray /dɪˈfreɪ/ *vt* 支付

defrayal /dɪˈfreɪəl/, **defrayment** /dɪˈfreɪmənt/ *ns* 支付

defrock /ˌdiːˈfrɒk/ *vt* 免去…的圣职

defrost /ˌdiːˈfrɒst/
A *vt* 1 (thaw) 使解冻 2 (remove ice from) 给…除霜 ‹*fridge, freezer*›; Amer (remove ice from a surface) 除去…上的冰霜 ‹*windscreen, window, car, lock*›
B *vi* 1 (thaw) «*frozen food*» 解冻 2 (lose ice) «*freezer, refrigerator*» 除霜; **our new fridge ~s automatically** 我们的新冰箱会自动除霜
C *v refl* **to ~ itself** «*refrigerator, freezer*» 自动除霜

defroster /ˌdiːˈfrɒstə(r)/ *n* 1 (of refrigerator) 除霜装置 2 Amer (of windscreen) (tool) 除霜器; (substance) 除霜剂

deft /deft/ *adj* 1 (dexterous) 熟练的 ‹*surgeon, carpenter*›; 灵活的 ‹*hands, feet*›; **to be ~ at sth./doing sth.** 在某事/做某事方面娴熟 2 (inventive) 巧妙的

deftly /ˈdeftli/ *adv* 熟练地

defunct /dɪˈfʌŋkt/ *adj* 不复存在的 ‹*custom, practice*›; 已废除的 ‹*law*›; 已停业的 ‹*company*›; 已解散的 ‹*organization*›

defuse /ˌdiːˈfjuːz/ *vt* 1 (remove fuse from) 拆除…的引信 ‹*bomb, explosive device*› 2 (make less tense) 平息 ‹*crisis, dispute*›; 缓和 ‹*situation*›

defy /dɪˈfaɪ/ *vt* 1 (disobey) 反抗 ‹*superior, government, authorities*›; 违抗 ‹*parent, teacher*›; 蔑视 ‹*law, convention, stereotype, rules*› 2 (challenge) 激; **to ~ sb. to do sth.** 激某人做某事; **I ~ you to prove me wrong** 我倒要看看你能否证明我是错的 3 (elude, resist) 使不可能; **to ~ sb.'s efforts/attempts to do sth.** 使某人做某事的努力不起作用; **to ~ belief/comprehension/description** 难以相信/理解/描述

degeneracy /dɪˈdʒenərəsi/ *n* [u] (of society) 倒退; (of person, way of life) 堕落

degenerate
A /dɪˈdʒenəreɪt/ *vi* «*health*» 恶化; «*appearance*» 蜕化; «*morals*» 堕落; **to ~ from ... into ...** 从…恶化成…; **to ~ into farce** 降格为闹剧

B /dɪˈdʒenərət/ *adj* **1** 堕落的 ‹*person, behaviour*›; 衰退的 ‹*society, system*› **2** Biol (reverted to a simpler form) 退化的

C /dɪˈdʒenərət/ *n* 堕落者

degeneration /dɪˌdʒenəˈreɪʃn/ *n* [u] **1** (of quality of life, goods, economy) 衰退; (of health) 恶化; **the ~ of society/the youth of today** 社会的倒退/当今年轻人的堕落 **2** (of the body) 退化; **~ of the spine** 脊椎退化

degenerative /dɪˈdʒenərətɪv/ *adj* 变性的 ‹*condition, process*›; **~ diseases/arthritis** 变性疾病/关节炎

degradation /ˌdegrəˈdeɪʃn/ *n* [u] **1** (humiliation) 屈辱 **2** (squalor) 落泊; **to live in utter ~** 过着潦倒的生活 **3** (of environment) 恶化; (of facilities) 毁坏 **4** (breakdown into simpler compounds) Biol 退化; Chem 降解

degrade /dɪˈgreɪd/

A *vt* **1** (humiliate) 使受辱; **to feel ~d** 感觉受屈辱 **2** Ecol 使恶化

B *vi* «*material, substance*» 降解; **this material will ~ on exposure to light** 这种材料遇光会降解

degrading /dɪˈgreɪdɪŋ/ *adj* 降低身份的; **to be ~** 有辱人格

degree /dɪˈgriː/ *n* **1** ▸**p. 814** [c] Geog, Math, Phys, Meteorol 度; **an angle of 45 ~s** 一个 45 度的角; **we were 35 ~s off course** 我们偏离航线 35 度; **one ~ Celsius** *or* **centigrade/Fahrenheit** 1摄氏度/华氏度 **2** [c] Univ 学位; **to have/get a ~** 拥有/获得学位; **to take** *or* **do a ~** 攻读学位; **first ~** 第一学位; **a ~ in history, a history ~** 历史学位 **3** [c] (amount, level) 程度; **by ~s** 渐渐地; **a high ~ of competence** 很强的能力; **he was not in the slightest ~ anxious** 他一点都不忧虑; **some/a ~ of autonomy** 一定程度的自治; **with varying ~s of success/accuracy** 以不同程度的成功/准确性; **to a** *or* **to some** *or* **to a certain ~** 在一定程度上; **to such a ~ that ...** 到这样的程度以至于…; **to a greater or lesser ~** 或多或少地; **the party was boring to a ~** Brit colloq 那次聚会相当无聊 **4** [c] Amer Jur [定罪量刑的] 等级; **murder in the first ~** 一级谋杀罪 **5** [u] archaic 地位; **a man of high/low ~** 上层/下层人

degree: ~ ceremony *n* Brit 学位授予仪式; **~ certificate** *n* Brit 学位证书; **~ course** *n* Brit 学位课程; **~ examinations** *npl* Brit 学位考试

dehumanization /ˌdiːhjuːmənaɪˈzeɪʃn, Amer -nɪˈz-/ *n* [u] 非人化

dehumanize /ˌdiːˈhjuːmənaɪz/ *vt* 使丧失人性

dehumidifier /ˌdiːhjuːˈmɪdɪfaɪə(r)/ *n* 除湿机

dehumidify /ˌdiːhjuːˈmɪdɪfaɪ/ *vt* 除去…的湿气

dehydrate /ˌdiːˈhaɪdreɪt, ˌdiːhaɪˈdreɪt/

A *vt* 使…脱水 ‹*substance, person, body*›

B *vi* «*person, animal, body, tissue*» 脱水

dehydrated /ˌdiːhaɪˈdreɪtɪd/ *adj* 脱水的; **~ vegetables/fruit** 脱水蔬菜/水果; **~ milk** 奶粉; **to be ~** «*person*» 失水; **to become/feel ~** 变得/感到口干舌燥

dehydration /ˌdiːhaɪˈdreɪʃn/ *n* [u] 脱水; **to suffer from ~** 受脱水之苦

de-ice /ˌdiːˈaɪs/ *vt* 除去…上的冰

de-icer /ˌdiːˈaɪsə(r)/ *n* **1** Aut 防冰装置 **2** Aviat 除冰器

deification /ˌdiːɪfɪˈkeɪʃn/ *n* [u] 奉若神明; **the ~ of the emperor** 皇帝的神化

deify /ˈdiːɪfaɪ/ *vt* 神化

deign /deɪn/ *vi* 降低身份; **to ~ to do sth.** 屈尊做某事; **she didn't even ~ to look up as we walked in** 我们进去时她甚至不屑抬头看一眼

deism /ˈdiːɪzəm/ *n* [u] 自然神论

deist /ˈdiːɪst/ *n* 自然神论者

deistic /diːˈɪstɪk/ *adj* 自然神论的

deity /ˈdiːəti/ *n* **1** [c] (god) 神; (goddess) 女神 **2** [u] (supreme being) 上帝; **the D~** 造物主 **3** [u] (divinity) 神性

déjà vu /ˌdeɪʒɑː ˈvuː/ *n* [u] 似曾经历; **a feeling of ~** 一种似曾相识的感觉

dejected /dɪˈdʒektɪd/ *adj* 垂头丧气的 ‹*person*›; 沮丧的 ‹*look, expression, mood*›; **to become** *or* **get ~** 变得情绪低落; **to look ~** 看上去无精打采

dejectedly /dɪˈdʒektɪdli/ *adv* 沮丧地

dejection /dɪˈdʒekʃn/ *n* [u] 沮丧; **a feeling/look of ~** 低落的情绪/垂头丧气的样子

dekaliter /ˈdekəliːtə(r)/ *n* Amer **= decalitre**

dekameter /ˈdekəmiːtə(r)/ *n* Amer **= decametre**

dekko /ˈdekəʊ/ *n* Brit colloq 看; **to have** *or* **take a ~ at sth.** 看一眼某物

Delaware /ˈdeləˌweə(r)/ *pr n* 特拉华州

delay /dɪˈleɪ/

A *vt* **1** (postpone, defer) 推迟; **we ~ed our journey until the weather improved** 我们把旅行推迟到了天气转好以后 **2** (make late or slow) 延误; **the bad weather ~ed our journey** 恶劣天气耽搁了我们的行程; **she was ~ed by a neighbour** 她被一个邻居拖住了

B *vi* 拖延; **we ~ed too long** 我们耽搁得太久了; **don't ~** 别磨蹭

C *n* **1** [u and c] (to transport, communications) 延误; **there will be ~s to flights** 会有航班延误 **2** [c] (time lapse) 延迟; **a few minutes' ~** 几分钟的延迟; **a slight ~ between transmission and reception** 发射和接收之间的短暂延时 **3** [u] (postponement, slowness) 推迟; **to do sth. without ~** 立即做某事; **she apologized for her ~ in replying** 她为回复晚了而道歉

delayed /dɪˈleɪd/ *adj* 延迟的; **the drug has a ~ effect** 这种药药效滞后

delayed action

A *n* 延迟作用

B delayed-action *adj* 定时的; **a delayed-action camera/shutter/bomb** 定时相机/快门/炸弹

delayering /ˌdiːˈleɪərɪŋ/ *n* [u] 减少员工层次

delaying tactics *npl* 拖延战术

delectable /dɪˈlektəbl/ *adj* **1** (delicious, tasty) 美味的 ‹*meal, dish, drink, food*› **2** (attractive, appealing) 迷人的 ‹*person, cottage, garment*›

delectation /ˌdiːlekˈteɪʃn/ *n* [u] 享受; **for the ~ of ...** 为了…的快乐

delegate

A /ˈdelɪgeɪt/ *vt* **1** (entrust) 委托 ‹*power, responsibility, task*›; **to ~ sth. to sb.** 把某事委托给某人; **he is reluctant to ~ authority** 他不情愿移交权力; **you've been ~d to make the tea** hum 你负责沏茶 **2** (send) 委派; **to ~ sb. to do sth.** 选派某人做某事

B /ˈdelɪgeɪt/ *vi* 授权; **a good manager must know how to ~** 好经理一定要知人善任

C /ˈdelɪgət/ *n* **1** (representative) 代表 **2** Amer Pol 州众议院议员

delegation /ˌdelɪˈgeɪʃn/ *n* **1** [u] (act of delegating) 委托 **2** [c] (representatives) 代表团; **members of the official ~** 官方代表团成员

delete /dɪˈliːt/ *vt* 删去; **to ~ sth. from sth.** 把某物从某处删除

delete key *n* 删除键

deleterious /ˌdelɪˈtɪərɪəs/ *adj* formal 有害的; **to be ~ to sb./sth.** 对某人/某物有害

deletion /dɪˈliːʃn/ *n* **1** [u] (act) 删除; **the accidental ~ of his name** 他名字的意外删除 **2** [c] (erased text) 删除部分

Delhi /ˈdeli/ *pr n* 德里

deli /ˈdeli/ *n* colloq **= delicatessen**

deliberate

A /dɪˈlɪbərət/ *adj* **1** (intentional) 故意的 ‹*mistake, insult, lie, act*› **2** (measured) 慎重的 ‹*decision, judgement, reasoning*›; 从容的 ‹*manner*›; **she has a ~ way of talking** 她说起话来不紧不慢的

B /dɪˈlɪbəreɪt/ *vi* **1** (discuss) 仔细讨论; **to ~ on** *or* **about** *or* **over sth.** 仔细讨论某事 **2** (reflect) 认真考虑; **to ~ on** *or* **about** *or* **over sth.** 仔细考虑某事

C /dɪˈlɪbəreɪt/ *vt* **1** (discuss) 仔细讨论 **2** (consider) 反复思考; **to ~ what to do/whether to do sth.** 认真考虑做什么/是否做某事

deliberately /dɪˈlɪbərətli/ *adv* **1** (intentionally) 故意地 **2** (slowly and carefully) 小心翼翼地

deliberation /dɪˌlɪbəˈreɪʃn/ *n* **1** [c and u] (reflection) 细想; **after careful/long ~** 经过仔细/长时间考虑 **2** [c] (discussion, debate) 商议; (of jury) 审议 **3** [u] (slowness) 从容; **with ~** 从容地

deliberative /dɪˈlɪbərətɪv/ *adj* **1** (with deliberating function) 审议的 ‹*assembly, council*› **2** (resulting from deliberation) 审慎的 ‹*conclusion, decision, judgement, speech*›

delicacy /ˈdelɪkəsi/ *n* **1** [u] (of beauty, features) 精致; (of colour, design) 雅致; (of embroidery, craftsmanship) 精湛; (of touch) 熟练 **2** [u] (of health) 娇弱 **3** [u] (awkwardness) 棘手; (of situation, subject) 微妙; **a matter of great ~** 一件非常棘手的事情 **4** [u] (tact of a person) 周到; **she handled the matter with considerable ~** 这件事她处理得相当周到 **5** [c] (food item) 佳肴; **a local ~** 当地的美味

delicate /ˈdelɪkət/

A *adj* **1** (fine, dainty) 精美的 ‹*embroidery*›; 精湛的 ‹*craftsmanship*›; 清秀的 ‹*beauty, features*›; 优雅的 ‹*steps, movement*›; **with a few ~ strokes of his brush** 他巧妙地勾画几笔 **2** (fragile) 易损的 ‹*silk*›; 易碎的 ‹*glass*›; 娇嫩的 ‹*flower, leaf*›; **~ fabrics** 精细织物 **3** (subtle) 柔和的 ‹*aroma, colour*›; 清香的 ‹*flavour*› **4** (light, gentle) 轻柔的 ‹*touch, caress*›; 轻巧的 ‹*footsteps, movement*› **5** (not robust) 纤弱的 ‹*heart, stomach, health*›; **I feel a bit ~ this morning** 我今天早上感觉有点虚弱; **he has a ~ stomach** 他的胃很娇气 **6** (finely tuned) 精密的 ‹*mechanism, instrument*›; **a ~ sense of taste and smell** 灵敏的味觉和嗅觉 **7** (requiring skill or tact) 需要小心处理的 ‹*operation, situation, question, subject*› **8** (tactful) 圆通的 ‹*manner, words*›; **her ~ handling of the problem** 她对这个问题的娴熟处理

B delicates *npl* 精细织物

delicately /ˈdelɪkətli/ *adv* **1** (finely, subtly) 精致地; **a ~ embroidered handkerchief** 精致的绣花手帕 **2** (sensitively, tactfully) 圆通地; **the letter was ~ phrased** 这封信措词得体 **3** (accurately, precisely) 精密地 **4** (carefully, gently) 小心翼翼地; **to be treated ~** 小心侍弄

delicatessen /ˌdelɪkəˈtesn/ *n* **1** (shop) 熟食店 **2** Amer (eating place) 餐饮店

delicious /dɪˈlɪʃəs/ *adj* **1** (having a very pleasant taste) 美味可口的 ‹*meal, cake, drink*›; 芬芳的 ‹*smell, flavour*›; **to taste ~** 味道很好; **a ~ recipe** 美味的烹饪法 **2** (pleasurable) 宜人的 ‹*sight*›; 令人愉快的 ‹*feeling, sound*›; **a ~ joke** 有趣的笑话

deliciously /dɪˈlɪʃəsli/ *adv* **1** (tastily) 可口地; **a ~ creamy soup** 美味奶油汤 **2** (delightfully) 宜人地; **the water was ~ cool** 水很凉爽

delight /dɪˈlaɪt/

A *n* **1** [u] 愉快; **to take ~ in sth./doing sth.** 以某事/做某事为乐; **it gives me great ~ to ...** …给我带来很大快乐; **(much) to my ~** 令我（很）高兴的是 **2** [c] (pleasurable thing) 高兴事; **it's a ~ to the senses/eyes** 这是一种感官/视觉的享受; **the ~s of camping** 野营度假的乐趣; **his singing is a ~ to hear** 他的歌声很动听; **he is the ~ of his family** 他是家里的开心果

B *vt* 使高兴; **to ~ sb. with sth.** 以某事愉悦某人; **it ~s me that ...** …使我愉快

C *vi* 感到高兴; **to ~ in sth./doing sth.** 以某事/做某事为乐

delighted /dɪˈlaɪtɪd/ *adj* 快乐的; **~ by** *or* **with** *or* **at** *or* **about sth.** 因某事感到高兴; **to be ~ to do sth./that ...** 很高兴做某事/…; **to be ~ with sb.** 对某人感到很满意; **I'm ~ for you** 我为你高兴; **(I should be) ~!** 很愿意! ; **~ to meet you** 很高兴见到你

delightedly /dɪˈlaɪtɪdli/ *adv* 高兴地

delightful /dɪˈlaɪtfl/ *adj* **1** (pleasant) 令人愉快的; **it is ~ to do/be doing sth.** 干某事令人愉快; **a ~ cottage** 可爱的小木屋 **2** (charming) 讨人喜欢的

delightfully /dɪˈlaɪtfəli/ *adv* 令人愉快地; **the sun was ~ warm** 太阳暖洋洋的; **he is ~ eccentric/shy** 他古怪/害羞得讨人喜欢

Delilah /dɪˈlaɪlə/ *pr n* **1** Bible 大利拉 [参孙的情妇] **2** (temptress) 妖妇

delimit /ˌdiːˈlɪmɪt/ *vt* 界定

delimitation /ˌdiːlɪmɪˈteɪʃn/ *n* [u] 界定; **species ~** 物种界定

delineate /dɪˈlɪnɪeɪt/ *vt* **1** (mark boundaries of) 勾画出…的轮廓 ‹*shape, mountain, building, features*› **2** (describe) 刻画 ‹*scene, character*›; 解释 ‹*plan, problem*›

delineation /dɪˌlɪnɪˈeɪʃn/ *n* [u and c] **1** formal (description, portrayal) (of problem, plan) 解释; (of character) 刻画 **2** (marking out of line, picture) 勾画轮廓; **to avoid neat ~ between fact and fiction** 避免对事实与虚构作简单的划分; **disagreements over the ~ of their shared frontier** 有关他们共同边界划分的分歧

delinquency /dɪˈlɪŋkwənsi/ *n* **1** [u and c] (minor crime) 轻罪 **2** [u] (criminal behaviour) 违法行为

delinquent /dɪˈlɪŋkwənt/
A *n* 罪犯
B *adj* 有违法倾向的

deliquesce /ˌdelɪˈkwes/ *vi* 潮解

deliquescence /ˌdelɪˈkwesns/ *n* [u] 潮解

deliquescent /ˌdelɪˈkwesnt/ *adj* 潮解的

delirious /dɪˈlɪrɪəs/ *adj* **1** Med 精神错乱的 ‹*patient*›; 神志不清的 ‹*hallucinations*›; **~ talk** 谵语; **to be in a ~ condition** 处于谵妄状态 **2** (wildly excited) 极度兴奋的 ‹*person, crowd*›; **~ with joy** 欣喜若狂的

deliriously /dɪˈlɪrɪəsli/ *adv* **1** Med 神经错乱地; **to rave ~** 说胡话 **2** (wildly) 极度兴奋地

delirium /dɪˈlɪrɪəm/ *n* [u] **1** Med 神志失常 **2** (wild excitement) 极度兴奋

delirium tremens /dɪˌlɪrɪəm ˈtriːmenz/ *n* [u] 震颤性谵妄

deliver /dɪˈlɪvə(r)/
A *vt* **1** (take to address, recipient) 递送 ‹*goods, package, message*›; **to ~ sth. to sb.** 把某物送到某人处; **to ~ a letter to an address** 把信投递到某个地址; **to have sth. ~ed** 让人送某物 **2** (hand over) 移交 ‹*goods, property, money*›; **to ~ sb./sth. over** *or* **up to sb.** 把某人/某物交给某人; **to ~ sth. into sb.'s care** 把某物交由某人保管 **3** (utter) 发表 ‹*speech, address*›; 作出 ‹*verdict, decision, reprimand*›; **to ~ a lecture** 作讲座; **to ~ a sermon** 布道; **to ~ (one's) lines** (in drama, lecture) 念台词; **to ~ an ultimatum** 发出最后通牒; **to ~ a sharp rebuke to sb.** 严厉训斥某人 **4** (throw) 投掷 ‹*ball*›; 发射 ‹*missile, bullet*›; 给予 ‹*blow, punch*›; **to ~ a nasty/fatal kick** 踢出危险的/致命的一脚 **5** (provide, achieve) 履行 ‹*promise*›; 实现 ‹*reform, improvement*›; **to ~ improved production levels** 提高生产水平; **the new model ~s speed and fuel economy** 这种新型号能提高速度并节约燃料; **to ~ the goods** fig colloq (fulfil a promise) 兑现承诺; (fulfil expectations) 不负所望 **6** Med, Vet 接生 ‹*baby, young animal*›; **to be ~ed by Caesarean section** 通过剖宫产手术出生; **to be ~ed of a baby** formal 分娩
B *vi* **1** Comm 送货 **2** Post 投递 **3** (fulfil a promise) 兑现承诺; (fulfil expectations) 不负所望; **they have failed to ~ on the issue of quality control** 他们在质量控制问题上令人失望; **the film promises much, but it doesn't ~** 这部电影让人期望很高, 但结果令人失望

deliverable /dɪˈlɪvərəbl/
A *adj* 可交付的
B *n* 可交付的产品

deliverance /dɪˈlɪvərəns/ *n* [u] 解脱; **~ from captivity** 摆脱囚禁; **to pray for ~** 祈祷得到拯救

deliverer /dɪˈlɪvərə(r)/ *n* **1** (of goods, groceries) 送货人 **2** (saviour) 拯救者

delivery /dɪˈlɪvəri/ *n* **1** [u] (of goods, milk) 发送; (of mail, newspaper) 投递; (to several houses) 分送; (to individual) 送交; **to take ~ of sth.** 收到某物; **to pay on ~** 货到付款; **free ~ to your home** 免费送货上门 **2** [c] (consignment) 发送物; **to make a ~** 送货 **3** [u and c] (of offspring) 分娩; **to have an easy/a difficult ~** 顺产/难产 **4** [u] (way of speaking) 演讲风格 **5** [u] (pronouncement) (of speech) 讲话; (of judgement, ruling) 宣布 **6** [u] (provision of sth. promised) 交出 **7** [u] (deliverance) 解救

delivery: ~ address *n* 送货地址; **~ charge** *n* 送货费; **~ man** ▸p. 409 *n* 送货人; **~ note** *n* 交货单; **~ room** *n* 产房; **~ service** *n* 送货服务; **~ suite** *n* Brit 产房; **~ time** *n* 送货期限; **~ van** *n* 厢式送货车

dell /del/ *n* liter 小山谷

delouse /ˌdiːˈlaʊs/ *vt* 消灭…的虱子

Delphic /ˈdelfɪk/ *adj* **1** Mythol 特尔斐的; **the ~ oracle** 特尔斐神谕 **2** (mysterious) 隐晦的; **a ~ utterance** 意义不明的话

delphinium /delˈfɪnɪəm/ *n* 翠雀属植物

delta /ˈdeltə/ *n* 三角洲; **the ~ of the Nile, the Nile ~** 尼罗河三角洲

delta wing *n* 三角翼

delta-winged *adj* 有三角翼的 ‹*aircraft*›

delude /dɪˈluːd/ *vt* 欺骗; **to ~ sb. into doing sth.** 哄骗某人干某事; **to ~ sb. with sth.** 用某事物欺骗某人; **we have been ~d with empty promises** 我们被空口诺言所骗; **to ~ oneself** 自欺; **to ~ oneself into believing that ...** 欺骗自己相信…

deluded /dɪˈluːdɪd/ *adj* 受骗的

deluge /ˈdeljuːdʒ/
A *vt* **1** lit ‹*rain*› 淹没 ‹*city, countryside*› **2** fig 使充满; **to be ~d with sth.** 因…应接不暇 ‹*enquiries, letters, complaints, offers*›
B *n* **1** lit (downpour) 暴雨; **a ~ of rain/water** 倾盆大雨/大洪水 **2** lit (severe flood) 洪水 **3** fig 蜂拥而至的事物; **a ~ of sth.** 汹涌而至的某物

delusion /dɪˈluːʒn/ *n* **1** [c] (false belief) 错觉; (symptom of mental disorder) 妄想; **you're under a ~!** 那是你的错觉! ; **to be under the ~ that ...** 怀有…的错觉; **to suffer from ~s** 患有幻想症; **~s of grandeur** 妄自尊大 **2** [u] (deluding) 欺骗

delusive /dɪˈluːsɪv/ *adj* 虚假的

de luxe /dəˈlʌks, -ˈlʊks/ *adj* (high quality) 高级的 ‹*car, caravan*›; (sumptuous) 豪华的 ‹*hotel, apartment*›; (improved) 精装的 ‹*edition, version*›

delve /delv/ *vi* **1** (research, inquire) 探索; **to ~ into sth.** 探究 ‹*memory, past*›; **to ~ further** *or* **deeper into the information/subject** 深入查找信息/钻研题目 **2** liter (dig) 挖掘; (search, rummage) 搜寻; **to ~ into sth.** 在某物里搜寻; **to ~ into one's pockets** fig 解囊

Dem *abbr* Amer = **Democrat, Democratic**

demagnetize /ˌdiːˈmæɡnɪtaɪz/ *vt* 使消磁

demagogic /ˌdeməˈɡɒɡɪk/ *adj* 蛊惑人心的 ‹*person*›; 煽动性的 ‹*address, manner, words*›

demagogue /ˈdeməɡɒɡ/ *n* 蛊惑人心的政客

demagogy /ˈdeməɡɒɡi/ *n* [u] **1** (practice) 蛊惑人心的行为; (methods) 煽动方法 **2** (rhetoric) 蛊惑人心的言论

de-man /ˌdiːˈmæn/ *vt* Brit 裁减…的人员 ‹*factory, mine*›

demand /dɪˈmɑːnd, Amer dɪˈmænd/
A *vt* **1** (request forcefully) 强烈要求; **to ~ one's money back** 坚决要求还钱; **to ~ sth. from sb.** 向某人索要某物; **I ~ to know the truth** 我一定要知道真相; **I ~ to be fed** 我要求吃饭; **to ~ that sb. do sth.** + *subjunctive* 强烈要求某人做某事; **we ~ that our employees be punctual** 我们严格要求我们的雇员守时; **to ~ of sb. that he/she** *etc.* + *subjunctive* 强烈要求某人…; **we ~ of our employees that they be punctual** 我们严格要求雇员守时; **she ~ed of him that he tell her his secret** 她极力要他把自己的秘密告诉她 **2** (insist on being told) 盘查; **she ~ed what I was doing** 她质问我在干什么 **3** (require) 需要 ‹*skill, time, patience, workers*›; **the qualities ~ed of a manager** 做经理应有的素质
B *n* **1** [c] (request) 要求; **to make a ~ for sth.** 要求得到某物; **a ~ for sb. to do sth.** 要某人做某事的呼声; **on ~** 一经要求; **payable on ~** 见票即付的 **2** [c] (requirement) [令人烦恼的] 要求; **I have many ~s on my time** 我的时间安排得很紧; **to make** *or* **put ~s on sb./sth.** 对某人/某事提出要求 **3** [c and u] Econ 需求; **supply and ~** 供求; **to be in ~** 需求大 **4** [c] (bill) 付款请求; **final ~** 最终付款请求

demand deposit *n* 活期存款

demanding /dɪˈmɑːndɪŋ, Amer -ˈmænd-/ *adj* **1** (not easily satisfied) 苛刻的; **to be ~ of sb.** 对某人要求苛刻; **he is a fussy and ~ child** 他是个挑剔而难缠的孩子 **2** (difficult) 费力的 ‹*work, task, activity*›; **military training is physically ~** 军训对体能要求高

demand note *n* 即期票据

demarcate /ˈdiːmɑːkeɪt/ *vt* **1** (mark out) 标出…的界线 ‹*space, area, plot*› **2** (distinguish) 区分 ‹*field, subject, discipline*›; **to ~ sth. from sth.** 区分某事物与某事物

demarcation /ˌdiːmɑːˈkeɪʃn/ *n* **1** [c] (physical boundary) 界线; **line of ~** 分界线 **2** [c] (distinction) 区别 **3** [u] (marking out) 划分; **the ~ of the maritime border** 海界的划分 **4** [u] Brit (of jobs) 分工

demarcation dispute *n* 分工争议

demean /dɪˈmiːn/
A *v refl* **to ~ oneself** 降低身份; **to ~ oneself to do sth.** 屈尊去做某事
B *vt* 使失去尊严; **such images ~ women** 这些形象有损妇女尊严

demeaning /dɪˈmiːnɪŋ/ *adj* 有失尊严的; **to be ~ for sb. to do sth.** 某人做某事有失体面

demeanour Brit, **demeanor** Amer /dɪˈmiːnə(r)/ *n* [u] (appearance) 外表; (behaviour) 举止

demented /dɪˈmentɪd/ *adj* **1** colloq (behaving irrationally) 焦躁不安的; **to become ~** 发狂; **to drive sb. ~** 把某人逼疯 **2** (suffering from dementia) 痴呆的

dementedly /dɪˈmentɪdli/ *adv* colloq 焦躁不安地

dementia /dɪˈmenʃə/ *n* [u] 痴呆

demerara /ˌdeməˈreərə/ *n* [u] **~ (sugar)** 德梅拉拉蔗糖

demerge /ˌdiːˈmɜːdʒ/ *vt* **1** (separate) 分拆 **2** (dissolve earlier merger) 合并后分拆

demerger /ˌdiːˈmɜːdʒə(r)/ *n* **1** (separation) 分拆 **2** (dissolution of an earlier merger) 合并后的分拆

demerit /ˌdiːˈmerɪt/ *n* **1** (fault, disadvantage) 短处; **the merits and ~s of sth.** 某事物的优缺点 **2 ~ (point)** Amer Sch 过失分

demigod /ˈdemɪɡɒd/ *n* **1** Mythol 半神半人 **2** (person) 受膜拜的人

demijohn /ˈdemɪdʒɒn/ *n* (bottle) 小口大酒瓶; (amount) 一小口大酒瓶的量

d

d

demilitarization /diːˌmɪlɪtəraɪˈzeɪʃn, Amer -rɪˈz-/ *n* [u] 非军事化

demilitarize /ˌdiːˈmɪlɪtəraɪz/ *vt* 使非军事化; **a ~d zone** 非军事区

demise /dɪˈmaɪz/ *n* formal or hum 1 (death) 死亡 2 (end) 终止 3 (failure) 失败

demisemiquaver /ˌdemɪˈsemɪkweɪvə(r)/ *n* Brit 32 分音符

demist /ˌdiːˈmɪst/ *vt* Brit 除去…的雾水

demister /ˌdiːˈmɪstə(r)/ *n* Brit [汽车挡风玻璃的] 除雾器

demo /ˈdeməʊ/ *n* (*pl* **~s**) colloq 1 Pol 示威游行; **to go on a ~ against sth.** 进行反对某事的游行 2 (exhibition and explanation) 示范; **I'll give you a ~** 我来给你演示一下 3 Mus (record, tape) 录音样带; **a ~ tape/CD** 录音样带/试样激光唱片

demobilization /diːˌməʊbɪlaɪˈzeɪʃn, Amer -lɪˈz-/ *n* [u] 复员

demobilize /ˌdiːˈməʊbɪlaɪz/ *vt* 使复员

democracy /dɪˈmɒkrəsi/ *n* 1 [u] (system of government) 民主政体 2 [u] (control by majority) 民主（制度） 3 [c] (country) 民主国家; **a multi-party ~** 多党制民主国家

Democrat /ˈdeməkræt/ *pr n* Amer (member) 民主党人; (supporter) 民主党支持者; **a ~ senator/politician** 民主党参议员/政治家

democrat /ˈdeməkræt/ *n* 民主主义者

Democratic /ˌdeməˈkrætɪk/ *adj* Amer 民主党的

democratic /ˌdeməˈkrætɪk/ *adj* 1 Pol 民主制度的 ‹*country, nation, principle*›; **a ~ constitution/election** 民主宪法/选举 2 (egalitarian) 平等的

democratically /ˌdeməˈkrætɪkli/ *adv* Pol 民主地; **a ~ elected government** 民主选举的政府; **a ~ appointed committee** 民主推举的委员会; **the decision was taken ~** 这是通过民主讨论作出的决定

Democratic Party *n* Amer 民主党

> **the Democratic Party**
>
> 民主党。美国两大政党之一，也是美国历史最悠久的政党。前身为民主共和党（Democratic Republican Party），由托马斯·杰斐逊（Thomas Jefferson）于 1792 年创立，1844 年简化为现有名称。和另一大党共和党（▸**the Republican Party**）相比，民主党倾向于社会改革，更受工会和少数族裔（minority）的支持。著名的民主党总统有托马斯·杰斐逊、富兰克林·D·罗斯福（Franklin D. Roosevelt）、约翰·F·肯尼迪（John F. Kennedy）等。民主党的标志是驴。

democratization /dɪˌmɒkrətaɪˈzeɪʃn, Amer -tɪˈz-/ *n* [u] 民主化

democratize /dɪˈmɒkrətaɪz/ *vt* 使…民主化 ‹*election, political system, country*›; 使…大众化 ‹*decision-making, music, art*›

demographer /dɪˈmɒɡrəfə(r)/ ▸**p. 409** *n* 人口学家

demographic /ˌdeməˈɡræfɪk/ *adj* 人口学的 ‹*study*›; **~ statistics** 人口统计资料

demography /dɪˈmɒɡrəfi/ *n* (study) 人口学; (statistics) 人口统计; **the social ~ of Africa** 非洲社会人口统计

demolish /dɪˈmɒlɪʃ/ *vt* 1 (knock down) 拆除 ‹*building, wall, fortifications*› 2 (refute) 驳倒 ‹*theory, belief, argument*› 3 Sport colloq (defeat) 彻底打败 4 Brit hum (devour) 狼吞虎咽地吃 ‹*food*›

demolition /ˌdeməˈlɪʃn/ *n* [u] 1 lit (knocking down) 拆除 2 fig (refutation) 驳倒 3 Sport colloq (defeat) 彻底打败

demolition: ~ area *n* 建筑物拆除区; **~ squad** *n* 爆破小组; **~ work** *n* [u] 建筑物拆除作业; **~ worker** ▸**p. 409** *n* 建筑物拆除工人; **~ zone** *n* = **~ area**

demon /ˈdiːmən/ *n* 1 (evil spirit) 恶魔 2 (compulsion, obsession) 邪念; (harmful person) 恶人; (harmful habit) 恶习; **the ~ of sexism/inflation/jealousy** 性别歧视/通货膨胀/嫉妒的恶魔; **the ~ drink** 含酒精饮料; **that child's a proper little ~** 那孩子是个十足的捣蛋鬼 3 colloq (energetic, devoted person) 精力充沛的人; **to be a ~ for sth.** 玩命地投入某事; **she's a ~ for work** 她是个工作狂 4 (expert, genius) 技艺出众的人; **to be a ~ at sth.** 是某方面的高手; **a ~ cook** 烹饪大师 5 Comput **= daemon**

demoniac /dɪˈməʊniæk/, **demoniacal** /dɪˈməʊniækl/ *adjs* **= demonic**

demonic /dɪˈmɒnɪk/ *adj* 1 (of or like demons) 恶魔般的 ‹*torments, cruelty, appearance*›; 邪恶的 ‹*army, horde*›; **~ possession** 恶魔附身 2 (frenzied) 狂热的 ‹*movement, activity*›

demonize /ˈdiːmənaɪz/ *vt* 把…妖魔化; **he was ~d by the right-wing press** 右翼媒体把他魔鬼化了

demonology /ˌdiːməˈnɒlədʒi/ *n* [u] 1 (study of demons) 鬼魔学 2 (set of beliefs) 魔鬼信仰

demonstrable /ˈdemɒnstrəbl, Amer dɪˈmɒnstrəbl/ *adj* 可论证的 ‹*fact, truth*›; 显而易见的 ‹*lie, inaccuracy*›; **a ~ need** 明显的需要

demonstrably /ˈdemɒnstrəbli, dɪˈmɒnstrəbli/ *adv* 可论证地 ‹*true, false*›; 明显地 ‹*better, worse, increase, decrease, grow*›; **~ unfair** 显失公平的

demonstrate /ˈdemənstreɪt/

A *vt* 1 (explain by showing) 示范操作 ‹*machine, gadget, equipment*›; **to ~ how to do sth.** 示范怎么做某事; **to ~ how sth. works** 说明某物的工作原理 2 (prove) 证明; **to ~ that ...** 证明…; **as ~d by this experiment** 如本试验所证明 3 (show) 表露 ‹*affection, dislike, indifference, feeling*›; **to ~ one's concern/support for sth.** 表明对某事的关心/支持; **as ~d by ...** 如…所表现的

B *vi* (protest) 游行示威; **to ~ for/against sth.** 进行支持/反对某事的示威游行

demonstration /ˌdemənˈstreɪʃn/ *n* 1 (of machine, gadget etc.) 示范操作; **to give a ~** 进行示范 2 (of emotion, support) 表达; **unrestrained ~s of affection** 爱的恣意表露 3 (protest) 示威游行; **to stage a ~** 举行示威游行; **to go on a ~ against/for sth.** 进行反对/支持某事的示威游行; **a human rights ~** 人权示威游行

demonstrative /dɪˈmɒnstrətɪv/

A *adj* 1 (unrestrained) 感情外露的; **a ~ child** 开朗的孩子 2 formal (indicative) **to be ~ of sth.** ‹*decision, law, action*› 表明某事 3 ▸**p. 193** Ling 指示的; **~ adjective/pronoun** 指示形容词/代词

B *n* Ling 指示代词

demonstrator /ˈdemənstreɪtə(r)/ *n* 1 (protestor) 示威者 2 Comm 产品示范者

demoralization /dɪˌmɒrəlaɪˈzeɪʃn, Amer dɪˌmɔːrəlɪˈzeɪʃn/ *n* [u] 意志消沉

demoralize /dɪˈmɒrəlaɪz, Amer -ˈmɔːr-/ *vt* 使泄气; **he ~s her with his constant criticism** 他不断批评她，使得她意志消沉

demoralizing /dɪˈmɒrəlaɪzɪŋ, Amer -ˈmɔːr-/ *adj* 使人泄气的; **poverty has a ~ effect on the whole community** 贫穷能使整个社会颓废

demote /ˌdiːˈməʊt/ *vt* 使降级; **he has been ~d to the rank of private** 他被降为二等兵

demotic /dɪˈmɒtɪk/ *adj* 1 formal (of ordinary people) 大众化的 ‹*art form, press, entertainment*› 2 (colloquial) 通俗的 ‹*language, speech, script*›; **a ~ idiom** 俗语

demotion /dɪˈməʊʃn/ *n* [c and u] (of person) 降职; (of sports team) 降级

demotivate /ˌdiːˈməʊtɪveɪt/ *vt* 使失去动力

demur /dɪˈmɜː(r)/ *vi* (*pres p etc.* **-rr-**) formal 表示反对; **to ~ at sth.** 反对某事

demure /dɪˈmjʊə(r)/ *adj* 端庄娴静的; **a ~ dress/woman/smile** 庄重的裙装/娴静的女士/矜持的微笑

demurely /dɪˈmjʊəli/ *adv* 端庄地

demurrage /dɪˈmʌrɪdʒ/ *n* Jur 1 (delay) 滞留; **goods in ~** 滞留货物 2 (compensation) 滞留费

demutualization /diːˌmjuːtʃʊəlaɪˈzeɪʃn/ *n* [住房信贷互助会等的] 改变拥有权

demutualize /ˌdiːˈmjuːtʃʊəlaɪz/ *vi* 改变拥有权

demystification /diːˌmɪstɪfɪˈkeɪʃn/ *n* [u] 非神秘化; **the ~ of the Bible stories** 《圣经》故事讲解

demystify /ˌdiːˈmɪstɪfaɪ/ *vt* 使明白易懂

demythologize /ˌdiːmɪˈθɒlədʒaɪz/ *vt* 去除…的神话色彩

den /den/ *n* 1 (of animals) 兽穴 2 pej (meeting place) 窝点; **~ of vice** *or* **iniquity** 不法之徒的窝点; **a drinking/gambling ~** 酗酒/赌博场所 3 (room) (for relaxation) 休息室; (for work) 工作室

denationalization /diːˌnæʃənəlaɪˈzeɪʃn, Amer -lɪˈz-/ *n* [u] 非国有化

denationalize /ˌdiːˈnæʃənəlaɪz/ *vt* 使非国有化

denaturalization /diːˌnætʃərəlaɪˈzeɪʃn, Amer -lɪˈz-/ *n* [u] 取消国籍

denaturalize /ˌdiːˈnætʃərəlaɪz/ *vt* 取消…的国籍

denature /ˌdiːˈneɪtʃə(r)/ *vt* 改变…的性质

denatured alcohol *n* [u] 变性酒精

Denbighshire /ˈdenbɪʃɪə(r)/ *pr n* 登比郡

dengue /ˈdeŋɡi/ *n* [u] 登革热

deniable /dɪˈnaɪəbl/ *adj* 可否认的

denial /dɪˈnaɪəl/ *n* 1 [c and u] (of accusation) 否认; (of request) 拒绝; **his ~ that he was the culprit** 他否认自己是罪犯; **a ~ of sth.** 对某事的否认; **a flat/firm ~** 断然/坚决的否认 2 [c and u] (refusal to believe) 拒绝相信 3 [c] (disowning) 脱离关系; **a traitor's ~ of his native land** 一个叛国者对祖国的背弃 4 [c and u] (withholding) 拒绝给予; **a ~ of basic human rights/resources** 基本人权/资源的剥夺 5 [u] Psych 拒绝接受; **in ~** 拒不承认; **I was an addict in ~** 我拒不接受我是瘾君子的事实

denial of service attack *n* 拒绝服务攻击

denier /ˈdenɪə(r)/ *n* [u] 旦 [测量丝线的纤度单位]; **15 ~ tights** Brit, **15 ~ pantyhose** Amer 15 旦的连裤袜

denigrate /ˈdenɪɡreɪt/ *vt* 诽谤; **to ~ one's own country/sb.'s success** 诋毁自己的国家/贬低某人的成就

denigration /ˌdenɪˈɡreɪʃn/ *n* [u] 诽谤; **the ~ of sb.'s achievements/passions** 对某人成就的贬低/热情的诋毁

denim /ˈdenɪm/

A *n* [u] 蓝粗棉布; **~ jeans** 牛仔裤

B **denims** *npl* 牛仔服

denizen /ˈdenɪzn/ *n* (person) [某地的] 居民; (animal) [某地的] 动物; **~s of the field and forest** 生活在田野和森林的动物

Denmark /ˈdenmɑːk/ *pr n* 丹麦

denominate /dɪˈnɒmɪneɪt/ *vt* [用某货币单位] 结算; **to be ~d in US dollars** 以美元计算

denomination /dɪˌnɒmɪˈneɪʃn/ *n* 1 Relig 教派; **various religious ~s** 各宗教派别 2 Fin 面值; **a high/low ~ coin/banknote** 高/低面值硬币/钞票

denominational /dɪˌnɒmɪˈneɪʃənl/ *adj* 教派的

denominational: ~ college *n* 教派学院; **~ school** *n* 教派学校

denominator /dɪˈnɒmɪneɪtə(r)/ *n* 分母

denotation /ˌdiːnəʊˈteɪʃn/ *n* **1** [c] (symbol used) 标记 **2** [u] (process of denoting) 表示

denote /dɪˈnəʊt/ *vt* **1** (stand for) «*object, symbol, drawing*» 表示 ‹*fact, event*› **2** (show proof of) 意味着 ‹*taste, intelligence*›

denouement /ˌdeɪˈnuːmɒŋ, Amer ˌdeɪmuː-ˈmɔːŋ/ *n* [小说、戏剧等的] 结局

denounce /dɪˈnaʊns/ *vt* **1** (inform on) 告发; **to ~ sb. to sb./sth.** 向某人/某处告发某人 **2** (criticize) 谴责; **to ~ sb. as a traitor/thief** 斥责某人是叛徒/小偷; **to ~ sb. for doing sth.** 谴责某人做了某事

dense /dens/ *adj* **1** Phys 密度大的 ‹*substance, rock, metal*› **2** (thick) 浓密的; **~ fog/smoke/liquid** 浓雾/浓烟/稠的液体 **3** (closely compacted) 茂密的 ‹*wood, thicket, undergrowth*›; (of high density) 密集的 ‹*housing, population*›; **a ~ crowd barred his access** 密集的人群挡住了他的路 **4** colloq (stupid) 愚笨的 **5** (condensed, concise) 难懂的 ‹*style, article*›

densely /ˈdensli/ *adv* 密集地; **~ populated/wooded** 人口密集/树木茂密的

denseness /ˈdensnɪs/ *n* [u] **1** = **density 2** **2** colloq (stupidity) 愚蠢

densimeter /denˈsɪmɪtə(r)/ *n* 密度计

densitometer /ˌdensɪˈtɒmɪtə(r)/ *n* **1** Phot 显像密度计 **2** Phys 光密度计

density /ˈdensəti/ *n* [c and u] **1** Phys, Electron 密度; **the ~ of a gas** 一种气体的密度; **a reduction in bone ~** 骨密度的降低 **2** (of population, objects) 密集度; **high/low ~ housing** 高/低密度住房

dent /dent/

A *n* **1** (depression) 凹痕; **to make a ~ in** 在…上弄出凹坑 ‹*wood, metal*› **2** (reduction) 削减; **to make a ~ in sth.** 削减某物的数量; **to make a ~ in one's finances** 消耗资金

B *vt* **1** (mark with a dent) 使…凹陷 ‹*metal object*›; **to ~ the furniture/table/car** 在家具/桌子/汽车上砸出坑 **2** (diminish) 削弱; **his pride/self-esteem has been ~ed** 他的自尊受到了伤害

dental /ˈdentl/

A *adj* **1** (relating to teeth) 牙齿的 ‹*problem, health, hygiene, decay*› **2** (relating to dentistry) 牙科的 ‹*examination, treatment*›; **sb.'s ~ records** 某人的牙科病历

B *n* Ling 齿音

dental: ~ appointment *n* 牙科预约; **~ assistant** *n* 牙医助理; **~ clinic** *n* 牙科诊所; **~ floss** *n* [u] 牙线; **~ hygienist** ▸**p. 409** *n* 牙科保健员; **~ nurse** ▸**p. 409** *n* 牙科护士; **~ plate** *n* 假牙床; **~ practitioner** ▸**p. 409** *n* 牙医; **~ receptionist** ▸**p. 409** *n* 牙科接待护士; **~ school** *n* 口腔医学院; **~ surgeon** ▸**p. 409** *n* 牙科医生; **~ surgery** *n* **1** [c] Brit (premises) 牙科诊所; **2** [u] (treatment) 牙科手术; **~ technician** ▸**p. 409** *n* 牙科技师

dentifrice /ˈdentɪfrɪs/ *n* [u] 洁齿剂; **a tube of ~** 一管牙膏

dentine /ˈdentiːn/, Amer **dentin** /ˈdentɪn/ *ns* [u] 牙质

dentist /ˈdentɪst/ ▸**p. 409** *n* 牙科医生; **to go to the ~('s)** 去看牙医

d

ℹ Demonstrative pronouns

■ 这／那, 这些／那些, 这里／那里, and 这儿／那儿 are demonstrative pronouns. In Chinese, demonstrative pronouns function as subject, object, attributive modifier, etc.

This and that

■ When 'this' and' that' function as subject or object, the Chinese equivalents are 这 and 那:

This is yours
= 这是你的

I'll take this with me
= 我把这个带走

That won't work
= 那不行

■ 这 and 那 can act as demonstrative adjectives to modify nouns, and are normally followed by a measure word. Where the context is sufficient, the modified noun may be omitted:

This lady is my sister
= 这位女士是我姐姐

That boy is my cousin
= 那个男孩是我的表弟

This one is mine
= 这个是我的

I want that one
= 我想要那个

■ When 'this' and 'that' function as adverbs, they must be translated as 这么 and 那么 instead of 这 and 那:

I have never been this late
= 我从来没这么晚过

The film was not that interesting
= 这部电影没那么有趣

These and those

■ 这些 (these) and 那些 (those) are plurals of 这 and 那 and function as subject, object or noun modifier:

These are theirs
= 这些是他们的

These books are mine
= 这些书是我的

Those are yours
= 那些是你们的

Those pictures are hers
= 那些照片是她的

She likes these but hates those
= 她喜欢这些，但讨厌那些

■ 'These ones' or 'those ones' can be (but are not always) translated into Chinese as 这些／那些. The modified noun can be omitted if there is enough context:

I will wear these ones
= 我会穿这些

These ones are more expensive than those ones
= 这些比那些贵

but

Which shoes do you think she will choose? — Those ones, I suppose
= 你认为她会选哪双鞋？—— 那双吧，我想

■ Where 'this' modifies an uncountable noun such as 'money' or 'luggage', it is translated as 这些 when the context suggests plurality:

This furniture belongs to my brother
= 这些家具是我弟的

This money is mine
= 这些钱是我的

That luggage is hers
= 那些行李是她的

That make-up is my sister's
= 那些化妆品是我姐的

■ When 'these' or 'those' are used with numbers, they must be translated as 这 and 那 as follows:

these five pencils
= 这 5 支铅笔

those six desks
= 那 6 张书桌

■ A possessive adjective always comes before 这 and 那 in Chinese in the examples below:

these three drawers of yours
= 你的这 3 个抽屉

these five envelopes of Mary's
= 玛丽的这 5 个信封

those two handbags of mine
= 我的那两个手提包

those six toy cars of Tom's
= 汤姆的那 6 个玩具车

Here and there

■ 'Here' is normally translated as 这里 or 这儿, and 'there' as 那里 or 那儿:

I live here
= 我住这儿

I'm leaving here
= 我要离开这里

I've been there
= 我去过那儿

Are you going there?
= 你去那里吗？

■ 'Be here' or 'be there' is translated into Chinese as 在这里／在这儿 or 在那里／在那儿:

She was here a moment ago
= 她刚才在这儿

He is there
= 他在那儿

■ Unlike English, 'here' or 'there' are placed before the noun they modify in Chinese. The order is '这里／这儿 or 那里／那儿 + 的 + noun'. Note that the particle 的 must be used:

People here like going to pubs
= 这儿的人喜欢去酒吧

The scenery there is beautiful
= 那里的风景很美

■ 'Here' and 'there' are not always translated as 这里／这儿 or 那里／那儿. Note the Chinese translation of these examples:

Here's Victor
= 维克托到了

Here comes the taxi
= 出租车来了

There's Sally. We've been waiting for her for almost two hours
= 萨莉可来了。我们等了她快两小时了

There goes the bus
= 公交车开走了

dentistry /ˈdentɪstri/ *n* [u] 牙科学; **to study ~** 学牙科

dentist: ~'s chair *n* 牙医椅; **~'s surgery** *n* 牙医诊所

dentition /denˈtɪʃn/ *n* [u] **1** (arrangement of teeth) 牙列 **2** (growth of teeth) 出牙

denture /ˈdentʃə(r)/

A *n* 假牙; **upper/lower ~** 上/下假牙; **a set of ~s** 一副假牙

B dentures *npl* 一副假牙

denude /dɪˈnjuːd, Amer -ˈnuːd/ *vt* 使…光秃 ‹*land, plant, rock*›; **the storm ~d the trees of their leaves** 暴风雨扫光了树上的叶子

denunciation /dɪˌnʌnsɪˈeɪʃn/ *n* 谴责

deny /dɪˈnaɪ/ *vt* **1** (declare untrue) 否认; **to ~ an accusation/a rumour/an account** 否认指责/谣言/说法; **to ~ doing** *or* **having done sth.** 否认做了某事; **to ~ all knowledge of sth.** 彻底否认知道某事; **there's no ~ing it/that ...** …无可否认 **2** (refuse to give) 拒绝给予; **to ~ sb. admittance to a building/club** 禁止某人进入大楼/拒绝接受某人加入俱乐部; **to ~ oneself** 自我克制; **to ~ oneself sth.** 戒绝某物; **he was denied bail** 他不得保释

deodorant /ˌdiːˈəʊdərənt/

A *n* [c and u] 除臭剂; **apply** *or* **use (a) ~** 使用除臭剂

B *adj* 除臭的; **~ foot powder** 除脚臭粉; **to have a ~ effect** 有除臭作用

deodorize /ˌdiːˈəʊdəraɪz/ *vt* 除去…的臭味

deoxidize /ˌdiːˈɒksɪdaɪz/ *vt* 使…脱氧 ‹*chemical compound*›

deoxygenate /ˌdiːˈɒksɪdʒəneɪt/ *vt* 使…脱氧 ‹*blood, air*›

deoxyribonucleic acid /diːˌɒksɪˌraɪbəʊnjuːˌkleɪɪk ˈæsɪd, Amer -nuː-/ *n* [u] 脱氧核糖核酸

depart /dɪˈpɑːt/

A *vi* **1** formal (leave) 出发; **to ~ from a place** 动身离开某地; **to ~ for a destination** 动身去某目的地 **2** (deviate) 背离; **you have ~ed from your original theory** 你违背了你最初的理论; **to ~ from one's usual routine** 一改通常的做法

B *vt* **to ~ this life** liter 去世

departed /dɪˈpɑːtɪd/ *adj* **1** ▸**p. 247** euph (dead) 亡故的; **the ~** 亡故者; **~ heroes** 已故的英雄们 **2** liter (vanished) 往昔的 ‹*joy, glory*›

department /dɪˈpɑːtmənt/ *n* **1** (of company, government) 部门; (of administration) 局; (within store) 部; **sales/personnel/service ~** 销售/人事/客服部 **2** (in hospital) 科; **x-ray ~** 放射科 **3** (in university) 系; (in secondary school) 教研室; **French ~** 法语系; **~ of electrical engineering** 电子工程系; **he's head of the maths ~** (in a school) 他是数学教研室主任 **4** (administrative district) [法国等国家的] 省

departmental /ˌdiːpɑːtˈmentl/ *adj attrib* **1** (of government) 部的; **her ~ colleagues** 她部里的同事 **2** (of organization) 部门的; **a ~ meeting** 部门会议

departmentalization /ˌdiːpɑːtˌmentəlaɪˈzeɪʃn, Amer -lɪˈz-/ *n* [u] 门类划分; **the ~ of sth.** 某物的分门别类; **the ~ of government** 政府的部门划分

departmentalize /ˌdiːpɑːtˈmentəlaɪz/ *vt* 将…划分部门

department: D~ for Business, Enterprise and Regulatory Reform *n* Brit 公司、企业及监管改革部; **D~ for Business, Innovation, and Skills** *n* Brit 商务、创新和技能部; **D~ for Children, Schools, and Families** *n* Brit 儿童、学校和家庭部; **D~ for Communities and Local Government** *n* Brit 社区与地方政府部; **D~ for Culture, Media, and Sport** *n* Brit 文化、媒体和体育部; **D~ for Energy and Climate Change** *n* Brit 能源和气候变化部; **D~ for Environment, Food, and Rural Affairs** *n* Brit 环境、食品与农村事务部; **D~ for Innovation, Universities and Skills** *n* Brit 创新、大学与技术部; **D~ for International Development** *n* Brit 国际发展部; **D~ for Transport** *n* Brit 交通部; **D~ for Work and Pensions** *n* Brit 工作与养老金部; **~ head** *n* **1** (administrative) 部门主管; **2** Univ 系主任; **~ manager** *n* **1** (of business) 部门经理; **2** (of store) 商店经理; **D~ of Defense** *n* Amer 国防部; **D~ of Health** *n* Brit 卫生部; **D~ of Health and Human Services** *n* Amer 卫生与公共服务部; **~ store** *n* 百货公司

departure /dɪˈpɑːtʃə(r)/ *n* **1** [c and u] (leaving) 出发; **~ from a place** 离开某地; **~ for a destination** 前往某目的地 **2** [c] (deviation) 背离; **a total ~ from traditional methods** 对传统方法的完全违背; **in a ~ from standard practice** 违背例行做法地 **3** [c] (start) 开端; **a new ~ in physics** 物理学上的新尝试

departure: ~ gate *n* 登机口; **~ lounge** *n* 候机室; **~ platform** *n* 发车站台; **~s board** *n* **1** (at airport) 出发时刻显示屏; **2** Rail 发车时间显示屏; **~ signal** *n* 发车信号; **~ time** *n* 出发时间

depend /dɪˈpend/ *vi* **1** (to rely on) 依靠; **to ~ on** *or* **upon sb./sth. (to do sth.)** 依靠某人/某物（做某事）; **you can't ~ on the bus arriving on time** 别指望公共汽车会准点到达; **to ~ on sb.** 靠某人养活 **2** (be sure of) 确信; **to ~ on** *or* **upon sb. to do sth.** 确信某人会做某事; **you can ~ on him to spoil the evening** 他一准会把晚会给搅了; **you can ~ upon it!** 放心吧！; **~ on it!** 没问题！ **3** (be determined by) 取决; **to ~ on** *or* **upon sth.** 取决于某事物; **that ~s, it all ~s** 那得看情况; **my arrival will ~ on the train times** 我到达的时间取决于火车班次的时间; **the temperature varies ~ing on the season** 气温随季节变化

dependability /dɪˌpendəˈbɪləti/ *n* [u] **1** (of machine, equipment) 可靠性 **2** (of person) 可信赖性

dependable /dɪˈpendəbl/ *adj* 可靠的 ‹*machine*›; 可信赖的 ‹*person*›

dependant /dɪˈpendənt/ *n* 受扶养者

dependence /dɪˈpendəns/ *n* [u] **1** (reliance) 依靠; **~ on ...** 对…的依赖; **emotional/financial/spiritual ~** 情感/经济/精神依赖 **2** (addiction) 瘾; **alcohol/drug ~** 酒瘾/毒瘾

dependency /dɪˈpendənsi/ *n* **1** [u] (reliance) 依赖; **his ~ on his mother/on heroin** 他对母亲的依赖/他的海洛因瘾 **2** [c] (territory) 附属国

dependency culture *n* [u] 依赖文化 [指依赖政府救助的生活方式]

dependent /dɪˈpendənt/ *adj* **1** (reliant) 依靠的; **to be ~ on** *or* **upon sb./sth.** 依靠某人/某物生活; **~ relatives** 受扶养的亲属; **a drug-~ patient** 依赖药物的病人 **2** *pred* (determined by) **to be ~ on sth.** 取决于 ‹*event, action*›; 受…影响 ‹*emotion*› **3** Ling 从属的 ‹*phrase, word*›; **a ~ clause** 从句

depersonalize /ˌdiːˈpɜːsənəlaɪz/ *vt* 使失去个性

depict /dɪˈpɪkt/ *vt* 描画

depiction /dɪˈpɪkʃn/ *n* [u and c] 描写; **a lively ~ of country life** 乡村生活的生动描写

depilate /ˈdepɪleɪt/ *vt* 使脱毛

depilatory /dɪˈpɪlətri, Amer -tɔːri/

A *n* 脱毛剂

B *adj* 脱毛的; **a ~ cream** 脱毛乳膏

deplane /ˌdiːˈpleɪn/ *vi* Amer 下飞机

deplete /dɪˈpliːt/ *vt* 耗尽; **reservoirs ~d of water** 枯竭的水库; **a lake ~d of fish** 鱼类资源已耗尽的湖

depleted uranium *n* [u] 贫化铀

depletion /dɪˈpliːʃn/ *n* [u] 耗尽; **a ~ of our fuel supplies** 我们的燃料供应的枯竭

deplorable /dɪˈplɔːrəbl/ *adj* (deserving condemnation) 应受谴责的 ‹*behaviour*›; (very bad) 糟透的 ‹*living conditions, state*›; **in a ~ condition** 在糟糕透顶的条件下

deplorably /dɪˈplɔːrəbli/ *adv* 糟透地; **~ late/impolite/bad** 迟得/无礼得/糟得令人吃惊

deplore /dɪˈplɔː(r)/ *vt* 强烈谴责; **to ~ the fact that ...** 强烈反对…这一事实

deploy /dɪˈplɔɪ/ *vt* **1** Mil 部署 ‹*soldiers, weaponry, equipment*›; **the general ~ed the tanks under the crest of the hill** 将军把坦克部队部署在山顶下 **2** (utilize) 有效利用 ‹*argument, resources*›

deployment /dɪˈplɔɪmənt/ *n* [u and c] **1** Mil 部署; **~ of nuclear missiles** 核导弹的部署 **2** (use) 有效利用

depolarization /diːˌpəʊləraɪˈzeɪʃn, Amer -rɪˈz-/ *n* [u] **1** Phys 消偏振 **2** Pol 折中; **signs of ~ in this dispute** 这次争论中妥协的迹象

depolarize /ˌdiːˈpəʊləraɪz/ *vt* **1** Phys 使…消偏振 ‹*particle, wave*› **2** Pol 使…折中 ‹*viewpoint, argument*›; 使…妥协 ‹*political party*›

deponent /dɪˈpəʊnənt/ *n* 宣誓证人

depopulate /ˌdiːˈpɒpjʊleɪt/ *vt* (reduce) 使人口减少; (remove) 驱除…的居民

depopulation /ˌdiːpɒpjʊˈleɪʃn/ *n* [u] 人口减少

deport /dɪˈpɔːt/ *vt* 把…驱逐出境 ‹*foreigner*›; 流放 ‹*native*›

deportation /ˌdiːpɔːˈteɪʃn/ *n* [c and u] (of foreigner) 驱逐出境; (of native) 流放

deportation order *n* 驱逐出境令

deportee /ˌdiːpɔːˈtiː/ *n* 被驱逐出境者

deportment /dɪˈpɔːtmənt/ *n* [u] **1** Brit formal (posture) 仪态 **2** esp Amer (behaviour) 行为

depose /dɪˈpəʊz/ *vt* **1** (remove from office) 废黜 ‹*king, head of state*›; **he was ~d from his post as managing director** 他被从总裁的位置上赶下来了 **2** Jur 宣誓证明; **to ~ the evidence** *or* **attestation** 宣誓作证

deposit /dɪˈpɒzɪt/

A *vt* **1** (put down) 放下 ‹*object*› **2** (lay) «*insect, fish*» 下 ‹*eggs*› **3** (entrust) 存放; **to ~ sth. with sb.** 把某物委托某人保管; **to ~ money at a bank** 把钱存入银行 **4** Geol «*river, glacier, wind*» 使…沉积 ‹*silt, rock, dust*›

B *n* **1** (into bank account) 存款; **to make a ~** 存一笔钱; **on ~** 储存着 **2** (part payment) 定金; **to put down a ~ on a house** 支付购房定金 **3** (against damage) 押金; (on bottle) 押瓶费 **4** Brit Pol 竞选保证金; **to lose one's ~** 失掉竞选保证金 **5** Geol 沉积层; **oil/coal ~s** 油藏/煤藏 **6** Chem 沉淀

deposit: ~ account *n* Brit 存款账户; **~ box** *n* 保险箱

deposition /ˌdepəˈzɪʃn/ *n* **1** [c and u] (formal statement) 证词; **to make/lodge a ~ (with sb.)** （为某人）作证 **2** [u] (of a head of state) 废黜

depositor /dɪˈpɒzɪtə(r)/ *n* 储户

depository /dɪˈpɒzɪtri, Amer -tɔːri/ *n* 仓库; **a book ~** 书库

deposit slip *n* 存款单

depot /ˈdepəʊ, Amer ˈdiːpəʊ/ *n* **1** (storehouse) 仓库; **an arms/a goods ~** 武器库/货物仓库 **2** (bus, train storage area) 车库; **bus/railway ~** 公共汽车/火车库 **3** Amer (bus station) 公共汽车站; (train station) 火车站

deprave /dɪˈpreɪv/ *vt* 使堕落

depraved /dɪˈpreɪvd/ *adj* 道德败坏的 ‹*person*›; 堕落的 ‹*behaviour*›; **this is the work of a ~ mind** 这是思想堕落者所为

depravity /dɪˈprævəti/ *n* **1** [u] (moral corruption) 堕落; **a life of ～** 腐化的生活 **2** [c] (immoral act) 堕落行为

deprecate /ˈdeprɪkeɪt/ *vt* 反对

deprecating /ˈdeprɪkeɪtɪŋ/ *adj* **1** (disapproving) 反对的 ‹*manner*› **2** (disparaging) 贬低的 ‹*criticism*›

deprecatory /ˌdeprɪˈkeɪtəri, Amer -tɔːri/ *adj* **= deprecating**

depreciate /dɪˈpriːʃɪeɪt/
A *vi* Fin 贬值; **sterling is depreciating against the euro** 英镑对欧元正在贬值
B *vt* **1** (belittle) 贬低 ‹*action, character*› **2** Fin 把…折旧; **the bank ～s PCs over a period of five years** 这家银行把个人计算机分 5 年折旧

depreciating /dɪˈpriːʃɪeɪtɪŋ/ *adj attrib* 贬值的 ‹*asset, investment*›

depreciation /dɪˌpriːʃɪˈeɪʃn/ *n* [u] 贬值; **currency ～** 通货贬值

depredation /ˌdeprəˈdeɪʃn/ *n* 劫掠

depress /dɪˈpres/ *vt* **1** (make unhappy) 使沮丧 **2** Comm, Fin 使…萧条 ‹*trading, market*›; 降低 ‹*price*› **3** (press) 按下 ‹*button*›; 压下 ‹*lever*›

depressant /dɪˈpresənt/
A *n* **1** Med 抑制药 **2** Econ 抑制作用
B *adj* Med, Econ 抑制的 ‹*drug, effect*›

depressed /dɪˈprest/ *adj* **1** (unhappy) 沮丧的 ‹*person, demeanour*› **2** Med 患抑郁症的 **3** Econ 不景气的 ‹*trade, area*›; 降低了的 ‹*prices*›

depressing /dɪˈpresɪŋ/ *adj* 令人沮丧的

depressingly /dɪˈpresɪŋli/ *adv* 令人沮丧地

depression /dɪˈpreʃn/ *n* **1** [u] ▸**p. 377** Med 抑郁症; **to suffer from ～** 患抑郁症 **2** [u] (unhappiness) 沮丧 **3** [u and c] Econ 萧条; **the (Great) D～** [二战前的] 大萧条 **4** [c] (hollow) 坑

depressive /dɪˈpresɪv/
A *adj* **1** Med 抑郁的 ‹*illness, state*› **2** Econ 抑制的 ‹*effect, policy*›
B *n* Med 抑郁症患者

depressurization /diːˌpreʃəraɪˈzeɪʃn, Amer -rɪˈz-/ *n* [u] 减压

depressurize /ˌdiːˈpreʃəraɪz/
A *vt* 使…减压 ‹*container, gas*›
B *vi* «*cabin, diver*» 减压

deprivation /ˌdeprɪˈveɪʃn/ *n* [u] **1** (withholding) 剥夺 **2** Psych 缺乏; **maternal ～** 母爱缺乏 **3** (poverty) 贫困; **to suffer from ～** 受穷

deprive /dɪˈpraɪv/ *vt* 剥夺; **to ～ sb. of sth.** 剥夺某人的某物; **he was ～d of his rights** 他被剥夺了权利

deprived /dɪˈpraɪvd/ *adj* 贫困的; **a ～ area/child** 贫困地区/穷苦的孩子

deprogramme /ˌdiːˈprəʊgræm/ *vt* 使放弃被灌输的理念

dept *abbr* **= department**

depth /depθ/
A *n* **1** [u] Meas 深度; **12 m in ～** 12 米深; **to be out of one's ～** lit 在水深没顶的地方; fig 非自己所能理解 **2** [u and c] (degree of intensity) 强烈; **the ～ of his despair/sorrow** 他强烈的绝望/深切的悲痛; **the ～ of her gratitude** 她深切的感激; **the ～ of his ignorance appalled me** 他那极端的无知令我震惊 **3** [u] (complexity) (of knowledge) 深奥; (of analysis, work) 深刻; **to examine** *or* **study sth. in ～** 深入研究某事物 **4** [u] (lowness of pitch) 低沉 **5** [u] Cin, Phot 立体感; **～ of focus** *or* **field** 景深
B **depths** *npl* **the ～s** 最深处; **the ～s of night** 深夜; **the ～s of winter** 隆冬; **in the ～s of his consciousness** 在他意识的最深层

depth charge *n* 深水炸弹

deputation /ˌdepjʊˈteɪʃn/ *n* 代表团

depute /dɪˈpjuːt/ *vt* formal **1** (instruct) 委派; **to ～ sb. for/to do sth.** 委派某人做某事 **2** (delegate) 把…交托给 ‹*task*›

deputize /ˈdepjʊtaɪz/ *vi* 担任代理; **to ～ for sb.** 代理某人

deputy /ˈdepjʊti/ *n* **1** (aide) 副手; (replacement) 代理; **～ to sb.** 某人的副手; **～ sales director** 销售副经理; **to act as (a) ～ for sb.** 代理某人 **2** Pol 议员 **3** Amer **～ (sheriff)** 警官

deputy: ～ chairman *n* 副主席; **～ chief constable** *n* Brit 副警察局长; **～ leader** *n* Brit 副领导人; **～ premier, ～ prime minister** *ns* 副首相; **～ president** *n* 副总统; **D～ Speaker** *n* Brit 副议长

derail /dɪˈreɪl/ *vt* 使…脱轨 ‹*locomotive*›; **the train has been ～ed** 火车出轨了

derailleur /dəˈreɪljə(r)/ *n* 换挡机构; **～ gears** 换挡齿轮

derailment /dɪˈreɪlmənt/ *n* [u and c] 脱轨

derange /dɪˈreɪndʒ/ *vt* 使精神错乱; **mentally ～d** 精神错乱的

derangement /dɪˈreɪndʒmənt/ *n* [u] 精神错乱

Derby /ˈdɑːbi, Amer ˈdɜːrbi/ *n* **1** Horse Racing **the ～** 德比马赛 **2** **derby** (competition) 体育比赛 **3** **derby** (hat) 圆顶高帽

Derbyshire /ˈdɑːbɪʃɪə(r)/ *pr n* 德比郡

derecognition /ˌdiːrekəgˈnɪʃn/ *n* [u] 撤销承认

derecognize /ˌdiːˈrekəgnaɪz/ *vt* 撤销对…的承认

deregulate /ˌdiːˈregjʊleɪt/ *vt* 撤销对…的管制 ‹*industry, prices, TV*›

deregulation /ˌdiːregjʊˈleɪʃn/ *n* [u] 撤销管制

derelict /ˈderəlɪkt/
A *adj* 破败的 ‹*building*›; 荒废的 ‹*farm, land*›; **to let sth. go ～** 使某物荒置
B *n* 社会弃儿

dereliction /ˌderəˈlɪkʃn/ *n* [u] **1** (dilapidation) 废弃; **to fall into ～** (land) 荒废; (building) 破败 **2** Jur 玩忽职守; **～ of duty** 渎职

derestrict /ˌdiːrɪˈstrɪkt/ *vt* 取消对…的限制 ‹*traffic speed, controls*›; **a ～ed road** Brit 无车速限制的道路

deride /dɪˈraɪd/ *vt* 嘲笑; **to ～ sb. for sth.** 因某事嘲笑某人; **to ～ sb. as old-fashioned/amateurish/an embarrassment** 嘲笑某人保守/外行/是个让人难堪的人

de rigueur /də rɪˈgɜː(r)/ *adj* (as etiquette) 合乎礼节的; (as fashion) 按照时尚的

derision /dɪˈrɪʒn/ *n* [u] 嘲笑; **to arouse ～** 引起嘲笑; **an object of ～** 嘲笑的对象

derisive /dɪˈraɪsɪv/ *adj* 嘲弄的; **～ laughter/comments** 嘲笑/讥评

derisively /dɪˈraɪsɪvli/ *adv* 嘲弄地

derisory /dɪˈraɪsəri/ *adj* **1** pej (small) 少得可笑的 ‹*offer, resources*› **2** **= derisive**

derivation /ˌderɪˈveɪʃn/ *n* [u] **1** (obtaining) 得到; **the ～ of scientific laws from observation** 基于观察的科学规律的获取 **2** Ling 派生; **to have its ～ in …** «*word, expression*» 由…派生而来

derivative /dəˈrɪvətɪv/
A *adj* **1** Ling 派生的; **a ～ word** 派生词 **2** Chem 衍生的; **a ～ compound** 衍生化合物 **3** Math 导数的; **a ～ function** 导函数 **4** pej (imitative) 缺乏独创性的 ‹*work, style, design*›
B *n* **1** Ling 派生词 **2** Chem 衍生物 **3** Math 导数 **4** Fin (金融) 衍生工具; **～s trading/trader** 衍生工具交易/交易商; **the ～s market** 衍生工具市场 **5** pej (imitation) 仿制品

derive /dɪˈraɪv/
A *vi* **to ～ from …** «*custom*» 起源于…; «*word*» 源自…
B *vt* **1** (obtain) 获得 ‹*benefit, joy*›; **to ～ sth. from sth.** 从某物中获得某物 **2** Ling 衍生; **'canine' is ～d from the Latin 'canis'** canine源自拉丁文词canis

dermatitis /ˌdɜːməˈtaɪtɪs/ ▸**p. 377** *n* [u] 皮炎

dermatologist /ˌdɜːməˈtɒlədʒɪst/ ▸**p. 409** *n* 皮肤病专家

dermatology /ˌdɜːməˈtɒlədʒi/ *n* [u] 皮肤病学

derogate /ˈderəgeɪt/ *vi* formal **1** (detract from) 减损 **2** (deviate from) 偏离; **to ～ from sth.** 偏离某物 **3** (disparage) 贬低 ‹*status*›

derogatory /dɪˈrɒgətri, Amer -tɔːri/ *adj* 贬低的 ‹*remark, article*›; 喜欢贬低他人的 ‹*person*›

derrick /ˈderɪk/ *n* **1** (crane) 转臂起重机 **2** (framework) 井架

derring-do /ˌderɪŋˈduː/ *n* [u] dated or hum 蛮勇

derringer /ˈderɪndʒə(r)/ *n* 大口径短筒手枪

derris /ˈderɪs/ *n* [u] 鱼藤酮 [一种植物杀虫剂]

derv /dɜːv/ *n* [u] Brit 车用柴油

dervish /ˈdɜːvɪʃ/ *n* 托钵僧

desalinate /ˌdiːˈsælɪneɪt/ *vt* 脱去…的盐分 ‹*sea water*›

desalination /diːˌsælɪˈneɪʃn/ *n* [u] 脱盐; **～ plant** 脱盐工厂

descale /ˌdiːˈskeɪl/ *vt* 除去…的水垢 ‹*kettle*›; **to ～ sb.'s teeth** 除掉某人的牙垢

descaler /ˌdiːˈskeɪlə(r)/ *n* [u] 除垢剂

descant /ˈdeskænt/ *n* 高于主音的旋律

descant recorder *n* 高音竖笛

descend /dɪˈsend/
A *vt* 走下 ‹*stairs, slope*›
B *vi* **1** (go down) «*person*» 下来; «*road, valley*» 下斜 **2** (move down scale) 递减; **in ～ing order of importance** 按重要性递减顺序 **3** (fall) «*atmosphere, darkness*» 降临; «*rain*» 降落; **gloom ～ed upon the group** 这群人突然变得沮丧起来 **4** (arrive) 突然涌来; **to ～ on** *or* **upon …** «*army*» 突袭…; «*visitors*» 蜂拥而至… **5** (be related to) 是后裔; **to ～ from …** 是…的后裔 **6** (originate from) 起源; **to ～ from …** «*customs, speech*» 起源于… **7** (sink) 堕落; **to ～ so low** *or* **far as to do sth.** 堕落到做某事的地步; **to ～ into** 逐渐陷入 ‹*chaos*›

descendant /dɪˈsendənt/ *n* 后代

descent /dɪˈsent/ *n* **1** [c] (downward motion) 下降; **to make one's/its ～** 下降 **2** [c] (down slope) 下坡; **a steep ～** 陡坡 **3** [u] (extraction) 血统; **of Irish ～** 爱尔兰血统的; **to trace one's ～** 追溯祖先; **to claim ～ from …** 声称是…的后代 **4** [u] fig (decline) 堕落; **～ into crime** 堕落到犯罪

descramble /ˌdiːˈskræmbl/ *vt* 解读

descrambler /ˌdiːˈskræmblə(r)/ *n* 解码器

describe /dɪˈskraɪb/ *vt* **1** (give details of) 描述 ‹*person, event*› **2** (characterize) 形容; **to ～ sb. as an idiot** 称某人为白痴; **it could be ～d as pretty** 这可以说是漂亮

description /dɪˈskrɪpʃn/ *n* **1** (account) 描述; **to answer to the ～ of …** 与…的描述相符; **to defy** *or* **be beyond ～** 无法形容 **2** (type) 种类; **of every** *or* **all ～(s)** 各种各样的

descriptive /dɪˈskrɪptɪv/ *adj* 描写的 ‹*passage, word*›; 记叙的 ‹*style*›

descriptive: ～ geometry *n* [u] 画法几何学; **～ linguistics** *npl + v sing* 描写语言学

descriptivism /dɪˈskrɪptɪvɪzəm/ *n* [u] 描述主义

descriptivist /dɪˈskrɪptɪvɪst/ *n* 描述主义者

descry /dɪˈskraɪ/ *vt* liter 看见

desecrate /ˈdesɪkreɪt/ *vt* **1** Relig 亵渎 ‹*church, altar*› **2** (spoil) 破坏

desecration /ˌdesɪˈkreɪʃn/ *n* [u] **1** Relig 亵渎神圣 **2** (spoiling) 破坏

desegregate /ˌdiːˈsegrɪgeɪt/
A *vt* 废除…的种族隔离 ‹*school, area*›; 废除…间的隔离 ‹*sexes*›
B *vi* «*school, area*» 废除种族隔离

desegregation /diːˌsegrɪˈgeɪʃn/ *n* [u] (racial) 废除种族隔离; (sexual) 废除性别隔离

deselect /ˌdiːsɪˈlekt/ *vt* Brit 取消…的候选资格 ‹*candidate*›

deselection /ˌdiːsɪˈlekʃn/ *n* Brit 取消候选资格

desensitize /ˌdiːˈsensɪtaɪz/ *vt* 使…脱敏 ‹*part of body*›; **to ~ sb. to sth.** 使某人对某物脱敏

desert¹ /ˈdezət/ *n* 1 Geog 沙漠; **~ region** 沙漠地区 2 fig (dull period) 荒凉时期; (dull place) 荒凉之地; **a cultural ~** 文化沙漠

desert² /dɪˈzɜːt/
A *vt* 1 (abandon) 抛弃 ‹*friend, cause*›; 遗弃 ‹*family*›; 离弃 ‹*land*›; **to ~ sb./sth. for sb./sth.** 抛弃某人/某物投向某人/某事 2 (fail) «*courage, resolve*» 背离 ‹*person*›; **our luck ~ed us** 我们的运气没了
B *vi* Mil 擅离; **to ~ to the enemy camp** 叛逃到敌营

desert: ~ boot *n* 沙漠靴; **~ crossing** *n* 穿越沙漠之旅

deserted /dɪˈzɜːtɪd/ *adj* 1 (abandoned) 废弃的 ‹*land, building*›; 被抛弃的 ‹*person*› 2 (empty) 空无一人的 ‹*street, valley*›

deserter /dɪˈzɜːtə(r)/ *n* 1 Mil 逃兵 2 (person who abandons sth./sb.) 背叛者

desertification /dɪˌzɜːtɪfɪˈkeɪʃn/ *n* [u] 沙漠化

desertion /dɪˈzɜːʃn/ *n* [u] 1 Mil 擅离职守 2 Jur 遗弃

desert island *n* 荒岛

deserts /dɪˈzɜːts/ *npl* (reward) 应得的奖赏; (punishment) 应得的惩罚; **to get** *or* **receive one's just ~** (punishment) 得到应有的惩罚; (reward) 得到应有的回报

deserve /dɪˈzɜːv/
A *vt* 应得; **it was no more than (what) he ~d** 他只是得到了他该得到的而已; **the idea ~s consideration** 这个想法值得考虑; **a richly ~d punishment** 活该得到的惩罚
B *vi* 应受; **to ~ to do sth.** 应该做某事; **she ~s to be promoted** 她应该得到提拔; **to be deserving of sth.** 应得某物; **to ~ better of sb.** 应受到某人更好的对待

deservedly /dɪˈzɜːvɪdli/ *adv* 理所当然地 ‹*unpopular, praised*›

deserving /dɪˈzɜːvɪŋ/ *adj* 1 (worthy) 值得赞助的 ‹*cause*›; 应得到帮助的 ‹*person*›; **to be ~ of sth.** 应得某物 2 *pred* (meriting) 值得的; **an issue ~ of attention** 值得注意的问题

desiccant /ˈdesɪkənt/ *n* 干燥剂

desiccate /ˈdesɪkeɪt/ *vt* 使…干燥 ‹*food, material*›

desiccated /ˈdesɪkeɪtɪd/ *adj* 脱水的; **~ coconut** 椰子干

desiccation /ˌdesɪˈkeɪʃn/ *n* [u] 脱水

desideratum /dɪˌzɪdəˈrɑːtəm/ *n* (*pl* **desiderata** /dɪˌzɪdəˈrɑːtə/) 想望的东西

design /dɪˈzaɪn/
A *n* 1 [c and u] (arrangement, conception) 设计; **a ~ for** *or* **of sth.** 某物的设计; **to be of faulty/poor design** 设计有问题/很差 2 [u] (art of designing) 设计艺术; **interior/theatre/industrial ~** 室内/舞台/工业设计 3 [c] (drawing, sketch, diagram) 设计图; **a set of ~s for sth.** 为某物设计的一套图样 4 [c] (decorative pattern) 图案 5 [c] (model, completed object) 款式; **this season's new ~s** 本季新款 6 [c and u] (intention) 意图; **to have ~s on sb./sth.** 企图占有某人/某物; **to have ~s against sb.** 算计某人; **by ~** 故意地
B *vt* (conceive, plan out, sketch) 设计; **to ~ sth. as sth.** 把某物设计成某物; **to be well/badly ~ed** 设计得好/不好; **a jug ~ed to hold** *or* **for holding water** 设计用来盛水的罐子

designate¹ /ˈdezɪgneɪt/ *vt* 1 (term) 命名; (classify) 指定; **to ~ sth. (as) sth.** 指定…为某物 ‹*land*›; **to ~ the area (as) a nature reserve** 把这个地区定为自然保护区; **to ~ sth. for sb./sth.** 为某人/某物指定某物 2 (appoint) 指派; **to ~ sb. as sth./to do sth.** 委任某人某职务/做某事

designate² /ˈdezɪgneɪt, -nət/ *adj* formal (appointed) 受委派而尚未上任的; (elected) 已当选而尚未就职的; **prime minister ~** 新当选而尚未上任的首相

designated driver /ˌdezɪgneɪtɪd ˈdraɪvə(r)/ *n* 指定司机 [指聚会时不饮酒以便开车送他人回家者]

designation /ˌdezɪgˈneɪʃn/ *n* 1 [c] (term) 名称 2 [u] (classification) 指定; **the ~ of sth. as** 指定某处为 ‹*smoking area, state park etc.*› 3 [u] (appointment) 委任

design: ~ award *n* 设计奖; **~ centre** *n* (for exhibiting) 设计展览中心; (for work) 设计中心; **~ consultant** ▸p. 409 *n* 设计顾问; **~ department** *n* 设计部; **~ engineering** *n* [u] 设计工程

designer /dɪˈzaɪnə(r)/ ▸p. 409
A *n* 设计师
B *modif* 名牌的; **~ jeans** 品牌牛仔服; **~ stubble** [为追求时尚留的] 特型胡子茬

designer: ~ baby *n* 设计婴儿 [指基因构造经过选择]; **~ drug** *n* 人造毒品

design: ~ fault *n* 设计缺陷; **~ feature** *n* 设计特点

designing /dɪˈzaɪnɪŋ/ *adj attrib* pej 工于心计的

design: ~ specification *n* 设计规范; **~ student** *n* 设计专业学生; **~ studio** *n* 设计室

desirability /dɪˌzaɪərəˈbɪləti/ *n* [u] 1 (value) 值得想望; **no one questions the ~ of cheaper fares** 没有人怀疑票价更便宜是件好事 2 (sexual appeal) 性感 3 (advisability) 可取性

desirable /dɪˈzaɪərəbl/ *adj* 1 (attractive, sought-after) 值得拥有的 ‹*gift, residence, job*›; **the qualities ~ in a secretary** 一个秘书应有的素质; **it is ~ that ...** 希望… 2 (sexually attractive) 性感的 3 (advisable) 明智的 ‹*decision*›; 可取的 ‹*action, plan*›

desire /dɪˈzaɪə(r)/
A *n* 1 [u and c] (wish) 渴望; **~ for sth.** 对某物的渴望; **to have no ~ to do sth.** 不想做某事; **her heart's ~** liter 她最心仪的东西 2 [u] (sexual longing) 情欲
B *vt* 1 (want) 渴望 ‹*object, event*›; **to ~ to do sth.** formal 想做某事; **to ~ sb. to do sth.** formal 期望某人做某事; **if you so ~** formal 如果你期望如此; **we ~ your presence** 我们期望您光临; **it leaves a lot to be ~d** 还有许多需要改进的地方 2 (want sexually) 对…产生性欲

desirous /dɪˈzaɪərəs/ *adj pred* formal **to be ~ of sth.** 渴望得到某物; **to be ~ that ...** 希望…

desist /dɪˈzɪst/ *vi* formal 停止; **to ~ from sth./doing sth.** 停止某事/做某事

desk /desk/
A *n* 1 (table) (in class) 课桌; (in office) 办公桌 2 (counter) 服务台; **reception ~** 接待处 3 Journ 编辑部; **the sports ~** 体育编辑部
B *modif* 台式的; **~ lamp** 台灯; **~ pad** (notepad) 记事簿; (blotter) 吸墨台; **~ job** 案头工作

desk: ~bound *adj* 终日伏案工作的; **~ clerk** *n* Amer 服务台接待员

deskill /ˌdiːˈskɪl/ *vt* 降低…的技术要求 ‹*process, job, task*›

deskilling /ˌdiːˈskɪlɪŋ/ *n* [u] (of workforce) 技能退化; (of process, job, task) 技术水准降低

desk: ~ research *n* [u] 案头研究; **~top** *n* 1 also Comput 桌面; **to save the shortcut to your ~top** 把快捷方式保存在桌面; 2 **= ~top computer**; **~top computer, ~top PC** *ns* 台式电脑; **~top publishing** *n* [u] 桌面排版

desolate /ˈdesələt/
A *adj* 1 (deserted) 无人居住的 ‹*place, building*› 2 (devastated) 荒芜的 ‹*land*›; 废旧的 ‹*building*› 3 (grief-stricken) 悲伤的 ‹*person, face*›; (forlorn) 孤独凄凉的
B *vt* 1 (devastate) 使…荒芜 ‹*land*›; 使…无人烟 ‹*town*› 2 (fill with grief) 使…悲伤 ‹*person*›

desolately /ˈdesələtli/ *adv* 悲伤地

desolation /ˌdesəˈleɪʃn/ *n* [u] 1 (devastation) 废墟; (emptiness) 荒凉; **a scene of utter ~** 满目疮痍的景象 2 (grief) 悲伤; (loneliness) 孤寂

despair /dɪˈspeə(r)/
A *n* [u] 1 (loss of hope) 绝望; **to be in ~ about** *or* **over sth.** 对某事物绝望; **to do sth. in ~** *or* **out of ~** 出于绝望做某事; **to be in the depths of ~** 陷于绝望的深渊 2 (cause of worry) **to be the ~ of sb.** 使某人感到绝望
B *vi* 绝望; **to ~ of ...** 对…绝望; **don't ~** 别灰心

despairing /dɪˈspeərɪŋ/ *adj* 绝望的

despairingly /dɪˈspeərɪŋli/ *adv* 绝望地

despatch *vt, n* **= dispatch**

desperado /ˌdespəˈrɑːdəʊ/ *n* (*pl* **~s** *or* **~es**) dated 亡命之徒

desperate /ˈdespərət/ *adj* 1 (hopeless) 绝望的 ‹*person, act*›; **to be ~ to do sth.** 拼命要做某事 2 (in great need) 极渴望的; **to be ~ for** 渴望得到 ‹*affection, help*›; **to be ~ to do sth.** 极想做某事 3 colloq (terrible) 极严重的; **a ~ shortage of teachers** 教师奇缺 4 (frantic) 孤注一掷的 ‹*act, attempt*› 5 (violent) 胆大妄为的; **a ~ criminal** 亡命之徒

desperately /ˈdespərətli/ *adv* 1 (hopelessly) 绝望地 ‹*glance*›; 拼命地 ‹*struggle, plead*› 2 (extremely) 极其 ‹*poor, sad*›; **~ in love** 疯狂地爱着; **~ disappointed** 极度失望的

desperation /ˌdespəˈreɪʃn/ *n* [u] 绝望; **in/out of (sheer) ~** 出于绝望; **in ~ she phoned the police** 在走投无路的情况下她打电话报警了; **to drive sb. to ~** 使某人陷入绝望

despicable /dɪˈspɪkəbl, ˈdespɪkəbl/ *adj* 卑鄙的; **to be ~ of sb. to do sth.** 某人做某事很卑鄙

despicably /dɪˈspɪkəbli, ˈdespɪkəbli/ *adv* 卑劣地

despise /dɪˈspaɪz/ *vt* 鄙视; **to ~ sb. for sth.** 因某事看不起某人; **to ~ sb.'s doing sth.** 鄙视某人做了某事

despite /dɪˈspaɪt/ *prep* 尽管; **we enjoyed ourselves, ~ the fact that we had no money** 我们虽然没有钱，但仍然过得很愉快; **~ oneself** 尽管自己不愿意; **he laughed, ~ himself** 他忍不住笑了出来

despoil /dɪˈspɔɪl/ *vt* liter 抢劫 ‹*house*›; 掠夺 ‹*nation*›

despondency /dɪˈspɒndənsi/ *n* [u] 沮丧

despondent /dɪˈspɒndənt/ *adj* 沮丧的

despondently /dɪˈspɒndəntli/ *adv* 沮丧地

despot /ˈdespɒt/ *n* 专制君主

despotic /deˈspɒtɪk/ *adj* 专横的 ‹*person, manner*›; **~ power/rule** 至高无上的权力/专制统治

despotically /deˈspɒtɪkli/ *adv* 专制地 ‹*rule*›; 霸道地 ‹*behave*›

despotism /ˈdespətɪzəm/ *n* [u] (government) 专制政府; (exercise of power) 专制统治

des res /ˌdez ˈrez/ *n* colloq hum 理想的房子

dessert /dɪˈzɜːt/ *n* （饭后）甜点

dessert: ~ apple *n* 作甜点的苹果; **~ chocolate** *n* [u] 作甜点的巧克力; **~ fork** *n* 糕饼叉; **~ knife** *n* 点心刀; **~ plate** *n* 点心碟; **~spoon** *n* 点心匙; **~ wine** *n* [u and c] 餐末甜酒

destabilization /ˌdiːsteɪbəlaɪˈzeɪʃn, Amer -lɪˈz-/ *n* [u] 不稳定

destabilize /ˌdiːˈsteɪbəlaɪz/ *vt* 使…不稳定 ‹*country, economy*›

destination /ˌdestɪˈneɪʃn/ *n* 目的地; **final ～** 最终目的地

destination wedding *n* 国外旅游结婚

destine /ˈdestɪn/ *vt* 指定; **to ～ sb./sth. for sth.** 指定某人/某物做某事; **her talent ～d her for popularity** 她的才能使她注定会走红

destined /ˈdestɪnd/ *adj* **1** (preordained) 注定的; **to be ～ for sth.** 注定有某结果; **it was ～ to happen** 这事注定会发生 **2** (bound for) «*person, vehicle*» 去往…的; «*letter, parcel*» 寄往…的; **to be ～ for sth.** 去往某地

destiny /ˈdestɪni/ *n* [u and c] 命运; **to be one's ～ to do sth.** 命中注定要做某事; **to achieve** *or* **fulfil** *or* **meet one's ～** 应验命中注定之事

destitute /ˈdestɪtjuːt, Amer -tuːt/ *adj* **1** (poor) 赤贫的; **to leave sb. ～** 使某人一贫如洗 **2** formal (lacking) **to be ～ of experience** 毫无经验

destitution /ˌdestɪˈtjuːʃn, Amer -tuːʃn/ *n* [u] 赤贫

de-stress /ˌdiːˈstres/ *vt* 使放松

destroy /dɪˈstrɔɪ/ *vt* **1** (obliterate) 破坏 ‹*object, place, evidence*›; 毁灭 ‹*evidence*› **2** (kill) 杀死; **we must ～ the enemy** 我们必须消灭敌人 **3** fig (ruin) 消除 ‹*influence*›; 摧毁 ‹*power, faith, happiness, love, hope, career*›; 破坏 ‹*atmosphere*›

destroyer /dɪˈstrɔɪə(r)/ *n* **1** Naut 驱逐舰; **a ～ escort** 护航驱逐舰 **2** Mil 歼击武器; **a tank ～** 坦克歼击车 **3** (person that destroys) 破坏者; (thing that destroys) 起破坏作用的东西; **sugar is the ～ of healthy teeth** 糖会蛀蚀健康的牙齿

destruct /dɪˈstrʌkt/
A *vt* 摧毁 ‹*missile, rocket*›
B *vi* «*missile, rocket*» 自毁

destructible /dɪˈstrʌktəbl/ *adj* 可破坏的

destruction /dɪˈstrʌkʃn/ *n* [u] (of object, place) 破坏; (of evidence) 毁灭; (of power, faith, happiness, love, hope, career) 摧毁; (of enemy) 消灭; **～ of character/reputation** 品格/声誉的破坏

destructive /dɪˈstrʌktɪv/ *adj* **1** lit 破坏性的 ‹*storm, weapon, behaviour*›; **to be ～ of** *or* **to sth.** 对某物具有破坏性; **a ～ child** 捣蛋的孩子 **2** fig 消极的 ‹*argument, comment, article, criticism*›

destructively /dɪˈstrʌktɪvli/ *adv* 消极地 ‹*speak, behave*›

destructiveness /dɪˈstrʌktɪvnɪs/ *n* [u] (of storm, weapon, behaviour) 破坏性; (of argument, comment, article, criticism) 消极

destructor /dɪˈstrʌktə(r)/ *n* **1** Brit (incinerator) 垃圾焚化炉 **2** Mil 自毁器

desultory /ˈdesəltri, Amer -tɔːri/ *adj* 随意的 ‹*reading*›; 散漫的 ‹*effort, friendship*›; **a ～ conversation** 随意闲聊

detach /dɪˈtætʃ/
A *vt* 使…分开 ‹*person, object*›; **to ～ sth. from sth.** 把某物从某物分开; **to ～ four soldiers for guard duty** Mil 派遣4个士兵去站岗
B *v refl* **to ～ oneself** 挣脱; **she ～ed herself from her friends** 她抽身离开朋友

detachable /dɪˈtætʃəbl/ *adj* 可拆卸的 ‹*handle*›; **～ collar/hood** 活领/活风帽

detached /dɪˈtætʃt/ *adj* **1** (separated) 单独的; **to become ～ from the group** 离群 **2** fig (objective) 公正的; (aloof) 冷漠的

detached: ～ garage *n* 独立车库; **～ house** *n* 独栋式住宅; **～ retina** *n* 视网膜脱落

detachment /dɪˈtætʃmənt/ *n* **1** [u] (separation) 分离; **～ of the retina** 视网膜脱落 **2** [u] (objectivity) 不偏不倚; (aloofness) 冷漠; **an air of ～** 冷漠的神态 **3** [c] Mil 分遣队

detail /ˈdiːteɪl, Amer dɪˈteɪl/
A *n* **1** [c] (piece of information, minor point) 细节 **2** [u] (facts) 详情; **in ～** 详细地; **to go into ～ (about sth.)** 详细叙述（某事） **3** [u and c] Art 细部 **4** [c] Mil (detachment) 特遣队; (assignment) 任务; **a guard ～** 警卫任务
B *vt* **1** (give facts about) 详述 ‹*event*›; 详细列举 ‹*items*› **2** Mil (assign) 派遣; **to ～ sb. to sth./to do sth.** 分派某人某事/派某人做某事

detail drawing *n* 详图

detailed /ˈdiːteɪld, Amer dɪˈteɪld/ *adj* **1** (comprehensive) 详细的 ‹*account, study*› **2** (intricate) 精细的 ‹*work*›

detain /dɪˈteɪn/ *vt* **1** (delay) 耽搁; **I won't ～ you any longer** 我不会再耽搁你了 **2** (arrest) 拘留 **3** (keep in hospital) 留…住院治疗; **he was ～ed for observation** 他被留院观察

detainee /ˌdiːteɪˈniː/ *n* 被拘留者

detect /dɪˈtekt/ *vt* **1** (find) 查明 ‹*evidence, plot*›; 发现 ‹*sign*›; **to ～ crime** 侦查犯罪活动 **2** (sense) 闻到 ‹*smell, gas*›; 察觉 ‹*mood*›

detectable /dɪˈtektəbl/ *adj* 可察觉的 ‹*trace, element, emotion*›

detection /dɪˈtekʃn/ *n* [u] **1** (discovery) 发现; **medical ～** 医学检测 **2** Police 侦查

detective /dɪˈtektɪv/ *n* 侦探; **a private/an amateur ～** 私人/业余侦探

detective: ～ constable *n* Brit 刑侦警探; **～ inspector** *n* Brit 探长; **～ sergeant** *n* Brit 刑侦队长; **～ story** *n* 侦探故事; **～ superintendent** *n* Brit 刑侦督察长; **～ work** *n* [u] 侦查工作

detector /dɪˈtektə(r)/ *n* 探测器

detector van *n* 有线电视用户探测车

détente /deɪˈtɑːnt/ *n* 缓和

detention /dɪˈtenʃn/ *n* **1** [u] (custody) 拘留; **to be held in ～** 被拘留 **2** [u and c] Sch [处罚性] 课后留校; **to give sb. (a) ～** 罚某人放学后留校; **to have (a) ～** 被罚放学后留校

detention centre Brit, **detention home** Amer *ns* **1** (for offenders) 感化中心 **2** (for refugees) 收容所

deter /dɪˈtɜː(r)/ *vt* (*pres p etc.* **-rr-**) **1** (dissuade) 威慑; **to ～ sb. from sth./doing sth.** 吓得某人不敢做某事; **nothing will ～ her** 什么都吓不住她 **2** (prevent) 防止

detergent /dɪˈtɜːdʒənt/
A *n* [u and c] 洗涤剂; **liquid ～** 洗涤液
B *adj attrib* 洗涤的; **～ powder/effect** 洗衣粉/洗涤效果

deteriorate /dɪˈtɪərɪəreɪt/ *vi* «*health, weather*» 恶化; «*mental powers*» 退化; «*fabric*» 磨损; «*food*» 变坏; «*work*» 质量下降; **to ～ into sth.** «*discussion*» 演变成 ‹*argument*›

deteriorating /dɪˈtɪərɪəreɪtɪŋ/ *adj attrib* 不断恶化的 ‹*weather, conditions, standards*›

deterioration /dɪˌtɪərɪəˈreɪʃn/ *n* [u] 恶化; **a ～ in** *or* **of sth.** 某事物的恶化; **a ～ of values** 价值观的堕落

determinable /dɪˈtɜːmɪnəbl/ *adj* **1** 可算出的 ‹*number*›; 可查明的 ‹*fact*› **2** Jur formal 可终止的

determinant /dɪˈtɜːmɪnənt/
A *adj* 决定性的 ‹*factor, effect*›
B *n* **1** Math 行列式 **2** (decisive factor) 决定因素

determination /dɪˌtɜːmɪˈneɪʃn/ *n* [u] 决心; **～ to do sth.** 做某事的决心

determine /dɪˈtɜːmɪn/ *vt* **1** (ascertain) 查明 ‹*cause, cost*›; **to ～ how/when** *etc.* 弄清楚如何/何时等; **to ～ that ...** 查清… **2** (decide, dictate) 确定 ‹*event, career*›; 作出 ‹*decision*›; **to ～ on** *or* **upon sth.** 决定某事; **to ～ to do sth.** 决定做某事; **the river ～s the boundary of our land** 这条河划定了我们国土的边界

determined /dɪˈtɜːmɪnd/ *adj* **1** (resolute) 下定决心的; **to be ～ to do sth.** 决心做某事; **to be ～ that ...** 下决心… **2** (with determination) 坚决的 ‹*manner, appearance*›

determiner /dɪˈtɜːmɪnə(r)/ *n* 限定词

determining /dɪˈtɜːmɪnɪŋ/ *adj attrib* 决定性的 ‹*factor, effect*›

determinism /dɪˈtɜːmɪnɪzəm/ *n* [u] 决定论

determinist /dɪˈtɜːmɪnɪst/
A *adj* 决定论的; **～ theory** 决定论
B *n* 决定论者

deterrent /dɪˈterənt, Amer -ˈtɜː-/
A *n* 威慑物; **a ～ to sth.** 对某事物的威慑; **to serve** *or* **act as a ～** 充当威慑物
B *adj* Jur 威慑的 ‹*effect, sentence*›

detest /dɪˈtest/ *vt* 憎恶; **to ～ doing sth.** 讨厌做某事

detestable /dɪˈtestəbl/ *adj* 令人厌恶的 ‹*person, behaviour*›; **it is ～ to act like that** 这样的行为真可恶; **it is ～ that ...** …令人憎恨; **it is ～ of sb. to do sth.** 某人做某事是可恶的

detestably /dɪˈtestəbli/ *adv* 可憎地

detestation /ˌdiːteˈsteɪʃn/ *n* [u] 憎恶; **to hold sb. in ～** 憎恶某人

dethrone /ˌdiːˈθrəʊn/ *vt* 废黜

dethronement /ˌdiːˈθrəʊnmənt/ *n* [u] 废黜

detonate /ˈdetəneɪt/
A *vt* 引爆 ‹*explosive, firework*›
B *vi* «*explosive, shell*» 爆炸

detonation /ˌdetəˈneɪʃn/ *n* [u and c] (act) 引爆; (result) 爆炸

detonator /ˈdetəneɪtə(r)/ *n* 引爆装置

detour /ˈdiːtʊə(r), Amer dɪˈtʊər/
A *n* 绕行; **to make** *or* **take a ～** 绕道
B *vi* «*person, vehicle*» 绕道
C *vt* esp Amer **1** (redirect) 使…绕行 ‹*traffic, car*› **2** (bypass) 绕过 ‹*obstacle, town*›

detox /ˌdiːˈtɒks/ colloq
A *vt, vi* **= detoxify**
B *n* **= detoxification**

detoxicate /ˌdiːˈtɒksɪkeɪt/ *vt, vi* **= detoxify**

detoxification /diːˌtɒksɪfɪˈkeɪʃn/, **detoxication** /diːˌtɒksɪˈkeɪʃn/ *n* [u] **1** (removing toxins) 解毒 **2** (purging the body of drugs) 戒毒; (purging the body of alcohol) 戒酒; **to be in ～** 在戒毒; **a ～ clinic** 戒毒所

detoxify /ˌdiːˈtɒksɪfaɪ/
A *vt* **1** (remove toxins from) 除去…的毒素 **2** (treat for addiction) (to drugs) 使戒毒; (to alcohol) 使戒酒
B *vi* 解毒

detract /dɪˈtrækt/ *vi* 减损; **to ～ from sth.** 减损某物; **the cracks in the vase ～ from its value** 花瓶上的裂纹会使其贬值

detractor /dɪˈtræktə(r)/ *n* 诋毁者

detrain /ˌdiːˈtreɪn/
A *vi* 下火车
B *vt* 使下火车

detriment /ˈdetrɪmənt/ *n* **1** [u] (state) 损害; **to the ～ of his health** 有害于他的健康; **without ～ to ...** 无损于… **2** [c] (cause) 有害物; **to be a ～ to sth.** 有损某物; **he is a ～ to the team** 他是害群之马

detrimental /ˌdetrɪˈmentl/ *adj* 有害的; **to be ～ to sth.** 对某事物有害; **smoking is ～ to health** 吸烟有损健康

detritus /dɪˈtraɪtəs/ *n* [u] **1** (gen) 残渣 **2** Geol 岩屑

deuce /djuːs, Amer duːs/ *n* **1** (in tennis) 局末平分; **～!** 平局! **2** (on dice) [骰子的] 两点 **3** colloq dated 到底; **what the ～!** 到底怎么回事!

deuterium /djuːˈtɪərɪəm/ *n* [u] 氘

Deutschmark /ˈdɔɪtʃmɑːk/ *n* Hist 德国马克

devaluate /ˌdiːˈvæljʊeɪt/ *vt* **= devalue A1**

devaluation /ˌdiːvæljʊˈeɪʃn/ *n* **1** Econ, Fin 贬值; **the ～ of sterling** 英镑的贬值 **2** (holding in low regard) 贬低

devalue /ˌdiːˈvæljuː/
A *vt* **1** Econ, Fin 使…贬值 ‹*currency*›; 使…下跌 ‹*shares*› **2** (gen) (consider of little worth) 贬低
B *vi* «*currency, property*» 贬值; «*shares*» 下跌; **the pound has ～d against the euro** 英镑对欧元贬值了

devastate /ˈdevəsteɪt/ *vt* **1** lit (destroy) 摧毁 ‹*town, enemy*›; 毁灭 ‹*population*›; (lay waste)

使…荒芜 ‹land› 2 fig (cause severe distress or shock to) 使极为悲痛

devastating /ˈdevəsteɪtɪŋ/ *adj* 1 (crushing, destructive) 毁灭性的 ‹*attack, storm, effect*›; **to be ~ for sb./sth.** 对某人/某事物是毁灭性的 2 (causing severe distress or shock) 令人震惊的 ‹*news, tragedy*›; **~ sorrow** 极度悲伤 3 (scathing) 尖刻的 ‹*wit, satire, comment*› 4 colloq (stunning, attractive) 令人倾倒的 ‹*beauty, charm*›

devastatingly /ˈdevəsteɪtɪŋli/ *adv* 1 (scathingly) 尖刻地 ‹*witty, amusing*› 2 colloq (stunningly) 令人倾倒地 ‹*beautiful, charming, attractive*›

devastation /ˌdevəˈsteɪʃn/ *n* [u] 1 (of land, town) 破坏; (of enemy) 毁灭; **the ~ caused by the bombing** 轰炸造成的破坏 2 (shock, trauma) 创伤

develop /dɪˈveləp/

A *vt* 1 (cultivate) 形成 ‹*idea, theme, theory, story, plan*› 2 (build up, expand) 建立 ‹*friendship*›; 发展 ‹*business enterprise*›; 习得 ‹*knowledge, understanding, intellect, skill*›; 培养 ‹*flair*›; 使…发达 ‹*body, muscle*› 3 (acquire) 养成 ‹*habit*›; 产生 ‹*feeling, sympathy*›; 出现 ‹*problem, trouble*›; 患上 ‹*illness*›; 显出 ‹*symptom, feature*›; 长出 ‹*limb, tail*›; **I'm ~ing a sore throat** 我嗓子开始疼了; **he's ~ed a liking for ouzo** 他逐渐喜欢上了茴香烈酒; **she's ~ed a fat behind** 她屁股大了; **the engine had ~ed a fault** 发动机出故障了 4 (convert, improve) 开发 ‹*land, site*›; **to ~ sth. into a business park** 把某地块开发成商业园区 5 (design and produce) 研制 ‹*device, machine, drug*›; 开发 ‹*PC game, software product*› 6 Phot 冲洗 ‹*film, negative, picture*›; 使…显现 ‹*image*›

B *vi* 1 (grow, evolve) «*animal, embryo, seed*» 发育; «*culture, civilization, theory*» 发展; «*skill, intelligence*» 提高; «*story, plot, argument*» 展开; **the caterpillar will eventually ~ into a butterfly** 毛虫最终会蜕变成蝴蝶; **the play ~s very slowly** 这出戏节奏很慢 2 (come into being) «*storm, crisis, friendship*» 形成; «*illness, symptom*» 显现 3 (progress, advance) «*battle, war, game, match*» 进展; **let's see how things ~** 让我们来看看事态如何发展吧; **he needs coaching to ~** 他需要培训以提高水平 4 (in size, extent) «*region, business, trade*» 扩展

developed /dɪˈveləpt/ *adj* 经济发达的 ‹*country, economy*›; **the ~ world** 发达国家

developer /dɪˈveləpə(r)/ *n* 1 (of property) 开发商 2 (designer) 开发者 3 Phot 显影剂 4 Psych, Sch 发育者; **a slow/late/early ~** 发育得慢/晚/早的人

developing /dɪˈveləpɪŋ/

A *adj attrib* 发展中的 ‹*country, economy, industry*›; 正在形成的 ‹*storm, crisis*›; 正在发育的 ‹*embryo*›

B *n* [u] Phot 显影

developing: ~ country *n* 发展中国家; **~ tank** *n* 显影槽

development /dɪˈveləpmənt/ *n* 1 [u] (evolution, growth) 发展; **physical/intellectual ~** 身体/智力发育; **emotional ~** 情感发展; **a stage in sb.'s ~** 某人的一个成长阶段 2 [u] (creation, invention) 开发; **research and ~** 研究和开发; **industrial ~** 工业开发 3 [c] (new buildings) 新开发区; **a housing ~** 新建住宅区 4 [u] (of idea, artistic work) 形成 5 [c] (event or innovation) 进展情况; **the latest ~s** 最新事态发展; **'new ~s in laser technology'** "激光技术新发展"

developmental /dɪˌveləpˈmentl/ *adj* 发展的 ‹*stage, process*›; 发育的 ‹*disorder*›

development: ~ area *n* 开发区; **~ bank** *n* 开发银行; **~ company** *n* 开发公司; **~ costs** *npl* 开发成本; **~ period** *n* 1 (of project) 开发期; 2 Biol 发育期; **~ potential** *n* 开发潜力

deviance /ˈdiːviəns/, **deviancy** /ˈdiːviənsi/ *n* [u] 异常

deviant /ˈdiːviənt/

A *adj* 异常的; **~ behaviour/sexual practices** 偏常行为/性行为

B *n* (person) 偏常者; (thing) 异常物

deviate /ˈdiːvieɪt/ *vi* 偏离; **to ~ from one's beliefs/principles** 背离信仰/原则; **to ~ from a path/the truth/the topic of a conversation** 偏离路线/事实/话题

deviation /ˌdiːviˈeɪʃn/ *n* 1 (from course, route) 偏离; **~ from sth.** 从某事物的偏离 2 (from norm, custom) 背离 3 (sexual practice) 性偏离 4 Stat 离差 5 (of compass needle) 偏差

deviationism /ˌdiːviˈeɪʃənɪzəm/ *n* [u] pej 路线背离

deviationist /ˌdiːviˈeɪʃənɪst/

A *n* pej 路线背离分子

B *adj* pej 路线背离分子的

device /dɪˈvaɪs/ *n* 1 (mechanical, electronic) 装置; **~ for sth./doing sth.** 用于某事/做某事的装置; **a ~ for measuring** 测量工具; **a labour-saving ~** 省力设备; **an explosive/incendiary ~** 炸弹/燃烧弹 2 esp Literat, Cin (for effect) 手法; **a rhetorical ~** 修辞手法; **one of the author's favourite ~s** 作者最喜欢的技巧之一 3 (means) 手段; **~ to do sth.** 做某事的策略; **a ~ to trick consumers** 欺骗顾客的花招; **to leave sb. to her/his own ~s** 听任某人自便 4 Herald 纹章图案

devil /ˈdevl/ ▸p. 325 *n* 1 (Satan) **the ~** *or* **D~** 撒旦; **speak** *or* **talk of the ~** 说到谁, 谁就到; **go to the ~!** dated colloq 见鬼去吧!; **to be caught between the ~ and the deep (blue) sea** 进退两难; **there'll be the ~ to pay (for this)** 那就有大麻烦了; **to have the luck of the ~** 非常走运; **the ~'s in the detail** 细微之处最易出问题; **the ~ finds work for idle hands** Prov 闲则生非; **the ~ looks after his own** Prov 恶人自有魔鬼保佑 2 (evil spirit) 魔鬼; **better the ~ you know (than the one you don't)** 熟悉的魔鬼总比陌生的好 [指宁可选择讨厌但熟悉的人或事物] 3 (used for emphasis) 究竟; **what/who/where** *etc.* **the ~ ...?** 究竟是什么/谁/在哪里等…?; **to work/run like the ~** 拼命地工作/跑; **what the ~!** 完了!; **come on, one drink won't hurt you! — oh, what the ~!** 来吧, 喝一杯酒不会伤着你的! ——唉, 那好吧!; **a ~ of a mess/noise/temper/problem** 一团糟/吵死人的噪音/极坏的脾气/棘手的问题; **the ~ you are!** 你敢!; **the ~ he has!** 鬼才信他!; **the ~ (only) knows!** 天晓得! 4 (expressing sympathy, affection, admiration) 家伙; **you poor/lucky/cheeky ~!** 你这个可怜的/幸运的/厚脸皮的家伙!; **I miss the old ~ now that he's gone** 现在他走了, 我倒挺想念这个老伙计; **you crafty ~!** 你这个滑头! 5 (mischievous person) 混蛋; (annoying thing) 讨厌的事物; **sth. is the** *or* **a ~ to do** 做某事要费九牛二虎之力; **this telephone is a ~ for going wrong** 这部电话动不动就坏; **a little ~** colloq 调皮鬼; **be a ~!** colloq 怕什么!

devilish /ˈdevəlɪʃ/ *adj* 1 (satanic) 魔鬼似的; **~ arts** 妖术 2 (heinous, evil) 恶毒的; **it is ~ of sb. to do sth.** 某人做某事很恶毒 3 (mischievous) 淘气的 ‹*trick, cunning, glee*› 4 (charming, rakish) 魔鬼般的 ‹*charm*›; 迷人的 ‹*smile, good looks*›

devilishly /ˈdevəlɪʃli/ *adv* 1 (wickedly, horribly) 骇人听闻地 ‹*cruel*› 2 (charmingly, rakishly) 迷人地

devilishness /ˈdevəlɪʃnɪs/ *n* [u] 1 (wickedness) 邪恶 2 (rakish charm) 魅惑

devilled /ˈdevɪld/ *adj* 加辣椒粉的 ‹*eggs, ham, kidneys*›

devil-may-care *adj* 逍遥自在的 ‹*attitude, lifestyle*›; 无所顾忌的 ‹*laugh*›

devilment /ˈdevlmənt/ *n* [u] Brit 恶作剧; **out of sheer ~** 纯属开玩笑地

devilry /ˈdevlri/ *n* [u] 1 (witchcraft, black magic) 妖术 2 **= devilment**

devil: ~'s advocate *n* 故意唱反调的人; **to play ~'s advocate** 故意唱反调; **~'s food cake** *n* esp Amer 浓巧克力蛋糕; **~'s own** *adj attrib* colloq 极其的; **to have the ~'s own trouble/luck** 麻烦透顶/十分幸运; **~ worship** *n* [u] 魔鬼崇拜

devious /ˈdiːviəs/ *adj* 1 (sly, underhand) 狡诈的 2 (winding) 迂回的 ‹*route, path*›

deviously /ˈdiːviəsli/ *adv* 狡诈地

deviousness /ˈdiːviəsnɪs/ *n* [u] 狡诈

devise /dɪˈvaɪz/ *vt* (create) 设计 ‹*plan, style*›; (invent) 发明 ‹*product*›; **of his/her** *etc.* **own devising** 他/她等自己的设计; **his problems are (entirely) of his own devising** 他的问题(完全)是他自己造成的

deviser /dɪˈvaɪzə(r)/ *n* (designer) 设计者; (inventor) 发明者

devoid /dɪˈvɔɪd/ *adj pred* **~ of sth.** 缺乏某物

devolution /ˌdiːvəˈluːʃn, Amer ˌdev-/ *n* [u] 1 esp Pol 权力下放; **~ of sth. (from sth.) to sth.** 某权力(从某机构)到某机构的下放; **~ of sth. on** *or* **on to sb.** 某权力向某人的移交 2 Brit Pol (decentralization) 分权制

> **devolution**
>
> 权力下放。指中央政府将部分权力下放给地方政府。20 世纪 90 年代末苏格兰和威尔士的民族政党——苏格兰民族党(Scottish National Party)和威尔士民族党(Plaid Cymru)强烈要求英国议会将权力下放。1997 年工党上台以后,苏格兰和威尔士举行全民公决(referendum),得到绝大多数人支持。1999 年,苏格兰议会(Scottish Parliament)和威尔士议会(Welsh Assembly)成立。苏格兰和威尔士的行政领导人称首席大臣(First Minister),其任命由议会提名,经英国君主批准。北爱尔兰自 1921 年起一直拥有自己的议会,但曾数次被暂停运作。北爱尔兰的行政领导人亦称首席大臣。英国中央政府保留的权力分别由苏格兰事务部(Scotland Office)、威尔士事务部(Wales Office)和北爱尔兰事务部(Northern Ireland Office)负责,负责人称事务大臣(Secretary of State)。

devolve /dɪˈvɒlv/

A *vt* 将…下放; **to ~ sth. (on** *or* **onto sb.)** 把某事移交(给某人); **ownership of the property will be ~d on to the survivor** 财产所有权将转给幸存者; **to ~ sth. (from sth.) to sth.** 把某权力(从某机构)下放给某机构

B *vi* 1 (become the responsibility of) «*powers, duties*» 被移交; **to ~ on sb.** 移交给某人 2 Brit Jur «*estate*» 转让; **to ~ on** *or* **to sb.** 转给某人

Devon /ˈdevən/ *pr n* 德文郡

Devonian /deˈvəʊniən/

A *adj* (of the period) 泥盆纪的; (of the rock system) 泥盆系的

B *n* **the ~** (period) 泥盆纪; (rock system) 泥盆系

devote /dɪˈvəʊt/ *vt* 1 (use) 把…专用于 ‹*time, energies, journalistic piece, money*›; **to ~ sth. to sth./doing sth.** 把某物用于某事/做某事; **they ~d all their thoughts to escaping** 他们光想着逃跑了; **a chapter ~d to ...** 专门讨论…的一章 2 (dedicate) 奉献; **to ~ sth. to sb.** 把某物奉献给某人; **to ~ sth. to sth./doing sth.** 把某物奉献给某事/做某事; **she ~d her life to her career/helping the poor** 她一生致力于事业/帮助穷人; **to ~ oneself to sth./doing sth.** 献身于某事/做某事

devoted /dɪˈvəʊtɪd/ *adj* 忠诚的 ‹*friend, disciple*›; 真诚的 ‹*friendship, service*›; **a ~ father** 慈爱的父亲; **~ to sb./sth.** 忠诚于某人/某事的

devotedly /dɪˈvəʊtɪdli/ *adv* 忠诚地

devotee /ˌdevəˈtiː/ *n* (of music, sport etc.) 爱好者；(of political cause) 献身者；(of person) 崇拜者；(of religious sect) 虔诚信徒

devotion /dɪˈvəʊʃn/
A *n* [u] 1 (loyalty) 忠诚；～ **to sth./sb.** 对某事/某人的忠诚；～ **to duty** 忠于职守 2 (deep affection) 挚爱；～ **to** *or* **for sb.** 对某人的挚爱 3 (act of giving) 投入；**the** ～ **of the family to the health of their friend** 全家人对朋友健康的关照 4 (piety) 虔诚
B **devotions** *npl* 宗教敬拜；**a book of** ～**s** 祈祷书；**to be at one's** ～**s** 在祈祷

devotional /dɪˈvəʊʃənl/ *adj* 祈祷的

devour /dɪˈvaʊə(r)/ *vt* 1 (consume) 吞食 ‹*food, prey*›；fig 耗尽 ‹*money, resources, petrol*› 2 (concentrate on) 如饥似渴地读 ‹*newspaper, book*›；**to** ～ **sb.'s words** 入迷地听某人讲话；**to** ～ **sb./sth. with one's eyes** 贪婪地盯着某人/某物看 3 (completely absorb or obsess) 使心神入迷；**to be** ～**ed by sth.** 心中充满某事物；**her entire being was** ～**ed by a desire for revenge** 她心中充满了复仇的欲望 4 (destroy) «*water, flames*» 吞没 ‹*village, building*›; «*plague*» 毁灭 ‹*population, civilization*›

devouring /dɪˈvaʊərɪŋ/ *adj attrib* 吞灭似的

devout /dɪˈvaʊt/ *adj* 1 (pious) 虔诚的 ‹*Christian, deed, prayer*› 2 (sincere) 真诚的；**it is my** ～ **hope** *or* **wish that ...** 我诚挚地希望…

devoutly /dɪˈvaʊtli/ *adv* 1 (piously) 虔诚地 2 (sincerely) 真诚地

devoutness /dɪˈvaʊtnɪs/ *n* [u] 虔诚

dew /djuː, Amer duː/ *n* [u] 露水

dewar /ˈdjuːə(r), Amer ˈduːər/ *n* 杜瓦瓶

dewdrop /ˈdjuːdrɒp, Amer ˈduː-/ *n* 露珠

Dewey decimal classification /ˈdjuːi/ *n* 杜威十进分类法

dew: ～**fall** *n* 结露；～**lap** *n* 垂肉；～**point** *n* 露点；～ **pond** *n* Brit [山丘上人造的] 露池

dewy /ˈdjuːi, Amer ˈduː-/ *adj* 带露水的

dewy-eyed *adj* 1 (sentimental) 易动感情的；(tearful) 泪汪汪的；**to get** *or* **go** ～ **about sth./sb.** 因某事/某人而眼泪汪汪 2 (naive) 天真轻信的；～ **about sth./sb.** 易轻信某事/某人的

dexter /ˈdekstə(r)/ *adj* [相对于佩戴者] 纹章盾形右侧的

dexterity /dekˈsterəti/ *n* [u] 1 (physical skill) 灵巧；～ **at** *or* **in sth./doing sth.** 在某事/做某事上的灵巧；～ **with leather/an axe** 制革/使用斧头的娴熟 2 (mental agility) 机敏；**mental** ～ 思维敏捷；～ **at** *or* **in sth./doing sth.** 在某事/做某事上的机敏

dexterous /ˈdekst(ə)rəs/ *adj* = **dextrous**

dexterously /ˈdekst(ə)rəsli/ *adv* = **dextrously**

dextrose /ˈdekstrəʊs, -əʊz/ *n* [u] 葡萄糖

dextrous /ˈdekstrəs/ *adj* 1 (physically skilful) 灵巧的 2 (mentally agile) 机敏的

dextrously /ˈdekstrəsli/ *adv* 1 (using physical skill) 灵巧地 2 (using mental skill) 机敏地

DFC *abbr* Brit = **Distinguished Flying Cross** 杰出飞行十字勋章

DG *abbr* = **director general**

Dhaka /ˈdækə/ *pr n* 达卡

dhow /daʊ/ *n* 阿拉伯三角帆船

DI *abbr* Brit = **detective inspector**

diabetes /ˌdaɪəˈbiːtiːz/ ▸p. 377 *n* [u] 糖尿病

diabetic /ˌdaɪəˈbetɪk/
A *adj* 糖尿病的 ‹*symptoms*›；适合糖尿病患者的 ‹*chocolate, beer*›；**a** ～ **patient** 糖尿病患者
B *n* 糖尿病患者

diabolic /ˌdaɪəˈbɒlɪk/ *adj* 魔鬼似的；**the** ～ **arts** 妖术

diabolical /ˌdaɪəˈbɒlɪkl/ *adj* 1 (wicked, cruel) 恶毒的 2 Brit colloq (terrible) 糟糕透顶的

diabolically /ˌdaɪəˈbɒlɪkli/ *adv* 1 (wickedly) 恶毒地 ‹*act, laugh*›；恶魔般地 ‹*cruel*› 2 Brit colloq (very badly) 糟糕透顶地 3 Brit colloq (excessively) 极其

diabolo /dɪˈæbələʊ, daɪ-/ *n* 1 [u] (game) 抖空竹 2 [c] (top) 空竹

diachronic /ˌdaɪəˈkrɒnɪk/ *adj* 历时的；**a** ～ **study/description of a language** 一种语言的历时研究/描述

diachronically /ˌdaɪəˈkrɒnɪkli/ *adv* 历时地

diacritic /ˌdaɪəˈkrɪtɪk/
A *n* 变音符
B *adj attrib* 变音的；**a** ～ **mark** 变音符

diacritical /ˌdaɪəˈkrɪtɪkəl/ *adj* = **diacritic B**

diadem /ˈdaɪədem/ *n* 王冠

diaeresis /daɪˈerəsɪs/ *n* (*pl* **diaereses** /daɪˈerɪsiːz/) 分音符

diagnose /ˈdaɪəgnəʊz, Amer ˌdaɪəgˈnəʊs/ *vt* 1 Med 诊断 ‹*illness, patient*›；**to** ～ **sth./sb. as sth.** 诊断某疾病/某人为某状况；**the doctor** ～**d him as being diabetic** 医生诊断他患有糖尿病；**to** ～ **that ...** 下诊断结论为… 2 (determine) 判断；**the mechanic** ～**d what was wrong with the car** 机修工查出了汽车的毛病；**to** ～ **our present economic ills as the result of poor planning** 判断我们目前的经济弊病是计划不周的结果

diagnosis /ˌdaɪəgˈnəʊsɪs/ *n* (*pl* **diagnoses** /ˌdaɪəgˈnəʊsiːz/) 1 Med (act of diagnosing) 诊断；(result of diagnosing) 诊断结果；(branch of medicine) 诊断法；～ **of sth.** 对某疾病的诊断；～ **of sth./sb. (as sth.)** 某疾病/某人（为某状况）的诊断；**to make a** ～ (act) 做诊断；(result) 下诊断结论；**a** ～ **that ...** …的诊断 2 (of a situation) 判断

diagnostic /ˌdaɪəgˈnɒstɪk/
A *adj* 诊断的
B *n* 1 Med 症状 2 Comput 诊断程序
C **diagnostics** *npl* + *v sing* 1 Med 诊断法 2 Comput 诊断

diagnostically /ˌdaɪəgˈnɒstɪkli/ *adv* 在诊断方面

diagnostician /ˌdaɪəgnɒˈstɪʃn/ *n* 诊断医师

diagonal /daɪˈægənl/
A *adj* (slanting) 斜的 ‹*lines, pattern*›；(connecting opposite corners) 对角的 ‹*line, plane*›；～ **to sth.** 与某物呈斜角的
B *n* 1 (row, stripe) 斜行 2 (line across rectangle, cube) 对角线 3 (in chess) 斜线

diagonally /daɪˈægənəli/ *adv* (at an angle) 斜向地；(from corner to corner) 沿对角线地

diagram /ˈdaɪəgræm/ *n* 1 (drawing) 示意图 2 (chart) 图表

diagrammatic /ˌdaɪəgrəˈmætɪk/ *adj* 图表的

diagrammatically /ˌdaɪəgrəˈmætɪkli/ *adv* 用图表

dial /ˈdaɪəl/
A *n* 1 (on telephone) 拨号盘 2 (of gauge, meter) 刻度盘 3 (of TV, radio) 调节器；(of other equipment) 控制器 4 (face of watch) 表盘；(clock face) 钟盘 5 Brit dated colloq (face) 脸
B *vt* (*pres p etc.* **-ll-** Brit, **-l-** Amer) 拨电话给 ‹*person, country*›；拨 ‹*number*›；**to** ～ **222 for sth./sb.** 做某事/找某人请拨222；**to** ～ **the wrong number** 拨错号
C *vi* (*pres p etc.* **-ll-** Brit, **-l-** Amer) 拨号；**you can** ～ **direct** 你可以直拨

dialect /ˈdaɪəlekt/ *n* 方言；**to speak** ～ 说方言；**a** ～ **of German** 德语方言

dialectal /ˌdaɪəˈlektl/ *adj* 方言的

dialect: ～ **atlas** *n* 方言地图；～ **geography** *n* [u] 方言地理学

dialectic /ˌdaɪəˈlektɪk/
A *n* 1 [u] (method of enquiry) 辩证法 2 [c] (argument, disputation) 逻辑论证 3 = **dialectics**
B *adj* 1 辩证的 ‹*method, philosopher*›；辩论的 ‹*skill*› 2 = **dialectal**

dialectical /ˌdaɪəˈlektɪkl/ *adj* 辩证的

dialectically /ˌdaɪəˈlektɪkli/ *adv* 辩证地

dialectical: ～ **materialism** *n* [u] 辩证唯物主义；～ **materialist** *n* 辩证唯物主义者

dialectics /ˌdaɪəˈlektɪks/ *npl* + *v sing* 辩证法

dialectologist /ˌdaɪəlekˈtɒlədʒɪst/ **p. 409** *n* 方言学家

dialectology /ˌdaɪəlekˈtɒlədʒi/ *n* [u] 方言学

dial-in *adj, n* = **dial-up**

dialling: ～ **code** *n* Brit 电话区号；**the** ～ **code for ...** …的电话区号；～ **tone** *n* Brit 拨号音

dialogue /ˈdaɪəlɒg, Amer -lɔːg/ *n* [c and u] 对话；**a** ～ **between A and B** A和B之间的对话；**to have a** ～ **(with sb.)** （与某人）进行对话；**the film contains much** ～ 这部电影对白很多

dialogue box *n* 对话框

dial-out
A *adj* 拨号上网的
B *n* 拨号上网

dial tone *n* Amer = **dialling tone**

dial-up
A *adj* 拨号上网的 ‹*service, user*›；～ **connection** 拨号连接
B *n* 拨号上网；**to be on** ～ 拨号上网

dialysis /daɪˈæləsɪs/ *n* (*pl* **dialyses** /ˌdaɪˈæləsiːz/) 透析

dialysis machine *n* 透析机

diamanté /ˌdaɪəˈmænti, ˌdɪəˈmɒnteɪ/ *adj* 珠光的 ‹*earrings*›；有闪光缀饰的 ‹*dress, fabric*›

diameter /daɪˈæmɪtə(r)/ *n* 直径；**the circle is 2 m in** ～ 这个圆的直径是2米

diametric /ˌdaɪəˈmetrɪk/, **diametrical** /ˌdaɪəˈmetrɪkl/ *adj* 截然相反的

diametrically /ˌdaɪəˈmetrɪkli/ *adv* 1 (completely) 完全地；(directly) 截然；**to be** ～ **opposed to ...** 与…完全相反 2 (at opposite ends) 在直径上 ‹*opposite*›；**at the** ～ **opposed point on the circle's circumference** 在圆周直径正对的一端

diamond /ˈdaɪəmənd/ *n* 1 (stone) 钻石 2 (shape) 菱形 3 (in cards) 方块；**the ace/five/king of** ～**s** 方块A/五/老K；**to play a** ～ 出一张方块 4 (in baseball) (entire field) 棒球场；(area bounded by the four bases) 内场

diamond: ～**back** *n* ～**back (rattlesnake)** 菱背响尾蛇；～ **cutter** *n* ▸p. 409 钻石切割工；～ **cutting** *n* [u] (action) 钻石切割；(craft) 钻石切割术；～ **jubilee** *n* 钻石大庆 [尤指国王或女王在位60周年纪念日]；～ **merchant** ▸p. 409 *n* 钻石商；～**-shaped** *adj* 菱形的；～ **wedding** *n* 钻石婚 [结婚60周年纪念]；～ **wedding anniversary** 钻石婚纪念日

diaper /ˈdaɪəpə(r), Amer ˈdaɪpər/ *n* 1 Amer (nappy) 尿布 2 Tex 菱形花纹织物

diaphanous /daɪˈæfənəs/ *adj* 轻薄透明的 ‹*fabric, veil, nightdress*›

diaphragm /ˈdaɪəfræm/ *n* 1 Anat 隔膜 2 (in acoustic system) 振动膜 3 Phot 光圈 4 (contraceptive) 子宫帽

diarist /ˈdaɪərɪst/ *n* 1 (author) 日记作者 2 (journalist) 专栏作者

diarrhea /ˌdaɪəˈrɪə/ *n* [u] Amer = **diarrhoea**

diarrheal /ˌdaɪəˈrɪəl/ *adj* Amer = **diarrhoeal**

diarrhoea /ˌdaɪəˈrɪə/ *n* [u] Brit 1 (condition, symptom) 腹泻；**to have** ～ 患腹泻；**chronic** ～ 慢性腹泻 2 (faeces) 水样粪便

diarrhoeal /ˌdaɪəˈrɪəl/ *adj* Brit 腹泻的

diary /ˈdaɪəri/ *n* 1 (for appointments) 记事簿；**to put sth. in one's** ～ 把某事记在记事簿里；**my** ～ **is full** 我的日程排满了；～ **pages** 工作日程页 2 (journal) 日记；**to keep a** ～ 记日记 3 (in newspaper) 专栏

diaspora /daɪˈæspərə/ *n* 1 [u] **the** ～ Hist (exile) [犹太人的] 大流散 2 **the** ～ *pl* (dispersed

Jews) 海外犹太人 [3] + *v sing or pl* (exiled people) 背井离乡的人们

diastolic /ˌdaɪəˈstɒlɪk/ *adj* 舒张的; **～ blood pressure** 舒张压

diatom /ˈdaɪətəm, Amer -tɒm/ *n* 硅藻

diatonic /ˌdaɪəˈtɒnɪk/ *adj* 用自然音阶的

diatribe /ˈdaɪətraɪb/ *n* 抨击; **a ～ against sth./sb.** 对某事物/某人的抨击

dibber /ˈdɪbə(r)/ *n* Brit **= dibble**

dibble /ˈdɪbl/ *n* 木铲

dibs /dɪbz/ *npl* Amer colloq, esp child lang 权利要求; **to have ～ on sth.** 有某物的所有权; **to have first ～ on sth.** 有某物的优先所有权

dice /daɪs/

[A] *n* (*pl* **dice**) (object) 骰子; (game) 掷骰游戏; **to throw** *or* **roll the ～** 掷骰子; **to play ～** 玩掷骰子游戏; **no ～!** colloq (refusal) 没门! ; (no luck) 没用!

[B] *vi* 掷骰子; **to ～ for sth.** 掷骰子赌某事物; **to ～ with death** 冒生命危险

[C] *vt* 将…切成丁

dicey /ˈdaɪsi/ *adj* colloq [1] (risky) 冒险的 [2] (uncertain) 不确定的; (unreliable) 不可靠的

dichotomy /daɪˈkɒtəmi/ *n* 一分为二; **a ～ between A and B** A和B之间的对立

dick /dɪk/ *n* [1] taboo sl (penis) 屌 offensive [2] Amer colloq dated (detective) 探子

dickens /ˈdɪkɪnz/ *n* colloq dated **where/who/what the ～ ...?** …到底在哪儿/是谁/是什么? ; **to have the ～ of a time doing sth.** 做某事很费劲

Dickensian /dɪˈkenzɪən/ *adj* [1] (of or concerning Charles Dickens) 狄更斯作品的 ‹*character, style*›; 狄更斯的 ‹*philosophy*› [2] (resembling Dickens's novels) 具有狄更斯小说特点的 ‹*novel*›; 类似狄更斯笔下的 ‹*character, slums, bureaucracy*›

dicker /ˈdɪkə(r)/ *vi* colloq esp Amer 讨价还价; **to ～ with sb. over** *or* **about sth.** 与某人就某价格争论不休; **to ～ for sth.** 为某物讨价还价

dickey /ˈdɪki/ *n* **= dicky**[1]

dickhead /ˈdɪkhed/ *n* Brit taboo sl 笨蛋 offensive

dicky[1] /ˈdɪki/ *n* 假衬衫

dicky[2] *adj* Brit colloq 虚弱的 ‹*health, heart*›; 不稳定的 ‹*situation, position*›

dicky: ～ bird *n* [1] child lang (bird) 小鸟; [2] Brit colloq (word) 话语; **I never heard a ～ bird** 我什么都没听到; **～ bow** *n* esp Brit colloq 蝶形领结

dicta /ˈdɪktə/ *pl* ▸ **dictum**

Dictaphone® /ˈdɪktəfəʊn/ *n* 口述录音机

dictate

[A] /dɪkˈteɪt, Amer ˈdɪkteɪt/ *vt* [1] (read out) 口述; **to ～ sth. (to sb.)** (向某人) 口授某事; **to ～ a letter into a dictating machine** 往口述记录机里口述一封信 [2] (prescribe) 强加 ‹*conditions*›; 支配 ‹*actions, attitude*›; **to ～ terms (to sb.)** (向某人) 发号施令; **to ～ that ...** 强行规定…; **lifestyle is ～d by income** 生活方式是由收入决定的

[B] /dɪkˈteɪt, Amer ˈdɪkteɪt/ *vi* [1] (read aloud) 口述; **to ～ to sb.** 向某人口述 [2] (boss sb. around) 发号施令; **to ～ to sb.** 向某人发号施令

[C] /ˈdɪkteɪt/ *n* [1] (decree) 命令 [2] **dictates** *pl* (promptings, precepts) 支配; **the ～s of sth.** 某物的支配; **to follow the ～s of one's conscience/passion** 凭良心办事/感情用事

dictating machine *n* 口述记录机

dictation /dɪkˈteɪʃn/ *n* [1] [c and u] (reading aloud) 口述; **to take ～** 记录口授 [2] [c and u] Sch 听写 [3] [u] (stipulation) 命令; **～ of sth. by sb./sth.** 某人/某物对某物的支配

dictation speed *n* 听写速度

dictator /dɪkˈteɪtə(r), Amer ˈdɪkteɪtər/ *n* [1] Pol 独裁者; **a military ～** 军事独裁者 [2] fig pej (autocratic person) 专横的人 [3] (arbiter) 权威; **a ～ of correct social behaviour** 倡导正确社会行为的权威

dictatorial /ˌdɪktəˈtɔːrɪəl/ *adj* [1] Pol 独裁的 ‹*rule, regime*› [2] pej (overbearing) 专横的 ‹*style*›

dictatorially /ˌdɪktəˈtɔːrɪəli/ *adv* [1] Pol 独裁地 [2] pej (overbearingly) 专横地

dictatorship /dɪkˈteɪtəʃɪp, Amer ˈdɪkt-/ *n* [1] [u] (form of government) 专政 [2] [c] (country) 独裁国家; (regime, government) 独裁政府

diction /ˈdɪkʃn/ *n* [u] [1] (articulation) 发音; **clear ～** 清晰的吐字 [2] (choice of words) 措词

dictionary /ˈdɪkʃənri, Amer -neri/ *n* 词典; **a chemistry ～, a ～ of chemistry** 化学词典

dictionary definition *n* 权威释义

dictum /ˈdɪktəm/ *n* (*pl* **～s** *or* **dicta**) [1] (saying) 格言 [2] (formal statement) 宣言; **the ～ that ...** …的正式声明; **a ～ on sth.** 对某事的权威意见

did /dɪd/ *pt* ▸ **do**[1] **A, B, C**

didactic /daɪˈdæktɪk, dɪ-/ *adj* [1] (educational, informative) 教导的 ‹*method, function*›; 道德说教的 ‹*literature, art*› [2] usu pej (excessively instructive) 好教训人的 ‹*person*›; 说教的 ‹*manner*›; **to be ～ in tone** 用说教的语气

didactically /daɪˈdæktɪkli, dɪ-/ *adv* [1] (for the purpose of teaching) 教导地 [2] usu pej (in an excessively instructive way) 说教性地

diddle /ˈdɪdl/ *vt* colloq [1] Brit (swindle) 哄骗 ‹*person*›; 骗取 ‹*money*›; **to ～ sb. out of sth.** 诈骗某人某物; **to ～ sb. into doing sth.** 哄骗某人做某事 [2] Amer (dawdle) 闲混

didgeridoo /ˌdɪdʒəriˈduː/ ▸ **p. 395** *n* 迪吉里杜管

didn't /ˈdɪdnt/ *abbr* colloq **= did not** ▸ **do**[1] **A, C**

die[1] /daɪ/ (*pres p* **dying,** *pt, pp* **died**)

[A] *vi* [1] (stop living, be killed) 死; fig (of extreme emotion) …得要死; **to ～ in one's sleep** 寿终正寝; **to ～ happy/poor** 在幸福/贫困中死去; **to ～ young** 夭亡; **to ～ a hero/martyr** 英勇/壮烈牺牲; **to ～ of cancer/a stroke** 死于癌症/中风; **to ～ of hunger/thirst/grief** 饿死/渴死/悲痛而死; **to ～ doing sth.** 做某事时死去; **we were going to rescue them or ～ in the attempt** 我们将不惜一切代价营救他们; **I'd sooner** *or* **rather ～ than ...** 我宁死也不愿…; **to ～ in one's bed** (of old age) 寿终正寝; (of illness) 病死; **nobody ever ～d of hard work** hum 工作累不死人; **never say ～!** 千万别放弃! ; **to ～ of boredom/embarrassment/shock/fright/shame** 无聊/窘迫/惊吓/恐惧/羞愧得要死; **I nearly ～d laughing when I heard the story** 我听到这故事时, 简直要笑死了; **a dress to ～ for** 漂亮得要命的连衣裙 [2] (wither) «*plant, tree, vegetable*» 枯死; «*flower*» 凋谢 [3] colloq (long) **to be dying for sth./to do sth.** 渴望某事物/做某事 [4] (go out) «*light, flame, candle*» 熄灭 [5] (fade) «*tradition, language*» 消亡; **the secret ～d with him** 这个秘密随着他一起入土了; **the words ～d on her lips** 她欲言又止; **to ～ hard** 很难消除; **old habits ～ hard** 积习难改 [6] hum (stop functioning) «*machine*» 停转; «*vehicle, engine*» 熄火; «*computer*» 死机; **the television has just ～d** 电视机刚刚坏了

[B] *vt* 以…的方式死去; **to ～ a violent/painful/natural death** 横死/痛苦地死去/寿终正寝; **he ～d a lingering death** 他拖了很久才死去; **he ～d a hero's death** 他死得英勇

Phrasal verbs

- **die away** *vi* «*sound, breeze, shock wave*» 渐渐消失
- **die back** *vi* «*plant, leaf, stem*» 回枯
- **die down** *vi* [1] (in intensity, severity) «*storm, pain, opposition, support*» 逐渐减弱; «*infection, swelling, enthusiasm*» 渐渐消退; «*rumour, excitement, fuss, campaign, reactions*» 逐渐平息 [2] (in volume) «*noise, sounds, cheering*» 逐渐减低 [3] (burn less strongly) «*flames*» 慢慢减弱
- **die off** *vi* [1] (die one by one) 相继死去 [2] (gradually wither away) «*plants*» 慢慢枯死
- **die out** *vi* [1] (become extinct) «*species, family*» 灭绝; **to ～ out with sb.** 随某人的死去而灭绝 [2] (fall out of use) «*ritual, practice*» 绝迹; «*tradition, language*» 消亡; «*skill*» 失传 [3] (ease off) «*rain, snow, showers*» 逐渐停止

die[2] *n* [1] (*pl* **dice**) (numbered cube) 骰子; **the ～ is cast (for better or worse)** (不论好坏,) 木已成舟 [2] (*pl* **～s**) Tech (for shaping metal) 模具; (for cutting metal) 冲模; (for stamping metal) 压模; **(as) straight as a ～** lit (absolutely straight) 笔直; fig (very honest) 非常诚实 [3] (*pl* **～s**) Tech (for screw thread) 板牙

die: ～-back *n* [u] 回枯; **～-cast** *adj* 压铸的; **～-casting** *n* [u] 压铸

diehard /ˈdaɪhɑːd/

[A] *n* 顽固分子

[B] *adj attrib* 顽固的; **a ～ fan** 死心塌地的狂热仰慕者

dieresis /daɪˈerəsɪs/ *n* (*pl* **diereses** /daɪˈerɪsiːz/) Amer **= diaeresis**

diesel /ˈdiːzl/ *n* [1] [u] (fuel) 柴油 [2] [c] (engine) 柴油机 [3] [c] (car) **～ (car)** 柴油车

diesel: ～-electric *adj* 内燃电力传动的; **～ engine** *n* 柴油机; **～ fuel, ～ oil** *ns* [u] 柴油; **～ train** *n* 内燃机车

die: ～ stamping *n* [u] 压凹凸印刷; **～stock** *n* 板牙扳手

diet[1] /ˈdaɪət/

[A] *n* [1] (food eaten) 日常饮食; **a ～ of sth.** 包括某物的饮食; **a healthy ～ of vegetables and whole grains** 蔬菜和全谷物的健康饮食; **the national ～** 全民饮食 [2] (limiting food) 节食; **to be on a special ～** 控制饮食; **I'm on a ～** 我在节食; **some control their blood sugar by ～ alone** 一些人单纯通过节制饮食控制血糖; **to stick to a ～** 坚持节食 [3] fig usu pej 大量单一的东西; **a ～ of sth.** 大量单一的某物; **the usual ～ of soap operas and situation comedies** 通常大量充斥的肥皂剧和情景喜剧

[B] *vi* 节食; **no cream, thank you. I'm ～ing** 不要奶油, 谢谢。我在节食; **to ～ (in order) to lose weight** 通过节食减轻体重

diet[2] *n* Pol [日本等国家的] 议会

dietary /ˈdaɪətri, Amer -teri/ *adj* [1] (relating to diet) 日常饮食的 [2] (by diet) 节食的

dietary: ～ fibre *n* [u] Amer 膳食纤维; **～ supplement** *n* 营养补充剂

dietetic /ˌdaɪəˈtetɪk/ *adj* 饮食营养的; **experienced ～ advice** 饮食经验之谈

dietetics /ˌdaɪəˈtetɪks/ *npl* + *v sing* 饮食学

dietician, dietitian /ˌdaɪəˈtɪʃn/ ▸ **p. 409** *n* 营养学家

differ /ˈdɪfə(r)/ *vi* [1] (be different) 有区别; **to ～ from sth.** 不同于某事物; **to ～ in sth.** 在某方面不同; **the two countries ～ed in the vote on climate change** 这两个国家在有关气候变化方面的表决有差别 [2] (disagree) 持不同看法; **to ～ with sb. (about** *or* **on sth.)** (在某事上) 不同意某人的看法; **I beg to ～** 我不敢苟同; **we must agree to ～** 我们保留不同意见吧

difference /ˈdɪfrəns/ *n* [1] [c and u] (dissimilarity) 差别; **age ～** 年龄差别; **what is the ～ between the two computers?** 这两台电脑有什么不同? ; **what's the ～?** 那有什么关系? ; **to tell the ～ between ... (and ...)** 区分… (和…) ; **I can't tell** *or* **see the ～** 我看不出有什么不同; **to make a/no ～ to sth.** 对某事有/没关系; **will it make any ～ (to you) if we come a little later?** 我们晚一点到 (对你) 有没有关系? ; **it makes all the** *or* **a world of ～** 这有天壤之别; **what ～ does it make if ...?** 如果…又有什么关系? ; **as near as makes no ～** 基本上一样; **with a ～** 与众不同; **this is an insurance scheme with a ～** 这个保险计划与众不同; **a ～ of approach** 方法上的不同; **the ～ in the personalities of the twins is remarkable** 这对双胞胎性格明显不一样 [2] [c and u]

(variation in level, cost, age, size) 差额; **to pay the ~** 支付差价; **to split the ~** 折中; **the ~ between ...** …之间的差额; **the ~ between the return on capital in the two markets** 两市场之间的资本回报差; **a ~ in sth.** 某事物上的差别; **the ~ in the growth rates** 增长率之差 **3** [c] (disagreement) 分歧; **a ~ of opinion** 观点分歧; **to settle one's ~s** 消除隔阂

different /ˈdɪfrənt/ *adj* **1** (dissimilar) 不同的; **~ from** *or* Brit **to** *or* Amer **than ...** 与…不同的; **you're no ~ from them** 你和他们没什么两样; **but I know ~** 但我知道的不是这样 **2** (other) 另外的; **to be/feel (like) a ~ person** (像是) 成为/感觉 (像) 是另外一个人; **I feel a ~ woman since I took up yoga** 自从练了瑜伽后我感觉整个人都变了 **3** (distinct) 各种的; **many ~ countries** 许多不同的国家 **4** (unusual) 不同寻常的; **he always has to be ~** 他非得与众不同

differential /ˌdɪfəˈrenʃl/

A *adj* **1** (varying) 差别的; **~ tariffs** 差别关税 **2** Math 微分的

B *n* **1** Brit (in pay) 级差; **pay** *or* **wage ~s** 工资级差 **2** Math 微分 **3** Aut 差动齿轮

differential: ~ calculus *n* 微分学; **~ equation** *n* 微分方程; **~ gear** *n* 差动齿轮; **~ pricing** *n* [u] 差别定价

differentiate /ˌdɪfəˈrenʃɪeɪt/

A *vt* **1** (tell the difference between) 区分; (make the difference between) 使不同; **~ sth. from sth.** 把某物和某物区分开; **the officers are ~d from the men by their uniform** 军官和士兵通过军服进行区别 **2** Math 求…的微分 ‹*quantity, expression*›

B *vi* **1** (tell the difference) 区分; **to ~ between A and B** 区分 A 和 B **2** (show the difference) 表明差别; **to ~ between A and B** 表明 A 和 B 之间的差别 **3** (discriminate) 区别对待; **to ~ between A and B** 区别对待 A 和 B

differentiation /ˌdɪfərenʃɪˈeɪʃn/ *n* **1** [u and c] (distinction, distinguishing) 区分; **product ~** 产品鉴别; **~ of/between ...** …的/之间的区分; **a clear ~ of roles/responsibilities** 职能/职责的明确划分; **~ between right and wrong** 是非的区分 **2** [u] Math 微分法

differently /ˈdɪfrəntli/ *adv* 不同地; **~ from** *or* Brit **to** *or* Amer **than ...** 与…不同地

difficult /ˈdɪfɪkəlt/ *adj* **1** (not easy) 困难的; **to be ~ to do sth.** 做某事难; **to be ~ for sb.** 对某人来说难; **to find it ~ to do sth.** 感到做某事难; **to prove ~** 证明是困难的; **what is so ~ about it?** 这事有什么难处? ; **the ~ thing is to ...** 困难的是…; **the job turned out to be too ~ for him** 结果证明这工作对他来说太难了 **2** (complex, inaccessible) 难懂的 ‹*work, concept*›; **~ authors like Dickens** 像狄更斯这样作品深奥的作家 **3** (awkward) 难取悦的 ‹*person, personality*›; **to be ~ about doing sth.** 在做某事上找茬; **it's a ~ area** 这是个棘手的领域 **4** (bad, tough) 艰难的 ‹*period, life, condition*›; **to be ~ for sb.** 对某人来说很艰难; **to make life ~ for sb.** 使某人的日子不好过; **to be ~ to live with** 难以忍受; **to be in a ~ position** 处境艰难

difficulty /ˈdɪfɪkəlti/ *n* **1** [u] (of task, activity) 困难; **the ~ of doing sth.** 做某事的难处; **to have ~ (in) doing sth.** 做某事有困难; **to have ~ with sth.** 在某事上有问题; **to have ~ with one's eyesight** 视力有问题; **to be under some ~** 在困难的条件下 **2** [u] (complexity) 难度; **the level of ~ of sth.** 某事的难办程度 **3** [u and c] (trouble) 麻烦; (obstacle) 障碍; **in ~** 处于麻烦中; **to create** *or* **make difficulties** 制造麻烦; **to meet difficulties** 遇到麻烦; **to run into difficulties** 碰到难题; **to have difficulties with sth.** 在某事上碰到麻烦

diffidence /ˈdɪfɪdəns/ *n* [u] **1** (lack of self-confidence) 缺乏自信; (shyness) 羞怯 **2** (modesty) 谦虚; **sb.'s ~ about sth.** 某人对某事的谦虚

diffident /ˈdɪfɪdənt/ *adj* **1** (lacking confidence) 缺乏自信的; (shy) 羞怯的 **2** (modest) 谦虚的; **to be ~ about sth.** 对某事谦虚

diffidently /ˈdɪfɪdəntli/ *adv* (without self-confidence) 缺乏自信地; (shyly, awkwardly) 羞怯地

diffract /dɪˈfrækt/ *vt* 使衍射

diffraction /dɪˈfrækʃn/ *n* [u] 衍射

diffraction grating *n* 衍射光栅

diffuse

A /dɪˈfjuːz/ *vt* **1** (spread out) 使…扩散 ‹*light, heat, liquid, gas*›; **to ~ sth. in sth.** 使某物在某物中扩散 **2** (disseminate) 传播 ‹*information*›; 散布 ‹*rumour*›; 普及 ‹*awareness*›; **to ~ sth. through sth.** 在某处传播某事

B /dɪˈfjuːz/ *vi* **1** 扩散; **to ~ in/through sth.** 在某处扩散 **2** (be disseminated) 传播; **to ~ through sth.** 通过某处传播

C /dɪˈfjuːs/ *adj* **1** (spread out) 弥散的 ‹*glow, warmth*› **2** (not concentrated) 分散的 ‹*effort, help*›; 松散的 ‹*organization, movement*› **3** (vague) 模糊的 ‹*sense, awareness*› **4** (lacking clarity) 冗赘的 ‹*argument, style*›; 行文芜蔓的 ‹*author*›

diffuseness /dɪˈfjuːsnɪs/ *n* [u] **1** (of light) 漫射 **2** (of organization) 松散; (of help, effort) 过度分散 **3** (of argument) 冗赘

diffuser /dɪˈfjuːzə(r)/ *n* **1** Phot 漫射屏 **2** (for hairdryer) 扩散装置

diffusion /dɪˈfjuːʒn/ *n* [u] **1** (of light, heat, liquid, gas) 扩散 **2** (of idea, feeling) 传播

dig /dɪɡ/

A *vt* (*pt, pp* **dug**) **1** (excavate) 掘 ‹*tunnel, ditch, trench, grave*›; (extract) 挖出 ‹*coal, peat, root vegetables*›; **to ~ oneself** *or* **one's way out (of sth.)** (从某物中) 挖出一条路来 **2** Hort (turn over) 翻松 ‹*soil, flower bed, vegetable patch, allotment*› **3** (embed) 用…刺 ‹*knife, needle*›; 用…戳 ‹*claws, fingernails*›; **to ~ sth. into sb./sth.** 用某物刺入某人体内/某物; **to ~ sb. in the ribs/back** 用手指戳某人的肋部/背部 **4** Amer colloq dated (like) 喜爱 **5** Amer colloq dated (look at) 瞧; **~ that, man!** 瞧那个, 老兄!

B *vi* (*pt, pp* **dug**) **1** (excavate) 挖掘; **to ~ into sth.** 掘入某物; **to ~ for sth.** 采掘 ‹*ore, coal, gold*›; **to ~ deep into one's savings/reserves** fig 动用大部分储蓄/储备 **2** Hort (turn over earth) 松土 **3** (search) 搜寻; **to ~ in** *or* **into one's handbag/pockets (for sth.)** 伸进手提包/口袋里摸寻 (某物)

C *n* **1** (poke, prod) 戳; **to give sb. a ~ in the ribs** 戳某人的肋部一下 **2** colloq (jibe) 挖苦; **to make a ~ at sb.** 挖苦某人; **a ~ about sth.** 对某事物的嘲讽 **3** Hort 翻地; **to give the ground/vegetable patch** *etc.* **a ~** 翻松土地/菜园等 **4** Archaeol 考古发掘; **to go on/take part in a ~** 进行/参加考古发掘

Phrasal verbs

- **dig in**

A *vi* **1** Mil 挖掩体; **we dug in (and prepared) for the battle** 我们挖掩体准备战斗 **2** colloq (eat heartily) 尽情地吃

B *vt* [**~ in sth., ~ sth. in**] **1** Hort (mix in) 翻土掺进 ‹*manure, fertilizer, sand*› **2** (embed) 用…刺 ‹*knife, spurs*›; 用…戳 ‹*claws, fingernails*›; 用…咬 ‹*teeth*›

- **dig into** *vt* **1** (probe) 探查 ‹*secret, origins, files*›; **to ~ into the past** 探究过去的情况 **2** colloq (eat heartily) 尽情地吃 **3** (press painfully) «*belt*» 勒进 ‹*flesh*›; «*nail*» 戳进 ‹*palm*›
- **dig out** *vt* [**~ out sth., ~ sth. out**] **1** (remove) 挖出; **to ~ a splinter out of one's finger** 把刺从手指中挑出来 **2** (ascertain) 查明 ‹*facts, the truth*›; 查到 ‹*detail, information, figure*› **3** colloq (bring out) 翻出 ‹*object*›
- **dig over** *vt* [**~ sth. over**] 翻挖 ‹*soil, flower bed, vegetable patch*›
- **dig up** *vt* [**~ sth. up, ~ up sth.**] **1** (remove from ground) 挖出 ‹*plant, roots, object, remains*› **2** (turn over) 翻挖 ‹*soil, flower bed, vegetable patch*› **3** fig (discover, uncover) 发现 ‹*information, fact*›; 查出 ‹*scandal*›

digest

A /daɪˈdʒest, dɪ-/ *vt* **1** (break down) 消化 ‹*food*›; **to be easy/difficult to ~** 容易/难消化 **2** fig (understand, assimilate) 理解 ‹*facts, information, implications*›

B /daɪˈdʒest, dɪ-/ *vi* «*food, meal*» 被消化

C /ˈdaɪdʒest/ *n* **1** (periodical) 文摘 **2** (summary of news, report) 摘要; **in ~ form** 以概要形式

digestible /dɪˈdʒestəbl/ *adj* **1** (able to be broken down) 可消化的 ‹*food*› **2** fig (easily understood, assimilated) 易理解的 ‹*book, form*›

digestion /daɪˈdʒestʃn, dɪ-/ *n* **1** [u] (of food) 消化 **2** [c] Anat (digestive system) 消化能力; **to have a good/poor ~** 消化功能好/不好 **3** [u] fig (of information, facts) 领悟

digestive /dɪˈdʒestɪv, daɪ-/

A *adj* **1** (relating to digestion) 消化的 ‹*process*›; (concerning the digestive system) 消化系统的; **the ~ organs** 消化器官; **~ disorders/problems** 消化紊乱/问题 **2** (aiding digestion) 助消化的

B *n* Brit **~ (biscuit)** 消化饼干

digestive: ~ juices *npl* 消化液; **~ system** *n* 消化系统; **~ tract** *n* 消化道

digger /ˈdɪɡə(r)/ *n* **1** (excavator) 挖掘机 **2** (worker) 挖掘工 **3** (miner) 矿工; (of gold) 掘金者 **4** (*also* **Digger**) colloq (Australian) 澳大利亚人

digging /ˈdɪɡɪŋ/

A *n* [u] **1** (in garden) 翻土; **to do some ~** 翻土 **2** (mining) 挖矿; (hollowing out) 挖掘; **~ for coal/gold** 挖煤/采金 **3** (searching) 挖寻; **~ for treasure** 挖宝

B **diggings** *npl* (material) 采掘物; (site) 矿区

digit /ˈdɪdʒɪt/ *n* **1** (number) [0到9中的任何一个] 数字; **a two-~ number** 两位数 **2** Anat (finger) 手指; (thumb) 拇指; (toe) 脚趾

digital /ˈdɪdʒɪtl/ *adj* **1** esp Comput 数字的 ‹*display*›; 数码的 ‹*recording*›; **a ~ watch** 数字式手表 **2** Anat (of fingers) 手指的; (of toes) 脚趾的

digital: ~ access lock *n* 数码锁; **~ audio tape** *n* 数码音频磁带; **~ camera** *n* 数码相机; **~ certificate** *n* 数字证书; **~ computer** *n* 数字计算机; **~ divide** *n* 数字鸿沟 [指能上网的人与没条件上网的人之间的差距]; **~ economy** *n* 数字经济; **~ fingerprinting** *n* [u] **1** (of fingerprints) 数字化指纹提取; **2** (of data) 数字指纹技术; **~ highway** *n* 数字公路; **~ image** *n* 数字图像

digitalis /ˌdɪdʒɪˈteɪlɪs/ *n* [u] **1** Bot 洋地黄 **2** Pharm 洋地黄制剂

digitalization /ˌdɪdʒɪtəlaɪˈzeɪʃn/ *n* [u] **= digitization**

digitalize /ˈdɪdʒɪtəlaɪz/ *vt* **= digitize**

digital lock *n* 数码锁

digitally /ˈdɪdʒɪtəli/ *adv* 以数字方式 ‹*broadcast, record*›; 以数码方式 ‹*scan, photograph*›

digital: ~ photo frame *n* 数字相框; **~ signature** *n* 数字签名; **~ television** *n* [u and c] 数字电视; **~ terrestrial television** *n* [u] 数字地面电视

digitization /ˌdɪdʒɪtaɪˈzeɪʃn/ *n* [u] 数字化

digitize /ˈdɪdʒɪtaɪz/ *vt* 使数字化; **a ~d map** 数字化地图

digitizer /ˈdɪdʒɪtaɪzə(r)/ *n* 数字转换器

dignified /ˈdɪɡnɪfaɪd/ *adj* **1** (worthy of respect) 尊贵的 ‹*person, position*› **2** (stately) 庄重的 ‹*bearing, bow*› **3** (self-respecting) 有尊严的 ‹*silence, behaviour*›; **it wasn't very ~ of me to scream at them like that** 我那么对他们大喊大叫有失体面

dignify /ˈdɪɡnɪfaɪ/ *vt* **1** (give dignity to) 使显贵; **the ceremony was dignified by the presence of the ambassador** 大使的光临为庆祝活动增辉 **2** (describe impressively) 抬高…的

d

身价; **to ~ sth. with the name of ...** 用…的名字美化某事物

dignitary /ˈdɪɡnɪtəri/ *n* 要人

dignity /ˈdɪɡnəti/ *n* [u] **1** (solemnity, importance) 尊贵 **2** (worthiness) 高尚; **the ~ of labour** 劳动的高尚 **3** (calmness, composure) 庄重; **the quiet ~ of the victims** 受害者表现出的无声的庄重 **4** (self-respect) 自尊; **to be beneath sb.'s ~** 有失某人的尊严; **to stand on one's ~** 要求受到应有的礼遇

digraph /ˈdaɪɡrɑːf, Amer -ɡræf/ *n* 二合字母 [如 ch, ea]

digress /daɪˈɡres/ *vi* 离题; **to ~ from sth.** 偏离某事物; **to ~ for a moment, ...** 暂时说点题外话，…

digression /daɪˈɡreʃn/ *n* 离题; **a ~ from sth.** 某事的题外话; **a ~ from the norm** 偏离常规; **let us make a brief ~ to consider** 我们扯远点考虑一下

dike /daɪk/ *n* = **dyke**

diktat /ˈdɪktæt/ *n* [c and u] usu pej 强制命令; **to rule by ~** 进行专制统治; **to refuse to accept the management's ~** 拒绝接受资方强加的规定

dilapidated /dɪˈlæpɪdeɪtɪd/ *adj* 破旧的 ‹*state, vehicle*›; 快要倒塌的 ‹*building, wall*›

dilapidation /dɪˌlæpɪˈdeɪʃn/
A *n* [u] 破旧; **a state of ~** 破旧状态
B dilapidations *npl* Jur 房屋的失修状况

dilate /daɪˈleɪt/
A *vt* 扩大 ‹*nostril, pupil*›; 扩张 ‹*blood vessel*›
B *vi* **1** (widen) «*pupil, cervix, nostril*» 扩大; «*blood vessel*» 扩张 **2** formal (speak or write at length) 详述; **~ on** *or* **upon sth.** 详述某事

dilation /daɪˈleɪʃn/ *n* [u] 扩大; **~ of the blood vessels** 血管的扩张; **the ~ of the pupil** 瞳孔的扩大

dilatoriness /ˈdɪlətərɪnɪs, Amer -tɔːrɪ-/ *n* [u] formal 拖延; **~ in doing sth.** 做某事上的拖拉

dilatory /ˈdɪlətəri, Amer -tɔːri/ *adj* formal **1** (slow) 拖拉的; **to be ~ in doing sth.** 做某事拖拉 **2** (time-wasting) 拖延的 ‹*tactics, behaviour*›

dildo /ˈdɪldəʊ/ *n* 人造阴茎

dilemma /daɪˈlemə, dɪ-/ *n* 窘境; **to be in a ~ (about sth.)** (在某事上) 进退两难; **to be caught on** *or* **be on the horns of a ~** 陷于左右为难的窘境

dilettante /ˌdɪlɪˈtænti/ *n* 半吊子

diligence /ˈdɪlɪdʒəns/ *n* [u] 勤奋; **to have** *or* **show ~ in sth./doing sth.** 在某事/做某事方面勤勉

diligent /ˈdɪlɪdʒənt/ *adj* **1** (hard-working) 勤奋的; **to be ~ in sth./doing sth.** 在某事/做某事方面孜孜不倦 **2** (committed, conscientious) 坚持不懈的

diligently /ˈdɪlɪdʒəntli/ *adv* 勤勉地; **to work** *or* **go about one's work ~** 勤奋工作

dill /dɪl/ *n* [u] 莳萝

dill pickle *n* [加了莳萝的] 腌黄瓜

dillydally /ˈdɪlɪdæli/ *vi* colloq **1** (dawdle) 磨蹭 **2** (be indecisive) 犹豫 **3** (waste time) 浪费时间

dillydallying /ˈdɪlɪdælɪŋ/ *n* [u] colloq **1** (dawdling) 磨蹭 **2** (indecisiveness) 犹豫 **3** (wasting time) 浪费时间

dilute /daɪˈljuːt, Amer -ˈluːt/
A *vt* **1** lit (make thinner) 稀释; **to ~ sth. with sth.** 用某物稀释某物; **to ~ to taste** 根据个人口味稀释后饮用 **2** fig 削弱 ‹*influence*›; 减少 ‹*responsibility*›
B *adj attrib* 稀释了的

dilution /daɪˈljuːʃn, Amer -ˈluːt-/ *n* **1** [u] lit 稀释 **2** [c] fig (of influence) 削弱; (of responsibility) 减少

dim /dɪm/
A *adj* **1** (not bright) 昏暗的 ‹*corner, spot, light, glow*› **2** (difficult to see) 朦胧的 ‹*shape, figure*› **3** (unclear, muffled) 模糊的 ‹*eyesight, feeling, sound*› **4** (not clearly defined or remembered) 不真切的 ‹*memory*›; **in the ~ and distant past** 在遥远的过去 **5** (not shiny) 无光泽的 ‹*brass, gloss*› **6** (not favourable) 暗淡的 ‹*prospect, outlook, future*›; **to take a ~ view of sth.** (disapprove of) 对某事物不太看好; (be annoyed by) 对某事物很恼火 **7** colloq (stupid) 愚蠢的 ‹*person, remark*›
B *vt* **1** (make less bright) 使…昏暗 ‹*light*› **2** (cause to fade) 使…减退 ‹*passion, memory, beauty*›; 使…暗淡 ‹*hope*› **3** (blur) 使…模糊 ‹*eyesight, eyes*› **4** Amer (dip) 使…变弱 ‹*headlights*›
C *vi* **1** (become less bright) «*lights, glow*» 变暗 **2** (fade) «*passion, memory, beauty*» 减退; «*hope*» 变暗淡 **3** (become blurred) «*eyesight, eyes*» 变模糊

dime /daɪm/ *n* Amer **1** (coin) [美国和加拿大的] 10 分硬币 **2** colloq (small amount of money) 少量的钱; **not worth a ~** 分文不值的; **they're a ~ a dozen** 它们太常见了，不值钱

dime novel *n* Amer 廉价通俗小说

dimension /daɪˈmenʃn, dɪ-/
A *n* **1** (measurement) 尺寸; **the ~s of the room** 房间的长宽高; **in two/three ~s** 二维/三维 **2** (aspect) 方面; **to take on a whole new ~** 呈现一个全新的特点; **to bring** *or* **add a new ~ to ...** 为…增添新的内容
B dimensions *npl* **1** (size) 面积 **2** fig (scope) 范围

dime store *n* Amer 廉价品店

diminish /dɪˈmɪnɪʃ/
A *vt* **1** (reduce) 减少 ‹*numbers, supplies, wealth, love, hope*› **2** (weaken) 削弱 ‹*influence, control, authority*› **3** (denigrate) 贬低 **4** Mus 减 ‹*interval*›
B *vi* **1** (decrease) «*numbers, supplies, wealth, love, hope*» 减少; **to ~ in value** 贬值 **2** (weaken) «*influence, control, authority*» 削弱

diminished /dɪˈmɪnɪʃt/ *adj* **1** 减少了的 ‹*income, support*›; **~ responsibility** 减轻的刑事责任 **2** (reduced in status) 被贬低的 ‹*person, rank*› **3** Mus 减的; **a ~ seventh (chord)** 减七和弦

diminishing /dɪˈmɪnɪʃɪŋ/ *adj* 逐渐减少的 ‹*supply, significance*›; **the law of ~ returns** 报酬递减律

diminuendo /dɪˌmɪnjʊˈendəʊ/
A *n* 渐弱
B *adj* 渐弱的
C *adv* 渐弱地

diminution /ˌdɪmɪˈnjuːʃn, Amer -ˈnuːʃn/ *n* 减少; **a ~ of** *or* **in sth.** 某物的缩减

diminutive /dɪˈmɪnjʊtɪv/
A *adj* **1** (very small) 极小的 **2** Ling 指小的 ‹*suffix, form*›
B *n* Ling 指小词

dimly /ˈdɪmli/ *adv* **1** (not brightly) 暗淡地 ‹*glow, shine*› **2** (faintly, vaguely) 隐约地 ‹*perceive*›; 模糊地 ‹*remember, be aware, recall*› **3** Brit colloq (stupidly) 愚蠢地

dimmer /ˈdɪmə(r)/ *n* **~ (switch)** 调光开关

dimness /ˈdɪmnɪs/ *n* [u] **1** (darkness) 昏暗; **the ~ of the evening** 傍晚的昏黑 **2** (of interior) 幽暗; (of light, lamp) 暗淡 **3** (dullness, lack of shine) 无光泽 **4** (of recollection, figure, outline) 模糊 **5** colloq (stupidity) 愚蠢

dimple /ˈdɪmpl/
A *n* (in flesh) 肉窝; (on chin, cheek) 酒窝; (in surface) 小坑
B *vt* 使出现酒窝; **a smile ~d her cheeks** 她笑出了酒窝
C *vi* «*cheeks, face*» 现笑靥; «*flesh*» 形成肉窝

dimpled /ˈdɪmpld/ *adj* **1** (marked with a dimple) 有酒窝的 ‹*cheek, chin*› **2** (marked with dimples) 有小坑的 ‹*surface, glass*› **3** (chubby) 有肉窝的 ‹*flesh*›; 肉乎乎的 ‹*hand*›

dim sum /dɪm ˈsʌm/ *n* [u] [中式] 点心

dim: ~wit *n* colloq 笨蛋; **~-witted** *adj* colloq 笨的

din /dɪn/
A *n* [u] (of people) 嘈杂声; (of machine) 轰鸣声
B *vt* **to ~ sth. into sb.** 反复叮嘱某人某事

dine /daɪn/
A *vi* (have dinner) 进餐; (to eat) 进食; **to ~ on/off sth.** 正餐吃某物; **we can't ~ on caviar and champagne every day** 我们不能每天都吃鱼子酱、喝香槟
B *vt* 宴请

Phrasal verbs
- **dine in** *vi* 在家就餐
- **dine out** *vi* 外出就餐; **to ~ out on a story/an anecdote** 总用某个故事/某则轶事来作笑谈

diner /ˈdaɪnə(r)/ *n* **1** (person) 就餐者 **2** Amer (restaurant) 小餐馆 **3** (in train) 餐车

dinette /daɪˈnet/ *n* [厨房旁边的] 小餐室

ding[1] /dɪŋ/
A *n* (sound) 叮当声
B *vi* 发叮当声; **the microwave ~ed** 微波炉发出叮的一声

ding[2] esp Amer
A *n* (dent) 凹痕
B *vt* 使…凹下 ‹*car*›

ding-a-ling /ˌdɪŋəˈlɪŋ/ *n* 丁零声

dingbat /ˈdɪŋbæt/ *n* colloq **1** Amer, Austral, NZ (idiot) 傻瓜; (eccentric) 怪人 **2** (symbol) 装饰字体

dingdong /ˈdɪŋdɒŋ/
A *n* **1** (sound) 叮咚 **2** Brit colloq (quarrel) 争吵
B *adj* Brit **1** (vigorous, heated) 激烈的 ‹*argument, fight*› **2** colloq (evenly matched) 难分难解的 ‹*contest*›

dinghy /ˈdɪŋɡi/ *n* **1** (for passengers) 小舢板; (with oars) 小划艇 **2** (inflatable) 橡皮筏

dinginess /ˈdɪndʒɪnɪs/ *n* [u] **1** (gloominess) 昏暗; **the ~ of his surroundings** 他周围环境的凄凉 **2** (shabbiness) 肮脏破旧 **3** (dullness of colour) 暗淡

dingo /ˈdɪŋɡəʊ/ *n* (*pl* **~** *or* **~es**) 澳洲野犬

dingy /ˈdɪndʒi/ *adj* **1** (gloomy) 昏暗的 ‹*streets, room*› **2** (shabby) 肮脏破旧的 ‹*curtains, material*› **3** (dull) 暗淡的 ‹*colour*›

dining: ~ car *n* 餐车; **~ chair** *n* 餐椅; **~ hall** *n* 餐厅; **~ room** *n* 餐厅; **~ table** *n* 餐桌

dinkum /ˈdɪŋkəm/ *adj* Austral, NZ colloq (genuine, true) 真正的; (honest) 诚实的

dinky /ˈdɪŋki/ *adj* colloq **1** Brit (small, cute) 小巧的 ‹*objects, gadgets*› **2** Amer (small, insignificant) 微不足道的

dinner /ˈdɪnə(r)/ *n* **1** (main meal) 正餐; (evening meal) 晚餐; **to have ~** 吃正餐; **to give the dog its ~** 喂狗; **at ~** 就餐; **to go out/be invited out to ~** 出去/被邀请出去吃饭; **to be invited to ~ at sb.'s** 受邀到某人家吃饭; **we'll be ten for ~** 我们有 10 个人就餐; **we're having chicken for ~** 我们正餐要吃鸡 **2** (banquet) 宴会; **to give a ~ for sb.** 设宴招待某人 **3** (baby food) 婴儿食品; (food for pet) 宠物食品

dinner: ~ bell *n* 午餐铃; **~ dance** *n* 餐后有舞会的正式宴会; **~ duty** *n* Brit [看管学生吃午饭的] 午餐值班; **~ fork** *n* 餐叉; **~ hour** *n* Brit (in school) 午餐时间; **~ jacket** *n* 无尾礼服; **~ knife** *n* 餐刀; **~ lady** *n* Brit [学校照顾孩子吃饭的] 午餐女服务员; **~ money** *n* [u] Brit 午餐费; **~ party** *n* 宴会; **~ party conversation** 宴会聊天; **~ plate** *n* 餐盘; **~ roll** *n* 正餐小圆面包; **~ service, ~ set** *ns* 成套西餐具; **~ table** *n* 餐桌; **~time** *n* 正餐时间; **~ tray** *n* 就餐托盘; **~ trolley** *n* 餐厅手推车; **~ware** *n* [u] Amer 餐具

dinosaur /ˈdaɪnəsɔː(r)/ *n* **1** lit 恐龙 **2** fig (person) 落伍的人; (thing) 过时的东西

dint /dɪnt/ *n* **by ~ of** 凭借; **by ~ of doing sth.** 靠做某事

diocesan /daɪˈɒsɪsn/ *adj* 教区的

d

diocese /'daɪəsɪs/ *n* 教区

diode /'daɪəʊd/ *n* **1** (semiconductor) 二极管 **2** (valve) 热离子管

dioptre Brit, **diopter** Amer /daɪ'ɒptə(r)/ *n* 屈光度

diorama /,daɪə'rɑːmə/ *n* **1** (model) 仿真模型 **2** (miniature film set) 透视缩影

dioxide /daɪ'ɒksaɪd/ *n* 二氧化物

dioxin /daɪ'ɒksɪn/ *n* 二噁英

Dip *abbr* = **diploma**

dip /dɪp/

A *vt* **1** (immerse) 浸; **to ~ sth. in** *or* **into sth.** 把某物在某液体中浸一下 **2** (put partially) 蘸; **to ~ sth. in** *or* **into sth.** 把某物在某液体中蘸一下 **3** Agric 给…洗药浴 ‹*sheep*› **4** Tech (plate, galvanize) 浸涂 ‹*metal*› **5** (lower, bend) 低 ‹*head*›; 屈 ‹*knee*› **6** Brit Aut 把…调为近光 ‹*headlights*›

B *vi* **1** (move downwards) «*bird, plane*» 俯冲; «*sun*» 下沉; «*head*» 低下 **2** (slope downwards) «*land, road*» 向下倾斜 **3** (decrease temporarily) «*rate, level, speed*» 暂时下降; **to ~ below sth.** 暂时下降到某水平以下 **4** (put one's hand into) 伸手掏; **to ~ into sth.** 伸手到某物中掏; **she will have to ~ into her savings to pay the bill** 她将不得不动用自己的积蓄来付账 **5** (browse) **to ~ into** 浏览 ‹*book, archives, records*›

C *n* **1** (short swim) 游一游; **I'm just going for a ~** 我只是去游个泳 **2** (hollow) 凹地; **there is a bit of a ~ in the road here** 路这里有点凹陷 **3** (of plane) 下落; (of head) 低下 **4** (decrease) 下降; **a sudden ~ in share prices** 股票价格的突然下跌 **5** Culin 蘸酱 **6** Phys 倾角; **magnetic ~** 磁倾角

diphtheria /dɪf'θɪərɪə/ ▸**p. 377** *n* [u] 白喉

diphthong /'dɪfθɒŋ, Amer -θɔːŋ/ *n* (sound) 二合元音; (letters) 双元音字母组合

diphthongize /'dɪfθɒŋaɪz, Amer -θɔːŋ-/ *vt* 使…二合元音化 ‹*vowel*›

diploid /'dɪplɔɪd/ *adj* 二倍体的

diploma /dɪ'pləʊmə/ *n* 毕业文凭

diplomacy /dɪp'ləʊməsi/ *n* [u] **1** Pol 外交 **2** (diplomatic skills) 外交技巧 **3** (tact) [处理人际关系的] 手腕

diplomat /'dɪpləmæt/ ▸**p. 409** *n* **1** Pol 外交官 **2** (tactful person) 有手腕的人

diplomatic /,dɪplə'mætɪk/ *adj* **1** (concerning international relations) 外交的 ‹*approaches*›; **a ~ presence** 出席的外交代表团; **through ~ channels** 通过外交渠道 **2** (concerning ambassadors) 外交人员的; **in ~ circles** 在外交界 **3** (showing tact) 得体的 ‹*behaviour*›; (tactful) 圆通的 ‹*person, reply, manner*›

diplomatically /,dɪplə'mætɪkli/ *adv* **1** Pol 在外交上; **it is hoped to settle the dispute ~** 希望通过外交途径解决这一争端 **2** (tactfully, discretely) 有策略地

diplomatic: ~ bag *n* Brit 外交邮袋; **~ corps** *n* [u] 外交使团; **~ immunity** *n* [u] 外交豁免; **~ passport** *n* 外交护照; **~ pouch** *n* Amer 外交邮袋; **~ relations** *npl* 外交关系; **~ service** *n* **the ~ service** 外事部门

diplomatist /dɪ'pləʊmətɪst/ *n* dated 外交官

dipole /'daɪpəʊl/ *n* **1** Elec, Phys 偶极子 **2** **~ (aerial)** 偶极天线

dipper /'dɪpə(r)/ *n* **1** Zool 河乌 **2** Amer (ladle) 长柄勺

dippy /'dɪpi/ *adj* colloq 傻的

dipso /'dɪpsəʊ/ *n* colloq 酒鬼

dipsomania /,dɪpsə'meɪnɪə/ *n* [u] 间发性酒狂

dipsomaniac /,dɪpsə'meɪnɪæk/ *n* 间发性酒狂患者

dipstick /'dɪpstɪk/ *n* Brit 油尺

dire /'daɪə(r)/ *adj* **1** (terrible) 可怕的 ‹*consequence, occurrence*› **2** (desperate) 急迫的 ‹*need, situation*›; (extreme) 极度的 ‹*misery, neglect, want*›; **to be in ~ need of sth.** 急需某物; **to be in ~ straits** 陷入极度困境 **3** (gloomy) 令人沮丧的 ‹*warning*› **4** colloq (of poor quality) 糟糕的 ‹*meal, lecture, outfit*›

direct /daɪ'rekt, dɪ-/

A *adj* **1** (without detour) 直的 ‹*course, road, line*›; 直系的 ‹*relative, ancestor, descendant*› **2** (without detour or changing) 直达的 ‹*flight, train*›; (without intermediary) 直接的; **in (no) ~ danger** (没) 有直接危险的; **a ~ line to sb.** 打给某人的直线电话; **~ sunlight** 直射阳光 **3** (straightforward, frank) 直率的 ‹*person*›; 直截了当的 ‹*approach, question, answer*›; **to be ~ with sb.** 对某人坦率直言 **4** (exact, clear) 截然的 ‹*comparison, contradiction, contrast*›; 直接的 ‹*evidence, quotation*›; **the ~ opposite of sth.** 与某物截然相反的一面

B *adv* **1** (without detour or changing) 直达地; **to go/travel ~** 直接去/作直达旅行; **to fly ~ to somewhere** 直飞某地 **2** (without intermediary) 直接地 ‹*speak, dial, negotiate, deal*›; **to pay sth. ~ into sb.'s account** 把某款项直接付到某人账户上

C *vt* **1** (show route, guide) «*person, sign, arrow*» 给…指路; **to ~ sb. to sth.** 给某人指到某处的路; **can you ~ me to the station?** 请问到车站怎么走? **2** Aut 指挥 ‹*traffic*› **3** (aim) 使…转向 ‹*car*›; 把…对准 ‹*gun, light, look*›; 使…集中 ‹*attention, attack, efforts*›; **he ~ed his gaze towards the picture** 他凝视着那张照片 **4** fig (address) 使…针对 ‹*appeal, remark, protest*›; 把…转到 ‹*enquiries, complaints*›; **to ~ sth. at** *or* **to sb.** 使某事物针对某人; **was your criticism ~ed at me?** 你的批评是冲我来的吗? **5** (control, organize) 管理 ‹*project, company, team*› **6** (instruct) 指示; **to ~ sb. to do sth.** 命令某人做某事; **to ~ that ...** 指示…; **(to be taken) as ~ed** 遵医嘱 (服用) **7** Cin, TV, Radio, Theat 导演 ‹*film, play, programme*›; 担任…的导演 ‹*performers, crew*›

D *vi* Cin, TV, Radio, Theat 担任导演; **I'd rather act than ~** 我宁愿演戏而不愿当导演

direct: ~ access *n* [u] 直接存取; **~ action** *n* [u] 直接行动 [指不通过会谈而直接罢工或示威等]; **~ current** *n* [u] 直流电; **~ debit** *n* 直接借记; **~ dialling** *n* [u] 直拨; **~ discourse** *n* [u] Amer = **~ speech**; **~ election** *n* 直接选举; **~ hit** *n* 直接命中; **to make a ~ hit** 直接射中

direction /daɪ'rekʃn, dɪ-/

A *n* **1** [c and u] lit (route) 方向; **in the ~ of ...** 在…方向; **in the right/wrong ~** 朝正确/错误的方向; **from all ~s** 从四面八方; **to have a good/bad sense of ~** 方向感好/不好 **2** [c and u] fig 动向; **a step in the right ~** 在正确方向上迈出的一步; **to lack ~** 迷失方向 **3** [u] Cin, Radio, TV, Theat 导演; Mus 指挥; **under the ~ of ...** 在…的指挥下; **stage ~** 舞台指示 **4** [u] (control, guidance) 指导; **under the ~ of ...** 在…的指导下

B **directions** *npl* **1** (for route) 指引; **to give sb. ~s** 给某人指路; **to ask for ~s to a place** 问路 **2** (for use) 指南; **~s for use** 用法说明

directional /daɪ'rekʃənl, dɪ-/ *adj* **1** (indicating direction) 指向的 ‹*marker*›; **~ signs** 路标 **2** Electron 定向的; **~ aerial** 定向天线

direction finder *n* 无线电测向仪

directive /daɪ'rektɪv, dɪ-/ *n* **1** (order) 命令; **a ~ on sth.** 有关某事的命令; **a ~ that sth. be** *or* **must be done** 必须完成某事的命令 **2** (guidance) 指示; **a ~ calling for sth.** 号召某事的指示; **to issue a ~** 发出指示; **to comply with** *or* **follow a ~** 遵从指示

direct labour *n* [u] 直接劳动力

directly /daɪ'rektli, dɪ-/

A *adv* **1** (in a direct line or manner) 直接地 ‹*move, expose, contact, quote*›; **to look ~ at sb.** 直视某人; **to be ~ descended from ...** 是…的直系后裔; **the two phenomena cannot be ~ compared** 这两种现象不能直接比较 **2** (exactly, completely) 恰好; **to be ~ proportional to ...** 与…成正比; **the front door opens ~ on to the road** 前门正对着马路; **she is ~ opposed to the proposal** 她断然反对这一提议 **3** (at once) 立刻; **she left ~ after the show** 表演一结束她就离开了; **he'll be back ~** 他马上就回来 **4** (frankly) 直截了当地

B *conj* Brit 一…就…; **~ he saw me, he stopped** 他一看见我就停下来了

direct: ~ mail *n* [u] 直接邮寄广告; **~ marketing** *n* [u] 直接营销; **~ method** *n* [u] [外语教学的] 直接教学法

directness /daɪ'rektnɪs, dɪ-/ *n* [u] **1** (of person, attitude) 坦率; (of play, work, writing) 直截了当 **2** (straightness of route, course) 笔直; (degree of straightness) 笔直程度

direct object *n* 直接宾语

director /daɪ'rektə(r), dɪ-/ *n* **1** Admin, Comm (member of board) 董事; (head of company, organization, programme) 主管; (manager) 经理; **D~ of Education/Social Services** 教育局局长/社会服务部干事 **2** (of project, investigation) 负责人 **3** Cin, TV, Radio 导演; (of orchestra, choir) 指挥; **~ of programmes** TV 节目编导 **4** Sch, Univ 院长; **~ of studies** 课程组长; **~ of admissions** 招生办主任

directorate /daɪ'rektərət, dɪ-/ *n* **1** (board) 董事会 **2** (government department) (政府) 部门

director general *n* (*pl* **directors general**) 总管

directorial /,daɪrek'tɔːrɪəl, ,dɪ-/ *adj* **1** Comm, Admin 主管的 ‹*responsibilities, attitudes, actions*› **2** Cin, Theat, TV 导演的; **~ debut** 作为导演的首部作品

director: D~ of Public Prosecutions *n* Brit 检察官; **~'s chair** *n* 折叠布椅; **~'s cut** *n* [电影的] 导演剪辑版

directorship /daɪ'rektəʃɪp, dɪ-/ *n* **1** (position) 董事职位; **to hold a ~** 任董事 **2** (period of office) 董事任期

director's report *n* 董事会报告

directory /daɪ'rektəri, dɪ-/ *n* **1** (book) 名录簿; **telephone ~** 电话号码簿; **trade ~** 商行名录 **2** Comput 目录

directory: ~ assistance *n* Amer = **~ enquiries**; **~ enquiries** *npl* Brit 电话号码查询台

direct: ~ primary *n* Amer 直接预选; **~ question** *n* 直接疑问句; **~ rule** *n* [u] 直辖; **~ sales** *npl* 直销; **~ selling** *n* [u] 直销; **~ speech** *n* [u] 直接引语; **~ tax** *n* 直接税; **~ taxation** *n* [u] 直接税收; **~ transfer** *n* 直接转账

dirge /dɜːdʒ/ *n* **1** (lament) 挽歌 **2** (mournful song) 哀伤的歌曲 **3** hum pej (slow, dull song) 缓慢无聊的歌曲

dirigible /'dɪrɪdʒəbl/ *n* = **airship**

dirt /dɜːt/ *n* [u] **1** (dirty substance) 尘垢; **to wash the ~ off one's face** 洗掉脸上的污垢; **to show the ~** 显脏; **to treat sb. like ~** 怠慢某人 **2** (soil) 泥土; **a pile of ~** 一堆土 **3** euph (faeces) 粪便; **dog ~** 狗屎 **4** colloq pej (gossip) 流言蜚语; **to dig up ~ on ...** 挖出…的丑闻; **to dish the ~ on** *or* **about sb.** 说某人的闲话; **to fling** *or* **throw ~ (at sb.)** 中伤 (某人) **5** (spoken obscenities) 下流话; (written obscenities) 色情描写

dirtbike /'dɜːtbaɪk/ *n* [适于在泥土路上行驶的] 轻型摩托车

dirt cheap colloq

A *adj* 非常便宜的

B *adv* 非常便宜地 ‹*buy, sell*›; **to travel/eat ~** 花很少旅费旅行/吃很便宜的东西

dirt farmer *n* Amer 自耕农

dirtily /'dɜːtɪli/ *adv* **1** (not cleanly) 肮脏地; **the children were ~ dressed** 孩子们穿着肮脏的衣服 **2** (dishonestly) 卑鄙地 ‹*act*›; **to**

behave ~ towards sb. 卑鄙地对待某人; to fight ~ 比赛时不讲体育道德

dirtiness /'dɜːtɪnɪs/ n [u] 1 lit 肮脏 2 fig (obscenity) 下流

dirt: ~ **road** n 土路; ~ **track** n 1 (road) = ~ **road**; 2 Sport (made of earth) 泥土平跑道; (made of cinders) 煤渣跑道

dirty /'dɜːti/

A adj 1 (covered or marked with unclean substance) 肮脏的; (slovenly) 邋遢的; (causing sb. to become unclean) 弄脏人的 ‹*work, task, chore*›; **to get/make sth. ~** 把某物弄脏; **to get ~** 变脏; **a ~ old tramp** 邋遢的老流浪汉; **a ~ job** 脏活儿 2 (unhygienic) 不卫生的 ‹*habit, behaviour*› 3 Med (infected) 受感染的 ‹*cut, wound, needle*› 4 (disgusting) 讨厌的; **look at the mess you've made, you ~ pig!** 瞧瞧你弄得一塌糊涂，你这头蠢猪！ 5 (greyish and dull) 灰暗的 ‹*colour, shade*›; **~ green** 暗绿色 6 (obscene) 色情的 ‹*book, film*›; 下流的 ‹*person, language, joke, behaviour*›; **don't get any ~ ideas!** 别想歪了！; **he has a ~ mind** 他满脑子下流事儿 7 (stormy) 狂风暴雨的 ‹*night*›; 恶劣的 ‹*weather*› 8 colloq (unfair, dishonest) 卑鄙的 ‹*action, liar*›; 没有体育道德的 ‹*player*›; 做了手脚的 ‹*contest, election*›; 非法所得的 ‹*money*›; **a ~ business** 卑鄙的事; **a ~ rascal** 臭无赖 9 colloq (unpleasant, distressing) 令人不愉快的 ‹*affair, business*›

B vt 弄脏

C adv colloq 1 (unfairly) 卑鄙地; **to fight/play ~** 出拳不择手段/恶意犯规 2 (obscenely) 下流地; **to talk ~** 讲下流话 3 (as intensifier) 非常; **she presented us with a ~ great bill** 她给了我们一张巨额账单

D n **to do the ~ on sb.** Brit colloq (cheat) 欺骗某人; (betray) 出卖某人; (behave in a mean way towards) 对某人耍卑鄙的手段

dirty: ~ **bomb** n 脏弹; ~ **look** n colloq 厌恶的表情; **to give sb. a ~ look** 狠狠地瞪某人一眼; ~ **mind** n colloq 肮脏的思想; **to have a ~ mind** 思想肮脏; **~-minded** adj colloq 思想肮脏的; ~ **old man** n pej 老色鬼; ~ **protest** n Brit 弄脏牢房以示抗议; ~ **trick** n 卑鄙手段; **to play a ~ trick on sb.** 对某人耍伎俩; ~ **tricks campaign** n 使用卑鄙伎俩的竞选运动; ~ **war** n 卑鄙战争 [指军方或警方为镇压革命者或恐怖分子而采取的暴力行动]; ~ **weekend** n Brit colloq 偷情周末; ~ **word** n 1 (word) 粗鄙字眼; 2 fig (concept) 忌讳想法; (thing) 讨嫌的东西; **'privatization' is a ~ word here** "私有化"在这儿遭人忌讳; ~ **work** n [u] 1 (dishonest activity) 卑鄙勾当; **don't get involved in his ~ work** 别卷进他的卑鄙勾当里去; 2 (unpleasant tasks) 苦活; **to do sb.'s ~ work (for them)** 帮某人干其不愿干的事

disability /ˌdɪsə'bɪləti/ n 1 ▸**p. 247** [u and c] (handicap, incapacity) 残疾; **a mental/physical ~** 心理缺陷/身体残疾; **multiple disabilities** 多重残疾; **~ for work** 无工作能力 2 [c] fig (disadvantage) 不利条件

disability: ~ **cover** n 伤残保险; ~ **pension** n 伤残抚恤金

disable /dɪs'eɪbl/ vt 1 Med ‹*illness, accident*› 使…伤残 ‹*person*› 2 (put out of action) 使…不能正常运转 ‹*computer, motor*›; Mil 使…丧失战斗力 ‹*tank*›; **the thieves ~d the alarm before breaking in** 贼人在闯入之前破坏了报警器 3 Jur (disqualify) 使无资格; **to be ~d from doing sth.** 无资格做某事

disabled /dɪs'eɪbld/ ▸**p. 247**

A adj 1 Med 有残疾的; **severely ~** 有严重残疾的; **to be mentally ~** 有心理缺陷 2 attrib Soc Admin 残疾人的 ‹*facility, equipment*› 3 (out of action) 无法启动的 ‹*computer*›; (damaged) 损坏的 ‹*ship, machinery*›

B npl **the ~** 残疾人

disabled: ~ **access** n [u] 残疾人通道; ~ **driver** n 残疾驾驶员; ~ **person** n 残疾人

disablement /dɪs'eɪblmənt/ n 残废

disabling /dɪs'eɪblɪŋ/ adj 严重妨碍健康的

disabuse /ˌdɪsə'bjuːz/ vt formal **to ~ sb. of sth.** 打消某人的某想法; **we'll soon ~ you of that notion!** 我们很快就会让你放弃那个念头的!

disadvantage /ˌdɪsəd'vɑːntɪdʒ, Amer -'væn-/

A n 1 [c] (drawback) 不利条件; **to be at a ~** 处于不利地位; **to get** or **catch sb. at a ~** 钻某人的空子; **to put sb. at a ~** 使某人处于不利地位 2 [u] (position of weakness) 不利地位; **to my/his ~** 对我/他不利; **to sell at a ~** 亏本卖出

B vt 使处于不利地位

disadvantaged /ˌdɪsəd'vɑːntɪdʒd, Amer -'væn-/

A adj 贫穷的 ‹*person, country*›

B npl **the ~** 下层社会

disadvantageous /dɪsˌædvɑːn'teɪdʒəs, Amer -væn-/ adj 不利的 ‹*situation, agreement*›; **~ to sb./sth.** 对某人/某事物不利的

disaffected /ˌdɪsə'fektɪd/ adj 不满的 ‹*citizen, soldier, member*›

disaffection /ˌdɪsə'fekʃn/ n 不满

disagree /ˌdɪsə'griː/ vi 1 (dissent) 不同意; **to ~ with sb. (about** or **over** or **on sth.)** (在某事上)与某人有分歧; **to ~ with sth.** 不同意 ‹*opinion, idea*›; **to agree to ~** 同意保留不同意见 2 (differ) «*people, ideas*» 有分歧; «*stories, statistics*» 不一致; **to ~ with sth.** 与某事物不符 3 (have adverse affect) «*food, climate*» 不适宜; **to ~ with sb.** 使某人不舒服; **work ~s with me** hum 我一工作就头痛

disagreeable /ˌdɪsə'griːəbl/ adj 难相处的 ‹*people*›; 令人不快的 ‹*situation*›; 难闻的 ‹*smell*›; 不合意的 ‹*taste*›; **to be ~ to sb.** «*food*» 不合某人的胃口

disagreeably /ˌdɪsə'griːəbli/ adv 讨厌地

disagreement /ˌdɪsə'griːmənt/ n 1 [u and c] (difference of opinion) 分歧; **a ~ (with sb./sth.) about** or **on** or **over sb./sth.** (与某人/某事)关于某人/某事的分歧 2 [c] (quarrel) 争吵; **a ~ between two people (on** or **about sth.)** 两个人之间(为某事)的争吵 3 [u] (inconsistency) 不符; **~ about sth./between two things** 在某事上/两件事之间的不一致

disallow /ˌdɪsə'laʊ/ vt 1 Sport 判…无效 ‹*goal*› 2 esp Jur 驳回 ‹*claim, appeal*›

disambiguate /ˌdɪsæm'bɪgjʊeɪt/ vt 消除…的歧义

disappear /ˌdɪsə'pɪə(r)/ vi 1 (vanish) 消失; **to make sth./sb. ~** 使某物/某人消失; **to ~ from view** 从视线里消失; **to ~ without trace** 消失得无影无踪; ▸**face A7** 2 (go missing) 失踪 3 (cease to exist) 不复存在; **the tension ~ed** 紧张气氛消失了; **this species will ~** 这个物种将会灭绝

disappearance /ˌdɪsə'pɪərəns/ n 1 (loss, theft) 丢失; (ceasing to be visible) 消失; **the ~ of sb./sth.** 某人的失踪/某物的丢失 2 (cessation, extinction) 灭绝

disappeared /ˌdɪsə'pɪəd/ npl **the ~** euph 失踪者

disappearing act, disappearing trick ns colloq 故意失踪; **to do a ~ act** or **trick** 玩故意失踪

disappoint /ˌdɪsə'pɔɪnt/ vt 1 (let down) 使…失望 ‹*person*› 2 (thwart) 使…破灭 ‹*hope, dream*›

disappointed /ˌdɪsə'pɔɪntɪd/ adj 失望的; **to be ~ about** or **at** or **in** or **with sb./sth.** 对某人/某事物失望; **to be ~ to see that ...** 看到…感到失望; **I'm ~ that you can't come** 你不能来，我感到很失望

disappointing /ˌdɪsə'pɔɪntɪŋ/ adj 令人失望的

disappointment /ˌdɪsə'pɔɪntmənt/ n 1 [u] (feeling) 失望; **to sb.'s ~** 使某人失望的是 2 [c] (thing causing upset) 使人失望的事; (person causing upset) 使人失望的人; **to be a ~ to sb.** 让某人扫兴

disapprobation /dɪsˌæprə'beɪʃn/ n [u] formal 反对; **~ of sb./sth.** 对某人/某事的反对

disapproval /ˌdɪsə'pruːvl/ n [u] 不赞成

disapprove /ˌdɪsə'pruːv/ vi 不赞成; **to ~ of sb./sth.** 不赞同某人/某事; **to ~ of sb. doing sth.** 不赞同某人做某事; **I ~ of noisy children in restaurants** 我不喜欢在饭店吵闹的孩子

disapproving /ˌdɪsə'pruːvɪŋ/ adj 不赞成的; **to give sb. a ~ look** 不满地看某人一眼

disapprovingly /ˌdɪsə'pruːvɪŋli/ adv 不赞成地

disarm /dɪs'ɑːm/

A vt 1 (take weapons from) 缴…的枪械 ‹*criminal*›; 解除…的武装 ‹*nation, armed force*› 2 fig (allay hostility of) 消除…的敌意 ‹*critic, opponent*›

B vi 裁军

disarmament /dɪs'ɑːməmənt/ n [u] 裁军; **a ~ conference/proposal** 裁军谈判/提议

disarming /dɪs'ɑːmɪŋ/

A adj 使人消气的 ‹*smile, manner*›; 使人消除敌意的 ‹*frankness, honesty*›

B n [u] 裁军

disarmingly /dɪs'ɑːmɪŋli/ adv 使人消气地 ‹*say, smile*›; 使人消除敌意地 ‹*candid*›; **~ frank/honest** 坦率/诚实得让人放心

disarranged /ˌdɪsə'reɪndʒd/ adj 乱糟糟的 ‹*hair, clothes*›

disarray /ˌdɪsə'reɪ/ n [u] 1 (disorder) 杂乱; **the room is in complete ~** 房间里一片狼藉 2 (confusion) 混乱; **in (complete) ~** 处于(彻底)混乱状态

disassemble /ˌdɪsə'sembl/ vt 拆卸 ‹*gun, machine*›

disassociate /ˌdɪsə'səʊʃɪeɪt/ vt, vi = **dissociate**

disassociation /ˌdɪsəˌsəʊʃɪ'eɪʃn/ n [u] = **dissociation**

disaster /dɪ'zɑːstə(r), Amer -'zæs-/ n 1 [c] (catastrophe) 灾难; **environmental ~** 环境灾难; **to be heading for ~** 走向灾难; **to be struck by ~** 遭受灾害 2 [u and c] (misfortune) 祸患; **to court** or **invite ~** 惹祸; **personal ~s** 个人的不幸 3 [c] colloq (failure) (event) 失败; (person) 失败者; **to be a (complete) ~** 是(彻底的)失败

disaster: ~ **area** n 1 lit 灾区; 2 fig colloq (place) 乱糟糟的地方; (situation) 灾难性局面; (person) 问题成堆的人; **this room is a ~ area** 这个房间乱七八糟; **you're a walking ~ area!** 你真是个灾星!; ~ **fund** n 赈灾基金; ~ **movie** n 灾难片; ~ **victim** n 灾民

disastrous /dɪ'zɑːstrəs, Amer -'zæs-/ adj 灾难性的 ‹*event, error, consequences*›

disastrously /dɪ'zɑːstrəsli, Amer -'zæs-/ adv 灾难性地; **her plans/the evening went ~ wrong** 她的计划/晚会弄得一团糟

disavow /ˌdɪsə'vaʊ/ vt formal 否认; **to ~ responsibility for sb./sth.** 拒绝为某人/某事承担责任

disavowal /ˌdɪsə'vaʊəl/ n formal 否认

disband /dɪs'bænd/

A vt 解散 ‹*group*›; 遣散 ‹*military unit*›

B vi 解散

disbelief /ˌdɪsbɪ'liːf/ n [u] 不信; **in ~** 怀疑地; **to be met with ~** 遭到怀疑

disbelieve /ˌdɪsbɪ'liːv/ vt 不相信

disbeliever /ˌdɪsbɪ'liːvə(r)/ n 持怀疑态度的人

disbelieving /ˌdɪsbɪ'liːvɪŋ/ adj 怀疑的 ‹*expression, tone*›

disburse /dɪs'bɜːs/ vt formal 支付

disbursement /dɪs'bɜːsmənt/ n formal 1 [u] (act) 支付 2 [c] (sum) 支出款额

disc /dɪsk/ *n* **1** (circular object) 圆盘 **2** (shape) 圆盘形 **3** Anat, Zool 椎间盘; **to slip a ~, to have a slipped ~** 椎间盘突出 **4** Mus dated 唱片 **5** (tag) 身份牌 **6** Comput **= disk 1**

discard /dɪs'kɑːd/
A *vt* **1** (get rid of) 丢弃 ‹*clothes, rubbish*› **2** (reject) 抛弃 ‹*idea, friend*› **3** (in cards) 垫出
B *vi* (in cards) 垫牌
C *n* **1** (person) 被抛弃的人; (thing) 抛弃物 **2** (in cards) 垫出的牌

disc brakes *npl* 盘式制动器

discern /dɪ'sɜːn/ *vt* **1** (see) 分辨出 ‹*object, person*›; **it was hard to ~ her features** 很难看清她的模样 **2** (perceive) 觉察到 ‹*fact, truth*›

discernible /dɪ'sɜːnəbl/ *adj* 看得清的 ‹*outline, difference*›

discernibly /dɪ'sɜːnəbli/ *adv* 明显地 ‹*different, offensive*›

discerning /dɪ'sɜːnɪŋ/ *adj* 有识别力的; **a ~ art critic** 有洞察力的艺术批评家

discernment /dɪ'sɜːnmənt/ *n* [u] 洞察力; **a person of ~** 有眼光的人

discharge
A /dɪs'tʃɑːdʒ/ *vt* **1** (release) 允许…出院 ‹*patient*›; 允许…退伍 ‹*serviceman, soldier*› **2** (dismiss) 解雇 ‹*employee*›; **to ~ sb. from their duties** 撤某人的职 **3** Jur 释放 ‹*prisoner, the accused*›; 解散 ‹*jury, juror*› **4** (emit) 排放 ‹*smoke, water, waste*› **5** Med 流出 ‹*blood, pus, mucus*› **6** Fin 清偿 ‹*debt*› **7** (perform) 履行 ‹*responsibility, obligation, duty*› **8** (unload) 卸下 ‹*cargo, load*›; 让…下来 ‹*passengers*› **9** (fire) 击发 ‹*gun, firearms*›; 使用 ‹*weapon*›; 发射 ‹*arrow*›
B /dɪs'tʃɑːdʒ/ *vi* **1** (flow) 流出; **the river ~s into the sea five miles down the coast** 那条河在海岸以南5英里处流入大海 **2** Med «*wound*» 流脓 **3** Elec 放电
C /'dɪstʃɑːdʒ, dɪs'tʃɑːdʒ/ *n* **1** [u] (release) (from hospital) 出院; (from employment) 解雇; (from military service) 退伍; **to get one's ~** 被解雇 **2** [c and u] (of liquid, gas) 排放 **3** [c] (substance released) 排放物 **4** [c and u] Med 分泌物; **bodily ~s** 身体分泌物 **5** [u] Fin 清偿; **in ~ of sth.** 作为对某项债务的清偿 **6** [u] (performance) 履行; **the ~ of his obligations** 他的义务的履行 **7** [u] (firing) 发射 **8** [u] Elec (electricity from charged object) 放电; (flow of electricity) 电流

disciple /dɪ'saɪpl/ *n* **1** (follower) 追随者; (pupil) 信徒 **2** Relig [耶稣的] 使徒

disciplinarian /ˌdɪsɪplɪ'neərɪən/ *n* (gen) 严守纪律者; Sch 严师

disciplinary /'dɪsɪplɪnəri, Amer -neri/ *adj* 惩戒性的 ‹*measure, action*›; **~ questions/matters** 种种违纪问题/事项

discipline /'dɪsɪplɪn/
A *n* **1** [u] (behaviour, state) 纪律 **2** [u] (punishment) 惩罚 **3** [c] Univ (subject) 学科
B *vt* **1** (train) 训导; **to ~ oneself** 自律; **to ~ a child** 管教孩子 **2** (punish) 惩罚

disciplined /'dɪsɪplɪnd/ *adj* (controlled) 纪律严明的; (trained) 训练有素的

disc jockey ▸p. 409 *n* 流行音乐节目主持人

disclaim /dɪs'kleɪm/ *vt* 否认 ‹*responsibility, knowledge, involvement*›

disclaimer /dɪs'kleɪmə(r)/ *n* 免责声明; **to issue a ~** 发表免责声明

disclose /dɪs'kləʊz/ *vt* **1** (make visible) 使…显露 ‹*scene, plaque*› **2** (make known) 透露 ‹*news, secret*›

disclosure /dɪs'kləʊʒə(r)/ *n* **1** [u] (act) 揭露; **~ of sth.** 某事的披露 **2** [c] (revelation) 揭露的事实

disco /'dɪskəʊ/ *n* colloq **1** [c] (event) 迪斯科舞会; **to go to a ~** 去参加迪斯科舞会 **2** [c] (club) **= discotheque 3** [u] **~ (music)** 迪斯科音乐

discography /dɪs'kɒgrəfi/ *n* 音乐作品目录

discoloration /ˌdɪskʌlə'reɪʃn/ *n* [u] 变色

discolour Brit, **discolor** Amer /dɪs'kʌlə(r)/
A *vt* «*smoking*» 使…变色 ‹*teeth*›; «*washing*» 使…褪色 ‹*blouse*›; **to be ~ed with age/by light** 因时间久远/光照而变色
B *vi* «*wood, metal*» 变色; «*fabric*» 褪色

discombobulate /ˌdɪskəm'bɒbjʊleɪt/ *vt* esp Amer hum colloq 使困惑

discomfit /dɪs'kʌmfɪt/ *vt* liter 使窘迫; **to be ~ed by sth.** 为某事物尴尬

discomfiture /dɪs'kʌmfɪtʃə(r)/ *n* [u] liter 窘迫

discomfort /dɪs'kʌmfət/
A *n* [u] **1** (lack of physical comfort) 不适; (pain) 轻微病痛 **2** (unease) 不安; **to cause sb. ~** 使某人不安
B *vt* 使不安

discomforting /dɪs'kʌmfətɪŋ/ *adj* **1** (causing slight pain) 引起轻微病痛的 **2** (causing unease) 使人不安的

disconcert /ˌdɪskən'sɜːt/ *vt* 使不安; **to be ~ed by sb./sth.** 被某人/某事物搅得不安

disconcerting /ˌdɪskən'sɜːtɪŋ/ *adj* 令人难堪的 ‹*attitude, habit, gaze*›

disconcertingly /ˌdɪskən'sɜːtɪŋli/ *adv* 令人难堪地; **to be ~ frank/self-assured** 直率/自信得令人难堪

disconnect /ˌdɪskə'nekt/ *vt* **1** (separate) 拔下 ‹*plug, hose*›; 使…分开 ‹*carriages*›; **to ~ sth. from sth.** 使某物从某物分离 **2** (unplug) 拔掉…的插头 ‹*appliance*›; 切断…的电源 ‹*lights*›; (cut off supply from) 停止供应 ‹*water*›; 切断…的服务 ‹*utilities, telephone*›; **to ~ the keyboard/printer from the computer** 把键盘/打印机从电脑上拔下来; **to ~ sb.'s water/gas** 切断某人的供水/煤气供应 **3** (on telephone) 切断…的电话 ‹*caller*›

disconnected /ˌdɪskə'nektɪd/ *adj* **1** fig 不连贯的 ‹*thoughts, remarks*› **2** lit 被切断服务的 ‹*utilities*›

disconsolate /dɪs'kɒnsələt/ *adj* 忧郁的

disconsolately /dɪs'kɒnsələtli/ *adv* 忧郁地

discontent /ˌdɪskən'tent/ *n* [u] 不满

discontented /ˌdɪskən'tentɪd/ *adj* 不满的; **to be ~ with sth.** 对某事物不满

discontentment /ˌdɪskən'tentmənt/ *n* [u] 不满

discontinuation /ˌdɪskəntɪnjʊ'eɪʃn/ *n* [u] 终止

discontinue /ˌdɪskən'tɪnjuː/ *vt* 终止

discontinuity /dɪsˌkɒntɪ'njuːəti/ *n* **1** [u] (incoherence) 不连贯 **2** [c] (interruption) 中断

discontinuous /ˌdɪskən'tɪnjʊəs/ *adj* 间断的

discord /'dɪskɔːd/ *n* **1** [u] (disagreement) 不一致; **a note of ~** 不和的征象; **to sew ~ among** *or* **within the group** 在群体中挑拨离间 **2** [c] Mus 不协和和弦

discordant /dɪ'skɔːdənt/ *adj* **1** (conflicting) 不一致的 ‹*opinion*›; **to strike a ~ note** 显得不协调 **2** Mus 不和谐的 ‹*note*›

discotheque /'dɪskətek/ *n* 迪斯科舞厅

discount
A /'dɪskaʊnt/ *n* [u and c] **1** (price reduction) 折扣; **to get/give a ~** 得到/给予折扣; **to get/give a ~ on sth.** 打折买/卖某物; **at a ~** 打折地; **~ for cash** 用现金有折扣; **to be sold at a ~** «*shares*» 低于票面值出售 **2** Fin 贴现
B /dɪs'kaʊnt, Amer 'dɪskaʊnt/ *vt* **1** (reject) 不予考虑 ‹*possibility, approach*› **2** (reduce price of) 打折出售 ‹*goods*› **3** Fin 把…贴现

discount: ~ card *n* 优惠卡; **~ flight** *n* 打折航班; **~ house** *n* **1** Brit Fin 贴现公司; **2** Amer **= ~ store**; **~ rate** *n* 贴现率; **~ store** *n* 折扣商店

discourage /dɪs'kʌrɪdʒ/ *vt* **1** (dishearten) 使灰心; **to become ~d** 变得沮丧; **don't be ~d!** 别泄气! **2** (deter) 阻拦; **to ~ sb. from doing sth.** 阻止某人干某事

discouragement /dɪs'kʌrɪdʒmənt/ *n* **1** [u] (despondency) 灰心 **2** [u] (dissuasion) 阻拦 **3** [c] (disincentive) 遏制因素; **a ~ to sb./sth.** 对某人/某事的阻遏

discouraging /dɪs'kʌrɪdʒɪŋ/ *adj* 令人泄气的

discourse formal
A /'dɪskɔːs/ *n* **1** [u] (debate) 辩论 **2** [c] (written thesis) 论文; (oral thesis) 演讲; **a ~ on** *or* **about sth.** 有关某事物的演讲 **3** [u] (conversation) 谈话 **4** [u] Ling 语篇
B /dɪ'skɔːs/ *vi* 论述; **to ~ on** *or* **about sth.** 论述某事物

discourse analysis *n* [u] 语篇分析

discourteous /dɪs'kɜːtɪəs/ *adj* 不礼貌的

discourteously /dɪs'kɜːtɪəsli/ *adv* 不礼貌地

discourtesy /dɪs'kɜːtəsi/ *n* **1** [u] (rudeness) 无礼; **to show ~** 表现得没礼貌; **a sign of ~** 失礼的表示 **2** [c] (rude remark) 失礼的话; (rude act) 失礼的举动; **to do sb. a ~** 对某人无礼

discover /dɪs'kʌvə(r)/ *vt* **1** (find out) 查明 ‹*truth*› **2** (come upon) 发现 ‹*person, place, thing*›; **a talent waiting to be ~ed** 有待赏识的天才 **3** (try) 初次接触 ‹*activity, thing*›; **to ~ Thai food** 初次品尝泰国菜

discoverer /dɪs'kʌvərə(r)/ *n* 发现者; **the ~ of America** 第一个发现美洲的人

discovery /dɪ'skʌvəri/ *n* [u and c] 发现; **a voyage of ~** 发现之旅

discredit /dɪs'kredɪt/
A *vt* **1** (damage reputation of) 败坏…的声誉 ‹*person, company*› **2** (cause to seem false) 使…不可置信 ‹*idea, evidence*›; **that theory has been ~ed** 那个理论已受到质疑
B *n* **1** [u] (loss of reputation) 名誉丧失; **to bring ~ on sb./sth.** 败坏某人/某机构的名声; **to bring ~ on the country** 败坏这个国家的声誉; **to sb.'s ~** 让某人丢脸的是; **to be to sb.'s ~** 使某人丢脸 **2** [c] (person bringing disgrace) 败坏名声的人; (thing bringing disgrace) 丢脸的事; **to be a ~ to sb.** 是某人的耻辱

discreditable /dɪs'kredɪtəbl/ *adj* 可耻的 ‹*conduct, deed*›

discreet /dɪ'skriːt/ *adj* **1** (tactful) 考虑周到的 ‹*person, remark*›; **be ~!** 审慎点! **2** (unobtrusive) 不唐突的 ‹*gesture*›; 低调的 ‹*handling*›; 朴素的 ‹*colour*›; **~ elegance** 素雅

discreetly /dɪ'skriːtli/ *adv* **1** (unobtrusively) 不唐突地 ‹*move, inform*›; 轻微地 ‹*cough*› **2** (subtly) 朴素地 ‹*dressed*›; **~ elegant** 素雅的

discrepancy /dɪs'krepənsi/ *n* 差异

discrete /dɪ'skriːt/ *adj* 分离的 ‹*steps*›; 不相关联的 ‹*meanings*›

discretion /dɪ'skreʃn/ *n* [u] **1** (tact) 谨慎; **the soul of ~** 谨慎的典范; **~ is the better part of valour** 谨慎即大勇 **2** (authority) 自行决定的自由; **to use one's (own) ~** 自行决定; **in** *or* **at my/his ~** 由我/他自行决定; **the age of ~** 责任能力年龄

discretionary /dɪ'skreʃənəri, Amer -neri/ *adj* 自由决定的 ‹*powers, measures*›

discriminate /dɪ'skrɪmɪneɪt/ *vi* **1** (show bias) 区别对待; **to ~ against sb.** 歧视某人; **to ~ in favour of sb./sth.** 偏爱某人/某物 **2** (distinguish) 区别; **to ~ between A and B** 区分A和B

discriminating /dɪ'skrɪmɪneɪtɪŋ/ *adj* 有识别力的 ‹*viewer, consumer*›; **a ~ collector of sth.** 有鉴赏力的某物的收藏者

discrimination /dɪˌskrɪmɪ'neɪʃn/ *n* [u] **1** (prejudice) 歧视; **racial ~** 种族歧视; **positive ~** 正面差别待遇 **2** (taste) 鉴赏力; **to show ~** 显示出鉴赏力 **3** (ability to differentiate) 识别力

discriminatory /dɪ'skrɪmɪnətəri, Amer -tɔːri/ *adj* 歧视性的 ‹*legislation, practice*›

d

discursive /dɪ'skɜ:sɪv/ *adj* 离题的 ‹*essay*›; 散漫的 ‹*style*›

discus /'dɪskəs/ *n* (*pl* **~es**) 铁饼; **the ~** (event) 掷铁饼比赛; **a ~ thrower** 铁饼运动员

discuss /dɪ'skʌs/ *vt* **1** (talk about, deliberate over) 讨论 ‹*topic, problem*›; **there's nothing to ~** 没什么好讨论的 **2** (in writing, lecture) 论述 ‹*problem, theory*›

discussion /dɪ'skʌʃn/ *n* **1** [u and c] (verbal exchange) 讨论; **a ~ about sb./sth.** 有关某人/某事物的讨论; **to be under ~** 在讨论中; **to be open to ~** 可以讨论 **2** [c] (in writing, lecture) 论述

discussion: ~ document, ~ paper *ns* 讨论文件; **~ group** *n* 讨论组

disdain /dɪs'deɪn/

A *n* 鄙视; **a sneer of ~** 鄙视的嘲笑; **to do sth. in** *or* **with ~** 蔑视地做某事; **to feel ~ for sb./sth.** 看不起某人/某事物

B *vt* **1** (look down on) 鄙视 ‹*person*›; 鄙弃 ‹*offer*› **2** (refuse) 不屑做; **to ~ to reply/join in** 不屑于回答/加入

disdainful /dɪs'deɪmfl/ *adj* 倨傲的 ‹*person*›; 轻蔑的 ‹*attitude, look*›; **to be ~ of sth.** 鄙视某事物

disdainfully /dɪs'deɪmfəli/ *adv* 鄙视地

disease /dɪ'zi:z/ *n* [u and c] **1** Med 病 **2** Hort 病害

diseased /dɪ'zi:zd/ *adj attrib* **1** (unhealthy) 患病的 ‹*person, tissue, animal, plant*› **2** (corrupt, abnormal) 病态的 ‹*mind, society*›

disembark /ˌdɪsɪm'bɑ:k/

A *vi* (from plane) 下飞机; (from ship) 下船; (from train) 下火车; **to ~ from sth.** 从某运输工具上下来

B *vt* 使…下来 ‹*passengers*›; 卸 ‹*vehicles*›

disembarkation /dɪsˌembɑ:'keɪʃn/ *n* (from plane) 下飞机; (from ship) 下船; (from train) 下火车

disembodied /ˌdɪsɪm'bɒdɪd/ *adj usu attrib* **1** (detached) 脱离肉体的; **a ~ spirit** 游魂 **2** (lacking physical source) 不见其人的 ‹*voice*›

disembowel /ˌdɪsɪm'baʊəl/ *vt* (*pres p etc.* **-ll-** Brit, **-l-** Amer) 取出…的内脏

disempower /ˌdɪsɪm'paʊə(r)/ *vt* **1** (make less powerful) 削弱…的力量 **2** (make less confident) 削弱…的自信心

disenchant /ˌdɪsɪn'tʃɑ:nt/ *vt* «*event, job*» 使…不抱幻想 ‹*person*›

disenchanted /ˌdɪsɪn'tʃɑ:ntɪd, Amer -'tʃænt-/ *adj* 失望的; **to be ~ with sb./sth.** 对某人/某事物不抱幻想

disenchantment /ˌdɪsɪn'tʃɑ:ntmənt, Amer -'tʃænt-/ *n* [u] 失望

disenfranchise /ˌdɪsɪn'fræntʃaɪz/ *vt* **1** (deprive of vote) 剥夺…的选举权 **2** (deprive of privilege, right) 剥夺…的权利

disengage /ˌdɪsɪn'geɪdʒ/

A *vt* 使脱离; **to ~ sb./sth. from sb./sth.** 使…与…脱离; **to ~ oneself from sb./sb.'s embrace** 挣脱某人/某人的怀抱; **to ~ the clutch** 松开离合器

B *vi* «*troops*» 撤离; «*clutch*» 松开

disengaged /ˌdɪsɪn'geɪdʒd/ *adj* formal 漫不经心的

disengagement /ˌdɪsɪn'geɪdʒmənt/ *n* [u] **1** (separation, release) 脱离; **~ from sth.** 与某物的脱离 **2** Mil (withdrawal) 撤军

disentangle /ˌdɪsɪn'tæŋgl/ *vt* **1** (remove knots from) 解开…的结 ‹*hair, thread*› **2** (extricate) 使摆脱; **to ~ sth. from sth.** 使…从某物松开 ‹*hair, fingers*› **3** fig (separate mentally) 理出; **to ~ sth. from sth.** 把…从某事中理出来 ‹*truth, fact*›

disequilibrium /ˌdɪsi:kwɪ'lɪbrɪəm/ *n* [u] 不平衡

disestablish /ˌdɪsɪ'stæblɪʃ/ *vt* **to ~ the Church** 废除国教 **to be ~ed** 被废除法定地位;

disestablishment /ˌdɪsɪ'stæblɪʃmənt/ *n* [u] 废除国教

disfavour Brit, **disfavor** Amer /dɪs'feɪvə(r)/ formal

A *n* [u] **1** (disapproval) 不赞成; **to look on** *or* **regard sb./sth. with ~** 不赞同地看待某人/某事 **2** (being disliked) 失宠; **to be in ~ (with sb.)** 受到（某人的）冷遇; **to fall into ~** 失宠

B *vt* 疏远

disfigure /dɪs'fɪgə(r), Amer dɪs'fɪgjər/ *vt* 使…变丑 ‹*person, face*›; 破坏…的面貌 ‹*landscape, building*›; **to be ~d (by sth.)** （因某物）破相

disfigurement /dɪs'fɪgəmənt, Amer dɪs'fɪgjə-/ *n* **1** [u] (spoiling) (of person) 毁容; (of place) 污损 **2** [c] (scar) 伤疤

disfranchise /dɪs'fræntʃaɪz/ *vt* **= disenfranchise**

disgorge /dɪs'gɔ:dʒ/ *vt* **1** (discharge) «*factory, river*» 大量排放 ‹*effluent, waters*› **2** fig «*station, theatre*» 涌出 ‹*crowd, fans*›; «*vehicle*» 涌下 ‹*passengers*› **3** (cough up) 吐出 ‹*bone*›; 呕出 ‹*vomit*›; 咳出 ‹*blood*›

disgrace /dɪs'greɪs/

A *n* **1** [u] (shame) 羞耻; **to bring ~ on sb.** 使某人蒙羞; **to be in ~** 丢脸; **there's no ~ in that** 那没什么丢脸的 **2** [c] (shameful thing) 丢脸的事; (shameful person) 让人丢脸的人; **to be a ~ to sb./sth.** 对某人/某物是个耻辱

B *vt* **1** (bring shame to) 使…蒙受耻辱 ‹*family, country*› **2** **to be ~d** (be dishonoured) «*politician, official*» 失势; «*general*» 被解职

C *v refl* **to ~ oneself** (behave badly) 出丑; (dishonour oneself) 使自己丢脸

disgraceful /dɪs'greɪsfl/ *adj* 可耻的 ‹*behaviour*›; 让人丢脸的 ‹*situation*›; **it's ~!** 真丢人!

disgracefully /dɪs'greɪsfəli/ *adv* 可耻地 ‹*behave*›; 很不像话地 ‹*dirty, underpaid*›

disgruntled /dɪs'grʌntld/ *adj* (dissatisfied) 不满的; (unhappy) 不高兴的

disguise /dɪs'gaɪz/

A *vt* **1** (camouflage) 伪装 ‹*person, appearance*›; **to be ~d as a priest** 化装成牧师; **to ~ one's voice** 伪装声音 **2** (hide) 掩盖 ‹*scar, fact, intentions*›

B *v refl* **to ~ oneself as sb./sth.** 把自己扮作某人/某物

C *n* **1** [u] (camouflage) 伪装; **in ~** 化了装; **to be a master of ~** 善于伪装 **2** [c] (costume) 化装用具

disgust /dɪs'gʌst/

A *n* (physical) 作呕; (moral) 厌恶; **to fill sb. with ~** 令某人恶心; **in ~** 厌恶地; **to sb.'s ~** 让某人厌恶的是

B *vt* 使厌恶

disgusted /dɪs'gʌstɪd/ *adj* (physically) 感到恶心的; (morally) 厌恶的; **to be ~ with sb. for sth.** 因为某事物厌恶某人

disgustedly /dɪs'gʌstɪdli/ *adv* (disapprovingly) 厌恶地; (angrily) 愤慨地

disgusting /dɪs'gʌstɪŋ/ *adj* 令人厌恶的 ‹*behaviour, language, sight*›; 令人恶心的 ‹*smell*›

disgustingly /dɪs'gʌstɪŋli/ *adv* **1** (revoltingly) 令人作呕地 ‹*smelly*›; **to be ~ dirty/fat** 脏得/肥得让人想吐 **2** colloq hum (extremely) 极其; **you're ~ fit/rich!** 你身体棒得令人眼红/富得流油!

dish /dɪʃ/

A *n* **1** (plate) 盘子 **2** (food) 一盘 **3** (recipe) 一道菜; **a hot/side ~** 热菜/小菜 **4** (receptacle) 碟状物; **a soap ~** 肥皂碟 **5** TV 抛物面天线 **6** colloq (good-looking person) 漂亮的人; (sexy person) 性感的人

B **dishes** *npl* 待洗餐具; **to do** *or* **wash the ~es** 洗碗

C *vt* esp Brit colloq dated 毁掉 ‹*chances*›; **to ~ the dirt about** *or* **on sb./sth.** 说某人/某事的闲话

Phrasal verbs

• **dish out** *vt* [**~ out sth., ~ sth. out**] **1** (serve) 把…分到盘里 ‹*food, helping*› **2** (distribute) 分发 ‹*money, leaflets*›; 布置 ‹*homework*› **3** (dole out) 提出 ‹*advice*›; 给予 ‹*punishment, insults*›; **to ~ it out** colloq 数落人

• **dish up** *vt* [**~ up sth., ~ sth. up**] **1** (serve) 端上; **to ~ up (the) dinner/the food** 端上晚饭/饭菜 **2** (come up with) 提出 ‹*argument, idea*›; 找出 ‹*excuse*›

disharmony /dɪs'hɑ:məni/ *n* [u] 不和谐

dishcloth /'dɪʃklɒθ/ *n* 洗碗布

dishearten /dɪs'hɑ:tn/ *vt* 使沮丧; **to be ~ed by sth.** 因某事物而沮丧; **don't be ~ed!** 别灰心!

disheartening /dɪs'hɑ:tnɪŋ/ *adj* 令人沮丧的 ‹*response, news*›

dishevelled Brit, **disheveled** Amer /dɪ'ʃevld/ *adj* 衣冠不整的 ‹*person*›; 凌乱的 ‹*hair*›; 不整洁的 ‹*clothes, appearance*›

dishonest /dɪs'ɒnɪst/ *adj* **1** (untrustworthy) 不诚实的 ‹*person*› **2** (deceptive) 欺骗性的 ‹*behaviour, practice*›

dishonestly /dɪs'ɒnɪstli/ *adv* 不诚实地 ‹*act, deal*›; 不正当地 ‹*acquire*›

dishonesty /dɪs'ɒnɪsti/ *n* [u] 不诚实

dishonour Brit, **dishonor** Amer /dɪs'ɒnə(r)/

A *n* [u] 耻辱; **to bring ~ on sb.** 使某人蒙受耻辱; **death before ~** 宁死不受辱

B *vt* **1** (bring disgrace on) 使…蒙受耻辱 ‹*person, group*› **2** (fail to respect) 违背 ‹*agreement*› **3** Fin 拒付 ‹*cheque*›

dishonourable Brit, **dishonorable** Amer /dɪs'ɒnərəbl/ *adj* 可耻的 ‹*person, act*›

dishonourable discharge *n* 开除军籍

dishonourably Brit, **dishonorably** Amer /dɪs'ɒnərəbli/ *adv* 可耻地 ‹*behave*›; 不诚实地 ‹*trade*›

dish: ~pan *n* Amer 洗碟盆; **~rag** *n* Amer **= dishcloth**; **~towel** *n* esp Amer 擦碗布; **~washer** *n* (machine) 洗碗机; (person) 洗碗工; **~washer detergent** *n* 洗碗机用洗涤剂; **~washer powder** *n* 洗碗机用洗涤粉; **~washer salt** *n* [u] 洗碗机用盐; **~washing liquid** *n* 洗涤液; **~water** *n* [u] **1** lit 洗碗水; **2** pej (weak drink) 淡而无味的饮料; **as dull as ~water** fig 极为乏味的

dishy /'dɪʃi/ *adj* esp Brit colloq (good-looking) 漂亮的; (sexy) 性感的

disillusion /ˌdɪsɪ'lu:ʒn/

A *vt* 使幻想破灭; **to ~ sb.** 打破某人的幻想; **to become ~ed with sth.** 对某事物不再抱幻想

B *n* 幻想破灭

disillusioned /ˌdɪsɪ'lu:ʒnd/ *adj* 不再抱幻想的; **to be ~ with sth./sb.** 对某事物/某人大失所望

disillusionment /ˌdɪsɪ'lu:ʒnmənt/ *n* [u] 幻想破灭

disincentive /ˌdɪsɪn'sentɪv/ *n* 遏制因素; **a ~ to sth.** 对某事物的遏制

disinclination /ˌdɪsɪnklɪ'neɪʃn/ *n* 不情愿; **(a) ~ to do sth.** 对做某事的不情愿; **to show a ~ to do sth.** 无意做某事

disinclined /ˌdɪsɪn'klaɪnd/ *adj* 不情愿的; **to be/feel ~ (to do sth.)** 不情愿（做某事）

disinfect /ˌdɪsɪn'fekt/ *vt* 为…消毒

disinfectant /ˌdɪsɪn'fektənt/

A *n* 消毒剂

B *adj* 消毒的

disinfection /ˌdɪsɪn'fekʃn/ *n* [u] 消毒

disinflation /ˌdɪsɪn'fleɪʃn/ *n* [u] 通货紧缩

disinformation /ˌdɪsɪnfə'meɪʃn/ *n* [u] 虚假信息

disingenuous /ˌdɪsɪn'dʒenjʊəs/ *adj* 不坦率的

disinherit /ˌdɪsɪn'herɪt/ *vt* 剥夺…的继承权

disintegrate /dɪsˈɪntɪɡreɪt/ *vi* «*cloth, wood*» 碎裂; fig «*family, relationship*» 破裂; «*aircraft, organization*» 解体; «*power*» 瓦解

disintegration /dɪsˌɪntɪˈɡreɪʃn/ *n* [u] (of cloth, wood) 碎裂; (of family, relationship) 破裂; (of aircraft, organization) 解体; (of power) 瓦解

disinter /ˌdɪsɪnˈtɜː(r)/ *vt* (*pres p etc.* **-rr-**) 挖出 ‹*body, corpse*›

disinterested /dɪsˈɪntrəstɪd/ *adj* **1** (impartial) 公正的 **2** (uninterested) 不感兴趣的

disinterment /ˌdɪsɪnˈtɜːmənt/ *n* 掘出尸骨

disinvest /ˌdɪsɪnˈvest/
A *vi* (withdraw) 撤资; (reduce holding) 减资
B *vt* (withdraw) 从…撤资 ‹*shares*›; (reduce holding of) 从…减资 ‹*shares*›

disinvestment /ˌdɪsɪnˈvestmənt/ *n* [u] 撤资

disjointed /dɪsˈdʒɔɪntɪd/ *adj* 不连贯的

disjunction /dɪsˈdʒʌŋkʃn/ *n* formal 分离

disk /dɪsk/ *n* **1** Comput 磁盘; **on ~** 存在磁盘上的 **2** Amer = **disc**

disk: ~ directory *n* 磁盘目录; **~ drive** *n* 磁盘驱动器

diskette /dɪˈsket/ *n* 软盘

disk: ~ management *n* [u] 磁盘管理; **~ operating system** *n* 磁盘操作系统; **~ player** *n* 磁盘播放器; **~ space** *n* [u] 磁盘空间

dislike /dɪsˈlaɪk/
A *vt* (feel distaste towards) 不喜欢; (feel hostility towards) 厌恶
B *n* **1** [u] (distaste) 不喜欢; (hostility) 厌恶; **to feel ~ for sb./sth.** 对某人/某事物反感; **to take a ~ to sb./sth.** 开始讨厌某人/某事物 **2** [c] (aversion) 不喜欢的事物; **likes and ~s** 好恶

dislocate /ˈdɪsləkeɪt, Amer ˈdɪsləʊkeɪt/ *vt* **1** Med 使…脱臼 ‹*shoulder, knee*› **2** formal (disrupt) 扰乱 ‹*system, traffic*›

dislocation /ˌdɪsləˈkeɪʃn, Amer ˌdɪsləʊˈkeɪʃn/ *n* **1** [c and u] (of shoulder, knee) 脱臼 **2** [u] formal (disruption) 混乱

dislodge /dɪsˈlɒdʒ/ *vt* 强行去除 ‹*object*›; 逐出 ‹*person*›

disloyal /dɪsˈlɔɪəl/ *adj* 不忠实的; **to be ~ to sb./sth.** 对某人/某事不忠

disloyalty /dɪsˈlɔɪəlti/ *n* [c and u] (lack of loyalty) 不忠; (particular instance) 不忠行为; **~ to sb./sth.** 对某人/某事的不忠

dismal /ˈdɪzməl/ *adj* **1** (gloomy) 阴沉的 ‹*day, morning*›; 沮丧的 ‹*mood, spirits*›; 暗淡的 ‹*future, prospect*› **2** (very bad) 十分差劲的; **as a father, he was a ~ failure** 作为父亲, 他很不称职

dismally /ˈdɪzməli/ *adv* **1** (expressing gloom) 沮丧地; (inducing gloom) 令人沮丧地 **2** (completely) 彻底地 ‹*fail*›

dismantle /dɪsˈmæntl/ *vt* **1** (take apart) 拆除 ‹*stand, scaffolding*›; 拆开 ‹*set, motor*› **2** (phase out) «*government, ministry, law*» 逐步废除 ‹*service, organization, system*›

dismast /dɪsˈmɑːst, Amer -ˈmæst/ *vt* 折断…的桅杆

dismay /dɪsˈmeɪ/
A *n* [u] 惊愕; **in ~** 诧异地; **to sb.'s ~** 使某人不安的是; **to fill sb. with ~** 令某人感到恐慌不安
B *vt* 使惊愕; **to be ~ed by** *or* **at sth.** 对某事物感到惊愕

dismayed /dɪsˈmeɪd/ *adj* 惊愕的; **to be ~ that ...** 对…感到震惊

dismember /dɪsˈmembə(r)/ *vt* **1** lit (remove limbs from) «*person*» 肢解 ‹*victim*›; «*animal*» 撕裂…的肢体 ‹*prey*› **2** fig (partition) 瓜分

dismemberment /dɪsˈmembəmənt/ *n* [u] **1** (removal of limbs) 肢解 **2** (partitioning) 瓜分

dismiss /dɪsˈmɪs/ *vt* **1** (reject) 对…不予考虑 ‹*idea, suggestion, possibility*›; **~ sth. as ...** 把某事物作为…而不予理会; **we ~ed that story as an idle rumour** 我们认为那说法是毫无根据的谣言而不予考虑 **2** (put out of mind) 彻底忘掉 ‹*thought, memory*›; 清除 ‹*fear*› **3** (remove from job) 解雇; **to be ~ed from one's post** 被免职 **4** (send out) 让…离开; **to ~ the class** 宣布下课; **the recruits were ~ed** 新兵们被解散了 **5** Jur «*judge*» 驳回 ‹*case, appeal, charges*› **6** Sport (in cricket) 迫使…退场

dismissal /dɪsˈmɪsl/ *n* **1** (rejection of idea, opinion etc.) 不予考虑 **2** (removal from job) (of employee, worker) 解雇; (of minister, director, manager) 撤职 **3** Jur (of appeal, claim) 驳回

dismissive /dɪsˈmɪsɪv/ *adj* 轻蔑的; **to be ~ of sb./sth.** 对某人/某物不屑一顾

dismissively /dɪsˈmɪsɪvli/ *adv* 轻蔑地

dismount /dɪsˈmaʊnt/
A *vi* (from bicycle, motorbike, etc.) 下车; (from horse) 下马
B *vt* **1** (cause to fall) «*horse*» 把…掀下来 ‹*rider*› **2** Mil 取下 ‹*gun*›

> **Disneyland®**
>
> 迪士尼乐园。美国大型游乐园，是世界第一个现代意义上的主题公园（theme park），位于加利福尼亚州的阿纳海姆（Anaheim）。创建人为华特·迪士尼（Walt Disney），1955 年建成。园内有美国主街（Main Street USA）、冒险世界（Adventureland）、边疆世界（Frontierland）和未来世界（Tomorrowland）等景观。1971 年，佛罗里达的迪士尼世界（Disney World）开始营业。目前东京、巴黎、香港都有类似的迪士尼主题公园。上海浦东也准备在近年动工兴建。

disobedience /ˌdɪsəˈbiːdiəns/ *n* [u] 不服从; **~ of the law** 违抗法律

disobedient /ˌdɪsəˈbiːdiənt/ *adj* 不服从的

disobey /ˌdɪsəˈbeɪ/
A *vt* 不服从; **to ~ one's parents** 忤逆父母; **to ~ an order** 违抗命令
B *vi* 不服从

disobliging /ˌdɪsəˈblaɪdʒɪŋ/ *adj* 冒犯的

disorder /dɪsˈɔːdə(r)/ *n* **1** [u] (state of confusion) 混乱; **to retreat in ~** Mil 溃退 **2** [u] (disturbance) 骚乱 **3** [c and u] (disease) 失调; **blood ~** 血液病; **eating ~** 进食障碍

disordered /dɪsˈɔːdəd/ *adj* 失调的

disorderly /dɪsˈɔːdəli/ *adj* **1** (untidy) 杂乱的 ‹*heap*›; (disorganized) 混乱的 ‹*system, arrangement*› **2** (uncontrolled) 目无法纪的 ‹*mob, demonstration, behaviour*›

disorderly conduct, disorderly behaviour *ns* [u] 妨害治安行为

disorganization /dɪsˌɔːɡənaɪˈzeɪʃn, Amer -nɪˈz-/ *n* [u] 缺乏组织

disorganized /dɪsˈɔːɡənaɪzd/ *adj* 杂乱无章的 ‹*plan, campaign, system*›; 缺乏条理的 ‹*person*›

disorient /dɪsˈɔːrient/ *vt* = **disorientate**

disorientate /dɪsˈɔːriənteɪt/ *vt* **1** (make lose sense of direction) 使迷失方向; (make lose sense of time) «*travel, jet lag*» 使失去时间感 **2** (confuse) 使迷惘

disown /dɪsˈəʊn/ *vt* **1** (refuse to acknowledge) 与…断绝关系 ‹*son, daughter, friend*› **2** (deny authorship of) 否认…为自己所写 ‹*article, play*›

disparage /dɪˈspærɪdʒ/ *vt* 贬低

disparagement /dɪˈspærɪdʒmənt/ *n* 贬低

disparaging /dɪˈspærɪdʒɪŋ/ *adj* 贬低的; **to be ~ about sb.** 贬损某人

disparagingly /dɪˈspærɪdʒɪŋli/ *adv* 以贬损的口吻

disparate /ˈdɪspərət/ *adj* **1** (incompatible) 迥然不同的 ‹*aspects, considerations, philosophies*› **2** (very different) 由不相干的成分组成的; **a ~ group** 三教九流的一帮人

disparity /dɪˈspærəti/ *n* 悬殊的差异

dispassionate /dɪˈspæʃənət/ *adj* **1** (impartial) 客观公正的 **2** (unemotional) 冷静的

dispassionately /dɪˈspæʃənətli/ *adv* **1** (impartially) 客观公正地 **2** (unemotionally) 冷静地

dispatch /dɪˈspætʃ/
A *vt* **1** (send) 派遣 ‹*messenger, troops, reinforcements*›; 发送 ‹*letter, report, goods*› **2** (deal with) 迅速完成 ‹*job*›; 迅速解决 ‹*problem*›; 迅速打败 ‹*opponent*› **3** (kill) 杀死 ‹*person, animal*›
B *n* **1** [c] (official report) 公文急件 **2** [c] (news report) 新闻报道 **3** [u] (sending of sb.) 派遣; (sending of sth.) 发送 **4** [u] (killing) 杀死

dispatch: ~ box *n* **1** (for documents) 公文箱; **2** **the D~ Box** Brit Pol [下议院中大臣站立时置于旁边的] 公文箱; **~ rider** *n* 通信员

dispel /dɪˈspel/ *vt* (*pres p etc.* **-ll-**) **1** formal (disperse) 驱散 ‹*mist, cloud, fog*› **2** (drive away) 消除 ‹*anxiety, illusion, rumour*›

dispensable /dɪˈspensəbl/ *adj* 可有可无的

dispensary /dɪˈspensəri/ *n* **1** Brit (chemist's) 药房 **2** (clinic) 诊所

dispensation /ˌdɪspenˈseɪʃn/ *n* formal **1** [u] (exemption) 豁免 **2** [u] (distribution) 分配; **the ~ of justice** 执法 **3** [c and u] (permission) 特许

dispense /dɪˈspens/ *vt* **1** (distribute) 分发 **2** formal (give out) 施与 ‹*charity*›; 给予 ‹*advice*› **3** Jur «*judge*» 执行 ‹*justice, law*› **4** Pharm 配发 ‹*medicine*›; 按…配药 ‹*prescription*›

Phrasal verb

- **dispense with** *vt* [**~ with sth.**] (manage without) 省掉; (get rid of) 摒弃; **let's ~ with the formalities** 咱们不必拘礼了; **to ~ with sb.'s services** 解雇某人

dispenser /dɪˈspensə(r)/ *n* **1** (machine) 自动发放机 **2** (person) 药剂师

dispensing: ~ chemist *n* Brit 药剂师; **~ optician** *n* 配镜师

dispersal /dɪˈspɜːsl/ *n* **1** (scattering) (of people, birds, fumes) 散布; (of seeds) 传播 **2** (breaking up) (of group of people) 疏散; (of group of things) 分散

dispersant /dɪˈspɜːsənt/ *n* 分散剂

disperse /dɪˈspɜːs/
A *vi* **1** (break up) «*crowd, onlookers, rally*» 散去 **2** (thin out) «*fumes, gases, fog*» 消散
B *vt* **1** (cause to thin out) 使…消散 ‹*fumes, gases*› **2** (send in different directions) 驱散 ‹*demonstrators, mob, crowd*› **3** Phys 使色散

dispersion /dɪˈspɜːʃn, Amer dɪˈspɜːrʒn/ *n* [u] **1** formal (of group of people, things) 分散 **2** Phys (of light) 色散

dispirit /dɪˈspɪrɪt/ *vt* 使沮丧; **to be ~ed by sth.** 因某事物而气馁

dispirited /dɪˈspɪrɪtɪd/ *adj* 沮丧的

dispiritedly /dɪˈspɪrɪtɪdli/ *adv* 沮丧地

dispiriting /dɪˈspɪrɪtɪŋ/ *adj* 令人沮丧的

displace /dɪsˈpleɪs/ *vt* **1** (expel) 使背井离乡 **2** (replace) 取代 ‹*leader, subject, runner*› **3** (dislodge) 使…脱位 ‹*component*›; 使…脱臼 ‹*bone, joint*› **4** Naut, Phys 排 ‹*amount of liquid*›; **an object will ~ its own weight in water** 物体的排水量相当于其本身的重量

displaced person *n* 难民

displacement /dɪsˈpleɪsmənt/ *n* **1** (of workers, population) 迁移 **2** (removal) 移位 **3** (replacement) 取代 **4** Naut, Phys 排水量 **5** Psych 情感转移

displacement: ~ activity *n* 替代活动 [人或动物在对立驱力作用下产生的无意识举动]; **~ pump** *n* 容积式泵; **~ tonnage** *n* 排水量吨位

display /dɪˈspleɪ/
A *n* **1** [u and c] Comm (goods for sale) 陈列品; (showing goods for sale) 陈列; **to put sth. on ~** 把某物陈列出来; **the ~s in the shoe shop window** 鞋店橱窗里的陈列品; **for ~ purposes only** 仅供陈列 **2** [u and c] (collection for looking at) 展品; **to be on ~** 被展出; **to go on**

～ 进行展出; **to put sth. on (temporary/permanent) ～** （临时/永久）展出某物; **for ～** 用来展出; **a beautiful floral ～** 漂亮的花卉展品; **do not touch the ～** 勿碰展品 [3] [c] (decorative arrangement) 展览; **to mount a ～** 举办展览 [4] [c] (demonstration) 表演; **to put on/mount a ～ (of sth.)** 进行（某节目的）表演; **an aerobatic ～ team** 特技飞行表演队 [5] [c] (intentional show) 表现; (unintentional show) 流露; **in a ～ of sth.** 作为某物的表现; **to make a ～ of sth.** 展示某物; **a ～ of might** 力量的显示 [6] [c] (pretence) [装出的] 样子; **to make a great ～ of ...** 极力装出…的样子 [7] [c] Zool 求偶炫耀 [8] [c] Print, Advertg 特排; **～ typeface/caption** 特排字体/说明文字 [9] [c] Electron, Comput, TV (representation) 显示; (information) 显示的信息; (monitor) 显示器; **digital ～** 数码显示; **the brightness of the ～** 显示屏的亮度; **a ～ screen/unit** 显示屏/装置

d

B *vt* [1] Comm 陈列 ‹*goods*› [2] (set out visibly) 张贴 ‹*notice, advertisement*›; 公布 ‹*list of winners*›; 悬挂 ‹*flag*›; 出示 ‹*permit, pass*›; 标示 ‹*time, price, words, figures, logo*› [3] (exhibit) 展出 ‹*object*› [4] Electron, Comput 显示 ‹*data, information*› [5] pej (flaunt) 炫耀 ‹*wealth, beauty, knowledge*› [6] (expose to view) 显示出 ‹*physical feature, colour*› [7] (give evidence of) 表现出 ‹*ignorance, emotion, virtue, strength*›

C *vi* (exhibit distinctive behaviour) «*male animal*» 求偶炫耀; (extend feathers) «*bird*» 展开尾羽; **these peacocks rarely ～** 这些孔雀难得开屏

display: ～ advertisement *n* [报纸、杂志上的] 大型广告; **～ cabinet, ～ case** *ns* 陈列柜; **～ panel** *n* [1] (for information) 公告板; [2] Electron 显示器; **～ rack** *n* 陈列架; **～ type** *n* 特排字体; **～ window** *n* 橱窗

displease /dɪs'pliːz/ *vt* (upset) 使不愉快; (annoy) 使生气

displeased /dɪs'pliːzd/ *adj* 不愉快的; **to be ～ with** *or* **at sb./sth.** 对某人/某事物感到不快

displeasing /dɪs'pliːzɪŋ/ *adj* 令人不快的

displeasure /dɪs'pleʒə(r)/ *n* [u] 不悦; **to show one's ～ at sth.** 对某事物表示不满; **to sb.'s great ～** 令某人深感不满的是; **much to sb.'s ～** 令某人很生气的是

disposable /dɪ'spəʊzəbl/

A *adj* [1] (throwaway) 一次性的 ‹*chopsticks, nappy, camera*› [2] (available) 可支配的 ‹*capital, time*›

B disposables *npl* 一次性用品

disposable: ～ assets *npl* 可支配资产; **～ income** *n* 可支配收入

disposal /dɪ'spəʊzl/ *n* [1] (removal) 处理 [2] (sale) 出售 [3] (availability for use) **at sb.'s ～** 供某人使用; **I am at your ～** 我听候你的吩咐

disposal value *n* 清算价值

dispose /dɪ'spəʊz/ *vt* [1] (encourage) 使倾向于; **to ～ sb. to sth./to do sth.** 使某人倾向于某事/做某事 [2] formal (arrange) 布置 ‹*furniture, ornaments*›; 部署 ‹*troops*›; **man proposes, but God ～s** Prov 谋事在人，成事在天

Phrasal verb

- **dispose of** *vt* [～ of sth./sb.]
[1] (get rid of) 清除 ‹*bomb*›; 销毁 ‹*evidence*›; 处理掉 ‹*rubbish, waste*› [2] (deal with) 解决; **to ～ of all the food** 把食物全吃光; **to ～ of the opposition in a decisive 4-0 win** 以4比0的绝对优势战胜对手 [3] (redistribute through sale) 卖掉; (redistribute as gift) 赠送 [4] (kill) 杀死; **to ～ of mice** 灭鼠

disposed /dɪ'spəʊzd/ *adj pred* [1] (inclined, willing) 愿意的; **to be/feel ～ to do sth.** 有意做某事; **should you feel so ～** formal 如果你愿意 [2] (having tendency towards sth.) 有倾向的; **to be ～ to sth./to do sth.** 倾向于某事物/做某事; **to be ill-/well-～ to** *or* **towards sb./sth.** 对某人/某事物没有/有好感

disposition /ˌdɪspə'zɪʃn/ *n* [1] (temperament) 性情; **to be of** *or* **to have a cheerful/an irritable ～** 性格开朗/急躁 [2] (tendency) 倾向; (inclination) 意向; **to have/show a ～ to sth./to do sth.** 对某事物/做某事有/表现出兴趣 [3] formal (arrangement) (of objects, people) 布置; (of troops) 部署

dispossess /ˌdɪspə'zes/ *vt* Jur 剥夺; **to ～ sb. of sth.** «*court, court order*» 剥夺某人的… ‹*wealth, home, land, property*›; **to be ～ed of sth.** 被剥夺某物; **a ～ed people** (poor) 一无所有的民族; (politically) 毫无前途的民族; **the ～ed** 被剥夺财产者

disproportion /ˌdɪsprə'pɔːʃn/ *n* 不成比例; **a ～ between sth. and sth.** 某物与某物之间不成比例

disproportionate /ˌdɪsprə'pɔːʃənət/ *adj* 不成比例的; **the quality is ～ to the price** 质量与价格不相称

disproportionately /ˌdɪsprə'pɔːʃənətli/ *adv* 不成比例地 ‹*large, small*›

disprove /dɪs'pruːv/ *vt* 证明…是虚假的

disputable /dɪ'spjuːtəbl/ *adj* 可质疑的; **it is ～ whether ...** 是否…可商榷

disputation /ˌdɪspjuː'teɪʃn/ *n* [c and u] formal 争论

disputatious /ˌdɪspjuː'teɪʃəs/ *adj* formal 好争论的

dispute /dɪ'spjuːt/

A *n* [1] [c and u] (quarrel) 争吵; (argument) 争论; **to have a ～ with sb. about** *or* **over sth.** 在某事上与某人发生纠纷 [2] [u] (disagreement) 争议; **to be in ～ with sb. about** *or* **over sth.** 在某事上与某人有争议; **beyond** *or* **without ～** 无可置疑地; **to be under ～** 处于争议中; **to be open to ～** 尚不确定

B *vt* [1] (argue) 就…发生争论 [2] (question) 对…表示怀疑 [3] (claim possession of) 争夺

C *vi* 争论; **to ～ with sb. (about sth.)** （为了某事物）与某人争论

disputed /dɪ'spjuːtɪd/ *adj* 有争议的 ‹*territory, property, claim*›

disqualification /dɪsˌkwɒlɪfɪ'keɪʃn/ *n* [1] [u] (from post, career) 取消资格; Sport 取消参赛资格; **～ from sth./doing sth.** 某事/做某事资格的取消; **～ from driving** 取消驾驶资格 [2] [c] (thing which disqualifies) 取消资格的原因

disqualify /dɪs'kwɒlɪfaɪ/ *vt* [1] (from post, career) 取消…的资格; **he's been disqualified (from driving)** 他被取消了（驾驶）资格 [2] Sport 取消…的参赛资格

disquiet /dɪs'kwaɪət/

A *n* [u] 不安

B *vt* **to be ～ed** 感到不安

disquieting /dɪs'kwaɪətɪŋ/ *adj* 令人不安的

disquietingly /dɪs'kwaɪətɪŋli/ *adv* 令人不安地

disquisition /ˌdɪskwɪ'zɪʃn/ *n* formal (oral) 专题讨论; (written) 专题论文; **a ～ on sth.** 某方面的专题论文

disregard /ˌdɪsrɪ'ɡɑːd/

A *vt* 不理会

B *n* [u] 忽视; **to show ～ for sth./sb.** 不顾及某事物/某人

disrepair /ˌdɪsrɪ'peə(r)/ *n* [u] 失修; **to be in/fall into ～** 破烂不堪

disreputable /dɪs'repjʊtəbl/ *adj* [1] (unsavoury) 不光彩的 ‹*behaviour*›; 名声不好的 ‹*person, place, establishment*› [2] (dishonest) 不名誉的 ‹*method, procedure*› [3] (unkempt) 邋遢的 ‹*person, clothing*›

disreputably /dɪs'repjʊtəbli/ *adv* 不名誉地

disrepute /ˌdɪsrɪ'pjuːt/ *n* [u] 名声不好; **to hold sb./sth. in ～** 对某人/某事物评价很低; **to bring sth. into ～** 使某事物蒙受耻辱; **to fall into ～** 名誉扫地

disrespect /ˌdɪsrɪ'spekt/ *n* 不尊敬; **to show ～ to** *or* **towards** *or* **for sb./sth. by doing sth.** 通过做某事表现出对某人/某事物的不敬; **no ～ (to you), but I think you're a little tired** 我（对你）没有不敬之意，只是觉得你有些累了

disrespectful /ˌdɪsrɪ'spektfl/ *adj* 无礼的; **to be ～ to** *or* **towards sb./sth.** 不尊敬某人/某物

disrespectfully /ˌdɪsrɪ'spektfəli/ *adv* 无礼地

disrobe /dɪs'rəʊb/ *vi* formal [1] (undress) 脱衣服 [2] (take off official robes) «*monarch*» 脱下王袍; «*judge*» 脱下黑袍; «*official*» 脱下制服; «*clergy*» 脱下法衣

disrupt /dɪs'rʌpt/ *vt* 使…中断 ‹*traffic, power supply*›; 扰乱 ‹*meeting, plans, lifestyle*›

disruption /dɪs'rʌpʃn/ *n* (of traffic, power supply) 中断; (of meeting, plans, lifestyle) 扰乱

disruptive /dɪs'rʌptɪv/ *adj* 引起混乱的

disruptiveness /dɪs'rʌptɪvnɪs/ *n* [u] 捣乱

diss /dɪs/ *vt* colloq 对…无礼

dissatisfaction /dɪˌsætɪs'fækʃn/ *n* [u] 不满; **～ with** *or* **at sb./sth.** 对某人/某事物的不满

dissatisfied /dɪ'sætɪsfaɪd/ *adj* 不满意的; **to be ～ with sb./sth.** 对某人/某事物不满

dissect /dɪ'sekt/ *vt* [1] (cut up) 解剖 ‹*body*› [2] (analyse) 剖析 ‹*article, speech*›

dissection /dɪ'sekʃn/ *n* [1] (cutting up) 解剖 [2] (analysis) 剖析

dissemble /dɪ'sembl/ *vi, vt* formal 掩盖

disseminate /dɪ'semɪneɪt/ *vt* 传播

dissemination /dɪˌsemɪ'neɪʃn/ *n* [u] 传播

dissension /dɪ'senʃn/ *n* [u] 纷争

dissent /dɪ'sent/

A *n* [u] [1] (disagreement) 异议; **～ from sth.** 对…的异议 ‹*policy, decision, opinion*›; **to brook** *or* **tolerate no ～** 不容许有异议 [2] Sport 不服裁判

B *vi* 持异议; **to ～ from sth.** 对某事持不同观点

dissenter /dɪ'sentə(r)/ *n* 持异议者

dissenting /dɪ'sentɪŋ/ *adj* 反对的 ‹*opinion, view*›; 持异议的 ‹*protester, voice, group*›

dissertation /ˌdɪsə'teɪʃn/ *n* [1] Brit Univ 学位论文; **a ～ on sb./sth.** 关于某人/某事物的学位论文 [2] (lengthy written discussion) 专题论文

disservice /dɪs'sɜːvɪs/ *n* 损害; **to do sb./sth. a ～, to do a ～ to sb./sth.** 对某人/某事物造成损害

dissidence /'dɪsɪdəns/ *n* [u] 持不同政见

dissident /'dɪsɪdənt/

A *n* 持不同政见者

B *adj attrib* 持不同政见的 ‹*writer, group, organization*›; 政见不同的 ‹*opinions, views, movement*›

dissimilar /dɪ'sɪmɪlə(r)/ *adj* 不同的; **to be ～ to** *or* **from sth.** 与某事物不相同

dissimilarity /ˌdɪsɪmɪ'lærəti/ *n* [1] [u] (difference) 不同; **the ～ between the two brothers/in age** 这两兄弟之间的/年龄的不同 [2] [c] (instance of difference) 不同之处; **the dissimilarities between the two novels** 这两本小说之间的不同点

dissimulate /dɪ'sɪmjʊleɪt/ *vi* formal 掩饰

dissipate /'dɪsɪpeɪt/

A *vt* [1] (disperse) 驱散 ‹*fog, mist, clouds*› [2] (dispel) 消除 ‹*fear, anxiety, suspicion*›; 平息 ‹*anger*›; 使…破灭 ‹*hope*› [3] (use up) 耗尽 ‹*energy, effort, resources*› [4] (waste) 浪费 ‹*fortune, talent*›

B *vi* (disperse) 消散; (disappear) 消失

dissipated /'dɪsɪpeɪtɪd/ *adj* 放荡的; **to lead a ～ life** 过花天酒地的生活

dissipation /ˌdɪsɪ'peɪʃn/ *n* [u] [1] (of fog, mist, clouds) 消散 [2] (of fear, anxiety, suspicion) 消除; (of anger) 平息; (of hope) 破灭 [3] (of energy, effort, resources) 耗尽 [4] (debauchery) 放荡

dissociate /dɪ'səʊʃɪeɪt/

A *vt* [1] (separate) 把…分开; **to ～ oneself from**

sb./sth. 和某人/某事物划清界线 **2** Chem 使…离解 ‹compound›
B *vi* **1** (separate) 分开 **2** Chem 离解

dissociation /dɪˌsəʊʃɪ'eɪʃn/ *n* **1** (separation) 分离 **2** Chem 离解 **3** Psych 分裂

dissolute /'dɪsəluːt/ *adj* 放荡的

dissolution /ˌdɪsə'luːʃn/ *n* **1** [c and u] (formal ending) (of parliament, assembly) 解散; (of partnership, marriage) 解除 **2** [u] (dissipation) 放荡

dissolve /dɪ'zɒlv/
A *vt* **1** (liquefy) 使溶解; **~ the sugar in water** 把糖溶于水中 **2** (break up) 解除 ‹*partnership, marriage*›; 解散 ‹*assembly, meeting, organization, parliament*›
B *vi* **1** (liquefy) 溶解; **salt ~s in water** 盐溶于水 **2** (disappear) «*hopes*» 破灭; «*fear, feelings*» 消失; «*courage*» 丧失; **to ~ into thin air** 消失得无影无踪; **to ~ in** *or* **into tears** 不禁潸然泪下 **3** (break up) «*assembly, meeting, parliament*» 解散 **4** Cin, TV 叠化; **one scene ~s into another** 一个镜头淡入另一个镜头
C *n* Cin, TV 叠化

dissonance /'dɪsənəns/ *n* **1** [c and u] (inharmonious sounds) 不和谐音 **2** [c and u] Mus 不协和音 **3** [u] (tension, clash) 不和谐

dissonant /'dɪsənənt/ *adj* **1** (inharmonious) 刺耳的 **2** Mus 不协和的 **3** (clashing) 不和谐的

dissuade /dɪ'sweɪd/ *vt* 劝阻; **to ~ sb. from sth./doing sth.** 劝某人放弃/不要做某事

dissuasion /dɪ'sweɪʒn/ *n* [u] 劝阻

distaff /'dɪstɑːf, Amer 'dɪstæf/ *n* 纺纱杆

distaff side *n* 母系; **on the ~** 母系的

distance /'dɪstəns/
A *n* **1** [u and c] (length of space between two points) 距离; (condition of being far off) 遥远; **at/from a ~** 在/从远处; **(in/into) the ~** (在/向) 远方; **the ~ of A from B** A 离开 B 的距离; **at a ~ of 10 metres** 在 10 米远; **some ~ (away)** 有相当距离地; **a short/long ~ away** 离得近/远地; **a ~ race** 长跑; **to be no ~** 很近; **to keep one's ~ (from sb./sth.)** (与某人/某物) 保持距离; **to remain at a safe ~ from sth.** 处在不受某物伤害的安全距离; **within walking/shouting ~** 在步行可达/能听见喊话的距离内; **~ lends enchantment (to the view)** Prov 距离产生美 **2** [u and c] (interval in time) 间隔; (condition of being far away in time) 久远; **from this ~** 隔了这么久; **at a ~ of 50 years** 相隔 50 年; **~ had blurred her memories** 时间隔得很久, 她的记忆已经模糊了 **3** [c] fig (gap) 差距; **the ~ between rich and poor** 贫富差距; **the ~ between fashion and art** 时尚与艺术的区别 **4** [u] (reserve) 冷淡; **his ~ is the result of shyness** 他态度冷淡是因为害羞 **5** [c] Sport (boxing) **the ~** 拳击比赛规定时间; **to go the (full) ~** «*boxer*» 打完回合; «*boxing match*» 打满全局; fig 坚持到底; **the striker may not go the ~** 前锋可能无法打完比赛
B *vt* (dissociate, alienate) 使疏远; **to ~ sb. from sb./sth.** 使某人疏远某人/某物; **to become ~d from sb.** 与某人的关系变得疏远; **to ~ one's remarks from the government view** 使言论与政府的观点保持距离
C *v refl* **to ~ oneself (from sb./sth.)** 疏远 (某人/某物)

distance: ~ learning *n* [u] 远程学习; **~ race** *n* 长跑比赛; **~ runner** *n* 中长跑运动员

distant /'dɪstənt/ *adj* **1** (remote) 远处的 ‹*sound*›; 久远的 ‹*time, event, memory*›; **twenty miles ~ from London** 离伦敦 20 英里远; **in the ~ past/future** 在遥远的过去/未来 **2** (far removed) 远房的 ‹*cousin, relation, relative*›; 远支的 ‹*descendant*› **3** fig (vague) 些微的 ‹*connection, relationship, resemblance*› **4** (cool, reserved) 冷淡的 ‹*person, manner, attitude*› **5** (dreamy) 恍惚的 ‹*look, gaze, smile*›

distantly /'dɪstəntli/ *adv* **1** (far away) 在远处 ‹*audible, visible*› **2** (not closely) 些微地 ‹*connected, associated, resemble*›; **to be ~ related to sb.** 和某人是远亲 **3** (coolly) 冷淡地 ‹*act, say, look, greet, smile*›

distaste /dɪs'teɪst/ *n* [u] (mild dislike) 反感; (aversion) 厌恶; **~ for sb./sth.** 对某人/某事物的反感; **to frown in ~** 厌恶地皱眉

distasteful /dɪs'teɪstfl/ *adj* 令人反感的; **to be ~ to sb.** 令某人反感

distemper[1] /dɪ'stempə(r)/
A *n* [u] **1** (paint) (for use on walls) 水性涂料; (for scene-painting) 胶画颜料 **2** (technique) 胶画法
B *vt* 用水性涂料涂刷 ‹*wall, room*›

distemper[2] *n* [u] Vet 瘟热

distend /dɪ'stend/
A *vt* 使膨胀
B *vi* 膨胀

distended /dɪ'stendɪd/ *adj* 鼓胀的 ‹*stomach, bladder*›

distension /dɪ'stenʃn/ *n* 鼓胀; **stomach ~** 胃胀

distich /'dɪstɪk/ *n* 押韵对句

distil Brit, **distill** Amer /dɪ'stɪl/ (*pres p etc.* **-ll-**)
A *vt* **1** (purify) 用蒸馏法提取; **to ~ water** 将水蒸馏净化; **to ~ sth. from sth.** 用蒸馏法从某物中提取某物 **2** (make) 用蒸馏法制造 ‹*whisky, spirit, vinegar*› **3** (extract essence from) 提炼 **4** (extract meaning from) 吸取…的精华 ‹*thought, wisdom*›
B *vi* «*company, person*» 用蒸馏法制造

Phrasal verb

- **distil off** *vt* [**~ off sth., ~ sth. off**] 用蒸馏法去除

distillation /ˌdɪstɪ'leɪʃn/ *n* **1** (of liquids) 蒸馏 **2** (essence) 精华; (reduction) 摘要

distilled /dɪ'stɪld/ *adj* **1** (purified) 蒸馏的 ‹*liquid*› **2** (comprising the essence) 凝炼的 ‹*wisdom, research*›

distilled water *n* [u] 蒸馏水

distiller /dɪ'stɪlə(r)/ *n* (person) 酿酒者; (company) 酿酒公司

distillery /dɪ'stɪləri/ *n* 酿酒厂

distinct /dɪ'stɪŋkt/ *adj* **1** (clearly visible) 清晰的; (easily perceived) 明显的 **2** *attrib* (indisputable) 确定无疑的 **3** (different) 不同的; **to be ~ from sth.** 与某事物不同

distinction /dɪ'stɪŋkʃn/ *n* **1** [c] (difference, contrast) 差别; **to draw** *or* **make a ~ between sb./sth. and sb./sth.** 把…和…区别开 **2** [u] (separation) 区分; **without ~ of rank** 不分级别地 **3** [u] (pre-eminence) 卓越; **to serve with ~** 服务优良; **a writer of ~** 优秀作家 **4** [u] (elegance) 优雅; (distinctive quality) 特质; **a woman of great ~** 气质优雅出众的女士 **5** [c] Sch, Univ (high pass grade) 优等成绩 **6** [c] (specific honour) 荣誉称号; (decoration) 奖章; **to win a ~ for bravery** 获得勇气勋章

distinctive /dɪ'stɪŋktɪv/ *adj* 特别的; **to be ~ of sth.** 是某物的特点

distinctly /dɪ'stɪŋktli/ *adv* **1** (clearly) 清晰地 ‹*speak, hear, see*› **2** (categorically) 确切地; **I ~ heard the sound of a door shutting** 我的确听见了关门声 **3** (decidedly) 确定无疑地; **he was looking ~ better** 他看起来确实好多了

distinguish /dɪ'stɪŋgwɪʃ/
A *vt* **1** (differentiate) 区分; **to ~ sb./sth. from sb./sth.** 将…和…区分开来; **to ~ right from wrong** 明辨是非 **2** (mark out) 使得以区分; (characterize) 是…的特征; **what ~es sport from games?** 体育何以有别于游戏? **3** (make out) 辨别出
B *vi* 区分; **to ~ between red and green** 分辨红色和绿色
C *v refl* **to ~ oneself by doing sth.** 因做某事而受人注目; **to ~ oneself as sth.** 作为…而享有盛名

distinguishable /dɪ'stɪŋgwɪʃəbl/ *adj* **1** (different) 可区分开的; **to be ~ from sth.** 可与某事物区分开 **2** (discernible) 可辨认出的

distinguished /dɪ'stɪŋgwɪʃt/ *adj* **1** (dignified) 优雅高贵的 ‹*person, appearance, manner*› **2** (famous) 著名的; (eminent) 显赫的; **a ~ career** 辉煌生涯

distinguishing /dɪ'stɪŋgwɪʃɪŋ/ *adj attrib* 区别性的 ‹*mark, feature*›

distort /dɪ'stɔːt/
A *vt* **1** (physically) 使…扭曲 ‹*face*›; 使…失真 ‹*voice*›; 使…变形 ‹*metal*› **2** (misrepresent or skew) 歪曲 ‹*truth, fact, history*›; 曲解 ‹*meaning, words, text*›; 篡改 ‹*result, figures, statistics*› **3** Electron 使…畸变 ‹*electrical signal, sound wave*›
B *vi* «*face*» 扭曲; «*voice*» 失真; «*metal*» 变形

distorted /dɪ'stɔːtɪd/ *adj* 扭曲的 ‹*features, face*›; 变形的 ‹*limb, metal, structure*›

distortion /dɪ'stɔːʃn/ *n* **1** (of metal) 变形; (of sound) 失真; (of features) 扭曲 **2** (of truth, fact, history) 歪曲; (of meaning, words, text) 曲解 **3** (of result, figures, statistics) 篡改

distract /dɪ'strækt/ *vt* **1** (break concentration of) 使…分心 ‹*person*›; (divert) 转移…的注意力 ‹*person*›; 转移 ‹*attention, thoughts*›; **to ~ sb. from doing sth.** 使某人不能专心做某事; **to ~ sb./sth. from sth.** 转移某人对某事物的注意力/把某种思绪从某事物上引开; **don't ~ me from my work** 别影响我专心工作 **2** (entertain) 给…以消遣

distracted /dɪ'stræktɪd/ *adj* **1** (unable to concentrate) 注意力分散的 **2** (very unhappy) 心烦意乱的; **to be ~ with sth.** 由于…而心烦意乱 ‹*grief, worry*›

distractedly /dɪ'stræktɪdli/ *adv* **1** (absent-mindedly) 心不在焉地 **2** (intensely) 强烈地; **to love sb. ~** 深爱某人; **to weep ~** 痛哭

distracting /dɪ'stræktɪŋ/ *adj* **1** (disturbing) 令人心烦意乱的 **2** (diverting) 令人忘忧的

distraction /dɪ'strækʃn/ *n* **1** [u] (inattention) 分心 **2** [c] (diversion) 分心之事 **3** [c] (entertainment) 娱乐 **4** [u] (madness) 精神错乱; **to drive sb. to ~** 把某人逼疯; **to love sb. to ~** 爱某人爱得发狂

distraint /dɪ'streɪnt/ *n* [u] 扣押财物

distraught /dɪ'strɔːt/ *adj* 心烦意乱的; **to be ~ with worry** 心烦意乱; **to be ~ at** *or* **over sth.** 为某事物烦心

distress /dɪ'stres/
A *n* [u] **1** (mental anguish) 痛苦; (physical pain) 疼痛; **to be in ~** (mentally) 感到痛苦; (physically) 感到疼痛; **~ at** *or* **over sth.** 为某事物痛苦; **to cause ~ to sb.** 给某人带来痛苦; **to sb.'s ~** 让某人痛苦的是 **2** (poverty) 贫困; **to live in ~** 生活贫困 **3** (danger) 危难; **a ship in ~** 遇险的船; **she was a damsel in ~** 她是位落难女子 **4** Med 不适; **to be in ~** 感到难受
B *vt* **1** (worry) 使苦恼; (upset) 使痛苦; **to ~ oneself** 犯愁 **2** (artificially age) 把…做旧 ‹*furniture, leather*›

distress call *n* (signal) 遇险求救信号; (phone call) 遇险求救电话

distressed /dɪ'strest/ *adj* **1** (upset) 苦恼的; (distraught) 痛苦的; **to be ~ at** *or* **by sth.** 为某事物痛苦 **2** (artificially aged) 做旧的 ‹*furniture, leather*›

distressing /dɪ'stresɪŋ/ *adj* **1** (worrisome) 令人苦恼的 **2** (upsetting) 使人痛苦的

distress: ~ rocket *n* 遇险信号火箭; **~ sale** *n* 亏本甩卖; **~ signal** *n* 遇险求救信号

distribute /dɪ'strɪbjuːt/ *vt* **1** (share out) 分发 ‹*alms, food, leaflets*›; 分配 ‹*profits, possessions*›; 散布 ‹*information*›; **to ~ sth. to sb.** 把某物分发给某人; **she ~d the money among the poor** 她把钱分给穷人; **to ~ the prizes** 颁发奖品 **2** Comm (supply, deliver) 分销 ‹*goods, supplies*› **3** (spread out) 分散 ‹*load, weight*›; **the cargo should be evenly ~d** 货物应该均匀放置 **4** (disperse) **to be ~d** «*flora, fauna, mineral deposits*» 分布; **fossil remains are ~d**

d

throughout the upper strata 化石遍布上部地层

distributed: ~ data processing *n* [u] 分布式数据处理; **~ system** *n* [u] 分布式系统

distribution /ˌdɪstrɪˈbjuːʃn/ *n* 1 [u] (of food) 分发; (of funds, resources, wealth) 分配; (of information) 散布; (of goods, supplies) 分销 2 [c] Geog (of flora, fauna, minerals) 分布 3 [u] (of weight, burden) 分散

distribution: ~ board *n* 配电盘; **~ cost** *n* 配送成本; **~ list** *n* 邮件发送列表

distributor /dɪˈstrɪbjʊtə(r)/ *n* 1 Comm 分销商 2 Aut 配电器

district /ˈdɪstrɪkt/ *n* 1 (region) 区域; (of country) 地区; **a mountainous ~** 山区 2 (of city, town) 区; **the business ~ of a city** 城市的商业区 3 (administrative area) 行政区; **an electoral ~** 选区; **a ~ councillor** 区政务委员会委员

district: ~ attorney *n* Amer 地方检察官; **~ council** *n* Brit 区政务委员会; **~ court** *n* Amer (federal court) 联邦地方法院; (state court) 州地方法院; **~ heating** *n* [u] 区域供热; **~ nurse** ▸**p. 409** *n* Brit [上门护理的] 区域护士; **D~ of Columbia** *pr n* 哥伦比亚特区

distrust /dɪsˈtrʌst/

A *vt* 不信任

B *n* [u] 不信任; **~ of sb./sth.** 对某人/某事物的怀疑

distrustful /dɪsˈtrʌstfl/ *adj* 不信任的; **to be ~ of sb./sth.** 不相信某人/某事物

disturb /dɪˈstɜːb/

A *vt* 1 (interrupt) 打扰; **'do not ~'** "请勿打扰" 2 (upset) «*news, event*» 使不安; **it ~s me to hear you say that** 听你说那样的话，我感到很不安; **to ~ the peace** Jur 扰乱治安 3 (disarrange) 弄乱 ‹*papers, bedclothes*›; 搅乱 ‹*water, sediment*›; **something had ~ed the surface of the lake** 有什么东西打破了湖面的平静

B *v refl* **to ~ oneself** 给自己带来麻烦; **don't ~ yourself on my account** 别为我麻烦了

disturbance /dɪˈstɜːbəns/ *n* 1 [u] (interruption, inconvenience) 打扰; (disarrangement) 弄乱; **he could brook no ~ of his routine** 他不能容忍自己的日常惯例被打乱 2 [c] (riot, outburst) 骚乱; **to cause a ~ of the peace** Jur 扰乱治安

disturbed /dɪˈstɜːbd/ *adj* 1 Psych 心理失常的; **she had an extremely ~ childhood** 她在童年时期心理极不正常 2 (restless) 烦躁的 ‹*night*›; 不安稳的 ‹*sleep*› 3 (disarranged) 弄乱了的 ‹*papers*›; 搅乱了的 ‹*water, sediment*›

disturbing /dɪˈstɜːbɪŋ/ *adj* 令人不安的 ‹*news, event, film*›

disturbingly /dɪˈstɜːbɪŋli/ *adv* 令人不安地

disunity /dɪsˈjuːnəti/ *n* [u] 不团结

disuse /dɪsˈjuːs/ *n* [u] 不用; **to fall into ~** «*machine, building*» 废弃

disused /dɪsˈjuːzd/ *adj* 废弃的 ‹*building, mine, railway line, factory*›

disyllabic /daɪˈsɪlæbɪk, dɪ-/ *adj* 双音节的

ditch /dɪtʃ/

A *n* 沟

B *vt* colloq 1 (get rid of) 抛弃 ‹*partner, friend*›; 丢弃 ‹*car, machinery*›; **to ~ one's boyfriend** 甩掉男友 2 Aviat (crash-land) «*pilot, crew*» 使…在海上迫降 ‹*plane*›

C *vi* Aviat colloq «*pilot, crew*» 作海上迫降

ditch: ~digger *n* 挖沟者; **~water** *n* [u] 沟中死水

dither /ˈdɪðə(r)/ colloq

A *vi* 犹豫不决; **to ~ over** *or* **about sth.** 在某事上犹豫不决; **don't just stand there ~ing!** 别站在那里犹豫不决!

B *n* **to be in a** *or* **all of a ~** 焦虑不安

ditherer /ˈdɪðərə(r)/ *n* colloq 优柔寡断的人

ditsy /ˈdɪtsi/ *adj* Amer colloq = **ditzy**

ditto /ˈdɪtəʊ/

A *n* 同上; **2 dozen knives, ~ forks** 两打刀子，同等数量的叉子

B *adv* colloq 1 (also) 同样地; **the food is awful and ~ the nightlife** 饭菜很糟糕，夜生活也一样 2 (expressing agreement) (I agree) 同意; (me too) 我也是; **I'm fed up — ~** 我真是受够了——我也是

ditto marks *npl* 表示"同上"的符号 ["]

ditty /ˈdɪti/ *n* (song) 小曲; (poem) 小诗

ditzy /ˈdɪtsi/ *adj* Amer colloq 没头脑的

diuretic /ˌdaɪjʊˈretɪk/

A *adj* 利尿的

B *n* 利尿剂

diurnal /daɪˈɜːnl/ *adj* 1 (of or during the day) 白天的 2 Zool 日间活动的 ‹*species*›

diva /ˈdiːvə/ *n* 著名女歌唱家

divan /dɪˈvæn, Amer ˈdaɪvæn/ *n* 1 (sofa) [无靠背和扶手的] 长沙发 2 **~ (bed)** 厚垫睡榻

dive /daɪv/

A *vi* (*pt* **~d**, Amer **dove**) 1 (into water) 跳水 2 (as hobby, job) 潜水; (underwater) «*submarine, fish, diver*» 下潜 3 (in air) «*aircraft, bird, flying insect*» 俯冲 4 (lunge) 猛冲; (move quickly) 猛地伸手; **to ~ under the bed/into the bushes** 急忙钻到床底下/灌木丛里; **to ~ into one's pocket/bag** colloq 突然把手伸进口袋/袋子; **he ~d into it with missionary zeal** fig 他以传教士般的热情投入其中 5 (drop suddenly) «*profit, price, sales*» 突然下降; «*hopes*» 突然失落; «*fortunes*» 突然转坏

B *n* 1 (plunge into water) 跳水 2 (swimming under sea) 潜水; (movement to deeper level) 下潜; **to be on a ~** 在潜水 3 (steep descent of aircraft, bird) 俯冲; **to go into a ~** 开始俯冲; **to pull out of a ~** 停止俯冲 4 (lunge) 猛扑; **to make a ~ for sth.** 扑向某物 5 Sport (in soccer) 假摔; (in boxing) 佯装被击倒; **to take a ~** «*boxer*» 佯装被击倒; «*footballer*» 假摔 6 (sudden drop) (in profits, prices) 突然下降; (of hopes) 突然失落; **to take a ~** 突然下降; **the party's fortunes have taken a ~** 该党的时运急转直下 7 colloq pej (bar) 低级酒馆; (club) 低级夜总会

Phrasal verbs

- **dive for** *vt* [**~ for sth.**]
  1 (in water) «*diver*» 潜水寻找 ‹*pearls, coral, wrecks*› 2 Sport **to ~ for the ball** «*player, goalkeeper*» 鱼跃扑球 3 (move quickly towards) 扑向 ‹*exit, door*›; **to ~ for cover** 冲向躲避处
- **dive in** *vi* 1 (into water) 跳入水中 2 (enter quickly) 冲进来 3 fig (act impulsively) 冲动行事

dive: ~-bomb *vt* «*plane, pilot*» 俯冲轰炸 ‹*town, building, target*›; **~-bomber** *n* 俯冲轰炸机; **~-bombing** *n* [u] 俯冲轰炸; **~master** *n* 潜水长

diver /ˈdaɪvə(r)/ ▸**p. 409** *n* 1 (for sport) 潜水员 2 Zool (animal) 潜水动物; (bird) 潜鸟

diverge /daɪˈvɜːdʒ/ *vi* 1 (separate) «*road, route, line*» 分叉; **their paths ~d** fig 他们分道扬镳了 2 (differ) 相异; **to ~ from sth.** 偏离某事物; **her approach to parenting ~d from her mother's** 她的育儿方式与她母亲不同

divergence /daɪˈvɜːdʒəns/ *n* 1 [u] (differentiation) 区别 2 [c] (difference) 分歧

divergent /daɪˈvɜːdʒənt/ *adj* 有分歧的 ‹*opinions*›; 不同的 ‹*interests, approaches*›

diverse /daɪˈvɜːs/ *adj* 1 (varied) 多种多样的 2 (different) 不同的

diversification /daɪˌvɜːsɪfɪˈkeɪʃn/ *n* [u] 多样化

diversify /daɪˈvɜːsɪfaɪ/

A *vt* 1 (vary) 使…多样化 ‹*skills, interests*› 2 (increase variety of) «*company*» 增加…的种类 ‹*range, services, investment*›

B *vi* «*company*» 从事多种经营; **to ~ into sth.** 在某方面拓展经营范围

diversion /daɪˈvɜːʃn, Amer daɪˈvɜːrʒn/ *n* 1 (redirection) 转向; **the ~ of the river** 河流的改道; **~ of funds** Fin 资金的转移; Jur 资金的挪用 2 (drawing attention away) 转移注意力的事物; **we need to create a ~ in order to escape** 为了逃走，我们需要制造事端来转移视线 3 (pastime) 消遣; **a ~ from sth.** 注意力从某事物上移开的消遣 4 Mil 佯攻; **to create a ~** 发动佯攻 5 Brit (of road traffic) 临时改道; (detour) 临时绕行路

diversionary /daɪˈvɜːʃənəri, Amer daɪˈvɜːrʒəneri/ *adj* 牵制性的 ‹*tactic, raid, action*›; 转移注意力的 ‹*argument, point, remark*›

diversion sign *n* Brit 改道标志

diversity /daɪˈvɜːsəti/ *n* 1 [u] (variety) 多样性; **the ~ in education** 教育的多元化 2 [c] (difference) 差异性; **a great ~ of opinions** 众说纷纭

divert /daɪˈvɜːt/ *vt* 1 (redirect) 使…转向 ‹*road, course*›; 使…改道 ‹*river*›; 使…绕道 ‹*traffic*›; 使…改变航向 ‹*aircraft, ship*›; 转移 ‹*attention*›; 转移…的话题 ‹*conversation*› 2 (reallocate) 改变…的用途 ‹*money, resources*›; **to ~ funds** Fin 转移资金; Jur 挪用资金 3 (amuse) 使愉悦; **her jokes ~ed me a while from my worries** 她讲的笑话把我逗乐了，让我暂时忘记了忧愁

diverting /daɪˈvɜːtɪŋ/ *adj* 有趣的

divest /daɪˈvest/ formal

A *vt* 1 (deprive, dispossess) 剥夺; **to ~ sb. of sth.** 剥夺某人的… ‹*power, rights, property*› 2 (deprive of quality) 使失去; **this production ~s the play of its charm** 这一制作使该剧魅力尽失

B *v refl* 1 **to ~ oneself of sth.** 脱掉 ‹*clothing*›; 摆脱 ‹*beliefs, ideas*› 2 Fin, Comm **to ~ itself of** (sell, dispose of) 处理掉; **the company ~ed itself of 45 per cent of its assets** 公司出售了 45% 的资产

divestiture /daɪˈvestʃə(r)/, **divestment** /daɪˈvestmənt/ *ns* 剥夺财产

divide /dɪˈvaɪd/

A *vt* 1 (split into parts) 分 ‹*food*›; 划分 ‹*area*›; 分隔 ‹*house, room*›; **to ~ the class into small groups** 把班级分成小组; **the world is ~d into rich and poor nations** 国分贫富 2 (share) 分配 ‹*money, time, work*›; **to ~ sth. between** *or* **among several people** 在几个人之间分配某物; **to ~ one's time between cooking and lecturing** 把时间一部分用在做饭上，一部分用在讲课上 3 (separate) 分开; **to ~ sth. from sth.** 把某物与某物分开; **to ~ sb. from** *or* **and sb.** 把某人和某人分开 4 Math 除 ‹*number*›; **to ~ X by Y** X 除以 Y; **X ~d by Y is Z** X 除以 Y 等于 Z; **to ~ Y into X** 用 Y 除 X 5 (cause to disagree, argue) «*row, disagreement, issue*» 使…产生分歧 ‹*friends, party, management*›; **to be ~d** 有分歧; **this issue has ~d the nation** 全国对这个问题意见不一 6 Brit Pol «*MP, government*» **to ~ the House** 把上下议院分为正反两方表决

B *vi* 1 (split) «*group, crowd*» 分开; «*road, river*» 分岔 2 Biol «*cell, organism*» 分裂 3 Math «*number*» 整除; **5 ~s into 10** 5 能整除 10; **10 ~s by 2 and 5** 10 能被 2 和 5 整除 4 Brit Pol «*the House*» 分正反两方表决 5 (cause division) 造成分歧; **to ~ and rule** *or* **conquer** 分而治之

C *n* 1 (split) 分歧; **the ~ between A and B** A 和 B 之间的分歧; **the North-South ~** 南北分歧 2 (boundary) 界限; **to cross the great ~** fig 死去 3 (turning point) 转折点 4 Amer Geog 分水岭

Phrasal verbs

- **divide off**

A *vt* [**~ sth. off, ~ off sth.**] «*barrier*» 把…分隔开 ‹*room, house, area of land*›

B *vi* «*person, couple*» 分开

- **divide out** *vt* [**~ out sth., ~ sth. out**] 分配
- **divide up** *vt* [**~ up sth., ~ sth. up**]
  1 (split up) 把…分开; **to ~ sth. up into sth.**

把某物拆分成某物 **2** (share) 分配 ‹*money, food, land*›

divided /dɪˈvaɪdɪd/ *adj* **1** (separated) 分开的 **2** (in disagreement) 有分歧的 ‹*opinion*›; 分裂的 ‹*nation, political party*›; **to be ~ on** *or* **over sth.** 对某事物意见不一; **~ loyalties** 难以两全的忠诚; **the family was sharply ~** 全家人意见极不一致

divided highway *n* Amer [有分车带的] 双向车道

dividend /ˈdɪvɪdend/ *n* **1** Fin (payment to shareholder) 股息; (payment in football pools) 彩金; **to pay ~s** 支付股息; **to declare a ~** 通告发放股息 **2** fig (bonus) 意外收获; (advantage) 收益; **to pay ~s** 产生收益; **you'll find it ~s dividends to exercise regularly** 你会发现经常锻炼大有好处 **3** Math 被除数

dividend: ~ cover *n* 赢利股息比率; **~ yield** *n* 股息收益率

divider /dɪˈvaɪdə(r)/ *n* **1** (in room) 隔板 **2** (in file) 分隔卡

dividers /dɪˈvaɪdəz/ *npl* 分线规; **a pair of ~** 一副分线规

dividing /dɪˈvaɪdɪŋ/ *adj attrib* 分隔用的 ‹*wall, fence, hedge*›

dividing line *n* 分界线; **to draw a ~ between sth. and sth.** 把某事物和某事物区分开来; **to cross the ~** 越过分界线

divination /ˌdɪvɪˈneɪʃn/ *n* [u] 占卜; **the art of ~** 占卜术

divine[1] /dɪˈvaɪn/ *adj* **1** (of God) 上帝的; (of a god) 神的; **~ will** 天意 **2** (concerning God) 献给上帝的; (concerning a god) 献给神的; **~ service** 礼拜仪式 **3** (deriving from God) 上帝赐予的; (deriving from a god) 神授的; **to believe in the ~ right of kings** 相信君权神授 **4** colloq (wonderful) 极好的; **you look simply ~!** 你看上去漂亮极了!

divine[2] *vt* **1** liter (intuit) 凭直觉发现; (guess) 猜到 **2** (foretell) 预言; **to ~ the future** 预卜未来 **3** (discover) [用占卜杖] 探寻 ‹*water, metal*›

divinely /dɪˈvaɪnli/ *adv* **1** (by God) 凭借上帝的力量; (by a god) 凭借神的力量; (in a godlike manner) 神一般地; **to be ~ inspired** 受到天启; **a ~ ordained event** 天命注定的事件 **2** colloq (wonderfully) 极好地; **~ simple** 极其简单的; **to sing ~** 唱得棒极了

diviner /dɪˈvaɪnə(r)/ *n* = **water diviner**

diving /ˈdaɪvɪŋ/ *n* [u] **1** (from a board) 跳水 **2** (swimming under the sea) 潜水

diving: ~ bell *n* 潜水钟; **~ board** *n* 跳板; **~ suit** *n* 潜水衣

divining /dɪˈvaɪnɪŋ/ *n* [u] = **water divining**

divining rod *n* 占卜杖

divinity /dɪˈvɪnəti/ *n* **1** [u] (of deity, person) 神性; **the ~ of Christ** 耶稣的神性 **2** [c] (deity) 神; **the D~** 上帝 **3** [u] (theology) 神学

divisible /dɪˈvɪzəbl/ *adj pred* **1** (capable of being divided) 可分的 **2** Math 可除尽的; **to be ~ by sth.** 可被某数除尽的; **24 is ~ by 8** 24 能被 8 除尽

division /dɪˈvɪʒn/ *n* **1** [u] (splitting) 分开; **the ~ of the country into North and South** 国家南部和北部的划分 **2** [u] (sharing) 分配; **~ between** *or* **among several people** 在几个人中的分配 **3** [u] Math 除法 **4** [c] Mil, Naut, Aviat 师 **5** [c] Comm (branch, sector) 部门; **the company's sales ~** 公司的销售部 **6** [c] Sport (in football) 级; **to be in ~ one, in the first ~** 在甲级队 **7** [u] (disagreement) 分歧 **8** [c] (difference) 差异 **9** [c] (section) 部分 **10** [c] Bot, Biol, Zool 部 **11** [c] Brit Pol 分组表决

divisional /dɪˈvɪʒənl/ *adj* **1** (departmental) 部门的; **a ~ manager** 部门经理 **2** Mil 师的; **the ~ commander** 师长 **3** Sport 分组的; **the ~ finals** 分组决赛

division: ~ bell *n* Brit 分组表决铃 [通知议员即将进行分组表决]; **~ of labour** *n* [u] 分工; **~ sign** *n* 除号

divisive /dɪˈvaɪsɪv/ *adj* (causing disagreement) 引起分歧的; (causing disunity) 制造分裂的; **to be socially ~** 引起社会不稳定

divisor /dɪˈvaɪzə(r)/ *n* 除数

divorce /dɪˈvɔːs/

A *n* **1** [c] Jur 离婚; **to file/sue for ~** 提起离婚诉讼; **to grant a ~** 准予离婚 **2** [u] fig 分离; **the ~ between the material and spiritual worlds** 物质世界与精神世界的分离

B *vt* **1** lit 与…离婚 ‹*spouse*›; 判…离婚 ‹*couple*›; **she ~d him, she was ~d from him** 她跟他离了婚; **they were ~d in 1987** 他们于 1987 年离婚 **2** fig (separate) 使分离; **to ~ sth. from sth.** 使某物脱离某物; **to ~ responsibility from power** 把责任与权力分开; **to ~ oneself from sth.** 使自己摆脱某物; **to be ~d from reality** 脱离现实

C *vi* Jur 离婚

divorce court *n* 离婚法庭

divorced /dɪˈvɔːst/ *adj* **1** Jur 离婚的; **he's ~** 他已经离婚 **2** fig (unconnected) 分离的; **his plans are ~ from reality** 他的计划脱离实际

divorcee /dɪˌvɔːˈsiː/ *n* 离了婚的人 [尤指女人]

divorce: ~ proceedings *npl* 离婚诉讼; **to start ~ proceedings** 提出离婚诉讼; **~ rate** *n* 离婚率; **~ settlement** *n* (conditions) 离婚协议; (sum of money) 离婚赔偿

divot /ˈdɪvət/ *n* [打高尔夫球时削起的] 小块草皮

divulge /daɪˈvʌldʒ/ *vt* 泄露 ‹*secret, information, details*›

divvy /ˈdɪvɪ/ *n* Brit colloq dated 红利

Phrasal verb

- **divvy up** *vt* [**~ sth. up, ~ up sth.**] Brit colloq 均分

Diwali /dɪˈwɑːli/ *pr n* 排灯节 [印度的宗教节日]

Dixieland /ˈdɪksilænd/ *n* [u] **~ (jazz)** 迪克西兰爵士乐

DIY *abbr* Brit = **do-it-yourself**

dizzily /ˈdɪzɪli/ *adv* 头晕目眩地 ‹*walk, rise, spin*›

dizziness /ˈdɪzɪnɪs/ *n* [u] 头晕目眩; **she felt an attack of ~ coming on** 她感到一阵眩晕

dizzy /ˈdɪzi/ *adj* **1** (physically) 头晕目眩的; **to suffer from ~ spells** 患有阵发性头晕 **2** (mentally) 困惑的; **to be ~ with sth.** 对某事不知所措; **to be ~ with success/despair** 因成功/绝望而昏了头 **3** *attrib* (extremely high) 使人头晕的 ‹*height*›; 极高的 ‹*price*›; 极快的 ‹*speed*› **4** (scatterbrained) 没头脑的; **a ~ young woman** 傻妞

DJ

A *abbr* **1** = **disc jockey** **2** Brit = **dinner jacket**

B *vi* 做流行音乐节目主持人

Djakarta /dʒəˈkɑːtə/ *pr n* 雅加达

Djibouti /dʒɪˈbuːti/ *pr n* 吉布提

DMZ *abbr* = **demilitarized zone** 非军事区

DNA *abbr* = **deoxyribonucleic acid**

DNA fingerprint, DNA profile *ns* DNA 指纹

DNA fingerprinting, DNA profiling *ns* [u] DNA指纹识别

D notice *n* Brit 国防机密通知

DNS *abbr* = **domain name system**

do[1] /duː/

A *vt* (*3rd pers sing pres* **does**; *pt* **did**; *negative pt* **did not** *or* colloq **didn't**; *pp* **done**) **1** (perform, be busy with) 做 ‹*housework*›; **what does he ~ for a living?** 他靠什么谋生?; **to ~ the ironing** 熨衣服; **to ~ some repairs** 修东西; **it was all I could ~ not to laugh** 我几乎忍不住笑出来; **what are you ~ing with yourself these days?** 最近你怎么打发时间的?; **she won't have anything to ~ with me** 她不肯理我; **what are you going to ~ for money?** 你打算怎么弄到钱?; **what's done is done** 木已成舟; **what's this dirty plate/pile of newspapers ~ing here?** 这只脏盘子/这堆报纸怎么会在这儿? **2** (make attractive) 使美观; **to ~ sb.'s hair/nails** 为某人做头发/修指甲; **to ~ one's teeth/face** 刷牙/洗脸; **to ~ the living room in pink** 把客厅装饰成粉红色; **she does the flowers in church on Sunday** 她周日去教堂布置鲜花 **3** (complete) 完成 ‹*job, masterpiece, term*›; **to be done ~ing sth.** colloq 做完; **are you done complaining/eating?** colloq 你抱怨完/吃完了吗?; **a woman's work is never done** Prov 女人的活永远做不完; **she did two years at college** 她在学院学习了两年; **to ~ a one-year sentence** 服刑一年; **he did his military service in the navy** 他曾在海军服役; **it's as good as done** 差不多完成了; **that's done it** (job completed) 行了; (in dismay) 完蛋了 **4** (study) 研究 ‹*book, author*›, 学习 ‹*subject*›; **he's ~ing an MA** 他在读文学硕士; **we're ~ing Shakespeare this year** 我们今年研读莎士比亚作品 **5** (write) 写作 ‹*critique, book*›; **to ~ a translation into Chinese** 把一些东西翻译成中文; **to ~ a biography of sb.** 写一部某人的传记 **6** (effect change on) 改变; **what have you done to the kitchen?** 你把厨房怎么动了一下?; **I haven't done anything with your pen!** 我没把你的笔怎么样!; **that hat does a lot/nothing for her** 她戴那顶帽子漂亮多了/没什么变化; **what am I to ~ with you!** 真拿你没办法! **7** (hurt) 伤害; **to ~ something to one's foot** 伤到脚; **what have you done to your leg?** 你的腿怎么了? **8** colloq (handle) 处理; (provide) 提供 ‹*service, meal*›; 出售 ‹*tickets*›; **the hairdresser can ~ you now** 美发师现在可以为您服务了 **9** (cook) 做 ‹*omelette*›; 烤 ‹*toast*›; 煮 ‹*noodles*› **10** (prepare) 洗切 ‹*vegetables*› **11** Theat 排演 ‹*play, programme*›; **to ~ a season of Brecht plays** 进行布莱希特戏剧季的演出 **12** (imitate) 模仿 ‹*celebrity, voice*›; **she can ~ Margaret Thatcher very well** 她能将玛格丽特·撒切尔模仿得惟妙惟肖 **13** (travel at) 以…的速度行驶; **this boat does 50 mph** 这艘小艇的速度达到每小时 50 英里; **I was ~ing 10 mph** 我正以每小时 10 英里的速度行进 **14** (cover distance of) 走完…的距离; **we've done 30 km since lunch** 午饭后我们已走了 30 公里路 **15** colloq (tour) 游览; **to ~ Venice** 游览威尼斯 **16** colloq (fill needs of) 适合; **will this pen ~ you?** 这支笔你用得上吗? **17** colloq (cheat) 欺骗; **to ~ sb. out of sth.** 从某人处骗走 ‹*money, job*›; **I've been done out of £20** 我被骗走了 20 英镑; **we've been done** 我们上当了 **18** colloq (sterilize) 骟; **to get the cat/dog done** 骟猫/骟狗 **19** colloq (rob) 抢劫; **to ~ a bank** 抢银行 **20** colloq (convict) 宣判…有罪; **to get done for sth.** 因…被判有罪 ‹*offence*›

B *vi* (*3rd pers sing pres* **does**; *pt* **did**; *negative pt* **did not** *or* colloq **didn't**; *pp* **done**) **1** (behave) 做; **~ as I ~** 照着我的样子做; **well done!** 干得好!; **~ unto others as you would have them ~ unto you** Prov 己所不欲, 勿施于人 **2** (be right) 合适; **that box will ~** 那个盒子能行; **these trousers will ~ for gardening** 这条裤子可以穿来侍弄花园; **this (really) won't ~!** 这(真的)不行!; **it wouldn't ~ to be late** 不可以迟到 **3** (be enough) 足够; **just a little will ~** 一点就够了; **that'll ~!** (as reprimand) 够了! **4** (get on) 进行; **how are you ~ing?** (regarding health) 你好!; (regarding progress) 你做得怎么样?; **how ~ you ~?** 你好!; **how did you ~ in your exams?** 你考得怎么样?; **his business is ~ing all right** 他的生意还不错; **the patient is not ~ing well** 病人恢复得不太好 **5** colloq (be active) 活跃; **to be up and ~ing again in no time** 马上又生龙活虎; **there is nothing ~ing in this town after nine** 9 点以后这镇上就死气沉沉了; **nothing ~ing!** 不行!

C *v aux* (*3rd pers sing pres* **does**; *pt* **did**; *negative* *pt* **did not** *or* colloq **didn't**; *pp* **done**) **1** (with questions, negatives) [用于疑问句和否定句]; **~ you agree?** 你同意吗？; **you don't have to answer** 你不必回答; **didn't he look great!** 他看上去很棒吧！ **2** (for emphasis) [用于强调]; **I ~ wish you'd let me help you** 我非常希望你会让我帮助你; **accidents like that ~ sometimes happen** 那种事故有时的确会发生 **3** (referring to other verb) [用于代替实义动词]; **I don't like cheese and neither does she** 我不喜欢奶酪，她也不喜欢; **either you did or you didn't see her** 你要么看到她了，要么就没看到 **4** (in requests, imperatives) [用于请求和祈使句中加强语气]; **may I take a leaflet? — ~** 我可以拿一份传单吗？——拿吧; **~ be careful!** 一定要小心！; **don't you tell me what to ~!** 用不着你来告诉我该怎么做！ **5** (in tag questions, responses) [用于附加疑问句和回答]; **he knows her, does he?** 他认识她，是吗？; **shall I tell him? — no, don't** 我该告诉他吗？——不，别告诉他 **6** (with inversion) [用于倒装句]; **only rarely does he write letters** 他极少写信; **little did he suspect that ...** 他几乎丝毫没有怀疑…

D *n* **1** Brit colloq (party) 聚会; **to have a ~ to celebrate passing one's exams** 为通过考试而庆祝一番; **a leaving ~** 告别晚会 **2** **~s and don'ts** colloq 注意事项; **too many ~s and don'ts** 规矩太多

Phrasal verbs

- **do away with** *vt* [**~ away with sth./sb.**] **1** (abolish, get rid of) 废除 ‹*rule, service*›; 拆掉 ‹*wall, building*› **2** colloq (kill) 干掉 ‹*person, animal*›
- **do down** *vt* [**~ sb./sth. down**] Brit colloq 贬低; **don't ~ yourself down** 别责怪自己
- **do for** *vt* [**~ for sb./sth.**] colloq «*illness*» 杀死 ‹*person*›; fig 毁掉 ‹*project, company*›; **I'm done for** fig 我完蛋了
- **do in** *vt* [**~ sb. in**] colloq **1** (kill) 杀死; **mobsters did him in** 匪徒们杀了他 **2** (exhaust) 使…筋疲力尽; **I feel done in** 我感觉浑身无力
- **do out** *vt* [**~ sth. out, ~ out sth.**] colloq 装饰 ‹*room*›; **to be done out in blue** 装饰成蓝色
- **do over** *vt* colloq **1** [**~ sb. over**] Brit 痛打; **they did him over for no reason whatsoever** 他们无缘无故痛打了他一顿 **2** [**~ sth. over**] (ransack) 寻遍; **thieves had done over the entire house** 盗贼翻遍了整栋房子 **3** [**~ sth. over**] Amer (redo) 重做; **the teacher told her to ~ it over (again)** 老师让她重做一遍
- **do up**

A *vt* [**~ sth. up, ~ up sth.**] **1** (fasten) 系好 ‹*clothes, laces, shoes*›; 拉上 ‹*zip*›; 扣好 ‹*buttons*› **2** (wrap) 捆扎 ‹*parcel*›; **the package was done up with string** 包裹是用细绳绑起来的; **to ~ one's hair (up) in a bun** 把头发扎成圆髻 **3** colloq (renovate) 翻新 ‹*house*›; **we are doing up the living room** 我们在翻修客厅 **4** colloq (adorn) 打扮; **to ~ oneself up in fine clothes** 穿上漂亮的衣服

B *vi* «*clothes*» 系牢; **to ~ up at the back/with a zip** 在后面/用拉链系起来

- **do with** *vt* **1** **to have to ~ with sth./sb.** (involve) 和…有关; **it has something/nothing to ~ with money** 这和钱有关/无关; **it has nothing to ~ with you** 这不关你的事 **2** Brit (tolerate) 忍受; **I can't be ~ing with loud music** 我受不了太响的音乐 **3** (need) 需要; **I could ~ with a holiday** 我得休假了; **what I could ~ with is ...** 我需要的是… **4** **to be done with** (have finished) 做完 ‹*work*›; 用完 ‹*tool*›; 吃完 ‹*meal*›; **it's all over and done with** 彻底完成了; **I used to gamble heavily, but I'm done with all that now** 我曾经赌博成瘾，但现在已经彻底洗手不干了
- **do without** *vt* [**~ without sth.**] 可以没有 ‹*food, luxuries*›; **I can't ~ without the car** 我不能没有车; **I can ~ without your advice** 我不需要你的劝告; **you'll have to ~ without!** 你只好将就了！

do² /dəʊ/ *n* = **doh¹**

doable /ˈduːəbl/ *adj* colloq 可行的; **the task is ~** 该任务可以完成

d.o.b. *abbr* = **date of birth** 出生日期

Dobermann (pinscher) /ˌdəʊbəmən ˈ(pɪnʃ(ə))/ *n* 杜宾犬 [一种德国种短毛猎犬]

doc /dɒk/ *n* **1** colloq = **doctor A1** **2** = **document A**

docile /ˈdəʊsaɪl, Amer ˈdɒsl/ *adj* 温顺的; **a ~ child** 听话的孩子

docility /dəʊˈsɪləti/ *n* [u] 温顺

dock¹ /dɒk/

A *n* **1** (area in harbour) 船坞; **to go into/to be in ~** 进入/停泊在船坞 **2** **the ~s** Naut (waterfront area) 港区 **3** Amer (wharf) 码头; (ship's berth) 泊位 **4** **the ~** Brit Jur 被告席; **the prisoner in the ~** 受审的囚犯; **to put sb./to be in the ~** fig 谴责某人/受到谴责

B *vt* **1** Naut «*pilot, helmsman, captain*» 使…进港 ‹*boat*›; **the ship was ~ed at Brest** 船停靠在布雷斯特 **2** Aerosp «*astronaut*» 使…对接 ‹*spacecraft*›

C *vi* **1** Naut (moor) 进港; **the ship ~ed at Southampton** 船停靠在南安普敦港 **2** Aerosp 对接; **to ~ with sth.** 与某航天器对接

dock² *vt* **1** Brit (reduce) 扣去 ‹*wages, pay, sum of money, proportion*›; 扣…的工资 ‹*person*›; **my salary was ~ed (by 15%)** 我的薪水被扣了（15%） **2** Vet (cut off) 剪掉 ‹*tail, ears*›; (cut short) 剪短 ‹*tail, ears*›

dock³ *n* Bot 酸模

docker /ˈdɒkə(r)/ ▸**p. 409** *n* 码头工人

docket /ˈdɒkɪt/

A *n* **1** esp Brit Comm (label) 标签; **a ~ for sth.** 某物上的标签 **2** Amer Jur 备审案件表

B *vt* esp Brit Comm **1** (fill out docket for) 给…加标签 ‹*parcel, package*› **2** (enter on a docket) 把…列在标签上 ‹*goods, contents*›

docking /ˈdɒkɪŋ/ *n* [u] 对接; **~ manoeuvres/procedures** 对接操作/程序

docking station *n* [手提电脑的] 扩展坞

dock labourer *n* = **dockworker**

dockland /ˈdɒklənd/ *n*, **docklands** *npl* 港区陆域; **the London D~s** 伦敦港区

dock: ~ leaf *n* 酸模叶; **~side** *n* 码头邻区; **~ strike** *n* 码头工人罢工; **~worker** ▸**p. 409** *n* 码头工人; **~yard** *n* 船厂

doctor /ˈdɒktə(r)/ ▸**p. 409**

A *n* **1** Med 医生; **to go to the ~** *or* **~'s** 去看医生; **to train as a ~** 学医; **D~ Jones** 琼斯医生; **just what the ~ ordered** 正需要的东西 **2** Univ 博士; **D~ of Law** 法学博士; **D~ Jones** 琼斯博士

B *vt* **1** (alter content of) 窜改 ‹*accounts, statistics, document*›; 伪造 ‹*evidence*› **2** (tamper with) 对…做手脚 ‹*machine, car, engine*› **3** Brit Vet (neuter) 阉割 ‹*animal*› **4** (add poison to) 将有害物掺入 ‹*drink, food, medicine*›; **to ~ sth. with sth.** 用某有害物掺入某物

doctoral /ˈdɒktərəl/ *adj attrib* 博士的 ‹*research, thesis, dissertation*›

doctor-assisted suicide *n* 医助自杀

doctorate /ˈdɒktərət/ *n* 博士学位; **a ~ in law** 法学博士学位

doctor: D~ of Divinity *n* 神学博士; **D~ of Philosophy** *n* **1** (degree) 博士学位; **2** (person) 博士; **~s and nurses** *n* 扮医生和护士游戏; **to play ~s and nurses** 玩扮医生和护士游戏; **~'s excuse** *n* Amer 病假条; **to provide a ~'s excuse for an absence** 提供缺勤病假条; **~'s note** *n* 病假条

doctrinaire /ˌdɒktrɪˈneə(r)/ *adj* pej 教条主义的 ‹*approach, response, practitioner*›

doctrinal /dɒkˈtraɪnl, Amer ˈdɒktrɪnl/ *adj* **1** Relig 教义的; Pol 主义的; Philos 学说的 **2** pej (doctrinaire) 教条主义的

doctrine /ˈdɒktrɪn/ *n* [c and u] Relig 教义; Pol 主义; Philos 学说

docudrama /ˈdɒkjʊdrɑːmə/ *n* 纪实电视剧

document /ˈdɒkjʊmənt/

A *n* also Admin, Comm, Jur, Comput 文件; **legal ~s** 法律文件; **travel/insurance ~s** 旅行证件/保险单据

B *vt* **1** (record, chart) 记录 ‹*event, situation, historical process*› **2** (support or prove with documents) 用文件证明; **the court case was not adequately ~ed** 该案件没有足够的书面证据; **a well ~ed report** 一份有大量文献佐证的报告; **a well/poorly ~ed fact** 证据充分/不充分的事实 **3** (provide with documents) 为…提供证明文件 ‹*student, employee, vehicle*›

documentary /ˌdɒkjʊˈmentri, Amer -təri/

A *n* Cin 纪录片; TV, Radio 纪实节目

B *adj attrib* **1** TV, Cin, Radio 纪实的 ‹*programme*›; 纪实性的 ‹*style, techniques, feel*›; **a ~ film** 纪录片 **2** (based on documents) 书面的 ‹*evidence, proof*›; 文件的 ‹*sources*›; **a ~ letter of credit** 跟单信用证

documentation /ˌdɒkjʊmenˈteɪʃn/ *n* [u] **1** (documents) 证明文件 **2** (act of recording) (of person, vehicle, goods) 登记; (of facts, historical process) 记录

document case *n* 公文包

documented /ˈdɒkjʊməntɪd/ *adj* 有文件可证明的 ‹*case, event*›

document: ~ holder *n* = **document case**; **~ reader** *n* 文件阅读器; **~ retrieval** *n* [u] 文件检索; **~ type definition** *n* 文件类型定义; **~ wallet** *n* = **document case**

docusoap /ˈdɒkjʊsəʊp/ *n* 纪实肥皂剧

dodder /ˈdɒdə(r)/ *vi* pej 蹒跚而行; **to ~ along/about** «*elderly person*» 颤巍巍地向前走/走来走去

dodderer /ˈdɒdərə(r)/ *n* pej 蹒跚而行的人; **an old ~** 步履蹒跚的老家伙

doddering /ˈdɒdərɪŋ/, **doddery** /ˈdɒdəri/ *adj* pej 步履蹒跚的 ‹*old person*›; 颤巍巍的 ‹*movement*›; 声音颤抖的 ‹*speech*›; **most of the country's leaders are ~ old men** 那个国家的大多数领导人都已经老态龙钟; **she's too ~ to be able to drive a car** 她太老了，不能开车

doddle /ˈdɒdl/ *n* Brit colloq 轻而易举的事情; **the exam was a ~** 这次考试易如反掌; **it's no ~** 这绝非易事

dodecahedron /ˌdəʊdekəˈhiːdrən, Amer -rɒn/ *n* 十二面体

dodge /dɒdʒ/

A *vt* **1** (move out of the way of) 闪身躲开 ‹*bullet, blow, oncoming vehicle, pursuers*› **2** fig (avoid dealing with) 回避 ‹*person, question, awkward situation*›; 逃避 ‹*school, military service, housework*›; **to ~ the rush hour traffic** 避开交通高峰; **to ~ paying one's taxes** 逃税

B *vi* 躲闪; **to ~ about** 东躲西闪; **the motorcyclist was dodging in and out of the traffic** 摩托车手在车流中穿进穿出

C *n* **1** (movement) 躲闪; **he made a quick ~ to the right** 他迅速向右一躲 **2** Brit colloq (trick) 诡计; **a ~ to avoid** *or* **for avoiding taxation** 逃税的花招; **to be up to all the ~s** 使出各种诡计

dodgem /ˈdɒdʒəm/ *n* Brit **~ (cars), the ~s** 碰碰车

dodger /ˈdɒdʒə(r)/ *n* colloq (trickster) 诡计多端的人; (shirker) 逃避者; **a fare ~** 逃票的人; **he's a crafty old ~** 他是一只狡猾的老狐狸; **he's a bit of a ~ when it comes to housework** 在做家务方面他有点爱偷懒

dodgy /ˈdɒdʒi/ *adj* Brit colloq **1** (untrustworthy, dubious) 可疑的; **he's a ~ bloke** 他是个狡猾

的家伙; **to sell ~ videos at the market** 在市场上出售来路不明的录像带; **that company is a bit ~** 那家公司有点不可靠 **2** (unsafe) 存在风险的 ‹*activity, plan, investment, machine*›; **I ate some ~ prawns last night** 我昨天吃的虾有问题 **3** (precarious) 不佳的; **the weather looks a bit ~** 天气看来会变; **I'm in a ~ financial situation at the moment** 我目前的财政状况岌岌可危

dodo /ˈdəʊdəʊ/ *n* (*pl* **~** *or* **~es**) 渡渡鸟; **as dead as a ~** colloq (dead) 死翘翘的; (no longer effective or valid) 完全失效的; (no longer interesting) 死气沉沉的

doe /dəʊ/ *n* (deer) 雌鹿; (rabbit, hare) 雌兔; (rat) 雌鼠; (ferret) 雌雪貂; (kangaroo) 雌袋鼠

doe-eyed *adj* 眼睛又大又黑的 ‹*woman, girl*›

doer /ˈduːə(r)/ *n* 做事的人; **I prefer to be a ~ rather than a talker** 我宁愿做实干家，而不做空谈者; **the subject of a sentence is the ~ of the action** 句子的主语是动作的执行者

does /dʌz, dəz/ *3rd pers sing pres* ▸**do¹ A, B, C**

doeskin /ˈdəʊskɪn/ *n* 母鹿皮; **in ~** 母鹿皮做的; **~ gloves** 母鹿皮手套

doesn't /ˈdʌznt/ colloq **= does not** ▸**do¹ C**

doff /dɒf, Amer dɔːf/ *vt* dated 脱; **to ~ one's hat to sb.** 脱帽向某人致敬

dog /dɒg, Amer dɔːg/

A *n* **1** (domesticated animal) 狗; **our pet ~** 我们的宠物狗; **it shouldn't happen to a ~** 这事太不像话; **I wouldn't give this food to a ~** 这种食物我连狗都不会喂的; **it's ~ eat ~** 竞争残酷无情; **it's a ~ eat ~ world** 这是个残酷无情的世界; **a ~ in the manger** 占着茅坑不拉屎的人; **to go and see a man about a ~** colloq 有点事儿出去一下; **to put on the ~** Amer colloq (behave in an unpleasant, grand way) 架子大; (show off) 要派头; **a ~'s dinner** *or* **breakfast** Brit colloq 一团糟; **to be dressed** *or* **got up like a ~'s dinner** Brit colloq pej 穿得花里胡哨; **a ~'s chance** 渺茫的机会 [一般用于否定句]; **they don't have a ~'s chance** 他们毫无机会; **love me, love my ~** 爱屋及乌; **every ~ has his** *or* **its day** Prov 人人皆有得意日; **give a ~ a bad name (and hang him)** Prov 人言可畏; **it's a ~'s life** 这是猪狗不如的生活; **to treat sb. like a ~** 待某人如猪狗; **you wouldn't put a ~ out on a night like this** 今晚天气太糟了; **to be as sick as a ~** colloq 呕吐得厉害; **like a ~ with two tails** 得意洋洋 **2** (wild animal of the dog family) 犬科动物 **3** (male dog, fox, wolf) 犬科雄兽; **a ~ fox/wolf** 公狐狸/公狼 **4** colloq pej (bad person) 卑鄙小人; **you dirty/vile ~!** 你这个无赖! **5** colloq (person of a specific kind) 家伙; **you lucky ~!** 你真走运! ; **he's a crafty old ~** 他老奸巨滑; **there's life in the old ~ yet** 人老心不老 **6** colloq pej (unattractive woman) 丑女 **7** esp Amer colloq (something of poor quality) 蹩脚货; **a ~ of a film** 粗制滥造的电影

B **dogs** *npl* **1** Brit Sport colloq **the ~s** 赛狗; **to bet on (the) ~s** 赌狗; **to go to the ~s** (lose good qualities) 堕落; (become unsuccessful) 衰败 **2** Amer colloq (feet) 双脚

C *vt* (*pres p etc.* **-gg-**) **1** (follow closely) 紧跟 ‹*person*›; **to ~ sb.'s footsteps** *or* **heels** 尾随某人 **2** (plague) 困扰; **to be ~ged by misfortune** 被灾祸困扰; **poor health ~ged his boyhood** 他儿时多病

dog: ~ basket *n* 狗睡觉用的篮子; **~ biscuit** *n* 狗食饼干; **~ breeder** ▸**p. 409** *n* 以养狗为生的人; **~ cart** *n* 双轮轻便马车; **~ collar** *n* **1** lit 狗项圈; **2** colloq hum (clerical collar) 牧师领 [牧师穿的白色硬领]; **~ days** *npl* esp liter **1** (hot weather) 三伏天; **2** (slack period) 淡季; **~-eared** *adj* 翻旧了的 ‹*book, magazine, exercise book*›; 折角的 ‹*pages*›; **~-end** *n* Brit colloq 烟头; **~fight** *n* **1** lit (between dogs) 斗狗; **2** Mil, Aviat 近距离空战; **3** (fierce struggle) 混战; **it was a real ~fight to get into the store** 人们为冲进商店你推我搡，乱作一团; **~fighting** *n* [u] 斗狗; **~fish** *n* (*pl* **~fish** *or* **~fishes**) 狗鲨; **~ food** *n* [u] 狗粮

dogged /ˈdɒgɪd, Amer ˈdɔːgɪd/ *adj* 顽强的; **~ persistence** 坚韧的毅力; **a ~ campaigner for human rights** 不屈不挠的人权运动人士

doggedly /ˈdɒgɪdli, Amer ˈdɔːg-/ *adv* 顽强地

doggedness /ˈdɒgɪdnɪs, Amer ˈdɔːg-/ *n* [u] 顽强

doggerel /ˈdɒgərəl, Amer ˈdɔːg-/ *n* [u] **1** pej (bad verse) 蹩脚诗 **2** (comic verse) 打油诗

doggie /ˈdɒgi,, Amer ˈdɔːgi/ *n* colloq **= doggy A**

doggo /ˈdɒgəʊ, Amer ˈdɔːgəʊ/ *adv* Brit colloq dated 隐蔽地; **to lie ~** 隐伏不动

doggone /ˈdɒgɒn, Amer ˈdɔːgɔːn/ Amer colloq

A *adj* (*also* **doggoned**) 该死的; **where's the ~ key?** 那该死的钥匙在哪儿?

B *adv* (*also* **doggoned**) 该死地; **don't drive so ~ fast!** 别他妈开这么快!

C *excl* **~ it!** 他妈的!

doggy /ˈdɒgi, Amer ˈdɔːgi/

A *n* child lang 狗狗

B *adj attrib* **1** (of a dog) 狗的; **a ~ smell** 一股狗气味 **2** colloq (fond of dogs) 爱狗的 ‹*person, family*›

doggy: ~ bag *n* 食品打包袋; **~-fashion** *adv* 狗刨式地 ‹*swim*›; 狗爬式地 ‹*make love, have sex*›; 像狗一样地 ‹*beg, eat*›

> **doggy bag**
>
> 食品打包袋，亦作 doggie bag。餐馆就餐后装剩饭带回家的袋子。字面意思为狗食袋，指带回家给宠物狗吃。食品打包在美国很常见，在英国则比较少见。

doggy-paddle

A *n* 狗刨式; **to do** *or* **swim (the) ~** 以狗刨式泳姿游泳

B *vi* 以狗刨式泳姿游泳

dog: ~ handler ▸**p. 409** *n* 驯狗员; **~house** *n* Amer (kennel) 狗窝; **(to be) in the ~house (with sb.)** colloq (in disgrace) （在某人那里）丢脸; (out of favour) （在某人那里）失宠; **~ licence** *n* 养狗许可证; **~like** *adj* (of a dog) 狗的; (like a dog) 像狗一样的 ‹*devotion, appearance, expression*›

dog in the manger

A *n* 占着茅坑不拉屎的人

B **dog-in-the-manger** *modif* 占着茅坑不拉屎的 ‹*attitude*›

dogleg /ˈdɒgleg/ *n* 急转弯

dogma /ˈdɒgmə, Amer ˈdɔːgmə/ *n* [u and c] (religious) 教义; (political) 信条

dogmatic /dɒgˈmætɪk, Amer dɔːg-/ *adj* **1** pej (laying down principles as undeniably true) 教条主义的; (not considering others' views) 武断的 **2** Relig (relating to dogma) 教义的; (based on dogma) 基于教义的 **3** Pol, Philos (relating to dogma) 信条的; (based on dogma) 基于信条的

dogmatically /dɒgˈmætɪkli, Amer dɔːg-/ *adv* pej 武断地

dogmatism /ˈdɒgmətɪzəm, Amer ˈdɔːg-/ *n* [u] pej 教条主义

dogmatist /ˈdɒgmətɪst, Amer ˈdɔːg-/ *n* pej 教条主义者

dogmatize /ˈdɒgmətaɪz, Amer ˈdɔːg-/ *vi* pej 教条地陈述

dognapping /ˈdɒgnæpɪŋ/ *n* [u and c] colloq 偷狗

do-gooder /duːˈgʊdə(r)/ *n* colloq pej 帮倒忙的人

dog: ~-paddle *n, vi* **= doggy-paddle**; **~ rose** *n* 犬蔷薇; **~sbody** *n* Brit colloq **(general) ~** 勤杂工; **~'s home** *n* 流浪狗收容所; **~show** *n* 狗展会; **D~ Star** *n* 天狼星; **~ tag** *n* **1** (for dog) 狗牌; **2** Amer Mil colloq 身份识别牌; **~-tired** *adj* colloq 极度疲乏的; **~track** *n* 赛狗跑道; **~trot** *n* 慢跑; **~watch** *n* 更换值班; **~wood** *n* 山茱萸

doh¹ /dəʊ/ *n* (first note) [大调音阶的第1音]; (eighth note) [大调音阶的第8音]

doh² *excl* colloq 哦; **~! why didn't I think of that?** 哦! 我怎么没想到?

Doha /ˈdəʊhɑː/ *pr n* 多哈

doily /ˈdɔɪli/ *n* 装饰垫

doing /ˈduːɪŋ/

A *pres p* ▸**do¹ A, B**

B *n* [u] **1** (thing done by sb.) 所做的事; (thing caused by sb.) 所造成的事; **to be sb.'s ~** 是某人干的 **2** [u] (effort) 努力; **to take some ~** 需要费点力 **3** **doings** *pl* esp Brit colloq (activities) 所作所为; **daily ~s** 日常事务; **the latest ~s of television stars** 电视明星们最近的社交活动

do-it-yourself *n* [u] esp Brit 自己动手; **a ~ bookcase kit** 一套自己装配的书橱部件; **a ~ store** DIY商店; **~ hairdressing** 自己动手做头发

do-it-yourselfer /ˌduːɪtjɔːˈselfə(r)/ *n* colloq 自己动手的人

doldrums /ˈdɒldrəmz/ *npl* **1** Geog **the ~** 赤道无风带 **2** Meteorol **the ~** [赤道无风带的] 无风天气 **3** fig (stagnation) 停滞; **the economy remains in the ~** 经济仍然不景气 **4** fig (depression) 消沉; **he's been in the ~ ever since she left him** 自从她离开他以后，他一直情绪消沉

dole /dəʊl/ *n* [u] **the ~** Brit colloq 失业救济金; **to be/go on the ~** 靠失业救济金生活/开始领失业救济金; **~ money/office** 失业救济金/办公室

Phrasal verb

• **dole out** *vt* [**~ out sth., ~ sth. out**] 发放 ‹*equipment, money, food*›; **to ~ sth. out to sb.** 发放某物给某人

doleful /ˈdəʊlfl/ *adj* 悲伤的; **a ~ face** 愁苦的脸

dolefully /ˈdəʊlfəli/ *adv* 悲伤地 ‹*smile*›

dole queue *n* colloq 领取失业救济金的队伍; **to join the ~** 加入失业者行列

doll /dɒl, Amer dɔːl/ *n* **1** (toy) 玩偶; **~s' clothes** 玩具娃娃的衣服 **2** colloq dated (attractive woman) 俊妞儿; **she's quite a ~!** 她真是个美人儿! **3** (nice person) 好心人; **would you be a ~ and set the table?** 你愿意帮忙摆放餐具吗?

Phrasal verb

• **doll up** *vt* [**~ up sb./sth., ~ sb./sth. up**] colloq 把…打扮得可爱迷人 ‹*child, animal*›; 把…装点得漂漂亮亮 ‹*furniture, building, food*›; **to ~ oneself up (in sth.)** （穿某种衣服）打扮自己; **I'm really going to ~ myself up tonight** 今晚我要好好打扮一番; **to ~ sb./sth. up in sth.** 用某物打扮某人/装点某物

dollar /ˈdɒlə(r)/ ▸**p. 174** *n* (money) 元; (US currency) 美元; **the ~ has fallen** 美元汇率下跌了; **to bet one's bottom ~ (on sth./that ...)** colloq （对…）打包票; **the sixty-four thousand ~ question** colloq 很难回答的大问题

dollar: ~ area *n* 美元区; **~ bill** *n* 一元钞票; **~ diplomacy** *n* [u] 金元外交; **~ gap** *n* 美元短缺; **~ sign** *n* 元的记号 [即$]

dollhouse /ˈdɒlhaʊs, Amer ˈdɔːlhaʊs/ *n* Amer **= doll's house**

dollop /ˈdɒləp/ *n* colloq 一团; fig 少许; **a ~ of sth.** 一小团某物

doll: ~'s hospital *n* 洋娃娃修理店; **~'s house** *n* 玩具小屋

dolly /ˈdɒli, Amer ˈdɔːli/ *n* **1** colloq (doll) 洋娃娃 **2** (mobile camera platform) 移动摄影机台架 **3** (to move heavy objects) 台车

dolly: ~ bird *n* Brit colloq dated 漂亮傻妞; **~ mixture** *n* 彩色什锦糖果

dolmen /ˈdɒlmən/ *n* 石板墓

d

dolomite /ˈdɒləmaɪt/ *n* [u] (mineral) 白云石; (rock) 白云岩

Dolomites /ˈdɒləmaɪts/ *pr npl* **the ～** 白云石山脉 [位于意大利东北部，属阿尔卑斯山脉]

dolphin /ˈdɒlfɪn/ *n* 海豚

dolphinarium /ˌdɒlfɪˈneərɪəm/ *n* (*pl* **～s** *or* **dolphinaria** /ˈdɒlfɪˈneərɪə/) 海豚馆

dolt /dəʊlt/ *n* 笨蛋

doltish /ˈdəʊltɪʃ/ *adj* 呆笨的

domain /dəʊˈmeɪn/ *n* [1] (sphere of activity, knowledge) 领域 [2] (lands, realm) 领土; (place under sb.'s/sth.'s domination) 领地; **the kitchen is my wife's ～; she doesn't like me going into it** 厨房是我妻子的领地；她不喜欢我进去 [3] Comput 域

domain: ～ name *n* 域名; **～ name system** *n* 域名系统

dome /dəʊm/ *n* [1] (part of a building) 穹顶 [2] (dome-shaped thing) 半球形物

domed /dəʊmd/ *adj* [1] Archit 有穹顶的 ‹*building, cathedral*› [2] (dome-shaped) 半球形的 ‹*roof, forehead, helmet, shell*›

Domesday Book /ˈduːmzdeɪ bʊk/ *n* Brit Hist 最终税册 [指英国1086年钦定土地调查清册]

domestic /dəˈmestɪk/ *adj* [1] (inside country) 国内的 ‹*market, news, flights*› [2] (of house) 家务的; (for use in the home) 家用的; (of family) 家里的 [3] (homely) 爱家的 ‹*person*›; 家庭的 ‹*comforts, scene, atmosphere*›; **she's very ～** 她非常恋家 [4] (tame) 驯养的; **a ～ cat** 家猫 [5] *attrib* (of servants in homes) 家庭雇用的; **～ staff** 家里的仆人

domestically /dəˈmestɪkli/ *adv* 在国内; **～ produced goods** 本国产品

domestic appliance *n* 家用器具

domesticate /dəˈmestɪkeɪt/ *vt* 驯化 ‹*animal, species*›

domesticated /dəˈmestɪkeɪtɪd/ *adj* [1] (tame) 驯养的 ‹*animal*› [2] (fond of home life) 恋家的

domestication /dəˌmestɪˈkeɪʃn/ *n* [u] 驯养

domestic help *n* [c and u] (person) 家政服务员; (service) 家政服务

domesticity /ˌdɒməˈstɪsəti, ˌdəʊ-/ *n* [u] 家庭生活

domestic: ～ science *n* [u] Brit dated 家政学; **～ servant** *n* 用人; **～ service** *n* [u] 家政服务; **～ violence** *n* [u] 家庭暴力

domicile /ˈdɒmɪsaɪl/ *n* formal 住所

domiciled /ˈdɒmɪsaɪld/ *adj* formal 定居的; **to be ～ in London** 在伦敦定居

dominance /ˈdɒmɪnəns/ *n* [1] (power, influence) 控制; **political/military ～** 政治/军事优势; **～ over sb./sth.** 对某人/某事物的支配; **the ～ of sth.** 对某事物的控制 [2] (importance) 支配地位

dominant /ˈdɒmɪnənt/

A *adj* [1] (most influential) 支配的 ‹*role*›; **the ～ power in Europe** 欧洲的头号强国 [2] (imposing) 高耸的 ‹*landmark*›; 显眼的 ‹*piece of furniture*› [3] (most important) 首要的 [4] Biol 显性的 ‹*characteristic, gene*› [5] Mus 属音的

B *n* Mus (fifth note) 属音; (chord) 属和弦; (key) 属调

dominate /ˈdɒmɪneɪt/

A *vt* [1] (have power over) 统治; (control) 控制 [2] (to be the most important element/person in sth.) 主宰; **her life is ～d by her children** 她的生活大部分被她的孩子占据 [3] (command attention over) «*building, monument*» 耸立于 ‹*area, city*›

B *vi* [1] (control others) 处于支配地位 [2] (predominate) 占优势

dominating /ˈdɒmɪneɪtɪŋ/ *adj* 专横的

domination /ˌdɒmɪˈneɪʃn/ *n* [1] (power over sth.) 统治; **under sb.'s ～** 在某人的统治之下; **world ～** 对世界的统治 [2] (dominance) 主宰; **American ～ of basketball** 美国在篮球运动中的霸主地位 [3] (control) 控制 [4] (sexual practice) 性主导

dominatrix /ˌdɒmɪˈneɪtrɪks/ *n* (*pl* **dominatrices** /dɒmɪˈneɪtrɪsiːz/ *or* **～es**) 女性施虐狂

domineer /ˌdɒmɪˈnɪə(r)/ *vi* pej 专横跋扈; **to ～ over sb.** 对某人专横跋扈

domineering /ˌdɒmɪˈnɪərɪŋ/ *adj* pej 专横跋扈的

Dominica /dəˈmɪnɪkə/ *pr n* 多米尼克

Dominican /dəˈmɪnɪkən/ ▸**p. 503**

A *adj* [1] Relig 多明我会的 [2] (of the Dominican Republic) 多米尼加共和国的; (of the people of the Dominican Republic) 多米尼加共和国人的 [3] (of Dominica) 多米尼克的; (of the people of Dominica) 多米尼克人的

B *n* [1] (monk) 多明我会修士 [2] (native of the Dominican Republic) 多米尼加共和国人 [3] (native of Dominica) 多米尼克人

Dominican Republic *pr n* **the ～** 多米尼加共和国

dominion /dəˈmɪnɪən/ *n* [1] [u] (sovereignty) 统治; (control) 支配; **under sb.'s ～** 在某人的统治下; **to have** *or* **hold ～ over sb./sth.** 统治某人/某事物 [2] [c] formal (territory) 领土 [3] [c] (*also* **Dominion**) (British colony) 英联邦自治领

domino /ˈdɒmɪnəʊ/ ▸**p. 307**

A *n* (block) 多米诺骨牌

B **dominoes** *npl* + *v sing* (game) 多米诺骨牌戏

domino: ～ effect *n* 多米诺骨牌效应; **～ theory** *n* 多米诺骨牌理论

don[1] /dɒn/ *vt* (*pres p etc.* **-nn-**) formal 穿上 ‹*clothes*›; 戴上 ‹*hat, gloves*›; fig 露出 ‹*smile, expression, air*›

don[2] *n* [1] Brit (university lecturer) [尤指牛津和剑桥的] 大学教师 [2] Amer (Mafia boss) 黑手党头目

donate /dəʊˈneɪt, Amer ˈdəʊneɪt/

A *vt* [1] (give) 捐赠; **to ～ sth. to sb./sth.** 捐赠某物给某人/某机构 [2] Med 捐献; **to ～ blood** 献血

B *vi* 捐赠; **to ～ to a charity** 向慈善团体捐赠

donation /dəʊˈneɪʃn/ *n* [1] [c] (contribution, gift) 捐赠物; **to make a ～ (to sb./sth.)** (向某人/某机构) 捐赠; **I made a ～ of fifty dollars to the earthquake relief fund** 我向地震救济基金捐了 50 美元 [2] [u] (giving) 捐赠; **the ～ of sth. to sb./sth.** 向某人/某机构捐赠某物

done /dʌn/

A *pp* ▸**do**[1] **A, B, C**

B *adj* [1] Brit colloq (acceptable) 合乎规矩的; **the ～ thing** 得体的事 [2] *pred* colloq (exhausted) 精疲力竭的 [3] *pred* (cooked) 煮熟的 [4] (finished) 完成; **I'm nearly done** 我马上就好 [5] *pred* (used up) 用完的; **the milk's nearly ～** 牛奶快喝光了; 完毕的 [6] *pred* (finished) **the battle is ～** 战斗结束了

C *excl* (agreeing deal) 行，好 [用以表示说话者接受提议]; **'～!'** "成交!"

doner kebab /ˌdəʊnə kəˈbæb/ *n* 土耳其卡巴 [面包夹烤羊肉和色拉而成]

dong /dɒŋ/ *n* taboo sl 屌 offensive

dongle /ˈdɒŋgl/ *n* 软件保护器

Dongting Lake /ˈdɒŋtɪŋ ˌleɪk/ ▸**p. 424** *pr n* 洞庭湖

donkey /ˈdɒŋki/ *n* [1] (animal) 驴; **～'s years** Brit colloq 很久; **(to be able) to talk the hind leg off a ～** Brit colloq 说话滔滔不绝 [2] colloq (stupid person) 蠢驴

donkey: ～ jacket *n* Brit 风雨衣; **～ ride** *n* 骑驴兜风; **～ work** *n* [u] Brit colloq 苦差事

donnish /ˈdɒnɪʃ/ *adj* Brit 学究气的

donor /ˈdəʊnə(r)/ *n* [1] Med 捐献者; **a blood ～** 献血者 [2] (of money) 捐赠者

donor: ～ card *n* 器官捐献卡; **～ organ** *n* 捐献的器官

don't /dəʊnt/ colloq = **do not** ▸**do**[1] **C**

don't know *n* 态度未定的人

donut /ˈdəʊnʌt/ *n* Amer = **doughnut**

doodad /ˈduːdæd/ *n* Amer colloq = **doodah**

doodah /ˈduːdɑː/ *n* Brit colloq 小玩意儿

doodle /ˈduːdl/

A *n* 涂鸦

B *vi* 信手乱涂

doofus /ˈduːfəs/ *n* (*pl* **～es**) Amer colloq 傻子

doolally /ˈduːlæli/ *adj* Brit colloq 发狂的; **to go ～** 发疯

doom /duːm/

A *n* [u] (of one person) 劫数; (of a country, group) 毁灭; **to go to/meet one's ～** 死亡

B *vt* 使在劫难逃; **to ～ sb./sth. to sth.** 使某人/某事注定遭受某事; **he/it was ～ed to failure** 他/这事注定要失败

doomed /duːmd/ *adj* 在劫难逃的

doom-laden *adj* 预示厄运的

doomsday /ˈduːmzdeɪ/ *n* [1] (time of crisis) 危机时刻; (crisis) 危难事件; **the ～ scenario** 可能出现的极糟糕局面 [2] Relig 世界末日; **we'll be here till ～** hum 我们将永远在这儿

Doomsday Book *n* = **Domesday Book**

door /dɔː(r)/ *n* [1] (barrier) 门; (doorway) 门道; **to knock at** *or* **on the ～** 敲门; **there's somebody at the ～** 门口有人; **the ～ to the kitchen** 通往厨房的门; **a four-～ car** 一辆四门汽车; **their house is a few ～s down** 隔几户人家就是他们的房子; **behind closed** *or* **locked ～s** 秘密地; **to see sb. to the ～** 把某人送到门口; **to go (from) ～ to ～** 挨家挨户敲门; **the journey takes about an hour ～ to ～** 全程要花大约一个小时; **out of ～s** 在户外; **to lay sth. at sb.'s ～** 把某事归咎于某人; **to lie at sb.'s ～** 归咎于某人; **at death's ～** 行将就木的; **to show sb. the ～** 向某人下逐客令 [2] (entrance) 门口; **to be on the ～** 守门; **'pay at the ～'** "门口交费" [3] (opportunity) 门路; **to open the ～(s) to sth.** 打开通向某事物的大门; **a foot in the ～** 成功的第一步; **to close** *or* **shut the ～ on** *or* **to sth.** 把某事的门堵死; **to leave** *or* **keep the ～ open (for sth.)** (为某事) 留有余地; **to shut** *or* **slam the ～ on sb.** *or* **in sb.'s face** lit 将某人拒之门外; fig 拒绝见某人; **when one ～ closes, another one opens** 当一扇门关闭时，另一扇就打开了

door: ～ bell *n* 门铃; **～ chime** *n* 门钟; **～ frame** *n* 门框; **～ handle** *n* 门拉手; **～ jamb** *n* 门边框; **～keeper** ▸**p. 409** *n* 门卫; **～ knocker** *n* 门环; **～knob** *n* 球形门拉手; **～man** /-mən/ ▸**p. 409** *n* 看门人; **～mat** *n* [1] (for wiping shoes) 门口地垫; [2] (submissive person) 受气包; **～nail** *n* 护门帽钉; **as dead as a ～nail** colloq 死翘翘的; **～ plate** *n* 门牌; **～post** *n* 门柱

doorstep /ˈdɔːstep/

A *n* [1] (step outside door) 门阶; **on the** *or* **one's ～** 在家门口 [2] Brit colloq (chunk of bread) 厚面包片

B *vt* Brit colloq (wait for interview) «*journalist*» 蹲守在…的门口 ‹*person*›

door: ～-stepping *n* [u] Brit colloq 蹲守 [指记者为了采访或照相候在某人的家门口]; **～stop** *n* [1] (to prevent slamming) 制门器; (to prevent door hitting the wall) 门吸; [2] (book) 厚书; **～-to-～** *adj attrib* 挨家挨户的; **a ～-to-～ salesman** 挨户兜售的推销员; **～way** *n* [1] (entrance) 门道; **in the ～way** 在门口; [2] (area in front of door) 门前; [3] fig (access) 门路; **the ～way to success** 通往成功之门

dopamine /ˈdəʊpəmiːn/ *n* [u] 多巴胺

dope /dəʊp/

A *n* [1] [u] colloq (illegal drugs) 毒品; **a ～ addict** 吸毒上瘾的人 [2] [u] (performance-enhancing drugs) 兴奋剂 [3] [u] colloq (information) 内幕消息; **the ～ on sth./sb.** 关于某事物/某人的内幕消息 [4] [c] pej colloq (fool) 笨蛋 [5] [u] (varnish) 飞机翼布涂料

B *vt* [1] Sport 给…服兴奋剂 ‹*person, animal*› [2] (drug) 给…服麻醉剂 ‹*person, animal*›; 在…中加麻醉剂 ‹*drink, food*›

doped up *adj* colloq 吸毒后昏昏沉沉的

dope peddler *n* 毒品贩子

dope test
A *n* 兴奋剂检查
B **dope-test** *vt* 对…做兴奋剂检查

dopey /'dəʊpi/ *adj* colloq **1** (stupid) 呆头呆脑的 **2** (sleepy) 昏昏沉沉的

doping /'dəʊpɪŋ/ *n* [u] 服用兴奋剂

doppelgänger /'dɒplgeŋə(r)/ *n* (apparition) 幽灵; (person) 面貌酷似的人

Doppler effect /'dɒplə(r) ɪˌfekt/ *n* 多普勒效应

dopy /'dəʊpi/ *adj* = **dopey**

Doric /'dɒrɪk/ *adj* [建筑风格] 多利斯式的

dork /dɔːk/ *n* colloq 呆子

dorm /dɔːm/ *n* colloq = **dormitory**

dormant /'dɔːmənt/ *adj* **1** (not active) 暂时搁置的 ‹*plan, idea, law*›; 暂时不用的 ‹*hereditary title*› **2** (latent) 潜在的 ‹*emotion, sexuality, conflict*› **3** Geol 暂停活动的; **a ~ volcano** 休眠火山 **4** Hort 休眠的 ‹*plant, seed*›

dormer /'dɔːmə(r)/ *n* **~ (window)** 老虎窗

dormice /'dɔːmaɪs/ *pl* ▸**dormouse**

dormitory /'dɔːmɪtri, Amer -tɔːri/ *n* **1** (shared bedroom) 宿舍 **2** Amer Univ (hall of residence) 宿舍楼

dormitory: ~ suburb *n* Brit 郊外住宅区; **~ town** *n* Brit [仅供人居住、其他功能弱化的] 居住性质城镇

dormouse /'dɔːmaʊs/ *n* (*pl* **dormice**) 榛睡鼠

dorsal /'dɔːsl/ *adj attrib* 背部的; **the ~ fin** 背鳍

Dorset /'dɔːsɪt/ *pr n* 多塞特郡

dory /'dɔːri/ *n* **1** Amer (boat) 平底小渔船 **2** Brit (fish) 海鲂

DOS /dɒs/ *n* = **disk operating system**

dosage /'dəʊsɪdʒ/ *n* **1** [c and u] (amount) 剂量 **2** [u] (administering of drug) 给药; **the ~ of patients with sedatives** 给病人服用镇静剂

dose /dəʊs/
A *n* **1** (of medicine) 一次的剂量; **to give** *or* **administer a ~ of cough mixture** 给服一剂咳嗽药; **in small/large ~s** 以小/大剂量; **I can only stand her in small ~s** 我只能忍受她一小会儿; **like a ~ of salts** colloq 很快地 **2** colloq **a ~ of sth.** (of sth. unpleasant) 一次 ‹*flu, deflation, conversation*›; (of sth. pleasant) 一点 ‹*optimism, originality, good luck, fresh air*›
B *vt* 给…服药; **to ~ sb. (up) with painkillers** 给某人服用止痛药
C *v refl* **to ~ oneself up** 服药; **to ~ oneself (up) with sleeping pills** 服用安眠药

dosh /dɒʃ/ *n* [u] Brit colloq 钱

doss /dɒs/ Brit colloq
A *vi* 将就过夜
B *n* **1** (easy task) 不费力的事; **my new job's a real ~** 我的新工作真轻松 **2** (place to sleep) [条件简陋的] 短暂过夜处

Phrasal verbs
- **doss about** *vi* Brit colloq 混时间
- **doss down** *vi* Brit colloq 将就过夜

dosser /'dɒsə(r)/ *n* colloq pej **1** (lazy person) 懒人 **2** (tramp) 流浪者

dosshouse /'dɒshaʊs/ *n* Brit colloq 廉价旅店

dossier /'dɒsɪə(r), -ɪeɪ/ *n* (file) 卷宗; (information) 资料汇编; **to build up** *or* **compile a ~ on sth./sb.** 汇编有关某事物/某人的资料

dot /dɒt/
A *n* **1** (small round mark) 小圆点; **the letter 'i' has a ~ on top** 字母 i 上面有一点; **the wallpaper is white with blue ~s** 墙纸是白底蓝点的; **on the ~** colloq 准时地; **the year ~** Brit colloq 很久以前 **2** (full stop) 句点; **three ~s indicate an omission** 3 个句点表示省略 **3** Mus (to lengthen note, indicate staccato) 附点 **4** (in Morse code) 点; **~ ~ dash** 点点划 **5** (faraway object) 点状物; **the helicopters looked like two black ~s** 直升机看上去像两个小黑点
B *vt* (*pres p etc.* **-tt-**) **1** (in writing) 在…上加点 ‹*an i*›; **~ the i's and cross the t's** 做最后的修改 **2** Mus 在…上加附点 ‹*musical note*› **3** (be scattered over) 散布于; (scatter) 使散布; **fishing villages ~ the coast** 渔村散布在海岸边; **we've ~ted a few chairs about** 我们在周围放了几把椅子 **4** Brit colloq (hit) 打; **I'll ~ you one!** 我要揍你一拳!

dotage /'dəʊtɪdʒ/ *n* [u] 衰老; **to be in one's ~** 年老糊涂; **to reach one's ~** 上了年纪

dot-com /dɒt'kɒm/ *n* 网络公司; **the bursting of the ~ bubble** 网络公司泡沫的破灭

dote /dəʊt/ *vi* 溺爱; **to ~ on sb./sth.** 溺爱某人/酷爱某物

doting /'dəʊtɪŋ/ *adj attrib* (showing a lot of love) 十分喜爱的; (showing too much love) 溺爱的; **a ~ son** 孝顺的儿子

dot matrix printer *n* 点阵式打印机

dotted /'dɒtɪd/ *adj* **1** *pred* (covered as with dots) 星罗棋布的; **the sky was ~ with stars** 天空繁星密布 **2** Mus 加附点的; **a ~ note** 附点音符

dotted line *n* 虚线; **to tear along the ~** 沿虚线撕开; **to sign on the ~** 在署名栏签名; fig 完全同意

dotty /'dɒti/ *adj* Brit colloq **1** (eccentric) 疯疯癫癫的 **2** *pred* (enthusiastic) 非常热情的; (infatuated) 着迷的; **she's ~ about her boyfriend** 她对男友很痴情

double /'dʌbl/ ▸**p. 288**
A *adj* **1** (intended for two) 供两者用的; **a ~ garage** 双车库; **a ~ ticket/invitation** 双人票/双人邀请 **2** (twice as much, twofold) 两倍的; **they earn ~ what you earn** 他们挣的是你的两倍; **it will take ~ the time** 那要花两倍时间; **she is ~ his age** 她的年纪比他大一倍; **a ~ helping of potato(es)** 双份的土豆; **four ~ whiskies** 4杯双份威士忌酒 **3** (consisting of two) 成双的 ‹*line, stripe, track*›; 双层的 ‹*lining, coat*›; 双写的 ‹*letter*›; **in ~ digits** 达两位数; **a ~-page advertisement** 双页广告; **a ~ murder** 一起两人丧命的谋杀案; **six four ~ three five** 64335 **4** (duplicitous) 双重的 ‹*purpose, advantage, meaning*›; **to lead a ~ life** 过双重生活; **to play a ~ game** 耍两面派 **5** Bot 重瓣的 ‹*flower*›
B *adv* **1** (twice as much) 两倍地; **this counts ~ for older people** 这一点对年长者来说倍加重要 **2** (so as to be twice as much) 重叠地; **to see ~** 看到重影; **to fold the blanket ~** 把毯子对折; **to be bent ~ with pain/laughter** 疼得/笑得弯下腰
C *pron* 两倍; **he paid me the ~ of what he owed me** 他把欠款加倍还给了我; **~ or quits** Brit, **~ or nothing** Amer 要么双倍赢钱, 要么输个精光
D *vt* **1** (increase twofold) 把…增加一倍 ‹*number, size, price, dose*› **2** (fold in two) 把…对折 ‹*cloth, paper*› **3** (in writing) 双写 ‹*letter, number*› **4** (clench) 握紧 ‹*fist*› **5** Mus [在高或低八度上] 重复 ‹*note*› **6** (in cards) 把…加倍 ‹*bid, stakes*›; **two hearts ~d** 两个红桃加倍
E *vi* **1** (increase twofold) 增加一倍; **to ~ in number/strength/size/value** 数量/力量/大小/价值翻倍 **2** (serve dual purpose) 兼作; **the sofa ~s (up) as a bed** 这张沙发兼作床用 **3** (have two jobs) 兼任; **to ~ as sth./sb.** 兼任某职位/某角色; **the actor ~d as the king in Act III** 这位演员在第三幕兼演国王一角 **4** Mus «*musician*» 兼奏; **to ~ on …** 兼奏… **5** Cin, Theat 做替身演员; **to ~ for sb.** 做某演员的替身 **6** (in bridge) 叫加倍
F *n* **1** (quick pace) **at the ~** Brit, **on the ~** Amer 步伐快速地 **2** (identical person) 酷似的人; **the ~ of sb.** 与某人一模一样的人 **3** Cin, Theat 替身演员 **4** (drink) 一杯双份的烈酒 **5** (sth. consisting of two) 双份物; **a ~** 双人间 **6** Horse racing 复式下注 **7** (in bridge) 叫加倍; (in darts) 双倍; (in dominoes, board games) 双点; **to throw a ~** (in darts) 投中一个双倍; (in dominoes, board games) 掷了一个双点 **8** Sport (two victories) 两次获胜
G **doubles** *npl* Sport 双打; **to play ~s** 打双打; **mixed ~s** 混合双打; **a ~s player/match** 双打运动员/比赛

Phrasal verbs
- **double back** *vi* **1** (return) 沿原路返回 **2** (turn sharply) «*road, river, queue*» 折回; **to ~ back on itself** 折回到原处
- **double over** *vt* [**~ sb./sth. over**] 把…对折 ‹*cloth, paper*›; 使…弯腰 ‹*person*›; **I was ~d over with pain** 我疼得直不起腰
- **double up**
A *vi* **1** (bend over) 弯腰; **to ~ up with pain/laughter** 疼/笑得弯下腰 **2** (share) 共用一物; **to ~ up with sb.** 和某人共用; **to ~ up on sth.** 共用某物
B *vt* [**~ sb. up, ~ up sb.**] 使…弯腰 ‹*opponent, audience*›; **to be ~d up (in** *or* **with pain/laughter)** (疼得/笑得) 直不起腰

double: ~ act *n* 双人表演; **~-acting** *adj* **1** (in two ways) 双动的; **2** (have two effects) 双效的; **~ agent** *n* 双重间谍; **~ album** *n* 双专辑; **~ bar** *n* 复纵线; **~-barrelled** Brit, **~-barreled** Amer *adj* **1** (with two barrels) 双管的 ‹*gun*›; **2** Brit (with two parts) 由两部分组成的 ‹*name, surname*›; **~ bass** ▸**p. 395** *n* 低音提琴; **~ bed** *n* 双人床; **~-bedded** *adj* 有双人床的; **~ bend** *n* S 形弯道; **~ bill** *n* 连场 [两个电视节目或两场电影的连续播放]; **~ bind** *n* 进退两难; **to find oneself** *or* **to be in a ~ bind** 处于两难的境地; **~-blind** *adj* 双盲的; **~ bluff** *n* 真话蒙人[指故意说真话让对方以为有假的骗术]; **~ boiler** *n* Amer = **~ saucepan**

double-book
A *vt* «*hotel, airline, company*» 重复预订 ‹*room, seat, flight*›
B *vi* «*hotel, airline, company*» 重复预订

double: ~ booking *n* [u and c] 重复预订; **~-breasted** *adj* 双排纽扣的

double-check
A *vt* 复查; **to ~ the figures** 复核数字
B *vi* 复查
C **double check** *n* 复查; **to do a double check (on sth.)** (对某事物) 进行复查

double: ~ chin *n* 双下巴; **~-chinned** *adj* 有双下巴的

double-click
A *vi* 双击鼠标
B *vt* 用鼠标双击

double: ~ consonant *n* 双辅音; **~ cream** *n* [u] Brit 高脂厚奶油

double-cross
A *vt* (cheat) 欺骗; (betray) 叛卖
B *n* (cheating) 欺骗; (betrayal) 叛卖

double-crosser *n* (sb. who cheats) 欺骗者; (sb. who betrays) 叛卖者

double date
A *n* Amer 两对男女一同参加的约会
B **double-date** *vi* 两对男女一起约会

double-dealer *n* 两面派

double-dealing
A *n* [u] 两面派行为
B *adj* 两面派的

double: ~-decker *n* **1** Brit (bus) 双层公共汽车; **2** (sandwich) 双层三明治; **~-declutch** *vi* Brit [换挡时] 踩两次离合器; **~ density** *adj* 双密度的; **~-digit** *adj* 两位数的; **a ~-digit number** 两位数; **~-dipper** *n* Amer colloq 拿两份工资的人; **~ dipping** *n* [u] Amer colloq 拿两份工资; **~ door** *n*, **~ doors** *npl* 双扇门; **~ Dutch** *n* [u] colloq 晦涩难懂的话; **to talk ~ Dutch** 说话莫名其妙; **to be ~ Dutch to sb.** 对某人来说如同天书; **~ eagle** *n* **1** Amer (coin) 双鹰金元 [价值20美元]; **2** (in golf) 双鹰 [比标准杆低3杆]; **~-edged** *adj* **1** (with two cutting edges) 双刃的 ‹*sword, knife, blade*›; **2** (ambiguous) 模棱两可的; **a ~-edged compliment**

d

意义双关的恭维话; **the consequences can be ~-edged** 结果可能是把双刃剑; **it's a bit of a ~-edged sword** 这有点像把双刃剑

double entendre /ˌdu:bl ɑ:n'tɑ:ndrə/ *n* (*pl* **double entendres** /ˌdu:bl ɑ:n'tɑ:ndrə/) **1** [c] (word, phrase) 双关语 **2** [u] (act, practice) 语义双关

double entry
A *n* 复式分录
B **double-entry** *modif* 复式分录的

double: ~ exposure *n* **1** [u] (act, process) 两次曝光; **2** [c] (photograph) 两次曝光的照片; **~-faced** *adj* **1** (reversible) 双面的 ‹*fabric, skirt, dress*›; **2** (deceitful) 两面派的; **a ~-faced liar** 向各方都说谎的人; **~ fault** *n* 双发失误; **to serve a ~ fault** 两次发球失误; **~ feature** *n* 双片连映; **~-figure** *adj attrib* 两位数的 ‹*inflation*›; **~ figures** *npl* 两位数; **in ~ figures** 达两位数; **~ first** *n* Brit 两门学科获优等成绩

double flat
A *n* **1** (sign) 重降号 **2** (note) 重降音
B **double-flat** *adj* 降两个半音的

double: ~-fronted *adj* 大门两边都有窗的; **~ game** *n* 两面派的花招; **~-glaze** *vt* 为…装双层玻璃 ‹*window*›; 为…装双层玻璃窗 ‹*house*›; **a ~-glazed window** 双层玻璃窗

double glazing
A *n* [u] 双层玻璃窗
B **double-glazing** *modif* 双层玻璃窗的

double: ~-header *n* esp Amer 一日连赛两场; **~ helix** *n* 双螺旋; **~ indemnity** *n* [u] 双倍赔偿; **~ jeopardy** *n* [u] 重复起诉; **~-jointed** *adj* 关节可前后弯曲的

double knit
A *n* [u] 双面针织物
B **double-knit** *modif* 双面针织的 ‹*fabric, material*›; 双面针织物做的 ‹*trousers, dress, jacket*›

double: ~ knot *n* 双交叉结; **~ lesson** *n* 双节课; **~ lock** *n* 双保险弹簧锁; **~ major** *n* Amer 双专业; **~ negative** *n* 双重否定; **~-page spread** *n* 横贯两版的文章

double-park
A *vi* 并排停车
B *vt* 并排停放 ‹*car, van, lorry*›

double: ~-parking *n* [u] 并排停车; **~ period** *n* = **~ lesson**; **~ pneumonia** ▸ **p. 377** *n* [u] 双侧肺炎

double-quick
A *adj* 极快的; **in ~ time** 飞快地
B *adv* 极快地; **get to it ~!** 马上动手!

double: ~ room *n* 双人房间; **~ saucepan** *n* 双层蒸锅

double sharp
A *n* **1** (sign) 重升号 **2** (note) 重升音
B **double-sharp** *adj* 升高两个半音的

double: ~-sided tape *n* [u] 双面胶带; **~-space** *vt* 使留出双倍行距; **~ spacing** *n* [u] 双倍行距; **~speak** *n* [u] (deceptive language) 假话; (ambiguous language) 模棱两可的话; **~ spread** *n* 横贯两版的文章; **~ standard** *n* 双重标准; **~ star** *n* (two stars apparently close together) 光学双星; (two stars actually close together) 物理双星; **~ take** *n* **to do a ~ take** 过一会才恍然大悟; **~ talk** *n* [u] esp Amer = **~speak**; **~ think** *n* [u] [同时接受两种相矛盾观念的] 双重思想; **~ time** *n* [u] **1** (rate of pay) 双倍工资; **2** Mil 行军快步; **to march in ~ time** 快步行军; **3** Mus 加倍拍; **~ vision** *n* [u] 复视; **~ wedding** *n* [同时为两对新人举行的] 双婚礼; **~ whammy** *n* colloq 双重打击; **~ yellow line** *n*, **~ yellow lines** *npl* Brit 双黄线 [表示不允许停车]

doubly /'dʌbli/ *adv* **1** (twice as much) 双倍地; **to be ~ careful** 加倍小心 **2** (in two ways) 两方面地; **she is ~ gifted as a writer and as an artist** 她兼有作家和艺术家的双重天赋

doubt /daʊt/
A *n* [u and c] 怀疑; **(there's) no ~ (about it)** (这事) 毫无疑问; **there is little/not much ~ about her guilt** *or* **that she is guilty** 几乎可以肯定她有罪; **there is a/some ~ about** *or* **as to ...** 对…有点/有些怀疑; **I have no ~ about her guilt** *or* **that she is guilty** 我确信她有罪; **to have (one's) ~s (about sth./doing sth.)** (对某事物/做某事) 心存疑虑; **to leave no ~ that .../about sth.** 对…毫无疑问; **to leave sb. in (no) ~ about** *or* **as to sth.** 使某人对某事物没有/有确切把握; **without (a) ~, without the slightest ~** 毫无疑问; **without a shadow of ~** 没有一丝怀疑; **beyond (a/any) ~, beyond all (possible) ~** 毫无疑问; **proof beyond ~** Jur 确凿证据; **to be in ~** «*outcome, future, event*» 不确定; «*honesty, innocence, guilt*» 令人怀疑; **if/when in ~, ...**: 如有疑问, …; **to cast** *or* **throw ~(s) on sth.** 对某事物产生疑问; **to raise ~s about sth.** 对某事物提出怀疑
B *vt* 怀疑 ‹*fact, person, honesty*›; **I ~ whether** *or* **if** *or* **that he'll know the answer** 我怀疑他是否会知道答案; **I ~ it** 我不信; **it cannot be ~ed that ...** …不容置疑; **to ~ one's own eyes/ears** 不敢相信自己的眼睛/耳朵

doubter /'daʊtə(r)/ *n* 持怀疑态度的人

doubtful /'daʊtfl/ *adj* **1** (unlikely) 不大可能的; **it's ~ if** *or* **whether** *or* **that they'll succeed** 他们未必会成功 **2** (unsure) 不确定的; **to feel ~ that .../whether .../about sth.** 对…拿不定主意 **3** (questionable) 令人生疑的 ‹*assertion, evidence, question*›; (uncertain) 难以预测的 ‹*future, benefit, weather*› **4** (dubious) 有问题的; **a ~ past** 令人生疑的过去; **his joke was in ~ taste** 他的笑话很庸俗

doubtfully /'daʊtfəli/ *adv* **1** (hesitantly) 犹豫地 **2** (sceptically) 怀疑地 **3** (not convincingly) 含糊地

doubtfulness /'daʊtfəlnɪs/ *n* [u] **1** (hesitancy) 犹豫 **2** (scepticism) 怀疑 **3** (dubiousness) 可疑

doubting Thomas /ˌdaʊtɪŋ 'tɒməs/ *n* 怀疑一切的人

doubtless /'daʊtlɪs/ *adv* (very probably) 很可能地; (without doubt) 无疑地

douche /du:ʃ/
A *n* **1** (device) (for the body) 冲洗器; (for internal body part) 灌洗器 **2** (jet of liquid) (for the body) 冲洗液; (for internal body part) 灌洗液 **3** (cleaning) (for the body) 冲洗; (for internal body part) 灌洗
B *vt* 冲洗 ‹*person, body, part of the body*›; 灌洗 ‹*vagina*›; **to ~ oneself** 自我清洗

dough /dəʊ/ *n* [u] **1** (for making bread, pastry etc.) 生面团 **2** colloq (money) 钱

doughnut /'dəʊnʌt/ *n* 甜甜圈; **it's dollars to ~s that ...** Amer colloq …十拿九稳

doughnut-shaped *adj* 环形的

doughty /'daʊti/ *adj* archaic or hum 强悍的

doughy /'dəʊi/ *adj* **1** (like dough) 又软又稠的 ‹*substance, mixture, texture*› **2** (not cooked properly) 夹生的 **3** (flabby, pale) 苍白的 ‹*skin, complexion, face*›

Douglas fir /ˌdʌgləs 'fɜ:(r)/ *n* 花旗松

dour /'daʊər/ *adj* **1** (stern) 严厉的 ‹*manner, look*›; (gloomy) 阴郁的 ‹*manner, look*›; 贫瘠的 ‹*landscape*›; 阴沉的 ‹*winter sky*›; (austere) 阴森森的 ‹*building*› **2** (stubborn) 顽强的 ‹*resistance, struggle*›; 激烈的 ‹*match, battle, meeting*›

dourly /'daʊəli/ *adv* **1** (sternly) 严厉地; (gloomily) 阴郁地 **2** (stubbornly) 顽强地

douse /daʊs/ *vt* **1** (put out) 浇灭 ‹*flames, fire*›; 熄灭 ‹*light, lamp*›; **nothing could ~ her euphoria** 没有什么能平抑她亢奋的情绪 **2** (pour water over) 往…上泼水 ‹*room*›; (pour another liquid over) 往…上泼液体; **to ~ the room with** *or* **in petrol** 在房间里浇汽油

dove[1] /dʌv/ *n* **1** Zool 鸽子 **2** esp Amer Pol 鸽派人物

dove[2] /dəʊv/ Amer *pt* ▸ **dive B**

dovecote, dovecot /'dʌvkɒt/ *n* 鸽房

dove-grey ▸ **p. 134**
A *adj* 鸽灰色的
B *n* [u] 鸽灰色

doveish /'dʌvɪʃ/ *adj* 鸽派的

dovetail /'dʌvteɪl/
A *n* **1** **~ (joint)** 鸠尾榫接头 **2** (part of joint) 鸠尾榫
B *vt* **1** fig 使吻合; **to ~ sth. with sth.** 使某物与某物吻合 **2** Constr 以鸠尾榫接合
C *vi* fig **to ~ (together)** 吻合; **to ~ with sth.** 与某物吻合

dovetail joint *n* = **dovetail A1**

dovish /'dʌvɪʃ/ *adj* = **doveish**

dowager /'daʊədʒə(r)/ *n* **1** (widow) [继承亡夫称号或财产的] 遗孀; **~ duchess** 公爵遗孀 **2** (elderly woman) 气度不凡的老妇

dowdiness /'daʊdɪnɪs/ *n* [u] (of a woman) 衣着过时; (of clothes) 过时

dowdy /'daʊdi/ *adj* 衣着过时的 ‹*woman*›; 过时的 ‹*dress, clothes*›

dowel /'daʊəl/
A *n* 暗榫
B *vt* (*pres p etc.* **-ll-** Brit, **-l-** Amer) 用暗榫接合

Dow Jones index, Dow Jones average /ˌdaʊ 'dʒəʊnz/ *ns* 道-琼斯平均指数

Dow Jones industrial average *n* 道-琼斯工业平均指数

> **the Dow-Jones average**
>
> 道-琼斯平均指数, 亦称道-琼斯指数 (Dow-Jones Index), 简称道指 (the Dow)。是世界上历史最悠久、影响最大的股价指数, 代表特定公司股票的平均价格, 反映纽约股票和证券市场的行情。道-琼斯公司是美国金融新闻出版商、为《华尔街日报》(*Wall Street Journal*) 的出版者。1882 年由查尔斯·道 (Charles Dow) 和爱德华·琼斯 (Edward Jones) 等创立, 1884 年开始编制并发布股价指数。道-琼斯指数以点而不是以美元计算, 现主要由四种指数构成, 分别为工业股价指数 (Industrial Average)、运输业股价指数 (Transportation Average)、公用事业股价指数 (Utility Average) 和综合股价指数 (Composite Average)。最具影响的工业股价指数由 30 种知名公司的股票价格平均数组成。

Down /daʊn/ *pr n* 唐郡

down[1] /daʊn/
A *adv* **1** (from higher to lower) 向下; (downstairs) 向楼下; **to read/climb ~** 往下读/爬; **to fall ~** (from standing) 跌倒; (from height) 掉下; **to put sth. ~** 把某物放下; **~!** (to dog) 趴下!; **is he ~ yet?** 他下楼了吗?; **3 ~** (in crossword) 第三竖行 **2** (in lower place) 在下面; **a car with the hood ~** 一辆前车盖合上的车; **the second shelf ~** 下面第二层架子; **~ below** 在底下; fig euph 在地狱; **50 metres ~** 地下 50 米深处 **3** (facing bottom) 朝下; **the bread fell with the buttered side ~** 面包掉落, 抹了黄油的一面朝下; **to lie face ~ on sth.** 趴在某物上 **4** (below horizon) 在地平线以下; **the sun will soon go ~** 太阳快要落山了 **5** (downstream) 向下游; **to row ~ towards the sea** 顺流而下划向大海 **6** (less in amount, price, volume) 减少; **sales are ~ again this quarter** 本季度的销售额又下降了; **to get the price ~ to £200** 将价格降到 200 英镑; **to get the article ~ to five pages** 把文章缩减到 5 页; **to get one's weight ~** 减轻体重; **she was watching TV with the sound ~** 她在看电视, 音量开得很低 **7** (making loss) 产生损失; **they were £200 ~ on what they'd hoped to make** 他们比期望的少赚了 200 英镑 **8** (left with) 仅剩下; **to be ~ to one's last few pounds** 只剩最后几英镑 **9** (in bad situation) 处于困境; **you don't hit** *or*

kick a man when he's ～ 不要落井下石 [10] Sport (behind) 落后; **to be 4 (points) ～** 落后 4 分; **she's ～ 15-40** 她 15 比 40 落后 [11] (along, to, at place) 在那一头; **my office is halfway ～** 我的办公室在靠走廊中间那里; **I saw him ～ at the shops** 我看到他在店铺那边 [12] (in south) 在南方; (to south) 向南方; **to go ～ south** 南下 [13] (away from city) 离开城市; **to go ～ from London** 从伦敦过来; **to go ～ to the village** 下乡; **to live ～ in the country/on the farm** 住在乡下/农场里 [14] (from earlier time) 从先到后; **～ through the ages** 古往今来 [15] (as deposit) 作为定金; **to pay £50 ～** 付 50 英镑定金 [16] (in writing) 以文字; **to put sth. ～ (on paper** *or* **in writing)** 写下某物; **it's ～ here in black and white** 白纸黑字写在这里 [17] (scheduled) [表示安排]; **to be ～ to do sth.** 安排好做某事; **you're ～ to speak next** 接下来就该你发言了; **you're ～ for Thursday** (for appointment) 你被排在周四; **you're ～ on the list** 名单上有你 [18] (in range) 以下; **from age 5 ～** 5 岁以下; **from the tenth century ～ to the present day** 从 10 世纪至今; **he described her exactly right ～ to the colour of her eyes** 他对她的描写详细到了她眼睛的颜色 [19] (finished) 完成; **5 ～ and 3 to go** 完成了 5 项，还差 3 项 [20] Brit (from university) 从大学结业 [尤指牛津或剑桥大学] [21] (sick) **to be ～ with the flu/a cold** 患流感/感冒病倒 [22] (attributable) **to be** *or* **come ～ to sb./sth.** 由某人/某事物引起; **her problems come ～ to the media** 她的诸多问题是媒体造成的; **it's ～ to you** 你看着办吧 [23] (away with) 打倒; **～ with corruption!** 消除腐败!

B *prep* [1] (from higher to lower point) 沿…向下; **she came ～ the stairs** 她走下楼梯; **he fell ～ the hole** 他跌进洞里; **tears ran ～ his face** 泪水顺着他的脸庞流下来; **a dress with buttons ～ the front** 正面有竖排纽扣的女装 [2] (at lower part of) 在…的下面; **farther ～ the hill** 在小山的更低处; **the kitchen is ～ those stairs** 厨房在那楼梯下面 [3] (downstream) 向…的下游; **to sail ～ the river** 顺河而下航行 [4] (along) 沿着; **to walk ～ a street** 沿街走过去; **halfway ～ the passage** 在过道中间; **they live ～ the road** 他们住在路的那头; **to look ～ sth.** 用…观看 ‹*telescope*›; 朝…里望去 ‹*tunnel*›; **I looked ～ the street** 我沿街望去 [5] (throughout) …以来; **～ the years/centuries** 多年/数百年以来 [6] Brit colloq (at) 在; (to) 去; **he's ～ the pub** 他在酒吧里; **she's gone ～ town** 她到市中心去了

C *adj* [1] *pred* colloq (depressed) 沮丧的; **to feel a bit ～** 有点闷闷不乐 [2] *attrib* (going downwards) 向下的 ‹*lift, escalator, arrow*› [3] *attrib* Brit Rail 下行的 ‹*train, line*› [4] *pred* Comput «*network*» 停止运行的; **the system was ～** 系统瘫痪了

D *vt* [1] (with blow, bullet) 打倒 ‹*opponent, prey*›; **he ～ed him with an uppercut** 他用一记上钩拳将他击倒 [2] (from air) 击落 ‹*aircraft*› [3] colloq (swallow) 一口气吞下; **he ～ed his beer** 他将啤酒一饮而尽

E *n* Brit colloq **to have a ～ on sb.** 厌恶某人

down[2] *n* [u] [1] (feathers) 绒羽 [2] (fine hair) 绒毛

down[3] *n* (*usu pl* **downs**) 丘陵地

down-and-out

A *adj* [1] (destitute) 穷困潦倒的 [2] (facing defeat) 面临失败的

B *n* 穷困潦倒的人

down at heel *adj* [1] (worn out) 鞋跟磨损的 ‹*shoe*› [2] (shabby) 破败的 ‹*town, hotel*›

downbeat /ˈdaʊnbiːt/

A *n* Mus 强拍

B *adj* [1] (gloomy) 忧郁的; (pessimistic) 悲观的 [2] (understated) 无热情的

down: ～cast *adj* [1] (looking down) 低垂的 ‹*eyes*›; [2] (despondent) 垂头丧气的; **～draught** *n* Brit 下沉气流

downer /ˈdaʊnə(r)/ *n* colloq [1] (depressing experience) 扫兴的经历; **to be on a ～** 心情沮丧 [2] (drug) 镇静药

downfall /ˈdaʊnfɔːl/ *n* [1] (ruin) 衰落; **the scandal led to his ～** 这桩丑闻使他身败名裂 [2] (cause of ruin) 衰落的原因; **drink was his ～** 酗酒使他堕落 [3] (of rain) 大阵雨; (of snow) 大阵雪

downgrade /ˈdaʊngreɪd/

A *vt* [1] (lower in rank) 使降职 [2] (reduce) 使降级; **the hotel has been ～d to a guest house** 这家宾馆已降格为招待所了

B *n* [1] (reduction in status or importance) 降低; (reduction in size) 缩小; (reduction in amount) 减少 [2] Amer (downward gradient) 下坡; **to be on the ～** 在走下坡路

downhearted /ˌdaʊnˈhɑːtɪd/ *adj* 消沉的; **don't be ～** 不要灰心丧气

downhill /ˌdaʊnˈhɪl/

A *adj* [1] *attrib* lit (sloping down) 下坡的 ‹*road*› [2] lit (going down) 下山的 ‹*walk*› [3] Sport (skiing) 滑降的 ‹*race*›; **～ skiing** 滑降滑雪 [4] *pred* fig (easy) 容易的; **it's all ～ from here** 从这以后就容易了 [5] *pred* fig (worsening) 每况愈下的; **be all ～, be ～ all the way** 每况愈下

B *adv* [1] lit (towards the bottom) 向山下; **to go ～** «*road*» 向下倾斜; «*person, vehicle*» 向下坡走 [2] fig (into a worsening state) 每况愈下地; **to go ～** 每况愈下

C *n* [1] (downward slope) 下坡 [2] (in skiing) 滑降比赛

down-home *adj* Amer 淳朴的

Downing Street /ˌdaʊnɪŋ ˈstriːt/ *pr n* [1] (street) 唐宁街; **(no.) 10, ～** 唐宁街 10 号 [2] Pol, Journ 英国政府

> **Downing Street**
>
> 唐宁街。英国伦敦威斯敏斯特市（City of Westminster）的一条街，1680 年前后由乔治·唐宁爵士（Sir George Downing）建成，故此得名。1735 年，英国第一任首相罗伯特·沃波尔（Robert Walpole）搬入唐宁街 10 号，此后 10 号一直为英国首相住所，"唐宁街"或"10 号"也因此成为英国首相或政府的代名词。唐宁街11号为英国财政大臣（Chancellor of the Exchequer）住所。

down-in-the-mouth *adj* 垂头丧气的

download /ˈdaʊnləʊd/

A *vt* 下载

B *n* [1] (copying of data) 下载 [2] (downloaded data) 下载的文件

downloadable /ˌdaʊnˈləʊdəbl/ *adj* 可下载的

downmarket /ˌdaʊnˈmɑːkɪt/ esp Brit

A *adj* 面向低端消费者的; **it's rather ～** 这是很低档的

B *adv* 面向低端消费者; **to go ～** 迎合低端市场

down: ～ payment *n* 首付款; **to make a ～ payment of £50** 首付 50 英镑; **a ～ payment on a house** 购房的首付款; **～pipe** *n* Brit 水落管; **～play** *vt* 对…轻描淡写; **～pour** *n* 倾盆大雨

downright /ˈdaʊnraɪt/

A *adj attrib* [1] (absolute) 完全的; **a ～ fool** 十足的傻瓜; **a ～ lie** 彻头彻尾的谎言; **a ～ refusal** 断然的拒绝 [2] (forthright) 直率的

B *adv* 完全地; **it makes me ～ angry** 这让我气愤之极; **it's ～ impossible** 这根本不可能

downriver /ˌdaʊnˈrɪvə(r)/

A *adj* (direction) 向下游的; (position) 在下游的

B *adv* 向下游; **to drift ～** 顺水漂下

downshift /ˈdaʊnʃɪft/

A *vi* [1] esp Amer (change gear) 换低挡 [2] fig (slow down) 放慢速度; **business was ～ing** 商业变得不景气 [3] (change lifestyle) 减慢生活节奏; **to ～ from full-time work** 从全日制工作换到比较悠闲的职位

B *n* [1] esp Amer (gear change) 换低速挡 [2] (change in lifestyle) 生活节奏的减慢

down: ～shifter *n* 减慢生活节奏的人; **～side** *n* 负面; **what's the ～side of this approach?** 这种方式的缺点是什么?

downsize /ˈdaʊnsaɪz/

A *vt* 精简 ‹*company, industry*›

B *vi* «*company, industry*» 缩小规模

down: ～sizing *n* [u] 缩小规模; **～spout** *n* Amer **= ～pipe**

Down's syndrome /ˈdaʊnz ˌsɪndrəʊm/ *n* [u] 唐氏综合征

downstage /ˈdaʊnsteɪdʒ/

A *adv* (position) 在舞台前部; (direction) 向舞台前部

B *adj* (position) 在舞台前部的; (direction) 向舞台前部的

downstairs /ˌdaʊnˈsteəz/

A *adv* (on lower floor) 在楼下; (to lower floor) 往楼下; **to go ～** 下楼; **the family ～** 楼下的人家

B *n* 楼下; **a ～ room/bathroom** 楼下的房间/浴室

C *adj attrib* 在楼下的; **the ～ toilet** 楼下的卫生间

downstate /ˈdaʊnsteɪt/

A *adv* Amer (location) 在州的边远地区; (direction) 向州的边远地区

B *adj attrib* 州的边远地区的; **～ New York** 纽约州的边远地区

downstream /ˈdaʊnstriːm/

A *adv* 向下游; **to go ～** 顺流而下

B *adj* (direction) 向下游的; (position) 在下游的; **～ regions** 下游地区

down: ～stroke *n* [1] (in writing) 向下的一笔; [2] (downward movement) (of wing) 向下的拍击; (of machine part) 下冲; **～swing** *n* [1] (in golf) 向下的挥动; [2] Econ 下降趋势; **～ time** *n* [u] [1] Comput 停机时间; [2] Amer (in workplace) 停工期; **everyone needs a little ～ time to relax** 人人都需要休息会儿放松一下; **～-to-earth** *adj* 务实的

downtown /ˈdaʊntaʊn/ esp Amer

A *adv* (location) 在市中心 ‹*live, work*›; (direction) **to go ～** 往市中心

B *adj* 市中心的; **～ New York** 纽约市中心; **～ stores** 闹市区的商店

C *n* [u] 市中心

down: ～trend *n* 下降趋势; **～trodden** *adj* 受压迫的; **～turn** *n* (in economy, career) 衰退; (in demand, profits) 下降; **～ under** *adv* colloq (in Australia) 在澳大利亚; (in New Zealand) 在新西兰; (to Australia) 往澳大利亚; (to New Zealand) 往新西兰

downward /ˈdaʊnwəd/

A *adj* [1] (moving, leading lower) 向下的 ‹*climb*› **to give a ～** 向下瞟一眼; **a ～ stroke with a brush** 画笔的向下一勾 [2] (decreasing in level) 下降的; **a ～ trend** 下降趋势; **a ～ movement of prices** 价格的下调 [3] (worsening in condition) 恶化的; **a ～ spiral** 每况愈下; **to be on the ～ path** 走下坡路

B *adv* **= downwards**

downward mobility *n* [u] [生活质量等的] 向下流动

downwards /ˈdaʊnwədz/ *adv* [1] (lower in position) 向下地; **the land slopes gently ～** 地面缓缓向下倾斜; **to read from the top ～** 自上而下读 [2] (face down) 朝下地; **to lie face ～** 俯卧 [3] (to lower level) 向低层次; **the long-term trend is ～** 从长远来看呈下降趋势; **to push prices ～** 把价格压低 [4] (in scale, degree, rank) 以下; **everybody from the boss ～** 上至老板，下至每个员工 [5] (from earlier time) 往后推移地; **from the 15th century ～** 自 15 世纪以来

downward trend *n* 下降趋势

downwind /ˌdaʊnˈwɪnd/

A *adv* 顺风地; **to sail ～** 顺风航行; **people living ～ of the fire** 住在火势下风处的人们

B *adj* 顺风的

downy /ˈdaʊni/ *adj* **1** (covered in soft hair) 毛茸茸的 **2** (soft and fluffy) 松软的

dowry /ˈdaʊəri/ *n* 嫁妆

dowse /daʊz/
A *vi* 用占卜杖探水源
B *vt* = **douse**

dowser /ˈdaʊzə(r)/ *n* 用占卜杖探水者

dowsing rod /ˈdaʊzɪŋ rɒd/ *n* [探测水源用的] 占卜杖

doyen /ˈdɔɪən/ *n* (most respected person) 元老; (most prominent person) 最杰出的人

doyenne /dɔɪˈen/ *n* (most respected woman) 女元老; (most prominent woman) 最杰出的女性

doz. *abbr* = **dozen 1**

doze /dəʊz/
A *vi* 打瞌睡
B *n* 瞌睡; **to have a ~** 打一会儿盹

Phrasal verb
- **doze off** *vi* 打瞌睡

d

dozen /ˈdʌzn/ ▸**p. 32** *n* **1** (twelve) 一打; **two ~ eggs** 两打鸡蛋; **a ~ people** 十二个人; **by the ~** 成打地 **2** colloq (a lot) 许多; **I've told you a ~ times!** 我已经告诉你好多遍了!; **~s of people** 很多人

dozy /ˈdəʊzi/ *adj* **1** (drowsy) 昏昏欲睡的 **2** Brit colloq (stupid) 愚笨的

DPhil *abbr* Brit = **Doctor of Philosophy**

DPP *abbr* Brit = **Director of Public Prosecutions**

Dr *abbr* = **doctor A**

drab /dræb/ *adj* 灰褐色的 ‹*colour, surroundings, house*›; 单调的 ‹*life, existence*›

drabness /ˈdræbnɪs/ *n* [u] (of colour, surroundings) 灰褐色; (of life) 单调

drachma /ˈdrækmə/ *n* (*pl* **~s** *or* **drachmae** /ˈdrækmiː/) Hist 德拉克马 [希腊旧货币单位]

draconian /drəˈkəʊnɪən/ *adj* 严苛的

draft /drɑːft, Amer dræft/
A *vt* **1** (make rough version of) 起草 **2** (select, appoint) 选派; **to ~ security staff from elsewhere** 从别处抽调保安人员 **3** Amer Mil (conscript) 征募; **to be ~ed into the army** 应征入伍
B *n* **1** (of letter, novel) 草稿; (of contract, plan) 草案; **the first/final ~** 初稿/定稿; **a ~ resolution** 决议草案; **a ~ letter** 信件草稿 **2** Fin 汇票 **3** esp Mil (detachment) 分遣队; (intake) 新兵 **4** Amer Mil (conscription) **the ~** 征兵 **5** Amer = **draught**

Phrasal verb
- **draft in** *vt* [**~ sb./sth. in, ~ in sb./sth.**] 抽调; **I was ~ed in to help with the tidying up** 我被派去帮忙整理

draft: **~ board** *n* Amer 征兵局; **~ card** *n* Amer 兵役应征卡; **~ dodger** *n* Amer 逃避兵役者

draftee /ˌdrɑːfˈtiː, Amer ˌdræf-/ *n* Amer 应征入伍者

drafthorse /ˈdrɑːfthɔːs, Amer ˈdræft-/ *n* Amer = **draught horse**

draftiness /ˈdrɑːftɪnɪs, Amer ˈdræftɪnɪs/ *n* [u] Amer = **draughtiness**

draftproof /ˈdrɑːftpruːf, Amer ˈdræft-/ *adj, vt* Amer = **draughtproof**

draftproofing /ˈdrɑːftpruːfɪŋ, Amer ˈdræft-/ *n* [u] Amer = **draughtproofing**

draftsman /ˈdrɑːftsmən, Amer ˈdræfts-/ *n* Amer = **draughtsman**

draftsmanship /ˈdrɑːftsmənʃɪp, Amer ˈdræft-/ *n* Amer = **draughtsmanship**

drafty /ˈdrɑːfti, Amer ˈdræfti/ *adj* Amer = **draughty**

drag /dræg/
A *vt* (*pres p etc.* **-gg-**) **1** (pull) 拖; **to ~ sth. to** *or* **towards sth.** 把某物拖向某处; **to ~ sth. along the ground** 在地上拖某物; **to ~ one's feet** *or* **heels** lit 拖着脚走; fig 故意拖拉; **to ~ one's feet over sth.** 在某事上迟迟不作决定; **to ~ its anchor** «*vessel*» 拖锚; **to ~ ass** Amer sl 别瞎磨蹭 **2** (force to go) 硬拉; **to ~ sb./sth. into/to sth.** 把某人/某事硬扯到某事中; **to ~ sb. from/out of sth.** 把某人从某处硬拉出来; **to ~ sb. to do sth.** 硬拉某人做某事; **they keep ~ging politics into sport** 他们谈体育时总是扯上政治; **to ~ sb. through the courts** fig 使某人受辱; **to ~ sb.'s name through the mud** *or* **mire** 诋毁某人的名声 **3** (search) 拖网搜索 ‹*lake, river*› **4** Comput (move across screen) 拖动 ‹*icon, mouse, image, highlighted text*›; **to ~ and drop sth.** 拖动（屏幕上）某东西
B *vi* (*pres p etc.* **-gg-**) **1** (move slowly) 拖沓地进行; **the first act was OK, but the second ~ged terribly** 第一幕还好，但第二幕拖沓得要命 **2** (trail) 拖着移动; **she let her fingers ~ in/through the water** 她的手指在水中划过 **3** colloq (smoke) 吸; **to ~ on a cigarette** 吸烟
C *n* **1** [c] (hindrance) 累赘; **to be a ~ on sth./sb.** 对某物/某人是个累赘 **2** [c] colloq (boring or tiresome person) 令人厌烦的人; (boring or tiresome thing) 乏味的事物; **to be a ~** 令人厌烦 **3** [c] colloq (puff) 抽一口; **to take a long ~ on one's cigarette** 深吸一口烟 **4** [u] Aviat, Phys 阻力 **5** [c] colloq (road) 道路; **the main ~** 主路 **6** [u] colloq (women's clothes) [男子穿的] 女装; **to dress up in ~** 穿娘们装 **7** [u] Amer colloq (influence) 影响力 **8** [c] (hook) 重型耙 **9** [c] Hunt (lure) 人工臭迹

Phrasal verbs
- **drag along**
A *vt* **1** [**~ sth. along**] (pull along) 拖着 **2** [**~ sb. along**] (force to come) 硬拉; **to ~ sb. along to a show/lecture** 硬拉某人去看演出/听讲座
B *v refl* **to ~ oneself along** 费力地移动
- **drag away**
A *vt* [**~ sb. away, ~ away sb.**] 拖走; **to ~ sb. away from sth.** 把某人从某处拉出来
B *v refl* **to ~ oneself away**; 勉强离开; **to ~ oneself away from the computer** 勉强离开电脑
- **drag behind** *vi* 拖沓地走在后面
- **drag by** *vi* «*time*» 慢慢过去
- **drag down**
A [**~ sb./sth. down, ~ down sb./sth.**] *vt* **1** (pull down) 拉下; **he ~ged her down to the ground** 他把她拉倒在地 **2** (bring to lower standard or level) 使…地位下降 ‹*person*›; 使…水平下降 ‹*object*›; **she didn't wish to be ~ged down to his level** 她不想被贬低到和他一个层次; **the economy is being ~ged down** 经济每况愈下
B [**~ sb. down, ~ down sb.**] *vt* (tire) «*illness*» 使…虚弱; (depress) «*weather*» 使…沮丧
- **drag in** *vt* [**~ sb./sth. in, ~ in sb./sth.**] **1** (pull in) 把…硬拉进来 **2** fig (introduce) 硬扯进 ‹*topic, reference*›
- **drag off** *vt* [**~ sb. off, ~ off sb.**] 把…硬拉走
- **drag on** *vi* 拖延太久; **the conflict ~ged on and on** 冲突没完没了地拖延着
- **drag out** *vt* **1** [**~ sb./sth. out, ~ out sb./sth.**] (force out) 拽出 **2** [**~ sth. out, ~ out sth.**] (extend) 拖延; **don't ~ it out, say what you have to say then sit down** 别拖泥带水，讲完该讲的就坐下 **3** **to ~ sth. out of sb.** (obtain) 迫使某人说出某事; **I'll get the truth if I have to ~ it out of them!** 哪怕对他们逼供我也得了解真相!
- **drag up**
A [**~ sth. up, ~ up sth.**] *vt* **1** (pull up) 把…拉过来 **2** fig colloq (mention) 提起某事物; **surely they aren't going to ~ all that up again?** 他们肯定不会把那档子事又抖出来吧?
B [**~ sb. up, ~ up sb.**] *vt* Brit colloq (bring up, educate) 把…拉扯大 ‹*child*›

drag: **~ and drop** *n* [u] 拖放; **~ coefficient, ~ factor** *ns* 阻力系数

draggy /ˈdrægi/ *adj* colloq 沉闷乏味的

drag: **~ lift** *n* 吊椅缆车; **~net** *n* **1** 全面搜捕; **to escape the police ~net** 逃避警方的罗网; **2** (for fishing, hunting) 拖网

dragon /ˈdrægən/ *n* **1** (mythical creature) 龙; **to chase the ~** colloq 吸食海洛因 **2** pej or hum (fierce woman) 悍妇

dragonfly /ˈdrægənflaɪ/ *n* 蜻蜓

dragoon /drəˈguːn/
A *n* Mil **1** Brit 王室禁卫队骑兵 **2** Hist (mounted infantryman) 骑马步兵
B *vt* 迫使; **to ~ sb. into doing sth.** 迫使某人做某事

drag: **~ queen** *n* colloq 模仿女性的男艺人; **~ race** *n* 短程高速赛车; **~ racer** *n* (car) 短程高速赛车; (driver) 短程高速赛车手; **~ racing** *n* [u] 短程高速赛车

dragster /ˈdrægstə(r)/ *n* 减重高速汽车

dragstrip /ˈdrægstrɪp/ *n* Amer 短程高速赛车道

drain /dreɪn/
A *n* **1** (sewer) 下水道; (waste water pipe) 下水管; (ditch) 排水沟; **to go down the ~** colloq (be wasted) 被浪费掉; (be ruined) 完蛋; **it's just money down the ~** 钱白白地扔进水里; **my plan for the summer holidays has just gone down the ~** 我的暑假计划泡了汤 **2** Brit (grating) 下水道格栅 **3** (burden, demand) 消耗; **a ~ on sth.** 对某物的耗费
B *vt* **1** (remove liquid from) 排空…的水 ‹*land, lake, radiator*› **2** Culin 沥干 ‹*vegetables*› **3** Med 为…引流 ‹*wound*› **4** (draw off, remove) 排出 ‹*liquid*›; **they've ~ed all the water from the swimming pool** 他们把游泳池的水排光了 **5** fig (sap) 耗尽 ‹*strength, funds*›; **working a full day at the office ~s me completely** 在办公室上一整天班让我精疲力竭; **to ~ a country of its resources** 耗尽一个国家的资源 **6** (drink up contents of) 喝光 **7** Geog «*river*» 容纳…的来水; **the Thames ~s the whole of southern Oxfordshire** 整个牛津郡南部地区的水流入泰晤士河
C *vi* **1** lit (flow away) «*liquid*» 流走; **the blood** *or* **colour ~ed from her face** 她脸色变得煞白; **the life is ~ing out of him** 他的生命渐渐枯竭 **2** (become dry) 沥干; **to leave sth. to ~** 让某物滴干水

Phrasal verbs
- **drain away** *vi* **1** (flow away) «*liquid*» 慢慢流走 **2** fig (fade, diminish) «*hope, strength*» 逐渐消失; **her money ~ed away** 她的钱慢慢花光了
- **drain off**
A *vi* «*liquid*» 流走
B *vt* [**~ sth. off, ~ off sth.**] 使…流走 ‹*liquid*›; **to ~ off any excess fat** 撇去多余的油脂

drainage /ˈdreɪnɪdʒ/ *n* [u] **1** (from land) 排水 **2** Med (from wound) 引流 **3** (system of pipes, ditches) 排水系统

drainage: **~ area, ~ basin** *ns* 流域; **~ board** *n* Amer = **draining board**; **~ tube** *n* 引流管

drainboard /ˈdreɪnbɔːrd/ *n* Amer = **draining board**

drained /dreɪnd/ *adj* 精疲力竭的

drainer /ˈdreɪnə(r)/ *n* 滤干器

draining board *n* Brit 滴水板

drainpipe /ˈdreɪnpaɪp/
A *n* **1** (for rain water) 排水管 **2** (for waste water, sewage) 下水管
B **drainpipes** *npl* Brit colloq = **drainpipe trousers**

drainpipe trousers *npl* Brit 瘦腿紧身裤

drake /dreɪk/ *n* 公鸭

dram /dræm/ *n* esp Scot 少量的酒; **a ~ of whisky** 少量威士忌

drama /ˈdrɑːmə/ *n* **1** [u] (genre) 戏剧; **modern ~** 现代戏剧 **2** [u] (acting) 戏剧表演; **to study ~ at college** 在大学学戏剧 **3** [c] (play) 戏

剧作品; **a television ～** 电视剧 **4** [c] (dramatic event) 戏剧性事件; **a human ～** 戏剧性的世间人事; **to make a ～ out of sth.** 对某事小题大做 **5** [u] (excitement) 激情; **her life was full of ～** 她的生活充满刺激

dramatic /drəˈmætɪk/ *adj* **1** Theat 戏剧的 ‹*work*› **2** (impressive, theatrical) 戏剧性的; **for ～ effect** 为达到戏剧性的效果 **3** (tense, exciting) 激动人心的 ‹*situation, event*› **4** (sudden, radical) 突发的 ‹*change, development*›; **there has been a ～ improvement in her condition** 她的健康状况有了惊人的好转

dramatically /drəˈmætɪkli/ *adv* **1** Theat 从戏剧角度 **2** (in a theatrical way) 戏剧性地; **she laid her hand ～ on her bosom** 她夸张做作地把一只手放在胸口上 **3** (causing excitement) 激动人心地 **4** (radically) 突发惊人地; **his influence declined ～** 他的影响力大减; **to deteriorate ～** 急剧恶化

dramatics /drəˈmætɪks/ *npl* **1** + *v sing* (dramatic art) 戏剧艺术; (performance) 戏剧表演 **2** + *v pl* pej (histrionics) 装腔作势

dramatic society *n* 戏剧社

dramatist /ˈdræmətɪst/ *n* 剧作家

dramatization /ˌdræmətaɪˈzeɪʃn, Amer -tɪˈz-/ *n* **1** [u] (act of dramatizing) 改编成戏剧 **2** [c] (dramatized version) 改编成的剧作 **3** [u] (exaggeration) 夸张

dramatize /ˈdræmətaɪz/

A *vt* **1** (adapt) 把…改编成戏剧; **a ～d documentary** 纪实剧 **2** (present vividly) 生动地表达 **3** pej (exaggerate) 夸张; **the press has ～d the whole affair** 新闻界把整个事件夸大了

B *vi* pej 装腔作势

drank /dræŋk/ *pt* ▸**drink A, B, C**

drape /dreɪp/

A *vt* **1** (cover, swathe) 悬挂 ‹*cloth*›; **he ～d his coat over the back of a chair** 他把上衣搭在椅背上; **to ～ a shawl around one's shoulders** 把披巾披在肩上; **to ～ oneself over sth.** 四肢舒展地躺在某物上 **2** (cover with) 覆盖 ‹*furniture*›; **walls ～d in ivy** 爬满常春藤的墙; **the entire room is ～d in** *or* **with silk hangings** 整间屋子挂满了丝绸帷幔

B *n* (cloth) 褶边

C **drapes** *pl* Amer (curtains) 窗帘

draper /ˈdreɪpə(r)/ *n* Brit dated 布商

drapery /ˈdreɪpəri/

A *n* [u] **1** (hanging cloth) 褶皱垂布 **2** Brit dated (cloth) 布料; (things made from cloth) 纺织品

B **draperies** *npl* Amer (curtains) 窗帘

drapery department *n* 纺织品部

drastic /ˈdræstɪk/ *adj* 极端的 ‹*measure, step*›; 剧烈的 ‹*change*›; **a ～ shortage of personnel** 人员的严重短缺

drastically /ˈdræstɪkli/ *adv* 剧烈地; **to ～ reduce employment prospects** 使就业机会急剧减少

drat /dræt/ *excl* colloq 见鬼; **～ (it)!** 见鬼!; **～ that man!** 那个讨厌的家伙!

dratted /ˈdrætɪd/ *adj attrib* colloq 讨厌的; **I can't get the ～ car to start** 这辆该死的车我就是发动不起来

draught /drɑːft, Amer dræft/ Brit

A *n* **1** [c] (current of air) 通风气流; **there's a terrible ～ in the room** 房间里有一股很大的穿堂风; **to sit in a ～** 坐在风口上; **to feel the ～** fig colloq 手头拮据 **2** [c] (to fire, furnace) 抽风 **3** [u] (of beer) **on ～** 散装的 **4** [c] (act of drinking) 一饮; (act of inhaling) 吸入; (amount swallowed) 一饮之量; (amount inhaled) 一口吸入的量; **she downed it in a single ～** 她一口把它喝光了; **to take long ～s of cool air** 大口大口地吸入凉爽的空气 **5** [c] (of ship) 吃水深度; **a vessel with a shallow ～** 吃水浅的船 **6** [c] Brit (piece in draughts) 国际跳棋棋子

B *modif* **1** (on draught) 散装的 ‹*beer*› **2** (used to pull loads) 拖曳重载的; **a ～ animal** 役畜

draught: ～board *n* Brit 国际跳棋棋盘; **～ excluder** *n* **1** [c and u] (strip inserted in a door or window) 防风条; **2** [c] (placed on the floor) 挡风物; **～ horse** *n* Brit 挽马

draughtiness /ˈdrɑːftɪnɪs, Amer ˈdræftɪnɪs/ *n* [u] Brit 有穿堂风

draughtproof /ˈdrɑːftpruːf, Amer ˈdræft-/ Brit

A *adj* 防风的

B *vt* 使…防风 ‹*door, window, room*›

draughtproofing /ˈdrɑːftpruːfɪŋ, Amer ˈdræft-/ *n* [u] Brit **1** (action) 防风处理 **2** (material) 防风材料

draughts /drɑːfts, Amer dræfts/ ▸**p. 307** *npl* + *v sing* Brit 国际跳棋; **to play ～** 下国际跳棋

draughtsman /ˈdrɑːftsmən, Amer ˈdræft-/ ▸**p. 409** *n* (*pl* **draughtsmen**) Brit **1** (person making technical drawings) 制图员 **2** (person skilled in drawing) 擅长绘画者 **3** Brit (piece in draughts) 国际跳棋棋子

draughtsmanship /ˈdrɑːftsmənʃɪp, Amer ˈdræft-/ *n* [u] Brit **1** (making technical drawings) 制图术 **2** (skill in drawing) 绘画技艺

draughty /ˈdrɑːfti, Amer ˈdræfti/ *adj* Brit 有穿堂风的; **I was sitting in a ～ seat** 我坐在风口上

draw /drɔː/

A *vt* (*pt* **drew**, *pp* **drawn**) **1** (on paper etc.) 画; fig (depict) 描绘; **to ～ sb. sth., to ～ sth. for sb.** 为某人画某物; **to ～ the line (at sth./doing sth.)** （在某事/做某事上）划定底线; **the line has to be drawn somewhere** 总得有个限度; **to ～ the line at downright disobedience** 完全不听话可不行; **a well-drawn character** 刻划得很成功的人物 **2** (pull) 拉; **the train was drawn by a steam engine** 火车由蒸汽机拉动; **to ～ one's handkerchief across one's brow** 用手帕擦额头; **he drew a comb through his wet hair** 他用梳子梳理湿发; **to ～ one's shawl round one's shoulders** 披上披肩; **to ～ the rope through the hole** 把绳子穿过孔眼; **to ～ one's bow** (in archery) 拉弓 **3** (attract to place, event) 吸引; (cause liking for) 使喜欢上; **to ～ sb. to do sth.** 吸引某人做某事; **to ～ sb. to/from sth.** 把某人吸引到某处/从某处吸引来; **to ～ (sb.'s) attention to sth./oneself** 把（某人的）注意力吸引到某事物上/自己身上; **our grief drew us together** 我们同病相怜; **she felt drawn to this mysterious stranger** 她对这个神秘的陌生人有好感 **4** (take out) 掏出; (pull out) 拔出 ‹*nail, thorn*›; **to ～ sth. from sth.** 从某处掏出某物; **to ～ a sword** 拔剑; **she drew a gun on me** 她拔出手枪对准我; **to ～ sb.'s/sth.'s teeth** *or* **fangs** fig 使某人/某物失去威力 **5** Sport, Games 以平局结束; **England drew their game against France** 英格兰队与法国队打成平局 **6** (in cards) 吊 ‹*card, trumps*› **7** Games (choose at random) 抽 ‹*card, straw*›; **to ～ sth. from sth.** 从某物中抽某物; **Italy has been drawn against Spain** *or* **to play Spain** 抽签结果是意大利队对西班牙队; **Smith drew Jones in the first round of the tournament** 锦标赛抽签结果是第一轮史密斯与琼斯对阵 **8** Fin (receive) 领取 ‹*salary, pension*›; (authorize) 开 ‹*bill of exchange*›; **the cheque was drawn on their joint account** 这张支票开到他们的共同账户上 **9** (pump, suck) 抽出 ‹*water, air*›; (take from supply) 取用 ‹*electricity, money*›; **to ～ water from the well** 从井中汲水; **his friends were drawn from all walks of life** 他的朋友来自社会各个阶层; **to ～ a bath** 放洗澡水 **10** (disembowel) 除去…的内脏 ‹*person, chicken*› **11** (derive) 得到 ‹*support, relief, strength*›; **to ～ comfort/encouragement/inspiration from sth.** 从某事中得到安慰/鼓励/灵感; **there is a moral to be drawn from this tale** 可以从这个故事中汲取教益 **12** (expound) 作出; **to ～ an analogy/a comparison/distinction/parallel between sth. and sth./with sth.** 在某事物与某事物之间/与某事物作类比/对照/区分/比较 **13** (produce as response) 引起; (cause to talk) 使…开口 ‹*person*›; **to ～ considerable praise** 赢得众多称赞; **she drew tears of laughter from the audience** 她把观众逗得眼泪都笑出来了; **she wouldn't be drawn into losing her temper** 她不肯发脾气; **to ～ sb. about** *or* **on sth.** 使某人透露某事 **14** (lead, guide) 带领 **15** Med 排出 ‹*pus, blood, abscess*› **16** Naut 吃水; **the ship ～s six metres** 这条船吃水 6 米 **17** Tech, Ind 拉拔 ‹*wire, rod*›; 轧制 ‹*plastic, glass, metal*›

B *vi* (*pt* **drew**, *pp* **drawn**) **1** (make picture) 绘画; **to ～ round** *or* **around sth.** 比着某物画 **2** (move) 移动; **to ～ alongside (sth.)** （与某物）并行; **to ～ level (with sth./sb.)** （与某物/某人）追平; **to ～ ahead (of sth./sb.)** 超过（某物/某人）; **we are ～ing ahead of our rivals** fig 我们就要领先对手了; **to ～ to an end** *or* **a close** 结束 **3** Sport, Games (achieve same score, finish with equal scores) 以平局结束; (finish at the same time) 同时到达; **to ～ with** *or* **against sb.** 与某人打成平局; **they drew 4-all** *or* **4-4 in the final** 他们在决赛中打成 4 平; **Smith and Jones drew for third place** 史密斯和琼斯并列第三名 **4** (take out weapon) 拔出武器; **to ～ on sb.** 拔出武器对准某人 **5** Sport, Games (make random choice) 抽签; **to ～ for sth.** 抽签决定某事 **6** Tech ‹*pump*› 抽水; ‹*vacuum cleaner*› 吸尘 **7** (infuse) ‹*tea*› 泡开

C *n* **1** Sport, Games (act of drawing lots) 抽签; (lottery, raffle) 抽彩; (sports match) 抽签赛; **the top half of the ～** 抽签赛的上半区 **2** Sport, Games (tie) 平局; **the match/game ended in a ～** 这场比赛以平局结束; **to hold sb. to a ～** 与某人打成平局 **3** (attraction) (person) 有吸引力的人; (thing, event) 有吸引力的事物 **4** (of gun) 拔枪; **to be quick/slow on the ～** lit 拔枪快/慢; fig 反应迅速/迟钝; **to beat sb. to the ～** lit 抢在某人前拔枪; fig 比某人抢先行动 **5** (on cigarette, pipe) 吸烟; **take a long ～ on one's pipe/at one's cigarette** 深吸一口烟斗/烟

Phrasal verbs

- **draw apart** *vi* **1** (move) 分开; **a small group had drawn apart from the rest** 一小群人与其他人分开了 **2** (become less intimate) 疏远; **the sect began to ～ apart from orthodox Judaism** 这个教派开始与正统犹太教分道扬镳了
- **draw aside**

A *vt* [**～ sth. aside, ～ aside sth.**] 把…拉到一边

B *vi* 退到一边

- **draw away**

A *vt* [**～ sb./sth. away, ～ away sb./sth.**] **1** (remove) 移开 **2** (withdraw, distract) 带…离开; (induce to leave) 吸引…离开; **they're trying to ～ her away from her present job** 他们正试图把她从目前的工作挖走 **3** (prevent from doing sth.) 使…分心; **don't let her ～ you away from your work** 别让她打扰你工作

B *vi* **1** Aut (move off) 驶出 **2** (move ahead) 超过; **he drew away from the rest of the field** 他甩开了其他参赛选手 **3** (recoil) 躲避; fig (dissociate oneself) 撇清关系

- **draw back**

A *vt* [**～ sth. back, ～ back sth.**] **1** (withdraw) 移开; (move away) 拉开 ‹*curtain*›; **her hair was drawn back in a bun** 她的头发向后梳成发髻 **2** (induce to return) 把…吸引回来

B *vi* **1** (recoil) 后退 **2** (refrain) 撤回; **she drew back at the last minute** 她在最后一刻罢手了

- **draw down** *vt* [**～ sth. down, ～ down sth.**] **1** (pull down) 拉下 **2** fig (attract, invite) 招来; **she had drawn shame down on her family** 她已经使家人蒙羞 **3** Fin 提取 ‹*money, loan, funds*›
- **draw in**

A *vt* [**～ sth. in, ～ in sth.**] **1** (add to picture) 把…画进去 **2** (pull in) 缩回; **the cat drew in its claws** 猫把爪子缩了进去 **3** (suck in) 吸入 **4** (earn) 挣得; **to ～ in**

d

huge sums of money 赚大钱 5 (attract) 吸引 6 (involve) 牵涉进; **I managed to avoid getting drawn into the argument** 我设法避免了卷入这场争论
B *vi* 1 (arrive) «*train*» 到站 2 (get shorter) «*days*» 渐短; «*evenings, nights*» 到来渐早

• **draw into**
A [**~ sb./sth. into sth.**] *vt*
1 (involve) 使…卷入…; (attract) 把…吸引到…; **neighbouring states were drawn into the battle** 邻国被卷入了这场战斗 2 (suck) 把…吸进 ‹*water, petrol, air, gas*›; **he was gradually drawn into a life of crime** 他逐渐陷入犯罪生涯 3 (lead, guide) 将…带入…; **she drew him into her arms** 她把他拉进怀里
B [**~ into sth.**] *vt* 到达 ‹*place*›; **the train drew into the station** 火车进站了

• **draw off**
A *vt* [**~ sth. off, ~ off sth.**]
1 (remove) 取下; **to ~ off one's gloves/the cover** 摘下手套/取下罩子 2 (extract) 抽出 ‹*liquid*›
B *vi* 1 (withdraw) 撤退 2 (move off) 出发

• **draw on**
A *vt* 1 [**~ sth. on, ~ on sth.**] (put on) 穿上 ‹*item of clothing*› 2 [**~ sb. on, ~ on sb.**] (encourage) 鼓励 3 [**~ on sth.**] (use, exploit) 利用 ‹*reserves, experience, knowledge*› 4 [**~ on sth.**] (puff, smoke) 吸 ‹*cigarette, pipe*›
B *vi* 1 (approach) «*time, season*» 临近; **night was ~ing on** 夜幕即将降临 2 (pass) 渐渐过去; **the months drew on, and there was still no word from her** 几个月过去了，她仍然杳无音信; **as the evening drew on, he became more talkative** 随着夜色渐深，他的话越来越多

• **draw out**
A [**~ sth. out, ~ out sth.**] *vt*
1 (take out) 拿出 2 (choose randomly) 随意抽取; **to ~ names out of a hat** 抽人名签 3 (pull out) 拔出 ‹*nail, splinter of glass*› 4 (pump or suck out) 抽出 ‹*dust, air*› 5 Fin 提取 ‹*money*› 6 (elicit) 诱出; **to ~ out a confession/secret** 引诱招供/套出秘密 7 Tech 拉拔 ‹*wire, plastic, glass, metal*› 8 (cause to last longer) 拖延; **he drew his meal out** 他一顿饭吃得磨磨蹭蹭
B [**~ sb. out, ~ out sb.**] *vt*
1 (cause or encourage to talk) 鼓励…讲话; **I managed to ~ him out of his silence** 我设法使他打破了沉默 2 (induce to come out) 把…吸引出来; **fine weather ~s people out of their houses** 好天气吸引人们出门
C *vi* 1 (leave) «*train*» 出站; (move out) «*vehicle*» 开出; **the lorry drew out into the middle of the road** 卡车斜插到路中央 2 (get longer) «*days*» 渐长; «*evenings, nights*» 到来渐晚

• **draw up**
A *vt* [**~ sth. up, ~ up sth.**]
1 (pull upwards) 提起 2 (devise) 起草 ‹*plan*›; 制订 ‹*course of action*› 3 (bring near) 拉近 ‹*chair, seat*› 4 (gather up) 系上 ‹*thread, string*› 5 (arrange) 排列 6 (bring to halt) 使…停下
B *v refl* **to ~ oneself up** 站得笔直
C *vi* 停下

• **draw upon** *vt* = **draw on**

draw: ~back *n* 缺点; **a ~back of** *or* **to sth./doing sth.** 某事/做某事的不利之处; **~bridge** *n* (over moat) 吊桥; (over river) 开合桥; **~cord** *n* 拉绳; *modif* **~cord waist/hem** 装有束带的腰部/褶边; **~down** *n* 1 Fin 提款; 2 Mil 裁军

drawee /drɔːˈiː/ *n* 受票人

drawer¹ /drɔː(r)/ *n* (in chest, cabinet) 抽屉

drawer² /ˈdrɔːə(r)/ *n* 1 (of pictures) 绘画人; (of technical drawings) 制图员 2 Fin 开票人

drawers /drɔː(r)z/ *npl* dated or hum 内裤

drawing /ˈdrɔːɪŋ/ *n* 1 [c] (picture) 图画; **a rough ~** 草图; **a ~ book** 绘图簿 2 [u] (artistic action, occupation) 绘画; (technical action, occupation) 制图

drawing: ~ board *n* 绘图板; **back to the ~ board** fig 从头再来; **to be still on the ~ board** fig 仍处于计划阶段; **~ book** *n* 图画本; **~ office** *n* 制图室; **~ pin** *n* Brit 图钉; **~ room** *n* 起居室

drawl /drɔːl/
A *vi* 拖腔拖调地说话
B *vt* 拖腔拖调地说
C *n* 拖腔拖调的说话方式

drawn /drɔːn/
A *pp* ▸**draw A, B**
B *adj* 1 (strained, haggard) 憔悴的 2 (ending in a draw) 打成平局的

drawn butter *n* [u] Amer 融化奶油

draw: ~ poker ▸**p. 307** *n* [u] Amer 暗扑克 [各发5张暗牌的扑克戏，下注后可要求换发手中不需要的牌]; **~string** *n* 拉绳; **~string trousers** 拉线裤; **~ ticket** *n* 抽奖券; **~-top table** *n* 抽拉式桌子

dray /dreɪ/ *n* 平板马车

dread /dred/
A *n* 1 [u] (fear) 恐惧; **to be** *or* **stand in ~ of sb./sth.** 畏惧某人/某事物 2 [c] (feared thing) 可怕的事物; **an impoverished old age is the ~ of many people** 老年贫困是很多人都害怕的事
B *vt* 惧怕; **to ~ doing sth.** 害怕做某事; **what would she say? — I ~ to think!** 她会怎么说？——我不敢去想！

dreaded /ˈdredɪd/ *adj attrib* 令人恐惧的

dreadful /ˈdredfl/ *adj* 1 (terrible) 可怕的 ‹*accident, news*›; 剧烈的 ‹*pain*› 2 (used emphatically) 极其的; **a ~ mistake** 大错; **what a ~ nuisance!** 真是讨厌透了！ 3 (unwell) 有病的; **to feel ~** 感觉不舒服; **to look ~** 看上去脸色不好 4 (embarrassed) 尴尬的; **to feel ~ about sth./doing sth.** 因为某事物/做某事感到难堪 5 (of poor quality) 糟糕透顶的 ‹*book, service*› 6 (disgraceful) 不光彩的; **I know it's ~ of me to refuse, but ...** 我知道我不应该拒绝，但是…

dreadfully /ˈdredfəli/ *adv* 1 (extremely) 非常; **it seems to have frightened her ~** 这似乎把她吓坏了 2 (very badly) 非常糟糕地 ‹*organized*› 3 (disgracefully) 不光彩地 ‹*behave, treat*›

dreadlocks /ˈdredlɒks/ *npl* "骇人"长发绺 [一种将湿发结成辫、四下散垂的发式]

dream /driːm/
A *n* 1 (while asleep) 梦; **to have a ~ (about sth./doing sth.)** 做梦（见到某物/做某事）; **to have a ~ that ...** 梦见…; **goodnight and sweet ~s!** 晚安，做个好梦！ 2 (while awake) 出神; **she's been going round in a ~ for the last few days** 最近几天她一直梦游似地到处转悠; **sorry, what did you say? I was in a ~** 对不起，你刚才说什么？我走神了 3 (hope) 梦想; **to have ~s of doing sth.** 梦想做某事; **to fulfil a ~** 圆梦; **to be (like) a ~ come true** （如）梦想成真; **in sb.'s wildest ~s** 某人无法想象的; **it's just an idle ~** 那只是痴心妄想; **in your ~s!** colloq 你做梦去吧！ 4 colloq (ideal, wonderful person) 梦一般美妙的人; (ideal, wonderful thing) 梦一般美妙的事物; **the machine is a ~ to operate** 这台机器操作起来棒极了; **her brother is a ~** 她哥哥帅呆了; **like a ~** 很完美
B *vi* (*pt, pp* **~ed** *or* **dreamt**) 1 (while asleep) 做梦; **to ~ about** *or* **of sb./sth./doing sth.** 梦见某人/某物/做某事 2 (while awake) 梦想; (fantasize) 幻想; (hope) 希望; **I must have been ~ing** 我一定是在做梦; **to ~ of** *or* **about sth./doing sth.** 幻想某事/做某事; **you'll never do it — well, I can ~, can't I?** 你永远不会成功的——嗯，我总可以抱希望吧，对吧？; **to ~ of fame and fortune** 向往名利; **~ on!** colloq 做梦去吧！ 3 (consider) 考虑; **sb. would not** *or* **never ~ of sth./doing sth.** 某人不会/绝不会考虑某事物/做某事; **are you going to apologize to her? — I wouldn't ~ of it!** 你准备向她道歉吗？——做梦！
C *vt* (*pt, pp* **~ed** *or* **dreamt**) 1 (while asleep) 梦见; **to ~ that ...** 梦见…; **I ~ed a strange dream last night** 我昨晚做了个奇怪的梦; **I never said that: you must have ~ed it!** 我从没说过那样的话——你肯定是胡思乱想出来的！ 2 (imagine) 想象; **to ~ that ...** 想象…; **I never ~ed he'd say yes!** 我从没想到他会同意！

Phrasal verbs

• **dream away** *vt* [**~ sth. away, ~ away sth.**] 在遐想中虚度 ‹*time, life*›

• **dream up** *vt* [**~ sth. up, ~ up sth.**] 凭空想出 ‹*plan, excuse, theory*›; 虚构出 ‹*plot, character*›

dreamboat /ˈdriːmbəʊt/ *n* colloq 意中人

dreamer /ˈdriːmə(r)/ *n* 1 (person dreaming) 做梦的人 2 (daydreamer) 做白日梦的人 3 (idealist, fantasist) 空想家

dreamily /ˈdriːmɪli/ *adv* 1 (in a dream) 恍惚地; **'I suppose so,' she said ~** "我想是的，"她心不在焉地说 2 (gently) 轻柔地 ‹*play, whisper*›; **a ~ peaceful scene** 安宁恬静的场景 3 colloq (delightfully) 妙不可言地

dreamland /ˈdriːmlænd/ *n* [u] 幻想世界

dreamless /ˈdriːmlɪs/ *adj* 无梦的

dreamlike /ˈdriːmlaɪk/ *adj* 如梦的; **the atmosphere of the place was ~** 这里的气氛如梦如幻

dreamt /dremt/ *pt, pp* ▸**dream B, C**

dream: ~ team *n* 梦之队; **~world** *n* (place of dreams) 梦乡; (fantasy world) 幻想世界; **he's living in a ~world** 他生活在幻想之中

dreamy /ˈdriːmi/ *adj* 1 (unrealistic) 不切实际的 ‹*idea, person*› 2 (distracted) 恍惚的; **she picked up the telephone in her ~ way** 她心不在焉地拿起电话 3 (vague) 模糊的 ‹*recollection*› 4 (gentle, soothing) 恬静的 ‹*music, voice*› 5 colloq (gorgeous) 妙不可言的; **a ~ little cottage** 绝妙的小屋

dreariness /ˈdrɪərɪnɪs/ *n* [u] 1 (dullness) 阴沉 2 (monotony) 枯燥乏味

dreary /ˈdrɪəri/ *adj* 1 (dull) 阴沉的 ‹*weather, scene*› 2 (monotonous) 枯燥乏味的 ‹*life, person*›

dredge¹ /dredʒ/
A *n* 1 (machine) 挖泥机 2 (boat) 挖泥船
B *vt* 疏浚 ‹*river, harbour*›; 用挖泥船挖掘 ‹*mud, silt*›
C *vi* (use a dredge) 用挖泥机挖掘; (use a dredger) 用挖泥船挖掘; **the ship has been dredging in the harbour** 那条船在港口清淤

Phrasal verb

• **dredge up** *vt* [**~ up sth., ~ sth. up**]
1 lit 挖掘出 ‹*sand, silt*› 2 fig 重提 ‹*forgotten story*›; 翻出 ‹*scandal, the past*›

dredge² *vt* Culin 撒; **to ~ the cake with icing sugar** 把糖霜撒在蛋糕上; **to ~ the flour over the meat** 在肉上撒面粉

dredger¹ /ˈdredʒə(r)/ *n* 1 (boat) 挖泥船 2 (machine) 挖泥机

dredger² *n* Culin 撒粉罐

dregs /dregz/ *npl* 1 lit (remnants) 残渣; **coffee ~** 咖啡渣; **to drink/drain sth. (down) to the ~** 喝光某物 2 fig pej (worst part or parts) 渣滓; **the ~ of society** 社会渣滓; **the ~ of humanity** 人间败类

drench /drentʃ/ *vt* 使湿透; **to get ~ed (to the skin)** 浑身湿透; **she ~ed the cake in brandy** 她把蛋糕用白兰地浸透; **she was ~ed in perfume** 她浑身洒满香水

drenching /ˈdrentʃɪŋ/
A *adj* 滂沱的; **~ rain** 瓢泼大雨
B *n* **to get a ~** 浑身湿透

dress /dres/
A *n* 1 [c] (item of women's clothing) 连衣裙 2 [u] (clothing) 衣服; **casual/formal ~** 便服/礼服
B *modif* 1 Tex 连衣裙的 ‹*material, pattern*›

2 (for formal occasions) 适于正式场合的 ‹*suit, uniform*›; **a ~ sword** 礼服用佩剑

C *vt* 1 (put clothes on) 给…穿衣服; (clothe) 为…提供衣服; **to get ~ed** 穿好衣服; **to ~ oneself in black** 穿黑色衣服; **to be well ~ed** 穿着体面; **he was ~ed as a woman** 他男扮女装; **I'm not ~ed for a hike** 我穿的衣服不适合远足; **she ~ed her twins in identical outfits** 她给她的双胞胎穿一模一样的衣服; **to be ~ed to kill** colloq 打扮得引人注目 2 (decorate) 装饰; **to ~ a shop window** 布置橱窗; **to be ~ed overall** Naut 挂满旗帜 3 Culin (prepare) 处理 ‹*poultry, shellfish*›; 调制 ‹*salad*›; **to ~ a chicken** 把鸡去毛开膛 4 Med 包扎 ‹*wound*› 5 (finish) 修整…的表面; **to ~ leather** 鞣皮 6 Agric (fertilize) 给…施肥 ‹*soil, plant*›

D *vi* 1 (put on clothes) 穿衣服; **I ~ed in my best clothes** 我穿上了自己最好的衣服 2 (wear particular kind of clothes) 穿衣; **to ~ comfortably** 穿得舒适; **he ~ed as a pirate to go to the fancy dress ball** 他装扮成海盗去参加化装舞会; **to ~ in red/a suit** 穿红色衣服/西服 3 (put on formal clothes) 穿礼服; **to ~ for dinner** 穿礼服赴宴 4 Mil 排列整齐; **squad, ~ right** 全班注意，向右看齐

Phrasal verbs

• **dress down**

A *vi* 穿着随便

B *vt* [**~ sb. down, ~ down sb.**] colloq 训斥

• **dress up**

A *vi* 1 (smartly) 穿上盛装; **don't bother to ~ up** 用不着穿礼服 2 (in fancy dress) 装扮; **he ~ed up as a policeman** 他装扮成警察; **she's ~ing up in her mother's dress** 她把母亲的连衣裙穿着玩

B *vt* 1 [**~ sb. up, ~ up sb.**] (in fancy dress) 给…化装打扮; **he ~ed himself up as a judge** 他装扮成法官 2 [**~ sth. up, ~ up sth.**] (improve) 装饰 ‹*clothing, object*›; fig 修饰 ‹*facts*›

dressage /ˈdresɑːʒ/ *n* [u] 盛装舞步

dress: ~ circle *n* Brit 楼厅前座; **~ coat** *n* 燕尾服; **~ code** *n* 着装规范; **~ designer** ▸**p. 409** *n* 服装设计师; **~-down Friday** *n* 可着便装的星期五

dresser[1] /ˈdresə(r)/ *n* 1 (person) 衣着…的人; **a stylish/sloppy ~** 穿着时髦/邋遢的人 2 ▸**p. 409** Theat 服装师

dresser[2] *n* 1 (sideboard for dishes) 碗橱 2 Amer (chest of drawers) 梳妆台

dressing /ˈdresɪŋ/ *n* 1 [u] (putting on clothes) 穿衣 2 [c] Med 敷料 3 [c and u] (for salad) 调料 4 [c and u] Amer (stuffing) 填料 5 [c and u] Agric, Hort (fertilizer) 肥料

dressing: ~ case *n* 梳妆盒; **~-down** *n* colloq 训斥; **the teacher gave me a right ~-down** 老师狠狠训了我一通; **~ gown** *n* 晨衣; **~ room** *n* 1 Theat 化妆间; 2 Sport 更衣室; 3 Amer (changing room) 试衣间; 4 (in house) 梳妆室; **~ table** *n* 梳妆台

dress: ~maker ▸**p. 409** *n* 女装裁缝; **~making** *n* [u] 女装制作; **~ parade** *n* 阅兵典礼; **~ rehearsal** *n* 1 Theat 彩排; 2 fig (practice) 预演; **~ sense** *n* [u] 选装意识; **~ shirt** *n* 礼服衬衫; **~ suit** *n* 正装; **~ uniform** *n* 军礼服

dressy /ˈdresi/ *adj* colloq 1 (smart) 考究的 ‹*clothes*› 2 (smartly dressed) 衣着讲究的 ‹*person*› 3 (requiring smart clothes) 须穿礼服的 ‹*occasion, party*›

drew /druː/ *pt* ▸**draw A, B**

dribble /ˈdrɪbl/

A *vi* 1 (run in drops) 滴下; (run in a thin stream) 细流 2 (drool) «*baby, person*» 流口水 3 Sport 运球

B *vt* 1 (allow to run) 使滴下; **she ~d saliva down her chin** 她的口水从下巴上淌下来; **he ~d cream into his coffee** 他把奶油滴入咖啡 2 Sport 运 ‹*ball*›

C *n* 1 [c] (stream of drops) 细流; (thin trickle) 小滴 2 [u] (saliva) 口水 3 [c] Sport 运球

Phrasal verb

• **dribble in** *vi* «*money, suggestions*» 零星地到来

dribbler /ˈdrɪblə(r)/ *n* 1 (person) 流口水的人 2 Sport 运球的人

driblet /ˈdrɪblɪt/ *n* 1 (drop of liquid) 一滴; (thin stream) 细流 2 (small amount of commodity, information, money) 少量

dribs and drabs /ˌdrɪbz ən ˈdræbz/ *npl* **in ~** 一点一点地

dried /draɪd/

A *pt, pp* ▸**dry B, C, D**

B *adj* Culin 脱水的 ‹*peas, herbs*›; **~ milk/fruit** 奶粉/干果

dried-up *adj* 1 (without liquid) 干涸的 ‹*river bed, well*› 2 (wrinkled) 年老干瘪的 ‹*person*›

drier /ˈdraɪə(r)/

A *n* = **dryer**

B *adj comp* ▸**dry A**

drift /drɪft/

A *vi* 1 (be carried by current, wind) «*floating object, person*» 漂流; «*balloon, cloud, smoke*» 飘 2 (go aimlessly) 顺其自然地发生; **I'm content to let things ~** 我喜欢顺其自然; **he ~ed through life/into marriage** 他漫无目的地度过了一生/不经意间结了婚; **to ~ around** *or* **about the house** 在房子里瞎转悠; **her gaze ~ed around the room** 她漫无目的地扫视一下房间; **the audience's attention was ~ing** 观众的注意力在转移 3 Naut, Aviat «*boat, aircraft*» 偏航; **to ~ off course** 偏离航线 4 Sport «*ball, stroke, shot*» 轻轻滑过 5 (pile up) «*snow, sand, leaves*» 吹积; **~ing snow** 堆积的雪; **~ing sand** 积成堆的沙

B *vt* 1 (carry or send on current) «*tide*» 使…漂流 ‹*floating object, raft*›; **a light wind ~ed the smoke in our direction** 烟随着轻风向我们飘来; **the logs are ~ed downstream to the mill** 原木顺流而下漂到木材加工厂 2 Sport 把…轻轻送到 ‹*ball, shot*›

C *n* 1 [u and c] (flow, movement) 流动; **a ~ away from sth.** 偏离某事物的变化; **a ~ back to sth.** 向某事物的恢复; **the ~ of the clouds through the sky** 云在天空的飘动; **the ~ of refugees across the border** 越过边界的难民流 2 [c] Geog 缓流; **the North Atlantic ~** 北大西洋缓流 3 [u] Naut, Aviat 偏航 4 [c] (pile, mass) (of snow, leaves, sand) 吹积物; (of smoke, mist) 团; **the snow was falling in ~s** 雪下得堆积起来 5 [c] (mass of flowers) 大丛的花 6 [c] (gist) 主旨; **to get** *or* **catch** *or* **follow sb.'s ~** 明白某人的意思

Phrasal verbs

• **drift apart** *vi* 逐渐疏远

• **drift away** *vi* **to ~ away from sth.** 慢慢离开 ‹*place, match*›; fig 慢慢摆脱 ‹*belief*›

• **drift in** *vi* 闲散地进来

• **drift off** *vi* 1 (doze) 入睡; **she ~ed off (to sleep)** 她迷迷糊糊地睡着了 2 (leave) 离开

• **drift out** *vi* 闲散地离开

drifter /ˈdrɪftə(r)/ *n* 1 Naut 流网渔船 2 (aimless person) 漂泊者

drift: ~ ice *n* [u] 流冰; **~net** *n* 流网; **~wood** *n* [u] 漂流木

drill[1] /drɪl/

A *n* 1 [c] (tool) 钻; (cutting tip) 钻头; **hand/power/pneumatic/dentist's ~** 手摇钻/电钻/风钻/牙钻 2 [u] Mil 训练 3 [u and c] Sch 练习; **pronunciation/grammar ~s** 语音/语法练习 4 [c] (practice) 演习; **fire/lifeboat/air-raid ~** 消防/救生艇/空袭演习 5 [u] colloq dated (correct procedure) 正确步骤; **what's the ~ for filling in time sheets?** 该怎样填写考勤表? 6 [u] Tex 粗斜纹布

B *vi* 1 (use rotating drill) 钻孔; **to ~ for oil** 钻井探油; **to ~ into sth.** 钻进某物; **his eyes ~ into me** 他眼睛直盯着我 2 Mil 训练

C *vt* 1 (make hole in) 钻; **to ~ a hole (in sth.)** (在某处) 钻孔 2 (riddle with bullets) 用子弹打穿 3 (teach by rigorous exercise) 训练; **to ~ sb. in sth.** 训练某人某方面的技能

Phrasal verb

• **drill down** *vi* 钻取数据

drill[2]

A *n* 1 (furrow) 条播沟 2 (machine) 条播机

B *vt* 条播 ‹*seed*›

drilling /ˈdrɪlɪŋ/ *n* [u] 钻孔

drilling: ~ derrick *n* 钻塔; **~ platform** *n* 钻井平台; **~ rig** *n* 1 (equipment) 钻探设备; 2 (platform) 钻台

drill sergeant *n* 操练军士

drily /ˈdraɪli/ *adv* 1 (with dry wit) 冷幽默地; **'how very observant,' he said ~** "真是明察秋毫啊，" 他不动声色地幽默了一句 2 (coldly) 冷冰冰地

drink /drɪŋk/

A *vt* (*pt* **drank**, *pp* **drunk**) 1 (consume) 喝; **to ~ sth. from** *or* **out of/through sth.** 从某物喝某物/用某器皿喝某物; **to have sth./nothing to ~** 有喝的/没有什么喝的; **to be fit to ~** 可饮用的; **to ~ sb. under the table** colloq 酒量胜过某人; **to ~ poison** 服毒 2 (in toasting sb./sth.) 为…祝酒; **to ~ a toast (to sb.)** (向某人) 祝酒; **to ~ to sb.'s health** *or* **the health of sb.** 为某人的健康干杯 3 colloq (absorb) «*plant, soil*» 吸收 ‹*moisture, water*›

B *vi* (*pt* **drank**, *pp* **drunk**) 1 (consume liquid) 喝; **to ~ from** *or* **out of sth.** 用某器皿喝 2 (consume alcohol) 喝酒; (consume habitually, and/or to excess) 酗酒; **don't ~ and drive** (slogan) 切勿酒后驾车 3 (drink a toast) 祝酒; **to ~ to sb./sth.** 向某人祝酒/为某事干杯; **I'll ~ to that!** 我完全同意!

C *v refl* (*pt* **drank**, *pp* **drunk**) **to ~ oneself to death/into a stupor** 喝到死/喝得神志不清; **to ~ oneself sick/unconscious/silly** 喝酒喝到病倒/不省人事/喝傻

D *n* 1 [c and u] (quantity of liquid) 一份; (liquid) 饮料; (mouthful) 一口; **a ~ of tea/lemonade** 一杯茶/柠檬水; **to give sb./sth. a ~** 给某人喝饮料/给某物浇水; **a hot/cold ~** 一杯热饮/冷饮; **canned/bottled ~s** 罐装/瓶装饮料; **to have a ~ of water/wine** 喝一口水/酒 2 [c and u] (quantity of alcohol) 一杯; **an after-dinner ~** 饭后酒; **a round of ~s** 一巡酒; **I need a ~!** 我需要喝杯酒壮壮胆! ; **to go out for a ~** 出去喝一杯 3 [u] (alcoholic liquor) 酒; **to drown one's sorrows in ~** 借酒消愁; **it's (just) the ~ talking** 那 (只) 是醉话 4 [u] (too much alcohol) 酗酒; **to take to ~** 开始酗酒; **to drive sb. to ~** 迫使某人酗酒; **those children of hers are enough to drive anybody to ~** hum 她那几个宝贝孩子真是人见人烦 5 [u] colloq (the sea) **the ~** 大海; **in the ~** 在海里

E **drinks** *npl* 酒会; **to have ~s (with sb.)** (与某人) 举行酒会

Phrasal verbs

• **drink away** *vt* [**~ sth. away, ~ away sth.**]
1 (forget) 借酒忘掉 ‹*sorrows, memories*› 2 (waste) 饮酒耗费 ‹*fortune, money*›; 饮酒损害 ‹*health*›; 饮酒虚度 ‹*life, time*›

• **drink down** *vt* [**~ sth. down, ~ down sth.**] 把…一饮而尽 ‹*medicine*›

• **drink in** *vt* [**~ sth. in, ~ in sth.**]
1 colloq (absorb) «*plant, soil*» 吸收 ‹*water, rain*› 2 (breathe) 愉快地吸入 ‹*fresh air*› 3 (savour) 尽情欣赏; **to ~ in the beauty of the scenery/every word** 陶醉于优美的景色/全神贯注地倾听每个词; **he sat in the corner, ~ing in everything around him** 他坐在角落里，沉醉于周围的一切

• **drink up**

A *vt* [**~ sth. up, ~ up sth.**] 把…喝完

B *vi* 干杯; **~ up!** 干杯!

drinkable /ˈdrɪŋkəbl/ *adj* 1 (safe to drink) 可饮用的 2 (pleasant to drink) 好喝的 3 (acceptable) 尚可一喝的

drink: **~-driver** *n* Brit 酒后驾车者; **~-driving** *n* [u] Brit 酒后驾车

drinker /'drɪŋkə(r)/ *n* **1** (person drinking) 常喝…的人; **a coffee ~** 常喝咖啡的人 **2** (person who drinks alcohol) 饮酒者; **a heavy ~** 酒鬼; **I'm not much of a ~** 我不怎么喝酒

drinking /'drɪŋkɪŋ/
A *n* [u] **1** (swallowing of liquid) 喝东西 **2** (consumption of alcohol) 喝酒; **accidents caused by ~ and driving** 酒后驾驶导致的事故
B *modif* **1** (involving alcohol consumption) 与饮酒有关的; **~ laws** 饮酒法; **a ~ friend** 酒友; **a ~ spree** 一次狂饮 **2** (used for drinking) 喝酒用的

drinking: **~ chocolate** *n* [u] Brit (powder) 巧克力粉; (drink) 巧克力热饮; **~ fountain** *n* 喷泉式饮水器; **~ problem** *n* = **drink problem**; **~ song** *n* 饮酒歌; **~-up time** *n* Brit 延长饮酒时间 [酒馆打烊后允许客人把余酒喝完的缓冲时间]; **~ water** *n* [u] 饮用水

drink problem *n* Brit 酗酒问题

drinks: **~ cabinet, ~ cupboard** *ns* Brit 酒柜; **~ dispenser, ~ machine** *ns* Brit 饮料自动售卖机; **~ party** *n* Brit 酒会

drip /drɪp/
A *vi* (*pres p etc.* **-pp-**) **1** (fall in drops) «*liquid*» 滴下 **2** (let drops fall) «*tap, wet object*» 滴下液体; **the rain has stopped, but the trees are still ~ping** 雨已经停了, 但树木还在滴水; **my face is ~ping with sweat** 我的脸上汗水淋淋 **3** fig **to ~ with sth.** 充满某物; **the women were ~ping with jewels** 那些女人浑身珠光宝气; **in a voice that ~ped with emotion** 用饱含深情的声音
B *vt* (*pres p etc.* **-pp-**) **1** (allow to fall in drops) 让…滴下 ‹*water, paint, blood*›; **to ~ sth. on to/down sth.** 把某物滴到某物上; **I ~ped some water down her back** 我在她背上滴了一些水 **2** fig (ooze) 溢出; **his voice ~ped smugness** 他的声音中透着自得
C *n* **1** (drop) 液滴 **2** (as action) 滴下; (as sound) 滴水声 **3** Med (device) 静脉滴注器; (solution) 滴液; **to be on a ~** 正在输液 **4** colloq pej (weak person) 软蛋

drip-dry
A *adj* 滴干免烫的 ‹*garment, fabric*›
B *vt* 把…滴干 ‹*garment*›
C *vi* «*garment*» 滴干

drip-feed
A /,drɪp'fiːd/ *vt* **1** Med 给…静脉滴注 ‹*patient*› **2** (add drop by drop) 滴注 ‹*oil, fluid*›
B /'drɪpfiːd/ *n* **1** Med 静脉滴注器 **2** (device) 滴注器

drip: **~ mat** *n* 杯垫; **~ pan** *n* 接油盘

dripping /'drɪpɪŋ/
A *n* [u] Culin 油滴
B *adj* **1** (letting drops fall) 滴水的 ‹*tap, branches*› **2** (very wet) 湿淋淋的 ‹*coat, hat*›; **to be ~ wet** 湿透

drivability /'draɪvə,bɪlɪti/ *n* [u] 驾驶性能

drivable /'draɪvəbl/ *adj* (in working order) 可驾驶的 ‹*car*›; (safe) 能安全驾驶的; (legal) 允许驾驶的; (easy to drive) 驾驶性能好的

drive /draɪv/
A *vt* (*pt* **drove**, *pp* **driven**) **1** Aut (be driver of) 开 ‹*vehicle*›; (convey) 开车送 ‹*person, goods*›; **we drove 500 km in one day** 我们一天行驶了500公里; **to ~ a vehicle into a garage/car park/space** 把车驶进车房/停车场/停车位; **he ~s tourists round the town** 他开车带游客参观这个镇子 **2** colloq (operate) 操作 ‹*machine*› **3** Electron, Mech, Tech 驱动 ‹*generator, mechanism, system*› **4** (push) 钉 ‹*nail, rivet*›; 拧 ‹*bolt*›; 打 ‹*stake, post*›; fig 推动 ‹*economy*›; «*wind*» 吹; «*water*» 冲; **huge waves drove the boat against the rocks** 巨浪把船打到礁石上; **the clouds were driven across the sky** 云朵被吹过天空; **to ~ sth. home** 把某物钉到位; **shortages are driving prices higher** 商品匮乏促使价格走高 **5** Sport (hit hard and straight) 猛击; (strike in golf) 从球座打出 **6** (force through or across) 辟出 ‹*road*›; 凿 ‹*tunnel*›; 打 ‹*well*›; **to ~ a passage through the enemy ranks** 从敌军队伍中杀出一条路 **7** (instil) 使…被理解 ‹*point, fact*›; **to ~ sth. into sb.'s head** 使某人记住某事物; **to ~ sth. home (to sb.)** 把某事(对某人)讲清楚 **8** (chase or herd) 驱赶 ‹*person, animal*›; **to ~ sb. from/out of sth.** 把某人从某地驱除出去; **to be driven out of the market** 被挤出市场; **to ~ sb. into a corner** 将某人逼入困境 **9** (expel) 打消; **to ~ evil thoughts from one's mind** 打消脑子里的坏念头; **he tried to ~ her out of his thoughts** 他试图不再想她 **10** (force, compel) 迫使; (cause to work, overwork) 迫使…过分劳累; **to ~ sb. into debt** 逼得某人负债; **to ~ sb. insane/mad/out of their mind** 把某人逼疯; **he was driven by jealousy** 他受了忌妒心的驱使; **he was finally driven to suicide** 他最后被迫自杀; **to ~ sb. to do sth.** 迫使某人拼命做某事; **to ~ the pupils very hard** 使学生的学习负担极为沉重
B *vi* (*pt* **drove**, *pp* **driven**) **1** Aut (be driver) 开车; (ride) 乘车; **he drove in luxury to the airport** 他乘豪华车去机场; **I drove into a ditch** 我把车开到沟里了 **2** Aut (be driven) «*vehicle*» 行驶; (operate) «*vehicle*» 操作; **a car had driven into the garden fence** 一辆汽车撞上了花园的栅栏; **it's not an attractive car, but it ~s well** 这部车不起眼, 但是很好开 **3** (move with force) «*wind, snow, waves*» 迅猛袭来; **the hail was driving in my face** 冰雹劈头盖顶地砸到我脸上; **the rain drove horizontally across the field** 大雨横扫田野 **4** Sport (hit a ball hard and straight) 抽球; (tee off) 发球
C *v refl* (*pt* **drove**, *pp* **driven**) **to ~ oneself to do sth.** 拼命做某事; **you're driving yourself too hard** 你把自己逼得太紧了
D *n* **1** [c] Aut (car journey) 驱车旅行; (car journey from A to B) 车程; **to go/come for a ~** 去/来开车兜风; **to take sb. for a ~** 开车带某人兜风 **2** [c] (path to house) 私人车道 **3** **Drive** (in road names) 路; **72 Queen's D~** 女王路72号 **4** [u and c] Aut, Mech, Tech 传动; **a belt/chain/fluid/electric ~** 皮带/链条/液压/电传动; **a car with right-/left-hand ~** 右/左座驾驶汽车; **he threw the car into ~** 他猛地给汽车挂上挡 **5** [c] Comput [磁盘的] 驱动器 **6** [c] Sport (hard, straight ball stroke) 抽球; (in golf) 发球; **an off ~** (in cricket) 正手抽球; **a strong forehand ~** (in tennis) 有力的正手击球; **he scored with a brilliant 25-yard ~** (in football) 他在25码外踢进漂亮一球; **a ~ to the baseline/into the corner of the net** 打到底线的/进网角的抽球; **a ~ off the tee** 球座发球 **7** [c] (herding, chasing) (of animals) 驱赶; **a grouse ~** 围赶松鸡 **8** [c] Mil 围攻 **9** [c] (campaign, effort) 运动; **a ~ to do/against/for/towards sth.** 做/反对/争取/为某事的运动; **a sales/charity ~** 推销/慈善活动; **an anti-sexism/-litter/-drugs ~** 反性别歧视/反乱丢垃圾/反毒品运动 **10** [u] (motivation, energy) 干劲 **11** [c] (instinct, need) 欲望; **a ~ for/to do sth.** 对某事物/做某事的欲望; **to have a ~ for perfection** 追求完美; **the ~ to win** 求胜的欲望; **sex** *or* **sexual ~** 性欲 **12** [c] Brit (gathering for game) 比赛; **a bingo/bridge/whist ~** 宾戈牌/桥牌/惠斯特牌比赛

Phrasal verbs

- **drive along**
A *vt* [**~ sth. along, ~ along sth.**] «*wind, current, tide*» 把…卷走 ‹*leaves, clouds, boat*›
B *vi* Aut 沿路行驶

- **drive at** *vt* [**~ at sth.**] 意指; **I wish I knew what she was driving at** 我真希望自己能明白她的意思

- **drive away**
A *vt* **1** [**~ sth. away, ~ away sth.**] (be driver of) 开走 ‹*vehicle*› **2** [**~ sb. away, ~ away sb.**] (convey) 开车送走 ‹*person*› **3** [**~ sb./sth. away, ~ away sb./sth.**] (repel) 赶走 **4** [**~ sth. away, ~ away sth.**] (get rid of) 消除 ‹*doubts, fears, care*›
B *vi* Aut **1** (drive vehicle away) 驱车离开 **2** (be driven away) «*vehicle*» 开走

- **drive back**
A *vt* [**~ sb./sth. back, ~ back sb./sth.**] **1** (be driver of) 开回 ‹*vehicle*› **2** (convey) 开车送回 ‹*person, passenger*› **3** (force withdrawal of) 把…赶回 ‹*people, animals*›
B *vi* 驱车返回

- **drive down**
A *vt* [**~ sth. down, ~ down sth.**] 压低 ‹*interest rates, prices, inflation*›
B *vi* Aut **1** (descend) 向下行驶 **2** (travel) (in a southerly direction) 驱车向南; (to a less important place) 驱车去小地方; **they drove down to the countryside** 他们开车去了乡下

- **drive forward** *vi* «*team*» 推进

- **drive in**
A *vt* [**~ sth. in, ~ in sth.**] **1** Aut 把…开进去 ‹*vehicle*› **2** (force in) 把…敲进去 ‹*nail, stake*›; 把…拧进去 ‹*bolt*›
B *vi* **1** (enter in vehicle) «*driver*» 开车进去; «*passenger*» 乘车进去 **2** (be driven in) «*vehicle*» 开进来

- **drive off**
A *vi* **1** Aut (leave in vehicle) 驱车离去; (be driven away) «*vehicle*» 开走 **2** Sport (in golf) 发球
B *vt* [**~ sth./sb. off, ~ off sth./sb.**] (repel) 把…赶走

- **drive on**
A *vi* Aut **1** (continue) 继续行驶 **2** (set off again) 重新上路
B *vt* [**~ sb. on, ~on sb.**] 激励

- **drive out**
A *vt* [**~ sth. out, ~ out sth.**] **1** Aut 把…开出来 ‹*vehicle*› **2** (expel) 把…赶走 ‹*people, animal, organization*›; **to ~ out evil spirits** 驱邪 **3** (dispel) 消除 ‹*feeling, thought, memory*›
B *vi* **1** (depart in vehicle) 开车离开 **2** (be driven out) «*vehicle*» 开出去

- **drive over**
A *vt* [**~ sb./sth. over, ~ over sb./sth.**] **1** (be driver of) 把…开过去 ‹*vehicle*›; **to ~ sth. over to sth.** 把…开到某处 ‹*vehicle*› **2** (convey) 开车送…过去 ‹*person, goods*›
B *vi* 开车过去; **to ~ over to sth.** 开车去某处

- **drive round** esp Brit
A *vt* **1** [**~ sth. round, ~ round sth.**] (be driver of) 把…开过去 ‹*vehicle*› **2** [**~ sb. round, ~ round sb.**] (convey) 开车送…过去; **to ~ sb. round to sth.** 开车送某人去某处 **3** [**~ sth. round, ~ round sth.**] Mech, Tech «*mechanism, wind, water*» 使…转动 ‹*wheel, propeller*›
B *vi* **1** (go in vehicle) 驱车过去 **2** (go in circles) «*driver*» 开车兜圈子 **3** (be driven in circles) «*vehicle*» 兜圈子

- **drive up**
A *vi* Aut **1** (ascend) 向上行驶 **2** (arrive in vehicle) **to ~ up to sth.** 驱车到达某处 **3** (be driven) «*vehicle*» 到达停靠 **4** (travel) (in a northerly direction) 驱车向北; (to a more important place) 驱车去大地方; **they drove up to London** 他们驾车去了伦敦
B *vt* [**~ sth. up, ~ up sth.**] 抬高 ‹*inflation*›; 提高 ‹*interest rates, wages*›

driveability /'draɪvə,bɪlɪti/ *n* [u] = **drivability**

driveable /'draɪvəbl/ *adj* = **drivable**

drive belt *n* 传动带

drive-by *adj attrib* 飞车进行的 ‹*killing, attack*›; **a ~ shooting** 飞车射杀

drive-in
A *adj attrib* 提供"免下车"服务的; **a ~ cinema** 汽车电影院
B *n* (cinema) 汽车电影院; (restaurant) 汽车餐馆

drivel /'drɪvl/ colloq
A *n* [u] (foolish nonsense) 蠢话; (meaningless words) 废话; **to talk ~** 胡说八道

B *vi* (*pres p etc.* **-ll-** Brit, **-l-** Amer) **to ∼ (on)** (talk nonsense) 说废话; (write nonsense) 写废话

driveline /ˈdraɪvlaɪn/ *n* Amer 动力传动系统

driven /ˈdrɪvn/

A *pp* ▸**drive A, B, C**

B *adj* 发奋的

driver /ˈdraɪvə(r)/ *n* **1** (person who drives a vehicle) 驾驶员; **a taxi ∼** 出租车司机; **John is a good ∼** 约翰车开得好 **2** (drover) 驱赶动物者; **a mule ∼** 赶骡人 **3** (golf club) 发球杆 **4** Comput 驱动程序 **5** (stimulus) 驱动因素

driver: ∼'s license *n* Amer **= driving licence**; **∼'s seat** *n* **= driving seat**

drive shaft *n* 驱动轴

drive-through Amer

A *adj attrib* 提供"免下车"服务的; **a ∼ pharmacy** 汽车药房

B *n* 汽车餐馆

drive: ∼ time *n* 交通高峰期; **∼-time music** *n* 交通高峰时播出的音乐; **∼train** *n* 动力传动系统; **∼ unit** *n* **1** Comput 驱动器; **2** Aut 驱动装置; **∼-up window** *n* Amer "免下车"服务窗口; **∼way** *n* 私人车道

driving /ˈdraɪvɪŋ/

A *n* [u] 驾驶; **dangerous ∼** Jur 危险驾驶; **his ∼ has improved** 他的车技有所提高

B *adj attrib* **1** (blown with great force) 猛烈的 ‹*hail*›; **∼ rain/snow** 暴雨/暴雪 **2** (forceful, strong) 强有力的 ‹*influence*›; **a ∼ ambition** 催人奋进的抱负; **a ∼ need for reform** 对改革的迫切需求 **3** Mech 驱动的

driving: ∼ examiner ▸**p. 409** *n* 驾照考官; **∼ force** *n* 驱动力; **∼ instructor** ▸**p. 409** *n* 驾驶教练; **∼ lesson** *n* 驾驶课程; **∼ licence** *n* Brit 驾驶执照; **∼ mirror** *n* 后视镜; **∼ range** *n* 高尔夫练球场; **∼ school** *n* 驾驶学校; **∼ seat** *n* 驾驶座; **to be in the ∼ seat** 处于控制地位; **this goal put the home team in the ∼ seat** 这一进球让主队控制了局面; **∼ test** *n* 驾照考试; **∼ wheel** *n* **1** (of train) 主动轮; **2** Mech 驱动轮

drizzle /ˈdrɪzl/

A *n* [u] 毛毛雨

B *v impers* 下毛毛雨; **it's drizzling** 正在下毛毛雨

C *vt* Culin 洒; **to ∼ the salad with oil** 往色拉上洒点儿油

drizzly /ˈdrɪzli/ *adj* 下毛毛雨的; **a ∼ morning** 一个细雨蒙蒙的早晨

drogue /drəʊg/ *n* **1** Naut, Aviat (for reducing speed) 减速伞 **2** (small parachute) (as brake) 刹车伞; (for pulling main parachute) 引导伞 **3** Aviat (for refuelling) 锥形管

droll /drəʊl/ *adj* **1** (amusing) 滑稽的 **2** dated (quaint, odd) 古怪的

dromedary /ˈdrɒmədəri, Amer -deri/ *n* 单峰驼

drone /drəʊn/

A *n* **1** (humming sound) (of insect, engine, voice) 嗡嗡声 **2** Zool 雄蜂 **3** fig (parasite) 寄生虫 **4** (pilotless aircraft) 无人驾驶飞机

B *vi* «*bee, insect*» 嗡嗡叫; «*aircraft, engine*» 嗡嗡响

C *vt* 低沉单调地说 ‹*speech*›; 低沉单调地唱 ‹*hymn*›

Phrasal verb

- **drone on** *vi* pej 喋喋不休; **to ∼ on about sth.** 喋喋不休地讲某事

drongo /ˈdrɒŋgəʊ/ *n* Austral, NZ colloq pej 傻蛋

drool /druːl/ *vi* **1** (dribble) 淌口水 **2** fig colloq (show admiration, desire) 垂涎; **to ∼ over sth./sb.** 对某物/某人垂涎欲滴; **to ∼ at the mouth** (in admiration, envy) 垂涎欲滴

droop /druːp/

A *vi* **1** (sag) «*head, shoulders, flower*» 下垂 **2** (slump) 垂头丧气; **the news made our spirits ∼** 这一消息使我们情绪低落

B *vt* 垂下 ‹*head, tail*›

C *n* [u] 下垂

droopy /ˈdruːpi/ *adj* 下垂的; **a ∼ moustache** 下垂的胡须; **the flowers are looking a bit ∼** 这些花看上去有些发蔫了

drop /drɒp/

A *vt* (*pres p etc.* **-pp-**) **1** (let fall by accident) 掉下; **to ∼ an easy catch** 未接住好接的球; **don't ∼ me!** 别把我掉了!; **to ∼ the ball** Amer fig 出错; **to ∼ a brick** *or* **clanger** Brit colloq 出言不慎; **to ∼ sb. in it** colloq 使某人尴尬 **2** (let fall on purpose) 放下; **∼ that gun!** 把枪放下! **3** (lower) 放低; (reduce) 降低; **she ∼ped her gaze** 她垂下目光; **∼ your voice a little** 小声点; **to ∼ one's trousers** colloq 故意拉低裤子 **4** (deliver) 捎带 ‹*goods*› **5** (allow to alight) 让…中途下车 **6** (give casually) 随口说出 ‹*word, remark, advice*›; 无意中透露 ‹*clue*› **7** (write) 写 ‹*letter, note, card, postcard*›; **to ∼ sb. a line** 给某人写封短信 **8** (exclude) 略去 ‹*syllable, word, figure*›; **to ∼ sb. from a team** 某人未被列入队员名单 **9** colloq (end contact with) 同…断绝关系 **10** (abandon, give up) 放弃 ‹*habit, subject*›; **to ∼ formalities** 免去俗套; **to ∼ charges** 撤销指控; **∼ everything! I need your help!** 放下所有事情! 我需要你帮助! **11** Sport (lose) 输掉 ‹*point, game*›; **to ∼ the first set** 输掉第一局 **12** colloq (knock or shoot down) 击落 ‹*bird*›; 击倒 ‹*animal, person*› **13** Aviat 空投 ‹*troops, supplies*› **14** colloq (take orally) 吞服 ‹*drug*› **15** Zool «*animal*» 产 ‹*young*›

B *vi* (*pres p etc.* **-pp-**) **1** (be dropped) 落下; (lower oneself) 低下身子; **the climber slipped and ∼ped to his death** 攀登者失足掉下去摔死了; **the rock ∼ped into the water** 岩石落到了水里; **to ∼ to the ground/into sb.'s arms** 卧倒在地/倒在某人怀中; **to ∼ into a local accent/a regular routine** 带出地方口音/渐渐变成例行公事 **2** colloq (collapse) 累倒; **to be/feel/look ready to ∼** 就要/感到要/看上去要累倒; **to work/dance/practise until** *or* **till one ∼s** 工作/跳舞/练到累垮为止; **to ∼ open** (in surprise or sleep) «*mouth, jaw*» 张开 **3** (move lower) «*gaze*» 垂下; **to ∼ open (in surprise** *or* **amazement)** «*mouth, jaw*» (惊讶地) 张开 **4** (stretch down) «*garment, curtain, skirt*» 下垂 **5** Geog (fall away) 陡降 **6** (move down scale) 下降; **interest rates have ∼ped to a five-year low** 利率已降到5年来的最低水平 **7** (come to end) «*subject*» 结束; **to let a matter/one's studies ∼** 搁置一件事/荒废学业; **you used to be so good at tennis: it's a pity you let it ∼** 你以前网球打得那么好——不练了真可惜

C *n* **1** (small globule of liquid) 滴; (small quantity) 少量; **∼s of sweat** 汗滴; **∼ by ∼** 一滴滴地; **not a ∼** 一点儿没有; **a ∼ in the ocean** Brit, **a ∼ in the bucket** Amer 沧海一粟; **just a ∼ (of sth.)** 就一点儿(某物); **not a bad ∼ of wine/whisky** 很好的葡萄酒/威士忌; **have a ∼ too much** colloq 喝醉; **he doesn't touch a ∼ during the week** colloq 他从星期一到星期五滴酒不沾 **2** (decrease) 下降; **a ∼ of 5%** 5%的下降幅度; **a ∼ in temperature/interest rates/consumer spending** 气温/利率/消费性开支的下降 **3** (jewel, ornament) 坠子 **4** (sweet, candy) 硬糖; **cough ∼s** 止咳糖 **5** (vertical distance) 垂直距离; (vertical slope or surface) 陡坡; **a sheer ∼ (of 200 m) to the rocks below** 距下面岩石(200米)的垂直落差 **6** Aviat (act of dropping people, supplies) 空投; (people dropped) 空投人员; (things dropped) 空投物资; (act of descending by parachute) 空降 **7** colloq (delivery by vehicle) 送货; **we've got three more ∼s to make** 我们还得送3次货 **8** (place to leave sth.) 藏匿处; (act of leaving sth.) 藏匿 **9** colloq (advantage) **to have/get the ∼ on sb.** 占某人的上风

D **drops** *npl* Med 滴剂

Phrasal verbs

- **drop away** *vi* **1** (diminish) «*attendance, numbers, interest*» 逐渐减少 **2** (fall steeply) «*land, shore, cliff*» 陡降
- **drop back** *vi* 落后; **∼ back: you're too close to the car in front** 开慢点儿, 你离前面的汽车太近了
- **drop behind** *vi* 落后
- **drop by** *vi* colloq 顺便访问; **Jim ∼ped by this afternoon** 吉姆今天下午来串门了
- **drop down**

A *vi* **1** (be dropped, become lower) 掉下 **2** (lower oneself) 低下身子

B *vt* [**∼ sth. down, ∼ down sth.**] 把…丢下来

- **drop in**

A *vt* [**∼ sth. in, ∼ in sth.**] **1** (let drop) 扔进; **I poured myself a cup of tea and ∼ped in a couple of sugar lumps** 我给自己倒了杯茶, 并放进几块方糖 **2** colloq (deliver) 递送

B *vi* colloq 顺便来访

- **drop off**

A *vi* **1** (decrease) 逐渐减少; **to show signs of ∼ping off** 呈现出下滑的迹象 **2** (fall asleep) 睡着

B *vt* **1** [**∼ off sth.**] (fall off) 从…掉下; **the blossom began to ∼ off the tree** 树上的花开始凋落 **2** [**∼ sth. off, ∼ off sth.**] (deliver) 捎带 **3** [**∼ sb. off**] (set down, allow to alight) 让…下车

- **drop out** *vi* **1** (fall out) 掉出; **the key must have ∼ped out of my pocket** 钥匙肯定从我口袋里掉出来了 **2** (withdraw) 退出; Sch, Univ 退学; Sociol 逃避现实; **to ∼ out (of school)** 退学; **he ∼ped out of politics** 他退出了政坛; **he ∼ped out of society** 他脱离了传统社会 **3** (disappear) 消失; **the coins will gradually ∼ out of circulation** 这些硬币将逐渐退出流通 **4** (straighten out) «*crease(s)*» 抻平
- **drop over** *vi* colloq **= drop round**
- **drop round** *vi* colloq 顺便访问; **(do) ∼ round some time** 有空来坐坐

drop: ∼-add period *n* Amer 选课期; **∼ cloth** *n* Amer **1** **= ∼ curtain**; **2** **= dust sheet**; **∼ curtain** *n* 垂幕; **∼-dead** *adv* colloq 令人绝倒地; **she was ∼-dead gorgeous** 她美艳惊人; **∼-down menu** *n* 下拉式菜单; **∼ forge** *n* 落锤锻; **∼ goal** *n* 抛踢球得分; **∼ hammer** *n* 落锤; **∼ handlebars** *npl* 下弯形车把; **∼ kick** *n* **1** (in rugby) 抛踢球; **2** (in martial arts) 飞踢; **∼ leaf** *n* 垂板; **∼-leaf table** *n* 有垂板的桌子

droplet /ˈdrɒplɪt/ *n* 小滴; **∼s of condensation on the window** 凝结在窗户上的小水珠

drop-off *n* 下降; **a ∼ in traffic** 车流量的减少; **a sudden ∼ in tourism** 旅游业的突然衰落

dropout /ˈdrɒpaʊt/ *n* **1** (from school) 退学者; **a college ∼** 大学肄业生; **∼ rate** 退学率 **2** (from society) 退出主流社会的人

dropped kerb *n* Brit 下斜路缘

dropper /ˈdrɒpə(r)/ *n* 滴管

droppings /ˈdrɒpɪŋz/ *npl* [鸟、昆虫等的] 粪

drop: ∼ shipment *n* 直达货运; **∼ shot** *n* 短吊; **∼ zone** *n* (for supplies etc.) 空投场; (for parachutist) 伞降区域

dross /drɒs/ *n* [u] **1** (rubbish) 糟粕 **2** (mineral waste) 浮渣

drought /draʊt/ *n* [c and u] 旱灾

drove /drəʊv/

A *pt* ▸**drive A, B, C**

B *n* **1** (herd, flock) 畜群; **a ∼ of cattle** 一群牛 **2** *usu pl* (large number) 大批; **∼s of sightseers** 成群的观光客; **in ∼s** 成群结队地

drover /ˈdrəʊvə(r)/ *n* 赶牲畜的人

drown /draʊn/

A *vi* 淹死; **she fell overboard and ∼ed** 她掉落船下, 溺水身亡; **he ∼ed in his own vomit/blood** 他被自己的呕吐物/血呛死了

B *vt* **1** (kill by immersion) 淹死; **to ∼ oneself** 投水自杀; **20 people were ∼ed in the accident** 事故中有20人溺水身亡; **to ∼ one's**

sorrows hum 借酒浇愁; **(to look) like a ~ed rat** colloq （看起来）像只落汤鸡 **2** (make inaudible) 压过 ‹*sound, speech*›; **the final words of the speech were ~ed in applause** 演讲的结尾被掌声淹没了 **3** (flood) 淹没 ‹*land, fields*›; **don't ~ it!** fig 别掺太多！

Phrasal verb

• **drown out** *vt* [**~ sth./sb. out, ~ out sth./sb.**] 压过 ‹*noise*›; 压过…的声音 ‹*person*›

drowning /ˈdraʊnɪŋ/
A *n* [c and u] 淹死
B *adj* 快要淹死的; **a ~ man will clutch at a straw** fig 病急乱投医

drowse /draʊz/ *vi* 打盹

drowsily /ˈdraʊzɪli/ *adv* 昏昏欲睡地

drowsiness /ˈdraʊzɪnɪs/ *n* [u] 昏昏欲睡

drowsy /ˈdraʊzi/ *adj* **1** (sleepy) 昏昏欲睡的; **to feel ~** 感觉困倦 **2** (sleep-inducing) 令人昏昏欲睡的 ‹*afternoon, atmosphere*›

d

drub /drʌb/ *vt* colloq 大胜 ‹*opponent*›

drubbing /ˈdrʌbɪŋ/ *n* colloq 彻底失败; **to give sb. a (good) ~** 把某人打得落花流水; **to take a ~** 遭到惨败

drudge /drʌdʒ/ *n* 做苦工的人

drudgery /ˈdrʌdʒəri/ *n* [u] 苦活; **household ~** 繁重乏味的家务活; **a life of ~** 劳累的一生

drug /drʌg/
A *n* **1** Pharm 药; **to be on/off ~s** 正在/停止用药; **the doctor has put me on a different ~** 医生给我开了另外一种药; **a ~ on the market** fig 滞销品 **2** (narcotic) 毒品; **to be on** *or* **to take ~s** 吸毒成瘾; **to do ~s** colloq 吸毒; **success is a (kind of) ~** 成功是种迷魂药
B drugs *npl* (medicines) 药品; (narcotics) 毒品; **a ~s bust** 缉毒搜查
C *vt* (*pres p etc.* **-gg-**) **1** (sedate) 用药麻醉 **2** (add drug to) 在…中投放麻醉药 ‹*food, drink*›

drug: ~ abuse *n* [u] 吸毒; **~ abuser** *n* 吸毒者; **~ addict** *n* 瘾君子; **~ addiction** *n* [u] 毒瘾; **~ culture** *n* [u] 毒品文化

drugged /drʌgd/ *adj* **1** (under the influence of medicine) 被药物控制的; **to be ~ up to the eyeballs** colloq 大量服药后变得精神恍惚; **she lay for hours in a ~ sleep** 她在药物的作用下睡了几个小时 **2** (poisoned) 下了毒的

druggist /ˈdrʌgɪst/ ▸**p. 409** *n* Amer (pharmacist) 药剂师; (retailer) 药商

druggy /ˈdrʌgi/ colloq
A *n* 瘾君子
B *adj* (caused by drugs) 毒品引起的; (involving drugs) 吸毒的; **he spent the day in a ~ haze** 他那天吸了毒，整天昏昏沉沉的

drug: ~ habit *n* 毒瘾; **~ peddler, ~ pusher** *ns* 毒品贩子; **~ rape** *n* 迷奸; **~-related** *adj* 与毒品有关的; **~ runner** *n* 毒品走私者; **~s charges** *npl* 与毒品有关的指控; **~ smuggler** *n* 毒品走私者; **~s offence** *n* 毒品犯罪; **~ squad, ~s squad** *n + v sing or pl* Brit 缉毒队; **~s raid** *n* 缉毒搜查; **~s ring** *n* 贩毒团伙; **~s scene** *n* 吸毒现场; **~store** *n* Amer 药房 [兼售化妆品等]; **~ taker** *n* 吸毒者; **~-taking** *n* [u] 吸毒; **~ test** *n* 药检; **~ trafficker** *n* 毒贩; **~ trafficking** *n* [u] 贩毒; **~ user** *n* 吸毒者

druid /ˈdruːɪd/ *n* 德鲁伊特 [古代凯尔特人的祭司]

drum /drʌm/
A *n* ▸**p. 395** **1** Mus 鼓; **Joe Morello is on ~s** 乔·莫雷洛担任鼓手 **2** (container) 大桶 **3** Tech, Aut 鼓轮; (in washing machine) 滚筒; **brake ~** 制动鼓 **4** (spool for rope, cable) 卷筒 **5** (sound) 敲击声; **the ~ of rain on the roof** 雨打在屋顶上的咚咚声
B *vi* (*pres p etc.* **-mm-**) **1** (beat drum) 打鼓 **2** (make drumming sound) 有节奏地敲击; **to ~ on the table with one's fingers** 用手指在桌上嗒嗒地敲击
C *vt* (*pres p etc.* **-mm-**) 用…有节奏地敲击; **to ~ one's feet on the floor** 有节奏地用脚跺地

Phrasal verbs

• **drum into** *vt* [**~ sth. into sb.**] 向…反复灌输…; **we had politeness ~med into us from a very early age** 我们从小就被反复灌输要讲礼貌; **I've managed to ~ a few words into their heads** 我反复强调，终于让他们记住了几句话

• **drum out** *vt* [**~ sb. out**] 开除

• **drum up** *vt* [**~ up sth./sb.**] 争取 ‹*support*›; 激起 ‹*enthusiasm*›; 招揽 ‹*customers, custom*›

drum: ~beat *n* 击鼓声; **~ brake** *n* 鼓形制动器; **~ kit** *n* 成套鼓乐器

drumlin /ˈdrʌmlɪn/ *n* 鼓丘

drum: ~ machine *n* 电子鼓; **~ major** *n* 行进乐队指挥; **~ majorette** *n* 行进乐队女指挥

drummer /ˈdrʌmə(r)/ ▸**p. 409** *n* **1** Mus 鼓手 **2** Amer colloq (sales representative) 旅行推销员

drumming /ˈdrʌmɪŋ/ *n* [u] **1** Mus (activity) 击鼓; (sound) 鼓声 **2** (of fingers, feet, rain) 咚咚声; **he kept up a constant ~ on the table** 他一直嗒嗒地敲着桌子

drum: ~ roll *n* 一连串击鼓声; **~stick** *n* **1** Mus 鼓槌; **2** Culin (of cooked chicken) 鸡腿; (of other fowl) 家禽腿

drunk /drʌŋk/
A *pp* ▸**drink A, B, C**
B *adj* **1** lit (inebriated) 醉的; **to get ~** 喝醉; **~ driving** 醉酒驾车; **dead** *or* **blind ~** 烂醉如泥的; **to be ~ and disorderly** Jur 酒后闹事; **as ~ as a lord** Brit hum colloq 酩酊大醉的 **2** fig 陶醉的; **to be ~ with sth.** 对某事物如痴如醉
C *n* (habitual) 酒鬼; (on a particular occasion) 醉汉

drunkard /ˈdrʌŋkəd/ *n* 酒鬼

drunken /ˈdrʌŋkən/ *adj* **1** (inebriated) 醉的; **a ~ driver** 喝醉的司机 **2** (alcoholic) 酗酒的 **3** (characterized by drunkenness) 纵情饮酒的 ‹*orgy, party*›; 酒后的 ‹*stupor, rage*›; **a ~ brawl** 酗酒滋事

drunkenly /ˈdrʌŋkənli/ *adv* **1** lit (in a drunken manner) 醉醺醺地 **2** fig (as if drunk) 蹒跚地 ‹*stagger, sway*›; **to lurch ~** 踉踉跄跄地走

drunkenness /ˈdrʌŋkənnɪs/ *n* [u] **1** (state) 醉酒 **2** (habit) 酗酒

dry /draɪ/
A *adj* **1** (not liquid, wet or moist) 干的 ‹*ink, paint*›; (not rainy) 干燥的 ‹*weather, place*›; (empty of water) 干涸的 ‹*river, well*›; **store in a cool, ~ place** 在凉爽干燥处储存; **~ bread** 不涂黄油的面包; **on ~ land** 在陆地上; **to keep (sth.) ~** （使某物）保持干燥; **to wipe sth. ~** 把某物擦干; **(as) ~ as a bone** 干透的; **there wasn't a ~ eye in the house** 全场无人不掉泪; **a ~ heat is much less tiring** 干热不会那么让人感到疲累; **to boil ~** «*kettle, food*» 烧干; **to run ~** «*river, well*» 干涸; fig «*funds, supplies*» 耗尽 **2** Physiol 干性的 ‹*skin, hair*›; **a ~ cough** 干咳 **3** (thirsty, thirst-making) 口渴的; **to be/feel ~** 口渴/感到口渴; **~ work** 令人口干舌燥的工作 **4** (without alcohol) 禁酒的 ‹*day, event, area*›; **the wedding was ~ — lemonade and fruit juice only** 婚礼上没有酒，只有柠檬水和果汁; **parts of the country are ~ on Sundays** 本国的一些地方星期天禁酒 **5** (not sweet) 干的; **a glass of ~ white wine** 一杯干白葡萄酒 **6** (subtle, ironical) 不形于色的 ‹*remark, humour*›; (unemotional) 冷淡的 ‹*voice, person, remark*›; **to make ~ asides** 一本正经地插科打诨 **7** (dull) 枯燥的 ‹*subject, lecture*›; **the ~ facts of the matter** 有关此事的干巴巴的事实; **(as) ~ as dust** 非常乏味的 **8** Brit Pol 保守党政客的
B *vt* (*3rd pers sing pres* **dries**; *pt, pp* **dried**) 弄干; **to ~ one's eyes** 擦干眼泪; **sun-dried tomatoes** 晒干的西红柿
C *v refl* (*3rd pers sing pres* **dries**; *pt, pp* **dried**) **to ~ oneself** 擦干身子
D *vi* (*3rd pers sing pres* **dries**; *pt, pp* **dried**) **1** (become dry) 变干 **2** Theat sl «*actor, speaker*» 忘词
E *n* (*pl* **dries** *or* **~s**) **1** (act of drying sth.) 弄干; **would you give those dishes a ~, please?** 请你把那些碟子擦干好吗？ **2** Brit Pol 保守党政客

Phrasal verbs

• **dry off**
A *vt* [**~ sb./sth. off, ~ off sb./sth.**] 把…擦干
B *v refl* **to ~ oneself off** 把自己擦干
C *vi* 变干

• **dry out**
A *vt* **1** [**~ sth. out, ~ out sth.**] (make dry) 使干透; **sunbathing will ~ out your skin** 日光浴会把你的皮肤晒得干燥 **2** [**~ sb. out, ~ out sb.**] (cure of alcoholism) 使戒酒
B *vi* **1** (become dry) 干透 **2** (undergo cure for alcoholism) 戒酒

• **dry up**
A *vi* **1** lit (become dry) «*river*» 干涸 **2** fig (run out) 耗尽 **3** Brit (dry dishes) 擦干餐具 **4** colloq (be unable to speak) 说不出话; Brit colloq (stop speaking) 住口; **oh, ~ up, will you!** 噢，你就不能住嘴！
B *vt* [**~ sth. up, ~ up sth.**] **1** (empty) «*sun, heat, drought*» 使…变干 ‹*water, puddles, river*› **2** Brit (wipe dry) 擦干 ‹*dishes*›

dry: ~-as-dust *adj* 枯燥无味的; **~ battery** *n* 干电池组; **~ cell** *n* 干电池; **~-clean** *vt* 干洗; **~-cleaner** ▸**p. 409** *n* (person) 干洗商; **the ~-cleaner's** 干洗店; **~-cleaning** *n* [u] 干洗; **~ dock** *n* 干船坞

dryer /ˈdraɪə(r)/ *n* **1** (tumble-dryer) 干衣机; (for hair) 电吹风 **2** (for paint, varnish) 催干剂

dry: ~-eyed *adj* 不哭的; **to be/remain ~-eyed** 不掉眼泪; **~ goods** *npl* Amer dated 干货; **~ ice** *n* [u] 干冰

drying /ˈdraɪɪŋ/
A *n* [u] (by machine) 烘干; (with cloth) 擦干
B *adj attrib* 使干燥的; **a ~ wind** 干燥的风; **it's a good ~ day** 今天洗衣服很容易晾干

drying: ~ rack *n* (for dishes) 晾碗架; (for clothes) 晾衣架; **~ room** *n* 晾衣室; **~-up** *n* [u] Brit 擦干餐具; **~-up cloth** *n* Brit 擦碗布

dryly /ˈdraɪli/ *adv* = **drily**

dry: ~ martini *n* 干马提尼酒; **~ measure** *n* 干量 [谷物等的计量单位]

dryness /ˈdraɪnɪs/ *n* **1** (of skin, weather, soil) 干燥 **2** (of manner, tone) 冷冰冰; (of wit, humour) 不动声色 **3** (of wine, sherry) 酸味

dry: ~ rot *n* [u] 干腐; **~ run** *n* 排练; **~ season** *n* 干季; **~ shampoo** *n* [c and u] 洗发粉; **~ shave** *n* 干刮脸; **~ shaver** *n* 电动剃须刀; **~ ski slope** *n* 人造滑雪坡; **~stone wall** *n* Brit 干砌石墙

DSc *abbr* = **Doctor of Science** 理学博士

DST *abbr* esp Amer = **daylight saving time**

DTD *abbr* = **document type definition**

DT's *abbr* colloq = **delirium tremens**

DTT *abbr* = **digital terrestrial television**

DTV *abbr* = **digital television**

DU *abbr* = **depleted uranium**

dual /ˈdjuːəl, Amer ˈduːəl/ *adj attrib* 双重的 ‹*role, function, purpose*›

dual: ~ admission *n* Amer [大学的] 双录取制; **a ~ admission student/program** 双录取制学生/项目; **~ carriageway** *n* Brit [中央有分隔带的] 双向车道; **~-control** *adj* 双重控制的; **~ controls** *npl* 复式控制装置; **~ national** *n* 有双重国籍的人; **~ nationality** *n* [u] 双重国籍; **~ ownership** *n* [u] 双方共有; **to have ~ ownership**

of sth. 双方共有某物; **~ personality** *n* [c and u] 双重人格; **~-purpose** *adj* 双重目的的; **a ~-purpose vehicle** 两用汽车; **~-use** *adj* 军民两用的 ‹*technology, product*›

dub /dʌb/ *vt* (*pres p etc.* **-bb-**) 1 (into foreign language) 为…配音; (add to soundtrack) 混录 ‹*sound effect*›; **the film had been ~bed into German** 这部电影已经用德语配了音 2 (nickname) 给…起绰号; (describe as) 把…称为 3 (knight) 封…为爵士; **to ~ sb. (a) knight** 封某人为爵士

Dubai /du:'baɪ/ *pr n* 迪拜

dubbin /'dʌbɪn/ *n* [u] Brit 护革油

dubbing /'dʌbɪŋ/ *n* [u] 1 (into foreign language) 配音 2 (sound mixing) 混录

dubious /'dju:bɪəs, Amer 'du:-/ *adj* 1 (doubtful) 犹疑的; **I am ~ about accepting** 我拿不准该不该接受 2 (arguable) 不确定的 ‹*point, question*› 3 (suspect) 可疑的 ‹*character, motive, origin*›; **a person of ~ reliability** 不大可靠的人 4 (equivocal) 不一定好的 ‹*honour, privilege*›; **he has the ~ distinction of being the only MP who has never made a speech in Parliament** 他是唯一一个从未在议会发言的议员，这算不上什么好名声

dubiously /'dju:bɪəsli, Amer 'du:-/ *adv* 1 (doubtfully) 犹疑地 2 (in a way that arouses doubt) 令人生疑地; **wildly expensive and ~ effective drugs** 价格昂贵但未必有效的药物

dubiousness /'dju:bɪəsnɪs, Amer 'du:-/ *n* [u] 1 (doubtfulness) 可疑 2 (equivocalness) 含糊

Dublin /'dʌblɪn/ *pr n* 都柏林

Dubliner /'dʌblɪnə(r)/ *n* 都柏林人

ducal /'dju:kl, Amer 'du:-/ *adj* 公爵的

duchess /'dʌtʃɪs/ *n* 1 (wife of duke) 公爵夫人 2 (woman holding ducal rank) 女公爵

duchy /'dʌtʃi/ *n* 公爵领地

duck /dʌk/

A *n* 1 [c] (*pl* **~s** *or* **duck**) Zool 鸭; **wild/domesticated ~** 野鸭/家鸭; **~s and drakes** 母鸭和公鸭; **to take to sth. like a ~ to water** 像鸭子入水般习惯某事; **to be like water off a ~'s back** «*remark*» 被当作耳旁风 2 [u] Culin 鸭肉 3 [c] Sport (in cricket) 零分; **to be out for a ~** 得零分出局; **to make a ~** 得零分; **to break one's ~** lit 首次得分; fig 首次成功 4 [c] (act of ducking) 低头

B *vi* 低下头; **to ~ (down) behind sth.** 弓身躲在某物后面; **to ~ into sth.** 低头钻进某处

C *vt* 1 (lower) 低下 ‹*head*› 2 (dodge) 躲避 ‹*blow, missile*›; fig colloq (avoid) 回避 ‹*issue*›; 逃避 ‹*duty*› 3 (push underwater) 把…按入水中 ‹*person, head*›

Phrasal verb

- **duck out** *vi* colloq **to ~ out of doing sth.** 逃避做某事; **to ~ out of seeing sb.** 躲着不见某人

duck-billed platypus *n* 鸭嘴兽

duckie /'dʌki/ *n* = **ducky**

ducking /'dʌkɪŋ/ *n* 浸入水中; **to give sb. a ~** 把某人按入水里

ducking stool *n* Hist 浸水椅 [一种刑具]

duckling /'dʌklɪŋ/ *n* 小鸭

duck: ~ pond *n* 鸭塘; **~s and drakes** *npl + v sing* Games 打水漂; **~weed** *n* [u] 浮萍

ducky /'dʌki/ *n* Brit colloq 宝贝儿

duct /'dʌkt/ *n* 1 Tech, Constr 管道 2 Anat 导管; **tear ~** 泪管

ductile /'dʌktaɪl, Amer -tl/ *adj* 可延展的

dud /dʌd/ colloq

A *n* 1 (malfunctioning machine or part) 不中用的东西; (defective or faulty item) 次品; (defective battery) 废电池 2 (defective firework) 未爆烟花; (defective shell) 哑弹 3 (fake coin, banknote) 假币 4 (bad cheque) 空头支票 5 (incompetent person) 窝囊废

B *adj* 1 (not working properly) 出故障的 ‹*motor, engine*›; **a ~ battery** 废电池 2 (defective) 有缺陷的 ‹*toy, product*› 3 (failing to ignite) 点不着的 ‹*firework*›; (failing to explode) 不能引爆的; **a ~ shell** 哑弹 4 (counterfeit) 伪造的; **a ~ banknote** 假钞 5 (dishonoured) 被拒付的; **a ~ cheque** 拒付支票

dude /dju:d, Amer du:d/ *n* esp Amer colloq 1 (man) 家伙; **hey, ~, what's up?** 喂，哥们，怎么啦？ 2 (stylish, confident person) 时髦自信的人 3 dated (dandy) 花花公子

dude ranch *n* Amer 度假牧场

dudgeon /'dʌdʒən/ *n* [u] **in (high) ~** 怒气冲冲地

due /dju:, Amer du:/

A *adj* 1 *pred* (payable) 到期的; **to be/fall ~** «*rent, instalment, payment*» 到期 2 *pred* (owed, entitled) 应有的; **to be ~ (for) sth.** 应得到 ‹*money, promotion*›; **to be ~ to sb./sth.** «*money, thanks*» 应给予 ‹*person, company*›; **to be ~ sb.** 归属某人; **I'm still ~ 10 days' leave** 我还应有 10 天的假期; **the debts ~ to the company** 公司的应收债款 3 *usu attrib* (appropriate) 适当的 ‹*reflection, praise, attention*›; **to pay ~ consideration** *or* **regard to sth.** 适当考虑某事物; **with all ~ respect** 恕我冒昧; **with all ~ regard** *or* **respect to sb./sth.** 充分考虑某人/某事物; **in ~ course** 在适当的时候; **he was charged with driving without ~ care and attention** 他被控鲁莽驾驶 4 *pred* (scheduled, expected) 预期应到的; **to be ~** «*event*» 预期发生; «*train, traveller*» 预期到达; **to be ~ to do sth.** 预定做某事; **to be ~ out** Transp 预定出发; Publg 预定出版; **to be ~ back** «*person, transport*» 预定返回; **when's the baby ~?** 宝宝什么时候出生？; **my essay's ~ next Wednesday** 我的文章下周三必须交; **the project is ~ for completion in 2010** 该项目预计 2010 年完工

B **due to** *pred* (caused by, because of) 因为; **~ to the fact that …** 由于…的事实; **to be ~ to sb.** 多亏某人; **~ to bad weather/a fall in demand/unforeseen circumstances** 由于恶劣天气/需求减少/不可预见的情况

C *adv* 正对着; **~ north/south/east/west** 正北/正南/正东/正西

D *n* fig (what is owed to sb.) 应得的东西; **to give sb. his/her ~** 给某人说句公道话; **he always tries to give folk their ~** 他总是尽量待人公平

E **dues** *npl* 应缴款; **to pay one's ~s** lit 交纳会费; fig (fulfil obligation) 尽责任; (experience difficulties) 经历苦难; **this drummer has paid his ~s with the best** 这个鼓手经历的苦难不比任何人少

due: ~ bill *n* Amer 借据; **~ date** *n* (for payment of a bill) 到期日; (for expected birth) 预产期; **~ diligence** *n* [u] 尽职审核

duel /'dju:əl, Amer 'du:-/

A *n* 1 lit (fight, contest) 决斗; **to have/fight/engage in a ~** 进行决斗; **a ~ to the death** 生死决斗; **to challenge sb. to a ~** 向某人挑战要求决斗 2 fig (struggle) 斗争; (competition) 竞争; **a ~ of wits** 斗智; **a verbal ~** 舌战

B *vi* (*pres p etc.* **-ll-**) 1 lit 决斗 2 fig (struggle) 斗争; (compete) 竞争

duellist /'dju:əlɪst, Amer 'du:-/ *n* 1 (fighter) 决斗者 2 (competitor) 对手

due process *n* [u] Amer **~ (of law)** 合法诉讼程序

duet /dju:'et, Amer du:-/ *n* (by two singers) 二重唱; (by two instrumentalists) 二重奏; (by two dancers) 双人舞

duff /dʌf/ *adj* Brit colloq 1 (defective) 出故障的 ‹*machine*› 2 (incompetent, worthless) 无能的 ‹*player, worker, character*› 3 (poorly executed, careless) 胡乱的 ‹*shot*›; 草率的 ‹*move*› 4 (stupid) 愚蠢的 ‹*idea, suggestion*›

Phrasal verb

- **duff up** *vt* [**~ sb. up, ~ sb. up**] Brit colloq 痛打

duffel /'dʌfl/ *n* [u] 起绒粗呢

duffel: ~ bag *n* 圆筒包; **~ coat** *n* 连帽粗呢大衣

duffer /'dʌfə(r)/ *n* colloq 1 (stupid person) 笨蛋 2 (ungifted person) 无能的人; **to be a ~ at sth.** 不擅长某事

duffle /'dʌfl/ *n* = **duffel**

dug /dʌg/ *pt, pp* ▸ **dig A, B**

dugong /'du:gɒŋ/ *n* (*pl* **~** *or* **~s**) 儒艮 [栖于印度洋海域的一种食草哺乳动物]

dugout /'dʌgaʊt/ *n* 1 (canoe) 独木舟 2 Sport (shelter) 球员席

duke /dju:k, Amer du:k/ *n* 公爵

dulcet /'dʌlsɪt/ *adj attrib* liter 悦耳的 ‹*tones*›

dulcimer /'dʌlsɪmə(r)/ ▸ **p. 395** *n* 1 (percussion instrument) **(hammered) ~** 扬琴 2 (plucked instrument) 杜西莫琴

dull /dʌl/

A *adj* 1 (not bright) 暗淡的 ‹*colour, shade*›; **a ~ blue** 暗蓝色 2 (overcast) 阴沉的 ‹*weather, sky, day*› 3 (muffled) 闷声的 ‹*thud, boom*› 4 (uninteresting) 乏味的 ‹*lecture, holiday*›; (lacking vivaciousness) 沉闷的 ‹*man, lecturer*›; **(as) ~ as ditchwater** *or* **dishwater** 非常单调乏味的 5 (blunt) 钝的 ‹*blade, edge, knife*› 6 (slow-witted) 愚钝的 7 (not intense) 隐隐的 ‹*ache, pain, throbbing*› 8 (vacant) 呆滞的 ‹*look, stare*›

B *vt* 1 (make matt) 使…变暗淡 ‹*lustre, brightness, finish*› 2 (muffle) 使…变低沉 ‹*sound*›; **to ~ sb.'s hearing** 使某人听力减退 3 (make slow, sluggish) 使…迟钝 ‹*wits, senses*› 4 (blunt) 使…变钝 ‹*blade, sharpness*›; **to ~ the edge of sb.'s appetite** 使某人没有胃口 5 (diminish) 减轻 ‹*suffering, pain*›; 减少 ‹*delight, pleasure*›

C *vi* 1 (become matt) «*lustre*» 变暗淡; **the manufacturers claim that the colour should not ~ for a long time** 厂商声称颜色可以保持很久 2 (become sluggish, slow) «*wits, senses*» 变迟钝 3 (grow blunt) «*blade, edge*» 变钝 4 (lose intensity) «*pain, anguish*» 减轻; «*delight, pleasure*» 减少

dullard /'dʌləd/ *n* dated pej 1 (idiot) 笨蛋 2 (dunce) 迟钝的人; **to be a ~ at school** 学业不开窍

dullness /'dʌlnɪs/ *n* [u] 1 (of colour, finish) 暗淡 2 (of weather, sky, day) 阴沉 3 (of sound) 低沉 4 (slow-wittedness) 愚钝 5 (tediousness) 乏味 6 (lack of vivacity, wit) 沉闷 7 (bluntness) 钝 8 (of ache, pain) 隐约 9 (of eyes) 呆滞

dullsville /'dʌlzvɪl/ *n* [u] esp Amer colloq 1 (dull place) 乏味的地方 2 (boring activity) 乏味的活动

dully /'dʌlli/ *adv* 1 (dimly) 昏暗地 ‹*glow, burn*› 2 (darkly) 阴沉地 3 (with a muffled sound) 低沉地 ‹*thump*› 4 (tediously) 乏味地 ‹*talk, perform*› 5 (vaguely, without intensity) 隐隐地 ‹*ache, throb*› 6 (vacantly) 呆滞地 ‹*look, stare*›

duly /'dju:li, Amer 'du:-/ *adv* 1 (in proper fashion) 适当地; **~ grateful** 适当地心存感激的 2 (predictably) 不出预料地 3 (at the expected time) 按时地

dumb /dʌm/ *adj* 1 (unable to speak) 哑的; **he's been ~ since birth** 他生来就是哑巴 2 (incapable of speech) 不能言语的; **~ animals** 哑巴牲口 3 *pred* (temporarily) 一时说不出话的; **to be struck ~ with astonishment** 惊讶得说不出话来 4 (resulting in speechlessness) 哑口无言的 ‹*terror, amazement*›; **to leave sb. in a state of ~ astonishment** 使某人惊讶得说不出话来 5 (uncommunicative) 不愿说话的; **~ incomprehension** 茫然不解 6 colloq (stupid) 愚蠢的; **to act ~** 装聋作哑; **a ~ ox** Amer 笨蛋

dumb: ~-ass *adj attrib* Amer colloq 愚蠢的; **~bell** *n* 1 Sport 哑铃; 2 Amer colloq (idiot) 笨蛋; **~ blonde** *n* colloq 金发傻妞

dumbfound /dʌm'faʊnd/ *vt* 使惊呆

dumbfounded /dʌm'faʊndɪd/ *adj* 惊呆的

dumbly /'dʌmli/ *adv* 一言不发地

dumbness /'dʌmnɪs/ *n* [u] 1 (inability to speak) 哑; **he was afflicted by ~** 他变哑了 2 colloq (stupidity) 愚蠢

dumbo /'dʌmbəʊ/ *n* colloq 笨蛋

dumbstruck /'dʌmstrʌk/ *adj* 惊呆的

dumb: ~ terminal *n* 哑终端; **~ waiter** *n* 1 (small lift, esp, in restaurant) 送菜升降梯; 2 Brit (food trolley) 上菜架; 3 Brit (revolving tray for displaying food) 圆转台

dumdum /'dʌmdʌm/ *n* **~ (bullet)** 达姆弹

dummy /'dʌmi/
A *n* 1 (human model) 人体模型; **wax ~** 蜡像 2 (ventriloquist's model) [口技表演用的] 假人 3 (imitation model) 仿制品 4 Publg, Print (mock-up) 装帧样本 5 Brit Sport 假动作; **to sell (sb.) a ~** 以假动作迷惑（某人） 6 colloq (stupid person) 笨蛋 7 Brit (for baby) 橡皮奶嘴
B *adj* 1 (fake) 假的 2 Sport 佯装的; **superb ~ moves** 漂亮的假动作 3 Mil (blank) 无炸药的; **~ bullets** 空包弹
C *vi* Brit Sport 做假动作

dummy: ~ pass *n* Brit 假传球; **~ run** *n* 1 (trial run) 试运行; 2 Aviat (practice attack) 演习

dump /dʌmp/
A *n* 1 (rubbish tip) 垃圾场; (rubbish heap) 垃圾堆 2 Mil 军需品临时存放处; **weapons ~** 临时军火库 3 colloq pej (unpleasant place) 讨厌的地方; **nobody wants to live in this ~ of a town** 没有谁愿意住在这个破镇上 4 Comput (copying of data) 转存; (file, printout) 转存文件 5 **to be down in the ~s** colloq 心情沮丧
B *vt* 1 倾倒 ‹*rubbish, waste*› 2 (sell abroad cheaply) [向国外] 倾销 3 colloq (get rid of) 抛弃; (end relationship with) 与…结束关系; **the company has ~ed him** 公司解雇了他; **to ~ one's girlfriend** 甩掉女朋友 4 colloq (set down) 猛地扔下; **she turned the handbag upside down and ~ed the contents on the table** 她将手提包倒过来，把里面的东西一股脑儿倒在桌上; **just ~ your case anywhere** 你把箱子随便放哪儿都行 5 Comput (copy) 转存 ‹*data*›; (print out) 转存打印 ‹*document*›
C *vi* Amer colloq **to ~ on sb.** 诘难某人

dumper /'dʌmpə(r)/ *n* = **dumper truck**

dumper truck, dump truck *ns* 自卸车

dumping /'dʌmpɪŋ/ *n* [u] 1 (disposal of waste) [垃圾的] 倾倒 2 Comm 倾销

dumping ground *n* (for waste) 垃圾场; fig (for rejects) 丢弃处

dumpling /'dʌmplɪŋ/ *n* 1 Culin (savoury) 饺子 2 Culin (dessert) 水果布丁 3 colloq (small, fat person) 矮胖子

dumpy /'dʌmpi/ *adj* 矮胖的

dun /dʌn/
A *adj* 灰褐色的
B *n* 1 [u] (colour) 灰褐色 2 [c] (horse) 灰褐色马

dunce /dʌns/ *n* (slow learner) 迟钝的学生; (stupid person) 愚笨的人

dunce's cap *n* 笨蛋高帽 [旧时学校中给差生戴的圆锥形纸糊帽]

dunderhead /'dʌndəhed/ *n* dated colloq 笨蛋

dune /dju:n, Amer du:n/ *n* 沙丘

dune buggy *n* = **beach buggy**

dung /dʌŋ/ *n* [u] 1 (faeces) 粪 2 (manure) 粪肥

dungaree /ˌdʌŋgə'ri:/
A *n* [u] (material) 粗棉布
B **dungarees** *npl* (trousers) 粗棉布工装裤

dung beetle *n* 蜣螂

dungeon /'dʌndʒən/ *n* 地牢

dung heap, dung hill *ns* 粪堆

dunk /dʌŋk/ *vt* 1 (dip) 把…浸入饮料 ‹*biscuit, bread*› 2 (immerse) 浸; **to ~ sth. in sth.** 把某物在某液体中浸一下; **the duck ~ed its head in** *or* **under the water** 鸭子把头入扎进水里

dunk shot *n* (in basketball) 扣篮

dunno /də'nəʊ/ *vi* colloq = **don't know** ▸ **know A, B**

dunnock /'dʌnək/ *n* = **hedge sparrow**

dunny /'dʌni/ *n* Austral, NZ colloq 茅厕

duo /'dju:əʊ, Amer 'du:əʊ/ *n* (*pl* **~s**) 1 Mus, Theat 一对表演者; **comedy ~** 喜剧搭档 2 Mus (by two singers) 二重唱; (by two instrumentalists) 二重奏; (by two dancers) 双人舞

duodecimal /ˌdju:əʊ'desɪml, Amer ˌdu:ə'desəml/ *adj* 十二进制的

duodenal /ˌdju:ə'di:nl, Amer ˌdu:ə'di:nl/ *adj* 十二指肠的

duodenum /ˌdju:ə'di:nəm, Amer ˌdu:ə'di:nəm/ *n* (*pl* **~s** *or* **duodena** /ˌdju:ə'di:nə/) 十二指肠

duopoly /dju:'ɒpəli, Amer du:-/ *n* 两强垄断

dupe /dju:p, Amer du:p/
A *vt* 欺骗; **to ~ sb. into doing sth.** 哄骗某人做某事; **to be ~d** 受骗
B *n* 易受骗的人; **to be a ~ of sb./sth.** 被某人/某事欺骗; **to make a ~ of sb.** 欺骗某人

duple /'dju:pl, Amer 'du:pl/ *adj* 双拍子的

duplex /'dju:pleks, Amer 'du:-/
A *adj* 双面打印的 ‹*printer*›
B *n* Amer, Austral 1 **~ (house)** 联式房屋 2 **~ (apartment)** 复式公寓

duplicate
A /'dju:plɪkeɪt, Amer 'du:plə-/ *vt* 1 (copy) 复制 ‹*document, sketch*›; 拷贝 ‹*film*›; (photocopy) 复印 ‹*document*›; **duplicating machine** 复印机 2 (repeat) 重复 ‹*action, feat*›; **to ~ the record** 平记录
B /'dju:plɪkət, Amer 'du:plə-/ *n* 1 (copy of document) 副本; (photocopy) 复印件; **in ~** 一式两份 2 (spare) 备用件
C /'dju:plɪkət, Amer 'du:plə-/ *adj* 复制的; **a ~ document** 文件的副本

duplication /ˌdju:plɪ'keɪʃn, Amer ˌdu:plə-/ *n* [u] 1 (copying) 复制; (photocopying) 复印 2 (repeating) 重复

duplicator /'dju:plɪkeɪtə(r), Amer 'du:plə-/ *n* 复印机

duplicitous /dju:'plɪsətəs, Amer du:-/ *adj* 骗人的

duplicity /dju:'plɪsəti, Amer du:-/ *n* [u] 1 (character trait) 表里不一 2 (deception) 欺骗

durability /ˌdjʊərə'bɪləti, Amer ˌdʊərə-/ *n* [u] 1 (of material, product) 耐用 2 (of relationship, peace) 持久

durable /'djʊərəbl, Amer 'dʊərə-/
A *adj* 1 耐用的 ‹*product, metal*›; **trousers made of ~ material** 耐穿的料子做成的裤子 2 持久的 ‹*relationship, peace*›
B **durables** *npl* 耐用品

duration /djʊ'reɪʃn, Amer dʊ-/ *n* [u] 持续时间; **a peace of long ~** 长久的和平; **for the ~ of the meeting** 在整个会议期间

duress /djʊ'res, Amer dʊ-/ *n* [u] 1 (gen) 强迫 2 Jur 胁迫; **under ~** 在胁迫之下; **I only agreed under ~** 我被迫无奈同意了

Durex® /'djʊəreks, Amer 'dʊə-/ *n* 杜蕾丝避孕套

Durham /'dʌrəm/ *pr n* 达勒姆; **(County) ~** 达勒姆郡

during /'djʊərɪŋ, Amer 'dʊə-/ *prep* 1 (throughout) 在…期间; **~ this time** 在此期间; **~ the course of sth.** 在某段时间里; **~ her lifetime** 她一生中 2 (within) 在…期间的某个时刻; **he was robbed ~ the journey** 他在旅行途中遭到抢劫

dusk /dʌsk/ *n* [u] 1 (twilight) 黄昏; **at ~** 在黄昏时分; **~ falls** 黄昏到来 2 liter (semi-darkness) 昏暗; **in the ~** 在昏暗中

dusky /'dʌski/ *adj* 1 (darkish) 黝黑的 ‹*skin, complexion*› 2 dated (with dark skin) 皮肤黝黑的 ‹*girl, woman*› 3 (of a darkish colour) 暗淡的 ‹*colour, blonde*›

dust /dʌst/
A *n* 1 (grime) 灰尘; **to gather ~** 积灰; fig 被忽视; **that idea has been gathering ~ since it was put forward** 那个计划从提出至今一直搁在一边; **to raise ~** 扬起灰尘 2 (earth, soil) 尘土; **a cloud of ~** 一片尘雾; **to raise a lot of ~** 扬起大片尘土; fig 引起骚乱; **to allow the ~ to settle** 让尘埃落下; fig 让事情平息; **to throw ~ in sb.'s eyes** fig 蒙蔽某人 3 (fine powder) 粉尘; **coal ~** 煤粉尘
B *vt* 1 (wipe dust from) 擦去…的灰尘 ‹*furniture, surface*› 2 (clean) 打扫 ‹*room, house*›; **to be (all) done and ~ed** colloq (completely finished) 完全结束; (completely ready) 准备就绪 3 (coat lightly) **to ~ sth. with sth.** 往…上撒某物 ‹*pastry*›; 往…上擦某物 ‹*face*›; **to ~ the cake with sugar** 把糖撒在蛋糕上 4 **to ~ sth. on to/over sth.** 把…撒在某物上 ‹*sugar*›; 把…擦在某物上 ‹*powder, make-up*›

Phrasal verbs
- **dust down** *vt* [**~ sth. down, ~ down sth.**] 擦去…的灰尘
- **dust off** *vt* [**~ sth. off, ~ off sth.**] 1 (brush off) 把…掸掉 ‹*dirt, crumbs*› 2 (remove dust from) 擦去…的灰尘 ‹*furniture, surfaces*›
- **dust out** *vt* [**~ sth. out, ~ out sth.**] 清扫…内部

dust: ~ bag *n* 集尘袋; **~ bath** *n* 沙浴

dustbin /'dʌstbɪn/ *n* Brit 垃圾箱; **~ man** 垃圾工

dustbin: ~ lid *n* 垃圾箱盖; **~ liner** *n* 垃圾袋

dust: ~ bowl *n* 干旱尘暴区; **~ cap** *n* 防尘盖; **~cart** *n* Brit 垃圾车; **~ cloth** *n* esp Amer 抹布; **~ cloud** *n* 尘雾; **~ cover** *n* 1 (on book) 护封; 2 (on furniture) 防尘罩; **~ devil** *n* 沙尘卷

duster /'dʌstə(r)/ *n* 1 Brit (cloth) 抹布 2 (for blackboard) 黑板擦

dustheap /'dʌsthi:p/ *n* lit, fig 垃圾堆; **to be thrown on the ~** 被彻底遗忘

dusting /'dʌstɪŋ/ *n* [u] 1 (cleaning) 擦灰; **to do the ~** 除尘 2 (powdery layer) 一薄层 3 Culin (of sugar, chocolate) 撒粉

dust: ~ jacket *n* 护封; **~man** /-mən/ ▸ **p. 409** *n* Brit 垃圾工; **~ mite** *n* 尘螨; **~pan** *n* 畚箕; **~proof** *adj* 防尘的; **~ sheet** *n* 防尘罩; **~ storm** *n* 沙尘暴; **~-up** *n* colloq 1 (quarrel) 争吵; **to have a ~-up (with sb.)** （与某人）争吵; 2 (fight) 打架; **to have a ~-up (with sb.)** （与某人）打架

dusty /'dʌsti/ *adj* 1 (covered with dust) 灰尘覆盖的; **the room was very ~** 房间里积了很多灰 2 (gritty, sandy) 满是尘土的 ‹*track, road*› 3 (full of dust) 尘土飞扬的 ‹*journey*› 4 Brit colloq (curt, abrupt) 生硬的 ‹*answer*› 5 (dull, muted) 灰暗的 ‹*colour*›

Dutch /dʌtʃ/ ▸ **p. 503, p. 426**
A *adj* (of the Netherlands) 荷兰的; (of the people) 荷兰人的; (of the language) 荷兰语的
B *n* 1 [u] + *v sing* (language) 荷兰语 2 **to go ~** 各付各的账
C *npl* **the ~** (people) 荷兰人

Dutch: ~ auction *n* 荷兰式拍卖 [逐渐降价直至有人购买为止]; **~ barn** *n* [无墙的] 干草棚; **~ cap** *n* 子宫帽; **~ courage** *n* [u] 酒后之勇; **I need (some) ~ courage** 我需要喝点酒壮壮胆; **~ elm disease** *n* [u] 荷兰榆树病; **~man** /-mən/ *n* 荷兰人; **~ oven** *n* 荷兰炖锅; **~woman** *n* 荷兰女人

dutiable /'dju:tɪəbl, Amer 'du:-/ *adj* 应征税的 ‹*goods*›

dutiful /'dju:tɪfl, Amer 'du:-/ *adj* 1 (obedient) 尽职的 ‹*husband, employee*›; 贤惠的 ‹*wife*›; 孝顺的 ‹*child*› 2 (conscientious) 出于责任感的 ‹*behaviour*›; **to be ~ of sb. to do sth.** 某人做某事很勤勉尽职

dutifully /ˈdju:tɪfəli, Amer ˈdu:-/ *adv* 1 (obediently) 恭顺地 ‹*behave, respond*› 2 (conscientiously) 尽职地 ‹*work, labour*›

duty /ˈdju:ti, Amer ˈdu:-/
A *n* (*pl* **duties**) 1 [u and c] (obligation) 责任; (task) 职责; **one's ~ to sb.** 对某人的责任; **to have a ~ to sb./to do sth.** 对某人有责任/有义务做某事; **to do one's ~ (by sb.)** (对某人)尽责任; **moral/legal/civic ~** 道德/法律/公民责任; **out of a sense of ~** 出于责任感; **to make it one's ~ to do sth.** 把做某事当作己任; **~ calls** 公务在身; **to be killed in the line/course of ~** 因公殉职; **she often gets up very early, but it's all in the line of ~** 她往往起床很早,但这都是工作需要; **to take up/neglect one's duties** 开始履行职责/玩忽职守 2 [u] (work) 值班; **the ~ doctor** 值班医生; **to be on/off (day/night) ~** 上/下(白/夜)班; **to go/come on/off ~** 上班/下班; **to report for ~** 上班签到; **to do ~ for sth.** 充当某物 3 [u and c] Tax 税; **customs/import duties** 关税/进口税; **to impose a ~ on sth.** 对某物征税; **to pay ~ on sth.** 为某物纳税; **to exempt sth. from ~** 对某物免税
B *modif* (done as duty) 礼节性的 ‹*visit*›

duty: ~-bound *adj* 责无旁贷的; **~ chemist** *n* [在非营业时间开门的] 尽责药房

duty-free
A *adj* 免关税的 ‹*goods*›
B *adv* 免关税地
C *n* [u] 免税货物

duty-free: ~ allowance *n* 免税定额; **~ shop** *n* 免税商店; **~ shopping** *n* [u] 免税购物

duty: ~ officer *n* 值勤官; **~-paid** *adj* 完税的; **~ roster, ~ rota** *ns* 值勤人员表; **~ solicitor** *n* Brit [提供免费服务的] 责任律师

duvet /ˈdu:veɪ/ *n* Brit 羽绒被

duvet cover *n* Brit 羽绒被套

DVD *abbr* = **Digital Versatile Disc** 数字影碟; **~ drive** 数字唯读光盘驱动器;

DVD: ~ audio *n* [u] DVD 音频格式; **~ burner** *abbr* = **~ writer**; **~ player** *n* DVD 播放器; **~ recorder** *n* DVD 刻录机; **~-ROM** *n* DVD 只读存储器; **~ video** *n* [u] DVD 视频格式; **~ writer** *n* DVD 刻录机

DVLA *abbr* Brit = **Driver and Vehicle Licensing Agency** 车牌发放局

DVT *abbr* = **deep-vein thrombosis**

dwarf /dwɔ:f/
A *n* (*pl* **~s** *or* **dwarves**) 1 (small person) 侏儒 2 Bot 矮生植物 3 Mythol 丑矮人
B *adj* 矮小的; **a ~ conifer** 矮针叶树
C *vt* 1 (make appear small) 使显得矮小; **the houses were ~ed by the tower block nearby** 这些房屋在旁边高楼大厦的映衬下显得很矮小 2 (overshadow) 使相形见绌; **this feat ~s all earlier achievements** 这个业绩盖过了以前所有的成就

dwarfish /ˈdwɔ:fɪʃ/ *adj* 矮小的

dwarves /dwɔ:vz/ *pl* ▸**dwarf A**

dweeb /dwi:b/ *n* esp Amer pej [不合群的] 书呆子

dwell /dwel/ *vi* (*pt, pp* **dwelt** *or* **~ed**) 1 formal or liter (live) 居住; **to ~ in ...** 居住在… 2 fig (lie, be found) 存在

Phrasal verb
• **dwell on, dwell upon** *vt* [**~ on sth.**] 1 (think about) 老是想着 2 (discuss at length) 详述 3 (look at) «*eyes, attention*» 停留在…身上

dweller /ˈdwelə(r)/ *n* 居住者; **cave ~** 穴居者; **city ~** 城市居民

dwelling /ˈdwelɪŋ/ *n* formal 住处

dwelling house *n* formal 住宅

dwelt /dwelt/ *pt, pp* ▸**dwell**

dwindle /ˈdwɪndl/ *vi* (in size) 逐渐变小; (in amount) 逐渐减少; (in strength) 逐渐减弱; **her voice ~d to silence** 她的声音越来越小,最后便听不见了

Phrasal verb
• **dwindle away** *vi* 逐渐消失; **our resources ~d away** 我们的资源渐渐耗尽了

dwindling /ˈdwɪndlɪŋ/
A *n* [u] (of amount) 逐渐减少; (of size) 逐渐缩小; (of enthusiasm, interest, strength) 逐渐减弱
B *adj* (growing smaller) 越来越少的; (becoming weaker) 越来越弱的

DWP *abbr* Brit = **Department for Work and Pensions**

dye /daɪ/
A *n* (substance) 染料; (synthetic colourant) 染液; **hair ~** 染发剂
B *vt* 给…染色; **to ~ one's hair** 染发; **to ~ sth. red** 把某物染成红色
C *vi* 被染色; **silk ~s well** 丝绸极易染色

dyed-in-the-wool *adj* (inveterate) 彻头彻尾的 ‹*conservative, traditionalist*›; (inflexible) 根深蒂固的 ‹*attitudes, beliefs*›

dyer /ˈdaɪə(r)/ *n* (person) 染色工; (company) 染印厂

dye: ~stuff *n* 染料; **~works** *npl + v sing* 染料厂

dying /ˈdaɪɪŋ/
A *adj* 1 (about to die) 将死的 ‹*person, animal*›; 即将枯萎的 ‹*plant*› 2 (terminally ill) 病入膏肓的; **to look like a ~ duck** colloq 看上去蔫头耷脑 3 (final) 临终的; **~ words** 临终遗言; **I will remember it till my ~ day** 我至死都不会忘记此事 4 (declining) 即将消亡的 ‹*industry, tradition*›
B *npl* **the ~** 临终者

dyke /daɪk/ *n* 1 (embankment) 堤 2 Brit (ditch) 沟 3 (bank of earth along a ditch) 土堤 4 sl offensive (lesbian) 女同性恋

dynamic /daɪˈnæmɪk/
A *adj* 1 (energetic, positive) 充满活力的 2 (characterized by change) 动态的 3 Tech, Phys 动力的
B *n* 动力
C **dynamics** *npl* 1 Phys 力学 2 (forces) 动态; **population ~s** 人口动态

dynamically /daɪˈnæmɪkli/ *adv* 1 (vigorously, energetically) 充满活力地 2 Tech 在动力上; **a ~ tested car** 经过动力测试的汽车

dynamic content *n* [u] 动态内容

dynamism /ˈdaɪnəmɪzəm/ *n* [u] 活力

dynamite /ˈdaɪnəmaɪt/
A *n* [u] 1 lit 黄色炸药 2 fig (cause of shock, excitement) 引起轰动的事物; **this issue is political ~** 这是个具有爆炸性的政治问题 3 (exciting person) 令人兴奋的人; **he's ~** (sexy) 他魅力十足; (dynamic) 他活力四射
B *vt* 用炸药炸开

dynamo /ˈdaɪnəməʊ/ *n* 1 Elec 发电机 2 fig colloq (person) 精力充沛的人

dynastic /dɪˈnæstɪk, Amer daɪ-/ *adj attrib* 王朝的; **~ succession** 朝代更迭

dynasty /ˈdɪnəsti, Amer ˈdaɪ-/ *n* 1 (line of rulers) 王朝; (period) 朝代; **to establish** *or* **found a ~** 建立一个王朝; **to overthrow a ~** 推翻一个王朝; **during the Tudor ~** 在都铎王朝时代 2 fig (family organization) 王朝; **oil ~** 石油王朝

dyne /daɪn/ *n* 达因 [力的单位]

dysentery /ˈdɪsəntri, Amer -teri/ ▸**p. 377** *n* [u] 痢疾

dysfunction /dɪsˈfʌŋkʃn/ *n* [c and u] 1 (maladjustment) 失衡; **family ~** 家庭关系失衡 2 Med 机能障碍

dysfunctional /dɪsˈfʌŋkʃənl/ *adj* 1 (maladjusted) 失衡的; **a ~ family** 不健全家庭 2 Med 机能障碍的

dyslexia /dɪsˈleksɪə, Amer -ˈlekʃə/ *n* [u] 诵读困难

dyslexic /dɪsˈleksɪk/
A *adj* 诵读困难的
B *n* 诵读困难患者

dyspepsia /dɪsˈpepsɪə/ ▸**p. 377** *n* [u] 消化不良

dyspeptic /dɪsˈpeptɪk/ *adj* 1 Med (suffering from dyspepsia) 患消化不良的; (related to dyspepsia) 消化不良的 ‹*symptoms*› 2 dated (irritable) 乖戾的

dysprosium /dɪsˈprəʊzɪəm/ *n* [u] 镝

dystopia /dɪsˈtəʊpɪə/ *n* 反面乌托邦

dystrophy /ˈdɪstrəfi/ ▸**p. 377** *n* [u] 营养障碍

Ee

e

E, e /iː/

A *n* (*pl* **Es** *or* **E's**) **1** (letter) [英语字母表的第5个字母] **2** Mus E 音, E 调 **3** Sch, Univ (grade) [学业成绩] 第五等

B *abbr* **1** **E** Geog = **east, eastern** **2** **E** colloq (drug) = **Ecstasy**

each /iːtʃ/

A *adj attrib* 每个的; **~ morning** 每天早晨; **~ and every day** 天天; **he lifted ~ box in turn** 他挨个提起箱子; **~ one was heavier than the last** 一个比一个重

B *pron* 每个; **~ despises the other** 互相谁都瞧不起谁; **~ is equally desirable** (of two) 两个都同样可取; (of several) 全都同样可取

C *adv* 各个; **I gave them a book ~** 我给了他们每人一本书; **two teams of ten players ~** 各有 10 名队员的两支运动队; **we ~ want something different** 我们各要不同的东西

each other *pron* 互相; **they know ~** 他们彼此认识

each way Brit

A *adv* 一注三赢地

B **each-way** *adj* 一注三赢的 ‹*bet*›

eager /ˈiːɡə(r)/ *adj* **1** (keen) 热切的; **to be ~ for sth.** 热切期待某事 **2** (filled with longing) 渴望的; **to be ~ to do sth.** 渴望做某事; **to be ~ for praise** 渴望得到赞许 **3** (impatient) 急切的; **they're ~ to leave** 他们急不可耐地想要离开 **4** (excited) 兴奋的 ‹*face, crowd*›; 高昂的 ‹*enthusiasm*›

eagerly /ˈiːɡəli/ *adv* **1** (keenly) 热切地; (with longing) 渴望地 **2** (impatiently) 急切地 **3** (excitedly) 兴奋地

eagerness /ˈiːɡənɪs/ *n* [u] **1** (keenness) 热切 **2** (longing) 渴望; **his ~ for affection was obvious** 很明显他想望关爱 **3** (impatience) 急切; **in my ~ to leave I forgot my coat** 我急着离开, 竟忘了外衣

eagle /ˈiːɡl/ *n* **1** Zool 鹰 **2** (in golf) 老鹰 [比标准杆少两杆]

eagle: ~ eye *n* (sharp) 锐利的目光; (watchful) 密切的注意; **~-eyed** *adj* 目光锐利的; **~ owl** *n* 雕鸮

eaglet /ˈiːɡlɪt/ *n* 小鹰

ear /ɪə(r)/ *n* **1** ▸**p. 71** [c] Anat, Zool 耳朵; **inner/middle/outer ~** 内耳/中耳/外耳; **an ~ infection** 耳部感染; **wet behind the ~s** fig colloq pej 乳臭未干的; **my ~s are burning** fig 有人在议论我呢; **to be all ~s** colloq 专心倾听; **to bend sb.'s ~ (about sth.)** colloq 向某人反复说 (某事); **to be out on one's ~** colloq (from job) 被迫离开工作岗位; (from home) 被赶出家门; **to be up to one's ~s in debt/work** colloq 负债累累/埋头工作; **to have a word in sb.'s ~** 和某人私下谈; **to go in one ~ and out the other** 左耳进, 右耳出; **to have** *or* **keep one's ~ to the ground** 关注动向; **to keep one's ~s open (for sth.)** (be quick to hear) 留意倾听 (某事); (find out about) 关注 (某事); **to lend** *or* **give a sympathetic ~** 同情地倾听; **to listen with half an ~** 心不在焉地听; ▸**deaf A2** **2** [u] (hearing, perception) 听觉; **pleasant to the ~** 悦耳的; **to the trained/untrained ~** 对于训练有素/缺乏训练的耳朵; **to play music by ~** 不看乐谱演奏乐曲; **to play it by ~** fig colloq 随机应变; **to have an ~ for music** 有音乐鉴赏力; **to have a good ~ for accents** 善于辨别口音 **3** [c] (of grain) 穗

ear: ~ache *n* [u] 耳痛; **~bashing** *n* colloq 喋喋不休的斥责; **to get an ~bashing** 被数落一通; **~drops** *npl* 耳药水; **~drum** *n* 鼓膜

earful /ˈɪəfʊl/ *n* colloq 长时间的训斥; **to give sb. an ~** 没完没了地责怪某人

earhole /ˈɪəhəʊl/ *n* 耳孔

earl /ɜːl/ *n* 伯爵; **the E~ of X** 某伯爵

earldom /ˈɜːldəm/ *n* 伯爵爵位; **to inherit an ~** 继承伯爵头衔

earlobe /ˈɪələʊb/ *n* 耳垂

early /ˈɜːli/

A *adj* **1** (before usual time) 提早的 ‹*arrival, retirement, holiday*›; **the ~ death of his mother** 他母亲的早逝; **daffodils are ~ this year** 今年黄水仙开得早 **2** (in period of time) 早的; **in the ~ hours (of the morning)** 在清晨; **the ~ bus** 早班公交车; **in the ~ morning/evening/spring/summer** *etc.* 在清晨/傍晚/早春/初夏等 **3** (near beginning) 初期的; **(in) ~ January/the ~ thirties** (在) 1 月/30 年代初; **in ~ pregnancy** 在妊娠早期; **it's ~ days (yet)** Brit 为时尚早 **4** *attrib* (in life) 早期的; **in ~ childhood** 在幼年; **at an ~ age** 在早年; **in one's ~ twenties** 在 20 岁出头; **the author's ~ novels** 该作家的早期小说 **5** *attrib* (happening soon) 不久的; **at an ~ date** 早日; **at the earliest** 最早; **at the earliest possible opportunity** 一有机会 **6** *attrib* Agric, Hort 早熟的 ‹*crop, vegetable, variety*›

B *adv* **1** (before expected time) 提早; **the strawberries ripened ~ this year** 草莓今年成熟得早; **to do sth. three weeks ~** 提前 3 个星期做某事 **2** (in period of time) 早地; **as ~ as possible** 尽早; **~ next year** 下一年年初; **~ on** 早先; **five minutes/three years earlier** 5 分钟/3 年以前; **as I said earlier, ...** 正如我先前所讲的, …; **as ~ as 1736** 早在 1736 年 **3** (near beginning of event, process) 初期; **~ in the war/match** 在战争/比赛初期; **~ in the book/meeting** 在书/会议的开头 **4** (in life) 早期; **~ (on) in life** 在早年; **~ (on) in one's career** 在职业生涯之初 **5** (referring to future) 早于; **not earlier than 10 o'clock/Monday/next week** 不早于 10 点钟/星期一/下周; **I can't get there earlier than five** 我 5 点钟以前赶不到那里

early: ~ bird *n* hum (person who gets up early) 早起的人; (person arriving early) 早到的人; **the ~ bird catches the worm** Prov 捷足者先登; **~ closing (day)** *n* Brit 提早打烊日; **~ days** *npl* Brit colloq 初期; **the ~ days of space exploration** 太空探索初期; **it's ~ days (yet)** 为时尚早; **~ night** *n* 很早的就寝; **to have an ~ night** 早早上床; **~ riser** *n* 惯于早起的人; **~ warning** *n* 预先警报; **~ warning system** *n* 预警系统; **pain is part of the body's ~ warning system** 疼痛是身体疾病的早期症状

ear: ~mark *vt* 指定…的用途; **to ~mark a sum of money for research** 拨出一笔款项作研究经费; **~muffs** *npl* 耳套

earn /ɜːn/ *vt* **1** lit 挣得; **to ~ sth. by doing sth.** 通过做某事挣得某物; **to ~ a** *or* **one's living** 谋生; **to ~ a living by writing** 靠写作谋生 **2** Fin ‹*stocks*› 生 ‹*interest*›; 获 ‹*profit*›; **those shares won't ~ you much** 那些股票获利不会很多 **3** fig (acquire) 获得; (deserve) 应得; **to ~ sb.'s respect** 赢得某人的尊敬; **he has ~ed respect/praise by his efforts** 他通过努力赢得了尊敬/称赞; **he's ~ed it!** 他当之无愧!

earned income *n* 劳动收入

earner /ˈɜːnə(r)/ *n* **1** (person) 挣钱者; **a high ~** 高收入的人 **2** colloq (source of money) 收入来源; **those shares aren't much of an ~** 那些股票不怎么赚钱; **a nice little ~** 摇钱树

earnest /ˈɜːnɪst/

A *adj* **1** (serious) 认真的 ‹*student*› **2** (sincere) 诚挚的 ‹*pledge, intention, desire*› **3** (fervent) 热切的 ‹*prayer, devotion*›; 热情的 ‹*invitation*› **4** (conscientious) 勤恳的 ‹*efforts, toil*›

B *n* **1** [u] (seriousness) 认真; **in ~** 认真地; **to begin** *or* **start in ~** 真正开始; **it was now snowing in ~** 雪真的下起来了; **to be in ~** 郑重其事; **this time I'm in ~** 这次我可是认真的 **2** [c] liter (guarantee) 保证; **he did it as an ~ of his sincerity** 他这样做以示诚意

earnestly /ˈɜːnɪstli/ *adv* **1** (seriously) 认真地 ‹*speak, promise*› **2** (sincerely) 诚挚地 ‹*hope, wish*› **3** (fervently) 热切地 ‹*pray, plead*› **4** (conscientiously) 勤恳地

earnestness /ˈɜːnɪstnɪs/ *n* [u] **1** (seriousness) 认真 **2** (sincerity) 诚挚 **3** (fervour) 热切 **4** (conscientiousness) 勤恳

earning power *n* [u] (of a person) 赚钱能力; (of a business) 赢利能力

earnings /ˈɜːnɪŋz/ *npl* **1** (income) 收入 **2** Fin (from shares) 收益

earnings: ~ growth *n* [u] 年均收益增长率; **~ related** *adj* 与收入挂钩的 ‹*pension, benefit, scheme*›

ear: ~, nose, and throat *n* **~, nose and throat (department)** 耳鼻喉科; **~phones** *npl* 耳机; **~piece** *n* (of telephone) 听筒; (of radio receiver etc.) 耳机

ear-piercing

A *n* 打耳洞

B *adj* 刺耳的

ear: ~plug *n* 耳塞; **~ring** *n* 耳环; **~shot** *n* [u] 听力所及范围; **to be out of/within ~shot** 在听力范围之外/之内; **she waited until he was out of ~shot before continuing** 她一直等到他听不见时才继续说; **~-splitting** *adj* 震耳欲聋的

earth /ɜːθ/

A *n* **1** [u and c] esp Astron (*also* **Earth**) (planet) 地球; **the ~'s crust/surface/core** 地壳/地表/地核; **to the ends of the ~** 到天涯海角; **how/what/why on ~ ...?** colloq 究竟如何/是什么/为什么…? ; **to cost the ~** Brit colloq 极其昂贵; ▸**face A7** **2** [u] (human world) 人世;

heaven/hell **on** ～ 人间天堂/地狱; **to feel/taste** *etc.* **like nothing on** ～ colloq 感觉/吃起来等糟透了 [3] [u] (ground) 陆地; **to come back** *or* **down to** ～ colloq 回到现实 [4] [u] (soil) 泥土 [5] [c and u] (lair, esp of fox) 兽穴; **to go to** ～ fig 躲藏起来; **to run sb./sth. to** ～ fig 终于追寻到某人/某物 [6] [c] Brit Elec 地线; ～ **wire** 地线

B vt Brit 使…接地 ‹*appliance, plug*›

Phrasal verb

- **earth up** vt [～ **up sth.**, ～ **sth. up**] 用土掩盖; **to** ～ **up the roots** 给根部壅土

earth: ～**bound** *adj* [1] (fixed on earth) 陆地上的; **a flightless,** ～**bound bird** 不会飞的地禽; [2] (approaching earth) 向地球移动的; **an** ～**bound meteor** 飞向地球的流星; **an** ～**bound astronaut** 返回地球途中的宇航员; ～ **closet** *n* Brit [用干土覆盖粪便的] 茅坑

earthen /'ɜ:θn/ *adj attrib* [1] (made of clay) 陶制的; **an** ～ **pot/dish** 陶罐/陶盘 [2] (made of earth) 泥土做的; **an** ～ **floor/wall** 泥地面/土墙

earthenware /'ɜ:θnweə(r)/ *n* [u] 陶器; **an** ～ **pot/dish** 陶罐/陶盘

earthly /'ɜ:θli/ *adj* [1] (worldly) 尘世的 ‹*life, existence, possessions, desire*› [2] colloq (conceivable) 可能的; **it's no** ～ **use** 这毫无用处; **there's no** ～ **reason why you should pay** 你根本不必付钱; **not have** *or* **stand an** ～ Brit colloq (chance) 毫无机会; (hope) 毫无希望; **not have an** ～ (clue) 毫无线索; (idea) 丝毫不知道

earth: ～**man** /-mæn/ *n* 地球人; ～ **mother** *n* [1] Mythol (goddess of fertility) 生育女神; (personification of the earth) 大地母亲; [2] fig (maternal woman) 母性十足的女人; ～**mover** *n* 推土机; ～**-moving equipment** *n* [u] 掘土机械

earthquake *n* 地震

earthquake-resistant *adj* 抗震的

earth: ～ **science** *n* [u] 地球科学; ～**shattering,** ～**shaking** *adjs* colloq 惊天动地的 ‹*news, discovery, experience*›; ～ **sign** *n* 土相星座; ～ **tremor** *n* 地颤动

earthward /'ɜ:θwəd/

A *adj* 向地球的 ‹*journey, flight, glance*›

B *adv* (*also* **earthwards**) 向地球 ‹*move, fly, look*›

earth: ～**work** *n* (*usu* ～**works**) 土垒; ～**worm** *n* 蚯蚓

earthy /'ɜ:θi/ *adj* [1] (of the soil) 泥土的; **the** ～ **smell of vegetables** 蔬菜的泥腥味儿; **these potatoes taste** ～ 这些马铃薯吃起来有泥腥味 [2] (unrefined) 粗俗的 ‹*person, joke, remark, sense of humour*›; (unspoilt) 朴实的 ‹*character*›; (down-to-earth) 脚踏实地的 ‹*person*›

ear: ～**wax** *n* 耳屎; ～**wig** *n* 蠼螋

ease /i:z/

A *n* [u] [1] (lack of difficulty) 容易; **with** ～ 轻易地; **for** ～ **of use** 为便于使用 [2] (feeling of relaxation and confidence) 轻松自在; **at** ～ **with sb./sth.** 与某人交往感到自在/处理某事得心应手; **my mind was at** ～ 我心情平静; **to put sb.'s mind at** ～ **(about sth.)** 使某人（对某事）稍安毋躁; **(stand) at** ～**!** Mil 稍息! [3] (confidence of manner) 自如 [4] (affluence) 安逸; **a life of** ～ 安逸的生活

B *vt* [1] (lessen) 减轻 ‹*pain, worry*› [2] (make easier) 使…更方便 ‹*communication, transition*› [3] (relieve anxiety) 使安心; **to** ～ **sb.'s mind** 使某人放心 [4] (move carefully) 小心地移动; **she** ～**d the car into the car park** 她把车慢慢开进停车场 [5] (slow) 慢慢减少 ‹*speed*› [6] (relax) 将…放松 ‹*grip*›

C *vi* [1] (lessen) «*tension*» 缓和; «*pain, congestion*» 减轻; «*rain*» 变小 [2] (become less difficult) «*situation*» 好转 [3] Fin «*share prices*» 下跌; «*interest rates*» 下降

D *v refl* **to** ～ **oneself into/out of sth.** 小心地进入/移出 ‹*bed, chair*›; 慢慢穿上/脱下 ‹*clothes*›; **to** ～ **oneself through** 慢慢通过 ‹*gap*›

Phrasal verbs

- **ease back** *vt* [～ **sth. back,** ～ **back sth.**]
  [1] (pull backwards) 轻轻往后拉 ‹*lever*›
  [2] (remove by pulling) 轻轻揭开 ‹*cover, bandage*›
- **ease off**

A *vi* [1] (lessen) «*situation, tension*» 缓和; «*pressure, pain*» 减轻; «*speed, pace*» 放慢 [2] (work less hard) 放松

B *vt* [～ **sth. off,** ～ **off sth.**] (remove gently) 轻轻揭开 ‹*bandage, lid*›; 轻轻脱下 ‹*boot*›

- **ease up** *vi* [1] (work less hard) 放松 [2] (lessen) «*situation, tension*» 缓和; «*pressure*» 减轻 [3] (be more moderate with) **to** ～ **up on sb./sth.** 对某人变宽容/使某事变宽松

easel /'i:zl/ *n* 画架

easily /'i:zɪli/ *adv* [1] (with no difficulty, readily) 容易地; **to get bored** ～ 易生厌倦 [2] (comfortably) 舒适地 ‹*sleep*›; 轻松地 ‹*talk*›; **to breathe more** ～ 更顺畅地呼吸 [3] (unquestionably) 肯定地; **she is** ～ **the tallest girl here** 她无疑是这里最高的女孩 [4] (probably) 很可能地; **it could** ～ **rain** 多半会下雨

easiness /'i:zmɪs/ *n* [u] [1] (lack of difficulty) 容易 [2] (comfort) 舒适 [3] (of attitude, manner) 从容

east /i:st/ ▸**p. 142**

A *n* [u] [1] (direction) 东; (position or location) 东方; (eastern part) 东部 [2] Pol, Geog **the E**～ 东方诸国; **out E**～ 在遥远的东方 [3] Hist (eastern Europe) **the E**～ 东欧 [4] Geog (eastern USA) **the E**～ 美国东部地区 [5] Geog (eastern Britain) **the E**～ 英国东部地区 [6] Hist **the E**～ (East Berlin) 东柏林; (East Germany) 东德 [7] Games 处在东首位置的一方玩家

B *adj* [1] (eastern) 东边的; **on the** ～ **side of the island** 在岛屿的东侧 [2] *attrib* (from the east) 来自东边的; **an** ～ **wind** 东风

C *adv* [1] (to the east, on the eastern side) 在东边; ～ **of sth.** 在某物的东边 [2] (towards the east) 向东; **due** ～ 向正东

East Africa *pr n* 东非

East African

A *adj* (of East Africa) 东非的; (of the people) 东非人的; (of language(s)) 东非语言的

B *n* 东非人

the East Coast

东海岸。指美国东海岸（the East Coast of the United States），亦作 Eastern Seaboard 或 Atlantic Seaboard。字面意思指美国东部大西洋沿岸各州，从南部的佛罗里达州（Florida）一直到北部的缅因州（Maine）。实际使用时常指这一区域的北段，即美国东北地区（Northeastern US），尤指从波士顿（Boston）、马萨诸塞（Massachusettes）到华盛顿特区之间人口稠密、城市高度发达的东北走廊（Northeast Corridor）地区。

east: **E**～ **Anglia** /ˌi:st 'æŋglɪə/ *pr n* 东英吉利; ～**bound** *adj* [1] 东行的 ‹*traffic, train, passenger*›; [2] 向东的 ‹*road, line, platform*›; **E**～ **End** *pr n* **the E**～ **End** 伦敦东区; **E**～ **Ender** *n* 伦敦东区人

the East End

伦敦东区。位于伦敦金融城（City of London）以东、泰晤士河北岸。伦敦的老码头多集中于此。20 世纪中期以前，居民大都是伦敦的码头工人。近年来经过重新开发（redevelopment），面貌已经发生彻底改变。码头区（Docklands）内的金丝雀码头大厦（Canary Wharf Tower）高 244 米，是欧洲最高的塔楼之一。东区的居民称 East Ender 或 cockney，以活泼、友善著称。▸**cockney**, ▸**the West End**。

Easter /'i:stə(r)/ *n* 复活节

Easter: ～ **bunny** *n* **the** ～ **bunny** 复活节小兔; ～ **Day** *n* = **Easter Sunday**; ～ **egg** *n* 复活节彩蛋

easterly /'i:stəli/ ▸**p. 142**

A *adj* [1] (in an eastward position) 东方的 ‹*point, area*› [2] (in an eastward direction) 向东的 ‹*aspect, course, journey*› [3] (from an eastward direction) 从东方吹来的; **an** ～ **wind** 东风

B *n* (*pl* **easterlies**) 东风

Easter Monday *n* 复活节星期一 [复活节后的星期一]

eastern /'i:stən/ ▸**p. 142** *adj attrib* [1] (of or in the east) 东方的; ～ **France** 法国东部 [2] (facing east) 向东的; (going towards east) 东行的 [3] (*also* **Eastern**) Pol, Geog (oriental) 东方的

Eastern: ～ **bloc** *n* Hist **the** ～ **bloc** 东欧集团; ～ **bloc country** *n* 东欧集团国家; ～ **Daylight Time** *n* [u] Amer 东部夏令时间

easterner /'i:stənə(r)/ *n* Amer 美国东部人

Eastern: ～ **Europe** *n* 东欧; ～ **European Time** *n* [u] 东欧时间

easternmost /'i:stənməʊst/ *adj* (furthest east) 最东的; (in or on the (most) eastern part) 在最东部的

Eastern Standard Time *n* [u] Amer 东部标准时间

Easter Sunday *n* 复活节

east-facing *adj* 朝东的

East German ▸**p. 503** Hist

A *adj* (of East Germany) 东德的; (of the people) 东德人的

B *n* 东德人

East Germany *pr n* Hist 东德

east-north-east ▸**p. 142**

A *n* 东东北

B *adj* [1] (in direction) 东东北的 ‹*position*› [2] (from direction) 从东东北吹来的 ‹*wind*›

C *adv* (to direction) 向东东北；(in direction) 在东东北

east-south-east ▸**p. 142**

A *n* 东东南

B *adj* [1] (in direction) 东东南的 ‹*position*› [2] (from direction) 从东东南吹来的 ‹*wind*›

C *adv* (to direction) 向东东南；(in direction) 在东东南

East: ～ **Sussex** /ˌi:st 'sʌsɪks/ *pr n* 东萨塞克斯郡; ～ **Timor** /ˌi:st 'ti:mɔ:(r)/ *pr n* 东帝汶

eastward /'i:stwəd/ ▸**p. 142**

A *adj* 向东的

B *adv* (*also* **eastwards**) 向东

east: ～**-west** *adj attrib* 东西向的 ‹*road, course*›; **in an** ～**-west direction** 沿东西方向; **the main** ～**-west rail route** 东西主干铁路线; **E**～**-West relations** *npl* 东西方关系

easy /'i:zi/

A *adj* [1] (not difficult) 容易的 ‹*job*›; 简单的 ‹*problem*›; 轻松的 ‹*journey*›; **an** ～ **climb** 不费力的攀爬; **it's an** ～ **car to drive** 那辆车容易开; **as** ～ **as pie** *or* **ABC** *or* **anything** colloq 极其容易; **to be** ～ **on the eye/ear** colloq 看起来/听上去不费力 [2] (comfortable) 舒适的 ‹*life, atmosphere*›; **to make life** *or* **things** *or* **it too** ～ **for sb.** 让某人过于舒服; **to have an** ～ **ride** colloq 一路顺风; **to live in** ～ **circumstances** 过宽裕的生活 [3] (relaxed) 自在的 ‹*smile*›; **to have an** ～ **manner** 举止洒脱; **to write in a relaxed,** ～ **style** 以平易流畅的风格写作; **to feel** ～ **(in one's mind) about sth.** 对某事物放心 [4] (vulnerable) 易受伤害的 ‹*victim*›; 易受攻击的 ‹*target*›; **he's** ～ **game** *or* **meat** 他容易上当 [5] colloq pej (promiscuous) 水性杨花的; **she's** ～ 她很容易到手 [6] Amer (lenient) 宽容的 ‹*teacher*›; 宽松的 ‹*standard*›; **dad was too** ～ **on him** 爸爸对他太纵容 [7] *pred* colloq (having no preference) 随和的; **shall we go? — I'm** ～ 我们走吗？——随便 [8] **easier** *pred, only in comp* (less intense) 程度

e

轻的; **to make the pain easier** 减轻疼痛; **is the pain any easier?** 疼得轻点了吗?

B *adv* **1** colloq (in relaxed way) 从容地; **to take it** *or* **things ~** 从容不迫; **take it ~!** 别着急! ; **~ come, ~ go** 来得容易去得快 **2** colloq (carefully) 小心地; **~ does it!** 轻点儿! ; **to go ~ on** *or* **with sth.** 轻手轻脚摆弄某物 **3** colloq (leniently) 宽容地; **to go ~ on** *or* **with sb.** 宽容地对待某人 **4** (without difficulty) 容易地; **easier said than done** 说时容易做时难 **5** Mil 放松地; **stand ~!** 稍息!

easy: ~-care *adj* 免熨烫的 ‹*fabric, article*›; **~ chair** *n* 安乐椅; **~-going** *adj* 随和的 ‹*person*›; 轻松自在的 ‹*atmosphere*›; **~ listening** *n* [u] 轻松悦耳的音乐; **~ money** *n* [u] 轻松得来的钱; **~ over** *adj* esp Amer 双面煎的 [指蛋]; **~ payments** *npl* 小额分期付款; **four ~ payments of just $49.99** 每次仅付 49.99 美元的四次分期付款; **~-peasy** /ˌiːziˈpiːzi/ *adj* colloq 十分简单的; **E~ Street** *n* [u] colloq 富裕; **to be on E~ Street** 过富足的日子; **~ terms** *n* **1** (rate of interest) 特惠利率; **to borrow money on ~ terms** 以低息借钱; **2** (relationship) 友好关系; **to be on ~ terms (with sb.)** (与某人) 关系友好

eat /iːt/ (*pt* **ate**, *pp* **eaten**)

A *vt* **1** (consume) 吃; **to be unfit to ~** 不宜食用; **to look good enough to ~** fig 秀色可餐; **to ~ one's words** fig 收回自己的话; **I could ~ a horse** colloq 我饿极了; **to ~ sb./sth. alive** lit 将某人/某物活活吃掉; fig (criticize) 对某人/某事物横加指责; fig (defeat) 彻底击败某人/某事物; **we were eaten alive by insects** fig colloq 虫子差点把我们活活吃了; **to ~ sb. out of house and home** colloq 把某人吃穷; **~ your heart out!** colloq 嫉妒去吧! ; ▸**pie** **2** colloq (use a lot of) «*car, machine*» 大量消耗 ‹*fuel*› **3** colloq (worry) 使烦恼; **what's ~ing you?** 你为何苦恼? ; **something's ~ing her** 她心事重重

B *vi* **1** (take food) 吃东西; **to ~ out of ...** 吃…中的食物 ‹*plate, bowl*›; **to ~ out of sb.'s hand** fig 对某人言听计从; **to ~ like a horse** colloq 食量大如牛 **2** (have meal) 吃饭

Phrasal verbs

- **eat away** *vt* [~ **away sth.**, ~ **sth. away**] **1** (by erosion) 侵蚀 **2** (chemically) 腐蚀 **3** (by nibbling) 蚕食
- **eat away at** *vt* [~ **away at sth.**] **1** (by erosion) 侵蚀 **2** (chemically) 腐蚀 **3** (by nibbling) 蚕食 **4** (use up) 消耗 ‹*savings, profits*› **5** (lessen) «*criticism, failure*» 使…逐渐丧失 ‹*confidence, self-esteem*›
- **eat into** *vt* [~ **into sth.**] **1** (chemically) 腐蚀 **2** (by nibbling) 蚕食 **3** (use up) «*bills, costs*» 消耗 ‹*savings, profits, funds*› **4** (encroach on) 占用 ‹*time, holiday*›
- **eat out** *vi* 下馆子
- **eat up**

A [~ **sth. up**, ~ **up sth.**] *vt* **1** (consume completely) 吃光 ‹*food*› **2** (use a lot of) «*car, heater*» 大量消耗 ‹*fuel*› **3** (use up) «*costs*» 耗尽 ‹*funds, savings*› **4** colloq (cover quickly) 迅速走过; **to ~ up the miles** 飞驰而过大段路程

B [~ **sb. up**, ~ **up sb.**] *vt* «*envy, guilt*» 困扰; **to be eaten up with** *or* **by ...** 因…而焦虑 ‹*envy, desire*›

C *vi* 吃光

eatable /ˈiːtəbl/

A *adj* 可吃的; **our school meals are barely ~** 我们学校的伙食简直难以下咽

B **eatables** *npl* colloq 可吃的东西

eaten /ˈiːtn/ *pp* ▸**eat**

eater /ˈiːtə(r)/ *n* **1** (person) 食者; **he is a big ~** 他食量很大; **a fussy/messy/small ~** 挑食/吃相邋遢/食量小的人 **2** (apple) 可生吃的苹果

eatery /ˈiːtəri/ *n* esp Amer colloq 餐馆

eating /ˈiːtɪŋ/ *n* [u] 吃; **healthy ~ is essential** 健康的饮食至关重要; **these apples make excellent ~** 这些苹果很好吃

eating: ~ apple *n* 可生吃的苹果; **~ disorder** *n* 饮食紊乱症; **~ habits** *npl* 饮食习惯; **~ house** *n* = **~ place**; **~ place** *n* 饮食店

eats /iːts/ *npl* colloq 小吃; **we can buy some ~ on the way** 我们可以在路上买些吃的

e-auction *n* 网上拍卖

eau de cologne /ˌəʊ də kəˈləʊn/ *n* [u] 古龙香水

eaves /iːvz/ *npl* 屋檐

eavesdrop /ˈiːvzdrɒp/ *vi* (*pres p etc.* **-pp-**) 偷听; **to ~ on** 偷听…的谈话 ‹*person*›; 偷听 ‹*conversation*›

eavesdropper /ˈiːvzdrɒpə(r)/ *n* 偷听的人; **he's a habitual ~** 他老爱偷听

eavestrough /ˈiːvztrɒf/ *n* Can 檐槽

e-bank *n* 网上银行

e-banking *n* [u] 网上银行业务

ebb /eb/

A *n* **1** lit (tide) 退潮; **the tide is on the ~** 正在退潮; **the ~ and flow of the tide** 潮水的涨落 **2** fig (decline) 衰退; **to listen to the ~ and flow of conversation** 听着时低时高的谈话声; **to be at a low ~** 处于低潮; **my spirits were at a low ~** 我当时情绪低落

B *vi* «*tide, tidewater*» 退落; **to ~ and flow** 潮涨潮落

Phrasal verb

- **ebb away** *vi* «*strength*» 衰退; «*fortunes*» 减少; **her enthusiasm was ~ing away** 她的热情渐渐消退下来

ebb tide *n* 落潮

e-billing *n* [u] 电子账单业务

EBM *abbr* = **evidence-based medicine**

Ebonics /eˈbɒnɪks/ *npl* + *v sing* 美国黑人英语

ebony /ˈebəni/ *n* [u] **1** (wood) 乌木; **an ~ casket/veneer/table** 乌木匣子/薄片镶饰/桌子 **2** ▸**p. 134** (colour) 乌黑色; **~ skin/hair** 黝黑的皮肤/乌黑的头发

e-book *n* 电子书

EBRD *abbr* = **European Bank for Reconstruction and Development**

ebullience /ɪˈbʌlɪəns, ɪˈbʊ-/ *n* [u] 热情洋溢

ebullient /ɪˈbʌlɪənt, ɪˈbʊ-/ *adj* 热情洋溢的

e-business /ˈiːˌbɪznɪs/ *n* **1** [u] (commerce) 电子商务 **2** [c] (company) 网上公司

EC *abbr* **1** = **European Commission** **2** = **European Community**

e-cash *n* [u] 电子现金

ECB *abbr* = **European Central Bank**

eccentric /ɪkˈsentrɪk/

A *adj* **1** (unconventional) 古怪的 ‹*person, appearance, habit*›; **~ clothes** 奇装异服 **2** Astron 不正圆的 ‹*orbit*›

B *n* **1** (odd person) 怪人 **2** Mech 偏心轮

eccentrically /ɪkˈsentrɪkli/ *adv* 古怪地

eccentricity /ˌeksenˈtrɪsəti/ *n* **1** [u] (of style, clothing, manner, ideas) 古怪 **2** [c] (act, habit) 怪癖

Eccles cake /ˈeklz ˌkeɪk/ *n* Brit 埃克尔斯果干馅饼

ecclesiastic /ɪˌkliːzɪˈæstɪk/ *n* formal [基督教的] 教士

ecclesiastical /ɪˌkliːzɪˈæstɪkl/ *adj* 基督教会的

ECG *abbr* **1** = **electrocardiogram** **2** = **electrocardiograph**

echelon /ˈeʃəlɒn/ *n* **1** (level) 阶层; **the higher** *or* **upper ~s of the business world** 商界高层 **2** Mil 梯队

echinoderm /ɪˈkaɪnədɜːm, ˈekɪn-/ *n* 棘皮动物

echo /ˈekəʊ/

A *n* (*pl* **~es**) **1** [u and c] (of sound, reverberation) 回声; **to cheer to the ~** 大声欢呼 **2** [c] fig (overtone) 暗示; **this book has many ~es of her previous one** 这本书和她的前一本书有多处相似 **3** [c] fig (of idea, opinion etc.) 附和; **his love for her found an ~ in her own feelings** 他对她的爱在她的情感中引起共鸣

B *vt* **1** (reflect) 使回响; **the walls of the cave ~ed their shouts** 他们的喊声在洞壁里回响; **the hills seemed to ~ their joy** 群山似乎也感染了他们的喜悦 **2** fig (repeat) 重复 ‹*words, opinions*›; 附和 ‹*attitudes*› **3** fig (resemble) 与…相似; **his style ~es T.S. Eliot** 他的风格像T. S. 艾略特

C *vi* **1** (reflect back) «*sound*» 回响; **her shouts ~ed through the valley** 她的喊声在山谷中回荡 **2** (resound) «*valley, hall, walls*» 产生回声; **the house ~ed to/with their music** 房子里回荡着他们的音乐 **3** fig (reappear) «*idea, theme*» 被重复

echo chamber *n* 回声室

echolocation /ˌekəʊləʊˈkeɪʃn/ *n* [u] 回声定位

echo sounder *n* 回声测深器

éclair /eɪˈkleə(r), ɪˈkleə(r)/ *n* 奶油泡芙

eclampsia /ɪˈklæmpsɪə/ ▸**p. 377** *n* [u] 子痫 [怀孕引起的高血压和惊厥]

eclectic /ɪˈklektɪk/

A *adj* 兼收并蓄的 ‹*approach, thinker, outlook*›; **universities offering an ~ mix of courses** 开设各种课程的大学

B *n* 兼收并蓄的人

eclecticism /ɪˈklektɪsɪzəm/ *n* [u] 折中主义

eclipse /ɪˈklɪps/

A *n* **1** Astron lit 食; **to be in/go into ~** «*sun*» 日食/进入日食; «*moon*» 月食/进入月食; **a partial/total/solar/lunar ~** 偏食/全食/日食/月食 **2** fig (overshadowing) 黯然失色; **Holland's power was in/went into ~** 荷兰队失势

B *vt* **1** Astron lit «*moon*» 遮住…的光 ‹*sun, planet*› **2** fig (overshadow) 使黯然失色; **she was ~d by an even more successful actress** 她被一位更为成功的女演员超越了

ecliptic /ɪˈklɪptɪk/ *n* 黄道

eco- /ˈiːkəʊ/ *combining form* 生态的

eco-audit *n* 生态审计

eco-aware *adj* 有环保意识的

ecocar /ˈiːkəʊkɑː(r)/ *n* 生态汽车

ecocatastrophe /ˈiːkəʊkəˌtæstrəfi/ *n* 生态灾难

ecocide /ˈiːkəʊsaɪd/ *n* [u] 生态破坏

eco-friendly *adj* 环保的

eco-label *n* 环保标签

eco-labelling *n* [u] 加贴环保标签

ecological /ˌiːkəˈlɒdʒɪkl/ *adj* 生态的 ‹*disaster, catastrophe, balance, damage*›; 生态学的 ‹*report, study*›

ecological footprint *n* 生态足迹 [测定人类对环境影响的指标，指需要多少土地和水来生产所需资源和吸纳废物]

ecologically /ˌiːkəˈlɒdʒɪkli/ *adv* 在生态方面

ecologist /iːˈkɒlədʒɪst/ *n* 生态学家

ecology /iːˈkɒlədʒi/ *n* [u] **1** (relations of organisms) 生态 **2** (study) 生态学

ecology: ~ movement *n* 生态保护运动; **E~ Party** *n* 生态党

e-commerce *n* [u] 电子商务

econometric /ɪˌkɒnəˈmetrɪk/ *adj* 计量经济学的

econometrician /ɪˌkɒnəməˈtrɪʃn/ ▸**p. 409** *n* 计量经济学家

econometrics /ɪˌkɒnəˈmetrɪks/ *npl* + *v sing* 计量经济学

econometrist /ɪˌkɒnəˈmetrɪst/ *n* = **econometrician**

economic /ˌiːkəˈnɒmɪk, ˌek-/ *adj* **1** (relating to economics) 经济学的 **2** (relating to the economy) 经济的; **to impose/lift ~ sanctions** 实行/

解除经济制裁 **3** (profitable) 有利可图的; **to make ～ sense** 有经济收益; **an ～ proposition** 能赚钱的事; **an ～ rent** 经济租金

economic: ～ aid *n* 经济援助; **～ analyst** ▸**p. 409** *n* 经济分析师; **E～ and Monetary Union** *n* 经济货币联盟

economical /ˌiːkəˈnɒmɪkl, ˌek-/ *adj* **1** (efficient) 经济的 ‹*use, system*›; **an ～ car** 节油型汽车; **this machine is very ～ on electricity** 这台机器很省电 **2** (thrifty) 节俭的 ‹*housewife, manager*›; **to be ～ with ...** 在…方面精打细算 **3** fig (sparing) 简洁的; **to be ～ with words** 用词简练; **to be ～ with the truth** euph 没把实话全说出来

economically /ˌiːkəˈnɒmɪkli, ˌek-/ *adv* **1** (efficiently) 经济地; **this machine is very ～ designed** 这台机器设计得很节能 **2** (in a thrifty manner) 节俭地 **3** (sparingly) 简洁地 ‹*constructed, write*› **4** (in an economic sense) 在经济上 ‹*strong, weak, viable*›; **the region is important ～** 这个区的经济地位很重要

economic: ～ forecast *n* 经济预测; **～ cost** *n* = **opportunity cost**; **～ development** *n* 经济发展; **～ geography** *n* [u] 经济地理学; **～ growth** *n* [u] 经济增长; **～ history** *n* [u] **1** (phenomenon) 经济历史; **2** (study) 经济历史学; **～ indicator** *n* 经济指标; **～ management** *n* [u] 经济管理; **～ refugee** *n* 经济难民

economics /ˌiːkəˈnɒmɪks, ˌek-/ *npl* **1** + *v sing* (social science) 经济学 **2** + *v pl* (financial aspects) 经济情况

economic: ～ system *n* 经济制度; **～ theory** *n* 经济理论

economist /ɪˈkɒnəmɪst, ˌek-/ ▸**p. 409** *n* 经济学家

economize /ɪˈkɒnəmaɪz/ *vi* 节约; **to ～ on sth.** 节约用某物

economy /ɪˈkɒnəmi/ *n* **1** [c and u] (saving) (careful management) 节约; **to practise ～** 厉行节约; **to make economies in sth.** 在某方面实行节约; **economies of scale** 规模效应; **it's an ～ to pay for quality, because it lasts** 买优质商品划得来，因为这类商品经久耐用 **2** [c] (financial system or state of a country) 经济; **the state of the ～** 经济状况; **a market/planned ～** 市场/计划经济

economy: ～ class *n* 经济舱; **～-class seat** 经济舱座位; **～-class syndrome** *n* [u] 经济舱综合征; **～ drive** *n* 节约运动; **～ pack** *n* 经济装; **～-size** *adj* 经济包装的; **an ～-size pack/bottle** 大包/经济装瓶; **～ version** *n* 经济型

ecosphere /ˈiːkəʊsfɪə(r)/ *n* 生态圈

ecosystem /ˈiːkəʊsɪstəm/ *n* 生态系统

ecoterrorist /ˈiːkəʊterərɪst/ *n* 生态恐怖主义者; **an ～ group/organization/attack** 生态恐怖团伙/组织/袭击

ecotourism /ˈiːkəʊtʊərɪzəm, -tɔːr-/ *n* [u] 生态旅游

ecotourist /ˈiːkəʊtʊərɪst, -tɔːr-/ *n* 生态旅游者

ecotoxic /ˈiːkəʊtɒksɪk/ *adj* 对环境产生毒害的

ecotype /ˈiːkəʊtaɪp/ *n* 生态型

eco-warrior *n* 生态保护斗士

ecstasy /ˈekstəsi/ *n* **1** [u and c] (overwhelming joy) 狂喜; **to be in ～** or **ecstasies (over sth.)** (对某事物) 欣喜若狂; **to go into ecstasies over sth.** 陶醉于某事物 **2** **Ecstasy** [u] (drug) 摇头丸

ecstatic /ɪkˈstætɪk/ *adj* **1** (joyful) 狂喜的 ‹*crowd, fan*›; **to be ～ about** or **over sth.** 对某事物欣喜若狂 **2** (rapturous) 狂热的 ‹*reception, welcome, cheers*›

ecstatically /ɪkˈstætɪkli/ *adv* 狂喜地; **～ happy** 欣喜若狂的; **the crowd cheered ～** 人群狂热地欢呼

ectomorph /ˈektəʊmɔːf/ *n* 外胚层体型者

ectopic pregnancy /ekˌtɒpɪk ˈpregnənsi/ *n* 宫外孕

ecu, ECU /eɪˈkuː/ ▸**p. 174** *n* Hist = **European Currency Unit** 欧洲货币单位

Ecuador /ˈekwədɔː(r)/ *pr n* 厄瓜多尔

Ecuadorian /ˌekwəˈdɔːrɪən/ ▸**p. 503**
A *adj* (of Ecuador) 厄瓜多尔的; (of the people) 厄瓜多尔人的
B *n* 厄瓜多尔人

ecumenical /ˌiːkjuːˈmenɪkl, ˈek-/ *adj* **1** (pan-Christian) 全基督教的 **2** (promoting unity) 基督教派合一的

ecumenism /iːˈkjuːmənɪzəm/ *n* [u] [推动基督教各派合一的] 大公主义

eczema /ˈeksɪmə, Amer ɪgˈziːmə/ ▸**p. 377** *n* [u] 湿疹

eddy /ˈedi/
A *n* 旋涡
B *vi* «*liquid*» 起旋涡; «*smoke*» 卷绕; «*crowd*» 环涌; **leaves swirled and eddied in the wind** 树叶在风中打转

edema /ɪˈdiːmə/ *n* Amer = **oedema**

Eden /ˈiːdn/ *pr n* **the Garden of ～** 伊甸园

edge /edʒ/
A *n* **1** [u and c] (outer limit) (of concrete object) 边缘; **the ～ of the cliff** 悬崖边; **on the ～ of one's seat with excitement** 异常兴奋; **to push sb. over the ～** fig 使某人发狂 **2** [u and c] (sharp side) (of knife) 刃; **to put an ～ on** 磨快 ‹*blade*›; **a knife with a sharp ～** 锋利的刀; **to take the ～ off** fig 减轻 ‹*anger, pain, hunger*›; **to take the ～ off one's appetite** 使食欲大减; **to give an ～ to** 刺激 ‹*appetite*› **3** [c] (narrow side) (of ruler, coin) 窄边 **4** [u] (brink) (of sth. bad) 边缘; **on the ～ of disaster** 濒临灾难; **to live on the ～** 生活在危险的边缘 **5** [u] (sharp tone) 尖声; **her voice had an ～ to it** 她的声音里带有怒气 **6** [u] (advantage) 优势; **to have a slight ～ over sb./sth.** 比某人/某事物略胜一筹; **who has the ～ now?** 目前谁占上风? ; **to have the ～ on** or **over sb./sth.** 胜过某人/某事 **7** [u] (strong, striking quality) 锋芒; **to lose one's ～** 失去锐气 **8** [u] **to be on ～** 紧张不安; **my nerves were all on ～** 我的精神紧张极了; **to be on ～ to do sth.** 急切地想做某事物; **to set sb.'s teeth on ～** 使某人恼火
B *vt* **1** (move slowly) 缓慢移动; **to ～ sth. towards sb./somewhere** 把某物慢慢地向某人/某处挪动 **2** (make border for) 给…镶边 ‹*handkerchief, blanket*› **3** (trim) 修剪…的边 ‹*lawn*›
C *vi* **1** (advance) 慢慢移动; **to ～ to** or **towards sb./sth.** 向某人/某物慢慢挪动; **she ～d to the front** 她慢慢挪到前面 **2** (make progress) 有所进展; **to ～ to** or **towards** 逐步走向 ‹*victory, independence, democracy*›

Phrasal verbs

- **edge out**
  A *vi* **to ～ out of ...** 从…慢慢出来 ‹*parking space, room*›; **he ～d out of the crowd** 他慢慢挤出了人群
  B *vt* [**～ sb./sth. out, ～ out sb./sth.**] 逐渐将…排挤出去 ‹*competitor, product*›; **to ～ sb./sth. out of sth.** 逐渐将某人/某物排挤出 ‹*power, company*›; **competing products ～d it out of the market** 竞争产品逐渐把它挤出市场
- **edge up** *vi* **1** (increase) «*prices, total*» 缓慢上升 **2** (approach) **to ～ up to sb./sth.** 慢慢靠近某人/某物

edgeways /ˈedʒweɪz/ Brit, **edgewise** /ˈedʒwaɪz/ Amer *advs* 侧着; **to get a word in ～** colloq 插话

edginess /ˈedʒɪnɪs/ *n* [u] **1** (nervousness) 紧张不安 **2** (irritability) 烦躁

edging /ˈedʒɪŋ/ *n* **1** [c] (border) 饰边 **2** [u] (making of a border) 饰边的制作

edging shears *npl* 修边剪刀

edgy /ˈedʒi/ *adj* **1** (nervous) 紧张不安的; **to be ～ about sth.** 对某事物感到紧张 **2** (irritable) 烦躁的

EDI *abbr* = **electronic data interchange** 电子数据交换

edible /ˈedɪbl/ *adj* 可食用的; **～ oil** 食用油

edict /ˈiːdɪkt/ *n* **1** Jur, Pol (official decree) 法令 **2** (any proclamation) 命令

edification /ˌedɪfɪˈkeɪʃn/ *n* [u] formal 教化; **to do sth. for sb.'s ～** 做某事以启迪某人

edifice /ˈedɪfɪs/ *n* **1** formal (building) 大厦 **2** fig (structure) 复杂体系; **the ～ of capitalism** 资本主义大厦

edify /ˈedɪfaɪ/ *vt* formal or hum 教化

edifying /ˈedɪfaɪɪŋ/ *adj* formal or hum 起教化作用的; **～ books** 有教化意义的书籍; **it was not an ～ spectacle/sight** 这场面/景象有失大雅

Edinburgh /ˈedɪnbərə/ *pr n* 爱丁堡

edit /ˈedɪt/
A *vt* **1** (check) 编辑 **2** (select and arrange) 选编 **3** (annotate) 给…作评注 ‹*text*›; 给…的作品作评注 ‹*author*› **4** TV, Cin 剪辑 **5** Journ 主编
B *n* **1** colloq (editing, change) 编辑 **2** Cin, TV 剪辑

Phrasal verb

- **edit out** *vt* [**～ out sth., ～ sth. out**] 删除 ‹*expletives, interference, interruptions*›

editing /ˈedɪtɪŋ/ *n* [u] **1** (checking for publication) 编辑 **2** (of essays, letters, author, collection, anthology) 选编 **3** (annotating) 评注 **4** TV, Cin (of film, tapes etc.) 剪辑 **5** Journ 主编

edition /ɪˈdɪʃn/ *n* **1** (printing) 一版印刷数; **the first ～ of the book was very small** 该书的初版印数很少 **2** (single copy) (of newspaper) 一份; (of book) 一册 **3** (particular version) 版本; **to bring out/issue an ～** 发行一版; **the revised ～** 修订版; **the hardback ～** 精装本 **4** (TV or radio programme) 一辑

edit key *n* 编辑键

editor /ˈedɪtə(r)/ ▸**p. 409** *n* **1** (of book, manuscript) 编辑 **2** (of anthology) 选编者 **3** (of dictionary) 编纂者 **4** (of writer, literary work) 评注者 **5** (of film, tape, etc.) 剪辑者 **6** (of newspaper, magazine, section) 主编 **7** Comput 编辑程序

editorial /ˌedɪˈtɔːrɪəl/
A *n* 社论
B *adj* 编辑的; **～ staff** 全体编辑人员

editorialist /ˌedɪˈtɔːrɪəlɪst/ *n* Amer 社论撰写人

editorship /ˈedɪtəʃɪp/ *n* 编辑工作; **under the ～ of ...** 经过…的编辑

EDP *abbr* = **electronic data processing** 电子数据处理

EDT *abbr* Amer = **Eastern Daylight Time**

educable /ˈedʒʊkəbl/ *adj* 可教育的

educate /ˈedʒʊkeɪt/ *vt* **1** (provide education for) 使接受学校教育; **to ～ one's children privately/at a state school** 送孩子上私立/公立学校 **2** (inform) 教育; **to ～ women about the dangers of smoking in pregnancy** 对妇女进行孕期吸烟危害的教育; **to be poorly ～d** 缺乏教养 **3** (refine) 培养 ‹*taste, judgement, skill*›

educated /ˈedʒʊkeɪtɪd/ *adj* **1** (having an education, taught) 受过教育的; **her parents are very ～** 她的父母很有学识; **a college-～ person** 受过大学教育的人; **self-～** 自修的 **2** (typical of an educated person) 有教养的; **an ～ voice** 斯文的声音 **3** (refined) 高雅的; **～ tastes in art** 高雅的艺术品味

educated guess *n* 有根据的猜测; **to make an ～** 进行有依据的猜测

education /ˌedʒʊˈkeɪʃn/ *n* **1** [u] (formal schooling) 教育; (knowledge acquired) 受到的教育; **to have a university/college ～** 接受大学教育; **adult/higher ～** 成人/高等教育; **～ standards** 教育水平; **my ～ is rather limited** 我没有受过多少教育 **2** [u] (field of study) 教育学;

e

～ **theory** 教育学理论; **a college of** ～ 教育学院 3 [u] (national system) 教育领域; **the Minister of E～, the E～ Minister** 教育部长 4 [u] (training) 培养; **physical/moral** ～ 体育/德育 5 [c] (revelation) 有益的经历; **he is a good workman; it is an** ～ **to watch him** 他是位好工人; 看他工作获益良多

Education Act *n* 教育法案

educational /ˌedʒʊˈkeɪʃənl/ *adj* 1 (of, providing education) 教育的; **what kind of** ～ **background does she have?** 她的教育背景如何? 2 (instructive) 起教育作用的; **an** ～ **toy** 寓教于乐的玩具 3 (enlightening) 有教育意义的 ‹*experience, event*›

educational adviser *n* 教育顾问

educationalist /ˌedʒʊˈkeɪʃənəlɪst/ *n* 教育家

educationally /ˌedʒʊˈkeɪʃənəli/ *adv* 在教育方面; **the book is** ～ **worthless** 这本书毫无教育价值; **to be** ～ **disadvantaged** 受教育条件差

educational: ～ **psychologist** ▸p. 409 *n* 教育心理学家; ～ **psychology** *n* [u] 教育心理学; ～ **television** *n* [u] 教育电视; **E～ Welfare Officer** *n* Brit 教育福利官员

education: ～ **authority** *n* 教育部门; ～ **department** *n* 1 (in central government) 教育部; 2 Brit (in local government) 教育局; 3 (in university, college) 教务处; ～ **officer** *n* Brit 教育局官员; ～ **system** *n* 教育体制

the UK and US education systems

英国和美国的教育制度。英国教育分成四大部分：小学（primary education）、中学（secondary education）、继续教育（further education）和高等教育（higher education）。3至5岁儿童接受学前教育，分幼儿园（nursery）和学前班（reception），称基础阶段（Foundation Stage）。义务教育大致从 5 岁开始，延续至 16 岁，从 1 年级（year）读到 11 年级，分为四个关键阶段（Key Stage）。第一、二阶段为小学，共 6 年。第三、四阶段为中学，共 5 年。毕业时需参加普通中等教育证书（General Certificate of Secondary Education，简称 GCSE）考试。此后，学生可以开始工作，也可以选择继续接受教育，以参加中学高级证书（Advanced Level，简称 A Level）考试。在英国上大学必须通过 A Level 考试。大学本科学制 3 年（苏格兰通常为 4 年），硕士学制一般 1 年，博士 3 年。

美国儿童 5 岁时必须进入幼儿园（kindergarten），一年后升入小学（elementary school）。小学学制 5 年。中学（high school）学制 7 年，分为初中（junior high school）和高中（senior high school）。高中也称为 high school，一般为 9 到 12 年级（grade）。毕业时要参加学术能力考试（Scholastic Aptitude Test，简称 SAT），相当于中国的高考。大学本科学制 4 年，硕士约 2 年，博士 3 到 6 年。

educative /ˈedʒʊkətɪv/ *adj* 教育的 ‹*process, experience, purpose, function*›

educator /ˈedʒʊkeɪtə(r)/ *n* 1 (teacher) 教育工作者 2 = **educationalist**

edutainment /ˌedjʊˈteɪnmənt/ *n* [u] 寓教于乐型产品

Edwardian /edˈwɔːdɪən/ *adj* 爱德华七世的 ‹*era, period*›; 爱德华七世时代的 ‹*gentleman, resort, society, building*›

EEC *abbr* = **European Economic Community**

EEG *abbr* 1 = **electroencephalogram** 2 = **electroencephalograph**

eel /iːl/ *n* 1 Zool 鳗 2 (person) 圆滑的人

e'er /eə(r)/ *adv* archaic *or* liter = **ever**

eerie /ˈɪəri/ *adj* 怪异恐怖的

eerily /ˈɪərɪli/ *adv* 怪异恐怖地

eeriness /ˈɪərɪnɪs/ *n* [u] 怪异恐怖

eery /ˈɪəri/ *adj* = **eerie**

EET *abbr* = **Eastern European Time**

eff /ef/ *vi* Brit euph sl 咒骂; **to** ～ **off** 滚开; **to** ～ **and blind** 咒骂

efface /ɪˈfeɪs/ *vt* 1 (erase) 擦去; **time and the weather** ～**d the inscriptions** 岁月和风雨磨掉了那些铭文 2 fig (obliterate) 冲淡; **she tried to** ～ **the memories** 她试图抹去那些记忆 3 **to** ～ **oneself** fig (make inconspicuous) 使自己不被人注意

effect /ɪˈfekt/

A *n* 1 [c and u] (result) 结果; **the** ～**s of medicine** 药效; **the beneficial** ～**s of exercise** 锻炼的益处; **the** ～ **of alcohol on the liver** 酒精对肝脏的影响; **to have a damaging** ～ **on sb./sth.** 对某人/某事物起破坏作用 2 [u] (efficacy) 效力; **of little/no** ～ 效力甚微/无效; **they took precautions, to no** ～ 他们采取了预防措施，但无济于事; **to take** ～ «*law*» 生效; «*medicine*» 见效; **to come into** ～ «*law*» 开始生效; **to put sth. into** ～ 实行 ‹*policy*›; **to put a new system into** ～ 实施新体制; **with** ～ **from ...** formal 从…起生效 3 [c and u] (impression) 效果; **to give/create the** ～ **of sth.** 产生某种效果; **the** ～ **on sb.** 给某人的印象; **for** ～ 为了加深印象; **a marbled** ～ 大理石效果; **an** ～ **of light** 灯光效果 4 [c] (basic meaning) 大意; **to this/that** ～ 有这/有那个意思; **... or words to that** ～ …或者类似的话 5 [c] Sci 效应; **the placebo** ～ 安慰剂效果

B **effects** *npl* 1 Cin, Radio, TV **special** ～**s** 特技效果 2 Jur **personal** ～**s** 个人财产

C **in effect** *adv phr* 1 (effectively) 实质上 2 (in use) 在实施中; **the regulations are not yet in** ～ 这些规定还没有实行

D *vt* formal 实行 ‹*reform*›; 实施 ‹*rescue*›; 引起 ‹*change*›; **to** ～ **a cure** 治愈; **to** ～ **a settlement of a dispute** 解决争端

effective /ɪˈfektɪv/ *adj* 1 (efficient) 有效的; ～ **measures to reduce unemployment** 减少失业人数的有效措施; **to be** ～ **against sth.** 对某事物有效 2 *pred* (operational) 生效的; **to become** ～ 生效; **this law is no longer** ～ 这条法规已经失效 3 (striking, impressive) 给人深刻印象的; **a very** ～ **colour scheme** 非常醒目的色彩布局; **an** ～ **speech** 精彩的演说 4 *attrib* (actual) 实际的 ‹*leader, amount, income*›; **to lose** ～ **power** 失去实权; **an** ～ **increase of 25%** 25%的实际增长 5 (fit for action) 有战斗力的 ‹*soldiers, army*›; 适于工作的 ‹*manpower*›

effectively /ɪˈfektɪvli/ *adv* 1 (successfully) 有成效地 ‹*work, solve, punish, campaign*› 2 (in effect) 实际上 3 (impressively) 引人注目地 ‹*perform, decorate, dress*›; 使人印象深刻地 ‹*describe*›; **the design works very** ～ 该设计十分醒目; **the statistics** ～ **demonstrate the failure of the policy** 这些统计数字有力地证明了该政策的失败

effectiveness /ɪˈfektɪvnɪs/ *n* [u] 1 (efficiency of measures, cure, person etc.) 有效性 2 (impressiveness) 引人注目

effects man *n* 特效师

effectual /ɪˈfektʃʊəl/ *adj* 有效的 ‹*method, system, cure*›; **he was not a very** ～ **ruler** 他是个平庸的统治者

effectuate /ɪˈfektjʊeɪt/ *vt* formal 使发生; **to** ～ **a plan** 实施计划; **to** ～ **a transfer of power** 实现权力的转移

effeminacy /ɪˈfemɪnəsi/ *n* [u] 女人气

effeminate /ɪˈfemɪnət/ *adj* 女人气的

effervesce /ˌefəˈves/ *vi* 1 lit (give off bubbles) «*liquid, powder, tablet*» 冒泡 2 fig (be vivacious) «*person*» 兴高采烈

effervescence /ˌefəˈvesns/ *n* [u] 1 lit (release of bubbles) 冒泡 2 fig (vivaciousness) 兴高采烈

effervescent /ˌefəˈvesnt/ *adj* 1 lit (bubbling) 冒泡的 2 fig (vivacious) 兴高采烈的

effete /ɪˈfiːt/ *adj* 1 pej (feeble, affected) 软弱做作的 ‹*dancer, artist*›; 女人气的 ‹*young man*› 2 (weak) 衰落的 ‹*civilization, empire*›

efficacious /ˌefɪˈkeɪʃəs/ *adj* formal 有效的 ‹*method, remedy*›

efficaciously /ˌefɪˈkeɪʃəsli/ *adv* formal 有效地

efficacy /ˈefɪkəsi/ *n* [u] formal 功效

efficiency /ɪˈfɪʃnsi/ *n* 1 [u] (of person, staff, method, organization) 效率; ～ **in doing sth.** 做某事的效率; **to improve/impair** ～ 提高/降低效率 2 [c] (action) 提高效率的行为; **the reforms will lead to efficiencies and savings** 这些改革将提高功效并节省开销 3 [u] (of machine, engine) 效率; **the machine has a high/poor/low** ～ **level** 这台机器效率高/差/低

efficiency apartment *n* Amer 公寓式小套房

efficient /ɪˈfɪʃnt/ *adj* 1 (competent and quick) 效率高的; **to be** ～ **at doing sth.** 做某事效率高; **an** ～ **secretary** 能干的秘书 2 (economical) 收效大的; **to make** ～ **use of energy** 有效利用能源

efficiently /ɪˈfɪʃntli/ *adv* 1 (competently and quickly) 效率高地 ‹*work, handle, deal*› 2 (in an economical manner) 收效大地 ‹*work, operate*›

effigy /ˈefɪdʒi/ *n* 1 (of famous person) 雕像 2 (of unpopular person) 模拟像

effing /ˈefɪŋ/ *adj* Brit euph sl 该死的

effloresce /ˌefləˈres/ *vi* 1 (become powdery) 粉化 2 (become coated) 霜化

efflorescence /ˌeflɔːˈresns/ *n* [u] 1 (becoming powdery) 粉化 2 (becoming coated) 起霜

efflorescent /ˌeflɔːˈresnt/ *adj* 粉化的

effluent /ˈeflʊənt/ *n* [u and c] 废水

effluvium /ɪˈfluːvɪəm/ *n* (*pl* **effluvia** /ɪˈfluːvɪə/) 1 (waste) 废料 2 (offensive gas) 臭气

effort /ˈefət/ *n* 1 [c and u] (energy) 努力; **to put a lot of** ～ **into sth.** 在某事上花费很多精力; **it's not worth the** ～ **to write** 不值得费心去写; **to spare no** ～ 不遗余力 2 [u and c] (difficulty) 费劲; **with/without** ～ 费力/不费力地; **it's an** ～ **to climb the stairs** 爬楼梯很吃力 3 [c] (attempt) 试图; **to make every** ～ 尽全力; **in an** ～ **to escape sth.** 为逃避某事; ～**s at sth./doing sth.** 做某事的尝试; **to thwart sb.'s** ～**s** 阻挠某人的企图 4 [c] (initiative) 有组织的活动; **the war** ～ 战事; **the United Nations peacekeeping** ～ 联合国维和行动 5 [c] (result) 成就; **sb.'s latest** ～ 某人的最新成果

effortless /ˈefətlɪs/ *adj* 1 (easy) 不需费力的; **he achieved the victory with** ～ **ease** 他轻松获胜 2 (innate) 天生的 ‹*skill, superiority, style*›

effortlessly /ˈefətlɪsli/ *adv* 轻松地

effortlessness /ˈefətlɪsnɪs/ *n* [u] 1 (ease) 轻松自如 2 (naturalness) 天生

effrontery /ɪˈfrʌntəri/ *n* [u] 厚颜无耻

effusion /ɪˈfjuːʒn/ *n* formal 1 [c] (emotional outpouring) 倾泻; **his letters were full of poetical** ～**s** 他的信洋溢着诗情 2 [u and c] (flowing of liquid) 流出; (flowing of gas) 喷出; **to stop the** ～ **of blood** 止血

effusive /ɪˈfjuːsɪv/ *adj* 过于热情的; ～ **welcome/praise/thanks** 热情洋溢的欢迎/极尽溢美之词的赞美/无比激动的道谢

effusively /ɪˈfjuːsɪvli/ *adv* 过分热情地 ‹*praise, welcome*›; **to thank sb.** ～ 对某人感谢万分

effusiveness /ɪˈfjuːsɪvnɪs/ *n* [u] 过分热情

EFL *abbr* = **English as a Foreign Language**

e-form *n* 电子表格

EFT *abbr* = **electronic funds transfer**

e

EFTA /'eftə/ *abbr* = **European Free Trade Association**

EFTPOS /'eftpɒs/ *abbr* = **electronic funds transfer at point of sale** 销售点资金电子转账

e.g. *abbr* = **exempli gratia** 例如

egalitarian /ɪ,gælɪ'teərɪən/
A *adj* 平等主义的
B *n* 平等主义者

egalitarianism /ɪ,gælɪ'teərɪənɪzəm/ *n* [u] 平等主义

egg /eg/ *n* [1] (of bird) 蛋; (of fish, reptile) 卵; **to put all one's ~s in one basket** fig 孤注一掷; **as sure as ~s is ~s** colloq 毫无疑问; **to have ~ on one's face** fig 丢脸; **to lay an ~** Amer 完全失败; ▸**goose A1, grandmother** [2] Biol (ovum) 卵子 [3] (egg-shaped object) 蛋状物; **a chocolate ~** 巧克力蛋

Phrasal verb
- **egg on** *vt* [~ **sb. on**] colloq 怂恿; **to ~ sb. on to do sth.** 鼓动某人做某事

egg: **~-and-spoon race** *n* 用汤匙端鸡蛋的赛跑; **~beater** *n* 打蛋器; **~ box** *n* 盛蛋盒; **~cup** *n* 蛋杯; **~ custard** *n* [u and c] 蛋奶糕; **~ donor** *n* 卵子捐献者; **~ flip** *n* [u and c] Brit = **~ nog**; **~ fried rice** *n* [u] 蛋炒饭; **~head** *n* colloq 学究; **~ nog** *n* [u and c] 蛋奶酒; **~plant** *n* Amer = **aubergine**; **~ roll** *n* Amer 炸蛋卷; **~s Benedict** *npl* (toast) 火腿蛋土司; (toasted muffin) 火腿蛋松饼; **~-shaped** *adj* 蛋形的

eggshell /'egʃel/
A *n* 蛋壳
B *modif* 略有光泽的; **~ paint/finish** 蛋壳漆/末道蛋壳漆

egg: **~ slicer** *n* 切蛋器; **~ timer** *n* 煮蛋计时器; **~ whisk** *n* 打蛋器; **~ white** *n* 蛋白

eggy /'egi/ *adj* (rich in egg) 含蛋多的; (covered in egg) 裹上蛋液的

egg yolk *n* 蛋黄

ego /'egəʊ, 'iːgəʊ, Amer 'iːgəʊ-/ *n* [1] (self-esteem) 自尊; **a blow to one's ~** 对自尊心的打击; **to have an inflated ~** 自负 [2] Psych 自我

ego booster *n* 增强自尊心的事

egocentric /,egəʊ'sentrɪk, 'iːg-, Amer 'iːg-/ *adj* 以自我为中心的

egocentricity /,egəʊsən'trɪsəti, ,iːg-, Amer ,iːg-/ *n* [u] 以自我为中心

egoism /'egəʊɪzəm, 'iːg-, Amer 'iːg-/ *n* [u] 利己主义

egoist /'egəʊɪst, 'iːg-, Amer 'iːg-/ *n* 利己主义者

egoistical /,egəʊ'ɪstɪkl, ,iːg-, Amer ,iːg-/, **egoistic** /,egəʊ'ɪstɪk, ,iːg-, Amer ,iːg-/ *adj* 自我主义的

egomania /,egəʊ'meɪnɪə, ,iːg-, Amer ,iːg-/ *n* [u] 极端利己

egomaniac /,egəʊ'meɪnɪæk, ,iːg-, Amer ,iːg-/ *n* 极端利己主义者

egotism /'egəʊtɪzəm, 'iːg-, Amer 'iːg-/ *n* [u] 自我中心

egotist /'egəʊtɪst, 'iːg-, Amer 'iːg-/ *n* 自我主义者

egotistical /,egəʊ'tɪstɪkl, ,iːg-, Amer ,iːg-/, **egotistic** /,egəʊ'tɪstɪk, ,iːg-, Amer ,iːg-/ *adj* 自我主义的

ego trip *n* colloq 自我表现; **to be on an ~** colloq 出风头

egregious /ɪ'griːdʒɪəs/ *adj* formal 极坏的 ‹*example*›; 极严重的 ‹*mistake, violation*›; 极糟糕的 ‹*cowardice*›; **an ~ lie** 弥天大谎; **~ incompetence** 极端的无能

egress /'iːgres/ *n* formal [1] [u] (action) 外出 [2] [c] (exit point) 出口

egret /'iːgrɪt/ *n* 白鹭

Egypt /'iːdʒɪpt/ *pr n* 埃及

Egyptian /ɪ'dʒɪpʃn/ ▸**p. 503, p. 426**
A *adj* (of Egypt) 埃及的; (of the people) 埃及人的; (of the ancient language) 古埃及语的
B *n* [1] [c] (person) 埃及人 [2] [u] (ancient language) 古埃及语

Egyptologist /,iːdʒɪp'tɒlədʒɪst/ ▸**p. 409** *n* 埃及学家

Egyptology /,iːdʒɪp'tɒlədʒi/ *n* [u] 埃及学

eh /eɪ/ *excl* colloq [用以询问、表示惊奇或征求同意等] 嗯; **simple, ~?** 很简单，是吧？

EIB *abbr* = **European Investment Bank**

eider /'aɪdə(r)/ *n* **~ (duck)** 绒鸭

eiderdown /'aɪdədaʊn/ *n* [1] [c] esp Brit (quilt) 鸭绒被 [2] **eider down** [u] (feathers) 鸭绒

eight /eɪt/ ▸**p. 15, p. 521, p. 831**
A *n* [1] (number, quantity) 八; **~ plus two equals ten** 8 加 2 等于 10; **in December nineteen hundred and ~** 在 1908 年 12 月; **we live at (number) ~, Victoria Road** 我们住在维多利亚路 8 号; **her phone number is two six double ~** 她的电话号码是 2688; **there are ~ of them** 他们有 8 个人 [2] (in time) 8 点钟; **at ~ (o'clock)** 在 8 点 [3] (on playing card) 8 点; **the ~ of diamonds** 方块 8 [4] (age) 8 岁 [5] (in rowing) 8 人划船队
B *adj* [1] (as quantity) 八的; **~ cats** 8 只猫; **~ books** 8 本书; **~ weeks** 8 周 [2] (in age) 8 岁的; **he's nearly ~** 他快 8 岁了; **our house is only ~ years old** 我们的房子才造了 8 年 [3] (in series) 第八的; **number ~** 8 号; **page ~** 第 8 页

eighteen /eɪ'tiːn/ ▸**p. 15, p. 521**
A *n* [1] (number, quantity) 十八 [2] (in age) 18 岁
B *adj* [1] (in number) 十八的; **~ metres** 18 米; **~ paintings** 18 张画 [2] (in age) 18 岁的; **to be ~ (years old)** 18 岁大; **to be over/under ~** 超过/不到 18 岁 [3] (in series) 第十八的; **size/number ~** 18 码/号

eighteenth /eɪ'tiːnθ/ ▸**p. 181, p. 521**
A *n* [1] (in sequence) 第十八个 [2] (in date) 18 日 [3] (fraction) 十八分之一
B *adj* [1] (in sequence) 第十八的 [2] (in name, title) 十八; **Louis the E~** 路易十八 [3] (as fraction) 十八分之一的
C *adv* 第十八

eighth /eɪtθ/ ▸**p. 181, p. 521**
A *n* [1] (in sequence) 第八 [2] (in date) 8 日 [3] (fraction) 八分之一
B *adj* [1] (in sequence) 第八的; **it's her ~ birthday** 这是她 8 岁生日; **on the ~ floor** 在 9 楼 [2] (in name, title) 八世; **Henry the E~ of England** 英王亨利八世 [3] (as fraction) 八分之一的
C *adv* 第八

eighth note *n* Amer 八分音符

eightieth /'eɪtɪəθ/ ▸**p. 521**
A *n* [1] (in sequence) 第八十个 [2] (fraction) 八十分之一
B *adj* [1] (in sequence) 第八十的 [2] (as fraction) 八十分之一的
C *adv* 第八十

eighty /'eɪtɪ/ ▸**p. 15, p. 521**
A *n* [1] (number, quantity) 八十; **there are ~ of us** 我们有 80 个人 [2] (in age) 80 岁
B *adj* [1] (in number) 八十的; **~ boys** 80 个男孩 [2] (in age) 80 岁的; **I'm nearly ~** 我快 80 岁了 [3] (in series) 第八十的

Eire /'eərə/ *pr n* 爱尔兰 [1937-1949年间爱尔兰共和国的官方名称]

eisteddfod /aɪ'stedfəd, -ðvɒd/ *n* (*pl* **~s** *or* **eisteddfodau** /,aɪ'stedfədaɪ, -ðvɒ-/) 威尔士音乐诗歌比赛

either /'aɪðə(r), 'iːðə(r)/
A *adj attrib* [1] (one or the other) 两者之中任一的; **take ~ road** 两条路随便走哪一条; **~ way, we can't win** 无论如何我们都赢不了 [2] (neither) 都没有 [用于否定句，不用作主语]; **there's no train on ~ day** 两天都没有火车 [3] (both) 两者的; **trees growing on ~ side of the road** 长在道路两侧的树; **~ end of the corridor** 走廊两头; **~ outcome is possible** 两种结果都有可能
B *pron* + *v sing* [1] (one or other) 两者中的任何一个; **I might marry ~ (of them)** 我可能和他们两人的其中一个结婚; **which book do you want? — either** 你想要哪一本书？——随便 [2] (neither) [用于否定句，不用作主语，表示两者都不]; **I don't like ~ of them** 两个我都不喜欢 [3] (both) 两者; **~ of us could win** 我们俩都可能赢
C *conj* [引导短语或句子，不常作主语; 或用于否定句，不用作主语]; **~ ... or ...** 或者…或者…; **~ by cheating or by lying** 要么通过欺骗，要么通过撒谎; **you ~ love him or hate him** 你不是爱他就是恨他; **put the gun down — it's ~ that or I'll call the police** 把枪放下——不然我就报警
D *adv* [1] (also) 也 [用于否定句句末]; **I can't sleep — I can't, ~** 我睡不着——我也睡不着; **there's no answer to that question ~** 那个问题也没有答案 [2] (moreover) 而且; **not only was it expensive, but it didn't work ~** 它不仅贵而且不管用

either/or *adj attrib* 非此即彼的; **an ~ question/choice/situation** 非此即彼的问题/选择/状况

ejaculate
A /ɪ'dʒækjʊleɪt/ *vt* [1] Physiol 射 ‹*semen*› [2] dated (exclaim) 突然说出 ‹*utterance*›
B /ɪ'dʒækjʊleɪt/ *vi* 射精
C /ɪ'dʒækjʊlət/ *n* [u] 射出的精液

ejaculation /ɪ,dʒækjʊ'leɪʃn/ *n* [1] [u] Physiol 射精 [2] [c] dated (exclamation) 叫喊; **an ~ of surprise** 惊讶的叫喊声

eject /ɪ'dʒekt/
A *vt* [1] (give out) 喷射; **lava ~ed from a volcano** 火山喷出的岩浆 [2] (throw out) 驱逐; **he was ~ed from the pub** 他被赶出了酒吧 [3] Audio 弹出 ‹*cassette, disk*›
B *vi* 弹出

eject button *n* 弹出键

ejection /ɪ'dʒekʃn/ *n* [u] [1] (of gases, waste, lava) 喷射; (of projectile) 弹射 [2] (of trouble-maker, intruder) 驱逐 [3] Aviat 弹出

ejection seat, ejector seat *ns* 弹射座椅

eke /iːk/

Phrasal verb
- **eke out** *vt* [**~ out sth., ~ sth. out**] [1] (by saving) 节约使用 ‹*provisions, materials*› [2] (by working hard) 竭力维持; **to ~ out a living/an existence** 勉强度日/糊口 [3] (by supplementing) 弥补…的不足; **he ~s out his earnings with odd jobs/by washing people's cars** 他靠打零工/帮人洗车来补贴收入

elaborate
A /ɪ'læbərət/ *adj* [1] (detailed) 精细的 ‹*task*›; 精密的 ‹*system, apparatus*›; 精心编造的 ‹*joke, excuse*› [2] (extravagant) 精美的 ‹*work of art, garment, pattern, meal*› [3] (complicated) 复杂的 ‹*ceremony, procedure, ritual*› [4] (carefully planned) 精心策划的 ‹*preparations, scheme*›
B /ɪ'læbəreɪt/ *vt* 详尽阐述 ‹*theory, scheme, hypothesis*›
C /ɪ'læbəreɪt/ *vi* 详尽阐述; **to ~ on a plan** 详细说明计划

elaborately /ɪ'læbərətli/ *adv* [1] (in great detail) 周详充分地 ‹*devised, constructed*›; (with careful attention to detail) 精心地 ‹*plan, conceive*› [2] (extravagantly) 精美地 ‹*patterned, ornamented*› [3] (in a complicated way) 复杂地 ‹*ritualized*›

elaborateness /ɪ'læbərətnɪs/ *n* [u] [1] (of task) 精细; (of system, apparatus) 精密 [2] (of a work of art, garment, pattern, meal) 精美 [3] (of a ceremony, procedure, ritual) 复杂 [4] (of preparations, scheme) 周详充分

elaboration /ɪ,læbə'reɪʃn/ *n* [u] 详尽阐述

e

elapse /ɪˈlæps/ *vi* «*time*» 流逝; **several years ～d before they returned** 过了几年他们才回来

elastic /ɪˈlæstɪk/
A *adj* **1** lit (stretchy) 有弹性的 **2** fig (flexible, able to change) 有伸缩性的 ‹*concept, definition, term*›
B *n* **1** [u] (material) 弹性材料 **2** [c] = **elastic band**

elasticated /ɪˈlæstɪkeɪtɪd/ *adj* 有松紧带的

elastic band *n* esp Brit 橡皮筋

elasticity /ˌelæsˈtɪsəti, Amer ɪˌlæs-/ *n* [u] **1** lit (of a material, thread) 弹性 **2** fig (flexibility) 灵活性

elate /ɪˈleɪt/ *vt* 使兴奋; **he was greatly ～d by his success** 他因成功而兴高采烈

elated /ɪˈleɪtɪd/ *adj* 兴高采烈的; **to be ～ about** *or* **at** *or* **by sth.** 因某事感到欢欣鼓舞

elation /ɪˈleɪʃn/ *n* [u] 兴高采烈; **to be filled with ～** 心里充满喜悦

elbow /ˈelbəʊ/
A *n* **1** (joint) 肘; **at sb.'s ～** 在某人近旁; **to give sb. the ～** Brit colloq 排斥某人; **to get the ～** 被排斥; **to be up to the ～s in sth.** colloq lit 把手臂深深地插入某物; fig 深深卷入某事; **to lift one's ～** colloq 纵酒 **2** (part of sleeve) 肘部; **out at the ～s** 邋遢的 **3** (sharp bend) 弯头
B *vt* 用肘推; **to ～ sb. aside** *or* **out of the way** 把某人挤到一旁; **to ～ sb. in the stomach** 用肘撞某人的腹部; **to ～ one's way forward/past** 用肘开路向前挤去/挤过
C *vi* 用肘推; **to ～ through sth.** 挤着穿过 ‹*crowd*›; **to ～ forward/past** 向前挤/挤过

elbow: ～ grease *n* [u] colloq 苦干; **～ joint** *n* 肘关节; **～ room** *n* [u] colloq **1** lit (room for moving the elbows freely) 自由伸展臂肘的空间; fig (room to move, work) 足够的活动空间; **2** fig (freedom) 行动的自由

elder[1] /ˈeldə(r)/
A *n* **1** (older person) 长者; **one's ～s and betters** 前辈和上级 **2** (in tribe etc.) 德高望重的人; **party ～s** 党内元老 **3** Relig 长老
B *adj* 较年长的; **his ～ sister/brother** 他的姐姐/哥哥; **Pitt the ～** 老皮特

elder[2] *n* Bot 接骨木

elder: ～berry *n* 接骨木果; **～berry wine** 接骨木果酒; **～care** *n* [u] Amer 老年保健; **～flower** *n* 接骨木花; **～flower wine** 接骨木花酒

elderly /ˈeldəli/ ▸**p. 15**
A *adj* 上年纪的; **an ～ couple** 一对老夫妻
B *npl* **the ～** 上年纪的人; **to take care of the ～** 照顾老人

elder statesman *n* (*pl* **elder statesmen**) [尤指政界] 元老

eldest /ˈeldɪst/ *adj* 年龄最大的; **the ～ son** 长子; **sb.'s ～ brother** 某人的大哥

elect /ɪˈlekt/
A *vt* 选举; **to ～ sb. (as) president** 选某人为总统; **to be ～ed to the Senate** 被选为参议员; **to ～ sb. to do sth.** 选某人做某事; **to ～ sb. from (among) ...** 从…中选出某人; **an ～ed representative** 当选的代表; **an ～ed office/post** 当选的要职/职位
B *vi* 选择; **to ～ to do sth.** 选择做某事
C *adj* 当选而尚未就职的; **the president-～** 候任总统

electable /ɪˈlektəbl/ *adj* 可能当选的 ‹*party, candidate*›

election /ɪˈlekʃn/ *n* **1** [c] (ballot) 选举; **to call an ～** 宣布举行选举; **to win/lose an ～** 在选举中获胜/失败; **to hold an ～ for sth.** 为某职位举行选举; **to stand for ～** 参加竞选; **～ campaign** 竞选运动 **2** [u] (appointment) 当选; **the ～ of sb. as sth./to do sth.** 选某人任某职/做某事 **3** [u] (act of choosing) 选择; **the ～ of sb./sth. as sth.** 选择某人/某物作为某物

election day *n* 选举日

electioneer /ɪˌlekʃəˈnɪər/ *vi* «*politician, candidate, activist*» 从事竞选活动

electioneering /ɪˌlekʃəˈnɪərɪŋ/ *n* [u] **1** (campaigning) 竞选活动; **an ～ speech** 竞选演讲 **2** (electoral gamesmanship) 竞选技巧

election results *npl* 选举结果

elective /ɪˈlektɪv/
A *adj* **1** (elected) 选举产生的 ‹*post, assembly*›; **an ～ official** 当选官员 **2** (empowered to elect) 有选举权的 ‹*role*› **3** esp Amer Sch, Univ (optional) 选修的
B *n* esp Amer Sch, Univ 选修课程

elector /ɪˈlektə(r)/ *n* **1** (voter) 选民 **2** Amer Pol 选举团成员

electoral /ɪˈlektərəl/ *adj* (relating to elections) 选举的; (relating to electors) 选举人的

electoral: ～ boundary *n* 选区分界; **～ college** *n* **1** (body of electors) 选举团; **2 E～ College** Amer 总统选举团; **～ district** *n* 选区; **～ division** *n* [较大的] 选区

electorally /ɪˈlektərəli/ *adv* 在选举中

electoral: ～ register, ～ roll *ns* 选民登记册; **～ vote** *n* Amer 总统选举团的选票

electorate /ɪˈlektərət/ *n* + *v sing or pl* 全体选民

electric /ɪˈlektrɪk/
A *adj* **1** (using electricity) 用电的; **an ～ light** 电灯; **an ～ toothbrush** 电动牙刷 **2** (relating to electricity) 电的; **～ current** 电流 **3** fig (emotionally charged) 紧张刺激的; **the atmosphere is ～** 气氛很热烈
B electrics *npl* Brit colloq 电路; **to check the ～s** 检查电路

electrical /ɪˈlektrɪkl/ *adj* **1** (relating to electricity) 电的; **～ power** 电力 **2** (using electricity) 用电的; **～ appliances** 电器

electrical: ～ engineer ▸**p. 409** *n* 电气工程师; **～ engineering** *n* [u] 电气工程; **～ fitter** ▸**p. 409** *n* 电工

electrically /ɪˈlektrɪkli/ *adv* 用电力; **an ～ powered car** 电动汽车

electrically charged *adj* 带电的

electrical storm *n* 雷暴

electric blanket *n* 电热毯

electric blue ▸**p. 134**
A *adj* 铁青色的
B *n* 铁青色

electric: ～ car *n* 电动汽车; **～ chair** *n* 电椅; **～ eel** *n* 电鳗; **～ eye** *n* colloq 电眼; **～ fence** *n* 电篱笆; **～ field** *n* 电场; **～ fire** *n* 电暖炉; **～ guitar** *n* 电吉他

electrician /ˌɪlekˈtrɪʃn/ ▸**p. 409** *n* 电工

electricity /ˌɪlekˈtrɪsəti/ *n* [u] **1** (form of energy) 电; **～ pylon/meter/bill/supply** 电缆塔/电流计/电费单/电力供应 **2** (supply) 供电; (electric current) 电流; **to cut off the ～** 断电

electric: ～ kettle *n* 电水壶; **～ motor** *n* 电动机; **～ shock** *n* 电击; **to get an ～ shock** 触电; **～ storm** *n* = **electrical storm**; **～ window** *n* 电动窗

electrification /ɪˌlektrɪfɪˈkeɪʃn/ *n* [u] 电气化

electrify /ɪˈlektrɪfaɪ/ *vt* **1** (convert to electricity) 使…电气化 ‹*railway, region*› **2** (charge with electricity) 使…通电 ‹*fence, machine*› **3** fig (excite) 使激动

electrifying /ɪˈlektrɪfaɪɪŋ/ *adj* 激动人心的

electro- /ɪˈlektrəʊ/ *combining form* [表示"电的"]; **～dynamic** 电动力的; **～metallurgy** 电冶金学

electrocardiogram /ɪˌlektrəʊˈkɑːdɪəgræm/ *n* 心电图

electrocardiograph /ɪˌlektrəʊˈkɑːdɪəgrɑːf, Amer -græf/ *n* 心电图仪

electrochemical /ɪˌlektrəʊˈkemɪkl/ *adj* 电化学的

electrochemistry /ɪˈlektrəʊˌkemɪstri/ *n* [u] 电化学

electroconvulsive /ɪˌlektrəʊkənˈvʌlsɪv/ *adj* 电休克的; **～ therapy** *or* **treatment** 电休克疗法

electrocute /ɪˈlektrəkjuːt/ *vt* **1** (injure) 使触电受伤; **to ～ oneself** 触电受伤 **2** (kill accidentally) 使触电死亡 **3** (execute in the electric chair) 用电刑处死

electrocution /ɪˌlektrəˈkjuːʃn/ *n* [u] **1** (injury) 触电受伤 **2** (death) 触电死亡

electrode /ɪˈlektrəʊd/ *n* 电极

electroencephalogram /ɪˌlektrəʊɪnˈsefələgræm/ *n* 脑电图

electroencephalograph /ɪˌlektrəʊɪnˈsefələgrɑːf, Amer -græf/ *n* 脑电图仪

electrolyse /ɪˈlektrəlaɪz/ *vt* **1** Chem 电解 ‹*solution, chemical*› **2** (remove) 用电蚀法除去 ‹*hair roots, blemish*›

electrolysis /ˌɪlekˈtrɒləsɪs/ *n* [u] 电解

electrolyte /ɪˈlektrəlaɪt/ *n* 电解液

electrolytic /ɪˌlektrəˈlɪtɪk/ *adj* 电解的; **～ cells/reaction** 电解电池/电解反应

electrolyze /ɪˈlektrəlaɪz/ *vt* Amer = **electrolyse**

electromagnet /ɪˌlektrəʊˈmægnɪt/ *n* 电磁铁

electromagnetic /ɪˌlektrəʊmægˈnetɪk/ *adj* 电磁的

electromagnetism /ɪˌlektrəʊˈmægnɪtɪzəm/ *n* [u] 电磁

electromechanical /ɪˌlektrəʊmɪˈkænɪkl/ *adj* 电动机械的

electrometer /ˌɪlekˈtrɒmɪtə(r)/ *n* 静电计

electromotive force /ɪˌlektrəʊˌməʊtɪv ˈfɔːs/ *n* 电动势

electron /ɪˈlektrɒn/ *n* 电子

electron gun *n* 电子枪

electronic /ˌɪlekˈtrɒnɪk/ *adj* 电子的

electronically /ˌɪlekˈtrɒnɪkli/ *adv* 用电子方法; **～ tested/operated** 用电子测试/驱动的

electronic: ～ data processing *n* [u] 电子数据处理; **～ directory** *n* 电子目录; **～ engineer** ▸**p. 409** *n* 电子工程师; **～ engineering** *n* [u] 电子工程学; **～ funds transfer** *n* 资金电子转账; **～ mail** *n* [u] 电子邮件; **to send a message by ～ mail** 通过电子邮件发信息; **～ mailbox** *n* 电子邮箱; **～ media** *npl* 电子媒体; **～ money** *n* [u] 电子货币; **～ music** *n* [u] 电子音乐; **～ news gathering** *n* [u] 电子新闻采集; **～ office** *n* 电子办公室; **～ organizer** *n* 电子记事簿; **～ paper** *n* [u] 电子纸; **～ payment** *n* 电子支付; **～ point of sale** *n* 电子销售点; **～ publishing** *n* [u] 电子出版

electronics /ˌɪlekˈtrɒnɪks/ *npl* **1** + *v sing* (branch of science, technology) 电子学 **2** + *v pl* (components) 电子器件; (circuits) 电子电路

electronic: ～ shopping *n* [u] 网上购物; **～ shopping basket** *n* 网上购物篮; **～ signature** *n* 电子签名; **～ storefront** *n* 电子店面; **～ surveillance** *n* [u] 电子监控; **～ tag** *n* 电子追踪标签; **～ tagging** *n* [u] 电子标签追踪

electron: ～ microscope *n* 电子显微镜; **～ volt** *n* 电子伏（特）

electroplate /ɪˈlektrəʊpleɪt/
A *vt* 电镀
B *n* [u] 电镀品

electroplating /ɪˌlektrəʊˈpleɪtɪŋ/ *n* [u] **1** (technique) 电镀术; (process) 电镀 **2** (coating) 电镀层

electroshock /ɪˈlektrəʊʃɒk/ *adj attrib* 电休克的; **to give sb. ～ treatment** *or* **therapy** 给某人进行电休克治疗

electroshock therapy, electroshock treatment *ns* [u] 电休克疗法

electrostatic /ɪˌlektrəʊˈstætɪk/ *adj* 静电的

electrostatics /ɪˌlektrəʊˈstætɪks/ *npl + v sing* 静电学

electrosurgery /ɪˌlektrəʊˈsɜːdʒəri/ *n* [u] 电外科

electrotechnology /ɪˌlektrəʊtekˈnɒlədʒi/ *n* [u] 电工学

electrotherapist /ɪˌlektrəʊˈθerəpɪst/ **▸p. 409** *n* 电疗医师

electrotherapy /ɪˌlektrəʊˈθerəpi/ *n* [u] 电疗

elegance /ˈelɪɡəns/ *n* [u] 1 (gracefulness) 优雅 2 (stylishness) 雅致 3 (of solution, proof) 简明

elegant /ˈelɪɡənt/ *adj* 1 (graceful, refined) 优雅的 ‹*movement, walk*›; 典雅的 ‹*design, piece of furniture, speech, prose*› 2 (stylish, fashionable) 高雅的 ‹*woman, circles, manners, society*›; 雅致的 ‹*dress*› 3 (neat) 简明的 ‹*solution, proof*›

elegantly /ˈelɪɡəntli/ *adv* 优雅地 ‹*walk, move*›; 雅致地 ‹*dress*›; 典雅地 ‹*write, prove, designed, furnished*›

elegiac /ˌelɪˈdʒaɪək/ *adj* 1 Literat (relating to an elegy) 挽歌的; (characteristic of an elegy) 挽歌体的 2 (mournful) 哀悼的; **the mood of the poem is ~** 这首诗的基调很伤感

elegy /ˈelədʒi/ *n* 1 Literat 挽歌 2 fig (lament) 悼文

element /ˈelɪmənt/ *n* 1 (constituent, characteristic part) 基本部分; **there are four ~s to the proposal** 本提案有四部分; **this controversy has all the ~s of an international crisis** 这一争端是非常典型的国际危机 2 (factor) 因素; **the time ~** 时间因素; **the key ~ in his success** 他获得成功的关键因素 3 (small part) 少量; **there was an ~ of truth in what she said** 她说的有点道理 4 + *v sing or pl* (constituent group) 一组; **the disruptive ~(s) in the class** 班上的一伙捣蛋分子 5 **elements** *pl* (rudiments) 基本原理; **the E~s of English Grammar** 英语语法入门 6 Chem 元素 7 (air, water etc.) 要素; **the four ~s** 四大要素 [即土、空气、水、火]; **to be in/out of one's ~** fig 适得其所/不得其所 8 **the elements** (weather) 恶劣天气; **to be exposed to the ~s** 经受风吹雨打; **to brave the ~s** hum 顶风冒雨 9 Elec 电热丝

elemental /ˌelɪˈmentl/ *adj* 1 (embodying the powers of nature) 自然力的; (strong) 强烈的; (primitive) 原始的; **the ~ fury of the storm** 暴风雨的肆虐; **~ passions** 强烈的感情; **~ drives** 原始的冲动 2 (fundamental) 基本的 ‹*truth, knowledge*› 3 Chem 元素的 ‹*form, state*›

elementary /ˌelɪˈmentri/ *adj* 1 (simple) 简单的 ‹*notion, principle, task, mistake*› 2 (rudimentary, intended for beginners) 初级的 ‹*class, level, student, arithmetic*› 3 esp Amer Sch 小学的 4 (basic, fundamental) 基本的

elementary: ~ particle *n* 基本粒子; **~ school** *n* Amer, Can 小学

elephant /ˈelɪfənt/ *n* (*pl* ~ *or* ~**s**) 大象

elephantine /ˌelɪˈfæntaɪn/ *adj* (huge) 巨大的; (heavy and clumsy) 笨重的

elevate /ˈelɪveɪt/ *vt* 1 lit (raise physically) 抬起 2 fig (morally, intellectually) 提高; **~ one's mind** 提高修养; **~ one's soul** 提升境界; **suffering ~s the spirit** 苦难可以磨炼意志 3 fig (cheer) 使…高昂 ‹*spirits*› 4 (in rank, status) 提升; **the college has been ~d to the status of a university** 该学院已经升格为大学; **to ~ sb. to the status of a star** 把某人捧为明星

elevated /ˈelɪveɪtɪd/ *adj* 1 (raised physically) 高的; **the house is in an ~ position** 这栋房子地势较高 2 (morally, intellectually) 高尚的 3 (in rank) 职位高的 4 (formal) 严肃的 ‹*style, language*›

elevated: ~ highway *n* Amer 高架公路; **~ railroad** *n* Amer 高架铁路

elevating /ˈelɪˌveɪtɪŋ/ *adj* 令人向上的 ‹*literature, experience, pursuit*›; **it is ~ to do sth.** 做某事可以陶冶情操

elevation /ˌelɪˈveɪʃn/ *n* 1 [u] (of celestial object, gun) 仰角; **the ~ of a star above the horizon** 恒星相对地平线的仰角 2 [c] (height) 海拔; **the city is at an ~ of 200 metres** 该城市海拔200米 3 [u] (act of raising) 抬起 4 [c] (high place) 高地 5 [u] (of mind, soul) 提高 6 [u] (of thought, spirit) 高尚 7 [u] (in rank, status) 提升 8 [c] Archit (facade) 立面; (drawing) 立面图

elevator /ˈelɪveɪtə(r)/ *n* 1 Amer (lift) 电梯 2 (hoist) 起重机 3 esp Amer (granary) 粮库 4 (of aircraft) 升降舵

eleven /ɪˈlevn/ **▸p. 15, p. 521, p. 831**

A *n* 1 (number, quantity) 十一 2 (in time) 11 点钟; **at ~ (o'clock)** 在 11 点 3 (in age) 11岁 4 + *v sing or pl* Sport 11 人队; **the football ~** 足球队; **to play for the first ~** 入选首发阵容

B *adj* 1 (in number) 十一的; **~ metres** 11 米; **~ paintings** 11 张画; **~ dogs** 11 只狗 2 (in age) 11 岁的; **to be ~ (years old)** 11 岁大; **to be over/under ~** 超过/不到 11 岁 3 (in series) 第十一的; **size/number ~** 11 码/号

eleven-plus *n* [u] Brit **the ~ (examination)** 十一岁儿童入学考试 [英国旧时举行的升中学甄别考试]

elevenses /ɪˈlevnzɪz/ *npl* Brit colloq 午前茶点

eleventh /ɪˈlevnθ/ **▸p. 181, p. 521**

A *n* 1 (in sequence) 第十一个 2 (in date) 11 日 3 (fraction) 十一分之一

B *adj* 1 (in sequence) 第十一的 2 (in name, title) 十一; **Louis the E~** 路易十一 3 (as fraction) 十一分之一的

C *adv* 1 (eleventhly) 第十一 2 (in eleventh position) 居第十一位

eleventh hour

A *n* 最后时刻; **at the ~** 在最后一刻; **to leave sth. to the ~** 把某事放到最后

B **eleventh-hour** *modif* 最后一刻的 ‹*decision, agreement*›

elf /elf/ *n* (*pl* **elves** /elvz/) 小精灵

elfin /ˈelfɪn/ *adj* 1 (elf-like) 小巧玲珑的 ‹*figure, features*›; 活泼淘气的 ‹*charm, smile*› 2 (relating to elves) 小精灵的 ‹*creature, laughter*›

elicit /ɪˈlɪsɪt/ *vt* 引出; **to ~ sth. from sb.** 从某人处诱出某物; **to ~ a response from sb.** 引导某人作出答复

elide /ɪˈlaɪd/ *vt* 省略 ‹*syllable, vowel*›

eligibility /ˌelɪdʒəˈbɪləti/ *n* [u] 资格; **sb.'s ~ to do sth./for sth.** 某人做某事/在某事上的资格

eligible /ˈelɪdʒəbl/ *adj* 1 (qualified, entitled) 有资格的; **to be ~ for sth./to do sth.** 有资格做某事; **he is ~ to vote** 他有投票资格 2 (desirable, marriageable) 合意的 ‹*bachelor, young man*›

eliminate /ɪˈlɪmɪneɪt/ *vt* 1 (omit from consideration) 排除 ‹*possibility, hypothesis, suspect*› 2 (eradicate) 消除 ‹*error, risk, waste, unnecessary expenditure*›; 消灭 ‹*disease*›; **to ~ slang words from an essay** 删除文章中的俚语 3 (kill) 除掉 ‹*enemy, opponent, rival*› 4 (from competition) 淘汰 5 Physiol (expel) 排出

elimination /ɪˌlɪmɪˈneɪʃn/ *n* [u] 1 (of possibility, hypothesis, suspect, etc.) 排除; **by a process of ~** 通过筛除 2 (of error, risk, waste, unnecessary expenditure) 消除; (of disease) 消灭 3 (of enemy, opponent, rival) 除掉 4 (of team, competitor, candidate) 淘汰 5 Physiol (of waste matter) 排出

elision /ɪˈlɪʒn/ *n* [u] 省音

elite /eɪˈliːt/

A *n + v sing or pl* 社会精英; **the ruling ~** 统治精英

B *adj* 高层次的 ‹*team, group*›; 精锐的 ‹*troops, corps*›; 上等的 ‹*restaurant, country club*›

élitism /eɪˈliːtɪzəm/ *n* [u] usu pej (of belief, attitude, behaviour) 精英主义; (rule by élites) 精英统治

élitist /eɪˈliːtɪst/

A *adj* usu pej (relating to élitism) 精英主义的; (snobbish) 自视甚高的 ‹*views, attitude, system, art*›

B *n* 精英主义者

elixir /ɪˈlɪksɪə(r)/ *n* (magical potion) 灵丹妙药; **the ~ of life** 长生不老药; **I have no magic ~ for solving the country's economic problems** fig (magical solution) 我没有解决国家经济问题的灵丹妙药

Elizabeth /ɪˈlɪzəbəθ/ *pr n* 伊丽莎白 [女性名及女王名]

Elizabethan /ɪˌlɪzəˈbiːθən/

A *adj* 伊丽莎白女王一世的 ‹*era, period*›; 伊丽莎白女王一世时代的 ‹*England, poetry, dress*›

B *n* 伊丽莎白女王一世时代的人

elk /elk/ *n* (*pl* ~ *or* ~**s**) 1 (European, Asian) 驼鹿 2 Amer (wapiti) 赤鹿

ellipse /ɪˈlɪps/ *n* 椭圆

ellipsis /ɪˈlɪpsɪs/ *n* (*pl* **ellipses** /ɪˈlipsiːz/) 1 Ling 省略 2 Print 省略号

ellipsoid /ɪˈlɪpsɔɪd/

A *n* 椭球

B (*also* **ellipsoidal** /ɪˌlɪpˈsɔɪdl/) *adj* 椭球的

elliptic /ɪˈlɪptɪk/ *adj* = **elliptical 1**

elliptical /ɪˈlɪptɪkl/ *adj* 1 Math, Astron (relating to an ellipse) 椭圆的; (having the form of an ellipse) 椭圆形的 2 Ling 省略的 3 (difficult to understand) 晦涩的 ‹*comment, allusion, clue*›

> **Ellis Island**
>
> 埃利斯岛。美国纽约曼哈顿外的一座小岛，与自由女神像（**▸the Statue of Liberty**）隔水相望。1892-1943 年间是美国主要的移民检查站。曾有 2000 多万移民在此处停留，等待移民局检查通过，以实现自己的美国梦。也有些人被拒入境，此岛因而成为许多人的"伤心岛"（Island of Tears）。1954 年关闭。后经大规模翻修，建成移民博物馆（Immigration Museum），1990 年开放。埃利斯岛是美国移民历史的象征，是自由女神像国家纪念碑（Statue of Liberty National Monument）的一部分。

elm /elm/ *n* 1 [c] (tree) 榆树 2 [u] (wood) 榆木

elocution /ˌeləˈkjuːʃn/ *n* [u] 演讲技巧

elongate /ˈiːlɒŋɡeɪt, Amer ɪˈlɔːŋ-/

A *vt* 使变长; **if you ~ a circle, you get an ellipse** 把圆拉长就得到椭圆

B *vi* 变长

elongated /ˈiːlɒŋɡeɪtɪd, Amer ɪˈlɔːŋ-/ *adj* 细长的

elongation /ˌiːlɒŋˈɡeɪʃən/ *n* [u] (act, process) 拉长; (amount of extension) 延长部分

elope /ɪˈləʊp/ *vi* 私奔

elopement /ɪˈləʊpmənt/ *n* [u] 私奔

eloquence /ˈeləkwəns/ *n* [u] 1 (of speaker, speech, style) 雄辩 2 (of gesture, silence, smile) 传神达意 3 (art of rhetoric) 修辞

eloquent /ˈeləkwənt/ *adj* 1 (fluent and persuasive) 雄辩的 ‹*speaker, speech, style*› 2 (expressive) 传神达意的 ‹*gesture, silence*›; **an ~ smile** 意味深长的微笑

eloquently /ˈeləkwəntli/ *adv* 1 (fluently and persuasively) 雄辩地 ‹*speak, argue, express*› 2 (expressively) 传神达意地

El Salvador /ˌel ˈsælvədɔː(r)/ *pr n* 萨尔瓦多

else /els/

A *adv* 1 (differently) 其他; **nobody/nothing ~** 没有别人/其他事物; **she's like no one ~** 她与众不同; **why can't you be like everyone ~?** 你为什么不能和大家一样呢？; **what ~ did he tell you?** 他还告诉了你什么？; **if all ~ fails, we can make a run for it** 如果别的都不行，我们可以逃跑 2 (in addition) 另外; **who ~ is coming?** 还有谁要来？; **there's not much ~ left to say** 没什么别的话可说;

if nothing ~, it should be amusing 即便没别的优点，它也应该是有趣的；▸ something A1, somewhere A1
B **or else** *conj phr* **1** (if not) 要不然；**do what you're told, or ~!** 要你干什么你就干什么，不然的话，哼！ **2** (alternatively) 或者；**either they didn't hear, or ~ they're out** 他们要么没听见，要么出去了

elsewhere /ˌelsˈweə(r)/
A *adv* (in another place) 在别处；(to another place) 到别处；(from another place) 从别处；**~ in China** 在中国其他地方
B *pron* 别处；**goods imported from ~ than the EU** 从欧盟以外的地方进口的货物

ELT *abbr* = **English Language Teaching**

elucidate /ɪˈluːsɪdeɪt/ *vt, vi* 阐明

elucidation /ɪˌluːsɪˈdeɪʃn/ *n* [u] 阐明；**this point requires further ~** 这一点需要进一步说明

elude /ɪˈluːd/ *vt* **1** (escape) 避开 ‹*attacker*›；逃避 ‹*police, capture*› **2** (be beyond the reach of) 使达不到；**the cure for the common cold still ~s us** 我们仍然没有找到感冒的治疗方法；**sleep ~d her** 她失眠了 **3** (fail to be understood by) 不为…所理解；(fail to be remembered by) 不为…所记得；(not be noticed by) 不为…所注意；**her name ~s me** 我想不起她的名字

elusive /ɪˈluːsɪv/ *adj* **1** (difficult to get hold of) 难以抓住的 ‹*criminal, fugitive, prey*›；难以找到的 ‹*businessman, official, celebrity*› **2** (difficult to attain) 难以获得的 ‹*prize, victory*›；难以实现的 ‹*goal*› **3** (difficult to define) 难以表述的 ‹*concept, quality*› **4** (difficult to remember) 难记的 ‹*thought, word, name*›

elusiveness /ɪˈluːsɪvnɪs/ *n* [u] **1** (of criminal, fugitive, prey) 难抓；(of businessman, official celebrity) 难找 **2** (of prize, victory) 难以获得；(of goal) 难以实现 **3** (of concept, quality) 难以理解；(of thought, word, name) 难以记住

elver /ˈelvə(r)/ *n* 幼鳗

elves /elvz/ *pl* ▸ **elf**

em /em/ *n* 全身 [西文排版行长单位]

'em /əm/ *pron* colloq = **them**

emaciated /ɪˈmeɪsieɪtɪd/ *adj* 消瘦的

emaciation /ɪˌmeɪsɪˈeɪʃn/ *n* [u] 消瘦

email, e-mail /ˈiːmeɪl/
A *n* [c and u] 电子邮件；**to send sb. an ~** 给某人发一封电子邮件；**to be on ~** 能够收发电子邮件；**~ address** 电子邮件地址
B *vt* 用电子邮件发送 ‹*information*›；给…发电子邮件 ‹*person*›

emanate /ˈeməneɪt/
A *vi* **1** (issue) 散发；**the smell of burning was emanating from next door's garden** 焦味从隔壁的花园传来 **2** (originate) 发源；**these superstitions ~ from old legends** 这些迷信源自古老的传说
B *vt* 发出；**he ~s self-confidence** 他显得自信

emanation /ˌeməˈneɪʃn/ *n* **1** [c] (emission) 散发的东西；**volcanic ~s** 火山喷发物 **2** [u] (process) 散发；**the risk of radon gas ~** 氡气泄漏的风险

emancipate /ɪˈmænsɪpeɪt/ *vt* 解放 ‹*women, mind, slave*›；使…不受约束 ‹*attitudes*›

emancipated /ɪˈmænsɪpeɪtɪd/ *adj* 解放了的 ‹*slave, mind*›；**an ~ young woman** 一位思想开放的年轻女士

emancipation /ɪˌmænsɪˈpeɪʃn/ *n* [u] 解放

e-marketing /ˈiːˌmɑːkɪtɪŋ/ *n* [u] 电子营销

emasculate /ɪˈmæskjʊleɪt/ *vt* **1** lit (deprive of masculinity) 使无男子气 **2** fig (make weaker) 削弱 ‹*opposition, trade unions, local government*›

emasculation /ɪˌmæskjʊˈleɪʃn/ *n* [u] **1** lit (of man) 失去男子气 **2** fig (weakening of opposition, trade unions, government) 削弱

embalm /ɪmˈbɑːm/ *vt* 对…进行防腐处理 ‹*body, corpse*›

embalmer /ɪmˈbɑːmə(r)/ ▸ **p. 409** *n* 尸体防腐员

embalming /ɪmˈbɑːmɪŋ/ *n* [u] 尸体防腐处理

embankment /ɪmˈbæŋkmənt/ *n* **1** (carrying railway, road) 路堤 **2** (holding back water) 堤岸

embargo /ɪmˈbɑːɡəʊ/
A *n* **1** (ban on trade) 贸易禁令；**to place** *or* **impose an ~ on sb./sth.** 对某人/某物实行贸易禁运；**to lift an ~** 解除贸易禁令；**an arms/oil/trade ~** 武器/石油/贸易禁运 **2** fig (official ban) 官方禁令；**to be under an ~** 被官方禁止
B *vt* **1** (impose trade ban on) 禁止 ‹*trade*›；禁止…的贸易 ‹*goods*›；对…实行贸易禁运 ‹*country*› **2** (ban publication of) 正式禁止…的刊登 ‹*information, news story*›；正式禁止…的发行 ‹*newspaper*›

embark /ɪmˈbɑːk/
A *vi* **1** (board a ship) 上船；**to ~ on a ship** 上船；**to ~ for France** 乘船去法国 **2** (begin) **to ~ on** *or* **upon sth.** 开始某事；**to ~ on a life of crime** 走上犯罪道路；**to ~ on a war** 发动战争；**to ~ on a serious discussion** 开始认真讨论
B *vt* «*officials, stewardess*» 使…上船 ‹*passengers*›；使…装船 ‹*cars*›

embarkation /ˌembɑːˈkeɪʃn/ *n* [u] (of passengers) 上船；(of vehicles) 装船

embarked /ɪmˈbɑːkd/ *adj pred* **to be ~ on sth.** 着手做某事

embarrass /ɪmˈbærəs/ *vt* 使尴尬；**it ~es me to have to admit that ...** 我不得不承认…，这使我很难堪

embarrassed /ɪmˈbærəsd/ *adj* 尴尬的 ‹*person, silence*›；**to be ~ about sth./doing sth.** 因某事/做某事而尴尬；**to feel ~ about sth./doing sth.** 对某事/做某事感到尴尬；**financially ~** 经济拮据的

embarrassing /ɪmˈbærəsɪŋ/ *adj* 令人尴尬的；**an ~ situation** 难堪的处境

embarrassingly /ɪmˈbærəsɪŋli/ *adv* 令人尴尬地；**to be ~ frank** 直率得令人难堪

embarrassment /ɪmˈbærəsmənt/ *n* **1** [u] (feeling) 尴尬；**to cause sb. ~** 使某人难堪；**financial ~** euph 财政困难 **2** [c] (person) 令人尴尬的人；(action) 令人尴尬的行为；(event) 令人尴尬的事；**to be an ~ to sb./sth.** 令某人/某机构难堪；**he's an ~ to his family** 他让家人难堪；**his resignation comes as an ~ to the government** 他的辞职让政府陷入难堪境地；**an ~ of riches** 多得难以选择的好东西

embassy /ˈembəsi/ *n* 大使馆

embattled /ɪmˈbætld/ *adj* **1** (beset by problems) 处境艰难的 ‹*politician, official, government*› **2** (involved in a war) 卷入战争的 ‹*city, country*›；参战的 ‹*forces*›

embed /ɪmˈbed/ *vt* (*pres p etc.* **-dd-**) **1** lit (fix firmly and deeply) 把…嵌入 **2** fig (in the mind) 使被铭记；**to ~ itself in sb.'s memory** 深深印在某人的记忆中；**these attitudes are ~ded in our society** 这些看法在我们的社会中根深蒂固 **3** fig (incorporate) 使并入；**clues to the identity of the author are ~ded in the poem** 关于作者身份的线索暗含在这首诗中

embedded /ɪmˈbedɪd/ *adj* **1** Ling, Math 嵌入的 ‹*expression, formula*›；**to be ~ in** *or* **within sth.** 嵌在某物中；**an ~ clause** 嵌套式从句 **2** Journ, Mil **an ~ journalist** 随军记者

embellish /ɪmˈbelɪʃ/ *vt* **1** (decorate) 装饰 ‹*building*›；润色 ‹*manuscript*› **2** (exaggerate) 渲染

embellishment /ɪmˈbelɪʃmənt/ *n* [u and c] **1** (of object) 装饰 **2** (of rhetoric, literary style, handwriting) 润色 **3** (of piece of music, musical performance) 装饰音 **4** (of story, description, truth) 渲染

ember /ˈembə(r)/ *n* **1** lit (glowing coal, piece of wood) 余烬 **2** **embers** *pl* fig (remains) 剩余物；**the dying ~s of their love** 他们残存的爱

embezzle /ɪmˈbezl/ *vt* 盗用…的资金 ‹*company, charity*›；贪污 ‹*funds*›；**£10,000 had been ~d from the bank** 该银行被盗用了1万英镑

embezzlement /ɪmˈbezlmənt/ *n* [u] (act) 盗用；(crime) 贪污罪

embezzler /ɪmˈbezlə(r)/ *n* 贪污者

embitter /ɪmˈbɪtə(r)/ *vt* 使…怨愤 ‹*person*›；使…恶化 ‹*feelings, relationship, dispute*›

embittered /ɪmˈbɪtəd/ *adj* 怨愤的 ‹*person*›；令人苦恼的 ‹*feelings, relationship*›；**an ~ old man** 牢骚满腹的老人

emblazon /ɪmˈbleɪzn/ *vt* **1** (display conspicuously) 醒目地展示；**his name is ~ed across the front pages of the tabloids** 他的名字醒目地印在那些通俗小报的头版上 **2** Herald (decorate) 用纹章装饰；(inscribe) 把纹章刻在…上

emblem /ˈembləm/ *n* 徽章；**the national ~** 国徽；**the heart is an ~ of love** 心形是爱的象征

emblematic /ˌembləˈmætɪk/ *adj* **1** (concerning emblems) 徽章的 **2** (serving as an emblem, symbolic) 象征的；**the results of the survey are ~ of changes in society** 调查结果彰显了社会的变化

embodiment /ɪmˈbɒdɪmənt/ *n* **1** [c] (incarnation of quality, idea) 化身 **2** [u] (incorporation) 包括

embody /ɪmˈbɒdi/ *vt* **1** (symbolize) 象征 **2** (give tangible form to) 使具体化；**the architect embodied his revolutionary theories in the church building** 建筑师把自己的革新理论应用到这座教堂的建筑中 **3** (incorporate) 包括；**many new features are embodied in the latest locomotives** 最新款的机车具有许多新特点 **4** (legally incorporate) 收录；**laws that would ~ the aspirations of the people** 将体现人民愿望的法律

embolden /ɪmˈbəʊldən/ *vt* 使更有胆量；**to be ~ed by wine** 借酒壮胆

embolism /ˈembəlɪzəm/ *n* 栓塞

emboss /ɪmˈbɒs/ *vt* 在…上压印浮凸图案 ‹*metal, wallpaper, fabric*›；凸印 ‹*design, pattern*›

embossed /ɪmˈbɒst/ *adj* 压花的 ‹*metal, wallpaper, fabric*›；凸印的 ‹*design, pattern*›

embrace /ɪmˈbreɪs/
A *vt* **1** lit (hug) 拥抱 **2** fig (include) 包括；**the report ~d a wide range of issues** 这篇报告涉及的问题非常广泛；**her generosity ~s the whole neighbourhood** 她的慷慨惠及四邻 **3** fig (espouse, adopt) 信奉 ‹*religion, cause, policy*› **4** fig (welcome) 欣然接受 ‹*offer, opportunity*›；**to ~ the challenge** 迎接挑战
B *vi* 互相拥抱
C *n* 拥抱；**to hold sb. in a warm ~** 热烈拥抱某人

embrasure /ɪmˈbreɪʒə(r)/ *n* **1** (for door) 斜面门洞；(for window) 斜面窗洞 **2** (for gun) 射击孔

embrocation /ˌembrəˈkeɪʃn/ *n* 止疼擦剂

embroider /ɪmˈbrɔɪdə(r)/
A *vt* **1** lit 在…上刺绣 ‹*dress, cloth*›；绣 ‹*pattern, lettering*› **2** fig 渲染 ‹*story, facts, truth*›
B *vi* **1** lit 刺绣 **2** fig 渲染；**to ~ on sth.** 对某事添枝加叶

embroidered /ɪmˈbrɔɪdəd/ *adj* 有刺绣的 ‹*cloth*›；绣上的 ‹*pattern, lettering*›

embroidery /ɪmˈbrɔɪdəri/ *n* [u] **1** (art) 刺绣 **2** (cloth) 刺绣品

embroidery: ~ frame *n* 绣框；**~ silk** *n* [u and c] 绣花丝线；**~ thread** *n* [u and c] 刺绣线

embroil /ɪmˈbrɔɪl/ *vt* 使卷入；**to ~ sb. with sb.** 使某人与某人发生纠纷；**to become ~ed in sth.** 卷入某事；**he was ~ed in a dispute with his colleague** 他与同事发生了争执

embryo /ˈembriəʊ/ *n* 1 Biol 胚胎 2 fig 萌芽状态; **in ~** 在萌芽时期; **my novel is still in ~** 我的小说还在酝酿之中

embryological /ˌembriəˈlɒdʒɪkl/ *adj* 胚胎学的

embryologist /ˌembrɪˈɒlədʒɪst/ ▸**p. 409** *n* 胚胎学家

embryology /ˌembrɪˈɒlədʒi/ *n* [u] 胚胎学

embryonic /ˌembrɪˈɒnɪk/ *adj* 1 Biol 胚胎的 2 fig 萌芽期的; **to be in the ~ stages of sth.** 处于某事的酝酿阶段; **an ~ plan** 酝酿中的计划

emcee /ˌemˈsiː/ Amer
A *n* 司仪
B *vt* 主持 ‹*show, event*›

em dash /ˈem dæʃ/ *n* = **em rule**

emend /ɪˈmend/ *vt* (correct) 校订; (make alterations in) 修改

emendation /ˌiːmenˈdeɪʃn/ *n* 1 [c] (correction) 校订的内容; (alteration) 修改意见 2 [u] (correcting) 校订; (altering) 修改

emerald /ˈemərəld/ ▸**p. 134**
A *n* 1 [c and u] (stone) 绿宝石 2 [u] (colour) **~ (green)** 翡翠绿
B *adj* 1 *attrib* (made of emeralds) 绿宝石制的 2 (in colour) 翡翠绿的

Emerald Isle *n* **the ~** 绿宝石岛［爱尔兰的别称］

emerge /ɪˈmɜːdʒ/ *vi* 1 lit (come out) 出现; (come up) 浮现; **the moon ~d from behind a cloud** 月亮从云朵后钻出来; **hours passed and still the diver did not ~** 几个小时过去了，潜水员还是没有浮出水面 2 fig (survive, recover from) 摆脱出来; **to ~ from an ordeal** 摆脱磨难; **to ~ from sth. as sth.** 作为某物从某事中兴起; **the USSR ~d from World War Two as a major world power** 苏联在第二次世界大战后崛起，成为世界强国 3 fig (become apparent) 出现; **no new ideas ~d from the talks** 这些谈话没有产生新的想法; **it ~s from his statement that ...** 他的陈述表明… 4 fig (come into existence) 形成; (become more prominent) 兴起; **nuclear weapons have ~d as a threat to the existence of the human race** 核武器的出现已经对人类的生存构成了威胁

emergence /ɪˈmɜːdʒəns/ *n* [u] 1 (of truth, ideas, problem) 出现 2 (of religion, movement, literary genre) 形成

emergency /ɪˈmɜːdʒənsi/ *n* [u and c] 1 (crisis) 紧急情况; **in an ~, in case of ~** 在紧急情况下; **in times of ~** 在非常时刻; **to take ~ measures** 采取紧急措施 2 Pol 紧急状态; **to declare a state of ~** 宣布进入紧急状态 3 (hospital case) 急症; **an ~ operation** 急诊手术

emergency: ~ aid *n* [u] 紧急援助; **~ ambulance service** *n* 急救服务; **~ blanket** *n* 急救毯; **~ call** *n* 应急电话; **~ case** *n* 急诊病人; **~ centre** *n* 紧急救援中心; **~ cord** *n* (on train) 紧急制动闸; **~ cover** *n* [u] 紧急救援; **~ exit** *n* 紧急出口; **~ landing** *n* 紧急着陆; **~ laws** *npl* 应急法规; **~ medical service** *n* Amer 急救服务; **~ number** *n* 应急号码; **~ powers** *npl* [非常时期政府的] 应急权力; **~ rations** *npl* 应急食品; **~ room** *n* Amer **= ~ ward**; **~ service** *n* 1 *usu pl* (public organization) **the ~ services** 应急服务机构; 2 (private facility) 应急设施; **~ stop** *n* 紧急停车; **to make** *or* **do an ~ stop** 紧急停车; **~ supplies** *npl* 应急物资; **~ surgery** *n* [u] 急诊手术; **~ switch** *n* 紧急开关; **~ ward** *n* 急诊室; **~ worker** *n* 急救人员

emergent /ɪˈmɜːdʒənt/ *adj* 新兴的 ‹*nation, industry, technology*›; 新生的 ‹*literary form*›

emerging /ɪˈmɜːdʒɪŋ/ *adj* = **emergent**

emerging market *n* [发展中国家的] 新兴市场

emeritus /ɪˈmerɪtəs/ *adj* 荣誉退休的; **an ~ professor of microbiology** 荣誉退休的微生物学教授; **the National Gallery's director ~** 荣誉退休的国家美术馆馆长

emery /ˈeməri/ *n* [u] 金刚砂

emery: ~ board *n* 指甲砂锉; **~ cloth** *n* 砂布; **~ paper** *n* 砂纸

emetic /ɪˈmetɪk/
A *n* 催吐剂
B *adj* 催吐的

emigrant /ˈemɪɡrənt/ *n* 移民; **an ~ family/worker** 移居外国的家庭/劳动者

emigrate /ˈemɪɡreɪt/ *vi* 移居国外

emigration /ˌemɪˈɡreɪʃn/ *n* [u] 移居外国

émigré /ˈemɪɡreɪ, Amer ˌemɪˈɡreɪ/ *n* [尤指因政治原因移居外国的] 流亡者

eminence /ˈemɪnəns/ *n* 1 [u] (distinction) 显赫; (fame) 著名 2 [c] (form of address) 最可敬的枢机 [天主教中对枢机主教的尊称]; **Your/His E~** 最可敬的枢机 3 [c] (hill) 山丘; (height) 高地

eminent /ˈemɪnənt/ *adj* 1 (distinguished) 名声显赫的 ‹*scholar, scientist, politician*› 2 (evident) 杰出的 ‹*qualities, virtues, achievements*›

eminently /ˈemɪnəntli/ *adv* 特别 ‹*sensible, qualified, practical*›

emir /eˈmɪə(r)/ *n* 埃米尔 [对伊斯兰教领袖的尊称]

emirate /ˈemɪərəɪt/ *n* 1 (lands) 埃米尔的管辖地 2 (rank) 埃米尔的职位 3 (reign) 埃米尔的统治

emissary /ˈemɪsəri/ *n* 密使

emission /ɪˈmɪʃn/ *n* 1 [c] (substance) 排放物; **noxious ~s from factory chimneys** 工厂烟囱排放的有害气体 2 [u] (act of emitting gases, smoke) 排放; (light, heat, sound, radiation) 发出; **~ of sth. from sth.** 从某物排放出某物

emission spectrum *n* 发射光谱

emissions trading *n* [u] 排放交易

emit /ɪˈmɪt/ *vt* 1 (discharge) 散发 ‹*smell, gas, vapour*›; 排出 ‹*smoke, fumes*›; 喷出 ‹*lava, ashes, dust*› 2 (radiate) 射出 ‹*light, heat, radiation, radio waves*› 3 (utter) 发出 ‹*sound, cry*›

emitter /ɪˈmɪtə(r)/ *n* (of gas) 排放者; (of radiation) 发射体

Emmy /ˈemi/ *n* (*pl* **~s**) 艾美奖 [美国每年颁发给优秀电视节目或电视演员的奖项]

emollient /ɪˈmɒlɪənt/
A *adj* 1 (conciliatory) 安慰性的 ‹*words, gesture*›; 使平静的 ‹*mood*› 2 (softening) 润肤的; **~ cream/ointment/effect** 润肤霜/润肤膏/润肤效果
B *n* [c and u] 润肤剂

emoluments /ɪˈmɒljʊmənts/ *npl* formal (salary) 薪水; (fee) 酬金

e-money /ˈiːˌmʌni/ *n* [u] = **electronic money**

emote /ɪˈməʊt/ *vi* 夸张地表现情感

emoticon /ɪˈməʊtɪkɒn, -ˈmɒtɪ-/ *n* 表情符号

emotion /ɪˈməʊʃn/ *n* 1 [c] (reaction such as anger, joy, fear) 情绪; (feeling such as love, hate, jealousy) 情感 2 [u] (passion as opposed to reason) 冲动 3 [u] (strong feeling) 激情

emotional /ɪˈməʊʃənl/ *adj* 1 Psych 情感的 ‹*problems, need, support*›; 情绪的 ‹*stability*› 2 (distressed) 沮丧的 ‹*person*›; 哀伤的 ‹*mood, response*›; 伤感的 ‹*farewell, reunion*› 3 (passionate) 令人激动的 ‹*appeal, speech*›; 感人的 ‹*music, film*›; 冲动的 ‹*person*›; **to get ~ about sth.** 因某事物变得情绪激动

emotionalism /ɪˈməʊʃənəlɪzəm/ *n* [u] 感情主义

emotionally /ɪˈməʊʃənəli/ *adv* 1 Psych (in connection with emotions) 情绪上; **~ fragile/unstable/deprived** 情感脆弱/不稳定/失落的 2 (governed by emotions instead of reason) 感情上; **to be ~ involved with sb.** 对某人动情 3 (passionately) 激动地 ‹*speak, embrace, thank*›; **an ~ worded tribute** 措词动人的赞扬

emotionally: ~ charged *adj* 充满激情的; **~ disturbed** *adj* 情绪紊乱的

emotionless /ɪˈməʊʃnlɪs/ *adj* 冷漠的

emotionlessly /ɪˈməʊʃnlɪsli/ *adv* 冷漠地

emotive /ɪˈməʊtɪv/ *adj* 有感染力的 ‹*word, term*›; 引起争论的 ‹*issue*›

empathize /ˈempəθaɪz/ *vi* 有同感; **to ~ with sb./sth.** 同情某人/对某事产生共鸣

empathy /ˈempəθi/ *n* [u] 同感; **to feel** *or* **have ~ with sb./sth.** 与…产生同感

emperor /ˈempərə(r)/ *n* 皇帝

emperor penguin *n* 帝企鹅

emphasis /ˈemfəsɪs/ *n* (*pl* **emphases** /ˈemfəsiːz/) 1 [u and c] (importance) 重要性; **to lay** *or* **place** *or* **put the ~ on sth.** 重视某事物; **to shift the ~ from sth. to sth.** 将重点从某事物转移到某事物上 2 [u and c] (vocal stress) 重音 3 [u] (urgency) 加重语气; **to speak with ~** 加重语气说话

emphasize /ˈemfəsaɪz/ *vt* 1 (give importance to) 强调; **to ~ that ...** 强调说…; **to ~ the importance of sth.** 强调某事物的重要性 2 (stress vocally) 重读 ‹*word, syllable*› 3 (highlight) 突出 ‹*feature, aspect, characteristic*›

emphatic /ɪmˈfætɪk/ *adj* 1 (clear) 明确坚决的 ‹*statement, gesture*›; **an ~ refusal/denial** 断然的拒绝/否认 2 (insistent, firm) 坚定的 ‹*person, voice, tone*›; **to be ~ about sth.** 强调某事物; **to be ~ that ...** 强调说… 3 (unambiguous) 明显的 ‹*victory, defeat*› 4 Ling (with emphasis) 重读的 ‹*pronoun, form, use*›

emphatically /ɪmˈfætɪkli/ *adv* 1 (vehemently) 强调地 ‹*speak, insist*›; 断然地 ‹*refuse, deny*› 2 (undeniably) 毫无疑问地 ‹*win, defeat*› 3 Ling (with emphasis) 重读地 ‹*use, pronounce*›

emphysema /ˌemfɪˈsiːmə/ ▸**p. 377** *n* [u] 肺气肿

empire /ˈempaɪə(r)/ *n* 1 (country or countries) 帝国 2 (commercial organization) 大企业 3 (petty domain of bureaucrat) 支配领域

empire: ~-builder *n* pej 扩张势力者; **~-building** *n* [u] pej 势力扩张

empirical /ɪmˈpɪrɪkl/ *adj* 以经验为依据的; **~ evidence/research/method** 实践经验的证据/以经验为基础的研究/经验主义的方法

empirically /ɪmˈpɪrɪkli/ *adv* 以经验为依据地; **~ tested/validated** 经实践检验的/证实的

empiricism /ɪmˈpɪrɪsɪzəm/ *n* [u] 经验主义

empiricist /ɪmˈpɪrɪsɪst/
A *n* 经验主义者
B *adj* 经验主义的

emplacement /ɪmˈpleɪsmənt/ *n* 炮台

employ /ɪmˈplɔɪ/
A *vt* 1 (give paid work to) 雇用; **to ~ sb. as sth.** 雇用某人任某职 2 (use) 使用 ‹*method, technique, equipment*›; 利用 ‹*resources, intelligence*›; **to ~ sth. as sth.** 将某物用作某物; **to ~ sth. to do sth.** 用某物做某事
B *n* [u] formal **in sb.'s ~** 受雇于某人

employable /ɪmˈplɔɪəbl/ *adj* 适宜雇用的

employed /ɪmˈplɔɪd/ *adj* 1 (in work) 有工作的 2 *pred* (busy) 忙碌的; **to be ~ (in) doing sth.** 忙于做某事

employee /ˌemplɔɪˈiː, ɪmˈplɔiː/ *n* 雇员

employer /ɪmˈplɔɪə(r)/ *n* 雇主

employment /ɪmˈplɔɪmənt/ *n* [u] 1 (state of being employed) 受雇; (action of employing sb.) 雇用; **to take up ~** 开始工作; **to seek/find ~** 找/找到工作; **to be in/without ~** 在职/失业; **conditions/place of ~** 雇用条件/工作地点; **the ~ of sb. as sth./to do sth.** 某人受雇任某职/做某事 2 (use) 运用; **~ of sth. as sth./to do sth.** 把某物用作某物/用某物做某事 3 (area of public policy) 就业; **~ law/policy** 就业法/政策

employment: ~ **agency** *n* 职业介绍所; ~ **contract** *n* 劳动合同; **E~ Minister, E~ Secretary** *ns* 劳工部长; ~ **office** *n* [政府] 就业办公室; ~ **statistics** *npl* 就业统计

emporium /ɪm'pɔːrɪəm/ *n* (*pl* ~**s** *or* **emporia** /ɪm'pɔːrɪə/) formal 大百货商场

empower /ɪm'paʊə(r)/ *vt* **1** (give legal rights to) 授权; **to ~ sb. to do sth.** 授权某人做某事; **to be ~ed to do sth.** 有权做某事 **2** (make feel stronger) 增加…的自主权; **to feel ~ed** 感到有更多的自主权

empowering /ɪm'paʊərɪŋ/ *adj* 给予自主权的

empowerment /ɪm'paʊəmənt/ *n* **1** (giving of power to) 授权 **2** (power to control lives) 增加信心和能力

empress /'emprɪs/ *n* **1** (wife of emperor) 皇后 **2** (female emperor) 女皇

emptiness /'emptɪnɪs/ *n* [u] **1** (desertedness) 空旷 **2** (insincerity, meaninglessness) 无意义 **3** (purposelessness) 空虚

empty /'empti/

A *adj* **1** (lacking contents) 空的 ‹*container, vehicle, shelf*›; 空白的 ‹*page*›; 未放物品的 ‹*table*›; 空着的 ‹*hand(s)*›; **to be ~ of sth.** 没有某物 **2** (lacking people) 无人的 ‹*room, building, street*›; 未载人的 ‹*vehicle, plane, boat*›; 空缺的 ‹*post*›; 无人做的 ‹*job*›; **to stand ~** «*house, office*» 空无一人 **3** (lacking food) 饿的; **on an ~ stomach** 空着肚子 **4** (insincere, meaningless) 空洞的 ‹*words, argument, promises*›; 虚张声势的 ‹*threats*›; 不现实的 ‹*dreams*›; ~ **of meaning** 没有意义 **5** (purposeless) 空虚的 ‹*life*›; 空闲的 ‹*hours, days, weeks*› **6** *pred* (exhausted) 疲乏的; **to feel ~** 感觉疲乏

B *vt* **1** (remove contents) 清空 ‹*container, pool, cupboard*›; 掏空 ‹*envelope, purse, pocket*›; 腾空 ‹*vehicle, ship*› **2** (pour) 倒空; **to ~ sth. into/on to sth.** 把…全部倒进某物里/倒在某物上 ‹*contents, water, rubbish*› **3** (clear) 将…清场 ‹*building, cinema, shop, street, bus*›

C *vi* **1** (discharge contents) «*container, tank, bin*» 腾空 **2** (pour out) 倒空; **to ~ into/on to sth.** «*contents, sand, rubbish*» 全部倒入某物/倒在某物上 **3** (flow) 流入; **to ~ into sth.** «*river, stream, water*» 流入某处 **4** (be vacated) «*building, theatre, shop, street, bus*» 被清场

D empties *npl* Brit colloq (bottles) 空瓶; (glasses) 空杯

Phrasal verb

• **empty out**

A *vt* [~ **out sth.**, ~ **sth. out**] (pour out) 倒空; (clear) 清空; **to ~ water out of one's boots** 把水从靴子里倒出来; **to ~ one's pockets out on to the table** 把衣袋里的东西全掏到桌子上

B *vi* **1** (leave a place) «*people*» 全部撤离 **2** (pour out of a container) «*contents*» 倒出; **the sand emptied out of the bag** 沙子从袋子里倒了出来 **3** (be vacated) «*building, bus*» 被清场

empty: ~**-handed** *adj pred* 空手的; **to come back ~-handed** 两手空空地回来; ~**-headed** *adj* 没头脑的

em rule /'em ruːl/ *n* 长破折号

EMS *abbr* **1** = **European Monetary System** **2** = **emergency medical service**

EMU *abbr* **1** = **Economic and Monetary Union** **2** = **European Monetary Union**

emu /'iːmjuː/ *n* 鸸鹋 [产于澳大利亚的一种不能飞的大型鸟]

emulate /'emjʊleɪt/ *vt* **1** formal (imitate) 模仿 ‹*performance, style, behaviour*› **2** (compete with) 同…竞争 ‹*rival*› **3** Comput 仿真

emulation /ˌemjʊ'leɪʃn/ *n* **1** 竞赛; **in ~ of sb./sth.** 以赶超某人/某物 **2** Comput 仿真

emulator /'emjʊleɪtə(r)/ *n* (software) 仿真程序; (hardware) 仿真器

emulsifier /ɪ'mʌlsɪfaɪə(r)/ *n* 乳化剂

emulsify /ɪ'mʌlsɪfaɪ/

A *vi* «*liquid, oil, starch*» 乳化

B *vt* 使…乳化 ‹*liquid, oil, starch*›

emulsion /ɪ'mʌlʃn/ *n* **1** Chem 乳化剂 **2** Phot 感光乳剂 **3** (paint) ~ **(paint)** 乳胶漆

en /en/ *n* 对开 [西文排版行长单位]

enable /ɪ'neɪbl/ *vt* **1** (give opportunity to) 使有机会; (give right to) 授权给; **to ~ sb. to do sth.** 使某人有机会做某事 **2** (facilitate) 使能够; **to ~ sb. to do sth.** 使某人有能力做某事 **3** Comput (make operational) 激活

enact /ɪ'nækt/ *vt* **1** (perform) 扮演 ‹*role, part*›; 上演 ‹*drama, scene*›; 举行 ‹*ritual*› **2** (put into practice) 实施 ‹*idea, suggestion*› **3** (put into law) 通过 ‹*bill, law, decree*›

enactment /ɪ'næktmənt/ *n* [u] **1** (of play) 演出 **2** (putting into law) 通过

enamel /ɪ'næml/

A *n* **1** [u] (decorative/protective substance) 瓷釉; ~ **pottery/tiles/brooch** 搪瓷陶器/琉璃瓦/珐琅胸针 **2** [u] (of teeth) 珐琅质 **3** [u] (paint) ~ **paint** 瓷漆 **4** [c] (as artwork) 瓷釉工艺品

B *vt* (*pres p etc.* **-ll-** Brit, **-l-** Amer) 给…涂瓷釉

enamelled, Amer **enameled** /ɪ'næmld/ *adj* 上了瓷釉的

enamelling, Amer **enameling** /ɪ'næmlɪŋ/ *n* [u] (process) 涂瓷釉; (artwork) 搪瓷工艺品

enamel: ~ **painting** *n* [u] 搪瓷画; ~**ware** *n* [u] 搪瓷器具; ~**work** *n* [u] **1** (craft) 搪瓷工艺; **2** (result) 搪瓷工艺品

enamoured Brit, **enamored** Amer /ɪ'næməd/ *adj pred* **1** **to be ~ of** *or* **with sth./sb.** (fond of) 喜欢某事物/某人 **2** **to be ~ of** *or* **with sb.** (in love) 迷恋某人

en bloc /ˌɒn 'blɒk/ *adv* 一起; **they left the meeting ~** 他们集体退出了会议

enc. = **encl.**

encamp /ɪn'kæmp/ *vi* **1** Mil 扎营 **2** (temporarily base oneself) 暂住

encampment /ɪn'kæmpmənt/ *n* **1** Mil 驻扎地 **2** (for nomads) 营地 **3** (prehistoric settlement) [尤指铁器时代的] 山堡

encapsulate /ɪn'kæpsjʊleɪt/ *vt* **1** (summarize) 概括 ‹*period of history, philosophy*› **2** (include, incorporate) 包含 ‹*information, scene*›

encase /ɪn'keɪs/ *vt* 包住; **to ~ sth. in sth.** 用某物把某物包起来

encash /ɪn'kæʃ/ *vt* Brit 兑现 ‹*bond, insurance policy*›

encephalitis /enˌsefə'laɪtɪs, -ˌkef-/ *n* [u] 脑炎

encephalomyelitis /enˌsefələʊmaɪə'laɪtɪs, -ˌkef-/ *n* [u] 脑脊髓炎

enchant /ɪn'tʃɑːnt, Amer -'tʃænt/ *vt* **1** (delight) 使陶醉 **2** (cast spell on) «*magician, magic wand*» 对…施魔法 ‹*person, place, object*›

enchanted /ɪn'tʃɑːntɪd, Amer -'tʃæntɪd/ *adj* **1** (delighted) 狂喜的; **to be ~ at** *or* **with sth.** 对某事物着迷 **2** (under spell) 中了魔法的

enchanting /ɪn'tʃɑːntɪŋ, Amer -'tʃænt-/ *adj* 迷人的

enchantingly /ɪn'tʃɑːntɪŋli, Amer -'tʃænt-/ *adv* 令人陶醉地 ‹*sing, smile*›; **she is ~ beautiful** 她美丽动人

enchantment /ɪn'tʃɑːntmənt, Amer -'tʃænt-/ *n* **1** (delight) 狂喜 **2** (spell) 着魔

enchantress /ɪn'tʃɑːntrɪs, Amer -'tʃænt-/ *n* **1** (sorceress) 女巫 **2** (temptress) 诱惑人的女子

enchilada /ˌentʃɪ'lɑːdə/ *n* 辣椒肉馅玉米卷饼 [墨西哥食品]

encircle /ɪn'sɜːkl/ *vt* «*fence, trees, belt*» 围绕 ‹*area, building*›; «*troops, police, guards*» 包围 ‹*building, crowd, army*›; **to ~ sth./sb. in** *or* **within sth.** 将某物/某人包在某物里; **to ~ sth./sb. with/by sth.** 用某物将某物/某人环绕

encirclement /ɪn'sɜːklmənt/ *n* 围绕

encircling /ɪn'sɜːklɪŋ/ *adj attrib* 围绕的

encl. *abbr* **1** = **enclosed** 随函附上的 **2** = **enclosure 4**

enclave /'enkleɪv/ *n* 飞地 [区域内文化或民族不同的部分]

enclitic /en'klɪtɪk/

A *n* 非重读后接成分

B *adj* 非重读后接成分的

enclose /ɪn'kləʊz/ *vt* **1** (surround) 围绕; **to ~ sth. in/within sth.** 把某物围在某物里; **to ~ sth. with sth.** 用某物将某物围住 **2** (insert in letter) 随函附上; **please find ~d ...** 兹附上…请查收

enclosed /ɪn'kləʊzd/ *adj* 封闭的; **an ~ space/garden** 封闭的空间/园子

enclosed order *n* 与世隔绝的修道会

enclosure /ɪn'kləʊʒə(r)/ *n* **1** [c] (for livestock or racehorses) 围场; (for activity) 活动场地; (for people) 观众席 **2** [c] (barrier) 围篱 **3** [u] (containment) 围住 **4** [c] (with letter) 附件 **5** [u] Brit Hist (process of making private property) 圈地

encode /ɪn'kəʊd/ *vt* **1** (put into code) 把…译成密码; **to ~ sth. into/in sth.** 把…译成某物 ‹*message, sentence, information*› **2** Comput 把…编码 ‹*data, characters, symbols*› **3** Biol 为…编码 ‹*protein*›

encoder /ɪn'kəʊdə(r)/ *n* 编码器

encoding /ɪn'kəʊdɪŋ/ *n* **1** (of message) 译成密码 **2** Comput 编码

encompass /ɪn'kʌmpəs/ *vt* **1** (include) 包含 ‹*subjects, facts, department*› **2** (cover) 围绕 ‹*surface, area, land*›

encore /'ɒŋkɔː(r)/

A *n* 加演的节目; **to give** *or* **play an ~** 应观众要求加演一个节目; **to get** *or* **receive an ~** 被观众要求加演

B *excl* 再来一个

C *vt* 要求…加演 ‹*singer, orchestra, performer, band*›

encounter /ɪn'kaʊntə(r)/

A *vt* **1** (be faced with) 遭遇 ‹*difficulties, resistance, danger*› **2** (meet) 偶然碰到 ‹*person, friend*›

B *n* 邂逅; **a brief/chance ~** 匆匆邂逅/巧遇; **an ~ with the enemy** 与敌人的遭遇战; **an ~ with** hum 触犯 ‹*the law*›; 撞上 ‹*a lamppost*›

encounter group *n* 交心治疗小组

encourage /ɪn'kʌrɪdʒ/ *vt* **1** (support) 鼓励; **to ~ sb. to do sth.** 鼓励某人做某事; **to ~ sb. in sth.** 在某事上支持某人 **2** (incite) 怂恿; **don't ~ bad habits in a child** 别助长小孩养成不良习惯 **3** (foster) 促使; **regular watering ~s healthy roots to develop** 定时浇水有助长出健壮的根

encouragement /ɪn'kʌrɪdʒmənt/ *n* **1** [u and c] (support) 鼓励; **to need no ~ to do sth.** 做某事不需要鼓励; **to give ~ to sb. (to do sth.)** 鼓励某人（做某事）; **to be an ~ to sb. to do sth.** 对某人来说做某事是个鼓舞 **2** [c] (incitement) 怂恿

encouraging /ɪn'kʌrɪdʒɪŋ/ *adj* 令人鼓舞的

encouragingly /ɪn'kʌrɪdʒɪŋli/ *adv* 令人鼓舞地

encroach /ɪn'krəʊtʃ/ *vi* **1** (intrude) 侵占; **to ~ on/into sth.** 插手某事; **to ~ on sb.'s privacy** 干涉某人的隐私; **to ~ on sb.'s territory** *or* **turf** 侵占某人的地盘; fig 干涉某人的事 **2** (advance) 侵蚀; **to ~ on/into sth.** «*sea*» 侵蚀 ‹*coast*›; «*housing*» 侵占 ‹*countryside*›

encroachment /ɪn'krəʊtʃmənt/ *n* **1** (on sb.'s rights) 侵犯; (on sb.'s privacy) 干涉 **2** (of sea, enemy) 蚕食

encrust /ɪn'krʌst/ *vt* 使在表面形成硬壳; **to ~ sth. with sth.** 使某物形成硬壳覆盖某物; **the wound was ~ed with dried blood** 伤口结了一层血痂

encrustation /ˌɪnkrʌ'steɪʃn/ *n* 1 [u] (action) 包外壳; (state) 结壳 2 [c] (of blood) 凝块; (of earth) 硬壳

encrypt /en'krɪpt/ *vt* 将…编码

encryption /en'krɪpʃən/ *n* 编码

encumber /ɪn'kʌmbə(r)/ *vt* 妨碍; **to be ~ed with sth.** 被某事物拖累

encumbrance /ɪn'kʌmbrəns/ *n* 1 (to movement, freedom) 妨碍; (obstacle) 障碍物 2 (burden) 负担; (person) 拖累; (possession) 累赘; **to be an ~ to sb./sth.** 对某人/某物是个累赘

encyclical /en'sɪklɪkl/ *n* 教皇通谕

encyclopedia, encyclopaedia /ɪnˌsaɪklə'piːdɪə/ *n* 百科全书

encyclopedic, encyclopaedic /ɪnˌsaɪklə'piːdɪk/ *adj* 1 (with information similar to that of an encylopedia) 百科全书式的 ‹*work, format, presentation*› 2 (comprehensive) 广博的 ‹*knowledge*›

end /end/

A *n* 1 (last part) 末尾; **the ~ of the year/month/week** 年终/月底/周末; **at the ~ of his life** 在他临终前; **the very ~** 最后 2 (finish) 结束; **'The End'** (of film) "剧终"; (of book) "全文完"; **by the ~ of sth.** 到…结束时 ‹*year, activity*›; **at the ~ of the day** colloq 说到底; **to be at the ~ of one's endurance/patience/strength** 忍无可忍/忍耐不住/筋疲力尽; **to be at** *or* **come to the/an ~** (be over) 结束; (be used up) 耗尽; **to bring sth. to an ~** 结束某事; **to put an ~ to sth.** 终止某事; **there is no ~ to sth.** 某事物无穷无尽; **to annoy sb. no ~** colloq 让某人大为恼怒; **to have no ~ of trouble** colloq 有许多麻烦; **to** *or* **till the ~ of time** liter 直到永远; **it's not the ~ of the world** fig colloq 这没什么大不了的; **that'll be the ~ of you!** 你完蛋了!; **that's the ~ of that!** 别再说了!; **in the ~** (finally) 最后; (in summary) 总的来说; **for hours/days/weeks on ~** 连续几个小时/几天/几星期 3 (extremity) 末端; (of road, place) 尽头; **the front/back ~ of the car** 车头/车尾; **the ~ of a piece of string/a branch/the bed** 线头/树梢/床头; **the ~ of the cat's tail** 猫的尾巴尖; **tie the two ~s together** 把两头系在一起; **from ~ to ~** 从一头到另一头; **(at) this/the other ~** (在)这一头/另一头; **the third from the ~** 倒数第三个; **~ to ~** 首尾相接地; **to look at sth. ~ on** 迎面看某物; **on (its) ~** 竖着; **the ~ of the road** *or* **line (for sb./sth.)** fig (某人/某事物的)结局; **to reach the ~ of the road** *or* **line** fig 走到尽头; **to make (both) ~s meet** fig colloq 仅够维持生活; **to get** *or* **have one's ~ away** Brit sl 做爱; ▸**candle, tunnel A1, stick**[1] **A1** 4 fig (side) 一方; **the other ~** 对方; **to keep up one's ~ of the conversation** colloq 尽量找话说以免冷场; **to keep one's ~ of the bargain** colloq 说到做到 5 fig (aspect) 方面; **the leisure ~ of the market** 市场的休闲产业 6 fig (in range) 一端; **a model from the cheaper ~ of the range** 该系列中的低端款式; **the upper ~ of this income bracket** 该收入阶层中的高端; **opposite ~s of the social scale** 社会等级中对立的两极 7 (aim) 目的; **for one's own ~s** 为了自己的目的; **to this/that ~** 为了这个/那个目标; **to be an ~ in itself** 本身就是目的; **a means to an ~** 达到目的的手段; **the ~ justifies the means** Prov 只要目的正当，可以不择手段 8 Sport 半边场地; **to change ~s** 交换场地 9 (death) 死亡; **to meet one's ~** liter 死亡; **to be nearing one's ~** 临终; **to come to a bad/untimely/cruel ~** 不得好死/英年早逝/惨死 10 Brit (scrap) 剩余物; **we found a few ~s of rope** 我们找到了一些绳头 11 Brit colloq (limit of what is tolerable) 可忍受的极限; **you really are the ~!** 真受不了你!; **that really is the ~!** 这真是太过分了!

B *vt* 结束; **to ~ sth.** 结束某事; **to ~ the month in the red** 到月底时欠债; **to ~ one's days in poverty** 在贫困中度过余生; **the party to ~ all parties!** 最出色的宴会!; **to ~ one's life,** colloq **to ~ it all** 自杀

C *vi* 1 (finish) 结束; **to ~ in/with sth.** 以某事物结尾; **to ~ in failure/an argument** 以失败告终/争吵收场; **where's it all going to ~?, where will it all ~?** 这一切结局会怎么样? 2 (finish in space) ‹*line, road*› 终止; **the queue ~s here** 队伍排到这里; **to ~ one metre from the house** 在离房子 1 米的地方到头 3 (have at extremity) **to ~ in** *or* **with sth.** …的末端是某物; **to ~ in a sharp point** ‹*stick, pencil*› 有个尖头 4 (expire) ‹*agreement, insurance*› 到期

Phrasal verb

- **end up** *vi* 结束; **to ~ up doing sth.** 最终做某事; **to ~ up with sb./sth.** 最终得到某人/某事物; **to ~ up (as) sth.** 以某事物结束; **I don't know how he'll ~ up** 我不知道他最后结果会怎样; **to ~ up behind a desk/on the stage** 结果做了案头工作/演员; **he ~ed up marrying his childhood sweetheart** 他最终娶了青梅竹马的恋人; **I wonder who'll ~ up with the booby prize** 我在想谁最终会得到末名奖; **the cake ~ed up burnt** 蛋糕结果烤焦了; **he ~ed up an alcoholic** 他最终成了个酒鬼

endanger /ɪn'deɪndʒə(r)/ *vt* 危害 ‹*health, environment, reputation, interests*›; 危及 ‹*life*›; **an ~ed species** 濒危物种

en dash /'endæʃ/ *n* **= en rule**

endear /ɪn'dɪə(r)/ *vt* 使受喜爱; **to ~ sb. to sb.** 使某人讨某人喜欢; **to ~ oneself to sb.** 讨某人喜欢; **she did not ~ herself to me** 她不讨我喜欢

endearing /ɪn'dɪərɪŋ/ *adj* 讨人喜欢的

endearingly /ɪn'dɪərɪŋlɪ/ *adv* 讨人喜欢地; **~ honest** 诚实得可爱

endearment /ɪn'dɪəmənt/ *n* 1 [u] (love, affection) 爱慕; **terms/words of ~** 爱称/情话 2 [c] (word, phrase) 爱慕的话语

endeavour Brit, **endeavor** Amer /ɪn'devə(r)/

A *vi* (try) 努力; **to ~ to do sth.** 努力做某事

B *n* 1 [c] (attempt) 尝试; **to make every ~ to do sth.** 想方设法做某事 2 [u] (striving) 努力 3 [c] (undertaking) 事业; **a political/military ~** 政治事业/军事活动

endemic /en'demɪk/ *adj* 地方性的; **to be ~ to a country/region** 在某国家/某地区流行

endgame /'endgeɪm/ *n* 残局

ending /'endɪŋ/ *n* 1 (final part of sth.) 结尾 2 (of a word) 词尾

endive /'endɪv, Amer -daɪv/ *n* 1 (curly lettuce) 苣荬菜 2 (blanched chicory) 菊苣

endless /'endlɪs/ *adj* 1 (unlimited) 无限的; **~ patience/energy/resources** 无限的耐心/无穷无尽的精力/取之不尽的资源; **to go to ~ trouble to do sth.** 不厌其烦地做某事 2 (interminable) 无休止的; **~ letters/complaints** 不计其数的信件/无休止的投诉; **an ~ journey/search** 没有尽头的旅程/不断的搜寻 3 (infinite) 无穷尽的 ‹*list, road*›; 无垠的 ‹*desert, ocean*›

endlessly /'endlɪslɪ/ *adv* 1 (unlimitedly, to infinity) 无限地 ‹*extend*›; **~ patient/tolerant** 极度耐心的/过度容忍的 2 (without stopping) 不停地 ‹*work, play, drive*›; 没完没了地 ‹*speak, cry*›

end matter *n* **= back matter**

endocrine /'endəʊkraɪn, -krɪn/ *adj* 内分泌的

endocrinologist /ˌendəʊkrɪ'nɒlədʒɪst/ ▸**p. 409** *n* 内分泌学家

endocrinology /ˌendəʊkrɪ'nɒlədʒɪ/ *n* [u] 内分泌学

end-of-term *adj attrib* 期末的 ‹*dance, revue, report, exam*›

endomorph /'endəʊmɔːf/ *n* 内胚层体型者

endorse /ɪn'dɔːs/ *vt* 1 (support) 支持 ‹*action, policy, candidate*› 2 (approve) 认可 ‹*document, invoice, claim*› 3 (recommend) 宣传 ‹*product, brand, clothes*› 4 Brit Jur (enter penalty points on) 在…上记录违章; **to have one's driving licence ~d** 驾照被记录违章 5 (sign) 背书 ‹*cheque*›

endorsement /ɪn'dɔːsmənt/ *n* 1 [c] (support) 支持 2 [c] (approval of invoice, claim) 认可 3 [c] (recommendation of product) 宣传 4 [c] Brit (on driving licence) 违章记录 5 [u] (signing of cheque) 背书

endoscope /'endəʊskəʊp/ *n* 内窥镜

endoskeleton /'endəʊskelɪtn/ *n* 内骨骼

endosperm /'endəʊspɜːm/ *n* 胚乳

endothermic /ˌendəʊ'θɜːmɪk/ *adj* 吸热的

endow /ɪn'daʊ/ *vt* 1 (donate) 向…捐赠 ‹*school, hospital, charity*› 2 (give) 赋予; **to ~ sb. with sth.** 赋予某人某品质; **to be ~ed with sth.** 生来具有某品质; **she is well-~ed** colloq 她天资聪颖 3 (establish) 设立 ‹*prize, academic post*›

endowment /ɪn'daʊmənt/ *n* 1 [u] (financing) 资助 2 [c] (money given) 捐款 3 [c] (talent, ability) 天赋

endowment: ~ insurance *n* [u] 人寿保险; **~ mortgage** *n* 人寿保险抵押; **~ policy** *n* 人寿保险单

end: ~paper *n* 衬页; **~ product** *n* 最终产品; **~ result** *n* 最终结果

endurable /ɪn'djʊərəbl, Amer -'dʊə-/ *adj* 可忍受的

endurance /ɪn'djʊərəns, Amer -'dʊə-/ *n* [u] 1 (tolerance for pain, hardship) 忍耐力; **past** *or* **beyond (all) ~** 忍无可忍 2 (durability) 耐用度

endurance test *n* 耐力测验; **Jane's party was a bit of an ~** fig hum 简的聚会像是在测试大家的耐心

endure /ɪn'djʊə(r), Amer -'dʊər/

A *vt* 忍耐; **to ~ doing sth.** 忍受做某事

B *vi* 持续

enduring /ɪn'djʊərɪŋ, Amer -'dʊə-/ *adj* 持续的

enduringly /ɪn'djʊərɪŋlɪ, Amer -'dʊə-/ *adv* 持续地

end user *n* 最终用户

endways /'endweɪz/ *adv* 1 (with end forwards) 末端向前地; (with end upwards) 末端朝上地 2 (end to end) 两端相接地

enema /'enəmə/ *n* 1 (procedure) 灌肠; **to give sb. an ~** 给某人灌肠 2 (syringe) 灌肠管 3 (fluid) 灌肠剂

enemy /'enəmɪ/ *n* 1 (person) 敌人; **to make enemies** 树敌; **to make an ~ of sb.** 与某人为敌; **public ~ number one** 头号公敌; **to be one's own worst ~** 自己害自己; **the ~ within** 内奸 2 Mil **the ~** + *v sing or pl* 敌军; **to go over to the ~** 投敌 3 fig (source of harm or weakness) 危害物

energetic /ˌenə'dʒetɪk/ *adj* 1 (requiring or having much energy) 运动量大的 ‹*activity, sport*›; 精力充沛的 ‹*child, animal, politician*› 2 (vigorous) 断然的 ‹*denial*›; 有力的 ‹*measures*›

energetically /ˌenə'dʒetɪklɪ/ *adv* 精力充沛地 ‹*work, play*›; 雄辩地 ‹*argue*›; 断然地 ‹*refuse*›

energize /'enədʒaɪz/ *vt* 1 (invigorate) 使…活跃 ‹*person, body, mind*›; **to feel ~d** 感觉精力充沛 2 Elec 使…通电 ‹*electrical device, wire*›

energizing /'enədʒaɪzɪŋ/ *adj* 提供能量的 ‹*foods*›; 增加体能的 ‹*vitamins*›; 令人振奋的 ‹*effect*›

energy /'enədʒɪ/ *n* 1 [u] (strength, vitality) 活力; **to have the ~ to do sth.** 有精力做某事; **to devote all one's ~ to sth./to doing sth.** 把全部精力投入到某事/做某事中 2 [c] **energies** *pl* (mental powers) 脑力; (physical powers) 体力; **to put all one's energies into sth./**

e

doing sth. 全身心投入某事/做某事 **3** [u] (power, fuel) 能源; **to save/waste ～** 节约/浪费能源; **Department of E～** 能源部 **4** [u] Phys 能量

energy: ～ audit *n* 能源审计; **～ conservation** *n* [u] 能源节约; **～ consumption** *n* [u] 能源消耗; **～ efficiency** *n* [u] 能源效率; **～-giving** *adj* 提供能量的 ‹*food*›; **～ performance certificate** *n* Brit 能效证书; **～ resources** *npl* 能源; **～-saving** *adj* 节能的 ‹*technology, measure*›

enervate /'enəveɪt/ *vt* 使无力

enervating /'enəveɪtɪŋ/ *adj* 使人乏力的 ‹*climate, atmosphere*›

enfant terrible /ˌɒnfɒn te'riːbl/ *n* (*pl* **enfants terribles** /ˌɒnfɒn te'riːbl/) 不可一世的人

enfeeble /ɪn'fiːbl/ *vt* 使…无力 ‹*body, muscles*›; 使…衰弱 ‹*nation, economy, institution*›

enfeebled /ɪn'fiːbld/ *adj* 虚弱的; **in his ～ state he found cooking difficult** 他身体虚弱，觉得煮饭很困难

enfold /ɪn'fəʊld/ *vt* **1** (envelop) «*darkness, mist, gloom*» 笼罩; **to ～ sb./sth. in sth.** 把某人/某物笼罩在某物中 **2** (embrace) 拥抱 ‹*person, body*›; **to ～ sb. in one's arms** 把某人搂在怀里

enforce /ɪn'fɔːs/ *vt* **1** (compel compliance with) 强制实施 ‹*law, regulation, policy, decision*›; 加强 ‹*discipline*›; **to ～ sth. on sb.** 强行对某人实施某措施; **the police ～ the law too strongly on some people** 警察对某些人执法过严 **2** (impose) 强迫 ‹*silence, obedience*›; **to ～ sth. on sb.** 把某事强加于某人

enforceable /ɪn'fɔːsəbl/ *adj* 可强制执行的

enforced /ɪn'fɔːst/ *adj* 被迫的

enforcement /ɪn'fɔːsmənt/ *n* **1** (of law, regulation) 强制实施; (of policy, decision) 强制执行; (of discipline) 加强; **～ action/measures** 强制行动/措施 **2** (of silence, obedience) 强迫

enfranchise /ɪn'fræntʃaɪz/ *vt* 给予…选举权

enfranchisement /ɪn'fræntʃaɪzmənt/ *n* [u] 选举权给予

engage /ɪn'geɪdʒ/

A *vt* **1** formal (interest, attract) «*situation, event*» 吸引 ‹*attention, person*›; 引起 ‹*interest*› **2** (involve) 使参加; **to ～ sb. in sth.** 使某人参与某事; **to be ～d in discussions/negotiations** 参与讨论/谈判; **to be otherwise ～d** 另有安排 **3** (employ) 雇用; **to ～ sb. as sth.** 雇用某人做 ‹*lawyer, cleaner, interpreter*›; **to ～ sb. to do sth.** 雇用某人做某事 **4** Mech «*machine operator, mechanism*» 使…啮合 ‹*gear, parts of a machine*›; **to ～ the clutch** «*driver*» 接上离合器 **5** Mil «*troops, forces*» 与…交战 ‹*enemy, troops, forces*›

B *vi* **1** (be or become involved) 从事; **to ～ in** 参与 ‹*debate, crime, campaign*› **2** **to ～ with sth./sb.** 对付某事/某人; (deal with) 处理 ‹*problem*›; 应付 ‹*situation, critics*› **3** Mil 交战; **to ～ with sb./sth.** «*army, enemy, troops, forces*» 与某人/某队伍交战 **4** Mech 啮合; **to ～ with sth.** «*machine part, clutch, gear*» 与某物啮合

engaged /ɪn'geɪdʒd/ *adj* **1** (having agreed to marry) 已订婚的; **to be/get ～ to sb.** 与某人订婚 **2** Brit (in use) 占用的 ‹*number, line, toilet*› **3** (busy) 忙碌的; **to be ～ with sb.** 忙于跟某人做某事; **the doctor is ～ with a patient at present** 医生现在正在看病人; **to be ～ in sth./doing sth.** 忙于某事/做某事

engaged signal, engaged tone *ns* Brit 忙音; **I keep getting an ～** 对方的电话一直占线

engagement /ɪn'geɪdʒmənt/ *n* **1** (agreement to be married) 订婚; **to break off an ～** 解除婚约 **2** formal (appointment, meeting) 约会; **a previous/prior ～** 前约/预约; **to break an ～** 取消预约 **3** (hiring) 雇用; **the ～ (of sb.) as ...** （某人）受雇为… **4** Mil (battle, skirmish) 交战; **an ～ with sb./sth.** 与某人/某部队的交战; **rules of ～** 开战规定

engagement: ～ book, ～ diary *ns* 预约簿; **～ party** *n* 订婚宴会; **～ ring** *n* 订婚戒指

engaging /ɪn'geɪdʒɪŋ/ *adj* 有吸引力的; **an ～ smile/manner/personality/novel** 迷人的微笑/动人的风度/令人愉快的性格/有趣的小说

engagingly /ɪn'geɪdʒɪŋli/ *adv* 有吸引力地; **she smiled ～** 她露出迷人的笑容

engender /ɪn'dʒendə(r)/ *vt* formal 导致 ‹*situation, phenomenon*›; 引发 ‹*feelings*›; **to ～ a sense of responsibility in sb.** 使某人产生责任感

engine /'endʒɪn/ *n* **1** (in car, train, aircraft, boat) 发动机 **2** (locomotive) 火车头

engine driver *n* Brit 火车司机

engineer /ˌendʒɪ'nɪə(r)/ ▸p. 409

A *n* **1** (professional) 工程师; **the (Royal) Engineers** Mil （皇家）工程兵 **2** (in factory) 机械师; (installer, repairer) 维修工; **heating/telephone ～** 供暖/电话技师 **3** (on ship) 轮机手; **chief ～** 轮机长 **4** Amer Rail 火车司机

B *vt* **1** (plot) 策划 ‹*plot, scheme*›; 谋划 ‹*revolt, conspiracy, downfall*› **2** (design, build) 设计制造 **3** (modify) 改变…的基因结构; **genetically ～ed plants** 转基因植物

engineering /ˌendʒɪ'nɪərɪŋ/ *n* [u] **1** (subject, science) 工程学; **civil/chemical ～** 土木/化学工程; **to study ～** 研习工程学; **an extraordinary feat of ～** 工程学上了不起的成就 **2** (industry) 机械制造业; **light/heavy ～** 轻型机械/重型机械制造业

engineering: ～ brick *n* 工程用砖; **～ company** *n* 工程公司; **～ course** *n* 工程学课程; **～ degree** *n* 工程学学位; **～ department** *n* 工程学系; **～ science** *n* 工程学; **～ student** *n* 工程学学生

engine: ～ failure *n* 发动机故障; **～ oil** *n* 机油; **～ room** *n* 轮机舱

England /'ɪŋglənd/ *pr n* 英格兰

English /'ɪŋglɪʃ/ ▸p. 503, p. 426

A *adj* (of England) 英格兰的 ‹*people, countryside, accent*›; (of the language) 英语的; **～ grammar/literature** 英语语法/英国文学; **an ～ teacher** 英语教师

B *n* [u] (language) 英语; **the King's** *or* **Queen's ～** 标准英语; **standard ～** 标准英语; **in plain/simple ～** 用简洁直率的语言

C *npl* **the ～** (people) 英国人

> **English breakfast**
>
> 英式早餐。英式早餐非常丰盛。常包括烤面包（抹黄油或果酱）、熏肉、煎鸡蛋、香肠、蘑菇、西红柿等。饮品一般有牛奶加麦片、果汁、咖啡或茶。英国许多宾馆的房费都包括了英式早餐。普通家庭中如此丰盛的早餐则较少见。相对而言，欧洲大陆式早餐（Continental breakfast）则比较简单，一般包括烤面包（抹黄油或果酱）、油酥糕点、果汁茶或咖啡等。

English: ～ as a Foreign Language *n* [u] 作为外语的英语; **～ as a Second Language** *n* [u] 作为第二语言的英语; **～ breakfast** *n* 英式早餐; **～ Channel** *n* **the ～ Channel** 英吉利海峡; **～ for Speakers of Other Languages** *n* [u] 面向操其他语言者的英语; **～ for Special Purposes** *n* [u] 专门用途英语; **～ Heritage** *pr n* Brit 英格兰遗产保护局; **～ Language Teaching** *n* [u] 英语教学

Englishman /'ɪŋglɪʃmən/ *n* (*pl* **Englishmen**) (native) 英格兰男子; (national) 英国人; **an ～'s home is his castle** Prov 英国人的家就是他的城堡

Englishness /'ɪŋglɪʃnɪs/ *n* [u] (of custom, behaviour etc.) 英国特色; (of person) 英国人作风

> **the English Civil War**
>
> 英国内战。从 16 世纪开始，英国资本主义开始迅速发展，新兴的资产阶级开始要求分享政治权力、限制王权、取消阻碍资本主义发展的封建专制制度。同时，清教徒（Puritan）认为英国国教会保留了太多的天主教传统，要求进一步改革，结果遭到迫害。1642 年，资产阶级和清教徒等组成的议会派（Parliamentarian，亦称圆颅党，Roundhead）和支持国王查理一世（King Charles I）的保皇派（Royalist，亦称骑士党，Cavalier）发生战争，英国内战开始。在马斯顿荒原（Marston Moor）和纳西比（Naseby）战役中，奥利弗·克伦威尔（Oliver Cromwell）率领的新模范军（New Model Army）击溃保皇派军队。1649 年，被俘的国王查理一世被处死，英国成立了共和国（Commonwealth）。克伦威尔后来成为"护国公"（Lord Protector）。克伦威尔死后，查理一世的儿子查理二世（Charles II）于 1660 年复辟。

English: ～ rose *n* 英国玫瑰少女 [指皮肤细嫩白皙的典型英国美貌少女]; **～ speaker** *n* 讲英语的人; **～-speaking** *adj* 讲英语的; **the ～-speaking world** 世界各地讲英语的国家; **～woman** *n* (native) 英格兰女人; (national) 英国女人

engrave /ɪn'greɪv/ *vt* «*person, machine*» 雕刻 ‹*inscription, stone, metal, wood*›; **to ～ sth. on/in sth.** 把某物刻在某物上/里; **to ～ sth. with sth.** 用某物刻某物

engraved /ɪn'greɪvd/ *adj pred* fig 印象深刻的; **to be ～ on/in sb.'s heart/mind** «*scene, words*» 被铭刻在某人心里/脑海中

engraver /ɪn'greɪvə(r)/ ▸p. 409 *n* 雕刻师

engraving /ɪn'greɪvɪŋ/ *n* **1** [u] (art) 雕刻术; (process) 雕刻 **2** [c] (print) 版画

engross /ɪn'grəʊs/ *vt* 使全神贯注; **to ～ sb. with sth.** 用某事物占据某人的全部注意力; **he ～ed his audience with tales of his expeditions** 他的探险故事深深地吸引了听众

engrossed /ɪn'grəʊst/ *adj* 全神贯注的; **to be ～ in sth.** 专注于某事; **to be ～ in conversation/work/the book/a TV programme** 聚精会神地谈话/工作/读书/看电视节目; **he was so ～ in his own problems that he neglected his family** 他光想着自己的事以至于疏忽了家人

engrossing /ɪn'grəʊsɪŋ/ *adj* 使人全神贯注的 ‹*book, game, work*›; **this novel is so ～ I can't put it down** 这部小说很有吸引力，让我读起来欲罢不能

engulf /ɪn'gʌlf/ *vt* **1** (cover, surround) «*fire, darkness*» 吞没 ‹*building, village*›; «*sea, waves*» 淹没 ‹*boat, land, coast*›; «*lava*» 吞噬 **2** (overwhelm) «*problems, emotion, crisis*» 严重影响 ‹*person, nation*›; **to be ～ed by hatred/grief** 陷入仇恨/悲伤之中

enhance /ɪn'hɑːns, Amer -'hæns/ *vt* **1** (improve) 提高 ‹*reputation, status, prospects, rights, quality, TV/radio reception, nutritional value*›; 提升 ‹*privileges, power, authority, tourist attraction*›; 改善 ‹*appearance, beauty*› **2** (increase) 增加 ‹*salary, pension, value*›

enhancement /ɪn'hɑːnsmənt, Amer -'hæns-/ *n* **1** [u] (improving) (of reputation, status, prospects, rights, quality, TV/radio reception, nutritional value) 提高; (of privileges, power, authority, tourist attraction) 提升; (of appearance, beauty) 改善; (of salary, pension, value) 增加 **2** [c] (instance) 改进手段; **software ～s** 软件增强手段; **various ～s have been made to the school facilities** 对学校设施进行了方方面面的改进

enigma /ɪ'nɪgmə/ *n* (thing) 谜; (person) 难以捉摸的人; **even after 20 years he's still an ～ to me** 甚至过了 20 年我仍然捉摸不透他; **why that never happened remains sth.**

of an ~ 为什么那事没有发生依然是个谜; **a mathematical ~** 一道数学难题

enigmatic /ˌenɪɡˈmætɪk/ *adj* 费解的 ‹*statement, remark*›; 神秘的 ‹*smile, figure*›; 难以捉摸的 ‹*personality, character*›

enigmatically /ˌenɪɡˈmætɪklɪ/ *adv* 难以捉摸地 ‹*behave*›; 神秘地 ‹*smile*›; 令人困惑地 ‹*reply*›

enjoin /ɪnˈdʒɔɪn/ *vt* **1** (urge, impose) 命令 ‹*silence, obedience, caution*›; **to ~ sb. to do sth.** 责令某人做某事; **to ~ sth. on sb.** 要求某人做到…; **this religion ~s chastity on all its followers** 这一宗教要求所有信徒保持忠贞 **2** (prohibit) 禁止; **to ~ sb. from doing sth.** «*person, judge, conscience*» 禁止某人做某事

enjoy /ɪnˈdʒɔɪ/

A *vt* **1** (get pleasure from) 享受; **to ~ the good weather** 享受好天气; **to ~ sth./doing sth.** 喜欢某事/做某事; **to ~ a film/concert** 欣赏电影/音乐会; **to ~ conversation** 喜欢交谈; **to ~ (playing) badminton/chess** 喜欢(打)羽毛球/(下)国际象棋; **to ~ one's day/life/stay** 过得很愉快/享受生活/待得很开心; **~ your meal!** 你吃好! **2** (benefit from) 享有 ‹*rights, advantage*›; **to ~ good health/success** 身体健康/取得胜利

B *v refl* **to ~ oneself** 玩得开心; **~ yourselves!** 你们好好玩吧!

C *vi* esp Amer colloq 享受 [通常用于祈使句]; **it's your birthday — ~!** 今天是你的生日——开心玩吧!

enjoyable /ɪnˈdʒɔɪəbl/ *adj* 令人愉快的 ‹*weekend, activity*›; 有趣的 ‹*occasion*›; 美味的 ‹*meal*›

enjoyably /ɪnˈdʒɔɪəblɪ/ *adv* 令人愉快地

enjoyment /ɪnˈdʒɔɪmənt/ *n* **1** [u] (pleasure) 愉快; **to get ~ from sth./doing sth.** 从某事/做某事中获得乐趣; **to do sth. for ~** 出于兴趣做某事; **to spoil sb.'s ~ of sth.** 破坏某人对某事物的兴致; **the pianist gave an encore, much to the ~ of the audience** 令观众十分愉快的是, 钢琴家加演了一曲 **2** [c] (enjoyable activity) 乐事; **gardening is one of her chief ~s in life** 园艺是她生活中的主要乐趣之一 **3** [u] formal (entitlement) 享有; **~ of rights/privileges/advantages** 权利/特权/有利条件的享有

enlarge /ɪnˈlɑːdʒ/

A *vt* **1** (expand) 扩大 ‹*building, business, gap, territory, empire, population*›; 增长 ‹*knowledge*›; 扩充 ‹*staff*›; 增补 ‹*edition*› **2** Phot 放大 ‹*photograph, document*›

B *vi* (say or write more) 详述; **to ~ on** *or* **upon sth.** 详细说明某事

enlarged /ɪnˈlɑːdʒd/ *adj* 扩大了的 ‹*territory*›; 肿大的 ‹*body part*›; 增补的 ‹*edition*›; 放大了的 ‹*image, photograph, document*›; **~ lymph nodes** 肿大的淋巴结

enlargement /ɪnˈlɑːdʒmənt/ *n* **1** [u] (of building, business, gap, territory, empire) 扩大; (of population) 增长; (of staff) 扩充; (of edition) 增补 **2** [c] (of photograph, document) 放大

enlarger /ɪnˈlɑːdʒə(r)/ *n* 放大机

enlighten /ɪnˈlaɪtn/ *vt* **1** (edify) 启迪 **2** (clarify) 阐明; **to ~ sb. on** *or* **about** *or* **as to sth.** 向某人指点某事

enlightened /ɪnˈlaɪtnd/ *adj* 有见识的 ‹*person*›; 开明的 ‹*opinions, attitudes*›; 明智的 ‹*ideas*›; **an ~ approach to teaching** 启发式教学法; **I'm no more ~ now than I was at the beginning** 我现在比开始时更糊涂了; **in these ~ days** iron 在当今的文明时期; **I'm waiting to be ~** iron 我等着接受点拨呢

enlightenment /ɪnˈlaɪtnmənt/ *n* **1** (edification) 启迪; **for your ~** 给你以启发 **2** (clarification) 阐明 **3** Hist (intellectual movement) **the (Age of) E~** 启蒙运动(时代)

enlist /ɪnˈlɪst/

A *vt* **1** Mil 使参军 **2** (engage) 谋求 ‹*help, support, cooperation*›; 争取…的帮助 ‹*people, helpers, volunteers*›

B *vi* 入伍; **to ~ in the army/as a soldier/for a commission** 参军/入伍当兵/任军职

enlisted man *n* Amer 士兵

enlistment /ɪnˈlɪstmənt/ *n* **1** Mil 征募 **2** (of help, support, cooperation) 谋求

enliven /ɪnˈlaɪvn/ *vt* **1** (enhance) 使…更有生气 ‹*discussion, party, decor, room*›; **to ~ sth. with sth.** 通过某事物使某事更有趣 **2** (animate) 使…更快活 ‹*person*›

en masse /ˌɒn ˈmæs/ *adv* 全体; **the committee resigned ~** 委员会集体辞职; **we left the meeting ~** 我们一起离开了会场

enmesh /ɪnˈmeʃ/ *vt* 缠住; **to be/become ~ed (in sth.)** 陷入(某事); **to be ~ed in a family feud** 卷入家族世仇

enmity /ˈenmətɪ/ *n* **1** [u] (hostility) 敌意; **~ towards sb.** 对某人的敌视; **~ between A and B** A与B之间的敌对 **2** [c] (disagreement, bad feeling) 不和; **family feuds and enmities** 家族世仇和怨恨

ennoble /ɪˈnəʊbl/ *vt* **1** (give title to) «*monarch, government*» 封…为贵族 ‹*person, commoner*› **2** (dignify) 使更高尚; **to ~ the person/spirit** 使人更高贵/使精神升华

enormity /ɪˈnɔːmətɪ/ *n* **1** [u] (of crime) 穷凶极恶; (of insult, threat) 肆无忌惮 **2** [u] (of task, problem) 巨大; **the ~ of a task/problem** 任务的艰巨/问题的棘手 **3** [c] (grave crime or sin) 滔天罪行

enormous /ɪˈnɔːməs/ *adj* 庞大的; **an ~ number of people/chairs** 很多人/椅子

enormously /ɪˈnɔːməslɪ/ *adv* 极其 ‹*heavy, funny*›; 非常 ‹*like, differ*›; 极大地 ‹*change*›

enough /ɪˈnʌf/

A *adj attrib and postpos* **1** (adequate amount or number of) 足够的; **is there ~ coffee left?** 剩下的咖啡够吗?; **I didn't get ~ sleep** 我睡眠不足; **she made ~ fuss about getting it** iron 她因达到了目的而大肆炫耀; **more than ~, ~ and to spare** 绰绰有余; **he's fool ~ to believe it** 他会相信这个, 真够傻的; **I go on ~ walks to keep fit** 我尽量步行以保持健康 **2** (too many or much) 太多的; **I've seen ~ television repeats** 我看够了电视重播; **as if that were not ~ ...** 好像那还不够似的

B *pron* **1** (adequate amount or number) 足够; **he's had quite ~ (to drink)** 他已经喝得够多的了; **I can't eat ~ of it** 这东西我怎么也吃不够; **it's ~ to make you weep** 这足以使你哭泣; **~ said** colloq 不必多说 **2** (too much or many) 太多; **I've had ~ of him/his rudeness** 他这个人/他的粗鲁无礼我受够了; **more than ~** 过多; **that's ~!** 够了!; **~ is ~** 凡事要适可而止

C *adv* **1** (sufficiently) 足够地; **the meat is not cooked ~** 肉没有熟透; **before he was old ~ to shave** 在他未到刮胡子的年龄时 **2** (fairly) 相当; **the meal was good ~** 这顿饭还过得去 **3** (very) 很; **the threat was plain ~** 威胁十分明显; **and sure ~** colloq 不出所料 **4** (for emphasis) [表示强调]; **funnily/strangely ~** 说来好玩/说来也怪

enquire /ɪnˈkwaɪə(r)/ *vt, vi* = **inquire**

enquirer /ɪnˈkwaɪərə(r)/ *n* = **inquirer**

enquiring /ɪnˈkwaɪərɪŋ/ *adj* = **inquiring**

enquiry /ɪnˈkwaɪərɪ, Amer ˈɪŋkwərɪ/ *n* = **inquiry**

enrage /ɪnˈreɪdʒ/ *vt* 激怒 ‹*person, animal*›; **to be ~d at/by sb./sth.** 对某人/某事非常愤怒

enraged /ɪnˈreɪdʒd/ *adj* 勃然大怒的 ‹*person, animal*›; 愤怒的 ‹*mob, roar*›

enrapture /ɪnˈræptʃə(r)/ *vt* «*person, beauty, music, fragrance, view*» 使欣喜若狂; **to be ~d (by sth.)** 陶醉(于某事)

enrich /ɪnˈrɪtʃ/ *vt* **1** (improve) 充实 ‹*mind, experience, civilization*›; 使…丰富 ‹*vocabulary*›; 使…肥沃 ‹*soil*›; 在…中添加营养成分 ‹*food*›; **to ~ sth. with sth.** 用某物充实某物 **2** (make wealthy) 使…富裕 ‹*person, country, company*› **3** Phys 使浓缩; **~ed uranium** 浓缩铀

enrichment /ɪnˈrɪtʃmənt/ *n* **1** (enhancement, improvement) 充实 **2** (of wealth) 致富 **3** Phys 浓缩

enrol Brit, **enroll** Amer /ɪnˈrəʊl/ (*pres p etc.* **-ll-**)

A *vt* (officially register) 注册; **to ~ sb. in/for a class** 把某人登记到班里; **to ~ sb. as a member (of) sth.** 将某人注册为某机构的成员; **to ~ sb. at a college** 招收某人进某学院

B *vi* «*student, member, participant*» 参加; **to ~ on a course/at a university** 注册学习某课程/上某大学; **to ~ in history** 报名学历史

enrolment Brit, **enrollment** Amer /ɪnˈrəʊlmənt/ *n* **1** [u] (on course, as member) 注册; **~ for evening classes/as a postgraduate student** 注册上夜校课程/读研究生 **2** [c] (numbers) 注册人数; **school ~s** 学校注册人数; **the drop in ~s** 注册人数的下降 **3** [c] Amer Sch, Univ 注册在校人数; **the school has an ~ of 800 students** 这所学校有在校学生800人

en route /ˌɒn ˈruːt/ *adv* 在路上; **~ for ...** 在去…的途中; **~ from ... to ...** 从…到…的途中; **she is ~ to stardom** 她已踏上了星途

en rule /ˈen ruːl/ *n* Brit 短划线

ensconce /ɪnˈskɒns/ *vt* 安置; **to be ~d/to ~ oneself** (in a room) 安顿下来; (in an armchair) 安坐

ensemble /ɒnˈsɒmbl/ *n* **1** (group of actors) 剧团; (group of musicians) 乐团; (group of dancers) 歌舞团 **2** (scene, passage) 合奏曲 **3** (set, group) [家具、服装、建筑物等] 协调搭配的一套

enshrine /ɪnˈʃraɪn/ *vt* **1** (preserve, protect) 珍藏; **to ~ sth. in sth.** 将…珍藏于某物 ‹*principle, tradition, idea*›; **the constitution ~s the rights of all citizens** 宪法保护所有公民的权利神圣不可侵犯; **to be ~d in sth.** 被神圣地记载入某物; **our nation's glorious history is ~d in the official records** 我们国家的光辉历史被庄严地载入官方文献; **a principle ~d in law** 受法律保护的原则 **2** Relig (put in shrine) **to ~ sth. in sth.** 把某物放在某物内供奉; **to be ~d in sth.** 放在某物内供奉; **the relics are ~d in a jewelled casket** 那些遗物供奉在一只镶宝石的匣子里

ensign /ˈensən/ *n* **1** (flag, standard) 旗 [尤指舰旗或军旗]; **to fly the ~** 升起军旗; **red/white/blue ~** 英国商船旗/英国皇家海军旗/蓝舰旗 **2** (officer) Amer Naut 海军少尉; Brit Mil 掌旗官; Hist 步兵少尉

enslave /ɪnˈsleɪv/ *vt* 使成为奴隶; fig 征服; **to be ~d by passion** 被激情所役使

enslavement /ɪnˈsleɪvmənt/ *n* 奴役; fig 征服; **~ by sb.** 某人的控制; **~ to sth.** 对某事的服从

ensnare /ɪnˈsneə(r)/ *vt* lit «*trap, net, hunter*» 诱捕 ‹*bird, animal*›; fig «*beauty, temptress*» 诱惑 ‹*person*›; **a fly had become ~d in the spider's web** 一只苍蝇被蜘蛛网缠住了; **he was ~d by her charms** 他被她的魅力迷住了

ensue /ɪnˈsjuː, Amer -ˈsuː/ *vi* 接着发生; **to ~ from sth.** «*consequences*» 紧接某事出现; «*death, defeat, events*» 紧接某事发生

ensuing /ɪnˈsjuːɪŋ, Amer -ˈsuː-/ *adj* 随后的 ‹*events, argument, period*›

en suite /ˌɒn ˈswiːt/ *adj* 与卧室配套的; **with bathroom ~, with an ~ bathroom** 带浴室

ensure /ɪnˈʃɔː(r), Amer ɪnˈʃʊər/ *vt* 保证; **to ~ sb. sth.** 向某人保证某事; **to ~ (that) ...** 保证…

ENT *abbr* = **ear, nose, and throat**

entail /ɪnˈteɪl/ *vt* **1** (involve) 须要 ‹*obligation, effort, discretion*›; 导致 ‹*changes, problems,*› *delays*›; **to ~ sb. doing sth.** 使某人必须做某事; **this will ~ her coming an hour earlier** 这意味着她得提前一小时到 **2** Jur 限嗣继承; **to ~ sth. on sb.** «*testator, will*» 限定某人继承 ‹*estate, land, property*› **3** Philos «*proposition*» 合乎逻辑地引出 ‹*proposition, consequence, conclusion*›

entangle /ɪn'tæŋgl/ *vt* **1** lit (become twisted) 缠住; **to ~ sth. in/with sth.** 把某物缠在某物里/用某物缠住某物; **to be ~d in sth.** 被缠在某物中 **2** fig (involve) 使卷入; **to ~ sb. in sth.** 使某人卷入某事; **to ~ oneself in complicated explanations** 纠缠于复杂的解释说明; **~ sb. with sth./sb.** 使某人卷入某事/与某人纠缠不清; **he is ~d with a woman half his age** 他和一个小他一半年龄的女人纠缠不清; **to be/become ~d in money problems/with the law** 陷入财政困难/法律纠纷

entanglement /ɪn'tæŋglmənt/ *n* **1** [u] (in net, wire, hedge) 缠住; **many dolphins die from ~ in fishing nets** 很多海豚被鱼网缠死 **2** [c] (complicated situation) 纠缠; **the legal ~s** 法律纠纷 **3** [c] Mil 铁丝网

enter /'entə(r)/

A *vi* **1** (come in) 进来; (go in) 进去 **2** Theat 上场 **3** (penetrate) «*bullet, water, gas*» 进入 **4** (register for event) 报名参加

B *vt* **1** (come or go into) (begin) 进入 ‹*room, stomach, airspace*›; 迈进 ‹*year, period*›; **to ~ a new phase** 进入一个新阶段; **it never ~ed** *or* **didn't ~ sb.'s head** *or* **mind** fig colloq 某人从未想到过 **2** (flow into) 流入 ‹*sea*› **3** (penetrate) «*bullet*» 穿入 ‹*body*›; «*water*» 灌进 ‹*boat*› **4** (join) 加入 ‹*group*›; 开始从事 ‹*profession*›; **to ~ the Church** 成为神职人员; **to ~ society** dated 正式进入社交界 **5** (take part in) 参加 ‹*competition, exam, event*›; **to ~ sb. in an event/competition** 为某人报名参加某比赛项目/某比赛; **to ~ one's dog in a show** 为狗报名参加表演 **6** (record) 记录; **to ~ sth. in the left-hand column/a ledger** 把某事物登记到左栏/分类账上; **to ~ sth. on the list/form** 把某事物登录到清单/表格上 **7** Comput 输入 ‹*data*› **8** (submit) 提出 ‹*proposal, testimony, bid*›; **to ~ a plea of not guilty** 提出无罪抗辩

Phrasal verbs

- **enter into** *vt* [~ into sth.]
  1 (embark on) 开始 ‹*discussion, negotiations*›; **there's no need to ~ into detail** 没必要讨论细节 **2** (commit to) 订立 ‹*agreement*›; **to ~ into a deal with a firm** 与某家公司达成一笔交易; **to ~ into an alliance** «*parties, nations*» 结成联盟 **3** (share in) 体谅 ‹*problem, distress*›; 分享 ‹*enthusiasm, mood*›; **to ~ into the spirit of sth.** 融入到某事物的乐趣中 **4** (be part of) «*factor*» 牵涉进 ‹*plans, situation*›; **to ~ into the way sb. handles sth.** 影响到某人处理某事物的方式; **don't let personal feelings ~ into it** 别把个人感情掺杂到这件事中
- **enter on** *vt* = **enter upon**
- **enter up** *vt* [~ up sth., ~ sth. up] 登录 ‹*details, total*›
- **enter upon** *vt* [~ upon sth.]
  1 formal (begin) 开始 ‹*career, war*› **2** Jur 正式占有 ‹*inheritance*›

enteric /en'terɪk/ *adj* **1** Anat 肠的; **~ virus/functions/disorders** 肠道病毒/功能/疾病 **2** Med 肠溶的 ‹*capsule*›

enteritis /ˌentə'raɪtɪs/ ▸**p. 377** *n* [u] 肠炎

enter key *n* 回车键

enterprise /'entəpraɪz/ *n* **1** [c] (company, firm) 企业 **2** [c] (project, undertaking) 事业; (venture) 有风险的计划; **a new business ~** 新的企业; **a hazardous ~** 有风险的事业 **3** [u] (entrepreneurial activity) 企业活动 **4** [u] (initiative) 创业精神

enterprise: ~ allowance *n* Brit 创业补贴; **~ culture** *n* [u] 企业文化; **~ zone** *n* 企业振兴区

enterprising /'entəpraɪzɪŋ/ *adj* 有事业心的 ‹*person, company*›; 有创新精神的 ‹*plan, venture*›

enterprisingly /'entəpraɪzɪŋli/ *adv* (showing business initiative) 有创新精神地; (showing resourcefulness) 有头脑地

entertain /ˌentə'teɪn/

A *vt* **1** (amuse, occupy) 使快乐; **to ~ sb. with sth.** 用某事物给某人带来快乐; **to keep sb. ~ed** 一直逗某人高兴 **2** (play host to) 款待; **to ~ sb. to dinner** 请某人吃饭 **3** (consider, nurture) 怀有 ‹*ambition, hope, thought*›; 考虑 ‹*suggestion, proposal*›

B *vi* 款待

entertainer /ˌentə'teɪnə(r)/ ▸**p. 409** *n* 表演者; **an all-round ~** 多才多艺的艺人

entertaining /ˌentə'teɪnɪŋ/

A *adj* 使人愉快的 ‹*performer, evening*›; 有趣的 ‹*play, film*›

B *n* [u] 款待; **they do a lot of ~** 他们经常请客

entertainingly /ˌentə'teɪnɪŋli/ *adv* 令人愉快地 ‹*present, recount, explain*›

entertainment /ˌentə'teɪnmənt/ *n* **1** [u] (amusement, enjoyment) 娱乐; **for sb.'s ~** 给某人助兴; **(much) to the ~ of sb.** 令某人(十分)愉快的是; **for one's own ~** 自娱自乐; **the world of ~, the ~ world** 娱乐界; **a place of ~** 娱乐场所 **2** [c] (performance, event) 娱乐活动 **3** [u] (hospitality) 款待; **the ~ of foreign visitors** 对外国游客的招待; **the company spends a lot of money on ~** 公司用于招待的开支很大

entertainment: ~ allowance *n* 酬酢津贴; **~ expenses** *npl* 招待费; **~ guide** *n* 休闲指南; **~ industry** *n* 娱乐业

enthral Brit, **enthrall** Amer /ɪn'θrɔːl/ *vt* (*pres p etc.* **-ll-**) «*woman, charms, scenery, performance*» 吸引住; **to be ~led by sb.'s beauty** 被某人的美貌所吸引

enthralling /ɪn'θrɔːlɪŋ/ *adj* 吸引人的 ‹*performance, novel*›; 迷人的 ‹*scenery, beauty*›

enthrone /ɪn'θrəʊn/ *vt* **1** lit (install on throne) 使…登基 ‹*monarch*›; 使…即位 ‹*bishop*› **2** fig (give authority to) 尊崇; **~d in the hearts of millions** 受数百万人敬仰

enthronement /ɪn'θrəʊnmənt/ *n* [u] 登基

enthuse /ɪn'θjuːz, Amer -'θuːz/ *vi* 充满热情; **to ~ about** *or* **over sth./sb.** 热衷于某事/对某人很热情

enthusiasm /ɪn'θjuːzɪæzəm, Amer -'θuːz-/ *n* **1** [u] (eagerness, interest) 热情; **to show ~ for** *or* **about sth./doing sth.** 表现出对某事/做某事的热情; **to arouse ~ in sb., to arouse sb. to ~** 激发某人的热情; **to fill sb. with ~** 使某人充满热情 **2** [c] (activity, hobby) 爱好; **gardening/cooking is his latest ~** 他最近爱上了园艺/做饭

enthusiast /ɪn'θjuːzɪæst, Amer -'θuːz-/ *n* 热衷者; **to be an ~ for sth.** 热衷于某事; **a rugby/tennis ~** 橄榄球/网球爱好者

enthusiastic /ɪnˌθjuːzɪ'æstɪk, Amer -ˌθuːz-/ *adj* 热情的; **to be ~ about sth./sb.** 对某人/某事物很感兴趣; **an ~ supporter** 热心的支持者

enthusiastically /ɪnˌθjuːzɪ'æstɪkli, Amer -ˌθuːz-/ *adv* 热情地 ‹*sing, help, support, work*›; 热烈地 ‹*discuss, cheer, welcome*›; 津津有味地 ‹*eat*›

entice /ɪn'taɪs/ *vt* 引诱; **to ~ sb. to do sth./into doing sth.** 诱使某人做某事; **to ~ sb. with sth.** 用某事物诱惑某人; **to ~ sb. somewhere** 诱骗某人去某处

Phrasal verb

- **entice away** *vt* [~ sb. away] «*lure, prospects, temptress, headhunter*» 把…引开; **to ~ sb. away from** 诱使某人放弃 ‹*activity, work*›

enticement /ɪn'taɪsmənt/ *n* **1** [c] (offer, incentive) 诱惑物; **an ~ to sb./to do sth.** 对某人/做某事的诱惑; **to offer sth. as an ~** 给予某物作为诱饵; **there were so many ~s that I could not refuse the job** 这工作很有诱惑力，我无法拒绝 **2** [u] (temptation) 引诱; **~ (of sb.) to do sth./into doing sth.** (对某人) 做某事的诱惑; **~ (of sb./sth.) with sth.** 用某物 (对某人/某物) 的引诱

enticing /ɪn'taɪsɪŋ/ *adj* 诱人的 ‹*menu, smell*›; 有吸引力的 ‹*offer, prospects*›; 迷人的 ‹*beauty, look*›

enticingly /ɪn'taɪsɪŋli/ *adv* 诱人地; **~ picturesque** 美丽动人的; **~ cool** 凉爽宜人

entire /ɪn'taɪə(r)/ *adj* **1** (whole, with no part left out) 全部的; **the ~ family/world** 全家/全世界; **the ~ weekend** 整个周末; **an ~ day** 一整天; **the text/collection is ~** 文本/收藏品很完整; **the ~ 50,000 dollars** 全部 5 万美元; **the ~ three million population** 整整 300 万人口 **2** (complete) 绝对的; **we are in ~ agreement with you** 我们完全同意你的意见; **our ~ support** 我们的全力支持

entirely /ɪn'taɪəli/ *adv* 完全地; **that's ~ up to you** 那完全由你决定; **not ~** 不完全地; **I was ~ to blame** 完全是我的责任; **~ free of additives** 绝对不含添加剂; **~ at your own risk** 风险完全由你承担

entirety /ɪn'taɪərəti/ *n* [u] 全部; **the ~ of sth.** 某事物的全部; **the film will be shown in its ~** 这部电影将放映完整版

entitle /ɪn'taɪtl/ *vt* **1** (authorize) 使享有权利; **to ~ sb. to sth./to do sth.** «*law, courts, government, passport, rank, position, qualifications*» 使某人享有某权利/做某事的权利; **to be ~d to sth./to do sth.** 有权获得某物/做某事; **I'm only claiming what I'm ~d to** 我只是要求得到属于我的东西; **to be ~d to one's own opinion** 有权发表自己的观点 **2** (call) 给…题名 ‹*book, play, music, painting*›; **the poem is ~d 'Love'** 这首诗的诗题是《爱》

entitlement /ɪn'taɪtlmənt/ *n* 权利; **~ to sth./to do sth.** 对某事物享有的权利/做某事的权利; **~ to vote** 投票资格

entity /'entəti/ *n* 实体; **a single/separate/political/legal ~** 单独的/独立的/政治/法人实体

entomb /ɪn'tuːm/ *vt* **1** lit (place in tomb) 埋葬; **to be ~ed in sth.** 被埋葬在某物中; **his body is ~ed in the crypt** 他的遗骸葬在教堂地下室 **2** fig (bury, trap) 困住; **many people were ~ed in the rubble of the earthquake** 很多人被掩埋在地震废墟中

entombment /ɪn'tuːmənt/ *n* **1** lit (placing in tomb) 埋葬 **2** fig (trapping) 掩埋; **the ~ of an entire village after an earthquake** 地震后整个村子的掩埋

entomological /ˌentəmə'lɒdʒɪkl/ *adj* 昆虫学的 ‹*research, classification*›; **an ~ specimen/society** 昆虫标本/昆虫学界

entomologist /ˌentə'mɒlədʒɪst/ ▸**p. 409** *n* 昆虫学家

entomology /ˌentə'mɒlədʒi/ *n* [u] 昆虫学

entourage /'ɒntʊrɑːʒ/ *n* 随从

entrails /'entreɪlz/ *npl* **1** lit (internal organs) 内脏 **2** fig (parts) 内部; (details) 细节; **to pick over the ~** 事后回顾; **to read the ~** 通过蛛丝马迹进行预测

entrain /ɪn'treɪn/ formal

A *vt* 使…上火车 ‹*troops, passengers*›

B *vi* «*troops, passengers*» 上火车

entrance¹ /'entrəns/ *n* **1** (door, gate, passage) 入口; **main ~** 大门 **2** (act of entering) 进入; **to make an ~** 进入; **a sudden ~** 突然闯入; **to force an ~** 强行进入 **3** (on to stage) 出场; **to make an/one's ~** 入场; **an actor must learn his ~s and exits** 演员必须学会如何出场和退场 **4** (right of way) 进入权; **to gain**

~ **to sth.** 获准进入 ‹*club*›; 被录取进入 ‹*university*›; **to deny** *or* **refuse sb.** ~ 拒绝某人加入 **5** (involvement) 卷入; ~ **into sth.** 参与某事; **my ~ into the world of high finance** 我涉足高级金融领域

entrance² /ɪn'trɑːns, Amer -'træns/ *vt* **1** (delight) 使…着迷 ‹*person, audience*›; **to be ~d at** *or* **by sth.** 对某事物着迷 **2** (cast spell on) 对…施魔法

entrance: ~ examination *n* Brit **1** Sch, Univ 入学考试; **2** (for civil service) 资格考试; **~ fee** *n* **1** (charge) 入场费; **2** (subscription to society, club etc.) 入会费; **~ hall** *n* 门厅; **~ requirements** *npl* 入学条件; **~ ticket** *n* 门票

entrancing /ɪn'trɑːnsɪŋ, Amer -'træns-/ *adj* 迷人的 ‹*beauty, music, vision*›

entrancingly /ɪn'trɑːnsɪŋli, Amer -'træns-/ *adv* 迷人地 ‹*dance, sing, smile*›; **she is ~ beautiful** 她美丽迷人

entrant /'entrənt/ *n* **1** (in race, competition) 参赛者; **to be an ~ for** *or* **in sth.** 参加某比赛 **2** (in exam) 考生 **3** (to profession) 新职员; **to be an ~ to sth.** 是某机构的新成员; **new ~s to the police force/diplomatic service** 新入职警察/新外交人员

entrap /ɪn'træp/ *vt* (*pres p etc.* **-pp-**) **1** (catch) 使入圈套; **to ~ sb. in sth.** 使某人陷入某事 **2** (trick) 诱骗; **to ~ sb. into doing sth.** 诱使某人做某事

entrapment /ɪn'træpmənt/ *n* 诱捕

entreat /ɪn'triːt/ *vt* 恳求; **to ~ sb. to do sth.** 乞求某人做某事; **to ~ sb. for sth., to ~ sth. of sb.** 向某人乞求某事; **spare his life, I ~ you!** 饶他一命吧, 我求求你了!

entreating /ɪn'triːtɪŋ/ *adj* 恳求的 ‹*look, voice*›

entreatingly /ɪn'triːtɪŋli/ *adv* 乞求地 ‹*look, kneel, wail*›

entreaty /ɪn'triːti/ *n* 恳求; **at sb.'s ~** 应某人的恳求; **a look/gesture/prayer of ~** 恳求的样子/姿势/祷告; **he was deaf to all entreaties** 他对所有的乞求置之不理

entrecôte /'ɒntrəkəʊt/ *n* 牛背肉

entrée /'ɒntreɪ/ *n* **1** (main course) 主菜 **2** Brit (dish) [鱼与肉两道正菜之间的] 小菜 **3** formal (into society) 进入权; **an ~ into high society** 进入上层社会的资格

entrenched /ɪn'trentʃt/ *adj* **1** (firmly established) 确立的; **to be ~ in sth.** 牢固确立于某物中; **he is ~ in his views** 他坚持自己的看法 **2** Mil 用壕沟围住的 ‹*camp, enemy, position*›

entrepôt /'ɒntrəpəʊ/ *n* 货物集散地

entrepreneur /ˌɒntrəprə'nɜː(r)/ *n* **1** (in business) 企业家 **2** (in entertainment) 倡导者

entrepreneurial /ˌɒntrəprə'nɜːrɪəl/ *adj* 企业家的 ‹*flair, initiative, mentality*›

entropy /'entrəpi/ *n* [u] 熵

entrust /ɪn'trʌst/ *vt* **1** (assign responsibility for) 委托; **to ~ sb. with sth., to ~ sth. to sb.** 把某事委托给某人; **to ~ sb. with the task of doing sth.** 把做某事的任务委托给某人 **2** (put into the care or protection of) 托付; **I ~ed the child to her (care)** 我把孩子托付给她 (照看); **the court ~ed the sergeant with the prisoner** 法庭指派这名警佐看管犯人

entry /'entri/ *n* **1** [u and c] (entrance) 进入; **to make an ~** 进入; **to gain ~ to** *or* **into sth.** 得以进入某处; **to force ~ to** *or* **into sth.** 强行闯入某处; **illegal ~** 非法闯入 **2** Theat, Sport 上场 **3** [c] (entranceway) 入口 **4** [u] (admission) 进入权; **~ by ticket only** 凭票入内; **~ (to sth.) is free** (某处) 免费进入; **to gain/be refused ~ (to sth.)** 获准/被拒绝进入 (某处); **right of ~** 入境权; **'No Entry'** (on door) "不得入内"; (in one-way street) "不得驶入" **5** [u] (participation) **~ into sth.** 加入 ‹*group*›; 从事 ‹*politics, profession*› **6** [u] (record) 登记 **7** [c] (recorded item) 记录; **to make an ~ of sth.** 记录某物; **to make an ~ in the log/one's diary** 写一条日志/一则日记 **8** Accts 入账 **9** [c] (in reference book) 条目 **10** [u] Comput 输入 **11** [u] (in competition) 参赛; **~ is open to everyone** 人人均可参赛 **12** [c] (competitor) 参赛者; **a late ~** 新参赛的选手 **13** [c] (item for competition) 参赛作品; **one's ~ for sth.** 参加某竞赛的作品 **14** [c] (number of competitors) 参赛人数

entry: ~ fee *n* 入场费; **~ form** *n* 加入申请表; **~-level** *adj* 初级的 ‹*position, job*›; **~ permit** *n* 入境许可; **E~phone®** *n* Brit 应门对讲机; **~ requirements** *npl* **= entrance requirements**; **~ word** *n* 词目; **~ wound** *n* 穿透伤

entwine /ɪn'twaɪn/ *vt* 缠绕 ‹*stems*›; **the stems/plants were ~d** 这些茎/植物缠绕在一起; **they were ~d in each other's arms** 他们臂挽着臂; **their lives/fates/fortunes were (inextricably) ~d** 他们的生活/命运/前途已是紧紧交织在一起

E-number /'iːˌnʌmbə(r)/ *n* Brit [注明食品中所含添加剂的] E数

enumerate /ɪ'njuːməreɪt, Amer -'nuː-/ *vt* **1** (list) 列举 **2** (count) 数

enumeration /ɪˌnjuːmə'reɪʃn, Amer -ˌnuː-/ *n* **1** (listing) 列举 **2** (counting) 数数

enunciate /ɪ'nʌnsɪeɪt/ *vt* **1** (pronounce) 清晰地读 **2** (state) 阐明

enunciation /ɪˌnʌnsɪ'eɪʃn/ *n* **1** (of sound, word) 清晰的发音 **2** (of facts, clause, principle, policy) 阐述 **3** (of law, problem) 宣告

envelop /ɪn'veləp/ *vt* **1** (cover) 盖住 ‹*person, ground*›; «*mist*» 笼罩 ‹*scene, mountain*›; **to ~ sb./sth. (in sth.)** (用某物) 把某人裹住/笼罩某物 **2** (conceal) 掩盖; **to be ~ed in sth.** 被隐藏在某物中 **3** Mil 包围

envelope /'envələʊp, 'ɒn-/ *n* **1** Post 信封; **to put sth. in an ~** 把某物装入信封; **in a sealed ~** 在密封的信封中; **a stamped (and) addressed ~** 贴了邮票有地址的信封; **drawn up on the back of an ~** 当场起草; **to push (the edge of) the ~** 发挥到极致 **2** (membrane) (gen) 膜 **3** Biol 包袋 **4** Bot 包被 **5** Zool 气囊 **6** Aviat (in balloon, airship) 气囊

enviable /'envɪəbl/ *adj* 令人羡慕的 ‹*position, beauty, affluence*›

enviably /'envɪəbli/ *adv* 令人羡慕地; **he was ~ slim/rich** 他身体修长/很富有, 令人羡慕

envious /'envɪəs/ *adj* 羡慕的; **to be ~ of sb./sth.** 忌妒某人/某物; **to make sb. ~** 使某人羡慕; **an ~ glance** 羡慕的一瞥

enviously /'envɪəsli/ *adv* 羡慕地

environment /ɪn'vaɪərənmənt/ *n* **1** (surroundings, conditions) 环境; **a friendly/working ~** 友好氛围/工作环境 **2** Ecol 生态环境; **the ~** 自然环境 **3** Comput 运行环境

environmental /ɪnˌvaɪərən'mentl/ *adj* **1** (of surroundings) 环境的; **~ noise/conditions** 周围的噪声/环境条件 **2** Ecol 自然环境的 ‹*changes, studies*›; **~ pollution/protection** 环境污染/保护

environmental: ~ audit *n* 环境审计; **~ footprint** *n* **= ecological footprint**; **~ health** *n* [u] **1** (field) 环境卫生; **2** **E~ Health** (department) 环境卫生部; **E~ Health Officer** *n* 环境卫生部官员

environmentalist /ɪnˌvaɪərən'mentəlɪst/ *n* 环境保护主义者; **~ movement/group/organization/party/policy** 环保运动/团体/组织/政党/政策

environmentally /ɪnˌvaɪərən'mentəli/ *adv* 在环境方面 ‹*damaging, beneficial, safe, sound, compatible*›; **~ friendly/aware** 对环境无害的/有环保意识的; **~ speaking** 从环境保护的角度说

Environmentally Sensitive Area *n* 环境敏感区

environmental: E~ Protection Agency *n* Amer 环境保护局; **~ science** *n* [u] 环境科学; **~ scientist** ▸**p. 409** *n* 环境科学家; **~ studies** *npl + v sing* 环境

environs /ɪn'vaɪərənz/ *npl* 周围地区; **in the ~ of ...** 在…附近

envisage /ɪn'vɪzɪdʒ/ *vt* **1** (anticipate) 展望; **to ~ sth.** 设想 ‹*failure, prosperity, situation, possibility*›; **it is ~d that ...** 预期… **2** (visualize) 想象 ‹*scene, outcome*›

envision /en'vɪʒn/ *vt* 想象

envoy /'envɔɪ/ *n* **1** (messenger, representative) 使者 **2** (diplomat) **~ (extraordinary)** 特命全权公使

envy /'envi/

A *n* [u] 忌妒; **to be the ~ of sb.** 是某人忌妒的对象; **to do sth. out of ~** 出于忌妒做某事; **to be green with ~** 十分忌妒

B *vt* 忌妒; **to ~ sb. sth.** 忌妒某人某事

enzyme /'enzaɪm/ *n* 酶

Eocene /'iːəsiːn, 'iːəʊ-/

A *adj* (of the period) 始新世的; (of the rock system) 始新统的

B *n* **the ~** (period) 始新世; (rock system) 始新统

eon /'iːən/ *n* **= aeon**

EP *abbr* **1** **= European Parliament** **2** **= extended-play** Mus 密纹唱片

EPA *abbr* Amer **= Environmental Protection Agency**

e-paper /'iːˌpeɪpə(r)/ *n* [u] 电子纸

epaulette, Amer also **epaulet** /'epəlet/ *n* (gen) 肩饰; Mil 肩章

ephemera /ɪ'femərə/ *npl* 生命短促的事物; **the ~ of everyday life** 日常生活的琐事; **popular ~** 流行一时的物品

ephemeral /ɪ'femərəl/ *adj* **1** fig (short-lived) 短暂的 ‹*pleasures, sunshine, season*› **2** Bot, Zool 短生的 ‹*insects, animals, plants*›

epic /'epɪk/

A *adj* **1** (heroic) 漫长而艰难的 ‹*journey*›; 坚苦卓绝的 ‹*task, struggle*›; 英勇的 ‹*deed*›; 巨大的 ‹*tragedy, achievement*› **2** Literat, Cin 史诗的 ‹*simile, verse*›; 史诗般的 ‹*hero*›; **an ~ poem/film/play/novel** 史诗/史诗式电影/史诗式戏剧/史诗式小说

B *n* **1** Literat (poem) 史诗; (film) 史诗式电影; (novel) 史诗式小说 **2** colloq hum (task, activity) 壮举; **our trip was an ~** 我们的旅行是一项壮举

epicentre Brit, **epicenter** Amer /'epɪsentə(r)/ *n* **1** lit (of earthquake) 震中 **2** fig (of situation, problem) 中心

epicure /'epɪkjʊə(r)/ *n* 美食家

epicurean /ˌepɪkjʊ'riːən/

A *adj* 爱享受的

B *n* 爱享受的人

epidemic /ˌepɪ'demɪk/

A *n* **1** lit (of infectious disease) 传染病; (disease occurring in such a way) 流行病; **an ~ of influenza/yellow fever** 流感/黄热病的流行 **2** fig (rapid spread) 蔓延; **an ~ of crime has infected the town** 犯罪活动在城里泛滥成灾

B *adj* 泛滥的; **the problem has reached ~ proportions** 该问题已到了泛滥成灾的程度

epidemiology /ˌepɪdiːmɪ'ɒlədʒi/ *n* [u] 流行病学

epidermis /ˌepɪ'dɜːmɪs/ *n* [u] 表皮

epidiascope /ˌepɪ'daɪəskəʊp/ *n* 透反射两用幻灯机

epidural /ˌepɪ'djʊərəl/ Med

A *n* 硬膜外麻醉

B *adj* 硬膜外的 ‹*injection, anaesthetic*›

epiglottis /ˌepɪ'glɒtɪs/ *n* 会厌 [喉头入口处的盖状软骨]

epigram /'epɪgræm/ *n* **1** (saying, remark) 警句 **2** (poem) 诙谐短诗

e

epigrammatic /ˌepɪɡrəˈmætɪk/, **epigrammatical** /ˌepɪɡrəˈmætɪkl/ *adjs* 简练精辟的; **an ~ style** 隽语式的风格

epigraph /ˈepɪɡrɑːf, Amer -ɡræf/ *n* 1 (quotation) 题词 2 (inscription) 铭文

epilepsy /ˈepɪlepsi/ ▸p. 377 *n* [u] 癫痫

epileptic /ˌepɪˈleptɪk/
A *n* 癫痫病患者
B *adj* 癫痫的; **an ~ fit** 癫痫发作

epilogue, Amer also **epilog** /ˈepɪlɒɡ/ *n* 1 Literat 后记 2 fig (conclusion) 总结

epiphany /ɪˈpɪfəni/ *n* 1 **Epiphany** Relig 显现节 [1月6日纪念贤士朝拜耶稣] 2 (revelation) 顿悟

episcopacy /ɪˈpɪskəpəsi/ *n* = **episcopate**

episcopal /ɪˈpɪskəpl/ *adj* 主教的

Episcopal Church *pr n* [苏格兰和美国的] 圣公会

Episcopalian /ɪˌpɪskəˈpeɪliən/
A *n* [苏格兰和美国的] 圣公会教徒
B *adj* 主教统辖制的

episcopate /ɪˈpɪskəpət/ *n* 1 (office of bishop) 主教职位; (term of bishop) 主教任期 2 (bishops) **the ~** 主教团

episode /ˈepɪsəʊd/ *n* 1 (event) 一个事件; (group of events) 一组事件 2 (instalment) (of book) 一节; (play, TV series) 一集 3 (finite period of illness) 发作期 4 Mus 插部

episodic /ˌepɪˈsɒdɪk/ *adj* 1 (in parts) 有许多片断的 2 (sporadic) 不定期的 3 (describing novel, book) 连载的; (describing drama) 连播的

epistemological /ɪˌpɪstɪməˈlɒdʒɪkl/ *adj* 认识论的

epistemology /ɪˌpɪstɪˈmɒlədʒi/ *n* [u] 认识论

epistle /ɪˈpɪsl/ *n* 1 formal 书信; **he wrote me a long ~ about his bunions** hum 他写了封长信告诉我他的脚肿了一块 2 **Epistle** (in Bible) 使徒书信 3 (in church service) 使徒书信摘录

epitaph /ˈepɪtɑːf, Amer -tæf/ *n* 墓志铭

epithet /ˈepɪθet/ *n* (adjective) 表述形容词; (descriptive phrase) 修饰语

epitome /ɪˈpɪtəmi/ *n* 典型; **the ~ of kindness** 仁慈的化身

epitomize /ɪˈpɪtəmaɪz/ *vt* 成为…的典范 ‹*person*›; 体现 ‹*quality, virtue*›

epoch /ˈiːpɒk, Amer ˈepək/ *n* 1 (period of time) 时代; **to mark the beginning of an ~** 标志着一个时代的开始; **the end/dawn of an ~** 一个时代的结束/开端 2 Geol 世

epoch-making *adj* 划时代的 ‹*discovery, event, invention*›

eponym /ˈepənɪm/ *n* 人名名称 [依据真人或神话人物的姓名命名的专有名词]

eponymous /ɪˈpɒnɪməs/ *adj* 同名的; **the ~ hero of the novel** 与小说同名的主人公

EPOS /ˈiːpɒs/ *abbr* = **electronic point of sale; ~ terminal** 电子销售终端

epoxy /ɪˈpɒksi/
A *n* **~ (resin)** 环氧树脂
B *adj* 环氧的; **~ cement** 环氧水泥
C *vt* 用环氧树脂胶合

eps *npl* = **earnings per share** 每股收益

Epsom salts /ˌepsəm ˈsɔːlts/ *npl* + *v sing* 泻盐

equable /ˈekwəbl/ *adj* 1 (moderate) 温差小的 ‹*climate, region*› 2 (even-tempered) 平和的 ‹*temperament, tones*›; 性情温和的 ‹*person*›

equably /ˈekwəbli/ *adv* 平和地 ‹*speak, answer*›

equal /ˈiːkwəl/
A *adj* 1 (same numerically) 相同的 ‹*number, quantity*›; **to be ~ to sth.** 等于…; **4 + 4 is ~ to 6 + 2** 4 加 4 等于 6 加 2 2 (equivalent, on same terms) 同样的 ‹*skill, delight, violence, pay, privileges*›; **to be about ~** 大致相当; **'~ work ~ pay'** "同工同酬"; **(all) other things being ~** 如果（所有）其他条件相同; **to be on an ~ footing (with sb.)** （与某人）地位相同; **to be on ~ terms (with sb.)** （与某人）处于同等条件; **to fight/compete on ~ terms** 在同等条件下对抗/竞争 3 (of people with same status) 平等的; **to be ~ before the law** 在法律面前平等 4 (able to do) **to be ~ to sth.** 胜任某事; **to be ~ to the task/challenge** 能胜任这项任务/能迎接挑战; **to be ~ to doing sth.** 能做某事
B *n* 相当者; **to be the ~ of sb., to be sb.'s ~** 与某人不相上下; **to be without/have no ~** 无与伦比; **to treat sb. as an/one's ~** 平等对待某人
C *adv* Sport 并列地 ‹*finish*›; **to come ~ third (with sb./sth.)** （与某人/某物）并列第三名
D *vt* 1 Math 等于; **1 + 2 ~s 3** 1 加 2 等于 3; **to let sth. ~ sth.** 设…等于… 2 (match) 比得上 ‹*achievement, record*›; **not to be ~led** 无与伦比; **there is nothing to ~ this painting** 这幅画举世无双 3 (result in) 导致; **health plus money ~s happiness** 拥有健康和金钱就拥有了幸福

equality /ɪˈkwɒləti/ *n* [u] 平等; **racial ~** 种族平等; **~ of opportunity** 机会均等

Equality and Human Rights Commission *n* Brit 平等及人权委员会

equalize /ˈiːkwəlaɪz/
A *vt* 使…相等 ‹*number*›; 使…均衡 ‹*distribution*›; 使…平等 ‹*opportunity*›
B *vi* Sport 扳平比分

equalizer /ˈiːkwəlaɪzə(r)/ *n* 1 (leveller) 使平等者; **education is the great ~** 教育对平等居功至伟 2 Sport 扳平比分的得分 3 Amer colloq (gun) 枪

equally /ˈiːkwəli/ *adv* 1 (in size) 平均地 ‹*divide, share, allocate*› 2 (in manner, degree) 同样地; **to be ~ right/wrong** 同样正确/错误 3 (in addition) 此外; **~, he could have a point** 此外, 他可能也有道理

equal: ~ opportunity, ~ opportunities *n* [u] 均等机会; **~ rights** *npl* 平等权利; **~s sign** Brit, **~ sign** Amer *n* 等号

equanimity /ˌekwəˈnɪməti/ *n* [u] 镇静

equate /ɪˈkweɪt/
A *vt* 1 (identify) 使等同; **to ~ sth. with sth.** 把某事物与某事物等同起来 2 (compare) 使相比较; **to ~ sth. to** *or* **with sth.** 将某事物与某事物相比较
B *vi* 相同; **to ~ to** *or* **with sth.** 相当于某事物

equation /ɪˈkweɪʒn/ *n* 1 Math 方程; **a quadratic/simple ~** 二次/一次方程 2 (process of equating) 等同; **the ~ of sth. with sth.** 把某事物与某事物等同起来

equator /ɪˈkweɪtə(r)/ *n* 赤道

equatorial /ˌekwəˈtɔːriəl/ *adj* (of or at the equator) 赤道的 ‹*rainforest, climate*›; (near the equator) 赤道附近的 ‹*countries*›

Equatorial Guinea /ekwəˌtɔːriəl ˈɡɪni/ *pr n* 赤道几内亚

equerry /ˈekwəri, ɪˈkweri/ *n* Brit 王室侍从官

equestrian /ɪˈkwestriən/
A *adj* 骑术的 ‹*event*›; **an ~ statue** 骑士塑像
B *n* 骑师

equestrianism /ɪˈkwestriənɪzm/ *n* [u] 马术

equidistant /ˌiːkwɪˈdɪstənt/ *adj* 等距离的; **to be ~ from A and B** 与 A 和 B 等距

equilateral /ˌiːkwɪˈlætərəl/ *adj* 等边的; **an ~ triangle** 等边三角形

equilibrium /ˌiːkwɪˈlɪbriəm/ *n* 1 (of forces, influences) 均衡; **to be in (a state of) ~** 处于均衡（状态） 2 (of mind) 平静 3 (physical balance) 平衡

equine /ˈekwaɪn/ *adj* 马的

equinoctial /ˌiːkwɪˈnɒkʃl, ˌek-/ *adj* 二分点的 ‹*tide*›; **an ~ point** 二分点 [春分或秋分]; **an ~ circle** *or* **line** 天体赤道; **an ~ year** 分至年

equinox /ˈiːkwɪnɒks, ˈek-/ *n* 二分点 [春分或秋分]

equip /ɪˈkwɪp/ *vt* (*pres p etc.* **-pp-**) 1 (with things) 装备; **to ~ sb./sth. with sth.** 为某物/某人装备某物; **to ~ sth. as sth.** 把某物装备成某物; **to ~ sb./sth. for sth.** 为某事装备某人/某物; **a fully ~ped kitchen** 设备齐全的厨房 2 (with qualities, skills) 使有能力; **a good education ~s one for life** 良好的教育会为人的一生打好基础; **to be well ~ped to deal with problems** 具备很强的处理问题的能力

equipment /ɪˈkwɪpmənt/ *n* [u] 1 (requisite items) 器械; **office/photographic/sports ~** 办公用品/照相器材/运动器械 2 Ind 设备; **a piece** *or* **an item of ~** 一件设备 3 Mil 装备 4 (fitting out) 配备

equitable /ˈekwɪtəbl/ *adj* 公正的 ‹*solution, share, result*›

equitably /ˈekwɪtəbli/ *adv* 公正地 ‹*share, divide*›

equity /ˈekwəti/
A *n* 1 [u] (fairness) 公正 2 [u] Fin (value of shares issued) 股本 3 [u] Jur 衡平法
B **equities** *npl* Fin 普通股

equity: ~ capital *n* [u] 股本; **~ financing** *n* [u] 股权融资; **~ market** *n* 证券市场

equivalence /ɪˈkwɪvələns/ *n* 相等

equivalent /ɪˈkwɪvələnt/
A *n* 相等物; **the ~ of sth.** 相当于某物的东西; **the English ~ of this word** 这个词的英语对应词
B *adj* 相等的 ‹*value, amount*›; **to be ~ to sth.** 相当于某事物

equivocal /ɪˈkwɪvəkl/ *adj* 1 (ambiguous) 模棱两可的 ‹*remarks, answer, attitude*› 2 (questionable) 难以理解的 ‹*behaviour, circumstances*›; 不肯定的 ‹*attitude*›

equivocally /ɪˈkwɪvəkli/ *adv* 模棱两可地

equivocate /ɪˈkwɪvəkeɪt/ *vi* 含糊其辞

equivocation /ɪˌkwɪvəˈkeɪʃn/ *n* 1 [u] (using ambiguous or vague statements) 含糊其辞; **without ~** 毫不含糊地 2 [c] (ambiguous expression) 搪塞的话; **the speech was full of contradictions and ~s** 这篇演讲全都是自相矛盾和模棱两可的话

ER *abbr* 1 = **Elizabeth Regina** 伊丽莎白女王 2 Amer = **emergency room**

er /ə, ɜː/ *excl* 嗯

era /ˈɪərə/ *n* 1 Hist 纪元 2 Geol 代 3 (in politics, fashion etc.) 时代; **to mark the end of an ~** 标志着一个时代的结束

eradicable /ɪˈrædɪkəbl/ *adj* 可根除的 ‹*disease*›

eradicate /ɪˈrædɪkeɪt/ *vt* 根除 ‹*disease, weeds, corruption, poverty*›; 杜绝 ‹*crime*›; 扫除 ‹*illiteracy, superstition*›

eradication /ɪˌrædɪˈkeɪʃn/ *n* (of disease, weeds, corruption, poverty) 根除; (of crime) 杜绝; (of illiteracy, superstition) 扫除

erase /ɪˈreɪz, Amer ɪˈreɪs/ *vt* 1 (rub out) 擦掉 ‹*writing, mark*› 2 Comput, Audio (wipe, delete) 删除 ‹*program, file*›; 抹去 ‹*recording*› 3 (obliterate) 消灭 ‹*poverty, disease*›; 销毁 ‹*carving*›; 毁灭 ‹*village*› 4 (blot out) 消除 ‹*fear*›; 忘却 ‹*thought, feeling*›; **to ~ the memory from one's mind** 忘却记忆中的事

eraser /ɪˈreɪzə(r), Amer -sər/ *n* (for paper) 橡皮擦; (for blackboard) 黑板擦

erasure /ɪˈreɪʒə(r)/ *n* 1 [u] (action) 擦除 2 [c] (word) 擦除的词; (mark) 擦痕

erbium /ˈɜːbiəm/ *n* [u] 铒

ere /eə(r)/ archaic *or* liter
A *prep* 在…之前; **~ long** 不久; **~ now** 刚才
B *conj* 在…之前

erect /ɪˈrekt/
A *adj* 1 (of posture, position) 直立的 ‹*posture*›; 竖直的 ‹*tail, pillar*›; **to hold oneself ~** 挺直

身子; **with head ～** 昂首 **2** Physiol 勃起的 ‹*penis*›; 挺起的 ‹*nipples, clitoris*›
B *vt* **1** (construct, build) 建造 ‹*building, monument, bridge*›; 竖立 ‹*statue, sign*›; 搭建 ‹*marquee, scaffolding*› **2** (set upright) 竖起 ‹*mast, pillar*› **3** (create, establish) 创立 ‹*theory, system*›

erectile /ɪ'rektaɪl, Amer -tl/ *adj* 能勃起的; **～ tissue/disorder** 勃起组织/功能紊乱

erectile dysfunction *n* [u] 勃起功能障碍

erection /ɪ'rekʃn/ **1** [u] (construction) (of building, monument, bridge) 建造; (of statue, sign) 竖立; (of marquee, scaffolding) 搭建 **2** (raising into a vertical position) (of mast, pillar) 竖起 **3** [c] Physiol (of penis) 勃起; (of nipples, clitoris) 挺起 **4** [c] pej (building) 建筑物

Erector Set® /ɪ ˊrektə(r) set/ *n* Amer 拼装玩具

erg /ɜːg/ *n* 尔格 [功和能量的单位]

ergo /'ɜːgəʊ/ *adv* formal 因此

ergonomics /ˌɜːgə'nɒmɪks/ *npl* + *v sing* 工效学

ergonomist /ɜː'gɒnəmɪst/ ▸**p. 409** *n* 工效学家

erhu /ɜː'huː/ ▸**p. 395** *n* 二胡

Eritrea /erɪ'treɪə/ *pr n* 厄立特里亚

Eritrean /erɪ'treɪən/
A *adj* 厄立特里亚的 ‹*culture, language, people*›
B *n* 厄立特里亚人

ERM *abbr* = **Exchange Rate Mechanism**

ermine /'ɜːmɪn/ *n* **1** [c] (*pl* **～** *or* **～s**) (animal) 白鼬 **2** [u] (fur) 白鼬毛皮

Ernie /'ɜːni/ *abbr* Brit = **electronic random number indicator equipment** 欧尼电子摇奖机

erode /ɪ'rəʊd/ *vt* **1** lit (wear away) «*water*» 侵蚀 ‹*coastline, cliff*›; «*wind*» 使…风化 ‹*stone*›; «*acid*» 腐蚀 ‹*metal*› **2** fig (diminish) 削弱 ‹*privileges*›; 消磨 ‹*self-esteem*›; 损害 ‹*rights, liberty*›; 削减 ‹*value*›

erogenous /ɪ'rɒdʒənəs/ *adj* 性敏感的 ‹*zone, area*›

erosion /ɪ'rəʊʒn/ *n* **1** lit (of coastline, cliff) 侵蚀; (of stone) 风化; (of metal) 腐蚀 **2** fig (of privileges) 削弱; (of self-esteem) 消磨; (of rights, liberty) 损害; (of value) 削减

erosive /ɪ'rəʊsɪv/ *adj* 侵蚀的 ‹*effect, action, power*›; 腐蚀性的 ‹*acid*›; **the wind and sea are ～ natural elements** 风和海是有侵蚀作用的自然因素

erotic /ɪ'rɒtɪk/ *adj* 性爱的 ‹*desire, feelings, pleasure, fantasy, dream*›; 色情的 ‹*verse, photograph*›; 淫秽的 ‹*scene*›

erotica /ɪ'rɒtɪkə/ *npl* **1** Literat 色情文学 **2** Cin, Art 色情艺术作品

eroticism /ɪ'rɒtɪsɪzəm/ *n* [u] 色情

err /ɜː(r)/ *vi* 犯错误; **to ～ in one's judgement** 判断出错; **to ～ is human** 犯错人皆难免; **to ～ on the side of caution** 宁可谨慎过头

errand /'erənd/ *n* 差事; **to go on** *or* **to run an ～ for sb.** 为某人跑腿; **to go/be sent on a fool's ～** 去/被派去做徒劳无益的事; **an ～ of mercy** 仁慈之事

errand boy *n* esp Brit dated 供差遣的童仆

errant /'erənt/ *adj* formal (straying) 出轨的; (misbehaving) 行为不端的; **an ～ husband** 出轨的丈夫

errata /e'rɑːtə/ *pl* ▸**erratum**

erratic /ɪ'rætɪk/
A *adj* 不稳定的 ‹*record, performance, temperament*›; 难以预测的 ‹*results*›; **a very ～ player** 状态很不稳定的选手
B *n* Geol 漂砾

erratically /ɪ'rætɪkli/ *adv* 不稳定地 ‹*play, perform*›; 不平稳地 ‹*drive*›

erratum /e'rɑːtəm/ *n* (*pl* **errata**) **1** (error) [印刷或书写中的] 文字错误 **2** **errata** (list) 勘误表; **a list of errata** 勘误单

erroneous /ɪ'rəʊnɪəs/ *adj* 错误的 ‹*idea, conclusion, statement*›

erroneously /ɪ'rəʊnɪəsli/ *adv* 错误地

error /'erə(r)/ *n* **1** [c] (mistake) 错误; **to commit** *or* **make an ～** 犯错; **an ～ of/in sth.** 某方面的错误; **an ～ of judgement** 判断错误; **a spelling/typing ～** 拼写/打字错误; **an ～ of 10%, a 10% ～** 10% 的误差 **2** [u] (being wrong) 犯错; **in ～** 弄错; **human ～** 人为错误; **there is no margin of** *or* **for ～** 这里绝对不允许出错; **a degree of ～** 错误程度; **to see the ～ of one's ways** 知错即改

error message *n* 出错信息

ersatz /'eəzæts, 'ɜːsɑːts/ *adj* 代用的; **～ tobacco/coffee/whiskey** 代用烟草/咖啡/威士忌; **～ culture** 虚假文化

erstwhile /'ɜːstwaɪl/ *adj attrib* liter 从前的 ‹*colleague, friend, associate*›

erudite /'eruːdaɪt/ *adj* 博学的

eruditely /'eruːdaɪtli/ *adv* 博学地

erudition /ˌeruː'dɪʃn/ *n* [u] 博学; **a display of (one's) ～** 对（自己）学识的炫耀

erupt /ɪ'rʌpt/ *vi* **1** lit «*volcano, geyser*» 喷发 **2** fig (break out) «*disease, riot, gunfire*» 爆发; «*laughter, howl, violence, hostilities*» 突然发出 **3** Med «*rash, pimple*» 突然长出

eruption /ɪ'rʌpʃn/ *n* **1** lit (of volcano, geyser) 喷发 **2** fig (of disease, riot, gunfire) 爆发; (of laughter, howl, violence, hostilities) 突然发出 **3** Med (of rash, pimple) 突然出现

ESA *abbr* **1** = **European Space Agency** **2** Brit = **Environmentally Sensitive Area**

escalate /'eskəleɪt/
A *vt* 使…上涨 ‹*prices*›; 使…升级 ‹*war, issue*›; 使…恶化 ‹*problem, fighting*›; 使…增加 ‹*demands*›; **he ～d the issue by informing the managing director** 他把这事上报了常务董事，使问题严重起来
B *vi* «*fighting, violence*» 恶化; «*prices, costs*» 不断上涨; «*demands*» 增加; «*inflation*» 加剧; **to ～ into a major crisis** 逐步升级为重大危机

escalation /ˌeskə'leɪʃn/ *n* (of fighting, violence) 恶化; (of inflation) 加剧; (of prices, costs) 上涨; (of demands) 增加; **the recent ～ in food prices** 最近食品价格的不断上涨

escalation clause *n* = **escalator clause**

escalator /'eskəleɪtə(r)/ *n* 自动扶梯

escalator clause *n* 伸缩条款 [合同中根据成本或费用变化而提高或降低支付额的条款]

escalope, escallop /'eskələʊp, ɪ'skæləp/ *n* 薄肉片

escapade /'eskəpeɪd, ˌeskə'peɪd/ *n* **1** (adventure) 冒险行为 **2** (prank) 恶作剧

escape /ɪ'skeɪp/
A *vi* **1** (break free) 逃跑; fig 消失; **to ～ to somewhere** 逃到某处; **to ～ from sb./sth.** 逃避某人/某事物; **to ～ from reality** 逃避现实; **to ～ by the skin of one's teeth** 侥幸逃脱; **to (manage to) ～ with one's life** （设法）逃命; **to ～ with a warning** 被训诫一通了事 **2** (leak) 泄漏; **to ～ from sth./somewhere** «*gas, air, liquid*» 从某物中/某处漏出; **to ～ through sth.** 通过某处漏出
B *vt* **1** (avoid) 逃脱 ‹*captivity*›; 避开 ‹*notice*›; 逃避 ‹*obligation, reality, punishment*›; **to ～ death/danger/persecution** 死里逃生/逃离危险/摆脱迫害 **2** (elude) 被忽略; **to ～ sb.'s attention** *or* **notice** 未被某人注意
C *n* **1** [u and c] lit (breaking free) 逃跑; **an ～ to somewhere/sth.** 逃到/逃进某处; **to make an** *or* **one's ～** 溜走; **to have a narrow/lucky ～** 死里逃生/幸运逃脱; **to make good one's ～** 成功逃脱 **2** [c] fig (refuge) 逃避; **an ～ from reality** 逃避现实 **3** [c] (leak of water, gas) 泄漏

escape: ～ artist *n* = **escapologist**; **～ character** *n* 转义字符; **～ clause** *n* 免责条款

escapee /ɪˌskeɪ'piː/ *n* (person escaped) 逃脱者; (from prison) 逃犯

escape: ～ hatch *n* 紧急出口; **～ key** *n* 退出键

escapement /ɪ'skeɪpmənt/ *n* [钟表的] 擒纵轮

escape: ～ road *n* 紧急避险岔道; **～ route** *n* 逃跑路线; **～ sequence** *n* 溢出序列; **～ velocity** *n* 逃逸速度 [指物体摆脱星球引力束缚所需的最低速度]; **～ wheel** *n* 擒纵轮

escapism /ɪ'skeɪpɪzəm/ *n* [u] 逃避现实; **sheer** *or* **pure ～** 纯粹的逃避; **a form of ～** 一种消遣形式

escapist /ɪ'skeɪpɪst/
A *adj* 逃避现实的 ‹*literature, film, fantasy*›
B *n* 逃避现实的人

escapologist /ˌeskə'pɒlədʒɪst/ ▸**p. 409** *n* 脱身术杂技演员

escapology /ˌeskə'pɒlədʒi/ *n* [u] 脱身术

escarpment /ɪ'skɑːpmənt/ *n* 悬崖

eschew /ɪs'tʃuː/ *vt* formal 戒绝 ‹*wine, drink*›; 避开 ‹*temptation, violence*›

escort
A /'eskɔːt/ *n* **1** Mil 护送部队; Naut 护航舰; Police 押送者; **a military/police/armed ～** 军队/警察/武装护送; **to put sb. under ～** 使某人得到护送 **2** (companion) 陪同者
B /ɪ'skɔːt/ *vt* 护卫 ‹*monarch, president*›; 护送 ‹*VIP*›; 押送 ‹*prisoner, captive*›; **to ～ sb. in/out** 护送某人进去/出来

escort: ～ agency *n* 社交陪伴服务社; **～ duty** *n* 护卫任务; **to be on ～ duty** 执行护卫任务; **～ vessel** *n* 护卫舰

escrow /e'skrəʊ/
A *n* Jur [u] 暂由第三方保管; **in ～** 由第三方代为保管
B *vt* esp Amer 将…暂交第三方保管 ‹*money, goods, document*›

escrow account *n* 托管账户

escutcheon /ɪ'skʌtʃən/ *n* 盾形徽章; **to be a blot on sb.'s ～** 玷污某人的名声

e-shopping /'iːˌʃɒpɪŋ/ *n* [u] = **electronic shopping**

Eskimo /'eskɪməʊ/ ▸**p. 503, p. 426**
A *adj* (of the people) 爱斯基摩人的; (of the language) 爱斯基摩语的
B *n* **1** [c] (person) 爱斯基摩人 **2** [u] (language) 爱斯基摩语

ESL *abbr* = **English as a Second Language**

ESOL *abbr* = **English for Speakers of Other Languages**

esophagus /ɪ'sɒfəgəs/ *n* Amer = **oesophagus**

esoteric /ˌiːsəʊ'terɪk, ˌe-/ *adj* 难懂的 ‹*poetry, language, style*›; 深奥的 ‹*argument, imagery*›

esoterica /ˌiːsəʊ'terɪkə, ˌe-/ *npl* **1** (subjects) 深奥的学科 **2** (publications) 专业书籍

ESP *n* **1** = **extrasensory perception** ▸**extrasensory** **2** = **English for Special Purposes**

espalier /ɪ'spælɪeɪ, Amer ɪ'spæljər/
A *n* **1** (tree, shrub) 墙树 **2** (trellis) 攀架
B *vt* 将…培育成墙树 ‹*tree, shrub*›

esparto /e'spɑːtəʊ/ *n* **～ (grass)** 细茎针茅

especial /ɪ'speʃl/ *adj attrib* **1** (better or greater than usual) 特别的 ‹*interest, importance*› **2** (belonging to one person or thing) 特有的

especially /ɪ'speʃəli/ *adv* **1** (particularly) 尤其; **why her ～?** 为何非得是她？; **he came ～ to see me** 他特地来看我 **2** (very much) 十分 ‹*cheerful, awkward, difficult*›

Esperanto /ˌespə'ræntəʊ/ ▸**p. 426** *n* [u] 世界语

e

espionage /ˈespɪənɑːʒ/ *n* [u] 谍报活动; **to engage in ~** 从事间谍活动

esplanade /ˌespləˈneɪd/ *n* 海滨空地

espouse /ɪˈspaʊz/ *vt* formal 支持 ‹*theory, cause*›; 拥护 ‹*ideology, belief*›

espresso /eˈspresəʊ/ *n* (*pl* **~s**) (coffee) 蒸馏咖啡; (a cup of) 一杯蒸馏咖啡

espy /ɪˈspaɪ/ *vt* liter 瞥见

Esq. *abbr* Brit dated or formal = **Esquire** 先生 [用于信头或信封]; **John Roberts ~** 约翰·罗伯兹先生

essay /ˈeseɪ/
A *n* **1** (piece of writing) 短文; Literat 散文 **2** formal or liter (endeavour) 尝试
B *vt* liter 试图; **to ~ sth.** 尝试某事

essayist /ˈeseɪɪst/ ▸**p. 409** *n* 散文作家

essence /ˈesns/ *n* **1** [u] (nature) 本质; **this is the very ~ of jazz** 这正是爵士乐的精髓; **of the ~** 至关重要的; **in ~** 实质上 **2** [c] Cosmet, Chem, Pharm (extract) 精油 **3** [c] Culin 香精

essential /ɪˈsenʃl/
A *adj* **1** (vital) 完全必要的; **to be ~ to sth./to doing sth.** 某事/做某事是必不可少的; **to be ~ that ...** 必须…; **to be ~ for sth.** 对某事物至关重要 **2** (basic) 本质的 ‹*characteristic, question*›; 基本的 ‹*quality, requirement*›
B *n* **1** (indispensable object) 必需品; **to be an ~** 是基本用品 **2** **essentials** *pl* (fundamental elements) 基本要素; **the ~s of English grammar** 英语语法基础; **to get down to ~s** 从基础着手; **in (all) ~s** 在（所有的）基本方面

essentially /ɪˈsenʃəli/ *adv* **1** (basically) 本质上 **2** (really, very) 非常 **3** (more or less) 大体上

essential oil *n* 精油

Essex /ˈesɪks/ *pr n* 埃塞克斯郡

EST *abbr* Amer = **Eastern Standard Time**

est. *abbr* = **established**

establish /ɪˈstæblɪʃ/ *vt* **1** (set up) 创立 ‹*business, company, factory*›; 建立 ‹*state, order, home*›; **to ~ a relationship with sb.** 与某人建立关系 **2** (prove) 证实 ‹*identity, guilt, innocence, need*›; **to ~ what/why/whether ...** 证明什么/为什么/是否…; **to ~ that sth. is the case** 证实某事; **to ~ a fact** 证明事实; **to ~ the cause of death** 确定死亡原因 **3** (gain acceptance for) 使…被接受 ‹*belief, claim*›; 使…得到认可 ‹*custom, practice*›; 确立 ‹*fame*›; **to ~ oneself as ...** 确立自己作为…的地位; **to ~ a reputation as sth.** 确立某声誉

established /ɪˈstæblɪʃt/ *adj* **1** (accepted, acknowledged) 已确立的; **an ~ fact** 毋庸置疑的事实 **2** (with a proven reputation) 知名的 ‹*artist, musician, politician*›; 已建立的 ‹*business, government, network*› **3** Relig 成为国教的 ‹*religion, faith*›; **the ~ church** 国教

establishment /ɪˈstæblɪʃmənt/ *n* **1** [u] (setting up) (of business) 创立; (of law, rule) 制定 **2** [c] (institution, organization) 机构 **3** [c] (shop, business) 企业 **4** [c] (staff) (of an organization) 编制; (of a household) 成员; **to be on/form part of the ~** 在编 **5** [u] (powerful group) **the E~** 权势集团; **a pillar of the E~** 统治阶级的中流砥柱 **6** [u] (influential group) 权威人士; **the literary/art/medical/legal ~** 文学/艺术/医学/法律界权威

estate /ɪˈsteɪt/ *n* **1** (house and park) 庄园 **2** esp Brit = **housing estate** **3** (assets) 财产 [尤指遗产]; **to divide (up) an ~** 分割财产; **to leave an ~** 留下遗产; **to liquidate an ~** 清算财产 **4** dated or liter (stage, state) 人生阶段; **the (holy) ~ of matrimony** （神圣的）已婚状况; **to reach man's ~** 成为成年男子 **5** (class, order) **~ of the realm** 政体阶层; **the three ~s of the realm** 构成上议院的三个阶层

estate: **~ agency** *n* esp Brit 房地产公司; **~ agent** *n* esp Brit 房地产经纪人; **~ car** *n* Brit 旅行轿车; **~ duty** *n* Brit dated 遗产税

esteem /ɪˈstiːm/
A *n* [u] 尊重; **to hold sb./sth. in low ~** 对某人/某事物评价低; **to hold sb./sth. in high/great ~** 非常尊重某人/看重某事物; **to go up/down in sb.'s ~** 得到某人更高/更低的评价
B *vt* **1** formal (admire) 尊重 ‹*person, opinion, quality*› **2** (think) 认为; **to ~ sth. an honour** 把某事看作是荣誉

esthete /ˈiːsθiːt, ˈes-/ *n* Amer = **aesthete**

esthetic /esˈθetɪk,/ *adj* Amer = **aesthetic**

estheticism /esˈθetɪsɪzm/ *n* [u] Amer = **aestheticism**

estimable /ˈestɪməbl/ *adj* formal 值得尊敬的

estimate
A /ˈestɪmət/ *n* **1** (assessment of size, cost, value) 估计; **to make an ~** 估算; **by one's ~** 按估计; **at a rough ~** 粗略估计一下 **2** Comm (written statement) 估价单; **to put in an ~ for sth.** 为某物估价 **3** (estimation) 评价; **to form an ~ of sb./sth.** 形成对某人/某事物的看法; **to revise one's ~ of sb./sth.** 改变对某人/某事的看法
B /ˈestɪmeɪt/ *vt* **1** (roughly calculate or judge) 估计 ‹*value, price, distance, speed*›; **to ~ that ...** 估计…; **to ~ sth. at/to be ...** 估计某物为… **2** (submit a probable price for) 为…估价; **to ~ a price for sth.** 估计某物的价格

estimate: **~d time of arrival** *n* 预计到达时间; **~d time of departure** *n* 预计出发时间

estimation /ˌestɪˈmeɪʃn/ *n* **1** (esteem) 尊敬; **to go up/down in sb.'s ~** 在某人心目中的地位提高/下降 **2** (judgement) 评价; **in sb.'s ~** 照某人看来 **3** (calculation) 估计

Estonia /ɪˈstəʊnɪə/ *pr n* 爱沙尼亚

Estonian /ɪˈstəʊnɪən/ ▸**p. 503, p. 426**
A *adj* (of Estonia) 爱沙尼亚的; (of the people) 爱沙尼亚人的; (of the language) 爱沙尼亚语的
B *n* **1** [c] (person) 爱沙尼亚人 **2** [u] (language) 爱沙尼亚语

estranged /ɪˈstreɪndʒd/ *adj* 疏远的; **to be ~ from sb.** 与某人不和; **her ~ husband** 她分居的丈夫

estrangement /ɪˈstreɪndʒmənt/ *n* **1** [u] (alienation) 疏远; **~ from sb.** 与某人的疏远 **2** [c] (rift) 分手; **an ~ between the two old friends** 两位老朋友的断交

estrogen /ˈiːstrədʒən/ *n* Amer = **oestrogen**

estrus /ˈiːstrəs/ *n* Amer = **oestrus**

estuary /ˈestʃʊəri, Amer -ʊeri/ ▸**p. 663** *n* 河口

Estuary English *n* [u] Brit usu pej 河口英语 [兼具标准发音和伦敦话的特点]

ETA *abbr* = **estimated time of arrival**

e-tailer /ˈiːˌteɪlə(r)/ *n* 网上零售商

e-tailing /ˈiːˌteɪlɪŋ/ *n* [u] 网上零售

et al. *abbr* = **and others** 等人

etc. *abbr* = **et cetera**

et cetera, etcetera /ɪt ˈsetərə, et-/ *adv* 等等

etch /etʃ/ *vt* 蚀刻; **to ~ sth. on** *or* **on to sth.** 在某物上蚀刻某物; **to be ~ed on sb.'s memory** *or* **mind** 被铭记在心

etching /ˈetʃɪŋ/ *n* **1** [u] (art) 蚀刻; (technique) 蚀刻法 **2** [c] (print) 蚀刻画

ETD *abbr* = **estimated time of departure**

eternal /ɪˈtɜːnl/ *adj* **1** (everlasting) 永远的 ‹*bliss, love*› **2** pej (ceaseless) 没完没了的 ‹*quarrelling, complaints, demands*› **3** Philos, Relig (unchanging) 永恒的 ‹*truth, principles, universe*›

eternally /ɪˈtɜːnəli/ *adv* 永久地; **~ grateful/indebted** 永远感激的

eternity /ɪˈtɜːnəti/ *n* [u] **1** (infinite time) 永恒; **for ~** 永远 **2** Relig 永生 **3** fig colloq (ages) 很长一段时间; **to wait for an ~** 等待漫长的一段时间

eternity ring *n* 永恒戒 [整圈镶满宝石的戒指，象征情谊永恒]

e-text /ˈiːˌtekst/ *n* 电子文本

ethane /ˈeθeɪn, ˈiːθ-/ *n* [u] 乙烷

ethanol /ˈeθənɒl/ *n* [u] = **ethyl alcohol**

ether /ˈiːθə(r)/ *n* [u] **1** Chem 乙醚 **2** colloq **the ~** (air as medium for radio) 以太

ethereal /ɪˈθɪərɪəl/ *adj* **1** (heavenly, spiritual) 超凡的 ‹*body, figure*›; 缥缈的 ‹*air, vision*›; 非人间的 ‹*region*› **2** (delicate, light) 优雅的 ‹*music, voice*›; 飘逸的 ‹*beauty, body*›

Ethernet /ˈiːθənet/ *n* 以太网

ethic /ˈeθɪk/ *n* 道德准则; **the puritan/hedonist ~** 清教徒/享乐主义道德观; **the Protestant ~** 新教伦理

ethical /ˈeθɪkl/ *adj* **1** (moral) 伦理的 ‹*issues, problem*›; 道德的 ‹*principles, standards*› **2** (morally correct) 合乎道德的 ‹*behaviour, business*›

ethical: **~ bank** *n* 道德银行 [对投资和放贷对象有所选择，关心随之带来的社会和环境影响]; **~ investment** *n* [c and u] 良知投资 [对符合道德规范的企业进行的投资]

ethically /ˈeθɪkli/ *adv* 道德上

ethics /ˈeθɪks/ *npl* **1** + *v sing* Philos 伦理学 **2** + *v pl* (moral principles) 道德准则; **professional/business ~** 职业/商业道德; **medical ~** 医德

Ethiopia /ˌiːθɪˈəʊpɪə/ *pr n* 埃塞俄比亚

Ethiopian /ˌiːθɪˈəʊpɪən/ ▸**p. 503**
A *adj* (of Ethiopia) 埃塞俄比亚的; (of the people) 埃塞俄比亚人的
B *n* 埃塞俄比亚人

ethnic /ˈeθnɪk/ *adj* **1** (as group) (national) 民族的; (racial) 种族的; (tribal) 部落的; **~ communities/traditions** 种族社区/民族传统 **2** (in origin) 源自民族文化的; **~ origin/background** 民族文化起源/背景 **3** (by birth, descent) 人种的; **~ Albanians** 阿尔巴尼亚后裔 **4** (non-Western) 非西方文化传统的; **~ dresses/music** 异国情调的服装/音乐

ethnically /ˈeθnɪkli/ *adv* 在种族方面

ethnic cleansing *n* [u] 种族清洗

ethnicity /eθˈnɪsətɪ/ *n* 种族特点

ethnic minority *n* 少数民族

ethnocentric /ˌeθnəʊˈsentrɪk/ *adj* 种族中心主义的

ethnographer /eθˈnɒɡrəfə(r)/ ▸**p. 409** *n* 人种志学者

ethnography /eθˈnɒɡrəfi/ *n* [u] 人种论

ethnologist /eθˈnɒlədʒɪst/ ▸**p. 409** *n* 人种学家

ethnology /eθˈnɒlədʒi/ *n* [u] 人种学

ethology /iːˈθɒlədʒi/ *n* [u] 动物行为学

ethos /ˈiːθɒs/ *n* [u] [社会、时代或文化的] 道德观; **the social ~** 社会风气

ethyl alcohol /ˈiːθaɪl ˈælkəhɒl, ˈeθɪl ˈælkəhɒl/ *n* [u] 酒精

ethylene /ˈeθɪliːn/ *n* [u] 乙烯

e-ticket *n* 电子机票

e-ticketing /ˈiːˌtɪkɪtɪŋ/ *n* [u] 电子票务

etiquette /ˈetɪket, -kət/ *n* [u] **1** (social propriety) 礼节 **2** (professional, diplomatic protocol) 规矩; **professional ~** 行业规矩 **3** (ceremonial formalities) 礼仪

etymological /ˌetɪməˈlɒdʒɪkl/ *adj* 词源（学）的

etymologically /ˌetɪməˈlɒdʒɪkli/ *adv* 在词源上

etymologist /ˌetɪˈmɒlədʒɪst/ ▸**p. 409** *n* 词源学学家

etymology /ˌetɪˈmɒlədʒi/ *n* **1** [u] (study of word origins) 词源学 **2** [c] (origin of word) 词源

EU *abbr* = **European Union**

eucalyptus /juːkəˈlɪptəs/ *n* (*pl* **~es** *or* **eucalypti** /juːkəˈlɪpti/) 1 Bot 桉树 2 Pharm 桉叶油

Eucharist /ˈjuːkərɪst/ *n* Relig **the ~** (service) 圣餐仪式; (consecrated elements) 圣餐面包和酒

euchre /ˈjuːkə(r)/ ▸ **p. 307** *n* [u] Amer 尤克牌戏

Euclidean /juːˈklɪdɪən/ *adj* 欧几里得的; **~ geometry** 欧几里得几何

eugenics /juːˈdʒenɪks/ *npl* + *v sing* 优生学

eulogize /ˈjuːlədʒaɪz/
A *vt* 称赞; **to be ~d as sth.** 被赞誉为某物
B *vi* 赞美; **to ~ over sth.** 赞美某事物

eulogy /ˈjuːlədʒi/ *n* 颂词

eunuch /ˈjuːnək/ *n* 1 (castrated man) 阉人 2 Hist (at oriental court) 太监 3 fig (ineffectual person) 无能者; **a bunch of political ~s** 一伙政治"阉人"

euphemism /ˈjuːfəmɪzəm/ *n* 委婉语

euphemistic /juːfəˈmɪstɪk/ *adj* 委婉的

euphemistically /juːfəˈmɪstɪkli/ *adv* 委婉地

euphonium /juːˈfəʊnɪəm/ *n* 尤风宁号

euphony /ˈjuːfəni/ *n* [u] 1 Mus 悦耳 2 Ling 变音倾向

euphoria /juːˈfɔːrɪə/ *n* [u] 狂喜; **in a state of ~** 兴高采烈

euphoric /juːˈfɒrɪk, Amer -ˈfɔːr-/ *adj* 狂喜的 ‹*feeling, mood*›; 兴高采烈的 ‹*state, crowd*›

EUR *abbr* = **euro**

Eurasia /jʊəˈreɪʒə/ *pr n* 欧亚大陆

Eurasian /jʊəˈreɪʒn/
A *adj* 欧亚的 ‹*continent, species*›
B *n* 欧亚混血儿

EURATOM /ˈjʊərətɒm/ *abbr* = **European Atomic Energy Community**

eureka /juːˈriːkə/ *excl* 我发现了

eurhythmics Brit, **eurythmics** Amer /juːˈrɪðmɪks/ *npl* + *v sing* 韵律体操

euro /ˈjʊərəʊ/ ▸ **p. 174** *n* 欧元

Eurobond /ˈjʊərəʊbɒnd/ *n* 欧洲债券

eurocentric /jʊərəʊˈsentrɪk/ *adj* 欧洲中心论的

eurocentrism /jʊərəʊˈsentrɪzəm/ *n* [u] 欧洲中心论

Eurocommunism /ˈjʊərəʊˌkɒmjuːnɪzm/ *n* [u] 欧洲共产主义

Eurocrat /ˈjʊərəʊkræt/ *n* colloq pej 欧盟官僚

Euro: ~currency *n* 欧洲货币; **the ~currency market** 欧洲货币市场; **~dollar** *n* 欧洲美元; **~land** /-lænd/ *pr n* 欧元区; **~market** *n* 1 Fin 欧洲货币市场; 2 (European Union) 欧盟市场; **in the ~market** 在欧盟市场; **~-MP** *n* 欧洲议会议员

Europe /ˈjʊərəp/ *pr n* 1 (continent) 欧洲 2 (mainland as distinct from the British Isles) 欧洲大陆 3 (European Union) 欧盟; **the UK went into ~ in 1973** 英国于 1973 年加入欧盟

European /jʊərəˈpɪən/
A *adj* (of the continent) 欧洲的; (of the European Union) 欧盟的
B *n* 1 (inhabitant) 欧洲人 2 (white-skinned person) 白人

European: ~ Atomic Energy Community *n* 欧洲原子能共同体; **~ Bank for Reconstruction and Development** *n* 欧洲复兴开发银行; **~ Central Bank** *n* 欧洲中央银行; **~ Commission** *n* 欧盟委员会; **~ Community** *n* 欧洲共同体; **~ Court of Human Rights** *n* 欧盟人权法院; **~ Court of Justice** *n* 欧盟法院; **~ Cup** *n* 欧洲杯; **~ Economic Community** *n* 欧洲经济共同体; **~ Free Trade Association** *n* 欧洲自由贸易联盟; **~ Investment Bank** *n* 欧洲投资银行

Europeanize /jʊərəˈpɪənaɪz/ *vt* 1 (in character) 使欧化; **to become ~d** 变得欧化 2 (integrate) 使加入欧盟

European: ~ Monetary Union *n* Hist 欧洲货币联盟; **~ Parliament** *n* 欧洲议会; **~ plan** *n* Amer 欧洲式收费制 [不包括餐费的宾馆收费制]; **~ Space Agency** *n* 欧洲航天局; **~ Union** *n* 欧洲联盟

europium /jʊəˈrəʊpɪəm/ *n* [u] 铕

Eurosceptic /ˈjʊərəʊskeptɪk/ Brit
A *n* (person who is opposed to European integration) 反对欧洲联盟者; (person who is sceptical of the European Union and its aims) 欧盟怀疑主义者
B *adj* (opposed to European integration) 反对欧洲联盟的; (sceptical of the European Union and its aims) 怀疑欧盟的

Euroscepticism /ˈjʊərəʊskeptɪsɪzəm/ *n* [u] Brit (disagreement with European integration) 反对欧洲联盟主义; (scepticism about the European Union and its aims) 欧盟怀疑主义

e

ℹ Euphemisms

■ Many euphemisms in English and Chinese are similar, although there are notable exceptions.

Death

He passed away last night
= 他昨晚去世了
or 他昨晚逝世了
or 他昨晚谢世了
or 他昨晚过世了

He is gone
= 他走了

He has departed
= 他离开了

He is in heaven
= 他归天了

He is no more
= 他不在了

He has found rest
= 他安息了

He has closed his eyes
= 他闭眼了

He has breathed his last
= 他咽气了

He has made the ultimate sacrifice
= 他牺牲了

Bodily functions

■ Going to the toilet:

Can I use your bathroom?
= 我可以用你的卫生间吗?

Where is the restroom?
= 洗手间在哪?

Where can I wash my hands?
= 在哪儿可以洗手?

to go to the ladies' room
or ***to go to the gentlemen's room***
= 去洗手间
or 去解手

to do a Number 2
= 解大手
or 去大号

to do a Number 1
or ***to pass water***
or ***to relieve oneself***
= 解小手
or 去小号

■ Menstruation:

She had her period
or ***She had a period***
= 她来例假了
or 她来好事了
or 她倒霉了

Disability

She is disabled
= 她行动不便

She is visually impaired
= 她有视力障碍

She is hard of hearing
= 她听觉不好
or 她听觉不灵

Other themes

■ Poverty:

He is hard up
or ***He is badly-off***
= 他手头紧
or 他很拮据
or 他囊中羞涩

She is down on her luck
= 她生活不宽裕

a person of modest means
= 没积蓄的人

■ Unemployment:

He's between jobs
= 他下岗了

■ Pregnancy:

She's expecting
= 她有了
or 她有喜了
or 她快要做妈妈了

■ Dustman:

sanitation worker
= 环卫工人

■ Mistress:

第三者 is a euphemism for a person who has a sexual relationship with a married man or woman.

■ Pornography:

adult magazines
= 成人杂志

blue movies
= 黄色电影

■ Obesity:

She is full-figured
= 她很丰满

He is getting bigger
= 他发福了

euro: E~star® *n* Transp 欧洲之星 [穿越英吉利海峡隧道的高速列车]; **E~vision** *n* 欧洲电视网; **~zone** *n* 欧元区

Eustachian tube /juːˌsteɪʃn ˈtjuːb, Amer ˈtuːb/ *n* 耳咽管

euthanasia /ˌjuːθəˈneɪzɪə, Amer -ˈneɪʒə/ *n* [u] 安乐死

euthanize /ˈjuːθənaɪz/ *vt* esp Amer 对…实施安乐死 ‹*animal*›

eutrophication /ˌjuːtrəfrˈkeɪʃn/ *n* [u] 富营养化

evacuate /ɪˈvækjʊeɪt/ *vt* 1 (leave, withdraw from) 撤出 ‹*place, house, vicinity, area*› 2 (to safe place) 撤走; **to ~ sb. from/to somewhere** 把…从某地疏散/疏散到某地 ‹*children, civilians*› 3 formal (remove) 抽空 ‹*air, water*› 4 formal (empty) 排空 ‹*bowels*›

evacuation /ɪˌvækjʊˈeɪʃn/ *n* 1 [c] (of place) 撤出 2 [u] (of people) 疏散 3 [u] (of bowels) 排空

evacuee /ɪˌvækjuːˈiː/ *n* 被疏散者; **~s from the battle area** 从战区撤离的人

evade /ɪˈveɪd/ *vt* 1 (escape, dodge) 逃脱 ‹*police, pursuer, capture*›; 躲避 ‹*attack, problem*› 2 (avoid) 逃避 ‹*military service, obligation*›; 规避 ‹*customs duty*› 3 (avoid answering) 回避 ‹*question, inquiry*›

evaluate /ɪˈvæljʊeɪt/ *vt* 评价 ‹*person, achievement, ability*›; 给…估值 ‹*damage, property*›; 评判 ‹*reasons*›

evaluation /ɪˌvæljʊˈeɪʃn/ *n* 评估

evanescent /ˌiːvəˈnesnt, Amer ˌev-/ *adj* liter 瞬息即逝的 ‹*fame, beauty, hope*›; 迅速消失的 ‹*mist, vision, bubble*›

evangelical /ˌiːvænˈdʒelɪkl/ *adj* 1 Relig 基督教福音主义的; (of Christian group emphasizing personal salvation) 基督教新教传统的 2 fig (zealous) 狂热鼓吹的

evangelism /ɪˈvændʒəlɪzəm/ *n* [u] 1 Relig 福音布道 2 fig (zeal) 狂热鼓吹

evangelist /ɪˈvændʒəlɪst/ *n* 1 lit (preacher, missionary) 福音布道者 2 (writer of Gospel) 福音作者; **St John the E~** 福音作者圣约翰 3 fig (zealous advocate) 狂热鼓吹者; **to be an ~ for sth.** 大力鼓吹某事; **he is an ~ for health foods** 他热衷推介健康食品

evangelize /ɪˈvændʒəlaɪz/
A *vt* 使皈依基督教
B *vi* 传播福音

evaporate /ɪˈvæpəreɪt/
A *vi* 1 lit (lose moisture) 蒸发 2 fig (disappear) 消失
B *vt* 使蒸发

evaporated milk *n* [u] 甜炼乳

evaporation /ɪˌvæpəˈreɪʃn/ *n* [u] 1 lit (of liquid) 蒸发 2 fig (of hope, fear, anger etc.) 消失

evasion /ɪˈveɪʒn/ *n* 1 [u] (of obligation) 逃避 2 [u] (avoidance) 回避 3 [c] (statement avoiding the issue) 托词

evasive /ɪˈveɪsɪv/ *adj* 含糊其辞的 ‹*answer*›; 回避的 ‹*manner*›; **to take ~ action** 采取回避行动

evasively /ɪˈveɪsɪvli/ *adv* 含糊其辞地 ‹*reply*›; 回避地 ‹*act*›

evasiveness /ɪˈveɪsɪvnɪs/ *n* [u] (remarks) 含糊其辞; (manner) 回避

eve /iːv/ *n* 前夕; **on the ~ of the election** 在选举前夕

even[1] /ˈiːvən/
A *adv* 1 (showing surprise) 竟然; **don't you ~ remember?** 你难道不记得了吗？; **she walked out without ~ apologizing** 她竟然没有道歉就走了出去 2 (emphasizing point) 即使; **~ now** 即便如此; **~ if** 即使; **don't tell anyone, not ~ your wife** 不要告诉任何人，连你妻子都不要告诉 3 (with comparative) 甚至; **I can't ~ swim, never mind dive** 我连游泳都不会，更不用说潜水了; **it's ~ colder today than it was yesterday** 今天甚至比昨天还要冷 4 liter (just) 恰好; **~ as I watched, the boat sank beneath the waves** 正当我注视着的时候，船被波浪淹没了
B **even though** *conj phr* 尽管; **he rents his house ~ though he's so rich** 他虽然很富有，却还是租房子住
C **even so** *adv phr* 虽然如此; **I didn't understand the lecture completely, but it was interesting ~ so** 我没有完全听懂讲座，但即便如此还是很有趣
D **even then** *adv phr* (at that time) 即使在那时; (all the same) 尽管如此

even[2]
A *adj* 1 (level) 平的; **~ surface/ground** 平面/平地; **to be ~ with sth.** 与某物齐平 2 (regular) 整齐的 ‹*teeth, hemline*›; 匀称的 ‹*features*›; 均匀的 ‹*colour, breathing*›; 稳定的 ‹*temperature, progress*› 3 (calm) 平和的 ‹*voice, disposition*› 4 (equal) 均等的 ‹*chance*›; 水平相当的 ‹*competitor*›; 势均力敌的 ‹*contest*›; 相等的 ‹*score*›; **it's ~ chances that ...** …输赢参半; **to break ~** 收支平衡 5 (fair) 公平的 ‹*exchange, distribution*›; **with an ~ hand** 不偏不倚地 6 *pred* (quits, not owing anything) 互不相欠的; **to be ~** 两清; **to get ~ with sb.** 向某人报复 7 (dividing without remainder) 除得尽的; (with even number) 偶数的，双数的 ‹*page, line*›; **an ~ number** 偶数 8 (exact) 整的; **an ~ number** 整数
B *vt* 拉平 ‹*score*›

Phrasal verbs

• **even out**
A *vi* 1 (become equal) «*prices*» 变均衡; «*supply, burden*» 变平均 2 (disappear) «*differences*» 消失
B *vt* [**~ sth. out, ~ out sth.**]
1 (make equal) 使…均衡 ‹*prices*›; 平均分配 ‹*supply, burden*› 2 (cancel out) 消除 ‹*disadvantage, variation*›

• **even up**
A *vt* [**~ sth. up, ~ up sth.**]
1 (make level) 平整 ‹*surfaces*› 2 (balance) 使…相等 ‹*numbers, amounts*›; **if he and I change sides, it will ~ things up** 如果他和我交换场地，就公平了
B *vi* Amer colloq 扯平; **to ~ up with sb.** 与某人扯平

even-handed *adj* 公正的 ‹*person, policy, handling, judgement*›; 一视同仁的 ‹*treatment*›

evening /ˈiːvnɪŋ/ ▸p. 831
A *n* 1 [u and c] (night) 晚上; **this ~** 今天晚上; **on Sunday ~** 在星期天晚上; **every Sunday ~, on Sunday ~s** 每逢星期天晚上; **all ~** 整个晚上; **during the ~** 晚间; **to work ~s** 上夜班 2 [c] (activity) 晚间活动; **a musical/theatrical ~** 音乐/戏剧晚会; **an ~ out/in** 在外面的/在家的一晚上 3 [c] fig (last years) 末期; **the ~ of one's life** 某人的晚年
B ▸p. 333 *excl* colloq **~!** 晚上好!
C **evenings** *adv* colloq 每天晚上

evening: ~ class *n* 夜校课程; **~ dress** *n* 1 [u] (formal clothes) 晚礼服; **in ~ dress** 穿着晚礼服; 2 [c] (gown) 女装晚礼服; **~ fixture, ~ game, ~ match** *ns* 晚间赛事; **~ meal** *n* 晚餐; **~ paper** *n* 晚报; **~ primrose** *n* 月见草; **~ shift** *n* 夜班; **~ showing** *n* 夜场; **~ star** *n* **the ~ star** 昏星 [指金星]

evenly /ˈiːvnli/ *adv* 1 (equally) 均匀地; **~ distributed** 平均分配的; **to be ~ matched** 势均力敌 2 (placidly) 心平气和地

even money
A *n* [u] 同额赌注
B **even-money** *modif* 输赢均等的 ‹*chance, favourite*›; **it's even-money that ...** …都是机会均等的

evenness /ˈiːvnnɪs/ *n* [u] (of ground, surface) 平坦; (of distribution, quality) 平均; (of breathing, movement) 平稳; (of temperament) 平和

evens /ˈiːvnz/ *npl* Brit 均等的输赢机会; **an ~ chance/favourite** 输赢均等的机会/输赢两可的有望夺魁者

evensong /ˈiːvnsɒŋ/ *n* [圣公会的] 晚祷

even-steven /ˌiːvnˈstiːvn/, **even-stevens** /-vnz/ colloq
A *adj* 均等的; **we're ~ now** 我们现在打平了
B *adv* 均等地; **we split the money ~** 我们平分了钱

event /ɪˈvent/ *n* 1 (incident) 事件; **a chain of ~s** 一连串的事件; **the course of ~s** 事态的发展; **to be wise after the ~** 事后聪明 2 (eventuality) 可能发生的事; **in the ~ of ...** 万一发生 ‹*fire, accident*›; **in the unlikely ~ that he should fail the exam** 万一他考试不及格; **in that ~** 如果是那样的话; **in either ~** 无论怎样; **in the ~** Brit (as things turned out) 结果; **in any ~** 无论如何; **at all ~s** 不管怎样 3 (special occasion) 社交场合; **it was quite an ~** 那场面真够壮观的 4 Sport 比赛项目; **track and field ~s** 田径赛项目; **a three-day ~** 为期 3 天的马术赛事

even-tempered *adj* 性情平和的

eventful /ɪˈventfl/ *adj* 充满大事的 ‹*period, year*›; 多姿多彩的 ‹*life, career, journey*›

eventing /ɪˈventɪŋ/ *n* [u] 综合马术比赛 [包括越野赛、超越障碍赛和盛装舞步]

eventual /ɪˈventʃʊəl/ *adj* 最终的 ‹*outcome, objective*›; 最后的 ‹*failure, success*›

eventuality /ɪˌventʃʊˈæləti/ *n* 可能发生的事; **in the ~ of sth.** 如果出现某事; **in the ~ of the job not being done** 如果工作没有完成

eventually /ɪˈventʃʊəli/ *adv* 最终

ever /ˈevə(r)/ *adv* 1 (at any time) 在任何时候; (at any previous time) 从来; **I don't think I'll ~ come back** 我想我再也不会回来了; **I'm unlikely ~ to go there** 我绝不可能到那里去; **if you ~ see one, buy it** 如果你什么时候见到了，就买下来; **I seldom** *or* **rarely, if ~, watch television** 我难得看电视; **we hardly ~ go out** 我们几乎从不出去 2 (when making comparisons) 以往任何时候; **better/worse than ~** 从来没有这么好/糟; **these are our worst results ~** *or* **worst ~ results** 这些是我们得到过最差的结果; **his first ~ cell phone** 他曾经拥有的第一部手机 3 (expressing anger, irritation, surprise) [表示恼怒、惊讶]; **why did I ~ leave?** (in exclamations) 我究竟为什么离开？; **don't you ~ listen?** (in imperatives) 你到底听不听啊？; **don't (you) ~ do that again!** (你) 绝对不能再这么做！; **well, did you ~?** colloq 哦，真的吗？ 4 (as intensifier) [表示强调]; **I was a fool ~ to believe her** 我真笨，居然会相信她; **all she ~ does is complain** 她一味抱怨; **what ~ is it?** 这到底是什么？; **~ so** Brit colloq 很; **I'm ~ so grateful** 我十分感激; **thanks ~ so (much)** 非常感谢 5 (always) 永远; **the same as ~** 一如既往; **she's fatter than ~** 她比任何时候都胖; **the danger is ~ present** 危险总是存在; **they lived happily ~ after** (conventional ending of fairy tales) 他们从此过上了幸福的生活; **the situation is growing ~ more dangerous** 情况变得越来越危险; **~-changing/-increasing** 不断变化/增长; **your ~-loving father** dated (closing a letter) 永远爱你的父亲 6 (in exclamations) colloq 极其; **do I ~!** 当然!

Everest /ˈevərɪst/ *pr n* **(Mount) ~** 埃佛勒斯峰 [即珠穆朗玛峰]

evergreen /ˈevəgriːn/
A *adj* 1 Bot 常青的 2 fig (popular) 长盛不衰的
B *n* (tree) 常青树; (plant) 常绿植物

everlasting /ˌevəˈlɑːstɪŋ, Amer -ˈlæst-/ *adj* 永恒的; **an ~ reminder** 永久的提醒; **life ~** 永生

every /ˈevri/ *adj attrib* 1 (each) 每一个; **insects of ~ kind** 各种昆虫; **I looked in ~ direction** 我四处张望; **they wiped up ~ bit of mud** 他们把泥点都擦掉了; **it gets worse**

~ year 一年不如一年; **give me** *or* **I prefer Australia ~ time** 我当然更喜欢澳大利亚 **2** (all possible) 所有的; **I have ~ confidence in her** 我对她有充分的信心; **you have ~ reason to be pleased** 你完全有理由感到满意; **at ~ opportunity** 一有机会; **I wished them ~ success** 我祝愿他们万事如意 **3** (indicating frequency) 每…的; **once ~ day/second day/few days** 每天/每隔一天/每隔几天一次; **change the oil ~ 5,000 miles** 每5,000英里换一次机油; **~ now and then, ~ now and again, ~ once in a while, ~ so often** 偶尔

everybody /'evrɪbɒdi/ *pron* **1** (each person) 每个人; **is ~ agreed?** 大家都同意吗?; **would ~ be quiet, please?** 请各位安静!; **~ thinks he/she is/they are worse off than ~ else** 人人都认为自己比别人艰难; **hello, ~!** 大家好! **2** (all people) 所有的人; **opera isn't to ~'s taste** 歌剧不是人人都喜欢的 **3** (many people) 很多人; **it's not ~ who can recite the whole poem** 很少有人能把整首诗背下来

everyday /'evrɪdeɪ/ *adj attrib* 日常的 ‹*life, language, routine*›; 每天的 ‹*task, activity*›; 通常的 ‹*occurrence, situation*›

Everyman /'evrɪmæn/ *n* 普通人

everyone /'evrɪwʌn/ *pron* **= everybody**

everyplace /'evrɪpleɪs/ *adv* Amer colloq **= everywhere**

everything /'evrɪθɪŋ/ *pron* **1** (each object) 每件东西; (each event or concept) 每件事; **~ (that) I have** 我所有的东西; **is ~ all right?** 一切都好吗?; **to be good at ~** 样样精通 **2** (all of importance) 最重要的东西; **money isn't ~** 金钱不是一切; **he meant ~ to her** 他对她来说比什么都重要; **they've got ~ going for them** 他们事事称心如意 **3** (all one has) 拥有的一切; **she lost ~ in the fire** 她在火灾中失去了一切 **4** colloq (life in general) 总体生活情况; **how's ~?** 最近怎么样?

everywhere /'evrɪweə(r)/
A *adv* 各处; **I've looked ~ for it** 我到处找它; **~ else** 其他任何地方; **she's been ~** 她什么地方都去过; **~ I go it's the same** 我去的每个地方情况都一样
B *n* [u] 所有地方; **they came from ~** 他们来自四面八方

evict /ɪ'vɪkt/ *vt* 驱逐; **to ~ sb. from somewhere** 将某人从某处赶走

eviction /ɪ'vɪkʃn/ *n* [c and u] 驱逐

eviction notice, eviction order *ns* 驱逐通告

evidence /'evɪdəns/
A *n* [u] **1** (gen) 证据; **there is ~ to suggest that ...** 有证据表明…; **there is no ~ that ...** 没有迹象显示…; **all the ~ is** *or* **suggests that ...** 所有的迹象表明…; **to believe the ~ of one's own eyes** 相信自己亲眼所见 **2** Jur (testimony) 证词; **to take** *or* **hear sb.'s ~** 听取某人的证词; **on the ~ of sb.** 根据某人的证言; **to give ~ (for/against sb.)** 给出(有利/不利于某人的)证词; **to turn King's/Queen's/State's ~** 提供同犯的罪证 **3** (sign, indications) 迹象; **on the ~ of sth.** 从某事来看; **to be (much) in ~** (经常)可看见; **she's not very much in ~ these days** 她这几天不太露面; **he was nowhere in ~** 哪儿都找不着他
B *vt* formal 证明; **(as) ~d by sth.** (正如)某事所证明的

evidence-based medicine *n* [u] 循证医学

evident /'evɪdənt/ *adj* 明显的; **to be ~ from sth. that ...** 从某事清楚地看出…; **it is ~ that ...** 显然…; **his fear is ~ in his behaviour/expression** 他的行为举止/话语中带着明显的恐惧

evidently /'evɪdəntli/ *adv* **1** (obviously) 明显地 **2** (apparently) 似乎; **they are going as well, ~** 看来, 他们也要去

evil /'iːvl/ ▸p. 325
A *adj* **1** (wicked) 邪恶的 ‹*person, purpose, spirit*›; **the E~ One** 恶魔; **an ~ deed** *or* **act** 恶行; **to give sb. the ~ eye** 恶狠狠地看某人; **the ~ hour/day** 倒霉的时刻/日子 **2** (foul) 令人厌恶的; **~ weather/an ~ smell** 讨厌的天气/难闻的气味
B *n* **1** [u] (wickedness) 邪恶; **to speak ~ of sb.** 说某人的坏话; **the root of all ~** 万恶之源; **to return good for ~** 以德报怨 **2** [c] (bad thing) 坏事; (of war or disease, social problem) 危害; (of doctrine, regime) 罪恶; **the ~s of drink/drugs** 酗酒/吸毒的害处; **the ~s of racism** 种族主义的罪恶; **social ~** 社会弊端; **the lesser of two ~s** 两害中较轻者

evil: ~-doer *n* liter 作恶者; **~-doing** *n* [u] liter 作恶; **~-minded** *adj* 恶毒的; **~-smelling** *adj* 难闻的

evince /ɪ'vɪns/ *vt* formal 表现 ‹*desire, surprise, joy*›; 显示 ‹*quality, talent*›

eviscerate /ɪ'vɪsəreɪt/ *vt* formal 除去…的内部器官

evocation /ˌevə'keɪʃn/ *n* 唤起; **the ~ of days gone by** 昔日重现

evocative /ɪ'vɒkətɪv/ *adj* 唤起记忆的; **to be ~ of sth.** 使人想起某事

evocatively /ɪ'vɒkətɪvli/ *adv* 唤起记忆地

evoke /ɪ'vəʊk/ *vt* **1** (bring to mind) 唤起 ‹*feeling, memory*› **2** (elicit) 引起 ‹*reaction, interest, sympathy*›; 激起 ‹*anger*› **3** (invoke) 召唤 ‹*spirit, deity*›

evolution /ˌiːvə'luːʃn/ *n* [u] **1** Biol 进化 **2** (gradual development) 演变

evolutionary /ˌiːvə'luːʃənəri, Amer -neri/ *adj* 进化的 ‹*theory*›; 演变的 ‹*process*›; **~ development** 进化发展

evolutionism /ˌiːvə'luːʃənɪzəm/ *n* [u] 进化论

evolve /ɪ'vɒlv/
A *vi* **1** Biol 进化 **2** (develop gradually) 逐步发展; **to ~ into sth.** 逐步发展成某物; **to ~ from sth.** 从某物演变而来
B *vt* 使…逐步形成 ‹*theory, policy, system, plan*›

ewe /juː/ *n* 母羊

ewer /'juːə(r)/ *n* 大口水壶

ex /eks/
A *prep* **1** Comm 在…直接交货; **~ works** Brit 在工厂直接交货; **~ ship** 在船上直接交货 **2** Fin 不包括; **~ dividend/interest** 不含红利/利息
B *n* colloq (former husband) 前夫; (former wife) 前妻; (former boyfriend) 前男友; (former girlfriend) 前女友

exacerbate /ɪg'zæsəbeɪt/ *vt* 使…恶化 ‹*disease, situation*›; 使…加剧 ‹*pain, difficulty*›

exact /ɪg'zækt/
A *adj* **1** (accurate, precise) 确切的 ‹*meaning*›; 准确的 ‹*time, description, measurement, number, amount*›; **one's ~ words** 原话; **to be (more) ~** (更)确切地说; **that's the ~ opposite of what she told me** 这与她告诉我的恰恰相反 **2** (careful) 严谨的 ‹*analyst, thinker, manager*› **3** (permitting precise measurements) 精密的 ‹*science*›
B *vt* **1** (demand and obtain) 索取; **to ~ sth. from sb.** 向某人索取 ‹*money, tribute*›; **to ~ obedience from sb.** 要求某人顺从 **2** (inflict) 施加; **to ~ revenge** *or* **vengeance on sb.** 报复某人; **to ~ retribution on a former lover** 报复前恋人

exacting /ɪg'zæktɪŋ/ *adj* **1** (demanding) 严格要求的 ‹*person*› **2** (requiring great attention) 需小心细致的 ‹*profession, task*› **3** (requiring great effort) 艰巨的 ‹*activity, work*›

exactitude /ɪg'zæktɪtjuːd, Amer -tuːd/ *n* [u] 精确性

exactly /ɪg'zæktli/ *adv* **1** (precisely) 确切地; **~ as promised** 正如所承诺的; **it would have been ~ the same** 情况本来会一模一样; **my feelings/opinion ~!** 恰恰是我的感觉/看法!; **not ~** (not at all) 根本不; (not quite) 不完全; **she wasn't ~ overjoyed/surprised** iron 她并不十分高兴/吃惊 **2** (with exactitude) 究竟; **what ~ are you looking for?** 你到底在找什么? **3** (as reply) 的确如此

exactness /ɪg'zæktnɪs/ *n* [u] 精确

exaggerate /ɪg'zædʒəreɪt/
A *vt* 夸大; **the dress ~s her height** 这件连衣裙使她显高
B *vi* 夸大; **to ~ about sth.** 对某事物言过其实

exaggerated /ɪg'zædʒəreɪtɪd/ *adj* 夸大的 ‹*account, version*›; 夸张的 ‹*picture, smile*›; 言过其实的 ‹*praise, criticism*›; 过分的 ‹*politeness*›; **he has an ~ sense of his own importance** 他自视过高

exaggeration /ɪgˌzædʒə'reɪʃn/ *n* [c and u] 夸大; **it's no ~ to say that ...** 说…并非言过其实; **..., and that's no ~** …一点也不夸张; **a bit of an ~** 有点夸张

exalt /ɪg'zɔːlt/ *vt* formal **1** (glorify) 高度赞扬 **2** (raise in rank) 提拔; (raise in power) 提升

exalted /ɪg'zɔːltɪd/ *adj* formal **1** (elevated) 尊贵的 ‹*person*›; 显赫的 ‹*position, rank*› **2** (jubilant) 兴高采烈的 ‹*mood, person*›; 兴奋的 ‹*shout, cry*› **3** (exaggerated, lofty) 夸张的; **to have an ~ opinion of oneself** 高估自己

e

exam /ɪg'zæm/ *n* colloq **= examination 1, 3**

examination /ɪgˌzæmɪ'neɪʃn/ *n* **1** Sch, Univ 考试; **to sit** *or* **take an ~** 参加考试; **to pass/fail an ~** 考试及格/不及格; **to resit an ~** 补考 **2** (inspection) 调查; **on ~** 经过查看; **under ~** 调查中; **after close/further ~** 经过仔细/进一步检查 **3** Med 检查; **to have an ~** 做体检; **to give sb. an ~** 为某人做体检 **4** Accts 审查 **5** Jur (of accused, witness) 审问; **under ~** 受审讯

examination: ~ board *n* 考试委员会; **~ paper** *n* 试卷; **~ script** *n* 答卷

examine /ɪg'zæmɪn/ *vt* **1** (inspect physically) 检查 ‹*patient, part of body, equipment, passport*› **2** (inspect intellectually) 调查 ‹*facts, problem, evidence*›; 审查 ‹*documents, accounts*› **3** Sch, Univ 对…进行考试 ‹*candidate, student*›; **to ~ sb. in** *or* **on sth.** 测试某人某课程 **4** Jur 审问 ‹*accused, suspect*›; 调查 ‹*case*›

examinee /ɪgˌzæmɪ'niː/ *n* 应试人

examiner /ɪg'zæmɪnə(r)/ *n* 考官

exam nerves *npl* 考试焦虑

example /ɪg'zɑːmpl, Amer -'zæmpl/ *n* **1** (fact, event, characteristic) 例子; **to offer sth. as an ~** 用某事举例; **for ~** 例如 **2** (person) 榜样; (thing) 范例; **to follow sb.'s ~** 效仿某人; **to set a good/bad ~** 树立一个好榜样/坏典型; **to learn by ~** 通过模仿学习 **3** (warning) 警诫; **to make an ~ of sb.** 惩罚某人以警诫他人

exasperate /ɪg'zæspəreɪt, Brit also -'zɑːsp-/ *vt* 使恼怒

exasperated /ɪg'zæspəreɪtɪd, Brit also -'zɑːsp-/ *adj* 恼怒的; **to be ~ at** *or* **by** *or* **with sb./sth.** 对某人/某事物感到恼火; **to become** *or* **grow** *or* **get ~** 变得恼火

exasperating /ɪg'zæspəreɪtɪŋ, Brit also -'zɑːsp-/ *adj* 使人恼火的 ‹*person, situation, day, wait*›

exasperatingly /ɪg'zæspəreɪtɪŋli, Brit also -'zɑːsp-/ *adv* 令人生气地; **~ clumsy/stupid** 笨拙/愚蠢得叫人恼火

exasperation /ɪgˌzæspə'reɪʃn, Brit also -'zɑːsp-/ *n* [u] 恼怒; **in ~** 恼怒地; **he stamped his foot in ~** 他气得直跺脚

excavate /'ekskəveɪt/
A *vt* **1** Constr 挖掘 ‹*ditch, hole*› **2** Archaeol 发掘 ‹*ruins, statue, site*›
B *vi* Archaeol 发掘

excavation /ˌekskəˈveɪʃn/ *n* **1** [u] (digging) (of land) 挖掘; (of tunnel) 开凿 **2** [c] Archaeol (site) 发掘现场

excavator /ˈekskəveɪtə(r)/ *n* **1** (machine) 挖掘机 **2** Archaeol (person) 发掘者

exceed /ɪkˈsiːd/ *vt* **1** (in number, size) 超过; (go beyond) 超出 ‹*limit, ability, authority*›; **when expenses ~ income** 当入不敷出时; **to ~ sth./sb. in sth.** 在某方面超过某物/某人; **his bid ~ed the others by £50** 他的出价比别人高了 50 英镑; **to ~ the speed limit** 超过限速 **2** (surpass) 超越; **to ~ all expectations** 完全出乎意料

exceedingly /ɪkˈsiːdɪŋli/ *adv* 非常

excel /ɪkˈsel/
A *vi* 突出; **to ~ at** *or* **in sth.** 擅长某事
B *v refl* **to ~ oneself** 超常发挥; **to ~ oneself at** *or* **in sth.** often iron 在某事上超水平发挥

excellence /ˈeksələns/ *n* [u] 优秀; **~ in** *or* **at sth.** 某方面的卓越

Excellency /ˈeksələnsi/ *n* 阁下; **Your/His/Her ~** 阁下

excellent /ˈeksələnt/
A *adj* 极好的 ‹*food, weather, journey*›; 极高的 ‹*language skills, standard*›; 杰出的 ‹*piece of work*›; **an ~ meal** 丰盛的一餐; **she speaks ~ Italian** 她的意大利语说得棒极了
B *excl* 好极了

excellently /ˈeksələntli/ *adv* 极好地

except /ɪkˈsept/
A *prep* 除…外; **nothing ~ her resignation will satisfy them** 除非她辞职，否则他们怎么都不会满意; **open every day ~ Monday** 除了星期一每天都营业
B *conj* **1** (other than) 除…之外; **everywhere ~ in Wales** 威尔士以外的所有地方; **~ if ...** 除非… **2** (but) 可是; **I'd tell him ~ he's in the bath** 我想告诉他，可是他在洗澡
C *vt* formal 把…除外; **~ed from the survey** 不在调查之列; **present company ~ed** 在场的诸位除外
D **except for** *prep phr* **1** (with the exception of) 除…之外; **everyone went ~ for me** 除我之外，所有人都去了 **2** (but for) 要不是; **I'd have left before ~ for the children** 要不是孩子，我之前就离开了

excepting /ɪkˈseptɪŋ/ *prep* 除…之外; **not** *or* **without ~ sb./sth.** 某人/某事物也不例外; **always ~ sb./sth.** 唯独某人/某事物除外

exception /ɪkˈsepʃn/ *n* **1** [c and u] (special case) 例外; **with the (possible) ~ of ...** （可能）不包括…在内; **without ~** 无一例外; **with some ~s** 有些例外; **to make an ~** 允许有例外; **an ~ to the rule** 规则的例外情况; **the ~ proves the rule** 例外反证规律 **2** [u] (dislike) 异议; **to take ~ to** 反对

exceptionable /ɪkˈsepʃnəbl/ *adj* 引起反对的

exceptional /ɪkˈsepʃənl/ *adj* **1** (unusual) 例外的 ‹*case*›; 不同寻常的 ‹*situation, circumstances, incident*›; 异常的 ‹*weather, temperature*› **2** (outstanding) 杰出的 ‹*person, achievement, talent*›; 出类拔萃的 ‹*quality, ability*›

exceptionally /ɪkˈsepʃənəli/ *adv* **1** (exceedingly) 特别 **2** (by way of exception) 例外地

excerpt /ˈeksɜːpt/ *n* (from book) 摘录; (from film, piece of music) 片段; **~s from a novel** 小说节选

excess /ɪkˈses/
A *n* **1** [u] (amount that is more than necessary or permitted) 过量; (lack of moderation) 过度; **to eat/drink to ~** 吃撑/喝多; **a life of ~** 无节制的生活; **in ~ of ...** 超过…; **she made in ~ of $1,000** 她的收入超过 1,000 美元; **the ~ of supply over demand** 供过于求 **2** [c] Brit (insurance) 免赔额
B **excesses** *npl* (immoderate behaviour) 放肆的行为; (overindulgence) 过分放纵
C *adj* **1** (surplus) 过多的 ‹*demand, food, production*›; **~ alcohol/speed/weight** 酒精超标/超速/超重; **~ water/fat** 多余的水分/脂肪 **2** Brit (additional) 额外的 ‹*charge*›

excess: ~ baggage *n* [u] 超重行李; **~ fare** *n* Brit 补票费

excessive /ɪkˈsesɪv/ *adj* 过高的 ‹*budget, price, level, enthusiasm, demand, expectation*›; 过重的 ‹*load*›; 过分的 ‹*politeness, severity*›; 过长的 ‹*working hours*›; **~ drinking** 酗酒

excessively /ɪkˈsesɪvli/ *adv* 过于 ‹*lenient, harsh, optimistic*›; 过多地 ‹*spend, worry*›; 非常 ‹*time-consuming, expensive*›; **to drink ~** 酗酒; **~ long/high** 过长/过高

excess: ~ luggage *n* [u] **= ~ baggage**; **~ postage** *n* [u] 欠资邮费; **~ profits** *npl* 超额利润; **~ profits tax** *n* 超额利润税

exchange /ɪksˈtʃeɪndʒ/
A *vt* 交换; **to ~ sth. for sth.** 用某物换取某物; **to ~ sth. with sb.** 与某人交换某物; **to ~ looks/blows (with sb.)** （与某人）互换眼色/打架; **to ~ words** 交谈几句
B *n* **1** (swap) 交换; **in ~ (for sth.)** 作为（对某物的）交换; **he is teaching her French in ~ for her teaching him English** 她教他英语，作为交换他教她法语; **~ of ideas/information** 想法/信息的交流 **2** Fin 兑换; **the rate of ~** 汇兑率; **bill of ~** 汇票 **3** (discussion) 争论; **a heated/an angry ~** 激烈/愤怒的争吵 **4** (reciprocal visit) 互访; **to go on an ~** 进行互访 **5** Fin (place of business) 交易所 **6** Telecom **(telephone) ~** 交换局

exchangeable /ɪksˈtʃeɪndʒəbl/ *adj* **1** Comm 可更换的 **2** (interchangeable) 可交换的 **3** Comput (removable) 可拆卸的; **~ disk** 可拆卸磁盘; **~ disk storage** 可拆卸磁盘存储

exchange control *n* 外汇管制

exchange control regulations *npl* 外汇管制条例

exchange rate *n* 汇率

Exchange Rate Mechanism *n* Hist 汇率机制

exchange: ~ student *n* 交换留学生; **~ teacher** *n* 交流教师; **~ visit** *n* 交流访问

exchequer /ɪksˈtʃekə(r)/ *n* **1** (state treasury) 国库 **2** **the Exchequer** Brit 财政部 **3** hum (funds) 个人的钱财

excise
A /ɪkˈsaɪz/ *vt* **1** Med 切除 ‹*tumour, tissue*› **2** (from text) 删除 ‹*passage, section*›; **to ~ sth. (from sth.)** 把某物（从某处）删除
B /ˈeksaɪz/ *n* [u] **~ (duty)** 消费税

excision /ɪkˈsɪʒn/ *n* formal **1** Med 切除 **2** (from text) 删除

excitable /ɪkˈsaɪtəbl/ *adj* 易激动的; **an ~ child** 易兴奋的孩子

excite /ɪkˈsaɪt/ *vt* **1** (make excited) 使…激动 ‹*person, oneself, animal*› **2** (stimulate sexually) 激发…的性欲 **3** (give rise to) 引起 ‹*suspicion, interest, envy*› **4** (incite) 激起; **to ~ sb. to sth.** 煽动某人参与 ‹*rebellion, revolution, insurrection*›; **to ~ sb. to do sth.** 鼓动某人做某事 **5** Phys 激发 ‹*atom, electron*›

excited /ɪkˈsaɪtɪd/ *adj* **1** (showing or feeling excitement) 兴奋的 ‹*children, crowd*›; 激动的 ‹*laughter, voice*›; **to be/get ~ about sth.** 因某事物而兴奋不已; **it's nothing to get ~ about!** 没有什么值得激动的！ **2** (sexually aroused) 性兴奋的 **3** (cross) 受刺激的; **don't get ~!** 别生气了！ **4** Phys 受激的 ‹*atom, electron*›

excitedly /ɪkˈsaɪtɪdli/ *adv* 激动地

excitement /ɪkˈsaɪtmənt/ *n* **1** [u] (emotion) 激动; **what ~!** 多么令人兴奋！; **the news caused great ~** 这消息引起一片哗然; **I want some ~ out of life** 我希望从生活中得到一些刺激; **to be in a state of great ~** 处于极度兴奋中 **2** [u] (sexual arousal) 性兴奋 **3** [c] (exciting experience) 令人激动的事

exciting /ɪkˈsaɪtɪŋ/ *adj* 令人激动的 ‹*news, story, discovery*›; 使人兴奋的 ‹*event, holiday, prospect*›

excitingly /ɪkˈsaɪtɪŋli/ *adv* 令人兴奋地 ‹*different, original*›

excl. *abbr* **= excluding**

exclaim /ɪkˈskleɪm/ *vi* 呼喊; **to ~ at** *or* **over ...** 对…喊起来; **everyone ~ed at** *or* **over how well he looked** 大家看到他气色那么好都欢呼起来; **to ~ in anger/surprise** 怒喊/惊叫

exclamation /ˌekskləˈmeɪʃn/ *n* 呼喊

exclamation mark Brit, **exclamation point** Amer *ns* 感叹号

exclamatory /ɪkˈsklæmətri, Amer -tɔːri/ *adj* 惊叹的; **an ~ sentence** 感叹句

exclude /ɪkˈskluːd/ *vt* **1** (deny access to) 拒绝…参加; **to ~ sb. from sth./doing sth.** 拒绝某人参与某事/阻止某人做某事 **2** (keep out) 不让…进入 ‹*air, water, draught*› **3** (rule out) 排除 ‹*possibility, doubt*› **4** (leave out) 对…不予考虑; **to ~ sth. from sth.** 把某事物排除在某事物之外 **5** (not include) «*price*» 不包括 ‹*accommodation, drinks, service*› **6** Brit (expel) «*school*» 开除 ‹*pupil*›

excluding /ɪkˈskluːdɪŋ/ *prep* 除…之外; **£38 ~ breakfast** 38英镑不包括早饭

exclusion /ɪkˈskluːʒn/ *n* **1** [u] (refusal of entry, participation) 排除在外; **the ~ of women from ...** 把女性排斥在…之外; **to the ~ of sth.** 除了某事物 **2** [c and u] Sch 开除 **3** [u] (ruling out) 排除; **the ~ of robbery as a motive** 排除抢劫动机

exclusion: ~ order *n* Brit 禁令; **~ zone** *n* 禁区

exclusive /ɪkˈskluːsɪv/
A *adj* **1** (high class, expensive) 高档的 ‹*restaurant, hotel*› **2** (private, select) 不接受新会员的 ‹*club, society*›; **an ~ school** 贵族学校 **3** (not found elsewhere) 独有的 ‹*style, design, problem, dress, product*›; 独家的 ‹*interview, coverage, story*›; (sole) 专有的 ‹*privileges*›; **to have ~ (marketing) rights for sth.** 拥有对某物的（营销）专营权; **to have ~ use of sth.** 独享某物 **4** (excluding all else) 唯一的 ‹*occupation, activity, interest, friendship*› **5** (incompatible) 排斥的; **mutually ~** 互不相容的 **6** (not including) 不包括…的; **~ of sb./sth.** 不包括某人/某事物
B *n* 独家新闻; **a BBC ~** 英国广播公司独家报道

exclusive economic zone *n* 专属经济区

exclusively /ɪkˈskluːsɪvli/ *adv* **1** (solely) 仅仅; **the style is ~ western** 这种风格是西方独有的 **2** Journ (as the only source) 独家地

exclusivity /ˌɪkskluːˈsɪvɪti/, **exclusiveness** /ɪkˈskluːsɪvnɪs/ *ns* [u] **1** (being high-class) 高档独特性 **2** (of contract, deal) 专有权 **3** (being closed) 排外性

excommunicate /ˌekskəˈmjuːnɪkeɪt/ *vt* 开除…的教籍

excommunication /ˌekskəˌmjuːnɪˈkeɪʃn/ *n* [u] 开除教籍

ex-con /ˌeksˈkɒn/ *n* colloq 前囚犯

excrement /ˈekskrɪmənt/ *n* [u] 粪便

excrescence /ɪkˈskresns/ *n* **1** (growth) 瘤 **2** (eyesore) 煞风景的东西

excreta /ɪkˈskriːtə/ *n* + *v sing or pl* formal 排泄物

excrete /ɪkˈskriːt/ *vt* 排泄 ‹*faeces, waste matter*›; 分泌 ‹*sweat*›; 排出 ‹*carbon dioxide*›

excretion /ɪkˈskriːʃn/ *n* **1** [u] (act of excreting) 排泄 **2** [c] (discharge) 排泄物

excretory /ɪkˈskriːtəri, Amer ˈekskrətɔːri/ *adj* 排泄的

excruciating /ɪkˈskruːʃɪeɪtɪŋ/ *adj* **1** (painful) 难以忍受的 ‹*pain, ache*›; 极痛苦的 ‹*suffering, feeling*› **2** colloq (awful) 糟糕透顶的 ‹*concert*›;

极讨厌的〈*noise*〉 **3** (tedious) 极度的〈*boredom, bore*〉 **4** (embarrassing) 令人尴尬的

excruciatingly /ɪk'skruːʃɪeɪtɪŋli/ *adv* **1** (extremely) 极其〈*painful, embarrassing, humiliating*〉; 十分〈*funny*〉 **2** (painfully) 痛苦地

exculpate /'ekskʌlpeɪt/ *vt* formal《*court*》证明…无罪〈*accused, defendant, prisoner*〉; 为…开脱〈*person*〉; **to ~ sb. from sth.** 给某人排除某罪名

excursion /ɪk'skɜːʃn/ *n* **1** (outing) 远足; **to go on/make an ~ to somewhere** 到某地去远足 **2** (exploration) 涉足; **an ~ into sth.** 涉猎某事物 **3** (digression) 离题

excursion: ~ ticket *n* [票价优惠的] 往返游览票; **~ train** *n* [票价优惠的] 游览列车

excusable /ɪk'skjuːzəbl/ *adj* **1** (forgivable) 可原谅的〈*rudeness, lateness, insolence, behaviour*〉 **2** (understandable) 可谅解的〈*mistake, ignorance, forgetfulness*〉

excuse ▸p. 29, p. 818

A /ɪk'skjuːs/ *n* **1** (pretext) 借口; **to make** *or* **find an ~** 找借口; **to look for an ~ to do sth.** 找借口做某事; **to make ~s (for sb./sth.)** (为某人/某事物) 找借口 **2** (justification) 理由; **an ~ for sth./doing sth.** 某事物/做某事的理由; **there is no ~ for sth./doing sth.** 某事物/做某事是毫无道理的; **without ~** 无故地; **it's just an ~ for a party** 那只是为聚会找个理由; **any ~ for a day off!** 只要能休息一天, 什么理由都行! **3** colloq (example) 蹩脚样本; **a poor ~ for a meal** 一顿不像样的饭; **a poor ~ for a manager** 无能的经理 **4** **to make one's ~s (to sb.)** (say one is leaving) (向某人) 表示歉意要离开 (say one is not coming) (向某人) 表示歉意不能来

B /ɪk'skjuːz/ *vt* **1** (forgive) 原谅〈*person, behaviour*〉; **please ~ the mess** 这里很乱, 请原谅; **to ~ sb. for sth./doing sth.** 原谅某人某事/做某事; **~ me** (asking sth.) 请问; (asking sb. to move) 劳驾; (bumping into sb.) 对不起; (interjecting, disagreeing) 抱歉; (apologizing) 请原谅; **~ me, you dropped your glove** 喂, 你的手套掉了; **~ me?** Amer 你说什么? **2** (justify) 为…辩解〈*action, person*〉; **nothing can ~ such arrogance** 这种傲慢是毫无道理的 **3** (allow to leave) 允许…离开; **to be ~d** (from table) 离席; Brit (from room) 去上洗手间; **if you'll ~ me** 请让我先走一步 **4** (exempt) 免除; **to ~ sb. from sth./doing sth.** 免除某人某事/做某事; **to ~ a debt** 免除债务; **to be ~d an entrance fee** 免收入场费; **to be ~d from games** 获准不用上体育课

C /ɪk'skjuːz/ *v refl* **to ~ oneself** **1** (when leaving) 请求准予离开; **to ~ oneself before leaving the table** 离席时表示一下歉意; **she ~d herself and left** 她说了句"不好意思"就走了; **it's time we ~d ourselves** 我们该走了 **2** (apologize) 请求得到原谅; **to ~ oneself for sth.** 请求原谅某事; **he ~d himself for being late** 他因迟到而请求原谅 **3** (beg off) 请求免除; **to ~ oneself from sth./doing sth.** 请求免除某事/做某事 **4** (justify oneself) 自我辩解; **to ~ oneself for sth./doing sth.** 为某事/做某事替自己辩解

ex-directory *adj* Brit 未列入电话簿的; **to go ~** 不列入电话簿

ex dividend

A *adj* 除股息的

B *adv* 除股息地

exec /ɪk'zek/ *n* Amer colloq = **executive B1**

execrable /'eksɪkrəbl/ *adj* formal 恶劣的〈*manners*〉; 极坏的〈*temper, weather*〉; 糟糕的〈*food, service*〉

executable file /ɪg'zekjʊtəbl ˌfaɪl/ *n* 可执行文件

execute /'eksɪkjuːt/ *vt* **1** (kill as legal punishment) 处死〈*murderer, traitor, spy*〉; **to be ~d for sth.** 因某事被处决 **2** formal (carry out) 执行〈*command, order, task*〉; 实施〈*plan, project*〉; 履行〈*duties*〉 **3** Jur (put into effect) 执行〈*will, person's wishes, judicial sentence*〉; (validate) 使…生效〈*deed, document, contract*〉 **4** formal (perform) 表演〈*dance, step*〉;《*musician*》演奏〈*piece of music*〉 **5** Comput 运行

execution /ˌeksɪ'kjuːʃn/ *n* **1** [c and u] (as legal punishment) 处决 **2** [u] (carrying out) 实行; (performance) 表演; **to put sth. into ~** 实施某事; **the ~ of his duty** 他职责的履行 **3** [u] (of will) 执行

executioner /ˌeksɪ'kjuːʃənə(r)/ *n* 行刑者

executive /ɪg'zekjʊtɪv/

A *adj* **1** (concerned with management) 经营管理的〈*powers, ability, talent, decision*〉; 决策的〈*position, post*〉; **~ authority** 决策当局 **2** (with the power to carry out) 有执行权的; **an ~ officer** 行政长官 **3** (luxurious) 高档的〈*car*〉

B *n* **1** (senior manager) 经理; **a top ~** 高层主管 **2** + *v sing or pl* (committee) 执行委员会 **3** **the ~** (branch of government) 行政部门

executive: ~ agreement *n* 行政协定; **~ arm** *n* 行政部门; **~ board** *n* 执行董事会; **~ branch** *n* = **~ arm**; **~ briefcase** *n* 公文包; **~ committee** *n* 执行委员会; **~ council** *n* 行政会议; **~ director** *n* 执行董事; **~ jet** *n* 公务机; **~ member** *n* 执委会成员; **~ officer** *n* 行政长官; **~ order** *n* Amer 行政命令; **~ privilege** *n* [u] Amer 行政官员豁免权; **~ producer** *n* 执行制片人; **~ secretary** *n* 行政秘书; **~ session** *n* Amer 行政会议; **~ suite** *n* 贵宾套房; **~ summary** *n* 行政报告摘要; **~ toy** *n* [总裁的] 办公桌小摆设

executor /ɪg'zekjʊtə(r)/ *n* 遗嘱执行者

exegesis /ˌeksɪ'dʒiːsɪs/ *n* (*pl* **exegeses** /-'siːz/) 注释

exemplar /ɪg'zemplə(r), -plɑː(r)/ *n* formal (typical example) 典型; (model, ideal) 模范; **an ~ of sth.** 某事物的范例

exemplary /ɪg'zempləri/ *adj* **1** (ideal, excellent) 可作楷模的〈*behaviour, model*〉; **an ~ student/father** 模范学生/父亲 **2** (serving as a deterrent) 惩戒性的 **3** Jur (exceeding compensation) 超过应得补偿的; **~ damages** 惩罚性的损害补偿金

exemplify /ɪg'zemplɪfaɪ/ *vt* **1** (typify) 是…的典型 **2** (illustrate, clarify) 举例说明

exempt /ɪg'zempt/

A *adj* 被免除的; **to be ~ from sth.** 免除某事物

B *vt* 免除; **to ~ sb./sth. from sth./doing sth.** 免除…某事物/做某事; **to ~ sth. from tax** 使某物免纳税

exemption /ɪg'zempʃn/ *n* **1** (dispensation) 免除; **~ from military service** 免服兵役 **2** Tax 免税

exemption clause *n* 免责条款

exercise /'eksəsaɪz/

A *n* **1** [u] (exertion) 锻炼; **to get** *or* Brit **take ~** colloq 锻炼身体 **2** [c] (activities) 体操; **breathing/keep-fit ~s** 吐纳/健身操 **3** [c] (task to develop skill) 练习; **piano ~s** 钢琴练习 **4** [c] (question) 习题; **a maths ~** 数学题 **5** [u] (application) 运用; **the ~ of power** 权力的行使; **in the ~ of one's duties** 在履行职责 **6** [c] (operation) 活动; **an academic/a marketing ~** 学术/营销活动; **an ~ in democracy/diplomacy** 民主运动/外交活动; **an ~ in futility** 白费劲的事 **7** [c] Mil 演习; **a military ~** 军事演习; **to go on (an) ~** 进行演习

B **exercises** *npl* Amer (ceremonies) 仪式; **graduation ~s** 毕业典礼

C *vt* **1** (train) 锻炼〈*body, mind*〉; 训练〈*dog*〉 **2** (use) 运用〈*skill, authority*〉; 行使〈*power, right*〉; 保持〈*patience, restraint*〉; 实施〈*control*〉; **to ~ considerable** *or* **a great deal of influence over sb./sth.** 对某人/某事物产生很大影响; **to ~ care in doing sth.** 小心做某事 **3** (worry) 使担忧; **to ~ sb.'s mind** 使某人伤脑筋

D *vi* 锻炼

exercise: ~ area *n* 活动区; **~ bicycle, ~ bike** *ns* 健身脚踏车; **~ book** *n* 练习本; **~ programme** *n* 健身计划

exerciser /'eksəsaɪzə(r)/ *n* esp Amer **1** (equipment) 体育器材 **2** (person) 锻炼者

exercise yard *n* [监狱内的] 放风场地

exert /ɪg'zɜːt/

A *vt* 施加〈*pressure, influence*〉; 利用〈*authority*〉; 运用〈*talent*〉; **to ~ sth. on sb./sth.** 给某人/某事施加某事; **to ~ a force on sth.** 向某物施加作用力; **to ~ every effort (to do sth.)** 尽一切力量 (做某事)

B *v refl* **to ~ oneself** 努力; **don't ~ yourself!** 别费劲儿了!

exertion /ɪg'zɜːʃn/ *n* **1** [c and u] (effort) 努力; **mental/physical ~** 智力/体力的竭尽 **2** [u] (application) (of pressure, influence) 施加; (of force, authority) 行使

exeunt /'eksɪənt/ *vi* 退场; **~ omnes** 全体退场

exfoliant /ˌeks'fəʊlɪənt/ *n* 去死皮磨砂膏

exfoliate /ˌeks'fəʊlɪeɪt/

A *vt* Cosmet 使…脱落〈*skin*〉

B *vi* 呈片状剥落

exfoliation /eksˌfəʊlɪ'eɪʃn/ *n* [u] 表皮剥落

ex gratia /ˌeks 'greɪʃə/ formal

A *adj* 作为恩惠的; **an ~ payment** 通融付款

B *adv* 优惠地

exhalation /ˌekshə'leɪʃn/ *n* **1** [u] (exhaling) (of air) 呼气; (of fumes, smoke) 散发 **2** [c] (quantity of air breathed out) 呼出的气 **3** [c] (fumes, gas) 散发物

exhale /eks'heɪl/

A *vi* 呼气

B *vt* 呼出

exhaust /ɪg'zɔːst/

A *vt* **1** (tire out) 使…精疲力竭〈*person*〉; **to ~ oneself** 累得筋疲力尽 **2** (use up) 用光〈*supplies, raw materials, resources*〉; 花光〈*finances*〉; 耗尽〈*patience*〉 **3** (drain, empty) 挖空〈*mine*〉; 抽干〈*oil well*〉; 用尽〈*reserves*〉 **4** (expound, explore fully) 详尽论述〈*subject, topic of conversation, problem*〉 **5** Tech (expel gas from) 使…成为真空〈*tank, boiler, flask*〉

B *n* **1** [u] (fumes) 废气 **2** [c] (pipe) 排气管

exhaust centre *n* 排气维修中心

exhausted /ɪg'zɔːstɪd/ *adj* **1** (fatigued) 精疲力竭的; **to be ~ by sth./from doing sth.** 因某事/做某事疲惫不堪 **2** (used up) 耗尽的〈*resources*〉 **3** (thoroughly explored) 讨论透彻的〈*subject*〉

exhaust emissions, exhaust fumes *npl* 尾气

exhausting /ɪg'zɔːstɪŋ/ *adj* 令人精疲力竭的

exhaustion /ɪg'zɔːstʃn/ *n* [u] **1** (tiredness) 精疲力竭 **2** (depletion) 耗尽

exhaustive /ɪg'zɔːstɪv/ *adj* 彻底的〈*survey, inquiry, search*〉; 全面的〈*analysis*〉; 详尽的〈*description, report*〉

exhaustively /ɪg'zɔːstɪvli/ *adv* 彻底地〈*search*〉; 全面地〈*study, research*〉; 详尽地〈*describe, comment*〉

exhaustiveness /ɪg'zɔːstɪvnɪs/ *n* [u] 彻底

exhaust: ~ pipe *n* 排气管; **~ system** *n* 排气系统

exhibit /ɪg'zɪbɪt/

A *vt* **1** (display) 展出〈*work of art*〉; 陈列〈*flowers, merchandise*〉 **2** (show) 表现出〈*endurance, courage, ingenuity, disappointment, concern*〉 **3** Jur (produce as evidence) 当庭出示〈*document, weapon*〉

B *vi*《*artist, craftsperson*》展出作品;《*company*》开展览会

C *n* **1** (work of art) 展览品; (object on display) 陈列品 **2** Amer (exhibition) 展览; **to be on ~** 在展出 **3** Jur (document) 证件; (object) 物证

exhibition /ˌeksɪ'bɪʃn/ *n* **1** (of art works, items) 展览; **an art ~** 艺术博览会; **to mount** *or*

e

stage/organize an ～ 举行/组织展览; to be on ～ 在展出; to make an ～ of oneself 出洋相 2 (of skill, technique) 展示 3 fig (of arrogance, rudeness) 显露 4 Brit Univ 奖学金

exhibition: ～ centre *n* 会展中心; **～ gallery** *n* 艺术品展览馆; **～ hall** *n* 展览厅

exhibitionism /ˌeksɪ'bɪʃənɪzəm/ *n* [u] 1 (desire to show off) 表现癖 2 Psych (mental condition) 裸露癖

exhibitionist /ˌeksɪ'bɪʃənɪst/
A *n* 1 (show-off) 好出风头的人 2 Psych 有裸露癖的人
B *adj* 1 (attention-seeking) 好出风头的 2 Psych 有裸露癖的

exhibition stand *n* 展位

exhibitor /ɪg'zɪbɪtə(r)/ *n* 参展者

exhilarate /ɪg'zɪləreɪt/ *vt* 使兴奋; to be ～d by sth. 因某事物兴奋; to be ～d at *or* by the thought of ... 一想到…就兴奋不已

exhilarating /ɪg'zɪləreɪtɪŋ/ *adj* 使人兴奋的 ‹*experience, music, contest*›

exhilaration /ɪgˌzɪlə'reɪʃn/ *n* [u] 兴奋; the ～ of doing sth. 做某事的激动心情; a feeling/sense of ～ 兴奋的感觉

exhort /ɪg'zɔ:t/ *vt* 规劝; to ～ sb. to sth./to do sth. 告诫某人做某事; to ～ sb. to action 敦促某人采取行动

exhortation /ˌegzɔ:'teɪʃn/ *n* 1 [u] (encouragement) 敦促 2 [c] (address) 告诫的话

exhumation /eksˌhju:'meɪʃn, Amer ɪgˌzu:m-/ *n* [c and u] formal 掘尸

exhume /eks'hju:m, Amer ɪg'zu:m/ *vt* formal 掘出 ‹*body, remains*›

ex-husband *n* 前夫

exigency /'eksɪdʒənsɪ/ *n* formal 1 [u] (urgency) 迫切 2 [c] (need) 急切需要; (demand) 迫切要求

exile /'eksaɪl/
A *n* 1 [c] (person) 背井离乡者; a tax ～ 移居低税国家的富人; a political ～ 政治流亡者 2 [u] (expulsion) 流放; to be in/go into ～ 在流放中/流亡; to live in ～ 过流亡生活; to be sent/driven *or* forced into ～ 被流放/被迫流亡; government-in-～ 流亡政府
B *vt* 流放; to ～ sb. from/to somewhere 将某人驱逐出/流放到某地; to ～ sb. for life 终生放逐某人

exist /ɪg'zɪst/ *vi* 1 (be) 存在; to continue to ～ 继续存在 2 (occur, be found) 出现; there ～s a custom that ... 有…的习俗 3 (survive) 存活 4 (live) 生存; to ～ on sth. 靠某物生活

existence /ɪg'zɪstəns/ *n* 1 [u] (being) 存在; in ～ 现存的; to come into/go out of ～ 产生/灭亡 2 [c] (way of life) 生活方式; to eke out an ～ 勉强度日 3 [u] (survival) 生存; to struggle for one's very ～ 为生计奔波

existent /ɪg'zɪstənt/ *adj* formal 存在的

existential /ˌegzɪ'stenʃl/ *adj* 1 (concerned with human existence) 与人类存在有关的; ～ crisis/question 生存危机/问题 2 (concerned with existentialism) 存在主义的 ‹*philosophy, proposition*›

existentialism /ˌegzɪ'stenʃəlɪzəm/ *n* [u] 存在主义

existentialist /ˌegzɪ'stenʃəlɪst/
A *n* 存在主义者
B *adj* 存在主义的

existing /ɪg'zɪstɪŋ/ *adj* 目前的 ‹*situation, circumstances*›; 现行的 ‹*system, legislation*›; 现有的 ‹*records*›

exit /'eksɪt/
A *n* 1 (way out, off a major road or roundabout) 出口; (in theatre, cinema) 安全门; 'no ～' "此路不通" 2 (departure) 离开; to make an ～ (gen) 离去; Theat 退场; Sport 退出; to make a quick *or* hasty ～ 匆匆离去; to make one's final ～ euph 辞世 euph
B *vi* 1 (go out, leave) 离开; to ～ from somewhere 离开某处 2 (leave the stage) «*actor, character*» 退场; to ～ stage left/right 从舞台左边/右边退场; '～ Hamlet' "哈姆雷特下" 3 Comput 退出; to ～ from a program 退出程序

exit: ～ permit *n* 出境签证; **～ point** *n* 出口; **～ poll** *n* 投票后民意调查; **～ ramp** *n* Amer 进出口匝道; **～ sign** *n* 出口标志; **～ visa** *n* 出境签证; **～ wound** *n* 穿透伤

Exocet /'eksəset/ *pr n* ～ (missile) [法国制造的] "飞鱼"反舰导弹

exodus /'eksədəs/ *n* (*pl* ～es) formal or hum 大批离开; a mass ～ 全体外出

ex officio /ˌeks ə'fɪʃɪəʊ/ formal
A *adv* 依据职权 ‹*attend, be present, serve*›
B *adj* 当然的 ‹*member, representative*›

exonerate /ɪg'zɒnəreɪt/ *vt* «*evidence*» 免除…的责任; «*court, judge*» 宣布…无罪; to ～ sb. from blame 使某人免受责备; an inquiry ～d those involved 经调查, 那些牵涉在内的人员是无罪的

exoneration /ɪgˌzɒnə'reɪʃn/ *n* [u] (of blame) 免除责任; (of criminal charge) 免除指控; ～ from sth. 免除对某事的责任

exorbitance /ɪg'zɔ:bɪtəns/ *n* [u] 过高

exorbitant /ɪg'zɔ:bɪtənt/ *adj* 过高的; to go to ～ lengths (to do sth.) (为做某事) 不遗余力; an ～ amount of time/money 多得离谱的时间/金钱; to an ～ degree 到过分的程度

exorcism /'eksɔ:sɪzəm/ *n* [c and u] 驱魔; to carry out an ～ of sth./on sb. 为某物/某人驱邪

exorcist /'eksɔ:sɪst/ *n* 驱魔法师

exorcize /'eksɔ:saɪz/ *vt* 1 (expel) 驱除 ‹*evil spirit*›; (free of evil spirit) 给…驱魔 ‹*person, place*› 2 (completely remove) 消除 ‹*memory, terror, spectre*›

exoskeleton /ˌeksəʊ'skelɪtn/ *n* 外骨骼

exosphere /'eksəʊsfɪə(r)/ *n* 外逸层

exothermic /ˌeksəʊ'θɜ:mɪk/ *adj* 放热的

exotic /ɪg'zɒtɪk/
A *adj* 1 (foreign) 来自异国的 ‹*plant, fruit, animal*›; 异国情调的 ‹*place*›; 异国风味的 ‹*cuisine*›; 奇异的 ‹*taste, smell*› 2 (attractive, striking) 异常迷人的 3 (erotic) 色情的
B *n* 1 (person) 外国人 2 (animal) 外来动物; (plant) 外来植物

exotica /ɪg'zɒtɪkə/ *npl* (unusual things) 奇异事物; (foreign things) 异族事物

exoticism /ɪg'zɒtɪsɪzəm/ *n* [u] 异国情调

expand /ɪk'spænd/
A *vt* 1 (increase, develop, enlarge) 扩大 ‹*trade, production*›; 扩展 ‹*business, operations*›; 拓展 ‹*horizons, knowledge*›; 详细阐述 ‹*ideas*›; 扩写 ‹*story*›; 扩张 ‹*lungs, chest, empire*›; 拉开 ‹*muscle*›; to ～ sth. into sth. 将某物发展成某物; the article was ～ed into a book 这篇文章被扩充成了一本书 2 Math 展开 ‹*fraction, expression*›
B *vi* 1 (increase) 增加; heat makes it ～ 它受热膨胀 2 (grow, develop) «*trade, possibilities*» 扩大; «*knowledge*» 拓展; «*industry, technology, relations*» 发展; «*population*» 增长; the company is ～ing into overseas markets 公司正在向海外市场拓展; to ～ on *or* upon sth. (give fuller account of) 详细阐述 ‹*topic, theme, point*› 3 (relax) «*person*» 放松

expandable /ɪk'spændəbl/ *adj* 1 可扩大的 ‹*container*›; 可伸缩的 ‹*suitcase*›; 可拉伸的 ‹*strap*› 2 Comput 可扩充的

expanded /ɪk'spændɪd/ *adj* 1 (extended, developed) 被扩展的 2 (having cellular structure) 发泡的; ～ plastic/polystyrene 泡沫塑料/发泡聚苯乙烯

expanding /ɪk'spændɪŋ/ *adj* 1 (growing, developing) 膨胀的 ‹*population*›; 发展的 ‹*market, industry, economy*›; 增加的 ‹*opportunities*› 2 (expandable) 可伸缩的 ‹*file, suitcase*›

expanse /ɪk'spæns/ *n* (of land, water) 广阔区域; (of flesh, fabric) 延伸部分

expansion /ɪk'spænʃn/ *n* 1 (increase in physical dimensions) 膨胀 2 (development, growth) (of business, production, economy etc.) 扩大; (of building, site) 扩建; (of population, membership, sales) 增长; rate of ～ 增长率 3 (elaboration of book, thesis, research) 扩充 4 (degree of growth, increase) 扩大程度 5 Math 展开

expansionary /ɪk'spænʃənərɪ/ *adj* 扩张性的

expansion: ～ board *n* 扩展卡 [可插入扩充槽内, 增加计算机的使用功能]; **～ bolt** *n* 伸缩栓; **～ card** *n* = ～ board

expansionism /ɪk'spænʃənɪzəm/ *n* [u] 扩张主义

expansionist /ɪk'spænʃənɪst/
A *adj* 扩张主义的
B *n* 扩张主义者

expansion: ～ joint *n* 伸缩接头; **～ programme, ～ scheme** *ns* 扩展计划; **～ slot** *n* 扩充槽; **～ tank** *n* 膨胀水箱

expansive /ɪk'spænsɪv/ *adj* 1 (effusive) 热情的 ‹*person, manner, welcome*›; 爽朗的 ‹*smile*›; 开朗的 ‹*mood*› 2 (extensive) 广阔的 ‹*plains, countryside*›; 宽大的 ‹*chest, waistcoat*›; 两手展开的 ‹*gesture*› 3 (covering large subject area) 全面的 ‹*definition*›; 洋洋洒洒的 ‹*writing style*›

expansively /ɪk'spænsɪvli/ *adv* 1 (effusively) 热情地 ‹*welcome, speak, greet*›; 爽朗地 ‹*smile*› 2 (widely) 两手展开地 ‹*gesture, wave*›

expansiveness /ɪk'spænsɪvnɪs/ *n* [u] (of person) 热情; (of gesture) 两手展开

expat /ˌeks'pæt/ *n* colloq = **expatriate A, B**

expatiate /ɪk'speɪʃɪeɪt/ *vi* formal 详尽阐述; to ～ on *or* upon sth. 详述某事

expatriate
A /ˌeks'pætrɪət/ *adj* 移居国外的
B /ˌeks'pætrɪət/ *n* 侨民
C /ˌeks'peɪtrɪeɪt/ *vt* «*government, state*» 把…逐出本国 ‹*citizen, national*›

expect /ɪk'spekt/
A *vt* 1 (anticipate) 预计; to ～ sb. to do sth. 预料某人会做某事; to ～ fine weather/trouble/good news 预计会有好天气/麻烦/好消息; to be ～ed 相当正常; to ～ the worst 做最坏的打算; to know what to ～ 知道将会发生什么; I ～ed as much 我就料到会这样; not as awful/good as I ～ed 没有我预计的那么糟糕/好; more/worse than ～ed 比预计的要多/差; I didn't ～ that of him 我没想到他会这样 2 (rely on) 指望; to ～ sb. to do sth. 指望某人做某事; to ～ sympathy/help from sb. 指望得到某人的同情/帮助 3 (await) 等待 ‹*guest, delivery*›; to ～ sb. to do sth. 期待某人做某事; to ～ a call/visit from sb. 等待某人的电话/来访; to be ～ed to arrive at six 应在 6 点钟到达 4 (require) 要求; to ～ sb. to do sth. 要求某人做某事; to ～ sth. from sb. 要求某人做到 ‹*high standards, commitment*›; to ～ a lot/too much of sb. 对某人要求很多/太高; to know what's ～ed (of one) 知道别人 (对自己) 的要求; it's too much to ～ 这要求太过分 5 colloq (suppose) 猜想; I ～ he's at home 我想他在家里 6 (be pregnant with) 怀着; she's ～ing her third child 她正怀着第三个孩子
B *vi* 1 (anticipate) 预计; to ～ to do sth. 预计会做某事; I didn't ～ to win 我没想到会获胜 2 (demand) 要求; I ～ to see you there 我要在那里见你 3 colloq (suppose) 猜想; will you be late? — I ～ so 你会迟到吗? —— 我想会的 4 to be ～ing (be pregnant) 怀孕

expectancy /ɪk'spektənsɪ/ *n* [u] 期望; an air/a look/a feeling of ～ 期盼的神情/样子/感觉

expectant /ɪk'spektənt/ *adj* 1 (eager, excited) 期盼的 ‹*silence, look, glance, faces*› 2 *attrib* (having a baby) 将有孩子的; **an ~ mother/father** 准妈妈/准爸爸

expectantly /ɪk'spektəntlɪ/ *adv* 期待地

expectation /ˌekspek'teɪʃn/ *n* **1** [c and u] (assumption, prediction) 预料; **the ~ of doing sth.** 做某事的预期; **contrary to** *or* **against all ~(s)** 出乎意料地; **to be in line with ~(s)** 不出所料; **it is my ~ that ...** 我预计…; **to have ~s of success** 有望成功; **beyond all ~(s)** 出乎意料 **2** [c] (aspiration, hope) 希望; (requirement, demand) 要求; **to live up to/fail to live up to sb.'s ~s** 达到/辜负某人的希望; **to come up to (sb.'s) ~s** 不负（某人）所望; **to have great ~s of sb./sth.** 对某人/某事物抱有很高的期望; **an atmosphere of ~** 期待的气氛; **to fail to meet one's ~s** 不理想

expected /ɪk'spektɪd/ *adj* 预料的

expected: ~ frequency *n* 期望频率; **~ value** *n* 期望值

expectorant /ɪk'spektərənt/ *n* 祛痰剂

expectorate /ɪk'spektəreɪt/ formal
A *vt* 咳出
B *vi* 吐痰

expediency /ɪk'spi:dɪənsɪ/, **expedience** /ɪk'spi:dɪəns/ *ns* [u] **1** (convenience) 适宜 **2** (gain) 眼前利益; **to act out of ~** 为了一时的利益行动

expedient /ɪk'spi:dɪənt/
A *adj* **1** (convenient) 适宜的 ‹*course of action, move, temporary solution*› **2** (advantageous) 出于私利考虑的 ‹*policy, course of action, solution*›
B *n* 应急的手段

expediently /ɪk'spi:dɪəntlɪ/ *adv* **1** (opportunely, conveniently) 适宜地 **2** (advantageously) 出于私利考虑地

expedite /'ekspɪdaɪt/ *vt* formal 加快 ‹*development, procedure, business, work*›

expedition /ˌekspɪ'dɪʃn/ *n* **1** (journey) 远征; **an ~ to/into ...** 去…的探险; **to go on an ~** 去探险 **2** (group) 远征队 **3** colloq (trip) 短途出行; **to go on a shopping ~** 上街购物; **a hunting/climbing ~** 去狩猎/登山

expeditionary force /ˌekspɪ'dɪʃnəri fɔ:s/ *n* 远征军

expeditious /ˌekspɪ'dɪʃəs/ *adj* formal 迅速而有效的

expeditiously /ˌekspɪ'dɪʃəslɪ/ *adv* formal 迅速而有效地

expel /ɪk'spel/ *vt* (*pres p etc.* **-ll-**) **1** (force to leave school or organization) 开除 ‹*pupil, party member*›; 取消…的比赛资格 ‹*athlete*›; **to ~ sb. from sth.** 把某人从某机构开除 **2** (force to leave country) «*government*» 驱逐…出境 ‹*foreign diplomats, invaders, dissidents*›; **to ~ sb. from the country** 把某人驱逐出境 **3** (eject) 排出 ‹*gas, liquid, smoke*›; **to ~ sth. from sth.** 从某处排出某物

expend /ɪk'spend/ *vt* **1** (devote, spend) 付出 ‹*effort, time, energy*›; 耗费 ‹*money, resources*›; **to ~ sth. on sth./doing sth.** (devote) 在某事/做某事上付出某事物; (spend) 在某事/做某事上花费某物 **2** (use) 耗费 ‹*resources, fuel, ammunition*›

expendable /ɪk'spendəbl/ *adj* **1** (unimportant, dispensable) 无足轻重的 ‹*person, labour force*› **2** (disposable) 一次性的 ‹*stationery, container*› **3** Mil 可牺牲的 ‹*troops*›; 可毁弃的 ‹*equipment*›

expenditure /ɪk'spendɪtʃə(r)/ *n* [u] **1** (amount spent) 开支; **~ on education/defence** 教育/国防经费; **income and ~** 收支 **2** (in bookkeeping) 支出额 **3** (act) (of spending) 花费; (of materials) 消耗; (of resources, energy, time) 耗费; **a useful ~ of time** 时间的有效使用

expense /ɪk'spens/
A *n* **1** [u] (cost) 费用; **at sb.'s ~** 由某人支付; **at public ~** 用公款; **to go to the ~ (of doing sth.)** 花钱（做某事）; **to spare no ~ (over sth.)** （在某事物上）不惜代价; **no ~ spared** 不惜代价; **to put sb. to the ~ of sth./doing sth.** 使某人花钱于某事物/做某事 **2** [u] (loss) 代价; **at the ~ of sb./sth.** 以某人/某事物为代价; **to make a joke/have a laugh at sb.'s ~** 拿某人开玩笑/作笑料 **3** [c] (cause for expenditure) 开销; (expensive item) 花钱的东西; **to cut down on ~s** 缩减开销; **to be too much of an ~** 是太大的一笔开销
B **expenses** *npl* 费用; **to cover sb.'s ~s** 支付某人的开销; **to get one's ~s paid** 报销费用; **all ~s paid** 费用全部报销的; **to claim ~s** 报销; **to fiddle ~s** colloq 虚报费用

expense account *n* 报销账目; **to put sth. on an ~** 把某物记入报销账目

expensive /ɪk'spensɪv/ *adj* 昂贵的 ‹*house, work of art, clothes*›; 奢侈的 ‹*hobby, lifestyle*›; 豪华的 ‹*restaurant, car*›; 代价高的 ‹*mistake*›; **~ to maintain** 保养费用高的

expensive-looking *adj* 看上去昂贵的

expensively /ɪk'spensɪvlɪ/ *adv* 昂贵地; **to be ~ dressed** 穿着奢华

expensiveness /ɪk'spensɪvnɪs/ *n* [u] 昂贵

experience /ɪks'pɪərɪəns/
A *n* **1** [u] (knowledge, skill) 经验; **to have ~ of sth./doing sth.** 有某事物/做某事的经验; **to have ~ in sth./doing sth.** 在某事物/做某事上有经验; **to have ~ with sb./sth.** 了解某人/某事物; **to learn by ~** 从经验中学习; **a question** *or* **matter of ~** 经验问题; **to acquire** *or* **gain ~** 获得经验 **2** [u] (things experienced) 经历; **from sb.'s own ~** 从某人的亲身经历中; **in my ~, ...** 据我的经验，…; **based on personal ~** 根据个人经历; **to judge from ~** 根据经验判断; **direct** *or* **first-hand ~ of poverty** 对贫穷的直接/亲身体验 **3** [c] (event) （一次）经历; **to have** *or* **go through an ~** 有某种体验; **that was quite an ~!** 那次经历不同寻常！; **the ~ of a lifetime** 难得的人生经历
B *vt* **1** (undergo) 经历 ‹*problems, change*›; **to ~ sth. at first hand** *or* **personally** 亲身经历某事; **to ~ difficulty doing sth.** 做某事遇到困难 **2** (feel) 体验 ‹*pain, fear*›; 体会 ‹*emotion*›; **to ~ pleasure** 感受愉悦; **to ~ profound relief** 感到极大的宽慰

experienced /ɪk'spɪərɪənst/ *adj* 有经验的; **to be ~ in sth./doing sth.** 在某事物上/做某事经验丰富

experiment /ɪk'sperɪmənt/
A *n* **1** [c] (scientific test) 实验; **to conduct** *or* **carry out** *or* **perform an ~** 做实验; **to do sth. as an ~** 以做某事为实验; **~s in chemistry/nuclear physics** 化学/核物理实验 **2** [u] (experimentation) 实验过程; **to learn by ~** 从实验中学习; **by way of ~** 通过实验 **3** [c] (attempt to do sth. new) 尝试; **an ~ with sth. new** 对某新事物的尝试
B *vi* **1** (carry out tests, research) 做实验; **to ~ on sb./sth.** 用某人/某物做实验; **to ~ with sth. on sb./sth.** 在某人/某物上做…的实验 **2** (try out) 尝试; **to ~ with sth.** 试用某物

experimental /ɪkˌsperɪ'mentl/ *adj* **1** (relating to science) 实验的 ‹*research, science, method*›; **on an ~ basis** 在实验基础上 **2** (innovative) 创新的 ‹*artist, film, teaching methods*› **3** (unfinalized, hypothetical) 试验性的; **at the ~ stage** 处于试验阶段

experimentally /ɪkˌsperɪ'mentəlɪ/ *adv* **1** (through experiment) 通过实验 ‹*establish, discover*› **2** (as an experiment) 试验性地 ‹*use, try*›

experimentation /ɪkˌsperɪmen'teɪʃn/ *n* [u] 实验; **small children learn by ~** 幼儿通过尝试学习; **~ is necessary for creativity to flourish** 实验对于发挥创造力是必要的

expert /'ekspɜ:t/
A *n* 专家; **to be an ~ on sth.** 是某方面的专家; **she is an ~ on ancient Greece** 她是古希腊学专家; **an ~ in sth.** 某方面的能手; **an ~ at sth./doing sth.** 某事/做某事的能手; **you're the ~!** 你是个高手！
B *adj* (skilled) 熟练的 ‹*craftsman, hands*›; 精湛的 ‹*skill, touch*›; (professional) 专业的 ‹*knowledge, advice, opinion, valuation*›; **to be ~ at doing sth.** 做某事在行; **an ~ cook/eye** 专业厨师/行家的眼光; **to require ~ handling** 要求操作娴熟

expertise /ˌekspɜ:'ti:z/ *n* [u] 专长; **~ in sth.** 在某方面的专长; **his ~ as a builder** 他作为建筑工人的专业技能; **to have/lack the ~ to do sth.** 具有/缺乏做某事的专业知识

expertly /'ekspɜ:tlɪ/ *adv* 熟练地

expertness /'ekspɜ:tnɪs/ *n* [u] 特别技能

expert: ~ system *n* 专家系统; **~ witness** *n* 专家证人

expiate /'ekspɪeɪt/ *vt* formal 为…接受惩罚 ‹*bad behaviour, wrong*›; 赎 ‹*sin, guilt*›

expiation /ˌekspɪ'eɪʃn/ *n* [u] formal (of crime, guilt, sin) 赎罪; (of fault) 补偿; **in ~ (of sth.)** 作为（对某事的）弥补

expiration /ˌekspɪ'reɪʃn/ *n* [u] (of contract, passport, treaty, current year) 期满; (of registration, application) 截止; (of term of office) 届满

expiration date *n* Amer = **expiry date**

expire /ɪk'spaɪə(r)/ *vi* **1** (end) «*passport, permit, licence, lease, contract*» 到期; «*time limit, period of time*» 结束; «*patent, prison sentence*» 期满; «*term of office*» 届满 **2** formal (exhale) «*person, animal*» 呼气; «*plant*» 释放气体 **3** formal (die) «*person, animal*» 死亡

expiry /ɪk'spaɪərɪ/ *n* [u] (of contract, time period) 期满; (of mandate, deadline) 终止

expiry date *n* **1** (of credit card, permit, passport, contract, lease, patent) 到期日 **2** (of perishable) 有效期

explain /ɪk'spleɪn/
A *vt* 解释 ‹*operation, meaning of word, thoughts, phenomenon, action, attitude*›; 说明 ‹*rules, plans, intentions*›; **to ~ sth. to sb.** 向某人说明某事; **to ~ what/how/that ...** 解释什么…/如何…/…; **that ~s it!** 原来是这样！
B *v refl* **to ~ oneself** 把自己的意思解释清楚

Phrasal verb

• **explain away** *vt* [**~ away sth., ~ sth. away**] 为…辩解 ‹*mistake, absence, failure*›

explainable /ɪk'spleɪnəbl/ *adj* 可解释的

explanation /ˌeksplə'neɪʃn/ *n* **1** (description, clarification) 解释; (giving of reasons) 说明; **by way of ~** 通过解释; **there is no ~** 无法解释; **it needs no ~** 这不需要解释; **an ~ for sth.** 对某事的说明 **2** (justification) 缘由; **in ~** 以作说明; **a plausible/an adequate/a convincing ~** 合理的/充足的/令人信服的理由

explanatory /ɪk'splænətrɪ, Amer -tɔ:ri/ *adj* 说明的 ‹*letter*›; 解释的 ‹*remarks, answer*›; **~ notes/diagram** 注释/图示

expletive /ɪk'spli:tɪv, Amer 'eksplətɪv/ *n* formal 咒骂语

explicable /ɪk'splɪkəbl, 'ek-/ *adj* 可解释的 ‹*phenomenon, motive*›; 可理解的 ‹*behaviour*›; **for no ~ reason** 无缘无故地; **to be ~ in terms of/in the light of ...** 可用…来说明

explicit /ɪk'splɪsɪt/ *adj* **1** (precise) 详述的 ‹*instructions, reasons, plan*›; 明确的 ‹*denial, purpose, prohibition, warning*›; **to be ~ about** *or* **on sth.** 对某事很明确 **2** (open) 直截了当的 ‹*criticism, opposition, support*›; **to be ~ about sth.** 对某事直言不讳 **3** (sexually graphic) 有露骨性爱场面的 ‹*film, description*›

explicitly /ɪk'splɪsɪtlɪ/ *adv* **1** (clearly, precisely) 明确地 ‹*warn, forbid, tell, deny*› **2** (openly) 坦率地 ‹*talk, admit*› **3** (graphically) 生动地 ‹*depict, display*›

explode /ɪk'spləʊd/
A *vi* **1** (blow up) «*bomb, rocket, gas, star*» 爆炸 **2** (be destroyed) «*aircraft, ship, building*» 被炸毁 **3** (expand) «*gas, chemical*» 剧烈膨胀 **4** (arise suddenly) «*violence*» 爆发; **to ~ into**

e

sth. «*crowd, audience*» 突然爆发出…; **to ~ into applause** 爆发出鼓掌喝彩声; **to ~ with** *or* **into rage/laughter** 勃然大怒/轰然大笑; **to be ready to ~** «*person*» 怒火一触即发 **5** (increase) «*population, birthrate*» 激增 **6** (appear suddenly) 突然出现; **to ~ on to the scene** 突然现身; **to ~ on to the musical/pop/theatrical scene** 突然出现在音乐界/流行音乐界/戏剧界

B *vt* **1** (detonate) 引爆 ‹*bomb*› **2** (refute) 戳穿 ‹*rumour, myth*›; «*publication*» 推翻 ‹*theory, assumption*›

exploded /ɪk'spləʊdɪd/ *adj* 分解的 ‹*diagram, drawing*›

exploit

A /'eksplɔɪt/ *n* 英雄业绩; **amorous ~s** hum 风流韵事

B /ɪk'splɔɪt/ *vt* **1** (make use of) 开发 ‹*resources, market, workforce*›; 发挥 ‹*skills, talent*› **2** (abuse, take advantage of) «*employer*» 剥削 ‹*employee*›; «*person, competitor*» 滥用 ‹*trust*›; (take advantage of) 利用 ‹*weakness, credulity, opportunity*›

exploitable /ɪk'splɔɪtəbl/ *adj* **1** (usable) 可利用的 ‹*resources, talents, contacts*› **2** (vulnerable to abuse) 易遭剥削的 ‹*person*›; 易被利用的 ‹*weakness, situation*›

exploitation /,eksplɔɪ'teɪʃn/ *n* [u] **1** (use of talent) 利用; (use of market, resources) 开发 **2** (abuse, taking advantage) (of employees) 剥削; (of weakness, situation) 利用

exploitative /ɪk'splɔɪtətɪv/ *adj* 剥削的

exploration /,eksplə'reɪʃn/ *n* **1** [c and u] (travel) 探索 **2** [c and u] (examination) 考察 **3** [u] (searching for resources) 勘探

exploratory /ɪk'splɒrətri, Amer -tɔːri/ *adj* **1** (investigative) 探索的 ‹*expedition, excavations, drilling*›; 探查的 ‹*surgery, X-rays*› **2** (preliminary) 试探性的 ‹*inquiries, discussions, calculations*›

explore /ɪk'splɔː(r)/

A *vt* **1** (travel over) «*group, expedition*» 勘察 ‹*region, outer space*›; **to set out to ~ sth.** 出发去勘探某事物 **2** (investigate) «*scientist, researcher*» 探索 ‹*alternatives, implications*›; **to ~ every avenue/path/possibility** 探索所有的手段/途径/可能性; **to ~ all eventualities** 探索所有的可能后果; **to ~ ways and means of doing sth.** 寻找做某事的方式方法 **3** (examine by touch) 探查 ‹*wound*›

B *vi* 勘察; **to ~ for oil/gas** 勘探石油/天然气; **to go (out) exploring** 去探险

explorer /ɪk'splɔːrə(r)/ *n* 探险者

explosion /ɪk'spləʊʒn/ *n* **1** (blowing up) 爆炸 **2** (outburst of activity, emotion etc.) 爆发 **3** (sudden increase) 激增; **an ~ in sth.** 某物的激增; **an ~ in the number of new HIV cases** 新艾滋病感染者数量的激增 **4** (of light, colour) 突然出现

explosive /ɪk'spləʊsɪv/

A *n* 炸药

B *adj* **1** (relating to explosions) 爆炸的 ‹*power, effect*›; (able to explode) 易爆的 ‹*material, weapon*›; **an ~ device** 爆炸装置 **2** (highly charged) 一触即发的 ‹*situation, political repercussions*›; 易引发冲突的 ‹*issue*› **3** (volatile) 暴躁的 ‹*temper, person*›; 激烈的 ‹*argument, debate*› **4** (sudden and dramatic) 急剧的 ‹*growth, development, expansion*›

exponent /ɪk'spəʊnənt/ *n* **1** (advocate) 倡导者 **2** (practitioner) 大师 **3** Math 指数

exponential /,ekspə'nenʃl/ *adj* **1** (becoming more rapid) 越来越快的 ‹*change, improvement*›; **~ growth** 呈几何级数的增长 **2** Math **an ~ curve/equation/expression** 指数曲线/方程/式

exponentially /,ekspə'nenʃəli/ *adv* 呈几何级数地

export

A /ɪk'spɔːt/ *vt* **1** (sell abroad) «*country, company*» 出口 ‹*goods, services*›; **to ~ sth. to somewhere** 向某地出口某物 **2** (spread) 传播 ‹*ideas, culture*›

B /ɪk'spɔːt/ *vi* «*country, firm*» 出口; **~ing countries** 出口国

C /'ekspɔːt/ *n* **1** [u] (exportation) (of goods, service) 出口; (of ideas, culture) 传播; **the ~ of sth.** 某物的出口; **for ~ (only)** (仅) 供出口 **2** [c] (commodity) 出口商品

exportable /ɪk'spɔːtəbl/ *adj* 可出口的 ‹*goods, services*›; 易于传播的 ‹*culture, ideas*›

export agent *n* 出口代理商

exportation /,ekspɔː'teɪʃn/ *n* [u] 出口; **for ~ only** 仅供出口

export: ~ controls *npl* 出口管制; **~ credit** *n* [c and u] 出口信贷; **~ drive** *n* 出口运动; **~ duty** *n* [u] 出口税; **~ earnings** *npl* 出口所得

exporter /ɪk'spɔːtə(r)/ *n* (person) 出口商; (firm) 出口公司; (country) 出口国

export: ~ finance *n* [u] 出口信贷; **~ goods** *npl* 出口产品; **~ house** *n* 出口公司; **~-import company** *n* 进出口公司; **~ licence** *n* 出口许可证; **~ manager** ▸**p. 409** *n* 出口部经理; **~ market** *n* 出口市场; **~-orientated, ~-oriented** *adj* 以出口为目的的; **~ permit** *n* = **~ licence**; **~ sales** *npl* 出口销售额; **~ trade** *n* 出口贸易

expose /ɪk'spəʊz/

A *vt* **1** (display) 暴露 ‹*chest, legs, arms*›; **to ~ to public view** 向公众展示 **2** (uncover) «*archaeological dig*» 发掘出 ‹*remains*›; «*low tide*» 使…显露 ‹*rocks, beach*›; 使…裸露 ‹*electrical connection, nerve*› **3** (make public) 揭穿 ‹*secrets, scandal, injustice*› **4** (reveal true nature of) 揭露 ‹*criminal, impostor*›; **to ~ sb. for what they are** 揭穿某人的真面目 **5** (make vulnerable) 使遭受; **to ~ sb./sth. to …** 让某人/某物遭受…; **to be ~d to attack/criticism/ridicule** 易受到袭击/抨击/嘲笑 **6** **to ~ sb. to sth.** (introduce to) 使某人了解 ‹*subject, idea, art form*›; (make experience) 使经受 ‹*influence, reality*› **7** Phot 将…曝光 ‹*film*›

B *v refl* **1** (display genitals) **to ~ oneself** 当众露阴 **2** (make oneself vulnerable) **to ~ oneself to sth.** 使自己易于遭受…

exposé /ek'spəʊzeɪ, Amer ,ekspə'zeɪ/ *n* 揭露

exposed /ɪk'spəʊzd/ *adj* **1** (bare) 裸露的 ‹*legs, arms, chest, breasts*›; 露出的 ‹*wire, connection, beam*›; **to be ~ to view** 暴露于视线下 **2** (unprotected) 无遮蔽的 ‹*position, hillside*› **3** (vulnerable) 易受攻击的 ‹*position, troops*›

exposition /,ekspə'zɪʃn/ *n* **1** [c and u] (description, explanation) 详细阐述 **2** [c] (exhibition) 博览会; **to hold/mount an ~ of sth.** 举办某物的展销会 **3** [c] (part of literary work) 提示部分 **4** [c] (part of musical composition) 呈示部

expostulate /ɪk'spɒstjʊleɪt/ formal

A *vi* 争论; **to ~ with sb. (about sth.)** (因为某事物) 与某人争吵

B *vt* 抗议

expostulation /ɪk,spɒstjʊ'leɪʃn/ *n* formal 抗议

exposure /ɪk'spəʊʒə(r)/ *n* **1** [c and u] (disclosure of crime, dishonesty etc.) 揭发; **to threaten with ~** 威胁要揭发 **2** [u] (subjection) 暴露; **~ to the wind and sun** 经受风吹日晒; **~ of children to radiation** 孩童暴露于辐射中 **3** [u] (physical condition) 受寒; **to suffer from ~** 受冻; **to die of ~** 冻死 **4** [u] (publicity) 亮相; (coverage) 报道; **to receive** *or* **get ~ in the media** 被媒体报道 **5** [u] (to financial losses) 承担金融风险 **6** [c and u] Phot (exposing a film to light) 曝光; (length of exposing time) 曝光时间; (picture) 底片; **to take an ~** 照一张相片; **a double ~** 二次曝光

exposure: ~ meter *n* 曝光表; **~ time** *n* 曝光时间

expound /ɪk'spaʊnd/

A *vt* (explain, interpret) 阐述 ‹*views, theory, reasoning, argument, philosophy, theory*›; «*judge*» 解释 ‹*the law*›; «*rabbi, priest*» 讲解 ‹*scriptures*›

B *vi* 详细说明; **to ~ on sth.** 详细说明某事物

ex-president *n* 前总统

express /ɪk'spres/

A *n* **1** [c] Rail 特快列车 **2** [u] Post 快递; **to send sth. by ~** 用快递寄送某物

B *adj attrib* **1** (rapid) 快速的 **2** Transp 特快的; **an ~ train/bus** 特快列车/公共汽车 **3** Post 快递的; **an ~ parcel** 快递包裹; **an ~ mail** 快件; **~ goods** 快运货物 **4** formal (explicit) 明确的 ‹*instructions, orders*›; **on the ~ understanding** *or* **condition that …** 明确的条件是…; **with/for the ~ purpose of doing sth.** 专门为了做某事

C *adv* 用快递 ‹*send*›

D *vt* **1** (say) 表达; **to ~ an opinion/gratitude** 表达观点/谢意; **words cannot ~ my feelings** 我的感情无以言表 **2** (show) 表示; **to ~ disapproval/grief** 表示反对/悲痛; **~ed in music** 从音乐中表现出来的 **3** Math 用符号表示 ‹*number, quantity*›; **to ~ sth. as a percentage** 以百分比表示某物; **to ~ sth. in decimal form** 用十进制表示某物; **to ~ sth. in its simplest form** 把某事物最简化; **to ~ sth. graphically** *or* **in a graph** 以图表表示某物 **4** formal (extract) 挤 ‹*milk*›; 榨 ‹*oil, juice*›; **to ~ sth. from** *or* **out of sth.** 从某物中榨出某物 **5** (send) 特快发送 ‹*goods*›; **to ~ sth. to sb.** 给某人快递某物

E *v refl* **1** **to ~ oneself** 表达自己的思想; **to ~ oneself (as) satisfied with/angry at sth.** 表示自己 (对某事物) 很满意/愤怒 **2** **to ~ itself** «*pleasure, disapproval*» 从…表现出来

expression /ɪk'spreʃn/ *n* **1** [c and u] (revealing one's thoughts, feelings) 表达; **to give ~ to sth.** 表达某事物; **he finds it hard to give ~ to his thoughts** 他觉得难以表达自己的想法; **freedom of ~** 言论自由; **beyond ~** 无法言传 **2** [c and u] (manifestation) (of emotion) 流露; (of friendship, gratitude etc.) 表现; **to accept sth. as an ~ of sth.** 接受某事物作为某事物的表示; **a spontaneous ~ of joy/gratitude** 喜悦/感激的不自觉流露; **to give ~ to sth.** 表露某事物; **to find ~ in sth.** 在某事物中得到表现 **3** [u] (feeling) 情感的表露; **to put ~ into sth.** 在某事物中注入感情; **to lack ~** 缺乏感情 **4** [c] (look) 表情; **with an ~ of horror/concern** 面带惧色/面露关切; **you could tell from her ~ that she wasn't happy** 她看上去不高兴 **5** [c] (choice of words) 措词; (phrase) 词语; **if you'll pardon the ~** 请原谅我这么说 **6** [u] formal (squeezing out) 榨出 **7** [c] Math 表达式

expressionism /ɪk'spreʃənɪzəm/ *n* [u] 表现主义

expressionist /ɪk'spreʃənɪst/

A *n* (painter) 表现主义艺术家; (writer) 表现主义作家

B *adj* 表现主义的

expressionless /ɪk'spreʃnlɪs/ *adj* **1** (blank) 毫无表情的 ‹*face*›; 呆板的 ‹*look*› **2** (monotonous) 单调的 ‹*voice*› **3** (without emotion) 没有激情的 ‹*style, playing*›

expressive /ɪk'spresɪv/ *adj* **1** (showing thought, feeling) 富有表情的 ‹*face, features*›; 生动的 ‹*language*›; 栩栩如生的 ‹*portrait*› **2** (communicative) 表达的 ‹*powers, ability*›; 意味深长的 ‹*look, grimace*›; 富有表现力的 ‹*piece of music, song, painting*› **3** (indicative of specific emotion or meaning) 有特殊意味的 ‹*silence, gesture*›; **to be ~ of despair** 意味着绝望

expressively /ɪk'spresɪvli/ *adv* 富有感情地 ‹*read, play, perform*›

expressiveness /ɪk'spresɪvnɪs/ *n* [u] (of face) 富有表情; (of words) 意味深长; (of work of art, performance) 富有表现力

expressly /ɪk'spresli/ *adv* **1** (explicitly) 明确地 ‹*say, forbid, refuse*› **2** (with specific intention)

特意地 〈*propose, undertake, legislate*〉; **to do sth. ~ (in order) to ...** 为了…特意做某事; **~ for sb.** 专为某人

expressway /ɪk'spreswer/ *n* Amer 高速公路

expropriate /ˌeks'prəʊprɪeɪt/ *vt* formal **1** (seize) 征用 〈*land*〉; 没收 〈*property, assets*〉 **2** hum (steal) 顺手偷走 〈*property, money*〉; 剽窃 〈*ideas*〉

expropriation /ˌeksˌprəʊprɪ'eɪʃn/ *n* [u] formal 没收

expulsion /ɪk'spʌlʃn/ *n* **1** [c and u] (expelling) (of pupil, member, player) 开除; (of diplomat, alien, dissident) 驱逐; **to face ~** 面临除名; **temporary ~** 暂时除名 **2** [u] (discharge) (of air, breath) 呼出; (of waste) 排出; (of foetus) 产出

expunge /ɪk'spʌndʒ/ *vt* formal 清除 〈*record*〉; 删除 〈*passage, name, clause*〉; 忘却 〈*offence, incident*〉; 抹去 〈*memory*〉; **to ~ sth. from sth.** 从某处删除某物

expurgate /'ekspəgeɪt/ *vt* formal 删除…中的不雅之处

exquisite /'ekskwɪzɪt, ɪk'skwɪzɪt/ *adj* **1** (lovely, perfect) 姣好的 〈*face, complexion, features*〉; 纤美的 〈*hands, figure*〉; 可爱的 〈*poise, sweetness*〉 **2** (finely crafted) 精致的 〈*brooch, embroidery*〉; 精湛的 〈*skill*〉 **3** (impeccable) 得体的 〈*manners, courtesy, tact*〉; 优雅的 〈*politeness, taste*〉 **4** (refined) 微妙的 〈*irony, sense of humour, wit*〉 **5** formal (acute) 剧烈的 〈*pain, agony*〉; 疯狂的 〈*revenge*〉; 极度的 〈*pleasure, relief*〉

exquisitely /ɪk'skwɪzɪtli/ *adv* **1** (delightfully) 优雅地 〈*dressed, groomed*〉; 光彩动人地 〈*beautiful, pretty*〉; 细腻地 〈*smooth, soft*〉 **2** (finely, delicately) 精致地 〈*carved, embroidered*〉 **3** (perfectly) 准确地 〈*timed, told*〉 **4** formal (acutely) 极度地 〈*sensitive, relieved*〉

ex-service *adj* esp Brit 退伍的

ex-serviceman *n* (*pl* **ex-servicemen**) esp Brit 退伍军人

ex-servicewoman *n* (*pl* **ex-servicewomen**) esp Brit 退伍女军人

extant /ek'stænt, Amer 'ekstənt/ *adj* (surviving) 尚存的 〈*manuscript, example*〉; (in force) 现行的 〈*law*〉

extemporize /ɪk'stempəraɪz/ formal
A *vi* «*speaker*» 即席讲话; «*performer*» 即兴表演
B *vt* «*speaker*» 即席发表 〈*speech*〉; «*performer*» 即兴表演 〈*melody*〉

extend /ɪk'stend/
A *vt* **1** (enlarge) 扩建 〈*building, road*〉 **2** (prolong) 延长 〈*deadline, opening hours, visit*〉; 延长…的期限 〈*visa*〉 **3** (expand) 扩大 〈*vocabulary, influence, power, authority*〉; 扩大…的适用范围 〈*law*〉; 扩展 〈*knowledge, meaning, idea, theory, story, business, market*〉; 增加 〈*services, demand*〉; **the list has been ~ed to include new members** 名单中已经增添了新成员 **4** (stretch) «*person*» 伸展 〈*limb*〉; «*bird*» 展开 〈*wing*〉; **to ~ one's hand** (in greeting) 伸出手 **5** formal (offer) 提供 〈*credit*〉; **to ~ sth. to sb.** 给某人提供 〈*loan, help*〉; 向某人发出 〈*invitation*〉; 向某人表示 〈*welcome*〉 **6** fig (push to limit) 使…竭尽全力 〈*pupil*〉; **to be fully ~ed** «*school, hospital*» 竭尽全力
B *vi* **1** (stretch) «*road, lake, grounds, premises*» 延伸; «*weather, influence*» 持续; **to ~ from sth. to sth.** 从某处延伸到某处; **to ~ all the way to/as far as sth.** 一直延伸到…; **to ~ beyond sth.** 超过某物; **to ~ over the whole country** 扩大到全国 **2** (last) 延续; **to ~ into May/late into the night** 延续到五月/深夜; **to ~ for five years** 持续五年; **to ~ over a month/a lifetime** 延续一个月/一生 **3** fig (reach) 涉及; **to ~ to sb./sth.** «*interest, authority, knowledge*» 涉及到某人/某事物; **to ~ beyond national boundaries** 超越国界; **her sympathy ~s to everyone** 她对每个人都抱有同情心 **4** fig (go as far as) 达到; **my charity doesn't ~ to writing you cheques** 我不会慷慨到给你开支票的地步
C *v refl* **to ~ oneself** 竭尽全力; **she's an able pupil, but she doesn't ~ herself** 她是个有能力的学生，但是她不肯尽全力

extendable /ɪk'stendəbl/ *adj* **1** (of adjustable length) 可伸缩的 〈*handle, couch, lamp*〉; **an ~ ladder** 伸缩梯 **2** (renewable) 可延期的 〈*visa, contract, permit, tenancy*〉

extended /ɪk'stendɪd/ *adj* 延长了的

extended family *n* 大家庭 [几代同堂的家庭]

extensible /ɪk'stensəbl/ *adj* 可扩展的; **~ markup language** 可扩展标记语言

extension /ɪk'stenʃn/ *n* **1** [c] (extra section) (of cable, table, road, track) 延长部分; (to building) 扩建部分 **2** [c] (prolongation) (of visa, permit, opening hours) 延期; (of deadline) 宽限期 **3** [c and u] (expansion) (of vocabulary, influence, power, authority) 扩大; (of law) 适用范围扩大; (of knowledge, meaning, idea, theory, story, business, market) 扩展; (of services, demand) 增加 **4** [c] (telephone line) 分机; (number) 分机号

extension: ~ cable *n* = **~ lead**; **~ course** *n* esp Amer [面向非全日制学生的] 进修课程; **~ ladder** *n* 伸缩梯; **~ lead** *n* 延长线; **~ tube, ~ ring** *ns* 近摄伸延管

extensive /ɪk'stensɪv/ *adj* **1** (wide-ranging) 大范围的 〈*selection, range of goods*〉; 分布广的 〈*markets, rail network, business operations*〉; 广泛的 〈*media coverage, contacts, research, debate, knowledge*〉; **~ reading** 泛读 **2** (substantial) 广阔的 〈*grassland, forests*〉; 大面积的 〈*gardens, damage, injuries, burns*〉; 巨大的 〈*losses, investment(s)*〉; 全面的 〈*repairs, alterations*〉

extensively /ɪk'stensɪvlɪ/ *adv* **1** (widely) 到处 〈*travel, read, advertise*〉 **2** (prolifically) 多产地 〈*write*〉 **3** (substantially) 大量地 〈*use, quote, modify*〉; 广泛地 〈*discuss*〉; 全面地 〈*alter*〉; 大面积地 〈*burned*〉

extensor /ɪk'stensə(r)/ *n* **~ (muscle)** 伸肌

extent /ɪk'stent/ *n* **1** (size) 大小; **over the whole ~ of sth.** 覆盖在某物上; **in ~** 在面积上 **2** (amount) (of damage) 严重性; (of knowledge, power, involvement) 范围 **3** (degree) 程度; **to what ~ ...?** 在多大程度上…？; **to a large/a certain/some ~** 在很大/一定/某种程度上

extenuating /ɪk'stenjʊeɪtɪŋ/ *adj* 情有可原的 〈*circumstances, factor*〉

exterior /ɪk'stɪərɪə(r)/
A *n* **1** (outside) 外部; **on the ~** 在外部 **2** (appearance) 外表
B *adj* **1** (outer) 外部的 〈*lighting, drains, paintwork, cleaning*〉; **'for ~ use'** "外用"; **~ walls/door** 外墙/外大门 **2** Cin, Phot (outdoor) 外景的 〈*shot, location*〉

exterior angle *n* 外角

exterminate /ɪk'stɜːmɪneɪt/ *vt* 消灭 〈*vermin*〉; 灭绝 〈*species, race*〉

extermination /ɪkˌstɜːmɪ'neɪʃn/ *n* [u] (of vermin) 消灭; (of species, race) 灭绝

extermination camp *n* 灭绝集中营

exterminator /ɪk'stɜːmɪneɪtə(r)/ *n* 灭害虫的人

extern /'ekstɜːn/ *n* Amer (doctor) 非住院医师; (other worker) 非住院工作人员

external /ɪk'stɜːnl/ *adj* **1** (outer) 外在的 〈*differences*〉; 表面的 〈*symptoms*〉; 外面的 〈*world*〉; **for ~ use/application (only)** (仅限) 外用; **~ appearance/injuries** 外表/外伤; **~ wall/skeleton** 外墙/外骨骼 **2** (from outside) 外界的 〈*influence, force, factors, events*〉 **3** Telecom 外线的 〈*telephone call*〉 **4** (outside the country) 对外的 〈*relations, trade, market*〉 **5** (outside the school) 校外的 〈*examiner, candidate*〉 **6** Comput 外置的 〈*data file, memory, disk drive*〉

external: ~ angle *n* = **exterior angle**; **~ degree** *n* Brit 校外生学位; **~ examiner** *n* 校外主考人

externalize /ɪk'stɜːnəlaɪz/ *vt* **1** formal (express in words, actions) 表露 〈*feelings, sense of failure, thoughts*〉 **2** Psych (project sth. on outside figure or object) 外化 〈*feelings, thoughts*〉

externally /ɪk'stɜːnəlɪ/ *adv* **1** (on the outside) 表面上 〈*calm, sound, cheerful*〉 **2** (from the outside) 从外部 〈*examined, investigated, funded, influenced*〉

external storage *n* [u] 外存

extinct /ɪk'stɪŋkt/ *adj* **1** (died out) 灭绝的 〈*species, plant, animal*〉; **to become ~** 绝种 **2** (inactive) 不再活跃的; **an ~ volcano** 死火山

extinction /ɪk'stɪŋkʃn/ *n* [u] **1** (of species) 绝种; **to be threatened with ~** 濒临灭绝 **2** (of debt) 偿清

extinguish /ɪk'stɪŋgwɪʃ/ *vt* **1** (put out) 扑灭 〈*fire*〉; 熄灭 〈*spark, candle, cigarette*〉; 关 〈*light*〉 **2** (destroy) 毁灭 〈*hopes, spirit, faith*〉; 压抑 〈*emotion, passion*〉 **3** (discharge) 偿清 〈*debt*〉

extinguisher /ɪk'stɪŋgwɪʃə(r)/ *n* = **fire extinguisher**

extirpate /'ekstəpeɪt/ *vt* formal **1** (pull up) 拔除 〈*weeds, growth*〉 **2** (eradicate) 使绝迹 〈*dissent, social evil*〉; 破除 〈*heresy, superstition*〉

extirpation /ˌekstə'peɪʃn/ *n* [u] formal **1** (pulling up) 拔除 **2** (eradication) 消灭

extn *abbr* = **extension 4**

extol, Amer also **extoll** /ɪk'stəʊl/ *vt* (*pres p etc.* **-ll-**) 赞美; **to ~ sb./sth. as sth.** 赞誉某人/某物为…; **he ~led her as a role model** 他称赞她为楷模; **to ~ sb./sth. to the skies** 大肆吹捧某人/某事物; **to ~ the virtues of ...** 宣扬…的好处

extort /ɪk'stɔːt/ *vt* **1** (obtain by threats) «*blackmailer*» 敲诈 〈*money*〉; «*corrupt official*» 强索 〈*favours*〉; **to ~ sth. from sb.** 向某人勒索某物 **2** (overcharge) «*seller, lender, bank*» 榨取 〈*high price, high rate of interest*〉; **to ~ every (last) penny from sb.** 榨干某人身上的每一分钱

extortion /ɪk'stɔːʃn/ *n* [u] 敲诈勒索

extortionate /ɪk'stɔːʃənət/ *adj* 过高的 〈*price, demand*〉

extortionist /ɪk'stɔːʃənɪst/ *n* 敲诈勒索者

extortion racket *n* colloq 敲诈勾当

extra /'ekstrə/
A *adj* **1** 额外的 〈*time, land, manpower*〉; **an ~ ...** 另外的…; **to incur/go to ~ expense** 带来额外花销/花额外费用 **2** (spare) 多余的 〈*rations, copies of document*〉; **we need an ~ chair (at the table)** 我们需要多一张椅子 (放到桌旁)
B *n* **1** (addition) 额外的事物 **2** (additional charge or cost) 另外收费的事物 **3** (actor) 临时演员
C *adv* 格外 〈*polite, kind, conscientious*〉; **to charge ~** 另外收费

extra charge *n* 额外收费

extract
A /ɪk'strækt/ *vt* **1** (pull out) 取出 〈*bullet*〉; 挑出 〈*splinter*〉; 拔出 〈*tooth*〉 **2** (obtain) 设法得到 〈*confession, promise, payment, information*〉; **to ~ sth. from sb.** (object) 设法从某人处取得某物; (information) 设法从某人处知悉某事情 **3** (derive) 获得 〈*pleasure, benefit*〉; 设法实现 〈*publicity*〉; 引申出 〈*idea, meaning, moral*〉; **the following ideas are ~ed from a variety of theories** 以下构思取自多个不同理论 **4** (obtain by chemical, physical process) 提取 〈*essence, dye, oil*〉; 榨取 〈*juice*〉; 采掘 〈*minerals, coal*〉; **copper is ~ed from copper ore by smelting** 铜是利用熔炼的方式从铜矿中提炼出来的 **5** (select, excerpt) 摘录 〈*article, passage, quotation*〉
B /'ekstrækt/ *n* **1** [c] (excerpt) 摘录 **2** [c and u] (preparation, solution) 萃取物

e

extraction /ɪk'strækʃn/ *n* 1 [c and u] (taking out) (of tooth) 拔出; (of bullet etc.) 取出; **a dental** ~ 拔牙 2 [u] (removal) (of mineral, peat) 开采; (of fumes, air, smell) 抽出; (squeezing of juice) 榨取 3 [u] (descent) 血统; **British/French** *etc.* **by** ~ 英裔/法裔等

extractor /ɪk'stræktə(r)/ *n* 1 (device) 提取器; **dust** ~ 吸尘器 2 = **extractor fan**

extractor fan *n* 排气扇

extra-curricular /ˌekstrəkə'rɪkjʊlə(r)/ *adj* 课外的 ‹*activities, sports, studies*›

extraditable /'ekstrədaɪtəbl/ *adj* 可引渡的 ‹*criminal, defendant, crime*›

extradite /'ekstrədaɪt/ *vt* 引渡; **to** ~ **(sb.) from a country** （把某人）从一个国家引渡; **to** ~ **sb. from the UK to the USA** 把某人从英国引渡至美国

extradition /ˌekstrə'dɪʃn/ *n* [c and u] 引渡; **to grant/oppose/fight the** ~ **of sb.** 批准/反对/反抗对某人的引渡

extradition: ~ **proceedings** *npl* 引渡程序; **to start** *or* **institute** ~ **proceedings** 启动引渡程序; ~ **treaty** *n* 引渡条约

extra: **~-dry** *adj* [香槟酒和起泡葡萄酒] 稍带甜味的; **~-fast** *adj* colloq 超快的; **~-fine** *adj* 超细的

extragalactic /ˌekstrəgə'læktɪk/ *adj* 银河系外的

extrajudicial /ˌekstrədʒu'dɪʃəl/ *adj* 未按法律程序的 ‹*execution, killing*›

extra-large *adj* 超大的 ‹*helping, portion*›; 特大的 ‹*size, garment*›

extramarital /ˌekstrə'mærɪtl/ *adj* 婚外的; ~ **affair** 婚外情; ~ **sex** 婚外性行为

extramural /ˌekstrə'mjʊərəl/ *adj* 1 Brit (outside school, university) 校外的 ‹*student, education, studies*› 2 (additional to study) 课外的; (additional to work) 工作之余的

extraneous /ɪk'streɪnɪəs/ *adj* 1 (irrelevant) 无关的 ‹*issues, information*›; **to be** ~ **to sth.** 与某事物无关 2 (external) 外部的 ‹*noise*›; 外来的 ‹*people*›; 外界的 ‹*idea, interference*›; ~ **material** 异物

extranet /'ekstrənet/ *n* 外联网

extraordinarily /ɪk'strɔːdnrəli, Amer -dənerɪli/ *adv* 异常地

extraordinary /ɪk'strɔːdnri, Amer -dəneri/ *adj* 1 (exceptional) 非凡的 ‹*success, career, courage, skill*›; 异常的 ‹*good fortune*›; 惊人的 ‹*violence*›; 反常的 ‹*behaviour*› 2 (remarkable) 奇特的 ‹*comment, event, coincidence, tale*›; **it was** ~ **that ...** 令人惊奇的是… 3 (not regular) 特别的 ‹*powers, revenues, item*›

extraordinary: ~ **general meeting** *n* 股东特别大会; ~ **rendition** *n* [u and c] 非常规引渡

extra pay *n* [u] 额外报酬

extrapolate /ɪk'stræpəleɪt/ *vt* 1 (estimate) 推断 ‹*future needs, future growth, future sales, results*›; **to** ~ **sth. from sth.** 从某事物推断某事 2 (draw by inferring) 外推 ‹*graph, curve*›

extrapolation /ɪkˌstræpə'leɪʃn/ *n* 推断; **on the basis of** ~ 在推断的基础上; **by** ~ 通过推断

extrasensory /ˌekstrə'sensəri, Amer -sɔːri/ *adj* 超感官的; ~ **perception** 超感知觉

extra: **~-special** *adj* colloq 超特别的; **~-strong** *adj* 特浓的 ‹*coffee*›; 味道超浓的 ‹*mints*›; 高浓度的 ‹*beer*›

extraterrestrial /ˌekstrətə'restrɪəl/

A *adj* 外星球的 ‹*being, life*›

B *n* 外星生物

extraterritorial /ˌekstrəˌterɪ'tɔːrɪəl/ *adj* 境外的 ‹*waters, trading*›; 治外法权的 ‹*privileges, jurisdiction*›; ~ **rights** 治外法权

extra time *n* [u] 加时赛; **in** ~ 在加时赛中

extravagance /ɪk'strævəgəns/ *n* 1 [u] (prodigality) 挥霍; (wastefulness) 铺张浪费 2 [c] (luxury) 奢侈品 3 [c] (excess) (of behaviour) 夸张举动; (of statement) 夸大其词 4 [u] (excessive elaboration) 奢华

extravagant /ɪk'strævəgənt/ *adj* 1 (profligate) 挥霍的 ‹*habits, shopping spree*›; (wasteful) 浪费的 ‹*habits, way of life*› 2 (costly) 昂贵的 ‹*luxuries, gifts*›; 过高的 ‹*prices*› 3 (exaggerated) 言过其实的 ‹*compliments, claims*›; 过分的 ‹*demands, behaviour*› 4 (unrealistic) 不切实际的 ‹*idea, theory*›

extravagantly /ɪk'strævəgəntli/ *adv* 1 (lavishly) 挥霍地 ‹*spend, live, treat*›; (wastefully) 浪费地 ‹*spend, consume*› 2 (elaborately) 奢华地 ‹*decorated, costumed, furnished*›

extravaganza /ɪkˌstrævə'gænzə/ *n* 1 (entertainment, show) 铺张华丽的娱乐表演 2 (lavish display) 奢华的展示

extravehicular /ˌekstrəviː'hɪkjʊlə(r)/ *adj* 航天器外的

extra virgin olive oil *n* 特级初榨橄榄油

extreme /ɪk'striːm/

A *adj* 1 (very great) 极度的; ~ **poverty** 赤贫; ~ **caution/pleasure/urgency** 极度的谨慎/快乐/紧迫 2 (unusual) 极端的; ~ **weather conditions** 极端恶劣的天气条件; **to go to** ~ **lengths to do sth.** 不遗余力地做某事; **to an** ~ **degree** 极端地 3 (extremist) 偏激的 ‹*political view*›; **the** ~ **right/left** 极右/左派 4 (farthest) 远端的; **in the** ~ **north/south** 在最北端/最南端

B *n* 1 (excess) 极端; **to go to** **~s** 走极端; **to take** *or* **carry sth. to** **~s** 把某事做得过头; **to be driven to** **~s** 被迫走极端; **to go to the other** *or* **opposite** ~ 走到另一个极端; **to go from one** ~ **to the other** 从一个极端走到另一个极端; **the** **~s** **of love and hatred** 爱与恨两种截然不同的感情; **~s** **of passion/cruelty** 热情/残酷之至 2 (greatest degree) 极度; **~s** **of cold/wind/rain** 严寒/狂风/骤雨; **~s** **of temperature** 酷热和严寒; **in the** ~ 极其

extremely /ɪk'striːmli/ *adv* 非常

extreme sport *n* 极限运动

extremism /ɪk'striːmɪzəm/ *n* [u] 极端主义

extremist /ɪk'striːmɪst/

A *n* 极端分子

B *adj pej* 极端主义的

extremity /ɪk'stremətɪ/ *n* 1 [c] (furthest point) 末端 2 **extremities** *pl* (hands and feet) 手足 3 [c and u] (dire situation) 绝境 4 [u] (intensity) (of disease) 严重; (of adversity) 糟糕; (of grief, joy) 极端

extricate /'ekstrɪkeɪt/ *vt* (from trap, net) 使脱离; (from situation) 使摆脱; **to** ~ **sb. from sth.** 使某人摆脱某事物

extrinsic /ek'strɪnsɪk/ *adj* 1 (not inherent) 外在的 ‹*advantage, factor, quality*› 2 (from outside) 外部的 ‹*stimuli, influence, circumstance*›

extroversion /ˌekstrə'vɜːʃn, Amer -'vɜːrʒn/ *n* [u] 性格外向

extrovert /'ekstrəvɜːt/

A *adj* 性格外向的

B *n* 性格外向的人

extrude /ɪk'struːd/ *vt* 1 (force out) 挤出 ‹*toothpaste, glue, icing*›; 压出 ‹*pasta*› 2 (shape) 压制 ‹*plastic, metal*›

extrusion /ɪk'struːʒn/ *n* 1 [u] (shaping process) 压制 2 [c] (component) 压制品 3 [c and u] Geol (movement of magma) 喷出; (igneous rock) 火成岩

exuberance /ɪg'zjuːbərəns, Amer -'zuː-/ *n* [u] (of person, greeting, speaker) 热情洋溢; (of music, performance, writing) 感情充沛

exuberant /ɪg'zjuːbərənt, Amer -'zuː-/ *adj* 1 (ebullient) 热情洋溢的 ‹*person, crowd, mood, performance, greeting*› 2 (lavish, extravagant) 过度的 ‹*compliment, eloquence, ornamentation*›; 词藻华丽的 ‹*account, narrative, style of writing*›; 炫目的 ‹*colour*›

exuberantly /ɪg'zjuːbərəntli, Amer -'zuː-/ *adv* 兴高采烈地 ‹*play, shout, describe*›; 词藻华丽地 ‹*write*›; 色彩绚丽地 ‹*paint*›; ~ **colourful** 光彩眩目的

exude /ɪg'zjuːd, Amer -'zuːd/

A *vt* 1 (discharge) 渗出 ‹*liquid, blood, sap*›; 分泌 ‹*sweat, resin, gum*›; 散发 ‹*smell, body odour, scent*› 2 (radiate) 流露 ‹*charm, energy, enthusiasm, confidence, vitality*›; 显露 ‹*fear, panic, despair, melancholy*›

B *vi* 1 (radiate) «*charm, energy, confidence, vitality*» 流露出来; «*fear, panic, despair, melancholy*» 显露出来 2 (be discharged) «*smell, body odour, scent*» 散发出来; «*liquid, blood, sap*» 渗出; «*sweat, resin, gum*» 分泌出来

exult /ɪg'zʌlt/ *vi* 兴高采烈; **to** ~ **at** *or* **in sth.** 因某事物而欢欣鼓舞

exultant /ɪg'zʌltənt/ *adj* 兴高采烈的; **to be** ~ **about** *or* **at sth.** 为某事物而欢欣鼓舞

exultantly /ɪg'zʌltəntli/ *adv* 兴高采烈地

exultation /ˌegzʌl'teɪʃn/ *n* [u] 兴高采烈; **with** *or* **in** ~ 欢悦地

exurbia /ˌeks'ɜːbɪə/ *n* Amer [富裕上班族居住的] 城市远郊

ex-wife *n* (*pl* **ex-wives**) 前妻

ex-works *adj* Brit (from the factory) 来自工厂的; (from the place of manufacture) 来自产地的

eye /aɪ/

A *n* 1 ▸**p. 71** Anat 眼睛; **blue/brown** **~s** 蓝/棕色眼睛; **to put** *or* **hold sth. to one's eye** 拿起某物看; **to have the sun in one's** **~s** 太阳刺眼; **there is joy/fear/love in sb.'s** **~s** 某人眼睛里透着喜悦/害怕/爱意; **that's one in the** ~ **for you!** colloq 这是你活该！; **as far as the** ~ **can see** 在目光所及之处; **to open sb.'s** **~s** **to sth.** 使某人意识到某事; **to do sth. with one's** **~s** **(wide) open** fig 有意识地做某事; **to keep one's** **~s/an** ~ **open** *or* **out (for sb./sth.)** colloq 留心（某人/某事物）; **to keep one's** **~s** **peeled** *or* **skinned (for sb./sth.)** colloq 密切注意（某人/某事物）; **to close** *or* **shut one's** **~s** **(to sth.)** fig （对某事物）视而不见; **to do sth. with one's** **~s** **closed** *or* **shut** fig 做某事毫不费力; **to go around with one's** **~s** **shut** fig 盲目地行动; **to only have** **~s** **for sb.** 只喜欢某人; **to make** **~s** **at sb.** 对某人抛媚眼; **to give sb. the** ~ 向某人抛媚眼; **to use one's** **~s** fig 睁大眼睛好好看看; **before** *or* **in front of one's (very)** **~s** （就）在某人的眼皮底下; **with one's own** **~s** 亲眼; **to be all** **~s** 专注地看; **to be up to one's** **~s** **in debt/work** colloq 债台高筑/忙得不可开交; **to see** ~ **to** ~ **(with sb.) (about** *or* **on sth.)** （与某人）（在某事物上）看法完全一致; **an** ~ **for an** ~ **(and a tooth for a tooth)** Prov 以眼还眼（以牙还牙）; **what the** ~ **doesn't see(, the heart doesn't grieve over)** Prov 眼不见心不烦; **dry A1, sore A1** 2 (vision) 视力; **to have weak/sharp** **~s** 视力差/眼尖; **to have one's** **~s** **tested** 检测视力; **don't you have (any)** **~s** **in your head?** 你没有留意到吗?; **to have** **~s** **in the back of one's head** fig 能觉察到周围发生的事; **a child's-~ view of the universe** 孩子心目中的宇宙 3 (gaze) 目光; **to raise/lower/avert one's** **~s** 抬起/垂下/转移目光; **all** **~s** **were on him/her** 所有的目光都落在了他/她身上; **under the watchful/anxious** ~ **of sb.** 在某人警惕/急切的目光下; **with a critical/anxious/jealous/curious** ~ 带着挑剔/焦急/嫉妒/好奇的眼光; **to run** *or* **cast one's** ~ **over sth.** 扫一眼某物; **to set** *or* **clap** *or* **lay** **~s** **on sb./sth.** colloq 看到某人/某物; **to run one's** ~ **down a list** 扫视名单; **this letter is for your** **~s** **only** 这封信只能你一个人看; **~s right/left/front!** Mil 向右/左/前看齐！ 4 (attention) 注意; **to catch sb.'s** ~ 引起某人的注意; **to keep an** *or* **one's** ~ **on sb./sth.** 留意某人/某事物; **to keep a close/strict** ~ **on sb./sth.** 密切注意某人/某事物; **to fix one's** **~(s)** **on sb./sth.** 紧紧盯住某人/某事物; **keep your** **~s** **on the road**

注意看清路面; **to keep an ~ on the time** 留意时间; **to keep one's ~ on the ball** Sport 眼睛盯着球; fig 注意手头的事情; **to take one's ~ off the ball** Sport 眼睛不盯住球; fig 不抓紧手头的事情; **to have one's ~ on sb./sth.** 盯上某人/某事物; **he's got his ~ on you for the director's job** 他已经考虑你来当经理; **to have** *or* **keep one** *or* **half an ~ on sb./sth.** 顺便留意某人/某事物; **to do one's homework with one ~ on the TV** 边做作业边看电视 **5** (intention) 打算; **with an ~ to sth./doing sth.** 有关于某事物/做某事的打算; **to do sth. with an ~ to future expansion** 做某事意图未来进行扩张 **6** (opinion) 观点; **in the ~s of sb., in sb.'s ~s** 在某人看来; **in the ~s of the law/church** 在法律/宗教上; **in the ~s of the world** 在世人的心目中; **to look at a problem through the ~s of sb.** 从某人的角度看问题; ▸**beholder** **7** (discernment) 眼力; **to have a good ~** 有好眼力; **to have an ~ for sth.** 对某事物很有眼力; **to have an ~ for a bargain** 有发现便宜货的眼光; **to the trained/expert/practised/experienced ~** 在训练有素的人/专家/老练的人/富有经验的人看来 **8** (of needle) 针眼 **9** (for hook) 钩眼 **10** (on potato) 芽眼 **11** (on peacock tail) 翎斑; (on butterfly wing) 翅斑 **12** Meteorol 风眼; **to be in the ~ of the storm** lit 处于暴风眼之中; **the ~ of the storm** fig (calm place) 避风港; (busy place) 风暴中心

B *vt* (*pres p* **eyeing** *or* **eying**) **1** (look at) 打量; **to ~ sb. up and down** *or* **from head to toe** 上下打量某人; **to ~ sb./sth. with ...** 以…的目光看某人/某事物 ‹*suspicion, envy, longing*›; **the dog was ~ing the biscuits** 那条狗正眼巴巴地看着饼干 **2** colloq (ogle) 色迷迷地看; **to ~ sb. up and down** 色迷迷地从头到脚打量某人

Phrasal verb

• **eye up** *vt* [**~ sb. up, ~ up sb.**] Brit colloq 色迷迷地看

eyeball /ˈaɪbɔːl/
A *n* 眼球; **~ to ~** 怒目相视
B *vt* 盯住

eye: ~ bank *n* 眼库; **~bath** *n* Brit 洗眼杯; **~bolt** *n* 眼螺栓

eyebrow /ˈaɪbraʊ/ *n* 眉毛; **to raise one's ~s/an ~** (in surprise) 惊奇地耸起眉毛; (in disapproval) 不屑地扬起眉头; **to raise a few ~s** (cause surprise) 令人吃惊; (cause disapproval) 令人不满; **to pluck one's ~s** 修眉

eyebrow: ~ pencil *n* 眉笔; **~ tweezers** *npl* 拔眉钳

eye: ~ candy *n* [u] colloq 中看不中用的东西; **~-catcher** *n* (person) 惹人注目的人; (thing) 惹人注目的事物; **~-catching** *adj* 惹人注目的; **~ contact** *n* [u] 目光接触; **to make ~ contact with sb.** 与某人目光交流

-eyed /aɪd/ *combining form* 有…眼睛的; **a brown~ brunette** 有褐色眼睛的褐发白人女子; **a one~ man** 独眼男子

eyedrops /ˈaɪdrɒps/ *npl* 眼药水

eyeful /ˈaɪfʊl/ *n* **1** (amount) 满眼; **to get an ~ of sth.** 把…弄了满眼 ‹*dust, sand*› **2** colloq (good look) 饱览; **to get an ~ of sth.** 好好看一看某物 **3** colloq (attractive thing) 好看的东西; (attractive person) 美人

eye: ~glasses *npl* Amer 眼镜; **~ hospital** *n* 眼科医院; **~lash** *n* 睫毛

eyelet /ˈaɪlɪt/ *n* 孔眼

eye level
A *n* [u] 视线的水平高度; **at ~** 与视线齐平
B **eye-level** *adj* 与眼睛齐平的

eye: ~lid *n* 眼皮; **~liner** *n* [u] 眼线笔; **~ make-up** *n* [u] 眼部化妆品; **~ make-up remover** 眼部卸妆水; **~ mask** *n* **1** (to aid sleep) 眼罩; **2** (to soothe eyes) 眼贴膜; **~-opener** *n* colloq **1** (revelation) 使人大开眼界的事物; **to be an ~-opener (for sb.)** 使（某）人大开眼界; **2** Amer (morning drink) 空腹酒; **~-patch** *n* 护眼罩; **~ pencil** *n* 眼线笔; **~piece** *n* 目镜; **~shade** *n* 遮光眼罩; **~ shadow** *n* [u] 眼影; **~sight** *n* [u] 视力; **to have good/poor ~sight** 视力好/差; **~ socket** *n* 眼窝; **~sore** *n* (ugly thing) 丑陋的东西; (structure) 碍眼的建筑; **~ specialist** ▸**p. 409** *n* 眼科专家; **~ strain** *n* [u] 眼疲劳; **~ surgeon** ▸**p. 409** *n* 眼外科医生; **~ test** *n* 眼部检查; **~tooth** *n* (*pl* **~teeth**) 上犬齿; **to give one's ~ teeth for sth./to do sth.** fig 为某物/做某事不惜一切代价; **~wash** *n* [u] **1** (liquid) 洗眼药水; **2** colloq (nonsense) 假话; **~-watering** *adj* fig 使人激动万分的 ‹*profit, sight*›; 令人心痛的 ‹*loss*›

eyewitness /ˈaɪwɪtnɪs/ *n* 目击者

eyrie /ˈeəri, ˈaɪəri/ *n* 猛禽巢

e-zine /ˈiːziːn/ *n* 电子杂志

F, f /ef/

A *n* (*pl* **Fs** *or* **F's**) 1 (letter) [英语字母表的第6个字母] 2 Mus F音, F调 3 Sch, Univ (grade) [学业成绩] 第六等

B *abbr* 1 **f = female** 2 **F = Fahrenheit**

FA *abbr* Brit **= Football Association** 足球协会

fa /fɑː/ *n* **= fah**

fab /fæb/ *adj* Brit colloq 绝妙的; **the F~ Four** 披头士乐队

Fabian /ˈfeɪbɪən/ *n* Brit 费边主义者

Fabian Society *pr n* Brit 费边社 [英国的社会主义者团体]

fable /ˈfeɪbl/ *n* 1 [c] Literat 寓言; **Aesop's ~s** 伊索寓言 2 [u and c] (legend) 神话; **the ~s of Greece and Rome** 希腊罗马神话; **gods made famous in ~** 传说中著名的众神 3 [c] (modern play, film) 神话情节 4 [u] (lies) 谎言; **to tell fact from ~** 辨别真伪

fabled /ˈfeɪbld/ *adj* 1 (mythical) 神话中的 ‹*creatures, cities, battles*› 2 (famous) 著名的 ‹*person, place*›

fabric /ˈfæbrɪk/ *n* 1 [u and c] (cloth) 织物 2 [u] (of a building) 结构 [即墙、地板和屋顶] 3 [u] fig (of society, culture) 基础; **the ~ of society** 社会基本结构

fabricate /ˈfæbrɪkeɪt/ *vt* 1 (invent) 伪造 ‹*evidence, excuse, accusation*› 2 (construct) 生产 ‹*system, goods*›; 制造 ‹*model*›

fabrication /ˌfæbrɪˈkeɪʃn/ *n* 1 [c] (lie) 谎言 2 [u] (construction) 制造

fabric conditioner, fabric softener *ns* [u and c] 织物柔顺剂

fabulous /ˈfæbjʊləs/ *adj* 1 colloq (wonderful) 极好的 ‹*performance, figure, match*› 2 (extraordinary) 惊人的 ‹*beauty*›; 巨大的 ‹*wealth, luxury*› 3 (very high) 极高的 ‹*price, income*› 4 (mythical) 传说中的 ‹*heroes, monsters*›

fabulously /ˈfæbjʊləsli/ *adv* 1 (extremely) 极其 ‹*rich, successful, happy*› 2 colloq (wonderfully) 极好地 ‹*get on*›

facade /fəˈsɑːd/ *n* 1 lit (of a building) 正面 2 fig (appearance) [尤指虚假的] 表面; **to see through sb.'s ~** 看清某人的真面目

face /feɪs/

A *n* 1 ▸p. 71 [c] 脸; **the muscles of the ~** 面部肌肉; **with tears streaming down one's ~** 泪流满面地; **a pretty/pale ~** 漂亮/苍白的面孔; **a round ~** 圆脸; **her ~ was red with embarrassment** 她窘得满脸通红; **she's a familiar ~** 她是个熟人; **there are some new ~s here tonight** 今晚在这里有一些新面孔; **he never forgets a ~** 他对见过的人过目不忘; **to lie ~ down** *or* **downwards/up** *or* **upwards** 俯卧/仰卧; **in sb.'s ~** 对着某人的脸; **the wind is blowing in our ~s** 风向着我们迎面吹来; **to sb.'s ~** 当着某人的面; **to criticize sb. to his/her ~** 当面批评某人; **to hide one's ~** lit 把脸藏起来; fig 躲起来; **he hid his ~ in his hands** 他用手蒙住了脸; **to show one's ~** fig 露面; **I'll never dare show my ~ in there again** 我再也不敢到那里去了; **~ to ~** 面对面; **I've never met the princess ~ to ~** 我从来没有面见过公主; **in your ~** colloq (blatantly aggressive); 咄咄逼人的; (provocative) 刺激的; **our music is loud and in your ~** 我们的音乐热闹刺激; **to get right in sb.'s ~** colloq 直言不讳; **to feed** *or* **fill** *or* **stuff one's ~** colloq 大吃一顿; **to set one's ~ against sth./doing sth.** 坚决反对某事/做某事; ▸**bury 5** 2 [c] (expression) 面容; **the children's happy, smiling ~s** 孩子们幸福的笑脸; **their ~s were sad/serious** 他们神情悲伤/严肃; **she looked at me with a puzzled ~** 她一脸困惑地看着我; **to have a long ~** 拉长着脸; **his ~ fell** 他的脸沉了下来; **to put on a brave** *or* **bold** *or* **good ~** 装出若无其事的样子; **to make** *or* **pull a ~** *or* **~s (at sb.)** (朝某人) 扮鬼脸; **he pulled a ~ when I asked him to lay the table** 我叫他摆桌子, 他做出一副苦相; **to make a disapproving ~** 显出不以为然的样子 3 [u] colloq hum (make-up) 化妆 4 [u] (respect) 面子; **to put one's ~ on** 化妆 4 [u] (respect) 面子; **to lose ~** 丢脸; **a loss of ~** 丢脸; **to save (one's) ~** 保全面子; **to save sb.'s ~** 保全某人的面子 5 [u] colloq dated (effrontery) 厚脸皮; **to have the ~ to do sth.** 有脸做某事; **they had the ~ to ask for more money!** 他们还有脸要更多的钱! 6 [c] (appearance, nature) 外表; **the changing ~ of the city** 不断变化的城市面貌; **on the ~ of it** 从表面上看 7 [c] (surface) 表面; **to disappear** *or* **vanish off the ~ of the earth** 消失得无影无踪 8 [c] (of mountain, rock, mine) 面; **the steep ~ of the rock** 陡峭的岩壁; **the north ~ of the Eiger** 艾格尔峰的北坡 9 (of clock, watch) 面; **the ~ of a watch/clock** 表面/钟面; **a dodecahedron has twelve ~s** 12 面体有12个面 10 [c] (front) 正面; **he put the cards ~ down on the table** 他把牌正面朝下放在桌子上; **the books are displayed ~ out** 书封面朝上摆放 11 [c] Print **= typeface** 12 [u] **in the ~ of sth.** (despite) 不顾某事物; (in direct confrontation) 面临某事物; **the peace conference went ahead in the ~ of the threats** 尽管有威胁, 和平会议仍然按计划举行; **she can't hope to win in the ~ of such opposition** 面对这样的反对力量, 她没有希望赢

B *vt* 1 (look towards) 面向; **they stood facing one another** 他们面对面站着; **he turned round to ~ the audience** 他转过身来面对观众; **the boy facing you** 面朝你的那个男孩; **the room ~s the sea** 房间朝海; **the house ~s west** 房子朝西; **~ the front!** 向前看! 2 fig (present itself to) 面临; **the problems ~d by one-parent families** 单亲家庭面临的问题 3 (have to deal with) 必须面对; **to be ~d with a difficult decision** 必须作出艰难的决定; **the company is facing a financial crisis** 公司正面临财务危机; **they ~ fines of up to £1000** 他们要支付高达1,000英镑的罚金; **to ~ spending the rest of one's life in prison** 不得不在监狱里度过余生; **if she wins this match she will ~ Steinberg in the final** 如果她赢了这场比赛, 她将在决赛中和斯坦伯格相遇 4 (tackle) 正视; **the problem will have to be ~d sooner or later** 这个问题迟早要解决; **to ~ one's responsibilities** 勇于承担责任; **they ~d the future with fear** 他们对未来忧心忡忡; **she turned to ~ her attackers** 她转过身来直面那些袭击她的人; **I can't ~ spending Christmas with my parents** 我真不愿意跟父母一起过圣诞节; **he can't ~ life without her** 没有她, 他活不下去; **they cooked me a lovely meal, but I couldn't ~ it** 他们为我做了一顿丰盛的饭菜, 但我实在没有胃口 5 (accept) 承认 ‹*truth, evidence*›; **to ~ (the) facts** 面对现实; **let's ~ it** colloq 让我们接受现实吧 6 (present) 使面对; **to ~ sb. with sth.** 使某人面对某事物; **to ~ sb. with the truth** 使某人面对事实; **to be ~d with the evidence** 面对证据 7 Print, Publg ‹*picture, diagram*› 正对; **facing page 12** 正对第12页 8 Constr 覆盖; **to ~ sth. with sth.** 用某物覆盖某物; **the wall was ~d with white marble** 墙壁贴了白色大理石 9 Sewing (trim, reinforce) 给…镶边; **to ~ sth. with sth.** 用某物给某物镶边; **a cloak ~d with white** 镶有白边的斗篷

C *vi* 1 (face or front the direction of) 面向; **she was facing towards the road** 她面朝着马路; **this room ~s towards the south** 这间屋子朝南; **when travelling on a train I prefer to ~ forwards** 我乘火车旅行时喜欢面朝前坐 2 Amer Mil 改变方向; **about/left/right ~!** 向后/左/右转!

Phrasal verbs

- **face down** *vt* [**~ sb./sth. down, ~ down sb./sth.**] 决然把…压倒; **she ~d down the protestors** 她挫败了反对者; **he ~d down some severe questioning** 他抗住了严厉的质问
- **face out** *vt* [**~ sb./sth. out**] 与…硬顶到底 ‹*person, critics*›; 在…中坚持到底 ‹*situation, crisis, matter*›
- **face up to** *vt* [**~ up to sb./sth.**] 勇于面对; **to ~ up to the fact that ...** 正视…的现实; **to ~ up to one's responsibilities** 勇于承担自己的责任

face: ~ache *n* 1 [u] Med (neuralgia) 面部神经痛; 2 [c] Brit sl (miserable person) 愁眉苦脸的人; **~book** *n* esp Amer 1 (brochure) 肖像花名册; 2 (online) 社交网站; **~ card** *n* Amer 人头牌; **~cloth** *n* Brit 洗脸毛巾; **~ cream** *n* [u and c] 面霜

-faced /feɪst/ *combining form* …脸的 ‹*person, animal*›; **a round~ child** 圆脸的孩子; **to be purple~ with rage** 因暴怒脸色发紫; **a long~ dog** 长脸的狗

face: ~ flannel [u] Brit 洗脸毛巾; **~guard** *n* 面罩

faceless /ˈfeɪslɪs/ *adj* (without a face) 无面孔的; fig (anonymous) 不具个人身份的 ‹*official, committee*›

face: ~lift *n* 1 lit (operation) 面部拉皮手术; 2 fig (of building, area) 翻新; **~ mask** *n* 1 (protective mask) 面罩; 2 (beauty treatment) 面膜; **~-off** *n* [冰球赛中的] 开球; **~ pack** *n* Brit 面膜; **~ paint** *n* [u and c] 脸彩; **~ painting** *n* [u] [儿童参加公共活动时的] 画脸; **~ powder** *n* [u and c] 扑面粉

face-saver *n* 保全面子的举动

face-saving
A *adj* 保全面子的 ‹*decision, lie*›; 体面的 ‹*compromise*›
B *n* [u] 保全面子

facet /ˈfæsɪt/ *n* **1** (of gemstone) 琢面 **2** (of case, problem) 方面 **3** (of personality) 特点

facetious /fəˈsiːʃəs/ *adj* 乱开玩笑的 ‹*person, remark*›

facetiously /fəˈsiːʃəsli/ *adv* 乱开玩笑地 ‹*reply*›

facetiousness /fəˈsiːʃəsnɪs/ *n* [u] 乱开玩笑

face-to-face
A *adj* 面对面的 ‹*discussion, confrontation*›
B **face to face** *adv* 面对面地 ‹*come, stand*›; **to meet sb. face to face** 与某人会面

face value *n* **1** Fin 票面价值 **2** fig (apparent value) 表面价值; **to take sth. at (its) ~** 对某事物信以为真

facial /ˈfeɪʃl/
A *adj* 面部的 ‹*expression, massage*›; **~ muscles/hair** 面部肌肉/毫毛
B *n* 美容; **to have a ~** 做美容

facile /ˈfæsaɪl, Amer ˈfæsl/ *adj* **1** (superficial, simplistic) 轻率的 ‹*salesmanship, solution*›; 肤浅的 ‹*writing, ideas*› **2** (simple) 简单的 ‹*style, painting*›

facilitate /fəˈsɪlɪteɪt/ *vt* 促进 ‹*negotiations*›; 加快 ‹*process*›; 使…便利 ‹*trend, matters*›

facilitator /fəˈsɪlɪteɪtə(r)/ *n* 协调人

facilities management *n* [u] 设备管理

facility /fəˈsɪləti/ *n* **1** [c] (buildings) 场所; **a health-care ~** 保健中心; **wastewater treatment facilities** 废水处理厂 **2** [c] Admin, Comm (service) 特色服务; **an overdraft ~** 透支服务; **he requested a loan ~ of £10,000** 他请求贷款 1 万英镑 **3** **facilities** [c] (services) 设施; **sports facilities** 体育设施; **cooking facilities** 厨具; **the theatre has no parking facilities** 该剧院没有停车场; **may I use your facilities?** euph dated 我可以用你的卫生间吗? **4** [c] Tech, Comput 特别功能; **a self-defrost/spell-check ~** 自动除霜/拼写检查功能 **5** [c] (opportunity) 便利; **we now have the ~ of controlling family size** 我们现在已有控制家庭人口的便利方法 **6** [u] (ease) 容易; **with ~** 不费力地; **to play the piano with great ~** 轻松自如地弹钢琴 **7** [c] (ability) 才能; **a ~ for problem-solving** 解决问题的能力; **he has a great ~ for (learning) languages** 他有很高的语言天赋

facing /ˈfeɪsɪŋ/ *n* **1** Constr 饰面 **2** (of neck, button-hole) 贴边; (decorative edging) 异色镶边

facsimile /fækˈsɪməli/
A *n* [u and c] **1** (of document) 摹本; **in ~** 精确复制地 **2** (of sculpture, illustrations) 复制品 **3** **= fax A**
B *modif* 摹本的 ‹*edition*›; 一模一样的 ‹*signature*›

fact /fækt/
A *n* **1** [c] 事实; **isn't it a ~ that the firm is losing money?** 公司正在亏损, 这难道不是事实吗?; **hard ~s** 事实真相; **~s and figures** 准确的信息; **a report full of ~s and figures** 资料翔实的报告; **to get one's ~s right** 把事实弄确切; **to face (the) ~s** 面对现实; **to know sth. for a ~** 确切地知道某事; **I know for a ~ that she's involved in something illegal** 我肯定她卷入了非法活动; **the ~s speak for themselves** 事实足以说明一切; **(and) that's a fact** colloq 事实就是这样; **is that a ~?** colloq (expressing interest or disbelief) 是真的吗?; **the ~s of life** [尤指对儿童讲的] 性知识 **2** [c] (existing situation, reality) 现实; **space travel is now a ~** 太空旅行已成为现实; **despite/owing to/apart from/in view of the ~ that ...** 尽管/由于/除了/鉴于…; **the ~ (of the matter) is that ...** 事实上是…; **a new car would be wonderful, but the ~ is that we can't afford one** 新车好是好, 不过实际情况是我们买不起; **after the ~** 事后; **a ~ of life** 生活的现实 **3** [u] (truth) 真实的事物; **~ and fiction** 真实和虚构; **this story is based on ~** 这个故事以真人真事为基础; **to accept sth. as ~** 把某事当真 **4** [u and c] Jur 事实; **a question of ~** 事实问题
B **as a matter of fact, in (actual) fact, in point of fact** *adv phr* **1** (when adding detail) 确切地说 [用以补充细节]; **we finished it yesterday, as a matter of ~** 其实, 这事我们昨天就完成了; **I used to live in France; in ~, not far from where you're going** 我以前住在法国; 确切地说, 离你要去的地方不远 **2** (when reinforcing point) 事实上 [用以强调]; **they promised to pay and in ~ that's what they did** 他们答应付钱, 事实上他们也这样做了; **does it in ~ matter very much?** 它真的关系重大吗? **3** (when summarizing) 总而言之; **he's dishonest, and ignorant: quite unsuitable in ~** 他这人既不诚实又无知: 总之很不合适 **4** (when contrasting, contradicting) 实际上 [用以对比]; **I don't mind at all; in ~ I'm delighted** 我一点都不介意, 实际上我很高兴

fact: ~finder *n* **1** (factsheet) 资料汇总; (website) 资讯检索站; **2** Jur 实情调查员; **~-finding** *adj attrib* 实情调查的 ‹*mission, trip*›; **~-finding committee** 实情调查委员会

faction /ˈfækʃn/ *n* **1** [c] (group) 派别 **2** [u] (discord) 派系斗争 **3** [u] TV 纪实与虚构相结合的节目

factional /ˈfækʃənl/ *adj* 派系的 ‹*in-fighting, disagreements*›

factious /ˈfækʃəs/ *adj* 宗派的 ‹*rivalry, quarrel*›

factitious /fækˈtɪʃəs/ *adj* 虚假的 ‹*demands, indignation*›

factor /ˈfæktə(r)/ *n* **1** (element) 因素; **to be an unknown ~** 是未知因素; **to be a ~ in sth.** 是某事的因素; **the human ~** 人的因素; **common ~** 共同的因素 **2** Math (divisor) 因子; (multiplier) 商; **(highest) common ~** (最大) 公因子 **3** Comm 代理商

Phrasal verb
- **factor in** *vt* [**~ sb./sth. in, ~ in sb./sth.**] 把…作为考虑因素

factor analysis *n* [u] 因子分析

factorial /fækˈtɔːrɪəl/
A *n* 阶乘
B *adj* (involving factors) 因子的; (involving factorials) 阶乘的 ‹*method, result*›

factorize /ˈfæktəraɪz/ *vt* 将…分解成因子

factory /ˈfæktəri/ *n* 工厂; **to open** *or* **set up a (new) ~** 开设一家 (新) 工厂

factory: F~ Acts *npl* Brit Hist 工厂法; **~ farm** *n* 工厂化农场; **~ farming** *n* [u] 工厂化饲养; **~ floor** *n* [u] lit, fig 劳方; **on the ~ floor** 在劳方; **~ inspector** ▸p. 409 *n* 工厂督察员; **~-made** *adj* 工厂批量生产的 ‹*goods, articles*›; **~ outlet** *n* 工厂直销店; **~ ship** *n* 捕捞加工船; **~ shop** *n* 工厂直销店; **~ unit** *n* 厂房出租区; **~ worker** ▸p. 409 *n* 工厂工人

factotum /fækˈtəʊtəm/ *n* (*pl* **~s**) 勤杂工; **general ~** 事务总管

fact sheet *n* 信息一览表

facts of life
A *npl* (information about sex) **the ~** 性知识
B **fact of life** *n* (unpalatable truth) 不容更改的现实; **the economic/political fact of life** 不容更改的经济/政治现实; **it's a fact of life that people must make their own mistakes** 人们都会犯错, 这是必须接受的事实

factual /ˈfæktʃʊəl/ *adj* 事实的 ‹*information*›; 事实性的 ‹*error*›; 如实的 ‹*account, description, report*›

factually /ˈfæktʃʊəli/ *adv* 事实上 ‹*incorrect, complete, misleading*›

faculty /ˈfæklti/
A *n* **1** (power) 官能; **to be in possession** *or* **command of/to possess all one's faculties** 拥有一切官能; **the ~ of speech/sight/reason** 言语能力/视力/推理能力 **2** (aptitude) 才能 **3** Univ (department) 院系; Amer (staff) 全体教师; **~ of Arts/Science** 文/理学院
B *modif* 全体教师的 ‹*meeting, housing, office*›

faculty: F~ Board *n* Brit 院务委员会; **~ lounge** *n* 教师休息室

> **the FA Cup**
>
> 英格兰足总杯, 全称 Football Association Challenge Cup。世界上历史最悠久的足球比赛, 每年举行, 开始于 1871-1872 赛季。参赛队伍包括英超联赛 (Premier League) 球队、足球联赛 (Football League, 分 Championship、League One 和 League Two, 即英冠、甲级和乙级联赛) 球队及其他非联赛 (non-league) 球队。比赛不设种子队, 通过抽签决定对手和主客场。半决赛以前的比赛出现平局时会进行重赛, 如再次打平则通过加时赛和点球决定胜负。英超和英冠等实力较强的球队可以跳过开始的一些轮次。比赛经常出现无名小队淘汰英超强队的局面。足总杯决赛传统上在温布利 (Wembley) 球场举行。

fad /fæd/ *n* **1** (craze) 一时的风尚 **2** (whim) 癖好

faddish /ˈfædɪʃ/ *adj* **1** (fashionable) 流行一时的 **2** (fickle) 捉摸不定的

faddy /ˈfædi/ Brit 挑剔的 ‹*person*›; 不断变化的 ‹*clothes*›

fade /feɪd/
A *vt* **1** (make paler) «*sun, washing, time*» 使…褪色 ‹*colours, curtains, clothes*› **2** Radio, Theat 使…逐渐消失 ‹*conversation, lights*›; **to ~ one scene/colour into another** 使某一场景/颜色淡出, 另一场景/颜色淡入
B *vi* **1** (lose colour) «*curtains, clothes*» 褪色; «*colour*» 变淡 **2** fig (grow faint, disappear) «*hope, smile, memory*» 逐渐消失; lit «*light*» 变暗; «*applause, music*» 渐低; **to ~ into sth.** 消失在某物中; **to ~ from sight** *or* **view** 从视线中消失 **3** (deteriorate, lose strength) «*faculty, memory, beauty*» 衰退; «*horse, runner*» 失去后劲; «*flowers*» 枯萎 **4** Cin, Radio, TV «*sound, music*» 变弱; «*scene, picture*» 变暗淡

Phrasal verbs
- **fade away** *vi* **1** (die down) «*sound, music*» 渐弱 **2** fig (decline physically) «*person*» 奄奄一息; **old soldiers never die, they only ~ away** 老兵永远不死, 他们只是凋零
- **fade in**
  A *vi* «*signal, music, lights*» 渐弱; «*image, scene*» 淡出
  B *vt* [**~ sth. in, ~ in sth.**] 使…渐强 ‹*music, dialogue, lighting*›; 使…淡入 ‹*picture, scene*›
- **fade out**
  A *vi* **1** (disappear) «*signal, music, lights*» 渐弱; «*image, scene*» 淡出 **2** fig «*person*» 淡出; «*custom, political movement*» 消失; **to ~ out (of the picture)** 淡出公众视线
  B *vt* [**~ sth. out, ~ out sth.**] 使…渐弱 ‹*music, dialogue, lighting*›; 使…淡出 ‹*picture, scene*›

faded /ˈfeɪdɪd/ *adj* **1** (discoloured) 褪了色的 ‹*material, wallpaper, photograph, ink*› **2** (declining) 韶华已逝的 ‹*person, beauty*›; 凋谢的 ‹*flower*›

fade: ~-in *n* (image) 淡入; (sound) 渐强; **~-out** *n* (image) 淡出; (sound) 渐弱

faecal /ˈfiːkəl/ *adj* 粪便的 ‹*bacteria*›; **~ blood** 便血

faeces /ˈfiːsiːz/ *npl* 粪便

faff /fæf/ *n* Brit colloq 忙乱

Phrasal verb
- **faff about, faff around** *vi* Brit colloq 磨蹭

f

fag /fæg/ *n* colloq **1** Brit (cigarette) 香烟 **2** Brit (chore) 苦差事 **3** Amer pej (homosexual) 男同性恋者

Phrasal verb

- **fag out** *vt* [**~ sb. out**] Brit colloq 累垮; **to be ~ged out** 累趴下

fag end *n* **1** Brit colloq (cigarette) 烟蒂 **2** fig colloq (of material) 边脚料; (of conversation, season) 收尾

faggot /ˈfægət/ *n* **1** Brit Culin 炸肉丸 **2** Amer colloq pej (homosexual) 男同性恋者

fah /fɑː/ *n* [大调音阶的第4音]

Fahrenheit /ˈfærənhaɪt/ ▸**p. 814**

A *adj* 华氏的 ‹*thermometer, scale*›; **80° ~** 80 华氏度

B *n* 华氏温标; **in ~** 以华氏温度

fail /feɪl/

A *vi* **1** (not succeed) 失败; **the treatment ~ed** 治疗没有效果; **to ~ in sth.** 未能做到某事; **to ~ in one's duty** 失职; **they ~ed in an attempt to break the record** 他们试图破纪录，但没能成功 **2** (not pass exam) 不及格; **he ~ed in chemistry/his exams** 他化学/考试不及格 **3** (stop working) «*engine, system*» 出故障; «*heart, kidney*» 衰竭; **his brakes ~ed as he was coming down the hill** 他下山时刹车失灵了; **the power ~ed throughout the area** 整个地区都停电了 **4** (become weak) 衰退; **his health has been ~ing over the years** 这些年来他的健康每况愈下; **I want to finish this picture before the light ~s** 我想在天黑之前完成这幅画 **5** (be insufficient) 缺乏; **the crops ~ed last year** 去年庄稼歉收; **the water supply ~ed during the drought** 干旱期间供水不足 **6** (go bankrupt) 破产; **several banks ~ed that year** 那年有数家银行倒闭了

B *vt* **1** (let down) 使失望; **he felt he had ~ed his family** 他感到辜负了家人; **his courage ~ed him** 他失去了勇气; **my memory often ~s me these days** 近来我经常忘事; **words ~ me!** 我不知道该怎么说! **2** (not meet standard) 未通过 ‹*exam, interview, test*›; 未通过…的考试 ‹*subject*›; 评定…为不及格 ‹*person*›; **to ~ French** 法语考试不及格; **the examiner ~ed all the candidates** 这位考官给所有的考生都打了不及格; **to ~ a drugs test** 没有通过药检 **3** (not complete, not do) 未能; **to ~ to do sth.** 未能做某事; **he ~ed to keep his word** 他没有信守诺言; **it never ~ed to irritate him that she was taller than he was** 她比他高，这一直让他耿耿于怀; **I ~ to understand why he is so aggressive** 我不明白他为何如此好斗; **she cannot have ~ed to be aware of it** 她不可能不知道这事; **the patient's ulcer ~ed to respond to treatment** 治疗对病人的溃疡不起作用

C *n* **1** Sch, Univ 不及格; **he got a pass in maths and a ~ in chemistry** 他数学及格了，但化学不及格 **2** **without ~** 必定; **she writes every week, without ~** 她每周都写，从不间断; **I promise to come, without ~** 我保证来，决不食言

failed /feɪld/ *adj* **1** (unsuccessful) 失败的 ‹*writer, bid, policy, marriage*›; **this is my fourth ~ attempt** 这是我第四次不成功的尝试; **he's a ~ playwright turned poet** 他从剧作家改行诗人不成功 **2** (broken) 出故障的 ‹*engine, brakes*›

failing /ˈfeɪlɪŋ/

A *n* (weakness) 弱点; (flaw) 缺点

B *adj* **1** (deteriorating) 衰退的 ‹*health, eyesight, heart*› **2** (unsuccessful) 失败的 ‹*business, relationship, economy, school*›

C *prep* 如果没有; **~ evidence to the contrary** 在没有相反证据的情况下; **~ all else ...** 万不得已…; **~ that, I don't know what to suggest** 如果那不行，我也不知道有什么可建议的

fail-safe *adj* **1** Tech 有自动保险装置的 ‹*mechanism, device, design*› **2** fig 万无一失的 ‹*system, procedure*›

failure /ˈfeɪljə(r)/ *n* **1** [u] (lack of success) 失败; **to end in ~** 以失败告终; **to be doomed to ~** 注定失败 **2** [c] (unsuccessful person) 失败者; (unsuccessful thing) 失败的事; **he'd always been a hopeless ~ at all kinds of sport** 在所有体育项目中，他一直是个不可救药的失败者; **to feel (like) a ~** 感觉自己（像）是个窝囊废; **the plan was a complete ~** 计划完全失败了 **3** [c] (omission) 未做; **I was angered by his ~ to reply to my letter** 他没有回信，我很生气; **~ to comply will result in a fine** 不遵守规定将被罚款 **4** [c] (of mechanism, system) 故障; **a brake ~** 刹车失灵; **a power ~** 停电 **5** [u] (weakening) 衰退; (of heart, liver) 衰竭; **~ of health** 健康恶化; **kidney ~** 肾衰竭 **6** [c] (insufficiency) 缺乏; **a ~ of concentration** 注意力的不集中; **crop ~s** 庄稼歉收 **7** [c] (of bank, business) 破产

faint /feɪnt/

A *adj* **1** (slight) 微弱的 ‹*sound, glow*›; **a ~ smell/breeze** 淡淡的气味/微风 **2** (vague) 渺茫的 ‹*hope, chance*›; **I haven't the ~est idea** colloq 我一点也不知道 **3** (weak) 虚弱的 ‹*voice, breathing*›; 淡淡的 ‹*smile*›; **~ heart never won fair lady** Prov 懦夫难赢美人心 **4** *pred* (dizzy) 眩晕的; **I'm ~ with hunger** 我饿得头昏眼花 **5** (ineffectual) 无效的 ‹*attempt, show, protest*›

B *n* [u] 昏厥; **to fall into a (dead) ~** （完全）昏厥

C *vi* 昏厥; **to ~ from ...** 因…昏厥

faint-hearted /ˌfeɪntˈhɑːtɪd/

A *adj* 怯懦的 ‹*person, attempt, defence*›

B *npl* **the ~** 懦夫

faint-heartedly /ˌfeɪntˈhɑːtɪdli/ *adv* 怯懦地 ‹*defend, fight*›

fainting fit *n* 昏厥; **he is subject to ~s** 他常常昏倒

faintly /ˈfeɪntli/ *adv* **1** (slightly) 微弱地 ‹*glow*›; 隐约地 ‹*call*›; 淡淡地 ‹*smell, tinge*›; (weakly) 虚弱地 ‹*breathe, smile*› **2** (vaguely) 稍微地 ‹*amused, disappointed, surprised*›; **to be ~ reminiscent of sth.** 使人依稀想起某事物

faintness /ˈfeɪntnɪs/ *n* [u] **1** (lack of clarity) 模糊 **2** (weakness) 虚弱 **3** (dizziness) 眩晕

fair¹ /feə(r)/

A *adj* **1** (just, impartial) 公正的; **a ~ trial** 公正的审判; **she's scrupulously ~** 她一丝不苟，秉公办事; **she's ~ to her employees** 她公平对待员工 **2** (reasonable) 合理的; **a ~ wage/question** 合理的工资/恰当的问题; **she wants her ~ share** 她想要她该得的那一份; **to be ~ (to them)** *or* **let's be ~ (to them), they were acting in good faith** 说句公道话，他们是出于好心; **it's only ~ that both sides should be heard** 双方的说法都应该听听才对; **~ enough** colloq (admitting sth. is reasonable) 有道理; (admitting sth. is acceptable) 可以; **I can't come — ~ enough** 我不能来了——行; **all this is ~ enough, but where is it leading?** 这些都很有道理，但目的是什么？; **to give sb. a ~ deal** *or* **a ~ shake** colloq 给某人公平待遇; **~ exchange is no robbery** 公平交易绝非抢夺; **it's a ~ cop** colloq 这是罪有应得; **to get a ~ crack at** *or* **of the whip** Brit colloq 得到合理机会; **~ dos** *or* **do's** Brit colloq 大家都要公平; **to be ~ game for sb.** 是某人的抨击目标; **she was ~ game for the critics** 她是评论家们的评论对象; **by ~ means or foul** 不择手段; **~'s ~** colloq 公平地说; **they didn't give me the job, but ~'s ~, they did interview me** 他们没有给我这个工作，但实事求是地讲，他们确实给了我面试; **(more than) one's ~ share of sth.** （超过）合理的数量; **I've had my ~ share of success in the past** 过去我已经获得了应有的成功; **she's had more than her ~ share of problems** 她遇到了太多的问题 **3** (reasonably good) 尚好的; **I have a ~ knowledge of French** 我的法语知识还算可以; **I'm afraid her school work is only ~** 很遗憾，她的功课只是一般般; **~ to middling** 马马虎虎 **4** *attrib* (good, high, large) 相当; **of a ~ size/length** 相当大的/长的; **to go at a ~ pace** 走得相当快; **she was a ~ way towards her goal** 她很有希望成功 **5** (fine) 晴朗的 ‹*weather*›; **the weather forecast was ~** 天气预报是晴天 **6** Naut 顺风的; **a ~ wind** 顺风 **7** (light-coloured) 浅色的; **a ~ complexion** 白皙的肤色; **he's ~** (fair-skinned) 他皮肤白皙; (fair-haired) 他长着浅色头发 **8** archaic (beautiful) 美丽的; **the ~ sex** dated hum 女性; **~ promises/words** 花言巧语/恭维话; ▸**faint A3**

B *adv* **1** (according to rules) 按照规则; **to play ~** 按规则行事 **2** **~ and square** colloq (honestly) 光明正大地; (with absolute accuracy) 精确地; **we won the match ~ and square** 我们光明正大地赢得了比赛; **the blame rests ~ and square on him** 责任完全由他承担 **3** colloq **= fairly 2**

fair² *n* **1** Brit (funfair) 露天游乐场 **2** (country market) 集市; **a cattle ~** 牛市 **3** (exhibition) 商品展销会; **an agricultural ~** 农产品展销会; **a book ~** 书展 **4** (event to raise funds for charity) 义卖会; **a church/Christmas ~** 教会/圣诞节义卖会

fair: ~ copy *n* 清稿; **to make a ~ copy of sth.** 誊清某书稿; **~ground** *n* 露天游乐场; **a ~ground ride/attraction** 乘坐游乐场设施的游览/游乐项目

fair-haired *adj* (with light-coloured hair) 浅色头发的; (with blonde hair) 金发的

fair-haired boy *n* Amer fig colloq [大众、媒体等的] 宠儿

fairing /ˈfeərɪŋ/ *n* 整流罩

fairly /ˈfeəli/ *adv* **1** (quite, rather) 相当 ‹*accurate, fast, well, soon*›; **I'm ~ sure that ...** 我有相当把握… **2** (justly) 公正地 ‹*treat, condemn, win*› **3** (reasonably) 合理地 ‹*describe, say, attribute*› **4** (actually) 简直; **the hours ~ flew past** 时光飞逝 **5** **~ and squarely = fair and square** ▸**fair¹ B2**

fair-minded /ˌfeəˈmaɪndɪd/ *adj* 公正的 ‹*person, approach*›

fairness /ˈfeənɪs/ *n* [u] **1** (justness) 公正; **in all ~** 说句公道话; **in ~ to sb.** 公正对待某人 **2** (lightness) (of complexion) 白皙; (of hair) 浅色

fair: ~ play *n* 公平办事; **to have a sense of ~ play** 公正无私; **~ play to them** Brit colloq 他们做得对; **~-sized** *adj* 相当大的 ‹*crowd, container, vehicle*›; **~-skinned** *adj* 皮肤白皙的; **~ trade** *n* [u] 公平贸易; **~ trade tea/coffee/cocoa** 公平贸易茶叶/咖啡/可可; **~-traded** *adj* 遵照互惠贸易原则产销的 ‹*product*›; **~way** *n* 球道; **~-weather friend** *n* 不能共患难的朋友

fairy /ˈfeəri/

A *n* **1** (magical being) 仙子; **she's away with the fairies** Brit colloq 她魂不守舍 **2** colloq pej (homosexual) 兔子 [指男同性恋者]

B *modif* 仙子的 ‹*wing*›; 飘逸的 ‹*costume, dance*›

fairy: ~ godmother *n* **1** (fictional character) 仙女婆婆 [给主人公带来意外好运的仙女]; **2** fig (benefactress) 女恩人; **~land** /-lænd/ *n* **1** (fictional place) 仙界; **2** fig 乐园; **~ lights** *npl* Brit 彩色小灯串; **~-like** *adj* 仙子般的 ‹*grace, creature, vision*›; **~ queen** *n* 仙界女王; **~ story** *n* **1** lit (children's story) 童话; **2** fig (untrue account) 不实之词

fairy tale

A *n* **1** lit (children's story) 童话 **2** fig (untrue account) 不实之词

B (*also* **fairy-tale, fairytale**) *modif* 童话般的 ‹*romance, wedding*›

faith /feɪθ/ *n* **1** [u] (confidence) 信心; (trust) 信任; **to have ~ in sb.** 相信某人; **to put one's ~ in sth.** 对某事物抱有信心; **to break/keep ~ with sb.** 对某人不守/守信用; **in good/**

f

bad ~ 真诚地/不诚实地 **2** [u] Relig (belief) 宗教信仰; **my ~ in God** 我对上帝的信仰 **3** [c] Relig (system of beliefs) 宗教; **the Christian, Jewish and Muslim ~s** 基督教、犹太教和伊斯兰教

faith crime *n* 信仰迫害罪

faithful /ˈfeɪθfl/

A *adj* **1** (loyal) 忠诚的 ‹*friend, ally, animal, servant*› **2** *attrib* (regular) 忠实的 ‹*listener*›; 兢兢业业的 ‹*worker*› **3** (monogamous) 忠贞的 ‹*husband, wife*›; **she was always ~ to you** 她一直对你忠贞不渝 **4** (accurate) 如实的 ‹*representation, description, account*›; 忠实于原著的 ‹*adaptation, translation*›; **~ to the original** 忠实于原著

B *npl* **1** lit (religious believers) **the ~** 信徒 **2** fig (supporters) **the ~** 支持者

faithfully /ˈfeɪθfəli/ *adv* **1** (loyally) 忠实地 ‹*follow, serve, stick by*›; **Yours ~** 您的忠实的 [正式商业信函结尾的套语] **2** (accurately) 如实地 ‹*represent, record, recreate*›

faithfulness /ˈfeɪθflnɪs/ *n* [u] **1** (loyalty) 忠诚; **~ to ...** 对…的忠诚 **2** (sexual fidelity) 忠贞 **3** (accuracy of representation) 如实; **~ to ...** 对…的如实反映

faith: **~ healer** *n* 信仰治疗者; **~ healing** *n* [u] 信仰疗法

faithless /ˈfeɪθlɪs/ *adj* **1** (disloyal) 不忠实的 ‹*friend, servant*›; 不忠贞的 ‹*wife*› **2** (non-religious) 无宗教信仰的 ‹*society*›

faith school *n* 教会学校

fake /feɪk/

A *n* **1** (jewel, work of art, etc.) 赝品 **2** (person) 假冒者

B *adj* 伪造的 ‹*picture, signature, passport, photograph*›; 人造的 ‹*furs, diamond*›; 做作的 ‹*emotion, sentiment*›

C *vt* **1** (forge, falsify) 伪造 ‹*picture, passport, signature, photograph*›; 仿造 ‹*furniture*›; 编造 ‹*story*›; 篡改 ‹*accounts, results*› **2** (feign) 假装 ‹*illness, injury, death, orgasm*›; **to ~ it** colloq 假装

D *vi* 假装

fakir /ˈfeɪkɪə(r), Amer fəˈkɪə(r)/ *n* [伊斯兰教的] 托钵僧

falafel /fəˈlæfl/ *n* [u] 炸豆丸子

falcon /ˈfɔːlkən, Amer ˈfælkən/ *n* 隼

falconer /ˈfɔːlkənə(r), Amer ˈfæl-/ *n* 训隼人

falconry /ˈfɔːlkənri, Amer ˈfæl-/ *n* [u] (sport) 放隼狩猎; (training falcons) 隼训练

Falkland Islander /ˌfɔːklənd ˈaɪləndə(r)/ *n* 福克兰群岛居民

Falklands /ˈfɔːkləndz/, **Falkland Islands** *pr npl* **the ~** 福克兰群岛

fall /fɔːl/

A *vi* (*pt* **fell**, *pp* **fallen**) **1** (come down vertically) 落下; **the vase fell and broke into a thousand pieces** 花瓶掉下来摔得粉碎; **the blow fell in the small of his back** 那一拳打在他的腰背部; **the axe has ~en on one of the company's subsidiaries** fig 公司的一家子公司歇业了; **the rain was ~ing steadily** 雨下个不停; **in early autumn, the leaves begin to ~ from** *or* **off the trees** 初秋，树叶开始凋落; **I fell out of bed last night** 我昨晚从床上摔了下来; **the handle of the suitcase fell off** 手提箱的把手掉了; **she fell into the river** 她掉进了河里 **2** (collapse) 倒下; **many trees fell in the storm** 在暴风雨中许多树都倒了; **she fell on her face** 她摔了个嘴啃泥; **six wickets fell before lunch** (in cricket) 午饭前有 6 个击球员被杀出局; **the bigger you are, the harder you ~** 人越高大，摔得越重; **the sales director has left — did he ~ or was he pushed?** fig 销售主管离职了——他是自己辞职的还是被解雇的？; **he fell to** *or* **on his knees and begged for mercy** 他跪下求饶; **they fell into each other's arms** 他们互相拥抱; **she fell into the chair, exhausted** 她筋疲力尽地跌坐在椅子上 **3** (move downwards) «*sun*» 下落; «*tide*» 消退; «*hands*» 垂落; **his arms fell to his sides** 他双臂下垂，放在身体两侧; **the curtain fell** Theat 幕落了 **4** (hang down) 下垂; **her hair fell over her shoulders** 她的头发披在肩上 **5** (occur) 发生; **my birthday ~s on a Wednesday** 我的生日适逢星期三; **Easter ~s early this year** 今年的复活节来得早 **6** (slope downward) «*land, path*» 向下倾斜; **the ground ~s gently for several hundred metres** 地面缓缓向下倾斜好几百米 **7** liter (perish in battle) 阵亡 **8** Mil, Pol (be captured) 失守; **Troy fell to the Greeks** 特洛伊城被希腊人攻陷; **a number of Labour seats have ~en to the Conservatives** 许多工党的席位落入了保守党的手中 **9** (be defeated) 被打败; (be removed) 下台; **the government fell after the revolution** 政府在那次革命之后垮台了 **10** fig (collapse) «*defence, theory*» 瓦解; «*future, career*» 垮掉; **to stand or ~ on sth.** 成败取决于某事物; **the case for the defence stands or ~s on this question** 被告的理由成立与否取决于对这个问题的回答 **11** fig (descend) «*hush, night, fear*» 降临; «*person, record, morale*» 下降; **a sudden silence fell over** *or* **among the waiting crowd** 等待的人群突然变得鸦雀无声; **darkness ~s quickly in the tropics** 热带地区天黑得很快; **great sadness fell upon them** 他们感到悲痛欲绝; **her spirits fell at the bad news** 她听到坏消息后情绪低落; **the band has ~en in popularity** 这个乐队的人气下降了; **she fell to third place** 她的排名降至第三 **12** (be uttered) 被说出; **not a word fell from his lips** *or* **mouth** 他一声不吭; **to let ~ sth.** *or* **to let sth. ~** 透露某事; **did he let ~ any hints about what he wants for his birthday?** 他暗示过他想要什么生日礼物吗？ **13** fig (land on) 落在; **a ray of light fell across his bed** 一束光线从他床上掠过; **the stress ~s on the first syllable** 重音落在第一个音节上; **my eye fell on a bloodstain on the carpet** 我突然看到地毯上有一处血迹; ▸**deaf A2** **14** (decrease) 下降; **prices have ~en on the stock market** 股市已经下跌; **the sound of the siren rises and ~s** 警报器的声音时高时低; **the value of the house has ~en by £20,000** 这幢房子贬值了 2 万英镑; **production fell to an all-time low last month** 上个月的产量降至历史最低; **don't let your speed ~ below five miles per hour** 别让你的车速低于每小时 5 英里 **15** (pass into specified state) 进入; **he fell under suspicion** 他受到了怀疑; **to ~ ill** *or* **sick** 生病; **she fell pregnant last May** Brit colloq 她是 5 月份怀的孕; **to ~ silent** *or* **quiet** 安静下来; **the book fell open at a picture of a spider** 书翻开在有蜘蛛插图的那一页; **to ~ to bits** *or* **pieces** 变成碎片; **my car is ~ing to pieces** 我的车要散架了; **their relationship has ~en to pieces** fig 他们的关系/婚姻已经破裂了; **to ~ into sth.** 陷入某种状态; **I fell into a deep sleep** 我陷入了沉睡; **they fell into bad habits** 他们养成了坏习惯; **moral standards are ~ing into decay** fig 道德标准每况愈下; **to ~ from power** 下台 **16** (move into specified place) 处于; **which category does this ~ into?** 这属于哪一类？; **an act that ~s in the grey area between attack and self-defence** 介于攻击与自卫之间的行为; **the lecture ~s naturally into three parts** 演讲自然地分为三个部分; **to ~ under sth.** 归于某事物之下; **that ~s under 'any other business'** 那属于"其他事项"; **to ~ outside/within sth.** 不在/在某事物的范围之内; **the question of finance ~s outside the scope of this inquiry** 财务问题不在本次调查的范围之内; **problems that ~ within my area of responsibility** 我责任范围内的问题 **17** Relig 堕落; **to ~ into temptation** 受到诱惑而堕落

B *n* **1** (act or instance of falling) 落下; **a heavy ~ of snow** 一场大雪; **a ~ of rocks had blocked the road** 滚落的岩石堵住了路; **winning or losing depends on the ~ of the dice** 输赢通过掷骰子来决定; **the rise and ~ of the tide** 潮水的涨落; **the ~ of the curtain signalled the end of the show** 落幕表示演出结束了 **2** (uncontrolled descent) 摔倒; **to have a bad ~** 重重地摔了一跤; **he was injured in a ~ from his horse** 他从马背上掉下来受了伤; **that was a nasty ~ — are you all right?** 这一跤摔得不轻——你还好吧？ **3** (distance fallen) 下落距离; **a ~ of 20 metres** 20 米的落差 **4** Sport (in wrestling) 双肩着地; (in judo) 体落 **5** (hang of fabric, hair) 下垂 **6** (collapse, defeat) 失守; **the ~ of Troy** 特洛伊城的沦陷 **7** (decline in power) (of person, president) 失势; (of government, regime) 垮台; (of empire, republic) 灭亡; **a ~ in popularity** 人气的下降 **8** (decrease) 下降; **a ~ in prices** 价格的下跌; **a sharp ~ in unemployment numbers** 失业人数的急剧减少; **a ~ in value of £3,000** 3,000 英镑的贬值 **9** (lowering in pitch) 降低; **the rise and ~ of the melody** 音调的升降 **10** (lapse into sin) 堕落; **the F~ (of Man)** 人类的堕落; **his ~ from grace** 他的堕落 **11** Amer (autumn) 秋天

C **falls** *npl* (waterfall) 瀑布; **the Niagara F~s** 尼亚加拉大瀑布

Phrasal verbs

- **fall about** *vi* **1** Brit colloq (be helpless with laughter) 捧腹大笑; **she looked so funny: he just fell about (laughing** *or* **with laughter)** 她看上去滑稽之极，让他笑得前仰后合 **2** (move awkwardly) 踉踉跄跄地走
- **fall apart** *vi* **1** (break) «*book, car*» 散架; «*house*» 倒塌; «*suitcase*» 破裂 **2** (disintegrate) «*relationship*» 破裂; «*country, organization*» 解体; «*plan*» 失败; **their marriage is ~ing apart** 他们的婚姻岌岌可危; **they couldn't raise the money, so the deal fell apart** 他们没能筹到钱，所以生意告吹了 **3** colloq (lose one's capacity to cope) 崩溃; **he fell apart when his wife died** 妻子死后他彻底垮了
- **fall away** *vi* **1** (become detached) 掉落; **to ~ away from sth.** 从某物上掉下来; **the paint is beginning to ~ away from the ceiling** 油漆开始从天花板上剥落 **2** (have slope) «*land, path*» 向下倾斜; **the field ~s sharply away to the river** 这块田在河边一带地势陡降 **3** (become fewer or less) 减少; **output fell away to an all-time low** 产量降至历史最低水平 **4** (withdraw support) «*supporters*» 离弃; **his friends began to ~ away** 他的朋友开始和他疏远了
- **fall back** *vi* **1** (move back) 后退; **the enemy fell back as our troops advanced** 我军向前挺进，敌军向后撤退; **she fell back in horror** 她吓得直往后退 **2** (lag behind) 落在后面; **they fell back from the main group** 他们落在大部队的后面
- **fall back on** *vt* [**~ back on sb./sth.**] 求助于; **your parents won't always be there to ~ back on** 你不可能总是依靠父母; **at least he's got his savings to ~ back on** 至少他还有积蓄可赖以生活; **they wanted me to do a computer course so that I'd have something to ~ back on** 他们希望我学习计算机课程，给自己多留一条出路
- **fall behind**

A *vi* **1** (move to a position behind others) 落在后面; **to ~ behind in the arms race** 在军备竞赛中落后 **2** (with payment) 拖欠; (with work or other activity) 没有及时做; **I had to sit up studying all night so as not to ~ behind** 我不得不整晚熬夜学习，以免落下功课; **to ~ behind with sth.** 拖欠某物; **to ~ behind with the rent** 拖欠租金; **I've ~en behind with my correspondence** 我积压了很多信没有回

B *vt* [**~ behind sb./sth.**] 落在某人/某事物的后面; **he has ~en behind his classmates**

f

in maths 他在数学方面落后于班上的其他同学; **their wages have ~en behind (earnings in) the private sector** 他们的工资比私营企业员工（的薪水）低

• **fall down** *vi* 1 (fall accidentally) «*person, animal*» 摔倒; «*object*» 掉落; **the poster has ~en down** 海报已经脱落了; **the tree fell down in the gale** 这棵树被大风吹倒了 2 (collapse) 倒塌; **the tent fell down in the middle of the night** 半夜里帐篷倒了; **the house was ~ing down** colloq 房子快塌了 3 fig (fail) 失败; **his argument ~s down on this point** 这一点就是他的论据的不足之处; **she fell down on music history** 她的音乐史考砸了

• **fall for** *vt* [~ **for sb./sth.**] colloq 1 (fall in love with) 爱上; **they fell for each other instantly** 他们一见倾心 2 (find attractive) 被…所吸引 ‹*charm, looks, house*› 3 (be tricked by) 对…信以为真; **he didn't ~ for the trick** 他没有中计; **they fell for my story** 他们听信了我的说法

• **fall in** *vi* 1 (tumble in) 掉进去; **the water's deep here, mind you don't ~ in!** 这里的水深，当心别掉下去！ 2 (give way) 塌陷; **the roof fell in** 屋顶塌了 3 Mil 站队; **you're late — ~ in immediately!** 你迟到了——立即入列！; **the sergeant ordered his men to ~ in** 中士命令士兵集合 4 (start walking next to) 跟着走; **I fell in alongside** *or* **beside the procession** 我在队伍旁边跟着走

• **fall in with** *vt* [~ **in with sb./sth.**] 1 (meet) 遇见; (join) 加入; (become involved with) 开始与…有牵连; **he fell in with bad company** 他结交了一帮不三不四的人 2 (agree with) 同意; **to ~ in with sb.'s plan** 赞成某人的计划

• **fall off** *vi* 1 (decrease in quantity) 减少; **business is ~ing off** 生意越来越清淡; **production fell off drastically during the strike** 罢工期间产量急剧下降 2 (deteriorate) «*standard, quality*» 下降

• **fall on** *vt* [~ **on sb./sth.**] 1 (attack) 袭击 2 (seize) 扑向 ‹*food, treasure*› 3 (be borne by) «*burden, cost*» 由…负担 ‹*person*›; **the duty of caring for her fell on the eldest daughter** 照顾她的任务落在大女儿的身上; **the blame always ~s on me** 出了错总是归咎于我; **it ~s on the retailer to replace faulty goods** 零售商有责任退换次品

• **fall out** *vi* 1 掉落; **his hair is starting to ~ out** 他的头发开始脱落; **don't lean out of the window too far — you might ~ out** 别探出窗户太远——你可能会摔出去; **she opened the book, and a faded photograph fell out** 她翻开那本书，一张褪色的照片掉了出来 2 (quarrel) 争吵; **we've ~en out** 我们吵架了; **to ~ out with sb.** 和某人争吵; **she's ~en out with her next-door neighbour** 她与隔壁邻居吵了一架; **to ~ out over sth.** 为某事物争吵; **they fell out over the issue of local government finance** 他们为地方政府的财政问题发生了争吵 3 Mil 原地解散; **~ out!** 原地解散！ 4 Brit (happen) 发生; **everything fell out as planned** 一切都按计划进行; **we were pleased with the way things fell out** 我们对事情的进展感到满意

• **fall over**

A *vi* (fall down) 倒下; **I tripped and fell over** 我绊了一下摔倒了; **the suit of armour fell over with a loud crash** 那套盔甲轰然倒地

B *vt* [~ **over sth.**] 1 (stumble over) 被…绊倒; **I fell over my own feet** 我自己把自己绊倒了 2 **to ~ over oneself to do sth.** fig colloq (be extremely keen) 迫不及待地做; (do everything within one's power) 不遗余力地做; **to be ~ing over each other to do sth.** 争先恐后地做某事; **banks are ~ing over each other to lend people money** 各家银行争着给人贷款

• **fall through** *vi* 落空; **our plan fell through** 我们的计划告吹了; **the sale has ~en through** 这笔买卖泡了汤

• **fall to**

A *vi* liter 开始; **she fell to with gusto** 她开始津津有味地吃起来; **to ~ to doing sth.** 开始做某事; **he fell to brooding about the problem** 他开始思考这个问题

B *vt* [~ **to sb.**] liter 该由…负责; **it fell to him** *or* **to his lot to organize the party** 组织晚会的任务落在了他的肩上

fallacious /fəˈleɪʃəs/ *adj* 谬误的 ‹*reasoning, assumption, logic, idea*›

fallaciously /fəˈleɪʃəsli/ *adv* 谬误地 ‹*argue, conclude, believe*›

fallaciousness /fəˈleɪʃəsnɪs/ *n* [u] 谬误

fallacy /ˈfæləsi/ *n* 1 [c] (belief) 谬论 2 [u] (false reasoning) 谬误推理

fallback position /ˈfɔːlbæk pəˌzɪʃn/ *n* 退路

fallen /ˈfɔːlən/

A *pp* ▸**fall A**

B *adj attrib* 1 (lying on the ground) 落下的 ‹*fruit, flower*›; 倒下的 ‹*person, tree*›; 倒塌的 ‹*building*›; **~ leaves** 落叶; **the ~ tree trunk** 倒伏在地的树干 2 (killed in battle) 阵亡的; **a monument to the ~ heroes of World War II** 二战烈士纪念碑 3 Relig or liter 堕落的; **Satan and his ~ angels** 撒旦和他的堕落天使们

C *npl* **the ~** formal or liter 阵亡者; **a monument to the ~ of World War I** 一战阵亡将士纪念碑

fallen arch *n* 足弓下陷; **to have ~es** 患足弓下陷

fall guy /ˈfɔːlgaɪ/ *n* Amer colloq 1 (dupe) 易上当的人 2 (scapegoat) 替罪羊

fallibility /ˌfæləˈbɪləti/ *n* [u] 1 (of person) 易犯错 2 (of method, memory) 不可靠性

fallible /ˈfæləbl/ *adj* 1 (prone to error) 易犯错的 2 (imperfect) 会出错的 ‹*memory, method*›

falling-off *n* (*pl* **fallings-off**) 1 (reduction in amount) 减少; (reduction in intensity) 减弱 2 (deterioration) 质量下降

falling-out *n* 争吵; **to have a ~** 发生争吵

falling star *n* 流星

fall-off *n* (*pl* **~s**) = **falling-off**

Fallopian tube /fəˈləʊpɪən ˌtjuːb, Amer ˌtuːb/ *n* 输卵管

fallout /ˈfɔːlaʊt/ *n* [u] 1 Nucl (radioactive material) 放射性坠尘 2 (other material) 污染性坠尘 3 fig (of event, action) 后果

fallout shelter *n* 放射性坠尘躲避所

fallow /ˈfæləʊ/ *adj* 休耕的 ‹*land, field*›; fig «*idea, thought*» 潜伏的; **to lie ~** «*land, field*» 休耕; **long ~ periods** 漫长的潜伏期

fallow deer *n* (*pl* **fallow deer**) 黇鹿

false /fɔːls/ *adj* 1 (incorrect) (fallacious) 错误的 ‹*idea, information, accusation, report*›; 证明有误的 ‹*rumour*›; **in a ~ position** (being misunderstood) 被人误解; (acting against principles) 违背自己原则地; **~ assumption/impression** 错误的假设/假象 2 (artificial) 假的 ‹*hem, nose, eyelashes, moustache*› 3 (insincere) 假惺惺的 ‹*tears, display, person*›; **~ modesty** 假谦虚 4 (deceitful) 骗人的 ‹*evidence, claims*›; **to bear ~ witness** Jur 作伪证 5 (illusory) 虚幻的 ‹*impression, scent, hope*›; **a ~ sense of security** 虚假的安全感 6 (fraudulent) 假的 ‹*coin, passport*› 7 (disloyal) 不忠实的; **to be ~ to sb.** 对…不忠实 ‹*friend, lover*›

false: ~ alarm *n* 1 lit 假警报; 2 fig 虚惊; **~ bottom** *n* 假底 [箱子等中为藏匿的夹层设计]; **~ dawn** *n* 1 lit 假曙光; 2 fig 虚幻的希望; **the latest signs of an economic recovery could be another ~ dawn** 最近的经济复苏迹象可能又是假象; **~ economy** *n* 假节约; **~ friend** *n* 假朋友 [指与母语形式相似但意义不同的外语词汇或表达式]

falsehood /ˈfɔːlshʊd/ *n* 1 [u] (dishonesty) 虚假; **to tell truth from ~** 辨别真假 2 [c] (lie) 谎言

false imprisonment *n* [u] 非法拘禁

falsely /ˈfɔːlsli/ *adv* 1 (wrongly) 不正确地 ‹*state, represent*›; (mistakenly) 错误地 ‹*assume, interpret*›; **~ accused** 被诬告; **to ~ imprison sb.** 非法拘禁某人 2 (deceitfully) 欺骗地 ‹*claim, pretend*›

false: ~ memory syndrome *n* [u] 虚妄记忆综合征; **~ move** *n* 不明智行为

falseness /ˈfɔːlsnɪs/ *n* [u] 1 (of a statement) 不正确; (of an assumption) 错误 2 (insincerity) 不真诚 3 (fraudulence) 欺骗

false: ~ note *n* 错误的音符; **to hit** *or* **strike a ~ note** fig 出错; **~ positive** *n* 假阳性; **~ pretences** *npl* 欺诈行为; **on** *or* **under ~ pretences** 用欺诈手段; **~ rib** *n* 弓肋; **~ start** *n* 1 Sport lit 抢跑; 2 fig 失败的开端; **~ step** *n* 1 lit 失足; 2 fig 失策; **~ teeth** *npl* 假牙

falsetto /fɔːlˈsetəʊ/

A *n* (*pl* **~s**) [男高音的] 假声

B *modif* 用假声发出的 ‹*tone, whine*›

falsies /ˈfɔːlsɪz/ *npl* colloq dated 衬垫义乳

falsification /ˌfɔːlsɪfɪˈkeɪʃn/ *n* [u] 1 [u] (of document, figures) 篡改 2 [c] (of truth, facts) 歪曲

falsify /ˈfɔːlsɪfaɪ/ *vt* 1 (alter) 篡改 ‹*records, details, document*› 2 (distort) 歪曲 ‹*issue, facts, story*›

falsity /ˈfɔːlsɪti/ *n* = **falseness**

falter /ˈfɔːltə(r)/

A *vi* 1 (lose strength) «*demand, interest*» 减少; «*engine*» 运转不畅; «*music*» 减弱; «*progress, memory*» 衰退 2 (waver) «*person, gaze*» 犹豫; «*team, courage*» 畏缩; «*voice*» 颤抖; **she never ~ed in her resolve** 她的决心从未动摇 3 (when speaking) 结巴 4 (when walking) «*steps*» 踉跄

B *vt* (when speaking) 结巴地讲出

faltering /ˈfɔːltərɪŋ/ *adj attrib* 踉跄的 ‹*steps*›; 不稳定的 ‹*demand, economy*›; 时有时无的 ‹*enthusiasm, interest, courage*›; 颤抖的 ‹*voice*›; **to make a ~ start** 艰难起步

falteringly /ˈfɔːltərɪŋli/ *adv* 支支吾吾地 ‹*speak, ask*›; 踉跄地 ‹*walk, advance*›

fame /feɪm/ *n* [u] 名气; **to rise to ~** 成名; **~ and fortune** 名利; **the road to ~** 成名之路

famed /feɪmd/ *adj pred* «*person, place*» 有名的; **to be ~ for ...** 因…著名; **to be ~ as ...** 作为…而闻名

familiar /fəˈmɪlɪə(r)/ *adj* 1 (well-known) 熟悉的 ‹*sight, face, voice, name*› 2 (customary) 常遇到的 ‹*complaint, excuse, protest*›; 常体验到的 ‹*feeling*› 3 *pred* (acquainted) 通晓的; **to be ~ with sth.** 通晓某事物 4 (intimate) 亲密的; **to be on ~ terms with sb.** 与某人交情好 5 pej (presumptuous) 放肆的 ‹*person, manner*›

familiarity /fəˌmɪlɪˈærəti/ *n* [u] 1 (of surroundings, place) 熟悉 2 (acquaintance) 通晓; **~ with ...** 对…的通晓 3 (intimacy) 亲密; **~ breeds contempt** Prov 亲不敬，熟生蔑 4 (presumptuousness) 放肆

familiarize /fəˈmɪlɪəraɪz/

A *vt* 使…了解 ‹*person*›; **to ~ sb. with sth.** 使某人熟悉某事物

B *v refl* 使通晓; **to ~ oneself with sth.** 使自己通晓某事

familiarly /fəˈmɪlɪəli/ *adv* 友好随便地 ‹*address, approach, behave*›

family /ˈfæməli/

A *n + v sing or pl* 1 (parents and children) 家庭; **to raise** *or* **feed** *or* **support a ~** 养家 2 (group of relatives) 大家庭 [包括父母子女及近亲]; **the Royal F~** 王室 3 (children) 子女; **to start a ~** 生孩子 4 (from common ancestor) 家族; **to run in the ~** 世代相传 5 (of plants, animals) 科; (of languages) 语族; (of peoples) 语族群;

the cat ～ 猫科; **the Indo-European ～ of languages** 印欧语系

B *modif* 1 (belonging to a family) 家庭的 ‹*estate, life, ties*›; **to be in the ～ way** colloq 有喜 2 (suitable for a family) 适合全家的 ‹*car, accommodation, activity*›

family: ～ business *n* 家族企业; **～ butcher** *n* 家庭肉商; **～ circle** *n* 家庭圈子; **～ court** *n* Amer 家庭法院; **～ doctor** *n* Brit 全科医生; **～ entertainment** *n* [u] 全家咸宜的娱乐; **～-friendly** *adj* 适合家庭的; **F～ Income Supplement** *n* Brit 低收入家庭补助; **～ man** *n* 1 (good father and husband) 顾家的男人; 2 (man supporting wife and children) 养家的男人; **～ name** *n* 姓; **～-owned** *adj* 家族所有的; **local ～-owned shops** 本地家庭店铺; **a ～-owned business** 家族企业; **～ practice** *n* Amer 全科医学; **～ practitioner** ▸**p. 409** *n* esp Amer 全科医生; **～ room** *n* 1 (in hotel) 家庭间; 2 (in pub) 儿童休息室; 3 (at home) 家庭娱乐室; **～-size, ～-sized** *adj* 家庭装的 ‹*pack, bottle, bag*›

family planning *n* [u] 计划生育; **～ advice** 计划生育指导

Family Planning Association *n* Brit 计划生育协会

family planning clinic *n* 计划生育指导站

family-style

A *adj* 餐者随意自取的 ‹*meal, eating*›

B *adv* 餐者随意自取地

family: ～ tree *n* 家谱图; **～ unit** *n* 家庭单位; **～ values** *npl* 家庭价值观; **～ viewing** *n* [u] **to be suitable for ～ viewing** 适合全家观看

famine /ˈfæmɪn/ *n* 饥荒

famished /ˈfæmɪʃt/ *adj* colloq 饿坏了的; **I'm ～** 我快饿死了

famous /ˈfeɪməs/ *adj* 著名的 ‹*person, building, institution*›; **to be ～ as sth.** 作为某事物很有名; **to be ～ for sth.** 以某事物闻名; **a ～ victory** colloq 辉煌的胜利; **～ last words!** colloq iron 说得倒很漂亮! iron

famously /ˈfeɪməsli/ *adv* 1 colloq (excellently) 极好地; **to get on** *or* **along ～** 相处极好 2 (as is well known) 出名地; **he once ～ stated that ...** 他有句名言说…

fan¹ /fæn/

A *n* 1 (electric) 电扇 2 (hand-held) 扇子

B *vt* (*pres p etc.* **-nn-**) 1 (cool) «*person*» 给…扇风; «*breeze*» 吹拂 ‹*face, arms*›; **to ～ oneself** 给自己扇风 2 (stimulate) «*person*» 扇 ‹*fire, embers*›; **his letter merely ～ned the flames** fig 他的信简直是火上浇油 3 (stir up) «*person, media*» 激起 ‹*anger, hatred*›

Phrasal verb

• **fan out**

A *vi* «*soldiers, policemen, searchers*» 成扇形散开

B *vt* [**～ sth. out, ～ out sth.**] «*person, peacock*» 成扇形展开 ‹*cards, feathers*›; **a wind ～ned her hair out behind her** 一阵风把她的头发吹得飘散在背后

fan² *n* (admirer) 狂热仰慕者; (enthusiast) 迷; **to be a ～ of sb.** 是某人的狂热仰慕者; **he's not one of her greatest ～s** iron 他没觉得她怎么样; **a pop music/jazz/football ～** 流行音乐/爵士乐/足球迷

fan-assisted oven *n* 风扇低温烤箱

fanatic /fəˈnætɪk/

A *n* 1 pej (extremist) 极端分子 2 colloq (enthusiast) 入迷者; **a sports/fitness/jazz ～** 运动迷/健身迷/爵士乐迷

B *adj* = **fanatical 1**

fanatical /fəˈnætɪkl/ *adj* 1 pej (over-zealous) 狂热的 ‹*disciple, extremist*› 2 (obsessive) 过度的 ‹*zeal, dedication, pursuit*›

fanatically /fəˈnætɪkli/ *adv* 狂热地 ‹*dedicated, enthusiastic*›

fanaticism /fəˈnætɪsɪzəm/ *n* [u] 狂热

fan belt *n* 风扇皮带

fanciable /ˈfænsɪəbl/ *adj* Brit colloq 性感的

fancier /ˈfænsɪə(r)/ *n* 饲养迷; **a dog/bird ～** 养狗迷/养鸟迷

fanciful /ˈfænsɪfl/ *adj* 1 (over-imaginative) 耽于空想的 ‹*person*›; 稀奇古怪的 ‹*name, story, tale*›; **to be ～** 爱空想 2 (unrealistic) 不现实的 ‹*idea, plan, suggestion*›; 不符合事实的 ‹*interpretation, explanation*› 3 (ornamental) 别出心裁的 ‹*design, sculpture*›

fancifully /ˈfænsɪfəli/ *adv* 1 (unrealistically) 毫无根据地 ‹*believe, suppose*›; 不合实际地 ‹*interpret, explain*›; **to think** *or* **imagine ～ that ...** 毫无根据地认为… 2 (whimsically) 别出心裁地 ‹*decorate, design*›; 奇怪地 ‹*name, describe*›

fancily /ˈfænsɪli/ *adv* 花哨地 ‹*decorated, dressed*›

fan club *n* lit 粉丝俱乐部; fig 粉丝

fancy /ˈfænsi/

A *vt* 1 Brit colloq (wish to have) 想要; (wish to do) 想做; **what do you ～ for lunch?** 午餐你想吃点什么?; **do you ～ a drink?** 想喝一杯吗?; **do you ～ going to the cinema this evening?** 今晚你想看电影吗?; **she doesn't ～ the idea of being in charge** 她不想当负责人; **a little of what you ～ does you good** dated 适当享受, 好处多多 2 colloq (find sexually attractive) 爱慕; **I rather ～ her** 我看上她了 3 (think) 认为; **I ～ it's going to rain today** 我觉得今天会下雨; **I ～ I've seen her somewhere before** 我觉得以前在哪里见过她 4 colloq (have high opinion of) **to ～ oneself** 自命不凡; **you ～ yourself in that hat, don't you?** 你觉得自己戴那顶帽子很漂亮, 是不是?; **to ～ oneself as ...** 自认为是…; **to ～ oneself as an expert on sth.** 自命为某方面的专家; **to ～ oneself with sth.** 自认为擅长某事; **she fancies herself with horses** 她自认为擅长骑马; **to ～ one's/sb.'s chances** Brit colloq 认为自己/某人会成功; **he's hoping to get the job but I don't ～ his chances** 他希望能得到那份工作, 但我觉得他没戏 5 *in imperative* [用于祈使句, 表示吃惊或难以置信等]; **～! they had nothing to eat for six days!** 真想不到! 他们有 6 天没吃东西!; **he's never been to London — ～ that!** 他从没去过伦敦——真是不可思议!; **～ him being a murderer!** 他居然是个杀人犯!; **～ meeting you here!** 真没想到在这儿遇到你! 6 colloq (regard as winner) 认为…会赢; **which horse do you ～ in the next race?** 下一场比赛你认为哪匹马会赢?; **I ～ him to win the tournament** 我认为他会赢得锦标赛

B *n* 1 [u and c] (whim) 一时的念头; **a passing ～** 心血来潮; **as** *or* **whenever the ～ takes sb.** 只要某人乐意; **I just go where the ～ takes me** 我想去哪里就去哪里; **he only paints when the ～ takes him** 他只在想画画时才动笔; **to take a ～ to sth.** 一时兴起想做某事 2 [u and c] (liking, desire) 一时的喜爱; **to catch** *or* **take sb.'s ～** 吸引某人; **the only thing that took my ～ at the auction was an antique writing desk** 拍卖会上我唯一中意的是一张古董写字桌; **they can do whatever takes their ～ with the money** 这笔钱他们可以想怎么花就怎么花; **to take a ～ to sth./doing sth.** 喜欢上某事物/做某事; **to take a ～ to sb.** 喜欢上某人; **he seems to have taken quite a ～ to your sister** 他似乎看上你妹妹了; **he gave the job to a young man who had taken his ～** 他把工作给了一个博得他好感的年轻人; **to have a ～ for sth.** 想要某物; **she has a ～ for antique jewellery** 她喜欢古董珠宝 3 [u] liter (imagination) 想象; (faculty of imagination) 想象力; **is it fact or ～?** 这是事实还是幻想?; **he paints whatever his ～ suggests** 他想到什么就画什么 4 [c] (supposed thing) 想象的事物; **did I really see it, or was it only a ～?** 我是真的看到了它, 还是只是幻觉?; **I had a ～ that something was going to go wrong** 我隐约预感到, 有什么事要出岔子; **I have a ～ that he said he would be late tonight** 我依稀记得他说过今晚会迟到 5 [c] (cake) 花色小蛋糕

C *adj* 1 (ornate) 有精美装饰的; **a ～ hat** 别致的帽子; **～ cakes** 花式蛋糕; **～ patterns** 精美的图案; **it's too ～ for my liking** 它太花哨了, 我不喜欢 2 (elaborate) 高级的 ‹*food, drink*›; fig 花言巧语的 ‹*excuse, explanation*›; **～ foreign food** pej 高档外国食品; **what do you want for lunch? — nothing ～: a cheese sandwich will do** 午饭你想吃点什么? ——简单点, 来个奶酪三明治就行了; **the wedding cake was very ～** 婚礼蛋糕做得非常精美 3 often pej colloq (extravagant, pretentious) 奢华的; **a ～ house** 豪宅; **a ～ restaurant** 高档餐厅; **why did you have to give the child such a ～ name?** 你干嘛非要给孩子起这么个怪名字? 4 colloq pej (expensive) 昂贵的 ‹*price*› 5 pej (high-flown) 不切实际的 ‹*idea*› 6 colloq (sophisticated) 复杂的 ‹*gadget, course, footwork*› 7 Amer (high-quality) 优质的 ‹*foodstuffs, groceries*› 8 Zool 珍奇的 ‹*animal, bird, plant*›

fancy dress

A *n* [u] 化装舞会服; **to go in ～** 穿化装舞会服出席

B **fancy-dress** *modif* 化装服的; **a ～ party/ball** 化装派对/舞会

fancy: ～-free *adj* (having no commitments) 逍遥自在的; (romantically unattached) 无恋爱对象的; **when she was young and ～-free** 她年轻未婚时; **～ goods** *npl* 小商品

fandango /fænˈdæŋɡəʊ/ *n* (*pl* **～s** *or* **～es**) 方丹戈舞

fanfare /ˈfænfeə(r)/ *n* lit 号角齐鸣; **in a ～ of publicity** fig 大张旗鼓地

fang /fæŋ/ *n* 1 (of dog, wolf) 尖牙 2 (of snake) 毒牙

fan: ～ heater *n* Brit 风扇电热器; **～jet** *n* 涡轮风扇发动机; **～ letter** *n* 粉丝来信; **～light** *n* 气窗; **～ magazine** *n* 粉丝杂志; **～ mail** *n* [u] 粉丝来信

fanny /ˈfæni/ *n* 1 Brit taboo sl (female genitals) 阴部 2 Amer colloq (buttocks) 屁股

fanny pack *n* Amer 腰包

fan: ～ oven *n* 风扇烤箱; **～-shaped** *adj* 扇形的 ‹*ornament, shell, window*›

fantasia /fænˈteɪzɪə, Amer -ˈteɪʒə/ *n* 1 Mus 幻想曲 2 Literat 幻想作品

fantasize /ˈfæntəsaɪz/

A *vt* 幻想

B *vi* 做白日梦; **to ～ about doing sth.** 幻想做某事

fantastic /fænˈtæstɪk/ *adj* 1 colloq (wonderful) 非常棒的 ‹*food, film, party*› 2 (unrealistic) 荒唐的 ‹*plan, project, idea*› 3 colloq (very high or large) 极快的 ‹*speed*›; 极大的 ‹*amount, rate, success, reductions*›; **the show/song was a ～ hit** 这个演出/这首歌曲一炮走红 4 (strange) 稀奇古怪的 ‹*dream, image, design*› 5 (incredible) 难以置信的 ‹*adventure, story*›

fantastically /fænˈtæstɪkli/ *adv* 1 colloq (wonderfully) 极好地; **everything went ～ (well)** 一切顺利 2 colloq (incredibly) 极大地 ‹*increase*›; 极其 ‹*large, high, wealthy, expensive*› 3 (fabulously) 稀奇古怪地 ‹*coloured, variegated, portrayed*›

fantasy /ˈfæntəsi/ *n* 1 [u] (imagination) (activity) 幻想; **to indulge in ～** 沉湎于幻想 2 [c] (dream) 梦想; **to act out a ～** Psych 把梦境表演出来 3 [c] (unrealistic idea) 不合实际的想法 4 [u and c] (story, film etc.) 幻想作品 5 [c] Mus 幻想曲

fantasy football *n* [u] 梦幻足球

fan vaulting *n* [u] 扇形穹顶

fanzine /ˈfænziːn/ *n* 爱好者杂志

FAO *abbr* = **Food and Agriculture Organization**

FAQ *npl, abbr* = **frequently asked questions** 常问问题

far /fɑː(r)/

A *adv* (*comp* **farther** *or* **further,** *superl* **farthest** *or* **furthest**) **1** (in distance) 远; **~ away** *or* **off** 在远处; **~ and wide** 到处; **to come from ~ and wide** 远道而来; **as ~ apart as ...** 像…这样相距遥远的; **to look down at the traffic ~ below** 远远地看下方的车流; **to go ~ into the jungle** 进入丛林深处; **as ~ as the eye can see** 极目所及; **~ be it from me to do that** 我决不会做某事; **to go ~** (be useful, extend) 足够; (become successful) 成功; **this food won't go very ~** 这点食物不够吃的; **she will go ~** 她会有出息的 **2** (in time) 久远; **~ away** *or* **off** 很遥远; **peace seems very ~ away** *or* **off** 和平看起来遥遥无期; **to look ~ ahead** 展望遥远的未来; **as ~ back as 1985** 早在 1985 年; **I can't plan ~ beyond next month** 我没法计划下个月之后太远的事; **to work ~ into the night** 工作到深夜; **to see ~ into the past/future** 看到遥远的过去/将来; **he's not ~ off 70** 他快到 70 岁了; ▸**few A1** **3** (to a great degree, very much) 非常; **~ too cold/busy/much** 太冷/太忙/太多; **~ faster/better/worse** 快/好/差得多; **not to be (too) far out** *or* **off** *or* **wrong** colloq «*opinion, guess, calculation*» 八九不离十; **far gone** colloq (ill) 奄奄一息的; (drunk) 烂醉如泥的; **I wouldn't trust him very ~** 我不太信任他; **to be ~ ahead** 遥遥领先 **4** (expressing specific degree, progress) [到某种程度]; **as** *or* **so ~ as possible** 尽可能; **as** *or* **so ~ as sb. can** 尽某人所能; **as** *or* **so ~ as sb. knows/can remember/can foresee** 就某人所知/所能记得/所能预见; **as** *or* **so ~ as sb. can see** 依某人看; **as** *or* **so ~ as sb. is concerned** (in sb.'s opinion) 依某人所见; **as** *or* **so ~ as sb./sth. is concerned** *or* **goes** (as regards sb. or sth.) 就某人/某事物而言; **as** *or* **so ~ as it goes** 在有限程度上; **how ~ gone** *or* **along** Amer **is she (in her pregnancy)?** 她怀孕多久了?; **how ~ is it possible to ...?** …的可能性有多大?; **how ~ have you got with that report?** 你那份报告写得怎么样了?; **I read as ~ as the third chapter** 我读到了第三章; **it's a good plan as ~ as it goes, but ...** 这计划本身还算不错，不过… **5** (to extreme degree) 过分地; **to go so ~ as to do sth.** 竟然做某事; **to go too ~** 做得过分; **to go so ~ as to apologize** 甚至都赔礼道歉; **I wouldn't go so ~ as to say that** 我倒不至于那样说; **she took** *or* **carried the joke too ~** 她这玩笑开得太过火了

B *adj attrib* (*comp* **farther** *or* **further,** *superl* **farthest** *or* **furthest**) **1** (remote in space) 遥远的; **the ~ north of Canada** 加拿大的最北端; **the ~ right of the photograph** 照片最右边; **to be a ~ cry from sb./sth.** fig 与某人/某事物截然不同 **2** (remote in time) 久远的; **the ~ future** 遥远的未来 **3** (more distant, other) 较远的 ‹*side, shore, bank*›; **at the ~ end of the room** 在房间的那一头; **a table in the ~ corner** 对面角落的桌子 **4** Pol 极端的; **the ~ right/left** 极右翼/极左翼

C **by far** *adv phr* (with comparative) …得多; (with superlative) 最…; **she's prettier by ~ than her sister** 她比她妹妹漂亮得多; **it's by ~ the nicest/the most expensive** 它是最好的/最贵的; **by ~ the quickest way** 最便捷的路径

D **far and away** *adv phr* 毫无疑问地; **she's ~ and away the better candidate** 她无疑是更好的候选人

E **far from** *prep phr* 完全不; **to be ~ from satisfied/certain** 根本不满意/毫无把握; **he's ~ from stupid** 他一点都不笨; **~ from complaining, I am very pleased** 我没有抱怨，相反却很高兴; **~ from it!** colloq 完全相反!; **are you angry? — ~ from it!** 你生气吗? ——一点都不!

F **so far** *adv phr* **1** (up till now) 到目前为止; **she's only written one book so ~** 她迄今只写了一本书; **so ~ so good** 到目前为止，一切还算顺利 **2** (to a certain extent) 到某一程度; **you can only trust him so ~** 你只能信任他到这个程度

G **thus far** *adv phr* formal 到现在为止; **thus ~ we don't have any information** 我们至今没有任何信息

farad /ˈfærəd/ *n* 法拉 [电容单位]

faraway /ˈfɑːrəweɪ/ *adj attrib* **1** lit 遥远的 ‹*land, place*› **2** fig 心不在焉的 ‹*look, voice*›

farce /fɑːs/ *n* **1** [c] Radio, Theat, TV 滑稽戏 **2** [u] (genre) 滑稽剧 **3** [c] fig 闹剧; **the trial was a ~** 这次审判纯属闹剧

farcical /ˈfɑːsɪkl/ *adj* 荒谬的 ‹*idea, situation*›

far: ~ cry *n* 截然不同的事物; **it's a ~ cry from what he promised** 这与他的许诺大相径庭; **~-distant** /ˌfɑːˈdɪstənt/ *adj* 遥远的; **~-distant mountains** 远处的山脉; **in the ~-distant future/past** 在遥远的将来/过去

fare /feə(r)/

A *n* **1** (cost of travelling) 票价; **a full/reduced ~** 全票/打折票; **~s please!** 请买票! **2** (taxi passenger) 出租车乘客 **3** [u] (food) 食物; **traditional ~** 传统菜肴; **bill of ~** 菜单

B *vi* «*person, team, party*» 进行; **how did you ~?** 你过得如何?

far: F~ East *pr n* 远东; **F~ Eastern** *adj* 远东的

fare: ~ dodger *n* 逃票者; **~-paying passenger** *n* 付费乘客; **~ stage** *n* [公共汽车的] 固定收费路段

farewell /ˌfeəˈwel/

A *n* [u and c] (act of departure) 告别; (parting good wishes) 告别话; **to say one's ~s** 道别; **to bid sb. ~** 和某人道别; **you can say ~ to your suitcase!** 你的手提箱一去不复返了!

B *modif* 告别的 ‹*gift, speech*›; **a ~ party** 欢送会

C *excl* archaic 再见

far: ~-fetched /ˌfɑːˈfetʃt/ *adj* 牵强的 ‹*example, story*›; **~-flung** *adj usu attrib* **1** (remote) 遥远的 ‹*area, outpost*›; **2** (widely distributed) 分布广的 ‹*countries, towns, regions*›; **~-flung trade connections** 广泛的贸易联系

farm /fɑːm/

A *n* 农场; **chicken/poultry ~** 养鸡场/家禽饲养场; **dairy ~** 奶牛场

B *vt* (for crops) 种植 ‹*land*›; (for animals) 饲养

C *vi* (for crops) 种植; (for animals) 养殖

Phrasal verb

• **farm out** *vt* [**~ sth. out, ~ out sth.**] **1** (subcontract) 包出 ‹*work, orders*›; **to ~ sth. out to sb.** 将某事务包给某人 **2** (entrust) 托人照顾 ‹*child, visitor*›; **to ~ sth. out to sb.** 把工作交给某人; **we ~ed the kids out to our neighbours** 我们把孩子交给邻居照看

farmer /ˈfɑːmə(r)/ ▸**p. 409** *n* (owner) 农场主; (worker) 农民

farmers' market *n* 农贸市场

farm: ~ gate price *n* 农产品产地价格; **~ hand** ▸**p. 409** *n* 农场工人

farmhouse /ˈfɑːmhaʊs/ *n* 农舍

farmhouse loaf *n* Brit 长白面包

farming /ˈfɑːmɪŋ/

A *n* [u] (agriculture) 农业; (raising livestock) 养殖业; **to take up** *or* **go into ~** 从事农业; **vegetable/fruit ~** 蔬菜/果树种植; **fish/mink ~** 养鱼/水貂养殖

B *modif* 农业的 ‹*resources, subsidies, community*›

farm: ~ labourer ▸**p. 409** *n* 农场工人; **~land** /-lænd/ *n* [u] 农田; **~ produce** *n* [u] 农产品; **~ shop** *n* 农产品商店; **~stead** *n* dated 农庄; **~ worker** ▸**p. 409** *n* 农场工人

farmyard /ˈfɑːmjɑːd/ *n* 农家庭院

farmyard chicken *n* 草鸡

Faroes /ˈfeərəʊz/, **Faroe Islands** /ˈfeərəʊ ˌaɪləndz/ *pr nspl* **the ~** 法罗群岛

far-off *adj* **1** (in space) 遥远的 ‹*land, place*› **2** (in time) 久远的; **in those ~ days** 在久远的往昔

far out *adj* colloq 标新立异的 ‹*theory, idea*›

farrago /fəˈrɑːgəʊ/ *n* 大杂烩; **a ~ of nonsense/lies** 胡言乱语/谎话连篇

far-reaching /ˌfɑːˈriːtʃɪŋ/ *adj* 影响深远的 ‹*consequences, effect, implications*›

farrier /ˈfærɪə(r)/ *n* Brit 蹄铁工

farrow /ˈfærəʊ/

A *n* **1** (litter of piglets) 一窝仔猪 **2** (act) 产仔猪

B *vi* «*sow*» 产仔

C *vt* 产 ‹*litter, piglets*›

far-sighted *adj* **1** (prescient) 有远见的 ‹*person, plan, policy*› **2** esp Amer Med 远视的

fart /fɑːt/ colloq

A *n* **1** (wind) 屁 **2** (stupid person) 讨厌的家伙

B *vi* 放屁

Phrasal verb

• **fart around,** Brit **fart about** *vi* colloq 闲荡

farther /ˈfɑːðə(r)/ (*comp of* **far**)

A *adv* **1** = **further A1** **2** = **further A2**

B *adj attrib* = **further B1**

farthest /ˈfɑːðɪst/ (*superl of* **far**)

A *adj* = **furthest A**

B *adv* = **furthest B**

farthing /ˈfɑːðɪŋ/ *n* Brit 法寻 [英国旧时硬币，等于1/4便士]; **I don't care** *or* **give a ~ for her** 我一点儿也不在乎她

fascia /ˈfeɪʃə/ *n* **1** Brit Aut (dashboard) 仪表板 **2** (over shop) 招牌

fascicle /ˈfæsɪkl/, **fascicule** /ˈfæsɪkjuːl/ *ns* [多卷册图书的] 分册

fascinate /ˈfæsɪneɪt/ *vt* 迷住; **she really ~s me** 她让我神魂颠倒

fascinated /ˈfæsɪneɪtɪd/ *adj* 入迷的 ‹*person, viewers*›

fascinating /ˈfæsɪneɪtɪŋ/ *adj* 迷人的

fascination /ˌfæsɪˈneɪʃn/ *n* **1** (interest) 入迷; **to have a ~ with sth.** 对某事物入迷; **in ~** 入迷地 **2** (attraction) 吸引力; **to have** *or* **hold a ~ for sb.** 对某人有吸引力

fascism /ˈfæʃɪzəm/ *n* [u] 法西斯主义

fascist /ˈfæʃɪst/

A *adj* (related to fascism) 法西斯主义的; (authoritarian) 独裁的

B *n* (member of fascist party) 法西斯分子; (authoritarian) 专横霸道的人

fashion /ˈfæʃn/

A *n* **1** [u and c] (vogue, trend) 时尚; **in/out of ~** 正在/不再流行; **the latest ~** 最新的时尚; **to be a slave to ~** 拼命赶时髦; **to be all the ~** 风行一时; **ladies' ~s** 新款女装 **2** (manner) 方式; **after a ~** 还算可以

B *modif* 流行的 ‹*accessory, jewellery*›

C *vt* **1** (mould) 使…成形 ‹*clay, wood*›; **to ~ sth. into sth.** 把某物做成某物 **2** (create) 制作 ‹*bowl, figure*›; **to ~ sth. out of** *or* **from sth.** 用某物制作某物

fashionable /ˈfæʃnəbl/ *adj* **1** (stylish) 时髦的 ‹*style, garment*›; 赶时髦的 ‹*person, society*› **2** (in vogue) 受人追捧的 ‹*resort*›; 流行的 ‹*topic, opinion, pastime*›; 作品畅销的 ‹*artist, writer*›; **to be ~ among ...** 在…中很受欢迎; **this restaurant is ~ among young people** 年轻人经常光顾这个餐馆; **long hair was ~ for men** 以前男人流行留长发

fashionably /ˈfæʃnəbli/ *adv* 时髦地 ‹*dressed*›

fashion: ~ business *n* [u] 时装业; **~ buyer** ▸**p. 409** *n* 时尚买手; **~-conscious** *adj* 赶时髦的; **~ designer** ▸**p. 409** *n* 时装设计师; **~ drug** *n* 时髦药; **~ editor** ▸**p. 409** *n* 时尚版编辑;

~ **house** *n* 时装公司; ~ **magazine** *n* 时尚杂志; ~ **model** ▸**p. 409** *n* 时装模特; ~ **parade** *n* 时装展示; ~ **show** *n* 时装秀; ~ **victim** *n* 时尚受害者

fast[1] /fɑːst, Amer fæst/

A *adj* 1 (speedy) 快的; **a ~ car** 速度快的汽车; **a ~ horse** 快马; **a ~ mover** fig colloq 动作快的人; **~ work** 迅速完成的工作; **a ~ worker** lit 做事麻利的人; fig [爱情关系中] 易受青睐的人; **he's a ~ talker** colloq 他能说会道; **to pull a ~ one (on sb.)** colloq 欺骗（某人） 2 (happening quickly) 迅速发生的; **a ~ trip to Paris** 匆促的巴黎之旅 3 (allowing quick movement) 可供快速运动的; **a ~ road/pitch** 快车道/平整的球场; **a ~ line** Rail 快车 4 *pred* (ahead of time) «*clock, watch*» 走得快的; **to be ten minutes ~** 快了十分钟 5 Phot 感光快的 ‹*film*›; **~ exposure** 快速曝光 6 pej (immoral) 放荡的; **to lead a ~ life** 过放荡不羁的生活; **a ~ woman** 荡妇 7 *pred* (fixed, attached) 牢固的; **the post has to be ~ in the ground** 柱子必须牢牢固定在地上; **to make the boat ~** 把船系牢 8 *attrib* liter (loyal) 可靠的 ‹*friend*›; **they formed a ~ friendship** 他们结下了牢不可破的友谊 9 Tex (permanent) 不褪色的 ‹*dye*›

B *adv* 1 (rapidly) 快速; **don't drive so ~!** 别把车开得这么快! ; **she ran off as ~ as her legs could carry her** 她拼命跑走了; **her heart beat ~er** 她的心跳加快了; **education is ~ becoming a luxury** 教育不久就要成为一种奢侈品了; **to play ~ and loose (with sb./sth.)** 玩弄（某人/某物） 2 (firmly) 牢固地; **the boat was stuck ~ in the mud** 船深陷在淤泥里动弹不得; **the door was shut ~** 门紧闭着; **to be ~ asleep** 沉睡; **to hold ~ to sth.** lit 抓紧某物; fig 坚持某事; **to stand ~** lit 屹立不动; fig 不让步; **to stand ~ by sb./sth.** 坚定不移地支持某人/某事物 3 (ahead) 快于标准时间; **that clock is running ~** 那钟快了 4 archaic **~ by** 就在…旁边; **~ by the tower** 就在塔楼旁边

fast[2]

A *vi* 禁食; **to ~ for sth.** 为某事而禁食; **do you ~ during Lent?** 你在大斋节期间斋戒吗?

B *n* (going without food) 禁食; (period of going without food) 禁食期; **to break one's ~** 开斋; **a ~ day** 斋戒日; **it's a time when Muslims observe a ~** 这是伊斯兰教徒斋戒的时期

fast: ~back *n* Brit 斜背式轿车; **~ breeder reactor** *n* 快中子增殖反应堆

fasten /ˈfɑːsn, Amer ˈfæsn/

A *vt* 1 (close, secure) 闩住 ‹*bolt*›; 系上 ‹*seat-belt, sandals*›; 扣上 ‹*button, necklace, dress*›; 盖上 ‹*lid, case*› 2 (attach) 粘上 ‹*paper, notice*›; 系 ‹*chain, lead*›; **she ~ed the ends together** 她把末端系在一起 3 fig (fix) 强加 ‹*blame, responsibility*›; **to ~ sth. on sb.** 把某事强加给某人 4 fig (direct) 集中; **to ~ one's gaze/eyes on sth.** 凝视/注视某物

B *vi* «*door, window*» 闩上; «*dress*» 系住; «*box*» 盖上

Phrasal verbs

• **fasten down** *vt* [**~ down sth., ~ sth. down**] 关上 ‹*flap, top*›; 闩上 ‹*peg, hatch*›

• **fasten on**

A *vt* [**~ on sth., to ~ sth. on**] 系上 ‹*strap, belt*›; 关上 ‹*top*›

B *vi* 1 **to ~ on to sb./sth.** (cling to) 抓住 ‹*person, arm*› 2 **to ~ on to sth.** (latch on to) 对…锲而不舍 ‹*idea, plan*›

• **fasten up**

A *vt* [**~ up sth., ~ sth. up**] 系上 ‹*dress*›; 盖上 ‹*case, box*›

B *vi* 系扣

fastener /ˈfɑːsnə(r), Amer ˈfæsnə(r)/, **fastening** /ˈfɑːsnɪŋ, Amer ˈfæsnɪŋ/ *ns* (button) 纽扣; (zip) 拉链; (clasp) 扣件; (lock) 锁; (hook) 钩; (press stud) 揿扣

fast: ~-flowing *adj* 湍急的 ‹*river*›; fig 变化万千的 ‹*thoughts*›; **~ food** *n* [u] 快餐

fast-forward

A *vt* 使…快进 ‹*tape, video*›; fig 快速推进 ‹*life, thoughts*›

B *vi* 快进; **to ~ through the adverts** 快跳过广告

fast-growing *adj* 快速发展的

fastidious /fæˈstɪdɪəs/ *adj* 1 (meticulous) 一丝不苟的 ‹*attitude*›; **to be ~ about sth.** 对某事过分讲究 2 (demanding) 挑剔的 ‹*critic, inspector*› 3 (about cleanliness) 讲究整洁的

fastidiously /fæˈstɪdɪəsli/ *adv* 过分讲究地 ‹*clean, check*›

fastidiousness /fæˈstɪdɪəsnɪs/ *n* [u] 1 (meticulousness) 过分讲究 2 (concern with cleanliness) 讲究整洁

fast: ~ lane *n* 快车道; **to live (life) in the ~ lane** fig 过快节奏的生活; **~ living** *n* [u] 放荡的生活; **~-moving** *adj* 快速进行的

fastness /ˈfɑːstnɪs, Amer ˈfæst-/ *n* 1 (speed) 快速 2 (of dye) 不褪色

fast: ~ rewind *n* 快速倒带; **~-talk** *vt* colloq 花言巧语地说服; **~-talking** *adj* colloq 花言巧语的

fast track

A *n* 快速晋升通道

B *modif* 快速的 ‹*promotion*›; 特快的 ‹*service*›

C *vt* 快速提拔 ‹*person*›; 加速…的进程 ‹*project*›

fat /fæt/

A *n* 1 [u] (in diet, on body) 脂肪; **the ham had too much ~ on it** 这块火腿肥肉太多; **excess body ~** 多余的体内脂肪; **foods which are low in ~** 低脂食物; **the ~'s in the fire** 要惹麻烦了; **to live off the ~ of the land** 生活奢侈 2 [u and c] Culin 食用油; **vegetable ~(s)** 植物油; **pork ~** 猪油

B *adj* 1 (overweight) 肥胖的; **to get ~** 长胖; **~ little legs** 胖胖的小腿儿; **you won't grow very ~ on that salary** fig colloq 那点薪水算不了什么 2 (fatty) 肥的; **~ meat** 肥肉 3 (full, swollen) 圆鼓鼓的; **a big ~ apple** 又大又圆的苹果; **a ~ wallet** 鼓鼓囊囊的钱包; **a ~ volume of verse** 厚厚的一册诗集 4 (substantial) 大量的; **to make a ~ profit** 获得暴利; **a nice ~ cheque** 大额支票; **a ~ job/salary** 肥缺/丰厚的薪水 5 colloq iron (not much) 算不上的; **a ~ chance he's got of escaping!** 他几乎不可能逃跑! ; **a ~ lot of good/use** 一点好处也没有/毫无用处; **a ~ lot of good that did!** 那样一点好处也没有! 6 liter (fertile) 肥沃的 ‹*land*›; 丰收的 ‹*year*›

fatal /ˈfeɪtl/ *adj* 1 (lethal) 致命的 ‹*accident, illness*›; 毁灭性的 ‹*delay, blow*›; **she sustained ~ injuries** 她受了致命伤 2 fig (disastrous) 灾难性的 ‹*mistake, decision, weakness*›; **to be ~ to sth.** 对某事物有毁灭性的影响

fatalism /ˈfeɪtəlɪzəm/ *n* [u] 宿命论; **to give way to ~** 听天由命

fatalist /ˈfeɪtəlɪst/ *n* 宿命论者

fatalistic /ˌfeɪtəˈlɪstɪk/ *adj* 听天由命的

fatality /fəˈtæləti/ *n* 1 [c] (person killed) 死者 2 [u] (death) 死亡; (deadliness) 致命性

fatally /ˈfeɪtəli/ *adv* 1 (mortally) 致命地; **to be ~ injured** 受致命伤 2 fig (disastrously) 灾难性地; **the design was ~ flawed** 该设计有致命缺陷

fat: ~back *n* [u] Amer [猪的] 背膘; **~ cat** *n* colloq pej 阔佬

fate /feɪt/ *n* 1 [u] (controlling power) 天数; **~ was on my side/against me** 天遂我愿/天不遂我愿; **to tempt ~** 冒险 2 [c] (destiny) 命运; **to be resigned to one's ~** 听天由命 3 [c] (death) 死亡; **to meet a sad ~** 死于非命

fated /ˈfeɪtɪd/ *adj* 1 *pred* (destined) 注定的; **to be ~ to do sth.** 注定做某事 2 (doomed) 注定没好结果的 ‹*love, trip*› 3 (decreed by fate) 命定的 ‹*existence, rise*›; **it was ~ that ...** 命定会…

fateful /ˈfeɪtfl/ *adj* 1 (momentous) 决定性的 ‹*event, night, moment*› 2 (portentous) 灾难性的 ‹*pronouncement, words, decision*›

fat: ~ farm *n* Amer colloq 瘦身中心; **~-free** *adj* 无脂的 ‹*diet, foods*›; **~head** *n* colloq pej 蠢货; **~-headed** /ˈfætˌhedɪd/ *adj* colloq pej 愚蠢的

Father /ˈfɑːðə(r)/ *n* Relig 1 (God) 上帝; **God the ~** 天父; **the** *or* **Our ~** (prayer) 天父 2 (title for priest) 神父; **~ Smith** 史密斯神父

father /ˈfɑːðə(r)/

A *n* 1 ▸**p. 419** (male parent) 父亲; **like ~ like son** Prov 有其父必有其子; **we had the ~ and mother of a row** fig colloq 我们吵得不可开交 2 liter (ancestor) 祖先 3 (originator) 创始人; **the ~ of the motor car** 汽车的发明者; **the ~ of English theatre** 英国戏剧之父

B *vt* 1 (be the parent of) «*man*» 是…的父亲 ‹*child, offspring, family*› 2 (be the creator of) 发明 ‹*invention*›; 创立 ‹*idea, project*›

father: F~ Christmas *pr n* Brit 圣诞老人; **~ confessor** *n* 告解神父; **~ figure** *n* 父亲般的人

fatherhood /ˈfɑːðəhʊd/ *n* [u] 父亲的身份

father: ~-in-law ▸**p. 419** *n* (*pl* **~s-in-law**) (father of one's husband) 公公; (father of one's wife) 岳父; **~land** /-lænd/ *n* 祖国 [尤用于希特勒当政时的德国]

fatherless /ˈfɑːðəlɪs/ *adj* 没有父亲的

fatherly /ˈfɑːðəli/ *adj* (resembling a father) 父亲般的 ‹*hug, affection*›; (of a father) 父亲的 ‹*concern, pride*›

father: F~'s Day *n* 父亲节; **F~ Time** *pr n* **(Old) F~ Time** 时间老人 [手持沙漏和大镰刀象征时间的老人形象]

fathom /ˈfæðəm/

A *n* 英寻 [水深量度单位，合6英尺或1.83米]

B *vt* 1 Naut 测量…的深度 2 **~ (out)** (understand) 弄懂

fathomless /ˈfæðəmlɪs/ *adj* 1 lit 深不可测的 ‹*depths, ocean*› 2 fig 神秘莫测的 ‹*truth, eyes*›

fatigue /fəˈtiːg/

A *n* [u] 1 (exhaustion) 疲劳 2 Tech [金属等的] 疲劳

B **fatigues** *npl* Mil 1 (clothing) 制服; **camouflage ~s** 迷彩服 2 (duties) 杂务

C *vt* (exhaust) 使疲惫不堪

fatigued /fəˈtiːgd/ *adj* 精疲力竭的

fatiguing /fəˈtiːgɪŋ/ *adj* 使人疲惫不堪的

fatless /ˈfætlɪs/ *adj* = **fat-free**

fatso /ˈfætsəʊ/ *n* colloq pej (man) 胖子; (woman) 肥婆

fat-soluble *adj* 脂溶的

fatten /ˈfætn/ *vt* 育肥 ‹*animal*›

Phrasal verb

• **fatten up** *vt* [**~ up sb./sth., ~ sb./sth. up**] 使…长肥

fattening /ˈfætnɪŋ/

A *adj* 使人发胖的 ‹*food*›

B *n* [u] 育肥

fattism /ˈfætɪzəm/ *n* [u] colloq 肥胖歧视

fatty /ˈfæti/

A *adj* 1 (containing fat) 脂肪的 ‹*tissue, deposit*›; **~ degeneration** 脂肪变性 2 (covered in fat) 富含脂肪的 ‹*chips, bacon, cooking*›; **~ food** 高脂食物

B *n* colloq pej (man) 胖子; (woman) 肥婆

fatty acid *n* 脂肪酸

fatuity /fəˈtjuːəti, Amer -ˈtuːəti/ *n* [u] 愚蠢昏庸

fatuous /ˈfætʃʊəs/ *adj* 愚蠢昏庸的

fatuousness /ˈfætʃʊəsnɪs/ *n* [u] 愚蠢昏庸

fatwa /ˈfætwɑː/ *n* 法特瓦 [伊斯兰国家的圣令]

faucet /ˈfɔːsɪt/ *n* Amer 水龙头

fault /fɔːlt/

A *n* 1 (defect) 缺点; **for all his ~s, he is very likeable** 尽管他有很多缺点，还是非常讨人

喜欢; **a structural/an electrical ~** 结构缺陷/电路故障; **to a ~** 过分地; **she is generous to a ~** 她过分慷慨 2 (responsibility, mistake) 过错; **it's her ~ that we're late** 我们迟到都怪她; **it happened through no ~ of mine** 发生这事错不在我; **to find ~ with sb./sth.** 找某人/某事物的错; **you're always finding ~** 你总是找岔子; **to be at ~ (in doing sth.)** (做某事) 有过错; **my memory was at ~** 我记错了; **you were at ~ in leaving it unlocked** 你没把它锁上是有责任的 3 Sport (in tennis) 发球失误; **to serve a (double) ~** (两次) 发球失误 4 Geol 断层

B *vt* 挑…的错; **I couldn't ~ his performance** 我认为他的表现无可挑剔; **you can't ~ him for being late — it was the traffic** 你不能指责他迟到——那是交通拥堵的原因

fault: ~-finder *n* 挑剔的人; **~-finding** *n* [u] 1 (criticism) 找茬儿; 2 Tech 故障检测

faultless /ˈfɔːltlɪs/ *adj* 无可挑剔的

faultlessly /ˈfɔːltlɪsli/ *adv* 无可挑剔地

fault: ~ line *n* 断层线; **~ plane** *n* 断层面

faulty /ˈfɔːlti/ *adj* 1 (defective) 有缺陷的 ‹*machine, system, wiring*› 2 (flawed, fallacious) 错误的 ‹*reasoning, argument*›; 靠不住的 ‹*memory, thinking*›

faun /fɔːn/ *n* 农牧神 [人身羊头的虚构动物]

fauna /ˈfɔːnə/ *n* [u and c] [某地区或某时期的] 动物群

faux pas /ˌfəʊ ˈpɑː/ *n* (*pl* **faux pas**) 失礼

favour Brit, **favor** Amer /ˈfeɪvə(r)/

A *n* 1 [u] (approval) 赞同; **to look on sth. with ~** *or* **to look with ~ on sth.** 赞同某事物; **to win ~ with sb.** *or* **to win sb.'s ~** 赢得某人的好感; **I tried in vain to win her ~** 我试图赢得她的芳心, 但没有成功; **to lose ~ with sb.** *or* **to lose sb.'s ~** 失去某人的好感; **he has lost ~ with the boss** 他已在老板面前失宠; **to find ~ (with sb./in sb.'s eyes)** (be approved of) 得到 (某人的) 赞同; (be liked) 受到 (某人的) 喜爱; **the proposal didn't find ~ with the workforce** 该提议没有得到劳工的支持; **ideas that are finding increasing ~ with young people** 越来越受年轻人青睐的观念; **he found ~ with the king** 他得到国王的宠信; **to fall from** *or* **out of ~ (with sb.)** (stop being approved of) 不再得到 (某人的) 赞同; (stop being liked) 不再受到 (某人的) 喜爱; **she has fallen out of ~ with the party leadership** 她已经失去了政党领导人的支持; **to be in/out of ~ with sb.** *or* **to be in/out of sb.'s ~** (be approved/disapproved of) 得到/不再得到某人的赞同; (be liked/disliked) 受到/不再受到某人的喜爱; (be in/out of fashion) 在某些人中流行/不再流行; **how can I get back into his ~?** 我怎样才能再次赢得他的好感?; **to be in ~ of sb./sth.** 赞同某人/某事物; **to be in ~ of sb. doing sth.** 赞同某人做某事; **all those in ~, raise your hands** 赞成的人请举手; **he spoke in ~ of the motion** 他发表讲话, 支持这项动议; **she hasn't got a word to say in her daughter-in-law's ~** 她从不夸奖她的儿媳妇 2 [u] (preferential treatment) 特殊照顾; **to show ~ to sb.** *or* **to show sb. ~** 偏袒某人 3 [u] (advantage) 好处; **the exchange rate is in your ~ at the moment** 现在的汇率对你有利; **he had youth and good looks in his ~** 他年轻英俊, 讨人喜欢; **the odds are in ~ of a June election** 6 月份举行选举的可能性较大; **the decision went in their ~** 这个决定对他们有利; **he turned down a well-paid job in ~ of voluntary work** 他放弃了待遇优厚的工作, 选择做志愿者 4 ▸ **p. 818** [c] (kindness) 善意行为; **she agreed to stay as a ~ to her father** 她同意留下是给她父亲一个面子; **to ask sb. a ~** *or* **to ask a ~ of sb.** 请某人帮个忙; **to do sb. a ~** *or* **to do a ~ for sb.** 帮某人一个忙; **you're not doing anyone any ~s by working all this unpaid overtime** 你加班加点还不要报酬, 这对任何人都没有好处; **do me a ~!** Brit colloq 得了吧!; **do yourself a ~ and stop smoking** 善待自己, 别再抽烟了; **to return a ~** 报答恩惠; **to owe sb. a ~** 欠某人一个人情 5 **favours** dated 同意性交

B *vt* 1 (prefer) 较喜欢; **the prime minister seems to ~ an October election** 首相似乎倾向于在 10 月举行选举; **she ~s trousers for warmth** 为了保暖, 她更喜欢穿裤子; **I ~ the Welsh team** 我支持威尔士队 2 (approve of) 赞同 ‹*proposal, plan*› 3 (treat preferentially) 偏袒; **teachers often ~ their brightest pupils** 老师们常常偏爱那些最聪明的学生 4 liter (prove advantageous to) 有利于; **the wind ~ed our voyage northwards** 我们向北航行是顺风的 5 formal (oblige) 赐予; **I should be grateful if you would ~ me with a prompt reply** 若蒙立即赐复, 鄙人将不胜感激; **do you think Paul will ~ us with his presence today?** iron 你认为保罗今天会赏光出席吗? 6 dated (resemble) 长得像; **he ~s his father** 他长得像他父亲

favourable Brit, **favorable** Amer /ˈfeɪvərəbl/ *adj* 1 (positive, good) 肯定的; **the book has had a number of ~ reviews** 这本书得到了许多好评; **I hope the reply will be ~** 我希望得到肯定的答复; **you made a ~ impression on the examiners** 你给考官留下了好印象; **they tried to present the organization in a ~ light** 他们试图展示这个机构的正面形象 2 *usu pred* (in agreement) 赞同的; **to be ~ to sth./sb. doing sth.** 赞同某物/某人做某事; **was she ~ to the suggestion?** 她赞成这个建议吗?; **my brother is not ~ to my borrowing his car** 我哥哥不同意我借他的车 3 (promising) 有利的; **she seems to have got her appetite back — that's a ~ sign** 她似乎又有了食欲——那是个好迹象; **this is a ~ result for the Italian team** 这个结果对意大利队有利 4 (suitable) 合适的; **~ weather for a picnic** 适合野餐的天气; **a ~ wind** 顺风; **to be ~ for** *or* **to doing sth.** 适合做某事

favourably Brit, **favorably** Amer /ˈfeɪvərəbli/ *adv* 1 (positively) 正面地; **he is ~ regarded by the board of directors** 他得到了董事会的赞许; **the book was ~ reviewed** 该书得到了好评; **his suggestions were ~ received** 他的建议被采纳了; **to react ~ to sth.** 对某事物反应积极; **to be ~ disposed to** *or* **towards sb./sth.** (like) 喜欢某人/某事物; (approve of, agree or consent to) 赞同某人/某事物 2 (well) 很好地; **I was ~ impressed by her performance** 她的表演给我留下了很好的印象; **to compare ~ with sth.** 与某事物相比好多了 3 (suitably) 合适地; **you couldn't have timed your resignation more ~** 你辞职的时机把握得再好不过了; **he is ~ placed to take action** 他占据了采取行动的有利位置

favoured Brit, **favored** Amer /ˈfeɪvəd/ *adj* 1 (preferred) 优先的; **privatization is the ~ option** 私有化是首选; **a ~ explanation** 更可取的解释; **the ~ candidate** 公众喜爱的候选人 2 (favourite) 受到偏爱的; **his ~ daughter** 他宠爱的那个女儿; **she is one of the ~ few** 她是少数受宠的人之一

favourite Brit, **favorite** Amer /ˈfeɪvərɪt/

A *adj attrib* 最喜欢的; **who's your ~ writer?** 你最喜欢的作家是谁?

B *n* 1 (favourite thing) 最喜爱的事物; (favourite person) 最喜爱的人; **this film is a great ~ of his** 这部电影是他特别喜爱的; **an old ~** 一直最喜欢的东西; **to be sb.'s ~** 是某人的最爱; **he is always a ~ with children** 他总是极受孩子们的喜爱 2 Sport 最有希望获胜者; **he is the ~ in the 100 metres** 他是 100 米赛夺冠呼声最高的选手

favourite son *n* 1 (successful man) 家乡的骄子 2 Amer (preferred candidate) 本州支持的总统候选人

favouritism Brit, **favoritism** Amer /ˈfeɪvərɪtɪzəm/ *n* [u] 偏爱

fawn¹ /fɔːn/ ▸ **p. 134**

A *n* 1 [c] Zool [未满一岁的] 幼鹿 2 [u] (colour) 浅黄褐色

B *adj* 浅黄褐色的

fawn² *vi* 1 (show affection) ‹*dog*› 摇尾乞怜; **to ~ on sb.** ‹*dog*› 向某人表示亲热 2 pej (flatter) ‹*courtier, hangers-on*› 讨好; **to ~ on sb.** 讨好某人

fawning /ˈfɔːnɪŋ/ *adj attrib* pej 阿谀奉承的

fax /fæks/

A *n* 1 [c] (copy) 传真件 2 [u] (method) 传真

B *vt* (contact by fax) 用传真联系; (send by fax) 用传真机发送; **to ~ sth. to sb.** 把某物用传真发送给某人

fax: ~ directory *n* 传真号码簿; **~ machine** *n* 传真机; **~ message** *n* 传真件; **~ number** *n* 传真号码

faze /feɪz/ *vt* colloq 烦扰

FBI *abbr* Amer = **Federal Bureau of Investigation**

> **the FBI**
>
> 联邦调查局, 全称 the Federal Bureau of Investigation。美国负责国内安全和情报的机关, 隶属于司法部 (Department of Justice)。主要职能包括调查触犯联邦法律的犯罪活动、反间谍及反恐等。成立于 1908 年, 始称调查局 (Bureau of Investigation), 1935 年 3 月改为现名。总部位于华盛顿, 在全国各地设有分支机构。局长 (director) 的任命需由总统提名, 经参议院批准, 任期最长 10 年。历史上最著名的局长为埃德加・胡佛 (Edgar Hoover)。

FCO *abbr* Brit = **Foreign and Commonwealth Office**

FDA *abbr* Amer = **Food and Drug Administration**

FE *abbr* Brit = **further education; ~ college** 进修学院

fealty /ˈfiːəlti/ *n* [u] Hist [对领主的] 忠诚; **to take an oath of ~** 宣誓效忠

fear /fɪə(r)/

A *n* 1 [u] (dread, fright) 害怕; **to show no ~** 毫无惧色; **to be unable to speak for** *or* **from ~** 吓得说不出话来; **to have a ~ of heights** 恐高; **have no ~!** liter or hum 别怕!; **he went about in ~ and trembling** 他战战兢兢地四处走动; **without ~ or favour** 不偏不倚地; **for ~ of** *or* **that ...** 唯恐…; **she hid away for ~ of being punished** *or* **punishment** 她因害怕受罚而躲起来了; **she said nothing, for ~ that he would be angry** 她什么也没说, 怕他生气; **to live** *or* **go in ~ of one's life** 一直害怕自己有生命危险 2 [c] (worry, apprehension) 担忧; **to have ~ for the future** 对未来忧心忡忡 3 [u] (reverent awe) 敬畏; **to put the ~ of God into sb.** 恐吓某人 4 [u] (possibility) 可能性; **there's not much ~ of her getting married soon** 她不太可能很快就结婚; **no ~!** colloq 绝不!

B *vt* 1 (be afraid of) 害怕; **to ~ death** 怕死; **he's a man to be ~ed** 他是个让人畏惧的人; **to ~ to do sth.** 害怕做某事; **he ~ed to speak in her presence** 在她面前他不敢说话; ▸ **angel 1** 2 (be worried about) 担忧; **I ~ (that) she may be dead** 我担心她可能已经死了; **we ~ the worst** 我们担心会发生最坏的情况; **she ~s our getting involved** 她担心我们受到牵连 3 (think) 恐怕; **is there any hope of their survival? — I ~ not** 他们还有幸存的希望吗? ——恐怕没有了; **is she seriously ill? — I ~ so** 她病得很重吗? ——我想是的; **you will be disappointed, I ~** 恐怕你会失望 4 (revere) 敬畏 ‹*God, deity*›

C *vi* formal 担忧; **to ~ for sb./sth.** 为某人/某事物担心; **I ~ for her health/safety** 我担心她的健康/安全; **never ~!** colloq 别怕!

fearful /ˈfɪəfl/ *adj* 1 (anxious) 担忧的 ‹*person, expression*›; **to be ~ of sb./sth.** 对某人/某事物担忧; **to be ~ for sb./sth.** 担心某人/某事物 2 (dreadful) 可怕的 ‹*noise, accident*› 3 fig colloq (very great) 极大的 ‹*nuisance, rage, heat*›; (very unpleasant) 极其烦人的 ‹*argument*›

fearfully /ˈfɪəfəli/ *adv* 1 (in fear) 胆怯地 ‹*cower, tremble*› 2 fig (terribly) 非常 ‹*late, hot*›; **I was ~ hungry** 我饿极了

fearless /ˈfɪəlɪs/ *adj* 无畏的

fearlessly /ˈfɪəlɪsli/ *adv* 无畏地

fearlessness /ˈfɪəlɪsnɪs/ *n* [u] 无畏

fearsome /ˈfɪəsəm/ *adj* 1 (frightening) 骇人的 ‹*sight, monster*›; (formidable) 惊人的 ‹*size*› 2 (very unpleasant) 十分讨厌的 ‹*business, task*›

feasibility /ˌfiːzəˈbɪləti/ *n* [u] 可行性

feasibility study *n* 可行性研究

feasible /ˈfiːzəbl/ *adj* 1 (practicable) 可行的 ‹*option, solution*› 2 colloq (probable) 可能的 ‹*explanation, excuse*›

feast /fiːst/
A *n* 1 (sumptuous meal) 盛宴; (formal, celebratory meal) 宴会; **enough is as good as a ~** 足食犹如筵席 [知足常乐之意]; **~ or famine** 不是太多就是太少 2 fig (for eyes, senses) 赏心悦目; **a ~ of music** 一场音乐的盛宴 3 Relig 节日; **a ~ day** 宗教节日
B *vi* 山吃海喝; **to ~ on** *or* **off sth.** 尽情享用某物
C *vt* 1 lit 设宴招待; **to ~ sb. on** *or* **with sth.** 用某物款待某人 2 fig 使…尽情享受 ‹*mind*›; **to ~ one's eyes on sth.** 尽情欣赏某物

feat /fiːt/ *n* 功绩; **a ~ of engineering** 非凡的工程

feather /ˈfeðə(r)/
A *n* 羽毛; **that's a ~ in your cap** fig 那是你值得骄傲的地方; **you could have knocked me down with a ~** fig 我惊讶得目瞪口呆; **that'll make the ~s fly** fig 这会引起争端; **to smooth ruffled ~s** fig 劝解
B *modif* 羽毛做的 ‹*boa*›; **a ~ mattress** 羽毛床垫
C *vt* 1 (in fixed expressions) **to ~ one's (own) nest** pej 中饱私囊; **to tar and ~ sb.** 严厉惩罚某人 2 (in rowing) 使…与水面平行 ‹*oar*› 3 Aviat 使…顺流交距 ‹*engine, propeller*›

feather: ~ bed *n* 羽毛褥垫; **~-bed** *vt* Brit 使…安逸 ‹*employee, staff*›; **~-brained** *adj* pej 呆头呆脑的; **~ duster** *n* 羽毛掸子

featherweight /ˈfeðəweɪt/
A *n* 次轻量级运动员
B *modif* 次轻量级的

feathery /ˈfeðəri/ *adj* 1 (light and soft) 轻软的 2 (in appearance) 羽毛状的

feature /ˈfiːtʃə(r)/
A *n* 1 (distinctive characteristic) 特征 2 (aspect) 方面; **to have no redeeming ~s** 没有可取之处 3 (of face) 面部特征; **with sharp ~s** 五官轮廓分明; **with coarse ~s** 面容粗犷 4 (of product) 附加部件; **built-in safety ~s** 内置的安全部件 5 Comm (special attraction) 特色商品 6 Cin (film) 正片 7 Journ (article) 特写; **she does a ~ in the Times** 她在《泰晤士报》撰写专题文章 8 TV, Radio 专题节目
B *vt* 1 (present) 突出介绍 ‹*article, interview*›; 由…主唱 ‹*singer, group*›; 以…为主打 ‹*song*›; 由…主演 ‹*actor*› 2 (have as a feature) «*machine, car*» 以…为特色 ‹*facility*›; **this model ~s several extras** 这个型号有好几个选配件
C *vi* 1 (figure) «*item, dish*» 占据重要位置; **to ~ in sth.** 在某事物中起重要作用; **several well-known names ~ on the list** 名单上有好几个著名人物 2 TV, Cin (perform) 出演主角; **to ~ in a new movie** 在一部新片中担任主角

feature: ~ article *n* 专题文章; **~ film** *n* 正片; **~-length** *adj* 与正片长度相当的

-featured /ˈfiːtʃəd/ *combining form* 有…面部特征的; **coarse~** 容貌粗犷的; **fine~** 眉清目秀的; **heavy~** 五官粗大的; **sharp~** 面部轮廓分明的

featureless /ˈfiːtʃəlɪs/ *adj* 无特色的

feature writer ▸p. 409 *n* 专栏作家

Feb /feb/ *abbr* = **February**

febrile /ˈfiːbraɪl/ *adj* 1 Med 发热的 ‹*patient, symptom*›; 发热引起的 ‹*cough*› 2 fig 狂热的 ‹*activity, behaviour*›

February /ˈfebrʊəri, Amer -ʊri/ ▸p. 490 *n* 二月; **last/this/next ~** 上个/本年/下个二月份; **in early/late ~** 二月上旬/下旬; **~ weather/morning** 二月的天气/早晨

fecal *adj* Amer = **faecal**

feces *npl* Amer = **faeces**

feckless /ˈfeklɪs/ *adj* 窝窝囊囊的 ‹*person, existence*›; 不负责任的 ‹*behaviour, attitude*›

fecund /ˈfiːkənd, ˈfekənd/ *adj* formal 多产的

Fed /fed/ *abbr* Amer 1 colloq (agent) 联邦政府官员 [尤指联邦调查局官员] 2 = **Federal Reserve**; **the ~** 联邦储备委员会

fed /fed/ *pt, pp* ▸**feed A, B**

federal /ˈfedərəl/ *adj* 1 Pol 联邦制的; **a country with a ~ system** 联邦制国家; **the ~ government** *or* **administration** Amer 联邦政府 2 Admin 联邦政府的 ‹*responsibility, level*›; **~ court** 联邦法院; **to make a ~ case out of sth.** Amer 过分夸大某事 3 **Federal** Amer Hist [南北战争时期] 北部联邦的

federal: F~ Bureau of Investigation *n* Amer 联邦调查局; **F~ Communications Commission** *n* Amer 联邦通讯委员会; **~ holiday** *n* Amer 法定假日

federalism /ˈfedərəlɪzəm/ *n* [u] (principle) 联邦主义; (system) 联邦制

federalist /ˈfedərəlɪst/
A *adj* 联邦主义的
B *n* 联邦主义者

Federal Land Bank *n* Amer 联邦土地银行

federally /ˈfedərəli/ *adv* Amer 由联邦政府

federal: F~ Republic of Germany *n* 德意志联邦共和国; **F~ Reserve** *n* Amer 联邦储备银行; **F~ Reserve System** *n* Amer 联邦储备系统; **F~ Trade Commission** *n* Amer 联邦贸易委员会

federate
A /ˈfedəreɪt/ *vi* 结成同盟
B /ˈfedəreɪt/ *vt* 使结成同盟
C *adj* /ˈfed(ə)rət/ 同盟的 ‹*armies, structure*›

federation /ˌfedəˈreɪʃn/ *n* 1 [c] (of states) 联邦 2 [c] (of clubs, societies) 联合会 3 [u] (action) 结盟

fedora /fɪˈdɔːrə/ *n* 浅顶软呢帽

fed up *adj pred* colloq (annoyed) 厌烦的; (discontented) 不愉快的; **to be ~ with sb./sth.** 对某人/某事物感到厌烦; **to be ~ to the (back) teeth** 烦透了; **to be ~ about sth.** 对某事感到不开心

fee /fiː/ *n* 1 (for professional, artistic service) 服务费; **for a ~** 有偿地 2 (for admission, membership) 费; **an annual membership ~** 年会费; **a registration ~** 注册费

feeble /ˈfiːbl/ *adj* 1 (weak) 有气无力的 ‹*person, gesture, movement*›; 虚弱的 ‹*brain, mind*›; 微弱的 ‹*pulse, light*› 2 (unconvincing) 站不住脚的 ‹*argument, excuse*›; 干巴巴的 ‹*performance, joke*›; 无益的 ‹*attempt*› 3 (spineless) 懦弱的 ‹*person*›

feeble-minded *adj* 1 (stupid) 愚笨的 2 (indecisive) 优柔寡断的

feebleness /ˈfiːblnɪs/ *n* [u] 1 (of person, gesture, movement) 有气无力; (of pulse, light) 微弱 2 (of argument, excuse) 无效

feebly /ˈfiːbli/ *adv* 1 (weakly, faintly) 乏力地 ‹*move, struggle*›; 轻微地 ‹*cry*› 2 (unconvincingly) 无说服力地 ‹*defend, protest*› 3 (spinelessly) 懦弱地 ‹*give in, accept*›

feed /fiːd/
A *vt* (*pt, pp* **fed**) 1 (supply with food) 给…食物; **to ~ a dog** 喂狗; **to ~ a large family/an army** 养活一大家人/一支军队; **I ~ the children on baked beans** 我给孩子们吃烘豆; **the child can ~ himself with a spoon** 这孩子能用勺子自己吃东西了; ▸**bite A1** 2 (give as food) 用…喂 ‹*food*›; 喂 ‹*person, animal*›; **she was ~ing bread to the birds** 她在用面包喂鸟; **to ~ the baby some more apple** 给婴儿再喂一点苹果 3 (supply) 供给; **the lake is fed by several rivers** 这湖是由几条河汇流而成的; **how is the printer fed with paper?** 这台打印机怎么进纸?; **a spy who fed secrets to his government** 一个为政府提供秘密情报的间谍; **to ~ coins into a meter** 把硬币投入停车计时收费器 4 fig (satisfy) 满足; (fuel) 助长; **to ~ a drug habit** 满足毒瘾; **this letter merely fed the flame of his passion** liter 这封信只是让他的激情更加高涨 5 Sport 传球给 ‹*player*›; 传 ‹*balls*›; **he fed the forwards a flow of passes** 他给前锋接连传了好几个球 6 Theat colloq 给…提词 ‹*actor*›
B *vi* (*pt, pp* **fed**) (take nourishment) 进食; **she had the infant ~ing at her breast** 她给婴儿哺乳; **to ~ on** *or* **off sth.** lit 以某物为食; fig 从某事物中得到滋养; **the horses usually ~ on oats** 这些马通常以燕麦为食; **vanity ~s on flattery** 奉承助长虚荣
C *n* 1 (meal for babies or animals) 一餐; **the baby was having five ~s a day** 这个婴儿那时一天要喂 5 次; **to give the horse a ~ of oats** 给马喂一次燕麦 2 Agric 饲料 3 colloq (hearty meal) 丰盛的一餐; **to have a good ~** 饱餐一顿 4 Tech (material) 进料; (pipe, channel) 进料装置; **the petrol ~ is blocked** 进油管堵住了; **sheet paper ~** Comput 进纸装置 5 Theat colloq (prompt) 提词; (actor) 提词员

Phrasal verbs

- **feed back** *vt* [**~ sth. back, ~ back sth.**] 反馈; **to ~ sth. back to sb.** 把某事物反馈给某人; **the results of the questionnaire were fed back to Head Office** 问卷调查的结果反馈给了总公司
- **feed in** *vt* [**~ sth. in, ~ in sth.**] 放入; **you ~ the paper in at this end** 你从这一端把纸放进去
- **feed up** *vt* [**~ up sb./sth., ~ sb./sth. up**] 1 (nourish) 养壮 ‹*person*› 2 colloq (fatten) 喂肥 ‹*animal*›

feedback /ˈfiːdbæk/ *n* [u] 1 (information about result, response) 反馈信息; **~ about sth.** 有关某事物的反应 2 Comput 反馈 3 Audio 反馈噪声

feeder /ˈfiːdə(r)/
A *n* 1 (person, animal) 进食者 2 (bib) 围涎 3 Brit (bottle) 奶瓶 4 Transp **~ (road/canal)** 支路 5 Rail **~ (line)** 支线 6 (for animals, birds) 给食器 7 (for printer) 进纸器
B *modif* 汇入主干道的 ‹*lane, pipe*›; 汇入主流的 ‹*stream*›

feeder school, feeder primary *ns* 直属小学

feeding: ~ bottle *n* Brit 奶瓶; **~ stuffs** *npl* 饲料; **~ time** *n* 1 (for animals) 喂食时间; 2 (for babies) 喂奶时间

feed pipe *n* 进料管

feedstuffs *npl* 饲料

fee income *n* [u and c] 收费收入

feel /fiːl/
A *vt* (*pt, pp* **felt**) 1 (touch deliberately) 触摸; **he felt the bump on her head** 他摸了摸她头上的肿块; **to ~ the weight of sth.** 掂某物的重量; **the police felt him all over for weapons** 警察搜他全身查找武器; **I want to ~ how cold the water is** 我想摸摸水有多冷; **to ~ one's way** lit 摸索着走; fig 谨慎行事; **I felt my way towards the door/out of the room** 我摸索着走向房门/走出屋子; **she's only just started this job: she's still ~ing**

f

her way (around) fig 她刚开始做这项工作，还在摸索着干 2 colloq (fondle) 抚弄; **to ~ oneself** 手淫; **to ~ sb. up** sl 猥亵某人 3 (have sensation of, be aware of) 感觉到; **he couldn't ~ anything in his left leg** 他的左腿失去了知觉; **he felt sth. crawling up his arm** 他觉得有东西顺着胳膊往上爬; **I can ~ a nail sticking into my shoe** 我感到有钉子扎进了鞋子; **she could ~ the warmth of the sun on her naked body** 她赤裸的身体感受到了阳光的温暖; **he likes to ~ the wind on his face** 他喜欢风吹在脸上的感觉; **she felt herself blush** 她感到自己脸红了; **I felt myself falling** 我觉得自己在往下掉; **I could ~ him staring at me** 我感到他在盯着我看; **I could ~ the tension in the room** 我感觉到了房间里的紧张气氛; **they don't ~ the necessity of paying their taxes** 他们觉得没有必要交税 4 (be affected physically) 对…有切身感受; **she really ~s the cold** 她很怕冷; **I'm ~ing the heat today** 今天我觉得特别热 5 (be affected emotionally) 意识到; **I felt a tremendous sense of loss** 我感到茫然不知所措; **he felt no bitterness towards her** 他一点儿都不恨她; **the loyalty I ~ to my former employer** 我对前一任雇主的耿耿忠心; **she no longer ~s anything for him** 她对他一点感觉都没有了; **I felt a sudden urge to jump into the water** 我突然很想跳进水里; **he felt the loss of his son very deeply** 他深陷丧子之痛; **the effects of the recession are being felt everywhere** 经济衰退的影响无处不在; **she'll ~ it when she has to do all her own cooking and cleaning** 当她不得不自己洗衣做饭时，她将体会到其中的辛苦 6 (think) 认为; **I felt his plan to be impractical** 我认为他的计划不切实际; **she felt she would succeed this time** 她相信自己这次会成功; **she felt that she had seen him before** 她觉得以前见过他

B *vi* (*pt, pp* **felt**) 1 (search with hand etc.) 摸索; **she felt in her bag for the key** 她在包里摸索着找钥匙; **she felt for the ledge with her foot** 她用脚探找岩石的突出部; **to feel around** *or* **about for sth.** 四处摸索寻找某物 2 (be capable of sensation) (physically) 有感觉; (emotionally) 有感情; **the dead cannot ~** 死人没有知觉 3 (give sensation) 给人…的感觉; **this bag ~s lighter than that one** 这个袋子给人的感觉比那个轻; **how does your leg ~? — a bit better** 你的腿感觉怎么样？——好点了; **it ~s cold/warm in here** 这儿很冷/暖和; **it ~s cooler today** 今天感觉凉快了一些; **it ~s like leather** 它摸上去像是皮革; **it ~s (to me) as if the bone is broken** （我）摸上去骨头好像断了; **it ~s like snow** *or* **as if it's going to snow** 好像要下雪; **it was only February, but it felt like April** 现在才 2 月份，但感觉是 4 月份了; **every day will ~ like Saturday when you've retired** 退休后，你会觉得每天都像星期六 4 (experience physically or emotionally) 感觉; **how are you ~ing?** *or* **how do you ~?** 你感觉怎么样？; **I don't ~ hungry** 我不觉得饿; **you're (only) as old as you ~** 心态有多年轻，你就有多年轻; **I felt as if I was going to be sick** 我感觉像要生病了; **how does it ~ to be a father?** 做父亲的感觉如何？; **to ~ oneself** 觉得身体好; **she doesn't ~ herself today** 她今天觉得身体不舒服; **I felt touched by their concern** 他们的关心让我感动; **I ~ (like) a fool in this costume** 穿这身衣服让我觉得自己像个傻瓜; **they made me ~ like a princess** 他们让我觉得自己像个公主; **he still ~s angry about it** 他对此仍然感到生气; **I ~ sure I've seen him somewhere before** 我敢肯定我以前在什么地方见过他; **I felt afraid to refuse** 我不敢拒绝; **how do you ~ about Sarah?** (do you love her) 你对萨拉有感觉吗？; (what do you think of her) 你觉得萨拉人怎么样？; **how do you ~ about capital punishment?** 你对死刑有什么看法？; **I don't ~ very strongly about it** 我对这件事不太在乎; **he ~s strongly about giving money to charity** 他对捐钱给慈善机构态度鲜明; **I didn't know you felt that way about it** 我不知道你对此有那种想法; **if that's the way she ~s, I won't offer to help again** 如果她那么想的话，我再也不会主动帮忙了; **I felt as though nobody cared** 我感觉好像没人在乎; **it ~s to me as though we're wasting our time** 我觉得我们好像在浪费时间 5 (be in the mood for) **to ~ like sth./doing sth.** 想要某物/做某事; **I ~ like a cup of tea/taking a nap** 我想喝杯茶/打个盹; **why didn't you go with them? — I didn't ~ like it** 你为什么不和他们一起走？——我不愿意; **sometimes I cycle to work, sometimes I walk: it all depends on what I ~ like** *or* **how I ~** 我有时骑车上班，有时走路去：完全取决于我的心情

C *n* 1 (act of touching) 触摸; **to have a ~ (of sth.)** *or* **give (sth.) a ~** 触摸（某物）; **he had a ~ in his pockets for his key** 他在口袋里摸钥匙; **let me have a ~** 让我摸一下 2 (sensation to the touch) 触觉; **you can tell it's leather by the ~ (of it)** 你一摸就知道它是皮的; **the rock was warm to the ~** 这块岩石摸上去热乎乎的; **she likes the ~ of the sun on her face** 她喜欢太阳照在脸上的感觉 3 (atmosphere, impression) 气氛; **I didn't like the ~ of the place** 我不喜欢这地方的气氛; **the cottage had a welcoming ~ about it** 这间村舍令人感到舒适; **it has the ~ of a French village** 它给人一种法国村庄的印象 4 (aptitude) 天赋; **to have a ~ for language** 有语言天赋; **she has a ~ for handling difficult people** 她天生善于同难缠的人打交道 5 (familiarity, understanding) 熟悉; **to get the ~ of sth./doing sth.** 开始熟悉某事物/做某事; **it takes a while to get the ~ of operating a different machine** 想要熟练操作另一台机器是要花时间的

Phrasal verbs

- **feel for** *vt* [**~ for sb.**] 同情
- **feel out** *vt* [**~ out sth., ~ sth. out**] colloq 把…摸清楚; **to ~ out the situation** 摸清形势
- **feel up to** *vt* [**~ up to sth.**] 有精力做; **I don't ~ up to cooking tonight** 我今晚没精力做饭; **after the accident she didn't ~ up to driving** 那次事故后，她不敢开车了

feeler /ˈfiːlə(r)/ *n* 1 (sense organ) 触角 2 fig (tentative proposal) 试探手段; **to put out ~s** 试探

feeler gauge *n* 测隙规

feelgood /ˈfiːlgʊd/ *adj attrib* 使人愉悦的; **the ~ factor** 愉悦感; **a ~ movie** 让人感到幸福美满的影片

feeling /ˈfiːlɪŋ/

A *n* 1 [u] (sense of touch) 触觉; **I've lost all ~ in my left foot** 我的左脚完全失去了知觉 2 [c] (physical sensation) 感觉; **I was aware of an itchy ~ at the back of my neck** 我感到脖子后面一阵发痒; **a ~ of warmth spread throughout her body** 一股暖意传遍她的全身; **I had a ~ of tightness in my chest** 我的胸部觉得憋闷 3 [c] (emotional or mental sensation) 感触; **I know the ~** colloq 我感同身受; **there never seems to be any money left at the end of the month — I know the ~** 每到月底似乎就没钱了——我也是; **they don't listen to a word I say — I know the ~** 他们对我说的话一句都不听——我也有同感; **his response gave her an uneasy ~** 他的反应让她感到不安; **a ~ of satisfaction** 满足感; **she had no ~s of regret** 她没有任何悔意 4 [u] (emotion) 情感; **the conflict between ~ and reason** 情感与理智的冲突; **he has a great deal of ~ for her** 他对她感情很深; **to put a bit more ~ into it** 多投入一点感情进去; **she plays the piano with great ~** 她演奏钢琴时十分投入 5 [u] (sensitivity) 感受; **a person of ~** 一个善感的人; **to have a ~ for sb.** 同情某人; **she has no ~ for others** 她对别人没有同情心 6 **feelings** *pl* (emotional responses) 感情; **to hurt sb.'s ~s** 伤害某人的感情; **to spare sb.'s ~s** 不使某人难过; **to hide/show one's ~s** 隐藏/表露自己的感情; **she doesn't seem to have any maternal ~s** 她似乎没有一点儿母性 7 [u] (instinct) 直觉; **she doesn't have much ~ for the beauty of nature** 她对大自然的美缺少鉴赏力 8 [u and c] (sentiment) 强烈情绪; **she spoke with ~ about the issue of equality** 她激动地谈论平等问题; **the council's decision has stirred up a lot of ~** 地方议会的决定激起了强烈反响; **~s are running high** 群情激愤 9 [u and c] (opinion) 意见; **popular ~** 公众的意见; **my own ~ is that it is too expensive** 我个人认为它太贵了; **what are your ~s on the matter?** 你对这事是什么态度？ 10 [c] (notion) 想法; **I've a ~ I forgot to lock the door** 我觉得我忘了锁门; **I had a ~ about her right from the start** 我从一开始就对她有看法; **I've got a bad ~ about this trip** 我对这次旅行有种不祥的预感; **I get the ~ that he doesn't like me** colloq 我觉得他不喜欢我 11 [c] (atmosphere) 气氛; **the house had a homely ~** 这房子给人一种温馨的感觉

B *adj* 有同情心的; **she is very ~ about other people** 她对他人极富同情心; **that wasn't a very ~ thing to say** 那么说可不太地道

feelingly /ˈfiːlɪŋli/ *adv* 1 (in a heartfelt way) 激动地; **he spoke ~ about environmental pollution** 他谈起环境污染问题时激动不已 2 (in a sympathetic way) 同情地

fee-paying *adj* 收费的 ‹*school*›

feet /fiːt/ *pl* ▸ **foot A**

feign /feɪn/ *vt* formal 假装

feint /feɪnt/

A *vi* 做假动作

B *n* 假动作

C *adj* 有隐格线的

feint-ruled *adj* 有隐格的; **~ paper** 隐格纸

feisty /ˈfaɪsti/ *adj* colloq 精神头十足的 ‹*woman*›; 好斗的 ‹*underdog*›

feldspar /ˈfeldspɑː(r)/ *n* [u] 长石

felicitations /fəˌlɪsɪˈteɪʃnz/ *npl* formal 祝贺; **~ on ...** 对…的祝贺

felicitous /fəˈlɪsɪtəs/ *adj* formal 恰当的 ‹*remark, example*›; 令人愉悦的 ‹*choice*›

felicity /fəˈlɪsəti/ *n* [u] formal 1 (appropriateness) 得体 2 (happiness) 幸福

feline /ˈfiːlaɪn/

A *adj* 1 (of or relating to the cat family) 猫科动物的 ‹*disease, behaviour*› 2 (cat-like) 似猫的 ‹*features, grace*›; **an irresistible ~ charm** 一种不可抗拒的娇柔魅力

B *n* 猫科动物

fell[1] /fel/ *pt, pp* ▸ **fall A**

fell[2] *vt* 1 (cut down) 砍伐 ‹*tree, forest*› 2 (knock down) 击倒 ‹*opponent, attacker*›

fell[3] *n* Brit [英格兰北部的] 荒野

fell[4] *adj* **with** *or* **at** *or* **in one ~ swoop** *or* **blow** 一下子

fellatio /fəˈleɪʃɪəʊ/ *n* [u] 吮吸阴茎

fellow /ˈfeləʊ/

A *n* 1 (man) 男人; **a nice ~** 好人; **an old ~** 老兄 2 (of society) 会员 3 Brit Univ (lecturer) 讲师; (postgraduate) 研究生 4 colloq (boyfriend) 男朋友 5 **fellows** *pl* (peers) 同辈 (colleagues) 同事; (compatriots) 同胞

B *modif* 同类的; **~ students** 同学

fellow: ~ citizen *n* 同胞; **~ countryman** *n* 同胞; **~ countrywoman** *n* 同胞姐妹; **~ creature** *n* (living thing) 其他生物; (person) 他人; **~ drinker** *n* 酒友; **~ feeling** *n* [u] 同感; **~ human being** *n*

他人; ~ **man** *n* 他人; ~ **member** *n* 成员; ~ **passenger** *n* 旅伴

fellowship /ˈfeləʊʃɪp/ *n* 1 [u] (companionship) 友情 2 [c] (association) 团体; (religious association) 团契 3 [c] Univ (post) 研究员职位; (funding) 研究基金

fellow: ~ **traveller** *n* 1 lit 旅伴; 2 Pol 同路人 [尤指同情共产党的非党人士]; ~ **worker** *n* 同事

fell-walking *n* [u] Brit 荒野漫步

felon /ˈfelən/ *n* 重罪犯

felony /ˈfeləni/ *n* [u and c] 重罪

felspar /ˈfelspɑː(r)/ *n* = **feldspar**

felt¹ /felt/ *pt, pp* ▸ **feel A, B**

felt² *n* [u] 1 (cloth) 毛毡 2 (for roof insulation) 油毡

felt-tip, felt-tip pen *ns* 毡头笔

female /ˈfiːmeɪl/

A *adj* 1 Biol 女性的 ‹*athlete, voice, sexuality*›; 雌性的 ‹*animal, plant*›; **a ~ cat** 母猫 2 Elec, Tech 内孔的 ‹*connection*›

B *n* Biol (person) 女性; (animal) 雌性动物; (plant) 雌性植物

female: ~ **circumcision** *n* [u] 女性割礼; ~ **condom** *n* 女用避孕套

Femidom® /ˈfemɪdɒm/ = **female condom**

feminine /ˈfemənɪn/

A *adj* 1 (female) 女性的; **the ~ side of his nature** 他性格中的阴柔一面 2 (unmasculine) 像女人的 ‹*build, voice*›; **that costume makes him look very ~** 他穿那套戏装看上去很女性化 3 Ling 阴性的 ‹*gender, noun, form*›

B *n* Ling 阴性; (word) 阴性词; (form) 阴性形式; **an adjective in the ~** 阴性形容词

femininity /ˌfeməˈnɪnəti/ *n* [u] 1 (feminineness) 阴柔 2 (femaleness) 女性气质

feminism /ˈfemɪnɪzəm/ *n* [u] (political belief) 女权主义; (social movement) 女权运动

feminist /ˈfemɪnɪst/

A *adj* 女权主义的

B *n* 女权主义者

feminize /ˈfemɪnaɪz/ *vt* 使女性化

femoral /ˈfemərəl/ *adj attrib* 股骨的

femur /ˈfiːmə(r)/ *n* (*pl* ~**s** *or* **femora** /ˈfemərə/) 股骨

fen¹ /fen/

A *n* [c and u] 沼泽

B the Fens *pr npl* [英格兰东部的] 沼泽地区

fen² ▸**p. 174** *n* (*pl* **fen**) (Chinese monetary unit) 分 [中国货币名，10分等于1角]

fence /fens/

A *n* 1 (barrier) 栅栏; **to sit on the ~** 骑墙; **to mend (one's) ~s** 捐弃前嫌 2 (in show jumping, horse racing) 围栏 3 colloq (receiver of stolen goods) 窝藏赃物者

B *vt* 1 (enclose) 把…用栅栏围起来 ‹*land, garden*› 2 colloq (sell) 销售 ‹*stolen goods*›

C *vi* 击剑

Phrasal verbs

- **fence in** *vt* 1 [~ **sth. in,** ~ **in sth.**] (surround) 把…用栅栏围起来 ‹*land, monument*› 2 [~ **sb./sth. in**] lit 使…无法挪动 ‹*person, car*›; fig (restrict) 限制
- **fence off** *vt* [~ **sth. off,** ~ **off sth.**] 把…用栅栏隔开

fencer /ˈfensə(r)/ *n* 击剑运动员

fencing /ˈfensɪŋ/

A *n* [u] 1 ▸**p. 307** Sport 击剑运动 2 (fences) 栅栏

B *modif* 1 Sport 击剑运动的; ~ **teacher** 剑术教练; ~ **mask/match** 击剑面罩/比赛 2 (type of barrier) 筑栅栏的 ‹*material, contractor*›

fend /fend/ *vi* **to ~ for oneself** 照料自己

Phrasal verb

- **fend off** *vt* [~ **off sb./sth.,** ~ **sb./sth. off**] 1 lit 抵挡 ‹*person, animal*› 2 fig (evade) 回避 ‹*criticism*›

fender /ˈfendə(r)/ *n* 1 (for fire) 火炉围栏 2 Amer Aut (mudguard) 挡泥板 3 Naut 护舷垫

fender bender *n* Amer colloq 轻微车祸

feng shui /ˌfeŋˈʃuːi, ˌfʌŋˈʃweɪ/ *n* 风水

fennel /ˈfenl/ *n* [u] 茴香

fenugreek /ˈfenuːgriːk/ *n* [u] 胡芦巴

feral /ˈfɪərəl, Amer ˈferəl/ *adj* 野生的 ‹*animal, population*›; **the ~ instinct** 野性

Fermanagh /fəˈmænə/ *pr n* 弗马纳郡

ferment

A /fəˈment/ *vt* 1 lit 使发酵 2 fig 挑起 ‹*trouble, unrest*›

B /fəˈment/ *vi* 发酵

C /ˈfɜːment/ *n* [u] 动乱; **to be in ~** 处于动乱中

fermentation /ˌfɜːmenˈteɪʃn/ *n* [u and c] 发酵

fern /fɜːn/ *n* [u and c] (*pl* ~**s** *or* ~) 蕨类植物

ferocious /fəˈrəʊʃəs/ *adj* 1 (fierce) 凶猛的 ‹*animal, warrior*›; 猛烈的 ‹*attack, criticism*›; 激烈的 ‹*competition, battle*›; 凶恶的 ‹*expression*›; 残忍的 ‹*behaviour*›; 恶劣的 ‹*weather*› 2 (dangerous) 锋利凶险的 ‹*knife, dagger, point, spike*› 3 colloq (very strong) 强烈的 ‹*sun*›; **a ~ headache** 剧烈的头痛; **the midday heat was ~** 中午的高温酷热难当

ferociously /fəˈrəʊʃəsli/ *adv* 1 lit (fiercely) 凶猛地 ‹*bark*›; 猛烈地 ‹*fight, attack*›; fig 激烈地 ‹*argue, campaign*› 2 colloq (extremely) 非常 ‹*difficult, bright, hot*›; **a ~ ambitious journalist** 一位雄心勃勃的记者

ferocity /fəˈrɒsəti/ *n* [u] (physical) 凶猛; (verbal) 激烈

ferret /ˈferɪt/

A *n* 雪貂

B *vi* (*pres p etc.* **-tt-**) 1 Hunt 用雪貂狩猎; **to go ~ing** 带雪貂去狩猎 2 (search) 搜寻; **to ~ about** *or* **around (in/among/through sth.)** (在某物中) 到处搜寻

Phrasal verb

- **ferret out** *vt* [~ **sth. out,** ~ **out sth.**] 查获 ‹*secret, information, facts*›

Ferris wheel /ˈferɪs wiːl, Amer hwiːl/ *n* esp Amer = **big wheel**

ferroconcrete /ˌferəʊˈkɒŋkriːt/ *n* [u] 钢筋混凝土

ferrous /ˈferəs/ *adj* 含铁的

ferrule /ˈferuːl, Amer ˈferəl/ *n* (metal) [手杖等顶端的] 金属包头; (rubber) [手杖等顶端的] 橡皮包头

ferry /ˈferi/

A *n* (small rowing boat) 渡船; (larger boat for vehicles etc.) 渡轮; **by ~** 乘渡船

B *modif* 摆渡的 ‹*services, sailing times*›

C *vt* 运送 ‹*people, goods*›; **to ~ sb. to school/the station** 送某人去学校/车站

ferryman /ˈferɪmæn/ *n* (*pl* **ferrymen**) 渡船人

fertile /ˈfɜːtaɪl, Amer ˈfɜːrtl/ *adj* 1 (rich in nutrients) 肥沃的 ‹*land, valley, soil*› 2 (capable of reproduction) 能生育的 ‹*person*›; 可繁殖的 ‹*animal, plant*›; ~ **egg** 受精卵 3 fig (inventive) 有创造力的 ‹*brain, mind*›; 丰富的 ‹*imagination*› 4 fig (likely to produce success) 提供发展可能的 ‹*area, situation*›; **a ~ environment for criminal activity** 滋生犯罪的环境

fertility /fəˈtɪləti/

A *n* [u] 1 (of human) 生育能力; (of animal, plant, seed) 繁殖力; (of land) 肥沃 2 fig (of mind, imagination) 丰富性

B *modif* 生育的 ‹*symbol*›; ~ **cult/rite** 生殖崇拜/仪式; ~ **rates are still declining** 生育率仍在下降

fertility: ~ **drug** *n* [促进女性排卵的] 催孕药; ~ **treatment** *n* 不育治疗

fertilization /ˌfɜːtɪlaɪˈzeɪʃn, Amer -lɪˈz-/ *n* [u] 1 (of woman, animal, plant, egg) 受精 2 (of land, soil, plant) 施肥

fertilize /ˈfɜːtɪlaɪz/ *vt* 1 Biol 使…受精 ‹*egg, female*›; 使…受粉 ‹*plant*› 2 Agric, Hort 给…施肥 ‹*land, crop*›

fertilizer /ˈfɜːtɪlaɪzə(r)/ *n* [u and c] 肥料

fervent /ˈfɜːvənt/ *adj* 热诚的 ‹*admirer, speech*›; 虔诚的 ‹*believer, belief*›

fervently /ˈfɜːvəntli/ *adv* 热诚地 ‹*believe, hope*›; 强烈地 ‹*oppose, denounce*›; 虔诚地 ‹*pray*›

fervid /ˈfɜːvɪd/ *adj* 充满激情的 ‹*imagination*›

fervour Brit, **fervor** Amer /ˈfɜːvə(r)/ *n* [u] 热忱

fest /fest/ *n* 1 (festival) 节日; (gathering) 集会; **media/jazz/film ~** 媒体艺术节/爵士音乐节/电影节 2 fig colloq 盛会; **what a celeb ~!** 真是名流云集啊！

fester /ˈfestə(r)/ *vi* 1 lit «*wound, cut, sore*» 溃烂 2 fig «*situation*» 恶化; «*feelings, resentment*» 加剧; «*person*» 健康恶化

festival /ˈfestɪvl/ *n* 1 (day or period of celebration) 节日 2 (arts event) 艺术节

festive /ˈfestɪv/ *adj* 节日的 ‹*atmosphere, meal, decorations*›; **the ~ season** 圣诞节

festivity /feˈstɪvəti/

A *n* [u] 欢庆

B festivities *npl* 庆祝活动; **wedding festivities** 婚庆活动

festoon /feˈstuːn/ *vt* 装饰 ‹*tree, room, garden, building*›; 打扮 ‹*person*›; **to ~ sth. with sth.** 用某物装饰某物

feta /ˈfetə/ *n* [u] [原产于希腊的] 羊奶干酪

fetal /ˈfiːtl/ *adj* 胎儿的 ‹*development, abnormality*›; **the ~ position** 胎姿

fetch /fetʃ/ *vt* 1 (bring) 接来 ‹*person*›; 取来 ‹*object*›; **to ~ sth. for sb., to ~ sb. sth.** 为某人取某物; **to ~ and carry for sb.** 为某人跑腿 2 (bring financially) 售得 ‹*sum, amount*›; **to ~ a good price** 卖得好价 3 colloq (hit) 给以; **to ~ sb. a blow** 打某人一拳

Phrasal verbs

- **fetch in** *vt* [~ **sth. in,** ~ **in sth.**] colloq 接来 ‹*person, animal*›; 取来 ‹*chair, washing*›
- **fetch out** *vt* [~ **sth. out,** ~ **out sth.**] colloq 取出 ‹*object*›; 赶走 ‹*person, animal*›
- **fetch up** *vi* colloq (arrive) 无意中到达; (end up) 告终

fetching /ˈfetʃɪŋ/ *adj* 迷人的 ‹*person, smile, charm*›; 惹人喜爱的 ‹*dress, hat*›

fetchingly /ˈfetʃɪŋli/ *adv* 迷人地 ‹*smile, move, pretty*›; 讨人喜欢地 ‹*say, look*›

fête, fete /feɪt/

A *n* 1 Brit (fair) 义卖会 2 Amer (celebration) 庆祝会

B *vt* 盛情款待; **the Princess was ~d wherever she went** 公主所到之处都受到了热情款待

fetid /ˈfetɪd, Amer ˈfiːtɪd/ *adj* 恶臭的 ‹*water, air, breath*›

fetish /ˈfetɪʃ/ *n* 1 (object) 迷恋物 2 (sexual interest) 恋物 3 (excessive devotion) 痴迷; **to have a ~ about sth.** 对某物痴迷; **to make a ~ of sth.** 对某物痴迷

fetishism /ˈfetɪʃɪzəm/ *n* [u] 1 (sexual obsession) 恋物癖 2 Relig, Sociol (belief) 物神崇拜

fetlock /ˈfetlɒk/ *n* 1 (joint) 肢关节 2 (tuft of hair) 距毛

fetter /ˈfetə(r)/ *vt* 1 (chain) 给…上脚镣 ‹*prisoner, slave, animal*› 2 fig (restrict) 束缚 ‹*union, activities, emotions*›

fetters *npl* 1 (of prisoner, slave) 脚镣; **in ~** 戴着脚镣 2 fig (restrictions) 束缚; **the ~ of authority/totalitarianism** 权威/极权主义的桎梏; **the ~ of poverty** 贫穷的羁绊

fettle /ˈfetl/ *n* [u] **to be in fine** *or* **good ~** 身心俱佳

fetus /ˈfiːtəs/ *n* (*pl* ~**es**) 胎儿

feud /fjuːd/

A *n* (long-standing dispute) 世仇; (violent hostilities) 夙怨; **a ~ with sb./a ~ between two groups**

f

与某人的/两个族群之间的夙怨; **a family ~** 家族世仇

B *vi* 长期争执; **to ~ with sb.** 与某人长期不和

feudal /ˈfju:dl/ *adj* 1 (relating to feudalism) 封建的 ‹*system, society, lord*› 2 fig (outdated) 陈腐的 ‹*idea, attitude, treatment*›

feudalism /ˈfju:dəlɪzəm/ *n* [u] 封建制度

fever /ˈfi:və(r)/ *n* 1 [u and c] Med (high temperature) 发烧; **to have a ~** 发烧; **to come** *or* **go down with a ~** 发烧病倒; **a high ~** 高烧 2 [u] (disease) 热病; **yellow ~** 黄热病; **scarlet ~** 猩红热; **hay ~** 枯草热 3 [u and c] (excited state) 亢奋; **to be in a ~ of expectation** 迫不及待 4 [u] (mass excitement) 群情激昂 5 (craze) 痴迷; **the ~ for sth.** 对某事物的痴迷

fevered /ˈfi:vəd/ *adj attrib* 1 (having a fever) 发烫的 ‹*chest, forehead*› 2 fig 亢奋的 ‹*imagination, activity*›; 按捺不住的 ‹*excitement*›

feverish /ˈfi:vərɪʃ/ *adj* 1 (having a fever) 发烧的 ‹*condition, person*›; **a ~ cold** 感冒发烧 2 (caused by fever) 发烧引起的 ‹*dreams, nightmares*› 3 (frenetic) 亢奋的 ‹*activity, excitement, pace, speculation*›

feverishly /ˈfi:vərɪʃli/ *adv* 心急火燎地 ‹*search, work, write*›

fever pitch /ˈfi:vəpɪtʃ/ *n* [u] 狂热; **to reach ~** 达到狂热; **to be at ~** 极度兴奋

few /fju:/ ▸**p. 32**

A *adj* 1 (not many) 极少的; **~ people came to the meeting** 与会者寥寥无几; **a man of ~ words** 沉默寡言的人; **to be ~ in number** 数量很少; **to be ~ and far between** 稀少; **such people/opportunities are ~ and far between** 这样的人/机会很少见 2 (some, several) 一些; **a ~** 一些; **quite a ~ people/sth.** 相当多的人/某物; **I would like a ~ more** 我还想要一些; **a good ~ people/things** Brit 相当多的人/东西; **a good ~ times** 多次; **a ~ weeks earlier/later** 几周前/后; **not a ~ people/things** formal 不少人/东西; **every ~ days** 每隔几天; **over the next ~ days/weeks** 在随后的几天/几周里

B *pron* 1 (not many) 极少; **as ~ as sth.** 只有几个某物; **as ~ as four people turned up** 只有区区 4 个人露面; **~ of us succeeded/survived** 我们当中成功者/幸存者寥寥无几; **so ~ were present** 到场的人如此之少; **there are four too ~** 缺少四个; **as ~ as possible** 尽可能少地; **the ~ who voted for him** 少数几个给他投票的人 2 + *v pl* (some, several) 一些; **a ~ of the soldiers/countries** 一些士兵/国家; **a ~ wanted to go on strike** 有些人想罢工; **quite a ~ of sb./sth.** 相当多的某些人/某物; **a good ~ of the houses were damaged** Brit 不少房屋被毁; **not a ~ of sb./sth.** formal 相当多的某些人/某物; **there are only a very ~ left** 所剩无几了; **to have had a ~ (too many)** colloq 酒喝多了

C *n* + *v pl* (people) 少数人; (things) 少数事物; **great wealth lay in the hands of the ~** 大量财富掌握在少数人手中

fewer /ˈfju:ə(r)/

A *adj* 更少的; **there are ~ trains on Sundays** 星期天的火车比较少; **~ and ~ people/opportunities** 越来越少的人/机会; **~ than 50 people** 不到 50 个人; **no ~ than** 不少于; **the ~ the better** 越少越好

B *pron* (people) 较少数人; (things) 较少数事物; **I have seen ~ recently** 我最近见得少了

fewest /ˈfju:ɪst/

A *adj* 最少的; **who had (the) ~ mistakes?** 谁的错误最少？; **the ~ accidents happened in this area** 这个区域发生的事故最少

B *pron* (people) 最少的人; (things) 最少的事物; **he sold the ~** 他卖的最少

fey /feɪ/ *adj* 神经兮兮的 ‹*person, behaviour, ideas*›

fez /fez/ *n* (*pl* **fezzes**) 土耳其毡帽

ff *abbr* = **following A2**

fiancé /fɪˈɒnseɪ, Amer ˌfi:ɑ:nˈseɪ/ *n* 未婚夫

fiancée /fɪˈɒnseɪ, Amer ˌfi:ɑ:nˈseɪ/ *n* 未婚妻

fiasco /fɪˈæskəʊ/ *n* (*pl* **~s**) 惨败; **to end in ~** 惨淡收场

fiat /ˈfaɪæt, Amer ˈfi:ət/ *n* formal 1 (decree) 法令; **government by ~** 法治政府 2 (authorization) 批准

fib /fɪb/ colloq

A *n* 无关紧要的谎话

B *vi* (*pres p etc.* **-bb-**) 撒小谎

fibber /ˈfɪbə(r)/ *n* colloq 惯撒小谎的人

fibre Brit, **fiber** Amer /ˈfaɪbə(r)/ *n* 1 [c] (filament, strand of yarn, wood, muscle, nerve) 纤维; **cotton ~(s)** 棉纤维; **a chain of nerve ~s** 一串神经纤维 2 [u and c] Tex (substance) 纤维质料; (cloth) 纤维布料; **a synthetic/artificial ~** 合成/人造纤维 3 Culin, Med (roughage) 纤维素; **a high ~ diet** 高纤维饮食 4 fig (strength) 人格力量

fibre: ~board *n* [u] 纤维板; **a ~ board base** 纤维板基; **~glass** *n* [u] 玻璃纤维; **a ~glass panel** 一块玻璃纤维板

fibre-optic *adj attrib* 光学纤维的; **a ~ camera/network/transmission** 光纤照相机/网络/传输

fibre-optic cable *n* 光缆

fibre optics *npl* + *v sing* [u] 纤维光学

fibre tip, fibre tip pen *ns* 纤维笔

fibril /ˈfɪbrɪl/ *n* 纤丝

fibrillation /ˌfaɪbrɪˈleɪʃn/ *n* [u] 纤维性颤动

fibroid /ˈfaɪbrɔɪd/

A *n* (benign tumour) 纤维瘤; (in wall of the womb) 子宫肌瘤

B *adj* 纤维性的; **a ~ tumour** 纤维瘤; **~ tissue** 纤维组织

fibrosis /faɪˈbrəʊsɪs/ ▸**p. 377** *n* [u] 纤维变性

fibrositis /ˌfaɪbrəˈsaɪtɪs/ ▸**p. 377** *n* [u] 纤维织炎

fibrous /ˈfaɪbrəs/ *adj* (containing fibres) 含纤维的; (resembling fibres) 似纤维的; **~ layer/tissue/structure** 纤维层/组织/结构; **a ~ root system** 纤维状根系

fibula /ˈfɪbjʊlə/ *n* (*pl* **~s** *or* **fibulae** /ˈfɪbjʊli:/) 腓骨

fiche /fi:ʃ/ *n* = **microfiche**

fickle /ˈfɪkl/ *adj* 1 不忠实的 ‹*person*›; 易变的 ‹*moods, public, market*›; **a ~ lover** 三心二意的情侣 2 fig 变幻莫测的 ‹*weather, fortune*›

fickleness /ˈfɪklnɪs/ *n* [u] (of lover, friend) 不忠实; fig (of weather, fortune) 易变; **the ~ of his moods** 他情绪的变化无常

fiction /ˈfɪkʃn/ *n* [u] 1 Literat (books and stories) 小说 2 [c] (delusion) 错觉 3 [u and c] (untruth) 虚构的事; **his address is a ~** 他的地址是假的; **the account was pure ~** 这个报道完全是杜撰的 4 [c] (pretence) 假象; **to keep up a ~ of being/doing sth.** 维持是某事物/做某事的假象

fictional /ˈfɪkʃənl/ *adj* 1 (imaginary) 虚构的 ‹*character, event, scenario*› 2 Literat 小说的 ‹*method, writing*›; **~ prose** 散文小说 3 (false) 虚假的 ‹*address, rumour, report*›; **the ~ belief that ...** …的幻觉

fictionalize /ˈfɪkʃənəlaɪz/ *vt* «*author, writer*» 把…写成小说 ‹*account, story*›; **~d history** 历史演义

fiction writer ▸**p. 409** *n* 小说作家

fictitious /fɪkˈtɪʃəs/ *adj* 1 (false) 虚假的 ‹*account, excuse*›; **a ~ name/address** 假名字/假地址 2 (imaginary) 虚构的 ‹*character, place, event*›

fiddle /ˈfɪdl/

A *n* 1 ▸**p. 395** Mus colloq (violin) 小提琴; **to be as fit as a ~** 非常健康; **a face like** *or* **as long as a ~** 拉长的脸; **to play second ~ to sb.** 给某人当副手 2 Brit colloq (dishonest scheme) 骗局; **to be on the ~** 行骗 3 Brit colloq (awkward task) 棘手的琐事; **inserting a tape is a bit of a ~** 装磁带有点麻烦

B *vt* colloq 篡改 ‹*books, accounts, figures*›; 虚报 ‹*expenses, tax return*›; 骗取 ‹*free ticket*›

C *vi* 1 (fidget) 拨弄; **to ~ with sth.** 拨弄某物; **to ~ about** *or* **around with sth.** 不停地拨弄某物 2 (adjust) 来回摆弄; **to ~ with sth.** 来回调整某物; **to ~ about** *or* **around with sth.** 不停摆弄某物 3 (interfere) 乱动; **to ~ with sth.** 乱动某物; **to ~ about** *or* **around (with sth.)** 乱动（某物） 4 Mus colloq 拉小提琴

Phrasal verb

- **fiddle about, fiddle around** *vi* 瞎混

fiddler /ˈfɪdlə(r)/ ▸**p. 395, p. 409** *n* colloq 1 Mus 小提琴手 2 Brit (crook) 造假者

fiddler crab *n* 招潮蟹

fiddlesticks /ˈfɪdlstɪks/ *excl* colloq dated 胡扯; **oh ~! the pen's run out!** 真讨厌！钢笔没水了！

fiddling /ˈfɪdlɪŋ/

A *adj* 1 (trivial) 琐碎的 ‹*details, job, problem*› 2 (fiddly) 烦琐的

B *n* [u] colloq 弄虚作假

fiddly /ˈfɪdli/ *adj* Brit colloq 烦琐的 ‹*job, task, tool, gadget*›

fidelity /fɪˈdeləti/ *n* [u] 1 (loyalty) 忠诚 2 (to sexual partner) 忠贞 3 (accuracy) 精确

fidget /ˈfɪdʒɪt/

A *vi* 1 (move restlessly) 坐立不安; **stop ~ing!** 不要动来动去！ 2 (be impatient) 烦躁; **to be ~ing to do sth.** 急不可耐要做某事 3 (fiddle) 来回拨弄; **to ~ with sth.** 来回拨弄某物

B *n* 坐立不安的人 [尤指小孩]

C **fidgets** *npl* 坐立不安; **to have** *or* **get the ~s** 坐立不安

Phrasal verb

- **fidget about, fidget around** *vi* 坐立不安

fidgety /ˈfɪdʒɪti/ *adj* 坐立不安的; **she's a ~ child** 她是一个好动的孩子

fiduciary /fɪˈdju:ʃəri/

A *adj* 信托的 ‹*obligation, relationship*›

B *n* 受信托者

fief /fi:f/ *n* 采邑

fiefdom /ˈfi:fdəm/ *n* 1 Hist 采邑 2 fig (of criminal, politician) 控制领域

field /fi:ld/

A *n* 1 [c] Agric (for crops) 田地; (for grazing) 牧场; **a ~ of wheat** 麦田; **an arable ~** 可耕地; **to work in the ~s** 在田间劳动 2 [c] (open area) 大片地方; **a lava ~** 熔岩区; **a large snow ~** 一大片雪原 3 [c] Geol, Miner 矿田; **an oil/gas ~** 油田/气田 4 [c] Sport (ground) 运动场; **a football/sports ~** 足球场/运动场; **to take to the ~** 上场 5 [u] Sport (group of contestants) 全体参赛者; **it's a strong ~** 这一组参赛选手实力很强; **to lead** *or* **be ahead of the ~** lit, fig 处于领先地位; **to play the ~** fig colloq 到处留情 6 [u] Mil 战场; **on the ~ of battle** 在战场上; **to die in the ~** 战死沙场; **to take the ~** 开始战斗; **to hold the ~** lit, fig 坚守阵地 7 [c] (real environment) 实地; **a ~ investigation** 实地调查; **to test sth. in the ~** 实地检验某物 8 [c] (area of knowledge) 领域; **in the ~ of medicine** 在医学领域; **to lead the ~ in cold fusion research** 在冷聚变研究领域处于领先地位; **his ~ is ...** 他的研究领域是…; **it's outside my ~** 这不属于我的专业领域 9 [c] (area of vision) 视野; **~ of vision** *or* **view** 视野 10 [c] Ling 语义域 11 [c] Phys 场; **a magnetic/force ~** 磁场/力场 12 [c] Comput 字段 13 [c] (design surface or background) [设计图案的] 底子

B *vt* 1 Sport 接 ‹*ball*› 2 (select) 选派…上场; **to ~ 10 players for a match** 派 10 名选手参加比赛 3 (supply) 把…投入使用 ‹*resources*›; **to ~ 5 helicopters and 100 men** 派出 5 架直升机和 100 个人 4 (answer) 应付; **she**

~ed the questions skilfully 她巧妙地回答了问题

field: ~ **ambulance** *n* 战地救护车; ~ **day** *n* 1 Sch, Univ (day of outdoor activity) 户外活动日; 2 Amer (sports day) 体育比赛日; 3 fig **to have a ~ day** (have fun) 尽情玩耍; (make money) 赚黑心钱; ~ **drain** *n* 田间排水沟

fielder /ˈfiːldə(r)/ *n* [板球、棒球等运动中的] 外场手

field: ~ **event** *n* 田赛项目; ~ **glasses** *npl* 双筒望远镜; ~ **goal** *n* Amer 定位球得分; ~ **gun** *n* 野战炮; ~ **hockey** *n* [u] Amer 曲棍球; ~ **hospital** *n* 野战医院; ~ **house** Amer *n* 1 (storage building) 体育用品贮藏室; 2 (sports centre) 体育中心; (sports hall) 体育馆; ~ **kitchen** *n* 移动式厨房; ~ **marshal** *n* 陆军元帅; **~mouse** *n* (*pl* **~mice**) 田鼠; ~ **officer** *n* 1 Mil 陆军校官; 2 (in company, organization) 工作人员; **~sman** /ˈfiːldzmən/ *n* Amer 外场手; ~ **sports** *npl* 野外运动 [指打猎、钓鱼、射击]; ~ **strength** *n* 场强; ~ **study** *n* 实地考察; ~ **test** *n* 现场测试; ~ **trials** *npl* 现场试验; ~ **trip** *n* 实地考察; **~work** *n* [u] 实地考察; **~worker** ▸**p. 409** *n* 实地考察工作者

fiend /fiːnd/ *n* 1 (cruel person) 恶人 2 colloq (mischievous person) 捣蛋鬼 3 colloq (fanatic) 痴迷者; **she's a real motorbike ~** 她是个地地道道的摩托车迷 4 Mythol 恶魔; **the ~** archaic 恶魔

fiendish /ˈfiːndɪʃ/ *adj* 1 (cruel) 恶魔似的 ‹*tyrant, cruelty*›; **a ~ smile** 狞笑; **to take a ~ delight in sth./in doing sth.** 从某事/做某事中得到残忍的乐趣; **he took a ~ delight in hiding their glasses** fig (mischievous) 他藏起了他们的眼镜, 从这一恶作剧中取乐 2 (ingenious) 巧妙复杂的 ‹*plan, plot, solution, device*› 3 colloq (difficult) 棘手的 ‹*problem, task*›

fiendishly /ˈfiːndɪʃli/ *adv* 1 (wickedly) 凶恶地 ‹*laugh, grin*›; **to smile ~** 狞笑 2 (extremely) 非常 ‹*difficult, cunning, expensive*›

fierce /fɪəs/ *adj* 1 (aggressive) 凶猛的 ‹*animal, person, battle*›; 恶狠狠的 ‹*expression, voice*› 2 (intense, forceful) 强烈的 ‹*resentment, desire*›; 坚定不移的 ‹*determination, loyalty*›; 猛烈的 ‹*attack*›; 激烈的 ‹*competition*› 3 (destructive) 狂暴的; **~ storms** 狂风暴雨; **~ heat** 酷暑; **a ~ wind** 狂风

fiercely /ˈfɪəsli/ *adv* 1 (angrily, aggressively) 凶狠地 ‹*react, speak, glare*›; 凶猛地 ‹*attack*› 2 (intensely, forcefully) 极其 ‹*determined, loyal, independent*›; 激烈地 ‹*argue, oppose*› 3 (ferociously) 猛烈地 ‹*burn, blow*›; **the bonfire blazed ~** 篝火熊熊燃烧; **the storm raged ~ all night** 暴风雨肆虐了一整夜

fierceness /ˈfɪəsnɪs/ *n* 1 (ferocity) (of animal) 凶猛; (of person, expression, voice) 凶狠; (of storm, battle, attack) 猛烈 2 (intensity) (of heat, flames, anger, criticism) 强烈; (of competition) 激烈; (of loyalty, determination) 坚定

fiery /ˈfaɪəri/ *adj* 1 (burning) 燃烧着的 ‹*gas, coals*› 2 (very hot) 灼热的 ‹*heat, sands*› 3 (strong, spicy) 辛辣的 ‹*drink, food*› 4 (bright red) 火红的 ‹*colour, sun*›; 火一般的 ‹*red*› 5 (passionate) 激情四溢的 ‹*speaker, speech, performance*› 6 (fierce) 暴躁的 ‹*person, temper*›

fiesta /fɪˈestə/ *n* 1 (religious festival) 宗教节日; (celebration) 狂欢节 2 (public event) 节日

FIFA /ˈfiːfə/ *abbr* = **Fédération Internationale de Football Association** 国际足联

fife /faɪf/ ▸**p. 395** *n* [军乐中与鼓合奏的] 横笛

fifteen /ˌfɪfˈtiːn/ ▸**p. 15, p. 521, p. 831**

A *n* 1 (number, quantity) 十五 2 (in age) 15 岁 3 (rugby team) [十五人组成的] 橄榄球队

B *adj* 1 (in number) 十五的; **~ metres** 15 米; **~ paintings** 15 张画 2 (in age) 15 岁的; **to be ~ (years old)** 15 岁大; **to be over/under ~** 超过/不到 15 岁 3 (in series) 第十五的; **size/number ~** 15 码/号

fifteenth /ˌfɪfˈtiːnθ/ ▸**p. 181, p. 521**

A *n* 1 (in sequence) 第十五个 2 (in date) 15 日 3 (fraction) 十五分之一

B *adj* 1 (in sequence) 第十五的; **in the ~ century** 在 15 世纪 2 (in name, title) 十五; **Louis the F~** 路易十五 3 (as fraction) 十五分之一的

C *adv* 1 (fifteenthly) 第十五 2 (in fifteenth position) 居第十五位

fifth /fɪfθ/ ▸**p. 181, p. 521**

A *n* 1 (in sequence) 第五 2 (in date) 5 日 3 (fraction) 五分之一

B *adj* 1 (in sequence) 第五的; **it's her ~ birthday** 这是她 5 岁生日; **on the ~ floor** 在 6 楼; **in the ~ century** 在 5 世纪 2 (in name, title) 五世; **Henry the F~ of England** 英王亨利五世 3 (as fraction) 五分之一的

C *adv* 1 (fifthly) 第五 2 (in fifth position) 居第五位

Fifth Amendment *n* Amer 《美国宪法修正案》第五条; **to invoke** *or* **plead** *or* **take the ~ Amendment** 拒绝作危害自己的证词

fifth: ~ **column** *n* 第五纵队 [泛指内奸]; ~ **columnist** *n* 内奸

fifthly /ˈfɪfθli/ *adv* 第五

fiftieth /ˈfɪftɪəθ/ ▸**p. 521**

A *n* 1 (in sequence) 第五十个 2 (fraction) 五十分之一

B *adj* 1 (in sequence) 第五十的 2 (as fraction) 五十分之一的

C *adv* 1 (fiftiethly) 第五十 2 (in fiftieth position) 居第五十位

fifty /ˈfɪfti/ ▸**p. 15, p. 521, p. 831**

A *n* 1 (number, quantity) 五十; **there are ~ of us** 我们有 50 个人 2 (in age) 50 岁

B *adj* 1 (in number) 五十的; **~ boys** 50 个男孩 2 (in age) 50 岁的; **I'm nearly ~** 我快 50 岁了 3 (in series) 第五十的

fifty-fifty /ˌfɪftiˈfɪfti/

A *adj* 1 对半的 ‹*division, share*›; **costs are to be shared on a ~ basis** 花费将平摊 2 (as likely to happen as not) 可能与不可能各半的; **to have a ~ chance** 有百分之五十的机会

B *adv* 各半 ‹*divide, share*›; **to go ~ on sth.** 平分某物

fig /fɪɡ/ *n* 1 (fruit) 无花果; **dried/fresh ~s** 干/新鲜无花果; **I don't give/care a ~ (for/about ...)** Brit colloq 我（对…）毫不在乎; **I don't give a ~ what they think!** 我才不在乎他们怎么想呢! 2 ~ (tree) 无花果树

fig. /fɪɡ/ *abbr* 1 = **figure A6; see ~ 3** 参看图 3 2 = **figurative 1**

fight /faɪt/

A *n* 1 (brawl) 打斗; Mil 战斗; **there was a ~ outside the pub last night** 昨晚在酒吧外面发生了一场打斗; **to get into** *or* **have a ~ with sb.** 和某人斗殴; **to ~ the good ~** 英勇战斗; **to be in a ~ to the death** 殊死搏斗 2 fig (struggle) 斗争; **a ~ for equality** 争取平等的斗争; **to put up a (good) ~** 进行（英勇）斗争; **sb.'s ~ against cancer** 某人与癌症的斗争 3 (in boxing) 拳击赛 4 (quarrel) 争吵; **to have a ~ with sb.** 跟某人争辩; **to pick a ~ (with sb.)** （与某人）吵架; **to have a ~ over money** 为钱争吵 5 (combative spirit) 斗志; **he had no ~ left in him** 他失去了斗志

B *vi* (*pt, pp* **fought**) 1 (brawl) 打斗; Mil 战斗; **to ~ with sb.** 和某人斗殴; **to ~ against sb.** Mil 与某人作战; Sport 与某人比赛; **to ~ for one's country** 为祖国而战; **to go down ~ing** 战斗到底; **soldiers who fought in the First World War** 参加过第一次世界大战的士兵 2 fig (struggle) 斗争; **to ~ (hard) to improve/change sth.** 为改善/改变某事物而（奋力）斗争; **to ~ against sleep** 撑着不睡着; **to ~ for one's life** 奋力求生 3 (quarrel) 争吵; **to ~ with sb. (over** *or* **about sth.)** 与某人（为某事）争吵 4 (compete against) 竞争; **to ~ against sb.** 与某人竞争

C *vt* (*pt, pp* **fought**) 1 (brawl with) 与…打斗; (in boxing) 与…搏击; Mil 与…战斗; **they fought the enemy on the streets of the capital** 他们在首都街头与敌人战斗 2 (struggle against) 与…作斗争 ‹*racism, cancer*›; **to ~ a fire** 扑火; **to ~ the urge to do sth.** 设法克制做某事的冲动; **to ~ a losing battle** 打一场无望取胜的仗; **to ~ a losing battle to stem the tears** fig 想忍住泪水, 却做不到 3 fig (battle) 努力开辟; **to ~ one's way (through)** 努力辟出一条路; **to ~ one's way to the front of the crowd** 奋力挤到人群的前面; **to ~ one's way to the top of the company** 努力奋斗登上公司的高位 4 (compete for) 竞争; **to ~ a seat/an election** 竞选席位/参加竞选 5 (run) 进行; **to ~ a campaign (against sth.)** 开展（反对某事物的）运动 6 Jur 打（官司）; **to ~ the case** 打这场官司

Phrasal verbs

• **fight back**

A *vi* 1 (retaliate) 还击; (resist) 抵抗; **the police were forced to ~ back** 警方不得不进行还击; **to ~ back against a disease** 与疾病抗争 2 Sport 反攻

B *vt* [**~ back sth.**] 忍住 ‹*laughter, tears*›

• **fight down** *vt* [**~ down sth.**] 抑制住 ‹*urge, impulse*›; **to ~ down the impulse to laugh** 尽力忍住不笑

• **fight off** *vt* [**~ off sb./sth., ~ sb./sth. off**] 1 lit 击退 ‹*attacker, troops, attack*› 2 (get rid of) 竭力摆脱; **to ~ off a cold** 治愈感冒; **to ~ off sleep** 克服睡意 3 (reject) 拒不接受 ‹*criticism, proposals*›

• **fight on** *vi* 继续战斗; fig 继续斗争

• **fight out** *vt* [**~ sth. out, ~ out sth.**] 1 lit 以斗争方式解决; **to ~ it out to the end** 斗争到底 2 fig 就…辩论出结果 ‹*disagreement*›; **let them ~ it out** 让他们去争个水落石出吧

fightback /ˈfaɪtbæk/ *n* 反击; **to mount a ~** 发起反击

fighter /ˈfaɪtə(r)/ *n* 1 (determined person) 斗士 2 Aviat, Mil **~ (plane)** 战斗机 3 Sport 拳击手

fighter: ~ **bomber** *n* 战斗轰炸机; ~ **pilot** ▸**p. 409** *n* 战斗机驾驶员

fighting /ˈfaɪtɪŋ/

A *n* [u] 1 (military combat) 战斗; **heavy ~** 鏖战; **hand to hand ~** 肉搏战 2 (in street, pub, school) 打斗

B *adj* 1 Mil 战斗的 ‹*troops, soldier*›; **a ~ man** 战士; **~ strength** 战斗力 2 (determined) 勇于战斗的; **~ spirit** 斗志

fighting: ~ **chance** *n* 经过努力才能成功的机会; **we've got a ~ chance of winning** 如果我们奋力一搏, 还有获胜的机会; ~ **cock** *n* 斗鸡; ~ **fit** *adj* 健壮的; ~ **words** *npl* colloq 1 (aggressive language) 挑衅性言论; 2 Amer (offensive remarks) 冒犯人的话

fig leaf *n* 1 lit (leaf) 无花果树叶 2 fig (cover) 遮羞布

figment /ˈfɪɡmənt/ *n* 臆想的事物; **a ~ of one's imagination** 凭空想象的事物

figurative /ˈfɪɡərətɪv, Amer ˈfɪɡjər-/ *adj* 1 Ling 比喻的 ‹*meaning, language, usage*›; **in the ~ sense** 在比喻的意义上 2 Art 具象的 ‹*artist, tradition, painting*›; **a ~ painter** 具象派画家

figuratively /ˈfɪɡərətɪvli, Amer ˈfɪɡjər-/ *adv* 比喻地; **~ speaking, ...** 打个比方说, …

figure /ˈfɪɡə(r), Amer ˈfɪɡjər/

A *n* 1 (number, amount) 数字; **unemployment ~s** 失业数字; **to put a ~ on sth.** 给出某事物的确切数字; **in round ~s** 以整数; **single/double ~s** 个位数/两位数; **a six-~ salary** 6 位数的薪水; **to sell for a high ~** 卖个高价; **the ~ 7** 数字 7; **there is a mistake in his ~s** (data) 他的数据中有一个错误 2 **~s**

pl Math 算术; **to be good at ~s** 擅长算术; **to have a head for ~s** 有算术头脑 **3** (personage, representative) 人物; **a leading/key/minor ~** 主要/关键/次要人物; **a public ~** 公众人物; **a ~ of authority** 权威人士; **a cult ~** 崇拜的偶像 **4** (human form) 人影; **a tall ~ approached me** 一个高个子人影朝我走来; **a familiar/imposing ~** 熟悉的/威严的身影; **to cut a sorry/fine ~** 显出可怜的样子/风度翩翩 **5** (body shape) 身材; **to have a good/awful ~** 身材好/不好; **to keep/lose one's ~** 保持身材/身材走样; **to watch one's ~** 注意保持体形; **a fine ~ of a man/woman** 体格健美的男人/身材窈窕的女人 **6** (illustration) 插图; (diagram) 图表; **see ~ 4** 见图表 4 **7** (outline) 图案; **to draw a ~ of an elephant** 画一头大象 **8** Math 图形; **a solid ~** 立体图形; **a six-sided ~** 六边形 **9** Art 人像; **a sculpture of two ~s embracing** 一尊两人相拥的雕像 **10** Dance, Sport 花式 **11** Mus 音型

B *vi* **1** (appear) 出现; **to ~ prominently on the music scene/in world politics** 在音乐界/国际政坛赫赫有名; **to ~ in a report** 列入报告 **2** colloq (make sense) 合乎情理; **that ~s** 那是合乎情理的; **it doesn't ~** 这没有道理; **it ~s that ...** …是理所当然的

C *vt* **1** esp Amer colloq (reckon) 认为; **I ~ I'd better leave** 我想我该走了; **that's what I ~d** 这就是我的看法 **2** (calculate) 计算 ‹*value, amount*› **3** (express pictorially) 以图表表示

Phrasal verbs

• **figure on** *vt* [~ **on sth.**] esp Amer colloq 指望; **I hadn't ~d on getting a prize** 我没有料到会得奖; **to ~ on doing sth.** (plan) 打算做某事

• **figure out**

A [~ **out sth.**, ~ **sth. out**] *vt*
1 (work out) 想出 ‹*answer, way*›; 算出 ‹*tax, sum*› **2** (understand) 弄明白 ‹*issue*›; **I can't ~ out what he's trying to say** 我弄不懂他想说什么; **to have one's future ~d out** 想清楚自己的未来

B [~ **sb. out**] *vt* 理解 ‹*person*›; **I can't ~ him out** 我一点儿都摸不透他

figurehead /ˈfɪɡəhed, Amer ˈfɪɡjər-/ *n* **1** (symbolic leader) 傀儡 **2** (of ship) 艏饰像

figure: ~ of eight Brit, **~ eight** Amer *ns* 8 字形; **to do a ~ of eight** 做 8 字形动作; **~ of speech** *n* (*pl* **figures of speech**) 修辞格; **it's just a ~ of speech** 这只是打个比方; **~ skater** *n* 花样滑冰运动员; **~ skating** ▸**p. 307** *n* [u] 花样滑冰

figurine /ˌfɪɡəˈriːn, Amer ˈfɪɡjəriːn/ *n* (carved) 小雕像; (moulded) 小塑像

Fiji /ˈfiːdʒiː/ *pr n* 斐济; **the ~ Islands** 斐济群岛

Fijian /fɪˈdʒiːən/ ▸**p. 503, p. 426**

A *adj* (of Fiji) 斐济的; (of the people) 斐济人的; (of the language) 斐济语的

B *n* **1** [c] (person) 斐济人 **2** [u] (language) 斐济语

filament /ˈfɪləmənt/ *n* **1** Elec 灯丝 **2** Tex 单纤维

filbert /ˈfɪlbət/ *n* **1** (tree) 欧洲榛 **2** (nut) 欧洲榛子

filch /fɪltʃ/ *vt* colloq 偷; **to ~ sth. from sth.** 从某处偷某物

file¹ /faɪl/

A *n* **1** (tool) 锉刀 **2** (for fingernails) 指甲锉

B *vt* «*person, file, tool, machine*» 锉 ‹*wood, metal, joint, tooth*›; **to ~ through sth.** 把某物锉断; **to ~ sth. away** 把某物锉掉; **to ~ down** 锉掉

file²

A *n* **1** (folder) 文件夹; (box file) 文件盒; (ring binder) 四眼活页夹; (card tray) 文件盘; (in filing cabinet) 文件柜 **2** Admin (record) 卷宗; **on ~** 存档; **to have/keep a ~ on sb.** 有/保存某人的档案; **to close/open a ~ on sth./sb.** 结束/建立某事物/某人的卷宗 **3** Comput 文件; **to create/edit/delete a ~** 创建/编辑/删除文件

B *vt* **1** Admin «*clerk, secretary*» 把…归档 ‹*notes, memo, bill, receipt*› **2** Jur «*employee, wife, creditor*» 提交 ‹*claim*›; **to ~ a lawsuit (against sb.)** 起诉（某人）; **to ~ a petition in bankruptcy** 提出破产申请 **3** Journ «*reporter, police officer*» 发送 ‹*report, story*›

C *vi* 提起诉讼; **to ~ for divorce** 起诉离婚

Phrasal verb

• **file away** *vt* [~ **sth. away**, ~ **away sth.**]
1 Admin 把…归档; **she ~d away her notes** 她整理了笔记 **2** fig (remember) 记住 ‹*fact, idea, information*›; **they listened attentively, filing it all away for future use** 他们仔细听着，为今后使用记住每一个细节

file³

A *n* 一行; **to walk in single ~** 单列行进; **a ~ of cars** 一溜汽车

B *vi* «*children, prisoners*» 排成纵列行进; **to ~ in/out** 鱼贯而入/出; **to ~ past** 列队走过

file: ~ cabinet *n* Amer 文件柜; **~ card** *n* 档案卡; **~ clerk** *n* 档案管理员; **~ copy** *n* **1** (of paper document) 文件副本; **2** Comput 文件复制; **~ extension** *n* 文件扩展名; **~ format** *n* 文件格式; **~ manager** *n* 文件管理器; **~ name** *n* 档案名称; **~ server** *n* 文件服务器; **~ sharing** *n* [u] 文件共享

filial /ˈfɪlɪəl/ *adj attrib* formal 子女的 ‹*responsibilities, love*›; **~ duty** 孝心

filibuster /ˈfɪlɪbʌstə(r)/

A *n* [采用冗长演说等的] 阻挠行动

B *vi* «*MP, senator, party*» [用冗长的演说等] 进行阻挠

C *vt* [用冗长的演说等] 阻挠…通过 ‹*bill*›

filigree /ˈfɪlɪɡriː/ *n* [u] 细工饰品; **~ silver** 银丝细工饰品

filing /ˈfaɪlɪŋ/ *n* **1** [u] Admin 存档 **2** Jur **~s** *pl* 提交备案; **tax/bankruptcy/divorce ~s** 纳税申报/破产/离婚档案

filing: ~ box *n* 文件盒; **~ cabinet** *n* 文件柜; **~ card** *n* 档案卡; **~ clerk** ▸**p. 409** *n* 档案管理员

filings /ˈfaɪlɪŋz/ *npl* 锉屑; **iron ~** 铁锉屑

filing: ~ system *n* 文件归档系统; **~ tray** *n* [办公桌上的] 文件盒

Filipino /ˌfɪlɪˈpiːnəʊ/ ▸**p. 503, p. 426**

A *adj* (of the Philippines) 菲律宾的; (of the people) 菲律宾人的; (of the language) 菲律宾语的

B *n* **1** [c] (person) 菲律宾人 **2** [u] (language) 菲律宾语

fill /fɪl/

A *vt* **1** (make full) 装满; **to ~ a box with books** 把盒子装满书; **to ~ sb. a bucket of water** 帮某人装满一桶水 **2** (plug) 填补; **to ~ a cavity** 填补龋洞; **to ~ a hole in the wall** 修补墙上的一个洞 **3** (occupy) 充满; **a church ~ed with flowers** 摆满鲜花的教堂; **the theatre is ~ed to capacity** 剧院座无虚席; **to ~ two seats** 占两个座位; **tears ~ed her eyes** 她的眼里噙满了泪水; **anger ~ed his heart** 他的心中充满了愤怒; **his life was ~ed with love** 他的一生充满了爱; **the idea ~ed me with excitement** 这个想法让我十分兴奋; **the film that is ~ing cinemas all over the country** 票房好得让全国的电影院都座无虚席的影片; **the next few days are ~ed with meetings** 接下来的几天时间都用于开会 **4** (pervade) 布满 ‹*room, hall, garden*›; **the smell of garlic ~ed the house** 房子里弥漫着大蒜的气味; **smoke ~ed the air** 空气中烟雾弥漫 **5** (use up) 耗去; **to ~ (the *or* one's) time doing sth.** 做某事打发时间 **6** (provide for) 满足 ‹*need, requirement*›; 填补 ‹*void, gap*›; **that ~s the bill** colloq 那正合适 **7** Naut «*wind*» 鼓起 ‹*sail*› **8** (stuff) 填充 ‹*pillow*›; **to ~ a turkey with stuffing** 给火鸡填入馅料 **9** (appoint sb. to) «*company, committee*» 派人担任 ‹*post*›; (accept a post) «*worker*» 充任 ‹*post*›; **the vacancy has been ~ed** 那个空缺已有人接任 **10** esp Amer (supply items for) 按…供应; **the waiter went to ~ the order** 侍者去上菜了; **the chemist was unable to ~ the prescription** 药剂师无法按处方配药 **11** (with food) = **fill up B1**

B *vi* **1** (become full) 变满; **the bath takes three minutes to ~** 浴缸蓄满水需要 3 分钟; **the theatre began to ~** 剧院开始满座; **his eyes ~ed with tears** 他的眼里噙满了泪水 **2** (with smell, light) 布满; **to ~ with smoke** «*room*» 布满烟雾 **3** Naut «*sail*» 鼓起

C *n* **1** (capacity) **to eat *or* have one's ~** 吃饱; **to drink *or* have one's ~** 喝足 **2** (limit) **to have had one's ~ of sth./doing sth.** 受够了某事物/做某事; **I've had my ~ of housework!** 家务活我已经干够了！

Phrasal verbs

• **fill in**

A [~ **in sth.**, ~ **sth. in**] *vt*
1 (plug) 填满 ‹*hole*›; **to ~ in a cavity** 补好龋洞 **2** (complete) 填写 ‹*form*›; (write in) 填入 ‹*information*›; **I ~ed in the form** 我把表格填好了 **3** (colour in) 给…着色 ‹*shape*›; **~ the circle in in red** 把圆圈涂成红色 **4** colloq (supply) 提供 ‹*information*›; **to ~ in a few details (for sb.)** （向某人）提供一些细节 **5** (occupy) **to ~ in time** 打发时间; **to ~ in a few hours shopping** 靠购物打发掉几个小时

B [~ **sb. in**] *vt* 向…通报; **to ~ sb. in on sth.** 向某人通告某事

C *vi* 临时代替; **to ~ in for sb.** 暂代某人工作

• **fill out**

A *vt* [~ **out sth.**, ~ **sth. out**] 开具 ‹*certificate, authorization*›; 填写 ‹*form, application*›; **to ~ out a prescription** 开处方

B *vi* 长胖

• **fill up**

A [~ **up sth.**, ~ **sth. up**] *vt*
1 (make full) 装满 ‹*container*›; **to be ~ed up to the brim** 注满到边缘上; **to ~ sth. up with sth.** 用某物装满某物; **to ~ the kettle up with water** 把水壶装满水 **2** (occupy entirely) 占据 ‹*space, room*›; **when people start to arrive, they'll ~ the room up** 人们到来后就会把房间挤满 **3** (occupy) 打发 ‹*time, day*›; **to ~ up (the) time with housework** 干家务活消磨时间 **4** Aut 加满 ‹*car, tank*›; **to ~ a car up with unleaded petrol** 把油箱加满无铅汽油

B [~ **sb. up**] *vt*
1 (make eat a lot) 让…吃饱 ‹*person*›; **to ~ sb./oneself up with sth.** 用某物喂饱某人/尽情吃某物; **don't ~ him up with beer!** 别给他灌饱啤酒; **don't ~ yourself up with biscuits!** 别用饼干填饱肚子 **2** (satisfy) «*food*» 使…饱足 ‹*person*›; **bread ~s me up** 我吃面包很容易饱

C *vi* **1** (become full) 变满; **to ~ up with sth.** 充满某物; **the bucket ~ed up with water** 桶里注满了水; **the theatre began to ~ up before the performance** 表演开始前，剧院开始满座 **2** Aut (with fuel) 加满油

-filled /fɪld/ *combining form* 充满…的; **feather ~ pillows** 羽毛枕头; **tear~ eyes** 泪眼

filler /ˈfɪlə(r)/ *n* **1** [u and c] (substance) 填料 **2** [c] Journ 补白 **3** [c] TV, Radio, Theat 凑数节目

filler cap *n* 加油口盖

fillet /ˈfɪlɪt/

A *n* [u and c] (meat) 去骨肉片; (fish) 剔骨鱼片

B *vt* «*butcher, chef, fishmonger*» 把…去骨切成片 ‹*meat, fish*›

fillet steak *n* 里脊牛排

fill-in *n* colloq 替工

filling /ˈfɪlɪŋ/

A *n* **1** [c] Dent 补牙填料; **to have a ~ (done)** 补牙 **2** [u and c] Culin 馅; **a pie with blackberry/meat ~** 黑莓/肉馅饼 **3** [u and c] (wadding) 填充物; **pillows with foam ~** 海绵枕头

B *adj* 易饱的 ‹*food*›

filling station *n* 加油站

fillip /ˈfɪlɪp/ *n* 推动; **to give a ~ to sth.** 促进某事

f

filly /ˈfɪli/ *n* [不满4岁的] 小母马

film /fɪlm/

A *n* **1** [c] Cin, TV 电影; **to see a ~** 看电影; **to make/shoot a ~** 制作/拍摄影片 **2** [u] (cinema) 电影业; **to be** *or* **work in ~** 从事电影业; **the ~ industry** 电影产业 **3** [u] (footage) 纪录片 **4** [u and c] Phot (for photos) 胶卷; (for movies) 胶片; **to develop a ~** 冲洗胶卷 **5** [c] (layer) 薄层; **a ~ of oil/dust** 薄薄的一层油/灰 **6** (thin plastic) 薄膜

B *vt* 拍摄 ‹*documentary, scene, wedding*›; 把…拍成电影 ‹*novel, story*›

C *vi* 拍摄电影

film: ~ archive *n* 电影档案馆; **~ award** *n* 电影奖; **~ award ceremony** 电影颁奖典礼; **~ badge** *n* 胶片式辐射计量器; **~ buff** *n* 电影迷; **~ camera** *n* 胶卷照相机; **~ club** *n* 电影俱乐部; **~ contract** *n* 电影合同; **~ coverage** *n* [u] 电视报道; **~ critic** ▸**p. 409** *n* 电影评论家; **~ director** ▸**p. 409** *n* 电影导演; **~ fan** *n* 电影迷; **~ festival** *n* 电影节; **~goer** *n* 常上电影院的人; **~ industry** *n* [u] 电影业; **~ laboratory** *n* 冲印室; **~ library** *n* **1** (building) 影片库; **2** (collection) 收藏的影片; **~ magazine** *n* 电影杂志; **~-maker** ▸**p. 409** *n* 电影摄制人员; **~-making** *n* [u] 电影摄制; **~ music** *n* [u] 电影音乐; **~ poster** *n* 电影海报; **~ premiere** *n* 电影首映; **~ producer** ▸**p. 409** *n* 电影制片人; **~ production** *n* [u] 电影制作; **~ rights** *npl* 电影版权; **~ script** *n* 电影剧本; **~ sequence** *n* 电影片段; **~ set** *n* 电影布景; **~set** *vt* (*pres p etc.* **-tt-**) 把…照相排版 ‹*article, paragraph*›; **~setter** *n* 照相排版工人; **~setting** *n* [u] 照相排版; **~ show** *n* 影片放映; **~ star** *n* 电影明星; **~ strip** *n* 幻灯片; **~ studio** *n* 电影制片厂; **~ test** *n* 试镜; **~ version** *n* 电影版

filmy /ˈfɪlmi/ *adj* **1** (thin) 轻薄透明的 ‹*night-dress, fabric, clouds*› **2** (cloudy) 雾蒙蒙的 ‹*glass, layer*›; **her eyes were dull and ~** 她的眼神呆滞蒙眬

filter /ˈfɪltə(r)/

A *n* **1** Sci, Tech (device) 过滤器; (material) 过滤材料; **an air/water ~** 空气/水过滤器; **an oil ~** 滤油器; **cigarettes with ~s** 过滤嘴香烟 **2** Electron 滤波器 **3** Phot 滤光镜 **4** Brit Transp 绿色分流信号灯

B *vt* «*person, equipment, system*» 过滤 ‹*petrol, water, air*›

C *vi* **1** (trickle) «*light, sound, music*» 透过; **to ~ in/through ...** 透进/透过 **2** (slowly become known) «*news, information*» 慢慢传开; **to ~ through/in/into ...** 慢慢传入… **3** (move slowly) 徐徐行进; **to ~ back/out** 慢慢回来/出去 **4** Brit Transp **to ~ (off)** «*vehicles, driver*» 在分流车道上行驶

Phrasal verb

- **filter out** *vt* [**~ out sth., ~ sth. out**] «*person, system, equipment*» 滤除 ‹*dirt, dust, impurities*›

filter: ~ bed *n* 滤床; **~ cigarette** *n* 过滤嘴香烟; **~ coffee** *n* [u and c] 滤纸冲泡式咖啡; **~ coffee machine** 滤纸冲泡式咖啡机; **~ funnel** *n* 过滤漏斗

filtering software *n* [u] 过滤软件

filter: ~ lane *n* Brit 分流车道; **~ light** *n* Brit 分流信号灯; **~ paper** *n* 过滤纸; **~ pump** *n* 过滤泵; **~ tip** *n* (cigarette) 过滤嘴香烟; (filter) 过滤嘴; **~-tipped** *adj* 过滤嘴的 ‹*cigarette*›

filth /fɪlθ/ *n* [u] **1** (dirt) 污物 **2** (vulgarity) 淫秽的言行

filthy /ˈfɪlθi/

A *adj* **1** (dirty) 肮脏的 **2** colloq (contemptible) 卑劣的; **a ~ trick** 卑鄙的花招 **3** (vulgar) 淫秽的 ‹*language, behaviour, book*›; **to have a ~ mind** 思想肮脏 **4** Brit (unpleasant) 恶劣的 ‹*weather, day*›

B *adv* colloq (as intensifier) 极度地; **~ dirty** 污秽不堪; **to be ~ rich** 富得流油

filtrate /ˈfɪltreɪt/ *n* 滤液

filtration /fɪlˈtreɪʃn/ *n* [u] 过滤

fin /fɪn/ *n* **1** Zool 鳍 **2** Aerosp, Naut 鳍状物 **3** Aut, Tech 散热片

finagle /fɪˈneɪgl/ esp Amer colloq

A *vt* **1** (wangle) 骗取 **2** (trick) 欺骗; **to ~ sb. into doing sth.** 欺骗某人做某事

B *vi* 使用欺诈手段

final /ˈfaɪnl/

A *adj* **1** *attrib* (last in series) 最后的 ‹*question, person, day*› **2** *attrib* (ultimate) 最终的 ‹*cost, result*› **3** (definitive) 决定性的 ‹*decision, answer, ruling*›; **that's ~!** colloq 就这么定了!; **to have the ~ word** 有最终决定权 **4** *attrib* (greatest) 最大的 ‹*penalty, irony*›

B *n* **1** Sport 决赛 **2** Journ [当天报纸的] 最后一次印刷; **the late ~** 最近更新版

C **finals** *npl* **1** Sport 决赛; **semi-~s** 半决赛 **2** Brit Univ 毕业考试

final: ~ approach *n* 最后进近 [飞机着陆前的最后一段飞行]; **~ demand** *n* 最后催款; **~ dividend** *n* 年终股息

finale /fɪˈnɑːli, Amer -næli/ *n* **1** (final part of performance, display) 最后一幕; **the grand ~** 大结局 **2** Mus 终曲

final invoice *n* 最终发票

finalist /ˈfaɪnəlɪst/ *n* 决赛选手

finality /faɪˈnæləti/ *n* [u] **1** (irreversibility) 定局; **the abrupt ~ of death** 死亡对一切的骤然终结 **2** (decisiveness) 决断态度; **with an air of ~** 以不容商量的态度

finalization /ˌfaɪnəlaɪˈzeɪʃn, Amer -lɪˈz-/ *n* 最后确定

finalize /ˈfaɪnəlaɪz/ *vt* 最后确定 ‹*preparations, contract, date, venue*›

finally /ˈfaɪnəli/ *adv* **1** (lastly) 最后 **2** (eventually) 终于 ‹*leave, realize, accept, decide*› **3** (conclusively) 彻底 ‹*resolve*›

final: ~ notice *n* 最后催款; **~ salary pension scheme, ~ salary pension plan** *ns* 最终薪酬退休金计划

finance /ˈfaɪnæns, fɪˈnæns/

A *n* [u] **1** (funds) 资金; **to get** *or* **obtain ~ for sth.** 为某事融资 **2** (banking, financial systems) 财政; **the world of high ~** 高级金融界; **an expert in ~** 金融专家

B *modif* 财政的; **the ~ page(s)** 财经版; **the ~ minister/ministry** 财政部长/部

C **finances** *npl* (of state) 财力; (of organization) 财务状况; (of person) 经济状况

D *vt* «*shareholders, entrepreneur, government*» 为…提供资金 ‹*company, project, purchase*›

finance: ~ bill *n* 拨款法案; **~ company** *ns* 信贷公司; **~ director** *n* 财务董事; **~ house** *n* = **~ company**

financial /faɪˈnænʃl, fɪ-/ *adj* 财政的 ‹*difficulties, chaos, support*›; 金融的 ‹*adviser, markets, situation*›; **~ aid** 助学金

financial: ~ backer *n* 出资人; **~ futures market** *n* 金融期货市场

financially /faɪˈnænʃəli, fɪˈn-/ *adv* 经济上

Financial: ~ Services Authority *n* Brit 金融服务局; **~ Times (Industrial Ordinary Share) Index** *n* 金融时报 (工业普通股) 指数; **~ Times Stock Exchange Index** *n* 金融时报 100 指数; **f~ year** *n* Brit 财政年度

financier /faɪˈnænsɪə(r), Amer ˌfɪnənˈsɪər/ *n* 金融家

financing /ˈfaɪnænsɪŋ, fɪˈnænsɪŋ/ *n* [u] 融资

finch /fɪntʃ/ *n* 雀科鸣鸟

find /faɪnd/

A *vt* (*pt, pp* **found**) **1** (discover by chance) 偶然发现; **I didn't expect to ~ you here!** 我没想到会在这里碰到你!; **he found an umbrella in the car park** 他在停车场捡到一把雨伞; **found: black-and-white kitten** (on notice) 失物招领: 一只黑白杂色的小猫; **to ~ sb./sth. doing sth.** 不期然发现某人/某物在做某事; **he woke up to ~ an intruder looking through his papers** 他醒来时发现一个闯入者在翻阅他的文件; **to ~ sb./sth. to be sth.** 后来发现某人/某物是某种状况; **the President was found to be dead** 总统被发现时已经死亡; **to leave sth. as one found it** 使某物保持原状; **to take sb. as one ~s them** 接受某人的现状; **we've only just got back from holiday so you must take us as you ~ us** 我们刚度假回来, 所以你得将就点 **2** (discover by searching) 找到; **she found his glasses for him** 她帮他找到了眼镜; **to ~ one's** *or* **the way** 找到正确的路; **to ~ one's feet** lit 站起来行走; fig 站稳脚跟 **3** (come up with) 求得 ‹*job, solution*›; 鼓起 ‹*courage*›; **you'll have to ~ a new secretary** 你得找个新秘书; **to ~ room for sth.** 找地方安置某物; **to ~ the energy to do sth.** 拿出做某事的干劲; **to ~ (the) time (for sth./to do sth.)** (为某事/为做某事) 挤出时间; **to ~ the money (for sth./to do sth.)** (为某事/去做某事) 弄到钱; **multiply the length by the width to ~ the area** 长宽相乘求得面积; **to ~ sth. for sb.** *or* **to ~ sb. sth.** 为某人找出某物; **wait there, I'll see if I can ~ you a seat** 在那儿等着, 我看看能不能给你找个座位; **let's ~ a vase for these flowers** 我们给这些花找个花瓶吧; **it's about time she found herself a husband** 她该给自己找个丈夫了; **all found** Brit dated (in advertisement) 食宿全包; **wages £75 a week all found** 周薪 75 英镑, 食宿全包 **4** (see present) 见到…的存在 ‹*animal, plant, thing*›; **tigers are found in Asia** 亚洲有老虎; **the portrait is to be found in the Louvre** 这幅肖像画可在卢浮宫见到 **5** (perceive, discover) 发觉; **to ~ sb./sth. (to be) sth.** 觉得某人/某事物 (是) 如何; **he ~s her difficult to get on with** 他觉得她很难相处; **I ~ her a bore** 我觉得她令人厌烦; **how did you ~ her new boyfriend?** 你觉得她的新男友怎么样?; **how did you ~ your mother yesterday?** 你母亲昨天身体怎么样?; **I think you will ~ that these tyres last longer** 我想你会发现这些轮胎寿命更长; **to ~ it hard/easy/necessary to do sth.** 认为做某事很难/很容易/有必要; **to ~ it encouraging/unfair that ...** 认为…令人鼓舞/不公平 **6** (experience) 感受到 ‹*happiness, satisfaction*›; **to ~ sth. (in sth./doing sth.)** (在某事/做某事中) 感受到某事; **she found comfort in prayer** 她在祈祷中找到了慰藉; **I found considerable satisfaction in proving him wrong** 我为成功证明他错误而感到相当满足 **7** (reach) 达到; **to ~ its mark** *or* **target** «*arrow, bullet*» 击中目标; **water ~s its (own) level** 水往低处流; **to ~ one's own level** fig 找到适合自己的位置; **rivers ~ their way to the sea** 江河流入大海; **the pamphlet soon found its way into the dustbin** 小册子很快就进了垃圾箱; **he found his way into a suitable occupation** 他无意中找到了适合自己的职业; **to ~ expression in sth.** «*feeling, idea*» 在某物中表达出来 **8** liter (in a particular condition, state) 发现…处于某状态; **Friday evening found him lying drunk on the floor** 星期五晚上他醉卧于地板上; **to ~ sb. in a good/bad mood** 发现某人心情不错/心情不好; **I hope this card ~s you in better health** formal 我希望您收到此卡片时身体会好些 **9** «*jury, court*» 裁决 ‹*person, accused*›; **to ~ sb. guilty/not guilty** 裁决某人有罪/无罪

B *v refl* (*pt, pp* **found**) **1** **to ~ oneself ...** (discover oneself in a situation) 突然发觉自己…; **I found myself in a deserted street** 我发觉自己来到了一条空荡荡的街道; **you are going to ~ yourself in trouble** 你在自找麻烦; **to ~ oneself trapped** *or* **stuck** 发觉自己被困; **to ~ oneself a prisoner/an**

f

outcast 发现自己竟成为囚犯/被抛弃者; **to ~ oneself doing sth.** 突然发觉自己在做某事; **before I knew what I was doing, I found myself kissing him** 我不知不觉吻起他来了 **2** (discover one's abilities, vocation etc.) **to ~ oneself** 发现自我; **he's just beginning to ~ himself** 他刚开始有自我认知; **she seems to have found herself at last** 她似乎终于找回了自我; **I really found myself when I started studying medicine** 我开始学医之后才真正找到了自己的位置

C *vi* (*pt, pp* **found**) «*court, judge, jury*» 裁决; **to ~ for/against sb.** 作出有利于/不利于某人的裁决

D *n* (of sth. valuable) [有价值的] 发现物; (of sb. useful or interesting) 人才; **an important archaeological ~** 一项重要的考古发现; **to make a ~** 淘到一件宝物; **a lucky ~** 碰巧发现的好东西; **this old bicycle was a lucky ~** 这辆旧自行车是碰巧买到的好东西; **a real ~** 被发现有才能的人; **Ted has turned out to be a real ~** 特德证明是难得的人才

Phrasal verb

• **find out** *vt* **1** [~ out sth., ~ sth. out] (discover) 查明 ‹*fact, price, cause*›; 发现 ‹*secret*›; **to ~ out about sth.** 弄清某事; **to ~ out where/who/how ...** 查清楚哪里/谁/如何…; **to ~ out that ...** 查明… **2** [~ sb. out] (detect wrong-doings of) 识破 ‹*person*›; 揭穿 ‹*deceit, lie*›; **her husband has found her out at last** 她丈夫最终发现了她的不忠

finder /ˈfaɪndə(r)/ *n* **1** (of treasure, lost thing) 发现者; **~s keepers (losers weepers)** colloq 谁找到归谁（谁丢谁倒霉） **2** (on telescope) [附加于天文望远镜上，用于测定天体位置的] 寻星镜

finding /ˈfaɪndɪŋ/ *n* **1** (conclusion) 调查结果; **they made the following ~s** 他们得出了下面的调查结论 **2** (discovery) 发现 **3** Jur (verdict) 裁决

fine¹ /faɪn/

A *n* 罚款; **a heavy ~** 巨额罚金; **to impose a ~ of £5,000 on the company** 对该公司处以5,000英镑的罚金; **to pay a £50 ~ for speeding** 因超速付50英镑罚款

B *vt* 处…以罚金; **to ~ sb. £50** 罚某人50英镑; **to be ~d £3,000** 被罚款3,000英镑; **to be ~d for speeding** 因超速被罚款

fine²

A *adj* **1** (excellent) 极好的 ‹*idea, place, season*›; (top quality) 优秀的 ‹*athlete, writer, pupil*›; **a ~ view** 美景; **a ~ performance** 精彩演出; **to be in ~ form** 处于极佳的竞技状态; **she has a ~ future ahead of her** 她前程似锦; **of the ~st quality** 最优质的 **2** (satisfactory) 很好的; (acceptable) 可以的; **how are you? — (I'm) ~** (in greetings) 你好吗？——（我）很好; **to feel/look ~** (healthy) 感觉/看上去身体很好; **I'm going now, OK? — yes, that's ~** 我要走了，可以吗？——行，没问题; **it's** *or* **that's ~ by** *or* **with me** 我没意见; **is that enough? — yes, that's ~** 那够吗？——是的，够了; **the cottage is ~ for four of us** 这小屋够我们4个人住 **3** iron [用作反语]; **a ~ friend you are!** 你真够朋友啊！; **this is a ~ mess we're in!** 我们的处境好狼狈啊！; **you're a ~ one to talk!** 没有你说话的份！; **it's all very ~ to say buy another one, but ...** 再买一个，说得倒轻巧，但是… **4** (elegant) 精美的; **~ crystal** 精致的水晶; **~ craftsmanship** 精巧的手艺; **a delicate face with ~ features** 清秀的娇小面孔 **5** (refined) 优雅的 ‹*manners*›; (beautiful) 华丽的 ‹*clothes, furnishings*›; **a man of ~ feelings** *or* **sentiments** 一个情感细腻的人 **6** (commendable) 高尚的 ‹*person*›; 高贵的 ‹*character*›; **he's a ~ young man** 他是一个好小伙子 **7** (sunny, clear) 晴朗的; **it's** *or* **the weather's ~** 天气很好; **I hope it stays ~ for the picnic** 我希望野餐那天还是晴天; **one ~ day** 晴朗的一天; **one of these ~ days** 总有一天 **8** (subtle) 细微的 ‹*detail, distinction*›; (exact) 精确的 ‹*adjustment*› **9** (thin) 纤细的; **a ~ thread** 细线; **~ rain/mist** 细雨/薄雾; **not to put too ~ a point on it** fig 不客气地说 **10** (of tiny grains) 颗粒细小的; **~ sand/powder** 细沙/细粉末 **11** (with small gaps) 细密的 ‹*net, sieve, comb*› **12** (of metal) 纯的; **~ silver** 纯银; **gold 18 carats ~** 18K金

B *adv* **1** colloq (well) 很好地; **keep going, you're doing ~!** 继续下去，你干得不错！; **to get on** *or* **along ~** 相处得很好; **that suits me ~** 那对我很合适 **2** (into tiny pieces) 细小地; **to cut/tear sth. quite ~** 把…切/撕得很细 ‹*peel, paper*›; **to cut it a bit ~** colloq 几乎不留余地; **he's cut it a bit ~ if he wants to catch the 10 o'clock ferry** 如果他想赶10点钟的渡船，时间就抠得太紧了

fine: ~ art *n* [u and c] 美术; **the ~ arts** 艺术; **to have** *or* **get sth. down to a ~ art** 依靠经验使某技能达到炉火纯青的地步; **~-drawn** *adj* **1** (subtle) 微妙的 ‹*distinction, arguments*›; **2** (delicate) 娇小玲珑的 ‹*features*›; **he had a ~-drawn face** 他容貌清秀; **~-grained** *adj* 细纹的 ‹*wood*›; 细的 ‹*salt, sugar*›; 颗粒的 ‹*rock*›

finely /ˈfaɪnli/ *adv* **1** (excellently) 极好地; **a ~ written book/speech** 文笔优美的书/演讲稿; **~ crafted** 制作精美的 ‹*jewellery, object*›; **a ~ executed performance** 精彩的演出 **2** (into tiny pieces) 细小地; **to chop up the meat ~** 把肉剁细; **~ chopped nuts** 切得很细的坚果 **3** (subtly, delicately) 精细地; **~ shaped features** 清秀的面容; **a ~ balanced argument** fig 不偏不倚的论点 **4** (exactly, precisely) 准确地; **a ~ adjusted piece of apparatus** 精确校准的器械 **5** (beautifully) 华丽地 ‹*furnished, dressed*›

fineness /ˈfaɪnnɪs/ *n* [u] **1** (of china, craftsmanship, features) 精致 **2** (of clothes, furnishings) 华丽 **3** (of detail, distinction) 细微 **4** (of adjustment, measurement) 精确 **5** (of thread) 纤细 **6** (of rain) 细; (of mist) 薄 **7** (of sand, powder) 微小 **8** (of mesh, net) 细密 **9** (of silver, gold) 纯度

fine print *n* [u] = **small print**

finery /ˈfaɪnəri/ *n* [u] 华丽服饰; **she was dressed in all her ~** 她穿戴华丽

finesse /fɪˈnes/

A *n* [u] **1** (gen) 策略; **with ~** 巧妙地 **2** (in cards) 飞牌

B *vt* **1** (in cards) 用…飞 ‹*card*› **2** (handle skilfully) 用策略对付

C *vi* (in cards) «*player*» 飞牌; **to ~ against sb.** 出小牌来飞某人的牌

fine: ~-tooth comb, ~-toothed comb *n* 细齿梳子; **to go over** *or* **through sth. with a ~-tooth comb** fig 仔细检查某物; **~-tune** *vt* 对…进行微调 ‹*equipment, economy*›; **~ tuning** *n* [u] 微调

finger /ˈfɪŋɡə(r)/

A *n* ▸p. 71 **1** [c] 手指; **first/second ~** 食指/中指; **third** *or* **ring ~** 无名指; **fourth** *or* **little ~** 小指; **to hold sth. between ~ and thumb** 用拇指和另一指拿着某物; **to snap one's ~s** 打响指; **to run one's ~s through one's hair** 用手指梳理头发; **to be all ~s and thumbs** Brit colloq 笨手笨脚; **to point a** *or* **one's ~ (at) sb.** 指责某人; **to point the ~ of scorn/suspicion at sb.** 对某人轻蔑地/怀疑地指指点点; **to put one's ~ on sth.** fig 确切指出某事物; **there's something wrong, but I can't quite put my ~ on it** 有什么事不对劲儿，但我说不出到底是什么不对劲儿; **to put the ~ on sb.** colloq 告发某人; **not lift** *or* **raise a ~ (to help)** 一点儿忙也不帮; **to lay a ~ on sb./sth.** (touch) 触碰某人/某物; (harm) 动某人/某物一根毫毛; **I didn't lay a ~ on her!** 我没有动过她一根毫毛！; **to twist** *or* **wrap sb. round one's little ~** 任意摆布某人; **let sth./sb. slip through one's ~s** 错过某事物/某人; **to keep one's ~s crossed (for sb.)** （为某人）祈求好运; **to have a ~ in every pie** fig 参与其中/处处插手; **to get one's ~s burnt** *or* **to burn one's ~s** (due to meddling) 因多管闲事而吃苦头; (due to lack of caution) 因不谨慎而吃亏; **to work one's ~s to the bone** fig 拼命干活; **I can count on the ~s of one hand the number of times he's taken me out to dinner** 他带我出去吃饭的次数屈指可数; **to put two ~s up (at sb.)** Brit colloq （对某人）手背向外竖两根手指 [表示轻蔑]; **to give sb. the ~** Amer colloq 向某人竖中指 [表示侮辱] **2** (of glove) [手套的] 指部 **3** (narrow strip) 狭长物; **a ~ of land jutting out into the sea** 一块伸向大海的狭长土地; **a chocolate ~** 巧克力条; **a ~ of toast** 长条吐司 **4** colloq (measure) 指幅; **two ~s of brandy** 两指幅的白兰地

B *vt* **1** (touch with fingers) 用手指触碰; (fiddle with) 摆弄; **to ~ one's beard** 捋胡子 **2** Amer colloq 告发

finger: ~ biscuit *n* 手指饼干; **~board** *n* [弦乐器的] 指板; **~ bowl** *n* 洗指碗; **~ buffet** *n* 手抓自助餐; **~ cymbal** *n* 指钹; **~ food** *n* 手抓食物; **~ hole** *n* 调音指孔

fingering /ˈfɪŋɡərɪŋ/ *n* [u] (technique, method) 指法; (in musical score) 指法符号

finger: ~less glove *n* 无指手套; **~ mark** *n* 指痕; **~nail** *n* 手指甲; **~ paint** *n* 指画颜料; **~ painting** *n* **1** [u] (technique) [儿童的] 指画法; **2** [c] (picture) 指画; **~ post** *n* 指路牌

fingerprint /ˈfɪŋɡəprɪnt/

A *n* 指纹; **to take sb.'s ~s** 取某人的指纹; **to leave (one's) ~s** 留下指纹

B *vt* **1** (take fingerprints of) 取…的指纹 ‹*suspect, prisoner*› **2** (dust for fingerprints) 在…上撒粉寻找指纹 ‹*table, gun, window*›

finger: ~printing *n* [u] 指纹提取; **~printing kit** 指纹工具箱; **~stall** *n* 护指套

fingertip /ˈfɪŋɡətɪp/ *n* 指尖; **to have sth. at one's ~s** 可方便地得到某事物; **do you have all the information at your ~s?** 你有所有资料吗？

fingertip control *n* 指尖操控

finial /ˈfɪnɪəl/ *n* **1** Archit 尖顶饰 **2** (on furniture) 装饰头

finicky /ˈfɪnɪki/ *adj* **1** (fussy) 过分讲究的 ‹*person, eater*›; **to be ~ about sth.** 对某事过分讲究 **2** (fiddly) 烦琐的 ‹*job*›

finish /ˈfɪnɪʃ/

A *vt* **1** (end) 结束 ‹*activity*›; (complete) 完成 ‹*task*›; **to ~ eating** 吃完; **let me ~ what I was saying** 让我把话说完; **to ~ writing an essay/reading a book** 写完一篇文章/读完一本书; **when was the Pompidou Centre ~ed?** 蓬皮杜中心是什么时候建成的？; **to put the ~ing touches to sth.** 对某物作最后的润色; **he ~es university next year** 他明年大学毕业; **to ~ work** (for the day) 下班; (retire) 退休 **2** (eat all of) 吃完; (drink all of) 喝完; (use all of) 用完; **are you going to ~ those potatoes?** 你会把那些土豆吃完吗？ **3** colloq (destroy) 毁掉; **the scandal ~ed her as an actress** 这一丑闻毁了她的演艺生涯; **any more stress will ~ him** 再多一点压力就会让他崩溃; **climbing that mountain almost ~ed me** 爬那座山差点儿把我累死 **4** (treat) 对…进行表面处理; **to ~ the shelves with furniture oil** 给架子刷家具漆

B *vi* **1** (conclude, end) 结束; **the meeting didn't ~ until ten o'clock** 会议直到10点才结束; **to ~ by announcing sth.** 以公布某事作为结束; **let me ~** 让我把话说完; **the film ~es on Saturday** 这部影片将于星期六停映 **2** (reach end of race) 跑完全程; **to ~ first** *or* **in first place** 跑了第一名; **to ~ badly/well** 比赛成绩不好/好

C *n* **1** (end) 最后阶段; **from start to ~** 自始至终; **to be in at the ~** fig 在最后阶段在场 **2** (of race, journey) 终点; **to arrive at the ~** 到达终点; **it's going to be a close ~** 比赛结果将难分上下; **to fight to the ~** 战斗到底; **a fight to the ~** 持续到最后一刻的搏斗 **3** (surface appearance) 成品表面; (paint, lacquer,

f

etc.) 末道漆; (veneer) 饰面; **an oil/a wax ～** 油/蜡涂饰; **paint with a gloss/matt ～** 亮光/亚光漆; **a mahogany/metal ～** 红木/金属饰面

Phrasal verbs

• **finish off**

A [**～ sth. off, ～ off sth.**] *vt*

1 (consume all of) 吃完 ‹*food*›; 喝光 ‹*drink*› **2** (complete) 完成 ‹*work, task*›; **to ～ off the letter/book** 把信/书写完; **to ～ off the week's work** 做完一周的工作 **3** (end) 结束 ‹*activity*›; **to ～ off the conference with the national anthem** 以国歌结束会议; **to ～ off one's talk by announcing the winners** 以宣布获胜者名单结束讲话

B [**～ sb. off**] *vt*

1 (kill) 杀死; **to ～ sb. off with one's sword** 用剑结果了某人 **2** fig (destroy) 毁掉; **a mistake that ～ed him off as a politician** 一个断送他政治生涯的错误; **the final sprint ～ed me off** 最后的冲刺要了我的命

• **finish up**

A *vt* [**～ sth. up, ～ up sth.**] 吃完 ‹*food*›; 喝光 ‹*drink*›

B *vi* Brit 终结; **to ～ up (by) doing sth.** 以做某事结束; **he wanted to be an architect but ～ed up as a teacher** 他原来想当建筑师，但最后却成了老师; **I took the wrong bus and ～ed up on the other side of town** 我上错了公共汽车，结果到了城区的另一头

• **finish with**

A [**～ with sth.**] *vt* 不再需用; **have you ～ed with that book?** 那本书你已经看完了吗?; **to be ～ed with sth.** (stop using) 不再需用某物; (stop participating in) 不再参与某事; **give me the pen when you're ～ed with it** 这支笔你用完后给我; **I'm ～ed with theatre/politics!** 我与戏剧/政治一刀两断了!

B [**～ with sb.**] *vt*

1 (cut relations with) 与…断绝关系; **she ～ed with her boyfriend** 她与男友分手了 **2** colloq (stop scolding) 不再责怪; **I haven't ～ed with you yet!** 我和你还没完呢!

finished /ˈfɪnɪʃt/ *adj* **1** *pred* (ended) 结束了的; (gone forever) 不复存在的; **to be almost ～** 差不多结束了; **his love for you is ～** 他已不再爱你 **2** *pred* (ruined) 被毁掉的; **her career as a musician is ～** 她的职业音乐人生涯被断送了; **if they take legal action, I'm ～** 如果他们提起诉讼，我就完蛋了; **I'm ～!** (exhausted) 我累死了! **3** (treated) 处理过的; **to be ～ in panelling** 用嵌板装饰; **to be ～ with oil/blue paint** 上了油/刷了蓝漆; **beautifully ～ furniture** 做工精美的家具 **4** *attrib* (completed) 完成了的; **a ～ product** 成品

finishing: ～ line *n* 终点线; **～ post** *n* 终点柱; **to beat sb. to the ～ post** fig 抢在某人之前完成; **～ school** *n* 淑女学堂 [教授上流社会少女社交礼仪的私立学校]; **～ touch** *n* 最后润色; **to put the ～ touches to sth.** 对某物作最后润色

finite /ˈfaɪnaɪt/ *adj* **1** 有限的 ‹*knowledge, amount*›; **～ set/number** Math 有限集合/有限数 **2** Ling 限定的 ‹*verb, mood*›

Finland /ˈfɪnlənd/ *pr n* 芬兰

Finn /fɪn/ ▸**p. 503** *n* 芬兰人

Finnish /ˈfɪnɪʃ/ ▸**p. 503, p. 426**

A *adj* (of Finland) 芬兰的; (of the people) 芬兰人的; (of the language) 芬兰语的

B *n* **1** [c] (person) 芬兰人 **2** [u] (language) 芬兰语

fiord /fɪˈɔːd/ *n* = **fjord**

fir /fɜː(r)/ *n* **～ (tree)** 冷杉

fir cone *n* 冷杉球果

fire /ˈfaɪə(r)/

A *n* **1** [u] (element, state) 火; **to catch** *or* **be on ～** 着火; **to set ～ to sth., to set sth. on ～** 点燃某物; **to play with ～** 玩火; **my throat is on ～** fig 我的喉咙火辣辣的; **to fight ～ with ～** fig 以其人之道还治其人之身 **2** [c] (conflagration) 失火; **a ～ started** *or* **broke out** 发生了火灾; **a forest ～** 森林大火; **to fight/put out a ～** 救火/把火扑灭; **to be damaged by ～** 被火烧毁; **～!** 着火啦! **3** [c] (for warmth) (indoors) 炉火; (outdoors) 篝火; (for cooking) 灶火; **a log/coal ～** 柴火/煤火; **to lay the ～** 准备生火; **to build** *or* **make a ～** 生火; **to light a ～** 点火; **in front of the roaring ～** 在熊熊炉火前 **4** [c] (heater) 取暖器; **to turn a ～ on** 打开暖气; **an electric/a gas ～** 电/煤气取暖器 **5** [u] Mil (shots) 炮火; (shooting) 射击; **a burst of machine gun ～** 一阵机枪射击; **to open ～ (on sb.)** (向某人) 开火; **to return (sb.'s) ～** 回击 (某人); **to exchange ～** 交火; **to hold one's ～** 停止射击; **to be/come under ～ (from sb.)** lit 遭到 (某人的) 炮火袭击; fig 遭到 (某人的) 攻击; **to be** *or* **get caught in the line of ～** lit 处于射程之内; fig 撞到枪口上; **to concentrate one's ～ on sb.** fig 集中全力抨击某人; **to hang** *or* **hold ～** 搁置 **6** [u] fig (passion) 激情; (anger) 愤怒; **to be on ～ with enthusiasm/love** 激情满怀/为爱痴狂; **to set the world on ～** colloq 引起轰动; **he'll never set the world on ～ with his paintings** 他的画永远不会引起轰动

B *vt* **1** Mil 开 ‹*cannon*›; 发射 ‹*rocket, missile*›; 射出 ‹*bullet*›; **who ～d the first shot?** 是谁开的第一枪?; **they ～d their guns at the crowd/into the air** 他们向人群开枪/朝天鸣枪; **to ～ a 21-gun salute** 鸣放21响礼炮; **to ～ an arrow at sth.** 向某物射箭 **2** fig (shoot) 急速发出; **to ～ questions at sb.** 向某人接二连三地提问; **to ～ remarks/insults at sb.** 对某人连珠炮似地说话/说侮辱的话 **3** fig (inspire) 激发 ‹*desire, enthusiasm*›; 使…充满激情 ‹*person*›; **to ～ one's imagination** 激发想象力; **to be ～d with renewed enthusiasm for the project** 重新燃起对这个项目的热情 **4** (dismiss) 解雇; **to be ～d (for sth.)** (因为某事) 被开除 **5** (heat) 点燃 ‹*kiln, furnace*› **6** (bake) 烧制 ‹*pot, glaze*›

C *vi* **1** Mil 射击; **to ～ at** *or* **on sb./sth.** 向某人/某物射击; **to ～ into the air** 朝天鸣枪; **the gun wouldn't ～** 这支枪打不响; **～!** 开火!; **～ away!** colloq (speak) 说吧!; (ask) 问吧! **2** Aut ‹*engine*› 点火; **to be firing on all cylinders** lit 所有汽缸一起点火; fig 全力以赴

Phrasal verbs

• **fire off** *vt* [**～ off sth., ～ sth. off**]

1 Mil 射出 ‹*bullet*›; 发射 ‹*missile*›; **to ～ off a few rounds** 打几发子弹 **2** fig 连珠炮似地发出 ‹*questions, information*›; **to ～ off a letter/report** 急速发出一封信/一份报告; **to ～ off names on a list** 一口气念出名单上的名字

• **fire up** *vt* **1** [**～ sb. up, ～ up sb.**] 充满激情; **to be all ～d up** 满怀热情 **2** [**～ sth. up, ～ up sth.**] 发动 ‹*engine*›

fire: ～ alarm *n* 火警报警器; **～-and-brimstone** *adj attrib* 用地狱烈火恐吓听众的 ‹*preacher, sermon*›; **～ appliance** *n* 消防车; **～arm** *n* 枪; **～ball** *n* **1** (ball of fire) 火球; **2** Astron 火流星; **3** Meteorol 球状闪电; **4** fig (person full of energy) 精力充沛的人; (hot-tempered person) 脾气火暴的人; **～base** *n* 重火力点; **～ bell** *n* 火警钟; **～boat** *n* 消防艇

firebomb /ˈfaɪəbɒm/

A *n* 燃烧弹

B *vt* (attack) 用燃烧弹进攻; (destroy) 用燃烧弹摧毁

fire: ～box *n* 机车锅炉炉膛; **～brand** *n* **1** (burning wood) 燃烧的木块; **2** fig (radical) 狂热分子; **～break** *n* 火障; **～brick** *n* 耐火砖; **～ brigade** *n* esp Brit (organization) 消防队; (people) + *v sing or pl* 消防人员; **～ chief** ▸**p. 409** *n* Amer 消防署署长; **～clay** *n* [u] 耐火黏土; **～ cover** *n* **1** Insur 火险; **2** (availability of emergency fire services) 紧急救火服务; **～cracker** *n* 爆竹; **～ curtain** *n* 防火幕; **～-damaged** *adj* 烧毁的 ‹*building, vehicle, stock*›; **～damp** *n* [u] 沼气; **～ department** *n* Amer = **～ brigade**; **～dog** *n* [成对的] 薪架; **～ door** *n* **1** (fire-resistant door) 防火安全门; **2** (emergency exit) 安全出口; **～ drill** *n* 消防演习; **～-eater** *n* 吞火表演者; **～ engine** *n* 消防车; **～ escape** *n* 太平梯; **～ exit** *n* 安全出口; **～ extinguisher** *n* 灭火器; **～fighter** ▸**p. 409** *n* 消防队员; **～fighting** *n* [u] 消防; **in a crisis the best staff are diverted to ～fighting** fig 在出现险情时，最好的人员被派去救火; **～fly** *n* 萤火虫; **～guard** *n* 炉栏; **～ hazard** *n* 火灾隐患; **～house** *n* Amer 消防站; **～ hydrant** *n* 消防栓; **～ insurance** *n* 火险; **～ irons** *npl* 火炉用具; **～light** *n* [u] 炉火光; **by ～light** 在炉火旁; **we sat telling stories by (the) ～light** 我们坐在炉火旁边讲故事; **～lighter** *n* [生炉子的] 引火物; **～man** /-mən/ ▸**p. 409** *n* 消防队员; **～ marshal** *n* **1** ▸**p. 409** Amer (fire service head) 消防署署长; **2** Brit (person delegated) 消防安全员; **～place** *n* 壁炉; **～ plug** *n* Amer 消防栓; **～ power** *n* [u] 火力; **financial ～power** fig 财力; **the team's lack of ～power this season** fig 该队本赛季攻击力的缺乏; **～ practice** *n* 消防演习; **～ prevention** *n* [u] 防火要求

fireproof /ˈfaɪəpruːf/

A *adj* **1** (fire-resistant) 防火的 ‹*clothing, door*› **2** Culin 耐火的 ‹*dish*›

B *vt* 使…防火 ‹*clothing, door*›; 使…耐火 ‹*dishes, furniture*›

fire: ～-raiser *n* Brit 纵火者; **～-raising** *n* [u] Brit 纵火; **～ regulations** *npl* 防火条例; **～ risk** *n* 火灾隐患; **～ sale** *n* 火灾后大甩卖; fig [尤指面临严重财务困境时的] 大甩卖; **～ screen** *n* 挡火隔板; **～ service** *n* 消防队; **～side** *n* 炉边; **to sit by the ～side** 坐在炉边; **a ～side chat** 炉边闲谈; **～ station** *n* 消防站; **～ tower** *n* 火警瞭望塔; **～trap** *n* 火灾陷阱 [指易失火或失火时难逃离的建筑物]; **～truck** *n* Amer 消防车; **～wall** *n* 防火墙; **～ warden** ▸**p. 409** *n* 消防员; **～water** *n* [u] colloq 烈酒; **～wood** *n* [u] 木柴

firework /ˈfaɪəwɜːk/

A *n* 烟火; **to let** *or* **set off a ～** 燃放烟火

B **fireworks** *npl* **1** lit 烟火燃放; **～s display** 烟火表演 **2** fig colloq (excitement) 精彩表演 **3** fig colloq (outburst of anger) 激烈言辞; **to wait for the ～s to die down** 等待纷争平息下来

firing /ˈfaɪərɪŋ/ *n* **1** [u] (of guns) 射击; **the ～ had been going on since dawn** 从拂晓起枪炮声一直不断 **2** [c and u] (of ceramics) 焙烧

firing: ～ line *n* 射击线; **to be in the ～ line** lit 处于射程以内; fig 易受攻击; **～ pin** *n* [枪的] 撞针; **～ squad** *n* 行刑队; **to face a ～ squad** 将被执行枪决

firm¹ /fɜːm/ *n* 商行; **a ～ of accountants** 会计师事务所; **a taxi ～** 出租车公司

firm²

A *adj* **1** (hard, solid) 坚硬的; **a ～ mattress** 硬床垫; **～ muscles** 结实的肌肉; **to be on ～ ground** lit 在坚实的地面上; fig 对事实确信无疑 **2** (forceful) 强力的; **to give sth. a ～ tap/tug** 用力拍/拉某物; **to get a ～ grip on sth.** 紧紧握住某物 **3** (strong) 牢固的 ‹*knot*›; (secure) 稳固的 ‹*base*›; **to hold sth. ～** 牢牢抓住某物; **to establish a ～ foothold in the market** fig 在市场上站稳脚跟; **to have a ～ hold on sth./sb.** fig 牢牢控制某事物/某人 **4** (definite) 确定的; **a ～ decision** 不能更改的决定; **a ～ offer** 实盘; **～ evidence** 确凿的证据; **the ～ favourite** (person, horse, etc.) 热门选手 **5** (resolute) 坚定的 ‹*person, voice, step, belief, support*›; 坚决的 ‹*attitude, resistance*›; 严格的 ‹*control, discipline*›; **to be ～ about sth./with sb.** 对某事物/某人态度坚决; **to stand ～ (against sb./sth.)** (对某人/某事物) 采取坚定立场; **a ～ belief/believer** 坚定的信念/信徒; **that child needs a ～ hand** 那个孩子需要严加管教 **6** Fin 坚挺的 ‹*currency*›; 稳定的 ‹*interest rate, investment*›; **to remain**

~ **against the dollar** «*currency*» 对美元保持坚挺
B *vt* 使坚实; ~ **the soil with your foot** 用脚把土踩实

Phrasal verb

• ~ **up** *vt* [~ **up sth.**, ~ **sth. up**]
1 lit 使…结实 ‹*muscles, body*›; 使…坚实 ‹*soil*› 2 fig 确定 ‹*appointment, deal*›; **to** ~ **up the details of a contract** 敲定合同的细节; **to** ~ **prices up** 稳定物价

firmament /'fɜːməmənt/ *n* liter 苍穹

firmly /'fɜːmli/ *adv* 1 (solidly) 密实地; ~ **packed soil/sugar** 压紧的泥土/食糖; **a** ~ **filled cushion** 塞得结结实实的垫子 2 (forcefully) 强有力地; **to tap** ~ **on sth.** 用力拍某物; **to shut the door** ~ 使劲关上门; **to grasp sth.** ~ 紧紧抓住某物 3 (strongly) 牢固地; (securely) 稳固地; **to be fixed** ~ **in place** 被牢牢地固定住; **the base stands** ~ **on four legs** 四根支柱稳稳地支撑着底座; **to be** ~ **rooted** *or* **embedded in sth.** 牢牢地扎根于某物; **to be** ~ **established (as sth.)** 稳固地确立（作为某物的）地位; **to keep one's feet** ~ **on the ground** fig 站稳脚跟 4 (resolutely) 坚定地 ‹*speak*›; 坚决地 ‹*maintain*›; 严格地 ‹*treat, handle*›; **I** ~ **believe that ...** 我坚信…; **to** ~ **insist that ...** 坚决要求…; **to deal** ~ **with sb./sth.** 严格对待某人/某物

firmness /'fɜːmnɪs/ *n* [u] 1 (of mattress, surface, ground) 坚硬; **the** ~ **of one's muscles** 肌肉的结实 2 (of push, tug, grip) 强力 3 (of knot) 牢固; (of base) 稳固 4 (of decision, offer) 确定 5 (of person, voice, belief, support) 坚定; **to treat sb. with** ~ 严格对待某人

firmware /'fɜːmweə(r)/ *n* [u] 固件

first /fɜːst/ ▸p. 181, p. 521
A *adj* 1 *usu attrib* (in sequence, placement) 第一的; (in time) 最早的; (initial) 最初的; **it's her** ~ **birthday** 这是她1岁生日; **on the** ~ **floor** 在2楼; **the** ~ **door on the right** 右边的第一扇门; **the** ~ **three pages** 前三页; **her** ~ **year at university** 她上大学的头一年; **the** ~ **symptoms of the disease** 这种疾病的初起症状; **one's** ~ **impression of sth.** 对某事物的第一印象; **the** ~ **thing that comes to mind** *or* **into one's head** 最先想到的事; **in the** ~ **place** (firstly) 首先; (immediately) 一开始; (anyway) 无论如何; **why didn't you phone the police in the** ~ **place?** 你为什么不先报警?; **he shouldn't have left the door open in the** ~ **place** 他根本就不应该让门开着; **to make the** ~ **move** 采取主动; **the** ~ **time** 第一次; **I warned him, not for the** ~ **time, that the current was very strong** 我不止一次警告过他，水流很急; **there's (got to be) a** ~ **time for everything** 凡事都有第一次; **to drink coffee** ~ **thing in the morning** 一大早就喝咖啡; **I'll do it** ~ **thing** 我马上就做 2 *usu attrib* (most important) 最重要的; (top) 第一流的; **my** ~ **duty** 我的首要任务; **my** ~ **choice** 我的首选; **to win** ~ **prize** 获得一等奖; **he was** ~, **I was second** 他第一名，我第二名; **~-division football** 足球甲级联赛; **F~ Lord of the Admiralty** 海军大臣; ~ **things** ~ 要事第一; **to put** ~ **things** ~ 先做要紧的事 3 *attrib* (in name, title) 一世; **Henry the F~ of England** 英王亨利一世; **Arthur Wellesley,** ~ **Duke of Wellington** 亚瑟·韦尔兹利，惠灵顿公爵一世 4 (slightest) 最起码的; **not to know the** ~ **thing about sb./sth.** 对某人/某事一无所知; **not to have the** ~ **idea what to do/where to go** 完全不知道该做什么/该去哪里
B *adv* 1 (before others) 最先; **he left** ~ 他第一个走了; **you (go)** ~! 你先请!; **ladies** ~! 女士优先!; **women and children** ~ 妇女和儿童优先; **she got there** ~ lit 她先到了; colloq fig 她抢先一步; **which comes** ~, **A or B?** A和B哪个在前?; ~ **come,** ~ **served** (for service) 先来先接待; (to receive sth.) 先到先得; **to be born head** ~ 出生时头先出来; **I'll leave this house feet** ~ fig 我死了才会离开这栋房子 2 (at top of ranking, firstly) 第一; **to come** *or* **finish** ~ 获得第一名; **to come** *or* **place** ~ **(in a competition)** （在比赛中）得第一名; **his career comes** ~ 他把事业放在第一位; **to put sb./sth.** ~ fig 首先考虑某人/某事; **to be a mother** ~ **and an accountant second** 首先是一位母亲，然后才是一名会计师; ~ **and last** colloq 从各方面看 3 (in first position) 居第一位 4 (for the first time) 第一次; **the play was** ~ **performed in 1845** 该剧的首次演出是在1845年; **when did the symptoms** ~ **appear?** 这些症状初次出现是什么时候? 5 (to begin with) 首先; ~ **we must decide ...** 首先我们必须决定…; ~ **you say you like it, then you say you don't** 你先是说喜欢它，然后又说不喜欢; ~ **of all** 首先 6 (initially) 最初; **when we were** ~ **married** 我们刚结婚时; **to be** ~ **used as sth.** 最初用作某物 7 (rather) 宁可; **move? I'd die** ~! 搬家? 我宁死也不搬!
C *n* 1 *sing* (first one) (in sequence) 第一; **I was the** ~ **to arrive** 我第一个到; **to be the** ~ **for 5 years** 是5年来的第一个; **Beethoven's** ~ 贝多芬第一交响曲 2 (of date) **the** ~ **of June, June the** ~ 6月1日 3 (the beginning) 开始; **at** ~ 最初; **from the (very)** ~ 从一开始; **from** ~ **to last** 自始至终 4 (notable event) 空前的成就; **to be a** ~ 是创举; **a** ~ **for the Australian team** 澳大利亚队的历史最好成绩 5 Aut 第一挡; **to be in** ~ «*car, driver*» 挂头挡 6 Brit Univ 优等成绩; **she got a** ~ **in physics** 她获得物理一级优等学位

first: ~ **aid** *n* [u] 急救; **to give sb.** ~ 对某人进行急救; **lessons in** ~ 急救课; **a** ~ **kit** 急救药箱; **~-aider** *n* 急救员; **~-aid officer** *n* 急救员; ~ **base** *n* 一垒; **not to get to** ~ **base** lit 未上一垒; fig 不能顺利开始

firstborn /'fɜːstbɔːn/
A *n* 头胎; **he was my** ~ 他是我的长子
B *adj* 头生的; **their** ~ **son/daughter** 他们的长子/长女

first class
A *n* 1 Tourism, Transp 头等; **a seat in** ~ 头等舱座位 2 Post 第一类邮件
B **first-class** *adj* 1 Tourism, Transp 头等的 ‹*cabin*›; 头等舱的 ‹*ticket, seat*› 2 Post 第一类的 ‹*mail*› 3 Brit Univ 一级优等的 ‹*honours, degree*› 4 (excellent) 极好的 ‹*hotel, cricket*›; **he was a** ~ **writer** 他是一流作家
C *adv* 1 Tourism, Transp (by train) 乘头等车 ‹*travel*›; (by plane, boat) 乘头等舱 ‹*travel*› 2 Post 作为第一类邮件

first: ~ **course** *n* 第一道菜; ~ **cousin** *n* (male) (paternal) 嫡堂兄弟; (maternal) 嫡表兄弟; (female) (paternal) 嫡堂姐妹; (maternal) 嫡表姐妹; ▸remove B14; **~-degree burns** *npl* 一度烧伤; **~-degree murder** *n* Amer 一级谋杀罪; ~ **edition** *n* (publication) 第一版; (copy) 第一版书刊; **~-ever** *adj attrib* 首次的

first floor
A *n* 1 Brit 二楼 2 Amer = **ground floor 1**
B **first-floor** *adj attrib* 1 Brit 二楼的 2 Amer 一楼的

first-foot Scot
A *vt* 作为新年第一位访客进入
B *n* 新年第一位访客

first: **~-footer** *n* Scot 新年第一位访客; **~-footing** *n* [u] Scot 拜新年; **to go ~-footing** 去拜新年; ~ **form** *n* Brit [中等学校的] 一年级; **~-former** *n* Brit [中等学校的] 一年级学生; ~ **fruits** *npl* fig 最初成果; ~ **gear** *n* [汽车等的] 第一挡; **~-generation** *adj* 第一代移民的 ‹*American*›; 第一代的 ‹*machine*›; ~ **grade** *n* Amer (class) 小学一年级; (pupils) 小学一年级全体学生

firsthand /ˌfɜːst'hænd/
A *adj attrib* 第一手的 ‹*information*›; 亲身的 ‹*experience*›
B **first hand** *n* **at** ~ 直接地
C *adv* 直接地 ‹*obtain*›

first: ~ **lady** *n* 1 Amer Pol 第一夫人; 2 (leading exponent) 女杰; **the** ~ **lady of sth.** 某行业中的女领袖; ~ **language** *n* 母语，第一语言; ~ **lieutenant** *n* 1 Brit 舰务官; 2 Amer 中尉; ~ **light** *n* [u] 破晓; **at** ~ **light** 在黎明时分

firstly /'fɜːstli/ *adv* 第一

first: ~ **mate** *n* [商船的] 大副; ~ **minister** *n* Brit 首席部长 [指苏格兰、威尔士和北爱尔兰地区的执政党领袖]; ~ **name** *n* 名字; **to be on** ~ **name terms with sb.** 与某人以名字相称; **F~ Nation** *n* Can 原部落居民 [指加拿大土著居民，不包括伊努伊特人或梅蒂人]; ~ **night** *n* (first performance) 首演; (evening of first performance) 首演之夜; *modif* ~ **night nerves** 首演的紧张感; ~ **night audience** 首场观众; ~ **offender** *n* 初犯; ~ **officer** *n* 大副; **~-past-the-post** *adj* Brit 得票最多者当选的 ‹*system*›; ~ **performance** *n* 首场演出; ~ **person** *n* 第一人称; **in the** ~ **person** 以第一人称的形式; ~ **person singular/plural** 第一人称单数/复数; ~ **person shooter** *n* 第一人称射击游戏; ~ **principles** *npl* 基本原理; **to go back to** ~ **principles** 回到基本原理上来; **~-rate** *adj* 第一流的; ~ **refusal** *n* 优先购买权; **to give sb.** ~ **refusal (on sth.)** 给某人（某物的）优先购买权; **to have** ~ **refusal (on sth.)** （对某物）拥有优先购买权; ~ **school** *n* Brit [5至9岁儿童上的] 第一学校; **~-strike** *adj* 第一次核打击的; **~-strike capability** 第一次核打击能力; **~-time buyer** *n* 初次购房者; **~-timer** *n* colloq 第一次做某事的人; **he's a ~-timer** 他是第一次做; ~ **violin** *n* 第一小提琴; ~ **water** *n* **of the** ~ **water** lit 第一水的 ‹*diamond*›; fig 第一流的 ‹*actor, musician*›; **F~ World** *n* 第一世界; ~ **year** *n* (group) 一年级; (pupil, student) 一年级学生; **a group of ~-year students** 一群一年级学生

firth /fɜːθ/ *n* 狭长海湾

fiscal /'fɪskl/ *adj* 财政的 ‹*policy*›

fiscal: ~ **drag** *n* [u] 经济活力减退; ~ **year** *n* Amer 财政年度

fish /fɪʃ/
A *n* 1 [u and c] (*pl* ~ *or* esp child lang or liter **~es**) Zool 鱼; **a shoal of** ~ 一大群鱼; **freshwater/sea/tropical** ~ 淡水鱼/海鱼/热带鱼; **to catch a** ~ 捕到一条鱼; **like a** ~ **out of water** colloq 如鱼离水; **to drink like a** ~ colloq 饮酒过度; **there are plenty more** *or* **of other** ~ **in the sea** colloq (available men or women) 天涯何处无芳草; **to have other** ~ **to fry** colloq 还有更重要的事要做 2 [u] Culin 鱼肉; **dried** ~ 鱼干; **a** ~ **market** 鱼市; **a** ~ **bone** 鱼刺; **a** ~ **fork** 鱼餐叉 3 [u] colloq (person) **an odd/a cold** ~ Brit 怪人/冷淡的家伙; **a big** ~ **in a little pond** 小池塘里的大鱼 [指只在小范围内有影响的人]
B *vi* 1 (with rod) 钓鱼; (with nets) 捕鱼; **to go (trout) ~ing** 去钓（鳟）鱼; **to** ~ **for salmon** 捕鲑鱼; **to** ~ **off the coast** 在离海岸不远处捕鱼; **to** ~ **in troubled waters** fig 混水摸鱼 2 fig (try to get) 转弯抹角地谋取; (try to find out) 旁敲侧击地打听; **to** ~ **for information/compliments** 转弯抹角地探听消息/谋取恭维; **stop ~ing!** 别再打听了!
C *vt* 1 (with rod) 在…中钓鱼 ‹*waters, river*›; (with nets) 在…中捕鱼 ‹*waters, sea*› 2 colloq (from bag, box) 掏出; (from water) 捞出; **to** ~ **sth. from one's pocket** 从口袋里掏出某物; **they ~ed a body from the canal** 他们在运河里捞上来一具尸体

Phrasal verbs

• **fish around** *vi* 找寻; **to** ~ **around for sth.** 摸找 ‹*object*›; 探求 ‹*information*›
• **fish out** *vt* [~ **sth. out,** ~ **out sth.**] (from bag, box) 掏出; (from water) 捞出

fish and chips *n* + *v sing or pl* 炸鱼薯条

fish: ~ and chip shop *n* Brit 炸鱼薯条店; **~bowl** *n* 金鱼缸; **~ cake** *n* 煎鱼饼

> **fish and chips**
>
> 炸鱼薯条。英国传统食品。炸鱼和薯条本来分开卖，大约在维多利亚时期合而为一，现已成为英国的标志之一。做法是将鳕鱼（cod）、鲽（sole）或黑线鳕（haddock）裹上面糊后油炸，和炸薯条（chip，美国英语作 French fries，简称 fries）一起就盐和醋食用，鱼上一般还会挤一些柠檬汁。炸鱼薯条在澳大利亚、新西兰等国也很受欢迎。经营炸鱼薯条的食品店也可称作 fish and chips，一般称 fish and chip shop，昵称为 chippy。人们通常将炸鱼薯条用纸包好，带走食用。

fisherman /ˈfɪʃəmən/ ▸**p. 409** *n* (as job) 渔民; (for sport) 垂钓者

fishery /ˈfɪʃəri/ *n* **1** [c] (area) 渔场 **2** [u] (occupation, industry) 渔业

fishery protection vessel *n* 渔业保护船

fish: ~-eye lens *n* 鱼眼镜头; **~ farm** *n* 养鱼场; **~ farming** *n* [u] 养鱼; **~ finger** *n* Brit [涂有面包粉煎炸的] 鱼条; **~ food** *n* 鱼食; **~ fry** *n* Amer 以吃炸鱼为主的野餐; **~ hook** *n* 鱼钩

fishing /ˈfɪʃɪŋ/ *n* [u] (as job) 捕鱼; (for sport) 钓鱼; **to go ~** 去钓鱼; **deep-sea ~** 深海捕鱼; *modif* **~ harbour/port** 渔港; **a ~ match/competition** 钓鱼比赛/竞赛

fishing: ~ boat *n* 渔船; **~ fleet** *n* 渔船队; **~ ground** *n* 渔场; **~ industry** *n* 渔业; **~ line** *n* 钓线; **~ net** *n* 渔网; **~ rod** *n* 钓竿; **~ tackle** *n* [u] 钓具; **~ village** *n* 渔村

fish: ~ kettle *n* 煮鱼锅; **~ ladder** *n* 鱼梯 [使鱼向上逐级游过水坝或瀑布的梯层水池]; **~ market** *n* 鱼市; **~ meal** *n* [u] [用作饲料或肥料的] 鱼粉

fishmonger /ˈfɪʃmʌŋɡə(r)/ ▸**p. 409** *n* Brit 鱼商; **the ~'s** 鱼店

fish: ~net *n* [u] 网眼织物; *modif* **a pair of ~net tights/stockings** 网眼裤袜/网眼长袜; **~ paste** *n* 鱼酱; **~pond** *n* 鱼塘; **~ restaurant** *n* 鱼味馆; **~ shop** Brit, **~ store** Amer *ns* 鱼店; **~ slice** *n* (for frying) 煎鱼锅铲; (for serving) 切鱼刀; **~ stick** *n* Amer [涂有面包粉煎炸的] 鱼条; **~ tank** *n* 玻璃鱼缸

fishy /ˈfɪʃi/ *adj* **1** lit 鱼腥的 ‹*taste*›; **there's a ~ smell in the fridge** 冰箱里有股鱼腥味 **2** fig colloq (suspicious) 可疑的 ‹*explanation, situation*›; **it sounds a bit ~ to me** 我觉得这事听起来有点可疑

fissile /ˈfɪsaɪl, Amer ˈfɪsl/ *adj* 可裂变的; **~ material** 可裂变材料

fission /ˈfɪʃn/ *n* [u] **(nuclear) ~** （核）裂变

fissure /ˈfɪʃə(r)/ *n* 裂缝

fist /fɪst/ *n* 拳; **to shake one's ~ at sb.** 向某人挥动拳头; **to clench one's ~** 捏紧拳头; **to make a ~** 握拳; **hand over ~** 快速大量地; **to make money hand over ~** 轻轻松松赚大钱; **to make a good/poor ~ of sth.** colloq 把某事做得很成功/不成功; **an iron ~ in a velvet glove** 外柔内刚

fist fight *n* 拳斗; **to have** *or* **get into a ~ with sb.** 与某人挥拳相斗

fistful /ˈfɪstfʊl/ *n* 一把; **a ~ of sth.** 一把某物

fisticuffs /ˈfɪstɪkʌfs/ *npl* 拳斗

fit[1] /fɪt/

A *adj* **1** (in trim) 健康的; **to keep (oneself) ~** 保持健康; **to look/feel ~** 看上去/感觉身体很好; **I am not ~ for work** 我身体不适，不能上班; **as ~ as a fiddle** colloq 非常健康的 **2** *pred* (suitable) 适合的; **to be ~ for the job** 能胜任工作; **a house/meal ~ for a queen** *or* **king** 富丽堂皇的房子/精致可口的食物; **this house is not ~ to live in** 这房子不适宜居住; **I'm not ~ to be seen** 我的样子无法见人; **not a ~ time to do sth.** 不是做某事的时候; **to be ~ and proper** formal 适宜; **to see** *or* **think ~ to do sth.** 认为做某事是妥当的; **to do as one sees** *or* **thinks ~** 做认为该做的事 **3** *pred* colloq (ready) 几乎要…的; **shouting/singing ~ to wake the dead** 叫声/歌声大得几乎能把死人吵醒; **she looked ~ to drop** 她看起来快要累垮了; **to laugh ~ to burst** 差点笑破肚子; **~ to be tied** colloq 非常恼火

B *vt* (*pres p* **fitting**, *pt, pp* **fitted** *or* Amer **fit**) **1** (be the right size for) 《*clothes, size*》 适合 ‹*person*›; **these trousers don't ~ me** 这条裤子我穿不合身; **to ~ one like a glove** 非常合身; **to ~ ages 3 to 5** 适合 3 至 5 岁的孩子穿; **one size ~s all** 均码; **to ~ the lock** 《*key*》 能开这把锁; **to ~ an A4 envelope** 可以装进一个 A4 信封 **2** (find room for) 找空间安置; **how are we going to ~ everyone into the hall?** 礼堂怎么容纳下所有的人呢？; **to ~ another plant on one's desk** 在桌上再放一盆植物; **to ~ three meetings into one day** 在一天中安排开三次会 **3** (install) 安装 ‹*attachment*›; (equip) 给…装配件 ‹*car, chair*›; **to ~ sth. into place** 把某物安装好; **to ~ a kitchen/garage with sth.** 为厨房/为车库配备某物; **I ~ted the car with an alarm** *or* **I ~ted an alarm to the car** 我在车上装了警报器 **4** (insert) 把…放入; **to ~ the key into the lock** 把钥匙插进锁孔 **5** (try on) 让…试 ‹*person*›; **to ~ sb. for a suit/dress** 让某人试穿西装/裙子; **to ~ sb. with sth.** 为某人调试 ‹*glasses, hearing aid*› **6** fig (match) 符合; (go with) 与…相称; **to ~ a description/theory** 符合描述/理论; **that chair doesn't ~ the room** 那把椅子与房间不相配; **the punishment should ~ the crime** 罚需当罪; **to ~ the bill** colloq 符合要求 **7** (qualify) 使合格; **your experience ~s you for the job** 你的经验使你胜任这份工作; **to be ~ted for the role of prime minister** 能担任首相一职 **8** (adjust) 使适应; **we must ~ our policies to the new circumstances** 我们必须根据新情况调整我们的政策

C *vi* (*pres p* **fitting**; *pt, pp* **fitted** *or* Amer **fit**) **1** (be the right size or shape) 合适; **the jacket doesn't ~** 这件夹克衫不合身; **to ~ like a glove** 《*clothes, size*》 非常合身; **a lid that ~s** 大小合适的盖子; **to ~ inside one another** 《*bowls*》 可以摞在一起; **all the jigsaw pieces ~ into place** 拼图的所有图块都安放到位 **2** (be accommodated in) 被容纳; **will the toys all ~ into the box?** 那个盒子装得下所有玩具吗？ **3** fig (tally, match) 符合; **his story doesn't ~** 他的说法不相符; **something doesn't ~ here** 这里有些不协调; **his statement doesn't ~ with the facts** 他的陈述与事实不符; **to ~ into one's lifestyle/philosophy** 符合自己的生活方式/理念

D *n* 合适; **to be a good ~** 《*garment*》 很合身; **to prefer a looser ~** 偏爱宽松的衣服; **the ~ is quite good** 大小正合适; **the plug is a perfect ~ for the sink** 这个塞子用在这个水槽正合适; **with seven of us it'll be a tight ~** 我们有 7 个人，会很挤的

Phrasal verbs

• **fit in**

A *vi* **1** (be inserted) 被放入; **the battery ~s in there** 电池可以装进那里 **2** (be accommodated) 被容纳; **seven people could ~ in (easily)** 可以（轻松）容纳 7 人; **these books won't ~ in** 这些书放不下 **3** fig (be compatible) 《*statement, plan*》 符合; ‹*person*› 相处融洽; **to ~ in with sb./sth.** 适合某人/某事物; **it didn't ~ in with our arrangements** 这与我们的安排有冲突; **to ~ in (with other people)** （与其他人）合得来; **I'll ~ in with your plans** 我会配合你的计划

B *vt* [**~ sth./sb. in, ~ in sth./sb.**] **1** (find room for) 找到空间安放; **can you ~ in another book?** 你能再放进一本书吗？ **2** fig (find time for) 安排时间见 ‹*person*›; 安排时间做 ‹*activity*›; **can you ~ me in at 10 o'clock tomorrow?** 你能安排明天上午 10 点与我见面吗？; **to ~ in a holiday next month** 下个月抽出时间去度假

• **fit out** *vt* **1** [**~ sth. out**] 为…提供所需物; **the kitchen is very well ~ted out** 这个厨房设备齐全; **to ~ out sth. as sth.** 把某物改装成某物; **to ~ the spare bedroom out as an office** 把闲置的卧室布置成办公室 **2** **to ~ sb. out with sth.** 给某人配备某物; **the optician will ~ you out with reading glasses** 这位眼镜技师将为你配阅读用眼镜

• **fit together**

A *vt* **to ~ A and B together** 把 A 和 B 组合在一起; **the tent poles have to be ~ted together** 帐篷支柱必须组装起来; **to ~ together the pieces of a puzzle** lit 把拼图的图块拼好; fig 理清难题

B *vi* 组合在一起

• **fit up** *vt* **1** = **fit out 2** **2** [**~ sb. up**] Brit colloq (incriminate) 诬陷

fit[2] *n* **1** Med (attack) 发作; (loss of consciousness) 昏厥; **to fall down in a ~** 突然昏倒; **to have an epileptic ~** 癫痫发作 **2** (burst of emotion, panic, etc.) 突发; **a ~ of coughing** 一阵咳嗽; **to do sth. in a ~ of rage** 一怒之下做某事; **she had a ~ of panic** 她感到一阵恐慌; **to be in ~s (of laughter)** colloq 大笑不止; **to have** *or* **throw a (blue) ~** colloq 大发雷霆; **by** *or* **in ~s and starts** 间歇地; **to progress by ~s and starts** 时断时续地进行

fitful /ˈfɪtfl/ *adj* 断断续续的 ‹*sleep*›; 一阵阵的 ‹*showers, breeze*›; 反复无常的 ‹*rage*›

fitfully /ˈfɪtfəli/ *adv* 断断续续地 ‹*sleep, work, rain*›

fitment /ˈfɪtmənt/ *n* Brit [嵌于墙壁的] 家具

fitness /ˈfɪtnɪs/ *n* [u] **1** (physical condition) 健康; **physical ~** 身体健康 **2** (suitability) 适合; **~ for sth./to do sth.** 适合某事/做某事; **to doubt sb.'s ~ for a job** 怀疑某人做工作是否称职

fitness: ~ consultant *n* 健身顾问; **~ fanatic** *n* 健身迷; **~ test** *n* 健康检查; **~ training** *n* [u] 健身锻炼

fitted /ˈfɪtɪd/ *adj* **1** Fashn 合身的 ‹*dress*› **2** esp Brit (built-in) 有订做配套设备的 ‹*kitchen*›; 订做的 ‹*wardrobe*›

fitted: ~ carpet *n* 铺满地面的地毯; **~ sheet** *n* 床笠 [边缘有松紧带的床单，可紧紧包裹住床垫]

fitter /ˈfɪtə(r)/ ▸**p. 409** *n* **1** (of machines, electrical equipment) 装配工 **2** (of carpets) **a (carpet) ~** 地毯安装工 **3** (of garment) 试衣裁缝

fitting /ˈfɪtɪŋ/

A *adj* (suitable) 恰当的 ‹*remark, behaviour, end*›

B *n* **1** (part) 配件; **a plastic light ~** 灯具塑料配件 **2** (for clothes) 试衣; (for hearing aid) 试听; **to go for/have a ~** 去试衣 **3** (shoe width) 鞋宽

C **fittings** *npl* (equipment) 可拆除装置; **furniture and ~s** 家具和可拆除装置

D **-fitting** *combining form* **well/badly/loose/tight~** 合身的/不合身的/宽松的/紧身的 ‹*garment*›

fittingly /ˈfɪtɪŋli/ *adv* 恰当地

fitting room *n* 试衣室

five /faɪv/ ▸**p. 15, p. 521, p. 831**

A *n* **1** (number, quantity) 五; **~ plus two equals seven** 5 加 2 等于 7; **in December nineteen hundred and ~** 在1905 年 12 月; **we live at (number) ~, Victoria Road** 我们住在维多利亚路 5 号; **her phone number is two six double ~** 她的电话号码是 2655; **there are ~ of them** 他们有 5 个人; **three ~s are fifteen** 三个 5 相加等于 15; **to take ~** esp Amer colloq 放松一下 **2** (figure, representation of a five) 表示五的符号 **3** (group, unit of five) 五个一组; **the horses paraded in ~s** 这些马每五匹一组列队前进 **4** (in time) 5 点钟; **at**

~ (o'clock) 在 5 点 **5** (on playing card) 5 点; (in series) 编号为 5 的东西; **the ~ of diamonds** 方块 5; **the ~ of hearts** 红心 5 **6** (age) 5 岁

B *adj* **1** (as quantity) 五的; 五个 ‹*people*›; **~ cats** 5 只猫; **~ books** 5 本书; **~ weeks** 5 周; **~ miles** 5 英里 **2** (in age) 5 岁的; **he's nearly ~** 他快 5 岁了; **our house is only ~ years old** 我们的房子才造了 5 年 **3** (in series) 第五的 ‹*lines, rooms*›; **number ~** 5 号; **page ~** 第 5 页

C **fives** *npl* Brit 墙手球 [用手或球拍对墙击球的球戏]

five: **~-and-dime** *n* Amer **~-and-dime (store)** 廉价商品店; **~-a-side** *n* [u] Brit **~-a-side (football)** 五人足球; **~-a-side matches** 五人足球赛; **~-barred gate** *n* 五栅门; **~-day week** *n* 一周五天工作制; **to work a ~-day week** 每周工作五日; **~-dollar bill** *n* Amer 五美元钞票

fivefold /ˈfaɪvfəʊld/

A *adj* 五倍的 ‹*increase, return*›

B *adv* 五倍地 ‹*increase, multiply*›

five: **~ o'clock shadow** *n* [早上刮过到傍晚又长出的] 胡子茬儿; **~ pence** *n* Brit 五便士硬币; **~-pound note** *n* Brit 五英镑钞票

fiver /ˈfaɪvə(r)/ *n* Brit colloq 五英镑钞票; Amer colloq 五美元钞票

five: **~-sided** *adj* 五面的; **~-star** *adj* 五星级的; **~-year plan** *n* 五年计划

fix /fɪks/

A *vt* **1** (attach, insert) 使…固定 ‹*picture*›; 安装 ‹*handle*›; **to ~ sth. to** *or* **on to sth.** 把某物固定在某物上; **to ~ a 'No Smoking' sign to the door** 在门上安一块"禁止吸烟"的牌子; **he ~ed his tie to his shirt with a pin** 他用领带夹把领带别在衬衫上; **to ~ sth. in** *or* **into ...** 把某物固定进…; **to ~ sth. into place** *or* **position** 把某物固定好; **to ~ things together** 把东西固定在一起; **to ~ the hammock to the tree** 把吊床固定在树上; **~ bayonets!** 上刺刀! **2** fig (assign) 把…归于 ‹*wrong-doing*›; **to ~ sth. on sb.** 把某事归咎于某人; **to ~ the blame on sb.** 怪罪某人; **to ~ the suspicion on sb.** 怀疑某人 **3** fig (imprint) 牢记 ‹*name, sight*›; **to ~ sth. in one's brain** *or* **mind** 牢记某事 **4** fig (concentrate visually) 使…对准 ‹*gaze*›; (gaze at) 盯住 ‹*person*›; **she ~ed her eyes on** *or* **upon the door** 她眼睛紧盯着门; **to ~ sb. with sth.** 以某种眼光注视某人; **he ~ed her with a stony look** 他冷冷地盯着她 **5** fig (focus) 使…集中 ‹*thoughts, attention, aim*›; **to ~ one's hopes on sth./doing sth.** 一心盼望某事/希望做某事 **6** (set, determine) 确定; **to ~ a time for sth./doing sth.** 确定某事/做某事的时间; **have you ~ed the rent yet?** 你定下房租了吗?; **the government has ~ed tax at 20%** 政府已经将税率定为 20% **7** (arrange) 安排 ‹*meeting, trip*›; **have you anything ~ed for Saturday evening?** 你周六晚上有事吗?; **they tried to ~ things so that they could travel together** 他们作了一些准备以便可以一起旅行; **if you really want to go to Greece I'll ~ it for you** 如果你真想去希腊, 我来替你安排 **8** (mend) 修理 ‹*object, equipment*›; 修补 ‹*puncture, hole*›; **I'll ~ the problem for you** 我来帮你解决问题 **9** esp Amer colloq (prepare) 准备 ‹*food, meal*›; **to ~ sb. sth., to ~ sth. for sb.** 为某人准备某物; **can I ~ you a drink?** 我替你弄杯饮品好吗? **10** esp Amer colloq (adjust) 整理 ‹*clothes, room*›; **to ~ one's make-up** 补妆; **I'll just go and ~ my hair/face** 我这就去梳个头/化个妆 **11** colloq (rig) 用不正当手段操纵 ‹*match, election*› **12** colloq (bribe) 买通 ‹*witness, judge*› **13** colloq (deal with) 向…报仇 ‹*bully, tormentor*›; **so that's her little game! I'll ~ her!** 她要这样的小花招! 我来收拾她! **14** colloq (kill) 干掉 ‹*criminal, gangster*›; (disable) 废掉; **I'll get him ~ed** 我要叫人干掉他 **15** Amer (neuter) 阉割 ‹*animal*›; **are you going to get him ~ed?** 你打算给它去势吗? **16** Art, Phot, Tex 使…定影 ‹*film*›; 使…固色 ‹*fabric, paper, pastel drawing*›; 使…固着 ‹*dye*› **17** Biol (assimilate) «*micro-organism, plant*» 使…不挥发 ‹*carbon dioxide*›; **bacteria that ~ nitrogen** 固氮菌 **18** Biol (stabilize) 固定 ‹*specimen, tissue, cells*› **19** colloq (inject) 为自己注射 ‹*heroin*›

B *vi* **1** colloq (arrange) 安排; **to ~ for sb. to do sth.** 安排某人做某事 **2** Amer (intend) 打算; **to ~ to do sth.** 打算做某事; **I'm ~ing to call the police** 我正打算报警 **3** colloq (inject heroin) 注射毒品

C *n usu sing* **1** colloq (quandary) 困境; **a fine** *or* **nice** *or* **pretty** *or* **real ~** 棘手的困境; **to be in/get into a ~** 处于/陷入困境 **2** colloq (drug dose) 一剂毒品; **a ~ of heroin** 一剂海洛因 **3** colloq (solution) 解决办法; **a quick ~** 即时的解决办法 **4** colloq (rigged arrangement) 受操纵的事; **the last race was definitely a ~** 最后一场赛跑肯定做了手脚 **5** Aviat, Naut 定位; **a radio ~** 无线电定位; **to take** *or* **get a ~ on sth.** 确定某物的方位; **let's get a ~ on the problem** 咱们来把问题搞清楚

Phrasal verbs

- **fix on**

A [**~ sth. on, ~ on sth.**] *vt* (fasten) 把…固定好; **to ~ the lid on firmly** 盖紧盖子; **he ~ed his glasses on his nose and started reading** 他把眼镜架上鼻梁后开始阅读; **she ~ed a new horseshoe on the mare's hoof** 她为母马的蹄子钉了新的马掌

B [**~ on sb./sth.**] *vt* (choose) 选定 ‹*person, place, date*›; 确定 ‹*amount*›; **to ~ on doing sth.** 确定做某事

- **fix up**

A [**~ sth. up, ~ up sth.**] *vt*

1 (arrange) 安排 ‹*holiday, date, meeting*›; **to ~ up to do sth.** 安排做某事; **we ~ed up that we'd go separately** 我们准备分头走; **I'll ~ up for you to accompany me** 我将安排你陪同我前去 **2** (put up) 把…挂起来 ‹*poster*›; 把…装上去 ‹*shelf, mirror*› **3** (hastily erect) 草草搭建 ‹*shelter, storage*›; 草草竖起 ‹*barrier*› **4** (decorate) 装修 ‹*building, home*›; (repair) 修理

B *vt* colloq (provide) **to ~ sb. up with sth.** 为某人准备某物; **we ~ed him up with a room/job** 我们给他准备了房间/安排了工作; **to ~ sb. up with sb.** 给某人介绍某人; **can you ~ me up with a date?** 你可以给我订一个日子吗?

fixated /fɪkˈseɪtɪd/ *adj* 异常迷恋的; **to be ~ on sb./sth.** 异常迷恋某人/某事物

fixation /fɪkˈseɪʃn/ *n* **1** [c] Psych 固恋 **2** [c] (obsessive interest) 异常迷恋; **to have a ~ with** *or* **about sb./sth.** 对某人/某事物过于着迷; **she has a ~ about cleanliness** 她有洁癖 **3** [u] Biol (of nitrogen, carbon dioxide) 固定

fixative /ˈfɪksətɪv/ *n* [c and u] **1** Dent, Tex 固定剂 **2** Art 定色剂

fixed /fɪkst/ *adj* **1** (fastened, not variable) 固定的; **~ income** 固定收入; **a ~ holiday** 日期固定的节日; **a ~-wing aircraft** 固定翼飞机; **to have no ~ ideas on sth.** 对某个问题没有定见; **to have the ~ menu** 点套餐 **2** (steady) 不变的; **a ~ smile** 呆板的微笑; **to hold sb. in a ~ gaze** 凝视某人 **3** (firm) 坚定不移的 ‹*aim, determination*› **4** *pred* colloq (situated) 处于某种境况的; **how are you ~ for time?** 你有多少时间?; **he is better ~ financially than me** 他的经济状况比我好

fixed: **~ assets** *npl* 固定资产; **~ charge** *n* 固定支出; **~ costs** *npl* 固定成本

fixedly /ˈfɪksɪdli/ *adv* 目不转睛地 ‹*stare*›; 僵硬地 ‹*smile*›

fixed: **~ point** *n* **1** Phys (固) 定点; **2** Comput, Math 定点; **~ rate financing** *n* [u] 固定利率融资; **~ term contract** *n* 定期合同

fixer /ˈfɪksə(r)/ *n* **1** [u] Phot 定影液 **2** [c] colloq (organizer) 作出安排者

fixings /ˈfɪksɪŋz/ *npl* **1** Brit (screws, bolts, etc.) 配件 **2** Amer Culin 配料

fixity /ˈfɪksəti/ *n* [u] 固定性; **the ~ of sth.** 某物的固定性; **~ of purpose** 目标的始终如一

fixture /ˈfɪkstʃə(r)/ *n* **1** Constr, Tech [房屋等的] 固定设施; **~s and fittings** 固定装置和可拆卸装置; **plumbing ~s** 管道装置 **2** Brit Sport 预定日期的体育赛事 **3** colloq (person) 长期驻守的人; (thing) 长期存在之物

fixture list *n* 体育赛事时间表

fizz /fɪz/

A *vi* **1** (effervesce) «*lemonade, champagne*» 冒气泡 **2** (make hissing sound) «*match, fireworks*» 发嘶嘶声

B *n* [u] **1** (of drink) 气泡嘶嘶声; **this lemonade has lost its ~** 这柠檬汽水跑气了 **2** (of match, firework) 嘶嘶声 **3** colloq (drink) 起泡饮料

Phrasal verb

- **fizz up** *vi* «*drink*» 冒着泡往上涌

fizzle /ˈfɪzl/ *vi* «*lemonade*» 发嘶嘶声; **the firework ~d and went out** 烟花发出嘶嘶声后熄灭了

Phrasal verb

- **fizzle out** *vi* **1** (stop burning) «*match, fire*» 嘶嘶着熄灭 **2** (peter out) «*event, plans*» 终成泡影; «*enthusiasm, interest*» 虎头蛇尾; **the game ~d out in the second half** 比赛到了下半场叫人失望

fizzy /ˈfɪzi/ *adj* 起泡的 ‹*drink, water*›

fjord /fɪˈɔːd/ *n* [尤指挪威海岸边的] 峡湾

FL *abbr* Amer = **Florida**

flab /flæb/ *n* [u] colloq 松弛的肌肉; **his muscles have gone to ~** 他的肌肉已经松弛了

flabbergast /ˈflæbəgɑːst, Amer -gæst/ *vt* 使大吃一惊; **to be ~ed at sth.** 对某事感到大吃一惊

flabby /ˈflæbi/ *adj* **1** (loose, fleshy) 松弛的 ‹*flesh, chin*› **2** (overweight) 肥胖的 ‹*person*› **3** fig (feeble) 软弱的 ‹*character*›; 无力的 ‹*excuse, argument*›

flaccid /ˈflæsɪd/ *adj* 松弛的 ‹*muscle*›; 萎软的 ‹*stem*›

flag[1] /flæg/

A *n* **1** (symbol of a country etc.) 旗; **the American ~** 美国国旗; **to hoist** *or* **raise** *or* **run up a ~** 升旗; **to fly a ~ at half mast** 下半旗; **to wave a ~** 挥舞旗子; **to strike the ~** 降旗表示投降; **loyalty to the ~** 对国家的忠诚; **to wrap oneself in the ~** Amer fig 炫耀爱国热情; **the ship was sailing under the Panamanian ~** 该船悬挂巴拿马国旗航行; **to put the ~(s) out** 悬旗庆祝; **to keep the ~ flying** 坚持传统; **to fly** *or* **wave the ~** (country) 表明拥护祖国; (party) 表明拥护政党; (movement) 表明拥护运动; **to show the ~** 露面; **to strike one's ~** fig 承认失败 **2** (as signal) 信号旗; **a ship flying the yellow ~** 悬挂检疫旗的船; **semaphore/signal ~s** 旗语旗/信号旗; **the chequered ~** (in motor racing) 黑白方格旗; **a warning ~** 警告旗; **the guard's ~** 铁路信号旗; **the white ~/~ of truce** 白色休战旗; **to show the white ~** 表现出胆怯; **with ~s flying** 英勇不屈地 **3** dated (on taxi) 空车牌; **the ~ was down** 空车牌是翻倒的 [表示有乘客] **4** (paper badge, on map) 小纸旗; **wear your ~ with pride!** 自豪地挂起旗子!; **the ~s mark military positions** 用小旗子标出阵地的位置 **5** Comput 标记

B *vt* (*pres p etc.* **-gg-**) **1** (mark with flags) 悬旗装饰 ‹*route, street*› **2** (mark with tab) 标示 ‹*item, text*›; **I've ~ged the most important paragraphs for you, Minister** fig 部长, 我已经为您标出了最重要的段落 **3** Comput 用标记标明 ‹*item, text, character, category*›

C *vi* (*pres p etc.* **-gg-**) Brit Sport «*official*» 举旗示意犯规; **the referee's assistant ~ged immediately** 助理裁判马上就举旗了

Phrasal verbs

- **flag down** *vt* [**~ sb./sth. down, ~ down sb./sth.**] 示意…停下 ‹*vehicle, driver*›; **let's ~ down a taxi** 我们拦一辆出租车吧
- **flag up** *vt* [**~ sth. up, ~ up sth.**] 使人们对…关注 ‹*problem, event, aspect*›

flag² *vi* 1 (tire) «*person, walker*» 疲乏; **I'm ~ging somewhat — let's have a rest** 我有点累，咱们休息一下吧 2 (diminish) «*interest, morale, strength*» 衰退; **her enthusiasm for the project was ~ging** 她对该项目的热情正逐渐减弱; **the conversation was ~ging** 谈话变得没了生气 3 (droop) «*plant, leaves*» 萎垂

flag³ *n* Bot 鸢尾

flag⁴ *n* = **flagstone**

flag: ~ carrier *n* 国家航空公司; **~ day** *n* 1 Brit 募捐日; 2 **F~ Day** Amer 国旗纪念日 [6月14日]

flagellate¹ /ˈflædʒəleɪt/ *vt* 1 Relig, Hist 鞭笞 2 (for sexual pleasure) 鞭打; **to ~ oneself** 鞭打自己

flagellate² /ˈflædʒələt, -eɪt/ *adj* 有鞭毛的

flagellation /ˌflædʒəˈleɪʃn/ *n* [u] 1 Relig, Hist 鞭笞 2 (for sexual pleasure) 鞭打

flagellum /fləˈdʒeləm/ *n* (*pl* **flagella** /fləˈdʒelə/) 鞭毛

flagged /flægd/ *adj* 地面铺石板的 ‹*hall*›; 石板铺就的 ‹*floor, pavement*›

flag of convenience *n* 方便旗 [指由于法律或经济原因挂的外国国旗]

flagon /ˈflægən/ *n* 1 (bottle) 大肚短颈瓶; (jug) 大酒壶 2 (bottleful) 一大肚短颈瓶; (jugful) 一大酒壶

flagpole /ˈflægpəʊl/ *n* 旗杆

flagrant /ˈfleɪgrənt/ *adj* 骇人听闻的 ‹*offence, violation, disregard*›; 丑恶可耻的 ‹*coward, offender*›; **a ~ case of media distortion** 媒体明目张胆的扭曲报道

flagrantly /ˈfleɪgrəntli/ *adv* 骇人听闻地 ‹*abuse, disregard, violate*›; 极端地 ‹*corrupt, illegal, incompetent*›

flag: ~ship *n* 旗舰; **a new ~ship store** fig 新开的旗舰店; **a ~ship project** fig 重点项目; **~staff** *n* 旗杆; **~stone** *n* 石板; **a ~stone path** 石板路; **~ stop** *n* Amer 招呼站; **~-waving** *n* [u] fig 强烈民族情绪; **a ~-waving speech** 沙文主义的讲话

flail /fleɪl/

A *vt* 1 (wave, swing) 拼命挥动 ‹*arms, hands*›; 乱踢 ‹*legs*› 2 (beat, flog) 猛打

B *vi* 胡乱摆动; **to ~ about** *or* **around** «*person*» 动来动去; «*arms, legs*» 胡乱摆动

C *n* 连枷 [旧时长柄脱粒农具]

flair /fleə(r)/ *n* [u] 1 (talent) 天赋; **a ~ for sth./doing sth.** 某方面/做某事的天赋; **she shows little ~ for conversation** 她不善于与人交谈 2 (discernment) 洞察力; **a ~ for sth./doing sth.** 对某事/做某事的鉴别力; **we need someone with her political ~** 我们需要一位有她这样政治眼光的人 3 (style) 魅力; **she designs clothes with tremendous ~** 她设计的服装非常有品位

flak /flæk/ *n* [u] 1 Mil 高射炮火 2 fig colloq (criticism) 严厉批评; **to get** *or* **take a lot of ~** 遭到广泛指责; **to take the ~ for sth.** 因某事遭到抨击

flake /fleɪk/

A *n* 1 (of snow, cereal, soap) 小薄片; (of paint, metal, rust) 薄层; **a bowl of oat ~s/corn~s** 一碗燕麦片/玉米片; **drifting snow~s** 飘飞的雪花; **~s of sth.** 某物的小薄片 2 Archaeol (of rock, flint) 原始石器

B *vi* «*paint, rock*» 剥落; «*skin*» 脱落

Phrasal verbs

- **flake off** *vi* = **flake B**
- **flake out** *vi* Brit colloq 1 (fall asleep) [疲倦得] 睡着 2 (collapse) [疲倦得] 倒下

flakey /ˈfleɪki/ *adj* = **flaky 3**

flak jacket *n* Brit 防弹背心

flaky /ˈfleɪki/ *adj* 1 (made up of flakes) 片状的 ‹*snow*›; 层状的 ‹*pastry*› 2 (tending to flake) 易剥落的 ‹*rock, paint*›; 易脱落的 ‹*skin*› 3 Amer colloq (eccentric) 古怪的 ‹*character*›; (feeble-minded) 意志薄弱的; (unreliable) 不可靠的 ‹*product*›

flaky pastry *n* [u] 酥饼

flamboyant /flæmˈbɔɪənt/ *adj* 1 (showy, exuberant) 炫耀的 ‹*person, speech, character*› 2 (bright) 艳丽的 ‹*clothes, colours*›

flame /fleɪm/

A *n* 1 [c and u] lit 火焰; **to be/go up in ~s** 着火; **to burst into ~s** 突然燃烧起来; **a naked ~** 明火; **over a low/high ~** Culin 用小火/大火; **to be shot down in ~s** fig «*plan, suggestion*» 被毁掉; **to commit sb./sth. to the ~s** 把某人烧死/某物烧掉 2 [c] fig 强烈感情; **to fan** *or* **fuel the ~s of love** 使爱情之火更为炽烈; **to fan the ~s of violence** 煽动暴乱; **an old ~** colloq 老相好 3 [c] colloq (on Internet) 含辱骂内容的邮件

B *vt* 1 Culin 在…上面浇酒并点燃 2 colloq (on Internet) 向…发送辱骂性邮件

C *vi* 1 (burn) «*fire*» 燃烧 2 (take on colour) «*cheeks, autumn leaves*» 变红; **his cheeks ~d with anger/embarrassment** 他气得/窘得面红耳赤 3 fig (flare up) «*passion, anger*» 爆发

Phrasal verb

- **flame up** *vi* 1 (burn high) «*fire, coals*» 烧得更旺 2 fig (flare up) «*passion, anger*» 爆发

flame gun *n* [用于烧除杂草等的] 喷火枪

flamenco /fləˈmeŋkəʊ/ *n* [u] 1 (dance) 弗拉门科舞; **~ dancer** 弗拉门科舞表演者 2 (music) 弗拉门科舞曲; **a ~ composer/singer** 弗拉门科舞作曲家/歌唱家

flameproof /ˈfleɪmpruːf/ *adj* 防火的 ‹*material, furniture*›; 耐火的 ‹*dish, ovenware*›

flamer /ˈfleɪmə(r)/ *n* 1 (gardening tool) 喷火除草机 2 colloq (on Internet) 侮辱性邮件发送者

flame retardant

A *n* 阻燃剂

B **flame-retardant** *adj* 阻燃的

flame-thrower *n* 火焰喷射器

flaming /ˈfleɪmɪŋ/ *adj* 1 (ablaze) 燃烧的 ‹*fire, timbers*› 2 fig (fiery red) 火红的 ‹*sky*›; **he fled with ~ cheeks** 他面红耳赤地逃开了 3 fig (heated) 强烈的 ‹*rage*›; 激烈的 ‹*argument*› 4 colloq (emphatic) 讨厌的; **it's a ~ nuisance!** 真让人讨厌!

flamingo /fləˈmɪŋgəʊ/ *n* (*pl* **~s** *or* **~es**) 红鹳

flammable /ˈflæməbl/ *adj* 易燃的; **highly ~** 极其易燃的

flan /flæn/ *n* 果馅饼

flange /flændʒ/ *n* (on wheel) 轮缘; (on pipe, tool) 凸缘; (on beam) 翼缘

flanged /flændʒd/ *adj* 有凸缘的; **a ~ wheel** 凸缘轮; **a ~ pipe** 法兰管; **a ~ beam** 工字梁

flank /flæŋk/

A *n* 1 (of animal) 胁腹 2 (side of hill, building) 侧面 3 Mil 侧翼; **the artillery was on the left ~** 炮兵部队在左翼

B *vt* 1 (be on each side of) 位于…的两侧 ‹*person, road*›; **the president was ~ed by two armed men** 总统的两旁有两个武装人员 2 (be on one side of) 位于…的一侧 ‹*building, road*›; **the town was ~ed by mountains to the north** 城镇的北面是山脉

flanker /ˈflæŋkə(r)/ *n* 1 (in rugby) 边锋 2 (in American football) 侧翼队员

flannel /ˈflænl/

A *n* 1 [u] Tex 法兰绒; **~ trousers** 法兰绒裤子 2 [c] Brit 毛巾 3 [u] Brit colloq (smooth talk) 兜圈子的话; **to talk a lot of ~** 说很多应付话

B *vi* (*pres p etc.* **-ll-**) Brit colloq 说应付话

flannelette /ˌflænəˈlet/ *n* [u] 绒布; **a pair of ~ sheets/pillowcases** 两条绒布被单/一对绒布枕套

flannels /ˈflænəlz/ *npl* 1 Clothg 法兰绒男裤 2 Sport 米色法兰绒板球裤

flap /flæp/

A *n* 1 (on pocket) 袋盖; (of envelope) 封盖; (of hat) 帽边; (of box) 口盖; (of tent) 门帘 2 (hinged section) (on table, bar) 折板; (of trapdoor) 活板 3 (movement of wings, sail) 拍打; (sound of wings, sail) 拍打声 4 Aviat 襟翼; **to raise/lower the ~s** 升起/降下襟翼 5 colloq (panic) 惊慌; **to be in a ~** 处于慌乱之中; **to get into a ~** 激动起来

B *vt* (*pres p etc.* **-pp-**) 1 (move about) «*bird*» 振动 ‹*wings*›; «*person*» 挥动 ‹*arms*› 2 (strike lightly) 拍打 ‹*person, paper*›; **to ~ sth. at sb./sth.** 用某物拍打某人/某物

C *vi* (*pres p etc.* **-pp-**) 1 (move) «*wings*» 振动; «*bird*» 振翅 2 (flutter, wave around) «*material, sail, flag*» 飘动; «*shutters*» 摆动 3 (strike lightly at) 拍打; **to ~ at sth.** 拍打某物 4 (fly) «*bird*» 振翅飞行 5 Brit colloq (panic) 惊慌; **stop ~ping!** 不要惊慌!

flapjack /ˈflæpdʒæk/ *n* 1 [u and c] Brit (biscuit) 甜燕麦饼 2 [c] Amer (pancake) 煎饼

flare /fleə(r)/

A *n* 1 (of match, lighter, firework) 火光 2 (on highway, runway) 照明灯 3 Mil (to illuminate) 照明弹; (warning signal) 闪光警告信号 4 Aviat, Naut (distress signal) 闪光报警信号 5 Astron 耀斑 6 Clothg 呈喇叭形展开; **a skirt with a slight ~** 微喇裙

B **flares** *npl* (trousers) 喇叭裤; **a pair of ~s** 一条喇叭裤

C *vi* 1 (burn briefly) «*match, torch*» 闪光; «*sunspot*» 闪耀 2 fig (erupt) «*tempers, violence*» 爆发 3 (widen) «*sleeves, skirt, trouser legs*» 呈喇叭形展开 4 (dilate) «*nostrils*» 张大

D *vt* 使…呈喇叭形展开 ‹*skirt, trouser legs*›; **a ~d skirt** 喇叭裙

Phrasal verb

- **flare up** *vi* 1 (burn brightly) «*candle, gas jet*» 旺烧起来; **the fire ~d up as I put on more sticks** 我加了些柴枝，火旺了起来 2 fig (erupt) «*trouble, epidemic, violence*» 爆发; **the unrest ~d up into a real revolt** 动荡的局面激化为真正的叛乱 3 fig (become angry) 突然发怒; **he suddenly ~d up** 他突然发起火来 4 (recur) «*disease, pain*» 复发; **my back trouble has ~d up again** 我的背又疼起来了

flare: ~ path *n* [夜间飞机起降用的] 照明跑道; **~-up** *n* 1 (burst of light, flame) 突然燃起; 2 (outburst of fighting, trouble) 爆发; **a ~-up of sth.** 某事的爆发; **a ~-up of tension between the two sides** 双方剑拔弩张; 3 (argument) 争吵; 4 (recurrence) (of emotion) 重现; (of disease, pain) 复发

flash /flæʃ/

A *n* 1 [c] (sudden burst of light or flame) 闪光; **a ~ of sth.** 某物的闪光; **a ~ of lightning** 一道闪电; **a ~ of colour** 一抹亮色; **in** *or* **like a ~** fig 瞬间; **quick as a ~** 飞快; **to be a ~ in the pan** 昙花一现 2 [c] fig (sudden idea, feeling) 闪现; **a ~ of sth.** 某物的闪现; **a ~ of merriment/laughter** 突然的一阵欢喜/笑声; **a ~ of inspiration** 灵感的闪现; **a ~ of understanding** 顿悟; **in a ~ of intuition, she realized that ...** 她突然有个直觉，认为…; **it came to him in a ~ that ...** 他突然想到… 3 [u and c] Phot 闪光灯; **with automatic ~** 备有自动闪光灯; **a built-in ~** 内置闪光灯 4 [c] TV, Radio 简讯 5 [c] Brit Mil (on uniform) 肩章 6 [c] (light patch or stripe) 一小块亮色; **a horse with a white ~ on its nose** 鼻子上有一块白斑的马 7 [u] colloq (ostentation) 炫耀; **eighties designer ~** 80 年代设计师华丽炫耀的设计风格 8 **F~** [u] Comput 矢量动画

B *vi* 1 (shine) «*light, jewel, metal, glass*» 闪光; «*indicator, warning light*» 闪烁; **his right indicator was ~ing, but he turned left** 他的右转向灯在闪，但他却向左转了 2 fig (blaze) «*eyes*» 闪耀; **her eyes ~ed as she turned**

f

to face her tormentors 她转身面对拷打自己的人时，眼中冒出怒火 3 (move quickly, appear suddenly) «*person, animal*» 飞奔; «*vehicle*» 飞驰; fig «*look, news, memory*» 闪现; «*time*» 飞逝; **the car ~ed past us** 那辆汽车从我们旁边飞驰而过; **a sudden thought ~ed through her mind** 她脑子里突然闪过一个想法; **to ~ through sb.'s mind that .../to do sth.** 某人脑中闪现…的念头/做某事的念头 4 colloq (expose oneself) 露阴

C *vt* 1 (shine) 使…闪光 ‹*light, mirror*›; **stop ~ing that torch at me/in my eyes** 别用手电闪我/我的眼睛; **why is that car ~ing its headlights at us?** 那辆车为什么朝咱们闪车头灯？ 2 (communicate by flashing light) 用车灯发出 ‹*signal, message*›; 用车灯向…发信号 ‹*person, vehicle*›; **the oncoming car ~ed him a warning** 迎面而来的汽车向他闪灯发出警告; **the police car ~ed them, and they had to pull in** colloq 警车向他们闪灯，于是他们不得不靠路边停下 3 fig (send) 闪现出 ‹*smile, warning, anger, resentment*›; **to ~ sth. at sb.** 向某人闪现出某物; **she ~ed a glance in his direction** 她朝他那边瞥了一眼; **he ~ed her an angry look** 他愤怒地看了她一眼; **her eyes ~ed fire** 她眼冒怒火 4 (transmit) 迅速发出 ‹*message, image*›; **they ~ed the news straight to their head office** 他们迅速把这条新闻直接发往总部; **the election results were ~ed on the screen** 选举结果显示在屏幕上 5 colloq (show) 亮出 ‹*identification card, papers, money*›; **to ~ sth. at sb.** 向某人亮出某物; **just ~ a fiver at the doorman and he'll let you in** 只要拿 5 英镑给看门人，他就会让你进去 6 colloq (show off) 炫耀 ‹*jewellery, money*›; **to ~ sth. at sb.** 向某人炫耀某物 7 colloq (expose oneself to) 对…露阴

D *adj* esp Brit colloq 1 (fancy) 华丽的 ‹*car*›; 奢华的 ‹*hotel*› 2 (ostentatiously rich) 炫富的 ‹*person*›; **he's so ~ always talking about his holidays in Barbados** 他非常爱炫富，总是谈论他在巴巴多斯岛度假的事

Phrasal verbs

- **flash about, flash around** *vt* [**~ sth. about**] colloq 到处炫耀 ‹*jewellery, money*›
- **flash back**

A *vi* 1 (return) «*mind, thoughts*» 突然浮现; **to ~ back to sth.** 回想起某事物 2 Cin, TV «*film, scene*» 闪回

B *vt* [**~ back sth., ~ sth. back**] 1 (send back) 闪现 ‹*message, image, news*› 2 colloq (say immediately) 立刻回答

- **flash by, flash past** *vi* «*person, animal, vehicle*» 飞奔而过; «*landscape*» 掠过; «*time*» 飞逝; **the hours ~ed by** 时间飞逝
- **flash up**

A *vi* «*news, message, image*» 闪现

B *vt* [**~ sth. up, ~ up sth.**] 使…闪现 ‹*news, message, image*›

flash: ~back *n* 1 (scene) (in film) 闪回; (in play, novel) 倒叙; 2 (memory) [往事的] 突然重现; **~bulb** *n* 闪光灯泡; **~ card** *n* 识字卡

flasher /ˈflæʃə(r)/ *n* 1 Aut (indicator) 闪光装置 2 colloq (exhibitionist) 露阴者

flash: ~ flood *n* 暴洪; **~-fry steak** *n* 速煎牛排; **~ gun** *n* 闪光枪

flashily /ˈflæʃɪli/ *adv* colloq 俗艳地 ‹*dressed*›

flashing /ˈflæʃɪŋ/ *n* [u] 防雨板

flash: ~light *n* 1 Phot 闪光灯; 2 Amer (torch) 手电筒; **~ memory** *n* [u] 闪存; **~ mob** *n* 快闪族 [起初互不相识，通过网络或手机聚集在某处进行无厘头的活动，时间一到即迅速四散的一群人]; **~ photography** *n* [u] 闪光摄影; **~point** *n* 1 [c] Chem 闪点; 2 [u and c] fig (explosive situation) 爆发点; **the crisis was nearing ~point** 危机一触即发

flashy /ˈflæʃi/ *adj* colloq 俗艳的 ‹*clothes, person*›

flask /flɑːsk, Amer flæsk/ *n* 1 (for tea, coffee) 瓶; (contents) 一瓶; **we drank a whole ~ of coffee** 我们喝了整整一瓶咖啡 2 Chem 烧瓶 3 (for oil, wine) 细颈瓶 4 (for alcohol) 扁平小酒瓶; **a ~ of whisky/brandy** 一小瓶威士忌/白兰地

flat¹ /flæt/

A *adj* 1 (horizontal, level and smooth) 水平的 ‹*ground, roof*›; 平坦的 ‹*road, surface*›; **a perfect, ~ lawn** 十分平坦的草坪; **to be ~ on one's back/face** *or* **stomach** 仰面平躺着/平趴着; **the sea was ~ and there was no wind** 海上风平浪静; **as ~ as a pancake** 完全平的 2 (not round) 平展的 ‹*stone*›; **slim hips and a ~ stomach** 窄臀平腹; **a ~ nose** 塌鼻子; **some early scientists believed that the earth was ~** 早期的一些科学家认为地球是平的; **a pan with a ~ base** 平底锅 3 (shallow) 浅的 ‹*dish, basket, box*› 4 (deflated, squashed) 瘪了的 ‹*ball*›; **my back tyre has gone ~** 我的后胎瘪了; **you've got a ~ tyre** 你有一个轮胎没气了; **to squash** *or* **press** *or* **squeeze** *or* **crush sth. ~** 把某物压扁; **to fold/pack sth. ~** 将某物折叠/包装成扁平状 5 *pred* (pressed close) 紧贴的; **with one's feet ~ on the floor** 双脚紧贴地板; **is the wardrobe ~ against the wall?** 衣柜贴住墙了吗？ 6 Clothg 平跟的 ‹*shoe*›; **a pair of sandals with ~ heels** 一双平跟凉鞋 7 **Flat** Horse racing 平地赛马的 ‹*meeting, racecourse*›; **the F~ season** 平地赛马季节 8 (no longer fizzy) 走了气的 ‹*alcoholic drink, lemonade*›; **to go ~** 走了气 9 Brit Elec 电用完的; **the battery must be ~** 电池肯定没电了; **to go ~** 电力耗尽 10 (lacking emotion) 平淡的 ‹*performance, party, tone*›; (lacking contrast) 反差小的 ‹*photograph*›; **his voice was ~ and monotonous** 他的声音平板而单调; **'she's dead,' he said in a ~ voice** "她死了，"他淡淡地说; **a ~ shade of grey** 单调的灰色 11 *usu pred* (insipid) 淡而无味的 ‹*food, drink*›; **to taste ~** 吃上去淡而无味 12 (depressed) 无精打采的; **to appear/feel/sound ~** 看起来/感觉/听起来无精打采的 13 Comm 不景气的 ‹*market, business*› 14 Mus (lower by a semitone) 降半音的; **E ~** 降 E 调 15 Mus (off-key) 音调偏低的 ‹*voice, instrument, note*›; **to go ~** 音调偏低 16 (absolute) 断然的 ‹*refusal, denial*›; 绝对的 ‹*contradiction*›; **she gave me a ~ rejection** 她断然拒绝了我; **and that's ~!** colloq 就这样定了！; **you're not going to the party, and that's ~!** 你不能去参加聚会，没有商量余地！ 17 *attrib* Comm 均一的 ‹*rate, charge, wage*›; **a ~ fare of £1.50** 车费一律 1.5 英镑; **I did the work for a ~ fee** 我做这个工作酬劳固定 18 (matt) 亚光的 ‹*colour, surface*›; **a ~ paint** 亚光漆 19 Phon 平舌的 ‹*vowel*› 20 *pred* Amer colloq (broke) 身无分文的; **to be ~** 一贫如洗

B *adv* 1 (so as to be horizontal or level) 平直地; **to hold one's hand out ~** 把手平伸; **to lay the blanket ~ on the floor** 把毯子平铺在地板上; **the bombing raid laid the village ~** 空袭将这个村庄夷为平地; **she knocked her opponent ~** 她将对手击倒在地; **to lie ~** 平躺; **~ on one's back/face** *or* **stomach** 仰面平躺/平趴着; **she hammered the metal ~** 她把金属锤平; **the pleats should lie ~ after you have pressed them** 熨烫过后这些衣褶应该很伏贴; **to fall ~** «*joke, plan*» 未达到效果; «*party, celebration*» 没意思 2 (in close contact) 紧贴地; **I pressed ~ against the wall** 我紧靠在墙上; **to rest the oars ~ on the water** 把桨平放在水面上 3 Mus 以降调 ‹*sing, play*› 4 colloq (absolutely) 断然地 ‹*turn down*›; **she told me ~ that I hadn't got the job** 她直截了当地告诉我说我没有得到这份工作; **he refused ~** 他断然拒绝 5 colloq (exactly) 正好; **in ... ~** 只用了…; **she drank the beer in five seconds ~** 她仅仅 5 秒钟就喝完了啤酒

C *n* 1 (flat surface of hand, blade, oar, etc.) 平面; **the ~ of sth.** 某物的平面; **he struck her with the ~ of his hand** 他扇了她一巴掌; **the ~ of a sword** 剑面 2 (area of flat ground) 浅滩; **mud/salt ~s** 淤泥滩/盐沼 3 Brit (flat ground) 平地; **on the ~** 在平地上 4 esp Amer colloq (deflated tyre) 瘪车胎; **to get a ~** 瘪了一个轮胎 5 esp Amer (shoe) 平跟鞋; **to wear ~s** 穿平跟鞋 6 **Flat** Brit Horse racing **the F~** 平地赛马 7 Mus (note) 降半音; (sign) 降半音符号 8 *usu pl* Theat 平面布景

flat² *n* Brit (set of rooms) 公寓; **a ~ on the top floor** 顶楼的一套公寓; **a service ~** 酒店式公寓; **a block of ~s** 公寓楼

flat: ~bed, ~bed lorry *ns* 平板卡车; **~bed scanner** *n* 平板扫描仪; **~bed truck** *n* 平板卡车; **~-bottomed** *adj* 平底的; **a ~-bottomed boat** 平底船; **~ broke** *adj* colloq 不名一文的; **~ cap** *n* 低顶圆帽; **~car** *n* Amer 平板货车; **~-chested** *adj* 平胸的 ‹*woman*›; **~ feet** *npl* 扁平足; **~fish** *n* 比目鱼; **~-footed** *adj* 1 lit 平足的 ‹*person*›; 2 fig colloq (awkward) 笨手笨脚的 ‹*person*›; 3 fig colloq (tactless) 不圆通的 ‹*person, manner*›; 不得体的 ‹*remark*›; 4 fig colloq (unprepared) 毫无准备的; **to catch sb. ~-footed** 乘其不备抓住某人; **~-hunting** *n* [u] Brit 搜房; **to go ~-hunting** 去搜房; **~ jockey** ▸p. 409 *n* 平地赛马骑师; **~lands** /-ləndz/ *npl* 平原地区

flatlet /ˈflætlɪt/ *n* Brit 小套房

flatline /ˈflætlaɪn/ *vi* colloq «*person*» 死亡; **to be flatlining in the polls** fig 在民意调查中处于低位

flatly /ˈflætli/ *adv* 1 (unemotionally) 漠然地 ‹*say, tell*› 2 (absolutely) 断然地 ‹*deny, reject*›; **I ~ refused to speak to her** 我断然拒绝与她谈话

flatmate /ˈflætmeɪt/ *n* Brit 合住公寓套间者

flatness /ˈflætnɪs/ *n* [u] 1 (of ground, roof) 平整; (of road, surface) 平坦 2 (of a stone) 平滑; (of stomach, nose) 扁平 3 (of dish, basket) 浅 4 (of ball, tyre) 瘪 5 (of shoe, heel) 平跟 6 (loss of fizziness) 走气 7 Elec (of battery) 电力耗尽 8 (of voice, style, event) 单调乏味; (of photograph) 无深浅反差 9 (lack of emotion) 平淡 10 Comm (of market, business) 萧条 11 Mus (of instrument, note) 音调偏低 12 (of refusal, denial) 直截了当 13 (of paint, colour, surface, finish) 亚光 14 Phon (of vowel) 平舌发音

flat: ~ out *adv* 1 Brit (as hard as possible) 竭尽全力地; (as fast as possible) 全速地 ‹*run, drive*›; **the whole team is working ~ out to meet the deadline** 整个小组都在竭力按期完成工作; 2 Amer (definitely) 断然; **I told him ~ out 'No'** 我直截了当地告诉他"不"; **~-pack** *adj* 扁平组件式的; **~ race** *n* 无障碍平地赛马; **~ racing** *n* [u] 无障碍平地赛马; **~ rate** *n* 1 (fixed charge) 统一价格; **the ~ rate state pension** 统一的国家养老金; 2 Tax 统一税率; **~ screen** *modif* 平面的 ‹*TV, monitor*›; **~ season** *n* 平地赛马赛季; **~-sharing** *n* [u] 公寓合住; **~ spin** *n* 1 Aviat 水平螺旋下降; 2 Brit fig colloq (panic) 惊惶失措; **to be in a ~ spin** 惊惶失措

flatten /ˈflætn/

A *vt* 1 colloq (level) «*wind*» 把…刮倒 ‹*crop, grass, tree*›; «*earthquake, bomb*» 夷平 ‹*building, town*›; «*person, punch*» 击倒 ‹*person*›; **the car skidded off the road and ~ed a garden fence** 汽车滑出路面，撞倒了花园的围栏; **that hat will ~ my hair** 那顶帽子会把我的发型压扁 2 (smooth out) «*machine*» 把…压平 ‹*ground, road, metal, paper*› 3 (deflate, squash) 把…弄瘪 ‹*ball, tyre*›; 把…压扁 ‹*fruit, animal, hat, box*›; fig colloq «*person, team*» 彻底击败 ‹*opponent*›; **exercises to ~ your stomach** 使小腹变平的运动 4 Elec 耗尽…的电力 ‹*battery*› 5 Mus 降低…的音高 ‹*note*› 6 fig colloq (humiliate) «*person, remark, event*» 羞辱 ‹*person*›

B *v refl* **to ~ oneself against sth.** «*person, animal*» 使自己紧贴某物

C *vi* «*ground, road, slope*» 变平; «*decline, growth*» 停止

Phrasal verb

- **flatten out**

A *vi* 1 (become level) «*ground, road, slope*» 变平; «*growth, decline*» 停止 2 Aviat «*pilot, aircraft*» 恢复平飞

B *vt* [~ **sth. out,** ~ **out sth.**] 使…变平 ‹*surface, ground, road, paper*›

flattening /ˈflætnɪŋ/ *n* 弄平; **the ~ of house prices** fig 房价的趋于稳定

flatter /ˈflætə(r)/

A *vt* 1 (compliment) 奉承; **to ~ sb. on** *or* **about sth.** 就某事讨好某人 2 (honour) 使…感到荣幸 ‹*person*›; **to be ~ed by sth.** 对某事深感荣幸; **to be/feel ~ed that ...** 很荣幸…; **they were ~ed to be invited** 承蒙邀请, 他们深感荣幸 3 (enhance) «*lighting, clothes*» 使…更漂亮 ‹*person, figure, skin*›; **that dress certainly ~s her** 她穿那条连衣裙的确漂亮多了 4 (show favourably) «*portrait, painter, photographer*» 美化 ‹*person*›; **this photograph does not ~ you** 这张照片没有你本人好看

B *v refl* **to ~ oneself** 自命不凡; **to ~ oneself on sth./being sth.** 自以为在…上/作为…了不起; **she ~s herself on her punctuality/on always being punctual** 她自以为很守时/一贯很守时; **to ~ oneself (that) ...** 自以为…; **he ~s himself that he is attractive to older women** 他自作多情地认为自己对年龄稍长的女性有吸引力

flatterer /ˈflætərə(r)/ *n* 阿谀奉承者; **she's a born ~** 她天生就会讨好

flattering /ˈflætərɪŋ/ *adj* 1 (full of praise, complimentary) 奉承的 ‹*words, comments*›; **he made some ~ remarks about her paintings** 他对她的画奉承了几句 2 (gratifying) 令人愉悦的 ‹*words*›; **it was very ~ to be invited to dine with someone so important** 承蒙邀请和这样的大人物共同进餐, 深感荣幸 3 (attractive) 增姿添彩的 ‹*clothes, lighting, portrait*›

flatteringly /ˈflætərɪŋli/ *adv* 奉承地 ‹*say, behave*›

flattery /ˈflætəri/ *n* [u] 奉承; **~ will get you nowhere** 阿谀奉承无济于事

flatties /ˈflætɪz/ *npl* Brit colloq 平跟鞋

flat-topped *adj* 平顶的 ‹*mountain, hat, rock*›

flatulence /ˈflætjʊləns/ *n* [u] 肠胃气胀

flatulent /ˈflætjʊlənt/ *adj* 肠胃气胀的 ‹*person*›; 引起肠胃气胀的 ‹*indigestion*›

flat: ~ware *n* [u] 1 (crockery) 扁平盘碟; 2 Amer (cutlery) 刀叉匙; **~worm** *n* 扁虫

flaunt /flɔːnt/

A *vt* 炫耀 ‹*wealth, knowledge, girlfriend*›; **to ~ sth. in front of sb.** 在某人面前炫耀某物; **she was ~ing her engagement ring in front of her colleagues** 她在同事面前炫耀她的订婚戒指

B *v refl* **to ~ oneself** (by behaviour) 动作性感撩人; (by dress) 衣着性感撩人; **they ~ed themselves in front of the judges** 他们在法官面前放荡不羁

flautist /ˈflɔːtɪst/ ▸ **p. 395, p. 409** *n* Brit 长笛手

flavour Brit, **flavor** Amer /ˈfleɪvə(r)/

A *n* [u and c] 1 (taste) 味道; **to bring out the ~** 使出味; **with a coffee ~** *or* **a ~ of coffee** 带咖啡味 2 fig (quality) 特色; (atmosphere) 气氛; **a** *or* **the ~ of sth.** 某物的特色; **the book captures the ~ of London** 这本书抓住了伦敦的风情; **~ of the month** colloq (person) 短期内风靡的人; (thing) 短期内风靡的事物

B *vt* «*cook, brewer*» 给…调味 ‹*food, drink*›; **to ~ sth. with sth.** 用某物给某物调味

flavour enhancer *n* 增味剂

flavouring Brit, **flavoring** Amer /ˈfleɪvərɪŋ/ *n* [u and c] 调味品

flavourless Brit, **flavorless** Amer /ˈfleɪvəlɪs/ *adj* 没有味道的 ‹*food, drink*›

flaw /flɔː/

A *n* 1 (imperfection) (in textile, gem) 瑕疵; (in glass, china, steel, timber) 裂缝; **a ~ in sth.** 某物的瑕疵 2 fig (mistake, weakness) 错误; **a ~ in sth.** 某事物的缺点; **there was a fatal ~ in their plan** 他们的计划有个致命错误 3 Jur (in contract) [使证件等无效的] 缺陷

B *vt* 1 (make imperfect) «*mark, imperfection*» 使…有瑕疵 ‹*article, piece of china, gem*›; 使…有裂缝 ‹*glass, metal, timber*› 2 (spoil, mar) 毁掉 ‹*masterpiece, beauty, character*› 3 (invalidate, weaken) «*mistake, problem*» 使…有缺陷 ‹*plan, argument*›

flawed /flɔːd/ *adj* 有缺陷的 ‹*character*›; 不完美的 ‹*logic, system, plan*›

flawless /ˈflɔːlɪs/ *adj* 完美的 ‹*performance, technique, argument, plan*›; **smooth, ~ skin** 光滑无瑕的皮肤

flax /flæks/ *n* [u] 1 (plant) 亚麻 2 (fibre) 亚麻纤维

flaxen /ˈflæksn/ *adj* 1 (made of flax) 亚麻制的; **~ thread** 亚麻线 2 liter (pale yellow) 亚麻色的 ‹*hair*›

flay /fleɪ/ *vt* 1 (remove skin) 剥…的皮 ‹*animal*› 2 (whip) 狠狠鞭打 ‹*person, animal*› 3 (criticize) 严厉批评 ‹*writer, system, policy*›

flea /fliː/ *n* 跳蚤; **to send sb. away with a ~ in their ear** colloq 用难听的话气走某人

flea: ~bag *n* colloq pej 1 Brit (person) 邋遢的人; (animal) 生蚤的动物; 2 Amer (hotel) 肮脏廉价的旅馆; **~ bite** *n* 1 lit 蚤咬的红斑; 2 fig (minor inconvenience) 小麻烦; (minor expense) 少量的花费; **~-bitten** *adj* 1 lit 被蚤咬过的 ‹*arms*›; 生蚤的 ‹*dog*›; 2 fig colloq (shabby) 破旧的 ‹*armchair, hotel*›; **~ collar** *n* [动物所戴有杀虫剂的] 灭蚤颈圈; **~ market** *n* 跳蚤市场; **~pit** *n* Brit colloq pej 蚤窝 [指破旧肮脏的电影院、剧院等]; **~ powder** *n* [u and c] 杀蚤粉

fleck /flek/

A *n* 1 (of colour) 色斑; (of light) 光斑; **~s of sth.** 某物的斑点 2 (of dust, soot) 微粒; (of dandruff) 屑; (of foam, milk) 泡沫

B *vt* «*colour, blood, paint*» 使…有斑点 ‹*material, clothes, plumage*›; **hair ~ed with grey** 花白头发; **the sky was ~ed with little clouds** 天空缀有点点云朵

fled /fled/ *pt, pp* ▸ **flee**

fledged /fledʒd/ *adj* 1 Zool 羽翼丰满的 ‹*bird, youngster*› 2 fig (established, qualified) 合格的; **she is now a fully ~ doctor** 她现在是个完全合格的医生

fledgling, fledgeling /ˈfledʒlɪŋ/ *n* 1 Zool 刚会飞的小鸟 2 fig (person) 初出茅庐的人; (organization) 无经验的组织; **~ nurses** 新护士; **a ~ tourist industry** 新兴旅游业

flee /fliː/ (*pt, pp* **fled**)

A *vt* 逃离 ‹*place, flood, danger*›

B *vi* 1 (escape, run away) 逃跑; **to ~ from sth.** 逃离某物; **to ~ to somewhere** 逃往某处; **to ~ before** *or* **in the face of ...** 面临…逃走; **to ~ in the face of danger** 遇到危险逃跑 2 hum (leave hastily) 匆忙离开

fleece /fliːs/

A *n* 1 [c] (of sheep, goat) 羊毛 2 [c] (wool from one sheep) 一只羊身上一次剪的羊毛 3 [u] (fabric) 绒头织物 4 [c] (garment) 绒头织物衣服

B *vt* colloq 1 (overcharge) 敲…的竹杠 2 (swindle) 欺诈; **to ~ sb. of sth.** 骗取某人某物

fleece-lined *adj* 绒头织物衬里的 ‹*coat, boots, gloves*›

fleecy /ˈfliːsi/ *adj* 1 (white, fluffy) 轻软如羊毛的 ‹*snow*›; **~ clouds** 朵朵轻云 2 (made of fleece) 羊毛制的; **a ~ blanket/jacket** 羊毛毯子/夹克

fleet /fliːt/ *n* 1 (of warships) 舰队; (of trawlers) 船队; (of vehicles) 车队; **a ~ of sixty warships** 由 60 艘战舰组成的舰队 2 (navy) **the ~** 海军

fleet: ~ admiral *n* Amer 海军五星上将; **~-footed** *adj* 脚步轻快的

fleeting /ˈfliːtɪŋ/ *adj* 1 (short-lived) 转瞬即逝的 ‹*beauty, memory, pleasure*› 2 (brief) 短暂的 ‹*visit, glance*›; **for a** *or* **one ~ moment** 刹那间

fleetingly /ˈfliːtɪŋli/ *adv* 短暂地 ‹*think, appear*›; 匆匆地 ‹*look*›

fleet of foot *adj pred* = **fleet-footed**

Fleet Street *pr n* 弗利特街 [以报馆集中著称, 指代英国新闻界]

flesh /fleʃ/ *n* [u] 1 (of human, animal) 肉; **they were eating human ~** 那时他们在吃人肉; **to put ~ on sth.** 加细节于某物; **it makes my ~ creep** *or* **crawl** 那让我心惊肉跳 2 (of fruit) 果肉; (of vegetable) 可食部分 3 (skin) 皮肤; **she revealed a lot of ~** 她穿着暴露 4 (body) 肉体; **~ and blood** 血肉之躯; **one's own ~ and blood** fig 亲骨肉; **to see sb. in the ~** 见到某人本人; **she's never seen him in the ~, only on the television** 她从未见过他本人, 只是在电视上见过 5 (human body and its needs) **the ~** 肉欲; **pleasures of the ~** 肉欲之乐; **sins of the ~** archaic hum 肉欲之罪; **(the spirit is willing but) the ~ is weak** 心有余而力不足

Phrasal verb

- **flesh out** *vt* [**~ sth. out, ~ out sth.**] 充实 ‹*speech, essay*›; **she ~ed out her speech with some statistics** 她用一些统计数据充实自己的讲话

flesh: ~ colour *n* [u] Brit 1 (colour) 肉色; 2 Art (pigment) 肉色颜料; **~-coloured** *adj* 肉色的 ‹*fabric*›; **~-eating** *adj* 食肉的 ‹*monster, bacteria*›; **~pots** *npl* 红灯区; **~ wound** *n* 皮肉之伤

fleshy /ˈfleʃi/ *adj* 1 (plump) 肥胖的 ‹*person, limbs*› 2 (pulpy) 肉质的 ‹*leaves, melon*›

flew /fluː/ *pt* ▸ **fly**[1] **A, B**

flex /fleks/

A *vt* 1 (contract) 使…收缩 ‹*muscles*›; **to ~ one's muscles** fig 显示力量 2 (bend and stretch) 屈伸 ‹*body, knees, legs*›

B *vi* (bend) 弯曲; **the stems ~ed in the wind** 茎给风吹弯了

C *n* [u and c] Brit 花线

flexibility /ˌfleksəˈbɪləti/ *n* [u] 1 (pliability) 柔韧性; **the ~ of the bar/wire/plastic** 棒/金属线/塑料的弹性 2 (adaptability) 灵活性; **to show** *or* **demonstrate ~** 表现出灵活性; **~ of approach is what we require** 我们要求方法灵活; **the ~ to do sth.** 做某事的变通性; **the plan has sufficient ~ to deal with all eventualities** 这个计划很灵活, 足以应付所有可能出现的情况

flexible /ˈfleksəbl/ *adj* 1 (pliable) 柔韧的 ‹*tubing, plastic*›; 柔软的 ‹*wire, sole*› 2 (adaptable) 可变通的 ‹*arrangement, timetable, people*›; 弹性的 ‹*working hours*›; 灵活的 ‹*plan, attitudes*›; **to be ~ about** *or* **over sth.** 在某方面很灵活; **whatever you decide, I'm ~** 无论你作何决定, 我都可以

flexible response *n* [u] 灵活反应战略

flexibly /ˈfleksəbli/ *adv* 灵活地 ‹*work, adapt*›

flexitime /ˈfleksɪtaɪm/ *n* [u] 弹性工作时间制; **to work** *or* **be on ~** 工作时间是弹性的

flexor /ˈfleksə(r)/ *n* 屈肌

flibbertigibbet /ˌflɪbətɪˈdʒɪbɪt/ *n* colloq pej 愚蠢而不负责任的人

flick /flɪk/

A *n* 1 (blow) (with fingers) 轻弹; (with cloth) 轻拂; (with whip) 轻抽; **to give sb./sth. a ~ (with sth.)** (用某物) 轻打某人/某物; **she gave her cigarette a ~ to knock off the ash** 她轻弹香烟把烟灰弹掉; **with a ~ of one's fingers** 用手指一弹 2 (movement) (of whip, cloth, fingers) 急速抖动; (of tongue) 急速伸缩; **with a ~ of sth.** 随着某物的抽动; **with a ~ of the wrist** 手腕一抖; **with a ~ of its tongue**

舌头猛地伸缩; **with a ~ of a whip** 鞭子一甩; **at the ~ of a switch** 一按开关; **a ~ of the ball** 拨球 **3** (turn of pages) 快速翻阅; **a ~ through a book** 浏览一本书 **4** Cin colloq 电影

B **flicks** *npl* Brit Cin colloq **the ~s** 电影院

C *vt* **1** (strike) (with finger) 轻弹; (with tail, cloth) 轻拂; (with whip) 轻抽; **to ~ sth./sb. with sth.** 以某物轻打某物/某人; **he ~ed me with his pen** 他用钢笔轻轻触了我一下; **she ~ed the crumbs off the table** 她弹去了桌面上的面包屑 **2** (extend and retract) 抖动 ‹*whip, cloth, implement*›; 伸缩 ‹*tongue*›; **to ~ sth. at/out of/round sth.** 朝某物抖动某物/把某物在某物外抖动/在某物周围抖动某物; **he ~ed the duster out of the window** 他在窗外抖了抖掸子; **the cow ~ed its tail at the flies** 母牛甩尾巴驱赶苍蝇 **3** (press) 啪地一按 ‹*switch*›; **he ~ed the catch and the door opened** 他啪地一拉门闩, 门开了; **to ~ a knife open** 啪地将刀刃弹出; **to ~ sth. on/off** 啪地打开/关闭某物 **4** Sport (with foot, hockey stick) 拨动 ‹*ball, puck*›; (with head) 轻顶 ‹*ball*›

D *vi* «*person, animal*» 快速移动; «*tongue*» 急速伸缩; **his head ~ed round** 他甩了甩头; **the frog's tongue ~ed in and out** 青蛙的舌头一伸一缩

Phrasal verbs

- **flick away** *vt* [**~ sth. away, ~ away sth.**] (with finger) 弹去 ‹*crumb, cigarette ash*›; (with implement, cloth, tail) 拂去 ‹*dust*›; **she quickly ~ed away a tear** 她迅速抹去一滴眼泪; **the horse ~ed the flies away (with its tail)** 马用尾巴赶走了苍蝇
- **flick off** *vt* [**~ sth. off, ~ off sth.**] (with finger) 弹掉 ‹*cigarette ash, crumb*›; (with implement, cloth, tail) 拂去 ‹*dust*›
- **flick out**

A *vt* [**~ sth. out, ~ out sth.**] 猛地伸出 ‹*arm, tongue, tail*›

B *vi* «*arm, tongue, tail*» 快速伸出; **the snake's tongue ~ed out** 蛇信子快速地吐出

- **flick over** *vt* [**~ sth. over, ~ over sth.**] 快速地翻 ‹*pages, paper*›
- **flick through** *vt* [**~ through sth.**] 快速翻阅 ‹*book, magazine, document*›

flicker /ˈflɪkə(r)/

A *vi* **1** (shine unsteadily) «*fire, light*» 闪烁 **2** (pass quickly) «*smile, hope, thought*» 闪现; **to ~ across** *or* **through sth.** 从某物中闪现; **a suspicion ~ed across** *or* **through his mind** 他脑中闪过一丝怀疑 **3** (move) «*tongue*» 伸吐; «*insects*» 振翅; «*shadows, needle*» 摆动; **to ~ towards/on/in sth.** 向某物/在某物上/在某物中快速一动; **her eyes ~ed towards the door** 她瞥了一眼门

B *n* **1** (of light, flame, candle) 闪烁 **2** (brief feeling, emotion) 闪现; **the ~ of a smile** 一闪而过的一丝微笑; **he felt a faint ~ of hope** 他心中闪过一丝微弱的希望 **3** (movement of eye) 转动; (of pointer, shadow) 摆动; **in the ~ of an eyelid** 一眨眼的工夫

flickering /ˈflɪkərɪŋ/ *adj* **1** (shining unsteadily) 闪烁的 ‹*light*›; 摇曳的 ‹*flame*› **2** (fluttering) 颤动的 ‹*eyelids*›; 来回摆动的 ‹*needle*›

flick knife *n* Brit 弹簧刀

flier /ˈflaɪə(r)/ *n* = **flyer**

flight /flaɪt/

A *n* **1** [u] (flying) 飞; **the history of space ~** 航天史; **in ~** 在飞行的; **birds in ~** 飞翔的鸟 **2** [c] (of bird, insect, projectile) (movement) 飞行; (distance) 飞行距离; (path) 飞行路线; **the ~ of sth.** 某物的飞行轨迹 **3** [c] (journey by air) 空中航行; **a smooth/comfortable/bumpy ~** 顺利的/舒适的/颠簸的航行; **a direct ~** 直航; **a maiden/test ~** 首航/试航; **a reconnaissance/scheduled/solo ~** 侦察飞行/定期航班/单人飞行; **to take a ~ from London to Sydney** 由伦敦乘飞机前往悉尼; **have a good ~!** 祝你飞行旅途愉快!; **what's our ~ number?** 我们的航班号是多少? **4** [c] (aircraft) 班机; **all incoming ~s were diverted** 所有到港的班机都改变了航线 **5** [c] Aerosp (journey through space) 宇宙飞行; **a crewed** *or* **manned ~** 载人宇航 **6** [c] (group) (of birds, insects, angels) 飞行的一群; (of arrows) 齐射的一组; **a ~ of arrows** 齐发的箭; **~s of migrating swans** 迁徙飞行的天鹅群; **in the top** *or* **first ~** 顶尖的 **7** [c] Aviat, Mil (air force unit) 空军小队 **8** [c] fig (of imagination, rhetoric) 奔放; **~(s) of sth.** 某物的迸发; **a ~ of fancy** 奇思怪想 **9** [c] (of steps, stairs, terraces) 一段; (of canal locks) 一系列; **a ~ of locks** 一系列船闸; **a short/steep ~ of stairs** 一小段楼梯/一段陡峭的楼梯 **10** [c] Sport (of hurdles) 一组跨栏 **11** [c] Sport (tail) (of dart) 镖尾; (of arrow) 箭尾 **12** [u and c] (fleeing) 逃走; **in a dangerous situation, would you prefer ~ to fight?** 在情况危险时, 你会宁愿逃走而不反抗吗?; **~ from sth.** 从…的逃离; **to put sb. to ~** formal 迫使某人逃跑; **to take (to) ~** 逃跑; **in sb.'s ~** 在某人逃走的过程中; **the ~ of capital abroad** 资本外撤 **13** [u] (movement, passage) 移动; **in full ~** 全力奔逃; **the striker was brought down in full ~** 这名前锋在飞速奔跑时被撞倒在地; **the speaker was in full ~ when ...** 演讲者正说得起劲, 这时…; **the rapid ~ of time** 时光的飞逝

B *vt* Brit Sport (football) 把…踢出漂亮的弧线 ‹*ball*›; (cricket) 把…击出漂亮的弧线 ‹*ball*›

flight: ~ attendant ▸p. 409 *n* 乘务员; **~ bag** *n* 航空旅行手提包; **~ control** *n* [u] 飞行控制; **~ crew** *n* 机组人员; **~ deck** *n* **1** Aviat 驾驶舱; **2** Naut [航空母舰上的] 飞行甲板; **~ engineer** ▸p. 409 *n* 随机工程师

flightless /ˈflaɪtlɪs/ *adj* 不能飞的 ‹*bird, insect*›

flight: ~ lieutenant *n* Brit 空军上尉; **~ log** *n* 飞行日志; **~ path** *n* 飞行路线; **~ plan** *n* 飞行计划; **~ recorder** *n* 飞行记录器; **~ sergeant** *n* 空军上士; **~ simulator** *n* 飞行模拟装置; **~-test** *n* 试飞; **~-test program** 试飞程式

flighty /ˈflaɪti/ *adj* **1** (frivolous) 不负责任的 ‹*person*›; 充满幻想的 ‹*mind*› **2** (fickle) 反复无常的 ‹*person, lover*›

flimflam /ˈflɪmflæm/ *n* [u] Amer colloq 废话

flimsily /ˈflɪmzɪli/ *adv* **1** (lightly) 单薄地 ‹*dressed*› **2** (weakly) 不结实地; **~ built** 造得不牢固的

flimsiness /ˈflɪmzɪnɪs/ *n* [u] **1** (of clothes, fabric) 轻而薄 **2** (of box, structure) 脆弱 **3** fig (of excuse, argument, evidence) 软弱无力

flimsy /ˈflɪmzi/ *adj* **1** (light, thin) 轻而薄的 ‹*clothes, material*› **2** (not strong) 不结实的 ‹*box, building*› **3** fig (feeble, weak) 站不住脚的 ‹*excuse, argument, evidence*›

flinch /flɪntʃ/ *vi* **1** (wince) 退缩; **she listened without ~ing as the judge pronounced her guilty** 她毫不畏惧地听着法官宣布她有罪; **to ~ at sth.** 因…而畏缩 ‹*criticism, insult*› **2** (avoid) 退开; **to ~ from sth./doing sth.** 回避某事物/做某事; **she never ~ed from doing her duty** 她从不逃避职责

fling /flɪŋ/

A *vt* (*pt, pp* **flung**) **1** (throw) 扔 ‹*ball, missile, garment, papers*›; **she flung her book at him, but missed** 她把自己的书朝他掷去, 但是没打中; **she was flung from her horse** 她从马上被抛了下来; **she flung him a look of contempt** 她轻蔑地看了他一眼; **to ~ sth. in sb.'s face** 用某事攻击某人 **2** (propel) 猛推 ‹*person*›; **he flung his opponent to the ground** 他将对手摔倒在地 **3** (move part of body) 猛甩 ‹*hands, head, hair*›; **she flung her arms around his neck/him** 她张开双臂搂住他的脖子/抱住他 **4** (send unceremoniously) «*person, authority, event*» 使突然陷入; **the prisoner was flung into the dungeons** 囚犯被投入地牢; **to ~ sb. into confusion** 使某人陷入困惑 **5** (hurl) 激烈地说出 ‹*remark*›; **they were ~ing abuse at each other** 他们激烈地互相辱骂

B *v refl* (*pt, pp* **flung**); **to ~ oneself** **1** (move forcefully) 扑; **she flung herself on the bed** 她扑倒在床上; **he flung himself over the wall** 他跃过墙; **the child flung herself into her father's arms** 孩子扑进父亲的怀抱 **2** (begin with commitment) 全身心投入; **to ~ oneself into sth./doing sth.** 全身心投入某事/全力以赴做某事

C *vi* (*pt, pp* **flung**) 猛冲; **he was ~ing about like a madman** 他像个疯子般横冲直撞

D *n* **1** (throw) 扔 **2** (spree) 一时的放纵; **to have a ~** 恣意行乐; **youth must have its ~** Prov 年轻人总要放纵一下 **3** (brief enthusiasm) 短暂的热情; **a brief ~ with Marxism** 对马克思主义的短暂热情 **4** colloq (attempt) 尝试; **to have** *or* **take a ~ at sth./doing sth.** 尝试某事/做某事 **5** Dance = **Highland fling**

Phrasal verbs

- **fling away** *vt* [**~ sth. away, ~ away sth.**] 丢弃; **she flung away the bouquet he had brought** 她扔掉了他带来的花; **she flung away her scruples** fig 她抛开顾虑
- **fling back** *vt* [**~ sth. back, ~ back sth.**] **1** (return) 扔回 **2** (remove, open) 猛地掀开 ‹*curtains, bedclothes*›; 猛地打开 ‹*door, window*› **3** (move backwards) 向后甩 ‹*head, hair*›; 向后挥 ‹*arm*›
- **fling down** *vt* [**~ sth. down, ~ down sth.**] 猛地扔下; **she flung his note down and stormed out** 她摔下他的字条, 气冲冲地走出去了
- **fling off** *vt* [**~ sth. off, ~ off sth.**] 匆忙脱下 ‹*garment*›; 匆忙掀掉 ‹*bedclothes*›; fig 摆脱 ‹*restraint, chains*›
- **fling on** *vt* [**~ sth. on, ~ on sth.**] 匆忙穿上 ‹*garment*›; 匆忙戴上 ‹*accessory*›; **she flung on a coat and ran out** 她匆忙穿了件外套, 跑了出去
- **fling open** *vt* [**~ sth. open, ~ open sth.**] 猛地打开 ‹*door, window*›
- **fling out**

A [**~ sth. out, ~ out sth.**] *vt* **1** (throw away) 扔掉 ‹*object*› **2** (extend quickly) 快速伸出 ‹*limb*› **3** (say aggressively) 语气激烈地说 ‹*remark*›

B [**~ sb. out, ~ out sb.**] *vt* 突然赶走 ‹*lover, troublemaker*›

- **fling up** *vt* [**~ sth. up, ~ up sth.**] 用力向上抛 ‹*object*›; 用力向上扬 ‹*arms, hands*›; **he flung up his hands in dismay/horror** 他沮丧地/惊恐地扬起双手

flint /flɪnt/ *n* **1** [u and c] (rock) 燧石; **she/he has a heart like ~** fig 她/他铁石心肠 **2** [c] (in lighter) 打火石

flintlock /ˈflɪntlɒk/ *n* 燧发枪

Flintshire /ˈflɪntʃɪə/ *pr n* 弗林特郡

flinty /ˈflɪnti/ *adj* **1** Geol (containing flint) 含燧石的 ‹*fields, rocks, soil*› **2** (hard) 坚硬的 ‹*material, bread*› **3** fig (harsh) 铁石般的 ‹*heart*›; 冷酷的 ‹*person, eyes*›

flip /flɪp/

A *vt* (*pres p etc.* **-pp-**) **1** (toss) 轻抛; **let's ~ a coin (to decide)** 咱们掷硬币决定吧; **to ~ sth. across** *or* **over/into ...** 把某物抛过/进…; **can you ~ me across a cigarette?** 扔给我一根香烟好吗? **2** (turn) 快速翻动 ‹*book, pancake, fish*›; **she ~ped the pancake over** 她把煎饼翻了个面; **to ~ one's lid** Brit colloq *or* **wig** esp Amer colloq 发火 **3** (flick) 按动 ‹*switch*›; 开关 ‹*light, engine*›; **to ~ sth. on/off** 把某物打开/关上; **to ~ sth. open/shut** 把某物打开/关上

B *vi* (*pres p etc.* **-pp-**) colloq **1** (get angry) 发火 **2** (go insane) 发疯 **3** (get excited) 变得激动

C *n* **1** [c] (with finger) 轻弹; **to give sth. a ~** 轻弹某物; **with a ~ (of the fingers), she sent the ball of paper flying** 她（手指）一弹, 把纸团弹飞了; **to decide sth. by** *or* **on the ~ of a coin** 抛硬币决定某事 **2** [c] (jerk)

急动; a ～ of the tail 尾巴的一下猛摆 [3] [c] (somersault) 空翻 [4] [u and c] (drink) 饮料酒; **egg ～** 鸡蛋酒

D *adj* 无礼的 ‹*comment, person*›

E *excl* Brit colloq **oh, ～!** 哦，讨厌!

Phrasal verbs

- **flip over**

A *vt* [**～ sth. over, ～ over sth.**] 把…翻过来; **he ～ped the pages over two at a time** 他一次两页地翻书; **a huge wave ～ped the boat over** 一个巨浪把小船打翻了

B *vi* 翻转; **the car hit a tree and ～ped over** 车撞到树上翻了

- **flip through** *vt* [**～ through sth.**] 快速翻阅 ‹*book, magazine*›

flipboard /ˈflɪpbɔːd/, **flipchart** /ˈflɪptʃɑːt/ *ns* 活动挂图

flip-flop

A *n* [1] (sandal) 人字拖鞋 [2] (flapping sound) 啪嗒啪嗒声 [3] Comput 触发器

B *vi* (*pres p etc.* **-pp-**) Amer colloq 来 180 度大转弯; **the government is ～ping a lot on this point** 政府在这一点上老是出尔反尔

flippancy /ˈflɪpənsi/ *n* [u] 轻率无礼; **the ～ of his reply** 他的回答的轻率

flippant /ˈflɪpənt/ *adj* 轻率无礼的 ‹*attitude, remark, person*›; **don't be ～!** 不得无礼!

flippantly /ˈflɪpəntli/ *adv* 轻率无礼地 ‹*say, remark*›

flipper /ˈflɪpə(r)/ *n* [1] Zool 鳍足 [2] (for swimmer) 脚蹼

flip phone *n* 翻盖式手机

flipping /ˈflɪpɪŋ/ Brit colloq

A *adj* 糟透的; **～ heck** 见鬼

B *adv* 非常 ‹*awful, stupid*›

flip: ～ side *n* [1] Mus (of record) 唱片反面; [2] fig (other side) 负面; **the ～ side of life in the capital is the noise and pollution** 首都生活的另一面是噪音和污染; **～-top** *adj* 翻盖的 ‹*bin, mobile phone*›; **a ～-top lid** 易拉盖

flirt /flɜːt/

A *vi* [1] (make romantic or sexual advances) 调情; **to ～ with sb.** 与某人调情 [2] (toy) 不认真地对待; **to ～ with sth./the idea of sth.** 玩似地考虑某事/某想法; **she ～ed with (the idea of) becoming a Buddhist** 她曾经一时兴起想过当佛教徒; **to ～ with danger/death** 冒险/玩命

B *n* 调情者

flirtation /flɜːˈteɪʃn/ *n* [1] [u] (flirting) 调情 [2] [c] (relationship) 短暂的风流韵事; **to have a ～ with sb.** 与某人一时风流 [3] [c] (interest) 一时的兴趣; **a brief ～ with Buddhism** 一时兴起信奉佛教

flirtatious /flɜːˈteɪʃəs/ *adj* 轻佻的 ‹*behaviour, person*›; **she threw him a ～ glance** 她挑逗地瞥了他一眼

flit /flɪt/

A *vi* (*pres p etc.* **-tt-**) [1] (fly) «*birds, butterfly*» 轻快地飞; **to ～ about** *or* **around** 轻快地四处飞 [2] (move quickly and lightly) «*person*» 轻快地移动; **to ～ about** 轻快地四处走动 [3] fig (flash) «*idea, image, expression*» 掠过; **a look of panic ～ted across his face** 他脸上掠过一丝惊慌 [4] (move restlessly) «*person, mind*» 频繁变化; **he ～s from one job to another** 他频繁跳槽

B *n* Brit colloq (house move) [为了躲债的] 搬家; **to do a (moonlight) ～** (夜间) 逃走

float /fləʊt/

A *vi* [1] (be suspended on liquid, in air) «*swimmer, object*» 浮; **wood ～s** 木头可以浮起来; **he was ～ing on his back** 他仰面浮在水上 [2] (move on liquid or in air) «*ship, log, swimmer*» 漂浮; «*feather, smoke, music*» 飘浮; fig «*ideas, visions*» 浮现; **the body ～ed (back) up to the surface** 尸体浮上水面; **clouds ～ed across the sky** 云在空中飘过; **thoughts of lazy summer afternoons ～ed through his head** fig 慵懒夏日午后的种种思绪浮现在他的脑海中; **the faint sound of voices came ～ing across the water** 微弱的说话声从水面的另一端飘来 [3] (move gracefully) 飘然走动; **she ～ed down the stairs** 她飘然走下台阶 [4] Fin «*currency*» 浮动

B *vt* [1] (suspend) 使…浮起 ‹*vessel, raft, log*›; **to ～ the cream on top of the soup** 使奶油浮在汤的表面 [2] (cause to move) «*current, person*» 使…漂流 ‹*boat, cargo, feather*›; **the trees are cut down, then ～ed downstream to the sawmill** 这些树被砍倒后顺流而下漂到锯木厂 [3] fig (propose) 提出 ‹*idea, project*› [4] Fin (offer shares in) «*person, company*» 发行 ‹*shares, securities*›; 使…上市 ‹*company*› [5] Fin (allow to vary) «*government, country*» 使…浮动 ‹*currency*›

C *n* [1] Fishg 浮子 [2] Brit (swimmer's aid) 浮板 [3] (in cistern, carburettor) 浮球 [4] Aviat 浮筒 [5] Biol 浮囊 [6] (decorated truck) 彩车; **a carnival ～** 狂欢节彩车 [7] Brit Aut 电动车; **a milk ～** 送奶电动车 [8] Brit (for expenses, in till) 备用零钱; **a cash ～** 备用现金 [9] Constr 镘刀 [10] Amer Culin 加冰激凌的饮料

Phrasal verbs

- **float about, float around** *vi* [1] (circulate) «*idea, news*» 传播; **there's a rumour ～ing about that he's going to be sacked** 有传闻说他将被解雇 [2] (move aimlessly) 闲荡; (move gracefully) 飘然走动; **he just ～s about the house all day** 他只是整天在屋子里游荡; **grandiose ideas were ～ing about in his mind** fig 他的头脑中浮现着一些华而不实的构想 [3] colloq (be somewhere) «*pen, glasses*» 在近处; **have you seen my keys ～ing about?** 你在附近看见我的钥匙了吗?
- **float away** *vi* [1] (on water) «*vessel, leaf*» 漂走; (in air) «*balloon, feather, leaf*» 飘走 [2] (move) «*person*» 飘然离去
- **float off**

A *vi* [1] **= float away** [2] Naut «*vessel, wreck*» 浮离; **we had to wait for the tide so that we could ～ off the reef** 我们必须等到涨潮才能浮离暗礁

B *vt* [**～ sth. off, ～ off sth.**] «*sailor, tide*» 使…浮离 ‹*vessel, wreck*›

floater /ˈfləʊtə(r)/ *n* [1] (in eye) 漂浮物 [2] Pol 游离选民 [3] Sport (footballer) 自由人 [4] Amer (employee) 临时工

floating /ˈfləʊtɪŋ/

A *adj* [1] (afloat) 漂浮的; **a ～ hotel** 水上旅馆; **a ～ bridge** 浮桥 [2] (mobile) 流动的 ‹*population*›

B *n* [u] [1] (of ship, logs) 漂浮 [2] Fin (of company) 上市; (of currency) 浮动

floating: ～ assets *npl* 流动资产; **～ capital** *n* [u] 流动资本; **～ currency** *n* 自由浮动货币; **～ debt** *n* 流动债务; **～ decimal, ～ decimal point** *ns* 浮点十进制; **～ dock** *n* 浮船坞; **～ exchange rate** *n* 浮动汇率; **～-point representation** *n* [u] 浮点表示法; **～ restaurant** *n* 水上餐馆; **～ vote** *n* Brit 游离票; **～ voter** *n* Brit 游离选民

flock[1] /flɒk/

A *n* [1] (of domestic animals) 畜群; (of birds) 鸟群; **～s of sheep** 一群群绵羊; **winter migrants arriving in ～s** 一群群飞来的冬季迁徙鸟 [2] (of people) 一大群人; **a ～ of people** 一大群人 [3] + *v sing or pl* Relig [属同一牧师所管的] 全体教徒; **a priest and his ～** 牧师与他的信众

B *vi* 群集; **to ～ to/into/out of ...** «*sightseers, birds*» 成群结队去/进/出…; **to ～ together** 聚集; **to ～ round (sb./sth.)** (把某人/某物) 团团围住

flock[2] *n* [1] [u] (soft material) 软填料; **～ wallpaper** 植绒壁纸; **a ～ mattress/cushion** 毛屑垫/靠垫 [2] [c] (fleecy tuft) 毛束

floe /fləʊ/ *n* **ice ～** 浮冰

flog /flɒg/ *vt* (*pres p etc.* **-gg-**) [1] (beat) 鞭打 ‹*offender*›; **to ～ sb. to death/to within an inch of his/her life** 把某人打死/打得半死; **to ～ sth. to death** fig colloq 好话说三遍，鸡狗不稀见; **to ～ a dead horse** Brit colloq 做徒劳无益的事; **advocates of capital punishment are ～ging a dead horse** 提倡死刑的人在做无用功 [2] Brit colloq (sell) 出售 ‹*car, furniture*›; **to ～ sb. sth., to ～ sth. to sb.** 把某物卖给某人

flogging /ˈflɒgɪŋ/ *n* [u and c] 鞭打; **to give sb. a ～** 把某人打一顿

flood /flʌd/

A *n* [1] [u and c] (large amount or excess flow of water) 洪水; **are you insured against ～?** 你投保水灾险了吗？; **to be in (full) ～** lit 泛滥; fig 正起劲; **the ～s have made many people homeless** 水灾使许多人无家可归; **we had a ～ in the kitchen** 我们的厨房漫水了; **the F～, Noah's F～** Bible 灭世洪水; **she burst into ～s of tears** fig 她突然泪如雨下 [2] [c] fig (overwhelming quantity) 大量; **～ of sth.** 大量的某物; **～s of visitors poured into the exhibition** 大批参观者涌入展览会; **a ～ of light illuminated the room** 一片强光照亮了房间; **a ～ of words** 滔滔不绝的一席话 [3] [u] (inflow of tide) 涨潮; **to be at the ～** «*tide*» 涨到最高点

B *vt* [1] (submerge) «*river, stream*» 淹没 ‹*valley, plain, town*›; «*burst pipe*» 使…灌满水 ‹*house, room*›; **the basement was ～ed when a pipe burst** 一根水管破裂，地下室被淹了 [2] (fill to overflowing) «*rain, storm*» 使…泛滥 ‹*river, stream*› [3] fig (fill or suffuse completely) «*papers, letters*» 大量涌向; «*light*» 充满 ‹*room, stage*›; **bills ～ed her letter box** 她的信箱塞满了账单; **the switchboard was ～ed with complaints** 总机接到了大量的投诉电话; **a blush ～ed her cheeks** 她的脸颊泛出红晕; **to ～ sth./sb. with sth.** 以某物充满某物/某人 [4] Comm «*producer*» 使…充斥 ‹*shops, country, market*›; **to ～ European markets with cheap imitations** 使欧洲市场充斥着廉价的仿制品 [5] Aut 使…溢流 ‹*carburettor*›; **to ～ the engine with too much petrol** 因加入太多汽油而使发动机溢油 [6] fig (overwhelm) «*feelings, thoughts*» 充溢; **childhood memories ～ed his mind** 童年的回忆涌上他的心头; **to be ～ed with sth.** 充满某物

C *vi* [1] (become submerged) «*valley, town, house*» 被水淹 [2] (overflow) «*river, tributary, stream*» 泛滥; «*sewer, bath, washing machine*» 漫水 [3] (spread, move) «*tears*» 涌出; «*flush, blush*» 涌现; **the news brought people ～ing into the streets** 这个消息使人们涌上街头; **sunlight ～ed into the room** 阳光洒满房间; **relief ～ed over him when he realized no one was hurt** 知道没有人受伤后，他深感宽慰

Phrasal verbs

- **flood back** *vi* «*emotions, memories, thoughts*» 涌上心头
- **flood in** *vi* «*people, contributions, gifts*» 大量涌入; **I threw back the shutters and let the light ～ in** 我猛地拉开百叶窗，让光线倾泻进来
- **flood out**

A *vt* [1] [**～ sb. out, ～ out sb.**] (force out) «*floodwater, burst pipe*» 迫使…离家 [2] [**～ sth. out, ～ out sth.**] «*water*» 淹没 ‹*house, room*›

B *vi* «*water, people*» 大量涌出

flood: ～ control *n* 防洪; **～ damage** *n* [u] 洪涝灾害; **～gate** *n* 防洪闸门; **to open the ～gates to sb./sth.** fig 使某人不受限制地进入/使某事一发不可收拾

flooding /ˈflʌdɪŋ/ *n* [u] [1] (floods) 洪涝; **the rain caused severe ～** 大雨引发严重水灾 [2] (overflowing of river) 泛滥

flood level *n* 洪水水位

floodlight /ˈflʌdlaɪt/
A *n* **1** [c] (powerful light) 泛光灯; **to play under ～s** 在泛光灯下比赛 **2** [u] (illumination) 泛光照明
B *vt* (*pt, pp* **floodlit** /ˈflʌdlɪt/) 用泛光灯照亮 ‹*buildings, match, theatre*›

flood: **～mark** *n* 高潮标记; **～plain** *n* 洪泛区; **～ tide** *n* 涨潮; **～water** *n* [u] **～waters** *npl* 洪水; **～way** *n* 泄洪道

floor /flɔː(r)/
A *n* **1** (of room) 地面; **an earth ～** Brit, **a dirt ～** Amer 泥土地面; **a concrete/wooden ～** 水泥/木质地面; **to sweep/scrub/mop the ～** 扫地/擦地/拖地; **from ～ to ceiling** 从地板到天花板; **at ～ level** 在底层; **to wipe the ～ with sb.** colloq 把某人打得一败涂地 **2** (of sea, valley, cave) 底; **on the ocean ～** 在海底; **the forest ～** 森林覆被 **3** (of vehicle, lift) 底板 **4** (storey) 楼层; **the ground ～** Brit 底楼; **to be** *or* **get in on the ground ～** fig colloq 从一开始就参与; **the first/second/third ～** Brit 二楼/三楼/四楼; Amer 一楼/二楼/三楼; **we live on the top ～** 我们住在顶楼; **the whole ～ has** *or* **have agreed to help** 这层楼的所有住户都同意帮忙 **5** Pol (main area of debating chamber) 议员席; **to speak on** *or* **from the ～** 在议员席上发言; **the Speaker will now take questions from the ～** 议长现在接受议员的提问; **to cross the ～ (of the House)** Brit 转而支持对方 **6** Pol (right to speak) 发言权; **to get/have/be given the ～** 获得/拥有/被给予发言权; **the ～ is yours** 你现在有权发言; **to take the ～** 发言 **7** **the ～** (for dancing) 舞池; (in factory) 车间; (of Stock Exchange) 交易厅; **several couples were already on the (dance) ～** 有几对已经在舞池中跳舞了; **shall we take the ～?** 我们跳舞吧? ; **the factory ～ has** *or* **have voted for a strike** 工人投票决定罢工; **trading on the ～ is brisk this morning** 今天上午交易厅交投活跃 **8** Econ, Fin 最低额; **a wage ～** 工资底限; **to fall through the ～** 跌破底限
B *vt* **1** Constr 给…铺地板 ‹*room, building*›; **to ～ sth. in** *or* **with sth.** 用某物给某物铺地面; **the kitchen was ～ed in red tiles** 厨房地面铺着红色瓷砖 **2** (knock down) 把…打倒在地 ‹*opponent, attacker, victim*›; **to ～ sb. with sth.** 以某物将某人打倒在地; **he ～ed him with a single blow** 他一拳把他打倒在地 **3** colloq (defeat) «*argument, remark*» 使…哑口无言; **his final words completely ～ed them** 他最后的话使他们彻底哑口无言 **4** colloq (stump) «*remark, discovery, suggestion*» 使…困惑; **I was ～ed by question five** 第5题把我难倒了 **5** Aut colloq 把…踩到底 ‹*accelerator*›

floor: **～ area** *n* 建筑面积; **～board** *n* 木地板条; **～ cloth** *n* Brit 擦地布; **～ covering** *n* 铺地板材料; **～ exercises** *npl* 自由体操

flooring /ˈflɔːrɪŋ/ *n* [u] 铺地面的材料

floor: **～ lamp** *n* Amer **= standard lamp**; **～ leader** *n* Amer 国会中的党派领袖; **～-length** *adj* 及地的 ‹*garment*›; **a ～-length window/mirror** 落地窗/镜; **～ manager** ▸**p. 409** *n* **1** TV 舞台总监; **2** Comm (in store) 楼面主管; **～ plan** *n* 楼层平面图; **～ polish** *n* 地板蜡; **～ polisher** *n* 地板打蜡机; **～ show** *n* [夜总会、餐馆等处的] 系列表演; **～ space** *n* 楼面面积; **～ trading** *n* [u] 场内交易; **～walker** ▸**p. 409** *n* Amer 铺面巡视员

floozie, floozy /ˈfluːzi/ *n* colloq pej 荡妇

flop /flɒp/
A *vi* (*pres p etc.* **-pp-**) **1** (move clumsily) 笨重地行动; (fall clumsily) 沉重地落下; **to ～ about** *or* **around** 扑腾; **the fish was ～ping around, gasping** 鱼扑腾着, 张着嘴喘着气; **the pile of magazines ～ped over on to the floor** 那堆杂志扑通一下散落在地板上 **2** (sit down heavily) 猛然坐下; (lie down heavily) 沉重地躺下; **to ～ down into a chair/on to the bed** 一屁股坐在椅子上/一下子倒在床上; **I'm ready to ～** colloq 我快累倒了 **3** (hang loosely) «*head, hair, ears*» 耷拉; **his head suddenly ～ped and he went to sleep** 他头突然一垂睡着了; **to ～ about** *or* **around** 摆来摆去; **can't you stop your hair ～ping about like that?** 你就不能别把头发那样甩来甩去吗? **4** colloq (fail) «*play, actor, book*» 搞砸 **5** colloq (sleep) [在某个地方] 睡觉
B *n* **1** (heavy movement) 扑腾; (heavy sound) 扑通声; **to sit down with a ～** 扑通一声坐下; **the ～ of fish in a pail** 鱼在桶里扑腾 **2** colloq (failure) 搞砸
C *adv* **1** (with flopping sound) 扑通一声 ‹*go, fall*›; **the ball fell ～ into the pond** 球咚的一声落进池子 **2** colloq (unsuccessfully) 彻底失败地; **the whole project just went ～ when the director left** 负责人离开后整个项目便告吹了

flophouse /ˈflɒphaʊs/ *n* Amer colloq 廉价旅馆

floppy /ˈflɒpi/
A *adj* 松软的 ‹*hat, clothes*›; **to let one's arm go ～** 垂下手臂; **toy rabbits with big ～ ears** 耷拉着大耳朵的玩具兔子
B *n* 软磁盘

floppy: **～ disk** *n* 软磁盘; **～ disk drive, ～ drive** *ns* 软盘驱动器

flora /ˈflɔːrə/ *n* [u] [尤指某地区或某时期的] 植物群; **～ and fauna** 动植物群

floral /ˈflɔːrəl/ *adj* **1** (made of flowers) 用花做的; **～ display/arrangements** 花展/插花; **～ tributes** (at funeral) 敬献的鲜花 **2** (decorated with flowers) 饰以花的; **a ～ skirt** 花裙子; **a ～ pattern** 花卉图案

floret /ˈflɒrɪt/ *n* [复花序中的] 小花

florid /ˈflɒrɪd, Amer ˈflɔːr-/ *adj* **1** (ornate) 过分华丽的 ‹*architecture, music*›; 词藻堆砌的 ‹*style, language*› **2** (ruddy) 红润的 ‹*complexion*›

Florida /ˈflɒrɪdə/ *pr n* 佛罗里达州

florist /ˈflɒrɪst, Amer ˈflɔːrɪst/ ▸**p. 409** *n* 花商; **the ～'s** 花店

floss /flɒs, Amer flɔːs/
A *n* [u] **1** (silk fibres) 丝线 **2** **= dental floss**
B *vt* 用牙线剔 ‹*teeth*›
C *vi* 用牙线剔牙

flotation /fləʊˈteɪʃn/ *n* **1** [u and c] Fin (of company) 发行股份; (of loan) 筹募; (of shares, stock, securities) 发行 **2** [u] (buoyancy) 漂浮

flotation: **～ bag** *n* 飘浮袋; **～ device** *n* Amer 救生漂浮用具; **～ tank** *n* 盐水浮力池

flotilla /fləˈtɪlə/ *n* **1** (of small boats) 小船队 **2** (of warships) 小型舰队

flotsam /ˈflɒtsəm/ *n* [u] 船只残骸; **～ and jetsam** lit (on water) 船只残骸; fig (odds and ends) 零碎杂物; fig (people) 流浪者

flounce /flaʊns/
A *vi* **1** (storm) [愤怒或不耐烦地] 急动; **to ～ in/out** *or* **off** 冲进/冲出; **she ～d angrily out of the room** 她忿忿地冲出房间 **2** (show off) 故作夸张地走动; **to ～ around** *or* **about** 动作夸张地走来走去; **she found her daughter flouncing around in her high heels** 她发现女儿穿着高跟鞋扭动着走来走去
B *n* 急动; **she left the room with a ～** 她猛一转身离开了房间; **with a ～ of her head she departed** 她一扭头离开了

flounder[1] /ˈflaʊndə(r)/ *vi* **1** (struggle) «*person, animal*» 挣扎; «*economy, career*» 困难重重; **many firms are ～ing** 许多公司举步维艰; **to ～ in the deep end** 在深水区挣扎; **to ～ about in the dark** 在黑暗中挣扎 **2** fig (falter) 支吾; **to ～ through a speech** 在整个讲话期间错误百出

flounder[2] *n* **1** Brit (specific flatfish) 鲽 **2** Amer (any flatfish) 比目鱼

flour /ˈflaʊə(r)/
A *n* [u] 面粉; **wheat/whole wheat/rye ～** 小麦粉/全麦粉/黑麦粉
B *vt* 在…上撒面粉; **to ～ a cake tin** 在烤饼锅上撒面粉

flour: **～ bin** *n* 面粉箱; **～ bomb** *n* 面粉弹 [为表示抗议而投掷的面粉包]

flourish /ˈflʌrɪʃ/
A *vi* **1** (prosper) «*business*» 兴旺; «*society*» 繁荣; **corruption ～es when everyone is badly paid** 当大家收入都很微薄时, 腐败就猖獗了 **2** (grow well, be healthy) «*plant, organism*» 茂盛; «*person*» 健康成长; **the family is ～ing** 全家人身体都很好 **3** (thrive) «*the arts, artist, school*» 处于全盛时期; **the Romantic Movement ～ed while Classicism declined** 浪漫主义运动盛行而古典主义衰落了
B *vt* 挥舞 ‹*certificate, tickets, flags*›
C *n* **1** (gesture) 夸张动作; **with a ～, she ushered them inside** 她做了个夸张动作领他们进去 **2** (curve) (in scrollwork) 流畅的曲线; (in handwriting) 花饰; **to sign sth. with a ～** 用花体在某物上签名

flourishing /ˈflʌrɪʃɪŋ/ *adj* **1** (prospering) 兴旺的 ‹*business*›; 繁荣的 ‹*society*›; **the country's ～ tourist industry** 国内蒸蒸日上的旅游业 **2** (blossoming) 茂盛的 ‹*garden*›

flour: **～ mill** *n* 面粉厂; **～ sifter** *n* 面粉筛子

floury /ˈflaʊərɪ/ *adj* **1** (covered in flour) 覆盖面粉的 ‹*loaf, dish*›; **～ hands** 沾了面粉的双手 **2** (powdery) 很面的 ‹*potatoes*›

flout /flaʊt/ *vt* 公然藐视 ‹*advice, the law*›

flow /fləʊ/
A *vi* **1** (move freely and steadily) «*liquid, air*» 流动; «*time*» 流逝; «*music*» 飘荡; **blood will ～** 会有人流血的; **most rivers ～ into the sea** 大多数河流汇入大海; **to ～ from sth.** lit 从某处流出; fig 源于某物; **blood was ～ing from a cut in her finger** 血正从她手指的伤口流出; **her actions ～ from a strong sense of justice** 她的行为源于强烈的正义感; **to ～ upwards/downwards** 向上/下流动; **to ～ over into sth.** fig 汇入某物; **the days ～ed past, one much like another** 岁月流逝, 日复一日; **the memories ～ed back** 往事一幕幕地浮现 **2** (move in system) «*adrenalin, energy*» 循环; «*electricity, data*» 流通; **ventilation channels keep the air ～ing** 通风管道保持空气流通; **Spanish blood ～ed through her veins** 她血管里流着西班牙人的血; **traffic is now ～ing freely again after the accident** 事故过后, 现在交通又畅通了 **3** fig (move in large numbers or amounts) «*money, messages*» 涌至; «*people*» 涌流; **to ～ in/out** 涌入/涌出; **skilled workers are now ～ing abroad** 熟练工人正大量涌向国外; **weeks after the disaster, money and help was still ～ing in** 灾难发生数周后, 资金和援助仍源源不断地涌入; **complaints/congratulations have been ～ing in** 投诉/贺词纷至沓来; **election results ～ed steadily in all night** 整个晚上选举结果不断传来 **4** (be continuous) «*conversation, ideas*» 流畅; **the writing does not ～** 文章不顺畅; **the sentences ～ed from his pen** 他下笔千言; **is the work ～ing smoothly?** 工作进展顺利吗? **5** Geog «*tide*» 涨; **to ebb and ～** 潮涨潮落; **the tide of public opinion is beginning to ～ in our favour** 公众的意见开始向我们倾斜 **6** (be available in large quantities) «*wine, money*» 大量供应; **to ～ with sth.** 有大量某物; **a land ～ing with milk and honey** Bible 丰饶之地 **7** (move gracefully) «*hair, clothing*» 飘垂 **8** Phys «*solid*» 变形
B *n* **1** [u and c] (movement of liquid, blood, gas, air) 流动; (rate of movement) 流速; **to measure the (rate of) ～** 测量流速; **increased ～s of water reached downstream areas** 上涨的水流到达了下游地带; **a woman's menstrual ～** 女性的月经; **the ～ of time** 时间的流逝 **2** [u and c] (movement in system) (of blood, adrenalin, energy) 循环; (of electricity, air, data) 流通; (of traffic, vehicles) 流动; **to impede traffic ～** 阻碍车流; **to increase the ～ of adrenalin** 提高肾上腺素水平; **a ～ of energy** 能量流; **data ～s** 数据流 **3** [u and c] (movement in large

numbers or amounts) 涌流; **the ~ of sth.** 源源不断的某物; **the ~ of refugees to the West** 涌往西部的难民潮; **the global ~s of capital** 全球的资本流通; **to go with the ~** colloq 随遇而安; **a cash-~ problem** 现金流问题 4 [u and c] (effusion) 流畅; **in full ~** 流畅地; **the elegant ~ of his prose** 他散文的优美流畅; **a ~ of subconscious imagery** 一连串潜意识的意象 5 [u] Geog (sea, tide, river) 涨潮; **the tide is on the ~** 正在涨潮 6 [u] Phys 变形

flow chart, flow diagram, flow-sheet *ns* 流程图

flower /ˈflaʊə(r)/
A *n* 1 (bloom) 花; **to be in/come into ~** 开花; **to be in full ~** lit 盛开; fig 盛行; **to arrange ~s** 插花; **a bunch or bouquet of ~s** 一束花; **'no ~s by request'** "不收花圈" 2 (plant) 开花植物; **wild ~s** 野花; **to plant/sow/grow ~s** 种花
B *vi* 1 lit «*plant, tree*» 开花 2 fig (develop) «*movement*» 繁荣; «*friendship, talent, young person*» 发展成熟; **she has ~ed into a great writer** 她已经成长为一位伟大的作家

flower: ~ arrangement *n* [u and c] 插花; **~ arrangement classes/exhibition** 插花班/展; **~ arranging** *n* [u] 插花; **~bed** *n* 花坛; **~ children, ~ people** *nspl* 佩花嬉皮士 [20世纪60年代主张博爱与和平、以花象征其信仰的人]

flowered /ˈflaʊəd/ *adj* 有花卉图案的 ‹*dress, material*›

flower: ~ garden *n* 花园; **~ head** *n* 头状花序

flowering /ˈflaʊərɪŋ/
A *n* [u] 1 (blooming) 开花; **the ~ of fruit trees** 果树的开花 2 fig (of idea, style, movement) 鼎盛
B *adj* 开花的 ‹*plants, shrubs*›; **early-/late-~** 开花早/晚的

flower: ~pot *n* 花盆; **~ power** *n* [u] Hist 花的力量; **~ seller** ▸**p. 409** *n* 花商; **~ shop** *n* 花店; **~ show** *n* 花展; **~ stall** *n* 花摊

> **flower power**
> 花的力量。20 世纪 60 年代嬉皮士（▸**hippie**）的反战口号。嬉皮士反对暴力，试图通过爱与和平来改变世界。嬉皮士认为花象征美与和平，他们佩戴或散发鲜花以表达自己的诉求和理想，因此也被称为"花童"（flower children 或 flower people）。

flowery /ˈflaʊəri/ *adj* 1 (covered with flowers) 多花的 ‹*meadow, field*› 2 (patterned with flowers) 有花卉图案的 ‹*material*›; **his ~ shirt** 他的花衬衣 3 (elaborate) 词藻华丽的 ‹*language, style*›

flowing /ˈfləʊɪŋ/ *adj* 1 (smooth) 流畅的 ‹*style, phrases, sentences*› 2 (streaming) 飘垂的 ‹*hair, robes*›

flown /fləʊn/ *pp* ▸**fly¹ A, B**

fl oz *abbr* = **fluid ounce**

flu /fluː/ ▸**p. 377** *n* [u] 流行性感冒; **to come or go down with (the) ~** 患流感病倒; **~ outbreak/vaccine/virus** 流感爆发/疫苗/病毒

flub /flʌb/ Amer colloq
A *vt* (*pres p etc.* **-bb-**) 把…搞糟
B *vi* (*pres p etc.* **-bb-**) 搞砸; **he ~bed on the first night** 他在首晚搞砸了
C *n* **~(-up)** 错误

fluctuate /ˈflʌktjʊeɪt/ *vi* 1 (rise and fall) «*price, temperature, demand*» 波动; **to ~ between sth. and sth.** 在某物与某物之间波动 2 (waver) «*people, attitudes, needs*» 摇摆不定; **to ~ between sth. and sth.** 在某物与某物之间摇摆不定; **her mood ~d between hope and despair** 她的情绪变化不定，时而充满希望，时而感到绝望

fluctuation /ˌflʌktjʊˈeɪʃn/ *n* [u and c] (change) 波动; **~ in or of sth.** 某物的波动; **price ~s** 价格的波动

flue /fluː/ *n* 烟道

flue gas *n* [u and c] 烟道废气

fluency /ˈfluːənsi/ *n* [u] 1 (in language) 流利; **~ in German** 德语说得流利 2 (of style, reading) 流畅; **the ~ of his writing** 他文笔的流畅; **with great ~** 非常流畅地

fluent /ˈfluːənt/ *adj* 1 (in language) 说话流利的 ‹*speaker*›; 流利的 ‹*French*›; **a ~ French speaker** 法语说得流利的人; **I speak ~ Greek** 我能说一口流利的希腊语; **she is ~ in Swahili** 她的斯瓦西里语说得很流利 2 (eloquent) 流畅的 ‹*style, speech, reading, essay*› 3 (articulate) 熟练自如的; **a ~ reader/speaker** 阅读流畅/说话流利的人

fluently /ˈfluːəntli/ *adv* 1 (in language) 流利地 ‹*write, speak, read, express*› 2 (eloquently) 流畅地

flue pipe *n* 烟道管

fluff /flʌf/
A *n* 1 [u] (waste, dust) 毛絮; **~ had accumulated under the beds** 床下积起了毛絮团 2 [u] (down) 绒毛 3 [c] colloq (mistake) (in play) 念错台词; (in playing music) 弹错音符; (in game) 失误; **to make a ~** 出错
B *vt* 1 (puff up) 拍松 ‹*pillow, cushion*›; «*bird*» 抖松 ‹*feathers*› 2 colloq (get wrong) «*actor*» 念错 ‹*lines, audition*›; «*musician*» 奏错 ‹*note, bar*›; «*player, student*» 把…搞砸 ‹*stroke, exam*›

Phrasal verb
- **fluff out, fluff up** *vt* [**~ sth. out, ~ out sth.**] 把…抖松

fluffy /ˈflʌfi/ *adj* 1 (soft, downy) 绒毛般的; (covered in fluff) 覆有毛绒的 ‹*blanket*›; **a ~ little kitten** 毛茸茸的小猫; **~ hair** 蓬松的头发; **a ~ toy** 毛绒玩具 2 (light) 松软的 ‹*cake, potato, rice*›

fluid /ˈfluːɪd/
A *n* [u and c] 1 (liquid) 液体; **to be on ~s (only)** (只) 吃流质; **body ~s** 体液 2 Chem, Tech 流体
B *adj* 1 (liquid) 流动的 ‹*substance*› 2 (changeable) 不稳定的 ‹*situation*›; 易变的 ‹*plans, ideas, opinions*› 3 (graceful) 流畅优美的 ‹*movements, style, drawing*›

fluid: ~ assets *npl* Amer 流动资产; **~ capital** *n* [u] Amer 流动资本

fluidity /fluːˈɪdəti/ *n* [u] 1 (of substance) 流动性 2 (of plans, ideas) 易变性; (of situation) 不稳定性 3 (of style, movement, lines) 流畅优美

fluid: ~ mechanics *npl + v sing* 流体力学; **~ ounce** *n* 液量盎司

fluke /fluːk/ *n* 1 colloq (chance) 侥幸; **by a (sheer) ~** (全) 靠侥幸; **that shot was a ~** 那次射门是侥幸成功 2 Naut (of anchor) 锚爪 3 (of harpoon, arrow) 倒钩

fluky, flukey /ˈfluːki/ *adj* 幸运的 ‹*coincidence*›; **that was a ~ shot!** 那是个运气球!

flume /fluːm/ *n* 1 (for transportation) 引水槽 2 (for entertainment) 滑水道

flummery /ˈflʌməri/ *n* 1 [u and c] Culin 蛋奶甜点心 2 [c] fig pej (nonsense) 废话; (flattery) 空洞的恭维话

flummox /ˈflʌməks/ *vt* colloq «*problem, situation*» 使困惑

flummoxed /ˈflʌməkst/ *adj* colloq 困惑的

flung /flʌŋ/ *pt, pp* ▸**fling A, B, C**

flunk /flʌŋk/ esp Amer colloq
A *vt* 1 (fail) «*student*» 没通过; **she ~ed biology/the biology exam** 她生物考试不及格 2 (give low grade to) «*teacher*» 给…打不及格分数; **she ~ed the whole class** 她给全班学生打了不及格的分数; **to be ~ed in sth.** 在某考试中不及格
B *vi* «*student*» 不及格

Phrasal verb
- **flunk out** *vi* colloq «*student*» 因不及格而退学; **to ~ out of college/school** 因不及格从学院/学校退学

flunkey, flunky /ˈflʌŋki/ *n* 1 Hist (servant) [穿制服的] 男仆 2 colloq pej (minion) 马屁精

fluorescence /flɔːˈresəns, Amer ˌflʊəˈr-/ *n* [u] 荧光

fluorescent /flɔːˈresənt, Amer ˌflʊəˈr-/ *adj* 1 (vivid) 发亮的 ‹*clothes, paint, badge*› 2 (emitting light) 发荧光的; **a ~ light/strip/tube** 荧光灯/带/管

fluoridate /ˈflɔːrɪdeɪt, Amer ˈflʊər-/ *vt* 在…中加入微量氟化物 ‹*water, toothpaste*›

fluoridation /ˌflɔːrɪˈdeɪʃn, Amer ˌflʊər-/ *n* [u] 饮用水氟化

fluoride /ˈflɔːraɪd, Amer ˈflʊəraɪd/ *n* [u] 氟化物; **~ toothpaste** 含氟牙膏

fluorinate /ˈflɔːrɪneɪt, Amer ˈflʊər-/ *vt* = **fluoridate**

fluorine /ˈflɔːriːn, Amer ˈflʊər-/ *n* [u] 氟

flurry /ˈflʌri/
A *n* 1 (bustle) 忙乱; **a ~ of activity** 一阵忙乱; **a ~ of excitement** 一阵哄动 2 (gust) 阵; **a ~ of rain/snow/wind** 一阵雨/雪/风 3 (of complaints, enquiries) 一连串事件
B *vt* 使…慌张 ‹*person*›

flush¹ /flʌʃ/
A *n* 1 (rosiness) (on cheeks, skin) 红晕; (in sky) 红光; **there was a ~ in her cheeks** 她双颊红扑扑的; **a rosy ~ in the eastern sky** 东方天空中一抹玫瑰色的红霞 2 (from fever, alcohol) [脸上的] 潮红 3 Med 潮热; **she has been suffering from hot ~es** 她一直有潮热发作 4 (surge of excitement, joy, enthusiasm) 一阵强烈感情; **in the first ~ of success/victory** 在成功/胜利之初的狂喜之中 5 (flow of water) 冲洗; **to give sth. a ~** 把某物冲洗一下 6 (toilet device) 冲水设备; **don't forget to pull the ~** 别忘了冲马桶; **a ~ toilet** 抽水马桶 7 (abundance) 生机勃勃; **a/the ~ of sth.** 某物的蓬勃生长; **in the first ~ of beauty/health/youth** 美丽/健康/青春正盛时; **in the full ~ of sth.** 在某物的鼎盛时期
B *vi* 1 (redden) «*face, cheeks*» «*person*» 脸红; **she ~ed angrily** 她气得涨红了脸; **to ~ crimson/bright-red** 脸变得通红; **to ~ with sth.** 因…脸红 ‹*embarrassment, delight*› 2 (operate) «*toilet*» 被冲洗; **the toilet doesn't ~** 马桶不能冲水了
C *vt* 1 (make red) 使发红; **fever ~ed her cheeks** 她烧得满脸通红 2 (clean with water) 冲洗 ‹*drain, toilet*›; **to ~ (out) a pipe/drain with water** 用水冲洗管道/下水道 3 (operate toilet) «*person*» 冲 ‹*toilet, lavatory*› 4 (dispose of) 冲水清除; **to ~ sth. down the toilet** 把某物冲下马桶

Phrasal verb
- **flush away** *vt* [**~ sth. away, ~ away sth.**] 冲洗掉 ‹*waste, unwanted items*›

flush² *adj* 1 (level) 完全齐平的 ‹*doors, fittings*›; **to be ~ with** 与…完全齐平 ‹*wall, surface*›; **to be ~ against sth.** 与某物紧挨; **the door is ~ against the wall** 门紧挨着墙 2 colloq (rich) 充裕的; **to be ~ with money** 很有钱

flush³ *vt* «*hunters*» 把…从隐蔽处赶出 ‹*birds, deer*›; **to ~ sth. from cover** 把某物从藏身处赶出; **the police finally ~ed the villains from their lair** 警察终于把那些流氓从他们的藏身处赶了出来

Phrasal verb
- **flush out** *vt* [**~ sb. out, ~ out sb.**] «*police*» 把…赶出来 ‹*criminals, spies, snipers*›; **to ~ sb./sth. out of shelter/hiding** 把某人/某物从躲避处/隐藏处赶出

flush⁴ *n* Games 同花 [同花色的一手牌]; **a royal ~** 同花大顺; **a straight ~** 同花顺

flushed /flʌʃt/ *adj* 1 (reddened) 发红的; **her face was ~ with shame** 她羞红了脸; **their cheeks were ~ with wine** 他们喝酒喝得满脸通红 2 (exhilarated) 容光焕发的; **~ with pride/excitement/success** 因自豪/兴奋/成功而容光焕发的

fluster /ˈflʌstə(r)/
A *vt* «*noise, person, questions*» 使慌乱; **to get** *or* **become** *or* **grow ~ed** 变得慌张
B *n* 慌乱; **(to be) in a ~** 心慌意乱

flute /fluːt/ ▸**p. 395** *n* **1** Mus (instrument) 长笛; **to play the ~** 吹长笛 **2** Mus (musician) 长笛演奏者 **3** Archit (groove) [柱子上装饰性的] 凹槽

fluted /ˈfluːtɪd/ *adj* 饰有凹槽的 ‹*column, bowl*›; 带褶子的 ‹*collar*›

flute: ~-maker *n* 长笛制作者; **~-player** *n* 长笛演奏者

flutist /ˈfluːtɪst/ ▸**p. 395, p. 409** *n* Amer **= flautist**

flutter /ˈflʌtə(r)/
A *vi* **1** (move quickly and lightly) «*wings*» 拍动; «*eyelashes*» 颤动; «*fan*» 晃动; «*leaf, paper, cloth*» 飘动; **flags ~ed in the breeze** 旗帜在微风中飘扬; **to ~ down** 飘落 **2** (fly) «*bird, butterfly, moth*» 振翅而飞; **to ~ about** *or* **around** 拍着翅膀飞来飞去; **to ~ away** 拍着翅膀飞走 **3** (beat irregularly) «*heart*» 怦怦乱跳; «*pulse*» 不规则地跳动; **to ~ with sth.** 因某事而怦怦乱跳; **her heart ~ed with excitement when he entered the room** 当他进屋时, 她激动得心怦怦乱跳
B *vt* **1** (flap) «*bird, butterfly, moth*» 拍打 ‹*wings*› **2** (move rapidly) 摇动 ‹*fan*›; 挥动 ‹*handkerchief*›; **to ~ one's eyelashes** 颤动着睫毛; **to ~ sth. at sb./sth.** 向某人/某物挥舞某物; **to ~ the dovecotes** colloq 引起惊慌
C *n* **1** [c] (rapid movement) (of wings) 拍动; (of bird, butterfly) 拍翅; (of flag, handkerchief, leaf) 飘动; (of eyelashes) 眨动; **with a ~ of his handkerchief, he waved goodbye** 他挥舞手帕告别; **with one ~ of her eyelashes, she captured his heart** 她睫毛一眨就掳获了他的心 **2** [u and c] (irregular beat) (of heart) 怦怦乱跳; (of pulse) 不规则跳动; **the ~ of his heart suggested that she was the girl for him** fig 他怦怦的心跳表明她就是他心仪的女孩; **heart ~** Med 心悸 **3** [c] (nervous state) 不安; (confusion) 困惑; (excitement) 激动; **to cause a ~** 引起慌乱; **a ~ of sth.** 一阵某种情绪; **he felt a ~ of excitement/panic as he stepped on to the platform** 走上讲台时, 他感到一阵激动/恐慌; **to be all of** *or* **in a ~** Brit 忐忑不安 **4** [c] (stir) 骚动; **to cause (quite) a ~** 引起 (很大的) 骚动; **to cause a ~ of activity** 引起一阵忙乱 **5** [c] Brit colloq (on horse, greyhound) 小赌; (on Stock Exchange) 小投资; **to have a ~ on sth.** 在某物上少量下注 **6** [u] (on recording) 放音失真 **7** [u and c] Aviat [尤指机翼的] 颤振

fluttering /ˈflʌtərɪŋ/
A *n* [u and c] **1** (rapid moving) (of wings) 拍动; (of bird, butterfly) 拍翅; (of flag, handkerchief, leaf) 飘动; (of eyelashes) 眨动; **there was a ~ in the chimney, and a bird flew out** 烟囱里有拍打翅膀的声音, 然后一只鸟飞了出来 **2** (irregular beating) (of heart) 怦怦乱跳; (of pulse) 不规则的跳动; Med 心悸
B *adj* **1** (moving rapidly) 拍动的 ‹*wings*›; 飞舞的 ‹*bird, butterfly*›; 飘动的 ‹*flag, handkerchief, leaf*›; 眨动的 ‹*eyelashes*› **2** (beating irregularly) 怦怦乱跳的 ‹*heart*›; 不规则的 ‹*heartbeat, pulse*›; Med 扑动的 ‹*heart*›

fluvial /ˈfluːvɪəl/ *adj* 河流的 ‹*deposits, sediment*›; **~ channel/system** 河道/河系

flux /flʌks/ *n* **1** [u] (uncertainty) 不断的变动; **in (a state of) ~** 处于不断的变动中 **2** [c] Phys 通量 **3** [u] Tech (for metals) 焊剂

fly¹ /flaɪ/
A *vi* (*pt* **flew**, *pp* **flown**) **1** (move through air) «*aircraft, insect, bird*»; fig liter «*hope, worries, cares*» 消失; **I can't sleep with a mosquito ~ing around** 有蚊子飞来飞去, 我睡不着; **to ~ into sth.** 飞进某物; **hopes of an early settlement have flown out of the window** 早日解决争端的希望破灭了; **rumours of her resignation were ~ing (around)** 她辞职的谣言正四处流传; **to ~ in the face of sth.** 违背某物; **to ~ in the face of all the evidence** 与所有证据相悖; **to ~ in the face of danger** 全然不顾危险; **to ~ in the face of authority** 违抗权威; **to ~ high** (ambitious) 雄心勃勃; (elated) 情绪高昂 **2** Aviat, Aerosp (as passenger) [乘坐飞机或航天器] 航行; (as pilot of aeroplane) 驾驶飞机; (as pilot of spaceship) 驾驶航天器; **have you ever flown in a helicopter?** 你乘坐过直升机吗?; **to ~ to the moon** 飞上月球 **3** (be propelled) «*person, animal*» 飞奔; «*projectile*» 飞行; «*spark*» 飞溅; **glass flew in all directions** 玻璃四处乱飞; **to go ~ing** 跌落; **the contents of the cupboard went ~ing** 碗柜里的东西掉落下来; **to send sb./sth. ~ing** 把某人打倒在地/四处乱抛某物; **the blow sent him ~ing** 这重重的一击将他打飞在地; **to ~ at sb.** (physically) 扑向某人; (verbally) 针对某人; **she flew at me, kicking and punching** 她扑向我, 对我拳打脚踢; **there's no need to ~ at me every time I ask you to do something** 你没必要每次我要你做事时都对我恶言相向; **to let ~ (at sb.) (with sth.)** (用某物) 击打 (某人); fig (用某物) 攻击 (某人); **she let ~ at him with a stream of abuse** 她连声辱骂他; **they let ~ (with) a hail of bullets** 他们射出一阵弹雨; **to make the sparks** *or* **fur** *or* **feathers ~** 引发激烈的争执; **to ~ into a rage/panic** 勃然大怒/突然惊慌失措 **4** (rush, hurry) «*person, animal*» 飞奔; «*vehicle*» 飞驰; **I must ~!** 我得快走了!; **the train flew by** *or* **past** 列车飞驰而过; **she came ~ing through the door** 她冲进门内; **to ~ open** «*door, box*» 猛地打开 **5** (pass quickly) «*period of time*» 飞逝; **time flies** 时光飞逝; **to ~ past** *or* **by** 过得飞快 **6** (flutter, wave) «*flag, scarf*» 飘扬; «*cloak, hair, kite*» 飘舞 **7** archaic (flee) 逃跑; **you must ~ for your life** 你必须逃命; **to ~ from sth.** 逃离某物
B *vt* (*pt* **flew**, *pp* **flown**) **1** (operate) 驾驶 ‹*aircraft, rocket*› **2** (transport by air) «*airline, carrier*» 空运 ‹*people, supplies*› **3** (cross by air) 飞越 ‹*the Atlantic, the Channel*›; **we ~ this route daily** 我们每天飞这条航线 **4** (use for flight) 乘坐…的飞机 ‹*company, airline*›; 乘坐 ‹*aircraft, model*› **5** (travel by air) «*person, aircraft, bird, insect*» 飞行 ‹*distance*›; **we flew thousands of miles** 我们飞了好几千英里 **6** (cause to fly) 使飞行; **to ~ a kite** 放风筝; **a group of small boys ~ing their model aeroplanes** 一群放飞飞机模型的小男孩 **7** (display) «*ship, building, organization*» 悬挂 ‹*flag, ensign*› **8** (raise) 升 ‹*flag*›
C *n* **1** (in men's clothes) (zip) 裤子拉链; (row of buttons) 裤子钮扣; (opening) 前裆开口 **2** (flap on tent) 帐篷的门帘
D **flies** *npl* **1** Brit **= C1** **2** Theat **the flies** 吊景区

Phrasal verbs

- **fly away** *vi* «*bird, insect, bat*» 飞走; **all your cares will ~ away** fig 你所有的烦恼都会烟消云散
- **fly in**
  A *vi* **1** (enter or arrive using wings) «*aircraft, bird, insect*» 飞来 **2** (arrive) «*aircraft, pilot*» 抵达; «*passenger*» 乘飞机到达
  B *vt* [~ **sb./sth. in**, ~ **in sb./sth.**] 用飞机运来 ‹*person, supplies*›
- **fly off** *vi* **1** (leave using wings) «*aircraft, bird, insect*» 飞走 **2** Aviat «*passenger*» 乘飞机离开; **we're ~ing off tomorrow** 明天我们将乘飞机离开 **3** (come off) «*hat, roof, top*» 脱落
- **fly out**
  A *vi* **1** Aviat 乘飞机去 **2** (extend) «*flag*» 飘扬; «*cloak, hair, kite*» 飘舞
  B *vt* [~ **sb./sth. out**, ~ **out sb./sth.**] 用飞机运走 ‹*person, supplies*›

fly² *n* **1** Zool 苍蝇; **fruit/tsetse ~** 果蝇/舌蝇; **to swat a ~** 打苍蝇; **to die** *or* **fall** *or* **drop like flies** 大批死掉; **he wouldn't hurt** *or* **harm a ~** fig 他连一只苍蝇都不愿伤害; **a ~ on the wall** fig 不被察觉的旁观者; **a ~ in the ointment** fig 美中不足之处; **(there are) no flies on him/her/you** fig colloq 他/她/你不会轻易上当; **to drink with the flies** Austral fig colloq 独自喝酒 **2** Fishg 假蝇

fly³ *adj* colloq **1** Brit (worldly-wise) 精明的 ‹*person*› **2** Amer (chic) 时尚的 ‹*person, place, clothing, art*›

fly: ~away *adj attrib* 细软的 ‹*hair*›; **~blown** *adj* 生蛆的 ‹*meat, carcass, wound*›; **~ button** *n* 门襟扣; **~by** *n* **1** (of planet, moon) 近天体探测飞行; **2** Amer **= ~past**

fly-by-night colloq
A *n* 无信用的人
B *adj* 无信用的 ‹*person, company*›

fly-by-wire *n* 线传操纵; **~ technology/aircraft** 线传操纵技术/飞机

fly-drive
A *n* 空陆联游
B *adj* 空陆联游的 ‹*break, holiday*›

flyer /ˈflaɪə(r)/ *n* **1** (pilot) 飞行员 **2** (air passenger) 飞机乘客 **3** (leaflet) 广告传单 **4** (bird) 飞鸟; (insect) 飞虫 **5** esp Amer colloq (fast-moving person) 能飞跑的人; (fast-moving thing) 快速移动的物体

fly: ~-fishing ▸**p. 307** *n* [u] 用假蝇钓鱼; **~ front** *n* 暗门襟

flying /ˈflaɪɪŋ/
A *n* [u] 飞行; **fear of ~** 对坐飞机的恐惧; **she decided to take up ~** 她决定从事飞行; **an hour's ~ time** 1 小时的飞行时间
B *adj attrib* **1** (able to fly) 会飞的; **an unidentified ~ object** 不明飞行物; **a ~ machine** 飞行器 **2** (moving through the air) 飞过来的 ‹*plate, book*›; **the ~ feet of the dancers** 舞者飞快舞动的脚; **to take a ~ leap** *or* **jump** 飞身一跃 **3** (passing quickly) 飞逝的 ‹*hours*› **4** (fluttering) 飞舞的 ‹*kite, hair, scarf, cloak*›

flying: ~ boat *n* 水上飞机; **~ bomb** *n* 飞弹; **~ buttress** *n* 拱扶垛; **~ colours** *npl* **with ~ colours** 出色地; **she passed her exam with ~ colours** 她以优异的成绩通过了考试; **~ doctor** *n* 乘飞机出诊的医生; **~ fish** *n* 飞鱼; **~ fox** *n* 狐蝠; **~ officer** *n* Brit 空军中尉; **~ picket** *n* Brit [罢工中的] 流动宣传员; **~ saucer** *n* 飞碟; **~ squad** *n* Brit 快速特警队; **~ start** *n* **1** Sport 快速起跑; **2** fig (good beginning) 好的开端; **to get off to a ~ start** 开端很好; **~ tackle** *n* **1** Sport 凌空抢球; **2** fig (bringing to ground) 扑倒; **she brought the thief to the ground with a ~ tackle** 她一个鱼跃, 把那个贼扑倒在地; **~ visit** *n* 闪电式访问

fly: ~leaf *n* [书籍前后的] 空白页; **~-on-the-wall** *adj* 写实的 ‹*technique, documentary*›; **~over** *n* **1** Brit Transp 立交桥; **2** Amer **= ~past**; **~paper** *n* [u and c] 粘蝇纸; **~past** *n* Brit 低空编队飞行; **~posting** *n* [u] 乱贴小广告; **~sheet** *n* **1** (tent cover) 防雨篷顶; **2** (handbill) 小传单; **~ spray** *n* 灭蝇喷射剂; **~ swatter, ~ swat** *ns* 蝇拍; **~tipping** *n* [u] Brit 非法倾倒垃圾; **~weight** *n* 次最轻量级拳击手; **~weight champion/tournament** 次最轻量级拳击冠军/锦标赛; **~wheel** *n* 飞轮; **~ whisk** *n* 驱蝇掸子

FM *abbr* **= frequency modulation**

FO *abbr* Brit **= Foreign Office**

foal /fəʊl/
A *n* 驹子; **to be in ~** 怀驹
B *vi* 产驹

foam /fəʊm/
A *n* **1** (on sea, drink, bath) 泡沫 **2** (sweat) 汗沫 **3** (saliva) 唾沫 **4** (chemical) 泡沫剂; **shaving ~** 泡沫剃须膏 **5** (rubber or plastic material) 泡沫材料; **cushions made of ~** 海绵垫子
B *vi* **1** (froth) «*beer, sea*» 起泡沫 **2** (from mouth) «*person, mouth*» 吐白沫; (as sweat) «*animal*» 冒汗; **to ~ at the mouth** lit 口吐白沫; fig 大怒

Phrasal verb

• **foam up** *vi* «*beer, fizzy drink*» 起泡沫

foam: ~ bath *n* 泡沫浴液; **~ insulation** *n* [u] 泡沫绝缘材料; **~ mattress** *n* 泡沫床垫; **~ rubber** *n* [u] 泡沫橡胶

foamy /ˈfəʊmi/ *adj* 起泡沫的 ‹*sea, beer*›

fob /fɒb/ *n* 1 (pocket) **~ pocket** 表袋 2 (chain) **~ chain** 怀表短链; **a watch ~** 表链; **a ~ watch** 带表链的怀表 3 (on key ring) 钥匙挂件

Phrasal verb

• **fob off** *vt* (*pres p etc.* **-bb-**) 1 [**~ off sb., ~ sb. off**] «*salesperson*» 哄骗 ‹*buyer, client*›; «*official*» 搪塞 ‹*enquirer*›; **I ~bed him off with an excuse** 我找了个借口搪塞他 2 **to ~ sth. off on (to) sb.** (give sth. inferior or different) «*salesperson*» 把某物骗售给某人

f.o.b. *abbr* = **free on board**

FOC *abbr* = **free of charge**

focal /ˈfəʊkl/ *adj* 1 (relating to focus) 焦点的 ‹*depth, field*› 2 (very important) 极其重要的

focal: ~ length, ~ distance *ns* 焦距; **~ plane** *n* 焦平面; **~ point** *n* 1 Phys, Optics 焦点; 2 (centre of interest) 活动的中心; **to be the ~ point of sth.** 是某物的中心; **a ~ point for sth.** 某物的活动中心; 3 (main concern) 关注的重点

fo'c'sle /ˈfəʊksl/ *n* = **forecastle**

focus /ˈfəʊkəs/

A *n* (*pl* **~es** *or* **foci** /ˈfəʊsaɪ/) 1 (focal point) 成像清晰点; **to be out of ~** 模糊不清; **to be in ~** 焦点对准; **to go out of ~** 焦点未对准; **to bring sth. into ~** 把焦点对准某物; **to come into ~** 变清晰 2 (device on lens) 调焦装置 3 fig (centre of interest) 关注的中心; **to be the ~ of sth.** 是某事的焦点; **to be the ~ of attention** 是注意的焦点 4 fig (emphasis) 重点; **the ~ will be on health** 重点将放在健康上

B *vt* (*pres p etc.* **-s-** *or* **-ss-**) 1 Phys 使…聚焦 ‹*beam, ray*›; **to ~ sth. on to sth.** 把某物聚焦到某物上; **to ~ sth. through sth.** 通过某物使某物聚焦 2 (adjust) 调节…的焦距 ‹*eye*›; **to ~ a lens on sth.** 将镜头对准 3 (concentrate, direct) 使集中; **to ~ one's mind/attention on sth.** 把精神/注意力集中于某事物; **to ~ one's eyes on sth./sb.** 把目光集中到某物/某人上

C *vi* (*pres p etc.* **-s-** *or* **-ss-**) 1 Phys «*rays, beams*» 聚焦; **to ~ on sth.** 聚焦在某物上 2 (adjust) «*photographer, camera, eye*» 调节焦距; **to ~ on sb./sth.** 把焦点调到某人/某物上; **without her glasses she cannot ~ properly** 她不戴眼镜就看不清楚 3 (concentrate) 集中; **to ~ on sth.** 集中于某物; **she was too tired to ~ on anything** 她太累了，干什么都不能集中精神; **all eyes ~ed on the Prime Minister** 所有的人都注视着首相 4 fig (emphasize) «*person, meeting, issue*» 侧重; **to ~ on sth./doing sth.** 侧重某事/做某事

focus group *n* 焦点小组 [向其征求对产品等反馈意见的有代表性的一群人]

fodder /ˈfɒdə(r)/ *n* [u] 1 (for livestock) 饲料 2 fig (raw material) 素材; **to ~ for the imagination** 供想象的素材; **the young soldiers were mere cannon ~** 这些年轻的士兵只不过是炮灰而已

FoE *n* = **Friends of the Earth**

foe /fəʊ/ *n* liter 敌人

foetal /ˈfiːtl/ *adj* Brit = **fetal**

foetid /ˈfetɪd/ *adj* = **fetid**

foetus /ˈfiːtəs/ *n* Brit = **fetus**

fog /fɒɡ/

A *n* 1 [u] Meteorol 雾; **a patch/blanket of ~** 一片/一层雾; **dense** *or* **thick ~** 浓雾 2 [c] fig (confusion) 困惑; **to be in a ~ about sth.** 对某物感到困惑; **a ~ of ignorance** 无知造成的困惑

B *vt* (*pres p etc.* **-gg-**) 1 (cover, obscure) **to ~ up** «*steam, condensation*» 使…蒙上雾 ‹*glasses, window*› 2 fig (confuse) «*person, instructions*» 使…困惑 ‹*person*›; **to ~ the issue** 使问题变得模糊不清

C *vi* (*pres p etc.* **-gg-**) **to ~ (up** *or* **over)** «*window, glasses*» 蒙上水汽; **your spectacles have ~ged (over)** 你的眼镜蒙上了一层雾

fog: ~ bank *n* 雾堤; **~bound** *adj* 1 (delayed) 因雾受阻的 ‹*passengers, plane*›; 2 (restricted) 因雾无法运行的 ‹*airport, harbour, town*›

fogey, fogy /ˈfəʊɡi/ *n* (*pl* **~s** *or* **fogies**) colloq 守旧者; **you old ~!** 你这个老顽固!

foggy /ˈfɒɡi/ *adj* 1 Meteorol 有雾的 ‹*weather, morning*›; **to be ~** 有雾; **to become** *or* **get ~** 起雾 2 fig (confused) 模糊的 ‹*idea, reasoning*›; **I haven't the foggiest (idea)** colloq 我完全蒙在鼓里

fog: ~horn *n* [向雾中的船只发警告用的] 雾角; **to have a voice like a ~horn** 嗓音像雾角一样刺耳; **~lamp, ~light** *ns* 雾灯; **~ patch** *n* 雾区

foible /ˈfɔɪbl/ *n* 怪癖; **everyone has their little ~s** 人人都有一些怪毛病

foil¹ /fɔɪl/ *n* 1 [u] (for wrapping) 箔; **a sheet of ~** 一张箔纸; **silver/gold ~** 银箔/金箔; **~-wrapped** 用箔纸包装的; **~ container** 箔制容器 2 [c] (contrast) 陪衬; **to be** *or* **act as a ~ to** *or* **for sb./sth.** 是某人/某物的陪衬

foil² *n* (in fencing) 花剑

foil³ *vt* 挫败 ‹*rival, plan, attempt*›; **to be ~ed in one's attempt to do sth.** 做某事的企图受挫

foist /fɔɪst/ *vt* 1 (impose) 把…强加于; **to ~ sth. on** *or* **on to sb.** 强迫某人接受 ‹*ideas, company*›; **she's always ~ing herself on me when I'd rather be alone** 当我想要独处的时候，她总是缠着我; **we didn't expect the whole family to ~ themselves on us** 我们没有料到那家人全都不请自来了 2 (force) 把…硬塞给; **to ~ sth. (off) on to** *or* **upon sb.** 把…硬塞给某人 ‹*task, goods*›

fold¹ /fəʊld/

A *n* 1 (of fabric, clothing, paper) 褶; (of skin) 褶皱; **the long skirt hung in soft, loose ~s** 长裙褶褶柔软而宽松; **she ironed the fabric to get the ~s out** 她把布料上的褶子熨平; **~s of flesh** 一层层的赘肉 2 esp Brit (hill) 山丘; (hollow) 山洼 3 Geol 褶皱

B *vt* 1 (crease, double) 折叠 ‹*paper, umbrella, bedding*›; **she ~ed the letter and put it in an envelope** 她将信折好，放进信封里; **a pile of ~ed sheets** 一摞折叠好的被单 2 (for storage, carrying) 用…包 ‹*paper, cloth, foil*›; 包 ‹*seeds, fragile object*›; **to ~ sth. round** *or* **around** *or* **over sth.** 用某物包住某物; **to ~ sth. in sth.** 把某物包在某物里; **the valley was ~ed in mist** fig 山谷笼罩在薄雾之中 3 (embrace) 抱; **to ~ sth./sb. in one's arms** 抱住某物/某人; **to ~ sb. to one's heart** 把某人抱到怀里 4 (intertwine) 交叉 ‹*arms, hands*›; «*bird, insect*» 收拢 ‹*wings*›; **he ~ed his arms across his chest** 他双臂交叉于胸前 5 (bend) 盘起 ‹*leg, tail*› 6 Culin 拌入; **to ~ sth. into sth.** 将某物拌入某物; **to ~ the flour into the mixture** 把面粉拌入混合料

C *vi* 1 (be collapsible) «*chair, bed, bicycle*» 可折叠 2 (bend) «*fingers*» 弯曲; **her hand ~ed over the letter before I could remove it** 我还没来得及把信拿走，她就抓在手里了 3 colloq (fail) «*business, company*» 倒闭; «*magazine, newspaper*» 停办; «*project*» 失败; «*play*» 停演

Phrasal verbs

• **fold away**

A *vt* [**~ away sth., ~ sth. away**] 将…折叠收起 ‹*clothes, bedding, umbrella*›

B *vi* «*bed, bicycle*» 可以折叠

• **fold back**

A *vt* [**~ back sth., ~ sth. back**] 收起 ‹*door, shutters*›; 折起 ‹*bedclothes*›; 卷起 ‹*sleeve, collar*›

B *vi* «*door, shutters*» 可收起

• **fold down**

A *vt* [**~ down sth., ~ sth. down**] 把…折下 ‹*corner of page, car seat, hood of pram, sofa bed, collar, flap*›

B *vi* «*car seat, hood of pram, sofa bed*» 可向下折

• **fold in** *vt* [**~ in sth., ~ sth. in**] 拌入 ‹*eggs, flour, cream*›

• **fold over** *vt* [**~ over sth., ~ sth. over**] 翻起

• **fold up**

A *vt* [**~ up sth., ~ sth. up**] 把…折叠起来 ‹*map, bed, bicycle, umbrella*›

B *vi* 1 (be collapsible) «*map, bed, bicycle, umbrella*» 可折叠; **the map ~s up very small** 这张地图可以折得很小 2 colloq (bend double) 弓起身子; **he ~ed up in agony** 他痛苦地蜷起身子

fold² *n* 1 Agric 羊栏 2 fig (group, church, family, party) 志同道合的人们; **to return** *or* **come back to the ~** 重返原组织; **the priest welcomed him back to the ~** 牧师欢迎他重返教会

-fold /fəʊld/ ▸p. 288 *n combining form* 1 (multiplied by) …倍的 ‹*increase, repay*›; **investors may expect a ten~ return on their investment** 投资者可望获得十倍的投资回报 2 (specifying number of parts) 有…部分的; **the problem is four~** 问题有四个部分

foldaway /ˈfəʊldəweɪ/ *adj attrib* 可折叠的; **a ~ bed** 折叠床

folder /ˈfəʊldə(r)/ *n* also Comput 文件夹

folding /ˈfəʊldɪŋ/ *adj* 可折叠的; **a ~ bicycle** 折叠式自行车; **a ~ chair** 折椅

folding: ~ door *n* 折叠门; **~ money** *n* colloq 纸币

fold-out

A *n* 1 (in book or magazine) 折页 2 (furniture) 折叠式家具

B *adj* 折叠式的; **a ~ map** 折叠地图

foliage /ˈfəʊlɪɪdʒ/ *n* [u] 叶子; **ornamental ~** 叶形饰; **a ~ plant** 观叶植物

folic acid /ˌfəʊlɪk ˈæsɪd/ *n* [u] 叶酸

folio /ˈfəʊlɪəʊ/ *n* 1 (sheet of paper) 对折纸 2 (book size) 对开本; **to publish a book in ~** 用对开本出版书; *modif* **a ~ volume** 对开本

folk /fəʊk/

A *npl* 1 colloq (people) 人们; **country/city ~** 乡下人/城里人; **old/young/poor ~** 老人/年轻人/穷人 2 **folks** *pl* colloq (relatives) 亲属; **the old ~s at home** 家中的老爸老妈 3 Mus 民间音乐

B *modif* **~ concert** 民间音乐会; **~ art** 民间艺术; **~ custom** 民俗

folk: ~ dance *n* 民间舞; **~ etymology** *n* 通俗词源; **~ hero** *n* 民间英雄

folkie /ˈfəʊki/ *n* colloq (singer) 民歌演唱者; (fan) 民歌迷; **~ ballads** 民谣

folk: ~lore *n* [u] 民俗学; **~ medicine** *n* [u] 民间医术; **~ memory** *n* 民间记忆; **~ music** *n* [u] 民间音乐; **~ rock** *n* [u] 民谣摇滚乐; **~ song** *n* 民歌

folksy /ˈfəʊksi/ *adj* colloq 1 (rustic) 有民间风味的 ‹*clothes, pottery, dialogue*› 2 (unpretentious) 质朴友好的 ‹*people*›

folk: ~ tale *n* 民间故事; **~ wisdom** *n* [u] 民间智慧

follicle /ˈfɒlɪkl/ *n* 1 (of hair) 毛囊 2 (in ovary) 囊状卵泡

follow /ˈfɒləʊ/

A *vt* 1 (move after) 跟随 ‹*person, vehicle*›; **the dog ~ed me all the way home** 那只狗一路跟着我回家; **his bodyguards ~ him wherever he goes** 他到哪儿，保镖就跟到哪儿; **~ me** 跟我来; **to ~ sb. in/out** 跟着某人进去/出来; **they'll ~ us on a later flight** 他们会乘较晚的航班跟上我们 2 (for surveillance) 跟踪 ‹*person, vehicle*›; **I think I'm being ~ed** 我想有人在跟踪我; **~ that car!**

f

跟着那辆车!; **to have sb. ~ed** 派人跟踪某人 **3** (do the same as) 追随 ‹*person*›; **he ~ed his mother to Oxford University** 他走母亲走过的路，也进了牛津大学 **4** (replace) 继承 ‹*person*›; (succeed) 接续 ‹*action, success*›; **she ~ed her 100 metres win with a gold medal in the 200 metres** 在 100 米赛跑中获胜后，她再接再厉又获得 200 米赛跑的金牌; **to be a hard** *or* **tough act to ~** 令人望尘莫及; **~ that!** 赶不上吧！ **5** (come after in time or in order) 接在…之后 ‹*event, period of time, person, item*›; **one misfortune ~ed another** 不幸接踵而来; **to ~ sth. with sth.** 做完某事后接着做某事; **we ~ed the training session with a swim in the pool** 上完培训课后，我们接着在游泳池里游泳; **the text is ~ed by a comprehensive index** 正文后面附有一份综合索引 **6** (go along/alongside) «*person, vehicle, path*» 沿着…行进 ‹*road, river*›; fig «*person, behaviour, event*» 按照…进行 ‹*pattern, line*›; **the border ~s the river** 以河为边界; **the government chose to ~ a more radical course of action** 政府选择采取更为激进的举措; **to let the disease ~ its course** 让这个病自然发展 **7** (be guided by) 遵照 ‹*clue, instruction, tradition*›; 听从 ‹*advice*›; **to ~ the signs to the town centre** 按照路标指示来到市中心; **~ing fashion can be rather expensive** 追求时尚是要花很多钱的; **to ~ one's instincts/heart** 按照本能/意愿行事 **8** (imitate) 仿效 ‹*person, organization*›; **to ~ sb.'s example** 学某人的样; **to ~ sb. in sth./doing sth.** 在某方面效仿某人/效仿某人做某事; **to ~ suit** lit (in card games) 跟牌; fig 跟着做 **9** (conform to) «*film, play*» 忠实于 ‹*text*›; **the translation ~s the original very closely** 这个译本非常忠实于原文 **10** (support, adhere to) 拥护 ‹*person*›; 信奉 ‹*religion, ideas, teachings*› **11** (have a continuing interest in) 密切关注 ‹*sport, career, stock exchange, court case, soap opera*›; **to ~ the fortunes of sb./sth.** 关注某人/某事物的命运 **12** (watch closely) 聚精会神地看 ‹*play, film*›; (listen to) 倾听 ‹*speech*› **13** (read to oneself) 默念 ‹*text, score, service*› **14** (understand) 理解 ‹*argument, plot*›; **I couldn't ~ the professor's explanation** 我听不懂教授的讲解; **do you ~ me?** 你听懂我说的话了吗？; **if you ~ my meaning** 如果你明白我的意思 **15** (practise) 从事 ‹*profession, hobby*›; **to ~ the teaching/medical profession** 从事教育工作/医务工作; **to ~ an isolated life** 过与世隔绝的生活

B *vi* **1** (move after) «*person, animal*» 跟随; «*cheque*» 随后到; **to ~ behind sb./sth.** 跟在某人/某物后面; **a group of children ~ed behind the procession** 一群孩子跟在队伍后面; **to ~ in sb.'s footsteps** 仿效某人; **invoice to ~ under separate cover** 发票随后另函寄到 **2** (come after in time or in order) «*event, period of time, course of meal*» 紧接; **what ~ed can only be described as a nightmare** 接下来发生的事只能用恶梦来形容; **the ... that ~ed** 接下来的…; **there's ice cream to ~** 接着有冰激凌; **as ~s** 如下 **3** (ensue) «*fight, death, success, advantage*» 随后发生; **to ~ from sth.** 因某事而产生 **4** (be logical consequence) 是必然结果; **it ~s that ...** 由此得出…; **she didn't come to work today, but it doesn't (necessarily) ~ that she's ill** 她今天没有来上班，但这并不（一定）说明她病了; **that ~s** 那是当然; **to ~ from sth.** 从某事得出结论 **5** (understand) 理解

Phrasal verbs

- **follow about, follow around** *vt* [**~ sb./sth. about**] 到处跟随; **he's been ~ing me about all day** 他整天跟在我后面
- **follow on** *vi* **1** (come later) 随后到 **2** (continue) «*lecture, programme, person*» 继续下去; **to ~ on from sth.** 从某事物继续下去 **3** (in cricket) «*team*» 继续击球
- **follow out** *vt* [**~ sth. out, ~ out sth.**] Amer 执行 ‹*order, instruction, rule*›; **when I give advice I expect you to ~ it out** 我提建议是希望你能听从
- **follow through**

A *vi* «*golfer, tennis player, footballer*» 做随球动作
B *vt* [**~ sth. through, ~ through sth.**] 坚持完成 ‹*project, plan, experiment*›; 施行 ‹*threat*›; 坚持 ‹*idea, argument*›

- **follow up**

A *vt* [**~ sth. up, ~ up sth.**] **1** (reinforce, confirm) 加强 ‹*effort, treatment*›; 对…采取进一步行动 ‹*visit, programme*›; 巩固 ‹*success, achievement, advantage, lesson*›; **to ~ sth. up with sth.** 以某事物进一步巩固 **2** (act on, pursue) 跟进 ‹*advertisement, article, idea*›; 追查 ‹*clue, lead, rumour*›; **I ~ed up her tip about investments** 我听从了她的投资建议
B *vi* 继续; **to ~ up with sth.** 进一步做某事

follower /ˈfɒləʊwə(r)/ *n* **1** (of religion, philosophy) 信徒; (of person) 追随者; **she's a dedicated ~ of fashion** 她热衷于赶时髦 **2** (of sport, team, person) 支持者; (of soap opera, strip cartoon) 爱好者; (of events) 关心者 **3** (of tradition, rule) 遵循者 **4** dated (admirer) 追求者

following /ˈfɒləʊwɪŋ/
A *adj* **1** (next in time) 接下来的; **the ~ day** 第二天; **the ~ September** 次年 9 月 **2** (next in order) **the ~** 下列的 ‹*name, item*› **3** (from the rear) 顺向的; **a ~ wind** 顺风
B *n* **1** (of leader, philosopher) 追随者; (of religion, philosophy, teaching) 信奉者; (of sport, team, person) 支持者; (of TV series) 喜爱者; **to have a large/small ~** 拥有一大批/少量追随者 **2** + *v sing or pl* (before list or explanation) **the ~** 下列
C *prep* **1** (as a result of) 由于 ‹*event, information, communication*›; **~ last month's terrorist attack, new security measures have been introduced** 由于上个月发生了恐怖袭击，新的安全措施被引入; **~ your letter of 5 October 2005, ...** formal 关于贵方 2005 年 10 月 5 日的来函，… **2** (after) 在…以后

follow: ~-my-leader ▸p. 307 *n* 学样 [一种儿童游戏，参加者模仿领头人的举动]; **to play ~-my-leader** 玩学样游戏; **~-on** *n* **1** (continuation) 后续; **as a ~-on from sth.** 作为某事的继续; **2** (in cricket) 继续击球; **~-through** *n* **1** Sport 随球动作; **2** (of project, plan, idea) 进行到底; **~-up** *n* **1** [c] (continuation, development) 后续; **to be a ~-up to sth.**

ℹ -fold

■ Two constructions are commonly used to express '-fold' in Chinese:

A is x times as big (thick, long, heavy ...) as B
= A 的大小（厚度、长度、重量…）是 B 的 X 倍
or A 比 B 大（厚、长、重…）X – 1 倍

A is x times bigger (thicker, longer, heavier ...) than B
= A 的大小（厚度、长度、重量…）是 B 的 X + 1 倍
or A 比 B 大（厚、长、重…）X 倍

■ In Chinese, 'x times' is expressed by using a cardinal number (either in Arabic numerals or in Chinese cardinal numbers) followed by 倍. There is no exact equivalent in Chinese for 'once', 'twice', or 'thrice':

This street is three times as wide as the other one
= 这条街的宽度是另一条街的 3 倍
or 这条街比另一条街宽两倍

My eldest brother is almost twice as old as me
= 我大哥的年纪几乎是我的两倍
or 我大哥年纪几乎比我大 1 倍

This box is five times heavier than the other one
= 这个箱子的重量是另一个的 6 倍
or 这个箱子比另一个重 5 倍

My new coat is exactly three times more expensive than hers
= 我的新大衣的价格正好是她的 4 倍
or 我的新大衣正好比她的贵 3 倍

■ Note the translations for the verbs 'double', 'treble', 'quadruple', etc.:

double
= 增加到（原来的）两倍
or 增加 1 倍

treble
= 增加到（原来的）3 倍
or 增加两倍

quadruple
= 增加到（原来的）4 倍
or 增加 3 倍

The price of petrol has almost doubled in the last five years
= 石油的价格在最近 5 年里几乎增长了 1 倍

The profits of our factory have trebled since the introduction of the new machines
= 自从引进了新机器，我们厂的利润增加了 2 倍

Student numbers at the university have quadrupled since 2000
= 这所大学的学生人数从 2000 年以来增加了 3 倍

Other phrases

Our living room is three times the size of theirs
= 我们的起居室是他们的 3 倍大

She is twice my size
= 她的块头是我的两倍

My father is three times my age
= 我父亲的年龄是我的 3 倍

I paid five times the usual price for the ticket
= 我付 5 倍于往常的价格买到了这张票

The rate of employment has increased by 40% in the last ten years
= 最近 10 年里就业率增加了 40%

Applications for the course have increased three times as compared with last year
= 申请这门课的人数增加到去年的 4 倍
or 申请这门课的人数比去年增加了 3 倍

The number of Internet users has increased by a factor of 7 since 2000
= 从 2000 年以来，互联网的使用人数增加了 7 倍

f

是某事的继续; **a ~-up study** 进一步的研究; **2** [u] (aftercare) 随访

folly /'fɒli/ *n* **1** [u] (foolishness) 愚蠢; **to be ~ to do sth.** 做某事很愚蠢; **the ~ of sb./sth.** 某人/某事的愚蠢; **an act of ~** 愚蠢之举 **2** [c] (foolish act) 蠢事; (foolish idea) 傻念头; **the follies of youth** 年轻时的荒唐事 **3** [c] Archit 大而无当的建筑

foment /fəʊ'ment/ *vt* 挑起 ‹*trouble, strife, rebellion*›

fond /fɒnd/ *adj* **1** *attrib* (affectionate) 深情的 ‹*gesture, embrace*›; **a ~ wife** 深情的妻子; **~ memories** 充满柔情的记忆; **absence makes the heart grow ~er** Prov 离别情更浓 **2** *attrib* (indulgent) 溺爱的 ‹*parents*› **3** *attrib* (deeply felt) 热切的 ‹*hope, ambition*› **4** *attrib* (foolishly optimistic) 盲目的 ‹*ambition, belief*›; **in the ~ hope that ...** 痴痴地希望… **5** *pred* (having a soft spot for) 喜欢的; **to be ~ of sb.** 喜欢某人 **6** *pred* (keen on) 爱好的; **to be ~ of sth./doing sth.** 爱好某事/做某事 **7** *pred* (irritatingly prone) 好…的; **to be ~ of doing sth.** 好做某事

fondle /'fɒndl/ *vt* 抚弄 ‹*child, hair, fur*›

fondly /'fɒndli/ *adv* **1** (lovingly) 深情地 ‹*gaze, smile, say*› **2** (naively) 天真地 ‹*believe, hope*›

fondness /'fɒndnɪs/ *n* 喜爱; **to have a ~ for sth./doing sth.** 喜爱某事物/做某事

fondue /'fɒndju:, Amer fɑ:n'du:/ *n* 火锅; **a Swiss cheese ~** 瑞士干酪火锅

font /fɒnt/ *n* **1** Relig 洗礼盆 **2** Print 字体

food /fu:d/ *n* **1** [u] (sustenance) (for animals and people) 食物; (for plants) 养料; **~ and drink** 饮食; **to cook** *or* **prepare ~** 做饭; **to grow/process ~** 种粮食/加工食物; **to be off one's ~** 没食欲; **to like one's ~** 有胃口; **the ~ industry** 食品工业 **2** [c] (foodstuffs) 某种食品; **health/junk/baby/pet ~** 保健/垃圾/婴儿/宠物食品 **3** [u] (cuisine) 菜肴; **Chinese ~** 中国菜 **4** [u] fig (mental fuel) 精神滋养; **~ for speculation/argument** 供思索/争论的材料; **~ for thought** 引人深思的事

food: ~ additive *n* 食品添加剂; **~ aid** *n* [u] 食物援助; **F~ and Agriculture Organization** *n* 粮食及农业组织; **F~ and Drug Administration** *n* Amer 食品及药物管理局; **~ chain** *n* 食物链; **~ crop** *n* 粮食作物

foodie, foody /'fu:di/ *n* colloq 美食家

food: ~ parcel *n* 救济食物包; **~ poisoning** *n* [u] 食物中毒; **~ processing** *n* [u] 食品加工; **~ processor** *n* 食品加工器; **~ science** *n* [u] 食品科学; **~ stamp** *n* Amer 食品券; **~stuff** *n* 食品; **~ subsidies** *npl* 食品补贴; **~ supply** *n* [u] 食物供应; **~ value** *n* [食物的] 营养价值

fool /fu:l/

A *n* **1** [c] pej (idiot) 蠢人; **to be an utter** *or* **absolute ~** 是个十足的傻瓜; **don't be such a ~, you'll get soaking wet** 别傻了，你会全身湿透的; **to be a ~ (not) to do sth.** （不）做某事很愚蠢; **he's a ~ to believe stories like that** 他真傻，竟然相信那样的故事; **(not) to be ~ enough to do sth.** （没有）蠢到做某事的程度; **he was not enough to agree, luckily** 还好，他并没傻到去同意的地步; **some ~ of a lawyer** colloq 一个愚蠢的律师; **any ~ can/could do sth.** 傻子都能做某事; **to be no ~** colloq 一点不傻; **(the) more ~ him/her/you!** colloq 他/她/你真傻！; **I gave her £50 — well, (the) more ~ you!** 我给了她 50 英镑——你真傻！; **not/never to suffer ~s gladly** 对蠢人没有/绝对没有耐心; **to act** *or* **play the ~** 扮傻逗乐; **a ~ and his money are soon parted** Prov 蠢人难聚财; **there is no ~ like an old ~** Prov 没有比老傻瓜更傻的人; **~s rush in where angels fear to tread** Prov 蠢人多鲁莽; **to live in a ~'s paradise** 生活在虚幻的乐园中; **we are living in a ~'s paradise of plentiful energy** 我们处于能源充足的美妙幻觉中; **to feel (like) a ~** 感到很愚蠢; **to make a ~ of oneself** 出丑; **to make a ~ (out) of sb.** 愚弄某人 **2** [c] Hist (jester) 弄臣 **3** [u and c] esp Brit Culin 奶油果泥; **fruit/rhubarb ~** 奶油水果泥/奶油大黄果泥

B *adj* colloq pej 愚蠢的

C *vi* 做蠢事; **stop ~ing and tell me the truth** 别胡闹了，告诉我实话; **no ~ing!** 不是开玩笑！

D *vt* «*person, promise, appearance*» 欺骗 ‹*person*›; **to ~ sb. out of sth.** 骗取某人某物; **to ~ sb. out of doing sth.** 骗某人不做某事; **to ~ sb. into sth./doing sth.** 骗某人某事物/做某事; **to have sb. ~ed** 使某人被骗

E *v refl* **to ~ oneself** 欺骗自己; **to ~ oneself into thinking ...** 自欺欺人地认为…; **to ~ oneself that ...** 自欺欺人地相信…

Phrasal verbs

- **fool around,** Brit **fool about** *vi* **1** (waste time) 闲荡 **2** (mess about) 瞎闹; **some boys were ~ing about** *or* **around in the pool** 一些男孩子在游泳池里耍闹; **to ~ about** *or* **around with sth.** 瞎摆弄 ‹*weapon, gadget, toy*› **3** **to ~ around with sb.** esp Amer (have relationship) 与某人胡搞
- **fool with** *vt* [**~ with sb./sth.**] **to ~ with sb./sth.** 与…鬼混/瞎掺和

foolery /'fu:ləri/ *n* [u] 蠢事

foolhardiness /'fu:lhɑ:dɪnɪs/ *n* [u] 鲁莽

foolhardy /'fu:lhɑ:di/ *adj* 鲁莽的 ‹*person, plan*›

foolish /'fu:lɪʃ/ *adj* **1** (silly, misguided) 愚蠢的 ‹*action, decision*›; **to be ~ enough to do ...** 做…真傻; **to be ~ of sb. to do sth.** 某人做某事很愚蠢; **that was a ~ thing to do** 那样做是不明智的 **2** (stupid) 显得难堪的 ‹*expression, smile*›; **to make sb. look ~** 使某人出洋相; **to look/feel ~** 出洋相/感到难堪

foolishly /'fu:lɪʃli/ *adv* **1** (unwisely) 愚蠢地 ‹*decide, remark, act*› **2** (in embarrassment) 难堪地 ‹*stand, look, grin*›

foolishness /'fu:lɪʃnɪs/ *n* [u] 愚蠢; **to be (sheer) ~ to do sth.** 做某事是（十分）愚蠢的

foolproof /'fu:lpru:f/ *adj* 不会出错的 ‹*method, plan, machine*›; **it's completely ~!** 这万无一失！

foolscap /'fu:lskæp/ *n* Brit 大裁 [书写纸规格]; **two dozen ~ envelopes** 两打大号信封

fool: ~'s errand *n* 徒劳的差事; **to go on/send sb. on a ~'s errand** 去做/派某人做徒劳无益的事; **~'s gold** *n* [u] 黄铁矿

foot /fʊt/

A *n* (*pl* **feet**) **1** ▸**p. 71** (of person, animal, insect) 脚; **to break a bone in one's ~** 折断脚骨; **my ~ hurts** 我的脚疼; **to have sore feet** 脚痛; **from head to ~** 从头到脚; **swift/light of ~** liter 步履敏捷/轻盈的; **to drag/stamp/shuffle one's feet** 拖着脚走/跺脚/把脚来回倒换; **in (one's) bare feet** 赤脚地; **in one's stocking** *or* **stockinged feet** 只穿袜子地; **to wipe one's feet** 把脚蹭干净; **to get one's feet wet** lit 把脚弄湿; fig 初次涉足; **on ~** 步行; **to set ~ in a place** 进入一个地方; **to be on one's feet** lit 站着; fig 恢复; **to rise** *or* **get to one's feet** 站起身来; **to bring sb. to his/her/their feet** 使他/她/他们站起来; **to keep one's feet** 站稳; **to get** *or* **be under sb.'s feet** 妨碍某人; **to help sb. to his/her/their feet** 扶他/她/他们站起来; **to put one ~ before the other** 行走; **to run** *or* **rush sb. off his/her feet** 使他/她疲于奔命; **to put one's feet up** colloq 休息; **I shall be only too pleased to retire and put my feet up** 我非常乐于退休，放松放松; **to sweep sb. off his/her/their feet** lit 使他/她/他们站立不稳; fig 使他/她/他们倾倒; **with his good looks and wealth he simply swept the girl off her feet** 他英俊富有，简直让这个女孩神魂颠倒; **to be quick on one's feet** 脚步灵活; **to take the weight off one's feet** 坐下; **to tie** *or* **bind sb. hand and ~** 捆住某人的手脚; **to wait on sb. hand and ~** 无微不至地伺候某人; **to leave somewhere feet first** fig 死着离开某地; **to have smelly feet** 脚臭; **to have flat feet** 有扁平足; **my ~!** colloq dated 胡说八道！; **to set sth. on ~** 开始某事; **to put** *or* **get sb./sth. on his/her/their feet again** 使他/她/他们恢复; **to put** *or* **get its feet again** 使某物复原; **to put one's ~ down** colloq 猛踩油门; fig 坚持立场; **to put one's ~ in it** *or* **in one's mouth** colloq 因说错话而冒犯别人; **to have a ~ in both camps** 脚踏两只船; **to put one's best ~ forward** (hasten) 赶快走; (do one's best) 全力以赴; **(not) to put a ~ wrong** （不）出错; **to get** *or* **start off on the wrong/right ~ (with sb.)** （和某人关系）一开始就不顺/很顺利; **to catch sb. on the wrong ~** 让某人措手不及; **to have one ~ in the grave** fig colloq 已经半截入土; **to be dying on one's feet** 气数将尽; **to be out** *or* **dead** *or* **asleep on one's feet** 筋疲力尽; **the boot** Brit *or* **shoe** Amer **is on the other ~** 情况相反; **to fall** *or* **land on one's feet** 安然脱离困境; **to sit at sb.'s feet** (as pupil or disciple) 受教于某人; **to lay the blame at sb.'s feet** 归咎于某人; **to stand on one's own (two) feet** 自立; **to have feet of clay** 有致命的缺点; **to get** *or* **have cold feet** 胆怯起来; **to shake the dust (of somewhere) off one's feet** 毫不惋惜地离开（某地）; **to pull the rug from under sb.'s feet** 拆某人的台; **to have itchy** *or* **itching feet** (eager to be on the move) 总想走动; (eager to change) 迫切求变; **to have two left feet** 脚步不灵活; **the patter of tiny feet** 婴儿的脚步声 [婴儿]; **to have** *or* **keep both** *or* **one's feet on the ground** fig 实事求是; **to have the ball at one's feet** fig 有机会成功; **to kick with the wrong ~** Scot, Ir 信仰与周围环境格格不入; **to walk/dance sb. off his/her feet** 使他/她/他们走得/跳舞跳得筋疲力尽; **not to let the grass grow under one's feet** 不浪费时间 **2** Zool (of reptile, amphibian) 足; (of horse, cow, sheep, goat, pig) 蹄; (of rabbit) 脚; (of bird, cat, dog) 爪; (of invertebrate) (locomotive) 运动器官; (adhesive) 吸附器官 **3** (covering for foot of sock, stocking or tights) 足部 **4** (of sewing machine) 压脚板 **5** (far end) (of bed, couch, grave) 放脚的一端; (of table) 下首位置; (of list, of page, of letter) 下端; **the ~ of sth.** 某物的下端; **at the ~ of the page** 在页脚; **the ~ of the bed** 床脚 **6** (lowest part) (of mountain, stairs, slope etc.) 底部; (of lamp) 底座; **the ~ of a hill** 山脚 **7** (of chair, table or stool) 脚 **8** (*pl* **feet** *or, after a numeral,* **foot**) ▸**p. 436** (measurement) 英尺; **6 feet** *or* **~ long/wide/high/deep** 6 英尺长/宽/高/深; **by the ~** 以英尺为单位 **9** Literat 音步

B *vt* **1** colloq (pay) 支付 ‹*bill, cost*› **2** (walk) 步行; **to ~ it** 步行

footage /'fʊtɪdʒ/ *n* [u] 连续镜头; **news ~** 一组新闻镜头

foot-and-mouth disease *n* [u] 口蹄疫

football /'fʊtbɔ:l/ ▸**p. 307** *n* **1** [u] (soccer) 足球运动; (American football) 橄榄球运动; **to play ~** Brit 踢足球; Amer 打橄榄球 **2** [c] (ball) Brit 足球; Amer 橄榄球

football: ~ coach ▸**p. 409** *n* 足球教练; **~ coupon** *n* Brit 足球彩票

footballer /'fʊtbɔ:lə(r)/ ▸**p. 409** *n* Brit 足球运动员; Amer 橄榄球运动员

football: ~ fan *n* 足球迷; **~ game** *n* Brit 足球比赛; Amer 橄榄球比赛; **~ kit** *n* 足球装备; **F~ League** *n* Brit 足球联合会; **~ player** ▸**p. 409** *n* Brit 足球运动员; Amer 橄榄球运动员; **~ pools** *npl* Brit 足球赌博; **~ season** *n* 足球赛季; **~ special** *n* Brit 足球迷专车; **~ supporter** *n* 足球队支持者

foot: ~bath *n* **1** (bowl, basin) 脚盆; **2** (liquid) 洗脚液; **~board** *n* **1** (on bed) 床脚竖板;

f

2▸ (on carriage) 踏脚板; ～ **brake** *n* 脚刹车; ～**bridge** *n* 人行桥

footer /ˈfʊtə(r)/ *n* **1**▸ Brit Sport colloq dated 足球运动 **2**▸ Print 脚注

footfall /ˈfʊtfɔːl/ *n* 脚步声

foot fault
A *n* 脚部犯规
B foot-fault *vi* «*player*» 脚部犯规
C foot-fault *vt* 判…脚部犯规 ‹*player*›

foot: ～**gear** *n* [u] 鞋类; ～**hills** *npl* 山麓丘陵; ～**hold** *n* **1**▸ (on rock face, ladder) 立足处; **to gain a/lose one's** ～**hold** 找到/失去踏脚处; **2**▸ fig (secure position) 稳固的地位; **to gain** *or* **get a** ～**hold** 取得稳固地位

footie /ˈfʊti/ *n* Brit colloq = **footy**

footing /ˈfʊtɪŋ/
A *n* **1**▸ (basis) 基础; **on a firm** ～ 在坚实的基础上; **to place** *or* **put sth. on a legal** ～ 使某事具有法律效力; **to be on an equal** *or* **even** ～ **with sb.** 与某人地位平等; **to be on a friendly** ～ **with sb.** 同某人很友好 **2**▸ (grip with one's feet) 站稳; **to keep/lose** *or* **miss one's** ～ 站稳/失足
B footings *npl* Constr 基脚

footle /ˈfuːtl/ *vi* Brit colloq **to** ～ **about** *or* **around** 闲混

footlights /ˈfʊtlaɪts/ *npl* 脚灯; **the lure of the** ～ fig 舞台生涯的吸引力

footling /ˈfuːtlɪŋ/ *adj attrib* 无足轻重的 ‹*task, amateur*›; 愚蠢的 ‹*question, excuse*›

foot: ～**loose** *adj* 自由自在的; ～**loose and fancy free** 自由自在, 无拘无束; ～**man** /-mən/ *n* 男仆; ～**mark** *n* 脚印; ～**note** *n* lit 脚注; fig 补充说明; ～ **passenger** *n* 徒步旅行者; ～**path** *n* (in countryside) 人行小径; (in town) 人行道; ～ **patrol** *n* 步行巡逻; **to be on** ～ **patrol** 在步行巡逻; ～**plate** *n* 司机室平台; ～**print** *n* **1**▸ (impression) 脚印; **2**▸ Comput [计算机硬件所占的] 台面空间; **3**▸ (environmental impact) 对环境的影响; ～ **pump** *n* 脚踏泵; ～**rest** *n* 搁脚物

Footsie /ˈfʊtsi/ *abbr* Brit colloq = **Financial Times Stock Exchange Index**

footsie /ˈfʊtsi/ *n* colloq 碰脚调情; **to play** ～ **with sb.** 与某人碰脚调情

footslog /ˈfʊtslɒg/
A *vi* (walk wearily) 费力地步行; (march wearily) 费力地行军
B *n* (walk) 长途跋涉; (march) 费力的长途行军

foot: ～ **soldier** *n* **1**▸ Mil 步兵; **2**▸ (worker) 起重要作用的小人物; ～**sore** *adj* [因走路过多而] 脚痛的; ～**step** *n* **1**▸ (movement) 脚步; (sound) 脚步声; **2**▸ fig (path, wake) 足迹; **to follow in sb.'s** ～**steps** 继承某人的事业; **to tread in sb.'s** ～**steps** 踩着某人的脚印走; **to dog sb.'s** ～**steps** 跟随某人; ～**stool** *n* 脚凳; ～**wear** *n* [u] 鞋类; ～**well** *n* 脚坑 [汽车或飞机前座供放脚的地方]; ～**work** *n* [u] 步法

footy /ˈfʊti/ *n* Brit colloq 足球运动

fop /fɒp/ *n* 纨绔子弟

foppish /ˈfɒpɪʃ/ *adj* 纨绔子弟特有的 ‹*manners, clothes*›; **a** ～ **man** 花花公子

for /fɔː(r), fə(r)/ ▸ **p. 487**
A *prep* **1**▸ (intended to be given to, be used by, to help to treat sth.) 给; (indicating purpose) 为; (in order to get sth.) 为得到; (indicating availability) 供; **these flowers are** ～ **you** 这些花是给你的; **medicine** ～ **a cold** 感冒药; **we treated her** ～ **asthma** 我们治疗了她的哮喘; **a play area** ～ **children** 儿童游乐区; **not** ～ **me, thanks** 我不需要了, 谢谢; **there's gratitude** ～ **you!** iron 这就叫感激! ; **to be in** ～ **it, to be** ～ **it** Brit colloq 会惹麻烦; **right, you're** ～ **it!** Brit colloq 没错, 你要遭殃了! ; **to have it in** ～ **sb.** colloq 讨厌某人; **what's this spring** ～**?** 这个弹簧有什么用? ; **I sent it away** ～ **repair** 我把它送去修理了; ～ **further information, write to ...** 欲知详情, 请致函…; **to be** ～ **sth.** 想做某事; **oh** ～ **a nice hot bath!** 要是能舒舒服服洗个热水澡该多好! ; ～ **sale/hire** 供出售/出租 **2**▸ (on behalf of, as representative, member, employee of) 代表; **I speak** ～ **everyone here** 我代表这里所有的人说话; **the MP** ～ **Oxford** 代表牛津的议员; **Minister** ～ **Foreign Affairs** (in UK) 外交大臣; (in other countries) 外交部长 **3**▸ (indicating destination) 向; **the train** ～ **London** 开往伦敦的火车; **they swam** ～ **the shore** 他们朝岸边游去 **4**▸ (equivalent to) 相当于; **T** ～ **Tom** T 代表汤姆; **red** ～ **danger** 红色表示危险; **what's the French** ～ **'boot'?** "靴子" 用法语怎么说? **5**▸ (in favour of) 赞成; (in support of) 支持; **to be** ～ **sth.** 赞成 ‹*peace, divorce, reunification*›; **to be** ～ **doing sth.** 想要做某事; **to be** ～ **or against sb./sth.** 支持或反对某人/某事; **are you** ～ **or against capital punishment?** 你支持还是反对死刑? ; **to be all** ～ **it** colloq 完全赞成; **a campaign** ～ **free education** 争取免费教育的运动 **6**▸ (as) 作为; **what would you like** ～ **a present?** 你想要一件什么礼物? **7**▸ (considering) 就…而言; **it's warm** ～ **the time of year** 在一年的这个时节这天气算是暖和的了; **she's very young** ～ **a doctor** 作为医生她很年轻 **8**▸ (as regards) 关于; **to have no ear** ～ **music** 对音乐一窍不通; **she's a great one** ～ **jokes** 她很会讲笑话; ～ **efficiency there is no better system** 论效率没有比这更好的系统了 **9**▸ (towards) 对; **her love** ～ **her children** 她对子女的爱; **to feel contempt** ～ **sb.** 看不起某人 **10**▸ (stressing appropriateness) 适合; **not** ～ **sb.** 不适合某人; **she's the person** ～ **the job** 她就是干这份工作的合适人选; **it's not** ～ **him to tell us what to do** 他没资格告诉我们该做什么 **11**▸ (indicating cost or value) 以…为代价; (in exchange for) 换取; **they bought the car** ～ **£6,000** 他们花 6,000 英镑买了那辆汽车; **he gave me one** ～ **nothing** 他白送了我一个; **I wouldn't do it** ～ **anything!** 无论给多少钱我都不干! ; **she wouldn't hurt him** ～ **anything** *or* ～ **the world** 她无论如何都不会去伤害他; **to exchange sth.** ～ **sth. else** 用某物换取另一物; **England were all out** ～ **200 runs** 英格兰队拼尽全力得了 200 分 **12**▸ (as part of ratio) [表示比例]; **one teacher** ～ **five pupils** 每 5 个学生有 1 个老师 **13**▸ (indicating duration) [表示时间段]; **the worst storm** ～ **years** 多年来最猛烈的暴风雨; **we haven't met** ～ **months** 我们好几个月没见面了 **14**▸ (indicating a deadline) 在…之前; **it will be ready** ～ **Saturday** 这要在周六之前准备就绪; **when is the essay** ～**?** 文章什么时候要? **15**▸ (indicating scheduled time) [表示安排]; (on the occasion of) 在…时; **the summit scheduled** ～ **next month** 计划于下个月举行的峰会; **an appointment** ～ **4 p.m.** 下午 4 点的约会; **he got a bike** ～ **his birthday** 他生日时得到了一辆自行车 **16**▸ (indicating distance) [表示距离]; **to drive** ～ **miles** 驱车几英里; **it rises** ～ **1,000m from the plain** 它矗立于平原之上高达 1,000 米 **17**▸ (as a result of) 由于; (indicating cause or reason) 因为; **you'll feel (all the) better** ～ **a rest** 你休息一下就会感觉好 (得多) 了; **I was unable to sleep** ～ **the pain/the noise** 我因为疼痛/噪音而难以入睡; ～ **one thing ... (and** ～ **another ...)** 首先… (其次…) **18**▸ Amer (after) 依照; **to name a child** ～ **sb.** 用某人的名字给孩子起名; **a plant named** ～ **a former viceroy** 用一位前总督的名字命名的植物 **19**▸ (indicating consequence) [表示结果]; **it's too cold** ～ **her to go out** 天冷得让她没法出门; **I haven't the patience** *or* **enough patience** ～ **sewing** 我没耐心做针线活 **20**▸ (indicating attitude) 对…来说; **the film was too earnest** ～ **me** 我觉得这部影片太严肃了; **what counts** ～ **them is ...** 他们看重的是…
B *conj* liter 因为; **she locked the door,** ～ **she was afraid of burglars** 她锁上了门, 因为她担心有窃贼

forage /ˈfɒrɪdʒ, Amer ˈfɔːr-/
A *n* **1**▸ [u] (cattle and horse food) 草料 **2**▸ [c] (search) 搜寻; **to go on a** ～ **for** 去搜寻 ‹*food*›; **to have a** ～ **(for sth.)** 搜寻 (某物)
B *vi* **1**▸ (for food) 搜寻食物; **to** ～ **(in sth.) for (sth.)** (在某处) 搜寻 (某物) **2**▸ fig (for object) 搜寻; **to** ～ **about** *or* **around for sth.** 四处搜寻某物

foray /ˈfɒreɪ, Amer ˈfɔːreɪ/
A *n* **1**▸ (first venture) 初步尝试; **to make a** ～ **into** 初次涉足 ‹*politics, acting, sport*› **2**▸ Mil (raid) 突袭; **to make a** ～ **against/into sth.** 对某处发动突袭
B *vi* Mil 进行突袭; **to** ～ **into ...** 对…进行突袭

forbade /fəˈbeɪd, -ˈbæd/, **forbad** /-ˈbæd/ *pt* ▸**forbid**

forbear /fɔːˈbeə(r)/ *vi* (*pt* **forbore,** *pp* **forborne**) formal 克制; **to** ～ **from sth./doing sth.** 克制住某事/不做某事; **to** ～ **to do sth.** 克制住不做某事

forbearance /fɔːˈbeərəns/ *n* [u] **1**▸ (patience) 耐心; **to show** ～ **(towards sb.)** (对某人) 显示出耐心 **2**▸ (tolerance) 宽容; **a policy of** ～ 宽大政策

forbearing /fɔːˈbeərɪŋ/ *adj* 宽容的 ‹*judge, parent*›

forbears /ˈfɔːbeəz/ *npl* liter 祖宗

forbid /fəˈbɪd/ *vt* (*pres p* **-dd-**; *pt* **forbade, forbad**; *pp* **forbidden**) **1**▸ (order not to) 禁止; **to** ～ **sb. to do sth.** 禁止某人做某事 **2**▸ (not allow) 不允许; **to** ～ **sb. sth., to** ～ **sth. to sb.** 不允许某人…; **to** ～ **sb. to do sth.** 不允许某人做某事; **entry to the park is strictly forbidden after 7.00 p.m.** 晚上 7 点钟以后严禁进入公园; **the doctor has forbidden him alcohol of any kind** 医生不许他喝任何酒 **3**▸ (prevent) 阻止; **to** ～ **sth.** 阻止某事; **his health** ～**s it** 他的健康状况不允许那样做; **God/Heaven** ～**!** 但愿上帝/老天别让这样的事情发生!

forbidden /fəˈbɪdn/
A *pp* ▸**forbid**
B *adj* 被禁止的 ‹*practice, food, subject*›; **a** ～ **area/book/place** 禁区/禁书/禁地; ～ **ground/territory** 忌讳事; ～ **fruit** 禁果; **the F**～ **City** 紫禁城

forbidding /fəˈbɪdɪŋ/ *adj* **1**▸ (threatening) 冷峻的 ‹*appearance, manner*›; 严峻的 ‹*prospect*› **2**▸ (ominous) 令人生畏的 ‹*sky, rocks, building*›; **to be/look** ～ 令人生畏/看上去险恶

forbiddingly /fəˈbɪdɪŋli/ *adv* 严峻地 ‹*frown, stare, rise*›; 令人望而生畏地 ‹*austere, long, complex*›

forbore /fɔːˈbɔː(r)/ *pt* ▸**forbear**

forborne /fɔːˈbɔːn/ *pp* ▸**forbear**

force /fɔːs/
A *n* **1**▸ [u] (physical strength, impact) 力; **brute** ～ 蛮力; **a** ～**-nine gale** 9 级大风; **to break the** ～ **of a fall/blow** 减弱下落/打击的力量; **the** ～ **of the earthquake** 地震的强度; **the destructive** ～ **of a bomb** 炸弹的破坏力 **2**▸ [u] (coercion) 暴力; **to use** *or* **employ** ～ **(against sb.)** (对某人) 使用暴力; **to do sth. by** ～ 强行做某事; **the threat/use of** ～ 武力的威胁/使用 **3**▸ [u and c] Phys 力; **(the)** ～ **of gravity** 地心引力 **4**▸ [u and c] (effect) 影响; **out of** *or* **from** ～ **of habit** 出于习惯; **the** ～**s of nature/destiny** 大自然/命运的威力; **the** ～**s of evil** 邪恶势力; **the** ～ **of popular opinion** 舆论的影响; **by** ～ **of sth.** 凭借某物; **by (sheer)** ～ **of numbers** (全) 凭人多势众; **by** ～ **of circumstance(s)** 因情势所迫 **5**▸ [c] (strong influence) (of person) 有影响的人; (of belief, ideology) 有影响的事物; **this country is no longer a world** ～ 该国不再是世界上举足轻重的国家了; **a** ～ **to be reckoned with** *or* **to reckon with** 必须认真对待的有影响力的人; **market** ～**s** 市场力; **a motivating** ～ 推动力 **6**▸ [u] (intensity of writing, style, speech, manner) 气势 **7**▸ [c] Mil, Police 部队; **air/exped-**

itionary/naval ～ 空军/远征军/海军; **the police ～** 警察部队; **the ～ +** *v sing or pl* Brit colloq 警察部门 **8** [c] + *v sing or pl* (organized group) [共同从事某种活动的] 一群人; **our sales ～** 我们的销售队伍; **to combine ～s** 联手 **9** [u] (binding effect) 效力; **to have the ～ of law** 具有法律效力; **to be in ～** 有效; **to come into ～** 开始生效 **10** [u] (large numbers) 大批; **in ～** 大批地; **the students attended the protest meeting in ～** 大批学生参加了抗议集会

B forces *npl* Mil 武装力量; **the armed ～s** 武装部队; **left-wing guerrilla ～s** 左翼游击队

C *vt* **1** (compel, oblige) 强迫; **the earthquake ～d the evacuation of hundreds of residents** 地震迫使数百名居民撤离; **to ～ sb. to do sth.** 强迫某人做某事; **to ～ sb. into sth./doing sth.** 迫使某人做某事 **2** (push, thrust) 强推; **she ～d him to his knees** 她摁他跪下; **the minister was ～d from** *or* **out of office after only three weeks** 仅仅3个星期后这名部长就被迫下台; **to ～ sb. into a corner** lit 把某人逼到角落; fig 使某人陷入困境; **he ～d it out of her hands** 他把那东西从她手中夺走; **to ～ sth. from** *or* **out of sb.** 强迫某人说出某事; **to ～ sth. down sb.** (make eat, drink) 强迫某人吞下某物; **to ～ a path** *or* **one's way through/into somewhere** 强行通过/进入某处; **the expedition had to ～ its way through the dense jungle** 探险队不得不在浓密的丛林中披荆斩棘前进; **to ～ an entry** 强行进入 **3** (impose) 把…强加于 ‹*object, course of action, result, views*›; **to ～ sth. on sb.** 把某事物强加于某人; **I didn't want to take the money, but she ～d it on me** 我不想拿钱，但是她非要我拿不可; **the team ～d a draw on their rivals** 球队逼平了对手 **4** (apply great pressure to) 强行打开 ‹*door, lock*›; **to ～ the** *or* **an issue** 强迫对方作出决定; **to ～ sb.'s hand** 强迫某人行动 **5** (make with effort) 勉强挤出 ‹*smile*›; 勉强发出 ‹*note*›; **to ～ a laugh** 勉强哈哈一笑; **it's forcing it a bit to call him a genius** 称他为天才有些牵强 **6** (artificially hasten) 人工加速…的生长 ‹*plant*›; 强行加快 ‹*pace*›; **don't ～ the engine of your new car for the first 500 miles** 头500英里，不要强行加快新车的发动机转速 **7** (rape) 强奸

D *v refl* **to ～ oneself 1** (push oneself) 强迫自己; **to ～ oneself to do sth.** 强迫自己做某事 **2** (impose oneself) 强行做某事 [尤指强奸]; **to ～ oneself on sb.** 强行和某人发生性关系

Phrasal verbs

- **force back** *vt* [～ sb./sth. back, ～ back sb./sth.]
  1 (push back) 迫使…后退 ‹*crowd, person*› **2** (hold back) 强忍住 ‹*emotion, tears, fear, anger*›
- **force down** *vt* [～ sth. down, ～ down sth.]
  1 Aviat 迫使…降落 ‹*aircraft*› **2** (eat reluctantly) 硬咽下 ‹*food, drink*› **3** (squash down) 硬塞 ‹*contents, objects*› **4** Econ 迫使…下降 ‹*prices, demand, inflation*›
- **force in** *vt* [～ sb./sth. in, ～ in sb./sth.]
  1 (make room for) 把…塞入 ‹*object*›; 使…挤入 ‹*person*› **2** (push in) 把…压进去 ‹*cork*›
- **force open** *vt* [～ sth. open, ～ open sth.] 强行打开 ‹*container, hand*›; 强行撬开 ‹*mouth*›; **his head ached, but he ～d his eyes open with an effort** 他头疼，但还是使劲睁开了眼睛
- **force out** *vt* [～ sb./sth. out, ～ out sb./sth.]
  1 (eject) 将…挤出 ‹*person, object*›; **the compressed air ～d the cork out** 压缩空气将软木塞顶了出来; **the minister has been ～d out of office** 这名部长已被迫离职 **2** (utter) 勉强说出 ‹*reply, apology, excuse*›
- **force through** *vt* [～ sth. through, ～ through sth.] 强行通过 ‹*legislation*›; 强制执行 ‹*policy, decision*›
- **force up** *vt* [～ sth. up, ～ up sth.] 迫使…上升 ‹*prices, demand, inflation*›

forced /fɔːst/ *adj* **1** (imposed) 强迫的; **～ labour** 强制劳动; **～ marriage** 强迫婚姻; **～ saving** 强制储蓄 **2** (false) 勉强的 ‹*smile*›; 牵强的 ‹*interpretation*›; **a ～ conversation** 没话找话的交谈 **3** (due to emergency) 不得已的 ‹*interval, break*›; **a ～ landing** 迫降 **4** Hort 人工促长的 ‹*vegetable, fruit, plant*›

forced march *n* 急行军

force: ～-feed *vt* (*pt, pp* **～-fed**) **1** lit (with food) 强迫…进食 ‹*person*›; 强制喂养 ‹*animal*›; **2** fig (with information, ideology) 强迫…接受; **her parents ～-fed her (on** *or* **with) Mozart** 父母强迫她听莫扎特的音乐; **～ field** *n* [科幻小说中的] 力障碍区

forceful /ˈfɔːsfl/ *adj* **1** (dynamic) 坚强的 ‹*person, character*›; 有力的 ‹*argument*› **2** (persuasive) 有说服力的 ‹*reasoning, argument*›

forcefully /ˈfɔːsfəli/ *adv* **1** (violently) 猛力地 ‹*hit, thrust*› **2** (with conviction) 有说服力地 ‹*express*›

forceps /ˈfɔːseps/ *npl* **1** (small) 镊子 **2** (large) 产钳; **a ～ delivery** 产钳分娩

forcible /ˈfɔːsəbl/ *adj* **1** (done by force) 强行的 ‹*entry*›; 强制的 ‹*feeding*› **2** (forceful) 强有力的 ‹*argument, deterrent*›

forcibly /ˈfɔːsəbli/ *adv* **1** (by force) 强行地 ‹*remove, detain, feed*› **2** (vigorously) 有力地 ‹*argue, recommend*›

ford /fɔːd/
A *n* 浅滩
B *vt* 涉过 ‹*river, stream*›

fore /fɔː(r)/
A *n* [u] 前部; **to be/come to the ～** 处于重要地位/变得重要; **to bring to the ～** 使…突出 ‹*talent, quality*›
B *adj attrib* 在…前部的 ‹*ship, plane, body*›; **the ～ and hind pairs of wings** 前对翅和后对翅
C *adv* 在船头; **～ and aft** 从船头到船尾
D *excl* (in golf) 前面当心 [挥杆时提醒别人以免被球击中]

forearm /ˈfɔːrɑːm/
A *n* 前臂
B *vt* **to be ～ed** 预作准备

forebears /ˈfɔːbeəz/ *npl* liter 祖宗

forebode /fɔːˈbəʊd/ *vt* liter «*cloud, event*» 预示 ‹*disaster*›

foreboding /fɔːˈbəʊdɪŋ/ *n* [对不祥之事的] 预感; **to have a ～ that …** 有一种…的预感; **to have ～s about sth.** 对某事有不好的预感; **to be full of ～** 充满不祥预感; **to fill with ～** 令有不祥之感; **a sense of ～** 一种不祥之感

forecast /ˈfɔːkɑːst, Amer -kæst/
A *n* **1** Meteorol 天气预报 **2** (prediction, estimation) 预测; **to make ～s about sth.** 对某事进行预测; **a racing ～** 赛马结果预测
B *vt* (*pt, pp* **forecast** *or* **～ed**) **1** Meteorol 预报; **sunshine is ～ for tomorrow** 预报明日天气晴好 **2** (predict, estimate) «*analyst, fortune teller*» 预测 ‹*profit, good luck, winner*›; **to ～ that …** 预测…; **to ～ sth.** 预测某事; **to be ～ to do sth.** 被预测会做某事; **as ～** 如预测的一样

forecaster /ˈfɔːkɑːstə(r), Amer -kæst-/ *n* **1** ▸ p. 409 *n* Meteorol 气象预报员 **2** (gen) 预测者

forecastle /ˈfəʊksl/ *n* 前部水手舱

foreclose /fɔːˈkləʊz/ *vi* «*bank, lender*» 取消抵押品赎回权; **to ～ on sb./sth.** 取消某人的抵押品赎回权/回赎某物的权利

foreclosure /fɔːˈkləʊʒə(r)/ *n* 抵押品赎回权的取消

forecourt /ˈfɔːkɔːt/ *n* **1** (of building) 前院 **2** Brit (of petrol station) 加油区

forefathers /ˈfɔːfɑːðəz/ *npl* 祖先

forefinger /ˈfɔːfɪŋgə(r)/ *n* 食指

forefoot /ˈfɔːfʊt/ *n* (*pl* **forefeet** /ˈfɔːfiːt/) [四足动物的] 前足

forefront /ˈfɔːfrʌnt/ *n* (leading position) 最前列; (most important position) 最重要的位置; **in** *or* **at/to/near the ～ of** 处于/进入/靠近…的最前列 ‹*change, research, debate*›; **it's in the ～ of my mind** 这是我首先要考虑的; **the issue should be brought to the ～** 这个问题应当成为关注的重点

foregather /fɔːˈgæðə(r)/ *vi* formal *or* hum «*people, delegates*» 预先集合; **I suggest we ～ in the pub for a quick drink before the party** 我建议在聚会前我们先集中到酒馆喝一杯

forego /fɔːˈgəʊ/ *vt* **= forgo**

foregoing /ˈfɔːgəʊɪŋ/
A *adj* 上述的 ‹*information, analysis, section*›
B *n* **the ～** 上述内容

foregone /ˈfɔːgɒn, Amer -ˈgɔːn/ *adj* 预先决定的; **to be a ～ conclusion** 是预料之中的必然结局

foreground /ˈfɔːgraʊnd/
A *n* **1** (of a situation) 突出的地位 **2** Art 前景; **in the ～** 在前景中
B *vt* 给予…突出的地位

forehand /ˈfɔːhænd/ *n* 正手击球; **a powerful ～ drive** 大力正手击球

forehead /ˈfɒrɪd, ˈfɔːhed, Amer ˈfɔːrɪd/ ▸ p. 71 *n* 额; **high/low ～** 高/低额头

foreign /ˈfɒrən, Amer ˈfɔːr-/ *adj* **1** (of, from or relating to another country) 外国的 ‹*culture, visitor*›; 在国外的 ‹*travel*›; 对外的 ‹*relations, trade, policy*›; **a ～ language/newspaper/currency** 外语/外报/外币; **in ～ parts** 在国外; **on the ～ market** 在国外市场上 **2** (alien, unknown) 陌生的 ‹*topic, concept*›; 非自身的 ‹*characteristic*›; **to be ～ to sb.'s nature** 不是某人的本性; **to be ～ to sb.'s experience** 是某人从未经历过的

foreign affairs *npl* 外交事务

foreign aid *n* [u] 外援; **to receive/benefit from ～** 接受/受益于外援; **to grant/offer/supply ～** 给予外援; **the American ～ program** 美国的外援项目; **～ budget** 外援预算

foreign: F～ and Commonwealth Office *n* Brit **the F～ and Commonwealth Office** 外交和联邦事务部; **～ body** *n* 异物; **～ correspondent** ▸ p. 409 *n* 驻外记者

foreigner /ˈfɒrənə(r)/ *n* 外国人

foreign exchange *n* [u] 外汇; **～ rates** 外汇汇率

foreign exchange: ～ dealer ▸ p. 409 *n* 外汇交易商; **～ market** *n* 外汇市场

foreign: ～ language assistant ▸ p. 409 *n* 外语口语助教; **F～ Legion** *n* 外籍军团; **～ minister** *n* 外交部长; **～ ministry** *n* 外交部; **F～ Office** *n* Brit **= Foreign and Commonwealth Office**; **～-owned** *adj* 外资的; **a ～-owned company** 外资公司; **～ policy** *n* 外交政策; **F～ Secretary** *n* Brit 外交大臣; **～ service** *n* 外交部门

foreknowledge /fɔːˈnɒlɪdʒ/ *n* 预知; **to have ～ of** 预先知道 ‹*crime, event*›

foreland /ˈfɔːlənd/ *n* 岬

foreleg /ˈfɔːleg/ *n* [四足动物的] 前腿

forelock /ˈfɔːlɒk/ *n* (of person) 额发; (of horse) 额毛; **to touch** *or* **tug one's ～** 必恭必敬

foreman /ˈfɔːmən/ ▸ p. 409 (*pl* **foremen**) **1** (supervisor) 工头 **2** Jur 陪审团团长

foremast /ˈfɔːmɑːst, -məst/ *n* 前桅

foremost /ˈfɔːməʊst/
A *adj* 最前面的 ‹*runner, position*›; 最重要的 ‹*expert, politician*›; **the issue is ～ in our minds** 这一问题是我们最优先考虑的
B *adv* 在最前; **first and ～** 首先

forename /ˈfɔːneɪm/ *n* 名

f

forensic /fəˈrensɪk, Amer -zɪk/ *adj* **1** (in crime detection) 法医的; ~ **evidence/test** 法医证据/检验 **2** fig (in debate) 辩论的 ‹*attack, skill*›; **with ~ eloquence** 雄辩地

forensic: ~ **medicine,** ~ **science** *ns* [u] 法医学; ~ **scientist** ▸p. 409 *n* 法医学家

forensics /fəˈrensɪks, Amer -zɪks/ *npl* **1** (tests) 法医检验; (techniques) 法医鉴定技术 **2** + *v sing or pl* colloq (laboratory, department) 法医室

forepaw /ˈfɔːpɔː/ *n* 前爪

foreplay /ˈfɔːpleɪ/ *n* [u] 前戏

forequarters /ˈfɔːkwɔːtə(r)/ *npl* [包括两前足的] 躯体前半部

forerunner /ˈfɔːrʌnə(r)/ *n* **1** (in job, post) 先驱; (institution, invention, model) 先导 **2** (sign) 预兆

foresail /ˈfɔːseɪl, -sl/ *n* 前桅帆

foresee /fɔːˈsiː/ *vt* (*pt* **foresaw**, *pp* **foreseen**) 预见 ‹*event, development*›

foreseeable /fɔːˈsiːəbl/ *adj* 可预见的 ‹*event, reaction*›; **for** *or* **in the ~ future** 在可预见的将来

foreshadow /fɔːˈʃædəʊ/ *vt* «*event, speech, achievement*» 预示 ‹*event, change*›

foreshore /ˈfɔːʃɔː(r)/ *n* 前滩

foreshorten /fɔːˈʃɔːtn/ *vt* «*artist, lens, distance, angle of vision*» 按透视法缩短 ‹*line*›; 用透视法缩小 ‹*object, form*›

foresight /ˈfɔːsaɪt/ *n* [u] 先见之明

foreskin /ˈfɔːskɪn/ *n* 包皮

forest /ˈfɒrɪst, Amer ˈfɔːr-/ *n* **1** (wooded area) 森林 **2** fig (dense mass) 一丛; **a ~ of chimneys** 林立的烟囱

forestall /fɔːˈstɔːl/ *vt* **1** (anticipate) 抢在…前行动 ‹*person, action, development*›; **we ~ed our competitors** 我们抢在了竞争对手之前 **2** (prevent) 预先阻止; **he will resign in order to ~ a vote of no confidence in him** 他将辞职以阻止对他的不信任投票

forested /ˈfɒrɪstɪd, Amer ˈfɔːr-/ *adj* 覆盖着森林的; **densely ~** 森林茂密的

forester /ˈfɒrɪstə(r), Amer ˈfɔːr-/ *n* 林务员

forest: ~ **fire** *n* 森林火灾; ~ **floor** *n* 森林覆被; ~ **management** *n* [u] 森林管理; ~ **ranger** *n* 护林官

forestry /ˈfɒrɪstri, Amer ˈfɔːr-/ *n* [u] **1** (speciality) 林学 **2** (industry) 林业

forestry: F~ Commission *n* Brit 林业委员会; ~ **worker** ▸p. 409 *n* Brit (maintenance) 林务员; (lumberjack) 伐木工

foretaste /ˈfɔːteɪst/ *n* 预先体验; **to have** *or* **get a ~ of sth.** 预先经历某事

foretell /fɔːˈtel/ *vt* (*pt, pp* **foretold**) «*person, oracle, stars*» 预言 ‹*event, outcome*›; **to ~ the future** 预言未来

forethought /ˈfɔːθɔːt/ *n* [u] 事先的考虑; **to show/have ~** 表现出/具有深谋远虑; **to have the ~ to do sth.** 事先考虑到做某事

foretold /fɔːˈtəʊld/ *pt, pp* ▸**foretell**

forever /fəˈrevə(r)/ *adv* **1** (for all future time) 永远; **I'll love you ~** 我永远爱你; **~ and ever** 永永远远; **~ afterwards** 以后永远 **2** (to infinity) 无尽地; **the desert seemed to go on ~** 沙漠似乎无边无际 **3** colloq (very long time) 长久地; (persistently) 老是; **it took ~ to find the book** 花了很长时间才找到这本书; **to be ~ doing sth.** 老是做某事; **she's ~ moaning** 她没完没了地呻吟 **4** (always) 始终; **they were ~ on the brink of achieving a breakthrough** 他们总是几近实现突破 **5** (in acclamations) 万岁; **Scotland ~!** 苏格兰万岁!

for ever *adv* Brit = **forever 1, 2, 3**

forevermore /fəˌrevəˈmɔː(r)/ *adv* liter 永远

forewarn /fɔːˈwɔːn/ *vt* 预先警告; **to ~ sb. of** *or* **about sb./sth.** 就某人/某事物预先警告某人; **~ed is forearmed** 有备无患

foreword /ˈfɔːwɜːd/ *n* 前言

forfeit /ˈfɔːfɪt/

A *vt* 丧失 ‹*life, freedom, right*›

B *n* **1** [u] (action, process) 丧失; **the ~ of freedom of speech** 言论自由的丧失 **2** [c] (penalty) 罚金; **to pay a ~** 交付罚金

C *adj pred* **to be ~** «*reputation, welfare*» 会丧失; **he knew his life was ~ if he did not do as he was told** 他知道如果他不遵命就会丧命

D forfeits *npl* + *v sing* (game) 罚物游戏

forfeiture /ˈfɔːfɪtʃə(r)/ *n* (of property, money) 没收; (of right) 丧失

forgather /fɔːˈgæðə(r)/ *vi* = **foregather**

forgave /fəˈgeɪv/ *pt* ▸**forgive**

forge /fɔːdʒ/

A *vt* **1** (fake) 伪造 ‹*passport, banknotes, cheque*›; 假冒 ‹*signature*›; **to ~ a painting** 伪造一幅画 **2** (in metal) 锻造 ‹*iron, horseshoe*› **3** (establish) 建立 ‹*friendship, links*›; 制定 ‹*plan*›; 订立 ‹*agreement*›

B *vi* 稳步前进; **to ~ ahead** 稳步前进; **to ~ ahead** *or* **forward with** 稳步实施 ‹*plan, idea*›; **to ~ into the lead** 加速跑到前头

C *n* **1** (smithy) 铁匠铺 **2** (furnace, hearth) 锻铁炉 **3** (workshop) 锻造车间 **4** (factory) 锻造工厂

forger /ˈfɔːdʒə(r)/ *n* 伪造者

forgery /ˈfɔːdʒəri/ *n* **1** [u] (faking) 伪造 **2** [c] (fake item) 伪造品

forget /fəˈget/ (*pres p* **-tt-**, *pt* **forgot**, *pp* **forgotten**)

A *vt* **1** (not remember) 记不起来 ‹*face, name, date, fact*›; **to ~ how to do sth.** 记不得如何做某事; **to ~ sth. in the heat of the moment** 盛怒之下忘记某事; **~ it!** (no way) 休想! ; (drop the subject) 别提它了! ; (think nothing of it) 不必在意! ; **once seen, never forgotten** 一见之下, 终生难忘 **2** (overlook) 忘记 ‹*person, situation, appointment*›; **I'm sorry, I always ~ your birthday!** 对不起, 我总是忘记你的生日! ; **to ~ to do sth.** 忘记做某事; **I'm in charge and don't you ~ it!** 是我负责, 你别忘了! ; **not ~ting** 还包括 **3** (put out of mind) 不再想 ‹*person, event, experience*›; **unpleasant experiences are best forgotten** 最好把不愉快的经历都忘掉 **4** (leave behind) 忘记带 ‹*umbrella, money*›

B *vi* 忘记; **an elephant never ~s** 大象什么事都不会忘记 [形容大象记忆力惊人]

C *v refl* **to ~ oneself** 举止不得体; **he seemed to ~ himself and started to swear and shout** 他好像不顾体面, 开始咒骂喊叫

Phrasal verb

- **forget about** *vt* [~ **about sb./sth.**] **1** (overlook) 忘记 ‹*person, event*› **2** (put out of mind) 不再想 ‹*person, event, situation*›; **if you're prepared to ~ about the matter, then so am I** 如果你准备不再提这件事, 那么我也一样

forgetful /fəˈgetfl/ *adj* **1** (absent-minded) 健忘的; **to become** *or* **grow ~** 变得健忘 **2** (negligent) 疏忽的; **to be ~ of one's duties** 玩忽职守

forgetfulness /fəˈgetflnɪs/ *n* [u] **1** (absent-mindedness) 健忘 **2** (negligence) 疏忽

forget: ~-me-not *n* 勿忘我; **~-me-not blue** ▸p. 134 *n* 浅蓝色

forgettable /fəˈgetəbl/ *adj* 易被忘记的 ‹*person, event*›

forgivable /fəˈgɪvəbl/ *adj* 可原谅的 ‹*mistake, remark*›

forgive /fəˈgɪv/ (*pt* **forgave**, *pp* **forgiven**) ▸p. 29

A *vt* **1** (pardon) 原谅 ‹*person, action, situation*›; **to ~ sb. sth.** 原谅某人某事; **to ~ sb. for doing ...** 原谅某人做…; **such a crime cannot be forgiven** 这种罪行不能饶恕; **to ~ and forget** 不念旧恶 **2** formal (excuse) 请原谅; **~ my curiosity, but ...** 请原谅我的好奇, 不过…

B *v refl* **to ~ oneself** 原谅自己; **to ~ oneself for doing/saying sth.** 原谅自己做了某事/说了某些话; **I'll never ~ myself for blaming her** 我责怪了她, 我决不能原谅自己

forgiveness /fəˈgɪvnɪs/ *n* [u] 原谅; **to ask/seek/beg (sb.'s) ~ (for sth.)** (为某事) 请求/寻求/乞求 (某人) 原谅; **to pray for (God's) ~** 祈求 (上帝的) 宽恕

forgiving /fəˈgɪvɪŋ/ *adj* 宽容的 ‹*nature, person*›

forgo /fɔːˈgəʊ/ *vt* (*pt* **forwent**, *pp* **forgone**) 放弃; **to ~ sth.** 放弃某物; **to ~ the chance** *or* **opportunity to do** *or* **of doing sth.** 放弃做某事的机会

forgot /fəˈgɒt/ *pt* ▸**forget**

forgotten /fəˈgɒtn/ *pp* ▸**forget**

fork /fɔːk/

A *n* **1** (for eating) 餐叉 **2** (for digging) 叉 **3** (division) (in railway, road) 岔口; (on bicycle) 车叉; (in tree) 杈

B *vt* 用叉叉 ‹*earth, manure, hay*›

C *vi* «*traveller*» 走岔路中的一条; «*road*» 分岔

Phrasal verbs

- **fork off** *vi* «*driver*» 走岔道; «*road*» 分岔
- **fork out** colloq

A *vi* [尤指不情愿地] 掏钱出来; **to ~ out for sth.** (不情愿地) 为某事物花费

B *vt* [~ **out sth.**] [尤指不情愿地] 花费

- **fork over** *vt* [~ **sth. over,** ~ **over sth.**] 用叉翻 ‹*soil, hay, manure, garden*›
- **fork up** *vi, vt* colloq = **fork out**

forked /fɔːkt/ *adj* 分叉的 ‹*branch, tongue*›; **to speak with a ~ tongue** fig 说谎话

forked lightning *n* [u] 叉状闪电

forkful /ˈfɔːkfʊl/ *n* 一叉; **a ~ of rice** 一叉米饭

fork: ~lift truck, ~lift *ns* Brit 叉车; **~ supper** *n* [用叉站着吃小份食物的] 轻自助餐

forlorn /fəˈlɔːn/ *adj* **1** (sad) 孤苦伶仃的 ‹*person, animal*›; **so what are you doing standing there all ~?** 你愁眉苦脸站在那儿做什么? **2** (cheerless) 荒凉的 ‹*place, landscape*› **3** (hopeless) 渺茫的 ‹*hope, attempt*›

forlornly /fəˈlɔːnli/ *adv* **1** (sadly) 可怜巴巴地 ‹*stand, weep*› **2** (cheerlessly) 凄凉地 ‹*appear, stand*› **3** (hopelessly) 渺茫地 ‹*hope, attempt*›

form /fɔːm/

A *n* **1** [u and c] (shape) (of object) 形状; (of person) 体型; **to take** *or* **assume the ~ of sth.** 呈现出某物的形状 **2** [c] (manifestation, substance) 形式; **in the ~ of sth.** 以某种形式; **to take the ~ of sth.** 以某种形式出现; **not in any shape or ~** 不论任何形式 **3** [c] (type, kind) 类型; **~ of sth.** 某物的种类; **what ~ of government do you think will ultimately emerge?** 你认为最终会出现何种政体? **4** [c] (document) 表格; **an application/tax ~** 申请表/税表; **a blank ~** 空白表格; **to fill in** *or* **fill out** *or* **complete a ~** 填写表格 **5** [u] (physical or mental condition) 状态; **in good/top ~** 竞技状态良好/极佳; **to be on/off ~** 状态良好/不佳; **to run** *or* **be true to ~** 一如既往; **on present ~** 从目前状况看; **he has shown an improvement in ~ recently** 最近他的状态有所改善 **6** [u and c] (of painting, building, music, literary work) 表现形式; **a sense of ~** 形式感; **the ~ and content of a novel** 小说的形式与内容; **the historical novel is a dying literary ~** 历史小说是一种濒临消失的文学样式 **7** [u] (etiquette) 礼貌; (behaviour) 习俗; **purely as a matter of ~** 纯粹依照惯例; **bad/good ~** 礼貌/不礼貌 **8** [c] Brit Sch dated 年级; **a third-~ pupil** 三年级学生; **to move** *or* **go up into the next ~** 升至下一年级; **F~ One/Two** 一/二年级; **~ captain/room/tutor** 级长/教室/年级导师 **9** [u and c] (prescribed set of words) 公式化语句; **in due ~** 以适当的惯用语言 **10** [c] Brit (bench) 无背长板凳 **11** [c] Brit (of hare) 窝 **12** [u] Brit sl (criminal record) 犯罪记录; **to have ~ (for sth.)** 有 (某罪行的) 案底 **13** [u and c] Ling 形式; **an adjectival/**

feminine/plural/negative ～ 形容词/阴性/复数/否定形式

B *vt* 1 (create) 制作 ‹*object, artefact*›; 建立 ‹*friendship, relationship*›; **to ～ one's letters** 组合字母; **he rolled up the paper to ～ a ball** 他将纸团成一个球; **how are stalactites ～ed?** 钟乳石是如何形成的？; **please ～ sentences using these words** 请用这些词造句; **to ～ sth. out of sth.** 用某物制成某物; **to ～ sth. from sth.** 由某物构成某物; **how do you ～ the future tense?** 怎样构成将来时态？; **she doesn't ～ her words properly** 她说话音不准; **to ～ the habit of doing sth.** 养成做某事的习惯 2 (make develop) «*water, rain*» 形成 ‹*puddle*›; «*people*» 排列成 ‹*queue, pattern*›; 编成 ‹*group*›; **to ～ words into a sentence** 将这些单词组成一个句子; **the general ～ed the troops into brigades** 将军把部队编成旅; **to ～ objects into patterns** 把物体摆成图案; **the workers ～ed themselves into unions** 工人们成立了工会 3 (conceive) 产生 ‹*impression, opinion*›; 构想出 ‹*plan, idea*›; **to ～ an image (of sb.)** 构想出（某人的）形象 4 (mould) 塑造 ‹*personality, taste, attitudes*›; **influential in ～ing public opinion** 对民意的形成颇具影响力的 5 (establish) 建立 ‹*society, party, government*› 6 (constitute) 构成 ‹*basis*›; **the trees ～ a windbreak** 树木构成一道防风墙; **young people ～ed the bulk of the protesters** 年轻人占抗议者的大多数; **to ～ (a) part of sth.** 构成某物的一部分; **to be ～ed from sth.** 由某物构成

C *vi* «*puddle, fog, cloud, idea*» 形成; **a scab had ～ed on his arm** 他的手臂上结了痂; **how do stalactites ～?** 钟乳石是怎样形成的？

Phrasal verb

• **form up**

A *vi* «*troops, procession, band*» 列队

B *vt* [～ **sth. up,** ～ **up sth.**] «*commander*» 使…列队 ‹*troops*›

formal /ˈfɔːml/ *adj* 1 (official) 正式的 ‹*occasion, investigation, invitation, request*› 2 (not casual) 拘谨的 ‹*person, manner*›; 整齐的 ‹*layout*› 3 (perfunctory) 敷衍的 ‹*greeting*›; 表面上的 ‹*resemblance*› 4 (structured) 有条理的 ‹*argument, logic*› 5 (officially sanctioned) 正规的 ‹*education, qualifications, training*› 6 (elevated) 高尚的 ‹*language, style, expression*› 7 Philos 形式的 ‹*argument, logic*›; 正式的 ‹*proof, demonstration*›

formaldehyde /fɔːˈmældɪhaɪd/ *n* [u] 甲醛

formal: ～ dress *n* 1 (at social event) 礼服; 2 Mil 制服; **～ garden** *n* 规整式花园

formalin /ˈfɔːməlɪn/ *n* [u] 福尔马林

formalism /ˈfɔːməlɪzəm/ *n* [u] 形式主义

formalist /ˈfɔːməlɪst/

A *n* 形式主义者

B *adj* 形式主义的

formality /fɔːˈmæləti/ *n* 1 [u] (of occasion, language) 正式; **with a minimum of ～** 尽量不拘谨; **the children were overawed by the ～ of the occasion** 这种庄重严肃的场面使孩子们感到惶恐 2 **formalities** *pl* (legal convention) 正式手续; (social convention) 俗套; **to dispense with** *or* **skip the formalities** 免去繁文缛节; **to observe the formalities** 遵守俗套; **legal formalities** 法律手续

formalize /ˈfɔːməlaɪz/ *vt* 1 (make official) 正式确定 ‹*arrangements, relationship, agreement*› 2 (give structure, shape to) 使定形

formally /ˈfɔːməli/ *adv* 1 (officially) 正式地 ‹*investigate, request, approved*› 2 (ceremoniously) 礼节性地 ‹*dine, address*›; **a duke should be ～ addressed as 'Your Grace'** 公爵应该被尊称为“阁下” 3 (in a structured way) 有条理地 ‹*argue*› 4 (in an elevated way) 高尚地 ‹*speak*›

format /ˈfɔːmæt/

A *n* 1 (layout) 样式 2 (size, style) 版式 3 TV, Radio 制式; **the standard VHS ～** 标准的 VHS 制式 4 Comput 格式; **standard display ～** 标准的显示格式

B *vt* (*pres p etc.* **-tt-**) Comput 为…编排格式 ‹*document, page*›; 格式化 ‹*disk*›

formation /fɔːˈmeɪʃn/ *n* 1 [u] (creation) 形成; **the ～ of the Arts Committee** 艺术委员会的组建; **the ～ of a child's character** 儿童性格的养成 2 [c] (shape, arrangement) 排列; **to fly in ～** 编队飞行; **a cloud ～** 云层结构

formation flying *n* [u] 编队飞行

formative /ˈfɔːmətɪv/ *adj* 1 (relating to development) 形成的 ‹*stage, experience*›; **the vital ～ years of a child's character** 儿童性格养成的关键时期; **Wagner had a ～ influence on Mahler's work** 瓦格纳对马勒的创作风格有重大影响 2 Ling 构词的 ‹*prefix, element*›

former /ˈfɔːmə(r)/

A *adj* 1 (earlier, previous) 以前的 ‹*glory, condition*›; **in ～ times** 在从前; **of ～ days** *or* **times** 从前的; **I'm sure I was a cat in a ～ life!** 我确信我前生是只猫！; **he's a shadow of his ～ self** 他衰弱得不成样子了 2 (no longer) 前任的 ‹*mayor*›; 一度的 ‹*palace, prison*›; **two ～ presidents** 两位前总统; **her ～ husband** 她的前夫 3 (first of two) 前者的 ‹*thing, method*›

B *n* 1 [u] (the first of two) 前者; **the ～ is simple, the latter is complex** 前者简单，后者复杂 2 [c] (for shaping) 模具

formerly /ˈfɔːməli/ *adv* 以前

Formica® /fɔːˈmaɪkə/ *n* [u] 福米加塑料贴面

formic acid /ˈfɔːmɪk/ *n* [u] 甲酸

formidable /ˈfɔːmɪdəbl, fɔːˈmɪd-/ *adj* 难克服的 ‹*obstacle*›; 难对付的 ‹*opponent, challenger*›; 令人钦佩的 ‹*intellect, qualifications*›

formless /ˈfɔːmlɪs/ *adj* 1 (lacking shape, form) 无定形的 ‹*figure, mass, garment*› 2 (vague) 杂乱的 ‹*piece of music, literary work*›; 模糊的 ‹*idea*›

form: ～ master *n* Brit dated 年级教师; **～ of address** *n* 称谓

Formosa /fɔːˈməʊsə/ *pr n* Hist 福摩萨［中国台湾岛的旧称］

formula /ˈfɔːmjʊlə/ *n* 1 (*pl* **～s**) (form of words) 惯用语句; **a legal ～** 法律惯用语 2 (*pl* **～s**) (method, pattern) 方案; **a ～ for sth.** 某事的方案 3 (*pl* **formulae**) Chem 分子式 4 (*pl* **formulae**) Math, Phys 公式 5 (*pl* **～s**) esp Amer (prescription) 配方; (substance) 配制物; **to make up a ～** 开处方 6 (*pl* **～s**) esp Amer (medicine) 处方药; (food) 配制食品; **baby ～** 婴儿配制食品

Formula One ▸p. 307 *n* 一级方程式赛车; **～ car/Grand Prix** 一级方程式赛车/国际汽车大奖赛

formulate /ˈfɔːmjʊleɪt/ *vt* 1 (devise) 构想 ‹*response, plan*›; 制订 ‹*policy, strategy*›; 创立 ‹*theory*› 2 (express concisely) 确切地表达 ‹*thoughts, treaty*›; **to ～ sth. in words** 用语言确切地表达某事

formulation /ˌfɔːmjʊˈleɪʃn/ *n* 1 [u] (of idea, reply) 构想; (of principle, strategy) 制订 2 [c] (particular expression) 确切的表达

fornicate /ˈfɔːnɪkeɪt/ *vi* formal *or* hum 通奸

fornication /ˌfɔːnɪˈkeɪʃn/ *n* [u] formal *or* hum 通奸; **to commit ～** 私通

forsake /fəˈseɪk/ *vt* (*pt* **forsook,** *pp* **forsaken**) formal «*God, person*» 抛弃 ‹*person, animal, home*›; 摒弃 ‹*habit*›

forsaken /fəˈseɪkən/

A *pp* ▸**forsake**

B *adj* 被抛弃的; **I felt utterly alone and ～** 我感到孤苦伶仃，为世人所弃

forsook /fəˈsʊk/ *pt* ▸**forsake**

forswear /fɔːˈsweə(r)/ *vt* (*pt* **forswore** /ˈfɔːˈswɔː(r)/; *pp* **forsworn** /ˈfɔːˈswɔːn/) formal 1 (renounce, reject) 发誓抛弃 ‹*person's company*›; 发誓放弃 ‹*ambition, wealth*›; 发誓戒除 ‹*gambling, drinking*› 2 Jur (deny) 发誓否认 ‹*knowledge, blame*›; 背弃 ‹*allegiance*›

forsythia /fɔːˈsaɪθɪə, Amer fərˈsɪθɪə/ *n* 连翘

fort /fɔːt/ *n* (enclosure or building) 堡垒; (strategic position) 要塞; **to hold the ～** fig 代他人尽责

forte /ˈfɔːteɪ, Amer fɔːrt/

A *n* 1 (strong point) 特长 2 Mus (passage played loudly) 用强音演奏的乐曲; (marked to be played loudly) 强音记号

B *adj* 强音的 ‹*marking, passage, playing*›

C *adv* 用强音 ‹*play*›

forth /fɔːθ/ *adv* liter 1 (onwards in time) 以后; **from this/that day ～** 从今天/那天起 2 *after v* (away from a place, out) 向外; **huge chimneys belched ～ smoke** 巨大的烟囱往外喷烟; **go ～ and preach the Word** 出去传道

forthcoming /fɔːθˈkʌmɪŋ/ *adj* 1 (happening soon) 即将到来的 ‹*event, elections, visit*›; **～ publications** 即将出版的书 2 *pred* (available) 可得到的; **no information was ～ from the government** 从政府那里得不到任何信息 3 *pred* (communicative) 乐于助人的; **to be ～ about sth.** 乐于提供某方面的消息; **his manner was not at all ～** 他的态度一点都不友善

forthright /ˈfɔːθraɪt/ *adj* 直率的 ‹*person, manner, answer*›; **in ～ terms** 以直截了当的语言

forthwith /fɔːθˈwɪθ, Amer -ˈwɪð/ *adv* formal 立即; **to become effective ～** 即刻生效

fortieth /ˈfɔːtɪɪθ/ ▸p. 521

A *n* 1 (in sequence) 第四十个 2 (fraction) 四十分之一

B *adj* 1 (in sequence) 第四十的; **on the ～ floor** 在 41 楼 2 (as fraction) 四十分之一的

C *adv* 居第四十位

fortification /ˌfɔːtɪfɪˈkeɪʃn/ *n* 1 [u] (fortifying) 设防 2 [c] (*usu* **fortifications** *pl*) (wall, ditch) 防御工事

fortify /ˈfɔːtɪfaɪ/

A *vt* 1 (strengthen) 加固 ‹*building, position*›; **to ～ sb./sth. against sb./sth.** 加强某人/加固某物以抵御某人/某物; **the militia fortified the town against enemy attack** 民兵在该镇设防，抵御敌人的进攻; **to ～ sb.** 使某人振奋起来 2 (add to food, wine) 提高…的酒精含量 ‹*wine*›; 给…添加营养成分 ‹*food, milk, diet*›; **fortified with vitamins** 添加维生素的

B *v refl* 增强; **to ～ oneself against sth.** 增强自己反对某事的信念; **to ～ oneself with sth.** 用某物使自己振作; **he fortified himself with half a bottle of whiskey** 他喝了半瓶威士忌来壮胆; **why don't you have a nice cup of tea to ～ yourself?** 你为什么不喝杯好茶提提神呢？

fortissimo /fɔːˈtɪsɪməʊ/

A *adj* 极强的

B *adv* 极强地

C *n* (*pl* **～s** *or* **fortissimi** /fɔːˈtɪsɪmi/) 用极强音演奏的片段

fortitude /ˈfɔːtɪtjuːd, Amer -tuːd/ *n* 坚韧; **to show (great) ～** 表现出（极大的）坚忍

Fort Knox /ˌfɔːtˈnɒks/ *pr n* 诺克斯堡［美国黄金储备的贮存处，位于肯塔基州北部］; **as secure as ～** 固若金汤

fortnight /ˈfɔːtnaɪt/ *n* Brit 两星期; **a today/tomorrow ～** 两星期后的今天/明天

fortnightly /ˈfɔːtnaɪtli/ Brit

A *adj* 每两星期一次的 ‹*publication, cycle*›

B *adv* 每两星期一次 ‹*meet, deliver*›

fortress /ˈfɔːtrɪs/ *n* 1 (stronghold) 要塞 2 fig (strong person) 不受外界影响的人; (strong thing) 不受外界影响的事物

fortuitous /fɔːˈtjuːɪtəs, Amer -ˈtuː-/ *adj* 偶然的 ‹*event, remark*›

fortuitously /fɔːˈtjuːɪtəsli, Amer -ˈtuː-/ *adv* 偶然地 ‹*happen, comment*›

fortunate /ˈfɔːtʃənət/ *adj* 1 (lucky) 幸运的; **I shall certainly ask her if I'm ～ enough to meet her** 如果有幸见到她，我一定会

问她的；**we were ～ in having glorious weather on holiday** 很幸运，我们度假时天气好极了；**he is ～ in that he doesn't have to work** 他不用工作，真有福气；**to count/consider oneself ～** 认为自己很幸运 2 (auspicious, favourable) 吉利的 ⟨*circumstance, action, event*⟩; **how ～!** 多好的运气啊！；**what a ～ coincidence!** 多么幸运的巧合！；**it was ～ for her that nobody noticed her absence** 算她运气好，没人注意到她的缺席

fortunately /ˈfɔːtʃənətli/ *adv* 幸运地；**she made two mistakes but ～ the examiner didn't notice** 她犯了两个错误，幸好考官没发现

fortune /ˈfɔːtʃuːn/ *n* 1 [u] (luck) 运气；**to have the good ～ to do ...** 有幸做…；**by good *or* great ～** 由于幸运；**a stroke of good ～** 好运；**ill ～** 厄运 2 [u] (chance) 命运；**to tell sb.'s ～** 给某人算命；**～ smiled on us** 我们交了好运；**～ favours the brave** 好运眷顾勇者；**to offer a hostage to ～** 以小损失碰运气 3 [c] (wealth) 大笔财产；**to spend/cost a ～** 花一大笔钱；**to seek fame and ～** 追求名利；**to go and seek one's ～** 去寻找发迹的机会；**to be worth a ～** 值一大笔钱；**to make a ～** 发财；**the family ～** 家产

fortune: ～ cookie *n* Amer 签饼 [中国餐馆的小脆饼，内有写着预言或格言的小纸条]；**～ hunter** *n* pej 猎财者 [专找富人结婚以求发财的人]；**～-teller** *n* 算命者；**～-telling** *n* [u] 算命

forty /ˈfɔːti/ ▸p. 15, p. 521

A *n* 1 (number, quantity) 四十；**there are ～ of us** 我们有 40 个人 2 (in age) 40 岁

B *adj* 1 (in number) 四十的；**～ boys** 40 个男孩 2 (in age) 40 岁的；**I'm nearly ～** 我快 40 岁了；**pushing ～** 年近四十的 3 (in series) 第四十的

forty-five /ˌfɔːtiˈfaɪv/ *n* 每分钟 45 转的密纹唱片

forum /ˈfɔːrəm/ *n* 1 (*pl* **fora** /ˈfɔːrə/) (Roman) 公共集会场所 2 (*pl* **～s**) (meeting on a specific topic) 专题讨论会；**to hold a ～** 举行专题讨论会；**in an open ～** 在公开的讨论会上 3 (*pl* **～s**) (medium for discussion) 论坛；**to be a ～ for sth.** 是讨论某事的论坛；**in open ～** 在公开论坛上

forward /ˈfɔːwəd/

A *adv* 1 (ahead in space) 向前 ⟨*rush, go*⟩; **to move sth. ～** 把某物向前移；**to be too far ～** 太往前了；**to reach/lean ～** 伸手/倾身向前；**we'd prefer seats facing ～** 我们想要面朝前的座位；**'～ march!'** Mil "开步走！"；▸**foot A1** 2 (from beginning to end) [从头至尾]；**to wind sth. ～** 向前卷绕 ⟨*cassette, tape, video*⟩; **a palindrome is a word that is spelled the same backward as it is ～** 回文指的是顺读倒读都拼写都相同的词 3 (ahead, in progress) 进展；**to go ～ with sth.** 启动某事；**a step ～ in her career** 她的事业向前迈进的一步；**there is no other way ～** 没有其他前进的道路 4 (towards the future) 向将来；(onwards in time) 往后；**to travel ～ in time** 向未来做时间旅行；**he doesn't tend to look very far ～** 他不会考虑得很长远；**from this/that day ～** 从今天/那天以后

B *adj* 1 (bold) 冒失的 ⟨*child, behaviour*⟩; **I hope you don't think I'm being too ～** 我希望你不要认为我过于冒昧 2 (towards the front) 向前的；**a ～ movement** 向前的移动；**the ～ gears** 前进挡；**～ troops** 先头部队 3 *pred* (advanced) 有进展的；**they're not very far ～ with the project** 这一项目他们未取得太大的进展 4 *attrib* formal (located at front) 前部的；**the ～ cabins** 前舱；**the plane's ～ door** 飞机的前舱门；**the ～ part of the train/procession** 火车的前部/队伍的前列 5 *attrib* Sport (attacking) 打前锋的；**～ players** 前锋球员；**the team's ～ line** 球队的前锋线 6 (ahead of time) 早的 ⟨*season*⟩; 早熟的 ⟨*plant*⟩; **he is very ～ in his reading** 他在阅读方面很早熟 7 *attrib* (relating to future) 未来的；**the ～ movement of history** 历史的未来发展 8 *attrib* Fin 预约的 ⟨*buying, delivery*⟩; 期货的 ⟨*market, price*⟩; 远期的 ⟨*rate*⟩

C *n* 前锋；**a rugby ～** 英式橄榄球前锋

D *vt* 1 (send on) 转递 ⟨*letter*⟩; **to ～ sth. to sb./sth.** 把某物转递给某人/到某处；**'please ～'** Post "请转递" 2 Comm formal (dispatch) «*person, firm*» 发送 ⟨*goods, information*⟩; **to ～ sth. to sb., to ～ sb. sth.** 把某物发送给某人；**I ～ed my CV to the company** 我把简历发给这家公司了；**to ～ a request/complaint** 提出要求/投诉 3 formal (further) 促进；**to ～ one's career** 发展事业

forwarding: ～ address *n* 转寄地址；**～ agent** *n* 货运代理商；**～ charges** *npl* 转运费用；**～ country** *n* 发送国；**～ instructions** *npl* 货物发送细则

forward: ～-looking *adj* 有远见的；**～ pass** *n* 前进传球 [指橄榄球中的犯规动作]；**～ planning** *n* [u] 预先规划；**～ roll** *n* 前滚翻

forwards /ˈfɔːwədz/ *adv* = **forward A**

forward slash *n* 正斜杠

fossil /ˈfɒsl/ *n* 1 Geol 化石 2 colloq hum (person) 老顽固

fossil fuel *n* 矿物燃料

fossilized /ˈfɒsəlaɪzd/ *adj* 1 Geol 变成化石的 ⟨*bones*⟩; **the ～ remains of a dinosaur** 一具恐龙化石 2 (incapable of change) 僵化的 ⟨*idea, person, constitution*⟩

foster /ˈfɒstə(r)/ *vt* 1 (encourage) 培养 ⟨*attitude, friendship*⟩; 树立 ⟨*conception, image*⟩; 促进 ⟨*activity, development*⟩; **we must ～ (the) demand for skilled employment** 我们必须促进对熟练工人的需求 2 (cherish) 抱有 ⟨*hope, plan, idea*⟩ 3 (act as parent to) 养育；**after ～ing the child for seven years they finally adopted her** 在照顾这个孩子 7 年之后，他们终于领养了她 4 Brit (place in care of) 寄养；**to ～ a child with sb.** 在某人处寄养孩子

foster: ～-brother *n* 义兄弟；**～ care** *n* [u] [儿童的] 寄养照顾；**to be (placed) in ～ care** 被寄养；**～-child** *n* 养子女；**～ family** *n* 寄养家庭；**～-father** *n* 养父；**～ home** *n* 寄养家庭；**～-mother** *n* 养母；**～-sister** *n* 义姊妹

fostering /ˈfɒstərɪŋ/ *n* [u] Brit 寄养

fought /fɔːt/ *pt, pp* ▸**fight B, C**

foul /faʊl/

A *adj* 1 (dirty, disgusting) 污秽的 ⟨*place*⟩; 污浊的 ⟨*water, air*⟩; 难闻的 ⟨*smell*⟩; 发臭的 ⟨*food*⟩; **I have an absolutely ～ taste in my mouth** 我嘴里有一股很恶心的味道；**my son says school meals are absolutely ～** 我儿子说学校的饭菜难吃极了；**this medicine tastes ～!** 这药很难吃！ 2 colloq (unpleasant) 令人不快的 ⟨*temper, frame of mind, time*⟩; **in a ～ mood** 心情糟透的 3 Meteorol 恶劣的 ⟨*weather, atmosphere*⟩; **it was a ～ day** 那天风雨交加 4 liter (evil) 邪恶的 ⟨*treachery, villain*⟩; **the criminal tried to conceal his ～ crimes/deeds** 罪犯企图掩盖他邪恶的罪行/行径；**a ～ traitor** 无耻的叛徒 5 (obscene) 下流的 ⟨*language, mind*⟩; **to have a ～ mouth *or* tongue** 嘴不干净 6 Sport 犯规的 ⟨*blow*⟩; **that was a ～ hit!** 那是犯规的一击！；**by fair means or ～** 不择手段

B *adv* 犯规地 ⟨*fight*⟩; **if you play ～, I'll never forgive you!** 如果你使坏，我决不原谅你！；**to fall *or* run ～ of sth./sb.** 与某事/某人发生冲突；**to fall ～ of the law** 触犯法律

C *n* 犯规；**to commit a ～** 犯规；**to be sent off for a ～** 因为犯规被罚下场

D *vt* 1 (pollute) 污染 ⟨*air, environment, water*⟩; 弄脏 ⟨*play area, path*⟩; **dogs must not ～ the pavement** 禁止狗在人行道上便溺；**it's an ill bird that ～s its own nest** Prov 恶鸟不渎巢；**to ～ one's own nest** fig 辱没家门 2 (become tangled with) «*rope, fishing net, seaweed*» 缠住 ⟨*anchor, engine*⟩; **to be ～ed on sth.** 被缠在某物上 3 (clog) «*dust, waste*» 使…壅塞 ⟨*device, chimney, pipe*⟩ 4 liter (dishonour) «*person, incident, action*» 玷污 ⟨*good name, reputation*⟩ 5 Sport 对…犯规 ⟨*opponent*⟩ 6 Naut «*vessel*» 碰撞 ⟨*vessel, bridge, rocks*⟩

Phrasal verb

• **foul up**

A *vt* [**～ sth. up, ～ up sth.**]

1 colloq (bungle) «*person, action, attitude*» 把…搞糟 ⟨*relationship, plan, prospect, system*⟩; **you've completely ～ed things up!** 你把事情彻底搞砸了！ 2 (block, entangle) «*rubbish, soot*» 使…壅塞 ⟨*chimney, pipe*⟩; «*weed*» 缠住 ⟨*engine, propeller*⟩

B *vi* colloq «*person, organization*» 搞砸

foul: ～ ball *n* Amer 界外球；**～ line** *n* Amer 边线；**～-mouthed** /faʊlˈmaʊðd/ *adj* 说话下流的 ⟨*person*⟩; 下流的 ⟨*language*⟩; **～ play** *n* [u] 1 (malicious actions) 暴行；**she suspected ～ play** 她怀疑是谋杀；2 Sport 犯规动作；**several instances of ～ play** 好几起犯规；**～-smelling** *adj* 难闻的 ⟨*chemicals, fumes, place*⟩; **～-tasting** *adj* 味道恶心的 ⟨*medicine, food*⟩; **～-up** *n* colloq [愚蠢错误引起的] 混乱；**a computer system ～-up** 计算机系统故障

found¹ /faʊnd/ *pt, pp* ▸**find A, B, C**

found² *vt* 1 (establish) 创建 ⟨*institution, business enterprise, political party*⟩; 兴建 ⟨*town*⟩ 2 (base) 把…基于 ⟨*philosophy, regime*⟩; **to be ～ed on sth.** 以某物为基础；**to be ～ed on fact** 以事实为根据；**I have ～ed my novel on my personal experience** 我的小说取材于我的个人经历 3 Tech 铸造 ⟨*metal*⟩; 熔制 ⟨*glass*⟩

foundation /faʊnˈdeɪʃn/ *n* 1 [u] (setting up) 创建 2 [c] lit (base) 地基；**to rest on firm ～s** 地基牢固；**to stand on a ～ of sth.** 建在某物做的地基上；**the building stands on a ～ of solid rock** 房屋建在坚实的岩石上；**to undermine the ～s** 破坏地基；**to lay the ～s for a building** 为建筑物打下地基 3 [c] fig (basis) 基础；**to lay the ～s for sth.** 为某事打下基础；**to rock *or* shake sth. to its ～s** 从根本上动摇某物；**the stock exchange crash rocked the company to its ～s** 股市暴跌使该公司元气大伤 4 [c] fig (truth) 根据；**to be/have a ～ for doing sth.** 是做某事的根据/做某事是有根据的；**without ～** 没有根据 5 [c] (*also* **Foundation**) (institution) 基金会 6 [u] fig (make-up base) 粉底霜

foundation: ～ course *n* Brit 基础课程；**～ stone** *n* 奠基石

founder /ˈfaʊndə(r)/

A *n* 创建者

B *vi* 1 (of a ship) 沉没；**the fishing vessel ～ed on the rocks** 渔船触礁沉没 2 (fail) «*plans, projects*» 失败；«*hopes*» 破灭；**to ～ on sth.** 在某事上失败；**the talks ～ed on the issue of reform** 会谈在改革这一问题上失败了

founder: ～ member *n* Brit 创建者之一；**F～'s Day** *n* Amer 创建者纪念日；**～s' shares** *npl* Brit 发起人股票

foundry /ˈfaʊndri/ *n* (workshop) 铸造车间；(factory) 铸造厂；**iron ～** 铸铁厂；**glass ～** 玻璃厂

foundry worker ▸p. 409 *n* 铸造厂工人

fount¹ /faʊnt/ *n* 1 (source) 源；**the ～ of all knowledge** 一切知识的源泉 2 liter (spring, fountain) 泉

fount² *n* Brit Print = **font**

fountain /ˈfaʊntɪn, Amer -tn/ *n* 1 (structure) 喷水池；**the ～s in Trafalgar Square** 特拉法尔加广场的喷水池 2 (jet) 喷泉；**the fireworks made ～s of coloured light in the sky** 烟花在空中绽放出多彩的光焰

fountain pen *n* 钢笔

four /fɔː(r)/ ▸p. 15, p. 521, p. 831

A *n* 1 (number, quantity) 四；**～ plus two equals six** 4 加 2 等于 6；**three ～s are twelve**

三四一十二; **in December nineteen hundred and ~** 在1904年12月; **we live at (number) ~, Victoria Road** 我们住在维多利亚路4号; **her phone number is two six double ~** 她的电话号码是2644; **there are ~ of them** 他们有4个人; **in ~s** 四个一组地; **~ out of ten applicants are rejected** 每10个申请者中有4人被拒绝; **you have ~ out of ten chances of succeeding** 你有四成的把握成功 **2** (symbol, digit) [4、IV、iv等表示四的符号]; **double ~** 两个4 **3** (in time) 4点钟; **at ~ (o'clock)** 在4点 **4** (on playing card) 4点; **the ~ of spades/diamonds** 黑桃/方块4 **5** (on dice, dartboard) 4点; **to throw a ~** 掷出一个4点 **6** (team) 四人的一组; **to make up a ~** 组成四人组 **7** (age) 4岁

B *adj* **1** (as quantity) 四的; **~ cats** 4只猫; **~ books** 4本书; **~ weeks** 4周; **~ times** 4次; **~ years** 4年; **~ people** 4个人; **to be ~ centimetres high/wide/long** 有4厘米高/宽/长; **to be in ~ figures** 有4位数; **to the ~ corners of the earth** 到天涯海角; **to proclaim one's opinions to the ~ winds** 把自己的意见公之于众; **the house was situated on high ground, open to the ~ winds** 房子位于高处，四面受风; **on all ~s** (on hands and knees) 趴着; (on all four feet) 四脚着地 **2** (in age) 4岁的; **he's nearly ~** 他快4岁了; **our house is only ~ years old** 我们的房子才造了4年; **to be ~ (years old)** 有4岁大 **3** (in series) 第四的; **number/volume ~** 4号/卷; **page ~** 第4页

four: ~-ball *n* 四人团体赛 [四人分为两组，每人一球，每组取最高得分]; **~-by-~** *n* 四轮驱动车; **~-dimensional** *adj* 四维的 ‹*space, space-time, world*›

four-door
A *adj* 四门的
B *n* 四门汽车

four: ~-engined *adj* 四个发动机的 ‹*aircraft, jet*›; **~-eyes** *n* colloq 四眼 [近视眼的绰号]

fourfold /ˈfɔːfəʊld/
A *adj* 四倍的 ‹*increase, decrease*›
B *adv* 四倍地 ‹*increase, decrease*›

four-four time *n* 4/4拍; **in ~** 以4/4拍

four: ~-handed *adj* **1** Mus 四手联奏的; **2** (card games) 四人参加的; **~-leaf clover, ~-leaved clover** *ns* 四叶苜蓿草 [一般为三叶，故被认为会带来好运]; **~-legged friend** *n* hum 四条腿的朋友 [指狗、猫、马等四足动物]; **~-letter word** *n* 粗俗下流词; **~-piece** *adj* 四人组成的 ‹*band*›; 四件套的 ‹*outfit*›; **~-ply** *adj* (four strands) 四股的 ‹*cashmere*›; (four layers) 四层的 ‹*bitumen*›; **~-poster, ~-poster bed** *ns* 有四根帷柱的床; **~-seater** *n* colloq Aut 四座汽车; (aeroplane) 四座飞机; (sofa) 四人沙发; **a ~-seater car** 四座汽车

foursome /ˈfɔːsəm/ *n* 四人一组; **to make (up) a ~** 组成四人小组

four-square
A *adj* **1** (square shape) 方形的 ‹*building, structure*›; (solid shape) 稳固的 **2** (firm, resolute) 坚定的 ‹*attitude, approach*›
B *adv* **1** (squarely) 端正地 ‹*stand, be set*›; (solidly) 稳固地 ‹*stand*›; **the tower stands ~ on the top of the hill** 那座塔屹立在山顶 **2** (firmly, resolutely) 坚定地

four-star
A *n* Brit **~ (petrol)** 四星汽油
B *adj* **1** Tourism (ranking) 四星级的 ‹*hotel, restaurant, rating*› **2** Amer Mil 四星军衔的; **a ~ general** 四星上将

four-stroke *adj* 四冲程的 ‹*engine*›

fourteen /ˌfɔːˈtiːn/ ▸**p. 15, p. 521**
A *n* **1** (number, quantity) 十四; **~ out of twenty** 20个中的14个 **2** (in age) 14岁; **a boy/girl of ~** 14岁的男孩/女孩
B *adj* **1** (in number) 十四的; **~ metres** 14米; **~ paintings** 14张画; **the garden is about ~ metres long** 花园长约14米 **2** (in age) 14岁的; **to be ~ (years old)** 14岁大; **to be over/under ~** 超过/不到14岁; **he's ~** 他14岁 **3** (in series) 第十四的; **page/chapter/volume ~** 第14页/章/卷; **size/number ~** 14码/号

fourteenth /ˌfɔːˈtiːnθ/ ▸**p. 181, p. 521**
A *n* **1** (in sequence) 第十四个 **2** (in date) 14日; **the ~ of July** 7月14日 **3** (fraction) 十四分之一
B *adj* **1** (in sequence) 第十四的; **to be ~ in sth.** 在某物中排第14; **for the ~ time** 第14次; **on the ~ floor** 在15楼 **2** (in name, title) 十四; **Louis the F~** 路易十四 **3** (as fraction) 十四分之一的
C *adv* **1** (fourteenthly) 第十四 **2** (in fourteenth position) 居第十四位

fourth /fɔːθ/ ▸**p. 181, p. 521**
A *n* **1** (in sequence) 第四 **2** (in date) 4日 **3** (fraction) 四分之一
B *adj* **1** (in sequence) 第四的; **It's her ~ birthday** 这是她4岁生日; **on the ~ floor** 在5楼; **for the ~ time** 第4次; **the ~ page** 第4页 **2** (in name, title) 四世; **Henry the F~ of England** 英王亨利四世 **3** (as fraction) 四分之一的
C *adv* **1** (fourthly) 第四; **to come** *or* **finish ~** 获得第四名 **2** (in fourth position) 居第四位

fourth: ~ dimension *n* [u] **1** (spatial dimension) 第四维; **2** (time) 时间; **~ estate** *n* [u] 第四等级 [指新闻业]

fourthly /ˈfɔːθli/ *adv* 第四

fourth-rate *adj* pej 蹩脚的 ‹*job, hotel, film*›

four-wheel drive *n* **1** [u] (system) 四轮驱动 **2** [c] (vehicle) 四轮驱动汽车

fowl /faʊl/ *n* **1** [c] (*pl* **~** *or* **~s**) (domestic) 家禽 **2** [u] (birds) 鸟; **to be neither fish nor ~** 非驴非马; **the ~ of the air** Bible 飞禽

fox /fɒks/
A *n* **1** Zool 狐狸 **2** colloq (sly person) 狡猾的人
B *adj* 狐皮的 ‹*coat, collar, hat*›
C *vt* colloq «*person, problem, situation*» 使迷惑; **that's got me ~ed** 那把我搞糊涂了

fox: ~ cub *n* 狐狸幼崽; **~ fur** *n* 狐裘; **a ~ fur hat** 狐皮帽; **~glove** *n* 毛地黄; **~hole** *n* 散兵坑; **~hound** *n* 猎狐犬; **~ hunt** *n* **1** (chase) 猎狐; **2** (association) 猎狐协会; **~ hunting** *n* [u] 猎狐; **~ terrier** *n* 猎狐㹴; **~trot** *n* **1** (dance) 狐步舞; **2** (music) 狐步舞曲

foxy /ˈfɒksi/ *adj* **1** (like fox) 似狐的 ‹*person, appearance*› **2** (crafty) 狡猾的 **3** Amer colloq (sexy) 狐媚的

foyer /ˈfɔɪeɪ, Amer ˈfɔɪər/ *n* 门厅

FPA *abbr* Brit **= Family Planning Association**

fracas /ˈfrækɑː, Amer ˈfreɪkəs/ *n* (*pl* **~** /ˈfrækɑːz/ *or* Amer **~es** /ˈfreɪkəsɪz/) (quarrel) 吵闹; (disturbance) 骚乱; **there's a bit of a ~ in the bar** 酒吧里一阵骚乱

fractal /ˈfræktl/ *n* 分形

fraction /ˈfrækʃn/ ▸**p. 521** *n* **1** Math 分数; **to express as a ~** 用分数表示; **to resolve a ~** 解分数 **2** (tiny amount) 一小部分; **a ~ of sth.** 某物的一小部分; **to miss by a ~** 差点打中; **to move a ~** 稍微挪一下

fractional /ˈfrækʃənl/ *adj* **1** (small, tiny) 极小的 ‹*difference*›; **he responded with a ~ movement of the head** 他微微地点了一下头作为回答 **2** Chem 分级的 ‹*process*›; **~ distillation** 分馏; **~ crystallization** 分离结晶

fractionally /ˈfrækʃənəli/ *adv* 略微地 ‹*different, out of tune, better, worse*›

fractious /ˈfrækʃəs/ *adj* 易怒的 ‹*mood, old person, child*›

fracture /ˈfræktʃə(r)/
A *n* **1** [c] Med 骨折; **to set a ~** 正骨 **2** [c] (crack, break) 裂缝; **a ~ in a rock** 岩石上的裂缝 **3** [u] (cracking, breaking) 断裂
B *vt* 使…断裂 ‹*rock, pipe*›; 使…折断 ‹*bone, nose, ankle*›
C *vi* «*rock, pipe, support*» 断裂; «*bone*» 折断

fragile /ˈfrædʒaɪl, Amer -dʒl/ *adj* **1** (breakable) 易碎的 ‹*porcelain, structure*› **2** (delicate) 娇嫩的 ‹*complexion, flower*› **3** (weak, tenuous) 脆弱的 ‹*economy, link, happiness*›; 虚弱的 ‹*person, animal, plant*›; **a ~ excuse** 站不住脚的借口; **to look/feel ~** 看起来/感到很虚弱

fragility /frəˈdʒɪləti/ *n* [u] 脆弱

fragment
A /ˈfrægmənt/ *n* **1** (of rock, shell, glass) 碎片; **to break into ~s** 裂成碎片 **2** (incomplete part) 片段; **~s of conversation** 谈话的只言片语
B /frægˈment/ *vt* 使…分开 ‹*land*›; 拆分 ‹*work*›; 分散 ‹*efforts, attention*›
C /frægˈment/ *vi* «*glass, windscreen*» 破碎; «*group, political party*» 分裂

fragmentary /ˈfrægməntri, Amer -teri/ *adj* 残破的 ‹*picture, pieces*›; 不完整的 ‹*evidence, recollections*›

fragmentation /ˌfrægmənˈteɪʃn/ *n* [u] (of rock) 碎裂; (of bomb) 爆裂; fig (of organization) 分裂

fragmentation bomb *n* 碎裂弹

fragmented /ˈfrægmentɪd/ *adj* 不完整的 ‹*story, dialogue*›; 支离破碎的 ‹*plot*›; 零零散散的 ‹*population*›

fragrance /ˈfreɪgrəns/ *n* **1** [u and c] (smell) 香味 **2** [c] Cosmet (perfume) 香水

fragrant /ˈfreɪgrənt/ *adj* 香的 ‹*flowers, herbs*›; **~ memories** liter 甜美的回忆

frail /freɪl/ *adj* **1** (delicate) 虚弱的 ‹*person, health*› **2** (fragile) 脆弱的 ‹*structure*›; 微弱的 ‹*hope*›; **a ~ excuse** 站不住脚的借口; **~ happiness/peace** 暂时的快乐/和平 **3** (morally weak) 意志薄弱的 ‹*human nature, person*›; 不坚定的 ‹*resolve*›

frailty /ˈfreɪlti/ *n* **1** [u] (of person, health) 虚弱; (of structure) 脆弱 **2** [u and c] (of morals, character) 弱点; **human frailties** 人性的弱点

frame /freɪm/
A *n* **1** [c] (of building, boat, roof) 构架; (of car, bicycle) 车架; (of racket) 框架; (of bed) 床架 **2** [c] (enclosing structure) 边框; **spectacles ~** 眼镜框 **3** [u] fig (basic structure) 基础结构 **4** [c] (body) 身躯; **huge/athletic ~** 巨大的身躯/健壮的体型 **5** [c] (of film, video) 画面; **to freeze a ~** 定格一帧画面
B *vt* **1** (enclose) 给…加框 ‹*picture, scene*›; **blonde hair ~d her lovely features** 金发衬着她可爱的面容; **the house was ~d against the sunset** fig 房子映衬在落日的余晖中 **2** (articulate in words) 表述 ‹*proposal, law*› **3** (devise) 构想出 ‹*plan, idea*›; 制定 ‹*policy*› **4** colloq (for a crime) «*person, police*» 作伪证诬陷

frame house *n* 木板房

frameless /ˈfreɪmlɪs/ *adj* 无框的 ‹*mirror, spectacles*›

frame: ~ of mind *n* 心态; **to be in the right/wrong ~ of mind for sth.** 有/没有兴致做某事; **~ of reference** *n* 参照标准; **cultural ~s of reference** 文化参照系; **~ rucksack** *n* 铝架背包; **~ tent** *n* esp Brit 框架式帐篷; **~-up** *n* colloq 诬陷; **~work** *n* **1** lit (support) 构架; **2** fig (of society, agreement, theory) 体系; (of novel, play) 结构; **within the ~work of the constitution** 在宪法的框架内

franc /fræŋk/ ▸**p. 174** *n* 法郎

France /frɑːns/ *pr n* 法国

franchise /ˈfræntʃaɪz/
A *n* **1** [u] (right to vote) **the ~** 选举权; **universal ~** 普选权; **to extend the ~** 扩大选举权 **2** [c] Comm 特许经销权; **to grant a ~** 授予特许经销权; **to hold a ~ for sth.** 拥有某商品的特许经销权; **to withdraw a ~** 撤销特

许经销权 3 [c] (business, service) 特许经销企业; *modif* **a ~ operation** 特许经销企业
B *vt* 给予…特许经销权 ‹*individual, firm*›; 给予经营…的特许经销权 ‹*product, service*›; **a ~d dealer** 特许经销商; **all the catering was ~d** 所有的餐饮业都是特许经营的

franchisee /ˌfræntʃaɪˈziː/ *n* 特许经营者

franchiser, franchisor /ˈfræntʃaɪzə(r)/ *n* 授予特许权者

Franciscan /frænˈsɪskən/
A *n* (friar) 方济各会修士; (sister) 方济各会修女
B *adj* 方济各会的 ‹*monastery, monk, nun*›; **the ~ order** 方济各会

francium /ˈfrænsɪəm/ *n* [u] 钫

francophile /ˈfræŋkəfaɪl/
A *adj* 亲法(国)的 ‹*person, organization, publication*›
B *n* 亲法者

francophone /ˈfræŋkəfəʊn/
A *adj* 操法语的
B *n* 操法语者

frank /fræŋk/
A *adj* 1 (honest, direct) 坦率的 ‹*person, manner, discussion*›; **to be perfectly ~, ...** 非常坦白地说… 2 (open) 不加掩饰的 ‹*curiosity, animosity*›
B *vt* 在…上盖邮资已付邮戳 ‹*letter, parcel*›; **the letter was ~ed in London** 这封信是在伦敦盖上的邮戳
C *n* 邮资已付戳

frankfurter /ˈfræŋkfɜːtə(r)/ *n* 熏猪牛肉香肠

frankincense /ˈfræŋkɪnsens/ *n* [u] 乳香

franking machine *n* 邮资机

frankly /ˈfræŋkli/ *adv* 1 (directly) 坦率地 ‹*discuss, confess*›; 不加掩饰地 ‹*hostile, rude*›; 显而易见地 ‹*appalling, ridiculous*›; **I'll tell you ~, I don't like your friends** 坦白告诉你，我不喜欢你的那些朋友 2 (bluntly) 坦率地说; **quite ~, I was pleased to leave** 老实说，我很高兴离开了

frankness /ˈfræŋknɪs/ *n* [u] 坦率

frantic /ˈfræntɪk/ *adj* 1 (wild) 发狂似的; **to be ~ with sth.** …得发狂 ‹*excitement, applause, weeping*›; **I'm nearly ~ with worry** 我都要愁死了; **to go ~** 发疯; **to drive sb. ~** 使某人发疯 2 (desperate) 狂乱的 ‹*activity, shout, effort*›; **after a ~ search we found the tickets** 经过一番狂找，我们找到了那些票

frantically /ˈfræntɪkli/ *adv* 1 (wildly) 发狂似地 ‹*wave, shout*› 2 (desperately) 拼命地 ‹*knock, struggle, search*›

fraternal /frəˈtɜːnl/ *adj* 1 (of brother) 兄弟的 ‹*feelings*›; (like brother) 兄弟般的 ‹*feelings, spirit*› 2 Biol 异卵双生的 ‹*twins*›

fraternity /frəˈtɜːnəti/ *n* 1 [u] (friendship, support) 友爱; **the ideals of liberty, equality, ~** 自由、平等、博爱的理想 2 [c] (group, community) 同仁; **medical/banking ~** 医务界/银行界同仁 3 [c] Amer Univ 男大学生联谊会

fraternization /ˌfrætənaɪˈzeɪʃn, Amer -nɪˈz-/ *n* [u] 亲善; **~ with the enemy** 亲敌

fraternize /ˈfrætənaɪz/ *vi* pej [尤指与不应该交往之人] 亲善; **to ~ with sb.** 与某人友好交往

fratricidal /ˌfrætrɪˈsaɪdl/ *adj* 自相残杀的 ‹*conflict, struggle, war*›

fratricide /ˈfrætrɪsaɪd/ *n* 1 [u] (killing) (of own brother) 杀兄弟的行为; (of own sister) 杀姐妹的行为; **to commit ~** 杀同胞手足 2 [c] (person killing brother) 杀兄弟的人; (person killing sister) 杀姐妹的人

fraud /frɔːd/ *n* 1 [u] (criminal deception) 诈骗; **to commit ~** 诈骗; **to be (found) guilty of ~** (被判决)犯诈骗罪; **by ~** 通过诈骗的手段; **computer/credit card ~** 电脑/信用卡诈骗 2 [c] (deceiver) 骗子; (deceptive thing) 骗人的东西; **to be a ~** 是个骗子; **to feel a ~** 感觉自己是在骗人

fraud squad *n* Brit 反诈骗科

fraudulence /ˈfrɔːdjʊləns, Amer -dʒʊ-/ *n* 1 = **fraud** 2 [u] (of contract, cheque, signature) 欺诈

fraudulent /ˈfrɔːdjʊlənt, Amer -dʒʊ-/ *adj* 欺诈性的 ‹*election, practice, claim*›; 假的 ‹*signature, contract*›; **~ gains** 欺诈所得

fraudulent conversion *n* [u] 欺诈侵占

fraudulently /ˈfrɔːdjʊləntli, Amer -dʒʊ-/ *adv* 欺诈地

fraught /frɔːt/ *adj* 1 *pred* (full) **to be ~ with** 充满 ‹*danger, difficulty*› 2 (tense) 忧虑的 ‹*person, look*›; 令人忧虑的 ‹*situation, atmosphere*›

fray /freɪ/
A *vt* 1 (wear away) 磨损 ‹*cloth, carpet, rope*› 2 fig (irritate, strain) 使…变得急躁 ‹*temper*›; 使…紧张 ‹*nerves*›
B *vi* 1 (unravel) «*garment, edges, rope*» 被磨损 2 fig (be strained) «*temper*» 变得急躁; «*nerves*» 变得紧张; **my patience is beginning to ~** 我越来越没有耐心了
C *n* formal 争斗; **to enter** *or* **join the ~** 介入争斗

frazzle /ˈfræzl/ colloq
A *n* 1 (exhausted) 疲惫; **to be worn to a ~** 精疲力竭 2 (completely burnt) 烧焦; **to be burnt to a ~** 被烧为灰烬
B *vt* 1 (wear out) 使疲惫; **to be ~d** 感到疲惫 2 (burn) 把…烧得皱缩; **she ~ my hair with curling tongs** 她用卷发钳给我烫头发

freak /friːk/
A *n* 1 (abnormal person) 畸形人; (abnormal thing) 畸形的东西; **a ~ of nature** 畸形 2 colloq pej (unconventional person) 怪人; **she's a ~ who goes everywhere barefoot** 她不论到哪儿都光着脚，真是个怪人 3 (occurrence) 怪事; **a ~ of fortune** 侥幸 4 colloq (enthusiast) 狂热爱好者; **he's a jazz/fitness ~** 他是个爵士乐/健身迷
B *adj* 反常的 ‹*weather, temperatures*›
C *vt* colloq = **freak out B**

Phrasal verb

• **freak out** colloq
A *vi* 发飙
B *vt* [**~ sb. out, ~ out sb.**] 使发飙

freakish /ˈfriːkɪʃ/ *adj* 1 (abnormal) 怪异的 ‹*person, appearance*› 2 (surprising) 反常的 ‹*event, weather*›

freak show *n* 1 Hist (sideshow, exhibition) 畸形秀 2 fig (spectacle) 荒诞景象

freaky /ˈfriːki/ *adj* colloq 怪异的 ‹*situation, atmosphere, event*›

freckle /ˈfrekl/
A *n* 雀斑
B *vi* «*person, skin*» 生雀斑

freckled /ˈfrekld/ *adj* 有雀斑的 ‹*face, person, skin*›

free /friː/
A *adj* 1 (from trap, wreckage, rubble) 未受困的; (from chains) 未受缚的; (from prison, captivity) 未受监禁的; (from slavery) 未受奴役的; **after 20 years in prison, he was a ~ man again** 坐了 20 年牢之后，他重获自由; **to set sb./sth. ~ (from sth.)** (从某处)释放某人/某物; **an attempt to set the hostages ~** 解救人质的尝试; **to cut sb./sth./oneself ~ (from sth.)** 使某人/某物/自己摆脱(某物的)束缚; **to pull sb./sth./oneself ~ (from sth.)** 把某人/某物/自己(从某物中)拉出来; **I managed to pull myself ~ from the rubble** 我设法爬出了瓦砾堆; **to break** *or* **get ~ (from sth.)** 挣脱(某物); **after struggling for hours, she managed to break ~** 挣扎了几个小时后，她成功脱身 2 (costing nothing) 免费的 ‹*ticket, health care*›; **~ admission** 免费入场; **~ delivery** 免费送货; **~ gift** Comm 赠品 3 *pred* (not prevented from doing sth.) «*person*» 不受限制的; **we are ~r than we were several centuries ago** 人类比几个世纪以前更自由; **to be ~ to do sth.** 可自由做某事; **guests are ~ to come and go as they please** 客人可以随意来去; **to set sb. ~ (to do sth./from sth.)** 使某人自由(做某事/摆脱某事); **to break ~ (of** *or* **from sth.)** 摆脱(某事); **feel ~!** colloq 请随意!; **feel ~ to make yourself a cup of coffee** 煮咖啡请自便; **as ~ as a bird** *or* **the air** *or* **the wind** 如鸟儿/风般自由 4 *usu pred* (not attached or trapped) 未系住的 ‹*rope, shoe, bag, boat*›; 未受束缚的 ‹*limb, foot, head, finger*›; 畅通的 ‹*movement, passage, flow*›; **he reached for the handle with his ~ arm** 他伸出空着的手臂去够把手; **to get hold of the ~ end of the rope** 抓住绳索松开的一端; **her heart is ~** fig 她的心无拘无束 5 *usu attrib* (not restricted) 自由的 ‹*press, election, choice, use, movement*›; 独立自主的 ‹*government*›; **~ translation** 意译; **the principle of ~ speech** 言论自由的原则; **she had ~ access to all our personal records** 她可以自由查阅我们所有的人事档案; **to draw a ~ likeness of sb.** 给某人随意画像; **it's a ~ country!** 这是个自由的国家!; **to have/get a ~ hand (in sth./doing sth.)** (在某事/做某事上)有自主权; **to allow** *or* **give sb. a ~ hand (in sth./doing sth.)** (在某事/做某事上)让某人自己作主 6 *pred* (not affected) «*person*» 不受影响的; **to be ~ from** *or* **of sth.** 免于某物; **to be ~ from debt** 没有债务; **to be ~ of infection** 不受感染; **an afternoon ~ of interruptions** 不受干扰的下午 7 *pred* (devoid) «*place, object, product*» 没有…的; **to be ~ from** *or* **of sth.** 无某事物; **to keep the lawn ~ from weeds for six months** 让草坪 6 个月不生杂草 8 *pred* Fin «*payment*» 免…的; **to be ~ of sth.** 免去某物; **the loan is ~ of interest** 贷款是免息的 9 *usu pred* (not busy) 有空的 ‹*person*›; (not booked up) 空闲的 ‹*day, time*›; **are you ~?** 你有空吗?; **to keep** *or* **leave sth. ~** 空出某个时间 10 (not in use) 未被占用的 ‹*room, toilet, bed*›; **is this seat ~?** 这个座位没人吧?; **your table is ~ now** 现在有空桌位给你了 11 *usu pred* (lavish) 滥用浪费的 ‹*person, organization*›; (generous) 慷慨的 ‹*person, organization*›; **to be a ~ spender** 花钱大手大脚; **to be ~ with sth.** 滥用某物; **don't be too ~ with the gin** 喝杜松子酒不要过量; **she's very ~ with her praise** 她不吝溢美之词; **they have always been ~ with money** 他们花钱总是大手大脚; **to make ~ with sth.** 擅自使用某物 12 Chem 游离的 ‹*element*›; 自由的 ‹*atom*› 13 Ling (independent) 自由的 ‹*form, vowel, syllable*›
B **the ~** *pl* 自由人; **land of the ~** 自由之邦
C *adv* 1 (at liberty, without restriction) 自由地 ‹*run, flow, swing*›; **the hostages were allowed to go ~** 人质获释; **the rapist walked ~ from the court** 强奸者被当庭释放 2 (without payment) 免费地 ‹*give, repair, travel*›; **children under five are admitted ~** 5 岁以下的儿童免费入场; **20% extra ~** 免费加送 20%; **for ~** colloq 免费地; **they seem to expect me to work for ~** 他们似乎想让我白干
D *vt* 1 (set at liberty) (from prison, captivity, slavery) «*person, organization*» 使…自由 ‹*animal, hostage*›; (release from chains, trap, wreckage, rubble) 救出; **to ~ a prisoner/slave** 释放囚犯/解放奴隶; **to ~ sb./sth. from sth.** 把某人/某物从某物中救出 2 (detach, release) 解开 ‹*rope, bag*›; 使…解脱 ‹*head, finger, end*›; **to ~ sth. from sth.** 使某物摆脱某物的束缚 3 (relieve) «*person, news, decision, exercise*» 使…摆脱 ‹*person, organization*›; **to ~ sb. from** *or* **of sth.** 使某人摆脱 ‹*care*›; **his decision ~d me of all responsibility** 他的决定免除了我所有责任 4 (clear) 清除; **to ~ sth. of** *or* **from sth.** 把某物从某物中除去; **he climbed up to ~ the gutter of leaves** 他爬上去清除檐槽里的树叶; **the council's latest campaign to ~ the streets of litter** 市议会最近旨在清除街面垃圾的运动 5 (make available)

«*person, organization, action*» 腾出 ‹*hands, time, resource*›; 使有时间 ‹*person*›; **to ~ sb./sth. for sth.** 为某事使某人腾出手来/腾出某物; **to ~ resources for education** 为教育腾出资源; **to ~ sb. for other duties** 让某人腾出手来处理其他事务; **to ~ sb./sth. to do sth.** 使某人腾出手来/腾出某物做某事

E *v refl* **to ~ oneself** **1** (get free from wreckage, rubble, chains, trap) «*person, animal, bird*» 脱身; **to ~ oneself from sth.** 从某处脱身; **I ~d myself from the cabin with difficulty** 我艰难地逃出机舱 **2** (get rid of sth.) **to ~ oneself from** *or* **of sth.** 摆脱某物; **to try to ~ oneself of prejudice** 努力让自己不存偏见

Phrasal verb

- **free up** *vt* [**~ up sth., ~ sth. up**] 腾出; **the organization ~d up resources for the earthquake victims** 该组织调拨资源用于援助地震灾民; **I've ~d up space on my hard drive for photos** 我在硬盘上为存放照片腾出了空间

free: ~ agent *n* 行动自由的人; **~ alongside ship** *adj* 船边交货的; **~ and easy** *adj* 无拘无束的; **the atmosphere in the office is quite ~ and easy** 办公室的气氛非常随意轻松; **they have a ~ and easy attitude to sex** 他们对待性的态度非常随便; **~ association** *n* [u] **1** (formation of group) 自由联合; **2** Psych (mental process) 自由联想

freebase /ˈfriːbeɪs/ *n* 精炼可卡因

freebie, freebee /ˈfriːbi/ *n* colloq 免费品; **a ~ lunch** 免费的午餐

freeboard /ˈfriːbɔːd/ *n* 干舷（高）

freebooter /ˈfriːbuːtə(r)/ *n* 劫掠者

free: F~ Church *n* 自由教会; **~ city** *n* 自由市; **~ climbing** *n* [u] 徒手攀岩; **~ collective bargaining** *n* [u] [劳资双方不受法律限制的] 自由集体谈判

freedom /ˈfriːdəm/ *n* **1** [u and c] (physical liberty) 自由; **to give sb./sth. his/her/its ~** 给某人/某物自由; **academic/artistic/personal/political/religious/financial ~** 学术/艺术/个人/政治/宗教/金融自由; **she decided to give the bird its ~** 她决定把鸟儿放飞; **after 27 years in prison, he was given his ~ yesterday** 在牢里度过27年后，他昨天被释放了; **~ of speech** 言论自由; **the ~ of a city** Brit 荣誉市民权; **to give sb. the ~ of sth.** 允许某人自由使用某物; **~ of the seas** Naut, Jur (right to sail) 公海自由航行权; (exclusive jurisdiction) 对公海上本国船只的专有司法权 **2** [u] Pol (of state, colony, people, region) 独立自主; **to gain** *or* **win** *or* **secure ~** 获得独立自主 **3** [u] (ability to move easily) 行动自如; **to allow the bolt ~ of movement** 让门闩活动自如 **4** [u] (absence) 免除; **~ from sth.** 某物的免除; **~ from pain** 解痛; **~ from hunger** 免于饥饿 **5** [u] (ease, expansiveness) 随意; **she discussed the scandal with surprising ~** 令人惊讶的是，她随意地谈论那件丑闻

freedom: F~ Charter *n* S Afr 《自由宪章》; **~ fighter** *n* [为实现政治目的奋斗的] 自由战士; **to be/become a ~ fighter** 是/成为自由战士; **to join the ~ fighters** 加入自由战士队伍; **~ of conscience** *n* [u] 信仰自由; **~ of religion** *n* [u] 宗教信仰自由

free: ~ enterprise *n* [u] 自由企业制; **~fall** *n* [u] 自由落体; **to be in ~fall** 呈自由落体状态; **the share price was in/went into ~fall** fig 股价猛跌不止; **~ fight** *n* 混战; **~ flight** *n* 惯性飞行; **~-flowing** *adj* 自由流动的 ‹*river, liquid*›; 顺畅的 ‹*conversation, traffic, game*›; **~ hair** 飘逸的头发

Freefone® /ˈfriːfəʊn/ *n* 免费电话业务

free-for-all *n* (fight) 混战; (argument) 群体争吵; **there was a ~ when the bus finally arrived** 当公交车终于到来时，大家一窝蜂地往上挤; **the meeting degenerated into a ~** 会议变成了一场大吵大闹

freehand /ˈfriːhænd/

A *adv* 徒手地 ‹*draw, paint*›

B *adj* 徒手画的 ‹*drawing, sketch, line, circle*›

free hit *n* 任意球

freehold /ˈfriːhəʊld/

A *n* [不动产的] 终身保有; **to have** *or* **own the ~ of sth.** 终身保有某物

B *adj* 可终身保有的 ‹*property, shop*›

C *adv* 终身地 ‹*own*›; **we bought the shop ~** 我们买下了这家商店，终身保有

free: ~holder *n* [不动产的] 终身保有者; **~ house** *n* Brit [可出售任何牌子酒的] 小酒馆; **~ kick** *n* 任意球

freelance /ˈfriːlɑːns, Amer -læns/

A *n* 自由职业者

B *adj* 自由职业的 ‹*artist*›; 自由职业者的 ‹*work, rates*›; **a ~ photographer/writer** 个体摄影师/自由作家; **on a ~ basis** 以自由职业者的工作方式

C *adv* 作为自由职业者 ‹*work*›; **to go ~** 成为自由职业者

D *vi* 当自由职业者

freelancer /ˈfriːlɑːnsə(r), Amer -lænsə(r)/ *n* 自由职业者

free: ~load *vi* colloq 吃白食; **to ~load from one's parents** 在父母处白吃白住; **~loader** *n* colloq 揩油者; **~ love** *n* [u] 自由性爱; **~man** /-mən/ *n* **1** (of city, borough) 荣誉市民; **to be made a ~man** 被授予荣誉市民; **2** Hist 自由民; **~ market** *n* 自由市场; **~ marketeer** *n* 主张自由市场者; **F~mason** *n* 共济会成员; **F~masonry** *n* [u] 共济会制

freely /ˈfriːli/ *adv* **1** (not being confined or obstructed) 自由地; **I can turn my head more ~ now** 现在我可以更自如地转头; **the traffic is flowing ~** 交通很通畅; **to breathe ~** 顺畅地呼吸; **thank heaven the inspector has gone away, I can breathe ~ again** fig 谢天谢地，检查员走了，我现在可以松口气了; **to talk** *or* **speak ~** 畅谈; **to be ~ available** ‹*goods, information*› 可随意获得 **2** (willingly) 自愿地 ‹*agree, sacrifice*›; **to admit sth. ~** 爽快承认某事; **to give one's consent ~** 自愿同意 **3** (abundantly) 大量地 ‹*give, use*›; **to spend money ~** 花钱大手大脚; **the plant grows ~ in the hedgerows** 植物在灌木树篱中生长茂盛 **4** (not strictly) 不紧扣原文地; **~ translated** 意译的

free of charge *adj, adv* 免费的（地）

free on board *adj, adv* 船上交货价的（地）

free: ~ period *n* 空课时; **F~phone** *n* 免费电话业务; **~ port** *n* **1** (port) 自由港; **2** (port area) 免税港区; **F~post** Brit *n* [u] 收件人邮资总付业务; *modif* 收件人邮资总付的 ‹*system, service, address*›; **~-range** *adj* 散养的 ‹*hens, pigs*›; 散养生产的 ‹*eggs, meat*›; **~ school** *n* 免费学校; **~ sheet** *n* 免费报纸

freesia /ˈfriːziə, Amer ˈfriːʒə/ *n* 小苍兰

free: ~ speech *n* [u] 言论自由; **~ spirit** *n* 特立独行的人; **~-spirited** *adj* 特立独行的; **~-standing** *adj* 独立式的 ‹*cooker, lamp, statue*›

freestyle /ˈfriːstaɪl/

A *n* (swimming) 自由泳; (wrestling) 自由式摔跤

B *modif* 自由式的 ‹*race, event*›

free thinker *n* 自由思想家

free-thinking

A *n* 自由思想

B *adj* 思想自由的

free-to-air *adj* 开路播出的 ‹*network, television, channel*›

Freetown /ˈfriːtaʊn/ *pr n* 弗里敦

free: ~ trade *n* [u] 自由贸易; **~ university** *n* 免费大学; **~ verse** *n* [u] 自由诗; **~ vote** *n* [议员的] 自由投票; **~ware** *n* [u] 免费软件; **~way** *n* Amer **1** (motorway) 高速干道; **2** (toll-free road) 免费公路

freewheel /ˌfriːˈwiːl, Amer -ˈhwiːl/

A *n* 飞轮

B *vi* **1** (coast) «*cyclist, bicycle*» 靠惯性滑行 **2** fig (relax) 随心所欲地行动

freewheeler /ˌfriːˈwiːlə(r), Amer -ˈhwiːlə(r)/ *n* 行动自由的人

freewheeling /ˌfriːˈwiːlɪŋ, Amer -ˈhwiːlɪŋ/ *adj* 随心所欲的 ‹*person, attitude, style*›

free will *n* [u] **1** Philos 自由意志论 **2** (choice) 自愿; **of one's own ~** 自愿地

freeze /friːz/

A *vi* (*pt* **froze,** *pp* **frozen**) **1** (become solid) «*liquid*» 冻结; fig «*blood*» 凝固; **water ~s at 0°C** 水在零摄氏度结冰; **to ~ solid** *or* **stiff** 冻得硬邦邦 **2** (preserve in freezer) «*food, vegetables*» 可冷藏 **3** (be covered with ice) «*river*» 被冰覆盖; (be blocked with ice) «*drain*» 被冰堵塞; **the mains water pipe has frozen** 总水管已经冻住; **when the pond ~s we go skating on it** 池塘结冰后，我们在上面滑冰 **4** (be fixed with ice) «*windscreen wiper, lock, mechanism*» 冻住; **to ~ to sth.** 冻结在某物上; **to ~ fast** 冻得很牢固 **5** (feel cold) 感到极冷; **to ~ with cold** 冻僵; **to ~ to death** 冻死; **my hands are freezing** 我的手快要冻僵了 **6** Meteorol 冰冻; **to ~ hard** 寒冷彻骨; **turn the heater on, it's freezing in here!** 打开暖气，这儿冷得要命！ **7** (become motionless) «*person, animal*» 呆住不动; **~! he shouted, pointing the gun at us** 不许动！他高喊道，同时用枪指着我们; **she froze with horror/surprise at the sight** 看到这个景象，她吓呆/惊呆了; **the words froze on her lips** fig 她话到嘴边又噎住了; **the smile froze on his face** fig 笑容在他的脸上僵住了 **8** Comput «*computer screen*» 冻结

B *vt* (*pt* **froze,** *pp* **frozen**) **1** (make solid) 使…冻结 ‹*liquid*› **2** (cover with ice) «*weather, cold*» 使…被冰覆盖 ‹*river*›; (block with ice) 使…被冰堵塞 ‹*drain*›; **the frost froze the pipes** 严寒的天气把管道都冻住了; **if this cold weather continues it will ~ the buds off the fruit trees** 如果这样寒冷的天气持续下去，就会冻掉果树上的花苞 **3** (fix with ice) «*cold, frost*» 使…冻住 ‹*mechanism, key, brakes*›; **the wind seemed to ~ her eyelids together** 寒风似乎要把她的眼皮冻在一起 **4** (preserve in freezer) 冷藏 ‹*food, vegetables, fruit*› **5** Econ, Fin «*bank, employer*» 冻结 ‹*interest rate, price, wages, account*›; **we should like to ~ car imports at their present level** 我们希望将汽车进口量固定在现有水平; **the new government has frozen all foreign assets** 新政府冻结了所有外国资产 **6** Cin, Theat «*director, camera*» 使…定格 ‹*action, scene*›; **~ it!** 定格！ **7** Med, Dent (render insensitive) 用冷冻法麻醉 ‹*part of body, tooth*› **8** Comput «*system problem*» 使…冻结 ‹*computer screen, window*›

C *n* **1** Meteorol colloq 冰冻期; **a big ~** 严寒期 **2** Econ, Fin (fixing of wages, prices etc.) 冻结; **a pay/price ~** 工资/价格冻结; **to impose a ~ on sth.** 冻结某物

Phrasal verbs

- **freeze out** *vt* [**~ sb./sth. out, ~ out sb./sth.**] colloq (force out) 逼走 ‹*person*›; (exclude) 排斥 ‹*person, foreign goods*›; **she had lied to her friends, so they froze her out** 她对朋友们说了谎，所以朋友们都疏远了她; **they froze out all newcomers** 他们排斥所有新来的人; **cheap imports are freezing out home-produced goods** 便宜的进口货正渐渐排挤掉国产商品
- **freeze over** *vi* 冰封; **when the pond froze over, we went skating on it** 池塘结冰时，我们在上面滑冰; **my bedroom window has frozen over** 我的卧室窗玻璃上结冰了; **when hell ~s over** 绝不可能

f

• **freeze up**
A *vi* «*pipe, car, mechanism, lock*» 冻住
B *vt* [**~ sth. up, ~ up sth.**] «*cold*» 使…冻住 ‹*pipe, car, mechanism, lock*›; **we were frozen up for several days last winter** fig 去年冬天，因为冰冻，我们有好几天不能外出

freeze: ~-dried *adj* 冷冻干燥的 ‹*food, coffee*›; **~-dry** *vt* 冷冻干燥保存 ‹*food, coffee*›; **~-drying** *n* [u] 冷冻干燥; **~ frame** *n* 1 [u] (facility) 定格设备; 2 [c] (image) 定格画面

freezer /ˈfriːzə(r)/ *n* 冷冻柜

freezer: ~ bag *n* 冷冻袋; **~ compartment** *n* 冷冻室; **~ trawler** *n* 冷冻拖网渔船

freeze-up *n* 严寒期

freezing /ˈfriːzɪŋ/ ▸**p. 814**
A *adj* 极冷的 ‹*room, weather*›; **I'm ~** 我快冻僵了
B *n* 冰点; **to be above/below ~** 在冰点以上/下

freezing: ~ cold *adj* colloq 极冷的; **~ point** ▸**p. 814** *n* 冰点

freight /freɪt/
A *n* 1 (goods) 货物; **to load/unload ~** 装/卸货; **to carry ~** 运输货物; **to handle ~** 搬运货物 2 (transport system) 货运; **air ~** 空运 3 (cost) 运费; **who pays the ~?** 谁付运费?
B *vt* 以货运运输 ‹*goods*›; **the bricks had been ~ed to the building site** 砖头运到了建筑工地

freight: ~ car *n* 货车; **~ charges** *npl* 运费; **~ costs** *npl* 运输成本; **~ elevator** *n* Amer = **goods lift**

freighter /ˈfreɪtə(r)/ *n* 1 Naut 货船 2 Aviat 运输机

freight: ~ forward *adv* Brit 运费到付; **~ forwarder, ~ forwarding agent** ▸**p. 409** *ns* 货运代理; **~ insurance** *n* [u] 运费保险; **F~liner®** *n* Brit 集装箱列车; **~ note** *n* 货运标签; **~ operator** ▸**p. 409** *n* 货运公司; **~ terminal** *n* 货运终点站; **~ train** *n* 货运列车; **~ yard** *n* 货场

French /frentʃ/ ▸**p. 503, p. 426**
A *adj* (of France) 法国的 ‹*town, river, tradition, food*›; (of the people) 法国人的 ‹*accent*›; (of the language) 法语的 ‹*word, proverb, idiom*›
B *n* [u] (language) 法语
C *npl* (people) **the ~** 法国人

French: ~ bean *n* Brit 菜豆; **~ bread** *n* [u] 法式长条面包

French Canadian ▸**p. 503, p. 426**
A *adj* (of the French-speaking part of Canada) 加拿大法语区的; (of the people) 法裔加拿大人的; (of the language) 加拿大法语的
B *n* 1 [c] (person) 法裔加拿大人 2 [u] (language) 加拿大法语

French: ~ chalk *n* 滑石; **~ door** *n* esp Amer **= ~ window**; **~ dressing** *n* [u] 1 (oil, vinegar dressing) [油和醋调成的] 法式色拉调料; 2 Amer (creamy dressing) [油、番茄酱和香料等制成的] 奶油色拉调料; **~ fries** esp Amer, **~ fried potatoes** Brit *npl* 炸薯条; **~ horn** ▸**p. 395** *n* 法国号; **~ kiss** *n* colloq 法式接吻; **~ knickers** *npl* 法式女灯笼裤; **~ leave** *n* [u] colloq dated 擅离职守; **to take ~ leave** 不辞而别; **~ letter** Brit colloq dated *n* 避孕套; **~ loaf** *n* 法式长条面包; **~man** /-mən/ *n* 法国男人; **~ marigold** *n* 万寿菊; **~ mustard** *n* [u] Brit 法式淡味芥末; **~ pleat** *n* 1 Sewing 窗帘褶裥; 2 (hairstyle) 卷筒形发式

French polish
A *n* [u] 罩光漆
B **french-polish** *vt* 给…涂罩光漆 ‹*furniture*›

French: ~ poodle *n* 卷毛狗; **~ Riviera** *n* 蓝色海岸; **~ stick** *n* 法式长条面包; **~ window** *n* **~ window(s** *pl*) 落地窗; **~woman** *n* 法国女人

frenetic /frəˈnetɪk/ *adj* 狂热的 ‹*activity, person, applause*›; 发狂似的 ‹*rhythm, joy*›; **an outburst of ~ anger** 一阵狂怒

frenetically /frəˈnetɪkli/ *adv* 发狂似地 ‹*dance, argue, shout*›

frenzied /ˈfrenzɪd/ *adj* 狂乱的 ‹*mob, activity*›; **to make a ~ attack on sb.** 对某人发动疯狂的进攻; **~ anger/delight** 狂怒/喜; **we had to make a ~ dash to the airport** fig 我们不得不发疯似地冲向机场

frenzy /ˈfrenzi/ *n* [u and c] 疯狂; **to be in a state of ~** 发狂; **cooking for ten sends me into a state of ~** hum 给十个人煮饭会让我发疯的; **to drive sb./sth. into a ~** 使…发疯 ‹*crowd*›; **media ~** 新闻媒体的疯狂报道; **to be in a ~ of anticipation** 热切地期盼; **to be in a ~ of joy/anxiety** 欣喜若狂/焦急万分

frequency /ˈfriːkwənsi/ *n* 1 [u] (rate of occurrence) 发生率; **in order of ~** 按发生率的大小顺序; **these incidents have been occurring with increasing ~** 这些事件越来越频繁地发生 2 [c and u] (rate of vibration, wave) 频率

frequency: ~ band *n* 频带; **~ distribution** *n* 频数分布; **~ hopping** *n* [u] 跳频; **~ modulation** *n* [u] 调频

frequent
A /ˈfriːkwənt/ *adj* 1 (common) 惯常的 ‹*custom, expression*›; **quite (a) ~ occurrence** 很常见的事情 2 (happening often) 频繁的 ‹*accident, rest, change*›; **to make ~ use of sth.** 频繁使用某物; **to be in ~ contact with sb.** 和某人经常联系 3 (of person) 惯常做某事的; **she's a ~ visitor to our house** 她是我们家的常客; **to be sb.'s ~ companion** 经常陪伴某人
B /frɪˈkwent/ *vt* 常去 ‹*place, party*›

frequenter /frɪˈkwentə(r)/ *n* 常客; **a ~ of pubs, clubs and discos** 酒馆、夜总会和迪厅的常客

frequent flyer *n* [搭乘飞机的] 常旅客

frequently /ˈfriːkwəntli/ *adv* 经常地; **we visit them ~** 我们常去拜访他们

fresco /ˈfreskəʊ/ *n* 1 [u] (method) 湿壁画技法; **to paint in ~** 作湿壁画 2 [c] (*pl* **~es**) (painting) 湿壁画

fresh /freʃ/
A *adj* 1 (not old or processed) 新鲜的 ‹*food, fruit*›; **~ milk/fish/meat/flowers** 鲜奶/鱼/肉/花; **to look/feel/taste/smell ~** 看上去/感觉/尝起来/闻起来新鲜; **to stay ~** 保鲜; **are the beans ~ or frozen?** 豆子是新鲜的还是冷冻的?; **~ from sth.** 刚从某处得到的; **milk ~ from the cow** 刚挤的牛奶; **apples ~ from the tree** 刚从树上摘下来的苹果; **bread ~ from the oven** 刚出炉的面包 2 usu attrib (new, additional) 另外的 ‹*supplies, drink*›; 新的 ‹*evidence, news, hope, attempt*›; **on a ~ sheet of paper** 在另一张空白纸上; **give the budgie some ~ water** 给这只虎皮鹦鹉换些新鲜水; **to take ~ heart** 重新振奋; **to make a ~ start** 重新开始 3 (recent) 新近的 ‹*mark, tracks*›; 新涂的 ‹*paint*›; **~ footprints in the snow** 雪地上新留下的足迹; **to be (still) ~ in sb.'s mind** or **memory** 某人记忆犹新 4 (recently arrived) 新到的 ‹*person, thing*›; **~ from** or **off** or **out of sth.** 刚从某处来的; **~ from their trip to America** 刚结束他们的美国之行回来的; **cars ~ off the production line** 刚下生产线的汽车; **~ to sth.** 刚到某处的; **she is ~ to television** 她刚刚接触电视业 5 (different, original) 新颖的 ‹*approach, attitude, manner*› 6 *pred* (energetic, alert) 精力充沛的; **I felt ~ after my holiday** 假期结束后我感到精神饱满; **as ~ as a daisy** 精神焕发的 7 Brit colloq (cool and windy) 凛冽的 ‹*wind, weather*›; **it's rather ~ out there** 外面挺冷的 8 (cool, refreshing) 凉爽的 ‹*air, day*›; 清凉的 ‹*water*›; **~ breeze** 清新的微风 9 (clean to the senses) 洁净的 ‹*clothes, cloth*›; 清爽的 ‹*smell, taste*›; **~ white sheets** 洁净的白床单; **~-looking/tasting/smelling** 相貌/味道/气味清新的 10 (bright) 鲜艳的 ‹*colour*› 11 (healthy) 光洁的 ‹*face, complexion, skin*› 12 *pred* colloq (overfamiliar) «*manner, person*» 无礼的; **to be** or **get ~ with sb.** 对某人放肆; **the clerk was a bit ~ with me** 这个职员对我有些无礼; **he started to get ~ and I slapped his face** 他开始放肆起来，我就打了他一个耳光
B *adv* 1 (recently) 刚 ‹*picked, caught, made*›; **~-cut flowers** 刚剪下的花; **~-baked bread** 刚烤好的面包; **~-frozen peas** 新鲜冷冻的豌豆; **~-ground coffee** 新磨的咖啡 2 colloq (completely) **to be ~ out of sth.** 刚用尽某物; **sorry, we're ~ out of melons** 很抱歉，瓜刚卖完

fresh air *n* [u] 新鲜空气; **in the ~** 在户外; **a breath of ~** lit 新鲜空气; fig 令人耳目一新者; **to go outside for a breath of ~** 到外面呼吸新鲜空气; **the new president was a breath of ~** 新总统给人耳目一新的感觉

fresh-air fiend *n* colloq hum 新鲜空气痴迷者

freshen /ˈfreʃn/
A *vi* «*weather*» 变冷; **the wind will ~ this evening** 今晚风力将会增强，气温下降
B *vt* 1 (make cooler) 使…清爽 ‹*atmosphere*› 2 (make cleaner) «*person, action*» 使…洁净 ‹*air, room, paintwork*›

Phrasal verb

• **freshen up**
A *vi* 梳洗; **would you like to ~ up before dinner?** 你想在晚餐前梳洗一下吗?
B *v refl* **to ~ oneself up** 梳洗打扮; **have I got time to ~ myself up?** 我有时间梳洗一下吗?
C *vt* [**~ sb./sth. up, ~ up sb./sth.**] 1 (enliven) «*rest, drink*» 使…精神焕发 ‹*person*› 2 (make cleaner) 使…洁净 ‹*air, room, dress, person*›

fresher /ˈfreʃə(r)/ *n* Brit colloq 大一新生

freshers' week *n* Brit colloq 欢迎新生周

fresh-faced *adj* 青春焕发的

freshly /ˈfreʃli/ *adv* 刚刚 ‹*made, cut, painted, ironed*›; **a glass of ~ squeezed orange juice** 一杯新榨的橙汁; **the smell of ~ brewed coffee** 新煮咖啡的味道

freshman /ˈfreʃmən/ *n* (*pl* **freshmen**) 1 Univ 大学一年级学生 2 Amer (at school) 中学一年级学生

freshness /ˈfreʃnɪs/ *n* [u] 1 (of food) 新鲜 2 (of news, evidence) 新; (of marks, tracks) 新近; (of paint) 新涂 3 (of approach, interpretation) 新颖 4 (energy, alertness) 精力充沛; **the ~ of youth** (energy) 年轻人的充沛精力; (inexperience) 年轻人的青涩 5 Brit colloq (of weather, water) 清凉 6 (of sheets, linen) 洁净; (of flavour, smell) 清新 7 (brightness) 鲜艳 8 (healthiness of complexion) 光洁

freshwater /ˈfreʃwɔːtə(r)/ *adj attrib* 淡水的

fret[1] /fret/
A *vi* (*pres p etc.* **-tt-**) 1 (be anxious) 苦恼; **to ~ about** or **over sth.** 担心某事; **to ~ at sth.** 为某事发愁 2 (cry) «*baby, child*» 哭闹; **to ~ for sb./sth.** 为得到某人/某物而哭闹; **the little boy was ~ting for his mother** 那个小男孩哭着要妈妈
B *n* esp Brit (annoyance) 苦恼; **to be/get in a ~** 陷入苦恼中; **to be/get in a ~ with sb.** 担心某人

fret[2] *n* Mus [吉他等弦乐器指板上定音的] 品

fretful /ˈfretfl/ *adj* 烦躁的 ‹*person*›; **he fell into a ~ sleep** 他睡得很不安宁

fretfully /ˈfretfəli/ *adv* 烦躁地 ‹*speak, cry*›; **to pace ~ to and fro** 烦躁地走来走去; **to cry ~** 烦躁地啼哭

fretsaw /ˈfretsɔː/ *n* 线锯

Freudian /ˈfrɔɪdɪən/
A *adj* (of or relating to Sigmund Freud) 弗洛伊德的; (of or relating to the methods of psychoanalysis) 弗洛伊德学说的

B *n* 弗洛伊德学说的信奉者; **my analyst is a ~** 我的心理分析师信奉弗洛伊德学说

Freudian slip *n* 失言; **to make a ~** 说漏了嘴

Fri. ▸p. 182 *abbr* = **Friday**

friable /ˈfraɪəbl/ *adj* 易碎的 ‹*soil, material*›

friar /ˈfraɪə(r)/ *n* 托钵修会修士

friary /ˈfraɪəri/ *n* 托钵修会

fricassee /ˈfrɪkəsiː/
A *n* 原汁煨肉块; **chicken ~** 原汁煨鸡块
B *vt* 把…烹制成原汁肉块

fricative /ˈfrɪkətɪv/
A *n* 摩擦音
B *adj* 摩擦的; **a ~ consonant** 摩擦辅音

friction /ˈfrɪkʃn/ *n* **1** [u] (resistance) 摩擦力 **2** [u] (rubbing) 摩擦 **3** [u and c] (discord) 不和; **there is growing ~ between management and workforce** 劳资双方之间的摩擦不断加剧; **there is a certain amount of ~ in any family** 任何家庭都有一定的矛盾

friction-driven *adj* 摩擦传动的 ‹*toy*›

Friday /ˈfraɪdi/ ▸p. 182 *n* 星期五; **on ~** 在星期五; **on ~s/every ~** 每周星期五; **~ morning/afternoon/night** 星期五早晨/下午/晚上; **this/last/next ~** 本周五/上周五/下周五

fridge /frɪdʒ/ *n* Brit colloq 冰箱

fridge-freezer *n* Brit 双门冰箱

fried /fraɪd/ *pt, pp* ▸**fry**¹

friend /frend/ *n* **1** (person one likes) 朋友; **to make ~s** 交朋友; **to make a ~ of sb.** 把某人变成朋友; **to make/be ~s with sb.** 和某人交朋友; **to be the best of ~s** 是最好的朋友; **let's be ~s!** (after quarrel) 我们和好吧！; **a ~ of the family** 亲友; **with ~s like him/her, who needs enemies?** 有他/她这样的损友，谁还需要敌人？; **a ~ in need is a ~ indeed** Prov 患难朋友才是真朋友 **2** fig (ally) 支持者; **the party has many ~s in industry** 该党在工业界有许多支持者; **to have ~s in high places** 有贵人相助; **to be a ~ of** *or* **to the poor** 是穷人的同情者 **3** (fellow member) 同志 **4** (patron) 赞助者; **F~s of the Cathedral** 大教堂之友 **5** (mode of address) 朋友 [用作称呼]; **come here, my ~, don't be shy** 到这儿来，我的朋友，别不好意思 **6** (with humorous or sarcastic reference) 老朋友 [含幽默或讽刺义]; **not forgetting our old ~ the taxman** iron 别忘了我们那位收税员老朋友 **7** fig (familiar object) 老朋友 [熟悉的有益事物]; **this book is an old ~** 这本书是位老朋友 **8** Brit Pol 朋友 [在议院中对同一政党成员的称呼]; **my honourable ~** 我尊敬的朋友 **9** Jur 同行; **my learned ~** 我渊博的同行

friendless /ˈfrendlɪs/ *adj* 无朋友的 ‹*person*›; 孤独无助的 ‹*situation*›

friendliness /ˈfrendlɪnɪs/ *n* [u] 友好

friendly /ˈfrendli/
A *adj* **1** (person, animal, behaviour) 友好的; **to be ~ to/towards sb.** 对某人友好; **to be ~ with sb.** 和某人友好; **to get** *or* **become ~ with sb.** 和某人有了情谊; **small shops often seem to be friendlier** 小商店往往看起来更亲切; **to be on ~ terms with sb.** 和某人相处融洽; **to have a ~ relationship with sb.** 和某人关系友好; **~ nations** 友邦; **~ matches** 友谊赛 **2** (supportive) 赞成的 ‹*parties, individuals*›; **to be ~ to sb./sth.** 支持某人/某事
B *n* Brit 友谊赛

friendly: ~ fire *n* [u] Mil euph 己方火力; **to be killed by ~ fire** 被本方火力误杀; **~ fire incident/death** 由己方火力造成的事件/死亡; **~ society** *n* Brit 互助会

friendship /ˈfrendʃɪp/ *n* **1** [c] (relationship) 友谊; **our ~ was very close/intimate** 我们是非常亲密的朋友; **to form ~s** 交朋友 **2** [u] (state or feeling) 友情; **to do sth. out of ~** 出于友情做某事

Friends of the Earth *pr n* “地球之友” [一环境保护组织]

fries /fraɪz/ *npl* Amer colloq 炸薯条

frieze /friːz/ *n* 饰带

frigate /ˈfrɪgɪt/ *n* 护卫舰

fright /fraɪt/ *n* [u and c] 惊吓; **to take ~** 受惊吓; **to have** *or* **get a ~** 吃惊; **to give sb. a ~** 让某人吃惊; **she gave a cry of ~** 她惊叫了一声; **to be paralyzed with ~** 被吓得不能动弹; **I had the ~ of my life!** 我吓得要命！; **to look a ~** colloq 看起来像个丑八怪

frighten /ˈfraɪtn/
A *vt* «*person, noise, sight, rumour*» 使…惊恐 ‹*person, animal*›; **to ~ sb. into doing ...** 使某人吓得做…; **to ~ sb. out of doing sth.** 吓得某人不敢做某事; **to ~ sb. off sth.** 吓得某人放弃某事; **to be ~ed of sb./sth.** 害怕某人/某事; **to ~ sb. into submission** 吓唬某人使其屈服; **to be ~ed to death** 吓得要死; **to be ~ed to death of sth.** 对某事怕得要命; **to be ~ed out of one's wits** 吓得魂飞魄散; **to ~ the life out of sb.** 把某人吓得要死
B *vi* 受惊吓; **I don't ~ easily** 我不易受惊吓

Phrasal verb

- **frighten away, frighten off** *vt* [**~ away sb./sth., ~ sb./sth. away**] 吓走 ‹*person, animal*›

frightened /ˈfraɪtnd/ *adj* 受惊的 ‹*person, animal*›; **to be ~** 感到害怕; **to be ~ that ...** 害怕…; **to be ~ about what might happen/about losing one's job** 为可能发生的事/失业担惊受怕; **to be ~ at the thought of doing ...** 想到做…而惊恐; **I've never been so ~ in my life** 我从来没有这样恐惧过

frightening /ˈfraɪtnɪŋ/ *adj* 骇人的 ‹*idea, sight, incident, quantity*›; **that story is ~** 那个故事很恐怖

frighteningly /ˈfraɪtnɪŋli/ *adv* 惊人地 ‹*simple, ugly, thin, expensive*›

frightful /ˈfraɪtfl/ *adj* **1** (shocking, terrifying) 可怕的 ‹*possibility, sight*› **2** colloq (serious) 严重的 ‹*mistake*›; **~ amount** 惊人的数量 **3** colloq (unpleasant) 讨厌的 ‹*book, smell, nuisance, speech*›; **he had a ~ time of it** 他因这事有一阵儿很不愉快

frightfully /ˈfraɪtfəli/ *adv* colloq dated 极其; **he was ~ tired** 他非常疲劳; **I'm not ~ keen** 我不太热衷

frigid /ˈfrɪdʒɪd/ *adj* **1** (temperature) 寒冷的 ‹*climate, wilderness, water*›; **~ zone** 寒带 **2** Med 性冷淡的 **3** (unfriendly) 冷淡的 ‹*look, atmosphere, silence*›

frigidly /ˈfrɪdʒɪdli/ *adv* 冷淡地 ‹*look, respond*›

frill /frɪl/
A *n* **1** Fashn 褶边 **2** Culin 纸卷饰
B **frills** *npl* 虚饰

frilled /frɪld/ *adj* 饰有褶边的 ‹*garment, curtain*›

frilly /ˈfrɪli/ *adj* **1** (having frills) 饰有褶边的 ‹*garment, curtain*› **2** (showy) 词藻华丽的 ‹*speech, style*›

fringe /frɪndʒ/
A *n* **1** Brit (of hair) 刘海 **2** (decorative trim) 流苏 **3** (edge) 边缘; **on the ~ of sth.** 在某物的外围; **on the ~(s) of society** 在社会的边缘
B *modif* **1** Theat 非主流的 ‹*actor*›; **she works in ~ theatre** 她在实验戏剧界工作 **2** Pol, Sociol 非正统的 ‹*element, views*›
C *vt* **1** (decorate, embellish) 装饰…的边缘; **the cloth was ~d with lace** 那块布镶有蕾丝花边 **2** (form border) «*trees, houses*» 构成…的边缘 ‹*pool, square, road*›; **palms ~d the oasis** 棕榈树环绕着绿洲

fringe benefit *n* 附加福利

frippery /ˈfrɪpəri/ *n* **1** [u] (showiness, ostentation) 虚饰; **I dislike ~ in architecture** 我不喜欢华丽的建筑风格 **2** [c] (tawdry thing) 俗丽的东西 **3** [c] (frivolous thing) 无价值的东西

frisbee® /ˈfrɪzbiː/ *n* 飞盘

frisk /frɪsk/
A *vi* «*animal, person*» 欢跃; **to ~ about** 活蹦乱跳
B *vt* colloq «*police officer*» 搜…的身 ‹*suspect*›

friskiness /ˈfrɪskɪnɪs/ *n* [u] 活泼

frisky /ˈfrɪski/ *adj* 活泼的 ‹*mood, lamb, puppy*›; **to feel ~** 觉得轻松活泼

fritillary /frɪˈtɪləri/ *n* **1** (plant) 贝母 **2** (butterfly) 豹纹蝶

fritter¹ /ˈfrɪtə(r)/

Phrasal verb

- **fritter away** *vt* [**~ away sth., ~ sth. away**] 浪费; **to ~ sth. away on ...** 把某物浪费在…上; **he ~s away his money on silly things** 他把钱浪费在一些傻事上

fritter² *n* 油炸馅饼; **apple/banana ~** 油炸苹果/香蕉馅饼

frivolity /frɪˈvɒləti/ *n* **1** [u] (light-heartedness) 轻浮 **2** [c] (frivolous action) 无聊行为; (frivolous thing) 无聊事; **she has no time for frivolities** 她没有时间做无聊的事情

frivolous /ˈfrɪvələs/ *adj* 轻浮的 ‹*person, behaviour, comment, activity*›

frivolously /ˈfrɪvələsli/ *adv* 轻浮地; **to behave ~** 举止轻浮; **to treat sb. ~** 对待某人很轻浮; **to treat sth. ~** 对待某事很敷衍

frivolousness /ˈfrɪvələsnɪs/ *n* [u] 轻浮

frizz /frɪz/
A *vt* 使拳曲; **to have one's hair ~ed** 把头发烫卷
B *n* 拳曲

frizzle /ˈfrɪzl/
A *vi* «*bacon, eggs*» [煎或烤得] 吱吱响
B *vt* (fry) 把…煎脆 ‹*bacon, eggs*›; (grill) 把…烤脆 ‹*bacon, eggs*›

frizzy /ˈfrɪzi/ *adj* 满是小卷儿的; **~-haired** 满头卷发的

fro /frəʊ/ *adv* ▸**to and fro**

frock /frɒk/ *n* **1** (dress) 连衣裙 **2** Relig (gown) 僧袍

frock coat *n* 男礼服大衣

frog /frɒg, Amer frɔːg/ *n* 青蛙; **to have a ~ in one's throat** colloq 失音

frog: ~man /-mən/ *n* 蛙人; **~march** *vt* «*soldiers, police officer*» 反扭双手押送 ‹*detainee, prisoner*›; **~spawn** *n* [u] 蛙卵

frolic /ˈfrɒlɪk/
A *vi* (*pres p* **~king,** *pt, pp* **~ked**) «*lamb, child, puppy*» 嬉戏; **to ~ about** *or* **around** 四处嬉戏; **to ~ in the waves** 戏浪
B *n* 欢乐的活动; **we let the children out for a ~ on the grass** 我们让孩子们出去到草地上嬉戏; **to her their affair was just a ~** 对她而言，他们的恋情不过是场游戏

frolicsome /ˈfrɒlɪksəm/ *adj* 嬉戏的 ‹*lamb, puppy, child*›; 欢乐的 ‹*mood*›

from /frɒm, frəm/ *prep* **1** (indicating place of origin, place of work) 来自; **a flight/train ~ Cardiff** 从加的夫来的航班/火车; **where is he ~?** 他是哪里人？; **butter ~ Denmark** 丹麦黄油; **a voice came ~ within/above** 从里面/上面传来一个声音; **an email ~ Paula** 葆拉发来的电子邮件; **a woman ~ the tax office** 税务所的女工作人员; **some girls ~ Year 6** 一些 6 年级女生 **2** (expressing distance, physical separation) 离; **10 km ~ the sea** 离海边 10 公里; **the journey ~ A to B** 从 A 地到 B 地的旅程; **to be away ~ home** 不在家; **to clear litter ~ the streets** 清除街头垃圾 **3** (indicating location, start of a process, original state) 从; (judging by) 依据; **~ the top of a bus** 从公共汽车顶上; **to rise ~ captain to colonel** 从上尉升为上校; **to translate ~ English into Spanish** 从英语译成西班牙语; **~ a practical point of view** 从实用的观点; **~**

f

what she said 据她所说; ~ her appearance you'd think she was only 20 从外表上看，你可能以为她只有 20 岁 4 (expressing starting time, point) 从…起; ~ today/July 从今天/七月起; ~ the 17th century on/9 o'clock onwards 从 17 世纪/9 点钟起; ~ morning till night 从早到晚; are these the photographs ~ last week? 这些是上周以来拍的照片吗？; wine ~ £5 a bottle 起价 5 英镑 1 瓶的葡萄酒; she's not back ~ work yet 她还没有下班回家 5 (using as basis, indicating source) [表示基础或来源]; to grow geraniums ~ seed 撒籽栽种天竺葵; I got no sympathy ~ him 我没有得到他的支持; you can tell him ~ me that ... 你可以转告给他，我说…; portraits ~ life 真人肖像 6 (among) 从…中; they were chosen ~ 100 competitors 他们是从 100 个竞争者中选出来的 7 (indicating raw material) 由; it's made ~ eggs 这是鸡蛋做的; it was carved ~ a large piece of wood 这是用一块大木料雕成的 8 (because of, owing to) 因为; to do sth. ~ necessity/laziness/nervousness 出于需要/懒惰/惶恐不安而做某事; I know ~ speaking to her that ... 我从与她的谈话中得知… 9 (in subtraction) 从…减去; 8 ~ 19 leaves 11 19 减 8 等于 11 10 (indicating attachment) [表示附着]; hanging ~ a pole 悬挂在柱子上; sticking out ~ the wall 从墙上伸出来 11 (indicating prevention) [表示防止]; he rescued her ~ drowning 他把她从水里救了上来; he was saved ~ the fire 他被人从火中救了出来 12 (indicating distinction) [表示区分]; he can't tell sugar ~ saccharine 他分不清糖和糖精; is Portuguese very different ~ Spanish? 葡萄牙语和西班牙语区别大吗？

frond /frɒnd/ *n* (of fern, palm) 叶; (of seaweed) 叶状体

front /frʌnt/

A *n* 1 [c] (forward-facing part) 前面; (main flat side) 正面; in ~ of sth. 在某物前面; there is a dent in the ~ of the car 车子前面有一个凹痕; the skirt fastens at the ~ 这条裙子在前面系扣; the book had a picture of an elephant on the ~ 书的封面有一张大象的图片; from the ~, it looks like ... 从正面看，它似乎…; the eyes are at the ~ of the head (of animal) 眼睛在头的正面; I'd like it a bit shorter at the ~, please (at hairdresser's) 我想要前面短一些 2 [c] (of person's body) 胸部; he spilt soup down his ~ 他把汤洒在了前胸上; I was lying on my ~ 我正趴着 3 [c] (furthest forward interior part) 前部; the teacher stood at the ~ of the room 老师站在房间前部; the pages at the ~ of the book 书的前几页; at the ~ of the plane 在飞机的前部; face the ~! 向前看！; out ~ 观众席 4 [c] (furthest forward part of procession, crowd) 前端; I was at the ~ of the queue *or* line 我在队列的最前面 5 [u] (position ahead of sb./sth.) 领先地位; to be in ~ (of sth./sb.) 领先（某物/某人）; if you want to stay in ~ of your competitors, you must ... 如果想保持领先你的对手，你必须… 6 [c] (initial position) 开始位置; at the ~ 在开始位置 7 [u] (presence) 面前; in ~ of sb. 在某人面前; not in ~ of the children! 不要当着孩子的面！ 8 [c] esp Brit (promenade) 海滨人行道; we went for a stroll along/on the ~ 我们沿着海滨路/在海滨路上漫步; on the river ~ 在滨河人行道上 9 [c] Meteorol 锋; a cold/warm/occluded ~ 冷锋/暖锋/锢囚锋 10 [c] Mil 前线; to open up a ~ 开辟一条战线 11 [c] (area of activity) 方面; on the ... ~ 在…范围内; on the political/fashion ~ 在政治/时尚领域 12 [c] (in names) 阵线; Popular F~ 人民阵线; the worker's/people's ~ 工人/人民阵线 13 [c] (outer appearance) 外表; to put on/show/present a bold/brave ~ 装出/显示出/呈现出大胆/勇敢的外表; to present a united ~ 表现出团结一致 14 [c] (cover) 掩护; a ~ for sth. 某物的掩护; the jewellery business was a ~ for a diamond-smuggling operation 珠宝生意被用作走私钻石的幌子 15 [u] (boldness) 放肆; he's got a bit of talent and a lot of ~ 他小有才华，但狂妄自大; he had the ~ to tell me I was wrong! 他竟厚颜无耻地对我说我错了！

B *adj attrib* 1 (facing street) 前面的 ‹*window, wall, gate, garden*›; (in the front) 前部的 ‹*wheel, wing*›; (furthest from rear) 前端的 ‹*carriage, seat, row*›; the piano is in the ~ room 钢琴在前厅; the ~ leg/foot/paw 前腿/足/爪; we sat in the ~ row 我们坐在前排; the ~ section of the book 书的第一部分; ~ teeth 门牙 2 Sport 领先的 ‹*athlete, car, horse*› 3 (head-on) 正面的 ‹*view, elevation*›

C *vi* 1 (face) «*house, window, garden*» 朝向; to ~ on to sth. Brit, to ~ on sth. Amer 面向某物; his office ~s on to the car park 他的办公室面对着停车场 2 (act as cover) 作掩护; to ~ for sb./sth. 掩护某人/某物

D *vt* 1 (face) «*house, garden*» 面向 ‹*beach, river, street*› 2 (be in front of) «*car park, wall, hedge*» 位于…前面 ‹*building*›; the house is ~ed by an attractive garden 房子前面是一个漂亮的花园 3 (provide with front) 为…装正面 ‹*building, monument, cupboard*›; to be ~ed with *or* by sth. 正面覆盖某物 4 colloq (lead) 领导 ‹*organization, group*› 5 TV, Radio colloq 主持 ‹*show, programme*›

frontage /ˈfrʌntɪdʒ/ *n* 1 [c] Archit (of house, shop) 正面 2 [u and c] (extent abutting on sth.) 毗邻面; a warehouse with river ~ 临河的仓库; the shop has ~s on two streets 该商店两面临街

frontal /ˈfrʌntl/

A *adj usu attrib* 1 (head-on) 正面的 ‹*assault, view, nudity*›; Cin, Phot 前面的 ‹*lighting*›; a ~ attack on the enemy 对敌人的正面进攻; the prime minister survived a ~ attack from the leader of the Opposition fig 首相顶住了反对党领袖的正面攻击 2 Anat 前额的; the ~ lobes of the brain 大脑额叶 3 Meteorol 锋面的 ‹*system, rainfall, cloud*›

B *n* 祭坛帷帘

front: ~ **bench** *n* [u] Brit 1 (seats) [议会下院中内阁和影子内阁成员坐的] 前座; 2 (members) 前座议员; the Opposition ~ bench 反对党的前座议员; **~bencher** /-ˈbentʃə(r)/ *n* Brit 前座议员; ~ **company** *n* 幌子公司; ~ **cover** *n* 封面; ~ **door** *n* 正门

front-end

A *n* 前端

B *modif* 前端的

frontier /ˈfrʌntɪə(r), Amer frʌnˈtɪər/

A *n* 1 (line, border) 边界 2 (district) 边疆 3 (limit of settled land) 边远地区; the wild ~ 蛮荒之地 4 (limit of knowledge) 前沿; the ~s of science 科学的新领域

B *modif* 边境的; ~ zone/town/spirit 边疆地带/边陲小镇/开拓精神

frontier: ~ **post** *n* 边防站; **~sman** /frʌnˈtɪəzmən/ *n* 边疆居民; **~swoman** *n* 边疆女居民

frontispiece /ˈfrʌntɪspiːs/ *n* 卷首插图

front line /ˈfrʌntlaɪn/

A *n* 1 Mil 前线; to be at *or* on the ~ 在前线 2 fig (position) 关键位置; to be in/on the ~ 在最重要的位置上

B **front-line** *modif* 前线的

Frontline States *npl* 前线国家

front: **~-loader** /-ˈləʊdə(r)/ *n* 1 (washing machine) 前开式滚筒式洗衣机; 2 (tractor) 前端式装载机; **~man** /-mæn/ *n* 1 (figurehead) 负责人; 2 ▸p. 409 *n* (TV presenter) 节目主持人; 3 ▸p. 409 *n* (lead musician) 首席乐师; (lead singer) 主唱; ~ **matter** *n* [u] 前页; ~ **money** *n* 预付款; ~ **office** *n* 管理部门

front of house Brit

A *n* （剧场）公众区

B **front-of-house** *modif* 公众区的

front page

A *n* 头版

B **front-page** *modif* 头版的; ~ headlines/news 头版头条/新闻

front: ~ **room** *n* = living room; ~ **runner** *n* 1 (contestant) 最可能获胜的竞争者; 2 (athlete, horse) 领先者; ~ **vowel** *n* 前元音; **~-wheel drive** *n* [u] 前轮驱动; a car with ~-wheel drive 前轮驱动车

frost /frɒst/

A *n* 1 [u] (weather condition) 霜冻; 10° of ~ 零下 10 度; a touch of ~ 轻微的霜冻 2 [c] (period of cold weather) 霜冻期; a hard *or* heavy *or* severe ~ 酷寒

B *vt* 1 (cover with frost) 使…结上霜; the garden was ~ed over 园子里结霜了 2 esp Amer Culin 在…上面撒糖霜

Phrasal verb

• **frost over, frost up** *vi* 结霜; the windshield has ~ed over 挡风玻璃结了霜

frost: **~bite** *n* [u] 冻伤; **~bitten** *adj* 冻伤的 ‹*feet, plants*›

frosted /ˈfrɒstɪd/ *adj* 1 (from cold) 结霜的 ‹*windscreen, window, garden*› 2 (textured) 磨砂的; ~ glass 毛玻璃

frosting /ˈfrɒstɪŋ/ *n* [u] 1 Amer Culin 糖霜 2 (on glass) 霜状表面

frost-resistant *adj* 抗霜冻的 ‹*plant, tile*›

frosty /ˈfrɒsti/ *adj* 1 (very cold) 严寒的 ‹*night, air*›; a spell of ~ weather 一段严寒天气 2 (covered with frost) 结霜的 ‹*pavement, lawn, roof*› 3 fig 冷淡的 ‹*atmosphere, welcome*›; to give sb. a ~ look 冷冷地看某人一眼

froth /frɒθ, Amer frɔːθ/

A *n* [u] 1 (in gas, liquid) 泡沫 2 (around the mouth) 口边白沫 3 fig (trivia) 无价值的事物

B *vi* 1 (form, contain bubbles) 起泡沫 2 (emit saliva) «*person, animal*» 口吐白沫; to ~ at the mouth lit 口吐白沫; fig 气得七窍生烟

frothy /ˈfrɒθi, Amer ˈfrɔːθi/ *adj* 1 (containing bubbles) 有泡沫的 ‹*liquid, beer*› 2 (trivial) 浅薄的 ‹*novel, talk, entertainment*›

frown /fraʊn/

A *n* 皱眉; to reply/say with a ~ 皱着眉头回答/说

B *vi* 皱眉; to ~ at sb./sth. 对某人/某事皱眉头; to ~ with concentration 全神贯注紧锁双眉

Phrasal verb

• **frown on, frown upon** *vt* [~ on sth.] 不赞成

frowzy, frowsy /ˈfraʊzi/ *adj* 邋遢的 ‹*clothes, person*›

froze /frəʊz/ *pt* ▸freeze A, B

frozen /ˈfrəʊzn/

A *pp* ▸freeze A, B

B *adj* 1 (covered with ice) 结冰的 ‹*lake, ground*›; to be ~ (over) 结冰; the ~ North 冰天雪地的北方 2 (hardened or blocked by ice) 冻住的 ‹*earth, pipe*›; to be ~ solid/through 被冻硬/透了 3 (preserved) 冷冻的 ‹*meat, vegetables, fruit*›; ~ food compartment 冷冻室 4 fig (extremely cold) 极冷的 ‹*person, hands, toes*›; to be ~ stiff/to the bone 冻僵 5 fig 吓呆的 ‹*person, animal*›; to be ~ with fear 被吓呆; to be ~ to the spot 被吓呆

FRS *abbr* Brit = Fellow of the Royal Society 皇家学会会员

frugal /ˈfruːɡl/ *adj* 1 (thrifty) 节俭的 ‹*housekeeper, life*›; to live in a ~ way/manner 节俭度日; to be ~ with one's modest income 因收入不高而节省 2 (inexpensive) 简单且花费少的 ‹*meal*›; a very ~ lunch 非常简单的中饭 3 (meagre) 份量少的 ‹*meal, portion*›

frugality /fruːˈɡæləti/ *n* [u] 1 (thriftiness) 节俭; the ~ of one's existence 俭朴的生活 2 (cheapness) 廉价; the ~ of her dinners

was notorious 她的晚餐之简单远近皆知 3 (meagreness) 量小

frugally /ˈfruːɡəli/ *adv* 节俭地 ‹*live, eat*›

fruit /fruːt/

A *n* 1 [c and u] (edible seed, seeds) 水果; **tropical ~s** 热带水果; **to grow ~** 种植水果; **to be in** *or* **bear ~** 结水果; **a piece of ~** 一块水果; **have some ~** 吃一些水果; **the ~s of the earth** 大地的果实 2 [c] (of other plants) 果实 3 [c] fig (result) 成果; **to bear ~** 取得成果; **the ~(s) of one's labours/of victory** 劳动成果/胜利果实; **the ~ of their union** liter 他们团结的产物

B *vi* «*tree*» 结果

fruit: ~ bowl *n* 果盆; **~ cake** *n* 1 Culin 水果蛋糕; 2 colloq hum 疯子; **to be as nutty as a ~cake** 完全疯了; **~ cocktail** *n* [罐装] 什锦水果; **~ cup** *n* 1 Brit (drink) 什锦果汁饮料; 2 Amer (fruit salad) 水果色拉; **~ dish** *n* 水果菜肴; **~ drop** *n* 1 [c] (sweet) 水果糖; 2 [u] (from tree) 落果

fruiterer /ˈfruːtərə(r)/ *n* ▸**p. 409** esp Brit dated 水果商

fruit: ~ farm *n* 果园; **~ farmer** ▸**p. 409** *n* 果农; **~ farming** *n* [u] 水果种植; **~ fly** *n* 果蝇

fruitful /ˈfruːtfl/ *adj* 1 lit 富饶的 ‹*earth, field*›; 丰产的 ‹*tree, plant*› 2 fig 富有成效的 ‹*discussion, collaboration*›; 成功的 ‹*experience, career*›; **a ~ line of enquiry** 有收获的询问方式

fruitfully /ˈfruːtfəli/ *adv* 1 (with positive results) 富有成效地 2 (usefully) 有效地

fruit gum® *n* 水果橡皮糖

fruition /fruːˈɪʃn/ *n* [u] (of hope, dream) 实现; (of project, plan) 完成; **to come to ~** 完成; **to bring sth. to ~** 使某事实现; **to be close to ~** 接近实现

fruit knife *n* 水果刀

fruitless /ˈfruːtlɪs/ *adj* 1 lit 不结果实的 ‹*tree, plant*› 2 fig 无成效的 ‹*efforts, negotiations*›; 无结果的 ‹*search, inquiry*›

fruit: ~ machine *n* Brit 老虎机; **~ salad** *n* 1 (dessert) 水果色拉; 2 Mil sl (decorations) 一排勋章; **~s of the forest** *npl* 丛林之果 [对浆果的称呼]; **~ tree** *n* 果树

fruity /ˈfruːti/ *adj* 1 (like or containing fruit) 果味的 ‹*wine, dessert*›; **a ~ smell/flavour** 果香味 2 (rich and deep) 圆润的 ‹*voice, tone, laugh*›

frump /frʌmp/ *n* pej 衣着过时的女人

frumpish /ˈfrʌmpɪʃ/ *adj* pej 衣着过时的

frustrate /frʌˈstreɪt, Amer ˈfrʌstreɪt/ *vt* 1 (prevent) «*weather, person*» 阻挠; **the storm ~d us in our attempt to land** 暴风雨使我们的降落意图落了空 2 (thwart) «*weather, opposition, person*» 挫败 ‹*efforts, plot*›; **to ~ sb.'s plans/hopes** 使某人的计划/希望落空 3 (annoy) «*money problem, difficulty, opposition, silence*» 使…心烦

frustrated /frʌˈstreɪtɪd, Amer ˈfrʌst-/ *adj* 1 (irritated) 恼怒的; **to be ~ at sth.** 对某事感到恼火; **to get ~** 恼火 2 (in job, role) 不满意的 3 (in attempt, effort) 受挫的 4 *attrib* (would-be) 不得志的 ‹*poet, actor, politician*› 5 (sexually) 性欲未获满足的

frustrating /frʌˈstreɪtɪŋ, Amer ˈfrʌst-/ *adj* 使人心烦的 ‹*problem, obstinacy, situation, experience*›; **it is ~ to be unable** *or* **not being able to do ...** 不能做…令人沮丧

frustratingly /frʌˈstreɪtɪŋli, Amer ˈfrʌst-/ *adv* 令人沮丧地

frustration /frʌˈstreɪʃn/ *n* 1 [u] (irritated feeling) 失望; **to suffer from ~** 感到失望; **~ at** *or* **with sth.** 对某事感到的失望; **to vent one's ~ (on sb./sth.)** (在某人/某物身上) 出气 2 [c] (irritating thing) 令人沮丧的事物; **the ~s of doing sth.** 做某事的不如意 3 (of attempt, effort) 沮丧 4 [u] (in job, role) 不满意 5 [u] (of plans, ambition) 受挫; **the ~ of sb.'s hopes** 某人希望的落空 6 (sexual) 性方面的不满足

fry¹ /fraɪ/ (*pt, pp* **fried**)

A *vt* 油煎; **to ~ eggs** 煎蛋

B *vi* «*fish, eggs*» 在油里煎

fry² *npl* (young fish) 鱼苗; (young animals) 幼小动物

frying pan Brit, **frypan** Amer *ns* 长柄平底煎锅; **to jump out of the ~ into the fire** fig 跳出油锅又落火坑

fry-up *n* Brit colloq 油煎菜; **to have a ~** 来一份油煎菜

FSA *abbr* Brit = **Financial Services Authority**

FT *abbr* Brit = **Financial Times**《金融时报》

ft *abbr* = **foot A8, feet**

FT index *n* = **FTSE index**

FTP

A *abbr* = **file transfer protocol** 文件传送协议

B *vt* (*pt* **FTP'd** *or* **FTPed,** *pres p* **FTPing**) 传送

FTSE index, FTSE 100 index *ns* = **Financial Times Stock Exchange Index**

fuchsia /ˈfjuːʃə/ *n* 倒挂金钟

fuck /fʌk/ taboo sl

A *n* 1 (act) 性交; **to have a ~** 性交 2 (person) 有性交技巧的人; **to be a good ~** 是个好床伴

B *excl* 他妈的 offensive; **~ you!** 滚你妈的蛋!; **~ it! it's broken!** 妈的! 坏掉了!; **~ me!** 我他妈的见鬼了!; **what the ~ is he doing here?** 他妈的, 他到底在这儿干什么?

C *vt* 1 lit 与…性交 ‹*person*› 2 (in exclamations) **I'm ~ed if I know!** 我要知道就不是人!; **~ knows!** 鬼才知道! 3 (damage, ruin) **it's ~ed** 坏了; **we're ~ed** 我们倒霉透了

D *vi* 性交

Phrasal verbs

- **fuck about, fuck around** taboo sl

A *vi* 瞎混; **stop ~ing about** *or* **around!** 别到处瞎混!

B *vt* [**~ sb. about/around**] 浪费…的时间 ‹*person*›

- **fuck off** *vi* taboo sl **~ off!** 滚开! offensive; **he told us to ~ off** 他叫我们滚
- **fuck up** *vt* taboo sl 1 [**~ up sb./sth., ~ sb./sth. up**] (mess up) 搞砸 ‹*task, job, project, challenge*› 2 [**~ up sb., ~ sb. up**] (confuse, damage emotionally) 使心绪不宁; **a ~ed-up kid** 糊涂的小子

fuck all *adv* Brit taboo sl 他妈的丝毫没有 offensive; **to know ~ about it** 他妈的对这个一点都不懂

fucking /ˈfʌkɪŋ/ taboo sl

A *adj* 该死的 offensive; **~ hell!** 他妈的见鬼!; **what a ~ shambles!** 真是乱成了一锅粥!; **you ~ idiot!** 你他妈的白痴!

B *adv* 他妈地 offensive; **you're ~ stupid!** 你真他妈愚蠢!

fuck-up *n* taboo sl 一团糟; **what a ~!** 真他妈一塌糊涂!

fuddle /ˈfʌdl/

A *n* colloq 糊涂; **in a ~** 糊里糊涂的

B *vt* [尤指酒精或毒品] 使糊涂

fuddled /ˈfʌdld/ *adj* 1 (confused) 糊里糊涂的 2 (from drinking) 醉醺醺的

fuddy-duddy /ˈfʌdidʌdi/

A *n* colloq 老古板; **you're such a ~!** 你真是个老顽固!

B *adj* 1 colloq (dull) 古板的; **a ~ idea** *or* **notion** 过时的观点 2 (fussy) 爱挑剔的 ‹*way, habit*›

fudge /fʌdʒ/

A *n* 1 [u] Culin (soft sweet) 乳脂软糖; **to have a piece of ~** 吃一块奶糖; **~ sauce** Amer 浓巧克力酱 2 [c] colloq (compromise) 蒙混; **a classic ~** 典型的弄虚作假

B *vt* 1 (evade) 回避 ‹*issue, problem*› 2 (falsify) 篡改 ‹*accounts, figures*›; 捏造 ‹*excuse, story*›

C *vi* 躲躲闪闪; **to ~ on sth.** 对某事含混其词

fuel /ˈfjuːəl/

A *n* 1 (for heat, power) 燃料; **to run/be out of ~** 用尽/没有燃料; **to take on ~** 加燃料; **~ prices/crisis** 燃料价格/危机 2 (food, drink) 营养物 3 (for anger, hatred) 刺激因素; **to add ~ to one's anger** 使某人更是怒火中烧; **to add ~ to the flames** *or* **fire** 火上加油

B *vt* (*pres p etc.* **-ll-,** Amer **-l-**) 1 (power) «*oil, gas, coal*» 用作…的燃料 ‹*furnace, vehicle*›; **to be ~led by oil/gas** 以石油/天然气为燃料 2 (put fuel into) 给…加燃料 ‹*plane, ship, rocket*› 3 fig (intensify) 使…加剧 ‹*inflation, crisis, unrest*›

C *vi* (*pres p etc.* **-ll-,** Amer **-l-**) «*driver, pilot, plane*» 加燃料; **a ~ling stop** 加油站

fuel: ~ cap *n* 油箱盖; **~ cell** *n* 燃料电池; **~ consumption** *n* 耗油量; **~-efficient** *adj* 油耗低的 ‹*motor, system, vehicle*›; **~-injected engine** *n* 电喷发动机; **~ injection** *n* [u] 燃料喷射; **~ injector** *n* 喷油器; **~ oil** *n* 燃油; **~ poverty** *n* [u] esp Brit 燃料贫困 [指无力支付家庭取暖燃料费]; **~ pump** *n* 燃油泵; **~ rod** *n* 燃料棒

fuel saving

A *n* [u] 节约燃料; **~ could increase profits** 节约燃料可以增加利润

B **fuel-saving** *adj* 节约燃料的

fuel tank *n* 油箱

fug /fʌɡ/ *n* Brit colloq 闷热污浊的室内空气; **a ~ of cigarette smoke** 污浊的香烟烟雾

fuggy /ˈfʌɡi/ *adj* Brit 闷热污浊的 ‹*room, atmosphere*›

fugitive /ˈfjuːdʒətɪv/

A *n* 逃亡者; **a ~ from justice** 逃犯

B *adj attrib* 1 (escaped) 逃跑的 ‹*robber*›; **a ~ criminal** 逃犯 2 liter (fleeting) 短暂的; **~ happiness/thoughts** 稍纵即逝的幸福/想法

fugue /fjuːɡ/ *n* 赋格曲

Fujian /ˌfuːˈdʒɪen/ ▸**p. 604** *pr n* **~ (Province)** 福建 (省)

fulcrum /ˈfʊlkrəm/ *n* (*pl* **fulcra** /ˈfʊlkrə/ *or* **~s**) 1 (of lever) 支点 2 fig (essential element) 支柱

fulfil Brit, **fulfill** Amer /fʊlˈfɪl/ *vt* (*pres p etc.* **-ll-**) 1 (realize, carry out) 实现 ‹*promise, prophecy, ambition*›; **to ~ one's potential** 发挥某人的潜力; **to ~ oneself** 充分发挥自己的才能 2 (satisfy) 满足 ‹*desire, need*›; 使…应验 ‹*dream, prayer*› 3 (meet) 符合 ‹*requirements, conditions*›; 履行 ‹*duty, obligation*›; 执行 ‹*command*›; **to ~ one's role/function as ...** 起到自己作为…的职责/作用

fulfilled /fʊlˈfɪld/ *adj* 感到满足的; **how ~ do you feel about your career?** 你对自己的事业满足感有多大?; **as a band we feel artistically ~** 作为一个乐队, 我们有艺术上的成就感

fulfilling /fʊlˈfɪlɪŋ/ *adj* 令人满足的 ‹*job, marriage*›

fulfilment Brit, **fulfillment** Amer /fʊlˈfɪlmənt/ *n* [u] 1 (realization, carrying out) 实现; **to come to ~** 实现; **this event was the ~ of an old prophecy** 这个事件应验了一个古老预言; **the ~ of one's hopes/prayers** 希望/祈祷的实现 2 (satisfaction) 满足; **to find ~ in sth.** 在某事中获得成就感; **to seek/find ~** 寻找/找到成就感; **~ still eluded her** 她仍然不满足 3 (of requirements) 符合; **~ of the statutory requirements** 法律要求的满足 4 (carrying out of role, duty, obligation) 履行

full /fʊl/

A *adj* 1 (completely filled, containing a significant amount) 装满的 ‹*box, glass, cupboard*›; 挤满人的 ‹*room, lift, bus*›; 满座的 ‹*theatre, cinema*›; 满房的 ‹*hotel*›; 塞满的 ‹*mouth, hand*›; Comput 刻录满的 ‹*disk*›; 录满的 ‹*tape*›; **~ sail** 满帆; **a ~ tank of petrol** 满满一箱汽油; **the bin**

f

is almost ~ 垃圾箱几乎满了; **'car park ~'** 车位已满; **~ to the brim** 满到边的; **~ to overflowing** lit 满得溢出的; **the train was ~ to overflowing** fig 火车上挤得水泄不通; **~ of sth.** 装满某物的; **a bucket ~ of water** 装满水的桶; **his arms were ~ of parcels** 他怀里抱满了包裹; **to have one's hands ~** 忙得不可开交; **don't speak** *or* **talk with your mouth ~** 嘴里塞满食物时不要讲话; **on a ~ stomach** 吃饱的; **my heart is ~** *or* **too ~ for words** 我激动得说不出话来; **with a ~ heart** 怀着激动的心情; **to be ~ of sth.** (be filled with) 充满某物; (focus on) 满脑子都是某物; **to be ~ of hope/fear** 充满希望/恐惧; **she's always ~ of good ideas** 她总是有很多好点子; **the papers are ~ of the plane crash** 报纸大肆报导这次坠机事件; **a letter ~ of spelling mistakes** 拼写错误连篇的信; **to be ~ of one's own importance** 自以为了不起 **2** *pred* (sated) «*person*» 吃饱的; **no thanks, I'm ~ (up)** 不, 谢谢, 我饱了; **I feel rather ~** 我感到有些撑; **to be ~ of sth.** 吃了很多某物 **3** (busy) 忙碌的 ‹*life, time*›; 排满的 ‹*diary*›; **his evenings are completely ~** 他每晚都很忙 **4** *attrib* (complete) 完整的 ‹*score, set, account, term*›; 全额的 ‹*sum, pension*›; 详尽的 ‹*details, information*›; **my grandfather still has a ~ set of teeth** 我祖父还有一口完整的牙齿; **in ~ uniform** 穿全套制服的; **students have to pay ~ fare** 学生必须付全价车费; **his ~ name** 他的全名; **a ~er understanding of the problem** 对这个问题更全面的理解; **to do a ~ week's work** 做整整一周的工作; **is he your ~ brother?** 他是你的同胞兄弟吗? ; **a book bound in ~ cloth/leather** 用全布面/全皮面装订的书 **5** *attrib* (officially recognized) 正式的 ‹*member, permit, citizenship*›; **a ~ professor** Amer Univ 正教授; **a ~ general/colonel** 将军/上校 **6** *attrib* (maximum) 最大的 ‹*volume, advantage*›; 最高的 ‹*score*›; **(at) ~ speed** *or* **tilt** *or* **pelt** (以) 全速; **~ speed** *or* **steam ahead** 全速前进; **they have been working ~ steam ahead all day** 他们一整天都在奋力工作; **~ employment** 充分就业; **to make ~ use of the facilities** 充分利用这些设施; **~ marks** lit 满分; **he deserves ~ marks for his loyalty** fig 他的忠诚值得褒奖; **~ marks to you for finding the key** 你找到了钥匙, 值得表扬; **to be at ~ stretch** 全力以赴 **7** *attrib* (emphasizing measurement) 整整 [表示强调]; **we waited a ~ hour** 我们等了整整一小时 **8** *attrib* (emphasizing magnitude) 全部的 ‹*responsibility*›; 绝对的 ‹*control, horror*›; **the ~ extent of the damage** 损坏的严重程度; **you have our ~ support in this campaign** 在这次活动中我们全力支持你; **the event received ~ TV coverage** 这个事件受到全面的电视报导; **in ~ possession of one's faculties** 神智十分清醒的; **in ~ view (of sb./sth.)** 被 (某人/某物) 尽收眼底 **9** *usu attrib* (rounded) 丰满的 ‹*figure, hips, breasts, lips*›; 胖乎乎的 ‹*face, thighs*› **10** Clothg 宽松的 ‹*skirt, sleeve, trousers, robe*› **11** Astron 满的; **a ~ moon** 满月 **12** (intense, rich) 深的 ‹*colour*›; 浑厚的 ‹*sound, voice*›; 浓郁的 ‹*flavour, body*› **13** (bright) 强烈的 ‹*sunshine, light*›; (direct) 直接的 ‹*sunshine, light*›; **to sit in the ~ sunlight** 坐在强烈的阳光下

B *adv* **1** (directly) 直接地; **to hit sb. ~ in the face/chest** 正中脸部/胸部; **~ in the centre** 在正中央; **to look sb. ~ in the face** 直盯着某人的脸 **2** dated (very) 非常; **I know ~ well what will happen** 我很清楚将要发生什么事 **3** (to the maximum) 最大程度地; **is the volume turned up ~?** 音量开到最大了吗? ; **~ on** 大开着; **the room heats up very quickly with the fire ~ on** 取暖器开到最大时, 房间很快就暖和起来; **the car's headlights were ~ on** 汽车的车头灯大开着; **she met the problem ~ on** 她全力对付这一问题

C *n* [u] **1** (complete form) 全部; **in ~** 完全地; **paid in ~** 付讫; **he has been repaid in ~ for his cruelty** 他的残忍遭到了彻底的报应 **2** (maximum) 最大程度; **to the ~** 充分地; **to enjoy** *or* **live life to the ~** 尽情享受生活

full: ~back *n* 后卫; **~ beam** *n* 远光; **~ blast** *adv* colloq 开足马力; **to turn on the radio (at) ~ blast** 开足收音机的音量; **to have the heater on (at) ~ blast** 把加热器调到最大档; **~-blooded** /ˌfʊlˈblʌdɪd/ *adj* **1** *attrib* (vigorous) 精力充沛的 ‹*person*›; 强有力的 ‹*argument*›; **a ~-blooded Socialist** 一位坚定的社会主义者; **~-blooded support/condemnation/onslaught** 大力支持/强烈谴责/猛烈攻击; **2** (pure bred) 纯血统的 ‹*person, animal*›; **~-blown** *adj* (fully developed) 充分发展的 ‹*plan, idea*›; 完全形成的 ‹*disease, disaster*›; 盛开的 ‹*rose*›; **~-blown Aids** 完全型艾滋病; **~ board** *n* [u] Brit 全食宿; **~-bodied** /ˌfʊlˈbɒdɪd/ *adj* 醇厚的 ‹*wine*›; 圆润的 ‹*sound*›; **~ colour** *n* [u] 全色; **illustrations in ~ colour** 彩色插图; **~-colour** *modif* 彩色的 ‹*picture, illustration, advertisement*›; **~-cream milk** *n* [u] 全脂牛奶

full dress

A *n* [u] 礼服; **officers in ~** 穿礼服的军官

B **full-dress** *modif* **1** Mil 穿礼服的 ‹*regiment, warrior*›; **full-dress uniform** 军礼服 **2** Pol 正式的 ‹*costume, reception*›

full: ~ face *adj* 正面的 ‹*picture, portrait*›; **~-fledged** *adj* Amer = **fully-fledged**; **~ house** *n* **1** Theat 满座; **to have a ~ house** 客满; **to play to a ~ house** 演出时座无虚席; **2** (in poker, bingo) 满堂红; **~-frontal** *adj* 裸露正面的 ‹*shot*›; **scenes of ~-frontal nudity** 正面全裸镜头; **~-grown** *adj* 完全成熟的

full-length /ˌfʊlˈleŋθ/

A *adj* **1** (of book, film) 标准长度的; **a ~ film/novel** 长片/足本小说 **2** (head to toe) 全身的; **~ window/mirror/portrait** 落地窗/穿衣镜/全身肖像 **3** (long) 及地的 ‹*nightdress, curtain*›; **a ~ skirt** 曳地长裙

B *adv* (*also* **full length**) 伸直地 ‹*fall, stretch out, sprawl*›; **she was lying ~ on the sofa** 她平躺在沙发上

full: ~ name *n* 全名; **~-nelson** *n* 双肩下握颈

fullness /ˈfʊlnɪs/ *n* [u] **1** (state of being filled) 满; **the ~ of the glass made it impossible to carry without spilling** 端这样满的玻璃杯不洒出去是不可能的 **2** (after eating) 饱; **a feeling of ~** 饱胀感 **3** (of details, information etc.) 充分; **the ~ of the information provided** 所提供信息的完整性; **the ~ of God's grace** 神恩浩荡; **in the ~ of time** liter 时机成熟时 **4** (of figure, lips, breasts, hips) 丰满 **5** (of skirt, sleeve) 宽松 **6** (of sound, voice) 圆浑; (of flavour) 醇厚

full: ~-page *adj* (in newspaper) 整版的 ‹*advertisement, picture*›; (in book or magazine) 全页的 ‹*article, illustration*›; **~ pay** *n* [u] 全薪; **~ price** *n* 全价; **to pay the ~ price** lit 付全价; fig 付出高昂的代价; **~-scale** *adj* 原尺寸的 ‹*drawing, model, replica*›; **~-size, ~-sized** *adj* **1** (large) 最大尺寸的; **2** (normal, standard) 正常尺寸的 ‹*bicycle, bed*›; **a ~-size violin** 全尺寸小提琴; **3** (actual size) 原尺寸的 ‹*replica, photo*›; **~ stop** *n* Brit **1** (in punctuation) 句号; **2** (as exclamation) 到此为止; **I'm not leaving, ~ stop!** 我不会走的, 不必多说了! ; **I find him a bit of a bore, ~ stop** 我发现他有些讨厌, 就是这话; **3** (in activity, situation) 完全停止; **to come to a ~ stop** 陷入僵局; **~-throated** *adj* 声音洪亮的; **to give a ~-throated laugh/cry** 放声大笑/哭; **~ time** *n* [u] 比赛结束; **to blow the whistle for ~ time** 吹响比赛结束的哨音

full-time

A *adj* 全职的 ‹*work, employee, employment*›; 全日制的 ‹*student, education*›; **it is a ~ job** lit 这是全职工作; fig 这是件费劲耗时的事情

B *adv* 全职地 ‹*write, teach, study*›; **she has been working ~ since Christmas** 从圣诞节以来她一直全职工作

full-timer *n* 全职人员

fully /ˈfʊli/ *adv* **1** (completely) 完全地; **you haven't ~ appreciated the dangers** 你并未充分认识到危险; **he ~ expected to lose his job** 他满以为自己会丢掉工作; **she hasn't ~ recovered** 她还没有完全康复; **a ~ automatic washing machine** 全自动洗衣机; **the apartment is ~ furnished** 这套公寓家具齐全; **a ~ illustrated guide** 配有详尽插图的指南 **2** (to the maximum) 充分地; **a ~ laden van** 一辆满载的货车; **my time is ~ occupied** 我的时间被占满了; **the valve must be ~ closed** 阀门必须关严; **to be ~ stretched** fig 竭尽所能 **3** (comprehensively) 深入地 ‹*study*›; 彻底地 ‹*investigate*›; 详尽地 ‹*describe*› **4** (at least) 整整 [用于强调]; **it took us ~ two hours to get there** 去那里花了我们整整 2 个小时

fully: ~-fashioned *adj* 合身的 ‹*stockings, knitwear*›; **~-fledged** *adj* Brit **1** (having grown all its feathers) 羽翼丰满的 ‹*bird*›; **2** (established, developed) 完全合格的 ‹*lawyer, doctor, accountant*›; 成熟的 ‹*religion, political party*›

fulmar /ˈfʊlmə(r)/ *n* 暴风鹱

fulminate /ˈfʊlmɪneɪt, ˈfʌl-/ *vi* 强烈抗议; **to ~ against sb./sth.** 强烈抗议某人/某事

fulmination /ˌfʊlmɪˈneɪʃn, ˌfʌl-/ *n* 强烈抗议

fulness /ˈfʊlnɪs/ *n* [u] = **fullness**

fulsome /ˈfʊlsəm/ *adj* 过分恭维的 ‹*appreciation*›; **to be ~ in one's compliments of sb./sth.** 大肆吹嘘某人/某物; **~ praise/apology** 溢美之词/低三下四的道歉

fulsomely /ˈfʊlsəmli/ *adv* 过分恭维地 ‹*praise, apologize*›

fulsomeness /ˈfʊlsəmnɪs/ *n* [u] 过分恭维

fumarole /ˈfjuːmərəʊl/ *n* [火山区的] 喷气孔

fumble /ˈfʌmbl/

A *vt* **1** (fluff, bungle) 笨拙地做; **I ~d my opening speech** 我把开场白念得结结巴巴; **to ~ one's entrance/answer** 跌跌撞撞地进来/结结巴巴地回答 **2** Sport 漏接 ‹*ball, throw*›

B *vi* **1** (fiddle clumsily) 笨拙地做事; **to ~ for/with sth.** 笨手笨脚地摸寻/摆弄某物 **2** fig (search for words) 笨嘴拙舌地说话; **to ~ for words** 结结巴巴找话说

Phrasal verb

- **fumble about, fumble around** *vi* 笨拙地摸索; **to ~ about in ...** 笨手笨脚地在…中摸索 ‹*bag, drawer*›

fume /fjuːm/

A *vi* **1** (emit smoke, gas, or vapour) «*embers, wreck, volcano*» 冒烟; «*liquid*» 冒出 **2** (feel, show anger) 发怒; **to ~ at sth./sb.** 为某事/对某人发怒; **to ~ with anger/ impatience** 怒气冲冲/极不耐烦

B **fumes** *npl* [刺鼻有害的] 气体; **to emit/inhale ~s** 发出/吸入有害气体; **petrol ~s** 汽油味; **exhaust ~s** 废气; **traffic/factory ~s** 汽车尾气/工厂废气

fumigate /ˈfjuːmɪgeɪt/ *vt* [为消毒或灭虫] 熏蒸 ‹*room, ward*›

fun /fʌn/

A *n* [u] **1** (amusement, enjoyment) 乐趣; **to have ~ doing sth.** 做某事很开心; **it is ~ to do sth., doing sth. is ~** 做某事很有趣; **for ~, for the ~ of it, in ~** 为了好玩; **to spoil sb.'s ~** 扫某人的兴; **to have a sense of ~** 有幽默感; **have ~!** 尽情玩吧! ; **~ and games** 嬉戏; **what ~!** 多么有趣! **2** (source of pleasure) 有趣的事物; **card games are great ~** 打牌非常有趣 **3** (playfulness) 风趣; **to be full of ~** 很风趣 **4** (good company) 有趣的人; **she is great ~ to be with** 同她在一起很开心 **5** (mockery) 嘲笑; **to make ~ of sb./sth.,**

f

to poke ~ at sb./sth. 嘲笑某人/某事; **to become a figure of ~** 成为取笑对象
B *adj attrib* 有趣的 ‹*person, activity*›; **it's a ~ thing to do** 这事做起来很有趣

function /ˈfʌŋkʃn/
A *n* 1 [c] (role) (of body, organ, tool) 功能; (of person) 职责; **to fulfil** *or* **perform a ~** 履行职责; **bodily ~s** 身体官能; **in her ~ as ...** 在她作为…的职责中 2 [u] (use, purpose) 用途; **designs that prioritize style over ~** 优先考虑式样而非实用性的设计 3 [c] (social event) 盛大的聚会; **to attend a ~** 出席大型社会活动; **a charity/an official/a social ~** 慈善/公务/社交活动 4 [c] fig (aspect, part) 应变量; **intelligence is partly a ~ of the speed of your brain** 智力水平有部分是取决于大脑活动的速度 5 [c] Comput 功能 6 [c] Math 函数; **an exponential ~** 指数函数
B *vi* 1 (work properly) «*machine, system, organization*» 运转; **the phone isn't ~ing** 电话坏了; **her brain/liver is ~ing normally** 她的大脑/肝脏功能正常 2 (perform as) 起作用; **to ~ as sb./sth.** 起某人/某物的作用; **to ~ as sb.'s administrative assistant** 担任某人的行政助理

functional /ˈfʌŋkʃənl/ *adj* 1 *attrib* (operational) 功能上的 ‹*efficiency, differences*›; **~ disorder** Med 机能紊乱; **~ dependence** 功能上的依赖 2 (in working order) 起作用的; **the museum will be ~ from May** 博物馆将从五月份开始开放; **all ~ machines are ready** 所有能用的机器都准备好了; **he's barely ~ before 10 o'clock** hum 他在10点钟以前无法工作 3 (practical, useful) 实用的 ‹*furniture, clothing, design*› 4 Math 函数的

functionalism /ˈfʌŋkʃənəlɪzəm/ *n* [u] 功能主义

functionality /ˌfʌŋkʃəˈnæləti/ *n* [u] 1 (practicality) 实用性 2 (purpose) 设计功能 3 Comput 功能

functionary /ˈfʌŋkʃənəri, Amer -neri/ *n* formal 公职人员; **a government ~** 政府官员

function: ~ key *n* 功能键; **~ room** *n* 功能厅; **~ word** *n* 功能词

fund /fʌnd/
A *n* 1 (cash reserve) 基金; **to establish** *or* **set up a ~** 设立基金; **to administer** *or* **manage a ~** 管理基金 2 fig (supply, store) 储备; **to have a ~ of sth. to draw on** 有某物可以利用; **to have a ~ of wisdom/wit/experience** 富有智慧/非常风趣/很有经验
B **funds** *npl* 资金; **to raise ~s for sth.** 为某事筹集资金; **to have the ~s to do sth.** 有钱做某事; **to be in ~s** 手头有钱; **insufficient ~s** 无存款 [银行通知开空头支票账户的用语]
C *vt* 为…提供资金 ‹*expansion, work*›; **publicly ~ed project** 公共资金资助的项目

fundamental /ˌfʌndəˈmentl/
A *adj* 1 (essential, crucial) 基本的 ‹*principle, concept, idea*›; **to be ~ to sth.** 对某事极为重要 2 (basic, total) 全然的; **a ~ incompatibility** 彻底的不相容; **these are ~ differences** 这些是根深蒂固的分歧 3 (central, primary) 根本的 ‹*change, mistake*›; 关键的 ‹*question*›; **to be of ~ concern/importance** 最为关心/重要
B **fundamentals** *npl* 基本原理; **the ~s of chemistry/weaving** 化学的基本原理/编织的基本知识; **to get down to ~s** 从最基本的问题着手

fundamentalism /ˌfʌndəˈmentəlɪzəm/ *n* [u] 1 (Christian) 基要主义 2 (Islamic) 原教旨主义

fundamentalist /ˌfʌndəˈmentəlɪst/
A *n* 1 (Christian) 基要主义者 2 (Islamic) 原教旨主义者
B *adj* 1 (Christian) 基要主义的 2 (Islamic) 原教旨主义的

fundamentally /ˌfʌndəˈmentəli/ *adv* 1 (essentially, crucially) 基本地; **~ incompatible/mistaken** 完全不相容/基本上错的 2 (basically) 根本地 ‹*change, transform*›; **what concerns me ~ is ...** 我最关心的是…; **he's ~ a socialist** 从本质上讲, 他是个社会主义者

fundi /ˈfʊndi/ *n* S Afr colloq 行家

funding /ˈfʌndɪŋ/ *n* [u] 资金; **~ from sb./sth.** 某人/某机构提供的资金; **~ for sth.** 为某事提供的资金; **~ for a project** 项目资金

funding body, funding agency *ns* 出资者

fund: ~ manager *n* 基金经理; **~ of ~s** *n* 母基金; **~-raiser** *n* (person) 资金筹集者; (event) 募捐活动

fund-raising
A *n* [u] 资金筹集
B *adj* 筹集资金的; **a ~ event/dinner** 募捐活动/宴会

funeral /ˈfjuːnərəl/ *n* 1 (ceremony) 葬礼; **to go to** *or* **attend a ~** 参加葬礼; **that's your/his/her ~!** 那是你/他/她自作自受! 2 dated (procession) 出殡的行列; **the ~ was going down the hill** 送葬的队伍正在下山

funeral: ~ director ▸**p. 409** *n* 殡仪员; **~ home** *n* esp Amer 殡仪馆; **~ march** *n* 哀乐; **~ oration** *n* 悼词; **~ parlour** *n* Brit 殡仪馆; **~ procession** *n* 送葬的队伍; **~ pyre** 火葬柴堆; **~ service** *n* [行宗教仪式的] 葬礼; **to attend/hold a ~ service** 参加/举行葬礼

funereal /fjuːˈnɪəriəl/ *adj* 悲哀肃穆的 ‹*atmosphere, tone*›

fun fair *n* esp Brit 游乐场

fungal /ˈfʌŋgl/ *adj* 由真菌引起的 ‹*disease, infection*›; 真菌的 ‹*growth*›

fungi /ˈfʌŋgaɪ, -dʒaɪ/ *pl* ▸**fungus 1, 2**

fungus /ˈfʌŋgəs/ *n* 1 [c] (*pl* **fungi** *or* **~es**) (plant) 真菌类植物 2 [c] (*pl* **fungi** *or* **~es**) (mould) 真菌 3 [u] (infection) [尤指鱼的] 真菌病 4 [u] fig (unpleasant growth, spread) 冒出来的丑陋东西; **a ~ of outbuildings behind the house** 房子后面冒出来的一批丑陋附属建筑物 5 [u] sl (facial hair) 胡须; **~ face** 大胡子 [称呼语]

funicular /fjuːˈnɪkjʊlə(r)/ *n* **~ (railway)** 缆索铁道

funk /fʌŋk/
A *n* 1 Mus 乡土爵士乐, 放克乐 2 Brit dated (fear, panic) 惊恐; **to be in a (blue) ~** 吓惨了
B *vt* colloq [因恐惧] 逃避; **I wanted to tell her but I ~ed it** 我想告诉她, 但我不敢

funky /ˈfʌŋki/ *adj* colloq 1 (in music) 节奏强劲的 ‹*music, sound*› 2 (stylish) 时髦的 ‹*car, hairstyle, clothes*›

fun-loving *adj* 喜欢玩乐的

funnel /ˈfʌnl/
A *n* 1 (for liquids) 漏斗 2 (on ship, engine) 烟囱
B *vt* (*pres p etc.* **-ll-** Brit, **-l-** Amer) 1 lit (direct) 使…流经漏斗形口子 ‹*liquid, gas, smoke, air*›; **to ~ sth. into/through/out sth.** 使某物流入/流过/流出某物 2 fig (channel) 输送 ‹*aid, funds, supplies*›
C *vi* (*pres p etc.* **-ll-** Brit, **-l-** Amer) 通过漏斗形空间; **to ~ into/through sth.** 挤进/挤过某物

funnies /ˈfʌnɪz/ *npl* Amer colloq 滑稽连环漫画

funnily /ˈfʌnɪli/ *adv* 1 (amusingly) 滑稽地 ‹*perform, recite*› 2 (oddly) 古怪地 ‹*behave, walk*›; **~ enough, ...** 真奇怪, …

funny /ˈfʌni/ *adj* 1 (amusing) 滑稽的 ‹*person, joke, story*›; **very ~!** iron 真好笑!; **don't try anything ~** 别玩鬼花样; **don't try to be ~!** 别开玩笑!; **don't get ~ with me!** 不要对我无礼!; **it's not ~** 这可不是儿戏 2 (odd) 古怪的 ‹*person, idea, noise*›; **it's ~ that ...** 真奇怪, …; **there's something ~ about ...** …有点蹊跷; **~ peculiar or ~ ha-ha?** 是稀奇古怪还是滑稽可笑? 3 colloq (unwell) 稍有不适的; **to feel ~** 感到有点不舒服; **to come over all ~** 感到头晕目眩

funny: ~ bone *n* colloq 麻筋儿 [肘端神经敏感节位]; **~ business** *n* [u] colloq 见不得人的勾当; **~ farm** *n* colloq **the ~ farm** 精神病院

fun run *n* colloq 募捐公益长跑

fur /fɜː(r)/
A *n* [u] 1 [u] (on animal) 软毛; **that'll make the ~ fly!** 那会闹得鸡飞狗跳! 2 [u and c] (for garment) 毛皮; **to be dressed in ~s** 穿着毛皮衣服; **a coat of fox ~** 一件狐皮大衣 3 [u] Brit (in kettle, pipes) 水垢; **a layer/deposit of ~** 一层水垢 4 [u] (on tongue) 舌苔
B *vi* (*pres p etc.* **-rr-**) Brit 积起沉淀物; **to ~ (up)** «*kettle, pipe*» 生水垢; «*tongue*» 生舌苔; «*artery*» 阻塞

furbish /ˈfɜːbɪʃ/ *vt* 翻新 ‹*room, building, furniture*›

furious /ˈfjʊəriəs/ *adj* 1 (angry) 狂怒的; **to be ~ at** *or* **with sb.** 对某人大发雷霆; **to be ~ about** *or* **at** *or* **over sth.** 对某事勃然大怒; **to be ~ with oneself** 生自己的气 2 fig (violent) 激烈的 ‹*battle, debate*›; **a ~ speed/storm/effort** 风驰电掣般的速度/狂风暴雨/巨大的努力; **the pace was fast and ~** 健步如飞; **the questions came fast and ~** 一个个问题连珠炮般地提出

furiously /ˈfjʊəriəsli/ *adv* 1 (angrily) 狂怒地 ‹*shout, rage*›; **~ angry** 大发雷霆 2 (energetically, violently) 激烈地 ‹*battle*›; **the sea was raging ~** 大海怒涛澎湃; **to struggle ~** 拼命搏斗

furl /fɜːl/ *vt* 卷起 ‹*sail, flag*›; 收拢 ‹*umbrella*›

furlong /ˈfɜːlɒŋ, Amer -lɔːŋ/ ▸**p. 436** *n* 浪 [长度单位, 相当于201米]; **a six-~ race** 6浪长的赛跑

furlough /ˈfɜːləʊ/ *n* 1 [u] (leave of absence) [尤指军人或传教士的] 休假; **to apply for ~** 申请休假; **to be on ~** 在休假 2 [c] (period of absence) 假期; **a six-week ~** 6周的假期

furnace /ˈfɜːnɪs/ *n* 1 (enclosed chamber) 熔炉 2 (appliance) 暖气炉 3 (place) 极闷热的地方; **to be like a ~** 热得像个火炉

furnish /ˈfɜːnɪʃ/ *vt* 1 (put furniture in) 为…配备家具 ‹*room, flat, office*›; **to ~ sth. with sth.** 用某物布置某处 2 (provide) 提供 ‹*information, equipment, supplies*›; **to ~ sb. with sth.** 为某人提供某物

furnished /ˈfɜːnɪʃt/ *adj* 配有家具的

furnishing /ˈfɜːnɪʃɪŋ/
A *n* [u] (supplying furniture) 配备; (decorating) 装饰; **~ fabrics** 装饰织物
B **furnishings** *npl* (furniture) 家具; (complete décor) 室内陈设

furniture /ˈfɜːnɪtʃə(r)/ *n* [u] 家具; **a piece of ~** 一件家具; **to be part of the ~** 成为习以为常的人或事物

furniture: ~ depot *n* 家具仓库; **~ polish** *n* 家具上光剂; **~ remover** ▸**p. 409** *n* Brit 搬家公司; **~ van** *n* 家具搬运车

furore /fjʊˈrɔːri/, Amer **furor** /ˈfjʊrɔːr/ *n* (acclaim) 轰动; (criticism) 公愤; **to cause a ~** (reaction, excitement, acclaim) 引起轰动; (outrage) 引起公愤; **there was a ~ over the photos** 因那些相片引起轰动

furred /fɜːd/ *adj* 1 (made of fur) 毛皮制成的 ‹*garment, material*›; (lined with fur) 毛皮衬里的 ‹*garment*›; (covered in fur) 毛皮覆盖的 ‹*coat*› 2 (with lime scale) 生水垢的 ‹*kettle, pipe*› 3 Brit Med 长舌苔的 ‹*tongue*›; 粥状硬化的 ‹*artery*›

furrier /ˈfʌriə(r)/ ▸**p. 409** *n* (vendor) 皮货商; (maker) 毛皮加工者

furrow /ˈfʌrəʊ/
A *n* 1 (in earth) 沟; **to plough a ~** 犁出一道沟 2 (on surface) 深痕 3 (on face) 皱纹
B *vt* 1 (make groove in the earth) 犁 ‹*earth, soil, field*› 2 (make groove on surface) 在…上留下深痕 ‹*wall, surface*› 3 (cause folds or lines) «*age, anxiety*» 使…起皱纹 ‹*brow, face, forehead*›; **to be ~ed with sth.** 由于某事而出现皱纹

furry /ˈfɜːri/ *adj* 1 (covered with fur) 毛皮覆盖的; **~ animals** 毛茸茸的动物 2 (soft in texture)

f

毛皮般柔软的 ‹coat, toy› **3** Brit Med 长舌苔的 ‹tongue›; 粥状硬化的 ‹artery›

further /ˈfɜːðə(r)/

A *adv* (*comp of* **far**) **1** (to or at a greater distance in space or time) 更远; **~ back/forward** 再往后/前; **~ away** *or* **off** 更远; **to get ~ and ~ away** 越来越远; **~ north/south** 再往北/南; **I can't go any ~** 我再也走不动了; **how much ~ is it?** 还有多远?; **the train doesn't go ~ than Bath** 火车最远只到巴斯; **a little ~ on** 再往前一点; **they ventured ~ into the jungle** 他们冒险深入丛林; **we must look ~ ahead** 我们必须目光放得再长远一点; **~ back than 1964** 早在1964年以前; **a year ~ on** 又过了一年后 **2** (at or to a more advanced point) 进一步; **to go ~** (proceed) 走得更远; (say more, develop argument) 进一步说; (last longer) 持续更久; (serve more people) 供更多人食用; **I haven't read ~ than page twenty** 我只读到20页; **to get ~ with the project** 在这个项目上取得进展; **as a family we grew ~ and ~ apart** 我们一家人越来越疏远了; **to sink ~ into debt** 更深地陷入债务; **your secret will go no ~** *or* **won't go any ~** 你的秘密不会外泄; **I'll go so far but no ~** 我就讲这么多，不多说了; **to take sth. ~** (take more serious action) 对某事采取进一步行动; (speak to sb. at a higher level) 向上级反映某事; **to take the matter ~** 进一步探讨这个问题; **nothing could be ~ from the truth** 事实远非如此; **nothing could be ~ from my mind** 我绝无此意 **3** (to a greater extent, even more) 在更大程度上; **she was ~ annoyed by his refusal to pay** 他拒不付款使得她更加恼怒了 **4** formal (in addition, furthermore) 此外; **the company ~ agrees to ...** 公司还同意…; **~, I must say that ...** 此外，我必须说…

B *adj attrib* (*comp of* **far**) **1** (more distant, other) 更远的; **the ~ end of the street** 街的那一头; **the ~ side of the road/river** 路的那一边/河对岸 **2** (additional) 进一步的 ‹reforms›; 更多的 ‹changes, increases, questions›; **a ~ 500 people** 另外的500人; **it will take a ~ month** 还要花一个月时间; **to take no ~ action** 不采取进一步行动; **the museum is closed until ~ notice** 博物馆闭馆，开馆时间另行通知

C *vt* 推动 ‹plan›; 促进 ‹cooperation›; 进一步发展 ‹career›; 增加 ‹chances›

D **further to** *prep phr* formal 关于; **~ to your letter of 2nd May** 按你方5月2日来函

furtherance /ˈfɜːðərəns/ *n* [u] formal 促进; **in the ~ of ...** 为促进…的发展

further education *n* [u] Brit 继续教育

furthermore /ˌfɜːðəˈmɔː(r)/ *adv* 而且

furthermost /ˈfɜːðəməʊst/ *adj* 最远的

furthest /ˈfɜːðɪst/ (*superl of* **far**)

A *adj* **1** (most distant in space) 最远的; **the houses ~ away from the river** 离河最远的房子; **at the ~** (distance) 最远; (at most) 至多; **it's only a couple of miles at the ~** 最多只有几英里远 **2** (at or to the most advanced point) 最大限度的; **it was the ~ thing from my mind** 我压根儿就没这个念头

B *adv* **1** (to or at the greatest distance in space) 最远; **which is the ~ north?** 哪里是最北边? **2** (to or at the greatest distance in time) 最久远; **the ~ ahead we can look is next week** 我们最多只能预见到下一周; **the ~ back I can remember is 1970** 我能记起的最早时间是1970年 **3** (at or to the most advanced point) 最大限度地; (to the greatest extent, most) 最大程度上; **the people ~ removed from the political process** 与政治进程最不相干的人

furtive /ˈfɜːtɪv/ *adj* 偷偷摸摸的; **~ drink/photograph/behaviour** 偷喝的酒/偷拍的照片/鬼鬼祟祟的行为; **to give sb. a ~ glance** 偷偷地瞥某人一眼

furtively /ˈfɜːtɪvli/ *adv* 偷偷摸摸地 ‹glance, behave›

furtiveness /ˈfɜːtɪvnɪs/ *n* [u] 鬼鬼祟祟

fury /ˈfjʊəri/ *n* **1** [u] (anger) 狂怒; **in ~** 狂怒地; **to vent one's ~ on** *or* **upon sb./sth.** 把怒气撒在某人/某物身上; **his ~ knew no bounds** 他怒不可遏 **2** [c] (surge of anger) 勃然大怒; **to fly into/be in a ~** 勃然大怒; **to put sb. into a ~** 使某人怒不可遏 **3** [u] fig (violent action) 狂暴; **the ~ of the storm/waves** 狂风暴雨/波涛汹涌

fuse /fjuːz/

A *n* **1** Elec 保险丝; **to blow a ~** lit 熔断保险丝; fig colloq 勃然大怒 **2** (for explosive device) 导火线; **to light a ~** 点燃导火索; **to arm** *or* **set a ~** 安导火索; **to be on a short ~** fig 动辄发怒 **3** (detonator) 引信

B *vt* **1** (join) «person, machine, heat» 使…熔接 ‹metal, wires, ends›; **to ~ sth. with/to sth.** 把某物同某物熔接在一起 **2** (unite, blend) 使…混合 **3** Elec (provide with fuse) 给…接上保险丝 **4** Brit Elec (cause to stop functioning) 把…的保险丝熔断

C *vi* **1** Chem, Tech «metals, chemicals» 熔接 **2** (merge) «companies, parties» 合并 **3** (blend) «images, flavours» 结合; **to ~ together** 结合在一起 **4** Brit Elec (stop working) «lights, television, plug» 保险丝熔断 **5** Phys 核聚变

fuse box *n* 保险丝盒

fuselage /ˈfjuːzəlɑːʒ, -lɪdʒ/ *n* 机身

fuse wire *n* 保险丝

fusillade /ˌfjuːzəˈleɪd, Amer -sə-/ *n* **1** lit (of guns, shots) 连发; **a ~ rang out** 响起了连续的射击声 **2** fig (of criticism, questions) 连续迸发; **a ~ of criticism/questions** 连珠炮似的批评/问题

fusion /ˈfjuːʒn/ *n* **1** [u] (of metals, cables) 熔合 **2** [u] (of companies, parties) 合并 **3** [c] (of flavours) 混合体; **a ~ of several styles** 几种风格的融合 **4** [u] Phys 核聚变 **5** [u] Mus 融合乐

fuss /fʌs/

A *n* **1** [u] (agitation) 大惊小怪; **I don't know what all the ~ was about** 我不明白有什么好激动的; **stop all this ~!** 别这么激动! **2** [c] (excessive display) 小题大做; **what a ~!** 真是小题大做!; **a big** *or* **great** *or* **terrible ~** 小题大做; **to make a ~ about** *or* **over sth.** 对某事小题大做; **to make a (big) ~ about nothing** 小题大做 **3** [c] (angry scene) 争吵; **there was a big ~ when she found out** 她发现后大吵大闹; **a ~ about** *or* **over sth.** 围绕某事的争吵; **to make a ~** 大发牢骚; **to kick up a ~** colloq 大吵大闹; **he didn't put up too much of a ~** colloq 他没有怎么争辩 **4** [u and c] (attention) 过分宠爱; **to make a ~ of** *or* **over sb.** 宠爱某人; **the dogs love to be made a ~ of** 狗喜欢人的宠爱

B *vi* **1** (worry) 烦恼; **to ~ about** *or* **over sth./sb.** 为某事/某人烦恼; **you shouldn't ~ so much about** *or* **over your appearance** 不要过分在意自己的外表 **2** (show attention) 过分关心; **please stop ~ing!** 请不要再过分关心!; **to ~ over sb.** 过于关爱某人 **3** (fiddle) 摆弄; **to ~ with sth.** 摆弄某物; **don't ~ with the computer** 不要乱动电脑

C *vt* colloq 烦扰; **I'm not ~ed where we sit** 我们坐在哪儿我都无所谓

Phrasal verb

- **fuss about, fuss around** *vi* 瞎忙一气; **she was ~ing about** *or* **around in the kitchen** 她在厨房里忙得团团转

fussbudget /ˈfʌsbʌdʒɪt/ *n* Amer colloq 大惊小怪的人

fussily /ˈfʌsɪli/ *adv* **1** (fastidiously) 挑剔地 **2** (over-elaborately) 过分装饰地 ‹decorated›; **to be ~ dressed** 穿得花里胡哨 **3** (meticulously) 大惊小怪地

fussiness /ˈfʌsɪnɪs/ *n* [u] **1** (choosiness) 挑剔; **~ about/over sth.** 对某事物的挑剔 **2** (of style) 过分装饰

fusspot /ˈfʌspɒt/ *n* Brit colloq **1** (finicky person) 好挑剔的人 **2** (worrier) 大惊小怪的人

fussy /ˈfʌsi/ *adj* **1** (difficult to please) 挑剔的; **to be ~ about food/details** 挑食/讲究细节; **I'm not ~** 我无所谓 **2** (over-elaborate) 过分装饰的 ‹clothes, furniture, style› **3** (overly meticulous) 大惊小怪的 ‹manner›; **~ parents** 瞎操心的父母

fusty /ˈfʌsti/ *adj* **1** (stale, stuffy) 腐臭的 ‹smell, odour›; 有霉湿味的 ‹room, house› **2** (old-fashioned) 守旧的 ‹person, attitude›

futile /ˈfjuːtaɪl, Amer -tl/ *adj* 无效的 ‹attempt, effort›; **it is ~ to call out** 叫喊是没有用的

futility /fjuːˈtɪləti/ *n* [u] (pointlessness) 无效; **the ~ of war/life** 战争的/生活的毫无意义

futon /ˈfuːtɒn/ *n* 日式床垫

future /ˈfjuːtʃə(r)/

A *n* **1** [u] (time) 将来; **in the ~** 在将来; **in ~** 今后; **in the near/distant/not too distant ~** 在不久的/遥远的/不太遥远的将来; **for the ~** 为将来; **the office/home/town of the ~** 未来的办公室/住宅/城镇; **to look to the ~** 考虑未来; **what the ~ holds** 将来要发生的事; **to look into the ~** 展望未来 **2** [u] (events) 未来的事; **to face the ~** 面对未来; **to see the ~** 预见未来的事; **to plan (out) the ~** 筹划未来 **3** [u and c] (prospect) 前途; **to have a/no ~** 有/没有前途; **to have a bright** *or* **promising** *or* **rosy ~** 前途光明; **there's no ~ (for me) here** (我)在这里毫无前途; **a sound ~** 良好的前景; **there's no ~ in it** colloq 那没戏 **4** [c] Ling (tense) 将来时; (verb form) 将来式; **the ~** 将来时

B **futures** *npl* Fin 期货; **coffee/currency/grain ~s** 咖啡/货币/谷物期货; **to deal in ~s** 做期货交易

C *adj attrib* **1** (of the future, intended) 未来的 ‹developments, investment, president›; **~ prospects are good** 前景良好; **~ generations** 后代; **at some ~ date** 在未来的某一天; **for ~ reference** 供日后参考; **my ~ husband** 我未来的丈夫; **a ~ life** Relig 来世 **2** Ling 将来时的 ‹tense, form›

future: ~ perfect *n* 将来完成时; **~-proof** *adj* 不会过时的 ‹solution, technology, system›; **~s contract** *n* 期货合同; **~s exchange** *n* 期货交易所; **~ shock** *n* 未来冲击; **~s market** *n* 期货市场; **~s options** *npl* 期权; **~s trader** ▸ p. 409 *n* 期货交易商

Futurism /ˈfjuːtʃərɪzəm/ *n* [u] 未来主义

Futurist /ˈfjuːtʃərɪst/

A *n* 未来主义者

B *adj* 未来主义的 ‹artist, painting, movement›

futuristic /ˌfjuːtʃəˈrɪstɪk/ *adj* 极其新潮的 ‹design, furniture, housing›

futurologist /ˌfjuːtʃəˈrɒlədʒɪst/ *n* 未来学家

futurology /ˌfjuːtʃəˈrɒlədʒi/ *n* [u] 未来学

Fuwa /ˈfuːwɑː/ *npl* 福娃 [2008年北京奥运会吉祥物]

fuze *n* = **fuse A2, A3**

fuzz /fʌz/ *n* **1** (mop of hair) 蓬松卷曲的毛发; (downy hair, beard) 绒毛 **2** **the ~** *pl* colloq (police) 警察

fuzziness /ˈfʌzɪnɪs/ *n* [u] **1** (of image, photograph) 模糊不清 **2** (of idea, understanding) 含混不清

fuzzy /ˈfʌzi/ *adj* **1** (frizzy) 毛茸茸的 ‹hair› **2** (indistinct) 模糊不清的 ‹picture, image, outline› **3** (vague) 含糊的 ‹distinction, difference› **4** (confused) 糊涂的 ‹thoughts, mind› **5** Comput, Philos 模糊的

fuzzy logic *n* [u] 模糊逻辑

fwd *abbr* = **forward**

F-word /ˈefwɜːd/ *n* colloq **the ~** 粗话 [指 fuck 一词]

FYI *abbr* = **for your information** 供参考

f

Gg

G, g /dʒiː/
A *n* (*pl* **Gs** *or* **G's**) **1** (letter) [英语字母表的第7个字母] **2** **G** Mus G 音，G 调
B **G** *abbr* Phys 重力

g. *abbr* = **gram(s)** 克

G7 *abbr* 7 国集团 [指7个工业强国]

G8 *abbr* 8 国集团 [指8个工业强国]

G20 *abbr* 20 国集团 [指20个工业强国]; **~ summit** 20 国集团峰会

GA *abbr* Amer = **Georgia 2**

gab /gæb/ colloq
A *vi* (*pres p etc.* **-bb-**) (chatter) 闲聊; (talk at length) 喋喋不休
B *n* **to have the gift of the ~** Brit 能说会道

gabardine /ˈgæbədiːn, -ˈdiːn/ *n* **1** [u] (fabric) 华达呢; **a ~ coat/raincoat** 华达呢外套/雨衣 **2** [c] (garment) 华达呢大衣 [尤指华达呢雨衣]

gabble /ˈgæbl/
A *n* [u] **1** (rapid speech) 急促不清的话; **a ~ of conversation** 一片急促不清的谈话声 **2** (gibberish) 废话; **meaningless ~** 毫无意义的废话
B *vt* 急促不清地说 ‹*message, words*›
C *vi* **1** (talk quickly) 急促不清地说话 **2** (talk unintelligibly) 说废话

Phrasal verbs
- **gabble away, gabble on** *vi* 含混不清地讲话; **to ~ away/on (about sth.)** 喋喋不休地谈论（某事物）
- **gabble out** *vt* [**~ out sth.**] 结结巴巴地说

gable /ˈgeɪbl/ *n* 三角墙

gabled /ˈgeɪbld/ *adj* 有三角墙的

gable: **~ end** *n* 山墙; **~ roof** *n* 三角形屋顶

Gabon /gəˈbɒn/ *pr n* 加蓬

Gabonese /ˌgæbəˈniːz/
A *adj* (of Gabon) 加蓬的; (of the people) 加蓬人的
B *n* 加蓬人

Gaborone /ˌgæbəˈrəʊni/ *pr n* 哈博罗内

gad /gæd/
Phrasal verb
- **gad about, gad around** *vi* (*pres p etc.* **-dd-**) colloq (go from place to place) 游荡; (in search of pleasure) 四处寻欢作乐

gadabout /ˈgædəbaʊt/ *n* colloq 四处寻欢作乐的人

gadfly /ˈgædflaɪ/ *n* **1** (insect) 牛虻 **2** fig (annoying person) 讨厌的人

gadget /ˈgædʒɪt/ *n* (appliance) 小机械; (device) 小装置

gadgetry /ˈgædʒɪtri/ *n* [u] 小机械

gadolinium /ˌgædəˈlɪnɪəm/ *n* [u] 钆

Gael geɪl/ *n* 盖尔人

Gaelic /ˈgeɪlɪk, ˈgæ-/ ►**p. 426**
A *adj* (of the people) 盖尔人的; (of the language) 盖尔语的; (of customs) 盖尔风俗的
B *n* [u] 盖尔语

> **Gaelic**
> 盖尔语。凯尔特语（Celtic language）的一种，主要在爱尔兰和苏格兰使用。爱尔兰盖尔语（Irish Gaelic）亦称爱尔兰语（Irish），和英语同为爱尔兰的官方语言。苏格兰盖尔语（Scottish Gaelic 或 Scots Gaelic）源自爱尔兰盖尔语。两者差别较大，但基本上可以互相理解。苏格兰盖尔语目前主要在苏格兰高地地区和西海岸使用——东南部低地地区使用的语言称苏格兰语（Scots或Scottish），属于英语的变种。

gaff[1] /gæf/
A *n* Fishg (prong) 鱼叉; (hook) 挽钩
B *vt* 用挽钩拉…上岸 ‹*fish*›

gaff[2] *n* [u] colloq (nonsense) 胡说; **that's just a lot of ~** 那简直是一派胡言

gaffe /gæf/ *n* (blunder) 失礼; (tactless remark) 失言; **I made a ~** 我失礼了

gaffer /ˈgæfə(r)/ *n* **1** Brit colloq (boss) 老板; (foreman) 工头 **2** dated colloq (old man) 老头儿

gaffer tape *n* [u] 强力防水胶带

gag /gæg/
A *n* **1** (piece of cloth) 塞口物 **2** fig (restriction) 言论箝制; **to put a ~ on democracy/free speech** 压制民主/言论自由 **3** colloq (joke) 笑话; (humorous story) 插科打诨; **to tell a ~** 讲笑话
B *vt* (*pres p etc.* **-gg-**) **1** (put a gag on) 塞住…的嘴; **to ~ sb. with a handkerchief** 用手绢塞住某人的嘴 **2** fig (restrict) 箝制…的言论 ‹*media, journalists*›
C *vi* (*pres p etc.* **-gg-**) 噎得想吐; **he ~ged on his soup** 他喝汤呛着了

gaga /ˈgɑːgɑː/ *adj* colloq **1** pej (senile) 老糊涂的; **to go ~** 老糊涂了 **2** (infatuated) 狂热的; **to go ~ over sb./sth.** 对某人/某事物着迷

gage /geɪdʒ/ *n, vt* Amer = **gauge**

gaggle /ˈgægl/ *n* **1** (flock of geese) （鹅）群; **a ~ of geese** 一群鹅 **2** colloq (disorderly group) 无秩序的人群; **a ~ of schoolchildren/tourists** 乱哄哄的一群学生/游客

gag law, gag rule *ns* Amer 言论箝制令

Gaia /ˈgaɪə/ *pr n* [u] **1** (system) [作为一个超级有机体的] 地球生态系; **the ~ theory/hypothesis** 盖亚理论/假说 **2** Mythol 盖亚 [希腊神话中的大地女神]

gaiety /ˈgeɪəti/ *n* [u] **1** (cheerfulness) 快乐 **2** (festivity) 庆祝活动

gaily /ˈgeɪli/ *adv* **1** (cheerfully) 快乐地 ‹*wave, laugh, chatter*› **2** (brightly) 鲜艳地; **~ decorated/dressed** 装饰花哨的/衣着艳丽的

gain /geɪn/
A *n* **1** [u and c] (profit) 收益; **to do sth. for financial/material/personal ~** 为金钱/物质/个人收益而做某事; **ill-gotten ~s** 不义之财; **to be to sb.'s ~** 有利于某人 **2** [c] (advantage) 收获; **~s and losses** 得失; **electoral/diplomatic ~s** 选举/外交方面的收获; **no pain, no ~** 不劳则无获 **3** [c] (increase in power, knowledge, weight) 增长; **to make ~s** 取得进展; **~s in efficiency** *or* **efficiency ~s** 效率的提高; **a ~ in time of 2.6 seconds** 时间上赢得 2.6 秒 **4** [c] Fin (increase in value of shares) 升值; **to make big ~s** «*shares*» 大涨
B *vt* **1** (acquire) 获得 ‹*experience, approval, freedom, support*›; **to ~ sb.'s goodwill** 博得某人的好感; **to ~ one's objective** 达到目标; **to ~ the impression (that) ...** 得到…的印象; **to ~ access to sb./sth.** 获得接近某人/某物的机会; **to ~ control/possession of sth.** 取得对某事物的控制/所有权; **to ~ sth. from sth.** 从某事物中获得某物; **the advantages to be ~ed from adopting this strategy** 采用这一策略将会赢得的优势; **we have nothing to ~ from this investment** 我们这项投资是不会获利的; **she ~ed an advantage by cheating** 她靠作弊取得了优势; **to ~ sth. by sth.** 靠某物获得某物; **to ~ time** 赢得时间; **to ~ ground** 取得进展 **2** (increase) 增加 ‹*momentum, height, weight*›; **to ~ speed** 加速; **to ~ X lbs/kg** 增重 X 磅/公斤; **my watch ~s ten minutes a day** 我的表每天快 10 分钟; **Smith has ~ed five yards over Jones** 史密斯领先琼斯 5 码; **the shares have ~ed several points** 股票涨了好几点 **3** (win) 赢得 ‹*seat, victory, position*›; **to ~ the day** 获胜; **to ~ the upper hand** 占上风 **4** (reach) 到达 ‹*destination, place, shore*›
C *vi* **1** (become fast) «*watch, clock*» 走快; **to ~ by five minutes** 快 5 分钟 **2** (improve) 增加; **to ~ in sth.** 增加 ‹*speed, weight, confidence, knowledge*›; **to ~ in value** 升值; **to ~ in prestige/popularity** 提高威望/人气 **3** (profit) 获利; **to ~ from sth.** 从某事物中获益

Phrasal verb
- **gain on** *vt* [**~ on sb./sth.**] 逼近 ‹*runner, vehicle, rival*›

gainer /ˈgeɪnə(r)/ *n* 得胜者

gainful /ˈgeɪnfl/ *adj* 赚钱的; **to be in ~ employment** 做有报酬的工作; **it's not a ~ occupation, it's a hobby** 这不是赚钱的工作，而是业余爱好

gainfully /ˈgeɪnfəli/ *adv* 赚钱地; **~ employed** 有酬雇用的

gainsay /ˌgeɪnˈseɪ/ *vt* (*pt, pp* **gainsaid** /ˌgeɪnˈsed/) formal 反驳 ‹*argument, account, statement*›; 否认 ‹*fact, evidence*›; **there's no ~ing it** 这无可否认

gait /geɪt/ *n* (of person) 步态; (of animal) 步法; **with an unsteady ~** 步履蹒跚地

gaiter /ˈgeɪtə(r)/ *n* 绑腿

gal /gæl/ *n* esp Amer colloq = **girl**

gal. /gæl/ *abbr* = **gallon**

gala /ˈgɑːlə/ *n* 盛会; **a swimming/sports/charity ~** 游泳运动会/体育盛会/慈善义演

galactic /gəˈlæktɪk/ *adj* 星系的 [尤指银河系的]

gala: **~ day** *n* 欢庆日; **~ dress** *n* 盛装; **~ night** *n* 欢庆之夜

Galapagos tortoise *n* 加拉帕戈斯象龟

galaxy /ˈgæləksi/ *n* **1** Astron 星系; **the ~** 银河系 **2** fig (group of people) 群英; **a ~ of stars/celebrities** 明星/名人荟萃

gale /geɪl/ *n* **1** Meteorol 大风; **a force 9 ~** 9 级大风; **~ force winds** 7 到 10 级的大风;

a ～ raged 狂风肆虐 2 ～(s) of laughter 阵阵笑声

gale warning *n* 大风警报

gall[1] /gɔːl/ *n* [u] 1 (impudence) 厚颜无耻; **to have the ～ to do sth.** 有脸皮做某事; **they haven't the ～ to say it straight out** 他们无脸直说 2 (bile) 胆汁

gall[2]
A *n* [u] (resentment) 恼怒; **to vent one's ～ on sb.** 对某人发火
B *vt* «*experience, incident*» 使恼怒; «*behaviour*» 使感到受羞辱; **it ～s sb. to do sth.** 做某事使某人感到恼火

gall[3] *n* 1 Bot (growth) 瘿 [指植物的非正常增生] 2 Vet (sore) 擦痛处

gallant /ˈgælənt/ *adj* 1 (brave) 勇敢的 ‹*person, deed, fight*› 2 (chivalrous) 侠义的 ‹*person, conduct*›; **it was ～ of you to do it** 你这样做真有骑士风度

gallantly /ˈgæləntli/ *adv* 1 (bravely) 勇敢地 ‹*fight, resist*› 2 (chivalrously) 侠义地 ‹*behave*›

gallantry /ˈgæləntri/ *n* [u] 1 (bravery) 英勇行为 2 (chivalry) 豪侠

gall bladder ▸p. 71 *n* 胆囊

galleon /ˈgælɪən/ *n* [15至17世纪的] 西班牙大帆船

gallery /ˈgæləri/ *n* 1 (public art venue) 美术馆 2 (room within museum) 陈列室 3 (private art venue) 画廊 4 Archit (at back) 楼座; (at side) 廊座; **the public ～ at the House of Commons/Law courts** 下议院/法庭的旁听席 5 Archit (balcony) 眺台 6 Theat (raised area) **the ～** 顶层楼座 7 Theat (spectators) 顶层楼座观众; **to play to the ～** 哗众取宠 8 (of mine, cave) 地下巷道 9 Amer (auction room) 拍卖大厅; (auction building) 拍卖大楼

galley /ˈgæli/ *n* 1 Hist (ship) [由奴隶或罪犯划桨的] 桨帆船 2 Aviat, Naut (kitchen) 厨房 3 Print ～ **(proof)** 长条校样

galley slave *n* 1 Hist 被罚划桨的人 2 fig (drudge) 做苦工者

Gallic /ˈgælɪk/ *adj* 法国式的 ‹*style, charm*›; ～ **wit/sophistication** 法国人的机智/世故; **the ～ Wars** 高卢战争

galling /ˈgɔːlɪŋ/ *adj* 令人恼怒的 ‹*affair, business*›; 令人感到屈辱的 ‹*incident, experience*›; **to be ～ to sb.** 使某人感到屈辱; **to find sth. ～** 感到某事物很令人恼火

gallium /ˈgælɪəm/ *n* [u] 镓

gallivant /ˈgælɪvænt/ *vi* colloq 游玩; **to ～ about** *or* **around (the country/world)** (在全国/世界各地) 游玩

gallon /ˈgælən/ *n* 加仑

gallop /ˈgæləp/
A *n* [u] 1 (of animal) 飞奔; **at a** *or* **the ～** 飞快地; fig 急速地; **to be at full ～** 以最快速度奔驰; **to break into a ～** 飞奔起来 2 Equit (ride) 骑马奔驰; **to go for a ～** 去骑马奔驰一番; **a ～ through European history** fig 欧洲历史概览
B *vt* Equit 使…飞奔 ‹*horse*›
C *vi* 1 Equit «*horse*» 飞奔; «*rider*» 策马飞奔; **to ～ away/back** 飞奔而去/来; **to go ～ing along/down/up the track** 沿着跑道策马飞奔 2 lit (run quickly) «*person*» 飞跑; **he came ～ing down the stairs** 他从楼梯上一路飞奔下来 3 fig (proceed quickly) 快速进展; **Japan is ～ing ahead in this field** 日本在这个领域遥遥领先; **to ～ through one's work** 匆匆做完工作

galloping /ˈgæləpɪŋ/ *adj* 1 (at a gallop) 飞奔的 ‹*horse*› 2 fig (increasing rapidly) 快速进展的; ～ **pneumonia/inflation** 迅速恶化的肺炎/失控的通货膨胀

gallows /ˈgæləʊz/ *n* (*pl* **gallows**) 绞刑架; **to die/end up on the ～** 死在绞刑架上; **to send sb. to the ～** 把某人送上绞刑架

gallows humour *n* [u] fig 大难临头时的幽默

gallstone /ˈgɔːlstəʊn/ *n* 胆石

Gallup poll® /ˈgæləp/ *n* 盖洛普民意测验

galore /gəˈlɔː(r)/ *adj postpos* 大量的; **clubs/flowers/prizes ～** 很多俱乐部/花/奖品

galoshes /gəˈlɒʃɪz/ *npl* 橡胶套鞋

galumph /gəˈlʌmf/ *vi* hum colloq 辟里啪啦地跑动; **to ～ about** *or* **around** (walk or run noisily) 辟里啪啦地走来走去; (walk or run clumsily) 笨拙地走来走去; **to go ～ing about** *or* **around** 辟里啪啦地跑动

galvanic /gælˈvænɪk/ *adj* 1 Elec 产生电流的; ～ **cell** 伏打电池 2 fig (dramatic) 使人震惊的; (stimulating) 激励人的

galvanization /ˌgælvənaɪˈzeɪʃn, Amer -nɪˈz-/ *n* [u] 1 Tech (coating) 镀锌 2 fig (of person, nation) 激励

galvanize /ˈgælvənaɪz/ *vt* 1 Tech (coat) 给…镀锌 ‹*iron, steel*› 2 fig (motivate, spur) 激励 ‹*person, nation*›; 激起 ‹*debate*›; **to ～ sb. into action/doing sth.** 激励某人行动起来/做某事

galvanometer /ˌgælvəˈnɒmɪtə(r)/ *n* 电流计

Gambia /ˈgæmbɪə/ *pr n* **(the)** ～ 冈比亚

Gambian /ˈgæmbɪən/ ▸p. 503
A *adj* (of the Gambia) 冈比亚的; (of the people) 冈比亚人的
B *n* 冈比亚人

gambit /ˈgæmbɪt/ *n* 1 (in chess) 开局让棋法; **to play/accept/decline a ～** 走/吃/拒吃弃兵局 2 fig (tactic) 开头一招; **opening ～** 第一招; **his resignation was a tactical ～** 他的辞职是很有策略的一招

gamble /ˈgæmbl/
A *n* 1 (bet) 赌博; **to have a ～ on sth.** 对某事物打赌 2 fig (risk) 冒险; **to take a ～** 有意冒一次险; **that's a bit of a ～** 那有一点冒险; **his ～ came/paid off** 他的冒险获得了成功
B *vt* 1 (bet) 以…为赌注 ‹*money*› 2 fig (risk) 冒险; **to ～ everything on sth.** 对某事物孤注一掷
C *vi* 1 (bet) 打赌; **to ～ on the horses/at cards** 赌马/赌纸牌 2 fig (take a chance) 冒险; **to ～ for high stakes** 冒巨大的风险; **to ～ on the Stock Exchange** 进行股票投机; **she ～d on his being there** 她想碰碰运气看看他会否在那里

Phrasal verb

- **gamble away** *vt* [～ **away sth.**, ～ **sth. away**] 输光 ‹*money*›; **to ～ the night away** 以赌博消磨一夜

gambler /ˈgæmblə(r)/ *n* 赌徒; **a heavy/hardened ～** 老赌棍

gambling /ˈgæmblɪŋ/ *n* [u] 赌博

gambling: ～ **debts** *npl* 赌债; ～ **den,** ～ **house** *ns* colloq 赌窟; ～ **joint** *n* Amer colloq 赌场; ～ **losses** *npl* 赌博损失; ～ **man** *n* 赌徒

gamboge /gæmˈbəʊʒ, -ˈbuːʒ/ *n* [u] 1 (resin) 藤黄胶脂 2 (colour) 橙黄色

gambol /ˈgæmbl/
A *vi* (*pres p etc.* **-ll-**, Amer **-l-**) 欢跳
B *n* 欢跳

game /geɪm/
A *n* 1 [c] (activity) 游戏; **to play a ～/～s** 玩游戏; **party ～s** 分组游戏; **a ～ of skill/chance** 技巧类/博弈类游戏; **a ～ for two players** 二人游戏; **the beautiful ～** 足球; **the fight ～** Amer 拳击; **it's only a ～!** 儿戏而已，何必当真！; **it's all in the ～** fig 万事皆如此; **to play the ～** 遵守游戏规则 2 [c] (session) 一场; **a ～ of chess/cards/Monopoly®** 一盘国际象棋/纸牌/大富翁游戏; **a ～ of cricket/snooker/darts** 一场板球/斯诺克台球/飞镖比赛; **to have** *or* **play a ～ (of sth.) (with** *or* **against sb.)** (和某人) 打一场 (某类) 比赛; **to be back in/get back into the ～ (again)** 将比分追上来; **a ～ of two halves** 上下半场两队表现迥异的比赛 3 [c] (section of match in tennis, badminton, bridge) 一局; **four ～s to one** (in tennis) 局分为四比一; ～ **to Edwards** 爱德华兹赢得本局比赛; ～, **set, and match (to Edwards)** 本局、本盘及整场比赛结束 (，爱德华兹获胜); **it's ～ all** 双方各胜一局; **we were two ～s all** 我们各胜两局; **21 points is ～** 比赛采用 21 分制 4 [c] (skill at playing) 比赛技巧; **I played my normal ～** 我发挥正常; **to raise/improve one's ～** 提高/改进比赛技巧; **she played a great ～ of chess** 她下了一局好棋; **to be off one's ～** 比赛发挥不佳; **to put sb. off his/her ～** 使某人比赛发挥不佳 5 [c] (set of equipment) (for fun) 游戏用品; (for sport) 比赛器具 6 [c] (lark) 儿戏; **this isn't a ～!** 这可不是儿戏！; **to play ～s** 闹着玩; **don't play ～s with me!** 别跟我打哈哈！ 7 [c] colloq (trick, scheme) 诡计; **I'm on to your little ～** 我已经看穿了你的小把戏; **to play sb.'s ～** 按某人的意愿行事; **to play the same ～** 采取同样的策略; **two can play (at) that ～** 这一套他会我也会; **to beat sb. at his/her own ～** 在某人擅长的领域击败某人; **what's your ～?** Brit 你要什么花招呢？; **to give the ～ away** 泄露秘密; **the ～ is up** 该收场了 [事情已经泄露了]; **the name of the ～** colloq 真正重要的东西 8 [c] colloq (occupation, business) 行业; **the publishing/insurance/marketing ～** 出版/保险/营销业; **I've been in this ～ for ten years** 这一行我干了 10 年 9 Brit colloq (prostitution) **the ～** 卖淫; **to be/go on the ～** 卖淫 10 [u] Hunt 猎物; **to hunt ～** 狩猎; **small/big ～** 小型/大型猎物 11 [u] Culin 野味 12 [u] (target) 目标; **to be easy/fair ～** 成为容易捕获的/恰当的目标
B *modif* 1 Hunt (referring to the catch) 可作为猎物的 ‹*bird, fish, animal*›; (referring to the sport) 狩猎的 ‹*park, reserve, laws, licence*› 2 Culin 野味的 ‹*pâté, stew, soup*›
C **games** *npl* 1 Brit Sch 体育课; **to be good at ～s** 体育好; **～s lessons/master/mistress/teacher** 体育课/教师/女教师/老师 2 (contest) 运动会
D *vi* 玩电脑游戏
E *adj* 1 *pred* (willing) 愿意的; **OK, I'm ～** 好吧，我乐意干; **to be ～ for sth./to do sth.** 愿意尝试某事物/做某事; **she's ～ for anything** 她什么都敢尝试; **he's always ～ for an adventure** 他随时愿意冒险 2 (plucky) 勇敢的 ‹*person, attempt*›

game: ～ **bird** *n* 猎鸟; ～ **fish** *n* 供垂钓的鱼; ～**keeper** ▸p. 409 *n* 猎场看守人; ～ **laws** *npl* 渔猎法规

gamely /ˈgeɪmli/ *adv* (bravely) 勇敢地; (with determination) 顽强地

game: ～ **park** *n* = ～ **reserve**; ～ **pie** *n* [u and c] 野味馅饼; ～ **plan** *n* Amer 对策; ～ **point** *n* 局点

gamer /ˈgeɪmə(r)/ *n* 1 (player) 玩游戏的人; **online ～** 网络游戏玩家 2 Amer Sport (enthusiastic participant) 体育爱好者

game: ～ **reserve** *n* (for preservation) 野生动物保护区; (for hunting) 禁猎区; ～**s console** *n* 游戏机; ～ **show** *n* 竞赛节目

gamesmanship /ˈgeɪmzmənʃɪp/ *n* [u] 比赛战术; **to be good at ～** 擅长耍花招; **a bit** *or* **piece of ～** 一个招数

games room *n* 游戏室

gamete /ˈgæmiːt/ *n* 配子

game: ～ **theory,** ～**s theory** *n* [u] 博弈论; ～ **warden** *n* 野生动物保护区管理员

gaming /ˈgeɪmɪŋ/ *n* [u] 1 = **gambling** 2 (on computer) 玩电脑游戏; **the popularity of online ～** 在线电脑游戏的普及

gaming: ～ **community** *n* (在线) 游戏社区; ～ **debt** *n* 赌债; ～ **house** *n* 赌场; ～ **laws** *npl* 赌场法规; ～ **machine** *n* 1 (slot machine) 投币式赌博机; 2 Comput 电子游戏机; ～ **site** *n* 游戏网站

gamma /ˈgæmə/
A *n* 1 (letter) 伽马 [γ，希腊语字母表的第3个字母] 2 Brit dated (grade) 丙等
B *modif* Phys γ射线的，伽马射线的

gamma: ~ particle *n* γ 粒子，伽马粒子；**~ radiation** *n* [u] γ 辐射，伽马辐射；**~ ray** *n* γ 射线，伽马射线

gammon /ˈgæmən/ *n* **1** [u] Brit (ham) 熏腿 **2** [c] (side of bacon) 熏猪肋肉；**~ steak/rashers** 熏猪排/熏肉薄片

gammy /ˈgæmi/ *adj* Brit colloq (injured) 受伤的；(lame) 跛的；**to have a ~ leg** 有一条腿跛

gamut /ˈgæmət/ *n* fig 整个范围；**the whole ~ of hopes/fears/crime** 所有的希望/恐惧/罪行；**a rich ~ of facial expressions** 极为丰富的面部表情；**to run the ~ of ...** 经历…的全过程

gamy /ˈgeɪmɪ/ *adj* 有膻腥味的 ‹*meat*›

gander /ˈgændə(r)/ *n* **1** Zool 雄鹅；▸**sauce A1** **2** Brit colloq (quick look) 一眼；**to take** *or* **have a ~ at sth.** 看一看某物

gang /gæŋ/ *n* **1** (criminal group) 一帮；**a ~ of criminals/hijackers** 一帮罪犯/一伙劫匪；**a terrorist/street ~** 恐怖主义集团/街头流氓团伙；**to join a ~** 加入团伙；**to go around in ~s** 成帮结伙四处走；**~ warfare** 帮派冲突 **2** colloq (social circle) 一伙人；**to be one of the ~** 成为大伙儿中的一员 **3** (team of workers) 一队 **4** (group of convicts) 一群

Phrasal verbs

- **gang together** *vi* 结成一伙；**if we ~ together, we can do it** 如果我们齐心协力，就能做成这件事
- **gang up** *vi* 联合起来；**to ~ up on** *or* **against sb.** 联手对付某人

gang bang *n* colloq **1** (rape) 轮奸 **2** (orgy) 集体淫乱活动

Ganges /ˈgændʒiːz/ ▸**p. 663** *pr n* **the ~** 恒河

gangfight /ˈgæŋfaɪt/ *n* 帮派火拼

gangland /ˈgæŋlænd/ *n* [u] 黑社会

gangland: ~ boss *n* 黑社会头目；**~ killing, ~ murder** *ns* 黑帮仇杀

gang leader *n* 黑社会头目

ganglia /ˈgæŋglɪə/ *npl* ▸**ganglion**

gangling /ˈgæŋglɪŋ/ *adj* 瘦长而笨拙的 ‹*youth, teenager*›

ganglion /ˈgæŋglɪən/ (*pl* **ganglia**) *n* **1** Anat 神经节 **2** fig (hub of organization, operation) 中心

gang: ~master *n* Brit 工头；**G~ of Four** *n* Hist 四人帮；**~plank** *n* 跳板

gang-rape *vt, n* 轮奸

gangrene /ˈgæŋgriːn/ ▸**p. 377** *n* [u] 坏疽

gangrenous /ˈgæŋgrɪnəs/ *adj* 生坏疽的；**to go ~** 生坏疽

gangsta rap /ˈgæŋstə ˌræp/ *n* [u] 匪帮说唱

gangster /ˈgæŋstə(r)/ *n* 匪徒

gangsterism /ˈgæŋstərɪzəm/ *n* [u] 匪徒行为

gangway /ˈgæŋweɪ/
A *n* **1** Brit (of bus, aircraft, cinema, theatre) 座间通道；**a ~ seat** 靠通道的座位 **2** Naut = **gangplank**
B *excl* **~!** 让路!

ganja /ˈgændʒə/ *n* [u] 大麻

gannet /ˈgænɪt/ *n* **1** Zool 塘鹅 **2** Brit hum (greedy person) 贪婪的人；**he's a real ~** 他真能吃

Gannt chart /ˈgænt tʃɑːt/ *n* 甘特进度图

Games and sports

■ In English, the verb 'play' is used for many different kinds of games. However, In Chinese, different games require different verbs.

Games

to play football
= 踢足球

to play basketball/badminton/table tennis
= 打篮球／羽毛球／乒乓球

to play bridge
= 打桥牌

to play chess
= 下象棋

to play hide-and-seek
= 捉迷藏

■ In English, some games take a singular form and others a plural. In Chinese the names of games have no separate singular or plural forms:

to play Scrabble
= 玩拼字游戏

to play backgammon
= 玩西洋双陆棋

to play marbles
= 打弹子游戏

to play cards
= 玩纸牌
or 打牌
or 打扑克

Players and events

The Chinese for 'player' is 选手, 运动员, 参加者, or 游戏者. 选手 refers to players who are selected to compete in a game or sports event, and means the same as 'contestant' or 'competitor' in English. 运动员 refers to professional athletes or sportsmen and sportswomen and competitors. 参加者 refers to both professional or non-professional players, and refers to any player who participates in any type of game. 游戏者 has no professional connotation, and refers to someone who plays a game for fun:

a footballer/football player
= 足球运动员
or 足球选手
or 足球队员

a table tennis player
= 乒乓球运动员
or 乒乓球选手

Scrabble players
= 拼字游戏参加者

I'm one of the players in this game of skittles
= 我是这场撞柱戏的游戏者之一

but

a chess player
= 棋手

■ Note also:

a game for four players
= 四人玩的游戏
or 四人游戏

board games
= 棋盘游戏

a game of Scrabble
= 拼字游戏

a game of football
= 足球比赛

tennis champion of the world
= 网球世界冠军

an Olympic champion
= 奥运会冠军

the British Tennis Championship
= 英国网球锦标赛

a chess tournament
= 象棋联赛

a football match
= 足球比赛

to play a tennis tournament
= 参加网球比赛
or 打网球比赛

the World Rally Championship
= 世界拉力锦标赛

the International Table Tennis Federation Pro-Tour
= 国际乒联职业巡回赛

the US Open Golf Championship
= 美国高尔夫球公开赛

the Volleyball World Grand Prix
= 世界排球大奖赛

Other phrases

She plays in the match on Friday
= 她星期五参加比赛
or 她星期五打比赛

Which team does he play for?
= 他代表哪个队参赛?
or 他为哪个队打比赛?

On Tuesday Lewis plays Robert
= 刘易斯星期二与罗伯特比赛
or 刘易斯星期二对阵罗伯特

Delia has played Dolly at chess
= 迪莉娅与多莉赛过象棋

Liverpool will play Manchester United
= 利物浦队将与曼联队比赛

I'll play chess with my friends
= 我要和朋友下象棋

She won the gold medal
= 她赢得了金牌

He won at chess
= 他下棋获胜
or 他赢了棋

Manchester won
= 曼彻斯特队赢了

He lost at chess
= 他下棋输了

I beat him at chess
= 我下棋赢了他

England drew 2-2 with Italy
= 英格兰 2 比 2 战平意大利

Manchester United narrowly beat Liverpool one-nil
= 曼联以 1 比 0 险胜利物浦

Brazil suffered a bitter defeat in the final against Argentina
= 在与阿根廷的决赛中，巴西队惨败

g

Gansu /ˌgæn'suː/ ▸**p. 604** *pr n* ～ **(Province)** 甘肃（省）

gantry /'gæntri/ *n* 1 (for crane) 龙门架; (for lights, signals) 路标架 2 Aerosp 竖立塔架

gaol /dʒeɪl/ *n, vt* Brit = **jail**

gaoler /'dʒeɪlə(r)/ *n* Brit = **jailer**

gap /gæp/ *n* 1 (empty space) 空白处; (empty distance) 空隙; **a ～ in sth.** 某物体中的缝隙; **a ～ between things** 物体间的缝隙; **to leave a ～** 留出间隙; **to fill in/stop up a ～** 填补/堵塞缝隙; **a ～ in the traffic** (of cars) 车流中的空隙; (of pedestrians) 行人中的空隙; **a ～ in the fence/wall/hedge** 篱笆/墙/树篱的缺口; **a ～ of several miles between villages** 村庄之间几英里宽的空地 2 fig (break) (in continuity, life, memory, understanding, market) 空白; (in record, account) 空缺; (in text, accounts) 脱漏; (in education, organization) 欠缺; **after a ～ of several months** 隔了数月之后; **her loss left a huge ～ in his life** 她的去世给他的生活留下了巨大的空白; **a communications ～** 交流障碍 3 fig (discrepancy) (in age, status, levels, standards) 差异; (in opinions, ideas, viewpoints) 分歧; (between people) 隔阂; (between scores) 差距; Econ, Fin 差额; **the generation ～** 代沟; **to bridge the ～ between rich and poor** 缩短贫富差距; **to close the ～ between two points of view** 消弥两种观点之间的分歧 4 Geog (in hills, mountains) 峡谷

gape /geɪp/
A *vi* 1 (stare) 张口结舌地瞪着; **to ～ at sth./sb.** 目瞪口呆地盯着某物/某人 2 (open the mouth) 《*person, bird*》 张着嘴 3 (open wide) 《*wound, seam*》 裂开; 《*mouth*》 张大; **his shirt ～d open** 他的衬衣敞开着
B *n* (stare) 张口呆看

gap financing *n* [u] 缺口融资

gaping /'geɪpɪŋ/ *adj attrib* 1 (open) 张开的 ‹*mouth*›; **to give a ～ yawn** 张嘴打呵欠 2 (wide) 裂开的 ‹*abyss, wound, seam*› 3 (staring) 目瞪口呆的 ‹*crowd, face*›

gappy /'gæpi/ *adj* colloq 1 (full of gaps) 多缺口的; **～ teeth** 齿缝很大的牙齿 2 (incomplete) 不足的 ‹*knowledge*›; 不完整的 ‹*record, text*›

gap: ～-toothed /'gæptuːθt/ *adj* 齿缝很大的; **～ year** *n* 间隔年 [中学毕业后与上大学前中断学业的一年]; **to take a ～ year** 休假一学年

garage /'gærɑːʒ, 'gærɪdʒ, Amer gə'rɑːʒ/
A *n* 1 (housing car) 车库 2 (filling station) 加油站 3 (for repairs, sales) 汽车车行
B *vt* 把…送入车库 ‹*motor vehicle*›

garage: ～ mechanic ▸**p. 409** *n* 汽车行修理工; **～ owner** *n* 汽车行老板; **～ rock** *n* [u] 车库摇滚; **～ sale** *n* Amer 宅前旧物出售; **～ start-up** *n* 车库新公司 [指创办于车库或后房的小公司]

garaging /'gærədʒɪŋ/ *n* [u] 汽车存放; **with/without ～** 可以/不可以存放汽车

garb /gɑːb/
A *n* [u] [尤指某职业特有的] 服装; **in peasant/clerical ～** 身着农民/牧师服装
B *vt* 给…穿衣; **to be ～ed in sth.** 穿上某衣物

garbage /'gɑːbɪdʒ/ *n* [u] 1 Amer (waste) 垃圾; **to dispose of/collect ～** 处理/收运垃圾; **to put the ～ out** 把垃圾带出去 2 colloq (nonsense) 废话

garbage: ～ can *n* Amer 垃圾箱; **～ chute** *n* Amer 垃圾通道; **～ collector** ▸**p. 409** *n* Amer 垃圾工; **～ disposal** *n* [u] Amer 垃圾处理机; **～ disposal unit** *n* Amer 垃圾处理装置; **～ man** ▸**p. 409** *n* Amer = **～ collector**; **～ truck** *n* Amer 垃圾车

garble /'gɑːbl/ *vt* 使…错乱 ‹*quotation, story, instructions, message*›

garbled /'gɑːbld/ *adj* 错乱的 ‹*quotation, story, instructions, message, account*›

garden /'gɑːdn/
A *n* [u and c] esp Brit (area around house) 花园; **to lead sb. up the ～ path** colloq 引诱某人出洋相; **everything in the ～'s rosy** Brit colloq 一切都称心如意; **～ flower/plant** 园艺花卉/植物
B **gardens** *npl* 公园; **botanical/zoological/municipal ～s** 植物园/动物园/城市公园

garden: ～ apartment *n* Amer 带花园的公寓; **～ centre** *n* 园艺品店; **～ city** *n* Brit 花园城市

gardener /'gɑːdnə(r)/ ▸**p. 409** *n* 园丁; **to be a keen ～** 热衷于园艺

garden: ～ flat *n* Brit 带花园的公寓; **～ fork** *n* 园艺叉; **～-fresh** *adj* 新采摘的 ‹*vegetables*›; 新出产的 ‹*produce*›; **～ gnome** *n* [花园中作装饰的] 侏儒塑像; **～ hose** *n* 浇花软管

gardening /'gɑːdnɪŋ/ *n* [u] 园艺活动

garden: G～ of Eden *n* 伊甸园; **～ of remembrance** *n* 纪念园; **～ party** *n* 花园招待会; **～ produce** *n* [u] 花园产品; **～ shears** *npl* 园艺剪刀; **～ snail** *n* 庭院蜗牛; **～ suburb** *n* Brit 园林化郊区; **～ waste** *n* [u] 花园垃圾

gargantuan /gɑː'gæntjʊən/ *adj* 巨大的; **a ～ appetite** 惊人的食欲

gargle /'gɑːgl/
A *vi* 含漱
B *n* 1 (act) 含漱; **to have a ～** 漱口 2 (liquid) 漱口液

gargoyle /'gɑːgɔɪl/ *n* 滴水兽

garish /'geərɪʃ/ *adj* 俗艳的 ‹*costume, colour, design*›

garishly /'geərɪʃlɪ/ *adj* 花里胡哨地 ‹*decorated, painted*›; **～ lit** 灯光刺眼的

garishness /'geərɪʃnɪs/ *n* [u] 花里胡哨; **the ～ of the city centre** 市中心的俗丽

garland /'gɑːlənd/ *n* 花环

garlic /'gɑːlɪk/ *n* [u] 大蒜

garlic: ～ bread *n* [u] 蒜蓉包; **～ butter** *n* [u] 大蒜味黄油

garlicky /'gɑːlɪki/ *adj* 有大蒜味的

garlic: ～ press *n* 压蒜泥器; **～ salt** *n* [u] 大蒜盐; **～ sauce** *n* [u] 蒜蓉酱

garment /'gɑːmənt/ *n* formal （一件）衣服

garner /'gɑːnə(r)/ *vt* 收集 ‹*information, facts*›; 获得 ‹*knowledge*›; 得到 ‹*support, approval*›; **to ～ sth. from sth.** 从某处获得某物

garnet /'gɑːnɪt/ *n* 石榴石

garnish /'gɑːnɪʃ/
A *n* [c and u] 装饰菜
B *vt* 在…上加装饰菜 ‹*meat*›; **the fish was ～ed with slices of lemon** 那道鱼配上了几片柠檬

garnishing /'gɑːnɪʃɪŋ/ *n* [u and c] 装饰菜

garret /'gærət/ *n* 阁楼

garrison /'gærɪsn/
A *n* + *v sing or pl* 卫戍部队
B *modif* 卫戍部队的 ‹*duty*›; 有驻军的 ‹*town*›; 驻防的 ‹*troops*›
C *vt* 1 (defend) 驻防 ‹*place*› 2 (station) 派…驻防 ‹*troops*›; **to be ～ed in ...** 被派往…驻防

garrotte Brit, **garrote** Amer /gə'rɒt/
A *vt* 1 (strangle) 勒死 2 (execute) 处…以铁环绞刑 ‹*prisoner*›
B *n* (wire) 勒杀用铁丝; (rope) 勒杀用绳; (metal collar) 绞刑铁环

garrulous /'gærʊləs/ *adj* 喋喋不休的

garrulously /'gærʊləsli/ *adv* 喋喋不休地

garter /'gɑːtə(r)/ *n* 1 (elasticated band) 袜带 2 Amer (suspender) 吊袜带 3 Brit (title) 嘉德勋位; (badge) 嘉德勋章; **Order/Knight of the G～** 嘉德勋位/嘉德勋骑士

garter: ～ belt *n* Amer = **suspender belt**; **～ snake** *n* 束带蛇

gas /gæs/
A *n* (*pl* **～es** *or* esp Amer **～ses**) 1 [c and u] Chem, Phys 气体 2 [u] (fuel) 燃气; **to cook with ～** 用煤气做饭; **to turn up/down the ～** 打开/关闭煤气; **on a low/medium/high ～** (in cooking) 用小火/中火/大火; **to use bottled ～** 使用罐装液化气 3 [u] (anaesthetic) 麻醉气; **to have ～** Dent 使用麻醉气; **～ and air** Med 混合气体镇痛剂 4 [u] Mil 毒气 5 [u] Amer (petrol) 汽油; **to stop for ～** 停车加油; **to step on the ～** lit 踩油门; fig 加快速度; **to take one's foot off the ～** lit 松开油门; fig 放慢速度 6 [u] Amer (in the alimentary canal) 肠气
B *vt* (*pres p etc.* **-ss-**) (poison with gas) 向…施放毒气; **she ～sed herself** 她开煤气自杀了
C *vi* (*pres p etc.* **-ss-**) Brit colloq (chatter) 闲聊; **to ～ away about sth.** 没完没了地聊某事

Phrasal verb

• **gas up** Amer colloq
A *vi* 加汽油
B *vt* [**～ up sth., ～ sth. up**] 给…加油 ‹*car*›

gas: ～bag *n* 1 colloq (chatterbox) 废话篓子; **a boastful ～bag** 夸夸其谈的人; 2 (container in balloon, airship) 气囊; **～ burner** *n* = **～ jet 1**; **～ carrier** *n* 燃气运输船; **～ chamber** *n* 毒气室; **～ cooker** *n* 煤气灶; **～-cooled** *adj* 气冷的

gaseous /'gæsɪəs, 'geɪsɪəs/ *adj* (composed of gas) 气体的; (related to gas) 气态的

gas: ～ explosion *n* 气体爆炸; **～ fire** *n* Brit 煤气取暖器; **～-fired** *adj* 以煤气为燃料的; **～-fired boiler** 燃气锅炉; **～ fitter** ▸**p. 409** *n* 煤气设备检修工; **～ fittings** *npl* 煤气设备; **～ guzzler** /'gæsˌgʌzlə(r)/ *n* Amer colloq 油老虎

gash /gæʃ/
A *n* 1 [c] (wound) 深长的伤口; (cut) 深长的切口; **to make a ～ in sth.** 在某物上划一条口子 2 [u] Brit colloq (rubbish) 垃圾
B *vt* 割破 ‹*arm, leg*›; 划开 ‹*leather, cloth*›; **to ～ one's leg/hand on sth.** 被某物割破腿/手

gas: ～ heater *n* 燃气取暖器; **～ hog** *n* Amer colloq = **～ guzzler**; **～holder** *n* = **gasometer**; **～ hydrate** *n* [u and c] 天然气水合物 [俗称"可燃冰"]; **～ jet** *n* 1 (burner) 煤气喷嘴; 2 (stream of gas) 煤气喷流

gasket /'gæskɪt/ *n* 密封垫; **to blow a ～** Aut 密封圈漏气; fig hum 勃然大怒

gas: ～ lamp *n* 煤气灯; **～light** *n* 1 [c] (lamp) 煤气灯; 2 [u] (light) 煤气灯光; **～ lighter** *n* 1 (for oven, fire) 煤气点火器; 2 (cigarette lighter) 气体打火机; **～ lighting** *n* [u] 煤气照明系统; **～lit** *adj* 用煤气灯照明的; **～ main** *n* 煤气总管; **～ man** ▸**p. 409** *n* (checking meters) 煤气表抄表员; (fitter) 煤气设备检修工; **～ mantle** *n* 煤气灯罩; **～ mark** *n* Brit (on gas oven) 温度标记; **～ mask** *n* 防毒面具; **～ meter** *n* 煤气表; **～ mileage** *n* [u] Amer 耗油里程数

gasohol /'gæsəhɒl/ *n* [u] Amer 汽油醇

gas oil *n* [u] 粗柴油

gasoline /'gæsəliːn/ *n* [u] Amer 汽油

gasoline-powered *adj* Amer 汽油驱动的 ‹*vehicle*›

gasometer /gæ'sɒmɪtə(r)/ *n* 大型储气罐

gas oven *n* 燃气灶

gasp /gɑːsp/
A *n* 喘气; **to let out** *or* **give a ～** 倒抽一口气; **to give a ～ of horror** 吓得倒吸一口气; **at the last ～** fig 在最后时刻; **to the last ～** fig 到最后一刻; **to be at one's last ～** lit 奄奄一息; fig 筋疲力尽
B *vi* 喘气; **to ～ for breath** *or* **air** 大口喘气; **to ～ in** *or* **with amazement** 惊愕地倒吸一口气; **to be ～ing for sth.** Brit fig colloq 渴望得到某物
C *vt* 喘着气说出; **she ～ed (out) a few words** 她好不容易憋出几个字

gas: ～ pedal *n* Amer 油门; **～-permeable** *adj* 透气的 ‹*contact lens*›; **～ pipe** *n* 燃气管; **～ pipeline** *n* 燃气管线;

～ poker *n* 煤气引火棒; **～-powered** *adj* **1** (burning propane, butane, etc.) 燃气驱动的 ‹*engine, vehicle*›; **2** Amer (burning petrol) 烧煤气的 ‹*lamp, appliance*›; **～ range** *n* [带烤箱的] 煤气灶; **～ ring** *n* Brit 环形轻便煤气灶; **～ station** *n* Amer = **filling station**; **～ stove** *n* 煤气炉

gassy /ˈgæsi/ *adj* **1** (filled with gas) 充满气体的; **a ～ drink/liquid** 含气饮料/液体 **2** Amer (flatulent) (肠胃) 胀气的

gas: ～ tank *n* Amer 油箱; **～ tap** *n* 气阀

gastric /ˈgæstrɪk/ *adj* 胃的; **～ flu** 胃肠炎; **～ juices/ulcer** 胃液/溃疡

gastritis /gæˈstraɪtɪs/ ▸**p. 377** *n* [u] 胃炎

gastroenteritis /ˌgæstrəʊˌentəˈraɪtɪs/ ▸**p. 377** *n* [u] 胃肠炎

gastrointestinal /ˌgæstrəʊɪnˈtestɪnl, -ˌɪntesˈtaɪnl/ *adj* 胃肠的

gastronome /ˈgæstrənəʊm/ *n* formal 美食家

gastronomic /ˌgæstrəˈnɒmɪk/ *adj* 美食的 ‹*feast, expert*›; 烹饪的 ‹*pleasures*›

gastronomist /gæˈstrɒnəmɪst/ *n* formal 美食家

gastronomy /gæˈstrɒnəmi/ *n* [u] 美食学

gastropod /ˈgæstrəpɒd/ *n* 腹足纲软体动物

gastropub /ˈgæstrəʊpʌb/ *n* 美食酒吧 [提供优质美食的酒吧]

gas: ～ turbine *n* 燃气轮机; **～ worker** ▸**p. 409** *n* 煤气工人; **～ works** *npl + v sing or pl* 煤气厂

gate /geɪt/ *n* **1** (barrier) (of garden, prison etc.) 大门; (of town) 城门; **to give sb. the ～** Amer colloq (fire) 解雇 ‹*employee*›; (dump) 甩掉 ‹*boyfriend*›; **to get the ～** Amer colloq (be fired) 被炒鱿鱼; (be dumped) 被抛弃 **2** (opening) 大门口 **3** (for controlling water) 闸门 **4** (entrance, exit) 出入口 **5** (at airport) 登机口 **6** Sport (number of spectators) 观众数; **a good** *or* **large/poor** *or* **small ～** 众多/很少的观众 **7** Sport (in skiing) 旗门

gateau /ˈgætəʊ, Amer gæˈtəʊ/ *n* [c and u] (*pl* **gateaux** /ˈgætəʊ, Amer gæˈtəʊ/ *or* **～s**) 奶油水果大蛋糕

gatecrash /ˈgeɪtkræʃ/ colloq

A *vt* (without invitation) 擅自参加 ‹*social event, party*›; (without paying) 无票观看 ‹*match, concert*›

B *vi* (without invitation) 擅自参加; (without paying) 无票观看

gate: ～crasher /ˈgeɪtkræʃə(r)/ *n* (at social event, party) 不速之客; (at match, concert) 无票混入者; **～house** *n* (at park, estate) 门房; (at lock) 闸门控制室; **～keeper** *n* 看门人; **～leg table** *n* 折叠式桌子; **～ lodge** *n* [豪宅等的] 门房; **～ money** *n* [u] 门票收入; **～post** *n* 门柱; **between you and me and the ～post** Brit colloq 你我私下说说

gateway /ˈgeɪtweɪ/ *n* **1** (entrance) 大门口 **2** Archit (frame) 门框; (arch) 门拱 **3** fig (place) 门户; **a ～ to** *or* **into a place** 通往某地的门户 **4** fig (means) 途径; **the ～ to success/fame** 通往成功之路/扬名的手段 **5** Comput 网关

gateway drug *n* 入门毒品 [可诱使吸毒者吸食更危险毒品]

gather /ˈgæðə(r)/

A *vt* **1** (draw together) 召集 ‹*pupils, followers, crowd*›; 集合 ‹*troops*›; 集齐 ‹*belongings, notes*› **2** (collect, harvest) 采集 ‹*berries, mushrooms, flowers*›; **to ～ wood** 拣柴禾 **3** (accumulate) 收集 ‹*facts, data, evidence*›; «*surface, object*» 积聚 ‹*dust, dirt*› **4** (increase in) 逐渐增加 ‹*speed, volume, strength*›; **the movement has been ～ing strength lately** 这项运动最近声势越来越大; **to ～ way** Naut 加速 **5** (infer, conclude) 推断; **to ～ that ...** 了解到…; **to ～ sth. from sth./sb.** 从某事中/某人处了解到某事; **you're leaving, I ～** 我想, 你是要走了吧; **I ～ed the impression that she wasn't happy** 我的印象是她不太高兴; **as far as I can ～** 根据我的了解 **6** fig (summon up) 鼓足 ‹*courage, strength*›; 集中 ‹*thoughts*› **7** Sewing 缝紧 ‹*sleeves, skirt, fabric*›; **a long dress ～ed under the bosom** 胸部以下收紧的长裙 **8** (draw in) 拉紧 ‹*shawl, skirt, cloak*›; **she had ～ed her hair into a bun** 她把头发束成一个结 **9** (embrace) 拥抱 ‹*person, child*›; **to ～ sb. in one's arms** 把某人抱进怀里 **10** liter (contract) 皱起 ‹*brows*› **11** Print 为…配页 ‹*sections of book*›

B *vi* **1** (come together) «*people, family*» 聚集; **tears ～ed in her eyes** 她眼泪盈眶 **2** (increase) «*clouds*» 积聚; **darkness was ～ing** 天色渐暗

C *v refl* **to ～ oneself** **1** (for an effort, a task) 做好准备 **2** (after a shock, an accident) 振作

D *n* 皱褶

Phrasal verbs

- **gather around** *vi* = **gather round**
- **gather in** *vt* [**～ in sth., ～ sth. in**]
  1 Agric 收割 ‹*harvest, crops*› **2** (collect) 收取 ‹*taxes, money*›; 收集 ‹*papers, essays*›
- **gather round** *vi* «*crowd*» 聚集; «*family*» 聚会
- **gather together**

A *vi* «*family, members, friends*» 聚会

B *vt* [**～ sth./sb. together, ～ together sth./sb.**]
1 (collect) 归拢 ‹*belongings, papers*›; 集合 ‹*people*› **2** (accumulate) 收集 ‹*facts, data, evidence*›

C *v refl* **to ～ oneself together** (after a shock, an accident) 镇定; (for an effort, a task) 做好准备

- **gather up**

A *vt* [**～ sth. up, ～ up sth.**]
1 (pick up) 收拾 ‹*toys, debris, remains*›; 总结 ‹*pieces of one's life*› **2** (summon up) 鼓足 ‹*strength, courage*›; 集中 ‹*thoughts*› **3** (draw in) 拉紧 ‹*shawl, skirt, cloak*›; **she had ～ed her hair up into a bun** 她把头发束成一个结

B *v refl* **to ～ oneself up** (mentally) 振作; (physically) 直起身

gathering /ˈgæðərɪŋ/

A *n* **1** [u] (collecting) (of berries, mushrooms, flowers) 采集; (of facts, data, evidence) 收集 **2** [c] (meeting) 聚会; **social/family ～** 社交/家庭聚会

B *adj attrib* 渐增的; **the ～ gloom/storm** 越来越暗的天色/越来越大的暴风雨; **the ～ clouds of war** fig 愈积愈厚的战争乌云

GATT /gæt/ *abbr* = **General Agreement on Tariffs and Trade** 关税及贸易总协定

gauche /gəʊʃ/ *adj* 不善交际的 ‹*person*›; 笨拙的 ‹*manner, behaviour*›

gaudily /ˈgɔːdɪli/ *adv* 俗艳地; **～ dressed** 穿着俗丽的; **a ～ painted banner** 五彩缤纷的旗帜

gaudy /ˈgɔːdi/ *adj* 俗艳的 ‹*decorations, jewellery*›; 花哨的 ‹*colours, shirt*›

gauge /geɪdʒ/

A *n* **1** (standard measure) (thickness) 标准厚度; (width) 标准宽度; **the ～ of the wire/screw** 金属丝/螺丝钉的直径; **the ～ of a sheet of metal/plastic** 一块金属/塑料板的厚度; **what ～ is the wool?** 这种毛线的隔距是多少?; **a 12-～ shotgun** 12 号口径的猎枪 **2** Rail 轨距 **3** (measuring instrument) 测量仪器; **oil/fuel/petrol ～** 油量计/燃油表/汽油表; **height ～** 高度计 **4** fig (way of judging) 判断方法; (way of estimating) 估计方法; **a good ～ of character** 衡量性格的好方法

B *vt* **1** (measure) 精确测量 ‹*diameter, temperature*› **2** (judge) 估计 ‹*strength, capacity*›; 判断 ‹*reaction, sentiments*›

gaunt /gɔːnt/ *adj* **1** (haggard) 憔悴的 ‹*face, look, person*› **2** (desolate) 荒凉的 ‹*landscape*›

gauntlet[1] /ˈgɔːntlɪt/ *n* **1** (in armour) 金属手套; **to throw down the ～** fig 发出挑战; **to pick up** *or* **take up the ～** fig 接受挑战 **2** Sport (protective glove) 防护手套

gauntlet[2] *n* **to run the ～** **1** fig (to be exposed to danger, anger or criticism) 受…攻击 **2** Hist 夹道鞭打刑罚

gauss /gaʊs/ *n* (*pl* **～** *or* **～es**) 高斯 [电磁感应单位]

gauze /gɔːz/ *n* **1** (fabric) 薄纱 **2** Med 纱布

gave /geɪv/ *pt* ▸**give A, B, C**

gavel /ˈgævl/ *n* [拍卖师或会议主席用的] 小木槌

gawk /gɔːk/ *vi* colloq 呆呆地看; **to ～ at sb./sth.** 盯着某人/某物傻看

gawky /ˈgɔːki/ *adj* 笨拙的

gawp /gɔːp/ *vi* Brit colloq = **gawk**

gay /geɪ/

A *adj* **1** (homosexual) 同性恋的 **2** dated (lively, bright) 愉快的 ‹*laughter, occasion*›; 快乐的 ‹*time*›; 欢快的 ‹*music, decorations*›; **the room was ～ with flowers** 房间里有了花显得生机盎然 **3** dated (carefree) 无忧无虑的 ‹*bachelor, life*›; **to do sth. with ～ abandon** 纵情做某事

B *n* 同性恋者; **～ rights** 同性恋者的权利; **～ club** 同性恋者俱乐部

gay: ～ liberation, ～ lib colloq *ns* [u] 同性恋解放运动; **～ marriage** *n* [c and u] 同性婚姻

gayness /ˈgeɪnɪs/ *n* [u] 同性恋

Gaza Strip /ˌgɑːzə ˈstrɪp/ *pr n* **the ～** 加沙地带

gaze /geɪz/

A *n* 凝视; **to hold sb.'s ～** 与某人长时间对视; **his ～ met mine** 他和我目光相遇

B *vi* 凝视; **to ～ at/into sth.** 凝视/直视某物; **to ～ out of the window/into the distance** 盯着窗外看/凝眸远眺; **he was just gazing into space** 他怔怔地望着前面

Phrasal verb

- **gaze about, gaze around** *vi* 左顾右盼; **to ～ around** *or* **about in wonder** 惊异地四处张望

gazebo /gəˈziːbəʊ/ *n* (*pl* **～s**) 凉亭

gazelle /gəˈzel/ *n* (*pl* **gazelle** *or* **～s**) 瞪羚

gazette /gəˈzet/ *n* **1** Brit (official journal) 公报 **2** Journ (in title) 报; **the Evening G～** 《晚报》

gazetteer /ˌgæzəˈtɪə(r)/ *n* 地名索引

gazump /gəˈzʌmp/ *vt* Brit colloq [房价议定后] 对…食言毁约

gazumping /gəˈzʌmpɪŋ/ *n* [u] Brit colloq [房价议定后的] 食言毁约

gazunder /gəˈzʌndə(r)/ *vt* Brit colloq 压价敲诈

gazundering /gəˈzʌndərɪŋ/ *n* [u] Brit colloq 压价敲诈

GB *abbr* **1** = **Great Britain** **2** Comput = **gigabyte**

GBH *abbr* = **grievous bodily harm**

GBP *abbr* = **Great Britain pound** 英镑

Gbyte *abbr* = **gigabyte**

GC *abbr* = **George Cross** 乔治十字勋章

GCE *abbr* Brit = **General Certificate of Education**

GCHQ *abbr* Brit = **Government Communications Headquarters** 政府通信总局

GCSE *abbr* Brit = **General Certificate of Secondary Education**

g'day /gəˈdeɪ/ *excl* Austral, NZ 你好

Gdns *abbr* = **garden B**

GDP *abbr* = **gross domestic product**

GDR *abbr* Hist = **German Democratic Republic**

gear /gɪə(r)/

A *n* **1** [u] (equipment) 用具; (machinery) 设备; **photography/gardening ～** 摄影/园艺用具; **fishing/cooking ～** 渔具/炊具; **steering ～** 转向装置; **winding/landing ～** 卷扬/降落装置 **2** [u] colloq (personal possessions, stuff) 所有物; **I'm going to pack my ～** 我要收拾东西了 **3** [u and c] Aut, Mech (specific setting) 排挡; **to put a car in** *or* **into ～** 给车挂上挡; **to be in/out of ～** 齿轮啮合/脱开; **to change ～** 换挡;

g

to slip *or* jump out of ～ 跳挡; to engage second ～ 挂二挡; reverse ～ 倒车挡; bottom/first ～ 最低挡/一挡; top *or* Amer high ～ 最高挡; to change *or* Amer shift into second/third ～ 换成二/三挡; keep in low ～ (on road sign) 保持低速行驶; you're in the wrong ～ 你挂错挡了; to get (oneself) into ～ for sth. fig 为某事做好准备 **4** [u] colloq (clothing) 衣服; football ～ 足球服; designer ～ 名牌服装 **5** [c] Mech (toothed wheel) 齿轮 **6** [u and c] Tech (set of wheels) 传动装置 **7** [u and c] fig (level) 速度; to change/move up a ～ 改变/提高速度; to move into high *or* top ～ 进入高速发展 **8** [u] Brit colloq (drugs) 毒品

B *vt* **1** (adapt) 使…适合于 ‹*system, timetable, country*›; to ～ sth. to do sth. 为做某事准备好某物; to ～ sth./sb. for sth. 使某物/某人为某事物做好准备; a nation ～ed for war 准备参战的国家; production was not ～ed to sudden fluctuations in demand 生产尚未做好应对需求突然波动的准备; we are not ～ed towards joining the single European currency 我们尚未做好加入单一欧洲货币体系的准备; to be ～ed to the cost of living 能应付生活支出 **2** Aut, Mech 设置…的排挡 ‹*vehicle, machine, wheel*›

C *vi* «*company, country*» 做准备; to ～ for sth. 为某事做好准备

Phrasal verb

- **gear up**

A *vi* «*person, company, country*» 做准备; to ～ up for sth./to do sth. 为某事/做某事做好准备

B *vt* [～ sth. up, ～ up sth.] 使…做好准备 ‹*company, country*›; to be ～ed up for sth./to do sth. 为某事/做某事做好准备

C *v refl* to ～ oneself up 做好准备; to ～ oneself up for sth./to do sth. 为某事/做某事做好准备

gear: **～box** *n* Brit 变速箱; **～ cable** *n* 刹车线; **～ change** *n* Brit 换挡

gearing /ˈgɪərɪŋ/ *n* **1** Tech (gears) 齿轮装置 **2** Brit Fin 资本负债比率

gear: **～ lever** *n* Brit 变速杆; **～ ratio** *n* 齿数比; **～ shift** *n* Amer **1** (lever) = **～ lever**; **2** (process) = **～ change**; **～ stick** *abbr* Brit = **～ lever**; **～ wheel** *n* 齿轮

gecko /ˈgekəʊ/ *n* (*pl* **～s** *or* **～es**) 壁虎

gee[1] /dʒiː/ *excl* Amer colloq **～ whizz** (in surprise) 咦; (in disappointment, commiseration) 哎呀; **～ it's good to see you** 哇, 见到你真高兴

gee[2] *excl* **～ up!** (to horse) 驾!

Phrasal verb

- **gee up** *vt* [～ sb./sth. up, ～ up sb./sth.] 让…快跑 ‹*horse*›; fig colloq (encourage) 激励 ‹*person*›

gee-gee /ˈdʒiːdʒiː/ *n* child lang 马儿

geek /giːk/ *n* colloq **1** (misfit) 闷蛋; (unfashionable person) 土包子 **2** (enthusiast) 痴迷者; **a computer/science ～** 电脑/科学迷

geek speak *n* [u] colloq 电脑术语

geese /giːs/ *npl* ▸ **goose A**

geezer /ˈgiːzə(r)/ *n* Brit colloq 家伙

Geiger counter /ˈgaɪgə ˌkaʊntə(r)/ *n* 盖格计数器

geisha /ˈgeɪʃə/ *n* **～ (girl)** 艺妓

gel /dʒel/

A *n* **1** Cosmet 胶状物; **bath/hair ～** 沐浴露/发胶 **2** Chem 凝胶体

B *vi* (*pres p etc.* **-ll-**) **1** (set) «*liquid*» 形成胶体 **2** fig (take shape) «*ideas*» 变得更清楚; «*plan*» 变得更明确; **to ～ into sth.** 具体化为某物

gelatin /ˈdʒelətɪn/, **gelatine** /ˈdʒelətiːn/ *n* [u] 明胶

gelatinous /dʒəˈlætɪnəs/ *adj* 凝胶状的

geld /geld/ *vt* 阉割

gelding /ˈgeldɪŋ/ *n* **1** [c] (horse) 阉过的动物 [尤指骟马] **2** [u] (castration) 阉割

gelignite /ˈdʒelɪgnaɪt/ *n* [u] 葛里炸药

gem /dʒem/ *n* **1** (precious stone) 宝石 **2** fig (outstanding person) 优秀的人; (outstanding thing) 精品; **a ～ of a village** 美丽的村庄; **the ～ of the collection** 收藏中的极品; **she's a ～** colloq (very pleasant) 她是个招人喜爱的人; (very capable) 她是个难能可贵的人

Gemini /ˈdʒemɪnaɪ, -niː/ *n* **1** [u] Astron 双子(星)座 **2** [u] Astrol (sign) 双子宫 [黄道第三宫] **3** [c] (*pl* **～s**) Astrol (person) 属双子(星)座的人

gemmology, gemology /ˌdʒemˈɒlədʒi/ *n* [u] 宝石学

gemstone /ˈdʒemstəʊn/ *n* [尤指未经雕琢的] 宝石

gen /dʒen/ *n* [u] Brit colloq 相关信息; **the ～ on sth.** 关于某事物的情况

Phrasal verb

- **gen up** Brit colloq

A *vi* **to ～ up on** *or* **about sth.** 获取某事物的详情

B *vt* **to ～ sb. up on** *or* **about sth.** 向某人提供某事物的相关信息; **to be ～ned up on** *or* **about sth.** 知道某事物

Gen. *abbr* = **general B1**

gender /ˈdʒendə(r)/ *n* [c and u] **1** (sexual classification) 性别; **male and female ～s** (of person) 男性和女性; (of animal) 雄性和雌性 **2** Ling 性; **in ～** 在性上; **common ～** 通性; **feminine ～** 阴性

gender: **～-bender** *n* colloq hum 易装癖者; **～ bias** *n* [u and c] 性别歧视; **～ gap** *n* 男女差别; **～-specific** *adj* 某一性别特有的; **to remove ～-specific language** 删除带有性别特点的语言

gene /dʒiːn/ *n* 基因; **to have sth. in one's ～s** 某人本性中有某品质

genealogical /ˌdʒiːnɪəˈlɒdʒɪkl/ *adj* 系谱的; **a ～ table/tree** 家谱表/家系树状图

genealogist /ˌdʒiːnɪˈælədʒɪst/ ▸ **p. 409** *n* 系谱学者

genealogy /ˌdʒiːnɪˈælədʒi/ *n* **1** [u] (study) 系谱学 **2** [c] (ancestry) 家系; (diagram) 系谱图

gene: **～ bank** *n* 基因库; **～ cluster** *n* 基因簇; **～ library** *n* 物种基因库; **～ mapping** *n* [u] = **genetic mapping**; **～ pool** *n* 种群基因库

genera /ˈdʒenərə/ *npl* ▸ **genus**

general /ˈdʒenrəl/

A *adj* **1** (widespread in application) 普遍的 ‹*interest, approval, opinion, chaos*›; 通常的 ‹*principle, axiom, conclusion*›; 全体的 ‹*meeting, strike*›; 群众性的 ‹*movement*›; **words in ～ use** 普遍使用的词汇; **the photocopier is for ～ use** 这台复印机是共用的; **～ consensus** 一致的赞成; **apple pie is a ～ favourite** 苹果馅饼是大家都喜欢的食品; **there was a ～ exodus** 众人一起撤离了; **the bad weather has been fairly ～** 各地几乎都是坏天气; **～ pandemonium** 一片混乱; **as a ～ rule** 通常 **2** *attrib* (overall, not detailed) 整体的 ‹*appearance, overview*›; 总体的 ‹*plan, condition, feeling, decline*›; 笼统的 ‹*description, statement, wording*›; 大致的 ‹*request, outline, direction*›; 泛泛的 ‹*discussion, conversation*›; **to improve one's ～ fitness** 改善总体健康状况; **a ～ view of the building** 大楼的概貌; **do you get the ～ idea?** 你理解大意了吗?; **I've got the ～ picture** 我了解了大致情况; **to talk in ～ terms** 笼统地谈; **this is the ～ plan of action** 这是大致的行动计划 **3** (not specialized) 非专门的 ‹*information, book, magazine, labourer*›; 普通的 ‹*education, linguistics, reader, office*›; 普及性的 ‹*science*›; 综合的 ‹*dealer*›; 杂项的 ‹*expenses, expenditure*›; **～ enquiries** 一般查询; **a ～ index** 总目; **～ office work** 办公室杂务; **～ household duties** 家务 **4** (normal, usual) 正常的 ‹*practice, solution, remedy*›; **in the ～ way of things** 通常情况下; **the ～ run of people** 普通人; **the ～ routine** 常规 **5** (chief) 首席的; **consul/inspector ～** 总领事/监察长; **Attorney/Governor/Secretary G～** 检察总长/总督/秘书长

B *n* **1** [c and u] Mil (officer) 将官; (rank) 将军; **～ of the army/air force** Amer 陆军/空军五星上将; **to make sb. a ～** 擢升某人为上将; **G～ Charles de Gaulle** 夏尔·戴高乐将军 **2** [u] **in ～** (for the most part, mostly, usually) 多数情况下; (referring to a wide-ranging group) 一般来讲

general: **～ anaesthetic** *n* [u and c] 全身麻醉剂; **G～ Assembly** *n* **1** (of UN) 联合国大会; **2** (governing body) 州议会; (group of representatives) 代表大会; **G～ Certificate of Education** *n* Brit 普通教育证书; **G～ Certificate of Secondary Education** *n* Brit 普通中等教育证书; **～ degree** *n* Brit 普通学士学位 [比荣誉学士学位低一级]; **～ delivery** *n* [u] Amer 存局候领; **to send sth. ～ delivery** 把某物寄到邮局候领; **～ election** *n* 大选; **～ headquarters** *npl + v sing or pl* 总司令部; **～ hospital** *n* 综合性医院

generalist /ˈdʒenrəlɪst/ *n* 多面手

generality /ˌdʒenəˈræləti/ *n* **1** [c] (general remark) 概括性的话; (general principle) 一般原则; (general issue) 一般性问题; **they talked of generalities** 他们谈的是一般性问题 **2** [u] (state of being general) 一般性; (vagueness) 笼统

generalization /ˌdʒenrəlaɪˈzeɪʃn, Amer -lɪˈz-/ *n* **1** [u] (act of generalizing) 概括 **2** [c] (statement) 推论; (principle) 普遍原则; **to make a ～** 作推论; **a ～ about sth.** 对某事物的归纳

generalize /ˈdʒenrəlaɪz/

A *vi* 概括; **to ～ about sth.** 对某事作概括总结

B *vt* **1** (make more widespread) 普及 ‹*education, use, practice*›; 推广 ‹*syllabus*› **2** formal (draw) 归纳出 ‹*conclusion, principle*›

generalized /ˈdʒenrəlaɪzd/ *adj* **1** (widespread) 普遍的 ‹*anxiety*›; 广泛的 ‹*effect*›; 全身的 ‹*malaise, sickness*› **2** (unspecific) 笼统的 ‹*statement*›; 概括性的 ‹*remark*›; 含糊的 ‹*criticism*›

general knowledge *n* [u] 常识; **a ～ question/quiz/test** 常识问题/问答比赛/考试

generally /ˈdʒenrəli/ *adv* **1** (usually) 一般地; **～ (speaking)** 一般来说; **it's ～ best to wait** 一般来说, 等待是最好的办法; **he ～ drives to work** 他通常开车上班 **2** (widely) 普遍地; **a ～ accepted definition of the term** 这一术语被普遍接受的定义; **the book is not ～ available** 此书不是随处都能买到的 **3** (on the whole) 总体上; **he's ～ unwell at the moment** 总体来看他目前身体状况欠佳; **the quality is ～ good** 总体质量不错; **she was dancing, drinking, and ～ enjoying herself** 她又跳舞又喝酒, 总之玩得很高兴; **I meant people ～** 我是泛指大家 **4** (in non-specific terms) 泛泛地 ‹*talk, speak, discuss*›

general: **～ manager** ▸ **p. 409** *n* 总经理; **～ meeting** *n* 全体会议; **～ officer** *n* 将级军官; **～ partner** *n* 普通合伙人; **～ partnership** *n* 普通合伙; **～ practice** *n* **1** [u] (field) 全科诊疗; **2** [c] (health centre) 全科诊所; **～ practitioner** ▸ **p. 409** *n* esp Brit 全科医生; **～ public** *n + v sing or pl* 公众; **～-purpose** *adj* 多用途的 ‹*detergent, drug*›; 多功能的 ‹*screwdriver, vehicle*›; **～ science** *n* [u] 科学通论; **a ～ science lesson** 一节科学通论课; **～ secretary** *n* 秘书长; **～ staff** *n + v sing or pl* 参谋部; **～ store** *n* 杂货店; **～ strike** *n* 总罢工; **～ studies** *npl + v sing* Brit 普通学科

generate /ˈdʒenəreɪt/ *vt* **1** Elec 产生 ‹*power*›; **to ～ electricity from fossil fuels** 用矿物燃料发电 **2** (produce, create) 带来 ‹*income, activity*›; 生成 ‹*paperwork*›; 创造 ‹*jobs*›; 引起 ‹*excitement, fears*›; **computers that ～ bank statements** 生成银行对账单的计算机

generating station /ˈdʒenəreɪtɪŋ ˌsteɪʃn/ *n* 发电站

generation /ˌdʒenəˈreɪʃn/ *n* **1** [c] (family group) 一代人; **all three ~s were present** 三代人都到场了; **a story handed down from ~ to ~** 世代流传的故事 **2** [c] (group of similar age) 同代人; **the younger/older/new ~** 年轻一代人/老一辈人/新一代人; **people of my ~** 我这一代人 **3** [c] (period of time) 一代人的时间 [通常为30年左右]; **a ~ ago** 一代人以前 **4** [c] (in product development) 一代 **5** [u] (of electricity) 产生 **6** [u] (of income) 带来; (of employment, wealth) 创造

generation gap *n* 代沟

generative /ˈdʒenərətɪv/ *adj* **1** (capable of producing) 生产的 ‹*power, process*› **2** Biol 生殖的 ‹*organs, capacity, cell*›

generative grammar *n* [c and u] 生成语法

generator /ˈdʒenəreɪtə(r)/ *n* **1** Elec 发电机 **2** (machine producing oxygen, sound, microwaves) 发生器 **3** (creator) 制造者

generic /dʒɪˈnerɪk/ *adj* **1** (common) 普通的; **a ~ term** 通称 **2** Comm 无注册商标的 ‹*food, product*›

generically /dʒɪˈnerɪkli/ *adv* **1** (with reference to type) 在类别上; **~ similar/distinct** 大类上相似/不同的 **2** Comm 作为通称

generic drug *n* 仿制药品

generosity /ˌdʒenəˈrɒsəti/ *n* [u] **1** (with money, gifts, food) 慷慨; **~ towards/with/in ...** 对…的/在…方面的慷慨; **such ~!** iron 如此大方! **2** (lavishness) 丰富; **the ~ of the gift** 礼物的丰厚 **3** (kindness) 宽宏大量; **~ of mind/spirit** 胸襟宽阔/灵魂高洁

generous /ˈdʒenərəs/ *adj* **1** (with money, gifts, food) 慷慨的 ‹*person, gesture, action*›; **to be ~ with sth.** 对…不吝啬 ‹*praise, time*›; **the most ~ person I know** 我所认识的最大方的人 **2** (lavish) 丰厚的 ‹*gift, donation*› **3** (magnanimous) 宽宏大量的 ‹*person, spirit*›; **he was ~ in defeat** 他并未因失败而心生怨恨 **4** (large) 巨大的 ‹*size, harvest*›; 丰足的 ‹*helping, supply*›; 丰盛的 ‹*meal*›

generously /ˈdʒenərəsli/ *adv* **1** (liberally) 慷慨地 ‹*give, offer*› **2** (lavishly) 大量地 ‹*provided*›; 丰富地 ‹*illustrated*› **3** (magnanimously) 宽宏大量地 ‹*forgive*›

genesis /ˈdʒenəsɪs/

A *n* (*pl* **geneses** /ˈdʒenəsiːz/) (origin) 起源; (formation) 形成

B **Genesis** *pr n* 《创世记》

gene therapy *n* [u and c] 基因疗法

genetic /dʒɪˈnetɪk/ *adj* **1** (relating to genes) 基因的 ‹*defect, make-up*› **2** (relating to genetics) 遗传学的 ‹*research, techniques*›

genetically /dʒɪˈnetɪkli/ *adv* **1** (through genes) 通过基因 ‹*determined, linked*› **2** (through genetics) 在遗传学上 ‹*altered, engineered*›

genetically modified, genetically manipulated *adjs* 基因改造的 ‹*plant, organism*›; 转基因的 ‹*food*›

genetic: ~ code *n* 遗传密码; **~ counselling** *n* [u] [向待生婴儿父母就是否有遗传疾病问题提供的] 遗传咨询; **~ engineering** *n* [u] 遗传工程学; **~ fingerprinting** *n* [u] 基因指纹识别; **~ ID card** *n* 基因识别卡

geneticist /dʒɪˈnetɪsɪst/ ▸**p. 409** *n* 遗传学家

genetic: ~ manipulation *n* [u and c] 基因操控; **~ map** *n* 遗传图; **~ mapping** *n* [u] 基因定位; **~ profile** *n* 基因图谱

genetics /dʒɪˈnetɪks/ *npl* **1** + *v sing* (field of study) 遗传学 **2** + *v sing or pl* (genetic properties) 遗传性; **determined by one's ~** 由自身的基因决定

genetic: ~ screening *n* [u] 遗传筛查; **~ testing** *n* [u] 基因测定

Geneva /dʒɪˈniːvə/ ▸**p. 424** *pr n* 日内瓦; **Lake ~** 日内瓦湖

Geneva Convention *n* **the ~** 日内瓦公约

genial /ˈdʒiːnɪəl/ *adj* (cheerful) 欢快的; (friendly) 友好的

geniality /ˌdʒiːnɪˈæləti/ *n* [u] 友善

genially /ˈdʒiːnɪəli/ *adv* (in a warm manner) 和蔼可亲地; (in a friendly manner) 友善地

genie /ˈdʒiːni/ *n* 精灵

genital /ˈdʒenɪtl/

A *adj* 生殖的 ‹*organ*›; 生殖器的 ‹*area, stimulation*›

B **genitals** *npl* 外生殖器

genital herpes ▸**p. 377** *n* [u] 生殖器疱疹

genitalia /ˌdʒenɪˈteɪlɪə/ *npl* 外生殖器

genitive /ˈdʒenɪtɪv/

A *n* 属格; **in the ~** 以所有格形式

B *adj* 属格的 ‹*ending, noun*›; **the ~ form of this noun** 这个名词的所有格形式

genito-urinary /ˌdʒenɪtəʊˈjʊərɪnəri, Amer -neri/ *adj* 生殖泌尿器的

genius /ˈdʒiːnɪəs/ *n* **1** [c] (*pl* **~es**) (person with exceptional talent) 天才人物; **a mathematical/musical ~** 数学/音乐天才 **2** [u] (exceptional creative ability) 天资; **his inventive ~** 他的创造性天赋 **3** [u] (great skill) 才干; **to have a ~ for sth./doing sth.** 有某方面/做某事的本领 **4** [u] (distinctive quality, spirit) 特征 **5** [c] (*pl* **genii** /ˈdʒiːnɪaɪ/) liter (spirit) 神灵; **sb.'s good/evil ~** 使某人得救的神灵/使某人毁灭的魔鬼

genocidal /ˈdʒenəsaɪdl/ *adj* 种族灭绝的

genocide /ˈdʒenəsaɪd/ *n* [u] 种族灭绝

genome /ˈdʒiːnəʊm/ *n* **1** (set of chromosomes) 基因组 **2** (genetic material) 全部遗传物质

genotype /ˈdʒenəʊtaɪp/ *n* (genetic constitution) 基因型; (group of organisms) 同遗传型小种

genre /ˈʒɑːnrə/ *n* 体裁; **~ painting** 风俗画

gent /dʒent/

A *n* **1** colloq (gentleman) 绅士; **this way, ~s!** 先生们, 这边走! **2** Brit (in shop titles) 男士; **~s' hairdresser's/clothing** 男士理发店/男装

B **Gents** *npl* **the G~s** Brit colloq (men's public toilet) 男厕所

genteel /dʒenˈtiːl/ *adj* **1** (respectable) 体面的; (well-bred) 有教养的; (refined) 高雅的; **to live in ~ poverty** 生活贫困但面子上却很讲究 **2** iron (affectedly refined) 假斯文的; (exaggeratedly refined) 过分雅致的; **she's too ~ for words** 她过于咬文嚼字了

gentian /ˈdʒenʃn/ *n* 龙胆属植物; **~ blue** 龙胆蓝色

gentian violet *n* [u] 龙胆紫

Gentile /ˈdʒentaɪl/

A *n* 非犹太人

B *adj* 非犹太人的

gentility /dʒenˈtɪləti/ *n* [u] **1** dated (respectability) 体面; (good breeding) 有教养; (refinement) 雅致 **2** (social superiority) 上流社会地位; iron or pej (affectation) 假斯文

gentle /ˈdʒentl/ *adj* **1** (kind, tender) 温柔的 ‹*person, nature, manner*›; **to be ~ with sb./sth.** 对某人温柔/轻轻摆弄某物; **the ~ sex** liter dated or iron 妇女 **2** (not harsh) 善意的 ‹*joke, fun*›; 和婉的 ‹*hint, reminder, rebuke*› **3** (quiet) 柔和的 ‹*voice*›; (calm) 和蔼的 ‹*look, eyes, expression*› **4** (light) 轻柔的 ‹*touch, push*›; 徐缓的 ‹*movement, progress*› **5** (moderate) 和缓的; **~ breeze/rain/heat** 和风/细雨/文火 **6** (gradual) 平缓的 ‹*slope*›; **to come to a ~ stop** 缓缓地停下来

gentleman /ˈdʒentlmən/ *n* (*pl* **gentlemen**) **1** (man) 先生; **gentlemen of the jury!** 陪审团的诸位先生们! **2** (well-bred man) 有教养的人; (courteous man) 彬彬有礼的人; **he's no ~** Brit 他可不是个正人君子; **one of nature's gentlemen** 绝对的绅士; **a ~ of leisure** 有钱的闲人 **3** Amer Pol (congressman) 男议员 **4** Brit Hist 富绅 **5** **Gentlemen** (sign) 男厕所

gentleman: ~-at-arms *n* Brit [举行仪式时] 国王的侍卫; **~-farmer** *n* 乡绅

gentlemanly /ˈdʒentlmənli/ *adj* **1** (courteous) 有礼貌的 ‹*manner, behaviour*› **2** (of a gentleman) 绅士的 ‹*appearance*›

gentleman's agreement *n* 君子协定

gentlemen /ˈdʒentlmən/ *npl* ▸**gentleman**

gentleness /ˈdʒentlnɪs/ *n* [u] **1** (kindness) (of person) 温柔; (of nature, manner) 温和 **2** (mildness) (of joke, fun) 善意; (of hint, reminder, rebuke) 和婉 **3** (quietness) (of voice) 柔和; (calmness) (of look, eyes, expression) 和蔼 **4** (lightness) (of touch) 轻柔; (of breeze) 徐缓 **5** (moderation) (of climate) 温和 **6** (gradualness) (of slope) 平缓

gently /ˈdʒentli/ *adv* **1** (kindly) 温柔地 **2** (mildly) 和婉地 ‹*hint, remind, rebuke*›; **to go ~ with** *or* **on sth.** colloq 小心地对待某物 **3** (quietly) 柔和地 ‹*speak*›; (calmly) 和蔼地 ‹*look*› **4** (lightly) 轻柔地 ‹*touch, push*›; 徐缓地 ‹*move*› **5** (moderately) 温和地 ‹*rain*› **6** (gradually) 平缓地 ‹*slope*›; 慢慢地 ‹*stop*›; **~!** Brit colloq 小心点儿!

gentrification /ˌdʒentrɪfɪˈkeɪʃn/ *n* [u] [地区、房屋等的] 中产阶级化

gentrify /ˈdʒentrɪfaɪ/ *vt* 使…中产阶级化 ‹*street, area, house*›

gentry /ˈdʒentri/ *n* [u and c] dated 绅士阶层; **a family of landed ~** 有地产的乡绅家庭

genuflect /ˈdʒenjuːflekt/ *vi* **1** Relig formal 跪拜 **2** fig pej (show deference) 卑躬屈膝; **to ~ to sb./sth.** 屈从于某人/某物

genuflexion Brit, **genuflection** Amer /ˌdʒenjuːˈflekʃn/ *n* [c and u] **1** Relig formal 跪拜; **to make a ~** 跪拜 **2** fig pej (act of deference) 卑躬屈膝

genuine /ˈdʒenjʊɪn/ *adj* **1** (authentic, real) 真的 ‹*antique, gem*›; 真迹的 ‹*manuscript, painting*›; 纯的 ‹*wool, gold*›; 真正的 ‹*bargain, reason*› **2** (sincere) 真诚的 ‹*belief, believer, concern*›; 真实的 ‹*emotion, fear, effort*›; **a ~ mistake** 确定无疑的错误

genuinely /ˈdʒenjʊɪnli/ *adv* **1** (in reality) 真正地 ‹*originate, prove*› **2** (sincerely) 真实地 ‹*feel, think*›; 真诚地 ‹*concerned, sorry*›

genuineness /ˈdʒenjʊɪnnɪs/ *n* [u] **1** (authenticity) 真实性 **2** (sincerity) 真诚

genus /ˈdʒiːnəs/ *n* (*pl* **genera** /ˈdʒenərə/) 属

geobiology /ˌdʒiːəʊbaɪˈɒlədʒi/ *n* [u] 地球生物学

geochemical /ˌdʒiːəʊˈkemɪkl/ *adj* 地球化学的

geochemist /ˌdʒiːəʊˈkemɪst/ ▸**p. 409** *n* 地球化学家

geochemistry /ˌdʒiːəʊˈkemɪstri/ *n* [u] 地球化学

geodesic /ˌdʒiːəʊˈdesɪk/ *adj* 曲面几何结构的; **~ structure/shape** 网格球顶结构/网格球形

geodesic: ~ dome *n* 网格球顶; **~ line** *n* 测地线

geodesy /dʒɪˈɒdɪsi/ *n* [u] 大地测量学

geodetic /ˌdʒɪəˈdetɪk/ *adj* 大地测量学的; **~ latitude/survey/system/data** 大地纬度/测量/坐标系统/测量数据

geoengineering /ˌdʒiːəʊendʒɪˈnɪərɪŋ/ *n* [u] 地质工程

geographer /dʒɪˈɒgrəfə(r)/ ▸**p. 409** *n* 地理学家

geographic /ˌdʒɪəˈgræfɪk/, **geographical** /ˌdʒɪəˈgræfɪkl/ *adj* 地理的 ‹*features, area*›; 地理学的 ‹*research, survey*›

geographically /ˌdʒɪəˈgræfɪkli/ *adv* 在地理上 ‹*distinct, separated*›; **~ speaking** 就地理上说; **~ remote areas** 偏远地区

geographical mile *n* 地理英里 [指赤道一分的弧长, 即海里]

g

geographic: ～ information system *n* 地理信息系统; **～ mile** *n* = **geographical mile**

geography /dʒɪˈɒɡrəfi/ *n* [u] 1 (field, subject) 地理学; **a ～ book/lesson** 地理书/课 2 (layout) 地形; **the ～ of the war zone** 交战区的地势; **to have a good/poor sense of ～** 有良好的/很差的方位感

geological /ˌdʒɪəˈlɒdʒɪkl/ *adj* 地质的 ‹*record, history*›; **～ formation/epoch** 地质构造/时期

geologist /dʒɪˈɒlədʒɪst/ **▸p. 409** *n* 地质学家

geology /dʒɪˈɒlədʒi/ *n* [u] 地质学; **she's doing a ～ course** 她正在学习一门地质学课程

geomagnetic /ˌdʒiːəʊmæɡˈnetɪk/ *adj* 地磁的 ‹*field, disturbance*›

geomagnetism /ˌdʒiːəʊˈmæɡnɪtɪzəm/ *n* [u] 1 (phenomenon) 地磁 2 (field of study) 地磁学

geomancy /ˈdʒiːəʊmænsi/ *n* [u] 风水术

geomarketing /ˌdʒiːəʊˈmɑːkɪtɪŋ/ *n* [u] 地理营销; **～ software/research** 地理营销软件/研究

geometric /ˌdʒɪəˈmetrɪk/, **geometrical** /ˌdʒɪəˈmetrɪkl/ *adj* 几何学的 ‹*problem, question*›; 几何的 ‹*lines*›; 几何图形的 ‹*design*›; **～ mean** 几何平均; **～ progression** *or* **series** 几何级数

geometrically /ˌdʒɪəˈmetrɪkli/ *adv* 按几何学原理 ‹*conceive, design*›

geometrician /ˌdʒiːəməˈtrɪʃn/ **▸p. 409** *n* 几何学家

geometry /dʒɪˈɒmətri/ *n* [u] 几何学; **a ～ book/lesson** 几何学书/课

geomorphic /ˌdʒiːəʊˈmɔːfɪk/ *adj* 地球形状的; **～ region** 地貌区

geomorphology /ˌdʒiːəʊmɔːˈfɒlədʒi/ *n* [u] 地形学

geophysical /ˌdʒiːəʊˈfɪzɪkl/ *adj* 地球物理学的 ‹*data, survey*›; 地球物理的 ‹*feature, phenomenon*›

geophysicist /ˌdʒiːəʊˈfɪzɪsɪst/ **▸p. 409** *n* 地球物理学家

geophysics /ˌdʒiːəʊˈfɪzɪks/ *npl* + *v sing* 地球物理学

geopolitical /ˌdʒiːəʊpəˈlɪtɪkl/ *adj* 地缘政治学的 ‹*research*›; 地缘政治的 ‹*conflict, factors*›

geopolitics /ˌdʒiːəʊˈpɒlətɪks/ *npl* + *v sing* 地缘政治学

Geordie /ˈdʒɔːdi/ *n* Brit colloq 1 [c] (person) 泰恩赛德人; **～ accent** 泰恩赛德口音 2 [u] (dialect) 泰恩赛德方言

Georgetown /ˈdʒɔːdʒtaʊn/ *pr n* 乔治敦

Georgia /ˈdʒɔːdʒə/ *pr n* 1 (country) 格鲁吉亚 2 (US state) 佐治亚州

Georgian /ˈdʒɔːdʒən/ **▸p. 503, p. 426**

A *adj* 1 (of the Republic of Georgia) 格鲁吉亚的 ‹*town*›; (of the people) 格鲁吉亚人的 ‹*customs*›; (of the language) 格鲁吉亚语的 ‹*grammar*› 2 Brit Hist 乔治王朝的 ‹*period*›; 乔治王朝时期的 ‹*culture*› 3 Archit 乔治王朝时期风格的 ‹*furniture, architecture*› 4 (of US state) 佐治亚州的

B *n* 1 [c] (native of the Republic of Georgia) 格鲁吉亚人 2 [c] (native of the US state) 佐治亚州人 3 [u] (language) 格鲁吉亚语

geoscience /ˌdʒiːəʊˈsaɪəns/ *n* [u] 地球科学

geoscientist /ˌdʒiːəʊˈsaɪəntɪst/ **▸p. 409** *n* 地球学家

geostationary /ˌdʒiːəʊˈsteɪʃənri, Amer -neri/ *adj* 与地球旋转同步的; **a ～ satellite/orbit** 同步卫星/同步轨道

geostrategic /ˌdʒiːəʊstrəˈtiːdʒɪk/ *adj* 地缘战略的 ‹*position, significance*›

geosynchronous /ˌdʒiːəʊˈsɪŋkrənəs/ *adj* = **geostationary**

geothermal /ˌdʒiːəʊˈθɜːml/ *adj* 地热的 ‹*spring, energy, power, heat*›

geothermally /ˌdʒiːəʊˈθɜːməli/ *adv* 通过地热 ‹*heated*›; **a ～ active area** 地热资源丰富的地区

geranium /dʒəˈreɪnɪəm/ *n* (genus Geranium) 老鹳草属植物; (genus Pelargonium) 天竺葵属植物

gerbil /ˈdʒɜːbɪl/ *n* 沙鼠

geriatric /ˌdʒerɪˈætrɪk/

A *adj* 1 Med 老年病学的; **～ care/medicine/ward** 老年病人护理/老年医学/老年病病房 2 colloq pej (decrepit) 衰老的 ‹*person*›; 破旧的 ‹*machine, vehicle*›

B *n* 1 (elderly patient) 老年病人 2 colloq pej (elderly person) 老年人

geriatrician /ˌdʒerɪəˈtrɪʃn/ **▸p. 409** *n* 老年病学专家

geriatrics /ˌdʒerɪætrɪks/ *npl* + *v sing* (field) 老年病学; (department) 老年病科

germ /dʒɜːm/ *n* 1 (microbe) 微生物; **to carry ～s** 携带病菌 2 Biol (seed) 种子; (embryo) 胚芽 3 fig (start) 开始; **the ～ of an idea** 一个想法的产生

German /ˈdʒɜːmən/ **▸p. 503, p. 426**

A *adj* (of Germany) 德国的 ‹*town, politics*›; (of the people) 德国人的 ‹*customs*›; (of the language) 德语的

B *n* 1 [c] (person) 德国人 2 [u] (language) 德语; **Low/Middle/High ～** 低地/中古/高地德语

German Democratic Republic *pr n* Hist 德意志民主共和国 [东德全称]

germane /dʒɜːˈmeɪn/ *adj* 有密切关系的 ‹*remarks, issues*›; **to be ～ to sth.** 同某事物密切相关

Germanic /dʒɜːˈmænɪk/ *adj* 1 (of German people) 德国的; (of German language) 德语的 2 (of the Germanic languages) 日耳曼语族的

germanium /dʒɜːˈmeɪnɪəm/ *n* [u] 锗

German: ～ measles ▸p. 377 *npl* + *v sing* 风疹; **～ sheepdog, ～ shepherd** *ns* 德国牧羊犬

Germany /ˈdʒɜːməni/ *pr n* 德国

germ: ～ carrier *n* 带菌者; **～ cell** *n* 生殖细胞; **～-free** *adj* 无菌的 ‹*environment*›

germicidal /ˌdʒɜːmɪˈsaɪdl/ *adj* 杀菌的 ‹*substance, property*›

germicide /ˈdʒɜːmɪsaɪd/ *n* [u and c] 杀菌剂

germinate /ˈdʒɜːmɪneɪt/

A *vi* 1 lit «*seed*» 发芽 2 fig «*idea*» 产生

B *vt* 1 lit 使…发芽 ‹*seeds, plants*› 2 fig 使…产生 ‹*idea, emotion*›

germination /ˌdʒɜːmɪˈneɪʃn/ *n* [u] 发芽

germ: ～-killer *n* 杀菌剂; **～-proof** *adj* 抗菌的 ‹*fabric, suit*›; **～ warfare** *n* [u] 细菌战

gerontocracy /ˌdʒerɒnˈtɒkrəsi/ *n* 1 [u] (government) 老人统治 2 [c] (state) 老人统治的国家; (society) 老人统治的社会

gerontologist /ˌdʒerɒnˈtɒlədʒɪst/ **▸p. 409** *n* 老年学专家

gerontology /ˌdʒerɒnˈtɒlədʒi/ *n* [u] 老年学

gerrymander /ˌdʒerɪˈmændə(r)/ pej

A *n* 不公正的选区划分

B *vi* 不公正地划分选区

C *vt* 不公正地划分 ‹*boundaries, constituency*›; 操纵 ‹*election result*›

gerrymandering /ˌdʒerɪˈmændərɪŋ/ *n* [u] 不公正的选区划分

gerund /ˈdʒerənd/ *n* 动名词

gestate /dʒeˈsteɪt/

A *vi* 1 Biol «*foetus, young*» 孕育 2 fig (develop) «*project, idea, relations*» 酝酿

B *vt* 1 Biol «*animal*» 孕育 ‹*young, offspring*› 2 fig (develop) 酝酿 ‹*plan, project*›

gestation /dʒeˈsteɪʃn/ *n* [u] 1 Biol (process) 妊娠; (period) 妊娠期 2 fig (development) 酝酿

gesticulate /dʒeˈstɪkjʊleɪt/ *vi* 做手势; **to ～ at sb.** 向某人打手势

gesticulation /dʒeˌstɪkjʊˈleɪʃn/ *n* 1 [u] (gesturing) 做手势 2 [c] (gesture) 示意动作; (hand movement) 手势

gesture /ˈdʒestʃə(r)/

A *n* [u and c] 1 (movement, sign) 示意动作; (hand movement) 手势 2 fig (act) 表示; **a ～ of goodwill/solidarity** 善意的/团结的表示; **that was a nice ～** 那是个很好的姿态; **to be (just) an empty ～** （只是）装装样子

B *vi* 用动作示意; **to ～ at** *or* **towards sth.** 对某物作示意动作; **to ～ to sb. (to do ...)** 向某人打手势示意（做…）

C *vt* 用手势表示; **to ～ one's assent** 用手势表示赞同; **to ～ sb. towards a chair** 示意某人在椅子上坐下

get /get/ (*pres p* **-tt-**; *pt* **got**; *pp* **got,** Amer **gotten**)

A *vt* 1 (acquire, receive, be given, achieve) 得到 ‹*chance, permission, help, custody*›; 收到 ‹*letter, signal*›; 获得 ‹*loan, mortgage*›; **to ～ lunch/enough sleep** 吃午餐/睡眠充足; **to ～ a divorce** 离婚; **to ～ what one pays for** 一分钱一分货; **London ～s a lot of tourists** 伦敦的游客很多; **to ～ good marks for maths/an A in physics** 数学考试取得好成绩/物理考试得 A; **～ yourself a good accountant/plumber** 给你自己找个好会计/水暖工; **to ～ digital channels** 收看数字频道; **the back of the house ～s all the sun** 屋子的背面阳光充足; **to ～ something for nothing** 不劳而获 2 (fetch sth.) 去取; (fetch sb.) 去带来; **to ～ sb. sth., to ～ sth. for sb.** 给某人拿来某物; **can you ～ the doctor for me?** 你能替我去叫医生来吗？; **I went to ～ raspberries from the garden** 我去园子里采山莓了 3 (buy) 买; **to ～ sb. sth.** 给某人买某物; **I got this DVD for £2** 我买这张数字影碟花了两英镑 4 (receive, earn) 挣得 ‹*pension, wealth*›; 赢得 ‹*fame, power*›; **to ～ money/a salary** 赚钱/挣工资; **this will ～ him a bad reputation** 这事会败坏他的名声; **Chelsea got £2,000,000 for him** 切尔西俱乐部准许他转会以换取 2 百万英镑 5 (catch hold of) 抓住; **reach up and ～ (me) an apple** 伸手上去（给我）摘个苹果; **～ him, boy!** (command to dog) 小家伙，去抓住他！ 6 (start to have) 开始有 ‹*belief, feeling*›; **don't ～ ideas!** 别想入非非的！; **he's got it bad (for her)** colloq 他（对她）着迷了; **to ～ religion** colloq 突然变得虔诚 7 (inherit) 继承; **to ～ sth. from sb.** 从某人处继承 ‹*money, property*›; 从某人身上遗传 ‹*trait, physical feature*›; **he ～s his musical talent from his mother** 他的音乐天赋是母亲遗传给他的 8 (encounter) 能遇见 ‹*type, phenomenon*›; **you ～ different kinds of ...** 你能见到各种各样的…; **you ～ snow in summer there** 那里夏季会下雪 9 (suffer, experience) 经受; **to ～ a surprise** 感到惊讶; **to ～ a bang on the head** 头上挨了一下; **to ～ three years in prison** 被判入狱三年; **you'll really ～ it this time!** colloq 你这次麻烦可大了!; **he got his car stolen** 他的汽车被偷了 10 Med 患上; **to ～ a headache/a bad back** 头痛/背部有毛病 11 Transp 乘坐 ‹*bus, taxi*›; **I got the eight o'clock train** 我乘坐的是 8 点那班火车 12 (subscribe to) 订阅 ‹*newspaper, periodical*› 13 (punish) 惩罚; (injure) 伤害; (kill) 杀死; **we'll ～ them yet!** colloq 我们会教训他们的！; **the sharks must have got him** 那些鲨鱼肯定把他弄死了 14 (hear) 听见; **I didn't ～ your name/what you said** colloq 我没听清你的名字/你的话; **～ this! he was arrested last night** colloq 听着！他昨晚被逮捕了; **～ her!** sl 听听她！ 15 (understand) 明白; **(I've) got it!** 明白了！; **now let me ～ this right/straight ...** 现在我来把这个说清楚… 16 colloq (hit) 击中; **the bullet got him in the chest** 子弹击中了他的胸部 17 Telecom (call by phone) 与…通电话; **～ me the police/fire brigade** 给我接警察局/消防队; **to ～ sb. on the phone** 和某人通电话 18 colloq (affect) «*words, music*» 感染; **that tune ～s me!** 那

支曲子打动了我！ **19** colloq (puzzle) 使困惑；**now you've got me** 你把我难住了 **20** (prepare) 准备；**to ~ sth. to eat** 弄某食物吃 **21** (deal with) 处理；**I'll ~ it!** (phone) 我来接！；(doorbell) 我来开门！ **22** colloq (hurt) 使疼痛；**the pain ~s me (right) here** 我（就）这儿疼；**it ~s you right there** 这使人心生柔情 **23** colloq (annoy) 使烦恼；**what ~s me is ...** 我感到烦恼的是… **24** colloq (look at) 瞧 [用作感叹语，表示鄙视]；**~ him in that hat!** 瞧他戴那顶帽子的样子！ **25** (put, take) 带…去；**to ~ sth. to sb.** 把某物带给某人；**could you ~ this card to my mother?** 把这贺卡带给我母亲好吗？；**to ~ a child to bed** 送孩子上床；**he's got you where he wants you** 他随意摆布你；**to ~ sb. somewhere/nowhere** 使某人有所/毫无进展；**rudeness won't ~ you anywhere** 动粗不会给你带来任何好处 **26** (cause, organize) 使；**to ~ sb./sth. doing sth.** 使某人/某物做某事；**to ~ the engine/dishwasher going** 让发动机/洗碗机运转起来；**his remark got me thinking** 他的话让我陷入沉思；**to ~ sth. done** 把某事做完；**to ~ sth./sb. ready** 把某事物/让某人准备好；**to ~ one's shoes repaired/mended** 把鞋子送去修补；**that won't ~ you promoted** 那不会让你得到提升的 **27** (persuade, make) **to ~ sb./sth. to do sth.** 说服…做某事 ‹*person*›；使…运转 ‹*machine*›；**can I ~ you to sign this, please** 请在这上面签字好吗？；**to ~ the car/engine to start** 把汽车/引擎发动起来 **28** (indicating possession, ownership) **to have got sth.** 具有某物；**have you got many friends here?** 你在这里有很多朋友吗？ **29** (must) 必须；**to have got to do sth.** 必须做某事；**you've got to realize/admit ...** 你必须认识到/承认…；**something has got to be done about it** 必须对这个采取措施

B *vi* **1** (become) 变得；**she's ~ting to be a bad influence** 她正带来负面影响；**how do people ~ like that?** 人们怎么变得那样？；**how lucky/stupid can you get?** 你怎么这么幸运/愚蠢啊？；**to ~ killed/hurt** 被杀死/受伤；**~ with it!** colloq 当心！；**he's ~ting (to be) a big boy now** Brit 他快成大男孩了；**to ~ done with sth.** 做完某事 **2** (reach) 到达；**to ~ somewhere** 到达某处；**how did that parcel ~ here?** 那个包裹怎么跑到这儿了呢？；**to ~ to sleep** 入睡 **3** (progress to) 达到；**I got as far as understanding the title** 我只能弄懂题目；**it got to 9 o'clock** 已经9点了；**algebra is hard, but I'm ~ting there** 代数很难，但我开始入门了；**I'm ~ting nowhere/somewhere with this essay** 我这篇文章毫无进展/有眉目了；**to ~ to the top** fig 达到巅峰；**to ~ nowhere fast** colloq 毫无进展 **4** (begin to) 开始；**to ~ to be sth.** 开始成为某事物；**we soon got to like them** 我们很快就喜欢上他们了；**~ moving!** 快动手！；**I got to thinking that ...** 我开始思考… **5** (have opportunity) 有机会；**to ~ to do sth.** 有机会做某事

C *v refl* **1** (move) **~ yourself over here immediately!** 马上过来！；**to ~ oneself to the station** 到车站 **2** (cause oneself to be) **you'll ~ yourself thrown out/arrested** 你会被赶出去的/被逮捕的

Phrasal verbs

- **get about**

A *vi* **1** (manage to move) [有困难地] 走动；**she ~s about quite well** 她腿脚挺利索 **2** (be spread) 传开；**it has got about that ...** 据传…

B *vt* [**~ about sth.**] 在…旅行；**to ~ about town** 在城里四处观光；**it has got about the village that ...** 村里纷纷传说…

- **get across**

A *vi* **1** (cross over) 到对面；**we finally managed to ~ across to the other side** 我们最后还是到达了对面 **2** **to ~ across to sb.** (establish communication with) ‹*person, message*› 传达给某人；**he didn't ~ across to the audience** 他没有让听众听明白

B [**~ across sth.**] *vt* (cross over) 到…的对面；**we got across the busy main road** 我们穿过了车水马龙的主干道

C [**~ sth. across, ~ across sth.**] *vt* (communicate) 把…讲清楚；**to ~ sth. across to sb.** 把某事对某人讲清楚；**I can't ~ it across that ...** 我无法让大家明白…

D [**~ sth. across**] *vt* (transport) 运送 ‹*goods*›；把…送过去 ‹*letter*›；**I'll ~ a copy across to you** 我给你送一份副本过去

- **get after** *vt* [**~ after sb./sth.**] 老是数落
- **get ahead** *vi* 获得成功；**to ~ ahead of sb./sth.** 开始领先某人/某物；**to ~ ahead of one's competitors** 胜过竞争对手；**let's not ~ ahead of ourselves** 咱们先别直奔主题
- **get along** *vi* **1** (progress) 进行；**how's your project ~ting along?** 你的项目进行得怎么样了？ **2** (cope) 对付过去；**we can ~ along without a computer** 没有电脑我们也能对付 **3** (be on friendly terms) 关系融洽；**to ~ along with sb.** 和某人相处很好 **4** colloq (go) 离开；**we must be ~ting along now** 我们现在得走了；**~ along with you!** Brit (go away) 滚开！；(I don't believe you) 胡说！
- **get around**

A *vi* **1** = **get about A** **2** (have different experiences) 阅历丰富；**she ~s around a lot** 她见多识广 **3** esp Amer = **get round A2**

B *vt* **1** = **get about B** **2** esp Amer = **get round D**

- **get at** *vt* [**~ at sb./sth.**]

1 (reach) 够得着；**(just) let me ~ at him!** （就）让我来教训他！ **2** (access) 接触；**he can't ~ at the money until he's 18** 他到18岁才能动用这笔钱 **3** (tamper with, spoil) 破坏；**somebody has got at the computer system** 有人弄坏了计算机系统 **4** (ascertain) 查明；**to ~ at sb.'s secret/the truth** 发现某人的秘密/查明真相 **5** colloq (intimidate, bribe) 威逼利诱；**he's been got at by government officials** 他受到政府官员的胁迫 **6** Brit colloq (criticize) 挖苦；**I hope you didn't think I was ~ting at you** 希望你不会认为我在挖苦你 **7** **to ~ at sb. to do sth.** Brit colloq (nag) 缠磨某人做某事；**she's always ~ting at him to buy her a diamond ring** 她总是缠着他给她买钻戒 **8** colloq (insinuate) 暗示；**what are you ~ting at?** 你是什么意思？

- **get away** *vi* **1** (escape) 逃走 **2** (leave) 离开；**I couldn't ~ away any sooner** 我巴不得马上离开；**~ away!** (go away) 走开！；(I don't believe you) 别胡说了！ **3** (go further ahead) 甩开
- **get away from**

A [**~ away from sb./sth.**] *vt*

1 (leave behind) 逃离 ‹*place, work*›；摆脱 ‹*pursuer*›；**to ~ away from it all** 躲清净 **2** fig (depart from) 背离；**to ~ right away from traditional methods** 完全违背传统方法 **3** (deny) 否认；**there's no ~ting away from it!** 这件事无法否认！ **4** (go further ahead than) 把…甩开

B [**~ sb./sth. away from sb./sth.**] *vt* 把…从…处带走 ‹*person*›；把…从…处赶走 ‹*animal*›；把…从…处夺走 ‹*object*›；**we couldn't ~ the knife away from him** 我们没法夺下他的刀子；**we must ~ him away from her/from her influence** 我们必须让他离开她/摆脱她的影响

- **get away with** *vt* [**~ away with sth.**]

1 (escape with) 携带…溜走 ‹*money, haul*› **2** (escape punishment for) 逃脱…的惩罚；(escape undesirable consequences of) 避免…的不良后果；**to ~ away with murder** fig colloq 逍遥法外；**she can ~ away with (wearing) bright colours** 她穿色彩鲜艳的衣服还可以 **3** (be let off with) 以…被从轻发落；**he got away with a £50 fine** 他交了50英镑罚款就了事了

- **get back**

A *vi* **1** (return to place or person) 返回；**to ~ back to work/the office** 回去工作/回到办公室；**when I ~ back to them** 当我回到他们中间时 **2** (return to former state) 恢复；**to ~ back to normal** 恢复正常；**to ~ back to sleep** 重新入睡；**when Labour got back (into power)** 当工党重新执政时 **3** **to ~ back to sth.** (return to earlier stage in discussion) 回到先前阶段；**to ~ back to your problem, ...** 再谈谈你的问题，… **4** **to ~ back to sb.** (contact again) 给某人回电话；**I'll ~ back to you** 我会给你回电话的 **5** (move backwards) 退后；**~ back!** 后退！

B [**~ sth. back, ~ back sth.**] *vt*

1 (have returned personally) 带回；(have returned by post etc.) 取回；**I went to the ticket office and got my money back** 我去售票处退了钱 **2** (obtain again) 重新获得 ‹*possessions, qualities*›；**to ~ back one's strength/old job** 恢复体力/原职；**to ~ one's own back** 报复 **3** (return to rightful place) 归还；**to ~ the book back to the library** 还书给图书馆 **4** (put back, replace) 把…放回原处；**to ~ the table back in the corner** 把桌子搬回角落 **5** (in racket games) 击回；**he got the ball back (over the net)** 他把球（从网上）打了回去

C [**~ sb. back**] *vt* (escort back) 把…送回

- **get back at** *vt* [**~ back at sb.**] 报复
- **get behind**

A *vi* **1** (fall behind) 落后；**we tried to keep up with others/the pace/the schedule, but we got behind** 我们努力尝试跟上其他人/节奏/进度，但我们落后了 **2** (fall into arrears) 拖欠；**to ~ behind with sth.** 拖延某物；**to ~ behind with one's work/payments** 拖延工作/拖欠款项

B *vt* [**~ behind sth./sb.**]

1 (move behind) 到…的后面；**to ~ behind the curtains/the sofa** 藏到窗帘/沙发后面 **2** (support) 支持；**the whole family got behind her/the idea** 全家都支持她/这个主意

- **get by**

A *vi* **1** = **get past A** **2** (survive, manage) 勉强维持；**to ~ by on sth.** 靠某物勉强对付；**to ~ by on a few pounds** 靠几英镑勉强过活；**to ~ by with sth.** 以某物将就；**we'll have to ~ by with what we have in stock** 我们将不得不靠库存勉强撑着 **3** (be good enough) 凑合；**his essay isn't very good but it will ~ by** 他的文章不是太好，但还过得去

B *vt* [**~ by sb.**]

1 (pass) 经过 **2** (escape unnoticed by) 逃过…的注意 ‹*guard, teacher*›

- **get down**

A *vi* **1** (descend, alight) 从…下来；**he got down from his horse** 他下了马 **2** (leave table) 离开餐桌；**may I ~ down?** 我可以离开吗？ **3** (sit down) 坐到地上；(lie down) 躺到地上；**to ~ down on one's knees** 跪下；**~ down!** 趴下！

B [**~ sth. down, ~ down sth.**] *vt*

1 (swallow) 吞下 **2** (record) 记下 ‹*notes, description*› **3** (reduce by elimination) 减少；**to ~ sth. down to sth.** 使人数/某物减少到某个水平；**we got the shortlist down to three** 我们把入围名单上的人数压缩到3人；**we got the number of participants down** 我们减少了参与者的人数

C [**~ sth./sb. down, ~ down sth./sb.**] *vt*

1 (bring down) 使下来；**to ~ the book/child down** 取下书/把孩子抱下来；**~ your trousers down** 脱下你的裤子 **2** (reduce by bargaining) 压低；**to ~ sb./the price down** 让某人降价/把价格压下来

D [**~ sb. down**] *vt* (depress) 使沮丧；**the weather's ~ting her down** 这天气使她感到压抑

E [**~ down sth.**] *vt* (descend) 从…下来；**to ~ down the stairs/mountain** 下楼/下山

- **get down to** *vt* [**~ down to sth.**]

1 (descend to) 下降到；**to ~ down to the pupils' level** fig 降到小学生的水平 **2** (attend to) 着手处理；**to ~ down to doing sth.** 着手做某事；**to ~ down to work/business** 开始工作/干正事

• **get in**
A *vi* **1** (arrive at destination) «*bus, plane*» 到达 **2** (enter, penetrate) 进入; **let the air ~ in** 让空气透进来 **3** (reach home) 到住所; **I ~ in at 6 o' clock** 我 6 点到家 **4** (be elected) «*candidate, party*» 当选 **5** (be admitted) «*candidate, student*» 被录取
B [**~ in sth.**] *vt*
1 (enter, penetrate) 进入; **the dust got in my eyes** 灰尘眯了我的眼睛; **how do you ~ in the museum?** 你是怎样进入博物馆的? **2** (fit in) 塞进; **that car will never ~ in that space** 那辆车无论如何都进不去那空位 **3** (develop) 开始有 ‹*mood, habit*›; **to ~ in a temper/panic** 发脾气/陷入恐慌
C [**~ sth. in, ~ in sth.**] *vt*
1 (bring in) 把…拿进来; **it's raining — ~ the tables/washing in** 下雨了，把桌子搬进来/衣服收进来 **2** (fit into space) 能把…塞进去; **to ~ the drawer in** 把抽屉推进去; **can you ~ these shoes in your suitcase?** 能否把鞋子塞进你的手提包内? **3** (deliver, hand in) 设法交出; **did you ~ your essay in on time?** 你按时交论文了吗? **4** (include in article, schedule) 设法增加; **he got in a reference to his new book** 他给自己的新书添加了参考书目; **to try to ~ in a little tennis** 争取打打网球; **I got mine in first** Amer colloq 我先下手报复 **5** (buy in) 购进 **6** Agric (collect) 收割 ‹*harvest, crops*› **7** (interpolate) 争取发言说; **to ~ a word in** 插话 **8** Agric, Hort (plant) 种植
D [**~ sb. in**] *vt*
1 (summon) 请来 ‹*police, doctor*› **2** (ensure admission of) 使进入; **this card will ~ you in** (to club) 凭此卡即可进去; **three As should be enough to ~ her in** (to school, university) 她得了三个 A，应该够录取条件 **3** Pol 使当选; **you must vote to ~ our candidate in** 你必须投票让我们的候选人当选

• **get in on** *vt* **1** [**~ in on sth.**] 参加; **to ~ in on the act** colloq [为了捞到好处] 插一手 **2** **to ~ sb. in on sth.** 使某人参与; **can you ~ me in on the deal?** 你能让我参加这次交易吗?

• **get into**
A [**~ into sth.**] *vt*
1 (enter) 进入; **water had got into the back of the cupboard** 水渗进了橱柜后面; **what's got into her?** fig 她是怎么回事? **2** (fit into) 能塞进; **the sofa wouldn't ~ into the alcove** 沙发放不进壁凹 **3** (be able to put on) 穿上 ‹*item of clothing*› **4** (be admitted to) 加入 ‹*club, team*›; 进入 ‹*school, university*› **5** (develop) 开始有 ‹*mood*›; 养成 ‹*habit*›; **to ~ into a temper/panic/bad habit** 发脾气/陷入恐慌/染上恶习 **6** (get involved in) 被牵扯进; **to ~ into debt/trouble** 负债/惹上麻烦 **7** (get interested in) 喜欢上 ‹*subject, pursuit*› **8** (get accustomed to) 熟悉; **to ~ into the way of doing sth.** 养成做某事的习惯; **he got into mountaineering** colloq 他喜欢上了登山运动 **9** Transp 到达 ‹*station, airport, city*› **10** (reach number) 数量是; **to ~ into the hundreds** 数以百计
B [**~ sb. into sth.**] *vt*
1 (cause to enter, ensure admission of) 使…进入; **she got me into the club** 她介绍我进了俱乐部; **the Hispanic vote got him into Congress** 拉丁裔选民的选票使他当选进入国会 **2** (make develop) 使…处于; **to ~ sb. into a good mood** *or* **humour** 让某人的情绪好起来 **3** (make accustomed) 使…习惯于; **to ~ sb. into the way of doing sth.** 使某人养成做某事的习惯 **4** (involve in) 使…陷入; **I'll ~ you into trouble with your dad** 我会让你爸爸管你的; **her boyfriend has got her into trouble** euph 她的男友把她肚子搞大了
C [**~ sb./sth. into sth.**] *vt* (make fit into space) 把…塞进; **to ~ the package into the post-box** 把包裹塞进邮筒; **to ~ sb./sth. into the picture** 把某人/某物拍进照片; **to ~ her into her uniform** 给她穿上制服

• **get in with** *vt* [**~ in with sb.**]
1 (gain favour with) 讨好 **2** (associate with) 结交

• **get off**
A *vi* **1** (alight from vehicle) 下车; **you need to ~ off at the next stop** 你要在下一站下车; **to tell sb. where he/she can ~ off** *or* **where to ~ off** fig colloq 叫某人别管闲事 **2** (descend) 下来; **~ off of that wall!** 快从那墙上下来! **3** (start on journey) 出发; **I aim to ~ off by seven o'clock** 我打算7点前出发; **to ~ off to a good/poor start** fig 有良好的/糟糕的开端 **4** (leave work) 下班; **can you ~ off tomorrow?** 你明天能不上班吗? **5** colloq (escape punishment) 免受处罚; (escape suffering) 免受罪; **to ~ off with a reprimand** 只是受到一番训斥就没事了; **he got off with just a scratch to his arm** 他只是手臂上擦破了一点皮 **6** Brit (fall asleep) 入睡; **to ~ off to sleep** 入睡 **7** **to ~ off with sb.** Brit colloq (start romantic relationship) 与某人谈恋爱; (start sexual relationship) 与某人发生关系; **John and Anne got off with each other** 约翰和安妮好上了 **8** (let go) 放开; **~ off!** 别碰! **9** **to ~ off on sth./doing sth.** colloq (get excited or aroused by) 对某事物/做某事感到兴奋; **she ~s off on leading men on** 她以吊男人的胃口为乐
B [**~ off sth.**] *vt*
1 (descend from) 从…上下来; **the cat got off my lap** 猫从我腿上跳了下去 **2** (alight from vehicle) 下车 **3** (remove oneself from) 离开; **~ off the floor!** 从地板上起来! ; **~ off my foot!** colloq 别踩我的脚! ; **to ~ off sb.'s back** fig 不去纠缠某人 **4** (depart from on purpose) 避开 ‹*subject*›; (depart from accidentally) 偏离 ‹*subject*›; **we've rather got off religion** 我们还是避开了宗教这个话题 **5** **to ~ off doing sth.** (avoid) 逃避做某事; **she got off without paying** 她没付钱溜了; **to ~ off doing homework/the washing up** 逃避做作业/洗碗 **6** (wean oneself off) 逐渐解除 ‹*drugs, heroin*›
C [**~ off sb.**] *vt* (let go of) 放开; **~ off me!** 别碰我!
D [**~ sth. off**] *vt*
1 (take off) 脱下 ‹*garment, shoes*›; 取下 ‹*top, tyre*›; **she can't ~ the ring off her finger** 她摘不掉手指上的戒指 **2** (clean away) 除掉; **to ~ the mud/dirt off** 除掉泥斑/灰尘; **to ~ the stain off the carpet** 除掉地毯上的污渍 **3** (bring down) 使下来; **he got the bottle off the top shelf** 他把瓶子从顶层搁板上拿了下来 **4** (take away) 移开; **~ your hands off!** 别碰! ; **~ your hands off my girl/husband!** 不许碰我的女友/丈夫! **5** (have as free time) 休息; **to ~ a day/week off** 休假一天/一周; **to ~ an hour off work** 工作时歇一小时 **6** **to ~ sth. off sb.** (receive, take) 从某人处得到某物; **~ his gun off him first** 先下了他的枪 **7** **to ~ sth. off sb.** (inherit) 从某人处经遗传获得某物; **he ~s his placidity off his mother** 他的温和性情是他母亲遗传的
E [**~ sth./sb. off**] *vt* (dispatch) 寄出 ‹*letter, parcel*›; 打发走 ‹*person*›; **to ~ sb. off to work/school** 打发某人上班/上学
F [**~ sb. off**] *vt*
1 **to ~ sb. off sth.** (force to leave) 迫使某人离开某处; **we tried to ~ them off our land** 我们试图把他们从我们的土地上赶走 **2** **to ~ sb. off sth.** (cause to stop discussing) 使某人停止谈论某事物; **you can't ~ him off the subject of cars** 一谈到汽车，你就没法让他停下来 **3** (send to sleep) 使入睡; **to ~ a child off to sleep** 让孩子入睡 **4** (cause acquittal of) 使免受处罚; **to ~ sb. off with a fine** 对某人罚款之后就了事 **5** **to ~ sb. off sth.** (wean from) 使某人戒掉 ‹*drug*›; 使某人戒除 ‹*habit*›
G *v refl* **to ~ oneself off** 准备离开; **I have to ~ myself off to work** 我必须去上班了

• **get on**
A *vi* **1** (board a bus, train) 乘坐上交通工具; **I got on at the last station** 我是上一站上车的 **2** (become late) 晚了; **to be ~ting on** 时间不早了; **it's ~ting on for teatime/towards bedtime** 快到茶点/睡觉时间了 **3** (progress) 进展; **how's Jo ~ting on these days?** 乔最近怎么样? ; **how are you ~ting on with the project?** 你的项目进展如何? **4** (be successful) 成功; **to ~ on in life** 飞黄腾达 **5** colloq (grow old) 年龄增长; **to be ~ting on** 年龄越来越大; **he's ~ting on for 40** 他将近40 岁了 **6** **to ~ on with sb.** (be on good terms with) 与某人和睦相处; **he's very difficult to ~ on with** 他这人很难相处 **7** (continue) **to ~ on with sth.** (continue after interruption) 继续某事; **~ on with your work** 继续干你的工作; **to ~ on to the next item** 进入下一项
B [**~ on sth.**] *vt*
1 (go aboard) 乘坐上; **to ~ on the bus/plane/ship** 乘上公共汽车/飞机/轮船 **2** (climb on to) 爬上; **we got on the roof** 我们爬了上屋顶 **3** (be appointed to) 入选; **to ~ on the board of governors/county council** 进入董事会/郡政务委员会
C [**~ sth. on, ~ on sth.**] *vt*
1 (put on) 穿戴上 ‹*clothes, hat, shoes*› **2** **to ~ sth. on sth.** (fit) 安上某物; **to ~ the lid on the jam jar** 盖上果酱罐的盖子
D *vt* **to ~ sth. on sb.** (obtain information) 从某处取得关于某人的资料
E **getting on for** *prep* Brit 接近; **she didn't arrive till ~ting on for eight** 她快 8 点时才到

• **get on to**
A [**~ on to sth./sb.**] *vt*
1 (go aboard) 乘上 ‹*bus, train, plane*› **2** (climb on to) 爬上 ‹*hill*›; 骑上 ‹*bicycle, horse*› **3** (start to discuss) 开始谈论 ‹*subject, topic*› **4** (discover) 觉察; **the police got on to him at once** 警察立刻识破了他 **5** (contact) 与…联系; **to ~ on to the authorities/gas company** 和官方/煤气公司取得联系 **6** (be appointed to) 入选 ‹*board, governing body*›
B [**~ sb. on to sth.**] *vt*
1 (cause to discuss) 使开始讨论; **don't ~ him on to morality!** 别让他谈论道德! **2** (ensure appointment to) 使入选; **he got her on to the committee** 他让她进入了委员会
C [**~ sb./sth. on to sth.**] *vt*
1 (make climb on to) 使登上 **2** (put aboard) 使乘坐上/把…放上; **he got his luggage on to the bus** 他把行李搬上巴士
D [**~ sb. on to sb./sth.**] *vt* (send to deal with) 派…去处理; **I'll ~ some more people on to this job** 我会增派一些人去做这项工作; **I'll ~ my big brother on to you!** Brit colloq 我会让我大哥去收拾你的!

• **get out**
A *vi* **1** (exit) 出去; **he got out through the window** 他从窗子爬出去; **~ out!** Amer colloq 不会吧! **2** (make social outing) 外出; **you should ~ out more and make friends** 你应该多外出结交朋友 **3** (escape) 逃跑; **to ~ out from under sth.** 摆脱某微妙局势 **4** (alight from car) 下车 **5** (move elsewhere) 离开; **she's lived there all her life, and can't wait to ~ out** 她在那里生活了一辈子，巴不得马上搬走呢 **6** (resign, withdraw) 退出 **7** (be let out) «*prisoner*» 获释; «*worker*» 下班 **8** (leak out) «*fact, news*» 泄露
B [**~ sth. out, ~ out sth.**] *vt*
1 (extract) 拔掉 ‹*tooth, cork*›; **I soon got the truth out of him** 我很快就逼他说出了真相 **2** (take on loan) 借出; **she's gone to the library to ~ some books out** 她到图书馆借书去了 **3** (erase) 除去 ‹*stain*›; **I can't ~ the mark out** 我弄不掉那个污渍; **I can't ~ the idea out of my mind** *or* **head** 我没法摆脱这个想法 **4** (bring out) 拿出; **he likes to ~ his photos out** 他喜欢给人看他的照片; **he got the money out of his wallet** 他从皮夹里拿出了钱 **5** (produce) 生产 **6** (utter) 勉强地说; **she couldn't ~ the words out** 她说不出话来
C [**~ sb./sth. out**] *vt*

g

1 (make go out) 使出去; **to ~ the sofa out the window/door** colloq 把沙发从窗户/门搬出去; **have you tried to ~ her out?** 你有没有试图把她撵走?; **~ that dog out of here!** 把那条狗赶走! 2 (cause to escape) 使逃出; **they planned to ~ him out of prison** 他们打算救他出监狱 3 (free from detention) 使自由; **his lawyer got him out (on bail)** 他的律师把他保了出来 4 (publish) 出版 5 Brit (solve) 解决 ‹*puzzle, mathematical problem*›

• **get out of** *vt* [**~ out of sth.**]
1 (exit from) 从…中出来; **I couldn't ~ out of the window/door** 我没法从窗户钻出去/没法出门 2 (move from) 离开; **~ out of my house!** 滚出我的房子!; **~ out of here!** Amer colloq 胡说! 3 (escape from) 从…逃出; **a lion has got out of the zoo** 一只狮子从动物园里跑出来了 4 (alight from) 从…下来; **to ~ out of the taxi/car** 从计程车/小汽车中出来 5 (withdraw from) 退出; **to ~ out of the European Union** 退出欧盟 6 (evade, avoid) 逃避 ‹*obligation, duty*›; 回避 ‹*fact*›; **to ~ out of doing sth.** 回避做某事; **I accepted the invitation, and now I can't ~ out of it** 我接受了邀请, 现在不能食言 7 (no longer do) 戒除 ‹*habit, practice*›

• **get over**
A *vi* 越过
B *vt* 1 [**~ over sth.**] (cross) 穿过; **to ~ over the river/mountain** 过河/翻过山; **the wall is too high to ~ over** 墙太高, 翻不过去 2 [**~ over sth./sb.**] (recover from) 从…中恢复过来/与…断绝关系后恢复过来; **to ~ over mumps/a cold** 腮腺炎/感冒痊愈; **she never really got over him** 与他分手后, 她从未真正恢复过来; **I can't ~ over the fact that ...** 我无法接受的是…
C [**~ sth. over, ~ over sth.**] *vt* (communicate) 讲清楚; **to ~ sth. over to sb.** 向某人讲清楚某事; **he couldn't ~ his ideas over to his readers** 他未能向读者说清楚他的想法
D *vt* 1 [**~ sb./sth. over**] (cause to cross) 使穿过; **to ~ sth./sb. over sth.** 使某人/某物穿过某物; **we couldn't ~ the car over the river/the mountains/the border** 我们没法驾车过河/翻山/越过边界; **~ it over the wall** 把它从墙上弄过去 2 **to ~ sth. over (with)** (finish) 结束某事; **to ~ exams/an operation over (with)** 结束考试/手术 3 **to ~ sb. over sth.** (cause to overcome) 使某人克服某事物; **counselling got her over the trauma** 心理咨询抚平了她的精神创伤 4 [**~ sb. over**] (cause to arrive) 让…来; **to ~ a plumber/doctor over** 请来水暖工/医生 5 [**~ sth. over**] (take, send) 送; **~ these documents over to Wall Street** 把这些文件送到华尔街
E *v refl* **to ~ oneself over (sth.)** 使自己到(某物)对面; **we got ourselves safely over the river** 我们安全地渡过了河; **she jumped at it and got herself over** 她从那上面一跃而过

• **get past**
A *vi* 通过; **let the convoy ~ past** 让车队通过
B [**~ past sb./sth.**] *vt*
1 (pass) 通过; **it won't ~ past the censors** 它通不过审查的 2 (go further than) 超过; **to ~ past the semi-finals** 闯过半决赛
C [**~ sth. past**] *vt* (take past) 带…通过; **we can't ~ the car past** 我们没法把汽车开过去; **to ~ sth. past sb./sth.** 带某物通过某处/某人; **to ~ the wine past customs** 带葡萄酒通过海关

• **get round**
A *vi* 1 (get past obstacle) 绕过; **we can't ~ round** 我们绕不过去 2 (come, go) 去; **~ round to the hospital straight away** 马上去医院
B [**~ round sth.**] *vt*
1 (move round) 围绕; **he got round the corner** 他绕过了拐角 2 (move about in or between) 在…周围到处走动; **she got round the shops in half an hour** 她花半小时转了转商店 3 fig (circumvent) 逃避 ‹*regulations, system*› 4 (spread through) 传遍; **it has got round the village that ...** 村里的人纷纷传说…
C [**~ round sb.**] *vt* (persuade) 说服
D [**~ sth. round**] *vt* (bring or send round) 把…送到; **to ~ sth. round to sb./sth.** 把某物送给某人/送到某处; **I'll ~ the boxes round to you** 我会把那些盒子给你送去
E [**~ sb. round**] *vt* (persuade) 说服; **to ~ sb. round to sth.** 就某事说服某人; **I'll soon ~ him round to my way of thinking** 我很快就会说服他同意我的想法的

• **get round to** *vt* **to ~ round to doing sth.** 抽时间做某事; **he finally got round to writing the article** 他最终抽出时间写这篇文章

• **get through**
A *vi* 1 (pass through) 通过 2 (transmit message) 传送到; **the news never got through** 这消息从未传到过; **he can't ~ through to his staff** 他无法和他的员工沟通 3 Telecom [用电话] 接通; **to ~ through to sth./sb.** 接通某处/某人的电话; **I can't ~ through to Oxford** 我没法打通牛津的电话 4 (make way through successfully) 顺利通过; **the team got through to the finals** 这个队进入了决赛; **do you think the regiment will ~ through?** 你认为这个团能顺利通过吗? 5 (survive) 熬过; **we got through thanks to ...** 由于…我们挺过来了
B [**~ through sth.**] *vt*
1 (pass through) 通过 ‹*window, jungle, traffic*›; **the sofa won't ~ through the front door** 沙发进不了前门 2 (reach the end of) 完成; **to ~ through the work/applications** 处理完工作/申请表 3 Pol, Jur 在…获得通过; **the bill hasn't got through Congress yet** 此议案尚未在国会通过 4 (survive) 挺过; **it was difficult to ~ through that time/the winter** 那段时间/那个冬天很难熬 5 (make way through successfully) 通过 ‹*exams, customs*› 6 colloq (consume, use) 消耗完; **he got through all the money/a pair of shoes** 他花光了所有的钱/穿坏了一双鞋
C [**~ sth./sb. through**] *vt*
1 (squeeze through) 使穿过; **to ~ the thread through the hole** 把线从孔里穿过; **the guide will ~ the unit through** 向导将带领分队通过 2 (transmit successfully) 把…传送到; **they got the signal through** 他们把信号发过去了; **can you ~ this message through to him/headquarters?** 你能把这条信息发给他/总部吗? 3 Telecom 接通…的电话; **~ me through to Paris at once** 马上给我接通巴黎的电话 4 (communicate) 清楚传达; **I can't ~ the idea through to him** 我没法让他明白这个意思 5 (help to pass or make way through) 帮助…通过; **the horses got the cart through the mud** 几匹马拉着马车通过泥地; **the coaching staff got their team through to the semi-final** 全体教练帮助他们的队进入了半决赛 6 (help to endure or overcome) 帮助…熬过; **counselling helped ~ him through** 心理咨询帮助他挺了过去; **card games got us through the long wait/afternoon** 我们靠打纸牌打发掉了漫长的等待/下午 7 Pol, Jur 使获得通过; **the government struggled to ~ its bill through** 政府艰难地要使议案得到通过

• **get to** *vt* [**~ to sb.**] colloq 使厌烦; **her constant chatter really ~s to me** 她不停地唠叨, 烦死我了

• **get together**
A *vi* 1 (meet socially) 聚会; **to ~ together with sb.**; 和某人约会 2 colloq (become romantically involved) **Jack and Jill have got together** 杰克和吉尔恋爱了 3 (unite, join forces) 联合起来; **to ~ together with sb.** 联合某人; **why don't we ~ together to buy her a present?** 我们为什么不凑份子给她买个礼物呢?
B *vt* [**~ sth./sb. together, ~ together sth./sb.**]
1 (accumulate, collect) 收集; **to ~ enough money together** 凑够钱; **to ~ one's thoughts together** 认真思考 2 (assemble from parts) 组织; **they got a rock band together** 他们组建了一支摇滚乐队; **to ~ one's act together** fig colloq 集中精力; **to ~ it together** colloq (get organized) 有条理; colloq (succeed) 成功 3 (assemble socially) 安排…会面; **they got together all their favourite people** 他们请来了所有他们最喜欢的人
C *v refl* **to ~ oneself together** (organize oneself) 控制自己; (compose oneself) 稳定情绪

• **get under**
A *vi* (go underneath) 到下面; (fit underneath) 放在下面; **you ~ under while I hold the wire up** 我掀着铁丝网, 你从底下钻过去
B [**~ under sth.**] *vt* (go underneath) 到…下面; (fit underneath) 放在…下面; **can you ~ under the fence?** 你可以到围栏下面吗?
C [**~ sth. under sth.**] *vt* 把…放到下面; **to ~ the box under the bed** 把盒子塞到床下

• **get up**
A *vi* 1 (get out of bed) 起床; **I got up early** 我很早就起了床 2 (rise to one's feet) 站起 3 **to ~ up on sth.** (mount) 登上某物; **she got up on her horse** 她跳上了她的马 4 (become strong or agitated) 增强; **a wind/the sea was ~ting up** 起风了/海上起浪了
B [**~ up sth.**] *vt*
1 (ascend) 爬上; **the old car just got up the steep incline** 那辆破旧的车刚刚爬上了陡坡 2 (penetrate) 上行进入; **water got up my nose** 水冲进了我的鼻子 3 (increase) 提高; **to ~ up speed** *or* **steam** 加速
C [**~ sb. up**] *vt*
1 (get out of bed) 叫…起床; **the nurse made sure to ~ the patient up** 护士保证会叫病人起床的 2 (make rise to feet) 使站起; **the doorbell got her up from her chair** 她听到门铃就从椅子上站了起来 3 (make go up) 使上去; **we got her up on the horse** 我们扶她上了马; **to ~ the car up the hill** 把汽车推上山坡 4 (dress up) 打扮; **her mother got her up as a fairy** 她母亲把她打扮成仙子
D [**~ sth. up**] *vt* (raise on end) 使竖起; **it ~s the hairs up on the back of my neck** 这令我毛骨悚然; **to ~ it up** sl 勃起; **~ 'em up!** colloq 举起手来!
E [**~ sth. up, ~ up sth.**] *vt* (organize) 组织; **to ~ up a petition/speech** 发起请愿/构思演讲; **to ~ up a crowd of protestors** 组织一群抗议者
F *v refl* **to ~ oneself up** (dress up) 打扮

• **get up to** *vt* [**~ up to sth.**]
1 (reach) 到达 ‹*stage, point*›; **I've got up to page 17** 我看到第17页了 2 (do) 忙于; **to ~ up to mischief** 调皮捣蛋; **what did you ~ up to today?** 你今天折腾什么了?

get: ~-at-able *adj* colloq 可去的 ‹*place*›; 可找到的 ‹*person*›; **is the attic ~-at-able?** 阁楼能上吗?; **~away** *n* 1 (escape) 逃跑; **to make a** *or* **one's ~away** 逃跑; **a ~away car** 逃跑用的汽车; 2 (start) 起跑; **a quick ~away** 快速的起跑; 3 colloq (holiday) 短假; **~-out** *n* Brit colloq (tactic) 逃避的办法; (excuse) 托词; **a ~-out clause** 退出条款; **~-rich-quick scheme** *n* colloq 投机计划; **~-together** *n* colloq 聚会; **to have a family ~-together** 举行家庭聚会; **~-tough** *adj attrib* colloq 强硬的 ‹*law, approach*›; **~-up** *n* 1 colloq (outfit) 穿戴; **what's that ~-up she's wearing?** 她穿的什么奇装异服?; 2 (presentation of a book or picture) 装帧; **~-up-and-go** *n* [u] colloq 干劲; **a ~-up-and-go attitude** 干劲十足的态度; **~-well card** *n* 祝愿康复卡

gewgaw /ˈgjuːgɔː/ *n* pej 花哨的廉价装饰品

geyser /ˈgiːzə(r)/ *n* 1 Geol 间歇喷泉 2 Brit (water heater) 热水器

G-force /ˈdʒiːfɔːs/ *n* 重力

Ghana /ˈgɑːnə/ *pr n* 加纳

Ghanaian /ɡɑːˈneɪən/ ▸p. 503
A *adj* (of Ghana) 加纳的 ‹*town, economy*›; (of the people) 加纳人的 ‹*customs*›
B *n* 加纳人

ghastly /ˈɡɑːstli, Amer ˈɡæstli/ *adj* **1** (dreadful) 可怕的 ‹*accident, scene*› **2** colloq (distasteful) 令人讨厌的 ‹*person, family*› **3** colloq (vulgar) 粗俗的 ‹*style, colour*› **4** colloq (unpleasant) 糟透的 ‹*sight, meal*› **5** (very ill) 病殃殃的 ‹*appearance, face, person*› **6** liter (unhealthily pale) 惨白的 ‹*light*›; 苍白的 ‹*pallor*›

gherkin /ˈɡɜːkɪn/ *n* [做泡菜用的] 嫩黄瓜

ghetto /ˈɡetəʊ/ *n* (*pl* **~s** *or* **~es**) **1** pej (slum) 贫民区; (minority quarter) 少数族裔聚居区 **2** Hist (Jewish quarter) 犹太人居住区

ghetto blaster /ˈɡetəʊblɑːstə(r)/ *n* colloq 大型手提收录机

ghettoization /ˌɡetəʊaɪˈzeɪʃn, Amer -əʊɪˈz-/ *n* [u] pej 隔离居住

ghettoize /ˈɡetəʊaɪz/ *vt* pej 使…隔离居住 ‹*black people, immigrants*›

ghost /ɡəʊst/
A *n* **1** ▸p. 325 (spectre) 鬼; **to believe in ~s** 相信有鬼 **2** fig (memory) 往事的阴影; **to lay the ~ of sth. (to rest)** 消除某事物留下的阴影 **3** fig (trace) 一丝; **the ~ of a smile** 一丝微笑; **you don't have a ~ of a chance of winning** 你毫无获胜的机会 **4** (spirit) 灵魂; **to give up the ~** «*person*» 死; «*vehicle*» hum 报废 **5** TV 重影
B *vt* = **ghostwrite A**

ghost image *n* 重影

ghostly /ˈɡəʊstli/ *adj* 像鬼似的 ‹*sound, footsteps*›

ghost: ~ site *n* 幽灵网站 [指无人更新或维护但仍可以访问的网站]; **~ story** *n* 鬼故事; **~ town** *n* 被废弃的城镇; **~ train** *n* Brit [游乐场里的] 撞鬼小火车

g

ghostwrite /ˈɡəʊstraɪt/ (*pt* **ghostwrote**, *pp* **ghostwritten**)
A *vt* 代…写作
B *vi* 代人写作; **to ~ for sb.** 为某人捉刀

ghostwriter /ˈɡəʊstraɪtə(r)/ *n* 代笔者

ghoul /ɡuːl/ *n* **1** (evil spirit) 食尸鬼 **2** pej (morbid person) [以死亡、灾难等为乐的] 暗黑怪客

ghoulish /ˈɡuːlɪʃ/ *adj* (of a ghoul) 食尸鬼的 ‹*stories*›; (like a ghoul) 食尸鬼似的 ‹*behaviour, laughter*›; (gruesome) 恐怖的 ‹*rumours, smile*›

GHQ *abbr* = **general headquarters**

GI *n* (*pl* **~s**) 美国兵

giant /ˈdʒaɪənt/
A *n* **1** Mythol 巨人 **2** (big person) 巨人; (big animal) 巨兽; (big plant) 巨型植物 **3** (big firm) 大公司; **American car ~s** 美国汽车业巨头 **4** (exceptional person) 卓越人物; **a ~ among ...** …中的巨擘
B *adj* **1** (huge) 巨大的 ‹*rock, packet, company, loss*›; **~ sale!** 超低价促销! ; **a ~ stride for the company** 公司的巨大进步 **2** Zool 特大的; **~ tortoise** 巨型陆龟

giant anteater *n* 大食蚁兽

giantess /ˈdʒaɪəntes/ *n* 女巨人

giant: ~-killer *n* Brit (person, team) 强手的克星; **~ panda** *n* 大熊猫; **~-size, ~-sized** *adjs* 特大的 ‹*hole, bag*›; **a ~-size crocodile** 巨型鳄鱼; **~ slalom** *n* [u and c] 大回转滑雪赛; **~ star** *n* 巨星

gibber /ˈdʒɪbə(r)/ *vi* **1** (talk incoherently) 急促不清地说话; **to ~ with terror/rage** 吓得/气愤得语无伦次 **2** pej (chatter) 瞎扯; **what's he ~ing on about?** 他在瞎扯些什么? ; **a ~ing idiot** 话都说不清的白痴

gibberish /ˈdʒɪbərɪʃ/ *n* [u] pej 胡扯; **it's total ~** 这完全是胡言乱语

gibbet /ˈdʒɪbɪt/ *n* 绞刑尸体示众架

gibbon /ˈɡɪbən/ *n* 长臂猿

gibbous moon /ˌɡɪbəsˈmuːn/ *n* 凸月

gibe /dʒaɪb/ = **jibe**[1]

giblets /ˈdʒɪblɪts/ *npl* 杂碎

Gibraltar /dʒɪˈbrɔːltə(r)/ *pr n* 直布罗陀

GI bride *n* 大兵娘子 [指美国军人在国外服役时所娶的外国女子]

giddily /ˈɡɪdɪli/ *adv* **1** (dizzily) 令人眩晕地 ‹*sway, rise*› **2** fig dated (frivolously) 轻浮地

giddiness /ˈɡɪdɪnɪs/ *n* [u] **1** (dizziness) 头晕; **a sudden feeling/attack of ~** 一阵眩晕 **2** fig dated (frivolity) 轻浮

giddy /ˈɡɪdi/ *adj* **1** (dizzy) 头晕的; **to feel ~** *or* **have a ~ feeling** 感到眩晕 **2** (causing dizziness) 使人头晕的 ‹*heights, speed*› **3** fig (exciting) 令人飘飘然的 ‹*pleasures, days*›; **the ~ delights of success** 令人陶醉的胜利喜悦 **4** fig dated (frivolous) 轻佻的 ‹*person, behaviour*› **5** *attrib* fig colloq dated [用于加强语气]; **it really is the ~ limit!** 这真正是极限了!

giddy: ~ spell *n* 一阵头晕; **~ up** *excl* 驾

Gideon Bible /ˌɡɪdɪən ˈbaɪbl/ *n* 基甸国际所赠的《圣经》

gift /ɡɪft/
A *n* **1** (present) 礼物; **a ~ from/for** *or* **to sb.** 某人送的/给某人的礼物; **a farewell/wedding ~** 临别/结婚礼物; **'free ~ inside'** "内有赠品"; **he thinks he is God's ~ to women** 他自以为是上帝赐给女人的礼物; **don't look a ~ horse in the mouth** Prov 白送的东西就不要挑剔 **2** (talent) 天赋; **to have a ~ for sth./doing sth.** 有某种/做某事的天赋 **3** esp Jur (bestowal) 赠与; **to make sb. a ~ of sth.** 把某物赠与某人; **by way of a ~** 通过赠送方式; **to be in sb.'s ~** formal 由某人授予; **a post in the sovereign's ~** 由君主授予的职位 **4** fig colloq (cheap purchase) 极便宜的东西; **at that price, it's a ~!** 那个价格简直是白送! **5** fig colloq (unmissable chance) 不可错过的机会; (sth. made easy) 极容易的事; **a ~ from the gods** 天赐良机; **it was a ~ of a goal** 这个进球不费吹灰之力
B *vt* **1** formal (give) 赠送 **2** *usu passive* (present) 提供 ‹*opportunity*›; **to be ~ed with a golden chance** 得到一个良机 **3** *passive* **to be ~ed with sth.** (endowed) 有某方面的天赋

gift: ~ certificate *n* Amer 礼券; **~ coupon** *n* [可换赠品的] 赠券

gifted /ˈɡɪftɪd/ *adj* (talented) 有天赋的 ‹*artist, musician*›; **a ~ child** 天资聪慧的孩子; **a linguistically/musically ~ student** 有语言/音乐天赋的学生

gift: ~ shop *n* 礼品商店; **~ token, ~ voucher** *ns* Brit 礼券

gift wrap
A /ˈɡɪftræp/ *n* [u] 礼品包装
B **gift-wrap** /ˌɡɪftˈræp/ *vt* (*pres p etc.* **-pp-**) **1** lit 用花纸包装 ‹*purchase, present*› **2** fig colloq 白送; **the opportunity came ~ped** 这个机会不费吹灰之力就得到了

gift wrapping *n* [u] = **gift wrap A**

gig[1] /ɡɪɡ/ *n* Mus colloq 演奏; **to do** *or* **play a ~** 举办演奏会

gig[2] *n* Naut (boat) 轻便快艇

gigabit /ˈɡɪɡəbɪt/ *n* 千兆比特

gigabyte /ˈɡɪɡəbaɪt/ *n* 千兆字节

gigaflop /ˈɡɪɡəflɒp/ *n* 每秒10亿次浮点运算

gigantic /dʒaɪˈɡæntɪk/ *adj* 巨大的 ‹*amount, size, success*›

gigawatt /ˈɡɪɡəwɒt/ *n* 千兆瓦

giggle /ˈɡɪɡl/
A *vi* 吃吃傻笑; **to ~ at sb./sth.** 对某人/某事物傻笑
B *n* **1** (laugh) 吃吃傻笑; **to give a nervous ~** 发出紧张的傻笑 **2** Brit colloq (joke) 玩笑; **to do sth. for a ~** 为了搞笑而做某事; **we had a good ~** 我们玩得很开心 **3** **the ~s** (continuous giggling) 咯咯的笑; **to get the ~s** 发出咯咯的笑声; **to have a fit of the ~s** 咯咯笑个不停

giggly /ˈɡɪɡli/ *adj* 动辄傻笑的 ‹*children, girl*›; 咯咯的 ‹*laughter*›; 咯咯傻笑的 ‹*behaviour*›

gigolo /ˈʒɪɡələʊ/ *n* (*pl* **~s**) 小白脸 [受雇于较年长女性的男伴]

gild /ɡɪld/ *vt* (*pt* **~ed**, *pp* **~ed** *or* **gilt**) **1** (gold-plate) 给…镀金 ‹*mirror, frame*›; **to ~ the lily** fig 画蛇添足 **2** fig liter (light up) «*sun, light*» 使…如金子般生辉 ‹*walls, face*›

gilding /ˈɡɪldɪŋ/ *n* [u] **1** (gold-plating) 镀金 **2** (material) 镀金用材料; (surface) 镀金饰面

gill[1] /ɡɪl/ *n* **1** Zool (of fish) 腮 **2** Bot (of mushroom) 菌褶 **3** **green at** *or* **about the ~s** 面如土色的

gill[2] /dʒɪl/ *n* Meas 及耳

gillie, gilly /ˈɡɪli/ *n* Scot [渔猎运动者的] 男侍从

gilt /ɡɪlt/
A *pp* ▸**gild**
B *n* **1** (gold leaf) 金箔; (paint) 金色涂层; **to take the ~ off the gingerbread** fig 煞风景 **2** **gilts** *pl* Brit Fin 金边证券 [由英国政府发行, 利率固定]

gilt-edged *adj* **1** lit 金边的 ‹*pages, design*› **2** fig (excellent) 极佳的 ‹*opportunity, proposition, investment*› **3** Fin 金边的 [指高度可靠的]; **~-edged securities/stocks** 金边证券/股票

gimbal /ˈdʒɪmbl, ˈɡɪmbl/ *n* (*usu pl* **~s**) 平衡环

gimcrack /ˈdʒɪmkræk/ *adj attrib* pej 华而不实的 ‹*ornaments, jewellery*›; **~ furniture** 花哨的劣质家具

gimlet /ˈɡɪmlɪt/ *n* 手钻; **to have eyes like ~s, to be ~-eyed** 目光犀利

gimmick /ˈɡɪmɪk/ *n* **1** (trick) [为引人注目而耍的] 花招; **his accent is just a ~** 他的口音只是一个噱头 **2** (gadget, novelty) 诡计; **a sales ~** 销售把戏

gimmickry /ˈɡɪmɪkri/ *n* [u] 耍花招; **to use/resort to ~** 耍花招/用伎俩

gimmicky /ˈɡɪmɪki/ *adj* 耍花招的 ‹*offer, style, advertising*›

gimp /ɡɪmp/ esp Amer colloq
A *n* **1** (limp) 跛行; **to have a ~** 有一条瘸腿 **2** (lame person) 瘸子
B *vi* 跛行; **he ~ed away** 他一瘸一拐地走了

gin[1] /dʒɪn/ *n* **1** [u] (drink) 杜松子酒 **2** [c] (serving) 一杯杜松子酒

gin[2] *n* **1** (machine) 轧棉机; **cotton ~** 轧花机 **2** (snare) **~ (trap)** 陷阱; **to set** *or* **lay a ~** 设圈套

gin: ~ and it *n* (*pl* **~ and its**) Brit 金合义 [杜松子酒和苦艾酒的混合饮料]; **~ and tonic** *n* (*pl* **~ and tonics**) 金汤尼 [杜松子酒加奎宁水调制的饮料]

ginger /ˈdʒɪndʒə(r)/ ▸p. 134 *n* [u] **1** Bot, Culin 姜; **flavoured with ~** 用姜调味的 **2** (colour) (of hair) 姜黄色 **3** colloq (energy) 精力; **to need a bit of ~ in one's life** 生活中需要一点活力

Phrasal verb
- **ginger up** *vt* [**~ up sb./sth., ~ sb./sth. up**] 使…有精神 ‹*person*›; 使…有生气 ‹*party, speech, evening*›

ginger: ~ ale *n* [u and c] 姜味汽水; **~ beer** *n* [u and c] 姜啤

gingerbread /ˈdʒɪndʒəbred/ *n* [u] 姜饼

gingerbread man *n* 人形姜饼

ginger group *n* Brit [政党或运动中的] 积极派

gingerly /ˈdʒɪndʒəli/
A *adv* 小心翼翼地 ‹*step, touch*›; **to tread ~** 谨慎地提及
B *adj attrib* 小心翼翼的 ‹*push, turn*›

gingernut, ginger snap *ns* 姜味硬饼干

gingery /ˈdʒɪndʒəri/ *adj* **1** Culin 姜似的 ‹*taste, smell*› **2** (reddish) 姜黄色的 ‹*hair, beard*›

gingham /ˈɡɪŋəm/ *n* [u] 格子布; 用格子布缝制的 ‹*dress, tablecloth*›

gingivitis /ˌdʒɪndʒɪˈvaɪtɪs/ ▸p. 377 *n* [u] 牙龈炎

gink /gɪŋk/ *n* esp Amer colloq 蠢货

ginseng /ˈdʒɪnseŋ/ *n* [u] [1] Bot 人参 [2] Pharm 人参制剂

gin sling *n* 金司令 [用杜松子酒加水和柠檬或酸橙汁调制的鸡尾酒]

gippo /ˈdʒɪpəʊ/ *n* (*pl* **~s**) Brit colloq offensive = **gyppo**

gippy tummy /ˌdʒɪpi ˈtʌmi/ *n* Brit colloq 热带腹泻; **to have a ~** 患热带腹泻

gipsy /ˈdʒɪpsi/ *n* = **gypsy**

giraffe /dʒɪˈrɑːf, Amer dʒəˈræf/ *n* 长颈鹿

gird /gɜːd/ liter

A *vt* (*pt, pp* **~ed** *or* **girt**) [1] (put on) 束; **~ around** *or* **on** 用…束上 ‹*belt, girdle*›; **~ (up) one's loins** fig 准备行动 [2] (fasten with belt) **~ on** 用带系上 ‹*sword, armour*›

B *v refl* **to ~ oneself for sth.** 为某事物做好准备

girder /ˈgɜːdə(r)/ *n* 大梁

girdle /ˈgɜːdl/

A *n* [1] (corset) 紧身褡 [2] (belt) 腰带

B *vt* [1] lit 在…上系腰带 ‹*waist, body*› [2] fig liter (surround) 环绕 ‹*island, lake*›

girl /gɜːl/ *n* [1] (female child) 女孩子; **~s' school** 女子学校; **the ~s' toilets** 女厕所 [2] (daughter) 女儿; **the Smith ~** 史密斯家的女儿 [3] (young woman) 姑娘 [4] dated (servant) 女仆 [5] (female employee) 女职员; **a factory/office ~** 工厂女工/女办事员

girl: ~ band *n* 女子流行乐队; **~ Friday** *n* 女助理; **~friend** *n* (partner) 女朋友; (friend) 女性朋友; **G~ Guide** *n* Brit 女童子军

girlhood /ˈgɜːlhʊd/ *n* [u] 少女时期

girlie[1] /ˈgɜːli/ *n* colloq 小姑娘

girlie[2] *adj* [1] pej (feminine) 女孩子气的 [2] (raunchy) 色情的

girlie: ~ mag, ~ magazine *ns* colloq 裸女色情杂志; **~ show** *n* colloq 裸女色情表演

girlish /ˈgɜːlɪʃ/ *adj* [1] (like a girl) 女孩子气的 ‹*behaviour, voice*›; (suitable for a girl) 适于少女的 ‹*dress, style*› [2] (effeminate) 女人气的 ‹*man, youth*›; 女孩子似的 ‹*body, gesture*›

girlishly /ˈgɜːlɪʃli/ *adv* 少女似地 ‹*laugh, giggle*›

girl: ~ power *n* [u] 女孩威力; **G~ Scout** *n* Amer 女童子军; **~s' wear department** *n* 女装部; **~ talk** *n* [u] colloq 女孩子的悄悄话; **~ trouble** *n* [u] colloq 与女友的矛盾; **he's having ~ trouble** 他在与女友闹矛盾

giro /ˈdʒaɪrəʊ/ *n* Brit [1] [u] (system) 电子转账; **a ~ transfer/payment** 汇划转账/支付 [2] [c] (cheque) 电子转账支票; (payment) 电子转账支付

girt /gɜːt/ *pt, pp* ▸**gird**

girth /gɜːθ/ *n* [1] [u] (measurement) (of waist) 腰围; (of tree) 干围; (of pillar) 周长 [2] [c] (waist) 腰身 [3] [c] Equit 肚带

GIS *abbr* = **geographic information system**

gismo /ˈgɪzməʊ/ *n* (*pl* **~s**) colloq = **gizmo**

gist /dʒɪst/ *n* [u] 主旨; **to get** *or* **gather the ~ of sth.** 获得某事的要点; **to give sb. the ~ of sth.** 把某事的要点告诉某人

git /gɪt/ *n* Brit sl pej 饭桶

give /gɪv/

A *vt* (*pt* **gave,** *pp* **given**) [1] (hand over) 给; **to ~ sth. to sb.** 把某物交给某人; **~ me that knife, please** 请把那把刀递给我; **the children were given balloons** 孩子们领到了气球 [2] (make gift of) 赠给; **to ~ a present to sb.** 把礼物赠送给某人; **to ~ sth. for ...** 赠送某物以庆祝 ‹*special occasion*›; **to ~ sth. as ...** 把某物作为…赠送 ‹*token, present, keepsake*› [3] (transfer ownership of) 送给; **to ~ property/land to sb.** 把财产/土地送给某人; **I gave him my heart** fig liter 我把心都交给他了; **my heart is given to another** fig liter 我已心有所属 [4] (donate) 捐赠 ‹*possessions, clothes, food*›; 无偿提供 ‹*aid*›; **to ~ blood** 献血; **to ~ sth. to sth./sb.** 把某物捐给某机构/某人; **to ~ alms (to the poor)** (向穷人)布施 [5] (supply) 提供; **to ~ food/drink/clothes/accommodation to sb.** 向某人提供食物/饮料/衣服/住宿; **to ~ the plants some water** 给花木浇点水; **have I given you enough room?** 我给你腾出的空间够吗?; **~ me ... (every time/any day)** 我宁可要…; **I can't stand modern music: ~ me Bach every time** 我受不了现代音乐: 我更喜欢巴赫; **I'll ~ you the lot for £20** 这堆东西我20英镑卖给你; **they gave us their car for the weekend** 他们把车借给我们周末使用; **she's given me her computer to fix** *or* **repair** 她把计算机交给我修理 [6] (allocate, distribute) 分给; **to ~ work/a task to sb.** 分配工作/任务给某人; **I gave him his fair share** 我把他应得的那份给他了; **I was given the guest room** 我被安排在客房; **we were given a translation to do** 我们留了翻译作业 [7] (pay) 支付 ‹*money, tip, salary, interest*›; **to ~ sth. to sb.** 付给某人某物; **to ~ sb. a pay rise/a discount** 给某人加薪/打折; **how much will you ~ me for this ring?** 这枚戒指你出多少钱? [8] (exchange) 拿…作交换; **he gave her a book in exchange for the record** 他给了她一本书来交换这张唱片; **to ~ anything for sth.** 渴望得到某物; **to ~ anything/it all/the lot to do sth.** 渴望做某事; **I'd ~ anything (for a chance) to go to India** 我非常想(有机会)去印度 [9] Med (provide) 提供; **to ~ sb. a new heart/liver** 为某人植入新的心脏/肝脏; **to ~ sb. a pacemaker/an artificial leg** 为某人安装心脏起搏器/假腿 [10] Med (administer) 给予; **to ~ sth. to sb.** 给某人服用 ‹*medicine*›; 给某人涂抹 ‹*ointment*›; 对某人进行 ‹*treatment, therapy*›; 给某人做 ‹*examination, massage, brain scan*›; **she gave me an injection** 她给我打了一针; **the doctor gave him a course of antibiotics** 医生用抗生素给他治疗了一个疗程; **can you ~ me anything for the pain?** 你能给我开些止疼药吗? [11] (be source of, yield) 产生 ‹*light, nutrient, result, interest*›; 得出 ‹*total, sum, answer*›; **cows ~ milk** 奶牛产奶; **the herd ~s a high yield** 牧群产量很高; **to ~ sth. to sb./sth.** 为某人/某物产出某物; **mixing yellow and blue paint ~s (you) green** 混合黄色和蓝色颜料就可以得到绿色 [12] (offer for holding) **to ~ sth. to sb.** 向某人伸出 ‹*hand, arm, leg, paw*› [13] dated (sanction marriage of) 同意把…嫁出 ‹*daughter*›; **he gave me his daughter's/his daughter's hand in marriage** 他把女儿嫁给我了 [14] (introducing name) 介绍; **I ~ you the next President** 让我为你们介绍下任总统; **I ~ you the bride and groom** 我提议诸位为新娘新郎干杯 [15] Telecom **to ~ sb. sth.** 为某人将电话接到 ‹*person, department, number*›; **~ me the police/extension 512** 请接警察局/512分机 [16] (sacrifice, devote) 献出 ‹*time*›; 牺牲 ‹*life, person*›; **to ~ thought/energy/time to sb./sth.** 把心思/精力/时间用于某人/某事物; **to ~ sth. all** *or* **everything one's got** colloq 尽全力做某事 [17] (allocate, allow) 留出; **~ me five minutes** 等我5分钟; **~ yourself time to think about it** 你抽空想想这件事; **about a metre, ~ or take a few centimetres** 大约一米, 误差不会超过几厘米 [18] colloq (predict to have) 估计出 ‹*length of time, weight*›; **how long do you ~ the new manager?** 你觉得新经理能干多长时间?; **the doctor gave her six months to live** 医生说她还能活6个月; **the polls ~ Labour a 5% lead** 民意调查显示工党领先5个百分点 [19] Sport 让 ‹*length of time, weight, height*›; **she could ~ her opponent five years** 她可以让对手5岁; **he was giving his opponent ten kilos** 他与比他重10公斤的对手比赛 [20] (award) 颁发 ‹*medal, award, honour*›; 加封 ‹*knighthood, title*›; Sch 给出 ‹*mark, grade*›; 给予 ‹*punishment, scholarship, bonus*›; Jur 判处 ‹*fine, sentence, damages, custody*›; **she was given the freedom of the city** 她获授该市荣誉市民; **I gave my poem the title 'Hope'** 我把诗的题目定为"希望"; **~ them a round of applause, ladies and gentlemen** 先生女士们, 请为他们鼓掌; **the prefect gave him 100 lines for being late** 他因迟到被级长罚写100行字; **judgement was given against the accused** 被告已经被宣判有罪了; **stop whimpering, or I'll ~ you something to cry about!** 别哭哭啼啼的, 不然我就把你揍得哭爹喊娘! [21] (administer) 施行; **to ~ sth. to sb./sth.** 施加某物于某人/某物; **~ your hands a (good) wash** 去(好好)洗洗手; **Spurs gave Arsenal a hammering** 热刺队给阿森纳队以迎头痛击; **he gave the door a coat of paint** 他给门刷上了一层漆; **to ~ it to sb.** colloq 责罚某人 [22] (perform, let out) 做出…的动作 ‹*shudder, wave, nod*›; 做出…的表情 ‹*smile, grin, frown*›; **she gave a bow and left the stage** 她鞠了躬, 离开了舞台; **he gave a start as the door slammed** 门砰地一响把他吓了一跳; **she gave a shrug of her shoulders** 她耸了耸肩; **the flame gave a final flicker** 火光最后闪了一下; **did you see the look he gave you?** 你看到他对你的表情了吗?; **she gave them a look of disgust** 她厌恶地看了他们一眼; **to ~ sb./sth. the green/red light** 给某人/某事物开绿/红灯; **to ~ sb./sth. the thumbs up/down** 赞同/反对某人/某事 [23] (utter, emit) 发出…的声音 ‹*cry, giggle, bark, squeak*›; **she gave a short laugh** 她浅笑了一声; **the duck gave a quack** 鸭子呷地叫了一声 [24] (proffer) 给出 ‹*advice, answer, information, name*›; 发出 ‹*alarm, warning*›; 作出 ‹*verdict*›; Mus 奏出 ‹*note*›; **I gave evidence at her trial** 我在她出庭受审时作证了; **she gave me her opinion that ...** 她给我的意见是…; **I gave her my word that I wouldn't tell anybody** 我向她保证不会告诉任何人; **to ~ sb./sth. a mention** 提及某人/某事物; **~ her my best wishes** 替我向她问好; **please ~ them my condolences** 请向他们转达我的哀悼; **I've been given my orders** hum 我已经领命; **she gave them her notice** 她向他们提出了辞职; **he gave her a good telling-off** 他狠狠地训斥了她一顿; **if she ~s me any more cheek, I'll ...** 如果她还是那么不要脸, 我就…; **don't ~ me that!** colloq 少来这一套!; **don't ~ me all that stuff about ...** colloq 少跟我说关于…的事; **I'll ~ you that** colloq 这一点我承认; **to ~ (sb.) as good as one gets** (对某人)以牙还牙 [25] Sport 判罚 ‹*corner, free kick, penalty*›; **the umpire gave the batsman out** (in cricket) 裁判把击球手罚出场; **to ~ the ball in** (in tennis) 判界内球 [26] (set out) 表示 ‹*quantity, time*›; **the number was given to seven decimal places** 该数字精确到小数点后7位; **~ the answer in metric units** 答案用公制单位表示 [27] (present in public) 举行 ‹*show, demonstration*›; 举办 ‹*concert, press conference, reception, party*›; **to ~ a lecture/speech** 做讲座/演讲; **she gave a magnificent performance as Lady Macbeth** 她演麦克白夫人演得太好了; **she ~s piano lessons** 她教钢琴课; **~ us a song!** 给我们唱首歌吧!; **to ~ a presentation to sb.** 为某人介绍情况; **to ~ interviews to journalists** 接受记者采访 [28] (cause physical effect) 引发; **to ~ sb. vertigo/asthma** 引起某人眩晕/哮喘发作; **to ~ sb. trouble** 给某人带来麻烦; **you nearly gave me a heart attack!** fig 你差点把我吓出心脏病来!; **to ~ sb. an electric shock/quite an appetite** 使某人受电击/胃口大开 [29] Med (pass on) 传染; **to ~ sth. to sb.** 把…传染给某人 ‹*cold, AIDS, disease, virus*›

g

30 (cause mental effect) **to ～ sb. pleasure/hope/a surprise** 使某人感到快乐/希望/惊奇; **it ～s me great pleasure to declare ...** 我很高兴地宣布…; **it gave them a feeling of insecurity** 这件事使他们产生了不安全感; **the long entries ～ me the most trouble** 长词条最让我头疼了; **the film gave him nightmares for weeks afterwards** 看过这部电影后，他做了几个星期的恶梦; **～ me strength!** colloq 我要坚持住! **31** (grant, cause to have) **to ～ sth. to sb./sth.** 给某人/某物以 ‹*opportunity, permission, authority, criticism*›; **he was given charge of 30 children** 他受命看管 30 个孩子; **the slave was given his freedom** 这个奴隶获得了自由; **it gave me something to think about** 这件事令我深思; **if you will ～ me your attention for a moment ...** 请听我说…; **you must ～ top priority to this project** 你一定要加倍重视这个项目; **the set ～s good reception/a clear picture** 这台电视机接收效果很好/图像很清晰 **32** colloq (care) 在意; **I don't ～ a damn** *or* **a hang** *or* **tuppence** 我才不在乎呢; **they didn't ～ two hoots about us** 他们根本没把我们放在心上

B *vi* (*pt* **gave,** *pp* **given**) **1** (contribute) 捐赠; **to ～ to sb./sth.** 向某人/某机构捐赠; **to ～ of one's best** formal 尽全力 **2** (bend, flex) «*mattress, floorboard, plank, branch, bridge*» 弯曲; «*cloth, leather, elastic, cable*» 伸展; **to ～ under** *or* **beneath sth./sb.** 在某物/某人的重压下变形 **3** (yield, break) «*bridge, roof, wall*» 垮塌; «*legs*» 支撑不住; «*rope, cable, hinge, fastening*» 崩断; **to ～ under** *or* **beneath sth./sb.** 在某物/某人的重压下支撑不住 **4** fig (concede, yield) «*person, group, side*» 让步; **something has to ～** 总要有所舍弃; **to ～ and take** 互相迁就 **5** Amer colloq (concede defeat) 认输 **6** colloq (happen) 发生; **what ～s?** 有什么事吗?

C *v refl* (*pt* **gave,** *pp* **given**) **to ～ oneself to sth.** 全身心投入某事; **the children really gave themselves to the play** 孩子们非常入戏

D *n* [u] (in cloth, leather, elastic, cable) 弹性; (in mattress, sofa, floorboard, bridge, plank, branch) 弯曲性; **this surface has more ～** 这个表面的弹力更大

Phrasal verbs

• **give away**

A [**～ sth. away, ～ away sth.**] *vt*

1 (out of kindness, to charity) 捐献 ‹*money, blood*›; (as gift) 赠送 ‹*possession, book*›; (for adoption) 把…送人 ‹*animal, child*› **2** Comm 免费送出 ‹*sample, mug, magazine, DVD*› **3** (present) 颁发 ‹*prize*› **4** (squander) 丧失 ‹*advantage, opportunity*›; 轻易输掉 ‹*game, match, point*›; **we don't want to ～ the contract away to our competitors** 我们不想把合同拱手让给竞争对手 **5** (reveal) 泄露 ‹*secret, answer, information*›; 暴露 ‹*identity*›; **～ nothing away to the press** 不要对新闻界透露任何消息; **to ～ the game** *or* **show away** 露馅 **6** Sport 有…的劣势 ‹*weight, height, length of time*›; **she is giving six years away to her opponent** 和对手相比，她有 6 岁的劣势

B [**～ sb. away, ～ away sb.**] *vt*

1 (in marriage) 把…交给新郎 ‹*bride, daughter, female relative*› **2** (betray) 供出 ‹*accomplice*›; 举报 ‹*escaped prisoner*›; «*sound, sign, clue, accent*» 暴露 ‹*person*›

C *v refl* **to ～ oneself away** 暴露

• **give back** *vt* [**～ sth./sb. back, ～ back sth./sb.**]

1 (return) 归还 ‹*book, pen*›; 退还 ‹*money, present*›; 送回 ‹*person, child, hostage*›; **～ it back to me at once!** 马上把它还给我! ; **satisfaction guaranteed, or we'll ～ you your money back** 保证满意，否则退款 **2** (restore) 恢复 ‹*sanity, confidence, freedom*›

• **give forth** *vt* [**～ forth sth.**] liter 发出 ‹*sound*›; 散发 ‹*smell*›

• **give in**

A *vi* **1** (admit defeat) 认输 **2** **to ～ in to sb./sth.** (comply with, obey) 对…妥协 ‹*person, demand, blackmail*› **3** **to ～ in to sth.** (succumb to) 屈从于 ‹*temptation, depression, impulse, desire*›; **they gave in to their animal instincts** 他们兽性大发

B *vt* [**～ sth. in, ～ in sth.**] Brit 上交 ‹*homework, exam paper*›; 交出 ‹*key*›; 发出 ‹*parcel, letter, petition*›; 递交 ‹*accounts, report, notice*›; **to ～ sth. in to sb.** 把某物交给某人; **you have to ～ your name in to the receptionist** 你得向前台报上姓名

• **give off** *vt* [**～ off sth.**] (emit) 发出 ‹*smell, heat, light, signal*›; 排放 ‹*noxious gas, fumes*›; 释放 ‹*oxygen, hydrogen*›

• **give on to** *vt* [**～ on to sth.**] Brit «*window, room*» 朝向 ‹*courtyard, street, garden, open space*›

• **give out**

A [**～ sth. out, ～ out sth.**] *vt*

1 (distribute) 分发 ‹*books, food, equipment*› **2** (announce) 公布 ‹*news, information, list, results*›

B [**～ out sth.**] *vt* (emit) 发出 ‹*heat, light, sound, signal*›

C *vi* **1** (run out) «*food, fuel, battery, strength*» 耗尽 **2** (break down) «*car, engine, machine, computer*» 瘫痪; «*fuse*» 熔断

• **give over**

A *vt* **1** (assign) **to ～ sth. over to sth., to ～ over sth. to sth.** 安排 ‹*place, period of time*›; **the afternoon was given over to private study** 下午的时间被安排用于自学; **to ～ sth. over to doing sth.** 把某物专用于做某事 **2** (devote) **to ～ sth. over to sth., to ～ over sth. to sth.** 付出 ‹*one's time, one's life*›; **to ～ sth. over to doing sth.** 付出某物来做某事; **he gave over the rest of his life to helping the poor** 他将余生致力于扶贫济困 **3** [**～ sth. over, ～ over sth.**] (hand over) 移交 ‹*place, business*›; **to ～ sth. over to sb.** 把某物托付给某人 **4** Brit colloq (stop) **to ～ over doing sth.** 停止做某事

B *vi* Brit colloq 停止; **～ over!** (stop doing sth.) 住手! ; (stop saying sth.) 住嘴!

C *v refl* **to ～ oneself over to sth./doing sth.** 致力于某事/做某事; **he gave himself over to the theatre/writing full-time** 他把所有时间都用来看戏/写作

• **give up**

A *vi* **1** (admit defeat) 认输; **don't ～ up** 别自暴自弃; **to ～ up on sth.** 放弃某事物; **I've given up on today's crossword** 今天的填字游戏我做不出来 **2** colloq (lose faith) 绝望; **to ～ up on sb.** 对某人失望; **don't ～ up on me** 不要对我失去信心

B [**～ sth./sb. up, ～ up sth./sb.**] *vt*

1 (surrender) 交出 ‹*passport, key, place, ticket*›; 说出 ‹*secret*›; 交出…的监护权 ‹*child*›; **they will not ～ up an inch of their territory** 他们寸土不让; **to ～ sth. up to sb., to ～ up sth. to sb.** 将某物交给某人; **she gave her seat up to an old man** 她把座位让给了一位老伯 **2** (part with) 卖掉 ‹*car, house, home*› **3** (abandon, drop) 放弃 ‹*job, right, hope, attempt*›; Sch 停止学习 ‹*subject*›; **Edward VIII gave up the throne for the woman he loved** 爱德华八世为了他爱的女人放弃了王位; **to ～ up doing sth.** 停止 ‹*writing, dancing, investigating, trying*› **4** (stop indulging in) 戒除 ‹*bad habit, smoking, meat*›; 停止 ‹*social life*›; **I'm giving up men!** hum 我再也不找男人了! **5** (sacrifice, devote) 付出 ‹*one's time, one's life*›; **to ～ up sth. to sth./doing sth.** 为某事/做某事投入某物

C [**～ sb. up, ～ up sb.**] *vt*

1 (deliver to authority) 交出 ‹*criminal, escaped prisoner, enemy soldier*› **2** (stop expecting to arrive) 认为…不会来; **to ～ sb. up for lost/dead** 不再期待某人出现/活着

D *v refl* **1** **to ～ oneself up** (surrender) 自首 **2** **to ～ oneself up to sth./doing sth.** (devote oneself) 致力于某事/做某事; (abandon oneself) 沉溺于某事/做某事; **she gave herself up to a life of crime** 她一生恶贯满盈

• **give way** *vi* **1** (collapse) «*bridge, ceiling, wall*» 垮塌; «*leg*» 支撑不住; «*rope, cable*» 崩断; fig «*strength, sanity, patience*» 丧失; **her health finally gave way** 她的身体最终垮掉了; **to ～ way under** *or* **beneath sth./sb.** 在某物/某人的重压下坍塌 **2** Brit (allow others to go first) «*person, vehicle, vessel*» 让路; **to ～ way to sb./sth.** 给某人/某物让路 **3** (obey, comply) **to ～ way to sb./sth.** 对…妥协 ‹*person, threat, demand, blackmail*› **4** (succumb) **to ～ way to sth.** 禁不住 ‹*temptation, fear, depression, desire*›; **I gave way to panic** 我恐慌不安 **5** (be replaced) **to ～ way to sth.** 被…所代替 ‹*feeling, conditions, environment, season*›; **the dark clouds gave way to bright sunshine** 乌云散去，明媚的阳光重新普照大地; **her discomfort gave way to anger** 她由不安转为愤怒; **winter ～s way to spring** 冬去春来

give and take

A *n* [u] **1** (mutual concession) 互相迁就; **it's a matter of ～** 这事得互相包涵 **2** (exchange) 交流; **the ～ of sth.** 在某方面的交流

B **give-and-take** *modif* 互相迁就的 ‹*attitude, affair, relationship, situation*›

giveaway /ˈɡɪvəweɪ/

A *n* **1** Comm 随赠品 **2** (revealing thing) 表明真相的事物; **the name is a ～** 观其名便可知其实; **a dead ～** colloq 使真相暴露无遗的事物; **oops, what a ～!** 嗬，这是多么明显的证据啊!

B *modif* **1** (free) 免费赠送的 ‹*mug, shampoo, DVD, magazine*› **2** (cheap) 低廉的 ‹*price*› **3** (revealing) 表明真相的 ‹*expression, action, words, clue*›

given /ˈɡɪvn/

A *pp* ▸**give A, B, C**

B *adj* **1** *usu attrib* (certain, specified) 特定的; **the ～ date** 规定日期; **at any ～ point** 在任意一点上; **a ～ level** 一定水平; **a stick of a ～ length** 已知长度的木棒 **2** *pred* (prone) 有倾向的; **I'm not ～ to losing my temper** 我不常发脾气; **the software is ～ to errors** 这款软件很容易出错

C *prep* **1** (in view of) 鉴于; **～ that ...** 因为…; **～ the state of the country at the moment** 鉴于当前的国内形势 **2** Math 已知; **～ the triangle ABC** 已知三角形 ABC; **～ that x = y + z** 已知 x = y + z **3** (with) 如果有; **～ the training** 如果接受培训; **～ a bit of encouragement, she will ...** 给她一点鼓励，她就会…; **the plants should flourish, ～ regular watering** 只要定期浇水，这些植物就会枝叶繁茂

D *n* 确定的情况; **attentive service is a ～** 殷勤的服务是理所当然的

given name *n* = **first name**

giver /ˈɡɪvə(r)/ *n* 给予者

give way sign *n* Brit 让车标志

gizmo /ˈɡɪzməʊ/ *n* (*pl* **～s**) colloq 小玩意儿

gizzard /ˈɡɪzəd/ *n* Zool 砂囊; Culin 肫; **to stick in sb.'s ～** fig colloq 使某人不高兴

glacé /ˈɡlæseɪ, Amer ɡlæˈseɪ/ *adj attrib* **1** Culin 糖渍的 ‹*fruit*›; **～ cherries** 蜜饯樱桃 **2** fig (smooth) 亮面的 ‹*leather, cloth*›

glacé icing *n* [u] [糖粉和水制成的] 糖衣

glacial /ˈɡleɪsɪəl, Amer ˈɡleɪʃl/ *adj* **1** Geol 冰川的 ‹*movement, deposit*›; 冰川形成的 ‹*valley, river*› **2** (cold) 冰冷的 ‹*wind, current*› **3** fig (hostile) 冷若冰霜的 ‹*manner, stare*›

glacial period *n* 冰川期

glaciated /ˈɡleɪsɪeɪtɪd/ *adj* 由冰川作用形成的; **a ～ valley** 冰蚀谷

glaciation /ˌɡleɪsɪˈeɪʃn/ *n* [u] 冰川覆盖; **the effects of ～** 冰川作用的影响

glacier /ˈɡlæsɪə(r)/ *n* 冰川

glaciological /ˌɡleɪsɪəˈlɒdʒɪkl/ *adj* 冰川的 ‹*effect, change*›; 冰川学的 ‹*expert*›

glaciologist /ˌgleɪsɪˈɒlədʒɪst/ ▸**p. 409** *n* 冰川学家

glaciology /ˌgleɪsɪˈɒlədʒi/ *n* [u] 冰川学

glad /glæd/ *adj pred* 高兴的; **to be ~ about sth.** 为某事物高兴; **I am ~ about your success** 我为你的成功感到高兴; **~ that ...** 很高兴⋯; **to be ~ to do sth.** 很高兴做某事; **I'll be ~ to help you** 我乐于帮助你; **only too ~ to ...** 非常乐意⋯

gladden /ˈglædn/ *vt* 使⋯高兴 ‹*person*›; 使⋯喜庆 ‹*occasion*›; **a story to ~ the heart** 令人高兴的故事; **a sight to ~ the eyes** 赏心悦目的景象

glade /gleɪd/ *n* 林中空地

glad: ~-hand *vt* esp Amer [尤指政客] 热情招呼; **~ hand** *n* (greeting) 热情招呼; **to give sb. the ~ hand** 热烈欢迎某人

gladiator /ˈglædɪeɪtə(r)/ *n* 角斗士

gladiatorial /ˌglædɪəˈtɔːrɪəl/ *adj* 角斗士的 ‹*sword, combat*›; **~ politics** fig 好斗政治

gladiolus /ˌglædɪˈəʊləs/ *n* (*pl* **gladioli** /ˌglædɪˈəʊlaɪ/ *or* **~es**) (plant) 剑兰; (flower) 剑兰花

gladly /ˈglædli/ *adv* (willingly) 乐意地 ‹*help, pay*›; (happily) 高兴地 ‹*accept*›

glad rags *npl* colloq hum 考究的衣服

glamor /ˈglæmər/ *n* [u] Amer = **glamour**

glamorize /ˈglæməraɪz/ *vt* 美化 ‹*person, place, job*›

glamorous /ˈglæmərəs/ *adj* 富有魅力的 ‹*woman*›; 令人向往的 ‹*occasion*›; **a ~ job/evening dress** 令人向往的工作/迷人的晚礼服

glamour /ˈglæmə(r)/ *n* [u] [1] (of woman) 魅力 [2] (of job, occasion) 诱惑力; (of travel, car) 吸引力; **to lend ~ to sth.** 为某事物增添魅力

glamour: ~ boy *n* colloq dated 迷人男子; **~ girl** *n* colloq dated 迷人女子; **a ~ girl calendar** 美女挂历; **~ model** *n* 性感美女模特; **~ photography** *n* [u] 魅态摄影

glance /glɑːns, Amer glæns/

[A] *n* 一瞥; **to have a ~ at sb./sth.** 对某人/某物匆匆看一眼; **to be able to tell sth. at a ~** 对某物一目了然; **to exchange ~s** 互相看一眼; **at first ~** 乍看上去; **to leave home without a backward ~** fig 义无反顾地离开家

[B] *vi* [1] (look) 匆匆一看; **to ~ at sb./sth.** 扫视某人/某物; **to ~ out of the window** 朝窗外瞥一眼; **to ~ down** 向下扫一眼; **to ~ around the room** 快速环视房间 [2] (read) 快速阅读; **to ~ at/through/over sth.** 浏览某物 [3] (be deflected) «*ball*» 斜擦而过; **to ~ off sth.** «*ball, bullet*» 掠过某物 [4] (be reflected) 闪烁; **to ~ off sth.** «*light, ray*» 在某物上反光

glancing /ˈglɑːnsɪŋ, Amer ˈglænsɪŋ/ *adj* 斜擦而过的; **a ~ blow/shot** 一记斜击拳/打偏的一枪

gland[1] /glænd/ *n* Med 腺; **to have swollen ~s** 腺体肿胀

gland[2] *n* Mech 密封套

glandular /ˈglændjʊlə(r), Amer -dʒʊ-/ *adj* 腺的; **~ illness/secretions** 腺体疾病/分泌

glandular fever ▸**p. 377** *n* [u] Brit 腺热

glare /gleə(r)/

[A] *n* [1] [c] (angry stare) 怒视; **to give sb. a ~** 瞪某人一眼; **he gave her an angry ~** 他对她怒目而视 [2] [u] (of lights, sun) 刺眼的强光 [3] [u] (attention) 密切关注; **in the ~ of publicity** 在众目睽睽之下

[B] *vi* [1] (stare angrily) 怒目而视; **to ~ at sb.** 怒视某人 [2] (of lights, sun) 发出刺眼的强光

glaring /ˈgleərɪŋ/ *adj* [1] (obvious) 明显的 ‹*error, omission, injustice*› [2] (dazzling) 耀眼的 ‹*light, colour*› [3] (angry) 凶狠的 ‹*expression, eyes, look*›

glaringly /ˈgleərɪŋli/ *adv* [1] (obviously) 显然 ‹*wrong, unfair*›; **it's ~ obvious** 这是显而易见的 [2] (dazzlingly) 耀眼地; **~ bright/white** 亮/白得刺目

glasnost /ˈglæznɒst/ *n* [u] 公开性 [前苏联采取的使政府更公开、新闻传播更自由的政策, 1985 年由戈尔巴乔夫发起]

glass /glɑːs, Amer glæs/

[A] *n* [1] [u] (substance) 玻璃; **a piece/pane of ~** 一片玻璃/一块窗玻璃; **mind the broken ~!** 当心碎玻璃! [2] [c] (drinking vessel) 玻璃杯; (glassful) 一玻璃杯; **a ~ of wine** 一玻璃杯葡萄酒 [3] [u] (glassware) 玻璃器皿 [4] [c] esp Brit dated (mirror) 镜子; (magnifying glass) 放大镜 [5] [c] (telescope) 望远镜 [6] [u] (of greenhouse, cold frame) 温室玻璃; **to cultivate sth. under ~** 在温室中种植某物

[B] **glasses** *npl* [1] 眼镜; **a pair of ~es** 一副眼镜; **he wears reading ~es** 他戴老花眼镜 [2] (binoculars) 双筒望远镜

Phrasal verbs

- **glass in** *vt* [**~ in sth., ~ sth. in**] 用玻璃罩住
- **glass over** *vt* = **glass in**

glass: ~ blower *n* 吹玻璃工; **~ blowing** *n* [u] 玻璃吹制; **~ ceiling** *n* fig 玻璃天花板; **~ cloth** *n* 玻璃砂布; **~ cutter** *n* (worker) 划玻璃工; (tool) 玻璃刀; **~ door** *n* 玻璃门; **~ eye** *n* 玻璃假眼; **~ factory** *n* = **~works**; **~ fibre** *n* [u] 玻璃纤维; **a ~-fibre seat** 玻璃纤维座位

glassful /ˈglɑːsfʊl, Amer ˈglæs-/ *n* 一杯; **three ~s of milk** 三杯牛奶

glass: ~house *n* Brit [1] (greenhouse) 玻璃暖房; **people in ~houses shouldn't throw stones** 自身毛病多, 勿与人交恶; [2] Mil colloq (prison) 监狱; **~ industry** *n* 玻璃业; **~making** *n* [u] 玻璃制造; **~ paper** *n* [u] 玻璃砂纸; **~ware** *n* [u] 玻璃器皿; **~ wool** *n* [u] 玻璃绒; **~works** *npl* + *v sing* 玻璃厂

glassy /ˈglɑːsi, Amer ˈglæsi/ *adj* [1] (resembling glass) 像玻璃的 [2] (slippery) (from ice) 光滑的 ‹*surface, road*›; (from rain) 湿滑的 ‹*surface, road*› [3] (smooth) 平静的 ‹*water, sea*› [4] (transparent) 清澈的 ‹*water, sea*› [5] (blank) 呆滞的 ‹*stare, eyes*›; (indifferent) 冷漠的 ‹*expression*›

glassy-eyed /ˌglɑːsɪˈaɪd, Amer ˌglæs-/ *adj* (blank) 目光呆滞的; (hostile) 怀有敌意的

Glaswegian /glæzˈwiːdʒən/

[A] *adj* 格拉斯哥的

[B] *n* 格拉斯哥人

glaucoma /glɔːˈkəʊmə/ *n* [u] 青光眼

glaze /gleɪz/

[A] *n* [1] (shiny coating) (on ceramics) 釉; (on leather) 研光; (on fabric) 轧光; (on paper) 上光 [2] (substance applied) (on ceramics) 釉料 [3] Culin (egg) 蛋浆; (milk) 奶浆; (icing) 糖浆; (on meat) 浓肉汁 [4] Amer (ice) 薄冰层

[B] *vt* [1] Brit (fit glass into) 给⋯装玻璃 ‹*door, window*›; 给⋯罩上玻璃 ‹*picture*› [2] (apply glaze to) 给⋯上釉 ‹*pottery, tiles*›; 给⋯上轧光 ‹*cotton, fabric*›; 给⋯上研光 ‹*leather*›; 给⋯浇亮汁 ‹*cake, pastry, meat*›; 给⋯上光 ‹*photographic paper*›; **potatoes ~d with butter** 浇了奶油亮汁的土豆

[C] *vi* **~ (over)** «*eyes, expression*» 变得呆滞

glazed /gleɪzd/ *adj* [1] (fitted with glass) 装上玻璃的 ‹*window*›; **a fully ~ door** 全玻璃门 [2] 上釉的 ‹*pottery, tiles*›; 研光的 ‹*leather*›; 轧光的 ‹*cotton*›; 上光的 ‹*paper*›; 浇了亮汁的 ‹*pastry, meat*› [3] fig (expressionless) 呆滞的 ‹*eyes, look, expression*› [4] Amer (ice-covered) 覆盖薄冰的 ‹*ground, water*›

glazier /ˈgleɪzɪə(r), Amer -ʒər/ *n* 装玻璃工

glazing /ˈgleɪzɪŋ/ *n* [u] [1] (fitting panes of glass) 装玻璃 [2] (panes of glass) 玻璃窗

glazing bar *n* 玻璃格条

gleam /gliːm/

[A] *n* [1] (of candle, lamp) 微光; (of sun, moon, stars) 光 [2] (of gold, glass) 闪光; (of sea, water) 反光 [3] (faint sign) 一丝; **a faint ~ of hope** 一线希望; **there was a malicious ~ in her eye** 她的眼中有一丝恶意

[B] *vi* [1] (shine) «*candle, lamp*» 发微光; «*sun, moon, stars*» 闪耀; fig «*eyes*» 闪烁; **his face ~ed with delight/mischief** 他脸上显露出欢乐/顽皮的神情 [2] (reflect light) «*knife, glass, metal*» 反光

gleaming /ˈgliːmɪŋ/ *adj* [1] (shining) 发光的 ‹*candle, lamp, sun, stars*›; fig 闪烁的 ‹*eyes*›; (shiny) 反光的 ‹*gold, sea, window*› [2] (clean, polished) 锃光瓦亮的 ‹*cooker, bathroom, car*›

glean /gliːn/ *vt* [1] (obtain) 搜集 ‹*information, news, fact*› [2] Agric lit 捡拾 ‹*grain*›

glee /gliː/ *n* [u] 高兴; **to shout with** *or* **in ~** 欢呼

glee club *n* Amer 合唱俱乐部; **a member of a ~** 合唱团成员

gleeful /ˈgliːfl/ *adj* 高兴的

gleefully /ˈgliːfəli/ *adv* 高兴地

glen /glen/ *n* [尤指苏格兰的] 峡谷; **a lonely ~** 幽谷; **G~ Urquhart** 厄克特峡谷

glib /glɪb/ *adj* 油腔滑调的

glibly /ˈglɪbli/ *adv* 油腔滑调地

glibness /ˈglɪbnɪs/ *n* [u] 油腔滑调

glide /glaɪd/

[A] *vi* [1] (move smoothly) «*person*» 滑动; «*car, boat*» 滑行; «*time*» 流逝; «*river, water*» 流动; **she ~d gracefully into/out of the ballroom** 她步履轻快优雅地进入/离开舞厅; **to ~ around the dance floor** 绕着舞池滑行; **the river ~s past the garden** 河水潺潺地流经花园 [2] (fly) «*bird, aircraft*» 滑翔 [3] (slide) «*skater, skier*» 滑行 [4] Mus, Phon 滑移

[B] *vt* 使⋯滑翔 ‹*aircraft*›

[C] *n* [1] (easy movement) 滑动 [2] (flight) 滑翔 [3] (in skating) 滑行; (in dancing) 滑步 [4] Mus, Phon 滑音

glide path *n* 下滑轨道

glider /ˈglaɪdə(r)/ *n* 滑翔机; **~ pilot** 滑翔机飞行员

gliding /ˈglaɪdɪŋ/

[A] *n* [u] 滑翔运动; **~ club** 滑翔俱乐部

[B] *adj* 滑动的

glimmer /ˈglɪmə(r)/

[A] *n* [1] (faint light) 闪烁的微光 [2] fig (trace) 一丝; **a ~ of hope** 一线希望

[B] *vi* «*torch, flare*» 微微闪光; «*lake, water*» 反射出微光; **a candle ~ed faintly in the darkness** 烛光在黑暗中摇曳着; **the lake ~ed in the moonlight** 月光下的湖面波光粼粼

glimpse /glɪmps/

[A] *n* [1] (sighting) 一瞥; **to catch a ~ of sth.** 瞥见某物 [2] fig (insight) 领略; **a ~ into the life of a ballet dancer** 对芭蕾舞演员生活的粗略了解

[B] *vt* [1] (catch sight of) 瞥见 [2] fig (understand) 领略; **I have just ~d the meaning of the poem** 我只是大致理解那首诗的意思

glint /glɪnt/

[A] *n* [1] (flash of light) 闪光 [2] (look in one's eye) [眼中某种感情的] 闪露; **an angry ~ in one's eye** 眼睛里露出的怒色

[B] *vi* «*knife, gold, glass*» 闪闪发亮; «*light, sun*» 闪闪发光; **the sunlight ~ed on the windows** 太阳照在窗户上闪闪发光; **his eyes ~ed with anger** 他的双眼闪着愤怒的光芒

glissando /glɪˈsændəʊ/ *n* (*pl* **glissandi** /glɪˈsændi/) 滑奏

glisten /ˈglɪsn/ *vi* 闪光; **to ~ with tears/sweat** 闪着泪光/汗珠

glitch /glɪtʃ/ *n* colloq [1] (malfunction) 失灵 [2] (minor problem) 小故障; (hitch) 小差错

glitter /ˈglɪtə(r)/

[A] *n* [u] [1] (sparkle) (of diamond, frost) 闪光 [2] fig (glamour) 魅力; **the superficial ~ of show business** 娱乐业的浅薄魅力 [3] (sparkling decoration) 亮片

[B] *vi* «*diamond, star, frost*» 闪闪发光; **her eyes ~ed with excitement** 她的双眼闪现出激

动兴奋的光彩; **all that ~s is not gold** 闪闪发光物，未必尽黄金

glitterati /ˌglɪtəˈrɑːti/ *npl* colloq [娱乐界等的]知名人士; **Hollywood's ~** 好莱坞的名流

glittering /ˈglɪtərɪŋ/ *adj* **1** (sparkling) 闪闪发光的 ‹*diamond, star, frost*› **2** (successful) 辉煌的 ‹*career, record*› **3** (impressive) 光彩夺目的; **a ~ array of stars** 一群闪耀的明星

glitz /glɪts/ *n* [u] colloq 浮华

glitzy /ˈglɪtsi/ *adj* colloq 耀眼的 ‹*jewellery*›; 浮华的 ‹*outfit, hotel*›; **~ ceremony** 华丽的典礼; **the ~ world of haute couture** 富丽堂皇的展示高档女装的地方

gloaming /ˈgləʊmɪŋ/ *n* [u] liter 黄昏; **in the ~** 薄暮时分

gloat /gləʊt/ *vi* 得意扬扬; **there's no need to ~** 没有必要沾沾自喜

gloating /ˈgləʊtɪŋ/ *adj* 得意扬扬的

glob /glɒb/ *n* colloq (of liquid, grease) 一滴; (of chewing gum) 一小团

global /ˈgləʊbl/ *adj* **1** (worldwide) 全球的 ‹*problem, competition*› **2** (comprehensive) 全面的; **to give sb. a ~ picture of ...** 给某人描述…的全貌 **3** Comput 整体的; **they sent a ~ email to all staff** 他们给全体员工群发了一封电子邮件

global economy *n* 全球经济

globalization /ˌgləʊbəlaɪˈzeɪʃən, Amer -lɪˈz-/ *n* [u] 全球化

globalize /ˈgləʊbəlaɪz/
A *vt* 使全球化
B *vi* 全球化

globally /ˈgləʊbəli/ *adv* **1** (worldwide) 在全球范围内; **to be ~ competitive** 具备全球竞争力 **2** (comprehensively) 全面地

global: ~ positioning system *n* 全球定位系统; **~ search** *n* 全程检索; **~ village** *n* **the ~ village** 地球村 [指通信技术将整个世界连接成一个单一的社区]; **~ warming** *n* [u] 全球变暖

globe /gləʊb/ *n* **1** (world) 地球; **the ~** 全球; **from all corners of the ~** 来自全球各个角落 **2** (model of planet earth) 地球仪 **3** (spherical object) 球状物

globe: ~ artichoke *n* 洋蓟; **~trotter** *n* colloq 环球旅行者; **~trotting** *n* [u] colloq 环球旅行

globular /ˈglɒbjʊlə(r)/ *adj* **1** (containing globules) 有小球的 ‹*substance, liquid*› **2** (spherical) 球状的 ‹*container, bead*›

globule /ˈglɒbjuːl/ *n* 小滴; **tiny ~s of water** 小水珠

glockenspiel /ˈglɒkənʃpiːl/ *n* 钟琴

gloom /gluːm/ *n* [u] **1** (darkness) 幽暗; **deepening ~** 越来越浓的夜色 **2** (despondency) 失望; **economic ~** 经济萧条; **to cast a ~ over sb./sth.** 使某人愁眉不展/使某物笼罩在忧郁的气氛中; **doom and ~** 悲观失望

gloomily /ˈgluːmɪli/ *adv* 沮丧地

gloomy /ˈgluːmi/ *adj* **1** (dark) 阴暗的 **2** (sad) 令人悲伤的 ‹*news, story*›; (despondent) 沮丧的 ‹*manner, expression*›; **to be ~ about sth.** 因为某事物而情绪低落

glorification /ˌglɔːrɪfɪˈkeɪʃn/ *n* [u] **1** (praise) 赞美; **the ~ of terrorism** 对恐怖主义的歌颂 **2** Relig (worship) 崇拜; **the ~ of sth.** 对某事物的颂扬

glorified /ˈglɔːrɪfaɪd/ *adj attrib* 美化的; **the studio was a ~ shack** 那间工作室其实是窝棚的美称

glorify /ˈglɔːrɪfaɪ/ *vt* **1** (praise) 赞美 ‹*battle, terrorism*›; **he denies that the film glorifies violence** 他否认那部电影美化了暴力 **2** Relig (worship) 崇拜

glorious /ˈglɔːrɪəs/ *adj* **1** (illustrious) 光荣的 ‹*victory*›; **a ~ chapter in our country's history** 我国历史上光辉的一页 **2** (magnificent) 壮丽的 ‹*cathedral, palace*›; 光辉的 ‹*example*› **3** (beautiful) 出色的 ‹*view*›; 美好的 ‹*evening*› **4** (very enjoyable) 极其愉快的 ‹*holiday, time*› **5** iron hum (dreadful) 极度的; **what a ~ mess!** 乱得真够呛!

gloriously /ˈglɔːrɪəsli/ *adv* **1** (with glory) 光荣地 ‹*win, succeed*› **2** (wonderfully) 极好地; **it was ~ sunny** 阳光明媚 **3** iron hum (dreadfully) 极度地; **to be ~ unsuccessful** 一败涂地

glory /ˈglɔːri/
A *n* **1** [u] (honour, distinction) 光荣; **to the greater ~ of sb./sth.** 为了给某人/某物增添荣耀; **to cover oneself in ~** 满载荣誉; **neither party particularly covered themselves in ~** 双方都没有获得什么特别的赞誉; **to bask/bathe in sb.'s reflected ~** 沐浴在某人的荣耀中 **2** Relig 赞颂; **~ be!** 多么伟大! [宗教仪式中的感叹句]; **~ to God in the highest** 在至高之处荣耀归于神 **3** [u] (splendour) (of person) 杰出; (of place) 壮丽; (of Heaven) 天国的荣耀; **in all one's ~** 在鼎盛时期 **4** [c and u] (source of pride) 带来荣耀的事; **the cathedral is the ~ of the city** 大教堂是城市的骄傲 **5** [c and u] (beauty) 美丽; **the ~ of the dawn sky** 黎明天空的绚丽
B **glories** *npl* **1** (splendours) 辉煌; **the glories of Venice** 威尼斯的辉煌 **2** (glorious deeds) 昔日的荣耀; **past glories** 昔日的荣耀
C *vi* **to ~ in sth.** (exult in) 因某事物而欣喜; (take pride in) 因某事物而骄傲

glory days *npl* 往日的美好时光

Glos. *abbr* Brit **= Gloucestershire**

gloss /glɒs/
A *n* **1** [u] (shine, lustre) 光泽; **to take the ~ off sth.** 使…失去光泽 ‹*wood, metal*›; fig 使…黯然失色 ‹*ceremony*› **2** [u] fig (facade) 虚饰; **to put a ~ on sth.** 粉饰某事物; **a ~ of respectability** 体面的假象 **3** [c] (shiny paint) 亮光漆 **4** [c] (explanation) 注释
B *vt* **1** (paint) 给…上光 ‹*metal, wood*› **2** (explain, clarify) 对…作注释 ‹*word, text*›

Phrasal verb

- **gloss over** *vt* [~ over sth.] 掩饰 ‹*defect, unpleasant truth, detail*›

glossary /ˈglɒsəri/ *n* 术语表

gloss: ~ coat *n* 清漆; **~ finish** *n* 上光; **~ paint** *n* [c and u] 光泽涂料; **~ paper** *n* [u] 光面纸

glossy /ˈglɒsɪ/
A *adj* **1** (shiny) 有光泽的 ‹*fur, hair*›; 光滑的 ‹*surface, metal, paper*›; 用亮光纸印的 ‹*photograph*›; **~ prints** 光面印刷品 **2** fig (stylish) 浮夸的 ‹*advertisement*›; 豪华的 ‹*apartment*›
B *n* colloq **= glossy magazine**

glossy magazine *n* 用有光纸印刷的杂志

glottal stop /ˈglɒtl ˌstɒp/ *n* 喉塞音

glottis /ˈglɒtɪs/ *n* 声门

Gloucestershire /ˈglɒstəʃə(r)/ *pr n* 格洛斯特郡

glove /glʌv/ *n* 手套; **to put on/take off one's ~s** 戴上/摘下手套; **the ~s are definitely off now** fig 恶斗已经开始了; **to be hand in ~ with sb.** 与某人勾结; ▸**fist**

glove: ~ box, ~ compartment *ns* 杂物箱; **~ factory** *n* 手套厂; **~ maker** *n* 手套制造商; **~ puppet** *n* Brit 手偶

gloved /glʌvd/ *adj* 戴手套的 ‹*hand*›

glow /gləʊ/
A *n* **1** (glimmer) 光亮; **the ~ of the evening sky** 晚霞 **2** fig (radiance) 容光焕发; **there was a ~ in her cheeks** 她双颊红润 **3** fig (feeling) 心满意足; **a ~ of self-satisfaction** 沾沾自喜的神情; **a warm ~** 暖洋洋的感觉
B *vi* **1** (emit light) 发光 **2** (redden) 发红; **to ~ with health** ‹*cheeks, face*› 容光焕发; **her cheeks ~ed with health** 她的脸颊泛出健康的红润 **3** (look vibrant) ‹*colour*› 焕发活力 **4** (look pleased) 喜形于色; **their eyes ~ed with delight** 他们的眼中闪烁着喜悦的光芒; **she was ~ing with pride/self-satisfaction/happiness** 她踌躇满志/洋洋自得/喜气洋洋

glower /ˈglaʊə(r)/ *n, vi* 怒视

glowering /ˈglaʊərɪŋ/ *adj* 怒视的 ‹*eyes*›; 阴沉的 ‹*expression*›

glowing /ˈgləʊɪŋ/ *adj* **1** (incandescent) 发光的 **2** (rich, warm) 鲜艳的 ‹*colour, tone*› **3** (flushed) 红润的 ‹*cheeks*›; 容光焕发的 ‹*face*› **4** (complimentary) 热情洋溢的 ‹*account, description*›; 热烈的 ‹*praise*›; **to paint a ~ picture of sth.** 对某事物作充满溢美之词的描述

glow-worm /ˈgləʊwɜːm/ *n* 萤火虫

glucose /ˈgluːkəʊs/
A *n* [u] **1** Chem, Biol 葡萄糖 **2** (syrup) 糖浆
B *modif* 含葡萄糖的 ‹*syrup, tablets, drink*›

glue /gluː/
A *n* [u and c] (paste) 胶; (liquid) 胶水; **to sniff ~** 吸胶毒
B *vt* **1** (stick) 用胶水粘; **to ~ sth. on/down/together** 用胶水把某物粘起来; **to ~ sth. back on/together** 把某物按原样粘合起来; **to ~ sth. (on) to sth.** 把某物粘到某物上 **2** fig colloq **to have one's eyes ~d to sb./sth.** 目不转睛地盯着某人/某物; **to have one's face/nose ~d to sth.** 把脸/鼻子紧贴着某物; **to be ~d to the spot** 呆立在原地; **to stay ~d to sb.'s side** 和某人形影不离

glue: ~ ear *n* [u] Brit 胶耳 [尤指儿童的咽鼓管堵塞]; **~ pen** *n* 胶水笔; **~-sniffer** *n* 吸胶毒者; **~-sniffing** *n* [u] 吸胶毒; **~ stick** *n* 胶棒

gluey /ˈgluːi/ *adj* 黏性的

glum /glʌm/ *adj* 忧郁的

glumly /ˈglʌmli/ *adv* 忧郁地

glumness /ˈglʌmnɪs/ *n* [u] 忧郁

glut /glʌt/
A *n* 供过于求; **a ~ of cheap videos on the market** 充斥市场的廉价录像带
B *vt* (*pres p etc.* **-tt-**) (oversupply) «*goods*» 充斥 ‹*market*›; (fill to excess) 充满; **the roads are ~ted with cars** 路上塞满了汽车

gluten /ˈgluːtn/ *n* [u] 面筋

gluten: ~ bread *n* [u] 面筋面包; **~ flour** *n* [u] 面筋粉; **~-free** *adj* 不含面筋的

glutinous /ˈgluːtənəs/ *adj* 黏性的 ‹*substance*›; **can you identify this ~ mess?** 你辨认得出这种黏乎乎的东西吗?

glutton /ˈglʌtn/ *n* **1** (voracious eater) 贪吃的人; (greedy person) 贪心的人 **2** fig (enthusiast) 入迷的人; **to be a ~ for sth.** 是酷爱某物的人; **a ~ for punishment/hard work** 喜欢自讨苦吃的人/吃苦耐劳的人

gluttonous /ˈglʌtənəs/ *adj* 贪吃的

gluttony /ˈglʌtəni/ *n* [u] 贪吃

glycerine /ˈglɪsəriːn, -rɪn/, **glycerin** /ˈglɪsərɪn/ *n* [u] 甘油

glycerol /ˈglɪsərɒl/ *n* [u] 丙三醇

glycogen /ˈglaɪkədʒn/ *n* [u] 糖原

glyph /glɪf/ *n* (character) 象形文字; (symbol) 象形符号

GM *abbr* **= genetically modified**

gm *abbr* **= gram(s)**

G-man /ˈdʒiːmæn/ *n* Amer colloq 联邦调查局探员

GMO *abbr* **= genetically modified organism** 转基因生物

GMT *abbr* **= Greenwich Mean Time**

gnarled /nɑːld/ *adj* 多节瘤的 ‹*tree, trunk*›; 粗糙的 ‹*face, hand*›

gnash /næʃ/
A *vt* [因愤怒而] 咬; **to ~ one's teeth (together)** 咬牙切齿
B *vi* 咬牙; **his teeth ~ed together** 他咬牙切齿

gnashing /ˈnæʃɪŋ/ *n* [u] (sound) 咬牙声; (act) 咬牙; **there was much ~ of teeth** fig 很多人都在咬牙切齿

gnat /næt/ *n* 叮人的小虫

gnat: ~ **bite** *n* 蚊虫叮伤; ~**catcher** *n* 蚋莺; ~**'s piss** *n* [u] colloq 虫尿 [指淡而无味的饮料]

gnaw /nɔː/
A *vt* 1 (chew) 啃 ‹*bone, wood*› 2 (bite) 咬 ‹*hole, opening*› 3 fig (torment) 折磨; ~**ed by guilt, he finally confessed** 在内疚的折磨下，他最后招认了
B *vi* 1 (chew) 啃; **to** ~ **at/on sth.** 啃某物 2 **to** ~ **at sb.** fig (torment) 折磨某人

Phrasal verbs
• **gnaw away**
A *vt* [~ **away sth.,** ~ **sth. away**] (destroy) 啃咬掉; (reduce) 慢慢消耗
B *vi* **to** ~ **away at sth.** 渐渐侵蚀某物
• **gnaw through** *vt* [~ **through sth.**] 咬穿

gnawing /ˈnɔːɪŋ/
A *n* [u] 啃; **can you hear that** ~ **sound?** 你听得见那个啃咬声吗?
B *adj* 折磨人的 ‹*pain, remorse, hunger*›

gneiss /naɪs/ *n* [u] 片麻岩

gnome /nəʊm/ *n* 1 (mythical dwarf) 土地神 2 (statue) [装饰花园的] 土地神塑像 3 colloq pej (financier) 资本大鳄

gnomic /ˈnəʊmɪk/ *adj* 1 (aphoristic) 格言式的 ‹*writing, remarks*› 2 (inscrutable) 难以理解的

gnosis /ˈnəʊsɪs/ *n* [u] formal 灵知

gnostic /ˈnɒstɪk/
A *adj* 1 灵知的 ‹*belief*›; ~ **writings** 灵异作品 2 Relig 诺斯替教的
B **Gnostic** *n* 诺斯替教徒

Gnosticism /ˈnɒstɪsɪzəm/ *n* [u] 诺斯替教

GNP *abbr* = **gross national product**

gnu /nuː/ *n* (*pl* **gnu** *or* ~**s**) 牛羚

GNVQ *abbr* Brit = **General National Vocational Qualification** 国家普通职业资格证书

go /gəʊ/ ▸p. 82
A *vi* (*3rd pers sing pres* ~**es,** *pt* **went,** *pp* **gone**) 1 (move, travel) 去; **to** ~ **for a walk/drink** 去散步/喝酒; **to** ~ **swimming/running** 去游泳/跑步; **to** ~ **to/for the doctor** 去看/请医生; **she has gone to China** 她去中国了; **we went economy class** 我们是乘坐经济舱去的; **to** ~ **on holiday** Brit 去度假; **to** ~ **to sb. for sth.** 为某事物去某人处; **she went to fetch them** 她去接他们了; ~ **and see if the bus has arrived** 去看看公交车来了没有; ~ **ask your mom** Amer colloq 去问你妈; **we went in jeans** 我们是穿牛仔裤去的; **where do we** ~ **from here?** fig 我们该往哪走?; **she knows where she's** ~**ing** fig 她有明确的人生目标; **this must** ~ **no further** 这件事一定得保密; **to** ~ **to it** Brit colloq 动手; **100 mph is really** ~**ing some!** colloq 100 英里的时速真叫快啊!; **who** ~**es there?** Mil 什么人?; **to** ~ **missing** 丢失 2 **to** ~ **to sth.** (attend, join) 进入某处; **to** ~ **to school/church** 上学/去教堂; **to** ~ **on the stage** 成为演员; **to** ~ **to work** 上班 3 (become, turn) 变得; **to** ~ **bankrupt** 破产; **my hair went grey** 我的头发变得花白了; **to** ~ **bad** 变坏 4 (perform action) 移动; **the car went skidding off the road** 汽车打滑偏离了公路; **the rabbit went hopping across the field** 野兔蹦跳着穿过田野; **she went like this with her fingers** 她这样动了动她的手指 5 (be conveyed) 被传递; **it can't** ~ **by post** 这个不能邮寄; **their proposal will** ~ **before the board** 他们的建议将提交给董事会 6 (depart) 离开; **we must** ~**, we must be** ~**ing** 我们必须走了; **the last train** ~**es at midnight** 最后一班火车午夜 12 点开出; **the boss will be sorry to see you** ~ 老板看到你离开会感到遗憾的; **two hot dogs to** ~ Amer 两份热狗，带走 7 (be destined, be about to) **to be** ~**ing to do sth.** 将要做某事; **I'm** ~**ing to be sick!** 我要吐了!; **is it** ~**ing to snow?** 要下雪了吗?; **this peace is not** ~**ing to last** 这种和平不会维持下去的 8 (intend to) **to be** ~**ing to do sth.** 打算做某事; **I was just** ~**ing to phone you** 我正要给你打电话呢; **I'm not** ~**ing to hurt you** 我不想伤害你; **I'm not** ~**ing to be treated like that!** 我不会容忍别人那么对待我的! 9 (when giving sth. wanted) **there you** ~ 给; **two sandwiches — there you** ~**!** 来两份三明治——给! 10 (showing confirmation, triumph, or resignation) **there you** ~ 怎么样; **there you** ~**, I told you he would come back** 怎么样，我告诉过你他会回来的 11 (disappear) 消失; (get lost) 丢失; (be used up) 用完; **summer is** ~**ing** 夏天快过去了; **my bike went from outside the house** 我的自行车在屋外丢了; **there** *or* **bang** ~**es our chance of winning first prize!** colloq 我们赢得头奖的机会告吹了! 12 (be spent) «*money*» 花掉; «*aid, tax*» 耗费; **I don't know where my salary** ~**es (to)!** 我不知道我的工资花到哪里去了! 13 (elapse) «*time, days, hours*» 流逝; **the hours went slowly** 时间过得很慢; **there are only three days to** ~ **before Christmas** 离圣诞节只有三天了 14 (be got rid of) «*person*» 被辞退; «*animal, object*» 被丢弃; «*building*» 被拆除; **he'll have to** ~ 他必须辞职; **that lampshade has to** ~ 那个灯罩一定得扔掉; **six down and four to** ~ 处理完了 6 个，还有 4 个要处理 15 (be sold) 被出售; (be let) 被出租; **it was** ~**ing cheap** 价格很便宜; **the house went to the highest bidder** 房子卖给了出价最高的人; ~**ing,** ~**ing, gone!** (at auction) 一次，两次，成交!; **I'm sorry, the room has gone** 对不起，房间租出去了 16 (become impaired) «*hearing, sight, strength*» 受损; **his hearing/eyesight is starting to** ~ 他的听力/视力开始衰退; **my voice has gone** 我说不出话了; **his health/mind is** ~**ing** 他的身体每况愈下/他越来越糊涂了 17 (stop working or being intact) «*support, roof*» 塌落; «*garment, machine, appliance*» 损坏; «*cable*» 断掉; **the brakes went** 刹车失灵了; **my legs went from under me** 我没站稳摔倒了; **the battery's** ~**ing** 蓄电池快用完了; **this jacket has gone at the elbows** 这件短外套肘部磨破了; **there** ~**es another button!** 又掉了一颗扣子! 18 (progress) 进行; (happen) 发生; **how's it** ~**ing?, how are things** ~**ing?, how** ~**es it?** 情况如何?; **the evening went very well** 晚会进行得很顺利; **what** ~**es?** Amer 出什么事了?; **the way things are** ~**ing, …** 看样子…; **he has something** ~**ing with one of his students** 他和他的一个学生有点关系暧昧; **to make the party** ~ **well** 把聚会办得成功 19 colloq (proceed recklessly, thoughtlessly, surprisingly) [表示强调] 竟然做; **now you've gone and done it!** 你竟然干出这种事!; **he only went and won the competition!** 他就那样赢得了比赛! 20 (take one's turn) 轮到; **you** ~ **first** 你先来; **whose turn is it to** ~**?** (in game) 轮到谁了? 21 (extend) 延伸; **the roots of the tree** ~ **very deep** 这棵树的根扎得很深; **this door/corridor** ~**es to the kitchen** 这扇门/这个走廊通往厨房; **volume 3 goes from M to R** 第 3 卷收录的是 M 字头到 R 字头的词条; **it's true as far as it** ~**es** 这还算真实; **these habits** ~ **very deep** 这些习惯根深蒂固; **a leg of lamb doesn't** ~ **very far among twelve people** 一条羊腿不太够 12 个人吃; **money does not** ~ **very far nowadays** 如今钱不太经用; **this** ~**es a long way towards explaining his attitude** 这能很好地解释他的态度; **to** ~ **one better (than sb.)** (比某人) 略胜一筹 22 (move towards certain point) 达到; **the boy will** ~ **far** 那个男孩会有出息的; **to** ~ **too far to back out** 陷得太深，没法退出; **I would even** ~ **as** *or* **so far as to say that …** 我甚至想说…; **to** ~ **further and admit that …** 进而承认… 23 (be bequeathed) 被遗赠; **to** ~ **to sb./sth.** 由…继承 ‹*heir*›; 被捐赠给 ‹*charity*›; **the house will** ~ **to his daughters** 这所房子将留给他的女儿们 24 (be given) 给予; **the judgement went in his favour** 裁决对他有利; **most of the credit should** ~ **to the designer** 大部分功劳应该归设计者; **the job went to a small builder** 这活儿给了一家小建筑公司 25 (move about) 移动; (live) 过活; **to** ~ **naked/armed** 光着身子/带着武器; **to** ~ **in fear of one's life** 总为性命担忧 26 (be on average) 一般而言; **he's not bad, as boys** ~ 和一般男孩子相比，他并不坏; **as things** ~ 就一般情形而言 27 (start) **to get** ~**ing on** *or* **with sth.** 开始做某事; **here** ~**es!, here we** ~**!** colloq 开始!; **there he** ~**es again!** 他又来了!; **ready, steady,** ~**!** Sport 各就位，预备，跑!; **from the word** ~ 从一开始 28 (operate, function) 运转; **to set** *or* **get sth.** ~**ing** 使某物运转起来; **to keep sb./sth.** ~**ing** 使某人坚持下去/让某事继续下去; **the engine won't** ~ 引擎坏了 29 (sound) «*bell, clock*» 响起; **the alarm went at 6** 6 点钟闹钟铃响了 30 (continue, last) 持续; **this strike's already been** ~**ing too long** 这次罢工持续时间太长了; **we can** ~ **days without seeing a soul** 我们能连着好几天看不见一个人 31 (have as content) 内容是; **as the saying** ~**es** 常言道; **the story/rumour** ~**es that …** 据说/有传言说…; **his theory** ~**es something like this** 他的理论大致是这样的; **I can't remember how the next line of the poem** ~**es** 我想不起这首诗的下一行是什么了 32 Mus 被演唱; **how does the song** ~**?** 这首歌是怎么唱的? 33 (contribute) 起作用; **everything that** ~**es to make a good teacher/school** 成为好教师/好学校的一切条件 34 (put oneself through) **to** ~ **to great expense/trouble** 花费很多钱/很大工夫 35 (resort, have recourse) 诉诸; **to** ~ **to war** «*country*» 开战; **to** ~ **to the relevant authority** 诉诸有关当局; **to** ~ **to law** Brit *or* **the law** Amer 诉诸法律; **to** ~ **to the country** Brit Pol 进行大选 36 (change to become) 变为; **to** ~ **vegetarian** 变成素食者; **to** ~ **metric** 实行公制; **the constituency went Conservative** 这个选区的选民转而支持保守党 37 (be, remain) 保持; **to** ~ **unnoticed/unpunished** 未被察觉/惩罚; **most of the population went hungry** 大多数人挨饿; **criminals were allowed to** ~ **free** 犯人们被释放了; **to** ~ **easy on sb.** 宽容地对待某人 38 (belong) 应放置; (be placed) 被放置; **this** ~**es under a different heading** 这个应放在其他标题下; **the suitcases will have to** ~ **in the back** 这些手提箱只能放在后面 39 (be on offer) 可供应; **to be** ~**ing** «*item for sale*» 能买到; «*job*» 可得到; **I'll have whatever's** ~**ing** 有什么我就吃什么; **there's a job** ~**ing at the London office** 伦敦办事处有一份工作空缺 40 colloq (urinate, defecate) 上厕所; **I need to** ~ **(really badly)** 我(憋不住)要上厕所了 41 (be accepted) 被接受; **what I say,** ~**es!** 凡是我说的都得照办!; **anything** ~**es these days** 如今无奇不有; **it** ~**es without saying that …** 不用说… 42 euph (die) 去世; **after I** ~ 我走了之后
B *vt* (*3rd pers sing pres* ~**es,** *pt* **went,** *pp* **gone**) 1 (travel) 走过 ‹*distance*›; 沿着 ‹*route*›; **we had gone only 3 km** 我们只走了 3 公里; **are you** ~**ing my way?** 你和我同路吗?; **to** ~ **one's own way** fig 我行我素 2 colloq (say) 说; (make sound) 出声; **so he** ~**es, 'what about my money?'** 于是他说: "我的钱呢?"; **the cat went miaow** 猫喵了一声 3 (bet, bid) 出 ‹*suit*›; 下…的赌注 ‹*sum of money*›; **I'm** ~**ing £10 on the red** 我给红方押 10 英镑; **he went three spades** 他出了 3 张黑桃 4 (proceed) **to** ~ **it** Brit colloq 干得起劲; **to** ~ **it alone** 独自行动
C *n* (*pl* ~**es**) 1 [u] Brit (energy) 精力; **to be full of** ~**, to be all** ~ 精力充沛; **she has no** ~ **in her** 她没有热情 2 [c] Brit (turn) 轮; **it's your** ~ **now** 轮到你了 3 [c] Brit (try) 尝试; **to have a** ~ **at sth.** 尝试做某事; **someone has had a** ~ **at this lock** 有人鼓捣过这把

g

锁; **to have a ~ at sb.** (criticize) 批评某人; (try to annoy) 招惹某人; **to have a ~ on sth.** 试一下某物 [4] [c] (spell of action) 一阵行动; **at one** *or* **a ~, in one ~** 一下子; **to do sth. in two ~es** 分两次做某事 [5] [u and c] (success) 成功; **to make a ~ of sth.** 在某事上取得成功 [6] [u] colloq dated (fashion) **to be all the ~** 十分流行 [7] [u] **on the ~** (busy) 忙碌; (active) 在进行; **to keep sb. on the ~** 让某人忙个不停

(Phrasal verbs)

- **go about**

A [~ **about sth.**] *vt*

[1] (undertake) 着手处理; **how do you ~ about losing weight?** 你是如何开始减肥的? [2] (be busy with) 忙于; **I'm just ~ing about my business** 我正忙着我的事呢 [3] (move round) 四处走动; **he ~es about town in a Rolls** 他开着一辆劳斯莱斯到处转

B *vi* [1] (associate) 交往; **he's ~ing about with an unpleasant set of people** 他结交了一帮不三不四的人; **she's ~ing about with Paul now** 她现在和保罗泡在一起 [2] **to ~ about doing sth.** (make habit of) 习惯于做某事; **he ~es about boasting about his new job** 他总是吹嘘他的新工作 [3] (circulate) 散布; **he caught a bug that's ~ing about** 他染上了一种流行传染病; **there's a story ~ing about that ...** 有传言说… [4] Naut 改变航程

- **go across**

A *vt* [~ **across sth.**] 穿过; **to ~ across the street/river** 穿过街道/过河

B *vi* 穿过; **she went across to Mrs Brown's** 她去了路对面布朗太太家

- **go after** *vt* [**to ~ after sth./sb.**]

[1] (chase) 追赶 [2] (aim for) 追求; **he's really ~ing after that job** 他确实在谋求那份工作

- **go against** *vt* [~ **against sth.**]

[1] (resist, oppose, conflict with) 违背; **it ~es against my conscience** 这有违我的良心; **to ~ against the tide** 逆潮流而动 [2] (prove unfavourable to) 对…不利; **the vote/verdict went against him** 投票/裁决对他不利; **if fate ~es against us** 如果我们不走运

- **go ahead** *vi* [1] (go in front) 走在前面; **~ ahead, I'll follow on** 你先走, 我随后就去 [2] **to ~ ahead of sb./sth.** (overtake) 领先某人/某物; **Arsenal went ahead of their rivals** 阿森纳队领先于对手 [3] (proceed) 开始进行; **to ~ ahead (with sth.)** 开始进行（某事）; **~ ahead and shoot!** 快开枪!; **next week's strike is to ~ ahead** 下个星期的罢工将照常进行; **to ~ ahead with the plan** 实行计划 [4] (progress) 继续进行; **work is ~ing ahead steadily** 工作正在稳步开展

- **go along**

A *vi* [1] (go as companion) 一起去; **he's asked me to ~ along (with him)** 他请我（跟他）一起去 [2] (move along) 沿某物向前移动 [3] fig (progress) 进行; **he's making it up as he ~es along** 他现编现讲

B *vt* [~ **along sth.**] (move along) 沿…向前移动; **to ~ along the road** 沿马路向前走

- **go along with** *vt* [~ **along with sth./sb.**]

[1] (obey) 服从; **I didn't agree, but I went along with her wishes** 我没有同意, 但我顺从了她的愿望 [2] (agree with) 赞同; **I can't ~ along with that** 那件事我不能同意

- **go around** *vi, vt* esp Amer = **go round**
- **go at** *vt* [~ **at sth./sb.**]

[1] (set to work on) 开始处理; **you're ~ing at it the wrong way** 你的方法错了 [2] (attack) 攻击; **the dog went at the postman** 那只狗扑向邮递员 [3] (eat greedily) 贪婪地吃 [4] (play, do energetically) 卖力干 [5] (be sold at) 以…的价格出售

- **go away** *vi* [1] (leave) 离开; **~ away and leave me alone!** 走开, 别烦我!; **don't ~ away thinking** *or* **with the idea that ...** 别以为…; **to ~ away (on holiday** Brit *or* **vacation** Amer**)** 去度假 [2] (disappear) «*problem*» 消失

- **go back** *vi* [1] (return, turn back) 返回; **they went back home** 他们回家了; **she won't ~ back to her husband** 她不肯回到她丈夫身边; **to ~ back on one's steps** 顺原路返回; **to ~ back on one's word** 食言; **this dress will have to ~ back** 这件连衣裙得退回去; **to ~ back to the beginning** 回到开始; **once you've committed yourself, there's no ~ing back** 你一旦作出承诺就不能反悔 [2] (extend backwards) 向后延伸; **the cave ~es back 300 metres** 这个洞进深 300 米 [3] **to ~ back to sth./doing sth.** (revert) 恢复某事物/做某事; **to ~ back to sleep** 再入睡; **to ~ back to the old system/one's former habits** 恢复旧制度/先前的习惯; **to ~ back to teaching** 重新执教 [4] (look back in time) 回忆; **my memory doesn't ~ so far back/back that far** 我记不起那么久远的事情; **to understand the problem we must ~ back fifty years** 要弄清这个问题, 我们必须回到 50 年以前 [5] (have history tracing back to) 追溯; **the family ~es back to the Norman Conquest** 这个家族可追溯到诺曼征服时期; **we ~ back a long way** 我们认识很久了

- **go before**

A *vt* [~ **before sb./sth.**]

[1] (go in front of) 到…前面; **the trumpeters went before the procession** 号手们走在队列前面 [2] Jur, Pol «*accused person*» 到…前 ‹*court*›; «*case*» 提交给; **the bill went before parliament** 这项议案提交给了议会 [3] (live earlier than) 在世时间早于

B *vi* [1] (happen earlier) 先发生; **all that has gone before** 先前发生的一切 [2] liter (go in front) 走到前面; **he went before to warn them** 他走上前去向他们提出警告

- **go below** *vi* Naut 到下层甲板
- **go by**

A *vi* [1] (elapse, pass) 过去; **as time ~es by** 随着时间流逝 [2] (move by) «*person*» 走过; «*vehicle*» 驶过 [3] (be lost) «*opportunity, chance*» 错失

B *vt* [~ **by sth./sb.**]

[1] (obey, proceed by) 按照; **to ~ by the position of the sun** 按照太阳的位置; **promotion ~es by seniority** 按照资历晋升 [2] (be lost to) 被…错过; **the opportunity went right by her** 机会和她擦肩而过 [3] (judge by) 以…判断; **to ~ by appearances** 凭外表判断; **~ing by her looks, she's under 20** 从她的外表来看, 她不到 20 岁; **if the trailer is anything to ~ by, it should be a good film** 如果预告片可信, 这应该是部好电影 [4] (be called by) 被叫做; **to ~ by another name** 叫另一个名字

- **go down**

A *vi* [1] (descend) «*person*» 下楼; «*vehicle*» 下行; «*road*» 向下延伸; **'~ing down!'** "下行!" [2] (fall) «*person, animal, building*» 倒下; «*aircraft*» 坠落 [3] (set) «*sun, moon*» 落下; **when the sun went down on the Roman Empire** 当罗马帝国最终灭亡时 [4] (sink) 沉没; **most of the passengers went down with the ship** 大多数乘客随船一起沉到水下 [5] (lessen) «*tide*» 退下; «*sea*» 退潮; «*water level, temperature*» 下降; **when the floods ~ down** 当洪水落下时; **his fever is ~ing down** 他正在退烧 [6] (lower body) 俯身; **to ~ down on all fours** «*person, animal*» 趴下 [7] (be swallowed) «*food*» 被吞下; «*drink*» 被喝下; **it went down the wrong way** 它咽到气管里了 [8] **to ~ down to sth.** (continue) 继续下去到某处; **if you ~ down to the bottom of the page you will see that ...** 如果你读到这一页的最下面你会看到…; **the championship went down to the last race** 直到最后一项比赛才决出冠军 [9] (extend) «*area of land, building*» 向前延伸; «*garment*» 垂下; **the skirt ~es down to the ankles** 这条裙子长及脚踝 [10] (deflate) «*tyre, balloon*» 瘪下去 [11] (get less swollen) «*ankle, knee*» 消肿 [12] (reduce in value, size, price) «*standard, quality, price*» 下降; «*commodity*» 降价; «*food*» 变差; «*shares, fund, value*» 贬值; «*amount, number*» 减少; «*weight*» 降低; **she's gone down in my estimation** 我对她的看法不如以前了; **the picture has gone down in value** 那幅画贬值了; **our readership has gone down** 我们的读者减少了; **I went down to 100 lbs** 我的体重降到了 100 磅 [13] (be downgraded) 降级; **the team went down to the second division** 这支队降到了乙级; **to ~ down a class** Sch 降一级 [14] (be defeated) «*competitor, team*» 被击败; **Spain went down to Holland 2-1** 西班牙队以 1:2 输给了荷兰队; **at least they went down fighting** 至少他们是战败的 [15] (go south) «*person, vehicle*» 南下; «*road*» 向南延伸; **we went down to Marseilles from Paris** 我们从巴黎南下到了马赛 [16] (go from capital) 离开首都; (go from centre) 离开中心地区; **to ~ down to the country/the sea** 去乡下/海边; **to ~ down from London** 离开伦敦 [17] Brit colloq (leave university) 离校 [尤指离开牛津或剑桥]; **he went down (from Oxford) in 1985** 他于 1985 年（自牛津）大学毕业 [18] Brit colloq (go to prison) 进监狱 [19] (be remembered) 被记住; **he will ~ down as a great statesman** 他作为一个伟大的政治家将名垂青史 [20] (be recorded) 被记录; **it all ~es down in his diary** 这都记在他的日记里 [21] (be received) 被接受; **to ~ down well/badly** 受到/不受欢迎 [22] Theat «*curtain*» 落下 [23] Comput «*computer, system*» 暂停运行 [24] colloq (happen) 发生; **I knew something was ~ing down** 我早知道有事会发生

B *vt* [~ **down sth.**]

[1] (move down) 下行; **the car was ~ing down the hill** 汽车正沿山坡下行; **a shiver went down my spine** 我背上一阵发冷 [2] (go to) 前去; **she's gone down the shops** 她去了商店

- **go down on** *vt* [~ **down on sb.**] taboo sl 对…口交
- **go down with** *vt* [~ **down with sth.**] 患…病; **to ~ down with flu/a cold** 患流感/感冒
- **go for** *vt* [~ **for sb./sth.**]

[1] (attack physically) 袭击; (attack verbally) 抨击; **the two youths went for him** 那两个年轻人揍了他; **~ for him, boy!** (to dog) 去咬他, 小家伙!; **his wife really went for him** 他妻子狠狠地数落了他 [2] (like) 喜欢; **he doesn't ~ for modern art much** 他不太喜欢现代艺术 [3] (choose) 选择; **designers have gone for a romantic look this year** 设计师们今年选择了浪漫的风格 [4] (attempt to achieve) 争取; **to ~ for gold/the world record** 争取得金牌/打破世界记录; **the company is ~ing for a new image** 公司正努力改变形象; **~ for it!** colloq 努力争取吧! [5] (apply to) 适用于; **the same ~es for Poland too** 波兰也是如此; **that ~es for me too** (applies to me) 我也一样; colloq (I agree) 我同意 [6] (be sold at) 以…的价格出售; **the house went for over £450,000** 这房子售价超过 45 万英镑 [7] **to have something/everything ~ing for one** (being favourable to) 有某些/一切有利条件; **he's got a lot ~ing for him** 他有很多优势

- **go forth** *vi* liter [1] (go out) 出发; (go onwards) 前进; **~ forth and multiply** (biblical command) 去繁衍生息吧 [2] (be issued) «*order, command*» 被传达
- **go forward** *vi* [1] (advance) 行进 [2] (progress) 取得进展; **to ~ forward to the final** 进入决赛 [3] (proceed) **to ~ forward with sth.** 开始某事; **to ~ forward with construction work** 开始施工
- **go in**

A *vi* [1] (enter, attend) 进入; **I don't have to ~ in (to work) today** 我今天不必去上班 [2] (fit) «*key, pin, box*» 放得进; **listen carefully: I want this to ~ in** fig 仔细听着: 我要你明白这个 [3] (go behind cloud) «*sun, moon*» 躲进云层 [4] Mil, Police 发动进攻; **the police went**

g

in to break up the demonstration 警察冲进来驱散示威群众

B *vt* [~ in sth.]

1 (enter) 进入 ‹*building, shop*› 2 (fit in) «*key, pin, box*» 放得进; **the box was too big to ~ in the cupboard** 这箱子太大, 放不进橱柜里

• **go in for** *vt* [~ in for sth.]

1 (be keen on) 热衷于; **he ~es in for opera in a big way** 他非常喜欢歌剧 2 Brit (enter for) 参加 ‹*competition, test*›

• **go into** *vt* [~ into sth.]

1 (enter place) 进入; **to ~ into hospital** 住院 2 (enter state) 进入…状态; **to ~ into a coma/deep sleep** 昏迷/陷入沉睡 3 (fit inside) 能放进; **will this ~ into the bag?** 这个能放进包里吗? 4 Math 能除尽; **6 ~es into 18 three times** 6 除 18 得 3 5 (hit) 撞上; **we went into a lamp post** 我们撞了一根灯柱 6 (examine, investigate) 调查; **to ~ into a question/case** 研究问题/调查案件 7 (explain) 解释; **I won't ~ into why I did it** 我不会解释我的动机的 8 (launch into, begin to do) 开始; **to ~ into a long explanation** 开始长篇大论地解释; **the car went into a skid** 汽车开始打滑 9 (be expended on) 花费在…上; **after all the money/work that has gone into this** 在这上面投入了这么多钱/做了这么多工作之后 10 Publg 以…形式出版; **to ~ into paperback/its tenth edition** 以简装本出版/出到第 10 版

• **go off**

A *vi* 1 (depart) 离开; **he went off to work** 他去上班了; **the goalkeeper had to ~ off** 守门员不得不退场 2 (be fired) «*gun*» 开火 3 (explode) «*bomb*» 爆炸 4 (sound) «*alarm*» 响起 5 (leave work) 下班 6 Theat (leave stage) 下场 7 Brit (go bad) «*food, drink*» 变质; **the wine/milk went off** 葡萄酒坏了/牛奶馊了 8 (cease to operate) 停止运作; **the power/light went off** 停电了/熄灯了 9 (fall asleep) 入睡 10 (deteriorate) 变坏; **the flowers are ~ing off now** 这些花蔫了 11 (grow less intense) 减轻; **the pain is ~ing off a bit** 疼痛有所缓解 12 (happen, take place) 进行; **the concert went off very well** 音乐会办得很成功 13 (enter state) **to ~ off into sth.** 进入某种状态; **she went off into a trance** 她陷入昏睡 14 (launch into) **to ~ off into sth.** 开始某事; **she went off into a monologue** 她开始长篇大论

B *vt* [~ off sb./sth.] Brit colloq 开始厌烦; **to ~ off one's boyfriend** 不再喜欢自己的男友

• **go off with** *vt* 1 [~ off with sth.] (take away) 擅自拿走; **he's gone off with my keys** 他顺手牵羊拿走了我的钥匙; **she went off with all his money** 她卷走了他所有的钱 2 [~ off with sb.] (leave with) 与…私奔; **he's gone off with my wife** 他和我老婆私奔了

• **go on**

A *vi* 1 (continue onwards) 继续行进; **you ~ on, we'll follow** 你先走, 我们随后; **after stopping at Carlisle, this train ~es on to Glasgow** 在卡莱尔停靠之后, 这趟列车接着开往格拉斯哥 2 (happen, take place) 发生; **what's ~ing on here?** 这里发生什么事了? 3 (continue) 继续; **we can't ~ on like this** 我们不能这样继续下去; **~ on, we're listening** 接着说, 我们听着呢; **the meeting went on into the afternoon** 会一直开到下午; **as the evening went on, he became more animated** 夜渐深, 他越发活跃了; **~ on, have a sherry!** 来, 喝杯雪利酒! ; **~ on (with you)!** colloq 去你的吧! ; **it went on raining** 雨不停地下着 4 **to ~ on to sth./to do sth.** (proceed to do) 继而做某事; **to ~ on to the next item** 接着处理下一项; **she went on to explain that ...** 她随后解释说… 5 (progress) 取得进展; **how's the patient/business ~ing on?** 病人/生意怎么样了? 6 **to be ~ing on (for) sth.** (be approaching) 接近某物; **it's ~ing on for 5 o'clock** 快 5 点了; **he's thirty, ~ing on thirty one** 他 30 岁了, 快到 31 7 (elapse) 过去 8 colloq (behave) 表现; **to ~ on in a dreadful way** 表现糟糕 9 (manage) 维持; **here's £50 to be ~ing on with** 眼下有 50 英镑可以将就 10 (keep talking) 唠叨; **'you know,' she went on, 'it's ridiculous'** "你知道," 她唠叨着说, "这很可笑"; **to ~ on and on** 唠叨个没完; **to ~ on at sb.** 对某人叨扰 11 Theat, Sport «*actor, substitute*» 上场; **A went on (for B) in the second half** A 在下半场上场 (替换了 B) 12 (fit) «*fitment, component*» 安装上; «*garment*» 穿上; «*piece of jewellery*» 戴上; **the ring won't ~ on** 戒指戴不上; **the top ~es on like this** 盖子是这样盖的 13 (begin to operate) «*machine*» 开始运作; **the heating ~es on at 6 o'clock** 6 点钟开始供暖

B *vt* [~ on sth.]

1 (fit) «*fitment, component*» 安装到…上; «*garment*» 穿到…上; «*piece of jewellery*» 戴到…上 2 (judge by) 依…判断; **the police had no clues to ~ on** 警方没有线索可循 3 (take part in) 参加; **she's gone on a training course** 她报名上了一门培训课 4 (undertake) 开始; **to ~ on a training regime** 开始常规训练 5 (be spent on) 花费在…上; **most of his money ~es on drink** 他的钱大部分都花在喝酒上了 6 **to be gone on sth.** colloq (like) 喜欢某物; **I'm really gone on that new car of his** 我真的喜欢他那辆新车 7 (ride on) 乘坐; **to ~ on the swing** 荡秋千 8 (be fuelled by) 以…为燃料; **to ~ on petrol/diesel** 以汽油/柴油为燃料

C **going on (for)** *prep phr* 将近; **it'll cost ~ing on (for) £70** 它要花将近 70 英镑

• **go on to** *vt* [~ on to sth.] «*component, lid*» 安装到…上; «*garment*» 适合…穿; «*piece of jewellery*» 适合…戴; **the ring won't ~ on to the right finger** 戒指没法戴到该戴的手指上

• **go out** *vi* 1 (go outside, leave) 出门; (for specific purpose) 外出做事; (socially) 出门交际; **to ~ out for a walk** 出去散步; **she likes ~ing out** 她喜欢外出参加社交活动; **to ~ out to the shops** 去商店; **to ~ out riding/shopping** 外出骑马/购物 2 **to ~ out to somewhere** (travel long distance) 到某地长途旅行; (travel to emigrate) 移居国外某地; **they went out to Nigeria** 他们去尼日利亚了 3 (be sent out, published, broadcast) «*information*» 发布; «*summons, invitation*» 发出; «*publication*» 发表; «*TV, radio programme*» 播放; **the magazine ~es out to all our subscribers** 这份杂志分发给我们所有的订阅者; **the news/word went out that ...** 有消息说/据说…; **a warrant has gone out for her arrest** 已对她发出逮捕令; **the programme is ~ing out live** 这个节目正在现场直播 4 **to ~ out with sb.** (have relationship with) 与某人约会; **he's been ~ing out with Jane** 他一直在和简约会; **they started to ~ out together** 他们开始相恋 5 **to ~ out to sb.** (be offered) «*sympathy, compassion*» 表露给某人; **my heart went out to him in his sorrow** 他伤心时我很同情他; **all our sympathy ~es out to you** 我们非常同情你 6 (recede) «*tide*» 退潮 7 (be extinguished) «*light, fire, cigarette*» 熄灭; **I went out like a light** 我立刻睡着了 8 (become unfashionable) «*fashion, activity*» 过时; **ankle-length skirts went out two years ago** 长及脚踝的裙子两年前就不时兴了 9 (be discontinued) «*custom, institution*» 消失; **gas lighting went out and was replaced by electricity** 煤气照明被电力取代, 不再使用了

• **go out of** *vt* [~ out of sth.]

1 (leave) 从…中出来; **the cat went out of the door** 猫从门出去了; **all my hopes went out of the window** 我的希望全破灭了 2 (disappear from) 从…中消失; **all the spirit seemed to have gone out of her** 她似乎丧失了一切斗志; **the romance had gone out of their relationship** 他们之间已经没有爱情了

• **go over**

A *vi* 1 (cross over) 穿过去; **he went over and asked her** 他走过去问她; **a plane went over** 一架飞机从上空飞过 2 (overturn) 倾覆; **the car hit the kerb and went right over** 汽车撞在路缘上一下子翻了 3 (be received) 受欢迎; **his speech went over well** 他的演讲很受欢迎; **to ~ over big** colloq 很成功

B *vt* [~ over sth.]

1 (visit, tour) 参观; **we went over the house with our hosts/the estate agent** 我们随主人/房地产经纪人看了房子; **there's no point in ~ing over old ground** 没有必要旧事重提 2 (check, inspect) 检查 ‹*report, accounts*› 3 (review) 回顾; **to ~ over the explanation again** 再解释一遍; **she went over the events of the day in her mind** 她把白天发生的事在脑子里过了一遍; **to ~ over one's lines** 复习台词 4 (clean) 打扫; **I went over the carpet with the vacuum cleaner** 我用吸尘器清理了地毯 5 (spend more than) 超出; **don't ~ over £40** 不要超过 40 英镑 6 (retrace) 润饰; **he went over the drawing in ink** 他用墨水把图描画了一遍

• **go over to** *vt* [~ over to sb./sth.]

1 (cross over to, travel to) 向…走过去; **she went over to him/the window** 她走到他身边/窗户前; **the ferry ~es over to Calais twice a day** 渡船每天去加来两次; **to ~ over to Washington for the latest news** 切换到华盛顿看最新消息 2 (desert to) 转投; **he went over to the Conservatives/the enemy** 他转向了保守党一边/投靠了敌人 3 (switch to) 转变到 ‹*system, function*›; **they've gone over to gas central heating** 他们已改用煤气中央供暖系统; **the factory went over to making doughnuts** 这家工厂改做甜甜圈了

• **go round**

A *vi* 1 (spin) «*wheel, propeller*» 转动; **the tape was still ~ing round** 磁带还在转 2 (move about) 到处走动; **to ~ round barefoot** 光着脚到处跑 3 (suffice) 足够分发; **there aren't enough books/there isn't enough food to ~ round** 书/食物不够分 4 (make detour) 绕道; **to ~ a/the long way round** 绕行很长的/这条很长的路; **we went round via Manchester** 我们绕道曼切斯特 5 (call round) 去拜访; **to ~ round to** *or* **and see sb.** 去看望某人; **we went round to Jim's house** 我们去吉姆家了 6 (associate) 经常在一起; **he's ~ing round with a bad bunch** 他和一帮坏人混在一起; **she's ~ing round with Paul now** 她正在和保罗谈恋爱 7 **to ~ round doing sth.** pej (make habit of) 习惯于做某事; **he ~es round boasting about his new job** 他总是吹嘘他的新工作 8 (circulate) 散布; **he caught a bug that's ~ing round** 他染上了一种流行传染病; **there's a story ~ing round that ...** 有传言说…

B *vt* [~ round sb./sth.]

1 (encircle) 围绕; **the belt wouldn't ~ round me** 这皮带的长度还不及我的腰围; **the rope went round the tree twice** 绳子绕树两圈 2 (move about) 在…到处走动; **he went round several companies trying to sell the idea** 他到几家公司游说他的想法 3 (turn) 绕过 ‹*corner, obstacle*›; **the car went round the roundabout the wrong way** 那辆车在环岛处拐错了方向

• **go through**

A *vi* 1 (move or travel through) 通过; **please ~ (on) through** 请进去吧 2 (be successfully completed) «*deal, transaction*» 达成 3 (progress) 往下进行; **they need only a draw to ~ through** 他们只需要打成平局就能进入下一轮比赛 4 Jur, Pol (be approved) 获得通过; **the bill failed to ~ through** 法案没有通过

B *vt* [~ through sth.]

1 (move or travel through) 通过; **to ~ through the gate/tunnel** 穿过大门/隧道; **to ~**

through the switchboard/the right authorities 经过交换台/通过正当的官方; the table won't ~ through the door 桌子没法通过这道门; it went through my mind that ... 我想起… 2 (search) 查遍 ‹*files*›; 搜遍 ‹*suitcase, drawer, possessions*›; to ~ through one's pockets/handbag 翻遍口袋/手提包 3 (inspect, check) 仔细检查 ‹*document, essay, mail*›; 仔细讲解 ‹*text*›; let's ~ through the points one by one 我们把这几点逐一研究一下吧 4 (read out, specify) 一一读出; to ~ through the register/list of names 点名; please ~ through exactly what's needed 请一一报出所需要的东西 5 (undergo) 经历 ‹*difficulties, war, period of time*›; 经受 ‹*test, interview*›; he went through several operations 他做过几次手术; we've all gone through difficult times 我们全都经历过艰难时刻; after all he's gone through 在他经历过这一切之后; he went through the day in a haze 他迷迷糊糊地度过了一天 6 (perform, accomplish) 完成; he went through the day's work in a couple of hours 他用了几个小时便做完了白天的工作; to ~ through the formalities 办手续 7 (rehearse) 排练; let's ~ through the whole scene once more 我们把这一场再排练一遍 8 (progress through) 经过 ‹*draft*›; the plan went through several stages 计划经过了几个阶段; this book has already gone through 13 editions 这本书已经连续出了13版 9 (consume, use up) 用完; we went through four bottles of wine 我们喝了4瓶葡萄酒; he has gone through four cars/secretaries hum 他开坏了4辆汽车/用过4个秘书 10 (make hole in) 磨破 11 Jur, Pol (be approved) 在…获得通过; the bill is going through the upper house 议案正在上院审议

- **go through with** *vt* [~ through with sth.] 努力完成; they went through with their marriage for appearances' sake 他们为了面子操办了婚礼
- **go together** *vi* 1 (harmonize, be compatible) «*furnishings*» 协调; «*clothes, people*» 相配; these colours don't really ~ together 这些颜色不十分搭配; lamb and mint sauce ~ well together 羊肉和薄荷汁很对味 2 (co-exist) 共存; poverty and crime often ~ together 贫穷和犯罪往往相伴而生
- **go towards** *vt* [~ towards sth.] 作为…的部分款项; the money will ~ towards a new car 这笔钱将用于购买新车
- **go under**

A *vi* 1 (sink, submerge) «*ship*» 沉没; «*person*» 沉入水中 2 (fail) 失败; his business finally went under 他的公司最终倒闭了
B *vt* [~ under sth.] 叫做; he ~es under the name of Brown 他名叫布朗

- **go up**

A *vi* 1 (ascend) 上去; the children went up to bed 孩子们上床了; '~ing up!' "上行!"; to ~ up in the world (in status) 飞黄腾达; (in wealth) 发迹 2 (rise up) 升起; a cloud of dust went up as they rode past 他们骑车经过时带起了一股灰尘 3 (continue) to ~ up to sth. «*account, book*» 延续到…; the series ~es up to 1990 这个系列写到1990年; I went up to £100 but I didn't get it (at auction) 我出价到100英镑,但没把它拍到手 4 (extend upwards) 向上延伸; (extend along) 向前延伸; the road ~es up as far as the summit 这条路向上通往山顶; the socks went up to his knees 这双袜子长及他的膝部 5 (be erected or installed) «*building*» 被建造; «*poster*» 被张贴; «*flag*» 升起; new office blocks are ~ing up 正在兴建新办公大楼 6 (increase) 增长; the house went up in value 这所房子升值了; our membership has gone up 我们的会员增加了 7 (be upgraded) 升级; the team went up to the first division 这支队升到了甲级; to ~ up a class Sch 升一级 8 (improve) 提高; standards are ~ing up 标准正在提高; he's gone up in my estimation 我对他的看法比以前好了 9 (go north) 北上; they've gone up to Scotland 他们北上苏格兰了 10 (go to capital) 前往首都; (go to centre) 前往中心; to ~ up to London 上伦敦去 11 (be destroyed by explosion) 被炸毁; (be destroyed by fire) 被烧毁; the house went up in flames/smoke 那所房子火光熊熊/烟雾腾腾 12 Brit colloq (start university) 上大学; (start term) 开学 13 (be emitted) «*noise*» 爆发; cheers/a shout went up from the crowd 人群中爆发出欢呼声/喊叫声 14 (approach) 走近 ‹*place, person*›; I went up to the bar 我走到酒吧柜台; he went up to Lewis and punched him 他走近刘易斯,打了他一拳
B *vt* [~ up sth.]
1 (ascend) 上到 ‹*mountain, hill*› 2 (go along) 沿…前行; she's just gone up the street 她刚刚沿街道走过去

- **go with**

A [~ with sth.] *vt*
1 (be compatible with) 与…相配; white wine ~es with fish better than red wine 白葡萄酒配鱼要比红葡萄酒更对味 2 (accompany) 与…并存; responsibility ~es with motherhood 为人母亲即意味着责任; the house ~es with the job 做这份工作能享用这所房子 3 (follow) 顺应; to ~ with the times/the crowd 合乎时代/随大溜
B [~ with sb.] *vt*
1 (accompany) 与…一起 2 colloq (spend time with) 和…相好

- **go without**

A *vt* [~ without sth.] 没有…而勉强应付; to ~ without food 挨饿; it ~es without saying that ... 显而易见…
B *vi* 没有也行; if you can't afford lunch, you'll have to ~ without 如果你买不起午饭,就只好将就着不吃了

goad /gəʊd/
A *n* [赶牛用的] 尖头棒
B *vt* 1 (prod) [用尖头棒] 驱赶 ‹*cattle*› 2 fig (provoke) 刺激; to ~ sb. to violence 驱使某人使用暴力

go-ahead
A *adj* 有进取心的 ‹*person, attitude*›; 开拓型的 ‹*organization, company*›
B *n* the ~ 批准; to get the ~ from sb. 得到某人许可; to give sb. the ~ (for sth./to do sth.) 批准某人(做某事)

goal /gəʊl/ *n* 1 Sport (area) 球门; (net) 球篮; to keep ~, to play in ~ 当守门员 2 Sport (point) 进球得分; to score/miss a ~ 进/失一个球; our team won by 6 ~s to 3 我们球队以6比3获胜 3 (objective) 目标; to achieve/attain/reach one's ~ 达到目标

goal area *n* 球门区

goalie /'gəʊli/ *n* colloq 守门员

goal: ~keeper *n* 守门员; **~ kick** *n* 球门球

goalless /'gəʊllɪs/ *adj* Brit 零进球的; a ~ match/draw 零比零的比赛/平局

goal: ~ line *n* 球门线; **~mouth** *n* 球门口; **~post** *n* 球门柱; to move the ~posts fig 改变规则; **~scorer** *n* 得分射手

goat /gəʊt/ *n* 1 [c] (animal) 山羊 2 [u] (as food) 山羊肉 3 [c] Brit colloq (fool) 蠢货; to act the ~ 干蠢事; silly old ~! 老笨蛋!; to get sb.'s ~ colloq 使某人恼火 4 [c] colloq (lecher) 色鬼 5 the G~ (Capricorn) 摩羯(星)座

goatee /gəʊ'tiː/ *n* 山羊胡子

goatherd /'gəʊthɜːd/ *n* 牧羊人

goatskin /'gəʊtskɪn/ *n* [c and u] 山羊皮; ~ rug/jacket 山羊皮小地毯/夹克

gob /gɒb/ sl
A *n* 1 [c] Brit (mouth) 嘴; you and your big ~! 都怪你那张大嘴! 2 [u] (spittle) 唾沫 3 [c] (soft mass) 黏糊糊的一团; a ~ of chewing gum 一团口香糖
B *vi* (*pres p etc.* -bb-) Brit 吐唾沫

gobbet /'gɒbɪt/ *n* (of meat, food) 一块; (of viscous matter) 一团

gobble[1] /'gɒbl/
A *vt* 大口吞吃
B *vi* 大口吞吃; eat it properly, don't ~! 注意吃相,不要狼吞虎咽!

Phrasal verbs

- **gobble down** *vt* [~ down sth., ~ sth. down] 大口吞下
- **gobble up** *vt* [~ up sth., ~ sth. up]
1 lit 大口吞吃 2 fig (use up) 很快消耗掉 3 fig (take over) 吞并

gobble[2]
A *vi* «*turkey*» 咯咯叫
B *n* 咯咯叫声

gobbledygook /'gɒbldɪguːk/ *n* [u] colloq 官样文章

gobbler /'gɒblə(r)/ *n* colloq 1 Amer (turkey) 雄火鸡 2 pej (person) 狼吞虎咽的人

go-between *n* (in love affair, marriage) 媒人; (in negotiation, business deal) 中间人

Gobi /'gəʊbi/ *pr n* 戈壁; the ~ desert 戈壁沙漠

goblet /'gɒblɪt/ *n* 高脚杯

goblin /'gɒblɪn/ *n* 小妖怪

gobsmacked /'gɒbsmækt/ *adj* Brit colloq 大吃一惊的; to be ~ at *or* by sth. 被某事物惊呆了

go-by *n* colloq the ~ 冷落; to give sb./sth. the ~ 怠慢某人/对某物视而不见

go-cart *n* 1 Amer (toy cart) 拉拉车 2 Motor racing = **go-kart**

god /gɒd/
A *n* 1 Relig (divine being) 神; Norse ~s 北欧诸神 2 (person) [被崇拜的] 偶像; (thing) 推崇备至的事物; to be sb.'s ~ 是某人的神圣要务; money is his ~ 他视钱如命
B **God** *pr n* 1 Relig (supreme being) (in Christianity) 上帝; (in Catholicism) 天主; so help me God 上天作证; would to God that ... 但愿…; a man of God 教士 2 colloq (in exclamations) (exasperated) 见鬼; (surprised) 居然这样; my God 天啊; by God 老天在上; God forbid he should find out! 但愿他不会查明真相!; she lives God knows where 天晓得她住在哪里; God knows I've tried! 请上天作证我已经努力了!; for God's sake 看在上帝的分上; God willing 如系天意

God Almighty
A *n* 全能的上帝
B *excl* colloq 我的天啊

god: ~-awful *adj* colloq 非常恐怖的 ‹*noise, place*›; 糟透的 ‹*film, food*›; **~child** *n* (boy) 教子; (girl) 教女

goddammit /'gɒddæmɪt/ *excl* Amer colloq 该死

goddamn /'gɒddæm/ colloq
A *n* 丝毫; not to give a ~ about sth. 毫不在乎某事物
B *adj* esp Amer 该死的
C *adv* 极其; don't be so ~ stupid! 别傻到那种地步!

goddaughter /'gɒddɔːtə(r)/ *n* 教女

goddess /'gɒdɪs/ *n* (divinity) 女神; (woman) 极受崇敬的女子; a screen ~ 银幕女神

god: ~father *n* 教父; **G~-fearing** *adj* 虔诚的; **~forsaken** *adj* 荒凉的 ‹*place*›; a ~forsaken existence 凄惨的生活

godless /'gɒdlɪs/ *adj* 1 (wicked) 邪恶的 ‹*person, institution*› 2 (atheistic) 不信神的 ‹*person*›; 无神论的 ‹*philosophy*›

godlike /'gɒdlaɪk/ *adj* 如神般的

godly /'gɒdli/ *adj* 虔诚的

god: ~mother *n* 教母; **~parent** *n* (male) 教父; (female) 教母; the ~parents 教父母; **~send** *n* 天赐之物; **G~ slot** *n* colloq 宗教节目; **~son** *n* 教子; **Godspeed** *excl* dated 一路顺风; to wish sb. Godspeed 祝某人一路顺风; **G~ squad** *n* colloq pej 上帝使团

The concepts of 'god' and 'devil'

■ Chinese and Western cultures have different concepts of 'god' and 'devil'. According to Chinese belief, 神 (god) is the maker of the universe and everything and anything in it. 神 can also represent an object or fetish to be worshipped. 鬼 has a superstitious connotation and can refer to both an evil spirit (like 'devil' in English) and the spirit of a dead person (like 'ghost' in English). In certain Chinese idioms, 神 and 鬼 appear together, representing something that is neither good nor bad.

■ In Chinese, 神 is not used as frequently as 'god' is in English. Thus, how 'god' is translated must depend on the context:

Apollo was the god of the sun
= 阿波罗是太阳神

I believe in God
= 我信仰上帝

Fame is her god
= 名誉是她的命

The house of God
= 教堂

It put the fear of God into him
= 这吓了他一大跳

God willing
= 如一切顺利
or 如事能如愿

Thank God I found my purse
= 谢天谢地，我的钱包找到了

■ The translation of 'devil' also depends on the context:

He believes in devils
= 他信鬼

Have another chilli. Go on, be a devil
= 再吃个辣椒吧。来，怕什么

Speak of the devil
= 说到某人，某人就到场
or 说曹操，曹操到

goer /'gəʊə(r)/
A *n* Brit colloq **1** pej (woman) 骚货; **she's a bit of a ～** 她有点水性杨花 **2** (fast mover) 能快速移动的东西; **this horse/car is a lovely little ～** 这匹马能跑得飞快/这辆车能开得飞快 **3** (lively person) 精力充沛的人 **4** (good idea) 可行的事; **his plan was a ～** 他的计划行得通
B -goer *combining form* 常去…的人; **theatre/cinema～** 常去看戏/看电影的人
goes /gəʊz/ ▸**go A, B**
go-faster stripes *npl* colloq [贴在车身上使车看起来更有动感的] 加速彩条
gofer /'gəʊfə(r)/ *n* esp Amer colloq 打杂的人; **Mr Brown's ～s** 为布朗先生跑腿的
go-getter *n* colloq 雄心勃勃的人
go-getting colloq
A *adj* 雄心勃勃的
B *n* [u] 进取心
goggle /'gɒgl/
A *vi* 瞪大眼睛看; **to ～ at sb./sth.** 瞪着某人/某物
B *n* 瞪视
C goggles *npl* **1** (protective glasses) 护目镜 **2** colloq hum (glasses) 眼镜
goggle: ～ box *n* Brit colloq 电视机; **～-eyed** *adj* colloq 瞪大眼睛的
go-go *adj attrib* **1** dated (erotic) 跳歌歌舞的 ‹*girl, bar*›; **～ dancing** 跳歌歌舞 **2** Amer (dynamic) 充满活力的; **an era of ～ optimism** 乐观活跃的时代 **3** Amer Econ, Fin 投机的; **the ～ market of the 1990s** 20 世纪 90 年代的投机市场
go-go dancer *n* 歌歌舞舞女
going /'gəʊɪŋ/
A ▸**go A, B**
B *adj* **1** *attrib* (profitable) 兴隆的; **a ～ concern** 生意兴隆的企业 **2** *attrib* (current) 现行的; **the ～ salary/rate of interest** 现行工资/利率 **3** *postpos* (existing, available) 现有的; **the best/worst ... ～** 目前最好的/最差的…; **it's the best machine ～** 这是目前最好的机器
C *n* **1** [u and c] (departure) 离去; **her ～ was a sad moment** 她的离别是个悲伤的时刻; **comings and ～s** 来来往往 **2** [u] (condition of ground for riding, walking) 地面状况; **the ～ is soft to heavy** 赛马场的地面软偏硬; **it's rough ～** 路面高低不平 **3** [u] fig (circumstances) 情况; **he got out while the ～ was good** 他趁机离开了; **when the ～ gets tough the tough get going** Prov 当条件变得艰苦时，有志者更加勇往直前 **4** [u] (progress) 进展; **that was good/slow ～** 进展很快/很慢; **the conversation/novel was heavy ～** 谈话进展缓慢/小说枯燥难懂; **her new job was hard ～** 她的新工作进展困难
D -going *combining form* 参加…活动的; **cinema/church～** 常去电影院/教堂的; **the theatre～ public** 常去剧院看戏的观众
going over *n* colloq **1** (check, examination) 彻底检查; **to give the house a ～** 仔细查看房子; **the doctor gave him/his heart a good ～** 医生对他/他的心脏进行了仔细检查 **2** (cleaning) 彻底清理; **the bedroom needs a real ～** 卧室需要彻底打扫 **3** (beating) 痛打 **4** (scolding) 痛骂 **5** (defeat) 彻底失败; **Pontypool gave them a 35 to 6 ～** 庞蒂浦队以 35 比 6 把他们打得一败涂地
goings-on *npl* **1** (events) 情况; **～ at home/backstage** 家里的情况/后台的活动 **2** (scandalous behaviour) 可耻勾当 **3** (weird behaviour) 异常行为; **there are strange ～ after dark** 天黑之后有异常活动
goitre Brit, **goiter** Amer /'gɔɪtə(r)/ *n* [u and c] 甲状腺肿
go-kart *n* 卡丁车
go-karting *n* [u] 卡丁车运动; **to go ～** 去参加卡丁车比赛
gold /gəʊld/
A *n* **1** [u] Miner 黄金; **pure ～** 纯金; **to be worth one's weight in ～** fig 非常有价值; **a heart of ～** fig 一颗金子般的心; **as good as ～** fig (of child) 规规矩矩的 **2** [u] (currency) 金币 **3** [u and c] Sport 金牌 **4** [u] (colour) 金色
B *modif* **1** Comm 金制的 ‹*jewellery*›; **a ～ watch/bar/tooth** 金表/金条/金牙 **2** Ind 含金的 ‹*ore, alloy*›; 采金的 ‹*miner*›
C *adj* 金色的; **to turn ～** ‹*leaves*› 变成金黄色
gold brick Amer colloq pej
A *n* **1** (shirker) 懒汉 **2** (worthless item) 假货
B goldbrick *vi* 偷懒
gold: ～ certificate *n* Amer 黄金证券 [可自由兑换黄金]; **G～ Coast** *n* Hist (Ghana) 黄金海岸 [加纳的旧称]; **～crest** *n* 戴菊莺; **～-digger** *n* **1** (miner) 淘金者; **2** fig colloq pej (woman) 以色相骗钱的女人; **～ disc** *n* 金唱片奖; **～ dust** *n* [u] 金粉; **to be like ～ dust** Brit 难以弄到
golden /'gəʊldən/ *adj* **1** (gold-coloured) 金色的; **～ hair** 金发; **～ sunset** 金灿灿的落日 **2** (made of gold) 金制的 ‹*object*›; **～ earrings** 金耳环; ▸**goose A1** **3** fig (fine) 美妙的 ‹*melody, tone*›; **sb.'s ～ voice** 某人的金嗓子 **4** fig (favourable) 非常有利的; **a ～ opportunity** 良机
golden: ～ age *n* (idyllic age) 黄金时代; (flourishing period) 鼎盛时期; **the ～ age of Spanish poetry** 西班牙诗歌的黄金时代; **～ anniversary** *n* **1** (of wedding) 金婚纪念 [50周年结婚纪念]; **2** (of event) **= ～ jubilee**; **～ boy** *n* colloq (popular) 大红人; (successful) 骄子; **the ～ boy of golf** 高尔夫金童
golden brown ▸**p. 134**
A *n* [u] 金棕色
B golden-brown *adj* 金棕色的
golden: ～ calf *n* **1** Bible 金牛犊 [古代以色列人崇拜的偶像]; **2** fig (as figure of worship) 膜拜物 [尤指钱财]; **～ eagle** *n* 金雕; **G～ Gate Bridge** *pr n* **the G～ Gate Bridge** 金门大桥; **～ girl** *n* colloq (popular) 大红人; (successful) 骄女; **the ～ girl of gymnastics** 体操玉女; **～ goal** *n* 金球 [足球、曲棍球加时赛中一方得分比赛即告结束赛制中的进球]; **～ goose** *n* 下金蛋的鹅 [不妥善利用就会枯竭的财富来源]; **to kill the ～ goose** 杀鸡取卵; **～ handshake** *n* colloq 退职金; **～ hello** *n* Brit colloq 丰厚的聘金; **～ jubilee** *n* 50 周年纪念; **～ mean** *n* **1** (happy medium) **the ～ mean** 中庸之道; **2** Art **= ～ section**; **～ oldie** *n* colloq 经典老作品; **～ parachute** *n* colloq 金降落伞 [公司被收购或兼并后发给高层人员的大笔遣散费]; **～ retriever** *n* 金毛寻回犬; **～ rule** *n* 重要原则; **～ section** *n* 黄金分割; **～ syrup** *n* [u] Brit 金黄色糖浆; **G～ Triangle** *n* **the G～ Triangle** 金三角; **～ wedding** *n* Brit 金婚纪念
golden yellow ▸**p. 134**
A *n* [u] 金黄色
B golden-yellow *adj* 金黄色的
gold: ～ exchange standard *n* 金汇兑本位制; **～ fever** *n* [u] 淘金热; **～field** *n* 金矿区; **～-filled** *adj* 填金的; **～ filling** *n* 黄金填料; **～finch** *n* 红额金翅雀
goldfish /'gəʊldfɪʃ/ *n* (*pl* **goldfish**) 金鱼
goldfish bowl *n* 金鱼缸; **it's like living in a ～!** fig 这就像生活在众目睽睽之下!
gold foil *n* [u] 金箔
Goldilocks /'gəʊldɪlɒks/ *pr n* **1** (character) 金发姑娘 [儿童故事《金发姑娘和三只熊》中的主人公] **2 goldilocks** colloq (person) 金发人
gold: ～ leaf *n* [u] 金叶; **～ medal** *n* 金牌; **a ～ medal winner** 金牌得主; **～ mine** *n* **1** lit 金矿; **2** fig (of wealth) 摇钱树; (of knowledge) 宝库; **to be sitting on a ～ mine** 坐在金山上; **a ～ mine of information** 知识宝库; **～ mining** *n* [u] 金矿开采; **～ note** *n* Amer **= ～ certificate**; **～ paint** *n* [u] 金色涂料
gold plate
A *n* [u] **1** (coating) 镀金层 **2** (objects) 镀金器具
B gold-plate *vt* 给…镀金
gold: ～-plated *adj* 镀金的; **～ record** *n* Amer **= ～ disc**; **～ reserve** *n* 黄金储备; **～ rush** *n* 淘金热; **～smith** ▸**p. 409** *n* 金匠; **～ standard** *n* **1** Hist, Econ 金本位制; **2** fig (model) 最佳标准; **～ star** *n* Amer 金星 [表示家庭或组织有成员战死的标志]; **a ～ star mother** 战死者的母亲
golf /gɒlf/ ▸**p. 307**
A *n* [u] 高尔夫球; **～ shoes/tournament** 高尔夫球鞋/锦标赛
B *vi* 打高尔夫球
golf ball *n* 高尔夫球
golf ball typewriter *n* 菊花轮打字机
golf: ～ club *n* **1** (stick) 高尔夫球杆; **2** (group, place) 高尔夫俱乐部; **～ course** *n* 高尔夫球场
golfer /'gɒlfə(r)/ *n* **1** (player) 高尔夫球手 **2** Brit dated (cardigan) 毛线衫
golf links *npl* + *v sing* **= links**
Goliath /gə'laɪəθ/
A *pr n* Bible 歌利亚 [被大卫杀死的非利士族巨人]

B goliath *n* fig (big person) 巨人; (big thing) 庞然大物

golliwog /ˈɡɒlɪwɒɡ/ *n* 黑脸布娃娃 [现常常被以为会冒犯黑人]

golly¹ /ˈɡɒli/ *excl* colloq dated 天哪

golly² *n* Brit colloq = **golliwog**

gonad /ˈɡəʊnæd/ *n* 性腺

gondola /ˈɡɒndələ/ *n* **1** (boat) 贡多拉 **2** (cabin) (under airship) 吊舱; (under balloon) 吊篮; (cable car) 缆车 **3** Brit (shelves) 货架 **4** Amer Rail ~ **(car)** 无盖货车

gondolier /ˌɡɒndəˈlɪə(r)/ ▸**p. 409** *n* 贡多拉船夫

gone /ɡɒn/

A *pp* ▸**go A, B**

B *adj pred* **1** (past) 过去的; **the days that are ~** 过去的日子; **~ are the days when ..., the days are ~ when ...** …的日子一去不复返了 **2** colloq (pregnant) 怀孕的; **to be 6 months ~** 怀孕 6 个月 **3** (not here) 消失的; **to be ~** «*person*» 不在; «*object, institution, building*» 不复存在; **my briefcase is ~!** 我的公文包不见了! **4** (consumed) 用光的; **the wine's all ~** 葡萄酒喝光了 **5** euph (dead) 去世的; **after I am ~** 我走之后; **to be long ~** 去世很久了 **6** colloq dated (fond) 着迷的; **to be ~ on sb./sth.** 迷恋某人/某物; **she's really ~ on him** 她确实迷恋上了他

C *prep* Brit 刚过; **it's just ~ seven o'clock** 刚过七点钟; **he was just ~ 70** 他刚过 70 岁

goner /ˈɡɒnə(r)/ *n* colloq (person) 无法挽救的人; (thing) 完蛋的事物; **the car's a ~** 汽车报废了; **it looks like he's a ~** 看上去他玩完了

gong /ɡɒŋ/ *n* **1** (metal disc) 锣; **to beat** *or* **sound a ~** 敲锣; **the dinner ~** 开饭锣 **2** Brit colloq (medal) 奖章

gonna /ˈɡɒnə/ colloq = **going to** ▸**go A7**

gonorrhoea Brit, **gonorrhea** Amer /ˌɡɒnəˈrɪə/ ▸**p. 377** *n* [u] 淋病

goo /ɡuː/ *n* [u] colloq **1** (gunge) 黏糊糊的东西 **2** fig pej (sentimentality) 过分多情

good /ɡʊd/

A *adj* (*comp* **better**, *superl* **best**) **1** (enjoyable) 好的 ‹*book, news*›; 愉快的 ‹*holiday, party, journey*›; **a ~ joke** 有趣的笑话; **did you have a ~ night?** 你那天晚上过得愉快吗?; **to have a ~ time** 玩得很高兴; **to be after a ~ time** colloq 寻欢作乐; **have a ~ trip/holiday!** 祝你旅途/假期愉快!; **the ~ things in life** 人生的乐趣; **it feels ~ to be alive** 活着真好; **this bed feels ~** 躺在这张床上感觉很舒服; **that's a ~ one!** 你真逗!; **have a ~ day!** 祝你度过愉快的一天!; **she came in a ~ second** (in contest) 她取得了第二的良好成绩; **to feel ~ (about sth./doing sth.)** (对某事/做某事) 感到愉快; ▸**riddance** **2** (high-quality) 优质的 ‹*product, furniture, tool*›; 肥沃的 ‹*land*›; 精彩的 ‹*performance*›; 上好的 ‹*meal, wine*›; 很好的 ‹*result, chance*›; 良好的 ‹*condition*›; 很高的 ‹*reputation*›; 高雅的 ‹*art, music, literature*›; 漂亮的 ‹*handwriting*›; **it's a ~ make** 这个品牌质量不错; **a ~-quality carpet** 高质量的地毯; **a ~ night's sleep** 通宵的酣睡; **a ~ honours degree in chemistry** 化学专业优等学位; **~ reviews** 好评; **to be in ~ health** 健康状况良好; **to be too ~ for sb./sth.** 太好而不适用于某人/某物; **I'm not ~ enough for her** 我配不上她; **~ thinking!** 好主意! **3** (healthy) 健康的 ‹*teeth, heart*›; 健全的 ‹*limb*›; **I don't feel (too) ~** 我感觉不 (太) 舒服; **you don't look (too) ~** 你气色不 (太) 好; **to have ~ hearing/eyesight/a ~ memory** 听力/视力/记忆力好; **he has a very ~ ear/eye** 他的听觉/视觉很灵敏 **4** *attrib* (prestigious) 有名望的 ‹*family, school*›; 体面的 ‹*job, position*›; **to make a ~ marriage** 与名门联姻; **to live in a ~ area/at a ~ address** 住在富人区/豪宅 **5** (fluent) 流利的 ‹*language*›; **she speaks ~ French** 她说一口流利的法语 **6** *attrib* (quality, not for everyday use) 高质量的 ‹*notepaper, tablecloth, china, cutlery*›; 重要场合穿着的 ‹*shoes, garment*› **7** (attractive) 漂亮的; **she looks ~ in that dress/in blue** 她穿那件裙子/蓝色衣服很漂亮; **to have a ~ figure** 有迷人的身材; **to look ~ with sth.** (match) 佩上…很漂亮 ‹*garment, accessory, colour, style*› **8** (tasty) 美味的 ‹*food, meal, drink*› **9** (virtuous) 正派的 ‹*person*›; (kind) 善良的 ‹*person*›; 良好的 ‹*example, influence*›; **she has led a ~ life** 她生活得规规矩矩; **the ~ guys** colloq 正面人物; **~ deeds** 善行; **to be ~ to sb.** 善待某人; **it was ~ of them to help** 他们能帮忙真好; **would you be ~ enough to do that, would/will you be so ~ as to do that** formal 请你那么做好吗; **to be ~ about sth.** 对…表现出宽容 ‹*mistake, accident, damage*›; **my ~ man** *or* **chap** *or* **fellow** dated 我的大好人 [一种居高临下的称呼]; **and how's your ~ lady?** dated 尊夫人还好吗?; **to be a ~ sort** colloq 是个好人; **to do sb. a ~ turn** 帮某人一个忙; **one ~ turn deserves another** Prov 投桃报李; **to do ~ works** dated 做慈善工作 **10** (in exclamations) **~ gracious** *or* **grief** *or* **heavens** *or* **Lord** *or* **God!** 天哪! **11** (obedient) 恭顺的 ‹*person, behaviour, conduct*›; 乖的 ‹*child*›; 驯良的 ‹*animal*›; **there's a ~ boy/girl!** 真乖!; **be a ~ boy and put your toys away** 乖, 把玩具整理好; **be ~!** 听话!; **to be as ~ as gold** 很乖 **12** (pleasant) 愉快的; **to be in a ~ mood** *or* **humour** *or* **temper** 心情愉快 **13** (reliable) 可靠的 ‹*person, shop, brand*›; 令人依恋的 ‹*place, country*›; **~ old John** 可靠的老约翰; **~ old Scotland** 苏格兰故土; **there's nothing like ~ old beeswax!** 没有什么比老牌子的蜂蜡更好用了! **14** (competent) 有能力的 ‹*accountant, hairdresser*›; 称职的 ‹*teacher, father, husband*›; **a ~ singer** 有实力的歌手; **I'm not a very ~ swimmer** 我游泳水平不太高; **you're not a very ~ liar** 你的撒谎技巧一般; **he's very ~ around the house** 他是操持家务的好手; **Dr Brown is very ~** 布朗医生医术高超; **to be ~ at sth./doing sth.** 擅长 ‹*school subject, DIY, dancing, solving problems*›; **something you're ~ at** 你擅长的事情; **to be ~ with sth.** 善于应付某事物; **she's ~ with horses** 她擅长驯马; **to be ~ with one's hands** 手巧; **to be ~ with sb.** 擅长和…打交道 ‹*old people, children*›; **to be ~ on sth.** 通晓某事; **to be ~ as sth.** 擅长扮演某角色; **she is so ~ as Ophelia** 她很会扮演奥菲利亚 **15** *pred* (beneficial) 有益的; **to be ~ for sb./sth.** 对…有好处 ‹*person, plant, skin*›; **exercise is ~ for your health** 锻炼有益健康; **it's not ~ for wine to be kept in a warm room** 葡萄酒不宜放在温暖的房间; **she eats more than is ~ for her** 她吃得过多, 对健康无益; **if you know what's ~ for you** 只要你知道好歹 **16** (effective) 好用的 ‹*tool, knife, shampoo*›; 有效的 ‹*way, pill, method*›; **to be ~ for sth./doing sth.** 对…有效 ‹*headaches, removing stains, sunburn*›; **to take ~ care of sb./sth.** 精心照顾某人/处理某事 **17** *attrib* (suitable) 合适的 ‹*book, time, place*›; 贴切的 ‹*example, name*›; **~ sailing weather** 适合从事帆船运动的好天气; **is this a ~ place to stop for lunch?** 可以在这里停下吃午饭吗?; **to be as ~ a time/place as any** 是最好的时机/地方 **18** (favourable, fortunate) 顺利的 ‹*year, day, time*›; 难得的 ‹*offer, opportunity, bargain*›; 吉利的 ‹*sign, omen, forecast*›; **that's ~!** 太好了!; **the ~ thing about sth./sb.** 某物/某人的优点; **in ~ time** 及早地; **all in ~ time!** 耐心点儿!; **it's a ~ job/thing that ...** colloq 幸好…; **to look ~** (promising) 看上去有希望; (impressive) 给人印象深; **to have never had it so ~** 境况从没像现在这样好过; **it's too ~ to be true** 这好得令人难以置信; **to have a ~ thing going** colloq 一切顺利; **too much of a ~ thing** 物极必反; **to come ~** colloq 有好结果 **19** (sensible, wise, valid) 明智的 ‹*idea, choice, investment*›; 合理的 ‹*excuse, argument*›; **to be a ~ thing/idea (to do sth.)** (做某事) 是明智的事/想法; **to have the ~ sense to do sth.** 机智地做某事; **it's ~ that ...** …是明智的; **(that's a) ~ point/question!** 说得/问得好!; **it's as ~ a reason as any** 这一理由足够了; **without ~ reason** 无缘无故地 **20** (close) 亲近的 ‹*relationship, terms, neighbour*›; **to be just ~ friends** 仅仅是好朋友而已 **21** (serviceable, valid) 有效的 ‹*cheque, ticket, credit, certificate*›; 能用的 ‹*car, machine, tyre*›; 能工作的 ‹*person*›; **to be ~ for sth.** 有效期为某时间; **my season ticket is ~ for two more months** 我的季票还能用两个月; **she's ~ for another 20 years!** colloq 她还能再干 20 年!; **the ball is ~** Sport 该球得分有效 **22** *pred* (able to provide) **to be ~ for sth.** «*person*» 能负担 ‹*loan, payment*›; «*lake*» 出产 ‹*salmon*›; «*newspaper*» 能提供 ‹*local news*› **23** (accurate) 准确的 ‹*description, spelling*›; 准的 ‹*clock, watch*›; **the photo is not a very ~ likeness** 这张照片不太像本人; **the shoes are not a very ~ fit** 这双鞋不太合脚; **to keep ~ time** «*clock, watch*» 走时准确 **24** (thorough) 充分的; **give the table a ~ polish** 彻底地擦一下桌子; **she gave him a ~ telling-off** 她狠狠地骂了他; **take a ~ look at this photograph** 好好看看这张照片; **a ~ long walk** 长途散步 **25** *attrib* (substantial) 相当大的 ‹*size, amount, chance, age*›; 相当长的 ‹*hour, distance*›; 相当高的 ‹*rate, salary*›; 相当多的 ‹*choice*›; **she weighs a ~ 70 kilos** 她体重足足 70 公斤; **he had eaten a ~ two-thirds of the cake** 他吃了整整三分之二的蛋糕; **to add a ~ pinch of salt** 撒一大把盐; **I'm feeling a ~ bit better** colloq 我感觉好多了; **a ~ many** *or* Brit **few ...** 相当多的 ‹*people*› **26** (virtually) **as ~ as** 几乎; **the match was as ~ as lost** 比赛几乎等于输掉了; **she as ~ as called me a thief** 她就差直接骂我是贼了; **it's as ~ as giving them a blank cheque** 这就等于给他们开了张空白支票; **to be as ~ as new** 和新的差不多 **27** **to make ~** (succeed) 取得成功 **28** **to make ~** (carry out) 履行 ‹*promise*›; 进行 ‹*threat*›; (repair) 弥补 ‹*damage, loss, deficiency*›; (reimburse) 偿付 ‹*expenses, money*›; (achieve) 实现 ‹*escape*›

B *excl* **1** (expressing pleasure, satisfaction, relief) **~!** 很好!; **jolly ~!** dated 太好了! **2** (encourage, approve) **very ~!** 太棒了!; **~ for her!** 她真是好样的!; **~ on you!** colloq 干得好! **3** (in assent) **very ~** 行啊

C *adv* colloq **1** (very) 非常; **~ and ...** 非常…; **we got up ~ and early** 我们一大早就起床了; **you messed that up ~ and proper** 你把事情彻底搞糟了 **2** esp Amer (well, thoroughly) 很好地 ‹*act, sing, dance*›; 彻底地 ‹*cook*›; **you listen ~** 好好听我说; **did I do ~, Pop?** 我做得对吗, 爸爸?; **go after that guy and fix him ~** 跟着那个人, 好好收拾他一顿

D *n* **1** [u] (virtue) 善; (virtuous deeds) 善行; **~ and evil** 善与恶; **to do ~** 行善; **the ~** 好事; **to be up to no ~** colloq 在做什么坏事; **to come to no ~** «*thing*» 没有好结果; «*person*» 没有好下场 **2** [u] (benefit) 好处; **to do sth. for one's (own) ~/for the ~ of sb.** 为了自己/某人好而做某事; **she's a bit too serious for her own ~** 她太严肃了, 这对她没有好处; **for the ~ of one's health** 为了健康; **to be not much/no ~** 没多少/没有效果; **to do sb./sth. ~** 给某人/某物带来好处; **it will do you ~ to sleep** 睡眠会对你有利; **to do sb. a power** *or* **world of ~** colloq 给某人带来很大好处; **no ~ can/will come of sth./doing sth.** 某事/做某事不会带来任何好处; **after paying for the car she was still £300 to the ~** Brit 买车后她手里还剩下 300 英镑; **to be (all) to the ~** (完全) 有利 **3** [u] (use) 用处; **what ~ will that do?** 那有什么用?; **what's the ~ (of doing that)?** (那么做) 有什么用?; **it's no ~, ...** 这没有用, …; **he's no ~ in emergencies** 他不擅长处理紧急情况; **to do not much/no/any/little ~**

g

没多少/没有/没有任何/很少有用处; **to do sb. not much/no ~** 对某人没多少/没有作用; **much ~ may it do you/them!** 但愿这会对你/他们有好处! ; **it's a fat lot of ~ telling me now!** colloq 现在跟我说没用! ; **a lot of ~ that will do!** 那有效果才怪! ; **to be not much/no ~ (to sb.)** (对某人) 没多大/没有用; **to be not much/no ~ for sth./doing sth.** 对某事/做某事没多大/没有用处 4 [u] (competence) 能力; **to be not much/no ~ (at sth./doing sth.)** 没有多大能力/没有能力 (处理某事/做某事) ; **I was never any ~ at (learning) English** 我根本不擅长 (学) 英语; **is the new secretary any ~?** 新来的秘书能力如何? 5 [u] (ever) **for ~** 永远; **she's coming home for ~** 她回到家就再也不走了; **for ~ and all** 永久地 6 + *v pl* (good people) **the ~** 好人; **the great and the ~** Brit iron 群贤; **the ~ die young** Prov 好人不长寿

good: ~ afternoon ▸p. 333 *excl* (greeting) 下午好; formal (farewell) 再见; **G~ Book** *n* **the G~ Book** 《圣经》

goodbye /ˌgʊd'baɪ/
A *excl* 再见; **to say ~ to sb.** 对某人说再见; **to say ~ to sth.** fig 对某物说再见
B *n* 告别; **to say a tearful ~** 洒泪道别; **we said our ~s** 我们已经道别了

good: ~ day ▸p. 333 *excl* formal dated (greeting) 你好; (farewell) 再见; **~ evening** ▸p. 333 *excl* formal (greeting) 晚上好; (farewell) 再见

good-for-nothing
A *n* 没用的人; **she's a ~** 她是个懒虫
B *adj* 没用的 ‹*son, girl*›; **her ~ husband** 她的饭桶丈夫

good: G~ Friday *n* 耶稣受难日; **~-hearted** *adj* 好心肠的 ‹*person*›; 善意的 ‹*teasing, manner*›; **~-humoured** Brit, **~-humored** Amer *adj* 1 (genial) 和蔼的 ‹*person, crowd*›; 2 (friendly) 友好的 ‹*gesture, remark, rivalry*›; **~-humouredly** Brit, **~-humoredly** Amer *adv* 友好地 ‹*smile, say*›

goodish /'gʊdɪʃ/ *adj* Brit colloq 尚好的; **to be in a ~ mood** 心情还不错; **a ~ helping of cream** 相当大的一份奶油点心

good: ~-looker *n* colloq 好看的人; **~-looking** *adj* 好看的; **he is ~-looking** 他长得帅; **a ~-looking girl** 漂亮女孩; **~ looks** *npl* 美貌

goodly /'gʊdli/ *adj attrib* dated 相当大的; **a ~ number of people** 相当多的人; **a ~ sum of money** 一大笔钱

good: ~ morning ▸p. 333 *excl* formal (greeting) 早上好; (farewell) 再见; **~-natured** *adj* 1 (warm-hearted) 性情温和的 ‹*person, animal*›; 2 (friendly) 和善的 ‹*smile, remark, discussion*›; **a ~-natured joke** 善意的玩笑; **~-naturedly** *adv* 和善地 ‹*smile, say*›

goodness /'gʊdnɪs/
A *n* [u] 1 (virtue) 美德 2 (kindness) 善良; **she did it out of the ~ of her heart** 她做这件事是出于好心; **would you have the ~ to open the window, please** formal 麻烦你开下窗户好吗 3 (nutritive value) 营养; **to be full of ~** 营养丰富; **the soil has lost much of its ~** 土壤里的大量养分已流失
B *excl* 上帝啊; **my ~!** 我的天啊! ; **~ gracious (me)!** 天哪! ; **surely to ~ you don't mean that ...** 你不会是说…吧; **thank ~** 谢天谢地; **I wish/hope to ~ that ...** 我真切地希望…; **~ (only) knows!** 天晓得! ; **for ~' sake** 看在老天爷的分上

goodnight /ˌgʊd'naɪt/ ▸p. 333 *excl* 晚安; **to give sb. a ~ kiss** 吻某人道晚安

goods /gʊdz/ *npl* 1 (merchandise) 商品; **~ and services** 商品与服务; **luxury ~** 奢侈品; **electrical ~** 电器; **stolen ~** 赃物; **to be caught with the ~** 人赃俱获 2 (property) 财产; **all my worldly ~** 我的一切财产; **~ and chattels** 全部动产 3 Brit Rail 运载的货物 4 fig colloq (desirable thing) 合意的东西; **she's the ~** Brit 她妩媚动人; **he's got the ~** 他有真本领; **to deliver/come up with the ~** 不负所望

Good Samaritan *n* 行善的人; **a ~ helped her** fig 一位好心人帮助了她

goods depot *n* Brit 商品仓库

good-sized *adj* 相当大的 ‹*room, object*›

goods: ~ lift *n* Brit 货梯; **~ train** *n* Brit 货物列车; **~ van** *n* Brit 有盖货车; **~ wagon** *n* Brit 敞车; **~ yard** *n* Brit 铁路货场

good: ~-tempered *adj* 1 (easy-going) 脾气好的 ‹*person*›; 2 (amicable) 和气的 ‹*discussion*›; **~-time girl** *n* colloq 寻欢作乐的女郎

goodwill /ˌgʊd'wɪl/ *n* [u] 1 (cooperation) 诚意; (kindness) 善意; **~ and cooperation** 亲善合作; **a man of ~** 好心人; **a ~ mission** 友好访问团; **a ~ gesture, a gesture of ~** 善意的举动; **to show ~ to** *or* **towards sb.** 对某人表示诚意; **in a spirit of ~** 以亲善精神; **to do sth. with ~** 善意地做某事 2 Comm 商誉

goody /'gʊdi/
A *n* colloq 1 *usu pl* (good eats) 好吃的东西 2 *usu pl* (desirable things) 好东西 3 Brit (hero) 好人
B *excl* child lang 好哇

goody bag *n* colloq 1 (for sweets, gifts) 糖果礼品袋 2 Comm (for samples) 样品袋

goody-goody colloq pej
A *n* 伪善的人; **she's a ~** 她是个假正经
B *adj* 伪善的 ‹*adult*›; 假装乖的 ‹*child*›

goody two shoes *n* colloq pej 假正经的人

gooey /'guːi/ *adj* colloq 1 lit 黏糊糊的 ‹*mess, face*› 2 fig pej 过分多情的 ‹*words, music*›; **she went all ~ around him** 她在他面前很娇弱多情

goof /guːf/ esp Amer colloq
A *n* 1 (blunder) 愚蠢的错误 2 (idiot) 傻瓜
B *vt* 搞糟; **to ~ one's lines** 把台词弄乱
C *vi* 搞糟; **she had a chance, but she ~ed** 她原有个机会, 但她错过了

Phrasal verbs
- **goof around, goof about** *vi* Amer colloq 闲荡
- **goof off** *vi* Amer colloq 偷懒
- **goof on** *vt* [**~ on sb.**] Amer colloq 戏弄
- **goof up** *vi* Amer colloq 犯愚蠢的错误

goof: ~ball *n* Amer colloq 1 (fool) 傻瓜; 2 (pill) 镇静剂药丸; **~-off** *n* Amer colloq 懒人; **~-up** *n* Amer colloq 愚蠢的错误

goofy /'guːfi/ *adj* esp Amer colloq 1 (silly) 愚蠢的 ‹*idea, person*›; 滑稽可笑的 ‹*hat*› 2 (odd) 古怪的 ‹*person, story*›

Google® /'guːgl/
A *n* [u] 谷歌 [网络搜索引擎]
B **google** *vt* 用网络搜索引擎搜索 ‹*person, subject*›
C **google** *vi* 用网络搜索引擎搜索

gook /guːk, gʊk/ *n* 1 [c] esp Amer sl pej (Asian person) 东方佬 2 [u] colloq (sticky mess) 黏糊糊的东西

goolies /'guːliːz/ *npl* Brit taboo sl 睾丸

goon /guːn/ *n* colloq 1 (fool) 傻子 2 Amer pej (thug) 打手; **a ~ squad** 打手队

goosander /guː'sændə(r)/ *n* 普通秋沙鸭

goose /guːs/
A *n* (*pl* **geese**) 1 [c] Zool 鹅; **a wild-~ chase** fig colloq 徒劳的追求; **to cook sb.'s ~** fig colloq 破坏某人的计划; **he/she wouldn't say boo to a ~** Brit 他/她非常羞怯; **to kill the ~ that lays the golden eggs** 杀鸡取卵; **all sb.'s geese are swans** 某人的鹅都是天鹅 [意指某人总是夸大其词]; ▸**sauce A1** 2 [u] Culin 鹅肉
B *vt* Amer colloq 戳…的屁股 ‹*person*›

gooseberry /'gʊzbəri, Amer 'guːsberi/ *n* 1 (fruit) 醋栗; **~ jam** 醋栗果酱 2 Brit colloq (third person) 电灯泡 [不识趣地夹在情侣中间的人]; **to play ~** 当电灯泡

gooseberry: ~ bush *n* 醋栗灌木丛; **~ fool** *n* [c and u] 醋栗奶油糖浆

goose: ~bumps *npl* esp Amer = **~ pimples**; **~flesh** *n* [u] = **~ pimples**; **~ pimples** *npl* 鸡皮疙瘩; **to have/get ~ pimples** 起鸡皮疙瘩

goose-step
A *n* 正步
B *vi* 正步走

GOP *abbr* Amer = **Grand Old Party**

gopher /'gəʊfə(r)/ *n* 囊地鼠

gorblimey /ˌgɔː'blaɪmi/ Brit colloq
A *excl* 竟然有这种事
B *adj* 低级的

Gordian Knot /ˌgɔːdɪən 'nɒt/ *n* fig 难题; **to cut the ~** 快刀斩乱麻; **it was his ~** 这件事把他难住了

gore[1] /gɔː(r)/ *vt* «*bull, boar*» 顶伤 ‹*person, animal*›; **to ~ sb. to death** 把某人顶死

gore[2] *n* [u] 凝固的血; **a scene of bloodshed and ~** 血腥的场面

gorge[1] /gɔːdʒ/ *n* 1 (valley) 峡谷 2 Anat archaic 咽喉; **to make sb.'s ~ rise** 使某人作呕

gorge[2]
A *v refl* **to ~ oneself** 狼吞虎咽; **to ~ oneself on** *or* **with sth.** 狼吞虎咽地吃某物
B *vi* 狼吞虎咽

gorgeous /'gɔːdʒəs/ *adj* 1 colloq (wonderful) 令人愉快的 ‹*time, day*›; **~ weather** 宜人的天气 2 colloq (attractive) 非常漂亮的; **a ~ blonde** 金发美女 3 (sumptuous) 华丽的 ‹*tapestry, dress*›; 绚丽的 ‹*colour, sunset*›

gorgeously /'gɔːdʒəsli/ *adv* 1 (attractively) 非常漂亮地 ‹*dressed*› 2 (sumptuously) 华丽地 ‹*decorated*›; 绚丽地 ‹*coloured*›

Gorgon /'gɔːgən/
A *pr n* Mythol **the ~** 戈耳工 [希腊神话中三个蛇发女怪之一, 人见之即化为石头]
B **gorgon** *n* fig (repulsive woman) 凶恶的丑女人

gorilla /gə'rɪlə/ *n* 1 (ape) 大猩猩 2 fig (man) 彪形大汉 3 fig colloq (bodyguard) 打手

gormandize /'gɔːməndaɪz/ *vi* formal pej 狼吞虎咽; **he loved to ~** 他喜欢大吃大喝

gormless /'gɔːmlɪs/ *adj* Brit colloq 愚蠢的 ‹*person*›; **a ~ boy** 傻小子

gorse /gɔːs/ *n* [u] 荆豆

gorse bush *n* 荆豆

gory /'gɔːri/ *adj* 1 liter (bloody) 沾满血污的; **a ~ monster** 血淋淋的妖怪; **the ~ details** 令人不快的详情 2 (gruesome) 暴力血腥的 ‹*film, sight*›; **a ~ battle** 血流成河的战役; **the ~ details of her divorce** fig hum 她离婚时的种种惨痛经历

gosh /gɒʃ/ *excl* colloq 啊呀; **~, it's freezing!** 啊呀, 天太冷了! ; **~! did you really do that?** 天哪! 你真的做了那事儿?

goshawk /'gɒshɔːk/ *n* 苍鹰

gosling /'gɒzlɪŋ/ *n* 小鹅

go-slow *n* Brit 怠工

gospel /'gɒspl/ *n* 1 *sing* Bible **the G~** (teachings) 福音; **to preach/spread the ~** 宣讲/传布福音 2 (*also* **Gospel**) [c] (book) 福音书; **St John's ~** 约翰福音; **the ~ story** 福音故事 3 [c] (philosophy) 准则; **health of body and mind is my ~** 保持身心健康是我的行为准则; **the ~ of self-reliance** 自力更生的信条 4 [u] **~ truth** colloq (truth) 真事; **is that ~?** 那是真的吗? ; **to take sb.'s words as ~** *or* **~ truth** 对某人的话深信不疑 5 [u] **~ music** 福音音乐

gossamer /'gɒsəmə(r)/
A *n* [u] 1 (cobweb) 蛛丝 2 (cloth) 薄纱
B *adj* (made of gossamer) 薄纱制的 ‹*drapes, handkerchief*›; (resembling gossamer) 状如薄纱的; **the ~ wings of a butterfly** fig liter 蝴蝶薄如轻纱的翅膀

g

gossip /ˈɡɒsɪp/
A n 1 [u] pej (rumours) 流言蜚语; **marketplace ～** 街谈巷议; **it's common ～ that ...** 大家议论纷纷说… 2 [u] (news) 小道消息; **the latest ～ about sb./sth.** 关于某人/某事的最新谣传 3 [c] colloq (chat) 闲聊; **to have a (good) ～ with sb.** 和某人闲聊（一通） 4 [c] pej (person) 爱传流言蜚语的人; **he's a terrible ～** 他特别爱说长道短
B vi 1 pej (spread rumours) 说长道短; **to ～ about sb.** 背后议论某人 2 colloq (chat) 闲聊; **I can't stand here ～ing all day** 我不能整天站在这儿闲聊; **to ～ with sb.** 和某人闲聊

gossip: ～ column n 漫谈专栏; **～ columnist** n 漫谈专栏作家

gossiping /ˈɡɒsɪpɪŋ/ pej
A n [u] 流言蜚语
B adj attrib 传布流言蜚语的 ‹person›

gossipmonger /ˈɡɒsɪpmʌŋɡə(r)/ n pej 爱传流言蜚语的人

gossipy /ˈɡɒsɪpi/ adj colloq pej 爱传流言蜚语的 ‹person›; 闲聊式的 ‹letter, article›; **a crowd of ～ old women** 一群爱说三道四的老太太

got /ɡɒt/ pp ▸**get A, B, C**

gotcha /ˈɡɒtʃə/ excl 1 colloq (grabbing sb.) 抓到你了 2 colloq (fooling sb.) **ha ha, ～!** 哈哈，你上当了！ 3 (expressing understanding) 我明白

Goth /ɡɒθ/ n 1 [c] Hist 哥特人 2 **goth** [c] (person) 哥特派成员; **a ～ girl** 哥特派的女孩; **～ make-up** 哥特派的化妆方式 3 **goth** [u] (music) 哥特摇滚乐

Gothic /ˈɡɒθɪk/ ▸**p. 426**
A n [u] 1 Archit 哥特式建筑 2 Print 哥特体黑体字 3 Ling 哥特语
B adj 1 Archit 哥特式的 ‹church› 2 Hist (of Goths) 哥特人的 ‹language› 3 Print 哥特体黑体字的 ‹lettering› 4 Literat 哥特派的 ‹novel›

gotta /ˈɡɒtə/ sl 1 **= have got to** ▸**get A29** 2 **= have got a** ▸**get A1**

gotten /ˈɡɒtn/ pp Amer ▸**get**

gouache /ɡʊˈɑːʃ/ n 1 [u and c] (paint) 水粉画颜料 2 [u] (method) 水粉画法 3 [c] (picture) 水粉画

Gouda /ˈɡaʊdə/ n [u] [荷兰产的] 豪达奶酪

gouge /ɡaʊdʒ/
A n 1 (tool) 半圆凿 2 (groove) [用半圆凿凿成的] 沟 3 (injury) 深长的伤口
B vt 1 (dig) 凿; **to ～ out a channel** «water» 冲刷出一条沟 2 Amer colloq (overcharge) 敲…的竹杠

Phrasal verb
• **gouge out** vt [**～ out sth., ～ sth. out**] 凿出 ‹groove›; 挖出 ‹eyes›

goulash /ˈɡuːlæʃ/ n [u] 匈牙利红烩牛肉

gourd /ɡʊəd/ n 1 Bot 葫芦 2 (container) 葫芦制容器; **a wine/water ～** 酒葫芦/水瓢

gourmand /ˈɡʊəmənd/ n 1 (gourmet) 美食家 2 pej (glutton) 贪吃的人

gourmet /ˈɡʊəmeɪ/
A n 美食家
B modif 美味的 ‹food›; 菜肴精美的 ‹restaurant›

gout /ɡaʊt/ ▸**p. 377** n 痛风

gov abbr Brit colloq **= guv**

govern /ˈɡʌvn/
A vt 1 Pol (administer) 治理 ‹nation›; (rule) 统治 ‹kingdom›; **to be ～ed by sb./sth.** 被某人/某组织统治 2 (control) «regulation, principle» 支配 ‹action, use›; **laws that ～ the manufacture of foodstuffs** 指导食品生产的法律 3 (determine) «factor, values» 决定 ‹behaviour, relationship›; **self-interest ～s all his actions** 他的所作所为皆取决于一己私利 4 fig (restrain) 抑制; **to ～ one's feelings** 克制情绪 5 Ling «verbs» 支配 ‹case› 6 Elec, Tech «valve» 调节 ‹flow, speed›
B vi 执政

governance /ˈɡʌvənəns/ n [u] formal 统治

governess /ˈɡʌvənɪs/ n 家庭女教师

governing /ˈɡʌvənɪŋ/ adj attrib 1 Pol 统治的 ‹class›; 执政的 ‹party› 2 (most important) 指导的 ‹principle›; 决定的 ‹factor›

governing body n 管理机构; **FIFA is the international ～ of association football** 国际足球联合会是英式足球的国际管理结构

government /ˈɡʌvənmənt/ n 1 [u] (exercise of authority) 统治; (power to govern) 统治权; **a party in ～** 执政党 2 [u] (system) 政体; **democratic/totalitarian ～** 民主/极权主义政体 3 [c] + v sing or pl (ruling body) 政府; **central/national ～** 中央/国民政府; **the British ～** 英国政府; **to form a ～** 建立政府; **～ policy/agency** 政府政策/机构

Government Accounting Office n Amer 美国审计署

governmental /ˌɡʌvənˈmentl/ adj 政府的

government: ～ bond n 公债; **～ contractor** n 政府承包商; **～ corporation** n Amer 政府公司; **～ employee** ▸**p. 409** n 政府雇员; **～-funded** adj 政府出资的 ‹healthcare, project›; **G～ House** n Brit 总督官邸; **～ office** n 公署; **～ official** ▸**p. 409** n 政府官员; **～ securities, ～ stocks** npl 公债券

governor /ˈɡʌvənə(r)/ n 1 (of province, town) 地方行政长官; **a provincial ～** 省长 2 (of colony) 总督 3 (of US state) 州长 4 (head of institution) 主管; **the G～ of the Bank of England** 英格兰银行总裁; **a prison ～** 典狱长 5 (board member) 董事; **the Board of ～s** 董事会 6 Brit colloq dated (employer) 老板; (father) 爸爸; **= guv** 7 Tech 调节器

Governor-General n (pl **Governors-General**) 总督

governorship /ˈɡʌvənəʃɪp/ n (office) 行政长官的职位; (jurisdiction) 行政长官的职责; (term) 行政长官的任期

govt. abbr **= government**

gown /ɡaʊn/ n 1 Fashn 女礼服; **a wedding ～** 新娘的结婚礼服 2 Jur, Univ 长袍; **a BA ～** 学士服 3 Med 罩衣

GP ▸**p. 409** abbr Brit **= general practitioner**

> **GP**
>
> 全科医生，全称 General Practitioner，亦称家庭医生（family doctor 或 family practitioner）。英国社区中负责初级保健（primary care）的医生，初步诊疗各种疾病。人们生病时一般都必须先去看全科医生。全科医生有处方权。在认为有必要时会开转诊单（referral），将病人转往专科医院，由专攻某一领域的医生作进一步的诊断治疗，称为二级保健（secondary care）。全科医生受雇于国民保健体系（NHS）下的政府卫生部门，一般在自己的诊所看病，有时也会出诊。

GPA abbr Amer **= grade point average**

GPS abbr **= global positioning system**

gr. abbr 1 **= gram(s)** 2 **= gross B1**

grab /ɡræb/
A vt (pres p etc. **-bb-**) 1 **～ (hold of)** lit (take hold of) 抓住 ‹handle, branch, sb.'s hand›; **to ～ hold of sth.** 抓住某物; **to ～ sb. by the arm** or **sb.'s arm** 抓住某人的胳膊; **to ～ sth. from sb./sth.** 从某人/某处抢走某物; **to ～ sth. from sb.'s hand** 抢走某人手里的某物; **to ～ sb. just as he is leaving** 在某人刚要离开时拦住他 2 fig (seize) 抓住 ‹chance, offer›; **to ～ sth. with both hands** 牢牢抓住某物 3 colloq (take illegally) 霸占 ‹land, resources›; 攫取 ‹power, leadership› 4 colloq (get quickly) 赶紧做; **to ～ some breakfast** 匆匆吃点早餐; **to ～ two hours' sleep** 抓紧时间睡两个小时 5 colloq (impress) 吸引; **the book doesn't ～ me** 这本书引不起我的兴趣; **how does the idea ～ you?** 你认为那个主意怎么样？
B vi (pres p etc. **-bb-**) 抓; **don't ～!** 别抢！; **to ～ at sb./sth.** 抓某人/某物; **to ～ at a chance** fig 抓住机会
C n 1 (snatch) 抓; **to make a ～ at** or **for sth.** 抓某物; **to make a ～ for power** 试图夺取权力; **up for ～s** colloq 可供争夺的; **the job is up for ～s** 这个工作人人都可以争取 2 Tech 抓具
D modif 用作抓握的; **～ rail** 三角拉手

grab bag n Amer 1 (lucky dip) 摸彩袋 2 colloq (holding unknown items) 混杂

grace /ɡreɪs/
A n 1 [u and c] (gracefulness, charm) 优雅; **to do sth. with ～** 优雅地做某事; **to have ～/no ～** 仪态优雅/粗鄙; **the social ～s** 社交风度 2 [u] Relig (kindness) 天恩; **by the ～ of God** 承蒙天恩; **(to be) in a state of ～** 怀着受天恩眷顾的心情; **there but for the ～ of God go I** 承蒙天恩，我幸免于难; **to fall from ～** lit 堕落; fig 失宠 3 [u] (time allowance) 宽限期; **to have/be given a week's ～** 有/获得一个星期的宽限; **a period of ～** 宽限期 4 [u] (graciousness) 大度; **(to do sth.) with good/bad ～** 心甘情愿/勉强地（做某事）; **to have the good ～ to do sth.** 通情达理地做某事 5 [c] (quality) 优点; **saving ～** 可取之处 6 [u and c] (prayer) 谢恩祷告; **to say ～** 做谢恩祷告 7 **Grace** [u] (title) 阁下 [对公爵、公爵夫人或大主教的尊称]; **His/Her/Your G～** 阁下
B **graces** npl 1 (affected mannerisms) **airs and ～s** 矫揉造作; **to give oneself/put on airs and ～s** 装腔作势 2 (favour) 宠爱; **to be in sb.'s good ～s** 得到某人的欢心 3 **the (Three) Graces** Mythol 美惠三女神
C vt 1 (decorate) 装饰 ‹room, building, page›; **to be ～d with sth.** «facade, square» 被装饰以某物 2 (honour) 给…带来荣耀 ‹person›; 使…增色 ‹occasion, event, ceremony›; **the Queen ～d us with her presence** 女王的驾临为我们带来了荣耀 3 (bless) **to be ～d with sth.** 天生具有 ‹beauty, intelligence›

grace-and-favour adj attrib Brit 钦赐的 ‹residence›

graceful /ˈɡreɪsfl/ adj 1 (elegant) 优雅的 ‹motion, style›; 端秀的 ‹writing›; **a ～ dancer** 动作优美的舞蹈演员 2 (dignified) 得体的 ‹exit, apology›; **a ～ refusal to an invitation** 对邀请的婉言谢绝

gracefully /ˈɡreɪsfəli/ adv 1 (elegantly) 优雅地 ‹move, shaped› 2 (with dignity) 得体地 ‹accept, worded›

gracefulness /ˈɡreɪsflnɪs/ n [u] 优雅

graceless /ˈɡreɪslɪs/ adj 1 (inelegant) 难看的 ‹dress›; **～ furniture** 粗笨的家具; **to be ～ in appearance** 外表丑陋 2 (ungracious) 无礼的 ‹remark›; **a ～ young man** 粗鲁的年轻人

grace note n 装饰音

gracious /ˈɡreɪʃəs/
A adj 1 (courteous) 亲切的 ‹smile, reply, manner, gentleman›; **to be ～ to sb. (about sth.)** （在某事上）对待某人很仁厚; **to be ～ in defeat** 豁达地面对失败; **to be ～ enough to apologize** 大度地道歉 2 attrib (in royal title) 仁慈的; **her ～ Majesty** 仁慈的女王陛下 3 (luxurious) 优裕的 ‹living›; 豪华的 ‹furniture›
B excl formal 天哪 [用于礼貌地表示惊讶]; **～ me!** 天哪！; **good** or **goodness ～!** 啊呀！

graciously /ˈɡreɪʃəsli/ adv 亲切地 ‹act, worded›; **to wave ～ at the crowds** 向人群亲切挥手

graciousness /ˈɡreɪʃəsnɪs/ n [u] 1 (courteousness) 有礼貌 2 (elegance) 和蔼可亲 3 (luxury) 豪华舒适

gradation /ɡrəˈdeɪʃn/ n 1 (scale) 等级 2 (stage) 阶段 3 (of colour) 层次; (of sound) 渐变; **a picture with subtle ～s in** or **of colour** 颜色细微渐变的一幅画 4 Meas 刻度

grade /ɡreɪd/
A n 1 Comm (of goods, produce) 等级; **high-～**

meat 优质猪肉; large-~ eggs 大号鸡蛋 **2** esp Amer (mark) 评分等级; to get good ~s 获得优良成绩; to be awarded *or* get two A ~s 得两个A **3** Amer (class, year) 年级 **4** (*also* **Grade**) Brit (examination, level of skill) 级别; ~ IV piano 钢琴四级 **5** Admin (in hierarchy) 级别; a salary ~ 工资级别; to make the ~ (reach the standard) 达到标准; (succeed) 成功 **6** Mil 军衔 **7** Amer (gradient) 斜坡; a steep ~ 陡坡

B *vt* **1** (categorize by quality, size) 将…按级分类 ‹*produce, accommodation, amenities*›; to be ~d by *or* according to size 按大小分等级 **2** (categorize by level of difficulty) 使…逐级变化 ‹*questions*›; ~d exercises for the piano 钢琴渐进练习 **3** esp Amer (mark) 给…评分 ‹*pupils, work, papers*›; the examination papers have been ~d 试卷已经评阅好了 **4** Civ Eng 把…筑平 ‹*road, land*›

grade: ~ book *n* Amer 考试成绩记录; **~ crossing** *n* Amer 平交道口; **~ inflation** *n* [u] Amer 分数贬值; **~ point average** *n* Amer 平均积点

grader /ˈɡreɪdə(r)/ *n* **1** (of produce) (machine) 分类机; (person) 分类者; to work as an egg ~ 做给鸡蛋分类的工作 **2** Civ Eng 平土机

grade school *n* Amer 小学

gradient /ˈɡreɪdɪənt/ *n* **1** (slope) 斜坡; a rising/falling ~ 上坡/下坡 **2** Meas (degree of slope) 坡度 **3** Math (on a graph) 斜率 **4** Phys (increase or decrease) 梯度

grading system *n* **1** (gen) 分级系统; (of wages, salaries) 分级制度 **2** Educ 评分体系

gradual /ˈɡrædʒʊəl/ *adj* **1** (slow) 逐渐的 ‹*improvement, change*›; a ~ process 渐进的过程 **2** (gentle) 平缓的 ‹*rise, incline, fall*›; a ~ slope 缓坡

gradualism /ˈɡrædʒʊəlɪzəm/ *n* [u] **1** Philos, Econ 渐进主义 **2** Biol 物种缓变论

gradualist /ˈɡrædʒʊəlɪst/

A *n* **1** Philos, Econ 渐进主义者 **2** Biol 物种缓变论者

B *adj* **1** Philos, Econ 渐进主义的 ‹*policy, politics, approach*›; 奉行渐进主义的 ‹*reformer*› **2** Biol 物种缓变论的 ‹*interpretation*›

gradually /ˈɡrædʒʊəli/ *adv* 逐渐地

graduate

A /ˈɡrædʒʊət/ *n* **1** Univ 学士学位获得者; a ~ in law, a law ~ 法学学士; a ~ of *or* from Oxford (University) 牛津大学毕业生 **2** Amer Sch 毕业生; a high school ~ 中学毕业生

B /ˈɡrædʒʊət/ *modif* 研究生的 ‹*studies, accommodation, centre*›; a ~ student 研究生

C /ˈɡrædjʊeɪt/ *vi* **1** Univ 获得学位; he ~d from Oxford in 1995 他 1995 年毕业于牛津大学; to ~ from *or* at the university of life fig hum 从生活这所大学毕业 **2** Amer Sch 毕业; to ~ from high school 中学毕业 **3** fig (progress) 渐进; to ~ (from sth.) to sth. (从某物) 渐变到某物; he started with motorbikes but has now ~d to his first car 他一开始骑的是摩托车, 但现在过渡到有了自己的第一辆小汽车

D /ˈɡrædjʊeɪt/ *vt* **1** Fin 将…分等级 ‹*contributions, payments*›; a ~d tax scheme 累进税制 **2** Tech 刻度数于 ‹*measure, vessel*›; a ruler ~d in inches 标有英寸刻度的尺子 **3** Amer (give degree to) 授予…学士; this college ~d fifty students last year 该学院去年有 50 名学生毕业

graduate: ~ assistant *n* Amer 研究生助教; **~ profession** *n* 文凭职业 [要求从业人员拥有学位的职业]; **~ recruit** *n* 有学位的新雇员; **~ school** *n* Amer 研究生院; **~ teacher** *n* 有学位的教师; **~ training scheme** *n* 大学毕业生职业培训计划

graduation /ˌɡrædʒʊˈeɪʃn/ *n* **1** [u] Univ (receiving a degree) 获得学位; where are you going to work after ~? 你毕业后将会在哪儿工作? **2** [u] Amer Sch (receiving a diploma) 毕业 **3** [c] Univ (ceremony) 毕业典礼; ~ day 毕业典礼日 **4** [c] (calibration) 刻度

graduation ceremony *n* (大学) 毕业典礼

graffiti /ɡrəˈfiːtiː/ *npl* + *v sing or pl* 涂鸦

graffiti artist *n* 涂鸦艺术家

graft[1] /ɡrɑːft, Amer ɡræft/

A *n* **1** Hort (shoot) 嫁接用的嫩枝; (joining) 嫁接 **2** Med (skin, bone, etc.) 移植物; (operation) 移植

B *vt* **1** Hort 嫁接; to ~ one variety of apple on to another 把一个苹果树种嫁接到另外一种上 **2** Med 移植 ‹*skin, organs*›; the new veins had been ~ed on to the heart 新的血管移植到了心脏上 **3** fig 使…紧密结合 ‹*ideas, system*›; to ~ sth. into/on to sth. 使某物并入某物; old values have been ~ed on to a new social class 旧的价值观已经植根于新的社会阶层

graft[2]

A *n* [u] **1** Brit colloq (hard work) 艰苦的工作; to put a lot of (hard) ~ into sth. 为某事付出巨大的努力 **2** esp Amer (corruption) 贿赂

B *vi* Brit colloq 卖力地工作

grafter /ˈɡrɑːftə(r), Amer ˈɡræftə(r)/ *n* **1** Brit colloq (hard worker) 卖力工作的人 **2** esp Amer (corrupt person) 腐败分子

graham /ˈɡreɪəm/: **~ cracker** *n* Amer 全麦饼干; **~ flour** *n* [u] Amer 全麦面粉

grail /ɡreɪl/ *n* **1** = **Holy Grail 1** **2** fig 努力追求的目标

grain /ɡreɪn/ *n* **1** [u and c] (commodity) 谷物; ~ prices 谷物价格 **2** [c] (single seed) 谷粒; a few ~s of rice 几粒大米 **3** [c] (tiny particle) 颗粒; a ~ of sand 一粒沙 **4** [c] (unit of weight) 格令 [重量单位, 等于0.065克] **5** [c] fig (of truth, hope, comfort) 少量; without a ~ of truth 没有一点真实性 **6** [u] (pattern) (in wood, stone, leather, paper, fabric) 纹理; to cut along the ~ 顺着纹路切; to go against the ~ (to do sth.) fig 违反常理 (做某事); it really goes against the ~ to have to go to the office at weekends 周末还得上班真是不合常情

grain: ~ alcohol *n* [u] [谷物酿制的] 乙醇; **~ elevator** *n* 谷物升运机

graininess /ˈɡreɪnɪnɪs/ *n* [u] 颗粒性

grainy /ˈɡreɪni/ *adj* **1** Phot 麻面的 **2** (granular) 粒状的

gram /ɡræm/ ▸**p. 909** *n* 克 [重量单位]

grammar /ˈɡræmə(r)/ *n* **1** [u] (study) 语法学; [c and u] (system) 语法; ~ exercise 语法练习 **2** [u] (notions of language) 语法规则 **3** [u] (person's use of language) 文理; to use bad ~ 遣词造句不当; errors in ~ 语法错误 **4** [c] a ~ (book) 语法书

grammar checker *n* 语法检验程序

grammarian /ɡrəˈmeərɪən/ *n* 语法学家

grammar school *n* **1** Brit Sch 文法学校 **2** Amer dated = **elementary school**

grammatical /ɡrəˈmætɪkl/ *adj* **1** (of or about grammar) 语法的 **2** (correct) 符合语法的 ‹*sentence, speech*›

grammaticality /ɡrəˌmætɪˈkæləti/ *n* [u] 符合语法

grammatically /ɡrəˈmætɪkli/ *adv* **1** (correctly) 符合语法地 ‹*speak, write*› **2** (syntactically) 在语法上 ‹*agree, disagree, accord*›; a ~ correct sentence 语法上正确的句子

grammaticalness /ɡrəˈmætɪklnɪs/ *n* [u] = **grammaticality**

gramme /ɡræm/ *n* Brit = **gram**

Grammy /ˈɡræmi/ *n* (*pl* ~s *or* **Grammies**) Amer 格莱美奖; the ~s 格莱美颁奖典礼

gramophone /ˈɡræməfəʊn/ *n* dated 唱机

gramophone: ~ needle *n* 唱针; **~ record** *n* 唱片

Grampians /ˈɡræmpɪənz/, **Grampian Mountains** *pr npl* the ~ 格兰扁山脉

gramps /ɡræmps/ *n* esp Amer colloq (grandfather) (on mother's side) 外公; (on father's side) 爷爷

gran /ɡræn/ *n* Brit colloq (grandmother) (on mother's side) 外婆; (on father's side) 奶奶

granary /ˈɡrænəri/ *n* 粮仓; Europe's ~ fig 欧洲的粮仓

granary: ~ bread *n* [u] Brit 全麦面包; **~ loaf** *n* Brit 全麦面包

grand /ɡrænd/

A *adj* **1** (impressive) 壮观的 ‹*building*›; (of great importance) 重要的 ‹*ceremony*›; (ambitious) 宏大的 ‹*design, concept*›; a ~ palace 雄伟的宫殿; on a ~ scale 大规模地; the wedding was a very ~ occasion 婚礼场面非常隆重; the ~ old man of English politics 英国政界的元老 **2** (self-important) 傲慢的 ‹*manner, action*›; to put on a ~ air 摆出一副了不起的样子; to make a ~ gesture 装腔作势 **3** colloq (fine, excellent) 极好的 ‹*adventure, weather*›; to have a ~ time 玩得很开心; he did a ~ job 他干得很出色

B *n* **1** (*pl* **grand**) colloq (sum of money) Brit 一千英镑; Amer 一千美元 **2** colloq (piano) 大钢琴

grand: ~child ▸**p. 419** *n* (son of son) 孙子; (daughter of son) 孙女; (son of daughter) 外孙; (daughter of daughter) 外孙女; **~dad** ▸**p. 419** *n* colloq (grandfather) (on mother's side) 外公; (on father's side) 爷爷; **~daddy** ▸**p. 419** *n* **1** colloq (grandfather) (on mother's side) 外公; (on father's side) 爷爷; **2** (greatest example, instance) 最突出的例子; the ~daddy of all headaches 最厉害的头痛病; **3** fig (precursor, originator) 老祖宗; **~daughter** ▸**p. 419** *n* (daughter of son) 孙女; (daughter of daughter) 外孙女; **~ duchess** *n* (wife of grand duke) 大公夫人; (female title holder) 女大公; **~ duchy** *n* 大公领地; **~ duke** *n* 大公

grandee /ɡrænˈdiː/ *n* 大人物

grandeur /ˈɡrændʒə(r)/ *n* [u] **1** (of scenery) 壮丽; (of building) 雄伟; (of style) 华丽 **2** (of power, status) 显赫; delusions of ~ 自以为了不起

grandfather /ˈɡrænfɑːðə(r)/ ▸**p. 419** *n* (on mother's side) 外祖父; (on father's side) 祖父

grandfather: ~ clause *n* Amer colloq 不溯既往条款; **~ clock** *n* 落地式大摆钟

grand finale *n* [终场演员的] 全体登台

grandiloquence /ˌɡrænˈdɪləkwəns/ *n* [u] formal 言辞浮夸

grandiloquent /ˌɡrænˈdɪləkwənt/ *adj* formal 言辞浮夸的 ‹*speaker, speech, style*›

grandiose /ˈɡrændɪəʊs/ *adj* **1** (imposing) 雄伟的 ‹*building*›; 壮丽的 ‹*style*› **2** (ambitious) 宏伟的 ‹*plan, project*›

grand: ~ jury *n* Amer 大陪审团; **~ larceny** *n* Amer 大盗窃罪; **~ma** *n* colloq (grandmother) (on mother's side) 外婆; (on father's side) 奶奶; **~ master** *n* 国际象棋大师

grandmother /ˈɡrænmʌðə(r)/ ▸**p. 419** *n* (on mother's side) 外婆; (on father's side) 奶奶; to teach one's ~ to suck eggs 班门弄斧

grandmother clock *n* 落地式摆钟 [大小约为落地式大摆钟 (grandfather) 的2/3]

grand: G~ National *n* Brit 全国赛马大会; **G~ Old Party** *n* Amer the G~ Old Party 老大党 [自1880年开始美国共和党的别称]; **~ opera** *n* 大歌剧; **~pa** ▸**p. 419** *n* colloq (grandfather) (on mother's side) 外公; (on father's side) 爷爷; **~parent** ▸**p. 419** *n* (father of mother) 外祖父; (mother of mother) 外祖母; (father of one's father) 祖父; (mother of father) 祖母; **~ piano** ▸**p. 395** *n* 大钢琴; **G~ Prix** /ˌɡrɒ̃ ˈpriː/ *n* (*pl* **G~s Prix**) (motor-racing) 国际汽车大奖赛; (motor-cycling) 国际摩托车大奖赛; **~ slam** *n* 大满贯 [桥牌比赛中指全赢13墩牌, 网球、高尔夫球等运动中指在一个赛季中赢得所有主要比赛]; **~son** ▸**p. 419** *n* (son of son) 孙子; (son of daughter) 外孙; **~ staircase** *n* 主楼梯; **~stand** *n* 大看台; **~stand ticket** 大看台门票; **~stand seat** 大看台座位; to have a ~stand view of sth. fig 看到某事物的全景;

g

~ **total** *n* 总计; **the ~ total for the repairs** 修理费用总额

grange /ɡreɪndʒ/ *n* Brit 庄园

granite /ˈɡrænɪt/ *n* [u] 花岗岩; **a heart of ~** fig 铁石心肠; **a man with ~ determination** fig 有坚定决心的人

granny, grannie /ˈɡræni/ *n* colloq (grandmother) (on mother's side) 外婆; (on father's side) 奶奶

granny: ~ flat *n* Brit colloq 老人套间; **~ knot** *n* 老奶奶结 [反向打的方结，容易散开]

grant /ɡrɑːnt, Amer ɡrænt/

A *vt* **1** (allow) 准予 ‹*favour, interview*›; 准许 ‹*bail*›; **to ~ sb. sth.** 将某物准予某人; **he ~ed him his request** 他答应了他的要求; **to ~ sb. permission (to do sth.)** 允许某人（做某事）; **permission ~ed!** 同意！; **I refused to ~ the men access to my home** 我拒绝让那些人进我的家门; **to ~ sb. an extension (of time)** 准许某人延期; **to ~ sb. one's time** 在某人身上花费时间 **2** (give formally or legally) 授予 ‹*land, right, power*›; 发放 ‹*visa, pension, compensation*›; **to ~ sb. asylum** 为某人提供政治避难; **he has been ~ed leave of absence** 他获准休假 **3** Fin 批准 ‹*loan, overdraft*› **4** (concede) 承认 ‹*truth, validity, statement*›; **to ~ (sb.) that ...** （向某人）承认…; **to ~ the truth of sth.** 承认某事的真实性; **he is, I ~ you, a convincing witness** 我承认，他是个有说服力的证人 **5** **to take sb./sth. for ~ed** (fail to appreciate) 对…不予重视 ‹*person, thing, circumstances*› **6** **to take it for ~ed that ...** (assume as true) 理所当然地认为…; **to take sth. for ~ed** 认为…是理所当然的 ‹*truth, validity, fact*›; **to take too much for ~ed** 过于想当然

B *n* **1** (award of money) 拨款; **a ~ to do sth.** 做某事的补助金; **a ~ towards sth./doing sth.** 某事/做某事的经费 **2** Jur (of land, property) 让渡; **a ~ of a patent** 专利权的转让; **a ~ of probate** 遗嘱检验权的授予

grant aid *n* [u] Brit 资助款

granted /ˈɡrɑːntɪd, Amer ˈɡræn-/ *adv* 诚然; **~, it's not an ideal situation, but ...** 的确，情况并不完美，可是…

grant-maintained *adj* Brit 由中央政府出资的 ‹*school, college*›

granular /ˈɡrænjʊlə(r)/ *adj* **1** (containing granules) 含颗粒的 ‹*substance, material*›; (granule-like) 粒状的 ‹*structure*› **2** (rough) 粗糙的 ‹*texture*›

granulate /ˈɡrænjʊleɪt/ *vt* (form into grains) 使…成粒状 ‹*substance, material*›; (make grainy in texture) 使变粗糙

granulated /ˈɡrænjʊleɪtɪd/ *adj* (formed into grains) 成粒状的; (with a grainy texture) 粗糙的; **~ sugar** 砂糖

granulation /ˌɡrænjʊˈleɪʃn/ *n* [u] (of substance) 形成颗粒; (of surface) 表面变得粗糙

granule /ˈɡrænjuːl/ *n* 颗粒

grape /ɡreɪp/ *n* 葡萄; **a bunch of ~s** 一串葡萄; **sour ~s** 酸葡萄; **~ juice** 葡萄汁

grapefruit /ˈɡreɪpfruːt/ *n* [c and u] 葡萄柚; **~ juice** 葡萄柚汁

grape: ~ hyacinth *n* 麝香兰; **~shot** *n* [u] 霰弹; **~ sugar** *n* [u] 葡萄糖; **~vine** *n* 葡萄藤; **to hear sth. on the ~vine** fig colloq 从小道消息听说某事物

graph /ɡrɑːf, Amer ɡræf/

A *n* **1** Math 图表; **a falling ~ of infant mortality** 婴儿死亡率下降的曲线图 **2** Ling 书写单位

B *vt* 用图表表示

graphic /ˈɡræfɪk/ *adj* **1** Art 平面艺术的 ‹*work, symbol*› **2** Comput 图形的; **~ information** 图形信息 **3** (vivid) 生动的 ‹*account, detail*›; **a ~ description of the horrors of war** 对战争惨状的逼真描写

graphical /ˈɡræfɪkl/ *adj* **1** (relating to visual art) 平面艺术的 **2** (relating to computer graphics) 图形的; **~ representation** 图示

graphical display *n* 图形显示

graphically /ˈɡræfɪkli/ *adv* **1** (diagrammatically) 以图表形式 **2** (vividly) 生动地; **he described the disaster ~** 他逼真地描述了那场灾难

graphical user interface *n* 图形用户界面

graphic: ~ art *n* [u] 平面艺术; **~ artist** ▸**p. 409** *n* 平面设计师; **~ arts** *npl* 平面造型艺术; **~ design** *n* [u] 平面造型设计; **~ designer** ▸**p. 409** *n* 平面造型设计师; **~ display** *n* = **graphical display**; **~ equalizer** *n* 图形均衡器

graphics /ˈɡræfɪks/ *npl* **1** + *v sing* Art (subject, speciality) 平面造型艺术 **2** + *v pl* Art (images, design) 图样 **3** Comput + *v pl* (images)（计算机）图形; + *v sing* (technique, method)（计算机）图形处理

graphics: ~ accelerator *n* 图形加速器; **~ board** *n* 显卡; **~ card** *n* 图形卡; **~ tablet** *n* 图形输入板

graphite /ˈɡræfaɪt/ *n* [u] 石墨; **a ~ drawing** 石墨画; **a ~ driver/shaft** 碳素杆/杆身

graphologist /ɡrəˈfɒlədʒɪst/ ▸**p. 409** *n* 笔迹学家

graphology /ɡrəˈfɒlədʒi/ *n* [u] 笔迹学

graph: ~ paper *n* [u] 方格纸; **~ plotter** *n* 绘图仪

grapnel /ˈɡræpnəl/ *n* = **grappling hook**

grapple /ˈɡræpl/ *vi* **1** lit (fight) 扭打; **to ~ with sb.** 与某人扭打 **2** fig (struggle) 努力对付; **to ~ with a problem** 努力解决问题

grappling hook, grappling iron /ˈɡræplɪŋ/ *ns* 抓钩

grasp /ɡrɑːsp, Amer ɡræsp/

A *n* **1** (hold, grip) 紧抓; **the pen fell from her ~** 钢笔从她手中掉落; **to take a firm/strong ~ on** *or* **of sth.** 紧紧地/有力地握住某物; **to tighten/loosen one's ~** 握紧手/松开手; **he held her in an iron ~** 他死死地抓住她 **2** fig (power, reach) (of person, organization) 掌握; (of emotion) 控制; **in the ~ of sb./sth.** 在某人/某物的控制之中; **to escape/slip from** *or* **out of sb.'s ~** 逃脱/摆脱某人的控制; **the prize has eluded her ~** 她没能获奖; **beyond the ~ of sb./sth.** 在某人/某物的掌控之外; **to have sb./sth. within one's ~** 掌握某人/某事物 **3** (understanding, imagination) 理解; **to have a good/sound ~ of sth.** 对某事物有充分/彻底的理解; **to have a poor ~ of sth.** 对某事物了解甚少; **within sb.'s ~** 在某人的理解范围内; **beyond sb.'s ~** 超出某人的理解范围

B *vt* **1** (seize) 抓住; **he ~ed me by the arm** 他揪住了我的胳膊; **to ~ the nettle** fig 知难而进; **to ~ the chance** *or* **opportunity** fig 抓住机会 **2** (understand) 理解; **she could never ~ what to do/how to do it** 她永远不明白该做什么/怎么做; **to ~ the seriousness/enormity/meaning of sth.** 理解某事的严重性/艰巨性/意思

C *vi* **to ~ at sth.** 试图抓住某物; **to ~ at straws** fig 抓救命稻草; **to ~ at the chance** *or* **opportunity** fig 尽力把握机会

grasping /ˈɡrɑːspɪŋ, Amer ˈɡræspɪŋ/ *adj* pej 贪婪的

grass /ɡrɑːs, Amer ɡræs/

A *n* **1** [u] (wild) 草; **a blade of ~** 一片草叶; **not let the ~ grow under one's feet** fig (in getting sth. done) 不拖拉; (in taking an opportunity) 不坐失良机; **to kick sth. into the long ~** fig colloq 把某事搁置一边 **2** [c] (as botanical classification) 禾本科植物 **3** [u] (lawn) 草地; (pasture) 草场; **keep off the ~!** 禁止踩踏草地！; **to mow** *or* **cut the ~** 割草; **the ~ is always greener on the other side (of the fence)** Prov 这山望着那山高; **to put ... out to ~** 赶…去吃草; fig hum 迫使…退休; **to play on ~** (in tennis) 在草地球场上打球 **4** [u] colloq (marijuana) 大麻 **5** [c] Brit colloq (informer) 向警方告密的人

B *vt* 在…上种草 ‹*garden, field, land*›

C *vi* Brit colloq pej 告密; **to ~ on sb., to ~ sb. up** 告发某人

grass: ~ box Brit, **~ catcher** Amer *ns* 集草箱; **~ court** *n* 草地球场; **~ cutter** *n* 割草机; **~ cuttings** *npl* 割下来的草

grass green ▸**p. 134**

A *n* 草绿色

B **grass-green** *adj* 草绿色的

grasshopper /ˈɡrɑːshɒpə(r), Amer ˈɡræs-/ *n* 蚱蜢; **knee-high to a ~** hum 十分幼小的

grassland /ˈɡrɑslənd, Amer ˈɡræs-/

A *n* [u] 草原

B **grasslands** *npl* 草场

grassroots

A *npl* (people) 基层群众; (level) 基层; **the ~ of the party** 党的基层组织

B **grass-roots** *modif* 基层群众的; **to win support at grass-roots level** 得到基层的支持; **a grass-roots movement** 群众运动

grass: ~ seed *n* [u and c] 草籽; **~ skiing** ▸**p. 307** *n* [u] 滑草运动; **~ skirt** *n* 草裙; **~ snake** *n* 游蛇; **~ widow** *n* dated hum 临时寡妇 [丈夫暂时不在身边的女人]

grassy /ˈɡrɑːsi, Amer ˈɡræsi/ *adj* 长满草的; **a ~ meadow** 草地

grate[1] /ɡreɪt/ *n* (fire-basket) 炉栅; (hearth) 炉膛

grate[2]

A *vt* 磨碎; **to ~ sth. into small pieces** 把某物磨成细末

B *vi* **1** (make a harsh noise) 发出刮擦声; **the hinges ~d as the gate swung open** 大门打开时，铰链吱嘎作响 **2** fig (annoy) 使人气恼; **to ~ on sb.'s nerves** 使某人心烦意乱; **her shrill voice ~s (on my ears)** 她尖厉的嗓音（对我来说）很刺耳

grateful /ˈɡreɪtfl/ *adj* 感激的; **to be ~ to sb. (for sth.)** （为某事）感激某人; **he was very ~ for my help** 他非常感谢我的帮助; **to be ~ for small mercies** 庆幸糟糕的情况没有变得更坏; **we are ~ that it is only two hours late** 让我们感到庆幸的是只晚了两个小时; **a ~ letter** 感谢信

gratefully /ˈɡreɪtfəli/ *adv* 感激地 ‹*accept, received*›

grater /ˈɡreɪtə(r)/ *n* 磨碎器

gratification /ˌɡrætɪfɪˈkeɪʃn/ *n* [u] (satisfaction) 满意; (pleasure) 满足; **much to one's ~ ...** 令人非常满意的是…; **sexual ~** 性满足

gratify /ˈɡrætɪfaɪ/ *vt* **1** (give satisfaction to) 使满意; (give pleasure to) 使高兴; **to be gratified at** *or* **by** *or* **with sth.** 对某事物感到满意 **2** (satisfy) 满足 ‹*desire, need*›; 纵容 ‹*passion*›

gratifying /ˈɡrætɪfaɪɪŋ/ *adj* (pleasing) 令人高兴的; (satisfying) 令人满意的

grating[1] /ˈɡreɪtɪŋ/ *n* 格栅

grating[2] *adj* 刺耳的 ‹*sound, noise, voice*›; **his ~ personality** fig 他那咄咄逼人的个性

gratis /ˈɡrɑːtɪs, ˈɡreɪtɪs/

A *adv* 免费地; **to work for sb. ~** 无偿为某人工作

B *adj* 免费的

gratitude /ˈɡrætɪtjuːd, Amer -tuːd/ ▸**p. 818** *n* [u] 感激之情; **to owe sb. a deep debt of ~ (for sth.)** （因某事）对某人感激不尽

gratuitous /ɡrəˈtjuːɪtəs, Amer -ˈtuː-/ *adj* (without good reason) 无理由的; (unnecessary) 不必要的; **a ~ insult** 无端的侮辱; **there is a lot of ~ violence on television** 电视里有很多无谓的暴力镜头

gratuitously /ɡrəˈtjuːɪtəsli, Amer -ˈtuː-/ *adv* (for no good reason) 无理由地; (unnecessarily) 不必要地; **to insult sb. ~** 无端地侮辱某人

gratuity /ɡrəˈtjuːəti, Amer -ˈtuː-/ *n* **1** formal (tip) 小费 **2** Brit (on retirement) 退休补贴

grave[1] /ɡreɪv/ *n* **1** (burial place) 坟墓; **to go to an early ~** 过早去世; **to drive sb. to an early ~** fig 使某人极为烦恼; **to go to one's ~ convinced that ...** 到死都相信…; **to**

dance on sb.'s ～ fig 因为自己不喜欢的某人死了而高兴; **somebody is walking over my** ～ fig 有人在我坟上走 [无故颤栗时的说法]; **to turn in one's** ～ fig 在九泉之下不得安宁; **to dig one's own** ～ fig 自掘坟墓; **to have one foot in the** ～ fig 离死不远; **from the cradle to the** ～ fig 从生到死 **2** fig (death) **the** ～ 死亡; **beyond the** ～ 死后; **as silent as the** ～ 死一般寂静的

grave² /greɪv/ *adj* **1** (serious) 严重的 ‹*consequences, mistake, danger*›; **a** ～ **risk of fire** 极大的火灾隐患 **2** (solemn) 严肃的 ‹*person, expression, look*›

grave³ /grɑːv/ *n* 沉音符

gravedigger /ˈgreɪvdɪgə(r)/ ▸**p. 409** *n* 掘墓人

gravel /ˈgrævl/

A *n* [u] 砂砾; **a** ～ **path** 石子路

B *vt* (*pres p etc.* **-ll-** Brit, **-l-** Amer) 用砂砾铺; **to** ～ **sth. over** 用碎石铺满某物

gravelly /ˈgrævəli/ *adj* **1** lit 由砂砾构成的 **2** fig 粗哑的 ‹*tone, voice*›

gravel pit *n* 采砾坑

gravely /ˈgreɪvli/ *adv* **1** (seriously) 严重地 ‹*hurt*›; **to be** ～ **mistaken** 大错特错; **to be** ～ **ill** 病得很重 **2** (solemnly) 严肃地 ‹*say, nod*›

graveness /ˈgreɪvnɪs/ *n* [u] **1** (of situation, illness, mistake) 严重 **2** (solemnity) 严肃

grave: ～**robber** *n* 盗墓贼; ～**side** *n* 坟墓边; ～**stone** *n* 墓碑

graveyard /ˈgreɪvjɑːd/ *n* 墓地; **the** ～ **of one's hopes** fig 希望破灭的地方

graveyard shift *n* 夜班

gravitas /ˈgrævɪtæs, -tɑːs/ *n* [u] formal 庄严; **a man of** ～ 举止庄严的人

gravitate /ˈgrævɪteɪt/ *vi* **to** ～ **towards** *or* **to sth./sb.** **1** Phys 受引力作用向某物/某人运动; **the deposit** ～**s to the bottom of the flask** 沉淀物沉到烧瓶底 **2** fig **to** ～ **towards** *or* **to sb.** /**sth.** (move towards) 移向某人/某物; (be attracted to) 受某人/某物吸引; **the conversation** ～**d to sport** 谈话的内容转到了运动方面

gravitation /ˌgrævɪˈteɪʃn/ *n* [u] (force) (万有) 引力; (movement) 引力作用下的运动; **the** ～ **of people towards the cities** fig 人们受吸引向城市的流动

gravitational /ˌgrævɪˈteɪʃənl/ *adj* (relating to gravity) (万有) 引力的; (resulting from gravity) 引力引起的; ～ **field** 引力场; **the** ～ **pull of the earth** 地球的引力; ～ **acceleration** 重力加速度

gravity /ˈgrævəti/ *n* [u] **1** Phys 重力; **the law of** ～ 万有引力定律; **the centre of** ～ 重心; ～ **feed** 重力供料 **2** (of offence, situation) 严重性 **3** (solemnity) 严肃; **to behave with due** ～ 表现出应有的庄重态度

gravy /ˈgreɪvi/ *n* [u] 肉汁

gravy: ～ **boat** *n* 船形肉汁盘; ～ **train** *n* colloq 可轻易发大财的手段; **to be/get on the** ～ **train** 得到轻松赚大钱的机会

gray /greɪ/ *adj, n, vt, vi* Amer = **grey**

grayish /ˈgreɪɪʃ/ *adj* Amer = **greyish**

graze¹ /greɪz/

A *vt* **1** (allow to eat grass) 放牧 ‹*cattle, sheep*› **2** (use as food) «*farmer*» 在…上放牧 ‹*grassland*›; «*animal*» 以…为食 ‹*grass*›

B *vi* **1** (eat grass) 吃草; **to put cattle/sheep out to** ～ 把牛/羊放出去吃草 **2** colloq (eat snacks) 吃零食; **to** ～ **on sweets** 吃糖果之类的零食

graze²

A *n* 擦伤; **to have a** ～ **on one's knee** 擦伤膝盖

B *vt* **1** (scrape) 擦伤; **to** ～ **one's knee** 擦伤膝盖 **2** (touch lightly) 擦过; **a bullet** ～**d his cheek** 一颗子弹擦过他的脸颊

C *vi* 轻擦; **our bumpers just** ～**d** 我们的保险杠轻轻碰了一下

grazing /ˈgreɪzɪŋ/ *n* [u] (grassland) 草场; (vegetation) 牧草

grazing: ～ **land** *n* [u] = **grazing**; ～ **rights** *npl* 放牧权

grease /griːs/

A *n* [u] **1** (lubricant) 润滑油; (oily substance) 油脂; **to put** ～ **on one's hair** 给头发抹上发油; **a** ～**-stained collar** 沾有油渍的领口 **2** Culin (animal fat) 动物油脂

B *vt* 给…加润滑油 ‹*machine part*›; 在…上涂油 ‹*cake tin*›; **like** ～**d lightning** colloq (very quickly) 飞快地 ‹*accept, disappear*›; (very quick) 飞快的 ‹*runner, driver*›; **to** ～ **sb.'s palm** fig colloq 向某人行贿; **to** ～ **the wheels** fig colloq 使事情顺利进行

grease: ～ **gun** *n* 滑脂枪; ～**paint** *n* [u] 化装油彩; ～**proof paper** *n* [u] Brit 防油纸

greaser /ˈgriːsə(r)/ *n* Brit colloq 长发飞车党

grease stain *n* 油渍

greasiness /ˈgriːsɪnɪs/ *n* [u] **1** lit 油腻 **2** fig (ingratiation) 虚伪圆滑

greasy /ˈgriːsi/ *adj* **1** (covered with grease) 沾满油脂的; (slippery) 滑溜的 ‹*hands, road surface*›; ～ **tools** 粘满油污的工具; **to climb the** ～ **pole** fig 面对激烈竞争夺取成功 **2** (oily) 油性的 ‹*hair, skin, complexion*› **3** Culin 油腻的 ‹*food*› **4** fig (ingratiating) 虚伪圆滑的; **a** ～ **smile** 假惺惺的笑

greasy spoon *n* colloq often pej [供应油炸食品的] 低级廉价饭馆

great /greɪt/

A *adj* **1** *usu attrib* (measurably large) 大的 ‹*size*›; 高的 ‹*temperature, percentage*›; 长的 ‹*time, distance*›; 强的 ‹*strength*›; **a** ～ **expanse of forest** 一大片森林; **at** ～ **speed** 高速地; **from a** ～ **height** 从很高的地方; **tortoises can live to a very** ～ **age** 龟的寿命很长 **2** *usu attrib* (large in quantity) 大量的; **a** ～**er proportion of houses** 多数房子; **the** ～ **majority of consumers** 绝大多数消费者; **a** ～ **deal (of)** 许多 (的) **3** *usu attrib* (large in general size) 非常大的; ～ **cliffs** 巍峨的悬崖; **a** ～ **shower of rain** 一阵大雨; **she heaved a** ～ **sigh of relief** 她宽慰地长吁了一口气 **4** *attrib* colloq (as intensifier) **you** ～ **buffoon!** 你这个十足的小丑! ; **a** ～ **long list of do's and don'ts** 长长的一串行为规范 **5** (extreme) 强烈的; **the heat is** ～**est at midday** 正午时最热; **the wind blew with** ～ **force** 风刮得很猛; **in** ～ **danger** 处于极度危险中 **6** (significant) 重大的 ‹*change, improvement, progress*›; 显著的 ‹*increase, decrease, difference, similarity*› **7** *usu attrib* (intensely felt) 深切的 ‹*emotion, need*›; **my** ～**est fear is that ...** 我最担心的是…; **it is with** ～ **pleasure** *or* **the** ～**est pleasure that I ...** 我满怀热情地…; **it gives me** ～ **pleasure to ...** …使我感到非常愉快 **8** *usu attrib* (considerably above average) 超乎寻常的; **a matter of** ～ **importance** 非常重要的事情; **she had** ～ **difficulty (in) finding a seat** 她找座位费了好大劲; **to describe sth. in** ～**er detail** 更详细地描述某物; **I'm in no** ～ **hurry (to leave)** 我不着急 (离开) ; **he's leaving — it's no** ～ **loss** 他要走了——没什么大不了的 **9** *usu attrib* (exceptionally competent) 杰出的 ‹*person, name*›; ～ **Scott!** dated 好家伙! **10** (important) (of people) 伟大的; (of things) 重大的; **Alexander the G**～ 亚历山大大帝; ～ **and/or small** 不论高低贵贱; **a** ～ **occasion** 盛大场面; **the** ～ **day/moment arrived** 重要的一天/时刻到来了; **the company has a** ～ **future (ahead of it)** 这家公司前途无量; **the** ～ **wines of Bordeaux** 著名的波尔多葡萄酒; **the** ～ **houses of England** 英格兰的豪门大宅 **11** colloq (excellent) 极好的; **what was the party like? —** ～**!** 晚会怎么样? ——棒极了! ; **it's** ～ **to be back!** 回来的感觉真好! ; **the town hall would be** ～ **as a venue** 地点设在市政厅再好不过了 **12** colloq (healthy, happy) 健康的 ‹*person*›; 良好的 ‹*eyesight, hearing*›; **to feel** ～ 感觉很好; **to look** ～ 气色不错; **he had a** ～ **memory** 他记性很好; **she has a** ～ **eye for detail** 她擅长观察细节; **not to feel** ～ **about sth./doing sth.** 对某事/做某事感到不安 **13** *pred* colloq (very attractive) **to look** ～ 很漂亮; **to look** ～ **with sth.** «*garment, accessory, colour*» 与某物搭配起来很漂亮 **14** colloq (admirable, likeable) 可爱的 ‹*person*›; **she's a** ～ **kid** 她是个好孩子; **it was** ～ **of them to lend us their caravan** 他们把篷车借给我们用了，真好; **to be** ～ **about sth.** 对…很大度; **he was** ～ **about the accident/misunderstanding/mistake** 他对这次意外/误会/失误并不在意 **15** *usu attrib* (enthusiastic) 痴迷的 ‹*walker, swimmer, angler*›; 狂热的 ‹*fan, admirer*›; **he's a** ～ **theatregoer** 他热衷于去剧院看戏; **her father's a** ～ **worrier** 她父亲对什么事情都不放心; **a** ～ **friend** 密友; **to be a** ～ **one for sth./doing sth.** colloq 对某事/做某事非常感兴趣 **16** colloq (very talented) 出色的 ‹*professional*›; **to be** ～ **at sth./doing sth.** 擅长某事/做某事; **to be** ～ **on sth.** 通晓某事; **to be** ～ **with sth.** 擅长应对某事; **to be** ～ **with sb.** 擅长和某人打交道 **17** colloq (very effective or suitable) 好用的 ‹*implement, gadget, tool*›; 有效的 ‹*medicine, method*›; 适宜的 ‹*day, season, weather, place*›; 贴切的 ‹*name, title*›; **to be** ～ **for sth./doing sth.** 适合某事/做某事; ～ **... for sth./doing sth.** 适合某事/做某事的…; **it's going to be a** ～ **weekend for fishing** 这个周末会很适合钓鱼; **this is a** ～ **place to keep the wine** 这个地方很适合保存葡萄酒 **18** *usu attrib* colloq (favourable, convincing) 极好的 ‹*opportunity, offer, idea, excuse*› **19** *attrib* (in names of places, animals, plants) 大的 [用于动植物名、地名、历史事件前]; ～ **auk** 大海鸦; ～**er celandine** 白屈菜; **G**～ **Russell Street** 罗素大街; **the G**～ **Rift Valley** 东非大裂谷

B **great-** *attrib* (in family relationship) [用于家族中的称呼]; ～**-grandmother** (on grandfather's side) 曾祖母; (on grandmother's side) 曾外祖母; ～**-**～**-grandmother** (on great-grandfather's side) 高祖母; (on great-grandmother's side) 高外祖母; ～**-**～**-**～**-grandmother** (on great-great-grandfather's side) 玄祖母; (on great-great-grandmother's side) 玄外祖母

C *adv* colloq 很好地; **I'm doing** ～ 我很好; **the machine's working** ～ **now** 机器现在运转正常; **everything's going** ～ 一切进展顺利

D *n* **1** + *v pl* formal or liter liter (great people) **the** ～ 伟人; **the** ～ **and the good** Brit iron 大人物 **2** colloq (sb. important) 要人; (sth. important) 重要的事物; **he was one of snooker's all-time** ～**s** 他是一位空前的斯诺克巨星; **one of the all-time** ～**s of the silent screen** 无声电影史上的巨作之一 **3** **greatest** + *v sing or pl* **the** ～**est** 最伟大的人; **we are the** ～**est!** 我们是最棒的!

E *excl* colloq **1** (expressing pleasure) 好极了 **2** iron (expressing displeasure) 真绝啊; **it's raining — oh** ～**, that's all I need!** 下雨了——好啊，偏偏给我来这一场雨!

great: ～ **ape** *n* 类人猿; ～**-aunt** *n* (sister of grandfather) 姑婆; (sister of grandmother) 姨婆; **G**～ **Barrier Reef** *pr n* **the G**～ **Barrier Reef** 大堡礁; **G**～ **Bear** *n* **the G**～ **Bear** 大熊座; **G**～ **Britain** *pr n* 大不列颠岛; ～ **circle** *n* 大圆; ～**coat** *n* (overcoat) 厚重长大衣; Mil 军大衣; **G**～ **Dane** *n* 大丹犬

Greater: ～ **London** *pr n* 大伦敦 [由伦敦城和32个区构成的行政区]; ～ **Manchester** /ˌgreɪtə ˈmæntʃestə(r)/ *pr n* 大曼彻斯特 [英格兰西北部的一都市郡，包括曼彻斯特市及周边地区]

greatest common divisor, greatest common factor *ns* 最大公因子

g

Great Britain

严格说来，Great Britain 是一个地理概念，指大不列颠岛，常称 Britain。它由英格兰、威尔士和苏格兰组成。英伦列岛（British Isles）除大不列颠岛之外，还包括爱尔兰岛和其他许多岛屿。1707 年，苏格兰和英格兰及威尔士合并，Great Britain 开始成为一个政治概念。1801 年，爱尔兰和大不列颠合并，组成大不列颠及爱尔兰联合王国（The United Kingdom of Great Britain and Ireland）。1922 年，爱尔兰南部宣布成立爱尔兰自由邦（Irish Free State），1949 年成为完全独立的爱尔兰共和国（Republic of Ireland）。英国全称也改为大不列颠及北爱尔兰联合王国（the United Kingdom of Great Britain and Northern Ireland），简称 the United Kingdom 或 the UK。目前在非正式场合，Great Britain 和 United Kingdom 都可以指英国。

great: ~-grandchild ▸**p. 419** *n* (son of grandson) 曾孙; (daughter of grandson) 曾孙女; (son of granddaughter) 曾外孙; (daughter of granddaughter) 曾外孙女; **~-granddaughter** ▸**p. 419** *n* (daughter of grandson) 曾孙女; (daughter of granddaughter) 曾外孙女; **~-grandfather** ▸**p. 419** *n* (on grandfather's side) 曾祖父; (on grandmother's side) 曾外祖父; **~-grandmother** ▸**p. 419** *n* (on grandfather's side) 曾祖母; (on grandmother's side) 曾外祖母; **~-grandparent** ▸**p. 419** *n* (on grandmother's side) (male) 曾外祖父; (female) 曾外祖母; (on grandfather's side) (male) 曾祖父; (female) 曾祖母; **~-grandson** ▸**p. 419** *n* (son of grandson) 曾孙; (son of granddaughter) 曾外孙; **~-hearted** *adj* dated 豪爽的; **G~ Lakes** ▸**p. 424** *npl* **the G~ Lakes** 五大湖; **G~ Leap Forward** *n* **the G~ Leap Forward** 大跃进; **~-nephew** ▸**p. 419** *n* (son of brother's son) 侄孙; (son of brother's daughter) 侄外孙; (son of sister's son) 甥孙; (son of sister's daughter) 甥外孙; **~-niece** ▸**p. 419** *n* (daughter of brother's son) 侄孙女; (daughter of brother's daughter) 侄外孙女; (daughter of sister's son) 甥孙女; (daughter of sister's daughter) 甥外孙女; **G~ Plains** *pr n* **the G~ Plains** 大平原; **G~ Power** *n* **the G~ Powers** 大国; **~-uncle** ▸**p. 419** *n* (younger brother of mother's father) 叔外公; (elder brother of mother's father) 伯外公; (younger brother of father's father) 叔祖父; (elder brother of father's father) 伯祖父; (brother of mother's mother) 舅外公; (brother of father's mother) 舅祖父; **G~ Wall of China** *pr n* **the G~ Wall of China** 中国万里长城

greatly /ˈgreɪtli/ *adv* 非常地; **the tragedy moved her ~** 这出悲剧深深打动了她; **the noise/problem was ~ reduced** 噪音大大降低了/问题大大简化了; **it is ~ to be regretted that ...** 很遗憾…

greatness /ˈgreɪtnɪs/ *n* [u] 伟大; **to achieve ~** 成大事

grebe /griːb/ *n* 䴙䴘

Grecian /ˈgriːʃn/ *adj* 古希腊的 ‹*warrior*›; 古希腊式的 ‹*architecture, beauty, profile*›

Greece /griːs/ *pr n* 希腊

greed /griːd/ *n* [u] **1** (for food) 贪食 **2** (for wealth, power) 贪婪

greedily /ˈgriːdɪli/ *adv* 贪婪地

greediness /ˈgriːdɪnɪs/ *n* = **greed 1**

greedy /ˈgriːdi/ *adj* **1** (for food) 贪食的; **~ guts** *or* **pig** colloq pej 贪吃的家伙 **2** (for wealth, power) 贪婪的; **a politician ~ for power** 贪图权力的政客; **a man ~ for success** 渴望成功的人

Greek /griːk/ ▸**p. 503, p. 426**

A *adj* (of Greece) 希腊的; (of the people) 希腊人的; (of the language) 希腊语的

B *n* **1** [c] (person) 希腊人; **beware of ~s bearing gifts** Prov 当心黄鼠狼给鸡拜年; **~ meets ~** 棋逢对手 **2** [u] (language) 希腊语; **it's all ~ to me** colloq 我完全不懂

Greek: ~ alphabet *n* 希腊语字母表; **~ Orthodox Church** *n* 希腊正教会

green /griːn/ ▸**p. 134**

A *adj* **1** (in colour) 绿色的 ‹*eyes, car, dress*›; **as ~ as grass** 青绿的 **2** (with vegetation) 青葱的 ‹*countryside, valley*›; **~ fields** 绿油油的田野 **3** (not ripe) 未成熟的; **~ tomatoes** 青西红柿 **4** Culin (not smoked) 未熏制的 ‹*bacon*›; **~ meat** 生肉 **5** (not dry) 未干透的; **~ wood does not burn well** 生柴不好烧 **6** fig (immature) 不成熟的; (inexperienced) 缺乏经验的; (easily fooled) 易受骗的; **I'm not as ~ as you think I am** 我并不像你想得那么幼稚 **7** colloq (pale) 苍白的; (sickly-looking) 有病容的; **to be/go ~ around the gills** colloq 脸色发青/变青; **~ with envy** 十分妒忌的 **8** fig 清晰的; **to keep sb.'s memory ~** 对某人永记不忘 **9** Ecol (ecologically sound) 环保的 ‹*product, building*› **10** **Green** Pol 赞成环境保护的 ‹*policies, politician, voter*›; **the G~ Party** 绿党

B *n* **1** [u and c] (colour) 绿色; **a girl dressed in ~** 穿绿衣服的女孩 **2** [c and u] (grassy area) 公共绿地; **a strip of ~** 一条绿化带 **3** [c] (in bowls) 草地滚球场; **against the rub of the ~** fig 事与愿违 **4** [c] (in golf) 球穴区 **5** [c] (snooker ball) 绿球 **6** [c] **Green** Pol 主张环保的从政者; **the success of the G~s in the European elections** 欧洲议会选举中绿党的胜利

C **greens** *npl* Brit (vegetables) 绿叶蔬菜

D *vt* **1** (make more verdant) 绿化 ‹*area, countryside*› **2** (make more environmentally friendly) 使…更环保 ‹*process, building*›

green: ~ audit *n* 绿色审计 [指对公司对环境的影响作出的评估]; **~back** *n* Amer colloq 美钞; **~ bean** *n* 青刀豆; **~ belt** *n* **1** esp Brit (around city) 绿带; **2** Sport 绿腰带; **G~ Beret** *n* "绿色贝雷帽" [指英军突击队成员或美国特种部队成员]; **~ card** *n* **1** Brit (insurance) 绿色保险证 [即汽车国外事故保险证]; **2** Amer (residence permit) 绿卡

green belt

绿带。城市周围带状的开放空间（包括森林、湿地、自然群落、农田等）。绿带上的房地产开发受到严格限制，以避免城市的无限扩张，同时为城市居民提供休闲娱乐的空间，亦用于保护农业用地。19 世纪末，倡导花园城市（garden city）理念的英国人埃比尼泽・霍华德（Ebenezer Howard）最早提出绿带概念。20 世纪 50 年代，大伦敦地区周围曾建起宽达 15 公里的绿带。美国的绿带通常是受城市保护的自然区域，多为大型公园。马里兰州的绿带镇（City of Greenbelt, Maryland）即是遵照花园城市理念建成，是 20 世纪 30 年代罗斯福新经济政策（New Deal）的产物。和绿带作用相似的是绿楔（green wedge），即城市楔形绿化带。

greenery /ˈgriːnəri/ *n* [u] (foliage) 青枝绿叶; (vegetation) 绿色植物

green: ~field *adj attrib* Brit 未开发地区的; **new factories built on ~field sites** 建在新地皮上的新工厂; **~finch** *n* 金翅 [产于欧洲的雀科鸣鸟]; **~ fingers** *npl* 绿手指 [指园艺技能]; **to have ~ fingers** 擅长种植; **~fly** *n* (*pl* **~fly** *or* **~flies**) 蚜虫; **~gage** *n* 西洋李; **~gage jam** 西洋李子酱; **~grocer** ▸**p. 409** *n* esp Brit 果菜商; **~grocer's (shop)** 蔬菜水果店; **~horn** *n* esp Amer colloq pej **1** (beginner) 新手; **2** (gullible person) 易受骗的人; **3** (newcomer) 新来者

greenhouse /ˈgriːnhaʊs/ *n* 温室

greenhouse: ~ effect *n* 温室效应; **~ gas** *n* 温室气体

greening /ˈgriːnɪŋ/ *n* [u] **1** (of an area) 绿化 **2** (of a party, city, industry) 环保化

greenish /ˈgriːnɪʃ/ ▸**p. 134** *adj* 淡绿色的; **~-brown eyes** 棕绿色的眼睛

greenkeeper /ˈgriːnkiːpə(r)/ *n* 球场看管人

Greenland /ˈgriːnlənd/ *pr n* 格陵兰（岛）; **the ~ Sea** 格陵兰海

Greenlander /ˈgriːnləndə(r)/ ▸**p. 503** *n* 格陵兰人

green light *n* **1** (traffic light) 交通绿灯 **2** fig 绿灯; **to give sb. the ~ (to do sth.)** 给某人开（做某事的）绿灯; **I gave him the ~ to go ahead with the project** 我准许他执行那个计划; **to get the ~ (to do sth.)** 获得许可（做某事）

greenness /ˈgriːnnɪs/ *n* [u] **1** (colour) 绿色; **the ~ of the English countryside in spring** 春天英国乡村的青葱翠绿 **2** (of fruit) 未成熟; (of timber) 未干透 **3** (of product, industry) 环保意识; (of party, policy) 注重环境保护 **4** (inexperience) 缺乏经验; (naivety) 天真

green: ~ onion *n* Amer 嫩洋葱; **G~ Paper** *n* Brit 绿皮书 [英国供议会讨论的政府提案文件]; **G~ Party** *n* **the G~ Party** Brit 绿党

the Green Party

绿党。世界上很多国家都有致力于环境保护的绿党。英国的绿党成立于 1973 年，始称人民党（People），后改称生态党（Ecology Party），1985 年又改称绿党。后来一分为三，成为各自独立的政党，即英格兰和威尔士绿党（Green Party of England and Wales）、苏格兰绿党（Scottish Green Party）和北爱尔兰绿党（Green Party in Northern Ireland）。美国绿党（The Green Party of the United States）是美国各州绿党的联合组织，前身是成立于 1996 年的各州绿党联合会（Association of State Green Parties），2001 年改为现名。

Greenpeace /ˈgriːnpiːs/ *pr n* 绿色和平组织

Greenpeace

绿色和平组织。致力于环境保护的国际性非政府组织。总部位于荷兰的阿姆斯特丹（Amsterdam）。目前在全世界 40 多个国家设有办事处。1971 年创立于加拿大，最初以非暴力方式阻止核试验，后来开始关注其他环境问题。其名称一般认为是由加拿大青年社会工作者比尔・达内尔（Bill Darnell）提出，表达了对地球的关注和对远离核武器的期盼。

green: ~ pepper *n* 青甜椒; **~ revolution** *n* **1** Agric 绿色革命 [指发展中国家推广的大规模改良农业的活动]; **2** Pol, Ecol 绿色革命[指工业国对日益恶化的环境问题的关注]; **~ room** *n* 演员休息室; **~ salad** *n* [u and c] 蔬菜色拉; **~stick fracture** *n* 青枝骨折 [指儿童的不完全骨折]; **~stuff** *n* [u] 绿叶蔬菜; **~ tea** *n* [u and c] 绿茶; **~ thumb** *n* Amer **to have a ~ thumb** 有园艺天分; **~wash** *n* [u] Amer 绿色外衣 [指机构为树立对环境负责的公众形象而散布的虚假信息]; **~way** *n* Amer 林荫道; **~-welly brigade** *n* Brit hum pej **the ~-welly brigade** 绿靴族 [住在乡下或喜欢去乡下消遣的有钱人]

Greenwich Mean Time /ˌgrenɪtʃ ˈmiːn taɪm/ *n* [u] 格林尼治（平均）时间

greet /griːt/ *vt* **1** (welcome) 迎接; **the delegation was ~ed warmly by the mayor** 代表团受到市长的热情接待 **2** (salute, acknowledge) 向…打招呼; **she ~ed him with a smile** 她微笑着向他打招呼 **3** (receive, react to) 对…作出反应; **the crowd ~ed the news with cheering** 人群对这一消息报以欢呼声; **the accused man ~ed the verdict with relief** 被告听到裁定松了一口气 **4** (confront) 突然被…感知; **an amazing sight ~ed me** 令人惊叹的一幕呈现在我眼前; **a lovely smell ~ed me** 我闻到一股香味

greeter /ˈgriːtə(r)/ *n* esp Amer 迎宾员

greeting /ˈgriːtɪŋ/ ▸**p. 333**

A *n* [c and u] (salutation) 招呼; **he waved at me in ~** 他挥手向我打招呼; **to exchange ~s** 互致问候

g

B **greetings** *npl* (on cards) 祝辞; **New Year ~s** 新年祝辞

greetings card Brit, **greeting card** Amer *n* 贺卡

gregarious /grɪ'geərɪəs/ *adj* **1** (sociable) 爱交际的 **2** Biol 群居的 ‹*birds, animals*›

gregariousness /grɪ'geərɪəsnɪs/ *n* [u] **1** (sociability) 爱交际 **2** Biol (of birds, animals) 群居

Gregorian: ~ calendar *n* 公历; **~ chant** *n* [u and c] 格列高利圣歌

gremlin /'gremlɪn/ *n* colloq [被认为造成机器故障等的] 小精灵; **the ~s have got into the computer** 计算机莫名其妙出了故障

Grenada /grə'neɪdə/ *pr n* 格林纳达

grenade /grə'neɪd/ *n* **1** (hand) **~** 手榴弹 **2** (fired from rifle or launcher) 枪榴弹

grenadier /,grenə'dɪə(r)/ *n* 英国近卫步兵团的士兵

grenadine /'grenədi:n/ *n* [u] 石榴汁糖浆

grew /gru:/ *pt* ▸ **grow**

grey /greɪ/ Brit ▸ **p. 134**

A *adj* **1** (colour) 灰色的 ‹*coat, eyes, hair, sky*› **2** (of face) 苍白的 ‹*face, complexion*› **3** (with grey hair) 头发灰白的; **to turn** *or* **go ~** 头发开始花白 **4** (dull) 昏暗的; **a cold, ~ day** 寒冷阴沉的一天 **5** fig (dreary) 沉闷的 ‹*existence, routine*› **6** (nondescript) 毫无吸引力的; **~, faceless men** 毫无吸引力、缺乏个性的男人

B *n* **1** (colour) 灰色; **to be dressed in ~** 穿灰色衣服; **the G~s** Mil 灰骑兵 [英国第二骑兵团的别称] **2** Equit (horse) 灰马

C *vt* 使…变灰白 ‹*hair*›; 使…变苍白 ‹*complexion*›

D *vi* «*hair*» 变灰白; «*complexion*» 变苍白; «*person*» 头发变灰白; «*animal*» 毛发变灰色; **to be ~ing at the temples** 两鬓斑白; **the population is ~ing** fig 人口正在老龄化

Phrasal verb

- **grey out** *vt* [**~ out sth., ~ sth. out**] 使…变灰隐去 ‹*menu, option*›

grey: ~ area *n* 灰色地带 [指难以归类和处理的问题或情况等]; **~ economy** *n* 灰色经济 [未纳入官方统计数字的经济活动]; **~ed command** *n* 灰色命令 [图形用户界面上变成灰色、不能操作的命令]; **~ eminence** *n* 幕后掌权者; **~-haired, ~-headed** *adjs* 头发灰白的

> **Greyhound bus**
>
> 灰狗巴士。灰狗公司（Greyhound Lines）的长途客车。灰狗公司是美国最大的城际长途客车运输公司，1914 年成立于明尼苏达州。因车身呈灰色，且线条流畅，被称为灰狗。1929 年开始称 Greyhound Corporation，并采用飞奔的灰狗作为标志。1930 年改为现名。灰狗公司票价低廉、乘坐方便，现已成为美国人生活的一部分。公司总部位于得克萨斯。其口号为：我们在路上（We're on the Way）。

greyhound /'greɪhaʊnd/ *n* 灵猩犬

greyhound: G~ bus *n* 灰狗巴士; **~ racing** ▸ **p. 307** *n* [u] 灵猩犬赛; **~ track** *n* 灵猩犬赛跑道

greyish /'greɪɪʃ/ ▸ **p. 134** *adj* Brit 浅灰色的

greylag goose /'greɪlæg ,gu:s/ *n* 灰雁

grey: ~ market *n* **1** (unofficial market) 灰市 [指未经厂商同意，进口并销售其产品的市场体系]; **2** Brit (elderly consumers) 老年市场; **~ matter** *n* [u] colloq (brain) 灰白质; (intelligence) 智力; **a boy without much ~ matter** 不太聪明的男孩; **to use one's ~ matter** 动脑筋; **~ seal** *n* 灰海豹; **~ squirrel** *n* 北美灰松鼠

grid /grɪd/ *n* **1** (grating) 格栅 **2** (pattern) 网格; **a ~ of intersecting streets** 棋盘式的街道布局 **3** (on map) 坐标方格 **4** Brit (network) 输电网 **5** Motor racing 赛车起跑线

griddle /'grɪdl/

A *n* 鏊子

B *vt* 用鏊子烹调

griddle cake *n* 烤饼

gridiron /'grɪdaɪən, Amer -aɪərn/ *n* **1** Culin 烤架 **2** Amer (in football) 橄榄球球场

gridlock /'grɪdlɒk/ *n* [u] **1** (traffic congestion) 交通大堵塞 **2** fig (stalemate) 僵局; **Congress is in ~** 国会因意见分歧而陷入僵局

grid: ~ map *n* 网格地图; **~ reference** *n* 格网座标

ℹ Greetings

Spoken greetings

■ Meeting someone:

Hello!
= 你好!
您好! (to show respect)

Hello! It's nice to see you again
= 你好，很高兴又见面了

Hi!
= 嗨!

Hi, Emma! What a pleasant surprise!
= 你好，埃玛! 真没想到会遇见你!

How are you?
= 你好吗?

How are you doing?
= 你过得怎么样?

Long time no see. How have you been?
= 好久不见了。你最近怎么样?
(very colloquial)

Good morning!/Morning!
= 早上好!
or 早!

Good afternoon!
= 下午好!

Good evening!
= 晚上好!

Good night!
= 晚安!

■ Responding to greetings:

I'm fine, thanks. How are you?
= 我很好，谢谢。你 / 您怎么样?

I'm just great. Thank you
= 我好极了，谢谢

I'm very well indeed, thank you
= 我确实很好，谢谢你 / 您

Not too bad, thanks
= 还好，谢谢

So-so. And you?
= 一般，你呢?
or 马马虎虎，你呢?

I'm OK, thanks
= 还可以，谢谢

Same as ever, thanks
= 和以前一样，谢谢

■ Meeting someone on special occasions:

Happy Birthday!
= 生日快乐!

Happy Christmas!
or ***Merry Christmas!***
= 圣诞快乐!

Happy New Year!
= 新年快乐!
or 新年好!

Congratulations!
= 恭喜!

Written greetings

■ For a birthday:

Happy Birthday!
= 生日快乐!

Wishing you all the best on your birthday!
= 为你的生日送上最美好的祝愿!
or 生日快乐，万事如意!

■ For a wedding:

Congratulations on your wedding day!
= 恭贺新婚!

All the best for your future together!
= 愿你们共享美好的未来!

■ For Christmas and the New Year:

With best wishes at Christmas!
= 让我在圣诞节之际致以最美好的祝愿!

Wishing you a Merry/Happy Christmas!
= 祝你圣诞快乐!

With best wishes for the New Year!
= 让我在新年之际献上最美好的祝福!

A Merry Christmas and a Happy New Year!
= 圣诞快乐，新年愉快!

■ On a 'Get Well' card:

Get well soon!
= 祝早日康复!

Hope you have a speedy recovery!
= 愿你早日恢复健康!

■ For Father's Day:

Happy Father's Day!
= 父亲节快乐!

With all my love on Father's Day!
= 在父亲节里献上我所有的爱!

■ For Mother's Day:

Happy Mother's Day!
= 母亲节快乐!

With love and best wishes to you today and always!
= 献上我对您永远的祝愿、永远的爱!

■ On Valentine's Day:

Happy Valentine's Day to my special Laura
= 愿我特别的劳拉情人节快乐

Just to say I love you forever and ever
= 只想说，我永远爱你

■ On a thank you card:

Thank you for the wonderful gift
= 非常感谢你精美的礼物

Thanks for being my true friend
= 谢谢你，我真正的朋友

I couldn't have done it without your support. Thank you!
= 没有你的支持我不会成功。谢谢了!

grief /griːf/
A *n* **1** [u] (sorrow) 悲伤; **to be overcome with ~** 悲痛欲绝; **to die of ~** 忧伤而死; **to come to ~** (have an accident) 出事故; (end in failure) 遭到失败; **several pedestrians came to ~ on the icy pavement** 几位行人在结了冰的人行道上摔倒了; **all his schemes for making a fortune came to ~** 他所有的发财计划都告吹了 **2** [c] (sad event) 伤心事 **3** [u] colloq (trouble, hassle) 麻烦; **to give sb. ~** 骚扰某人
B *excl* **good ~!** 哎呀!

grief-stricken *adj* 极度悲伤的

grievance /ˈgriːvns/ *n* **1** (cause for complaint) 不平的事; **the employees' ~s against the management** 雇员对资方的抱怨 **2** (feeling) 委屈; **to air one's ~s** 发牢骚; **to harbour** *or* **nurse a ~ against sb.** 对某人心怀不满

grievance procedure *n* 投诉程序

grieve /griːv/
A *vi* 感到悲伤; **to ~ for sb.** 为某人伤心; **to ~ over sb./sth.** 为某人/某事物悲伤
B *vt* liter 使伤心; **it grieves me** *or* **I am ~d that you cannot accept my proposal** 你不能接受我的提议，我感到很难过

grievous /ˈgriːvəs/ *adj* **1** (causing sorrow) 令人悲伤的; **to receive ~ news** 收到噩耗 **2** liter (severe) 极严重的; **to do sb. a ~ wrong** 极大地伤害某人; **a ~ crime** 滔天罪行 **3** (showing sorrow) 显示悲痛的; **to utter a ~ cry** 悲号

grievous bodily harm *n* [u] 严重人体伤害

grievously /ˈgriːvəsli/ *adv* **1** (cruelly) 令人痛苦地 ‹*insult, offend*› **2** liter (seriously) 极严重地; **to be ~ mistaken/wounded** 大错特错/受重伤

griffin /ˈgrɪfɪn/, **griffon** /ˈgrɪfən/ *n* 狮身鹰首兽

grill /grɪl/
A *n* **1** Brit (on cooker) [烤炉内的] 烤架; (on barbecue) [置于火上的] 烧烤架 **2** Culin (dish) 一盘烤菜; **a mixed ~** 什锦烤肉 **3** **grill-room** (restaurant) 烧烤店 **4** **= grille**
B *vt* **1** Culin 烤炙 ‹*meat, fish*› **2** fig (warm) 使受高温烤炙; **to sit ~ing oneself in front of a fire** 坐着烤火 **3** fig colloq (interrogate) 盘问; **the police ~ed him for three hours** 警察盘问了他三个小时
C *vi* 烤炙; **steaks ~ing over a barbecue** 在烤架上烤着的牛排

grille /grɪl/ *n* 格栅; **an iron ~** 铁栅; **a radiator ~** 散热器面罩

grilled /grɪld/ *adj* **1** Culin 烤炙的; **charcoal-~ prawns** 炭烤对虾 **2** (having a grille) 有格栅的

grilling /ˈgrɪlɪŋ/ *n* colloq 盘问; **to give sb. a ~** 盘问某人

grill pan *n* Brit 烤盘

grim /grɪm/ *adj* **1** (serious) 严肃的 ‹*expression*›; **to be ~-faced** 表情严肃 **2** (unrelenting) 严酷的 ‹*contest, battle*›; **a ~ struggle for survival** 无情的生存竞争 **3** (depressing) 令人沮丧的 ‹*news, outlook, facts*›; **her future is ~** 她的未来令人堪忧 **4** (steadfast) 坚定的; **~ determination** 不屈不挠的决心; **to hold on to sb. like ~ death** Brit 死死抓住某人不放 **5** (horrific) 恐怖的 ‹*story, sight*›; (black) 黑色的 ‹*humour, joke*›; **a ~ silence** 可怕的寂静 **6** (forbidding) 阴森的; **the ~ walls of the prison** 阴森森的监狱四壁 **7** *pred* colloq (ill) 生病的; **I'm feeling pretty ~** 我觉得很不舒服

grimace /grɪˈmeɪs, ˈgrɪməs/
A *n* (of pain) 脸部扭曲; (of disgust) 怪相; (in fun) 鬼脸; **her face was contorted in a ~ of pain** 她痛得脸都扭曲了
B *vi* (involuntarily) 脸部扭曲; (pull a face) 做鬼脸; **he ~d with** *or* **in disgust** 他做出厌恶的表情

grime /graɪm/ *n* [u] 污垢

grimly /ˈgrɪmli/ *adv* **1** (gloomily) 严肃地 ‹*frown, speak*› **2** (relentlessly) 坚定地 ‹*fight, struggle*›; **he battled ~ up the icy slope** 他奋力爬上结了冰的斜坡

grimness /ˈgrɪmnɪs/ *n* [u] (of expression) 严肃; (of words) 严厉; (of situation, battle) 严峻; (of story, news) 可怕; (of landscape, town) 阴森

Grim Reaper *n* **the ~** 狰狞的持镰收割者 [指死神]

grimy /ˈgraɪmi/ *adj* 沾满污垢的

grin /grɪn/
A *vi* (*pres p etc.* **-nn-**) 露齿而笑; **to ~ at sb.** 向某人咧着嘴笑; **to ~ from ear to ear** 笑得合不拢嘴; **to ~ and bear it** 默默忍受; **to ~ like a Cheshire cat** 咧着嘴傻笑
B *n* 露齿的笑; **wipe that (silly) ~ off your face!** 别嬉皮笑脸的!

grind /graɪnd/
A *vt* (*pt, pp* **ground**) **1** (crush) 磨碎; **to ~ corn into flour** 把玉米磨成粉; **to ~ sth. to dust** 把某物碾成碎末 **2** (produce by crushing) 磨成 ‹*flour*›; **to ~ coffee from beans** 把咖啡豆磨成咖啡 **3** Amer Culin 绞碎 ‹*meat*› **4** fig (oppress) 压迫 ‹*person, nation*›; **to ~ sb. into submission** 迫使某人屈从 **5** (polish) 打磨 ‹*surface, lens, gem*›; (sharpen) 磨快 ‹*blade*›; **he ground the blade to a sharp edge** 他把刀磨得很锋利; **to ~ sth. on** *or* **with sth.** 用某物打磨某物; **to have an axe to ~** fig 别有企图 **6** (rub together noisily) 把…磨得吱吱响; **to ~ one's teeth** 磨牙 **7** (press firmly) 用力压; **to ~ sth. into sth.** 把某物用力压入某物; **dirt ground into the carpet** 踩进地毯里的尘土; **to ~ facts/information into sb./sth.** fig 向某人/某物灌输事实/信息; **to ~ the faces of the poor (into the dust)** 压榨剥削穷人 **8** (turn) 摇动 ‹*handle*›; 摇动手柄操作 ‹*coffee mill, pepper mill*›; 摇动手柄演奏 ‹*barrel organ*›
B *vi* (*pt, pp* **ground**) **1** (be crushed) 被磨碎; **to ~ to** *or* **into sth.** 被磨碎成某物; **to ~ easily** 容易磨碎 **2** (work by crushing) «*mill, machine*» 磨 **3** (make harsh sound) «*machine, engine*» 发出刺耳的摩擦声; fig 运行不畅; **to ~ to a halt** *or* **standstill** «*machine*» 嘎吱嘎吱地停下来; fig «*campaign, dispute*» 渐渐停止 **4** Amer colloq (swot) **to ~ at sth.** 埋头苦读 **5** colloq (dance erotically) 跳色情舞; **to bump and ~** 跳磨臀摆身舞
C *n* **1** (act of grinding) 研磨; (sound of grinding) 研磨声; **the slow ~ of the legal system** fig 法律体系的缓慢施压 **2** (size after grinding) 磨细的等级; **fine/coarse ~** 细磨/粗磨; **different ~s of coffee** 大小不同的咖啡颗粒 **3** colloq (hard work) 苦差; **a long, hard ~** 漫长、艰苦的工作; **a real/an awful ~** 极苦的差事; **the daily ~** 单调的日常工作 **4** Amer colloq pej (swot) 书呆子

Phrasal verbs

- **grind away**
A *vt* [**~ away sth., ~ sth. away**] 磨掉 ‹*rough edge, metal, excess material*›
B *vi* **1** (make harsh noise) «*machine, engine, vehicle*» 发出刺耳的摩擦声 **2** colloq (work hard) 埋头苦学; **to ~ away at sth.** 埋头做某事; **he is ~ing away at his essay/maths** 他正在埋头写文章/学数学

- **grind down** *vt* **1** [**~ down sth., ~ sth. down**] (crush finely) 磨碎 **2** [**~ down sth., ~ sth. down**] (smooth) 磨光 ‹*material, metal, irregularities*› **3** [**~ sb. down, ~ down sb.**] (wear down) 压迫 ‹*person, opposition, nation*›; **to be ground down by poverty** 苦于贫寒

- **grind off** *vt* [**~ off sth., ~ sth. off**] 磨光 ‹*material, metal, rough edge*›

- **grind on** *vi* «*project, negotiation*» 单调地进行; «*speaker*» 单调地说

- **grind out** *vt* [**~ out sth., ~ sth. out**] **1** Culin 摇动手柄加工出 ‹*pepper, coffee*› **2** pej (produce laboriously) 费力地写出 ‹*books, novels*›; 单调地输出 ‹*facts, data*› **3** (extinguish) 碾灭 ‹*cigarette*›

- **grind up** *vt* [**~ up sth., ~ sth. up**] 磨碎

grinder /ˈgraɪndə(r)/ *n* **1** (crushing device) 研磨器械; **a coffee ~** 磨咖啡机 **2** (person) 研磨者; **a knife-~** 磨刀匠 **3** Anat (tooth) 臼齿

grinding /ˈgraɪndɪŋ/
A *adj* **1** (harsh) 刺耳的; (complete) 完全的; **to bring sth./come to a ~ halt** (使某事物) 完全停下来; **the strike brought industry to a ~ halt** fig 罢工使工业趋于停滞 **2** (oppressive) 难于忍受的; **~ poverty** 极度贫困
B *n* 刺耳的噪声

grinding wheel *n* 砂轮

grindstone /ˈgraɪndstəʊn/ *n* 磨石; **to keep one's nose to the ~** 一刻不停地苦干

gringo /ˈgrɪŋgəʊ/ *n* (*pl* **~s**) Amer colloq 外国佬 [拉丁美洲人用来称呼英语国家的白人]

grip /grɪp/
A *n* **1** (hold) 抓牢; **to lose one's ~** 松手; **to tighten one's ~ on sth.** 将某物抓得更紧; **to relax one's ~ on sth.** 松手放开某物; **to have a firm ~ (on sth.)** 牢牢地抓住（某物）; **to come** *or* **get to ~s with sb./ sth.** lit 开始与某人/某物搏斗; fig (begin to deal with) 开始处理某人/某事; (begin to understand) 开始理解某人/某事 **2** (manner of holding) 抓牢的方式; (in tennis) 握拍法; (in golf) 握杆法; (in wrestling) 擒拿法; (power of holding) 握力; **a weak** *or* **feeble ~** 无力的一握; **to hold sb./sth. in a tight ~** 紧紧抓住某人/某物 **3** (ability to hold) 抓力; **the tyres lost their ~** 这些轮胎已经不防滑了 **4** fig (control) 控制; **to get** *or* **take a ~ on** *or* **of oneself** 控制住自己; **to lose one's ~** (become unable to understand) 无法认清自己的处境; (become unable to control) 无法掌控局面; **I feel I'm losing my ~** 我感到自己无能为力; **he lay in the ~ of despair** 他绝望地躺着 **5** (handle) 柄 **6** Brit (for hair) 发夹 **7** esp Amer (bag) 旅行袋
B *vt* (*pres p etc.* **-pp-**) **1** (take or have firm hold) «*person*» 抓牢; «*vice*» 夹牢; «*animal*» 咬住; **to ~ a handrail with both hands** 用双手紧紧抓住扶手; **to ~ sth. between one's teeth** 紧紧咬住某物 **2** (adhere to) «*tyres, brakes*» 抓住 ‹*road, rails*› **3** fig (captivate) «*film, story*» 吸引住; (have a strong or adverse effect on) 攫住; **she was ~ped by a feeling of excitement** 她激动万分; **the country was ~ped by recession** 该国陷入了经济衰退
C *vi* (*pres p etc.* **-pp-**) «*tyres, brakes, shoes*» 抓地; **the tyres failed to ~ on the ice** 轮胎在冰上打滑了

gripe /graɪp/
A *vi* **1** colloq (complain) 抱怨; **to ~ about sb./sth.** 抱怨某人/某事物 **2** Med «*stomach*» 患胃绞痛; «*intestines*» 患肠绞痛
B *vt* esp Amer colloq 惹恼
C *n* **1** colloq (complaint) 抱怨; **to have a (good) ~** (大) 发牢骚 **2** Med (in stomach) 胃绞痛; (in intestines) 肠绞痛

gripe water *n* [u] Brit 止痛水

griping /ˈgraɪpɪŋ/ colloq
A *n* [u] (complaining) 抱怨
B *adj* Med 绞痛的

gripper rail /ˈgrɪpə reɪl/ *n* 地毯定位条

gripping /ˈgrɪpɪŋ/ *adj* 吸引人的; **a ~ story** 扣人心弦的故事

grip tape *n* [u] 防滑定位胶带

grisly /ˈgrɪzli/ *adj* 恐怖的; **the ~ remains of a body** 令人毛骨悚然的尸体残骸

grist /grɪst/ *n* [u] **1** (grain) 制粉用谷物 **2** (useful material) 有用材料; **to be ~ to the mill** 是有利的东西

gristle /ˈgrɪsl/ *n* [u] [肉里的] 软骨

gristly /ˈgrɪsli/ *adj* (gristle-like) 似软骨的 ‹*texture*›; (full of gristle) 多软骨的 ‹*meat*›

g

grit /grɪt/
A *n* [u] **1** (grains of stone, sand) 沙子 **2** (courage) 勇气; (resolve) 毅力
B *vt* (*pres p etc.* **-tt-**) Brit 在…上撒沙子 ‹*road, pavement*›; **to ~ one's teeth** lit 咬紧牙关; fig 下定决心

grits /grɪts/ *npl* Amer 粗玉米粉

gritter /'grɪtə(r)/ *n* Brit 撒沙车

gritting /'grɪtɪŋ/ *n* [u] Brit 撒沙砾; **a ~ lorry** 撒沙车

gritty /'grɪti/ *adj* **1** (grit-like) 沙子般的 ‹*texture, feel*›; (covered with grit) 覆盖着沙子的 ‹*road, surface*›; (containing grit) 含沙子的 ‹*seafood, flour*›; **my eyes feel ~** 我感到眼睛里进了沙子; **this cake has a ~ taste** 这块蛋糕有点牙碜 **2** fig (courageous) 勇敢的 ‹*competitor, fighter*›; 坚毅的 ‹*upholder of sth., champion*›; 坚定的 ‹*performance*› **3** fig (realistic, tough) 真实的 ‹*portrayal, film, tale*›

grizzle /'grɪzl/ *vi* Brit colloq (cry) 哭闹; (complain) 抱怨

grizzled /'grɪzld/ *adj* 头发花白的 ‹*person*›; 花白的 ‹*hair, beard*›

grizzly /'grɪzli/
A *adj* **1** Brit colloq (fretful) 哭闹的 **2** (grey) 花白的 ‹*beard, hair*›
B *n* **~ (bear)** 灰熊

groan /grəʊn/
A *vi* **1** (in pain) 呻吟; (in protest, pleasure) 发哼声; **to ~ in** *or* **with pain** 痛苦地呻吟; **he always ~s at my jokes** 他总是对我讲的笑话报以哼声; **to ~ inwardly** 暗自叫苦; **'I've been hit!' he ~ed** "我被打中了！" 他呻吟着说 **2** (complain) 抱怨; **to ~ about** *or* **over sb./sth.** 抱怨某人/某事物; **poor people ~ing beneath harsh taxation** 被苛捐杂税压得透不过气来的贫民 **3** (creak) 发吱嘎声; **to ~ under the weight of sth.** 在某物的重压下吱嘎作响 **4** fig (be laden with) 受重压; **a table ~ing with food** 摆满食物的桌子
B *n* **1** (of pain) 呻吟; (of pleasure, protest) 哼声; **to give a ~ of dismay** 发出灰心的叹息声 **2** (complaint) 抱怨声 **3** fig (creaking sound) 吱嘎声

groats /grəʊts/ *npl* 去壳谷物

grocer /'grəʊsə(r)/ ▸**p. 409** *n* 食品杂货商; **~'s (shop)** 食品杂货店

groceries /'grəʊsərɪz/ *npl* 食品杂货

grocery /'grəʊsəri/ *n* **~ (shop)** Brit, **~ (store)** Amer 食品杂货店; **the ~ business** 食品杂货业; **~ shopping** 食品杂货采购

grog /grɒg/ *n* [u] 格罗格酒 [一种掺水烈酒]

groggy /'grɒgi/ *adj* (weak and unsteady) 眩晕无力的; (sleepy) 昏昏沉沉的

groin /grɔɪn/ ▸**p. 71** *n* **1** Anat 腹股沟 **2** colloq (genital region) 阴部 **3** Archit 穹棱 **4** Amer = **groyne**

grommet /'grɒmɪt/ *n* (metal) 金属扣眼; (rubber) 垫圈

groom /gru:m/
A *n* **1** (bridegroom) 新郎 **2** (for horse) 马夫
B *vt* **1** (clean by brushing) 刷洗 ‹*horse, dog*› **2** «*monkey*» 为…梳毛 **3** (prepare) 使作好准备; **he was being ~ed for the presidency** 他正在为就任总统作准备; **to ~ sb. as one's successor** 培养某人作为自己的接班人

groomed /gru:md/ *adj* 打扮好的 ‹*person*›; 刷洗好的 ‹*pet*›; 修剪过的 ‹*lawn*›; **he was immaculately ~** 他打扮得很整洁

grooming /'gru:mɪŋ/ *n* [u] (of a person) 打扮; (of horse, dog) 刷洗

groomsman /'gru:mzmæn/ *n* (*pl* **groomsmen**) Amer 伴郎

groove /gru:v/
A *n* **1** (in wood, metal, stone) 槽 **2** (on record) 纹路 **3** fig (routine) 常规; **to be stuck in a ~** 墨守成规; **to be in/get into the ~** colloq «*athlete, pitcher*» 表现出色 **4** Mus colloq (rhythm) 节奏; **to be in the ~** (playing well) 演奏得出色; (with a good rhythm) 节奏强烈; **in the ~** (enjoying oneself) 玩得开心
B *vt* 在…上开槽 ‹*wood, metal, stone*›; **deep lines ~d her face** 她的脸上布满了深深的皱纹
C *vi* colloq **1** (dance) 随着舞曲跳舞 **2** Mus (play well) 出色地演奏音乐; (with a good rhythm) 节奏强烈地演奏音乐

groovy /'gru:vi/ *adj* colloq dated or hum (excellent) 顶呱呱的 ‹*music, club*›; (attractive) 吸引人的 ‹*clothes, haircut*›; **a ~ party** 令人愉快的晚会; **I'm feeling ~** 我感觉棒极了

grope /grəʊp/
A *vi* lit, fig 摸索; **he ~d for the door-handle** 他摸索着找门把手; **to ~ for words** 搜寻字眼
B *vt* **1** (feel) 摸索; **to ~ one's way down the dark staircase** 摸索着走下黑暗的楼梯 **2** colloq (fondle) 猥亵
C *n* colloq 抚摸

Phrasal verb
- **grope about, grope around** *vi* 到处摸索; **he ~d about for the light switch** 他到处摸索着找电灯开关

groper /'grəʊpə(r)/ *n* colloq 咸猪手 [指猥亵他人身体的人]

gross /grəʊs/
A *adj* **1** (coarse) 粗俗的; **~ language** 污言秽语; **a ~ eater** 吃相不雅的人 **2** (serious) 严重的 ‹*neglect, error, injustice, ignorance*›; 粗略的 ‹*generalization, simplification*›; **~ inequality** 极端的不平等 **3** Fin, Tech (before deductions) 总的; **~ income** 总收入; **the ~ weight** 毛重 **4** colloq (disgusting) 令人厌恶的; **that is just ~!** 那真恶心 **5** colloq (obese) 过度肥胖的
B *n* **1** (*pl* **gross**) (twelve dozen) 罗 [等于12打] **2** (*pl* **~es**) (profit) 毛利; (income) 总收入
C *vt* (make gross profit of) 获得…毛利; (have gross income of) 获得…总收入; **to ~ two million dollars** 总共赚得 200 万美元

Phrasal verbs
- **gross out** *vt* [**~ sb. out**] esp Amer colloq 使厌恶; **to ~ out one's parents** 冒犯父母
- **gross up** *vt* [**~ up sth.**] 返计还原 [指使净收入等增长至税前毛额] ‹*income, interest*›

gross: ~ domestic product *n* 国内生产总值; **~ indecency** *n* [u] 严重猥亵

grossly /'grəʊsli/ *adv* **1** (extremely) 极度地; **~ overweight/exaggerated** 严重超重的/过分夸张的 **2** (crudely) 粗俗地

gross national product *n* 国民生产总值

grossness /'grəʊsnɪs/ *n* [u] **1** (vulgarity) 粗俗 **2** (obesity) 过度肥胖 **3** colloq (disgusting nature) 令人厌恶

gross: ~ ton ▸**p. 909** *n* 长吨 [等于1016公斤]; **~ tonnage** *n* 总吨位

grot /grɒt/ *n* [u] Brit colloq (dirt) 脏东西; (of poor quality) 劣质品

grotesque /grəʊ'tesk/ *adj* **1** (ugly) 奇形怪状的; **dancers wearing ~ masks** 戴着奇异面具跳舞的人 **2** (outrageous) 荒谬的; **a ~ distortion of the truth** 对事实的无理歪曲 **3** (offensive) 怪诞的; **the ~ sight of an old man flirting with a young girl** 老头儿与少女调情的那种恶心样子

grotesquely /grəʊ'teskli/ *adv* **1** (in an ugly way) 风格奇特地 ‹*disfigured, dressed*› **2** (outrageously) 荒唐地 ‹*exaggerated, overstate*›

grotto /'grɒtəʊ/ *n* (*pl* **~s** *or* **~es**) 人工洞室

grotty /'grɒti/ *adj* Brit colloq **1** (squalid) 破破烂烂的 ‹*clothes, hotel*›; (of poor quality) 低劣的 ‹*film, food*›; 恶劣的 ‹*weather*› **2** *pred* (ill) 不舒服的; **to feel ~** 感到不适

grouch /graʊtʃ/
A *n* **1** (person) 好抱怨的人 **2** (complaint) 抱怨; **to have a ~ about sth.** 抱怨某事物 **3** (cause for complaint) 不满的原因; **to have a ~ against sb./sth.** 对某人/某事物不满
B *vi* 抱怨; **to ~ about sth.** 抱怨某事物

grouchy /'graʊtʃi/ *adj* colloq 愠怒的; **to look ~** 看上去愤愤不平

ground[1] /graʊnd/
A *n* **1** [u] (surface underfoot) **the ~** 地面; **to sit/lie (down) on the ~** 坐/躺在地上; **get up off the ~!** 爬起来！; **to fall/drop/crash to the ~** 落/掉/坠落到地上; **from the ~ up** fig 彻底地; **to hit the ~ running** fig colloq 雷厉风行; **to burn to the ~** «*building, town*» 被大火夷为平地; **to raze sth. to the ~** «*army, enemy*» 将…夷为平地 ‹*building, town*›; **that suits me down to the ~** fig colloq 那对我再合适不过了; **that's her down to the ~** fig colloq 这是她的一贯作风; **above/below (the) ~** 在地面上/下; **to be thick/thin on the ~** 为数众多/不多; **to run sth. into the ~** 弄坏 ‹*car, machine, engine*›; 搞砸 ‹*business, organization*›; **to run** *or* **drive/work oneself into the ~** 把自己累垮 **2** [u] Brit (floor) **the ~** 地板 **3** [u] (earth, soil) 土壤; **the ~ is still frozen** 土还冻结着; **a hole in the ~** 地下的洞穴; **the ~ must be carefully prepared before sowing the grass seed** 播种草籽之前必须仔细平整土地; **the house was built on marshy ~** 房子建在了湿软的土地上; **the ~ is rather stony** 土里石头很多; **to break new** *or* **fresh ~** fig 开创新局面; **to prepare the ~ (for sth.)** fig (为某事物) 奠定基础; **to go to ~** «*animal*» 逃入洞穴; fig «*person*» 潜逃 **4** [u] (land) 土地; (territory) 领土; **a piece of ~** 一块地; **to cover a lot of ~** 走长路; **on level/hilly/high/rocky ~** 在平坦/陡峭/高耸/多岩石的地段; **holy ~** 圣地; **neutral ~** 中立国领土; **on sb.'s own ~** lit 在某人的土地上; fig (in sb.'s area of expertise) 在某人熟知的领域内; fig (on sb.'s terms or conditions) 按某人提出的条件; **to gain ~ (on sb./sth.)** lit 逼近 (某人/某物); fig «*country, organization*» 追上 (某人/某物); **to gain ~** fig «*idea*» 流行; **to lose ~ (to sb./sth.)** lit (对某人/某物的) 优势缩小; fig (向某人/某物) 作出让步; **to give** *or* **yield ~ (to sb./sth.)** (向某人/某物) 让步; **to hold** *or* **stand one's ~** lit 坚守阵地; fig 坚持立场; **to make up** *or* **regain lost ~** lit 收复失地; fig 东山再起; **to change** *or* **shift one's ~** fig 改变立场 **5** [u] fig (area of knowledge) 领域; **to cover a lot of/the same ~** 涉及很多领域/同一话题; **to be on firm** *or* **sure ~** 有可靠依据; **to be on shaky ~** 依据不足; **to be on dangerous/safe/delicate ~** 处于危险/安稳/微妙的境地; **the ~ is shifting** 态势变幻不定 **6** [c] (enclosed or defined area) 场地; **cricket/rugby ~** Brit 板球/橄榄球场; **burial ~** 墓地; **hunting/fishing ~(s)** 猎场/渔场; **a good training ~ for young actors** 年轻演员很好的训练场; **a dumping ~** 垃圾场; **a breeding ~ for terrorists** 恐怖分子滋生地 **7** [c] (reason) 理由; **~ for doing sth./to do sth.** 做某事的理由; **on the ~ that ...** 因为… **8** [c] Art (base, plain surface) 底色 **9** [u] Amer Elec = **earth A6**
B **grounds** *npl* **1** (of house, institution) 庭园; **private ~s** 私人宅邸; **in the ~s of the university** 在大学校园内 **2** (motive, reasons) 原因; **to have good/no ~s for complaint** 有充分理由/没有理由抱怨; **on what ~s?** 为什么？; **on religious/personal ~s** 出于宗教/个人原因; **on the ~s of ill health/cost** 以健康状况不佳/成本为由; **~s for sth.** …的理由 ‹*hope, divorce*›; **on the ~s that ...** 因为… **3** (dregs) 沉淀物; **coffee ~s** 咖啡渣
C *modif* 陆生的 ‹*plant*›; 陆栖的 ‹*animal*›
D *vt* **1** Aviat 使…停飞 ‹*aircraft, pilot*› **2** colloq (keep at home) 不准…外出 ‹*child, teenager*› **3** Naut 使…搁浅 ‹*ship*› **4** (teach) **to ~ sb. in sth.** 为…进行某方面的基础训练 ‹*student*›; **to be well ~ed in sth.** 在某方面基础很好 **5** (base) **to ~ sth. on sth.** 将…建立在某事物的基础上 ‹*opinion, assumption, policy*›; **to be ~ed on the fact that ...** 建立在…这一

g

事实的基础上; **a well-~ed theory** 依据充分的理论; **to ~ sth. in sth.** 使…以某事物为依据 ‹*right, truth, understanding*› 6 (put on ground) 将…放在地上 ‹*golf club, weapon*›; **he didn't ~ the ball** (in rugby) 他未能使球触地; **to ~ arms** 放下武器 7 Amer Elec 将…接地; **to be soundly ~ed** 接地良好; **a ~ed plug** 接地插头
E *vi* «*ship*» 搁浅

ground²
A *pt, pp* ▸**grind A, B**
B *adj* 1 (powdered) 磨碎的 ‹*coffee, pepper*›; **~ rice** 米粉 2 Amer 绞碎的 ‹*meat*› 3 (rubbed) 磨砂的; **~ glass** 毛玻璃

ground: ~ almonds *npl* 杏仁粉; **~ attack** *n* 地面进攻; **~bait** *n* [u] 水底诱饵; **~-based** *adj* 陆基的; **~ beef** *n* [u] Amer 牛肉糜; **~ clearance** *n* [u] [车辆的] 离地间隙; **~ cloth** *n* Amer = **~sheet**; **~ control** *n* [u] (people) 地面控制人员; (place) 地面控制

ground cover *n* [u] 地被植物

ground cover plant *n* 地被植物

ground: ~ crew *n* 地勤人员; **~ floor** *n* esp Brit 1 (of building) 底楼; **her room is on the ~ floor** 她的房间在一楼; **a ~-floor bedroom** 一楼的卧室; 2 colloq fig (early stages) 开始阶段; (lowest level) 最低级别; **to get in on the ~ floor** 在开始时参与; **he worked his way up from the ~ floor** 他从最底层的工作干起, 慢慢升了上去; **~ forces** *npl* 地面部队; **~ frost** *n* [u and c] Brit 地面霜; **~ glass** *n* [u] 1 (opaque) 磨砂玻璃; 2 (crushed) 玻璃粉

groundhog /ˈgraʊndhɒg/ *n* Amer 土拨鼠

Groundhog Day *n* Amer 土拨鼠日 [2月2日, 据说土拨鼠在这一天结束冬眠出洞]

ground hostess ▸p. 409 *n* 女地勤人员

grounding /ˈgraʊndɪŋ/ *n* 1 (in academic subject) 基础教学; (in practical, physical skill) 基础训练; **to have a good** *or* **thorough ~ in sth.** 在某学科领域具有坚实的基础 2 Aviat 停飞 3 Naut 搁浅 4 Amer Elec 接地

groundkeeper /ˈgraʊndkiːpə(r)/ *n* Amer = **groundsman**

groundless /ˈgraʊndlɪs/ *adj* (without foundation) 无根据的; (without good reason) 无理由的; **~ rumours** 无稽之谈; **~ fears** 无缘无故的恐惧

ground level *n* [u] 1 (level of land) 地平面 2 (floor of building) 底层

groundnut /ˈgraʊndnʌt/ *n* 1 Brit (peanut) 花生 2 Amer Bot 野豆

groundnut oil *n* [u] Brit 花生油

ground: ~ plan *n* 底层平面图; **~ rent** *n* [u and c] [付给房地产主的] 地租; **~ rule** *n usu pl* 基本原则; **to lay down the ~ rules** 定下基本原则

groundsel /ˈgraʊnsl/ *n* [u] 千里光属植物

ground: ~sheet *n* 防潮布; **~sman** /ˈgraʊndzmən/ *n* Brit (of sports facility) 运动场地管理员; (of park, gardens) 庭园管理员; **~ speed** *n* 地速 [飞机相对于地面的速度]; **~ staff** *n* [u] 1 Aviat 地勤人员; 2 Sport 场地管理人员; **~swell** *n* [u] 1 Naut lit 海涌; 2 fig (upsurge) 迅速高涨; **there was a ~swell of opinion for reform** 要求改革的呼声越来越高; **~-to-air missile** *n* 地对空导弹; **~-to-~ missile** *n* 地对地导弹; **~ troops** *npl* 地面部队; **~water** *n* [u] 地下水; **~ wire** *n* Amer 地线; **~work** *n* [u] 基础工作; **to lay** *or* **do the ~work for sth.** 为某事物打基础; **~ zero** *n* [u] (of nuclear explosion) 爆心投影点; **G~ Zero** (of 9/11 terrorist attack) 世贸中心废墟

group /gruːp/
A *n* + *v sing or pl* 1 (of people or things) 群; **a ~ of houses** 一片房子; **the lower income ~** 低收入人群; **the Germanic ~ of languages** 日耳曼语系; **a ~ photograph** 合影 2 (people with same interests or objectives) 群体; **a drama ~** 戏剧团体; **~ discussion** 小组讨论 3 Comm 集团 4 Mus (band) 流行组合 5 Art 群像
B *vt* **~ (together)** 使成群; **to ~ sth. according to price** 将某物按价格归类
C *vi* 聚集; **to ~ (together) round sb./sth.** 聚集在某人/某物周围; **~ together in threes!** 三人一组!

group: ~ booking *n* 团体预订; **~ captain** *n* Brit 空军上校

grouper /ˈgruːpə(r)/ *n* 石斑鱼

groupie /ˈgruːpi/ *n* colloq (of pop star) 流行歌星迷; (of other celebrity) 追星族

grouping /ˈgruːpɪŋ/ *n* 1 [c] (group, alliance) 小集团 2 [u] (putting together) 分组

group: ~ insurance *n* [u] esp Amer 团体保险; **~ interview** *n* 集体面试; **G~ of Seven/Eight/Twenty** *n* 七国/八国/二十国集团; **~ practice** *n* 联合医疗; **~ sex** *n* [u] 群交; **~ therapy** *n* [u] 群体治疗; **~ware** *n* [u] 群件; **~ work** *n* [u] 小组作业

grouse¹ /graʊs/ *n* (*pl* **grouse**) 1 [c] (bird) 松鸡 2 [u] (meat) 松鸡肉

grouse² colloq
A *n* (complaint) 牢骚
B *vi* 抱怨; **to ~ about sb./sth.** 抱怨某人/某事物

grouse: ~ moor *n* 松鸡猎场; **~ shooting** *n* [u] 猎松鸡

grout /graʊt/
A *n* [u and c] [用来填砖、石缝隙的] 浆液
B *vt* 给…灌浆 ‹*joints, tiles*›

grouting /ˈgraʊtɪŋ/ *n* [u] [尤指变硬后的] 灌浆

grove /grəʊv/ *n* 树丛

grovel /ˈgrɒvl/ *vi* (*pres p etc.* **-ll-**, Amer **-l-**) 1 fig (act obsequiously) 卑躬屈膝; **to ~ to sb. for sth.** 低声下气地向某人要求某物 2 lit (lie) 匍匐; (crawl) 匍匐前进; **get up and stop ~ling!** 站起来, 别趴着!; **to ~ on (one's) hands and knees** 四肢着地爬行

grovelling, Amer **groveling** /ˈgrɒvlɪŋ/ *adj* 卑躬屈膝的; **a ~ letter of apology** 一封低声下气的道歉信

grow /grəʊ/
A *vi* (*pt* **grew**, *pp* **grown**) 1 (increase in size naturally) 生长; **her hair had grown very long** 她的头发长得很长了; **to ~ X inches/centimetres** 长X英寸/厘米; **to ~ (to) more than 20 feet long** *or* **to a length of more than 20 feet** 长到 20 多英尺长; **to let one's hair/nails ~** 蓄发/留指甲; **to ~ from sth.** 从…生长起来 ‹*seed, bulb, acorn*› 2 (increase in measurable way) «*business, money, profits*» 增长; «*membership, family*» 增多; **the queue is ~ing** 队列越排越长了 3 fig (increase, develop) «*pressure, ability, confidence*» 增强; «*friendship, love*» 加深; «*anger, fear, crisis*» 加剧; **she continues to ~ as an artist** 身为艺术家, 她在不断成长; **as I listened, my anger grew** 我越听越生气; **to ~ in strength/authority/importance/confidence** 在力量/权力/重要性/自信心方面得以增强; **she has grown in beauty/popularity** 她比以前更美丽/更受欢迎了 4 (become) 渐渐变成; **to ~ old** 渐渐变老; **to ~ dark/light** 慢慢暗下来/亮起来; **the weather is ~ing hot** 天越来越热; **to ~ impatient** 越来越不耐烦; **to ~ used to sth./doing sth.** 逐渐适应某事/做某事; **to ~ like sb.** 变得像某人 5 (reach stage) 开始; **to ~ to like sb.** 开始喜欢某人; **to ~ to expect sth. of sb.** 开始对某人的某事习以为常
B *vt* (*pt* **grew**, *pp* **grown**) 1 (allow to grow) 使…生长 ‹*part of body, cells*›; **to ~ one's hair/a beard** 蓄发/蓄须; **to ~ one's nails long** 留长指甲; **the lizard grew a new tail** 蜥蜴长出了一条新尾巴 2 Agric, Hort 种植 ‹*fruit, vegetables, crop*›; **to ~ flowers from cuttings/seed** 用插条/种子培育这些花 3 Comm 拓展 ‹*business, market*›; 提高 ‹*sales, production*›

Phrasal verbs

- **grow apart** *vi* 变得疏远; **to ~ apart from sb.** 疏远某人
- **grow away** *vi* 变得疏远; **to ~ away from sb.** 逐渐疏远某人; **they had grown away from each other** 他们之间逐渐疏远了
- **grow from** *vt* [**~ from sth.**] 1 (arise out of) 源于 ‹*activity, condition, earlier stage or form*›; **her scepticism grew from her early experiences** 她怀疑的态度源于年少时的经历 2 (change from) «*person*» 由…成长而来; «*place, business*» 由…演变而来; **the city grew from a small village** 这座城市是由一座小村庄发展起来的 3 (increase from) «*number, amount, deficit*» 增长; «*population, crime*» 增多; Comm «*sales, profits*» 上涨; **to ~ from sth. to sth.** 从…发展到某程度 ‹*figure, level*›; **the school grew from 400 to 900 pupils** 在校学生人数从 400 名上升到 900 名
- **grow in** *vi* «*nail*» 向内生长
- **grow into** *vt* [**~ into sth.**] 1 (become) 进入 ‹*adult*›; **~ into sth. larger/older** 长得更大/更老; **~ into sb./sth. different** 变成不同的人/东西 2 (fit into) 长得适合于穿着 ‹*garment, shoes*›; **the coat's too big for him now, but he'll ~ into it** 这件外套他现在穿太大, 但他长高后可以穿 3 fig (become accustomed to) 适应 ‹*role, job*›; 养成 ‹*habit*› 4 (become embedded) «*bone, nail*» 长进…里 ‹*skin, flesh*›
- **grow on** *vt* [**~ on sb.**] 1 (become ingrained in) «*habit, characteristic*» 深深影响 ‹*person*› 2 (become more appealing to) 越来越受…的喜爱 ‹*person*›; **the music was starting to ~ on me** 我越来越喜欢听这种音乐了
- **grow out**
  A *vi* «*perm, colour, curls*» 长长后被剪掉
  B *vt* [**~ sth. out, ~ out sth.**] 等…长长后剪掉 ‹*perm, colour, curls*›
- **grow out of** *vt* [**~ out of sth.**] 1 (no longer fit into) 长得穿不下 ‹*garment, shoes*› 2 (become too mature for) 随成熟而放弃 ‹*practice, activity, liking*›; **most children ~ out of tantrums by the time they're three** 多数孩子到三岁就不会乱发脾气了; **to ~ out of the habit of doing sth.** 随成熟而放弃做某事的习惯 3 (develop from) 源于 ‹*experience, activity, earlier stage or form*›
- **grow together** *vi* 1 (become more intimate) 变得更亲近 2 (join) «*branches, bones, plants*» 长到一起; **a tangle of bushes which had grown together** 一团纠缠蓬乱的灌木
- **grow up** *vi* 1 (become adult) 长大; **to ~ up into sth.** 长大成人; **he grew up into a handsome young man** 他长成了英俊的小伙子; **to ~ up to do sth.** 长大做某事; **he grew up to play in the World Cup** 他长大后参加了世界杯 2 (spend childhood) 度过童年; **to ~ up in London/believing that ...** 儿时在伦敦度过/儿时就相信… 3 (act more sensibly) 变得成熟; **oh, ~ up!** 哎, 成熟点好不好! 4 (develop) «*city, business, movement*» 逐渐发展; «*idea, friendship, custom, feeling*» 形成

grow bag *n* Brit 栽培袋

grower /ˈgrəʊə(r)/ *n* 种植者; **a fruit ~** 果农

growing /ˈgrəʊɪŋ/
A *n* 种植; **a fruit-~ area** 水果种植区
B *adj* 1 (maturing) 生长的; (becoming larger) 增大的; **a ~ baby** 正在发育的婴儿; **a club with a ~ membership** 会员不断增多的俱乐部 2 (increasing) 增长的 ‹*number, amount, demand*›; 增强的 ‹*feeling, pressure, criticism*›; **a ~ crisis** 日益严重的危机; **there is ~ concern about cyber security** 人们对网络安全越来越担心

growing: ~ pains *npl* 1 lit [儿童的] 发育期痛; 2 fig (of firm, project) 发展时期的困难; **~ season** *n* [植物的] 生长季节

g

growl /graʊl/
A *vi* **1** (of dog) 低声吼叫; **the dog ~ed at me** 那条狗冲我狺狺狂吠 **2** (speak angrily) 气冲冲地说; **the man ~ed at him** 那人冲他怒吼 **3** (rumble) 发轰隆声; **his stomach ~ed** Amer 他饥肠辘辘
B *vt* 粗暴地说; **'get out!', he ~ed** "出去!" 他怒吼道
C *n* 怒吼声; **to give a ~** 发出一声咆哮

grown /grəʊn/
A *pp* ▸**grow**
B *adj* (mature) 成熟的; (adult) 长大的; **a ~ man** 成年男子

grown-up
A /ˌgrəʊn'ʌp/ *adj* **1** (mature) 成熟的; (adult) 长大的; **a ~ son** 成年的儿子; **to be ~ for one's age** 比实际年龄要成熟 **2** (suitable for adults) 适于成人的; (typical of adults) 成人特有的; **a ~ party** 成人晚会
B /'grəʊnʌp/ *n* 成年人

growth /grəʊθ/ *n* **1** [u] (of person) 成长; (of plant, hair, nails) 生长; **intellectual ~** 智力发育 **2** [u] (increase in amount) 增长; (increase in intensity) 增强; **a ~ in crime** 犯罪行为的增多; **economic ~** 经济发展 **3** [u] (thing growing) 生长物; **a thick ~ of weeds** 一片浓密的野草; **a week's ~ of beard** 一周未刮的胡子 **4** [c] Med (tumour) 肿瘤; **a small ~ on his finger** 他手指上的小肉瘤; **a benign ~** 良性瘤

growth: ~ area *n* 快速增长区; **~ factor** *n* 生长因子; **~ hormone** *n* [u and c] 生长激素; **~ industry** *n* 迅速发展的行业; **~ rate** *n* (of economy, population) 增长率; (of person, animal, plant) 生长率; **~ ring** *n* 年轮

groyne /grɔɪn/ *n* 防波堤

grub¹ /grʌb/ *n* **1** [c] (larva) 幼虫 **2** [u] colloq (food) 食物; **~'s up!** 饭好了!

grub² *vi* 翻掘; **to ~ for sth.** 翻找某物

Phrasal verbs
- **grub about, grub around** *vi* **to ~ about** *or* **around for sth.** 四处翻寻某物
- **grub up** *vt* [**~ sth. up, ~ up sth.**] 掘出; **birds ~bing up insects** 刨虫子的鸟

grubbiness /'grʌbɪnɪs/ *n* [u] (dirtiness) 肮脏; fig (dishonesty) 卑鄙

grubby /'grʌbi/ *adj* (dirty) 肮脏的 ‹*room, clothes, face*›; fig (dishonest) 卑鄙的 ‹*campaign, affair*›

grub screw *n* Brit 无头螺丝

grudge /grʌdʒ/
A *n* 积怨; **to bear** Brit *or* **hold a ~ (against sb.)** (对某人) 怀有积怨; **a ~ fight** Sport 冤家对头之间的拳击赛
B *vt* (do sth. unwillingly) 勉强做; (give sth. unwillingly) 勉强给; (resent) 嫉妒; **to ~ sb. sth./sb. doing sth.** 妒忌某人有某物/某人做某事; **to ~ doing sth.** 不情愿做某事

grudging /'grʌdʒɪŋ/ *adj* 勉强的; **to be ~ in** *or* **with sth.** 在某事上很不情愿

grudgingly /'grʌdʒɪŋli/ *adv* 勉强地 ‹*admit, give*›

gruel /'gru:əl/ *n* [u] 燕麦粥

gruelling, Amer **grueling** /'gru:əlɪŋ/ *adj* 使人筋疲力尽的

gruesome /'gru:səm/ *adj* (horrifying) 恐怖的; (disgusting) 令人厌恶的

gruff /grʌf/ *adj* 粗哑的 ‹*voice*›; 粗鲁的 ‹*person*›

gruffly /'grʌfli/ *adv* 粗哑地 ‹*spoken, say*›; 粗鲁地 ‹*mannered*›

gruffness /'grʌfnɪs/ *n* [u] (of voice) 粗哑; (of person) 粗鲁

grumble /'grʌmbl/
A *vi* **1** (complain) 抱怨; **to ~ at sb.** 冲某人发牢骚; **to ~ to sb.** 在某人面前发牢骚; **to ~ about sb./sth.** 抱怨某人/某事物 **2** (rumble) ‹*thunder*› 发轰隆声; ‹*stomach*› 咕咕叫
B *n* **1** [c] (complaint) 抱怨; **to have a ~ about sb./sth.** 抱怨某人/某事物 **2** [u] (of thunder) 轰隆声; (of stomach) 咕咕声

grumbler /'grʌmblə(r)/ *n* colloq 发牢骚的人

grumbling /'grʌmblɪŋ/
A *n* [u] **1** (complaining) 抱怨; **~ at** *or* **about sb./sth.** 对某人/某事的抱怨 **2** (of thunder) 轰隆声; (of stomach) 咕咕声
B *adj attrib* **1** (complaining) 抱怨的 ‹*old man*› **2** (rumbling) 轰隆作响的 ‹*thunder*› **3** Med (intermittently painful) 间歇性疼痛的

grump /grʌmp/ *n* colloq **1** (person) 脾气坏的人 **2** (bad mood) 脾气的发作; **to have the ~s, to be in a ~** 发脾气

grumpily /'grʌmpɪli/ *adv* 生气地

grumpiness /'grʌmpɪnɪs/ *n* [u] 脾气坏

grumpy /'grʌmpi/ *adj* 脾气坏的

grunge /grʌndʒ/ *n* [u] **1** colloq (dirt) 污垢 **2** Mus 垃圾摇滚乐 **3** (fashion style) 垃圾摇滚风格 [与垃圾摇滚乐相关的一种不修边幅的时尚风格]

grungy /'grʌndʒi/ *adj* **1** colloq (dirty) 肮脏的 **2** Mus 垃圾摇滚乐的 ‹*music, rock*› **3** Fashn 垃圾摇滚风格的 ‹*clothes, fashion*›

grunt /grʌnt/
A *vi* **1** (of animal) 发呼噜声 **2** (of person) 咕哝; **to ~ with** *or* **in pain** 痛苦地哼哼
B *vt* 咕哝着说
C *n* (made by animal) 呼噜声; (made by person) 咕哝声; **he gave a ~ of disapproval** 他咕哝一声表示不赞成

gryphon /'grɪfən/ *n* = **griffin**

GSM *abbr* = **Global System for Mobile (Communications)** 全球移动通信系统 [一种移动通信技术标准]

G: ~-string *n* **1** Clothg 丁字裤; **2** Mus G 弦; **~-suit** *n* 重力防护服

Gt *abbr* = **Great**

Guangdong /ˌgwæŋ'dʊŋ/ ▸**p. 604** *pr n* **~ (Province)** 广东 (省)

Guangxi /ˌgwæŋ'ʃi:/ ▸**p. 604** *pr n* **~ (Zhuang Autonomous Region)** 广西 (壮族自治区)

Guangzhou /ˌgwæŋ'dʒəʊ/ *pr n* 广州

guano /'gwɑ:nəʊ/ *n* [u] 鸟粪

guanxi /ˌgwæn'ʃi:/ *n* [u] 关系 [指中国有助于办事的人际网络]; **~ can affect a person's success in employment** 关系网会影响一个人事业的成败; **to develop** *or* **cultivate/expand one's ~** 培养关系/扩大关系网

guarantee /ˌgærən'ti:/
A *n* **1** [u and c] Comm (warranty, document) 保修单; **to be under ~** Brit 在保修期内; **without/with no ~** 无担保地; **the watch comes with** *or* **carries** *or* **has three years ~** 这块表保修期为 3 年; **to be covered by (the manufacturer's) ~** 在 (生产商) 保修范围内; **a money-back ~** 退货保证; **there is a one year's ~ on the vehicle** 这辆汽车有一年的保修期; **a certificate of ~** 质保证书; **a written ~** *or* **a ~ in writing** 书面保证; **~ card/form** 质保卡/表格 **2** [c] (promise) 保证 **3** [c] Jur (undertaking) = **guaranty** **4** [u and c] Jur (person) = **guarantor**
B *vt* **1** (assure, make certain) 保证; **his presence ~s that the event will be a success** 他在场可保证此次活动成功举办; **it's ~d to rain!** 天准会下雨!; **her new novel is a ~d best seller** 她的新小说肯定畅销; **there's no ~ing ...** 无法保证… **2** Comm 为…提供质量保证 ‹*product, service, transaction*›; **to be ~d against rust** 保证不生锈; **to be ~d for 18 months** 保质期 18 个月; **to ~ to refund sb.'s money** 保证退某人的款; **to ~ sth. to be genuine** 保证某物为真品 **3** Jur 为…提供担保 ‹*debt, cheque, bill of exchange, person*›; **to ~ sb. for a loan** 为某人贷款作担保; **to ~ sb.'s good conduct** *or* **behaviour** 保证某人行为规矩

guaranteed: ~ interest *n* [u] 保证利息; **~ loan** *n* 担保贷款; **~ price** *n* **1** (minimum price) 保证价格; **2** (fixed price) 固定价格

guarantor /ˌgærən'tɔ:(r)/ *n* 保证人; **to stand ~ for sb.** 为某人作担保

guaranty /'gærənti/ *n* 担保

guard /gɑ:d/
A *n* **1** [c and u] Mil (sentinel) 警卫; (sentry duty) 警戒; **to put a ~ on sb./sth.** 派警卫保护某人/某物; **a soldier on ~** 站岗的士兵; **under (close) ~** 处于 (严密) 戒备状态; **to keep** *or* **stand ~** 守卫; **to mount (a) ~ over sb./sth.** 守卫某人/某物 **2** [u] + *v sing or pl* (group of soldiers) 警卫队; **the changing of the ~** 卫队换岗; **to double the ~** 派双岗 **3** [u] (defensive position) 防御姿势; **to drop/keep up one's ~** 收起/保持防御姿势; **to let one's ~ slip** fig 丧失警惕 **4** [u] (watchfulness) 警惕; **to be on one's ~** 提防; **to be off (one's) ~** 不提防; **to catch sb. off ~** 使某人措手不及 **5** **Guards** *pl* Brit (regiment) 近卫军 **6** [c] esp Amer (in prison) 监狱看守人 **7** [c] Brit (railway official) 列车长 **8** [c] (apparatus) 防护装置; **the safety ~ on the saw** 锯子上的防护罩
B *vt* **1** (protect) 保卫; fig 保护 ‹*reputation*›; (control access to) 守卫 ‹*building, vault*› **2** (prevent from escaping) 看守 ‹*prisoner, hostage*›; fig 保守 ‹*secret*›; **to be closely ~ed** 被严加看守; **to ~ one's tongue** 言语谨慎

Phrasal verb
- **guard against** *vt* [**~ against sth.**] 防止; **to ~ against disease** 预防疾病; **dangers to be ~ed against** 需要防范的危险

guard: ~ dog *n* 警卫狗; **~ duty** *n* [u] 警卫任务

guarded /'gɑ:dɪd/ *adj* **1** (protected) 守护着的 **2** (cautious) 谨慎的

guardedly /'gɑ:dɪdli/ *adv* 谨慎地

guardedness /'gɑ:dɪdnɪs/ *n* [u] 谨慎

guardhouse /'gɑ:dhaʊs/ *n* (for soldiers) 警卫室; (for prisoners) 禁闭室

guardian /'gɑ:dɪən/ *n* **1** (defender) 保卫者 **2** Jur (of juvenile or patient) 监护人

> **The Guardian**
> 《卫报》。英国全国性日报。1821 年创刊于曼彻斯特, 始称《曼彻斯特卫报》(The Manchester Guardian)。起初为周报, 1855 年起改为日报 (星期日除外)。1959 年改名The Guardian。该报持自由派观点, 政治立场偏左。

guardian angel *n* lit 守护天使; fig 守护者

guardianship /'gɑ:dɪənʃɪp/ *n* [u] 监护权 **under the ~ of sb.** 在某人的监护下

guard: ~ of honour *n* 仪仗队; **~ rail** *n* (on building, cliff) 护栏; Amer (crash barrier) 防撞护栏; **~room** *n* (for soldiers) 警卫室; (for prisoners) 禁闭室; **~sman** /'gɑ:dzmən/ *n* 近卫军士兵; **~'s van** *n* Brit [列车上护车人员乘坐的] 守车

Guatemala /ˌgwɑ:tə'mɑ:lə/ *pr n* 危地马拉

Guatemalan /ˌgwɑ:tə'mɑ:lən/ ▸**p. 503**
A *adj* (of Guatemala) 危地马拉的; (of the people) 危地马拉人的
B *n* 危地马拉人

guava /'gwɑ:və, Amer 'gwɔ:və/ *n* (tree) 番石榴树; (fruit) 番石榴

gubbins /'gʌbɪnz/ *npl* Brit colloq **1** + *v sing or pl* (paraphernalia) 各色小物件 **2** + *v sing* (gadget) 小装置

gubernatorial /ˌgu:bənə'tɔ:rɪəl/ *adj* formal 州长的

gudgeon pin /'gʌdʒən pɪn/ *n* 活塞销

Guernsey /'gɜ:nzi/
A *pr n* Geog 格恩西岛
B *n* (*pl* **~s**) Agric 格恩西奶牛

guerrilla /gə'rɪlə/
A *n* 游击队员
B *adj* 游击队的 ‹*fighter, organization*›; **a ~ attack/tactic** 游击进攻/战术

guerrilla: ~ war *n* 游击战; **~ warfare** *n* [u] 游击战争

guess /ges/

A n 猜测; **to have** *or* **make** *or* **take** *or* **hazard a ~ (at/as to sth.)** （对某事物）进行猜测; **I'll give you three ~es!** 我让你猜三次！; **my ~ is that ...** 我猜…; **one's best ~** 最乐观的估计; **a good/lucky/wild ~** 正确/侥幸正确/胡乱的猜测; **your ~ is as good as mine** 我跟你一样没把握; **anybody's** *or* **anyone's ~** 大家都拿不准的事情; **what will happen now is anybody's ~** 没人知道会发生什么; **at a (rough) ~** 凭（大致）猜测

B vt [1] (intuit) 猜测; (estimate correctly) 猜对; **she ~ed the girl's age at 14 or 15** 她猜那个女孩的年龄有 14 或 15 岁; **he ~ed her to be about thirty** 他推测她大概 30 岁; **can you ~ what I've brought for you?** 你能猜出我给你带来了什么吗？; **~ what/who!** 你猜怎么回事/是谁！; **you'll never ~ who has come to see us** 你肯定猜不出谁来看我们了; **I ~ed as much** 如我所料 [2] esp Amer colloq (suppose, think) **I ~ that ...** 我想…; **I ~ so/not** 我想是这样/不是

C vi 猜测; **to ~ at** *or* **as to sth.** 猜测 ‹*outcome, number, plan*›; **one can but ~ at the number of casualties** 人们只能估计一下伤亡人数; **to ~ right** *or* **correctly** 猜对; **to ~ wrong** 猜错; **I can't begin to ~!** 我怎么知道！; **you'll never ~!** 你无论如何也想不到！; **how did you ~?** 你怎么知道的？; **try and ~!** 猜猜看！; **to keep sb. ~ing** colloq 让某人捉摸不定

guesstimate, guestimate /ˈgestɪmət/ n colloq 约略估计

guesswork /ˈgeswɜːk/ n [u] (process) 猜测; (results) 猜测的结果

guest /gest/

A n [1] (at party, wedding, ceremony) 客人; (in one's house) 访客; **an uninvited ~** 不速之客; **a wedding ~** 婚礼宾客; **the ~ of honour** 贵宾; **be my ~!** colloq 请便！; **we had ~s for the weekend** 周末我们有客人到访; **the ~ list** 宾客名单 [2] (in hotel) 旅客; (in boarding house) 宿客 [3] (performer) 客串演员; **a ~ appearance** 客串出场 [4] (participant) 特邀嘉宾; **~ speaker** 特邀演讲者

B vi colloq 客串

guest: ~ artist n 特邀艺人; **~book** n [1] (for visitors) 来宾登记簿; [2] (on website) 留言簿; **~house** n 家庭旅馆; **~ room** n 客房; **~worker** n 外籍工人

guff /gʌf/ n [u] colloq 胡说八道

guffaw /gəˈfɔː/

A n 大笑; **to give** *or* **let out a ~** 发出一阵狂笑

B vi 大笑

GUI *abbr* **= graphical user interface**

Guiana /gaɪˈænə/ *pr n* **the ~s** 圭亚那地区

guidance /ˈgaɪdns/ n [u] [1] (advice) 指导; (leadership) 领导; (direction) 引导; **~ as to how to do sth./how sth. should be done** 关于如何做某事的指导; **~ from sb.** 来自某人的指导; **to be under sb.'s ~** 受某人的指导; **to give (sb.) ~** 指导（某人） [2] (of missile, aircraft) 制导; **a laser ~ system** 激光制导系统

guide /gaɪd/

A n [1] (person leading climbers, explorers) 向导; (person leading tourists) 导游; **a tour ~** 导游 [2] (adviser) 指导者; **a spiritual/moral ~** 精神导师/道德指导者; **let reason be your ~** 做事要靠理智 [3] (indication) 指示; **this figure is only meant to be a ~** 这一数字只是起指导作用; **to give sb. a ~ as to sth.** 给某人有关某事的指示; **to treat sth. as a ~** 以某事为指导; **as a rough ~** 大致上; **to be no/little ~** 没有/几乎没有指导意义 [4] (guidebook) 旅行指南; (reference book) 手册; **a ~ to Greece** 希腊旅行指南; **a user's ~ to sth.** 某物的用户手册; **a weekly TV ~** 电视节目周报 [5] esp Brit (member of youth organization) 女童子军; **a Brownie/Ranger G~** 初级/高级女童子军; **Queen's/King's G~** Brit 皇家女童子军 [最高级别的女童子军]; **to be in the G~s** 是女童子军成员; **to join the G~s** 参加女童子军 [6] Tech 导向装置

B vt [1] (lead) 为…引路 ‹*visitor, blind person*›; **he ~d her through the crowd/to the garden** 他领着她穿过人群/走向花园; **he ~d the country through the war/to victory** 他领导全国度过战争时期/走向胜利; **he ~d the conversation away from personal matters** 他把话题从私事上扯开 [2] (direct) 牵引 ‹*rope, cable, thread*›; 驾驶 ‹*ship*› [3] (influence) 指导 ‹*person, behaviour, action*›; **let your common sense ~ you** 依照常识行事吧; **be ~d by my advice** 听我的建议吧 [4] Aerosp, Mil 导引 ‹*rocket, missile, spacecraft*›

guide: ~ book n 指南; **~d missile** n 导弹; **~ dog** n 导盲犬; **~d tour** n 有导游带领的游览; **~line** n 指导方针; **~post** n esp Amer 指导原则; **~ rail** n 导轨; **~ rope** n 导向绳

guiding /ˈgaɪdɪŋ/ adj 指导性的; **a ~ principle** 指导原则; **a ~ light** lit 指路明灯; fig 指路人

guild /gɪld/ n [1] (in Middle Ages) 同业公会 [2] (in modern times) 协会

guildhall /ˈgɪldhɔːl/ n [1] (in Middle Ages) 同业公会会馆 [2] Brit (town hall) 市政厅

guile /gaɪl/ n [u] 奸诈; **a man without ~** 厚道的人

guileful /ˈgaɪlfl/ adj 奸诈的

guileless /ˈgaɪllɪs/ adj 不奸诈的

guillemot /ˈgɪlɪmɒt/ n 海鸽

guillotine /ˈgɪləti:n/

A n [1] (for execution) 断头台 [2] (for paper, metal) 裁切机 [3] Brit Pol (time limit) 规定截止辩论的时限

B vt [1] (execute) 把…送上断头台 ‹*prisoner*› [2] (cut) 切断 ‹*paper, metal*› [3] Brit Pol «*government*» 限制…的辩论时间 ‹*bill*›

guilt /gɪlt/ n [u] [1] (for a crime) 有罪; **to admit ~** 认罪; **to establish/prove sb.'s ~** 认定/证实某人有罪 [2] (for a situation, problem) 过错; **where does the ~ lie?** 何人之过？ [3] (anxiety, unhappiness) 内疚; **to be tormented** *or* **racked by ~** 深感内疚; **a ~ complex** 内疚情结

guiltily /ˈgɪltɪli/ adv 内疚地

guiltless /ˈgɪltlɪs/ adj formal 无辜的

guilty /ˈgɪlti/ adj [1] (of a crime) 有罪的; **to be ~ of sth.** 犯有某罪的; **the ~ party** 有罪的一方; **to plead ~/not ~** 认罪/不认罪; **to be found ~/not ~ (of sth.)** 被判决有（某）罪/没有犯（某）罪 [2] (for a problem) 有过错的 [3] (for one's actions) 内疚的 ‹*expression, look*›; **to feel ~ about sb./sth.** 对某人/某事感到内疚; **a ~ conscience** 内疚

Guinea /ˈgɪni/ *pr n* [1] (republic) 几内亚 [2] dated (region) 几内亚地区

guinea /ˈgɪni/ n Brit 几尼 [英国旧时的一种金币]

Guinea-Bissau /ˌgɪnɪbɪˈsaʊ/ *pr n* 几内亚比绍

guinea: ~fowl (*pl* **~fowl**), **~ hen** *ns* 珠鸡; **~-pig** n [1] (animal) 豚鼠; [2] (in experiment) 试验对象

Guinness® /ˈgɪnɪs/ n [u and c] 健力士黑啤酒

guise /gaɪz/ n (appearance) 外表; (facade) 伪装; **under the ~ of sth.** 以某物为幌子; **in various** *or* **different ~s** 以不同的形式

guitar /gɪˈtɑː(r)/ ▸**p. 395** n 吉他; **to play the ~** 弹吉他; **a ~ player** 吉他弹奏者

guitarist /gɪˈtɑːrɪst/ ▸**p. 395, p. 409** n 吉他弹奏者

Guizhou /ˌgweɪˈdʒəʊ/ ▸**p. 604** *pr n* **~ (Province)** 贵州（省）

Gujarat /ˌguːdʒəˈrɑːt/ *pr n* (state) 古吉拉特邦; (region) 古吉拉特地区

Gujarati /ˌguːdʒəˈrɑːti/ ▸**p. 426** n [1] [c] (person) 古吉拉特人 [2] [u] (language) 古吉拉特语

gulch /gʌltʃ/ n Amer 冲沟

gulf /gʌlf/ n [1] (area of sea) 海湾; **the G~ of Mexico** 墨西哥湾 [2] (difference, division) 鸿沟; **the ~ between rich and poor** 贫富差距 [3] **the Gulf** (the Persian Gulf) 波斯湾; (neighbouring states) 波斯湾沿岸诸国 [4] liter (chasm) 深渊

Gulf: ~ States *pr npl* [1] Brit (in Middle East) **the ~ States** 海湾国家 [指波斯湾沿岸产油诸国]; [2] Amer (in Americas) **the ~ States** 美国濒墨西哥湾诸州; **~ Stream** *pr n* **the ~ Stream** 墨西哥湾流

Gulf War *pr n* **the ~** (1980-1988) 两伊战争; (1991) 海湾战争; (2003) 美伊战争

Gulf War syndrome ▸**p. 377** n [u] 海湾战争综合征

gull¹ /gʌl/ n 海鸥

gull² vt 欺骗

gullet /ˈgʌlɪt/ n 食管; **the words stuck in my ~** 那些话卡在我的嗓子眼里说不出来

gulley /ˈgʌli/ n **= gully**

gullibility /ˌgʌləˈbɪləti/ n [u] 轻信

gullible /ˈgʌləbl/ adj 易受骗的

gull-wing door n 鸥翼式车门

gully /ˈgʌli/ n [1] (ravine) 冲沟 [2] (channel) 水沟

gulp /gʌlp/

A n [1] (when swallowing) 吞咽; (nervous action) 哽塞; **he finished his drink in one** *or* **at a ~** 他将酒一饮而尽 [2] (noise) (when swallowing) 吞咽声; (when nervous) 哽塞声 [3] (mouthful) 一大口; **to have** *or* **take a ~ of sth.** 吞下一大口某物

B vt [1] (swallow) 狼吞虎咽; **they were ~ing brandy** 他们正大口地喝着白兰地 [2] (breathe in) 大口地吸 ‹*air*› [3] (say with emotion) 哽塞地说

C vi (swallow) 吞咽; (breathe) 倒吸气; **to ~ for air** 大口呼吸

Phrasal verbs

- **gulp back** vt [**~ back sth., ~ sth. back**] 忍住 ‹*sobs, jealousy*›
- **gulp down** vt [**~ down sth., ~ sth. down**] 大口吞下 ‹*food, drink*›
- **gulp in** vt [**~ in sth.**] 大口地吸 ‹*air*›

gum¹ /gʌm/ n Anat 牙龈

gum²

A n [1] [u] (from tree) 树胶 [2] [u] (glue) 胶 [3] [u] (chewing gum) 口香糖; (bubble gum) 泡泡糖 [4] [c] (sweet) 橡皮糖 [5] [u and c] (tree) 胶树

B vt (*pres p etc.* **-mm-**) (spread with glue) 在…上涂胶; (join with glue) 用胶粘; **~med label** 带粘胶的标签; **to ~ sth. to** *or* **on to sth.** 把某物粘在某物上; **to ~ sth. and sth. together** 把某物和某物粘在一起

Phrasal verbs

- **gum down** vt [**~ sth. down, ~ down sth.**] 用胶粘牢
- **gum up** vt [**~ up sth., ~ sth. up**] (clog up) 使…运转不灵 ‹*mechanism, system*›; fig colloq (disrupt) 搞糟 ‹*plans, arrangements*›; **to ~ up the works** fig 使制度不能运转

gum arabic n [u] 阿拉伯树胶

gumbo /ˈgʌmbəʊ/ n [1] [u] (okra) 秋葵 [2] [u and c] (soup) 秋葵汤

gum: ~boil n 牙龈脓肿; **~boot** n esp Brit dated 高筒胶靴; **~ disease** ▸**p. 377** n [u] 牙龈病; **~drop** n 橡皮糖

gummy¹ /ˈgʌmi/ adj (sticky) 黏性的

gummy² adj (toothless) 露齿龈的

gumption /ˈgʌmpʃn/ n [u] colloq 进取心

gum: ~shield n 牙套; **~shoe** n Amer colloq 侦探; **~ tree** n 胶树; **to be up a ~ tree** 陷入困境

gun /gʌn/

A n [1] (hand weapon) 枪; (artillery weapon) 炮; **to fire a ~ at sb.** 向某人开火; **to draw a ~ on sb.**

掏出枪对准某人; **a 12-～ salute** 12 响礼炮; **big ～** fig colloq 大人物; **top ～** fig colloq 头号人物; **to go great ～s** fig colloq 进展顺利; **to stick to one's ～s** colloq 坚持己见; **to spike sb.'s ～s** fig colloq 破坏某人的计划; **under the ～** fig colloq 在巨大压力下 **2** Sport (starting pistol) 发令枪; (signal) 起跑信号; **to jump the ～** colloq 过早行动 **3** (tool) 喷枪; **a paint/glue ～** 油漆喷枪/热熔胶枪
B *vt* (*pres p etc.* **-nn-**) colloq 加大…的油门 ‹*engine, motor*›
C *vi* **to be ～ning for sb.** (attack) 伺机攻击某人; (criticize) 伺机批评某人; **to be ～ning for sth.** 竭力谋求 ‹*job, prize*›

Phrasal verb
- **gun down** *vt* [**～ sb. down, ～ down sb.**] (kill) 枪杀; (injure) 开枪打伤

gun barrel *n* (of pistol, rifle) 枪管; (of artillery weapon) 炮筒
gunboat /ˈɡʌnbəʊt/ *n* 炮艇
gunboat diplomacy *n* [u] 炮舰外交
gun: ～ carriage *n* 炮架; **～dog** *n* 猎狗; **～fight** *n* 枪战; **～fire** *n* [u] 炮火
gunge /ɡʌndʒ/ *n* [u] Brit colloq 黏糊糊的东西

Phrasal verb
- **gunge up** *vt* [**～ sth. up, ～ up sth.**] Brit colloq (block) 以黏性物阻塞; (encrust) 在…上结起黏糊糊的一层

gung ho /ˌɡʌŋˈhəʊ/ *adj* colloq 狂热的
gunk /ɡʌŋk/ *n* [u] colloq 黏糊糊的东西
gun: ～ laws *npl* 枪支法; **～ licence** *n* 持枪证; **～man** /-mən/ *n* 持枪歹徒
gunnel /ˈɡʌnl/ *n* **= gunwale**
gunner /ˈɡʌnə(r)/ *n* Brit 炮兵
gunnery /ˈɡʌnəri/ *n* [u] 火炮学; *modif* 重炮的; **a ～ expert/officer** 重炮专家/指挥官
gunnery sergeant *n* Amer 枪炮军士
gunny /ˈɡʌni/ *n* **1** [u] (fabric) 黄麻布 **2** [c] (sack) 黄麻袋 **3** [c] Amer sl (gunnery sergeant) [美国海军陆战队的] 枪炮军士
gunnysack /ˈɡʌnɪsæk/ *n* Amer 黄麻袋
gun: ～play *n* [u] 交火; **～point** *n* [u] 枪口; **to do sth. at ～point** *«robber»* 用枪胁迫做某事; *«hostage, victim»* 在枪口威胁下做某事; **to hold sb. up at ～point** 用枪威胁某人
gunpowder /ˈɡʌnpaʊdə(r)/ *n* [u] 火药
Gunpowder Plot *pr n* Hist 火药阴谋
gun: ～runner *n* 军火走私者; **～running** *n* [u] 军火走私; **～ship** *n* 武装直升机
gunshot /ˈɡʌnʃɒt/ *n* **1** [c] (bullet) 射出的枪弹; (shell) 射出的炮弹; **the sound of ～s** 枪炮声 **2** [u] archaic (range) 射程; **to be within/out of ～** 在射程之内/外
gunshot wound *n* 枪伤
gun: ～sight *n* 瞄准具; **～slinger** /ˈɡʌnslɪŋə(r)/ *n* Amer colloq 快枪手; **～smith** ▸**p. 409** *n* (maker) 造枪工; (repairer) 修枪匠; **～ turret** *n* 回转炮塔
gunwale /ˈɡʌnl/ *n* 舷缘; **to load** *or* **fill sth. to the ～s** 把某物装得满满的
guppy /ˈɡʌpi/ *n* 虹鳉
gurgle /ˈɡɜːɡl/
A *n* (of water) 汩汩声; (of baby) 咯咯声
B *vi «water, stream»* 发汩汩声; *«baby»* 发咯咯声
Gurkha /ˈɡɜːkə/ *n* 廓尔喀兵
guru /ˈɡʊruː, Amer ɡəˈruː/ *n* **1** (Hindu spiritual leader) 古鲁 **2** fig (teacher) 导师; (authority) 权威; **a management ～** 管理大师
gush /ɡʌʃ/
A *n* **1** (of water, oil, blood) 涌出; (of gas) 喷出; **the oil came out in** *or* **with a ～** 油喷涌而出 **2** (of enthusiasm, pleasure) 迸发
B *vi* **1** (flow) *«water, oil, blood»* 涌出; *«gas»* 喷出 **2** fig pej (talk) 滔滔不绝地说话; **to ～ over sb./sth.** 滔滔不绝地谈论某人/某事物
C *vt* **1** (discharge) 使涌出 ‹*oil, water, blood*› **2** (say) 滔滔不绝地说

Phrasal verbs
- **gush in** *vi «water»* 涌入
- **gush out** *vi «water, oil, blood»* 涌出

gusher /ˈɡʌʃə(r)/ *n* colloq 自喷井
gushing /ˈɡʌʃɪŋ/ *adj* **1** (flowing) 喷涌而出的 ‹*water, oil*› **2** (effusive) 过分热情的; **to pay sb. ～ compliments** 对某人大加吹捧
gushy /ˈɡʌʃi/ *adj* 装腔作势的 ‹*person, letter, manner*›
gusset /ˈɡʌsɪt/ *n* **1** (in garment) 衬料 **2** Tech 角撑板
gust /ɡʌst/
A *n* (of wind) 一阵狂风; (of air, rain, snow) 一阵; **the wind blows in ～s** 风一阵阵刮着
B *vi «wind»* 一阵阵吹; *«rain, snow»* 一阵阵下
gusto /ˈɡʌstəʊ/ *n* [u] (enjoyment) 乐趣; (enthusiastic vigour) 热情; **to eat with ～** 津津有味地吃
gusty /ˈɡʌsti/ *adj* 刮阵风的 ‹*day, weather*›; 一阵阵吹的 ‹*wind*›
gut /ɡʌt/
A *n* **1** **guts** *pl* colloq (insides) 内脏; **to have a pain in one's ～s** colloq 肚子疼; **to hate sb.'s ～s** fig colloq 对某人恨之入骨; **to have sb.'s ～s for garters** Brit hum 严惩某人; **to work** *or* **slog** *or* **flog** *or* **sweat one's ～s out** colloq 拼命工作; **to bust a ～** fig colloq 竭尽全力 **2** **guts** *pl* (of machine) 内部结构; (of speech) 要点 **3** **guts** *pl* colloq (courage) 勇气; **to have the ～s to do sth.** 有胆量做某事; **sb. with ～s** 有魄力的某人; **to take (a lot of) ～s to do sth.** 做某事需要（很大的）勇气 **4** [c] (intestine) 肠 **5** [c] colloq (abdomen) 肚子; **a beer ～** 啤酒肚 **6** **guts** *pl + v sing* colloq (greedy person) 贪心鬼 **7** [u] (thread) 肠线
B *modif* (instinctive) 本能的 ‹*reaction, response*›; **a ～ feeling** 直觉
C *vt* (*pres p etc.* **-tt-**) **1** (remove intestines from) 取出…的内脏; **to ～ a fish** 挖出鱼的内脏 **2** (destroy) 彻底毁坏…的内部; **the fire ～ted the warehouse** 大火把仓库烧得只剩下了骨架
gutless /ˈɡʌtlɪs/ *adj* colloq 怯懦的
gutsy /ˈɡʌtsi/ *adj* colloq **1** (courageous) 勇敢的 ‹*fighter*›; 充满激情的 ‹*performance*› **2** fig (strongly flavoured) 很有风味的 ‹*food, drink*› **3** (greedy) 贪婪的
gutta-percha /ˌɡʌtəˈpɜːtʃə/ *n* **1** [u] (substance) 杜仲胶 **2** [c] (tree) 杜仲树
gutter /ˈɡʌtə(r)/
A *n* **1** [c] (on roof) 檐槽 **2** [c] (in street) 排水沟 **3** [u] (way of life) **the ～** 贫贱生活; **to rise from the ～** 从贫民区成长起来; **the language of the ～** 粗鄙的语言
B *vi «candle»* 摇曳不定
guttering /ˈɡʌtərɪŋ/ *n* [u] 排水系统
gutter: ～ press *n* [u] pej 市井小报; **～snipe** *n* pej 小瘪三
guttural /ˈɡʌtərəl/ *adj* (produced in the throat) 喉中发出的; (harsh-sounding) 粗嘎的; **a ～ consonant** 颚辅音
guv /ɡʌv/ *n* Brit colloq 先生 [男子对男子的称谓]; **thanks ～!** 谢谢，先生!
guv'nor /ˈɡʌvnə(r)/ *n* Brit colloq **= guv**
guy[1] /ɡaɪ/ *n* **1** colloq (man) 家伙; **the good/bad ～** 好人/坏蛋; **her ～** 她的男人; **you ～s!** 伙计们! **2** Brit (effigy) 盖伊模拟像; **penny for the ～** “给盖伊的便士” [孩子们在篝火之夜说的话，讨来零钱买鞭炮]
guy[2]
A *n* (rope) **= guyrope**
B *vt* 用牵索固定
Guyana /ɡaɪˈænə/ *pr n* 圭亚那
Guyanese /ˌɡaɪəˈniːz/ ▸**p. 503**
A *adj* (of Guyana) 圭亚那的; (of the people) 圭亚那人的
B *n* 圭亚那人
Guy Fawkes Night /ˈɡaɪ fɔːks naɪt/ *n* Brit **= Bonfire Night**
guyrope /ˈɡaɪrəʊp/ *n* 牵索
guzzle /ˈɡʌzl/
A *vt* (eat) 暴食; (drink) 狂饮; **this car ～s petrol** fig 这辆车很耗油
B *vi* (eat) 暴食; (drink) 狂饮

Phrasal verb
- **guzzle down** *vt* [**～ sth. down, ～ down sth.**] (eat) 暴食; (drink) 狂饮

Gwynedd /ˈɡwɪneð/ *pr n* [英国威尔士的] 圭内斯郡
gybe /dʒaɪb/ Brit
A *vi «boat, crew»* 转帆
B *vt* 使…从一舷转至另一舷 ‹*sail, boom*›
C *n* 转帆
gym /dʒɪm/ ▸**p. 307** *n* **1** [c] (gymnasium) 体操馆 **2** [u] (gymnastics) 体操
gymkhana /dʒɪmˈkɑːnə/ *n* 赛马会
gymnasium /dʒɪmˈneɪzɪəm/ *n* 体操馆
gymnast /ˈdʒɪmnæst/ *n* 体操运动员
gymnastic /dʒɪmˈnæstɪk/ *adj* 体操的
gymnastics /dʒɪmˈnæstɪks/ ▸**p. 307** *npl* **1** + *v sing* (sport, form of exercise) 体操 **2** + *v pl* (agility) 技巧; **mental ～** 思维的敏捷
gym: ～ shoe *n* 体操鞋; **～slip** *n* Brit 体操衫
gynaecological Brit, **gynecological** Amer /ˌɡaɪnəkəˈlɒdʒɪkl/ *adj* 妇科的 ‹*problem, procedure*›
gynaecologist Brit, **gynecologist** Amer /ˌɡaɪnəˈkɒlədʒɪst/ ▸**p. 409** *n* 妇科学家
gynaecology Brit, **gynecology** Amer /ˌɡaɪnəˈkɒlədʒi/ *n* [u] 妇科学
gyp /dʒɪp/ *n* [u] Brit colloq 疼痛; **to give sb. ～** (cause pain) 使某人痛苦不堪; (scold) 严厉责骂某人
gyppo /ˈdʒɪpəʊ/ *n* (*pl* **～s**) Brit colloq offensive 吉普赛人
gypsum /ˈdʒɪpsəm/ *n* [u] 石膏
gypsy /ˈdʒɪpsi/ *n* **1** (nomad) 吉卜赛人; **it must be the ～ in me** 那一定是因为我内心有一种浪迹天涯的冲动; **a ～ caravan/camp** 吉卜赛马拉篷车/营地; **the ～ life** 流浪生活 **2** (free-spirited person) 四海为家的人
gypsy cab *n* Amer colloq 流动揽客的出租车
gyrate /ˌdʒaɪˈreɪt, Amer ˈdʒaɪreɪt/ *vi* 旋转
gyration /ˌdʒaɪˈreɪʃn/ *n* 旋转
gyratory /ˈdʒaɪrətri, ˌdʒaɪˈreɪtri/ *adj* 旋转的; **～ system** Brit 环形交通系统
gyro /ˈdʒaɪərəʊ/ *abbr* colloq **1** **= gyroscope** **2** **= gyrocompass**
gyrocompass /ˈdʒaɪrəʊkʌmpəs/ *n* 陀螺罗经
gyroscope /ˈdʒaɪrəskəʊp/ *n* 陀螺仪
gyroscopic /ˌdʒaɪrəˈskɒpɪk/ *adj* 陀螺仪的
gyrostabilizer /ˌdʒaɪrəʊˈsteɪbəlaɪzə(r)/ *n* 陀螺稳定器

Hh

H, h /eɪtʃ/

A *n* (*pl* **Hs** *or* **H's**) (letter) [英语字母表的第8个字母] **to drop one's 'h''s** Brit 漏发"h"音

B **h** *abbr* = **hard** [铅笔芯硬度符号]; **a 2~ pencil** 2H 的铅笔

ha¹ /hɑː/ *excl* 1 (to show triumph, scorn) 哈; **~! got you!** 嘿！逮住你了！ 2 **~! ~!** (laughter) 哈哈; iron 哼; **~ ~, very funny** 哼，真好笑

ha² *abbr* = **hectare**

habeas corpus /ˌheɪbɪəs ˈkɔːpəs/ *n* [u] 人身保护令

haberdasher /ˈhæbədæʃə(r)/ ►**p. 409** *n* 1 Brit (selling sewing articles) 缝纫用品店店主 2 Amer (selling men's clothing) 男装店店主

haberdashery /ˈhæbədæʃəri/ *n* 1 [u] Brit (sewing items) 缝纫用品 2 [c] Brit (shop selling sewing items) 缝纫用品店 3 [c] Amer (shop selling men's clothing) 男装店

habit /ˈhæbɪt/ *n* 1 [c and u] (usual behaviour) 习惯; **to be in the ~ of doing sth., to make** *or* **have a ~ of doing sth.** 有做某事的习惯; **to fall** *or* **get into the ~ of doing sth.** 养成做某事的习惯; **to fall** *or* **get out of the ~ of doing sth.** 改掉做某事的习惯; **to do sth. out of ~** *or* **from force of ~** 出于习惯做某事; **history has a ~ of repeating itself** 历史经常重演; **a ~ of mind** 惯常的心态 2 [u] (addiction) 瘾; **to kick the ~** colloq (of smoking) 戒烟; (of drugs) 戒毒 3 [c] Relig 修道服

habitable /ˈhæbɪtəbl/ *adj* 适于居住的; **this house is no longer ~** 这房子已经不能住人了

habitat /ˈhæbɪtæt/ *n* 栖息地

habitation /ˌhæbɪˈteɪʃn/ *n* [u] 居住; **unfit for human ~** 不适合人居住

habit-forming *adj* 易上瘾的 ‹*drug*›; 易成习惯的 ‹*activity*›

habitual /həˈbɪtʃʊəl/ *adj* 1 (usual) 通常的; **his ~ dress** 他常穿的衣服 2 (constant) 习惯性的 ‹*behaviour, smile*›; **a ~ late sleeper** 惯常晚睡的人 3 (as habit) 已养成习惯的; **to be/become ~** «*drinking, lying*» 有瘾/上瘾; **a ~ smoker** 有烟瘾的人; **a ~ liar** 撒谎成性的人; **a ~ offender/criminal** 惯犯

habitually /həˈbɪtʃʊəli/ *adv* 1 (out of habit) 习惯性地 ‹*drink, offend*›; **a person who lies ~** 撒谎成性的人 2 (constantly) 惯常地; **he's ~ late for work** 他上班迟到惯了

habituate /həˈbɪtʃʊeɪt/ *vt* formal **to ~ oneself/sb. to sth./to doing sth.** 使自己/某人习惯于某事/做某事; **he has ~d himself to extremely hard work** 他已习惯于极艰苦的工作

hack¹ /hæk/

A *n* 1 (blow) (with axe, knife) 砍; (with sword, hand) 劈; (with stick) 打; **to take a ~ at sb./sth.** 砍某人/某物; **to cut through sth. with a single ~** 一下子砍断某物 2 Sport pej (kick) 踢; (hit) 打; **a ~ on sb.** 踢某人; **to give sb. a ~ on sth.** 踢某人某部位一脚 3 (cough) 干咳

B *vt* 1 (chop) 砍; **to ~ sb./sth. with sth.** 用某物砍某人/某物; **to ~ sb. to death** 把某人砍死; **to ~ sb./sth. to pieces** lit 把某人/某物砍成碎片; **to ~ the article to pieces** fig 把这篇文章删得支离破碎 2 (clear) 劈出; **to ~ a path through/out of/into sth.** 劈出一条穿过/离开/进入某处的路; **to ~ one's way through/out of/into sth.** 开辟出一条穿过/离开/进入某处的路 3 Sport pej (kick) 踢; (hit) 打 4 colloq (cope with) **I can't ~ it** 我应付不了; **how long can he ~ it?** 他能撑多久？ 5 Comput colloq 窃取; **to ~ secret data from computers** 从计算机里窃取机密资料

C *vi* 1 (chop) 砍; **to ~ through sth.** 砍伐 ‹*branch, vine*›; **to ~ at the coalface** 在采煤区挖煤 2 Sport pej «*footballer*» 踢; «*golfer*» 击; **to ~ at one's ball in a bunker** 在沙坑里击球 3 Comput colloq 非法入侵; **to ~ into the system** 入侵系统 4 (cough) 干咳 5 esp Brit Equit 骑马; **to go ~ing** 去骑马

Phrasal verbs

- **hack about** *vt* [**~ sth. about**] 胡乱删改 ‹*text, book*›
- **hack around** *vi* Amer colloq 闲逛
- **hack away**

A *vt* [**~ sth. away, ~ away sth.**] 砍去 ‹*branches, trees*›

B *vi* 1 **to ~ away at sb./sth. (with sth.)** (cut) (用某物) 砍某人/某物; **to ~ away with a pick** 用镐不停地刨 2 (cough) 干咳

- **hack down** *vt* [**~ sth. down, ~ down sth.**] 砍倒 ‹*tree*›
- **hack off** *vt* 1 [**~ sth. off, ~ off sth.**] (remove) 砍去 ‹*limb*› 2 [**~ sb. off, ~ off sb.**] Brit colloq (annoy) 惹恼
- **hack out** *vt* [**~ sth. out, ~ out sth.**] 凿出 ‹*trail, path*›
- **hack up** *vt* [**~ sth. up, ~ up sth.**] 把…剁成大块

hack² *n* 1 pej (writer) 雇佣文人; **a literary ~** 雇佣作家 2 pej (worker) 杂务工; **a party ~** 政党杂务人员 3 Equit (riding horse) 供人骑乘的马; (old horse) 老马 4 Amer colloq (taxi) 出租车

hacked off *adj* Brit colloq 非常恼火的

hacker /ˈhækə(r)/ *n* colloq 1 Comput 黑客 2 (person) 劈砍者; (tool) 劈砍工具

hacker-proof *adj* colloq 防黑客的 ‹*system, software*›

hackette /hæˈket/ *n* colloq pej [尤指平庸的] 女记者

hacking /ˈhækɪŋ/ *n* [u] Comput colloq 黑客入侵

hacking cough *n* [u] 急促频繁的干咳

hackle /ˈhækl/

A *n* 细长颈羽

B **hackles** *npl* lit 后颈毛; **to raise its ~s** 竖起后颈毛; **to get one's ~s up** fig 发怒; **to make sb.'s ~s rise** fig 激怒某人; **with one's ~s up** fig 怒气冲冲地

hackney cab /ˌhækni ˈkæb/ *n* Brit formal 出租汽车

hackneyed /ˈhæknɪd/ *adj* 陈腐的 ‹*expression*›; **a ~ phrase** 陈词滥调; **~ old sayings** 老生常谈

hack: **~ reporter** *n* pej 平庸记者; **~saw** *n* 弓锯; **~work** *n* [u] pej 平庸作品; **~ writer** *n* pej 1 (for hire) 雇佣文人; 2 (second-rate writer) 平庸作家; (second-rate journalist) 平庸记者; **~ writing** *n* [u] pej 1 (for hire) 雇佣文人炮制的作品; 2 (second-rate writing) 平庸作品; (second-rate journalism) 平庸报道

had /hæd, həd/ *pt, pp* ►**have**

haddock /ˈhædək/ *n* (*pl* **haddock**) 黑线鳕

Hades /ˈheɪdiːz/ *pr n* [u] Mythol 冥界; **in ~** 在阴间

hadn't /ˈhædnt/ colloq = **had not** ►**have**

Hadrian's Wall /ˌheɪdrɪənz ˈwɔːl/ *n* 哈德良长城 [位于英格兰北部，公元2世纪罗马人所建]

haematite /ˈhiːmətaɪt/ *n* [u] Brit 赤铁矿

haematologist /ˌhiːməˈtɒlədʒɪst/ ►**p. 409** *n* Brit 血液学家

haematology /ˌhiːməˈtɒlədʒi/ *n* [u] Brit 血液学

haematoma /ˌhiːməˈtəʊmə/ *n* (*pl* **~s**) Brit 血肿

haemodialysis /ˌhiːmədaɪˈæləsɪs/ *n* [u] Brit 血液透析

haemoglobin /ˌhiːməˈgləʊbɪn/ *n* [u] Brit 血红蛋白

haemophilia /ˌhiːməˈfɪlɪə/ ►**p. 377** *n* [u] Brit 血友病

haemophiliac /ˌhiːməˈfɪlɪæk/ *n* Brit 血友病患者

haemorrhage /ˈhemərɪdʒ/

A *n* Brit 1 [u and c] Med 出血; **a brain** *or* **cerebral ~** 脑出血 2 [c] fig 大量流失; **a steady ~ of qualified teachers** 合格教师的不断流失

B *vi* Med 大出血

C *vt* fig «*company*» 大量失去 ‹*cash*›

haemorrhoids /ˈhemərɔɪdz/ *npl* Brit 痔

hafnium /ˈhæfnɪəm/ *n* [u] 铪

haft /hɑːft/

A *n* 柄

B *vt* 给…装柄 ‹*blade, axe*›

hag /hæg/ *n* 1 pej (old woman) 丑老太婆 2 (witch) 女巫

haggard /ˈhægəd/ *adj* 憔悴的 ‹*person, expression*›; **to look ~ (and drawn)** 看上去很憔悴

haggis /ˈhægɪs/ *n* [u and c] Scot (*pl* **~** *or* **~es**) 杂碎肚 [用羊或小牛杂碎加香料等制成]

haggle /ˈhægl/ *vi* «*shopkeeper, buyer*» 争论; **to ~ about** *or* **over sth.** 为某事物争论不休; **to ~ with sb. over the price** 与某人讨价还价

hagiographer /ˌhægɪˈɒgrəfə(r)/ ►**p. 409** *n* 圣徒传作者

hagiography /ˌhægɪˈɒgrəfi/ *n* 1 [u] Relig 圣徒传 2 [u] fig pej (biographical writing) 吹捧性的传记写作 3 [c] fig pej (biography) 吹捧性的传记

hag-ridden *adj* (by nightmares) 常做恶梦的; (by anxieties) 忧心忡忡的

Hague /heɪg/ *pr n* **the ~** 海牙

ha-ha /ˈhɑːhɑː/ *n* 界沟

hail¹ /heɪl/

A *n* 1 [u] (frozen rain) 雹; (storm) 雹暴 2 [c] (barrage) [雹子般的] 一阵; **a ~ of bullets/blows** 一阵弹雨/乱打; **a ~ of curses/criticism** 连珠炮似的咒骂/批评

B *v impers* 下冰雹; **it's ~ing** 正在下冰雹

C *vt* 使冰雹般落下; **to ~ curses on sb.** 痛骂

h

某人; **to ~ blows on an opponent** 把对手乱打一通

Phrasal verb

- **hail down**

A *vi* «*blows, bullets*» 雹子般落下; «*abuse, criticism*» 连珠炮似地攻击

B *vt* **to ~ down sth. on sb./sth.** «*attacker*» 使…雹子般落在某人/某物上 ‹*blows*›; «*critic*» 连珠炮似地发表 ‹*criticism*›

hail²

A *vt* [1] (call) 招呼 ‹*person, ship*›; **within ~ing distance** 在听得见招呼的距离内 [2] (flag down) 打手势叫住 ‹*taxi, driver*› [3] (acclaim) 称颂; **to be ~ed as sth.** 被誉为 ‹*a masterpiece, the hero*›; **to be ~ed as the new leader** 被拥立为新领袖

B *vi* **to ~ from ...** «*person, ship*» 来自…

C *excl* archaic 欢迎; **~ the conquering hero!** 向所向披靡的英雄致敬!

hail: ~-fellow-well-met *adj* 亲热随和的 ‹*person, manner*›; **H~ Mary** *n* 万福马利亚 [天主教祈祷词]; **~stone** *n* 雹块; **~storm** *n* 雹暴

Hainan /ˌhaɪˈnæn/ ▸**p. 604** *pr n* **~ (Province)** 海南（省）

hair /heə(r)/ ▸**p. 71** *n* [1] [u] (on head) 头发; (on body, animal) 毛; **to have long/short ~** 留着长发/短发; **grey/white ~** 灰白的头发/白发; **thick/thin ~** 浓密/稀疏的头发; **a fine head/coat of ~** 一头秀发/一身漂亮的毛; **to have** *or* **get one's ~ cut/done/trimmed/dyed** 理发/做头发/剪头发/染发; **to wear one's ~ in plaits** Brit *or* **in braids** Amer 梳着辫子; **to put/keep one's ~ up/down** 盘起头发/披着头发; **to lose one's ~** 脱发; **body/facial ~** 体毛/脸毛; **to remove unwanted ~** 祛毛; **to get in sb.'s ~** colloq 把某人惹毛; **to let one's ~ down** colloq 放松一下; **to make sb.'s ~ stand on end** colloq 令某人毛骨悚然; **to tear one's ~ (out)** colloq (in anger) 气得吹胡子瞪眼; (with anxiety) 急得抓耳挠腮; **keep your ~ on!** Brit colloq 保持冷静! [2] [c] (single strand) (on head) 一缕头发; (on body, animal) 一撮毛; **not a ~ out of place** 十分整洁; **by a ~** *or* **a ~'s breadth** 以极小量; **to win a race by a ~** 以微弱优势赢得比赛; **to escape death by a ~'s breadth** 险些丧命; **not to turn a ~** 面不改色; **to split ~s** 斤斤计较; **the ~ of the dog (that bit you)** colloq 解醉酒; **to not harm** *or* **touch a ~ on sb.'s head** 不伤某人的毫发 [3] [c] Bot [植物叶茎上的] 茸毛

hair: ~ ball *n* 毛团; **~band** *n* 束发带; **~brush** *n* 发刷; **~care** *n* [u] 头发护理; **~care products** 护发产品; **~clip** *n* 发夹; **~ clippers** *npl* 理发推子; **~ conditioner** *n* 护发素; **~ cream** *n* 发乳; **~ curler** *n* 卷发器; **~cut** *n* (act) 理发; (style) 发型; **~do** *n* colloq (style) 发型; (process) 做头发; **~dresser** ▸**p. 409** *n* (person) 美发师; **the ~-dresser('s)** (place) 美发店; **~dressing** *n* [u] (business) 美发业; (art) 美发技术; **~drier** *n* (hand-held) 电吹风; (hood) 帽式吹发器; **~ dye** *n* 染发剂; **~ extension** *n* 接长的假发; **~ follicle** *n* 毛囊; **~ gel** *n* 发胶; **~grip** *n* Brit 发夹; **~ implant** *n* [1] [u] (implantation) 假发植入; [2] [c] (hair implanted) 植入的假发

-haired /ˈheəd/ *combining form* 有…头发的

hairless /ˈheəlɪs/ *adj* 无头发的 ‹*person*›; 光秃的 ‹*head*›; 无毛的 ‹*animal, chest*›; 无胡子的 ‹*chin*›

hairline /ˈheəlaɪn/ *n* 发际线; **a receding ~** 后移的发际线

hairline: ~ crack *n* 细小的裂纹; **~ fracture** *n* 细微骨裂

hair: ~ lotion *n* [u and c] 护发素; **~net** *n* 发网; **~ oil** *n* [u and c] 发油; **~piece** *n* (toupee) [男士戴的] 假发; (added section) [使女士头发更显浓密的] 装饰假发

hairpin /ˈheəpɪn/ *n* 发叉

hairpin: ~ bend *n* Brit 急转弯; **~ turn** *n* Amer 急转弯

hair: ~-raising *adj* 使人毛骨悚然的 ‹*sight, story*›; **~ remover** *n* [u] 脱毛剂; **~ restorer** *n* [u] 生发剂; **~ roller** *n* 卷发筒; **~'s breadth** *n* **by a ~'s breadth** 以毫末之差; **~-slide** *n* Brit 小发夹; **~-splitter** *n* 纠缠细节的人; **~ splitting** *n* [u] 纠缠细节; **a ~-splitting argument** 纠缠于琐碎细节的争论; **~spray** *n* [u and c] 喷发胶; **~spring** *n* [手表内的] 游丝; **~ straightener** *n* 直发器; **~style** *n* 发型; **~ stylist** ▸**p. 409** *n* 发型师; **~ transplant** *n* 植发

hair trigger

A *n* 微力扳机

B **hair-trigger** *modif* 一触即发的; **a ~ temper** 火暴脾气

hairy /ˈheəri/ *adj* [1] (covered in hair) 多毛的 ‹*chest, person, animal*›; Bot 长有绒毛的 ‹*stem, roots*›; (rough) 毛糙的 ‹*blanket, coat*›; **~ arms** 汗毛浓密的手臂 [2] fig colloq (dangerous) 惊险的 ‹*moment, experience*›

Haiti /ˈheɪti/ *pr n* 海地

Haitian /ˈheɪʃn/ ▸**p. 503, p. 426**

A *adj* (of Haiti) 海地的; (of the people) 海地人的; (of the language) 海地克里奥尔语的

B *n* [1] [c] (person) 海地人 [2] [u] (language) 海地克里奥尔语

hake /heɪk/ *n* (*pl* **~** *or* **~s**) 无须鳕

halal /hɑːˈlɑːl/ *adj* 合乎伊斯兰教教法的 ‹*meat*›; **~ food** 清真食品

halcyon /ˈhælsɪən/ *adj* 幸福美好的; **the ~ days of youth** 美好的青春年华

hale /heɪl/ *adj* **~ and hearty** 精神矍铄的

half /hɑːf, Amer hæf/

A *n* (*pl* **halves**) [1] (equal part) 一半; **the top/left ~** 上/左半部分; **to cut/tear/break sth. in ~** 将某物切/撕/破成两半; **to increase/cut by ~** 增加/削减一半; **to go halves (with sb.) (on sth.)** (share food) （与某人）平分（某物）; (share expense) （与某人）平摊（某）费用; **a ... and a ~** colloq (great) 棒极了; (big) 极大的…; **a meal/job and a ~** 丰盛可口的一餐/一件费时费力的工作; **too clever/friendly** *etc.* **by ~** 过于聪明/友善等; **not to do things** *or* **anything by halves** 做任何事都不半途而废; **she doesn't know the ~ of it** colloq 她不懂得最重要的方面; **sb.'s better** *or* **other ~** colloq hum 某人的另一半 [指配偶]; **how the other ~ lives** colloq (richer) 富人如何生活; (poorer) 穷人如何生活; **to give sb./sth. ~ a chance** 给某人/某事一点点机会; **to have ~ a mind to do sth.** 可能会做某事 [2] Math 零点五; **twelve and a ~ per cent** 百分之十二点五 [3] (in age) 半; **two and a ~** 两岁半 [4] Sport (period, area) 半场; **the first/second ~** 上/下半场 [5] Sport **= halfback** [6] Brit colloq (bus fare) 半价票; **(a) ~ to the station, please** 请给我一张到车站的半价票 [7] Brit colloq (half pint) 半品脱; **two halves of bitter** 两份半品脱的苦啤酒

B *adj* [1] (50%) 一半的; **~-litre** 半升的; **~ the price/the size** 一半的价格/尺寸; **~ a minute** *or* **second** *or* **moment** colloq 一会儿 [2] (most of) 很大部分; **a woman ~ sb.'s age** 一个小某人很多岁的女人; **~ the time/fun/trouble** 大部分时间/主要乐趣/最大的麻烦; **two and a ~ years old** 两岁半

C *pron* [1] (50%) 一半; **out of 30 students, only ~ passed** 在30个学生之中，只有一半人及格 [2] (a large number) 很大部分; **~ of them can't even spell their names properly** 他们当中很多人甚至不能正确拼写出自己的名字

D *adv* [1] (50%) 有一半; **to be ~ full/empty/over** 满/空/过了一半; **~ as much/many** 一半那么多; **~ as big/old** 一半大/老的; **~ as much/big** *etc.* **again** Brit, **~ again as much/big** *etc.* Amer 原来数量/大小等的一倍半; **to be ~ Italian** 有一半意大利血统 [2] (partly) 部分地; **~ awake/asleep** 睡眼惺忪/半睡半醒; **to be ~ drowned/drunk** 淹得半死/喝得半醉; **~-cooked/-digested/-remembered** 半熟的/未完全消化的/记忆不全的; **to be only ~ listening** 只是漫不经心地听着 [3] (in time expressions) 半小时; **~ past four,** colloq **~ four** 4点半; **~ past** colloq 半点; **to run at ~ past the hour** «*buses*» 每隔半点发车

E **not half** *adv phr* [1] (not nearly) 远非; **the hole's not ~ deep enough** 洞远远不够深 [2] colloq (not at all) 一点也不; **that hat doesn't look ~ bad** 那顶帽子很漂亮 [3] Brit colloq (extremely) 非常; **it doesn't ~ stink!** 它奇臭无比!

half a dozen *n, adj* **= half-dozen**

half-and-half

A *adj* 各占一半的

B *adv* 各半

half: ~-arsed /ˈhɑːfɑːst/ Brit, **~-assed** /ˈhæfæst/ Amer *adj* taboo sl 蹩脚的 ‹*idea*›; 不够格的 ‹*attempt, effort*›; **~back** *n* 前卫; **~-baked** *adj* colloq 考虑不周的 ‹*plan, idea*›; **~-blood** *n* [1] (brother of same mother) 同母异父兄弟; (brother of same father) 同父异母兄弟; (sister of same mother) 同母异父姐妹; (sister of same father) 同父异母姐妹; [2] Amer pej **= ~-breed**; **~-board** *n* [u] Brit 半食宿 [包括早餐和晚餐的住宿]; **~ boot** *n* 半高筒靴; **~-bred** *adj* offensive 混血的 ‹*person*›; **~-breed** *n, adj* offensive 混血儿（的）; **~ brother** *n* (of same father) 同父异母兄弟; (of same mother) 同母异父兄弟; **~-caste** *n, adj* offensive 混血儿（的）; **~ century** *n* [1] (period) 半个世纪; [2] Sport 50分 [尤指板球击球手的得分]; **~-cock** *n* **at ~-cock** lit [枪的] 处于半击发状态; fig (unprepared) 准备不充分地; (premature) 时机不成熟地; **to go off at ~-cock** fig 操之过急; **~-cocked** *adj* [1] lit 半击发状态的 ‹*gun*›; [2] fig (half ready) 准备不充分的 ‹*plan, event*›; **to go off ~-cocked** (act when only partly ready) 仓促行事; (speak when only partly ready) 仓促表态; **~-conscious** *adj* 半清醒的; **~-crown, ~-a-crown** *ns* Brit 二先令六便士硬币; **~-cup** *adj attrib* 半罩杯的 ‹*bra*›; **~-cut** *adj* Brit colloq 醉的; **~ day** *n* (of holiday) 半天休假日; (of work) 半天工作日; **~-dead** *adj* [1] lit 半死的; [2] fig colloq 筋疲力尽的; **~-dollar** *n* Amer (coin) 50美分硬币; (value) 50美分

half-dozen

A *n* 半打

B *adj attrib* **~ eggs/people** 6个蛋/人; **~ times** 6次

half: ~-fare *n* 半价; **to travel (at** *or* **for) ~-fare** 买半价票旅行; **~-hardy** *adj* 半耐寒的 ‹*plant, annual*›; **~-hearted** *adj* [1] (without effort) 半心半意的 ‹*attempt, manner*›; **a ~-hearted smile** 勉强的微笑; **a ~-hearted attitude** 敷衍了事的态度; [2] (apathetic) 缺乏热情的; **~-heartedly** *adv* [1] (lacking effort) 半心半意地 ‹*try, work*›; [2] (apathetically) 缺乏热情地 ‹*wave, say*›; **to ~-heartedly agree** 勉强同意; **~-heartedness** *n* [u] 半心半意; **~-hitch** *n* 半结 [一种绳结]; **~ holiday** *n* 半天休假日; **~-hour** *n* [1] (*also* **half an hour**) (30 minutes) 半小时; [2] (half past) 半点钟; **on the ~-hour** 在半点钟; **a ~-hour lesson/shift** 半小时的课程/轮班

half-hourly

A *adj* 半小时一次的 ‹*bulletin, flight, update*›

B *adv* 半小时一次地 ‹*run, fly, update*›

half-jokingly *adv* 半开玩笑地

half-length

A *adj* [1] Art 半身的 ‹*portrait*› [2] (half usual length) 一半长的; **~ boots** 半高筒靴; **a ~ jacket** 半长夹克

B *n* Art (portrait) 半身肖像; (photo) 半身照片; (sculpture) 半身塑像

half: ~-life *n* 半衰期; **~-light** *n* [u] 昏暗光线; **in the ~-light** 在昏暗的光线下; **~ marathon** *n* 半程马拉松; **~-mast** *n* **at ~-mast** (of flag) 下半旗; **~ measures** *npl* 不强硬的折中政策

half-moon
A *n* **1** (first quarter phase) 上弦; (last quarter phase) 下弦; (moon at first quarter) 上弦月; (moon at last quarter) 下弦月 **2** (of fingernail) 指甲弧影
B *modif* 半月形的

half: ~-naked *adj* 半裸的; **~-nelson** *n* [摔跤中的] 侧面肩下扼颈; **to put/hold sb. in a ~-nelson** 使某人失去招架之力; **~-note** *n* esp Amer 二分音符; **~-open** *adj* 半睁着的 ‹*eyes*›; 半张开的 ‹*mouth*›; 半开着的 ‹*door*›; **~ pay** *n* [u] 半薪; **to be on ~ pay** 支取半薪; **~penny** /ˈheɪpni/ *n* (*pl* **~pence** *or* **~pennies**) Brit **1** (coin) 半便士硬币; **a ~penny coin** 一枚半便士硬币; **2** fig (small amount) 一丁点钱; **I haven't got a ~penny** 我身无分文; **~pennyworth** /ˈheɪpnɪwɜːθ/ *n* Brit **1** (amount) 值半便士的量; **2** fig (small amount) 一丁点; **a ~pennyworth of sth.** 一丁点某物; **~-pint** *n* 半品脱; **a ~-pint of milk** 半品脱牛奶; **a ~-pint glass** 半品脱容量的杯子

half-price
A *n* [u] 半价; **at ~** 以半价(买卖)
B *adv* 以半价 ‹*buy, sell, get in*›
C *adj* 半价的

half: ~ rest *n* Amer 二分休止; **~ sister** *n* (of same mother) 同母异父姐妹; (of same father) 同父异母姐妹

half-size
A *n* (of shoe) 半号尺码
B *adj* (*also* **half-sized**) 一半尺寸的 ‹*bed, copy*›

half: ~ smile *n* 淡淡的微笑; **~-staff** *n* Amer **= ~-mast**; **~-starved** *adj* **1** lit 饿得半死的; **2** fig colloq 饿得要命的; **~ term** *n* [u and c] Brit **1** (holiday) 期中假; **at ~-term** 在期中假; **2** (period) 半学期; **~-timbered** *adj* 露明木架的 ‹*house*›

half-time
A *n* [u] **1** Sport 中场休息; **the score at ~** 上半场比分; **~ break** 中场休息 **2** Ind **on ~** 上半班; **a ~ worker** 上半班的工人
B *adv* 以一半时间 ‹*operate, teach*›; **work ~** 上半班

half-time score *n* 上半场比分

half: ~-title *n* (title) 副标题; (section title) 章节标题; (page) 附书名页; **~-tone** *n* **1** Phot (process) 网目版; **~-tone illustrations** 网目版插图; **2** esp Amer Mus **= semitone**; **~-track** *n* 半履带式车辆; **~-truth** *n* 半真半假的陈述; **~-volley** *n* 半截击

halfway /ˌhɑːfˈweɪ, Amer ˌhæf-/
A *adv* **1** (in distance) 在中间; **sth. ~ between A and B** 在A和B中间的某物; **~ down the page** 在下半页中间部分 **2** (in journey) 在中途; **to stop ~** 在半路上停下 **3** (in time, process) 到一半; **~ through the meal** 饭吃到一半时 **4** fig 部分地; **to be ~ there** 成功了一半; **to go ~ to** *or* **towards sth./doing sth.** 做某事完成了一部分; **to meet sb. ~** 对某人让步; **to meet trouble ~** 预先考虑到麻烦 **5** colloq (fairly) 相当地 ‹*decent, competent*›
B *adj* 中途的 ‹*mark*›; 中间的 ‹*point, stage*›

halfway: ~ house *n* **1** (for former prisoners) 过渡教习所; (for patients) 过渡疗养地; **2** (compromise) 折中办法; **~ line** *n* 中场线

half: ~wit *n* pej colloq 笨蛋; **~-witted** *adj* pej colloq 愚蠢的; **~-year** *n* 半年

half-yearly
A *adj* 半年一次的 ‹*trip, report*›
B *adv* 半年一次地 ‹*pay, report, meet*›

halibut /ˈhælɪbət/ *n* (*pl* **halibut**) 大比目鱼

halitosis /ˌhælɪˈtəʊsɪs/ *n* [u] 口臭

hall /hɔːl/ *n* **1** (in house) 门厅; (corridor) 走廊 **2** (for public events) 礼堂; **a school ~** 学校礼堂 **3** Brit Univ (accommodation) 学生宿舍; (refectory) 学生食堂 **4** Brit (manor house) 大庄园府第

hallelujah /ˌhælɪˈluːjə/ *excl* 哈利路亚 [表示赞美上帝]

hallmark /ˈhɔːlmɑːk/
A *n* **1** (distinctive feature) 特点; **to bear the ~** *or* **~s of sb./sth.** 带有某人/某事物的特征 **2** Brit (on metal) 纯度印记
B *vt* 给…打上纯度印记 ‹*ring*›

hallo /həˈləʊ/ *n, excl* **= hello**

hall: H~ of Fame *n* esp Amer **1** (place) [纽约市的] 美国名人纪念堂; **2** (group) 杰出人物; **the hockey H~ of Fame** 曲棍球明星; **~ of residence** *n* Brit 学生宿舍

halloo /həˈluː/
A *excl* 嘿 [用以引起注意或促狗快跑]
B *vi* (*3rd pers sing pres* **~s**; *pt, pp* **~ed**) Hunt 喊出"嘿"声

hallow /ˈhæləʊ/ *vt* **1** lit 使神圣; **(to be buried in) ~ed ground** (被安葬在)圣地; **~ed precincts** 神圣的场所 **2** fig (revere) 尊崇; **a ~ed memory** 辉煌的往昔岁月; **a ~ed tradition** 崇高的传统

Halloween /ˌhæləʊˈiːn/ *n* [u] 万圣节前夕

hallstand /ˈhɔːlstænd/ *n* 门厅衣帽架

hallucinant /həˈluːsɪnənt/ *n* 致幻剂

hallucinate /həˈluːsɪneɪt/ *vi* 产生幻觉

hallucination /həˌluːsɪˈneɪʃn/ *n* 幻觉

hallucinatory /həˈluːsɪnətri, Amer -tɔːri/ *adj* 引起幻觉的; **a ~ experience** 一次幻觉经历; **a ~ drug** 致幻药

hallucinogen /həˈluːsɪnədʒn/ *n* 致幻剂

hallucinogenic /həˌluːsɪnəˈdʒenɪk/ *adj* 引起幻觉的 ‹*drug*›; 幻觉的 ‹*experience*›

hallway /ˈhɔːlweɪ/ *n* **= hall 1**

halo /ˈheɪləʊ/ *n* (*pl* **~s** *or* **~es**) **1** (circle of light) 光轮 **2** fig (glory) 荣光; **his ~ is a bit tarnished** 他的光辉形象受到了一点玷污; **my ~ has slipped!** hum 我已经声名扫地! **3** Astron [日、月等发光体的] 光晕

halo effect *n* 光环效应

halogen /ˈhælədʒn/ *n* 卤素

halogen lamp *n* 卤素灯

halon /ˈheɪlɒn/ *n* 哈龙 [一种惰性气体化合物]

halt /hɔːlt/
A *n* **1** (stop) 停止; **to come to a (screeching) ~** (吱的一声)停下来; **to call a ~ to sth.** 叫停某事; **a ~ in production** 停产 **2** (pause for rest) 暂停前进; **to have a (short/brief) ~** 短暂休息 **3** Brit Rail 小站
B *vt* **1** (stop) 使…停下 ‹*person, vehicle*› **2** (block) 阻止 ‹*progress, inflation*›
C *vi* 停止; **to ~ for a rest** 停下来休息; **platoon, ~!** Mil 全排停止前进!

halter /ˈhɔːltə(r)/ *n* **1** Equit 缰绳 **2** (of dress, top) **a ~ dress/top** 绕颈式露背连衣裙/吊带衫

halterneck /ˈhɔːltənek/ *n* 绕颈式露背装; **a ~ dress/top** 绕颈式露背连衣裙/吊带衫

halting /ˈhɔːltɪŋ/ *adj* 迟疑不决的 ‹*reply*›; 结结巴巴的 ‹*speech, English*›; 蹒跚的 ‹*steps, progress*›; **~ verse** 不流畅的韵文

haltingly /ˈhɔːltɪŋli/ *adv* 迟疑不决地 ‹*reply*›; 结结巴巴地 ‹*express*›; 蹒跚地 ‹*advance*›

halt sign *n* 停车标志

halve /hɑːv, Amer hæv/ *vt* **1** (divide in two) 对半分; **to ~ an apple** 把一个苹果分成两半; **to ~ the work** 对半分担工作 **2** (reduce by half) 把…减半 ‹*time, sales*› **3** (in golf) 以同杆数打完; **they ~d the tenth** 他们以相同的杆数打完了第十洞

halves /hɑːvz, Amer hævz/ *pl* ▸**half A**

halyard /ˈhæljəd/ *n* 升降索

ham /hæm/
A *n* **1** [u] (meat) 火腿肉 **2** [c] (pig leg) 火腿 **3** [c] **hams** *pl* (back of thigh) 大腿根部; (buttocks) 股臀部 **4** [c] colloq (actor) 表演过火的演员; **a ~ actor** 一个表演过火的演员 **5** [c] colloq (radio) **~** 业余无线电爱好者
B *vt* colloq (*pres p etc.* **-mm-**) «*actor*» 过火地表演 ‹*part, role*›
C *vi* colloq (*pres p etc.* **-mm-**) 装腔作势

Phrasal verb
- **ham up** *vt* [**~ sth. up, ~ up sth.**] colloq 过火地表演 ‹*role*›; **to ~ it up** 表演得过火

ham and eggs *n* [u] 火腿蛋

hamburger /ˈhæmbɜːgə(r)/ *n* 汉堡包

ham-fisted /ˌhæmˈfɪstɪd/ Brit, **ham-handed** Amer /ˌhæmˈhændɪd/ *adjs* colloq pej 笨手笨脚的

hamlet /ˈhæmlɪt/ *n* 小村庄

hammer /ˈhæmə(r)/
A *n* **1** (tool) 锤子; **to knock sth. in with a ~** 用锤子把某物钉入; **to be** *or* **go at it** *or* **each other ~ and tongs** fig 激烈地争斗 **2** (of piano) 音锤 **3** (on firearm) 击铁 **4** (auctioneer's gavel) [拍卖时用的] 木槌; **to come** *or* **go under the ~** 被拍卖 **5** Sport (ball attached to wire) 链球; (event) 链球比赛; **to throw the ~** 掷链球 **6** (bone in ear) 锤骨
B *vt* **1** (hit with tool) 锤击; **to ~ a nail into sth.** 把钉子锤进某物 **2** (shape with tool) 锤打 ‹*metal*›; **to ~ sth. straight** *or* **flat** 把某物锤平; **to ~ sth. into shape** 把某物锤打成型; **to ~ sb. into shape** 培养某人成材 **3** (beat with hand) 反复敲打; **to ~ sth. against the wall/with one's fist** 在墙上反复摔打某物/用拳头反复击打某物 **4** (kick hard) 猛击; **to ~ the ball into the net** 将球猛击入网 **5** fig (criticize) 严厉批评; **to ~ sb. for sth./doing sth.** 因为某事物/做某事严厉批评某人 **6** (utterly defeat) 彻底击败; **Chelsea ~ed Stoke 5-0** 切尔西以5比0彻底击败斯托克 **7** fig (adversely affect) «*recession, unemployment*» 使…受负面影响 ‹*district, group*›; **to be ~ed by recession** 因经济不景气而受挫 **8** **to ~ sth. into sb.** (instil) 把某事灌输给某人; **to ~ some sense into sb.** 让某人懂事一些
C *vi* **1** (use hammer) 锤击 **2** (pound) 敲打; **to ~ at** *or* **on sth. (with one's hand/fist)** (用手/拳头)敲打某物; **to ~ on** *or* **against sth.** «*rain, hail*» 噼里啪啦地打在…上 ‹*roof, window*› **3** (thump) «*heart*» 剧烈跳动

Phrasal verbs
- **hammer away** *vi* **1** (with tool or hand) 反复敲打; **to ~ away at sth./sb.** 反复敲打某物/某人; **I could hear him ~ing away at the door** 我可以听到他一直在敲门 **2** fig (insist) 作不懈努力; **to ~ away at the problem/point** 致力于解决这个问题/反复强调这一点
- **hammer down** *vi* colloq «*rain, hail*» 噼里啪啦地落下
- **hammer home** *vt* [**~ sth. home, ~ home sth.**] **1** (with tool) 将…完全钉入 ‹*nail*› **2** fig (emphasize) 着重把…讲清楚 ‹*point, argument*› **3** (score with) 用力踢…得分 ‹*ball*›; **to ~ the ball home** 把球猛踢进球门得分
- **hammer in** *vt* [**~ sth. in, ~ in sth.**] **1** (with tool) 钉入 ‹*nail*› **2** fig (cause to be learned) 反复灌输 ‹*idea, message*›
- **hammer out** *vt* [**~ sth. out, ~ out sth.**] **1** (with tool) 敲平 ‹*dent*› **2** (play) [尤指在钢琴上] 敲打出 ‹*tune*› **3** fig (achieve) 反复讨论出; **to ~ out a compromise/decision** 反复磋商后达成妥协/作出决定

hammer: ~ and sickle *n* **the ~ and sickle** 锤子镰刀图案; **~ beam** *n* 悬臂托梁; **~ blow** *n* **1** lit 锤击; **2** fig 巨大的打击; **~ drill** *n* **1** (rock drill) 风动冲击凿岩机; **2** (hand drill) 冲击钻; **~head** *n* **~head (shark)** 槌头双髻鲨

hammering /ˈhæmərɪŋ/ *n* [u] **1** (striking) 锤击; (sound) 锤击声 **2** fig colloq (defeat) 惨败; **to take** *or* **get a ~** 遭到惨败 **3** fig colloq (criticism) 抨击; **to give sth. a ~** 猛烈抨击 ‹*film*›

h

hammer toe *n* [u and c] 锤状趾
hammock /ˈhæmək/ *n* 吊床
hamper¹ /ˈhæmpə(r)/ *n* 1 (basket) 有盖的大篮子; **picnic ~** Brit 野餐食品篮; **laundry** *or* **clothes ~** Amer 洗衣篮 2 Brit (as a gift) 礼品盒
hamper² *vt* 阻碍 ‹*movement, progress*›
Hampshire /ˈhæmpʃɪə(r)/ *pr n* 汉普郡
ham radio *n* [u] 业余无线电
hamster /ˈhæmstə(r)/ *n* 仓鼠
hamstring /ˈhæmstrɪŋ/
A *n* (of human) 腘绳肌腱; (of animal) 后腿腱; **to pull a ~** 扭伤腿筋
B *vt* (*pt, pp* **hamstrung** /ˈhæmstrʌŋ/) 1 lit 挑断…的脚筋 2 fig **to be hamstrung (by sth.)** (因某事物而)变得无能为力; **to be hamstrung by a lack of sth.** 因缺乏某物而无能为力
Han /hæn/ *n* 1 [u] (dynasty) 汉朝 2 [c] (ethnic group) 汉族
hand /hænd/
A *n* 1 ▸**p. 71** Anat 手; **the palm/back of the ~** 手掌/手背; **in one's ~** 在手中; **gun/money in ~** 手里拿着一把枪/钱; **with both ~s** 用双手; **to seize an opportunity with both ~s** fig 紧紧抓住机会; **by ~** lit 用手; (on envelope) 亲手递交; **from ~ to ~** 从一个人到另一个人; **to be good with one's ~s** 手巧; **to hold sb.'s ~** lit 牵着某人的手; fig 支持某人; **to hold ~s (with sb.)** (与某人)手牵手; **to join ~s** 手拉着手; **to take sb.'s ~, take sb. by the ~** 拉某人的手; **to be on one's ~s and knees** 四肢着地趴着; **to put one's ~s together** (to pray) 双手合十; (to clap) 鼓掌; **to put one's ~ up** 举手; **~s up!** (in class, vote) 请举手！; (to surrender) 举起手来！; **~s down!** 放下手！; **~s off (sb./sth.)!** lit 不许碰(某人/某物)！; fig 不许干涉(某人/某物)！; **to keep one's ~s off sb./sth.** 不碰某人/不拿某物; **to lay** *or* **get one's ~s on sb./sth.** 抓住某人/获取某物; **to put one's ~s on sth.** 找到某物; **to have one's ~s full** lit 手里拿满了东西; fig 忙得不可开交; **to give sb. one's ~ (on sth.)** 握手答应某人(某事); **to stay one's ~** formal 罢手; **to win ~s down** colloq 轻易取胜; **to win sth. ~s down** colloq 轻易赢得某物; **with one ~ (tied) behind one's back** fig colloq 轻而易举地; **to know sth. like the back of one's ~** 对某事物了如指掌; **at the ~s of sb.** 由于某人的作用; **our defeat at the ~s of the French team** 我们败在法国队手里的事实; **many ~s make light work** Prov 人多好办事; **the left ~ doesn't know what the right ~ is doing** 左手不知道右手在干什么 [指组织内部缺乏沟通]; **to ask for sb.'s ~ (in marriage)** dated 向某人求婚; **to win sb.'s ~** dated 向某人求婚成功; ▸**bird 1**, ▸**bite A1**, **= bury 5, devil 1** 2 (of ape, monkey) 前爪 3 (handwriting) 书写; **in sb.'s own ~** 某人亲笔所书; **to write** *or* **have a neat/legible ~** 字迹工整/清晰 4 (applause) 鼓掌; **to give sb. a big ~** 给某人热烈鼓掌; **to get a big ~ (from sb.)** 获得(某人的)热烈鼓掌 5 (possession) **to be in/out of sb.'s ~s** 受/不受某人控制; **to place** *or* **put sth. in sb.'s ~s** 把某物交给某人处理; **to change ~s** 易主; **to get/come/fall into sb.'s ~s** 落入某人手中; **to put oneself in sb.'s ~s** 把自己交给某人; **the children are in safe ~s** 孩子们有人妥善照看; **to be in private ~s** 由私人拥有; **to play (right) into sb.'s ~s** 正中某人下怀 6 colloq (help) **to want/need a ~ (with sth.)** (在某方面)需要帮忙; **to offer/give sb. a ~ to do/with sth.** 帮某人做某事; **to lend (sb.) a ~ (with sth.)** (在某方面)帮(某人的)忙; **a helping ~** 帮忙 7 (responsibility) **to have sb./sth. on one's ~s** 有某人需要照管/有某事需要处理; **to have sth. on/off sb.'s ~s** 某人需要面临某事/不再负责某事; **to offer to take sth. off sb.'s ~s** 建议某人不再负责某事; **to get/have sb./sth. off one's ~s** 使某人不再照顾某人/负责某事 8 (involvement) **the ~ of God** 上帝之手; **to have a ~ in sth./doing sth.** 参与某事/做某事 9 (skill) **to try one's ~ at sth./doing sth.** 尝试某事/做某事; **to turn** *or* **set one's ~ to sth./doing sth.** 开始进行/着手做某事; **to get/keep one's ~ in** 通过练习获得/保持技能 10 Games (cards dealt) 一手牌; **a lousy/winning ~** 一手烂牌/要赢的好牌; **to throw in one's ~** lit 认输; fig 放弃; **to show one's ~** lit 亮牌; fig 公开自己的真正意图 11 (skilled person) **to be a good/poor ~ at sth./doing sth.** 擅长/不擅长某事/做某事 12 (worker) 工人; (sailor) 船员; **all ~s on deck!** 全体船员甲板集合！; fig 大家都来帮忙！ 13 Games (game) 一局; **a ~ of bridge** 一盘桥牌 14 (side) **on every/either ~** liter 在各方面/任何方面; **on sb.'s right/left ~** 在某人的右边/左边 15 (aspect) **on (the) one ~ ...** 一方面…; **on the other ~ ...** 另一方面… 16 (source) **(at) first/second ~** (经过)第一手/第二手; **to get information second ~** 得到二手信息 17 (available) **to be on ~** 在近旁; **to be (close** *or* **near) at ~** (in space) 在附近; (in time) 即将到来; **to** *or* **on ~** 在手边; **to have sth. to** Brit *or* **on** Amer **~** 将某物放在手边; **the first thing to come to ~** 到手的第一件东西; **to be on ~ to help sb.** 随时都可以帮某人 18 (on clock, dial) 指针; **the hour/minute ~** 时针/分针 19 Equit 一掌之宽; **12 ~s in height** 高度为12掌宽 20 (bunch) 串; **a ~ of bananas** 一串香蕉
B in hand *adv phr* 1 (under control) 在控制中; **to have/get sth. in ~** 掌控某事物/使某事物在掌握中; **to take sb./sth. in ~** 管束某人/控制某事物 2 (under way) «*job*» 在处理中; «*preparations*» 在进行中 3 (to spare) 可使用; **time in ~** 可用的时间; **stock in ~** 现有存货 4 Brit Sport 待进行; **Liverpool have two games in ~** 利物浦队还有两场比赛要打
C out of hand *adv phr* 1 (out of control) 不受控制; **to get/be out of ~** «*inflation, people*» 失去/不受控制 2 (thoughtlessly) 不假思索
D *modif* 1 Anat 手的; **a ~ gesture** 手势 2 Cosmet 手部的; **~ care** 手部护理 3 (operated by hand) 用手操作的 ‹*tool, puppet*›
E *vt* 递; **to ~ sth. to sb.** 把某物递给某人; **you've got to ~ it to him/her** fig colloq 你不得不佩服他/她

(Phrasal verbs)

- **hand around** *vt* Brit [**~ sth. around, ~ around sth.**]
 1 (distribute) 分发 2 (circulate) 传递
- **hand back** *vt* 1 [**~ sth. back, ~ back sth.**] (return) 归还 ‹*object, land, colony*›; **to ~ sth. back to sb.** 把某物归还给某人 2 **to ~ sb. back to sb.** Radio, TV 让某人听(某人)报道 [记者在某地报道结束时, 让演播室的主持人继续主持节目的用语]; **I'll ~ you back to Michael** 现在让我们回来听迈克尔报道
- **hand down** *vt* [**~ sth. down, ~ down sth.**]
 1 (pass to lower level) 把…往下递 ‹*object*›; **to ~ sth. down to sb.** 把某物往下递给某人 2 (bequeath) 把…遗赠给 ‹*property*›; **to ~ sth. down to sb.** 把某物遗赠给某人; **~ed down from father to son** 父子相传的 3 (pass on after use) 把旧的…传下去 ‹*clothes*›; **to ~ sth. down to sb.** 把使用过的某物传给某人 4 Jur «*judge*» 宣布 ‹*verdict, sentence*›
- **hand in** *vt* [**~ sth. in, ~ in sth.**]
 1 (submit) 交 ‹*homework*›; 递交 ‹*petition, one's resignation*› 2 (return) 交还 ‹*library book, found item*›
- **hand on** *vt* [**~ sth. on, ~ on sth.**]
 1 (transmit) 传递 ‹*object, skill*›; **to ~ sth. on to sb.** 把某物传递给某人; **to be ~ed on from parent to child** 由父母传授给孩子 2 (delegate) 交付 ‹*problem, responsibility*›; **to ~ sth. on to sb.** 把某事物交给某人处理
- **hand out** *vt* [**~ sth. out, ~ out sth.**]
 1 (distribute) 分发 ‹*leaflets, gifts*›; **to ~ sth. out to sb.** 把某物分发给某人 2 pej (offer) 提供 ‹*advice*›; **to ~ sth. out to sb.** 向某人提供某物; **to ~ out words of wisdom** 传播至理明言 3 (impose) 给予 ‹*punishment, fine*›
- **hand over**
A *vt* [**~ sb./sth. over, ~ over sb./sth.**]
 1 (surrender) 交出 ‹*money, hostage*›; **to ~ sb./sth. over to sb.** 向某人交出某人/某物 2 (transfer) 将…移交 ‹*criminal, power, territory*›; **to ~ a suspect/stolen goods over to the police** 将疑犯/赃物移交给警方 3 (entrust) 托付; **to ~ the children/valuables over to sb.** 把这些孩子托付给某人照顾/把贵重物品交给某人看管 4 **to ~ sb. over to sb.** (on radio, TV, telephone) 让某人听另一人讲话; **I'm ~ing you over to our sports correspondent** 现在请听本台体育记者的报道 5 (to be addressed) 把…交由另一人应对; **I'll ~ you over to our guest speaker** 我会把你的问题交给我们的演讲嘉宾回答
B *vi* 1 **to ~ over to sb.** (transfer power) [把权力、责任等] 移交给某人 2 **to ~ over to sb.** (allow to speak) 让另外的某人应对; **I'll ~ over to my colleague to take you through ...** 现在请我的同事带大家了解… 3 Radio, TV **to ~ over to sb.** 把报道时间交给 ‹*reporter, presenter*›
- **hand round** *vt* Brit **= hand around**
- **hand up** *vt* [**~ sth. up, ~ up sth.**] 把…递上去; **to ~ sth. up to sb.** 把某物递上去给某人

handbag /ˈhændbæg/ Brit
A *n* 手提包
B *vt* colloq hum 臭骂
hand: ~ baggage *n* [u] esp Amer 手提行李; **~ball** ▸**p. 307** *n* [u] 墙手球运动; **a ~ball player** 墙手球运动员; **~basin** *n* Brit [带水龙头、固定的] 台盆; **~bell** *n* 手摇铃; **~bill** *n* 传单; **~book** *n* (manual) 手册; (for travel) 旅游指南; **~brake** *n* Brit (brake) 手刹; (lever) 手刹杆; **~car** *n* Amer [检修铁路时用的] 手摇车; **~cart** *n* (pulled) 手拉车; (pushed) 手推车; **~clap** *n* 鼓掌; **a slow ~clap** 稀稀拉拉的鼓掌 [表示不赞成或不耐烦]; **~clasp** *n* Amer 握手
handcraft /ˈhændkrɑːft, Amer -kræft/
A *n* **= handicraft**
B *vt* 手工制作
hand cream *n* [u and c] 护手霜
handcuff /ˈhændkʌf/
A handcuffs *npl* 手铐; **to put ~s on sb.** 把某人铐起来
B *vt* 给…戴上手铐; **to ~ sb. to sth.** 把某人铐在某物上
hand-dryer, hand-drier *n* 干手器
-handed /ˈhændɪd/ *combining form* 1 (indicating number or type of hands) [表示有或需要几只手或什么样的手]; **a one~ man** 只有一只手的男子; **a two~ tool/job** 双手操作的工具/工作 2 (indicating number of people) [表示需要的人手]; **a four~ game of cards** 4个人玩的纸牌游戏
handful /ˈhændfʊl/ *n* 1 (fistful) 一把; **a ~ of peanuts** 一把花生; **by the ~, in ~s** 一把一把地 2 (few) 少量; **a ~ of sth.** 少量的某物; **a ~ of people** 少数几个人 3 colloq (difficult person) 难管束的人; (difficult animal) 难驯服的动物; **that child is quite a ~** 那孩子真难管
hand: ~ grenade *n* 手榴弹; **~grip** *n* 1 (handle) 柄; 2 (grasp) 握; **~gun** *n* 手枪
handheld /ˌhændˈheld/
A *adj* 手提式的 ‹*camera, tool*›; 手持的 ‹*flare, shower*›
B *n* **= handheld device**
handheld device *n* 1 (device) 手提设备 2 Comput 掌上电脑
hand: ~hold *n* 可以抓手的地方; **~-hot** *adj* 温热的 ‹*water*›

handicap /ˈhændɪkæp/
A *n* 1 (physical disability) 残障; (mental disability) 智障 2 (disadvantage) 障碍; **(to be) a ~ to sb./sth.** （是）对某人/某事物的障碍 3 Sport (race) 让步赛 4 Sport (penalty) [比赛中给较强选手设置的] 不利条件; **a time/weight ~** 让时间/让磅 5 (in golf) 差点 [指球手打球的平均杆数和标准杆数的差距]; **to have a ~ of three** 差点为 3
B *vt* (*pres p etc.* **-pp-**) 1 lit 使残废; **to be ~ped by injury** 因伤致残 2 fig 妨碍; **to be ~ped by not being able to read** 吃了不识字的亏

handicapped /ˈhændɪkæpt/
A *adj* (physically disabled) 残障的; (mentally disabled) 智障的
B *npl* **the ~** (physically) 残障人士; (mentally) 智障者; **the visually ~** 视障人士

handicraft /ˈhændɪkrɑːft, Amer ˈhændɪkræft/ *n* [u and c] 1 (skill) 手工艺 2 (object) 手工艺品

handily /ˈhændɪlɪ/ *adv* 1 (conveniently) 近便地 ‹*located*› 2 Amer (easily) 轻易地 ‹*defeated*›

handiness /ˈhændɪnɪs/ *n* [u] 1 (convenience) (of place) 近便 2 (usefulness) (of object) 好用; **the ~ of a pocket calculator** 袖珍计算器的便利 3 (skilfulness) (of person) 手巧; **his ~ with mechanical objects** 他善于摆弄机械物件

hand in hand *adv* 1 lit 手牵手地 2 fig 相关联地; **prejudice often goes ~ with ignorance** 偏见常常伴随着无知

handiwork /ˈhændɪwɜːk/ *n* [u] 1 (article(s) made by hand) 手工艺品; **is this graffiti your ~?** iron 这些涂鸦是你的大作吗？ 2 (work) 所作所为; **the ~ of an arsonist** 纵火犯的恶行

handjob /ˈhænddʒɒb/ *n* taboo sl [尤指他人对男性实施的] 手淫; **to give sb. a ~** 为某人手淫

handkerchief /ˈhæŋkətʃɪf, -tʃiːf/ *n* (cloth) 手帕; (paper) 纸巾; **the size of a ~** fig 巴掌大的

hand-knitted *adj* 手织的

handle /ˈhændl/
A *n* 1 (of door, drawer, suitcase) 把手; **to hold** *or* **take sth. by the ~** 抓着某物的把手; **to turn a ~** 旋转把手 2 (of tool, knife, cup) 柄; **to start a car on** *or* **with the ~** 摇手柄发动汽车; **to fly off the ~** fig colloq 大发雷霆 3 fig (hold) 理解; **to get a ~ on sb./sth.** 弄懂某人/某事的意思; **to give sb. a handle (on sth.)** 使某人弄懂（某事）; **to use sth. as a ~ (against sb.)** 利用某事物作为（反对某人的）手段 4 colloq (name) 称呼 5 colloq (title) 头衔; **to have a ~ to one's name** 名字前冠有头衔
B *vt* 1 (touch) 碰; **'~ with care'** Post "小心搬运"; **to ~ the ball** (in football) 以手触球 2 (treat) 对待; **to ~ sb./sth. roughly/gently** 粗暴/温和地对待某人/某事物 3 (manage) 管理 ‹*person, animal*› 4 (cope with) 应付 ‹*situation, pressure*›; **to ~ the crisis/pace** 处理危机/控制速度; **this car ~s bends well** 这辆车转弯很灵活; **to ~ sb. with tact** 有技巧地应对某人; **can you ~ another drink?** colloq 你还能再喝一杯吗？; **to be too hot to ~** fig «*situation*» 太棘手，不好处理 5 (take care of) 负责 ‹*business, work*› 6 (process) 处理 ‹*goods, procedures*›; **the subway network ~s over a million passengers a day** 地铁网每天可运送上百万名乘客 7 (buy or sell) 经营; **to ~ imports** 经营进口商品; **to ~ stolen goods** 收受赃物 8 (operate) 操纵 ‹*vehicle, aircraft*›; **to ~ the car/gun with great skill** 娴熟地驾驶汽车/使用枪支 9 Art, Literat, Mus 涉及 ‹*subject, composition*›; **to ~ all aspects of the subject** 论及这个问题的各个方面
C *vi* Aut **to ~ well/badly** 容易/难以驾驶

handle: ~bar moustache *n* 翘八字胡; **~bars** *npl* 把手

-handled /ˈhændld/ *combining form* 有…手柄的; **short/long~** 短/长手柄的

handler /ˈhændlə(r)/ *n* 1 (of animal) 驯兽师; (of police dog) 警犬训练员 2 (worker) 处理者; **a baggage ~** 行李搬运工; **a food ~** 从事食品加工的人 3 (celebrity agent) 经纪人; (political agent) 顾问 4 (dealer) **a ~ of stolen goods** 销赃者

handling /ˈhændlɪŋ/ *n* [u] 1 (touching) 触摸; **gentle/rough ~** 轻拿轻放/野蛮搬弄 2 (way of dealing with sth.) 处理方式; **a sensitive ~ of the theme** 对主题的细腻处理 3 (managing) 管理; **the horse needs firm ~** 这匹马需要严加训练 4 (processing) 处理; **~ of air traffic** 航空管制 5 (operation) 操纵; **a car designed for easy ~** 为便于驾驶而设计的汽车 6 Comm (processing fee) 手续费 7 Comm (shipping) 运输; (cost of shipping) 运费

handling charge *n* 1 (processing) 手续费 2 (transporting) 运费

hand: ~ lotion *n* [u and c] 润手露; **~ luggage** *n* [u] esp Brit 手提行李; **~made** *adj* 手工制作的; **~maid, ~maiden** *ns* 1 archaic (servant) 女仆; 2 fig (subservient person) 起辅助作用者; (subservient thing) 起辅助作用的事物; **~-me-down** *n* colloq 使用过的旧物; **to wear a ~-me-down from one's elder sister** 穿姐姐的旧衣服

handout /ˈhændaʊt/ *n* 1 (payment) 捐款; (gift) 捐赠物; **to live off/rely on ~s** 靠别人的施舍生活 2 (document) (at meeting) [分发的] 材料; (to students) 讲义 3 (leaflet) 宣传单

handover /ˈhændəʊvə(r)/ *n* 移交; **during the ~ period** 在移交期间

hand: ~-painted *adj* 手绘的; **~-pick** *vt* 仔细挑选; **a team of ~-picked players** 由精选队员组成的队伍; **~print** *n* 手印; **~rail** *n* 1 (on stairs) 扶手; 2 (on balcony, pier) 栏杆; **~-reared** *adj* 人工饲养的 ‹*animal*›; **~saw** *n* 手锯; **~set** *n* 电话听筒

hands-free *adj* 免提的 ‹*phone, calling*›

hands-free: ~ headset *n* 免提耳机; **~ kit** *n* 免提套件

hand: ~shake *n* 握手; **~shaking** *n* [u] 1 (greeting) 握手; 2 Comput 信号交换; **~ signal** *n* 手势信号; **~s-off** *adj* 不插手的 ‹*policy*›; **a ~s-off management style** 放手式管理风格

handsome /ˈhænsəm/ *adj* 1 (good-looking) 英俊的 ‹*man*›; **~ is as ~ does** Prov 行为美才是真美 2 (striking) 端庄健美的 ‹*woman*› 3 (fine) 俊美的 ‹*horse*›; 堂皇的 ‹*building*›; 美观的 ‹*furniture*› 4 (generous) 慷慨的; **a ~ present** 厚礼; **a ~ compliment** 高度的赞扬 5 (substantial) 可观的; **a ~ profit** 相当大的利润; **a ~ price** 相当高昂的价格; **a ~ majority** 绝大多数

handsomely /ˈhænsəmlɪ/ *adv* 1 (elegantly) 漂亮地 ‹*decorated*›; **a ~ styled chair** 造型美观的椅子 2 (generously) 慷慨地 ‹*behave, respond*›; **to compliment sb. ~** 高度赞扬某人 3 (amply) 可观地 ‹*repay, reward*›

hand: ~s-on *adj* (practical) 实际的 ‹*training, job*›; (involved) 亲身实践的; **~s-on experience** 实际经验; **a ~s-on leader** 事必躬亲的领导; **~spring** *n* 前手翻腾越; **~stand** *n* 手倒立

hand-to-hand
A *adj* 直接交手的 ‹*combat*›; **a ~ fight** (with weapons) 白刃战; (with hands) 肉搏战
B *adv* 直接交手地 ‹*fight*›

hand-to-mouth
A *adj* 勉强糊口的; **a ~ existence** 勉强维持的生计
B **hand to mouth** *adv* 勉强糊口地

hand: ~ towel *n* 擦手巾; **~work** *n* [u] 手工; **~-woven** *adj* 手织的; **~writing** *n* [u] 1 (style) 笔迹; 2 (writing by hand) 书写; **~written** *adj* 手写的

handy /ˈhændi/ *adj* 1 (useful) 好用的 ‹*tool*›; **a ~ hint** *or* **tip** 有益的提示; **to come in ~** colloq 派得上用场 2 (convenient) 近便的 ‹*spot*›; **the hotel is ~ for the shops** 旅馆离商店很近 3 (on hand) 手边的 ‹*tool*›; **to have/keep sth. ~** 有/将某物放在手边 4 colloq (skilful) 手巧的; **to be ~ with a paintbrush** 擅长油画; **to be ~ about the house** 擅长家里的修修补补

handyman /ˈhændɪmæn/ *n* (amateur) [擅长家庭修补的] 巧手; (professional) 杂务工

hang /hæŋ/
A *vt* (*pt, pp* **hung**) 1 (suspend) 悬挂 ‹*light, picture*›; (drape) 挂 ‹*clothes, rug*›; (dangle) 吊 ‹*line, string*›; **to ~ sth. on** *or* **from sth.** 把某物悬挂在某物上; **to ~ the lamp from a hook in the ceiling** 把灯悬挂在天花板上的钩子上; **to ~ sth. over** *or* **above sth.** 把某物悬挂在某物上方; **to have sth. hung around one's neck** 脖子上挂着某物; **to ~ the washing on the clothes horse/line** 把洗干净的衣物挂在晾衣架上/晒衣绳上; **to ~ a rope out of the window** 把绳子搭在窗外 2 (droop) 垂着 ‹*arm, leg*›; **to ~ one's head (in shame/sorrow** *etc.***)** （羞愧地/悲伤地等）垂着头 3 Art 展出 ‹*painting, exhibition*› 4 (decorate) 悬挂装饰; **to ~ sth. with sth.** 悬挂…装饰某物 ‹*flags, garlands*›; **a room hung with tapestries** 挂有壁毯的房间 5 (stick to wall) 贴 ‹*wallpaper*› 6 Constr 用铰链装 ‹*door*› 7 Culin 晾挂 ‹*meat*› 8 (*pt, pp* **~ed**) (execute) 绞死; **to be ~ed for sth.** 因某事被绞死; **to ~ sb. from sth.** 在某物上绞死某人; **to be ~ed, drawn and quartered** 先被绞死，然后开膛破肚，再大卸四块 9 Brit colloq dated (damn) 该死; **~ it/him/the expense!** 该死！/让他见鬼去吧！/别管花多少钱！; **I'll be ~ed!** 真让人吃惊！
B *vi* (*pt, pp* **hung**) 1 (be suspended) 悬挂; (be draped) «*clothes, rug*» 挂; **to ~ on** *or* **from** *or* **around sth.** 悬挂在某物上; **to ~ over** *or* **above sth.** 悬挂在某物上方; **towels ~ing on the rail/line** 挂在架子/绳子上的毛巾 2 (dangle) «*hair, arm*» 垂下; **to ~ from/out of sth.** 从某处垂下/垂在某物外面; **the children were ~ing out of the window** 孩子们大半个身子探出窗外; **to ~ by a thread** *or* **hair** fig 岌岌可危; **his life is ~ing by a thread** 他命悬一线 3 (drape) «*curtain, dress*» 飘垂; **this fabric ~s better than that one** 这种布料垂挂起来比那种感觉好; **to ~ loosely on sb.** 松松垮垮地挂在某人身上 4 liter (float) «*fog, smell*» 漂浮; **to ~ over sth.** «*mist*» 笼罩在某物上空 5 Art «*painting, photograph*» 被展出; «*artist*» 作品被展出; **his paintings ~ in the Louvre** 他的油画在卢浮宫展出 6 Culin «*meat, pheasant*» 被晾挂 7 (*pt, pp* **~ed**) (be executed) 被绞死; **to be found ~ing from the rafters** 发现被吊死在斜梁上; **sb./sth. can go ~** Brit colloq dated 让某人/某事见鬼去吧
C *v refl* (*pt, pp* **~ed**) **to ~ oneself** 自缢
D *n* 1 colloq (knack) 诀窍; **to get the ~ of sth.** (learn how) 掌握做某事的做法; (understand) 开始懂得某事的意义; **to get the ~ of doing sth.** 学会做某事 2 (of fabric) 垂落; **the ~ of the skirt** 裙子的垂感 3 colloq dated (damn) **not to give** *or* **care a ~ (about sb./sth.)** 一点也不在乎（某人/某事物）

Phrasal verbs

- **hang about** *vi* Brit colloq 1 (be slow) 慢悠悠; **he wasn't ~ing about!** 他做事雷厉风行！ 2 (wait) 等一下; **~ about! I'm not ready yet** 且慢！我还没准备好 3 = **hang around** A1
- **hang about with** *vt* Brit colloq = **hang around with**
- **hang around** colloq
A *vi* 1 (waiting) 等待; **they kept me ~ing around for three hours** 他们让我等了 3 个小时 2 (loitering) 闲荡; **to ~ around on street corners** 在街头闲荡
B *vt* 1 [**~ around sth.**] (loiter at) 在…闲荡; **to ~ around the door** «*fans*» 在门口徘徊 2 [**~ around sb.**] usu pej (associate with) 缠着
- **hang around with** *vt* [**~ around with sb.**] 与…厮混在一起

• **hang back** *vi* 1 (stay behind) 留下来 2 (hesitate) 踌躇不前; **to ~ back from doing sth.** 做某事犹豫不决
• **hang down** *vi* «*hair, hem*» 垂下
• **hang in** *vi* colloq 坚持不懈; **~ in there!** 顶住!
• **hang off** *vi* «*door*» 松脱; «*head*» 耷拉
• **hang on**
A *vi* 1 (clutch) 紧紧抓住; **to ~ on (to sth.) with one's hands** 双手抓紧 (某物); **~ on tight!** 抓紧! 2 colloq (wait) 等候; **they've kept me ~ing on for days** 他们让我等了好几天了; **~ on a minute: I've got a better idea** 稍等片刻, 我想到了一个更好的点子 3 colloq (on phone) 稍等, 不挂断 4 (survive) 坚持
B *vt* [**~ on sth.**]
1 (listen carefully) 倾听; **to ~ on sb.'s words** *or* **sb.'s every word** 仔细听某人说的话 2 (depend on) «*outcome*» 取决于 ‹*decision, results*›
• **hang on to** *vt* [**~ on to sb./sth.**]
1 (clutch) 紧紧抓住 ‹*person, branch*›; **~ on to your hat!** lit 抓住你的帽子! ; fig 准备看好戏吧! 2 fig colloq (retain) 保留 ‹*possession, power, values*›; **sth. worth ~ing on to** 值得保留的某物
• **hang out**
A *vt* [**~ sth. out, ~ out sth.**]
1 (for drying) 把…晾挂出去 ‹*washing*› 2 (display) 悬挂出 ‹*banner*›
B *vi* 1 (protrude) 伸出; **sb.'s/sth.'s tongue is ~ing out** lit «*dog*» [因天热] 伸出舌头; fig «*person*» 非常渴望; **to let it all ~ out** colloq 玩个痛快 2 colloq (spend time) 消磨时间; **the pub where students ~ out** 学生常泡的酒吧
• **hang over** *vt* [**~ over sb./sth.**] «*threat, danger*» 逼近; «*doubt, suspicion*» 困扰
• **hang together** *vi* 1 (be consistent) «*statements, evidence*» 前后一致; **that argument doesn't ~ together** 那个论据前后矛盾 2 (cooperate) «*people*» 同心协力
• **hang up**
A *vt* [**~ sth. up, ~ up sth.**]
1 (suspend, drape) 挂起 ‹*picture, clothes*›; **to ~ sth. up in the hall/wardrobe** 把某物挂在门厅里/衣柜里; **to ~ sth. up to dry** 把某物挂起来晾干 2 Telecom 挂断 ‹*phone*›; **to ~ up the receiver** 挂上听筒 3 fig hum (stop using) 搁置; **to ~ up one's skis/gloves/spade** 将滑雪板/手套/铁铲束之高阁
B *vi* 挂断电话
• **hang up on** *vt* [**~ up on sb.**] 挂断…的电话

hangar /'hæŋə(r)/ *n* 飞机库

hangdog /'hæŋdɒg/ *adj* 羞愧的 ‹*look, expression*›

hanger /'hæŋə(r)/ *n* 衣架

hanger-on *n* colloq pej 马屁精

hang: ~-glider *n* 1 (craft) 悬挂式滑翔机; 2 (pilot) 悬挂式滑翔机运动员; **~-gliding** ▸p. 307 *n* [u] 悬挂式滑翔运动; **to go ~-gliding** 去玩悬挂式滑翔

hanging /'hæŋɪŋ/
A *n* 1 [u] (action of executing) 绞死 2 [c] (instance of executing) 绞刑; **to be sentenced to death by ~** 被判处绞刑 3 [c] (drape on wall) 壁挂; (curtain) 帷幔
B *adj* 1 *attrib* Jur 应处以绞刑的 ‹*crime*›; Hist 惯于判处绞刑的 ‹*judge*›; **it's not a ~ matter** fig colloq 这不是什么大不了的事 2 *pred* (undecided) **the matter/story was left ~** 事件悬而未决/故事仍未结束

hanging: ~ basket *n* 吊花篮; **~ committee** *n* 参展作品遴选委员会; **H~ Gardens of Babylon** *pr npl* **the H~ Gardens of Babylon** [古巴比伦的] 空中花园; **~ valley** *n* 悬谷

hang: ~man /-mən/ *n* 1 [c] (executioner) 执行绞刑的刽子手; 2 ▸p. 307 [u] (game) "绞架" 猜词游戏 [猜词者每猜错一次则多画一笔, 绞架画成则猜词者失败]; **~nail** *n* [指甲旁的] 倒刺; **~-out** *n* colloq (usual place) 常去的地方; (home) 住处; **~over** *n* 1 lit 宿醉; 2 fig 遗留物; **a ~over from sth.** 从某事物沿袭下来的东西; **a ~over from his schooldays** 他学生时代的遗存

Hang Seng Index /hæŋ 'seŋ ɪndeks/ *n* 恒生指数

hang-up *n* colloq 1 (neurosis) 困扰; **to have a ~ about one's appearance** 为自己的外貌感到苦恼; **a ~ about spiders** 对蜘蛛的恐惧 2 Amer (issue) 烦恼事

hank /hæŋk/ *n* 1 (bundle) 一束; (loop) 一卷; **a ~ of hair** 一绺头发 2 Meas (of cloth, yarn) 亨克 [每单位质量的布或纱线的长度单位]

hanker /'hæŋkə(r)/ *vi* 渴望; **to ~ after** *or* **for sth.** 渴求某物; **to ~ to do sth.** 渴望做某事

hankering /'hæŋkərɪŋ/ *n* 渴望; **a ~ for sth./to do sth.** 对某事物/做某事的渴求

hankie, hanky /'hæŋki/ *n* colloq 手帕

hanky-panky /,hæŋki'pæŋki/ *n* [u] colloq hum (sexual) 调情; (legally dubious) 花招

Hanoi /hæ'nɔɪ/ *pr n* 河内

Hanoverian /,hænə'vɪərɪən/ *adj* Brit 汉诺威王室的

Hansard /'hænsɑːd/ *n* [u] [英国、加拿大、澳大利亚、新西兰或南非议会的] 议会议事录

ha'pence /'heɪpəns/ *npl* = **halfpenny**

ha'penny /'heɪpni/ *n* (*pl* **ha'pence** *or* **ha'pennies**) Brit = **halfpenny**

haphazard /hæp'hæzəd/ *adj* (unorganized) 杂乱的 ‹*arrangement, plan*›; (random) 随意的 ‹*discovery*›; **a ~ world** 无秩序的世界; **in a ~ fashion** 乱七八糟地

haphazardly /hæp'hæzədli/ *adv* 1 (untidily) 杂乱地 ‹*arrange, work*›; **he stuffed the bills ~ at the back of the drawer** 他把账单胡乱塞进抽屉深处 2 (casually) 随意地

hapless /'hæplɪs/ *adj attrib* 不幸的 ‹*person, victim*›

haploid /'hæplɔɪd/ *adj* 单倍体的 ‹*cell, organism*›

happen /'hæpən/ *vi* 1 (occur) 发生; **it had to** *or* **was bound to ~** 这件事原本就是要发生的; **whatever ~s** 无论发生什么事; **success doesn't just ~!** 成功不是偶然的! ; **a person who makes things ~** 可以成事之人; **these things ~** colloq 这种事在所难免; **what's ~ing?** sl 谁来了? 2 (result) 产生结果; **what ~s if ...?** 如果…会怎样? ; **the reforms never ~ed** 改革没有实行 3 (chance) 碰巧; **to ~ to do sth.** 碰巧做某事; **it ~s that ...** 碰巧…; **as it ~s, I can speak French** 我正好会说法语 4 (used indignantly) [表示愤怒或异议]; **he just so ~s to be the best ...** 他偏偏是最优秀的…; **sorry, but I ~ to disagree** 恕我不敢苟同

Phrasal verbs

• **happen on** *vt* [**~ on sth.**] dated 偶然发现; **I ~ed on a restaurant** 我碰巧来到一家餐馆
• **happen to** *vt* [**~ to sb./sth.**]
1 (befall) 使遭遇; **death is something that ~s to us all** 我们每个人都会死的 2 (become of) 发生于; **what ~ed to all those promises?** 那些承诺都怎么样了? 3 (come to harm) 伤害; **I hope nothing ~s to her** 我希望她不要出什么事
• **happen upon** *vt* dated = **happen on**

happening /'hæpənɪŋ/ *n* 1 (occurrence) 发生的事情; **recent ~s** 最近发生的事; **there have been some strange ~s** 发生了一些怪事 2 (performance) 即兴表演

happenstance /'hæpənstəns/ *n* [u and c] esp Amer 偶然情况; **by ~** 碰巧

happily /'hæpɪli/ *adv* 1 (cheerfully) 快乐地; **a ~ married man** 婚姻幸福的男人; **to live ~ ever after** 从此以后过上幸福的生活 2 (luckily) 幸运地 3 (willingly) 情愿地 4 (appropriately) 恰当地

happiness /'hæpɪnɪs/ *n* [u] 幸福; **a feeling of ~** 幸福感; **it is with great ~ that ...** 非常荣幸…

happy /'hæpi/ *adj* 1 (cheerful) 快乐的 ‹*person, smile, nature*›; **to be ~ to do** *or* **doing sth.** 因做某事感到高兴; **to be ~ for sb.** 替某人感到高兴; **to be ~ that ...** 很高兴…; **as ~ as a sandboy** colloq *or* **as Larry** Brit colloq *or* **as a clam** Amer colloq 极高兴的 2 (giving pleasure) 幸福的 ‹*day, memory*›; 令人愉快的 ‹*atmosphere*›; **a ~ childhood/marriage** 幸福的童年/婚姻 3 (satisfied) 满意的; **to be ~ about sth.** 对某事物满意; **to be ~ with sb./sth.** 对某人/某事物满意; **to keep sb. ~** 一直让某人满意 4 (willing) 乐意的; (glad) 高兴的; **to be ~ to do sth.** 愿意做某事; **to be ~ for sb. to do sth.** 为某人做某事感到高兴 5 (in greetings) 愉快的; **H~ Christmas!** 圣诞快乐! ; **many ~ returns (of the day)!** 长命百岁! 6 *attrib* (lucky) 幸运的 ‹*coincidence, chance*›; **to be in the ~ position of having no debts** 很幸运没负债; **the ~ few** 幸运的少数 7 (suitable) 适当的 ‹*choice, balance*›; **a ~ turn of phrase** 恰当的措词 8 colloq (tipsy) 醉醺醺的

> **Happy Birthday to You**
>
> 《祝你生日快乐》。生日歌, 通常在吹灭生日蜡烛之前由在场的人一起唱。源自1893年面世的幼儿园歌曲《大家早上好》(*Good Morning to All*), 词作者为美国教育家帕蒂·S·希尔 (Patty S. Hill), 曲作者为其姐姐米尔德丽德·J·希尔 (Mildred J. Hill)。1935年, 歌词经过改编, 变成了现在的生日歌。

happy: ~ couple *n* **the ~ couple** 新婚夫妇; **~ ending** *n* 美满的结局; **~ event** *n* 喜事 [指生孩子]; **~ families** ▸p. 307 *npl* + *v sing* **to play ~ families** 玩快乐家庭游戏 [一种儿童纸牌游戏, 牌上有 "家庭" 成员像]; **~-go-lucky** *adj* 乐天的 ‹*person, attitude*›; **~ hour** *n* 快乐时间 [指酒吧等低价供应饮料的时段]; **~ hunting ground** *n* 幸福乐土; **to be a ~ hunting ground for sb.** 是某人的乐园; **~ medium** *n* 中庸之道; **to strike a ~ medium between ... and ...** 在…和…之间找到折中的办法; **~ slapping** *n* [u] "开心掌掴" [指掌掴毫无戒备的受害者, 同伙将过程拍摄下来取乐的行为]

hara-kiri /,hærə'kɪri/ *n* [u] 切腹自杀; **to commit ~** 切腹自杀

harangue /hə'ræŋ/
A *vt* (*pres p* **haranguing**) (politically) 向…作慷慨激昂的演讲; (morally) 滔滔不绝地教训
B *n* (political) 慷慨激昂的演讲; (moral) 冗长的训话; **a ~ about sth.** 对某事义愤填膺的谴责

Harare /hə'rɑːri/ *pr n* 哈拉雷

harass /'hærəs, Amer hə'ræs/ *vt* 1 (beleaguer) 不断骚扰 ‹*enemy*› 2 fig (worry) 烦扰; (intimidate) «*police, boss*» 恐吓; **to be ~ed by guilt** 时时受到良心的谴责

harassed /'hærəst, Amer hə'ræst/ *adj* 疲惫的; **a ~ housewife** 疲惫不堪的家庭主妇

harassment /'hærəsmənt, Amer hə'ræsmənt/ *n* [u] (action) 骚扰; (result) 烦扰; **sexual ~** 性骚扰; **a victim of ~** 被骚扰者

harbinger /'hɑːbɪndʒə(r)/ *n* liter (thing) 前兆; (person) 预告者; **swallows are the ~s of summer** 燕子是夏天的信使

harbour Brit, **harbor** Amer /'hɑːbə(r)/
A *n* [u and c] 1 lit 港口; **to enter/leave ~** 入港/离港 2 fig 避风港; **a safe ~** 安全的港湾
B *vt* 1 (shelter) 藏匿 ‹*criminal*›; (provide place for) 有…居住; **to ~ dangerous animals** «*forest*» 有危险动物出没 2 (nurse) 心怀 ‹*suspicion, grudge*› 3 (contain) 藏有 ‹*insect, germs*›

harbour: ~ arm *n* [伸入港湾的] 防波堤; **~ dues, ~ fees** *nspl* 港务费; **~ master**

h

▸p. 409 *n* 港务长; ~**side** *n* 港边地区; **a ~ cafe** 港畔咖啡馆; ~ **station** *n* 港口火车站

hard /hɑːd/

A *adj* [1] (difficult) 困难的 ‹problem, choice›; **it's ~ (for sb.) to do sth.** （某人）做某事很难; **to find sth. ~ to do** 感到某事很难做; **it's ~ to believe that ...** 很难相信…; **a ~ person to get on** *or* **along with** 难于相处的人; **to play ~ to get** colloq 故意拿架子 [2] (rigid) 坚硬的 ‹substance, surface›; **~ muscles** 结实的肌肉; **to go** *or* **get** *or* **become** *or* **grow ~** 变坚硬; **as ~ as iron** *or* **(a) rock** *or* **(a) stone** 像钢铁/石头一样坚硬; ▸**nut A1** [3] (demanding) 辛苦的 ‹day›; 艰苦的 ‹life, childhood›; **to be ~ to do sth.** 做某事很费劲; **to be too much like ~ work** iron 太费劲了; **~ work never hurt** *or* **killed anybody** 辛苦的工作有益无害; **to be ~ going** «trip, task» 费力; «text» 难懂 [4] (diligent) 辛勤的 ‹worker›; **he's a very ~ worker** (student) 他非常勤奋; (employee) 他工作很努力 [5] (forceful) 用力的 ‹blow, push›; **to take a ~ fall** 砰然落地 [6] (unpleasant) 艰难的 ‹year›; **to deal sb./take a ~ blow** 给某人以/遭受沉重打击; **life is ~** colloq iron 生活很艰辛; **it's a ~ life being a millionaire** iron 做百万富翁不容易; **it's a ~ world** 这是个残酷的世界; **to fall on ~ times** 经历艰难时期; **to give sb. a ~ time** colloq 为难某人; **to have a ~ time (of it)** 经历艰难困苦; **to learn sth.** *or* **to find sth. out the ~ way** 通过吃苦头认识某事物; **no ~ feelings** 不再怨恨; **~ lines!** Brit colloq (sympathetic) 真不幸！; (unsympathetic) 活该倒霉！ [7] (jarring) 刺眼的 ‹light, colour›; 刺耳的 ‹sound› [8] (stark) 生硬的 ‹outline› [9] (very cold) 严寒的; **a ~ winter/frost** 严冬/寒冷的霜冻 [10] (stern) 冷酷无情的 ‹person, look›; **a ~ heart** 硬心肠; **there were ~ words between us** 我们相互苛责; **to be ~ on sb./sth.** (harsh) 对某人/某事物苛刻; (unfair) 对某人/某事物不公平; (damaging) 伤害某人/损坏某物; **to be ~ on one's shoes/feet** 穿鞋很费/挤脚; **to be ~ on the nerves** 使人焦虑不安 [11] colloq (tough) 强健的 ‹body›; 坚强的 ‹mind›; **you think you're really ~, don't you?** 你以为你真的有种，是不是？ [12] (reliable) 确凿的 ‹facts, evidence›; 确切的 ‹news› [13] Chem **~ water** 硬水 [14] (potent) 烈性的 ‹drink, liquor› [15] (explicit) 极度淫秽的 ‹pornography› [16] Pol **the ~ left/right** 极左派/极右派 [17] Phon 硬的 ‹sound›; **a ~ consonant** 硬辅音

B *adv* [1] (rigidly) 结实地; **to set/freeze/bake ~** 变结实/冻得结结实实/烤得硬梆梆的 [2] (forcefully) 用力地 ‹push›; **to slam the door ~** 使劲关上门; **to fall ~ against** *or* **on sth.** 重重地撞在某物上 [3] (diligently) 努力地; **no matter how ~ I tried, ...** 不管我多努力，…; **as ~ as one can** 竭尽全力; **to work ~** 辛勤工作; **to be ~ at work** *or* colloq **at it** 忙于干活 [4] (carefully) 仔细地 ‹think, look› [5] (heavily) 大量地; **to rain/snow very ~** 雨/雪下得很大 [6] (intensely) 剧烈地; **to laugh/cry ~** 大笑/痛哭 [7] fig (deeply) 严重地; **to hit sb./sth. ~** 给某人/某事以沉重打击; **to be ~ hit (by sth.)** 受到（某事的）严重影响 [8] (sharply) 急剧地; **to turn ~ to the right** 向右急转; **go ~ astern!** 全速倒退！; **~ a-port/a-starboard** 左/右满舵 [9] (with difficulty) 困难地; **to be ~ put (to it) to do sth.** 做某事很难 [10] (badly) **to take sth. ~** 为某事难过 [11] (unfairly) **~ done by** 受到不公平待遇; **to look ~ done by** 看起来很委屈 [12] (close) **~ behind** 紧随在后; **~ on** *or* **upon sth.** 紧随某事之后; **~ by (sth.)** dated 在（某物）近旁

hard: ~ and fast *adj* 不容改变的 ‹rule›; 明确无误的 ‹distinction, conclusion›; **~-ass** *n* Amer taboo sl 厉害角色

hardback /ˈhɑːdbæk/, **hardcover** /ˌhɑːdˈkʌvə(r)/

A *ns* 精装书; **to be published in ~** 以精装本形式出版

B *modif* 精装的 ‹novel, book, atlas›; 精装书的 ‹sales›

hard: ~ball *n* [u] Amer 棒球运动; **to play ~ball** lit 打棒球; fig colloq 采取强硬手段; **~-bitten** *adj* 久经磨炼的; **a ~-bitten war reporter** 久经沙场的战地记者; **~board** *n* [u] 硬质纤维板; **~board wall** 纤维板墙; **~-boiled** *adj* [1] lit 煮老的 ‹egg›; [2] fig colloq 不动感情的 ‹person›; 风格冷峻的 ‹drama, novel›; **a ~-boiled criminal** 冷酷强悍的罪犯; **~ cash** *n* [u] 现金; **~ cheese** *excl* Brit colloq 倒霉［用于表示对小事的同情，通常具有讽刺意味］; **I haven't got enough money — well, ~ cheese!** 我的钱不够——哦，太糟糕了！; **~ copy** *n* [u and c] 打印件; **~ core** *n* [1] [c] + *v sing or pl* (committed group of protestors) 中坚; (of employees) 骨干; (of the poor, unemployed) 固定人员; [2] [u] Constr 路基碎砖石; [3] **~core** [u] (pornography) 顶级色情; **~core pornography** 顶级色情作品; [4] **~core** [u] Mus 硬核音乐［以高音量和猛烈的表现方式为特点］; **~ court** *n* 硬地网球场; **~ currency** *n* 硬通货

hard disk *n* 硬盘

hard disk drive *n* 硬驱

hard: ~-drinking *adj attrib* 酗酒的; **the ~-drinking culture of the city in the 1950s** 20世纪50年代该城市的酗酒文化; **~ drive** *n* 硬盘驱动器; **~-earned** *adj* 辛苦挣来的 ‹money›; 来之不易的 ‹title, place›

harden /ˈhɑːdn/

A *vt* [1] (make rigid) 使…变硬 ‹substance, surface›; **to ~ one's muscles/the skin** 使肌肉变结实/使皮肤硬化 [2] (make serious) 使…更严肃 ‹expression›; **to ~ one's voice/face** 声音严厉起来/脸沉下来 [3] (toughen physically) «time, event» 使变强壮; **to ~ sb. to the cold** 使某人能抵御寒冷 [4] (toughen mentally) «time, event» 使冷酷无情; **to ~ sb. to the suffering of others** 使某人对别人的苦痛无动于衷; **to ~ sb.'s/one's heart (to** *or* **towards sb.)** 硬下心肠（对待某人） [5] (intensify) 使…强硬 ‹idea, resolve›; **to ~ one's opposition to sth.** 更加坚定地反对某事

B *vi* [1] (become rigid) «substance» 变硬; **this varnish ~s quickly** 这种清漆干得很快 [2] (become serious) «expression» 变严肃; **sb.'s face/voice ~s** 某人的脸色沉下来/声音严厉起来 [3] (become physically tougher) 变强壮 [4] (become mentally tougher) 变得冷酷无情 [5] (intensify) «stance, resolve» 变得坚定; **her dislike ~ed into a feeling of contempt** 她的态度由厌恶变为轻蔑 [6] Fin «market, economy» 变得坚挺

Phrasal verb

• **harden off**

A *vt* [**~ sth. off, ~ off sth.**] 使…变得耐寒 ‹plant›

B *vi* «plant» 变得耐寒

hardened /ˈhɑːdnd/ *adj* [1] lit (toughened, set) 硬化的 ‹glue, skin›; 淬火的 ‹steel› [2] fig (inured) 久经磨炼的; **to be ~ to sth.** 对某事无所谓; **to become ~ to sth.** 对某事变得无所谓; **~ police officers** 老练的警官 [3] *attrib* fig (inveterate) 积习难改的 ‹drinker, addict›; 怙恶不悛的 ‹terrorist›; **a ~ criminal** 惯犯 [4] (strengthened) 经加固有核防护设施的 ‹silo, bunker›

hardening /ˈhɑːdnɪŋ/ *n* [u] [1] lit (of varnish, glue, muscle) 硬化; (of steel) 淬火 [2] fig (of attitude) 冷漠化; (of resolve) 强硬化

hard: ~-faced *adj* 面目冷峻的; **~ feelings** *npl* ［用以指生气、厌恶、怨恨、恶意等］; **there are no ~ feelings between us** 我们之间没有敌意; **to leave without ~ feelings** 心平气和地离开; **to bear sb. no ~ feelings** 不生某人的气; **no ~ feelings?** (offence) 不生气吧？; (objection) 不介意吧？; **~-fought** *adj* 激烈的 ‹battle›; 势均力敌的 ‹game, election›; **~ hat** *n* [1] Constr 安全帽; [2] Equit 头盔; **~-headed** *adj* 冷静精明的 ‹person, approach›; **a ~-headed businessman** 头脑冷静的商人; **~-hearted** *adj* 硬心肠的 ‹person, attitude›; **~-heartedness** *n* [u] 无情; **to have a reputation for ~-heartedness** 以铁石心肠著称; **~-hitting** *adj* 直言不讳的 ‹speech, criticism›

hardiness /ˈhɑːdɪnɪs/ *n* [u] [1] (robustness) 吃苦耐劳 [2] Hort 耐寒

hard: ~ labour *n* [u] 苦役; **~ landing** *n* Aerosp［航天器的］硬着陆; Econ［经济的］硬着陆; **~ line** *n* 强硬路线; **to take a ~ line (on sth./with sb.)** （对某事/某人）采取强硬态度; **~-line** *adj* [1] (diehard) 顽固不妥协的 ‹socialist, Democrat›; **the ~-line minority** 顽固的少数人; [2] (rigid) 强硬的 ‹position, policy›; **~-liner** /ˌhɑːdˈlaɪnə(r)/ *n* 主张强硬路线者

hard luck Brit colloq

A *excl* **~!** (sympathetic) 真不幸！; (unsympathetic) 活该倒霉！

B *n* [u] 厄运; **it's ~ on sb. (to do sth.)** （做某事）是某人的不幸; **it'll be ~ on the spectators if it rains** 如果下雨观众就倒霉了; **it was ~ on him to break his leg** 他不幸折断了腿; **it's ~ that ...** 真不幸，…; **that's sb.'s ~** 那是某人倒霉

hard-luck story *n* ［向他人诉说以博取同情的］倒霉事

hardly /ˈhɑːdli/ *adv* [1] (scarcely) 几乎不; **to ~ ever do sth.** 几乎从不做某事; **there's ~ any milk left** 牛奶差不多没了; **I could ~ keep my eyes open** 我眼睛都快睁不开了; **I ~ know him** 我不怎么认识他; **~ a day goes by without sb. doing sth.** 某人几乎天天做某事 [2] (not really) 不十分; **it's ~ likely/surprising** 这不大可能/不足为奇; **you can ~ expect him to trust you** 你可别指望他会相信你; **is she going to win? — ~!** 她会赢吗？——没门！; **I need ~ say that ...** 我不消说…; **I can ~ wait!** also iron 我等不及了！ [3] (barely) 刚刚; **~ had he opened the newspaper when the telephone rang** 他刚打开报纸，电话就响了

hardness /ˈhɑːdnɪs/ *n* [u] [1] (rigidity) 坚硬; **level of ~** 硬度 [2] (difficulty) (of problem) 困难; (of physical work) 艰辛; (of life) 艰苦 [3] (force of blow, fall) 力度 [4] (sternness) 冷酷无情; **~ of heart** 铁石心肠 [5] colloq (toughness) 坚强 [6] (harshness of light) 刺眼; (harshness of sound) 刺耳 [7] (starkness of line) 生硬 [8] Chem 硬度

hard-nosed *adj* colloq 冷静精明的 ‹businessman, journalist›

hard of hearing

A *adj pred* 耳背的

B *npl* **the ~** 耳背的人

hard-on *n* taboo sl 勃起

hard: ~ palate *n* 硬腭; **~ porn** *n* [u] colloq 硬色情; **~-pressed, hard-pushed** *adjs* 处于困境的; **to be ~-pressed to do sth.** 勉强能做某事; **to be ~-pressed for time** 时间很紧; **to be ~-pressed (for money)** 手头很紧; **a ~-pressed worker** 工作压力太大的工人; **~ rock** *n* [u] 硬摇滚

hard sell

A *n* (act) 强行推销; (technique) 强行推销术; **to give sb. the ~, to do a ~ on sb.** 向某人强行推销

B **hard-sell** *modif* 强行推销的 ‹approach, tactic›

hardship /ˈhɑːdʃɪp/ *n* [1] [u] (suffering, poverty) 穷困; **to bear ~ with fortitude** 坚韧地忍受穷困 [2] [u and c] (difficulty) 艰难; **it's no ~ for me (to do sth.)** 我（做某事）毫不费力 [3] [c] (ordeal) 磨难; **to suffer ~s** 吃苦

hardship fund *n* 贫困援助基金

hard: ~ shoulder *n* Brit 硬质路肩; **~ standing** *n* [u] Brit ［用于停放车辆等的］硬地面; **~ stuff** *n* [u] colloq **the ~ stuff** 烈酒; **you're on the ~ stuff, are you?** 你喝烈酒，是吧？; **~top** *n* (car) 硬顶汽车; (roof) 可卸式硬顶; **a ~top convertible** 硬顶敞篷车

hard up *adj* colloq **1** (short of money) 手头紧的 **2** **to be ～ for sth.** (lacking) 缺少 ‹*ideas, work*›; **why don't you take up flower arranging? — I'm not that ～!** 你为什么不学学插花？——我没那么无所事事！; **she must be really ～ to be considering going out with him** 她如果考虑和他约会，那她肯定是到了饥不择食的地步了

hardware /ˈhɑːdweə(r)/ *n* [u] **1** (in house) 五金制品 **2** Comput 硬件; **～ design/company** 硬件设计/公司 **3** Mil 重武器 **4** (equipment) 设备

hardware: **～ dealer** ▸p. 409 *n* Amer 五金商人; **～ shop, ～ store** *ns* 五金店

hard: **～-wearing** *adj* 经久耐用的 ‹*tyre, shoes*›; 耐磨的 ‹*carpet*›; **～-wired** *adj* **1** Electron, Comput 硬连线的 ‹*network, device*›; **2** fig colloq 遗传的 ‹*response, behaviour*›; **～-won** *adj* 来之不易的; **a ～-won contract** 费尽周折签订的合同; **～wood** *n* **1** [u and c] (wood) 硬木; **～wood floor** 硬木地板; **2** [c] (tree) 硬木树; **～ worker** *n* 工作勤勉的人; **～-working** *adj* 努力工作的

hardy /ˈhɑːdi/ *adj* **1** (robust) 强壮的; **the children are very ～** 孩子们非常结实; **a ～ constitution** 强壮的体格 **2** Bot 耐寒的 ‹*plant*›

hardy: **～ annual** *n* 一年生耐寒植物; **～ perennial** *n* 多年生耐寒植物

hare /heə(r)/

A *n* **1** [c] Zool 野兔; **mad as a March ～** hum colloq 疯疯癫癫; **to run with the ～ and hunt with the hounds** pej 两面讨好 **2** [u] Culin 野兔肉

B *vi* Brit 飞奔

Phrasal verbs

- **hare about** *vi* Brit 东奔西跑; **stop haring about** 别老是奔来奔去
- **hare off** *vi* Brit 飞奔而去

harebrained /ˈheəbreɪnd/ *adj* colloq 轻率的 ‹*person, idea*›

hare: **～ coursing** *n* [u] 猎野兔; **～lip** *n* [u and c] 唇裂

harem /ˈhɑːriːm/ *n* **1** (wives) 妻妾 **2** (women's quarters) 内室 **3** Zool 雌性配偶群

haricot /ˈhærɪkəʊ/ *n* Brit **～ (bean)** 扁豆

hark /hɑːk/ *vi* liter 听; **～ at him!** Brit colloq 瞧他那副德行！

Phrasal verb

- **hark back to** *vt* [**～ back to sth.**] **1** (recall) «*person*» 回忆起 **2** (evoke) «*thing*» 使人想起

harken /ˈhɑːkən/ *vi* archaic = **hearken**

harlequin /ˈhɑːlɪkwɪn/

A *n* (*also* **Harlequin**) [传统哑剧中穿色彩斑斓菱形花纹服装的] 丑角

B *adj* 色彩斑斓的

Harley Street /ˈhɑːli striːt/ *pr n* Brit 哈莱街 [英国伦敦一街道，许多著名医生在此设有诊所]; **a ～ doctor** 哈莱街的医生

harm /hɑːm/

A *n* [u] 损害; **to do** *or* **cause ～** 伤害; **to come to ～** 受损害; **to do ～ to sb./sth., to do sb./sth. ～** 对某人/某事物有害; **to mean ～ to sb., to mean sb. ～** 有意伤害某人; **I didn't mean him any ～** 我对他并无恶意; **there is no ～ in doing that** 做那事没什么坏处; **it would do no ～ to do sth.** (there's nothing to lose) 不妨做某事; (it would be a good idea) 做某事也不错; **some hard work wouldn't do him any ～** iron 他干点儿重活不会累坏的; **out of ～'s way** 在安全的地方; **to do more ～ than good** 害多益少; **where's the ～ in it?** 这有什么坏处？; **no ～ done!** 没事！

B *vt* **1** (injure) 伤害 ‹*person*›; 损坏 ‹*object*›; 危害 ‹*crop*›; **he wouldn't ～ a fly!** 他连只苍蝇都不会伤害！ **2** (affect adversely) 损害 ‹*reputation, economy*›

harmful /ˈhɑːmfl/ *adj* 有害的 ‹*substance, chemical*›; 不良的 ‹*habit, side effect, influence*›; **to be ～ to sb./sth.** 对某人/某物有害; **to be ～ to one's health** 对身体有害; **to be ～ to do sth.** 做某事是有害的

harmless /ˈhɑːmlɪs/ *adj* **1** (not dangerous) 无害的; **to be ～ to sth./sb.** 对某事物/某人无害; **it's ～ to do sth.** 做某事没害处 **2** (inoffensive) 无恶意的 ‹*person, joke*›; **a little ～ fun** 无恶意的取乐; **he's ～!** hum 他是个好好先生！

harmonic /hɑːˈmɒnɪk/

A *adj* **1** Mus 和声的 ‹*sequence*› **2** Math 调和的 ‹*series*›

B *n* **1** Mus 泛音 **2** Phys 谐波

harmonica /hɑːˈmɒnɪkə/ ▸p. 395 *n* 口琴

harmonics /hɑːˈmɒnɪks/ *npl* + *v sing* 乐音学

harmonious /hɑːˈməʊnɪəs/ *adj* **1** (tuneful) 悦耳的 ‹*voice, tune, melody, laughter*› **2** (amicable) 和谐的 ‹*relationship, atmosphere*› **3** (combining pleasingly) 协调的 ‹*colours, tones*›

harmoniously /hɑːˈməʊnɪəsli/ *adv* **1** (tunefully) 悦耳地 ‹*sing, play*› **2** (amicably) 和谐地 ‹*live, work*› **3** (pleasingly) 协调地 ‹*blend, combine*›

harmonium /hɑːˈməʊnɪəm/ ▸p. 395 *n* 簧风琴

harmonize /ˈhɑːmənaɪz/

A *vt* **1** Mus 为…配和声 ‹*tune*› **2** (reconcile) 调和 ‹*relations, theories, ideas*›; **they are unable to ～ their ideas** 他们无法达成共识 **3** (systematize) 使…一致 ‹*law, text*›; **to ～ sth. with sth.** 使某物与某事物一致 **4** (coordinate) 使…协调 ‹*colours*›

B *vi* **1** Mus «*singer*» 以和声唱; «*instrument*» 以和声演奏 **2** (be in accord) «*idea, personality*» 相符合 **3** (be consistent) «*text, version*» 相一致 **4** (coordinate) «*colour, plan, arrangement*» 协调; **to ～ with sth.** 和某事物协调

harmony /ˈhɑːməni/ *n* **1** [u and c] Mus 和声 **2** [u] (accord) 和谐; **in ～ (with sb.)** (与某人) 协调一致; **perfect ～** 十分融洽; **domestic ～** 家庭和睦 **3** [u] (pleasing combination) 协调

harness /ˈhɑːnɪs/

A *n* (for animal) 挽具; (for person) 保护带; **safety ～** 安全带; **to work in ～ (with sb.)** fig (与某人) 合作; **to die in ～** fig 工作时死去

B *vt* **1** (put harness on) 给…上挽具 ‹*animal*›; 给…系保护带 ‹*person*› **2** (attach with harness) 用挽具套 ‹*animal*›; 用保护带系 ‹*person*›; **to ～ the ox to the cart** 把牛套到大车上; **I ～ed myself into the seat** 我坐到座位上，系上了安全带 **3** (channel) 利用 ‹*power, resources*›

harp /hɑːp/ ▸p. 395 *n* 竖琴

Phrasal verb

- **harp on** colloq

A *vi* **to ～ on about sth.** 喋喋不休地谈论某事; **she ～ed on about her children** 她老是念叨她的孩子们

B *vt* [**～ on sth.**] 喋喋不休地谈论; **to ～ on the subject** 反复谈论这个话题

harpist /ˈhɑːpɪst/ ▸p. 395, p. 409 *n* 竖琴演奏者

harpoon /hɑːˈpuːn/

A *n* 鱼叉; **～ gun** 捕鲸炮

B *vt* 用鱼叉叉 ‹*whale, fish*›

harpsichord /ˈhɑːpsɪkɔːd/ ▸p. 395 *n* 拨弦键琴

harpsichordist /ˈhɑːpsɪkɔːdɪst/ ▸p. 395, p. 409 *n* 拨弦键琴演奏者

harpy /ˈhɑːpi/ *n* **1** Mythol 鸟身女妖 **2** pej (unscrupulous woman) 泼妇

harridan /ˈhærɪdən/ *n* pej 泼妇

Harrier /ˈhærɪə(r)/ *n* **～ (jump jet)** "鹞式"战斗机

harrier /ˈhærɪə(r)/ *n* 鹞

Harris tweed® /ˌhærɪs ˈtwiːd/ *n* [u] 海力斯粗花呢

> **Harrods**
>
> 哈罗兹公司。位于伦敦市中心的骑士桥（Knightsbridge）区，在海德公园（Hyde Park）南面。创始人为亨利·查尔斯·哈罗德（Henry Charles Harrod）。起初只是伦敦东区的一家食品杂货店。1849 年迁至现址。经过百余年的发展，已成为世界知名的奢侈品商店，也是世界最大的百货公司之一。经营口号为 omnia, omnibus, ubique（为任何地方的任何人提供任何服务）。

harrow /ˈhærəʊ/

A *n* 耙

B *vt* 耙 ‹*field*›

harrowing /ˈhærəʊɪŋ/ *adj* 悲惨的 ‹*experience*›

harry /ˈhæri/ *vt* **1** (pursue) «*animal*» 对…紧追不舍 ‹*prey*› **2** (harass) «*person*» 不断烦扰 ‹*victim*›; **his creditors are constantly ～ing him** 他的那些债主不断向他催债 **3** Mil 不断攻击

harsh /hɑːʃ/ *adj* **1** (severe) 严厉的 ‹*judgement, punishment, law, expression, criticism, person*›; 严格的 ‹*rule*›; 严酷的 ‹*regime*›; **to be ～ with** *or* **to sth./sb.** 对某事/某人严厉 **2** (difficult) 恶劣的 ‹*climate*›; 艰苦的 ‹*conditions, life*›; 严寒的 ‹*winter*› **3** (rough) 粗糙的 ‹*cloth*› **4** (grating) 刺耳的 ‹*sound, voice*› **5** (glaring) 刺眼的 ‹*colour, light*›

harshly /ˈhɑːʃli/ *adv* 严厉地 ‹*speak, treat*›; 刺眼地 ‹*contrast*›

harshness /ˈhɑːʃnɪs/ *n* **1** (of judgement, punishment, law, expression, criticism, person) 严厉; (of rule) 严格; (of regime) 严酷 **2** (of climate) 恶劣; (of winter) 严寒; (of conditions, life) 艰苦 **3** (of cloth) 粗糙 **4** (of sound, voice) 刺耳 **5** (of colour, light) 刺眼

hart /hɑːt/ *n* (*pl* **～** *or* **～s**) 雄赤鹿

harum-scarum /ˌheərəmˈskeərəm/ colloq

A *adj* 鲁莽的 ‹*behaviour, person*›; 草率的 ‹*scheme*›

B *n* 冒失鬼

harvest /ˈhɑːvɪst/

A *n* **1** (gathering) (of crops) 收割; (of fruit) 收获 **2** (yield) 收成; **a good/poor ～** 丰收/歉收 **3** fig (result) 结果; **to reap the ～** fig (benefit) 收获成果; (suffer) 尝到苦果

B *vt* **1** lit 收割 ‹*crops*›; 收获 ‹*fruit*› **2** fig 收集 ‹*facts, information*› **3** Med 分离 ‹*cells, organ*›

C *vi* (gather crops) 收割庄稼; (gather fruit) 收获水果

harvester /ˈhɑːvɪstə(r)/ *n* **1** (machine) 收割机 **2** (person) 收割者

harvest: **～ festival** *n* 秋收感恩节; **～ home** *n* **1** (gathering) 收获归仓; **2** (festival) 收获节祝宴; **～man** /-mən/ *n* 盲蜘蛛; **～ moon** *n* 获月 [秋分后的第一次满月]; **～ mouse** *n* 巢鼠; **～ time** *n* [u] 收获季节

has /hæz, həz/ *3rd pers sing pres* ▸**have**

has-been *n* colloq pej 过气名人; **a political ～** 风光不再的政治人物

hash[1] /hæʃ/

A *n* **1** [u and c] Culin 回锅肉丁 **2** [c] fig colloq (mess) 一团糟; **to make a ～ of sth.** 把某事弄糟

B *vt* Culin 把…切碎 ‹*meat*›

Phrasal verb

- **hash up** *vt* [**～ up sth., ～ sth. up**] **1** Culin 把…切碎 **2** fig colloq 把…弄糟

hash[2] *n* = **hash sign**

hash[3] *n* [u] colloq = **hashish**

hash browns *npl* esp Amer 洋葱土豆煎饼

hashish /ˈhæʃiːʃ/ *n* [u] 大麻麻醉剂

hash: **～ key** *n* 井号键; **～ sign** *n* 井号

hasn't colloq = **has not** ▸**have**

hasp /hɑːsp/ *n* 搭扣

hassle /ˈhæsl/

A *n* colloq **1** [u and c] (trouble) 麻烦; **to be a ～ to do sth.** 做某事很麻烦; **legal ～s** 法律程序

h

的繁复 **2** [c] (dispute) 争吵 **3** [u] (pestering) 纠缠; **don't give me any ~!** 别跟我顶嘴!
B *vt* 不断烦扰; **to ~ sb. to do sth.** 缠着某人做某事; **to feel ~d about sth.** 对某事物感到烦心; **to ~ sb. with complaints** 老是向某人抱怨; **stop hassling me!** 别老烦我!

hassock /ˈhæsək/ *n* 跪垫

haste /heɪst/ *n* [u] 匆忙; **in ~** 匆忙地; **make ~** dated 快点; **to make ~ to do sth.** 急忙做某事; **marry in ~, repent at leisure** Prov 草率结婚后悔多; **more ~, less speed** Prov 欲速则不达

hasten /ˈheɪsn/
A *vi* 赶紧; **to ~ to sth.** 赶往某地; **to ~ to do sth.** 赶紧做某事; **they ~ed away** 他们匆匆离去了
B *vt* 催促 ‹*reply, departure*›; 加快 ‹*step*›; **to ~ sb.'s response** 催某人快点作出反应

hastily /ˈhæstɪli/ *adv* **1** (quickly) 匆忙地 **2** (rashly) 草率地

hasty /ˈheɪsti/ *adj* **1** (hurried) 匆忙的; **a ~ sketch of sth.** 某物的草图; **to have a ~ meal** 急急忙忙用餐 **2** (rash) 草率的 ‹*words, decision*›

hat /hæt/ *n* 帽子; **to put on/take off one's ~** 戴上/脱下帽子; **to pass the ~ around** (to buy gift) fig 凑份子; (for entertainer) 收钱; **~ in hand** fig 卑躬屈膝地; **~s off to sb.** fig 让我们向某人表示敬意; **to take off one's ~ to sb.** fig 向某人表示敬佩; **to keep sth. under one's ~** fig 对某事保密; **to wear two ~s** fig 同时担任两个职务; **I'm wearing my legal ~ now** fig 我现在是律师身份; **at the drop of a ~** fig 一发出信号

hat: ~band *n* 帽带; **~box** *n* 帽盒

hatch[1] /hætʃ/
A *n* **1** Naut, Aviat 舱口; **under ~es** Naut 在甲板下; **batten down the ~es** Naut 封住舱口; fig 作好应对危机的准备; **down the ~** fig colloq 干杯 **2** (in house) 开口; **a dining ~ in the kitchen wall** 厨房墙上传递菜肴的小窗口 **3** (brood) 一窝; **a ~ of young birds** 一窝小鸟
B *vt* **1** lit 孵 ‹*eggs*›; ▸**chicken A1** **2** fig (conspire to devise) 策划 ‹*plot*›

hatch[2] *vt* Art 在…上画影线

hatchback /ˈhætʃbæk/ *n* **1** (car) 掀背式汽车 **2** (door) 掀开式车门

hat: ~check girl *n* Amer 衣帽间女服务员; **~check man** *n* Amer 衣帽间男服务员

hatchery /ˈhætʃəri/ *n* 孵化场

hatchet /ˈhætʃɪt/ *n* 短柄小斧; **bury the ~** fig 言归于好

hatchet: ~ face *n* colloq pej 棱角分明的瘦削脸; **~-faced** *adj* colloq pej 脸瘦削而严厉的 ‹*person*›; **~ job** *n* fig colloq 恶毒攻击; **to do a ~ job on sb./sth.** 诋毁某人/某事物; **~ man** /-mæn/ *n* colloq 刀斧手 [指受雇执行不光彩任务的人]

hatching[1] /ˈhætʃɪŋ/ *n* [u] **1** (incubation) 孵化 **2** (emergence) 孵出

hatching[2] *n* [u] Art 影线法

hatchling /hætʃlɪŋ/ *n* 刚孵出的卵生动物

hatchway /ˈhætʃweɪ/ *n* 舱口

hate /heɪt/
A *vt* **1** (detest) 憎恶; (intensely) 恨; **to ~ sb. for sth./for doing sth.** 因某事物而恨某人/因某人做某事而恨某人; **they ~ each other** 他们相互仇视 **2** (not enjoy) 讨厌; **to ~ doing** *or* **to do sth.** 讨厌做某事; **I ~ it when people complain** 我厌烦别人抱怨; **I ~ to see her cry** 我不喜欢看到她哭; **to ~ sb. to do sth.** 不愿某人做某事 **3** (regret) 不愿; **I ~ to interrupt you, but ...** 抱歉打断你一下, …; **I ~ (having) to say it but ...** 我不想提这事, 但是…
B *n* **1** [u] (dislike) 憎恶; (intense) 仇恨 **2** [c] colloq (person) 所憎恶的人; (thing) 所憎恶的事; **cooking is my pet ~** 我特别厌恶做饭

hate campaign *n* 仇恨运动

hated /ˈheɪtɪd/ *adj* 憎恶的

hateful /ˈheɪtfl/ *adj* **1** (full of hatred) 充满仇恨的 ‹*glance, words*› **2** colloq (very unpleasant) 可恶的; **to be ~ to sb.** 对某人很凶

hate: ~ mail *n* [u] 诋毁信件; **a threatening ~ mail** 恐吓信; **~monger** /ˈheɪt,mʌŋɡə(r)/ *n* 煽起仇恨者

hatless /ˈhætlɪs/ *adj* 不戴帽子的

hat: ~pin *n* 女帽饰针; **~rack** *n* (shelf) 挂帽架; (pegs) 挂帽钩

hatred /ˈheɪtrɪd/ *n* [u] (hate) 仇恨; (intense dislike) 厌恶; **out of ~** 出于仇恨; **ancient ~** 宿仇; **~ for sb./sth.** 厌恶某人/某事物

hat: ~shop ▸**p. 409** *n* 帽店; **~ stand** Brit, **~ tree** Amer *ns* 立式衣帽架

hatter /ˈhætə(r)/ ▸**p. 409** *n* 帽商; **mad as a ~** colloq 疯疯癫癫

hat trick *n* 帽子戏法 [一人连得3分或连续3次取胜]; **to score a ~** 上演帽子戏法

haughtily /ˈhɔːtɪli/ *adv* 傲慢地

haughtiness /ˈhɔːtɪnɪs/ *n* [u] 傲慢

haughty /ˈhɔːti/ *adj* 傲慢的

haul /hɔːl/
A *n* **1** (stolen goods) 大批赃物; **a £2m ~** 一批价值 200 万英镑的赃物; **a ~ of jewellery** 大批偷来的珠宝 **2** (found by police) 大量非法物品; **a ~ of weapons** 大批非法武器 **3** Fishg 渔获量; **a fine ~ of fish** 满满一网鱼 **4** Sport (winnings) 得分总数 **5** (journey) 旅程; **a ~ to/from sth.** 前往/离开某处的行程; **it's going to be a long ~** colloq 长路漫漫; **the long ~ to recovery** Med 漫长的恢复过程; Econ 漫长的复苏过程 **6** (time) 一段时间; **a long/short ~ to sth.** 距离某事很长/很短的一段时间
B *vt* **1** (drag, tow) 拖 ‹*goods, barge*›; **to ~ ass** Amer sl (hurry) 赶紧; (move fast) 开足马力 **2** (transport) 运输 ‹*goods, coal*›
C *vi* Naut (head into wind) «*ship, vessel*» 逆风航行; (alter course) 改变航向
D *v refl* **to ~ oneself out of/on to sth.** 爬出/爬上某物

Phrasal verbs

- **haul down** *vt* [**~ down sth., ~ sth. down**] 降下 ‹*flag, sail*›
- **haul in** *vt* [**~ in sth., ~ sth. in**] 收 ‹*net*›; 把…拉上来 ‹*fish, catch*›
- **haul out** *vt* [**~ out sb./sth., ~ sb./sth. out**] 将…拖出 ‹*net, body*›
- **haul up** *vt* [**~ up sb./sth., ~ sb./sth. up**] **1** (pull up) 升起 ‹*flag, sail*›; 把…拖上来 ‹*person, boat*› **2** colloq (make appear in court) 传讯; **to be ~ed up before** *or* **in front of the judge** 接受法官的传讯

haulage /ˈhɔːlɪdʒ/ *n* [u] **1** (transport) 陆路货运 **2** (cost) 运费

haulage: ~ company *n* 陆路货运公司; **~ contractor** *n* (business) 陆路货运承包商; (haulier) 陆路货运公司

haulier /ˈhɔːlɪə(r)/ Brit, **hauler** /ˈhɔːlə(r)/ Amer ▸**p. 409** *ns* (owner) 陆路货运商; (firm) 陆路货运公司

haunch /hɔːntʃ/ *n* **1** [c] *usu pl* Anat (of human) 臀胯部; (of animal) 腰腿; **to squat on one's ~es** 蹲着 **2** [u] Culin 腰腿肉

haunt /hɔːnt/
A *vt* **1** lit «*ghost*» 经常出没于 ‹*place, house*› **2** fig (frequent) «*person*» 常去 ‹*place*› **3** fig (trouble, disturb) «*memory, guilt*» 缠绕 ‹*mind, person*›; **the sight ~ed me for years** 数年来那情景总是浮现在我眼前; **to be ~ed by the fear of dying** 心头萦绕对死亡的恐惧
B *n* (of people) 常去的地方; (of animals) 生息地; **the ~ of thieves** 小偷经常出没的地方

haunted /ˈhɔːntɪd/ *adj* **1** lit 鬼魂出没的; **a ~ house** 凶宅 **2** fig 忧心忡忡的 ‹*expression, person*›

haunting /ˈhɔːntɪŋ/
A *adj* 萦绕于心的 ‹*doubt*›; 难忘的 ‹*memory, melody*›; 久久不散的 ‹*perfume*›
B *n* [u] 闹鬼

hauntingly /ˈhɔːntɪŋli/ *adv* 令人难忘地 ‹*familiar, beautiful*›

Havana /həˈvænə/
A *pr n* 哈瓦那
B *n* (cigar) 哈瓦那雪茄

have /hæv/
A *vt* (*3rd pers sing pres* **has**; *pt, pp* **had**) **1** **~ (got)** (possess, own) 有; **~ you (got) a pen?** 你有钢笔吗?; **I ~ no doubts that he's guilty** 我毫不怀疑他有罪; **she has (got) black hair** 她一头黑发; **I've nothing against sport** 我不讨厌体育运动; **to ~ had it** colloq (be in bad condition) 情形很糟; (be in trouble) 惹上麻烦了; (be unlikely to survive) 没法幸免了; **this car/TV has had it** 这辆汽车/这台电视机修不好了; **when your father finds out, you've had it!** 等你爸爸知道了, 有你好受的!; **oh Lord, we've had it now!** 天哪, 我们这下完蛋了!; **to ~ had it (up to here) (with sb./sth.)** colloq 受够了 (某人/某物); **I've had it up to here with my job** 我的工作没法干下去了; **to ~ (got) sb./sth. to oneself** 独占某人/某物; **to ~ (got) it in for sb.** colloq 跟某人过不去; **I've got it!** 我明白了!; **to ~ it off** *or* **away (with sb.)** Brit sl (与某人) 性交; **and what ~ you** colloq 诸如此类; **to ~ (got) it in one (to do sth.)** colloq 有能力 (做某事); **she doesn't ~ it in her to be nasty** 她凶不起来; **and the ayes/noes ~ it** 投赞成票/反对票的赢了 **2** **~ (got)** (consist of) 由…组成; **in 1999 the party had 10,000 members** 该党在 1999 年时拥有 10,000 名党员 **3** **~ (got)** (be able to make use of sth. available) «*person, organization*» 能利用 ‹*time, money*›; **we had no alternative** 我们别无选择; **he hasn't (got) long to live** 他活不长了 **4** **~ (got)** (know) 通晓; **he has good French but only a little Spanish** 他的法语很好, 但只懂一点儿西班牙语 **5** **~ (got)** (need to do) 有必要; **to ~ (got) sth. to do** 有某事要做; **I ~** *or* colloq **I've got letters to write** 我有几封信要写; **I ~ (got) an essay for tomorrow** 我明天要交一篇短文 **6** **~ (got)** (be with) 同…在一起; **he had a friend with him** 他和一位朋友在一起 **7** (receive, obtain) 得到; (accept) 接受; **you can ~ it if you want it** 你如果想要就拿去吧; **I've had no news from him** 我没有得到他的消息; **to ~ it (from sb.) that ...** 听 (某人) 说…; **these are the best skates to be had** 这种冰鞋是市场上最好的; **I'll ~ tea please** 我点茶; **will you ~ this woman to be your wife?** 你想娶这位女子为妻吗? **8** (perform, do) 做; **to ~ a walk/dream/read** 散步/做梦/阅读; **~ a look at this one!** 看看这个! **9** (exhibit quality, emotion) 表现出 ‹*temerity, courtesy, mercy*›; **they ~ a lot of courage** 他们很勇敢; **she had the good sense to refuse** 她很明智地拒绝了; **I had pity on them** 我可怜他们 **10** (produce) 产生 ‹*influence, result*›; **the colour green has a restful effect** 绿色使人感到宁静 **11** (organize, hold) 举办 ‹*party, exhibition*›; 召集 ‹*meeting*›; 进行 ‹*conversation, talks, enquiry, interview*› **12** **~ (got)** (be responsible for) 担负 ‹*duties*›; **he has the job of cutting the hedge** 他的工作是修剪树篱; **she has overall direction of the project** 她负责这个项目的总体指导 **13** (consume) 吃 ‹*food*›; 喝 ‹*drink*›; 吸 ‹*cigarette*› **14** **~ (got)** (suffer from) 患; **to ~ (a) toothache** 牙痛; **to ~ measles/a cold** 患麻疹/感冒 **15** (experience) 经受 ‹*shock, heart attack*›; 接受 ‹*operation, checkup*›; **he had a crash in his new car** 他开新车出了车祸; **to ~ a boring day** 度过乏味的一天; **~ a nice day!** 祝你度过愉快的一天!; **a good time was had by all** 大家都过得很愉快; **to ~ sth. done** 遭受某事; **he had his car/watch**

stolen 他的汽车/手表被偷了; **I've (got) a pupil coming in 10 minutes** 我约了个学生10分钟以后来; **~ you got** *or* **do you ~ a cold coming on?** 你是不是要感冒了? **16** (accept into home) 接; **we're having the kids for the weekend** 我们这个周末要接孩子们回家; **we've (got) students living in the house** 我们家里有寄住学生 **17** (entertain) 在家招待; **we had some friends to dinner last night** 我们昨晚请了一些朋友来家里吃晚饭 **18** (cause or tell) 使; **to ~ sb. do sth.** 让某人做某事; **she's always having the builders in to do something or other** 她总是让建筑工人来家里做这做那; **the court had him pay the full costs** 法庭判他支付全部费用; **we'll soon ~ everything ready** 我们很快就会把一切准备就绪的; **to ~ sth. done** 让他人为自己做某事; **to ~ one's hair cut** 去理发; **they like to ~ stories read to them** 他们喜欢听别人给他们读故事; **to ~ sb./sth. doing sth.** 使某人/某物做某事; **he had his audience listening attentively** 他抓住了听众的注意力; **as luck/chance would ~ it** 幸运/碰巧的是; **rumour has it that ...** 据传… **19** (allow) 容忍; **I won't ~ this kind of behaviour!** 我不会容忍这种行为的!; **we can't ~ them staying in a hotel** 我们不能让他们住在旅馆里; **he won't ~ it that ...** 他拒绝接受… **20** **~ (got)** (hold) 拿着; **she had the glass in her hand** 她手里拿着玻璃杯; **she had him by the throat/by the arm** 她卡住了他的喉咙/抓住了他的胳膊 **21** **~ (got)** (put, keep in a position) 保持; **he had (got) his back to me** 他背对着我; **she had (got) her hands over her eyes** 她用手捂着双眼 **22** (be dealing with) 处理; **what we ~ here is a small group of extremists** 我们要对付的是一小撮极端分子; **over here, we ~ a painting by Picasso** 这边是毕加索的一幅画 **23** (become parent of) 生育 ‹*child, offspring*›; **she's having a baby (in May)** 她（五月份）要生孩子了; **our cat has had kittens** 我们的猫生小猫了 **24** **~ (got)** colloq (enjoy complete power over) 胜过; (baffle) 使迷惑不解; **I ~ (got) him now** 我把他制服了; **to ~ (got) sb. where you want them** 完全控制住某人; **I'll ~ you!** 我会收拾你的!; **you ~** *or* colloq **you've got me there!** 你把我问住了! **25** colloq (trick) 欺骗; **I'm afraid you've been had!** 恐怕你上当了! **26** colloq (have sex with) 和…上床

B *modal aux* (*3rd pers sing pres* **has**; *pt, pp* **had**) **1** (must) 必须; (be obliged to) 不得不; (giving advice, recommendation) 得 [用于提出劝告或建议]; **to ~ (got) to do sth.** 不得不做某事; **you don't ~ to** *or* **you haven't got to leave so early** 你不必这么早离开; **I ~ to admit, the idea of marriage scares me** 我得承认, 一想到结婚我就害怕; **to ~ (got) to do sth.** esp Brit 得做某事; **you simply ~ to get a new job** 你就是得找份新工作 **2** (expressing certainty, inevitability) 必定; **to ~ (got) to do sth.** esp Brit 必定做某事; **there has to be a reason for his strange behaviour** 他的古怪行为一定事出有因 **3** (expressing exasperation) 非得; **to ~ to do sth.** 非得做某事; **just tonight the bus had to be early** 偏偏今晚公共汽车非得早开; **why in the world did this ~ to happen?** 为什么就非得出这事呢?

C *v aux* (*3rd pers sing pres* **has**; *pt, pp* **had**) **1** (in perfect tenses) [用于完成时]; **she has lost her bag** 她把包丢了; **I've never been to Greece** 我从来没去过希腊; **to ~ done with sth.** esp Brit 结束某事 [指不愉快的事]; **let's ~ done with this silly argument!** 我们停止这种无聊的争吵吧! **2** (in conditional clauses) [用于条件句]; **if I had known** 如果我早知道的话; **had I taken the train, this would never ~ happened** 如果我坐了火车, 这事绝对不会发生

D **having** *aux* **1** (after) [与过去分词连用, 表示主要动词之前的动作]; **having finished his breakfast, he went out** 他吃完早饭就出去了 **2** (because, since) [与过去分词连用, 表示原因]; **I was cautious, having been deceived before** 由于以前受过骗, 我很谨慎 **3** (although) [与过去分词连用, 表示让步]; **having said that, I still think he's the best person for the job** 虽然话是那么说, 我仍然认为他是这个工作的最佳人选

Phrasal verbs

- **have back**

A [**~ sth. back, ~ back sth.**] *vt* 收回; **can we ~ our ball back?** 把球还给我们好吗?

B [**~ sb. back**] *vt* **1** (allow to return) 重新接纳; **she won't ~ him back** 她不肯与他重修旧好 **2** (invite in return) 回请

- **have down** *vt* [**~ sb. down**] **1** (from north) 邀请…南下; **we had the in-laws down from Scotland for the weekend** 这个周末我们请众位姻亲从苏格兰南下做客 **2** (from larger place) 邀请…来小地方; **we had friends down from London last week** 上星期我们邀请伦敦的朋友到舍下小聚

- **have on**

A *vt* (*also* **have got on**) **1** [**~ sth. on, ~ on sth.**] (be wearing) 穿着; **to ~ nothing on** 光着身子 **2** [**~ sth. on**] (be using) 开着 ‹*radio, light, heating, engine, music*› **3** [**~ sth. on**] (have arranged to do) 安排做

B [**~ sb. on**] *vt* Brit colloq (tease) 哄骗; **it's not true: he's only having you on** 那不是真的, 他只是在哄你

- **have out** *vt* [**~ sth. out**] **1** (cause to be removed) 拔掉 ‹*tooth*›; 切除 ‹*appendix*› **2** (settle) 把…讲个明白; **to ~ sth. out with sb.** 与某人把某事说明白; **we'd better ~ the matter out** 我们最好把这件事说清楚

- **have over** *vt* [**~ sb. over**] 请…来家里; **we had them over yesterday evening** 我们昨天晚上请他们来家里了

- **have round** *vt* Brit = **have over**

- **have up** *vt* [**~ sb. up**] Brit colloq 使出庭受审; **to be had up for sth.** 因某事出庭受审; **he was had up for dangerous driving** 他因危险驾驶被送上法庭

have-a-go *adj* Brit colloq 见义勇为的 ‹*hero*›

haven /ˈheɪvn/ *n* **1** Naut 避风港 **2** fig (refuge) 避难所; **a ~ of peace** 安宁的处所; **a ~ for wildlife** 野生生物的栖息地

have-nots *npl* colloq **the ~** 穷人; **the widening gap between the haves and the ~** 日益扩大的贫富差距

haven't /ˈhævnt/ colloq = **have not** ▸**have**

haver /ˈheɪvə(r)/ *vi* **1** Scot (talk nonsense) 胡说 **2** Brit (dither) 犹豫不决; (prevaricate) 支吾搪塞

haversack /ˈhævəsæk/ *n* 背包

haves /hævz/ *npl* colloq 富人; **the ~ and the have-nots** 富人与穷人

havoc /ˈhævək/ *n* [u] **1** (destruction) 大破坏; **to wreak ~ on sth.** 对…造成严重破坏 ‹*building, landscape*›; **to make ~ of sth.** 摧毁某物; **to cry ~** 警告灾祸将临 **2** fig (confusion) 大混乱; **to play ~ with sth.** 严重扰乱 ‹*plans, system*›; **junk food plays ~ with my digestion** 垃圾食品使我消化不良

haw¹ /hɔː/ *n* 山楂果

haw² *vi* 发"呃"声; **to hum** *or* **hem and ~** 支支吾吾

Hawaii /həˈwaɪi/ *pr n* 夏威夷州

Hawaiian /həˈwaɪən/ ▸**p. 503, p. 426**

A *adj* 夏威夷的; **the ~ Islands** 夏威夷群岛

B *n* **1** [c] (person) 夏威夷人 **2** [u] (language) 夏威夷土语

Hawaiian shirt *n* 夏威夷衬衫

hawk¹ /hɔːk/

A *n* **1** Zool 鹰; **to have eyes like a ~** 目光犀利 **2** Pol 鹰派人物

B *vi* 带鹰狩猎

hawk² *vi* colloq 大声清嗓

Phrasal verb

- **hawk up** *vt* [**~ sth. up**] 咳出 ‹*phlegm*›

hawk³ *vt* (sell) (door-to-door) 推销; (in street) 叫卖

hawker /ˈhɔːkə(r)/ *n* (in street) 叫卖小贩; (door-to-door) 上门推销员

hawk-eyed *adj* (sharp-eyed) 目光犀利的; (vigilant) 警惕的

hawkish /ˈhɔːkɪʃ/ *adj* **1** (hawk-like) 似鹰的; **his ~ nose** 他的鹰钩鼻; **keep a ~ eye on sth.** 密切关注某事物 **2** Pol 鹰派的 ‹*position, person*›; **take a ~ attitude** 采取强硬的态度

hawk moth *n* 天蛾

hawser /ˈhɔːzə(r)/ *n* (of jute) 缆索; (of steel) 钢缆

hawthorn /ˈhɔːθɔːn/ *n* 山楂树; **a ~ hedge** 山楂树篱; **~ berry/blossom** 山楂果/花

hay /heɪ/ *n* [u] 干草; **to hit the ~** colloq 上床睡觉; **to make ~ while the sun shines** lit 趁有太阳时晒干草; fig 趁热打铁; **to have a roll in the ~** colloq 交欢

hay: **~cock** *n* 小堆干草; **~ fever** ▸**p. 377** *n* [u] 枯草热; **~ fork** *n* 干草叉; **~ loft** *n* 干草厩楼; **~maker** *n* **1** (machine) 干草翻晒机; **2** (person) 制干草的工人; **3** colloq (blow) 重击; **~making** *n* [u] 干草制备; **~rick** *n* = **~stack**; **~seed** *n* esp Amer colloq pej 乡巴佬; **~stack** *n* 大干草堆

haywire /ˈheɪwaɪə(r)/ *adj pred* colloq **1** (malfunctioning) **to be/go ~** «*machine*» 出故障 **2** (spoiled) **to be/go ~** «*plan*» 乱了套 **3** Amer (crazy) **to be/go ~** 发疯

hazard /ˈhæzəd/

A *n* **1** [c] (danger) 危险; **a fire ~** 火灾隐患; **smoking is a ~ to health** 吸烟有害健康 **2** [c] (in golf) 障碍物 **3** [u] Games 掷骰子游戏

B *vt* **1** (endanger) 使冒风险; **to ~ one's life** 冒生命危险 **2** (venture) 试着说出 ‹*reply, opinion*›; **I can only ~ a guess** 我只能猜猜看

hazard lights *npl* 示警灯

hazardous /ˈhæzədəs/ *adj* 危险的 ‹*job, journey*›; 有害的 ‹*substance, weather conditions*›; 有风险的 ‹*venture*›

hazardous waste *n* [u] 有害废物

haze¹ /heɪz/ *n* **1** [c and u] (mist, cloud) 雾霭 **2** [c] fig (state of confusion) 迷糊; **in an alcoholic ~** 处于醉酒的迷糊状态; **I'm in a bit of a ~** 我脑子有点昏昏沉沉

Phrasal verb

- **haze over** *vi* 变得雾蒙蒙

haze² *vt* Amer sl (harass, humiliate) 捉弄

hazel /ˈheɪzl/

A *n* **1** (shrub) 榛树 **2** (nut) 榛子

B ▸**p. 134** *adj* 淡褐色的

hazelnut /ˈheɪzlnʌt/ *n* 榛子

haziness /ˈheɪzɪnɪs/ *n* [u] **1** (cloudiness) 雾蒙蒙 **2** (vagueness) 模糊

hazing /ˈheɪzɪŋ/ *n* [u] Amer sl 捉弄

hazy /ˈheɪzi/ *adj* **1** (misty, cloudy) 雾蒙蒙的; **a ~ moon** 朦胧的月亮; **it is very ~ today** 今天雾气很重 **2** fig (vague) 模糊的 ‹*idea, recollection, history*›; **to be ~ about sth.** 对某事物不明确; **I'm a little ~ about what to do next** 我有一点拿不准下一步该做什么

H: **~-beam** *n* 工字梁; **~ bomb** *n* 氢弹

HC *abbr* = **hot and cold water** 冷热水

HDTV *abbr* = **high-definition television** 高清晰度电视

HE *abbr* **1** = **high explosive** **2** (title) = **His/Her Excellency** 阁下

he /hiː, hi/

A *pron* **1** (referring to man, boy) 他 **2** (referring to male animal) 它 **3** dated (referring to person without specifying sex) 他 [现代英语中这一表达方式常以he/she或they代替]; (referring to animal) 它; **every-one may do what ~ likes** 每个人都可以做自己想做的事 **4** dated (referring to any person) 他 [指任何人]; **~ who hesitates is lost** Prov

h

当断不断，必受其患 **5** **He** (referring to God) 他 [指上帝]

B *n* **1** (man) 男子; (boy) 男孩; **is the baby a ～ or a she?** 婴儿是男的还是女的? **2** (male animal) 雄性动物; **the dog's definitely a ～** 这条狗绝对是公狗

head /hed/ ▸**p. 71**

A *n* **1** [c] Anat 头; **to nod/shake one's ～** 点头/摇头; **the top of one's ～** 头顶; **a man with a good ～ of hair** 长着一头好头发的男子; **to get/have one's ～ down** 低下头; Brit fig (sleep) 睡觉; (work hard) 埋头工作; **to keep one's ～ down** lit 低着头; fig 保持低姿态; **with one's ～ in one's hands** 双手抱头; **from ～ to foot** *or* **toe** 从头到脚; **to count ～s** 清点人数; **to go over sb.'s ～** (go to sb.'s superior) 越过某人; **to stand on one's ～** 倒立; **to do sth. standing on one's ～** 轻而易举地做某事; **to stand** *or* **turn sth. on its ～** 推翻 ‹*theory, idea*›; **on your (own) ～ be it!** 后果自负! ; **to turn ～s** 引人注目; **not to be able to make ～(s) or tail of sth.** 完全不理解某事物; **to bite sb.'s ～ off** colloq 对某人大喊大叫; **to laugh/sneeze/talk** *etc.* **one's ～ off** colloq 狂笑不止/猛打喷嚏/聊个没完等; **off the top of one's ～** 不假思索地; **to give sb. their ～** 让某人随意行事; **to give a horse its ～** 放松缰绳让马飞奔; **to give (sb.) ～** taboo sl (对某人) 行口交; ▸**lion 1, sore A1** **2** [c] (size of head) 一个头; **to be a/half a ～ taller than sb., to be taller than sb. by a/half a ～** 高出某人一/半个头; **to win by a ～** 以一个马头的优势获胜; fig 以微弱的优势获胜; **to be ～ and shoulders above sb.** 比某人好得多 **3** [c] (mind) 头脑; **to get sth. into sb.'s ～** 使某人明白某事; **to get it into sb.'s ～ that ...** 使某人明白…; **to get sth. into one's ～** 偏偏相信某事; **to get it into one's ～ that ...** 偏偏相信…; **to put sth. into sb.'s ～** 使某人相信某事; **to take it into one's ～ to do sth.** 心血来潮想做某事; **to get** *or* **put sth. out of one's ～** 把某事物忘掉; **to go (right) out of one's ～** colloq (立刻) 被忘记; **to do sth. in one's ～** 在考虑某事; **what's going on in her ～?** 她在想什么?; **use your ～!** colloq 动动脑子! ; **to be** *or* **go over sb.'s ～** 超出某人的理解力; **to talk over sb.'s ～** 说话使某人费解; **to bother** *or* **worry one's ～ about sth.** colloq 担心某事; **to put their/our/your ～s together** colloq 集思广益; **to keep/lose one's ～** 保持头脑冷静/惊慌失措; **to turn sb.'s ～** 使某人得意忘形; **to go to sb.'s ～** «*alcohol*» 使某人上头; «*success*» 冲昏某人的头脑; **to go off one's ～** Brit colloq 发疯; **out of one's ～** colloq 发疯; **to be weak** *or* **soft in the ～** colloq 愚蠢; **not right in the ～** colloq 头脑不正常; **two ～s are better than one** Prov 两人智慧胜一人 **4** [c] (ability) **to have a ～ for sth.** 有某方面的头脑; **to have a ～ for figures** 长于算术; **to have a good/no ～ for heights** 不恐高/恐高 **5** [c] colloq (headache) 头痛; **to have a bad ～** 头痛得厉害 **6** [u] (number of people) 人数; (number of animals) 头数; **a** *or* **per ～** 每人; **10 ～ of cattle** 10 头牛 **7** [c] (tip of pin, nail, match) 头; (tip of spear, tool, racket, club) 端头; ▸**nail A1** **8** [c] Hort, Culin (of flower) 头状花序; (of cabbage) 叶球 **9** [c] (front) 前头; **the ～ of the queue** 队首 **10** [c] (top) (of list, column, mast) 顶端; (of valley) 上端; (of river, lake) 源头; (of glacier) 低端; **the ～ of the stairs/page** 楼梯顶上/页面上方; **the ～ of the table/bed** 桌子头/床头; **the ～ of the pier/jetty** 码头/突堤的前端 **11** [c] (leader) 领导; **the ～ of the family** (of nuclear family) 一家之主; (of clan) 大家长; **the ～ of government/state/the tribe** 政府首脑/国家元首/部落首领; **～ of department** Comm 部门经理; Admin 部长; Sch 系主任; **with sb. at the ～** 以某人为首 **12** [c] Sch (**～ teacher**) 校长 **13** [c] Audio, Comput 磁头 **14** [c] (on beer) 酒头; **to have a good ～** 有不少泡沫 **15** [c] Med (on boil) 脓头; **to come to a ～** lit «*spot*» 出脓头; fig «*situation*» 到了紧要关头; **to bring sth. to a ～** 使…到达紧要关头 ‹*crisis*› **16** [c] (water pressure) 水压; (height of water) 水位; **an 8 m ～ of water** 高 8 米的水位 **17** [c] Mech **a ～ of steam** lit 蒸汽压力; fig 充沛的精力; **to have a good ～ of steam** 发展良好 **18** [c] (heading, topic) 主题; **these questions can be grouped under three ～s** 这些问题可归入三个主题 **19** [c] (promontory) 岬

B **heads** *n* [u] [硬币的] 正面; **～s or tails?** 正面还是反面? ; **～s I win; tails you lose** 无论如何都是我赢

C *modif* **1** Anat 头部的 ‹*injury*› **2** (chief) 领头的; **a ～ cook/gardener** 厨师长/首席园艺师

D *vt* **1** (be at top of) 排在…的前头 ‹*queue, parade, list*› **2** (lead) 主管 ‹*company*›; 负责 ‹*investigation*›; 带领 ‹*team*›; 领导 ‹*rebellion*›; **a delegation ～ed by the chairman** 由主席率领的代表团 **3** (give title to) 给…加标题; **to ～ a chapter/article with sth.** 给章节/文章加某标题; **to ～ a letter with one's address** 将地址写在信的最上面; **to be ～ed 'confidential'** 给标上 "confidential" (密件) **4** (steer) 使朝某方向行进; **to ～ sb./sth. towards/away from sth.** 使某人/某物朝某处行进/离开某处; **to ～ the sheep towards the gate** 朝大门赶羊; **to ～ the boat into the wind** 驾船迎风行驶; **to be ～ed ...** 朝…移动; **to be ～ed this/sb.'s way** 朝这边来/朝某人走去 **5** Sport **to ～ the ball** 用头顶球

E *vi* 朝某方向行进; **to ～ home** 回家; **to ～ west/in the wrong direction** 朝西/朝错误的方向前进; **to be ～ing this/sb.'s way** 朝这边来/朝某人走去; **bad weather is ～ing this way** 坏天气要来了

Phrasal verbs

- **head for** *vt* [**～ for sb./sth.**]
  1 (move towards) 朝…移动; **we were ～ing** *or* **～ed for the coast** 我们那时正向着海岸进发 **2** fig (approach) 即将遇到; **to be ～ing for disaster/a breakdown** 将遭遇灾难/快要精神崩溃; **the economy is ～ed for recession** 经济面临衰退; **to be ～ed for success** 即将获得成功
- **head off**
  A *vi* (move off) 朝…移动; **to ～ off for/in the direction of/across the village** 朝村庄走去/朝村庄方向走去/穿过村庄
  B *vt* [**～ sb./sth. off, ～ off sb./sth.**]
  1 (intercept) 拦截 **2** fig (forestall) 阻止; **to ～ off an argument** 制止一场争执
- **head up** *vt* [**～ sth. up, ～ up sth.**] 领导 ‹*department, team*›

headache /ˈhedeɪk/ ▸**p. 377** *n* **1** 头痛; **to have a ～** 头痛; **to give sb. a ～** 使某人头痛 **2** fig (thing) 令人头痛的事物; (person) 令人头痛的人; **the new airport security system is a real ～** 新机场的安全系统非常令人头痛

headachy /ˈhedeɪki/ *adj* colloq 头痛的; **to feel ～** 感到头痛

head: ～band *n* 头带; **～banger** *n* colloq **1** (fan) 重金属音乐爱好者; (performer) 重金属音乐演奏者; **2** (eccentric person) 疯子; **～board** *n* 床头板; **～ boy** *n* Brit 男生代表

headbutt /ˈhedbʌt/

A *n* 用头的顶撞; **he was knocked down by a ～** 他被一头撞倒在地

B *vt* 用头顶撞

head: ～ case *n* colloq 疯子; **～ cheese** *n* [u] Amer 碎头肉冻; **～ cold** ▸**p. 377** *n* 头伤风; **～ cook and bottle washer** *n* hum 勤杂工; **～count** *n* **1** (act of counting) 点人数; **to do a ～count** 清点人数; **2** (total staff) 总人数; **～dress** *n* 头饰

headed /ˈhedɪd/ *adj* 有信头的 ‹*paper, stationery*›

-headed /ˈhedɪd/ *combining form* (of particular colour, type) 有…头的; (with a particular number) 有…个头的; **a black～ bird** 黑头鸟; **a scaly ～ reptile** 头部有鳞的爬行动物; **a three～ monster** 三头怪兽

header /ˈhedə(r)/ *n* **1** (in soccer) 头球 **2** (text) 眉头词 **3** colloq (dive) 头朝下的一跳; (falling) 头朝下的跌落; **to take a ～ off from/into sth.** 头朝下从某物上跳下/跳入某物 **4** Constr (brick) 露头砖; (stone) 露头石

header tank *n* 上水箱

head: ～first *adv* **1** lit (headlong) 头朝前地; **to fall ～first down the stairs** 一头栽下楼梯; **2** fig (without thinking) 仓促地; **to rush ～first into marriage** 轻率地结婚; **～ gasket** *n* 汽缸盖垫片; **～ gear** *n* [u] 头戴之物; **～ girl** *n* Brit 女生代表; **～ height** *n* [u] 一人的高度; **the shelf was at ～ height** 搁板在一人高处

headhunt /ˈhedhʌnt/

A *vt* (seek to recruit) 物色; (recruit successfully) 挖到

B *vi* 挖人

head: ～hunter *n* **1** Comm (agency) [物色人才的] 猎头公司; (person) 物色人才者; **2** (tribe member) 猎头族人; **～hunting** *n* [u] **1** Comm 猎头; **2** (tribal practice) 猎取敌人首级

headiness /ˈhedɪnɪs/ *n* [u] **1** (exhilaration) 令人兴奋 **2** (of alcoholic drink) 上头 **3** (of scent) 浓烈

heading /ˈhedɪŋ/ *n* **1** (title of text) 标题; (at top of stationery) 信头 **2** (division, topic) 主题; **philosophy comes under the ～ of 'Humanities'** 哲学属于 "人文学科" **3** Aviat 航向; Naut 艏向

head: ～lamp *n* = **headlight**; **～land** /-lənd/ *n* 岬角

headless /ˈhedlɪs/ *adj* **1** (with no head) 无头的 ‹*corpse, ghost, animal*›; **like a ～ chicken** 惊慌失措地; **to run around like a ～ chicken** 像无头苍蝇一样瞎忙 **2** Tech 无头的 ‹*nail, tack*› **3** (having lost its head) 头掉了的 ‹*pin, flower*›

headlight /ˈhedlaɪt/ *n* 前灯

headline /ˈhedlaɪn/

A *n* **1** Journ 大标题; **to hit the ～s** colloq 登上头条新闻; **to make the ～s** 成为重要新闻; **～ news** 头条新闻 **2** **headlines** Radio, TV (part of a news broadcast) 摘要新闻; (replacing a full news programme) 新闻摘要

B *vt* **1** Journ 给…加标题 ‹*article, feature*› **2** Mus (lead) 担当…的主角 ‹*concert*›

C *vi* 担当主角

headline: ～-grabber *n* colloq 有重要新闻价值的题材; **～-grabbing** *adj* colloq 有重要新闻价值的; **～ inflation** *n* [u] 整体通货膨胀率

headlong /ˈhedlɒŋ/

A *adv* **1** (headfirst) 头朝前地; **to fall ～ into the lake** 一头栽进湖中 **2** (rapidly) 迅猛地 **3** fig (without thinking) 莽撞地; **don't rush ～ into marriage** 不要草率结婚

B *adj attrib* **1** (headfirst) 头朝前的; **a ～ dive** 俯冲跳水 **2** (rapid) 迅猛的; **a ～ flight** 高速飞行 **3** fig (hasty) 莽撞的; **a ～ rush to do sth.** 仓促去做某事

head: ～ louse *n* (*pl* **～ lice**) 头虱; **～man** /-mæn/ *n* 头领; **～master** ▸**p. 409** *n* esp Brit 男校长; **～mistress** ▸**p. 409** *n* esp Brit 女校长; **～ nurse** *n* Amer 护士长; **～ office** *n* **1** (office) 总部; **2** (managers) 总部经理人员

head-on

A *adv* **1** (front-to-front) 头对头地; **the two trains crashed ～** 两列火车迎头相撞; **we collided ～ in the corridor** 我们在走廊里迎面相撞 **2** (with the front of a vehicle) 正面地; **her car hit the wall ～** 她的汽车一头撞在墙上 **3** fig (directly) 直接地; **to meet sth. ～** 直面某事物; **to tackle a problem ～** 毫不回避地应对问题

B *adj* **1** lit (front-to-front) 头对头的; **a ～ collision** 正面相撞 **2** fig (direct) 直接的; **a ～**

approach to the problem 直截了当处理问题的态度

head: ~phones *npl* 耳机; **a pair of ~phones** 一副耳机; **~quarters** *npl* + *v sing or pl* 1 (of a company) 总部; 2 Mil 司令部; **~rest** *n* (gen) 头靠; Aut 头枕; **~ restraint** *n* 头枕; **~room** *n* [u] 1 (for person) 内部高度; **we haven't got enough ~room to sit comfortably** 高度不够，我们坐得不舒服; 2 (for vehicle) 净空高度; **max ~room 4 metres** 限高4米; **~sail** /ˈhedseɪl, -səl/ *n* 艏斜帆; **~scarf** *n* 头巾; **~set** *n* 头戴式受话器

headship /ˈhedʃɪp/ *n* esp Brit 1 [c] (position) 校长职务 2 [u] (state of being head) 领导地位; **under her ~** 在她的领导下

head: ~shrinker *n* colloq 1 esp Amer pej (psychiatrist) 精神病医师; (psychoanalyst) 精神分析学家; 2 Hist (headhunter) 猎头族人; **~square** *n* 头巾; **~stand** *n* 倒立; **to do a ~stand** 做一个竖蜻蜓动作; **~ start** *n* (gen) 先发优势; Sport 先起动; **to give sb. a ~ start on** *or* **over sb.** 使某人比某人领先一步; **to have a ~ start** 领先一步; **~stone** *n* 1 (on grave) 墓碑; 2 Archit 拱顶石; **~strong** *adj* 固执任性的; **~ tax** *n* 人头税; **~ teacher** ▸p. 409 *n* esp Brit 校长

head-to-head
A *adj attrib* 正面对抗的; **a ~ battle** 正面战斗
B *adv* 正面对抗地; **to come ~** 对峙
C *n* 正面对抗

head: ~-up display *n* 平视显示; **~ waiter** ▸p. 409 *n* 领班; **~waters** *npl* 上游源头; **~way** *n* [u] 1 lit 前进; **to make ~way** 前进; 2 fig 进展; **to make ~way** 取得进展; **~wind** *n* 顶头风; **to fly against a ~wind** 逆风飞行; **~word** *n* 词目

heady /ˈhedi/ *adj* 1 (exhilarating) 令人兴奋的 ‹*experience, victory*›; **to be ~ with success** 因成功而感到飘飘然; **the ~ days of youth** 令人陶醉的青少年时代 2 (intoxicating) 上头的 ‹*drink*› 3 (strong) 浓烈的 ‹*perfume, fragrance*›

heal /hiːl/
A *vt* 1 lit 治愈 ‹*person, injury, wound*› 2 fig (alleviate) 减轻 ‹*suffering, pain*›; **time ~s all sorrows** 时间会抚平所有的伤痛 3 fig (make right) 纠正; **to ~ a breach** *or* **rift** 弥合裂痕
B *vi* «*wound, cut*» 愈合; «*rash*» 痊愈

Phrasal verbs
- **heal over** *vi* 痊愈
- **heal up** *vi* = **heal B**

healer /ˈhiːlə(r)/ *n* 1 (practitioner of alternative health practices) 另类治疗师 2 = **faith healer** 3 (sth. that alleviates a situation) 缓解物; **time is a great ~** 时间是良药

healing /ˈhiːlɪŋ/
A *n* [u] 1 (of person) 康复 2 (of wound, cut) 愈合
B *adj attrib* 有疗效的; **to have a ~ effect** 有疗效; **the ~ process** 康复过程; **the gift of ~ hands** 手到病除的本领

health /helθ/ *n* [u] 1 (physical or mental condition) 健康状况; **mental ~** 心理健康; **be in good/bad ~** 身体好/不好 2 (well-being) 健康; **she was glowing with ~** 她身体健康，容光焕发; **Ministry of H~** 卫生部 3 (in toasts) **to drink (to) sb.'s ~** 为某人的健康干杯; **(here's) to your (good) ~!** Brit 祝你健康! 4 fig (of economy, finances, environment etc.) 状况

health: ~ and safety *n* [u] 健康与安全; **H~ and Safety Executive** *n* Brit 健康与安全管理局; **H~ and Safety Inspector** ▸p. 409 *n* Brit 健康与安全检查员; **H~ Authority** *n* Brit 卫生局; **~ benefits** *npl* 1 (good effects on health) 对健康的益处; 2 (money) 健康保险金; **~ card** *n* Can 健康卡; **~care** *n* [u] 医疗保健; **~ centre** *n* Brit 医疗中心; **~ check** *n* 体检; **~ clinic** *n* = **~ centre**; **~ club** *n* 健身俱乐部; **~ education** *n* [u] 健康教育; **~ farm** *n* esp Brit 健身庄; **~ food** *n* [c and u] 保健食品; **~ food shop** *n* 保健食品商店

healthful /ˈhelθfl/, **health-giving** /ˈhelθɡɪvɪŋ/ *adjs* 有益健康的

health hazard *n* 健康危害物

healthily /ˈhelθɪli/ *adv* 1 (in a healthy manner) 健康地 ‹*live, eat*› 2 (in good way) 正常合理地 ‹*suspicious, unimpressed, sceptical*›

health: ~ inspector ▸p. 409 *n* Brit 社区卫生检查员; **~ insurance** *n* [u] 健康保险; **~ officer** ▸p. 409 *n* 卫生官员; **~ resort** *n* 疗养胜地; **~ risk** *n* = **health hazard**; **H~ Secretary** *n* Brit 卫生部长; **H~ Service** *n* Brit 公共医疗卫生服务; **~ spa** *n* 疗养地; **~ tourism** *n* [u] (to improve one's health) 保健旅游; (for medical treatment) 求医旅游; **~ visitor** ▸p. 409 *n* Brit 家访护士; **~ warning** *n* 健康警告

healthy /ˈhelθi/ *adj* 1 (in good health) 健康的 ‹*person, animal*›; 茁壮的 ‹*tree, crop*›; (manifesting good health) 显示健康的 ‹*skin, hair*›; **to have a ~ appetite** 胃口好 2 (good for the health) 有益健康的 3 (successful, working well) 兴旺发达的 ‹*economy*›; 运转良好的 ‹*machinery*›; **his finances are none too ~** 他的经济状况一点儿都不好; **your car doesn't sound very ~** hum 你的车听声音不太正常 4 (good, reasonable) 正常合理的; **a ~ interest in sth./doing sth.** 对某事/做某事的正当兴趣; **to have a ~ respect for sb./sth.** 对某人/某事表现出应有的尊重

heap /hiːp/
A *n* 1 (pile) 堆; **to pile sth. up in a ~/in ~s** 把某物堆成一堆/许多堆; **to fall** *or* **collapse in an exhausted ~** 累得瘫倒; **at the top/bottom of the ~** colloq (of an organization or society) 在高层/底层 2 colloq (a lot) 大量; **~s of** (plenty) 许多; (too much) 太多; **that child is a (whole) ~ of trouble** 那孩子是个大麻烦 3 colloq pej (car) 破汽车
B **heaps** *adv* Brit colloq 非常; **to feel ~s better** 感觉好多了; **~s more room** 大得多的空间; **thanks ~s** 非常感谢
C *vt* 1 (pile) = **heap up** 2 fig (shower) 倾注; **to ~ scorn on sb.** 对某人大加嘲弄; **they ~ed honours on him** 他们授予他种种荣誉

Phrasal verb
- **heap up** *vt* [**~ sth. up, ~ up sth.**] 堆放; **to ~ sb. up with sth.** 大量地给予某人某物; **to ~ sth. up with sth.** 在某物上堆满某物; **she ~ed up the food on our plates** 她在我们的盘子里盛满了食物

heaped /hiːpt/ *adj* 堆满的; **a ~ spoonful** 满满的一匙; **a dish ~ with cakes** 装满糕点的盘子

hear /hɪə(r)/
A *vt* (*pt, pp* **heard** /hɜːd/) 1 (perceive with ears) 听到; **can you ~ me?** 你能听到我说话吗?; **to ~ sb./sth. do** *or* **doing sth.** 听到某人/某物在做某事; **he was heard to boast** 有人听到他吹牛; **to ~ sth. done** 听到有人做某事; **the first time I heard the violin played** 我第一次听到小提琴演奏; **to ~ him talk, you'd think (that) ...** 听他讲话，你会以为…; **we'll never ~ the end of it** 这事没完没了; **to ~ the end** *or* **last of sb./sth.** 最后一次听到关于某人/某事物的消息; **to make oneself** *or* **one's voice heard** lit 大声说话; fig 发表见解; **I can't ~ myself think** 我都给吵昏头了; **let's ~ it for ...** colloq 让我们为…鼓掌 2 (find out about) 听说 ‹*news*›; **to ~ the results** 得知成绩; **to ~ (it said) (that) ...** 听说…; **so I ~** 我听说了; **I've heard it all before** 这话我听得多了; **I've heard that one before!** (heard that excuse) 别蒙我了!; **to ~ tell (of sth.)** formal 听说(某事物) 3 (listen to) 听 ‹*lecture, music*›; **to ~ sb. do sth.** 听某人做某事; **to ~ what sb. has to say** 听某人要说的话; **do you ~ (me)?** 听清楚没有? 4 Jur 审理 ‹*case*›; 听取 ‹*plea, testimony*›; 听取…陈述 ‹*defendant*›; **to ~ the evidence** 听证 5 formal (grant) «*God, king*» 倾听并接受 ‹*prayer, plea*›; **~ my prayer** 请倾听并接受我的祈求
B *vi* (*pt, pp* **heard**) 听见; **I can't** *or* **don't ~ very well** 我耳背
C *excl* **~! ~!** 是啊! 是啊! [表示同意某人所说的话]

Phrasal verbs
- **hear from** *vt* [**~ from sb.**]
1 (get news from) 得到…的消息; **I look forward to ~ing from you** (in letter) 盼望收到你的信; **you'll be ~ing from me!** (threat) 你等着吧! 2 Radio, TV 听…发表观点 ‹*politician*›; 听…讲述经历 ‹*eyewitness*›
- **hear of** *vt* [**~ of sb./sth.**]
1 (find out about) 得知 ‹*news, vacancy*›; **the first/last I heard of him ...** 我最初/最后一次听到关于他的消息…; **he hasn't been heard of since** 此后再也没有关于他的消息 2 (become aware of) 知道; **I've never heard of anything so stupid!** 我从未听说过如此荒唐无聊之事!; **haven't you heard of asking permission?** 你不知道要征得同意吗? 3 (consider) 同意; **I won't ~ of it!** 我不会允许的!
- **hear out** *vt* [**~ sb. out**] 听…说完

hearer /ˈhɪəre(r)/ *n* 听者; **his ~s were enthralled** 他的听众被迷住了

hearing /ˈhɪərɪŋ/ *n* 1 [u] (sense, faculty) 听觉; **his ~ is not very good** 他听力不太好; **~ loss/damage/test** 听觉丧失/损伤/测试 2 [u] (earshot of a person or sound) 听得见的距离; **in** *or* **within/out of sb.'s ~** 在某人听力所及的范围之内/之外; **I called his name, but he was already out of ~** 我叫他的名字，但是他已经走远听不到了 3 [c] (chance to be heard) 被倾听的机会; **to get a ~** 获得发言的机会; **to give sb./sth. a ~** 听某人/某方的申诉 4 [c] Jur 审讯; **a preliminary ~ before the magistrates** 地方法官的预审

hearing aid *n* 助听器

hearing-impaired
A *adj* 听觉受损的
B *npl* **the ~** 听觉受损的人

hearken /ˈhɑːkən/ *vi* archaic 倾听; **to ~ to sth.** 倾听某事

hearsay /ˈhɪəseɪ/ *n* [u] 传闻; **it's only ~** 这只是道听途说

hearsay evidence *n* [u] 传闻证据

hearse /hɜːs/ *n* 灵车

heart /hɑːt/ *n* 1 [c] Anat, Zool (organ) 心脏; **~ muscle** 心肌; **to have a ~ condition** 有心脏病; **my ~ missed** *or* **skipped a beat** 我的心跳停顿了一下; **his ~ stopped beating** lit 他的心脏停止了跳动; fig 他吓得要命; **to learn/know sth. by ~** 背诵/熟记某事 2 [c] Anat (part of chest) 胸前; **hand on ~**, **with one's hand on one's ~** lit, fig 手放胸前发誓 3 [u and c] Culin 心; **chicken/sheep's ~** 鸡心/羊心 4 [c] (site of emotion, love) 爱心; **his ~ was troubled** liter 他忧心忡忡; **to give sb. one's ~, to give/lose one's ~ to sb.** liter 爱上某人; **to win/capture/steal sb.'s ~** 赢得/获得/博得某人的喜爱; **to take sb. to one's ~** 喜欢上某人; **to break sb.'s ~** 使某人心碎; **to cry fit to break one's ~** 伤心痛哭; **it does one's ~ good to do sth.** 做某事令人心情愉快; **with a heavy/light ~** 心情沉重/轻松; **to sing/play one's ~ out** 尽情歌唱/演奏; **to sob one's ~ out** 痛哭; **one's ~ goes out to sb.** 同情某人; **the way to sb.'s ~** 赢得某人欢心的方法; **the way to a man's ~ is through his stomach** Prov 想要征服男人的心，首先要征服男人的胃; **two ~s that beat as one** 心心相印; ▸**cockle 2, rule B3, sleeve A1** 5 [u and c] (mind, feelings, nature) 内心; **to have what one's ~ desires** 拥有心中想要的东西; **to put one's ~ into one's work** 专心致志地工作; **at ~** 本质上; **I'm a Londoner at ~** 骨子里我是伦敦人; **to have sth. at ~** 关心某事物; **to have sb.'s**

h

(best) interests at ～ 关心某人的利益; **in one's** ～ **(of** ～**s)** 在内心深处; **from the (bottom of one's)** ～ 衷心地; **to come from the** ～ 出自真心; **to open one's** ～ **to sb.** 向某人敞开心扉; **to take sth. to** ～ 把某事物放在心上; **don't take it to** ～ 别往心里去; **to follow one's** ～ 按照心意做事; **with all one's** ～ 全心全意地; **to wish/hope with all one's** ～ **that ...** 衷心祝愿/希望…; **sb.'s** ～ **is not in sth.** 某人心思不在某事物上; **to set one's** ～ **on sth./doing sth.** 一心想得到某物/做某事; **to be close** *or* **dear** *or* **near to sb.'s** ～ (important) 在某人看来十分重要; (dear) 为某人所爱; **sb. after one's own** ～ 中意的某人; **to do sth. to one's** ～**'s content** 尽情地做某事; **to have a change of** ～ 态度有所变化; **to have a cold/soft** ～ 性情冷酷/温和; **to have a warm/hard/kind** ～ 心肠热/硬/好; **to have no** ～ 残酷无情; **to be all** ～ iron 心肠太好了; **not to have the** ～ **(to do sth.)** 不情愿（做某事）; **to find it in one's** ～ **to do sth.** 愿意做某事; **sb.'s** ～ **is in the right place** 某人的心地是善良的; **have a** ～**!** colloq 发发善心吧！ 6 [u and c] (courage) 勇气; **to lose** ～ 灰心; **to take** ～ **(from sth.)** 受到（某事物的）鼓舞; ▸**faint A3** 7 [c] (essence) 实质; **the** ～ **of the matter** 事情的实质; **to get** *or* **go to the** ～ **of sth.** 触及某事的核心; **to lie at the** ～ **of sth.** 是某事物的核心 8 [c] (middle) 中心; **in the** ～ **of sth.** 在某物的中心; **an oasis in the** ～ **of the desert** 沙漠中间的一片绿洲; **in the** ～ **of winter** 在隆冬 9 [c] (of lettuce, artichoke, celery) 菜心 10 [c] (shape) 心形 11 [c] (in cards) 红桃; **the ace/five/king of** ～**s** 红桃 A/五/老 K; **to play a** ～ 出一张红桃

heart: ～**ache** *n* [c and u] (gen) 痛心; (romantic) 伤心; **divorce may involve considerable** ～**ache** 离婚可能令人很伤心; ～ **attack** *n* 心脏病发作; **to have a** ～ **attack** lit, fig 心脏病发作; **she nearly had a** ～ **attack when she heard the news** 听到那个消息时她差点儿心脏病发作; ～**beat** *n* 心跳; ～ **block** *n* [u] 心传导阻滞; ～**break** *n* [u] 心碎; ～**breaker** *n* 令人心碎的人; **she's a** ～**breaker** 她是个水性杨花的人; ～**breaking** *adj* 令人心碎的; **it was** ～**breaking to see him leave** 看到他离去令人心碎; ～**broken** *adj* 心碎的; **to be** ～**broken** 伤心至极; ～**burn** *n* [u] 胃灼热; ～ **disease** *n* [u and c] 心脏病

-hearted /ˈhɑːtɪd/ *combining form* 有…之心的; **a pure/generous**～ **person** 心地纯洁的/宽宏大量的人

hearten /ˈhɑːtn/ *vt* 使振作

heartening /ˈhɑːtnɪŋ/ *adj* 令人振奋的

heart: ～ **failure** *n* [u] 心力衰竭; ～**felt** *adj* 衷心的 ‹*sympathy, gratitude, wish*›; 诚挚的 ‹*appeal, plea, prayer*›

hearth /hɑːθ/ *n* 壁炉炉床; **by the** ～ 在壁炉旁; ～ **and home** liter 温暖舒适的家庭生活; **a longing for** ～ **and home** 对温馨家庭生活的渴望

hearth rug *n* 壁炉前地毯

heartily /ˈhɑːtɪli/ *adv* 1 (warmly) 热情友好地 ‹*welcome, greet*› 2 (enthusiastically) 热诚地 ‹*approve, support*›; **he** ～ **agreed with her** 他由衷地赞同她 3 (vigorously) 起劲地 ‹*kick, slap, work*›; 尽情地 ‹*play, cry*›; **to laugh/sing** ～ 开怀大笑/放声歌唱 4 (healthily) 胃口好地; **to eat** ～ 放开肚子大吃 5 (strongly) 强烈地 ‹*resent, dislike, disapprove*›; (extremely) 极其 ‹*glad, relieved*›; **to be** ～ **sick of sth.** 对某事物极其腻烦

heartiness /ˈhɑːtɪnɪs/ *n* [u] 1 (warmth of greeting, reception) 热情友好 2 (whole-heartedness of approval, support) 热诚 3 (vigour) (of person) 健壮; (of voice, laugh) 尽情; (of manner) 快活; **the** ～ **of his appetite** 他食欲的旺盛

heartland /ˈhɑːtlænd/ *n* (*also* **heartlands,** *pl*) 中心区域; **the desert** ～**(s)** 沙漠腹地; **the industrial** ～**(s) of the north** 北方的工业中心

heartless /ˈhɑːtlɪs/ *adj* 无情的; **a** ～ **father** 狠心的父亲; ～ **treatment (of sb./sth.)**（对某人/某物的）冷酷对待

heartlessly /ˈhɑːtlɪsli/ *adv* 无情地

heartlessness /ˈhɑːtlɪsnɪs/ *n* [u] 无情

heart: ～**-lung machine** *n* 人工心肺机; ～ **monitor** *n* 心脏监测器; ～ **murmur** *n* 心杂音; **to have a** ～ **murmur** 心脏有杂音; ～ **rate** *n* 心率; ～**rending** *adj* 令人心碎的; ～**-searching** *n* [u] 内省; **after much** ～**-searching** 考虑再三之后; ～**-shaped** *adj* 心形的; ～**-stopping** *adj* 惊心动魄的; **a** ～**-stopping moment** 令人心悸的一刻; **it was a** ～**-stopping final** 这场决赛非常刺激; ～**strings** *npl* **to pluck** *or* **tug** *or* **pull (at) sb.'s** ～**strings** 拨动某人的心弦; ～ **surgeon** ▸**p. 409** *n* 心脏外科医生; ～ **surgery** *n* [u] 1 (branch of medicine) 心脏外科学; 2 (surgery on the heart) 心脏外科手术; ～**-throb** *n* colloq 大众情人; **he's a real** ～**-throb** 他是个真正的万人迷

heart-to-heart

A *adj attrib* 真诚坦率的 ‹*discussion, conversation, chat*›; **a** ～ **talk** 倾心交谈

B *adv* 真诚坦率地 ‹*talk, discuss*›

C *n* 真诚坦率的交谈; **to have a** ～ **(with sb.)**（与某人）谈心

heart: ～ **transplant** *n* 心脏移植手术; ～ **trouble** *n* [u] 心脏病; **to have** ～ **trouble** 有心脏病; ～**-warming** *adj* 暖人心房的; **a** ～**-warming sight** 感人的场面; ～**wood** *n* [u] 心材

hearty /ˈhɑːti/ *adj* 1 (warm, friendly) 热情友好的 2 (enthusiastic) 热诚的 ‹*approval, support, agreement*› 3 (jolly and vigorous) 快活的 ‹*person, manner*›; 尽情的 ‹*laugh*›; 有力的 ‹*voice, kick*›; **a** ～ **slap** 猛的一拍 4 (healthy, strong) 健壮的 ‹*person*› 5 (robust, healthy) 旺盛的 ‹*appetite*›; 胃口好的 ‹*eater*›; (substantial) 丰盛的 ‹*meal*› 6 (extreme) 强烈的 ‹*dislike, disapproval*›

heat /hiːt/

A *n* 1 [u and c] (high temperature) 热; **intense** ～ 灼热; ～ **rises** 热量上升; **if you can't stand the** ～**, get out of the kitchen** fig 怕热就别进厨房 2 [u and c] (level of temperature) 温度; **the** ～ **in the greenhouse** 暖房里的温度 3 [u and c] (hot weather) 炎热天气; **summer** ～ 夏日酷暑; **to suffer from the** ～ 饱受酷暑之苦; **a dry/sticky** ～ 燥热/潮湿闷热的天气 4 [u and c] Culin (of oven, stove) 炉火; **to turn the** ～ **up/down** 将炉火调高/低; **to cook at a low/moderate** ～ 用低温/中温烹饪 5 [u] (heating) 暖气; **to turn** *or* **put the** ～ **on/off** 打开/关闭暖气; **to turn the** ～ **up/down** 将暖气开大/关小 6 [u] fig (passion) 激情; **in the** ～ **of the moment** 在紧迫的情势下; **to take the** ～ **out of sth.** 平息 ‹*situation, dispute*› 7 [u] fig (pressure) 压力; **to put** *or* **turn the** ～ **on sb. (to do sth.)** 对某人施加压力（做某事）; **to turn up the** ～ **(on sb.)** 增加（某人的）压力; **to take the** ～ **off sb./of sth.** 解除某人/某事的压力 8 [c] Sport (round) 预赛; **a qualifying** ～ 资格赛 9 [u] Zool 发情期; **to be/come on** Brit *or* **in** Amer ～ 处于/进入发情期

B *vt* 1 (provide heating for) 给…供暖 ‹*room, pool*› 2 Culin 加热 ‹*food*›; **to** ～ **sth. to boiling** 把某物煮开; **to** ～ **the oven to 350°** 把烤炉加热到 350 度 3 Med 高温处理 ‹*blood*›

C *vi* «*place, pot*» 变热; «*oven*» 加热

Phrasal verbs

• **heat through**

A *vt* [～ **sth. through**] 充分加热 ‹*food*›

B *vi* «*food*» 热透; «*house*» 变暖

• **heat up**

A *vt* [～ **sth. up,** ～ **up sth.**] 1 (make warm) 使…变暖 ‹*room*› 2 Culin 加热 ‹*food, leftovers, oven, grill*›

B *vi* 1 (become warm) «*air, room*» 变暖 2 Culin «*food, drink*» 变热 3 (reach required temperature) «*heater, engine, iron*» 加热停当 4 fig (intensify) «*situation, contest*» 激化; **things are** ～**ing up in the election** 选举渐渐趋于白热化

heat capacity *n* [u] 热容量

heated /ˈhiːtɪd/ *adj* 1 lit 加温的; **a** ～ **swimming pool** 温水游泳池 2 fig 激烈的 ‹*argument, debate*›; 愤怒的 ‹*denial, defence*›

heatedly /ˈhiːtɪdli/ *adv* 激烈地 ‹*argue, discuss*›; 愤怒地 ‹*deny, defend*›

heat: ～ **efficiency** *n* [u] 热效率; ～ **engine** *n* 热机

heater /ˈhiːtə(r)/ *n* 加热器; **a gas water** ～ 燃气热水器

heat: ～ **exchanger** *n* 热交换器; ～ **exhaustion** *n* [u] 中暑虚脱

heath /hiːθ/ *n* 1 [c] (area) 灌木丛生的荒野 2 [u] (vegetation) 低矮灌木; (heather) 石南属植物

heat haze *n* 热霾［天气炎热时空气中产生的雾翳］

heathen /ˈhiːðn/

A *adj* 1 usu pej (irreligious) 不信教的; (pagan) 异教徒的 2 colloq pej dated (uncivilized) 未开化的

B *n* 1 (non-believer) 不信教的人; (non-Christian) 异教徒 2 colloq (uncivilized person) 未开化的人

heathenism /ˈhiːðənɪzəm/ *n* [u] 异教信仰

heather /ˈheðə(r)/ *n* [c and u] 1 (Eurasian heath) 欧石南 2 (any similar plant) 石南属植物

Heath Robinson /ˌhiːθ ˈrɒbɪnsən/ *adj* Brit 复杂而不实用的

heating /ˈhiːtɪŋ/ *n* [u] (device) 暖气设备; (system) 供暖系统; **to turn the** ～ **on/off** 打开/关闭暖气; ～ **apparatus** 供热设备

heating: ～ **engineer** ▸**p. 409** *n* 供暖工程师; ～ **plant** *n* 大型供暖设备; ～ **system** *n* 供暖系统

heat: ～ **lamp** *n* 取暖灯; ～ **lightning** *n* [u]［尤指在热天出现的］无雷声闪电; ～ **loss** *n* [u] 热损耗; ～**-proof** *adj* 隔热的 ‹*mat, layer, clothing*›; 耐高温的 ‹*dish*›; ～ **pump** *n* 热泵; ～ **rash** *n* 痱子; ～**-resistant** *adj* 隔热的 ‹*tile, mat*›; 耐高温的 ‹*dish*›; 不易热的 ‹*clothing*›; **a** ～**-resistant handle** 不传热的手柄

heat seal

A *n* 热封

B **heat-seal** *vt* 热塑封

heat: ～**-seeking** *adj attrib* 寻热的 ‹*missile*›; ～**-sensitive** *adj* 热敏的; ～ **shield** *n*［航天器的］热屏蔽装置; ～ **stroke** *n* [u] 中暑; ～**-treated** *adj* 1 (heat-strengthened) 经过热处理的 ‹*metal, material*›; 2 (heat-sterilized) 加热消毒过的 ‹*milk, food*›; ～ **treatment** *n* [u] 1 Med 热疗法; 2 Metall 热处理; ～ **wave** *n* 持续高温天气

heave /hiːv/

A *vt* (*pt, pp* ～**d**) 1 (lift) 用力举起; (pull, drag) 用力拉动; **I** ～**d myself up in bed** 我从床上费力地坐起来 2 (throw) 抛; **to** ～ **a brick through a window** 把砖头扔出窗外 3 (let out, breathe) 发出; **to** ～ **a sigh of relief** 如释重负地松一口气

B *vi* (*pt, pp* ～**d**) 1 (rise and fall) «*chest, sea*» 有节奏地起伏; **on the heaving deck** 在颠簸的甲板上; **her shoulders** ～**d with laughter** 她笑得双肩抖动 2 (pull) 用力拉; **to** ～ **away at sth.** 用力拉某物 3 colloq (retch) 恶心; (vomit) 呕吐; **it made my stomach** *or* **me** ～ 它使我反胃 4 (*pt, pp* **hove**) **to** ～ **in** *or* **into sight** *or* **view** 进入视野; **a ship hove in view** 一艘船出现了

C *n* 1 (effort to pull) 用力拉; (effort to lift) 用力拿起 2 esp liter (swell of chest, sea) 起伏; **the** ～ **of the ocean** 大海的汹涌翻腾

Phrasal verb

• **heave to** (*pt, pp* **hove**)

A *vt* [～ **sth. to**] 顶风停航 ‹*ship*›

B *vi* «*ship*» 顶风停航; «*crew*» 顶风停船

h

heave-ho /ˌhiːvˈhəʊ/
A *excl* 嘿哟嗬
B *n* colloq hum 解雇; to give sb. the (old) ~ 解雇某人; to get the ~ 被解雇

heaven /ˈhevn/ *n* 1 [u] (*also* Heaven) (place) 天堂; ~ and earth 天与地; to move ~ and earth to do sth. fig 竭尽全力做某事; the kingdom of ~ 天国; ~s (above)! dated 天啊! [表示惊恐]; good ~s! dated 天哪! [表示惊讶] 2 [u] (God) 上帝; (the gods) 众天神; the will of ~ 天意; for ~'s sake 看在上帝的份上; for ~'s sake, don't let on that you know 看在老天爷面上, 别跟人家说你知道; ~ forbid! 但愿不要这样!; ~ forbid she should realize! 但愿她不会意识到!; ~ (only) knows! 天晓得!; ~ knows he's got plenty of money 他确实有很多钱; what in ~'s name are you up to? colloq 你究竟想干什么? 3 [c and u] colloq (state of bliss) 极乐; (place where one is happy) 乐土; (a) ~ on earth 人间天堂; that dress is sheer ~! 那条裙子漂亮极了!; to be in seventh ~ 高兴极了 4 liter (sky) the ~s 天空; the ~s opened 下了一场倾盆大雨

heavenly /ˈhevənli/ *adj* 1 (of heaven) 天堂的; (of God) 上帝的; H~ Father 天父 2 (of the sky) 天空的; ~ body 天体 3 colloq (wonderful) 绝妙的; what a ~ hat! 多漂亮的帽子!; this place is ~ 这个地方好极了

heaven-sent *adj* 天赐的

heavenward /ˈhevnwəd/, **heavenwards** /ˈhevnwədz/ *adv* (towards heaven) 向着天国; (towards the sky) 朝天空; to raise *or* cast one's eyes ~ 举目望天

heavily /ˈhevɪli/ *adv* 1 (with considerable weight) 沉重地; a ~ loaded lorry 重载卡车; trees ~ laden with fruit 硕果累累的树木 2 (thickly) 浓重地; to be ~ made-up 化着浓妆 3 (powerfully) 强壮地; to be ~ built 身体魁梧 4 (abundantly, seriously) 大量地; to lose ~ (lose money) 损失惨重; (lose game) 惨败; to be ~ in debt 负债累累; to be ~ armed 全副武装; to be too ~ dependent on sth. 过度依赖某物; to be ~ into sth. colloq 对…上瘾 ‹*drugs*›; 沉醉于 ‹*music*› 5 (loudly) to sigh/breathe ~ 重重地叹气/喘粗气 6 (deeply) 沉沉地; to be sleeping ~ 正在酣睡 7 (forcefully) 重重地 ‹*fall, sit, lean, press*›; 笨重地 ‹*move, walk*› 8 (severely) 严厉地; to come down ~ on sb./sth. 严厉地批评某人/某事物

heaviness /ˈhevɪnɪs/ *n* [u] 1 (weight) 重量 2 (thickness) (of line) 粗; (of features) 粗犷 3 (bulkiness) (of fabric) 粗厚; (of shoes, furniture) 粗笨 4 (largeness of build) 强壮 5 (of perfume, make-up) 浓 6 (large amount) (of expense, debt) 高额; (of casualties, bleeding, drinking) 大量 7 (large degree) (of accent, penalty) 重; (of loss, defeat) 惨重; (of irony) 强烈; (of fighting) 激烈 8 (deepness of breathing, sleep) 深沉 9 (severity of symptoms) 严重 10 (difficulty of work) 繁重 11 (of food) 难消化 12 (clay content of soil) 黏硬 13 (of rain, snow) 大; (of fog, frost) 浓; (of dew) 重 14 (force of blow, fall, movement) 沉重 15 (sadness) ~ of heart 沉重的心情

heavy /ˈhevi/ ▸p. 909
A *adj* 1 (having great weight or density) 重的 ‹*object, liquid*›; how ~ is sth./sb.? 某物/某人有多重?; gas is heavier than air 天然气比空气重 2 (thick) 粗的 ‹*line*›; 粗犷的 ‹*features*›; ~ type 粗体; to wear ~ make-up 化浓妆 3 (bulky) 厚的 ‹*coat*›; 笨重的 ‹*shoes, furniture*› 4 (large) 重型的 ‹*artillery, machinery*›; a man of ~ build 一个身材粗壮的男子 5 (in amount) 大量的 ‹*cuts, demands, bleeding*›; 高额的 ‹*expenditure, debt, crop*›; ~ traffic/trading/gunfire 拥挤的交通/繁忙的交易/密集的炮火; there are ~ casualties 伤亡很惨重; a ~ smoker/drinker 烟瘾/酒瘾大的人 6 (in degree) 重的 ‹*accent, penalty, sentence*›; 重大的 ‹*responsibility, issue*›; 繁重的 ‹*workload*›; 强烈的 ‹*irony*›; a ~ loss/defeat 惨重的损失/失败; ~ fighting/security 激烈的战斗/严密的安全措施; to lay ~ emphasis on sth. 格外强调某事; to be ~ going fig «*person*» 难以打交道; «*thing*» 难以理解 7 (strong, dense) 浓烈的 ‹*smell, wine*› 8 (deep) 深沉的 ‹*sigh*›; a ~ sleep 沉睡 9 (severe) 严重的 ‹*symptoms*›; a ~ cold 重感冒; to have ~ periods 月经过多 10 (too filling) 太撑人的 ‹*meal*›; 难消化的 ‹*food*›; (rich) 油腻的 ‹*cake*› 11 (full of clay) 黏硬的 ‹*soil*› 12 Equit (muddy) 泥泞难走的 ‹*track*› 13 Meteorol 大的 ‹*rain, snow*›; 浓的 ‹*fog, frost*›; 重的 ‹*dew*›; 阴沉的 ‹*sky*›; 密布的 ‹*cloud*›; to make ~ weather of sth./doing sth. 把某事/做某事小题大做 14 (tired) 疲乏的 ‹*limbs, eyes*› 15 (sad) 沉痛的; with a ~ heart 心情沉重地 16 (forceful) 沉重有力的 ‹*movement, thud, fall*›; a ~ blow lit 重击; fig 沉重的打击 17 (surging) 波涛汹涌的 ‹*sea*› 18 liter (full) 满的; to be ~ with sth. 充满 ‹*perfume, resentment*›; branches ~ with fruit 果实累累的树枝; ~ with meaning 意味深长 19 colloq (using a lot) to be ~ on sth. 消耗大量的… ‹*petrol, electricity*› 20 (profound) 晦涩难懂的 ‹*book, film*› 21 pej (boring) 乏味的 ‹*article, lecture*› 22 (strenuous) 费力的 ‹*work, task*› 23 (busy) 繁忙的 ‹*day, schedule*› 24 colloq (strict) 过于严厉的; to be ~ with sb. 对某人过分严格 25 colloq (serious) 难应付的; to get ~ (difficult) 变得难以处理
B *n* colloq 1 (bodyguard) 保镖 2 (criminal) 打手 3 Brit (newspaper) 严肃报纸
C *adv* 1 (with great weight) 重重地; to lie *or* weigh ~ on sb./sth. 重重地压在某人/某物上; the pudding lay ~ on my stomach 布丁吃到我肚子里沉甸甸的 2 (worryingly) 令人忧虑地; to lie *or* weigh ~ on sb./sth. 让某人/某物不安; the issue weighed ~ on her mind 这个问题让她心绪不宁 3 (slowly) 缓慢地; time hangs *or* lies ~ on sb.'s hands 某人百无聊赖

heavy: ~ **breathing** *n* [u] 喘气声; ~ **cream** *n* [u] Amer = double cream; ~ **crude** *n* [u] ~ crude (oil) 重质原油; ~**-duty** *adj* (very strong) 厚重耐穿的 ‹*uniform, boots*›; 耐磨的 ‹*rubber, carpet*›; 耐用的 ‹*tool, battery*›; (for industrial use) 重载的 ‹*tyre*›; 重型的 ‹*equipment, machine*›; ~ **goods vehicle** *n* Brit 重型货车; ~**-handed** *adj* 1 (tactless) 笨拙的; ~-handed remarks 笨口拙舌的话; 2 (using too much) 大手大脚的; don't be ~-handed with the flour 不要放太多的面粉; 3 (using unnecessary force) 暴虐的 ‹*regime, policy*›; 严厉的 ‹*treatment, person*›; ~-handed police methods 警察的高压手段; ~**-hearted** *adj* 心情沉重的; ~ **industry** *n* [u and c] 重工业; ~ **metal** *n* 1 [u] Mus 重金属摇滚乐; ~ metal band 重金属乐队; 2 [c] Metall 重金属; ~ **mob** *n* Brit colloq the ~ mob 一伙暴徒; ~ **oil** *n* [u] 重油; ~ **petting** *n* [u] colloq 性爱抚; ~ **water** *n* [u] 重水

heavyweight /ˈhevɪweɪt/ *n* 1 Sport (boxer) 最重量级拳击手; (wrestler) 最重量级摔跤运动员; (class) 最重量级 2 fig colloq (influential person) 有影响力的人; (influential thing) 有影响力的事物; a political ~ 政界要人; a ~ issue 重大问题 3 (heavy person) 特别重的人; (heavy thing) 特别重的物件; a ~ coat 厚重的大衣

Hebei /ˌhɜːˈbei/ ▸p. 604 *pr n* ~ (Province) 河北(省)

Hebraic /hiːˈbreɪɪk/ *adj* 1 (of or in Hebrew) 希伯来语的 2 (of the Hebrews) 希伯来人的

Hebrew /ˈhiːbruː/ ▸p. 426
A *adj* 1 (of the Hebrews) 希伯来人的 2 (of or in Hebrew) 希伯来语的
B *n* 1 [c] (person) 希伯来人 2 [u] (language) 希伯来语

Hebrides /ˈhebrɪdiːz/ *pr npl* the ~ 赫布里底群岛

heck /hek/ colloq
A *n* 1 [用以表示惊讶或恼怒等]; what the ~ is going on? 究竟发生了什么事?; what the ~ are you doing there? 你到底在那儿干什么? 2 [用以加强语气]; he earns a ~ of a lot colloq 他挣钱很多; he's made a ~ of a mess 他搞得一塌糊涂; it means I'll be late for work, but what the ~! 这意味着我上班会迟到, 不过管它的呢!
B *excl* 见鬼; oh ~! 真见鬼!

heckle /ˈhekl/
A *vi* 起哄
B *vt* 对…起哄

heckler /ˈheklə(r)/ *n* 起哄者

heckling /ˈheklɪŋ/ *n* [u] 起哄

hectare /ˈhekteə(r)/ *n* 公顷

hectic /ˈhektɪk/ *adj* (very busy) 忙乱的; (frantic) 狂乱的; a ~ schedule 安排很满的日程表; they made ~ attempts to contact her 他们拼命设法和她取得联系

hectogram, esp Brit **hectogramme** /ˈhektəgræm/ ▸p. 909 *n* 百克

hectolitre /ˈhektəliːtə(r)/ *n* 百升

hector /ˈhektə(r)/ *vi, vt* 威吓

he'd /hiːd/ colloq 1 = he had ▸have 2 = he would ▸would

hedge /hedʒ/
A *n* 1 Hort, Agric 树篱; to look as if one has been dragged through a ~ backwards fig colloq 看上去蓬头垢面 2 fig (against financial loss) 保值措施; (against other adverse circumstances) 防范措施
B *vt* 1 (plant a hedge around) 用树篱围住; to ~ sth. off, to ~ off sth. 用树篱隔开某物 2 fig (evade) 回避; to ~ the issue 回避问题 3 (protect against financial loss) 对冲防止…损失; to ~ one's bets (avoid committing oneself) 避免明确表态; (reduce the risk) 对冲止损 4 (limit, qualify) 限定; (restrict, confine) 束缚; his proposals were ~d about with difficulties 他的提议受制于种种困难
C *vi* 1 (equivocate) 避免正面回答; we pressed him to say, but he just ~d 我们催促他说, 但他只是闪烁其词; he ~d on *or* at every new question 他回避每一个新问题 2 (reduce risk) to ~ against sth. 对冲防止 ‹*inflation, loss*›

hedge: ~**-clippers** *npl* 树篱修剪器; ~ **fund** *n* 对冲基金; ~-fund manager 对冲基金经理; ~**hog** *n* 刺猬; ~**-hop** *vi* (*pres p etc.* -pp-) 掠地飞行; ~**row** *n* 灌木篱墙; ~row plant 篱墙植物; ~ **sparrow** *n* 篱雀; ~ **trimmer** *n* 树篱修剪器

hedonism /ˈhiːdənɪzəm/ *n* [u] 1 (pursuit of pleasure) 追求享乐 2 (ethical theory) 享乐主义

hedonist /ˈhiːdənɪst/
A *n* 享乐主义者
B *adj* 享乐主义的

hedonistic /ˌhiːdəˈnɪstɪk/ *adj* 享乐主义的

heebie-jeebies /ˌhiːbɪˈdʒiːbɪz/ *npl* colloq 紧张不安; to give sb. the ~ 使某人坐立不安

heed /hiːd/
A *vt* 留心 ‹*person, warning*›; 听从 ‹*advice, remarks*›
B *n* [u] 注意; he paid no ~ to my warnings 他对我的警告不予理睬; to take ~ of the doctor's advice 听从医嘱

heedless /ˈhiːdlɪs/ *adj* (thoughtless) 不加注意的; (carefree) 漫不经心的 ‹*laugh, song, remark*›; to be ~ of sth. 不注意某事物

heedlessly /ˈhiːdlɪsli/ *adv* 不加注意地; she bicycled ~ through the crowd 她冒冒失失地骑车穿过人群

heehaw /ˈhiːhɔː/
A *vi* «*donkey, mule*» 叫
B *n* (produced by donkey) 驴鸣; (produced by mule) 骡叫声

heel¹ /hiːl/
A *n* 1 (of foot) 脚后跟; to turn *or* spin *or* swing round on one's ~ 突然转身; at the ~s of

sb. 紧随某人; **(close** *or* **hard** *or* **hot) on the ~s of sb./sth.** (in pursuit) 紧追在某人/某物后面; (soon after) 紧接着某人/某事物; **on the ~s of their defeat came more troubles** 他们失败后更多的麻烦接踵而来; **to take to one's ~s** 拔腿逃走; **to show (sb.) a clean pair of ~s** 溜之大吉; **to bring a dog to ~** 让狗跟着; **to bring sb. to ~** fig 迫使…就范 ‹*rebel*›; 让…听话 ‹*child*›; **to come to ~** lit «*dog*» 跟着; fig 就范; **to cool** *or* Brit **kick one's ~s** 空等; **to dig in one's ~s** *or* **dig one's ~s in (over sth.)** (在某事上) 固执己见; **to fall** *or* **go head over ~s** lit 头朝下跌倒; **to be/fall head over ~s in love with sb.** 爱某人爱得神魂颠倒/神魂颠倒地爱上某人; **to kick up one's ~s** esp Amer colloq 放松享乐 **2** (of shoe) 鞋跟; **shoes with a low/high ~** 低跟/高跟鞋; **to click one's ~s** Mil 立正 **3** (of sock) 后跟 **4** Anat (of hand) 手掌根 **5** Culin (of loaf) 面包头 **6** Bot (of plant) 踵 **7** fig liter (power) 统治; **under the ~ of sb.** 在某人的统治下; **the iron ~ of oppression** 压迫的铁蹄 **8** colloq dated (unpleasant or untrustworthy person) 浑蛋

B **heels** *npl* 高跟鞋

C *excl* 跟着 [唤狗用语]; **~, boy!** 小家伙, 跟着!

D *vt* **1** (repair) 给…装鞋跟 ‹*shoe*› **2** Sport 用脚跟向后传 ‹*ball*›

Phrasal verb

• **heel in** *vt* [**~ sth. in, ~ in sth.**] 埋植 ‹*plant*›

heel² Naut

A *vi* «*boat*» 倾侧

B *n* **1** (instance) [船的] 倾侧 **2** (degree) 倾侧度

Phrasal verb

• **heel over** *vi* **1** Naut «*boat*» 倾侧; **the ship was ~ing over several degrees** 船倾侧了几度 **2** (tip over) «*lorry, wardrobe, crane*» 翻倒; **the tree slowly ~ed over** 树慢慢倒下了

heel bar ▸**p. 409** *n* (shop) 立等可取的修鞋店; (counter in shop) 立等可取的修鞋柜台

heft /heft/ *vt* colloq **1** (lift up) 举起 **2** (assess weight of) 掂…的重量

hefty /'hefti/ *adj* **1** (powerfully built) 高大健壮的 ‹*person*›; 粗壮的 ‹*arms, legs*› **2** (forceful) 有力的; **a ~ blow** 重重的一击 **3** (large) 很大的 ‹*portion, piece*› **4** (considerable) 可观的; **a ~ salary** 高薪; **a ~ bill** 巨额账单

Hegelian /her'gi:lɪən/

A *adj* 黑格尔的 ‹*dialectic, philosophy*›; 黑格尔哲学的 ‹*synthesis*›

B *n* 黑格尔派哲学家

hegemony /hɪ'dʒeməni, Amer 'hedʒeməʊni/ *n* [u] formal (leadership) 领导权; (dominance) 支配权; **military ~** 军事霸权

heifer /'hefə(r)/ *n* 小母牛

heigh-ho /ˌher'həʊ/ *excl* colloq 嗨呵 [表示厌烦、惊讶、高兴或顺从]; **~! it's back to work!** 唉! 又开始上班了!

height /haɪt/ ▸**p. 436**

A *n* **1** [u and c] (tallness) (of person) 身高; (of table, tower, tree, mountain) 高; **a woman of average** *or* **medium ~** 中等身高的女人; **to be 1 metre in ~** 高 1 米; **to draw oneself up** *or* **rise to one's full ~** 挺直身体站立 **2** [c and u] (distance from ground) 高度; **at a ~ of 200 metres** 在 200 米高处; **~ above sea-level** 海拔高度; **(at) head/knee ~** 齐头/膝高; **to gain/lose ~** «*aircraft*» 上升/下降; **to clear a ~ of 2.5/5 metres** 跳过 2.5/5 米高度 **3** [c] (high place) 高处; **to fall/jump from a great ~** 从高处落下/向下跳; **to be afraid of ~s** 恐高; **fear of ~s** 恐高 **4** [c] fig (peak of excitement, crisis) 顶点; (peak of festivities) 高潮; **to reach its ~** «*event*» 达到高潮; **the ~ of one's career/success** 事业/成功的巅峰; **to reach the dizzy ~s of television stardom** 达到电视明星的显赫地位; **the ~ of rush hour** 交通高峰期; **at** *or* **in the ~ of summer** 在盛夏; **the ~ of the season** 旺季 **5** [c] (utmost) 极度; **the ~ of fashion/folly/rudeness** 最时髦/愚不可及/无礼至极

B **heights** *npl* **1** lit (cliffs) 峭壁; **snowy ~s** 白雪覆盖的悬崖 **2** fig (high level) 极高水平; **to rise to** *or* **reach new ~s** 达到新高

heighten /'haɪtn/

A *vt* **1** (make higher) 加高 **2** (intensify) 增强; **the wait ~ed our tension** 等待让我们变得更紧张了; **illustrations will ~ the interest** 插图可以增加趣味

B *vi* 增强; **his colour ~ed** 他的脸红了

Heilongjiang /ˌheilʊŋ'dʒjæŋ/ ▸**p. 604** *pr n* **~ (Province)** 黑龙江 (省)

heinous /'heməs/ *adj* formal 十恶不赦的

heir /eə(r)/ *n* 继承人; **to be the ~ to sth.** 是某物的继承人; **~ to the throne** 王位继承人; **to make sb. one's ~** 立某人为继承人; **~ apparent** 当然继承人; **~ presumptive** 假定继承人 [继承权会因另一个继承人出生而丧失]; **he is the ~ apparent to the chief executive** 他肯定会继任总裁

heiress /'eərɪs/ *n* 女继承人; **to be the ~ to sth.** 是某物的女继承人

heirloom /'eəlu:m/ *n* 传家宝

heist /haɪst/ Amer colloq

A *n* 抢劫

B *vt* 盗窃

held /held/ *pt, pp* ▸**hold A, B, C**

helical /'helɪkl, 'hi:lɪkl/ *adj* 螺旋形的

helices /'helɪsi:z, 'hi:-/ *pl* ▸**helix**

helicopter /'helɪkɒptə(r)/

A *n* 直升机; **to travel by ~** 乘直升机旅行

B *vt* 用直升机载运

Phrasal verbs

• **helicopter in** *vt* [**~ sth./sb. in, ~ in sth./sb.**] 用直升机将…运入

• **helicopter out** *vt* [**~ sth./sb. out, ~ out sth./sb.**] 用直升机将…运出

helicopter: ~ base *n* 直升机基地; **~ gunship** *n* 武装直升机; **~ patrol** *n* [c and u] 直升机巡逻; **~ pilot** ▸**p. 409** *n* 直升机驾驶员; **~ rescue** *n* 直升机救援; **~ station** *n* 直升机基地; **~ view** *n* fig colloq 概述; **to gain a ~ view of the workings of the company** 了解公司运营的概况

helideck /'helɪdek/ *n* 直升机甲板

heliograph /'hi:lɪəgrɑ:f, Amer -græf/ *n* **1** (signalling device) 日光反射信号器 **2** (message) 日光反射信号 **3** Astron [拍摄太阳用的] 太阳照相仪

heliostat /'hi:lɪəstæt/ *n* 定日镜

heliotrope /'hi:lɪətrəʊp/

A *n* 天芥菜

B *adj* 淡紫色的

helipad /'helɪpæd/ *n* 直升机停机坪

heliport /'helɪpɔ:t/ *n* 直升机机场

helium /'hi:lɪəm/ *n* [u] 氦

helix /'hi:lɪks/ *n* (*pl* **helices**) **1** (spiral shape) 螺旋形物 **2** (chain of atoms) 螺旋结构

hell /hel/ *n* **1** [c] (*also* **Hell**) Relig 地狱; **to be in ~** 身处地狱; **go to ~!, to ~ with you!** sl 见鬼去吧!; **~'s bells** *or* **teeth!** Brit sl 真见鬼!; **(oh) ~!** sl 哦, 见鬼!; **I'll see him in ~ first** 我再也不要见到他; **there's not a hope in ~ (of doing sth.)** colloq 毫无希望 (做某事); **to raise (merry) ~ (with sb.)** colloq (与某人) 大闹起来; **to play (merry) ~ with sb./sth.** Brit colloq 给某人/某事物造成大麻烦; **until** *or* **till/when ~ freezes (over)** colloq 永不; **all ~ broke** *or* **was let loose** colloq 突然一片混乱; **come ~ or high water** 无论有什么困难; **there will be ~ to pay** colloq 要有大麻烦了; **(just) for the ~ of it** colloq 只是闹着玩; **to give sb. ~** colloq (scold) 大声责骂某人; (cause trouble for) 给某人惹麻烦; **to beat the ~ out of sb./sth.** colloq 痛打某人/某物; **to scare/annoy the ~ out of sb.** colloq 把某人吓得半死/烦得要死; **the neighbour/holiday from ~** colloq 恶邻/最糟糕的假期; **to be ~ on the knees/the car's suspension** colloq 对膝盖/车子的悬架有害; **to catch ~** Amer colloq 受责备; **not to have** *or* **stand a snowball's chance in ~ (of doing sth.)** colloq 决不可能 (做某事); ▸**cat 1** **2** [u] (bad experience) 磨难; **how was the trip? — sheer ~!** 旅行如何? ——糟糕透了!; **to have been to ~ and back** colloq 经历了一番磨难; **to make sb.'s life ~, to make life ~ for sb.** 使某人的生活苦不堪言; **to go through ~ doing sth.** 做某事历尽磨难 **3** [u] colloq (as intensifier) **as/like ~** 非常; **run like ~!** 快跑!; **to hurt like ~** 疼得要命; **it sure as ~ wasn't me** 那肯定不是我; **like ~ I will/you are!** 我才不愿意/你才不是!; **a** *or* **one ~ of a sb./sth.** 极其的某人/某事物; **a ~ of a cold day** 特冷的一天; **a ~ of a guy** 一个不错的家伙; **to be a ~ of a lot worse** 更糟糕; **I got a ~ of a shock** 我吓了一大跳; **to have one ~ of a time (doing sth.)** (good) (做某事) 很愉快; (bad) (做某事) 很痛苦; (difficult) (做某事) 很困难; **what the ~!** (in surprise) 哎呀!; (in dismissal) 管它呢!; **to get the ~ out (of sth.)** 赶紧离开 (某地)

he'll /'hi:əl/ colloq **1** **= he shall** ▸**shall** **2** **= he will** ▸**will¹**

hell-bent /ˌhel'bent/ *adj pred* 不顾一切的; **she is ~ on leaving** 她执意要离开; **he is ~ on destruction** 他顽固地走向毁灭

hellcat /'helkæt/ *n* 泼妇

Hellenic /he'li:nɪk, Amer he'lenɪk/ *adj* **1** (of Greeks) 希腊人的; (of Greece) 希腊的 **2** Archaeol 古希腊的

hellfire /ˌhel'faɪə(r)/ *n* [u] 地狱之火; **a ~ sermon** 宣讲罚入地狱的布道

hell-for-leather

A *adv* 飞快地; **to work ~** 拼命工作; **to go ~** 全力以赴

B *adj* colloq 飞快的

hellhole /'helhəʊl/ *n* colloq 地狱般的地方

hellish /'helɪʃ/

A *adj* **1** (hell-like) 地狱般的; (of hell) 地狱的; (from hell) 来自地狱的; **~ groans** 撕心裂肺的呻吟声 **2** Brit colloq (terrible) 极不愉快的; **the ~ noise in the factory** 工厂里可怕的噪声; **I had a ~ time getting here** 我费了九牛二虎之力才到这儿

B *adv* Brit colloq 极端地; **it's ~ dark in here** 这里黑得要命; **it was ~ difficult** 这极度困难

hellishly /'helɪʃli/ *adv* Brit colloq **1** (terribly) 极其恶劣地; **it hurt ~** 痛得非常厉害 **2** (extremely) 极端地; **he drove ~ fast** 他开车快得要命; **it was ~ cold outside** 外面冷得够呛

hello /hə'ləʊ/

A *n* 问候

B *excl* **1** ▸**p. 333** (greeting) 你好; (on phone) 喂 **2** Brit (in surprise) 嘿

Hell's angel /ˌhelz 'eɪndʒl/ *n* 地狱天使 [指成帮结伙骑摩托车飙车的男青年]

helluva /'heləvə/ *n* sl **= hell of a** ▸**hell 3**

helm /helm/ *n* **1** Naut 舵; **to take the ~** 开始掌舵; **to be at the ~** 掌舵 **2** fig (position of control) 领导地位; **to take the ~** 开始掌握大权; **to be at the ~ of the state** 担任国家领导人

helmet /'helmɪt/ *n* 头盔

helmeted /'helmɪtɪd/ *adj* 戴着头盔的

helmsman /'helmzmən/ *n* 舵手

help /help/

A *vt* **1** (assist) 帮助; **to ~ sb. (to) do sth.** 帮助某人做某事; **to ~ sb. with the children/their bag** 帮某人照看孩子/拎包; **may I ~ you?** (in shop) 要帮忙吗?; (on phone, at desk) 您有什么事?; **I can't ~ you** 我帮不上你的忙 **2** (financially) 资助; **to ~ the poor** 救济穷人; **to ~ sb. with the mortgage** 帮某

h

人偿还按揭款 3 (in emergency) 救助; **God/heaven ~ us/them!** colloq 我们/他们要靠上帝了！; **so ~ me (God)** Jur 上帝作证; (in anger) 我发誓 [用于表达愤怒情绪或表示说到做到]; **God ~s those who ~ themselves** Prov 天助自助者 4 (in moving) 协助; **to ~ sb. up** (pull) 拉某人起来; (support) 扶某人起来; **to ~ sb. to their feet** 扶某人站起来; **to ~ sb. out of the car/down the steps** 扶某人下车/走下台阶; **he ~ed me in with the bed** 他帮我把床搬了进来 5 (improve) 改善 ‹*situation, relations*›; «*medicine*» 使…好转 ‹*illness*›; «*medicine*» 减轻 ‹*pain*›; **he didn't ~ matters by writing that letter** 他写那封信于事无补 6 (contribute) 有助于; **to ~ (to) keep prices down** «*policy*» 有助于平抑价格上涨; **to ~ brighten up the room** «*carpet*» 使房间变得更加漂亮 7 (serve) **to ~ sb. to sth.** 给某人送上 ‹*food*›; **he ~ed his guests to wine** 他为客人们斟酒 8 (prevent) **sb. can't ~ sth.** 某人控制不住 ‹*feelings*›; 某人忍不住 ‹*laughing*›; **I can't ~ but believe her** 我不得不相信她; **I can't ~ it if ...** 如果…我也没办法; **it can't be ~ed** 这是没办法的事情; **she can't ~ being stupid** 她总是犯傻

B *vi* 1 (assist) 帮忙; **to ~ with sth.** 帮忙做某事 2 (be useful) 有帮助; **every little bit ~s** 点滴皆有用 3 (give money) 资助; **to ~ with the expenses** 分担费用 4 (in emergency) 救助 5 (be of benefit) 改善状况; **doing that won't ~** 做那事没用; **would it ~ if I turned the light on?** 我打开灯会有用吗？

C *v refl* 1 (serve) **to ~ oneself** 自己取用; **to ~ oneself to fruit** 自己拿水果吃; **~ yourselves!** 请自便！; **~ yourselves to coffee** 喝些咖啡吧 2 colloq (steal) 顺手牵羊; **to ~ oneself from the till/to the apples** 捞走出纳机里的钱/这些苹果 3 (prevent oneself) **I tried not to laugh/cry, but I couldn't ~ myself** 我想忍住不笑/不哭出来，但是忍不住

D *n* 1 [u and c] (assistance) 帮助; **with the ~ of sb.** 在某人的帮助下; **to be a great ~ to sb.** 对某人大有帮助; **do you need ~?** 你需要帮忙吗？; **to be more of a hindrance than a ~** 成事不足，败事有余 2 [u] (aid, support) 援助; **to seek financial/medical ~** 寻求经济/医疗援助; **to get ~ with housing/food** 获得住房/食物补助 3 [u] (in emergency) 救助; **to come/go to sb.'s ~** 来/去救助某人; **to shout** *or* **cry for ~** 呼救; **to be beyond** *or* **past (all) ~** «*person*» 无药可救 4 [u and c] (use) 用处; **to be of ~ (to sb.)** «*money, advice*» (对某人) 有用; **with the ~ of sth.** 借助 ‹*stick, atlas*›; **the map isn't much ~** 这张地图用处不大; **it's a ~ having two cars** 有两辆车很方便; **there's no ~ for it** esp Brit 没法子了 5 [c] (helper) 帮手; **he's a big ~** 他是个大帮手; **you're a great ~!** iron 你可真够帮忙的！ 6 **Help** [u] Comput 帮助文档

E *excl* 1 (calling for aid) 救命; **~! I'm drowning!** 救命！我快淹死了！; **~! I'm stuck!** 救命！我被卡住了！ 2 (expressing dismay) 糟糕; **~! I've spilt the wine** 糟糕！我把葡萄酒弄洒了

Phrasal verbs

- **help along** *vt* [**~ sb./sth. along**]
  1 (assist in moving) 搀扶…向前走 ‹*person*›; «*tide, push*» 推动 ‹*car, ball*›; **the wind ~ed the boat along** 风吹动小船前行 2 (facilitate) 促进 ‹*project, negotiations*›
- **help out**

A *vi* 1 (assist) 帮忙做; **to ~ out with sth.** 帮忙做某事; **to ~ out with the housework** 帮忙做家务 2 (financially) 资助; **to ~ out with the mortgage** 帮忙偿还按揭款 3 (in crisis) 帮忙摆脱困境; **she's always there to ~ out** 她总是急人之难

B *vt* [**~ sb. out**]
1 (assist) 帮助; **to ~ sb. out with sth.** 帮助某人做某事; **to ~ sb. out with the gardening** 帮某人干园艺活 2 (financially) 资助; **to ~ sb. out with the rent/mortgage** 帮某人付房租/抵押贷款 3 (in emergency) 帮助…摆脱困境; **to ~ each other out in times of trouble** 在困难时互相帮助

- **help through** *vt* [**~ sb. through sth.**] 帮…度过 ‹*difficult time, divorce*›

helpdesk /'helpdesk/ *n* 服务台

helper /'helpə(r)/ *n* 帮助者; **where's my little ~?** 我的小助手在哪儿？

helpful /'helpfl/ *adj* 1 (obliging) 乐于帮忙的 ‹*person*›; (handy) 便于使用的 ‹*machine, gadget*›; **I was only trying to be ~!** 我只是想帮忙！; **to be ~ to sb.** 乐于帮助某人 2 (useful) 有用的; **you've been most ~** 你帮了大忙; **to be ~ to sb.** 对某人有用; **to be ~ for doing sth.** 有益于做某事; **the computer is very ~ for keeping stock records** 电脑用来做库存记录非常方便 3 (effective, of use) 有效的; **a ~ remedy for seasickness** 治晕船的良方

helpfully /'helpfəli/ *adv* 1 (obligingly) 乐于助人地; **she ~ showed me** 她热心地给我演示 2 (usefully) 有用地; **this road is ~ signposted** 这条路上设置了有用的路标 3 (so as to help) 为了帮助人; **the path had been ~ cleared of snow** 路上的积雪已被清除，给行人带来了方便

helpfulness /'helpflnɪs/ *n* [u] 1 (willingness to help) 乐于助人 2 (usefulness) 有用 3 (effectiveness) 有效

helping /'helpɪŋ/ *n* 一份; **a ~ of peas** 一客豌豆

helping hand *n* 帮助; **to give** *or* **lend a ~ to sb.** 帮助某人; **to give** *or* **lend sb. a ~ with sth.** 就某事对某人提供帮助

Help key *n* [电脑键盘上的] 帮助键

helpless /'helplɪs/ *adj* 1 (powerless) 无助的; **to feel ~** 感到无助; **she was ~ in this matter** 这件事她帮不上忙; **I was ~ to prevent his leaving** 我没能阻止他离开 2 (incapacitated) 抑制不住的; **they were ~ with laughter** colloq 他们情不自禁地大笑起来 3 (incapable, dependent) 不能自立的; **a ~ invalid** 生活不能自理的病人; **as ~ as a child/baby/new-born babe** 像小孩/婴儿/新生儿一样无助 4 (defenceless) 不能自卫的; **the ~ victims of war** 手无寸铁的战争受害者

helplessly /'helplɪsli/ *adv* 1 (powerlessly) 徒劳地; **she tried ~ to persuade them** 她试图说服他们，但没有成功; **we looked on ~** 我们无奈地看着 2 (uncontrollably) 抑制不住地; **to laugh ~** 情不自禁地大笑 3 (unable to help oneself) 不能自立地; **to lie ~ on the floor** 无力地躺在地板上; **they were ~ drunk** 他们醉得一塌糊涂 4 (defencelessly) 不能自卫地

helplessness /'helplɪsnɪs/ *n* [u] 1 (powerlessness) 无助 2 (inability to help oneself) 无自立能力 3 (defencelessness) 不能自卫

help: ~line *n* 服务热线; **~mate** *n* dated 伴侣

Helsinki /hel'sɪŋki/ *pr n* 赫尔辛基

helter-skelter /ˌheltə'skeltə(r)/

A *adv* 仓促忙乱地; **to run ~** 乱哄哄地跑

B *adj* 仓促忙乱的 ‹*rush*›; 杂乱无章的 ‹*description, arrangement*›

C *n* 螺旋滑梯

hem¹ /hem/

A *n* Clothg (bottom edge) 下摆; (folded material) 褶边; **to take up/let down the ~ on (a garment)** (把衣服) 改短/改长

B *vt* (*pres p etc.* **-mm-**) 缝…的褶边

Phrasal verb

- **hem in** *vt* [**~ sb./sth. in, ~ in sb./sth.**]
  1 lit 把…围起来; **the troops ~med us in** 军队把我们团团围住; **a park ~med in by oaks** 橡树环绕的公园 2 fig 限制; **he felt ~med in (by convention)** 他感觉受到 (社会习俗的) 束缚

hem²

A *excl* 嗯 [吸引注意或表示犹豫等的轻咳或清嗓子声]

B *vi* (*pres p etc.* **-mm-**) **~ and haw** ▸**haw²**

he-man *n* 男子汉

hematologist /ˌhiːmə'tɒlədʒɪst/ *n* Amer = **haematologist**

hematology /ˌhiːmə'tɒlədʒi/ *n* Amer = **haematology**

hematoma /ˌhiːmə'təʊmə/ *n* (*pl* **~s**) Amer = **haematoma**

hemiplegia /ˌhemɪ'pliːdʒɪə/ *n* [u] 偏瘫; **to suffer from ~** 患半身不遂

hemiplegic /ˌhemɪ'pliːdʒɪk/

A *adj* 偏瘫的

B *n* 偏瘫病人

hemisphere /'hemɪsfɪə(r)/ *n* 1 (half of a sphere) 半球体 2 (of the brain) 大脑半球 3 (of the earth) 半球; **the western ~** 西半球

hemline /'hemlaɪn/ *n* 底边; **~s are going up/coming down** 现在流行较短/较长的衣裙

hemlock /'hemlɒk/ *n* 1 [c] (plant) 毒芹 2 [c] (tree) **~ fir** *or* **spruce** 铁杉 3 [u] (poison) 毒芹毒素

hemodyalysis /ˌhiːmədaɪ'æləsɪs/ *n* Amer = **haemodialysis**

hemoglobin /ˌhiːmə'gləʊbɪn/ *n* [u] Amer = **haemoglobin**

hemophilia /ˌhiːmə'fɪlɪə/ *n* [u] Amer = **haemophilia**

hemophiliac /ˌhiːmə'fɪlɪæk/ *n* [u] Amer = **haemophiliac**

hemp /hemp/ *n* [u] 1 (plant) 大麻 2 (fibre) 大麻纤维 3 (drug) 大麻

hemstitch /'hemstɪtʃ/

A *n* 抽丝线迹

B *vt* 为…抽丝做花边

hen /hen/

A *n* 1 (female chicken) 母鸡 2 (female bird) 雌禽 3 (female lobster) 雌龙虾; (female crab) 雌蟹

B *adj* 雌性的; **a ~ pheasant** 雌雉

Henan /ˌhɜː'næn/ ▸**p. 604** *pr n* **~ (Province)** 河南 (省)

hence /hens/ *adv* formal 1 (therefore, for this reason) 因此; **she was slimmer and ~ more active** 她更苗条了，也因此更有活力了; **there is a strike, ~ the delay** 发生了罢工，所以耽搁了 2 (from now) 从现在起; **three days ~** 3 天以后

henceforth /ˌhens'fɔːθ/, **henceforward** /hens'fɔːwəd/ *advs* formal (from now on) 从此以后; (from then on) 从那以后

henchman /'hentʃmən/ *n* (*pl* **henchmen**) 1 pej (of gangster, dictator) 亲信 2 archaic (squire) 侍从

hen: ~ coop *n* 鸡棚; **~ harrier** *n* 白尾鹞; **~house** *n* 鸡舍

henna /'henə/

A *n* [u] 散沫花染剂

B *vt* (*3rd pers sing pres* **~s**; *pt, pp* **~ed**) 用散沫花染剂染 ‹*hair*›

hen: ~ party *n* 女性聚会; **~-pecked** *adj* 常受老婆责骂的; **he is a ~-pecked husband** 他是个 "妻管严"; **~ run** *n* 养鸡场

hepatitis /ˌhepə'taɪtɪs/ ▸**p. 377** *n* [u] 肝炎

heptagon /'heptəgən, Amer -gɒn/ *n* 七边形

heptathlete /hep'tæθliːt/ *n*

heptathlon /hep'tæθlən, -lɒn/ ▸**p. 307** *n* (女子) 七项全能

her /hɜː(r), hə(r)/ ▸**p. 487**

A *pron* 1 (referring to woman, girl) 她; dated (referring to ship, country) 她; **is that HMS Victory? — that's ~** 那是皇家海军胜利号吗？——是她 2 colloq (referring to female animal, car) 它; **give ~ a respray and she'll be as good as new** 再喷一次漆，它就会像新车一样

B *det* 1 (of woman, girl) 她的; dated (of ship, country) 她的; **~ crew were eager for some shore**

h

leave 全体船员急于上岸休假 2 colloq (of female animal, car) 它的; **~ engine's a little rusty** 它的发动机有点生锈了

herald /ˈherəld/

A *n* 1 Hist (messenger) 传令官; (at a tournament) 宣令调度官 2 Brit Hist (official) 司宗谱纹章的官员 3 (harbinger) 预报者; **the cuckoo, ~ of spring** 布谷鸟，春天的使者

B *vt* 1 (*also* **~ in**) (be a sign of) 预示…的来临; **to ~ the new age** 宣告新时代的到来; **much ~ed visit/publication** 大加宣传的访问/发布 2 (acclaim) **to ~ (sb./sth.) as sth.** 宣称（某人/某物）为某物

heraldic /heˈrældɪk/ *adj* 纹章的

heraldry /ˈherəldri/ *n* [u] 1 (study, history) 纹章学 2 (pomp) 盛典

herb /hɜːb, Amer ɜːrb, hɜːrb/ *n* 1 (plant) 草本植物 2 (for cooking) 香草; (with medicinal properties) 药草

herbaceous /hɜːˈbeɪʃəs/ *adj* 1 Bot 草本的 ‹*plant*› 2 (containing perennials) 有多年生草本植物的; **~ border** 多年生草本植物花坛

herbal /ˈhɜːbl/

A *adj* 草本植物的; **~ medicine** 药草学

B *n* 草药志

herbalist /ˈhɜːbəlɪst/ ▸**p. 409** *n* 1 (person) (selling herbs) 药草商; (studying herbs) 草本植物学家 2 (shop) 草药店

herbarium /hɜːˈberɪəm/ *n* (*pl* **herbaria** /hɜːˈberɪə/) 1 (collection) 植物标本集 2 (room) 植物标本室; (building) 植物标本馆

herb garden *n* 百草园

herbicide /ˈhɜːbɪsaɪd/ *n* 除草剂

herbivore /ˈhɜːbɪvɔː(r)/ *n* 食草动物

herbivorous /hɜːˈbɪvərəs/ *adj* 食草的

herb tea, herbal tea *n* [u and c] 草药茶

Herceptin® /hɜːˈseptɪn/ *n* [u] 赫赛汀 [抗癌药]

Herculean /ˌhɜːkjʊˈliːən/ *adj* (possessing enormous strength) 力大无比的; (demanding enormous strength) 费力的; **a ~ struggle** 艰苦的斗争; **a ~ task** 艰巨的任务

Hercules /ˈhɜːkjʊliːz/ *pr n* 1 Mythol 赫拉克勒斯 [大力神] 2 (person) 大力士

herd /hɜːd/

A *n* 1 [c] (group of animals) 兽群; **a ~ of cattle** 一群牛 2 [c] pej (group of people) 人群; **a ~ of joggers** 一群慢跑者 3 [u] (ordinary people) 民众; **the common ~** 普通百姓; **to follow the ~** 随大溜

B *vt* 1 (drive) «*person, dog*» 把…赶在一起 ‹*animals, people*›; **they ~ed the prisoners into one room** 他们把犯人赶进了一间屋子 2 (keep or look after) 放牧; **the boy was ~ing goats** 男孩在放山羊

C *vi* 成群移动; **to ~ into sth.** 成群进入某处

herd instinct *n* [u] 群体本能

herdsman /ˈhɜːdzmən/ ▸**p. 409** *n* (owner) 牧主; (keeper) 牧人

here /hɪə(r)/ ▸**p. 193**

A *adv* 1 (at or in this place) 在这里; **we're over ~** 我们在这里; **in/up ~** 在这里面/上面; **down ~ in the valley** 在这下面的山谷里; **around** *or* **round** *or* **about** Brit **~** 这附近; **~ and there** 到处; **there's been some criticism ~ and there** 各方提出了一些批评; **~, there, and everywhere** 四处; **~ today and gone tomorrow** (soon over or forgotten) 稍纵即逝; (short-lived) 短暂的; **with acting, you're ~ today and gone tomorrow** 做演员往往让人昙花一现; **~'s to sb./sth.!** 为某人/某事干杯!; **~ we go** colloq 开始了; **~ we go (again)** colloq 又来了 [尤指坏事]; **~'s hoping** 我希望; **neither ~ nor there** 无关紧要; **~ lies ...** (on tombstone) 这里安葬的是… 2 (to this place) 到这里; **come over ~** 过来吧; **can you bring it ~?** 你把它带过来好吗? 3 (identifying person or thing close by) [指近处的人或物]; (in piece of writing) 这里; **ask this lady ~** 问一问这位女士吧; **this paragraph ~ needs to be deleted** 这一段得删除; **this ~ contraption** colloq 这个奇怪的玩意儿; **it says ~ that he was hanged** 这里写道，他被绞死了; **~ below** 下文 4 (indicating a person's role in a situation) [表示某人的作用]; **~ to do sth.** 来做某事; **I'm ~ to help you** 我是来帮助你的 5 (on telephone) [电话用语]; **hello, it's Anne ~** 喂，我是安妮 6 (in roll-call) 到; **Matthew Brown? — ~!** 马休·布朗? ——到! 7 (indicating arrival) 来了; **~'s my brother** 我弟弟来了; **~ we are at last** 我们终于到了; **~ comes the bus** 公共汽车开过来了 8 (when introducing sth.) [用以进行介绍]; **~ is the news** 下面播送新闻; **~'s a dish that's easy to make** 这是一道简单易做的菜; **~'s why** 这就是原因; **~ goes** colloq 看我的 9 (when giving sth.) [给东西时说]; **~ are your tickets** 这是你的票; **where's the knife? — ~ it is** 刀子在哪里? ——给; **~ we** *or* **you are! a nice hot cup of tea for you** 给! 为你沏的一杯热茶; **~ you go!** colloq 给! 10 (on this topic) 在这一点上; **~ I disagree with you** 在这一点上，我和你看法不同 11 (now) 此时; **the countdown to Christmas starts ~** 现在开始圣诞节倒计时; **~'s our chance to escape** 我们逃跑的机会来了

B *excl* 1 Brit (attracting attention) 喂; **~, hang on a minute!** 喂，等一下! 2 (said when offering sth.) [表示主动提议]; **~, take this one** 来，拿着这一个

hereabout /ˈhɪərəbaʊt/ Amer, **hereabouts** /ˈhɪərəbaʊts/ Brit *advs* 在这附近; **is there a post office ~?** 这一带有没有邮局?

hereafter /ˌhɪərˈɑːftə(r)/

A *n* 死后的生活; **the/a ~** 来世

B *adv* formal 此后

here and now

A *n* 1 (present) 现在; **a poet of the ~** 一位当代诗人 2 (life before death) 现世生活; **the ~** 此生

B *adv* 马上; **settle this ~** 马上处理这件事

hereby /hɪəˈbaɪ/ *adv* formal 特此; **I ~ promise that ...** 我在此承诺…

hereditary /hɪˈredɪtri, Amer -teri/ *adj* 1 (by inheritance) 世袭的 ‹*title, monarch*› 2 (by genetic factors) 遗传的 ‹*disease, characteristic*›

heredity /hɪˈredəti/ *n* [u] 1 (genetics) 遗传 2 (ancestry) 遗传特征

Herefordshire /ˈherɪfədʃɪə(r)/ *pr n* 赫里福德郡

herein /ˈhɪərɪn/ *adv* formal (in this document or book) 于此; (in this statement or fact) 在这方面; **~ lies the problem** 问题就在这里

hereinafter /ˌhɪərɪnˈɑːftə(r)/ *adv* formal 在下文

hereof /ˌhɪərˈɒv/ *adv* formal 在本文件中; **the provisions ~** 在本文件中的条款

heresy /ˈherəsi/ *n* 1 Relig 异教 2 fig (unorthodox opinion) 异端邪说; **saying that is ~** 说那样的话真是离经叛道

heretic /ˈherətɪk/ *n* 1 Relig 异教徒 2 fig (holder of unorthodox opinion) 离经叛道者

heretical /hɪˈretɪkl/ *adj* 1 Relig 异教的 2 fig (unorthodox) 离经叛道的

hereto /ˌhɪəˈtuː/ *adv* formal 于此; **attached ~** 在此附上; **the parties ~** 当事各方

heretofore /ˌhɪətuːˈfɔː(r)/ *adv* formal 在此之前

herewith /ˌhɪəˈwɪð/ *adv* formal 随同此信

heritable /ˈherɪtəbl/ *adj* 1 Biol 可遗传的 2 Scot Jur 可继承的

heritage /ˈherɪtɪdʒ/ *n* [u] 1 dated or formal (legacy) 遗产; **the dreadful ~ of war** fig 可怕的战争后遗症; **the ~ of revolution** fig 革命的产物 2 (cultural) 文化遗产

heritage: ~ centre *n* 文化遗产中心; **~ tourism** *n* [u] 文化遗产旅游

hermaphrodite /hɜːˈmæfrədaɪt/

A *n* (plant) 雌雄同株植物; (animal) 雌雄同体动物; (person) 两性人

B *adj* 雌雄同株的 ‹*plant*›; 雌雄同体的 ‹*animal*›; 两性的 ‹*person*›

hermeneutic /ˌhɜːmɪˈnjuːtɪk/

A *adj* (of the Bible) 《圣经》注解学的; (of literary texts) 阐释学的

B **hermeneutics** *npl* + *v sing* (of the Bible) 《圣经》注解学; (of literary texts) 阐释学

hermetic /hɜːˈmetɪk/ *adj* 1 (airtight) 密封的 2 fig (closed) 不受外界影响的; **a ~ society** 封闭的社会; **the ~ world of the theatre** 与世隔绝的戏剧世界

hermetically /hɜːˈmetɪkli/ *adv* 密封地

hermit /ˈhɜːmɪt/ *n* 隐士

hermitage /ˈhɜːmɪtɪdʒ/ *n* 隐居处

hermit crab *n* 寄居蟹

hernia /ˈhɜːnɪə/ *n* 疝

hero /ˈhɪərəʊ/ *n* (*pl* **~es**) 1 (courageous person) 英雄; (man one admires) 受崇拜的男人; **a ~'s welcome** 英雄般的欢迎; **he died a ~'s death** 他死得很英勇; **my ~** 我崇拜的偶像 2 (chief male character) 男主角 3 Mythol 神人

heroic /hɪˈrəʊɪk/ *adj* 1 (courageous) 英勇的; **he was ~ under fire** 他受到炮火攻击时表现得很英勇 2 (determined) 坚决的; (desperate) 用极端办法的; **to make ~ attempts to do sth.** 拼尽全力做某事; **~ efforts** 不懈的努力 3 Mythol 关于古代英雄的; **the ~ myths and legends** 英雄神话与传说 4 (grand) 宏大的; **a ~ tenor** 洪亮的男高音; **this was foolishness on a ~ scale** hum 这真是愚蠢至极 5 Literat 史诗体的; **~ verse** 英雄诗体

heroically /hɪˈrəʊɪkli/ *adv* 1 (courageously) 英勇地 2 (determinedly) 坚决地

heroics /hɪˈrəʊɪks/ *npl* 英雄行为

heroin /ˈherəʊɪn/ *n* [u] 海洛因; **to come off ~** 戒断海洛因毒瘾; **to be on ~** 有海洛因毒瘾

heroin: ~ addict *n* 海洛因瘾君子; **~ addiction** *n* [u] 海洛因毒瘾

heroine /ˈherəʊɪn/ *n* 1 (courageous woman) 女英雄; (woman one admires) 受崇拜的女人; **her teenage ~** 她少年时的偶像 2 (chief female character) 女主角

heroism /ˈherəʊɪzəm/ *n* [u] 英勇精神; **an act of ~** 英雄行为

heron /ˈherən/ *n* 鹭

hero sandwich Amer 大号三明治

hero-worship

A *n* [u] 偶像崇拜

B *vt* (*pres p etc.* **-pp-**, Amer **-p-**) 崇拜

herpes /ˈhɜːpiːz/ ▸**p. 377** *n* [u] 疱疹

herpesvirus /ˈhɜːpiːzvaɪərəs/ *n* 疱疹病毒

herring /ˈherɪŋ/ *n* (*pl* **~** *or* **~s**) 鲱

herringbone /ˈherɪŋbəʊn/ *n* [u] 1 (fabric) 人字呢 2 (design) 人字形图案; **~ weave** 人字形编织样式

herringbone stitch *n* 人字形缝法

herring gull *n* 银鸥

hers /hɜːz/ ▸**p. 487** *pron* 1 (belonging to woman, girl) 她的; **she took my hand in ~** 她握住我的手 2 colloq (belonging to female animal, car) 它的 3 dated (belonging to ship, country) 她的

herself /həˈself/ *pron* 1 (reflexive gen) 她自己; **she's cut ~** 她割伤了自己; **the dog hurt ~** 那条母狗弄伤了自己; **(all) by ~** (alone, unaided) 她独自; **(all) to ~** 由她独用; **she wants a room all to ~** 她想要一个完全属于自己的房间 2 (emphatic gen) 她本人; (female animal) 它本身; (ship, country) 她本身; **she ~ didn't know** 她本人并不知道 3 (in normal state) [表示状况正常]; **she's not/she doesn't seem ~ today** 她今天不舒服; **she wasn't feeling ~** 她感觉身体不适 4 (not influenced by others) [表示不受他人影响]; **she needed space to be ~** 她需要自己的独立空间

Hertfordshire /ˈhɑːtfədʃɪə(r)/ *pr n* 赫特福德郡

Herts. /hɑːts/ *abbr* Brit = **Hertfordshire**

hertz /hɜːts/ *n* (*pl* **hertz**) 赫兹

he's /hiːz/ colloq **1** = **he is** ▸**be** **2** = **he has** ▸**have**

hesitancy /ˈhezɪtənsi/ *n* [u] 不愿; **to have some ～ about doing sth.** 对是否做某事迟疑不决

hesitant /ˈhezɪtənt/ *adj* 犹豫的 ‹*reply, voice, step*›; **to be ～ about doing sth.** 对是否做某事犹豫不决; **his reading was ～** 他读得结结巴巴

hesitantly /ˈhezɪtəntli/ *adv* 犹豫地 ‹*reply*›; 步履蹒跚地 ‹*walk*›; 结结巴巴地 ‹*read*›

hesitate /ˈhezɪteɪt/ *vi* **1** (pause) 犹豫; **he jumped in without hesitating** 他毫不犹豫地跳了进去; **he who ～s is lost** Prov 当断不断，必受其患; **to ～ over sth.** 对某事拿不定主意; **to ～ at nothing** 什么都干得出来 **2** (be reluctant) 有顾虑; **he ～d to spoil the mood** 他怕破坏气氛; **don't ～ to telephone** 尽管打电话来

hesitation /ˌhezɪˈteɪʃn/ *n* **1** [c and u] (delay) 犹豫; **there is no room for ～** 没有踌躇的余地; **without the slightest** *or* **a moment's ～** 毫不犹豫地 **2** [u] (doubt) 疑虑; (reluctance) 不愿; **to have no ～ in doing sth.** 欣然做某事

hessian /ˈhesɪən, Amer ˈheʃn/ *n* [u] 粗麻布

hetero /ˈhetərəʊ/ *adj, n* (*pl* **～s**) colloq = **heterosexual**

heterodox /ˈhetərədɒks/ *adj* 非正统的 ‹*belief, doctrine*›; 持非正统观点的 ‹*person*›

heterodoxy /ˈhetərədɒksi/ *n* [u] (holding of different views) 持非正统观点; (beliefs) 非正统信仰

heterogeneous /ˌhetərəˈdʒiːnɪəs/ *adj* 各种各样的; **a ～ population** 由不同族裔组成的人口; **these designs are too ～** 这些图案太混杂了

heterosexual /ˌhetərəˈsekʃʊəl/

A *adj* 异性间的 ‹*attraction*›; 异性恋的 ‹*person, behaviour, couple*›

B *n* 异性恋者

heterosexuality /ˌhetərəˌsekʃʊˈæləti/ *n* [u] (sexual attraction) 异性恋; (sexual activity) 异性性行为

het up /ˌhetˈʌp/ *adj pred* colloq 生气的; **why are they all so ～?** 为什么他们全都那样生气?

heuristic /hjʊəˈrɪstɪk/

A *adj* 启发式的

B *n* 启发

C **heuristics** *npl + v sing* 启发法

hew /hjuː/ (*pt, pp* **hewn** /hjuːn/ *or* **～ed**)

A *vt* **1** (chop, cut) 砍 ‹*wood*›; 凿 ‹*stone*›; 采 ‹*coal*›; **to ～ a path through the forest** 在森林中辟出一条路来 **2** (to make, shape) 砍成; fig (make) 奋斗出 ‹*career, position*›; **a rough-hewn bench** 粗劈成的长凳; **statues hewn from marble** 用大理石凿刻成的雕像

B *vi* Amer (to adhere) **to ～ to sth.** 坚持某事

Phrasal verb

- **hew out** *vt* [**～ sth. out, ～ out sth.**] 凿成 ‹*monument, statue*›; fig 干出一番 ‹*career*›; 晋升 ‹*position*›

hex /heks/ Amer colloq

A *vt* 施魔法于

B *n* 魔法; **to put a ～ on sth./sb.** 对某物/某人施魔法

hexadecimal /ˌheksəˈdesɪml/

A *adj* 十六进制的

B *n* 十六进制

hexagon /ˈheksəgən, Amer -gɒn/ *n* 六边形

hexagonal /hekˈsægənl/ *adj* 六边形的

hexagram /ˈheksəgræm/ *n* 六角星形

hexameter /hekˈsæmɪtə(r)/ *n* [c and u] 六音步诗行

hey /heɪ/ *excl* colloq **1** (call for attention) 嗨; **～ you!** 喂! 我说你哪! **2** (in protest) 嘿; **～, that's mine!** 嘿，那是我的!

heyday /ˈheɪdeɪ/ *n* 全盛期; **in my ～** (my best) 在我年富力强之时; (the peak of one's success) 在我名声最盛时

hey presto /ˌheɪ ˈprestəʊ/ *excl* 变 [表示戏法变成功或完成某事易如反掌]; **press the start button and, ～, a copy comes out the other end** 按下开始键，嘿，一份复印件就从另一端出来了

H grade *n* Scot = **higher grade** 高级的

HGV *abbr* Brit = **heavy goods vehicle**

HI *abbr* Amer = **Hawaii**

hi /haɪ/ ▸**p. 333** *excl* colloq 嗨; **～, how are you?** 嗨，你好吗? ; **～ there!** 喂!

hiatus /haɪˈeɪtəs/ *n* (*pl* **～es** *or* **～**) **1** Ling 元音连读 **2** formal (break) 间断

hibernate /ˈhaɪbəneɪt/ *vi* «*animal*» 冬眠; hum «*person*» 蛰居; **I ～ in January** 我 1 月份待在家里不出门

hibernation /ˌhaɪbəˈneɪʃn/ *n* [u] 冬眠; **to go into ～** 进入冬眠; **to emerge from** *or* **come out of ～** 结束冬眠

hibiscus /hɪˈbɪskəs, Amer haɪ-/ *n* (*pl* **～es**) 木槿

hiccup, hiccough /ˈhɪkʌp/

A *n* **1** lit 呃逆; **to have** *or* **get (the) ～s** 打嗝 **2** fig (setback) 小问题

B *vi* (*pres p etc.* **-p-**) 打嗝

hick /hɪk/ Amer colloq pej

A *n* 乡巴佬

B *adj* (unsophisticated) 乡巴佬似的; (provincial) 乡下的; **a ～ town** 小乡镇

hickey /ˈhɪki/ *n* esp Amer sl 吻痕

hickory /ˈhɪkəri/ *n* **1** [c] (tree) 山核桃树 **2** [u] (wood) 山核桃木

hid /hɪd/ *pt* ▸**hide**¹ **A, B**

hidden /ˈhɪdn/ *pp* ▸**hide**¹ **A, B**

hide¹ /haɪd/

A *vt* (*pt* **hid,** *pp* **hidden**) **1** (conceal) 把…藏起来 ‹*money, book, person*›; **to ～ one's blushes** 不让别人看见自己脸红; **to ～ one's anger** 掩饰愤怒; **a hidden meaning** 言外之意; **to ～ one's light under a bushel** Prov 不露锋芒 **2** (keep secret) 掩盖; **to ～ a fact from sb.** 对某人隐瞒事实; **to have nothing to ～** 没什么可隐瞒的 **3** (obscure from view) 遮掩; **the house was hidden by the trees** 房子被树丛遮住了; **the future is hidden from us** 对我们来说，未来难以预料 **4** (cover) 遮盖; **she hid her face in his shoulder** 她把脸埋在他的肩膀上

B *vi* (*pt* **hid,** *pp* **hidden**) (conceal oneself) 躲藏; hum «*thing*» 隐藏; **a place to ～** 藏身之处; **to ～ behind sb./sth.** lit, fig 藏在某人/某物后面; **to ～ from the police** 躲开警察; **where are my keys hiding?** 我的钥匙放到哪里去了?

C *n* Brit 藏身处

Phrasal verbs

- **hide away**

A *vt* [**～ sth. away, ～ away sth.**] 把…藏起来

B *vi* 躲藏

- **hide out** Brit, **hide up** Amer *vi* 躲藏起来; **where have you been hiding out since April?** hum 从4月以来你藏哪儿去了?

hide² *n* **1** [c] (skin) 兽皮; **I've not seen ～ nor hair of him** 我连他的影子也没有看到 **2** [u] (leather) 皮革; **a ～ suitcase** 皮箱

hide: ～ and seek Brit, **～-and-go-seek** Amer ▸**p. 307** *ns* [u] 捉迷藏游戏; **～away** *n* (secret place) 躲藏处; (retreat) 退隐处; **～bound** *adj* 迂腐守旧的

hideous /ˈhɪdɪəs/ *adj* **1** (ugly) 极其丑陋的; (very unpleasant) 令人厌恶的; **a truly ～ vase** 十分难看的花瓶; **～ noise** 讨厌的噪声 **2** (terrible) 令人惊骇的; **a ～ mistake** 可怕的错误; **a ～ murder** 骇人听闻的谋杀案

hideously /ˈhɪdɪəsli/ *adv* **1** (repulsively) 令人厌恶地; (grotesquely) 极其丑陋地 **2** colloq (very) 非常 ‹*expensive, embarrassing*›

hideout /ˈhaɪdaʊt/ *n* 藏身处

hiding¹ /ˈhaɪdɪŋ/ *n* [u] (concealment) 躲藏; **to go into ～** 躲藏起来; **to be in ～** 躲藏着; **to emerge from** *or* **come out of ～** 从躲藏处出来

hiding² *n* (beating) 痛打; **to give sb. a (good) ～** 痛打某人一顿; **to be on a ～ to nothing** Brit colloq 毫无成功希望

hiding place *n* (for person) 藏身处; (for object) 隐藏处

hierarchic /ˌhaɪəˈrɑːkɪk/, **hierarchical** /ˌhaɪəˈrɑːkɪkl/ *adj* **1** (of a hierarchy) 等级制度的 **2** (arranged in a hierarchy) 分等级的; **a ～ society** 阶级社会

hierarchy /ˈhaɪərɑːki/ *n* **1** (system) 等级制度 **2** (people) 统治集团 **3** (classification) 等级体系; **the ～ of the invertebrates** 无脊椎动物的级系

hieroglyph /ˈhaɪərəglɪf/ *n* **1** (pictograph) 象形文字; (symbol) 象形符号 **2** (incomprehensible symbol) 难以理解的符号

hieroglyphic /ˌhaɪərəˈglɪfɪk/

A **hieroglyphics** *npl* **1** (writing in hieroglyphs) 象形文字 **2** (illegible writing) 难以辨认的文字

B *adj* 用象形文字写成的

hifalutin /ˌhaɪfəˈluːtɪn/ *adj* colloq = **highfalutin**

hi-fi /ˈhaɪfaɪ/

A *adj* 高保真的; **a ～ system** 高保真系统

B *n* 高保真音响设备

higgledy-piggledy /ˌhɪgldɪˈpɪgldi/

A *adj* 杂乱无章的; **a ～ collection of houses** 一片杂乱错落的房屋

B *adv* 杂乱无章地; **all the shoes were lying ～ by the door** 所有的鞋子都乱七八糟地放在门口

high /haɪ/ ▸**p. 436**

A *adj* **1** (tall) 高的; **the ～est mountain in the world** 世界上最高的山; **a shoe with a ～ heel** 高跟鞋; **how ～ is it?** 它有多高? ; **to be 10 feet ～** 高 10 英尺; **a 3-metre-～ wall** 3 米高的墙 **2** (far from bottom) 在高处的; **a room with a ～ ceiling** 天花板很高的房间; **a jumper with a ～ neck** 高领针织衫; **to fly at a ～ altitude** 在高空飞行; **a ～ plateau** 高原; **how ～ (up) are we?** 我们距地面有多高? ; **an 8-foot-～ ceiling** 8 英尺高的天花板 **3** (above usual level) 上涨的 ‹*sea, tide*›; **the river is ～ today** 今天河水上涨了 **4** (at or near top of scale) 居高的; **a ～ price/speed/temperature** 高价/高速/高温; **a ～ standard** 高水平 **5** (great) 高度的 ‹*praise*›; **a state of ～ anxiety** 极度焦虑的状态; **a moment of ～ drama** 极具戏剧性的时刻; **to be at ～ risk of heart disease** 极易罹患心脏病; **it's ～ time (that) ...** colloq 是（…的）时候了; **it's ～ time she faced facts** 她该面对事实了 **6** Aut (gear) 高速的; **in ～ gear** 以高速挡 **7** Games 点数大的; **a ～ card** 大牌 **8** (plentiful) 含量高的; **to have a ～ iron content** 富含铁; **foods ～ in fat** 高脂肪食物 **9** *usu attrib* (noble) 崇高的 ‹*ideals, principles*› **10** *usu attrib* (favourable) 十分赞许的; **to have a ～ opinion of sb./sth.** 对某人/某事物评价很高; **to be held in (very) ～ regard by sb.** （很）受某人的敬重 **11** *usu attrib* (in rank, status) 高层的; **the ～est authority** 最高当局; **a ～er court** 上级法院; **to hold ～ office** 担任要职; **to be ～ up (in sth.)** （在某组织中）地位很高; **in ～ places** fig 身居高位; **corruption in ～ places** 高层腐败; **to have friends in ～ places** 认识有权有势的人; **to go on to ～er things** fig colloq 升到更高的职位 **12** *attrib* (advanced) 高级的; **the ～er plants/animals** 高等植物/动物; **to study for a ～er degree** 攻读更高的学位 **13** *attrib* (strong) 强劲的 ‹*wind*› **14** (at peak) 全盛的 ‹*period*›; **in ～ summer** 在盛夏;

h

~ Gothic 哥特风格的鼎盛时期 15 (flushed) **to have a ~ colour** 脸色红润 16 Geog **at ~ latitudes** 高纬度 17 (in pitch) 高音的; **the ~ notes** 高音符; **to speak in a ~ voice** 尖声讲话 18 *pred* (mature) 开始变质的〈*cheese, meat*〉; **the fish smells rather ~** colloq euph 这鱼闻起来很不新鲜 19 *pred* colloq (euphoric) 非常高兴的; (on drug) 表现兴奋的; **to be/get ~ on heroin** 因吸食海洛因而神志恍惚; **to be ~ on success** 因获胜而兴高采烈 20 Ling 舌位高的; **a ~ vowel** 高元音

B *adv* 1 (to great height) 高高地; **to build the wall ~** 把墙筑高; **to be piled ~**《*papers*》堆得高高的 2 (toward great height) 向高处; (at great height) 在高处; **to climb ~er and ~er** 越爬越高; **to write the address ~er up** 把地址写高一点; **to fly ~** lit 在高空飞行; fig 洋洋自得; **to run ~**《*river*》上涨;《*emotions, tempers*》激昂; **to hold one's head (up) ~** lit 昂首; fig 感到骄傲; **to search ~ and low** fig 到处找 3 (in cost, amount) **to be/go as ~ as ...**《*inflation*》高达…; **to creep ~er**《*prices*》逐步攀升 4 (to high level) **to turn sth. up ~** 把…调高〈*volume*〉; 把…的音量调高〈*radio, TV*〉; 把…开大〈*gas, heating*〉 5 (in importance) 处于高层; **to take sth. ~er** 把…呈交上级处理〈*case, appeal*〉; **to get ~ up in the company** 在公司里担任要职 6 (at high pitch) 音调高地; **I can't sing that ~** 我唱不了那么高

C *n* 1 (high level) 高水平; **an all-time** *or* **a record ~** 历史最高水平; **to rise to** *or* **hit** *or* **reach a new ~** 创下新高 2 Meteorol (pressure system) 高气压区; (temperature) 最高气温 3 colloq (euphoria) 兴奋感; **to give sb. a ~**《*drug*》给某人带来快感;《*success, compliment*》让某人十分开心; **to be on a ~** (drug-induced) 正经历快感; (happy) 处于兴奋状态 4 Amer Sch colloq = **high school 1**

D on high *adv phr* 1 liter (in high place) 在高处; **from on ~** 从高处; **the stars on ~** 高空的星星 2 Relig liter 在天上; **from on ~** 来自上天的; **the order came down from on ~** hum 指示是上头下达的

high: ~ altar *n* 主祭台; **~ and dry** *adj* 1 (stranded) 不在水里的; **the yacht was ~ and dry on a sandbank** 游艇搁浅在沙洲上; 2 fig (without help, resources) 孤立无援的; **his Dad left them ~ and dry years ago** 他的父亲多年前就抛弃了他们; **some businesses have been left ~ and dry** 一些企业陷入了困境; **~-angle shot** *n* 高角度拍摄; **~ball** *n* Amer 高杯酒; **~ beam** *n* [u] Amer 远光; **~boy** *n* Amer 高脚五斗橱

highbrow /ˈhaɪbraʊ/
A *n* 趣味高雅的人
B *adj* 趣味高雅的

high chair *n* 高脚椅

High Church
A *n* [u] 高派教会
B *adj* 高派教会的

high: ~-class *adj* 1 (high-quality) 高级的; 2 (of a high social class) 上流社会的; **~ comedy** *n* [u] 高雅喜剧; **~ command** *n* [u] 最高指挥部; **~ commission** *n* 高级专员公署; **~ commissioner** ▸p. 409 *n* 高级专员; **~ court** *n* 最高法院; **H~ Court (of Justice)** *n* Brit 高等法院; **~ day** *n* Brit dated 宗教节日; **~-definition** *adj* 高清晰度的; **~-definition television** *or* **TV** 高清晰度电视; **~-density** *adj* 1 (high-capacity) 大容量的〈*disc, tape*〉; 2 Phys, Tech 高密度的〈*plastic, metal*〉; 3 (with many buildings) 建筑物密集的〈*area*〉; **~-density housing** *n* [u] 高密度住房; **~-dependency** *adj* 需特别护理的; **~ diver** *n* 高台跳水运动员; **~ diving** ▸p. 307 *n* [u] 高台跳水; **~-energy physics** *n* + *v sing* 高能物理学

Higher /ˈhaɪə(r)/ *n* Scot 教育高级证书

high: ~er education *n* [u] 高等教育; **~er mathematics** *npl* + *v sing* 高等数学; **Higher National Certificate** *n* Brit 国家高级证书; **Higher National Diploma** *n* Brit 国家高等技术学校毕业证书; **~er-up** *n* colloq 上级; **~est common factor** *n* 最大公约数; **~ explosive** *n* [c and u] 烈性炸药

highfalutin /ˌhaɪfəˈluːtɪn/, **highfaluting** /ˌhaɪfəˈluːtɪŋ/ *adj* colloq 装模作样的

high: ~ fashion *n* [u] 高级时装业; **~-fibre** *adj* 高纤维的

high fidelity
A *n* [u] 高保真
B high-fidelity *modif* 高保真的

high: ~ finance *n* [u] 巨额融资; **~ five** *n* esp Amer colloq 举手击掌 [表示庆贺或打招呼]; **to give sb. a ~ five** 与某人举手击掌; **~-flier** *n* (someone very successful) 大获成功的人; (someone with potential) 有成功潜力的人; **~-flown** *adj* usu pej 好高骛远的〈*ideas*〉; 言过其实的〈*phrases, speech, style*〉; **~-flyer** *n* = **~-flier**; **~-flying** *adj* 1 (successful) 大获成功的〈*executive*〉; (ambitious) 很有抱负的; **a ~-flying plan** 雄心勃勃的计划; 2 Aviat 在高空飞行的; **~-frequency** *n* 高频; **~-grade** *adj* (high-quality) 高级的〈*product*〉; 纯度高的〈*mineral, ore*〉; **~ ground** *n* [u] 1 lit (elevated land) 高地; 2 fig (moral position) 优势; **to seize** *or* **claim** *or* **take the (moral) ~ ground** (道义上)处于有利地位; **~-handed** *adj* 专横的; **~-handedly** *adv* 以高压手段〈*govern*〉; 专横地〈*behave, speak*〉; **~-handedness** *n* [u] 专横; **the ~-handedness of the government's action** 政府的高压行动; **~ hat** *n* 踩钹 [鼓的配件]; **~-heeled** *adj* 高跟的; **~ heels** *npl* 1 (heels) 高跟; 2 (shoes) 高跟鞋; **~-impact** *adj* 1 (strong) 抗冲击的〈*plastic*〉; 2 Sport 高强度的〈*activity, sport*〉; 3 (violent) 猛烈的〈*crash, collision*〉; 严重的〈*injury*〉; 4 (powerful) 影响力巨大的〈*advertising, publication, news*〉; **~-income** *adj* 高收入的; **~-intensity** *adj* 1 (very bright) 高亮度的〈*light*〉; 2 (intense) 高强度的〈*training, game*〉; **~-interest** *adj* 高利息的; **~ jinks** /ˌhaɪ ˈdʒɪŋks/ *npl* colloq 狂欢作乐; **we had ~ jinks at the office party** 我们在办公室聚会上玩得很痛快; **~ jump** ▸p. 307 *n* 1 Sport 跳高; 2 Brit colloq **to be for the ~ jump** 将受到严厉惩罚; **~ jumper** *n* 跳高运动员; **~ kick** *n* [舞蹈或武术中的] 大踢腿

highland /ˈhaɪlənd/
A *n* 高地
B highlands *npl* 高原地区; **the H~s** (of Scotland) 苏格兰高地
C *modif* 高地的〈*region, vegetation*〉

Highlander /ˈhaɪləndə(r)/ *n* (Scottish) 苏格兰高地人

highlander /ˈhaɪləndə(r)/ *n* 高地人

Highland: ~ fling *n* 苏格兰高地舞; **to do the ~ fling** 跳高地舞; **~ Games** *npl* 苏格兰高地运动会; **~ Region** *pr n* **the ~ Region** 苏格兰高地

> **the Highlands**
>
> 苏格兰高地。苏格兰北部多山地区,欧洲著名的风景区。该名称是相对东南部的低地(Lowlands)而言。苏格兰盖尔语(▸**Gaelic**)使用者主要集中于这一地区。区域内的本尼维斯山(Ben Nevis)海拔 1343 米,是英国的最高峰;尼斯湖(Loch Ness)因传说中的尼斯湖怪(Loch Ness Monster 或 Nessie)而闻名于世。高地服装(Highland dress)是苏格兰男子的传统服装,也是英国军队中苏格兰士兵的军装。主要包括格子花呢短褶裙(tartan kilt)、裙子前挂的毛皮袋(sporran)和格子花呢披风(tartan plaid,披于左肩)。苏格兰高地人称作Highlander。

high: ~-level *adj* 1 (involving people of high rank) 高层的〈*meeting*〉; 高级别的〈*officials, committee*〉; 2 Comput 高级的〈*language, programming*〉; **~ life** *n* [u] 豪华的生活

highlight /ˈhaɪlaɪt/
A *n* 1 Art 强光部分 2 (in hair) 挑染的头发; **to put ~s in one's hair** 挑染头发 3 (best part) (gen) 最精彩的部分; (of match, show, event) 最精彩的片段
B *vt* 1 Art (accentuate)《*artist*》用强光突出〈*form, point of interest*〉;《*light*》突出〈*form, point of interest*〉 2 (draw attention to) 强调〈*issue, needs*〉 3 (mark with highlighter) 用荧光笔标出 4 (bleach) 挑染〈*hair*〉

high: ~lighter /ˈhaɪlaɪtə(r)/ *n* 荧光笔; **~ living** *n* [u] 豪华生活

highly /ˈhaɪli/ *adv* 1 (very) 非常; **~ important** 极为重要的; **~ developed** 高度发达的; **~ classified** 绝密的; **a ~ educated young man** 受过高等教育的年轻人 2 (enthusiastically, favourably) 高度赞许地; **to speak ~ of sb.** 对某人大加称赞; **to praise sb. ~** 高度赞扬某人; **to be ~ regarded** 受到很高的评价 3 (with a large amount) 大量地; **~ priced** 价格高昂的

highly: ~-charged *adj* 高度紧张的〈*atmosphere*〉; 非常激烈的〈*game, debate*〉; 饱含激情的〈*narrative*〉; **~-coloured** *adj* 1 (bright, colourful) 色彩鲜亮的; 2 (exaggerated) 添枝加叶的〈*story, account*〉; **~-paid** *adj* 高收入的; **~-placed** *adj* 职位高的; **~-polished** *adj* 高度抛光的; **~-principled** *adj* 节操高尚的; **~-sexed** *adj* 性欲过强的; **~-strung** *adj* 紧张不安的; **~-trained** *adj* 受过高水平训练的

high-minded *adj* 高尚的

highness /ˈhaɪnɪs/ *n* 1 **Highness** (title) **his/her/your (Royal) ~** 殿下 2 (of building) 高; (of voice, sound) 尖

high: ~ noon *n* [u] 1 (midday) 正午; **at ~ noon** 在正午; 2 fig (decisive event) 决定性事件; **~-occupancy vehicle** *n* Amer 高乘载车辆; **~-octane** *adj* 1 Aut, Aviat 高辛烷值的〈*fuel*〉; 2 fig (dynamic) 富有活力的〈*style, match*〉; **~-performance** *adj* 高性能的〈*car, computer*〉; 高精确性的〈*technology, material*〉; **~-pitched** *adj* 很高的〈*sound, note*〉; 尖厉的〈*voice, whistle, scream*〉; **~ point** *n* = **~ spot**; **~-powered** *adj* 1 (powerful) 大功率的〈*engine*〉; 大马力的〈*car*〉; 高倍的〈*telescope, microscope*〉; 2 fig (important) 重要的〈*business, course*〉; 责任重大的〈*job*〉; (dynamic) 精力充沛的〈*executive, official*〉

high pressure
A *n* [u] 高气压
B high-pressure *modif* 1 Meteorol 高气压的〈*area, system*〉; Tech 高压的〈*system, gas, hose*〉 2 fig (aggressive) 使用强制手段的〈*salesman*〉; **high-pressure sales tactics** 强行推销术 3 fig (stressful) 压力大的〈*job, work*〉

high: ~-priced *n* 昂贵的〈*goods, housing*〉; **~ priest** *n* 1 Relig (chief priest) 大祭司; (in Judaism) 祭司长; 2 fig (chief proponent) 领袖; **the ~ priest of existentialism** 存在主义的领军人物; **one of the ~ priests of modern technology** 现代科技的领头人之一; **~ priestess** *n* 1 Relig 女大祭司; 2 fig (chief proponent) 女领袖; **the ~ priestess of fashion** 引领时尚的女人; **~-principled** *adj* 节操高尚的; **~-profile** *adj* 广受关注的; **~-protein** *adj* 含高蛋白的; **~-ranking** *adj* 职位高的〈*official*〉; 显要的〈*position*〉; **~-resolution** *adj* 高清晰度的〈*image, screen*〉

high-rise
A *adj* 高层的; **a ~ office block** 高耸的办公大楼
B *n* 高层建筑

high: ~-risk *adj* 1 (dangerous) 高风险的〈*occupation, sport*〉; 2 (in danger) 高度危险的; **a ~-risk patient/group** 高危病人/群体; **~ road** *n* 1 Brit dated (main road) 主干道; 2 fig (direct way) 最直接的方式; **the ~ road to success/fame/fortune** 通向成功/出名/

发大财的最佳途径; **3** Amer fig (morally superior approach) 高尚途径; **he took the ~ road in his campaign** 他在竞选中走的是正大光明的路线; ~ **roller** *n* colloq (big spender) 挥金如土的人; (gambler) 豪赌者; ~ **school** *n* **1** Amer (secondary school) 中学; **2** Brit (grammar school) 文法学校; **~-scoring** *adj* 得高分的 ‹*player, striker, game*›; ~ **seas** *npl* 公海; **on the ~ seas** 在公海上; ~ **season** *n* [u] esp Brit [旅游的] 旺季; **in (the) ~ season** 在旺季; **~-season prices** 旺季的价格; **~-security** *adj* 戒备森严的 ‹*jail, cell*›; 高度安全的 ‹*fence, vault*›; **~-sided vehicle** *n* [卡车等] 高帮汽车; ~ **society** *n* [u] 上流社会; **~-sounding** *adj* pej 虚夸的 ‹*language, ideas*›; **~-speed** *adj* **1** (fast) 高速的 ‹*train, plane, printer, machine, transport*›; **2** Phot 高感光度的 ‹*film*›; 高速的 ‹*camera, lens*›; **~-spending** *adj* 高消费的 ‹*lifestyle, person*›; 开销很大的 ‹*project, government*›; **~-spirited** *adj* **1** (lively) 兴高采烈的 ‹*person*›; **2** (difficult to control) 烈性的 ‹*horse*›; ~ **spirits** *npl* 欢欣; **to be in ~ spirits** 兴高采烈; ~ **spot** *n* (most exciting) 最精彩的部分; (most enjoyable) 最好玩的部分; **to hit the ~ spots** 游玩主要景点

high street Brit
A *n* [市镇商业区的] 大街; **in the ~** 在商业大街
B **high-street** *modif* 商业大街的; **high-street fashion/prices** 大众款式/市场价格

high-street: ~ **bank** *n* 商业大街上的银行; ~ **shop** *n* 商业大街上的商店; ~ **spending** *n* [u] 商业大街上的花销

high: **~-strung** *adj* Amer = **highly-strung**; ~ **summer** *n* [u] 盛夏; ~ **table** *n* **1** [c] (at function) [要人的] 高台餐桌; **2** [u] Brit Univ [院长、导师与贵客的] 贵宾桌; **~tail** *vi* esp Amer colloq 急忙离开; **to ~tail it** 迅速离开; **to ~tail out of a place** 迅速逃离某地; ~ **tea** *n* [u and c] Brit 傍晚茶

high tech /ˌhaɪ ˈtek/
A *n* [u] **1** (high technology) 高科技 **2** (style) 高技术室内装饰
B **high-tech** *adj* **1** (using high-technology) 高科技的 ‹*equipment, company*›; ~ **gadgets for the home** 高科技家用器具 **2** (modern) 现代化的 ‹*design, decor*›; 使用现代化材料的 ‹*furniture, house*›

high: ~ **technology** *n* [u] 高科技; **~-tension** *adj* 高（电）压的; ~ **tide** *n* [u and c] (level) 高潮; (time) 高潮时期; ~ **treason** *n* [u] 叛国罪; **~-up** *n* colloq 高官; **~-velocity** *adj* 高速的; **~-visibility jacket,** colloq **~-vis jacket** /ˌhaɪˈvɪz/ *n* 高能见度反光夹克; ~ **voltage** *n* 高（电）压; **~-voltage** *adj* 高（电）压的 ‹*cable, current*›

high water *n* [u] (level) 高潮; (time) 满潮时刻

high-water mark *n* **1** lit (artificial, natural) 高水位线 **2** fig 顶峰

highway /ˈhaɪweɪ/ *n* **1** esp Amer (main road) 公路 **2** Brit (public road) 公用通道

highway: **H~ Code** *n* Brit 公路法规; ~ **engineer, ~s engineer** ▸p. 409 *n* 公路工程师; ~ **maintenance** *n* [u] 公路维护; **~man** /-mən/ *n* [骑马持枪的] 拦路强盗; ~ **patrol** *n* Amer 公路巡警; ~ **robbery** *n* [u] lit 公路抢劫; fig 漫天要价; **H~s Department** *n* [地方政府的] 公路部

high wire *n* [杂技演员走的] 高空绳索

hijack /ˈhaɪdʒæk/
A *vt* **1** (illegally seize) 劫持 ‹*aircraft, bus, car*›; 拦路抢劫 ‹*cargo*› **2** fig (take over) 把持 ‹*meeting, organization*›
B *n* 劫持

hijacker /ˈhaɪdʒækə(r)/ *n* (of plane) 劫机者; (of bus, car) 劫持者

hijacking /ˈhaɪdʒækɪŋ/ *n* [c and u] 劫持; **the recent rise in ~s** 最近劫持事件的增多

hike /haɪk/
A *n* **1** (walk) 远足; **to go on** *or* **for a ~** 去远足 **2** (sharp increase) 大幅度上升; **wage/price ~** 工资/价格大幅上涨
B *vi* 远足; **they ~d all round Italy** 他们环意大利徒步旅行
C *vt* colloq **1** (*also* ~ **up**) (pull up) 拉起 ‹*trousers, socks*› **2** (increase) 大幅提高 ‹*price, rent*›

hiker /ˈhaɪkə(r)/ *n* 远足者

hiking /ˈhaɪkɪŋ/ ▸p. 307 *n* [u] 远足; **a ~ holiday** 徒步旅行的假期

hiking boot *n* 旅行靴

hilarious /hɪˈleərɪəs/ *adj* 极其滑稽的; **we had a ~ time** 我们玩得非常快活; **he's ~ in that film** 他在那部电影里十分滑稽

hilariously /hɪˈleərɪəslɪ/ *adv* 极其滑稽地; ~ **funny** 滑稽可笑

hilarity /hɪˈlærətɪ/ *n* [u] 狂欢

hill /hɪl/ *n* **1** (raised land) 小山; **a range of ~s** 一片丘陵; **to take to the ~s** 逃跑后躲起来; **as old as the ~s** 古老的; **to be over the ~** fig 在走下坡路; **over ~ and dale** liter 漫山遍野; **up ~ and down dale** liter 到处; **over the ~s and far away** 遥远的 **2** (hillside) 山坡; (slope, incline) 斜坡

hillbilly /ˈhɪlbɪlɪ/ *n* Amer colloq pej 山区乡巴佬

hill: ~ **climb** *n* [汽车或摩托车] 爬坡比赛; ~ **farming** *n* [u] Brit 山地牧业

hilliness /ˈhɪlɪnɪs/ *n* [u] 多丘陵

hillock /ˈhɪlək/ *n* 小丘

hill: **~side** *n* 小山坡; **on the ~side** 在山坡上; ~ **station** *n* [印度的] 山区避暑小镇; **~top** *n* 小山顶; **a ~top settlement** 小山顶上的定居点; **~walker** *n* 丘陵远足者; **~walking** *n* [u] 丘陵远足

hilly /ˈhɪlɪ/ *adj* 多丘陵的 ‹*landscape, country*›; 陡的 ‹*road, garden*›

hilt /hɪlt/ *n* (of weapon) 柄; **(up) to the ~** fig 完全地; **to be mortgaged up to the ~** 全部被抵押; **I'm up to the ~ in debt** 我负债累累; **to back sb. (up) to the ~** 全力支持某人

him /hɪm/ *pron* **1** (referring to man, boy) 他 **2** (referring to male animal) 它 [指雄性动物] **3** **Him** (referring to God) 他 [指上帝]; **praise Him!** 赞美主吧!

Himalayas /ˌhɪməˈleɪəz/ *pr npl* **the ~** 喜马拉雅山脉

himself /hɪmˈself/ *pron* **1** (reflexive gen) 他自己; **he introduced ~** 他作了自我介绍; **the cat was sunning ~** 那只猫在晒太阳; **(all) by ~** (alone, unaided) 他独自; **(all) to ~** 由他独用; **he has the house to ~ during the week** 从周一到周五他一个人住着这所房子 **2** (emphatic gen) 他本人; (male animal) 它本身; **he ~ didn't know** 他本人并不知道 **3** (in normal state) [表示状况正常]; **he's not/he doesn't seem ~ today** 他今天不舒服; **he isn't feeling ~** 他感觉身体不舒服 **4** (not influenced by others) [表示不受他人影响]; **he wanted the freedom to be ~** 他想自由自在

hind[1] /haɪnd/ *adj* 后面的; ~ **legs** 后腿; **to talk the ~ leg off a donkey** fig 唠叨个没完没了

hind[2] *n* 雌鹿 [尤指3岁以上的赤鹿或梅花鹿]

hinder /ˈhɪndə(r)/ *vt* (hamper) 妨碍 ‹*person*›; (delay) 阻挡 ‹*activity, progress*›

Hindi /ˈhɪndɪ/ ▸p. 426
A *n* [u] 印地语
B *adj* 印地语的

hindmost /ˈhaɪndməʊst/ *adj* 最后面的; **(the) devil take the ~** 要鬼捉不到，抢在人前逃

hindquarters /ˌhaɪndˈkwɔːtəz/ *npl* [四足动物的] 后腿及臀部

hindrance /ˈhɪndrəns/ *n* (thing) 阻碍物; (person) 阻碍者; **to be a ~ to sb./sth.** 是某人的累赘/某事的障碍; **he's more of a ~ than a help** 他没帮上忙，反而成了累赘

hindsight /ˈhaɪndsaɪt/ *n* [u] 事后聪明; **with (the benefit of) ~** 事后一想

Hindu /ˌhɪnˈduː, ˈhɪnduː/
A *n* 印度教教徒
B *adj* 印度教的 ‹*religion, civilization, people*›; 印度教的 ‹*gods, philosophy*›

Hinduism /ˈhɪnduːɪzəm/ *n* [u] 印度教

Hindustani /ˌhɪndʊˈstɑːnɪ/ ▸p. 426
A *n* [u] **1** (group of languages) 印度斯坦语 **2** (specific dialect) 德里方言
B *adj* 印度西北部文化的

hinge /hɪndʒ/
A *n* 铰链; **to come off one's ~s** 铰链脱落; fig 精神异常
B *vt* 给…装铰链; **the box had a ~d lid** 箱子有个带铰链的盖子
C *vi* **1** lit «*door, lid*» 靠铰链转动; **to ~ on sth.** 铰接在某物上 **2** fig (depend) 依赖; **to ~ on sb./sth.** «*result, outcome*» 取决于某人/某事物

hint /hɪnt/
A *n* **1** (insinuation) 暗示; **a broad ~** 明显的示意; **to drop a ~ (about sb./sth.) to sb.** 给某人（关于某人/某事物的）暗示; **to take a/the ~** 领会暗示; **some people just can't take a ~!** 有些人就是不会看眼色! **2** (sign) 迹象; **at the first ~ of trouble** 一发现不妙的迹象 **3** (clue) 提示; **to give sb. a ~** 给某人提示 **4** (of flavour, emotion, accent) 少许; **white with a ~ of pink** 略呈粉红的白色; **a ~ of impatience** 有点儿不耐烦 **5** (tip) 建议; **handy ~s for gardeners** 园艺妙诀
B *vt* 暗示; **to ~ (to sb.) that ...** （向某人）暗示说…
C *vi* 暗示; **to ~ at sth.** 暗示某事; **to keep ~ing about sth.** 一直在暗示某事物

hinterland /ˈhɪntəlænd/ *n* **1** (remote area) 偏僻地区; **the mountainous ~** 偏僻的山区 **2** (area beyond town, river) 腹地

hip[1] /hɪp/ *n* **1** ▸p. 71 Anat 髋; **to break one's ~ in a fall** 摔断髋骨; **to stand with one's hands on one's ~s** *or* **with hands on ~s** 双手叉腰站着 **2** **hips** (area below waist) 臀部; **to have large ~s** 臀部大 **3** Archit 屋脊; **a ~ roof** 有斜背的屋顶

hip[2] *n* Bot 野蔷薇果

hip[3] *excl* (in exclamations) 嘿 [欢呼喝彩声]; **~ ~ hurrah!** 嘿，嘿，万岁!

hip[4] *adj* colloq (fashionable) 时髦的 ‹*clothes, style, music*›

hip: ~ **bath** *n* 坐浴盆; **~bone** *n* 髋骨; ~ **flask** *n* [可随身携带的] 小扁酒瓶; ~ **hop** *n* [u] 嘻哈音乐; ~ **joint** *n* 髋关节; ~ **measurement** *n* 臀围

hippie /ˈhɪpɪ/ *n* 嬉皮士; **a ~ lifestyle** 嬉皮士生活方式

> **hippie**
>
> 嬉皮士，亦作 hippy。20 世纪六七十年代西方反传统的年轻人。美国加利福尼亚州的旧金山是他们的文化中心。hippie 源于形容词 hip（时髦的），后者用于形容 20 世纪 50 年代垮掉的一代（Beat Generation）成员。为了表示和传统道德习俗格格不入，嬉皮士常常身着奇装异服、留长发、性生活放纵，甚至吸毒。他们常常多人混居，称为公社（commune）。嬉皮士反对越战，相信爱与和平能够改变世界，常被称为“花童”（flower children，▸**flower power**）。

hippo /ˈhɪpəʊ/ *n* (*pl* ~ *or* **~s**) colloq = **hippopotamus**

hip pocket *n* 后口袋

Hippocratic oath /ˌhɪpəkrætɪk ˈəʊθ/ *n* 希波克拉底誓言 [表明医生的职业操守]

hippopotamus /ˌhɪpəˈpɒtəməs/ *n* (*pl* **~es** *or* **hippopotami** /ˌhɪpəˈpɒtəmaɪ/) 河马

hippy *n* = **hippie**

hip replacement *n* [c and u] 髋关节置换; **to have a ~** 做髋关节置换手术

hipster /ˈhɪpstə(r)/
A *adj* Brit 低腰的; **a pair of ~ jeans** 一条低腰牛仔裤
B **hipsters** *npl* (trousers) 低腰长裤; (jeans) 低腰牛仔裤

hire /ˈhaɪə(r)/
A *n* [u] 租用; **car/boat/video ~** 汽车/船只/录像出租; **on** *or* **for ~** 供出租
B *vt* esp Brit 租用 ‹*vehicle, equipment*›; 雇用 ‹*person*›; **a ~d killer** 雇佣杀手; **to take on ~d help** 招收雇工

Phrasal verb
- **hire out**
A *vt* [**~ sth. out, ~ out sth.**] 出租
B *v refl* **to ~ oneself out** 受雇; **he ~d himself out as a van driver** 他受雇当了客货车司机

hire: ~ car *n* (rented) 租用的汽车; (for rent) 供出租的汽车; **~ charge** *n* 租金; **~ company, ~ firm** *ns* 出租公司

hired hand *n* 雇工

hireling /ˈhaɪəlɪŋ/ *n* pej 可受雇干杂活的人

hire purchase *n* [u] Brit **on ~** 以分期付款方式; **a ~ agreement** 分期付款协议

hirsute /ˈhɜːsjuːt, Amer -suːt/ *adj* formal or hum 多毛的 ‹*face, limbs*›; 体毛多的 ‹*person*›

his /hɪz/ ▸**p. 487**
A *pron* **1** (referring to man, boy) 他的; **he took my hand in ~** 他握住我的手 **2** (referring to male animal) 它的 [指雄性动物的] **3** **His** (referring to God) 祂的 [指上帝的]; **the glory is His** 荣耀属于上帝
B *det* **1** (of man, boy) 他的 **2** (of male animal) 它的 [指雄性动物的] **3** **His** (of God) 祂的 [指上帝的]

Hispanic /hɪˈspænɪk/
A *adj* 西班牙的 ‹*man, immigrant, population, origin, culture*›; 说西班牙语的 ‹*community, American*›
B *n* 西语裔美国人 [尤指拉丁美洲人后裔]

> **Hispanic**
> 西语裔美国人，尤指来自讲西班牙语的拉丁美洲国家或有拉丁美洲血统的美国人。亦常被称为 Latino（拉美裔美国人）。西语裔美国人第一语言多为西班牙语，是美国最大的少数民族，主要居住在加利福尼亚（California）、得克萨斯（Texas）、纽约（New York）和佛罗里达（Florida）等地。Hispanic 多用复数，该词最早见于 20 世纪 70 年代。

hiss /hɪs/
A *vt* «*audience, group*» 对…发嘘声 ‹*actor, public figure, performance*›; **he was ~ed off the stage** 他在嘘声中被轰下台
B *n* **1** [c] (of gas, snake) 嘶嘶声; (showing disapproval) 嘘声 **2** [u and c] (on recording) 嘶嘶的摩擦声
C *vi* **1** (make hissing sound) «*gas, snake, cat*» 发嘶嘶声; «*audience*» 发嘘声; **to ~ at sb.** 朝某人发嘘声 **2** (speak in menacing tone) 带嘘声说话; (whisper loudly) 大声地耳语

hissy fit /ˈhɪsɪ fɪt/ *n* esp Amer colloq 发脾气; **to throw a ~** 发脾气

histamine /ˈhɪstəmiːn/ *n* [u and c] 组胺

histogram /ˈhɪstəgræm/ *n* 矩形图

histologist /hɪˈstɒlədʒɪst/ ▸**p. 409** *n* 组织学家

histology /hɪˈstɒlədʒi/ *n* [u] 组织学

historian /hɪˈstɔːrɪən/ ▸**p. 409** *n* 历史学家

historic /hɪˈstɒrɪk, Amer -ˈstɔːr-/ *adj* **1** (remarkable, significant) 历史性的 ‹*event, battle*›; 有历史意义的 ‹*period, site, building*›; **of ~ importance** 有重要历史意义的; **on this ~ occasion** 在这个历史性时刻 **2** Ling 历史的; **past ~** 过去时; **in the ~ present** 用历史现在时

historical /hɪˈstɒrɪkl, Amer -ˈstɔːr-/ *adj* **1** (belonging to the past) 历史的; **~ background/record** 历史背景/记载; **a ~ novel** 历史小说 **2** (concerning past events) 有关历史的 ‹*events, study*›; **a ~ fact** 史实

historically /hɪˈstɒrɪkli, Amer -ˈstɔːr-/ *adv* **1** (referring to past) 历史上; **~ accurate** 符合史实的; **~ based** 基于历史的 **2** (from a historical point of view) 从历史角度; **viewed/speaking ~** 从历史角度看/说

historicism /hɪˈstɒrɪsɪzm, Amer -ˈstɔːr-/ *n* [u] **1** (theory) 历史决定论 **2** esp pej (in art, architecture) 历史主义

historiography /hɪˌstɔːrɪˈɒgrəfi/ *n* [u] 历史编纂学

history /ˈhɪstri/ *n* **1** [u] (study of past events) 历史学; **~ of art** 艺术史; **ancient/modern/military ~** 古代史/近代史/军事史; **~ books** 历史学书籍 **2** [u] (the past) 历史; **the course of ~** 历史的进程; **far back in recorded ~** 早在刚有历史记载时; **to make/rewrite ~** 创造/重写历史; **to make ~ by doing sth.** 因做某事而青史留名; **to go down in ~ as …** 作为…载入史册; **~ repeats itself** 历史时常重演; **that's ancient/past ~** 那是古时候/过去的事了; **the rest is ~** 余下的大家都知道，不需要说了 **3** [c] (background) 经历; **a family ~** 家族史; **medical ~** 病史; **to have a ~ of heart trouble/violence** 有心脏病史/有过暴力行为 **4** [c] (account) 历史记载; (book) 历史著作

histrionic /ˌhɪstrɪˈɒnɪk/
A *adj* 矫揉造作的
B **histrionics** *npl* 矫揉造作; **cut out the ~s!** 别装腔作势了!

hit /hɪt/
A *vt* (*pres p* **-tt-**; *pt, pp* **hit**) **1** (strike) 击; **to ~ the ball out of the court** 把球打出场外; **to ~ the nail with the hammer** 用锤子敲钉子; **to ~ sb. on the back** 拍某人的背; **he didn't know what ~ him** fig 他惊得目瞪口呆; **to ~ sb. (straight** *or* **right) between the eyes** fig 对某人来说一目了然; **to ~ it off (with sb.)** fig colloq （与某人）一见如故; ▸**nail A1** **2** (reach target) 击中; Sport 击中得分; **to ~ the target** 命中目标; **to fire and ~ sb.** 开枪打中某人; **to ~ a home run** 打出本垒打; **to ~ sb./sth. where it hurts** colloq 击中某人/某事物的要害 **3** (collide with) 碰撞; **to ~ one's head on sth.** 头碰到某物; **to ~ the roof** *or* **ceiling** fig colloq 勃然大怒 **4** (press) 按 ‹*button, switch*›; 踩 ‹*brakes*› **5** (attack) 攻击 **6** fig (affect adversely) 对…造成不良影响; **to be ~ by strikes/bad weather** 受到罢工打击/恶劣天气的影响; **his death ~ me badly** 他的死对我打击很大 **7** fig (reach) 到达; **to ~ town** 到镇上来; **to ~ the main road** 上主干道; **to ~ the spot** colloq 切合需要; **to ~ 40°** «*temperature*» 达到 40 度; **to ~ a record high** «*currency*» 创下历史新高; **to ~ the high notes** 唱高音; **to ~ the big time** colloq 一举成名 **8** fig colloq (go out to) 去; **to ~ the town/pub** 去城里/去酒吧 **9** fig (feature in) «*news, story*» 是…的重要新闻 ‹*papers*›; **to ~ the headlines** 上头版头条 **10** fig (encounter) 遇到 ‹*bad weather, problem*›; **to ~ the worst of the rush hour** 赶上交通最拥挤的时候 **11** fig colloq (become apparent to) 使突然意识到; **it suddenly ~ me** 我突然记起来; **the full horror ~ me** 我突然感到非常恐惧 **12** fig colloq (raid) 抢劫 ‹*bank, shop*› **13** fig sl (kill) 行凶杀死; (mug) 行凶抢劫
B *vi* (*pres p* **-tt-**; *pt, pp* **hit**) **1** (occur) «*tornado*» 突然袭来 **2** (attack) «*army*» 发动进攻
C *n* **1** Sport 击; **to give the ball a tremendous ~** 大力击球; **to score a ~** Sport 击中; fig colloq 一炮打响 **2** (strike on target) 击中; **to take a ~** lit 受到损坏; fig 受到严重影响 **3** (popular person) 受欢迎的人; (popular song) 流行歌曲; **to be a big** *or* **smash ~** «*show*» 风靡一时; «*record*» 十分畅销; **to be a (big) ~ with sb.** colloq （极）受某人喜爱 **4** sl (dose) [毒品的] 一剂 **5** sl (murder) 谋杀 **6** Comput (visit to a website) 点击; (in search results) 搜索结果; **to get 10,000 ~s a day** 日访问量 1 万次
D *modif* 畅销的 ‹*song, record*›; 风靡一时的 ‹*film, series*›

Phrasal verbs
- **hit back**
A *vt* **1** [**~ sb. back**] (strike in return) 回击 **2** [**~ sth. back, ~ back sth.**] Sport 把…击回 ‹*ball, shot*›
B *vi* **to ~ back at sb./sth.** **1** (strike, criticize) 反击某人/某事物 **2** (retaliate) 报复某人/某事物
- **hit out** *vi* **to ~ out at sb./sth.** lit 猛打某人/某物; fig 猛烈抨击某人/某事物; **to ~ out in all directions** 朝四面八方乱打一气
- **hit on** *vt* **1** [**~ on sth.**] (think of) 突然想到 ‹*idea, solution*›; **she ~ on the perfect title** 她灵机一动，想到了这个理想的标题 **2** [**~ on sth.**] (find) 偶然找到 ‹*gift*› **3** [**~ on sb.**] esp Amer colloq (chat up) 挑逗
- **hit upon** *vt* = **hit on 1, 2**

hit: ~-and-miss *adj* 欠考虑的 ‹*method*›; 无计划的 ‹*arrangements*›; 随意的 ‹*ideas*›; 漫不经心的 ‹*attitude*›; **the way they run things is pretty ~-and-miss** 他们的管理方法十分杂乱无章; **~-and-run** *adj* 肇事逃逸的 ‹*driver*›; 打了就撤的 ‹*attack*›; **a ~-and-run accident** 肇事者逃逸的交通事故

hitch /hɪtʃ/
A *n* **1** (problem) 暂时问题; **to pass off without a ~** 顺利地完成 **2** (knot) [某种] 结; **a clove ~** 卷结
B *vt* **1** (fasten, harness) 拴住 ‹*boat*›; 系 ‹*rope*›; 套住 ‹*horse, wagon*›; 挂上 ‹*tractor, trailer*› **2** colloq (when travelling) **to ~ a ride** *or* **lift** 搭便车 **3** colloq **to get ~ed** (get married) 喜结连理
C *vi* colloq (hitch-hike) 免费搭车; **to ~ to Paris** 免费搭车到巴黎

Phrasal verb
- **hitch up** *vt* [**~ up sth., ~ sth. up**] **1** (pull up) 拉起 ‹*skirt, socks*›; **to ~ a bag up on to one's back** 扛起袋子 **2** (harness) 套上 ‹*horse, wagon*›; (attach) 挂上 ‹*tractor, trailer*›

hitched up *adj* 提起的 ‹*clothing*›; 挂住的 ‹*rope*›; 挽起的 ‹*hair*›

hitch: ~-hike *vi* 免费搭便车; **to ~-hike round the world** 搭便车作环球旅行; **~-hiker** *n* 免费搭便车者; **~-hiking** *n* [u] 免费搭便车

hi-tech *adj* = **high tech B**

hither /ˈhɪðə(r)/ *adv* archaic or liter (to this place) 到此处; (towards this place) 向此地; **~ and thither** 四处

hitherto /ˌhɪðəˈtuː/ *adv* formal (up until now) 迄今; (up until then) 直到那时; **a ~ unrecognized talent** 迄今仍未被承认的天才

Hitler /ˈhɪtlə(r)/
A *pr n* 希特勒
B *n* fig 希特勒式的人; **a little ~** 小希特勒

hit: ~ list *n* 暗杀名单; **~ man** *n* colloq 职业杀手; **~ parade** *n* dated [每周] 畅销唱片排行榜; **~ single** *n* 畅销单曲; **~ squad** *n* 职业杀手团伙

HIV *abbr* = **human immunodeficiency virus** 艾滋病病毒

hive /haɪv/ *n* **1** (place) 蜂房 **2** (bees) 蜂群 **3** fig 忙碌的场所; **a ~ of activity** 繁忙的地方

Phrasal verb
- **hive off** *vt* [**~ sth. off, ~ off sth.**] esp Brit (sell off) 卖掉 ‹*part of business*›

HIV: ~-infected *adj* 感染艾滋病病毒的; **~-negative** *adj* 艾滋病病毒呈阴性的; **~-positive** *adj* 艾滋病病毒呈阳性的

hiya /ˈhaɪjə/ *excl* colloq 你好

HK *abbr* = **Hong Kong**

HKD *abbr* = **Hong Kong dollar** 港元

hl *abbr* = **hectolitre(s)** 百升

HM *abbr* = **His Majesty, Her Majesty** 陛下

hm *abbr* = **hectometre(s)** 百米

HMG *abbr* Brit = **His/Her Majesty's Government** 英国政府

HMS *abbr* Brit = **His/Her Majesty's Ship** 英国皇家海军舰艇; ～ **Victory** 皇家海军胜利号

HMSO *abbr* Brit = **His/Her Majesty's Stationery Office** 英国皇家文书局

HNC *abbr* Brit = **Higher National Certificate**

HND *abbr* Brit = **Higher National Diploma**

hoagie /ˈhəʊgi/ *n* Amer [夹肉、干酪、色拉等的] 长条三明治

hoard /hɔːd/

A *n* (of treasure) 聚藏; (of provisions) 贮藏; **a miser's** ～ 守财奴聚藏的钱财

B *vt* 1 (accumulate) 聚藏 ‹*treasure*›; 贮藏 ‹*provisions*›; **to** ～ **money** 积聚钱财 2 (refuse to throw away) 收集

hoarder /ˈhɔːdə(r)/ *n* 贮藏者; **to be a** ～ **of sth.** 贮藏某物; **I'm a terrible** ～ 我非常爱好收集东西

hoarding /ˈhɔːdɪŋ/ *n* Brit 1 (for advertisements) 大幅广告牌 2 (fence) [建筑工地等的] 临时围篱

hoar frost /ˈhɔːfrɒst, Amer -frɔːst/ *n* [u] 冰霜

hoarse /hɔːs/ *adj* 沙哑的; **to shout/laugh oneself** ～ 把嗓子喊哑/笑哑

hoarsely /ˈhɔːsli/ *adv* 沙哑地

hoarseness /ˈhɔːsnɪs/ *n* [u] 沙哑

hoary /ˈhɔːri/ *adj* 1 (with white or grey hair) 灰白的 ‹*hair, beard*›; 头发灰白的 ‹*head, man*›; 胡须灰白的 ‹*face*› 2 fig (old, trite) 老掉牙的 ‹*joke, topic*›; 陈腐的 ‹*problem*›

hoax /həʊks/

A *n* 1 (practical joke) 恶作剧; **to play** ～**es on sb.** 戏弄某人 2 (deception) 骗局

B *vt* 1 (joke) 戏弄; **to** ～ **sb. into doing sth.** 哄骗某人做某事 2 (deceive) 欺骗

hoax call *n* 恶作剧电话

hoaxer /ˈhəʊksə(r)/ *n* 1 (joker) 搞恶作剧者 2 (deceiver) 骗子

hob /hɒb/ *n* 1 Brit (on cooker) 炉盘 2 (on open fire) 壁炉搁架

hobble /ˈhɒbl/

A *vi* (limp) 跛行; **to** ～ **in/out/along** 一瘸一拐地走进/走出/向前走

B *vt* (fetter) 捆缚…的腿 ‹*horse*›

C *n* 1 (limp) 跛行 2 (strap) 缚在牲口腿上的绳索

hobby /ˈhɒbi/ *n* 业余爱好; **hobbies and interests** 业余爱好与兴趣

hobby horse *n* 1 (toy) 马头杆 2 (rocking horse) 摇摆木马 3 (model) 马形道具 4 (favourite topic) 喜爱的话题

hobbyist /ˈhɒbɪɪst/ *n* 业余爱好者

hobgoblin /ˈhɒbgɒblɪn/ *n* 1 (in folklore) 淘气的小妖精 2 fig (obsession, preoccupation) 着魔; (fear) 骇人的东西

hobnail /ˈhɒbneɪl/ *n* 平头靴钉; ～ **boots** 平头钉靴子

hobnob /ˈhɒbnɒb/ *vi* (*pres p etc.* **-bb-**) colloq 亲近; **to** ～ **with sb.** 与某人过从甚密

hobo /ˈhəʊbəʊ/ *n* (*pl* ～**s** *or* ～**es**) Amer (migratory worker) 季节工人; (tramp) 流浪者

Hobson's choice /ˌhɒbsənz ˈtʃɔɪs/ *n* 无余地的选择; **it's** ～ 那是不得已的选择

hock[1] /hɒk/ *n* 1 [c] (leg joint) [动物后腿的] 跗关节 2 [u] (meat) 后腿肉

hock[2] *n* [u] Brit (German wine) 霍克酒 [莱茵干白葡萄酒]

hock[3]

A *n* [u] colloq 1 (pawn) 抵押; **to be in** ～ (pawned) 被典当; **to put sth. in** ～ 把某物当掉; **to get sth. out of** ～ 把某物赎回 2 (in debt) 欠债; **to be in** ～ **to sb.** 欠某人债

B *vt* (pawn) 抵押 ‹*valuables*›

hockey /ˈhɒki/ ▸ **p. 307** *n* [u] 曲棍球

hockey: ～ **player** *n* 曲棍球球员; ～ **stick** *n* 曲棍球球棍; **she's rather jolly** ～ **sticks** fig colloq 她还真有点童子军精神

hocus-pocus /ˌhəʊkəsˈpəʊkəs/ *n* [u] 1 (conjuror's skill) 魔术戏法 2 pej (deception) 骗术 3 pej (jargon) 故弄玄虚的行话; **political** ～ (activity) 政治花招; (words) 政治鬼话

hod /hɒd/ *n* V 型砖斗

hodgepodge /ˈhɒdʒpɒdʒ/ *n* esp Amer = **hotchpotch**

Hodgkin's disease /ˈhɒdʒkɪnz dɪˌziːz/ *n* [u] 何杰金氏病

hoe /həʊ/

A *n* 长柄锄

B *vt* 用锄头松 ‹*soil*›; 用锄头给…除草松土 ‹*plants*›; 用锄头除 ‹*weeds*›

hoedown /ˈhəʊdaʊn/ *n* Amer 1 (folk dance) 方形舞 2 (social event) [热烈喧闹的] 方形舞舞会

hog /hɒg/

A *n* 1 Brit (castrated pig) 阉猪 2 (feral pig) 野猪; (other wild species) 野生猪科动物 3 fig colloq (greedy person) 贪婪的人; **to go the whole** ～ 挥霍

B *vt* (*pres p etc.* **-gg-**) colloq 1 (monopolize) 独占 ‹*sofa, bathroom*›; **to** ～ **the limelight/attention** 抢镜头/出风头 2 (eat a lot of) 多占 ‹*food*›

Hogmanay /ˈhɒgməneɪ/ *n* Scot [苏格兰12月31日的] 除夕

hog: ～**-tie** *vt* Amer 1 (bind) 捆绑…的四肢 ‹*person, animal*›; 2 fig (hinder) 阻碍; ～**wash** *n* [u] colloq (nonsense) 废话; **that's a load of** ～**wash!** 那真是胡说八道!

hoick /hɔɪk/ Brit colloq

A *vt* **to** ～ **(up)** 猛提 ‹*skirt, bag*›; 猛拉 ‹*rope*›

B *n* 猛拉; **to give sth. a** ～ 猛地一拉某物

hoi polloi /ˌhɔɪ pəˈlɔɪ/ *npl* pej 草民

hoist /hɔɪst/

A *vt* 1 (raise) [用绳索和滑轮] 升起 ‹*sail, flag*›; **to be** ～**ed with one's own petard** fig 搬石头砸自己的脚 2 (haul up) 举起 ‹*wreckage, car, trunk*›; **to** ～ **sth. into position** 将某物抬到位

B *n* 1 (apparatus) (for people) 升降机; (for things) 起重机 2 (raising) 升起; **to give sb. a** ～ **(up)** 向上推某人一下

hoity-toity /ˌhɔɪtɪˈtɔɪti/ *adj* colloq pej 傲慢的 ‹*manner, air*›; 势利的 ‹*behaviour*›

hokey-cokey /ˌhəʊkɪˈkəʊki/ *n* **the** ～ 霍基－科基舞

hokum /ˈhəʊkəm/ *n* [u] colloq 1 (nonsense) 废话; **that's just a load of** ～ 那只是一派胡言 2 (in a film, play, book) (situation) 做作情节; (dialogue) 煽情对话

hold /həʊld/

A *vt* (*pt, pp* **held**) 1 (clasp in hand) 握着 ‹*stick, gun*›; (clasp in arms) 抱着 ‹*person, animal*›; **to** ～ **a coin** 攥住一枚硬币; **to** ～ **a pen** 握笔; **she held me by the sleeve** 她抓住我的衣袖 2 (clasp in mouth) «*person, animal*» 咬住; «*bird*» 衔住; **it held the worm in its beak** 它用喙衔着小虫; **the dog was** ～**ing a ball in its mouth** 那条狗嘴里叼着一个球 3 (embrace) 拥抱; **to** ～ **sb. in one's arms** 抱着某人; **to** ～ **each other tight** 紧紧相拥 4 (use as support) 抓住 ‹*handrail, branch*› 5 (keep in place) 使保持不动; **to** ～ **sth. in place** *or* **position** 把某物固定住; **to** ～ **the door open/shut** 把门开着/关着; **to** ～ **the camera steady** 拿稳相机; **to** ～ **a ladder (for sb.)** （为某人）扶住梯子; **to** ～ **one's head forward/back** 头向前探/头向后仰; **to** ～ **a knife to sb.'s throat** 用刀抵着某人的喉咙 6 (grasp in pain) 捂住 ‹*head, stomach*›; **she was** ～**ing her head** 她抱着头 7 (support) 承受 ‹*weight, load*›; 承受…的重量 ‹*person, object*› 8 (restrain) 阻止; **we held the thief** 我们看住了小偷; **there's no** ～**ing him/her** fig colloq 他/她要大展宏图 9 (keep in check) = **hold back A2** 10 (detain) 扣留; **to** ～ **suspects (for questioning)** 拘留嫌犯（审讯）; **to** ～ **sb. prisoner/hostage** 囚禁某人/把某人扣为人质 11 (contain) «*box*» 装着 ‹*valuables*›; (accommodate) «*theatre, room*» 容纳 ‹*spectators, people*›; **the tank** ～**s 5 litres** 这个油箱能装 5 升汽油; **the car** ～**s five (people)** 这辆车能坐下 5 个人 12 (possess) 持有 ‹*licence, passport, PhD*›; 拥有 ‹*territory, title*›; **to** ～ **the record (for sth.)** 保持（某比赛的）纪录; **to** ～ **a fascination for sb.** 对某人有很大的吸引力 13 (consume without getting drunk) 能喝下; **to** ～ **one's drink** *or* **liquor** 酒量很大; **he can't** ～ **his drink** 他是一喝就醉 14 (occupy) 担任 ‹*position, office*›; 掌握 ‹*power*› 15 (have charge of) 保管 ‹*document, money*›; «*computer*» 保存 ‹*information*› 16 (defend successfully) «*army*» 守住 ‹*city, fort*›; «*party, team*» 保住 ‹*seat, title*› 17 (have reserved) 保留 ‹*seat, booking*› 18 (delay) 推迟 ‹*flight*› 19 (stop) 停止处理 ‹*order*›; 暂缓 ‹*phone call*›; 延后投递 ‹*letter*›; ～ **it!** colloq (wait) 等一下!; (don't move) 别动!; ～ **the onions** colloq (at restaurant) 不加洋葱; ～ **everything!** colloq 快停下! 20 Mus «*player, instrument*» 延长 ‹*note, chord*›; «*singer*» 继续唱 ‹*note, chord*›; **a minim is held for two beats** 一个二分音符延续两拍 21 Telecom **to** ～ **the line** 不挂断电话 22 Aut **to** ～ **the road** «*vehicle*» 抓地; **these tyres don't** ～ **the road well in rain** 这些轮胎在下雨天抓地性能差 23 (engage) 吸引 ‹*interest, attention*› 24 Aviat, Naut «*ship, plane*» 沿…航行 ‹*course*› 25 (maintain) 保持 ‹*lead, speed, pose*›; 守住 ‹*position*›; **to** ～ **spending to £2 billion** 使开支保持在 20 亿英镑; **he held the class spellbound** 他使全班学生听得入了神 26 (stage) 举行 ‹*meeting, talks*›; 举办 ‹*exhibition, party*›; 进行 ‹*election, enquiry*›; **to** ～ **a service** 做礼拜; **to** ～ **a conversation (with sb.)** （与某人）进行交谈 27 (be sure of) 坚持 ‹*view*›; **to** ～ **the idea/opinion that ...** 认为…; **a firmly held belief** 坚定的信念 28 formal (regard as) 认为; **to** ～ **sb. responsible (for sth.)** 认为某人应该（对某事物）负责; **to** ～ **sb./sth. in high esteem** *or* **regard** 非常尊重某人/高度重视某事物; **she is held to be an expert** 她被视为专家 29 (in tennis) **to** ～ **one's serve** 保住发球局

B *vi* (*pt, pp* **held**) 1 (remain intact) «*dam, shelf, rope*» 支撑得住; «*glue*» 粘得牢; **to** ～ **fast** «*anchor*» 牢牢地吃住不动 2 (continue) 保持不变; **to** ～ **until tomorrow** «*weather*» 持续到明天; **his luck held** 他一直走运 3 Telecom 等待; **please** ～ **a moment** 请稍等 4 (be valid) 合乎逻辑; **to** ～ **true** «*theory, principle*» (be true) 正确; (be valid) 适用; **his argument doesn't** ～ 他的论点站不住脚 5 (remain available) «*offer, promise*» 有效; **to** ～ **good** 有效 6 (be applicable) **to** ～ **for sb./sth.** «*rule, law*» 适用于某人/某事物 7 (remain in place) 保持不动; ～ **still!** 不要动! 8 (hold on) 抓住; ～ **tight!** 抓紧!

C *v refl* (*pt, pp* **held**) 1 (physically) **to** ～ **oneself well** 保持端正的姿势; **to** ～ **oneself upright** 挺直身体 2 (mentally) **to** ～ **oneself ready for sth.** 准备好做某事

D *n* 1 [u] (grasp with hand) 抓; (grasp with arms) 抱; **to get** *or* **take** *or* **lay** ～ **of sb./sth.** 抓住某人/某物; **to keep (a)** ～ **of sb./sth.** 抓着某人/某物不放; **to relax** *or* **release one's** ～ **on sb./sth.** 放开某人/某物; **to catch** ～ **of sth. as it falls** 接住坠落的某物 2 [c] (in wrestling) 擒拿法; **to have sb. in a** ～ 用擒拿法控制住某人 3 [c] (in climbing) 支撑点 4 [u] fig (control) 控制; **to have a** ～ **over** *or* **on sb.** 能左右某人; **get a** ～ **of yourself!** 镇定一点!; **she needs to get a** ～ **of herself** 她该重新振作起来了; **to take** ～ «*epidemic, fear*» 蔓延开来; «*habit*» 变得根深蒂固; **to take** ～ **of sb./sth.** «*panic, urge*» 完全控制某人/某事物 5 [u] (possession) **to get** ～ **of sth.** 得到某物; **he got** ～ **of another ticket** 他又搞到了一张票; **where did he get** ～ **of that idea?** 他怎么会有这样的想法? 6 [u] (contact) **to get** ～ **of**

sb. (locate) 找到某人; (communicate with) 与某人联系上 7 [u] (for hair) 定型力; **a long-lasting ~** 持久定型 8 [c] Aviat, Naut (for storage) 货舱

E **on hold** *adv phr* 1 Telecom 待接; **to put sb. on ~** 让某人等待; **to put a call on ~** 让电话待接 2 (postponed) 推迟; **to put sth. on ~** 暂停 ‹*plan, project*›; **to put one's career on ~ (to do sth.)** 中断事业（做某事）

Phrasal verbs

• **hold against** *vt* [~ **sth. against sb.**] 因…降低对…的评价; **I never held that against you** 我从没有因为那件事而轻视你

• **hold back**

A [~ **back sb./sth.**, ~ **sb./sth. back**] *vt*
1 (restrain) 阻止 ‹*person*›; **to ~ sb. back from doing sth.** 阻止某人做某事; **to ~ back a crowd** 拦住人群 2 (keep in check) «*wall, dam*» 挡住 ‹*animals, mob, water*› 3 (keep in place) «*person, clip*» 固定 ‹*hair*› 4 fig (suppress) 抑制 ‹*emotions*›; **to ~ back one's laughter/anger** 忍住不笑/压住怒火 5 (block) 妨碍; **to ~ back the tide of reform** 阻挡改革的浪潮; **to be held back in one's career** 在事业上受阻 6 (not reveal) 向某人隐瞒 ‹*information, truth*›; **to ~ back the results of the investigation** 对调查结果秘而不宣; **she's ~ing something back from us** 她有什么事瞒着我们 7 (not give) 扣住 ‹*payment, goods*›

B [~ **sb. back**] *vt* (deter) 阻止; **consideration for her held him back from saying what he really thought** 考虑到她的感受，他没有说出自己的真实想法

C *vi* 犹豫; **to ~ back from signing a contract** 犹豫着不签合约; **I held back** (hesitated) 我犹豫着; (waited) 我等着

• **hold down** *vt* [~ **sb./sth. down**, ~ **down sb./sth.**]
1 (keep from moving) **to ~ sb./sth. down** 按住; **to be held down with tacks** 被大头钉钉住了 2 (by pressing) 压住 ‹*key, switch, lever*›; 踩住 ‹*pedal*› 3 (keep level) 控制 ‹*prices, expense, number*› 4 (have) 有 ‹*job*›; (keep) 保住 ‹*job*›; **to ~ down two jobs at once** 同时做两份工作 5 fig (oppress) 压制; **a dictator who held his people down** 压迫人民的独裁者

• **hold forth** *vi* pej 夸夸其谈; **to ~ forth on** *or* **about sth.** 滔滔不绝地谈论某事物

• **hold in** *vt* [~ **sth. in**, ~ **in sth.**]
1 (pull in) 收缩; **to ~ one's stomach/chest in** 收腹/含胸 2 (restrain) 抑制 ‹*emotions, temper*›; **to ~ one's feelings in** 克制感情; **I couldn't ~ in my anger** 我压不住自己的怒火

• **hold off**

A *vi* (not happen) «*rain, snow*» 不下; «*winter*» 不来临; **the storm held off until we got home** 我们到家之后暴风雨才来

B *vt* [~ **off sb./sth.**, ~ **sb./sth. off**]
1 (repel) 抵挡住 ‹*attacker, attack*› 2 (beat) 战胜 ‹*challenger, competitor*›; 赢得 ‹*challenge*› 3 (stall) 拖住 ‹*creditors, reporters*› 4 **to ~ off doing sth.** (delay) 推迟做某事; **we held off telling her for a few days** 我们推迟了几天才告诉她

• **hold on**

A *vi* 1 (wait) 等待; **~ on! let me get my breath back!** 等一下！让我喘口气！; **~ on! I'll get him** 稍等！我去叫他来 2 (grip) 抓牢; **~ on tight!** 抓紧！; **to ~ on with both hands** 双手抓紧; **the dog held on (with its teeth)** 这条狗（用牙齿）紧紧咬住不松口 3 (endure) 坚持; **~ on! Help is on its way** 坚持住！救援马上就到

B *vt* [~ **sth. on**] 固定; **to be held on with glue** 用胶水粘住

• **hold on to** *vt* [~ **on to sb./sth.**]
1 (grip) 抓牢; **to ~ on to one's hat** 按住帽子; **~ on to the dog** 把狗牵好 2 (keep) 保有 ‹*object, property*›; **this is worth ~ing on to** 这值得保留 3 fig (retain) 保持 ‹*hope, dreams, position*›; **to ~ on to one's lead** 保持领先; **he held on to his belief that …** 他坚持认为… 4 (look after) 保管 ‹*money, keys*›; **to ~ on to sth. for sb.** 为某人保管某物

• **hold out**

A *vt* 1 [~ **out sth.**, ~ **sth. out**] (stretch out, offer) 伸出 ‹*hand*›; 递出 ‹*object*›; **to ~ one's hand out for a cup** 伸手去拿一个杯子; **to ~ out a cup to sb.** 递给某人一个杯子 2 [~ **out sth.**, ~ **sth. out**] (retain) **to ~ out hope for sth.** 一直对某事物抱希望; **I don't ~ out much hope of them paying** 我对他们付钱的事不抱多大希望 3 [~ **out sth.**] (provide) 提供 ‹*chance*›; 带来 ‹*hope*›; **to ~ out the prospect of sth.** 使某事有可能

B *vi* 1 (last) «*stocks, fuel*» 维持 2 (resist) **to ~ out (against sb./sth.)** 抵抗 ‹*enemy, attack*›; 抵制 ‹*changes, reform*›; **to ~ out against sb.'s threats** 面对某人的威胁拒不妥协

• **hold out for** *vt* [~ **out for sth.**] 坚持要求 ‹*pay rise, better conditions, improved offer*›

• **hold out on** *vt* [~ **out on sb.**] colloq 瞒着; **she's ~ing out on you!** 她一直瞒着你！

• **hold over** *vt* [~ **sth. over**, ~ **over sth.**]
1 (postpone) 推迟 ‹*decision, programme*› 2 (continue to show) 延长…的演出期 ‹*play*›; 延长…的放映期 ‹*film*›; 延长…的开放期 ‹*exhibition*›; **the show was held over for five more performances** 这场表演又续演 5 场了

• **hold to** *vt* [~ **to sth.**]
1 (maintain) 坚持 ‹*belief, principle, decision*›; **to ~ to one's promise** 恪守诺言 2 [~ **sb. to sth.**] (make sb. fulfil sth.) 使履行 ‹*agreement, contract*›; **he held her to her promise** 他要求她恪守诺言; **I'll ~ you to that!** 你要说话算话！

• **hold together**

A *vi* 1 (not break) 保持完整; **this car is scarcely ~ing together** 这辆车快要散架了 2 (remain united) «*group*» 保持团结; **to ~ together in times of crisis** 在危难时刻团结一致

B *vt* [~ **sth. together**] 使…保持完整 ‹*car, machine*›; 使…连在一起 ‹*papers, pieces*›; **to be held together with a paper clip** 用回形针别在一起; **to ~ the family together** 使全家人凝聚在一起

• **hold up**

A *vt* [~ **sth. up**, ~ **up sth.**]
1 (support) 支撑 ‹*roof, tent*›; **her trousers were held up by a drawstring** 她的裤子是用拉带系着的 2 (lift) 举起 ‹*object*›; **~ your hand up**, **~ up your hand** 举手; **~ your head up** 把头抬起来; **to ~ up two fingers** 竖起两根手指 3 **to ~ sb./sth. up as sth.** (present) 将某人/某事物作为…举例; **to ~ sb. up as a model of good behaviour** 拿某人作良好表现的榜样; **to ~ sb./sth. up to ridicule/scorn** 嘲笑/鄙视某人/某事物 4 (delay) 延误 ‹*departure*›; (obstruct) 拦住 ‹*procession*›; **to ~ up the traffic** 阻碍交通; **sorry we're late: we were held up** 很抱歉我们迟到了：我们被耽搁了 5 (rob) [尤指持枪] 抢劫 ‹*person, bank*›

B *vi* 1 (remain intact) 保持完好; **the hut held up** 小屋仍完好地矗立着; **these shoes will not ~ up much longer** 这些鞋子穿不了太久了 2 (remain valid) «*argument, theory*» 站得住脚; **his excuse didn't ~ up under scrutiny** 他的理由经不起推敲 3 (remain strong) «*person*» 保持健康; «*support*» 依然有力; «*currency*» 仍然坚挺; **the Labour vote held up well** 工党的得票总数保持高态势

• **hold with** *vt* [~ **with sth.**] 赞成 ‹*idea, system*›; **I don't ~ with keeping animals in cages** 我反对把动物关在笼内

holdall /ˈhəʊldɔːl/ *n* Brit 大旅行袋

holder /ˈhəʊldə(r)/ *n* 1 (of passport, degree, key) 持有者; (of shares) 股东; **a credit card/season ticket/passport/permit ~** 信用卡/季票/护照/通行证持有人; **~s of high office** 高级官员 2 Sport (of title) 获得者; **world record ~** 世界纪录保持者; **the world cup ~s** 世界杯获得者 3 (container) 储物器; (stand) 支托物; **plant-pot ~** 花盆支架; **credit-card ~** 信用卡套

holding /ˈhəʊldɪŋ/ *n* 1 (property, assets) 拥有的财产; (stocks) 股份; **a 40% ~ in the company** 公司 40% 的股份 2 (area of land) 租用的土地 3 (of library) 藏书; (commodities) 收藏品

holding: **~ company** *n* 控股公司; **~ operation** *n* 维持现状的行动; **~ pattern** *n* [飞机在机场上空待降时的] 等待航线; **~ tank** *n* 储存槽

hold-up *n* 1 (delay) 停顿; (on road) 交通堵塞 2 (robbery) 抢劫

hole /həʊl/

A *n* 1 (aperture) 洞; **to have ~s in one's tights** 连裤袜上有破洞; **a ~ in the ozone layer** 臭氧层空洞; **to need sth. like a ~ in the head** fig colloq 绝对不需要某物 2 (hollow, depression) (in road, man-made) 坑洼; (pothole) 壶穴; **to dig a ~** 挖一个坑 3 (of mouse, fox, rabbit) 洞穴 4 (in golf) (target) 球洞; (division of course) 球座到球洞的区域; **a nine-~ golf course** 有 9 个洞的高尔夫球场; **to get a ~ in one** 一杆打入球洞 5 fig (flaw) 漏洞; **to pick** *or* **knock ~s in an argument** 从论证中找出破绽 6 fig (shortage) 短缺; (financial loss) 财政窘境; **to make a (big) ~ in profits** 用掉（大量的）利润 7 colloq (awkward situation) 窘境; **to get oneself into/out of a ~** 陷入/摆脱困境 8 colloq pej (unpleasant place) 狭小简陋的地方; **a dreadful ~** 糟糕的鬼地方

B *vt* 1 (make hole in) 在…上打洞 ‹*ship, defences*› 2 (in golf) 把…打入球洞 ‹*ball, shot*›

Phrasal verbs

• **hole out** *vi* 1 (in golf) 击球入洞 2 (in cricket) «*batsman*» 击球被接出局

• **hole up** *vi* 躲藏; **they were ~d up in the hills** 他们躲在山里

hole: **~-and-corner** *adj* 秘密的; **~ in the heart** *n* 先天性心膜缺损; **~ in the wall** *n* Brit colloq 自动提款机; **~ punch** *n* 纸张打孔机

holey /ˈhəʊli/ *adj* colloq 有洞的 ‹*clothes*›

holiday /ˈhɒlədeɪ/ esp Brit

A *n* 1 (vacation) 假期; **the summer/winter ~s** 暑假/寒假; **to go/be on ~** 去/在休假; **a busman's ~** fig colloq 照常工作的假日; **high days and ~s** liter 节假日; **a ~ atmosphere** 欢乐的气氛 2 esp Brit (time off work) 休假日; **four weeks' ~ with pay** 4 周的带薪假期; **a national/public/religious ~** 全国假日/公共假日/宗教节日 3 (in payments) 宽限期; **a payment ~** 付款宽限期

B **holidays** *npl* Amer (Christmas, New Year) 节日假期; **Happy Holidays!** 节日快乐！

C *vi* 度假; **to ~ in France** 在法国度假

holiday: **~ camp** *n* Brit 度假营地; **~ centre** *n* Brit 度假中心; **~ home** *n* Brit 度假别墅; **~ job** *n* Brit [大学生的] 假期打工; **~maker** *n* Brit 度假者; **~ resort** *n* Brit [常指海边的] 度假胜地; **~ season** *n* Brit 度假季节 [常指夏季]; **~ traffic** *n* [u] Brit 假日交通; **~ village** *n* Brit 度假村

holier-than-thou /ˌhəʊlɪəðənˈðaʊ/ *adj* pej 自命清高的 ‹*attitude, look*›

holiness /ˈhəʊlɪnɪs/ *n* 1 [u] (of person, life) 神圣 2 [c] (title) 宗座 [教皇、东正教主教的头衔或尊称]; **His/Your H~** 宗座

holism /ˈhɒlɪzəm, ˈhəʊl-/ *n* [u] 1 Philos 整体论 2 Med 整体观

holistic /hɒˈlɪstɪk, ˈhəʊl-/ *adj* 整体论的 ‹*philosophy*›; 全面的 ‹*view, approach*›; 整体性的 ‹*treatment, therapy*›

Holland /ˈhɒlənd/ *pr n* 荷兰

holler /ˈhɒlə(r)/ colloq

A *vi* 大声叫喊; **stop ~ing at me — I'm not deaf!** 别冲我嚷嚷——我不是聋子！

B *vt* 大声喊出

C *n* 大声叫喊

hollow /ˈhɒləʊ/

A *adj* 1 (not solid) 中空的 ‹*tree, tooth, tube*›;

the wall sounds ~ 墙壁听起来是空心的; **to beat sb. ~** fig colloq (in game) 彻底打败某人 **2** (sunken) 凹陷的 ‹*cheeks, eyes*›; 憔悴的 ‹*look*› **3** (concave) 凹面的 ‹*valley, depression*› **4** (booming) 低沉的 ‹*sound, cough*›; (echoing) 空响的 ‹*voice, clang*› **5** fig (insincere) 虚伪的 ‹*friendship, words*›; 空洞的 ‹*promise*›; **to give a ~ laugh** 干笑一声 **6** fig (empty) 徒有其表的 ‹*pleasures, joys*›; 无价值的 ‹*victory*›

B *n* **1** (depression) (in tree, hillside) 凹陷处; (of hand, back) 坑 **2** Geog (small valley) 山谷

Phrasal verb

- **hollow out** *vt* [**~ sth. out, ~ out sth.**] 挖空 ‹*wood, tree, bank, ground*›; 挖成 ‹*canoe, nest*›; **the centre of the log had been ~ed out** 圆木心挖空了

hollow: ~-cheeked *adj* 面颊凹陷的; **~-eyed** *adj* 眼睛凹陷的

hollowly /ˈhɒləʊli/ *adv* 空洞地 ‹*sound, ring*›; 干巴巴地 ‹*laugh*›

holly /ˈhɒli/ *n* **1** [c] (tree) 冬青树 **2** [u] (wood) 冬青木 **3** [u] (branches, foliage) 冬青枝 [用于装饰房屋]

hollyhock /ˈhɒlɪhɒk/ *n* 蜀葵

holmium /ˈhəʊlmɪəm/ *n* [u] 钬

holocaust /ˈhɒləkɔːst/ *n* **1** (mass destruction) [尤指火灾或核战争引起的] 大毁灭 **2** Hist **the H~** [第二次世界大战期间纳粹对犹太人的] 大屠杀

Holocene /ˈhɒləsiːn/

A *adj* (of the period) 全新世的; (of the rock system) 全新统的

B *n* **the ~** (period) 全新世; (rock system) 全新统

hologram /ˈhɒləgræm/ *n* **1** (image) 全息图 **2** (photograph) 全息照片

holographic /ˌhɒləˈgræfɪk/ *adj* (connected with holography) 全息术的; (produced by holography) 用全息术制作的

holography /həˈlɒgrəfi/ *n* [u] 全息学

hols /hɒlz/ *npl* Brit colloq 假期

holster /ˈhəʊlstə(r)/ *n* [系在腰带或腋下的] 手枪皮套

holy /ˈhəʊli/ *adj* **1** (sacred) 神圣的 ‹*day, writings, place*›; **a ~ picture** 宗教图画; **on ~ ground** 在圣地 **2** (pious) 圣洁的 ‹*person*›; **to lead a ~ life** 过圣洁的生活 **3** colloq dated (expressing surprise, dismay) 天哪; **~ cow!** 天哪!

holy: ~ city *n* 圣城; **H~ Communion** *n* **= communion 2, 3**; **H~ day** *n* 圣日; **H~ Father** *n* 教宗; **H~ Ghost** *n* **= Holy Spirit**; **H~ Grail** *n* **1** Relig (cup) **the H~ Grail** [耶稣在最后晚餐时用的] 圣杯; **2** **~ grail** fig (sought-after thing) 努力追求之物; **H~ Land** *n* **the H~ Land** 圣地 [指地中海东海岸地区]; **~ of holies** *n* fig **the ~ of holies** 至圣所; **~ orders** *npl* 圣秩; **to take ~ orders** 领受圣秩; **H~ Roman Empire** *pr n* **the H~ Roman Empire** 神圣罗马帝国; **H~ See** *n* **the H~ See** 圣座 [指教宗职位或罗马教廷]; **H~ Spirit** *n* **the H~ Spirit** 圣灵; **H~ Trinity** *n* **= trinity 2**; **~ war** *n* 圣战; **H~ Week** *n* 圣周 [复活节前的一周]; **H~ Writ** *n* [u] **1** (Bible) 《圣经》; **2** fig (writings) 至高无上的权威著作; (sayings) 箴言

> **the Holy Grail**
>
> 圣杯（或圣盘），亦作 the Grail。传说中耶稣在最后的晚餐上用的杯子或盘子，耶稣被钉上十字架后曾用圣杯接过他的血。圣杯的传说多见于中世纪传奇及寓言故事。寻找圣杯是亚瑟王圆桌骑士（Knights of the Round Table）传奇的重要组成部分。最终，唯一完美无瑕的爵士加拉哈（Sir Galahad）找到了圣杯。加拉哈死后，人们看见圣杯也随之升天。圣杯亦用来比喻人们孜孜以求却又难以得到的东西。

homage /ˈhɒmɪdʒ/ *n* [u] 敬词; **to pay ~ to sb.** 向某人表示敬意; **in ~ to sb./sth.** 为向某人/某事物表示敬意

homburg /ˈhɒmbɜːg/ *n* 洪堡毡帽 [卷边男用毡帽]

home /həʊm/

A *n* **1** [u and c] (one's house, flat) 家; **to leave ~** (to go out, go to work etc.) 离开家; (move out) 搬出去; **to set up ~** Brit 建立家庭; **to make one's ~ somewhere** 在某处定居; **to be away from ~** (on business) 外出工作不在家; (travelling) 外出旅行不在家; Sport Brit 在客场比赛; **close to** *or* **near (to) ~** fig (accurate) 正中要害; (affecting one directly) 有直接影响; **his questions were a bit too close to ~** 他的问题有点过于直截了当; **a ~ from** Brit *or* **away from** Amer **~** 舒适如家的地方; **~ sweet ~** 可爱的家; **there's no place like ~** Prov 家总是家啊; **~ is where the heart is** Prov 心在哪儿，家就在哪儿 **2** [c] (family base) 家庭; **'good ~ wanted'** "为宠物寻找好人家" **3** [c] Comm (property) 房子; **low-cost ~s** 廉价住宅 **4** [u and c] (one's town or district) 家乡; (one's country) 祖国; (where one lives) 居住地; **to make a place one's ~** 在一处地方安家; **my spiritual ~** 我的精神家园 **5** [c] (place of origin) 发祥地; **Greece, the ~ of democracy** 希腊，民主的发祥地; **Wimbledon, the ~ of tennis** 温布尔登，网球的发源地 **6** [u and c] (plant habitat) 产地; (animal habitat) 栖息地; **this region is the ~ of many species of wild flower** 这个地区有很多种类的野花; **the Rockies are ~ to bears and mountain lions** 落基山脉地区是熊和美洲狮的栖息地 **7** [c] colloq (place for keeping sth.) 存放地; **to find a ~ for sth.** 找到存放某物的地方 **8** [c] (place of residential care) (for old people) 养老院; (for children) 保育院; (for the mentally ill) 精神病院; (for the sick) 疗养院; Brit (for pets) 收养所

B *modif* **1** (of the place where one lives) 家的 ‹*surroundings*›; 家庭的 ‹*background, troubles, furnishings*›; (for use in one's own house) 家用的 ‹*appliance, computer*›; **a free ~ delivery service** 免费送货上门服务; **an increase in ~ repossessions** 房屋收回数量的增长 **2** esp Brit (national) 国内的 ‹*affairs, news, market*› **3** Sport 主场的 ‹*match, player, crowd*› **4** Amer Comm 总部的 ‹*office*›

C *adv* **1** (to one's house, flat) 到家; (in one's house, flat) 在家; **to see/drive sb. ~** 送某人/开车送某人回家; **on the journey ~** 在回家途中; **when will he be ~ from work?** 他什么时间下班回到家?; **to be nothing to write ~ about** fig colloq 平平常常; **to be ~ and dry** Brit, **to be ~ free** Amer 成功 **2** (to one's town) 向家乡; (to one's country) 向祖国 ‹*go, come, return*› **3** (in one's town) 在家乡; (in one's country) 在祖国; **it's great to be ~ and seeing all my old friends again** 回到家乡再次见到所有老朋友太好了; **I wonder how everyone's getting on back ~ in England** 我想知道大家在英格兰老家的情况 **4** Sport (in race) 向终点; **the favourite romped ~ 3 lengths ahead** 那匹热门马以领先 3 个马身的优势轻松到达终点 **5** (into position) 到位; **to hammer the nail ~** 用锤子把钉子敲到头; **to drive the ball ~** 踢球破门; **the torpedo struck ~ on the hull of the ship** 鱼雷正中船身 **6** fig (creating awareness) 深刻地; **to hit** *or* **strike ~** 正中要害; **her remark really struck ~** 她的话的确说到了点子上; **to drive** *or* **hammer sth. ~ (to sb.)** (给某人) 把某事讲透彻; **the television pictures brought ~ to us the full horror of the attack** 电视画面使我们清楚真切地了解到袭击的恐怖; **to come ~ to sb.** 使某人完全明白

D **at home** *adv phr* **1** (in one's house) 在家里 ‹*work, stay*›; **to live at ~** 和父母一起生活 **2** (comfortable) 舒适自在地; **he feels very at ~ on a horse** 他骑马得心应手; **he's not really at ~ on the stage** 他在台上有点拘束; **to make oneself at ~** 不拘束 **3** (in one's town) 在本地; (in one's country) 在本土 (in one's town, country); **at ~ and abroad** 在国内外 **4** Sport (on own ground) 《*team*》 在主场 ‹*win, lose, draw*› **5** dated (receiving visitors) 准备好接待客人; **I'm not at ~ to anyone today** 我今天不接待任何人

Phrasal verb

- **home in on** *vt* [**~ in on sth.**] **1** (move towards) 《*missile*》 导向 ‹*target*›; **sharks can ~ in on tiny amounts of blood in the sea** 鲨鱼在海里能精确定位极少量的血 **2** (focus on) 注意到某事物; **the FBI has begun to ~ in on the Guatemalan connection** 联邦调查局已经盯上了危地马拉的贩毒网络

home: ~ address *n* 家庭住址; **~-baked** *adj* 自家烘烤的; **~ banking** *n* [u] 家庭银行系统; **~ birth** *n* 家中分娩; **~body** *n* esp Amer colloq 恋家的人; **~bound** *adj* esp Amer **1** (housebound) [由于年老或疾病而] 困居家中的; **2** (heading home) 回家的 ‹*traveller, flight*›; **~ brew** *n* [u] 家酿酒; **~ buyer** *n* 购房者; **~ buying** *n* [u] 买房; **~ center** *n* Amer 家用建筑材料销售中心; **~ cinema** *n* [u] 家庭影院; **~ cinema system/kit/speakers** 家庭影院系统/套装/扬声器; **~ comforts** *npl* 家里舒适的条件; **~coming** *n* 回家; **~ computer** *n* 家用计算机; **~ cooking** *n* [u] (at home) 家常便饭; (in restaurant) 家常菜; **H~ Counties** *npl* Brit **the H~ Counties** 伦敦周围各郡; **~ country** *n* 祖国; **~ economics** *n* [u] 家政学; **~ entertainment** *n* [u] 家庭娱乐; **~ front** *n* (during war) (civilian population) 后方民众; (civilian support) 后方的支前活动; **on the ~ front** 在大后方; **~ ground** *n* **1** [c] Sport 主场场地; **to win on one's ~ ground** 在主场获胜; **2** [u] fig (familiar territory) 熟悉的地盘; (familiar subject) 熟悉的领域; **~-grown** *adj* **1** (in own garden) 自家种的; (in own country) 本国出产的 ‹*fruit, vegetables*›; **~-grown apples and pears** 国产苹果和梨; **2** fig 土生土长的 ‹*talent, idea, star*›; **H~ Guard** *n* Brit Hist **the H~ Guard** 地方军; **~ help** *n* Brit [尤指地方当局雇的] 家务帮手; **~ information pack** *n* Brit 房产资料册

homeland /ˈhəʊmlænd/ *n* **1** (native country) 祖国 **2** (state) (autonomous) 自治国家; (semi-autonomous) 半自治国家

homeland security *n* [u] Amer 国土安全 [防止恐怖袭击的行动及机构]

home leave *n* [u] 探亲假; **to be on ~** 休探亲假

homeless /ˈhəʊmlɪs/

A *adj* 无家的

B *npl* **the ~** 无家可归的人

homelessness /ˈhəʊmlɪsnɪs/ *n* [u] 无家可归

home life *n* [u] 家庭生活

homeliness /ˈhəʊmlɪnɪs/ *n* [u] **1** Brit (cosiness) (of room, atmosphere) 如家一般舒适 **2** (unpretentious nature) (of food) 家常; (of person) 朴实 **3** Amer pej (plainness) 相貌平平

home: ~ loan *n* 住房贷款; **~-loving** *adj* 爱待在家里的

homely /ˈhəʊmli/ *adj* **1** Brit (cosy, welcoming) 如家一般舒适的 ‹*pub, atmosphere*› **2** Brit (unpretentious) 朴实无华的 **3** Amer (plain, unattractive) 相貌平平的 ‹*appearance, face*›; 一般的 ‹*style of dress*›

home: ~-made *adj* 家里做的; **~-made bread/wine** 自制的面包/家酿酒; **~maker** *n* (woman) 主妇; (woman or man) 操持家务者; **~-making** *n* [u] 持家; **~ movie** *n* 自制电影; **H~ Office** *n* Brit **the H~ Office** 内政部

homeopath /ˈhəʊmɪəpæθ/ *n* 顺势疗法医生

homeopathic /ˌhəʊmɪəˈpæθɪk/ *adj* 顺势疗法的

homeopathy /ˌhəʊmɪˈɒpəθi/ *n* [u] 顺势疗法

home: ~ owner *n* 房主; **~ ownership** *n* [u] 拥有住房; **~ page** *n* 主页; **~ plate**

n 本垒板; ~ **port** *n* 船籍港; ~ **rule** *n* [u] [尤指1870-1914年爱尔兰主张的] 地方自治; ~ **run** *n* 本垒打; **H~ Secretary** *n* Brit the H~ Secretary 内政大臣; ~ **shopping** *n* [u] 家居购物 [通过电话、电子邮件等购买物品]; ~**sick** *adj* (for home) 想家的; (for country) 思乡的; ~**sickness** *n* [u] (for home) 想家; (for country) 思乡; ~ **side** *n* = ~ **team**

homespun /ˈhəʊmspʌn/
A *adj* [1] (of cloth, yarn) 家纺的 [2] fig (simple, unsophisticated) 朴实的 ‹*person*›; 朴素的 ‹*lifestyle, philosophy*›
B *n* [u] 手工纺织呢

home: ~**stead** /ˈhəʊmsted/ *n* [1] (house and land) 家宅; [2] (farm) 农庄; [3] Amer Hist (land) [分给定居者的] 公地; ~ **straight,** ~ **stretch** *ns* [1] (of racecourse) [终点线前的] 直线跑道; [2] fig (of activity, campaign) 最后冲刺阶段; ~ **team** *n* [比赛中的] 主队; ~**time** *n* [u] 放学在家时间; ~ **town** *n* 家乡; ~ **truth** *n* [尤指别人指出的] 令人不快的事实; **I'll tell him a few ~ truths** 我要跟他讲几句大实话; ~ **video** *n* [1] [c] (recording) 自制录像; [2] [c] (camera) 业余录像设备; (video recorder) 家庭摄像机; [3] [c] (rented film) 在家中观看的录像; [4] [u] (rental business) 家庭音像业; ~ **visit** *n* [医生、护士等的] 家访

homeward /ˈhəʊmwəd/
A *adj* 回家的
B *adv* (*also* **homewards**) 向家; **to go** *or* **head** *or* **travel ~(s)** 朝家里走; **~-bound commuters** 下班回家的通勤者

home: ~**work** *n* [u] [1] (school work) 家庭作业; [2] fig (preparatory research) 准备工作; **to do one's ~work** 做准备; [3] (piecework) 在家做的工作 [尤指低报酬计件工作]; ~**worker** *n* 在家工作的人; ~**working** *n* [u] 在家做的工作

homey /ˈhəʊmi/ *adj* Amer = **homely 3**

homicidal /ˌhɒmɪˈsaɪdl/ *adj* 杀人的 ‹*tendencies, person*›

homicide /ˈhɒmɪsaɪd/ *n* [1] [u] (act) [蓄意] 杀人罪 [2] [c] (case) 杀人案 [3] [c] dated (murderer) 杀人犯

homicide bureau *n* + *v sing or pl* Amer [警察局的] 凶杀重案组

homily /ˈhɒmɪli/ *n* [1] (sermon) 布道 [2] fig (moralizing discourse) 道德说教

homing /ˈhəʊmɪŋ/ *adj attrib* 自导引的 ‹*missile, system*›; **a ~ device** 自导引装置

homing: ~ **instinct** *n* 返巢本能; ~ **pigeon** *n* 信鸽

hominy grits /ˈhɒmɪni ɡrɪts/ *npl* Amer 玉米糁

homo /ˈhəʊməʊ/ *n* (*pl* ~**s**) sl offensive 同性恋者

homoeopath /ˈhəʊmɪəpæθ/ *n* = **homeopath**

homoeopathic /ˌhəʊmɪəˈpæθɪk/ *n* = **homeopathic**

homoeopathy /ˌhəʊmɪˈɒpəθi/ *n* = **homeopathy**

homoerotic /ˌhəʊməʊɪˈrɒtɪk/ *adj* 同性恋的 ‹*film, behaviour, desire*›

homogeneity /ˌhɒmədʒɪˈniːɪti/ *n* [u] 同质

homogeneous /ˌhɒməˈdʒiːnɪəs/ *adj* 同种族的 ‹*population, group*›; 同质的 ‹*nature, structure*›

homogenize /həˈmɒdʒənaɪz/ *vt* [1] Culin 使均质; ~**d milk** 均质牛奶 [2] fig (make similar) 使…相似 ‹*society, attitudes*›

homograph /ˈhɒməɡrɑːf, Amer -ɡræf/ *n* 同形异义词

homologous /həˈmɒləɡəs/ *adj* Biol 类似的 ‹*cell, sequence*›; 同源的 ‹*gene, chromosome*›

homologue Brit, **homolog** Amer /ˈhɒməlɒɡ/ *n* formal 同系物

homonym /ˈhɒmənɪm/ *n* 同形同音异义词

homonymy /hɒˈmɒnəmi/ *n* [u] 同形同音异义

homophobe /ˈhɒməfəʊb/ *n* 仇同性恋者

homophobia /ˌhɒməˈfəʊbɪə/ *n* [u] 仇同性恋

homophobic /ˌhɒməˈfəʊbɪk/ *adj* 仇同性恋的

homophone /ˈhɒməfəʊn/ *n* (different spelling) 同音异形词; (different meaning) 同音异义词

homophony /həˈmɒfəni/ *n* [u] 同音异形

Homo sapiens /ˌhəʊməʊ ˈsæpɪenz/ *n* [u and c] (species) 智人; (humans) 人类

homosexual /ˌhɒməˈsekʃʊəl/
A *adj* 同性恋的
B *n* 同性恋者; **practising** *or* **active ~s** 有同性恋行为的人

homosexuality /ˌhɒməˌsekʃʊˈæləti/ *n* [u] 同性恋

Hon *abbr* [1] (in official title) = **honourable 4** [2] (in job title) = **Honorary** 名誉的; **the ~ Secretary** 名誉秘书长

honcho /ˈhɒntʃəʊ/ *n* (*pl* ~**s**) colloq 头头; **he's the head ~** 他是老板

Honduran /hɒnˈdjʊərən/ ▸ **p. 503**
A *adj* (of Honduras) 洪都拉斯的; (of the people) 洪都拉斯人的
B *n* 洪都拉斯人

Honduras /hɒnˈdjʊərəs/ *pr n* 洪都拉斯

hone /həʊn/
A *vt* [1] (sharpen) 把…磨快 ‹*razor, blade*› [2] fig (polish, perfect) 修饰 ‹*style, essay*›
B *n* (stone) 磨石

honest /ˈɒnɪst/
A *adj* [1] (truthful) 诚实的 ‹*person*›; **to be ~ about sth.** 在某事上是诚实的; **the ~ truth** 真理 [2] (frank, genuine) 坦诚的 ‹*confession*›; 坦率的 ‹*answer, explanation*›; **an ~ opinion** 真实意见; **to be ~ with oneself/sb.** 直视自己的想法/对某人坦诚; **to be ~, …** 坦率地讲, … [3] (legal, fairly earned) 正当的 ‹*profit, work*›; 辛苦挣得的 ‹*money*›; **by ~ means** 通过正当手段; **to make an ~ living** 踏踏实实地过日子; **he's never done an ~ day's work** 他从未认认真真干过一天活儿; **to earn** *or* **turn an ~ penny** 老老实实赚钱
B *excl* 真的; ~ **to God** *or* **goodness!** 老天爷作证!

honest broker *n* 公正调解人

honestly /ˈɒnɪstli/ *adv* [1] (truthfully) 诚实地 ‹*answer, behave*› [2] (sincerely) 真诚地 ‹*admit, believe*›; **quite ~, …** 十分坦率地讲, … [3] (fairly, legally) 正当地 ‹*obtain, earn*› [4] colloq (really) 的确 [表示不耐烦、不赞成、吃惊等]; **~, I mean it!** 说实在的, 我是认真的!

honest-to-God
A *adj attrib* colloq 真正的
B *adv* 真正地; **~, I didn't know!** 真的, 我原本不知道!

honest-to-goodness *adj attrib* 真正的

honesty /ˈɒnɪsti/ *n* [u] (truthfulness) 诚实; (integrity) 正直; (sincerity) 真诚; **to have the ~ to admit sth.** 坦诚地承认某事; **in all ~** 说实话; **~ is the best policy** 诚实为上策

honesty box *n* 诚信投币箱 [购物者凭诚信度投币购物]

honey /ˈhʌni/ *n* [1] [u and c] (food) 蜂蜜 [2] [u] fig (sweetness) 甜蜜; **a taste of ~** 甜美的滋味 [3] [c] esp Amer colloq (darling) 亲爱的; **hi, ~! I'm home!** 嗨, 宝贝, 我到家了! [4] [c] esp Amer colloq (good thing) 好东西; **your present was a real ~!** 你的礼物真是太棒了!

honey: ~**bee** *n* 蜜蜂; ~**bunch,** ~**bun** *ns* esp Amer colloq 亲爱的

honeycomb /ˈhʌnɪkəʊm/
A *n* [1] (in hive) 蜂巢 [2] (structure) 蜂窝状物
B *vt* 使…成蜂窝状 ‹*bank, hillside*›; **to ~ sth. with sth.** 用某物使某物成蜂窝状

honeycombed /ˈhʌnɪkəʊmd/ *adj* [1] (filled with holes) 多洞的; (filled with passages) 多孔道的; **~ with tunnels** 多孔道的 [2] fig (riddled) 遍布的; **to be ~ with sth.** 充满某物 [3] (patterned) 蜂窝状的 ‹*appearance, texture*›

honeydew /ˈhʌnɪdjuː/ *n* [u] (from aphids) 蜜露; (from plants) 蜜汁

honeydew melon *n* [c and u] 蜜瓜

honeyed /ˈhʌnɪd/ *adj* [1] Culin (coated with honey) 涂蜂蜜的; (tasting of honey) 蜂蜜味的 [2] (flattering) 甜言蜜语的 ‹*words, compliments*›

honeymoon /ˈhʌnɪmuːn/
A *n* [1] (period after wedding) 蜜月; **to be on one's ~** 在度蜜月; **to go on ~ to …** 去…度蜜月 [2] fig (initial period) ~ **(period)** [新工作、新关系等初期的] 和谐时期; **the ~ period for the government is over** 这届政府的蜜月期已经过去了
B *vi* 度蜜月

honeymoon couple *n* 新婚夫妇

honeymooner /ˈhʌnɪmuːnə(r)/ *n* 度蜜月者

honeymoon suite *n* 蜜月套房

honey: ~**pot** *n* 储蜜罐; ~**suckle** *n* [u and c] 忍冬

Hong Kong /ˌhɒŋ ˈkɒŋ/ *pr n* 香港; ~ **Special Administrative Region** 香港特别行政区

honied /ˈhʌnɪd/ *adj* = **honeyed**

honk /hɒŋk/
A *vi* «*goose*» 叫; «*horn*» 鸣响; **to ~ at sb./sth.** 朝某人/某物鸣喇叭
B *n* (of goose) 鹅叫声; (of horn) 汽车喇叭声

honky-tonk /ˈhɒŋkɪtɒŋk/ *n* [1] [u] (music) 雷格泰姆钢琴曲; **a ~ rhythm** 雷格泰姆节拍 [2] [c] Amer colloq (club) 低级嘈杂的夜总会; (bar) 低级嘈杂的酒吧; (dance hall) 低级嘈杂的舞厅; **a ~ beach cafe** 低级嘈杂的海滩咖啡馆

honor /ˈɒnə(r)/ *n, vt* Amer = **honour**

honorable /ˈɒnərəbl/ *adj* Amer = **honourable**

honorably /ˈɒnərəbli/ *adv* Amer = **honourably**

honorarium /ˌɒnəˈreərɪəm/ *n* (*pl* **honoraria** /ˌɒnəˈreərɪə/) 酬金

honorary /ˈɒnərəri, Amer ˈɒnəreri/ *adj* [1] (conferred as an honour) 荣誉的 ‹*degree*›; 名誉的 ‹*fellowship, member*› [2] Brit (voluntary) 义务的 ‹*president, post, secretary*›

honorific /ˌɒnəˈrɪfɪk/
A *adj* 表示尊敬的
B *n* [尤指东方语言中的] 尊称

honour /ˈɒnə(r)/ Brit
A *n* [1] [u] (high principles) 正义感; **a sense of ~** 廉耻心; **a man of ~** 品德高尚的人; **to give (sb.) one's word of ~** (向某人) 郑重承诺; **a matter/point of ~** 道义上的事; **to be on one's ~ (to do sth.)** 以人格担保 (做某事); **~ is satisfied** dated or hum 双方都保住了尊严; **on** *or* **upon one's ~** dated 以人格担保; **(there is) ~ among thieves** Prov 盗亦有道 [2] [u and c] (glory, reputation) 荣誉; **a medal/title of ~** 荣誉勋章/称号; **it is a matter of ~** 这事事关荣辱; **to be buried with full military ~s** 以隆重的军葬礼下葬; **to do the ~s** colloq 履行社交职责 [3] [c] (credit) 光荣; **an ~ to the profession** 这一行业的光荣 [4] [c] formal (privilege) 荣幸; **to have the ~ of meeting sb.** 有幸见到某人; **it is a great ~ (for me) to be invited** 承蒙邀请, 不胜荣幸; **will you do me the ~ of dining with me?** 你能赏光与我共进晚餐吗?; **to what do I owe this ~?** formal or hum 我缘何享此殊荣? [5] [u] (respect) 崇敬; **to be seated in the place of ~** 坐在上席; **(to do sth.) in ~ of sb./sth.** 为了向某人/某事物表示敬意 (做某事); **a ceremony in ~ of sth./sb.** 为某事物/某人举行的仪式; **flags were flying in ~ of the occasion** 旗帜飘扬, 庆祝这一盛会 [6] [c] (title) **His/Her/Your ~** (judge) 法官大人; Amer (mayor) 市长阁下
B **honours** *npl* [1] Univ (course) 优等生课程;

h

(grade) 优异成绩; **to graduate with ~s** 以优异成绩毕业 **2** (in cards) 最大点数的牌

C *vt* **1** (respect) 尊敬; **our ~ed guests** 我们的贵宾; **to ~ sb.'s memory** 缅怀某人 **2** (give glory to) 给…以荣誉; **to be ~ed with a knighthood (for sth.)** (因某事)荣获爵士头衔 **3** formal (make proud, pleased) 使感到荣幸; **I feel highly ~ed by her trust in me** 她对我的信任让我感到万分荣幸; **will you ~ us with a visit some time?** 如蒙光临，荣幸之至 **4** (fulfil, be bound by) 履行 ‹*promise, contract*›; 执行 ‹*policy*›; 承认…有效 ‹*signature*› **5** Fin 承兑 ‹*cheque, draft*›; 承还 ‹*debt*›; 承付 ‹*bill*›

honourable /ˈɒnərəbl/ *adj* **1** (principled) 正直的 ‹*person*›; 高尚的 ‹*action, deed*›; **it is/it is not ~ to do sth.** 做某事很光荣/不光彩 **2** (worthy) 体面的 ‹*defeat, victory*› **3** (estimable) 值得尊敬的 ‹*deed, profession*› **4** **Honourable** (in titles) 尊敬的; **the H~ Mr Justice Jones/Gentleman/Lady** 尊敬的琼斯法官阁下/先生/女士

honourable: ~ discharge *n* 荣誉退役; **~ mention** *n* 荣誉奖

honourably /ˈɒnərəbli/ *adv* 光荣地 ‹*act, fight*›; 光明磊落地 ‹*behave, acquit oneself*›

honour: ~-bound *adj pred* 为荣誉必须做的; **to be/feel ~-bound to do sth.** 做某事是/感觉是关乎荣誉的; **~ killing** *n* [u and c] 荣誉谋杀; **~s course** *n* Brit 优等生课程; **~s degree** *n* Brit 优等学位; **~s list** *n* Brit 受表彰人员名单; **~s system** *n* 诚信制度 [指支付或考试中出于信任而不加监督的制度]

the honours system

英国的勋誉体系历时久远，迄今已有 650 余年的历史。英国的君主是勋誉之源（fountain of honour），各类勋誉一般都要由国王或女王在白金汉宫亲自颁授。英国现今通常每年授勋两次，授勋对象主要根据英国内阁办公室（▸**the civil service**）的推荐名单确定。新年颁授的勋誉称新年勋誉（New Year Honours），6 月女王的官方生日时颁授的称寿辰勋誉（Birthday Honours）（女王真正的生日在 4 月）。通过这两次授勋活动，有些人获封为终身贵族（life peerage，不能继承），有些人获封为爵士（knight），其他人则获得一些次要的勋誉。许多勋誉都和骑士勋位（order of chivalry）有关。嘉德勋位（Order of the Garter）是英国历史最悠久、等级最高的骑士勋位，始设于 1348 年，授予英国和其他王室成员及最多不超过 24 名其他人士。比较常见的英帝国勋位（Order of the British Empire）设立于 1917 年，共设五个级别，依次为：英帝国大十字爵士勋位（Knight/Dame Grand Cross of the British Empire，简称 GBE）、英帝国二级爵士勋位（Knight/Dame Commander of the British Empire，男性简称 KBE，女性简称 DBE）、英帝国高级勋位或英帝国三等勋位（Commander of the British Empire，简称 CBE）、英帝国官佐勋位或英帝国四等勋位（Officer of the British Empire，简称 OBE）、英帝国员佐勋位或英帝国五等勋位（Member of the British Empire，简称 MBE）。

hooch /huːtʃ/ *n* [u] esp Amer colloq 烈酒 [尤指非法蒸馏的威士忌]

hood /hʊd/ *n* **1** (for head) 风帽; **a jacket with/without a ~** 带/不带兜帽的夹克 **2** Zool (on falcon) 羽冠; (on cobra) 颈部皮褶 **3** (on machinery) 防护罩; (on stove, cooker) 排风罩; (on camera) 遮光罩 **4** Brit (on car, pram) 折叠式车篷; **to put the ~ up/down** 把篷盖打开/放下 **5** Amer Aut (bonnet) 引擎罩 **6** Amer sl (gangster, delinquent) **= hoodlum** **7** esp Amer colloq (neighbourhood) **the ~** 街区

hooded /ˈhʊdɪd/ *adj* **1** (having a hood) 有风帽的 ‹*coat, cloak*›; (wearing a hood) 戴风帽的 ‹*monk*›; 戴面罩的 ‹*robber, gunman*› **2** (of eyes) 眼皮耷拉的

hoodie /ˈhʊdi/ *n* colloq (garment) 兜帽上衣; (youth) 爱穿兜帽上衣的年青人

hoodlum /ˈhuːdləm/ *n* (violent criminal) 暴徒; (hooligan) 小流氓; (juvenile delinquent) 小阿飞

hoodoo /ˈhuːduː/ colloq

A *n* (*pl* **~s**) **1** [u] (witchcraft) 魔法 **2** [c] (bad luck) 厄运 **3** [c] (jinx) (person) 带来厄运的人; (thing) 不祥之物

B *vt* (cast spell on) 使遭厄运; (bewitch) 施巫术于

hoodwink /ˈhʊdwɪŋk/ *vt* 欺诈; **to ~ sb. into doing sth.** 哄骗某人做某事

hooey /ˈhuːi/ *n* [u] colloq 胡言八道; **that's a load of ~!** 那是一派胡言!

hoof /huːf/

A *n* (*pl* **~s** or **hooves**) **1** (of mammal) 蹄; **on the ~** 未屠宰的 ‹*cattle*›; fig (without preparation) 草草地 ‹*act, decide*›; **he delivered his speech on the ~** 他随口说了几句 **2** colloq (of human) 脚丫子

B *vt* colloq **1** (go on foot) 步行; **to ~ it** 走路 **2** (kick) 猛踢

hoof and mouth disease *n* [u] Amer 口蹄疫

hoofed /huːft/ *adj* 有蹄的

hoo-ha /ˈhuːhɑː/ *n* [u] colloq 激动; **they made a real ~ about it** 他们对此过于大惊小怪

hook /hʊk/

A *n* **1** (for clothes, picture) 挂钩; **by ~ or by crook** fig colloq 千方百计地 **2** Fishg 鱼钩; **to fall for sth. ~, line, and sinker** colloq 完全被某事物欺骗; **to be off the ~** fig 摆脱责任; **to get/let sb. off the ~** fig 使/让某人摆脱责任; **to get one's ~s into sb.** fig 使某人上钩 **3** (in sewing) 钩眼扣 **4** (on arm) 钩状假手 **5** Telecom **off the ~** 不挂上; **to take/leave the phone off the ~** 摘下电话听筒 **6** Agric 镰刀 **7** (in boxing) 钩拳 **8** (in golf, cricket) 曲线球 **9** fig (bait) 诱惑; **to look for a sales ~** 寻找卖点

B *vt* **1** (hang) 用钩挂; (fasten) 钩住; **to ~ sth. to the back of the car** 把某物挂在汽车尾部; **to be** or **get ~ed on a nail** (accidentally) 被钉子钩住 **2** (bend) 使成钩状; **to ~ one's finger** 屈指; **to ~ one's foot under a stool** 用脚从底下钩住凳子 **3** Fishg 钓 ‹*fish*› **4** fig hum (acquire) 钓到 ‹*spouse*› **5** Sport (in rugby) 用脚钩…给队友 ‹*ball*›; **to ~ the ball** (in golf, cricket) 打出曲线球

C *vi* **1** (be fastened) 用钩固定; **to ~ at the back** «*garment*» 在背部用钩眼扣扣住 **2** (be hung) 用钩挂; **to ~ over the roof ridge** «*ladder*» 钩挂在屋脊上 **3** (be bent) 弯成钩状; **to ~ around sb.'s neck** «*arm*» 勾住某人的脖子

Phrasal verbs

- **hook on**

A *vi* «*attachment, trailer*» 钩住

B *vt* [**~ sth. on, ~ on sth.**] 挂上 ‹*trailer, lamp*›

- **hook together**

A *vt* [**~ sth. together**] 用钩连接 ‹*pieces, wagons*›

B *vi* «*pieces, wagons*» 用钩连接

- **hook up**

A *vi* **1** (be fastened) «*garment*» 用搭扣扣住 **2** **to ~ up with sb.** fig colloq (meet up) 与某人碰头; (work together) 与某人搭档

B *vt* [**~ up sb./sth., ~ sb./sth. up**] **1** (fasten) 扣上…的钩眼扣 ‹*dress*›; **can you ~ me up?** 你能帮我扣上扣子吗? **2** **to ~ sb./sth. up to sth.** (attach, connect) 把某人/某物与某物连接; **the computer is ~ed up to the printer** 计算机与打印机相连接; **she was ~ed up to an IV drip** 她在输液 **3** (join with hook) 用钩连接 ‹*trailer, wagon*›; **to ~ up the caravan to the vehicle** 把活动住房挂到汽车上 **4** Radio, TV 把…装接起来 ‹*stations*›

hookah /ˈhʊkə/ *n* 水烟袋

hook and eye *n* 钩眼扣

hooked /hʊkt/ *adj* **1** (curved) 钩状的; **a ~ nose/beak** 鹰钩鼻/钩喙 **2** (having a hook or hooks) 带钩的 ‹*stick*› **3** fig colloq (enthusiastic) 入迷的; (addicted) 成瘾的; **to be ~ on sth.** 对…上瘾 ‹*heroin*›; 对…着迷 ‹*series, activity*›

hooker /ˈhʊkə(r)/ *n* **1** esp Amer sl (prostitute) 妓女 **2** (in rugby) [并列争球的] 钩球队员

hookey, hooky /ˈhʊki/ *n* [u] Amer colloq **to play ~** 逃学

hook: ~ nose *n* 鹰钩鼻; **~-nosed** *adj* 长鹰钩鼻的; **~-up** *n* [尤指与电源、通信或广播设备的] 连接

hooligan /ˈhuːlɪɡən/ *n* 小流氓; **soccer ~s** 足球流氓

hooliganism /ˈhuːlɪɡənɪzəm/ *n* [u] 流氓行为

hoop /huːp/ *n* **1** (a round barrel) 箍 **2** (of metal, wood etc.) 环; **to put sb. through the ~s** fig 使某人经受磨炼; **to go through the ~s** fig 受苦难; **to jump through ~s** fig 付出巨大努力 **3** (in croquet) 拱门 **4** (toy) 滚环; **to roll** or **bowl** or **trundle a ~ down the street** 在街上滚圆环

hoopla /ˈhuːplɑː/ ▸**p. 307** *n* [u] Brit [游乐场的] 投环套物游戏

hooray /hʊˈreɪ/ *excl* **= hurrah**

Hooray Henry /hʊˌreɪ ˈhenri/ *n* Brit colloq pej 纨绔子弟

hoosegow /ˈhuːsɡaʊ/ *n* Amer colloq 监狱

hoot /huːt/

A *n* **1** (of owl) 鸣叫声 **2** (of train, horn, siren) 鸣响声; (of car) 喇叭声 **3** (of derision) 嘲笑; (of laughter) 大笑; **this was greeted with ~s of laughter** 这引起了阵阵哄笑 **4** colloq (amusing person) 滑稽可笑的人; (amusing thing) 滑稽可笑的事物 **5** colloq (in exclamations) **I don't give a ~** or **two ~s!** 我一点儿也不在乎!

B *vi* **1** (cry mournfully) «*owl*» 鸣叫 **2** (toot) «*train, horn, siren*» 鸣响; «*driver*» 按汽车喇叭 **3** (laugh derisively) 蔑视地笑; **to ~ with laughter** 哄堂大笑

C *vt* **1** (toot) 使…鸣响 ‹*horn*›; **to ~ one's horn (at sb.)** (向某人)鸣喇叭 **2** (jeer) 嘲笑 ‹*actor, speaker*›; **my suggestion was ~ed down by the other committee members** 我的建议受到其他委员会委员的嘘声反对

hootch /huːtʃ/ *n* **= hooch**

hootenanny /ˌhuːtəˈnæni/ *n* esp Amer colloq [非正式的] 民歌演唱会

hooter /ˈhuːtə(r)/ *n* **1** Brit (siren) 警笛; (car horn) 喇叭 **2** Brit colloq (nose) [尤指大的] 鼻子 **3** **hooters** *pl* Amer taboo sl (breasts) 奶子

Hoover® /ˈhuːvə(r)/

A *n* Brit 真空吸尘器

B **hoover** *vt, vi* 用吸尘器打扫

hooves /huːvz/ *pl* ▸**hoof A**

hop[1] /hɒp/

A *vi* (*pres p etc.* **-pp-**) **1** (on one leg) 单足跳行; **to ~ up/down the path** 单脚跳着沿路跑上去/跑下来 **2** (move on both feet) «*animal, bird*» 齐足跳行 **3** (jump) 跳跃; **to ~ off a wall** 从墙上跳下; **to ~ over a puddle/ditch** 跃过水坑/沟渠; **to ~ up and down with rage/delight** fig 气得跳脚/高兴得跳来跳去; **to be ~ping mad** fig colloq 暴跳如雷; **to ~ into bed with sb.** colloq 和某人上床 **4** (move speedily) 快速移动; **to ~ on a plane** 登上飞机; **to ~ off a bus** 跳下公共汽车 **5** colloq (travel) 作短途旅行; **to ~ over to ...** 到…作短途旅行; **we ~ped across the Atlantic to New York for the weekend** 我们飞越大西洋到纽约去度周末

B *vt* (*pres p etc.* **-pp-**) **1** (jump over) 跳过 **2** (go away) **~ it!** colloq 走开!

C *n* **1** (on one leg) 单足跳; **to be (kept) on the ~** fig colloq 忙忙碌碌; **to catch sb. on the ~** fig colloq 使某人措手不及 **2** (on both feet) 齐足跳; **in a series of little ~s** 蹦蹦跳跳地 **3** colloq (short journey) 短途旅行; (short distance) 短距离 **4** colloq (dance) [非正式的] 舞会

h

Phrasal verbs

- **hop about, hop around** *vi* 四处蹦蹦跳跳
- **hop off** *vi* colloq 快速离开

hop²
A *n* **1** (plant) 啤酒花藤 **2** **hops** *pl* (flowers) 啤酒花
B *vt* 用啤酒花给…加味 ‹*beer*›

hope /həʊp/
A *n* **1** [u and c] (expectation, optimism) 希望; **a glimmer** *or* **ray of ~** 一线希望; **to have great ~s of winning** 很有希望获胜; **to give up/lose ~** 放弃/失去希望; **to live in ~ (of sth.)** （对某事物）抱有希望; **to place** *or* **put** *or* **set** *or* **pin (all) one's ~s on sb./sth.** 把（所有的）希望寄托在某人身上/某事物上; **to build up** *or* **raise sb.'s ~s** 激起某人的希望; **don't get your ~s up** 别抱太大希望; **to be beyond ~ (of sth.)** 毫无（…的）希望; **~ springs eternal in the human breast** Prov 人心永远充满希望; **to see some ~ for the future** 看到未来的一些希望 **2** [c] (aspiration) 期望; **to have high ~s for one's children** 对孩子寄予厚望; **my only ~ is that he will be happy** 我唯一的希望是他可以幸福 **3** [u and c] (that which gives hope) 希望所在; (chance) 可能性; (promising person) 有前途的人; **you're my last ~!** 你是我最后的希望！; **her only ~ of survival** 她生存的唯一希望; **there's not much ~ that he'll come** 他来的可能性不大; **not to have a ~ in hell (of doing sth.)** colloq 毫无机会（做某事）; **not** *or* **what a ~!** Brit colloq, **some ~!** colloq 不可能！
B *vt* **1** (want, expect) 希望; **to ~ to make a lot of money** 指望赚大钱; **what is it you ~ to achieve?** 你想达到什么目的？ **I ~ he comes today** 但愿他今天来; **hoping to hear from you** (in letter) 期盼你的回信 **2** (expressing polite wish, disapproval) **to ~ (that) ...** 但愿…; **I ~ we didn't disturb you** 但愿我们没有打扰你
C *vi* 希望; **I ~ so/not** 希望如此/但愿不会; **to ~ against ~ (that ...)** （对…）仍然抱一线希望; **to ~ for the best** 尽量往好处想; **to ~ for good weather on Sunday** 盼望星期天天气好; **all we can do now is ~** 现在我们能做的就是期待

hope chest *n* Amer 嫁妆柜

hopeful /ˈhəʊpfl/
A *adj* **1** (filled with hope) 抱有希望的 ‹*mood, attitude*›; **to be ~ about sth.** 对某事物抱有希望; **to be ~ of sth./doing sth.** 对某事物/做某事抱有希望; **he is ~ that he will win** 他希望自己能赢 **2** (encouraging) 给人以希望的 ‹*sign, situation*›
B *n* (ambitious person) 希望获得成功的人; (promising person) 有望成功的人

hopefully /ˈhəʊpfəli/ *adv* **1** (with hope) 抱有希望地 ‹*say, smile*› **2** (with luck) 但愿; **~, he'll pay** 但愿他会付钱

hopeless /ˈhəʊplɪs/ *adj* **1** (desperate) 绝望的 ‹*tears, sigh*›; 没有希望的 ‹*struggle, situation, dilemma*› **2** (useless) 没用的; **it's ~ trying to escape** 试图逃走是徒劳的 **3** (incompetent) 无能的 ‹*teacher, gardener, parent*›; **to be ~ at sth./doing sth.** 不能胜任某事/做某事; **to be ~ with sb./sth.** 对某人/某事物无能为力; **he was ~ as a manager** 他当经理不称职 **4** (irreparable, incorrigible) 无可救药的 ‹*case, liar*›; 糟糕透顶的 ‹*muddle, work*›; **you're ~!** (affectionately) 你真是不可救药！

hopelessly /ˈhəʊplɪsli/ *adv* **1** (despairingly) 绝望地 ‹*speak, weep*› **2** (irretrievably) 不可挽回地; (irremediably) 无可救药地; **to be ~ lost** 彻底失败; **to be ~ in love** 爱得不能自拔; **to be ~ in debt** 债台高筑; **to be ~ confused** 完全糊涂了 **3** (extremely) 极度地 ‹*naive, incompetent, extravagant*›

hopelessness /ˈhəʊplɪsnɪs/ *n* [u] **1** (despair) 绝望 **2** (futility) 无用

hopfield /ˈhɒpfiːld/ *n* 啤酒花藤田

hopper /ˈhɒpə(r)/ *n* **1** (container for grain, coal etc.) 漏斗 **2** (railway truck) **~ (car)** 底卸式货车

hop: **~-picker** ▸p. 409 *n* **1** (person) 啤酒花采摘工; **2** (machine) 啤酒花采摘机; **~-picking** *n* [u] 采摘啤酒花; **the ~-picking season** 采摘啤酒花的季节; **~ pole** *n* 啤酒花藤支柱; **~scotch** ▸p. 307 *n* [u] 跳房子［一种儿童游戏］

horde /hɔːd/ *n* **1** usu pej (large group) 一大群人 **2** (nomadic tribe) 游牧部落; (nomadic army) 游牧队

horizon /həˈraɪzn/ *n* **1** (skyline) 地平线; **on the ~** (visible) 在地平线上; fig (imminent) 即将发生; **the only cloud on the ~** 唯一能起破坏作用的因素 **2** fig (possibility, potential) 范围; **to open up new ~s** 开启新的领域; **to widen** *or* **broaden one's ~s** 开阔眼界

horizontal /ˌhɒrɪˈzɒntl, Amer ˌhɔːr-/
A *adj* 水平的; **a dress with ~ stripes** 横纹连衣裙
B *n* (line) 水平线; (plane) 水平面; **at an angle of twenty degrees to the ~** 以与水平线成20度的角度

horizontal: **~ bar** *n* 单杠; **~ integration** *n* [u] 横向联合

horizontally /ˌhɒrɪˈzɒntəli, Amer ˌhɔːr-/ *adv* 水平地

hormonal /hɔːˈməʊnl/ *adj* 激素的

hormone /ˈhɔːməʊn/ *n* [c and u] 激素; **female/male ~** 雌性/雄性激素; **growth ~** 生长激素

hormone: **~ replacement therapy** *n* [u] 激素替代疗法; **~ rooting powder** *n* [u] 激素生根粉; **~ therapy, ~ treatment** *ns* [u and c] 激素治疗

horn /hɔːn/ *n* **1** [c] (bony outgrowth) 角; (for drinking) 角质容器; **to draw** *or* **pull in one's ~s** fig (reduce spending) 减少开支; (reduce activities) 行为检点; **to lock ~s with sb.** fig (in business) 与某人发生冲突; (in argument) 同某人辩论; **to take the bull by the ~s** fig 勇敢应对困难 **2** [u] (substance) 角质; **~ spoons/buttons** 角质勺子/纽扣 **3** [c] fig (on moon) 月牙钩; (on anvil) 尖角 **4** [c] (of snail) 触角; (of owl) 角羽 **5** ▸p. 395 [c] Mus 号; **to play the ~** 吹号 **6** [c] (warning device) (of car) 喇叭; (of ship) 汽笛; **to blow** *or* **sound the** *or* **one's ~** 按喇叭; **to blow one's own ~** fig 自吹自擂 **7** **the ~** Brit taboo sl (erection) 勃起的阴茎

horn: **~beam** *n* **1** [c] (tree) 鹅耳枥; **2** [u] (wood) 鹅耳枥木; **~bill** *n* 犀鸟

horned /hɔːnd/ *adj* 有角的; **long-/short-~ sheep** 长/短角羊

hornet /ˈhɔːnɪt/ *n* 大黄蜂; **a ~'s nest** 困境; **to stir up a ~'s nest** fig 招惹麻烦

horn: **~ of plenty** *n* 丰饶角［盛满水果、蔬菜等的羊角状物］; **~pipe** *n* 号笛舞［流行于水手中的单人舞］; (music) 号笛舞曲; **~-rimmed** *adj* 角质镜架的 ‹*glasses, spectacles*›

horny /ˈhɔːni/ *adj* **1** (made of horn) 角质的; (hornlike) 角一样坚硬的; **a ~ beak** 角质喙 **2** (hard, rough) 粗硬的 ‹*hands, skin*› **3** sl (sexually aroused) 欲火中烧的; **to feel ~** 欲火中烧

horology /həˈrɒlədʒi/ *n* [u] **1** (science) 计时学 **2** (clockmaking) 钟表制造术

horoscope /ˈhɒrəskəʊp, Amer ˈhɔːr-/ *n* **1** (chart) 天宫图 **2** (forecast) 占星术 **3** (in newspaper) 星象预测

horrendous /hɒˈrendəs/ *adj* 骇人的 ‹*injury, situation*›; 令人震惊的 ‹*price, cost*›; 可怕的 ‹*traffic jam, noise*›; 糟透了的 ‹*taste, colour*›

horrendously /hɒˈrendəsli/ *adv* **1** (in a horrific manner) 可怕地 **2** (extremely) 极度 ‹*expensive, ugly*›

horrible /ˈhɒrɪbl, Amer ˈhɔːr-/ *adj* **1** (shocking) 令人恐惧的 ‹*sight, scream, accident*›; 骇人听闻的 ‹*crime*›; **he died in ~ agony** 他在极度痛苦中死去 **2** (unpleasant) 十分讨厌的 ‹*place, colour, sensation, thought, person*›; 可恶的 ‹*weather, sound, smell*›; **to be ~ to sb.** 令某人极为不快; **she had a ~ suspicion that they were lost** 她感觉不妙，怀疑他们迷路了

horribly /ˈhɒrɪbli, Amer ˈhɔːr-/ *adv* **1** (shockingly, dreadfully) 令人恐惧地 ‹*scream, die, tortured, injured, murdered*› **2** (extremely) 极度 ‹*afraid, embarrassed*›

horrid /ˈhɒrɪd, Amer ˈhɔːr-/ *adj* **1** (very unpleasant) 极讨厌的 ‹*day, weather, thought, taste*›; **the food tasted ~** 饭菜味道很糟糕 **2** (nasty) 恶意的; (unkind) 极不友好的; **it was ~ of him to say that** 他那么说太可恶了 **3** dated (terrible) 令人恐惧的 ‹*crime, sight*›

horrific /həˈrɪfɪk/ *adj* 令人恐惧的 ‹*accident, wound*›; 骇人的 ‹*disaster, fire, crime*›

horrified /ˈhɒrɪfaɪd, Amer ˈhɔːr-/ *adj* **1** (shocked, offended) 充满恐惧的 ‹*expression, stare*›; **a ~ silence** 弥漫着恐怖的寂静 **2** (appalled) 震惊的; **to be ~ at sth.** 对某事物感到震惊; **to be ~ to hear that ...** 听到…感到震惊

horrify /ˈhɒrɪfaɪ, Amer ˈhɔːr-/ *vt* **1** (shock, offend) 使恐惧 **2** (appal) 使震惊; **to be horrified by sth.** 对某事感到震惊

horrifying /ˈhɒrɪfaɪɪŋ, Amer ˈhɔːr-/ *adj* **1** (terrifying, frightening) 令人恐惧的 ‹*sight, experience, film*› **2** (appalling) 令人震惊的 ‹*rudeness, ignorance, cost*›

horrifyingly /ˈhɒrɪfaɪɪŋli, Amer ˈhɔːr-/ *adv* 令人震惊地

horror /ˈhɒrə(r), Amer ˈhɔːr-/
A *n* **1** [u] (intense fear) 恐惧; **to sb.'s ~** 令某人惊恐地; **to have a ~ of sth./doing sth.** 对某物/做某事恐惧; **to recoil in ~** 恐惧地退缩 **2** [u] (fear, loathing) 强烈的反感; **to have a ~ of sth.** 嫌恶某事物 **3** [c] (horrifying event) 恐怖性; **the ~s of war** 战争的恐怖 **4** [c] (bad experience) (causing fear) 可怕经历; (causing repugnance) 令人不快的经历; **the ~s of flat-sharing** 合住公寓的不堪回首的经历 **5** [c] colloq (dislikeable person) 讨厌鬼［尤指孩子］; (dislikeable thing) 讨厌的东西; **the new office building is a complete ~** 新办公大楼难看极了 **6** [c] colloq (feeling of fear) **the ~s** 一阵极度的紧张不安; **to give sb. the ~s** 令某人非常紧张 **7** [c] colloq hum (in exclamations) 糟糕; **~ of ~s!** 糟糕透了！
B *modif* 恐怖的; **a ~ movie/story** 恐怖电影/故事

horror-struck, horror-stricken *adjs* 惊恐的

horse /hɔːs/ *n* **1** [c] Zool 马; **to mount/ride a ~** 跨上/骑着马; **the ~s** colloq 赛马; **to back the wrong ~** fig 支持失败一方; **to change** *or* **swap ~s in midstream** fig 中途改变支持对象; **(straight) from the ~'s mouth** fig （直接）来自有关人士的; **to get** *or* **be on one's high ~** fig 举止傲慢; **a ~ of a different** *or* **another colour** fig 风马牛不相及的事物; **to flog a dead ~** fig colloq 白费劲; **hold your ~s!** fig colloq 耐心点！; **you can take a ~ to water but you can't make it drink** Prov 老牛不饮水，不能强按头; **wild ~s wouldn't drag it out of me** fig colloq 我一定守口如瓶 **2** [c] (stallion) 成年公马 **3** [u] Mil 骑兵马; **light ~** 轻骑兵 **4** [c] (in gymnastics) 鞍马

Phrasal verb

- **horse about, horse around** *vi* colloq 胡闹

horseback /ˈhɔːsbæk/
A *n* [u] 马背; **on ~** 骑着马; **~ riding** Amer 骑马
B *adv* Amer 在马背上; **to ride ~** 骑马

horse: **~box** *n* Brit 运马拖车; **~ brass** *n* 黄铜马饰; **~ breeder** ▸p. 409 *n* 马夫; **~ chestnut** *n* **1** (tree) 七叶树; **2** (fruit) 马栗; **~ collar** *n* 马颈圈; **~ dealer** ▸p. 409 *n* 贩马商; **~ doctor** ▸p. 409 *n* 马医; **~-drawn** *adj* 马拉的; **~fly** *n* 虻; **H~ Guards** *npl* Brit **the H~ Guards** 皇家

骑兵卫队; **~hair** *n* [u] (mane) 马鬃; (tail) 马尾毛; **a ~hair mattress/sofa** 马鬃床垫/沙发; **~hide** *n* [u and c] (skin) 马皮; (leather) 马革; **~ latitudes** *npl* **the ~ latitudes** 副热带无风带; **~man** /-mən/ *n* 骑手; **~manship** /ˈhɔːsmənʃɪp/ *n* [u] 骑术; **~meat** *n* [u] 马肉; **~ opera** *n* Amer colloq 西部片; **~play** *n* [u] 喧闹嬉戏; **~power** *n* [u] 马力; **a 90 ~power engine** 90马力的发动机; **~ race** *n* 赛马; **~ racing** ▸**p. 307** *n* [u] 赛马运动; **~radish** *n* [u] **1** (plant) 辣根; **2** (root) 辣根的根; **~radish sauce** 辣根沙司; **~riding** ▸**p. 307** *n* [u] Brit 骑马; **~ sense** *n* colloq 基本常识; **~shit** *n* [u] esp Amer sl **1** (manure) 马粪; **2** fig (nonsense) 废话; **a load of ~shit** 一堆屁话

horseshoe /ˈhɔːsʃuː/ *n* **1** (for horse) 马掌 **2** (symbol of luck) 马蹄形吉祥物 **3** (shape) 马蹄形物; **a ~ bend** U形弯曲

horseshoe crab *n* 鲎

horse: ~ show *n* 马术比赛; **~ trader** ▸**p. 409** *n* **1** lit 贩马商; **2** fig (hard bargainer) 善于讨价还价的人; **a political ~ trader** 精明的政客; **~-trading** *n* [u] **1** lit 马匹买卖; **2** fig (bargaining) [尤指政治中的] 精明交易; **~ trials** *npl* 马术竞赛

horsewhip /ˈhɔːswɪp/

A *n* 马鞭

B *vt* (*pres p etc.* **-pp-**) 用马鞭抽打

horsewoman /ˈhɔːswʊmən/ *n* 女骑手

horsey, horsy /ˈhɔːsi/ *adj* **1** colloq (interested in horses) 爱马的; **the ~ set** 热衷马赛的圈子 **2** pej colloq (like a horse) 像马的; **she has a ~ face** 她长着一张马脸

horticultural /ˌhɔːtɪˈkʌltʃərəl/ *adj* 园艺的 ‹*society, show*›

horticulturalist /ˌhɔːtɪˈkʌltʃərəlɪst/ ▸**p. 409** *n* = **horticulturist**

horticulture /ˈhɔːtɪkʌltʃə(r)/ *n* [u] (activity) 园艺; (science) 园艺学

horticulturist /ˌhɔːtɪˈkʌltʃərɪst/ ▸**p. 409** *n* 园艺家

hose /həʊz/

A *n* **1** [c and u] (for garden, cleaning) 软管; **a length of ~** 一段软管 **2** [c and u] (for firefighting) **(fire) ~** 水龙带 **3** [u] formal = **hosiery**

B *vt* 用软管浇 ‹*garden*›; 用软管冲洗 ‹*vehicle, building*›; 用水龙带浇灭 ‹*fire*›

Phrasal verbs

- **hose down** *vt* [**~ sth. down, ~ down sth.**] 用软管彻底冲洗 ‹*vehicle, floor, driveway*›
- **hose out** *vt* [**~ out sth., ~ sth. out**] 用软管冲洗 ‹*shed, outhouse, barn*›

hosepipe /ˈhəʊzpaɪp/ *n* Brit 软管; **a ~ ban** 软管禁令 [禁止用软管浇花园、植物或洗车]

hosiery /ˈhəʊzɪəri, Amer ˈhəʊʒəri/ *n* [u] formal 袜类; **the ~ department** 袜类部

hospice /ˈhɒspɪs/ *n* 临终安养院

hospitable /hɒˈspɪtəbl/ *adj* **1** (friendly) 友好的 ‹*person, gesture, invitation*›; (welcoming) 好客的 ‹*family, host*› **2** (pleasant, favourable) 有利的 ‹*conditions*›; 适宜的 ‹*circumstances, terrain*›; 宜人的 ‹*climate*›

hospitably /ˈhɒspɪtəbli, ˌhɒˈspɪt-/ *adv* 热情友好地 ‹*welcome, receive*›

hospital /ˈhɒspɪtl/ *n* 医院; **to/from (the) ~** 到/从医院; **to be taken** *or* **admitted to ~ with ...** 因…被医院收治; **to be released** *or* **discharged from (the) ~** 出院

hospital: ~ administrator ▸**p. 409** *n* 医院管理者; **~ case** *n* 医院病人

hospitality /ˌhɒspɪˈtæləti/ *n* [u] 款待; **to extend** *or* **offer** *or* **show ~ (to sb.)** 殷勤招待（某人）

hospitality tent *n* [社交或商业聚会的] 招待帐篷

hospitalize /ˈhɒspɪtəlaɪz/ *vt* 送…入院治疗

hospital: ~ porter ▸**p. 409** *n* Brit 医院搬运工; **~ service** *n* 医院服务; **~ ship** *n* 医院船 [尤用于接治伤病士兵]; **~ trust** *n* Brit 信托医院 [指由信托机构管理的医院]

Host *n* Relig **the ~** 祭饼

host¹ /həʊst/

A *n* **1** (at home) 主人; (at conference, ceremony) 主持人; **to be** *or* **play ~ to sb.** 招待某人 **2** (town, country, institution) 东道主; **to be** *or* **play ~ to sth.** 做…的东道主; **the ~ nation/city** 主办国/城市 **3** Radio, TV 节目主持人 **4** Bot, Zool 寄主 **5** Comput 主机

B *vt* **1** (gen) 主办 ‹*conference, contest*› **2** Radio, TV 主持 ‹*show, programme*›

host² *n* (large number) 许多; **~s** *or* **a ~ of sth.** 大量的某物

hostage /ˈhɒstɪdʒ/ *n* 人质; **to take/hold sb. ~** 将某人扣为人质; **to give a ~ to fortune** *or* **fate** 招惹麻烦

hostage-taker *n* 劫持人质者

host: ~ computer *n* 主机; **~ country** *n* 主办国

hostel /ˈhɒstl/

A *n* **1** (accommodation) [提供廉价食宿的] 招待所 **2** = **youth hostel**

B *vi* [尤指假期] 住招待所

hosteler /ˈhɒstələ(r)/ *n* Amer = **hosteller**

hosteling /ˈhɒstəlɪŋ/ *n* [u] Amer = **hostelling**

hosteller /ˈhɒstələ(r)/ *n* Brit 住青年旅社的旅行者

hostelling /ˈhɒstəlɪŋ/ *n* [u] Brit 住青年旅社

hostelry /ˈhɒstəlri/ *n* archaic or hum (inn) 旅店; (public house) 酒馆

hostess /ˈhəʊstɪs/ *n* **1** (at home) 女主人; (at conference) 女主持人 **2** (in club, bar, dance hall) 女侍 **3** (on aircraft, train) 女乘务员 **4** Radio, TV 节目女主持

hostile /ˈhɒstaɪl, Amer ˈhɒstl/ *adj* **1** (unfriendly) 不友善的 ‹*expression, manner, person*›; (antagonistic) 有敌意的 ‹*attack, audience, crowd*›; **to be ~ to** *or* **towards sb./sth.** 对某人/某事物怀有敌意 **2** (opposed) 反对的 ‹*criticism, opinion, attitude*› **3** (unwelcoming) 不利的 ‹*situation, conditions, environment*› **4** Mil 敌人的 ‹*aircraft, artillery fire, forces*›; **we came under ~ fire** 我们遭遇敌方炮火攻击

hostility /hɒˈstɪləti/

A *n* **1** (unfriendliness) 不友善; (antagonism) 敌意; **to show ~ to** *or* **towards sb./sth.** 对某人/某事物表现出敌意 **2** (opposition) 反对; **~ to** *or* **towards sb./sth.** 对某人/某事物的抵制

B **hostilities** *npl* 战争行为

host name *n* 主机名

hot /hɒt/ ▸**p. 814** *adj* **1** (very warm) 热的; (feeling heat) 感觉热的; **~ weather** 炎热的天气; **a ~ bath** 热水浴; **to be too ~ to drink/touch** 太烫，不能喝/摸; **to be ~ from the oven** ‹*bread*› 新鲜出炉; **the sun was ~ on my back** 太阳火辣辣地照在我的背上; **to get sb. into ~ water** fig colloq 使某人惹上麻烦; **to blow ~ and cold (about sth.)** fig colloq （对某事）出尔反尔; **I am** *or* **feel ~** 我觉得很热; **to be ~ with embarrassment** «*face*» 窘得发烫; **to go ~ and cold** lit 感觉一阵冷一阵热; fig 突然感到害怕; **to get all ~ and bothered** fig colloq 变得焦虑不安; ▸**cat 1, iron A3** **2** (making sb. feel heat) 使人感到热的; **digging is ~ work** 挖地让人全身发热; **a long, ~ journey** 走起来很热的长途旅程 **3** (spicy) 辣的 ‹*spice, curry, dish*› **4** (fresh) 最新的 ‹*news, gossip*› **5** *pred* (newly arrived) 刚到达的; **~ off the press** «*news*» 刚见报的; **to be ~ from the factory** «*product*» 刚出厂; **she was ~ from the New York conference** 她刚参加完纽约研讨会 **6** (intense) 激烈的 ‹*competition, debate*›; 热门的 ‹*issue, topic*›; **the pace is getting ~ter** 节奏越来越快 **7** (fiery) 易发怒的; **to have a ~ temper** 脾气暴躁 **8** colloq (good) 极好的; **the team is ~** 这个队很棒; **a ~ tip** 内部消息; **to be the ~ favourite (for sth.)** 是（某项赛事）最被看好的选手; **to be on a ~ streak** Amer 连连取得成功; **to be ~ on sth.** (knowledgeable) 通晓某事; (keen) 擅长某事; **not so** *or* **too** *or* **all that ~** (quality) 不太好的; (health) 不太舒服的 **9** (close) 紧跟的; **to be ~ on sb.'s trail** *or* **tracks** 紧跟某人; **to set off in ~ pursuit (of sb.)** 出发紧追（某人）; **to be ~ on the trail of sth.** 即将找到某物 **10** *pred* colloq (in games) **you're getting ~** (finding sth.) 你快找到了; (guessing answer) 你快猜中了 **11** colloq (popular) 当红的 ‹*star, band*›; 广受欢迎的 ‹*club, show*› **12** *pred* colloq (rigorous) **to be ~ on sth.** 对…要求严格 ‹*grammar, manners*›; **he's ~ on environmental protection** 他很重视环保 **13** colloq (difficult, dangerous) 艰难的 ‹*situation*›; **to make it** *or* **things ~ for sb.** 让某人日子不好过; **things are getting ~** 形势越来越严峻 **14** colloq (stolen) 偷来的 **15** *usu attrib* (bright) 鲜亮的 ‹*colour*›; **~ red** 鲜红色 **16** colloq (erotic) 色情的 ‹*movie, scene*›; (sexy) 性感的 ‹*guy, girl*›; **to look ~** 看上去性感 **17** Mus 节奏强的 ‹*jazz*› **18** colloq (radioactive) 强放射性的

Phrasal verb

- **hot up** (*pres p etc.* **-tt-**) Brit colloq

A *vi* **1** (get exciting) «*match, campaign*» 变得激烈起来; «*party*» 变得活跃起来; **things are really ~ting up** 形势的确越来越紧张 **2** (get faster) «*pace, chase*» 加快 **3** (intensify) «*competition, raids*» 加剧; «*trade*» 剧增

B *vt* [**~ sth. up, ~ up sth.**] **1** (make exciting) 使…变得激烈起来 ‹*campaign, contest*›; 使…变得活跃起来 ‹*broadcast, speech*›; **to ~ the music up** 使音乐变得活泼欢快 **2** (make faster) 加快 ‹*pace*› **3** (intensify) 加强 ‹*raids, surveillance*›

hot air *n* [u] colloq 夸夸其谈; **he's talking ~** 他在夸夸其谈; **it's just a load of ~!** 这不过是一堆空话!

hot air balloon *n* 热气球

hot: ~bed *n* (for plants) 温床; **to be a ~bed of rumours/revolt** fig 是谣言/叛乱的温床; **~-blooded** *adj* 血气方刚的 ‹*person*›; 急躁的 ‹*action, behaviour*›; 激动的 ‹*response*›; **~ button** *n* Amer colloq 热点话题; **a ~-button issue/topic/question** 热点问题/热门话题/争论不休的问题; **~ cake** *n* Amer 薄煎饼; **to sell like ~ cakes** fig 非常抢手; **her books sell like ~ cakes** 她的书很畅销

hotchpotch /ˈhɒtʃpɒtʃ/ *n* Brit 杂乱无章的一堆东西; **to be a ~ of sth.** 是某物的大杂烩

hot cross bun *n* 十字面包

hot: ~-desking /ˈhɒtˌdeskɪŋ/ *n* [u] 办公桌轮用; **~ dog** *n* 热狗; **a ~ dog stand** *or* **stall** 热狗售卖亭

hotel /həʊˈtel/ *n* 旅馆; **to stay at** *or* **in a ~** 住旅馆; **to check out of/into a ~** 登记入住/结账离开旅馆

hotelier /həʊˈtelɪə(r)/ ▸**p. 409** *n* (owner) 旅馆老板; (manager) 旅馆经理

hotel: ~keeper ▸**p. 409** *n* = **hotelier**; **~ manager** ▸**p. 409** *n* 旅馆经理; **~ receptionist** ▸**p. 409** *n* 旅馆接待员; **~ room** *n* 旅馆房间; **~ staff** *n* 旅馆员工; **~ work** *n* [u] 旅馆工作

hot flush Brit, **hot flash** Amer *ns* 热潮红 [女性更年期出现的一种突然而短暂的发热感]

hotfoot /ˈhɒtfʊt/

A *adv* 匆忙地 ‹*run, go, come*›

B *vt* colloq 急走; **to ~ it** 快跑; **to ~ it down to the pub** 匆匆跑到酒馆

hot: ~ hatch, ~ hatchback *ns* Brit colloq [高性能的] 掀背式轿车; **~head** *n* 鲁莽的人

hot-headed /ˌhɒtˈhedɪd/ *adj* 鲁莽的 ‹*person, behaviour*›

hot-headedly /ˌhɒtˈhedɪdli/ *adv* 鲁莽地; **to rush ~ into things** 仓促行事

hot-headedness /ˌhɒtˈhedɪdnɪs/ *n* [u] 鲁莽

hothouse /ˈhɒthaʊs/ *n* **1** lit (for plants) 温室 **2** fig 有利于迅速发展的环境; **the school**

was a ~ for bright pupils 这所学校有利于聪明学生快速成长

hothouse plant *n* 1 Bot 温室植物 2 fig (frail person) 脆弱的人; (frail thing) 脆弱的事物

hot: ~ key *n* 快捷键; **~line** *n* 1 (for specific purpose) 热线; 2 (for customer support) 咨询服务专线; **to place an order on the sales ~line** 通过销售专线电话订货; **~link** *n* (dynamic connection) 热链接; (hyperlink) 超文本链接; **~list** *n* 1 (of fashionable people) 走红人物名单; (of items) 热点物品清单; (of places) 热点地区名录; 2 Comput 热门网页列表

hotly /ˈhɒtli/ *adv* 1 (passionately) 激动地 ‹*dispute, exclaim*›; (vehemently) 热烈地 ‹*debate, argue*›; (resolutely) 坚决地 ‹*deny, retort*› 2 (closely) 激烈地 ‹*contested*›; **~ pursued by the police** 被警察紧紧追赶

hot: ~ money *n* [u] 短期流动资金; **~ pants** *npl* 女式热裤; **~plate** *n* [炉灶上的]加热板; **~pot** *n* [u] Brit 焖罐 [内装炖煮的肉、蔬菜和土豆]; **~ potato** *n* fig colloq (issue) 棘手问题; (situation) 尴尬处境; **to drop sth./sb. like a ~ potato** 像扔烫手山芋一样丢掉某物/某人; **~ rod** *n* 改装成的高速汽车

hots /hɒts/ *npl* colloq 情欲; **to have the ~ for sb.** 对某人欲火中烧

hot: ~ seat *n* colloq **the ~ seat** 责任重大的位置; **to be in the ~ seat** 处于困境; **~ shoe** *n* 热靴 [照相机的闪光灯接口]; **~shot** *n* colloq 1 (able person) 能人; (important person) 大佬; 2 (sports player) 运动高手; **~ spot** *n* 1 (small area) [同周围相比] 气温较高的地区; 2 colloq (nightclub) 热闹的夜总会; (place of entertainment) 热闹的娱乐场所; 3 fig (place of danger) 多事之地; **a political ~ spot** 政治热点地区; 4 (on screen) 热点区 [屏幕上点击后即可启动程序的区域]; 5 (*also* **~spot**) (for wireless access) 热点; **~ spring** *n* 温泉; **~ stuff** *n* [u] colloq 1 (outstanding person) 技艺高超的人; (outstanding thing) 了不起的事物; **to be ~ stuff at tennis** 是网球高手; 2 (attractive person) 性感的人; **~-swap** *vt* colloq 热插拔 [指在不切断电源的情况下安装或更换部件]; **~-tempered** /ˈhɒtˌtempəd/ *adj* 易怒的; **~ ticket** *n* colloq (person) 炙手可热的人; (thing) 炙手可热的事物; **this show is the current ~ ticket** 这个节目现在很火; **~ tub** *n* [休闲或理疗的] 热水浴池; **~-water bottle** *n* 热水袋

hot-wire
A *vt* colloq 热线发动
B *adj attrib* 热线式的

hoummos, houmous, houmus /ˈhʊməs/ *ns* [u] = **hummus**

hound /haʊnd/
A *n* 1 (hunting dog) 猎狗; **to ride** *or* **follow the ~s** 骑马纵狗打猎 2 colloq hum (other dog) 狗 3 colloq (despicable person) 卑鄙的人
B *vt* 纠缠

Phrasal verbs
- **hound down** *vt* [**~ sb. down, ~ down sb.**] 紧追
- **hound out** *vt* [**~ sb. out, ~ out sb.**] 赶走 ‹*rival, politician*›; **to be ~ed out of town/politics** 被赶出镇子/政界

hour /aʊə(r)/ ▸p. 831
A *n* 1 (60 minutes) 小时; **a solid** *or* **full ~** 整整1小时; **within** *or* **inside the ~** 在1小时内; **a one-~ examination** 1小时的考试; **an ~ (away) from London** 距离伦敦有1小时的路程; **to be paid by the ~** 按小时付报酬 2 (top of the hour) 整点; **the clock struck the ~** 钟整点敲响; **the bus leaves on the ~** 公共汽车整点发车 3 (part of day) 时段; **at an early ~** 清早时分; **who can that be at this ~?** 这时候会是谁呢? 4 (point in time) 时刻; **in sb.'s ~ of need** 在某人困难的时候; **the country's finest ~** 国家最繁盛的时期; **his last ~ was at hand** 他大限将至
B **hours** *npl* 1 (a long time) 很长时间; **to wait for ~s** 等很久; **it took ~s to get there** 花了好长时间才到那里 2 (opening time) (for offices) 工作时间; (for shops) 营业时间; **business/office ~s** 营业/办公时间; **after ~s** (of shop, pub) 打烊后; (of office) 下班后; **visiting ~s** (in hospital) 探视时间 3 (as schedule) **to keep early/late ~s** 早睡早起/晚睡晚起; **to keep regular/strange ~s** 作息有规律/怪异 4 (part of day) 时段; **the early** *or* **small** *or* Amer colloq **wee ~s (of the morning)** 凌晨; **at all ~s** 在任何时间; **to do sth. at all ~s of the day and night** 不分昼夜随时做某事; **till all ~s** 到很晚 5 (on 24-hour clock) 点钟; **the train leaves at 1400 ~s** 列车于14点发车 6 Relig [天主教的] 祈祷礼拜; **a book of ~s** 祈祷书

hour: ~glass *n* 沙漏; **an ~glass figure** 腰细的身材; **~ hand** *n* 时针

hourly /ˈaʊəli/
A *adj* 1 (every hour) 每小时一次的 ‹*service, bulletin, visit*› 2 (per hour) 按小时计算的 ‹*earnings, rate, quota*›; **on an ~ basis** 按小时计的
B *adv* 1 (every hour) 每小时一次地 ‹*depart, run, apply*› 2 (per hour) 按小时计算地

house
A /haʊs/ *n* (*pl* **~s** /ˈhaʊzɪz/) 1 [c] (home) 房子; **at my ~** 在我家; **to help in the ~** 帮忙做家务; **to keep ~ (for sb.)** (为某人)料理家务; **to set up ~ (together)** (共同)安家; **to put** *or* **set one's (own) ~ in order** fig 把自己的事管好; **to get on** Brit *or* **along** Amer **like a ~ on fire** fig colloq 打得火热; **to play ~** colloq 玩"过家家"游戏; ▸**eat A1** 2 [c] (household) 一家人; **the whole ~** 全家人 3 [c] **the H~** Pol 议院 4 [c] (in debate) **the** *or* **this ~** 参与议院辩论的人; **to urge the ~ to do sth.** 呼吁参与辩论的诸位做某事 5 [c] (firm) 公司; **a fashion/banking/publishing ~** 时装公司/银行/出版社; **in/out of ~** 在/不在公司 6 [c] (establishment) 店家; **the speciality of the ~** 本店的特色菜; **on the ~** 由店家免费提供 7 [c] Theat (audience) 观众; (seating) 观众席; **'full ~'** (on notice) "满座"; **to play to full/empty ~s** 演出满座/观众寥寥无几; **to bring the ~ down** fig colloq 博得满堂彩 ▸**dry A1** 8 [c] (family line) 望族; **the H~ of Windsor** 温莎王室 9 [c] Brit Sch (dorm) 宿舍; (team) 小组 10 [c] Astrol 黄道宫 11 [u] Mus **~ (music)** 货仓音乐 [一种电子乐器演奏的快节奏流行舞曲]
B /haʊz/ *vt* 1 (give lodging to) 给…提供住处; **to be badly** *or* **poorly ~d** 居住条件差; **to ~ refugees in the church** (temporarily) 将难民安置在教堂里 2 (store) 收藏; **to ~ works of modern art** ‹*museum*› 收藏现代艺术作品 3 *passive* **to be ~d in the old courthouse** (be set up in) 设在旧法院大楼里

house: ~ agent ▸p. 409 *n* Brit = **estate agent**; **~ arrest** *n* [u] 软禁; **to be kept under ~ arrest** 受到软禁; **to put sb. under ~ arrest** 软禁某人; **~boat** *n* 船屋

housebound /ˈhaʊsbaʊnd/
A *adj* 出不了门的 ‹*person, invalid*›
B *npl* **the ~** 出不了门的人

house: ~break *vt* Amer = **~-train**; **~breaker** *n* Brit 入室行窃者; **~breaking** *n* [u] Brit 入室行窃; **~broken** *adj* Amer 养成良好卫生习惯的 ‹*dog, pet*›; **~ call** *n* (visit) 登门拜访; (by doctor) 出诊; **~clean** *vi* 1 Amer (clean) 打扫房屋; 2 fig ‹*firm, business*› 整顿; **~cleaning** *n* [u] 1 Amer (cleaning of house) 打扫房屋; **she pays someone to do the ~cleaning** 她雇人来大扫除; 2 fig (at company, business) 整顿; **~ clearance sale** *n* 清仓大甩卖; **~coat** *n* 家居女袍; **~fly** *n* 家蝇

houseful /ˈhaʊsfʊl/ *n* 一屋子; **a ~ of guests/cats/jumble** 满屋子客人/猫/乱七八糟的东西; **you've got quite a ~ today!** 今天你屋子里人可不少!

house guest *n* 在家小住的客人

household /ˈhaʊshəʊld/ *n* 1 (house plus occupants) 一家人; **the whole ~** 全家人; **a large/small ~** 大/小家庭; **~ accounts/expenditure/goods** 家庭账目/开支/用品 2 (occupants) 家庭; **the head of the ~** 户主

household: ~ appliance *n* 家用电器; **H~ Cavalry** *n* [u] Brit 皇家骑兵团

householder /ˈhaʊshəʊldə(r)/ *n* 1 (owner) 房主; (tenant) 住户 2 (head of household) 户主

household name, household word *ns* (person) 家喻户晓的人物; (thing) 家喻户晓的事物

the Houses of Parliament

1. 英国议会。英国最高权力和立法机关。1215年签署的《大宪章》(Magna Carta)确立了英国现代议会制度的基本原则。14世纪,上下两院开始形成。上院(House of Lords)由贵族和僧侣组成,称贵族院;下院(House of Commons)由骑士、市民代表等组成,称平民院。1688年"光荣革命"(Glorious Revolution)后,议会成为凌驾于国王之上的国家最高权力机关。下院掌握立法、财政和监督政府等权力。通常所说的英国议会(Parliament)即指下院。议员(Member of Parliament,简称MP)也指下院议员,由各个选区(constituency)的选民直接选举产生。上院主要负责审查、修改下院通过的法案,同时还是英国最高的上诉法院(Court of Appeal)。

2. 英国议会大厦。位于泰晤士河畔。曾为王宫,现仍称威斯敏斯特宫(Palace of Westminster)。最古老的建筑为威斯敏斯特大厅(Westminster Hall),始建于11世纪。议会大厦1834年经历大火,仅威斯敏斯特大厅等少数建筑幸存,后用了30年左右时间重建,采用了哥特式建筑风格。1941年下院遭到德军轰炸,战后依原样重建。议会大厦北侧为大本钟(▸**Big Ben**)。

house: ~-hunt *vi* 找房子; **~-hunting** *n* [u] 找房子; **to go ~-hunting** 去找房子; **~ husband** *n* 操持家务的丈夫; **~ journal** *n* = **~ magazine**; **~keeper** ▸p. 409 *n* 管家 [通常指女性]; **~keeping** *n* [u] 1 (cleaning, washing, etc.) 家务; **he enjoys ~keeping** 他喜欢料理家务; 2 (management) 家务管理; 3 (money) 家务开支; 4 (at company, business) 整理工作; **~ lights** *npl* 观众席照明灯; **~ magazine** *n* 公司内部出版物; **~ maid** ▸p. 409 *n* [家庭的] 女佣; **~ maid's knee** *n* [u] 髌前囊炎 [常因跪着干活引起]; **~man** /-mən/ ▸p. 409 *n* Brit = **~ officer**; **~ manager** *n* 剧院经理; **~martin** *n* 家马丁鸟; **~master** *n* Brit 男舍监; **~mistress** *n* Brit 女舍监; **~ music** *n* = **house A11**; **~ of cards** *n* 1 (structure) 纸牌搭成的房子; 2 fig (situation) 不可靠的形势; **H~ of Commons** *pr n* Brit **the H~ of Commons** 下议院; **~ officer** ▸p. 409 *n* Brit 实习医师; **H~ of God** *n* **the H~ of God** 教堂; **H~ of Keys** *pr n* **the H~ of Keys** [马恩岛立法议会中的] 下议院; **H~ of Lords** *pr n* Brit **the H~ of Lords** 上议院; **H~ of Representatives** *pr n* Amer **the H~ of Representatives** 众议院; **~owner** *n* 房主; **~ painter** ▸p. 409 *n* 房屋油漆工; **~ party** *n* 乡村府邸聚会; **~ physician** ▸p. 409 *n* Amer 内科住院医师; **~plant** *n* 室内盆栽植物; **~ prices** *npl* 房价; **~-proud** *adj* 讲究家居整洁的; **~ red** *n* [u] [饭店或酒吧中的] 最便宜的红葡萄酒; **~room** *n* [u] (space) 家里的空间; (accommodation) 家里的房间; **to not give sth. ~room** Brit 不喜欢把某物留存在家里; **~ sales** *npl* 房屋销售; **~-sit** *vi* 代为照看房子; **~-sitter** *n* 代为照看房子的人; **~-sitting** *n* [u] 代为照看房子; **H~s of Parliament** *n* Brit 1 (Houses of Lords and Commons) 议院; 2 (Palace of Westminster) 议会大厦; **~ sparrow** *n* 家麻雀; **~ style** *n* [公司书面材料的]

h

版面设计风格; ~ **surgeon** ▸**p. 409** *n* Amer 住院外科医师; Brit 高级住院外科医师

house-to-house

A *adj* 挨家挨户的 ‹*search, enquiries, sales, collection*›

B *adv* 挨家挨户地 ‹*search, enquire, sell*›

house: ~top *n* = **rooftop**; **~-train** *vt* Brit 训练…养成良好卫生习惯 ‹*pet, cat*›; fig hum 教…有教养 ‹*person*›; **~-trained** *adj* Brit 养成良好卫生习惯的 ‹*pet, cat*›; fig hum 教养好的 ‹*person*›; **~wares** *npl* formal [尤指厨房中的] 家用器皿; **~-warming** *n* 乔迁聚会; **to have** *or* **give** *or* **throw a ~-warming party** 举行乔迁聚会; ~ **white** *n* [u] [饭店、酒吧中] 最便宜的白葡萄酒; **~wife** *n* 家庭主妇

housewifely /'haʊswaɪflɪ/ *adj* 勤俭持家的 ‹*skills, virtues*›; 家庭主妇的 ‹*thrift, economy*›

house: ~ wine *n* [u] [饭店、酒吧中] 便宜的葡萄酒; **~wives** *npl* ▸**~wife**; **~work** *n* [u] 家务劳动; **to do the ~work** 做家务

housey-housey, housie-housie /ˌhaʊsɪ'haʊsɪ/ ▸**p. 307** *n* Brit dated = **bingo A**

housing /'haʊzɪŋ/ *n* **1** [u] (dwellings) 住房 **2** [u] (provision of dwellings) 住房供给; ~ **shortage/policy** 住房短缺/政策 **3** [c] (of machine, engine) [机器部件等的] 外壳

housing: ~ association *n* Brit 房屋协会 [为有住房需求者提供低价房]; ~ **benefit** *n* [u] Brit 住房补贴; ~ **development** *n* = ~ **estate**; ~ **estate** *n* Brit [同一建筑商或市政府建造的] 住宅区; ~ **project** *n* Amer [政府为低收入家庭建造的] 住宅区; ~ **stock** *n* [包括移动住房在内的] 居住单元总数

HOV *abbr* Amer = **high-occupancy vehicle**

hove /həʊv/ *pt, pp* ▸**heave A, B**

hovel /'hɒvl/ *n* 肮脏简陋的住所

hover /'hɒvə(r)/ *vi* **1** (remain stationary) 盘旋; **to ~ around/over sb./sth.** 盘旋在某人/某物周围/上方; **a question/smile ~ed on his lips** 他意欲问一个问题/一丝笑容挂在他嘴边 **2** (vacillate) 处于不稳定状态; **a country ~ing on the brink of war** 处于战争边缘的国家; **to be ~ing between life and death** 在生死间徘徊 **3** (linger) 踌躇 **4** (remain at level) «*prices, profits, inflation*» 徘徊

hover: ~craft *n* 气垫船; **~fly** *n* 食蚜虻; **~port** *n* 气垫船站; **~train** *n* 气垫列车

how /haʊ/

A *adv* **1** (enquiring about health, general situation, progress) 如何 [用以询问健康状况、大致情况或进展]; **~ are you?** 你好吗?; **~'s your foot?** 你的脚怎么样了?; **~ did the exam go?** 考试考得怎么样?; **~ are things?** 一切都好吗?; **~'s it going?** 情况如何?; **~ do you do?** formal (as greeting) 你好! **2** (in what way, by what means) 怎样 [询问方式]; **~ to do sth.** 怎样做某事; **~ is it spelt?** 它是怎么拼写的?; **~ do you mean?** 你是什么意思?; **he did not know ~ he ought to behave** 他不懂规矩 **3** (enquiring about enjoyment) 怎样 [询问是否愉快]; **~ was the film/book?** 电影/书好看吗?; **~ did you like the party/house?** 你觉得聚会/这房子好吗? **4** (in questions about number, quantity) 多少; (in questions about degree) 多么; **~ much can you eat?** 你能吃多少?; **~ many do you want?** 你要多少个?; **~ long is the rope?** 绳子有多长?; **~ big is the garden?** 这座花园有多大?; **~ old are you?** 你几岁了? **5** (in exclamations) **~ horrible!** 真可怕!; **~ I dislike her!** 我很讨厌她!; **~ you've grown!** 你长得真高! **6** (expressing annoyance, disbelief) 怎么 [表示生气、疑惑]; **~ could you? after all I've done for you!** 我为你做了这么多, 你怎么能这样!; **~ can he say that?** 他怎么能说那种话?; **~ is it that ...?** 怎么会…呢?

B *conj* **1** (that, the way in which) **you know ~ he always arrives late** 你知道他总是迟到; **it's funny ~ people always remember him** 奇怪的是人们总是记着他 **2** (in whatever way) 以任何方式; **you can dress ~ you like** 你随便穿什么衣服都行

C and how *adv phr* colloq 当然了; **did you miss me? — and ~!** 你想我了吗? ——太想了!; **did your mother tell you off? — and ~!** 你妈妈训你了吗? ——可不是么!

D how come *adv phr* colloq 为什么; **~ come you always arrive first?** 你为什么总是第一个到?

E how so *adv phr* 怎么会; **he refused — how so?** 他拒绝了——怎么会呢?

F how's that *adv phr* colloq **1** (what do you think) 怎么样; **I'll take you home, ~'s that?** 我送你回家, 如何?; **I'll tuck you in; ~'s that? comfortable?** 我来给你掖一掖被子, 怎么样? 舒服吗?; **~'s that for an interesting job?** 这份工作够有趣吧? **2** (why) 为什么 **3** (pardon) 你说什么; **he's called Nicholas — ~'s that?** 他叫尼古拉斯——叫什么?

G *n* 方法; **the ~ and the why of sth.** 某事的方法和原因

how-do-you-do /ˌhaʊdəju:'du:/, **how-de-do** /ˌhaʊdɪ'du:/, **how-d'ye-do** /ˌhaʊdjə'du:/ *ns* colloq 麻烦事; **this is a fine** *or* **real ~!** 这事可难办了!

howdy /'haʊdɪ/ *excl* Amer colloq 你好

however /haʊ'evə(r)/ *adv* **1** (nevertheless) 然而; **we thought the figures were correct; ~, we have discovered some errors** 我们原以为数据是正确的; 不过我们发现了一些错误; **most people like it; not me, ~** 大多数人喜欢它; 可是我不喜欢 **2** (no matter how) 不管怎样; **~ fast I go** 不管我走得多快; **~ difficult the task is** *or* **may be, we can't give up** 无论任务有多困难, 我们都不能放弃 **3** (in whatever way) 无论以什么方式; **you can do it ~ you like** 你想怎么做都行; **~ that may be** 尽管如此

howitzer /'haʊɪtsə(r)/ *n* 榴弹炮

howl /haʊl/

A *n* **1** (of animal) 长嚎; **to let out** *or* **give a ~** 发出一声嗥叫 **2** (of person) 喊叫声; **a ~ of pain/rage** 一阵痛苦/愤怒的喊叫声; **~s of protest/laughter** 阵阵抗议的呼声/大笑 **3** (of wind) 怒号 **4** (of electronic device) 啸鸣

B *vi* **1** «*dog, wolf*» 嚎叫 **2** «*baby, person*» 叫喊; «*monster*» 吼叫; **to ~ with rage/terror** 怒吼/惊嚎; **to ~ with laughter** 大笑 **3** «*wind*» 怒号; **listen to the gale ~ing in the trees** 倾听风在树丛中的呼啸 **4** «*electronic device*» 啸鸣

Phrasal verb

- **howl down** *vt* [**~ sb. down, ~ down sb.**] «*audience, crowd*» 以怒吼声压倒 ‹*speaker, politician*›

howler /'haʊlə(r)/ *n* colloq 愚蠢可笑的错误

howling /'haʊlɪŋ/

A *adj attrib* **1** 嗥叫的 ‹*animal*›; 呼啸的 ‹*wind*›; 哀嚎的 ‹*person*› **2** fig colloq 极大的 ‹*mistake, success, failure*›

B *n* [u] (of animal) 嗥叫; (of wind) 怒号; (of baby) 嚎哭声; (of crowd) 怒吼声

hoy /hɔɪ/ *excl* 嗨

hp, HP *abbr* **1** = **horsepower** **2** = **hire purchase**

HQ *abbr* = **headquarters**

HR *abbr* = **human resources**

hr *abbr* = **hour**

HRH *abbr* = **Her** *or* **His Royal Highness** 殿下 [间接提及时用]

HRT *abbr* = **hormone replacement therapy**

HT *abbr* = **high-tension**

HTML *abbr* = **hypertext markup language**

HTTP *abbr* = **hypertext transfer protocol**

hub /hʌb/ *n* **1** (on wheel) 轮毂 **2** fig (centre) 中心 **3** Aviat 枢纽机场 **4** Comput 集线器

hubbub /'hʌbʌb/ *n* **1** (noise) 喧闹声 **2** (situation) 骚动

hubby /'hʌbɪ/ *n* colloq 丈夫

hubcap /'hʌbkæp/ *n* 轮毂盖

Hubei /ˌhu:'beɪ/ ▸**p. 604** *pr n* ~ **(Province)** 湖北 (省)

hubris /'hju:brɪs/ *n* [u] liter 傲慢自大

huckleberry /'hʌklbərɪ, Amer -berɪ/ *n* **1** (fruit) 黑浆果 **2** (plant) 黑果木

huckster /'hʌkstə(r)/ *n* Amer (pedlar) 小贩; (door-to-door salesperson) 上门推销员

huddle /'hʌdl/

A *vi* **1** (crowd together) 挤在一起; **to ~ around sth.** 围聚在…周围 ‹*fire, radio, speaker*›; **to ~ round** 围聚 **2** (curl up) 蜷缩; **to ~ over a fire/in a corner/under the bushes** 蜷缩在炉火旁/角落里/灌木丛下

B *n* (of people) 挤在一起的人; (of things) 挤在一起的物品; **they were in a ~ around the radio** 他们围聚在收音机旁; **to go into a ~ (with sb.)** (和某人) 凑在一起交头接耳

Phrasal verbs

- **huddle together** *vi* «*people, birds, animals*» 挤成一团
- **huddle up** *vi* 蜷缩

huddled /'hʌdld/ *adj* 挤在一起的 ‹*people, animals*›; **~ in sth.** 蜷缩在…里的 ‹*chair, bed, car*›; **houses ~ around the square** fig 围聚在广场四周的房子

hue /hju:/ *n* **1** (colour) 色彩; (shade) 色调; **a warm/light/deep/bright ~** 暖/淡/深/亮色调 **2** fig (aspect, character) 类型; **people of all political ~s** 拥有各种政治信仰的人们

hue and cry *n* (shouting) 大声叫嚷; (public outcry) 公众的强烈抗议; **to raise a ~ against** *or* **about sth.** 对某事物提出强烈抗议

huff /hʌf/

A *vi* **1** (breathe heavily) 气喘吁吁 **2** (show annoyance) 发怒; **to ~ and puff** lit 气喘吁吁; fig 发脾气

B *n* 气恼; **to be in a ~** 怒气冲冲; **to go** *or* **get into a ~** 发怒

huffiness /'hʌfɪnɪs/ *n* [u] 发怒

huffish /'hʌfɪʃ/ *adj* (annoyed) 恼怒的; (irritable) 易怒的; (sulky) 郁郁不乐的 ‹*mood, temper*›

huffy /'hʌfɪ/ *adj* colloq (annoyed) 怒冲冲的 ‹*person, voice*›; (prickly) 易生气的 ‹*person*›; **to get (all) ~ (with sb.)** (对某人) 生气

hug /hʌg/

A *vt* (*pres p etc.* **-gg-**) **1** (embrace) 拥抱 ‹*person*›; 抱着 ‹*toy*› **2** (hold tightly) 抱紧 **3** (fit tightly) «*trousers, jeans, dress*» 紧裹; **figure-~ging** 紧身的 **4** (keep close to) 紧挨着 ‹*shore, ground, boundary*›; **to ~ the coast/walls** 紧靠海岸/墙壁

B *v refl* (*pres p etc.* **-gg-**) **to ~ oneself** 沾沾自喜

C *n* 拥抱; **to give sb. a ~** 拥抱某人; **a bear ~** 熊抱

huge /hju:dʒ/ *adj* **1** (in size, area) 极大的; **China is a ~ country** 中国是个幅员辽阔的国家; **a ~ smile** 开心的笑 **2** (in amount) 极多的 ‹*numbers, debts, quantity*› **3** fig (in scale) 巨大的 ‹*success, disappointment, effort*›; 程度高的 ‹*increase, demand*›; 大规模的 ‹*enterprise*›

hugely /'hju:dʒlɪ/ *adv* 极其 ‹*excited, successful, expensive, disappointed*›; 极大地 ‹*increase, vary*›

hugeness /'hju:dʒnɪs/ *n* [u] 巨大

hugger-mugger /'hʌgəmʌgə(r)/

A *adj* **1** (confused) 混乱的 ‹*arrangement, scheme, plan*› **2** (secret) 秘密的 ‹*meeting, trial, wedding*›

B *adv* **1** (in confused way) 混乱地 ‹*happen, occur*› **2** (secretly) 秘密地 ‹*dispatch, assassinate, marry*›

h

Huguenot /ˈhjuːɡənəʊ/
A *n* 胡格诺派教徒［指16至17世纪法国基督教新教徒］
B *modif* 胡格诺派的 ‹*tradition, church, emigrant*›

huh /hə/ *excl* (in surprise, inquiry) 啊; (in derision, disgust) 噢

hulk /hʌlk/ *n* 1 (abandoned ship) [船的] 残骸 2 (disused structure) 庞大的废弃物 3 (unwieldy boat) 庞大笨重的船; (unwieldy object) 大而笨的物体 4 (person) 高大粗笨的人

hulking /ˈhʌlkɪŋ/ *adj* colloq 高大粗笨的 ‹*person, animal*›; 庞大的 ‹*building, instrument*›; **a great ~ brute** (man) 彪形蠢汉; (dog) 大笨狗

hull /hʌl/
A *n* 1 (of ship) 船体 2 (of pea, bean) 荚; (of grain) 皮; (of strawberry) 花萼
B *vt* 剥掉…的荚 ‹*peas, beans*›; 除去…的皮 ‹*grain*›; 摘掉…的花萼 ‹*strawberry*›

hullabaloo /ˌhʌləbəˈluː/ *n* [u] colloq 喧闹; **she made a great ~ about being refused entry** 她因被禁止进入而大吵大闹

hullo /hʌˈləʊ/ *excl* = **hello B1**

hum¹ /hʌm/
A *vi* (*pres p etc.* **-mm-**) 1 (buzz) «*insect*» 发嗡嗡声; «*machine, traffic*» 发隆隆声 2 (sing with closed lips) 哼曲子; **to ~ along to a tune** 随曲调低声哼唱; **to ~ to oneself** 轻声哼唱; ▸**haw²** 3 colloq (bustle) «*place, town, business*» 活跃; **to ~ with activity/life** 忙碌/活跃 4 Brit colloq (emit smell) «*person, drains, dustbin*» 发臭
B *vt* (*pres p etc.* **-mm-**) 哼 ‹*melody*›; **to ~ a tune to/for sb.** 对着/为某人哼曲子
C *n* (low sound) 嘈杂声; (of insect) 嗡嗡声; (of machine, traffic) 隆隆声

hum² *excl* 嗯

human /ˈhjuːmən/
A *adj* 1 (not animal) 人的 ‹*existence, behaviour*›; **~ body** 人体 2 (susceptible) 人本性的 ‹*frailty, pride, stupidity*›; **~ weakness** 人性的软弱; **it's only ~ to do sth.** 做某事是人之常情 3 (compassionate) 通人情的; **to lack/need the ~ touch** 缺乏/需要同情心; **the milk of ~ kindness** 人的善良天性
B *n* 人

human: ~ being *n* 人; **~ chain** *n* 1 (line) [传递东西时结成的] 人链; 2 (circle) [抗议、示威或防御时结成的] 人墙

humane /hjuːˈmeɪn/ *adj* 1 (compassionate) 富于同情心的 ‹*person, attitude, act*› 2 (without cruelty) 人道的 ‹*method, treatment, killing*›

human ecology *n* [u] 人类生态学

humane killer *n* 牲口无痛屠宰机

humanely /hjuːˈmeɪnli/ *adv* 1 (compassionately) 富于同情心地 2 (without cruelty) 人道地 ‹*treat, kill*›

human engineering *n* [u] 人机工程学

humane trap *n* 牲口麻醉捕捉机

human: ~ geography *n* [u] 人类地理学; **~ interest** *n* [u] [新闻报道等的] 人情味; **a ~ interest story** 有人情味的报道

humanism /ˈhjuːmənɪzəm/ *n* [u] 人文主义

humanist /ˈhjuːmənɪst/
A *n* 人文主义者
B *adj* 人文主义的 ‹*ideal, education, philosophy*›

humanistic /ˌhjuːməˈnɪstɪk/ *adj* 人文主义的 ‹*values, beliefs*›; **~ materialism** 人本学唯物主义

humanitarian /hjuːˌmænɪˈteərɪən/
A *adj* 人道主义的 ‹*ideals, work, concerns*›
B *n* 人道主义者

humanity /hjuːˈmænəti/
A *n* [u] 1 (human race) 人类 2 (kindness) 人道 3 (human condition) 人性
B humanities *npl* (subject) 人文学科

humanize /ˈhjuːmənaɪz/ *vt* 1 (make humane, civilize) 使更人道 2 (give human character to) 使具有人的属性; **a ~d mouse** 人性化了的老鼠

humankind /ˌhjuːmənˈkaɪnd/ *n* [u] 人类

humanly /ˈhjuːmənli/ *adv* 1 (within human ability) 在人力所能及的范围内; **it is not ~ possible to run that fast** 人不可能跑那么快 2 (in human manner) 以人的方式

human nature *n* [u] 人性; **it's only ~ to do sth.** 做某事不过是人之常情

humanoid /ˈhjuːmənɔɪd/
A *adj* (in appearance) 有人形的; (in character) 有人的特性的
B *n* (robot) 人形机器人; (being) 类人动物

human: ~ race *n* **the ~ race** 人类; **~ relations** *npl* 人际关系

human resources *npl* 人力资源

human resources manager ▸**p. 409** *n* 人力资源部经理

human rights *npl* 人权

human rights: ~ activist *n* 人权活动家; **~ campaign** *n* 人权运动; **~ campaigner** *n* 人权活动家; **~ group** *n* 人权组织; **~ movement** *n* 人权运动; **~ record** *n* 人权记录

human shield *n* 人体盾牌

humble /ˈhʌmbl/
A *adj* 1 (meek) 谦逊的 ‹*person, attitude, remarks*› 2 (deferential) 谦恭的; **please accept my ~ apologies** formal 请接受鄙人的歉意; **in my ~ opinion** iron 依拙见; **your ~ servant** formal 您谦卑的仆人; ▸**pie** 3 (lowly) 低下的 ‹*position, status*›; 卑下的 ‹*occupation*›; 卑微的 ‹*birth, origins*› 4 (unpretentious) 简陋的 ‹*home, dwelling*›; 寒碜的 ‹*meal, offering*›
B *vt* 1 (lower dignity of) 使…感到卑微 ‹*person, group*› 2 (defeat, abase) 击败 ‹*enemy, opponent*›; 压制 ‹*the rich, the powerful, arrogant individual*›
C *v refl* **to ~ oneself** 低声下气; **to ~ oneself before ...** 在…面前表现卑微; **to ~ oneself to do sth.** 低声下气地做某事

humble-bee *n* dated = **bumblebee**

humbleness /ˈhʌmblnɪs/ *n* [u] 1 (humility) 谦逊 2 (low rank) 卑微; **despite the ~ of her birth** *or* **origins** 尽管她出身卑微

humbling /ˈhʌmblɪŋ/ *adj* 羞辱的; **a ~ experience/defeat/job** 令人羞愧的经历/失败/工作

humbly /ˈhʌmbli/ *adv* 1 (meekly) 谦逊地 ‹*request, bow, suggest*› 2 (modestly) 卑微地 ‹*live, die, raised*›; **~ born** 出身卑微的

humbug /ˈhʌmbʌɡ/ *n* 1 [u] (deceitful behaviour) 欺骗行为 2 [c] (hypocrite) 伪君子 3 [c] Brit (sweet) 薄荷硬糖

humdinger /ˌhʌmˈdɪŋə(r)/ *n* colloq (person) 了不起的人; (thing) 出色的事物; **a ~ of a match/an argument** 扣人心弦的比赛/精彩的辩论

humdrum /ˈhʌmdrʌm/
A *adj* 乏味的 ‹*chores, activities*›; 单调的 ‹*life, routine*›
B *n* [u] (of activity) 乏味; (of life, routine) 单调

humerus /ˈhjuːmərəs/ *n* (*pl* **humeri** /ˈhjuːməraɪ/) 肱骨

humid /ˈhjuːmɪd/ *adj* 湿热的

humidex /ˈhjuːmɪdeks/ *n* Can 湿热指数

humidifier /hjuːˈmɪdɪfaɪə(r)/ *n* 加湿器

humidity /hjuːˈmɪdəti/ *n* [u] 1 (dampness) 潮湿 2 (in atmosphere) 湿度

humiliate /hjuːˈmɪlɪeɪt/ *vt* 羞辱

humiliating /hjuːˈmɪlɪeɪtɪŋ/ *adj* 耻辱的 ‹*experience, defeat, failure*›; 羞辱的 ‹*behaviour, comment*›

humiliatingly /hjuːˈmɪlɪeɪtɪŋli/ *adv* 羞辱地

humiliation /hjuːˌmɪlɪˈeɪʃn/ *n* 1 [u] (feeling) 耻辱 2 [c] (act) 羞辱

humility /hjuːˈmɪləti/ *n* [u] 谦逊; **in all ~** 十分谦虚地

humming /ˈhʌmɪŋ/ *n* 1 (of insect) 嗡嗡声; (of machine, traffic) 隆隆声 2 (of person) 哼唱

humming: ~ bird *n* 蜂鸟; **~ top** *n* 响声陀螺

hummock /ˈhʌmək/ *n* 小丘

hummus /ˈhʊməs/ *n* [u] 鹰嘴豆泥 [中东开胃食品]

humor /ˈhjuːmə(r)/ *n* [u] Amer = **humour**

humorist /ˈhjuːmərɪst/ *vt, n* (writer) 幽默作家; (artist) 诙谐艺术家

humorless /ˈhjuːməlɪs/ *adj* Amer = **humourless**

humorlessly /ˈhjuːməlɪsli/ *adv* Amer = **humourlessly**

humorous /ˈhjuːmərəs/ *adj* 幽默的 ‹*story, writer*›; 滑稽有趣的 ‹*entertainer, artist*›

humorously /ˈhjuːmərəsli/ *adv* 幽默地

humour /ˈhjuːmə(r)/ Brit
A *n* [u] 1 (quality) 幽默; **the ~ of the situation** 这情景的滑稽之处; **to have a/no sense of ~** 有/无幽默感 2 (mood) 心情; **to be in good/bad ~** 情绪好/不佳; **when the ~ takes me** 当我有兴致时
B *vt* 迁就 ‹*child, person*›; 顺应 ‹*wish, desire*›

humourless /ˈhjuːməlɪs/ *adj* Brit 无幽默感的

humourlessly /ˈhjuːməlɪsli/ *adv* Brit 无幽默感地

humous /ˈhʊməs/ *n* [u] = **hummus**

hump /hʌmp/
A *n* 1 (on camel) 峰; (on person) 驼背 2 (mound) 土墩; (hillock) 小丘; **to be** *or* **get over the ~** 度过最困难阶段 3 Brit colloq (bad temper) 恼怒; **to have** *or* **get the ~** 感到恼怒
B *vt* 1 Brit colloq (lift, carry) 背负; **to ~ sth. on** *or* **on to one's shoulder/back** 把某物扛在肩上/背在背上 2 (make hump-shaped) 使隆起 3 sl (have sex with) 与…性交

humpback /ˈhʌmpbæk/ *n* 1 **~ (whale)** 座头鲸 2 = **hunchback**

humpback bridge *n* Brit 弓形桥

humpbacked /ˈhʌmpbækt/ *adj* = **hunchbacked**

humph /hʌmf/ *excl* 哼

humus /ˈhjuːməs/ *n* [u] 腐殖质

Hun /hʌn/ *n* 1 (nomadic Asian) 匈奴人 2 pej sl (German) [尤指第一或第二次世界大战时的] 德国佬

Hunan /ˌhuːˈnæn/ ▸**p. 604** *pr n* **~ (Province)** 湖南 (省)

hunch /hʌntʃ/
A *vt* 弓起 ‹*back*›; 耸起 ‹*shoulders*›
B *vi* 弓身; **to ~ over one's desk/work** 俯在写字台上/伏案工作; **to ~ up** *or* **down** 蜷缩成一团
C *n* (feeling) 直觉; (guess) 预感; **to work on a ~** 凭直觉工作; **to have a ~ that ...** 预感到…; **to play a** *or* **follow one's ~** 凭直觉行事

hunch: ~back *n* 1 (deformity) 驼背; 2 (person) 驼子; **~backed** *adj* 驼背的

hunched /hʌntʃt/ *adj* 驼背的 ‹*figure, person*›; 弓着的 ‹*back*›; 耸起的 ‹*shoulders*›; **he was ~ up in the corner** 他蜷缩在角落里

hundred /ˈhʌndrəd/ ▸**p. 32, p. 521**
A *n* 1 [u] (number) 一百; **a ~ to one** 可能性极大; **sold in ~s** *or* **by the ~** 大批出售的; **to turn up in one's ~s** 大批出现; **in nineteen ~** 在 1900 年; **the sixteen ~s** 17 世纪 2 [c] fig colloq (very many) 许多; **~s of times/girlfriends** 很多很多次/女朋友 3 [u] colloq (speed in miles per hour) **a ~** 每小时一百英里; (speed in km per hour) 每小时一百公里; **to do a ~** 每小时开 100 公里 4 [c] (degrees) **a ~** 一百华氏度
B *adj* 1 *attrib* (in number) 一百的; **about a ~ people/metres** 大约 100 人/米; **to live to be a ~ (years old)** 活到 100 岁; **to be a ~ per cent correct** 百分之百正确 2 *pred* (in age) 百岁的; **to be over/under a ~**

h

年纪为 100 多岁/不到 100 岁 **3** *postpos* (in series) 第一百的; **page one ~** 第一百页 **4** (in combinations) 一百…的; **a ~-litre container** 100 升的容器
C *pron* **1** (denoting number) 一百 **2** (denoting age) 百岁

hundred-and-first *adj* 第一百零一的
hundred-and-one ▸ **p. 521**
A *adj* **1** lit 一百零一的 **2** fig hum (many) 许多; **she had a ~ things to do** 她有一大堆事情要做
B *pron* 一百零一

hundredfold /'hʌndrədfəʊld/ ▸ **p. 288**
A *adj* 百倍的 ‹*growth, increase*›
B *adv* 百倍地 ‹*grow, bigger, multiply*›

hundreds and thousands *npl* Brit [装饰糕点等用的] 着色珠子糖

hundredth /'hʌndrətθ/ ▸ **p. 521**
A *n* **1** (item, person) 第一百 **2** (fraction) 百分之一; **three ~s (of sth.)** 百分之三（某物）
B *adj* 第一百; **for the ~ time** lit 第一百次; fig colloq 无数次了; **~ birthday/anniversary** 百岁诞辰/一百周年纪念

hundredweight /'hʌndrədweɪt/ ▸ **p. 909** *n* (*pl* **~** *or* **~s**) 英担 [相当于1吨的20分之一]

hundred-year-old ▸ **p. 15** *adj* 百岁的

Hundred Years War *pr n* 百年战争 [1337-1453年英法两国间的战争]

hung /hʌŋ/
A *pt, pp* ▸ **hang A, B**
B *adj* **1** (after election) 各党势均力敌的 ‹*parliament, council*› **2** Jur 不能取得一致意见的 ‹*jury*›

Hungarian /hʌŋ'geərɪən/ ▸ **p. 503, p. 426**
A *adj* (of Hungary) 匈牙利的; (of the people) 匈牙利人的; (of the language) 匈牙利语的
B *n* **1** [c] (person) 匈牙利人 **2** [u] (language) 匈牙利语

Hungary /'hʌŋgəri/ *pr n* 匈牙利

hunger /'hʌŋgə(r)/
A *n* [u] **1** (lack of food) 饥饿 **2** fig (craving, desire) 渴望; **sb.'s ~ for sth./sb.** 某人对某事物/某人的渴求
B *vi* 渴望; **to ~ for** *or* **after sb./sth.** 渴望某人/某事物

hunger: ~ march *n* Brit [尤指英国20世纪20至30年代失业者举行的] 反饥饿示威游行; **~ strike** *n* [尤指囚犯的] 绝食抗议; **to go/be on ~ strike** 进行绝食抗议; **~ striker** *n* 绝食抗议者

hung-over *adj* colloq 宿醉; **to be** *or* **feel ~** 有宿醉

hungrily /'hʌŋgrɪlɪ/ *adv* **1** (ravenously) 饥肠辘辘地 ‹*eat, devour, stare*› **2** (eagerly) 如饥似渴地 ‹*seek, kiss, seize*›

hungry /'hʌŋgrɪ/ *adj* **1** (lacking food) 饥饿的; **to be** *or* **feel ~** 感到饥饿; **to make sb. ~** 勾起某人的食欲; **to go ~** (from necessity) 挨饿; (by choice) 绝食挨饿 **2** fig (craving, desiring) 渴望的; **to be** *or* **feel ~ for sth./sb.** 渴望某事物/某人 **3** *attrib* (causing hunger) 使人饥饿的; **~ work** 让人容易饥饿的工作

hung-up *adj pred* colloq **1** (emotionally confused) 心神不宁的 **2** (obsessed) 着迷的; **to be ~ about** *or* **on sb./sth.** 念念不忘某人/某事物

hunk /hʌŋk/ *n* **1** (large piece) 大块 **2** colloq (man) 猛男

hunker /'hʌŋkə(r)/ *vi* **~ (down)** 蹲坐

hunkers /'hʌŋkəz/ *npl* colloq 腚; **to sit/be on one's ~** 蹲坐/蹲着

hunky /'hʌŋki/ *adj* colloq 结实性感的 ‹*man*›

hunky-dory /,hʌŋki'dɔːri/ *adj* colloq 平安无事的; **is everything ~?** 一切都好吗?

hunt /hʌnt/
A *n* **1** (search) 寻找; **to be on the ~ for sth.** 在寻找某物; **to launch a ~ for sb.** 开始追捕某人; **the ~ is on for a candidate** 正在物色人选 **2** (for animals) 打猎; **a lion ~** 猎狮 **3** Brit (for foxes) 猎狐; (hunting group) 猎狐队
B *vt* **1** (try to catch) «*police*» 追捕 ‹*criminal*›; «*criminal*» 追杀 ‹*victim, witness*› **2** Zool «*predator*» 猎食 ‹*prey*› **3** «*hunter, hounds*» 追猎 ‹*game, fox*›; **to ~ and kill whales** 捕杀鲸鱼 **4** Brit «*rider, hound*» 猎狐; **to ~ an area** 在某区域猎狐 **5** (drive out) 驱逐; **to ~ sb. out of** *or* **off sth.** 把某人赶出某地
C *vi* **1** (look) 寻找; **to ~ for a new job** 找新工作; **to ~ high and low (for sth.)** 到处寻找（某物） **2** (try to catch) 追捕; **to ~ for sb.** 追捕 ‹*criminal*›; 追杀 ‹*victim*› **3** Zool «*predator*» 猎食 **4** (for animals) 打猎; **to ~ for foxes/tigers** 猎狐/猎虎

Phrasal verbs

- **hunt down** *vt* [**~ down sb./sth., ~ sb./sth. down**]
1 (try to capture) 追捕 ‹*criminal, terrorist*›; 追杀 ‹*victim*›; **to be finally ~ed down** 终于被捉拿归案 **2** (try to find) 寻找 ‹*object*›; **I ~ed down my tax records** 我查到了我的纳税记录 **3** Hunt 追猎 ‹*game*›; **they ~ed the tiger down to its lair** 他们把老虎追进了虎穴
- **hunt out** *vt* [**~ out sth., ~ sth. out**] 找到 ‹*clothes, letter*›; **she ~ed out some old photographs** 她找出一些旧照片
- **hunt up** *vt* [**~ up sb./sth., ~ sb./sth. up**] 寻找 ‹*person, lost object*›

hunted /'hʌntɪd/ *adj* **1** (pursued) 被追捕的; (sought) 被搜寻的 **2** (harassed) 疲惫焦虑的

hunter /'hʌntə(r)/ *n* **1** (person) 猎人; (animal) 猎兽 **2** (collector) 搜集人; **a fossil/souvenir ~** 搜集化石/纪念品的人 **3** **Hunter** (constellation) **the H~** 猎户星座

hunter: ~-gatherer *n* 采猎者 [主要靠打猎、捕鱼和采集野生植物为生的游牧部族成员]; **~-killer** *n* 反潜潜艇; **~'s moon** *n* 猎月 [获月后的第一个满月]

hunting /'hʌntɪŋ/ *n* [u] 打猎; **to go ~** 去打猎; **to live by ~** 以狩猎为生

hunting: ~ ground *n* 猎场; fig 可以找到所寻觅东西的地方; **a happy ~ ground** 大显身手的地方; **~ horn** *n* 猎号; **~ knife** *n* 猎刀; **~ lodge** *n* 猎人留宿屋; **~ season** *n* 狩猎期

hunt saboteur *n* 阻挠捕猎者

huntsman /'hʌntsmən/ *n* 狩猎者

hurdle /'hɜːdl/
A *n* **1** Sport 栏架; **to clear a ~** 跨过栏架 **2** **hurdles** *pl* (race) 跨栏赛; **the 100m ~s** 100 米跨栏赛 **3** fig (obstacle) 障碍; **to clear** *or* **get over** *or* **sail over a ~** 克服障碍 **4** Agric 临时围栏
B *vi* Sport 参加跨栏比赛
C *vt* 跨过 ‹*fence, obstacle*›

hurdler /'hɜːdlə(r)/ *n* 跨栏运动员

hurdling /'hɜːdlɪŋ/ ▸ **p. 307** *n* [u] 跨栏赛跑

hurdy-gurdy /,hɜːdi'gɜːdi/ ▸ **p. 395** *n* **1** (musical instrument) 手摇弦琴 **2** colloq (barrel organ) 手摇风琴

hurl /hɜːl/
A *vt* **1** (throw) 猛扔 ‹*book, stone, ball*›; 用力推 ‹*person*›; **to ~ sth. at** *or* **against/through ...** 向…用力扔某物/通过…将某物抛出; **she was ~ed through the windscreen** 她被从挡风玻璃处抛出来 **2** (direct) 大声说出; **to ~ insults/accusations at sb.** 厉声辱骂/谴责某人
B *v refl* **to ~ oneself** (throw oneself, jump) 扑; **to ~ oneself against** *or* **at** *or* **into sb./sth.** 扑向某人/某物; **he ~ed himself into his work** fig 他全身心投入工作

hurling /'hɜːlɪŋ/ *n* [u] 爱尔兰曲棍球

hurly-burly /,hɜːli'bɜːli/ *n* [u] 喧闹

hurrah /hə'rɑː/, **hurray** /hə'reɪ/
A *excls* 好哇; **~ for Paul!** 为保罗喝彩!
B *ns* 喝彩声

hurricane /'hʌrɪkən, Amer -keɪn/ *n* (cyclone) 飓风; **~ force wind** 飓风级大风

hurricane lamp *n* 防风灯

hurried /'hʌrɪd/ *adj* (hasty, rushed) 匆忙的 ‹*action, departure, glance*›; 匆忙完成的 ‹*work*›; 仓促的 ‹*decision*›

hurriedly /'hʌrɪdli/ *adv* 匆忙地

hurry /'hʌri/
A *n* [u and c] **1** (haste) 急忙; **what's (all) the ~?** 急什么? ; **in my ~, I forgot** 匆忙间我忘记了; **(to be) in a ~** 匆忙; **to do sth. in a ~** 匆忙做某事; **to leave in a ~** 赶忙离开; **to be in a ~ to do sth.** 急于做某事; **to be in a ~ to grow up** 恨不得一下子长大; **to be in no ~ (to do sth.), not to be in any ~ (to do sth.)** (have time) 有时间（做某事）; (be unwilling) 不想（做某事）; **I'm not in any ~** 我没什么急事; **they won't do that again in a ~** colloq 他们再也不愿做那事; **I won't forget that in a ~!** colloq 我不会忘记那件事的! **2** (need for haste) 紧急; **there's no ~** 不用着急
B *vi* **1** (act quickly) 急忙; **to ~ over sth.** 匆忙做 ‹*work, homework*›; 匆忙吃 ‹*meal*›; **don't ~!** 别急! ; **to make sb. ~** 催某人加快速度; **~ or you'll miss the bus** 抓紧时间，否则就赶不上汽车了; **~ and open your present** colloq 快点打开礼物 **2** (rush) **to ~ out/in/away** 匆匆出去/进来/离开; **to ~ home** 急匆匆赶回家
C *vt* **1** (do hastily) 仓促完成 ‹*task*›; 匆忙吃 ‹*meal*›; **careful planning cannot be hurried** 精细的规划急不得 **2** (press) 催促; **to ~ sb. into sth./doing sth.** 催促某人某事/做某事; **don't ~ me** 不要催我; **to be hurried into (making) an unwise choice** 在催逼之下作出不明智的选择 **3** (hasten) 使加快; **to ~ sb. in** 让某人赶快进来; **to ~ sb. to their seat** 迅速带某人到他的座位; **to ~ sb. out of/away from sth.** 迅速带某人离开某处

Phrasal verbs

- **hurry along**
A *vi* 快走; **~ along there, please!** 请快点!
B *vt* [**~ along sth., ~ sth. along**] 加快 ‹*process*›; **to ~ dinner along a bit** 快点准备好晚餐
- **hurry away** *vi* 迅速离开; **don't ~ away!** 别忙着走!
- **hurry back** *vi* **1** (to home) 赶快回家; **~ back!** 赶快回来! **2** (to other place) 迅速返回; **to ~ back to school/the office** 赶紧回学校/办公室
- **hurry off** *vi* 匆忙离开; **to ~ off without saying goodbye** 没说再见就匆忙离开
- **hurry up**
A *vi* 赶快做; **~ up! we'll be late** 快点! 我们要迟到了; **I wish the bus would ~ up and come** 我希望公交车能快一点来; **~ up with the scissors!** 快点把剪刀拿来!
B *vt* [**~ sb./sth. up**] 催促 ‹*person*›; 使…加快 ‹*process*›; **to ~ sb. up a bit** 催某人快点; **to ~ the order up** 让订的东西快点送来

hurt /hɜːt/
A *vt* (*pt, pp* **hurt**) **1** (injure) 使受伤; **to ~ one's shoulder in a fall** 摔伤肩膀; **to be seriously/slightly ~** 受重伤/轻伤; **somebody's going to get ~** 有人会受伤的 **2** (cause pain to) 使…疼痛 ‹*person*›; **these shoes ~ my feet** 这双鞋子我穿着脚疼; **my shoulder has been ~ing me for days** 我的肩膀已经疼了好几天了; **it ~s him to bend his knee** 他的膝盖一弯就疼 **3** (wound emotionally) 伤害; **to ~ sb.'s feelings/pride** 伤某人的心/伤害某人的自尊心; **to get ~** 感情受到伤害; **her remarks ~ me deeply** 她的话让我很伤心 **4** (affect adversely) 损害; **to ~ sb.'s reputation** 损害某人的名誉; **a dry summer will ~ the farmers** 干旱的夏季将给农民造成损失 **5** *with negative* iron (harm) **it wouldn't ~ her to apologize** 道个歉对她来说也无伤大雅; **getting up early never ~s anybody** 早起绝不会有坏处
B *vi* (*pt, pp* **hurt**) **1** (be painful, cause pain) 疼痛; **my foot ~s** 我脚疼; **my shoes ~** 我的鞋子

h

穿着脚疼; **it ~s when I turn my head** 我的头一转动就疼 **2** (be upsetting) «*truth, insult*» 使人伤心; **her indifference ~s** 她的冷漠让人难过; **what really ~ was that she had lied** 真正令人伤心的是她说了谎 **3** colloq (feel upset) 感到伤心; **he was ~ing (badly)** 他感到（非常）伤心 **4** (have adverse effect) «*sanctions, taxes*» 有不良影响 **5** **to be ~ing for sth.** Amer colloq (be in need of) 急需某物; **to be ~ing (for money)** 缺钱花 **6** *with negative* (do harm) 有妨害; **it won't ~ to check** 检查一下没有坏处的; **one little chocolate won't ~** 吃一点巧克力不碍事的; **it won't ~ to postpone the meeting** 会议延期没什么大不了的
C *v refl* (*pt, pp* **hurt**) **to ~ oneself** 受伤; **I fell, but I didn't ~ myself** 我摔倒了，但没有受伤
D *adj* 受伤的 ‹*look, feelings*›; **to sound** *or* **look ~** 听起来/看上去很伤心; **she was ~ not to have been invited** 她没有受到邀请，感到很难过
E *n* [u and c] 伤害; **there was ~ and anger in her voice** 她的语气显得既难过又生气

hurtful /ˈhɜːtfl/ *adj* 伤感情的

hurtfully /ˈhɜːtfəli/ *adv* 伤感情地

hurtfulness /ˈhɜːtfəlnɪs/ *n* [u] 伤害

hurtle /ˈhɜːtl/
A *vi* 猛冲; **to ~ down sth.** 从某物上冲下来; **to ~ along a road/through the air** 在大道上飞驰/从空中飞过
B *vt* 猛投

husband /ˈhʌzbənd/
A ▸**p. 419** *n* 丈夫; **to live as ~ and wife** 像夫妻一样共同生活; **to work as a ~ and wife team** 夫妻搭档工作; **to take a ~** dated 嫁人
B *vt* 节俭使用 ‹*resources, money, energy*›

husbandry /ˈhʌzbəndri/ *n* [u] **1** (of crops, animals) 农牧业; **animal/crop ~** 畜牧业/种植业 **2** (of resources) 节俭使用

hush /hʌʃ/
A *vt* **1** (silence) 使…安静下来 ‹*noise, din*›; 使…停止 ‹*students, crowd*› **2** (pacify) 使平静 ‹*baby*›
B *vi* 安静 [尤用于发出命令]
C *n* [u] 寂静; **a ~ fell over the crowd** 人群变得鸦雀无声

Phrasal verb
• **hush up** *vt* **1** [**~ sth. up, ~ up sth.**] (hide information about) 掩盖 ‹*scandal, case*› **2** [**~ sb. up, ~ up sb.**] (make be quiet) 使…住嘴

hushed /hʌʃt/ *adj* 寂静的 ‹*street, theatre, courtroom*›; 轻的 ‹*voice, tone, whisper*›

hush: **~-~** *adj* colloq (secret) 秘密的 ‹*arrangements, document*›; **to keep sth. ~-~** 对某事保密; **~ money** *n* [u] colloq 封口费; **~ puppy** *n* Amer 炸玉米饼

husk /hʌsk/
A *n* **1** (of seed) 外壳; (of fruit) 外皮 **2** (coating) 外衣
B *vt* 除去…的外壳 ‹*grain, nuts*›

huskily /ˈhʌskɪli/ *adv* 沙哑地 ‹*speak, whisper*›

huskiness /ˈhʌskɪnɪs/ *n* [u] 沙哑

husky[1] /ˈhʌski/ *adj* **1** (hoarse) 沙哑的 ‹*voice, cough*› **2** (burly) 粗壮有魅力的

husky[2] *n* (dog) 爱斯基摩犬

hussy /ˈhʌsi/ *n* colloq 荡妇

hustings /ˈhʌstɪŋz/ *n* (*pl* **hustings**) **1** (meeting) [竞选前候选人的] 演讲集会 **2** fig (campaigning) **the ~** 竞选活动

hustle /ˈhʌsl/
A *vt* **1** (force) 推搡; **to ~ sb. into/through/out of sth.** 将某人推进/推过/推出某处 **2** (urge) 强迫; (hurry) 催促; **to ~ sb. into sth./doing sth.** 迫使某人卷入某事/做某事 **3** Amer colloq (obtain) 靠欺诈获得 ‹*goods*›
B *n* **1** [u] (activity) 忙碌喧嚣; **~ and bustle** 拥挤喧嚣 **2** [c] Amer colloq (illegal activity) 欺诈行为
C *vi* (push, shove) 推; **to ~ over** *or* **through/in** 挤过/挤进

hustler /ˈhʌslə(r)/ *n* Amer colloq **1** (swindler) 骗子 **2** (prostitute) 妓女

hut /hʌt/ *n* **1** (native type) 简陋小屋 **2** (in shanty town) 棚屋 **3** (on building site) 工棚 **4** (in garden, on beach) 木屋

hutch /hʌtʃ/ *n* **1** (for animals) 笼; **rabbit ~** 兔笼 **2** Amer (storage chest) 贮存箱 **3** Amer (cupboard, dresser) 柜

hutong /ˈhuːtɒŋ/ *n* [北京的] 胡同

hyacinth /ˈhaɪəsɪnθ/ *n* **1** (plant) 风信子 **2** (gemstone) 红锆石

hyaena /haɪˈiːnə/ *n* = **hyena**

hybrid /ˈhaɪbrɪd/
A *n* **1** (of plant) 杂交植物; (of animal) 杂种动物 **2** (of different elements) 混合物
B *adj* **1** (crossbred) 杂种的; **a ~ race** 混血种族 **2** (mixed) 混合的 ‹*system, method*›

hybrid: **~ bike** *n* 公路山地两用自行车; **~ bill** *n* Brit 混合法案; **~ car** *n* 混合动力车; **~ circuit** *n* 混合电路

hybridization /ˌhaɪbrɪdaɪˈzeɪʃn, Amer -dɪˈz-/ *n* [u] **1** (cross-breeding) 杂交 **2** fig (combination) 混合

hybridize /ˈhaɪbrɪdaɪz/
A *vt* 使…杂交 ‹*plant, animal*›
B *vi* «*plant, animal*» 杂交

hybrid system *n* [半手动半计算机化的] 混合系统

hydrangea /haɪˈdreɪndʒə/ *n* 绣球属植物

hydrant /ˈhaɪdrənt/ *n* 消防栓

hydrate /ˈhaɪdreɪt/
A *n* 水合物
B *vt* 使成水合物

hydraulic /haɪˈdrɔːlɪk/ *adj* 水力的; **~ power/steering/brakes/suspension** 水力/液压转向/水力闸/液压悬架

hydraulic: **~ engineer** ▸**p. 409** *n* 水力工程师; **~ ram** *n* 水锤泵

hydraulics /haɪˈdrɔːlɪks/ *npl* **1** + *v sing* (science) 水力学 **2** + *v pl* (systems) 水力系统

hydro /ˈhaɪdrəʊ/ *n* Can 电力

hydrobiology /ˌhaɪdrəʊbaɪˈɒlədʒi/ *n* [u] 水生生物学

hydrocarbon /ˈhaɪdrəkɑːbən/ *n* 碳氢化合物; **~ compounds** 碳氢化合物

hydrochloric /ˌhaɪdrəˈklɔrɪk/ *adj* 氯化氢的; **~ acid** 盐酸

hydrodynamics /ˌhaɪdrəʊdaɪˈnæmɪks/ *npl* + *v sing* 流体动力学

hydroelectric /ˌhaɪdrəʊɪˈlektrɪk/ *adj* 水力发电的; **a ~ plant/power** 水力发电站/水力发出的电

hydroelectricity *n* [u] 水力电

hydrofoil /ˈhaɪdrəfɔɪl/ *n* **1** (boat) 水翼船 **2** (foil) 水翼

hydrogen /ˈhaɪdrədʒən/ *n* [u] 氢

hydrogen: **~ bomb** *n* 氢弹; **~ peroxide** *n* [u] 过氧化氢

hydrographic /haɪˈdrɒgrəfɪk/ *adj* 水文的

hydrography /haɪˈdrɒgrəfi/ *n* [u] 水文地理学

hydrological /ˌhaɪdrəˈlɒdʒɪkl/ *adj* 水文学的 ‹*data, study*›; 水文的 ‹*change, survey*›

hydrology /haɪˈdrɒlədʒi/ *n* [u] 水文学

hydrolysis /haɪˈdrɒləsɪs/ *n* [u] 水解

hydrometer /haɪˈdrɒmɪtə(r)/ *n* 液体比重计

hydropathic /ˌhaɪdrəˈpæθɪk/ *adj* 水疗的

hydrophobia /ˌhaɪdrəˈfəʊbɪə/ *n* [u] **1** (fear of water) 恐水 **2** (rabies) 狂犬病

hydrophobic /ˌhaɪdrəˈfəʊbɪk/ *adj* **1** (afraid of water) 恐水的 **2** (repelling water) 疏水的 **3** (rabid) 患狂犬病的

hydroplane /ˈhaɪdrəpleɪn/ *n* **1** (boat) 水上滑行艇 **2** (on submarine) 水平舵 [用于使潜艇上浮或下潜]

hydroplaning /ˈhaɪdrəpleɪnɪŋ/ *n* [u] 湿路打滑

hydroponics /ˌhaɪdrəˈpɒnɪks/ *npl* + *v sing* 溶液栽培

hydrotherapy /ˌhaɪdrəˈθerəpi/ *n* [u] 水疗法; **a ~ pool** 水疗池

hydroxide /haɪˈdrɒksaɪd/ *n* 氢氧化物

hyena /haɪˈiːnə/ *n* **1** Zool 鬣狗 **2** fig (person) 阴险贪婪的人

hygiene /ˈhaɪdʒiːn/ *n* [u] 卫生; **in the interests of ~** 为卫生起见; **public/social/personal/sexual ~** 公共/社会/个人/性卫生

hygienic /haɪˈdʒiːnɪk/ *adj* 卫生的

hygienist /ˈhaɪdʒiːnɪst/ ▸**p. 409** *n* 卫生保健专家; **an industrial ~** 工业卫生师; **a (dental) ~** 牙科保健专家

hymen /ˈhaɪmen/ *n* 处女膜; **to rupture the ~** 使处女膜破裂

hymn /hɪm/ *n* (song) 圣歌; (poem) 赞美诗

hymn: **~ book** *n* 赞美诗集; **~ sheet** *n* **1** Mus 颂歌歌单; **2** fig (manifesto) 宣言; **to sing from the same ~ sheet** Brit colloq 口径一致

hype /haɪp/ colloq
A *n* [u] **1** (publicity, promotion) 不实宣传; **media ~** 夸张的媒体广告 **2** (deception) 宣传骗局
B *vt* (publicize, promote) 夸张地宣传

Phrasal verb
• **hype up** *vt* [**~ sb./sth. up, ~ up sb./sth.**] colloq (publicize, promote) 夸张地宣传 ‹*person, exports*›; (exaggerate) 夸大 ‹*reputation, membership*›

hyped up /ˌhaɪptˈʌp/ *adj* colloq **1** (over-publicized, over-promoted) 过分宣扬的 ‹*reputation, product, performance*› **2** (over-excited) 十分兴奋的 ‹*person*›

hyper /ˈhaɪpə(r)/ *adj* colloq 亢奋的

hyperacidity *n* [u] 胃酸过多

hyperactive *adj* **1** Psych 多动的 ‹*child*› **2** Med 异常活跃的 ‹*pituitary gland*›; 亢进的 ‹*thyroid*›

hyperactivity *n* [u] 多动症

hyperbola /haɪˈpɜːbələ/ *n* (*pl* **hyperbolae** /haɪˈpɜːbəli/ *or* **~s**) 双曲线

hyperbole /haɪˈpɜːbəli/ *n* [u] 夸张

hyperbolic /ˌhaɪpəˈbɒlɪk/ *adj* **1** Math 双曲线的 ‹*function, tangent*› **2** (exaggerated) 夸张的 ‹*statement, praise*›

hypercorrection /ˌhaɪpəkəˈrekʃn/ *n* [u] 矫枉过正

hypercritical /ˌhaɪpəˈkrɪtɪkl/ *adj* 吹毛求疵的 ‹*person, remark, attitude*›

hyperdrive /ˈhaɪpərdraɪv/ *n* 超光速推进系统

hyperinflation /ˌhaɪpərɪnˈfleɪʃn/ *n* [u] 恶性通货膨胀

hyperlink /ˈhaɪpəlɪŋk/ *n* 超链接

hypermarket /ˈhaɪpəmɑːkɪt/ *n* Brit 超大型自助商场

hypermedia /ˈhaɪpəmiːdɪə/ *n* [u] 超媒体

hypernym /ˈhaɪpənɪm/ *n* 上义词

hypersensitive /ˌhaɪpəˈsensətɪv/ *adj* 过敏的; **to be ~ to pollen/criticism** 对花粉过敏/受不了批评

hypersonic /ˌhaɪpəˈsɒnɪk/ *adj* 高超音速的 ‹*speed, flight, aircraft*›

hyperspace /ˈhaɪpəspeɪs/ *n* [u] **1** Phys 超空间 **2** (in science fiction) 超光速状态

hypertension /ˌhaɪpəˈtenʃn/ *n* [u] 高血压

hypertext /ˈhaɪpətekst/ *n* [u] Comput **1** (system) 超文本 **2** (text) 超文本文档

hypertext: ~ markup language *n* [u] 超文本标记语言; **~ transfer protocol** *n* 超文本传输协议

hyperthermia /ˌhaɪpəˈθɜːmɪə/ *n* [u] 高热

hypertrophy /haɪˈpɜːtrəfi/ *n* [u] [器官或组织的] 肥大

hyperventilate /ˌhaɪpəˈventɪleɪt/ *vi* 过度换气

hyperventilation /ˌhaɪpəventɪˈleɪʃn/ *n* [u] 换气过度

hyphen /ˈhaɪfn/
A *n* 连字符
B *vt* = **hyphenate**

hyphenate /ˈhaɪfəneɪt/ *vt* 用连字符连接

hyphenated /ˈhaɪfəneɪtɪd/ *adj* 带连字符的 ‹*word, surname*›

hyphenated American *n* Amer colloq 归化入美国籍的人

hyphenation /ˌhaɪfəˈneɪʃn/ *n* [u] 连字符使用

hypnosis /hɪpˈnəʊsɪs/ *n* [u] 催眠状态; **in a state of** *or* **under ~** 处于催眠状态

hypnotherapy /ˌhɪpnəˈθerəpi/ *n* [u] 催眠疗法

hypnotic /hɪpˈnɒtɪk/ *adj* **1** (inducing hypnosis) 催眠的 ‹*state, trance, effect, drug*› **2** (compelling, fascinating) 迷人的 ‹*scent, personality, eyes*›

hypnotism /ˈhɪpnətɪzəm/ *n* [u] 催眠术

hypnotist /ˈhɪpnətɪst/ *n* 催眠术士

hypnotize /ˈhɪpnətaɪz/ *vt* **1** Med 对…施催眠术; **to ~ sb. into doing sth.** 施催眠术让某人做某事 **2** (beguile, fascinate) 使着迷

hypo-allergenic /ˌhaɪpəʊæləˈdʒenɪk/ *adj* 不致过敏的 ‹*textile, metal, pillow*›

hypochondria /ˌhaɪpəˈkɒndrɪə/ *n* [u] 疑病症

hypochondriac /ˌhaɪpəˈkɒndrɪæk/ *n* 疑病症患者

hypocrisy /hɪˈpɒkrəsi/ *n* [u] 伪善

hypocrite /ˈhɪpəkrɪt/ *n* 伪君子

hypocritical /ˌhɪpəˈkrɪtɪkl/ *adj* 伪善的; **to be ~ (of sb.) to say/do sth.** （某人）虚伪地说/做某事

hypocritically /ˌhɪpəˈkrɪtɪkli/ *adv* 伪善地

hypodermic /ˌhaɪpəˈdɜːmɪk/
A *adj attrib* 皮下的 ‹*infection, injection*›; 皮下注射用的 ‹*needle, syringe, drug*›
B *n* 皮下注射器

hyponym /ˈhaɪpənɪm/ *n* 下义词

hypotension /ˌhaɪpəʊˈtenʃən/ *n* [u] 低血压

hypotenuse /haɪˈpɒtənjuːz, Amer -nuːs/ *n* [直角三角形的] 弦

hypothalamus /ˌhaɪpəˈθæləməs/ *n* (*pl* **hypothalami** /ˌhaɪpəˈθæləmaɪ/) 下丘脑

hypothermia /ˌhaɪpəʊˈθɜːmɪə/ *n* [u] 体温过低

hypothesis /haɪˈpɒθəsɪs/ *n* (*pl* **hypotheses** /haɪˈpɒθəsiːz/) **1** (supposition) 假设 **2** Philos 假说

hypothesize /haɪˈpɒθəsaɪz/
A *vt* 假设 ‹*idea, theory*›
B *vi* 假设; **to ~ that ...** 假定…

hypothetical /ˌhaɪpəˈθetɪkl/ *adj* **1** (of a hypothesis) 假设的 ‹*question, argument, statement*›; **this is purely ~** 这纯粹是假设的; **a ~ planet** 假想的星球 **2** Philos 假言的 ‹*statement*›; **a ~ syllogism** 假言三段论

hypothetically /ˌhaɪpəˈθetɪkli/ *adv* 假设地 ‹*speak, possible*›

hysterectomy /ˌhɪstəˈrektəmi/ *n* 子宫切除

hysteria /hɪˈstɪərɪə/ *n* [u] **1** (great emotion) 歇斯底里; **mass ~** 集体歇斯底里症 **2** Psych 癔病

hysterical /hɪˈsterɪkl/ *adj* **1** (emotional) 歇斯底里的 ‹*patient, weeping, shouting*›; **~ laughter** 狂笑; **to get** *or* **become ~ about sth.** 因某事物而发狂 **2** colloq (funny) 极可笑的 **3** Psych 癔病的

hysterically /hɪˈsterɪklɪ/ *adv* **1** (emotionally) 歇斯底里地 ‹*weep, laugh, scream*› **2** colloq **~ funny** 极可笑

hysterics /hɪˈsterɪks/ *npl* **1** (laughter) 狂笑; **to be in** *or* **to have ~** 捧腹大笑 **2** Psych 歇斯底里发作; **to have** *or* **go into ~** 歇斯底里发作; **to be on the verge of ~** 几乎要发疯了

Hz *abbr* = **hertz**

h

Ii

I[1], **i** /aɪ/ *n* (*pl* **Is** *or* **I's**) [英语字母表的第9个字母]
I[2] *pron* 我
IA *abbr* Amer = **Iowa**
IAEA *abbr* = **International Atomic Energy Agency**
iambic /aɪˈæmbɪk/ *adj* 抑扬格的; ~ **pentameters** 抑扬格五音步
IBAN /ˈiːbæn/ *abbr* = **International Bank Account Number** 国际银行账户号码
Iberian /aɪˈbɪərɪən/
A *adj* (of the Iberian peninsula) 伊比利亚半岛的; (of the people) 伊比利亚人的; (of the languages) 伊比利亚半岛语的
B *n* **1** [c] (person) 伊比利亚人 **2** [u] (languages) 伊比利亚半岛语
Iberian peninsula *pr n* **the** ~ 伊比利亚半岛
ibex /ˈaɪbeks/ *n* 北山羊
ibid /ˈɪbɪd/ *abbr* = **ibidem** 同上
ibis /ˈaɪbɪs/ *n* (*pl* ~**es**) 鹮
Ibiza /ɪˈbiːθə/ *pr n* 伊维萨岛
IBRD *abbr* = **International Bank for Reconstruction and Development**
ibuprofen /ˌaɪbjuːˈprəʊfn/ *n* [u] 布洛芬 [消炎止痛药]
ICBM *abbr* = **intercontinental ballistic missile**
ice /aɪs/
A *n* **1** [u] (gen) 冰; (on roads) 冰层; (in drinks) 冰块; **a show on** ~ 冰上表演; **a whisky with** ~ 加冰块的威士忌; **as cold as** ~ 冷得像冰一样; **to put sth. on** ~ lit 冰镇某物; fig 暂时搁置某事; **'danger! thin** ~**'** "薄冰, 危险!"; **to be skating on thin** ~ fig 如履薄冰; **to break the** ~ fig 消除拘谨; **to cut no** ~ **(with sb.)** fig (对某人) 不起作用 **2** [c] Brit (ice cream) 冰激凌; (ice lolly) 冰棒 **3** [u] colloq (diamonds) 钻石; (diamond jewellery) 钻石首饰
B *vt* (cover with icing) 在…上挂糖霜
Phrasal verbs
- **ice over** *vi* «*window, road, pond*» 结冰
- **ice up** *vi* «*water pipe, windscreen wiper, lock*» 结冰

ice age
A *n* 冰川期
B **ice-age** *modif* 冰川期的
ice: ~ **axe** *n* 冰镐; ~ **beer** *n* [u and c] 冰啤
iceberg /ˈaɪsbɜːg/ *n* 冰山
iceberg lettuce *n* 卷心莴苣
ice blue
A *n* [u] 淡蓝色
B **ice-blue** *adj* 淡蓝色的
ice: ~**-bound** *adj* (blocked by ice) 冰封的 ‹*port, road*›; (surrounded with ice) 被冰困住的 ‹*ship*›; ~**box** *n* **1** Brit (freezer compartment) 冷冻室; **2** Amer (fridge) 冰箱; **3** (cool box) 冰盒; ~**breaker** *n* **1** Naut 破冰船; **2** fig (word) 活跃气氛的话; (action) 活跃气氛的行为; ~ **bucket** *n* 冰桶; ~**cap** *n* 冰冠; ~**-cold** *adj* 冰冷的
ice cream *n* **1** [u] (dessert) 冰激凌 **2** [c] (portion) 一份冰激凌
ice-cream: ~ **cone,** ~ **cornet** *ns* 蛋筒冰激凌; ~ **parlour** *n* 冰激凌店; ~ **seller** ▶**p. 409** *n* 卖冰激凌的人; ~ **soda** *n* Amer 冰激凌苏打水; ~ **sundae** *n* 冰激凌圣代; ~ **van** Brit, ~ **truck** Amer *ns* 冰激凌销售车
ice cube *n* 小冰块
iced /aɪst/ *adj* 冰镇的 ‹*tea, coffee*›
ice: ~ **dancer** *n* 冰上舞蹈演员; ~ **dancing** ▶**p. 307** *n* [u] 冰上舞蹈; ~ **field** *n* 冰原; ~ **floe** *n* 浮冰; ~ **hammer** *n* 冰锤; ~ **hockey** ▶**p. 307** *n* [u] 冰球
Iceland /ˈaɪslənd/ *pr n* 冰岛
Icelander /ˈaɪsləndə(r)/ ▶**p. 503** *n* 冰岛人
Icelandic /aɪsˈlændɪk/ ▶**p. 503, p. 426**
A *adj* (of Iceland) 冰岛的; (of the people) 冰岛人的; (of the language) 冰岛语的
B *n* [u] (language) 冰岛语
ice: ~ **lolly** *n* Brit 冰棒; ~ **machine** *n* 制冰机; ~**man** /-mæn/ *n* Amer (seller) 卖冰人; (shipper) 送冰人; ~ **pack** *n* 冰袋; ~ **pick** *n* **1** (for climbing) 冰镐; **2** Culin 碎冰锥; ~ **piton** *n* 冰锥; ~ **rink** *n* 溜冰场; ~ **shelf** *n* 冰架; ~ **show** *n* 冰上表演
ice skate
A *n* **1** (boot) 溜冰鞋 **2** (blade) 冰刀
B **ice-skate** *vi* 溜冰
ice: ~ **skater** *n* 溜冰运动员; ~**-skating** ▶**p. 307** *n* [u] 溜冰; ~ **storm** *n* Amer 冰暴; ~ **tray** *n* 冰格盘; ~ **water** *n* [u] Amer 冰水; ~ **yacht** *n* 冰帆
I Ching /ˌiːˈtʃɪŋ/ *n* 《易经》
ichthyologist /ˌɪkθɪˈɒlədʒɪst/ ▶**p. 409** *n* 鱼类学家
ichthyology /ˌɪkθɪˈɒlədʒi/ *n* [u] 鱼类学
icicle /ˈaɪsɪkl/ *n* 冰柱
icicle lights *npl* 冰柱形装饰灯
icily /ˈaɪsɪli/ *adv* 冷冰冰地 ‹*say, stare*›
icing /ˈaɪsɪŋ/ *n* [u] **1** Culin 糖衣; **the** ~ **on the cake** fig 装饰点缀之物 **2** (on aircraft, ship, vehicle) 结冰
icing sugar *n* [u] Brit 糖粉
icky /ˈɪki/ *adj* colloq **1** (dirty, unpleasant) 脏兮兮的 ‹*hand, clothes*› **2** (sticky) 黏糊糊的 ‹*fingers*› **3** (distastefully sentimental) 矫情得令人作呕的 ‹*story*›
icon /ˈaɪkɒn/ *n* **1** Art (painting) 画像; (carved sculpture) 雕像; (moulded sculpture) 塑像 **2** Relig 圣像 **3** Comput 图标 **4** fig (person) 偶像; (object) 标志; **a feminist** ~ 女权主义者的偶像
iconify /aɪˈkɒnɪfaɪ/ *vt* 使图标化
iconoclast /aɪˈkɒnəklæst/ *n* **1** (attacking traditions) 反传统者 **2** Hist 捣毁圣像者
iconoclastic /aɪˌkɒnəˈklæstɪk/ *adj* 反传统的
iconography /ˌaɪkəˈnɒgrəfi/ *n* **1** [u] Art (symbolic images) 肖像学 **2** [c and u] (set of recognized images) 标志
ICT *abbr* = **information and communications technology** 信息与通信技术
icy /ˈaɪsi/ *adj* **1** (very cold) 冰冷的; **in an** ~ **draught** 在寒风中 **2** (covered in ice) 结冰的 **3** fig 冷冰冰的 ‹*tone, manner*›
icy-cold *adj* 冰冷的
ID[1]
A *abbr* = **identification, identity** 身份; **to establish** *or* **prove one's** ~ 证明身份
B *vt* (*pres* **ID's**; *pres p* **ID'ing**; *pt, pp* **ID'd**) 核查身份
ID[2] *abbr* Amer = **Idaho**
id /ɪd/ *n* **the** ~ 本我
I'd /aɪd/ colloq **1** = **I had** ▶**have** **2** = **I should** ▶**should** **3** = **I would** ▶**would**
Idaho /ˈaɪdəhəʊ/ *pr n* 爱达荷州
IDD *abbr* Brit = **International Direct Dialling** 国际长途直拨
idea /aɪˈdɪə/ *n* **1** (plan) 主意; **she's full of good** ~**s** 她足智多谋; **that's an** ~**!** 那是个好主意! ; **it's just an** ~ 这只是个设想; **a sensible** ~ 明智的想法; **to hit on an** ~ 无意中想到一个主意 **2** (expectation) 期望; **to get** ~**s** 想入非非; **to give sb.** ~**s** 使某人想入非非; **don't give the boy** ~**s** 不要让孩子空抱希望; **to put** ~**s into sb.'s head** 让某人想入非非; **you can get** *or* **put that** ~ **out of your head!** 你想都别想! **3** (intention, purpose) 目的; **the** ~ **of the game is to get rid of all your cards** 这个游戏的目标是把牌全部出完; **what's the** ~ **of this handle?** 这个把手是做什么用的? ; **what's the big** ~**?** colloq 这都是为了什么? **4** (prospect) 预期; **I don't fancy the** ~ **of sharing the flat with another family** 我不想与另一户人家同住一套公寓; **the very** ~**!** 多么荒谬的想法! ; **what an** ~**!** 多荒唐的想法! **5** (opinion, notion) 看法; **very old-fashioned** ~**s about education** 非常陈旧的教育观; **she got the** ~ **that I didn't really want to go** 她认为我并不是真的想去; **whatever gave you that** ~**!** 你怎么会那样想! ; **don't run away with the** ~ **that this is an easy job** 别误以为这事很容易 **6** (concept) 概念; **to have a clear** ~ **of what sb. is trying to achieve** 清楚某人要达到什么目的; **to have no** ~ **of the difficulties of sth.** 想象不出某事的难处; **the book gives the reader a better** ~ **of life in prison** 这本书让读者更好地了解监狱里的生活; **his** ~ **of a good salary is at least £40,000 a year** 他心目中的高工资是至少年薪4万英镑 **7** (knowledge) 知晓; **she had no** ~ **that he was married** 她不知道他已经结婚了; **he hasn't got much** ~ **about running a business** 他不大懂得如何经营企业; **not to have the faintest** *or* **foggiest** *or* **slightest** *or* **least** *etc.* ~ 一点儿也不知道; **to get the** ~ 明白
ideal /aɪˈdiːəl/
A *adj* **1** (best possible) 理想的 ‹*weather, companion, marriage*› **2** (most suitable) 最适合的 ‹*location, circumstances, strategy*›; **to be** ~ **for sb./sth.** 最合适某人/某事物 **3** (perfect) 完美的 ‹*world, system*›
B *n* **1** (model) 典范; **the feminine/Christian** ~ 女性/基督教的典范 **2** (principle) 原则 **3** Philos 理念

i

Ideal Home Exhibition *n* Brit 理想家居用品展

idealism /aɪˈdɪəlɪzəm/ *n* [u] **1** (lack of realism) 空想 **2** (belief in ideals) 理想主义 **3** Philos 唯心主义

idealist /aɪˈdɪəlɪst/ *n* **1** (unrealistic person) 空想家 **2** (principled person) 理想主义者 **3** Philos 唯心主义者

idealistic /ˌaɪdɪəˈlɪstɪk/ *adj* **1** (visionary, unrealistic) 空想的 **2** (principled) 理想主义的

idealize /aɪˈdɪəlaɪz/ *vt* 把…理想化

ideally /aɪˈdɪəli/ *adv* **1** (preferably) 理想地; **~, we'd like a house/to stay** 我们最好有一幢房子/能留下来; **what would you like, ~?** 你最想要的是什么? **2** (perfectly) 最适合地; **to be ~ suited to doing sth.** 最适合做某事; **to be ~ located** *or* **situated** 处于最佳位置

ideas man *n* colloq 谋士

identical /aɪˈdentɪkl/ *adj* 相同的; **to be ~ to** *or* **with sth.** 与某事物相同; **they look ~** 他们长得一模一样

identically /aɪˈdentɪkli/ *adv* 相同地; **to be ~ alike** 一模一样

identical twin *n* 同卵双胞胎之一

identifiable /aɪˌdentɪˈfaɪəbl/ *adj* **1** (recognizable) 可辨别的; **he was easily ~ by his red beard** 他长着红胡子，很好认 **2** (visible) 显而易见的

identifiably /aɪˌdentɪˈfaɪəbli/ *adv* **1** (recognizably) 可辨认地 **2** (visibly) 显而易见地

identification /aɪˌdentɪfɪˈkeɪʃn/ *n* **1** [c and u] (of body, species, person) 辨认; (of problem) 鉴定; **to make an ~ of a criminal** 辨认一名罪犯的身份 **2** [u] (empathy) 认同; **~ with sb./sth.** 对某人/某事物的认同

identification: **~ disc** *n* 身份牌; **~ mark** *n* 识别标志; **~ papers** *npl* 身份证明; **~ parade** *n* Brit 列队认人; **~ tag** *n* 身份牌

identifier /aɪˈdentɪfaɪə(r)/ *n* **1** (unique code) 识别码 **2** Comput 标识符

identify /aɪˈdentɪfaɪ/

A *vt* **1** (establish identity of) 辨认 ‹*criminal, body*› **2** (pick out) 认出 ‹*person, place, object*› **3** (consider as equivalent) 认为…等同; **to ~ money with happiness** 认为金钱就是幸福 **4** (associate) 联系; **to ~ sth. with sb.** 把某事与某人联系起来

B *vi* **to ~ with sb.** 与某人产生共鸣

C *v refl* **1** (establish identity) **to ~ oneself (as ...)** 自称（是…） **2** (sympathize with) **to ~ oneself with sb.** 同情某人

identikit /aɪˈdentɪkɪt/

A *n* (*also* **Identikit®, identikit picture**) [嫌疑犯等的] 容貌拼图

B *adj* pej 千篇一律的 ‹*pop group*›

identity /aɪˈdentəti/ *n* **1** [c] (being specific person) 身份; **to change** *or* **alter one's ~** 改变身份; **to protect/reveal sb.'s ~** 保护/透露某人的身份; **proof of ~** 身份证明; **to establish the ~ of sb./sth.** 确定某人/某物的身份; **a case of mistaken ~** esp Jur 一例身份判断错误 **2** [c and u] (individual characteristics) 特点; (of person) 个性; **a (strong) sense of personal ~** （强烈的）个人特性认同感; **national/religious ~** 民族/宗教的特性; **sexual ~** 性取向

identity: **~ bracelet** *n* 身份手镯 [军人或初生婴儿佩戴]; **~ card** *n* 身份证; **~ crisis** *n* 自我认同危机; **~ disc** *n* 身份牌; **~ number** *n* **1** Admin 身份编号; **2** Comput 用户账号; **~ papers** *npl* 身份证明; **~ parade** *n* Brit 列队认人; **~ theft** *n* [u] 身份盗窃

ideogram /ˈɪdɪəgræm/, **ideograph** /ˈɪdɪəgrɑːf, Amer -græf/ *ns* (sign or symbol) 表意符号; (in writing system) 表意文字

ideological /ˌaɪdɪəˈlɒdʒɪkl/ *adj* 意识形态的

ideologically /ˌaɪdɪəˈlɒdʒɪkli/ *adv* 在意识形态方面

ideologist /ˌaɪdɪˈɒlədʒɪst/, **ideologue** /ˈaɪdɪəlɒg/ *ns* **1** (proponent of an ideology) 意识形态倡导者 **2** (theorist) 理论家; (idealist) 空想家

ideology /ˌaɪdɪˈɒlədʒi/ *n* **1** Pol, Econ 意识形态 **2** (beliefs of social group, individual) 思想体系

idiocy /ˈɪdɪəsi/ *n* **1** [u] (stupidity) 愚蠢; **a piece of ~** 一桩蠢事 **2** [c] (stupid act) 愚蠢的行动; (stupid remark) 蠢话

idiolect /ˈɪdɪəlekt/ *n* 个人语型

idiom /ˈɪdɪəm/ *n* **1** [c] (set phrase) 成语 **2** [u and c] (language natural to a group of speakers) [某语言群体的] 语言 **3** [c] (characteristic language) (of speakers) 方言; (of theatre, sport) 行话 **4** [c] (of music, art, architecture) 风格; **rock/folk/jazz ~** 摇滚乐/民谣/爵士乐风格

idiomatic /ˌɪdɪəˈmætɪk/ *adj* 符合语言习惯的; **an ~ expression** 惯用语

idiomatically /ˌɪdɪəˈmætɪkli/ *adv* 符合语言习惯地; **the expression is ~ correct** 这种表达很地道

idiosyncrasy /ˌɪdɪəˈsɪŋkrəsi/ *n* **1** (of person or animal) 习性; (of machine, system) 特点 **2** hum (foible) 癖好

idiosyncratic /ˌɪdɪəsɪŋˈkrætɪk/ *adj* 独特的

idiot /ˈɪdɪət/ *n* 傻瓜; **to act/talk like an ~** 做事/说话像个傻瓜; **to feel like an ~** 感觉像个傻瓜; **that ~ Martin** 马丁那个傻瓜

idiot: **~ board** *n* colloq [电视台给播音员等用的] 提示板; **~ box** *n* Amer colloq 电视机

idiotic /ˌɪdɪˈɒtɪk/ *adj* 十分愚蠢的; **an ~ grin** 一脸傻笑

idiotically /ˌɪdɪˈɒtɪkli/ *adv* 十分愚蠢地

idle /ˈaɪdl/

A *adj* **1** (unoccupied) 空闲的 ‹*moments, time*›; 闲散的 ‹*person*› **2** (unemployed) 无工作的; **to make employees/staff ~** 使雇员/工作人员失业; **the ~ rich** 有闲富人阶层; **to lead an ~ life** 混日子 **3** pej (lazy) 懒惰的; **an ~ layabout** 游手好闲的懒鬼; ▸**devil 1** **4** (not functioning) 闲置的 ‹*factory, machine, capital*›; **to lie** *or* **stand ~** 处于闲置状态 **5** (without evidence) 无根据的 ‹*gossip*›; (without reason) 无端的 ‹*threat, fears*› **6** (vain, pointless) 无意义的 ‹*words, thought*›; **it would be ~ to attempt to do that** 企图那么做是徒劳的

B *vi* **1** (do nothing) 游手好闲 **2** (tick over) «*engine, machine*» 空转

Phrasal verbs

- **idle about** *vi* 游手好闲
- **idle away** *vt* [**~ away sth., ~ sth. away**] 消磨 ‹*time*›

idleness /ˈaɪdlnɪs/ *n* [u] **1** (inactivity) 闲散; **enforced ~** 被迫的闲散 **2** (laziness) 懒散

idler /ˈaɪdlə(r)/ *n* **1** (slacker) 懒汉; (loiterer) 游手好闲者 **2** Tech (idle wheel) 惰轮; (pulley) 滑轮

idle wheel *n* 惰轮

idly /ˈaɪdli/ *adv* **1** (not doing anything) 无所事事地; **to sit** *or* **stand ~ by** 袖手旁观 **2** (lazily) 懒洋洋地 ‹*sit, lie*› **3** (aimlessly) 漫无目的地 ‹*talk, look*› **4** (without evidence) 无根据地 ‹*speculate, gossip*›

idol /ˈaɪdl/ *n* **1** Relig 神像 **2** (hero) 偶像; **a football/fallen ~** 足球/陨落的明星

idolater /aɪˈdɒlətə(r)/ *n* pej 偶像崇拜者

idolatrous /aɪˈdɒlətrəs/ *adj* pej 偶像崇拜的

idolatry /aɪˈdɒlətri/ *n* [u] pej **1** (worship of idols) 偶像崇拜 **2** (excessive admiration) 盲目崇拜

idolize /ˈaɪdəlaɪz/ *vt* 崇拜

idyll /ˈɪdɪl, Amer ˈaɪdl/ *n* **1** Literat 田园诗 **2** (perfect time) 良辰美景

idyllic /ɪˈdɪlɪk, Amer aɪˈd-/ *adj* **1** (bucolic) 田园风光的; (happy) 快乐无忧的 ‹*life, marriage*›; (simple and peaceful) 质朴宜人的 ‹*peace, calm*›; **an ~ scene** 一派田园风光 **2** Literat 田园诗风格的; **~ poetry** 田园诗

i.e. *abbr* = **that is** 即; **soft drinks, ~ lemonade and tomato juice** 软饮料，即柠檬汁和番茄汁

IED *abbr* = **improvised explosive device** 临时爆炸装置

> **IELTS**
>
> 雅思，即国际英语水平测试，全称为 International English Language Testing System。前身为 1980 年开始的英语测试服务（English Language Testing Service，简称 ELTS）。现由英国剑桥大学考试委员会（Cambridge Assessment）、英国文化协会（British Council）和澳大利亚教育国际开发署（International Development Program of Australian Universities and Colleges）共同举办。该测试旨在考查希望前往英语国家学习或生活的考生的语言能力，分培训类（General Training Module）和学术类（Academic Module）两种，前者多适用于移民，后者多适用于留学。成绩从 1 分至 9 分不等，包括总分以及听力、阅读、口语和写作 4 个单项的分数。雅思考试已得到多个国家的认可。

if /ɪf/ ▸**p. 147**

A *conj* **1** (in the event that, supposing that) 假如; **~ it snows, I can't go** 要是下雪的话，我就走不了; **~ so** 如果是这样的话; **~ and when** 万一; **~ and when we meet** 倘若我们见面; **~ I were you** 换了我 **2** (on condition that) 只要; **I'll help you ~ you pay me** 你给我钱，我就帮你; **I'm not coming ~ you invite her** 你要是邀请她，我就不来 **3** (whenever) 每当; **~ you mention him, she cries** 每次提到他，她都会哭; **~ in doubt** 一旦有疑问 **4** (whether) 是否; **find out ~ it's true** 搞清楚这是不是真的; **he asked ~ I am coming** 他问我来不来 **5** (despite being, despite the possibility that) 尽管; **it's good, ~ a bit expensive** 这虽然有点儿贵，但还不错; **it's interesting, ~ nothing else** 起码它很有趣; **a correct ~ conventional reaction** 常规但却是正确的反应; **~ it takes me all night, I'll do it** 哪怕这件事要花我一晚上的时间，我也会去做; **I don't care ~ he is married** 即使他结婚了我也不在乎 **6** (and perhaps not) 即使; **he has few, ~ any, supporters** 他的支持者即便有也寥寥无几 **7** (expressing minor point) 要说; (expressing opinion) 如果; **~ she has any weakness, it is ...** 要说她有什么弱点，那就是…; **~ you don't mind my saying so, ...** 如果你不介意我这么说的话，…; **~ you ask me, ...** 依我看，… **8** (in polite requests) [表示请求]; **~ you'll just sign here** 请在这儿签字; **~ I could interrupt ...** 请容许我打断一下… **9** (expressing surprise) **~ it isn't Frank!** 那不是弗兰克吗!

B *n* colloq 不确定的情况; **it's a big ~** 这是个很大的疑问; **there are too many ~s** 有太多的不确定因素; **~s and buts** 不确定因素; **I don't want any ~s and buts about it** 不要找借口

C **if anything** *adv phr* **1** (speaking tentatively) [用于试探性地表达观点]; **he's like his father, ~ anything** 如果说像谁的话，他像他的父亲 **2** (saying the opposite is true) 恰恰相反; **she's not thin: ~ anything, she's plump** 她不瘦，其实她挺丰满

D **if not** **1** *conj phr* (or else) 否则; **are you ready? ~ not, I'm leaving** 你准备好了吗？要不然我就走了 **2** *adv phr* (maybe even) 甚至; **hundreds, ~ not thousands** 几百，甚至几千; **come tomorrow, ~ not sooner** 明天就过来吧，早点更好

E **if only** *conj phr* **1** (expressing wish) 但愿; **~ only I were rich!** 但愿我很有钱！; **~ only I'd listened to you!** 要是我听了你的话就好了！ **2** (for no other reason than) 只是; **don't go, ~ only for my sake** 别走，就算是给我面子; **~ only because ...** 只是因为…

i

iffy /ˈɪfi/ *adj* esp Brit colloq **1** (uncertain) 不确定的〈*outcome, future*〉; **he's a bit ~ about going** 他对去不去有点犹豫 **2** (of doubtful quality or legality) 有问题的; **that meat smells a bit ~ to me** 我闻着那肉有点变味了

igloo /ˈɪgluː/ *n* [爱斯基摩人的] 冰屋

igneous /ˈɪgnɪəs/ *adj* **1** (formed by volcanic action) 火成的; **~ rock** 火成岩 **2** (of volcano) 火山的〈*activity*〉

ignite /ɪgˈnaɪt/

A *vt* **1** (set fire to) 点燃〈*combustible material, bomb*〉; 《*fire, spark*》引燃〈*fuel*〉 **2** fig (arouse, inflame) 激发〈*temper*〉; 引起〈*controversy, debate*〉; **to ~ tensions** 引发紧张局势

B *vi* **1** (catch fire) 着火 **2** fig 《*anger*》爆发

ignition /ɪgˈnɪʃn/ *n* **1** [c] Aut (mechanism) 点火装置; **to switch on/off the ~** 打开/关上点火开关 **2** [u] Aut (igniting of fuel) 点火; **electronic ~** 电子点火 **3** [u] (combustion) 着火

ignition: ~ coil *n* 点火线圈; **~ key** *n* 点火开关钥匙; **~ point** *n* 燃点; **~ switch** *n* 点火开关; **~ temperature** *n* 点火温度

ignoble /ɪgˈnəʊbl/ *adj* **1** formal (dishonourable) 不光彩的; (despicable) 卑鄙的 **2** liter (humble) 卑微的〈*birth, origin*〉

ignominious /ˌɪgnəˈmɪnɪəs/ *adj* formal **1** (humiliating) 耻辱的〈*defeat, concession*〉 **2** (disgraceful) 不光彩的〈*conduct*〉

ignominiously /ˌɪgnəˈmɪnɪəsli/ *adv* formal 耻辱地

ignominy /ˈɪgnəmɪni/ *n* [u] formal 耻辱; **with ~** 可耻地; **she lived on in ~** 她在耻辱中苟活

ignoramus /ˌɪgnəˈreɪməs/ *n* pej 无知的人

ignorance /ˈɪgnərəns/ *n* [u] **1** (lack of knowledge) 不知情; **~ of** *or* **about sth.** 对某事物的不了解; **to do sth. out of** *or* **through ~** 由于不知情而做某事; **to keep sb. in ~ of sth.** 不让某人知道某事物; **~ is bliss** 无知是福 **2** (lack of education) 蒙昧; **~ of science** 对科学的无知

ignorant /ˈɪgnərənt/ *adj* **1** (of a subject) 不知情的; **to be ~ of** *or* **about sth.** 对某事物不知情; **to have ~ ideas** *or* **notions about sth.** 不了解某事物 **2** (uneducated) 蒙昧的〈*person, society*〉; **she's not stupid, just ~** 她并不傻，只是没有学识; **to be pig ~** sl pej 极其无知 **3** (boorish) 粗鲁的〈*person, behaviour, remark*〉

ignorantly /ˈɪgnərəntlɪ/ *adv* **1** (without knowledge) 不知情地 **2** (boorishly) 粗鲁地

ignore /ɪgˈnɔː(r)/ *vt* **1** (take no notice of) 忽视 **2** (intentionally disregard) 无视; **to ~ personal danger** 不顾个人安危 **3** (disobey) 不理会〈*advice, warning notice, command*〉

iguana /ɪgˈwɑːnə/ *n* 鬣蜥

ikon /ˈaɪkɒn/ *n* = **icon**

IL *abbr* Amer = **Illinois**

ilk /ɪlk/ *n* **1** (type, class) 种类; **of that/his/her/their ~** 那/他这/她这/他们一类的; **fascists, racists, and others of that ~** 法西斯分子、种族主义者之流 **2** Scot archaic **of that ~** 同名的地方的; **Moncreiffe of that ~** 蒙克里夫的蒙克里夫

ill /ɪl/

A *adj* **1** (having particular illness) 有病的; **to fall ~** 生病; **to be taken ~** 病倒; **she's ~ with flu** 她得了流感; **terminally ~ patients** 病入膏肓的人 **2** (unwell) 不舒服的; **to feel ~** 感到不舒服; **to look ~** 气色不好 **3** (harmful, hostile) 坏的; **to suffer no ~ effects** 未受不良影响; **it's an ~ wind (that blows nobody any good)** Prov 害于此者利于彼

B *adv* formal (scarcely) 几乎不; **it ~ becomes them to criticize us** 他们无权批评我们; **he ~ deserves your praise** 他不值得你表扬

C *n* **1** [u] (misfortune) 厄运; **to wish sb. ~** 希望某人倒霉; **for good or ~** 不论好坏 **2** [c] (problem) 问题; **the ~s of city life/old age** 城市生活的种种弊病/老年的种种苦恼

D *npl* **the ~** 病人

I'll /aɪl/ colloq **1** = **I shall** ▸ **shall 2** = **I will** ▸ **will¹**

ill: ~-advised *adj* 不明智的; **he would be ~-advised to wait** 他要是等待就不明智了; **~-assorted** *adj* **1** (badly mixed) 杂乱的; **2** (badly matched) 不相配的〈*couple, pair*〉; **~ at ease** *adj* 局促不安的; **~-bred** *adj* 缺乏教养的〈*person*〉; 粗鲁的〈*behaviour, remark*〉; **~ breeding** *n* [u] 无礼貌; **~-concealed** *adj* 外露的〈*emotion*〉; **~-conceived** *adj* 考虑不周的〈*plan, attempt*〉; **~-considered** *adj* 考虑不周的〈*action, remark*〉; **~ deed** *n* liter 恶行; **~-defined** *adj* **1** (not having a clear limit) 轮廓不清的; **2** (not having a clear description) 不明确的; **~-disposed** *adj* 不友好的; **to be ~-disposed towards sb./sth.** (unfriendly towards) 对某人/某物不友好; (not in favour of) 不赞同某人/某事; **~ effect** *n* 不良后果

illegal /ɪˈliːgl/ *adj* **1** (unlawful, outlawed) 非法的〈*regime, trade union*〉; **to be ~ to do sth.** 做某事是违法的; **~ publication** (book) 非法出版物; (act of publishing) 非法出版; **~ operation/character** Comput 非法操作/字符 **2** Sport, Games 犯规的〈*pass, move, tackle*〉 **3** (not enforceable in law) 无法律效力的〈*contract, claim*〉

illegal immigrant *n* 非法移民

illegality /ˌɪlɪˈgæləti/ *n* **1** [u] (unlawfulness) (of regime, trade union) 不合法 **2** [u] Sport (of pass, move, tackle) 犯规 **3** [u] (of contract, claim) 无法律效力 **4** [c] (unlawful act) 非法行为

illegally /ɪˈliːgəli/ *adv* 非法地

illegible /ɪˈledʒəbl/ *adj* 无法辨认的

illegibly /ɪˈledʒəbli/ *adv* 无法辨认地

illegitimacy /ˌɪlɪˈdʒɪtɪməsi/ *n* [u] **1** (unlawfulness) 非法性 **2** (being born out of wedlock) 私生; **the rate of ~** 非婚生育率 **3** (of argument, claim) 不合理

illegitimate /ˌɪlɪˈdʒɪtɪmət/ *adj* **1** (unlawful, unauthorized) 违规的 **2** (born out of wedlock) 私生的〈*child*〉; **to have been born ~** 是私生子 **3** (invalid, unsound) 不合理的〈*argument, claim*〉

illegitimately /ˌɪlɪˈdʒɪtɪmətli/ *adv* **1** (unlawfully, without authorization) 违规地 **2** (out of wedlock) 私生地; **he was ~ born** 他是私生的; **he was ~ descended from ...** 他是…的私生后裔 **3** (incorrectly, unsoundly) 不合理地〈*argue, claim*〉

ill: ~-equipped *adj* (lacking equipment) 装备不足的; (lacking qualities) 能力欠缺的; **they are ~-equipped to cope emotionally** 他们无法抑制感情; **~-fated** *adj* (having bad luck) 倒霉的〈*day, person*〉; (having an undesirable outcome) 注定不成功的〈*marriage, attempt*〉; **~-favoured** *adj* 丑陋的; **~ feeling** *n* [u] 敌意; **~-fitting** *adj* 不合身的〈*clothes*〉; 不合脚的〈*shoes*〉; **~-founded** *adj* 缺乏根据的〈*argument, assumption*〉; **~-gotten** *adj* 来路不正的; **~-gotten gains** dated or hum 不义之财; **~ health** *n* [u] 病弱体质; **to be in a state of** *or* **to suffer from ~ health** 体质差; **~ humour** *n* [u] 恶劣心情; **to be in an ~ humour** 心情不佳; **~-humoured** *adj* 脾气不好的; **he made an ~-humoured remark about ...** 他就…说了些气话

illiberal /ɪˈlɪbərəl/ *adj* **1** (intolerant, narrow-minded) 狭隘的〈*person, attitude*〉 **2** (restricting freedom, thought, or behaviour) 不开明的〈*society, environment*〉; 专制的〈*regime, law*〉

illicit /ɪˈlɪsɪt/ *adj* **1** (illegal) 违法的〈*activity, means*〉; 违禁的〈*substance*〉 **2** (not approved of) 不正当的〈*relationship, deal*〉; (secret) 私自的〈*agreement, encounter*〉; **~ sex** 通奸

illicitly /ɪˈlɪsɪtli/ *adv* **1** (illegally) 违法地 **2** (secretly) 私自地

ill-informed *adj* 了解不够的; **~ opinions** 孤陋寡闻之见

Illinois /ˌɪlɪˈnɔɪ/ *pr n* 伊利诺伊州

illiteracy /ɪˈlɪtərəsi/ *n* [u] **1** (inability to read or write) 文盲; **to wipe out** *or* **eliminate ~** 扫盲 **2** (ignorance) 无知; **scientific/political ~** 科学盲/政治盲

illiterate /ɪˈlɪtərət/

A *adj* **1** (unable to read or write) 文盲的; **the country is 40 per cent ~** 该国40%的人口是文盲 **2** (badly written) 行文拙劣的 **3** (ignorant, uncultured) 缺乏知识的; **scientifically ~** 科学盲的

B *n* 文盲

ill: ~-judged *adj* 考虑不周的; **~ luck** *n* [u] 不幸; **~-mannered** *adj* 举止粗鲁的; **~-natured** *adj* 脾气坏的

illness /ˈɪlnɪs/ *n* **1** [c] (disease) 疾病; **a minor/serious ~** 小病/重病 **2** [u] (being ill) 患病; **she has a history of mental ~** 她有精神病史; **time lost through ~ has decreased** 员工因病耽误的工时减少了 **3** [c] (period of being ill) 患病期; **she died after a long ~** 她久病不愈而亡

illogical /ɪˈlɒdʒɪkl/ *adj* **1** (irrational) 乖戾的〈*person, action*〉; 不合理的〈*idea, approach*〉 **2** (lacking sound reasoning) 不合逻辑的〈*argument, line of thought*〉

illogicality /ɪˌlɒdʒɪˈkæləti/ *n* [u] **1** (of person, approach, action) 不合理性 **2** (of argument, reasoning) 不合逻辑性

illogically /ɪˈlɒdʒɪkli/ *adv* **1** (irrationally) 乖戾地 **2** (with unsound reasoning) 不合逻辑地

ill: ~-omened *adj* 不吉利的〈*journey, marriage*〉; **~-prepared** *adj* 未准备好的; **~ repute** *n* [u] 恶名; **a house of ~ repute** archaic or hum 妓院; **~-starred** *adj* formal **1** (destined to fail or end badly) 注定要失败的〈*mission, operation, marriage*〉; **2** (unlucky) 时运不济的〈*person*〉; **~ temper** *n* [u] (permanent characteristic) 暴躁脾气; (temporary state) 发怒; **~-tempered** *adj* (permanently angry) 脾气暴躁的; (temporarily angry) 发怒的; (rude) 粗鲁的〈*behaviour, gesture*〉; **~-timed** *adj* 不合时宜的; **~-treat** *vt* 虐待; **~ treatment** *n* [u] 虐待

illuminate /ɪˈluːmɪneɪt/ *vt* **1** (light up) 《*light*》照亮〈*room, place*〉; fig 《*smile*》使…容光焕发〈*face, eyes, expression*〉 **2** fig (elucidate) 阐明〈*subject, theory*〉; (enlighten) 启发〈*person*〉 **3** Art 华丽地装饰〈*manuscript, prayer book*〉 **4** (decorate with lights) 用彩灯装饰

illuminated /ɪˈluːmɪneɪtɪd/ *adj* **1** (lit up) 被照亮的〈*sign, advertisement*〉 **2** Art 装饰华丽的〈*manuscript, book*〉 **3** (decorated with lights) 用彩灯装饰的

illuminating /ɪˈluːmɪneɪtɪŋ/ *adj* 富有启发性的〈*explanation, analysis, comment*〉; **it was ~ to listen to his theories** 听他的理论很有启发

illumination /ɪˌluːmɪˈneɪʃn/

A *n* [u] **1** (lighting) 照明 **2** (enlightenment) 启示 **3** (of manuscript) 彩饰

B illuminations *npl* Brit 彩灯

illuminator /ɪˈluːmɪneɪtə(r)/ *n* 书稿彩饰师

illumine /ɪˈluːmɪn/ *vt* liter 照亮

ill use *n* [u] formal 虐待

ill-use /ˌɪlˈjuːz/ *vt* formal 虐待

illusion /ɪˈluːʒn/ *n* **1** (false belief) 幻想; **to have no ~s about the future** 对未来不抱有任何幻想; **to be** *or* **labour under the ~ that ...** 误以为… **2** (false appearance of space, depth, speed etc.) 假象; **an ~ of space** 空间的假象 **3** (magic trick) 幻术 **4** Psych (false perception) 错觉

illusionist /ɪˈluːʒənɪst/ *n* 幻术师

illusive /ɪˈluːsɪv/ *adj* liter = **illusory**

illusory /ɪˈluːsəri/ *adj* **1** (delusory) 虚幻的〈*feeling, hope*〉 **2** (deceptive) 虚假的〈*situation, vision*〉

illustrate /ˈɪləstreɪt/ *vt* **1** (provide with pictures) 给…加插图 **2** (explain, make clear) 说明; **to ~ a point/how ...** 说明一个观点/如何… **3** (exemplify) 举例说明; **to ~ the fact that ...** 举例说明…的事实

illustrated /ˈɪləstreɪtɪd/ *adj* 有插图的; **an ~ talk** 有图片演示的演讲

illustration /ˌɪləˈstreɪʃn/ *n* **1** [c] (picture) 插图; **in-text ~s** 文内插图 **2** [c and u] (example) 例证; **by way of ~** 通过举例; **as an ~ of what I mean** 作为说明我意思的例证 **3** [u] (act of illustrating a text) 插图制作

illustrative /ˈɪləstrətɪv, Amer ɪˈlʌs-/ *adj* 说明性的; **to be ~ of sth.** 说明某事; **for ~ purposes only** 只供说明之用

illustrator /ˈɪləstreɪtə(r)/ ▸**p. 409** *n* 插图画家

illustrious /ɪˈlʌstrɪəs/ *adj* **1** (famous, distinguished) 著名的; **an ~ name** 赫赫大名 **2** formal (glorious) 伟大的 ‹*emperor, ancestor*›; 辉煌的 ‹*victory*›; 隆重的 ‹*banquet, gathering*›

illustriously /ɪˈlʌstrɪəsli/ *adv* 隆重地

ill will *n* [u] 恶意; **I bear them no ~** formal 我对他们没有敌意

ILO *n* = **International Labour Organization**

Illnesses, aches, and pains

Where does it hurt?

■ 疼 and 痛 are most commonly used in Chinese to express pain:

Where does it hurt?
= 哪儿疼?
or 哪儿痛?

Tell me where it hurts
= 告诉我哪里痛
or 告诉我哪儿疼

My back hurts
or ***My back is hurting me***
or ***I have a pain in my back***
or ***I have backache***
= 我背痛

My ear aches
or ***I have earache***
= 我耳朵疼

I'm aching all over
= 我浑身痛

My eyes are sore
or ***I have sore eyes***
= 我眼痛

I've been suffering various aches and pains
= 我一直饱受各种疼痛之苦

I felt a sharp pain in my back
= 我感到背上一阵剧痛

I've got a slight ache in my leg
= 我的腿有点疼

Accidents

Ella hurt her back
= 埃拉伤了背

Adam was slightly injured in the crash
= 亚当在撞车事故中受了轻伤

He sustained multiple injuries in the accident
= 他在事故中多处受伤

He was badly burnt in the fire
= 他在火灾中严重烧伤

She broke her left leg
= 她弄断了左腿

She sprained her ankle
= 她扭伤了脚踝

It was a bad sprain
= 扭伤很严重

Chronic conditions

He has a weak heart
= 他心脏不好

He has a weak stomach
= 他胃不好

He has a bad back
= 他背痛得厉害

He has bad teeth
= 他有蛀牙
or 他的牙不好

He has liver trouble
= 他有肝病

Being ill / falling ill

■ The verb 'to have' is used in English to express suffering from a particular illness. In Chinese, the verbs 患, 有 and others are used:

to have skin cancer
= 患有皮肤癌

to have diarrhoea
= 患腹泻
or 拉肚子 (colloquial)

to have bronchitis
= 有支气管炎

to have asthma
= 患哮喘

■ In Chinese, the verbs 染上, 感染上, 得 or 患 are used to express 'to get', 'to catch', 'to contract' or 'to develop' a particular disease:

to get/contract Aids
= 感染艾滋病

to get/contract measles
= 患麻疹

to get/contract malaria
= 得疟疾

to develop rheumatism
= 患风湿

to catch a cold
= 患感冒

to get food poisoning
= 食物中毒

■ 突发, 发作 or 一阵 are used in Chinese to denote an attack of an illness, as in the examples below:

to have a bout of flu
= 突发流感

to have an attack of asthma
= 哮喘病发作

to have a heart attack
= 心脏病发作

to have a coughing fit
= 一阵咳嗽

to have an epileptic fit
= 癫痫发作

■ Note that the indefinite article is included in the English examples below, but not in the Chinese:

to get an inflammation of the eye
= 眼部发炎

to have a stomach ache
= 肚子痛

to contract pneumonia
= 得肺病

to have a headache
= 头痛

Treatment

She is being treated for breast cancer
= 她正接受乳腺癌的治疗

He took some cough medicine
= 他吃了些咳嗽药

I was prescribed painkillers
= 我给开了止痛药

This medicine is only available on prescription
= 这种药有处方才能买

The surgeon is operating on her injured leg
= 外科医生正在为她受伤的腿做手术

He had an operation on his shoulder
= 他肩部做过手术

He has insulin injections every day
= 他每天打胰岛素针

The nurse gives him insulin injections every day
= 护士每天给他注射胰岛素

to be vaccinated against chickenpox
= 接种水痘疫苗
or 注射水痘疫苗

to have a vaccination against measles
= 接种麻疹疫苗
or 注射麻疹疫苗

to be immunized against polio
= 接种小儿麻痹症疫苗
or 注射小儿麻痹症疫苗

capsules for colds/cold relief capsules
= 感冒胶囊

sachets of powder for flu/sachets of flu powder
= 流感冲剂

vitamin tablets/pills
= 维生素片

travel sickness tablets
= 晕车药

sleeping pills
= 安眠药

allergy tablets
= 抗过敏药

eye drops
= 眼药水

cough syrup
= 止咳糖浆

acupuncture therapy
= 针灸疗法

throat spray
= 喉咙喷剂

burn treatment cream
= 烧伤药膏

I'm /aɪm/ colloq = **I am** ▸**be A, B, D**

image /ˈɪmɪdʒ/

A *n* **1** (conception) 印象；(mental picture) 想象；(notion) 概念；**the popular ~ of life in the north** 对北方生活的普遍印象；**a preconceived ~ of sth.** 对某物的先入之见 **2** TV, Video, Phot, Comput 图像；**the moving ~** 动态影像 **3** (optical appearance) 图像；**microscopic ~s** 显微图像 **4** (carved representation) 雕像；(moulded representation) 塑像；**a wooden ~ of Christ** 木雕基督像 **5** (public perception) 形象；(epitome) 典型；**to project/promote/improve a public ~** 树立/提升/改善公众形象；**the ~ of the successful working mother** 成功职业母亲的典型 **6** Literat (simile, metaphor) 意象 **7** (likeness of a person) 酷似的人；(likeness of a thing) 酷似的物；**God created man in his own ~** 上帝按照自己的模样创造了人；**he is the (spitting) ~ of you** 他长得酷似你 **8** (portrayal) 生动描述；**the author creates a haunting ~ of the American war in Vietnam** 作者把美国越战塑造得可怕且难以忘却

B *vt* 塑造…的形象

image: ~-conscious *adj* 注意形象的；**~ consultant** *n* 形象顾问；**~ processing** *n* [u] 图像处理

imagery /ˈɪmɪdʒəri/ *n* [u] **1** Literat (descriptive, figurative language) 意象；**poetic ~** 诗的意象 **2** (visual images) 图像；**satellite ~** 卫星影像 **3** (visual symbolism) 视觉象征手法

imaginable /ɪˈmædʒɪnəbl/ *adj* 可想象的；**you're the best mum ~!** 你是天下最好的妈妈！；**we've got all the time ~** 我们有的是时间；**by every means ~, by every ~ means** 用一切可能的方法

imaginary /ɪˈmædʒɪnəri, Amer -əneri/ *adj* **1** (fictitious) 虚构的 **2** (unreal, fanciful) 虚幻的 **3** (hypothetical) 假想的 **4** Math, Geog 虚的 ‹*point, line*›

imaginary number *n* 虚数

imagination /ɪˌmædʒɪˈneɪʃn/ *n* **1** [c] (faculty) 想象力；**to have a vivid ~** 想象力活跃；**to defy (the) ~** 难以想象；**to leave sth. to sb.'s ~** 让某人自己想象某事物；**not by any stretch of the ~ could he be considered handsome** 他无论如何也算不上英俊；**you shouldn't let your ~ dwell too much on that** 你不应该总想着那事 **2** [u] (fancy) 幻想；**there's nothing there, it's just your ~** 那儿什么也没有，那只是你的幻觉而已；**it's all in your ~, she's not cheating on you** 都是你在胡思乱想，她并没有对你不忠；**to catch sb.'s ~** 使某人觉得有趣 **3** [c] (ability to be creative or resourceful) 创造力；**to have a fertile ~** 有丰富的创造力；**to stir** *or* **fire** *or* **capture sb.'s ~** 激发某人的兴趣；**to use one's ~** 动脑筋

imaginative /ɪˈmædʒɪnətɪv, Amer -eɪtɪv/ *adj* 富于想象力的；**an ~ answer** 有创意的回答

imaginatively /ɪˈmædʒɪnətɪvli, Amer -eɪtɪvli/ *adv* **1** (creatively) 富于想象力地；**he paints ~** 他的绘画富于想象力 **2** (inventively) 有创意地；**an ~ devised scheme** 别出心裁的方案

imaginativeness /ɪˈmædʒɪnətɪvnɪs, Amer -eɪtɪvnɪs/ *n* [u] **1** (creativity) 富于想象力 **2** (inventiveness of approach, policy, device, etc.) 独创性

imagine /ɪˈmædʒɪn/ *vt* **1** (picture, visualize) 想象；**just ~ how disappointed I was** 想象一下我当时是多么失望；**you can't/you can (well) ~ my horror!** 你想象不出/你（完全）能够想象到我有多恐惧！ **2** (believe wrongly) 幻想；**there's nothing there, you're just imagining it!** 那里什么都没有，只是你的幻觉而已！；**don't ~ you're going to succeed without a lot of hard work** 别幻想不付出艰苦努力就能获得成功 **3** (suppose) 料想；**I ~ he's still alive** 我想他还活着；**she mistakenly ~d she would get the job** 她误以为自己会得到那份工作；**you'd never ~ anyone would be so unpleasant** 你绝对不会想到居然有人会这么讨厌

imaging /ˈɪmɪdʒɪŋ/ *n* [u] **1** Med 放射造像 **2** Comput 成像

imaginings /ɪˈmædʒɪnɪŋz/ *npl* 想象；**beyond one's ~** 出乎想象

imam /ɪˈmɑːm/ *n* 伊玛目 [伊斯兰教长称号]

imbalance /ˌɪmˈbæləns/ *n* [u and c] 不平衡；**an ~ between A and B** A 和 B 之间的失衡；**to correct** *or* **redress an ~** 纠正不平衡；**an ~ of wealth** 贫富不均

imbecile /ˈɪmbəsiːl, Amer -sl/ colloq

A *n* 傻瓜；**(you) ~!**（你这）傻瓜！

B *adj* 愚蠢的 ‹*remark, behaviour*›

imbecility /ˌɪmbəˈsɪləti/ *n* **1** [u] (stupidity) 愚蠢；**it's sheer ~ to do that** 做那事简直愚蠢透顶 **2** [c] (foolish act) 愚蠢的行为；(foolish remark) 蠢话

imbibe /ɪmˈbaɪb/

A *vt* **1** formal or hum (drink) 喝 **2** formal (assimilate) 吸收 ‹*information*›；接受 ‹*idea*›

B *vi* formal or hum 酗酒

imbroglio /ɪmˈbrəʊlɪəʊ/ *n* formal 错综复杂的尴尬局势

imbue /ɪmˈbjuː/ *vt* formal 使充满；**to ~ sb./sth. with sth.** 给某人灌输某事/使某物中充满某物；**~d with patriotism, they fought to the last man** 他们满怀爱国之情，战斗到了最后一人

IMF *abbr* = **International Monetary Fund**

imitate /ˈɪmɪteɪt/ *vt* **1** (copy) 仿效；(mimic) 模仿 ‹*person, mannerism*›；模拟 ‹*sound*›；**to ~ a cock crowing** 学公鸡啼叫；**art ~s life** 艺术是对生活的仿制 **2** (reproduce) 复制；**to ~ sb.'s signature** 模仿某人的签名 **3** (simulate) 仿制；**synthetic fabrics can now ~ everything from silk to rubber** 如今可以用合成纤维仿制从丝绸到橡胶的任何东西

imitation /ˌɪmɪˈteɪʃn/

A *n* **1** [u and c] (copying) 效仿；(impersonation) 模仿；**to learn by ~** 通过模仿学习；**to do ~s** *or* **an ~ of sb.** 学某人的样子；**in ~ of sb./sth.** 模仿某人/某物；**~ is the sincerest form of flattery** Prov 仿效方为真恭维 **2** [c] (reproduction) 仿制品；**beware of ~s!** 谨防赝品！

B *modif* 人造的 ‹*fur, jewellery, leather, pearl*›

imitation: ~ gold *n* [u] 仿金；**~ marble** *n* [u] 人造大理石

imitative /ˈɪmɪtətɪv, Amer -teɪtɪv/ *adj* **1** (tending to mimic) 善于模仿的 ‹*animal, bird*›；**to be ~ of sth.** 模仿某物；**the flute can produce sounds ~ of bird cries** 笛子可以模仿鸟叫 **2** pej (derivative) 因袭他人的 ‹*writer, artist*›；因袭的 ‹*idea, style*›；仿造的 ‹*work of art*›

imitator /ˈɪmɪteɪtə(r)/ *n* **1** (mimic) 模仿者 **2** (copier of artefact) 仿制品

immaculate /ɪˈmækjʊlət/ *adj* **1** (very clean or tidy) 整洁的 ‹*clothes, room*›；干净利落的 ‹*person*›；无污迹的 ‹*manuscript, paint*›；**to keep sth. ~** 保持某物整洁 **2** (flawless) 完美的 ‹*appearance, performance*›；精准的 ‹*technique, timing*›；**car for sale, in ~ condition** 汽车待售，车况完好 **3** Relig 德操无瑕的 ‹*person, life*›；**the I~ Conception**（圣母马利亚）无沾成胎说

immaculately /ɪˈmækjʊlətli/ *adv* **1** (very cleanly or tidily) 整洁地 ‹*dressed*› **2** (flawlessly) 完美地 ‹*behave, arrange*›；精准地 ‹*copy, draw*›

immanent /ˈɪmənənt/ *adj* formal 内在的 ‹*quality*›；天生的 ‹*beauty*›；**~ presence** 无所不在

immaterial /ˌɪməˈtɪərɪəl/ *adj* **1** (unimportant) 无关紧要的 ‹*fact, factor*›；**to be ~ to sth./sb.** 与某事/某人不相干；**it's ~ (to me) whether you like it or not** 你喜不喜欢（我）无所谓 **2** (intangible) 无形的 ‹*soul, apparition*›；**~ beings** 无形体

immature /ˌɪməˈtjʊə(r), Amer -tʊər/ *adj* **1** (not fully developed) 发育未全的 ‹*animal, organism*›；未成熟的 ‹*fruit, plant*› **2** (childish) 孩子气的；**he's being ~** 他在耍小孩子脾气；**to be ~ for one's age** 幼稚得与年龄不相称

immaturity /ˌɪməˈtjʊərəti, Amer -tʊər-/ *n* [u] **1** (lack of development) (of animal, organism) 发育未全；(of fruit, plant) 未成熟 **2** (childishness) 孩子气

immeasurable /ɪˈmeʒərəbl/ *adj* **1** (vast) 极大的 ‹*benefit, damage*›；**~ desire/pleasure** 无餍的欲望/极乐 **2** (incalculable) 无法计量的 ‹*height, distance*›

immeasurably /ɪˈmeʒərəbli/ *adv* **1** (incalculably) 无法计量地；**to benefit ~ from sth.** 从某事中获益无穷；**an ~ wealthy family** 资财多得数不清的人家 **2** (immensely) 极大地；**it's all ~ sad** 无比哀痛

immediacy /ɪˈmiːdɪəsi/ *n* [u] 即时性；**a sense of ~** 即时感；**the ~ of the threat** 威胁的迫在眉睫

immediate /ɪˈmiːdɪət/ *adj* **1** (without delay) 立即的 ‹*action*›；**the drug took ~ effect** 这药马上就见效了 **2** (needing urgent attention) 迫切的 ‹*task, problem*›；紧急的 ‹*measure, steps*›；**~ concerns** 当务之急；**the patient is not in ~ danger** 该病人暂时没有危险 **3** *attrib* (near) 紧邻的 ‹*area*›；最近的 ‹*objective*›；**an ~ neighbour** 近邻；**one's ~ successor/predecessor** 前/后一任；**his ~ family** 他的直系亲属；**in the ~ vicinity** 近在咫尺；**on my ~ left/right** 就在我的左边/右边；**in the ~ future** 短期内 **4** *attrib* (direct) 直接的 ‹*knowledge, connection, effect, influence*›；**the ~ cause of death** 直接死因

immediately /ɪˈmiːdɪətli/

A *adv* **1** (at once) 立刻；**~ at** *or* **to hand** 就在手头；**he was ~ recognizable** 一眼就能认出他来 **2** (now) 现在 ‹*effective, available*›；**he is not ~ at risk** 他现在没有危险；**the new law is to come into force ~** 这部新法令即刻就生效 **3** (near) 紧邻地；**~ next door** 就在隔壁；**~ opposite/to the left/under the window** 就在对面/左边/窗子下面；**~ after/before sth.** 就在某物后面/前面 **4** (directly) 直接 ‹*concern, affect, related*›

B *conj* Brit 一…就；**he left ~ he received the call** 他接到电话后立刻就离开了

immemorial /ˌɪməˈmɔːrɪəl/ *adj* 古老的 ‹*custom, usage*›；**since** *or* **from time ~** 自古以来

immense /ɪˈmens/ *adj* 巨大的 ‹*space, distance, wealth*›；无限的 ‹*possibilities*›；十分的 ‹*popularity*›；艰巨的 ‹*problem, task*›；严重的 ‹*damage*›；**a project/problem of ~ importance** 极其重要的项目/问题

immensely /ɪˈmensli/ *adv* 极其 ‹*rich, popular, generous, large*›；**I enjoyed the play ~** 我非常喜欢看这部戏；**I was ~ pleased to hear the news** 我听到这个消息高兴极了

immensity /ɪˈmensəti/ *n* [u] **1** (large size) (of damage, loss) 巨大；(of problem, task) 艰巨 **2** (large expanse) 无边无际 **3** (large amount) 大量

immerse /ɪˈmɜːs/

A *vt* **1** (submerge) 浸泡；**to ~ sth. in sth.** 把某物浸泡于某液体中 **2** fig (absorb, engross) 使…沉浸 ‹*person*›；**to be ~d in sth.** 深陷于某事 **3** Relig 给…施浸礼

B *v refl* **to ~ oneself (in sth.)** 专心于（某事）

immersion /ɪˈmɜːʃn, Amer -ʒn/ *n* [u] **1** (submersion) 浸没 **2** fig (engrossment) 沉浸 **3** Relig 浸礼；**baptism by total ~** 全身入水的浸礼

immersion: ~ course *n* 浸入式强化训练课程；**~ heater** *n* Brit 浸入式加热器

immigrant /ˈɪmɪɡrənt/ *n* （外来）移民；**an illegal ~** 非法移民；**~ population/community/labour** 侨民人口/社区/劳动力；**an ~ worker** 侨民劳工

immigrate /ˈɪmɪɡreɪt/ *vi* （从外地）移居；**to ~ to (somewhere)** 移居至（某地）

i

immigration /ˌɪmɪˈɡreɪʃn/ *n* [u] 移民入境; **to go** *or* **pass through ～** (at airport, border) 通过移民局检查

immigration: ～ authorities *npl* 移民局; **～ control** *n* 1 [u and c] (mechanism) 移民控制; 2 [u] (office) 移民局检查站; **～ laws** *npl* 移民法; **～ officer, ～ official** *ns* 移民局官员; **～ service** *n* 移民处

imminence /ˈɪmɪnəns/ *n* [u] 迫近

imminent /ˈɪmɪnənt/ *adj* 迫近的 ‹*danger, storm, revolution*›; 即将作出的 ‹*confession, declaration*›

immobile /ɪˈməʊbaɪl, Amer -bl/ *adj* 1 (motionless) 静止的; **to remain ～** 保持不动; **to sit/stand ～** 一动不动地坐着/站着 2 (unable to move) 无法移动的

immobility /ˌɪməˈbɪləti/ *n* [u] 1 (motionlessness) 静止不动; **to freeze into ～** 冻僵 2 (inability to move) 无法移动; **muscular ～** 肌肉僵硬; **～ of labour** 劳动力的不流动

immobilize /ɪˈməʊbɪlaɪz/ *vt* 1 (prevent from operating or moving) «*weather conditions, circumstances*» 使无法行动; «*strike, jam*» 使…陷入瘫痪 ‹*city, traffic*› 2 (render immobile) «*authorities*» 禁止…行驶 ‹*vehicle*›; «*device*» 锁住 ‹*vehicle*› 3 Med (keep still) «*plaster, cast, splint*» 固定 ‹*limb, joint*› 4 Fin 变…为固定资本 ‹*capital, assets*›

immobilizer /ɪˈməʊbɪlaɪzə(r)/ *n* 汽车防盗器

immoderate /ɪˈmɒdərət/ *adj* formal 无节制的 ‹*conduct, desire, use*›; 过分的 ‹*demands, pride*›

immodest /ɪˈmɒdɪst/ *adj* 1 (improper) 不合适的 ‹*dress, suggestion*›; 不正经的 ‹*behaviour, talk*› 2 (boastful) 自负的 ‹*person, statement*›; **～ boasting/claims** 狂妄的吹嘘/贪求

immodestly /ɪˈmɒdɪstli/ *adv* 1 (improperly) 不端庄地 ‹*dressed*›; 不正经地 ‹*talk, behave*› 2 (boastfully) 自负地 ‹*boast*›

immodesty /ɪˈmɒdɪsti/ *n* [u] 1 (impropriety) 不端庄 2 (boastfulness) 自负; **I can claim, without ～, that ...** 我敢毫不自夸地说…

immolate /ˈɪməleɪt/ formal
A *vt* 用…作燔祭
B *v refl* **to ～ oneself** 自焚

immoral /ɪˈmɒrəl, Amer ɪˈmɔːrəl/ *adj* 1 (morally wrong, unethical) 不道德的 ‹*act, remark, activity*›; 堕落的 ‹*person*›; 邪恶的 ‹*system*› 2 (dissolute) 放荡的 ‹*person, lifestyle*›; **to live off ～ earnings** 以卖淫为生

immorality /ˌɪməˈræləti/ *n* [u] 1 (being morally wrong, unethical) 不道德 2 (immoral behaviour) 不道德的行为 3 (dissoluteness) 伤风败俗; **a life of ～** 淫荡的生活

immortal /ɪˈmɔːtl/
A *adj* 1 (undying) 永生的 ‹*god, person, being, soul*› 2 (timeless, deserving to be remembered forever) 不朽的 ‹*person, fame, glory, masterpiece*›
B *n* 1 (god) 神; **the ～s** 众神 2 (person deserving to be remembered forever) 不朽的人物; **～s of stage and screen** 千古留名的舞台银幕人物

immortality /ˌɪmɔːˈtæləti/ *n* [u] 1 (eternal life) 永生 2 (timelessness, fame) 不朽; **to achieve ～** 取得不朽的声望

immortalize /ɪˈmɔːtəlaɪz/ *vt* 1 (make enduringly famous) 使…千古留名 ‹*person, place, event, deeds*› 2 (render immortal) 使…永生 ‹*person, soul*›

immovable /ɪˈmuːvəbl/ *adj* 1 (immobile) 固定的 ‹*object, obstacle*› 2 (steadfast) 坚定不移的 ‹*determination, decision*›; 意志坚定的 ‹*person, government*› 3 (fixed, unchangeable) 根深蒂固的 ‹*prejudice, conservatism*›; 执着的 ‹*purpose, intention*›

immovably /ɪˈmuːvəbli/ *adv* 无法移动地

immune /ɪˈmjuːn/ *adj* 1 (resistant to disease) 有免疫力的; (relating to immunity) 免疫的 ‹*reaction*›; **to be ～ to** *or* **against sth.** 对某疾病有免疫力; **～ system** 免疫系统 2 (protected) 受保护的; **to be ～ from** *or* **to sth.** 不受某事影响 3 (exempt) 豁免的; **to be ～ from prosecution** 免于起诉 4 (unaffected) 不受影响的; **to be ～ to flattery/temptation** 不为奉承/诱惑所动

immune therapy *n* [u] 免疫治疗

immunity /ɪˈmjuːnəti/ *n* 1 [u] Med 免疫力; **natural/acquired ～** 自然/获得性免疫力; **to develop (an) ～ to sth.** 对某疾病产生免疫力 2 [u] (exemption) 豁免; **tax/legal ～** 税收/法律上的豁免 3 [u and c] (privilege of exemption) 豁免权; **diplomatic/parliamentary ～** 外交/议会豁免权; **to be given** *or* **granted ～ from prosecution** 获得豁免权 4 [u] (insusceptibility to influence) 不受影响; **～ to criticism** 对批评的无动于衷

immunization /ˌɪmjʊnaɪˈzeɪʃn, Amer -nɪˈz-/ *n* [u and c] 免疫; **mass ～** 大规模免疫接种

immunize /ˈɪmjuːnaɪz/ *vt* 使免疫; **to ～ sb. against sth.** 给某人接种抗某病的疫苗

immunodeficiency /ˌɪmjʊnəʊdɪˈfɪʃənsi/ *n* 免疫缺陷

immunodeficient /ˌɪmjʊnəʊdəˈfɪʃənt/ *adj* 有免疫缺损的 ‹*person*›

immunoglobulin /ˌɪmjʊnəʊˈɡlɒbjʊlɪn/ *n* [u] 免疫球蛋白

immunological /ɪˌmjuːnəˈlɒdʒɪkl/ *adj* 免疫系统的 ‹*disease, reaction*›; 免疫学的 ‹*research*›; **the ～ system** 免疫系统

immunologist /ˌɪmjʊˈnɒlədʒɪst/ ▸**p. 409** *n* 免疫学专家

immunology /ˌɪmjʊˈnɒlədʒi/ *n* [u] 免疫学

immunostimulant /ˌɪmjʊnəʊˈstɪmjʊlənt, ɪˌmjuːnəʊ-/ *n* 免疫刺激剂

immunosuppression /ˌɪmjʊnəʊsəˈpreʃn, ɪˌmjuːnəʊ-/ *n* [u] 免疫抑制

immunosuppressive /ˌɪmjʊnəʊsəˈpresɪv, ɪˌmjuːnəʊ-/ *adj* 免疫抑制的; **～ drugs** 免疫抑制类药物

immunotherapy /ˌɪmjʊnəʊˈθerəpi, ɪˌmjuːnəʊ-/ *n* [u] 免疫治疗

immure /ɪˈmjʊə(r)/ *vt* formal 监禁; **to ～ sb. in sth.** 在某处监禁某人

immutable /ɪˈmjuːtəbl/ *adj* formal 不可改变的 ‹*fact, decision*›

immutably /ɪˈmjuːtəbli/ *adv* formal 永久地 ‹*established, settled*›; 不可改变地 ‹*decided*›

imp /ɪmp/ *n* 1 fig (child) 顽童; **a little ～** 小淘气 2 (sprite) 小恶魔

impact
A /ˈɪmpækt/ *n* [u and c] 1 (violent contact) 冲撞; **on ～** 受冲撞时; **the bomb will explode on ～** 这炸弹一撞即爆; **the point of ～** 撞击点; **under the ～ of sth.** 在某物的撞击下 2 (force of blow, collision, explosion) 冲击力; **the full ～ of the blast** 爆炸的全部冲击力 3 (impression) 影响; **to have** *or* **make an ～ on sb./sth.** 对某人/某事产生影响 4 (effect) 作用; **a social/revolutionary/technological ～** 社会的/革命性的/技术方面的作用
B /ɪmˈpækt/ *vt* 1 esp Amer (affect) 深刻影响 2 (press firmly) 压紧
C /ɪmˈpækt/ *vi* 产生深刻影响; **to ～ on sth.** 对某事产生深刻影响; **high interest rates have ～ed on spending** 高利率极大影响了消费

impacted /ɪmˈpæktɪd/ *adj* 阻生的 ‹*wisdom tooth*›; **～ fracture** 嵌入骨折

impair /ɪmˈpeə(r)/ *vt* 削弱 ‹*mobility, strength*›; 降低 ‹*efficiency*›; 损害 ‹*health, sight*›

impaired /ɪmˈpeəd/ *adj* 受损的 ‹*health*›; 被削弱的 ‹*strength, mobility*›

impairment /ɪmˈpeəmənt/ *n* [u and c] 损伤; **mental/physical/visual ～** 智力低下/身体损伤/视力损伤; **～ of hearing** 听力受损

impala /ɪmˈpɑːlə/ *n* 黑斑羚

impale /ɪmˈpeɪl/
A *vt* 刺穿 ‹*person, head, fish, animal*›; **to ～ sth./sb. on sth.** 将某物/某人钉在某物上
B *v refl* **to ～ oneself (on sth.)** 被刺穿 (在某物上)

impalpable /ɪmˈpælpəbl/ *adj* formal 无形的 ‹*horror, presence, aura*›

impart /ɪmˈpɑːt/ *vt* 1 (communicate) 传授 ‹*knowledge, skill*›; 传达 ‹*information*›; 透露 ‹*news*›; **to ～ sth. to sb.** 将…赋予某人 ‹*wisdom*›; 向某人传授 ‹*knowledge*› 2 (add) 带来 ‹*atmosphere, flavour*›; **wine ～s elegance to a meal** 葡萄酒能给进餐带来优雅的氛围

impartial /ɪmˈpɑːʃl/ *adj* 公正的 ‹*judge, judgement, decision, inquiry, investigation*›; 中立的 ‹*report, reporter, observer*›

impartiality /ɪmˌpɑːʃɪˈæləti/ *n* [u] (of judge, judgement, decision, inquiry, investigation) 公正; (of report, reporter, observer) 中立

impartially /ɪmˈpɑːʃəli/ *adv* 公正地 ‹*act, investigate, judge, decide, treat*›; 中立地 ‹*mediate*›

impassable /ɪmˈpɑːsəbl, Amer -ˈpæs-/ *adj* 不可逾越的 ‹*barrier*›; 无法通行的 ‹*river, road, terrain*›

impasse /ˈæmpɑːs, Amer ˈɪmpæs/ *n* 僵局; **to reach an ～** 陷入僵局; **to find a way out of an ～** 找到打破僵局的办法

impassioned /ɪmˈpæʃnd/ *adj* 热切的 ‹*appeal*›; 热烈的 ‹*debate*›; 热情的 ‹*speech*›

impassive /ɪmˈpæsɪv/ *adj* 1 (expressionless) 面无表情的 ‹*person*›; 木然的 ‹*features*› 2 (emotionless) 冷漠的 ‹*attitude, response*›

impassively /ɪmˈpæsɪvli/ *adv* 1 (without visible emotion) 无表情地 ‹*watch, wait, stand*› 2 (without feeling emotion) 泰然地 ‹*carry on, reply*›

impatience /ɪmˈpeɪʃns/ *n* [u] 1 (irritation at delay) 不耐烦; **with ～** 不耐烦地 2 (intolerance) 难以忍受; **～ with sb./at sth.** 对某人/某事的不容忍 3 (eagerness) 急切; **～ to do sth./for sth.** 做某事/要得到某物的迫不及待

impatient /ɪmˈpeɪʃnt/ *adj* 1 (quick-tempered) 急躁的 ‹*person*›; 不耐烦的 ‹*glance*›; **to become** *or* **get ～ with sb.** 对某人不耐烦 2 (intolerant) 不宽容的 ‹*person, reply, gesture*›; **to be ～ at sth./with sb.** 对某事/某人无法忍受; **to be ～ of sth./sb.** 不能容忍某人/某事 3 (eager) 急切的; **to be ～ to do sth./for sth.** 迫不及待地要做某事/要得到某物; **to be ～ for sth. to happen** 热切期待某事发生

impatiently /ɪmˈpeɪʃntli/ *adv* 焦急地 ‹*wait*›; 不耐烦地 ‹*reply*›

impeach /ɪmˈpiːtʃ/ *vt* 1 Brit (charge with crime against the state) 控告; **to ～ sb. for sth./doing sth.** 控告某人有某罪/犯有某罪 2 Amer (charge with misconduct) 弹劾 ‹*person, public official, president*› 3 (call into question) 质疑 ‹*honesty, testimony*›

impeachment /ɪmˈpiːtʃmənt/ *n* 1 Brit (for crimes against the state) 控告 2 Amer (of public official) 弹劾; **to face ～ for sth./doing sth.** 因某事/做某事面临弹劾 3 (questioning of character, integrity, honour, motives) 质疑; **～ of sth.** 对某事的质疑

impeccable /ɪmˈpekəbl/ *adj* 无可挑剔的 ‹*appearance, style, behaviour, manners, credentials, language*›; 无瑕疵的 ‹*record*›

impeccably /ɪmˈpekəbli/ *adv* 无可挑剔地 ‹*dress, behave, write, tidy*›

impecunious /ˌɪmpɪˈkjuːnɪəs/ *adj* formal 一文不名的; **to be in ～ circumstances** 一贫如洗

impedance /ɪmˈpiːdəns/ *n* [u] 阻抗

impede /ɪmˈpiːd/ *vt* 阻碍 ‹*action, advance*›; 阻塞 ‹*traffic*›; «*long hair, clothes*» 妨碍 ‹*person, movement*›; «*lack of money*» 拖延 ‹*progress*›; **to ～ success** 阻碍成功

impediment /ɪm'pedɪmənt/ *n* 1 (hindrance) 阻碍; **to be an ～ to sth.** 是对某事的妨碍 2 (speech defect) 言语障碍; **to overcome an ～** 克服言语障碍 3 Jur (to marriage, contract) 障碍; **an ～ to sth.** 对某事的障碍

impedimenta /ɪm,pedɪ'mentə/ *npl* formal 辎重

impel /ɪm'pel/ *vt* (*pres p etc.* **-ll-**) 1 (force, drive) 迫使; **poverty ～led him into crime** 贫穷逼得他犯罪 2 (urge) «*fear*» 驱使 〈*person*〉; «*ambition*» 激励 〈*person*〉; **to ～ sb. into sth./into doing** *or* **to do sth.** 驱使某人做某事

impending /ɪm'pendɪŋ/ *adj* 即将到来的 〈*visit, meeting, examination*〉; 临近的 〈*danger, death, storm*〉

impenetrability /ɪm,penɪtrə'bɪləti/ *n* [u] 费解

impenetrable /ɪm'penɪtrəbl/ *adj* 1 (solid, unbreakable) 无法穿透的 〈*substance, wall*〉; 无法通过的 〈*barrier, fortress*〉; 刺不穿的 〈*armour, shield*〉; **to be ～ to sth.** 无法穿透某物 2 (opaque) 无法透视的 〈*gloom, fog*〉; 混浊的 〈*waters*〉; **～ darkness** 漆黑 3 (unfathomable) 费解的 〈*problem, expression*〉 4 (dense) 茂密的 〈*forest, undergrowth*〉

impenitent /ɪm'penɪtənt/ *adj* formal 无悔意的

imperative /ɪm'perətɪv/
A *adj* 1 (crucial, urgent) 迫切的 〈*need*〉; **to have an ～ desire to do sth.** 急欲做某事; **it is ～ that she (should) write** 她必须写; **it is ～ to act promptly** 必须立刻行动 2 *attrib* (commanding, imperious) 必须服从的 〈*order, command*〉; 命令式的 〈*tone of voice, gesture*〉 3 *attrib* Ling 祈使的; **～ mood** 祈使语气
B *n* 1 (priority) 紧迫之事; **the first ～** 当务之急; **to be an ～ to do sth.** 迫切需要做某事; **it is an ～ for the government that it win the battle against inflation** 政府亟须打赢抵制通货膨胀这一仗 2 Ling (verb) 祈使语气动词; **the ～** (mood) 祈使语气; **commands in the ～** 祈使语气的命令

imperatively /ɪm'perətɪvli/ *adv* 1 (urgently) 迫切地 〈*need, require*〉; 极其 〈*important, urgent*〉 2 Ling 祈使地; **to use a verb ～** 以祈使语气使用动词

imperceptible /,ɪmpə'septəbl/ *adj* 难以察觉的 〈*change, difference, increase*〉; **to be ～ to the ear/eye** 难以听见/看见

imperceptibly /,ɪmpə'septəbli/ *adv* 难以察觉地 〈*change, merge*〉

imperceptive /,ɪmpə'septɪv/ *adj* 缺乏感知力的

imperfect /ɪm'pɜːfɪkt/
A *adj* 1 (faulty) 有缺陷的 〈*article, logic*〉 2 (not fully formed) 不完全的 〈*knowledge, understanding*〉; **to speak ～ Cantonese** 说疙疙瘩瘩的粤语 3 Ling 未完成时的; **the ～ tense** 未完成时
B *n* Ling 未完成时; **to use a verb in the ～** 用动词的未完成时

imperfection /,ɪmpə'fekʃn/ *n* 1 [u] (faultiness) 有缺陷 2 [c] (fault, defect) 缺陷

imperfectly /ɪm'pɜːfɪktli/ *adv* 不完善地 〈*function, operate*〉; 不完全地 〈*understand, integrated*〉

imperial /ɪm'pɪərɪəl/ *adj* 1 (of empire) 帝国的; **I～ China** 中华帝国 2 (of emperor) 皇帝的 3 Brit Meas 英制的 〈*gallon, pound, quarto*〉

imperialism /ɪm'pɪərɪəlɪzəm/ *n* [u] 帝国主义; **economic/cultural ～** 经济/文化扩张主义

imperialist /ɪm'pɪərɪəlɪst/
A *adj* 帝国主义的
B *n* 帝国主义者

imperil /ɪm'perəl/ *vt* (*pres p etc.* **-ll-** Brit, **-l-** Amer) 危及 〈*life, project, future*〉

imperious /ɪm'pɪərɪəs/ *adj* formal 专横的 〈*command, demand*〉; 傲慢的 〈*look, manner*〉

imperiously /ɪm'pɪərɪəsli/ *adv* 蛮横地

the Imperial System

英制度量衡。英国传统上采用的度量衡制度。1825 年开始实施。1965 年起，英国开始采用公制度量衡（metric system），英制单位逐渐淡出。1995 年开始，英国所有的包装说明都必须使用公制单位。但为了照顾传统人士，法律允许同时标注英制单位。在日常生活中，人们仍用英尺（foot）、英寸（inch）表示身高，如 5 feet 7，表示 5 英尺 7 英寸。路标上仍用英里（mile）表示里程。表示体重仍常用英石（stone，等于 14 磅，6.35 公斤）。美国的传统单位（customary unit，亦称 standard unit，即标准单位）来源于英制单位，但稍有区别，目前仍在使用，而公制单位只用于科学研究中。

imperishable /ɪm'perɪʃəbl/ *adj* 1 (not subject to decay) 不会腐烂的 〈*material*〉 2 (enduring) 永存的 〈*memory, truth*〉

impermanent /ɪm'pɜːmənənt/ *adj* 临时的 〈*arrangement, situation*〉

impermeable /ɪm'pɜːmɪəbl/ *adj* 不可渗透的 〈*substance, membrane*〉

impermissible /,ɪmpə'mɪsəbl/ *adj* 不允许的 〈*means, experimentation*〉

impersonal /ɪm'pɜːsənl/ *adj* 1 (objective) 客观的 〈*assessment, criticism*〉; 中立的 〈*decision, selection*〉 2 (formal) 不带个人色彩的 〈*letter, meeting*〉 3 (aloof, cold) 冷淡的 〈*manner, stare*〉 4 (anonymous) 平常无奇的 〈*building, room*〉 5 Ling 无人称的 〈*verb*〉

impersonality /ɪm,pɜːsə'næləti/ *n* [u] 1 (objectivity) 客观 2 (coldness of person, manner, style) 冷淡 3 (anonymity of building, room) 平常无奇

impersonally /ɪm'pɜːsənəli/ *adv* 1 (objectively) 客观地 〈*assess, account, choose, decide*〉 2 Ling 无人称地 〈*use*〉

impersonate /ɪm'pɜːsəneɪt/ *vt* 1 (imitate) 模仿 〈*person, animal*〉; 模拟 〈*sound*〉 2 (pretend to be) 冒充 〈*person*〉

impersonation /ɪm,pɜːsə'neɪʃn/ *n* [u and c] 模仿; **to do an ～ (of sb.)** 作模仿（某人的）表演

impersonator /ɪm'pɜːsəneɪtə(r)/ *n* 滑稽模仿秀演员

impertinence /ɪm'pɜːtɪnəns/ *n* [u] 不礼貌; **to be the height of ～ to do sth.** 做某事无礼至极; **to have the ～ to do sth.** 无礼地做某事

impertinent /ɪm'pɜːtɪnənt/ *adj* 不礼貌的; **to be ～ to sb.** 对某人不礼貌; **to be ～ to do sth.** 做某事不礼貌

impertinently /ɪm'pɜːtɪnəntli/ *adv* 不礼貌地

imperturbable /,ɪmpə'tɜːbəbl/ *adj* 冷静的; **to remain ～** 保持镇定

imperturbably /,ɪmpə'tɜːbəbli/ *adv* 冷静地; **～ calm** 镇定自若的; **～ polite** 沉着有礼貌的

impervious /ɪm'pɜːvɪəs/ *adj* 1 (impermeable) 不能渗透的 〈*substance, layer*〉; **to be ～ to sth.** 防某物渗透 2 (unaffected) 不为所动的; **to be ～ to pain/fear/threats** 能忍受疼痛/不畏惧/不怕威胁; **to be ～ to criticism/reason** 能忍受批评/不可理喻

impetigo /,ɪmpɪ'taɪgəʊ/ ▸ **p. 377** *n* [u] 脓疱病

impetuosity /ɪm,petʃʊ'ɒsəti/ *n* [u] 冲动

impetuous /ɪm'petʃʊəs/ *adj* 鲁莽的 〈*person, personality, action, behaviour, response*〉

impetuously /ɪm'petʃʊəsli/ *adv* 鲁莽地 〈*act, behave, respond*〉; **it was an ～ foolhardy thing to do** 做那事真是冲动莽撞

impetuousness /ɪm'petʃʊəsnɪs/ *n* [u] **= impetuosity**

impetus /'ɪmpɪtəs/ *n* 1 [u] Phys 动力; **to give (an) ～ to sth.** 推动某物; **to gain ～** 加大动力; **under its own ～** 依靠自身惯性 2 [u] fig (momentum) 推动力; **to gain/lose ～** 加大/减弱势头 3 [u and c] fig (stimulus) 促进因素; **to give (an) ～ to sth.** 促进某事; **a financial ～ to industrial development** 促进产业发展的财政因素

impiety /ɪm'paɪəti/ *n* [u] formal 1 Relig (lack of reverence) 不敬神 2 (disrespect) 失敬

impinge /ɪm'pɪndʒ/ *vi* 1 **to ～ upon** *or* **on sb./sth.** (restrict) «*situation, event*» 妨碍某人/某事; **to ～ upon sb.'s free time/weekend** 侵占某人的业余时间/周末 2 **to ～ on** *or* **upon sb./sth.** (affect) «*noise, policy*» 影响某人/某事

impious /'ɪmpɪəs/ *adj* 1 Relig (irreverent) 不敬神的 2 (disrespectful) 失礼的 〈*person, act*〉

impish /'ɪmpɪʃ/ *adj* 顽皮的 〈*child, grin, charm*〉

implacable /ɪm'plækəbl/ *adj* 无法消解的 〈*hatred, fury*〉; 坚决的 〈*demands*〉; **an ～ enemy/opponent** 死敌/死对头

implacably /ɪm'plækəbli/ *adv* 坚决地 〈*force, oppose*〉; 毫不留情地 〈*cruel, hostile*〉; **to be ～ opposed to sth.** 坚决反对某事

implant
A /ɪm'plɑːnt, Amer -'plænt/ *vt* 1 (instil) 灌输 〈*idea, principle*〉; 将…埋藏于心 〈*desire, fear*〉; **to ～ a sense of justice in students** 培养学生的正义感 2 Med 移植 〈*organ*〉; 植入 〈*electrode*〉; **to ～ sth. in sb.** 把某物植入某人体内
B /'ɪmplɑːnt, Amer -plænt/ *n* 移植物; **to have an ～** 接受移植

implantation /,ɪmplɑː'nteɪʃn, Amer -plænt-/ *n* [u] 移植

implausible /ɪm'plɔːzəbl/ *adj* 不合情理的 〈*story, excuse*〉; **an ～ liar** 难以自圆其说的撒谎者

implausibly /ɪm'plɔːzəbli/ *adv* 不合情理地 〈*claim, maintain*〉

implement
A /'ɪmplɪmənt/ *n* 工具; **a farm/household/gardening ～** 农具/家庭用具/园艺工具; **a set of ～s** 一套工具; **an ～ for sth./doing sth.** 用于某事/做某事的工具
B /'ɪmplɪment/ *vt* 实施 〈*plan, scheme*〉; 实践 〈*promise, suggestion, idea*〉; 执行 〈*policy, contract, decision*〉

implementation /,ɪmplɪmen'teɪʃn/ *n* [u and c] (of plan, scheme) 实施; (of promise, suggestion, idea) 实践; (of law, policy, contract, decision) 执行

implicate /'ɪmplɪkeɪt/ *vt* 1 (incriminate) «*person, evidence*» 牵连 〈*person*〉; **to ～ sb. in a crime/in espionage** 使某人卷入犯罪/谍报活动 2 **to be ～d in sth.** (be involved in) 与某坏事有牵连; **viruses are ～d in certain cancers** 病毒与某些癌症有关

implication /,ɪmplɪ'keɪʃn/ *n* 1 [u and c] (suggestion) 暗示; **by ～** 暗指地; **the ～ is that ...** 含意是… 2 [c] (consequence) 可能的结果; **to have serious** *or* **grave ～s (for sth.)** （对某事）可能产生严重后果 3 [u] (involvement) **～ in sth.** 某坏事的牵连

implicit /ɪm'plɪsɪt/ *adj* 1 (implied) 含蓄的 〈*criticism, contempt*〉; **～ consent** *or* **agreement** 默许; **to be ～ in sth.** 暗含于某事中 2 (absolute) 绝对的 〈*faith, trust, confidence*〉 3 (inherent) 内在的 〈*meaning, emotion*〉; 内含的 〈*knowledge*〉; **the values ～ in the school ethos** 校风中蕴含的价值观

implicitly /ɪm'plɪsɪtli/ *adv* 1 (by implication) 含蓄地; **to be ～ against sth.** 含蓄地反对某事 2 (completely) 绝对地; **to trust sb./sth. ～** 完全相信某人/某事

implied /ɪm'plaɪd/ *adj* 含蓄的 〈*criticism, approval*〉; **～ consent** 默许

implode /ɪm'pləʊd/ *vi* 1 (collapse inwards) 内爆 2 (fail completely) «*organization, system*» 崩溃

implore /ɪm'plɔː(r)/ *vt* 1 (plead with) 恳求; **to ～ sb. to do sth.** 恳求某人做某事 2 liter (beg) 恳求得到 〈*mercy*〉; **I ～ your forgiveness** 我恳求你原谅

i

imploring /ɪmˈplɔːrɪŋ/ *adj* 恳求的 ‹*look, tone, voice*›

imploringly /ɪmˈplɔːrɪŋli/ *adv* 恳求地; **to look at sb.** ～ 哀求地看着某人; **to ask sb.** ～ **to do sth.** 恳求某人做某事

implosion /ɪmˈpləʊʒn/ *n* 1 (collapse) 内爆 2 (failure of organization, system) 崩溃

imply /ɪmˈplaɪ/ *vt* 1 (insinuate, suggest) 暗示 ‹*attitude, decision*›; **to** ～ **that ...** 暗示… 2 (entail, indicate) 意味着; **rights** ～ **obligations** 权利意味着义务; **to** ～ **that ...** 意味着…; **her success implies that she has some ability** 她的成功说明她有一定的能力 3 (mean) «*term, word*» 表示; **iron meteorites are, as their name implies, composed mainly of iron** 铁陨石, 顾名思义, 其主要成分是铁

impolite /ˌɪmpəˈlaɪt/ *adj* 不礼貌的; **to be** ～ **to sb.** 对某人不礼貌; **to be** ～ **of sb. to do sth.** 某人做某事是不礼貌的

impolitely /ˌɪmpəˈlaɪtli/ *adv* 不礼貌地

impoliteness /ˌɪmpəˈlaɪtnɪs/ *n* [u] 不礼貌

impolitic /ɪmˈpɒlɪtɪk/ *adj* 不明智的; **to be** ～ **to do sth.** 做某事是不明智的

imponderable /ɪmˈpɒndərəbl/
A *adj* 难以估量的 ‹*factor*›; 难以预料的 ‹*consequences*›
B *n* 难以衡量的事物

import
A /ˈɪmpɔːt/ *n* 1 [c] Comm (act of importing) 进口; (item of merchandise imported) 进口货物; (service) 输入劳务; **the volume/level of** ～**s** 进口量/进口水平; ～ **surplus** 入超; ～ **surcharge** 进口附加税; ～ **quota** 输入限额 2 [c] (cultural borrowing) 文化输入物 [如词语、观念等] 3 [u] formal (meaning) 含义; **the** ～ **of sth.** 某事的含义 4 [u] formal (importance) 重要性; **of no (great) political** ～ 政治上不(很)重要的; **to be of** ～ **to sth.** 对某事重要
B /ɪmˈpɔːt/ *vt* 1 Comm 进口 ‹*goods, services*› 2 (introduce) 引进 ‹*word, ideas*› 3 Comput 输入 ‹*data, file*›

importance /ɪmˈpɔːtns/ *n* [u] 1 (significance) 重要性; **to be of national/strategic/historic** ～ 有全国性/战略上/历史上的重要性; **the** ～ **of sth. to sth.** 某物对某事的重要性; **it is of vital** ～ **to us that the pound should remain stable** 保持英镑稳定对我们来说至关重要; **to assume growing** ～ 具有越来越强的重要性; **to attach** *or* **lend** *or* **give** ～ **to sth.** 赋予某物重要性; **a matter of (great)** ～ 一桩(十分)要紧的事 2 (high rank, status) 重要地位; **a person of** ～ 要人; **a position of** ～ 重要地位; **a figure of no** ～**, nobody of any** ～ 无足轻重的人; **to be full of one's own** ～ 妄自尊大

important /ɪmˈpɔːtnt/ *adj* 1 (of great significance) 重要的; **to be** ～ **to do sth.** 做某事很重要; **not to be at all** *or* **in the least** ～ 毫不重要; **I earn good money, but, more** ～**, I enjoy my work** 我赚钱很多, 但更重要的是, 我干得很开心; **an** ～ **point** 要点; **the** ～ **thing is that ...** 重要的是…; **to be** ～ **for sb./sth.** 对某人/某事很重要; **to be** ～ **for sb. to do sth.** 做某事对某人来说很重要; **it is** ～ **to sth./sb. that ...** …对某事/某人来说很重要 2 (influential, of high rank) 重大的 ‹*event*›; 地位高的 ‹*person*›; **to look** *or* **appear** ～ 显得重要; **to feel** ～ 感到自己很重要

importantly /ɪmˈpɔːtntli/ *adv* 1 (significantly) 重要地; **most/more** ～**, it means ...** 最/更重要的是, 这意味着… 2 (pompously) 自命不凡地 ‹*behave, boast*›

importation /ˌɪmpɔːˈteɪʃn/ *n* [u] 1 Comm 进口 2 (introduction of culture, custom) 引进

import duty *n* [u and c] 进口关税

imported /ɪmˈpɔːtɪd/ *adj* 进口的

importer /ɪmˈpɔːtə(r)/ *n* (person, company) 进口商; (country) 进口国; **a car/oil** ～ 汽车/石油进口公司; **a net** ～ **of sth.** 某商品的净进口国

import-export
A *adj attrib* 进出口的 ‹*merchant, trade*›
B *n* [u] 进出口业

importing /ɪmˈpɔːtɪŋ/ *adj attrib* 进口的; **an oil-**～ **country/company** 石油进口国/公司

import licence *n* 进口许可证

importunate /ɪmˈpɔːtʃʊnət/ *adj* formal 再三的 ‹*demand*›; 胡搅蛮缠的 ‹*person*›

importune /ˌɪmpɔːˈtjuːn/ *vt* formal 纠缠; **to** ～ **sb. with sth.** 因某事对某人胡搅蛮缠; **to** ～ **sb. for sth.** 再三向某人要求某物; **to** ～ **sb. to do sth.** 强求某人做某事

impose /ɪmˈpəʊz/
A *vt* 1 (enforce) 强制实行 ‹*restriction, penalty, sanctions*›; 强行收取 ‹*charge, fine*›; **to** ～ **sth. on sb.** 把某事强加于某人; **to** ～ **a sentence of five years on sb.** 判处某人5年徒刑; **to** ～ **silence on the class** 硬让全班安静下来; **to** ～ **a tax** 征税 2 (force on others) 将…强加于人; **to** ～ **one's opinions on sb.** 勉强某人接受自己的想法; **to** ～ **one's presence on sb.** 让某人意识到自己在场
B *vi* 利用; **to** ～ **on sb.'s kindness/hospitality** 利用某人的仁慈/好客; **I do hope I'm not imposing** 真希望我没有添麻烦
C *v refl* **to** ～ **oneself on sb.** 使某人接受自己

imposing /ɪmˈpəʊzɪŋ/ *adj* 壮观的 ‹*ceremony, landscape*›; 雄伟的 ‹*building, facade*›; 使人印象深刻的 ‹*appearance, personality*›

imposition /ˌɪmpəˈzɪʃn/ *n* 1 [u] (of sanctions, restraints, penalties) 施加; (of tax) 征收 2 [c] (unwelcome demand) 过分的要求; **it was rather an** ～ *or* **something of an** ～ 这很过分

impossibility /ɪmˌpɒsəˈbɪləti/ *n* 1 [u] (state of being impossible) 不可能; **the** ～ **of doing sth.** 做某事的不可能性 2 [c] (impossible thing) 不可能的事; **a physical/logical** ～ 实际上/逻辑上不可能的事; **it's a near** ～ **that he'll get out of the city alive** 他几乎不可能活着出城

impossible /ɪmˈpɒsəbl/
A *adj* 1 (not possible) 不可能完成的 ‹*task, plan*›; **it is** ～ **(for sb.) to do sth.** (某人)做某事是不可能的; **to become** ～ 变得不可能 2 (implausible) 不合情理的 ‹*story, excuse*›; (absurd, unreasonable) 荒唐的 ‹*suggestion, notion*›; **(that's)** ～**! I can't believe it!** (那)太荒唐了! 我无法相信! 3 (unattainable) 遥不可及的 ‹*dream, goal*› 4 (very difficult) 极艰难的 ‹*situation, life*›; 过分的 ‹*demand, pressure(s)*› 5 colloq (awkward, unreasonable) 难对付的 ‹*person*›
B *n* [u] **the** ～ 不可能的事; **to achieve the** ～ 达到不可能实现的目标

impossibly /ɪmˈpɒsəbli/ *adv* 1 (inconceivably) 难以置信地; **to be** ～ **difficult/expensive** 难得/贵得令人难以置信 2 (extremely) 极度地 ‹*crazy, rude*›; 非常 ‹*exciting, beautiful*›

impost /ˈɪmpəʊst/ *n* Amer 税

impostor, imposter /ɪmˈpɒstə(r)/ *n* 冒名顶替者

imposture /ɪmˈpɒstʃə(r)/ *n* 冒名行骗

impotence /ˈɪmpətəns/ *n* [u] 1 (powerlessness) 无能 2 (lack of sexual power) 阳痿

impotent /ˈɪmpətənt/ *adj* 1 (powerless) 无能的; **to be** ～ **to do sth.** 无能力做某事; **the air attack rendered our forces** ～ 空袭令我方部队束手无策 2 (lacking in sexual power) 阳痿的; **to be/become** ～ 阳痿/变得阳痿

impound /ɪmˈpaʊnd/ *vt* 扣押 ‹*goods, property*›

impoverish /ɪmˈpɒvərɪʃ/ *vt* 使…贫穷 ‹*people, society*›; 使…贫瘠 ‹*soil*›

impoverished /ɪmˈpɒvərɪʃt/ *adj* 贫穷的 ‹*person, society, area*›; 贫瘠的 ‹*soil*›; **culturally** ～ 文化贫乏的

impoverishment /ɪmˈpɒvərɪʃmənt/ *n* [u] 贫穷

impracticability /ɪmˌpræktɪkəˈbɪləti/ *n* [u] 不可行

impracticable /ɪmˈpræktɪkəbl/ *adj* 不可行的 ‹*scheme, suggestion*›; **to be** ～ **to do sth.** 做某事不可行

impractical /ɪmˈpræktɪkl/ *adj* 1 (unworkable) 不现实的 ‹*plan, suggestion*› 2 (without practical skills) 无实践能力的 ‹*person*› 3 (unsuitable for use) 不适合穿的 ‹*clothes*›

impracticality /ɪmˌpræktɪˈkæləti/ *n* [u] 1 (unworkability of plan, idea) 不现实 2 (lack of practical skills) 无实践能力 3 (unsuitability of clothes) 不宜穿着

imprecation /ˌɪmprɪˈkeɪʃn/ *n* formal 咒语

imprecise /ˌɪmprɪˈsaɪs/ *adj* 不准确的 ‹*term, estimate*›; 含糊的 ‹*notion, idea*›

imprecision /ˌɪmprɪˈsɪʒn/ *n* [u] 不精确

impregnable /ɪmˈpregnəbl/ *adj* 1 (impenetrable) 坚不可摧的 ‹*fortress*›; 攻不破的 ‹*defences*›; **to be** ～ **to attack** 坚不可摧 2 (unassailable) 不可动摇的 ‹*self-confidence, self-assurance*›; **(to build up) an** ～ **lead** (逐步建立起)不可动摇的领先地位 3 (irrefutable) 无可辩驳的 ‹*argument, truth*›

impregnate /ˈɪmpregneɪt, Amer ɪmˈpreg-/ *vt* 1 (soak, saturate) «*marinade*» 腌 ‹*food*›; «*detergent*» 浸泡 ‹*clothes*›; «*rain, dew*» 湿润 ‹*soil, wood*›; **to be** ～**d with sth.** 浸透某物; **to** ～ **sth. with sth.** 以某物浸渍某物 2 fig liter (pervade) 充满; **an atmosphere** ～**d with tension** 十分紧张的气氛 3 formal (make pregnant) 使妊娠

impregnation /ˌɪmpregˈneɪʃn/ *n* [u] 1 (of wood, material) 浸透 2 formal (of female, egg) 受精

impresario /ˌɪmprɪˈsɑːrɪəʊ/ *n* 经理

impress /ɪmˈpres/
A *vt* 1 (arouse respect in) 使钦佩; **to** ～ **sb. with sth.** 因某事物令某人敬佩; **to be** ～**ed by** *or* **with sb./sth.** 对某人/某事物印象深刻; **she** ～**ed the examiners** 她给考官们留下了好印象; **we were greatly** ～**ed by his footballing skills** 他踢足球的技巧让我们赞叹不已; **we were not** ～**ed by his feeble excuses** 我们不为他那些站不住脚的借口所动; **this child** ～**ed me as unusually mature** 这孩子异乎寻常地成熟, 给我留下了深刻的印象 2 **to** ～ **sth. on** *or* **upon sb.** (emphasize to sb.) 使某人铭记 ‹*importance, value, danger*›; **I must** ～ **on you the need to study hard** 我必须让你认识到努力学习的必要性; **the teacher** ～**ed on** *or* **upon us that we should be punctual** 老师让我们记住应当守时 3 (imprint) 压印; **to** ～ **a pattern on (the surface of) a plate** 在盘子(的表面)上压印图案; **to** ～ **a seal in the wax** 在蜡上盖印章
B *vi* 留下好印象; **he only did it to** ～ 他这么做只是为了哗众取宠; **his efforts/the film failed to** ～ 他的努力/这部电影没有引起注意
C *n* 1 (act of impressing) 压印; **bluish marks made by the** ～ **of his fingers** 他用手指按下的浅蓝色印记 2 (mark) 压痕; **the** ～ **of a seal in the soft wax** 印章在软蜡上留下的戳记

impression /ɪmˈpreʃn/ *n* 1 (impact, perception) 印象; **to make a good/bad** ～ **(on sb.)** (给某人)留下好/坏印象; **to make** *or* **create a good** ～ **at (the) interview** 面试时给人留下好印象; **his singing made quite an** ～ **on us** 他的演唱给我们留下了深刻印象; **what is your** ～ **of the new secretary?** 你对新秘书印象如何?; **she gives an** ～ **of vulnerability** 她给人的印象是弱不禁风; **first** ～**s are often deceptive** 第一印象往往靠不住 2 (vague idea or belief) 感觉; **she had the** ～ **that she had seen him before** 她觉得以前见过他; **to be under the** ～ **that ...** 以为… 3 (imitation) 滑稽模仿; **to do** ～**s/an** ～ **(of sb./sth.)** (对某人/某事物)进行滑稽模仿 4 (representation) 印象画; **an artist's** ～ **of the attacker** 画家为袭击者画的印象画 5 (difference) 效果; **the floor was too dirty**

i

for the mop to make much (of an) ～ 地板太脏了，用拖把拖不干净 **6** (of foot, finger, seal, etc.) 压痕; **to leave an ～ in the mud** 在泥地上留下痕迹 **7** Print, Publg (unaltered reprint) 重印本; (process) 重印; (total number of copies) 印数

impressionable /ɪmˈpreʃənəbl/ *adj* 易受影响的; **at an ～ age** 处于易受外界影响的年龄

Impressionism /ɪmˈpreʃənɪzəm/ *n* [u] 印象派

Impressionist /ɪmˈpreʃənɪst/
A *n* Art 印象派画家; Mus 印象派作曲家; Literat 印象派作家
B *adj* 印象派的

impressionistic /ɪmˌpreʃəˈnɪstɪk/ *adj* **1** (based on impressions) 凭印象的 ‹*view, description*› **2** **Impressionistic** Art 印象派的

impressive /ɪmˈpresɪv/ *adj* (making a strong impression) 令人印象深刻的; (big, important) 很大的 ‹*number*›; 使人敬畏的 ‹*position*›

impressively /ɪmˈpresɪvli/ *adv* 令人印象深刻地

imprimatur /ˌɪmprɪˈmeɪtə(r), -ˈmɑːtə(r)/ *n* formal or hum 正式批准; **to give sth. one's ～** 对某事物表示同意

imprint
A /ɪmˈprɪnt/ *vt* **1** (stamp, mark) 压印 ‹*seal, foot*›; 留下…的印记 ‹*tyre mark, footprint*›; 在…上盖印 ‹*letter, product*›; **to ～ sth. in/on sth.** 在某物上印下某物; **to ～ sth. with a stamp** 在某物上盖印 **2** (make firm) 铭刻 ‹*image, idea*›; **the day ～ed itself forever in his memory** 这一天永远铭刻在他的记忆中
B /ˈɪmprɪnt/ *n* **1** (mark) 印记 **2** (deep impression) 深刻影响; **to leave an ～** 留下持久的影响; **to bear the ～ of sth.** 有某事物的印记 **3** Publg (on title page) 出版说明; (publishing house) [出版社的] 品牌; **to be published under the Clarendon ～** 以克拉伦登的品牌出版

imprinting /ɪmˈprɪntɪŋ/ *n* [u] 印刻作用 [动物生命早期的一种学习机能]

imprison /ɪmˈprɪzn/ *vt* 关押; **to be ～ed for sth./doing sth.** 因某事物/做了某事而遭监禁; **to be ～ed for ten years** 被囚 10 年; **I was ～ed in the office until midnight** (trapped) 我被关在办公室里一直到半夜

imprisonment /ɪmˈprɪznmənt/ *n* [u] 监禁; **to be sentenced to ten years'/life ～** 被判 10 年/终身监禁

improbability /ɪmˌprɒbəˈbɪləti/ *n* **1** [u] (of sth. happening or being true) 不大可能性 **2** [c] (unlikely event) 不大可能的事; **a statistical ～** 统计学上来说不太可能的事

improbable /ɪmˈprɒbəbl/ *adj* **1** (unlikely to happen) 不大可能发生的; **it is ～ that ...** …是不太可能发生的 **2** (unlikely to be true) 未必真实的 **3** (unexpected and inauthentic) 奇异的 ‹*name, statue*›

improbably /ɪmˈprɒbəbli/ *adv* 不大可能地; **her hair was ～ red** 她的头发居然是红的; **still more ～, the results show that ...** 更出人意料的是，结果表明…

impromptu /ɪmˈprɒmptjuː, Amer -tuː/
A *adj* (improvised) 即兴的 ‹*performance, speech*›; (last-minute) 临时的 ‹*party, change of plan*›
B *adv* 即兴地
C *n* 即兴曲

improper /ɪmˈprɒpə(r)/ *adj* **1** (inappropriate) 不合时宜的; (indecent) 不得体的 ‹*conduct, story, joke*› **2** (illegal) 非法的 **3** (incorrect) 不正确的; (unfit) 不适用的 ‹*tool, drug*›; (non-standard) 非标准的 ‹*term, usage*›; Sport 犯规的 ‹*tactics*›

improper: ～ fraction *n* 假分数; **～ integral** *n* 广义积分

improperly /ɪmˈprɒpəli/ *adv* **1** (inappropriately) 不合适地; (indecently) 不体面地 **2** (illegally) 违法地 **3** (incorrectly) 不正确地

impropriety /ˌɪmprəˈpraɪəti/ *n* [c and u] **1** (misconduct) 不当行为; **to commit an ～** 做出欠妥的事; **to behave with ～** 行为欠妥 **2** (indecency) 不得体的话 **3** (irregularity) 不正当行为; **financial ～** 财政问题

improve /ɪmˈpruːv/
A *vt* **1** (qualitatively) 改善; **to ～ a service/the soil/the kitchen** 改进服务/改良土壤/整修厨房; **to ～ one's memory** 增强记忆力; **to ～ one's German** 提高德语水平; **the new arrangements did not ～ matters** 那些新的安排于事无补 **2** (quantitatively) (by increasing) 增加 ‹*pay, yield*›; (by decreasing) 减少 ‹*fuel consumption, unemployment figures*›; **to ～ wages** 加薪; **to ～ efficiency/productivity** 提高效率/生产率; **to ～ delivery times/the mortality rate** 缩短送货时间/降低死亡率 **3** (make better in character, education) 提高…的修养; (make better in social status, wealth) 改善…的境况; **young offenders are rarely ～d by imprisonment** 监禁很少使青少年罪犯改邪归正; **I was anxious to ～ myself** 我急于提高自己
B *vi* **1** (qualitatively) 改善; **her handwriting hasn't ～d** 她的书写没有长进; **the town ～s on closer acquaintance** 这座城市熟悉之后给人的感觉更好; **most good wines ～ with age** 大多数好的葡萄酒愈陈愈香; **she is slowly improving in health, her health is slowly improving** 她的健康状况在慢慢好转 **2** (quantitatively) (by increasing) «*productivity, rate*» 增加; (by decreasing) «*fuel consumption, unemployment figures, delivery times*» 减少; **teachers' pay has ～d** 教师的工资提高了; **the value of the house is improving all the time** 房子一直在升值

Phrasal verb
- **improve on, improve upon** *vt* [～ **on** *or* **upon sth.**] 比…更好; **she has ～d on last year's performance** 她的业绩超过了去年

improvement /ɪmˈpruːvmənt/ *n* [c and u] **1** (in quality) 改善; **an ～ in East-West relations** 东西方关系的改善; **she has shown some ～ in maths** 她的数学成绩有所提高; **there has been no further ～ in her condition** 她的病情没有进一步好转; **there's room for ～ in your work** 你的工作仍有改进的余地 **2** (in quantity) (increase) 增加; (decrease) 减少; **a significant ～ in the sales figures** 销售数字的大幅增长; **there has been an ～ in the infant mortality rate** 婴儿死亡率降低了 **3** (better condition) 改进之处; (sth. better) 改善的事物; **what do you think of my new hairstyle? — it's an ～** 你觉得我的新发型怎么样？——比原来的好; **the new edition is a considerable ～ on the old one** 新版本较旧版本有了很大的改进 **4** (to building, road) 整修; **to make/carry out ～s to the house** 对房屋进行整修; **a road ～ scheme** 道路修缮计划

improvement grant *n* Brit 物业维修补助金

improver /ɪmˈpruːvə(r)/ *n* Brit **1** (student) 中级学习者 **2** (in flour, soil) 改良剂

improvidence /ɪmˈprɒvɪdəns/ *n* [u] formal **1** (lack of foresight) 缺乏远见 **2** (lack of thrift) 挥霍

improvident /ɪmˈprɒvɪdənt/ *adj* formal **1** (lacking foresight) 缺乏远见的; **an ～ lifestyle** 不顾未来的生活方式 **2** (lacking thrift) 挥霍的

improvisation /ˌɪmprəvaɪˈzeɪʃn, Amer *also* ɪmˌprɒvəˈzeɪʃn/ *n* **1** [u] (extemporization) 即兴创作 **2** [u] (act of improvising) 临时拼凑; **an instance of clever ～** 急中生智的拼凑 **3** [c] (work of art) 即兴作品; (improvised solution) 临时拼凑之物

improvise /ˈɪmprəvaɪz/
A *vt* **1** (extemporize) 即兴创作 ‹*song, poem, tune*›; 即兴表演 ‹*scene, play*›; **an ～d speech/accompaniment** 即兴演讲/伴奏 **2** (make from available materials) 临时做 ‹*meal, stretcher*›; **an ～d table** 临时搭的桌子
B *vi* «*poet, composer*» 即兴创作; «*performer*» 即兴表演

imprudence /ɪmˈpruːdns/ *n* [u] 轻率; **the ～ of sth./doing sth.** 某事/做某事的不谨慎

imprudent /ɪmˈpruːdnt/ *adj* 轻率的; **it is ～ (of sb.) to do sth.** （某人）做某事不明智

imprudently /ɪmˈpruːdntli/ *adv* 轻率地

impudence /ˈɪmpjʊdəns/ *n* [u] 粗鲁无礼

impudent /ˈɪmpjʊdənt/ *adj* 粗鲁的

impudently /ˈɪmpjʊdəntli/ *adv* 粗鲁地

impugn /ɪmˈpjuːn/ *vt* formal 置疑

impulse /ˈɪmpʌls/ *n* **1** [c and u] (spontaneous urge) 冲动; **to have a sudden ～ to do sth.** 突然心血来潮想做某事; **to act on (an) ～** 凭一时冲动行事 **2** [c] (stimulus) 推动力; **an ～ towards economic recovery** 经济复苏的推动力; **to give an ～ to sth./doing sth.** 促进某事/做某事 **3** [c] Physiol 神经冲动; **nerve ～s** 神经冲动 **4** [c] Elec 脉冲; **an electrical ～** 电脉冲

impulse: ～ buy, ～ purchase *ns* 冲动购买的物品; **～ buying** *n* [u] 冲动购买

impulsion /ɪmˈpʌlʃn/ *n* 冲动; **a strong ～ to do sth.** 做某事的强烈欲望

impulsive /ɪmˈpʌlsɪv/ *adj* **1** (impetuous) 冲动的 ‹*remark, action*›; 易冲动的 ‹*person, character*› **2** Phys 脉冲的; **an ～ force** 脉冲力

impulsively /ɪmˈpʌlsɪvli/ *adv* 冲动地

impulsiveness /ɪmˈpʌlsɪvnɪs/ *n* [u] 冲动

impunity /ɪmˈpjuːnəti/ *n* [u] 免于惩处; **to do sth. with ～** 有恃无恐地做某事

impure /ɪmˈpjʊə(r)/ *adj* **1** (polluted) 不纯的 ‹*liquid*›; 受污染的 ‹*air*› **2** (adulterated) 含杂质的 ‹*metal, chemical*›; 劣质的 ‹*cocaine*›

impurity /ɪmˈpjʊərəti/ *n* **1** [c] (contaminant) 杂质 **2** [u] (contamination) 污染 **3** [u] (adulteration) 不纯

imputation /ˌɪmpjuːˈteɪʃn/ formal **1** [u] (attribution) 归咎; **the ～ of sth. to sb.** 将某事归咎于某人; **no ～ of guilt or blame is intended by this remark** 这话并非指责谁有罪或须负责 **2** [c] (accusation) 指责

impute /ɪmˈpjuːt/ *vt* formal 归咎; **to ～ blame/a crime to sb.** 归咎/归罪于某人

IN *abbr* Amer = **Indiana**

in /ɪn/ ▸**p. 487**
A *prep* **1** (within enclosed space) 在…里; (within flat space) 在…上; (within sth. abstract) 在…中; **～ the dictionary/newspaper/film** 在词典里/报纸上/电影中; **～ bed/the street** 在床上/街上; **～ a group/collection** 在团队/收藏品中; **～ the city** 在市内; **～ China** 在中国; **a country ～ Africa** 一个非洲国家; **there are 31 days ～ May** 5 月有 31 天; **there are 100 centimetres ～ a metre** 1 米等于 100 厘米 **2** (into) 到…里; **to put sth. ～ one's pocket** 把某物放入口袋; **to dip a brush ～ paint** 把刷子蘸进油漆 **3** (within conditions of) 在…之中; (indicating state of) 处于…状态; **～ the darkness** 在黑暗之中; **to go out ～ the rain** 冒雨出去; **to be ～ love** 恋爱; **to be ～ full bloom** 盛开; **to be ～ good repair** 状况良好; **to put things ～ order** 把东西收拾整齐 **4** (indicating occupation) 从事; **to be ～ the army** 当兵; **to be ～ politics** 从政; **to work ～ insurance** 从事保险工作 **5** ▸**p. 181** (during) 在…期间; (within period of) 在…之内; **～ spring/May** 在春天/5 月份; **～ 1987/the twenties** 在 1987 年/20 年代; **at four ～ the morning** 在凌晨 4 点钟; **to do sth. ～ two weeks** 在两个星期之内完成某事; **～ a matter of seconds** 刹那间 **6** (at end of) 在…之后; **to be back ～ half an hour** 半个小时后回来; **～ a week** *or* **week's time** 一周以后 **7** (for) 有…之久; (since) 自…以来; **it hasn't rained ～ weeks** 已经有好几个星

期没有下雨了; **it's the first letter I've had ~ ten days** 这是我 10 天来收到的第一封信 **8** (amidst) 在…过程中; **~ the confusion, he escaped** 他趁乱逃跑了; **~ his hurry he forgot his keys** 他匆忙之间忘了钥匙 **9** (present or inherent in) 存在于; **I see his father ~ him** 我在他身上看到了他父亲的影子; **he hasn't got it ~ him to succeed** 他没有成功的气质; **there's something ~ what he says** 他所说的话有点道理; **we lost a friend ~ Jim** 我们失去了吉姆这位朋友 **10** (referring to colour, material) [表示颜色、材质]; **available ~ black/several colours** 有黑色/几种颜色供挑选; **bags ~ leather and canvas** 用皮革和帆布做成的包 **11** (indicating size) [表示尺寸]; **~ size 16** 16 号的; **~ a smaller/larger size** Clothg 尺码更小/更大的; Print, Ind 规格更小/更大的 **12** (wearing) 穿着 ‹*jeans*›; **~ a hat** 戴着帽子的; **men ~ uniform** 身穿制服的男人; **to be dressed ~ black** 穿着黑色的衣服 **13** (by means of, through the medium of) 以; **to write ~ pencil** 用铅笔书写; **to pay ~ cash** 用现金支付; **to speak ~ German** 说德语; **a book ~ Chinese** 一本中文书; **peaches ~ brandy** 用白兰地酒拌的桃子; **~ A major** 用A大调; **to speak ~ a high voice** 高声说话 **14** (as regards) 在…方面; **an expert/a class ~ physics** 物理专家/物理课; **to be rich/lacking ~ sth.** 富含/缺乏某物; **10 cm ~ length** 长 10 厘米; **equal ~ weight** 重量相等 **15** (by) 正当…; **~ doing sth.** 正当做某事的时候; **~ trying to save the child ...** 在试图营救那孩子的时候…; **~ doing so** 通过这么做 **16** (indicating range, age) 在…范围内; **to be the tallest building ~ the world** 是世界上最高的建筑物; **to be ~ the thirties** «*temperature*» 在 30 多度; **to be ~ one's twenties** 20 多岁 **17** (by units of) 按; **~ rows of 3** 3 个一排地; **~ bundles** 按束; **what is it ~ centimetres?** 按厘米算是多少? **18** (in arrangement of) [表示形状或组合] **~ a circle** 成环状; **to cut sth. ~ three** 把某物切成三部分; **a novel ~ four parts** 由四部分组成的小说 **19** (in ratios) [表示比率]; **a gradient of 1 ~ 4** 1 比 4 的倾斜度; **a one ~ five chance** 五分之一的机会; **a tax of 22 pence ~ the pound** 每英镑 22 便士的税率 **20** Brit (approximately within) [表示约数]; **~ the** *or* **their hundreds/thousands** 数以百计/千计

B *adv* **1** (into) 进入; **please come ~** 请进; **to ask** *or* **invite sb. ~** 请某人进来; **to fall ~** 掉进去; **to stir** *or* **blend sth. ~** 掺入某物 **2** (inside) 在里面; **coffee with milk ~** 加了牛奶的咖啡 **3** (at home) 在家; **to be ~** 在家; **to have an evening ~** 在家度过一个夜晚 **4** (at work) 在上班; **to come ~ early** 很早就来上班; **to come ~ two days a week** 每周来上两天班 **5** fig colloq (included) **to be ~ on sth.** 了解 ‹*secret*›; 参与 ‹*plan*›; **I wasn't ~ on it** 我对此一无所知; **to be ~ at the start** 出现在起跑线; **to be (well) ~ with sb.** (friendly) 与某人(十分)友好; (for illicit purposes) 与某人勾结(甚深) **6** fig colloq (about to experience) **to be ~ for sth.** 将经受某事; **to be ~ for a shock/surprise** 即将感到震惊/吃惊; **to be ~ for a storm** 将要遭遇暴风雨; **you're ~ for a great time** 你马上就会玩得很开心 **7** (in prison) 在监狱; **to be ~ for murder** 因犯谋杀罪而被关押 **8** (in hospital) 住院; **to be ~ for sth.** 因患某病住院; **she's ~ for a biopsy** 她住院接受活组织切片检查 **9** (arrived) **to be ~ (at six)** «*train, bus*» (6 点钟)到站; «*ferry*» (6 点钟)到码头 **10** (at high point) **to be ~** «*sea*» 涨潮; **when the tide is ~** 涨潮时 **11** Sport (within line) «*ball, shot*» 在界内; (batting) «*team, player*» 击球 **12** (gathered) 收获; **the harvest/wheat is ~** 庄稼/小麦收割了 **13** (available) 有储备; **we don't have any ~** 我们一点储备也没有; **to get sth. ~** 准备某物 **14** (submitted) 交来; **to be handed ~** «*application*» 被提交; **homework has to be ~ tomorrow** 明天必须交作业 **15** (in power) 当权; **how long have Labour been ~?** 工党当政有多长时间了?

C *adj* colloq 流行的; **short skirts are ~ again** 短裙又流行起来了; **to be the ~ thing/colour** 很时髦/是流行色

D *n* colloq **1** (access) 途径; **an ~ to sth.** 获取某物的门路 **2** (influence) 影响; **to have an ~ with sb.** 能支配某人

E **in and out** *prep phr* 进进出出; **to be ~ and out of prison all one's life** 一辈子进出监狱; **to be ~ and out of hospital a great deal** 成为医院里的常客; **to weave ~ and out of** 来回穿行于 ‹*traffic*›

F **in that** *conj phr* formal 由于; **I'm fortunate ~ that ...** 我很幸运, 因为…

G **ins** *npl* colloq **the ~s and outs (of sth.)** (某事的)详情; **to know the ~s and outs of a job** 了解工作的全部细节

in. *abbr* = **inch(es)** 英寸

inability /ˌɪnəˈbɪləti/ *n* [u] 无能; **~ to do sth.** 做某事的无能

in absentia /ˌɪn æbˈsentɪə/ *adv* formal 缺席

inaccessibility /ˌɪnæksesəˈbɪləti/ *n* [u] **1** (unreachableness) (of place) 难以到达; (of person) 难以见到 **2** (unapproachableness of person) 难以接近 **3** (abstruseness of text, theory, work) 难以理解

inaccessible /ˌɪnækˈsesəbl/ *adj* **1** (out of reach) 难以到达的 ‹*place*›; (difficult to meet) 难以见到的 ‹*person*›; (difficult to access) 难以得到的 ‹*information*›; (difficult to use) 难以使用的 ‹*data*› **2** (unapproachable) 难以接近的 ‹*person*› **3** (hard to grasp) 难以理解的 ‹*theory, writing*›

inaccuracy /ɪnˈækjərəsi/ *n* **1** [u] (of report, account, estimate, term) 不准确; (of person) 马虎; (of weapon) 不精准 **2** [c] (in account, estimate) 差错; **the report is full of inaccuracies** 这份报告错误百出

inaccurate /ɪnˈækjʊrət/ *adj* 不准确的 ‹*report, account, estimate, term*›; 马虎的 ‹*person*›; 不精准的 ‹*weapon*›

inaccurately /ɪnˈækjʊərətli/ *adv* 不准确地; **known ~ as ...** 不确切地称为…

inaction /ɪnˈækʃn/ *n* [u] (lack of action) 无行动; (state of idleness) 不活跃

inactivate /ɪnˈæktɪveɪt/ *vt* 使…失活 ‹*virus, bacteria*›; 使…失去爆炸力 ‹*bomb*›

inactive /ɪnˈæktɪv/ *adj* **1** (not active) 不活动的 ‹*person, animal*›; 懒散的 ‹*life*›; 不活跃的 ‹*mind, member of a society*›; **politically ~** 对政治不热衷的 **2** (not working) 不运转的 **3** (dormant) 休眠的 ‹*volcano*›

inactivity /ˌɪnækˈtɪvəti/ *n* [u] **1** (idleness) 无活动 **2** (inaction) 不作为; **government ~** 政府的不作为

inadequacy /ɪnˈædɪkwəsi/ *n* **1** [u] (insufficiency) 不充足; **the ~ of sth.** 某物的短缺 **2** [c] (defect) 缺点; **the inadequacies of your essay** 你的文章的不足之处

inadequate /ɪnˈædɪkwət/ *adj* **1** (insufficient) 不充分的 ‹*excuse, knowledge*›; 贫乏的 ‹*resources*›; **to be ~ to do sth./for sth.** 不足以做成某事/应付某事 **2** Psych 不胜任的; **to feel ~ to do sth.** 对做某事感到力不从心

inadequately /ɪnˈædɪkwətli/ *adv* 不充分地 ‹*expressed, planned, prepared, heated*›; 不足地 ‹*paid, rewarded*›; **it is ~ staffed** 人手不够; **~ trained** 缺乏训练的; **the presentation was ~ prepared** 讲课准备不充分

inadmissible /ˌɪnədˈmɪsəbl/ *adj* formal **1** (unacceptable) 不能接受的 ‹*proposal*›; 不允许的 ‹*behaviour*› **2** Jur 不可采纳的 ‹*evidence*›

inadvertent /ˌɪnədˈvɜːtənt/ *adj* **1** (caused by lack of attention) 粗心的 ‹*omission, error*› **2** (unintentional) 无意的 ‹*insult*›; **~ manslaughter** 过失杀人

inadvertently /ˌɪnədˈvɜːtəntli/ *adv* 不经意地

inadvisability /ˌɪnədvaɪzəˈbɪlɪti/ *n* [u] 不明智

inadvisable /ˌɪnədˈvaɪzəbl/ *adj* 不明智的; **it is ~ (for sb.) to do sth.** (某人)做某事欠妥; **~ haste** 冒失

inalienable /ɪnˈeɪlɪənəbl/ *adj* 不可剥夺的 ‹*right*›; 不可分割的 ‹*part of territory*›

inamorata /ˌɪnæməˈrɑːtə/ *n* liter or hum 情妇

inane /ɪˈneɪn/ *adj* **1** (silly) 愚蠢的 ‹*laughter, grin*› **2** (without meaning or intelligence) 无聊的 ‹*remark, chatter, conversation*›

inanely /ɪˈneɪnli/ *adv* **1** (in a silly way) 愚蠢地 ‹*grin*› **2** (without meaning) 无聊地 ‹*chatter*›

inanimate /ɪnˈænɪmət/ *adj* 无生命的 ‹*object, person*›

inanity /ɪˈnænəti/ *n* **1** [u] (of laughter, grin) 愚蠢 **2** [c] (meaningless remark) 蠢话; (meaningless act) 愚蠢的行为

inapplicable /ɪnˈæplɪkəbl, ˌɪnəˈplɪk-/ *adj* 不相干的 ‹*remark*›; 不适用的 ‹*rule*›; **to be ~ to sth./sb.** 不适用于某事/某人

inappropriate /ˌɪnəˈprəʊprɪət/ *adj* **1** (unsuitable or not useful) 不合适的 ‹*clothes*›; **to be ~ for sth.** 不适合某事; **an ~ choice for leader** 不合适的领导人选 **2** (improper) 不恰当的 ‹*behaviour, remark*›; **it is ~ (for sb.) to do sth.** (某人)做某事是不合适的 **3** (incorrect) 不适当的 ‹*title, site, treatment, advice*›

inappropriately /ˌɪnəˈprəʊprɪətli/ *adv* **1** (unsuitably) 不合适地; **to be ~ dressed** 穿着不得体 **2** (improperly) 不恰当地 ‹*behave, remark*› **3** (incorrectly) 不适当地

inappropriateness /ˌɪnəˈprəʊprɪətnɪs/ *n* [u] **1** (unsuitability) 不合适 **2** (impropriety) 不恰当 **3** (incorrectness) 不适当

inapt /ɪnˈæpt/ *adj* 不恰当的

inarticulate /ˌɪnɑːˈtɪkjʊlət/ *adj* **1** (unable to express oneself) 不善言辞的 ‹*person*›; **she was ~ with rage** 她气得语无伦次 **2** (indistinct) 含糊不清的 ‹*speech, sound*› **3** (defying expression) 难以言喻的 ‹*feeling, suffering*›

inartistic /ˌɪnɑːˈtɪstɪk/ *adj* **1** (without artistic ability) 缺乏艺术修养的 ‹*person*› **2** (lacking artistic value) 缺乏艺术性的 ‹*work*›

inasmuch as /ˌɪnəzˈmʌtʃəz/ *conj* formal **1** (in so far as) 由于; **he is guilty ~ he stole the necklace** 他偷了项链, 因此他有罪 **2** (considering that) 在…范围内; **he is an unusual musician ~ he is deaf** 他耳朵失聪, 从这点上来说, 他是个了不起的音乐家

inattention /ˌɪnəˈtenʃn/ *n* [u] 不注意

inattentive /ˌɪnəˈtentɪv/ *adj* 不注意的; **to be ~ to ...** 漠视…

inattentively /ˌɪnəˈtentɪvli/ *adv* 不注意地

inaudible /ɪnˈɔːdəbl/ *adj* 听不见的

inaudibly /ˌɪnˈɔːdəblɪ/ *adv* 听不见地

inaugural /ɪˈnɔːgjʊrəl/ *adj* **1** (first in series) 首次的 **2** (of an inauguration) 就职的

inaugurate /ɪˈnɔːgjʊreɪt/ *vt* **1** (begin, open) 为…举行开幕式 ‹*exhibition, festival, conference*› **2** (admit to office) 使…就职 ‹*bishop, official*› **3** formal (introduce) «*person, invention*» 开创 ‹*era*›; «*government*» 开始施行 ‹*policy, scheme*›

inauguration /ɪˌnɔːgjʊˈreɪʃn/ *n* [u and c] **1** (admission into office) 就职; (ceremony) 就职仪式; **~ ceremony** 就职典礼 **2** (of exhibition) 开幕式; (of era, tradition) 开端

Inauguration Day *n* Amer 总统就职日 [1月20日]

inauspicious /ˌɪnɔːˈspɪʃəs/ *adj* 不吉利的; **~ omen/wind** 凶兆/妖风

inauspiciously /ˌɪnɔːˈspɪʃəsli/ *adv* 不吉利地

in-between *adj* 中间的; **an ~ colour/state** 中间色/中间状态

i

inboard /ˈɪnbɔːd/
A *adj* 舱内的 ‹*engine, entertainment, service*›
B *adv* (towards interior) 向舱内; (inside) 在舱内

inborn /ˈɪnbɔːn/ *adj* **1** (innate) 天生的 ‹*quality, ability*›; 先天的 ‹*characteristic, propensity*› **2** (inherited) 遗传的

in-box *n* (电子邮件) 收件箱

inbred /ˌɪnˈbred/ *adj* **1** (innate) 天生的 **2** (produced by inbreeding) 近亲繁殖的

inbreeding /ɪnˈbriːdɪŋ/ *n* [u] (in animals) 同系交配; (in humans) 近亲繁殖

inbuilt /ˌɪnˈbɪlt/ *adj* **1** (ingrained) 根深蒂固的 ‹*belief, bias*›; 内在的 ‹*tendency, trait*› **2** (built-in) 内置的 ‹*microphone*›

Inc. *abbr* Amer = **incorporated** 公司; **Macron ～** 麦卡隆公司

Inca /ˈɪnkə/ *n* 印加人

incalculable /ɪnˈkælkjʊləbl/ *adj* 极大的 ‹*harm, loss, damage*›; 不可估量的 ‹*amount, value*›

incandescence /ˌɪnkænˈdesns/ *n* [u] (giving off light when heated) 白炽; (light produced through heat) 白炽光

incandescent /ˌɪnkænˈdesnt/ *adj* **1** (with heat) 炽热的 ‹*coal, glow*›; 白炽的 ‹*bulb*› **2** formal (passionate) 激情的 ‹*person*›; 激动的 ‹*emotion*›; **he was ～ with rage** 他怒不可遏

incandescent lamp *n* 白炽灯

incantation /ˌɪnkænˈteɪʃn/ *n* **1** [c] (chant) 咒语 **2** [u] (chanting) 念咒

incapability /ɪnˌkeɪpəˈbɪlɪtɪ/ *n* [u] **1** (gen) 无能力 **2** Jur 无资格

incapable /ɪnˈkeɪpəbl/ *adj* **1** (lacking ability) 无能力的; **to be ～ of sth./doing sth.** 无能力做某事 **2** (incompetent) 不能胜任的 **3** (incapacitated) 无行动能力的; **mentally ～** 脑损伤的; **drunk and ～** Jur 酒醉后无行为能力的 **4** formal **～ of sth.** (not admitting of) 不容许某事的; **actions ～ of justification** 无正当理由的行动 **5** **～ of sth.** (too caring or moral to do) 对某事不忍心的; **he is ～ of stealing** 他下不了手去偷

incapacitate /ˌɪnkəˈpæsɪteɪt/ *vt* **1** (weaken or disable) «*sickness, injury*» 使…无行动能力 ‹*person*›; **severely ～d** 严重伤残的 **2** Jur 使无资格

incapacity /ˌɪnkəˈpæsəti/ *n* [u] **1** (inability) 无能力; **～ for working** *or* **for work** 工作能力的缺乏 **2** Jur 无资格

incapacity benefit *n* [u] Brit 伤残补助金

in-car *adj attrib* 车内的; **～ stereo/entertainment system** 车内立体声/娱乐系统

incarcerate /ɪnˈkɑːsəreɪt/ *vt* formal 关押; **to ～ sb. (in sth.)** 囚禁某人 (于某处)

incarceration /ɪnˌkɑːsəˈreɪʃn/ *n* [u] formal 关押

incarnate formal
A /ɪnˈkɑːnət/ *adj usu postpos* **1** (of spirit, deity) 化身的; **the devil ～** 魔鬼的化身 **2** (in perfect or extreme form) 极端的; **here is capitalism ～** 这就是资本主义的极致
B /ˈɪnkɑːneɪt/ *vt* formal **1** (give bodily form to) 将…具体化 ‹*spirit, quality*›; **to be ～d in** *or* **as sth.** 化身为某物 **2** (embody) «*person*» 体现 ‹*virtue, tyranny*›

incarnation /ˌɪnkɑːˈneɪʃn/ *n* **1** (embodiment) 体现; **to be the ～ of sth.** 是某物的化身 **2** (life) 生命; **in a previous ～** 在前世; **her earlier ～ as a lawyer** hum 她先前的律师身份 **3** Relig **the I～** 道成肉身

incautious /ɪnˈkɔːʃəs/ *adj* 轻率的

incautiously /ɪnˈkɔːʃəsli/ *adv* 轻率地

incendiary /ɪnˈsendɪəri, Amer -dɪeri/
A *adj attrib* **1** (combustible) 能燃烧的; **～ bombs/grenades** 燃烧弹/燃烧手榴弹 **2** formal (inflammatory) 煽动性的 ‹*rhetoric, remark*›
B *n* 燃烧弹

incendiary: ～ attack *n* 火攻; **～ device** *n* 燃烧装置

incense[1] /ɪnˈsens/ *vt* 激怒; **to be ～d by** *or* **at sth.** 被某事物激怒

incense[2] /ˈɪnsens/ *n* [u] 香

incense burner *n* 香炉

incensed /ɪnˈsenst/ *adj* 大怒的

incentive /ɪnˈsentɪv/ *n* **1** [c and u] (motivation) 刺激; **to give sb. the ～ to do sth.** 刺激某人做某事; **there are no ～s for people to save** 没有鼓励人们储蓄的措施 **2** [c] Fin, Comm 优惠; **export/tax ～** 出口/税收优惠

incentive: ～ bonus, ～ payment *ns* 奖金; **～ scheme** *n* 奖励计划

incentivize /ɪnˈsentɪvaɪz/ *vt* 激励; **to ～ sb. to do sth.** 激励某人做某事

inception /ɪnˈsepʃn/ *n* [u] 开始; **from** *or* **since its ～ in 1962** 自其 1962 年创立以来

incertitude /ɪnˈsɜːtɪtjuːd/ *n* [u] formal (lack of certainty) 犹豫; (doubt) 怀疑

incessant /ɪnˈsesnt/ *adj* 持续不断的; **～ rain** 连续不断的降雨

incessantly /ɪnˈsesntli/ *adv* 持续不断地; **the wind blew ～** 风刮个不停

incest /ˈɪnsest/ *n* [u] 乱伦; **to commit ～ with sb.** 与某人乱伦

incestuous /ɪnˈsestjʊəs, Amer -tʃʊəs/ *adj* **1** (involving or guilty of incest) 乱伦的 ‹*relationship, pair*› **2** pej (excessively close) 过分亲密的 ‹*group of people*›; 排外的 ‹*society, business*›

inch /ɪntʃ/ ▸ **p. 436**
A *n* **1** Meas 英寸; **8 ～es of rain/snow** 8 英寸的降雨量/降雪量 **2** fig (small amount) 少许; **～ by ～** 一点一点地; **I cannot see an ～** 我一点儿也看不见; **to be within an ～ of death** *or* **one's life** 险些丧命; **to miss being run over by ～es** 险些被碾压; **to know every ～ of sth.** 对某事物了如指掌; **she won't give** *or* **budge an ～** 她不会作出丝毫让步; **he's every ～ an aristocrat** 他是个地地道道的贵族; **give him an ～ and he will take a mile** 他会得寸进尺
B *vi* 缓慢移动; **to ～ towards sth.** 向某物缓慢移动; **to ～ one's way along/across sth.** 一点一点地沿某处前行/穿过某处
C *vt* 使缓慢移动; **to ～ sth. in/out** *etc.* 慢慢将某物挪进来/挪出去等

Phrasal verb

- **inch up** *vi* «*inflation, interest rate, price*» 缓慢上升

inchoate /ɪnˈkəʊət, ˈɪn-/ *adj* formal **1** (rudimentary) 初步的 ‹*plan, democracy*› **2** (confused, incoherent) 混乱的 ‹*desire*›; 动摇的 ‹*feeling, thought*›

incidence /ˈɪnsɪdəns/ *n* [c and u] (occurrence) 发生; (rate of occurrence) 发生率

incident /ˈɪnsɪdənt/
A *n* **1** [c] (event in life or narrative) 发生的事; **several amusing ～s** 几桩趣事 **2** [u] (drama, excitement) 枝节; **without ～** 平安无事; **to be full of ～** 充满波折 **3** [c] (disturbance) 暴力事件; (between countries) 冲突; **a border/diplomatic/stabbing ～** 边境冲突/外交冲突/持刀伤人事件
B *adj* **1** formal **to be ～ on sth.** (result from) 由某事物导致; **the pains ～ to growing up** 成长的烦恼 **2** Phys 入射的 ‹*light, ray, beam*›

incidental /ˌɪnsɪˈdentl/
A *adj* **1** (occurring as minor consequence) 次要的; **it is ～ to my purpose** 这不是我的主要目的 **2** (attendant on) 不可避免的 ‹*responsibilities, risks*›; **to be ～ to sth.** 伴随某事物而来 **3** (minor) 附带的 ‹*remarks*›
B **incidentals** *npl* (occurrences) 杂事; (sundries) 杂项

incidental: ～ damages *npl* 附带损失; **～ expenses** *npl* 杂费

incidentally /ˌɪnsɪˈdentli/ *adv* **1** (by the way) 附带地; **～, did you see ...?** 顺便提一句, 你见过…吗?; **who, ～, owes me £10?** 顺便问一下, 谁欠了我10英镑? **2** (by chance) 偶然

incidental music *n* [u] 配乐

incident room *n* [警察局的] 专案室

incinerate /ɪnˈsɪnəreɪt/ *vt* 焚毁

incineration /ɪnˌsɪnəˈreɪʃn/ *n* [u] 焚毁

incinerator /ɪnˈsɪnəreɪtə(r)/ *n* 垃圾焚化炉

incipient /ɪnˈsɪpɪənt/ *adj* 刚开始的 ‹*uprising, quarrel*›; 早期的 ‹*disease, enmity*›

incise /ɪnˈsaɪz/ *vt* **1** (cut) 切开 ‹*wound, skin*› **2** (engrave) 雕刻 ‹*decoration, figure*›; 刻 ‹*letter*›

incision /ɪnˈsɪʒn/ *n* **1** [c] (surgical cut) 切口; (mark, decoration) 雕刻 **2** [u] (cutting) 切割

incisive /ɪnˈsaɪsɪv/ *adj* **1** (clear-thinking) 头脑敏锐的 ‹*person*›; 敏锐的 ‹*mind*› **2** (decisive) 果断的 ‹*tone, voice*› **3** (accurate, sharp) 切中要害的 ‹*report, speech, advice*›

incisively /ɪnˈsaɪsɪvli/ *adv* **1** (clearly) 头脑敏锐地 ‹*reason, analyse*› **2** (decisively) 果断地 ‹*speak, say*› **3** (accurately) 切中要害地 ‹*present, write, advise*›

incisiveness /ɪnˈsaɪsɪvnɪs/ *n* [u] **1** (clarity) (of person) 头脑敏锐; (of mind) 敏锐 **2** (decisiveness) (of tone, voice) 果断 **3** (accuracy, sharpness) (of report, advice) 切中要害

incisor /ɪnˈsaɪzə(r)/ *n* 门齿

incite /ɪnˈsaɪt/ *vt* **1** (urge, encourage) 煽动; **to ～ sb. to do sth.** 煽动某人做某事 **2** (stir up) 激起 ‹*anger, mutiny, hatred*›

incitement /ɪnˈsaɪtmənt/ *n* [u] 煽动; **～ to sth.** 对某事的刺激

incivility /ˌɪnsɪˈvɪləti/ *n* **1** [u] (rudeness) 粗鲁 **2** [c] (rude remark) 粗鲁的言语

incl. **1** = **including** 包括 **2** = **inclusive** 包括一切的; **£911 ～** 总计 911 英镑

inclement /ɪnˈklemənt/ *adj* formal 恶劣的 ‹*weather, climate*›; 寒冷的 ‹*winter*›

inclination /ˌɪŋklɪˈneɪʃn/ *n* **1** [c and u] (liking) 意愿; **to have no ～ to do sth.** 无意做某事; **to follow one's own ～(s)** 随心所欲; **she has an ～ for a quiet life/towards being on her own** 她想过安静的生活/独立自主; **my own ～ is to pay** 我本人倾向于付款 **2** [c] (disposition) 性格; **to be lazy by ～** 生性懒惰 **3** [c and u] (degree of slope) 坡度; **an ～ of 45°** 45 度的坡度 **4** [c] (bow) 弯腰; (nod) 点头; **an ～ of one's head** 点头

incline
A /ɪnˈklaɪn/ *vt* **1** (bend) 弯下 ‹*part of body*›; **to ～ one's head** 点头 **2** **to ～ sb. to do sth.** (dispose) 使某人倾向于做某事; **his sincerity ～d us to trust him** 他的真诚使我们愿意相信他 **3** (predispose) «*character trait*» 使…倾向于 ‹*person*›; **his deafness ～s him to shout** 他因为耳聋, 说起话来常常大喊大叫的 **4** (tilt) 使…倾斜 ‹*object*›
B /ɪnˈklaɪn/ *vi* **1** (bow) 弯腰; (bend the head) 点头 **2** (lean) 倾斜 **3** (tend) 倾向; **to ～ towards the opinion that ...** 倾向于认为…; **the colour of his eyes ～s to green** 他的眼珠带点绿色
C /ˈɪŋklaɪn/ *n* (slope) 斜坡; **a steep/gentle ～** 陡峭/平缓的斜坡

inclined /ɪnˈklaɪnd/ *adj* **1** (minded) 有愿望的; **to be ～ to do sth.** 想做某事; **I'm ～ to agree with you** 我打算同意你的意见 **2** (disposed, liable) 有倾向的; **to be ～ to do/be sth.** 倾向于做/是某事 **3** (with a specified talent) 有天赋的; **to be artistically/musically** *etc.* **～** 有艺术/音乐等天赋; **he is that way ～** colloq 他好那口儿; **if you feel so ～** 如果你想这样

inclined plane *n* 斜面

inclose /ɪnˈkləʊz/ *vt* = **enclose**

inclosure /ɪnˈkləʊʒə(r)/ *n* = **enclosure**

include /ɪnˈkluːd/ *vt* 1 (incorporate) 包括; **children ∼d** 包括孩子们 2 (put in, make part of) 把…算入; **the guests ∼d Jason** 贾森算在宾客中; **does that ∼ me?** 算上我了吗？; **breakfast is ∼d in the price** 价格含早餐

including /ɪnˈkluːdɪŋ/ *prep* 包括; **up to and ∼ Monday** 直到且含周一; **∼ Mary/not ∼ Mary, we'll be six** 算上/不算玛丽，我们一共6个人

inclusion /ɪnˈkluːʒn/ *n* 1 [u] (incorporation) 包括; **the ∼ of a woman in the committee** 吸纳一名女成员进入委员会; **advertisements for ∼ in next week's issue** 下周发行的一期将刊出的广告 2 [c] (included item) 被包括的项目; (included person) 被包括的人; **there were some surprising ∼s in the list** 名单包括了一些意想不到的人

inclusive /ɪnˈkluːsɪv/ *adj* 1 (with everything included) 全包括的 ‹*charge, price*› 2 (including, counting) 包括的; **sth. (not) ∼ of sth.** (不)包括某物的某物 3 (including the specified limits) 首末项包含在内的; **those aged 17-24 ∼** 年龄在17至24岁（含）的那些人 4 (not excluding any group) 不排斥任何群体的 ‹*society, policy*›

inclusively /ɪnˈkluːsɪvli/ *adv* 1 (so as to include) 全包括地; **they charged ∼ for meals** 他们的收费包括餐费 2 (including the specified limits) 包括首末项地; **occurring between 1985 and 2001 ∼** 发生在1985至2001年之间的

incognito /ˌɪŋkɒgˈniːtəʊ, Amer ɪŋˈkɒgnətəʊ/
A *adj* 化名的; **to be ∼** 使用化名; **to remain ∼** 一直隐姓埋名
B *adv* 化名地

incoherence /ˌɪŋkəʊˈhɪərəns/ *n* [u] 语无伦次

incoherent /ˌɪŋkəʊˈhɪərənt/ *adj* 1 (illogical, muddled) 不连贯的 ‹*message, style*›; 无条理的 ‹*report, account*› 2 (unintelligible) 语无伦次的 ‹*person, ramblings*›

incoherently /ˌɪŋkəʊˈhɪərəntli/ *adv* 1 (illogically, unclearly) 不连贯地 2 (unintelligibly) 语无伦次地

incombustible /ˌɪŋkəmˈbʌstəbl/ *adj* 不燃的

income /ˈɪŋkʌm/ *n* [c and u] 收入; **a (profitable) source of ∼** (赚钱的)收入来源; **to live within one's ∼** 量入为出; **to live beyond one's ∼** 入不敷出; **low-/high-/middle-∼ households** 低/高/中等收入家庭; **loss of ∼** 收入损失; **gross ∼** 总收入; **to be on an ∼ of £20,000 per year** 年薪2万英镑

income bracket, income group *ns* 收入档次

incomer /ˈɪnkʌmə(r)/ *n* esp Brit 外来者

income: ∼s policy *n* 收入政策; **∼ support** *n* [u] 低收入补助; **to be on ∼ support** 靠领取补助金度日; **∼ tax** *n* [u] 所得税; **∼ tax form** *n* 所得税申报表; **∼ tax inspector** ▸p. 409 *n* 所得税检查员; **∼ tax return** *n* 所得税申报表

incoming /ˈɪnkʌmɪŋ/
A *adj* 1 (arriving) 即将到达的 ‹*plane, passengers, ship*›; **∼ flights** 进港航班 2 (newly elected) 新当选的 ‹*official, president*›; (newly chosen) 新任的 ‹*member*›; **the ∼ government/administration** 新一届政府/行政当局 3 (received) 刚收到的 ‹*message*›; (coming in) 逼近的 ‹*tide, fire, missiles*›; **∼ mail/phone calls** 寄来的邮件/打进来的电话
B incomings *npl* 收入

incommensurable /ˌɪŋkəˈmenʃərəbl/ *adj* formal 不能相比的; **to be ∼ with sb./sth.** 与某人/某事物大相径庭

incommensurate /ˌɪŋkəˈmenʃərət/ *adj* formal 1 (disproportionate) 不相称的; (inadequate) 不足的; **to be ∼ with ...** 与…不相称; **her talents are ∼ to her ambition** 她志大才疏 2 **= incommensurable**

incommode /ˌɪŋkəˈməʊd/ *vt* formal dated 妨碍

incommunicable /ˌɪŋkəˈmjuːnɪkəbl/ *adj* 无法表达的

incommunicado /ˌɪŋkəˌmjuːnɪˈkɑːdəʊ/ *adj pred* (not allowed to communicate) 不得与外界接触的; (not able to communicate) 无法与外界接触的; (not wanting to communicate) 不愿与外界接触的; **he's currently ∼** 他现在联系不上

incomparable /ɪnˈkɒmprəbl/ *adj* 1 (without equal) 无与伦比的 ‹*beauty, talent*›; 绝美的 ‹*hair, eyes*›; 绝佳的 ‹*prose, food*›; **the ∼ Greta Garbo** 举世无双的葛丽泰·嘉宝 2 (totally different) 完全不同的; **it's ∼ with what it was** 它完全不同于以往

incomparably /ɪnˈkɒmprəbli/ *adv* 无与伦比地; **∼ the best** 绝佳的; **∼ beautiful** 美丽绝伦的

incompatibility /ˌɪŋkəmˌpætəˈbɪləti/ *n* [u] 1 (inability to harmonize) (of people) 不和睦; (of wishes, attitudes, aims) 不一致; (of colours, styles) 不协调 2 (inconsistency) 矛盾; **the ∼ of sth. with sth.** 某物与某物的矛盾 3 Med (of blood groups) 不相容; (of drugs) 配伍禁忌 4 Comput 不兼容

incompatible /ˌɪŋkəmˈpætɪbl/ *adj* 1 (not in harmony) 有冲突的 ‹*attitudes, intentions*›; 不和睦的 ‹*people*›; 不协调的 ‹*colours, styles*›; **her wishes are ∼ with his intentions** 她的愿望与他的意图相互冲突 2 (inconsistent) 矛盾的 ‹*arguments, proposals*›; 互斥的 ‹*propositions*› 3 Med 配伍禁忌的 4 Comput 不兼容的

incompetence /ɪnˈkɒmpɪtəns/, **incompetency** /ɪnˈkɒmpɪtənsɪ/ *ns* [u] 1 (ineptitude) (of professional) 不称职 2 Jur (of witness) 无资格; (of child) 无能力; (of patient) 机能不全

incompetent /ɪnˈkɒmpɪtənt/
A *adj* 1 (inept) 无能力的 ‹*doctor, plumber*›; 拙劣的 ‹*performance, leadership, attempt*›; **to be ∼ to do sth.** 无能力做某事 2 Jur 无资格的 ‹*witness*›; 无效的 ‹*testimony*›; 无行为能力的 ‹*child, patient*›
B *n* 无能的人

incompetently /ɪnˈkɒmpɪtəntli/ *adv* 无能力地

incomplete /ˌɪŋkəmˈpliːt/ *adj* 1 (unfinished) 未完成的 ‹*work*›; 未结束的 ‹*narrative*› 2 (lacking parts) 不完整的 ‹*set, collection, series*› 3 (imperfect) 不彻底的 ‹*success, victory*›

incompletely /ˌɪŋkɒmˈpliːtli/ *adv* 1 (unfinished) 未完成地 2 (with parts missing) 不完整地 3 (imperfectly) 不彻底地

incompleteness /ˌɪŋkəmˈpliːtnɪs/ *n* [u] 1 (being unfinished) 未完成 2 (having parts missing) 不完整 3 (being imperfect) 不彻底

incomprehensible /ɪnˌkɒmprɪˈhensəbl/ *adj* 1 (that cannot be understood) 无法理解的 ‹*reasoning, motives, attitude, actions*› 2 (unintelligible) 难懂的 ‹*person, speech, words*›

incomprehensibly /ɪnˌkɒmprɪˈhensəbli/ *adv* 1 (inconceivably) 无法理解地; **∼, she didn't react** 难以理解的是，她没有回应 2 (unintelligibly) 难懂地

incomprehension /ɪnˌkɒmprɪˈhenʃn/ *n* [u] 不理解; **to look at sb. in ∼** 茫然不解地看某人

inconceivable /ˌɪŋkənˈsiːvəbl/ *adj* (unbelievable) 难以置信的 ‹*number, size*›; (unimaginable) 不可思议的 ‹*success, happiness*›; **it is ∼ that ...** 难以置信的是…; **to be ∼ for sb. to do sth.** 某人做某事匪夷所思

inconceivably /ˌɪŋkənˈsiːvəbli/ *adv* 难以置信地

inconclusive /ˌɪŋkənˈkluːsɪv/ *adj* (without a conclusion) 无结论的 ‹*debate, argument*›; (indecisive) 非决定性的 ‹*vote*›; (unconvincing) 无说服力的 ‹*outcome, evidence*›; **the test results were ∼** 测试结果无定论

inconclusively /ˌɪŋkənˈkluːsɪvli/ *adv* 无结果地

incongruity /ˌɪŋkɒŋˈgruːəti/ *n* 1 [u] (of appearance, behaviour) 不合时宜; (of situation) 不协调 2 [c] (of act, event) 不相称

incongruous /ɪnˈkɒŋgrʊəs/ *adj* 不协调的 ‹*sight, sound*›; 不适宜的 ‹*remark, act*›; **it seems ∼ that ...** …似乎不合适; **a building ∼ with its surroundings** 与环境格格不入的建筑

incongruously /ɪnˈkɒŋgrʊəsli/ *adv* 不协调地; **to be ∼ modern** 现代得不合时宜

inconsequential /ɪnˌkɒnsɪˈkwenʃl/ *adj* 无关紧要的 ‹*detail, event*›; 离题的 ‹*question, conversation*›

inconsiderable /ˌɪŋkənˈsɪdrəbl/ *adj* **not ∼** 巨大的; **a not ∼ sum/reward/force** 可观的总数/不菲的奖赏/巨大的力量

inconsiderate /ˌɪŋkənˈsɪdərət/ *adj* (selfish) 不为他人着想的 ‹*person, action*›; (thoughtless) 考虑不周的 ‹*remark, reply*›; **to be ∼ towards sb.** 不为某人着想; **that was a very ∼ thing to say** 说那样的话很欠考虑

inconsiderately /ˌɪŋkənˈsɪdərətli/ *adv* 考虑不周地

inconsistency /ˌɪŋkənˈsɪstənsi/ *n* 1 [c and u] (being self-contradictory) 前后矛盾; (instance of self-contradiction) 前后矛盾处; **this report contains a number of inconsistencies** 这份报告有很多前后不一致的地方 2 [u] (variability) 反复无常; **the ∼ of her behaviour** 她的行为的变化无常

inconsistent /ˌɪŋkənˈsɪstənt/ *adj* 1 (conflicting) 反常的 ‹*actions, attitudes*›; 不一致的 ‹*statements, results*›; **to be ∼ with sth.** 与某事物相悖 2 (self-contradictory) 前后矛盾的 ‹*reasoning, account*› 3 (erratic) 反复无常的 ‹*person, behaviour*›

inconsolable /ˌɪŋkənˈsəʊləbl/ *adj* (despairing) 伤心欲绝的 ‹*person*›; **∼ grief/emotion** 极度的悲伤/悲情

inconsolably /ˌɪŋkənˈsəʊləbli/ *adv* 伤心欲绝地 ‹*cry, weep*›; 极度地 ‹*miserable, distressed*›

inconspicuous /ˌɪŋkənˈspɪkjʊəs/ *adj* 不显眼的; **to try to be ∼** 力图保持低调

inconspicuously /ˌɪŋkənˈspɪkjʊəsli/ *adv* 不显眼地

inconstancy /ɪnˈkɒnstənsi/ *n* formal 1 [u] (changeability) 多变 2 [c and u] (fickleness) 不忠实

inconstant /ɪnˈkɒnstənt/ *adj* formal 1 (changeable) 多变的 ‹*conditions, temperature*› 2 (fickle, faithless) 不忠实的 ‹*lover, friend*›; 不专一的 ‹*love, friendship*›

incontestable /ˌɪŋkənˈtestəbl/ *adj* 无可争辩的

incontinence /ɪnˈkɒntɪnəns/ *n* [u] [大小便的]失禁

incontinence pad *n* 失禁垫

incontinent /ɪnˈkɒntɪnənt/ *adj* [大小便] 失禁的

incontrovertible /ˌɪŋkɒntrəˈvɜːtəbl/ *adj* 无可争辩的 ‹*evidence, fact*›

incontrovertibly /ˌɪŋkɒntrəˈvɜːtəbli/ *adv* 无可争辩地; **it is ∼ true that ...** …无可置疑

inconvenience /ˌɪŋkənˈviːnɪəns/
A *n* 1 [u] (trouble) 不便; **to put sb. to (great** *or* **a great deal of) ∼** 给某人带来（极大的）不便; **to cause sb. ∼** 给某人造成麻烦; **to go to a great deal of ∼ to do sth.** 费尽周折做某事; **we apologize for any ∼ (caused)** 我们对（所造成的）任何不便表示道歉 2 [c] (disadvantage) 缺点; (nuisance) 麻烦事
B *vt* 给…造成不便 ‹*person*›

inconvenient /ˌɪŋkənˈviːnɪənt/ *adj* 1 (causing difficulty) 不方便的 ‹*place, arrangement*›; **the house is ∼ for working in** 这房子在里面工作很不方便 2 (inopportune) 不合适的 ‹*time, moment*›; 不凑巧的 ‹*visitor, telephone call*›; **to be ∼ for sb. (to do sth.)** 对某人来说（做某事）不合时宜 3 euph (embarrassing) 令人为难的 ‹*fact, incident*›

i

inconveniently /ˌɪŋkənˈviːnɪəntli/ *adv* 1 (awkwardly) 令人不便地 ‹*designed, located*› 2 (inopportunely) 不合时宜地 ‹*arrive, happen*›; **~ early/late** 过早/过晚

inconvertible /ˌɪŋkənˈvɜːtəbl/ *adj* 1 (not convertible to another currency) 不能兑换外币的 2 (not exchangeable to coin) 不能兑换硬币的 ‹*bank note*›

incorporate /ɪnˈkɔːpəreɪt/ *vt* 1 (include) 纳入 ‹*thoughts, suggestions*›; 收录 ‹*revision, feature*› 2 Comm, Jur 合并 ‹*business, company*›

incorporated /ɪnˈkɔːpəreɪtɪd/ *adj* 组成公司的; **Smith and Brown I~** 史密斯和布朗公司

incorporation /ɪnˌkɔːpəˈreɪʃn/ *n* [u] 1 (inclusion) 吸收; **the ~ of sth. into sth.** 某物对某物的吸收; **to collect information for ~ into sth.** 收集信息以纳入某物 2 Comm, Jur 合并

incorporeal /ˌɪŋkɔːˈpɔːrɪəl/ *adj* formal (without material form) 无形的 ‹*spirit, fear*›; (without a body) 无形体的 ‹*deity, being*›; **~ property** Jur 无形财产

incorrect /ˌɪŋkəˈrekt/ *adj* 1 (false, inaccurate) 不正确的 2 (improper, unsuitable) 不得体的 ‹*dress, behaviour*›

incorrectly /ˌɪŋkəˈrektli/ *adv* 1 (falsely) 不正确地; **we assumed ~ that ...** 我们错误地认为… 2 (improperly, unsuitably) 不得体地 ‹*dressed, behave*›

incorrectness /ˌɪnkəˈrektnɪs/ *n* [u] 1 (inaccuracy) 不正确 2 (impropriety) 不适当

incorrigible /ɪnˈkɒrɪdʒəbl, Amer -ˈkɔːr-/ *adj* 屡教不改的; **she's an ~ romantic** pej 她不可救药地耽于幻想

incorrigibly /ɪnˈkɒrɪdʒəbli, Amer -ˈkɔːr-/ *adv* 屡教不改地

incorruptible /ˌɪŋkəˈrʌptəbl/ *adj* 1 (honest, unbribable) 廉洁的 ‹*official, lawyer*› 2 (imperishable) 不会腐蚀的 ‹*substance*›

increase

A /ɪnˈkriːs/ *vi* 1 (become larger) 增加; **the population has ~d from 70,000 to 90,000** 人口已经从7万增长到了9万; **the value of the house has ~d by 25%** 房子增值了25%; **to ~ in speed** 加速; **petrol has ~d in price** 汽油价格上涨了 2 (become more intense) 增强; **her anger ~d** 她怒气更大了; **the pain is increasing (in intensity)** 越来越疼了; **the rain ~d** 雨下大了; **the darkness ~d** 天越来越黑了 3 (in knitting) 放针

B /ɪnˈkriːs/ *vt* 1 (make greater) 增加; **to ~ the value of a property** 使某房产升值; **giving up smoking may ~ life expectancy by 10 years** 戒烟可以使预期寿命延长10年; **she ~d her speed from 60 to 70 mph** 她把速度从每小时60英里提高到70英里 2 (intensify) 增强; **to ~ volume** 调高音量; **the news ~d our anxiety** 这一消息使我们更加焦虑 3 (in knitting) 放; **to ~ one stitch** 放一针

C /ˈɪŋkriːs/ *n* 1 (in amount) 增加; **a price/pay ~** 涨价/加薪; **a massive ~ in unemployment** 失业人数的大幅增长; **a 5% ~, an ~ of 5%** 5%的增长; **(to be) on the ~** 正在增加; **the problem of illiteracy is on the ~** 文盲问题越来越严重 2 (in intensity) 增强; **a further ~ in effort is needed** 需要更加努力; **an ~ in support for sb./sth.** 对某人/某事物更多的支持; **(to be) on the ~** 正在增强

increased /ɪŋˈkriːst/ *adj* (in size, amount, weight, etc.) 增加的; (in intensity) 增强的; **an ~ risk of cancer/injury** 患癌症/受伤的更大风险; **the bomb attacks led to ~ security** 炸弹袭击使安全措施变得更加严密

increasing /ɪŋˈkriːsɪŋ/ *adj* 1 (growing) 正在增加的; **an ~ number of people** 越来越多的人; **the ~ value of the investment** 不断增长的投资价值 2 (intensifying) 正在增强的; **an atmosphere of ~ tension** 越来越紧张的气氛; **the ~ pain** 不断加剧的疼痛

increasingly /ɪŋˈkriːsɪŋli/ *adv* 1 (more and more) 越来越; **~ fierce competition** 日益激烈的竞争 2 (more and more frequently) 越来越频繁地; **~, companies are having to put up prices** 各家公司不得不愈加频繁地涨价

incredible /ɪnˈkredəbl/ *adj* 1 (beyond belief) 难以置信的 ‹*behaviour, size, story*› 2 colloq (wonderful) 美妙的

incredibly /ɪnˈkredəbli/ *adv* 1 (extremely) 极其 ‹*large, beautiful*› 2 (unbelievably) 难以置信地; **~, she didn't hear a thing** 真是难以置信，她什么也没听见

incredulity /ˌɪŋkrɪˈdjuːləti, Amer -duː-/ *n* [u] 不相信; **a look** *or* **expression of ~** 一副怀疑的表情; **sb.'s ~ at sth.** 某人对某事物的怀疑; **~ that sth. could happen/has happened** 对某事能发生/已发生的怀疑

incredulous /ɪnˈkredjʊləs, Amer -dʒə-/ *adj* 不相信的 ‹*look, expression*›; **he was ~ at your success** 他对你的成功表示怀疑; **I was ~ that ...** 我不相信…

incredulously /ɪnˈkredjʊləsli, Amer -dʒə-/ *adv* 不相信地

increment /ˈɪŋkrəmənt/ *n* 1 (on salary) 加薪; (in value) 增值; **an unearned ~** 自然增值 2 (addition) 增加; **an ~ in growth** 增长

incremental /ˌɪŋkrəˈmentl/ *adj* 递增的; **~ increases** 递增

incremental: ~ backup *n* 增量备份; **~ cost** *n* 增加的成本; **~ scale** *n* 增量规模

incriminate /ɪnˈkrɪmɪneɪt/

A *vt* «*evidence, witness*» 表明…有罪 ‹*accused*›; **to ~ sb. in sth.** 表明某人在某案中有罪

B *v refl* **to ~ oneself** 受到牵连

incriminating /ɪnˈkrɪmɪneɪtɪŋ/ *adj* 显示有罪的 ‹*evidence, circumstances*›

incrimination /ɪnˌkrɪmɪˈneɪʃn/ *n* [u] 显示有罪

incriminatory /ɪnˈkrɪmɪneɪtəri, -nətri, Amer -tɔːri/ *adj* 显示有罪的 ‹*testimony, statement, evidence*›

in-crowd *n* colloq 时尚一族; **to be in with the ~** 属于时尚一族

incrust /ɪnˈkrʌst/ *vt* = **encrust**

incrustation /ˌɪŋkrʌˈsteɪʃn/ *n* = **encrustation**

incubate /ˈɪŋkjʊbeɪt/

A *vt* 1 (sit on) «*bird*» 孵化 ‹*egg*› 2 (grow) «*scientist, chemist*» 培养 ‹*bacteria, embryo*› 3 Med «*person*» 携带 ‹*disease*›

B *vi* 1 (develop into young) «*eggs*» 被孵化 2 Biol «*bacteria, embryo*» 被培养 3 Med «*disease*» 潜伏; **the disease takes four weeks to ~** 这种疾病潜伏期为4周

incubation /ˌɪŋkjʊˈbeɪʃn/ *n* [u] 1 (of eggs) 孵化 2 (of germs, bacteria) 培养 3 Med (of disease) 潜伏

incubation period *n* 潜伏期

incubator /ˈɪŋkjʊbeɪtə(r)/ *n* 1 (for eggs, embryos) 孵化器; (for bacteria) 恒温器 2 (for child) 恒温箱

incubus /ˈɪŋkjʊbəs/ *n* (*pl* **incubi** /ˈɪnkjʊbaɪ/) 1 (devil) 梦淫妖 [欧洲传说中与熟睡妇人交合的妖怪] 2 (cause of distress or anxiety) 精神负担

inculcate /ˈɪnkʌlkeɪt, Amer ɪnˈkʌl-/ *vt* formal 1 (instil) 灌输 ‹*ideas, beliefs*›; **to ~ sth. in** *or* **into sb.** 向某人灌输某思想 2 (teach) 教导 ‹*pupil, followers*›; **to ~ sb. with sth.** 教导某人某事

inculcation /ˌɪnkʌlˈkeɪʃn/ *n* [u] formal 思想灌输

incumbency /ɪnˈkʌmbənsɪ/ *n* formal (position) 现任职位; (period) 任期; **during his ~ at the ministry** 他在部里任职期间

incumbent /ɪnˈkʌmbənt/

A *adj* 1 (morally obligatory) **it is ~ on** *or* **upon sb. to do sth.** 某人有责任做某事 2 *attrib* (in office) 在任的

B *n* Admin, Pol 任职者; **the present ~ of the White House** 现任美国总统

incur /ɪnˈkɜː(r)/ *vt* (*pres p etc.* **-rr-**) 1 Comm, Fin 招致 ‹*risks, loss*›; **to ~ debts** 带来债务 2 (provoke) 引起 ‹*hostility*›; (be subject to) 遭受 ‹*blame*›

incurable /ɪnˈkjʊərəbl/ *adj* 1 Med 无法治愈的 ‹*patient*›; **an ~ disease** 不治之症 2 (incorrigible) 不可改变的 ‹*optimism, optimist, romanticism, romantic*›; **~ habits** 难改的积习

incurably /ɪnˈkjʊərəbli/ *adv* 1 Med 不可治愈地; **to be ~ ill** 病入膏肓 2 (incorrigibly) 无法改变地; **to be ~ romantic/inquisitive** 浪漫/好奇得无可救药

incurious /ɪnˈkjʊərɪəs/ *adj* 不感兴趣的 ‹*person*›; 漫不经心的 ‹*look, glance*›

incursion /ɪnˈkɜːʃn, Amer -ʒn/ *n* 1 Mil 袭击; **to make an ~ into (enemy territory** *etc.***)** 袭击（敌方领土等） 2 (intrusion) 干扰; **to make ~s into sb.'s spare time** 侵占某人的业余时间

indaba /ɪnˈdɑːbə/ *n* S Afr 1 (meeting) 重要会议 2 colloq (concern) 关心的事; (problem) 问题; **that's her ~** 那是她的事

indebted /ɪnˈdetɪd/ *adj* 1 (grateful) 蒙恩的; **to be ~ to sb. for sth./for doing sth.** 因某事/因做某事而感激某人 2 Econ, Fin 欠债的; **to be ~ to sb. (for sth.)** （因某事物）欠某人钱

indebtedness /ɪnˈdetɪdnɪs/ *n* [u] 1 (gratitude) 感激; **~ to sb. (for sth.)** （为某事物）对某人的感激 2 Econ, Fin 欠债; **the ~ of the bankrupt firm** 这家破产商号的债务

indecency /ɪnˈdiːsnsi/ *n* 1 [u] (lack of decency) 不体面 2 [u] Jur (offence) 猥亵; **gross ~** 严重猥亵 3 [c] (indecent act, gesture) 下流行为; (indecent words) 下流话

indecent /ɪnˈdiːsnt/ *adj* 1 (obscene, offensive) 下流的 ‹*remark, behaviour*›; 淫秽的 ‹*poster, photograph*› 2 (unseemly) 不适当的; **an ~ amount of work/money** 不适当的工作量/钱数; **he remarried with ~ haste** 他仓促再婚，不合礼数

indecent: ~ assault *n* [u] 猥亵罪; **~ exposure** *n* [u] 猥亵暴露罪

indecently /ɪnˈdiːsntli/ *adv* 1 (offensively) 下流地; **~ dressed** 衣着暴露的 2 (inappropriately) 不适当地; **they got married ~ soon** 他们很快便草率结了婚; **~ early/greedy** 过早/过贪的

indecipherable /ˌɪndɪˈsaɪfrəbl/ *adj* 难以破译的 ‹*code*›; 难以辨认的 ‹*scribble*›; 难懂的 ‹*writing*›

indecision /ˌɪndɪˈsɪʒn/ *n* [u] 迟疑不决; **~ about sth.** 对某事的优柔寡断; **after months of ~** 迟疑了几个月之后

indecisive /ˌɪndɪˈsaɪsɪv/ *adj* 1 (hesitant) 迟疑不决的 ‹*leader, thinker, manner*›; **he's an ~ person** 他是个优柔寡断的人 2 (inconclusive) 非结论性的 ‹*answer, reply*›; 非决定性的 ‹*battle, discussion*›

indecisively /ˌɪndɪˈsaɪsɪvli/ *adv* 1 (hesitantly) 犹豫不决地 ‹*behave, speak*› 2 (inconclusively) 非决定性地 ‹*defeated, end*›

indeclinable /ˌɪndɪˈklaɪnəbl/ *adj* 不变格的

indecorous /ɪnˈdekərəs/ *adj* formal 不得体的

indecorously /ɪnˈdekərəsli/ *adv* formal 不得体地 ‹*dressed, behave*›; 不雅地 ‹*skimpy, low-necked*›

indeed /ɪnˈdiːd/ *adv* 1 (emphasizing statement or answer) 确实; **it is ~ likely that ...** 的确有可能…; **it's unfair — ~!** 这不公平——确实如此！; **are you going? — I am ~!, yes ~!** 你去吗？——当然！; **that's very good news ~** 那可真是个好消息; **to yell very loudly ~** 叫喊的声音确实非常大 2 (in fact) 实际上; **she is polite, ~ charming** 她彬彬

有礼，更确切地说，是很迷人；**if ~ I did forget ...** 如果我真的忘了… **3** iron (expressing surprise, contempt) [表示惊讶或轻蔑] **he knows you — does he ~?** 他认识你——是吗？；**a bargain ~! it's a rip-off!** 这么贵！简直是敲诈！ **4** (repeating question) 是呀；**who is she? — who ~?** 她是谁啊？——是呀，是谁？

indefatigable /ˌɪndɪˈfætɪɡəbl/ *adj* 不知疲倦的；**~ diligence** 不懈的勤奋

indefatigably /ˌɪndɪˈfætɪɡəbli/ *adv* 不知疲倦地 ‹*work*›；不屈不挠地 ‹*campaign*›；不懈地 ‹*persevere*›

indefensible /ˌɪndɪˈfensəbl/ *adj* **1** (inexcusable) 不可原谅的 ‹*behaviour, crime*› **2** (unsustainable) 站不住脚的 ‹*argument, theory*› **3** Mil (undefendable) 无法防守的 ‹*territory, fort*›

indefensibly /ˌɪndɪˈfensəbli/ *adv* 不可原谅地

indefinable /ˌɪndɪˈfaɪnəbl/ *adj* 难以解释的

indefinably /ˌɪndɪˈfaɪnəbli/ *adv* 难以解释地；**to be ~ mysterious** 说不出地神秘

indefinite /ɪnˈdefɪnət/ *adj* **1** (vague) 含糊的 ‹*answer*›；模糊的 ‹*ideas, feelings*›；(ill-defined) 不明确的 ‹*responsibilities, plans*› **2** (without limits) 期限不定的 ‹*duration*›；不定的 ‹*number*›；**an ~ ban** Sport 无限期禁赛；**~ detention** 无限期拘留 **3** Ling 不定的；**the ~ article** 不定冠词

indefinitely /ɪnˈdefɪnətli/ *adv* 无限期地

indelible /ɪnˈdeləbl/ *adj* **1** (that cannot be erased) 不褪色的 ‹*ink*›；笔迹擦不掉的 ‹*pen*›；擦不掉的 ‹*marks*› **2** (unforgettable) 无法忘记的 ‹*impression, memory*›；**an ~ part of sth.** 某事难以忘怀的一部分

indelibly /ɪnˈdeləbli/ *adv* **1** (permanently) 无法擦除地 ‹*marked, printed*› **2** (unforgettably) 无法忘记地 ‹*impressed*›

indelicacy /ɪnˈdelɪkəsi/ *n* [u] 粗率

indelicate /ɪnˈdelɪkət/ *adj* 粗率的；**it was ~ of her to mention it** 她提起此事真是有欠考虑

indemnification /ɪnˌdemnɪfɪˈkeɪʃn/ *n* **1** [u] (protection) 保障；**~ for sth.** 对某事的保障；**~ against sth.** 免受某损害的赔偿保证 **2** [c] (act of compensation) 赔偿；(thing as compensation) 赔偿物

indemnify /ɪnˈdemnɪfaɪ/ *vt* **1** (secure against legal responsibility) 使免予受罚；**to ~ sb. against** *or* **from sth.** 使某人免于承担某责任 **2** (compensate) 赔偿 ‹*employee, person*›；**to ~ sb. for sth.** 为某事物赔偿某人

indemnity /ɪnˈdemnəti/ *n* **1** [u] (protection) 保障；**~ against sth.** 针对某事的保障 **2** [c] (sum of money) 赔款；(goods) 赔偿物 **3** [c and u] Jur (exemption) 免于惩罚；**act of ~** 免罪法

indemnity: ~ fund *n* 赔偿基金；**~ insurance** *n* [u] 损失补偿保险

indent

A /ɪnˈdent/ *vt* **1** (make notches in) 使…成锯齿状 ‹*edge, coast*›；**an ~ed coastline** 崎岖的海岸线 **2** (dent) 在…上打出凹口 **3** Print 缩排 ‹*text*›；**new paragraphs should be ~ed** 新段落须首行缩进

B /ˈɪndent/ *n* **= indentation 4**

indentation /ˌɪndenˈteɪʃn/ *n* **1** [u] (indenting) 造成凹陷 **2** [c] (depression) 凹陷 **3** [c] (notch, recess) 锯齿 **4** [c and u] Print 缩排

indenture /ɪnˈdentʃə(r)/ Hist

A *n* (of apprentice) 师徒契约；(of servant) 主佣契约

B *vt* 以契约约束 ‹*apprentice, servant*›；**to be ~d to sb.** 《*apprentice*》 签契约给某人做学徒；《*servant*》 签契约给某人做用人

independence /ˌɪndɪˈpendəns/ *n* [u] **1** (self-sufficiency, self-reliance) 自立；**a spirit of ~** 自立精神 **2** Pol 独立；**to achieve/gain/win ~ from ...** 从…取得/获得/赢得独立

Independence Day *n* Amer [美国] 独立纪念日 [7月4日]

independent /ˌɪndɪˈpendənt/

A *adj* **1** (self-reliant) 有主见的 ‹*thinker, attitude*› **2** (self-supporting) 自立的；**to be/become ~ of one's parents** 独立于/变得独立于父母 **3** *attrib* (sufficient to make one independent) 足够独立生活的；**~ means/income** 衣食无忧的财富/收入 **4** (not state-run) 私立的 ‹*school*›；私营的 ‹*television, broadcasting*› **5** Pol (self-governing) 独立的 ‹*state*› **6** (autonomous) 独立运作的 ‹*company*›；(unconnected to a political party) 无党派的 ‹*member of parliament, newspaper*› **7** (separate, unconnected) 不相关的 ‹*evidence*›；独立进行的 ‹*investigation*›；独立得出的 ‹*conclusion*› **8** (impartial) 客观公正的 ‹*report, jury*›

B *n* Pol 无党派人士；**to stand for election as an ~** 以独立候选人身份参选

> **The Independent**
>
> 《独立报》，英国全国性日报。1986 年创刊。姊妹报《星期日独立报》（*The Independent on Sunday*）1990 年创刊。该报号称政治上超越党派观念，保持独立。

independent clause *n* 独立分句

independently /ˌɪndɪˈpendəntli/ *adv* **1** (without help) 单独地 ‹*act*›；自立地 ‹*live*› **2** (separately) 独立地 ‹*work, operate*›；**to act ~ of sb./sth.** 不依赖某人/某物行动 **3** (impartially) 客观公正地 ‹*investigate, monitor*›

independent: ~ suspension *n* [u] 独立悬架；**~ variable** *n* 自变量

in-depth *adj* 深入的；**~ analysis of the figures** 对数据的深入分析

indescribable /ˌɪndɪˈskraɪbəbl/ *adj* 无法形容的

indescribably /ˌɪndɪˈskraɪbəbli/ *adv* 无法形容地；**to be ~ dirty/beautiful/sad** 肮脏/美丽/悲哀得无法形容；**an ~ boring film** 无比乏味的电影；**~ happy** 说不出地高兴

indestructible /ˌɪndɪˈstrʌktəbl/ *adj* 不可毁坏的 ‹*furniture, machine*›；坚不可摧的 ‹*friendship, trust*›

indeterminable /ˌɪndɪˈtɜːmɪnəbl/ *adj* 无法确定的

indeterminate /ˌɪndɪˈtɜːmɪnət/ *adj* 不确定的 ‹*size, amount*›；模糊的 ‹*colour, sound*›

index /ˈɪndeks/

A *n* (*pl* **~es** *or* **indices**) **1** (in book) 索引 **2** (card catalogue) 卡片索引 **3** (indication) 标志；**to be an ~ of sth.** 是某事的指标 **4** Econ, Fin 指数；**cost-of-living ~** 生活成本指数

B *vt* **1** (provide an index to) 为…编索引；**this book is badly ~ed** 这本书的索引很乱 **2** (record in an index) 将…编入索引 ‹*terms, data*›；**to be ~ed under sth.** 在索引中被编入某条目下 **3** Econ 《*government*》 使…与指数挂钩 ‹*salaries, interest rates*›；**to ~ sth. to sth.** 使某物与某物挂钩

indexation /ˌɪndekˈseɪʃn/ *n* 指数化；**the ~ of sth. to sth.** 某物与某物在指数上的挂钩

index: ~ card *n* 索引卡片；**~ figure** *n* 指数；**~ finger** *n* 食指；**~-linked** *adj* 与指数挂钩的 ‹*interest rates, salaries*›；**~ number** *n* 指数；**~ print** *n* 照片索引

India /ˈɪndiə/ *pr n* 印度

India ink *n* [u] Amer **= Indian ink**

Indian /ˈɪndiən/ **▸p. 503**

A *adj* **1** (of India) 印度的 **2** dated or offensive (native American) 印第安人的；**an ~ reserve/reservation** 印第安人居留地

B *n* **1** (from India) 印度人 **2** dated or offensive (native American) 印第安人 **3** colloq (Indian meal) 印度菜；**to go for an ~** 去吃印度菜

Indiana /ˌɪndɪˈænə/ *pr n* 印第安纳州

Indian: ~ club *n* （体操）棒；**~ corn** *n* [u] esp Amer 印第安玉米；**~ elephant** *n* 印度象；**~ file** *n* [u] 单列纵队；**to advance in ~ file** 排成单列纵队前进；**~ ink** *n* [u] [尤用于绘画的] 墨汁；**~ Ocean** *pr n* **the ~ Ocean** 印度洋；**~ rope-trick** *n* 攀岩悬空绳索杂技；**~ summer** *n* **1** (warm period in autumn) 小阳春；**2** fig (period of success) 兴旺的晚期；(period of happiness) 晚年幸福

India rubber *n* [u] 天然橡胶

indicate /ˈɪndɪkeɪt/

A *vt* **1** (designate) 指示 ‹*direction, object*›；**to ~ to sb. that ...** 向某人指示…；**please ~ to the organizers where you would like to sit** 请向组织者说明你想坐在何处 **2** (suggest) 暗示 ‹*feelings*›；**to ~ the presence/approach of sth.** 暗示某事物的存在/临近；**sth. ~s that ...** 某事物表明…；**it ~s how ashamed he feels** 这暗示着他感觉有多羞愧 **3** (show) 标示 ‹*weight, temperature*›；**the speedometer ~d 100** 速度表的读数是 100 **4** **to be ~d** Med 《*treatment, action*》 被暗示；**surgery is usually ~d in such cases** 这种情况通常建议动手术 **5** (make known) 表明 ‹*intentions, plans*›；**to ~ (to sb.) that one is going to do sth.** （向某人）表明自己要做某事 **6** Aut 打…的转向信号；**to ~ left/right** 打左转/右转信号；**she ~d that she was turning left** 她打出了左转信号

B *vi* 打转向信号

indication /ˌɪndɪˈkeɪʃn/ *n* 迹象；**to be an ~ of sth.** 是某事的端倪；**he gave no ~ that ...** 他没有表示…；**there is every ~ that ...** 所有迹象表明…；**an ~ of how much remains to be done** 剩余工作量的标志

indicative /ɪnˈdɪkətɪv/

A *adj* **1** 指示的；**to be ~ of sth.** 表明某事；**to be ~ (of the fact) that ...** 表明…（这一事实） **2** Ling 陈述的；**the ~ mood/verb form** 陈述语气/动词形式

B *n* Ling **the ~** 陈述语气；**the verb is in the ~** 这个动词用了陈述语气

indicator /ˈɪndɪkeɪtə(r)/ *n* **1** (device) 指示器；**a speed/pressure ~** 速度/压力表 **2** esp Brit Aut 转向灯 **3** Rail **~ (board)** 指示牌；**an arrivals/departures ~** 到达/出发指示牌 **4** (measure) 指示物；**a good ~ of the government's popularity** 政府受欢迎程度的有效标志 **5** Chem 指示剂

indices /ˈɪndɪsiːz/ *pl* **▸index A**

indict /ɪnˈdaɪt/ *vt* esp Amer 控告；**to be ~ed for sth./on a charge of sth.** 因某事受到指控/受到某指控

indictable /ɪnˈdaɪtəbl/ *adj* 可起诉的；**to be ~ for sth.** 因某事可被提起公诉

indictment /ɪnˈdaɪtmənt/ *n* **1** [c] Jur (written statement) 公诉书；**an ~ against sb. (for sth.)** 状告某人（犯有某罪）的起诉书；**to bring an ~ against sb.** 控告某人；**a bill of ~** 诉状 **2** [u] Jur 起诉；**to be under ~ for murder** 被控犯有谋杀罪 **3** [c] fig (proof that sth. deserves condemnation) 罪证；(critical statement) 声讨；**an ~ of sth./sb.** 某事/某人的罪证；**to deliver a stinging ~** 提出严厉声讨

indie /ˈɪndi/ *adj* colloq 非主流的；**~ music/label** 非主流音乐/唱片公司

indifference /ɪnˈdɪfrəns/ *n* [u] **1** (lack of concern) 漠不关心；**it is a matter of ~ to him** 这事对他无关紧要；**~ about** *or* **to** *or* **towards sth.** 对某事物的漠不关心；**to affect** *or* **feign ~** 装作不在乎 **2** (mediocrity) 平庸

indifferent /ɪnˈdɪfrənt/ *adj* **1** (unconcerned) 漠不关心的；**to be ~ as to** *or* **about sth./sb.** 不在乎某事物/某人 **2** (mediocre) 一般的 ‹*wine, food*›；平庸的 ‹*writer, performer*›；较差的 ‹*quality, ability*›

indifferently /ɪnˈdɪfrəntli/ *adv* **1** (without caring) 漠不关心地 ‹*look on*›；不屑一顾地 ‹*shrug*› **2** (in a mediocre way) 平庸地 ‹*play, sing, draw*›

indigence /ˈɪndɪdʒəns/ *n* [u] formal 贫困

indigenous /ɪnˈdɪdʒɪnəs/ *adj* 当地的 ‹*plant, animal*›；本地的 ‹*culture, language, people*›；土著的 ‹*race, tribe*›

indigent /ˈɪndɪdʒənt/ *adj* formal 贫穷的

indigestible /ˌɪndɪˈdʒestəbl/ *adj* 1 lit 难消化的 ‹*food*› 2 fig (difficult to understand) 难懂的

indigestion /ˌɪndɪˈdʒestʃn/ *n* [u] 消化不良; **to suffer from ~** 患消化不良症; **to give sb. ~** 引起某人消化不良; **an ~ sufferer/tablet** 消化不良症患者/消食药片

indignant /ɪnˈdɪɡnənt/ *adj* 义愤的; **to be ~ at** *or* **over** *or* **about sth.** 对某事愤愤不平

indignantly /ɪnˈdɪɡnəntli/ *adv* 义愤地

indignation /ˌɪndɪɡˈneɪʃn/ *n* [u] 愤慨; **~ at** *or* **over** *or* **about sth.** 对某事的愤慨; **(much) to his ~** 令他（十分）愤慨; **righteous ~** 义愤

indignity /ɪnˈdɪɡnəti/ *n* 1 [u] (shame) 羞辱; **the ~ of having to do sth.** 被迫做某事的羞辱 2 [c] (humiliation) 侮辱性的行为

indigo /ˈɪndɪɡəʊ/ ▸**p. 134**
A *n* 1 [u] (colour) 靛蓝色 2 [u] (dye) 靛蓝色染料 3 [c] (plant) 木蓝属植物
B *adj* 靛蓝色的; **~ blue** 靛蓝

indirect /ˌɪndɪˈrekt, -daɪˈr-/ *adj* 1 (not straight) 迂回的 ‹*route*› 2 (oblique) 拐弯抹角的 ‹*answer*›; 闪烁其词的 ‹*criticism*› 3 (incidental, through intermediaries) 间接的 ‹*effects, communication*›

indirect: **~ advertising** *n* [u] 间接广告; **~ costs** *npl* 间接成本; **~ labour** *n* [u] 间接人工; **~ labour costs** *npl* 间接人工成本; **~ lighting** *n* [u] 间接照明

indirectly /ˌɪndɪˈrektli, -daɪˈr-/ *adv* 1 (by indirect means, incidentally) 间接地 ‹*affect*›; **to lead ~ to sth.** 间接导致某事 2 (obliquely) 拐弯抹角地 ‹*answer*›; **to refer ~ to sth.** 拐弯抹角地提及某事物

indirect: **~ object** *n* 间接宾语; **~ proof** *n* [u and c] 归谬法; **~ speech** *n* [u] 间接引语; **~ tax** *n* 间接税; **~ taxation** *n* [u] 间接课税

indiscernible /ˌɪndɪˈsɜːnəbl/ *adj* 1 (imperceptible) 隐约的 ‹*object, sound*› 2 (inscrutable) 难以理解的 ‹*reasons, expression*› 3 (indistinguishable) **to be ~ from sth.** 无法与某物区分开来

indiscipline /ɪnˈdɪsɪplɪn/ *n* [u] 无纪律

indiscreet /ˌɪndɪˈskriːt/ *adj* 不慎重的; **it is ~ of sb. to do sth.** 某人做某事是不审慎的

indiscretion /ˌɪndɪˈskreʃn/ *n* 1 [u] (lack of discretion) 不慎重 2 [c] (act) 不检点行为; (remark) 不审慎的言语; **youthful ~s** 年轻人的鲁莽; **sexual ~s** 性生活的不检点

indiscriminate /ˌɪndɪˈskrɪmɪnət/ *adj* 1 (undiscriminating) 不加分析的 ‹*reader, reading*›; 盲目的 ‹*admiration*›; **to be ~ in ...** 在…方面不加判断 2 (random) 恣意的 ‹*violence, killing, punishment*›

indiscriminately /ˌɪndɪˈskrɪmɪnətli/ *adv* 1 (without distinction) 不加分析地 ‹*read*›; 盲目地 ‹*admire*› 2 (randomly) 恣意地 ‹*punish, kill*›

indispensable /ˌɪndɪˈspensəbl/ *adj* 不可或缺的; **to be ~ to sb./sth.** 对于某人/某事是必不可少的; **to be ~ for doing sth.** 对于做某事不可或缺; **an ~ necessity** 必备之物

indisposed /ˌɪndɪˈspəʊzd/ *adj* formal 1 (ill) 微恙的; **an ~ performer/speaker** 因病缺席的演员/演讲者 2 (unwilling) 不愿意的; **to be ~ to do sth.** 不愿做某事

indisposition /ˌɪndɪspəˈzɪʃn/ *n* [c and u] formal 1 (illness) 微恙 2 (unwillingness) 不愿意; **to feel** *or* **have an ~ to do sth.** 不愿做某事

indisputable /ˌɪndɪˈspjuːtəbl/ *adj* 无可争辩的

indisputably /ˌɪndɪˈspjuːtəbli/ *adv* 无可争辩地; **to be ~ the greatest/greater** 毫无疑问是最/更伟大的

indistinct /ˌɪndɪˈstɪŋkt/ *adj* 不清晰的 ‹*sound, photograph*›; 模糊的 ‹*memories, features, shape*›

indistinctly /ˌɪndɪˈstɪŋktli/ *adv* 不清楚地 ‹*see, hear, speak*›; 模糊地 ‹*feel, remember*›

indistinguishable /ˌɪndɪˈstɪŋɡwɪʃəbl/ *adj* 1 (identical) 难以分辨的; **to be ~ from sth. (else)** 难以与（其他的）某物区分开 2 (indiscernible) 不易察觉的 ‹*difference, change*›; 模糊的 ‹*sound, figure*›

indistinguishably /ˌɪndɪˈstɪŋɡwɪʃəbli/ *adv* 1 (identically) 难以分辨地 2 (imperceptibly) 不易察觉地

indium /ˈɪndiəm/ *n* [u] 铟

individual /ˌɪndɪˈvɪdʒuəl/
A *adj* 1 (single, separate) 单独的; **each ~ person/article** 每个人/每件物品 2 (of one person) 个人的 ‹*freedom, pursuit*›; (for one person) 单人的 ‹*sport, portion*› 3 (distinctive, original) 独特的 ‹*charm, manner, style, way*›
B *n* 1 (person) 个人; **each ~** 每个人; **donations from private ~s** 私人捐助 2 colloq, esp pej (type of person) 一类人; **she's a lazy ~** 她是个懒鬼 3 (original person) 有个性的人; **he's a real ~** 他是个很有个性的人

individualism /ˌɪndɪˈvɪdʒuəlɪzəm/ *n* [u] 1 (independence, self-reliance) 个性特征 2 (social theory) 个人主义

individualist /ˌɪndɪˈvɪdʒuəlɪst/ *n* 1 (independent person) 我行我素的人 2 (supporter of individualism) 个人主义者

individualistic /ˌɪndɪˌvɪdʒuəˈlɪstɪk/ *adj* 我行我素的

individuality /ˌɪndɪˌvɪdʒuˈæləti/ *n* [u] 1 (uniqueness) 个体特征; **the ~ of sth.** 某物的特性; **a novel of marked ~** 具有鲜明特点的小说 2 (separate existence) 个体

individualize /ˌɪndɪˈvɪdʒuəlaɪz/ *vt* 使个性化

individually /ˌɪndɪˈvɪdʒuəli/ *adv* 1 (separately) 单独地; **~ priced/designed** 单独标价的/个别设计的 2 (for or by oneself) 亲自 3 (distinctively) 独特地

indivisibility /ˌɪndɪˌvɪzɪˈbɪləti/ *n* [u] 1 (inseparability) 不可分割 2 Math 除不尽

indivisible /ˌɪndɪˈvɪzəbl/ *adj* 1 (inseparable) 不可分割的; **to be ~ from sth.** 不能与某事物割裂开 2 Math 除不尽的; **six is ~ by five** 6 不能被 5 整除

indivisibly /ˌɪndɪˈvɪzəbli/ *adv* 不可分割地

Indo-China /ˌɪndəʊˈtʃaɪnə/ *pr n* 印度支那半岛

Indo-Chinese /ˌɪndəʊtʃaɪˈniːz/
A *adj* 印度支那的
B *n* 印度支那人

indoctrinate /ɪnˈdɒktrɪneɪt/ *vt* pej 向…灌输; **to ~ sb. with sth.** 把某思想灌输给某人; **to ~ sb. against sth.** 灌输给某人反对某事的思想

indoctrination /ɪnˌdɒktrɪˈneɪʃn/ *n* [u] pej 灌输; **~ of sb.** 对某人的思想灌输; **~ with** *or* **in sth.** 某思想的灌输; **~ against sth.** 反对某事的思想灌输

Indo-European /ˌɪndəʊˌjʊərəˈpiːən/
A *adj* 印欧语系的
B *n* [u] 印欧语系

indolence /ˈɪndələns/ *n* [u] formal 懒惰

indolent /ˈɪndələnt/ *adj* formal 懒惰的 ‹*person*›; 懒洋洋的 ‹*gesture, expression*›

indolently /ˈɪndələntli/ *adv* formal 懒惰地

indomitable /ɪnˈdɒmɪtəbl/ *adj* 坚定的 ‹*spirit, will*›; 意志坚定的 ‹*person*›; 不可动摇的 ‹*pride, character*›; **~ courage** 不屈不挠的勇气

indomitably /ɪnˈdɒmɪtəbli/ *adv* 坚定地 ‹*persevere, optimistic*›; 不屈不挠地 ‹*fight*›

Indonesia /ˌɪndəʊˈniːzjə/ *pr n* 印度尼西亚

Indonesian /ˌɪndəʊˈniːzjən/ ▸**p. 503, p. 426**
A *adj* (of Indonesia) 印度尼西亚的; (of the people) 印度尼西亚人的; (of the languages) 印度尼西亚语的
B *n* 1 [c] (person) 印度尼西亚人 2 [u] (languages) 印度尼西亚语

indoor /ˈɪndɔː(r)/ *adj attrib* 室内的; **~ and outdoor sports facilities** 户内外的运动设施; **~ shoes/clothes** 室内穿的鞋子/衣服

indoors /ˌɪnˈdɔːz/ *adv* 往室内 ‹*go*›; 在室内 ‹*stay*›; **~ and outdoors** 在室内外

indorse /ɪnˈdɔːs/ *vt* Amer **= endorse**

indubitable /ɪnˈdjuːbɪtəbl, Amer -ˈduː-/ *adj* formal 不容置疑的; **~ signs** 明确无疑的迹象

indubitably /ɪnˈdjuːbɪtəbli, Amer -ˈduː-/ *adv* formal 不容置疑地

induce /ɪnˈdjuːs, Amer -ˈduːs/ *vt* 1 (persuade) 劝说; **to ~ sb. to do sth.** 劝某人做某事 2 (cause) **to ~ sb. to do sth.** 导致某人做某事; **to ~ illness/fatigue/panic in sb.** 使某人生病/疲乏/恐慌; **to ~ sleep** 使人入睡 3 Med 催产; **to ~ labour** 引产; **she was ~d** 她接受了引产 4 Elec, Phys 感应 ‹*electric current, electromotive force*›

inducement /ɪnˈdjuːsmənt, Amer -ˈduː-s/ *n* 1 [c] (promised reward) 奖励; euph (bribe) 贿赂物; **financial ~** 经济奖励; **as an ~ to first-time buyers** 作为对首次购买者的奖励; **to be an ~ (for sb.) to do sth.** 是（某人）做某事的动力 2 [u] (incentive) 刺激; **there is little/no ~ for them to work harder** 几乎没有/没有让他们更加努力工作的激励措施

induct /ɪnˈdʌkt/ *vt* 1 (inaugurate) 使…正式就职 ‹*priest, official*›; **to be ~ed into sth.** 正式就任某职 2 (introduce to) ‹*teacher, priest*› 传授 ‹*priesthood, mystery*›; **to ~ sb. into sth.** 使某人了解某事物 3 Amer Mil (enlist) 征召…入伍

inductance /ɪnˈdʌktəns/ *n* [u] 电感

induction /ɪnˈdʌkʃn/ *n* 1 [c and u] (act of inauguration) 就职; (ceremony of inauguration) 就职仪式 2 [u] (bringing about) 引起; **the ~ of sleep/hypnosis** 引起睡眠/催眠 3 [u] (introduction to job) 入门; **the ~ of sb. into sth.** 某人对某领域的入门 4 [u] Med (of labour) 催产 5 [u] Amer Mil (enlistment) 征兵 6 [u] Elec, Phys 电磁感应

induction: **~ coil** *n* 感应线圈; **~ course** *n* 入门课程; **~ heating** *n* [u] 感应加热; **~ motor** *n* 感应电动机

inductive /ɪnˈdʌktɪv/ *adj* 1 (using reasoning) 归纳的 2 Elec, Phys 感应的

indulge /ɪnˈdʌldʒ/
A *vt* 1 (spoil) 纵容 ‹*children, lover*›; **she was ~d as a child** 她小时候被宠坏了 2 (satisfy) 满足 ‹*desire, curiosity*›; **to ~ a longing** 满足愿望
B *vi* colloq (allow a pleasure) 沉溺; (allow drinking) 沉迷饮酒; **to ~ in sth./doing sth.** 沉溺于某事/做某事; **do you ~?** 你喜欢喝酒吗?
C *v refl* **to ~ oneself with sth.** 尽情享受某事物; **to ~ oneself by doing sth.** 尽情做某事

indulgence /ɪnˈdʌldʒəns/ *n* 1 [c] (luxury) 嗜好; **it is my only ~** 这是我唯一的爱好 2 [u] (tolerance) 纵容; **if I may beg your ~** formal 我恳求您包涵 3 [u] (act of indulging) 沉溺; **~ in food** 暴食; **~ in nostalgia** 怀旧

indulgent /ɪnˈdʌldʒənt/ *adj* 纵容孩子的 ‹*person*›; 宽容的 ‹*pat, smile*›; **to be (too) ~ to** *or* **towards sb.** 对某人（太）迁就

indulgently /ɪnˈdʌldʒəntli/ *adv* 宽容地

Indus /ˈɪndəs/ *pr n* **the ~** 印度河

industrial /ɪnˈdʌstrɪəl/ *adj* 1 (relating to industry) 工业的 ‹*spy, espionage, output, development*›; 工业领域的 ‹*analyst*›; **~ accident/wealth/worker/insurance** 工伤事故/劳动创造的财富/产业工人/劳动保险 2 (for use in industry) 工业用的 3 (with highly developed industries) 工业发达的

industrial: **~ action** *n* [u] Brit 劳工行动; **to take ~ action** 罢工; **~ archaeology** *n* [u] 工业考古学; **~ arts** *npl* Amer 工艺课; **~ base** *n* 工业基础; **~ democracy** *n* [u] 工业民主; **~ design** *n* [u] 工业设计; **~ designer** ▸**p. 409** *n* 工业设计师; **~ diamond** *n* 工业金刚石;

i

~ **disease** *n* 职业病; ~ **dispute** *n* 劳资纠纷; ~ **engineering** *n* [u] 企业管理学; ~ **estate** *n* Brit 工业区

industrialism /ɪn'dʌstrɪəlɪzəm/ *n* [u] 产业主义

industrialist /ɪn'dʌstrɪəlɪst/ *n* 工业家, 实业家

industrialization /ɪn,dʌstrɪəlaɪ'zeɪʃn, Amer -lɪ'z-/ *n* [u] 工业化

industrialize /ɪn'dʌstrɪəlaɪz/
A *vt* 使工业化
B *vi* 工业化

industrial: ~ **park** *n* 工业园区; ~ **psychologist** ▸p. 409 *n* 工业心理学家; ~ **psychology** *n* [u] 工业心理学; ~ **rehabilitation** *n* [u] 职工康复中心; ~ **relations** *npl* 劳资关系; **I~ Revolution** *n* 工业革命; **~-strength** *adj* 强大的; ~ **tribunal** *n* Brit 劳资裁判庭; ~ **union** *n* 产业工会; ~ **unrest** *n* [u] 行业动荡; ~ **vehicle** *n* 工业车辆; ~ **waste** *n* [u] 工业废弃物

industrious /ɪn'dʌstrɪəs/ *adj* 勤奋的 ‹*students*›; 勤劳的 ‹*workers, bees*›

industriously /ɪn'dʌstrɪəsli/ *adv* 勤奋地

industriousness /ɪn'dʌstrɪəsnɪs/ *n* [u] 勤勉

industry /'ɪndəstri/ *n* **1** [u] (manufacturing) 工业; **heavy/light** ~ 重/轻工业 **2** [c] (particular form of production) 企业; **the catering/advertising** ~ 饮食业/广告业 **3** [c] fig pej 专题研究; **the Shakespeare/Joyce** ~ 莎士比亚/乔伊斯研究 **4** [u] formal (diligence) 勤奋

inebriate /ɪ'ni:brɪət/ *n* formal or hum 酗酒者

inebriated /ɪ'ni:brɪeɪtɪd/ *adj* formal or hum 喝醉的

inebriation /ɪ,ni:brɪ'eɪʃn/ *n* [u] formal 醉酒; **in a state of** ~ 醉醺醺地

inedible /ɪn'edɪbl/ *adj* **1** (because poisonous) 不能吃的 ‹*plant, mushroom*› **2** (because of poor quality) 不宜食用的

ineducable /ɪn'edʒʊkəbl/ *adj* [因智障等] 不可教育的

ineffable /ɪn'efəbl/ *adj* liter 难以形容的; ~ **beauty** 妙不可言的美

ineffective /,ɪnɪ'fektɪv/ *adj* 无效的 ‹*law, remedy*›; 无能的 ‹*teacher, sales person*›

ineffectively /,ɪnɪ'fektɪvli/ *adv* 无效地

ineffectiveness /,ɪnɪ'fektɪvnɪs/ *n* [u] (of law, remedy) 无效; (of teacher, sales person) 无能

ineffectual /,ɪnɪ'fektʃʊəl/ *adj* **1** (ineffective) 无效的 ‹*policy, attempt, leadership*› **2** (lacking ability) 无能的 ‹*politician, president*›

ineffectually /,ɪnɪ'fektʃʊəli/ *adv* 无效地

inefficacious /,ɪnefɪ'keɪʃəs/ *adj* formal 无效的

inefficacy /ɪn'efɪkəsi/ *n* [u] formal 无效

inefficiency /,ɪnɪ'fɪʃnsi/ *n* **1** [u] (of person) (incompetence) 不称职; (lack of organization) 低效能 **2** [u] (of machine, method, system) 低效率 **3** [c] (instance) 低效率现象

inefficient /,ɪnɪ'fɪʃnt/ *adj* 效率低的 ‹*measures, management, machine*›; (incompetent) 不称职的 ‹*person, worker*›

inefficiently /,ɪnɪ'fɪʃntli/ *adv* 低效率地

inelastic /,ɪnɪ'læstɪk/ *adj* **1** (not stretchable) 无弹性的 ‹*material*› **2** fig (inflexible) 不灵活的 ‹*schedule*› **3** Econ 无弹性的 ‹*price structure, market*›

inelegant /ɪn'elɪgənt/ *adj* 不雅的 ‹*gesture, stance, style*›; 粗俗的 ‹*phrasing*›

inelegantly /ɪn'elɪgəntli/ *adv* 不雅地 ‹*stand, seated, perched*›; 粗俗地 ‹*phrased*›

ineligibility /ɪn,elɪdʒə'bɪləti/ *n* [u] (for job) 不合格; Pol 无资格; ~ **for benefit/to vote** 无资格获得补贴/没有资格投票

ineligible /ɪn'elɪdʒəbl/ *adj* (for job) 不合格的; (for election, competition, benefit, award) 无资格的; **to be** ~ **to vote/for candidacy** 无资格投票/当候选人

ineluctable /,ɪnɪ'lʌktəbl/ *adj* formal 不可避免的 ‹*fact*›; 无法躲避的 ‹*fate*›

inept /ɪ'nept/ *adj* **1** (incompetent) 无能的 ‹*diplomat, negotiator, manager*›; (clumsy) 笨拙的 ‹*behaviour, handling*› **2** (tactless) 不恰当的 ‹*remark, reply, intervention*›

ineptitude /ɪ'neptɪtju:d, Amer -tu:d/, **ineptness** /ɪ'neptnɪs/ *ns* [u] **1** (inefficiency, incompetence) 无能; (clumsiness) 笨拙 **2** (tactlessness) 不恰当

ineptly /ɪ'neptli/ *adv* **1** (incompetently) 缺乏技巧地 ‹*negotiated, managed*›; (inefficiently) 无能地 ‹*deal with*›; (clumsily) 笨拙地 ‹*handle*› **2** (tactlessly) 不恰当地 ‹*remark, reply, intervene*›

inequality /,ɪnɪ'kwɒləti/ *n* [u and c] 不平等

inequitable /ɪn'ekwɪtəbl/ *adj* formal 不公平的

inequity /ɪn'ekwəti/ *n* formal **1** [u] (unfairness) 不公平 **2** [c] (unfair action) 不公正的行为; (unfair matter) 不公正的事

ineradicable /,ɪnɪ'rædɪkəbl/ *adj* formal 无法根除的 ‹*disease, prejudice*›; 无法改变的 ‹*fault, tendency*›

inert /ɪ'nɜ:t/ *adj* **1** (unable to move) 不活动的 ‹*matter, object*›; 一动不动的 ‹*body*›; **she lay** ~ **on the bed** 她躺在床上一动不动 **2** Chem, Phys (unreactive) 惰性的

inert gas *n* 惰性气体

inertia /ɪ'nɜ:ʃə/ *n* [u] **1** (inactivity) 不活动; **bureaucratic** ~ 官僚主义惰性 **2** Phys (incapability of self-movement) 惯性; (resistance to change) 惰性

inertial /ɪ'nɜ:ʃl/ *adj* 惯性的; ~ **mass/system/navigation** 惯性质量/坐标系/导航

inertia: ~ **reel seatbelt** *n* 惯性卷筒式安全带; ~ **selling** *n* [u] Brit 惰性销售

inertly /ɪ'nɜ:tli/ *adv* 呆滞地

inescapable /,ɪnɪ'skeɪpəbl/ *adj* 必然的 ‹*conclusion, consequence, fate*›; 不可逃避的 ‹*fact, truth*›

inessential /,ɪnɪ'senʃl/
A *adj* 非必需的; ~ **luxuries** 不必要的奢侈品
B *n* 可有可无之物

inestimable /ɪn'estɪməbl/ *adj* formal 难以估量的; **a treasure of** ~ **value** 无价之宝

inevitability /ɪn,evɪtə'bɪləti/ *n* [u] 必然性

inevitable /ɪn'evɪtəbl/
A *adj* (bound to happen) 必然发生的 ‹*consequence, event*›; 难以避免的 ‹*disaster*›; (predictable) 照例必有的; **it was** ~ **that he would do that** 按照惯例他要做那件事
B *n* 必然发生的事; **the** ~ **happened** 逃不掉的事情发生了; **to bow to the** ~ 接受必然发生的事

inevitably /ɪn'evɪtəbli/ *adv* **1** (certainly) 必然地; (unavoidably) 不可避免地 **2** (as one would expect) 不出所料地

inexact /,ɪnɪg'zækt/ *adj* 不精确的 ‹*account, measurement, science*›; 不准确的 ‹*description, information, translation*›

inexactitude /,ɪnɪg'zæktɪtju:d, Amer -tɪtu:d/ *n* **1** [u] (inexactness) 不精确 **2** [c] (inaccuracy) 不准确

inexactly /,ɪnɪg'zæktli/ *adv* 不精确地 ‹*measure*›; 不准确地 ‹*describe, relate*›

inexcusable /,ɪnɪk'skju:zəbl/ *adj* 不可宽恕的; **it is** ~ **of sb. to do sth.** 某人做某事不可原谅

inexcusably /,ɪnɪk'skju:zəbli/ *adv* 不可宽恕地

inexhaustible /,ɪnɪg'zɔ:stəbl/ *adj* 用之不竭的 ‹*store, resource, energy*›; 无穷无尽的 ‹*supply*›; 无限的 ‹*patience*›

inexorable /ɪn'eksərəbl/ *adj* **1** (impossible to stop) 不可阻挡的 ‹*march, trend*›; (impossible to change) 无法改变的 ‹*doom, fate, logic*› **2** (unrelenting) 无情的 ‹*tyrant, tormentor, opponent*›

inexorably /ɪn'eksərəbli/ *adv* 不可阻挡地

inexpedient /,ɪnɪk'spi:dɪənt/ *adj* formal 不适当的

inexpensive /,ɪnɪk'spensɪv/ *adj* 不昂贵的; **a good but** ~ **wine** 质优价廉的葡萄酒

inexpensively /,ɪnɪk'spensɪvli/ *adv* 便宜地

inexperience /,ɪnɪk'spɪərɪəns/ *n* [u] (lack of practical experience) 缺乏经验; (lack of knowledge) 缺乏知识

inexperienced /,ɪnɪk'spɪərɪənst/ *adj* 缺乏经验的

inexpert /ɪn'ekspɜ:t/ *adj* 缺乏技巧的 ‹*cooking, typing, sewing, etc.*›; 不熟练的 ‹*cook, typist, gardener, etc.*›; **to the** ~ **eye** 在外行人看来

inexpertly /ɪn'ekspɜ:tli/ *adv* 不熟练地 ‹*handle, produce, organize*›; 不内行地 ‹*guide, advise*›

inexplicable /,ɪnɪk'splɪkəbl/ *adj* 无法解释的; **for some** ~ **reason** 由于某种莫名其妙的原因

inexplicably /,ɪnɪk'splɪkəbli/ *adv* 无法解释地

inexpressible /,ɪnɪk'spresəbl/ *adj* 难以表达的 ‹*dismay, grief*›; 无法形容的 ‹*joy, relief*›

inexpressibly /,ɪnɪk'spresəbli/ *adv* 无法形容地

inexpressive /,ɪnɪk'spresɪv/ *adj* 毫无表情的

inextinguishable /,ɪnɪk'stɪŋgwɪʃəbl/ *adj* 不可遏止的 ‹*longing*›; 永不衰减的 ‹*good humour, optimism*›

inextricable /ɪn'ekstrɪkəbl, ,ɪnɪk'strɪk-/ *adj* **1** (inseparable) 分不开的; **sth. is** ~ **from sth.** 某事物与某事物密不可分; **her story is** ~ **from that of her country** 她的故事与她的国家紧密相关; **(there is) an** ~ **connection between ... and ...** …和…之间（存在着）千丝万缕的联系 **2** (inescapable) 无法摆脱的 ‹*dilemma, difficulties*›

inextricably /ɪn'ekstrɪkəbli, ,ɪnɪk'strɪk-/ *adv* 解不开地 ‹*entangled*›; 分不开地 ‹*linked*›

infallibility /ɪn,fælə'bɪləti/ *n* [u] 无过失; **the** ~ **of sth./sb.** 某事/某人的绝对可靠

infallible /ɪn'fæləbl/ *adj* 绝对可靠的 ‹*instinct, memory, intuition*›; 不可能错的 ‹*reasoning, person*›; 绝对有效的 ‹*remedy, method*›; **doctors are not** ~ 医生也是会犯错的

infallibly /ɪn'fæləbli/ *adv* **1** (faultlessly) 绝对地 ‹*correct, exact*›; ~ **accurate** 绝对精确 **2** (always) 一贯 ‹*late, early*›

infamous /'ɪnfəməs/ *adj* **1** (notorious) 臭名昭著的 ‹*monarch, traitor, locality*›; **to be** ~ **for sth./doing sth.** 因某事/做某事而名声狼藉 **2** (abominable) 无耻的 ‹*conduct, deed*›

infamy /'ɪnfəmi/ *n* **1** [u] (notoriety) 臭名昭著; **the** ~ **of (sth.)** （某事物）的臭名 **2** [c and u] (evil act, behaviour) 恶行

infancy /'ɪnfənsi/ *n* [u] **1** (young childhood) 婴儿期; **from (one's)** ~ 自幼; **in early** ~ 在襁褓中 **2** fig (early stage) 初期; **in the** ~ **of the movement/his career** 在运动的初期/在他职业生涯的初始阶段; **the company/project is in its** ~ 公司刚创建/项目刚起步

infant /'ɪnfənt/
A *n* **1** (baby) 婴儿; (young child) 幼儿; **a newborn** ~ 新生儿 **2** Brit (schoolchild) 学童
B *modif* **1** (related to early childhood) 婴儿的 **2** fig (at an early stage) 初期的

infanticide /ɪn'fæntɪsaɪd/ *n* [u] **1** (crime) 杀婴罪; **to commit** ~ 犯杀婴罪 **2** (custom) 杀婴习俗

infantile /'ɪnfəntaɪl/ *adj* **1** pej (childish) 孩子气的 ‹*behaviour, person*› **2** Med 婴儿的 ‹*disease, condition*›

infant: ~ **mortality** *n* [u] 婴儿死亡率; ~ **prodigy** *n* 神童

infantry /'ɪnfəntri/ *n* 步兵

i

infantryman /ˈɪnfəntrɪmən/ *n* 步兵

infant school *n* Brit [招收7岁以下儿童就读的] 幼儿学校

infatuate /ɪnˈfætʃʊeɪt/ *vt* 使沉迷

infatuated /ɪnˈfætʃʊeɪtɪd/ *adj* 痴迷的; **to be/become ~ with sb./sth.** 迷恋某人/痴迷某事物

infatuation /ɪnˌfætʃʊˈeɪʃn/ *n* [c and u] 痴迷; **to develop an ~ for sb.** 开始迷恋某人; **a passing ~** 转瞬即逝的痴迷

infect /ɪnˈfekt/ *vt* 1 (cause disease in) 传染; **to ~ sb./sth. with sth.** 使某人/某物感染某病 2 (contaminate, pollute) «*factory, bacteria, effluent*» 污染 ‹*water, atmosphere, food*› 3 fig (influence) 影响; **to ~ sb. with one's enthusiasm** 用热情感染某人

infection /ɪnˈfekʃn/ *n* 1 [u] (of wound, organ) 感染; (of person, blood) 传染; **to be exposed to ~** 暴露于易受感染的环境 2 [c] (disease) 传染病; **to have an ~** 患传染病

infectious /ɪnˈfekʃəs/ *adj* 1 Med 传染性的 ‹*disease*›; 患有传染病的 ‹*person*› 2 fig 富有感染力的 ‹*laughter, emotion, idea*›

infectiousness /ɪnˈfekʃəsnɪs/ *n* [u] 1 Med 传染性 2 fig 感染力

infer /ɪnˈfɜː(r)/ *vt* (*pres p etc.* **-rr-**) 推理; **to ~ sth. from sth.** 从某事推断某事; **to ~ that sth. is the case** 断定某情况如此

inference /ˈɪnfərəns/ *n* 1 [u] (act, process) 推断; **by ~** 通过推理 2 [c] (conclusion) 推断结果; **the ~ is that ...** 结论是…; **to draw an ~ from ...** 从…得出推论

inferential /ˌɪnfəˈrenʃl/ *adj* 推理的 ‹*proof, method*›

inferior /ɪnˈfɪərɪə(r)/

A *adj* 1 (lower in quality) 较差的 ‹*goods, product, workmanship*›; (lower in rank) 级别较低的 ‹*status*›; **to make sb. feel ~** 使某人自惭形秽; **to be ~ to sb./sth.** 比不上某人/某事物 2 Jur 下级的; **an ~ court** 初级法院 3 Print 下标的

B *n* 级别较低的人

inferiority /ɪnˌfɪərɪˈɒrəti, Amer -ˈɔːr-/ *n* [u] 低等; **~ to sb./sth.** 低某人/某物一等; **feelings of ~** 自卑感

inferiority complex *n* 自卑情结

infernal /ɪnˈfɜːnl/ *adj* 1 (of hell) 地狱的 ‹*pit*›; **the ~ regions** 阴间; **~ heat** fig 酷热 2 (wicked) 穷凶极恶的; **~ cruelty** 极度残酷 3 colloq (annoying, infuriating) 讨厌的

infernally /ɪnˈfɜːnəli/ *adv* 极讨厌地; **it's ~ hot today!** 今天热死了!

inferno /ɪnˈfɜːnəʊ/ *n* 1 (conflagration) 熊熊烈火 2 fig (chaos) 混乱场面

infertile /ɪnˈfɜːtaɪl, Amer -tl/ *adj* 1 (sterile) 不育的 ‹*person, animal*›; 不结果实的 ‹*plant*› 2 (unproductive) 贫瘠的 ‹*land, soil*›

infertility /ˌɪnfəˈtɪləti/ *n* [u] 1 (of person, animal) 无生育能力 2 (of land, soil) 贫瘠

infertility: ~ clinic *n* 不孕症诊所; **~ treatment** *n* [u] 不孕症治疗

infest /ɪnˈfest/ *vt* 大批出没于; **clothing ~ed with lice** 长满虱子的衣服; **to be ~ed with rats** 老鼠成灾

infestation /ˌɪnfesˈteɪʃn/ *n* 大量滋生; **an ~ of cockroaches** 蟑螂成灾

infidel /ˈɪnfɪdəl/

A *n* (adhering to a different religion) 异教徒; (non-believer) 无宗教信仰者

B *adj* 异教徒的

infidelity /ˌɪnfɪˈdeləti/ *n* 1 [u] (state) 不忠 2 [c] (action) 不忠行为

infighting /ˈɪnfaɪtɪŋ/ *n* [u] 内讧

infill /ˈɪnfɪl/

A *n* [u] (buildings) 空隙填料

B *vt* 1 (fill) 填实 ‹*space, hole*› 2 (with buildings) 在…间隙处添建新房

infiltrate /ˈɪnfɪltreɪt/

A *vi* «*liquid, light, troops*» 潜入; **to ~ through/into sth.** 潜入某地

B *vt* 1 Mil, Pol «*troops, political agents*» 潜入 ‹*territory, party*›; (gain access to) 悄悄进入; **police ~d the organization** 警方潜入了该组织; **to ~ spies into the country** 派特务潜入这个国家 2 (pass slowly into) «*scientist, technician*» 使…渗入 ‹*liquid, gas, substance*›; **to ~ sth. into sth.** 使某物渗透到某物中; **to ~ sth. with sth.** 用某物渗透某物

infiltration /ˌɪnfɪlˈtreɪʃn/ *n* [u] 1 Mil, Pol 潜入 2 (of gas, liquid) 渗透

infinite /ˈɪnfɪnət/ *adj* 1 (boundless) 无限的 ‹*space, region, extent*›; **God in his ~ wisdom** 无比智慧的上帝 2 (immense) 极大的 ‹*pains, patience, variety*›; **to give ~ pleasure to sb.** 给某人无尽的快乐; **with ~ care** 极其小心地 3 Math 无穷大的 ‹*series*›

infinitely /ˈɪnfɪnətli/ *adv* 1 (endlessly) 无限地 ‹*large, small, numerous*› 2 (very much) …得多 ‹*worse, wiser*›; 非常 ‹*preferable, desirable*›

infinitesimal /ˌɪnfɪnɪˈtesɪml/ *adj* 1 (extremely small) 极小的 ‹*amount, increase, decrease*› 2 Math 无穷小的 ‹*quantity, number, variable*›

infinitesimal calculus *n* [u] 微积分

infinitesimally /ˌɪnfɪnɪˈtesɪməli/ *adv* 微乎其微地 ‹*larger, change*›

infinitive /ɪnˈfɪnətɪv/ *n* 动词不定式

infinitude /ɪnˈfɪnɪtjuːd, Amer -tuːd/ *n* [u] formal 无限

infinity /ɪnˈfɪnəti/ *n* 1 [u] (boundlessness) 无限 2 [u] (infinite distance) 无限远的距离; **into ~** 至无限远 3 [u] Phot 无限远聚焦区 4 [u] Math 无穷大; **to ~** 直至无穷 5 [c] (huge, endless amount) 无限大的量; **an ~ of sth.** 数不清的某物

infirm /ɪnˈfɜːm/

A *adj* 体弱的 ‹*person*›; 虚弱的 ‹*appearance, step*›

B *npl* **the ~** 病弱的人

infirmary /ɪnˈfɜːməri/ *n* 1 (hospital) 医院 2 (in school, prison) 医务室

infirmity /ɪnˈfɜːməti/ *n* 1 [u] (physical weakness) 体弱 2 [c] (illness) 疾病

in flagrante delicto /ɪn flæˌgrænteɪ deɪˈlɪktəʊ/ *adv phr* formal 当场 [尤指捉奸]; **he was caught ~ with his secretary** 他在和秘书私通时被当场抓住

inflame /ɪnˈfleɪm/ *vt* 1 (exacerbate) 使…恶化 ‹*situation*› 2 Med «*infection*» 使…红肿 ‹*eye*›; «*disease*» 使…发炎 ‹*throat, organ, joint*› 3 (to anger) 使…愤怒 ‹*person*›; (provoke sb. to strong emotions) «*action, words, imagination*» 激起…的强烈感情 ‹*crowd, audience, followers*›; **to ~ sb. to anger** 激怒某人; **to be ~d with desire** 被勾起欲望

inflamed /ɪnˈfleɪmd/ *adj* 1 Med 红肿的 ‹*eye*›; 发炎的 ‹*throat, organ, joint*› 2 (roused) 非常激动的 ‹*crowd, audience, followers*›; (angry) 愤怒的 ‹*crowd, mob*›

inflammable /ɪnˈflæməbl/ *adj* 易燃的

inflammation /ˌɪnfləˈmeɪʃn/ *n* [u and c] 发炎

inflammatory /ɪnˈflæmətri, Amer -tɔːri/ *adj* 1 (provocative) 煽动性的 ‹*words, remarks*› 2 Med 发炎的

inflatable /ɪnˈfleɪtəbl/

A *adj* 可充气的

B *n* (dinghy) 充气小艇; (toy) 充气玩具

inflate /ɪnˈfleɪt/

A *vt* 1 (fill with air or gas) 给…充气 ‹*object*›; 使…胀大 ‹*lungs*› 2 fig (exaggerate) 夸大; **flattery ~s one's ego** *or* **self-esteem** 赞扬吹捧使人自高自大 3 Econ «*government*» 使…膨胀 ‹*economy*›; «*company*» 使…上涨 ‹*bill*›; **~ prices** 抬高物价

B *vi* 充气

inflated /ɪnˈfleɪtɪd/ *adj* 1 (with air or gas) 充气的 ‹*object*›; 胀大的 ‹*lungs*› 2 fig (overblown) 夸张的; **to have an ~ ego** 自命不凡 3 (flowery) 华而不实的 ‹*language, prose*› 4 Econ 上涨的 ‹*price, bill*›; 膨胀的 ‹*economy, currency*›

inflation /ɪnˈfleɪʃn/ *n* [u] 1 Econ 通货膨胀; **with ~ (running) at 10%** 通胀率达 10% 2 (of object) 充气

inflation-adjusted *adj* 随通货膨胀调整的

inflationary /ɪnˈfleɪʃnri, Amer -neri/ *adj* 通货膨胀的

inflation rate *n* 通胀率

inflect /ɪnˈflekt/

A *vt* 1 Ling 使屈折变化; **to be ~ed with 'ed'** 屈折变化形式为添加"ed" 2 (vary intonation of) 变 ‹*voice*›; 转 ‹*tone, intonation*›

B *vi* «*verb, noun, adjective, language*» 屈折变化

inflected /ɪnˈflektɪd/ *adj* 屈折变化的

inflection /ɪnˈflekʃn/ *n* [c and u] esp Brit 1 Ling 屈折变化 2 (of voice, tone) 语调抑扬变化

inflectional /ɪnˈflekʃənl/ *adj* 有屈折变化的

inflexibility /ɪnˌfleksəˈbɪləti/ *n* [u] 1 (of material, structure) 刚性 2 (of attitude, will, rule, stance) 坚定不移; (of system, method, policy) 不可改变

inflexible /ɪnˈfleksəbl/ *adj* 1 (unable to bend) 不可弯曲的 ‹*material, structure*› 2 (unwilling to change) 坚定不移的 ‹*will, purpose*›; 不可动摇的 ‹*attitude, stance*› 3 (unchangeable, unadaptable) 僵化的 ‹*rule, system, policy*›

inflexion /ɪnˈflekʃn/ *n* esp Brit **= inflection**

inflexional /ɪnˈflekʃənl/ *adj* esp Brit **= inflectional**

inflict /ɪnˈflɪkt/ *vt* 1 (cause to be suffered) 带来 ‹*punishment, pain, defeat*›; **to ~ sth. on sb.** 使某人遭受某事物 2 (impose) 强加 ‹*presence, beliefs*›; **to ~ sb./sth. on** *or* **upon sb.** 把某人/某事物强加给某人; **to ~ oneself on** *or* **upon sb.** 打扰某人

infliction /ɪnˈflɪkʃn/ *n* [u] 施加; **the ~ of severe penalties** 严惩; **the ~ of pain on sb.** 某人遭受痛苦

in-flight *adj attrib* 飞行中提供的 ‹*magazine, entertainment*›

inflow /ˈɪnfləʊ/ *n* [u] 1 (of cash, goods, people) 涌入 2 (of liquid) 注入; (of air) 流入

inflow pipe *n* (for liquid) 注入管; (for air) 进气管

influence /ˈɪnflʊəns/

A *n* 1 [u] (power to affect) 影响力; **to be under the ~ of sb./sth.** 受到某人/某事物的影响; **to have a good/bad ~ (on sb.)** (对某人) 有好/坏影响; **his parents no longer have any real ~ over him** 他的父母对他不再有任何真正的约束力了; **the young king was under the ~ of his chief minister** 这位年轻的国王受到总理大臣的控制; **under the ~** colloq 喝醉酒的; **to drive under the ~** 醉酒驾车 2 [c] (sb. or sth. that exercises power) 影响; **those friends are a bad ~ on her** 那些朋友对她有负面影响; **we are subject to many ~s in life** 我们一生中受到诸多因素的影响 3 [u] (ability to obtain favourable treatment) 势力; **he used his ~ to get his son the position** 他凭借权势为儿子谋得这一职位; **she has great ~ with the manager** 她能够对经理施加巨大影响 4 [c and u] (of climate, magnetic field, gravity, planet) 作用; **the ~ of the moon on the tides** 月球对潮汐的作用

B *vt* 影响; **to ~ sb. in his choice/decision/opinion** 影响某人的选择/决定/意见; **what on earth ~d you to behave in that way?** 究竟是什么使你作出那样的举动?

influence peddling *n* [u] 权势贩卖 [利用地位或政治影响力谋取钱财或关照]

influential /ˌɪnflʊˈenʃl/ *adj* 1 (persuasive) 有影响力的; **to be ~ in sth./doing sth.** 对某事物/做某事有影响 2 (powerful) 有权势的; **to have ~ friends** 交有权势的朋友

influenza /ˌɪnflʊˈenzə/ ▸**p. 377** *n* [u] 流感

influx /ˈɪnflʌks/ *n* 1 (of people, money) 大量涌入 2 (of liquid) 流入

info /ˈɪnfəʊ/ *n* [u] colloq 信息

infoglut /ˈɪnfəʊglʌt/ *n* colloq 信息过剩

infomania /ˌɪnfəʊˈmeɪnɪə/ *n* [u] colloq 信息狂躁症 [指持续处理电子信息导致的注意力下降]

infomercial /ˌɪnfəʊˈmɜːʃl/ *n* colloq 商业信息广告片

inform /ɪnˈfɔːm/
A *vt* 1 (notify, tell) 通知; **to ~ sb. of** *or* **about sth.** 通知某人某事; **why wasn't I ~ed?** 为什么没有告诉我?; **to keep sb. ~ed of** *or* **as to ...** 随时向某人报告…; **I am pleased/sorry to ~ you that ...** 我很高兴/遗憾地告诉你…; **to ~ sb. if/when ...** 告诉某人如果/何时… 2 (pervade, give essential features to) 赋特征于; **the sense of justice which ~s all her writings** 充溢于她所有作品中的正义感
B *vi* (denounce) 告发; **to ~ against** *or* **on sb.** 告发 ‹*gang, criminal*›

informal /ɪnˈfɔːml/ *adj* 1 (relaxed) 轻松友好的 ‹*atmosphere, mood, occasion, manner*› 2 (casual) 随便的 ‹*dress, attire*›; **~ clothes** 便服 3 (unofficial) 非正式的 ‹*announcement, communication, visit, invitation*›; **on an ~ basis** 非正式地 4 (in tone, style) 非书面的 ‹*language, term, style*›; 非正式的 ‹*letter*›

informality /ˌɪnfɔːˈmæləti/ *n* [u] 1 (lack of ceremony) 不拘礼节; (unofficial status) 非官方; (relaxed feel) 轻松友好; **I liked the ~ of the ceremony** 我喜欢典礼的轻松气氛 2 (of language) 非书面

informally /ɪnˈfɔːməli/ *adv* 1 (without ceremony) 不拘礼节地 ‹*dress, speak, act*› 2 (unofficially) 非正式地 ‹*announce, instruct, invite, suggest*›

informant /ɪnˈfɔːmənt/ *n* 1 (provider of information) 提供消息的人 2 Ling, Anthrop 资料提供者

informatics /ˌɪnfəˈmætɪks/ *npl* + *v sing* 信息学

information /ˌɪnfəˈmeɪʃn/ *n* [u] 1 (facts, details) 消息; **~ on** *or* **about sb./sth.** 有关某人/某事物的消息; **a piece** *or* **bit** *or* **an item of ~** 一则消息; **to give/receive/pass on ~** 发布/接收/传递信息; **for further** *or* **additional** *or* **more ~** 欲知详情; **for ~** 供参考; **for your ~** 需要说明的是; **a mine of ~** 知识宝库 2 Amer Telecom 电话号码查询台; **to call ~** 打电话给查号台 3 (data) 数据; **genetically transmitted ~** 基因遗传信息

information: ~ bureau *n* 问讯处; **~ centre** *n* 信息中心; **~ content** *n* [u] 信息量; **~ desk** *n* 问讯台; **~ economy** *n* 信息经济; **~ exchange** *n* 信息交流; **~ office** *n* = **~ bureau**; **~ officer** ▸**p. 409** *n* 1 (PR person, press officer) 情报员; 2 (person responsible for IT) 信息管理员; **~ pack** *n* 信息包; **~ processing** *n* [u] 信息处理; **~ retrieval** *n* [u] 信息检索; **~ retrieval system** *n* 信息检索系统; **~ revolution** *n* 信息革命; **~ room** *n* 情报室; **~ science** *n* [u] 信息学; **~ scientist** *n* ▸**p. 409** 信息学家; **~ service** *n* 信息服务; **~ superhighway** *n* 信息高速公路; **~ system** *n* 信息系统; **~ technology** *n* [u] 信息技术; **~ theory** *n* [u] 信息论; **~ transfer** *n* [u] 信息传送

informative /ɪnˈfɔːmətɪv/ *adj* 提供有用信息的

informed /ɪnˈfɔːmd/ *adj* 1 (having or showing knowledge) 有见识的 ‹*person, opinion, critic*› 2 (based on understanding) 有依据的 ‹*opinion, judgement*›; **he is very well-/ill-~** 他消息灵通/闭塞

informer /ɪnˈfɔːmə(r)/ *n* 告密者

infotainment /ˌɪnfəʊˈteɪnmənt/ *n* [u] colloq 信息娱乐片

infotech /ˈɪnfəʊtek/ *n* [u] colloq 信息技术

infowar /ˈɪnfəʊwɔː(r)/ *n* colloq 信息战

infraction /ɪnˈfrækʃn/ *n* formal 违法; **a minor ~** 轻微触犯

infra dig /ˌɪnfrəˈdɪg/ *adj* dated colloq 有失身份的

infrared /ˌɪnfrəˈred/
A *adj* 红外线的
B *n* [u] 1 **the ~** (region) 红外线区 2 (radiation) 红外线辐射

infrared sensor *n* 红外传感器

infrasonic /ˌɪnfrəˈsɒnɪk/ *adj* 次声的

infrasound /ˈɪnfrəsaʊnd/ *n* [u] 次声

infrastructure /ˈɪnfrəstrʌktʃə(r)/ *n* [c and u] 基础设施

infrequency /ɪnˈfriːkwənsi/ *n* [u] 罕见

infrequent /ɪnˈfriːkwənt/ *adj* 罕见的; **~ visits** 少有的拜访; **~ trains** 稀少的火车

infrequently /ɪnˈfriːkwəntli/ *adv* 罕见地

infringe /ɪnˈfrɪndʒ/
A *vt* 1 (break) 违背 ‹*agreement*›; 触犯 ‹*law*› 2 (violate) 侵犯 ‹*liberty, rights*›
B *vi* (encroach) **to ~ on** *or* **upon sth.** 侵犯某权益

infringement /ɪnˈfrɪndʒmənt/ *n* [c and u] (of rule) 违反; (of rights, liberty) 侵犯; (of law) 触犯

infuriate /ɪnˈfjʊərɪeɪt/ *vt* 使大怒; **to be ~d with** *or* **by sb./sth.** 被某人/某事物激怒

infuriating /ɪnˈfjʊərɪeɪtɪŋ/ *adj* 令人极为恼火的

infuriatingly /ɪnˈfjʊərɪeɪtɪŋli/ *adv* 令人极为恼火地; **~ slow** 慢得叫人火冒三丈的

infuse /ɪnˈfjuːz/
A *vt* 1 (instil, pervade) 使充满; **to ~ a project with enthusiasm** 在项目中倾注热情; **the movement was ~d with new life** 这一运动被注入了新的活力 2 Culin 浸泡; **vinegar ~d with tarragon** 浸泡龙蒿叶的醋
B *vi* «*tea, herbs*» 被浸泡

infusion /ɪnˈfjuːʒn/ *n* 1 [c] (drink, remedy) 泡剂 2 [u and c] (process) 泡制 3 [u and c] (of element, quality) 注入; **an ~ of sth. into sb./sth.** 将某观念向某人的灌输/将某资源向某处的注入; **an ~ of new capital into a company** 对公司的新资金注入

ingenious /ɪnˈdʒiːnɪəs/ *adj* 心灵手巧的 ‹*person*›; 精巧的 ‹*device, instrument, mechanism*›; 别出心裁的 ‹*idea, scheme, solution*›; **to be ~ at doing sth./sth.** 做某事/在某方面机敏

ingeniously /ɪnˈdʒiːnɪəsli/ *adv* 灵巧地 ‹*act*›; 机敏地 ‹*behave*›; **~ designed** 设计巧妙的

ingénue /ˈænʒeɪnjuː, Amer ˈændʒənuː/ *n* 1 (innocent young woman) 天真少女 2 (role, part) 扮演天真少女的演员

ingenuity /ˌɪndʒɪˈnjuːəti, Amer -ˈnuː-/ *n* [u] 心灵手巧; **to use one's ~** 发挥聪明才智

ingenuous /ɪnˈdʒenjʊəs/ *adj* 天真的 ‹*person, facial expression*›; 单纯的 ‹*action, look*›; 坦诚的 ‹*nature, attitude*›

ingenuously /ɪnˈdʒenjʊəsli/ *adv* 天真地

ingenuousness /ɪnˈdʒenjʊəsnɪs/ *n* [u] 天真

ingest /ɪnˈdʒest/ *vt* 1 (eat, absorb) 咽下 ‹*food*›; 喝下 ‹*drink*› 2 fig (take in) 吸取 ‹*information, facts*›

ingestion /ɪnˈdʒestʃn/ *n* [u] 1 (of food, drink) 摄入 2 fig (of information, facts) 吸收

inglenook /ˈɪŋglnʊk/ *n* 壁炉边

inglorious /ɪnˈglɔːrɪəs/ *adj* liter 可耻的

ingot /ˈɪŋgət/ *n* 铸块; **gold ~s** 金锭

ingrained /ɪnˈgreɪnd/ *adj* 1 (deep-rooted) 根深蒂固的 ‹*habit, prejudice, hatred*›; **to be deeply ~ in ...** 深深地积存在… 2 (difficult to remove) 难以清除的 ‹*stain, mark, grease*›

ingratiate /ɪnˈgreɪʃɪeɪt/ *v refl* pej 讨好; **to ~ oneself with sb.** 巴结某人

ingratiating /ɪnˈgreɪʃɪeɪtɪŋ/ *adj* pej 奉承的 ‹*words, smile*›; 讨好的 ‹*demeanour, behaviour*›

ingratitude /ɪnˈgrætɪtjuːd, Amer -tuːd/ *n* [u] 忘恩负义

ingredient /ɪnˈgriːdɪənt/ *n* 1 Culin 原料; **a list of ~s** 配料表 2 (element) 因素; **the ~s of a successful novel** 一部成功小说的要素

ingress /ˈɪŋgres/ *n* [u] formal (entering) 进入; (right to enter) 进入权; **right of ~** 入境权; **to have free ~ into ...** 可自由进入…

in-group *n* 小集团

ingrowing toenail, ingrown toenail *ns* 嵌甲

ingrown /ˈɪngrəʊn/ *adj* 1 (innate) 天生的 ‹*habit*› 2 (grown into the flesh) 长进肉里的 ‹*hair, toenail*› 3 (inward-looking) 关注内部的 ‹*society*›

inhabit /ɪnˈhæbɪt/ *vt* lit «*people*» 居住于 ‹*house, country, town*›; «*animals, birds*» 栖息于 ‹*burrow, region, nest*›

inhabitable /ɪnˈhæbɪtəbl/ *adj* 可居住的 ‹*house, area, planet*›

inhabitant /ɪnˈhæbɪtənt/ *n* (person) 居民; (animal) 栖息动物

inhalant /ɪnˈheɪlənt/ *n* 1 (medicine) 吸入剂 2 (solvent for drugs) 溶解物

inhalation /ˌɪnhəˈleɪʃn/ *n* [u and c] 吸入

inhalator /ɪnˈheɪlətə(r)/ *n* 气雾吸入器

inhale /ɪnˈheɪl/
A *vt* 吸入
B *vi* (breathe in) 吸气; (when smoking) 吸烟

inhaler /ɪnˈheɪlə(r)/ *n* 吸入器

inherent /ɪnˈhɪərənt, ɪnˈherənt/ *adj* 内在的 ‹*weakness, virtue*›; 固有的 ‹*problem, characteristic, danger*›; **with its ~ risks** 由于其本身的危险; **to be ~ in sth.** 是某事物固有的

inherently /ɪnˈhɪərəntli, ɪnˈher-/ *adv* 内在地 ‹*inefficient, dangerous, risky*›

inherit /ɪnˈherɪt/ *vt* 1 (receive as heir) 继承; **to ~ sth. from sb.** 从某人处继承某物 2 (receive genetically) 经遗传获得 ‹*temperament, complexion*› 3 fig (be left with) «*person, institution*» 接手 ‹*problem*›; (maintain) 沿袭 ‹*tradition, custom*›

inheritance /ɪnˈherɪtəns/ *n* 1 [c] (thing inherited) 继承物; **to come into an ~** 得到遗产 2 [u] (succession) 继承; **by** *or* **through ~** 通过继承 3 [u] Biol 遗传

inheritance tax *n* [u and c] Amer 遗产税

inherited /ɪnˈherɪtɪd/ *adj* 遗传的 ‹*characteristic, disorder, disease*›; 继承的 ‹*wealth, debt, tradition*›

inheritor /ɪnˈherɪtə(r)/ *n* 继承人

inhibit /ɪnˈhɪbɪt/ *vt* 1 (restrain, hinder) 抑制 ‹*impulse*›; 妨碍 ‹*person, behaviour*›; 阻碍 ‹*process, activity*›; **to ~ sb. from doing sth.** 妨碍某人做某事 2 Physiol, Biol 抑制

inhibited /ɪnˈhɪbɪtɪd/ *adj* 拘谨的; **to be ~ by sth.** 因某事而拘谨; **she is ~ by inexperience** 她因缺乏经验而羞涩

inhibiting /ɪnˈhɪbɪtɪŋ/ *adj* 抑制的

inhibition /ˌɪnhɪˈbɪʃn, ˌɪnɪˈb-/ *n* 1 [c] (feeling) 拘谨; **to get rid of one's ~s** 克服自己的拘束感 2 Psych, Biol 抑制

inhibitor /ɪnˈhɪbɪtə(r)/ *n* 1 Biol 抑制因子 2 Med 抑制剂

in-home *adj* 上门的 ‹*service, activity*›

inhospitable /ˌɪnhɒˈspɪtəbl/ *adj* 1 (unfriendly, unwelcoming) 不友好的 2 (harsh and difficult to live in) 严酷的 ‹*climate, environment*›; 不适合居住的 ‹*region*›; 荒凉的 ‹*desert*›

inhospitably /ˌɪnhɒˈspɪtəbli/ *adv* 1 (unwelcomingly) 不友好地 ‹*receive, greet*› 2 (unpleasantly) 不宜人地; **~ barren and dry** 贫脊、干旱，不适合居住

inhospitality /ɪnˌhɒspɪˈtæləti/ *n* [u] 1 (of person) 不好客 2 (of environment) 不宜居住

in-house *adj* 机构内部的 ‹*training, guidelines*›; **~ editor** 社内编辑

i

inhuman /ɪn'hjuːmən/ *adj* 冷酷无情的〈*violence*〉; 不人道的〈*cruelty, treatment*〉; 非人的〈*behaviour*〉

inhumane /ˌɪnhjuː'meɪn/ *adj* 不人道的〈*treatment, law, decision*〉; 残忍的〈*person, weapon*〉

inhumanity /ˌɪnhjuː'mænəti/ *n* [u] 残忍; **man's ~ to man** 人类相残

inimical /ɪ'nɪmɪkl/ *adj* **1** (hostile) 不友好的〈*action, area*〉; 不利的〈*climate, species*〉; **to be ~ to sb./sth.** 对某人有敌意/对某事物不利 **2** (obstructive, harmful) 有害的〈*policy, legislation*〉; **to be ~ to sb./sth.** 有损于某人/某事物

inimitable /ɪ'nɪmɪtəbl/ *adj* 无法仿效的; **in her own ~ way** 以她独特的方式

iniquitous /ɪ'nɪkwɪtəs/ *adj* **1** (wicked) 邪恶的〈*system, regime, practice, policy*〉 **2** (unjustly high) 奇高的〈*price, tax*〉

iniquity /ɪ'nɪkwəti/ *n* **1** [u] (wickedness) 邪恶; (unfairness) 不公正; **a den of ~** 藏污纳垢之地 **2** [c] (wicked act) 恶劣行为; (unjust act) 不公正行为

initial /ɪ'nɪʃl/
A *n* 首字母; **what's your first/second ~?** 你名字的第一个/第二个首字母是什么？; **to put one's ~s on sth.** 在某物上签上自己姓名的首字母; **my ~s are MOC** 我的姓名首字母是 MOC
B *adj* 开始的〈*problem, capital*〉; 最初的〈*reaction, investment, expenditure*〉; **~ letter** 首字母; **in the ~ stages** 在初始阶段
C *vt* (*pres p etc.* **-ll-** Brit, **-l-** Amer) 用姓名首字母签署〈*page, letter, document*〉

initially /ɪ'nɪʃəli/ *adv* 起初

initial public offering *n* 首次公开招股

initiate
A /ɪ'nɪʃieɪt/ *vt* **1** (cause to begin) 开始〈*talks, project, scheme, process*〉; **to ~ proceedings against sb.** 起诉某人 **2** (admit into membership) 使…加入〈*novice, applicant*〉; **to ~ sb. into a religious sect/secret society** 接纳某人加入宗教教派/秘密会社 **3** (instruct) 传授; **to ~ sb. into sth.** 使某人了解某事物
B /ɪ'nɪʃiət/ *n* 新加入组织的人; **~s of the cult** 新加入异教团体的人

initiated /ɪ'nɪʃieɪtɪd/ *npl* **the ~** 知情人士

initiation /ɪˌnɪʃi'eɪʃn/ *n* **1** [u] (of talks, project, scheme, process) 开始 **2** [u] (admission) (into sect) 入会; (into knowledge) 入门; **sb.'s ~ into sth.** 某人初次涉足某领域 **3** [c] (ceremony) 入会仪式

initiative /ɪ'nɪʃətɪv/ *n* **1** [u] (ability to think and act on one's own) 主动性; **use your ~!** 自己想办法吧!; **on one's own ~** 主动地 **2** [c] (first move) 主动行为; **to take the ~** 采取主动; **peace ~(s)** 和平倡议 **3** [u] (upper hand) 主动权; **to lose the ~** 丧失先机 **4** [c] Pol 立法提案程序

initiative test *n* 主动性测试

initiator /ɪ'nɪʃieɪtə(r)/ *n* 发起者

inject /ɪn'dʒekt/ *vt* **1** 注射〈*drug*〉; 给…注射〈*patient*〉; 注入〈*liquid, gas*〉; **to ~ sb. with penicillin** 给某人注射青霉素; **~ foam into the cavity wall** 将泡沫剂注入空心墙 **2** fig (introduce) 引入〈*thoughts*〉; 投入〈*cash, enthusiasm*〉; **to ~ funds into sth.** 为某事投入资金; **to ~ a new spark of life into the city** 给这座城市注入新的活力

injection /ɪn'dʒekʃn/ *n* **1** [u and c] Med (act or instance of injecting) 注射; **the morphine was administered by ~** 吗啡已经注射入体内; **to give sb. an ~** 给某人打针; **an ~ of sth. into sb.** 某药注射入某人体内 **2** [c] fig (introduction) 投入; **an ~ of cash into the company** 对公司的现金投入

injection: ~-moulded *adj* 注塑成型的; **~-moulded plastic** 注塑塑料; **~ moulding** *n* [u] 注塑

injector /ɪn'dʒektə(r)/ *n* 喷油器

in-joke *n* 圈子里的笑话

injudicious /ˌɪndʒuː'dɪʃəs/ *adj* 不明智的

injudiciously /ˌɪndʒuː'dɪʃəsli/ *adv* 不明智地

injunction /ɪn'dʒʌŋkʃn/ *n* **1** Jur 禁制令; **to seek an ~** 请求强制令 **2** (admonition) 警告; (order) 命令; **an ~ to do sth.** 做某事的命令

injure /'ɪndʒə(r)/ *vt* **1** (hurt) 使受伤; **to ~ oneself by doing sth.** 做某事使自己受伤; **to ~ one's arm (playing football)** (踢足球时)手臂受伤 **2** fig (damage) 损害〈*reputation, self-esteem*〉; **to ~ sb.'s feelings** 伤害某人的感情

injured /'ɪndʒəd/
A *adj* **1** Med 受伤的 **2** fig (damaged, wronged) 受损的〈*party, reputation*〉; 受委屈的〈*person, look, tone*〉; 受伤的〈*pride, self-esteem, feelings*〉
B *npl* **the ~** 伤员
C *modif* 伤员的; **to be on the ~ list** 在伤员名单上

injurious /ɪn'dʒʊəriəs/ *adj* formal **1** (harmful) 造成伤害的〈*practice, effect*〉; **smoking is ~ to one's health** 吸烟有害健康 **2** (abusive) 不公正的〈*treatment, comment*〉; 诽谤的〈*remark*〉

injury /'ɪndʒəri/ *n* **1** [c] Med 受伤; **to do sb./oneself an ~** 弄伤某人/自己; **head injuries** 头部受伤 **2** [c] fig (to reputation, self-esteem) 伤害; **injuries to sb.'s pride/reputation** 对某人自尊/名誉的损害 **3** [c] Jur 伤害行为; **insurance against ~** 伤害险

injury: ~ benefit *n* Brit 工伤抚恤金; **~ time** *n* [u] 伤停补时; **in ~ time** 在伤停补时阶段

injustice /ɪn'dʒʌstɪs/ *n* **1** [u] (lack of justice) 不公正 **2** [c] (unjust act) 不公正行为; **to do sb. an ~** 冤枉某人

ink /ɪŋk/
A *n* **1** [u and c] (for writing, painting) 墨水; **in ~** 用墨水写; **as black as ~** 漆黑 **2** [u] (of octopus, squid) 墨汁
B *vt* 给…上油墨〈*roller, type*〉

Phrasal verb
- **ink in** *vt* [**~ in sth., ~ sth. in**] 用墨水描画

inkblot /'ɪŋkblɒt/ *n* 墨迹

ink: ~blot test *n* 墨迹测验 [受测者说出对各种墨迹的联想]; **~ drawing** *n* 钢笔画; **~jet printer** *n* 喷墨打印机

inkling /'ɪŋklɪŋ/ *n* 粗浅认识; **to have an/no ~ of sth.** 对某事物略知一二/一无所知; **to give (sb.) an/no ~ of sth.** 对某事物给予/不给予(某人)暗示; **that was my first ~ that ...** 那是我第一次隐约感觉到…

ink: ~pad *n* 印台; **~pot** *n* 墨水瓶; **~stand** *n* 墨水台; **~well** *n* 墨水池

inky /'ɪŋki/ *adj* **1** lit 沾有墨水的 **2** fig 漆黑的; **~ blackness** *or* **darkness** 一片漆黑

inlaid /ˌɪn'leɪd/
A *pt, pp* ▸ **inlay B**
B *adj* 嵌饰的〈*pattern, brooch, table, floor*〉; **~ work** 镶嵌细工

inland
A /'ɪnlənd/ *adj* **1** (not coastal) 内陆的〈*area, town, harbour*〉; **~ navigation/waterways** 内河航行/内陆水路 **2** Brit (domestic) 国内的〈*mail, transport*〉
B /ˌɪn'lænd/ *adv* 向内陆〈*go, retreat, advance*〉; 在内地〈*live, settle*〉; **to move further ~** 深入内陆地区

inland: ~ bill *n* Brit 国内汇票; **I~ Revenue** *n* [u] Brit 国内税收署; **~ sea** *n* 内陆海

in-laws /'ɪnlɔːz/ *npl* (parents) (on wife's side) 岳父母; (on husband's side) 公婆; (other relatives) 姻亲

inlay
A /'ɪnleɪ/ *n* (design) 镶嵌装饰; (pattern) 镶嵌图样; **a brooch with enamel ~(s)** 镶嵌着珐琅的胸针
B /ˌɪn'leɪ/ *vt* (*pt, pp* **inlaid**) 镶嵌; **to ~ sth. with sth.** 用某物镶嵌某物; **to ~ sth. in(to) sth.** 把某物镶入某物

inlet /'ɪnlet/ *n* **1** (of sea, river) 水湾 **2** Tech (for fuel, air) 注入口 **3** (in garment) 嵌片

inlet: ~ pipe *n* 注入管; **~ valve** *n* 进给阀

in-line: ~ skates *n* 滚轴溜冰鞋; **~ skating** ▸ **p. 307** *n* [u] 滚轴溜冰

in loco parentis /ɪn ˌləʊkəʊ pə'rentɪs/ *adv, adj* 代替家长责任(的)

inmate /'ɪnmeɪt/ *n* (of institution) 同住者; (of hospital, mental hospital) 同院病人; (of prison) 同狱犯人

inmost /'ɪnməʊst/ *adj* = **innermost**

inn /ɪn/ *n* 小旅店

innards /'ɪnədz/ *npl* colloq **1** (entrails) 内脏 **2** fig (internal workings) 内部结构

innate /ɪ'neɪt/ *adj* 天生的〈*beauty, talent, ability, honesty, stupidity*〉; 固有的〈*attribute, tendency*〉

innately /ɪ'neɪtli/ *adv* 天生地〈*beautiful, talented, honest, stupid*〉

inner /'ɪnə(r)/
A *adj attrib* **1** (inside) 里面的; **an ~ room/courtyard/wrapping** 内室/内院/内包装 **2** fig (exclusive) 核心的; **the ~ circle** 核心集团 **3** (intimate) 内心的〈*thoughts, feelings*〉
B *n* (in archery, shooting) 内圈; (shot) 内圈命中

inner circle *n* 核心集团

inner city
A *n* **the ~** 市中心区
B **inner-city** *modif* 市中心的〈*housing, slums*〉

inner: ~ ear *n* 内耳; **~ lane** *n* 内车道; **~ man** *n* **1** (soul) [男子的] 灵魂; **2** hum (stomach) [男子的] 胃

Inner Mongolia ▸ **p. 604** *pr n* **~ (Autonomous Region)** 内蒙古(自治区)

innermost /'ɪnəməʊst/ *adj attrib* **1** (most intimate) 内心深处的〈*feelings, thoughts, fears*〉; **his ~ self** *or* **being** liter 他内心深处的自我 **2** (deepest) 最里面的; **the ~ depths of ...** …的最深处

inner: ~ sanctum *n* (in church, temple) 圣坛; (secret place) 隐秘之地; (private place) 私人领地; **~ sole** *n* 鞋内底; **~ tube** *n* [气胎的] 内胎; **~ woman** *n* **1** (soul) [女子的] 灵魂; **2** hum (stomach) [女子的] 胃

inning /'ɪnɪŋ/ *n* Amer [棒球运动的] 局

innings /'ɪnɪŋz/ *n* + *v sing* Brit **1** (in cricket) 局 **2** fig 活跃期; **to have had a good ~** (in life) 终养天年; (in one's career) 事业有成

innkeeper /'ɪnkiːpə(r)/ *n* 旅店老板

innocence /'ɪnəsns/ *n* [u] **1** Jur (of accused) 清白; **to prove one's ~** 证明自己无罪 **2** (guilelessness) 天真; **he had an air of childlike ~** 他看上去有一种孩童般的单纯 **3** (naivety) 缺乏经验; **in my ~, I thought that ...** 我幼稚地以为…

innocent /'ɪnəsnt/
A *adj* **1** Jur (not guilty) 无罪的; **(to be) ~ of a crime** (是)无罪的; **~ in the eyes of the law** 从法律的角度看是清白的 **2** (blameless) 无辜的〈*victim, bystander*〉 **3** (innocuous) 无害的〈*pastime, mistake*〉; 无恶意的〈*question, remark*〉 **4** (naive) 天真无邪的〈*face, expression*〉; **to put on an ~ air** 故作天真
B *n* 天真无邪的人; **they're no ~s!** 他们并不幼稚!

innocently /'ɪnəsntli/ *adv* 天真地〈*ask, say, behave*〉

innocuous /ɪ'nɒkjuəs/ *adj* **1** (inoffensive) 无意冒犯的〈*remark, words, statement*〉 **2** (harmless) 无害的〈*drug, substance*〉

Inn of Court *n* Brit (legal society) 律师学院 [英国有权授予大律师资格的机构]; (building) 律师学院楼

innovate /'ɪnəveɪt/ *vi* 革新

innovation /ˌɪnə'veɪʃn/ *n* **1** [c] (new method) 新方法; **to make ~s in sth.** 在某方面进行

创新 **2** [u] (introduction of new ideas, methods, etc.) 革新

innovative /ˈɪnəvətɪv/ *adj* 革新的 ‹*product, approach, technology, design*›; 富有创新精神的 ‹*company*›; 有创意的 ‹*idea, concept*›

innovator /ˈɪnəveɪtə(r)/ *n* 革新者

innovatory /ˌɪnəˈveɪtəri/ *adj* = **innovative**

innuendo /ˌɪnjuːˈendəʊ/ *n* [c and u] (*pl* **~s** *or* **~es**) (hint) 暗示; (remark) 影射; **to make ~es about** *or* **against sb.** 含沙射影地指责某人; **a campaign of ~ and lies** 一系列影射和谎言; **a song full of sexual ~** 充满性暗示的歌曲

innumerable /ɪˈnjuːmərəbl, Amer ɪˈnuː-/ *adj* 数不清的 ‹*people, objects*›; 很多的 ‹*benefits, reasons, excuses*›

innumeracy /ɪˈnjuːmərəsi, Amer ɪˈnuː-/ *n* [u] 不会计算

innumerate /ɪˈnjuːmərət, Amer ɪˈnuː-/ *adj* 不会计算的

inoculate /ɪˈnɒkjʊleɪt/ *vt* 给…接种; **to ~ sb. with/against sth.** 为某人注射某预防针/某疾病的预防针

inoculation /ɪˌnɒkjʊˈleɪʃn/ *n* [u and c] 预防接种

inoffensive /ˌɪnəˈfensɪv/ *adj* 不伤人的 ‹*remark*›; 不讨人嫌的 ‹*appearance, person*›

inoperable /ɪnˈɒpərəbl/ *adj* **1** Med 不宜动手术的 ‹*illness, tumour*› **2** (unworkable) 行不通的; (impractical) 不实用的

inoperative /ɪnˈɒpərətɪv/ *adj* 无效的 ‹*law, rule*›; 不能运营的 ‹*bus service, train service, ferry service*›

inopportune /ɪnˈɒpətjuːn, Amer -tuːn/ *adj* **1** (inappropriate) 不合适的 ‹*remark, request*› **2** (untimely) 不适宜的 ‹*moment, time*›

inopportunely /ɪnˈɒpətjuːnli, Amer -tuːn-/ *adv* **1** (inappropriately) 不合适地 **2** (in an untimely manner) 不合时宜地

inordinate /ɪnˈɔːdɪnət/ *adj* 超出合理限度的 ‹*size, quantity*›; 过分的 ‹*demands, passion, delays*›; **an ~ amount of time** 过多的时间; **an ~ number of people** 过多的人数

inordinately /ɪnˈɔːdɪnətli/ *adv* 过分地 ‹*hot, heavy*›; 极其 ‹*angry, rich*›; **to be ~ fond of sth.** 非常喜欢某事物

inorganic /ˌɪnɔːˈgænɪk/ *adj* **1** (not of animal or plant origin) 无生物的 **2** Chem 无机的

inorganic chemistry *n* [u] 无机化学

in-patient *n* 住院病人

input /ˈɪnpʊt/

A *n* **1** [c] (of money, resources) 投入; (of energy) 输入; **the ~ of sth. in** *or* **into sth.** 对某事物投入某资源 **2** [c] (contribution) 贡献 **3** [c] Phys, Electron (energy) 输入能量; **the ~ is a low-frequency signal** 输入的是低频信号 **4** [c] Electron (device, port) 输入端; **the ~ is located by the keyboard** 输入端口在键盘上 **5** [u] Comput 输入; **the ~ of new information and data** 新信息与数据的输入

B *vt* (*pres p* **-tt-**; *pt, pp* **input** *or* **inputted**) 输入; **to ~ data into a computer** 把数据输入计算机

input: ~ data *n* [u] 输入数据; **~-output** *adj attrib* 输入一输出的

inquest /ˈɪŋkwest/ *n* **1** Jur (into an incident, event) 审讯 **2** Brit Jur (into a death) 验尸; **the coroner is holding an ~** 验尸官正在进行验尸 **3** colloq (discussion of outcome) 结果讨论

inquire /ɪnˈkwaɪə(r)/

A *vt* 询问; **to ~ sth. of** *or* **from sb.** 向某人打听某事物

B *vi* 打听; **to ~ about sb./sth.** 打听某人/某事物; **to ~ after sb.** 问候某人; **to ~ into the truth of an allegation** 调查一项指控的真相; **~ within** 欲知详情请进内询问; **to ~ at the information desk** 在问讯台查问

inquirer /ɪnˈkwaɪərə(r)/ *n* 询问者

inquiring /ɪnˈkwaɪərɪŋ/ *adj* 爱探索的 ‹*intellect*›; 探询的 ‹*look, expression*›; **to have an ~ mind** 有好奇心

inquiringly /ɪnˈkwaɪərɪŋli/ *adv* 探询地

inquiry /ɪnˈkwaɪəri, Amer ˈɪŋkwəri/ *n* **1** [c] (request for information) 询问; **to make an ~ about** *or* **into sth.** 查问某事; **on ~, it was discovered that ...** 调查时发现…; **'all inquiries to ...'** "所有查询事宜请到…"; **in answer to** *or* **with reference to your ~** 作为对您所咨询问题的答复 **2** [c] (official investigation) 调查; **to hold** *or* **conduct an ~ into sth.** 对某事展开调查 **3** [u] (informal investigation) 打听; **on ~** 通过探问; **a fruitful line of ~** 成效不错的探听线索

inquiry: ~ response system *n* 查询反馈系统; **~ terminal** *n* 查询终端

inquisition /ˌɪnkwɪˈzɪʃn/

A *n* formal or hum (inquiry) 盘问; **an ~ into sth.** 对某事的详尽探究; **why the ~?** hum 为何盘问不休?

B **Inquisition** *pr n* Relig, Hist **the I~** 宗教裁判所

inquisitive /ɪnˈkwɪzətɪv/ *adj* **1** (curious, inquiring) 好奇的 ‹*mind*›; 爱钻研的 ‹*person*› **2** (prying) 好打听的 ‹*person, habit*›

inquisitively /ɪnˈkwɪzətɪvli/ *adv* 好打听地

inquisitiveness /ɪnˈkwɪzətɪvnɪs/ *n* [u] **1** (curiosity) 好奇心 **2** (nosiness) 包打听

inquisitor /ɪnˈkwɪzɪtə(r)/ *n* **1** (person making inquiry) 盘问者 **2** **Inquisitor** Relig Hist [异端审问的] 裁判人

inquisitorial /ɪnˌkwɪzɪˈtɔːrɪəl/ *adj* (like an inquisitor) 审判官似的; (of an inquisitor) 审判官的

inquisitorial system *n* 纠问制 [主要由主审法官负责提问并作事实认定的诉讼制度]

inquorate /ɪnˈkwɔːreɪt/ *adj* 未达到法定人数(而无法继续进行)的 ‹*meeting, assembly*›

inroad /ˈɪnrəʊd/ *n* **to make ~s into sth.** (advance into) 在某事上取得进展; (encroach on) 削弱某事物; **the firm is beginning to make ~s into the UK market** 该公司开始进军英国市场; **his extravagance has made ~s into his savings** 他的挥霍耗去他不少积蓄

inrush /ˈɪnrʌʃ/ *n* (of air) 涌入; (of water) 流入; **an ~ of visitors into the area** 涌入该地区的参观者

insalubrious /ˌɪnsəˈluːbrɪəs/ *adj* 肮脏破旧的

insane /ɪnˈseɪn/

A *adj* **1** (mentally ill) 精神失常的; **to go** *or* **become ~** 变得精神错乱 **2** (irrational) 疯狂的; (foolish) 愚蠢的 ‹*plan*› **3** (angry, distracted) 发怒的; **to drive sb. ~** 把某人逼疯; **the noise from next door was driving us ~** 隔壁的噪音快把我们逼疯了

B *npl* **the ~** 精神失常的人

insanely /ɪnˈseɪnli/ *adv* colloq 疯狂地; **to be ~ jealous** 妒忌得发疯

insanitary /ɪnˈsænɪtri, Amer -teri/ *adj* 不卫生的

insanity /ɪnˈsænəti/ *n* [u] **1** (madness) 精神失常; **to enter a plea of ~** 提出精神失常的抗辩 **2** (extreme foolishness) 极端愚蠢

insatiable /ɪnˈseɪʃəbl/ *adj* (voracious) 贪得无厌的 ‹*greed, thirst*›; (unsatisfiable) 不能满足的 ‹*appetite, curiosity, desire, lust*›

insatiably /ɪnˈseɪʃəbli/ *adv* 贪得无厌地

inscribe /ɪnˈskraɪb/ *vt* (write) 题写; (engrave) 刻写; **to ~ sth. on/in sth.** 把某文字刻在某物上/里; **to ~ sth. with a verse, to ~ a verse on sth.** 在某处题诗

inscription /ɪnˈskrɪpʃn/ *n* (gen) 铭文; (on stone, metal) 铭刻; (in book) 题名

inscrutability /ɪnˌskruːtəˈbɪləti/ *n* [u] 高深莫测

inscrutable /ɪnˈskruːtəbl/ *adj* 难以捉摸的 ‹*expression, remark*›; 不可思议的 ‹*person*›; 神秘莫测的 ‹*face, smile*›

insect /ˈɪnsekt/ *n* **1** (arthropod) 昆虫 **2** (small many-legged creature) 爬虫

insect: ~ bite *n* 昆虫叮咬; **~ eater** *n* 捕食昆虫者

insecticide /ɪnˈsektɪsaɪd/ *n* [c and u] 杀虫药

insectivore /ɪnˈsektɪvɔː(r)/ *n* 食虫动物

insectivorous /ˌɪnsekˈtɪvərəs/ *adj* 食虫的

insect: ~ powder *n* 杀虫粉; **~ repellent** *n* 驱虫剂; **~ spray** *n* 喷雾杀虫剂

insecure /ˌɪnsɪˈkjʊə(r)/ *adj* **1** (lacking confidence) 缺乏信心的; **to be ~ about sth.** 对某事没有把握 **2** (not reliable) 无保障的 ‹*career, job, future*›; 不可靠的 ‹*plan, arrangement*› **3** (loose) 不牢固的 ‹*bolt, nail, screw*›; (unsafe) 不安全的 ‹*rope, structure, foothold*› **4** (inadequately protected) 不牢靠的 ‹*lock, door*›; 易被非法侵入的 ‹*computer, network, system*›

insecurity /ˌɪnsɪˈkjʊərəti/ *n* [u] **1** (lack of confidence, anxiety) 缺乏信心; **to suffer from feelings of ~** 感到惶恐不安 **2** (unreliability of situation, income) 不稳定; **financial ~** 金融风险

inseminate /ɪnˈsemɪneɪt/ *vt* 使受精

insemination /ɪnˌsemɪˈneɪʃn/ *n* [u] 授精

insensibility /ɪnˌsensəˈbɪləti/ *n* [u] **1** (lack of physical feeling) 无感知能力; **~ to pain** 对疼痛无感觉 **2** (lack of awareness) 麻木不仁; **sb.'s ~ to sth.** 某人对…无动于衷 **3** (unconsciousness) 失去知觉

insensible /ɪnˈsensəbl/ *adj* **1** (without physical feeling) 无感觉的 **2** (unconscious) 失去知觉的; **to be ~ to pain** 对疼痛无感觉; **to drink oneself ~** 喝酒喝得不省人事 **3** (unaware) 未察觉的; **to be ~ of sth.** 未察觉到某事物; **he was ~ of the dangers/risks** 他没有意识到危险/风险 **4** (imperceptible) 难以察觉的 ‹*change, shift*›

insensitive /ɪnˈsensətɪv/ *adj* **1** (tactless) 漠然的; (unfeeling) 漠不关心的; **an ~ attitude/remark** 冷漠的态度/话语 **2** (to pain, criticism) 无感觉的; **to be ~ to heat and cold** 感觉不到冷热; **to be ~ to criticism** 对批评无动于衷

insensitivity /ɪnˌsensəˈtɪvəti/ *n* [u] **1** (tactlessness) 漠然; **~ to sth.** 对某事物的漠然 **2** (to pain, cold, etc.) 无感觉; **~ to sth.** 对某事物无感觉

inseparable /ɪnˈseprəbl/ *adj* 形影不离的 ‹*friends*›; 不可分离的 ‹*team, part*›

inseparably /ɪnˈseprəbli/ *adv* 不可分离地 ‹*linked, joined*›

insert

A /ɪnˈsɜːt/ *vt* 插入; **to ~ sth. in** *or* **into sth.** 把某物插入某物中; **to ~ a hyphen/space between two words** 在两个词中间插入连字符/空格

B /ˈɪnsɜːt/ *n* **1** = **insertion 2** **2** (in dress, shoe) 嵌饰

insertion /ɪnˈsɜːʃn/ *n* **1** (action of inserting) 插入 **2** Journ (enclosed page, leaflet) 插页; (advertisement) 散页广告; (amendment) 更正页 **3** (in dress, shoe) 嵌饰

insertion mark *n* 插入符号

in-service *adj attrib* 在职进行的

in-service training *n* [u] 在职培训

inset /ˈɪnset/

A *n* **1** (thing inserted) 嵌入物 **2** (picture) 套印小图; (map) 套印小地图 **3** Publg, Journ 插页 **4** (in sewing) 镶料

B *vt* (*pres p* **-tt-**; *pt, pp* **inset**) 插入 ‹*word, diagram*›; 嵌入 ‹*ornamentation*›

INSET day /ˈɪnset ˌdeɪ/ *n* Brit 教师在职培训日

inshore /ˌɪnˈʃɔː(r)/

A *adj* 近海的 ‹*lifeboat, current*›; **an ~ wind** 向岸风; **weather forecasts for UK ~ waters** 英国近海水域的天气预报

B *adv* 向海岸 ‹*swim, blow*›

inside /ˈɪnsaɪd/
A *n* **1** (inner part) 里面; **the ~ of the car** 汽车内部; **to be locked on** *or* **from the ~** «*door, house*» 从里面锁上 **2** (inner surface of box, window, leg etc.) 内侧; **on the ~** 在内侧; **the ~ as well as the outside** 内外两侧; **the ~ of his arm** 他的胳膊内侧 **3** (of road) [靠近路边的] 慢车道 **4** Sport (of track) 内圈; **on the ~** 在内圈上 **5** (of pavement) [离马路较远的] 人行道内侧 **6** fig (of organization) 内幕; **to know an organization from the ~** 了解某个组织的内幕; **someone on the ~** 内部人士; **our sources on the ~** 我们的内线 **7** fig colloq (prison) 监狱; **life on the ~** 监狱里的生活
B *prep* (*also* esp Amer **~ of**) **1** (within) 在…里; **~ the box there is …** 盒子里有…; **conditions ~ the refugee camp** 难民营里的条件; **contacts ~ the company** 在公司内的熟人; **~ China** 在中国国内 **2** (toward interior of) 到…里; **put it ~ the envelope** 把它放入信封 **3** (behind) 在…后面; **to stand ~ the gate** 站在大门里面 **4** (within body) 在…体内; (within mind) 在…内心; **anger surged up ~ me** 我怒火中烧 **5** Sport 在…内侧; **to go** *or* **cut ~ sb.** 切到某人的内侧 **6** (under) 在…以内; **to be ~ the speed limit** 在限速范围内; **~ an hour/a year** 在不到一小时/一年的时间里; **to be ~ the world record** 打破世界纪录
C *adj attrib* **1** (interior) 里面的; **the ~ pages of the paper** 报纸的内页 **2** fig (first-hand) 第一手的 ‹*information*›; (within organization) 内部的; **an ~ story/source** 内情/内部信息来源; **it was clearly an ~ job** 这显然是内部人干的
D *adv* **1** (within object, structure) 在里面; **she's ~** 她在屋里; **to wait ~** 在里面等; **to have sth. ~** 里面有某物 **2** (into object, structure) 到里面; **to go/come ~** 进屋; **to bring sth. ~** 把某物拿进来; **to look ~** 往里看 **3** fig (within organization) 在内部; **to have someone ~** 有内应 **4** (within body) 在体内; (within mind) 在内心; **to know sth. deep down ~** 内心深处明白某事 **5** Brit colloq (in prison) 在狱中; **he's been ~** 他坐过牢; **to put sb. ~** 将某人关进监狱
E **insides** /ɪnˈsaɪdz/ *npl* colloq 内脏; **it upset his ~s** 这使他感到肠胃不适; **my ~s hurt** 我肚子疼
F **inside out** *adv phr* 里面朝外; **to wear a T-shirt ~ out** 反穿着T恤衫; **to blow an umbrella ~ out** «*wind*» 把雨伞吹翻; **to turn sth. ~ out** (reverse) 把…翻过来 ‹*coat, jacket*›; (ransack) 把…翻个底朝天 ‹*room, closet*›; (transform) 彻底改变 ‹*life*›; **to know sb./sth. ~ out** 彻底了解某人/某事物; **to know one's subject ~ out** 对科目了如指掌

inside: ~ angle *n* 内角; **~ forward** *n* 内锋; **~ information** *n* [u] 内部消息; **~ lane** *n* **1** Sport (of track) 内侧跑道; **2** (of road) 慢车道; **~ left** *n* 左内锋; **~ leg** *n* 下落裆; **~ leg (measurement)** 裤腿内侧长度

insider /ɪnˈsaɪdə(r)/ *n* **1** (gen) 圈内人 **2** Fin, Comm 知情者

insider: ~ dealer *n* = **~ trader**; **~ dealing** *n* [u] = **~ trading**

inside right *n* 右内锋

insider: ~ trader *n* 内幕交易者; **~ trading** *n* [u] 内幕交易

inside track *n* 内圈跑道; **to be on the ~** fig 占据有利地位

insidious /ɪnˈsɪdɪəs/ *adj* 潜伏的 ‹*disease, illness*›; 暗中滋生的 ‹*jealousy*›; 有隐患的 ‹*flattery, promises, problem*›; 阴险的 ‹*enemy*›

insidiously /ɪnˈsɪdɪəsli/ *adv* 潜在地 ‹*harmful*›; 暗中进行地 ‹*spread*›

insight /ˈɪnsaɪt/ *n* **1** [c] (enlightening fact, revealing glimpse) 洞悉; **to give an ~ into sth.** 对某事物提出深刻见解; **to gain an ~ into sth.** 深入了解某事物 **2** [u] (perceptiveness, intuition) 洞察力; **to have/show ~ into sth.** 具有/表现出对某事物的洞察力

insightful /ˈɪnsaɪtfʊl/ *adj* 有深刻见解的 ‹*analysis, criticism*›; 富有洞察力的 ‹*analyst, critic*›

insignia /ɪnˈsɪgnɪə/ *npl* **1** (symbols of office) 证章 **2** Mil 徽章

insignificance /ˌɪnsɪgˈnɪfɪkəns/ *n* [u] **1** (unimportance) 无足轻重; **to pale** *or* **fade into ~** 逐渐变得无足轻重 **2** (negligibility) 微不足道

insignificant /ˌɪnsɪgˈnɪfɪkənt/ *adj* **1** (unimportant) 地位低微的 ‹*person*›; 无足轻重的 ‹*detail, fact, factor, part*› **2** (negligible) 微不足道的 ‹*quantity, cost*›

insincere /ˌɪnsɪnˈsɪə(r)/ *adj* 不诚恳的 ‹*person, opinion*›; 虚伪的 ‹*remark, smile*›; **to be ~ in sth./doing sth.** 在某事上/做某事缺乏诚意

insincerity /ˌɪnsɪnˈserəti/ *n* [u] (of person, opinion) 无诚意; (of remark, smile) 虚伪

insinuate /ɪnˈsɪnjʊeɪt/
A *vt* 暗示; **to ~ that …** 旁敲侧击地暗示…
B *v refl* **to ~ oneself into sth.** 巧妙获取某事物; **to ~ oneself into sb.'s favour** 巧妙地逐渐取得某人的宠信

insinuating /ɪnˈsɪnjʊeɪtɪŋ/ *adj* 旁敲侧击的 ‹*remark*›; 暗示的 ‹*tone*›; 含沙射影的 ‹*language*›

insinuation /ɪnˌsɪnjʊˈeɪʃn/ *n* 影射; **to make ~s about sb./sth.** 含蓄地批评某人/某事物; **to make an ~ that …** 暗示…

insipid /ɪnˈsɪpɪd/ *adj* **1** (lacking flavour) 淡而无味的 **2** (lacking interest, vigour) 枯燥乏味的

insist /ɪnˈsɪst/
A *vt* **1** (demand forcefully) 坚决要求; **I ~ you tell me!** 我一定要你告诉我! **2** (maintain forcefully) 坚持认为; **they ~ed that it was true** 他们坚持说那是真的
B *vi* 坚决主张; **to ~ on sth./doing sth.** 坚决主张某事/做某事; **to ~ on sb. doing sth.** 坚决要求某人做某事; **I won't ~** 随你的便; **all right, if you ~** 好吧，如果你坚持的话

insistence /ɪnˈsɪstəns/ *n* [u] 坚决要求; **to do sth. at sb.'s ~** 在某人的坚持下做某事; **~ on sth./doing sth.** 对某事/做某事的坚持

insistent /ɪnˈsɪstənt/ *adj* **1** (demanding) 坚决要求的; **to be ~ about** *or* **on sth.** 在某事上很坚持; **he was most ~ that we should attend** 他十分坚决地要求我们参加 **2** (regular, repeated) 持续的; **the child's ~ whining** 孩子没完没了的哭泣

insistently /ɪnˈsɪstəntli/ *adv* **1** (in a demanding manner) 坚持地 **2** (repeatedly) 持续地

insofar as /ˌɪnsəˈfɑːr æz/ *conj* **~ …** 在…范围内; **~ I know/I can** 就我所知/所能; **~ sth. is concerned** 就某事物而言

insole /ˈɪnsəʊl/ *n* 鞋垫

insolence /ˈɪnsələns/ *n* [u] 粗鲁无礼

insolent /ˈɪnsələnt/ *adj* 粗鲁无礼的

insolently /ˈɪnsələntli/ *adv* 粗鲁无礼地

insolubility /ɪnˌsɒljʊˈbɪləti/ *n* [u] **1** (of problem) 不能解决的问题; (of mystery) 无法解释的事 **2** Chem 不溶解性

insoluble /ɪnˈsɒljʊbl/ *adj* **1** (incapable of being solved) 不能解决的 ‹*problem*›; 无法解释的 ‹*mystery*› **2** Chem 不溶解的

insolvency /ɪnˈsɒlvənsi/ *n* [u and c] 破产; **an ~ expert** 处理破产问题的专家

insolvent /ɪnˈsɒlvənt/ *adj* 破产的; **to declare oneself ~** 宣布自己破产

insomnia /ɪnˈsɒmnɪə/ *n* [u] 失眠症; **to suffer from ~** 患失眠症

insomniac /ɪnˈsɒmnɪæk/ *n* 失眠患者

insomuch /ˌɪnsəʊˈmʌtʃ/ *adv* formal **~ as …** (to the extent that) 到…程度; (seeing that) 由于…; **~ that …** 由于…

insouciance /ɪnˈsuːsɪəns/ *n* [u] formal 无忧无虑

insouciant /ɪnˈsuːsɪənt/ *adj* formal 无忧无虑的

inspect /ɪnˈspekt/ *vt* **1** (examine) 检查 ‹*ticket, luggage*›; 审查 ‹*document, passport, publication*›; 检阅 ‹*troops*›; 巡视 ‹*school*›; **to ~ sth. for defects** 检验某物有无缺陷 **2** (assess, survey) 视察

inspection /ɪnˈspekʃn/ *n* [c and u] (of ticket, machinery) 检查; (of document, passport, publication) 审查; (of troops) 检阅; (of school) 巡视; **to make** *or* **carry out an ~** 进行检查; **on closer ~** 经仔细检查

inspection: ~ certificate *n* 检验合格证; **~ chamber** *n* 检修井; **~ copy** *n* 样书; **~ cover** *n* 检查盖; **~ pit** *n* 检修坑井

inspector /ɪnˈspektə(r)/ *n* **1** (gen) 检查员 **2** Brit (policeman) 巡官 **3** Brit (of schools) 督学 **4** Brit (on bus, train) 检票员

inspectorate /ɪnˈspektərət/ *n* 检查团

inspiration /ˌɪnspəˈreɪʃn/ *n* **1** [u] (stimulus) 灵感; **the ~ to do sth.** 做某事的灵感; **to draw ~ from sth.** 从某事物汲取灵感; **a flash of ~** 瞬间的灵感 **2** [c] (inspiring person) 启发灵感的人; (inspiring thing) 启发灵感的事物; **she is an ~ to us all!** 她是我们所有人的灵魂! **3** [c] (sudden idea) 妙计; **to have a (sudden) ~** (突然) 想到个好主意

inspirational /ˌɪnspəˈreɪʃənl/ *adj* 鼓舞人心的

inspire /ɪnˈspaɪə(r)/ *vt* **1** (motivate) 鼓舞; **to ~ sb. to do sth.** 激励某人做某事; **to ~ sb. to greater efforts** 激励某人更加努力 **2** (give rise to) 使产生 ‹*thought, feeling*›; **what ~d you to suggest that?** 是什么使你想到那个建议的? **3** (arouse) 激起; **to ~ love/respect/trust in sb.** 唤起某人的爱/尊敬/信任; **to ~ sb. with hope/courage** 激起某人的希望/勇气

inspired /ɪnˈspaɪəd/ *adj* **1** (filled with creative power) 富有灵感的 ‹*person*› **2** (of extraordinary quality) 品质卓越的; **an ~ guess** 得自灵感的猜测

inspiring /ɪnˈspaɪərɪŋ/ *adj* 鼓舞人心的 ‹*person, leadership, speech, vision*›; 启发灵感的 ‹*example, story*›

inst. /ɪnst/ *abbr* dated (in business letters) = **instant** 本月的; **we have received your letter of the 15th ~** 我方已收悉贵方本月15日来函

instability /ˌɪnstəˈbɪləti/ *n* **1** (gen) 不稳定; **a time of great political ~** 政治大动荡时期 **2** Psych 精神变化无常; **mental ~** 精神不稳定

instal, install /ɪnˈstɔːl/ *vt* (*pres p etc.* **-ll-**) **1** (place in position) 安装 ‹*equipment, machine, device*›; **to have sth. ~led** 请人安装某物 **2** (place in official post) 正式任命 ‹*chancellor, president*›; **to ~ sb. in office** 任命某人就职 **3** (settle) 安置; **to ~ sb./oneself in sth.** 将某人/自己安顿在某处; **he is comfortably ~led before the TV** 他舒舒服服地坐在电视机前

installation /ˌɪnstəˈleɪʃn/ *n* **1** [u] (act of) (placing in position) 安装 **2** [c] (instance of placing in position or official post) 就职 **3** [c] (equipment) 装备 **4** [c] (military, industrial facility) 设施 **5** [c] (art exhibit) 展品

installation disk *n* 安装盘

instalment, Amer also **installment** /ɪnˈstɔːlmənt/ *n* **1** (partial payment) 一期付款; **by monthly/annual ~s** 按月/年分期付款; **to pay for sth. in** *or* **by ~s** 以分期付款方式支付某款项 **2** (of serial) 一集; (of story, novel) 一节; **to publish sth. in weekly ~s** 以每周连载方式刊登某文

instalment: ~ credit *n* [u] 分期清偿信用贷款; **~ plan** *n* Amer 分期付款购货法; **to buy sth. on an ~ plan** 用分期付款法购买某物

instance /ˈɪnstəns/
A *n* **1** (case) 情况; **in the first ~** 首先; **in this**

～ 在这种情况下 **2** (example) 例子; **for ～** 例如; **as an ～ of ...** 作为…的例证
B *vt formal* 举…为例

instant /'ɪnstənt/
A *adj* **1** (immediate) 立刻的; **～ success/relief/hot water** 一举成功/即刻减轻/即开即热水 **2** *attrib* (processed to allow quick preparation) 立即可食的; **～ coffee/food/soup** 速溶咖啡/即食食品/速食汤 **3** (urgent) 紧急的; **～ help** 紧急援助
B *n* **1** (moment) 片刻; **at that (very) ～** （就）在那时; **for an ～** 一瞬间; **in an ～** 立刻; **an ～ later** 不一会儿; **come here this ～!** 马上过来！ **2** *colloq* (coffee) 速溶咖啡

instantaneous /ˌɪnstən'teɪnɪəs/ *adj* 瞬间发生的; **an ～ reaction** 即时反应

instantaneously /ˌɪnstən'teɪnɪəsli/ *adv* 即刻

instant camera *n* 拍立得照相机

instantly /'ɪnstəntli/ *adv* 立即 ‹*vanish, respond*›; **an ～ recognizable voice** 极易识别的声音; **to be killed ～** 当场身亡

instant messaging *n* [u] 即时通讯

instant replay *n* 即时回放; **to show an ～ of a goal** 即时重放进球

instead /ɪn'sted/
A *adv* 作为替代; **we didn't go home, we went to the park ～** 我们没有回家，而是去了公园; **I was going to phone but wrote ～** 我原本想打电话的，结果却写了信
B **instead of** *prep phr* 而不是; **you should be helping us ～ of moaning!** 你现在应该帮助我们而不是抱怨！; **you can go ～ of me** 你可以替我去

instep /'ɪnstep/ *n* (of foot) 足背; (of shoe) 鞋面; **to have a high ～** 足弓高

instigate /'ɪnstɪgeɪt/ *vt* 进行 ‹*action, inquiry*›; 发起 ‹*attack, strike*›; **to ～ proceedings** 提起诉讼

instigation /ˌɪnstɪ'geɪʃn/ *n* [u] 鼓动; **at the ～ of sb., at sb.'s ～** 在某人的鼓动下

instigator /'ɪnstɪgeɪtə(r)/ *n* 煽动者

instil, instill /ɪn'stɪl/ *vt* (*pres p etc.* **-ll-**) 使…逐渐形成 ‹*feeling, courage*›; 逐渐灌输 ‹*idea, values*›; **to ～ a sense of awe/fear in** *or* **into sb.** 逐渐使某人产生敬畏/恐惧感

instinct /'ɪnstɪŋkt/ *n* **1** [c] (inborn tendency, natural reaction) 本能; **to have an ～ for sth.** 具有某种天性; **to have an ～ for doing sth.** 具有做某事的天性; **my first ～ was to ...** 我本能的反应就是…; **the killer ～** *lit* 嗜杀本性; *fig* 拼杀本能 **2** [u] (intuition) 直觉; **to follow your ～(s)** (when making decision) 跟着感觉走; **by ～** 凭直觉; **to act on ～** 凭直觉行事

instinctive /ɪn'stɪŋktɪv/ *adj* 本能的 ‹*reaction, fear, understanding*›; 天生的 ‹*ability, talent*›

instinctively /ɪn'stɪŋktɪvli/ *adv* 本能地 ‹*understand, realize*›; 凭直觉地 ‹*act, react*›

institute /'ɪnstɪtju:t, *Amer* -tu:t/
A *n* (organization) 机构; **the Women's I～** 妇女协会; **a research ～** 研究院
B *vt* 开始实行 ‹*rule, scheme*›; **to ～ (legal) proceedings against sb.** 对某人提起诉讼; **to ～ inquiries into sth.** 着手调查某事

institution /ˌɪnstɪ'tju:ʃn, *Amer* -'tu:ʃn/ *n* **1** [c] (custom, practice) 习俗; **a long-established ～** 长期形成的惯例 **2** [c] (hospital, care home) 社会福利机构; **to live in an ～** 在福利院生活; **an ～ for the handicapped** 残疾人福利机构 **3** [c] Fin (company, organization) 金融机构 **4** [c] *fig* (person) 知名人士; (object) 众所周知的事物; **she has become a national ～** 她已经成为举国皆知的人物了 **5** [u] (initiation) 设立; **～ of legal proceedings** 诉讼程序的启动

institutional /ˌɪnstɪ'tju:ʃənl, *Amer* -'tu:-/ *adj* **1** (of an institution) 福利机构的 ‹*meals, education, food*›; (like an institution) 具有公共机构特征的; **～ life** 墨守成规的生活; **to be put in ～ care** «*child*» 被送到社会福利机构 **2** Comm, Fin 金融机构的 ‹*shares, advertising, activity*› **3** (in the form of an institution) 机构的; **～ racism** 制度性种族歧视

institutionalize /ˌɪnstɪ'tju:ʃənəlaɪz, *Amer* -'tu:-/ *vt* **1** (place in special care) 将…送入收容机构 ‹*patient, elderly, insane*› **2** (establish officially) 使…制度化 ‹*procedure, custom, practice*›; **～d religion** 制度化的宗教

institutionalized /ˌɪnstɪ'tju:ʃənəlaɪzd, *Amer* -'tu:-/ *adj* **1** (unable to live independently) 缺乏自理能力的 ‹*inmate, patient*› **2** (established) 成惯例的 ‹*procedure, practice*›; **～ racism** 由来已久的种族偏见

in-store
A *adj attrib* 商店内的; **an ～ bakery** 设在商店里的面包店
B *adv* 在商店内

instruct /ɪn'strʌkt/ *vt* **1** (teach) 教导 ‹*pupil, learner*›; 训练 ‹*apprentice, recruit*›; **to ～ sb. in** 教某人 ‹*subject, discipline, craft*›; **to ～ sb. how to do sth.** 教某人如何做某事 **2** (direct) 吩咐; **to ～ sb. to do sth.** 吩咐某人做某事; **to ～ sb. about sth.** 告诉某人某事 **3** Brit Jur (engage) 委托 ‹*solicitor, counsel*› **4** Brit Jur (give directions to) «*solicitor*» 指示 ‹*barrister*›

instruction /ɪn'strʌkʃn/
A *n* **1** [u] (teaching) 教导; **to give sb. ～ in sth.** 给某人以某方面的指导; **to receive ～ in sth.** 在某事上接受训练 **2** [c] (direction) 命令; **to issue** *or* **give ～s to sb. to do sth.** 向某人发布做某事的命令; **to receive/carry out ～s** 接到/执行命令; **to be under ～s to do sth.** 受命做某事; **according to ～s** 按照指示; **failing ～s to the contrary** 如果没有相反的指令 **3** [c] Comput 指令
B **instructions** *npl* (for product use) 使用说明; **to follow the ～s** 按照使用说明操作; **～s for use** 操作指南

instructional /ɪn'strʌkʃənl/ *adj* 教学的

instruction: ～ book, ～ leaflet *ns* 说明书; **～ manual** *n* 使用手册; **～ set** *n* 指令集; **～ sheet** *n* 使用说明

instructive /ɪn'strʌktɪv/ *adj* 有教益的 ‹*film, report, book, lecture*›

instructor /ɪn'strʌktə(r)/ ▸p. 409 *n* **1** (teacher) 教师; (trainer) 指导者; (military) 教官; (in sports) 教练 **2** Amer Univ 讲师

instructress /ɪn'strʌktrɪs/ ▸p. 409 *n* **1** (teacher) 女教师; (trainer) 女指导者; (military) 女教官; (in sports) 女教练 **2** Amer Univ 女讲师

instrument /'ɪnstrʊmənt/ *n* **1** (tool, implement) 器械; **an ～ of torture** 刑具; **to be an ～ for good** 能产生好的影响 **2** Mus 乐器; **to play an ～** 演奏乐器 **3** (measuring device) 仪表; **to fly on ～s** 靠仪表导航飞行 **4** *fig* (pawn) 被他人利用的人; **to be the ～ of fate** 受命运摆布的人 **5** (means) (person) 促成某事的人; (thing) 促成某事的手段; **the ～ of change** 促成变革的措施; **the ～ for doing sth.** 做某事的手段 **6** (formal document) 文书

Musical instruments

Playing a musical instrument

■ Different musical instruments collocate with different verbs in Chinese. These verbs are normally associated with the action performed, such as 拉, 弹, 打, 吹 etc.

■ Unlike English, there is no definite article between the verb and the musical instrument in Chinese:

to play the guitar
= 弹吉他

to play the cello
= 拉大提琴

to play the trumpet
= 吹喇叭

to play the drums
= 打鼓

Players

■ In Chinese, 家 or 手 are added to the name of the instrument to denote the player. 家 has a more professional connotation than 手:

a violinist/violin player
= 小提琴演奏家 / 小提琴手

She is a renowned cellist
= 她是位知名的大提琴演奏家

■ However, for players of certain instruments, 手 is always used and not 家:

a drummer
= 鼓手

a trumpeter
= 小号手

■ 演奏者 can usually be used in all cases:

a concert cellist
= 音乐会大提琴演奏者

a recorder player
= 竖笛演奏者

a pianist/piano player
= 钢琴家 / 钢琴演奏者

■ There are two typical constructions in Chinese to express how well or how badly someone plays a musical instrument:

He plays the erhu well
= 他的二胡拉得很好
or 他二胡拉得很好

She plays the piano badly
= 她的钢琴弹得很糟
or 她钢琴弹得很糟

Combinations

violin lessons
= 小提琴课

a violin solo
= 小提琴独奏

a violin sonata
= 小提琴奏鸣曲

a piano concert
= 钢琴音乐会

piano scores
= 钢琴谱

a piano teacher
= 钢琴老师

instrumental /ˌɪnstrʊˈmentl/
A *adj* **1** **to be ~ in sth./doing sth.** (have important role) 对某事物/对做某事起重要作用; **to play an ~ part** *or* **role in sth.** 在某事物中起重要作用; **to be ~ in sb.'s downfall** 成为某人垮台的主要原因 **2** Mus 器乐的; **~ music** 器乐曲
B *n* 器乐曲

instrumentalist /ˌɪnstrʊˈmentəlɪst/ *n* 器乐演奏者

instrumentation /ˌɪnstrʊmenˈteɪʃn/ *n* **1** Mus (combination of instruments) 乐器组; (arrangement, composition) 器乐谱写 **2** (measuring instruments) 测量仪器

instrument panel *n* 仪表板

insubordinate /ˌɪnsəˈbɔːdɪnət/ *adj* 不服从的; **~ behaviour** 违抗命令的行为

insubordination /ˌɪnsəˌbɔːdɪˈneɪʃn/ *n* [u] **1** (gen) 不服从 **2** Mil 违抗命令

insubstantial /ˌɪnsəbˈstænʃl/ *adj* **1** (flimsy) 不坚固的 ‹*structure, construction*›; 软弱无力的 ‹*argument, accusation*› **2** (unreal) 非真实的 ‹*figure, creature*›; 虚幻的 ‹*form, vision*› **3** (lacking nutritional value) 缺乏营养的 ‹*meal, diet*›

insufferable /ɪnˈsʌfrəbl/ *adj* **1** (too extreme) 难以忍受的 ‹*heat, cold, conditions*› **2** (annoying) 极其讨厌的; **an ~ bore** 讨厌鬼; **~ arrogance/rudeness** 难以容忍的傲慢/粗鲁

insufferably /ɪnˈsʌfrəbli/ *adv* 难以忍受地 ‹*hot, cold, stuffy*›; 令人厌恶地 ‹*rude, conceited, arrogant*›

insufficiency /ˌɪnsəˈfɪʃnsi/ *n* **1** [u] (lack) 不充足 **2** [c] (deficiency) 缺陷 **3** [u] Med 机能不全

insufficient /ˌɪnsəˈfɪʃnt/ *adj* 不足的 ‹*food, resources, light*›; 不充分的 ‹*information, evidence*›; 不全面的 ‹*protection, training*›; **to be ~ for/to do sth.** 不足以…

insufficiently /ˌɪnsəˈfɪʃntli/ *adv* 不全面地 ‹*protected, trained*›; 不充足地 ‹*provided, resourced*›; **~ supported** 未得到全力支持

insular /ˈɪnsjʊlə(r), Amer -sələr/ *adj* **1** (narrow-minded) 狭隘的 ‹*attitude, frame of mind*›; 保守的 ‹*person, view, outlook*›; 只关心本国利益的 ‹*nation, society*› **2** (isolated) 与世隔绝的 **3** Geog 岛屿的; **an ~ climate** 海岛气候; **an ~ way of life** 海岛生活方式

insularity /ˌɪnsjʊˈlærəti, Amer -səˈl-/ *n* [u] (of nation, society, group) 岛国性质; (of person, view, outlook) 偏狭

insulate /ˈɪnsjʊleɪt, Amer -səl-/ *vt* **1** (against cold, heat, noise) 使隔绝; **the apartment block had been ~d against sound** 这幢公寓大楼是隔音的 **2** Elec 使…绝缘 ‹*wire*›; **the electrical cables had been ~d with rubber** 这些电缆线已用橡胶进行了绝缘处理 **3** fig (protect) 使免除; (segregate) 使分离; **to ~ sb./sth. from** *or* **against sth.** 将某人/某物与某物隔开

insulated /ˈɪnsjʊleɪtɪd, Amer -səl-/ *adj* (against cold) 保温的; (against heat) 隔热的; (against noise) 隔音的; **a well-~ house** 隔热性能好的房子

insulating /ˈɪnsjʊˌleɪtɪŋ, Amer -səˈl-/ *adj attrib* 绝缘的 ‹*tape, layer*›; 起隔绝作用的 ‹*case, compound*›; **~ material** 绝缘材料

insulation /ˌɪnsjʊˈleɪʃn, Amer -səˈl-/ *n* [u] **1** (act of insulating) (thermal) 隔热; (acoustic) 隔音; (electrical) 绝缘 **2** (material) (thermal) 隔热材料; (acoustic) 隔音材料; (electrical) 绝缘材料

insulator /ˈɪnsjʊleɪtə(r), Amer -səl-/ *n* (thermal) 隔热物; (acoustic) 隔音物; (electric) 绝缘体

insulin /ˈɪnsjʊlɪn, Amer -səl-/ *n* [u] 胰岛素

insulin: ~-dependency *n* [u] 胰岛素依赖; **~-dependent** *adj* 胰岛素依赖的; **~-dependent diabetes** *n* [u] 胰岛素依赖型糖尿病; **~ level** *n* 胰岛素水平; **~ shock** *n* [u] 胰岛素休克; **~ treatment** *n* [u] 胰岛素治疗

insult
A /ˈɪnsʌlt/ *n* (remark) 辱骂; (action) 侮辱; **to make ~s about sb./sth.** 辱骂某人/某事物; **to hurl ~s at sb.** 大声辱骂某人; **an ~ to sb.'s intelligence/memory** 对某人智力/记忆力的侮辱; **to add ~ to injury** 雪上加霜
B /ɪnˈsʌlt/ *vt* (verbally) 辱骂; (by one's behaviour) 侮辱

insulting /ɪnˈsʌltɪŋ/ *adj* 侮辱性的 ‹*behaviour, remark, language*›

insultingly /ɪnˈsʌltɪŋli/ *adv* 侮辱性地 ‹*behave, speak*›; 无礼地 ‹*answer, reply*›; **the exam was ~ easy** 这考试太容易了，简直是侮辱人

insuperable /ɪnˈsuːpərəbl, ɪnˈsjuː-/ *adj* 难以克服的 ‹*difficulty, problem*›; 不可逾越的 ‹*barrier, obstacle*›

insupportable /ˌɪnsəˈpɔːtəbl/ *adj* **1** (unbearable) 不能承受的 ‹*burden, strain, heat*›; 难以容忍的 ‹*behaviour*› **2** (unjustifiable) 无根据的

insurable /ɪnˈʃɔːrəbl, Amer -ˈʃʊər-/ *adj* 可保险的; **an ~ risk/interest/event** 可保风险/权益/事故

insurance /ɪnˈʃɔːrəns, Amer -ˈʃʊər-/ *n* **1** [u] (arrangement, practice) 保险; **~ for the house/car** 房屋/汽车保险; **to take out ~ against sth.** 办理某种保险 **2** [u] (payments) 保险费; **to pay the ~ on sth.** 付某物的保险费; **to pay £500 in ~ on the car** 支付 500 英镑的汽车保险费; **when her husband died she received £50,000 ~** 丈夫死后她得到了 5 万英镑的保费 **3** [u] (profession) 保险业; **he works in ~** 他从事保险工作 **4** [c] fig (safeguard) 安全保证; **I see my investments as a form of ~ against inflation** 我把投资当成抵御通货膨胀的一种保障形式

insurance: ~ adjuster ▸**p. 409** *n* esp Amer = **loss adjuster**; **~ agent** ▸**p. 409** *n* 保险代理人; **~ assessor** ▸**p. 409** *n* 险损估价人; **~ broker** ▸**p. 409** *n* 保险经纪人; **~ certificate** *n* 投保证明; **~ charge** *n* 保险费; **~ claim** *n* 保险索赔; **~ company** *n* 保险公司; **~ money** *n* [u] 保险金; **~ office** *n* 保险事务所; **~ plan** *n* Amer 保费分期支付计划; **~ policy** *n* lit 保险单; fig (safeguard) 保障; **~ premium** *n* 保险费; **~ salesman** ▸**p. 409** *n* 保险推销员; **~ scheme** *n* 保险方案

insure /ɪnˈʃɔː(r), Amer -ˈʃʊər/
A *vt* 给…保险; **to ~ sb./sth. against sth.** 为某人/某物投保某险; **to ~ oneself** *or* **one's life** 为自己投保人寿险
B *vi* **1** (take out insurance) 投保; **to ~ against sth.** 投保某险; **to ~ against interest fluctuations/sickness/injury** 投保利息浮动险/疾病险/伤害险 **2** (take precautions) 采取预防措施; **to ~ against delay/disappointment** 采取措施以避免耽误/失望

insured /ɪnˈʃɔːd, Amer -ˈʃʊərd/
A *n* **the ~** 被保险人
B *adj* 上过保险的 ‹*person, property, car, life*›; 在保险范围内的 ‹*risk*›; **a parcel ~ for £50** 投保 50 英镑的包裹

insured party *n* 被保险人

insurer /ɪnˈʃɔːrə(r), Amer -ˈʃʊər-/ *n* (company) 保险公司; (person) 承保人

insurgent /ɪnˈsɜːdʒənt/
A *n* 造反者; **an attack by armed ~s** 武装叛乱分子的进攻
B *adj* 叛乱的 ‹*troops, force*›; 暴动的 ‹*mob, group*›

insurmountable /ˌɪnsəˈmaʊntəbl/ *adj* 无法克服的 ‹*problem, difficulty*›; 无法逾越的 ‹*obstacle, barrier*›

insurrection /ˌɪnsəˈrekʃn/ *n* **1** [u] (violent action) 叛乱 **2** [c] (uprising) 起义

insurrectionary /ˌɪnsəˈrekʃənəri, Amer -neri/ *adj* 叛乱的 ‹*troops, forces*›; 起义的 ‹*group, faction*›

insurrectionist /ˌɪnsəˈrekʃənɪst/
A *n* 造反者
B *adj* 暴动的 ‹*group, propaganda, action*›

int. *abbr* = **international A**

intact /ɪnˈtækt/ *adj* 完好无损的 ‹*object*›; 未受损害的 ‹*reputation*›; **to survive ~** 未受损伤地幸存下来; **to keep their traditional way of life ~** 保持传统生活方式不受外界影响

intaglio /ɪnˈtɑːlɪəʊ/ *n* (*pl* **~s**) **1** (design) 凹雕 **2** (gem) 阴雕宝石 **3** (seal) 凹雕图章 **4** (printing process) 凹版印刷

intake /ˈɪnteɪk/ *n* **1** [u] (consumption) 摄取量; **a high sugar ~** 高糖摄取量 **2** [u] (inhalation) 吸入; **an ~ of breath** 倒吸一口气 **3** [c] (inlet) 入口; **an air/a fuel ~** 进气口/进油口 **4** [c] (number admitted) Sch, Univ 新生; Mil 新兵; (into profession) 新员工

intake valve *n* (for air) 进气阀; (for fuel) 进油阀

intangible /ɪnˈtændʒəbl/
A *adj* **1** (indefinable) 不易度量的 ‹*benefit, value*›; 难以界定的 ‹*quality*›; 难以理解的 ‹*concept*›; **an ~ air** *or* **atmosphere** 说不出的气氛 **2** Econ, Fin 无形的; **~ assets/property** 无形资产/财产
B *n* 无形的事物

integer /ˈɪntɪdʒə(r)/ *n* 整数

integral /ˈɪntɪgrəl/
A *adj* **1** (essential) 必需的; **to be an ~ part of sth.** 是某事物必不可少的一部分; **to be ~ to sth.** 对某事物是不可或缺的 **2** (whole) 完整的 ‹*system*›; **an ~ design** 整体设计 **3** (built-in) 内置的 ‹*power source, component, motor*› **4** Math 整数的; **an ~ number** 整数
B *n* 积分; **a definite/an indefinite ~** 定积分/不定积分

integral calculus *n* [u] 积分学

integrate /ˈɪntɪgreɪt/
A *vt* **1** (incorporate) 使成为一体; **to ~ sth. into** *or* **with sth.** 使某物与某物成为一体; **to be well ~d with its surroundings** 与环境融为一体 **2** (blend, combine) 使融入; **to ~ sb. into** *or* **with sth.** 使某人融入某群体; **to ~ two systems** 合并两个系统 **3** Math 求…的积分 ‹*number, quantity, expression*›
B *vi* 成为一体

integrated /ˈɪntɪgreɪtɪd/ *adj* 种族融合的 ‹*school, neighbourhood*›; 整体的 ‹*plan*›; 综合的 ‹*design, transport scheme*›

integrated: ~ circuit *n* 集成电路; **~ data network** *n* 综合数据网; **~ services digital network** *n* 综合业务数字网

integration /ˌɪntɪˈgreɪʃn/ *n* [u] **1** Sociol, Pol 整合; Sch 种族融合; Comm 一体化; **the ~ of ethnic minorities into the community** 少数族裔在社区的融入 **2** Math 积分法

integrity /ɪnˈtegrəti/ *n* [u] **1** (honesty) 正直; **a man of ~** 诚实的人 **2** (wholeness) 完整; **territorial ~** 领土完整

intellect /ˈɪntəlekt/ *n* **1** [u] (intelligence, faculty of reasoning) 思维能力; **a man of great ~** 很有头脑的人 **2** [c] (person) 才智出众的人 **3** [c] (mental powers) 智力

intellectual /ˌɪntəˈlektʃʊəl/
A *adj* **1** (relating to the intellect) 智力的; **~ faculties/powers** 智力; **children need ~ stimulation** 孩子需要激发智力 **2** (appealing to or requiring the intellect) 用脑力的; **an ~ contest** 智力竞赛 **3** (possessing intellect) 智力发达的
B *n* 知识分子

intellectualism /ˌɪntəˈlektʃʊəlɪzəm/ *n* [u] 理智主义

intellectualize /ˌɪntəˈlektʃʊəlaɪz/
A *vt* 使理智化
B *vi* (through discussion) 理性地谈论; (in written word) 理性地写作; (through thought) 理性地思考; **to ~ about sth.** 对某事物作纯理性的探讨

intellectually /ˌɪntəˈlektʃʊəli/ *adv* 理智地

i

intellectual: ~ property *n* [u] 知识财产; **~ property rights** *npl* 知识产权

intelligence /ɪnˈtelɪdʒəns/ *n* [u] **1** 智力; **to be of low/high ~** 智力低/高; **use your ~!** 动动脑筋!; **that's an insult to my ~!** 那是对我智力的侮辱! **2** (information) 情报; **according to the latest ~** 根据最新情报 **3** (secret service) 情报机构; **military/naval ~** 军事/海军情报机构; **to be in ~** 从事情报工作

intelligence: ~ agent *n* 间谍; **I~ Corps** *n* Brit 情报部队; **~ quotient** *n* 智商; **~ service** *n* 情报部门; **~ test** *n* 智力测验

intelligent /ɪnˈtelɪdʒənt/ *adj* 有才智的; **an ~ baby** 聪明的婴儿; **an ~ question/answer** 机智的问题/回答; **an ~ animal** 有智力的动物

intelligent: ~ agent *n* 智能代理; **~ design** *n* [u] 神创论

intelligently /ɪnˈtelɪdʒəntli/ *adv* 聪明地 ‹*speak, act*›; 机智地 ‹*respond, behave*›

intelligentsia /ɪnˌtelɪˈdʒentsɪə/ *n + v sing or pl* **the ~** 知识阶层

intelligent terminal *n* 智能终端

intelligibility /ɪnˌtelɪdʒəˈbɪləti/ *n* [u] 明白易懂

intelligible /ɪnˈtelɪdʒəbl/ *adj* 明白易懂的 ‹*speech, language*›; 可理解的 ‹*description, explanation*›

intelligibly /ɪnˈtelɪdʒəbli/ *adv* 明白易懂地 ‹*speak, communicate, converse*›; 可理解地 ‹*express*›

intemperance /ɪnˈtempərəns/ *n* [u] formal 无节制

intemperate /ɪnˈtempərət/ *adj* formal **1** (unrestrained) 无节制的; **~ rage/remarks/zeal** 极度愤怒/过激的言语/过分热情 **2** (given to or characterized by excess) 过度放纵的 ‹*appetite, habits*›; (in consumption of alcohol) 酗酒的 ‹*person, lifestyle*›

intend /ɪnˈtend/ *vt* **1** (have as one's purpose) 想要; **to ~ doing sth.** *or* **to do sth.** 想做某事; **to ~ being** *or* **to be sb./sth.** 想当某人/从事某职业; **I ~ed no harm** 我并无恶意; **it has turned out exactly as I ~ed** 事情的结果正如我所愿; **to ~ sb. to do sth.** 打算让某人做某事; **to ~ that ...** 打算… **2** (design, destine) 计划; **to ~ sth. as sth.** 计划使某事物成为某事物; **to ~ sth. for sb.** 为某人准备某物; **the flowers are ~ed for my mother** 这些花是送给我母亲的; **the present was ~ed as a surprise** 送这件礼物是为了给对方一个惊喜; **I ~ed my remark as a joke** 我说这话只是想开个玩笑; **that remark was ~ed for you!** 那句话是说给你听的!; **a dictionary ~ed for schoolchildren** 供小学生使用的词典; **an exchange ~ed to cement cultural ties** 旨在巩固文化关系的交流活动 **3** (mean) 意指; **to ~ sth. by sth.** 通过…表达某种意思; **what did he ~ by that remark?** 他说那话是什么意思?

intended /ɪnˈtendɪd/
A *adj* **1** (meant, desired) 预期的 ‹*result, outcome, purpose*›; **the ~ meaning** 想要表达的意思 **2** (deliberate) 故意的 ‹*insult, rebuff*›
B *n* dated or hum (man one plans to marry) 未婚夫; (woman one plans to marry) 未婚妻

intense /ɪnˈtens/ *adj* **1** (great) 强烈的 ‹*frustration*›; **~ heat/cold/darkness/light/pain** 酷热/严寒/漆黑/强光/剧痛; **~ pleasure/anger/anguish** 十分快乐/极端愤怒/极为苦恼 **2** (serious) 紧张的 ‹*tone, expression, activity*›; 激烈的 ‹*competition*›; **~ interest** 浓厚的兴趣 **3** (prone to strong emotions) 热切的

intensely /ɪnˈtensli/ *adv* 极度地 ‹*hot, cold, unpleasant*›; 非常 ‹*moving, irritating, frustrating, passionate*›; **~ competitive** 竞争极为激烈的; **to ~ dislike sb./sth.** 极讨厌某人/某事物

intensification /ɪnˌtensɪfɪˈkeɪʃn/ *n* (of efforts) 增强; (of crisis) 加剧

intensifier /ɪnˈtensɪfaɪə(r)/ *n* 强调成分

intensify /ɪnˈtensɪfaɪ/
A *vt* 加强 ‹*efforts, campaign*›; 增强 ‹*sound*›; 加大 ‹*tension, pressure*›; 加剧 ‹*crisis, conflict*›
B *vi* «*efforts, process*» 加强; «*emotion, dispute, competition, crisis, conflict*» 加剧; «*tension, pressure*» 加大

intensity /ɪnˈtensəti/ *n* [u] 强烈; **to speak with ~** 强有力地说

intensive /ɪnˈtensɪv/
A *adj* **1** (concentrated) 集中的 ‹*action*›; 密集的 ‹*bombardment*›; 加强的 ‹*struggle, search*›; **an ~ course in French** 法语强化课程 **2** Agric 集约的; **~ farming/production** 集约农业/生产 **3** Ling 加强词义的
B -intensive *combining form* …密集的; **energy~** 能源密集型的; **technology~** 技术密集型的

intensive: ~ care *n* [u] 重症监护; **to be in ~ care** 在特别护理病房; **to be in need of ~ care** 需要特别护理; **~ care unit** *n* 重症监护室

intensively /ɪnˈtensɪvli/ *adv* 集约地 ‹*farmed*›; 集中地 ‹*developed*›; 密集地 ‹*bombed*›

intent /ɪnˈtent/
A *n* [u] (intention) 意图; **a declaration of ~** 意向声明; **to all ~s and purposes** 几乎完全; **a man who was to all ~s and purposes illiterate** 十足的文盲; **to all ~s and purposes his attempt has failed** 他的尝试实际上已经失败了; **with ~ (to kill)** Jur 故意（杀人）
B *adj* **1** (earnest, eager) 热切的 ‹*expression, look*› **2** (attentively occupied) 专心的; **to be ~ on one's work** 专心致志地工作 **3** (resolved) **to be ~ on** *or* **upon sth./doing sth.** 决意于某事物/要做某事; **he's ~ on getting a promotion** 他一心想要得到晋升; **to be ~ on** *or* **upon revenge** 下定决心复仇

intention /ɪnˈtenʃn/ *n* 意图; **with the ~ of doing sth.** 打算做某事; **the ~ is to ...** 计划是…; **have no ~ of doing sth.** 无意做某事; **with good ~s** 善意地; **with the best of ~s** 一片好心; **to be full of good ~s** 满怀善意; ▸ **road 1**

intentional /ɪnˈtenʃənl/ *adj* 有意的

intentionally /ɪnˈtenʃənəli/ *adv* 有意地

intently /ɪnˈtentli/ *adv* 专注地

inter /ɪnˈtɜː(r)/ *vt* 埋葬

interact /ˌɪntərˈækt/ *vi* **1** (act reciprocally) «*substances, things*» 相互作用; (act socially) 交流; **to ~ with sb.** 与某人沟通 **2** Comput 交互

interaction /ˌɪntərˈækʃn/ *n* [u and c] **1** (gen) 交流; Phys 相互作用; **the ~ of A with B** A 与 B 的相互影响; **an ~ between A and B** A 和 B 之间的互动 **2** Comput 交互

interactive /ˌɪntərˈæktɪv/ *adj* **1** (gen) 相互作用的 ‹*substances*›; 相互影响的 ‹*ideas*›; 合作的 ‹*groups*› **2** Comput 交互的; **an ~ computer/display/map** 交互式计算机/显示/地图

interactive: ~ computing *n* [u] 交互式计算; **~ gaming system** *n* 交互式游戏系统; **~ learning** *n* [u] 交互式学习

interactively /ˌɪntərˈæktɪvli/ *adv* 互动地

interactive: ~ mode *n* 交互方式; **~ television** *n* [u] 互动式电视; **~ terminal** *n* 交互式终端机; **~ video** *n* [u and c] 交互式视频

interactivity /ˌɪntərækˈtɪvəti/ *n* [u] 互动

interbreed /ˌɪntəˈbriːd/
A *vt* 使…杂交繁殖 ‹*animals, plants*›
B *vi* «*people, animals, plants*» 杂交繁殖

interbreeding /ˌɪntəˈbriːdɪŋ/ *n* [u] 杂交繁殖

intercalate /ɪnˈtɜːkəleɪt/ *vt* formal **1** (in calendar) 设置 ‹*day*› **2** (insert) 插入 ‹*verse, narrative, year*›

intercede /ˌɪntəˈsiːd/ *vi* formal 说情; **to ~ with sb. (for** *or* **on behalf of sb.)** （代某人）向某人说情

intercept
A /ˌɪntəˈsept/ *vt* 拦截
B /ˈɪntəsept/ *n* 窃听

interception /ˌɪntəˈsepʃn/ *n* [u and c] **1** Telecom 窃听 **2** Sport 截球

interceptor /ˌɪntəˈseptə(r)/ *n* 截击机

intercession /ˌɪntəˈseʃn/ *n* [u] formal 说情

interchange
A /ˈɪntətʃeɪndʒ/ *n* **1** [u and c] (exchange) 交换 **2** [c] (on motorway) 立体交叉道 **3** (between transport systems) 公交枢纽
B /ˌɪntəˈtʃeɪndʒ/ *vt* (exchange) 交换; (change positions of) 使互换位置; **to ~ sth. with sb.** 与某人交换某物
C *vi* 交替发生; **to ~ with sb./sth.** 与某人/某物交替

interchangeable /ˌɪntəˈtʃeɪndʒəbl/ *adj* 可交换的

interchangeably /ˌɪntəˈtʃeɪndʒəbli/ *adv* 可交换地

intercity /ˌɪntəˈsɪti/
A *adj* 城市间的
B *n* Brit (*also* **InterCity®**) 城际铁路运输; **to travel by ~** *or* **InterCity** 乘城际列车旅行

intercollegiate /ˌɪntəkəˈliːdʒət/ *adj* 校际的

intercom /ˈɪntəkɒm/ *n* 内部通话系统; **on** *or* **over the ~** 通过内部通话系统

intercommunicate /ˌɪntəkəˈmjuːnɪkeɪt/ *vi* «*people*» 相互联系; «*rooms*» 相通

intercommunication /ˌɪntəkəˌmjuːnɪˈkeɪʃn/ *n* [u] 相通; **a means of ~** 互通方式

interconnect /ˌɪntəkəˈnekt/
A *vi* «*components, computers, systems*» 相互连接; «*rooms*» 相通
B *vt* 使相互联系

interconnecting /ˌɪntəkəˈnektɪŋ/ *adj attrib* 相通的 ‹*rooms, apartments, compartments*›; 相互连接的 ‹*cable*›

interconnection /ˌɪntəkəˈnekʃn/ *n* [c and u] 相互连接

intercontinental /ˌɪntəˌkɒntɪˈnentl/ *adj* 洲际的

intercontinental ballistic missile *n* 洲际弹道导弹

intercooler /ˈɪntəkuːlə(r)/ *n* 中间冷却器

intercourse /ˈɪntəkɔːs/ *n* [u] **1** (social) 交流; **social ~** 社交; **business ~** 生意往来 **2** (sexual) 性交

intercultural /ˌɪntəˈkʌltʃərəl/ *adj* 跨文化的; **~ communication** 跨文化交际

interdenominational /ˌɪntədɪˌnɒmɪˈneɪʃənl/ *adj* 各教派间共有的

interdepartmental /ˌɪntəˌdiːpɑːtˈmentl/ *adj* **1** Admin, Comm 各部门间的 **2** Univ 各系间的

interdependence /ˌɪntədɪˈpendəns/ *n* [u] 相互依赖

interdependent /ˌɪntədɪˈpendənt/ *adj* 相互依赖的

interdict
A /ˈɪntədɪkt/ *n* **1** esp Scot Jur 禁令 **2** (in Roman Catholic church) 禁行圣事令
B /ˌɪntəˈdɪkt/ *vt* **1** esp Amer (prohibit) 禁止 **2** (intercept, prevent movement of) 阻断

interdiction /ˌɪntəˈdɪkʃn/ *n* **1** esp Scot Jur 禁令 **2** (in Roman Catholic church) 禁行圣事 **3** (interception) 阻断

interdisciplinary /ˌɪntəˌdɪsɪˈplɪnəri, Amer -neri/ *adj* 跨学科的 ‹*studies, course*›; 多学科的 ‹*degree, qualification*›

interest /ˈɪntrəst, ˈɪntrest/
A *n* **1** [u and c] (concern, curiosity) 兴趣; **to feel** *or* **take** *or* **have (an) ~ in sb./sth.** 对某人/某事物感兴趣; **to show (an) ~ in sb./sth./doing sth.** 对某人/某事物/做某事表现出兴趣; **to**

arouse *or* **provoke** *or* **stimulate ~** 激起兴趣; **she takes a great ~ in her pupils** 她非常关注自己的学生; **with ~** 有兴趣地; **just for ~** 仅仅是出于兴趣; **to attract** *or* **catch sb.'s ~** 吸引某人的注意; **that is of no ~ to me** 我对那一点也不感兴趣; **economic history holds no ~ for me** 我对经济史不感兴趣 **2** [u] (quality arousing concern, curiosity) 趣味; (power to hold attention) 引人关注的性质; **suspense adds ~ to a story** 悬念可以增强故事的趣味; **to be of public ~** 为公众所关注 **3** [c] (pursuit, pastime) 爱好; **she has wide ~s** 她爱好广泛 **4** [c] (advantage, benefit) 利益; **to look after** *or* **protect** *or* **safeguard one's (own) ~s** 保护自己的利益; **to promote** *or* **further** *or* **advance one's (own) ~s** 促进自己的利益; **to act in sb.'s ~(s)** 行事为某人着想; **to have sb.'s ~s at heart** 为某人的利益着想; **in the ~s of safety** 为了安全; **in the public ~** 为了公众的利益 **5** [c] (financial stake) 权益; **business ~s** 企业股份; **American ~s in Europe** 在欧洲的美国权益; **he sold his ~ in the company** 他卖掉了自己在公司的股份 **6** [c] (personal connection) 利益关系; **to declare one's ~** 申明利益关系; **I have an ~ in this matter** 这件事和我有利益关系 **7** [u] Fin 利息; **the monthly rate of ~** 月利率; **you will be charged ~ at 10%** 将按10%的利率征收利息; **a loan with ~** 有息贷款; **to pay ~ charges on a loan** 支付贷款利息

B **interests** *npl* (people engaged in the same business) 利益集团; **powerful business ~s** 强大的企业集团; **banking/landed ~s** 银行业者/土地所有者阶层

C *vt* **1** (excite curiosity of) 使感兴趣; **to ~ oneself in sth.** 对某事物有兴趣; **to ~ sb. in sth.** 使某人对某事物产生兴趣; **it may ~ you to know** *or* **to learn that ...** 或许你有兴趣知道… **2** (arouse curiosity or desire in) 使愿意参与; **can I ~ you in our latest computer?** 我向您介绍一下我们最新的计算机好吗？; **I tried to ~ him in helping with the preparations** 我试图让他来帮忙做准备工作 **3** formal (cause to give attention) 使关心; **the future of endangered species ~s us all** 我们大家都很关注濒危物种的未来

interest-bearing *adj* 附息的

interested /ˈɪntrəstɪd, ˈɪntrestɪd/ *adj* **1** (taking or showing interest) 感兴趣的; **to be ~ in sb./sth.** 对某人/某事物感兴趣; **he had an ~ look on his face** 他脸上露出好奇的表情; **he is ~ in history** 他喜欢历史; **I shall be ~ to know what happens** 我想知道会发生什么事 **2** (not impartial) 有利害关系的; **as an ~ party, I was not allowed to vote** 作为利害相关的一方，我不得投票; **the ~ parties** Jur 各当事人

interest-free
A *adj* 免息的
B *adv* 免息地

interest-free loan *n* 免息贷款

interest group *n* 利益集团

interesting /ˈɪntrəstɪŋ, -tres-/ *adj* **1** (holding the attention) 有趣的; **he was not very ~ to talk to** 和他交谈没什么意思; **it must have been quite ~ for you** 你对这事一定很关注; **did you meet the author? how very ~!** 你见到那位作家了？真是太棒了！ **2** (promising to be profitable) 会赢利的 ‹*bid, offer*›; 有益的 ‹*proposition*›

interestingly /ˈɪntrəstɪŋli, -tres-/ *adv* **1** (in an interesting manner) 有趣地; **he talked most ~ on the subject** 他把这个话题讲得妙趣横生; **it was an ~ constructed building** 那幢大楼结构奇特 **2** (in a way that is worthy of note) 值得注意地; **she was there, but ~ her husband was not** 她在那儿，但值得注意的是她丈夫却没在那儿

interest rate *n* 利率

interface /ˈɪntəfeɪs/
A *n* **1** (junction, meeting point) 接合点; fig 相互作用点 **2** Comput 接口 **3** Phys 界面
B *vi* 连接; **to ~ with sb./sth.** 与某人互相配合/与某物连接; **to ~ with other computers/networks/systems** 与其他电脑/网络/系统连接
C *vt* 使接合

interfacing /ˈɪntəfeɪsɪŋ/ *n* [u] 内衬

interfere /ˌɪntəˈfɪə(r)/ *vi* **1** (involve oneself) 插手; (intervene) 干涉; **to ~ in** 干涉 ‹*internal affairs, private life*› **2** **to ~ with sth.** (tamper with) 弄坏某物 **3** (hinder, obstruct) 妨碍; **to ~ with** 扰乱 ‹*family life, freedom, right*› **4** Brit euph **to ~ with sb.** (assault) 对…进行性骚扰 ‹*child*› **5** Phys 干扰

interference /ˌɪntəˈfɪərəns/ *n* [u] **1** (by people, organization, bureaucracy) 干涉; **~ in/with sth.** 对某事的介入/妨碍; **~ from sb.** 某人的干涉 **2** Radio, TV, Phys 干扰

interfering /ˌɪntəˈfɪərɪŋ/ *adj attrib* 爱管闲事的

interferon /ˌɪntəˈfɪərɒn/ *n* [u] 干扰素

intergalactic /ˌɪntəgəˈlæktɪk/ *adj* 星系际的

intergovernmental /ˌɪntəˌgʌvnˈmentl/ *adj* 政府间的

interim /ˈɪntərɪm/
A *n* **in the ~** 在此期间
B *adj attrib* **1** (temporary) 临时的 ‹*government, arrangement*›; 暂时的 ‹*measure*›; **the ~ period** 过渡阶段; **an ~ loan** 短期贷款 **2** esp Brit Fin 期中的; **~ dividend** 期中红利

interior /ɪnˈtɪərɪə(r)/
A *n* **1** (of room, building, vehicle) 内部 **2** (of country, continent) 内陆; **people from the ~** 内地来的人 **3** **the I~** Pol (nation's own affairs) 内政; **Minister of the Interior** 内政部长 **4** (in painting, stage set) 内景; **the curtain opens on an ~** 帷幕拉开，出现的是室内场景
B *adj attrib* **1** (inside) 室内的 **2** Cin, TV 内景的; **an ~ shot/scene** 室内镜头/内景 **3** (inland) 内地的 **4** (in the mind) 内心的

interior: ~ angle *n* 内角; **~ decoration** *n* [u] 室内装饰; **~ decorator** ▸p. 409 *n* 室内装饰设计师; **~ design** *n* [u] 室内设计; **~ designer** ▸p. 409 *n* 室内设计师; **~-sprung** *adj* 内装弹簧的

interject /ˌɪntəˈdʒekt/ *vt* 插入; **to ~ a remark** 插话

interjection /ˌɪntəˈdʒekʃn/ *n* **1** (exclamation) 感叹语 **2** (interruption) 插话

interlace /ˌɪntəˈleɪs/
A *vt* **1** (interweave) 使…交错 ‹*patterns*›; 使…交叉 ‹*fingers*› **2** (intersperse) 在…中夹杂 ‹*talk, conversation*›; **a speech ~d with jokes** 夹杂玩笑的演说
B *vi* ‹*threads, branches*› 交错; ‹*fingers*› 交叉

interleave /ˌɪntəˈliːv/ *vt* 插入; **to ~ sth. with sth.** 把某物插入某物

interlibrary loan *n* [u and c] （图书馆）馆际互借

interline /ˌɪntəˈlaɪn/ *vt* 加内衬于

interlinear /ˌɪntəˈlɪnɪə(r)/ *adj* 写于行间的

interlining /ˈɪntəlaɪnɪŋ/ *n* [u] 内衬材料

interlink /ˌɪntəˈlɪŋk/ *vt* 使连接; **the teaching course is ~ed with a research project** 该教学课程与一个研究项目相联系; **the two processors are ~ed** 这两个处理器是连在一起的

interlock /ˌɪntəˈlɒk/ *vi* 相扣

interlocutor /ˌɪntəˈlɒkjʊtə(r)/ *n* formal 对话者

interloper /ˈɪntələʊpə(r)/ *n* 闯入者; **an ~ at the party** 聚会的不速之客

interlude /ˈɪntəluːd/ *n* **1** (pause in events) 间歇; **in the ~** 在这期间 **2** Cin, Theat (interval) 幕间休息 **3** (brief entertainment) 幕间节目 **4** (episode) 穿插事件

intermarriage /ˌɪntəˈmærɪdʒ/ *n* [u and c] **1** (between groups) 通婚 **2** (within a family) 近亲结婚

intermarry /ˌɪntəˈmæri/ *vi* **1** (between groups) [不同种族或部落间的] 通婚 **2** (within a family) 近亲结婚

intermediary /ˌɪntəˈmiːdɪəri, Amer -dɪeri/
A *n* 中间人
B *adj attrib* 调解的; **an ~ agent** 调解人; **to play an ~ role** 做调解人

intermediate /ˌɪntəˈmiːdɪət/ *adj* **1** (in-between) 中间的; **an ~ stage/step/form** 中间阶段/中间步骤/过渡形式 **2** Educ 中级的; **an ~ course/level/exam** 中级课程/水平/考试

intermediate: ~ range *adj* 中程的; **an ~ range missile** 中程导弹; **~ technology** *n* [u] 中间技术

interment /ɪnˈtɜːmənt/ *n* [u and c] 埋葬

intermezzo /ˌɪntəˈmetsəʊ/ *n* (*pl* **intermezzi** /ˌɪntəˈmetsi/ *or* **~s**) **1** (short piece) 间奏曲 **2** (connecting movement) 幕间表演

interminable /ɪnˈtɜːmɪnəbl/ *adj* 无休止的 ‹*speech, wait, debate, argument*›; 没完没了的 ‹*flight*›; 冗长的 ‹*list*›

interminably /ɪnˈtɜːmɪnəbli/ *adv* 无休止地; **~ long** 长得没完没了

intermingle /ˌɪntəˈmɪŋgl/
A *vt* 使混合; **to ~ fact with fiction** 使事实与虚构交织在一起
B *vi* 混合; **the guests ~d with each other** 客人们聚在一起

intermission /ˌɪntəˈmɪʃn/ *n* **1** (pause) 间歇; **to work on without ~** 不间断地工作 **2** (in play, film) 幕间休息

intermittent /ˌɪntəˈmɪtənt/ *adj* 间歇的 ‹*flash*›; 断断续续的 ‹*use, fault*›; **~ rain** 阵雨; **~ bursts of gunfire** 一阵阵的炮火

intermittently /ˌɪntəˈmɪtəntli/ *adv* 间隔地 ‹*publish, appear*›; 断断续续地 ‹*hear, see*›

intern
A /ɪnˈtɜːn/ *vt* 拘留
B /ˈɪntɜːn/ *n* esp Amer 实习医师

internal /ɪnˈtɜːnl/ *adj* **1** (inner) 里面的; **the machine's ~ workings** 机器的内部运转情况; **~ angle** 内角; **~ consistency** 内在的一致性 **2** Med 体内的; **~ bleeding** 内出血 **3** (of the mind) 内心的 **4** (within organization) 内部的; **~ financing** 内部融资 **5** (within country) 国内的; **~ affairs** 内政; **~ fighting** 内战

internal: ~ combustion engine *n* 内燃机; **~ examiner** *n* Brit 校内考官; **~ exile** *n* [u] 国内流放

internalize /ɪnˈtɜːnəlaɪz/ *vt* 使内在化; **to ~ values** 认同并接受价值观

internally /ɪnˈtɜːnəli/ *adv* **1** (inside) 在里面; **~, the building needs major renovation** 这座楼房内部需要大修 **2** (in the body) 在体内; **has she been injured ~?** 她受内伤了吗？; **not to be taken ~** 不可内服 **3** (in the mind) 在内心 **4** (within organization) 在内部 **5** (in country) 在国内

internal: ~ market *n* 国内市场; **I~ Revenue Service** *n* Amer 国内税务署; **~ storage** *n* [u] 内存

international /ˌɪntəˈnæʃnəl/
A *adj* (existing between countries) 国际的; **~ law/rights/sport/trade/flight** 国际公法/权利/体育运动/贸易/航班
B *n* Brit (game) 国际体育比赛; (player) 国际体育比赛选手

International: ~ Atomic Energy Agency *n* 国际原子能机构; **~ Bank for Reconstruction and Development** *n* 国际复兴开发银行; **~ Court of Justice** *n* 国际法院

Internationale /ˌɪntənæʃəˈnɑːl/ *n* **the ~** 国际歌

The International Herald Tribune

《国际先驱论坛报》，纽约时报公司拥有的国际性英文报纸，简称 IHT，总部位于巴黎。前身为《纽约先驱报》（*New York Herald*）的欧洲版《巴黎先驱报》（*Paris Herald*），创刊于 1887 年，1967 年改为现名。新闻报道以严肃、全面著称。报纸销售至全球 180 多个国家。

internationalism /ˌɪntəˈnæʃnəlɪzəm/ *n* [u] 1 (cooperation between nations) 国际主义 2 (state of being international) 国际性; **the ~ of popular music** 流行音乐的国际性

internationalist /ˌɪntəˈnæʃnəlɪst/ *n* 国际主义者

internationalization /ˌɪntəˌnæʃnəlaɪˈzeɪʃn, Amer -lɪˈz-/ *n* [u] 国际化

internationalize /ˌɪntəˈnæʃnəlaɪz/ *vt* 使国际化

International Labour Organization *n* 国际劳工组织

internationally /ˌɪntəˈnæʃnəli/ *adv* 在国际上; **an ~ known writer** 国际知名作家; **the invasion has been ~ condemned** 这一侵略行径受到了世界各国的谴责

international: I~ Monetary Fund *n* 国际货币基金组织; **~ money order** *n* 国际汇票; **I~ Organization for Standardization** *n* 国际标准组织; **I~ Phonetic Alphabet** *n* 国际音标; **~ relations** *npl + v sing* 国际关系; **~ reply coupon** *n* 国际回信券; **I~ Standard Book Number** *n* 国际标准书号

internecine /ˌɪntəˈniːsaɪn/ *adj* 1 (mutually destructive) 两败俱伤的 2 (relating to internal conflict) 内讧的

internee /ˌɪntɜːˈniː/ *n* 拘留犯

Internet /ˈɪntənet/ *n* **the ~** 互联网; **to be on the ~, to be connected to the ~** 在上网; **to buy/find sth. on the ~** 网上购买/找到某物

Internet: ~ access *n* [u] 互联网接入; **to have ~ access** 可以上网; **~ access provider** *n* 互联网接入提供商; **~ address** *n* 互联网地址; **~ advertising** *n* [u] 互联网广告; **~ banking** *n* [u] 网络银行业; **~ cafe** *n* 网络咖啡屋; **~ chat** *n* [u] 网络聊天; **~ commerce** *n* [u] 互联网商务; **~ connection** *n* 互联网连接; **~ content provider** *n* = **content provider**; **~-enabled** *adj* 连接互联网的; **~ host** *n* 联网主机; **~ hosting** *n* [u] 联网主机服务; **~-illiterate** *adj* 网络盲的; **~-literate** *adj* 会使用互联网的; **~ phone** *n* 网络电话; **~ presence provider** *n* 网络平台供应商; **~ protocol** *n* 网络协议; **~ relay chat** *n* [u] 互联网接力聊天室; **~ search** *n* [c and u] 互联网搜索; **~ service provider** *n* 互联网服务提供商; **~ site** *n* 网站; **~ start-up** *n* 新上网网络公司; **~ user** *n* 互联网用户

internist /ɪnˈtɜːnɪst/ *n* Amer 内科医师

internment /ɪnˈtɜːnmənt/ *n* [u] 拘留

internship /ɪnˈtɜːnʃɪp/ *n* Amer 1 (position) 实习职位 2 (period of time) 实习期

interpersonal /ˌɪntəˈpɜːsənl/ *adj attrib* 人际的; **~ skills/dynamics** 人际交往技巧/互动

interplanetary /ˌɪntəˈplænɪtri, Amer -teri/ *adj* 行星际的

interplay /ˈɪntəpleɪ/ *n* [u] 相互作用; **the ~ of colours in the painting** 图画中色彩的相互映衬

Interpol /ˈɪntəpɒl/ *pr n* 国际刑警组织

interpolate /ɪnˈtɜːpəleɪt/ *vt* formal 1 (insert) 插入 2 (add) 添加 3 (interject) 插嘴说; **to ~ a remark** 插一句话

interpolation /ɪnˌtɜːpəˈleɪʃn/ *n* formal 1 [u] (adding, inserting) 插入 2 [c] (addition, insertion) 插入文字 3 [c] (interjection) 插话

interpose /ˌɪntəˈpəʊz/ formal
A *vt* 1 (insert) 插入; **to ~ sth. between A and B** 把某物置于A和B之间 2 (interject) 插嘴说
B *vi* 干预

interpret /ɪnˈtɜːprɪt/
A *vt* 1 (explain, clarify) 解释; **to ~ a dream** 解梦 2 (understand) 理解; **to ~ sb.'s silence as consent** 把某人的沉默看作是同意 3 (perform) 演绎 ‹*role, song*›
B *vi* 做口译; **to ~ for sb.** 为某人口头翻译

interpretation /ɪnˌtɜːprɪˈteɪʃn/ *n* 1 [u and c] (act of understanding) 理解; **to be open to ~** 可作各种解释 2 [c] (explanation) 说明; **to place an ~ on sth.** 对某事作出解释 3 [c] (translation) 口译 4 [c] (of painting, song, role) 演绎

interpretative /ɪnˈtɜːprɪtətɪv/ *adj* 解释的 ‹*approach, method*›; 说明性的 ‹*style, hypothesis*›

interpreter /ɪnˈtɜːprɪtə(r)/ *n* 1 (translator) 口译者; **to communicate through an ~** 通过口译员交流 2 (of theory, dream, situation) 解释者 3 (actor, singer, musician) 演绎者 4 Comput 解释程序

interpreting /ɪnˈtɜːprɪtɪŋ/ *n* [u] 口译; **simultaneous ~** 同声传译

interracial /ˌɪntəˈreɪʃl/ *adj* 种族间的

interregnum /ˌɪntəˈregnəm/ *n* (*pl* **interregna** /ˌɪntəˈregnə/) (between reigns) 空位期; (between leaders) 过渡期

interrelate /ˌɪntərɪˈleɪt/
A *vt* 使相互关联; **these events are ~d** 这些事件是相互关联的
B *vi* 相互关联

interrelation /ˌɪntərɪˈleɪʃn/, **interrelationship** /ˌɪntərɪˈleɪʃnʃɪp/ *ns* (of facts, events) 相互关联; (of people, groups) 相互联系

interrogate /ɪnˈterəgeɪt/ *vt* 1 (question) 审讯 ‹*suspect, prisoner*› 2 Comput 查询

interrogation /ɪnˌterəˈgeɪʃn/ *n* [c and u] 审问; **to carry out** *or* **conduct an ~** 进行审讯; **to have sb. under ~** 对某人进行审讯; **he confessed under ~** 他在审讯中招供了

interrogative /ˌɪntəˈrɒgətɪv/
A *adj* 1 (questioning) 询问的 ‹*tone, glance*› 2 Ling 疑问的
B *n* 疑问词; **in the ~** 以疑问形式

interrogatively /ˌɪntəˈrɒgətɪvli/ *adv* 1 (questioningly) 询问地 2 Ling 疑问地; **the word is used ~ here** 该词在此用作疑问词

interrogator /ɪnˈterəgeɪtə(r)/ *n* 审问者

interrogatory /ˌɪntəˈrɒgətri, Amer -tɔːri/ *adj* 疑问的

interrupt /ˌɪntəˈrʌpt/
A *vt* 1 (cut in on) 打断 ‹*person, speech*› 2 (disturb) 暂停 ‹*programme*›; 中断 ‹*trade*› 3 (break up) 遮挡 ‹*view*›; **the skyline was ~ed by pylons** 地平线被塔楼遮挡了
B *vi* 打断; **stop ~ing!** 别打岔!

interruption /ˌɪntəˈrʌpʃn/ *n* 1 (in speech, conversation) 插嘴; **without ~s** 不被打断 2 (in continuity) 阻断; **an ~ to trade** 贸易中断

intersect /ˌɪntəˈsekt/
A *vt* 1 (gen) 横断; **a field ~ed by ditches** 沟壑纵横的田野 2 Math 和…相交
B *vi* 1 (cross) 交叉; **to ~ with ...** 与…交叉; **two ~ing paths** 两条交叉的小路 2 Math 相交

intersection /ˌɪntəˈsekʃn/ *n* 1 (point of connection) 交点 2 (road junction) 十字路口 3 Math 相交

interservice /ˌɪntəˈsɜːvɪs/ *adj attrib* 各军种间的

intersession /ˈɪntəseʃn/ *n* Can 短学期 [大学两个学期之间5到6周的强化学习时间，需要学完13周的课程]

intersperse /ˌɪntəˈspɜːs/ *vt* 1 (scatter) 散布; **houses ~d among the trees** 分布在树丛中的房子; **laughter ~d between sarcastic comments** 夹杂在尖刻话语中的笑声 2 (diversify with other things) 点缀; **a lawn ~d with flower beds** 点缀着花坛的草坪; **sunshine ~d with showers** 晴间或有阵雨

interstate /ˌɪntəˈsteɪt/ Amer
A *adj attrib* 州际的
B *n* **~ (highway)** 州际公路

interstellar /ˌɪntəˈstelə(r)/ *adj attrib* 星际的

interstice /ɪnˈtɜːstɪs/ *n* formal 缝隙

intertwine /ˌɪntəˈtwaɪn/
A *vt* 使缠绕在一起
B *vi* 缠绕在一起; **intertwining branches** 缠绕在一起的枝条; **their fates were ~d** 他们的命运紧密相连

interurban /ˌɪntərˈɜːbən/ *adj attrib* 市际的

interval /ˈɪntəvl/ *n* 1 (in time, space) 间隔; **at regular ~s** 每隔一定时间; **at weekly ~s** 每隔一周; **he is fed at four-hourly ~s** 他每 4 个小时喂食一次; **bright ~s** Meteorol 间有晴天; **to have lucid ~s** Med 有时清醒 2 Brit Theat 幕间休息; Sport 中场休息 3 Mus 音程; **an ~ of a third** 三分之一音程

intervene /ˌɪntəˈviːn/ *vi* 1 (take action) 介入; **to ~ on sb.'s behalf** 代表某人出面干预; **to ~ in a dispute** 调解争端 2 (happen) 阻碍; **if nothing ~s** 如果没有任何阻扰的话

intervening /ˌɪntəˈviːnɪŋ/ *adj attrib* (coming between) 期间发生的 ‹*events*›; 其间的 ‹*period, years*›; (situated in between) 位于其中的; **in the ~ 10 years** 在这期间的 10 年里; **he could see across the ~ fields to the hills** 他能看见田野那边的山丘

intervention /ˌɪntəˈvenʃn/ *n* [c and u] 干涉; **an ~ on my behalf** 代表我的介入; **government ~** 政府干预

interventionist /ˌɪntəˈvenʃənɪst/
A *adj* 干涉主义的
B *n* 干涉主义者

intervention price *n* 干预价格 [农产品低于此价格时欧盟会介入购买]

interview /ˈɪntəvjuː/
A *n* 1 (for job etc.) 面试; **to be called/invited for (an) ~** 接到通知/受邀面试 2 (on TV, radio) 采访; **to hold** *or* **conduct an ~ with sb.** 采访某人; **in an ~ with ...** 在对…的采访中 3 (formal discussion) 面谈; **a career's ~** 择业咨询面谈 4 (by police) 审问 5 (in survey) 访谈
B *vt* 1 (for job etc.) 对…进行面试 ‹*applicant*› 2 (on TV, radio) 采访 3 (question formally) «*police*» 问讯 ‹*suspect*› 4 (in survey) 访谈
C *vi* 面试表现; **to ~ well/badly** 面试表现好/差

interviewee /ˌɪntəvjuːˈiː/ *n* 1 (for job) 被面试者 2 (on TV, radio) 被采访者 3 (in survey) 访谈对象

interviewer /ˈɪntəvjuːə(r)/ *n* 1 (for job) 面试官 2 (on TV, radio) 采访者 3 (in survey) 访谈人员

intervocalic /ˌɪntəvəˈkælɪk/ *adj* 元音间的

interwar /ˌɪntəˈwɔː(r)/ *adj attrib* 两次世界大战之间的; **during the ~ years** 在两次世界大战之间的岁月里

interweave /ˌɪntəˈwiːv/ (*pt* **interwove** /-ˈwəʊv/; *pp* **interwoven** /-ˈwəʊvn/)
A *vt* 1 (weave together) 交错编织 ‹*threads*› 2 fig (blend, mix) 使…交织在一起 ‹*destinies, themes, stories*›
B *vi* 交织在一起

intestate /ɪnˈtesteɪt/ *adj* 未留遗嘱的; **to die ~** 死时没留下遗嘱

intestinal /ɪnˈtestɪnl, ˌɪntesˈtaɪnl/ *adj* 肠的; **an ~ blockage** 肠梗阻

intestine /ɪnˈtestɪn/ *n* 肠

intimacy /ˈɪntɪməsi/
A *n* 1 [u] (closeness) 亲密 2 [c and u] formal or Jur

i

(sexual relations) 性行为; **there had been no ~ between them** 他们之间没发生过性关系
B intimacies *npl* (gestures) 亲密行为; (words) 亲密的言语

intimate¹ /ˈɪntɪmət/
A *adj* **1** (close) 亲密的; **to have an ~ relationship with sb.** 与某人关系密切; **to be on ~ terms with sb.** 与某人来往密切 **2** euph (sexual) 有性关系的; **to be ~ with sb.** formal *or* Jur 与某人有性关系 **3** (personal) 私密的; **~ feelings** 内心的感情; **~ details** 隐私细节; **sb.'s ~ life** 某人的私人生活; **an ~ conversation** 私下交谈 **4** (cosy) 宜于密切关系的; **an ~ restaurant** 幽静的餐馆 **5** (detailed, deep) 详尽的; **to have an ~ knowledge of/acquaintance with sth.** 对某事物了如指掌
B *n* 密友

intimate² /ˈɪntɪmeɪt/ *vt* **1** (hint) 暗示; **to ~ that ...** 透露… **2** formal (announce) 宣布; **to ~ that ...** 通知…

intimately /ˈɪntɪmətli/ *adv* **1** (closely) 密切地 **2** euph (sexually) 在性关系上; **to be ~ involved with sb.** 与某人关系暧昧 **3** (personally, privately) 隐秘地 ‹*write, converse*› **4** (strongly, closely) 紧密地; **to be ~ acquainted with sth.** 谙熟某事物; **to be ~ aware of sth.** 对某事物了解详尽; **to be ~ involved in** *or* **connected with sth.** 与某事物联系紧密

intimation /ˌɪntɪˈmeɪʃn/ *n* 暗示; **an ~ of danger/disaster** 危险/灾难的征兆

intimidate /ɪnˈtɪmɪdeɪt/ *vt* 恐吓; **to ~ sb. into doing sth.** 胁迫某人做某事; **to feel ~d** 被吓住

intimidating /ɪnˈtɪmɪdeɪtɪŋ/ *adj* 令人胆怯的

intimidatingly /ɪnˈtɪmɪdeɪtɪŋli/ *adv* 令人胆怯地

intimidation /ɪnˌtɪmɪˈdeɪʃn/ *n* [u] 恐吓; **the ~ of witnesses** 对证人的威胁

into /ˈɪntu:/ *prep* **1** (to location within) 到…里; **to go ~ the room/building** 走进房间/建筑物; **to go ~ town** 进城; **to get ~ bed** 上床; **to get ~ a car** 钻进汽车; **to go ~ hospital** Brit *or* **the hospital** Amer 去医院; **to go ~ the shade** 到阴凉处; **to rush out ~ the night** 冲到外面的夜幕中; **to disappear ~ the mist** 消失在薄雾中 **2** (towards centre of) 向…内; **to go ~ sth./sb.** «*knife*» 扎进某物/捅到某人身上; «*nail*» 掐进某物/某人皮肤; **to soak ~ sth.** «*oil, dye*» 渗入某物; **to bite ~ sth.** 咬一口某物 **3** (in direction of) 向着; **to look straight ~ the sun** 盯着太阳看; **to speak ~ a microphone** 对着麦克风讲话; **to see ~ the future** 洞察未来 **4** (against) 碰上; **to bump/crash ~ sth.** 撞到/猛撞到某物 **5** (indicating change of state) 进入…状态; **to fall ~ a heavy sleep** 陷入沉睡; **to get ~ bad habits** 养成坏习惯; **to be scared ~ silence** 吓得不敢出声; **to rush ~ marriage** 草率结婚; **to fall ~ a new job** 找到新工作 **6** (to form, shape, style of) 成为; **to change sth. ~ sth.** 把某物变成某物; **to change ~ a butterfly** 变成蝴蝶; **to translate sth. ~ Chinese** 把某作品翻译成中文; **to make sth. ~ a film** 把某作品改编成电影; **to roll sth. ~ a ball** 把某物卷成团; **to break ~ pieces** 摔碎; **to change ~ jeans** 换上牛仔裤 **7** (expressing the result of an action) 以…为结果; **to be shocked ~ a confession** 被吓得招认 **8** (concerning) 关于; **to research ~ sth.** 对某事物进行研究; **an investigation ~ sth.** 有关某事物的调查 **9** (at a point within a period of time) 到 [一段时间的某一点]; **several minutes ~ the second half** 下半场开始后几分钟; **she is ~ the fourth month of her pregnancy** 她已进入孕期的第四个月了; **to be well ~ 2011** 早已进入 2011 年; **he is well ~ his forties** 他四十好几了 **10** (to a point within a period of time) 延续到; **to continue or last well ~ 2006** 一直持续到 2006 年; **to do sth. far** *or* **long ~ the night** 做某事直到深夜 **11** Math 除; **5 ~ 20 is 4** 5 除 20 等于 4 **12** colloq (keen on) 迷上; **to be ~ sth.** 迷上某物; **to be ~ sb.** 十分喜欢某人; **she's ~ art in a big way** 她痴迷于艺术; **to be ~ drugs** 有毒瘾; **to be ~ everything** «*child, kitten, puppy*» 对什么都好奇

intolerable /ɪnˈtɒlərəbl/ *adj* 无法容忍的; **it is ~ to see her suffer** 看到她受苦让人受不了; **it is ~ that he should have to go through that** 他不得不有那种经历真可怕

intolerably /ɪnˈtɒlərəbli/ *adv* 难以忍受地; **it was ~ hot/cold/humid** 天气热/冷/潮湿得无法忍受

intolerance /ɪnˈtɒlərəns/ *n* **1** [u] (gen) 不宽容; **~ of/to** *or* **towards sb./sth.** 对某人/某事物无法容忍 **2** Med 过敏; **~ to** *or* **of sth.** 对某物的过敏; **~ to alcohol** 酒精过敏

intolerant /ɪnˈtɒlərənt/ *adj* **1** (bigoted, narrow-minded) 偏执的; **to be ~ of sb./sth.** 不能容忍某人/某事物 **2** Med 过敏的; **to be ~ to** *or* **of sth.** 对某物过敏; **to be alcohol ~** 酒精过敏

intolerantly /ɪnˈtɒlərəntli/ *adv* 偏执地 ‹*behave, react*›; **~ bigoted** 偏执得令人无法忍受

intonation /ˌɪntəˈneɪʃn/ *n* **1** [c] Ling 语调 **2** [c] Mus 音准 **3** [u] (intoning, reciting) 吟诵

intone /ɪnˈtəʊn/ *vt* **1** (speak solemnly) 缓慢庄重地说 **2** (recite) 吟诵

intoxicant /ɪnˈtɒksɪkənt/
A *n* 麻醉剂
B *adj* 麻醉的

intoxicate /ɪnˈtɒksɪkeɪt/ *vt* **1** (inebriate) 使醉 **2** fig 使陶醉

intoxicated /ɪnˈtɒksɪkeɪtɪd/ *adj* **1** (drunk) 喝醉的; **to drive while ~** 酒醉开车 **2** fig 陶醉的; **~ by** *or* **with success** 被成功冲昏了头脑的

intoxicating /ɪnˈtɒksɪkeɪtɪŋ/ *adj* **1** lit 醉人的 **2** fig 令人陶醉的

intoxication /ɪnˌtɒksɪˈkeɪʃn/ *n* [u] **1** lit 醉酒; **in a state of ~** 喝醉了 **2** fig 陶醉

intractability /ɪnˌtræktəˈbɪləti/ *n* [u] **1** (of person, disposition) 倔强 **2** (of problem, situation) 难对付; (of illness) 难治疗

intractable /ɪnˈtræktəbl/ *adj* **1** (stubborn) 倔强的 ‹*person, disposition*› **2** (difficult to control) 棘手的 ‹*problem, situation*›; 难治疗的 ‹*illness*›

intranet /ˈɪntrənet/ *n* 内联网

intransigence /ɪnˈtrænsɪdʒəns/ *n* [u] 不妥协; **~ about** *or* **over sth.** 对某事的毫不妥协

intransigent /ɪnˈtrænsɪdʒənt/ *adj* 固执己见的 ‹*person*›; 不妥协的 ‹*behaviour, attitude*›

intransitive /ɪnˈtrænsətɪv/
A *adj* 不及物的
B *n* 不及物动词

intransitively /ɪnˈtrænzətɪvli/ *adv* 不及物地; **the verb is used ~ in this sentence** 该动词在这个句中用作不及物动词

intrapreneur /ˌɪntrəprəˈnɜ:(r)/ *n* 内部策划经理

intrauterine /ˌɪntrəˈju:təraɪn/ *adj* 子宫内的

intrauterine device *n* 宫内节育器

intravenous /ˌɪntrəˈvi:nəs/ *adj* 注入静脉的; **an ~ drip/injection** 静脉滴注/注射

intravenously /ˌɪntrəˈvi:nəsli/ *adv* 通过静脉

in-tray *n* 收件篮

intrepid /ɪnˈtrepɪd/ *adj* 勇敢的 ‹*person*›; 无畏的 ‹*exploits, character*›

intrepidly /ɪnˈtrepɪdli/ *adv* 勇敢地

intricacy /ˈɪntrɪkəsi/
A *n* [u] 错综复杂; **the ~ of a plot/story** 情节/故事的复杂
B intricacies *npl* **1** (of story) 错综复杂的事物 **2** (of law) 纷繁难懂的细节

intricate /ˈɪntrɪkət/ *adj* 错综复杂的

intricately /ˈɪntrɪkətli/ *adv* 错综复杂地

intrigue
A /ɪnˈtri:g/ *vt* (fascinate) 引起…的好奇心; **I'm ~d to know whether ...** 我很想知道是否…; **she was ~d by his story** 她被他的故事迷住了
B /ɪnˈtri:g/ *vi* 密谋; **to ~ (with sb.) against sb.** (与某人) 密谋策划加害某人
C /ˈɪntri:g, ɪnˈtri:g/ *n* **1** [u] (plotting) 密谋策划 **2** [c] (plot) 阴谋; **a political ~** 政治阴谋; **to be involved in an ~** 参与一个阴谋

intriguing /ɪnˈtri:gɪŋ/ *adj* 引起兴趣的; **an ~ smile** 迷人的微笑; **an ~ thought** 有趣的想法; **an ~ story** 引人入胜的故事

intriguingly /ɪnˈtri:gɪŋli/ *adv* 引人入胜地; **the announcement was ~ worded** 公告的措词非常有趣; **~, she said nothing** 令人不解的是，她什么也没说

intrinsic /ɪnˈtrɪnzɪk, -sɪk/ *adj* 本质的 ‹*quality*›; 本身的 ‹*part*›; 固有的 ‹*merit, value*›; 真正的 ‹*interest*›; **this problem is ~ to the situation** 这是局势本身的问题

intrinsically /ɪnˈtrɪnzɪkli, -sɪk-/ *adv* 本质上 ‹*superior, valuable*›; 就本身而言 ‹*flawed*›; 真正地 ‹*significant*›

intro /ˈɪntrəʊ/ *n* colloq **1** Mus 前奏 **2** (gen) 介绍

introduce /ˌɪntrəˈdju:s, Amer -ˈdu:s/ *vt* **1** (make known, present) 介绍 ‹*person*›; 使…相互认识 ‹*two people*›; **to ~ sb. to sb.** 把某人介绍给某人; **he was ~d to the queen** 他被引见给女王; **I'm sorry, I don't think we've been ~d** 抱歉，我想我们还不认识呢; **to ~ oneself** 做自我介绍; **he ~d himself as Dr Edwards** 他自称是爱德华兹博士 **2** TV, Radio (announce) 主持 ‹*programme, item*› **3** (occur at start of) 引出 ‹*piece, article, film*›; **to ~ sth. with sth.** (provide an opening explanation to) 用某事物作…的开场白 ‹*lesson, programme, article*›; **each chapter is ~d by a quotation** 每章的开头都有一段引文; **the scene that ~s Act 5** 第 5 幕开始的那一场; **she ~d her talk with a short film** 她播放了一个电影短片作为谈话的引子 **4** (bring to attention of) 使初次了解; **to ~ sb. to sth.** 使某人初次接触某事物; **the foundation course ~s students to the basics** 基础课程向学生介绍基础知识; **she has ~d many people to the pleasures of wine-tasting** 她使很多人体会到了品尝葡萄酒的乐趣; **it was her brother who ~d her to smoking** 是她哥哥教会她吸烟的 **5** (mention for first time) 初次提及; **two new characters are ~d in Chapter 6** 第 6 章出现了两个新人物; **to try to ~ the subject into the conversation** 试图将话题引入到谈话中 **6** (bring in for the first time) 引入 ‹*person, animal, plant*›; 传入 ‹*disease*›; 添加 ‹*uncertainty, excitement*›; (surreptitiously) 偷偷带入 ‹*camera, bomb*›; **let's ~ a bit of colour** 我们来添加一点色彩; **it ~d a bit of drama into our lives** 它为我们的生活带来了一些戏剧性 **7** (bring into use or operation) 推行; **new legislation has just been ~d** 新法律刚刚开始实施; **the company is introducing a new model next year** 公司明年将推出一种新型产品; **computers were first ~d into schools in the 1970s** 计算机于 20 世纪 70 年代首次在学校中使用 **8** Pol 将…提交讨论; **to ~ a bill** 提交议案 **9** (insert) 插入 ‹*needle, tube*›; 添入 ‹*substance*›

introduction /ˌɪntrəˈdʌkʃn/ *n* **1** [c] (presentation) 介绍; **to do/make/perform the ~s** 作介绍; **she was hoping for an ~ to the president** 她希望被引见给总统; **our next guest needs no ~** 我们的下一位客人就无需介绍了; **a letter of ~** 介绍信; **this document was my ~ to high society** 这份文件是我进入上流社会的敲门砖 **2** [c] (background information) 开场白; **by way of ~** 作为开场白 **3** [c] (to book, article, speech) 序言 **4** [c] Mus (preceding main section) 前奏; (opening passage) 序曲

i

5 [c] (first experience of sth.) 初次经历; **this concert was my ~ to classical music** 这场音乐会使我第一次接触到古典音乐; **an ~ to Paris nightlife** 对巴黎夜生活的初次体验 6 [c] (beginner's guide) 入门书; **An Introduction to Latin** 《拉丁语入门》 7 [u] (mentioning for first time) 初次提及; **the ~ of these new characters complicates the plot** 这些新人物的出现令情节变得复杂了 8 [u] (insertion of needle, tube) 插入; (addition of substance) 添入 9 [u and c] (bringing in) (of species, plant) 引进; (of disease) 传入 10 [u] (bringing into use or operation) 推行; **the ~ of the new legislation/product** 新法律的实施/新产品的推出; **issues arising from the ~ of new technology** 采用新技术引发的问题 11 [u] Pol 提交讨论; **the ~ of the bill** 议案的提交 12 [c] (thing newly brought in) 新推行的事物; **the procedure is a new ~** 该程序是新推出的; **these exotic vegetables are recent ~s to our supermarkets** 这些进口蔬菜是我们超市新进的

introduction agency *n* 婚姻介绍所

introductory /ˌɪntrəˈdʌktəri/ *adj* 1 (preliminary) 介绍的; **an ~ letter/chapter** 介绍信/序篇; **to make a few ~ remarks** 说几句开场白 2 Comm 试销的; **an ~ offer/promotion** 特价试销/试销推广

introspection /ˌɪntrəˈspekʃn/ *n* [u] 反省

introspective /ˌɪntrəˈspektɪv/ *adj* 好反省的

introversion /ˌɪntrəˈvɜːʃn, Amer -ˈvɜːrʒn/ *n* [u] 内向

introvert /ˈɪntrəvɜːt/
A *n* 内向的人
B *adj* = **introverted**

introverted /ˈɪntrəvɜːtɪd/ *adj* 1 内向的 2 (inward-looking) 封闭的

intrude /ɪnˈtruːd/
A *vi* 1 (meddle, interfere) 侵扰; **to ~ into sb.'s affairs** 干涉某人的私事; **to ~ on** *or* **upon sb.'s privacy/grief** 侵犯某人的私生活/搅扰某人的伤心事 2 (encroach) 闯入; **I don't want to ~ on a family gathering** 我不想贸然闯入家庭聚会 3 (have unwelcome effect) 扰乱
B *vt* 强加; **to ~ one's views on** *or* **upon ...** 把意见强加给…; **to ~ oneself into ...** 硬挤进…

intruder /ɪnˈtruːdə(r)/ *n* 侵入者; **we were made to feel like ~s** 我们被弄得觉得自己像是不速之客

intruder alarm *n* 侵入报警器

intrusion /ɪnˈtruːʒn/ *n* [c and u] 1 (interruption, unwelcome arrival) 闯入; **she apologized for the ~** 她对径自闯入表示抱歉 2 (interference) 干涉; **an ~ into sb.'s affairs** 对某人私事的侵扰

intrusive /ɪnˈtruːsɪv/ *adj* 1 (disturbing) 打扰的 2 (indiscreet) 烦扰的; **I found his questions rather ~** 我觉得他的问题有点唐突

intuit /ɪnˈtjuːɪt, Amer -ˈtuː-/ *vt* 凭直觉知道; **to ~ that ...** 凭直觉感到…

intuition /ˌɪntjuːˈɪʃn, Amer -tuː-/ *n* [c and u] 直觉; **to have an ~ that ...** 有…的直觉; **to know sth. by ~** 通过直觉知道某事

intuitive /ɪnˈtjuːɪtɪv, Amer -ˈtuː-/ *adj* 1 (instinctive) 凭直觉的; **~ knowledge** 直观知识 2 (easy to use) 使用简便的 ‹*software, interface*›

intuitively /ɪnˈtjuːɪtɪvli, Amer -ˈtuː-/ *adv* 凭直觉地

Inuit /ˈɪnjuːɪt, ˈɪnʊɪt pl ▸**p. 426**
A *n* 1 [c] (*pl* ~ *or* **~s**) (person) 伊努伊特人 2 [u] (language) 伊努伊特语
B *adj* (of the people) 伊努伊特人的; (of the language) 伊努伊特语的

inundate /ˈɪnʌndeɪt/ *vt* 1 (flood, submerge) 淹没 2 fig (overwhelm) 使不胜负荷; **I was ~d with invitations** 众多的邀请弄得我应接不暇

inundation /ˌɪnʌnˈdeɪʃn/ *n* 淹没

inure /ɪˈnjʊə(r)/ *vt* 使习惯; **to ~ sb./oneself to sth.** 使某人/自己适应某事物; **to become ~d to sth.** 习惯于某事物

invade /ɪnˈveɪd/ *vt* 1 (enter by force) 侵略 ‹*country*› 2 (enter in large numbers) 大批涌入; **the resort was ~d by tourists** 度假胜地涌入了大批游客; **doubts ~d his mind** 他满腹狐疑 3 (disturb) 侵扰; **to ~ sb.'s privacy** 侵犯某人的隐私

invader /ɪnˈveɪdə(r)/ *n* 侵略者

invading /ɪnˈveɪdɪŋ/ *adj attrib* 侵略的 ‹*forces, army*›; **the ~ Germans** 入侵的德国人

invalid[1] /ˈɪnvəlɪd, ˈɪnvəliːd/
A *n* (ill person) 病弱者; (disabled person) 残疾人
B *modif* (ill) 病弱的; (disabled) 残疾的
C *vt* 令…退役; **he was ~ed out of the army** 他因伤病退役; **he was wounded in the battle and ~ed home** 他在战斗中负伤，后退役回家

invalid[2] /ɪnˈvælɪd/ *adj* 1 (void, not officially acceptable) 无效的 ‹*will, passport, judgement, marriage*›; 作废的 ‹*ticket, contract*› 2 (not true) 无根据的 ‹*conclusion*›; 站不住脚的 ‹*argument*›

invalidate /ɪnˈvælɪdeɪt/ *vt* 1 (render void) 使…无效 ‹*will, passport, judgement, marriage*›; 使…作废 ‹*ticket, contract*› 2 (render unsound or erroneous) 证明…错误 ‹*argument, conclusion*›

invalidity /ˌɪnvəˈlɪdəti/ *n* [u] 1 Brit (of person) 病弱 2 (state of being unsound) 站不住脚 3 (state of being void) 无效

invalidity benefit *n* [u] Brit 病残救济金

invaluable /ɪnˈvæljʊəbl/ *adj* 无法估价的 ‹*collection, item, jewellery*›; 非常宝贵的 ‹*advice, help, assistant*›

invariable /ɪnˈveərɪəbl/ *adj* 恒定的 ‹*pressure, amount*›; 不变的 ‹*habit*›; 始终如一的 ‹*routine, helpfulness, comment*›; **~ courtesy/an ~ practice** 一贯的彬彬有礼/做法

invariably /ɪnˈveərɪəbli/ *adv* 一贯地

invasion /ɪnˈveɪʒn/ *n* 1 (by armed forces) 侵略 2 (incursion in large numbers) 大批涌入; **an ~ of tourists/locusts** 游客的纷至沓来/蝗虫的大肆侵害 3 (intrusion) 侵扰; **an ~ of sb.'s privacy** 对某人隐私的侵犯

invasive /ɪnˈveɪsɪv/ *adj* 1 (spreading harmfully) 肆意蔓延的 ‹*plant*›; 扩散性的 ‹*disease, cancer cells*› 2 Med 开刀的; **minimally ~ surgery/treatment** 微创手术/治疗 3 (intrusive) 侵扰的; **~ questions/sound** 侵犯隐私的问题/扰人的声音

invective /ɪnˈvektɪv/ *n* [u] 咒骂; **to hurl ~ at sb.** 对某人破口大骂

inveigh /ɪnˈveɪ/ *vi* formal 痛斥; **to ~ against sb./sth.** 猛烈抨击某人/某事物

inveigle /ɪnˈveɪgl/ *vt* formal pej 引诱; **to ~ sb. into doing sth.** 诱骗某人做某事

invent /ɪnˈvent/ *vt* 1 (create, design) 发明 ‹*machine, device, game*› 2 (make up) 捏造 ‹*story, excuse*›; **an ~ed name** 虚构的名字

invention /ɪnˈvenʃn/ *n* 1 [c] (something invented) 发明物 2 [u] (action of inventing) 发明 3 [c] (lie, fabrication) 虚构; **the story is a malicious ~** 这个说法属恶意编造 4 [u] (creative ability) 创造力

inventive /ɪnˈventɪv/ *adj* 1 (indicative of creativity) 有创意的 ‹*design, device*› 2 (having creative ability) 有创造力的 ‹*person*›; 善于创造的 ‹*powers*›

inventiveness /ɪnˈventɪvnɪs/ *n* [u] (of person) 创造力; (of design, device) 创意

inventor /ɪnˈventə(r)/ *n* 发明者

inventory /ˈɪnvəntri, Amer -tɔːri/
A *n* 1 (list) 存货清单; **an ~ of fixtures and fittings** 夹具和配件清单 2 (quantity in stock) 库存
B *vt* 1 (make list of) 列出…的清单 ‹*stock*› 2 (enter in list) 把…编目 ‹*items*›

inventory control *n* [u] 库存管理

inverse
A /ˌɪnˈvɜːs/ *adj* 1 Math 反的; **~ function** 反函数 2 (gen) 相反的 ‹*ratio, relation*›; **in ~ order** 按逆序; **in ~ proportion to ...** 与…成反比
B /ˈɪnvɜːs/ *n* 1 Math 倒数 2 (gen) 相反的事物

inversely /ɪnˈvɜːsli/ *adv* 相反地

inversion /ɪnˈvɜːʃn, Amer ɪnˈvɜːrʒn/ *n* 1 [u] (inverting) 倒转 2 [c] (instance of inverting) 颠倒

invert /ɪnˈvɜːt/ *vt* 1 (upend) 倒置 2 (reverse) 颠倒 ‹*order*›

invertebrate /ɪnˈvɜːtɪbrət/
A *adj* 无脊椎的
B *n* 无脊椎动物

inverted: ~ commas *npl* esp Brit 引号; **in ~ commas** 加引号的; **~ snob** *n* [蔑视财富和社会地位的] 倒转势利眼; **~ snobbery** *n* [u] 倒转势利眼 [指对财富和社会地位的蔑视]

invert sugar /ˈɪnvɜːt ˌʃʊgə(r)/ *n* [u] 转化糖

invest /ɪnˈvest/
A *vt* 1 (commit) 投资 ‹*funds, capital*›; **to ~ £50,000 in shares** 投资5万英镑购买股票 2 (expend) 投入 ‹*time, energy*›; **we've ~ed a lot of effort in this project** 我们在这个项目上耗费了很多精力 3 (install) 使…就职 ‹*prince, president*›; **to ~ sb. as sth.** 使某人就任某职位; **to ~ sb. with sth.** 授给某人某物 4 (provide, bestow) 赋予; **to be ~ed with significance** 被赋予意义
B *vi* 1 (commit funds) 投资; **to ~ in shares** 投资股票 2 (spend money on purchase) 花钱; **to ~ in sth.** 花钱买某物

investigate /ɪnˈvestɪgeɪt/
A *vt* 1 (inquire into) 调查 ‹*crime, accident*›; **they are being ~d** 他们正在受调查 2 (find out details about) 审查 ‹*candidate, motives, suspect, applicant*› 3 (study) 调研 ‹*market, possibilities*›; **it's worth investigating whether ...** 值得调查一下是否…
B *vi* 进行调查

investigation /ɪnˌvestɪˈgeɪʃn/ *n* [c and u] 1 (inquiry) 侦查; **the crime is still under ~** 这一罪行还在侦查中; **he is under ~** 他在接受审查; **a criminal ~** 罪案侦查 2 (study) 调查研究; **the matter under ~** 研究中的事; **on (further) ~** 经(进一步)研究; **an ~ is under way** 正在进行调查研究

investigative /ɪnˈvestɪgətɪv, Amer -geɪtɪv/ *adj* 调查研究的 ‹*method, work*›; **a piece of ~ journalism** 一篇调查研究报道; **an ~ reporter** 采访记者

investigator /ɪnˈvestɪgeɪtə(r)/ *n* 调查者

investiture /ɪnˈvestɪtʃə(r), Amer -tʃʊər/ *n* 1 [u] (act) 授衔; **the ~ of sb. as sth.** 授予某人某职务 2 [c] (ceremony) 授衔仪式

investment /ɪnˈvestmənt/ *n* 1 [u] (act of investing) 投资; **he called for more government ~ in industry** 他呼吁政府对工业增加投资 2 [c] (sum, amount) 投资额; **a good/bad ~** 良性/不良投资 3 [c] (commodity) 投资物; **those antiques were bought as an ~** 这些古董是作为投资买下的 4 [u and c] (commitment) 投入; **the ~ of time and energy in sth.** 对某事时间和精力的投入; **a huge emotional ~** 大量的情感投入

investment: ~ analyst ▸**p. 409** *n* 投资分析师; **~ bank** *n* Amer 投资银行; **~ income** *n* 投资收入; **~ management** *n* [u] 投资管理; **~ manager** ▸**p. 409** *n* 投资经理; **~ trust** *n* 投资信托公司

investor /ɪnˈvestə(r)/ *n* 投资者

inveterate /ɪnˈvetərət/ *adj attrib* 1 (long-standing) 根深蒂固的 ‹*hatred, prejudice*›; **~ drunkenness** 长年酗酒 2 (confirmed) 积习难改的; **an ~ liar/smoker/drunkard** 惯于说谎的人/烟鬼/酒鬼

i

invidious /ɪnˈvɪdɪəs/ *adj attrib* **1** (incurring resentment) 引起反感的; **I was in the ~ position of having to sack him** 我不得不解雇他，这会得罪人 **2** (unfairly discriminating) 厚此薄彼的 ‹*choice, distinction*›; **such comparisons are ~** 这样的比较是不公平的

invigilate /ɪnˈvɪdʒɪleɪt/ Brit
A *vi* 监考; **to ~ at an exam** 监考
B *vt* **to ~ a test/an examination** 监考

invigilator /ɪnˈvɪdʒɪleɪtə(r)/ *n* Brit 监考人

invigorate /ɪnˈvɪɡəreɪt/ *vt* «*drink, fresh air, climate, exercise*» 使…精神焕发 ‹*person*›; **to feel ~d** 感到精神焕发

invigorating /ɪnˈvɪɡəreɪtɪŋ/ *adj* 使人精神焕发的 ‹*air, climate, exercise*›

invincibility /ɪnˌvɪnsəˈbɪləti/ *n* [u] (of person, army, team) 不可战胜; (of will, belief) 坚定不移

invincible /ɪnˈvɪnsəbl/ *adj* **1** (undefeatable) 不可战胜的 ‹*army, force, team*› **2** (unchangeable) 不动摇的; **an ~ belief** *or* **conviction** 坚定不移的信念; **an ~ will to survive/win** 求生的坚定信念/必胜的愿望

inviolability /ɪnˌvaɪələˈbɪləti/ *n* [u] formal (of rights) 不可侵犯; (of law, oath, treaty) 不容违背

inviolable /ɪnˈvaɪələbl/ *adj* formal 不可侵犯的 ‹*rights*›; 不容违背的 ‹*law, oath, treaty*›

inviolably /ɪnˈvaɪələbli/ *adv* formal (so as not able to be broken) 不容违背地 ‹*pledged*›; (so as not able to be dishonoured) 不可侵犯地 ‹*sacred*›

inviolate /ɪnˈvaɪələt/ *adj usu pred* 未违背的 ‹*treaty, oath*›; 未受侵犯的 ‹*right, sovereignty*›

invisibility /ɪnˌvɪzəˈbɪləti/ *n* [u] 看不见; **the magic potion gave her temporary ~** 这种神奇药水让她暂时隐身

invisible /ɪnˈvɪzəbl/ *adj* **1** (not visible) 看不见的; **~ to the naked eye** 肉眼看不见的; **the fairy made herself ~** 仙子隐身了 **2** (concealed) 隐藏的 ‹*object, landmark*›; **the tower was ~ because of the fog** 那座塔隐没在雾中 **3** fig (ignored) 被忽视的 **4** Econ 无形的 ‹*earnings, trade*›

invisible: ~ exports *npl* 无形输出; **~ ink** *n* [u] 隐形墨水; **~ mending** *n* [u] 无痕织补

invisibly /ɪnˈvɪzəbli/ *adv* **1** (not visibly, imperceptibly) 看不见地; **the fairy lurked ~ in the woods** 仙子隐藏在树林中; **that myth has ~ influenced our lives** 那个神话无形中影响了我们的生活 **2** (so as not to show) 察觉不到地 ‹*mended, repaired*›; **my coat's been ~ mended** 我的外套已经织补好了

invitation /ˌɪnvɪˈteɪʃn/ *n* **1** (request, act of inviting) 邀请; **to extend** *or* **issue** *or* **send an ~** 发出邀请; **to send out ~s** 发出邀请; **to accept/decline an ~** 接受/婉拒邀请; **an ~ to dinner** 参加晚餐的邀请; **an ~ to bid for funds/places** 争取资金/职位的邀请; **at sb.'s ~** 应某人的邀请; **by ~ (only)** （仅）凭请柬; **a letter of ~** 邀请函 **2** fig (encouragement) 鼓励; **unlocked doors are an open ~ to burglars** 门不上锁会引贼入室

invitation card *n* 请柬

invite
A /ɪnˈvaɪt/ *vt* **1** (informally, socially) 邀请; **to ~ sb. to do sth.** 邀请某人做某事; **to ~ sb. back** 回请某人; **to ~ sb. in** 邀请某人来家里做客; **to ~ sb. over** *or* **round (to one's house)** 邀请某人（到家中）作客; **to ~ sb. to a party/for a drink** 请某人参加聚会/喝酒; **to ~ sb. for interview** 约请某人参加面试 **2** (request, elicit) 征求 ‹*opinions*›; **to ~ subscriptions** 征订; **he ~d questions from the audience** 他请观众提问 **3** fig (encourage) 招致; **why ~ trouble?** 为何自找麻烦？
B /ˈɪnvaɪt/ *n* colloq 邀请; **don't forget to bring the ~** 别忘了把请柬带上

inviting /ɪnˈvaɪtɪŋ/ *adj* 诱人的 ‹*prospect, meal, place, aroma*›; 迷人的 ‹*smile*›

invitingly /ɪnˈvaɪtɪŋli/ *adv* 诱人地

in vitro /ˌɪn ˈviːtrəʊ/
A *adj* 在生物体外的
B *adv* 在生物体外; **to be fertilized ~** 体外受精

in vitro fertilization *n* [u] 体外受精

invocation /ˌɪnvəˈkeɪʃn/ *n* formal **1** (appeal) 祈祷 **2** (prayer) 祷文

invoice /ˈɪnvɔɪs/
A *n* 发票; **to make out** *or* **issue** *or* **send an ~ for sth.** 开某物的费用清单
B *vt* 给…开发票 ‹*client, customer*›; **to ~ sb. for sth.** 给某人开某物的发票

invoke /ɪnˈvəʊk/ *vt* **1** (cite or appeal to sb. or sth.) 援引 ‹*act, law, principle, tradition*› **2** (call up) 唤起 ‹*memories*›; **the film ~s an atmosphere of nostalgia** 这部电影营造出怀旧的氛围 **3** (call upon) 祈求…保佑 ‹*god, muse*›; 祈求 ‹*help, assistance*›; **to ~ vengeance on sb.** 祈求神明让某人遭报应 **4** (summon) 用法术召唤 ‹*spirit, devil, genie*›

involuntarily /ɪnˈvɒləntrəli, Amer -terɪli/ *adv* **1** (without conscious control) 不由自主地 **2** (without consent) 非自愿地

involuntary /ɪnˈvɒləntri, Amer -teri/ *adj* **1** (without conscious control) 不由自主的; **an ~ exclamation/movement/spasm** 不由自主的惊叹/动作/抽搐 **2** (without consent) 非自愿的; **~ retirement** 强制性退休; **~ exposure to cigarette smoke** 被动吸烟

involuntary manslaughter *n* [u] 过失杀人

involve /ɪnˈvɒlv/ *vt* **1** (entail) 需要; **the game ~s more luck than skill** 在这项运动中，运气比技巧重要; **a certain degree of risk is ~d** 有一定程度的风险 **2** (affect) 影响; **this doesn't ~ you: mind your own business!** 这事与你无关：管好你自己的事！; **more than 20 vehicles were ~d in the accident** 事故涉及20多辆车; **the people ~d** 有关人员; **the future of the company is ~d** 事关公司的前途 **3** (participate, cause to participate) 使参与; **several ministers were ~d in the scandal** 几位部长卷入了丑闻; **they should ~ themselves more in the community** 他们应该多参与社区事务; **there's no need to ~ the police** 没有必要让警察介入; **she got ~d in a heated argument with the manager** 她与经理发生了激烈的争论 **4** (implicate) 牵连; **the witness's statement ~s you in the robbery** 证人的陈述表明你与抢劫案有牵连 **5** (oblige to do) **to ~ sb. in sth.** «*task, problem, journey*» 使某人承担某事; **the repairs will ~ them in a lot of expense** 这些维修会花掉他们一大笔钱; **it will ~ you in too much extra work** 这会给你增加太多额外的工作 **6** (engross, absorb) 吸引 ‹*reader, audience, viewer*›; **to be/get ~d (with** *or* **in sth.)** 专注（于某事物）; **the reader becomes totally ~d in** *or* **with the plot** 读者完全被情节吸引住了; **she's too ~d with her family to have any time for her friends** 她一心扑在家庭上，没有时间顾及朋友 **7** (become attached) 使投入感情; **to be/get** *or* **become ~d (with sb./sth.)** （对…）投入感情 ‹*person, problem, situation*›; **to be/get ~d (with sb.)** (romantically) （与某人）有恋爱关系; (sexually) （与某人）有性关系; **he's too ~d to be able to judge objectively** 他感情投入太深，以至不能作出客观的判断; **he was getting emotionally ~d** 他逐渐坠入情网 **8** (associate) 使加入; **to be/get** *or* **become ~d with sb.** 是/成为某类人中的一员; **she got ~d with a bad crowd** 她与一伙坏人混在一起

involved /ɪnˈvɒlvd/ *adj* 十分复杂的; **a highly ~ plot** 极为复杂的情节

involvement /ɪnˈvɒlvmənt/ *n* **1** [u] (participation) 参与; **she tried to avoid ~ in her colleagues' arguments** 她试图避免卷入到同事的争执中去 **2** [u] (act of involving sb.) 牵连; **the ~ of the police** 警方的介入 **3** [u] (engrossment) 投入; **the children's ~ in the film** 孩子们对这部电影的着迷 **4** [u] (commitment) 专注; **~ in/with sth.** 对某事物的专注; **my ~ with the Red Cross** 我对红十字会工作的投入 **5** [u and c] (emotional attachment) 感情投入; (romantic attachment) 恋爱; (sexual attachment) 性爱; **counsellors must avoid ~ with their clients** 律师必须避免与委托人发生感情纠葛; **an ~ with one's secretary** 与秘书的恋情 **6** [u] (connections with person, group, organization) 关系; **~ with sb./sth.** 与某人/某机构的关系

invulnerability /ɪnˌvʌlnərəˈbɪləti/ *n* [u] **1** lit 不受侵害 **2** fig (safety, security) 安全

invulnerable /ɪnˈvʌlnərəbl/ *adj* **1** lit 不受侵害的; **the fortress seemed ~ to attack** 该要塞似乎固若金汤 **2** fig (safe, secure) 安全的 ‹*status*›; **to put oneself in an ~ position** 使自己立于不败之地

inward /ˈɪnwəd/
A *adj attrib* **1** (towards the inside) 向内的; **an ~ curve** 内弯 **2** (inner) 内心的; **man's ~ nature** 人的心性
B *adv* = **inwards**

inward: ~-bound *adj* 入港的; **~ investment** *n* [u and c] 对内投资; **~-looking** *adj* 关心自己的; **she's too ~-looking** 她对别人漠不关心

inwardly /ˈɪnwədli/ *adv* 在内心; **he was ~ furious** 他怒火中烧

inwards /ˈɪnwədz/ *adv* **1** (towards the inside) 向内 **2** (towards the mind, soul) 向内心; **her thoughts turned ~** 她的思想转向了内省

in-your-face *adj* 咄咄逼人的 ‹*approach, attitude, style*›; 露骨的 ‹*advertising*›

IOC *abbr* = **International Olympic Committee** 国际奥林匹克委员会

iodine /ˈaɪədiːn, Amer -daɪn/ *n* [u] **1** Chem 碘 **2** Med 碘酒

IOM *abbr* Brit = **Isle of Man**

ion /ˈaɪən/ *n* 离子

Ionic /aɪˈɒnɪk/ *adj* 爱奥尼亚柱式的

ionize /ˈaɪənaɪz/ *vt* 使离子化

ionizer /ˈaɪənaɪzə(r)/ *n* 负离子发生器

ionosphere /aɪˈɒnəsfɪə(r)/ *n* [u] 电离层

iota /aɪˈəʊtə/ *n* 极少量; **she hasn't changed one** *or* **an ~** 她一点儿都没变

IOU *abbr* = **I owe you** 借据; **an ~ for £500** 500英镑的借据; **unpaid bills and ~s** 未付的账单和欠条

IOW *abbr* Brit = **Isle of Wight**

Iowa /ˈaɪəʊə/ *pr n* 艾奥瓦州

IP *abbr* = **Internet protocol**

IPA *abbr* = **International Phonetic Alphabet**

IPO *abbr* = **initial public offering**

iPod® /ˈaɪpɒd/ *n* 苹果mp3播放器

IQ *abbr* = **intelligence quotient** 智商; **to test sb.'s ~** 测试某人的智商; **to have an ~ of ...** 有…的智商

IRA *abbr* = **Irish Republican Army**

Iran /ɪˈrɑːn/ *pr n* 伊朗

Iranian /ɪˈreɪnɪən/ ▸p. 503, p. 426
A *adj* (of Iran) 伊朗的; (of the people) 伊朗人的; (of the languages) 伊朗语系的
B *n* **1** [c] (person) 伊朗人 **2** [u] (languages) 伊朗语系

Iraq /ɪˈrɑːk/ *pr n* 伊拉克

Iraqi /ɪˈrɑːki/ ▸p. 503, p. 426
A *adj* (of Iraq) 伊拉克的; (of the people) 伊拉克人的; (of the language) 伊拉克阿拉伯语的
B *n* **1** [c] (person) 伊拉克人 **2** [u] (language) 伊拉克阿拉伯语

Iraq War *n* 伊拉克战争

irascibility /ɪˌræsəˈbɪləti/ *n* [u] (tendency) 易怒; (behaviour) 发怒

i

irascible /ɪ'ræsəbl/ *adj* **1** (easily angered) 易怒的 **2** (angry) 发怒的; **she was in an ~ mood** 她正在生气

irascibly /ɪ'ræsəbli/ *adv* 发怒地 ‹*react, behave*›

irate /aɪ'reɪt/ *adj* 极其愤怒的; **to be ~ about sth.** 对某事物极度愤怒; **an ~ phone call** 怒气冲冲的电话

IRBM *abbr* = **intermediate-range ballistic missile** 中程弹道导弹

IRC *abbr* = **Internet relay chat**

ire /'aɪə(r)/ *n* [u] 愤怒; **to provoke** *or* **incur** *or* **arouse the ~ of sb.** 激怒某人

Ireland /'aɪələnd/ *pr n* 爱尔兰

iridescence /ˌɪrɪ'desns/ *n* [u] 色彩斑斓

iridescent /ˌɪrɪ'desnt/ *adj* 色彩斑斓的; **the sparkling ~ colours of the precious stones** 宝石闪烁的奇光异彩

iridium /aɪ'rɪdɪəm/ *n* [u] 铱

iris /'aɪərɪs/ *n* (*pl* **~es**) **1** Anat 虹膜 **2** Bot 鸢尾属植物

Irish /'aɪərɪʃ/ ▸p. 503, p. 426
A *adj* (of Ireland) 爱尔兰的; (of the people) 爱尔兰人的; (of the language) 爱尔兰语的
B *n* [u] (language) 爱尔兰语
C *npl* **the ~** (people) 爱尔兰人

Irish: ~ coffee *n* [u and c] 爱尔兰咖啡; **~man** /-mən/ *n* 爱尔兰男人; **~ Republic** *pr n* = **Republic of Ireland**; **~ Republican Army** *pr n* 爱尔兰共和军; **~ Sea** *pr n* **the ~ Sea** 爱尔兰海; **~ stew** *n* 洋葱土豆炖羊肉; **~woman** *n* 爱尔兰女人

> **the IRA**
>
> 爱尔兰共和军，全称 the Irish Republican Army。北爱尔兰准军事组织。目标是结束英国在北爱尔兰的统治，建立南北统一的爱尔兰共和国。该组织成立于 1919 年，前身为争取独立的“爱尔兰义勇军”（Irish Volunteers）。1969 年分裂为正统派（Official IRA）和临时派（Provisional IRA，简称 the Provisionals 或 the Provos），前者在 1972 年以后放弃武装斗争，后者则继续通过爆炸、暗杀等暴力活动争取统一。通常所说的爱尔兰共和军即指临时派。2005 年 7 月，爱尔兰共和军发表声明，宣布停止使用暴力，转而通过政治方式解决北爱尔兰问题。新芬党（Sinn Fein）是爱尔兰共和军的政治组织。

irk /ɜːk/ *vt* «*behaviour, situation*» 使恼怒; **his arrogance ~ed me** 他的傲慢让我很生气

irksome /'ɜːksəm/ *adj* 令人恼怒的 ‹*duty, situation, pain*›; **an ~ task** 令人厌烦的工作

iron /'aɪən, Amer 'aɪərn/
A *n* **1** [u] (metal) 铁; **the ~ and steel industry** 钢铁工业; **old/scrap ~** 旧/废铁; **to strike while the ~ is hot** fig 趁热打铁; **the ~ had entered his soul** fig 他极端怨愤不平; **a man of ~** (determined) 意志坚强的人; (cruel) 冷酷的人; **a will of ~** 钢铁般的意志 **2** [c] (for smoothing clothes) 熨斗; **to run the ~ over sth., to give sth. an ~** 熨烫某物 **3** [c] (tool) 铁器; **to have a lot of ~s in the fire** fig 同时有许多事情要做 **4** [c] (in golf) 铁头球棒
B **irons** *npl* Hist 镣铐; **to put sb. in ~s** 给某人戴上镣铐
C *modif* **1** (made of iron) 铁制的 **2** fig (strong and determined) 刚强的; **a man with an ~ will** 意志坚强的男子 **3** fig (harsh) 严酷的; **~ rule** 暴虐的统治
D *vt* 熨烫
E *vi* 熨平衣物

Phrasal verb

- **iron out** *vt* [**~ out sth., ~ sth. out**] **1** lit (remove) 熨平 ‹*creases, wrinkles*› **2** fig (smooth over) 解决 ‹*problem, difficulty*›; 消除 ‹*misunderstanding*›

Iron Age *pr n* **the ~** 铁器时代; *modif* 铁器时代的 ‹*village, burial, artefact*›

iron-clad
A *adj* fig 牢不可破的 ‹*argument, defence*›
B *n* Hist (ship) 铁甲舰

iron: I~ Curtain *n* Hist **the I~ Curtain** 铁幕; **an I~ Curtain country** 铁幕国家; **~ filings** *npl* 铁屑; **~ fist** *n* fig 铁拳; **to rule with an ~ fist** 进行铁腕统治; **an ~ fist in a velvet glove** 戴天鹅绒手套的铁拳 [喻外柔内刚]; **~ foundry** *n* 铸铁厂

iron grey
A *n* 铁灰色
B **iron-grey** *adj* 铁灰色的 ‹*hair, colouring*›

iron hand *n* = **iron fist**

ironic /aɪ'rɒnɪk/, **ironical** /aɪ'rɒnɪkl/ *adjs* **1** (using irony) 讽刺的; **an ~ smile** 嘲讽的微笑 **2** (odd, amusing) 令人啼笑皆非的

ironically /aɪ'rɒnɪkli/ *adv* **1** (paradoxically) 令人啼笑皆非地; **~, she never replied** 具有讽刺意味的是，她并未答复 **2** (using irony) 讽刺地; **I was speaking ~** 我带着挖苦的语气说话

ironing /'aɪənɪŋ, Amer 'aɪərn-/ *n* [u] **1** (task, activity) 熨烫; **to do the ~** 熨衣服 **2** (clothes, fabric) 待熨烫的衣物

ironing board *n* 熨衣板

ironmonger /'aɪənmʌŋgə(r), Amer 'aɪərn-/ ▸p. 409 *n* Brit 五金商人; **~'s (shop)** 五金商店

ironmongery /'aɪənmʌŋgəri, Amer 'aɪərn-/ *n* [u] Brit 五金器具

iron: ~-on *adj* 可烫附于织物的; **~ ore** *n* [u] 铁矿; **~ pyrites** *n* [u] 黄铁矿; **~ rations** *npl* （野战）应急口粮; **~stone** *n* [u] 硬质陶器; **~ work** *n* [u] 铁制品; **~works** *n + v sing or pl* 钢铁厂

irony /'aɪərəni/ *n* **1** [u] (for humorous or sarcastic effect) 反语; **a touch** *or* **hint of ~** 一丝嘲讽 **2** [c] (incongruity) 具有讽刺意味的事; **the ~ is that many people agree with her** 讽刺的是，许多人同意她的看法; **it's just one of life's little ironies** 那只是生活的一个小小的嘲弄

irradiate /ɪ'reɪdɪeɪt/ *vt* **1** Med (expose to radiation) 使受放射线照射 **2** (to kill microorganisms) 使…受 γ 射线照射 ‹*food*› **3** (illuminate) 照亮

irradiation /ɪˌreɪdɪ'eɪʃn/ *n* [u] (irradiating) 放射线照射; (being irradiated) 受放射线照射

irrational /ɪ'ræʃənl/ *adj* **1** (illogical) 不合逻辑的; (unreasonable) 不合理的; **it is ~ to do sth.** 做某事没有道理; **to be/become quite ~ about sth.** 在某事上非常不可理喻/变得非常不可理喻; **an ~ belief** 荒谬的信念; **he had an ~ fear of losing his job** 他无端地害怕会失去工作 **2** (lacking power of reason) 无理性的 **3** Math 无理的; **an ~ number** 无理数

irrationally /ɪ'ræʃənəli/ *adv* (illogically) 不合逻辑地; (unreasonably) 无理性地; **to behave ~** 表现得没有理性

irreconcilable /ɪ'rekənsaɪləbl, ɪˌrekən'saɪləbl/ *adj* **1** (implacably hostile) 势不两立的 **2** (incompatible) 不相容的 ‹*ideas, actions*›; 不可调和的 ‹*disagreement, conflict, differences*›; **to be ~ with sth.** 和某事物不相容; **his account is ~ with the known facts** 他的陈述与已知事实不符

irrecoverable /ˌɪrɪ'kʌvərəbl/ *adj* (not able to be recovered) 不能挽回的 ‹*loss*›; (not able to be remedied) 无法补救的 ‹*error*›; **an ~ debt** 收不回的烂账

irredeemable /ˌɪrɪ'diːməbl/ *adj* **1** Fin 不能清偿的 ‹*securities, shares, loan*› **2** (incapable of being reformed) 不可挽救的 ‹*criminal*› **3** (incapable of being corrected) 无法改正的 ‹*wrong, mistake*› **4** (unrestorable) 不可补救的 ‹*loss, failure, misfortune*›

irredeemably /ˌɪrɪ'diːməbli/ *adv* 不能挽救地

irreducible /ˌɪrɪ'djuːsəbl, Amer -'duːs-/ *adj* **1** (in size) 不能缩减的; **~ expenditure** 最低花费 **2** (not able to be simplified) 无法简化的 ‹*complexity, problem*›

irrefutable /ɪ'refjʊtəbl, ˌɪrɪ'fjuː-/ *adj* 无可辩驳的 ‹*proof, evidence, testimony*›

irregular /ɪ'regjʊlə(r)/ *adj* **1** (in shape) 不规则的 ‹*outline, pattern*›; 不平整的 ‹*surface*› **2** (intermittent) 无规律的; **at ~ intervals** 不定期地; **an ~ heartbeat** 不齐的心律; **he's very ~ in his attendance at my class** 我的课他经常缺席 **3** (in practice, routine) 不合常规的; **~ financial dealings** 违规金融交易; **to keep ~ hours** 作息时间不正常 **4** Ling 不规则的; **an ~ verb** 不规则动词

irregularity /ɪˌregjʊ'lærəti/ *n* **1** [u] (state, quality) (of shape, pattern) 不规则; (of surface) 不平整; (intermittency) 无规律; (in practice, routine) 不合常规 **2** [c] (instance) (in shape, pattern) 不规则物体; (of surface) 不平整表面; (intermittency) 无规律的事物; (in practice, routine) 不合常规的行为; **financial irregularities** 财务违规行为

irregularly /ɪ'regjʊləli/ *adv* **1** (unevenly) 不规则地 **2** (at varying intervals) 无规律地 **3** (improperly) 不合常规地

irrelevance /ɪ'reləvəns/, **irrelevancy** /ɪ'reləvənsi/ *ns* **1** [u] (lack of importance) 无关紧要 **2** [c] (unimportant thing) 无关紧要的事物

irrelevant /ɪ'reləvnt/ *adj* **1** (unimportant) 无关紧要的; **to be ~ to sth.** 对某事物无关紧要 **2** (unconnected) 不相关的 ‹*remark, fact, question*›; **to be ~ to sth.** 与某事物不相关

irrelevantly /ɪ'reləvəntli/ *adv* 不相关地 ‹*say, ask*›

irreligious /ˌɪrɪ'lɪdʒəs/ *adj* **1** (having no interest in religion) 漠视宗教的 **2** (hostile to religion) 敌视宗教的

irremediable /ˌɪrɪ'miːdɪəbl/ *adj* formal 不可挽回的 ‹*loss*›; 无法补救的 ‹*harm, damage, error*›

irreparable /ɪ'repərəbl/ *adj* 不可弥补的 ‹*damage, harm*›; 无法挽回的 ‹*loss*›

irreparably /ɪ'repərəbli/ *adv* 不可弥补地 ‹*damage, harm*›; 无可救药地 ‹*spoiled*›

irreplaceable /ˌɪrɪ'pleɪsəbl/ *adj* 不能替代的; **the vase is absolutely ~** 这个花瓶实属孤品

irrepressible /ˌɪrɪ'presəbl/ *adj* 控制不住的 ‹*person, humour, high spirits*›; **~ confidence** 十足的信心; **the little boy is just so ~** 这个小男孩野得很

irrepressibly /ˌɪrɪ'presəbli/ *adv* 控制不住地

irreproachable /ˌɪrɪ'prəʊtʃəbl/ *adj* 无可指责的 ‹*character, conduct*›

irresistible /ˌɪrɪ'zɪstəbl/ *adj* **1** (strong, compelling) 不可抗拒的 ‹*temptation, force*›; 不可遏制的 ‹*desire, impulse, urge*› **2** (alluring) 极其诱人的; **she's utterly ~** 她极富魅力

irresistibly /ˌɪrɪ'zɪstəbli/ *adv* 无法抗拒地; **~ charming** 极其迷人的

irresolute /ɪ'rezəluːt/ *adj* 优柔寡断的

irresolutely /ɪ'rezəluːtli/ *adv* 优柔寡断地

irresoluteness /ɪ'rezəluːtnəs/ *n* [u] 优柔寡断

irrespective of /ˌɪrɪ'spektɪv ɒv/ *prep* 不考虑; **~ race** 不分种族; **~ whether it rains** 不管是否下雨

irresponsibility /ˌɪrɪˌspɒnsə'bɪləti/ *n* [u] **1** (of behaviour, conduct) 不负责任 **2** (of temperament) 无责任感

irresponsible /ˌɪrɪ'spɒnsəbl/ *adj* **1** (not showing a sense of responsibility) 不负责任的 ‹*action, behaviour*› **2** (in temperament) 无责任感的 ‹*person*›

irresponsibly /ˌɪrɪ'spɒnsəbli/ *adv* 不负责任地

irretrievable /ˌɪrɪ'triːvəbl/ *adj* 不可挽回的; **an ~ loss** 不可弥补的损失

irretrievably /ˌɪrɪ'triːvəbli/ *adv* 不可挽回地

irreverence /ɪ'revərəns/ *n* [u] 不尊敬

irreverent /ɪ'revərənt/ *adj* 不尊敬的; **~ remarks** 无礼的言辞

irreverently /ɪ'revərəntli/ *adv* 不尊敬地

irreversible /ˌɪrɪ'vɜːsəbl/ *adj* **1** (permanent) 不可逆转的 ‹*damage, decline, change*› **2** (final, definitive) 不可撤回的 ‹*decision, judgement*›

irreversibly /ˌɪrɪ'vɜːsəblɪ/ *adv* 不可逆转地

irrevocable /ɪ'revəkəbl/ *adj* 不可撤回的; **the committee's decision is ~** 委员会的决定是不可改变的

irrevocably /ɪ'revəkəbli/ *adv* 不可撤回地

irrigate /'ɪrɪgeɪt/ *vt* **1** Agri 灌溉 ‹*fields, crops*› **2** Med 冲洗 ‹*wound, body part*›

irrigation /ˌɪrɪ'geɪʃn/ *n* [u] **1** Agric 灌溉; **to be under ~** 在灌溉; **a complex ~ system** 复杂的灌溉系统 **2** Med 冲洗

irritability /ˌɪrɪtə'bɪləti/ *n* [u] 易怒

irritable /'ɪrɪtəbl/ *adj* 易怒的; **to feel/look ~** 感到/看上去恼怒; **to get** *or* **grow ~** 变得恼火; **she was in an ~ mood** 她心情烦躁

irritable bowel syndrome ▸**p. 377** *n* [u] 肠易激综合征

irritably /'ɪrɪtəbli/ *adv* 易怒地; **'please be quiet,' she said ~** "请保持安静，"她烦躁地说

irritant /'ɪrɪtənt/ *n* **1** (annoyance, irritation) 令人烦恼的事物; **to be an ~ to sb.** 令某人烦恼 **2** (substance) 刺激物

irritate /'ɪrɪteɪt/ *vt* **1** (annoy) 使恼怒; **they were ~d by the persistent noise** 持续的噪音让他们很心烦 **2** Med 刺激

irritating /'ɪrɪteɪtɪŋ/ *adj* 令人恼怒的

irritatingly /'ɪrɪteɪtɪŋli/ *adv* 令人恼怒地; **the noise is ~ persistent** 噪音持续不断，让人心烦

irritation /ˌɪrɪ'teɪʃn/ *n* **1** [u] (annoyance, anger) 恼怒; **~ at sb./sth.** 对某人/某事物的恼火; **a constant source of ~** 总让人生气的事 **2** [c] (aggravation) 恼人的事 **3** Med 发炎

IRS *abbr* Amer = **Internal Revenue Service**

> **the IRS**
>
> 国内税务署，全称 the Internal Revenue Service。美国联邦政府负责税收的机构。隶属于财政部（Department of the Treasury），总部位于华盛顿。前身为 1862 年林肯总统下令成立的Bureau of Internal Revenue。1953 年重组，改为现名。负责确定、评估并征收个人、企业等的税收。国税局局长（commissioner）由总统提名，经参议院确认。

is /ɪz/ *3rd pers sing pres* ▸**be**

ISA /'aɪsə/ *abbr* Brit = **Individual Savings Account** 个人储蓄账户

ISBN *abbr* = **International Standard Book Number**

ISDN *abbr* = **integrated services digital network**

isinglass /'aɪzɪŋglɑːs, Amer -glæs/ *n* [u] 鱼胶

Islam /'ɪzlɑːm, -læm, -'lɑːm/ *n* [u] **1** Relig 伊斯兰教 **2** (all Muslims) 伊斯兰教徒; (the Muslim world) 伊斯兰教国家

Islamabad /ɪs'lɑːməbæd/ *pr n* 伊斯兰堡

Islamic /ɪz'læmɪk/ *adj* (of the religion) 伊斯兰教的; (of Muslims) 伊斯兰教徒的; (of Muslim countries) 伊斯兰教国家的

Islamism /'ɪzlæmɪzəm/ *n* [u] 伊斯兰教

Islamist /'ɪzlæmɪst/

A *n* **1** (scholar) 伊斯兰教学者 **2** (fundamentalist) 伊斯兰教徒

B *modif* 伊斯兰教的 ‹*fundamentalism, group, movement*›

Islamophile /ɪz'læməfaɪl/ *n* 亲伊斯兰教及穆斯林者

Islamophobe /ɪz'læməfəʊb/ *n* 恐伊斯兰教及穆斯林者

Islamophobia /ɪzˌlæmə'fəʊbɪə/ *n* [u] 恐伊斯兰症

Islamophobic /ɪzˌlæmə'fəʊbɪk/ *adj* 恐伊斯兰教及穆斯林的

island /'aɪlənd/ *n* **1** (in sea, ocean) 岛屿; **on an ~** 在岛上; **a deserted** *or* **uninhabited ~** 荒岛; **~ races** 岛屿民族 **2** (for pedestrians) = **traffic island** **3** (on roundabout) 环岛中央 **4** (peaceful place) **an ~ of calm/tranquillity** 安静/宁静的地方

islander /'aɪləndə(r)/ *n* 岛民

island-hopping *n* [u] 列岛旅行

isle /aɪl/ *n* 岛; **a desert ~** 荒岛

Isle of Man *pr n* **the ~** 马恩岛

Isle of Wight /waɪt/ *pr n* **the ~** 怀特岛

Isles of Scilly /'sɪli/ *pr npl* = **Scillies**

islet /'aɪlɪt/ *n* 小岛

ism /'ɪzəm/ *n* colloq 主义

isn't /'ɪznt/ colloq = **is not** ▸**be**

ISO = **International Organization for Standardization**

isobar /'aɪsəbɑː(r)/ *n* 等压线

isogloss /'ʌɪsəglɒs/ *n* 同言线［地图上表示某语言特点的区域线］

isolate /'aɪsəleɪt/ *vt* **1** (separate physically) 使脱离; **to ~ sb. from sth.** 使某人从某团体孤立出来 **2** (treat separately) 将…剔出 **3** Biol, Chem 分离 ‹*genes, acid*› **4** Med (keep apart) 隔离 ‹*patient*› **5** (undermine support for) 使…孤立 ‹*leadership, management, opponent*›

isolated /'aɪsəleɪtɪd/ *adj* **1** (set apart physically) 隔离的; **their farm is very ~** 他们的农场非常偏僻; **we live an ~ life** 我们过着与世隔绝的生活 **2** (lonely) 孤单的; **to feel ~** 感到孤独 **3** (single) 单独的; **an ~ incident** 个别事件

isolation /ˌaɪsə'leɪʃn/ *n* [u] **1** (physical separation) 隔离; **the ~ of the village makes life there a bit dull** 村子地理位置偏僻使得那儿的生活有一些单调 **2** (solitude, separateness) 孤立; **elderly folk living in ~ and poverty** 生活在孤独和贫困中的老人 **3** Biol, Chem 分离

isolation hospital *n* Brit 隔离病院

isolationism /ˌaɪsə'leɪʃənɪzəm/ *n* [u] 孤立主义

> **isolationism**
>
> 孤立主义。美国曾长期奉行的传统外交政策，即避免同他国结盟或卷入他国事务。1796 年，华盛顿总统在离职前的《告别演说》（*Farewell Address*）中，告诫美国在同他国发展贸易关系的同时，应尽量避免与他国建立政治或军事同盟。这种孤立主义的政策后来为其他总统继承，并一直延续到 20 世纪中期。因为孤立主义的影响，美国在两次世界大战初期都避免卷入战争。二战以后，美国放弃了这一政策。

isolationist /ˌaɪsə'leɪʃənɪst/

A *n* 孤立主义者

B *adj* 孤立主义的

isolation ward *n* Brit 隔离病房

isomorphic /ˌaɪsə'mɔːfɪk/ *adj* (identical in form) 同形的; (identical in structure) 同构的

isosceles /aɪ'sɒsəliːz/ *adj* 等腰的 ‹*triangle*›

isotherm /'aɪsəθɜːm/ *n* 等温线

isotonic drink /ˌaɪsə'tɒnɪk drɪŋk/ *n* 等渗饮料

isotope /'aɪsətəʊp/ *n* 同位素

ISP *abbr* = **Internet service provider**

Israel /'ɪzreɪl/ *pr n* **1** (country) 以色列 **2** (nation) 希伯来民族

Israeli /ɪz'reɪli/ ▸**p. 503**

A *adj* (of Israel) 以色列的; (of the people) 以色列人的

B *n* 以色列人

Israelite /'ɪzrɪəlaɪt, -rəlaɪt/ *n* Hist 希伯来人

issue /'ɪʃuː, 'ɪsjuː/

A *n* **1** [c] (point in question) 问题; **a major political ~** 重大的政治问题; **she raised the ~ of security** 她提出了安全问题; **that's not the ~** 这不是问题所在; **to face the ~** 正视问题; **to avoid** *or* **evade** *or* **dodge the ~** 回避问题; **to cloud** *or* **confuse the ~** 混淆问题; **to force the ~** 迫使对该问题作出决定; **to make an ~ of sth.** 对某事物小题大做; **at ~** 讨论中的; **what he wants to do with the money is not at ~** 他打算将这笔钱派什么用场不是讨论的要点; **to take ~ with sb./sth.** 向某人/对某事物提出异议 **2** [c] (copy of newspaper, journal, magazine etc.) 期; **the April ~ of the magazine** 杂志的四月号 **3** [u] (allocation) (of blankets, food, arms, uniforms, etc.) 分发; (of passport, licence, credit card, etc.) 发放; (of summons, writ, etc.) 发出; **standard army-~ boots** 制式军靴 **4** [c] (set of items that is allocated) 发行物; **the latest ~ of shares** 最新发行的股份; **~s of food and blankets to the refugees** 发给难民们的食品和毛毯 **5** [u] (distribution of stamps, coins, banknotes, shares) 发行 **6** [u] Jur (progeny) 子女; **to die without ~** 死后无子嗣

B *vt* **1** (allocate) 分发 ‹*blankets, food, arms, uniform*›; 发放 ‹*passport, licence, credit card*›; 发出 ‹*summons, writ*›; **to ~ sth. to sb., to ~ sb. with sth.** 把某物发给某人; **we were ~d with maps and compasses** 我们配发了地图和指南针 **2** (make public) 发布 ‹*instructions, proclamation*›; 发出 ‹*invitation, ultimatum, warning*›; 发表 ‹*statement, press release*› **3** (release officially) 发行 ‹*stamps, coins, banknotes, shares*› **4** (publish) 出版

C *vi* **to ~ from sth.** 从某处出来; **a stream of abuse ~d from the kitchen** 从厨房里传来的一连串辱骂声

Istanbul /ˌɪstæn'bʊl/ *pr n* 伊斯坦布尔

isthmus /'ɪsməs/ *n* (*pl* **~es**) 地峡

IT *abbr* = **information technology**

it /ɪt/

A *pron* **1** (thing, animal) 它; **what is ~?** 这是什么东西？; **where's the car? — ~'s in the garage** 车在哪儿？——在车库里 **2** (person) (of unspecified sex) **who is ~?** 谁啊？; **she hopes ~'ll be a boy** 她希望是个男孩儿; **~'s me** 是我 **3** (fact, situation) 情况; **what is ~?** (occurrence) 出了什么事？; (problem) 怎么回事？; **how was ~?** 怎么样了？; **yes, I was home: what about ~?** 是的，我到家了，怎么啦？; **to hear all about ~** 听说事情的全部情况; **stop ~!** (doing sth.) 住手！; (saying sth.) 打住吧！; **that's ~** (correct) 对啦; (the end) 就这样了; (the issue) 问题就在这里; (enough) 行了; **this is ~** (feared event) 该来的就要来了; (awaited event) 终于来了; (main point) 正是这样; **the best/worst of ~ is that ...** 好在/最糟糕的是… **4** (things in general)［指一般情况］; **how's ~ going?** colloq 一切都好吗？; **if ~'s convenient** 如果方便的话; **I like ~ here** 我喜欢这里的环境 **5** (when referring to time, distance, weather)［指时间、距离或天气］ **~'s six o'clock/Friday** 现在是 6 点/今天是星期五; **~'s two miles to town** 到城里有两英里; **~'s raining** 下雨了 **6** (as anticipatory subject)［用作先行主语］ **~'s no use shouting** 喊叫根本没用; **~ appears that he is sleeping** 看来他睡了 **7** (for emphasis)［表示强调］ **~'s Spain that he went to, not Portugal** 他去的是西班牙，不是葡萄牙

B *n* [u] **1** Games 捉人者 **2** colloq 所需的素质; **either you've got ~ or you haven't** (talent) 你要么是好样的，要么一无是处; (sex appeal) 你要么很性感，要么没有吸引力

Italian /ɪ'tæljən/ ▸**p. 503, p. 426**

A *adj* (of Italy) 意大利的; (of the people) 意大利人的; (of the language) 意大利语的

B *n* **1** [c] (person) 意大利人 **2** [u] (language) 意大利语

Italianate /ɪ'tæljəneɪt/ *adj* 意大利风格的

i

italic /ɪ'tælɪk/
A *adj* 斜体的 ‹*script, nib, type*›
B **italics** *npl* 斜体

italicize /ɪ'tælɪsaɪz/ *vt* (print in italics) 用斜体印刷; (write in italics) 用斜体书写

Italy /'ɪtəli/ *pr n* 意大利

itch /ɪtʃ/
A *n* **1** lit 痒; **to relieve an ~** 止痒 **2** fig colloq (long) 渴望; **to have an ~** *or* **feel for sth./to do sth.** 渴望得到某物/做某事
B *vi* **1** lit 发痒; **I was ~ing like mad** 我奇痒难熬 **2** fig colloq (long) 渴望; **to ~ for sth./to do sth.** 渴望得到某物/做某事

itching /'ɪtʃɪŋ/
A *n* [u] 痒
B *adj attrib* 发痒的; **I had an ~ arm** 我手臂发痒; **to have an ~ palm** 贪财

itching powder *n* [u] 致痒粉

itchy /'ɪtʃi/ *adj* 发痒的; **I have an ~ back** 我后背发痒; **to have ~ feet** fig 酷爱旅行; **to have ~ fingers** fig 想偷东西

it'd /'ɪtəd/ colloq **1** = **it had** ▸**have B** **2** = **it would** ▸**would**

item /'aɪtəm/ *n* **1** (article, object) 一件物品; **an ~ of furniture** 一件家具; **household ~s** 家用物品 **2** (on agenda) 项目; **the next ~ on the agenda** 议程的下一项; **~ nine** 第九项; **~ by ~** 一项一项地 **3** Journ, Radio, TV 一条新闻; **the main ~ in the news** 主要新闻; **an ~ about sth./sb.** 有关某事物/某人的一则新闻

itemize /'aɪtəmaɪz/ *vt* 列出…的清单; **I have ~d the morning's tasks** 我已经逐条列出了上午要做的事情; **an ~d phone bill** 电话明细账单

iterative /'ɪtərətɪv/ *adj* 迭代的 ‹*process, approach, algorithm*›

itinerant /aɪ'tɪnərənt, ɪ-/
A *adj* 巡回的; **~ workers** 流动工人; **to lead an ~ life** 过漂泊不定的生活
B *n* 流动者; **a homeless ~** 无家可归的流浪者

itinerary /aɪ'tɪnərəri, ɪ-, Amer -reri/ *n* 旅行日程

it'll /'ɪtl/ colloq = **it will** ▸**will**[1]

ITN *abbr* Brit = **Independent Television News** 独立电视新闻公司

its /ɪts/ ▸**p. 487** *det* **1** (of thing, animal) 它的; **turn the camera on ~ side** 把相机侧过来; **the dog lost ~ collar** 狗的项圈丢了 **2** (of baby) **a baby in ~ mother's womb** 母亲子宫里的胎儿

it's /ɪts/ colloq **1** = **it is** ▸**be** **2** = **it has** ▸**have B**

itself /ɪt'self/ *pron* **1** (reflexive gen) 它自己; **to come on by ~** «*light*» 自动开启; **to stand by ~** «*tree*» 独自矗立; **to present ~** «*problem*» 自行出现; **to fend for ~** «*animal*» 自生自灭; **to earn ~ a reputation** «*company*» 为自己赢得声誉; **sth. that curves back on ~** 自身弯曲的某物; **sth. that replicates ~** 自我复制的某物 **2** (per se) 本身; **the town ~ is not large** 镇子本身并不大; **that's an achievement in ~** 这本身就是一项成就; **the library is not in the university ~** 图书馆并不在大学里面 **3** (for emphasis) [表示强调]; **he was kindness ~** 他非常善良

ITV

独立电视台，全称 Independent Television，亦称 ITV1。1955 年成立。目的是为 BBC 提供竞争对手（▸**the BBC**）。1990 年，《广播法案》（*Broadcasting Act 1990*）规定其为第三频道（Channel Three）。ITV 拥有 15 份区域性电视播放许可证，在成立初期分属不同的公司。经过兼并，2004 年成立的独立电视有限公司（ITV plc）获得其中 11 份许可证。该独立电视台是英国最大的商业电视网络，可以播出广告，因此和 BBC 不同。独立电视台的监管机构在 2003 年以前是独立电视委员会（Independent Television Commission），之后由通信管理局（Ofcom）取代。

ITV *abbr* Brit = **Independent Television** 独立电视台

IUD *abbr* = **intrauterine device**

IV *abbr* = **in vitro A**

I've /aɪv/ colloq = **I have** ▸**have**

IVF *abbr* = **in vitro fertilization**

ivory /'aɪvəri/ ▸**p. 134**
A *n* **1** [u] (substance) 象牙 **2** [c] (ornament) 象牙制品 **3** [u] (colour) 象牙色
B **ivories** *npl* colloq (piano keys) 钢琴键; **to tickle the ivories** 弹钢琴
C *modif* **1** (made of ivory) 象牙制的; **an ~ handle** 象牙把手 **2** (in colour) 象牙色的 ‹*skin, complexion*›

Ivory Coast *pr n* **the ~** 象牙海岸 [即科特迪瓦]

ivory tower *n* 象牙塔; **to live in an ~** 生活在象牙塔中

ivy /'aɪvi/ *n* 常春藤

Ivy League *pr n* Amer **the ~** 常春藤联盟; **the ~ colleges** 属于常春藤联盟的大学

the Ivy League

常春藤联盟。在美国，邻近的大学和学院常组成联合会（conference），进行体育竞赛等活动。其中最负盛名的是美国东北地区的常春藤联盟。由 8 所历史悠久的大学组成，包括：哈佛大学（Harvard University）、耶鲁大学（Yale University）、宾夕法尼亚大学（the University of Pennsylvania）、普林斯顿大学（Princeton University）、哥伦比亚大学（Columbia University）、布朗大学（Brown University）、达特茅斯学院（Dartmouth College）和康奈尔大学（Cornell University）。因这些大学的古老建筑上多爬满常春藤，20 世纪 30 年代，体育记者斯坦利·伍德沃德（Stanley Woodward）最先使用Ivy League的说法。常春藤联盟的成员在学术上享有盛誉，因此常春藤大学常用作顶尖大学的代名词。

Jj

J, j /dʒeɪ/ *n* (*pl* **Js** *or* **J's**) [英语字母表的第10个字母]

jab /dʒæb/
A *vt* (*pres p etc.* **-bb-**) **1** (thrust) 戳; **to ~ a needle/one's finger in** *or* **into sth./sb.** 用针/用手指戳某物/某人; **to ~ one's finger at sb.** 用手指戳某人 **2** (poke) 捅 ‹*person, object*›; **to ~ sb./sth. with a stick/one's elbow** 用棍子/胳膊肘捅某人/某物
B *vi* (*pres p etc.* **-bb-**) **1** (poke) 捅; **to ~ at sth.** 捅某物 **2** Sport «*boxer*» 出刺拳
C *n* **1** (poke) 捅; **to give sb. a ~** 戳某人一下 **2** (punch) 刺拳; **to land/throw a ~** 出刺拳打中/打出刺拳 **3** Brit colloq (injection) 打针; (vaccination) 打预防针; **to have one's ~** 打预防针; **to give sb. a ~** 给某人打针

jabber /ˈdʒæbə(r)/ *vi* **1** (chatter) 喋喋不休地说; **to ~ (away) about sth.** 喋喋不休地谈论某事物 **2** (talk unintelligibly) 叽里咕噜地说; (talk on and on) 絮絮叨叨地说; **to ~ away** *or* **on** 叽里咕噜说个不停

jabbering /ˈdʒæbərɪŋ/ *n* [u] **1** (chatter) 喋喋不休 **2** (incomprehensible talk) 叽里咕噜

jack /dʒæk/ *n* **1** (for car wheel) 千斤顶 **2** (in cards) J牌，杰克; **the ~ of clubs/spades** 梅花J/黑桃J **3** (in bowling) 靶子球 [白色，较其他球小] **4** colloq **to be a ~ of all trades (and master of none)** 样样通，样样松; **before you could say J~ Robinson** 刹那间; **I'm all right, J~** 老兄，我过得很好 [表达一种自满自得的态度]; **every man ~** 每个人; **every man ~ of them** 他们中的每个人; **on one's ~** Brit sl 孤零零地; ►**play C1**

Phrasal verbs
- **jack in** *vt* [**~ in sth., ~ sth. in**] Brit colloq 停止干 ‹*job, work*›
- **jack off** *vi* Amer taboo sl 手淫 [常指男性]
- **jack up** *vt* [**~ up sth., ~ sth. up**]
  1 (raise) 用千斤顶抬高 ‹*vehicle*› **2** fig colloq (raise the level of) 提高 ‹*taxes, prices, wages*›

jackal /ˈdʒækl/ *n* 豺

jack: ~ass *n* **1** (ass) 公驴; **2** fig (fool) 笨蛋; **~boot** *n* **1** (boot) 长筒军靴; **2** fig 暴政; **~boot tactics** 高压手段

jackdaw /ˈdʒækdɔː/ *n* 寒鸦

jacket /ˈdʒækɪt/ *n* **1** (garment) 夹克; **~ pocket** 夹克口袋 **2** Tech (insulating cover) 保温套 **3** (of book) 护封 **4** Amer (of record) 唱片套; **5** (of potato) 土豆皮; **a ~ potato** 带皮烤的土豆

jack: J~ Frost *pr n* 霜冻 [拟人化称呼]; **~hammer** *n* esp Amer 风钻; **~-in-the-box** *n* (*pl* **~-in-the-boxes**) 玩偶匣 [揭开匣盖即有玩偶跳起]

jackknife /ˈdʒæknaɪf/
A *n* (*pl* **jackknives**) 大折刀
B *vi* «*lorry, trailer*» 弯折成V字形; «*person*» 弓腰

jackknife dive *n* 屈体跳水

jackleg /ˈdʒækleg/ *n* Amer colloq **1** (incompetent person) 不称职的人; **a ~ carpenter/plumber** 蹩脚的木匠/管子工 **2** (dishonest person) 不诚实的人; **a ~ lawyer** 品行不端的律师

jack: ~ plug *n* [尤指音响设备的] 插头; **~pot** *n* (prize) 头奖; (accumulated stake) 累积奖金; **to hit the ~pot** lit 赢得一大笔钱; fig 获得巨大成功; **~rabbit** *n* 长耳大野兔; **J~ the Lad** *n* (*pl* **J~ the Lads**) Brit colloq 浪荡少年

Jacobean /ˌdʒækəˈbɪən/ *adj* 英王詹姆斯一世时期的 ‹*literature, mansion*›

Jacobite /ˈdʒækəbaɪt/
A *n* 英王詹姆斯二世的追随者
B *adj* 英王詹姆斯二世党人的 ‹*sympathies, rising*›

jacuzzi® /dʒəˈkuːzi/ *n* (*pl* **~s**) 冲浪按摩浴缸

jade /dʒeɪd/ ►**p. 134**
A *n* [u] **1** (stone) 玉; **jewellery made of ~** 玉石首饰; **~ ring/ornaments** 玉石戒指/饰物 **2** (colour) 绿玉色
B *adj* 绿玉色的 ‹*dress, eyes*›

jaded /ˈdʒeɪdɪd/ *adj* **1** (sated, bored) 厌倦了的 ‹*critic, listener*›; 腻烦的 ‹*appetite, ear*› **2** (tired) 精疲力竭的 ‹*person, look*›

jade green ►**p. 134**
A *n* [u] 绿玉色
B *adj* 绿玉色的

jag *n* esp Amer colloq 一阵; **a crying/drinking ~** 一阵哭泣/狂饮

jagged /ˈdʒægɪd/ *adj* 有尖突的 ‹*rocks*›; 锯齿状的 ‹*edge*›; 凹凸不平的 ‹*tear, hole*›

jaguar /ˈdʒægjʊə(r)/ *n* 美洲豹

jail /dʒeɪl/
A *n* 监狱; **to be in ~ (for sth.)** （因某事）坐牢; **to go to ~** 进监狱; **to serve time in ~** 在狱中服刑
B *modif* 监禁的; **the ~ buildings** 监狱大楼; **a ~ sentence/term** 徒刑/刑期
C *vt* 监禁 ‹*offender*›; **to ~ sb. (for sth.)** （为某事）监禁某人; **to be ~ed for life** 被终身监禁

jail: ~bait *n* [u] + *v sing or pl* colloq 祸水妞儿 [与之发生性关系即构成强奸罪的未成年女子]; **~bird** *n* colloq 惯犯; **~break** *n* 越狱

jailer /ˈdʒeɪlə(r)/ *n* 监狱看守

jalopy /dʒəˈlɒpi/ *n* colloq 老爷车

jalousie /ˈʒæluziː/ *n* 百叶窗

jam¹ /dʒæm/
A *n* **1** [c] (congestion) (of people, animals) 拥挤; (of vehicles) 堵塞; **~s formed at all the exits** 所有出口都给堵住了 **2** [c] (blockage of machine) 卡住 **3** [c] (bottleneck in system) 障碍 **4** [c] colloq (difficult situation) 困境; **to get into/find oneself in a ~** 陷入/发现自己陷入困境; **to be in/get into/get out of a ~** 处于/陷入/摆脱困境 **5** [c] Mus **a ~ (session)** 即兴演奏会
B *vt* (*pres p etc.* **-mm-**) **1** (push) 用力推; **to ~ sth. into** *or* **in sth.** 把某物塞入某物; **reporters were ~ming microphones in our faces** 记者们把话筒塞到我们面前; **to ~ one's foot on the brake** 用力踩刹车; **he ~med his hat on his head** 他把帽子使劲往头上一扣 **2** (stuff, pile) 塞; **we were ~med together like sardines** 我们像沙丁鱼一样挤在一起 **3** (fix firmly, wedge) 使卡住; **to ~ sb./sth. between sb./sth.** 把某人/某物卡在某人/某物中间; **to ~ sth. against sth.** 用某物抵住某物; **to ~ sth. open/shut** 卡住某物使之敞开/关闭; **I got a finger ~med** *or* **~med a finger in the door** 我的手指被门夹住了; **to ~ the lock/gun/switch/door** 把锁/枪/开关/门卡住 **4** (block) 堵塞; **to be ~med solid with sb./sth.** 被某人/某物挤得水泄不通; **viewers ~med the switchboard with complaints** 观众的投诉把总机打爆了 **5** Radio, Telecom 干扰 ‹*frequency, transmission, programme*›
C *vi* (*pres p etc.* **-mm-**) **1** (become stuck) «*lock, gun, switch, door*» 卡住; **the printer keeps ~ming** 打印机总是卡纸; **the valve has ~med shut** 阀门卡死了 **2** Mus 即兴演奏

Phrasal verbs
- **jam in**
  A *vt* [**~ sb./sth. in, ~ in sb./sth.**]
  1 (pack in) 把…塞进; **there were 30 people ~med into the room** 30个人挤在这间屋子里 **2** (wedge in) 使动弹不得; **her car was ~med in** 她的车被堵住了
  B *vi* 挤进来; **a large crowd had ~med in to see the band play** 一大群人挤进来观看乐队演奏
- **jam on** *vt* [**~ sth. on, ~ on sth.**] 猛按 ‹*handbrake*›; 猛踩 ‹*brakes*›
- **jam up** *vt* [**~ sth. up, ~ up sth.**]
  1 (block) 堵住 ‹*road*› **2** (cause to stop moving) 卡住 ‹*lock, gun, switch, door*›

jam² *n* [u and c] 果酱; **strawberry/apricot ~** 草莓酱/杏果酱; **you want ~ on it!** Brit colloq hum 你的要求过分了！; **~ tomorrow** Brit 许而不予的好东西; **a ~ sandwich** 果酱三明治

Jamaica /dʒəˈmeɪkə/ *pr n* 牙买加

Jamaican /dʒəˈmeɪkən/ ►**p. 503**
A *adj* (of Jamaica) 牙买加的; (of the people) 牙买加人的
B *n* 牙买加人

jamb /dʒæm/ *n* (of door, window) 门窗边框; (of fireplace) 壁炉侧柱

jamboree /ˌdʒæmbəˈriː/ *n* **1** (party) 狂欢聚会 **2** (for Scouts) 童子军大会

jam: ~-full *adj* = **~-packed**; **~jar** *n* 果酱罐

jamming /ˈdʒæmɪŋ/ *n* [u] Radio, Telecom 干扰

jammy /ˈdʒæmi/ *adj* **1** (sticky with jam) 沾满果酱的 ‹*finger, food*› **2** Brit colloq (lucky) 幸运的 ‹*person*›

jam: ~-packed *adj* 挤得水泄不通的 ‹*room, street*›; 塞得满满的 ‹*box, case*›; **to be ~-packed with** 挤满了 ‹*people*›; 塞满了 ‹*clothes*›; **~pot** *n* = **~jar**

Jan *abbr* = **January**

jangle /ˈdʒæŋgl/
A *vi* «*bell, keys, chains*» 发出叮当声; «*alarm clock, phone*» 发出丁零声
B *vt* **1** lit 使…发出叮当声 ‹*bell, keys, chains*› **2** fig (irritate) «*noise, accident*» 烦扰 ‹*nerves*›
C *n* [u] (of bell, keys, chains) 叮当声; (of alarm clock, phone) 丁零声

jangling /ˈdʒæŋglɪŋ/
A *n* [u] = **jangle C**
B *adj* 叮当作响的 ‹*bell, chains, bracelets*›; 鸣响的 ‹*alarm*›

janitor /ˈdʒænɪtə(r)/ *n* esp Amer 看门人

January /ˈdʒænjʊəri, Amer -jʊeri/ ▸p. 490 *n* 一月; **last/this/next ~** 上个/本年/下个一月份; **in early/late ~** 一月上旬/下旬; **~ weather/morning** 一月的天气/早晨

Jap /dʒæp/ *n* colloq offensive 日本佬 pej

Japan /dʒəˈpæn/ *pr n* 日本

japan /dʒəˈpæn/
A *n* [u] 黑亮漆
B *vt* (*pres p etc.* **-nn-**) 在…上面涂黑亮漆; **a ~ned tray/bowl** 黑漆盘子/碗

Japanese /ˌdʒæpəˈniːz/ ▸p. 503, p. 426
A *adj* (of Japan) 日本的; (of the people) 日本人的; (of the language) 日语的
B *n* **1** [c] (person) 日本人; **the ~** *pl* 日本人民 **2** [u] (language) 日语

jape /dʒeɪp/ *n* dated 恶作剧

japonica /dʒəˈpɒnɪkə/ *n* 贴梗海棠

jar[1] /dʒɑː(r)/
A *n* **1** (jolt, shock) 震动 **2** (noise) 刺耳声
B *vi* (*pres p etc.* **-rr-**) **1** (make noise) «*voice, instrument*» 发出刺耳声; **to ~ on sth.** 刺激某物; **to ~ on one's ears/nerves** 使某人感到刺耳/烦躁 **2** (rattle) «*machine, window*» 轧轧作响; **to ~ against sth.** 轧轧响着碰撞某物 **3** fig (clash) «*notes, colours*» 不协调; «*ideas, comments*» 冲突; **her opinion ~red with mine** 她和我意见相左
C *vt* (*pres p etc.* **-rr-**) «*blow, blast, fall*» 撞击 ‹*person, knee, building*›

jar[2] *n* **1** (glass container) 广口瓶; **a ~ of sth.** 一瓶某物 **2** (pottery container) 罐子; **a ~ of oil** 一罐油 **3** Brit colloq (glass of beer) 一杯啤酒; **to have a ~** 喝一杯

jargon /ˈdʒɑːgən/ *n* [u] 行话; **to use/lapse into ~** 用术语/开始讲行话

jarring /ˈdʒɑːrɪŋ/ *adj* **1** (irritating) 恼人的 ‹*vibration, experience*› **2** (discordant) 刺耳的 ‹*sound, music*›; **to strike a ~ note** lit 弹出刺耳的音; fig 引起反感 **3** (clashing) 不和谐的 ‹*notes, colours*›

jasmine /ˈdʒæzmɪn/ *n* 茉莉

jasper /ˈdʒæspə(r)/ *n* [u] 水苍玉

jaundice /ˈdʒɔːndɪs/ ▸p. 377 *n* [u] 黄疸病

jaundiced /ˈdʒɔːndɪst/ *adj* **1** lit (affected with jaundice) 患黄疸病的 **2** fig (bitter, cynical) 刻薄的 ‹*look, attitude, remark*›

jaunt /dʒɔːnt/ *n* 短途旅行; **to go for a ~** 去游玩; **a ~ into town** 到城里的游玩

jauntily /ˈdʒɔːntɪli/ *adv* 得意扬扬地 ‹*stride*›; 快活地 ‹*greet, whistle*›

jauntiness /ˈdʒɔːntɪnɪs/ *n* [u] 快活

jaunty /ˈdʒɔːnti/ *adj* 得意扬扬的 ‹*appearance, person, stride*›; 快活的 ‹*greeting, whistle*›; **she was wearing her hat at a ~ angle** 她俏皮地歪戴着帽子

Java /ˈdʒɑːvə/
A *pr n* Geog 爪哇岛
B **Java®** *n* Comput Java语言

java /ˈdʒɑːvə/ *n* [u] Amer colloq 咖啡

Javanese /ˌdʒɑːvəˈniːz/ ▸p. 503, p. 426
A *adj* (of Java) 爪哇的; (of the people) 爪哇人的; (of the language) 爪哇语的
B *n* **1** [c] (person) 爪哇人 **2** [u] (language) 爪哇语

javelin /ˈdʒævlɪn/ *n* **1** (weapon) 投枪 **2** ▸p. 307 Sport 标枪; **the ~** 掷标枪项目; **to throw the ~** 投标枪

javelin: ~ thrower *n* 标枪运动员; **~ throwing** ▸p. 307 *n* [u] 掷标枪（项目）

jaw /dʒɔː/
A *n* **1** [c] (of person, animal) 颌; **the upper/lower ~** 上颌/下颌 **2** [c] (lower part of face) 下巴; **his ~ dropped** fig 他惊讶不已; **to set one's ~** fig 咬牙坚持 **3** [u] colloq (tedious talk) 说教 **4** [u] colloq (chat) 闲谈; **to have a good ~** 好好聊一聊
B **jaws** *npl* **1** (of person, animal) 口部 **2** (of valley, canyon, vessel) 狭窄入口 **3** (of tool) 钳口 **4** fig (clutches) 险境; **the ~s of death/hell** 鬼门关
C *vi* colloq 闲谈

jaw: ~bone *n* 颌骨; **~breaker** *n* colloq **1** (word) 难念的词; **2** esp Amer (candy) 大块硬糖; **~-dropping** *adj* colloq 惊人的 ‹*beauty, view*›; **~line** *n* 下颌的轮廓

jay /dʒeɪ/ *n* 松鸦

jay: ~walk *vi* «*pedestrian*» 乱穿马路; **~walker** *n* 乱穿马路的人; **~walking** *n* [u] 乱穿马路

jazz /dʒæz/ *n* [u] **1** Mus 爵士乐 **2** colloq (energy) 热情奔放 **3** colloq (talk) 胡扯; **to give sb. a lot of ~ about sth.** 对某人胡吹某事物 **4** colloq **and all that ~** 以及诸如此类的东西

Phrasal verb
- **jazz up** *vt* [**~ up sth., ~ sth. up**] **1** Mus «*musician, band*» 使…具有爵士乐风格 ‹*tune, classic*› **2** colloq (liven up) 使…更有生气 ‹*design, building, decor*›; 使…更出彩 ‹*film, magazine*›

jazz dance *n* [u] 爵士舞; **a ~ class** 爵士舞班

jazzy /ˈdʒæzi/ *adj* **1** colloq (bright) 艳丽的 ‹*colours, clothes*›; 花哨的 ‹*decor, design*›; 张扬的 ‹*tastes, look*› **2** Mus 爵士乐的 ‹*beat, solo*›

JCB® *n* 挖掘装载机

JCS *abbr* Amer = **Joint Chiefs of Staff**

jealous /ˈdʒeləs/ *adj* **1** (envious) 嫉妒的 ‹*glance, remark*›; 吃醋的 ‹*spouse, lover*›; **to be** *or* **feel ~ of sb.** 妒忌某人; **to be ~ of sb.'s success** 妒忌某人的成功; **to make sb. ~** 使某人嫉妒; **~ suspicion/hatred** 猜忌/嫉恨 **2** (protective) 小心守护的 ‹*person*›; **to keep a ~ eye on sb./sth.** 小心守护着某人/某事物

jealously /ˈdʒeləsli/ *adv* **1** (enviously) 嫉妒地 **2** (protectively) 小心地 ‹*defend*›; **a ~ guarded secret** 被严守的秘密

jealousy /ˈdʒeləsi/
A *n* [u] (feeling) 嫉妒; **a fit of ~** 一阵嫉妒
B **jealousies** *npl* (acts) 嫉妒的行为; (remarks) 嫉妒的言语

jeans /dʒiːnz/ *npl* 牛仔裤

jeep® /dʒiːp/ *n* 吉普车

jeer /dʒɪə(r)/
A *vi* 嘲弄; **to ~ at sb./sth.** 嘲弄某人/某事物
B *vt* 嘲笑 ‹*effort, attempt*›
C *n* 嘲弄

jeering /ˈdʒɪərɪŋ/
A *adj attrib* 嘲笑的 ‹*mob, face*›; **a ~ laugh** 嘲笑
B *n* [u] 嘲笑

Jehovah /dʒɪˈhəʊvə/ *pr n* 耶和华

Jehovah's Witness *pr n* 耶和华见证人 [基督教非传统教派，相信世界末日将临，只有其教徒才可以获得救赎]

jejune /dʒɪˈdʒuːn/ *adj* liter pej **1** (naive) 幼稚的 ‹*view, idea*› **2** (dull) 枯燥乏味的 ‹*writings, platitudes*›

jejunum /dʒiːˈdʒuːnəm/ *n* 空肠

Jekyll and Hyde /ˌdʒekɪl ən ˈhaɪd/ *n* 具有双重人格的人; *modif* 具有双重人格的 ‹*character, existence*›

jell /dʒel/ *vi* **1** Culin «*pudding, liquid*» 凝胶 **2** (take shape) «*ideas, plan*» 开始成形 **3** (begin to work well) 起作用

jellied /ˈdʒelɪd/ *adj* 凝成胶状的 ‹*fish*›; **~ meat** 肉冻

jello, Jell-O® /ˈdʒeləʊ/ *ns* Amer = **jelly 1**

jelly /ˈdʒeli/ *n* [u] **1** esp Brit (sweet gelatin) 果冻; **to shake like (a) ~** 害怕得发抖; **to turn to ~** fig «*legs*» 发软 **2** (meat gelatin) 肉冻 **3** (fruit preserves) 果酱 **4** (gel-like substance) 胶状物; **petroleum ~** 矿脂 **5** colloq = **gelignite**

jelly: ~ baby *n* Brit 胶糖娃娃 [娃娃形状的果味凝胶软糖]; **~ bean** *n* 软心豆粒糖; **~fish** *n* (*pl* **~fish** *or* **~fishes**) 水母; **~ mould** *n* 果冻模子; **~ roll** *n* Amer 果冻卷

jemmy /ˈdʒemi/ *n* Brit 短撬棍

jeopardize /ˈdʒepədaɪz/ *vt* 危及 ‹*safety, future, project*›

jeopardy /ˈdʒepədi/ *n* [u] 危险; **to be in ~** 处于危险中; **to put** *or* **place sb./sth. in ~** 使某人/某事物处于危险之中

Jeremiah /ˌdʒerɪˈmaɪə/
A *pr n* 耶利米 [希伯来先知]
B *n* (person who foretells misfortune) 预言灾难的人; **don't be such a ~!** 别这么悲观！; **the ~s who predicted complete economic collapse were proved wrong** 预言经济会全面崩溃的杞人忧天者被证实是错的

Jericho /ˈdʒerɪkəʊ/ *pr n* 耶利哥

jerk /dʒɜːk/
A *n* **1** [c] (jolt) 突然的一动; **a sharp ~** 突然的一动; **to give sth. a ~, to give a ~ on sth.** 猛推某物一下; **with a ~** 猛地一下; **the car moved forward in a series of ~s** 汽车一颠一颠地前行; **with a ~ of sth.** 猛然晃动某物 **2** [c] (twitch of muscle, limb) 抽搐 **3** [c] colloq (annoying person) 蠢人; **shut up, you ~!** 闭嘴，傻瓜！ **4** [u] Culin (meat) 烤腌肉; **~ meat/chicken** 烤肉/烤鸡
B *vt* **1** (move in particular direction) 使突然一动; **to ~ sth. around** 将某物摇来摇去; **to ~ sth. away (from sb./sth.)** (从某人/某处)猛地拿走某物; **he ~ed the child to his feet** 他猛地把孩子拽起来; **the door was ~ed open by the impact** 门被猛地撞开了 **2** (jolt) 突然拉动
C *vi* **1** (jolt) 突然一动; **to ~ along** «*vehicle*» 一颠一颠地前行; **to ~ around** 猛然转身; **to ~ to a halt** «*vehicle*» 猛然停下来; **to ~ (bolt) upright** 猛然起身 **2** (twitch) «*muscle, limb*» 抽搐; «*head*» 扭动; «*arm*» 拽动

Phrasal verbs
- **jerk around** *vt* [**~ sb. around**] Amer colloq 刁难
- **jerk off** esp Amer taboo sl
  A *vi* 手淫
  B *vt* [**~ sb. off**] 为…手淫; **to ~ oneself off** 手淫
- **jerk out** *vt* [**~ out sth., ~ sth. out**] 猛地抽出 ‹*gun, knife*›; **she suddenly ~ed the money out of my hand** 她突然从我手里把钱抢走了

jerkily /ˈdʒɜːkɪli/ *adv* 断断续续地 ‹*speak*›; 颠簸地 ‹*move*›; 忽动忽停地 ‹*swim*›

jerkin /ˈdʒɜːkɪn/ *n* **1** Fashn 坎肩 **2** Hist 男式皮马甲

jerky /ˈdʒɜːki/ *adj* 颠簸的 ‹*movement*›; 忽动忽停的 ‹*steps*›; 断断续续的 ‹*phrases, speech*›

jeroboam /ˌdʒerəˈbəʊəm/ *n* 大酒瓶

jerry /ˈdʒeri/: **~-building** *n* [u] pej 偷工减料的建筑; **~-built** *adj* pej 草率建成的 ‹*building*›; **~can** *n* 扁平大金属罐

Jersey /ˈdʒɜːzi/
A *pr n* 泽西岛
B *n* (*pl* **~s**) **~ (cow)** 泽西奶牛

jersey /ˈdʒɜːzi/ *n* **1** [c] (for sports) 运动衫 **2** [c] Brit (sweater) 毛衣 **3** [u] (fabric) 平针织物

Jerusalem /dʒəˈruːsələm/ *pr n* 耶路撒冷

Jerusalem artichoke *n* 菊芋

jest /dʒest/
A *n* [c and u] (sth. amusing said) 俏皮话; (sth. amusing done) 玩闹; **in ~** 开玩笑地; **that story was told in ~** 那故事是说着玩的; **many a true word is spoken in ~** Prov 笑谈之中有至理
B *vi* 开玩笑; **to ~ about sth.** 取笑某事物

jester /ˈdʒestə(r)/ *n* **1** Hist (court clown) 弄臣 **2** (joker) 爱开玩笑的人

Jesuit /ˈdʒezjʊɪt, Amer ˈdʒeʒəwət/ *n* 耶稣会会士; **the ~ Order** 耶稣会

Jesuitical /ˌdʒezjʊˈɪtɪkl, Amer ˌdʒeʒʊ-/ *adj* **1** Relig 耶稣会的 **2** pej (equivocating) 闪烁其词的 ‹*reply*›; 狡诈的 ‹*practice, plan*›

J

Jesus /ˈdʒiːzəs/
A *pr n* 耶稣; ~ **Christ** 耶稣基督
B *excl* sl ~! 天哪!

Jesus: ~ **freak** *n* colloq pej 耶稣迷; ~ **sandals** Brit, ~ **shoes** Amer *nspl* 凉鞋

jet[1] /dʒet/
A *n* **1** (aircraft) 喷气式飞机 **2** (stream of water or flame) 喷射流 **3** (from gas ring, engine) 喷嘴
B *vi* **1** (spurt) «*water, gas*» 喷射 **2** (travel) 乘坐喷气式飞机; **to ~ (off) to ...** 坐喷气式飞机去…; **to ~ around the world** 乘喷气式飞机周游世界

jet[2] *n* [u] **1** (stone) 黑玉; **a ~ necklace** 黑玉项链 **2** (colour) ~ **(black)** 乌黑; ~ **black hair** 乌黑的头发

jet: ~ **aircraft** *n* 喷气式飞机; ~ **engine** *n* 喷气式发动机; ~ **fighter** *n* 喷气式战斗机; ~**foil** *n* 喷流水翼船; ~ **fuel** *n* [u] 喷气燃料; ~**lag** *n* [u] 时差反应; ~**lagged** *adj* 有时差反应的; ~**liner** *n* 喷气式客机; ~**-propelled**, ~**-powered** *adjs* 喷气推进的; **a ~-propelled aircraft/car** 喷气式飞机/汽车; ~ **propulsion** *n* [u] 喷气推进

jetsam /ˈdʒetsəm/ *n* [u] ▸**flotsam**

jet: ~ **set** *n* colloq **the ~ set** [乘喷气式飞机到处旅行的] 富豪一族; **the ~ set lifestyle** 乘喷气式飞机到处旅游的阔佬生活方式; ~**-setter** *n* colloq 乘喷气式飞机到处旅游的阔佬

jet ski
A *n* 喷气式滑艇
B **jet-ski** *vi* 乘喷气式滑艇滑水

jet: ~**-skiing** ▸**p. 307** *n* [u] 乘喷气式滑艇滑水; ~ **stream** *n* 高空急流

jettison /ˈdʒetɪsn/ *vt* **1** Naut «*ship, crew*» 丢弃 ‹*cargo*› **2** Aviat «*aircraft, spacecraft, crew*» 投弃 ‹*cargo, fuel, rocket*› **3** colloq (discard) 扔掉 ‹*old things*› **4** fig (abandon) 放弃 ‹*plan, responsibility*›

jetty /ˈdʒeti/ *n* (of stone) 防波堤; (of wood) 码头

Jew /dʒuː/ *pr n* **1** (ethnically Jewish person) 犹太人; (practising Jew) 犹太教徒 **2** **jew** dated pej colloq (miser) 吝啬鬼

jewel /ˈdʒuːəl/ *n* **1** (gem) 宝石 **2** *usu pl* (piece of jewellery) 珠宝; **valuable/priceless ~s** 贵重/无价的珠宝 **3** (in watch) 宝石轴承 **4** fig (person) 典范; (thing) 珍品; **she is a ~ of a nurse** 她是一名优秀的护士; **the ~ in the crown** 最珍贵的东西

jewel case *n* 光盘盒

jewelled Brit, **jeweled** Amer /ˈdʒuːəld/ *adj* 镶宝石的 ‹*crown, sword, ring*›

jeweller Brit, **jeweler** Amer /ˈdʒuːələ(r)/ ▸**p. 409** *n* 珠宝商

jewellery /ˈdʒuːəlri/ *n* [u] Brit 珠宝; **a piece of ~** 一件珠宝首饰; **a ~ shop** 珠宝店

jewellery: ~ **box** *n* 首饰盒; ~ **case** *n* 首饰匣; ~ **store** *n* esp Amer 珠宝店

jewelry /ˈdʒuːəlri/ *n* [u] Amer = **jewellery**

Jewish /ˈdʒuːɪʃ/ *adj* (of the Jews) 犹太人的 ‹*name, language*›; (of Judaism) 犹太教的 ‹*scholar, writings*›; **the ~ community/diaspora** 犹太人群体/大流散

Jewish calendar *n* **the ~** 犹太历

Jewry /ˈdʒʊəri/ *n* [u] 犹太人 [总称]

Jew's harp *n* 单簧口琴

Jiangsu /ˌdʒæŋˈsuː/ ▸**p. 604** *pr n* ~ **(Province)** 江苏 (省)

Jiangxi /ˌdʒæŋˈʃiː/ ▸**p. 604** *pr n* ~ **(Province)** 江西 (省)

jiao /dʒaʊ/ ▸**p. 174** *n* (*pl* **jiao**) 角 [中华人民共和国货币单位, 10角等于1元, 1角等于10分]

jib /dʒɪb/
A *n* **1** Naut 艏三角帆 **2** (of crane) 悬臂
B *vi* (*pres p etc.* **-bb-**) **1** (stop) «*horse, mule*» 逡巡不前; **to ~ at sth.** 面对…畏缩不前 ‹*jump, fence*› **2** fig (baulk) 不愿接受; **to ~ at sth./at doing sth.** 拒绝某事物/做某事

jib: ~ **boom** *n* 艏斜帆桁; ~ **crane** *n* 悬臂起重机

jibe[1] /dʒaɪb/
A *n* (insulting or mocking remark) 嘲讽
B *vi* 嘲讽

jibe[2] *n, vi, vt* Amer Naut = **gybe**

jibe[3] *vi* Amer colloq «*accounts, description*» 符合; **to ~ with sth.** 与某物一致

jiffy /ˈdʒɪfi/, **jiff** /dʒɪf/ *ns* colloq 瞬间; **in a ~** 即刻

Jiffy bag® /ˈdʒɪfi bæg/ *n* Brit 厚层信封

jig /dʒɪg/
A *n* **1** (dance) 吉格舞; **to dance** *or* **do a ~** 跳吉格舞; **the ~ is up** Amer 把戏被拆穿了 **2** Mus 吉格舞曲 **3** Tech 夹具
B *vi* (*pres p etc.* **-gg-**) **to ~ up and down** 又蹦又跳; **to ~ about** *or* **around** 来回晃动
C *vt* (*pres p etc.* **-gg-**) 摇晃 ‹*baby, feet*›; **to ~ sb./sth. up and down** 不停地摇晃某人/某物

jigger /ˈdʒɪgə(r)/ *n* (measure) 吉格 [一种液量单位, 约1.5盎司]; (glass) [容量为1.5盎司的] 小量杯

jiggered /ˈdʒɪgəd/ *adj* Brit colloq **1** (broken) **to be ~** «*object*» 受损; **well I'm** *or* **I'll be ~!** 太不可思议了! **2** *pred* (tired) «*person*» 精疲力竭的

jiggery-pokery /ˌdʒɪgərɪˈpəʊkəri/ *n* [u] Brit colloq 骗局

jiggle /ˈdʒɪgl/
A *vt* 晃动 ‹*tooth*›; 转动 ‹*key, handle*›
B *vi* **to ~ (about** *or* **around)** «*person, car*» 晃动

jigsaw /ˈdʒɪgsɔː/ *n* **1** ~ **(puzzle)** (picture) 拼图 **2** Tech (tool) 线锯 **3** fig (mysterious situation) 谜团

jihad /dʒɪˈhɑːd/ *n* 伊斯兰圣战

Jilin /ˌdʒiːˈlɪn/ ▸**p. 604** *pr n* ~ **(Province)** 吉林 (省)

jilt /dʒɪlt/ *vt* 抛弃 ‹*sweetheart*›; **a ~ed lover** 被抛弃的情人

Jim Crow /ˌdʒɪm ˈkrəʊ/ *n* Amer **1** [u] Hist (policy) 种族隔离; ~ **laws** 种族隔离法律 **2** [c] dated offensive (person) 黑鬼 offensive

jim-jams /ˈdʒɪmdʒæmz/ *npl* Brit colloq 睡衣

jimmy /ˈdʒɪmi/ *n* Amer = **jemmy**

jin /dʒɪn/ ▸**p. 909** *n* (*pl* **jin**) 斤

jingle /ˈdʒɪŋgl/
A *n* **1** [u] (sound) 叮当声; **the ~ of sth.** 某物发出的叮当声 **2** [c] (tune) 广告短歌; (verse) 广告短句
B *vi* «*bells, coins, keys*» 发出叮当声
C *vt* 使…发出叮当声 ‹*bells, coins, keys*›

jingo /ˈdʒɪŋgəʊ/ *excl* dated **by ~!** (as declaration) 我发誓!; (in approval) 没错!

jingoism /ˈdʒɪŋgəʊɪzəm/ *n* [u] pej 沙文主义

jingoist /ˈdʒɪŋgəʊɪst/ *n* pej 沙文主义者

jingoistic /ˌdʒɪŋgəʊˈɪstɪk/ *adj* pej 沙文主义的 ‹*attitude, remarks*›; 鼓吹沙文主义的 ‹*person, crowd*›

jink /dʒɪŋk/ *vi* esp Brit 躲闪; **to ~ (to the left/right)** (往左/右) 快速闪开

jinx /dʒɪŋks/
A *n* **1** (curse) 厄运; **to put a ~ on sb./sth.** 让某人厄运缠身/让某事物受诅咒 **2** (person bringing bad luck) 不祥之人; (thing bringing bad luck) 不祥之物
B *vt* *usu passive* colloq 给…带来厄运 ‹*person, team*›; 使…遭到诅咒 ‹*machine, project*›

jitter /ˈdʒɪtə(r)/ *vi* colloq 紧张不安; **stop ~ing! you're making me feel nervous too!** 别慌! 你把我也弄得紧张了!

jitters /ˈdʒɪtəz/ *npl* **the ~** colloq 紧张不安; **to have** *or* **get the ~** 焦躁不安

jittery /ˈdʒɪtəri/ *adj* colloq 紧张不安的 ‹*person*›

jive /dʒaɪv/
A *n* [u] **1** (dance) **the ~** 牛仔舞 **2** (music) 摇摆乐; ~ **music** 摇摆乐 **3** Amer dated sl (glib talk) 花言巧语 **4** Amer sl ~ **(talk)** 俚语
B *vi* **1** (dance) 跳牛仔舞 **2** Amer colloq (talk nonsense) 胡扯
C *vt* Amer colloq **to ~ sb.** 取笑某人

Jnr *abbr* = **junior A4**

Job /dʒəʊb/ *pr n* 约伯 [《圣经》人物]; **to have the patience of ~** 有极大的忍耐力

job /dʒɒb/
A *n* **1** (post) 工作; **to have a ~** 有工作; **to have a ~ in local government/at a hospital** 在当地政府任职/在一家医院工作; **a teaching/civil service/temporary/permanent/part-time/full-time ~** 教学/公务员/临时/固定/兼职/全职工作; **to get/look for a ~** 找到/找工作; **to take a ~ as a waitress/shop assistant** 当服务员/店员; **to apply for a ~** 求职; **to give/offer sb. a ~** 为某人提供工作; **to give up one's ~** 辞去工作; **to lose one's ~/be out of a ~** 失业; **to know one's ~** 做工作在行; **to do one's ~** 做分内事; **on the ~** (working) 在工作时; Brit colloq (having sex) 在性交; **to lie down** *or* **fall asleep on the ~** fig 怠工; **~s for the boys** Brit colloq pej 为亲信安排的工作; ~ **losses** 失业 **2** (piece of work) 活儿; **to have a ~ for sb. (to do), to find a ~ for sb. (to do)** 有活儿给某人(做); **to find sb. a ~ (to do), to find a ~ for sb. (to do)** 给某人找事情做; **she found little ~s to do to keep herself busy** 她找了些零活干, 为的是不让自己闲下来 **3** (matter) 事情; **the ~ in hand** 手头的事情 **4** (assignment) 任务; **to have the ~ of doing sth.** 承担做某事的任务; **to give sb. the ~ of doing sth.** 把做某事的任务分派给某人; **to do a ~ for sb.** 为某人做事; **to do the ~** colloq 管用; **I need something to steady the table with — ah, this book should do the ~** 我要用东西把桌子垫稳——啊, 这本书应该管用 **5** (result of work) 成果; **a good/poor/lovely ~** 干得不错/干得很糟/招人喜欢的活儿; **to make** *or* **do a good** *or* **great ~ of sth./doing sth.** 把某事/做某事做得很棒; **to do a good ~ of work** Brit 干得不错; **just the ~!** Brit colloq 要的就是这个! **6** (duty) 职责; **it's sb.'s ~ to do sth.** 该由某人负责做某事; **that's not my ~** 这件事不归我管 **7** (function) 作用; **to have the ~ of doing sth.** 具有做某事的作用; **the ~ of the liver is to ...** 肝脏的功能是… **8** colloq (situation) 情况; **it's a good ~ (that) ...** esp Brit 幸好…; **(and a) good ~ too!** esp Brit 真是件好事!; **to give sb./sth. up as a bad ~** 因没有希望而放弃某人/某事物; **to make the best of a bad ~** 在困难条件下尽力而为 **9** (difficult activity) 难做的事; **a real ~** 很费力的事情; **quite a ~** 很难做的事情; **to have a ~ doing sth.** *or* **to do sth.** 费力地做某事; **to be a ~ doing sth.** *or* **to do sth.** 做某事很费力; **he had a hard ~ to make himself heard** 他颇费了些力气才让别人听到他讲话; **you've got a real ~ on there!** 这回你可得费点劲儿了! **10** colloq (object) 东西; **the car was a fast-looking ~** 那辆车看上去跑得很快 **11** colloq (crime) 犯罪行为 [尤指盗窃或抢劫]; **to do a ~** 行窃; **to pull off a ~** 抢劫; **an inside ~** 内部人员作的案; **a bank ~** 银行抢劫案 **12** Comput [作为单元处理的] 作业; **you need to cancel all pending print ~s** 你得取消所有待打印任务
B *vi* (*pres p etc.* **-bb-**) **1** (do casual work) 打零工; **she's just ~bing at the moment** 她眼下正在打零工 **2** (do piece-work) 做计件工作

job advertisement, Brit colloq **job advert** *ns* 招聘广告; **he looked through the ~s, but there was nothing he could apply for** 他浏览了招聘广告, 但没什么他能做的工作

jobbing /ˈdʒɒbɪŋ/ *adj attrib* 临时的 ‹*work*›; 打零工的 ‹*gardener, builder*›

job: Job Centre *n* Brit 就业服务中心; ~ **control language** *n* 作业控制语言; ~ **creation** *n* [u] 提供就业机会; **a ~ creation scheme** *or* **project** 创造就业计划;

~ **description** *n* 岗位描述; ~ **evaluation** *n* 岗位评价; ~**holder** *n* 有固定职业的人; ~**-hunt** *vi* 求职; ~**-hunter** *n* 求职者; ~**-hunting** *n* [u] 求职

jobless /'dʒɒblɪs/
A *npl* **the** ~ 失业者; **the** ~ **rate** 失业率
B *adj* 失业的 ‹*person*›

joblessness /'dʒɒblɪsnɪs/ *n* [u] 失业

job: ~ **lot** *n* **1** lit (articles) 成堆出售的杂货; **2** fig (things) 一堆次品; (people) 一帮庸才; ~ **offer** *n* 聘用; ~ **queue** *n* 作业排队; ~ **satisfaction** *n* [u] 工作满意度; ~ **security** *n* [u] (guarantee) 工作保障; (feeling) 职业安全感

jobseeker /'dʒɒbsi:kə(r)/ *n* 求职者

jobseeker's allowance *n* [u] Brit 求职津贴

job-share
A *n* 工作分担 [两个兼职者合做一份全职工作]; **to do a job on a** ~ **basis** 合做一份工作
B *vi* 合做一份工作

job: ~ **sharing** *n* [u] 工作分担制; **on a** ~**-sharing basis** 以工作分担的方式; ~**sheet** *n* 工作纪录表

jobsworth /'dʒɒbzwɜ:θ/ *n* Brit colloq pej 行事刻板的官僚

job title *n* 职衔

Jock /dʒɒk/ *n* Brit colloq offensive 苏格兰佬 pej

jock /dʒɒk/ *n* Amer colloq **1** = **jockstrap** **2** (athlete) [尤指缺少其他兴趣的] 男运动狂

jockey /'dʒɒki/
A *n* (*pl* ~**s**) 赛马骑师
B *vi* 运用手段图谋; **to** ~ **for position** lit 抢占有利位置; fig 谋取职位; **to** ~ **for advantage** 为得到优势耍手段
C *vt* 哄骗 ‹*customer, opponent*›; **to** ~ **sb. into sth./doing sth.** 哄骗某人接受某事物/做某事; **to** ~ **sb. out of sth./doing sth.** 耍手腕使某人放弃某事物/做某事

Jockey: ~ **Club** *n + v sing or pl* **the** ~ **Club** 赛马总会; ~ **shorts®** *n* Amer 男用紧身内裤

jockstrap /'dʒɒkstræp/ *n* [男子运动时穿的] 下体护身

jocose /dʒə'kəʊs/ *adj* formal **1** *usu attrib* (playful) 诙谐的 ‹*vicar, teacher*› **2** (humorous) 滑稽的 ‹*remarks, response*›

jocular /'dʒɒkjʊlə(r)/ *adj* **1** (cheerful) 乐天派的; (fond of joking) 爱逗乐的 ‹*person*› **2** (playful) 风趣的 ‹*remark, manner, fashion*›

jocularity /,dʒɒkjʊ'lærəti/ *n* [u] 风趣

jocularly /'dʒɒkjʊləli/ *adv* 风趣地 ‹*say*›; **to be** ~ **known as** *or* **called ...** 被风趣地称为···

jocund /'dʒɒkənd/ *adj* formal 欢乐的 ‹*person, group, laughter*›

jodhpurs /'dʒɒdpəz/ *npl* 马裤

Joe: ~ **Bloggs** /,dʒəʊ 'blɒgz/ *pr n* colloq 普通人; ~ **Public** *pr n* [u and c] Brit colloq 普罗大众

joey /'dʒəʊɪ/ *n* (*pl* ~**s**) Austral (young kangaroo) 幼袋鼠; (young wallaby) 幼沙袋鼠

jog /dʒɒg/
A *vt* **1** (*pres p etc.* **-gg-**) (nudge) 轻推 ‹*table, glass*› **2** fig colloq (stir) «*person, event, sight*» 刺激; **to** ~ **sb.'s memory** 唤起某人的记忆; **to** ~ **sb. into action** 促使某人行动起来
B *vi* (*pres p etc.* **-gg-**) **1** (as form of exercise) 慢跑健身 **2** (trot) «*animal, child*» 小跑
C *n* **1** (nudge) 轻推; **to give sb./sth. a** ~ 轻轻推一下某人/某物 **2** (as form of exercise) 健身慢跑; **to go for a** ~ 去慢跑 **3** ~ **(trot)** 小跑; **to set off at a** ~ «*person*» 慢跑着出发; «*horse*» 小跑着出发 **4** fig (push) 刺激; **to give sth. a** ~ 激发某物

Phrasal verb
- **jog along, jog on** *vi* **1** lit 一路小跑 **2** fig «*person*» 平静生活; «*life*» 波澜不兴; «*work*» 平稳进展

jogger /'dʒɒgə(r)/
A *n* 慢跑健身者
B **joggers** *npl* 宽松慢跑裤

jogging /'dʒɒgɪŋ/ ▸p. 307
A *n* [u] 健身慢跑
B *modif* 用于慢跑的 ‹*kit*›; 一起慢跑的 ‹*companion*›; ~ **shoes/clothes** 慢跑鞋/慢跑服; ~ **bottoms,** Amer ~ **pants** 慢跑裤

joggle /'dʒɒgl/ esp Amer colloq
A *vt* 轻轻摇晃 ‹*baby, glasses*›
B *vi* **to** ~ **(about)** 轻轻摆动
C *n* 摇晃; **to give sth./sb. a** ~ 摇晃某物/某人

jog trot *n* = **jog C3**

Johannesburg /dʒəʊ'hænɪsbɜ:g/ *pr n* 约翰内斯堡

john /dʒɒn/ *n* Amer sl **1** **the** ~ (toilet) 厕所; **to go to the** ~ 上厕所 **2** (prostitute's client) 嫖客

John: ~ **Bull** *n* dated **1** [u] (England) 英国; **2** [c] (Englishman) 英国人; ~ **Doe** *n* Amer **1** colloq (ordinary person) 普通人; **2** Jur 无名氏 [指诉讼案中不知名的原告]

johnny /'dʒɒni/ *n* (*pl* **johnnies**) colloq **1** (chap) 家伙; (man) 男人 **2** (condom) **(rubber)** ~ 避孕套

johnny-come-lately *n* (*pl* **johnny-come-latelies**) **1** (newcomer) 新来的人 **2** (upstart) 暴发户

John Q. Public *n* Amer colloq = **Joe Public**

join /dʒɔɪn/
A *vt* **1** (connect) 连接; **to** ~ **two pieces together** 把两部分接在一起; **to** ~ **two points** 将两点连接起来; **to** ~ **one end to another** *or* **the other** 把一头和另一头相接; **the island is** ~**ed to the mainland by a bridge** 这个岛与大陆由桥相连; **to** ~ **hands (with sb.)** (和某人) 手拉手; fig (和某人) 联手 **2** (merge with) «*road, railway*» 与···会合 ‹*motorway, main line*›; **the river** ~**s the sea at Avonmouth** 这条河在阿芬默斯汇入大海 **3** (be with, associate with) 加入; **he** ~**s his unit tomorrow after a week's leave** 休假一周后, 他将于明日回到工作岗位; **he's flown out to** ~ **his family in India** 他已经乘飞机前往印度与家人会合了; **may I** ~ **you?** 我可以坐在你这桌吗? ; **to** ~ **sb. for sth.** 和某人一起享用 ‹*dinner, drink*›; **to** ~ **sb. in sth.** 和某人一起 ‹*walk, drink*›; **to** ~ **sb. in sth./doing sth.** 与某人一起做某事; **to** ~ **forces (with sb./sth.) (to do sth.)** (与某人/某物) 合力 (做某事); **please** ~ **me in wishing Peter every success in his new job** 请与我一起祝福彼得新工作一切顺利 **4** Brit (board) 上 ‹*train, ship, plane*›; (start to travel along) 走上 ‹*road*› **5** (become a member of) 进入 ‹*society, company*›; 加入 ‹*political party, police*›; ~ **the club!** colloq 彼此彼此! ; **if you're confused,** ~ **the club!** 如果你被搞糊涂了, 那我也一样! **6** (take part in) 参加 ‹*procession, demonstration, strike, feast*›; **to** ~ **battle (with sb.) (over sth.)** formal lit (与某人) (为某事物) 展开搏斗; fig (与某人) (就某事物) 展开争论 **7** (go to the end of) 排在···的最后 ‹*line, queue, row, list*› **8** formal (unite in marriage) «*priest*» 使···结为夫妻 ‹*couple, bride and groom*›; **to be** ~**ed in marriage** 结为夫妻

Jobs

What is your job?

What's your job?
= 你干什么工作?

What's your occupation?
or 你的职业是什么?
or 你从事哪种职业?
or 你干哪一行?

What do you do (for a living)?
= 你从事什么工作?
or 你干什么工作 (谋生)?

What sort of work do you do?
= 你干哪种工作?

Talking about jobs

■ Note that no article is used in Chinese when discussing jobs or professions:

He is a lawyer
or ***He works as a lawyer***
= 他是律师
or 他当律师

He is a professional photographer
= 他是职业摄影师

He is an eye specialist
= 他是眼科专家

She is a financial consultant
= 她是金融顾问

He works as a freelance writer
= 他是自由撰稿人

■ Note the translations of these examples:

I run a grocery business
= 我经营一家食品杂货店

I am with an international company
= 我在一家跨国公司做事

I work in a bank
= 我在一家银行工作
or 我在银行工作

I work for a computer company
= 我为一家电脑公司工作

■ Other phrases:

I work full-time
= 我做全职工作

I work part-time
= 我做兼职工作

I work freelance
= 我做自由职业

She's got a temporary job as an editor
= 她找到了一份做编辑的临时工

I have secured a permanent job
= 我找到了一份固定工作

She has recently lost her job
= 她最近失业了

He has applied for a job with a school
= 他向一所学校求了职

I have been out of work for six months
= 我下岗有六个月了

I have been unemployed for two years
= 我失业两年了

I have been jobless for the past year
= 我已经失业一年了

B *vi* **1** (be connected) «*pieces, pipes*» 接合; **to ~ together** 连接起来; **the wires ~ inside the junction box** 电线在接线盒内连接起来 **2** (meet) «*rivers, roads*» 会合 **3** (become a member) 入会; **it costs £20 to ~** 入会费为20英镑 **4** (form association) 联合; **to ~ to do sth.** 联合起来做某事; **to ~ together (in doing** *or* **to do sth.)** 联合起来（做某事）
C *n* 接合点

Phrasal verbs

- **join in**

A *vi* **to ~ in with sb./sth.** 加入某人/参与某事; **she listens, but she never ~s in** 她只是听，但从不搭腔; **I wish he would ~ in with the other children** 我希望他能加入到其他孩子中间; **I ~ed in with the carols** 我和大家一起唱颂歌
B *vt* [**~ in sth.**] 加入 ‹*game, discussion, demonstration, campaign*›; **let's ~ in the fun** 我们一起玩吧

- **join on**

A *vi* **to ~ on to sth.** «*part*» 连接到某物上
B *vt* [**~ sth. on, ~ on sth.**]
1 (attach) 接上 **2** (add) 添加; **two extra carriages were ~ed on at York** 在约克站又加挂了两节车厢

- **join up**

A *vi* **1** Brit Mil (enlist) 参军 **2** **to ~ up with sb.** (meet up) 与某人会合 **3** **to ~ up with sb./sth.** (unite) «*group, organization, business*» 与某人/某机构联合 **4** **to ~ up with sth.** (come together with) «*track, railway line*» 与某物交会; «*river*» 与某物交汇; **this is where our line ~s up with the main line to London** 我们的铁路线在这里与通向伦敦的干线交会
B *vt* [**~ up sth., ~ sth. up**] 连接 ‹*pieces, wires, characters, dots*›; **~ed-up writing** 连笔字

joined-up government *n* [u] Brit 合作政府

joiner /ˈdʒɔɪnə(r)/ ▸**p. 409** *n* 细木工人

joinery /ˈdʒɔɪnəri/ *n* [u] **1** (skill) 细木工手艺; (trade) 细木工行业 **2** (wooden components) 细木工制品

joint /dʒɔɪnt/
A *n* **1** Anat 关节; **elbow/knee/ankle/shoulder/wrist ~** 肘/膝/踝/肩/腕关节; **to dislocate a ~** 使关节脱臼; **out of ~** (dislocated) 脱臼的; (not operating normally) 混乱的; **to put one's shoulder out of ~** 使某人肩膀脱臼; **to put sb.'s nose out of ~** colloq 使某人心烦意乱; **a ~ problem/pain/replacement** 关节毛病/关节痛/关节置换术 **2** (in woodwork, metalwork, of framework, pipework) 接合处; (of suit of armour, doll, puppet) 活动接点 **3** Brit Culin (piece of meat, beef, pork, lamb, mutton) 大块肉; **the Sunday ~** 星期天烤肉 **4** colloq (public meeting place) 公共场所; **a fast-food/burger/pizza ~** 快餐店/汉堡店/比萨饼店 **5** colloq (cannabis cigarette) 大麻烟卷
B *adj attrib* 联合的 ‹*programme, negotiations, measure*›; 共同的 ‹*obligation, resolution, responsibility*›; 并列的 ‹*winners*›; **~ manoeuvres/statement** 联合演习/声明; **they came ~ third** 他们并列第三名
C *vt* 把…切成大块 ‹*meat, poultry*›

joint: ~ account *n* 联名账户; **~ agent** *n* Brit 联合代理人; **~ agreement** *n* [u and c] 联合协议; **~ and several** *adj* Jur 连带的 ‹*liability, guarantee*›; **~ author** *n* 合著者; **~ beneficiary** *n* 共同受益人; **J~ Chiefs of Staff** *npl* Amer 参谋长联席会议; **~ committee** *n* 联合委员会; **~ custody** *n* [u] [夫妻离婚以后] 对子女的共同监护; **to have ~ custody of sb./sth.** 共同监护某人/联名保管某物

jointed /ˈdʒɔɪntɪd/ *adj* **1** (articulated) 有活动关节的 ‹*puppet, doll*› **2** (joining together) 有接头的 ‹*rod, pole*›

joint: ~ effort *n* 共同努力; **~ heir** *n* 共同继承人; **~ honours** *npl* Brit 双荣誉学位; **a ~ honours degree/course** 双荣誉学位/双荣誉学位课程

jointly /ˈdʒɔɪntli/ *adv* 共同地 ‹*publish, own, agreed, funded*›

jointly and severally *adv* Jur 连带地 ‹*liable, responsible*›; **to be ~ liable to pay the costs** 对支付费用负有连带责任

joint: ~ management *n* 联合管理; **~ meeting** *n* 联席会议; **~ owner** *n* 共同所有人; **~ ownership** *n* [u] 共同所有权; **to have ~ ownership of sth.** 共同拥有某物; **to be in ~ ownership** 属于共同所有; **~ resolution** *n* Amer [参众两议院的] 共同决议; **~-stock company** *n* 合股公司; **~ venture** *n* 合资企业

joist /dʒɔɪst/ *n* 托梁

jojoba /həʊˈhəʊbə/ *n* **1** [u] **~ (oil)** 霍霍巴油 **2** [c] (shrub) 霍霍巴灌木

joke /dʒəʊk/
A *n* **1** (amusing story) 笑话; **a ~ about sth.** 关于某事物的笑话; **a bad ~** lit 无聊的笑话; fig 令人不快的情况; **it's a private ~** 这是两个人之间的笑话; **to tell a ~** 讲笑话; **to make** *or* **crack a ~** 说笑话; **to make** *or* **crack a ~ at sb.'s expense** 拿某人开玩笑; **dirty ~s** 下流的笑话; **I don't get the ~** 我没明白这个笑话 **2** (laughing matter) 可笑之处; **I only did/said it as** *or* **for a ~** 我做那事/说那话只是开开玩笑; **to make a ~ of sth., to turn sth. into a ~** 拿某事当玩笑; **to see the ~** 领会可笑之处; **the ~ is that ...** 可笑的是…; **to be no ~** 不是闹着玩的; **it's no ~ having noisy neighbours** 邻居爱吵闹可是个大麻烦; **to be** *or* **get beyond a ~** 超出开玩笑的限度 **3** (prank) 玩笑; **to play a ~ on sb.** 同某人开玩笑; **be unable to take a ~** 经不起开玩笑; **to carry** *or* **take a ~ too far** 开玩笑开过了头; **the ~'s on you** colloq 开玩笑开到自己身上 **4** colloq (ridiculous person) 荒唐可笑的人; (ridiculous thing) 荒唐可笑的事; **it's a ~!** 真荒唐！; **our boss is a ~!** 我们的老板真荒唐！ **5** (object of scorn, ridicule) 笑柄; **she is the ~ of the neighbourhood** 她成了邻居取笑的对象
B *vi* **1** (make jokes) 说笑话; **to ~ with sb.** 和某人开玩笑; **to ~ about sth.** 拿某事物开玩笑 **2** colloq (not be serious) 说着玩; **you must** *or* **have (got) to be joking!** 你一定是说着玩的吧！
C *vt* **1** (say as joke) 打趣地说 **2** (not say seriously) 调侃说; **she ~d that she only loved him for his money** 她调侃说她爱他只是因为他有钱

joker /ˈdʒəʊkə(r)/ *n* **1** (joke teller) 爱开玩笑的人; **a practical ~** 恶作剧者 **2** colloq (fool) 笨蛋 **3** (in cards) 百搭; **the ~ in the pack** fig (unpredictable factor) 不确定因素; (unpredictable person) 难以捉摸的人

jokey /ˈdʒəʊki/ *adj usu attrib* colloq 滑稽的 ‹*remark, name*›; 戏谑的 ‹*attitude*›

joking /ˈdʒəʊkɪŋ/
A *adj attrib* 开玩笑的 ‹*person, remark, manner*›; **it's no ~ matter** 这可不是闹着玩儿的
B *n* [u] 开玩笑; **~ apart** *or* **aside** 言归正传; **~ apart, I do hope you will come and see us occasionally** 说正经的，我希望你时不时能来看我们

jokingly /ˈdʒəʊkɪŋli/ *adv* 开玩笑地

joky /ˈdʒəʊki/ *adj* = **jokey**

jollification /ˌdʒɒlɪfɪˈkeɪʃn/ *n* [u] 欢闹

jollity /ˈdʒɒləti/ *n* [u] 欢乐

jolly /ˈdʒɒli/
A *adj* **1** (happy) 欢乐的 ‹*person, manner, occasion, mood*› **2** dated (enjoyable) 令人愉快的 ‹*time*› **3** (drunk) 有几分醉意的
B *adv* Brit colloq 非常 ‹*good, nice*›; **~ well** 当然 [生气时用于加强语气]; **she should ~ well hurry up!** 她当然得赶紧！
C *n* Brit colloq (outing) 游玩; (party) 欢宴

Phrasal verb

- **jolly along** *vt* [**~ sb. along**] colloq 鼓励

Jolly Roger *n* (*pl* **Jolly Rogers**) 骷髅旗

jolt /dʒəʊlt/
A *vt* **1** (rock) «*vehicle, movement*» 使…震动 ‹*person, load*› **2** (jar) «*person, movement*» 撞击 ‹*person, arm, train*› **3** fig (shock) «*pain, event*» 使…震惊 ‹*person*›; **to ~ sb. out of/into sth.** 使某人从某事物中猛然醒悟过来/猛然醒悟而做某事
B *vi* «*vehicle, load*» 震动
C *n* **1** (jerk) 震动; (blow) 撞击 **2** fig (shock) 震惊; **to give sb. a ~** 使某人大吃一惊

jolty /ˈdʒəʊlti/ *adj* 颠簸的 ‹*vehicle, ride, road*›

jonquil /ˈdʒɒŋkwɪl/ *n* 长寿花

Jordan /ˈdʒɔːdn/ ▸**p. 663** *pr n* **1** (country) 约旦 **2** **the ~, the River ~** Brit, **the ~ River** Amer 约旦河

Jordanian /dʒɔːˈdeɪnɪən/ ▸**p. 503**
A *adj* 约旦的
B *n* 约旦人

josh /dʒɒʃ/ esp Amer colloq
A *vt* (tease) 戏弄
B *vi* (joke) 开玩笑

joss stick /ˈdʒɒstɪk/ *n* 线香

jostle /ˈdʒɒsl/
A *vt* 推挤
B *vi* **1** (push) 挤; **to ~ against sb.** 推挤某人 **2** (push through) 挤来挤去; **to ~ (with sb.) to do sth.** 为做某事（与某人）挤来挤去 **3** fig (compete) 争抢; **to ~ (with sb.) for position/attention** （与某人）争抢职位/抢出风头

jot /dʒɒt/
A *n* 一点儿; **not one ~** 一点儿都不
B *vt* (*pres p etc.* **-tt-**) = **jot down**

Phrasal verb

- **jot down** *vt* [**~ sth. down, ~ down sth.**] 草草记下 ‹*notes, ideas*›

jotter /ˈdʒɒtə(r)/ *n* Brit 便笺簿

jottings /ˈdʒɒtɪŋz/ *npl* 便条

joule /dʒuːl/ *n* 焦耳

journal /ˈdʒɜːnl/ *n* **1** (periodical) 期刊 **2** (daily newspaper) 日报; (weekly newspaper) 周报 **3** (private diary) 日记; (official diary) 备忘录 **4** (business record) (account book) 流水账 **5** Tech **~ (bearing)** 轴颈

journalese /ˌdʒɜːnəˈliːz/ *n* [u] 新闻文体

journalism /ˈdʒɜːnəlɪzəm/ *n* [u] **1** (as profession) 新闻业 **2** (as product) 新闻报道

journalist /ˈdʒɜːnəlɪst/ *n* 新闻记者

journalistic /ˌdʒɜːnəˈlɪstɪk/ *adj attrib* 新闻业的 ‹*integrity, standards*›; 新闻记者的 ‹*experience, profession*›

journey /ˈdʒɜːni/
A *n* **1** (trip) 旅行; **to make** *or* **go on a ~** 去旅行; **to reach the end of one's ~** *or* **~'s end** 到达旅途终点; fig 到达生命尽头; **to break one's ~** 中断旅行; **one's ~ through life** 生命的旅程 **2** (distance) 路程; **a ~ of fifty miles** 50英里的路程 **3** (time taken) 行程; **the ~ time** 行程时间
B *vi* 旅行

journeyman /ˈdʒɜːnɪmən/ *n* (*pl* **journeymen**) **1** (craftsman) 出师的学徒工; **a ~ baker/printer** 满师的面包师/印刷工 **2** (worker) 熟手; **a ~ actor** 熟练演员

joust /dʒaʊst/
A *vi* **1** Hist 骑马比武 **2** fig 竞争
B *n* Hist 骑马比武

jovial /ˈdʒəʊvɪəl/ *adj* 快乐的 ‹*person, mood, smile*›; 友好的 ‹*manner*›

joviality /ˌdʒəʊvɪˈæləti/ *n* [u] 快乐

jowl /dʒaʊl/ *n usu pl* (jaw) 下颌; (fleshy fold) 双下巴; **heavy ~s** 肥厚的双下巴; **cheek by ~** 紧挨着

-jowled /ˈdʒaʊld/ *combining form* 下颌…的; **heavy~** 下颌肥厚的; **square~** 方下颌的

joy /dʒɔɪ/ *n* **1** [u] (delight) 高兴; **to dance/jump/shout** *etc.* **with** *or* **for ~** 高兴得跳起舞来/跳起来/叫起来等; **to do sth. for the (sheer** *or* **pure) ~ of it** （纯粹）出于喜欢做某事; **to find** *or* **take ~ in sth./doing sth.** 在某事物/做某事中得到快乐; **to sb.'s great ~** 使某人非常高兴的是; **I wish you ~ (of it)** iron 我向你道喜啦 **2** [c] (person that brings joy) 开心果; (thing that brings joy) 乐事; **the ~s of sth./doing sth.** 某事物/做某事的乐趣; **to be full of the ~s of spring** 兴高采烈 **3** [u] esp Brit colloq (satisfaction) 满足; **to have** *or* **get no ~ from** *or* **out of sth./sb.** 从某事物/某人那里得不到满意的结果

joyful /ˈdʒɔɪfl/ *adj* 快乐的 ‹*celebration, expression*›; 使人高兴的 ‹*news, event*›; **to be ~ about** *or* **over sth.** 为某事物感到高兴

joyfully /ˈdʒɔɪfəli/ *adv* 高兴地

joyfulness /ˈdʒɔɪflnɪs/ *n* [u] 快乐

joyless /ˈdʒɔɪlɪs/ *adj* 不快乐的 ‹*marriage, existence, people*›

joyous /ˈdʒɔɪəs/ *adj* esp liter 快乐的 ‹*celebration, occasion, spirit, song*›

joyride /ˈdʒɔɪraɪd/ *n* **1** (in stolen car) 开偷来的车兜风 **2** (fun ride) (in vehicle) 驾车兜风; (in aircraft) 开飞机兜风

joyrider /ˈdʒɔɪraɪdə(r)/ *n* 偷车兜风者

joyriding /ˈdʒɔɪraɪdɪŋ/ *n* [u] 偷车兜风

joystick /ˈdʒɔɪstɪk/ *n* **1** Aviat 驾驶杆 **2** (in video games) 游戏杆

JP *abbr* Brit = **Justice of the Peace**

Jr *abbr* = **junior A4**

jubilant /ˈdʒuːbɪlənt/ *adj* 欢腾的 ‹*crowd, shout*›; 喜气洋洋的 ‹*face, mood*›; **to be ~ about** *or* **at sth.** 为某事物欢欣鼓舞

jubilation /ˌdʒuːbɪˈleɪʃn/ *n* [u] **1** (joy) 欢腾; **~ about** *or* **at sth.** 为某事物欢欣鼓舞 **2** (rejoicing) 欢庆

jubilee /ˈdʒuːbɪliː/ *n* 周年庆祝; **the ~ celebrations** 周年欢庆

Judaic /dʒuːˈdeɪɪk/ *adj* **1** (of the ancient Jews) 希伯来人的 ‹*tradition, law*› **2** (of Judaism) 犹太教的 ‹*study, thought*›

Judaism /ˈdʒuːdeɪɪzəm, Amer -dɪɪzəm/ *n* [u] 犹太教

Judas /ˈdʒuːdəs/ *pr n* **1** Bible 犹大; **~ Iscariot** 加略人犹大 **2** fig (traitor) 叛徒

judder /ˈdʒʌdə(r)/ Brit
A *vi* «*train, machine, wheel*» 剧烈震动; **to ~ to a halt** 在剧烈震动中停下来
B *n* 剧烈震动

judge /dʒʌdʒ/
A *n* **1** Jur 法官; **to appear before a ~** 出庭受审; **J~ Brown** 布朗法官 **2** (in competition, sporting event, show) 裁判; **a panel of ~s** 评委会 **3** fig (authority) 鉴定人; **to be a good/bad ~ of sth.** 是鉴别某物的行家/外行; **an excellent ~ of character** 很善于鉴人者; **to be no ~ (of sth.)** （对某事）不在行; **I'll be** *or* **let me be the ~ of that** 让我来判断吧
B *vt* **1** (consider) 判断; **to ~ sb./sth. by** *or* **on sth.** 根据某事物判断某人/某事物; **to ~ sb./sth. (to be) sth.** 认为某人/某事物是某事物; **the operation was ~d a great success** 手术被认为非常成功; **we ~d it right to tell you** 我们认为应该告诉你; **I could not ~ whether this remark was an insult or a compliment** 我判断不出这句话是侮辱还是恭维; **to ~ a book by its cover** fig 以貌取人 **2** (estimate) 估计; **I ~d him to be about fifty** 我估计他年龄在 50 岁左右; **to ~ the moment well** 准确判断时机 **3** (in competition) 担任…的裁判; **a panel of experts will ~ the entries** 专家小组将对参赛作品作出评判 **4** (pass judgement on) 评价; **who are you to ~ others?** 你有什么资格对别人评头论足? **5** Jur (decide) «*judge, court*» 审理 ‹*case, matter*› **6** Jur (give verdict on) «*judge, court*» 判决 ‹*defendant, prisoner*›; **she was ~d innocent of murder** 法庭判决她的谋杀罪名不成立
C *vi* **1** (form opinion) 判断; **to ~ by** *or* **from sth.** 根据某事物来判断; **to ~ for oneself** 自己作出判断; **as far as I can ~, all of them are to blame** 依我看，他们都有责任 **2** (pass judgement) 评价; **who are you to ~?** 你有什么资格进行评价? **3** (in competition, sporting event, show) 担任裁判 **4** Jur 判案; **to ~ leniently/harshly** 判案宽松/苛刻

judge advocate *n* 军事检察官

judgement, judgment /ˈdʒʌdʒmənt/ *n* **1** [u] (discernment) 判断力; **to have sound ~** 有正确的判断力; **to lack ~** 缺乏判断力; **a lack of ~** 判断力的不足; **an error of ~** 判断错误; **to use one's (own) ~** 发挥（自己的）判断力; **he succeeded, more by luck than by ~** 他成功了，主要是靠运气而非判断力 **2** [u and c] (opinion) 看法; **to make a ~ about sb./sth.** 对某人/某事物作出评价; **I think you made an unfair ~ of his character** 我觉得你对他品格的评价不公正; **to give one's ~ on sb./sth.** 对某人/某事物给予评价; **in my ~, ...** 依我看，…; **my (personal) ~ is that ..., it is my (personal) ~ that ...** 依我（个人）来看…; **to reserve ~** 暂时不作评论; **to do sth. against one's better ~** 违心地做某事; **who am I to pass ~ on her behaviour?** 我有什么资格对她的行为说三道四呢? ; **to sit in ~ on** *or* **over sb./sth.** 参加对某人/某事物的评判 **3** [u and c] Jur 判决; **the claimant obtained ~ in his favour** 原告得到了有利于他的判决; **to hand down** *or* **pronounce** *or* **pass ~ (on sb.)** 宣布（对某人的）判决; **the court has yet to pass ~** 法庭尚未宣布判决结果; **the judge decided to reserve ~ on the case** 法官决定暂不对本案作出判决 **4** [c] formal (punishment, retribution) 报应; **some saw her sudden blindness as a ~ on her behaviour** 有些人认为她眼睛突然失明是她所作所为的报应; **divine ~** Relig 天谴

judgemental, judgmental /ˌdʒʌdʒˈmentl/ *adj* **1** (critical) 苛刻的 ‹*person, remark, attitude*› **2** (showing judgement) 下结论的 ‹*person*›; 判断的 ‹*remark*›

Judgement Day, Judgment Day *n* [上帝的] 最后审判日

judicial /dʒuːˈdɪʃl/ *adj attrib* **1** (legal) 司法的 ‹*system, process*›; **to bring ~ proceedings against sb.** 对某人正式提起诉讼 **2** (of a judge) 法官的 ‹*review, inquiry, appointment*› **3** (impartial) 公正明断的 ‹*mind, faculty*›

judicial: ~ murder *n* [u and c] 合法但不公正的死刑判决; **~ review** *n* [u] **1** Brit 案件复审; **2** Amer [最高法院的] 司法审查

judiciary /dʒuːˈdɪʃɪəri, Amer -ʃieri/ *n* [u] **1** (system) 司法系统 **2** + *v sing or pl* (judges) 法官; **the federal ~** Amer 联邦法官

judicious /dʒuːˈdɪʃəs/ *adj* 审慎的 ‹*remark, investment, selection*›; **it would be ~ to ...** …是明智的

judiciously /dʒuːˈdɪʃəsli/ *adv* 审慎地 ‹*remark, invest, select*›; **a ~ worded letter** 一封措词审慎的信

judo /ˈdʒuːdəʊ/ ▸**p. 307** *n* [u] 柔道; **a ~ champion/contest** 柔道冠军/比赛

jug /dʒʌg/
A *n* **1** [c] Brit (pitcher) 壶; (amount) 一罐; **a ~ of cream/juice** 一罐奶油/果汁 **2** [c] Amer (jar) 大罐 **3** [u] colloq (prison) 监狱
B **jugs** *npl* Amer taboo sl 奶子
C *vt* (*pres p etc.* **-gg-**) **1** Culin 炖 ‹*meat*›; **~ged hare** 炖野兔 **2** Amer colloq (imprison) 把…关进监狱

jug: ~ band *n* 即兴坛罐乐队 [用罐子等粗陋的临时性乐器演奏爵士乐、蓝调、乡村音乐等]; **~-eared** *adj* pej 长着招风耳的

jugful /ˈdʒʌgfʊl/ *n* Brit 一罐

juggernaut /ˈdʒʌgənɔːt/ *n* **1** Brit (large, heavy vehicle) 重型卡车 **2** fig 不可抗拒的力量

juggle /ˈdʒʌgl/
A *vi* **1** lit «*juggler*» 玩抛接杂耍; **she's learning to ~ with clubs** 她正在学习玩甩棒 **2** **to ~ with sth.** fig (manage simultaneously) 同时应付某事物 **3** fig (manipulate) **to ~ with sth.** 篡改 ‹*figures, budget*›; 把…调来调去 ‹*schedule, hours*›; **to ~ with the accounts** 在账目上搞鬼
B *vt* **1** lit «*juggler*» 抛接 ‹*balls, clubs*› **2** fig (cope with) 同时应付 ‹*roles, demands*›; **to ~ a career and a family** 兼顾事业与家庭; **to ~ three girlfriends** 周旋在 3 个女朋友之间 **3** fig (manipulate) 篡改 ‹*figures, facts*›; (play with) 把…调来调去 ‹*schedule, hours*›

juggler /ˈdʒʌglə(r)/ *n* 抛接杂技演员

Jugoslav /ˈjuːgəslɑːv/ *adj, n* Hist = **Yugoslav**

Jugoslavia /ˌjuːgəˈslɑːvɪə/ *pr n* Hist = **Yugoslavia**

jugular /ˈdʒʌgjʊlə(r)/
A *n* 颈静脉; **to go (straight) for the ~** （直接）攻击要害
B *adj attrib* 颈的; **the ~ vein** 颈静脉

juice /dʒuːs/
A *n* **1** [u and c] (of fruit) 果汁; (of vegetable) 蔬菜汁; **~s** (of meat) 肉汁 **2** [u] (sap) [植物的] 汁液 **3** [c] **~s** *pl* (in stomach) 胃液 **4** [u] colloq (petrol) 汽油 **5** [u] colloq (electricity) 电; **to turn on the ~** 接通电源
B *vt* 榨出…的汁 ‹*fruit, vegetable*›

Phrasal verb

• **juice up** *vt* [**~ sth. up, ~ up sth.**] Amer colloq 使生动有趣

juice extractor *n* = **juicer**

juicer /ˈdʒuːsə(r)/ *n* 榨汁机

juiciness /ˈdʒuːsɪnɪs/ *n* [u] 多汁

juicy /ˈdʒuːsi/ *adj* **1** Culin 多汁的 ‹*fruit, meat*› **2** fig (racy) 富于刺激性的 ‹*scenes, details*›; **~ gossip** 绯闻; **a ~ story** 花边趣闻 **3** colloq (interesting) 生动有趣的 ‹*problem, part*› **4** colloq (profitable) 利润丰厚的 ‹*deal, contract*›

ju-jitsu, jujitsu /dʒuːˈdʒɪtsuː/ ▸**p. 307** *n* [u] 柔术

jujube /ˈdʒuːdʒuːb/ *n* **1** (berry) 枣子 **2** (shrub) **~ (bush)** 枣树

jukebox /ˈdʒuːkbɒks/ *n* 投币式自动点唱机

Jul *abbr* = **July**

julep /ˈdʒuːlɪp/ *n* esp Amer 冰镇薄荷酒

Julian /ˈdʒuːlɪən/
A *pr n* 朱利安
B *adj attrib* **the ~ calendar** 儒略历 [古罗马尤利乌斯・恺撒执政时期开始使用的历法]

July /dʒuːˈlaɪ/ ▸**p. 490** *n* 七月; **last/this/next ~** 上个/本年/下个七月份; **in early/late ~** 七月上旬/下旬; **~ weather/morning** 七月的天气/早晨

jumble /ˈdʒʌmbl/
A *vt* **1** lit 胡乱堆放 ‹*objects*›; **to be ~d (up)** 乱成一团 **2** fig 混淆 ‹*facts, images*›; 使…混乱 ‹*feelings*›
B *n* **1** [c] (of objects) 杂乱的一堆; (of ideas, feeling) 混乱 **2** [u] Brit (for sale) [待义卖的] 一堆旧杂物

jumble sale *n* Brit 旧杂物义卖

jumbo /ˈdʒʌmbəʊ/
A *n* **1** child lang (elephant) 大象 **2** colloq = **jumbo jet**
B *modif* 特大的 ‹*bag, size*›

jumbo jet *n* 巨型喷气式飞机

jump /dʒʌmp/
A *vi* **1** (leap) 跳; **to ~ over sth.** 翻越 ‹*gate, fence, wall*›; **to ~ across sth.** 跨过 ‹*ditch, gap, stream*›; **to ~ into sth.** 跳入 ‹*air, river, pit*›; **to ~ into bed with sb.** colloq 直接和某人上床; **to ~ on to sth.** 跳到…上 ‹*roof, table, bus*›; **to ~ out of sth.** 跳出 ‹*bed, window, tower*›; **to ~ from sth.** 从…上跳下

j

‹plane, car›; **to ~ clear (of sth.)** 逃离（某事物）; **I managed to ~ clear of the oncoming truck** 我跳到一边避开了后面开来的卡车; **to ~ for joy** lit 高兴得手舞足蹈; fig 欢欣鼓舞; **to ~ down sb.'s throat** colloq 愤怒地反驳某人; **go and ~ in the lake** or **river!, go and take a running ~!** colloq dated 滚开！; **to ~ up and down** lit 上窜下跳; fig colloq (be angry) 暴跳; (be upset) 躁动不安; (be excited) 手舞足蹈; **to ~ in line** Amer 插队 **2** (move or act quickly) 快速行动; **to ~ at sb.'s command** 听到某人命令后迅速行动; **to ~ to one's feet** 一跃而起; **~ to it!** colloq 赶快行动！; **to make sb. ~** 促使某人行动; **to ~ to conclusions** 匆忙下结论; **to ~ to sb.'s defence** 积极为某人辩护 **3** (start) 吃惊; **to make sb. ~** 使某人大吃一惊; **sb.'s heart ~s** 某人心中一惊; **to ~ out of one's skin** colloq 大吃一惊 **4** (increase suddenly) «*amount, value, profits, expenditure*» 激增; **dividends ~ed by 20 per cent that year** 那年的红利猛增了 20%; **sales ~ed from £2.7 billion to £3.5 billion** 销售额从 27 亿英镑猛增到 35 亿英镑 **5** (change suddenly) 迅速转变; **to ~ from one topic to another** 从一个话题跳到另一个话题 **6** (move or jerk suddenly) 突然跳动; **the needle ~ed across the dial** 指针在刻度盘上乱摆 **7** **to be ~ing** Amer colloq 非常活跃; **the joint is really ~ing tonight** 今晚店里真热闹

B *vt* **1** (leap over) 跳过 ‹*ditch, gap, stream*›; 翻过 ‹*gate, fence, wall*›; **to ~ the gun** colloq (in race) «*runner, athlete*» 抢跑; (act prematurely) 贸然行动; **to ~ the lights** Brit colloq «*person, car*» 闯红灯; **to ~ ship** «*sailor*» 未经允许离船; (leave organization) 擅自离职; **to ~ the queue** Brit 插队 **2** (cause to leap) 使跃起; **she ~ed her horse over the hedge** 她策马越过了树篱 **3** (cover by leaping) 跳越 ‹*distance*›; **she has ~ed 2.2 metres** 她跳过了 2.2 米 **4** (omit) 略去 ‹*step*›; **to ~ a stage** (in promotion hierarchy) 越级; (in argument) 省略步骤 **5** (be dislodged from) «*carriage*» 脱离 ‹*track*›; **to ~ the rails** «*train*» 出轨 **6** esp Amer (board) 跳上 ‹*train, bus*›

C *n* **1** (leap) 跳; **to give a ~ for joy** 高兴得跳起来; **she cleared the distance in one ~** 这个距离她一跳而过; **to be one ~ ahead (of sb.)** 领先（某人）一步; **to get** or **have the ~ on sb.** colloq 抢在某人之前 **2** Sport (barrier) 障碍物 **3** (sudden movement) 惊跳; **I woke with a ~** 我突然惊醒了; **to give a ~ (of fright)** 吓了一跳 **4** (sudden increase) 突升; **a huge ~ in profits/expenditure** 利润/支出的激增 **5** (sudden transition) 突然跨越; **the great ~ forward to a new technological era** 步入新技术时代的巨大飞跃; **she's made the ~ from deputy to director** 她从副手一下子晋升为主任

Phrasal verbs

- **jump at** *vt* [**~ at sth.**] 欣然接受 ‹*offer, opportunity, suggestion*›
- **jump back** *vi* **1** (leap back) 迅速后退; **to ~ back from sb./sth.** 迅速离开某人/某物 **2** (return to position) ‹*lever, spring*› 归位
- **jump down** *vi* 跳下来; **to ~ down from** or **off sth.** 从…上跳下来 ‹*wall, steps, ladder*›
- **jump in** *vi* **1** (leap into water, pool, hole) 跳入; **she liked swimming but was nervous of ~ing in** 她喜欢游泳，但是害怕跳水 **2** colloq (get in car) 跳上车 **3** colloq (interrupt) 插话; **before she could finish, he ~ed in with an objection** 她话还没说完，他就插嘴反对
- **jump off**

A *vt* [**~ off sth.**] 从…上跳下来 ‹*steps, diving board, bus*›
B *vi* 跳下来

- **jump on**

A *vt* [**~ on sb./sth.**]
1 colloq (get on quickly) 跳上 ‹*bus, train, horse*› **2** (leap on) 跳到…上面 ‹*bed*› **3** (attack physically) 突然袭击 **4** colloq (criticize) 训斥; **she ~ed on me for answering her back** 她因为我跟她顶嘴就训了我一通
B *vi* colloq 跳上; **as soon as the train drew up, they ~ed on to get a seat** 火车刚刚停下，他们就跳上车抢占座位

- **jump out** *vi* **1** (leap out) 跳出; **to ~ out of the window** 跳窗而出 **2** **to ~ out of sth.** colloq (get out quickly) 从…上跳下来 ‹*bed, train, bus*› **3** **to ~ out in front of sb./sth.** (appear suddenly) 突然出现在某人/某物面前; **a figure suddenly ~ed out from behind the tree** 一个身影突然从树后跳了出来; **she just ~ed out in front of me** 她一下子出现在我面前
- **jump out at** *vt* [**~ out at sb.**]
1 (surprise, attack) 突如其来地冲向 **2** (be obvious) 极易引起…的注意; **the mistakes in the figures ~ed out at me** 我一眼就看出数字有错误
- **jump up** *vi* **1** (stand up from seat, bed, floor) 突然站起来; **he ~ed up immediately and offered me his seat** 他立刻站起来给我让座 **2** **to ~ up on (to) sth.** (leap upwards) 跳上某物

jump cables *npl* Amer = **jump leads**

jumpcut /ˈdʒʌmpkʌt/
A *n* 跳切 [指电影或电视中场景的跳跃式切换]
B **jump-cut** *vi* 跳切

jumped-up *adj attrib* colloq 妄自尊大的 ‹*clerk, official*›

jumper /ˈdʒʌmpə(r)/ *n* **1** Brit (sweater) 针织套衫 **2** Amer = **pinafore dress** **3** (person) 跳跃者; (animal) 跳跃动物

jumper cables *npl* Amer = **jump leads**

jumping: ~ bean *n* **(Mexican) ~ bean** 跳豆; **~ jack** *n* **1** esp Amer (jump) 立定跳远; **he's good at doing ~ jacks** 他擅长立定跳远; **2** (toy) 提线木偶; **3** Brit dated (firework) 跳爆竹; **~-off place, ~-off point** *ns* 起点

jump: ~ jet *n* 垂直起降喷气机; **~ jockey** ▸p. 409 *n* 障碍赛马骑手; **~ leads** *npl* Brit 跨接引线; **~-off** *n* 障碍赛马决胜赛; **~ rope** *n* Amer 跳绳; **~ seat** *n* esp Amer [汽车或飞机里的] 折叠式座椅

jump-start
A /ˌdʒʌmpˈstɑːt/ *vt* **1** Aut (push-start) 助推启动; (with leads) 用跨接引线启动 **2** fig (kick-start) 推动 ‹*career, economy, market*›
B /ˈdʒʌmpstɑːt/ *n* **1** Aut (push-starting) 助推启动; (with leads) 跨接引线启动; **to give sb. a ~** 帮助某人推车启动 **2** fig (impetus) 推动力; **to give sth. a ~** 推动某事物发展

jump suit *n* [女式] 连衫裤

jumpy /ˈdʒʌmpi/ *adj usu pred* 紧张不安的

Jun *abbr* = **June**

junction /ˈdʒʌŋkʃn/ *n* **1** (point where two or more things join) 会合处 **2** (of roads) 交叉路口 **3** Rail 枢纽站

junction box *n* 分线盒

juncture /ˈdʒʌŋktʃə(r)/ *n* formal 关头; **at this (critical) ~** 在此（紧急）时刻

June /dʒuːn/ ▸p. 490 *n* 六月; **last/this/next ~** 上个/本年/下个六月份; **in early/late ~** 六月上旬/下旬; **~ weather/morning** 六月的天气/早晨

June bug *n* 六月鳃金龟

Jungian /ˈjʊŋɪən/ *adj* 荣格的; **~ psychology/analysis** 荣格心理学/分析法

jungle /ˈdʒʌŋgl/ *n* **1** lit 热带丛林; **the law of the ~** 丛林法则; **~ tribes/plants** 热带丛林部落/植物 **2** (tangled mass) 杂乱的一堆; **a ~ of flowers** 乱蓬蓬的一丛花 **3** fig (difficult situation) 弱肉强食; (confusion) 混乱; **a ~ of regulations** 乱七八糟的规章

jungle: ~ fever *n* [u] 丛林热; **~ fowl** *n* (*pl* **~ fowl**) 原鸡; **~ gym** *n* Amer 儿童攀爬架; **~ juice** *n* [u] colloq 家酿烈酒; **~ music** *n* [u] 丛林音乐; **~ warfare** *n* [u] 丛林战

junior /ˈdʒuːnɪə(r)/
A *adj* **1** (younger) 较年幼的; **to be ~ to sb. by two years** 比某人小两岁 **2** (low-ranking) 级别较低的 ‹*official, partner*›; **to be ~ to sb. (in sth.)** （在某方面）地位比某人低 **3** *attrib* (for youth) 适合青少年的 ‹*division, fashion*›; 少年组的 ‹*league, player*› **4** (*also* **Junior**) esp Amer (in name) 小; **Bob Mortimer ~** 小鲍勃·莫蒂默
B *n* **1** (younger person) 年少者; **to be x years sb.'s ~, to be sb.'s ~ by x years** 小某人 X 岁 **2** (low-ranking worker) 职位较低者; **the office ~** 办公室初级文员 **3** Amer colloq (as form of address) 大儿子 **4** Brit Sch (junior school student) 小学生 **5** Amer Sch, Univ (third-year student) [四年制中学或大学的] 三年级学生

junior: ~ clerk *n* 低级文员; **~ college** *n* Amer 两年制专科学校; **~ doctor** *n* Brit 见习医生; **~ high school** *n* Amer 初级中学; **~ management** *n* [u] 初级管理; **~ manager** *n* 助理经理; **~ minister** *n* 助理部长; **~ partner** *n* 低级合伙人; **~ rating** *n* Brit 初级水手; **~ school** *n* Brit 小学; **~ seaman** *n* Brit [海军] 列兵; **~ technician** *n* Brit [空军] 初级技师

juniper /ˈdʒuːnɪpə(r)/ *n* **~ (bush)** 杜松; **~ berry** or **berries** 杜松子

junk¹ /dʒʌŋk/ colloq
A *n* [u] **1** (garbage) 垃圾; **~ dealer/market** 废品商/市场 **2** (second-hand items) 二手货; (poor quality items) 次品 **3** pej (stuff) 破烂货 **4** fig (nonsense) 胡说八道 **5** sl (drugs) 毒品 [尤指海洛因]
B *vt* 丢弃 ‹*objects*›; 抛弃 ‹*ideals, friends*›

junk² *n* (boat) 中国式帆船

junk: ~ bond *n* 垃圾债券; **the ~ bond market** 垃圾债券市场; **~ DNA** *n* [u] 垃圾 DNA [指不能编码蛋白质、看似无用的DNA序列]; **~ email** *n* 垃圾（电子）邮件

junket /ˈdʒʌŋkɪt/
A *n* **1** [u] (pudding) 乳冻甜食 **2** [c] colloq pej (paid trip) [政府官员的] 公费旅游 **3** [c] colloq pej (party) 欢宴
B *vi* colloq **1** pej (travel) 公费旅游 **2** (celebrate) 花公费庆祝

junketing, junketting /ˈdʒʌŋkɪtɪŋ/ *n* [u] colloq pej **1** (trips) 公费旅游 **2** (celebrating) 公费庆典

junk food *n* [u] 垃圾食品

junkie /ˈdʒʌŋki/ *n* colloq 上瘾的人; **a TV/news ~** 电视迷/新闻迷

junk: ~ mail *n* [u] 垃圾邮件; **~ shop** *n* 旧货店

junky /ˈdʒʌŋki/ *n* colloq = **junkie**

junkyard /ˈdʒʌŋkjɑːd/ *n* Amer 废品站

junta /ˈdʒʌntə/ *n* + *v sing or pl* usu pej [以武力夺取政权的] 军人集团

Jupiter /ˈdʒuːpɪtə(r)/ *pr n* 木星

Jurassic /dʒʊəˈræsɪk/
A *adj* (of the period) 侏罗纪的; (of the rock system) 侏罗系的
B *n* **the ~** (period) 侏罗纪; (rock system) 侏罗系

jurisdiction /ˌdʒʊərɪsˈdɪkʃn/ *n* **1** [u] Jur (power) 司法权 **2** [u] Jur (sphere) 管辖权; **to come within** or **under/to fall outside a court's ~** 在法院的管辖权之内/外 **3** [c] Admin 权限; **to come within** or **under/to fall outside sb.'s ~** 在某人的权限之内/外 **4** [c] (territory) 管辖区域

jurisprudence /ˌdʒʊərɪsˈpruːdns/ *n* [u] formal **1** (theory of law) 法学 **2** (precedents) 法庭判例

jurist /ˈdʒʊərɪst/ ▸p. 409 *n* **1** (expert) 法学家 **2** Amer (lawyer) 律师; (judge) 法官

juror /ˈdʒʊərə(r)/ *n* 陪审员

jury /ˈdʒʊəri/ *n* + *v sing or pl* **1** Jur 陪审团; **trial by ~** 陪审团审判; **the ~ is out** lit 陪审团尚未作出裁定; fig 争端悬而未决 **2** (at competition) 评委会

jury: ~ box *n* 陪审团席; **~ duty** *n* [u] 参与陪审期; **~man** /-mən/ *n* 男陪审员; **~-rigged** *adj* esp Amer 临时凑成的; **~ service** *n* Brit **= ~ duty**; **~ system** *n* 陪审员制度; **~woman** *n* 女陪审员

just[1] /dʒʌst/

A *adv* 1 (exactly, precisely) 恰好; **~ then, ~ at that moment** 就在那时; **~ in time** 刚好及时; **not ~ yet** 这会儿还不; **~ here/there** 就在这儿/那儿; **that's ~ it** *or* **the trouble!** 问题就在这里！; **that's ~ the point!** 就是这个意思！; **~ by the library** 就在图书馆旁边; **she looks ~ like her mother** 她看上去跟她母亲一模一样; **~ what do you think you're doing?** 你以为你在干什么？; **~ how many there are isn't known** 究竟有多少还不清楚; **~ as I thought: he was lying** 果然不出我所料：他在撒谎; **it's ~ on six** Brit 现在是6点整; **he likes everything to be ~ so** 他喜欢什么事情都井井有条; **~ so!** formal (expressing agreement) 没错！; **~ as you wish** formal 由你决定 2 (very recently) 刚才; **it has ~ been varnished** 这东西刚上过清漆; **you've missed him: he's ~ left** 你没赶上，他刚走; **I've only ~ noticed it** 我才注意到它; **I'm ~ back** 我刚回来 3 (at this or that very moment) 此刻; **to be ~ doing sth.** 正在做某事; **I'm ~ finishing the letter** 这封信我快写完了; **I'm ~ off!** 我走了！ 4 (in a few moments) 马上; **to be ~ about to do sth.** 正要去做某事; **to be ~ going to do sth.** 正打算去做某事; **I was ~ going to tell you when ...** 我刚要告诉你，这时… 5 (shortly) 不久; **he arrived ~ after** 他随后就到了; **~ before/after midnight** 就在午夜前/午夜后; **I get nervous ~ before, but once I'm on stage, I'm fine** 就在刚才我还很紧张，但是一上了台，我就没事了 6 (simply) 只是; **it's not ~ my imagination** 这并非只是我的想象; **there's ~ one method** 只有一种方法; **I'm not angry, ~ disappointed** 我没有生气，只是失望; **~ for fun** *or* **a laugh** 只是好玩; **~ two days ago** 就在两天前; **I'd ~ like to say ...** 我只是想说…; **I was ~ wondering if ...** 我只是在想，是否…; **I ~ can't remember** 我根本想不起来; **she ~ won't listen** 她就是不愿意听; **~ my luck!** 我就是这么倒霉！; **he did it ~ to annoy us** 他这么做完全是为了惹我们生气; **~ in case** 以防万一; **~ a moment** *or* **minute** *or* **second** (please wait) 请稍等; (when interrupting, disagreeing) 且慢 7 (barely) 勉强地; **he's ~ 20** 他刚满20岁; **he only ~ passed the exam** 他考试勉强及格 8 (slightly) 稍微; **~ over 20 kg** 20公斤刚过; **~ beyond** *or* **past** *or* **after the station** 刚过车站; **the skirt comes ~ below the knee** 裙子刚过膝 9 (absolutely) 确实; **that was ~ wonderful/delicious** 那简直太棒了/味道好极了; **that's ~ typical!** iron 果然与众不同啊！; **that's ~ great!** (enthusiastically) 棒极了！; (ironically) 真了不起！ 10 (easily) 轻易地; **I can ~ imagine it** 我很容易想象这事; **I can ~ smell the pine forests** 我一下子就闻到了松林的味道 11 (possibly) 也许; **it might** *or* **could ~ be true** 这件事也许是真的 12 (equally) 正好; **~ as big/well as ...** 正好和…一样大/好; **I can ~ as easily walk** 我一样可以毫不费力地步行; **~ as well** 无妨; **we might ~ as well have stayed at home** 我们当初还不如待在家里呢; **I'd ~ as soon stay in as go out tonight** 我今晚出去也行，待在家里也行; **I'd ~ as soon you didn't mention it to anyone** 我希望你不要把这件事告诉任何人 13 (with imperatives) [用于祈使句]; **~ keep quiet!** 请保持安静！; **~ think! you could have been hurt!** 好好想想吧！你原本会受伤的！; **~ look at the time!** 请看看时间吧！; **~ you dare!** 你敢！ 14 (in requests) [用于请求]; **if I could ~ interrupt you** 打搅一下; **if you could ~ hold this box** 请拿着这个盒子; **could you ~ wait five minutes?** 请等5分钟好吗？ 15 (in excuses) [表示歉意]; **I've ~ got a few things to do first** 我得先处理几件事 16 (expressing agreement) [表示同意]; **he's adorable! — isn't he ~!** 他真可爱！——可不是吗！

B just about *adv phr* 1 (almost) 几乎; **~ about cooked/finished** 差不多熟了/快完工了; **are you ready? — ~ about** 你准备好了吗？——快了; **~ about everything/anything** 几乎每件事/任何事; **I can ~ about see it/reach it** 我几乎看得见它/够得着它; **it's ~ about the most boring book I've ever read** 这几乎是我读过的最乏味的书 2 (approximately) 大概; **it's ~ about 10 o'clock** 现在大约是10点钟; **I've had ~ about enough!** 我差不多吃饱了！; fig 我受够了！ 3 (barely) 刚刚; **~ about enough for two** 刚刚够两个人的; **will we catch the plane? — ~ about!** 我们赶得上飞机吗？——勉强可以！

C just now *adv phr* 1 (at the moment) 此刻; **I'm busy ~ now** 我正忙着呢 2 (a short time ago) 刚才; **I saw him ~ now** 我刚见到过他

D just as *conj phr* 在…的同时; **he arrived ~ as I was leaving** 就在我要离开的时候，他到了

just[2]

A *adj* 1 (fair) 公正的 ‹*monarch, ruler*›; **it is only ~ to do sth./that ...** 做某事/…是公平合理的; **to be ~ in one's dealings with sb.** 在和某人打交道时保持公正 2 (morally right) 正义的; **to fight for a ~ cause** 为正义的事业而斗争 3 (deserved) 应得的 ‹*punishment, reward*›; **to get one's ~ desserts** 得到应有的惩罚 4 (well-founded) 有依据的 ‹*suspicion, comment, criticism*›; **without ~ cause** 无充分理由地 5 Jur 合法的 ‹*claim, title, request, inheritance*›

B the just *npl* 正派人; **to sleep the sleep of the ~** 踏实地睡觉

justice /'dʒʌstɪs/ *n* 1 [u] (fair treatment) 公正 2 [u] (fairness) 公平; **in ~ to sb.** 出于对某人的公平; **to do ~ to sb./sth., to do sb./sth. ~** 公平对待某人/某事物; **to do ~ to a meal** 尽情享用一餐; **to do oneself ~** 充分发挥能力 3 [u] (the law) 司法; **a court of ~** 法院; **to obstruct the course of ~** 妨碍司法; **to bring sb. to ~** 将某人绳之以法 4 [c] Brit (judge) 法官; **Mr J~ Brown** 布朗法官先生 [对高等法院法官的称呼] 5 [u] (retribution) 惩罚

Justice: ~ Department *n* Amer 司法部; **~ Minister, Minister of ~** *ns* 司法部长; **~ of the Peace** *n* (*pl* **~s of the Peace**) Brit 治安法官

justifiable /'dʒʌstɪfaɪəbl/ *adj* 有理由的 ‹*anger, concern*›; 无可非议的 ‹*action*›; 可证明为正当的 ‹*use, claim*›

justifiable homicide *n* [u] 正当杀人 [出于自卫等原因]

justifiably /'dʒʌstɪfaɪəbli/ *adv* 情有可原地 ‹*angry, upset*›; 有理由地 ‹*proud, contented, cautious, happy*›

justification /ˌdʒʌstɪfɪ'keɪʃn/ *n* 1 [u] (reason) 理由; **~ of** *or* **for sth.** 做某事的理由; **with some/without any ~** 有几分理由地/无任何理由地 2 [u and c] (explanation) 辩解; **a ~ for sth.** 对某事物的辩解; **in ~ (of** *or* **for sth.)** 作为（对某事物的）解释 3 [u] Print 齐行

justified /'dʒʌstɪfaɪd/ *adj* 1 (having or done for a good reason) 有正当理由的 ‹*criticism, suspicion, actions*›; **to be quite/fully** *or* **completely ~ (in sth./in doing sth.)** （在某事中/做某事）颇有/完全有理由 2 Print 齐行的 ‹*text, line*›

justify /'dʒʌstɪfaɪ/ *vt* 1 (be reason for) «*events, facts*» 是…的正当理由 ‹*actions, decisions*›; **the end justifies the means** 只要目的正当，可以不择手段 2 (explain) «*person*» 为…辩解 ‹*actions, remark*›; **to ~ oneself** 为自己辩解; **to ~ doing sth.** 证明做某事是有道理的 3 Print 使…齐行 ‹*margin, text*›

just-in-time *adj attrib* «*manufacturing, production, stock control*» 适时制的 [指在需要时才将原料或部件送达以降低库存的做法]

justly /'dʒʌstli/ *adv* 1 (equitably) 公正地 ‹*administer, act, treat*› 2 (justifiably) 有理由地 ‹*criticized, angry*› 3 (deservedly) 应得地 ‹*punished, rewarded*›

justness /'dʒʌstnɪs/ *n* [u] 1 (aptness) 恰当 2 (reasonableness) 正当

jut /dʒʌt/ *vi* (*pres p etc.* **-tt-**) **to ~ (out)** «*bone, rock, chin, jaw*» 突出; **to ~ (out) over sth.** «*balcony*» 伸出到某物上方; **to ~ (out) into sth.** «*structure, wall*» 伸入某处; **to ~ (out) from sth.** «*rock*» 从某处突出

jute /dʒuːt/ *n* [u] 黄麻纤维; **~ rope** 黄麻绳索; **a ~ mill** 麻纺厂

jutting /'dʒʌtɪŋ/ *adj attrib* 突出的 ‹*bone, rock, chin, jaw*›

juvenile /'dʒuːvənaɪl/

A *n* 1 esp Jur 少年 2 Zool (animal) 幼兽; (bird) 雏鸟

B *adj* 1 *attrib* (young) 少年的 ‹*novel, arthritis*› 2 pej (childish) 幼稚的 ‹*behaviour, joke*› 3 Zool 幼兽的 ‹*behaviour*›; 雏鸟的 ‹*plumage, markings*›

juvenile: ~ court *n* 少年法庭; **~ crime** *n* [u] 少年犯罪; **~ delinquency** *n* [u] 少年犯罪; **~ delinquent** *n* 少年犯; **~ lead** *n* 青少年主角; **~ offender** *n* 少年犯

juxtapose /ˌdʒʌkstə'pəʊz/ *vt* formal 把…并列 ‹*photographs, materials, colours, styles*›; **to ~ sth. with sth.** 把某物和某物并列

juxtaposition /ˌdʒʌkstəpə'zɪʃn/ *n* [u] formal 并列; **in ~ with sth.** 与某物并列; **the ~ of different ideas** 不同观念的并列

Kk

K, k /keɪ/
A *n* (*pl* **Ks** *or* **K's**) [英语字母表的第11个字母]
B *abbr* **1** **K** colloq **= thousand(s)** 一千; **he earns £50～** 他挣5万英镑 **2** **k** Meas (of distance) **= kilometre(s)** 千米 **3** **K** Comput **= kilobyte(s)** 千字节; **64～ of memory** 64K内存 **4** ▸**p. 814 K** Meas (of temperature) **= kelvin**

Kabbalah /kəˈbɑːlə, ˈkæbələ/ *n* [犹太教的]神秘释经学

Kabbalistic /ˌkæbəˈlɪstɪk/ *adj* 神秘的

Kabul /ˈkɑːbl/ *pr n* 喀布尔

kaffeeklatsch /ˈkæfeɪklætʃ/ *n* Amer 咖啡叙谈会

kaffir /ˈkæfə(r)/ *n* offensive 卡菲尔人 [对非洲黑人的蔑称]

Kafkaesque /ˌkæfkəˈesk/ *adj* 卡夫卡式的

kaftan /ˈkæftæn/ *n* (dress) 宽大长袖女袍; (belted tunic) [男式束腰带的] 阿拉伯长袍

kagoul, kagoule /kəˈguːl/ *n* **= cagoule**

Kalahari /ˌkæləˈhɑːri/ *pr n* **the ～** 卡拉哈里沙漠

kale /keɪl/ *n* [u] **(curly) ～** 羽衣甘蓝

kaleidoscope /kəˈlaɪdəskəʊp/ *n* **1** (toy) 万花筒 **2** fig (colourful scene, changing pattern) 千变万化

kaleidoscopic /kəˌlaɪdəˈskɒpɪk/ *adj* 千变万化的 ‹*scenes, visions, patterns*›; 万花筒般的 ‹*images*›

kamikaze /ˌkæmɪˈkɑːzi/
A *n* **1** (aircraft) 神风突击机 [二战时期日本的自杀式战机] **2** (pilot) 神风队飞行员
B *adj* 自杀式的; **a ～ pilot/plane** 神风队飞行员/神风突击机

Kampala /kæmˈpɑːlə/ *pr n* 坎帕拉

Kampuchea /ˌkæmpʊˈtʃɪə/ *pr n* Hist **= Cambodia**

Kampuchean /ˌkæmpʊˈtʃɪən/ *adj, n* Hist **= Cambodian**

kangaroo /ˌkæŋgəˈruː/ *n* 袋鼠

kangaroo court *n* 袋鼠法庭 [指非法私设的法庭]

kanji /ˈkændʒi/ *n* [u] [日语中的] 汉字

Kansas /ˈkænzəs/ *pr n* 堪萨斯

kaolin /ˈkeɪəlɪn/ *n* [u] 高岭土

kapok /ˈkeɪpɒk/ *n* [u] 木棉

kaput /kæˈpʊt/ *adj pred* colloq 坏了的; **to go ～** 坏掉; **my heater and new kettle went ～ on the same day** 我的取暖器和新水壶在同一天坏了

karaoke /ˌkærɪˈəʊki, -keɪ/ *n* [u] 卡拉OK; **to sing ～** 唱卡拉OK; **a ～ machine** 卡拉OK机

karat /ˈkærət/ *n* Amer **= carat 1**

karate /kəˈrɑːti/ ▸**p. 307** *n* [u] 空手道

karma /ˈkɑːmə/ *n* **1** [u] Relig [佛教和印度教的] 羯磨 **2** [u and c] fig colloq (destiny) 命相; (good or bad luck resulting from one's actions) 因果报应; **good/bad ～** 善因缘/恶因缘

karst /kɑːst/ *n* [u] 喀斯特地貌

kart /kɑːt/ *n* 卡丁车

karting /ˈkɑːtɪŋ/ ▸**p. 307** *n* [u] 卡丁车比赛

Kashmir /kæʃˈmɪə(r)/ *pr n* 克什米尔

Kashmiri /kæʃˈmɪəri/ ▸**p. 503, p. 426**
A *adj* (of Kashmir) 克什米尔的; (of the people) 克什米尔人的; (of the language) 克什米尔语的
B *n* **1** [c] (person) 克什米尔人 **2** [u] (language) 克什米尔语

Kathmandu /ˌkætmænˈduː/ *pr n* 加德满都

kayak /ˈkaɪæk/
A *n* [有顶棚的] 独木舟
B *vi* 划独木舟

kayaker /ˈkaɪækə(r)/ *n* 划独木舟者

Kazakh /kəˈzæk, ˈkæzæk/ ▸**p. 503, p. 426**
A *adj* (of Kazakhstan) 哈萨克斯坦的; (of the people) 哈萨克斯坦人的; (of the language) 哈萨克斯坦语的
B *n* **1** [c] (person) 哈萨克斯坦人 **2** [u] (language) 哈萨克斯坦语

Kazakhstan /ˌkæzəkˈstɑːn/ *pr n* 哈萨克斯坦

kazoo /kəˈzuː/ *n* 卡祖笛

KB, Kb *abbr* **= kilobyte(s)** 千字节

kbyte *abbr* ▸**kilobyte**

KC *abbr* Brit **= King's Counsel**

kebab /kɪˈbæb/ *n* 烤肉串

kedgeree /ˈkedʒəriː, ˌkedʒəˈriː/ *n* [u] Brit 鱼蛋烩饭

keel /kiːl/ *n* 龙骨; **on an even ～** lit, fig 平稳地

Phrasal verb

- **keel over** *vi* **1** Naut «*ship*» 倾覆 **2** fig colloq «*tree, mast, person*» 倒下; «*structure*» 倒塌

keelhaul /ˈkiːlhɔːl/ *vt* Hist 把…拖过船底

keen[1] /kiːn/ *adj* **1** esp Brit (eager) 渴望的; **to be ～ (that) sb. should do sth., to be ～ on sb.'s doing sth., to be ～ for sb. to do sth.** 很希望某人做某事; **to look ～** 显出渴望的样子 **2** esp Brit (enthusiastic) 热心的; **to be ～ on sth.** 热衷于某事物; **to be ～ on doing sth.** *or* **to do sth.** 热衷于做某事; **my wife wants to go, but I'm not too ～** *or* **less than ～** 我妻子想去, 但我不太想去; **a ～ sportsman/supporter** 热心体育运动的人/热心支持者 **3** **to be ～ on sb./sth.** esp Brit colloq (attracted to) 对…着迷 ‹*person*›; 喜欢 ‹*idea*›; **to be mad ～ on sb./sth.** 对某人/某事物极度着迷; **I'm not too ～** *or* **not over-～ on the idea** 我不太喜欢这个主意 **4** (intense) 强烈的 ‹*desire, interest*›; **a ～ sense of loss/tradition** 强烈的失落感/传统意识 **5** (acute) 灵敏的 ‹*ear, sight, sense of smell*›; 敏锐的 ‹*mind, intelligence, powers of observation*›; **to have a ～ eye for sth.** 对某事物有灵敏的识别力 **6** (competitive) 激烈的 ‹*competition, debate*› **7** liter (sharp) 锋利的 ‹*blade, point*›; 寒冷刺骨的 ‹*wind, air*› **8** Brit (low) 低廉的 ‹*prices*›

keen[2] *vi* dated 恸哭; **to ～ over sb.** 为某人恸哭

keenly /ˈkiːnli/ *adv* **1** (eagerly) 渴望地; **the ～ awaited moment** 渴望已久的时刻 **2** (intensely) 强烈地 ‹*desired, interested*›; **his death will be ～ felt** 他的去世会让人深感悲痛 **3** (acutely) 敏锐地; **to be ～ aware of sth.** 深知某事物 **4** (passionately) 激烈地 ‹*fought, argued*›; **a ～ contested match** 竞争激烈的比赛 **5** (closely) 仔细地 ‹*watch, observe*›

keenness /ˈkiːnnɪs/ *n* [u] **1** (eagerness) 热切; **his ～ to share the joke** 他想把笑话讲给大家听的迫切心情 **2** (intensity) 强烈; **the ～ of one's grief/desire/ interest** 自己强烈的悲痛/渴望/兴趣 **3** (acuity) 敏锐 **4** (sharpness) 锋利; **the ～ of the wind** liter (coldness) 寒风的凛冽

keep /kiːp/
A *vt* (*pt, pp* **kept**) **1** (cause to remain) 使保持; **to ～ sth. clean/dry** 使某物保持清洁/干燥; **to ～ sb. awake/amused** 使某人醒着/开心; **to ～ sth. in one's head** 记住某事物; **to ～ sb. in suspense** 吊某人的胃口; **she kept her hands over her eyes** 她双手捂住了眼睛; **the hostages were kept in a cellar** 人质关在地窖里; **there's nothing to ～ me here** 已经没有什么理由能让我留在这里了 **2** (retain) 保留; **to ～ sb.'s attention** 保持某人的注意力; **～ the change** 不用找零钱; **to ～ a car for two days** 用两天车; **you can ～ sth.** colloq iron 某物你留着好了 **3** (reserve) 预留; **to ～ sth. for sb., to ～ sb. sth.** 为某人留某物; **she kept him a piece of cake** 她给他留了一块蛋糕; **to ～ some of the sandwiches for later** 留点儿三明治晚些时候再吃 **4** (put, store) 存放; **to ～ sth. in a box/drawer** *etc.* 把…放在箱子里/抽屉里等 ‹*object, money*›; **a place where the tools are kept** 放工具的地方 **5** (sustain) 使继续进行; **to ～ sth. going** 让…不熄灭 ‹*fire*›; 让…延续 ‹*tradition, discussion*›; **to ～ sb. waiting/talking/laughing** 让某人一直等/不停说话/笑个不停; **to ～ the water flowing** 让水保持流动; **to ～ sb. going** fig colloq 使某人坚持下去; **it was his work that kept him going** 他的工作是他活下去的动力; **a sandwich will ～ you going** 吃块三明治能顶饿 **6** (detain) 耽搁; **I won't ～ you (but) a minute** 我不会耽误你很久; **to ～ sb. for questioning** 拘留某人问话; **what kept you?** 什么事把你耽搁了? **7** (stock) 备有 ‹*products, goods*› **8** (own) 经营 ‹*store, shop*› **9** (maintain) 料理; **to ～ house** 料理家务; **the house was not badly kept** 房子收拾得不错; **she ～s two cars** 她有两辆汽车 **10** (raise and look after) 饲养 ‹*animal, pet*› **11** (support) 供养; **to ～ sb. in style** 供养某人过阔绰的生活; **he can afford to ～ servants** 他雇得起用人 **12** (maintain as record) 记录; **to ～ the accounts** 记账; **to ～ a diary** 写日记; **to ～ a note of sth.** 记下某事; **to ～ one's records up-to-date** 及时更新记录 **13** (honour, fulfil) 遵守; **to ～ the law** 遵守法律; **to ～ one's appointment/promise/word** 践约/遵守诺言/信守诺言 **14** (observe) 庆祝 ‹*holiday*›; 纪念 ‹*anniversary*› **15** Mus **to ～ time** *or* **the beat** 合着节拍 **16** archaic (protect) 保护; **the Lord bless thee and ～ thee** 愿主赐福予你, 保佑你; **to ～ sb./sth. from ...** 使某人/某事物免受…的侵害
B *vi* (*pt, pp* **kept**) **1** (maintain state) 保持状态; **to ～ warm/calm/fit** 保持温暖/镇静/健康; **to ～ on good terms with sb.** 与某人保持良好关系 **2** (continue) 继续; **to ～ doing sth.** 继续做某事; **to ～ going** (working) 继续工作下去;

k

(living) 坚持生活下去 3 (continue going) 一直前行; **to ～ straight on** 径直向前走; **to ～ west** 一直向西; **to ～ left** 靠左走 4 (do repeatedly) 反复做; **to ～ interrupting/forgetting** 老是插嘴/忘记; **the phone kept ringing** 电话响个不停 5 (remain in place) 留在某处; **to ～ indoors** 待在室内; **to ～ out of the rain** 躲雨 6 (stay fresh) 保持新鲜; **strawberries don't ～ very well** 草莓不易保鲜; **the meat will ～ for a few days** 这些肉可以保持几天不变质 7 (wait) 能耽搁; **this is very important: it won't ～!** 这很重要: 耽搁不得!; **I've got something to tell you — will it ～ till tomorrow?** 我有话对你说——等明天再说好吗? 8 colloq **how are you ～ing?** (how is your health?) 你身体好吗?; **he's been ～ing well lately** 他最近很健康

C *v refl* (*pt, pp* **kept**) 1 (maintain) **to ～ oneself clean/healthy** 使自己干净/健康 2 (support) **to ～ oneself** 养活自己

D *n* 1 [u] (maintenance) 生活费用; **to pay for sb.'s ～** 支付某人的生活费; **to work for one's ～** 为糊口而工作; **to earn one's ～** 自食其力; **that old horse isn't worth its ～** 那匹老马吃得多, 干得少 2 [c] Archit 城堡主楼

E for keeps *adv phr* colloq 永远; **I'm home for ～s this time** 这次回到家我再也不离开了

Phrasal verbs

• **keep after** *vt* [**～ after sb./sth.**]
1 (pursue) 紧紧追赶 ‹*thief, vehicle*› 2 (nag) 不断催 ‹*debtor*›; 唠唠叨叨地催 ‹*child*›

• **keep at** *vt* 1 [**～ at sth.**] (persevere at) 坚持 ‹*work, studies*›; **～ at it!** 加油! 2 **to ～ sb. at ...** (make persevere at) 使坚持 ‹*work, studies*›; **she kept him at his scales** 她让他一直练习音阶 3 [**～ at sb.**] colloq (nag) 缠住…不放

• **keep away**

A *vt* [**～ sb./sth. away**]
1 (repel) 赶走; **to ～ sb./sth. away from sb./sth.** 不让某人/某物接近某人/某物; **～ the flies away from the food** 别让苍蝇靠近食物 2 (prevent from going somewhere or doing sth.) 阻碍; **to ～ sb./sth. away from sb./sth.** 阻碍某人/某物接近某人/某物; **bad weather kept the tourists away** 恶劣的天气阻碍了游客前来旅游; **am I ～ing you away from your work?** 我妨碍你工作了吗?; **to ～ sth. away from small children** 把某物放在小孩拿不到的地方

B *vi* **to ～ away (from sb./sth.)** 避开 (某人/某事物); **～ away from the edge/that man** 离边缘/那个男人远一点

• **keep back**

A *vt* [**～ sb./sth. back, ～ back sb./sth.**]
1 (hold back) 阻挡 ‹*fans, cattle*›; **to ～ one's hair back with an elastic band** 用橡皮筋把头发束在脑后; **to ～ the crowd back from the stage** 阻挡观众靠近舞台 2 (restrain) 忍住 ‹*tears, laughter*› 3 (retain) 留出 ‹*money, food*› 4 (conceal) 隐瞒 ‹*information*›; **to ～ back the results of the survey** 不公布调查结果 5 (prevent) 妨碍 ‹*person*›; **don't let me ～ you back** 别让我误了你的事 6 Sch (cause to repeat year) 使…留级 ‹*student*›; **he was kept back a year** 他留了一级 7 Brit Sch (as punishment) 罚…留下 ‹*pupil*›; **to be kept back after school** 放学后被罚留在学校

B *vi* **to ～ back (from sb./sth.)** 不靠近 (某人/某事物); **～ back from the fire** 不要接近火; **he warned spectators to ～ well back** 他警告观众远远靠后站

• **keep down**

A *vt* [**～ sb./sth. down, ～ down sb./sth.**]
1 (hold down) 压住; **I put bricks on the corners of the tarpaulin to ～ it down** 我用砖压住油布的四角不让它翘起来; **～ that dog down!** 别让那只狗乱跳! 2 (repress) 压迫 ‹*person*›; **he won't be kept down** 他很难制服; **you can't ～ a good man down** 有志向的人是什么困难都压不倒的 3 (control) 控制 ‹*costs, pollution*›; **to ～ the weeds down** 除草 4 (reduce) 降低 ‹*interest rates, noise*›; **～ your voice down!** 小声点! 5 (hold in stomach) 不呕吐出来 ‹*food, liquid*›; **she couldn't ～ anything down** 她吃什么就吐什么 6 Brit Sch (cause to repeat year) 使…留级 ‹*student*›

B *vi* **～ down!** 蹲下!; **we kept down while the security patrol passed by on the other side of the wall** 保安巡逻队经过墙的另一边时, 我们蹲了下来

• **keep from**

A *vt* 1 **to ～ from doing sth.** (refrain) 忍住不做某事; **she couldn't ～ from laughing** 她忍俊不禁 2 **to ～ sb. from sth./doing sth.** (prevent) 使某人避免某事物/阻止某人做某事; **am I ～ing you from your work/doing your work?** 我耽误你工作了吗?; **the thing that kept me from dismissing her was ...** 我没解雇她的理由是… 3 [**～ sb./sth. from sth.**] (protect) 使…免受…侵害; **God will ～ you from harm** 上帝保佑你不受伤害; **to be kept from temptation** 远离诱惑 4 [**～ sth. from sb.**] (conceal) 对…隐瞒 5 [**～ sth. from sth.**] (stop from affecting) 使…不受…影响; **she could not ～ the dismay from her voice** 她声音里不禁透出沮丧

B *v refl* **to ～ oneself from doing sth.** 忍住不做某事; **I couldn't ～ myself from yawning** 我忍不住打起了哈欠

• **keep in**

A *vt* [**～ sb./sth. in, ～ in sb./sth.**]
1 (cause to stay indoors) 把…关在屋里 ‹*person*›; **the rain kept us in all day** 雨下了一整天, 我们无法出门; **to ～ sb. in for observation** (in hospital) 让某人留院观察 2 Sch (as punishment) 罚…课后留校 ‹*pupil*› 3 (wear) 不摘下 ‹*dentures, contact lenses*› 4 (hold in) 使收进来; **to wear a corset to ～ one's stomach in** 戴束腹以收紧肚子; **～ your elbows in!** 收起胳膊肘! 5 (restrain) 控制 ‹*emotions*› 6 **to ～ sb. in sth.** (provide with) 向某人供给某物; **he can't afford to ～ the children in shoes** 他连给孩子们买鞋的钱都没有

B *vi* **～ in!** 在路内侧走!

• **keep in with** *vt* [**～ in with sb.**] Brit colloq 与…保持良好关系

• **keep off**

A [**～ off sth.**] *vt*
1 (stay away from) 勿靠近 ‹*flowerbed, property*›; **'please ～ off the grass'** "请勿践踏草坪" 2 (not consume) 不吃 ‹*fatty foods*›; **to ～ off alcohol/drugs** 不喝烈性酒/吸毒 3 (not mention) 不提起 ‹*topic*›

B [**～ sth. off**] *vt* (not wear) 暂时不穿 ‹*shoes, clothes*›; **～ your hat off until you come out of the church** 出了教堂再把帽子戴上

C [**～ sth. off, ～ off sth.**] *vt* (keep from damaging) 不让…接近 ‹*pests*›; 不让…弄脏 ‹*rain, paint*›; **～ the paint off the glass** 别让油漆弄脏了玻璃; **this sheet ～s the dust off** 这张单子能挡灰尘; **～ the football off the flowerbeds** 不要把足球踢进花圃

D [**～ sb. off sth.**] *vt*
1 (stop from mentioning) 使…不提起; **～ her off the subject of money** 不要让她提钱的事 2 (stop from consuming) 使…不吃 ‹*fatty foods*›; **to ～ sb. off alcohol/cigarettes** 使某人戒酒/戒烟

E *vi* 1 (stay away) 不靠近; **～ off!** 离远点! 2 (not start) «*snow, storm*» 不下; **if the rain ～s off, we'll have lunch in the garden** 如果不下雨, 我们就在花园里吃午餐

• **keep on**

A *vi* **to ～ on doing sth.** (do repeatedly) 反复做某事; **to ～ on reminding sb.** 不断提醒某人

B *vt* [**～ sth./sb. on**]
1 (hold in place) 固定 ‹*hat, lid*› 2 (wear) 继续穿着 ‹*shoes, coat*›; **can I ～ my hat on?** 我可以不脱帽子吗? 3 (retain) 继续雇用 ‹*employee, worker*›; 继续使用 ‹*house, car*›; **she kept the flat on after she left London** 她离开伦敦后并没有把公寓退掉

C *vi* 1 (continue) **to ～ on with sth., to ～ on doing sth.** (not stop) 继续做某事; **to ～ on with one's studies** 继续学习; **the alarm kept on ringing** 闹铃响个不停 2 (continue on course) 继续前行; **～ on till you get to the station** 一直往前走到车站; **～ on past the station** 一直走过车站 3 **to ～ on about sb./sth./about doing sth.** pej (harp on) 就某人/某事物/做某事唠唠叨叨; **to ～ on about the exam** 老说考试的事情; **he does ～ on!** 他真够啰唆的!

• **keep on at** *vt* **to ～ on at sb. (to do sth.)** 纠缠某人 (做某事); **he kept on at me to take him to the funfair** 他缠着我要我带他去游乐场

• **keep out**

A *vi* 1 (not enter) 留在外面; **'～ out!'** "严禁入内!"; **to ～ out of sth.** 不进入 ‹*place*›; **to ～ out of the war zone** 不进入战区; **to ～ out of sb.'s way** *or* **out of the way of sb.** (not hinder) 不妨碍某人; (avoid) 避免与某人相见 2 **to ～ out of sth.** (avoid involvement in) 不卷入 ‹*argument, fight*›; **～ out of this!** 别管这事!; **he can't ～ out of mischief** 他动不动就搞恶作剧 3 **to ～ out of the sun/rain** (avoid exposure to) 避免日晒/避雨

B *vt* [**～ sb./sth. out**]
1 (stop from entering) 使不进入; **to ～ sb./sth. out of sth.** 阻止某人/某物进入 ‹*place*›; **～ that dog out of my bedroom!** 别让那条狗进我的卧室!; **to ～ sb./sth. out of sb.'s way** *or* **out of the way of sb.** (prevent from hindering) 使某人/某事物不妨碍某人; (prevent from being seen) 使某人见不到某人/某事物; **～ those toys out of my way!** 别让那些玩具挡我的路!; **～ the cat out of your brother's way** 别让你弟弟看见猫 2 **to ～ sb./sth. out of sth.** (prevent involvement in) 使某人/某事物不卷入某事; **～ him out of trouble!** 别让他惹麻烦! 3 (protect against) 抵御; **to ～ out the cold/rain** 御寒/挡雨; **to ～ the sun out of one's eyes** 让眼睛免受阳光直射 4 **to ～ sb./sth. out of sth.** (prevent exposure to) 使…不接触某事物 ‹*person, animal, plant*›; **～ the children out of danger** 让孩子们远离危险

• **keep to**

A [**～ to sth.**] *vt*
1 (follow) 不偏离 ‹*road*›; **to ～ to the path** 顺着小路走; **to ～ to the left** 靠左边走 2 (not deviate from) 执行 ‹*schedule, plan*›; 不背离 ‹*one's beliefs*›; **to ～ to the facts/the point** 坚持实事求是/不跑题; **～ to the script!** 按剧本表演! 3 (be bound by) 履行 ‹*promise, contract*›; 遵守 ‹*law*› 4 (stay in) 不离开 ‹*place*›; **to ～ to one's bed/room** 卧床不起/留在房间内; **to ～ to oneself** 不与人往来

B [**～ sb./sth. to sth.**] *vt*
1 (cause to follow) 使…不偏离 ‹*road*›; **to ～ sb. to the official route** 让某人不偏离官方指定路线 2 (cause to adhere to) 使…执行 ‹*schedule, plan*› 3 (bind by) 使履行 ‹*promise, contract*›; 使…遵守 ‹*law*› 4 (restrict) 使限制在…内 ‹*size, speed*›; **to ～ the new version to the same length as the original** 保持新版本与原版长度一致 5 **to ～ sth. to oneself** (not share) 不泄露 ‹*information, secret*›; **～ your opinions to yourself!** 把你的意见收起来吧!; **～ your hands to yourself!** colloq 放尊重点!

• **keep together**

A *vi* 1 (in group) 在一起; **～ together as we go through the cave** 穿过山洞时我们不能走散 2 (remain synchronized) 协调一致

B *vt* [**～ sb./sth. together**]
1 (in group) 使在一起; **～ these papers together in a folder** 把这些文件放在一个文件夹里 2 (synchronize) 使…协调一致 ‹*orchestra, crew, dancers*›

• **keep up**

A *vi* 1 (progress at same speed) «*person, animal, car*» 跟上; **I managed to ～ up by taking work home in the evenings** 我把工作带回家晚上做才跟上了进度 2 (develop at same rate) «*nation, industry, rival*» 保持同步 3 (learn at same rate) 跟上功课; **to have no difficulty**

k

~ing up 跟上功课毫无困难 **4** (increase at same rate) «*prices, wages, production*» 同步增长; **inflation is rising so fast that wages can't ~ up** 通货膨胀迅速加剧，工资很难同步增长 **5** (continue) «*bad weather, rain*» 持续不停 **6** fig (follow) 理解; **she changes her mind so often, I can't ~ up** 她主意变来变去，让我无所适从

B [**~ sth. up, ~ up sth.**] *vt*
1 (hold up) 使不下落; **you won't be able to ~ your umbrella up in this wind** 风这么大，你没法打伞的; **six pillars ~ the roof up** 6 根柱子支撑着屋顶 **2** (continue) 使…继续下去 ‹*friendship, attack*›; 继续 ‹*studies, lessons*›; 沿袭 ‹*tradition, custom*›; **I can't ~ this up for long** 我坚持不了多久; **to ~ up the bombardment all night** 持续轰炸一整夜; **to ~ up a correspondence with sb.** 与某人保持书信来往; **to ~ up the payments** 按时分期付款; **~ up the good work!** 继续好好干!; **~ it up!** 再接再厉! **3** (maintain at high level) 保持 ‹*strength*›; **to ~ one's spirits up** 保持高昂的情绪; **to ~ up moral standards** 维持道德标准; **to ~ up the pressure (on sb.) (for sth.)** (为某事物) (对某人) 继续施加压力

C [**~ sb. up**] *vt* (prevent from sleeping) 使不能睡觉; **I hope I haven't kept you up** 希望我没有耽误你睡觉

• **keep up with** *vt* [**~ up with sb./sth.**]
1 (progress at same speed as) 跟上…的速度 ‹*person, animal*›; **to ~ up with the car in front** 跟上前面那辆车; **to have difficulty ~ing up with the others** 很难跟上其他人 **2** (avoid backlog of) 同步完成 ‹*work, requests*›; **to ~ up with orders** 按期为订单供货 **3** (develop at same rate as) 与…同步进展 ‹*competitors*›; **to ~ up with the Joneses** 与人攀比 **4** (increase at same rate as) 与…同步增长 ‹*inflation, demand*›; **pensions are barely ~ing up with the cost of living** 养老金的增加跟不上生活费用的增长速度 **5** (learn at same rate as) 和…同步学习 ‹*person, class*›; **to ~ up with the rest of the class** 跟上班里其他同学的功课 **6** (understand) 理解 ‹*person, explanation*›; **are you ~ing up with me?** 你们明白我的意思吗? **7** (know about) 保持了解; **to ~ up with the latest fashions** 赶时髦; **to ~ up with the times** 与时俱进 **8** (stay in contact with) 与…保持联系 ‹*friend*› **9** (pay on time) 按时支付 ‹*bills*›; **to ~ up with the payments** 按期付款

keeper /ˈkiːpə(r)/ *n* **1** (in zoo) 饲养员 **2** Sport (in football) 守门员; (in cricket) 捕手 **3** (curator) 管理员 **4** (guard) 看守; **the ~ of the gate** 看门人 **5** (person in charge of sb. else) 监护人; **to be sb.'s ~** 担任某人的监护人

keep-fit *n* 健身运动; **a ~ teacher** 健身教练

keep-fit exercises *npl* 健身操

keeping /ˈkiːpɪŋ/
A *n* [u] 保管; **in sb.'s ~, in the ~ of sb.** 由某人保管; **to put** *or* **leave sb./sth. in sb.'s ~** 把某人/某事物交给某人照管
B **in keeping with** *prep phr* 与…相一致 ‹*law, image, tradition*›; **to be in ~ with the surroundings** 与周围浑然一体; **not in ~ with what we expected** 与我们的预期不一致
C **out of keeping with** *prep phr* 与…不一致 ‹*image, style, occasion*›; **to be quite out of ~ with sb.'s character** 与某人的性格大相径庭

keepsake /ˈkiːpseɪk/ *n* 纪念品

keg /keg/ *n* **1** [c] (for liquid) 小桶; (for gunpowder) 炸药桶 **2** [u] Brit colloq = **keg beer**

keg beer *n* [u and c] Brit 桶装啤酒

kelp /kelp/ *n* [u] 巨藻

kelvin /ˈkelvɪn/ *n* ▸**p. 814** 开; **at 10 degrees ~** 开尔文温度为 10 度

ken /ken/
A *n* [u] **beyond** *or* **outside sb.'s ~** 在某人知识范围之外
B *vt* (*pt, pp* **kent** *or* **kenned**) Scot = **know A**

kennel /ˈkenl/
A *n* **1** (for dog) 狗窝 **2** **kennels** + *v sing or pl* Brit (establishment) 养狗场; **to put a dog in ~s** 把狗放进养狗场
B *vt* (*pres p etc.* **-ll-**) 把…圈入狗窝

Kent /kent/ *pr n* 肯特郡

kent /kent/ *pt, pp* ▸**ken B**

Kentucky /kenˈtʌki/ *pr n* 肯塔基州

Kenya /ˈkenjə/ *pr n* 肯尼亚

Kenyan /ˈkenjən/ ▸**p. 503**
A *adj* (of Kenya) 肯尼亚的; (of the people) 肯尼亚人的
B *n* 肯尼亚人

kept /kept/
A *pt, pp* ▸**keep A, B, C**
B *adj* **a ~ woman** 被包养的女人

keratin /ˈkerətɪn/ *n* [u] 角蛋白

kerb /kɜːb/ *n* esp Brit 路缘; **to pull into/away from the ~** 驶入/驶出路缘

kerb: ~ crawler *n* Brit 路边慢驶招妓者; **~ crawling** *n* [u] Brit 路边慢驶招妓; **~ drill** *n* [u] Brit 安全过街规则; **~ market** *n* 场外证券市场; **~side** *n* 马路牙子; **~stone** *n* Brit 路缘石; **~ weight** *n* Brit 全装备重量

kerchief /ˈkɜːtʃɪf/ *n* dated (square scarf) 方围巾; (triangular scarf) 三角围巾

kerfuffle /kəˈfʌfl/ *n* [u] Brit colloq 瞎闹腾; **what's all the ~ about?** 这乱哄哄的是怎么回事?

kernel /ˈkɜːnl/ *n* **1** (of nut, pine cone) 仁 **2** (whole seed) 籽 **3** fig (core) 核心 **4** Comput 内核

kernel sentence *n* 核心句

kerosene, kerosine /ˈkerəsiːn/ *n* [u] **1** Amer, Austral (paraffin) 煤油 **2** (aircraft fuel) 航空煤油

kestrel /ˈkestrəl/ *n* 红隼

ketch /ketʃ/ *n* 双桅帆船

ketchup /ˈketʃəp/ *n* [u] 番茄酱

ketone /ˈkiːtəʊn/ *n* [u] 酮

kettle /ˈketl/ *n* **1** (for boiling water) 水壶; **to boil the ~** 烧开水 **2** (for cooking fish) 锅; **a different ~ of fish** colloq (person) 截然不同的人; (thing) 完全不同的事物; **a fine** *or* **pretty ~ of fish** colloq 尴尬的局面; ▸**pot¹ A1**

kettledrum ▸**p. 395** *n* 定音鼓

key¹ /kiː/
A *n* **1** (for lock, door, car, clock, toy) 钥匙; **a front-door ~, a ~ to the front door** 前门钥匙; **a spare ~** 备用钥匙; **to put a ~ into a lock/the ignition** 把钥匙插进锁眼/点火器; **to turn a ~ in a lock/door** 转动钥匙开锁/门; **to have a duplicate ~ cut** 配一把钥匙 **2** (for radiator) 销子 **3** fig (crucial point) 关键; **the ~ to success/happiness** 成功/幸福的关键; **to hold the ~ to the mystery** 掌握解开这个谜团的关键 **4** (on map) 图例 **5** (to abbreviations) 略语表 **6** (for code) 密码本 **7** (set of answers) 答案; **a ~ to the exercises** 练习答案 **8** Mus 调; **the ~ of D major/minor** D 大调/小调; **a piece of music in the ~ of E flat** 一首降E调乐曲; **to change ~** 变调; **to sing in/off ~** 唱歌搭调/走调 **9** (on musical instrument, computer, phone, etc.) 键; **the white ~s** (on piano) 白色琴键; **to press** *or* **strike** *or* **hit a ~** 按键 **10** fig (general tone) 基调; **to be all in the same ~** 千篇一律
B *adj* 关键的 ‹*figure, role, issue*›
C *vt* **1** (input) 键入 ‹*text, data*› **2** (roughen) 将…弄毛糙 ‹*wall, surface*›

Phrasal verb

• **key in** *vt* [**~ sth. in, ~ in sth.**] 键入 ‹*text, data*›

key² *n* (island) [尤指加勒比海中的] 低岛

keyboard /ˈkiːbɔːd/ ▸**p. 395**
A *n* **1** (of computer, typewriter) 键盘 **2** Mus (set of keys) 乐器键盘; (instrument) 键盘乐器; **~ music** 键盘音乐
B **keyboards** *npl* **who played ~s on Bob Dylan's new CD?** 鲍勃·迪伦的新唱片谁是键盘手?
C *vt* 用键盘输入 ‹*data*›
D *vi* 用键盘输入信息

keyboarder /ˈkiːbɔːdə(r)/ *n* 键盘输入员

keyboarding /ˈkiːbɔːdɪŋ/ *n* [u] 键盘输入

keyboard: ~ instrument *n* 键盘乐器; **~ operator** *n* = **keyboarder**; **~ shortcut** *n* 快捷键; **~ skills** *npl* **1** Comput 键盘操作技能; **2** Mus 键盘乐器弹奏技能; **~ player** *n* 键盘乐器手

key: ~ card *n* [宾馆用的] 门卡; **~ combination** *n* 组合键

keyed-up *adj* 激动不安的

key holder *n* **1** (person) 掌管钥匙的人 **2** (case) 钥匙包; (chain) 钥匙链

keyhole /ˈkiːhəʊl/ *n* 锁孔

keyhole: ~ saw *n* 栓孔锯; **~ surgery** *n* [u] 微创手术

keying /ˈkiːɪŋ/ *n* [u] 数据输入

key: ~logging *n* [u] 按键记录; **~ money** *n* [u] **1** Brit (as advance payment for key) [新房客付的] 钥匙押金; **2** colloq (as inducement) [向房东付的] 小费

keynote /ˈkiːnəʊt/ *n* **1** Mus 主音 **2** fig (main theme) 基调

keynote: ~ lecture *n* 主题报告; **~ speaker** *n* 主题发言人; **~ speech** *n* 主题发言

key: ~pad *n* 小键盘; **~ ring** *n* 钥匙圈; **~ signature** *n* 调号; **~stone** *n* **1** Archit 拱顶石; **2** fig (central principle) 主旨; **~stroke** *n* 按键; **~word** *n* **1** (to a code) 解密关键词; **2** (essential concept) 关键概念; **3** (in search engine, index) 关键词; **~ worker** *n* 关键工作人员

kg *abbr* = **kilogram(s)** 千克, 公斤

KGB *abbr* Hist 克格勃 [前苏联国家安全委员会]

khaki /ˈkɑːki/
A *n* [u] **1** Tex 卡其布 **2** (colour) 暗绿色
B **khakis** *npl* (clothing) 卡其服装
C *adj* 暗绿色的

Khartoum /kɑːˈtuːm/ *pr n* 喀土穆

Khmer /kmeə(r)/ ▸**p. 503, p. 426**
A *adj* (of the people) 高棉人的; (of the language) 高棉语的
B *n* **1** [c] (person) 高棉人 **2** [u] (language) 高棉语

Khyber Pass /ˌkaɪbəˈpɑːs/ *pr n* 开伯尔山口

kHz *abbr* = **kilohertz**

kia ora /ˌkiːəˈɔːrə/ *excl* NZ 你好

kibbutz /kɪˈbʊts/ *n* (*pl* **kibbutzim** /ˌkɪbʊˈtsiːm/) 基布兹 [以色列的集体农场]

kibitz /ˈkɪbɪts/ *vi* Amer colloq **1** (spectate and give advice) [尤指纸牌游戏旁观者] 指手画脚 **2** (chat) 闲聊

kibitzer /ˈkɪbɪtsə(r), kɪˈbɪtsə(r)/ *n* Amer colloq 指手画脚的旁观者

kibosh /ˈkaɪbɒʃ/ *n* [u] **to put the ~ on sth.** colloq 结束某事

kick /kɪk/
A *vt* **1** (strike) 踢; **to ~ sb. on** *or* **in sth.** 踢中某人的某部位; **he ~ed me on the shin** 他踢到了我的胫骨; **to ~ sb. in the teeth** fig colloq 使某人受到重创 **2** (propel) 踢走; **to ~ sth. away** 把某物踢走; **to ~ sb./sth. down the stairs/over a wall/under the bed** 把某人/某物踢下楼梯/踢过墙/踢到床下; **he ~ed dust into my face** 他把尘土踢到了我脸上; **to ~ the ball into touch** (in rugby) 把球踢出边线 **3** (create by striking) 踢出 ‹*hole, dent*›; **to ~ a hole in sth.** 在某物上踢出一个洞 **4** (flail) 踢腾 ‹*feet*›; **to ~ one's legs in the air** «*baby, dancer*» 踢腿 **5** (in rugby) 踢…球得

k

分; to ～ two conversions/penalties 踢两个触地/罚球得分 ⑥ colloq (give up) to ～ the habit 戒除恶习 ⑦ Amer sl to ～ (some) ass (act forcefully) 用强硬手段摆平; (be excellent) that soundtrack really ～s ass 那配乐真棒

B vi ① (strike) 踢; to ～ at sb./sth. 向某人/某物踢去; alive and ～ing «person» 活蹦乱跳的; bigotry is still alive and ～ing 偏执思想仍大行其道 ② Sport (propel ball) 踢球; to ～ for touch (in rugby) 把球踢出边线 ③ (move legs) 踢腿; to ～ hard with one's feet 奋力踢腿; to ～ for home «athlete, swimmer, racehorse» 向终点冲刺 ④ (recoil) 后冲; this gun really ～s when you fire it 这支枪射击时后坐力很大

C v refl to ～ oneself colloq 自责; to ～ oneself for doing sth. 懊悔做某事

D n ① [c] (blow with foot) 踢; to give sb./sth. a ～ 踢某人/某物一脚; to get a ～ on the shin (from sb./a horse) 被（某人/马）踢到胫骨; a ～ up the backside or in the pants colloq lit 对屁股的一踢; fig 突如其来的猛力鞭策; to deserve a good ～ up the backside 应该受敲打; a ～ in the teeth fig colloq (rebuff) 使人丢脸的回绝; (setback) 重挫 ② [c] Sport 踢球; to blast the ～ wide 踢大脚球; to aim a ～ at goal 射门 ③ [c] (leg movement) (of swimmer) 蹬水; (of dancer) 踢腿 ④ [c] colloq (thrill) 极大的乐趣; to get a ～ out of or from sth./doing sth. 从某事物/做某事中得到极大乐趣; to do sth. for ～s 做某事寻求刺激; to give sb. a ～ 给某人带来极大乐趣 ⑤ [u and c] colloq (strong effect) 刺激性; a drink with a lot of ～ in it 劲儿大的酒 ⑥ [u] colloq (vigour) 活力; he still has plenty of ～ in him 他仍然活力十足 ⑦ [c] colloq (craze) 一时的狂热; to be on a health-food ～ 心血来潮热衷于健康食品 ⑧ [u and c] (of firearm) 后冲; this gun has quite a ～ 这支枪后坐力很大

Phrasal verbs

- **kick about** vt = kick around
- **kick against** vt [～ against sb./sth.] 竭力反抗 ‹parents, system›; to ～ against the rules 违反规则
- **kick around**

A [～ sth. around] vt ① (play with) 把…踢着玩 ‹toy›; to ～ a ball around 踢球玩 ② (discuss) 随便谈谈 ‹idea› ③ (treat badly) 粗暴对待; I won't be ～ed around by anyone 我不会让任何人欺负的 ④ (treat roughly) 胡乱摆弄 ‹books, toys›

B [～ around sth.] vt colloq ① (wander around) 在…四处游荡 ‹town, school› ② (lie unused in) 被闲置在 ‹house, garden›

C vi colloq ① (wander) 四处游荡 ② (lie unused) 被闲置; there's a pen ～ing around on my desk 我的桌上有一支多余的钢笔 ③ (exist) 存在; that idea's been ～ing around for years 那个想法都提出好几年了

- **kick back** vi ① (recoil) «firearm» 反冲 ② esp Amer colloq (relax) 放松
- **kick down** vt [～ sth. down, ～ down sth.] 踢倒 ‹door, barrier›
- **kick in**

A vt ① [～ sth. in, ～ in sth.] (smash in) 踢破 ‹door, box›; ～ sb.'s teeth or face in colloq 猛揍某人 ② [～ in sth.] Amer colloq (contribute) 捐出 ‹money, amount›

B vi colloq ① (start working) «machinery» 开始运转; «regulation» 开始生效; the reforms will ～ in later this year 改革将于今年晚些时候开始推行 ② Amer (contribute) 捐助

- **kick off**

A vi ① Sport 开球 ② to ～ off with sth. colloq (start) 从某事物开始; to ～ off with a few comments 先说几点意见

B vt [～ off sth., ～ sth. off] ① (remove) 踢掉 ‹shoes› ② colloq (start) 开始 ‹event, tour, discussion›; to ～ off the season with ... 以…开始本赛季的比赛

- **kick out** vt [～ sb. out, ～ out sb.] colloq ① (eject) 撵出 ‹intruder, troublemaker, drunk› ② (expel, dismiss) 开除 ‹member, employee›
- **kick out at** vt [～ out at sb./sth.] ① lit 猛踢; she ～ed out at her attacker 她猛踢袭击她的人 ② fig (rebel against) 对…反应强烈; to ～ out at the injustices of the government 强烈质疑政府的不公正行为
- **kick over** vt [～ sth. over, ～ over sth.] 踢翻 ‹vase, bucket›
- **kick up** vt [～ up sth.] 踢起 ‹dirt, dust›; to ～ up clouds of dust 踢得尘土飞扬; to ～ up a fuss or stink about sb./sth. fig colloq 就某人/某事物起哄

kick: ～back n ① colloq (payment) 回扣; ② (recoil) 反冲; **～boxer** n 跆拳道运动员; **～boxing** n [u] 跆拳道

kicker /ˈkɪkə(r)/ n ① Sport 踢球的运动员 ② (animal) 爱踢腿的动物

kicking /ˈkɪkɪŋ/ n ① (repeated kicks) 反复踢打; to give sb. a good ～ 狠踢某人一顿 ② fig colloq (sound defeat) 溃败

kick: ～-off n ① Sport 开球; ② fig colloq 开始; **～stand** n [自行车或摩托车的] 撑脚架

kickstart /ˈkɪkstɑːt/

A n ① (on motorbike) 脚踏启动器 ② fig (boost) 推动; new investment will provide a ～ 新的投资将起到推动作用

B vt ① lit 用脚踏启动器启动 ‹motorbike› ② fig (boost) 推动

kickstarter /ˈkɪkstɑːtə(r)/ n = kickstart A1

kid /kɪd/

A n ① [c] Zool (young goat) 小山羊; (young antelope) 小羚羊 ② [u] (goatskin) 山羊皮; ～ shoes/bag 羊皮鞋/包 ③ [c] colloq (child) 小孩; ～s' stuff 小儿科

B vt (pres p etc. -dd-) colloq ① (playfully deceive) 戏弄; I ～ you not 我不骗你 ② (tease) 取笑; to ～ sb. about sth. 为某事物取笑某人 ③ (fool) 欺骗; if they think that, they're ～ding themselves 如果他们这样想的话，那是在欺骗自己

C vi (pres p etc. -dd-) colloq (tease) 逗弄; no ～ding! 真的！

kid brother n esp Amer colloq 弟弟

kiddy /ˈkɪdi/ n colloq 小家伙

kid glove n 羊皮手套; to handle or treat sb./sth. with ～s fig 小心谨慎地对待某人/某事物; modif ～ treatment 小心谨慎的对待

kidnap /ˈkɪdnæp/

A n 绑架罪; ～ victim(s) 被绑架者

B vt (pres p etc. -pp-) 绑架

kidnapper /ˈkɪdnæpə(r)/ n 绑匪

kidnapping /ˈkɪdnæpɪŋ/ n [c and u] 绑架

kidney /ˈkɪdni/ n ① Anat 肾 ② Culin 腰子; lamb/beef ～s 羊/牛腰子

kidney: ～ bean n 云豆; **～ dialysis** n [u] 肾透析; **～ dish** n [做手术用的] 肾形盘; **～ donor** n 捐肾者; **～ failure** n [u] 肾衰竭; **～ machine** n (artificial kidney) 人工肾; (dialysis machine) 血液透析机; **～-shaped** adj 肾形的; **～ specialist** n 肾脏专家; **～ stone** n 肾结石; **～ transplant** n 肾脏移植

kid sister n esp Amer colloq 妹妹

Kiev /kiˈev/ pr n 基辅

Kigali /kɪˈɡɑːli/ pr n 基加利

kill /kɪl/

A vt ① (cause to die) 杀死; to ～ sb./sth. with a weapon/with poison 用武器杀死/毒药毒死某人/某物; to be ～ed by sb./sth. 被某人/某事物杀死; she was ～ed by the disease 她死于这种疾病; to be ～ed in a fire/accident 在火灾/事故中遇难; to be ～ed in action or battle 战死; to be ～ed outright 当场死亡; (even) if it ～s me! colloq 不管有多难！; I could have ～ed her! colloq 我恨不得杀了她！; to ～ sb./sth. with kindness 宠坏某人/某物; ►goose A1; to kill two birds with one stone Prov 一石二鸟 ② usu pres p colloq (cause discomfort) 使极不舒服; my feet are ～ing me 我的脚疼死了; the suspense is ～ing me 这悬念让我坐立不安 ③ (destroy) 扼杀 ‹interest›; 毁灭 ‹hopes›; 破坏 ‹feeling›; 使…无法进行 ‹conversation›; to ～ sb.'s chances/appetite 使某人失去机会/没了胃口 ④ (stop) 否决 ‹project, proposal›; 撤销 ‹bill, law›; 挫败 ‹attempt›; 阻止…流传 ‹story, rumour› ⑤ (deaden) 消除; to ～ the pain/sound/smell 止痛/消音/除味 ⑥ colloq (overexert) «action» 使过度疲累; it won't or wouldn't ～ sb. (to do sth.) 对某人来说（做某事）没有什么大不了的 ⑦ colloq (turn off) 关掉 ‹machine, light› ⑧ colloq (delete) 删去 ‹line, file› ⑨ colloq (spend) to ～ time (doing sth.) （做某事）消磨时间; I have two hours to ～ 我有两个小时需要打发 ⑩ colloq (amuse) 使笑个不停; you ～ me! the things you say! 你说的那些话笑死我了！

B vi 致死; tiredness while driving can ～ 疲劳驾驶会出人命的; a murderer who ～s in cold blood 冷血杀手

C v refl to ～ oneself 自杀; fig colloq 使自己精疲力竭; to ～ oneself doing or to do sth. 拼命做某事; don't ～ yourself! iron 可别累着自己！; to ～ oneself laughing Brit 笑得缓不过劲儿来

D n ① (slaughter) 杀死; to make a ～ 杀死猎物; to close in or move in or go in for the ～ lit 逼近以杀死; fig 采取果断行动以求达到目的; to be in at the ～ lit 猎物被杀时在场; fig 获胜时在场 ② (prey) 猎获物; lions feeding on their ～ 正在吃猎物的狮子

Phrasal verb

- **kill off** vt [～ off sth./sb., ～ sth./sb. off] ① (destroy) 大量杀死 ‹pests, species›; 大量毁掉 ‹crops› ② (murder) 屠杀 ‹person›; to ～ off the heroine fig 让女主人公死去 ③ colloq (destroy) 使…停止 ‹project, scheme›; 消灭 ‹opposition›

killer /ˈkɪlə(r)/ n ① (person) 杀手; (illness, poison, etc.) 致命之物; cancer is a major ～ 癌症是一大致命杀手; ～ virus/bees 致命病毒/杀人蜂; sharks can be vicious ～s 鲨鱼有时会变成残忍的杀手 ② colloq (sth. difficult) 棘手的事; this hill is a ～! 这座山可难爬了！; the exam was a real ～! 这考试真让人头疼！ ③ colloq (sth. funny) 十分有趣的事; that joke's a ～! 那个笑话真逗！

killer: ～ application n 杀手级应用程序 [指特别有用的计算机程序，使消费者愿意为这种程序购买其他产品]; **～ cell** n 杀伤细胞; **～ disease** n 致命的疾病; **～ instinct** n ① lit 嗜杀的本性; ② fig 残酷无情; **～ satellite** n 截击卫星; **～ whale** n 逆戟鲸

killing /ˈkɪlɪŋ/

A n [u and c] 杀戮; the ～ of civilians/elephants 对平民/大象的杀戮; to make a ～ fig colloq 发大财

B adj ① colloq (exhausting) 令人精疲力竭的 ‹pace, work, journey› ② dated (amusing) 十分好笑的

killing fields npl 杀戮战场

killingly /ˈkɪlɪŋli/ adv colloq 极其 ‹funny›

killjoy /ˈkɪldʒɔɪ/ n 令人扫兴的人

kill or cure adj 孤注一掷的

kiln /kɪln/ n 窑; a pottery ～ 瓷窑

kilo /ˈkiːləʊ/ ►p. 909 n 公斤

kilo- /ˈkɪləʊ, ˈkiːləʊ/ combining form 千; ～gram 千克; ～metre 千米

kiloampere /ˈkiːləʊæmpeə(r)/ n 千安培

kilobit /ˈkɪləbɪt/ n 千比特

kilobyte /ˈkɪləbaɪt/ n 千字节

kilocalorie /ˈkɪləˌkæləri/ n 千卡

kilogram, Brit also **kilogramme** /ˈkɪləɡræm/ ►p. 909 n 千克，公斤

kilohertz /ˈkɪləhɜːts/ n 千赫兹

kilojoule /ˈkɪlədʒuːl/ n 千焦耳

kilolitre Brit, **kiloliter** Amer /ˈkɪləliːtə(r)/ n 千升

kilometre /kɪˈlɒmɪtə(r)/ Brit, **kilometer** /ˈkɪləmiːtə(r)/ Amer ►p. 436 n 千米，公里

kiloton /ˈkɪlətən/ ►p. 909 n 千吨

k

kilovolt /ˈkɪləvɒlt/ *n* 千伏特

kilowatt /ˈkɪləwɒt/ *n* 千瓦

kilowatt-hour *n* 千瓦时

kilt /kɪlt/ *n* 苏格兰短褶裙

kilted /ˈkɪltɪd/ *adj* 穿苏格兰短褶裙的

kilter /ˈkɪltə(r)/ *n* [u] colloq **out of ~** 不一致; **to be out of ~ with sth.** 与某事物不一致

kimono /kɪˈməʊnəʊ, Amer -nə/ *n* **1** (Japanese robe) 和服 **2** (dressing gown) 和服式晨衣

kin /kɪn/ *n* [u] + *v pl* formal 亲属

kind[1] /kaɪnd/

A *n* **1** [u and c] (type) 种类; **all** *or* **various ~s of people/activities, people/activities of all** *or* **various ~s** 各种各样的人/活动; **I like tennis, squash, that ~ of thing** 我喜欢网球、壁球之类的运动; **that's the ~ of person I am** 我就是这种人; **that's my ~ of film!** 这正是我喜欢的那类电影！; **she's not the marrying ~** 她不是那种适合结婚的女人; **ideas of a dangerous/subversive ~** 危险/具破坏性的想法; **what ~ of talk is that?** 那叫什么话啊？; **he must be some ~ of idiot** 他一定有点儿白痴; **would you like a drink of some ~?** 你要喝点儿什么吗？; **of its ~** 在其同类中; **the only one of its ~** 绝无仅有; **one of a ~** 独一无二; **two/three** *etc.* **of a ~** (same) 两个/三个等完全一样的; (similar) 两个/三个等非常相似的; (in card games) 两张/三张等相同点数的; **they're two of a ~** 他们俩一个样; **something of the** *or* **that ~** 类似的事情; **he's resigning — I expected something of the ~** 他要辞职了——我料到会有这样的事; **nothing** *or* **not anything of the ~** 完全不是那么回事; **he's an idiot — he's nothing of the ~!** 他是个傻瓜——他才不傻呢！; **of a ~** pej 徒有其名; **it's wine of a ~** 这葡萄酒不怎么样 **2** [c] **a ~ of** (sth. resembling) 几分; **a ~ of toy/genius** 玩具类的东西/有几分像天才的人; **to feel a ~ of apprehension** 感到几分担心 **3** [c] (classified type) 某类人; **I know his ~** 我了解他这类人; **one's (own) ~** 同类的人

B **in kind** *adv phr* **1** (in goods) **to pay in ~** 以实物支付 **2** (in same way) **to repay sb. in ~** (with good deed) 以德报德; (with bad deed) 以牙还牙; **to respond in ~** 以其人之道还治其人之身 **3** (in essence) 在本质上; **the regions differ in size, but not in ~** 这些地区大小不同，但实际上并无区别

C **kind of** *adv phr* colloq 有几分; **I ~ of like him** 我有点喜欢他; **I ~ of thought/heard that ...** 我倾向于认为/好像听说…; **did you have fun? — ~ of** 你玩得高兴吗？——还行吧; **did you have a row? — ~ of** 你是不是打架了？——差不多算是吧

kind[2] *adj* **1** (characterized by friendliness and generosity) 友好的 ‹*person, voice, face*›; **a ~ act** 善行; **to be ~ to animals** 善待动物 **2** (favourable) 有利的; **life has/has not been ~ to me** 生活一直对我很眷顾/很不公; **candlelight is ~ to the complexion** 烛光衬托下的肤色很好看 **3** (gentle) 温和的; **soap that is ~ to one's hands** 不刺激手的肥皂; **rollers that are ~ to hair** 不伤头发的卷发筒 **4** (expressing gratitude) 令人感激的; **you're too ~!** 你太好了！; **have another! — that's very ~ of you** 再吃一个吧！——谢谢; **to be ~ of sb. to do sth.** 某人做某事令人感激; **she was ~ enough to give me a hand** 多亏她帮我 **5** *pred* formal (in requests) [用于礼貌的请求或命令]; **would you be ~ enough** *or* **so ~ as to ...** 请您…好吗 **6** formal (in correspondence) [用于信件的结束敬语中]; **(with) ~ regards** 衷心祝好

kinda /ˈkaɪndə/ *adv* colloq = **kind of** ▸**kind**[1] **C**

kindergarten /ˈkɪndəgɑːtn/ *n* 幼儿园

kind: ~-hearted *adj* 善良的; **~-heartedly** *adv* 善良地; **~-heartedness** *n* [u] 善良

kindle /ˈkɪndl/

A *vt* **1** (set light to) 点燃 ‹*wood, grass*›; 燃起 ‹*fire*› **2** fig (arouse) 激起 ‹*anger, passions*›; 唤起 ‹*hope*›; 激发 ‹*interest*›

B *vi* 着火; **his eyes seemed to ~ with fire** fig 他的眼睛像在冒火

kindliness /ˈkaɪndlɪnɪs/ *n* [u] 和善

kindling /ˈkɪndlɪŋ/ *n* [u] 引火柴

kindly[1] /ˈkaɪndli/ *adv* **1** (in a kind, nice way) 和善地 ‹*say, behave*›; **thank you ~** dated 衷心感谢你 **2** (obligingly) 好心地; **she ~ opened the door for him** 她好心地为他开门 **3** (favourably) 赞许地; **to look ~ on sb./sth.** 正面地看待某人/某事物; **to think ~ of sb./sth.** 赞同某人/某事物; **to take ~ to sb./sth.** 喜欢某人/某事物; **not to take ~ to doing sth.** 不乐意做某事; **to speak ~ of sb./sth.** 对某人/某事物有好评价 **4** (please) 请; **~ close the door** 烦请关上门

kindly[2] *adj* 和善的 ‹*person, smile, manner, nature*›; 好心的 ‹*advice, interest*›

kindness /ˈkaɪndnɪs/ *n* **1** [u] (quality) 好意; **to show sb. ~, to show ~ to** *or* **towards sb.** 向某人表示善意; **to show sb. nothing but ~** 以一片善意对待某人; **to treat sb. with ~** 友善地对待某人; **~ to animals** 对动物的友善; **an act of ~** 善行; **out of ~** 出于善意; **out of the ~ of one's heart** 出于内心的善意; **to kill sb. with ~** fig 宠坏某人; **to kill a plant with ~** 因过分打理而把植物养死 **2** [c] (act) 友好举动; **his many ~es to me** 他对我的很多帮助; **to do sb. a ~** 帮某人一个忙; **you're not doing him a ~ by keeping quiet** 你保持沉默对他并没有好处; **it's a/no ~ (to sb.) to do sth.** 做某事（对某人来说）有/没有好处

kindred /ˈkɪndrɪd/

A *n* [u] **1** + *v pl* (family) 家人 **2** + *v sing* (blood relationship) 血缘关系; **ties of ~** 亲属关系

B *adj attrib* **1** (related) 有血缘关系的 ‹*family*›; 同族的 ‹*tribe*›; 同源的 ‹*language*› **2** (similar) 类似的 ‹*idea, activity*›

kindred spirit *n* 志趣相投的人

kinetic /kɪˈnetɪk/ *adj* 运动的

kinetic: ~ art *n* [u] 动态艺术; **~ energy** *n* [u] 动能

kinetics /kɪˈnetɪks/ *npl* + *v sing* 动力学

king /kɪŋ/ *n* **1** (monarch) 国王; **a ~ in waiting** 下任国王; **to live like a ~** 过国王般奢华的生活; **the K~ of K~s** (God) 上帝; (title of oriental monarchs) 万王之王 **2** fig (best or most important person or thing) 首屈一指的人; **in Italy football is ~** 在意大利，足球的地位至高无上 **3** (in chess) 王; (in cards) 老 K; (in draughts, checkers) 王棋

king cobra *n* 眼镜王蛇

kingdom /ˈkɪŋdəm/ *n* **1** (monarchy) 王国 **2** (division of the natural world) 界; **the plant/animal ~** 植物界/动物界 **3** fig (realm) 领域; **the ~ under the waves** 大海; **the ~ of God** *or* **Heaven** Bible 天堂; **till** *or* **until ~ come** colloq 永远; **to ~ come** colloq 到来世; **the explosion blew them all to ~ come** colloq 爆炸把他们通通送上了西天

king: ~fisher /ˈkɪŋfɪʃə(r)/ *n* 翠鸟; **K~ James Bible, K~ James Version** *pr ns* 钦定版《圣经》; **~maker** *n* 有权支配要职的人; **~ of beasts, ~ of the jungle** *ns* 百兽之王 [指狮子]; **~ of the castle** *n* [u] Brit (children's game) 山寨大王; fig (person) 大王; **~ penguin** *n* 王企鹅; **~pin** *n* 转向立轴; fig 关键; **~ post** *n* 中柱; **~ prawn** *n* 宽沟对虾; **K~'s Counsel** *n* 王室法律顾问 [国王在位时称]; ▸**Queen's Counsel**; **K~'s English** *n* 标准英语 [国王在位时称]; ▸**Queen's English**; **K~'s evidence** *n* 对同案犯不利的证据 [国王在位时称]; ▸**Queen's evidence**; **K~'s highway** *n* [国王保护下的] 国道; ▸**Queen's highway**

kingship /ˈkɪŋʃɪp/ *n* [u] (being a king) 国王身份; (position of king) 王位

king-size, king-sized *adj* 特大号的 ‹*bed, chocolate bar*›

Kingston /ˈkɪŋstən/ *pr n* 金斯顿

Kingstown /ˈkɪŋztaʊn/ *pr n* 金斯敦

kink /kɪŋk/

A *n* **1** (in pipe, hair) 绞缠; (in road) 弯曲 **2** fig (in personality) 怪癖 **3** fig (flaw) 缺陷

B *vi* «*wire, rope, hair*» 绞缠

C *vt* 使…绞缠 ‹*wire, rope, hair*›

kinky /ˈkɪŋki/ *adj* colloq (perverted) 性行为反常的 ‹*person*›; 变态的 ‹*tastes, sex*›; (provocative) 撩人的 ‹*underwear*›

kinsfolk /ˈkɪnzfəʊk/ *npl* formal 亲戚

Kinshasa /kɪnˈʃɑːsə/ *pr n* 金沙萨

kinship /ˈkɪnʃɪp/ *n* **1** [u] (blood relationship) 亲属关系 **2** [c] fig (empathy) 投契; (close relationship) 密切关系; (sympathetic feeling) 亲切感

kinship term *n* 亲属称谓

kinsman /ˈkɪnzmən/ *n* (*pl* **kinsmen**) formal 男性亲戚

kinswoman /ˈkɪnzwʊmən/ *n* (*pl* **kinswomen**) formal 女性亲戚

kiosk /ˈkiːɒsk/ *n* **1** (stand) 售货亭 **2** Brit Telecom 公用电话亭

kip /kɪp/ Brit colloq

A *n* [c and u] (sleep) 睡觉; **to have a ~, to get some ~** 睡一会儿

B *vi* (*pres p etc.* **-pp-**) **to ~ (down)** 睡觉

kipper /ˈkɪpə(r)/

A *n* (smoked herring) 熏鲱鱼; (dried herring) 腌鲱鱼

B *vt* (by smoking) 熏制; (by drying) 腌晒

Kirghiz /ˈkɜːgɪz/ ▸**p. 503, p. 426** *n, adj* = **Kyrgyz**

Kirghizia /kɜːˈgiːzɪə/ *pr n* = **Kyrgyzstan**

Kirghizstan /ˌkɜːgɪˈstæn, ˌkɪəgɪ-, -stɑːn/ *pr n* = **Kyrgyzstan**

Kiribati /ˌkɪrɪˈbɑːti, ˈkɪrɪbæs/ *pr n* 基里巴斯

kirk /kɜːk/ *n* Scot 教堂; **the K~** 苏格兰教会

kiss /kɪs/

A *vt* **1** (touch with lips) 亲吻; **to ~ sb. on the lips/cheek** 亲吻某人的双唇/面颊; **to ~ sb. goodnight** 亲吻某人并道晚安; **the two lovers ~ed each other** 这对恋人相互亲吻; **to ~ hands** (ceremoniously) 行吻手礼; **to ~ the ground** 匍匐在地 [向所到国表示问候]; **to ~ sth. better** colloq 亲一亲某处就好了; **to ~ sth. goodbye, to ~ goodbye to sth.** colloq 承认对某事物无能为力; **you can ~ that money goodbye!** 那笔钱你就别想要回来了！; **to ~ (sb.'s) arse** Brit *or* Amer **ass** taboo sl 拍（某人的）马屁; **~ my arse** Brit *or* Amer **ass!** taboo sl 见鬼去吧！ **2** (in snooker, billiards) 轻轻擦过

B *vi* **1** (touch with lips) 亲吻; **to ~ and make up** 亲吻以示和好; **to ~ and tell** 宣扬自己的风流韵事 **2** (in snooker, billiards) «*balls*» 轻碰

C *n* 吻; **to give sb. a ~** 亲某人一下; **a ~ on the lips** 唇吻; **a goodnight ~** 晚上告别时的吻; **love and ~es** (in letter) 爱你吻你

kiss: ~-and-tell *adj attrib* 宣扬自己的风流韵事的; **~ curl** *n* 一绺卷发

kisser /ˈkɪsə(r)/ *n* **1** (person) 接吻的人; **she's a good ~** 她善于接吻 **2** sl (mouth) 嘴

kiss: ~ of death *n* fig 导致毁灭的行为; **~-off** *n* colloq (dismissal) 突然解雇; (rejection) 粗暴拒绝; **~ of life** *n* 口对口人工呼吸

kissogram /ˈkɪsəgræm/ *n* 贺吻 [在祝贺的同时亲吻受贺者]

kit /kɪt/ *n* **1** [c] (set of tools) 成套工具; **a survival ~** 救生包 **2** [c and u] Brit (gear) 全套装备; (clothes) 全套服装; **to get one's ~ off** colloq 脱光衣服 **3** [c] (set of parts for assembly) 配套组件; **in ~ form** 以成套组件形式 **4** [u] Mil 装备; **in full ~** 全副武装; **~ inspection** 装备检查

k

(Phrasal verb)
• **kit out** *vt* [~ **out sb./sth.**, ~ **sb./sth. out**] Brit 使装备齐全

kit: ~**bag** *n* Brit [士兵的] 行囊; ~**car** *n* 组装车

kitchen /ˈkɪtʃɪn/ *n* 厨房; **a fitted** ~ 整体厨房; *modif* **a** ~ **knife** 菜刀

kitchen: ~ **area** *n* 厨房区; ~ **cabinet** *n* **1** lit 橱柜; **2** Pol 厨房内阁 [政府首脑的私人顾问团]; ~**-diner** *n* 餐厨两用间

kitchenette /ˌkɪtʃɪˈnet/ *n* (small room) 小厨房; (part of room) [房间里的] 厨房区

kitchen: ~ **foil** *n* [u] 厨房用铝箔; ~ **garden** *n* 家庭菜园; ~ **maid** *n* 帮厨女佣; ~ **paper** *n* [u] 厨房用卷纸; ~ **porter** *n* 厨房杂务工; ~ **range** *n* 炉灶; ~ **roll** *n* [u and c] 厨房用卷纸; ~ **scales** *npl* 厨房用秤

kitchen sink *n* 厨房洗涤池; **everything but the** ~ colloq 能想到的一切

kitchen sink drama *n* Brit 激进现实主义戏剧

kitchen: ~ **soap** *n* [u] 厨房洗手皂; ~ **tea** *n* Austral, NZ [给新人送厨具的] 茶会; ~ **unit** *n* 全套厨具; ~**ware** *n* [u] 厨房用具; ~ **waste** *n* [u] 厨房泔水

kite /kaɪt/ *n* **1** (toy) 风筝; **to fly a** ~ lit 放风筝; fig 试探舆论; **to be as high as a** ~ colloq (intoxicated by alcohol) 烂醉如泥; (intoxicated by drug) 因吸毒飘飘然; (overexcited) 如痴如狂 **2** (bird) 鸢

kite: ~**board** *n* 风筝滑板; ~**boarding** *n* [u] 风筝滑板运动; ~**boarder** *n* 风筝滑板手; ~**-flying** *n* [u] **1** Sport 放风筝; **2** fig (public testing) 试探舆论反应; **they indulged in a little** ~**-flying before launching the new product** 他们推出新产品之前试探了一下公众的反应

Kitemark® /ˈkaɪtmɑːk/ *n* Brit 风筝标记 [商品质量和安全认证标志]

kite: ~**surf** *vi* 去玩风筝冲浪; ~**surfer** *n* 风筝冲浪手; ~**surfing** *n* [u] 风筝冲浪运动

kit furniture *n* [u] 组装家具

kith /kɪθ/ *n* [u] ~ **and kin** 亲朋

kitsch /kɪtʃ/
A *n* [u] (art) 庸俗艺术; (objects) 俗气的物品; (design) 低俗的设计
B *modif* 俗气的

kitten /ˈkɪtn/ *n* 小猫; **to have** ~**s** Brit fig colloq 焦躁不安

kittiwake /ˈkɪtɪweɪk/ *n* 三趾鸥

kitty[1] /ˈkɪti/ *n* **1** (communal fund) 凑集的钱 **2** (in card games) [纸牌戏中的] 全部赌注

kitty[2] *n* colloq 猫咪

kiwi /ˈkiːwiː/ *n* **1** (bird) 鹬鸵 **2** **Kiwi** colloq (person) 新西兰人 **3** colloq = **kiwi fruit**

kiwi fruit *n* [c and u] 猕猴桃

KKK *abbr* = **Ku Klux Klan**

Klansman /ˈklænzmən/ *n* 三 K 党成员

klaxon® /ˈklæksn/ *n* 高音报警器

Kleenex® /ˈkliːneks/ *n* [c and u] 纸巾

kleptomania /ˌkleptəˈmeɪnɪə/ *n* [u] 偷窃癖

kleptomaniac /ˌkleptəˈmeɪnɪæk/
A *n* 有偷窃癖的人
B *adj* 偷窃癖的 ‹*tendencies*›

klutz /klʌts/ *n* esp Amer colloq 愚笨的人

km *abbr* = **kilometre(s)**

kmh *abbr* = **kilometres per hour** 千米/小时

knack /næk/ *n* **1** (skill) 技能; **there's a** ~ **in** *or* **to unlocking this cupboard** 打开这个碗橱有一个窍门儿 **2** (tendency) 习惯; **he has a** ~ **of getting himself into trouble** 他总是给自己惹麻烦

knacker /ˈnækə(r)/
A *n* 屠宰老残家畜的人
B **knackers** *npl* taboo sl 睾丸
C *vt* Brit sl **1** (exhaust) 使…精疲力竭 ‹*person, animal*› **2** (damage) 损坏 ‹*car, machinery*›

knacker's yard *n* 老残家畜屠宰场

knapsack /ˈnæpsæk/ *n* 背包

knave /neɪv/ *n* **1** (playing card) [纸牌中的] 杰克 **2** archaic (dishonest person) 无赖

knead /niːd/ *vt* **1** (work with the hands) 揉 ‹*dough*›; 捏 ‹*clay*› **2** (massage) 按摩 ‹*muscles, back*›

knee /niː/
A ▸**p. 71** *n* **1** Anat (joint) 膝关节; **to fall to** *or* **on to one's** ~**s** 跪下; **on bended** ~**(s)** 跪着; **to go weak at the** ~**s** 两腿发软; **the strike brought the country to its** ~**s** 罢工使国家陷入瘫痪 **2** (lap) [坐下时] 大腿朝上的面; **to learn at one's mother's** ~ 在孩提时期学习; **to put a child over** *or* **across one's** ~ 把小孩脸朝下放在腿上打屁股 **3** (part of garment) [裤子的] 膝部
B *vt* 用膝盖撞击; **to** ~ **sb. in the groin** 用膝盖顶某人的下身

kneecap /ˈniːkæp/
A *n* 膝盖骨
B *vt* 击碎…的膝盖骨

kneecapping /ˈniːkæpɪŋ/ *n* [c and u] 击碎膝盖骨

knee-deep
A *adj* 齐膝深的; **to be** ~ **in sth.** fig 深陷于某事物中
B *adv* 齐膝地; **to go in** ~ 走入齐膝深处

knee-high *adj* 齐膝的; ~ **to a grasshopper** colloq 小不点儿

knee-jerk
A *n* 膝跳反射
B *adj attrib* fig pej 本能地作出的 ‹*reaction, response*›

kneel /niːl/ *vi* (*pt, pp* **knelt** *or* esp Amer ~**ed**) **to** ~ **(down)** 跪下

knee: ~**-length** *adj* 及膝的; ~**-pad** *n* 护膝; ~**s-up** *n* Brit colloq 欢闹的聚会

knell /nel/ *n* **1** (sound of bell) 丧钟声; **to sound** *or* **toll the** ~ 敲响丧钟 **2** fig 破灭的预兆; = **death knell**

knelt /nelt/ *pt, pp* ▸**kneel**

knew /njuː, Amer nuː/ *pt* ▸**know A, B**

knickerbocker glory /ˌnɪkəbɒkə ˈglɔːri/ *n* esp Brit 彩宝圣代 [盛在高玻璃杯里的水果冰激凌]

knickerbockers /ˈnɪkəbɒkəz/ *npl* 灯笼裤

knickers /ˈnɪkəz/
A *npl* **1** Brit (underwear) 女式内裤; **to get one's** ~ **in a twist** colloq 恼火 **2** Amer (knickerbockers) 灯笼裤
B *excl* Brit colloq 讨厌; **oh,** ~ **to the lot of them!** 啾，让他们那伙人见鬼去吧！

knick-knack /ˈnɪknæk/ *n* colloq 小摆设

Kinship terms

Chinese kinship terms are the product of a complex and hierarchical family system and are considerably more specific than English kinship terms. All the terms below are still in common use today in the Chinese-speaking world.

English term		Chinese term
grandfather	paternal grandfather	祖父／爷爷
	maternal grandfather	外祖父／外公
grandmother	paternal grandmother	祖母／奶奶
	maternal grandmother	外祖母／外婆
grandson	son's son	孙子
	daughter's son	外孙
granddaughter	son's daughter	孙女
	daughter's daughter	外孙女
uncle	father's elder brother	伯父
	father's younger brother	叔父
	father's sister's husband	姑父／姑夫
	mother's brother	舅父
	mother's sister's husband	姨父／姨夫
aunt	father's elder brother's wife	伯母
	father's younger brother's wife	叔母／婶婶
	father's sister	姑母／姑妈
	mother's brother's wife	舅母／舅妈
	mother's sister	姨母／姨妈
brother	elder brother	哥哥
	younger brother	弟弟

English term			Chinese term
sister	elder sister		姐姐
	younger sister		妹妹
brother-in-law	elder sister's husband		姐夫
	younger sister's husband		妹夫
sister-in-law	elder brother's wife		嫂子
	younger brother' s wife		弟媳／弟妇／弟妹
cousin	father's brother's son	older	堂兄／堂哥
		younger	堂弟
	father's brother's daughter	older	堂姐
		younger	堂妹
	father's sister's son	older	姑表哥
		younger	姑表弟
	father's sister's daughter	older	姑表姐
		younger	姑表妹
	mother's brother's son	older	舅表哥
		younger	舅表弟
	mother's brother's daughter	older	舅表姐
		younger	舅表妹
	mother's sister's son	older	姨表哥
		younger	姨表弟
	mother's sister's daughter	older	姨表姐
		younger	姨表妹

knife /naɪf/
A *n* (*pl* **knives**) **1** (gen) 刀; **like a ～ through butter** 轻而易举地; **to go** *or* **be under the ～** colloq 接受手术; **the knives are out (for sb.)** （对某人）磨刀霍霍; **to get** *or* **stick the ～ into sb.** colloq (be vindictive or malicious) 对某人怀恨在心; (try to harm) 加害某人; **to turn** *or* **twist the ～ (in the wound)** 在伤口上撒盐; **the tension was so thick you could cut it with a ～** 局势剑拔弩张，空气似乎都凝滞了; **his accent is so thick you could cut it with a ～** 他的口音很重 **2** Ind (blade) 刀片
B *vt* 用刀砍; **he was ～d in the chest** 他胸口被砍了一刀

knife: ～ block *n* 刀架; **～-edge** *n* **1** lit 刀刃; **2** fig 紧张局势; **to be on a ～-edge** 胜负难料; **～ grinder** *n* 磨刀匠; **～ pleat** *n* 刀形窄褶; **～point** *n* 刀尖; **at ～point** 在刀子的威胁下; **he was robbed at ～point** 他遭到了持刀抢劫; **～ rest** *n* 刀叉架; **～ sharpener** *n* 磨刀器

knifing /ˈnaɪfɪŋ/ *n* [c and u] 持刀行凶

knight /naɪt/
A *n* **1** Hist 骑士; **the K～s of the Round Table** [亚瑟王传奇中的] 圆桌骑士; **a ～ in shining armour** fig 救人于危难之中的男子 **2** (holder of title 'Sir') 爵士 **3** (in chess) [国际象棋中的] 马
B *vt* Brit 封…为爵士

knight errant *n* Hist 游侠骑士

knighthood /ˈnaɪthʊd/ *n* 爵士头衔

knightly /ˈnaɪtli/ *adj* 骑士的 ‹*virtues, ideals*›

knit /nɪt/ (*pt, pp* **～ted**, **knit**)
A *vt* **1** (make) 编织; **to ～ sb. a sweater** 为某人织毛线衣 **2** fig (join together) 使紧密结合; **a closely-～ family** 关系融洽的家庭; **to ～ one's brows** 皱眉
B *vi* **1** (make with wool) 编织 **2** (join together) «*bones*» 愈合

Phrasal verbs

• **knit together**
A *vt* [**～ sth. together, ～ together sth.**]
1 lit 编 ‹*strands*› **2** fig (bring together) 使…紧密融合 ‹*ideas*› **3** fig (unite) 使…紧密团结 ‹*members of group*›
B *vi* **1** (join) «*bones*» 愈合; «*eyebrows*» 紧皱 **2** fig (unite) «*members of group*» 紧密团结

• **knit up**
A *vt* [**～ sth. up, ～ up sth.**] 编织 ‹*wool, yarn, garment*›
B *vi* «*yarn, wool*» 编织成衫

knitter /ˈnɪtə(r)/ *n* 编织者

knitting /ˈnɪtɪŋ/ *n* [u] **1** (process) 编织 **2** (material) 编织物 **3** (of bones etc.) 愈合

knitting: ～ bag *n* 装编织物的口袋; **～ machine** *n* 编织机; **～ needle** *n* 编结针; **～ wool** *n* [u] 毛线

knitwear /ˈnɪtweə(r)/ *n* [u] 针织品

knives /naɪvz/ *pl* ▸ **knife A**

knob /nɒb/ *n* **1** (handle) (of door, drawer) 球形把手; **the same to you with (brass) ～s on!** Brit colloq 你也一样，甚至更严重！ **2** (decoration) (on furniture, walking-stick etc.) 圆球饰 **3** (control button) 按钮 **4** (small lump) 小块; **a ～ of butter** 一小块黄油 **5** taboo sl (penis) 阴茎

knobbly /ˈnɒbli/ Brit, **knobby** /ˈnɒbɪ/ Amer *adjs* 多疙瘩的 ‹*vegetable*›; 有节的 ‹*wood*›; **～ knees/hands** 骨节突出的膝盖/手

knock /nɒk/
A *vt* **1** (strike) 碰撞; **to ～ one's head/arm on sth.** 把头/胳膊碰到某物上; **to ～ the egg against the side of the bowl** 在碗沿上把鸡蛋磕开 **2** (collide with) = **knock into** **3** (tap with knuckles or tool) 敲打; **to ～ sth. on the head** Brit fig (stop) 阻止…实施 ‹*plan*›; 扼杀 ‹*hope*›; (disprove) 打破 ‹*myth, belief*›; **to ～ sb.'s suggestion on the head** 对某人的建议横加指责 **4** (stun) 打昏; **to ～ sb. unconscious** *or* **cold** *or* **senseless** 打昏某人 **5** (cause to move) 敲动; (cause to fall) 碰落; **to ～ sb./sth. to the ground/floor** 把某人/某物撞倒在地; **to ～ sb./sth. flying/overboard** 把某人/某物击飞/打下船; **to ～ sb. flat** 把某人打倒在地; **to ～ sb./sth. across/over/down/into sth.** 把某人/某物打到某物的对面/另一面/下面/里面; **to ～ a ball over the wall** 把球打过墙; **to ～ a peg into the ground** 把桩子砸进地里; **to ～ a ball back and forth** 来来回回地打球; **to ～ sb./sth. against sth.** 使某人/某物撞到某物上; **to ～ sb./sth. off/out of sth.** 把某人/某物从某物上撞落/撞出某物; **to ～ sb./sth. out of the way** 把某人/某物推到一边; **the blow ～ed me off balance** *or* **off my feet** 这一下把我给撞倒了 **6** (produce by hitting) 打; **to ～ a hole/dent in sth.** 在某物上凿出一个洞/撞出一个凹痕; **to ～ two rooms into one** Brit 把两间房打通 **7** fig colloq (beat) 打击; **to ～ some sense/politeness into sb.** 迫使某人变得理智些/学得礼貌些; **to ～ sth. off/out of sb./sth.** 迫使某人/某事物停止某事物; **I'll ～ that smile off his face!** 我去揍他，看他还笑得出来！ **8** colloq (criticize) [尤指不公正地] 批评; **she's always ～ing the way I look** 她总是对我的外表评头论足; **to ～ modern art** 对现代艺术横加指责; **don't ～ it!** hum 嘴下留情啊！
B *vi* **1** (to call attention) 敲; **to ～ on** *or* **at sth.** 敲 ‹*door, window*› **2** (bang) 发出碰撞声 **3** Aut «*engine*» 突突响 **4** fig (in fear) «*knees*» 打颤; «*heart*» 怦怦跳
C *n* **1** (to call attention) 敲击声; **a ～ at** *or* **on sth.** 敲在…上的声音 ‹*door, window*›; **to give sb. a ～** (to awaken) 敲门叫醒某人; **～! ～!** 当当当！当当当！ **2** (blow) 碰撞; **to get a ～ on the head** 撞了一下头; **to give the ball quite a ～** 用力击球; **to give the car a bit of a ～** 刮碰到汽车 **3** fig (setback) 打击; **to take the ～s** 承受打击; **it gave his confidence a ～** 这件事打击了他的信心

Phrasal verbs

• **knock about** *vt, vi* Brit = **knock around**

• **knock against** *vt* [**～ against sb./sth.**] 撞上; **to ～ against each other** «*bottles*» 互相碰撞

• **knock around** colloq
A [**～ sth. around**] *vt* **1** (damage) 粗暴使用; **to ～ the furniture around** 对家具不爱惜 **2** Sport **to ～ the ball around** 把球踢来踢去 **3** (discuss) 非正式讨论 ‹*idea*›
B [**～ around sth.**] *vt* **1** (wander) 在…闲逛 ‹*area*›; **trousers for ～ing around the house in** 家居裤 **2** Brit (be lying around in) «*object*» 放在 ‹*house*›
C [**～ sb. around**] *vt* (beat) 虐待 ‹*person*›; **to ～ sb. around a bit** 折磨某人
D *vi* **1** (wander) 闲逛; **he's ～ed around a bit** 他游历甚广 **2** Brit (be present) 在…地方; **where's Jane? — she's ～ing around somewhere** 简在哪里？——她就在附近; **to ～ around together** 一起厮混; **to ～ around with sb.** 常与某人厮混

• **knock back**
A [**～ back sth., ～ sth. back**] *vt*
1 Sport 把…打回去 ‹*ball*› **2** colloq (drink) 猛喝; **to ～ back a couple of pints of beer** 猛喝几品脱啤酒
B [**～ sb. back**] *vt* colloq **1** (cost) **to ～ sb. back £50** 花了某人 50 英镑; **the court case ～ed me back a year's salary** 这场官司花了我一年的薪水 **2** Brit (surprise) 使吃惊

• **knock down** *vt* [**～ sb./sth. down, ～ down sb./sth.**]
1 (cause to fall) 撞倒 ‹*person, post*›; 打倒 ‹*victim, opponent*›; 碰落 ‹*object*›; 撞开 ‹*door*›; fig 排除 ‹*barrier*›; **to be ～ed down by lightning/a wave** 被雷电击倒/被大浪冲倒 **2** (demolish) 拆掉 ‹*building*›; fig 驳倒 ‹*opinion, argument*› **3** colloq (reduce) 减少; **to ～ the bill down by a few pounds** 把账单金额减少几英镑; **to ～ the price down 5%** 杀价 5%; **they're ～ing down all their prices** 他们正在全线降价; **to ～ one's fee down £20** 把收费降低 20 英镑; **the charges have been ～ed down (by) 15%** 收费降低了 15%; **to ～ sth. down (from/to sth.)** （从/到某数额）杀低 ‹*charge*›; **to ～ the price down from £100 to £75** 把要价从 100 英镑砍到 75 英镑 **4** colloq (get reduction from) 得到减价; **to ～ sb. down (to/from sth.)** 使…（从/到某数额）降价 ‹*seller*›; **to ～ the landlord down from £200 to £150** 把房东的要价从 200 英镑还到 150 英镑; **to ～ sb. down by a few pounds** 把某人的要价杀低几镑 **5** (sell at auction) 击槌卖出 ‹*painting, vase*›; **lot 36 was ～ed down at £180** 第 36 号拍品以 180 英镑拍出; **they can't ～ it down for less than the reserve price** 他们不能低于底价拍出这件东西

• **knock in** *vt* [**～ sth. in, ～ in sth.**]
1 (force in) 把…敲进去 ‹*nail, peg*›; **～ the bung in as far as it will go** 把塞子尽量塞得深一些 **2** (cause to break) 砸破 ‹*door, skull*›; **I'll ～ your teeth in!** 我要打掉你的牙！

• **knock into** *vt* [**～ into sb./sth.**] 撞到 ‹*person, table*›; **he staggered along, ～ing into people** 他在人群中跌跌撞撞地往前走; **to ～ into each other** 相撞

• **knock off**
A *vt* [**～ sb./sth. off, ～ off sb./sth.**]
1 (cause to fall) 打落 ‹*object*›; 撞倒 ‹*person*›; **the blow ～ed her glasses off** 这一拳把她的眼镜打掉了 **2** (break) 碰掉 ‹*end, handle*› **3** colloq (deduct) 减去 ‹*amount, percentage*›; **she wouldn't ～ anything off (the price)** 她一点也不肯降价; **they ～ off 10% if you pay cash** 若你付现金，他们就会给予 10% 的优惠; **to ～ 20% off the total** 把总价降低 20% **4** colloq (produce quickly) 匆匆完成; **on a good day she can ～ off 5,000 words** 她灵感突现的时候一天能写 5,000 字; **a poem I ～ed off** 我草草写成的一首诗 **5** colloq (finish) **to ～ off work** 下班 **6** **to ～ off doing sth.** colloq (stop) 停止做某事; **to ～ off smoking** 戒烟; **～ it off!** (stop making noise) 别吵了！ **7** Brit colloq (steal) 偷走; **to ～ off some pens from the office** 从办公室顺走几支钢笔 **8** colloq (murder) 谋杀; **he had his wife ～ed off** 他雇凶杀妻; **to get ～ed off in the final act** 在最后一幕中被杀了 **9** Brit colloq (have sex with) 与…上床; **he ～ed off the bridesmaid** 他和女傧相上了床
B *vi* colloq 收工

• **knock on**
A *vi* **1** **to be ～ing on (a bit)** Brit colloq (growing old) 变老; **the car's ～ing on a bit** 这辆汽车有点旧了 **2** (in rugby) 以手击球
B *vt* **1** Brit colloq (be nearly) **to be ～ing on 90** 快 90 岁了; **it was ～ing on midnight when we left** 我们离开的时候差不多半夜了 **2** (in rugby) **to ～ the ball on** 用手击球

• **knock out**
A [**～ sb. out, ～ out sb.**] *vt*
1 (stun) 打晕 ‹*person*›; **he nearly ～ed me out** 他差点把我打昏 **2** Sport 击倒 ‹*boxer*›; 摔倒 ‹*wrestler*›; **nobody has ever ～ed him out** 还没有人打倒过他 **3** colloq (exhaust) 使精疲力竭; **this heat really ～s you out** 这种炎热真让人乏力 **4** colloq (impress greatly) «*film, achievement*» 给…留下深刻印象; «*beauty, talent*» 迷住; «*news, results*» 使狂喜; **the view from the top of the mountain ～ed me out** 从山顶看到的美景让我着迷 **5** colloq (astonish) «*news, event*» 使惊讶 **6** Sport (eliminate) 淘汰 ‹*person, team*›; **France ～ed Argentina out of the World Cup** 法国队把阿根廷队淘汰出了世界杯比赛
B [**～ sth. out, ～ out sth.**] *vt*
1 (dislodge) 敲出 ‹*peg*›; 打破 ‹*window*›; 打掉 ‹*nail, tooth*›; **to ～ the contents out** 把里面的东西磕出来 **2** (destroy) «*hurricane, bomb*» 毁坏 ‹*factory, tank*›; **to be ～ed out by the storm** 被暴风雨摧毁 **3** (straighten) 敲平 ‹*dent, metal*› **4** colloq (produce) 快速完成 ‹*amount, book*›; **to ～ out five books a year**

k

(easily) 每年轻松写出五本书; **to ～ out a thousand words a day** (hurriedly) 每天赶写一千字

C *v refl* **to ～ oneself out** (with blow) 失去知觉; colloq (with drugs, alcohol) 陷入昏迷; colloq (with exertion) 精疲力竭; **don't ～ yourself out** 你别累坏了

• **knock over** *vt* [**～ sb./sth. over, ～ over sb./sth.**]
1 (cause to fall) 碰倒 ‹*person, object*›; **he nearly ～ed me over** 他差点把我撞了个跟头 **2** (run over) «*vehicle, driver*» 撞倒 ‹*pedestrian*›

• **knock through** *vi* (remove wall) 拆除隔墙; (create hole) 打通隔墙; **to ～ through between two bedrooms** 打通两间卧室

• **knock together**

A *vi* «*objects, elbows*» 碰到一起; **her knees were ～ing together** 她两只膝盖直哆嗦

B *vt* [**～ sth. together, ～ together sth.**]
1 (hit) 使…相碰 ‹*sticks, shoes*› **2** Brit (remove wall between) 把…打通 ‹*rooms, buildings*›; **two cottages ～ed together** 两栋打通的村舍

• **knock up**

A [**～ sth. up, ～ up sth.**] *vt* Brit (make) 草草做成; **a makeshift shelter had been ～ed up** 草草搭了一个临时窝棚; **I'll go into the kitchen and see what I can ～ up** 我去厨房看看能凑合着做点什么饭

B [**～ sb. up**] *vt*
1 colloq (make pregnant) 使怀孕 **2** colloq (exhaust) 使精疲力竭 **3** Brit colloq (wake) 敲门窗唤醒

C *vi* Sport 赛前练习

knockdown /ˈnɒkdaʊn/

A *n* 击倒; **he suffered repeated ～ blows** 他被连续的重拳击倒

B *adj attrib* colloq 低廉的; **at a ～ price** 以低价

knocker /ˈnɒkə(r)/

A *n* **1** (on door) 门环 **2** colloq (critic) 吹毛求疵的人

B **knockers** *npl* sl 奶子

knock-for-knock *adj* **a ～ agreement** 汽车互撞理赔协议

knocking /ˈnɒkɪŋ/ *n* [u] (gen) 敲击声; (in engine) 敲缸声

knocking copy *n* [u] [针对竞争对手产品的] 诋毁性广告

knocking-off time *n* [u] colloq 下班时间

knocking shop *n* Brit colloq 窑子

knock: ～-kneed *adj* 膝内翻的; **～ knees** *npl* 膝内翻

> **knock-knock joke**
>
> 敲门问答笑话。英语中常见的一种笑话，为甲、乙对答，共五句。前两句格式固定，甲以"Knock! Knock!"开始，乙问"Who's there?"。第三句甲回答"xx"（常常为人名），当中暗含包袱。第四句乙追问"xx who?"。最后一句为抖包袱（punch line），多为利用第三句回答的谐音制造喜剧效果。例："Knock! Knock!" "Who's there?" "Mary." "Mary who?" "Merry (Mary) Christmas!"

knock-on *n* (in rugby) 手臂向前击球

knock-on effect *n* esp Brit 连锁反应; **to have a ～** 产生连锁反应

knockout /ˈnɒkaʊt/

A *n* **1** (in boxing) (act) 击倒; (blow) 击倒对手的一拳 **2** colloq (impressive person) 引人注目的人; (impressive thing) 令人印象深刻的东西; **his girlfriend is a ～** 他的女友令人倾倒 **3** (tournament) 淘汰赛

B *modif* **1** Sport 击倒对手的 ‹*punch*›; **this news came as a ～ blow** 传来了这个令人震惊的消息 **2** colloq (brilliant) 精彩的 ‹*performance*›; **that's a ～ idea!** 这主意太棒了! **3** Brit esp Sport 淘汰的; **a ～ tournament** 淘汰赛

knock-up *n* 赛前热身

knoll /nəʊl/ *n* 圆丘

knot /nɒt/

A *n* **1** (fastening) 结; **to tie a ～** 打个结; **to cut the (Gordian) ～** fig 快刀斩乱麻; **to tie the (marriage) ～** colloq 结婚; **to tie sb. up in ～s** fig 使某人困惑不解 **2** (tied decoration) 花结 **3** (tangle in hair or string) 缠结 **4** (in wood) 节子 **5** (group) 一小群 **6** (tense feeling) 紧揪感; **he had a ～ in his stomach** 他感到心里一阵紧揪 **7** Naut, Aviat 节 [速度计量单位]; **at a rate of ～s** Brit colloq 飞快地

B *vt* (*pres p etc.* **-tt-**) **1** (tie in a knot) 把…打成结; **to ～ one's tie** 打领带 **2** (make tense) 使…紧揪 ‹*stomach*›

C *vi* (*pres p etc.* **-tt-**) **1** (form a knot) 打结 **2** (become tense) 紧揪

Phrasal verb

• **knot together** *vt* [**～ sth. together, ～ together sth.**] 把…打结

knothole /ˈnɒthəʊl/ *n* [木板的] 节孔

knotty /ˈnɒti/ *adj* **1** (gnarled, full of knots) 多节的 ‹*plank, pine*›; 骨节突出的 ‹*fingers, joints*›; 纠结的 ‹*hair*› **2** fig (complicated) 棘手的 ‹*problem, question*›

know /nəʊ/

A *vt* (*pt* **knew,** *pp* **known**) **1** (be aware of) 知道; **I ～ what I'm doing** colloq 我知道我在做什么; **you ～ perfectly well what I mean** 我的意思你心知肚明; **to let sb. ～ sth.** 告知某人某事; **to let it be known that one is dissatisfied (with sth.)** 公开表示（对某事物）不满; **to ～ what's what** colloq 见闻广博; **to ～ what's what about politics** 熟谙政治; **to ～ sth. about sb./sth.** 了解有关…的某事 ‹*person, event*›; **I don't ～ anything about art, but I ～ what I like** 我对艺术一窍不通，但我知道自己喜欢什么; **sb. is/was not to ～ (that) ...** 某人不会知道…; **to ～ to do sth.** 知道必须做某事; **I knew not to mention the war** 我知道不能提战争; **to ～ sb./sth./oneself to be sth.** 知道某人/某事物/自己是某情况; **I knew him to be a coward** 我知道他是个懦夫; **it's known that ...** 众所周知…; **it became known that ...** …的消息传开了; **it is not known how he died** 他死因不明; **not much is known about his early life** 关于他早年的生活大家知之甚少; **to make sth. known (to sb.)** （向某人）表明 ‹*views*›;（向某人）说明 ‹*information*›; **you ～ as well as I do** 你我都明白; **I'll have you ～ (that) ...** (emphatic) 我要让你明白…; **and don't I ～ it!** 我又何尝不知道!; **(do) you ～ what** *or* **something?** colloq 你知道吗?; **I ～ what!** 我明白了!; **(well,) what do you ～!** iron （哟，）真想不到!; **... and I don't ～ what** …以及诸如此类的东西; **you ～ what/who/where** *etc.* colloq (keeping secret) 你知道是什么/谁/哪里等; **God** *or* **heaven** *or* **goodness (only) ～s what/why/how** *etc.* colloq 天知道是什么/为什么/怎样等; **who ～s what/why/how** *etc.* 谁知道什么/为什么/怎样等; **to ～ one's place** 有自知之明; ▸**devil 2** **2** (be privy to) 知情; **you ～ something, don't you?** 你察觉到了什么，是不是? **3** (be sure about) 确知; **(not) to ～ for certain** *or* **sure what/how/where** *etc.* （不）确定什么/怎样/在哪里等; **it'll rain: I ～ it will** 要下雨了，肯定会下的; **to ～ sth. for a fact** 对某事物有把握; **I ～ for a fact that ...** 我肯定…; **I don't ～ that ...** 我没有把握…; **I don't ～ that I'm in favour of ...** 我不清楚是否应该赞成…; **I don't ～ what to think** 我拿不定主意; **there's no ～ing what/how** *etc.* 谁也不知道什么/怎样等; **he doesn't ～ what to do with himself** 他不知道该怎样打发时间; **you don't ～ what to do with yourself today, do you?** 你今天无所事事，是吗?; **not ～ where to put oneself** colloq 感到非常尴尬; **not ～ where** *or* **which way to look** 被眼前的景象弄得不知所措; **not ～ where** *or* **which way to turn** fig 不知所措; **not ～ whether one is coming or going** colloq 不知如何是好; **I'm so busy, I don't ～ whether I'm coming or going** 我忙得晕头转向 **4** (have in memory) 记得; **not ～ one's lines** 记不住台词; **to really ～ one's classical history** 在古典史方面造诣很深; **to ～ sth. by heart** 背诵 ‹*poem, part*› **5** (be able to speak) 懂得 ‹*language, Chinese*›; **to ～ enough Arabic to get by** 掌握的阿拉伯语能应付日常生活 **6** (possess ability at) 会; **to ～ what one is doing** 胜任所做的事; **he obviously didn't ～ what he was doing** 他显然不称职; **he certainly ～s how to upset people!** iron 他真会扰人不安! **7** (have experience of) 经历过; **to have known both poverty and wealth** 经历过贫穷和富有; **you have to ～ sorrow to ～ what happiness is** 要体会快乐就要先经历悲痛; **to ～ what it's like (to do sth.)** 体会过（做某事的）感受; **I ～ what it is to be hungry** 我尝过挨饿的滋味; **to ～ nothing/a lot/all** *etc.* **about sth.** 对某事物毫无/有深刻的/有刻骨的等体会 **8** (have seen) 见过; (have heard) 听说过; **I've never known him to lose his temper** 我从未见他发过脾气; **he has never been known to break a promise** 从未听说过他违背诺言; **it has been known (for sb./sth.) to do sth.** （某人/某物）做某事有其先例; **it has been known to snow in July** 七月飞雪确有其闻 **9** (be acquainted with) 认识; **you say you knew Mary: how well did you ～ her?** 你说你认识玛丽：你对她了解多少?; **to be known to sb.** 为某人所知; **to get to ～ sb.** 渐渐了解某人; **to ～ sb. by name/reputation/sight** 叫得出某人的名字/了解某人的声誉/与某人面熟; **to ～ the right people** 认识管用的人; **it's not what you ～ but who you ～** 本事大不如熟人多; **to ～ sb. to speak/talk to** 和某人熟悉到可以攀谈; **I ～ you!** 你就是这样! **10** (be familiar with) 熟悉; **(not) to ～ sth. very well** 对某事（不太）熟悉; **to get to ～ sth.** 渐渐熟悉某事物; **to ～ the/one's way (to sth.)** 熟悉（去某处的）路; **to ～ one's way around (sth.)** 熟悉（某处的）环境; fig 熟悉（某事物）; **he already ～s his way around** 他已经轻车熟路了; **to ～ what sb./sth. is** 熟悉某人/某事物的特性; **... as we ～ it** 我们所熟悉的…; **the end of civilization as we ～ it** iron 我们所熟悉的文明的终结; ▸**devil 2** **11** (recognize) 认出; **I hardly knew him** 我几乎认不出他来了; **I ～ an Irish accent when I hear one** 爱尔兰口音我一听就能听出来; **to ～ sb./sth. from sb./sth.** 能够把…和…区别开; **he ～s right from wrong** 他能分辨是非; **to ～ sb./sth. by sth.** 根据某特征认出某人/某事物; **I knew her by her voice** 我听到她的声音就知道是她; **it takes one to ～ one** hum 彼此彼此 **12** (use name for) 称呼; **to ～ sb./sth. as ...** 将某人/某事物称作…; **the disease that we ～ as German measles** 我们称之为风疹的疾病; **to be known as sb./sth. (to sb.), to be known (to sb.) as sb./sth.** （被某人）称为某人/某物; **Edward, better known as Ted** 爱德华，大家常称其为特德; **he is known to his employees as 'the Chief'** 他的雇员们管他叫"头儿" **13** (regard) 视为; **to ～ sb./sth. as** *or* **to be sth.** 把某人/某事物看作是某事物; **to be known as** *or* **to be sth.** 被视作某事物; **this kind of car is known to be unreliable** 这种汽车被认为性能不可靠; **to ～ sb./sth. for sth.** 认为某人/某事物是某情况; **they all knew him for a cheat** 他们都认为他是个骗子; **to be known for sth./doing sth.** 以某事/做某事而著称; **he's not known for (his) tolerance** iron 他的耐性可不好

B *vi* (*pt* **knew,** *pp* **known**) **1** (be aware) 知道; **to ～ about sb./sth.** 知道关于某人/某事物的情况; **to ～ about the change in the law** 知道对法律所作的修订; **to ～ of sb./sth.** 知道某人/某事物; **to ～ of sb. who can help** 知道某人能帮忙; **I don't ～ her, but I ～ of her** 我不认识她，但听说过她; **not that I ～**

of 据我所知没有; **to let sb. ~ (of** *or* **about sth.)** 告知某人（关于某事物的情况）; **I'll let you ~ as soon as I can** 我一有消息就通知你; **thank you, we'll let you ~** (polite refusal) 谢谢你，以后再说吧; **I ~** (agreeing, sympathizing) 我明白; (acknowledging) 我知道了; (introducing idea) 我有个主意; **it's your fault — I ~** 那是你的错——我知道; **I ~! let's go and see a film** 我有主意了！咱们去看电影吧; **I wouldn't ~** 我怎么知道呢; **how should I ~?** 我怎么会知道呢？; **if you must ~** 既然你非要知道; **I'll** *or* **I'd have you ~!** colloq 我告诉你吧！; **wouldn't you like** *or* **love to ~!** colloq 就不告诉你！; **as you ~** 如你所知; **the failure rate is very high, as you ~** 失败率很高，这一点你是知道的; **as well he ~s, as he well ~s** (from knowledge) 这一点他是知道的; (from experience) 这一点他是有体会的; **you ~** colloq (adding information) 你知道的; (emphasizing) 你要知道; **it's all a bit ..., you ~, ... under-the-counter** 这事有点，嗯，你知道，嗯，见不得人; **you ~, she could be telling the truth** 我觉得嘛，她说的可能是实话; **you ~, that's the first time I've seen ...** 真奇怪，那是我头一回看到…; **if you do that, you'll ~ about it** colloq 不要那样做，不然后果严重; **if the brakes fail, you'll ~ about it** 如果刹车失灵，后果不堪设想; **God** *or* **heaven** *or* **goodness (only) ~s** colloq 天知道; **who ~s?** colloq 谁知道呢？; **to ~ better** (know the truth) 知道真相; **to ~ better (than to do sth.)** (be sensible) 明事理（不至于做某事）; **he doesn't ~ any better** 他不懂事理 2 (be certain) 确知; **to ~ for certain** *or* **sure** 确定; **I think she's lying, but I don't ~** 我觉得她在撒谎，但我不能肯定; **I don't ~** (in disagreement) 我说不准; (in exasperation) 真是的; **he won't win — oh, I don't ~** 他不会获胜——哦，我可说不准; **I don't ~ about that** colloq 让我想想; **can I borrow your car? — oh, I don't ~ about that!** 我能借你的车吗？——哦，让我想想吧！; **is it useful? — I don't ~ about useful, but it's cheap** 这东西有用吗？——有没有用我不敢说，但它很便宜; **I don't ~ about you** (your opinion) 我不知道你怎么想; **there's no ~ing** 谁也不知道

C *n* **in the ~** colloq 知情; **to be in the ~ about sth.** 知晓某事物的内情

knowable /'nəʊəbl/ *adj pred* 可知的; **the total number is not ~** 总数不得而知

know-all *n* esp Brit colloq 自以为无所不知的人; **~ politicians** 自以为无所不知的政客

knowbot /'nəʊbɒt/ *n* 知识机器人软件

know: ~-how *n* colloq 实际知识; **~-it-all** *n* esp Amer colloq = **know-all**

knowing /'nəʊɪŋ/ *adj usu attrib* 1 (showing knowledge) 会意的 ‹*look, smile, wink, nod, glance*› 2 (deliberate) 故意的; **a ~ offence** 故意犯罪; **a ~ violation of the rules** 明知故犯的违规行为

knowingly /'nəʊɪŋli/ *adv* 1 (with knowledge) 会意地 ‹*look, smile, wink, nod*› 2 (deliberately) 故意地 ‹*deceive, offend*›; **to ~ risk sb.'s life** 在知情的情况下拿某人的生命冒险

knowledge /'nɒlɪdʒ/ *n* [u] 1 (store of factual information) 知识; (learning) 学问; **to have a wide/superficial ~ of sth.** 在某方面知识渊博/肤浅; **the sum of human ~** 人类知识的总和; **all branches of ~** 所有知识门类; **a thirst for ~** 对知识的渴求 2 (awareness) 了解; **to have ~ of sth.** 对某事物有了解; **to have no ~ of good or evil** 不能分辨善恶; **with the ~ that ...** 得知…; **to sb.'s ~** 据某人所知; **to bring sth. to sb.'s ~** formal 让某人了解某事物; **it has come to my ~ that ...** formal 我已经了解到…; **with sb.'s full ~, with the full ~ of sb.** 在某人完全知情的情况下; **without sb.'s ~, without the ~ of sb.** 在某人不知情的情况下 3 (grasp) 语言能力; **to have a working ~ of five languages** 会使用五种语言; **my ~ of Italian is limited** 我对意大利语知之甚少 4 (familiarity) 熟悉程度; **one's ~ of the city/legislation** 对这个城市/这项法规的熟悉程度

knowledgeable /'nɒlɪdʒəbl/ *adj* 博学的; **to be ~ about sth.** 对某事物很在行

knowledgeably /'nɒlɪdʒəbli/ *adv* 很有见识地 ‹*speak, write*›

knowledge: ~-based system *n* 知识库系统; **~ economy** *n* 知识经济; **~ engineer** ▸p. 409 *n* 知识工程师; **~ engineering** *n* [u] 知识工程; **~ management** *n* [u] 知识管理; **~ worker** ▸p. 409 *n* 知识工作者

known /nəʊn/

A *pp* ▸**know A, B**

B *adj* 1 (recognized) 为人所知的 ‹*fact, cure, danger*›; **~ to sb./sth.** 为某人/某事物所知的; **little ~ to sb./sth.** 某人/某事物知之甚少的 2 *attrib* (publicly acknowledged) 出了名的 ‹*criminal, liar*›; 知名的 ‹*expert*› 3 Math 已知的; **a ~ quantity/variable** 已知量/已知变量

knuckle /'nʌkl/ *n* 1 (of person) 指关节; **to get a rap on** *or* **over the ~s** lit 被敲打指关节; fig 挨批评; **near the ~** Brit colloq 近乎下流 2 Culin (of lamb, pork) 蹄

Phrasal verbs

- **knuckle down** *vi* colloq 开始认真工作; **to ~ down to sth.** 开始努力做某事
- **knuckle under** *vi* colloq 认输

knuckle: ~bone *n* 指节骨; **~bones** ▸p. 307 *n* 抛接子游戏; **~-duster** *n* 指节铜套; **~head** *n* colloq 笨蛋; **~ joint** *n* 1 Anat 指节; 2 Mech 铰链接合

knurl /nɜːl/ *n* (in wood) 木节; (in metal) 滚花

knurled /nɜːld/ *adj* 有滚花的; **this coin has a ~ edge** 这枚硬币边上有滚花

KO Boxing

A *abbr* = **knockout A1**

B *vt* = **knock out A2**

koala /kəʊ'ɑːlə/ *n* **~(bear)** 树袋熊

kohlrabi /ˌkəʊl'rɑːbi/ *n* [c and u] 球茎甘蓝

kook /kuːk/ *n* Amer colloq (crazy person) 怪人; (fool) 蠢人

kookaburra /'kʊkəbʌrə/ *n* 笑翠鸟

kooky, kookie /'kuːki/ *adj* Amer colloq 愚蠢的 ‹*person*›; 荒诞的 ‹*character, idea*›; 怪异的 ‹*charm*›

kopek, kopeck /'kəʊpek/ *n* 戈比 [俄罗斯辅币名，100戈比合1卢布]

Koran /kə'rɑːn/ *n* **the ~** 《古兰经》

Koranic /kə'rænɪk/ *adj attrib* 《古兰经》的

Korea /kə'rɪə/ *pr n* 朝鲜半岛

Korean /kə'rɪən/ ▸p. 503, p. 426

A *adj* 1 (of South Korea) 韩国的; (of the people) 韩国人的 2 (of North Korea) 朝鲜的; (of the people) 朝鲜人的 3 (of the South or North Korean language) 朝鲜语的

B *n* 1 [c] (South Korean person) 韩国人; (North Korean person) 朝鲜人 2 [u] (South or North Korean language) 朝鲜语

korfball /'kɔːfbɔːl/ *n* [u] 合球 [类似篮球，比赛双方各6男6女]

korma /'kɔːmə/ *n* 拷玛 [一种印度菜，用肉或鱼浸在酸奶里制成]

kosher /'kəʊʃə(r)/ *adj* 1 Relig 合礼的 ‹*food, restaurant*› 2 colloq (legitimate) 合法的

Kosovar /'kɒsəvɑː(r)/, **Kosovan** /'kɒsəvn/ ▸**p. 503**

A *adj* 科索沃的

B *n* 科索沃人

Kosovo /'kɒsəvəʊ/ *pr n* 科索沃

Kowloon /kaʊ'luːn/ *pr n* 九龙

kowtow /kaʊ'taʊ/ *vi* 卑躬屈膝; **to ~ to sb./sth.** 在某人/某事物面前唯唯诺诺; **to ~ to convention** 屈从于习俗

kph *abbr* = **kilometres per hour** 千米/小时; **a speed of 60 ~** 时速 60 公里

Kremlin /'kremlɪn/ *pr n* **the ~** (building) 克里姆林宫; (Russian government) 俄罗斯政府; (former USSR government) 苏联政府

krill /krɪl/ *n* (*pl* **krill**) 磷虾

Krishna /'krɪʃnə/ *pr n* 克利须那 [印度教中的至尊神]

krona /'krəʊnə/ ▸p. 174 *n* Fin 1 (*pl* **kronor** /'krəʊnə/) (of Sweden) 克朗 [瑞典货币单位，1克朗合100欧尔] 2 (*pl* **kronur** /'krəʊnə/) (of Iceland) 克朗 [冰岛货币单位，1克朗合100奥拉]

krone /'krəʊnə/ ▸p. 174 *n* (*pl* **kroner** /'krəʊnə/) (of Denmark, Norway) 克朗 [丹麦和挪威货币单位，1克朗合100欧尔]

krypton /'krɪptɒn/ *n* [u] 氪

KS *abbr* Amer = **Kansas**

Kt *abbr* = **knight A**

Kuala Lumpur /ˌkwɑːlə 'lʊmpʊə(r)/ *pr n* 吉隆坡

kudos /'kjuːdɒs/ *n* [u] (honour and glory) 荣誉; (credit) 赞扬; (prestige) 声望

Ku Klux Klan /ˌkuː klʌks 'klæn/ *n* 三 K 党 [美国白人极端种族主义组织]

kumquat /'kʌmkwɒt/ *n* (fruit) 金柑; (tree) 金柑树

kung fu /ˌkʊŋ 'fuː/ ▸p. 307 *n* 功夫; *modif* **a ~ film** 武打片

Kuomintang /ˌkwəʊmɪn'tæŋ/ *n* [中国] 国民党

Kurd /kɜːd/ *n* 库尔德人

Kurdish /'kɜːdɪʃ/ ▸p. 503, p. 426 *adj* (of the people) 库尔德人的; (of the language) 库尔德语的

Kurdistan /ˌkɜːdɪ'stæn/ *pr n* 库尔德斯坦

Kuwait /kʊ'weɪt/ *pr n* 科威特; **~ City** 科威特城

Kuwaiti /kʊ'weɪti/ ▸p. 503

A *adj* (of Kuwait) 科威特的; (of the people) 科威特人的

B *n* 科威特人

kW *abbr* = **kilowatt(s)** 千瓦

kwashiorkor /ˌkwæʃɪ'ɔːkɔː(r)/ ▸p. 377 *n* [u] 夸希奥科病 [缺乏蛋白质引起的热带儿科病]

kWh *abbr* = **kilowatt-hour(s)** 千瓦时

KY *abbr* Amer = **Kentucky**

Kyrgyz /'kɜːgɪz/ ▸p. 503, p. 426

A *adj* (of Kyrgyzstan) 吉尔吉斯斯坦的; (of the people) 吉尔吉斯斯坦人的; (of the language) 吉尔吉斯斯坦语的

B *n* 1 [c] (person) 吉尔吉斯斯坦人 2 [u] (language) 吉尔吉斯斯坦语

Kyrgyzstan /ˌkɜːgɪ'stæn, ˌkɪəgɪ-, -stɑːn/ *pr n* 吉尔吉斯斯坦

Ll

L, l /el/

A *n* (*pl* **Ls** *or* **L's**) [英语字母表的第12个字母]

B *abbr* **1** **L = Lake L Windermere** 温德米尔湖 **2** **L = learner-driver** **3** **L = large** 大号的 **4** **l = left** 左 [用于书面] **5** **l = line** 诗行 **6** **l = litre(s)** Brit, **liter(s)** Amer 升

LA *abbr* Amer **1** **= Los Angeles** 洛杉矶 **2** **= Louisiana**

la /lɑː/ *n* **= lah**

lab /læb/ *n* colloq 实验室; **the science/research ~** 科学/研究实验室

Lab. /læb/ *abbr* Brit **= Labour A; H. Moore ~** 工党的H·穆尔

lab coat *n* 实验室白大褂

label /ˈleɪbl/

A *n* **1** (on clothing, jar, luggage, diagram) 标签; **a price/warning ~** 价格标签/警示标示; **an address ~** 地址签条; **to put a ~ on sth.** 在某物上贴标签 **2** fig 称号; **I hated the ~ 'housewife'** 我讨厌"家庭主妇"这个称谓; **his critics hung** *or* **stuck the ~ (of) 'superficial' on his work** 评论家给他的作品扣上了"肤浅"的帽子 **3** Mus 唱片公司 **4** Fashn 时装品牌 **5** Comput 标识符 **6** (in dictionary) 标注

B *vt* (*pres p etc.* **-ll-**) **1** (attach label to) 贴标签于; **a machine for ~ling wine bottles** 给酒瓶贴标签的机器; **the air-freshener was ~led 'ozone-friendly'** 这种空气清新剂标明"对臭氧层无害" **2** fig 把…归类; **her work is difficult to ~ accurately** 她的作品很难准确归类; **he is usually ~led as an Impressionist** 人们通常称他为印象派艺术家 **3** (tag in dictionary) 给…加标注

labelling /ˈleɪblɪŋ/ *n* [u] (act) 加标签; (information) 标签信息

labia /ˈleɪbɪə/ *npl* 阴唇

labial /ˈleɪbɪəl/ *adj* **1** Anat 唇的 **2** Ling 唇音的

labiodental /ˌleɪbɪəʊˈdentl/ *adj* 唇齿音的

labiovelar /ˌleɪbɪəʊˈviːlə(r)/ *adj* 圆唇软颚音的

labor /ˈleɪbə(r)/ *n, vi, vt* Amer **= labour**

laboratory /ləˈbɒrətri, Amer ˈlæbrətɔːri/ *n* 实验室; **a chemistry/physics ~** 化学/物理实验室

laboratory: ~ assistant *n* 实验室助理; **~ technician** *n* 实验室技术员

Labor Department *n* Amer 劳工部

labored /ˈleɪbəd/ *adj* Amer **= laboured**

laborer /ˈleɪbərə(r)/ *n* Amer **= labourer**

laborious /ləˈbɔːrɪəs/ *adj* **1** (requiring a lot of effort) 艰巨的 ‹*task*›; 艰难的 ‹*process, journey*› **2** (showing signs of great effort) 生硬的 ‹*style, speech*›

laboriously /ləˈbɔːrɪəsli/ *adv* 艰苦地

labor union *n* Amer 工会

Labour /ˈleɪbə(r)/

A *pr n* Brit 工党; **to vote ~** 投工党的票

B *modif* 工党的 ‹*MP, government, policy*›; **the ~ vote** 投给工党的选票

labour /ˈleɪbə(r)/ Brit

A *n* **1** [c and u] (work) 劳动; **manual ~** 体力劳动; **the division of ~** 分工; **to withdraw one's ~** 罢工; **a ~ of love** 出于热爱而做的工作; **the ~s of Hercules** 异常艰巨的任务 **2** [u] (workers) 劳工; **cheap ~** 廉价劳动力; **skilled/unskilled ~** 熟练/非熟练工人 **3** [c and u] Med 分娩; **to go into** *or* **begin ~** 开始分娩; **to be in ~** 正在分娩; **an easy/difficult ~** 顺产/难产

B *modif* 劳动力的 ‹*costs, shortage*›; 劳资的 ‹*dispute*›; 工会的 ‹*leader*›; **the graduate ~ market is changing** 毕业生就业市场正在发生变化

C *vi* **1** (work hard) 努力; **he's been ~ing at** *or* **over the report since Wednesday** 自星期三以来他一直忙着写这份报告; **to ~ to do sth.** 努力做某事; **they were ~ing to finish the job on time** 他们正努力争取按时完成工作 **2** (have difficulties) 费力地做; Aut «*engine*» 缓慢运转; **he was ~ing to breathe** 他吃力地呼吸着; **the car ~ed up the hill** 这辆车费力地爬上了山 **3** (suffer) **to ~ under a misapprehension/a handicap** 为误会/障碍所蒙蔽; **he's ~ing under the delusion that he is going to be offered the job** 他有一种错觉，以为自己会得到这份工作; **we must not ~ under the illusion that we are safe** 我们一定不要误以为我们是安全的

D *vt* **to ~ the point** 一再重复已说明的事; **if you keep ~ing the point, your arguments become less effective** 如果你总是重复，你的论点就会变得没有说服力

labour: ~ camp *n* 劳改营; **L~ Day** *n* (May 1) 国际劳动节; Amer, Can (first Monday of September) 劳工节

laboured /ˈleɪbəd/ *adj* Brit **1** (difficult) 缓慢困难的 ‹*movement, breathing*› **2** (cumbersome) 生硬的 ‹*introduction, style*›

labourer /ˈleɪbərə(r)/ ▸**p. 409** *n* Brit 体力劳动者; **a farm ~** 农场工人

labour: L~ Exchange *n* Brit dated **= Job Centre**; **~ force** *n* 劳动力; **~-intensive** *adj* 劳动密集型的 ‹*industry, process, work*›

Labourite /ˈleɪbəraɪt/ *n* Brit often pej 工党支持者

labour: ~ law *n* **1** [u] (body of laws) 劳动法规; **2** [c] (single law) 劳动法; **~ movement** *n* 工人运动; **~ pains** *npl* 分娩阵痛; **L~ Party** *n* Brit **the L~ Party** 工党; **~ relations** *npl* 劳资关系; **~-saving** *adj* 省力的 ‹*device, machinery*›; **~ ward** *n* 产房

> **the Labour Party**
>
> 工党，亦称 Labour。英国三大政党之一，成立于1900年，始称"工人代表委员会"（Labour Representation Committee），1906年改为现名。1924年首次组阁，取代自由党的地位，与保守党交替执政。工党代表工人阶级的利益，传统上得到工会的支持。20世纪80至90年代，工党放弃了以前的一些左倾政策，开始走第三条道路（▸**the third way**），转型成为"新工党"（New Labour）。1997年，工党在大选中大获全胜，在野多年后成为执政党。

labrador /ˈlæbrədɔː(r)/ *n* 拉布拉多犬; **a ~ retriever** 拉布拉多寻回犬

lab technician *n* colloq **= laboratory technician**

laburnum /ləˈbɜːnəm/ *n* 金链花

labyrinth /ˈlæbərɪnθ/ *n* 迷宫; **a ~ of dark corridors** 迷宫似的昏暗走廊; **a veritable ~ of procedures** fig 复杂烦琐的手续

labyrinthine /ˌlæbəˈrɪnθaɪn, Amer -θɪn/ *adj* 错综复杂的 ‹*structure, law, procedure*›

lace /leɪs/

A *n* **1** [u] (fabric) 花边; **a piece of ~** 一条花边; **edged** *or* **trimmed with ~** 镶花边的 **2** [c] (of shoe, boot, dress) 鞋带; (of tent) 系带; **to tie one's ~s** 系鞋带

B *modif* 蕾丝的 ‹*curtain, handkerchief*›; **~ industry** 蕾丝编织业

C *vt* **1** (fasten, tie) 系上 ‹*dress*›; **to ~ sb. into sth.** 帮某人束紧 ‹*corset*›; **to ~ one's shoes** 系鞋带 **2** (add substance to) 为…调味 ‹*drink, food*›; **to ~ a drink with alcohol/poison** 在饮料中掺入酒精/毒药

Phrasal verb

• **lace up**

A *vt* [**~ sth. up, ~ up sth.**] 系上 ‹*dress, boots, corset*›; **to ~ up one's shoes** 系鞋带

B *vi* 系带; **a dress that ~s up at the back** 从后面系带的连衣裙

lace: ~-maker ▸**p. 409** *n* 蕾丝制造商; **~-making** *n* [u] 蕾丝编织

lacerate /ˈlæsəreɪt/ *vt* **1** lit (cut) 割裂 **2** fig (rip into) 抨击 ‹*film, person*›; 挫伤 ‹*feelings*›

laceration /ˌlæsəˈreɪʃn/ *n* [c and u] 割裂; **facial ~s** 面部裂伤; **~s to ...** …处的割伤 ‹*arm, leg*›

lace-up

A *n* 系带的鞋

B *adj* 系带的 ‹*shoe, garment*›

lack /læk/

A *n* 缺乏; **a/no ~ of sth.** 某物的缺乏/不缺乏; **there is a ~ of parking spaces in the town** 城里停车位不够用; **there is no ~ of PhDs in universities** 大学里不缺博士; **for** *or* **through ~ of** 因缺乏 ‹*funds, evidence*›

B *vt* 缺乏 ‹*confidence, funds, talent, time*›; **to ~ a sense of proportion** 不知分寸; **to ~ the courage of one's convictions** 没有勇气坚持自己的信念

C *vi* 缺乏; **to be ~ing** «*clothing, food, funding*» 短缺; **to be ~ing in** 缺少 ‹*humour, experience, raw materials*›; …不足 ‹*ability*›; **to ~ for nothing** 什么也不缺

lackadaisical /ˌlækəˈdeɪzɪkl/ *adj* 懒散的 ‹*person, attitude*›; **to be ~ about sth.** 对…不热心 ‹*studies, work*›

lackey /ˈlæki/ *n* **1** (servant) [尤指穿制服的] 男仆 **2** fig pej 走狗

lacking /ˈlækɪŋ/ *adj pred* colloq 缺乏的; **as a scholar, you will find him somewhat ~** 你会发现他作为学者能力一般

lacklustre Brit, **lackluster** Amer /ˈlæklʌstə(r)/ *adj* 枯燥乏味的 ‹*speech, performance*›; **~ eyes** 黯淡的眼神

laconic /ləˈkɒnɪk/ *adj* 简洁的 ‹*style, remark*›; 谈吐简洁的 ‹*speaker*›

lacquer /ˈlækə(r)/

A *n* **1** (on metal, wood) 漆; **a coat of ~** 一层漆 **2** dated **(hair) ~** 喷发胶

B *vt* 用漆涂 ‹*wood, metal*›; 给…喷发胶 ‹*hair*›

lacrosse /ləˈkrɒs, Amer -ˈkrɔːs/ ▸**p. 307** *n* [u] 长曲棍球

lacrosse stick *n* 长曲棍球球棍

lactate /lækˈteɪt/ *vi* 泌乳

lactation /lækˈteɪʃn/ *n* 泌乳

lactic acid /ˌlæktɪk ˈæsɪd/ *n* 乳酸

lacto-ovo-vegetarian /ˌlæktəʊˌəʊvəʊˌvedʒɪˈteərɪən/ *n, adj* 乳蛋素食者（的）

lactose /ˈlæktəʊz, -s/ *n* [u] 乳糖

lacto-vegetarian /ˌlæktəʊˌvedʒɪˈteərɪən/ *n, adj* 乳品素食者（的）

lacuna /ləˈkjuːnə/ *n* (*pl* **lacunae** /ləˈkjuːniː/) (missing section) 脱漏; (gap) 空白; **to fill a ~ in sth.** 填补某领域的空白

lacy /ˈleɪsi/ *adj* (made out of lace) 蕾丝的 ‹*clothing, tablecloth*›; (trimmed with lace) 镶花边的 ‹*petticoat, underwear*›; (resembling lace) 网眼状的 ‹*fabric, cloud, pattern*›

lad /læd/ colloq

A *n* **1** (boy) 男孩; (young man) 男青年; **come in, ~** 进来吧，小伙子 **2** Brit (lively man) 浪荡子; **Tony was a bit of a ~ — he always had an eye for the women** 托尼真是个花花公子——总是很会欣赏女人 **3** Equit (stable worker) 马夫

B **lads** *npl* 哥们儿; **to go out with the ~s** 和伙伴们一起出去玩; **come in, ~s** 进来吧，哥们儿

ladder /ˈlædə(r)/

A *n* **1** (for climbing) 梯子; **to climb up/down a ~** 爬上/爬下梯子; **the property ~** fig 房产阶梯 [指房产市场]; **to work one's way up** *or* **to climb to the top of the social/career ~** 费力地爬到社会顶层/最高职位; **to be at the bottom/top of the ~** lit 在梯子底端/顶端; fig 在最底/最高层 **2** Brit (in tights, stockings) 抽丝; **to have a ~ in one's tights/stockings** 裤袜/长统袜有一处抽丝

B *vt* Brit 使…抽丝 ‹*tights, stockings*›

C *vi* Brit «*tights, stockings*» 抽丝

ladderproof /ˈlædəpruːf/ *adj* Brit 防抽丝的 ‹*tights, stockings*›

laddie /ˈlædi/ *n* esp Scot colloq (boy) 男孩; (young man) 小伙子

laddish /ˈlædɪʃ/ *adj* colloq pej 小男孩似的 ‹*behaviour, manner, humour, bloke, boyfriend*›; 适合小男孩的 ‹*TV programme, magazine*›

laden /ˈleɪdn/ *adj* 满载的 ‹*cart, lorry*›; **~ with sth.** 装满…的 ‹*supplies, fruit*›; **~ in bulk** Comm 散装满载的

ladette /læˈdet/ *n* Brit colloq 狂放女人

la-di-da /ˌlɑːdɪˈdɑː/ *adj* colloq pej 做作的 ‹*airs, voice*›

ladies': ~ night *n* 女士之夜 [夜总会面向女士的免费或优惠场]; **~ room** *n* 女洗手间

ladle /ˈleɪdl/

A *n* **1** Culin 长柄勺 **2** Ind 铸勺

B *vt* 用大勺舀 ‹*soup, cream*›; **to ~ sth. into/over sth.** 把某物舀到某物里/舀起浇在某物上

Phrasal verb

- **ladle out** *vt* [**~ sth. out, ~ out sth.**] **1** Culin 用大勺舀 ‹*soup, food*› **2** fig colloq 慷慨地给予 ‹*money*›; **he's not one to ~ out praise** 他不轻易夸赞别人

lad mag *n* colloq 男性向杂志

lady /ˈleɪdi/

A *n* **1** (woman) 女士; **ladies first** 女士先请; **ladies and gentlemen** (at the start of a speech) 女士们，先生们; **his young ~** dated 他的女友; **your good ~** dated 尊夫人; **my old ~** colloq 我老婆; **look here, young ~!** colloq 喂，小姐！; **the ~ of the house** 主妇; **a little old ~** 一个小老太太; **hey ~! — you can't park there!** Amer colloq 嘿，女士！——不能在那里泊车！; **a ~ doctor/writer** 女医生/作家 **2** (woman of good manners) 淑女 **3** **Lady** Brit (in titles) (wife of some nobles) 夫人; (daughter of some nobles) 小姐; **L~ Churchill** 丘吉尔夫人; **L~ Philippa (Stewart)** 菲利帕（·斯图亚特）小姐 **4** **Lady** (in official titles) 阁下; **the L~ Mayoress** 市长女士阁下 **5** Relig **Our Lady** 圣母

B **Ladies** *npl + v sing or pl* Brit **the Ladies** 女洗手间

lady: ~bird Brit, **~bug** Amer *ns* 瓢虫; **L~ Chapel** *n* [大教堂内的] 圣母堂; **~ friend** *n* dated [多指男子的] 女友; **~-in-waiting** *n* [皇室的] 女侍臣; **~-killer** colloq *n* 女性杀手 [善于勾引女子的帅男]

ladylike /ˈleɪdɪlaɪk/ *adj* 淑女般的; **~ behaviour** 文静娴雅的举止; **it is not ~ to do …** 做…不文雅

ladylove /ˈleɪdɪlʌv/ *n* dated 情妇

Ladyship /ˈleɪdɪʃɪp/ *n* (woman) 夫人; (girl) 小姐; **Your/Her ~** (woman) 夫人; (girl) 小姐; **Her ~ wants you!** iron hum (woman) 夫人要见您！; (girl) 小姐要见您！

lady's maid *n* 贴身女侍

lag¹ /læg/

A *n* (time period) (lapse) 时间间隔; (delay) 延搁; **a (time) ~ of half an hour** 半个小时的间隔

B *vi* (*pres p etc.* **-gg-**) «*person, price, wages*» 落后

Phrasal verb

- **lag behind**

A *vi* 落后

B *vt* [**~ behind sb./sth.**] 落后于; **wages are ~ging behind prices** 工资没有物价涨得快

lag² *vt* (*pres p etc.* **-gg-**) 给…装隔热材料 ‹*boiler, roof*›; 给…加保暖层 ‹*pipes, hot-water tank*›; **to ~ the roof with fibreglass** 给屋顶铺玻璃纤维以隔热

lag³ *n* colloq (convict) 囚犯

lager /ˈlɑːgə(r)/ *n* **1** [u and c] 拉格啤酒 [一种多泡沫的淡啤酒] **2** [c] (glass of) 一杯拉格啤酒; (pint of) 一品脱拉格啤酒

lager lout *n* Brit colloq pej 耍酒疯的男青年

laggard /ˈlægəd/ *n* dated 落后者; **he's no ~ when it comes to asking for money** 他要钱的时候可一点都不含糊

lagging /ˈlægɪŋ/ *n* [u] 隔热材料

lagoon /ləˈguːn/ *n* 环礁湖

lah /lɑː/ *n* [大调音阶的第6音]

laid /leɪd/ *pt, pp* ▸**lay¹ A, B**

laidback /ˌleɪdˈbæk/ *adj* colloq 悠闲放松的 ‹*temperament, music, atmosphere*›; **he is very ~ about everything** 他对一切事都漫不经心的

lain /leɪn/ *pp* ▸**lie¹ A**

lair /leə(r)/ *n* **1** (of animal) 兽穴 **2** fig 藏身处

laird /leəd/ *n* Scot 地主

lake /leɪk/ *n* 湖; **the Great L~s** 五大湖; **go and jump in the ~!** colloq 滚开！

lake: L~ Baikal /ˌleɪk baɪˈkɑːl/ *pr n* 贝加尔湖; **~ dweller** *n* 湖上居民; **~ dwelling** *n* 湖上木排屋; **L~ Erie** /ˌleɪk ˈɪəri/ *pr n* 伊利湖; **L~ Huron** /ˌleɪk ˈhjʊərɒn/ *pr n* 休伦湖; **L~ Michigan** /ˌleɪk ˈmɪtʃɪgən/ *pr n* 密歇根湖; **L~ Ontario** *pr n* 安大略湖

lakeside /ˈleɪksaɪd/

A *n* 湖边; **by** *or* **on the ~** 在湖边

B *modif* 湖边的 ‹*path, cottage, village*›

Lake: ~ Superior *pr n* 苏必利尔湖; **~ Victoria** *pr n* 维多利亚湖

la-la-land /ˈlɑːlɑːlænd/ *n* [u] Amer colloq **1** (Hollywood) 拉拉城 [指好莱坞或洛杉矶] **2** (dreamworld) 幻想世界

lam /læm/ *vt* colloq 重击 ‹*object, ball*›; 痛打 ‹*person*›; **one more word and I'll ~ you!** 再说一个字我就揍扁你！

Phrasal verb

- **lam into** *vt* [**~ into sb./sth.**] (physically) 重击; (verbally) 抨击

lama /ˈlɑːmə/ *n* 喇嘛

lamasery /ˈlɑːməsəri, ləˈmɑːsəri/ *n* 喇嘛寺

lamb /læm/

A *n* **1** [c] (animal) 羔羊; **like a ~ to the slaughter** 不加反抗地; **sacrificial ~** lit 燔祭用的羔羊; fig 牺牲品; ▸**sheep 1** **2** [u] Culin 羔羊肉; **leg of ~** 羔羊腿肉; **spring ~** 早春嫩羊肉 **3** [c] colloq (term of endearment) 宝贝;

ℹ Lakes

■ There are many different words for 'lake' in Chinese such as 湖 (hu), 池 (chi), 泊 (po), 海 (hai), 潭 (tan), 淀 (dian), etc. 湖 is the most often used. Note that 湖, 池, etc. always come after the name of the lake in Chinese:

Lake Tai
or ***Tai Hu***
or ***Lake Taihu***
or ***Taihu Lake***
= 太湖

Lake Qinghai
or ***Qinghai Lake***
or ***Qinghai Hu***
= 青海湖

Lake Wudalianchi
or ***Wudalian Chi***
= 五大连池

Dian Lake
or ***Lake Dianchi***
or ***Dian Chi***
= 滇池

Lake Luobu Po
or ***Luobu Po Lake***
or ***Luobu Po***
= 罗布泊

the Black Sea
= 黑海

Erhai Lake
= 洱海

Lake Jingyue
or ***Jingyue Lake***
or ***Jingyuetan***
= 净月潭

Lake Baiyangdian
or ***Baiyangdian***
= 白洋淀

■ In English, the word 'lake' sometimes appears before the name and sometimes after it. In Chinese, 湖 always follows the name of the lake:

Lake Victoria
= 维多利亚湖

Lake Superior
= 苏必利尔湖

Lake Baikal
= 贝加尔湖

Bear Lake
= 贝尔湖

my little ～! 我的小乖乖！; the ～ of God 耶稣
B vi «ewe» 产羔

lambaste, lambast /læm'beɪst, -'bæst/ vt colloq 狠批

lambing /'læmɪŋ/ n [u] 产羔; ～ time or the ～ season 产羔期

lambskin /'læmskɪn/ n 羔皮; a ～ coat 羔皮大衣

lamb's wool n 羔羊毛; a ～ jumper 羔羊毛套衫

lame /leɪm/
A adj 1 (unable to walk) 瘸腿的 ‹person, animal›; to go ～ 腿瘸了; to be ～ in the left/right leg 左/右腿瘸了; to be slightly ～ 腿稍微有点瘸 2 fig (poor) 缺乏说服力的 ‹excuse, explanation, argument›
B vt 使…腿瘸 ‹person, animal›; he was ～d in a riding accident 他在一次坠马事故中瘸了腿
C npl the ～ 瘸腿的人

lamé /'lɑːmeɪ/
A n [u] 金银锦缎
B modif 金银锦缎的 ‹material, dress, suit›

lame duck
A n 跛脚鸭 [指处于困境需要帮助的人、事物或机构]
B modif Amer 将届满卸任的 ‹government, president›

lamely /'leɪmli/ adv 缺乏说服力地 ‹argue, say, excuse oneself›; a ～ worded argument/apology 苍白无力的论点/道歉

lameness /'leɪmnɪs/ n [u] 1 (of person, animal) 瘸腿 2 fig (of argument, excuse) 缺乏说服力

lament /lə'ment/
A n 1 (expression of grief) 悲痛 2 (song) 挽歌; (poem) 哀诗; a funeral ～ (song) 葬礼挽歌; (poem) 葬礼悼词; a ～ to sb. or sth. (song) 悼念某人/某事物的挽歌; (poem) 悼念某人/某事物的哀诗
B vt 1 (grieve over) 为…感到悲痛 ‹sb.'s death, disappearance of sb. or sth., loss›; the late ～ed John Adams 新近辞世的约翰·亚当斯; to ～ one's dead friend 哀悼亡友; to ～ one's fate or misfortune 悲叹自己的不幸 2 (complain about) 抱怨 ‹lack of sth.›; to ～ that … 抱怨…
C vi 1 (grieve) 感到悲痛; to ～ for or about sb./sth. 为某人/某事物感到悲痛 2 (complain) 抱怨; to ～ about sth. 抱怨某事物

lamentable /'læməntəbl/ adj 令人惋惜的 ‹state, incident, loss, result›

lamentably /'læməntəbli/ adv 令人惋惜地 ‹inadequate, ignorant, behave, fail›

lamentation /ˌlæmən'teɪʃn/ n 1 [u] (grieving) 悲痛 2 [c] (expression of grief) 恸哭; the wails and ～s 号啕痛哭

laminate
A /'læmɪneɪt/ vt 1 (cover with protective material) 给…压膜 ‹card, book jacket›; 给…覆盖保护膜 ‹tabletop› 2 (build up in thin sheets) 粘合 ‹plastic, wood, glass› 3 (beat) 把…锤打成薄片 ‹metal›; (roll) 把…碾压成薄片 ‹metal›
B /'læmɪnət/ n [u and c] 层压材料

laminated /'læmɪneɪtɪd/ adj 1 (covered with protective material) 压膜的 ‹card, book jacket›; 覆膜的 ‹tabletop› 2 (made of thin sheets) 层压的 ‹plastic, wood, glass› 3 (beaten) 锤打成箔的 ‹metal›; (rolled) 碾压成箔的 ‹metal›

lamp /læmp/ n 灯; to light a ～ 点灯; a street/table/sun ～ 路灯/台灯/太阳灯

lamp: ～ bracket n 壁灯座; **～ light** n [u] 灯光; to read by ～light 在灯光下读书; **～lighter** n 点灯人

lampoon /læm'puːn/
A n 讽刺诗文
B vt «person, cartoon, poem» 嘲讽 ‹person, institution, government›

lamppost /'læmppəʊst/ n 路灯柱

lamprey /'læmpri/ n 七鳃鳗

lampshade /'læmpʃeɪd/ n 灯罩

lamp standard n 路灯柱

LAN /læn/ abbr = local area network

Lancashire /'læŋkəʃɪə(r)/ pr n 兰开夏郡

lance /lɑːns, Amer læns/
A n 1 (weapon) 长矛 2 Med 柳叶刀
B vt 用柳叶刀切开 ‹abscess, boil›

lance corporal n Brit 一等兵

lancet /'lɑːnsɪt, Amer 'læn-/ n 柳叶刀

lancet: ～ arch n 桃尖拱; **～ window** n 尖头窗

Lancs. abbr Brit = Lancashire

land /lænd/
A n 1 [u] (terrain, not sea) 陆地; flat/mountainous ～ 平地/山地; back on dry ～ 重返陆地; to reach or make ～ 到岸; to travel by ～ 陆路旅行; the war on ～ 陆战; how the ～ lies fig 目前情况 2 [u] (area of ground) 地产; private/public ～ 私有/公共地产; forest/building ～ 林地/建筑用地 3 [u] (farmland) 田地; arable ～ 可耕地; the fruits of the ～ 土地的产出; to live off the ～ 靠土地生活; to work the ～ 种地 4 [u] (countryside) 农村; to live on/leave the ～ 住在/离开农村 5 [c] (country) 国家; the finest orchestra in the ～ 国内最好的管弦乐队; foreign ～s 外国; throughout the ～ 全国各地; the ～ of opportunity 机遇之乡
B modif 1 Agric, Constr 土地的 ‹clearance, prices, law›; 地面的 ‹drainage›; a ～ worker 农场工人 2 (in contrast to sea, water) 陆地上的; the ～ battle/forces 陆战/地面部队; ～ transport 陆地交通; a ～ animal 陆生动物
C vt 1 Aerosp, Aviat 使…着陆 ‹aircraft, spacecraft, passenger›; 卸下 ‹cargo›; Naut 使…上岸 ‹passenger› 2 Fishg (with net) 捕到; (with rod) 钓到 3 fig colloq (secure) 得到; to ～ a prize 获奖; to ～ a job/contract 找到工作/揽到一份合同 4 colloq (burden) 给…强加; to ～ sb. with sth. 把…推给某人 ‹task, problem›; I was ～ed with the children/with washing the car 照看孩子/洗车的任务落在了我头上 5 colloq (cause to be in) 使陷于; to ～ sb. in court 把某人送上法庭; to ～ sb. in it 给某人惹上麻烦; now you've really ～ed her in it or in a fine mess! 这下你可真给她惹出大麻烦了! 6 colloq (deliver) 打 ‹blow, punch›; she ～ed him one (in the eye) 她打了他(的眼睛)一拳
D vi 1 (end up) 落下; he fell and ～ed at the bottom of the stairs 他摔下来，跌到了楼梯底部; the petition ～ed on my desk 请愿书放到了我的桌上; the punch ～ed on his chin 这一拳打在他的下巴上; to ～ in hot water fig 陷入困境 2 Aerosp, Aviat «aircraft, spacecraft, passenger» 着陆; Naut «passenger» 上岸
E v refl to ～ oneself in 陷入 ‹difficult situation›; he ～ed himself in jail/hospital 他进了监狱/住进了医院; to ～ oneself with colloq 承担 ‹task, problem›; she ～ed herself with an unpleasant task 她揽下了一份苦差事

Phrasal verb
- **land up** vi colloq 告终; to ～ up in prison 最终落得个锒铛入狱的下场; he ～ed up with the bill 账单最终由他付; she ～ed up doing everything herself 她最后自己做了所有的事

land: ～ agent ▸p. 409 n 1 (on estate) 地产管理人; 2 (broker) 地产经纪人; **～ bank** n 1 (land holdings) 土地储备; 2 Fin 地产银行; **～ breeze** n 陆风; **～ bridge** n 陆桥; **～ claim** n Can [原住民的] 土地权要求; **～ drain** n 地面排水沟

landed /'lændɪd/ adj attrib 拥有大量土地的 ‹gentry, proprietor›; the ～ classes 地主阶级; ～ estates or properties 地产

landed cost n 到岸成本

lander /'lændə(r)/ n 着陆舱

land: ～fall n 到达陆地; to make ～fall «person» 踏上陆地; «boat» 到达陆地; **～fill** n 1 [u] (disposal) 垃圾填埋; to dispose of waste by ～fill 用填埋法处理垃圾; 2 [c] (site) **～fill (site)** 垃圾填埋地; 3 [u] (waste) 填埋的垃圾; **～form** n 地貌; **～ grant** n Amer, Can 政府赠地; **～ holder** n 土地所有者

landing /'lændɪŋ/ n 1 [u] (of people) 上岸; (of cargo) 到岸卸货 2 [c] (on runway) 着陆; (by troops, from boat, on planet) 登陆; (from plane, by parachute) 降落; (in the sea) 坠落; to make a ～ 着陆; a smooth/bumpy/hard ～ 平稳着陆/颠簸着陆/硬着陆; a paratroop ～ 伞兵空降; the Normandy/D-day ～s 诺曼底/开始进攻日登陆; moon ～ 登月 3 (of animal, athlete, hang-glider) 落地; (of parachutist, bird, insect) 落下; a hard ～ 摔落 4 (on stairs) 楼梯平台; (corridor) 楼层; on the next ～ 在下一层楼

landing: ～ beacon n 着陆信标; **～ beam** n 着陆导航波束; **～ card** n Aviat 入境申报卡; Naut 离船登岸证; **～ craft** n 登陆艇; **～ field** n 飞机场; **～ gear** n [u] 起落架; **～ lights** npl (on plane) 着陆灯; (on airfield) 着陆指示灯; **～ net** n 抄网; **～ party** n 登陆小分队; **～ place** n [尤指浮码头的] 登陆处; **～ platform** n 降落平台; **～ speed** n 着陆速度; **～ stage** n 码头 [尤指浮码头]; **～ strip** n 简易机场; **～ wheel** n 起落轮

landlady /'lændleɪdi/ n 1 (of flat, house, room) 女房东; (of land, farm) 女地主; (wife of landlord of flat, house) 房东太太; (wife of landlord of land, farm) 地主婆 2 (of boarding house) 女店主 3 Brit (woman running a pub) 女老板; (wife of the landlord of a pub) 老板娘

landless /'lændlɪs/ adj 无土地的 ‹farmer, labourer›

land: ～ line n 陆地线路; **～locked** adj 1 (body of water) 陆围的 ‹lake›; a ～locked sea 内海; a ～locked harbour 天然港; 2 (country, region) 内陆的; Switzerland is ～locked 瑞士是内陆国家; **～lord** n 1 (of flat, house, room) 房东; (of land, farm) 地主; 2 (of boarding house) 店主; 3 Brit (of pub) 老板; **～lubber** /'lændlʌbə(r)/ n colloq hum 旱鸭子 [不谙或不好航海的人]; **～mark** n 1 (building, natural feature) 地标; 2 fig (event, invention, important point) 里程碑; a ～mark in sth. 某方面的里程碑; a ～mark discovery/decision/reform 重大发现/决定/改革; **～ mass** n 陆块; **～mine** n 地雷; **～ office** n Amer 地政局; **～owner** n 土地所有人; **～-owning** adj attrib 拥有土地的 ‹class, group, people›; **～ reform** n [u] 土地改革; **～ registry** n 地政局

landscape /'lændskeɪp/
A n 1 (scenery, terrain) 陆上风景; to admire the ～ 欣赏风景; a bleak ～ 荒凉的景色 2 Art (painting, drawing) 风景画; (photograph) 风景照片
B modif 1 (scenery, terrain) 风景画的 ‹painter, artist›; 风景的 ‹photographer›; ～ painting/art/photography 风景画/风景画艺术/风景摄影 2 Archit, Hort 园林的 ‹design, construction›; ～ gardening 园艺
C vt 对…作景观美化 ‹garden, park, site›

landscape format n [宽超过高的] 风景画版式

landscapist /'lændskeɪpɪst/ ▸p. 409 n (painter) 风景画家; (photographer) 风景摄影师

landslide /'lændslaɪd/ n 1 Geol 山崩; to set off a ～ 引发塌方 2 Pol 压倒性胜利; to win by a ～ 以压倒多数的选票获胜; a ～ victory/majority 压倒性的选举胜利/压倒性的选举多数

land: ～slip n 滑坡; **～sman** /'lændzmən/ n 旱鸭子 [指不谙航海者]; **～ tax** n 土地税; **～ use** n [u] 土地用途

landward /'lændwəd/
A adj 1 Naut (closest to land) 朝陆地的 ‹side›; 最接近陆地的 ‹boat, island› 2 usu attrib (from

coast or sea) 向陆地的 ‹*direction, movement, wind*›
B (*also* **landwards**) *adv* 向陆地 ‹*face, sail, turn*›

land yacht *n* 快艇车

lane /leɪn/ *n* **1** (narrow country road) 小路; ▸**memory 2 2** (narrow town road) 小巷; **Church L~** 教堂巷 **3** Transp (strip of road) 车道; **a three-~ road** 三车道公路; **the inside** *or* **near side ~** 慢车道; **the slow/fast/overtaking ~** 慢/快/超车道; **to keep in ~** Brit 禁止越线; **'get in ~'** Brit 注意选择车道 **4** Sport (on track) 跑道; (in pool) 泳道; **in ~ four** 在第四道

lane: ~ closure *n* 车道关闭; **~ discipline** *n* [u] 行车纪律; **~ markings** *npl* 车道线

language /ˈlæŋgwɪdʒ/
A *n* **1** [u and c] (system, of particular nation) 语言; **~ skills/acquisition** 语言技能/习得; **the English ~** 英语; **one's native ~** 母语; **a foreign/dead ~** 外语/死语言; **to enter** *or* **pass into the ~** 融入语言; **to speak the same ~** fig 志趣相投; **bad** *or* **strong** *or* **foul ~** 脏话; **to put sth. in one's own ~** 用自己的语言表述某事物 **2** [c] (words used by a particular group) 专用语; **the ~ of science** *or* **scientific language** 科学术语; **formal/legal ~** 正式/法律用语 **3** [u] (manner of expressing oneself) 措词; **mind your ~!** 注意你的言辞!; **don't use that ~ with me!** 别对我那样说话! **4** [u and c] (system of signs) 表达方式; **the ~ of flowers** 花语 **5** [c] Comput 计算机语言
B *modif* 语言的 ‹*ability, learner, teacher, use*›

language: ~ barrier *n* 语言障碍; **~ course** *n* 语言课程; **~ engineering** *n* [u] 语言工程; **~ laboratory, ~ lab** *ns* 语言实验室; **~ school** *n* 语言学校; **~ student** *n* 外语学生

languid /ˈlæŋgwɪd/ *adj* 慢悠悠的 ‹*movement*›; 无精打采的 ‹*voice, look, gesture*›

languidly /ˈlæŋgwɪdlɪ/ *adv* 慢悠悠地 ‹*move*›; 无精打采地 ‹*speak, gesture, smile*›

languish /ˈlæŋgwɪʃ/ *vi* **1** (lose vitality) «*person, organization*» 失去活力; **to ~ in the heat** 热得懒洋洋的; **the motor industry ~ed for years because of lack of investment** 多年来汽车业由于缺少投资而停滞不前 **2** (remain neglected) «*person*» 被忽视; **a composer who ~ed in obscurity all his life** 一生默默无闻的作曲家 **3** (suffer hardship) «*person, population*» 受苦; **to ~ in ...** 在…中受苦 ‹*prison, poverty*›; **to ~ under sth.** 受某事物的煎熬; **a country ~ing under foreign domination** 在外国统治下饱受煎熬的国家

languishing /ˈlæŋgwɪʃɪŋ/ *adj* 含情脉脉的 ‹*glance, sigh, posture, gesture*›

languor /ˈlæŋgə(r)/ *n* [u] **1** (listlessness) 倦怠; **a feeling of ~ crept over him** 一种懒洋洋的感觉渐渐传遍他的全身 **2** (peacefulness) 恬静; **music that induces a delicious ~** 使人心旷神怡的音乐

languorous /ˈlæŋgərəs/ *adj* **1** (listless) 倦怠的 ‹*feeling, movement*›; **2** (peaceful) 恬静的 ‹*sound, music*›; **a ~ afternoon** 懒洋洋的下午

lank /læŋk/ *adj* 平直而无光泽的 ‹*hair*›

lanky /ˈlæŋki/ *adj* 瘦长的 ‹*person, figure*›

lanolin /ˈlænəlɪn/ *n* [u] 羊毛脂

lantern /ˈlæntən/ *n* 灯笼

lantern: L~ Festival *n* 元宵节; **~-jawed** *adj* 下巴瘦长突出的 ‹*man, face*›

lanthanum /ˈlænθənəm/ *n* [u] 镧

lanyard /ˈlænjəd/ *n* **1** Naut (rope) 收紧索 **2** (cord round neck) 颈带 [用以系小刀、哨子等]

Lao /ˈlɑːɒ, laʊ/
A *adj* (of Laos) 老挝的; (of the people) 老挝人的; (of the language) 老挝语的
B *n* **1** [c] (person) 老挝人 **2** [u] (language) 老挝语

Laos /ˈlɑːɒs, laʊs/ *pr n* 老挝

Laotian /ˈlɑːɒʃn, ˈlaʊʃɪən/ *n, adj* **= Lao**

lap /læp/
A *n* **1** (area of body) 大腿部; **the child was sitting in** *or* **on her mother's ~** 孩子坐在她妈妈的腿上; **in the ~ of the gods** 结果难以预料; **all we can do is to wait, now; it's in the ~ of the gods** 现在我们能做的只有等待; 这事非人力所能左右; **in the ~ of luxury** 生活优裕; **to drop** *or* **dump a problem in sb.'s ~** 把问题推给某人 **2** Sport 一圈; **on the last ~** lit 在最后一圈; fig 在最后阶段; **to run a ~ of honour** 绕场一周欢庆胜利 **3** (part of journey) 一段; (part of a project, task) 阶段; **the next ~ of the journey** 下一段旅程
B *vt* (*pres p etc.* **-pp-**) **1** (drink) 舔食 **2** Sport (go one lap ahead of) 比…领先一圈; (go two or more laps ahead of) 比…领先数圈 **3** (overlap) 部分重叠于…之上; **each row of tiles ~s the one below** 每一排瓦都搭接在下一排之上
C *vi* (*pres p etc.* **-pp-**) **1** (splash) 轻轻拍打; **the lake ~ped gently on the shore** 湖水轻拍着湖岸 **2** (overlap) **to ~ over** 部分重叠; **the tiles ~ped over like a jalousie window** 瓦片互相搭接, 像是一扇百叶窗 **3** Sport 跑完一圈

Phrasal verb
- **lap up** *vt* [**~ up sth., ~ sth. up**]
1 lit 舔食; **the fox was ~ping up water from the pond** 狐狸正从池塘里舔水喝 **2** fig (accept eagerly) 欣然接受; **the world's media is ~ping up the news** 全球的媒体都在争相报道这条新闻

lap and shoulder belt *n* 斜挎式安全带

laparoscope /ˈlæpərəskəʊp/ *n* 腹腔镜

laparoscopy /ˌlæpəˈrɒskəpi/ *n* (technique) 腹腔镜检查技术; (use of the technique) 腹腔镜检查

La Paz /ˌlæ ˈpæz, ˌlɑː ˈpɑːz/ *pr n* **1** (capital of Bolivia) 拉巴斯 [玻利维亚首都] **2** (city in Mexico) [墨西哥南部的] 拉巴斯

lap: ~ belt *n* 安全腰带; **~ dance** *n* 脱衣舞; **~ dancer** *n* 脱衣舞演员; **~ dancing** *n* [u] 脱衣舞; **~dog** *n* **1** (pet dog) 叭儿狗; **2** (person) 走狗; **he's her ~dog** 他对她唯命是从

lapel /ləˈpel/ *n* 翻领; **to grab sb. by his** *or* **her ~s** colloq 揪住某人的衣领

lapel microphone *n* 领夹式话筒

lapis lazuli /ˌlæpɪs ˈlæzjʊlaɪ, -li/ *n* [u] **1** (gem) 杂青金石 **2** (pigment) 天青石颜料 **3** (colour) 天青石色

lap joint *n* 搭接

Lapland /ˈlæplænd/ *pr n* 拉普兰

Laplander /ˈlæplændə(r)/ *n* 拉普兰人

Lapp /læp/ ▸**p. 503**
A *adj* (of Lapland) 拉普的; (of the people) 拉普人的; (of the language) 拉普语的
B *n* **1** [c] (person) 拉普人 **2** [u] (language) 拉普语

lap robe *n* Amer 旅行毛毯

lapse /læps/
A *n* **1** (slip) 小错; **a ~ of memory** 记错; **a ~ in concentration** 走神 **2** (moral error) 行为

ℹ Languages

■ In Chinese, the name of a language is normally used as a noun, and not an adjective.

■ There are different ways for expressing the names of languages in Chinese:

Chinese
= 汉语
or 中国话
or 中文

汉语 is the general term for 'the Chinese language', in either its written or spoken form. 中国话 usually means spoken Chinese, while 中文 mostly refers to the written language.

Similarly,

Japanese
= 日语
or 日本语
or 日文

German
= 德语
or 德文

English
= 英语
or 英文

■ Note that where 'in' is used in English, 用 is usually used in Chinese:

read in English
= 用英语读

speak in English
= 用英语说

a book in English
= 用英语写的书

a class in English
= 用英语上的课

Note the Chinese translation of these examples:

a teacher of English
= 教英语的老师

a book on English
= 关于英语的书

■ In Chinese, 'language nouns' can be used as modifiers to modify another noun:

an English phrase
= 英语短语

a French novel
= 法语小说

the Spanish language
= 西班牙语

a Chinese teacher
= 汉语老师

■ Other phrases:

She speaks English
= 她说英语
or 她讲英语

She speaks fluent English
= 她说一口流利的英语

She speaks English without an accent
= 她讲英语不带任何口音

He speaks with a broad Scottish accent
= 他说话时有很重的苏格兰口音

He's got a strong American accent
= 他有很浓的美国口音

Joseph speaks with a slight London accent
= 约瑟夫说话时带点儿伦敦口音

Jed writes perfect English
= 杰德的英文写得非常好

His written English is excellent
= 他的英语写得好极了

失检; **a ~ from** 对…的违反 ‹*virtue, standards*›; **a ~ into sin** 堕入罪孽; **a momentary** *or* **temporary ~** 一时的失足 **3** (interval) 时间间隔; **a ~ of 6 months** *or* **a 6-month ~** 半年的间隔 **4** (of right, patent, policy) 期满终止

B *vi* **1** (fail to maintain position or standard) «*person*» 背弃; «*standard, ideal*» 降低; **to ~ from** 背离 ‹*virtue, standards, principle*› **2** (sink or drift) «*person*» 衰退; «*custom*» 消失; **to ~ into sth.** 陷入 ‹*silence, sleep, unconsciousness*›; **to ~ into bad habits** 染上恶习; **to ~ into dialect** 说起方言 **3** Jur (expire) «*right, law*» 期满终止

laptop /ˈlæptɒp/ *n* 手提电脑; **a ~ computer** 笔记本电脑

lapware /ˈlæpweə(r)/ *n* [u] 幼儿教育娱乐软件

lap welding *n* [u] 搭焊

lapwing /ˈlæpwɪŋ/ *n* 凤头麦鸡

larceny /ˈlɑːsəni/ *n* 盗窃罪; **a case of grand/petty ~** 重大/轻微盗窃案件

larch /lɑːtʃ/ *n* 落叶松

lard /lɑːd/

A *n* [u] 猪油

B *vt* **1** Culin [烤肉前] 给…加腌肉片 **2** fig (embellish) 给…添枝加叶; **a speech ~ed with learned quotations** 夹杂着高深引语的讲话

larder /ˈlɑːdə(r)/ *n* 餐柜

large /lɑːdʒ/

A *adj* **1** (big, substantial) 大的; **a ~ country** 幅员辽阔的国家; **a ~ horse** 高头大马; **to take a ~ size** 穿大号; **a ~ fortune** 一大笔财产; **a ~ population** 众多的人口; **to be out in ~ numbers** 蜂拥而出; **~r than life** 夸大的; **she has a ~r than life personality** 她个性夸张惹人注目; **as ~ as life** hum 亲自; **he turned up two days later (as) ~ as life!** 两天后他本人出现了! **2** euph (fat) 发福的; (big) 高大的; **a ~ lady** 丰满的女士 **3** (extensive) 广泛的; **the buffet sells a ~ selection of sandwiches** 这家自助餐厅出售多种三明治; **in ~ measure** *or* **to a ~ extent** 在很大程度上; **by and ~** 总的来说

B **at large** *adj phr* **1** (free) 在逃的; **to be/remain at ~** «*killer, convict*» 在逃; «*wild animal*» 未被捕获 **2** (in general) 大多数; (as a whole) 整个; **the population at ~** 大多数人; **society at ~** 整个社会; **in the country at ~** 在全国

large: ~-hearted *adj* 宽厚的; **~ intestine** *n* 大肠

largely /ˈlɑːdʒli/ *adv* 主要地; **what you say is ~ true** 你的话多半是对的

large-scale *adj* **1** (major, important) 大规模的 ‹*investigation, project, production, development*› **2** (in proportion) 大比例尺的 ‹*map, model*›

largesse /lɑːˈdʒes/ *n* [u] **1** (generosity) 慷慨解囊 **2** (money, gifts) 捐赠

large white *n* **1** (pig) 大白猪 **2** (butterfly) **= cabbage white**

largish /ˈlɑːdʒɪʃ/ *adj* 相当高大的 ‹*person*›; 相当大的 ‹*sum, town, house, crowd*›

largo /ˈlɑːgəʊ/

A *adv* 缓慢庄严地 ‹*play*›

B *adj* 广板的; **~ movement/finale** 广板乐章/广板终曲

C *n* 广板乐曲

lariat /ˈlærɪət/ *n* esp Amer (for catching a horse) 套马索; (for tethering a horse) 系马绳

lark¹ /lɑːk/ *n* Zool 百灵鸟; **to be** *or* **get up with the ~** 清晨早起; **to sing like a ~** 歌声甜美; **as happy as a ~** 非常幸福的

lark² *n* colloq **1** (fun) 嬉戏; **to be a great ~** *or* **a bit of a ~** Brit 非常好玩; **to do sth. for a ~** 做某事闹着玩; **to have a ~** 玩耍 **2** (unpleasant business) 讨厌的事; **I don't think much of this dieting/weeding ~** 我可不太喜欢节食/除草这档子事

Phrasal verb

- **lark about, lark around** *vi* esp Brit colloq 闹着玩; **stop ~ing about** *or* **around and go to sleep!** 别闹了, 睡觉去!

larkspur /ˈlɑːkspɜː(r)/ *n* 飞燕草

larrikin /ˈlærɪkɪn/ *n* Austral 不守规矩的人

larva /ˈlɑːvə/ *n* (*pl* **larvae** /ˈlɑːviː/) 幼虫

larval /ˈlɑːvəl/ *adj* 幼虫的 ‹*stage, form*›

laryngitis /ˌlærɪnˈdʒaɪtɪs/ ▸**p. 377** *n* [u] 喉炎

larynx /ˈlærɪŋks/ *n* 喉

lasagne /ləˈzænjə/ *n* 宽面条

lascivious /ləˈsɪvɪəs/ *adj* 淫荡的 ‹*person*›; 淫秽的 ‹*image, thoughts*›; 猥亵的 ‹*smile, act, wink*›

lasciviously /ləˈsɪvɪəsli/ *adv* 猥亵地 ‹*look, smile, wink*›

laser /ˈleɪzə(r)/ *n* 激光; **~ technology** 激光技术

laser: ~ beam *n* 激光束; **~disc** *n* 光盘; **~-guided** *adj* 激光制导的 ‹*missile, weapon*›; **~ gun** *n* **1** (for reading a bar code) 激光条码扫描仪; (for determining distance) 激光测速仪; **2** (in science fiction) 激光枪; **~ pointer** *n* 激光指示器; **~ printer** *n* 激光打印机; **~ show** *n* 激光表演; **~ surgery** *n* [u] 激光手术; **~ treatment** *n* [u and c] 激光治疗

lash /læʃ/

A *n* **1** (eyelash) 睫毛 **2** (whip stroke) 鞭打; fig (of wind, rain, etc.) 猛击; **the sailor was given 40 ~es** 这个水手挨了40鞭; **to feel the ~ of sb.'s tongue** 领教某人那张利嘴 **3** (part of whip) 鞭梢 **4** (flogging) **the ~** 鞭刑; **to be sentenced to the ~** 被判笞刑

B *vt* **1** lit (whip) 鞭打; **to ~ the horses with a whip** 用鞭子抽打马匹 **2** fig (batter) 猛击; **the typhoon is ~ing the coastal area** 台风在沿海地区肆虐 **3** (swish) 甩动 ‹*tail*› **4** (secure) 捆牢; **to ~ two things together** 把两件东西捆在一起; **they ~ed the cargo to the deck with a stout rope** 他们用一根粗绳把货物系在甲板上; **the kidnappers ~ed their victim to a chair** 绑匪把受害人绑在椅子上

Phrasal verbs

- **lash about** *vi* 剧烈扭动
- **lash down**

A *vi* 猛下; **the rain was ~ing down** 大雨倾盆; **hailstones ~ed down on the roof** 冰雹猛烈地打在屋顶上

B *vt* [**~ sth. down, ~ down sth.**] 捆住; **~ those barrels down!** 把桶捆好了!

- **lash out** *vi* **1** (hit out) 猛烈攻击; **the horse ~ed out with its back legs** 这匹马用后腿猛踢; **to ~ out at sb./sth.** lit 猛烈攻击某人/某物; fig 猛烈抨击某人/某事物 **2** colloq (spend freely) 大手大脚地花钱; **let's ~ out and have dinner at a restaurant** 咱们挥霍一下, 去饭店吃饭吧; **to ~ out on sb./sth.** 为某人/某事物解囊; **I ~ed out on a new car** 我不惜重金买了一辆新车
- **lash up** *vt* [**~ up sth., ~ sth. up**] 用绳捆牢; **the rowing boat was ~ed up to the landing stage** 划艇牢牢地系在码头上

lashing /ˈlæʃɪŋ/

A *n* **1** (flogging) 鞭打; **to get a ~** 遭鞭打; **to give sb./sth. a ~** 鞭打某人/某物 **2** fig (scolding) 斥责; **he got a verbal ~ from the teacher** 他遭到了老师的训斥 **3** (fastening) 捆绳

B **lashings** *npl* Brit colloq **~s of ...** 大量的 ‹*cream, food*›

lass /læs/ *n* esp Scot and N Eng (girl) 少女; (young woman) 年轻女子

lassie /ˈlæsi/ *n* esp Scot 女孩

lassitude /ˈlæsɪtjuːd, Amer -tuːd/ *n* [u] formal 疲乏

lasso /læˈsuː/

A *n* (*pl* **~s** *or* **~es**) 套索

B *vt* 用套索套捕 ‹*horse, cattle*›

last¹ /lɑːst, Amer læst/

A *adj* **1** (final in series) 最后的; **the ~ house on the right** 右边尽头的房子; **sb.'s ~ name** 某人的姓; **the ~ person in the queue** 队伍末尾的那个人; **this was her ~ novel** 这是她最后一本小说; **sb.'s ~ days** 某人临终的日子; **that's the ~ time I'll ask him for advice!** 这是我最后一次向他征求意见!; **why are you always ~?** 为什么你总是最晚?; **you shouldn't eat cheese ~ thing at night** 晚上临睡前不应该吃奶酪; **I'll get my revenge, if it's the ~ thing I do!** 我无论如何都要复仇! **2** *attrib* (previous, most recent) 最近的; **the ~ village we went through** 我们刚刚经过的那个村庄; **in my ~ job** 做上一份工作时; **~ time she went on a plane she was airsick** 她上次坐飞机时晕机了; **in the ~ three years** 在过去3年里; **~ night/month/year/Tuesday/April/Christmas** 昨天晚上/上个月/去年/上星期二/去年四月/去年圣诞节 **3** *attrib* (final remaining) 仅剩的; **this is our ~ bottle of wine** 这是我们最后一瓶葡萄酒; **he drank his beer (down) to the ~ drop** 他把啤酒喝得一干二净; **we spent every ~ penny we had on the house** 我们把所有的钱都花在房子上了; **every ~ one of the eggs is broken** 那些鸡蛋全都破了 **4** (in a race or competition) 最差的; **to be ~** 是最后一名; **to finish in ~ place** 得最后一名 **5** (least likely) 最不可能的; (least desirable) 最不想要的; **that was the ~ thing we expected him to do** 那是我们最不希望他做的事; **he's the ~ person I'd ask!** 我才不会问他呢!

B *n* **1** (final person) 最后的人; (final thing) 最后的事物; **she was the ~ of my classmates to find a job** 她是我的同学中最后一个找到工作的 **2** **at (long) ~** (finally) 终于; **at the (very) ~** 在最后一刻; **she converted to Catholicism at the very ~** 她临终前皈依了天主教; **to** *or* **till the (very) ~** 直到最后一刻; **she protested her innocence to the very ~** 她至死都辩称自己无罪; **to leave sb./sth. till ~** 把某人/某事物留到最后处理; **to wait till ~** 等到最后; **to hear/see the ~ of sb./sth.** 与某人撇清关系/了结某事物; **I don't think we've seen the ~ of him** 我认为他不会就此罢休; **we thought we'd heard the ~ of that issue** 我们原以为那件事已经了结; **that was the ~ I saw of her** 那是我最后一次看见她; **to look one's ~ on sb./sth.** 看某人/某物最后一眼 **3** (previous or most recent person) 最近的人; (previous or most recent thing) 最近的事物; **the night/week before ~** 前天晚上/上上周; **his new novel is better than the ~** 他的新小说比上一本要好; **the ~ we heard of him, he was living in Spain** 我们最近听到的消息是他住在西班牙 **4** (all that remains) **the ~ (of sth.)** (某物中) 仅剩的部分; **these are the ~ of our apples** 这是我们仅剩的一些苹果; **she gave the cat the ~ of the milk** 她把剩下的牛奶给猫喝了 **5** (least likely person) 最不可能的人; (least likely thing) 最不可能的事物; **to be the ~ to do sth.** 是最不可能做某事的人; **he'd be the ~ to refuse an offer like that!** 他绝不可能拒绝那样的提议!

C *adv* **1** (in final position) 在最后; (finally) 最后; **he came ~ and left first** 他来得最晚, 走得最早; **do this ~ of all** 最后做这个; **~, I'd like to thank you all for coming** 最后, 我想感谢各位的光临 **2** (most recently) 最近; **when did you see her ~?** 你最近什么时候见过她?; **I washed up ~** 上一次是我洗的碗; **~ in, first out** 后来者先走 **3** (in competition) 最末; **to rank ~** 名列末位; **to come (in)** *or* **finish ~** 得最后一名; **to put sb./sth. ~** 把某人/某事物摆在最不重要的位置

last²

A *vi* **1** (extend in time) 持续; **their marriage didn't ~ long** 他们的婚姻没有维持太久; **the film ~ed (for) three hours** 这部电影演了3个小时 **2** (maintain condition) 持久; **the material will ~** 这种材料耐用; **that meat won't ~ unless it's in the fridge** 那些肉如

果不放在冰箱里就会变质 **3** (survive) 坚持; **no one ～s long in this company** 这家公司里没人呆得下去; **she caught pneumonia and didn't ～ long after that** 她得了肺炎，不久就死了

B *vt* 够…之用; **enough food to ～ us (for) four days** 足够我们吃 4 天的食物; **you've got enough clothes there to ～ you a lifetime** 你的衣服够穿一辈子了

Phrasal verb

• **last out**

A *vi* **1** (not run out) 《*supplies, food*》 够用 **2** (survive) 存活; **how long will she ～ out?** 她还能活多久? **3** (persist) 坚持; **she says she's given up smoking, but she'll never ～ out!** 她说自己已经戒烟了，但她绝对坚持不了!

B *vt* [**～ sb./sth. out, ～ out sth.**]
1 (survive for) 活过 ‹*period of time*›; **I don't think she'll ～ out the night** 我认为她活不过今晚; **can we ～ out a month on these supplies?** 我们靠这些补给品能坚持 1 个月吗? **2** (be sufficient for) 够…之用 ‹*person, period of time*›; **my savings should ～ the year out** 我的积蓄够今年用; **the water should ～ us out until we get home** 这些水应该够我们用到回家

last³ *n* (for making shoes) 鞋楦

last: ～-ditch *adj* 孤注一掷的 ‹*attempt, effort, fight*›; **a ～-ditch stand against sth.** 对某事物孤注一掷的抵抗; **～-gasp** *adj* 最后一刻达成的 ‹*score, try*›

lasting /ˈlɑːstɪŋ, Amer ˈlæstɪŋ/ *adj* 持久的 ‹*effect, peace, value, damage, relationship*›; **it's to her ～ credit that ...** …让她一直享有好名声

Last Judgement *n* 末日审判

lastly /ˈlɑːstli, Amer ˈlæstli/ *adv* 最后; **～, don't forget to take the pills** 最后一点，别忘了吃药

last: ～-mentioned *n* formal (person) 最后提到的人; (thing) 最后提到的事物; **～-minute** *adj* 最后一刻的 ‹*preparations, attempt, changes*›; **～-named** *n* (person) 最后提到的人; (thing) 最后提到的事物; **～ number redial** *n* [u] 末码重拨; **～ post** *n* Brit **the ～ post** (each evening) 军营熄灯号; (at military funerals) 军人葬礼号; **～ rites** *npl* **the ～ rites** 临终圣礼; **to give sb. the ～ rites, to administer the ～ rites to sb.** 为某人举行临终圣事; **L～ Supper** *n* **the L～ Supper** 最后晚餐; **～ word** *n* **1** (unsurpassable thing) **the ～ word (in sth.)** (在某方面) 达到极致的事物; **it's the ～ word in luxury!** 这真是极尽奢华!; **2** (final contribution) 最后发言; (final decision) 最终决定; **to have the ～ word** 说了算; **the demonstrators put up a fight, but the police had the ～ word** 游行示威者开始动武，但警方最终控制了局面; **3** (final statement) 最后一句话; (final opinion) 定论; **get out! that's my ～ word to all of you!** 我对你们这帮人最后说一遍，滚!; **the dictionary claims to be the ～ word on English** 那本词典号称是英语的终极权威; **～ words** 临终遗言

latch /lætʃ/

A *n* **1** (bar) 门闩; **to lift/drop the ～** 拨起/放下门闩 **2** (spring lock) 弹簧锁; **to put the door on the ～** 把门关上但没有锁

B *vt* (with a bar) 把…闩上 ‹*door, gate*›; (with a spring lock) 用弹簧锁锁上 ‹*door, gate*›; **it wasn't properly ～ed** 门没锁好

Phrasal verbs

• **latch on** *vi* colloq 明白; **I kept hinting, but he didn't ～ on** 我不断地暗示，可他没领会

• **latch on to** colloq

A [**～ on to sth.**] *vt*
1 (seize on) 热情接受 ‹*idea*›; **she always ～es on to the latest trend/fashion** 她总是紧跟最新潮流/时尚 **2** (exploit) 揪住…不放 ‹*mistake, error, weakness*› **3** (realize) 了解 ‹*secret, method*›; **she did not ～ on to what was happening** 她当时没弄懂发生了什么

B [**～ on to sb.**] *vt* (become constant companion of) 纠缠

latchkey /ˈlætʃkiː/ *n* 弹簧锁钥匙; **a ～ child** *or* **kid** colloq 挂钥匙的孩子

late /leɪt/

A *adj* **1** (after expected time) 晚的; **he was 20 minutes ～ for school** 他上学迟到了 20 分钟; **it's ～** 时间不早了; **she's had too many ～ nights recently** 她最近熬夜太多; **a ～ breakfast/spring** 晚进的早餐/来迟的春天; **to get off to a ～ start** 晚于预定时间开始; **there's ～ opening on Fridays** 星期五营业时间会延长; **～ essays will not be marked** 迟交的作文将不予评分; **the tomatoes are ～ this year** 今年西红柿成熟得晚 **2** *attrib* (near end of period or process) 近末期的; **in ～ summer/January** 在夏末/一月底; **the ～ afternoon/evening** 下午/晚上晚些时候; **the ～st date for applications** 申请的截止日期; **Shakespeare's ～ works** 莎士比亚的晚期作品; **a ～ film** 夜场电影; **in the ～ 1950s** 在 20 世纪 50 年代末; **we'd better get the roof repaired, before it's too ～** 我们最好在屋顶还能修的时候把它修好; **it's never too ～ to stop smoking** 任何时候戒烟都不算晚; **in ～r life** (from middle age onwards) 晚年; (from now on) 日后; **a man in his ～ forties** 年近 50 的男子; **in the ～ Middle Ages** 在中世纪末期; **～ Renaissance art** 文艺复兴晚期的艺术; **at this ～ stage** 在收尾阶段 **3** **later** *comp, attrib* (following in series) 后来的; **the matter will be dealt with at a ～r meeting** 这个问题将在之后的会议中讨论 **4** *attrib* (very recent) 最近的; **an item of ～ news** 一条最新消息; **a ～ addition to this range of gardening tools** 本套园艺工具中的新增产品 **5** *attrib* (deceased) 已故的; **my ～ husband** 我已去世的丈夫; **the ～ President** 已故总统 **6** *attrib* Agric, Hort 晚熟的 ‹*fruit, crop*›; 花期晚的 ‹*flower*›

B *adv* **1** (after expected time) 晚; **to arrive ～** 迟到; **to go to bed ～r** 晚一些上床睡觉; **I'm running ～ already** 我已经晚了; **to start three months ～** 迟了3个月开始; ▸ **too 1, never A1** **2** (towards end of time period) 接近末尾; **till ～** 直到深夜; **to leave sth. ～** 推迟做某事; **～ next year/last week** 明年年底/上周末; **～ in the morning/afternoon** 上午/下午晚些时候; **～ in the day** (towards the end of the working day) 快下班的时候; (towards the end of the day) 晚些时候; (later than desirable) 为时已晚; (in the final stages) 在最后阶段; **to work ～ into the night** 工作到深夜; **he died six months ～r** 6 个月后他去世了; **we learnt ～r that ...** 我们后来才知道…; **he might prove helpful ～r (on) in your career** 他可能对你以后的事业有帮助; **it must be ready no ～r than Friday** 必须在星期五之前准备好; **at the ～st** 最晚; **to marry ～** 结婚晚; **to start learning Italian ～ in life** 年纪挺大才开始学意大利语; **see you ～r!** 再见! **3** (recently) 最近; **this law was still in force as ～ as 1968** 这条法律直到 1968 年仍然有效; **as ～ as yesterday** 就在昨天; **of ～** 最近以来; **he's been rather depressed of ～** 他最近相当沮丧 **4** formal (formerly) 以前; **Miss Evans, ～ of the Foreign Office** 埃文斯小姐，以前任职于外交部; **David Green, ～ of Kingston** 大卫・格林，以前住在金斯敦

latecomer /ˈleɪtkʌmə(r)/ *n* **1** (to meeting, event) 迟到者 **2** (to profession, activity) 新手; **to be a ～ to sth.** 是…方面的新手 ‹*profession, gardening, sport*›

late developer *n* **1** (mentally) 智力发展晚的孩子 **2** (physically) 身体发育晚的孩子 **3** hum (adult) 大器晚成的人

lately /ˈleɪtli/ *adv* 近来; **have you seen her ～?** 你最近见过她吗?; **has anything interesting happened? — not ～** 有什么趣事么? ——最近没有

latency /ˈleɪtnsi/ *n* **1** Comput 等待时间 **2** Med (state) 潜伏; (period) 潜伏期; **asbestos-related diseases with a ～ of twenty years or more** 潜伏期为 20 年或更长的石棉有关疾病

lateness /ˈleɪtnɪs/ *n* [u] **1** (of person, train etc.) 迟到 **2** (of time) 晚; **I apologize for the ～ of my visit** 我很抱歉这么晚来拜访; **the ～ of the hour** formal 深更半夜

late-night *adj* 深夜的 ‹*film, shopping*›

latent /ˈleɪtnt/ *adj* 潜在的 ‹*quality, tension*›

latent: ～ heat *n* 潜热; **～ period** *n* 潜伏期

later /ˈleɪtə(r)/ *comp* ▸ **late**

lateral /ˈlætərəl/ *adj* 侧面的 ‹*branch*›; fig 横向的 ‹*thinking, development*›; **～ artery** 侧动脉

laterally /ˈlætərəli/ *adv* 侧面地 ‹*shoot, bud*›; fig 横向地 ‹*grow, develop, think*›

late riser *n* 起床晚的人

latest /ˈleɪtɪst/

A *superl* ▸ **late**

B *n* [u] **1** (news, etc.) 最新消息; **the ～ on sth.** 某事的最新报道; **for the ～ on the earthquake in Wenchuan, here's Luo Jing** 下面由罗京实地报道汶川地震的最新消息 **2** (work, book, film, etc.) 最新作品; (idea) 最新想法; **have you read her ～?** 你看了她的新作没有? **3** hum (lover) 现任情人; **her ～** 她的现任情人

C *adj* 最新的 ‹*development, fashion, film, figure*›

D **at the latest** *adv phr* 最晚; **I want you home by 11 at the ～** 我要你最迟 11 点到家

latex /ˈleɪteks/ *n* (produced by plants) 胶乳; (synthetic) 合成乳胶

lath /lɑːθ, Amer læθ/ *n* **1** [c] (thin strip of wood) 木板条 **2** [u] (building material) 板条; **～-and-plaster wall** 灰板墙

lathe /leɪð/ *n* 车床

lather /ˈlɑːðə(r), esp Amer ˈlæðə(r)/

A *n* **1** (of soap) 泡沫; **to work up a ～** 弄起泡沫 **2** (frothy sweat) 汗沫; **the horse was in a ～** 这匹马满身冒汗 **3** fig colloq (state of agitation) 焦躁不安; **to be in a ～** 焦躁不安; **don't get in a ～!** 别激动!; **he was in a real ～** 他大动肝火; **to be in a ～ about sth./doing sth.** 因某事/做某事紧张

B *vt* **1** (coat with lather) 在…上涂皂沫 ‹*face, chin*› **2** colloq (hit) 狠揍 ‹*person*›; fig (in competition) 大败 ‹*person*›

C *vi* 《*soap, powder*》 起泡沫

Latin /ˈlætɪn, Amer ˈlætn/ ▸ **p. 426**

A *adj* (of the people) 讲拉丁语的 ‹*nation, people*›; 拉丁人的 ‹*culture, temperament*›; (of the language) 拉丁语的 ‹*author, grammar, lesson, text*›

B *n* **1** [c] (person) 拉丁人 [尤指拉丁美洲人] **2** [u] (language) 拉丁语; **low/late/vulgar ～** 中古/后期/俗拉丁语; **dog ～** 不正规的拉丁语

Latina /læˈtiːnə/

A *adj* 拉丁美洲裔的 ‹*woman, girl*›; 拉丁美洲裔女性的 ‹*student, author*›

B *n* esp Amer 拉丁美洲裔女子

Latin America *pr n* 拉丁美洲

Latin American

A *adj* 拉丁美洲的 ‹*country, culture, people, studies*›

B *n* 拉丁美洲人

Latino /læˈtiːnəʊ/

A *adj* 拉丁美洲裔的 ‹*family, population, community*›; 拉丁美洲的 ‹*culture*›

B *n* esp Amer 拉丁美洲裔男子

latish /ˈleɪtɪʃ/

A *adj* 相当晚的; **it was ～ when we arrived** 我们到时已很晚了

B *adv* 相当晚地 ‹*arrive, leave*›

latitude /ˈlætɪtjuːd, Amer -tuːd/ *n* **1** [c] Geog 纬度; **at a ～ of 57 degrees north** *or* **at 57 degrees ～ north** 在北纬 57 度 **2** (**latitudes**, *pl*) (region) 纬度地区 **3** [u] (freedom)

自由; **to allow sb. ~ in sth.** 在某方面给某人自由

latrine /lə'triːn/ *n* [尤指兵营、宿营地的] 厕所

latte /'lɑːteɪ, 'læteɪ/ *n* 拿铁咖啡

latter /'lætə(r)/

A *adj* **1** (second) 后者的 **2** (later) 后半期的; **in the ~ part of the evening** 在后半夜; **in his ~ years** 在他的后半生

B *n* **the ~** 后者

latter-day *adj attrib* 当今的; **a ~ version/equivalent of sb./sth.** 某人/某事物的现代翻版/对等者

latterly /'lætəli/ *adv* **1** (recently) 近来 **2** (in later times) 后来

lattice /'lætɪs/ *n* 格子框架 [用作屏障、篱笆，或供植物攀附]; **a ~ of tall reeds** fig 高芦苇篱笆

lattice: ~ girder *n* 格构大梁; **~work** *n* [u] 网格结构

Latvia /'lætvɪə/ *pr n* 拉脱维亚

Latvian /'lætvɪən/ ▸**p. 503, p. 426**

A *adj* (of Latvia) 拉脱维亚的; (of the people) 拉脱维亚人的; (of the language) 拉脱维亚语的

B *n* **1** [c] (person) 拉脱维亚人 **2** [u] (language) 拉脱维亚语

laud /lɔːd/ *vt* formal 赞美

laudable /'lɔːdəbl/ *adj* 值得赞美的

laudably /'lɔːdəbli/ *adv* 值得赞美地

laugh /lɑːf, Amer læf/

A *vi* 笑; **to ~ out loud** *or* **aloud** 放声大笑; **to have to ~** 不由得笑起来; **to make sb. ~** 逗某人发笑; **don't make me ~!** 别开玩笑了！; **to ~ about** *or* **over sth.** 觉得某事物可笑; **we were angry at the time, but we ~ed about it afterwards** 我们当时很生气，但后来觉得这事好笑; **to ~ to oneself** 暗自好笑; **to be ~ing** colloq 占优势; **even if they only sell five a week, they're ~ing** 即使一周只卖5件，他们也赢利; **to ~ like a drain** colloq 放声大笑; **to ~ in sb.'s face** 当面取笑某人; **to ~ in the face of sth.** 对某事物一笑置之; **to ~** *or* **be ~ing on the other side of one's face** 转喜为悲; **he who ~s last ~s longest** Prov 谁笑在最后，谁笑得最久; **~ and the world ~s with you, weep and you weep alone** Prov 笑时万众附和，哭时独自垂泪; **to ~ all the way to the bank** 轻松赚大钱

B *vt* 笑; **'of course not!' she ~ed** "当然不是！"她笑着说; **he ~ed a triumphant laugh** 他得意地笑了; **we ~ed ourselves hoarse** 我们笑得嗓子都哑了; **to ~ oneself silly** colloq 笑个不停

C *n* **1** (amused noise) 笑声; (act of laughing) 笑; (response) 发笑; **to give a ~** 大笑一声; **to have the last ~** 获得最后胜利; **I had the last ~ over my rivals** 我最终战胜了竞争对手; **to get a ~** 引人发笑 **2** (sth. amusing) 令人发笑的事物; (target of ridicule) 笑柄; (sb. amusing) 风趣的人; **she likes a ~** 她喜欢开玩笑; **let's go to the party: it'll be a ~** 咱们去参加聚会吧：会很开心的; **to have a ~** 觉得有趣; **to give sb. a ~** 让某人发笑; **to be good for a ~** 令人发笑; **(just) for a ~, (just) for ~s** (只是) 为了取乐; **her brother is a real ~** 她哥哥真是个活宝; **her, offer to pay? that's a ~!** 她，主动付账？简直是笑话！

Phrasal verbs

- **laugh at** *vt* [~ **at sb./sth.**]
1 (be audibly amused by) 因…而笑; **she ~ed at his joke** 听了他的笑话，她笑了起来; **what are you ~ing at?** 你们在笑什么？ **2** (feel amused by) 对…感到好笑; **stop ~ing at me!** 别再取笑我了！; **to ~ at oneself** 自嘲; **to ~ with sb., not at them** 和某人一起笑，而不是取笑某人 **3** (mock) 嘲笑 ‹*person, thing*› **4** (express defiance of) 对…一笑置之; **they ~ed at our warnings** 他们对我们的警告不以为然
- **laugh off** *vt* [~ **sth. off**, ~ **off sth.**] 对…一笑置之 ‹*incident, crime*›

laughable /'lɑːfəbl, Amer 'læf-/ *adj* 荒唐可笑的 ‹*attempt, plan, suggestion*›; 少得可笑的 ‹*sum, amount, wages*›; **it is ~ to think you will succeed** 还以为你会成功，真是荒唐可笑

laughably /'lɑːfəbli, Amer 'læf-/ *adv* 荒唐可笑地

laughing /'lɑːfɪŋ, Amer 'læfɪŋ/ *adj* 大笑的 ‹*person*›; 含笑的 ‹*face, eyes, expression*›; **it's no ~ matter** 这可不是开玩笑的事; **he's in no ~ mood** (in bad temper) 他脾气不好; (in low spirits) 他情绪低落

laughing gas *n* [u] 笑气

laughingly /'lɑːfɪŋli, Amer 'læf-/ *adv* **1** (jokingly) 开玩笑地; **he said/explained ~ that ...** 他开玩笑地说/解释… **2** (inappropriately) 可笑地 ‹*described, named*›

laughing stock *n* 笑柄; **to make sb./sth./oneself a ~** *or* **to make a ~ of sb./sth./oneself** 使某人/某事物/自己成为笑柄

laughter /'lɑːftə(r), Amer 'læf-/ *n* [u] (act) 笑; (sound) 笑声; **to roar** *or* **howl with ~** 哈哈大笑; **to be doubled up with ~** 笑弯了腰; **hearty/derisive/convulsive ~** 尽情大笑/讥笑/狂笑; **the hall was full of ~** 满堂欢笑; **a fit of ~** 一阵大笑

laughter line Brit, **laugh line** Amer *ns* 笑纹

launch /lɔːntʃ/

A *n* **1** (motor boat) 大型汽艇 **2** (of ship, boat) 下水; (for first time) 首次下水 **3** (of spacecraft, satellite, missile) 发射 **4** fig (of campaign) 发起; (of attack) 发动; (of scheme) 实施 **5** fig (of product) 上市; (of publication) 发行

B *vt* **1** (move into water) 使…下水 ‹*ship, boat*›; (for first time) 使…首次下水 ‹*ship*›; **to ~ the dinghy** 把小划艇放下水; **the ship was ~ed by the Queen** 这艘船的下水仪式是由女王主持的 **2** (propel) 发射 ‹*missile, torpedo, satellite*›; **he ~ed a blow at his attacker** 他朝袭击者打了一拳; **to ~ sth. at** *or* **against sb./sth.** 朝某人/某物推进某物; **to ~ oneself at sb.** 朝某人扑过去 **3** (start) 发起 ‹*campaign*›; 发动 ‹*attack*›; 实施 ‹*scheme*›; **she is well and truly ~ed on her new career** 她的新事业已经成功开展起来了 **4** (release) 使…上市 ‹*product*›; 发行 ‹*newspaper*›; **to ~ a new model** 推出新型号

C *vi* **to ~ into, to ~ forth into** 开始; **I ~ed (forth) into a lengthy explanation** 我开始长篇大论地解释起来

Phrasal verb

- **launch out** *vi* 开始创业; **to ~ out on one's own** 开始自己创业; **he left the company and ~ed out on his own** 他离开公司，自己创业; **the company ~ed out into the overseas market** 公司开始涉足海外市场

launch complex *n* 综合发射设施

launcher /'lɔːntʃə(r)/ *n* 发射装置

launching /'lɔːntʃɪŋ/ *n* **1** (of ship, boat) 下水; (for first time) 首次下水 **2** (of spacecraft, satellite, missile) 发射 **3** (of campaign) 发动; (of product) 上市; (of publication) 发行; (of scheme, project) 启动

launching: ~ ceremony *n* 新船下水典礼; **~ pad** *n* 发射平台; **~ site** *n* **= launch site**

launch: ~ pad *n* 发射平台; **~ party** *n* 发布会; **~ platform** *n* (for spacecraft) 航天器发射台; (for missiles) 导弹发射台; **~ site** *n* (for spacecraft) 航天器发射场; (for missiles) 导弹发射场; **~ vehicle** *n* 运载火箭; **~ window** *n* 最佳发射时段

launder /'lɔːndə(r)/ *vt* **1** (wash) 洗熨 ‹*clothes, linen*› **2** (conceal the origin of) 把…转为合法 ‹*funds, profit*›; **to ~ money through a company** 通过某公司洗钱

launderette, laundrette /lɔːn'dret, ˌlɔːndə'ret/ *n* Brit 投币式自助洗衣店

laundress /'lɔːndrɪs/ *n* 洗衣女工

Laundromat® /'lɔːndrəmæt/ *n* Amer **= launderette**

laundry /'lɔːndri/ *n* **1** [c] (shop) 洗衣店 **2** [c] (room in hotel, house) 洗衣房 **3** [u] (washed linen) 已洗熨的衣物; (linen to be washed) 需洗熨的衣物; **dirty ~** 需洗熨的脏衣物; **to do the ~** 洗衣

laundry: ~ basket, Amer **~ hamper** *n* 洗衣篮; **~ detergent** *n* Amer **= washing powder**; **~ van** *n* 洗衣店货车; **~ worker** ▸**p. 409** *n* 洗衣工

laureate /'lɒrɪət, Amer 'lɔːr-/ *n* **1** (distinguished person) 获奖者; **a Nobel ~** 诺贝尔奖得主 **2** Brit (court poet) **the poet ~** 桂冠诗人

laurel /'lɒrəl, Amer 'lɔːrəl/

A *n* **1** (tree) 月桂树 **2** (**laurels,** *pl*) (wreath of leaves) 桂冠; **to crown sb. with ~s** 给某人戴上桂冠 **3** (**laurels,** *pl*) (honours) 荣誉; **to win one's ~s** 赢得荣誉; **to look to one's ~s** 惜护荣誉; **to rest on one's ~s** 不思进取

B *modif* 月桂枝叶做的 ‹*wreath*›; **a ~ crown** 桂冠

lav /læv/ *n* Brit colloq 厕所

lava /'lɑːvə/ *n* [u] 熔岩

lava: ~ bed *n* 熔岩层; **~ field** *n* 熔岩原; **~ flow** *n* 熔岩流; **~ lamp** *n* 熔岩灯

lavalier /lɑː'vɑːlɪə(r)/ *n* Amer 宝石坠饰

lavatorial /ˌlævə'tɔːrɪəl/ *adj* 粗秽的

lavatory /'lævətri, Amer -tɔːri/

A *n* **1** (toilet) 抽水马桶; **to flush sth. down the ~** 把某物冲下抽水马桶 **2** (room) 厕所

B *modif* (of a toilet) 抽水马桶的 ‹*brush*›; (of the room) 厕所的 ‹*door, attendant*›; 粗秽的 ‹*humour*›; **~ paper** 卫生纸; **a ~ bowl** 抽水马桶桶身

lavender /'lævəndə(r)/ ▸**p. 134**

A *n* **1** [u and c] (plant) 薰衣草 **2** [u] (dried flowers) 干薰衣草花 [用以熏香衣物] **3** [u] (colour) 淡紫色

B *adj* 淡紫色的; **~ blue** 薰衣草蓝色

lavish /'lævɪʃ/

A *adj* **1** (generous) 大方的 ‹*person*›; 慷慨给予的 ‹*praise, money, gifts*›; **to be ~ with sth.** 对某物大手大脚; **to be ~ in one's praise for** *or* **in praising sth./sb.** 对某事/某人赞不绝口 **2** (plentiful) 巨大的 ‹*expenditure*›; 奢华的 ‹*reception, lifestyle, surroundings*›; **a ~ amount of food and drink** 大量食品饮料; **their hospitality was ~** 他们非常好客

B *vt* **to ~ sth. on sb./sth.** 慷慨地将…给予某人/某事 ‹*praise, money, affection*›

lavishly /'lævɪʃli/ *adv* 大量地 ‹*provide, spend, give*›; 奢华地 ‹*furnished, decorated, illustrated*›

law /lɔː/ *n* **1** [u] (body of rules) 法律; **to obey/break the ~** 守/犯法; **that's against the ~** 那是违法的; **to be above the ~** 凌驾于法律之上; **the ~ is on our side** 我们是有法律依据的; **the ~ as it stands** 现行法律; **by ~** 按照法律规定; **his word is ~** 他的话就是金科玉律 **2** [c] (rule) 法规; **there is no ~ against it** 尚无规定禁止这事; **to be a ~ unto oneself/itself** 我行我素 **3** [u] (justice) 司法; **in the eyes of the ~** 根据法律; **to go to ~ about** *or* **over sth.** 为某事物打官司; **to take the ~ into one's own hands** 滥用私刑 **4** [u] colloq (police) **the ~** 警察; **I'll have the ~ on you!** 我要报警了！ **5** [u] (academic discipline) 法学; **to read/study ~ at university** 在大学攻读法律; **to practise ~** 当律师 **6** [c] (principle) 定律; **the ~ of gravity** 万有引力定律 **7** [c and u] (code of conduct) 行为规范; **the ~s of etiquette** 礼仪规范; **the ~s of football** 足球比赛规则

law: ~-abiding *adj* 守法的; **~ and order** *n* [u] 法治; **~breaker** *n* 违法者; **~-breaking** *n* [u] 违法; **~ centre** *n* Brit 免费法律咨询中心; **~ clerk** ▸**p. 409** *n* Amer 律师助理; **~ court** *n* 法庭

law enforcement *n* [u] 执法

law enforcement: ~ agency *n* 执法机构; **~ officer** ▸**p. 409** *n* 执法官

law: Law Faculty *n* 法学院; **~ firm** *n* 律师事务所

lawful /ˈlɔːfl/ *adj* 合法的; **to go about one's ~ business** 做合法生意; **to do sth. without ~ authority** 在无合法授权的情况下做某事

lawfully /ˈlɔːfəli/ *adv* 合法地

lawless /ˈlɔːlɪs/ *adj* 没有法律的 ‹*period, country*›; 目无法纪的 ‹*mob, youth*›

lawlessness /ˈlɔːlɪsnɪs/ *n* [u] (of period, country) 没有法律; (of gang, youth) 目无法纪

law: Law Lord *n* Brit 上议院司法议员; **~maker** *n* 立法者; **~man** /-mæn/ *n* Amer 执法官

lawn /lɔːn/ *n* 草坪

lawn: ~ edger *n* 草坪修边器; **~ mower** *n* 割草机; **~ tennis** ▸**p. 307** *n* [u] formal 网球

law: ~ school *n* esp Amer 法学院; **~ student** *n* 法律专业学生

> **law school**
>
> 法学院。美国培养律师和法律工作人员的机构。全美共有 200 余所法学院，一般附属于大学或学院，仅有少数为独立机构。学制三年，兼职学习为四年。学生必须拥有本科文凭（first degree），并通过法学院入学考试（Law School Admissions Test，缩写为 LSAT），才有可能被录取。法学院毕业后获得法律博士（doctor of jurisprudence，缩写为 JD）学位，可参加律师资格考试（bar examination），以取得执业资格。获得法律博士学位后，再经过一年的学习，可获取法学硕士（master of laws，缩写为 LLM）学位。比法学硕士学位更高的是法学博士（doctor of juridical science，缩写为 SJD）学位。

lawsuit /ˈlɔːsuːt/ *n* 诉讼; **to bring a ~ against sb.** 对某人提起诉讼

lawyer /ˈlɔːjə(r)/ ▸**p. 409** *n* 律师; **to consult one's ~s** 咨询自己的律师

lax /læks/ *adj* **1** (not strict) 不严谨的 ‹*person*›; 不严格的 ‹*discipline*›; 败坏的 ‹*morals*›; 不检点的 ‹*behaviour*›; **to be ~ about sth.** 对某事物不严格; **to be ~ in** *or* **about doing sth.** 做某事不严格 **2** (of pronunciation) 松弛的 ‹*sound*›; **a ~ vowel** 松元音

laxative /ˈlæksətɪv/
A *n* 轻泻剂
B *adj* 通便的 ‹*effect, pill*›

laxity /ˈlæksɪti/ *n* [u] **1** (slackness) 松弛; **ligament ~** 韧带松弛 **2** fig 宽松; **fiscal ~** 财政宽松

lay[1] /leɪ/
A *vt* (*pt, pp* **laid**) **1** (place carefully) 安放; **he laid a plank across the stream** 他在小溪上搭了一块木板; **I laid a wreath at the foot of the monument** 我在纪念碑下献了个花圈; **she laid the baby in the cot** 她把婴儿放到小床上; **to ~ the blanket on the ground** 把毯子铺在地上 **2** (place in specified position) 放 ‹*part of one's body*›; **she laid her head on his shoulder** 她把头靠在他的肩上; **the dog laid its paw on my knee** 狗把爪子搭在我的膝盖上; **to ~ a finger/hand on sb.** (strike) 打某人; (harm) 伤害某人; (molest) 骚扰某人; **if you ever ~ a finger on my daughter again, I'll kill you!** 你再碰我女儿一下，我就宰了你！; **to ~ one on sb.** colloq 给某人一拳 **3** (spread out) 涂 ‹*paint, concrete, plaster*›; 铺 ‹*straw, newspaper*› **4** (put in) 铺 ‹*carpet, paving stones, turf*›; 铺设 ‹*railway line, cable*›; 埋设 ‹*mine*›; 砌 ‹*bricks*›; **to ~ the foundation stone** 奠基; **to ~ the foundations** lit 打地基; fig 打基础 **5** (set for meal) 摆放; **to ~ the table** 摆好餐具; **you haven't laid a place for Anna** 你没有给安娜摆放餐具 **6** **to ~ a fire** 摆放燃料生火 **7** Zool (produce) 产; **the hens have laid 15 eggs** 母鸡下了 15 个蛋 **8** (place, impose) 把…施加于; **to ~ a curse on sb.** 诅咒某人; **to ~ charges against sb.** 指控某人; **to ~ emphasis** *or* **stress on sth.** 强调某事物; **to ~ the blame (for sth.) on sb.** (把某事物) 归咎于某人; **to ~ it on the line** colloq 直说 **9** (in gambling) 押; **to ~ a bet** 下赌注; **I'll ~ you two to one it'll rain tomorrow** 我一赔二跟你打赌，明天要下雨 **10** (present) 提交; **he laid his proposal before the committee** 他向委员会递交了提议 **11** (prepare) 奠定 ‹*foundation*›; 留下 ‹*trail*›; 制定 ‹*plan*›; 设置 ‹*trap, snare*› **12** (settle) 消除 ‹*fears, doubts*›; **to ~ a rumour** 辟谣 **13** (expose) 使…处于特定状态 ‹*person*›; **we have laid ourselves open to criticism** 我们处于受批评的境地 **14** sl (have sex with) 与…性交; **he has been ~ing the boss's wife** 他一直和老板的老婆睡觉 **15** Agric, Hort 编制 ‹*hedge*›; 用…编制篱笆 ‹*branches, trunks*›
B *vi* (*pt, pp* **laid**) 产卵; **the hens are not ~ing well** 母鸡现在不爱下蛋
C *n* **1** (position) 放置方式; (direction) 放置方向 **2** sl (sexual partner) 性交的女方; **she's an easy ~** 她是个荡妇 **3** sl (sex act) 性交

Phrasal verbs

- **lay about** *vt* [**~ about sb./sth.**]
  1 (attack violently) 猛打; **she laid about me, punching and kicking** 她对我拳打脚踢; **he laid about the horse with a whip** 他用鞭子狠抽这匹马 **2** (strike out wildly) **to ~ about sb. (with sth.)** (用某物) 向某人乱打; **he laid about him with a stick** 他挥棒向他乱打
- **lay aside** *vt* [**~ aside sth., ~ sth. aside**]
  1 lit (put to one side) 把…放在一边 **2** fig (set aside) 留存…备用; **he has laid a bit of money aside for his old age** 他存了点儿钱防老 **3** fig (abandon, relinquish) 放弃; **to ~ aside the cares of office** 不再为公务烦恼; **to ~ aside one's personal feelings** 将个人情感置之度外
- **lay back** *vt* [**~ sb./sth. back**] 使…向后倾斜; **~ your head back** 头向后仰; **the nurse laid the patient back gently** 护士轻轻扶病人躺下
- **lay by** *vt* [**~ sth. by**] (set aside) 留存…备用; **she's got a bit of money laid by** 她存了一点儿钱
- **lay down**
  A [**~ sb./sth. down**] *vt* (put horizontally) 把…放平; **he laid the baby down on the settee** 他把婴儿平放在长椅上; **to ~ the blanket down on the floor** 把毯子铺在地板上
  B [**~ down sth., ~ sth. down**] *vt*
  1 (put down) 放下; **he laid his racket down on the floor beside him** 他把球拍放在身旁的地板上 **2** (relinquish) 放弃; **to ~ down one's arms** 放下武器 **3** Constr 铺设 ‹*cable, drain*›; 铺筑 ‹*road, railway*›; **to ~ down the foundations** 打地基 **4** (establish) 制定 ‹*rule, policy*›; 确定 ‹*price, wage*›; **it is laid down in the constitution that the president must be elected by the people** 宪法规定，总统必须由民选产生; **to ~ down the law** 制定法律
- **lay in** *vt* [**~ in sth., ~ sth. in**] 储存; **to ~ in food for Christmas** 为圣诞节储备食物
- **lay into** *vt* [**~ into sb.**] colloq **1** (attack violently) 狠打; **to ~ into sb. with sth.** 用某物狠打某人; **the champion laid into his opponent** 冠军猛烈地攻击对手; **she laid into me with her umbrella** 她用雨伞拼命打我 **2** (attack verbally) 抨击; **he laid into me, calling me a cheat** 他大骂我是骗子
- **lay off**
  A [**~ sb. off, ~ off sb.**] *vt* (make redundant) (temporarily) 使下岗; (permanently) 解雇; **to start ~ing people off** 开始裁员; **she was laid off from her job at the bakery** 她失去了面包房的工作
  B [**~ off sb./sth.**] *vt*
  1 (leave alone) 停止打扰; **~ off her! it wasn't her fault!** 别再责罚她了！那不是她的错！; **~ off that poor animal!** 别再欺负那可怜的动物了！; **I told him to ~ off my daughter** 我告诉他别再骚扰我女儿 **2** (refrain from) **to ~ off sth./doing sth.** 停止使用某物/做某事; **to ~ off cigarettes/smoking** 戒烟; **~ off drinking my whisky!** 别再喝我的威士忌!
  C *vi* colloq 停止; **~ off! you're messing up my hair!** 住手！你把我的头发弄乱了！
- **lay on** *vt* [**~ on sth., ~ sth. on**]
  1 (apply) 用一层…覆盖 ‹*glue*›; **he laid on the plaster, layer after layer** 他把灰泥一层层地涂上去 **2** Brit (install) 安装 ‹*gas, water*›; **you can reclaim the cost of ~ing on electricity and water** 你可以报销安装水电的费用 **3** (provide) 提供 ‹*food, transport*›; **the organizers of the event had laid on free refreshments** 活动的组织者提供了免费的茶点; **the Council is ~ing on extra bus services in the run-up to Christmas** 圣诞前市政会安排加开公交车 **4** (organize) 安排 ‹*event*›; **the villagers laid on a display of traditional dancing** 村民们安排了传统舞蹈表演 **5** fig colloq (exaggerate) 使…过分 ‹*praise, gratitude, sarcasm*›; **she was ~ing on the sweetness and flattery** 她极尽甜言蜜语、阿谀奉承之能事; **to ~ it on thick** 过分地夸大某事物; **sometimes he ~s it on a bit thick with the sympathy** 有时候他那种同情的表情做得有点太夸张了
- **lay out**
  A [**~ out sth., ~ sth. out**] *vt*
  1 (spread out ready for use) 将…摊开放好; **they laid out all the items for sale on the stall** 他们把所有待售商品都散开摆放在摊位上 **2** (spread out to full extent) 展开 ‹*map, garment, fabric*›; **he laid the map out on the table** 他在桌上摊开地图; **to ~ the material out flat** 把布料摊平; **a green and brown carpet was laid out in the entrance area** 入口处铺着一块绿色和棕色相间的地毯 **3** (design) 版面设计 ‹*magazine, page, advertisement*›; **the volume is attractively designed and laid out** 这卷书的设计排版很吸引人 **4** (set out according to a plan) 设计 ‹*town, garden, building*›; **the suburb was laid out in 1937 by the town planners** 该近郊住宅区是由城市规划师在 1937 年设计的 **5** (explain) 阐明 ‹*reasons, argument, demands, facts*›; **all the terms and conditions are laid out in the contract** 所有的条款与条件在合同中都已清楚地列明 **6** colloq (spend) 花 ‹*sum of money*›; **he laid out a fortune on a new car** 他花了一大笔钱买新车
  B [**~ out sb., ~ sb. out**] *vt*
  1 (prepare for burial) «*undertaker*» 为…作殡葬准备 ‹*body*› **2** colloq (knock unconscious) 把…打昏; **he was laid out by a blow to the left temple** 他的左太阳穴被打了一下，昏了过去
- **lay up**
  A [**~ up sth., ~ sth. up**] *vt*
  1 (store) 储存; **to ~ up fuel for the winter** 为过冬储存燃料 **2** (take out of service) 将…搁置不用; **my car's laid up** 我的车停开了; **the ship was laid up for repairs** 船进坞检修
  B [**~ sb. up**] *vt* (confine to bed) 使卧床不起; **she was laid up with flu** 她得了流感，卧病在床

lay[2] *pt* ▸**lie**[1] **A**

lay[3] *n* Literat 叙事诗

lay[4] *adj attrib* **1** Relig 在俗的 ‹*member*›; **a ~ brother/sister/reader** 平信徒修士/修女/读经员 **2** (non-expert) 外行的 ‹*mind, opinion*›

layabout /ˈleɪəbaʊt/ *n* colloq pej 懒汉

layaway /ˈleɪəweɪ/ *n* Amer 预付定金购货法; **to buy** *or* **purchase sth. on ~** 以预付定金方式购买某物

lay-by *n* Brit 路侧停车带

L

layer /ˈleɪə(r)/

A *n* 1 层; **the bottom/outer/top ~** 底层/外层/顶层; **~ upon ~** 一层又一层; **many ~s of meaning** fig 多层意义 2 (hen) 生蛋鸡; **a good/poor ~** 生蛋多/少的鸡

B *vt* (in hairdressing) 把…修剪出层次 ‹*hair*›; (arrange in layers) 把…分层堆放 ‹*metal, fabric*›

layer cake *n* 夹层蛋糕

layette /leɪˈet/ *n* 新生儿全套用品

layman /ˈleɪmən/ *n* (*pl* **laymen**) 1 (Christian) 平信徒 [指非神职人员] 2 (non-expert) 外行

lay: ~off *n* 1 (permanent) 解雇; (temporary) 暂时解雇期; 2 (period of inactivity) 休养期; **~out** *n* (in graphic design) 排版; (of architecture, landscape) 布局; (of machine) 设计; **~over** *n* 中途短暂停留; **~person** *n* 1 (Christian) 平信徒; 2 (non-expert) 外行

lay-up *n* 1 [u] Naut 闲置 2 [c] (in basketball) 单手上篮

laze /leɪz/ *vi* 懒散; **to ~ in the sun** 懒洋洋地晒太阳

Phrasal verbs

- **laze about, laze around** *vi* 懒散; **to ~ about in bed** 懒洋洋地躺在床上
- **laze away** *vt* [**~ sth. away, ~ away sth.**] 懒散地打发 ‹*time*›; **to ~ one's life away** 虚度人生; **to ~ away an afternoon** 懒散地度过下午

lazily /ˈleɪzɪli/ *adv* 懒惰地 ‹*work*›; 懒散地 ‹*drift, wander*›; 缓慢地 ‹*comb, stroke*›

laziness /ˈleɪzɪnɪs/ *n* [u] 懒惰

lazy /ˈleɪzi/ *adj* 1 pej (unwilling to exert oneself) 懒惰的 ‹*person*› 2 (done without effort) 懒洋洋的 ‹*yawn, manner*›; **a ~ day/holiday**; 懒散的一天/一个假期 3 (moving slowly) 缓慢的 ‹*movement*›; 流动缓慢的 ‹*river, current*› 4 pej (slapdash) 马虎的 ‹*idea, attempt*›; **~ thinking** 随随便便的思考

lazybones /ˈleɪzɪbəʊnz/ *n* colloq 懒骨头

lb *abbr* = **pound(s)** 磅

LBO *abbr* = **leveraged buyout**

lbw *abbr* = **leg before wicket** 腿截球 [击球员犯规出局的情况]

lc *abbr* = **lower case**

LCD *abbr* = **liquid crystal display**

L-driver *n* Brit 见习驾驶员

LEA *abbr* Brit = **local education authority**

leach /liːtʃ/

A *vt* 滤去; **to ~ sth. from sth.** 滤去某物中的某物; **to ~ minerals/nutrients from the soil** 滤去土壤中的矿物质/营养成分

B *vi* ‹*chemical, pollutant*› 被滤去

lead¹ /liːd/

A *vt* (*pt, pp* **led**) 1 (guide, escort) 为…带路; (take by hand or bridle) 牵领; **I led the children across the road** 我领孩子们过马路; **they led us into a trap** 他们引我们进了圈套; **to ~ the way** 带路; **the criminal was led away to the police station** 罪犯被押到了警察局; **he led the camel by a rope** 他用绳子牵着骆驼 2 (be at the front of) 走在…的前列 ‹*procession, march*› 3 (be leader of) 领导; **to ~ a discussion** 主持讨论; **she led the Democrats to victory** 她带领民主党人获得了胜利; **she led the audience in a cheer** 她领着观众欢呼; **to ~ an operation** 组织活动 4 (be ahead in race, competition) 在…中领先 ‹*race, league, market*›; 领先于 ‹*opponent, competitor*›; **she is ~ing her rival by 15 metres** 她领先对手 15 米; **to ~ the field** 处于领先地位; **to ~ the world in cancer research** 在癌症研究方面走在世界前列; **to ~ the way (in sth.)** (在某方面) 领先 5 (go in direction of, open on to, bring to) 引…通往; **this road led us to the station** 我们沿这条路到了车站; **this door should ~ us into the library** 我们从这扇门应该可以进入图书馆; **the tiger's footprints led the hunters to its lair** 猎人顺着老虎的脚印找到了它的巢穴 6 (steer, bring) 引导; **to ~ the conversation away from religion** 把谈话从宗教话题上引开; **this course of action could ~ them to disaster** 这种做法可能把他们引向灾难; **that line of investigation led them nowhere** 那种调查方式使他们一无所获 7 (cause, influence) 影响; **what led you to this decision?** 是什么让你做出了这个决定?; **the house was smaller than I had been led to believe** 那幢房子比我原以为的要小一些; **she's too easily led** 她太容易受人左右 8 (conduct, have) 过; **to ~ a miserable/lazy life** 过悲惨/懒散的生活 9 (in cards) 先出; **he led the ace of clubs** 他先出了一张梅花A 10 (in dancing) 领舞

B *vi* (*pt, pp* **led**) 1 (guide others) 带路; **you ~, we'll follow** 你领路，我们跟着 2 (go first) 走在前列 3 (be ahead in competition) 领先; **Germany are ~ing 2-0** 德国队 2 比 0 领先; **he was ~ing by nine seconds** 他领先 9 秒; **to ~ in the opinion polls** 在民意测验中领先 4 (go, provide access) 通向; **the track ~s from the farm to the village** 这条小路从农场通向村庄; **this door ~s into the garden** 这道门通向花园 5 (result in) **to ~ to sth./doing sth.** 导致某事物/做某事; **worn tyres may ~ to an accident** 磨损的轮胎可能引发事故; **one thing led to another** 一件事引出另一件事 6 Journ **to ~ with sth.** 把某事物作为头条新闻; **the Guardian led with the teachers' strike** 《卫报》把教师罢工作为头条新闻 7 (in boxing) 出击; **to ~ with one's right** 用右拳出击 8 (in cards) 先出牌

C *n* 1 (position at front of group) 前面的位置; **in the ~** 在前面 2 (example) 榜样; **to follow sb.'s ~** 效仿某人; **to give (sb.) a ~** (为某人) 树立榜样 3 (initiative) 领导; **to take the ~ (in doing sth.)** 带头 (做某事) 4 (winning position or advantage in race, competition) 领先地位; **to be in the ~** 处于领先地位; **to take the ~** 领先; **to go** *or* **move into the ~** 进入领先地位; **to lose the ~** 失去领先地位; **they have the ~ in laser technology** 他们在激光技术方面处于领先地位 5 (winning margin) 领先幅度; **he increased his ~ to 10 metres** 他把领先距离拉大到了 10 米; **he has a ~ of 12 seconds over the former champion** 他领先上届冠军 12 秒 6 (clue) 线索; **the police have a number of ~s to follow** 警方有很多条追查的线索 7 Theat, Cin (principal role) 主角; (performer) 扮演主角的演员; **to play/sing the ~** 演/唱主角 8 Journ (story) 头条新闻 9 (in cards) (action of leading) 先出牌; (right to lead) 先出牌权; (card led) 先出的牌; **it's Jane's ~** 该简先出牌 10 Brit (for dog) 牵狗带; **dogs must be kept on a ~** 狗必须牵住 11 Elec (wire) 电源线

D *modif* 1 (principal) 主要的; **she is their ~ singer** 她是他们的主唱 2 Journ 头条的; **a ~ item/article** 头条新闻/文章

Phrasal verbs

- **lead off**

A *vt* [**~ sth. off, ~ off sth.**] 开始; **to ~ off a discussion** 带头发言开始讨论; **he led off the debate with an attack on the committee** 他对委员会的抨击，拉开了辩论的序幕

B *vi* 开始; **to ~ off with sth.** 以某事物开始; **she led off with a Haydn sonata** 她以海顿的一首奏鸣曲作为开始

- **lead on** *vt* [**~ sb. on**] 1 (give false hope to) 诱惑; (sexually) 勾引 2 (influence) 怂恿; **to ~ sb. on to do sth.** 怂恿某人做某事
- **lead up to** *vt* [**~ up to sth.**] 1 (precede) 在…之前; **in the weeks ~ing up to the election** 选举前的几个星期里 2 (culminate in) 是导致…的原因; **the negotiations that led up to the release of the hostages** 使人质得以获释的谈判 3 (introduce) 迂回地引向; **he led up to the subject as tactfully as he could** 他尽可能巧妙地引出这个话题

lead² /led/

A *n* 1 [u] (metal) 铅; **~ content** 含铅量; **to fill** Brit *or* **pump** Amer **sb. full of ~** colloq 向某人连续扫射 2 [c] (in pencil) 铅笔芯 3 [c] Naut (for sounding) 测深锤

B *modif* (made of lead) 铅制的; (containing lead) 含铅的 ‹*paint*›; **a ~ pipe** 铅管; **to go down like a ~ balloon** fig colloq 毫无效果

lead counsel *n* 主控律师

leaded /ˈledɪd/ *adj* 1 (framed with lead) 铅框的 ‹*glass, windows*› 2 (with added lead) 加铅的 ‹*petrol*›

leaded light *n* 菱形铅条玻璃窗

leaden /ˈledn/ *adj* 1 dated (made of lead) 铅制的 ‹*pipe, strip*› 2 (lead-coloured) 铅灰色的 ‹*clouds, sky*› 3 (heavy and slow) 缓慢沉重的 ‹*footsteps, pace*› 4 (gloomy) 沉闷的 ‹*atmosphere, silence*›

leader /ˈliːdə(r)/ *n* 1 (of procession) 带队者; (climber) 先导登山者 2 Sport (in race or competition) 领先的选手; (in horse-racing) 领先的赛马; (of team) 领先的参赛队; **to be among the ~s** 领先 3 (organizer, instigator) (of expedition) 领队; (of strike, rebellion, movement) 领导者; (of project, operation) 带头人 4 (chief, head) (of nation, political party, religious sect) 领袖; (of council, club, group, team, trade union) 负责人; (of army, troops) 首长; (of gang) 头目; **a meeting of world ~s** 世界领导人会议 5 (in market, field) 领先者; **to be a ~ in sth.** 在某方面领先; **a world ~ in car manufacturing** 世界汽车制造业的领先企业 6 (of pack, herd) 领群兽; **the ~ of the flock** 领头羊 7 Brit (in orchestra) 首席小提琴手 8 Brit Journ (newspaper article) 社论 9 (on tape) 空段 10 (tree shoot) 顶枝

leader: ~ board *n* 选手积分榜; **L~ of the House of Commons** *n* Brit 下议院议长; **L~ of the House of Lords** *n* Brit 上议院议长; **L~ of the Opposition** *n* Brit 议会反对党领袖

leadership /ˈliːdəʃɪp/

A *n* [u] 1 (of party, state, company) 领导职位; **~ of the party** 政党领导; **to be elected to the ~** 被选为领导 2 (fact of being leader) 领导; **during/under her ~** 在她领导期间/之下 3 (quality) 领导才能 4 (group of leaders) 领导层

B *modif* 领导的 ‹*quality, potential, challenge*›

leadership contest *n* 领导地位的角逐; **to hold a ~** 举行领导人竞选

lead-free /ˈledfriː/ *adj* 无铅的 ‹*petrol, paint*›

lead-in /ˈliːdɪn/ *n* (introduction) 引子; (in piece of music) 序曲; **a ~ to sth.** 某事物的序曲

leading /ˈliːdɪŋ/ *adj* 1 (at the front) 最前头的 ‹*animal, vessel, vehicle*›; **the ~ carriages of the train** 列车的头几节车厢 2 (in race, competition, league) 领先的 ‹*athlete, team, horse, boat*› 3 (most important or famous) 最杰出的 ‹*writer, artist, lawyer, politician*›; 最著名的 ‹*brand, product*›; 占主导地位的 ‹*company, bank, industry*› 4 (main) 主要的 ‹*part, cause, idea*›; **to play a ~ role in sth.** 在某事物中起主要作用

leading article *n* Brit 社论

leading edge

A *n* 1 (vanguard) 最前沿; **at the ~ of sth.** 在…的最前沿 ‹*technology*› 2 (of wing) 前缘; (of propeller blade) 导边

B **leading-edge** *modif* 最前沿的 ‹*technology, project*›

leading: ~ lady *n* 女主演; **~ light** *n* 重要人物; **~ man** *n* 男主演; **~ question** *n* 诱导性问题; **~ rein** *n* 1 (for horse) 缰绳; 2 (for child) 学步带; **~ seaman** *n* Brit 上等水兵

lead /led/: **~ pencil** *n* 铅笔; **~ poisoning** *n* [u] 铅中毒; **~ shot** *n* [u] 铅弹

lead /liːd/: **~ story** *n* 头条新闻; **~ time** *n* (in production) 投产前研制周期; (in delivery) 订货交付时间

leaf /li:f/
A n (pl **leaves** /li:vz/) **1** (of plant) 叶子; **lettuce/autumn leaves** 生菜叶/秋叶; **to come into ~** 长叶; **to shake like a ~** 吓得哆嗦 **2** (of paper) 张; (of book) 页; **to take a ~ from** *or* **out of sb.'s book** fig 效仿某人; **to turn over a new ~** fig 重新开始 **3** (of gold, silver) 箔 **4** (of table) 活动面板
B vi 长叶
C **-leafed** /li:fd/; *combining form* **four~** 四叶的 ‹*clover*›; **red~** 红叶的 ‹*lettuce*›; **broad~** 宽叶的 ‹*ivy, grass*›

Phrasal verb
- **leaf through** vt [**~ through sth.**] 匆匆翻阅 ‹*pages, book*›

leaf bud n 叶芽
leafless /'li:flɪs/ adj 无叶的
leaflet /'li:flɪt/
A n **1** (for advertising, propaganda) 传单 **2** (little leaf) 小叶
B vt 向…散发传单 ‹*homes, houses*›; 在…内散发传单 ‹*town, area*›
C vi 散发传单; **a ~ing campaign** 散发传单的宣传活动
leaf: ~ mould n [u] 腐叶土; **~ spinach** n [u] 菠菜叶; **~ tobacco** n [u] 烟叶; **~ vegetable** n 叶菜
leafy /'li:fi/ adj **1** (with lots of leaves) 叶茂的 ‹*branch*› **2** (with lots of trees) 多树木的 ‹*glade, suburb*›
league /li:g/
A n **1** [c] (alliance) 联盟; **L~ of Nations** Hist 国际联盟 **2** [u] (collaboration) 联合; **to be in ~ with sb.** 与某人勾结 **3** [c] Brit (in football) 联赛 **4** [c] fig colloq (class) 等级; **to be out of one's ~** 才能难以胜任自己的职位; **I'm not in his ~** 我远不如他; **to be in the big ~** 位列高层; **to be at the top of the exports/employment ~** 在出口/就业方面领先 **5** [c] archaic (unit of distance) 里格
B *modif* 联赛的; **the L~ Cup** [英国] 联赛杯
league: ~ standings npl 联赛排名榜; **~ table** n **1** Brit (in football) 联赛排名榜; **2** (in competitive field) 排名榜
leak /li:k/
A n **1** (crack) 裂缝; (hole) 漏洞; **to plug** *or* **stop a ~** 堵塞漏洞; **to spring a ~** 出现裂缝 **2** (escape) 漏出物; **a gas/radiation ~** 煤气/辐射泄漏; **to go for** *or* **take a ~** colloq 撒尿 colloq **3** fig (accidental disclosure) 泄露; (deliberate disclosure) 透露; **the source of the ~** 泄密者; **I don't want any ~s** 我不希望走漏任何风声
B vi **1** (allow liquid in or out) 漏; **the roof ~s** 屋顶漏了; **the petrol tank is ~ing** 汽油箱在漏油 **2** (seep) «*liquid*» 渗漏; «*gas, radioactivity*» 泄漏; **to ~ away** 漏掉 **3** fig (be accidentally disclosed) 泄露; (be deliberately disclosed) 透露
C vt **1** (allow out) 漏; **the tank has been ~ing petrol** 油箱一直在漏汽油 **2** fig (disclose accidentally) 泄露; (disclose deliberately) 透露; **details of the project were ~ed to the press** 项目的细节被透露给了新闻界

Phrasal verbs
- **leak in** vi 渗入
- **leak out** vi **1** (escape accidentally) 泄漏 **2** fig (be accidentally disclosed) 被泄露; (be deliberately disclosed) 被透露; **this is sure to ~ out** 这肯定会泄露出去; **it ~ed out that there was a secret deal** 据消息透露，有一宗秘密交易

leakage /'li:kɪdʒ/ n **1** [u] (process) 泄漏 **2** [c] (liquid, gas) 泄漏量
leaker /'li:kə(r)/ n 泄密者
leak-proof adj 防漏的
leaky /'li:ki/ adj 渗漏的 ‹*pipe, boat, shoe*›; **a ~ roof** 漏雨的屋顶
lean[1] /li:n/
A adj **1** (not fat) 瘦的 ‹*person, body, face*›; **~ meat** 瘦肉 **2** fig (difficult) 不景气的 ‹*times*›; **to have a ~ time of it** 日子不好过; **to have a ~ year** 经历荒年 **3** (efficient) 效率高的 ‹*company*›
B n [u] 瘦肉
lean[2]
A vt (pt, pp **~ed** *or* Brit **leant**) 使倾斜; **to ~ one's head on sb.'s shoulder** 把头靠在某人肩上; **to ~ one's elbows on sth.** 把胳膊肘撑在某物上; **to ~ a bike/ladder against a wall** 把自行车/梯子斜靠在墙上; **to ~ one's back against the wall** 背靠着墙
B vi (pt, pp **~ed** *or* Brit **leant**) (to be sloping) «*wall, building*» 倾斜; (for support) «*ladder, bicycle*» 斜靠; «*person*» 背靠; **to ~ against a wall** 靠在墙上

Phrasal verbs
- **lean across**
A vi 俯身过来; **to ~ across to do sth.** 俯身过来做某事
B vt [**~ across sth.**] 俯身探过 ‹*desk, table*›
- **lean back**
A vi 向后靠; **to ~ back in one's chair** 靠在椅背上
B vt [**~ sth. back**] 使…后倾 ‹*chair*›; 使…后仰 ‹*head*›
- **lean down** vi 俯身向下
- **lean forward**
A vi 身体前倾
B vt [**~ sth. forward**] 使…前倾 ‹*head, body*›
- **lean on**
A [**~ on sth.**] vt 倚靠在…上 ‹*arm, windowsill*›
B [**~ on sb.**] vt
1 lit 倚靠在…身上; fig 依靠; **to ~ on sb. for support** lit 靠在某人身上; fig 依靠某人获得支持 **2** fig (pressurize) 对…施加压力; **to ~ on sb. for sth.** 为获得某物而向某人施压; **to ~ on sb. to do sth.** 向某人施压要其做某事
- **lean out**
A vi 探出上半身; **to ~ out of sth.** 探身到某物外
B vt [**~ sth. out**] 探出; **to ~ one's head/shoulder out of the window** 把头/肩膀探到窗外
- **lean over** vi «*tower, post, tree*» 倾斜; «*person*» (forwards) 俯身向前; (sideways) 倾斜上半身; **to ~ over backwards** 身体后屈; **he leant over backwards to be helpful** fig 他竭尽全力帮忙
- **lean towards** vt [**~ towards sb./sth.**]
1 lit 斜靠在…上 ‹*person, window*› **2** fig 倾向于 ‹*party, opinion, socialism*›; 倾向于…的观点 ‹*person*›

lean-burn adj 稀燃的; **a ~ engine** 稀燃发动机; **~ technology** 稀燃技术
leaning /'li:nɪŋ/
A adj 倾斜的; **the ~ Tower of Pisa** 比萨斜塔
B n 倾向; **a L~ towards sth.** 对某事物的倾向; **do you have artistic ~s?** 你有艺术爱好吗?
leant /lent/ pt, pp Brit ▸**lean**[2]
lean-to n (small building) 单坡顶小屋; (shed) 单坡顶棚子; **a ~ garage** 单坡顶车库
leap /li:p/
A vi (pt, pp **~ed** *or* Brit **leapt**) **1** (jump) 跳跃; **to ~ across** *or* **over the stream** 跃过小溪; **the flames were ~ing into the air** 火焰蹿向空中; **to ~ to one's feet** 赶紧站起来; **the tiger leapt on its prey** 老虎扑向猎物; **to ~ at sth.** fig 赶紧抓住 ‹*opportunity*›; 迫不及待地接受 ‹*offer*›; **to ~ to conclusions** 草率下结论; **his heart leapt** 他的心怦怦跳 **2** (go quickly) 迅速移动; **he leapt into the car and drove off** 他跳上车开走了; **he leapt out from behind the tree** 他从树后面跳出来; **he leapt upstairs** 他冲上楼; **to ~ to stardom** fig 一举成名 **3** (increase dramatically) «*price, stock market*» 猛涨; «*profit*» 剧增
B vt (pt, pp **~ed** *or* Brit **leapt**) 跳过; **he tried to ~ the hedge on his horse** 他试图骑马跃过树篱
C n **1** (jump) 跳跃; **to take a ~** 跳跃; **he made it across with one ~** 他一跃而过; **by** *or* **in ~s and bounds** fig 非常迅速地; **a ~ in the dark** fig 冒险举动; **a great ~ forward** fig 一大进步 **2** (dramatic increase) 激增; **the ~ in petrol prices** 汽油价格的猛涨

Phrasal verbs
- **leap about, leap around** vi 跳来跳去
- **leap out** vi 引人注目; **to ~ out at sb.** 一下子进入某人的视线
- **leap up** vi **1** (jump up) 跳起来; **the dog leapt up at the intruder** 狗扑向闯入者 **2** (rise) «*prices, rates, inflation*» 猛涨

leapfrog /'li:pfrɒg/ ▸**p. 307**
A n [u] 跳背游戏
B vt (pres p etc. **-gg-**) **1** (jump over) 分腿跳过 ‹*fence, wall, person*› **2** (overtake) 超过 ‹*rival, opponent*›
C vi (pres p etc. **-gg-**) **1** (jump) 分腿跳; **to ~ over sb./sth.** 分腿跳过某人/某物 **2** (overtake) 超越; **to ~ over one's rival** 超过对手; **she ~ged into a senior sales position** 她蹿升到了高级营销员的职位
leapt /lept/ pt, pp Brit ▸**leap A, B**
leap year n 闰年
learn /lɜ:n/ (pt, pp **~ed** *or* Brit **learnt**)
A vt **1** (through study, practice) 学习 ‹*language, skill*›; **it's time you ~ed better manners!** 你该懂点礼貌! ; **to ~ sth. by heart** 记住某事物; **to ~ to swim** 学游泳; **I've ~ed my lesson** 我吸取了教训 **2** (discover) 得知 ‹*news, facts*›; **I never ~ed her name** 我从来没有听说过她的名字; **we'll soon ~ whether she succeeded** 我们很快就会知道她是否成功了 **3** Brit sl (teach) 教训; **I'll soon ~ you!** 我很快就要你好看!
B vi **1** (acquire knowledge) 学习; **to ~ about sth.** 学习关于某事物的知识; **to ~ from sb.** 向某人学习; **to ~ by** *or* **from one's mistakes** 从错误中吸取教训; **it's never too late to ~** 活到老，学到老; **you'll ~!** 你等着瞧! ; **I've learnt better since then** 自那之后我学聪明了 **2** (hear information) 听说; **to ~ about** *or* **of sth.** 得知某事物; **we only ~ed about** *or* **of the accident today** 我们今天才听说了这次事故
learned[1] /'lɜ:nɪd/ adj **1** (having much knowledge) 博学的; **a ~ person** 学者; **my ~ friend** Brit Jur 我这位法律同仁 **2** attrib (scholarly) 学术的 ‹*book, article, journal, society*› **3** (displaying knowledge) 深奥的 ‹*remark, speech*›
learned[2] /lɜ:nd/ adj Psych 学来的
learner /'lɜ:nə(r)/ n 学习者; **to be a fast/slow ~** 学得快/慢
learner-driver n Brit 学习驾车者
learning /'lɜ:nɪŋ/
A n [u] **1** (erudition) 学问; **book ~** 书本知识; **a man of (considerable) ~** 学者; **a little ~ is a dangerous thing** 丁点学问，为害颇深 **2** (process) 学习
B *modif* 学习的; **~ resources** 学习参考资料
learning: ~ curve n 学习曲线; **~ difficulties** npl Brit 学习障碍; **~ disability** n 学习无能; **~ disabled child** n Amer 无学习能力儿童; **~ resources centre** n 学习资料中心; **~ support teacher** ▸**p. 409** n Brit 学习辅助教师
learnt /lɜ:nt/ pt, pp Brit ▸**learn**
lease /li:s/
A n **1** (contract) 租约; **to take out a ~ on sth.** 办理某物的租约; **to take out a ~ on an apartment** 租一套公寓房; **to hold/renew a ~** 签有/续签租约; **they have the building on ~** 他们租用了这幢楼; **the land was held under (a) ~** 这地租出去了 **2** (period of time) 租期; **to be on a long ~** «*land, building*» 被长租; **the ~ has expired** *or* **run out** 租期到了 **3** **a new ~ of life** Brit *or* **on life** Amer (for person) 更愉快的生活; (for thing) 更好的使用; **the operation gave her a new ~ of life** 手术后她重获新生; **the city has**

been given a new ~ of life 这座城市焕然一新

B *vt* 1 (to take lease on) 租用 2 (let) 出租; to ~ (out) an apartment 出租公寓房

leaseback /ˈliːsbæk/ *n* 售后回租; a ~ agreement 售后回租协议

leasehold /ˈliːshəʊld/

A *n* 1 [c] (property) 租赁的地产 2 [u] (tenure) 租赁权; to have sth. on ~ 租用某物

B *adj* 租赁的 ‹*property, land*›

C *adv* 以租赁方式 ‹*have, hold*›; they let the building out ~ 他们出租那幢楼

leaseholder /ˈliːshəʊldə(r)/ *n* 租赁人

leash /liːʃ/ *n* 1 lit (for dog) 牵狗带; to be on a ~ ‹*dog*› 用皮带拴着 2 fig (restraint) 限制; to keep sb. on a short *or* tight ~ 严格限制某人; to be straining at the ~ ‹*person*› 迫不及待

leasing /ˈliːsɪŋ/

A *n* [u] 租赁

B *modif* 租赁的 ‹*agreement, arrangement*›

least /liːst/ *superl* ▸ little

A *adj* 1 (smallest) 最小的; (smallest amount of) 最少的; he has (the) ~ money/food 他的钱/食物最少; the ~ expensive car 最便宜的汽车; the ~ thing upsets her 一点小事都会使她不开心 2 (in negative constructions) 最轻微的; she didn't have the ~ difficulty 她没有遇到一丁点困难; I haven't the ~ idea what she's talking about 我一点也不明白她在说什么; the ~ bit 丝毫; she wasn't the ~ bit cross/frightened 她一点也不生气/害怕

B *pron* the ~ 最少量; nobody has much food, but you have the ~ 大家的食物都不多，但你的最少; it's the ~ I can do 这是我所能做的最起码的事; that's the ~ of our worries 那是我们最不在乎的事; I was annoyed, to say the ~ 至少可以说我很恼火; in the ~ 丝毫; it doesn't matter in the ~ 一点也不要紧; we didn't in the ~ expect it 我们根本没有预料到这件事; not in the ~! 一点也不!

C *adv* 最低限度地; one of the ~ known areas 最鲜为人知的地区之一; when you are ~ expecting it 在你最意料不到的时候; he did it ~ easily of all 这件事他干得最艰难; ~ of all 尤其不; nobody complained, ~ of all the parents 没有人抱怨，尤其是家长们; ~ of all would I wish to offend him 我尤其不想得罪他; not ~ 特别; not ~ because ... 尤其是因为…; last but not ~ 最后但同样重要地

D **at least** *adv phr* 1 (not less than, if nothing else) 至少; it cost at (the) ~ 50 euros 它花了至少 50 欧元 2 (anyway) 无论如何; he's ill, at ~ that's what he says 他病了，反正他是这么说的

leastways /ˈliːstweɪz/, **leastwise** /ˈliːstwaɪz/ *advs* Amer colloq 至少

leather /ˈleðə(r)/

A *n* 1 (material) 皮革 2 (used for cleaning) (wash) ~ 油鞣革

B *modif* 皮革的; a ~ jacket/wallet 皮夹克/皮夹

C **leathers** *npl* 皮衣

leather: **~-bound** *adj* 皮面装帧的; **~ goods** *npl* 皮革制品; **~jacket** *n* Brit 大蚊幼虫; **~wear** *n* [u] 皮衣

leathery /ˈleðəri/ *adj* 皮革般粗糙的 ‹*skin, face*›; 皮革般嚼不动的 ‹*meat*›

leave /liːv/

A *vt* (*pt, pp* **left**) 1 (move away from) 离开; to ~ home/the country 离家/出国; to ~ the plane 下飞机; to ~ school (go home from school) 放学; (finish one's education) 毕业离校; the plane ~s Rome for Madrid at 11.30 罗马到马德里的飞机于 11 点 30 分起飞; he hasn't left his bed for five days 他已经 5 天没下床了; please don't ~ me on my own 请不要留下我一个人; I'll have to ~ you now 我现在得走了; I left her cleaning her car 我离开时她正在洗车; I left the pie to cool 我把馅饼放着让它凉一凉; to ~ sb./sth. standing colloq 远远胜过某人/某事物; she set off at a pace that left the others standing 她出发的速度比其他人快得多; to ~ the track ‹*train*› 出轨; the words had scarcely left her lips when ... 她的话刚一出口…; we left the subject of finance and went on to discuss the schedule 我们把资金问题搁下，接着讨论日程安排; the smile left her face 她脸上的笑容消失了 2 (resign from) 辞去 ‹*job*›; 离开 ‹*company*›; she has left the teaching profession 她已经不再教书了 3 (leave behind) 丢弃; (abandon) 抛弃; she left him to find his own way home 她丢下他让他自己找路回家; he left his wife for another woman 他为另一个女人抛弃了妻子 4 (be survived by) 遗下; he ~s a widow and three children 他死后留下寡妻和3个孩子 5 (cause to remain) 使处于; they left him waiting for 10 minutes 他们让他等了10分钟; she left the baby crying 她听任孩子哭个不停; I made a couple of mistakes, but I left them 我犯了几个错误，但是没有更正; to ~ the door open 让门开着; to ~ it at that 就到此为止; to ~ it that ... 做…的安排; we left it that he would let us know if he couldn't come 我们的安排是，如果他不能来就通知我们; how shall we ~ it? 我们该怎样安排? 6 (cause) 使得; (result in) 结果是; the illness left him with chronic bronchitis 这场病让他患上了慢性支气管炎; I was left with the impression that they didn't care 留给我的印象是他们不在乎; I was left speechless by her reply 她的回答弄得我哑口无言; the accident left him an orphan 事故之后他成了孤儿; she was left with no alternative but to sell the car 她别无选择，只能卖车; the accident left a scar on her face 事故之后她脸上留下了一道伤疤 7 (allow to remain) 剩下; she left most of her breakfast 她的早餐剩了一大半没吃; ~ some wine for Jane 给简留一些葡萄酒; you've (got) eight minutes left 你还剩 8 分钟 8 Math 余下; seven from ten/ten minus seven ~s three 10 减 7 得 3 9 (leave in place) (deliberately) 留下; (forgetfully) 忘记带; she left the letter on his desk 她把信留在他的书桌上; don't ~ your toys all over the floor! 不要把玩具丢得地板上到处都是! ; she left her gloves on the bus 她把手套落在公共汽车上了; we left the notice up for several days 我们把通知贴了好几天; the postman left the parcel with my neighbour 邮差把包裹留给了我的邻居; he left a note for his mother 他给母亲留了张条子; he didn't ~ his name 他没有留下姓名 10 (give over for safekeeping) 托付; (entrust) 交托; the children were left in my care 孩子们托付给我照看; he left his watch with his father while he went for a swim 他去游泳时把手表交给父亲保管; he left the matter in our hands 他把这件事交给我们处理; I left the report for her to write 我把报告交给她写; ~ it to *or* with me: I'll see to it 这事交给我吧：我来处理; how the money is spent is left up to the project leader 钱如何使用由项目主管决定 11 (bequeath) 遗留; she left all her money to charity 她把所有的钱都遗赠给了慈善机构; my grandfather left me £1,000 我祖父遗留给我 1,000 英镑 12 (not accept) 不接受; to take sb./sth. or ~ sb./sth. 对某人/某事物持无所谓的态度; what do you think of Jenny? — I can take her or ~ her 你觉得珍妮怎么样? ——无所谓好不好 13 (postpone) 推迟; ~ it for now: you can finish it off tomorrow 把这事暂搁一下：你可以明天完成; let's ~ the washing-up till tomorrow 把餐具留到明天再洗吧 14 (let be, neglect) 不做; should I try and fix it? — no, ~ it 我试着修一下好吗? ——不用，放着吧; his homework often gets left 他经常不做家庭作业 15 (not interfere with) 不干预; ~ that! it's dirty! 别碰那个! 脏! ; to ~ sb. to himself/herself 不打扰某人; people need to be left to themselves at times like this 在这种时候人们需要独处; children should be left to discover things for themselves 应当让孩子们自己去探索; to ~ sb. to it 让某人独立完成工作 16 (let go) to ~ hold/go of sth./sb. 放开某物/某人; the dog wouldn't ~ go of my arm 狗咬住我的手臂不放; don't ~ hold! 别松手!

B *vi* (*pt, pp* **left**) 1 (depart) 离开; don't ~ without me 不要丢下我; it's time we left 我们该走了; the plane left for Paris at 9.45 飞机 9 点 45 分起飞前往巴黎了 2 (resign) 辞职; he left for another firm 他跳槽了

C *v refl* (*pt, pp* **left**) to ~ oneself (with) sth. 留给自己某事物; to ~ oneself short of money/time 没有给自己留足够的钱/时间

D *n* [u] 1 (holiday) 假期; (through illness) 病假; Mil 休假; annual ~ 年假; to take three days' ~ 休假 3 天; to be/go on ~ 休假; he was granted ~ of absence 他获准休假 2 formal (permission) 许可; he was granted ~ to address the meeting 他获准在会上发言; by *or* with your ~ 请允许我; without so much as a by your ~ colloq 未经许可 3 (departure) 告别; to take one's ~ (of sb.) formal（向某人）告别; the guests took their ~ 客人们告辞了

Phrasal verbs

- **leave about, leave around** *vt* [~ sth. about *or* around] (carelessly) 乱放; (deliberately) 放置; he always ~s his clothes around his bedroom 他总是把衣服扔得卧室里到处都是; I need a place where I can ~ my tools around 我需要一个可以放工具的地方
- **leave aside** *vt* [~ aside sth., ~ sth. aside] 不考虑; leaving aside the cost, do we actually need a second car? 且不说费用，我们真的还需要一辆车吗?
- **leave behind** *vt* [~ sb./sth. behind] 1 (outstrip) 把…抛在后面; to ~ the competitors behind 超过竞争对手; you'll have to walk a bit faster if you don't want to get left behind 如果你不想落在后面，就得走快一些; the teacher left us behind halfway through the first lecture 第一堂课讲到一半我们就跟不上老师了 2 (move away from) 离开; (put behind) 抛开; the boat sailed away, leaving the coast behind 船驶离海岸; to ~ one's family behind 离开家人; you must ~ all that behind you and start afresh 你必须抛开那一切，重新开始 3 (forget to bring) 忘记带; (not take) 不带; he left his briefcase behind on the train 他把公文包落在火车上了; anything that is too heavy to carry will have to be left behind 搬不动的重物都必须留下; don't ~ me behind 别把我丢下 4 (cause) 使处于; the storm left a trail of destruction behind it 暴风雨过后满目疮痍
- **leave in** *vt* [~ sth. in, ~ in sth.] 1 (cause to remain) 留下; you shouldn't ~ the plug in when you clean an electrical appliance 清洁电器的时候不应该插着插头 2 (retain) 保留; do you think I should take this paragraph out? — no, ~ it in 你看我应该把这段删掉吗? ——别，留着吧
- **leave off**

A [~ sth. off, ~ off sth.] *vt* 1 (not wear, not keep on) 不穿 ‹*coat, shoes*›; 不戴 ‹*hat, glasses*›; 不盖 ‹*blanket*›; I usually ~ off the eiderdown in the summer 夏天我通常把鸭绒被拿掉 2 (not replace) 不重新装上; (not attach) 不装上; I think you should ~ the door off 我认为你不应该装门 3 (omit) 遗漏; I deliberately left off my telephone number 我特意没写电话号码; his name had been left off the register 登记簿上漏掉了他的名字 4 colloq (stop) to ~ off doing

sth. 停止做某事; **I wish he would ~ off whistling that tune** 我希望他不要再吹那个曲子了
B [**~ sth. off**] *vt* (not switch on) 不开
C *vi* 停止; **has the rain left off yet?** 雨停了吗?; **~ off!** colloq 停!

• **leave on**
A [**~ sth. on, ~ on sth.**] *vt* (continue to wear) 继续穿着 ‹*coat, shoes*›; 继续戴着 ‹*hat, glasses*›; **I'm glad I left my boots on** 我很高兴没有脱掉靴子; **she left her make-up on when she went to bed** 她睡觉时没有卸妆
B [**~ sth. on**] *vt*
1 (not remove) 不拿掉; **~ the lid on** 不要揭开盖子; **she left the pan on and set fire to the kitchen** 她任平底锅一直烧着, 结果把厨房烧着了 2 (not switch off) 开着; **somebody left the kitchen light on** 有人没关厨房的灯

• **leave out**
A [**~ out sth., ~ sth. out**] *vt*
1 (fail to include) (deliberately) 忽略; (accidentally) 遗漏; **she left out a word when she dictated the address** 她口述地址时漏掉了一个词; **the results of the experiment were left out of the report** 报告中没提实验结果; **he left out a vital screw when he reassembled the engine** 重装发动机时, 他漏装了一个关键的螺丝钉; **the cake will taste awful if you ~ the sugar out** 如果不加糖, 蛋糕会很难吃 2 (fail to consider) 没有考虑 ‹*fact, possibility*›; **to ~ sth. out of one's calculations/the reckoning** 没有考虑某事物; **~ it out!** Brit colloq (stop doing that!) 行啦!; (expressing disbelief) 别逗了! 3 (not bring in) 让…留在室外; **to ~ the wet clothes out** 把湿衣服晾在外面 4 (not put away) 不拿走; **I left the milk and sugar out on the table** 我把牛奶和糖留在桌子上
B [**~ sb. out, ~ out sb.**] *vt* (from social group, activity) 不包括; **there are 25, not 24: I left Sarah out** 有 25 个人, 不是 24 个: 我刚才没算萨拉; **you can ~ me out of your quarrel** 别把我拉入你们的争吵中; **to feel left out** 感到受冷落; **Barton has been left out of the team** 巴顿未能入选参赛名单

• **leave over** *vt* 1 **to have sth. left over** (as remainder) 剩下某物; **he had just 45 pence left over** 他只剩 45 便士了 2 [**~ sth. over**] (postpone) 推迟; **let's ~ this over till tomorrow** 这事明天再说吧; **I don't like leaving things over** 我做事不喜欢拖拖拉拉

-leaved /li:vd/ *combining form* = **leaf C**

leaven /'levn/ *vt* 1 (cause to ferment) 在…中加入酵母 ‹*bread, mixture*› 2 fig (enliven) 使…渐渐有趣 ‹*culture*›

leaves /li:vz/ *npl* ▸**leaf A**

leave-taking *n* [u] 告别

leaving /'li:vɪŋ/
A *n* (departure) 离开
B *modif* 离职的 ‹*present, party*›
C **leavings** *npl* (left-overs) 剩饭菜; (rubbish) 废弃物

Lebanese /ˌlebə'ni:z/ ▸**p. 503**
A *adj* (of Lebanon) 黎巴嫩的; (of the people) 黎巴嫩人的
B *n* 黎巴嫩人

Lebanon /'lebənən/ *pr n* **(the) ~** 黎巴嫩

lech /letʃ/
A *n* colloq pej 好色之徒
B *vi* 好色; **to ~ for** *or* **after sb.** 对某人起色心

lecher /'letʃə(r)/ *n* 色鬼

lecherous /'letʃərəs/ *adj* 好色的 ‹*man*›; 色迷迷的 ‹*look, grin*›

lecherously /'letʃərəsli/ *adv* 色迷迷地 ‹*leer, grin, stare*›

lechery /'letʃəri/ *n* [u] 好色

lectern /'lektɜ:n/ *n* (in church) 诵经台; (for lecture notes) (斜面) 讲台

lecture /'lektʃə(r)/
A *n* 1 (public talk) 讲座; **to give/attend a ~** 作/听讲座; **a ~ about** *or* **on sth.** 关于某主题的讲座 2 (scolding) 训斥; **to give sb. a ~ about honesty** 训诫某人要诚实
B *vt* 训斥 ‹*person*›; **to ~ sb. for having done sth.** 因某人做了某事对其加以训斥
C *vi* 讲课; **he ~s on Spanish literature/in law** 他讲授西班牙文学/法律; **to ~ to a large audience** 对众多的听众作讲座

lecture: ~ hall *n* 报告厅; **~ notes** *npl* (by student) 讲课笔记; (used by lecturer) 讲义

lecturer /'lektʃərə(r)/ ▸**p. 409** *n* 1 (speaker) 讲演者 2 Brit (university teacher) 讲师; **a maths ~** *or* **a ~ in maths** 数学讲师

lecture room *n* Brit 大教室

lectureship /'lektʃəʃɪp/ *n* Brit 讲师职位; **a ~ in lexicography** 词典学讲师职位

lecture theatre *n* 阶梯教室

LED *n* = **light-emitting diode**

led /led/ *pt, pp* ▸**lead¹ A, B**

ledge /ledʒ/ *n* 1 (in house) 壁架 2 (on mountain, cliff) 岩架 3 (under sea) 暗礁; **a reef ~** 礁脉

ledger /'ledʒə(r)/ *n* 分类账簿

ledger line *n* [五线谱上方或下方标示音高的] 加线

lee /li:/ *n* 背风处; **in** *or* **under the ~ of ...** 在…的背风面; **~ side** 背风面

leech /li:tʃ/ *n* 1 (worm) 水蛭; **to cling to sb. like a ~** 紧紧缠住某人 2 pej (person) 榨取他人血汗者

leek /li:k/ *n* 韭葱

leer /lɪə(r)/
A *vi* 色迷迷地斜睨; **to ~ at sb.** 色迷迷地斜睨某人
B *n* 色迷迷的目光

leery /'lɪəri/ *adj* colloq 猜疑的; **to be ~ of sth./sb.** 对某事物/某人有疑虑; **to be ~ about sth.** 对某事谨慎

lees /li:z/ *npl* 酒渣

leeward /'li:wəd, 'lu:əd/
A *n* [u] 背风面; **to ~** 向下风处
B *adj* 背风的
C *adv* 背风地

leeway /'li:weɪ/ *n* [u] 1 (margin of safety) 安全裕度; (margin of error) 容许的误差; **there is little ~ if anything goes wrong** 一旦出错, 则几乎没有挽救余地了 2 (room) 余地; **to give** *or* **leave sb. ~** 给某人留余地; **five minutes' ~ to change trains** 换乘火车的 5 分钟富余时间 3 (make up for lost time) **to make up (the) ~** 努力赶上 4 (drift of vessel) 偏航

left¹ /left/ *pt, pp* ▸**leave A, B, C**

left²
A *n* ▸**p. 905** 1 [u] (side, direction) 左边; **on** *or* **to the/sb.'s ~** 在左边/在某人的左边; **to the/sb.'s ~** 向左边/向某人的左边; **to keep to the ~** Aut 靠左行驶; **on the ~ of sth.** 在某物的左边; **the third turning on the** *or* **your ~** 左边的第三个拐弯; **on** *or* **to your ~ is the town hall** 在你的左边是市政厅 2 [c] (road) 左侧道路; **the first/second ~** 左侧第一/第二条道路 3 [c] (turn) 左转弯; **to make a ~** 向左转弯; **to hang a ~** Amer colloq 向左拐弯 4 **Left** [u] (grouping, wing of party) **the L~** 左派; **to be on the L~** 是左派; **to the ~ of sb.** 比某人更左 5 [c] (in boxing) (punch, fist) 左手拳; **you need to use your ~ more** 你得多用你的左手拳; **he caught me with a ~** 他左手一拳打中了我
B *adj* 左边的; **~ eye/ear/hand/arm/shoulder** 左眼/左耳/左手/左臂/左肩; **on my ~ hand** 在我的左边; **the ~ side** 左边; **my ~ foot** 我的左脚; **the ~ bank** 左边的岸; **take a ~ turn at the intersection** 在十字路口左拐
C *adv* (on the left side) 靠左面; (to the left side) 向左 ‹*look*›; **go** *or* **turn ~ by the pub** 在酒馆处向左转; **keep ~** Aut 靠左行驶; **eyes ~!** Mil 向左看齐!; **~, right and centre** 到处; **new shops are springing up ~, right, and centre** 到处有新店铺在迅速开业; **stage ~** Theat 舞台左侧

left back *n* 左后卫

left-click
A *n* 点击鼠标左键; **a double ~** 双击左键
B *vi* 点击鼠标左键
C *vt* 点击…的左键 ‹*mouse*›; 用鼠标左键点击 ‹*icon*›

left-hand *adj attrib* 左边的; **a ~ turn/page** 左转/页面左边; **the ~ side** 左边

left-hand drive
A *n* 1 [u] (steering system) 左侧驾驶 2 [c] (vehicle) 左侧驾驶的车辆
B *adj* 左侧驾驶的 ‹*vehicle, car*›

left-handed /ˌleft'hændɪd/
A *adj* 惯用左手的 ‹*person*›; 左手用的 ‹*golf clubs, scissors, tool*›; **she is ~** 她是个左撇子
B *adv* 用左手 ‹*play, write*›

left: ~-handedness /-'hændɪdnɪs/ *n* [u] 惯用左手; **~-hander** /-'hændə(r)/ *n* 1 (person) 左撇子; 2 colloq (blow) 左手拳

leftie /'lefti/ *n* colloq 左派人士

leftist /'leftɪst/
A *n* 左派分子
B *adj* 左派的

left: ~ luggage *n* [u] Brit 1 (luggage) 寄存的行李; 2 (room) 行李寄存处; 3 *modif* 寄存行李的; **a ~ luggage office** 行李寄存处; **~-of-centre** *adj* 中间偏左的

leftover /'leftəʊvə(r)/
A *n* 1 **leftovers** *pl* (remaining food) 剩饭菜; (other remaining things) 剩余物 2 (remnant) 遗留物; **this habit is a ~ from her childhood** 这个习惯是从她童年时期遗留下来的
B *adj* 剩余的

left wing
A *n* 1 Pol **the ~** 左翼 2 Sport 左路; **to play on the ~** 打左路
B **left-wing** *adj* 左翼的 ‹*view, person*›

left-winger *n* 1 Pol 左翼人士 2 Sport 左路队员

leg /leg/
A *n* 1 ▸**p. 71** (of person, animal) 腿; **my grandmother has a bad ~** 我祖母有一条腿行动不便; **to stand on one ~** 单腿站立; **my ~s won't go any further** 我的腿再也走不动了; **to give sb. a ~ up** (to mount a horse) 扶某人上马; (to mount a high object) 扶某人登上高处; fig 帮某人改善处境; **she doesn't have a ~ to stand on** fig 她的论点站不住脚; **to pull sb.'s ~** fig 同某人开玩笑; **break a ~!** Theat fig 祝你好运!; **shake a ~!** fig colloq 快点!; **to get one's ~ over** Brit sl (have sex) 性交 2 Culin [动物的] 腿; **a roast ~ of lamb** 烤羊腿; **spicy hot chicken ~s** 香辣鸡腿 3 (of furniture) [家具的] 腿; **a table ~** 桌腿 4 (of clothing) 裤腿; **a trouser ~** 一条裤腿 5 (of journey, process, etc.) 一段; **the longest ~ of the journey/race** 行程/赛程中最长的一段; **the final ~ of the election campaign** 竞选活动的最后阶段 6 Sport (in darts) 一局; (in football) 一场; (in running, cycling) 赛段; (in sailing) 一段航程
B *vt* (*pres p etc.* **-gg-**) **to ~ it** colloq (go on foot) 步行; (walk quickly) 疾走; (run) 跑; (run away) 逃跑; **I ~ged it to the station as fast as I could** 我以最快速度跑到车站

legacy /'legəsi/
A *n* 1 (inheritance) 遗产; **a small/sizable ~** 一小笔/一大笔遗产; **to leave sb. a ~** 留给某人一笔遗产 2 (lasting consequence) 遗存; **a ~ of hope/faith** 希望/信念的遗存; **a ~ from Victorian days** 维多利亚时代的遗风
B *modif* 老式的; **~ software/hardware** 陈旧的软件/硬件

legal /'li:gl/ *adj* 1 (relating to the law) 法律的 ‹*representative, procedure, system*›; **to take** *or* **get ~ advice** 咨询律师; **to take ~ action against sb.** 起诉某人; **to be awarded ~**

costs 免于承担诉讼费用; **what is the ~ position?** 相关法律怎么说的? **2** (recognized by the law) 法定的 ‹*right, currency, limit*›; **~ capacity** 法定资格; **it is ~ (for sb.) to do ...** (某人) 做…是合法的; **it is your ~ duty to do ...** 做…是你的法定义务; **the ~ age for drinking/driving** 饮酒/驾驶的法定年龄

legal: ~ aid *n* [u] 法律援助; **~ eagle** *n* colloq [尤指精明的] 律师; **~ entity** *n* 法人

legalese /ˌliːɡəˈliːz/ *n* [u] colloq 法律行话

legal holiday *n* Amer 法定假日

legalistic /ˌliːɡəˈlɪstɪk/ *adj* pej 拘泥于法规的

legality /liːˈɡæləti/ *n* [u and c] 合法性

legalization /ˌliːɡəlaɪˈzeɪʃn, Amer -lɪˈz-/ *n* [u] 合法化

legalize /ˈliːɡəlaɪz/ *vt* 使合法化

legally /ˈliːɡəli/ *adv* **1** (in the eyes of the law) 在法律上; **to be ~ represented/qualified** 有法定代理人/法律资格; **to be ~ responsible for sth.** 对某事物负法律责任; **to be ~ entitled to do sth.** 享有做某事的法定权利; **this contract is ~ binding** 这一合同具有法律约束力; **~, the matter is complicated** 从法律上讲, 这个问题很复杂 **2** (in accordance with the law) 合法地 ‹*act, administer*›

legal: ~ practice *n* [c] (office) 律师事务所; [u] (exercise of law) 律师业务; **~ practitioner** *n* 法律界从业人员; **~ proceedings** *npl* 法律诉讼; **to instigate** *or* **institute ~ proceedings against sb.** 对某人提起诉讼; **~ profession** *n* 法律界人士; **~ tender** *n* [u] 法定货币

legation /lɪˈɡeɪʃn/ *n* **1** (diplomat) 公使馆全体人员 **2** (residence) 公使馆 **3** (diplomats) 外交人员

legend /ˈledʒənd/ *n* **1** [c] (story) 传奇故事; **the ~ of Jason** 关于伊阿宋的传奇故事 **2** [u] (mythology) 传说; **~ has it that ...** 传说… **3** [c] (famous person) 传奇人物; **a rock and roll ~** 摇滚乐界的传奇人物; **a living ~** 当世传奇名人 **4** [c] (inscription) 铭文 **5** [c] (on map, picture) 图例

legendary /ˈledʒəndri, Amer -deri/ *adj* **1** (very famous) 赫赫有名的 ‹*pirate, achievements, feat*›; 众所周知的 ‹*patience, stubbornness*›; **a ~ reputation** 鼎鼎大名 **2** (of legend) 传说中的 ‹*hero*›; **the ~ account of sb./sth.** 关于某人/某事物的传说

legerdemain /ˌledʒədəˈmeɪn/ *n* **1** [u] (skilful performance) 戏法 **2** [c and u] (deception, trickery) 花招

-legged /ˈleɡɪd/ *combining form* 有…腿的; **three~** 三条腿的 ‹*stool, table*›; **four~** 四条腿的 ‹*animal*›; **long~** 长腿的 ‹*person, animal*›; **bare~** 光着腿的 ‹*person*›

leggings /ˈleɡɪŋz/ *npl* (for walker, farmer) 绑腿; (for woman, baby) 紧身弹力裤

leggy /ˈleɡi/ *adj* **1** (long-legged) 腿修长的 ‹*woman*›; pej (ungainly) 腿过长的 ‹*youth, player*› **2** colloq 细长茎的 ‹*plant*›

legibility /ˌledʒəˈbɪləti/ *n* [u] 清晰; **poor ~** 不清晰

legible /ˈledʒəbl/ *adj* 清晰的 ‹*handwriting, script*›

legibly /ˈledʒəblɪ/ *adv* 清晰地 ‹*write*›

legion /ˈliːdʒən/

A *n* **1** (group of soldiers) 军团; (in Roman empire) 古罗马军团 **2** (multitude) 大批的人; **a ~** *or* **~s of ...** 一大批…

B *adj pred* 大量的; **his crimes are ~** 他的罪行罄竹难书

legionary /ˈliːdʒənəri, Amer -neri/ *n* (in Roman empire) 古罗马军团士兵; (modern soldier) 军团士兵

legionnaire /ˌliːdʒəˈneə(r)/ *n* [尤指法国的] 外籍军团成员

legionnaire's disease ▸p. 377 *n* [u] 军团病

leg iron *n* 脚镣

legislate /ˈledʒɪsleɪt/ *vi* **1** (make laws) «*government, parliament*» 立法; **to ~ against sth.** 制定法律禁止 ‹*discrimination, pornography*› **2** (predict) **to ~ for/against sth.** *or* **for/against sth. happening** 预测并应对/阻止…发生 ‹*circumstance, occurrence, behaviour*›

legislation /ˌledʒɪsˈleɪʃn/ *n* [u] **1** (body of laws) 法律; **a piece of ~** 一条法律; **new ~ against sth./to do sth.** 禁止某事/做某事的新法律; **to adopt/present/introduce** *or* **bring in ~** 通过/提交/推行法律 **2** (process of lawmaking) 立法

legislative /ˈledʒɪslətɪv, Amer -leɪtɪv/ *adj* **1** (relating to legislation) 立法的 ‹*procedures, reforms, priorities*›; **~ drafting** Amer 法律起草 **2** (able to make laws) 拥有立法权的 ‹*authorities, council, status*›; **the country's supreme ~ body** 国家最高立法机关; **~ powers** 立法权

legislator /ˈledʒɪsleɪtə(r)/ *n* 立法者; **a state ~** Amer 州议会议员

legislature /ˈledʒɪsleɪtʃə(r)/ *n* 立法机构; **the Illinois ~** Amer 伊利诺伊州议会

legit /lɪˈdʒɪt/ *adj* colloq = **legitimate A1**

legitimacy /lɪˈdʒɪtɪməsi/ *n* [u] **1** (of law, measure) 合法性 **2** (of comment, conclusion) 合理性; **to give ~ to sth.** 为某事提供正当理由 **3** (of birth) 婚生子身份

legitimate

A /lɪˈdʒɪtɪmət/ *adj* **1** (in accordance with the law) 合法的 ‹*authority, right, spouse*›; **to make sth. ~** 使某事物合法 **2** (justifiable) 合理的 ‹*reason, request, argument*›; **it is ~ for me to do this** 我这么做是合理的; **the ~ killing of another human being** 合理致人死亡 **3** 婚生的 ‹*child*›

B /lɪˈdʒɪtɪmeɪt/ *vt* = **legitimize**

legitimately /lɪˈdʒɪtɪmətli/ *adv* **1** (legally) 合法地 ‹*authorize, act*› **2** (with justification) 合理地 ‹*act, argue, blame*›; **one might ~ wonder whether ...** 人们有理由想知道是否…

legitimization /lɪˌdʒɪtɪmaɪˈzeɪʃn/, **legitimation** /lɪˌdʒɪtɪˈmeɪʃn/ *ns* [u] **1** (making legal) 合法化 **2** (justification) 合理化

legitimize /lɪˈdʒɪtɪmaɪz/ *vt* **1** (legalize) 使…合法 ‹*organization, practice*› **2** formal (justify) 使…合理 ‹*action, policy*›; **being poor doesn't ~ stealing** 贫穷不是偷窃的理由

legless /ˈleɡlɪs/ *adj* **1** lit 无腿的 **2** colloq (drunk) 醉醺醺的

leg: ~-pull *n* colloq 捉弄; **~-pulling** *n* [u] colloq 捉弄; **~room** *n* [u] [座位前的] 伸腿处

legume /ˈleɡjuːm/ *n* **1** (plant) 豆科植物 **2** (edible pod) 豆荚; (edible seed) 荚果

leguminous /lɪˈɡjuːmɪnəs/ *adj* 豆科植物的

leg: ~-warmers /-wɔːməz/ *npl* 暖腿套; **~work** *n* [u] colloq 跑腿活儿; **to do the ~work for sb.** 为某人跑腿

Leicestershire /ˈlestəʃɪə(r)/ *pr n* 莱斯特郡

leisure /ˈleʒə(r), Amer ˈliːʒə(r)/

A *n* [u] 空闲; **the ~ for** *or* **to do sth.** 做某事的空闲时间; **to do sth. at ~** 不慌不忙地做某事; **to do sth. at one's ~** 趁闲暇时做某事; **the guide to ~, sport and tourism** 休闲、体育和旅游活动指南; **a gentleman/lady of ~** hum 有闲男士/女士; **to lead a life of ~** 逍遥度日

B *modif* 空闲的 ‹*moments, period*›; 业余的 ‹*activities, pursuits*›; 休闲的 ‹*facilities, services*›

leisure: ~ centre *n* Brit 休闲活动中心; **~ class** *n* **1** Sociol 有闲阶级; **2** (evening class) [无正式考试的] 闲暇夜校课程; **~ complex** *n* 休闲运动中心

leisured /ˈleʒəd, Amer ˈliːʒəd/ *adj attrib* 有闲暇的; **the ~ classes** 有闲阶级

leisure industry *n* 休闲产业

leisurely /ˈleʒəli, Amer ˈliːʒ-/

A *adj* **1** (unhurried) 慢悠悠的 ‹*stroll, lunch, progress*›; 不慌不忙的 ‹*person, eater*›; 慢吞吞的 ‹*service, worker*›; **to do sth. in a ~ way** *or* **at a ~ pace** 从容不迫地做某事 **2** (not strenuous) 休闲的 ‹*activity, sport*›; 轻松的 ‹*job*›

B *adv* 慢悠悠地 ‹*stroll, eat*›; 慢吞吞地 ‹*work*›

leisure: ~ park *n* 游乐场; **~ society** *n* 休闲社会; **~ suit** *n* Amer 休闲套装; **~ time** *n* [u] 闲暇时间; **~ traveller** *n* 休闲旅行者; **~wear** *n* [u] 休闲装

leitmotif, leitmotiv /ˈlaɪtməʊtiːf/ *n* 主题

lekker /ˈlekə(r)/ *adj* S Afr colloq 好的

lemma /ˈlemə/ *n* **1** Math 辅助定理 **2** (heading) 标题 **3** Ling 词目

lemmatize /ˈlemətaɪz/ *vt* 把…按屈折变化形式归类

lemme /ˈlemi/ colloq = **let me** 让我; **~ go/have a look!** 让我走/看看!

lemming /ˈlemɪŋ/ *n* 旅鼠; **a ~-like rush to do sth.** 为做某事盲目地一拥而上

lemon /ˈlemən/ ▸p. 134

A *n* **1** [c and u] (fruit) 柠檬 **2** [u] (colour) 淡黄色; **do you have the coat in ~?** 这件外套有淡黄色的吗? **3** [c] colloq hum (idiot) 傻冒; **to look/feel a ~** 看上去/感到自己像个傻瓜 **4** [c] colloq (disappointing book, car, film etc.) 蹩脚货

B *modif* 柠檬的 ‹*peel, pip*›; 柠檬味的 ‹*drink, ice-cream*›; 柠檬树的 ‹*blossom, grove*›

C *adj* 淡黄色的

lemonade /ˌleməˈneɪd/ *n* [u and c] **1** (carbonated) 柠檬汽水 **2** (still) 柠檬汁饮料

lemon: ~ balm *n* [u] 柠檬薄荷; **~ cheese, ~ curd** *ns* [u] Brit 柠檬酪 [用柠檬、糖、鸡蛋、黄油等制成]; **~ drop** *n* 柠檬硬糖; **~-flavoured** *adj* 柠檬味的; **~ grass** *n* [u] 柠檬草; **~ juice** *n* **1** [u] (juice of lemon) 柠檬汁; **2** [u and c] (drink made from lemons) 柠檬汁饮料; **~ squash** *n* [u and c] Brit 柠檬味饮料; **~ squeezer** *n* Brit 柠檬榨汁器; **~ tea** *n* [u and c] 柠檬茶; **~ tree** *n* 柠檬树

lemon yellow ▸p. 134

A *adj* 淡黄色的

B *n* [u] 淡黄色

lemur /ˈliːmə(r)/ *n* 狐猴

lend /lend/ (*pt, pp* **lent**)

A *vt* **1** (to a friend, colleague, relative) 借出; **to ~ sb. sth.** *or* **to ~ sth. to sb.** 把…借给某人 ‹*book, money, tool*›; **I've been lent a bicycle** 我借到了一辆自行车; **I can ~ you Sarah for the afternoon** 我下午可以把萨拉让给你 **2** Fin 贷; **to ~ sb. sth., to ~ sth. to sb.** 把…贷给某人 ‹*money, funds*›; **to ~ money at 10%** 以 10% 的利息放贷 **3** (add, confer) 增添 ‹*significance, credibility, respectability*›; **his presence lent dignity to the occasion** 有他出席, 这一场合更显庄严; **you can also ~ a nice personal touch by sending flowers** 你也可以通过送花营造一种温馨的个人情调 **4** (provide, offer) 提供 ‹*expertise*›; **to ~ support to sth.** 支持某事; **to ~ an ear (to sb./sth.)** 倾听 (某人/某事); **to ~ sb. a (helping) hand (with sth.)** (在某事上) 帮某人的忙; **to ~ one's name to sth.** 出面支持 ‹*campaign, protest*›; **to ~ one's voice to sth.** (speak in support of) 声援 ‹*appeal, cause*›; (provide the voice for) 为…配音 ‹*character*›

B *vi* 贷款; **to ~ against sth.** 以…作抵押进行贷款 ‹*property, gold*›; **to ~ at 15%** 以 15% 的利率进行贷款

C *v refl* **to ~ itself to sth.** 适合于某事物; **her voice ~s itself to blues singing** 她的嗓子适合唱蓝调; **the system ~s itself to abuse** 这个制度容易被滥用

Phrasal verb

- **lend out** *vt* [**~ sth. out, ~ out sth.**] 借出; **to ~ sth. out to sb.** 把某物借给某人

lender /ˈlendə(r)/ *n* 放款人

lending /ˈlendɪŋ/ *n* [u] 放贷

lending: ~ library *n* 外借图书馆; **~ limit** *n* 借贷上限; **~ rate** *n* 贷款利率

L

length /leŋθ/

A *n* **1** [c and u] (linear measurement) 长度; **a river 500 kilometres in ~** 一条 500 公里长的河流; **this room is twice the ~ of the other** 这个房间的长度是另一个的两倍 **2** [u] **the ~ of ...** (all the way along) 全长; **the whole ~ of the street was planted with trees** 整条街上都种了树; **ice had formed along the ~ of the plane's wing** 整个机翼都结了冰 **3** [c] (of swimming pool) 游泳池长度; **to swim/do a ~ (of the pool)** 游一个游泳池长度的距离; **he does 20 ~s every morning** 他每天早晨游 10 个来回 **4** [c] (in race) 自身长度; **the horse is two ~s ahead** 那匹马领先两个马身的距离; **I was two car ~s behind the other vehicle** 我在另一辆车后面两个车身远 **5** [c] (piece, section) 一段; **a ~ of rope** 一根绳子; **to be sold in ~s of five metres** 5 米一段出售; **a dress ~** 一块够做一条连衣裙的布料 **6** [c and u] (size, extent) 篇幅; **a book 200 pages in ~** 一本 200 页的书; **a book the ~ of War and Peace** 一本篇幅像《战争与和平》一样长的书 **7** [c and u] (duration) 时间的长短; **the film is three hours in ~** 这部影片长 3 小时; **the whole ~ of sth.** 某事的全部时间; **a considerable ~ of time** 很长一段时间; **the ~ of time between two events** 两件事之间的间隔 **8** [u] (quality of being long) 长; **I was struck by the ~ of his fingernails** 他的指甲那么长，让我很吃惊; **a war of such ~** 一场如此旷日持久的战争 **9** **at ~** (for a long time) 长时间地; (at last) 最后; **he went on at tedious ~ about his favourite hobby** 他啰啰唆唆地谈论他最大的爱好 **10** [c and u] (of vowel, syllable) 音长

B **lengths** *npl* (extent, measures) 程度; **to go to great/any/such ~s (to do sth.)** (为做某事) 不遗余力; **they went to absurd ~s to keep the affair secret** 他们为了对这件事保密无所不用其极; **to go to the ~s of doing sth.** 到做某事的程度; **he even went**

ℹ Length, width, and height

■ The metric system is commonly used in Chinese-speaking countries and communities.

Metric system

1 kilometre (km) 公里 / 千米
= 1,000 metres 米
= 0.621 mile 英里

1 metre (m) 米
= 100 centimetres 厘米 / 公分
= 1.094 yards 码

1 centimetre (cm) 厘米 / 公分
= 10 millimetres 毫米
= 0.394 inch 英寸

Imperial system

1 inch (in) 英寸
= 2.54 centimetres 厘米 / 公分

1 foot (ft) 英尺
= 12 inches 英寸
= 30.48 centimetres 厘米 / 公分

1 yard (yd) 码
= 3 feet 英尺
= 0.914 metres 米

1 mile (ml) 英里
= 1760 yards 码
= 1.609 kilometres 公里 / 千米

Length

How long is the cable?
= 这根电线多长?
or 这根电线有多长?

It is twelve metres long
= 有 12 米长

Cables are sold by the metre
= 电线是按米卖的

A is longer than B
= A 比 B 长

A is two metres longer than B
= A 比 B 长 2 米

A is two metres too long
= A 长了 2 米

A is shorter than B
= A 比 B 短

A is one yard shorter than B
= A 比 B 短 1 码

A is one yard too short
= A 短了 1 码

A is as long as B
or ***A is the same length as B***
or ***A and B are the same length***
or ***A and B are equal in length***
= A 和 B 一样长

A is not as long as B
= A 没有 B 长

A and B are not the same length
or ***A and B are different lengths***
= A 和 B 长度不同

■ The Chinese construction with 的 always comes before the noun it modifies:

a washing line four metres long
or ***a four-metre-long washing line***
= 一根 4 米长的晾衣绳

a canal 20 kilometres long
or ***a twenty-kilometre-long canal***
= 一条 20 公里长的运河

Width

What width is the table?
or ***How wide is the table?***
= 桌子多宽?
or 桌子有多宽?

It's fifty inches wide
= 有 50 英寸宽

A is wider than B
= A 比 B 宽

A is two inches wider than B
= A 比 B 宽 2 英寸

A is two inches too wide
= A 宽了 2 英寸

A is narrower than B
= A 比 B 窄

A is ten centimetres narrower than B
= A 比 B 窄 10 厘米

A is ten centimetres too narrow
= A 窄了 10 厘米

A is as wide as B
or ***A is the same width as B***
or ***A and B are the same width***
or ***A and B are equal in width***
= A 和 B 一样宽

A is not as wide as B
= A 没有 B 宽

A and B are not the same width
= A 和 B 不一样宽

A and B are not different widths
= A 和 B 宽度没有不同

■ The Chinese construction with 的 always comes before the noun it modifies:

a street eight metres wide
= 一条 8 米宽的街道

a tablecloth eighty centimetres in width
= 一块 80 厘米宽的桌布

Height

■ In Chinese, 高 (tall or high) and 矮 / 低 (short/low) can be used to refer to both people and things. 小 (small) is usually used to refer to people:

How tall is she?
= 她有多高?

She's 1 m 58 (cm)
= 她身高一米五八

He is 6' 3" tall
or ***He is 6' 3"***
or ***He's six foot/feet 3 inches***
= 他身高为六英尺三
or 他身高为 6 英尺 3 英寸

Miss McDonald is a small girl
= 麦克唐纳小姐个子小

Mr. Blair is very tall
= 布莱尔先生个子很高

a six-foot-tall girl
= 一位 6 英尺高的姑娘

a man 2 metres in height
= 一个身高 2 米的男子

How high is the tree?
— It's over 8 metres high
= 这棵树有多高? —— 8 米多高

The chair is 80cm high
= 椅子 80 公分高

a 100-metre-high building
= 一座 100 米高的建筑物

an iron tower about 300 metres high
= 一座大约 300 米高的铁塔

A is taller/higher than B
= A 比 B 高

B is shorter/smaller/lower than A
= B 比 A 矮 / 低

A is as tall/high as B
= A 和 B 同样高

B is not as tall/high as A
= B 没有 A 高

Giving dimensions

The table is 0.8 metres (wide) by 1.2 metres (long)
or ***The table is 1.2 metres long and 0.8 metres wide***
or ***The table is 1.2 metres in length and 0.8 metres in width***
= 桌子长 1.2 米，宽 0.8 米

The bed is two metres long, 1.5 metres wide, and 0.7 metres high
= 床长 2 米，宽 1.5 米，高 0.7 米

to the ~s of writing to the Queen 他甚至给女王写了信

lengthen /ˈleŋθən/
A vt **1** 加长 ‹wall, shelf, distance›; 放长 ‹skirt, trousers›; **to ~ sth. from X metres to Y metres** 把某物从 X 米加长到 Y 米 **2** (prolong) 延长 ‹period, visits›; **to ~ sth. from X years to Y years** 使…从 X 年延长到 Y 年 **3** Phon 拖长 ‹vowel, pronunciation›
B vi **1** (increase in length) «queue, waiting list» 变长; «bone, stem» 长长; «shadow» 伸长; **to ~ from X cm to Y cm** 从 X 厘米变长为 Y 厘米 **2** (last longer) «days, nights» 变长; «intervals, visits» 延长; **the average life-span has ~ed from 70 to 75 years** 平均寿命从 70 岁延长到了 75 岁

lengthily /ˈleŋθɪli/ adv 长时间地; **she spoke ~ in defence of her client** 她为当事人做了长篇辩护

length mark n 元音长度符号

lengthways /ˈleŋθweɪz/, **lengthwise** /ˈleŋθwaɪz/
A adv 纵向地 ‹lay, cut, fold›
B adj 纵向的 ‹cut, fold›

lengthy /ˈleŋθi/ adj **1** (long) 长时间的 ‹visit, illness, negotiations› **2** (too long) 冗长的 ‹speech, document, novel›

leniency /ˈliːnɪənsi/, **lenience** /ˈliːnɪəns/ ns [u] (of judge, ruler) 仁慈; (of punishment, treatment) 宽大; **to show (sb.) ~** (对某人) 表现出宽容

lenient /ˈliːnɪənt/ adj 仁慈的 ‹judge, ruler, attitude›; 宽大的 ‹punishment, treatment›; 宽松的 ‹marking›; **to be ~ with sb.** 对某人宽宏大量

leniently /ˈliːnɪəntli/ adv 仁慈地 ‹govern, judge›; 宽大地 ‹treat›; 宽松地 ‹mark›

Lenin /ˈlenɪn/ pr n 列宁

Leninism /ˈlenɪnɪzəm/ n [u] 列宁主义

Leninist /ˈlenɪnɪst/
A adj 列宁主义的 ‹doctrines, party, politician›
B n 列宁主义者

lens /lenz/ n **1** (in optical instruments) 透镜; (in spectacles) 镜片; (in camera) 镜头; **a concave/convex ~** 凹/凸透镜; **to have strong/weak ~es** (of glasses) 度数深/浅 **2** Anat (of eye) 晶状体 **3** (contact lens) 隐形眼镜

lens: ~ cap n 镜头盖; **~ hood** n 遮光罩

Lent /lent/ n [u] 大斋节 [指复活节前为期40天的斋戒和忏悔]; **to observe ~** 守大斋节; **to give up sth. for ~** 在大斋节期间戒除 ‹meat, sex, smoking›

lent /lent/ pt, pp ▸**lend**

lentil /ˈlentl/ n 小扁豆; **~ soup** 小扁豆汤

lentivirus /ˈlentɪvaɪərəs/ n 慢病毒 [感染后潜伏一段时间才发作的逆转录病毒]

Leo /ˈliːəʊ/ n **1** [u] Astron 狮子(星)座 **2** [u] Astrol (sign) 狮子宫 [黄道第五宫] **3** [c] (pl ~s) Astrol (person) 属狮子(星)座的人 **4** (name) 利奥; (of lion) **~ the Lion** 狮子王雷欧

leopard /ˈlepəd/ n 豹; **a ~ cannot change its spots** Prov 本性难移

leopard cub n 豹崽

leopardess /ˈlepədes/ n 母豹

leopardskin /ˈlepədskɪn/
A n [u and c] 豹皮
B modif (made from real leopardskin) 豹皮制成的; (with leopardskin pattern) 豹纹的 ‹coat, top, design›

leotard /ˈliːətɑːd/ n 紧身连衣裤

leper /ˈlepə(r)/ n **1** (person with leprosy) 麻风病患者 **2** fig (outcast) 被排斥的人; **a social ~** 社会弃儿

leper colony n 麻风病隔离区

leprechaun /ˈleprəkɔːn/ n [爱尔兰民间传说中的] 调皮小精灵

leprosy /ˈleprəsi/ n [u] 麻风病

lepton /ˈleptɒn/ n 轻子

lesbian /ˈlezbɪən/
A n 女同性恋者
B adj 同性恋的 ‹woman›; 女同性恋者的 ‹sex, relationship, tendencies, bar›; **she is openly ~** 她公开承认自己是同性恋

lesbianism /ˈlezbɪənɪzəm/ n [u] 女同性恋

lesion /ˈliːʒn/ n 损伤; **a ~ of the left lung/on his arm** 左肺/他手臂的损伤

Lesotho /lɪˈsuːtʊ, ləˈsəʊtʊ/ pr n 莱索托

less /les/ (comp of **little**) ▸**p. 140**
A det (smaller in quantity) 较少的; **I have ~ money than you** 我的钱比你的少; **~ noise please!** 请安静些! ; **he knows little German and ~ Russian** 他几乎不懂德语, 对俄语更是一窍不通; **of ~ importance** 次要的; **to grow ~** 减少
B adv (to a smaller extent) 较少; **no ~** (surprise) 竟然; (large number) 多达; **no ~ a person than the Prime Minister** 竟然是首相本人; **nothing ~ than** 不折不扣的; **it's nothing ~ than disgraceful** 这真可耻; **she's no ~ intelligent than you** 她和你一样聪明; **~ and ~** 越来越少; **to work ~ and ~ carefully** 工作越来越马虎; **~ than** 根本不; **I'm ~ than happy about her** 我对她一点也不满意
C prep 减去…之前; **he earns £1000 per month ~ tax** 他的税前月薪为 1000 英镑; **they finished the project in a year ~ 4 days** 他们用一年差 4 天完成了这个项目
D pron **1** (smaller portion) 较少部分; (smaller amount) 较少量; **she's eating ~ than usual** 她吃的比平时少; **~ than 5 people/£5** colloq 不到 5 人/5 英镑; **children aged 7 or ~** 7 岁或 7 岁以下的儿童; **in ~ than no time** 马上; **~ of ...** 不那么多…; **you're ~ of a fool than your sister** 你不像你姐姐那么傻; **~ of it!** colloq 够了! ; **could we have ~ of that noise?** 安静一下好吗? **2** (sth. of smaller importance) 次要的事物; **people have been shot for ~** 人们曾因为小事而遭到枪杀

lessee /leˈsiː/ n 承租人

lessen /ˈlesn/
A vt 减轻 ‹pain, impact, pressure›; 降低 ‹noise, cost, likelihood, risk›; **to ~ the need for sth.** 减少对某物的需求
B vi «anger, pain, pressure» 减轻; «risk» 降低; «difficulties» 减少; **her fever has ~ed** 她的烧退了

lessening /ˈlesnɪŋ/ n [u] (of pain, impact, pressure) 减轻; (of noise, cost, likelihood, risk) 减小

lesser /ˈlesə(r)/ adj attrib **1** (not so great) 较小的; (not so important) 次要的; **to a ~ degree** or **extent** 在较小程度上; **a ~ offence** or **crime** 较轻的罪行 **2** (lower in rank) 较低的; (lower in quality) 较差的; **~ mortals** or **beings like us** hum 像我们这样的小人物

lesson /ˈlesn/ n **1** (teaching period) 一节课; **Spanish/tennis ~** 西班牙语/网球课; **to give/have ~s** 讲/听课; **to take ~s** (teacher) 授课; (student) 听课; **to be in a ~** 授课 **2** (**lessons**, npl) (parts of school day) 上课; **to have ~s** 上课 **3** (in textbook) 课; **~ one** 第一课 **4** Relig (in church service) 圣经选读 **5** (sth. learned from experience) 教训; **let that be a ~ to you!** 记住这次教训! ; **to learn one's ~** 吸取教训; **I'm going to teach him a ~!** 我要教训他一顿!

lesson plan n 教案

lessor /leˈsɔː(r)/ n 出租人

lest /lest/ conj formal **1** (for fear that) 以免; **he wrote down the address ~ he forget it** 他把地址写下来以免忘记; **he took his umbrella ~ it (should** or **might) rain** 他怕下雨, 就带了伞 **2** (in case that) 万一; **~ anyone should ask you, tell them ...** 若有人问你, 你就说…; **'~ we forget'** "永志不忘" **3** (after expressions of fear) 担心; **I was afraid ~ he (might** or **should) die** 我担心他会死

let¹ /let/
A vt (pres p **-tt-**, pt, pp **let**) **1** (allow) 允许; **don't ~ the fire go out** 别让火熄灭; **I can't go because she won't ~ me** 我不能去, 因为她不肯同意; **~ me (help you)** 让我来(帮你)吧; **~ him have it** colloq (give it to him) 把东西给他; (shoot at him) 让他吃枪子; **they were late home, and their mother ~ them have it** 他们回家晚了, 于是母亲骂了他们一通 **2** (allow to go or be) 让…过去; **~ me through** or **past** 让我过去; **the curtains ~ the light through** 这些窗帘透光; **the headmaster ~ the children go home early** 校长让孩子们早回家 **3** Brit (lease out) 出租; **'To Let'** "房屋招租"; **to ~ a field to a farmer** 把田租给一位农民 **4** (expressing command, proposal, threat, criticism) 让; **~ it be known that ...** 要让大家知道…; **~ there be no mistake about this** 这个不能有差错; **~ me see** or **think** 让我想一想; **~ him say what he likes, I don't care** 随便他说什么吧, 我不在乎 **5** (introducing a postulate) 假设; **~ the line AB intersect the line CD** 假设直线 AB 与直线 CD 相交; **~ X equal 2** 设 X 等于 2 **6** (when making suggestion) [用于提出建议, 涉及说话者和听众]; **~'s** or **~ us do it** 我们做这事吧; **~ us pray** 我们祈祷吧; **don't ~'s start yet, ~'s not start yet** 咱们先别开始吧; **it costs more than, ~'s say, a dishwasher** (for example) 比如说, 它的价钱要比洗碗机贵
B **let alone** conj phr, used after negative 更不用说; **she can't even talk, ~ alone sing** 她甚至不会说话, 更不用说唱歌了
C n Brit 租借期; **a long/short/2-year ~** 长期/短期/两年期租借

Phrasal verbs

• **let alone** vt [**~ sb./sth. alone**] 不打扰; **please ~ that kitten alone** 请不要碰那只小猫; **to ~ well alone** 别管闲事

• **let down**
A [**~ sth. down, ~ down sth.**] vt
1 (lengthen) 放长 ‹item of clothing›; **I've ~ the skirt down by 2 centimetres** 我把裙子放长了 2 厘米 **2** (lower) 放下 ‹bucket, basket›; **as the other car drew alongside he ~ down the window** 当另一辆车开上来的时候, 他把窗玻璃降了下来 **3** (deflate) 给…放气 ‹tyre›
B [**~ sb. down, ~ down sb.**] vt 使失望; **my watch never ~s me down** 我的手表一向走得很准; **to ~ sb. down gently** 委婉地把不幸的消息告诉某人

• **let drop** vt [**~ drop sth., ~ sth. drop**] 把…说漏嘴; **she ~ drop the fact that they were already married** 她无意中说出了他们已经结婚的事

• **let fly** vi (physically) 打; (verbally) 骂; **he ~ fly with his right foot** 他飞起右脚踢了一下; **she really ~ fly at me for forgetting the biscuits** 因为我忘了买饼干, 她狠狠骂了我一顿

• **let go**
A vi lit 松手; fig 忘掉; **I ~ go, and the balloon floated away** 我松开手, 气球飘走了; **to ~ go of the rope** 松开绳子; **~ go of me!** 放开我! ; **he just can't ~ go** fig 他就是忘不了
B vt [**~ sb./sth. go**]
1 (free) 让…离开; **they ~ the hostages go** 他们让人质离开 **2** (release hold on) 放开 ‹person, arm›; **to ~ go the reins** 松开缰绳; **~ me go!** 放开我!; **she made a sarcastic comment, but he just ~ it go** 她挖苦了一句, 但他没有理会 **3** (stop worrying about) 不再担心; **we'll ~ it go at that** 这事到此为止吧; **you must ~ the past go** 你一定要忘掉过去 **4** euph (from a job) 解雇; **unfortunately, we have to ~ you go** 很遗憾我们只能让你走人
C v refl **to ~ oneself go** (relax) 自我放松; (neglect one's appearance) 不修边幅; **unwind and ~ yourself go** 放松一下

• **let in** vt [**~ sth./sb. in, ~ in sb./sth.**]

1 (allow inside) 让…进来; **he ~ himself in with a key** 他用钥匙把门打开进来 2 (allow in) «*tent, window*» 漏 ‹*water, light*›; **the roof ~s the rain in** 屋顶漏雨 3 **to ~ oneself/sb. in for sth.** colloq (create trouble for) 卷入某事/使某人卷入某事; **she ~ herself in for a lot of problems** 她惹了一身麻烦 4 **to ~ sb. in on sth.** (allow to share) 向某人透露 ‹*secret*›; **I agreed to ~ him in on the news** 我同意告诉他这个消息

- **let into** *vt* 1 **to ~ sth. into sth.** (set into surface) 把…嵌入; **a statue ~ into the wall** 嵌进墙壁的雕像 2 **to ~ sb. into sth.** (allow to share) 向某人透露 ‹*secret*›
- **let off**

A [**~ sth. off, ~ off sth.**] *vt* (detonate) 引爆; **to ~ off fireworks/a gun** 放烟火/开枪

B [**~ sb. off**] *vt* (punish lightly) 从轻处罚; (not punish at all) 放过; **to ~ sb. off lightly** 轻易放过某人; **she was ~ off with a fine** 她只是被罚款了事; **I'll ~ you off your homework** 我会免了你的家庭作业的

- **let on**

A *vi* colloq 说出秘密; **don't ~ on!** 别告诉别人啊！; **don't ~ on about what they did** 不要把他们干的事说出去

B *vt* **to ~ on that ...** 假装…; **he ~ on that he was a tourist** 他装作是游客

- **let out**

A [**~ out sth.**] *vt* (emit) 发出; **to ~ out a shriek** 发出一声尖叫

B [**~ sb./sth. out, ~ out sb./sth.**] *vt* 1 (show out) 送…出门; **he ~ himself out quietly** 他悄悄出了门 2 (make wider) 放宽; **to ~ one's belt out by 2 holes** 把皮带放宽两个孔 3 Brit (reveal) **to ~ out that ...** 透露…; **she ~ out that he'd given her a lift home** 她透露了他捎带她回家的事 4 (release) 放…出去; **~ me out!** 放我出去！; ▸**cat 1** 5 (allow to flow out) 使…泄漏; **to ~ the air out of a tyre** 给轮胎放气; **she ~ out a sigh** 她叹了口气

- **let up** *vi* 1 (stop, slow down) 停下; **the rain didn't ~ up all night** 雨下了整整一夜 2 (ease off) 放松; **he never ~s up** 他从不懈怠; **what a chatterbox she is, she never ~s up!** 她真是个话匣子，嘴没有闲着的时候！; **to ~ up on sb.** colloq 对某人更宽容

let² *n* 1 Sport (in tennis, etc.) 擦网球; **~!** 擦网！; **to play a ~** 擦网重发 2 formal (obstruction) **without ~ or hindrance** 毫无阻碍; **the right to travel without ~ or hindrance** 旅行不受阻碍的权利

let-down *n* 失望; **it was a bit of a ~** 那有些令人失望

lethal /'li:θl/ *adj* 1 (fatal) 致命的 ‹*attack, disease, weapon*›; **a ~ dose** 致死剂量; **to deal a ~ blow (to sb.)** fig 给予（某人）致命的打击 2 (dangerous) 危险的 ‹*vehicle, equipment, toy*› 3 (with firearm, in boxing, football) 精准的 ‹*shot, punch*›; **he's ~ with that bow and arrow** 他射箭百发百中 4 colloq hum (extremely intoxicating) 极易醉人的 ‹*spirit, cocktail*›; **a ~ combination** *or* **mixture** 极易醉人的混合酒

lethargic /lɪ'θɑ:dʒɪk/ *adj* 没精打采的; **to feel** *or* **become ~** 倦怠; **to make sb. ~** «*weather*» 使某人无精打采

lethargically /lɪ'θɑ:dʒɪkli/ *adv* 没精打采地

lethargy /'leθədʒi/ *n* [u] 没精打采

let-out clause *n* 不适用条款

let's /lets/ colloq = **let us** 让我们; **~ meet up for a drink sometime** 咱们什么时候一起喝一杯吧

Lett /let/ *n* dated 列托人 [拉脱维亚人的旧称]

letter /'letə(r)/

A *n* 1 (item of correspondence) 信; **a ~ of intent** 意向书; **a ~ of introduction/apology/resignation** 介绍信/道歉信/辞职信; **are there any ~s for me?** 有我的信吗？; **to write/send (sb.) a ~** （给某人）写/寄信; **to inform sb. by ~** 函告某人 2 (of alphabet) 字母; **the ~ A** 字母 A; **to write a word in capital ~s** 用大写字母写单词; **to have a lot of ~s after one's name** Brit colloq 拥有多个学术头衔; **to keep** *or* **stick to the ~ of sth.** 严格遵守 ‹*law*›; **to do sth. to the ~** 严格按照规定做某事; **to carry out one's duties to the ~** 一丝不苟地履行职责; **to follow the instructions to the ~** 严格按照指示行事

B **letters** *npl* 1 (literature) 文学; **the world of ~s** 文学界; **a man/woman of ~s** 男/女文学家 2 Amer (award) 校名首字母标志; **to award ~s to the members of the school baseball team** 授予校棒球队员校名首字母标志

C **letters** *modif* 读者来信的; **the ~s page/column** 读者来信页/专栏; **the ~s editor** 读者来信编辑

D *vt* 用字母标明; **the rows are ~ed from A to X** 排数从 A 标到 X

letter: **~ bomb** *n* 邮件炸弹; **~ box** *n* Brit 1 (in door) 投信口; 2 (at entrance) 信箱; 3 (pillar box) 邮箱; **~ card** *n* 邮简; **~head** *n* 信头

lettering /'letərɪŋ/ *n* [u] [刻印的] 字; **ornamental ~** 装饰字

letter: **~man** /-mən/ *n* Amer 字母荣誉学生 [指在体育比赛等表现优异获得校名首字母的学生]; **~ of credit** *n* 信用证; **~ opener** *n* 拆信刀; **~-perfect** *adj* Amer 一字不差的 ‹*copy, speaker*›; 台词一字不差的 ‹*performance, actor*›; **~ post** *n* [u] 信件邮递; **~press** *n* [u] 1 (text) [有别于插图的] 印刷文字; 2 (printing method) 凸版印刷; **~-quality** *adj* 优质打印的; **~s page** *n* 读者来信版; **~-writer** *n* 写信者; **he's a keen/not much of a ~-writer** 他非常喜欢/不太喜欢写信

letting agent *n* Brit 房屋中介

lettuce /'letɪs/ *n* [u and c] 生菜; **a head of ~** 一棵生菜

let-up /'letʌp/ *n* [c and u] 1 (lull) 暂停; **there will be no ~ in my efforts** 我会不懈努力的 2 (respite) 片刻休息; **without a ~** 一刻不歇地

leucocyte /'lu:kəsaɪt/ *n* 白细胞

leukaemia Brit, **leukemia** Amer /lu:'ki:mɪə/ ▸**p. 377** *n* [u] 白血病

leukocyte /'lu:kəsaɪt/ *n* esp Amer = **leucocyte**

levee /'levi/ *n* esp Amer 1 (man-made) 防洪堤 2 (natural) 冲积堤

level /'levl/

A *adj* 1 (not at an angle) 水平的; (not bumpy) 平坦的; **I don't think this bed is ~** 我认为床不平; **~ ground** 平地; **a ~ teaspoonful of salt** 一平茶匙盐 2 (at equal height) 等高的; **the curtains are not hanging ~** 窗帘挂得不一样高; **when the water is ~ with this mark, the tank is half-full** 当水与这个标记平齐时，水箱就装满了一半 3 (abreast) 并排的; **the police car drew ~ with the taxi** 警车追上来与出租车并排行驶; **a ~ race** 一场势均力敌的比赛 4 (equal in achievement, rank) 不相上下的; **supply should keep ~ with demand** 应该保持供需平衡; **at half-time the score was ~** 中场休息时比分相同; **France scored the first two goals, but Italy soon drew ~** 法国队先进两球，但意大利队很快将比分扳平; **to do one's ~ best** 竭尽全力 5 *attrib* (fixed) 逼人的 ‹*gaze*› 6 (steady) 平静的 ‹*voice, tone*›; **to keep a ~ head** 保持头脑冷静

B *n* 1 (equal plane) 水平面; (horizontal line) 水平线; **on the ~** 在平地上; **the garden is on a ~ with the floor** 花园和地板在同一水平面上 2 (floor) 楼层; (layer) 层; **she parked the car on ~ 2** 她把车停在 2 楼 3 (height) 高度; **the ~ of the river** 河流的水位; **to be at shoulder-~** 齐肩高; **to be on a ~ (with sth./sb.)** (at the same height) （与某物/某人）一样高; (abreast) （与某物/某人）并排 4 (degree) 程度; (amount) 数量; (intensity) 强度; (concentration) 浓度; **the ~ of alcohol in the blood** 血液中的酒精含量; **the ~ of illiteracy among school-leavers** 辍学者中的文盲人数; **the ~ of customer satisfaction** 顾客的满意度 5 (of a course, etc.) 等级; (standard of competence) 水平; **elementary/intermediate/advanced ~** 初级/中级/高级; **to reach new ~s of excellence** 达到新的优秀水平; **the course is below your ~** 这门课程难度低于你的水平; **her reading ability is on a ~ with that of a nine-year-old** 她的阅读能力相当于一个 9 岁的孩子; **I could have retaliated, but I refused to descend to his ~** 我本来可以报复，但是我不愿降低身份同他一般见识; **the conversation soon sank to its customary low ~** 谈话很快就变得同往常一样庸俗了 6 (position in hierarchy) 级别; **decisions that are taken at board ~** 由董事会作出的决定; **the system was first implemented at a local ~** 该制度首先在地方实施 7 fig (plane) 层次; **~s of language** 语言的各个层面; **the poem can be interpreted on various ~s** 这首诗可以在不同层面上进行阐释 8 colloq **on the ~** (trustworthy) 诚实的; (legal) 合法的 9 Tech (tool) 水平仪

C *vt* (*pres p etc.* **-ll-, -l-** Amer) 1 (make horizontal) 使保持水平; (make flat) 使平坦; **to ~ the ground** 平整地面 2 (raze to ground) 夷平 ‹*building, forest*›; **the enemy ~led the village** 敌人将村庄夷为平地 3 colloq (knock down) 击倒; **the punch ~led her attacker** 她一拳击倒了袭击她的人 4 (make equal) 使相等; **to ~ the score** 扳平比分 5 (aim) 以…瞄准; **he ~led his gun at my chest** 他举枪瞄准我的胸膛 6 (direct) 使针对; **he ~led an icy stare at his wife** 他冷冷地注视着妻子; **to ~ a charge at** *or* **against sb.** 对某人提出控告 7 (in surveying) 对…作水平测量 ‹*land*›

Phrasal verbs

- **level off**

A *vt* [**~ sth. off, ~ off sth.**] (make horizontal) 使…保持水平; (make flat) 把…弄平 ‹*pile, mound*›; **~ the surface off by rubbing it with sandpaper** 用砂纸将表面磨平

B *vi* 1 Aviat «*aircraft, pilot*» 水平飞行 2 (become horizontal) «*curve*» 走平; «*slope, road*» 变得平坦 3 (stabilize) 呈稳定状态; **the rate of inflation has ~led off at 8%** 通货膨胀率稳定在了 8%

- **level out**

A *vt* [**~ sth. out, ~ out sth.**] (make horizontal) 使…保持水平; (make flat) 把…弄平 ‹*pile, mound*›

B *vi* ▸**level off B2**

- **level up** *vt* [**~ up sth., ~ sth. up**] (by raising lower object) 把…升高到平齐; (by moving either object) 把…调整到平齐; **some of the pictures need ~ling up** 有些图片需要对齐
- **level with** *vt* [**~ with sb.**] colloq 对…说实话; **~ with me: what are my chances of success?** 实话告诉我：我成功的机会有多大？

level: **~ crossing** *n* Brit 平面交叉; **~-headed** *adj* 头脑冷静的

levelling screw *n* 校平螺旋

lever /'li:və(r), Amer 'levər/

A *n* 1 (handle) 控制杆; **to pull a ~** 拉起控制杆 2 (lifting device) 杠杆; **I used the spade as a ~ to lift the box** 我用铲子作杠杆撬起了箱子 3 fig (means) 施压手段; **to have one's hands on the ~s of power** 拥有利用权力施压的手段 [指通过融资收购企业]

B *vt* 1 (manipulate with lever) 撬动; **to ~ sth. into/out of/off of sth.** 把某物撬进/出/离某处; **to ~ sth. open/into position** 把某物撬开/撬入位 2 fig (manoeuvre) 操控; **to ~ sb. into/out of sth.** 用手段使某人进入/离开某处; **he**

l

was ~ed out of the chairmanship 他的主席位置被人搞掉了

Phrasal verb

- **lever up** *vt* [~ up sth., ~ sth. up] 撬起 ‹*lid, rock*›; **she ~ed herself up on her elbows** 她用胳膊肘撑着身体

leverage /ˈliːvərɪdʒ, Amer ˈlev-/ *n* [u] 1 Phys (force) 杠杆作用 2 fig (influence) 影响力; **to have ~ with sb.** 能影响某人; **to exert (one's) ~ on sb.** 对某人施加影响 3 Fin 资本负债比率

leveraged /ˈlevərɪdʒd *adj* 举债的; **highly ~** 高度举债的

leveraged: ~ buyout *n* 杠杆收购 [指通过融资收购企业]; **~ management buy-out** *n* 管理层杠杆收购

leveret /ˈlevərɪt/ *n* 小野兔

leviathan /lɪˈvaɪəθn/ *n* 庞然大物; **the multinationals are ~s that devour smaller companies** 跨国公司是吞并小公司的庞然大物

levitate /ˈlevɪteɪt/
A *vi* [尤指借助魔力] 悬浮
B *vt* 使悬浮

levitation /ˌlevɪˈteɪʃn/ *n* [u] [尤指借助魔力的] 悬浮; **to rise/float in the air by ~** 悬浮升空/在空中悬浮

levity /ˈlevəti/ *n* [u] 轻率; **this is no occasion for ~** 这可不是闹着玩的

levy /ˈlevi/
A *n* 税; **to impose a ~ on sth./sb.** 对某物/向某人征税
B *vt* 征收 ‹*duty*›; **to ~ a tax on sb./sth.** 向某人/对某物征税; **to ~ sth. from sb./sth.** 从某人处/从某物处收取 ‹*fine, subscription*›

lewd /ljuːd, Amer luːd/ *adj* 淫荡的 ‹*gesture, behaviour, grin*›; 淫秽的 ‹*joke, remark, pictures*›; **a ~ song** 下流歌曲

lewdly /ˈljuːdli, Amer ˈluːdli/ *adv* 淫荡地

lewdness /ˈljuːdnɪs, Amer ˈluːd-/ *n* [u] (of person, behaviour) 淫荡; (of joke, remark, picture) 淫秽

lexical /ˈleksɪkl/ *adj* 词汇的

lexicalize /ˈleksɪkəlaɪz/ *vt* 使…进入词汇 ‹*foreign word, trade name*›; **to become fully ~d** 完全成为本族语词汇

lexicographer /ˌleksɪˈkɒɡrəfə(r)/ ▸p. 409 *n* 词典编纂者

lexicographical /ˌleksɪkəˈɡræfɪkl/ *adj* 词典编纂的

lexicography /ˌleksɪˈkɒɡrəfi/ *n* [u] 词典编纂

lexicological /ˌleksɪkəˈlɒdʒɪkl/ *adj* 词汇学的

lexicologist /ˌleksɪˈkɒlədʒɪst/ ▸p. 409 *n* 词汇学家

lexicology /ˌleksɪˈkɒlədʒi/ *n* [u] 词汇学

lexicon /ˈleksɪkən, Amer -kɒn/ *n* 1 (glossary) 词汇表; **a ~ of architectural terms** 建筑学术语词汇表 2 (dictionary) [尤指古代语言的] 词典 3 Ling (vocabulary) [与语法相对的] 词汇

liability /ˌlaɪəˈbɪləti/ *n* 1 [c] (drawback) 不利条件; **the house has become a ~ for them** 这套房子成了他们的累赘; **the goalkeeper is a real ~ to his team!** 这名守门员完全是球队的拖累! 2 **liabilities** *pl* Fin (debts) 负债; **to meet one's liabilities** 偿付债务 3 [u] Jur (responsibility) 责任; **to deny ~ for sth.** 不承认对…负有责任 ‹*debt, damage*›; **the ~ for tax** *or* **paying tax** 纳税的义务

liable /ˈlaɪəbl/ *adj pred* 1 (likely) 可能的; **to be ~ to do sth.** 很可能会做某事; **the plan is ~ to fail** 该计划可能会失败; **we're ~ to be arrested** 我们会被捕的 2 (prone) 有…倾向的; **to be ~ to sth.** 可能遭受某事; **the contract is ~ to changes** 合同可能有变; **the area is ~ to flooding** 该地区易发洪水 3 Jur (responsible) 负有法律责任的 ‹*person, company*›; **parents are ~ for their children** 父母要对孩子的行为负责; **to be ~ for damages/sb.'s debts** 有责任赔偿损失/偿付某人的债务 4 Jur (legally subject) 应受罚的 ‹*person*›; (answerable) 有义务的 ‹*person, company*›; **to be ~ for tax** «*profits, person, company*» 必须纳税; **to be ~ for duty** «*imports, goods*» 必须缴纳关税; **to be ~ for military service** 有服兵役的义务; **offenders are ~ to heavy fines/loss of citizenship** 违者处以高额罚款/失去公民资格

liaise /lɪˈeɪz/ *vi* 联络; **to ~ with sb.** 与某人联络

liaison /lɪˈeɪzn, Amer ˈlɪəzɒn/ *n* 1 [u] (cooperation) 联络; **~ with sb.** 与某人的联络; **who is responsible for ~ with the press?** 谁负责与新闻界联络? 2 [c] (affair) 私通; **to have a ~ with sb.** 和某人私通; **they had a brief ~** 他们有过一段短暂的风流韵事

liaison committee *n* 联络委员会

liang /lɪˈæŋ/ ▸p. 909 *n* (*pl* **liang**) 两

Liaoning /ˌljaʊˈnɪŋ/ ▸p. 604 *pr n* ~ **(Province)** 辽宁（省）

liar /ˈlaɪə(r)/ *n* 说谎者; **a good/bad ~** 善于/不善于撒谎的人

Lib /lɪb/ *abbr* Brit = **liberal A3**

lib /lɪb/ *n* [u] colloq = **liberation** 解放运动; **women's ~** 妇女解放运动

Lib Dem /ˌlɪb ˈdem/ *n, adj* Brit = **Liberal Democrat**

libel /ˈlaɪbl/
A *n* 1 [u] (act of defamation) 诽谤罪; **to bring an action for ~ against sb.** *or* **to sue sb. for ~** 控告某人犯诽谤罪 2 [c] (article, statement) 诽谤性文字 3 [c] (insult) 诽谤; **a ~ on sb.** 对某人的诽谤
B *modif* 诽谤罪的 ‹*case, damages*›
C *vt* (*pres p etc.* **-ll-**, Amer **-l-**) 诽谤

libellous Brit, **libelous** Amer /ˈlaɪbələs/ *adj* 诽谤性的 ‹*statement, allegation*›

liberal /ˈlɪbərəl/
A *adj* 1 (open-minded, tolerant) 宽容的 ‹*person*›; 开明的 ‹*intellectual, attitude, school, laws*› 2 Pol (favouring liberty and moderate reform) 自由的 ‹*views, regime*›; **a ~ democratic party** 自由民主党 3 **Liberal** Pol (relating to party) 自由党的 ‹*politician, supporter, policy*› 4 (generous) 大量的 ‹*supply, helping, quantity*›; 慷慨的 ‹*person, offer, donation*›; **to be ~ with sth.** 慷慨给予某物; **he's very ~ with his money** 他花钱很大方; **to make ~ use of sth.** 大量使用某物; **some examiners were too ~** 有些考官给分太松; **~ coating** 厚厚的涂层 5 (not literal) 不拘泥字面的 ‹*account*›; **a ~ translation** 灵活的翻译
B *n* 1 (tolerant person) 宽容大度的人; **I'm a ~ as far as marriage is concerned** 我在婚姻问题上很开明 2 Pol (sb. favouring liberty and moderate reform) 自由主义者 3 **Liberal** Pol (member) 自由党党员; (supporter) 自由党支持者

liberal: ~ arts *npl* esp Amer 文科; **~ democracy** *n* 自由民主; **L~ Democrat** *n* Brit 自由民主党人; **the L~ Democrats** 自由民主党

> **the Liberal Democratic Party**
>
> 自由民主党，亦称 the Liberal Democrats，非正式简称为 the Lib Dems。为保守党（▸**the Conservative Party**）和工党（▸**the Labour Party**）之后的英国第三大政党。1988 年由自由党（Liberal Party）和社会民主党（Social Democratic Party）合并而成。政策上中间偏左。

liberalism /ˈlɪbərəlɪzəm/ *n* [u] 1 Pol (belief in liberty and moderate reform) 自由主义 2 Pol (party politics) 开明政治; (party ideology) 开明的意识形态 3 Econ 经济自由主义 4 = **liberality**

liberality /ˌlɪbəˈræləti/ *n* [u] 1 (generosity) 慷慨大方; **~ with sth.** 在给予某物方面的慷慨大方 2 (open-mindedness) 开明

liberalization /ˌlɪbərəlaɪˈzeɪʃn, Amer -lɪˈz-/ *n* [u] 自由化

liberalize /ˈlɪbərəlaɪz/ *vt* 使…自由化 ‹*economy, society*›; 使…开明 ‹*attitude, law*›; **an agreement to ~ trade** 贸易自由化协定

liberally /ˈlɪbərəli/ *adv* 1 (generously) 大量地 ‹*apply, supply*›; 宽松地 ‹*mark*› 2 (not literally) 灵活地 ‹*translate, interpret*› 3 (tolerantly) 开明地 ‹*govern, think*›; 宽容地 ‹*treat*›

liberal: L~ Party *n* **the L~ Party** 自由党; **~ studies** *npl* Brit 通识教育科

liberate /ˈlɪbəreɪt/ *vt* 1 (make free) 解放 ‹*women, mankind, slave, country*› 2 (release) 解救 ‹*prisoner, hostage*› 3 colloq hum (steal) 偷盗 ‹*money, goods*› 4 Fin 释放 ‹*capital, funds*› 5 Chem 释出 ‹*gas*›

liberated /ˈlɪbəreɪtɪd/ *adj* 1 (made free) 获得解放的 ‹*country, people*› 2 (liberalized) 思想开放的 ‹*person*›

liberating /ˈlɪbəreɪtɪŋ/ *adj* 令人感到解脱的 ‹*activity, experience*›

liberation /ˌlɪbəˈreɪʃn/ *n* [u] 1 (act of freeing) 解放; **the ~ of women from male oppression** 妇女从男权压迫下的解放 2 (liberating event) 解脱; **the divorce was an enormous ~ for her** 离婚对她来说是一大解脱

liberation: ~ army *n* 解放军; **~ front** *n* 解放阵线; **~ movement** *n* 解放运动; **~ war** *n* 解放战争

liberator /ˈlɪbəreɪtə(r)/ *n* 解放者

Liberia /laɪˈbɪərɪə/ *pr n* 利比里亚

Liberian /laɪˈbɪərɪən/ ▸p. 503
A *adj* (of Liberia) 利比里亚的; (of the people) 利比里亚人的
B *n* 利比里亚人

libertarian /ˌlɪbəˈteərɪən/
A *adj* 1 (advocating libertarianism) 自由论的 ‹*philosophy, view*› 2 (liberal) 持自由论观点的 ‹*person, thinker*›
B *n* 自由论者

libertarianism /ˌlɪbəˈteərɪənɪzəm/ *n* [u] 自由论

libertine /ˈlɪbətiːn/ *n* liter 放荡不羁的人

liberty /ˈlɪbəti/ *n* 1 [u] (freedom in society) 自由 2 [c] (right) 自由权 3 [u] (physical freedom) 人身自由; **to deprive sb. of his/her ~** 剥夺某人的人身自由; **to be at ~** 不受监禁; **to set sb. at ~** 释放某人; **to be at ~ to do sth.** 可以随意做某事 4 [c] (presumptuous remark or action) 放肆; **to take the ~ of doing sth.** 肆意做某事; **to take liberties with sb.** 对某人过分亲昵; **to take liberties with sth.** 任意改动 ‹*text, script*›; **it is a bit of a ~ to turn up uninvited** 不请自来有些失礼; **what a ~!** colloq 胡闹!

libidinous /lɪˈbɪdɪnəs/ *adj* 好色的 ‹*person*›; 淫荡的 ‹*glance, behaviour*›

libido /lɪˈbiːdəʊ, ˈlɪbɪdəʊ/ *n* (*pl* **~s**) 1 [c and u] (sexual desire) 性欲; **loss of ~** 性欲的丧失 2 [u] Psych 力比多 [指性本能]

Libra /ˈliːbrə/ *n* 1 [u] Astron 天秤（星）座 2 [u] Astrol (sign) 天秤宫 [黄道第七宫] 3 [c] (*pl* **~s**) Astrol (person) 属天秤（星）座的人

Libran /ˈlɪːbrən/
A *adj* 属天秤（星）座的 ‹*person*›; 有天秤（星）座特点的 ‹*character, temperament*›
B *n* 属天秤（星）座的人; **he's a ~** 他是天秤座的

librarian /laɪˈbreərɪən/ ▸p. 409 *n* 图书管理员

librarianship /laɪˈbreərɪənʃɪp/ *n* [u] 图书管理学

library /ˈlaɪbrəri, Amer -breri/
A *n* 1 (institution) 图书馆 2 (collection) 馆藏品; **a newspaper/record ~** 馆藏报纸/唱片 3 (in private house) 私人收藏室; **the men retired to the ~ for a drink** 男人们回到书房小酌一杯 4 Comput **(software) ~** 软件库
B *modif* 1 (of institution) 图书馆的 ‹*book, staff*›;

a ～ card *or* ticket 借书证 2 Comput 软件库的 ‹*disk, program*›

library: ～ **edition** *n* 图书馆版 [指精装大开本图书]; ～ **pictures** *npl* [说明历史资料的] 移动字幕; ～ **science** *n* [u] 图书馆学

librettist /lɪ'bretɪst/ *n* 歌剧剧本作者

libretto /lɪ'bretəʊ/ *n* (*pl* **～s** *or* **libretti** /lɪ'breti/) 歌剧剧本

Libreville /'li:brəvɪl/ *pr n* 利伯维尔

Libya /'lɪbɪə/ *pr n* 利比亚

Libyan /'lɪbɪən/ ▸**p. 503**

A *adj* (of Libya) 利比亚的; (of the people) 利比亚人的

B *n* 利比亚人

lice /laɪs/ *npl* ▸**louse 1**

licence /'laɪsns/ *n* Brit 1 [c] (permit) 许可证; **a fishing/private detective's ～** 捕鱼许可证/私家侦探执照; **to issue sb. with** *or* **to grant sb. a ～** 给某人发放许可证; **a ～ to practise as a doctor** 执业医师执照; **a ～ certificate** 许可证; **a vehicle ～** 车辆牌照; **to lose one's (driving) ～** 驾照遭到没收; **the restaurant doesn't have a ～ (for alcohol)** 该饭店没有酒类专卖证; **a ～ to print money** fig 一本万利 2 [u] (permission) 许可; **to sell/manufacture sth. under ～ (from sb.)** 经（某人）许可售卖/生产某产品; **to be married by special ～** 经特许结婚; **your success doesn't give you a ～ to criticize others** fig 你的成功并不意味着你有权随便批评别人 3 [u] (freedom to deviate from fact) 不拘一格; **artistic ～** 艺术上的自由发挥 4 [u] dated pej (immoral behaviour) 放纵

licence: ～ **agreement** *n* 许可协议; ～ **fee** *n* 牌照费; ～ **number** *n* 1 (of car) 车牌号码; 2 (of driver) 驾照号码; **～-payer** *n* Brit 付费电视用户; ～ **plate** *n* 车辆牌照

license /'laɪsns/

A *vt* 1 (authorize) 给…发许可证; **to ～ sb. to do sth.** 许可某人做某事; **commercial radio stations have to be ～d by the local authority** 商业电台必须获得地方当局颁发的许可证 2 (register) 得到…的许可证 ‹*vehicle, gun, drug*›; **dogs no longer have to be ～d** 养狗不再需要办许可证了 3 (use under licence) 准许使用; **the software is ～d from X** 该软件在X的授权下使用

B *n* Amer = **licence**

licensed /'laɪsnst/ *adj* 1 (holding a licence) 有许可证的 ‹*gun owner, dog-handler*›; 有执照的 ‹*doctor, pilot, security firm*›; **the shop is ～ for the sale of** *or* **to sell tobacco** 这家店有烟草经销执照; **to be ～ to carry a gun** 有持枪证 2 (allowed by a licence) 获准拥有的 ‹*firearm, taxi*›; 有牌照的 ‹*vehicle*› 3 (to sell alcohol) 有售酒许可证的 ‹*hotel, restaurant*›; ～ **premises** Brit 许可售酒的场所

licensed victualler *n* Brit 有许可证的酒商

licensee /ˌlaɪsən'si:/ *n* 1 (to sell alcohol) 售酒执照持有人 2 (manufacturer) 有生产许可证的企业

license plate, license tag *ns* Amer 车牌

licenser /'laɪsnsə(r)/ *n* = **licensor**

licensing: ～ **authority** *n* 许可证发放部门; ～ **hours** *npl* esp Brit 售酒时段; ～ **laws** *npl* esp Brit 售酒法; ～ **magistrate** *n* Brit 许可证发放官 [负责为售酒及娱乐场所颁发许可证]

licensor /'laɪsnsə(r)/ *n* (person) 许可证发放官; (organization) 许可证发放机构

licentious /laɪ'senʃəs/ *adj* 淫荡的

lichen /'laɪkən/ *n* [c and u] 地衣

lichgate /'lɪtʃgeɪt/ *n* 停柩门

lick /lɪk/

A *vt* 1 (with tongue) 舔; **to ～ sth. clean** 把某物舔干净; **to ～ one's lips** *or* colloq **chops** lit 舔嘴唇; fig (at prospect) 热切期盼; **the children ～ed their lips as the cake was cut** 切蛋糕时孩子们都馋得直舔嘴唇; **she's ～ing her chops at the thought of spending all that money!** 她一想到能花那一大笔钱都迫不及待了; **to ～ sth./sb. into shape** 使某事物/某人变得更好; **the old house has been ～ed into shape** 这幢旧房子修缮好了; **the manager has a year to ～ the team into shape** 主教练有一年的时间把球队调教好 2 (remove with tongue) 舔掉; **to ～ sth. off, to ～ off sth.** 把某物舔掉; **to ～ blood from a cut/honey off a spoon** 舔掉伤口上的血/调羹上的蜂蜜 3 colloq (defeat) 打败; (outperform) 超过; **to get ～ed** 被打败; **to ～ a problem** 解决问题; **this puzzle has got me ～ed** 这个难题把我难住了 4 (touch lightly) 轻轻触及; **the waves were ～ing the seashore** 波浪轻拍着海岸

B *n* 1 (with tongue) 舔; **to give sth. a ～** 舔某物一下; **the child gave the bowl a good ～** 孩子把碗舔得干干净净; **to give sb.** *or* **let sb. have a ～ (of sth.)** 让某人舔一口（某物）; **a ～ and a promise** colloq 草草了事; **to give the room a ～ and a promise** colloq 马马虎虎打扫一下房间 2 fig colloq (quick application) 一点; **a ～ of paint** 薄薄的一层油漆 3 colloq (speed) 速度; (fast speed) 快速; **at a fair (old) ～** 快速地; **at (quite) a ～** 迅速地; **to drive at full ～** 全速驾驶

Phrasal verb

- **lick up** *vt* [**～ up sth., ～ sth. up**] 舔食; **the cat ～ed up the milk** 猫把牛奶舔光了

lickety-split /ˌlɪkətɪ'splɪt/ *adv* Amer colloq 火速地 ‹*go, drive*›

licking /'lɪkɪŋ/ *n* colloq (defeat) 惨败; **to take** *or* **get a (good** *or* **right) ～** 遭到惨败; **to give sb. a (good** *or* **right) ～** 把某人打得一败涂地

licorice /'lɪkərɪs/ *n* Amer = **liquorice**

lid /lɪd/ *n* 1 (of container) 盖子; (of piano) 盖; **to open/close the ～** 打开/合上盖子; **a dustbin ～** 垃圾箱盖; **to keep a/the ～ on sth.** colloq (restrict) 控制住某事物; (block information) 对某事物保密; **to put a/the ～ on** colloq 终止; **to take** *or* **lift** *or* **blow** *etc.* **the ～ off sth.** 揭露关于某事物的真相; **an article that lifts the ～ on the world of professional boxing** 一篇揭露职业拳击界内幕的文章 2 (eyelid) 眼皮

lido /'li:dəʊ, 'laɪdəʊ/ *n* (*pl* **～s**) Brit (pool) 露天游泳池; (beach) 海滨浴场

lie¹ /laɪ/

A *vi* (*pres* **～s**; *pres p* **lying**; *pt* **lay**; *pp* **lain**) 1 (in horizontal position) «*person*» 躺; «*animal*» 趴; **the child lay fast asleep on the bed** 孩子躺在床上睡得很熟; **the dog lay at its master's feet** 狗卧在主人脚边; **to ～ on one's back/front/side** 仰卧/俯卧/侧卧; **to ～ low** 躲藏; **to ～ in ambush** 埋伏 2 (be buried) 被埋葬; **'here ～s John Smith'** "约翰·史密斯长眠于此" 3 (rest flat) 平放; **a fallen tree lay across the path** 一棵砍倒的树横挡在路上 4 (remain in position) 处于某位置; (remain in state) 处于某状态; **a rug lay in front of the hearth** 一块地毯铺在壁炉前面; **I'd rather spend my money than leave it lying idle in the bank** 我宁愿把钱花掉也不愿闲置在银行里; **the book lay open on his desk** 书摊开放在他的书桌上; **to ～ in sb.'s/sth.'s way** 妨碍某人/某事物; **the house lay empty for several months** 房子空了好几个月; **all his dreams lay shattered** 他所有的梦想都破碎了; **to let sth. ～** 不再管某事物 5 (as covering) «*snow*» 堆积起来; **the snow lay thick on the ground** 地上积雪很厚 6 Naut 停泊; **to be lying at anchor** 抛锚停泊 7 fig (rank in race, competition) 名列; **to ～ first/second** *or* **in first/second place** 名列第一/第二 8 (be situated) 位于; **the village lay at the foot of the mountain** 村庄坐落在山脚下; **who knows what ～s around the next corner?** fig 谁知道将要发生什么事? 9 (extend) 延伸; **you are still young; your whole life ～s before you!** 你还年轻; 整个人生还长着呢! ; **on one side lay the mountains; on the other lay the sea** 一边是连绵群山，一边是汪洋大海; **danger lay all around him** 他周围危机四伏 10 (reside, rest) 存在; **the burden of responsibility ～s on his shoulders** 责任的重担落在他的肩上; **our strength ～s in our members' sense of duty** 我们的力量源于所有成员的责任感; **to ～ with sb.** 在于某人; **the blame ～s with them** 责任在他们身上; **the decision ～s with the manager** 决定应由经理作出; **she explained where the problem lay** 她解释了问题之所在; **to ～ behind sth.** 是某事物的原因 11 Jur (be admissible) «*action, appeal*» 可受理

B *n* 1 (position) 位置; (direction) 方向; (manner) 方式; **the ～ of the streets/of the land** 街道/田地的布局 2 (in golf) 球停位置

Phrasal verbs

- **lie about, lie around** *vi* 无所事事地混日子; **she just ～s about all day** 她一整天都无所事事; **to ～ around the house** 在家里闲着
- **lie back** *vi* 1 (horizontally) 平躺 2 (lean back) 仰靠
- **lie down** *vi* «*person*» 躺下; «*animal*» 平卧; **she lay down on the bed** 她躺在床上; **the technology is dead, but it won't ～ down** 这种技术已经过时了，但还不会被弃用; **to ～ down on the job** 怠工; **to take sth. lying down** fig 甘心忍受某事物; **the electorate will not take this lying down** fig 选民不会对此逆来顺受的
- **lie in** *vi* 睡懒觉
- **lie up** *vi* 躲藏

lie²

A *n* (falsehood) 谎言; **to tell a ～** 说谎; **it's all ～s!** 一派胡言! ; **a pack** *or* **tissue of ～s** 一派谎言; **I tell a ～** Brit colloq 我说错了; **to give the ～ to sth.** 证明某事不实; **to live a ～** 过骗人的生活

B *vi* (*pres p* **lying**) 1 (tell a lie) 说谎; **to ～ about one's age** 谎报年龄; **to ～ to sb.** 对某人说谎; **to ～ through one's teeth** colloq 睁着眼睛说瞎话 2 (give false impression) 造成假象; **appearances sometimes ～** 外表有时不可靠; **the camera never ～s** 相机从不作假

C *vt* (*pres p* **lying**) 谎称; **'that dress really suits you,' I ～d** "那条连衣裙真的很适合你，" 我违心地说; **she ～d her way out of trouble** 她靠说谎摆脱了麻烦

Liechtenstein /'lɪktənstaɪn/ *pr n* 列支敦士登

lie: ～ **detector** *n* 测谎器; **a ～ detector test** 测谎试验; **～-down** *n* Brit colloq 小憩; **to have a ～-down** 小憩片刻; **～-in** *n* Brit colloq 懒觉; **to have a ～-in** 睡懒觉

lieu /lju:, Amer lu:/ *n* **in ～ (of sth.)** 替代（某事物）; **some people choose to do community work in ～ of military service** 有些人选择做社区工作，以替代服兵役; **a free holiday or £500 cash in ～** 一次免费度假或代之以 500 英镑现金发放

Lieut. *abbr* = **lieutenant**

lieutenant /lef'tenənt, Amer lu:'t-/ *n* 1 (in UK army) 陆军中尉; (in UK or US navy) 海军上尉 2 (in US police) 中尉 3 (assistant) 助理官员

lieutenant governor *n* (deputy governor) 副州长; (deputy to the Governor General) 副总督

life /laɪf/

A *n* (*pl* **lives**) 1 [c and u] (of people, animals, plants) 生命; (existence) 生存; **～ and death** 生与死; **to bring sb./sth. (back) to ～** (revive sb./sth. appearing to be dead) 使某人/某物苏醒; (revive sb./sth. that has died) 使某人/某物复活; **to come (back) to ～** (return from death) 复活; (become lively) 变得活跃; **to frighten the ～ out of sb.** 把某人吓得魂飞魄散; **the journalists had been pestering the ～ out of him** 那些记

l

者一直纠缠他，令他不胜其烦; **his ~ is at stake** 他性命堪忧; **to risk one's ~** 冒生命危险; **to lose one's ~** 丧生; **4,000 lives were lost in the earthquake** 有 4,000 人在这场地震中丧生; **to take sb.'s ~** 杀死某人; **to take one's (own) ~** 自杀; **to take one's ~ in one's hands** 冒生命危险; **to lay down one's ~ (for sb./sth.)** （为某人/某事物）牺牲自己的生命; **to lay down one's ~ for one's country** 为国捐躯; **to give one's ~** 献出生命; **for one's ~, for dear ~** 拼命地; **for the ~ of me/him** *etc.* colloq 无论如何; **not on your ~!** colloq 决不！; **to make an attempt on sb.'s ~** 企图杀死某人 **2** [u] (living things) 生物; **there was no sign of ~** 没有生命迹象; **plant/animal ~** 植物/动物; **bird/insect/human ~** 鸟类/昆虫类/人类 **3** [c and u] (period from birth to death) 一生; (part of this period) 一生中的部分时间; **the insect has a relatively short ~** 昆虫的寿命较短; **all one's ~** 一辈子; **adult/early ~** 成年/幼年; **the rest of one's ~** 余生; **to start a new ~** 开始新生活; **in this ~ and the next** 今生和来世; **at sb.'s time of ~** 在某人这个年纪; **for ~** 终身; **she gave him the shock of his ~** 她让他感到了前所未有的震惊; **the time of one's ~** 特别愉快的时光; **the children were having the time of their lives** 孩子们玩得特别高兴 **4** [c and u] (social activity, lifestyle) 生活经历; **to have a hard ~** 生活艰难; **private/family ~** 私生活/家庭生活; **the man/woman in sb.'s ~** 某人生活中的男人/女人; **the ~ and times of sb.** 某人的生平; **modern/country/college/political ~** 现代/乡村/大学/政治生活; **way of ~** 生活方式; **this is the ~!** 这才叫生活！; **that's the ~ for me!** 那就是我的生活方式！; **what a ~!** 生活不易啊！ **5** [c] (purpose of one's existence) 人生目的; **singing is her ~** 唱歌是她的生命; **his son is his ~** 儿子是他的命根子 **6** [u] (as general concept) 生活; **~ in general** 日常生活; **how's ~?** 最近过得怎么样？; **don't make ~ too difficult for yourself** 不要自找麻烦; **~ had passed her by** 她没有得到生活的眷顾; **~ goes on, ~ must go on** 生活还是要继续; **that's ~!** 生活就是这样！; **such is ~!** 这就是生活！; **~ is too short for sth./for doing sth.** 人生苦短，不应浪费在某事物/做某事上 **7** [u] (ways of living) 社会生活; **to see ~** 见世面; **from all walks of ~** 来自各行各业 **8** [u] Art (model) 实物; **to draw from ~** 写生 **9** [u] (animation, vigour) 活力; **there was no ~ in her voice** 她的声音有气无力; **to bring sth. to ~** (make lively) 使某事物更生动; (make realistic) 使某事物显得逼真; **the actor brought the character to ~** 那位演员把人物演活了; **to come to ~** (become animated) 变得活跃; (become realistic) 显得逼真; **exhibitions that make history come to ~** 生动再现历史的展览; **the engine roared into ~** 引擎隆隆几声发动起来; **to put ~ into sb./sth.** 为某人/某物注入活力 **10** [u] (useful duration) (of machine, clothes, vehicle) 使用期; (of organization, institution) 存在期; (of licence) 有效期; **battery ~** 电池的寿命; **during the ~ of the last government** 在上届政府执政期间; **how much ~ is left in them?** 它们还能用多久？ **11** [u] colloq (life imprisonment) 无期徒刑; **to give sb. ~** 判某人无期徒刑; **to do ~** 服无期徒刑 **12** [c] (biography) 传记; **a ~ of sb.** 某人的传记 **13** [c] Games 命 [指玩家出局前的机会]; **I've got two lives left** 我还剩 2 条命
B *modif* 终身的; **~ membership** 终身会员身份

life: ~-and-death *adj* 生死攸关的 ‹*decision, struggle*›; **~ assurance** *n* [u] **= ~ insurance**; **~belt** *n* 救生带; **~blood** *n* [u] **1** lit (blood) 生命必需的血液; **2** fig (vital element) 命脉; **~boat** *n* 救生艇; **~boatman** /-mən/ ▸ **p. 409** *n* 救生艇救生员; **~boat station** *n* (on land) 救生艇停泊处; (on ship) 救生艇架; **~buoy** *n* esp Brit 救生圈; **~ class** *n* 人体写生课; **~ coach** ▸ **p. 409** *n* 人生规划师; **~ cycle** *n* 生活周期; **~ drawing** *n* **1** [u] (action) 写生; **2** [c] (picture) 写生作品; **~ event** *n* 人生大事; **~ expectancy** *n* [c and u] **1** Biol 预期寿命; **2** Tech 预期使用寿命; **~ force** *n* (vital force) 活力; (spirit) 生命力; **~ form** *n* 生物; **~-giving** *adj* 维持生命的; **~guard** ▸ **p. 409** *n* 救生员; **~ history** *n* **1** Biol 生活史; **2** (life story) 生平; **~ imprisonment** *n* [u] 无期徒刑; **~ insurance** *n* [u] 人寿保险; **to take out ~ insurance** 投保人寿保险; **~ jacket** *n* 救生衣

lifeless /ˈlaɪflɪs/ *adj* **1** (dead) 死的 ‹*person, animal, plant*›; **a ~ body** 尸体 **2** (inanimate) 无生命的 ‹*matter, machine*› **3** (appearing dead) 失去知觉的 ‹*person, animal*›; 枯萎的 ‹*plant*› **4** (without life) 无生命的 ‹*planet, land, pool*› **5** fig (lacking vitality) 死气沉沉的 ‹*performance, plot, voice*›

life: ~like *adj* 栩栩如生的; **~line** *n* **1** (for climbing) 保险绳; (on ship) 救生索; **2** fig (indispensable aid) 生命线; **the telephone was her ~line** 电话是赖以生存的依靠; **the economic ~line of the surrounding communities** 周围地区的经济命脉; **~long** *adj* 终身的 ‹*companion, habit, work*›; 一生的 ‹*friendship, love, ambition*›; **sb.'s ~long wish** 某人的终身愿望; **~-or-death** *adj* **= ~-and-death**; **~ peer** *n* Brit [爵位不能世袭的] 终身贵族; **~ preserver** *n* **1** Amer Naut 救生设施; **2** Brit (stick) 护身棒

lifer /ˈlaɪfə(r)/ *n* colloq 无期徒刑犯

life: ~ raft *n* 救生筏; **~saver** *n* **1** Austral, NZ (lifeguard) 海滩救生员; **2** fig (thing) [帮助解除困境的] 救助物; (person) 帮大忙的人; **you're a ~saver!** 你真是帮了大忙了！

lifesaving /ˈlaɪfseɪvɪŋ/
A *n* [u] (for swimmers) 救生术; (first-aid) 急救
B *modif* **1** (in swimming) 救生的 ‹*skills, techniques*›; (using first aid) 实施急救的 ‹*skills, techniques*› **2** Med 急救的 ‹*drugs, treatment, equipment*›

life: ~ sciences *npl* **the ~ sciences** 生命科学; **~ sentence** *n* 无期徒刑; **~-size** *adj* 与真人一样大小的 ‹*painting, sculpture*›; 与实物一样大小的 ‹*model, replica*›; **~ span** *n* **1** (duration) 寿命; **2** (expectancy) 使用寿命; **~ story** *n* **1** (biography) 传记; **2** (account) 生平经历

lifestyle /ˈlaɪfstaɪl/
A *n* 生活方式
B *modif* 与向往的生活方式有关的 ‹*magazine, product*›; **~ drug** 生活品质改善药

life support
A *n* [u] **1** Med, Aerosp (provision of care) 生命支持 **2** Med (equipment) 生命支持设备; **she has been on ~ for 2 days** 两天来她靠机器维持生命
B **life-support** *modif* Med, Aerosp 维持生命的 ‹*system, equipment, machine*›

life: ~'s work *n* 毕生的事业; **~-threatening** *adj* 危及生命的 ‹*disease, condition*›

lifetime /ˈlaɪftaɪm/
A *n* **1** (from birth to death) 一生; **the work of a ~** 毕生的事业; **in her ~** 在她的一生中; **she has had a ~'s experience of poverty** 她一生贫寒; **the chance/holiday of a ~** 千载难逢的机会/假日; **it felt like a ~** 真觉得恍如隔世 **2** (extended period) 漫长的时间 [通常指从学校毕业到退休之间]; **she has given a ~ of service to the company** 她为公司服务了一辈子 **3** (shelf life of object) 使用期限
B *modif* 终身的 ‹*ban, subscription*›

life vest *n* esp Amer 救生衣

lift /lɪft/
A *vt* **1** (pick up) 拿起 ‹*plate, glass, book*›; 抱起 ‹*child*›; 提起 ‹*suitcase*›; **the piano was too heavy for us to ~** 这架钢琴太重了，我们抬不动; **these containers can be ~ed only by the most powerful cranes** 这些集装箱只有最强力的起重机才能吊起来; **she ~ed the heavy box down from the shelf** 她把那个重盒子从架子上搬了下来; **one, two, three, ~!** 一、二、三，起！ **2** (raise) 抬起 ‹*leg, head*›; 举起 ‹*arm, hand*›; **he ~ed his feet off the stool** 他把脚从凳子上放下来; **he never ~ed his head from his book** 他一直埋头看书 **3** Mil (airlift) 空运; **three men were ~ed off the burning ship by helicopter** 有 3 个人被直升机从燃烧的船上吊起救走了 **4** (end) 撤销 ‹*ban, sanctions, curfew*›; 解除 ‹*embargo, siege*› **5** (remove) 去除; **this reprieve ~s a great deal of the pressure off him** 这份缓刑令让他感觉轻松了不少; **I feel as if a great weight has been ~ed from my mind** 我觉得思想上好像卸掉重负 **6** (boost) 鼓舞; **this piece of luck ~ed his spirits** 这点运气振奋了他的情绪; **to ~ the football team** 鼓舞足球队的士气 **7** Brit colloq (steal) 偷盗; **he ~ed the document from my briefcase** 他从我的公文包里偷走了那份文件 **8** (plagiarize) 剽窃; **to ~ an idea from another author** 剽窃另一位作者的观点; **she ~ed her article from another magazine** 她的文章是从另一本杂志上抄来的 **9** Sport (win) 赢得 ‹*trophy, title*› **10** (improve) 改进 ‹*game, performance*›
B *vi* **1** (improve) 受到鼓舞; **her spirits began to ~** 她的情绪开始好转; **my heart ~ed at the news** 这个消息让我很高兴 **2** (end) «*depression, bad mood*» 消失; «*headache*» 停止 **3** (dissipate) «*fog, clouds*» 消散
C *n* **1** [c] Brit (elevator) 电梯; **to take the ~ to the sixth floor** 乘电梯到7楼 **2** [c] (ride) 免费乘车; **to give sb. a ~** 让某人搭车; **to get a ~ from** *or* **off** *or* **with sb.** 搭某人的车; **I thumbed** *or* **hitched a ~ (home/to the railway station)** 我搭了便车（回家/去火车站） **3** [c] (boost) 鼓舞; **to give sb. a tremendous ~** 给某人极大的鼓舞 **4** [c] Sport (in weightlifting) 举; **each competitor has three ~s** 每位选手有 3 次试举机会 **5** [u] Aviat 升力

Phrasal verbs

• **lift off**
A *vi* «*rocket, spaceship*» 发射
B *vt* [**~ sth./sb. off, ~ off sth./sb.**] 揭掉 ‹*lid, cover, roof*›; 吊起 ‹*person*›; **we carefully ~ed the beam off his leg** 我们小心翼翼地把那根屋梁木从他腿上移开了; **the climbers had to be ~ed off by helicopter** 攀登者只得由直升机吊起救走

• **lift up**
A *vt* [**~ up sth., ~ sth. up**] 举起 ‹*trophy, arm*›; 抱起 ‹*person*›; 撩起 ‹*skirt*›; 掀起 ‹*carpet*›; 抬起 ‹*head, foot, elbow*›; **~ that box up on to the shelf** 把那只箱子搬到架子上
B *vi* «*lid*» 被揭开; «*flap*» 被掀起; «*seat*» 被抬起

lift: ~ attendant ▸ **p. 409** *n* Brit 电梯服务员; **~ cage** *n* Brit 电梯轿厢; **~gate** *n* Amer [旅行车后部的] 升降式车门

lifting equipment, lifting gear *ns* [u] 起重设备

lift: ~-off *n* 发射; **~-off from the moon** 在月球进行的发射; **we have ~-off!** 发射成功！; **~ shaft** *n* Brit 电梯井

ligament /ˈlɪɡəmənt/ *n* 韧带; **~ injury** 韧带损伤

ligature /ˈlɪɡətʃə(r)/ *n* **1** Med 结扎线 **2** (restraint) 结扎 **3** (character) 连字 [如æ、œ、Æ、Œ 等]

light¹ /laɪt/
A *n* **1** [u] (brightness) 光亮; (from a source) 光线; **by the ~ of the sun** 借着阳光; **the ~ is too bright/dim** 光线太亮/暗; **to cast** *or* **shed** *or* **throw ~ (on sth.)** 投射光线（在某物上）; **to stand with one's back to the ~** 背光站着; **to be/stand/sit in sb.'s ~** 挡住某人的光线; ▸ **tunnel A1** **2** [c] (gleam, bright point) 光点; **she saw a ~ in the distance** 她看见远处有一点亮光; **the ~s of the city** 城市的灯火 **3** [c] fig (aspect) 角度; **in a good/favourable/new/different ~** 从好的/有利的/新的/

l

不同的角度; **they saw him in the worst ~** 他们看到了他最糟糕的一面; **in the ~ of sth.** fig 考虑到某事物; **the decision was made in the ~ of previous experience** 决定是根据以前的经验作出的 **4** [u] (daylight) 日光; **to go home in the ~** 在天黑前回家; **the ~ was beginning to fail** 天色渐暗; **the ~ of day** lit 日光; fig 光天化日; **things may be different in the ~ of day** 第二天醒来事情也许会有所不同 **5** [c] (electrical appliance) 灯; (brightness of appliance) 灯光; **to put** *or* **turn** *or* **switch a ~ on** 开灯; **to put** *or* **turn** *or* **switch a ~ off** *or* **out** 关灯; **no talking after ~s out** 熄灯后禁止说话; **to turn a ~ up/down** 把灯光调亮/暗; **to go** *or* **be out like a ~** colloq (fall asleep quickly) 很快入睡; (become unconscious) 失去知觉 **6** **lights** *pl* (headlights) 车灯; **to put** *or* **turn** *or* **switch one's ~s on/off** 打开/关上车灯 **7** (traffic light) 交通信号灯; **to go through a red ~** 闯红灯; **the ~s are green** 现在是绿灯; **the ~s were against me** 我遇到了红灯 **8** **lights** *pl* (decorative display) 彩灯; **the Christmas ~s** 圣诞节灯饰 **9** [c and u] (flame) 火; **to set ~ to sth., to put a ~ to sth.** 点燃某物; **to strike a ~** 划出火来; **have you got a ~?** 你有火吗? **10** [c] (glint in eye) 目光; **there was a mischievous ~ in her eyes** 她目光中透着一丝顽皮 **11** [u] fig (enlightenment) 启发; **to see the ~** (understand) 明白过来; (in religion) 改变信仰; **to cast** *or* **shed** *or* **throw ~ on sth.** fig 使某事物更容易理解; **this research has cast new ~ on the causes of the disease** 这项研究使人们对这种疾病的病因有了新的认识 **12** [u] **to bring sth. to ~** (reveal) 披露某事物; **our investigation brought to ~ some important facts** 我们的调查揭露了一些重要的事实; **to come to ~** 为人所知; **the conspiracy came to ~** 阴谋败露了 **13** [u] (happiness) 幸福; (hope) 希望; **he brought ~ into their lives** 他给他们的生活带来了快乐; **the ~ of sb.'s life** 某人的最爱 **14** **lights** *pl* **according to one's ~s, by one's (own) ~s** (in conformity with one's beliefs) 根据自己的看法; (in conformity with one's attitudes) 根据自己的态度; (in conformity with one's ability) 根据自己的能力; **to do one's best according to one's ~s** 尽力而为 **15** [c] Constr (window) 窗; (opening) 采光孔; (division of a window) 窗格; (pane of glass) 窗格玻璃

B *adj* **1** (bright) 光线充足的 ‹*place*›; 有日光的 ‹*morning, sky*›; **a ~ room** 明亮的房间; **it isn't ~ enough to take a photograph** 光线不足, 无法拍照; **it gets ~ earlier at this time of year** 一年中的这个时节, 天亮得比较早; **it's ~** 天亮了 **2** ▸**p. 134** (pale) 浅色的; **to wear ~ colours** 穿浅色衣服; **a ~-blue flower** 淡蓝色的花; **their skin is ~er** 他们的肤色浅一些

C *vt* (*pt, pp* **lit** *or* **lighted**) **1** (illuminate) 照亮; **the headlamps lit the road ahead** 车头灯照亮了前方的路; **to ~ the way with a torch** 用手电筒照路 **2** (set fire to) 点燃; **to ~ a match/a bonfire** 划燃一根火柴/燃起篝火 **3** (switch on) 打开 ‹*light, torch, sign*›

D *vi* (*pt, pp* **lit** *or* **lighted**) 开始燃烧; **the oven won't ~** 炉子点不着

Phrasal verb

• **light up**

A *vt* [~ **up sth.**, ~ **sth. up**] **1** (illuminate) 照亮; **the shop windows were lit up** 商店橱窗灯火通明 **2** (set fire to) 点燃 ‹*cigarette, cigar, pipe*› **3** fig (make animated) 使发亮; **a rare smile lit up his stern features** 他严肃的面庞上露出了难得一见的笑容; **his face was lit up with happiness** 他脸上喜气洋洋

B *vi* **1** (become illuminated) «*light, panel*» 发光; **the lamps lit up** 灯亮了 **2** (light cigarette) 开始吸烟 **3** fig (become animated) 面露喜色; **she opened the present, and her face lit up** 她打开礼物, 面露喜色; **her eyes lit up with excitement** 她眼中闪着兴奋的光

light²

A *adj* **1** (not heavy) 轻的; **(as) ~ as a feather** 轻如羽毛 **2** (not great in amount) 少量的; (not great in intensity) 不猛烈的; **a ~ rain** 小雨; **~ mist** 薄雾; **the winds are much ~er today** 今天风小了许多; **the traffic was ~** 车辆稀少; **business has been fairly ~ recently** 最近生意相当清淡 **3** (made of thin material) 轻薄的 ‹*clothes*›; **~ canvas shoes** 轻便帆布鞋 **4** (small and manoeuvrable) 轻型的 ‹*machinery, vehicle, weapon*› **5** Agric 轻质的 ‹*soil*› **6** (easily disturbed) 不沉的 ‹*sleep*›; **I'm a ~ sleeper** 我睡觉容易醒 **7** (not loud) 轻声的; **a ~ knock on the door** 轻轻的敲门声 **8** (small) 少量的 ‹*meal*›; **a ~ snack** 小吃; **lunch was fairly ~** 午餐食品量很少 **9** (aerated, fluffy) 松软的 ‹*cake, pastry*› **10** (easy to digest) 清淡的 ‹*soup, sauce*› **11** (not tiring) 轻松的; **to take some ~ exercise** 做些运动量小的运动; **to make ~ work of sth./sb.** 轻而易举地做成某事/打败某人; **many hands make ~ work** Prov 人多好办事 **12** (graceful) 轻盈的 ‹*movement, step*›; (gentle) 轻柔的 ‹*touch, kiss*›; **a ~ tap** 轻轻的一拍; **to be ~ on one's feet** 步履轻快 **13** (not demanding) 消遣性的 ‹*reading*›; **a ~ programme** 娱乐性节目; **~ music** 轻音乐 **14** (not important) 不重要的; **to make ~ of sth.** 对某事物等闲视之; **he made ~ of his injury** 他不把自己的伤当回事 **15** (not severe) 不严厉的 ‹*punishment, criticism*›; 不严重的 ‹*cold, stomach upset*›; **to get a ~ sentence** 被轻判 **16** (cheerful) 轻松愉快的 ‹*mood*›

B *adv* **to travel ~** 轻装旅行

light³

Phrasal verb

• **light on, light upon** *vt* (*pt, pp* **lighted** *or* **lit**) [~ **on** *or* **upon sth.**] 偶然发现 ‹*object*›; **the detective's eyes ~ed on the revolver** 侦探无意中看见了那把左轮手枪

light: ~ ale *n* [u and c] 淡麦芽啤酒; **~ box** *n* 灯箱; **~ bulb** *n* 灯泡; **~-coloured** Brit *adj* 淡色的; **~-emitting diode** *n* 发光二极管

lighten¹ /ˈlaɪtn/

A *vt* **1** (make brighter) 照亮 ‹*room, sky, darkness*› **2** (make paler) 使…颜色变淡 ‹*hair, skin*›; 使…变淡 ‹*colour*›

B *vi* **1** (grow brighter) «*sky, darkness*» 变亮 **2** (grow paler) «*hair, skin*» 颜色变淡; «*colour*» 变淡

lighten²

A *vt* **1** (make less intense) 减轻 ‹*burden, workload, pressure*›; **the tax burden has been considerably ~ed** 税收负担减轻了很多 **2** (reduce weight of) 减轻…的重量 ‹*load, baggage, package*› **3** (make more cheerful) 缓和 ‹*atmosphere*›; 使愉悦 ‹*mood*›

B *vi* **1** (become less intense) «*burden, workload, pressure*» 减轻 **2** (become more cheerful) «*face, expression*» 露出喜色; «*atmosphere*» 缓和; «*mood*» 变愉快

Phrasal verb

• **lighten up** *vi* colloq 愉快起来; **~ up!** 开心点!

lightener /ˈlaɪtnə(r)/ *n* (for hair) 脱色剂; (for skin) 增白剂

light entertainment *n* [u] 轻娱乐

lighter /ˈlaɪtə(r)/ *n* **1** (for cigarette) (hand-held) 打火机; (in car) 点烟器 **2** (for gas cooker) 点火器

lighter: ~ fuel *n* [u] 打火机燃料; **~ socket** *n* 点烟器插座

light: ~-fingered *adj* 惯偷的; **a ~-fingered thief/pickpocket** 惯偷/惯扒; **~ fitting** *n* 灯具; **~-footed** *adj* 步态轻盈的 ‹*runner, dancer, animal*›; **~-haired** *adj* 淡色头发的 ‹*person*›; 淡色皮毛的 ‹*animal*›

light-headed *adj* **1** (dizzy) 眩晕的 ‹*person, feeling*›; **to feel ~** 感到头晕目眩 **2** (frivolous, absent-minded) 没头脑的 **3** (excited) 兴奋的; **to be ~ with sth.** 因某事物而兴奋

light-headedness *n* [u] 眩晕

light-hearted *adj* **1** (happy) 无忧无虑的 ‹*person, atmosphere, laughter*› **2** (not serious) 轻松的 ‹*remark, teasing, banter*›

light-heartedly *adv* **1** (happily) 无忧无虑地; **to ~ discuss a number of topics** 愉快地讨论许多话题 **2** (casually) 漫不经心地; **this is not to be done ~** 这事做起来马虎不得 **3** (jokily) 轻松地; **the songs are delivered ~** 这些歌曲唱得很随便

light-heavyweight

A *n* 轻重量级拳击手 [体重为75-81公斤]

B *modif* 轻重量级拳击的 ‹*bout, champion*›

lighthouse /ˈlaɪthaʊs/ *n* 灯塔

lighthouse keeper *n* 灯塔看守人

light industry *n* [u and c] 轻工业

lighting /ˈlaɪtɪŋ/ *n* [u] **1** (lights) 照明设备; (illumination) 灯光 **2** Theat 照明; Phot 布光

lighting: ~ director ▸**p. 409** *n* 灯光技术指导; **~ effects** *npl* 灯光效果; **~ engineer** ▸**p. 409** *n* 灯光师; **~-up time** *n* 规定开灯时间

lightly /ˈlaɪtli/ *adv* **1** (not heavily or excessively) 少许地 ‹*eat, season*›; 轻盈地 ‹*move, run, walk*›; **~ perfumed** 有淡淡香气的; **to sleep ~** 睡得不实; **to dress ~** 衣服穿得薄; **it began to snow ~** 开始下小雪了 **2** (gently, delicately) 轻轻地 ‹*kiss, tap, touch, knock*› **3** Culin 稍稍地 ‹*fry, toast, grilled*›; **a ~ boiled egg** 煮得很嫩的蛋 **4** Mil 以轻武器 ‹*armed, equipped*› **5** (frivolously) 轻率地 ‹*treat, decide, undertake*›; (casually) 随便地 ‹*dismiss, joke, say*› **6** colloq (with little punishment) **to get off ~** 只受轻罚; **to let sb. off ~** 从轻发落某人

light meter *n* 曝光表

lightness¹ /ˈlaɪtnɪs/ *n* [u] **1** (brightness) 明亮 **2** (paleness) 淡色

lightness² *n* [u] **1** (in weight) 轻; **the ~ of the parcel** 包裹之轻 **2** (of movement, touch) 轻盈

lightning /ˈlaɪtnɪŋ/

A *n* [u] (instance, phenomenon) 闪电; (striking sth.) 雷击; **a flash/blot of ~** 一道闪电; **like (a flash of) ~** *or* **as quick as ~** 飞快地 ‹*run, think*›; **like greased ~** *or* **a streak of ~** 一溜烟地 ‹*run*›; **to be struck by ~** 遭雷击; **~ never strikes twice in the same place** Prov 倒霉的事不会重复发生

B *adj attrib* 闪电般的 ‹*speed, response, raid, visit*›; 伴有雷电的 ‹*storm*›; 雷电造成的 ‹*damage*›

lightning: ~ bug *n* Amer 萤火虫; **~ conductor** Brit, **~ rod** Amer *ns* 避雷针; **~ strike** *n* Brit 闪电式罢工; **~ stroke** *n* Amer 一道闪电

light: ~ opera *n* [c and u] 轻歌剧; **~ pen** *n* **1** (for computer screen) 光笔; **2** (to read barcode) 条形码识读器; **~ railway** *n* 轻轨; **~ relief** *n* [u] (words) 缓和气氛的话; (actions) 缓和气氛的行为; **~-sensitive** *adj* 光敏的 ‹*film, paper*›; **~ship** *n* 灯船 [停泊在海中, 用以警示或导航]; **~ show** *n* 灯光表演; **~-skinned** *adj* 肤色浅的; **~ switch** *n* 电灯开关; **~ therapy** *n* [u] 光照疗法

lights /laɪts/ *npl* 牲畜肺脏

lights wave *n* 光波

lightweight /ˈlaɪtweɪt/

A *adj* **1** (lighter than average) 轻便的 ‹*suit, tent, camera, coat*› **2** fig pej (not serious) 无足轻重的 ‹*politician, newspaper*›

B *n* **1** Sport 轻量级拳击手 [体重为57-60公斤] **2** fig pej 无足轻重的人; **an intellectual ~** 才智平庸的人

C *modif* 轻量级拳击的 ‹*bout, champion*›

light year *n* **1** Astron (distance) 光年 **2** **light years** colloq fig (considerable distance) 极远的距离; (considerable time) 很长时间; (considerable amount) 极大的数量; **to be ~s ahead of sb.** 遥遥领

先于 ‹*rivals*›; **it was ~s ago** 那是很久很久以前了; **retirement seemed ~s away** 退休似乎遥遥无期

lignite /ˈlɪɡnaɪt/ *n* [u] 褐煤; **~ mine** 褐煤矿; **~ industry** 褐煤采矿业

like¹ /laɪk/

A *prep* **1** (similar to, resembling) 像; **to be ~ sb./sth.** 像某人/某物; **you know what she's ~!** 你知道她的为人了吧!; **what's the film ~?** 那部电影怎么样?; **it looks ~ rain** 看样子要下雨了; **it seemed ~ hours** 似乎过了好几个小时 **2** (in the manner of) 像…一样; **she spoke ~ an aristocrat** 她说起话来像个贵族; **~ me, she loves swimming** 她像我一样喜欢游泳; **it happened ~ this ...** 事情是这样的…; **don't talk ~ that!** 不许那么说话! **3** (typical of) 符合…的特点; **that's just ~ him!** 他就是这么一个人!; **it's not ~ her to be late** 她才不会迟到呢; **~ father, ~ son** 有其父必有其子 **4** (close to, approximately) 大约; **it will cost something ~ £100** 这大概要花 100 英镑; **it'll cost more ~ £200** 更确切地说, 这要花差不多 200 英镑; **he's called Rufus or Rudolph or something ~ that** 他好像叫鲁弗斯或鲁道夫之类的名字 **5** (such as, for example) 例如; **big countries ~ India** 印度这类大国; **the basic necessities of life ~ food and drink** 诸如食物和饮料之类的基本生活必需品

B *adj attrib* 类似的; **people of ~ minds** 志趣相投的人; **eating, drinking, and ~ activities** 吃喝之类的活动; **to be of ~ mind on this issue** 在这个问题上意见一致

C *conj* **1** (in the same way as) 像…一样; **do it ~ I do** 照我的做; **you don't know him ~ I do** 你不像我那么了解他; **~ I said, I wasn't there** 正如我说过的, 我当时不在那儿; **to tell it ~ it is** 实话实说 **2** colloq (as if) 好像; **he behaved ~ he was afraid** 他表现得好像很害怕; **it looks ~ it's going to rain** 看起来像要下雨

D *adv* **1** (nearly) 差不多; **the sequel is nothing ~ as good as the original** 续集远远不如原作; **if it's anything ~ as cold as today ...** 要是像今天这样冷…; **more ~** colloq 倒更像是; **champagne? sparkling wine, more ~!** colloq 香槟? 倒更像是汽酒吧! **2** colloq (so to speak) 可以说; **I felt embarrassed, ~** 可以这么说, 我觉得尴尬; **it was, ~, Christmas, so we wanted to have some fun** 这么说吧, 那天是圣诞节, 所以我们想找点乐子

E *n* **1** (similar thing) 类似的事物; (similar person) 类似的人; **did you ever see the ~ (of it)?** 你见过这种东西吗?; **and the** *or* **such ~** 诸如此类; **judges, lawyers, and the ~** 法官、律师等人士; **the ~ of which** 如此这般; **to compare ~ with ~** 同类相比; **the ~s of ...** …之类; **she doesn't associate with the ~s of us!** colloq 她才不愿意跟我们这种人扯在一起! **2** (something liked) 爱好; **sb.'s ~s and dislikes** 某人的好恶

like² *vt* **1** (find agreeable) 喜欢; **the boss won't ~ it if you're late** 你要是迟到, 老板会不高兴的; **he is well ~d by his colleagues** 他的同事都很喜欢他; **to ~ swimming/to swim** 喜欢游泳; **if the manager ~s the look of you** 如果经理喜欢你的长相; **well, I ~ that!** iron 哦, 说得好啊!; **I ~ his cheek** *or* **nerve!** 亏他说得出口!; **~ it or not** 不管喜欢与否; **~ it or lump it** 不管你高兴与否 **2** (want) 想要; **I would** *or* **should ~ some coffee, please** 请给我来点咖啡; **I ~ people to be punctual** 我希望人们守时; **to ~ to do sth.** 想做某事; **I don't ~ to disturb her** 我不想打扰她; **if you ~** (willingly agreeing) 你要是愿意的话; (reluctantly agreeing) 也可以这么说; (when making suggestion) 如果你愿意的话; (as possibility) 可以说; **it's a change, an improvement if you ~** 那是一种变革, 也可以说是一种进步; **if you ~ that kind** *or* **sort of thing** 如果你想要那种玩意儿的话; **as you ~** 随你的便; **just as you ~, sir/madam** 请便, 先生/女士; **he can say what he ~s, I won't change my mind** 让他随便说去吧, 我不会改变主意的

likeable /ˈlaɪkəbl/ *adj* 讨人喜欢的 ‹*person, animal*›; 感动人的 ‹*character, lead*›; 好看的 ‹*film, novel*›; 好听的 ‹*music*›; 好喝的 ‹*wine*›

like-for-like *adj* 同比的; **~ sales/growth** 同比销售额/增长

likelihood /ˈlaɪklɪhʊd/ *n* [u] 可能性; **in all ~** 十有八九; **the ~ is that ...** 很可能…; **there is some/little/no ~ of peace** 和平是有些可能的/几乎没有可能的/没有可能的; **to increase/reduce the ~ of his finding out** 增大/降低他发现的可能性

likely /ˈlaɪkli/

A *adj* **1** *attrib* (probable) 可信的 ‹*outcome, explanation, reason*›; 可望成功的 ‹*candidate*›; **a ~ story** *or* **tale!** colloq iron 说得倒像煞有介事!; **a ~ excuse!** colloq iron 真是个好借口!; **he is the ~ thief/victim** 他应该就是窃贼/受害者 **2** *pred* (expected) 可能的; **to be ~ to do sth.** 有可能做某事; **it is/seems ~ that ...** …是/似乎是可能的 **3** *attrib* (promising) 合适的 ‹*place, hotel, location*›; (potential) 潜在的 ‹*client, customer*›; **she looks like a ~ buyer** 她看似有意购买; **the likeliest river for fishing** 最适合捕鱼的河流

B *adv* 很可能地; **as ~ as not, it will rain** 天很可能下雨; **not ~!** Brit colloq 决不可能!

like-minded *adj* 志趣相投的

liken /ˈlaɪkən/ *vt* **to ~ sb./sth. to ...** 把某人/某事物比作…

likeness /ˈlaɪknɪs/ *n* **1** [c and u] (similarity) 相像; **family ~** 家庭成员的相像; **to bear a ~ to ...** 与…相像 **2** [c] (picture, painting) 画像; (photo) 照片; **to be a true** *or* **good ~** ‹*photo, painting*› 很像; **he has caught the ~** (in painting) 他画得很逼真; (in photo) 他拍的照片很像

likewise /ˈlaɪkwaɪz/ *adv* **1** (similarly) 同样地; **I'm leaving and I suggest you do ~** 我要走了, 建议你也走; **~, students feel that ...** 学生们同样感到… **2** (also) 也; **I'm well and my parents ~** 我很好, 我父母也是; **pleased to meet you! — ~** 很高兴见到你——我也是!

liking /ˈlaɪkɪŋ/ *n* [u] 喜爱; **to take a ~ to sb./sth.** 对某人/某物产生好感; **to have/develop a ~ for ...** 喜爱/喜欢上…; **to be to sb.'s ~** 中某人的意; **this will be more to your ~** 这会更合你意的; **he's too smart for my ~** 他太精明, 我不喜欢

lilac /ˈlaɪlək/

A *n* **1** [c and u] (bush) 丁香 **2** [u] (blossom) 丁香花

B ▸**p. 134** *adj* 淡紫色的

lilo, Li-lo® /ˈlaɪləʊ/ *n* 气垫

lilt /lɪlt/ *n* **1** (of tune) 轻快旋律 **2** (of accent) 抑扬顿挫; **to have a Scottish ~** 讲话带抑扬顿挫的苏格兰口音

lilting /ˈlɪltɪŋ/ *adj* 轻快的 ‹*music, voice, sound*›

lily /ˈlɪli/ *n* (plant) 百合; (flower) 百合花

lily: ~-livered *adj* pej 胆怯的 ‹*person, actions*›; **~ of the valley** *n* 铃兰; **~ pad** *n* 睡莲的漂浮叶; **~ pond** *n* 睡莲池; **~-white** *adj* 白皙的 ‹*skin, cheeks, hand*›

Lima /ˈliːmə/ *pr n* 利马

lima bean /ˈliːmə biːn, Amer ˈlaɪmə/ *n* 利马豆

limb /lɪm/ *n* **1** (of human, animal) 肢体; **fore/hind/upper/lower ~** 前/后/上/下肢; **to stretch one's ~s** 舒展四肢 **2** (of tree) 主枝; **to be** *or* **go out on a ~** (not supported by others) 使自己孤立无援; (take different view to the majority) 与大多数人观点相左; **to tear sb. ~ from ~** (dismember) 肢解某人; fig (criticize severely) 猛烈抨击某人

limber up /ˌlɪmbərˈʌp/

A *vi* 做准备活动

B *vt* 活动 ‹*arms, legs, fingers*›

limbic system /ˈlɪmbɪk ˌsɪstəm/ *n* 大脑边缘系统

limbless /ˈlɪmlɪs/ *adj* 无四肢的 ‹*person, body*›; 无枝桠的 ‹*tree*›

limbo /ˈlɪmbəʊ/ *n* [u] **1** (state of uncertainty) 待定状态; (state of neglect or isolation) 被遗忘状态; **to be in (a state of) ~** ‹‹*affairs, case*›› 尚待决定; **he found himself in political ~** 他发现自己在政治上被孤立了 **2** (dance) [西印度群岛的] 林波舞

limbo: ~ dancer *n* 跳林波舞的人; **~ dancing** *n* [u] 跳林波舞

lime¹ /laɪm/ *n* **1** [c and u] (citrus fruit) 酸橙 **2** [c] (citrus tree) 酸橙树 **3** [u] (drink) 酸橙汁饮料

lime²

A *n* [u] **1** (quicklime) 生石灰 **2** (slaked lime) 熟石灰

B *vt* 给…撒石灰 ‹*soil*›; 在…上涂粘鸟胶 ‹*twigs, branches*›

lime³ *n* (linden tree) 椴树

lime: ~-green ▸**p. 134** *n, adj* 酸橙绿的; **~ juice** *n* [u] 酸橙汁; **~ kiln** *n* 石灰窑

limelight /ˈlaɪmlaɪt/ *n* [u] **1** (on stage) 聚光灯; **to be in the ~** 在聚光灯的照射下 **2** (the centre of attention) 公众注意的中心; **to be in/out of the ~** 为/不为公众瞩目; **to avoid** *or* **shun the ~** 避免引人注目; **to hog the ~** pej 出风头

limerick /ˈlɪmərɪk/ *n* 五行打油诗

lime: ~scale *n* [u] Brit 水垢; **~stone** *n* [u] 石灰岩; **~ tree** *n* (citrus) 酸橙树; (linden) 椴树

Limey /ˈlaɪmi/ Amer, Austral colloq

A *n* (*pl* **~s**) 英国佬

B *adj* 英国的

limit /ˈlɪmɪt/

A *n* **1** (maximum extent) 极限; **to go to any ~s (to do sth.)** 竭尽全力(做某事); **he has pushed my patience to the** *or* **its ~s** 他已让我忍无可忍了; **this is/you're the ~!** colloq 太过分了/你太过分了! **2** (legal restriction) 限制; **height ~** 限高; **public spending ~s** 公共开支限额; **safety ~s** (人体)安全限值; **to be over/under the ~** 超出/未超出限制; **to do sth. within ~s** 在一定限度内做某事 **3** (boundary) (of territory, universe) 边界; (of power, science) 界限; (of enclosed area) 范围; **to do sth. within (the) ~s** 在能力范围内做某事; **to be beyond the ~(s) of experience** 超出经验; **to be off ~s (to the public)** 不(对公众)开放; **my private life is off ~s** fig 禁止谈论我的私生活

B *vt* 限制; **to be ~ed to doing sth.** 仅限于做某事; **we must ~ our budget to £100** 我们必须把预算控制在 100 英镑以内

C *v refl* **to ~ oneself to ...** 把自己限制在…之内 ‹*amount, quantity*›; **he ~s himself to one cup of tea per day** 他限定自己每天只喝一杯茶

limitation /ˌlɪmɪˈteɪʃn/ *n* **1** (restriction) 限制; **a ~ on sth.** 对某事物的限制; **to impose** *or* **place ~s on sth.** 对…加以限制 ‹*right, freedom, power*› **2** (shortcoming) 局限; **to know one's (own) ~s** 清楚自己的短处

limited /ˈlɪmɪtɪd/ *adj* **1** (small, poor or inadequate) 有限的 ‹*space*›; (in short supply) 限量的; (restricted) 受限的; **to be of ~ ability/intelligence** 能力/才智有限; **there is only a ~ number of these cars available** 这些车中仅有一些可用; **these flowers are ~ to the south of Spain** 这些花仅生长在西班牙南部 **2** Brit (in company names) 有限责任的

limited: ~ company *n* Brit 有限责任公司; **~ edition** *n* 限定版; **~ liability company** *n* Brit 有限责任公司

limitless /ˈlɪmɪtlɪs/ *adj* 无边的 ‹*ocean, horizon, view*›; 无限的 ‹*wealth, power, patience*›

limo /ˈlɪməʊ/ *n* (*pl* **~s**) colloq = **limousine**

limousine /ˈlɪməziːn, ˌlɪməˈziːn/ *n* 豪华轿车; **an airport ~** 机场客车

limp[1] /lɪmp/ *adj* **1** (not stiff or firm) 无力的 ‹*body, hand, handshake*›; **to let oneself/one's arm go ～** 浑身松松垮垮/手臂耷拉着 **2** (without vigour) 无精神的 ‹*person*›; 蔫的 ‹*vegetable, flower*›; 无生气的 ‹*literary style*›

limp[2]

A *vt* **1** (walk with difficulty) «*person, animal*» 跛行 **2** (proceed with difficulty) «*vessel, vehicle*» 艰难行驶; **we ～ed back to port** 我们艰难地返回了港口

B *n* [u] 跛行; **to walk with** *or* **have a ～** 走路一瘸一拐; **to have a slight ～ in one's left leg** 左腿稍微有点跛

limpet /ˈlɪmpɪt/ *n* 帽贝

limpet mine *n* 附着水雷

limpid /ˈlɪmpɪd/ *adj* **1** (clear, unclouded) 清澈的 ‹*water*›; 明亮的 ‹*eyes*› **2** (lucid) 清晰顺畅的 ‹*style, writing*›

limply /ˈlɪmpli/ *adv* 无力地 ‹*move, speak*›

limp-wristed /ˌlɪmpˈrɪstɪd/ *adj* colloq pej 女人气的

linchpin /ˈlɪntʃpɪn/ *n* **1** Mech, Civ Eng 制轮楔 **2** fig (person) 关键人物; (thing) 关键因素; **the ～ of the organization/government** 组织/政府的支柱

Lincolnshire /ˈlɪŋkənʃɪə(r)/ *pr n* 林肯郡

Lincs. *abbr* Brit = **Lincolnshire**

linctus /ˈlɪŋktəs/ *n* (*pl* **～es**) Brit 润喉止咳糖浆; **cough/throat ～** 止咳/润喉糖浆

line[1] /laɪn/

A *n* **1** (mark made by pen, paintbrush, etc.) 线; (mark occurring naturally) 纹; **a curved/broken/double ～** 曲线/虚线/双线; **to put a ～ through sth.** 在某物上划一条线; **paper with ～s** 横格纸; **dots and ～s on a butterfly's wing** 蝴蝶翅膀上的斑点和纹路 **2** Aut 交通指示线; **a single white/yellow ～** 单白线/单黄线 **3** Sport 场地线; **the start/finish ～** 起跑/终点线; **to be the first off the ～** 起跑速度最快 **4** (indentation) 线状凹痕; **an engraved ～** 刻线 **5** (wrinkle) (on face) 皱纹; (on palm of hand) 掌纹 **6** TV 行 **7** (general shape) (of face, ship, car, building) 轮廓; (of skirt, trousers) 线条; **sb.'s slender ～s** 某人苗条的身材 **8** fig (notional limit) 界线; **to divide along political ～s** 按照政治界线划分; **the (dividing) ～ between ...** …之间的（分）界线; **the ～ where the sea meets the sky** 海天相接处的地平线 **9** (row) 排; **a ～ of sth.** 一排 ‹*trees, lampposts, hills*›; **a double ～ of stitching** 双排针脚; **a ～ of people queuing** 排队的一行人; **in straight ～s** 成直线排列 ‹*plant, arrange, sit*›; **to stand in** *or* **form a ～** 站成一排; **to be in/out of ～** 成/不成直线; **to put** *or* **place sth. in ～** 将某物摆放成一排; **to be in ～ with sth.** 与某物在一条直线上; **to get (back) into ～** （重新）列队 **10** (conformity) 一致; **in ～** 一致的; **to be in/out of ～ (with sth./sb.)** （与某事物/某人）一致/不一致; **to keep sb./sth. in ～** 使某人/某事物保持一致; **the teacher kept the class in ～** 这位老师把班里的学生管得规规矩矩的; **to bring sth./sb. into ～ (with sth./sb.)** 使某事物/某人（与某事物/某人）一致; **to come** *or* **fall** *or* **move** *or* **get into ～ (with sth./sb.)** （与某事物/某人）取得一致; **if the children get out of ～, ...** 如果孩子们不守规矩，…; **she'll come back into ～ (with our way of thinking)** 她会接受（我们的想法）的; **his behaviour is/you're out of ～** colloq 他的行为太离谱/你太过分了; **to step out of ～** 出轨 **11** Amer (queue) 队; **a ～ of people** 一队人; **to stand** *or* **wait in ～** 排队; **to be second in ～** 排队站在第二; **to cut the ～** 插队 **12** (order of precedence) 顺序; **～ of precedence/succession** 优先/继承顺序; **to be first in ～ to the throne/for promotion** 是王位的第一继承人/是晋升的第一人选 **13** (in genealogy) 家族; **to found** *or* **establish a ～** 建立家族; **the male/female ～** (ancestors) 男性/女性祖先; (descendants) 男性/女性后裔; **the Tudor ～** 都铎王朝; **a long ～ of Republican presidents** 历届共和党总统; **the royal ～** 皇族; **～ of descent** 后代; **to trace one's (family) ～ back to sb.** 家谱追溯到某人; **to trace a ～ down to sb.** 家族延续至某人; **to come from a (long) ～ of ...** 出身于…世家 ‹*doctors, miners*› **14** Ind 生产线; **the workers on the (production) ～** 生产线上的工人; **to roll off the ～s** «*products*» 下线 **15** Mil 防线; **the Maginot L～** 马其诺防线; **behind enemy ～s** 在敌后 **16** (in prose) 行; (in verse) 诗句; (in music) 乐句; **page 5, ～ 3** 第 5 页，第 3 行; **to give sb. 200 ～s** Brit 罚某人抄写句子 200 遍; **to miss a ～** 漏一行; **to start a new ～** 重起一行; **a ～ of verse** *or* **poetry** 一行诗; **the opening ～ of her speech** 她演讲的开场白 **17** Theat 台词; **to learn one's ～s** 背诵台词; **a throwaway ～** 信口说出的台词 **18** colloq (in letters) 便条; **to write a few ～s about sth.** 简单写几句谈谈某事; **just a ～ to say thanks** 只是一张致谢的留言条 **19** Mus 旋律; **the treble/bass ～** 高音/低音旋律 **20** Fishg 钓鱼线; **to cast one's ～** 抛钓钩 **21** (rope, wire, etc.) 绳子; **to throw sb. a ～** 把绳子抛给某人; **to hang sth. on the ～ to dry** 把某物挂在晾衣绳上晾干 **22** Telecom (cable) 电话线; (link) 通讯线路; **the ～s are down/out of order** 电话线断了/出故障了; **to have a direct ～ to sb.** 可与某人直接通话; **the ～ is dead/engaged** 线路不通/占线; **this is a terrible ～** 线路通话质量很糟; **dial 9 to get an outside ～** 按 9 拨打外线; **to give sb. a ～** «*switchboard operator*» 为某人转接电话; **to have sb. on the ～** 让某人不挂断电话; **to get on/off the ～** colloq 接通/挂断电话; **to be on the ～ to sb.** 在和某人通话; **at the other end of the ～** 在电话的另一端; **a crossed ～** 串线的电话; **to hold the ～** 不挂断电话 **23** Elec 电缆 **24** Electron 电子信号线 **25** (pipe) 管道; **an oil/a gas ～** 输油管/天然气管道 **26** Rail (track) 铁路; (system) 铁路线; **repairs to the ～** 铁路保养; **to stop at every station along the ～** «*train, express*» 沿途各站均停靠; **the Shanghai-Nanjing ～** 沪宁线 **27** (route, course) 路线; **in straight ～s** 沿直线; **the ～ of flight of a projectile** 抛射物的飞行轨道; **～ of vision** 视线; **to be in sb.'s ～ of vision** 在某人的视线内; **～ of sight** 视线; **to be in ～ for sth.** (be likely to get sth.) 有望获得某物; (be a candidate for sth.) 有望就任某职位; **he's in ～ for redundancy** 他很可能被解雇 **28** fig (direction) 方式; **～ of investigation/thought/development** 调查/思维/发展方式; **～ of research/reasoning/argument** 研究/推理/论证方法; **what's your ～ of thinking here?** 你有什么看法?; **all along the ～** 完全地; **(right) down the ～** (affecting all people or things) 彻底地; (happening all the time) 始终; **somewhere along the ～** (in time) 不知何时; (in place) 不知何处; **along** *or* **on the ～s of sth.** 类似某物的; **along** *or* **on these/those ～s** 像这些/那些的; **to do sth. along** *or* **on traditional/familiar/the same ～s** 按照传统/类似/同样模式做某事; **her theory ran along the following ～s: ...** 她的理论如下: …; **on the right ～s** 接近正确 **29** (stance) 态度; **the Party ～** 党的方针; **a ～ on sth.** 对某事的态度; **to take a hard/firm/similar ～ (with sb./on sth.)** （对某人/某事物）采取强硬/坚决/类似的立场 **30** (type of work) 行业; **～ of business** *or* **work** 行业 **31** (profession) 专业; **to be (in) sb.'s ～** (suit sb.'s skills and interests) 与某人专业对口; (be enjoyable) 为某人所喜爱 **32** Comm (product) 产品; (range of products) 产品系列; **a ～ in sth.** 某类产品 **33** (type, kind of thing) 种类; **something in the sports ～/in that ～** 体育用品/那类东西 **34** colloq (piece of information) 消息; **to have/get a ～ on sb./sth.** 有/得到关于某人/某事物的消息; **to give sb. a ～ on** *or* **about sb./sth.** 告诉某人关于某人/某事物的信息; **don't give me that ～!** 别找借口了! **35** **to be on the ～** (at risk) 面临危险; (at issue) 受到争议

B *vt* **1** (stand along) 沿…排列成行 ‹*wall, street, room*›; **to be ～d with trees/cars/spectators** «*route, avenue*» 两边树木成行/沿途车辆川流不息/两边观众成排 **2** (mark with lines) 在…上画线 ‹*paper, pad*›; **a ～d exercise book/notebook** 横格练习本/笔记本 **3** (mark with wrinkles) 使…起皱纹 ‹*face, forehead, skin*›; **～d hands** 布满皱纹的手; **to be ～d with sth.** 因…而起皱纹 ‹*age, worry*›

Phrasal verb

- **line up**

A *vt* **1** [**～ sb./sth. up, ～ up sb./sth.**] (side by side) 使排成行; (one behind the other) 使排成列; **to be ～d up** 排成队 **2** **to ～ sth. up (with sth.)** (align) 使某物（与某物）对齐; **to be ～d up (with sth.)** （与某物）对齐 **3** **to ～ sb./sth. up (for sth./sb.)** (arrange) （为某人/某事物）安排 ‹*performer, speaker, task*›; (organize) （为某人/某事物）组织 ‹*event, project*›; (prepare) （为某人/某事物）准备 ‹*questions*›; **to have a lot ～d up for this week/next term** 把这星期/下学期安排得很满

B *vi* **1** (side by side) 排成行; (one behind the other) 排成列; **～ up!** 列队!; **to ～ up for inspection** «*soldiers*» 列队接受检阅; **to ～ up in rows/teams** 排成数排/数队 **2** esp Amer (queue) «*people, cars*» 排队 **3** (take sides) «*people, group, nation*» 联合起来; **to ～ up alongside** *or* **with sb./sth.** 站在某人/某事物一边; **to ～ up behind sb./sth.** 联合起来支持某人/某事物; **to ～ up against sb./sth.** 联合起来反对某人/某事物

line[2] /laɪn/ *vt* (add layer of material to) 给…加内衬; **to ～ sth. with sth.** 用某物给某物加衬; **to ～ the walls and ceilings** 贴墙和天花板; **to be ～d with books** «*wall, room*» 摆满书

lineage /ˈlɪnɪɪdʒ/ *n* 家系; **of noble** *or* **proud ～** 有贵族血统的; **to trace one's ～ to sb.** 宗谱追溯到某人

lineal /ˈlɪnɪəl/ *adj* 直系的 ‹*succession*›; **～ descent from sb.** 某人的直系后裔

linear /ˈlɪnɪə(r)/ *adj* 直线的; **～ pattern/design** 线条花纹/图案; **～ relationship/sequence** 直系关系/线性顺序

linear equation *n* 线性方程

lined /laɪnd/ *adj* **1** (marked with lines) 有皱纹的 ‹*face, skin, hands*›; **～ paper** 横格纸 **2** (faced with material) 带衬里的

line: **～ dance** *n* 队列舞; **～-dance** *vi* 跳队列舞; **～ dancer** *n* 跳队列舞者; **～ dancing** *n* [u] 跳队列舞; **～ drawing** *n* 线条画; **～ feed** *n* [u] 换行; **～-item veto** *n* Amer 单项条款否决权; **～ judge** *n* 边线裁判员; **～man** /-mən/ ▸ **p. 409** *n* **1** Rail 巡线工人; **2** Amer Elec, Telecom 架线工; **3** Amer Sport［美式橄榄球］线上球员; **～-manage** *vt* 分线管理; **～ management** *n* [u] 部门经理层; **～ manager** *n* 部门经理

linen /ˈlɪnɪn/

A *n* [u] **1** (fabric) 亚麻布; **to wear ～** 穿亚麻衣服 **2** (household items) 日用织品; (underwear) 内衣裤; **to change the bed ～** 换床单; **to wash sb.'s dirty ～ in public** fig 外扬家丑

B *modif* 亚麻纺织的 ‹*industry*›; 亚麻布的 ‹*jacket, sheet*›

linen: **～ basket** *n* 待洗衣物筐; **～ closet** *n* Amer 家用织品壁橱; **～ cupboard** *n* esp Brit 家用织品壁橱

line: **～ of argument** *n* 一系列理由; **～ of attack** *n* lit 进攻路线; fig 解决问题的方式; **～ of credit** *n* 信贷最高限额; **～ of descent** *n* 家族谱系; **～ of duty** *n* **in the ～ of duty** 在执行公务过程中; **to be killed in the ～ of duty** 殉职; **～ of fire** *n* 发射线; **in the ～ of fire** 在发射线内; **～ of flight** *n* 飞行线; **～ of latitude** *n* 纬线; **～ of longitude** *n* 经线; **～ of**

l

thought *n* 思路; ~ **of vision** *n* 视线; **in** *or* **within/out of one's ~ of vision** 在视线内/外; ~ **of work** *n* 行业; **we are in the same ~ of work** 我们是同行; **~-out** *n* 界外球; ~ **printer** *n* 行式打印机

liner¹ /ˈlaɪnə(r)/ *n* (ship) 邮轮

liner² *n* **1** (disposable protective layer) 衬套; **black plastic bin ~s** 黑色塑料垃圾袋 **2** (of pipe, chimney, etc.) 衬里

linesman /ˈlaɪnzmən/ *n* Brit **1** (in tennis) 司线员; (in football, hockey) 边线裁判员 **2** ▸**p. 409** Elec, Telecom 架线工

line-spacing *n* 行间距

line-up *n* **1** (of sports team, pop group) 阵容 **2** (personnel) 团队; **the management ~** 全体管理人员 **3** (list of acts, programmes etc.) 系列节目; **a ~ of cabaret acts** 卡巴莱歌舞系列表演 **4** (identification parade) 列队认人; **a police ~** 嫌疑犯列队认人 **5** Amer (queue) 排队

ling /lɪŋ/ *n* 石南

linger /ˈlɪŋɡə(r)/ *vi* «*person, gaze*» 逗留; «*smell, suspicion*» 留存; **she ~ed beside the grave** 她在墓旁徘徊; **let your eyes ~ over the view** 慢慢欣赏美景吧; **he ~ed for another few weeks** 他又拖了几个星期; **the painful memory ~ed (on) for years** 痛苦的记忆延续了多年; **doubt still ~ed in his mind** 他仍然心存疑虑

Phrasal verb

- **linger over** *vt* [~ **over sth.**] 缓慢做; **they ~ed over their meal** 他们慢条斯理地吃饭

lingerie /ˈlænʒəriː, Amer ˌlɑːndʒəˈreɪ/ *n* [u] 女式内衣

lingering /ˈlɪŋɡərɪŋ/ *adj* **1** (residual) 存留的 ‹*scent, doubt, memory*›; 持续的 ‹*pain, decline*›; ~ **regret/fear** 余恨/余悸 **2** (slow) 拖延的; **a painful, ~ death** 痛苦而缓慢的死亡

lingo /ˈlɪŋɡəʊ/ *n* colloq 语言

lingua franca /ˌlɪŋɡwə ˈfræŋkə/ *n* 通用语

linguist /ˈlɪŋɡwɪst/ *n* **1** (sb. who studies languages) 语言学家 **2** (sb. who is skilled in languages) 通晓多种语言的人; **I'm no ~** 我不擅长学语言

linguistic /lɪŋˈɡwɪstɪk/ *adj* 语言的 ‹*minority, diversity, community*›; ~ **ability** 语言能力; ~ **borrowing** 外来词

linguistics /lɪŋˈɡwɪstɪks/
A *npl + v sing* 语言学
B *modif* 语言学的 ‹*course, lecturer, student*›

liniment /ˈlɪnɪmənt/ *n* [u] 止痛搽剂

lining /ˈlaɪnɪŋ/ *n* **1** (for garment, bag) 衬里; ▸**cloud A1** **2** Physiol 内膜; **the ~ of the womb** 子宫内膜 **3** Aut 制动鼓衬层

lining paper *n* (for decorating) 衬纸; (for shelves) 衬纸板

link /lɪŋk/
A *n* **1** (of chain) 环 **2** Transp 交通路线; **a road/rail ~ between A and B** A 地与 B 地之间的公路/铁路交通; **an air/a bus ~** 航线/公交线; **a fixed ~** 英吉利海峡隧道 **3** Telecom, Radio 通讯联系; **a TV/telephone ~** 电视频道/电话线路; **a ~ by satellite to Shanghai** 与上海的卫星连线 **4** (between nations, companies, etc.) 关系; **to forge ~s between ... and ...** 在…与…之间建立关系; **to break off** *or* **sever/renew/strengthen ~s with ...** 断绝/恢复/加强与…的关系; **to have ~s with terrorist groups** 勾结恐怖组织 **5** (connection between facts, events) 联系; **the ~ between A and B** A 与 B 之间的联系; **to be the weak ~ in ...** 是…的薄弱环节 ‹*team, plan, argument*› **6** Comput 链接
B *vt* **1** (connect physically) 连接 ‹*place, machine*›; 挽住 ‹*hand, arm*›; **to ~ A to B** *or* **A with B** *or* **A and B** 连接 A 和 B; **to be ~ed by ...** 通过…连接 ‹*bus, bridge, cable*›; **five ~ed circles** 五连环 **2** (establish connection between) 联系 ‹*facts, events*›; **the crimes are ~ed** 这些犯罪活动互相关联; **evidence ~ing sb. to sth.** 把某人与某事物联系起来的证据; **they are romantically ~ed** 他们恋爱了 **3** Comput 连接 ‹*computers, server*›; **to ~ sth. to** *or* **with sth.** 把某物与某物连接 **4** TV, Radio 给…建立通讯联系 ‹*places*›; **to be ~ed to Moscow by satellite** 通过卫星与莫斯科联络

Phrasal verb

- **link up**
A *vi* **to ~ up with sth./sb.** «*person, company*» 与某处/某人联系; «*army*» 与某队伍/某人汇合; **to ~ up with** 与…取得联系 ‹*person, city, space station*›
B *vt* [~ **up sth./sb.,** ~ **sth./sb. up**] 连接 ‹*computers, cities, people, networks*›

linkage /ˈlɪŋkɪdʒ/ *n* **1** [u] (between ideas, events) 联系 **2** [c] (in machine) 联动装置

link: ~man /-mæn/ *n* 串联节目男主持; ~ **road** *n* Brit 连接路

links /lɪŋks/ *npl + v sing* 高尔夫球场

link-up /ˈlɪŋkʌp/ *n* 连接; **a satellite ~** 卫星连线; **a ~ with ...** 与…的结合

linkwoman /ˈlɪŋkwʊmən/ *n* 串联节目女主持

linnet /ˈlɪnɪt/ *n* 赤胸朱顶雀

lino /ˈlaɪnəʊ/ *n* [u] 油地毡

linocut *n* [c and u] 油毡浮雕图案

linoleum /lɪˈnəʊlɪəm/ *n* [u] 油地毡

lino print *n* 油毡浮雕图案

linseed /ˈlɪnsiːd/ *n* [u] 亚麻籽

linseed oil *n* [u] 亚麻籽油

lint /lɪnt/ *n* [u] **1** Med 卫生纱布 **2** esp Amer (fluff) 棉绒

lintel /ˈlɪntl/ *n* 过梁

lion /ˈlaɪən/ *n* **1** 狮子; **the ~'s den** lit 狮穴; fig 绝境; **to put one's head into the ~'s mouth** fig 有把握地冒险; **the ~'s share (of sth.)** fig (某物) 最大的一份; **to twist the ~'s tail** *or* **the ~ by his tail** fig 出其不意地骚扰强敌 **2** fig (person) 名人; **a literary ~** 文豪

lion cub *n* 幼狮

lioness /ˈlaɪənes/ *n* 母狮

lion: ~hearted *adj* 勇敢的; ~ **hunter** *n* lit 猎狮者; fig pej 攀附名流者

lionize /ˈlaɪənaɪz/ *vt* 把…视为名人

lion tamer ▸**p. 409** *n* 驯狮员

lip /lɪp/ *n* **1** [c] Anat 嘴唇; **to kiss sb. on the ~s** 吻某人的嘴唇; **to read sb.'s ~s** 唇读某人的话; **read my ~s!** 不要非让我把难听的话说出来!; **the name on everyone's ~s** fig 大家都在谈论的人; **my ~s are sealed!** fig 我不会说出来的!; **to bite one's ~** fig (hold back one's tears) 忍住眼泪; (hold back one's words) 忍住要说的话; **to smack one's ~s at ...** 对…垂涎; **to go** *or* **pass from ~ to ~** «*story, news*» 流传开来; **to keep a stiff upper ~** fig 坚定沉着 **2** [c] (of cup, basin, crater) 边缘; (of jug) 口 **3** [u] colloq (insolence, cheek) 傲慢无礼的话; **to give sb. ~** 顶撞某人; **enough of your ~!** 不得无礼!

lip gloss *n* [u and c] 唇彩

lipid /ˈlɪpɪd/ *n* 脂质

liposuction /ˈlaɪpəʊsʌkʃn, ˈlɪpəʊ-/ *n* [u] 脂肪抽吸术

lippy /ˈlɪpi/
A *adj* 傲慢无礼的 ‹*teenager, trainee, recruit*›; **don't get ~ with me!** 不许跟我顶嘴!
B *n* [u and c] colloq 口红

lip: ~-read *vi* 唇读; **~-reader** *n* 唇语者; **~-reading** *n* [u] 唇读法; **~salve** *n* [u and c] Brit 护唇膏; ~ **service** *n* [u] 空口的应酬话; **to pay ~ service to ...** 仅仅口头支持 ‹*human rights, equality, feminism*›; **~stick** *n* [u and c] 口红

lip-sync /ˈlɪpsɪŋk/
A *vi* 对口型
B *vt* 对口型说 ‹*speech*›; 对口型唱 ‹*song, lyrics*›

liquefaction /ˌlɪkwɪˈfækʃn/ *n* [u] 液化

liquefied petroleum gas /ˈlɪkwɪfaɪd/ *n* [u] 液化石油气

liquefy /ˈlɪkwɪfaɪ/
A *vt* 使…液化 ‹*solid, gas*›
B *vi* «*solid, gas*» 液化

liqueur /lɪˈkjʊə(r), Amer -ˈkɜːr/ *n* [u and c] 烈性甜酒

liqueur: ~ brandy *n* [u and c] 白兰地甜酒; ~ **chocolate** *n* [u and c] 酒心巧克力; ~ **coffee** *n* [u and c] 掺酒咖啡; ~ **glass** *n* 甜酒杯

liquid /ˈlɪkwɪd/
A *n* **1** (substance) 液体 **2** Phon 流音
B *adj* **1** (fluid) 液态的 ‹*wax*›; ~ **ammonia/hydrogen** 液态氨/氢 **2** (clear) 清澈的 ‹*eyes, gaze*›; 清脆的 ‹*sound*›; 行云流水般的 ‹*movement*›

liquid assets *npl* 流动资产

liquidate /ˈlɪkwɪdeɪt/ *vt* **1** (wind up the affairs of) 清算 ‹*company, business, partnership*› **2** (pay off) 清偿 ‹*debt, claim*› **3** (convert into cash) 变卖 ‹*asset, shares*› **4** colloq (murder) 杀掉 ‹*rival, enemy*›

liquidation /ˌlɪkwɪˈdeɪʃn/ *n* [u and c] (of company) 清算; (of assets) 变现; (of debt) 清偿; **to go into ~** 破产

liquidator /ˈlɪkwɪdeɪtə(r)/ *n* 清算人

liquid crystal *n* 液晶

liquid: ~ crystal display *n* 液晶显示; ~ **diet** *n* 流质饮食; **to put sb. on a ~ diet** 规定某人吃流质食品

liquidity /lɪˈkwɪdəti/ *n* [u] (资产) 流动性

liquidize /ˈlɪkwɪdaɪz/ *vt* Brit 将…打成泥 ‹*food, strawberries*›; **~d carrots** 胡萝卜泥

liquidizer /ˈlɪkwɪdaɪzə(r)/ *n* Brit 搅拌器

liquid: ~ lunch *n* colloq hum 液体午餐 [指在酒吧喝酒]; **to have a ~ lunch** 以酒代午餐; ~ **measure** *n* **1** (vessel) 液体量器; **2** (amount) 酒的分量; **3** (dispenser) 量酒器; **L~ Paper®** *n* [u] 涂改液; ~ **soap** *n* [u] 液体肥皂

liquor /ˈlɪkə(r)/ *n* [u] **1** (alcoholic drink) 酒; **hard** *or* **strong ~** 烈性酒; **he can't hold his ~** 他容易喝醉 **2** Culin [烹调食物时的] 汁

Phrasal verb

- **liquor up** Amer colloq
A *vi* 喝醉
B *vt* [~ **sb. up**] 灌醉

liquorice /ˈlɪkərɪs/ *n* [u] Brit **1** (plant) 甘草 **2** (substance) 甘草糖

liquorice: ~ allsorts /ˌlɪkərɪs ˈɔːlsɔːts/ *npl* 什锦甘草糖果; ~ **root,** ~ **stick** *ns* 干草根

liquor store *n* Amer 酒品店

lira /ˈlɪərə/ ▸**p. 174** *n* (*pl* **lire** /ˈlɪərə, ˈlɪəreɪ/) Hist 里拉 [意大利前货币单位]

Lisbon /ˈlɪzbən/ *pr n* 里斯本

lisp /lɪsp/
A *n* 咬舌; **to talk with** *or* **have a ~** 说话咬舌
B *vt* 咬着舌说出 ‹*answer, words*›
C *vi* 说话咬舌

lissom /ˈlɪsəm/ *adj* 苗条柔美的

list¹ /lɪst/
A *n* (of names) 名单; (of items) 清单; **to be on a ~** «*names*» 在名单上; «*items*» 在清单上; **to put sb./sth. on a ~** 把某人列入名单/把某事物列入清单; **to take sb./sth. off a ~** 从名单中除去某人/从清单中删去某事物; **to be at the head** *or* **top of the ~** «*name*» 列在名单之首; «*item*» 列在清单之首; **to be high/low on one's ~ of priorities** 需要/不需要优先考虑; **to draw up/run through a ~** 制表/浏览目录
B *vt* **1** 列出 ‹*names, articles, prices*›; **to be ~ed**

l

under sth. 被列在某类别下; **to be ~ed in sth.** 被列在…里 ‹*directory, phone book*›; **to be ~ed as missing** «*person*» 被列入失踪人员名单; **he is ~ed among the greatest painters of his age** 他被认为是他那个时代最伟大的画家之一 [2] Fin 将…挂牌上市; **to be ~ed on the Stock Exchange** 在伦敦证券交易所挂牌上市

[C] *vi* Comm 被列入价目表; **what does ~ it at** *or* **for?** 它定价多少?

list² Naut

[A] *vi* «*ship, boat*» 倾斜

[B] *n* 倾斜; **to develop a ~** «*ship, boat*» 开始侧倾

listed /ˈlɪstɪd/ *adj* Brit 列入文物保护范围的 ‹*building*›

listen /ˈlɪsn/

[A] *vi* [1] (to words, music, sounds) 听; **to ~ to sb./sth.** 听某人/某物; **to ~ to sb. singing/playing the violin** 听某人唱歌/拉小提琴; **to ~ at the door** 把耳朵凑在门上听; **~ to this!** 请听!; **sorry, I wasn't ~ing** 对不起，我没听清楚; **'you're ~ing to ...'** Radio "您正在收听的是…" [2] (take notice) 听从; **to ~ to ...** 听…的话 ‹*adviser, teacher*›; **to ~ to reason** 服理; **you just never ~** 你就是不听; **~, can you come tomorrow?** 听着，你明天能来吗?; **to ~ for sth.** 留心听 ‹*voice, sound, signal*›

[B] *n* 听; **to have a ~ to sth.** 听一听某物

Phrasal verbs

- **listen in** *vi* [1] (eavesdrop) 偷听; **to ~ in on sth.** 偷听 ‹*conversation, phone call, meeting*› [2] Radio 收听; **to ~ in to sth.** 收听 ‹*show, programme*›
- **listen out** *vi* **to ~ out for sth.** 留心听 ‹*information, signals*›
- **listen up** Amer colloq *vi* 听; **hey, ~ up a minute!** 嘿，注意听着!

listenable /ˈlɪsnəbl/ *adj* [1] (audible) 容易听清的 ‹*talk, soundtrack*› [2] (entertaining) 好听的 ‹*record, speech*›

listener /ˈlɪsnə(r)/ *n* [1] (gen) 听者; **to be a good/bad ~** 认真听/不认真听; **a ready ~** 乐于听人倾诉的人 [2] Radio 听众

listening /ˈlɪsnɪŋ/ *n* [u] 听; **it makes interesting/exciting ~** 它听起来很有趣/很带劲; **'happy ~!'** "听得开心!"

listening: ~ device *n* [1] (for the hard-of-hearing) 助听装置; [2] (for eavesdropping) 窃听装置; **~ post** *n* 监听哨; **~ skills** *npl* 听力; **~ station** *n* 监听站

listeria /lɪˈstɪərɪə/ *n* [u] [1] (bacterium) 利斯特菌 [2] colloq (illness) 利斯特菌病

listeriosis /lɪˌstɪərɪˈəʊsɪs/ *n* [u] 利斯特菌病

listing /ˈlɪstɪŋ/

[A] *n* also Fin 登记项目; **Stock Exchange ~s** 证券交易所挂牌表; **he has no ~ in the telephone directory** 电话簿里找不到他

[B] **listings** *npl* (in newspaper, magazine) [报刊上刊登的] 演出信息

listless /ˈlɪstlɪs/ *adj* 无精打采的

listlessly /ˈlɪstlɪsli/ *adv* 无精打采地

listlessness /ˈlɪstlɪsnɪs/ *n* [u] 无精打采

list price *n* 价目表价格

lit¹ /lɪt/ *pt, pp* ▸**light¹ C, D**

lit² *n* colloq (literature) 文学

litany /ˈlɪtəni/ *n* [1] Relig 连祷文 [2] fig (of complaints etc.) 枯燥冗长的陈述; **a long ~ of complaints** 没完没了的抱怨

litchi /ˈlaɪtʃiː, ˌlaɪˈtʃiː/ *n* = **lychee**

lite /laɪt/

[A] *adj* 低热量的 ‹*yogurt, cream*›; **~ beer** 淡啤酒

[B] *n* [u] (低热量、低酒精度的) 淡啤酒

liter /ˈliːtə(r)/ *n* Amer = **litre**

literacy /ˈlɪtərəsi/ *n* [u] [1] (of population, individual) 读写能力; **~ skills** 读写能力; **~ level/rate** 基本文化水平/普及率; **to teach ~** 教人读写; **100% adult ~** 100%的成人识字率 [2] (in a specific subject) 专业知识; **computer ~** 计算机知识

literacy: ~ campaign *n* 提高文化水平运动; **~ hour** *n* Brit 读写课; **~ programme** *n* [1] (project) 提高文化水平计划; [2] TV, Radio 文化课节目; **~ target** *n* [教师、公务员等必须达到的] 文化程度目标; **~ test** *n* 文化水平测验

literal /ˈlɪtərəl/ *adj* [1] (basic) 字面的 ‹*meaning, sense*› [2] (word for word) 逐字的 ‹*interpretation*›; **~ translation** 直译 [3] (exactly copied) 如实的 ‹*performance, adaptation*›; pej 缺乏想象力的 [4] (actual, real) 确确实实的 ‹*ruin, starvation, truth*› [5] colloq (absolute) 绝对的; **her marriage was five years of ~ hell** 她五年的婚姻生活着实让她吃尽苦头

literally /ˈlɪtərəli/ *adv* [1] (exactly as written or said) 逐字地; **to take sth./sb. ~** 照字面意义理解某事物/某人说的话 [2] (without exaggeration) 确确实实地; **they quite ~ danced all night** 他们真的整晚都在跳舞 [3] colloq (emphatic) 简直; **he ~ exploded with rage** 他简直气炸了

literal-minded *adj* pej 缺乏想象力的

literary /ˈlɪtərəri, Amer ˈlɪtəreri/ *adj* [1] (of literature) 文学的; **a ~ prize** 文学奖; **~ talent/style** 文才/文风; **~ ambitions** 作家梦 [2] (scholarly) 博学的 ‹*person*›; **a ~ giant** 饱读诗书之士; **he's a bit too ~** 他书卷气有些太重了

literary: ~ agent ▸**p. 409** *n* 作家代理人; **~ critic** ▸**p. 409** *n* 文学批评家; **~ criticism** *n* [u] 文学批评; **~ theory** *n* [u] 文学理论

literate /ˈlɪtərət/ *adj* [1] (able to read and write) 有读写能力的; **he is barely ~** 他几乎不识字 [2] (cultured) 有文化修养的 ‹*person*›; 显示出文化修养的 ‹*style, prose, vocabulary*› [3] (knowledgeable) 精通的; **to be ~ in sth.** 精通某事; **an emotionally ~ person** 通达人情世故的人

literati /ˌlɪtəˈrɑːti/ *npl* 文人学士

literature /ˈlɪtrətʃə(r), Amer -tʃʊər/

[A] *n* [u] [1] (literary writings) 文学; **a work of ~** 文学作品 [2] (pamphlets) 宣传册; **campaign/sales ~** 宣传/推销资料 [3] (publications) 专题文献; **the ~ on sth.** 某方面的文献

[B] *modif* 文学的; **a ~ course/lecturer/student** 文学课/文学老师/学文学的学生

lithe /laɪð/ *adj* 肢体柔韧的 ‹*person, animal*›; 柔韧的 ‹*body*›

lithium /ˈlɪθɪəm/ *n* [u] 锂

lithium: ~ battery *n* 锂电池; **~ ion battery** *n* 锂离子电池

lithographic /ˌlɪθəˈɡræfɪk/ *adj* 平版印刷的; **~ prints** 平板印刷品

lithography /lɪˈθɒɡrəfi/ *n* [u] 平版印刷术

Lithuania /ˌlɪθjuːˈeɪnɪə/ *pr n* 立陶宛

Lithuanian /ˌlɪθjuːˈeɪnɪən/ ▸**p. 503, p. 426**

[A] *adj* (of Lithuania) 立陶宛的; (of the people) 立陶宛人的; (of the language) 立陶宛语的

[B] *n* [1] [c] (person) 立陶宛人 [2] [u] (language) 立陶宛语

litigant /ˈlɪtɪɡənt/ *n* 诉讼当事人

litigation /ˌlɪtɪˈɡeɪʃn/ *n* [u] 诉讼; **to come to ~** 提起诉讼; **to be the subject of ~** 是诉讼的主题

litigious /lɪˈtɪdʒəs/ *adj* 好诉讼的 ‹*person*›; 可提起诉讼的 ‹*matter, subject, topic*›

litmus /ˈlɪtməs/ *n* [u] 石蕊

litmus: ~ paper *n* [u] 石蕊试纸; **~ test** *n* 石蕊试验; **to be a ~ test** fig 是立见分晓的检验; **a ~ test of her principles** 检验她道德原则的试金石

litre /ˈliːtə(r)/ *n* Brit 升; *modif* 一升容量的 ‹*bottle, measure*›

litter /ˈlɪtə(r)/

[A] *n* [1] [u] (rubbish) 垃圾; **to drop ~** 乱扔垃圾; **no ~** 禁止乱扔垃圾 [2] [u] (random collection) 乱放的杂物; **a ~ of ...** 一堆乱七八糟的… ‹*books, toys, beer cans*› [3] [c] (group of young animals) 一胎幼崽; **to have a ~ of kittens** 生一窝小猫 [4] [u] (bedding for farm stock) 褥草; (in toilet tray) 猫砂

[B] *vt* 乱扔; **to ~ a house with sth.** 在房子里乱扔 ‹*toys, clothes, rubbish*›; **to ~ the floor/ground with sth.** 在地板上/地上到处扔某物; **to be ~ed with leaves/corpses** «*field, ground*» 到处都是落叶/尸体; **to be ~ed with allusions/references** fig 满是典故/参考引文

[C] *vi* «*animal*» 产崽

litter: ~ basket *n* 废纸篓; **~ bin** *n* Brit 垃圾箱; **~ box** *n* Amer 垃圾箱; **~bug** *n* 乱丢垃圾者; **~ lout** *n* Brit 乱丢垃圾者; **~ tray** *n* 宠物便盆

little /ˈlɪtl/

[A] *adj* [1] (small) 小的 ‹*person, animal, thing*›; **a ~ house/dog** 小屋/小狗; **a ~ old lady** 小老太太; **the ~ toe** 小脚趾; **I need a ~ something to eat** colloq 我要吃点东西 [2] (young) 年幼的; **my ~ ones** 我年幼的孩子们; **the polar bear and her ~ ones** 那头北极熊和它的幼崽; **when I was ~** 我小时候 [3] (feeble, weak) 不明显的 ‹*gesture, nod*›; 微弱的 ‹*voice*›; **a shy ~ smile** 一丝羞怯的笑 [4] (expressing scorn, contempt) 讨厌的 ‹*people, things*›; **she's a snobbish ~ woman** 她是个势利小人; **a poky ~ flat** 简陋狭窄的公寓 [5] (short) 很短的 ‹*time, distance*›; 小的 ‹*bit, piece*›; **a ~ nap/break** 小睡/短暂的休息; **to walk a ~ way** 走一小段路; **after a ~ while** 过了一小会儿

[B] *det* (*comp* **less**, *superl* **least**) 很少的 ‹*point, sense*›; 微不足道的 ‹*damage*›; 很小的 ‹*hope, chance, influence*›; **he speaks ~ German** 他几乎不会说德语; **there's ~ time** 时间很紧; **to have ~ money** 钱很少; **with no ~ difficulty** 很困难地; **I see ~ of Paul these days** 我最近很少见到保罗

[C] *pron* 一点; **to taste a ~ of sth.** 尝一小口某物; **a ~ of the money** 这笔钱的很少一部分; **to remember very ~ about sth.** 几乎不记得某事物; **he gave her what ~ he had** 他把仅有的一点给了她; **~ of what he says is true** 他没说真话; **there's ~ I can do/to worry about** 我做不了什么/没什么好担心的; **~ of note** 无足轻重的事; **she did ~ to help** 她没怎么帮忙; **I got ~ out of the lecture** 我从这场讲座中获益不多; **to do as ~ as possible** 尽可能少做事; **age has ~ to do with it** 这和年纪没什么关系; **~ or nothing** 几乎没有什么; ▸**too 1**

[D] *adv* [1] (rarely) 很少 ‹*go, say, read, sleep*›; **she visits them as ~ as possible** 她尽量不拜访他们 [2] (hardly, scarcely) 几乎不; **to be ~ changed** 几乎没有改变; **to be ~ better** 好不了多少; **it's ~ short of madness to do sth.** 做某事简直是疯了; **a ~-known novel** 鲜为人知的长篇小说 [3] (not at all) 完全不; **I ~ thought** *or* **supposed that ...** 我根本不认为…; **~ do you know!** 你完全想不到!

[E] *in adv phrs* [1] **a little (bit)** (slightly) 有点; **to be a ~ (bit) anxious at sth.** 对某事有点焦虑; **a ~ less/more ...** 更少/更多一点…; **to stay a ~ longer** 呆得再稍微久些; **could you move over a ~?** 劳驾能往那边挪一点儿吗?; **not a ~ surprised/proudly** 极其惊讶的/骄傲地 [2] **little by little** (gradually, slowly) 渐渐地 [3] **as little as** (only as much as) 仅仅; **it cost as ~ as £60** 它只要60英镑; **I like Luna as ~ as you do** 我和你一样不喜欢卢娜

little: L~ Bear *pr n* Brit **the L~ Bear** 小熊星座; **L~ Dipper** *pr n* Amer **the L~ Dipper** 小熊星座; **~ end** *n* Brit [连杆体与活塞销相连接的] 小头; **L~ Englander** *n* pej 英格兰本土主义者; *modif* 英格兰本土主义的 ‹*mentality, views*›; 信奉英格兰本土主义的 ‹*party*›; **~ finger** *n* 小指; **to wrap** *or* **twist sb. round one's ~ finger** 能随意差遣某人;

~ **hand** *n* 时针; ~ **people** *npl* **1** (common people) 平民; **2** (mythical beings) 小精灵族; **3** (children) 小孩

liturgical /lɪ'tɜːdʒɪkl/ *adj* 礼拜仪式的

liturgy /'lɪtədʒi/ *n* 礼拜仪式

livable /'lɪvəbl/ *adj* **1** (inhabitable) 可居住的 ‹*house, room, building*›; **the flat is small but** ~ 这套公寓很小但还能住 **2** (bearable) 可忍受的 ‹*life, situation*›; **he's not** ~ **with** colloq 他太难相处了; **the pain is** ~ 疼痛可以忍受

live[1] /lɪv/

A *vt* 过; **to** ~ **one's life** 生活; **to** ~ **a normal/peaceful life** 过正常/平静的生活; **to** ~ **a life of luxury/crime** 过奢华/罪恶的生活; **to** ~ **the life of a recluse/a saint** 过隐士/圣徒般的生活; **to** ~ **one's faith/politics** 按照信仰/政治立场生活; **to** ~ **the part** *or* **role (of sb.)** 生活中亦如演出（某角色）一般; **to** ~ **sth. down** 让人忘记某事物; **I'll never** ~ **it down!** hum 我永远都无法让人忘记这件事!

B *vi* **1** (dwell) «*person, animal*» 居住; **where do you** ~? 你住哪里?; **a place to** ~ 居住地; **to** ~ **in ...** «*person*» 住在 ‹*countryside, town, street*›; «*animal*» 生活在 ‹*fresh water, forest*›; **to** ~ **at home/number 15/Buckingham Palace** 住在家里/15号/白金汉宫; **he** ~**s at the betting shop/in those jeans** colloq hum 他整天泡在投注站里/穿着那条牛仔裤; **he** ~**s by the canal/over the shop** 他住运河边/店铺楼上; **to** ~ **with sb.** 与某人住一起; **he's not very easy to** ~ **with** 与他同住不是件容易的事; **to** ~ **together** «*family, friends*» 同住; «*couple*» 同居; **to** ~ **apart** 分居; **to** ~ **alone** *or* **on one's own** 独居; **the tea towels** ~ **in that cupboard over there** colloq 茶巾通常放在那边那个橱柜里 **2** (lead one's life) 生活; **to** ~ **well/dangerously** 过殷实/危险的生活; **to** ~ **in luxury/poverty** 生活奢侈/贫困; **we** ~ **in the computer age** 我们生活在计算机时代; **to** ~ **in hope/fear (of sb./sth./doing sth.)** 生活在（对某人/某事物/做某事的）希望/恐惧之中; **to** ~ **in peace with sb.** 与某人和平相处; **to** ~ **for sth./sb.** 为…而活着 ‹*sport, work, pastime, family*›; **to** ~ **through sth.** 经历 ‹*war, depression*›; **to** ~ **without sth./sb.** 在没有…的情况下生活 ‹*person, luxury, substance*›; **they** ~**d happily ever after** 后来他们便一直过着幸福的生活; **to** ~ **like a king/lord/pig** 像国王/老爷/猪一样生活; **to** ~ **by** 遵照…生活 ‹*standards, beliefs, rules*›; **to** ~ **from day to day** 一天天过日子; **to** ~ **and let** ~ 互相宽容; **you** ~ **and learn** 活到老，学到老 **3** (be alive) 活着; **he** ~**d to be ninety-three** 他活到了93岁; **as long as I** ~**, I'll ...** 只要我还活着，我就会…; **he's only got six months to** ~ 他只能活6个月了; **I don't think all the quintuplets will** ~ 我认为五胞胎不会都活下来; **I'll** ~**!** hum 我死不了!; **I've got nothing left to** ~ **for** 我活着没什么盼头了; **to make the characters** ~ 把人物塑造得栩栩如生 **4** (survive) 存活; **to** ~ **to do sth.** 活到做某事; **you may** ~ **to regret this** 你总有一天要为这件事后悔的; **long** ~ **sb./sth.!** 某人/某事物万岁!; **the memory will** ~ **in my heart forever** 这份记忆将永远留在我心中; **to** ~ **through winter/the night** 活过冬季/今晚; **to** ~ **to fight another day** 存活下来以期再战; **to** ~ **to tell the tale** 活下来讲述危险的经历 **5** (maintain existence) 生存; **I barely earn enough to** ~ 我赚的钱勉强够养活自己; **to** ~ **by doing sth.** 靠做某事为生; **to** ~ **on** 以吃…为生 ‹*food*›; 靠…过活 ‹*wage, charity*›; **to** ~ **on fresh air** 不吃不喝; **to** ~ **off** 靠…过活 ‹*interest, profits*›; **to** ~ **out of** 靠吃…里的食物过活 ‹*freezer, cans*› **6** (put up with) **to** ~ **with sth.** 忍受某事物; **to** ~ **with the consequences** 接受后果; **how can you** ~ **with the knowledge that ...?** 既然知道…，你怎么还能坐视不理?; **to** ~ **with the fact that ...** 接受…的事实; **to learn to** ~ **with sth.** 努力忍受某事物; **to** ~ **with oneself** 感到心安; **I couldn't** ~ **with myself** *or* **my conscience** 我良心上过不去 **7** colloq (experience life) 享受生活; **this is what I call living!** 这才是我所谓的享受生活呢!; **she's really** ~**d!** 她真正享受了生活!; **you haven't** ~**d until you've ...** 你只有…才算享受过人生的乐趣; ~ **a little!** 享受一下生活吧!; **to** ~ **it up** 狂欢

Phrasal verbs

- **live in** *vi* 住在工作的地方; **most of the teachers/students** ~ **in** 大多数老师/学生住校; **most of the workers** ~ **in** 多数工人住在厂区
- **live on** *vi* «*person, animal*» 继续存活; fig «*fame, memory, work*» 继续存在
- **live out**

A *vi* 不住在工作的地方

B *vt* [~ **out sth.**] **1** (survive) 活过 ‹*season, day, week*› **2** (spend) 度过; **to** ~ **out the rest of one's days somewhere** 在某处度过余生 **3** (enact) 实现 ‹*fantasies*›

- **live up to** *vt* [~ **up to sth.**] 不辜负 ‹*expectations*›; 符合 ‹*standards, advertising, hype*›; **to** ~ **up to one's reputation (as ...)** （作为…）名符其实

live[2] /laɪv/

A *adj* **1** (not dead) 活的; **experiments on** ~ **animals** 活体动物实验; **a** ~ **birth** 活产; **a real** ~ **...** colloq 活生生的 ‹*explorer, film star*› **2** Radio, TV (not recorded) 现场的 ‹*audience, performance, recording*›; 即时的 ‹*communications*›; **a** ~ **broadcast from ...** 来自…的实况转播 **3** Elec 通电的 ‹*switch, piece of metal*›; **the bare wire is** ~ 裸线有电 **4** (unused) 可点燃的 ‹*matches*›; 可爆炸的 ‹*ammunition*›; ~ **bullets** 实弹 **5** (burning) 燃烧着的 ‹*coal, embers, cigarette end*› **6** (topical) 当前所关注的 ‹*issue, topic*›

B *adv* 在现场 ‹*broadcast, transmit*›; **speaking** ~ **from Beijing is ...** 从北京进行现场报道的是…

live bait /laɪv 'beɪt/ *n* [u] 活钓饵

lived-in /'lɪvdɪn/ *adj* (homely) 家居的 ‹*house, flat, room*›; fig 饱经风霜的 ‹*face*›

livelihood /'laɪvlɪhʊd/ *n* 生计; **to lose one's** ~ 失业; **my** ~ **depends on it** 我靠它维持生计

liveliness /'laɪvlɪnɪs/ *n* [u] (of person, group) 精力充沛; (of place) 热闹; (of style) 轻快; (of discussion, argument) 热烈; (of account, narrative) 生动; (of imagination, mind) 活跃

livelong /'lɪvlɒŋ, Amer 'laɪvlɔːŋ/ *adj* liter **all the** ~ **day** 一整天

lively /'laɪvli/ *adj* **1** (vivacious) 充满活力的 ‹*person, group*› **2** (busy) 热闹的 ‹*market, restaurant, atmosphere*› **3** (stimulating) 热烈的 ‹*discussion*›; 生动的 ‹*narrative*›; 愉快的 ‹*afternoon*›; 活跃的 ‹*imagination, mind*› **4** (fast) 轻快的 ‹*pace, music, dance*›; ~ **breeze** 轻风; **look** ~**!** colloq 动作快点! **5** colloq (out of control) 闹哄哄的 ‹*party, group*›

liven up /'laɪvn ʌp/

A *vt* [**liven up sth., liven sth. up**] 使…活跃 ‹*social occasion, atmosphere, person*›; **to liven things up** 活跃气氛

B *vi* «*person, party, atmosphere*» 活跃起来; **things are livening up** 气氛活跃起来了

liver[1] /'lɪvə(r)/ *n* **1** [c] Anat 肝脏 **2** [u] (as food) 肝; **fried** ~ 煎肝

liver[2] *n* (person) [以某方式] 生活的人; **a clean/loose/fast** ~ 洁身自好/生活放荡/生活纷乱的人

live rail /laɪv 'reɪl/ *n* 带电铁轨

liver complaint *n* 肝病

liveried /'lɪvərɪd/ *adj* 穿制服的 ‹*servant, footman*›

liver pâté *n* 肝酱

Liverpudlian /ˌlɪvə'pʌdlɪən/

A *adj* 利物浦的; **the** ~ **accent** 利物浦口音

B *n* 利物浦人

liver: ~ **salts** *npl* 治肝盐; ~ **sausage** *n* [u and c] esp Brit 肝泥香肠; ~ **spot** *n* 雀斑; ~ **trouble** *n* [u] 肝病; ~**wort** /'lɪvəwɜːt/ *n* [u] 叶苔

livery /'lɪvəri/ *n* **1** (servants' uniform) 仆从制服 **2** (colour scheme, design) 公司专用色彩; **BA planes now have a new** ~ 英国航空公司的飞机采用了新的专用色彩

lives /laɪvz/ *pl* ▸**life A**

livestock /'laɪvstɒk/ *n* [u] 牲畜

live wire /laɪv/ *n* 富有进取心的人

livid /'lɪvɪd/ *adj* **1** (furious) 大怒的; **to be** ~ **with sb.** 对某人发火; **to be** ~ **at sth.** 因某事大怒; **to be** ~ **with rage** 大发雷霆 **2** (dark and angry) 乌青色的 ‹*sky, scar, face*›; **a** ~ **bruise** 淤青

living /'lɪvɪŋ/

A *adj* **1** (alive) 活的 ‹*person, animal, organism*›; **is your grandmother still** ~? 令祖母还健在吗?; **to be** ~ **proof/a** ~ **example of sth.** 是某事物的鲜活证明/生动例证; **a** ~ **hell** 人间地狱; **there wasn't a** ~ **soul about** 那儿一个人影也没有; **he's the** ~ **image of his father** 他酷似父亲; **he's a** ~ **legend** 他是当今的传奇人物; **the** ~ **dead** 活死人 [指僵尸、吸血鬼等] **2** (used or practised today) 现存的 ‹*culture, tradition*›; **a** ~ **language** 现用语言; **the** ~ **word of God** 福音; **in** *or* **within** ~ **memory** 在当今人们的记忆中

B *n* [u] **1** (livelihood) 生计; **to earn** *or* **make a** ~ **by doing sth.** 靠做某事为生; **an honest/a meagre** ~ 规矩/贫困的生活; **to scratch a** ~ 勉强维持生活; **what do you do for a** ~? 你以何为生?; **it's not much of a** ~ 这收入不高; **some of us have to work for a** ~**!** hum 我们不能都干坐着啊! **2** (lifestyle) 生活方式; **easy/loose/fast/high** ~ 自在/淫荡/放浪/豪奢的生活方式 **3** Relig (position) 有薪俸的神职 **4** **the** ~ *pl* (people who are alive) 生者; **to be still in the land of the** ~ hum (alive) 还活着; (awake) 还醒着

living: ~ **conditions** *npl* 生活条件; ~ **death** *n* [u] 活受罪; ~ **expenses** *npl* 生活开支; ~ **quarters** *npl* 住处; ~ **room** *n* 起居室; ~ **space** *n* [u] 居住面积; ~ **standards** *npl* 生活水平; ~ **wage** *n* 基本生活工资; ~ **will** *n* 生前意愿 [重症患者为防止失去思维或语言能力而签立的文件，声明在救治无望时不采用人工设备维持生命]

lizard /'lɪzəd/ *n* 蜥蜴

lizardskin /'lɪzədskɪn/ *n* [u] 蜥蜴皮

Ljubljana /ˌluːblj'ɑːnə/ *pr n* 卢布尔雅那

llama /'lɑːmə/ *n* **1** [c] (animal) 美洲驼 **2** [u] (wool) 美洲驼绒呢

lo /ləʊ/ *excl* liter ~ **(and behold)!** 你瞧!

load /ləʊd/

A *n* **1** (sth. carried) 负荷; **a** ~ **of coal** 一车煤; **a lorry-/plane-**~ **of sth.** 一卡车/一飞机的某物; **to have a heavy** ~ **to bear** fig 负担重; **to shed its** ~ «*vehicle, vessel*» 卸货; **to take a** ~ **off sb.'s mind** 使某人放心 **2** Tech, Mech (weight) 装载量; **this beam has a** ~ **of 10 tonnes** 这根梁承重10吨; **axle** ~ 轴荷; **do not exceed maximum** ~ (sign on lift, crane, etc.) 请勿超载 **3** (batch) 一批; **four** ~**s of washing** 4缸洗涤的衣物 **4** Elec 供电量; **lines carrying a** ~ **of 10,000 volts** 输送1万伏电的电力网 **5** fig (amount of work) 工作量; **to lighten sb.'s** ~ 减轻某人的负荷; **to spread the** ~ 分摊工作量 **6** **a** ~ colloq (a lot) 大量; **a** ~ *or* **a whole** ~ **of books/people** 很多书/人; **a** ~ **of rubbish** 一派胡言; **get a** ~ **of this** *or* **that!** (watch) 一饱眼福吧!; (listen) 竖起耳朵听吧!

B **loads** *npl* colloq 很多; ~**s of people/photos/flowers** 很多人/照片/花; ~**s of champagne/**

l

time 大量的香槟酒/时间; **to have ~s of energy** 精力充沛; **to have ~s of work** 工作堆积如山; **to have ~s of money** 有万贯家财

C vt **1** (place cargo on) 给…装货 ‹*ship, van*›; 让…驮上货物 ‹*animal*›; 让…负重 ‹*person*›; (place on lorry, ship, etc.) 装载 ‹*machinery, food*›; **they ~ed the lorry with scrap metal** 他们把废金属装到卡车上; **they are ~ing coal on to the ship** 他们正把煤装上船; **to ~ sb. with** fig 给某人大量的 ‹*presents, honours, medicine*› **2** (insert) 装上 ‹*film, bullet*›; 放入 ‹*clothes*›; **to ~ a gun/washing machine/camera** 给枪装子弹/把衣物放进洗衣机/给照相机装胶卷 **3** Comput 载入 ‹*program, software*›; **ready to ~** 准备安装 **4** Elec 使…超负荷 ‹*system, power line*› **5** (tamper with) **to ~ the dice against sb.** fig 使某人背运

D vi ‹*ship, lorry, cart*› 装货

Phrasal verbs

- **load down** vt [~ **sb./sth. down,** ~ **down sb./sth.**] 使…负担过重 ‹*person*›; 使…载荷过重 ‹*van, lorry, car*›; **to be ~ed down with shopping/work** 提着很多购买的物品/工作繁重
- **load up** vt [~ **sb./sth. up,** ~ **up sb./sth.**] 将…上的货物摞得很高 ‹*van, lorry, car*›; **he ~ed me up with books** 他让我搬起高高的一摞书

load-bearing *adj* 承重的; **a ~ wall/beam** 承重墙/承重梁

loaded /ˈləʊdɪd/ *adj* **1** (full, laden) 装满的 ‹*tray, vehicle*›; 装有弹药的 ‹*gun*› **2** (weighed down) 受重压的; **to be ~ (down) with boxes** 提着许多盒子; **to be ~ with honours/medals** fig 拥有许多荣誉/奖牌 **3** fig colloq (rich) 富有的 **4** (charged with meaning) 诱导性的 ‹*question*›; 含蓄的 ‹*word*›; **a statement ~ with meaning** 意味深长的话 **5** Amer colloq (drunk) 喝醉了的

loading bay *n* 货物装卸区

load line *n* 载重线

loaf /ləʊf/ *n* (*pl* **loaves**) **1** Culin 一条; **a ~ of bread** 一条面包; **half a ~ is better than no bread** 有一点总比没有好 **2** colloq (head) 脑袋; **use your ~** 动动脑筋

Phrasal verb

- **loaf about, loaf around** *vi* colloq 游手好闲

loafer /ˈləʊfə(r)/ *n* **1** (idler) 游手好闲者 **2** (shoe) 懒汉鞋

loaf tin Brit, **loaf pan** Amer *ns* 烤模

loam /ləʊm/ *n* 壤土

loamy /ˈləʊmi/ *adj* 壤土性的; **~ soil** 壤土

loan /ləʊn/

A *n* **1** [c] (money) 借款; **a £20,000 ~, a ~ of £20,000** 2万英镑的借款; **to take out/ask for/give a ~** 获得/申请/发放贷款 **2** [u] (use, services) 借用; **to give sb./have the ~ of sth.** 借给某人某物/借用某物; **to be on ~ to sth./sb.** 借给某机构/某人

B vt 借出 ‹*money, books, work of art*›; 借调 ‹*personnel*›

loan: ~ account *n* 贷款账户; **~ agreement** *n* 贷款协议; **~ facility** *n* 贷款融通; **~ shark** *n* pej colloq 放高利贷者; **~ translation** *n* 借译词语; **~ word** *n* 外来词

loath /ləʊθ/ *adj* 不愿意的; **to be ~ to do sth.** 不情愿做某事

loathe /ləʊð/ *vt* 厌恶; **to ~ doing sth.** 很不喜欢做某事

loathing /ˈləʊðɪŋ/ *n* [u] 厌恶; **to have a ~ for sb./sth.** 厌恶某人/某事物; **to have a ~ of sth.** 厌恶某事物

loathsome /ˈləʊðsəm/ *adj* 讨厌的

loaves /ləʊvz/ *pl* ▸**loaf**

lob /lɒb/

A *n* 高球

B vt (*pres p etc.* **-bb-**) 以高弧线抛出 ‹*ball, stone*›; 以高弧线射出 ‹*missile*›

C vi (*pres p etc.* **-bb-**) 吊高球

lobby /ˈlɒbi/

A *n* **1** (of house) 门厅; (of hotel) 大堂; (of theatre) 大厅 **2** (for politicians) 民众接待厅 **3** Brit (place where MPs vote) **(division)** ~ 议员分组投票厅 **4** (pressure group) 游说团体 **5** (campaign) 游说活动

B vt 游说 ‹*person, group*›; 游说使…得以通过 ‹*bill*›

C vi 游说; **to ~ for sth.** 游说争取某事物

lobby: ~ correspondent *n* 议会新闻记者; **~ group** *n* 游说团体

lobbyist /ˈlɒbɪɪst/ *n* 说客; **political ~** 政治说客

lobe /ləʊb/ *n* **1** (rounded projection) 耳垂 **2** (of brain, lung, etc.) 叶; **the frontal ~ of the brain** 大脑额叶

lobelia /ləˈbiːljə/ *n* 半边莲

lobotomy /ləʊˈbɒtəmi/ *n* 脑叶切断术

lobster /ˈlɒbstə(r)/ *n* **1** [c] (living creature) 龙虾 **2** [u] (as food) 龙虾肉

lobster: ~ pot *n* 诱捕龙虾的笼; **~ thermidor** *n* [u] 焗烤龙虾

local /ˈləʊkl/

A colloq *n* **1** (resident) 本地人 **2** (pub) 住处附近的酒吧 **3** (newspaper) 本地报纸 **4** (train) 市郊列车; (bus) 市内公共汽车

B *adj* **1** (neighbourhood) 邻近的; **the ~ curry house** 附近的咖喱菜馆 **2** (of the town, country) 本地的; (regional) 地方性的; **~ time** 当地时间; **~ news** 本地新闻; **~ businesses** 当地的商业机构; **~ bus service** 当地的公交系统 **3** (on body part) 局部的 ‹*pain, swelling*›

local: ~ anaesthetic *n* 局部麻醉; **~ area network** *n* 局域网; **~ authority** *n* Brit + *v sing or pl* 地方当局; **~ authority schools/grant** 地方政府创办的学校/地方政府拨款; **~ call** *n* 本地电话; **~ colour** *n* [u] 地方特色; **~ council** *n* Brit = **~ authority**; **~ derby** *n* 当地球队间的比赛

locale /ləʊˈkɑːl, Amer -ˈkæl/ *n* 发生地点; **a ~ for a film** 电影拍摄现场

local: ~ education authority *n* Brit + *v sing or pl* 地方教育局; **~ election** *n* 地方选举; **~ government** *n* 地方政府

locality /ləʊˈkæləti/ *n* **1** (local area) 地区; **shops in the ~** 本地商店 **2** (place) 地点

localization /ˌləʊkəlaɪˈzeɪʃn/ *n* [u] 本地化

localize /ˈləʊkəlaɪz/ *vt* **1** (pinpoint) 确定…的地点; **bats ~ objects using ultrasound** 蝙蝠用超声波定位物体 **2** (restrict to one area) 使局部化 **3** (adapt to locality) 使…本土化 ‹*software, website*› **4** (give power to locality) 把…交给地方政府负责 ‹*control, education*›

localized /ˈləʊləlaɪzd/ *adj* 局部的 ‹*pain, problem*›; 局部地区的 ‹*weather*›; 本地的 ‹*government, control*›

locally /ˈləʊkəli/ *adv* 在当地; **the magnificent mountain is known ~ as 'The Rock'** 这座巍峨高山被当地人称作"石头山"; **the products we sell are ~ produced** 我们销售的产品是本地生产的

locate /ləʊˈkeɪt, Amer ˈləʊkeɪt/

A vt **1** (find) 找出…的准确位置 **2** (situate) 把…设置在; **the factory is ~d in an industrial park** 工厂建于工业园内; **the film is ~d in Italy** 影片的外景地设在意大利

B vi ‹*mechanical part, fitment*› 安装到位

location /ləʊˈkeɪʃn/ *n* **1** (place) 地方; (position) 位置 **2** (filming site) 外景拍摄地; **to go on ~** 去拍摄外景; **the movie was filmed on ~** 电影是在外景地拍摄的

locative /ˈlɒkətɪv/

A *n* **~ (case)** 方位格

B *adj* 方位格的; **a ~ noun** 方位名词

loch /lɒk, lɒx/ *n* Scot (lake) 湖; (narrow sea inlet) 狭长海湾

lock[1] /lɒk/

A *n* **1** (mechanism) 锁; **to fasten a ~** 把锁锁上; **to pick a ~** 撬锁; **under ~ and key** 妥善保管着 **2** (on canal, river) 闸; **the ~ filled with water** 水闸内放满了水 **3** (in wrestling, fighting) 夹; **arm/leg ~** 夹臂/抱腿 **4** (rugby) **~ (forward)** 第二排前锋 **5** Aut 前轮转向角度; **on half/full ~** 转向打到一半/打到底的; **3.5 turns from ~ to ~** 3.5 轮的满转向角度; **to have a good/bad ~** 转向良好/不好 **6** Comput (on file) 加密锁 **7** archaic (on firearm) 保险栓; **~, stock, and barrel** fig 完全地

B vt **1** (close securely) 锁上 ‹*door, window, drawer*›; **to ~ sth. in a drawer** 把某物锁在抽屉里; **~ed and barred** *or* **bolted** 锁得严严实实的 **2** Comput 对…加锁 ‹*file*› **3** (become fixed) 紧紧抓住; **to ~ horns** lit ‹*animals*› 扭打; fig ‹*people*› 争执; **to be ~ed in combat** ‹*enemies, armies, countries*› 陷入战斗; **to be ~ed in an embrace** ‹*lovers, friends*› 紧紧拥抱

C vi **1** (close securely) ‹*door, drawer*› 被锁上 **2** (seize up) ‹*steering wheel*› 卡住; ‹*wheels*› 刹住; ‹*brakes*› 抱死

Phrasal verbs

- **lock away** vt [~ **sb./sth. away,** ~ **away sb./sth.**] 把…锁起来 ‹*valuables, documents, money*›; 关押 ‹*person*›
- **lock in** vt [~ **sb./sth. in**] 把…锁在里面; **to ~ oneself in** 把自己锁在里面
- **lock on to** vt [~ **on to sth.**] ‹*radar, bomb*› 锁定 ‹*target, building*›
- **lock out** vt [~ **sb./sth. out**] 把…关在门外; **to ~ oneself out** 把自己锁在门外
- **lock together** vi ‹*components, pieces*› 结合
- **lock up**

A vi **1** (when leaving) 锁好门窗 **2** ‹*wheels*› 刹住; ‹*brakes*› 抱死

B vt [~ **up sb./sth.,** ~ **sb./sth. up**] 把…锁起来 ‹*valuables, documents, money*›; 关押 ‹*person*›; **he should be ~ed up!** colloq 他应该被关起来!

lock[2] *n* (hair) 一绺头发; **a ~ of hair** 一绺头发; **wavy/curly ~s** 波浪发/卷发

lockdown /ˈlɒkdaʊn/ *n* 把犯人关入牢房

locker /ˈlɒkə(r)/ *n* 可上锁的衣物柜; **to go to Davy Jones's ~** 葬身鱼腹

locker room

A *n* 衣物间

B *modif* 粗俗的 ‹*humour, joke*›

locket /ˈlɒkɪt/ *n* 盒式项链坠

lock: ~ gate *n* 闸门; **~-in** *n* **1** (in a pub) [酒吧打烊后的] 留滞顾客续饮期; **2** (exclusive agreement) 锁定协议 [规定只可与某一公司谈判或交易]; **~jaw** *n* [u] 破伤风; **~ keeper** ▸**p. 409** *n* 船闸管理员; **~nut** *n* 防松螺母; **~-out** *n* 闭厂; **~smith** ▸**p. 409** *n* 锁匠; **~ stitch** *n* 连锁缝; **~-up** *n* **1** Brit (garage) 独立车库; (store) 独立仓库; **a ~-up shop** 店主和店员不在内居住的小商店; **2** dated (prison) 拘留所

loco[1] /ˈləʊkəʊ/ *adj* colloq (mad) 发疯的

loco[2] *n* Brit colloq (train) 机车

locomotion /ˌləʊkəˈməʊʃn/ *n* [u] (movement) 运动; (ability to move) 运动力

locomotive /ˌləʊkəˈməʊtɪv/

A *n* 火车头

B *adj* 运动的

locomotive shed *n* 机车棚

locum /ˈləʊkəm/ *n* Brit (cleric) 代理牧师; (doctor) 代班医生

locust /ˈləʊkəst/ *n* **1** (insect) 蝗虫; **a plague of ~s** 蝗灾 **2** **~ (tree)** 角豆树; **~ bean** 角豆

lode /ləʊd/ *n* 矿脉

loden /ˈləʊdn/ *n* **1** [u] (fabric) 洛登缩绒厚呢 **2** [c] (coat) 洛登缩绒厚呢大衣

lodestone /ˈləʊdstəʊn/ *n* 天然磁石

l

lodge /lɒdʒ/
A *n* 1 (for gatekeeper, caretaker) 门房; **entrance ～** 门房 2 (for country sports) [供参加户外运动者暂住的] 乡间小屋 3 (in Freemasonry) (building) 地方分会集会处; (group) 地方分会 4 (of beaver) 穴
B *vt* 1 (accommodate) 为…提供住宿 ‹*guests, friends*› 2 (file) 正式提出 ‹*appeal, protest*›; **to ～ a complaint** 正式提出投诉 3 (deposit) 存放; **to ～ the money with the court** 把钱交法庭保管
C *vi* 1 (reside) 寄宿; **to ～ with sb.** 在某人家寄宿 2 (stick) 嵌入; **the bullet has ～d in his shoulder** 子弹射入了他的肩膀; **a bone ～d in his throat** 一根骨头卡在他的喉咙里; **it ～d in her memory** fig 这事留存在她的记忆中

lodger /ˈlɒdʒə(r)/ *n* esp Brit 房客

lodging /ˈlɒdʒɪŋ/
A *n* (accommodation) 寄宿; **board and ～** 膳宿
B **lodgings** *npl* (room) 寄宿舍; **to take ～s with sb.** 租住在某人家中

loess /ˈləʊes/ *n* [u] 黄土

loft¹ /lɒft, Amer lɔːft/ *n* 1 [c] (attic) 阁楼; **pigeon ～** 鸽舍 2 [c] (in church) 楼厢; **the organ ～** [教堂内的] 管风琴台 3 [u] (of fabric) 松软 4 [u] (of golf club) [球杆头的] 倾斜角度

loft² *vt* 向高处击

loft: ～ bed *n* Amer 高架床; **～ conversion** *n* 用阁楼改装的居室; **～ hatch** *n* 阁楼入口

loftily /ˈlɒftɪli, Amer ˈlɔːft-/ *adv* 高傲地

loftiness /ˈlɒftɪnɪs, Amer ˈlɔːftɪnɪs/ *n* [u] 1 (of building) 高耸; (of ideals) 崇高 2 (disdain) 高傲

loft ladder *n* 折叠式阁楼梯

lofty /ˈlɒfti, Amer ˈlɔːfti/ *adj* 1 (tall) 高耸的; (high-minded) 崇高的; **～ sentiments** 高尚的情操 2 (disdainful) 高傲的 ‹*manner, tone*›

log¹ /lɒg, Amer lɔːg/
A *n* 1 (of wood) 原木; **to sleep like a ～** fig 睡得死沉; **as easy as falling off a ～** colloq 非常容易 2 (record) **～ (book)** 日志; **a ship's ～** 航海日志; **to keep a ～ of people's comings and goings** 记录人们的来往情况 3 Naut (to measure speed) 计程仪
B *vt* (*pres p etc.* **-gg-**) 1 (record) 记录 2 (clock up) 记录达到…水平; **I have ～ged 10 hours of work** 我工作的时间长达 10 小时 3 (cut trees in) 采伐…的树木 ‹*forest, area*›

Phrasal verbs
- **log in** *vi* 登录
- **log off** *vi* 退出
- **log on** *vi* 登录; **to ～ on to the system** 登录系统
- **log out** *vi* 退出; **to ～ out of the system** 退出系统
- **log up** *vt* = **log¹ B2**

log² *n* Math = **logarithm**

loganberry /ˈləʊgənbəri, Amer -beri/ *n* 洛根莓; **～ jam/juice** 洛根莓酱/洛根莓汁

logarithm /ˈlɒgərɪðəm/ *n* 对数

logarithmic /ˌlɒgəˈrɪðmɪk/ *adj* 对数的

log: ～ book *n* 1 Naut 航海日志; 2 (of car) 行驶日志; **～ cabin** *n* 小木屋; **～ fire** *n* 柴火

log cabin

小木屋。用圆形实木筑成的简易小屋，屋角处用近似榫合的方式固定，不用钉子。17世纪由瑞典人引入北美地区，常见于美国拓荒时代的边疆地区。林肯等数位美国总统都出生在小木屋内。后来的政客往往以出生于小木屋自诩，标榜自己出身寒微。

logger /ˈlɒgə(r)/ *n* 伐木工人

loggerheads /ˈlɒgəhedz/ *npl* **to be at ～ (with sb.)** (be on bad terms) （与某人）不和; (be in serious disagreement) （与某人）有严重分歧

loggerhead turtle *n* 蠵龟

logging /ˈlɒgɪŋ/ *n* [u] (activity) 伐木; (business) 伐木业

logic /ˈlɒdʒɪk/ *n* [u] 1 (science) 逻辑学; (method) 推理法 2 (reason) 理由; (sense) 道理; **I can see the ～ of selling it** 我能明白卖掉它是有正当理由的 3 (power of reasoning) 推理能力; **to chop ～** 强词夺理

logical /ˈlɒdʒɪkl/ *adj* 1 (relating to logic) 逻辑的; **～ thought/reasoning** 逻辑思考/推理 2 (reasonable) 合理的 ‹*solution, conclusion*›

logically /ˈlɒdʒɪkli/ *adv* 合乎逻辑地; **～ speaking** 从逻辑上说

logic: ～ bomb *n* 逻辑炸弹 [一种电脑病毒]; **～ circuit** *n* 逻辑电路

logician /ləˈdʒɪʃn/ *n* 逻辑学家

login /ˈlɒgɪn/ *n* 1 (act) 登录 2 (password) 登录密码

logistical /ləˈdʒɪstɪkl/, **logistic** /ləˈdʒɪstɪk/ *adj* Comm 物流的; Mil 后勤的

logistically /ləˈdʒɪstɪkli/ *adv* Comm 从物流方面; Mil 从后勤方面

logistics /ləˈdʒɪstɪks/ *npl* + *v sing or pl* Comm 物流; Mil 后勤

log jam *n* 1 (in river) 漂浮原木造成的堵塞 2 (in work) [因事情太多而造成的] 延误

logo /ˈləʊgəʊ/ *n* (*pl* **～s**) 标识

logoff /ˈlɒgɒf/ *n* 退出

logon /ˈlɒgɒn/ *n* = **login**

logout /ˈlɒgaʊt/ *n* 退出

log: ～ pile *n* 原木堆; **～rolling** *n* [u] Amer colloq 互投赞成票; **～ tables** *npl* 对数表

loin /lɔɪn/
A *n* [u] (cut of meat) 腰肉
B **loins** *npl* dated (lower back) 腰部; euph (sexual organs) 下身; **to gird up one's ～s** 准备行动

loincloth /ˈlɔɪnklɒθ/ *n* [用来遮羞的] 腰布

loiter /ˈlɔɪtə(r)/ *vi* 闲逛; **to ～ with intent** Brit Jur 徘徊观望伺机作案

loitering /ˈlɔɪtərɪŋ/ *n* [u] 闲荡; **～ with intent** Brit Jur 徘徊观望伺机作案

loll /lɒl/ *vi* «*person*» 懒洋洋地倚靠; «*part of body*» 垂下

lollipop /ˈlɒlɪpɒp/ *n* 1 (sweet) 棒棒糖 2 colloq (music) 轻松的古典音乐短曲

lollipop: ～ lady *n* Brit colloq 女交通安全员; **～ man** *n* Brit colloq 男交通安全员

lolly /ˈlɒli/ *n* Brit 1 [c] (lollipop) 棒棒糖; (ice lolly) 棒冰 2 [c] Austral, NZ (sweet) 糖果 3 [u] colloq dated (money) 钱

London /ˈlʌndən/ *pr n* 伦敦

Londonderry /ˈlʌndənderi/ *pr n* 伦敦德里郡

Londoner /ˈlʌndənə(r)/ *n* 伦敦人

lone /ləʊn/ *adj attrib* 1 (unsupported) 孤身的; **a ～ mother** 单身母亲 2 (isolated) 孤零零的 ‹*tree, building*› 3 (single) 唯一的; **a ～ friend came to his aid** 只有一个朋友来帮助他; **a ～ voice** 唯一的声音

loneliness /ˈləʊnlɪnɪs/ *n* [u] 1 (of person) 孤独 2 (of position) 偏僻

lonely /ˈləʊnli/ *adj* 1 (lacking friends) 孤独的 ‹*person, life*›; **she felt very ～** 她感到非常寂寞; **I am ～ for my family** 我思念我的家人 2 (isolated) 偏僻的 ‹*place, building*›; **to walk a ～ road** 选择离群索居

lonely: ～ hearts' club *n* 征友俱乐部; **～ hearts' column** *n* 征友专栏

lone parent *n* (male) 单身父亲; (female) 单身母亲

loner /ˈləʊnə(r)/ *n* 独来独往的人

lonesome /ˈləʊnsəm/ *adj* 孤单的; **to be ～ for sth./sb.** 思念某物/某人; **to be all on one's ～** Brit, **to be all by one's ～** Amer 独自一人

lone wolf *n* 独来独往的人

long¹ /lɒŋ, Amer lɔːŋ/ ▸ **p. 436**
A *adj* 1 (lengthy, protracted) 长的; **twenty metres/minutes ～** 20 米/20 分钟长; **～ thin sausages** 细长的香肠; **to get** *or* **grow ～** 变长/长长; **to be ～ in the leg** 腿长; **to be ～ in the tooth** colloq 年迈; **to be ～ on sth.** colloq 颇具某特性; **～ on brawn, short on brains** 肌肉发达，头脑简单; **to have a ～ face** 愁眉苦脸; **to make** *or* **pull a ～ face** 表情郁闷; **not by a ～ chalk** *or* **shot** colloq 绝不 2 **a ～ way** (in distance) 长距离的; **to be a ～ way away** *or* **off (sth.)** （离某处）很远; **they're a ～ way away from satisfying all the requirements** 他们还远不能满足所有要求; **a ～ way down the road/up to the top/out to sea** 沿路过去/往山顶/到海洋远处的很长距离; **you have to go a ～ way down the list before ...** 你必须顺着名单往下找很久，才能…; **to be a ～ way out** 相去甚远; **to have come a ～ way since those days** 从那时到现在取得了长足的进步; **to go a ～ way** (be successful) «*person*» 获得成功; (last long time) «*quantity, amount*» 够维持很长时间; **to go a ～ way towards sth./doing sth.** 对某事物/做某事大有帮助; **to have a ～ way to go (to ...** *or* **before ...)** （离…）有很大差距 3 (in time) 长时间的; **a ～ holiday** 长假; **it's been a very ～ day** 真是漫长的一天; **to take a ～ hard look at sth.** 仔细严格地检视某物; **a ～ hard stare** 长时间的审视; **she took a ～ drink from the flask** 她拿着保温杯喝了一大口水; **a ～ kiss** 深深的一吻; **to heave a ～ heavy sigh** 长叹一声; **to take the ～ view** 从长远考虑; **a ～ time** 长时间; **I'm sorry I've been such a ～ time returning your call** 我很抱歉这么久才回你电话; **for a ～ time** 很久以来; **a (very) ～ time ago** （很久）很久以前; **to take a ～ time (for sb.) to do sth.** 做某事花（某人）很长时间; **to be a ～ way away** *or* **off (sth.)** （离某时间）尚早; **to wait a ～ time before ...** 等待很久才…; **～ time no see** hum 久违了
B *adv* 1 (extended period of time) 长久地 ‹*last, go on, continue*›; **I shan't be ～** 我很快就好; **will you be ～?, how ～ will you be?** 你要很久吗? /你需要多久? ; **don't be ～ getting ready, please** 请马上准备好; **it's been so ～ since we last met** 我们已经很久没见面了; **it's not that ～ until Christmas** 很快就是圣诞节了; **it wasn't ～ before people began to arrive** 人们很快就开始到来了; **I don't have** *or* **haven't got ～** 我的时间不多了; **you won't have ～ to wait** 你们不用等很久; **she hasn't got ～ before her exams start** 她很快就要开始考试了; **～ live the King!** 国王万岁! ; **he stayed just ～ enough to meet us** 他只待到和我们见了个面; **to take ～er than expected** 比预期的要长; **not to take ～ to do sth.** 做某事没用很长时间; **at the ～est it only lasted one second** 它最长只持续1秒钟; **before ～** (in future) 马上; (in past) 不久前; **(not) for ～** （不）长久地; **will you be gone for ～?** 你要去很久吗? ; **he's happy now but not for ～** 他现在很高兴，可惜好景不长; **(not to do sth. until) ～ after** 很久以后（才做某事）; **it's ～ after your bedtime** 你的就寝时间早就过了; **～ ago** 很久以前; **it's not so ～ ago that you ...** 不久以前，你还…; **～ before ...** 在…之前很久; **～ before the end/we were married** 在结束前/我们结婚前很久; **it wasn't ～ before he realized** 他很快便意识到了; **he left not ～ before you arrived** 你到时他刚离开不久; **～ since** 很久以前; **they've ～ since gone home** 他们早就回家了; **not ～ since** 没过多久; **a ～-since discredited theory** 早就受到质疑的理论; **no ～er** 不再; **I can't stand it any ～er** 我再也无法忍受了; **five minutes, no ～er** 只给 5 分钟; **I'll be no ～er than five minutes** 我 5 分钟之内就好; **so ～** colloq 再见 2 (over a period of time) 很早以前; **I had ～ wished to meet him** 我早就想见他; **he is**

~ **gone** 他早走了 **3** (expressing duration) 整个地; **all day/night** ~ 一整天/一整夜; **her whole life** ~ 她的一辈子

C **as long as** *conj phr* **1** (in time) **borrow it for as ~ as you like** 你爱借多久就多久 **2** (provided that) **as** *or* **so ~ as** 只要; **as ~ as possible/necessary** 只要有可能/有必要; **as ~ as I live** 只要我一息尚存; **as ~ as you're safe** 只要你安全

D *n* **1** (essential points) **that's the ~ and the short of it** 情况就是这样; **the ~ and the short of it is that ...** 总而言之… **2** (syllable, signal) 长音节; (in Morse Code) 长画

long^{2} *vi* 渴望; **to ~ for sth./sb.** 渴望某事物/思念某人; **I've been ~ing for a chance to tell you** 我一直盼着有机会告诉你; **to ~ to do sth.** 渴望做某事

long: ~-awaited *adj* 等待已久的; **~boat** *n* 大划艇; **~bow** /-bəʊ/ *n* 大弓; **~-delayed** *adj* 延误已久的

long-distance

A *adj* 长距离的; **a ~ runner** 长跑运动员; **a ~ call/flight** 长途电话/飞行

B *adv* 长距离地; **to phone sb. ~** 给某人打长途电话

long: ~ division *n* [u and c] 长除法; **~-drawn-out** *adj* 持续很久的; **a ~-drawn-out trial** 旷日持久的审判; **~ drink** *n* 大杯饮料; **~ed-for** *adj* 期待已久的; **~-established** *adj* 建立已久的; **a ~-established custom** 由来已久的风俗

longevity /lɒn'dʒevəti/ *n* (of person, animal) 长寿; (of idea, tradition) 持久

long: ~-haired *adj* 长发的 ‹*person*›; 长有长毛的 ‹*animal*›; **~hand** *n* 普通书写; **in ~hand** 用手写; **~-haul** *adj* 长距离的; **a ~-haul flight** 长途飞行

longing /'lɒŋɪŋ, Amer 'lɔːŋɪŋ/

A *n* [u] 渴望; **to have a ~ for sth./sb.** 渴望某事物/思念某人; **to have** *or* **feel a ~ to do sth.** 渴望做某事

B *adj* 渴望的 ‹*look*›

longingly /'lɒŋɪŋli, Amer 'lɔːŋ-/ *adv* 渴望地 ‹*look*›

longish /'lɒŋɪʃ, Amer 'lɔːŋɪʃ/ *adj* 稍长的; **it's a ~ hop from here to London** 从这儿去伦敦有点远

longitude /'lɒndʒɪtjuːd, Amer 'lɔːndʒɪtuːd/ *n* 经度; **to be located at ~ 19° east** 位于东经 19 度

longitudinal /ˌlɒndʒɪ'tjuːdɪnl, Amer ˌlɔːndʒɪ'tuːdnl/ *adj* (relating to longitude) 经度的; (vertical) 纵向的 ‹*stripes, line*›

long: ~ jump ▸p. 307 *n* Brit 跳远; **~ jumper** *n* Brit 跳远选手; **~-lasting** *adj* 持久的; **~-legged** *adj* 腿长的; **~-life milk** *n* [u] 常温奶; **~-limbed** *adj* 四肢长的; **~ lost** *adj* 长久不见的 ‹*relative, brother*›; **L~ March** *n* **the L~ March** 长征; **~-overdue** *adj* 迟到很久的; **~-overdue reforms** 早该进行的改革; **~-playing record** Brit, **~play record** Amer *ns* 慢转唱片; **~-range** *adj* **1** (long distance) 远程的 ‹*missile, rocket*›; **2** (in future) 长远的; **a ~-range weather forecast** 远期天气预报; **~-running** *adj* 长期连播的 ‹*series*›; 长期的 ‹*dispute*›; **~ship** *n* 狭长快速战船; **~shoreman** /'lɒŋʃɔːmən/ *n* Amer 码头工人; **~ shot** *n* **1** Sport 获胜可能性极小的参赛者; **2** (risky attempt) 不太可能成功的尝试; **this plan is a ~ shot** 这一计划成功率极低; **~-sighted** *adj* **1** Brit (suffering from hypermetropia) 远视的; **2** (having foresight) 有远见的; **~-sleeved** *adj* 长袖的; **a ~-sleeved shirt/dress** 长袖衬衫/连衣裙; **~-standing** *adj* 存在已久的 ‹*agreement, tradition*›; **~-stay car park** *n* Brit 长期停车场; **~-suffering** *adj* 耐苦的 ‹*parents, wife*›; **~-term** *adj* 长期的 ‹*plan, solution*›; **~-time** *adj* 为时甚久的; **a ~-time friend** 老朋友; **~ ton** ▸p. 909 *n* 长吨; **~ trousers** *npl* 长裤

long wave

A *n* [u] 长波; **on ~** 用长波

B **long-wave** *modif* 长波的; **a long-wave broadcast/signal** 长波广播/信号

longways /'lɒŋweɪz, Amer 'lɔːŋ-/ *adv* 纵向地

long: ~ weekend *n* [三天或更长的] 周末长假; **~-winded** *adj* 啰唆的

loo /luː/ Brit colloq

A *n* (toilet) 抽水马桶; (room) 洗手间

B *modif* 洗手间的; **~ paper** 卫生纸; **a ~ seat/roll** 马桶盖/卷筒纸

loofah, luffa /'luːfə/ *n* 丝瓜络

look /lʊk/

A *vi* **1** (direct one's eyes) 看; **I waved at you, but you weren't ~ing** 我向你挥手, 可你却没注意; **oh, ~!** 哦, 瞧! ; **~ (over) there!** 瞧那儿! ; **to ~ along/around/down/up/over sth.** 顺着某物看/往某物四周看/顺某物往下看/顺某物往上看/往某物远处看; **to ~ into sb.'s eyes** 直视某人的眼睛; **to ~ over sb.'s shoulder** 越过某人的肩膀看去; **he ~ed over his shoulder** 他回头看; **I ~ed up and down the street** 我仔细打量这条街; **to ~ down one's nose at sb./sth.** 看不起某人/某事物; **to ~ on the bright side** 抱乐观态度; **to ~ the other way** lit 往另一边看; fig 装作没看见 **2** (search) 寻找; **he ~ed everywhere for his keys** 他到处找他的钥匙; **to ~ in the dictionary** 查词典 **3** (face) «*building, window*» 朝向; **the balcony ~s north/over the garden** 阳台朝北/俯瞰花园; **to ~ on to sth.** 面向某物 **4** (intend) 打算; **to be ~ing to do sth.** 正试图做某事 **5** (appear, seem) «*person, thing*» 看起来; **to ~ one's age** 相貌与年龄相符; **you ~ very good in blue** 你穿蓝色衣服真好看; **to ~ well** 看起来气色很好; **how did he ~?** 他气色如何? ; **to ~ one's best** 表现出最佳状态; **to ~ the part** (seem appropriate) 看上去得体; (dress appropriately) 穿着得体; **you ~ a complete idiot in that hat** 你戴上那顶帽子样子傻透了; **does the meat ~ done to you?** 你觉得肉煮熟了吗? ; **to ~ bad** 看起来糟糕; **it'll ~ very bad if ...** 如果…, 那就显得很糟糕了; **to ~ good** (beautiful) 漂亮; (successful) 顺利; (attractive) 诱人; **it doesn't ~ as if ...** 看起来不像是…; **it ~s (to me) as if** *or* **as though ...** (在我) 看来似乎; **they ~ to be gaining on us** 他们似乎快要追上我们了; **there ~s to be more trouble in store** 似乎要有更多的麻烦了; **~ alive!** 快点! ; **~ sharp** *or* **smart** *or* **snappy!** 赶快! ; **~ sharp about it!** 赶快!

B *vt* **1** (gaze, stare) 注视; **to ~ sb. (straight) in the eye** 直视某人; **I'll never be able to ~ her in the face again** fig 我永远都无法再面对她了; **to ~ sb. up and down** 上下打量某人; **to ~ one's last on sth.** 看某物最后一眼 **2** (pay attention) 注意; **~ what you're doing with that knife** 瞧你是怎么用那把刀的; **if you don't ~ where you're going, ...** 如果你走路不留神, …; **~ who's here!** 看谁来了! ; **~ what arrived in the post this morning** 注意今天上午的邮件

C *excl* **1** (attracting attention) **~!** 喂! **2** (protesting) **(now) ~ here!** 听着!

D *n* **1** (act of looking) 看; **the church is worth a ~** 这个教堂值得一看; **one last ~ and then we must go** 我们最后看一眼就得走了; **to have** *or* **take a ~ at sb./sth.** 看看某物/某人; **to have** *or* **take another ~/a good ~ at sb./sth.** 再看一眼/好好看看某物/某人; **to get a good ~ at sb./sth.** 看清楚某物/某人; **to take one ~ at sb./sth.** 看某物/某人一眼; **to take a quick ~ at sth.** 瞥一眼某物; **to have** *or* **take a ~ around (sth.)** (在某处) 四处看看; **to have** *or* **take a ~ inside/outside (sth./somewhere)** 在 (某物/某处) 里面/外面看看; **to have** *or* **take a ~ through** 用…观看 ‹*telescope, binoculars*›; **to take a ~ ahead to next week's programmes** 看看下星期的节目预告; **to have a quick ~ through sth.** 迅速翻阅某物; **I had a ~ in the newspaper** 报纸我看过了; **to give sth. a ~** 检查某物 **2** (search) 寻找; **to have a ~ for sth./sb.** 寻找某物/某人; **we've had several ~s** 我们已找找过好几遍了; **to take another ~/a ~ around** 再找一次/四下寻找; **to have a good ~ through sth.** 仔细翻检某物 **3** (facial expression) 表情; **a ~ of fear/anger/amusement** 恐惧/愤怒/愉悦的表情; **a kind/questioning/penetrating ~** 和善/疑问/犀利的目光; **to give sb. a ~ of ...** 以…的目光看某人 ‹*disdain, disbelief*›; **to get some odd** *or* **funny ~s** 被人投以奇怪的目光; **he gave me an odd ~** 他神情古怪地看了我一眼; **he had a malicious ~ in his eye** 他眼带凶光; **if ~s could kill ...** 如果眼神可以杀人… **4** (appearance) (of person) 外貌; (of thing) 外观; **he had a ~ of profound melancholy about him** 他显得十分忧郁; **he has the ~ of a military man** 他长得像个军人; **the ~ typical of a psychotic** 典型的精神病患者的样子; **to like the ~(s) of sb./sth.** 喜欢某人/某物的样子; **I don't like the ~ of that** 我感觉不妙; **by** *or* **from the ~(s) of sb.** 从某人的外表看; **by** *or* **from the ~(s) of it** 看样子; **you can't go** *or* **judge by ~s** 不能仅凭外表判断 **5** (fashion) 款式; **the ~ for men** 男装的款式

E **looks** *npl* 容貌; **good ~s** 美貌; **to keep/lose one's ~s** 容颜不改/不再

(Phrasal verbs)

- **look after** *vt* [**~ after sb./sth.**]
  1 (care for) 看护 ‹*invalid*›; 养护 ‹*equipment, possessions*›; 招待 ‹*guests*›; **~ after yourself!** 保重! **2** (be responsible for) 照管 ‹*child, pet, business, suitcase*›; 保管 ‹*money*›; **to ~ after sth. for sb.** 为某人照看某物; **to ~ after the shop/house** 看店/看房子; **to ~ after sb.'s interests** 维护某人的利益 **3** (attend to) 处理 ‹*financial matters, legal business*›; 解决 ‹*needs*›; **to ~ after customer enquiries** 处理客户咨询
- **look ahead** *vi* 为将来打算; **to ~ ahead to sth.** 为某事物做打算; **to be ~ing ahead four years** 为今后的 4 年作打算
- **look around**
  A *vi* **1** (turn one's head) 四下看 **2** (search) 四处寻找; **to ~ around for sb./sth.** 四处寻找某人/某事物 **3** (view) 四处看看; **I'd just like to ~ around, please** 哦, 我只是想随便看看
  B *vt* [**~ around sth.**] 参观 ‹*building, town, exhibition*›
- **look at** *vt* [**~ at sth.**]
  1 (observe) 看; **~ at the mess/you!** 瞧瞧这一堆乱摊子/你自己! ; **to ~ at sb. doing** *or* **do sth.** 看某人做某事的样子; **he's a wrestler, but you'd never think it to ~ at him** 他是摔跤手, 但是看他的样子你怎么都想不到; **she's not much** *or* **she's nothing to ~ at** 她相貌平平 **2** (glance briefly at) 浏览 ‹*newspaper, report*› **3** (consider) 考虑 ‹*problem, implications, proposal*›; **~ at where she is now/what happened to her!** 想想她现在在哪儿吧/她的遭遇吧! **4** (regard) 看待 ‹*life, situation, event*›; **~ at it this way** 这样看这件事; **~ed at another way, ...** 换个角度看, …
- **look back** *vi* **1** (look behind one) 回头看; **to ~ back at sth./sb.** 回头看某物/某人; **since then he's never ~ed back** fig 自那以后, 他的事业蒸蒸日上 **2** (reflect, reminisce) 回顾; **to ~ back on/to sth.** 回顾某事
- **look down** *vi* **1** 向下看; **to ~ down at sth.** 向下看某物 **2** (dominate) «*fortress, tower*» 俯瞰 ‹*town, valley*› **3** (despise) 小看; **to ~ down on sth./sb.** 轻视某事物/某人
- **look for** *vt* [**~ for sb./sth.**]
  1 (search for) 寻找 ‹*person, object, opportunity*›
  2 (expect) 期待 ‹*result, promise, commitment*›
- **look forward** *vi* **to ~ forward to sth.** 期待 ‹*event, reunion, visit*›; **I ~ forward to**

hearing from you soon (in letter) 我希望能很快收到你的回信

- **look in** *vi* 1 (peer) 往里面看; **to ~ in at the window/through a crack** 在窗边/从一条缝隙往里面看 2 (pay a short call) **to ~ in at a place** 短暂拜访某处; **we could ~ in at Sarah's/at the library on the way** 我们可顺便去萨拉家/图书馆; **to ~ in on sb./sth.** 短暂拜访某人/某处; **I'll ~ in on you later** 我晚些时候再来找你
- **look into** *vt* [**~ into sth.**] 调查 ‹*cause, case, problem*›; **to ~ into sb.'s accounts/financial position** 审查某人的账目/财务状况
- **look like** *vt* [**~ like sb./sth.**] 看似; **what does he/it ~ like?** 他长/它是什么样子?; **he doesn't ~ at all like his father** 他一点都不像他父亲; **that ~s very much like my wallet** 那看起来很像是我的钱包; **it ~s to me like a forgery** 我看它像是赝品; **are you having trouble? — what does it ~ like?** 你有麻烦吗? ——看着像吗?; **it ~s like rain** 看来要下雨; **~s like trouble, I'm afraid** 恐怕有麻烦; **you ~ like being the only man here** 你好像是这里唯一的男人
- **look on**

A *vt* [**~ on sb./sth.**] 看待; **they ~ed on her with the deepest suspicion** 他们对她充满怀疑; **to ~ on sb./sth. as ...** 视某人/某事物为…; **they ~ed on him as ideal for the job** 他们认为他是这份工作的理想人选

B *vi* 旁观; **we did all the work, while they ~ed on** 我们做了所有工作, 他们只是袖手旁观; **we will not sit back and ~ on while our allies are attacked** 我们的盟友受袭时, 我们不会坐着袖手旁观

- **look out**

A *vi* 1 (take care) 注意; **~ out!** 当心!; **~ out behind you!** 当心身后!; **they'd better ~ out** 他们最好当心点; **to ~ out for sth.** 当心某事物 2 (keep watch) 留意寻找; **to ~ out for sb./sth.** 留心寻觅某人/某物 3 (stare, gaze) 向外看; **we could ~ out over the town** 我们可以向外俯瞰全城; **to ~ out of sth.** 从某物向外望; **she was ~ing out of an upstairs window** 她正从楼上窗户向外看

B *vt* [**~ out sth.**] Brit 找出 ‹*back numbers, old clothes*›; **to ~ sth. out for sb.** 为某人找出某物

- **look over** *vt* [**~ over sth., ~ sth. over**] 浏览 ‹*essay, report*›
- **look round** *vi, vt* Brit **= look around**
- **look through** *vt* 1 [**~ through sth., ~ sth. through**] (read through quickly) 浏览 ‹*book, script, notes*› 2 [**~ through sth.**] (search) 在…中查找 ‹*cupboards, drawers*›; 翻查 ‹*files, records*›; **I've ~ed through my wardrobe** 我在衣柜里找过了; **we've ~ed through the accounts for that year** 我们查过那年的账了 3 [**~ through sb.**] (ignore) 无视 ‹*person*›
- **look to** *vt* 1 [**~ to sb.**] (rely on) 指望; **to ~ to sb./sth. for sth.** 指望从某人/某事物处取得某物; **to ~ to sb./sth. to do sth.** 指望某人/某事物做某事; **people ~ to us for advice** 人们希望从我们这里得到建议 2 [**~ to sth.**] formal (take care of) 注意; **a sovereign nation must ~ to its own defences** 一个主权国必须确保自己的国防安全
- **look up**

A *vi* 1 (direct gaze) 抬头看; **to ~ up from sth.** 从某物抬头往上看; **he ~ed up from his work/newspaper (to talk to us)** 他停下手中的工作/放下手中报纸, 抬起头 (, 和我们说话) 2 colloq (improve) 好转; **things are ~ing up for us** 对我们来说情况正在好转; **business may ~ up a little** 生意可能会有些起色

B *vt* 1 [**~ sth. up, ~ up sth.**] (try to find) 查找 ‹*word, name, date*› 2 [**~ sb. up, ~ up sb.**] (visit) 看望 ‹*friend*›; **~ me up if you're ever in Shanghai** 你若来上海就来看我吧

- **look upon** *vt* **= look on A**
- **look up to** *vt* [**~ up to sb./sth.**] 敬重; **I've always ~ed up to him as someone of great integrity** 我一直敬重他是个正人君子

look: ~-alike *n* 长得很像的人; **~ed-for** *adj attrib* 盼望的 ‹*event, result*›

looker /ˈlʊkə(r)/ *n* colloq (woman) 美女; (man) 帅哥

looker-on *n* (*pl* **lookers-on**) 旁观者

look-in *n* colloq 1 (short visit) 顺道访问; **to give sb. a ~** 顺道拜访某人 2 Brit (chance, opportunity) 机会; **to get a ~** 得到机会; **I didn't get a ~** 我没得到机会; **to give sb. a ~** 给某人机会

looking-glass *n* liter 镜子

look: ~out *n* 1 (surveillance) 留神观察; **to be on the ~out for sth./sb.** 注意某事物/某人; **to keep a ~out for sth./sb.** 当心某事物/某人; 2 (person) 观察员; 3 (surveillance post) 观察所; *modif* **a ~out post** 瞭望哨; 4 (prospect) 前景; 5 Brit colloq (one's own concern) 自己的事; **that's his ~out** 那是他自己的事; **~-over** *n* 查看; **to give sth. a ~-over** 查看某物; **~-see** *n* colloq 飞快一瞥; **to have** *or* **take a ~-see** 看一眼; **~-up** *n* [u] 查表

loom /luːm/

A *n* 织布机

B *vi* 1 (appear menacingly) 令人生畏地隐现; **to ~ (up) from/through sth.** 从某处/通过某处赫然出现 2 (threaten) 阴森地逼近; **to ~ over sth.** 逼近某物; **to ~ large** 令人忧虑

loon /luːn/ *n* colloq 傻瓜; **he is a bit of a ~** 他有点儿蠢

loonie /ˈluːni/ *n* Can colloq 一加元硬币

loony /ˈluːni/

A *n* colloq 1 (eccentric) 怪人 2 (deranged person) 疯子

B *adj* colloq 1 (eccentric) 古怪的 2 (deranged) 发疯的

loony bin *n* colloq pej 疯人院

loop /luːp/

A *n* 1 (circular shape) 环形; **he attached a ~ of wire to the post** 他把导线绕在柱子上; **to be in/out of the ~** fig colloq 属圈内/圈外人士; **to keep somebody out of/in the ~** fig colloq 不让/让某人知情 2 (of plane) 筋斗; **to ~ the ~** 翻筋斗特技飞行 3 (repeat of film) 循环电影胶片; (repeat of tape) 循环音像磁带 4 (closed circuit) 回路 5 (in computer programming) 循环 6 (contraceptive) 节育环

B *vt* 使成环; **to ~ sth. around sth.** 用某物环绕某物

C *vi* 成环形; **the river ~s across the plain** 那条河盘绕着流过平原

loophole /ˈluːphəʊl/ *n* 1 (let-out) 漏洞; **to close** *or* **plug a ~** 堵漏洞; **to find/exploit a ~** 找到/利用漏洞 2 (in fortification) (for defence through) 枪眼; (as window) 透光孔

loopy /ˈluːpi/ *adj* colloq (mad) 疯狂的; (silly) 愚蠢的

loose /luːs/

A *adj* 1 (not firmly tied or secured) 松动的 ‹*tooth, nail, joint, brick*›; 松散的 ‹*knot, page, thread*›; **my shoelace is ~** 我鞋带松了; **the post is very ~ in the ground** 柱子松松地埋在地里; **I've got a ~ button on my shirt** 我衬衣上有一颗纽扣松了; **a ~ connection** Elec 接触不良; **to come** *or* **get** *or* **work ~** «*nail, brick, handle*» 松动; «*knot, bonds*» 松散; **to work** *or* **make ~** 使…松动 ‹*nail, brick, handle*›; 使…松散 ‹*knot, bonds*›; **to hang ~** «*reins, rope, thread*» 垂下; «*hair*» 披散; **hang ~, man!** Amer colloq 放松, 老兄!; **to be at a ~ end** 无所事事; **to tie up any** *or* **the ~ ends** 做收尾工作 2 (not confined, free) 不受束缚的 ‹*animal, person*›; **there's a tiger ~ at the zoo** 动物园里有一只放养的老虎; **to get ~** 挣脱束缚; **to let** *or* **set** *or* **turn ~** 释放 ‹*animal, prisoner*›; **to let the dogs ~ on sb.** 放狗袭击某人; **to let sb. ~ on sth.** 让某人随意使用某物; **to roam/run ~** 闲散地游荡/奔跑 3 (separate) 零散的 ‹*fragments, sheet of paper*›; 散装的 ‹*biscuits, cheese, vegetables*›; **~ stones** 碎石子; **~ change** 零钱; **to sell sth. ~** 零卖某物 4 (not tight or constricting) 宽松的 ‹*clothing*›; 松弛的 ‹*skin*›; **leave the scarf ~** 把围巾系得松些; **a ~ fold of skin** 松弛的皱皮 5 (not compact) 疏松的 ‹*soil, earth*›; 松软的 ‹*chippings*›; 松散的 ‹*grouping, organization*›; **a ~ scrum** (rugby) 乱集团争球; **to have ~ links with sb.** 与某人关系疏远 6 (imprecise) 不准确的 ‹*translation, rendering, definition*›; 不严谨的 ‹*style, wording, thinking, argument*›; 松散的 ‹*structure, discipline*› 7 pej (dissolute) 放荡的 ‹*person, living*›; 堕落的 ‹*morals*›; 轻率的 ‹*talk*› 8 Med 腹泻的; **to have ~ bowels** 拉肚子

B *n* **to be on the ~** 不受约束; **a convict/puma on the ~** 逍遥法外的罪犯/到处乱跑的美洲狮

C *vt* 1 liter (set free) 放开 ‹*animal, person*›; **he ~d their bonds** 他为他们松了绑 2 (shoot) 射 ‹*arrow*›; **to ~ a volley** 齐射

Phrasal verb

- **loose off**

A *vt* [**~ off sth.**] 1 (fire, discharge) 放 ‹*gun*›; 射 ‹*arrow*›; 发射 ‹*shells*› 2 fig (verbally) 不受约束地表达; **he ~d off a volley of abuse** 他大骂一通

B *vi* 1 (shoot) 射击; **to ~ off at sb./sth.** 朝某人/某物射击 2 fig (verbally) 谩骂; **to ~ off at sb./sth.** 对某人/某事物大骂一通

loose: ~ cannon *n* 大炮 [指举止无法预料的人]; **~ cover** *n* Brit (for chair) 椅子套; (for sofa) 沙发套; **~-fitting** *adj* 宽松的 ‹*jeans, clothes*›; **~-knit** *adj* 1 (loosely made) 织法宽松的 ‹*sweater, jumper*›; 2 **= loosely knit**; **~-leaf** *adj* 活页的; **a ~-leaf folder** *or* **binder** 活页夹

loosely /ˈluːsli/ *adv* 1 (not tightly) 松散地; **a ~ woven fabric** 质地稀疏的织物 2 (roughly) 不精确地; **the film is ~ based on that novel** 这部电影大致是根据那本小说改编的

loosely knit *adj* 组织松散的 ‹*group*›

loosen /ˈluːsn/

A *vt* 1 (make less tight) 使变松; **to ~ one's tie** 松开领带; **to ~ a knot** 解结; **to ~ stiff muscles** 放松僵硬的肌肉; **to ~ one's grip** *or* **hold on sth.** lit 松开某物; fig 放松对某事物的控制; **to ~ family ties** 疏远家庭关系; **alcohol ~s the tongue** 酒后话多 2 (soften) 使…通畅 ‹*bowels*›; 使…松软 ‹*earth, soil*›

B *vi* 变松; **my grip ~ed on the steering wheel** 我松开了方向盘; **family ties have ~ed** 家庭关系疏远了

Phrasal verb

- **loosen up**

A *vi* 1 (relax muscles) «*person*» 放松肌肉; «*muscle, joint*» 放松 2 (become mentally relaxed) 放松心情; **they ~ed up after a few drinks** 他们喝过几杯酒之后变得随便了

B *vt* [**~ up sth./sb., ~ sth./sb. up**] 使放松

looseness /ˈluːsnɪs/ *n* [u] 1 (of knot, fastening, joint) 松动; (of rope) 松弛; (of clothing) 宽松 2 (of translation) 不精确; (of argument, thinking) 不严谨 3 (laxity of morals, behaviour) 放纵 4 (of structure, organization) 松散

loot /luːt/

A *n* [u] 1 (stolen goods) 赃物; (from enemy in war) 战利品; (taken during riot) 掠夺物 2 colloq (money) 钱

B *vt* 抢劫 ‹*shop, house, valuables*›

C *vi* 抢劫; **to go ~ing** 去抢劫

looter /ˈluːtə(r)/ *n* 抢劫者

looting /ˈluːtɪŋ/ *n* [u] 抢劫

lop /lɒp/ (*pres p etc.* **-pp-**) *vt* 修剪…的树枝

Phrasal verb

- **lop off** *vt* [**~ sth. off, ~ off sth.**] 1 砍掉 ‹*branch*› 2 fig colloq 减掉; **the new road ~s half an hour off the journey** 有了新修的公路, 路程缩短了半小时

l

lope /ləʊp/
A *n* 轻松的大步子
B *vi* (walk) «*person*» 轻松地大步走; (run) «*tiger, wolf*» 轻松地大步跑

lop-eared /ˈlɒpɪəd/ *adj* 有垂耳的; **a ~ rabbit** 垂耳兔

lopsided /ˌlɒpˈsaɪdɪd/ *adj* 向一侧倾斜的; **he gave a ~ smile** 他撇嘴一笑

lopsidedly /ˌlɒpˈsaɪdɪdli/ *adv* 向一边倾斜地

loquacious /ləˈkweɪʃəs/ *adj* formal 健谈的

loquacity /ləˈkwæsəti/, **loquaciousness** /ləˈkweɪʃəsnɪs/ *ns* [u] formal 健谈

lord /lɔːd/
A *n* **1** (ruler) 君主; **to be ~ of sth./sb.** 是某国/某人的君主; **the ~ of the manor** 庄园主 **2** **Lord** Brit (nobleman) 勋爵; **the (House of) L~s** 上议院; **drunk as a ~** 酩酊大醉的 **3** Brit (form of address) 大人 **4** Relig 主 **5** colloq (in exclamations) 天哪; **good ~!** 老天!; **~ (only) knows!** colloq (只有)天晓得!
B *vt* **to ~ it over sb.** colloq 对某人逞威风

Lord Chancellor *n* Brit 大法官

lordly /ˈlɔːdli/ *adj* 高傲的 ‹*manner*›

Lord Mayor *n* Brit 市长大人; **the ~ of London** 伦敦市市长

lordship /ˈlɔːdʃɪp/ *n* Brit **1** (*also* **Lordship**) (title) 大人 **2** formal dated (authority) 贵族的权力; **to have ~ over sb./sth.** 统治某人/某物

Lord: ~'s Prayer *n* **the L~'s Prayer** 主祷文; **~'s Supper** *n* **the L~'s Supper** 圣餐

lore /lɔː(r)/ *n* [u] (traditional beliefs) 学问; (stories) 传说; **plant ~** 植物方面的知识; **Celtic ~** 凯尔特人的传说

lorry /ˈlɒri/ *n* Brit 卡车; **it fell off the back of a ~** colloq hum 它是从车后面掉下来的 [偷盗者的托词]

lorry: ~ driver ▸**p. 409** *n* Brit 卡车司机; **~-load** *n* Brit 一卡车; **a ~-load of soldiers** 一卡车士兵; **~-loads of money** fig colloq 很多钱

> **the Los Angeles Times**
> 《洛杉矶时报》。美国报纸，1881 年创刊，总部位于洛杉矶。曾多次获得普利策奖（▸**Pulitzer Prize**），是美国最优秀的报纸之一。

lose /luːz/ (*pt, pp* **lost**)
A *vt* **1** (be unable to find) 丢失 ‹*thing*›; 弄丢 ‹*person*›; **to ~ one's way** lit (become disoriented) 迷路; fig (morally) 迷失 **2** (be deprived of) 失去 ‹*limb, confidence, territory*›; 损失 ‹*heat, power, money, value*›; **to ~ the use of** 丧失…的功能 ‹*limb, muscle, eye*›; **she's lost a lot of blood** 她失血很多; **to ~ weight** 减轻体重; **to ~ interest in sth./sb.** 失去对某事物/某人的兴趣; **to ~ sound quality** 影响音质; **the poem has lost a lot in translation** 这首诗翻译后失色不少; **we're losing oil/speed** 我们在漏油/减速; **Labour has lost London** 工党在伦敦的竞选中失利; **I lost thousands at poker** 我玩扑克输了几千块; **200 jobs will be lost** 将裁减 200 个工作岗位; **we're losing a lot of business to our competitors** 我们的很多生意都让竞争对手夺走了; **to ~ members to other sectors** 向其他部门流失人员; **she lost her husband recently** 她新近丧夫; **many lives were lost in the disaster** 许多人在这场灾难中丧生; **to ~ a patient** 没救活病人; **the ship was lost with all hands** 这艘船失事了，船员无一生还; **to be lost at sea** 死于海难; **to have nothing to ~** colloq 不会损失什么; **try it, you've got nothing to ~** 试试吧，你又不会损失什么; **I daren't risk it, I've got too much to ~** 我不敢冒险，否则损失会很大; **to (totally** *or* **completely) ~ it** colloq (lose one's temper) (大)发脾气 **3** (miss, waste) 失去 ‹*opportunity*›; 浪费 ‹*time*›; **there's no time/not a moment to ~** 没有时间/片刻时间可以浪费; **he lost no time in replying** 他立刻作出答复; **this allusion was not lost on him** 他领会了这个暗示 **4** (not hear, understand) 听不到 ‹*remark, word*›; 使…迷惑 ‹*person*›; **the speech was lost in the din** 讲话被喧闹声淹没; **you've lost me there** colloq 你把我弄糊涂了 **5** (not see) 看不见 ‹*target, aircraft, ball*› **6** colloq (get rid of) 甩掉 ‹*unwanted person, pursuer, car*› **7** esp Amer colloq (rid oneself of) 扔掉 ‹*unwanted object*›; 处理掉 ‹*money*›; 辞掉 ‹*jobs, worker*›; 改掉 ‹*habit*›; **~ the box somewhere** 把那盒子找个地方扔了; **~ the tie!** 摘掉领带! **8** (become slow) «*watch, clock*» 走慢 ‹*minute, seconds*› **9** (be defeated in) 输掉 ‹*battle, game, case, debate*›; **we lost the motion/election** 我们的动议没有通过/我们在选举中失败了 **10** (cause to lose) **to ~ sb. sth.** 使某人失去某物; **his speech lost the party a million votes** 他的演讲让该党损失了 100 万张选票
B *v refl* **to ~ oneself in sth.** 全神贯注于某事物; **to ~ oneself in a book/newspaper** 埋头看书/读报
C *vi* **1** (be defeated) «*team, player, competitor*» 输掉; **we lost 3-0/by a large margin** 我们以 0 比 3/大比分落败; **to ~ to sb./sth.** 输给某人/某物 **2** (be worse off) 遭受损失; **you can't ~ by letting her try her method** 让她试试她的方法，你不会损失什么; **to ~ (heavily) on a transaction** 在一笔交易中亏损(严重); **the novel ~s in translation** 小说经过翻译就失色了; **the story doesn't ~ in the retelling** 这个故事百讲不厌 **3** (go too slowly) «*clock, watch*» 走慢

Phrasal verb

- **lose out** *vi* **1** (be deprived of an opportunity) 失去机会; **to ~ out on** 错过 ‹*opportunity, chance*›; **to ~ out on a deal** *or* **bargain** 在交易中赔钱 **2** (be the loser) 失败; **to ~ out to** 输给 ‹*rival, person, team*›

loser /ˈluːzə(r)/ *n* **1** (person defeated or receiving no benefit) 失败者; **to be a good/bad ~** 输得起/输不起; **you won't be the ~ by it** 你不会因此而吃亏的 **2** colloq (unsuccessful person) 老是失败的人; **a born ~** 天生背运的人

losing /ˈluːzɪŋ/ *adj* 失败的 ‹*team, side*›; **to be on a ~ streak** 连连失败; **it's a ~ battle** 这是必败之仗; **to fight a ~ battle against sth.** 徒劳地与某事物斗争

loss /lɒs, Amer lɔːs/ *n* [c and u] **1** (gen) 损失; Comm, Fin 亏损; **~ of blood** 失血; **weight ~** 体重减少; **heat ~** 热损耗; **~ of income** *or* **earnings** 收入的减少; **there was great ~ of life** 很多人丧生; **you should report the ~ of your credit card immediately** 信用卡丢失后应立即挂失; **~ of sound/vision** TV 声音/图像的消失; **with the ~ of 300 jobs** 在减少 300 个工作岗位的情况下; **he is a great ~ to the arts** 他的离去对文艺界来说是一大损失; **a sense of ~** 失落感; **to make a ~ on sth.** 在某事上亏损; **to trade at a ~** 做亏本买卖; **to suffer heavy ~es** Comm 亏损严重; Mil 伤亡惨重; **the party suffered heavy ~es in the elections** 该党在选举中失去了大量席位 **2** **to be at a ~** (puzzled) 感到困惑; (helpless) 不知所措; **he was at a ~ for words** 他不知说什么好; **I'm at a ~ to explain what went wrong** 我无法解释出什么问题了

loss: ~ adjuster ▸**p. 409** *n* 损失理算员; **~ leader** *n* [为招揽顾客而低价出售的] 亏本商品; **~-maker** *n* (product) 亏损产品; (company) 亏损公司; **~-making** *adj* 亏损的; **a ~-making product/company** 亏损产品/公司

lost /lɒst, Amer lɔːst/
A *pt, pp* ▸**lose**
B *adj* **1** (unable to be found) 遗失的 ‹*key, wallet, treasure*›; 走失的 ‹*pet*›; **a ~ article** 失物; **her watch is** *or* **got ~** 她的手表丢了; **get ~!** colloq 快滚!; **to give sb./sth. up for ~** 认定某人已死/某事没有希望 **2** (gone, vanished) 逝去的 ‹*youth, happiness*›; 消逝的 ‹*civilization*›; 失传的 ‹*art, craft, skill*›; **to be ~ to sth.** 不再属于某物; **a promising talent ~ to the sport** 体育界失去的未来之星 **3** (missed, wasted) 错失的 ‹*opportunity, chance*›; 浪费的 ‹*time*›; **to be ~ on sb.** (make no impression) 未被某人注意; (be wasted) 未被某人理解 **4** (astray) 迷路的; **to get ~** 迷路 **5** (uncomprehending, bewildered) 困惑的 ‹*look, expression*›; **I was completely ~** 我彻底糊涂了; **I'd be ~ without you/the dictionary** 没有你/词典的话，我会不知所措; **I felt ~ after she left** 她走之后我感到迷惘; **to be ~ for words** 无言以对 **6** *pred* (rapt, absorbed) 专注的; **to be ~ in thought/meditation** 陷入沉思/冥想; **to be ~ in a book/newspaper** 专心致志读书/看报; **to be ~ in wonder at sth.** 对某物惊叹不已; **to be ~ to the world** 对周围的事浑然不觉 **7** (doomed) 毁灭的; **all is ~** 全完了; **like a ~ soul** 失魂落魄地; **a ~ cause** 败局已定的事

lost and found *n* **1** [u] (items) 失物 **2** [c] (office) 失物招领处 **3** [c] (newspaper column) 失物招领栏

lost property Brit *n* = **lost and found 1, 2**

lot¹ /lɒt/
A *pron* **1** (great deal) **a ~** 很多; **to get a ~ out of sth.** 从…中获益良多 ‹*book, activity*›; **to do a ~ to help sb./to improve sth.** 尽力帮助某人/改进某事物; **there's not a ~ to tell** 没有多少可讲的; **to give a ~ to be able to do sth.** 付出很多努力才能做某事; **it says a ~ about sb./sth.** 上面说了很多关于某人/某事物的事; **it has a ~ to do with sth.** 这主要和某事物有关; **an awful ~** colloq 非常多; **quite a ~** 相当多; **to mean quite a ~ to sb.** 对某人来说相当重要; **to know a ~ about sth.** 十分熟悉某事物; **such a ~** 这么多 **2** colloq (entire amount) **the ~** 全部; **she ate the (whole) ~** 她全都吃了; **the police will confiscate the ~!** 警方将把这些东西全部充公!; **I'll write you a cheque for the ~** 我会把所有的费用给你开成一张支票; **the best speech of the ~** 所有演讲中最精彩的; **I've had heartburn, cramps, the ~!** 我烧心、抽筋等全都一一经历了 **3** colloq (specific group of people) 一群人; **the best/nicest of the ~** 这一群人里最好/最善良的; **that ~** pej 那帮家伙; **your/my ~** 你们/我们这些人; **he's a bad ~** 他是个坏蛋; **it's the best of a bad ~** 这是差中之优了
B *n* **1** (great deal) **a ~ of** 很多的; **a ~ of money/time/women** 很多钱/时间/女人; **not a ~ of cars/people** 不多的汽车/人; **to see a ~ of sb.** 经常见到某人; **to do a ~ of sth.** 做大量的某事; **an awful ~ of time/responsibility** colloq 很多时间/很大责任; **what a ~ of entries/books!** 词条/书真多啊! **2** colloq (entire group) 全部; **the (whole) ~ of you/them** 你们/他们所有人
C **lots** *npl* colloq **~s (and ~s) of** 很多(很多)的; **there are ~s of things to do** 有许多事要做; **..., and ~s more** …，以及许多其他的; **has he got any DVDs? — yes, ~s!** colloq 他有 DVD 吗? ——有，多着呢!
D **lots** *adv* 很; **~s better/more interesting** 好/有趣得多
E **a lot** *adv phr* (by far) 很大程度地; (much) 很多地; (often) 经常; **a ~ easier/more useful** 容易/有用得多; **to talk a ~ about sth.** 大谈某事; **to improve/worry a ~** 大有改善/非常担心; **you're smoking an awful ~** colloq 你抽烟抽得太凶了; **he travels abroad such a ~** 他三天两头出国

lot² *n* **1** (fate) 命运; (quality of life) 生活状况; **to be happy with one's ~** 乐天安命; **to improve sb.'s ~** 改善某人的生活状况; **to throw in one's ~ with sb.** 决心与某人共命运 **2** Amer (piece of land) 地块; **a vacant ~** 空地; **a car ~** 停车场; **the farmland was**

divided up into ~s 这块耕地被分割成小块 **3** (at auction) 拍卖品; **~ (No.) 28** 第 28 号拍品; **to be sold in ten ~s** 被分作 10 批拍卖 **4** (decision-making process) 抽签; **to draw** *or* **cast ~s** 抽签; **to be chosen/decided/allocated by ~** 以抽签方式选择/决定/分配; **it fell to my ~ to ...** 我命中注定要… **5** Cin (studio) 露天片场 **6** colloq (batch, group of goods, people) 一批; **a ~ of apples/tourists** 一批苹果/游客

loth /ləʊθ/ *adj* = **loath**

lotion /ˈləʊʃn/ *n* [u and c] 护肤液; **sun ~** 防晒霜; **cleansing/moisturizing ~** 洁肤/润肤乳液

lottery /ˈlɒtəri/ *n* lit 抽彩; fig 碰运气的事; **~ winner** 中彩者; **~ ticket** 彩票

lotto /ˈlɒtəʊ/ ▸**p. 307** *n* 乐透 [一种抽号码赌博游戏]

lotus /ˈləʊtəs/ *n* (*pl* **~es**) 莲

lotus position *n* [u] 莲花坐 [做瑜伽或冥想的坐姿]

louche /luːʃ/ *adj* 声名狼藉的

loud /laʊd/

A *adj* **1** (noisy) 声音巨大的 ‹*explosion*›; 大声的 ‹*scream*›; 喧闹的 ‹*music, noise*›; 响亮的 ‹*laugh, voice*› **2** (emphatic) 呼声强烈的 ‹*protest, objection*›; **to be ~ in one's praise/condemnation of sth.** 竭力称赞/谴责某事 **3** pej (vulgar) 俗丽的 ‹*clothes, colour*›; 招摇的 ‹*manner, person*›

B *adv* 大声地 ‹*talk, laugh, cry*›; **out ~** 大声地; **I am receiving you ~ and clear** Radio 我听到你的声音，清晰响亮; colloq hum 你的话我听得一清二楚

loudhailer /ˌlaʊdˈheɪlə(r)/ *n* Brit 扩音器

loudly /ˈlaʊdli/ *adv* **1** (noisily) 大声地; **the audience sang along ~** 观众齐声高歌 **2** (garishly, vulgarly) 俗丽地 ‹*dress*›; 粗俗地 ‹*behave*›

loud: ~mouth *n* colloq pej 说话大声大气的人; **~mouthed** *adj* colloq pej 说话大声大气的

loudness /ˈlaʊdnɪs/ *n* [u] (of voice, laughter, applause, protest) 响亮程度; (of music, sound, radio) 音量

loudspeaker /ˈlaʊdspiːkə(r)/ *n* **1** (for announcements) 扩音器; **a ~ van/announcement** 广播车/通知 **2** (for hi-fi) 扬声器

Louisiana /luːˌiːzɪˈænə/ *pr n* 路易斯安那州

lounge /laʊndʒ/

A *n* **1** (in house) 客厅 **2** (in hotel) 休息室; **a TV ~** 电视放映室; **a cocktail ~** [供应鸡尾酒等饮料的] 休息室 **3** **(airport) ~** 候机厅

B *vi* (sprawl) 懒洋洋地躺着; (stand) 懒洋洋地站着

Phrasal verb

- **lounge about, lounge around**

A *vi* 闲逛

B *vt* [**~ about** *or* **around sth.**] 在…闲逛; **to ~ about** *or* **around the house** 在屋子里走来走去

lounge: ~ bar *n* Brit 高级酒吧; **~ lizard** *n* colloq 花花公子; **~ suit** *n* Brit 日常西装; **'~ suit'** (on invitation) “请穿西服”; **~ suite** *n* Brit 沙发三件套

louse /laʊs/ *n* **1** (*pl* **lice**) (insect) 虱 **2** (*pl* **~s**) colloq pej (person) 讨厌鬼

Phrasal verb

- **louse up** *vt* [**~ sth. up, ~ up sth.**] sl 把…弄糟

lousy /ˈlaʊzi/ *adj* **1** colloq (very bad) 非常糟糕的; **to be ~ at sth.** 对某事物很不擅长; **to feel ~** 感觉很不舒服; **a ~ trick** 卑鄙的诡计 **2** (louse-infested) 长满虱子的 **3** colloq (teeming) **to be ~ with sth.** 充斥着某物

lout /laʊt/ *n* 举止粗野的人; **a clumsy ~** 笨手笨脚的家伙

loutish /ˈlaʊtɪʃ/ *adj* **1** (bad-mannered) 粗鲁的 **2** (rowdy, violent) 粗暴的

louvre Brit, **louver** Amer /ˈluːvə(r)/ *n* 百叶窗; **a ~ window/door** 百叶窗/门

lovable /ˈlʌvəbl/ *adj* 可爱的 ‹*child, puppy*›

love /lʌv/

A *n* **1** [u] (affection, devotion) 爱; **a ~ letter/token** 情书/定情物; **~ at first sight** 一见钟情; **~ for sb.** 对某人的爱; **to marry for ~** 为爱而结婚; **to do sth. for ~ of sb.** *or* **out of ~ for sb.** 为了某人做某事; **I wouldn't do that for ~ or** *or* **nor money** 我决不会做那事; **for the ~ of God!** 看在上帝份上！; **for the ~ of Mike!** Brit colloq dated 看在上帝份上吧！; **to be in ~ (with sb.)** （与某人）恋爱; **to be in ~ with the idea** 非常喜欢这个主意; **to fall in/out of ~ with sb.** 爱上/不再爱某人; **to make ~ (to sb.)** （与某人）做爱; **to give sb. one's ~** 向某人转达问候; **Sarah sends her ~** 萨拉向你（们）问好; **~ to Mary and the kids** 向玛丽和孩子们问好; **with ~ from Jason/~, Jason** (in letter) 爱你（们）的贾森 [用于书信末尾]; **there's no ~ lost between them** 他们互相厌恶 **2** [u and c] (great interest, pleasure) 喜爱; **(to develop) a ~ of** *or* **for sth.** （萌发）对某事物的喜爱; **to be/fall in ~ with sth.** 喜欢/喜欢上某物; **to do sth. simply for the ~ of it** 仅仅是出于爱好做某事 **3** [c] (object of affection) 爱恋的对象; **sb.'s first ~** (person) 某人的初恋情人; (thing) 某人最大的爱好; **to be the ~ of sb.'s life** 是某人一生的挚爱 **4** [c] Brit colloq (term of address) 亲爱的 **5** [c] colloq (pleasant person) 宝贝; **be a ~ and fetch me the matches** 乖，把火柴拿给我; **little ~s** 小宝贝们 **6** [u] (in tennis) 零分; **15 ~/~ 15** 15比0/0比15; **to win the game to ~** 使对手未得分赢得比赛

B *vt* **1** (feel affection for) 爱; **to ~ sb. for sth.** 因为某事物而爱某人; **to ~ each other** 彼此相爱; **I must ~ you and leave you, I'm afraid** hum 恐怕我得告辞了; **he/she ~s me, he/she ~s me not** 他/她爱我，他/她不爱我 [占卜情事时反复念叨之语]; **~ me, ~ my dog** Prov 爱屋及乌 **2** (enjoy, appreciate) 喜欢; **to ~ doing** *or* **to do sth.** 喜欢做某事; **I'd ~ to do it** 我很乐意那样做; **I'd ~ to help him, but I can't** 我对他爱莫能助; **dance? — I'd ~ to!** 跳支舞吧？——乐意奉陪！; **I ~ the way you hold me** 我喜欢你抱着我的感觉; **I'd ~ it if ...** 我很想…

love affair *n* (with person) 风流韵事; (with place, car, era) 热爱

lovebird

A *n* Zool 情侣鹦鹉 [产于非洲]

B **lovebirds** *npl* hum (lovers) [热恋中的] 情侣

love: ~bite *n* 爱痕 [情人在皮肤上咬或吮吸后留下的红色痕迹]; **~ child** *n* 私生子; **~-hate relationship** *n* 爱恨交加的关系; **~-in** *n* colloq dated 爱的聚会 [20世纪60年代的嬉皮士聚会，所有与会者一起分享爱的体验或做爱]; **~-in-a-mist** *n* 黑种草; **~ interest** *n* **1** [u] (romantic subplot) 爱情情节; **2** [c] (character, role) 扮演主角恋人的演员

loved one *n* **1** (beloved, lover) 情人 **2** (close family member) 至亲 **3** (dead relation) 死去的亲人

love handles *npl* colloq 腰间赘肉

loveless /ˈlʌvlɪs/ *adj* **1** (without love) 无爱的 ‹*marriage, home*› **2** (unloved) 没有人爱的 ‹*person*›

love life *n* 爱情生活

loveliness /ˈlʌvlɪnɪs/ *n* [u] 美丽

lovelorn /ˈlʌvlɔːn/ *adj* 单相思的

lovely /ˈlʌvli/

A *adj* **1** (beautiful) 美丽的 ‹*girl, hair, eyes, view*›; 可爱的 ‹*baby*›; 悦耳的 ‹*voice*›; 优美的 ‹*song, poem, story*›; **you look ~ in pink** 你穿粉红色衣服真漂亮 **2** (pleasant) 美好的 ‹*time, idea, party*›; 亲切和善的 ‹*person*›; 美味的 ‹*meal*›; **to smell ~** 闻上去很香; **to taste ~** 味道很好; **it was ~ to see you** 见到你真好

B *n* colloq 美女; **my ~** 我的美人儿

love: ~making *n* [u] 做爱; **~ match** *n* 天作之合; **~ nest** *n* colloq 爱巢 [情人幽会处]; **~ potion** *n* 春药

lover /ˈlʌvə(r)/ *n* **1** (sexual partner) 情人 **2** (person in love) 恋人; **young ~s** 年轻的情侣; **~s' vows** 海誓山盟 **3** (enthusiast) 爱好者; **a ~ of fast cars/fine wines** 喜欢开快车/美酒的人

lover boy *n* colloq (lover) 情夫; (woman-chaser) 风流男子

lovesick *adj* 害相思病的

lovey /ˈlʌvi/ *n* Brit colloq 亲爱的

lovey-dovey /ˌlʌvɪˈdʌvi/ *adj* Brit colloq 情意绵绵的

loving /ˈlʌvɪŋ/

A *adj* **1** (affectionate) 充满爱的; **they exchanged ~ looks** 他们深情地相互看了看; **from your ~ son John** (in letter-writing) 爱你们的儿子约翰 **2** (attentive, careful) 细心周到的

B **-loving** *combining form* **football/music~** 爱好足球/音乐的; **peace/freedom~** 热爱和平/自由的

lovingly /ˈlʌvɪŋli/ *adv* **1** (with love) 充满爱地 **2** (painstakingly) 细心周到地; **every detail of the scene has been ~ recorded** 现场的每个细节都做了详细记录

low¹ /ləʊ/ ▸**p. 436**

A *adj* **1** (close to the ground) 低的 ‹*ceiling, attitude, level*›; 低矮的 ‹*hill, building, table*›; **~ cloud** 低云; **~ ground/wall** 低地/矮墙; **a ~ point on the scale** 标尺的小刻度; **to make a ~ bow** 深鞠一躬; **to be ~ at the front/back** ‹*dress*› 前胸/后背开得低; **to be ~ in the sky** ‹*sun, moon*› 低悬在天空; **the ship was ~ in the water** 这艘船吃水很深; **the return was very ~ over the net** (in tennis, badminton etc.) 回球几乎擦网而过; **~ beam** 低梁，小心碰头; **a ~ blow** (in boxing) 对下身的击打 **2** (minimal, less than normal) 低的 ‹*rate, temperature, speed, price*›; 少的 ‹*quantity*›; 小的 ‹*pressure, number, percentage*›; 轻的 ‹*weight*›; **a ~ IQ** 低智商; **to be in the ~ forties** 40岁出头; **~est common multiple** 最小公倍数; **to be (a bit) on the ~ side** （有些）偏低; **to be ~ in ...** …含量低 ‹*salt, polyunsaturates*›; **to be ~ on** 缺少 ‹*petrol, staff, team spirit*›; **stocks are ~** 存货不足; **to get** *or* **run ~** (of water, ammunition) 即将耗尽; (of stocks of goods) 短缺; **to run ~ on sth.** 缺乏某物 **3** (inferior) 低的 ‹*grade, standard, expectation*›; 差的 ‹*quality, morale*›; **a ~ achiever** 成绩不佳的人; **it was the ~ point in our relationship** 那是我们关系的低谷 **4** (humble, unimportant) 低微的 ‹*origin*›; 低等的 ‹*rank*›; **an official in a ~ grade job** 从事低级工作的官员; **~ in the hierarchy** 职级低的; **to be a ~ priority (for sb.)** （对某人来说）不重要; **to be ~ on the list of things sb. has to do** 不是某人的当务之急 **5** (base, vulgar) 卑劣的 ‹*character, behaviour*›; 低俗的 ‹*humour, comedy*›; **a person of ~ morals** 小人 **6** (depressed physically) 衰弱的; (depressed psychologically) 消沉的; **to feel ~** 消沉; **to lay sb. ~** (knock sb. down) 把某人击倒在地; (make sb. feel weak) 使某人病倒 **7** (deep in pitch) 低的; (quiet, soft) 轻的; **a ~ note** 低音; **at the ~ end of my range** 在我音域的下限; **in a ~ voice** 轻声地; **at ~ volume** 用低音量; **he gave a ~ laugh/whistle** 他轻声一笑/轻轻吹了声口哨 **8** (dim) 微弱的 ‹*light, glow*›

B *adv* **1** (near the ground) 低地; **to come/go in ~** 屈身进来/过去; **to swoop/fly/pass ~ over sth.** 从低空掠过/飞过/越过某物; **the moon hung ~ (down) in the eastern sky** 月亮低悬于东方天际; **to bend/bow ~** 深深地弯腰/鞠躬; **to keep ~** 保持低姿势; **~ down on the page** 在页面下方; **~er down the hill/valley** 更靠近山脚/谷底的; **the dress is cut ~ at the front** 这条连衣裙的前胸开得很低; **to be brought ~** (defeated) 被打败; (destroyed) 被摧毁; **I wouldn't sink** *or* stoop so ~ as to do sth. 我才不会堕落到做某事的地步 **2** (at a reduced level) 低水平地; **to buy ~** 买得便宜; **to mark sth. ~** 给…打低分 ‹*essay*›; **to rate sb. pretty ~** 对某人评价颇低; **to stand ~ in sb.'s esteem** 在某人心目中地位很低; **to fall ~** «*stocks, reserves*» 减少; **the fire was burning ~** 火要燃尽了; **to turn the radio/lights/heating down ~** 调低收音机音量/调暗灯光/关小暖气 **3** (at a deep pitch) 用低音调 ‹*sing, play*›; **to go ~** 降低声调 **4** (quietly, softly) 轻声地 ‹*speak, sing*›; **to leave the television on ~** 把电视机音量调低开着; **to whisper sth. ~ in sb.'s ear** 在某人耳边低语某事

C *n* **1** Meteorol 低气压区 **2** (low point) 低点; **my career has had its highs and its ~s** 我的事业起起伏伏; **to be at/to hit an all-time** *or* **a record ~** 处于/达到历史最低点; **the dollar has reached** *or* **sunk to a new ~** 美元汇价降到了新低

low² *vi* «*cow*» 哞哞叫

low: ~-alcohol *adj* 酒精度低的; **~-angle shot** *n* 低角度镜头

lowbrow pej
A *adj* 文化艺术修养低的
B *n* 文化艺术修养低的人

low: ~-budget *adj* 低预算的; **~-calorie** *adj* 低热量的 ‹*food, diet*›; **~-carbon** *adj* 低碳的; **~-cost** *adj* 低成本的; **~-cost housing** 低价房; **Low Countries** *pr npl* **the Low Countries** 低地国家 [指欧洲西北部，包括荷兰、比利时和卢森堡]; **~-cut** *adj* 低胸的 ‹*dress*›

low-down
A *adj* 不光彩的; **a ~ trick** 卑鄙的伎俩
B *n* 真相; **to give sb. the ~ (on sth.)** 把（关于某事物的）实情告诉某人

low-end *adj* 低端的 ‹*computer, audio*›

lower¹ /ˈləʊə(r)/
A *adj* 较低的; **the ~ back/jaw/decks** 下背部/下颌/下层甲板; **on the ~ floor** 在下一楼层; **to be demoted to a ~ rank** 被降职
B *vt* **1** (bring or let down) 放下 ‹*curtain, weapon, newspaper*›; 垂下 ‹*gaze*›; 降低 ‹*ceiling*›; **to ~ one's eyes/head/arms** 垂下目光/低下头/放下手臂; **to ~ sb./sth. down/into/on to ...** 把某人/某物放到…下面/里面/上面; **to ~ the flag to half mast** 降半旗 **2** (reduce) 降低 ‹*price, standards, temperature*›; 调暗 ‹*light*›; 调低 ‹*volume*›; 减少 ‹*value*›; **to ~ one's voice** 压低嗓音; **to ~ (sb.'s) morale** 打压（某人的）士气; **to ~ one's guard** 放松警惕; **to ~ sb.'s resistance** Med 降低某人的抵抗力 **3** (abolish) 取消 ‹*trade barrier*› **4** Naut 放下 ‹*lifeboats*›; 降下 ‹*mast, sail*›
C *v refl* **to ~ oneself** **1** (demean oneself) 降低身份 **2** (into a position) 小心翼翼地坐下; **to ~ oneself into sth.** 小心翼翼地坐到…中 ‹*water, bath*›; 小心翼翼地坐到…上 ‹*seat, chair*›

lower² /ˈlaʊə(r)/ *vi* **1** (look threatening or angry) 面露愠色; **~ing eyes** 阴沉的目光 **2** (look dark and threatening) «*sky*» 变阴沉; **black clouds ~ed on the horizon** 天边乌云密布

lower case
A *n* 小写字体
B **lower-case** *modif* 小写的 ‹*script*›; **a lower-case letter** 小写字母

Lower Chamber *n* 下议院

lower class
A *n* **the ~, the ~es** 下层阶级
B **lower-class** *adj* 下层阶级的

lower: ~ court *n* 下级法院; **~ house** *n* 下议院

lower middle class
A *n* **the ~, the ~es** 下层中产阶级
B **lower middle-class** *adj* 下层中产阶级的

lower: ~-ranking *adj* 低级的; **a ~-ranking army officer** 下级军官; **~ school** *n* 低年级部 [学校中五年级以下的学部]; **~ sixth** *n* Brit **1** (year) 低六年级 [英国中学的最低年级] **2** + *v sing or pl* (pupils) 低六年级生; **to be in the ~ sixth** 是低六年级生

lowest common denominator *n* **1** Math 最小公分母 **2** fig pej (audience) 品位低俗的观众; (consumer group) 最平庸的消费者群体; **a new form of television, ruled by the ~** 迎合大众品味的新的电视形式

low: ~-fat *adj* 低脂肪的; **~-flying** *adj* 低空飞行的; **~-frequency** *adj* 低频的; **~-grade** *adj* (poor quality) 低级的 ‹*ore*›; 劣质的 ‹*steel, meat*›; (minor) 低级别的 ‹*official*›; (less serious) 不严重的 ‹*illness*›; **a ~-grade malignancy** 低度恶性肿瘤; **~-heeled** *adj* 低跟的; **a pair of ~-heeled shoes** 一双低跟鞋; **~-income** *adj* 低收入的 ‹*family*›; 廉价的 ‹*housing*›; **~-key** *adj* 低调的

lowland /ˈləʊlənd/
A *n* 低地
B *modif* 低地的; **~ Scots** 低地苏格兰语

low: ~-level *adj* **1** Aviat 低空的; **~-level flying** 低空飞行; **2** (minor) 低级别的 ‹*delegation, talks*›; 低级的 ‹*job*›; **3** Comput 低级的 ‹*language*›; **4** Nucl 低放射性的 ‹*waste*›; **~ life** *n* **1** [u] (underworld) 下层社会的生活及行为; **2** [c] (*pl* **~ lifes**) colloq (person) 社会渣滓; **~light** *n* **1** **~ lights** (dark streaks) 颜色较深的发绺; **2** (dull moment) 索然无味的事; **~-loader** *n* [火车的] 低架式挂车

lowly /ˈləʊli/
A *adj* 低下的 ‹*position, status*›; 卑微的 ‹*birth, origin*›
B *adv* 低地; **~ paid workers** 低薪工人

low: ~-lying *adj* 低洼的; **~-necked** *adj* 低领的 ‹*dress*›; **~-nicotine** *adj* 低尼古丁的

low-paid
A *adj* 低薪的 ‹*job*›; 挣钱少的 ‹*worker*›
B *npl* **the ~** 低薪阶层

low: ~-pitched *adj* **1** Mus 低沉的; **2** Archit 缓坡的 ‹*roof*›; **~-priced** *adj* 低价的

low-profile
A *n* 低姿态; **to keep a ~** 保持低调
B *adj* **1** (discreet) 低调的; **a ~ approach** 不引人注目的方式 **2** Aut 低断面的 ‹*tyre*›

low-quality *adj* 劣质的

low-rise
A *adj* 低层的 ‹*building*›
B *n* 低层建筑

low: ~-risk *adj* 低风险的 ‹*investment, operation*›; **~-scoring** *adj* 比分低的; **~ season** *n* 淡季; **~-slung** *adj* 矮帮的 ‹*shoes*›; 低腰的 ‹*jeans*›; 低车身的 ‹*car*›; 低矮的 ‹*building, sofa*›; **~-start mortgage** *n* Brit 低启动累进按揭

low-tar
A *adj* 低焦油的
B *n* 低焦油香烟

low: ~-tech *adj* 低技术的; **~ tide** *n* 低潮; **at ~ tide** 退潮时

low voltage
A *n* 低电压
B **low-voltage** *adj* 低电压的

low-water mark *n* **1** (water level) 低水位线 **2** fig (nadir) 最低点

lox /lɒks/ *n* [u] Amer 熏鲑鱼

loyal /ˈlɔɪəl/ *adj* 忠实的 ‹*friend, supporter, servant*›; **to be ~ to one's socialist ideals** 忠于社会主义理想; **to be ~ to sb.** 对某人忠诚

loyalist /ˈlɔɪəlɪst/
A *n* (supporter) [对政府或统治者] 忠诚的人
B **Loyalist** *pr n* Pol 支持大不列颠和北爱尔兰联合的人

loyally /ˈlɔɪəli/ *adv* 忠心耿耿地 ‹*serve, support*›

loyalty /ˈlɔɪəlti/ *n* **1** [u] (faithfulness) 忠诚; **to swear an oath of ~** 宣誓效忠 **2** [c] (allegiance) 忠心; **to have divided** *or* **conflicting loyalties** 两面效忠; **a man of fierce loyalties** 忠贞不二的人

loyalty card *n* 忠诚卡 [顾客凭卡中的消费积分购物可享优惠]

lozenge /ˈlɒzɪndʒ/ *n* **1** (medicine tablet) [尤指用于治疗咳嗽和喉痛的] 糖锭 **2** (shape) 菱形

LP *abbr* = **long-playing record**

LPG *abbr* = **liquefied petroleum gas**

L-plate *n* Brit 红L字牌 [学驾驶时置于车上的标志]

LPN *abbr* Amer = **licensed practical nurse** 持执照临床护士

LSAT *abbr* Amer = **Law School Admission Test** 法学院入学考试

LSD *abbr* [u] = **lysergic acid diethylamide** 麦角酸酰二乙胺 [一种致幻药]

L-shaped *adj* L形的 ‹*room, desk*›

Lt *abbr* = **lieutenant**

Ltd *abbr* Brit = **limited (liability)** 有限责任公司

Luanda /luːˈændə/ *pr n* 罗安达

lubricant /ˈluːbrɪkənt/ *n* [c and u] 润滑剂

lubricate /ˈluːbrɪkeɪt/ *vt* (oil) 使润滑; fig 使顺畅; **whisky ~s his tongue** 喝了威士忌后他的话多了起来

lubricating oil *n* [u and c] 润滑油

lubrication /ˌluːbrɪˈkeɪʃn/ *n* [u] 润滑

lubricator /ˈluːbrɪkeɪtə(r)/ *n* (substance) 润滑剂; (person) 加油工

lubricious /luːˈbrɪʃəs/ *adj* pej 淫荡的

lucid /ˈluːsɪd/ *adj* **1** (clear, understandable) 明白易懂的 **2** (sane, clear-headed) 头脑清晰的

lucidity /luːˈsɪdəti/ *n* [u] **1** (clearness) 明白易懂 **2** (sanity) 头脑清晰

lucidly /ˈluːsɪdli/ *adv* 明白易懂地

lucifer /ˈluːsɪfə(r)/ *n* **1** **Lucifer** (Satan) 撒旦; **as proud as L~** 非常高傲 **2** Brit archaic (match stick) 火柴

luck /lʌk/ *n* [u] **1** (fortune) 运气; **good/bad** *or* **ill ~** 好运/厄运; **to be bad/good ~ to do sth.** 做某事走运/不走运; **to bring (sb.) good/bad ~** （给某人）带来好运/厄运; **I've had nothing but bad ~ with that car** 这辆汽车尽让我倒霉; **to have the good/bad ~ to do sth.** 做某事运气真好/不好; **~ is on our side** 我们走运了; **as ~ would have it, ...** 碰巧，…; **good ~!** 祝你好运！; **better ~ next time!** 祝你下次运气好些！; **I wish you all the best of ~** 祝你一切顺心如意; **bad** *or* **hard ~!** 真不幸！; **just my ~!** 我总是不走运！; **worse ~!** 真倒霉！; **to be down on one's ~** 穷困潦倒; **to try one's ~** 碰运气; **it's the ~ of the draw** 此事全凭运气; **to depend on the ~ of the draw** 凭运气 **2** (good fortune) 好运; **with ~, ...** 幸运的话，…; **he hasn't had much ~ with women** 他女人缘不佳; **to wear sth. for ~** 穿戴某物以求好运; **by a bit** *or* **stroke of ~** 碰巧; **what a stroke of ~!** 真是巧了！; **to have the ~ to do sth.** 有幸做某事; **any ~ with the job hunting?** 工作找得有眉目了吗？; **have you found it? — no ~ yet** 找到了吗？——还没有; **no such ~!** 才没这样的好运气呢！; **to have the devil's own ~** 非常幸运; **to be in/out of ~** 运气好/不好; **to run out of ~** 不再走运; **my ~'s in!** 我运气来了！; **he did 20 press-ups and one for ~** 他做了 20 个俯卧撑，又做了一个图个吉利

Phrasal verb
- **luck out** *vi* Amer colloq 走运

luckily /ˈlʌkɪli/ *adv* 幸运地; **~ for him, the mistake was not serious** 他很幸运，错误并不严重; **I was late but ~ so was the boss** 我迟到了，但幸好老板也迟到了

luckless /ˈlʌklɪs/ *adj* 运气不好的 ‹*attempt*›; 不幸的 ‹*person*›

l

lucky /ˈlʌki/ *adj* **1** (fortunate) 幸运的; **to be ~ to do/be sth.** 做某事/是某状况很幸运; **to be ~ enough to do sth.** 做某事够幸运的; **to have a ~ escape** 幸运地逃脱; **~ you!** 你真走运！; **you ~ thing** *or* **devil** *or* **dog!** colloq 你这个走运的家伙！; **you'll be ~ to get a taxi** 但愿你能打到出租车; **I/you should be so ~!** colloq 我/你没那么走运吧！; **you should think** *or* **count yourself ~ that ...** 你该暗自庆幸了, …… **2** (bringing good luck) 带来好运的 ‹*mascot, person*›; **~ charm/colour/number/day** 吉祥饰物/幸运色/幸运数字/吉日; **(to get a** *or* **one's) ~ break** （获得）机遇; **to thank one's ~ stars** 感谢上苍; **you can thank your ~ stars that ...** colloq 多亏你运气好，才……; **third time ~** colloq 第三次会交好运的

lucky dip *n* Brit 摸彩游戏

lucrative /ˈluːkrətɪv/ *adj* 赚大钱的 ‹*market, deal*›

lucre /ˈluːkə(r)/ *n* [u] colloq dated 钱财; **filthy ~** 不义之财

Luddite /ˈlʌdaɪt/ *n* (in workplace) 勒德分子 [强烈抵制技术革新的人]; (in general) 反对技术革新的人

ludicrous /ˈluːdɪkrəs/ *adj* 荒唐可笑的 ‹*idea, suggestion*›

ludicrously /ˈluːdɪkrəsli/ *adv* 荒唐可笑地 ‹*happy, expensive, long*›

ludo /ˈluːdəʊ/ ▸p. 307 *n* [u] Brit 卢多 [一种用骰子和筹码玩的板上游戏]

luff /lʌf/
A *n* 纵帆前缘
B *vt* 使…迎风行驶 ‹*boat*›

lug /lʌg/
A *n* **1** (on jug, pot, dish) 把手 **2** (on beam, frame) 凸耳 **3** Brit colloq (ear) 耳朵
B *vt* (*pres p etc.* **-gg-**) (carry) 吃力地搬运; (drag or pull) 用力拖

luge /luːʒ/ *n* **1** [c] (toboggan) 平底雪橇 **2** [u] (sport) 平底雪橇比赛

luggage /ˈlʌgɪdʒ/ *n* [u] esp Brit 行李

luggage: ~ handler ▸p. 409 *n* 行李处理员; **~ label** *n* 行李标签; **~ rack** *n* 行李架; **~ van** *n* Brit 行李车

lughole /ˈlʌgəʊl/ *n* Brit colloq 耳朵

lugubrious /ləˈguːbrɪəs/ *adj* 悲伤的

lugubriously /ləˈguːbrɪəsli/ *adv* 悲伤地

lukewarm /ˌluːkˈwɔːm/ *adj* **1** (tepid) 温热的; **~ water** 温水 **2** fig (unenthusiastic) 不热情的 ‹*reception, support*›

lull /lʌl/
A *n* 间歇; **a ~ in the conversation** 谈话中的沉寂; **the post-Christmas ~** 圣诞节后的生意清淡期; **the ~ before the storm** fig 暴风雨前的宁静
B *vt* 使平静; **to ~ sb. to sleep** 哄某人入睡; **to be ~ed into a false sense of security** 受麻痹而产生一种虚假的安全感

lullaby /ˈlʌləbaɪ/ *n* 摇篮曲

lumbago /lʌmˈbeɪgəʊ/ *n* [u] 腰痛

lumbar /ˈlʌmbə(r)/ *adj* 腰的; **the ~ region** 腰部; **~ puncture** 腰椎穿刺

lumber /ˈlʌmbə(r)/
A *n* [u] **1** esp Amer (timber) 木材 **2** Brit dated (junk) 废旧杂物
B *vt* **1** Brit colloq (burden) 迫使…承担; **to be ~ed with sth.** 受到某事的拖累 **2** Amer (log) 采伐…的林木 ‹*area, forest*›
C *vi* 缓慢吃力地移动; **a tank ~ed past me** 一辆坦克从我身旁隆隆驶过

lumber company *n* Amer 木业公司

lumbering /ˈlʌmbərɪŋ/ *adj* 缓慢沉重的

lumber: ~jack ▸p. 409 *n* 伐木工; **~jacket** *n* 厚短夹克衫; **~man** /-mæn/ ▸p. 409 *n* esp Amer 伐木工; **~ mill** *n* esp Amer 锯木厂; **~ room** *n* Brit 杂物间; **~yard** *n* esp Amer 贮木场

luminary /ˈluːmɪnəri, Amer -neri/ *n* 杰出人物

luminesce /luːmɪˈnes/ *vi* 发冷光

luminescence /ˌluːmɪˈnesns/ *n* [u] 发光

luminosity /ˌluːmɪˈnɒsəti/ *n* [u] 发光

luminous /ˈluːmɪnəs/ *adj* **1** (brilliant, radiant) 发光的; **her eyes were ~ and sparkling** 她的眼睛闪闪发光 **2** (bright in colour) 鲜亮的; **a ~ green** 翠绿色

lump /lʌmp/
A *n* **1** (of rock, cheese, concrete) 块; **to get** *or* **take one's ~s** fig 吃苦头 **2** (on body) 肿块; **she had a ~ in her breast** 她乳房里长了个肿块; **to have a ~ in one's throat** fig 喉咙哽住 **3** colloq pej (person) 傻大个
B *vt* 把…归并在一起; **these two things shouldn't be ~ed together** 这二者不应该混为一谈; **to ~ it** colloq 将就; **like it or ~ it** colloq 不管高兴不高兴

lumpenproletariat /ˌlʌmpənˌprəʊlɪˈteərɪət/ *n* 流氓无产阶级

lump: ~ sugar *n* [u] 方糖; **~ sum** *n* 一次总付的钱款; **~-sum payment** 一次性付款

lumpy /ˈlʌmpi/ *adj* (full of lumps) 多块状物的; (covered in lumps) 为块状物覆盖的; **a ~ mattress** 凹凸不平的床垫; **to go ~** «*sauce*» 结块

lunacy /ˈluːnəsi/ *n* [u] **1** (foolishness) 疯狂愚蠢的行为 **2** dated (insanity) 精神错乱

lunar /ˈluːnə(r)/ *adj* 月亮的; **~ landing** 登月; **~ month** 朔望月; **~ calendar** 阴历

lunatic /ˈluːnətɪk/
A *n* **1** pej or hum (foolish person) 疯狂愚蠢的人; **he drives like a ~!** 他开车像个疯子！ **2** dated (mentally ill person) 精神病患者
B *adj* **1** (foolish) 疯狂愚蠢的 ‹*idea, behaviour*› **2** dated (insane) 精神错乱的

lunatic: ~ asylum *n* dated 疯人院; **~ fringe** *n* pej **the ~ fringe** 极端分子

lunch /lʌntʃ/
A *n* [c and u] 午餐; **to have ~** 吃午饭; **to eat sth. for ~** 吃某物作午餐; **~!, time for ~!** 吃午饭了！; **the bar does good ~es** 那个小吃店提供的午餐很可口; **out to ~** colloq (crazy) 发疯的; **there's no such thing as a free ~** 天下没有免费的午餐
B *vi* 吃午餐; **to ~ with sb.** 同某人一起吃午饭; **to ~ at home/the pub/a restaurant** 在家/酒吧/餐馆吃午饭; **to ~ on** *or* **off sth.** 午饭吃某物

lunch: ~ box *n* **1** (container) 午餐盒; **2** Brit colloq hum (male genitals) 男性生殖器; **~break** *n* 午餐时间

luncheon /ˈlʌntʃən/ *n* formal 午餐

luncheon: ~ meat *n* [u] 午餐肉; **~ voucher** *n* Brit 午餐券

lunch: ~ hour *n* 午餐时间; **~time** *n* 午餐时间

lung /lʌŋ/ *n* 肺; **to have a good pair of ~s** hum 声音洪亮; **~ transplant** 肺移植

lung cancer *n* 肺癌

lunge /lʌndʒ/
A *n* **1** (movement) 猛冲; **to make a ~ for sth.** 向某物猛扑过去; **she made a ~ for him with a knife** 她挥刀向他扑过去; **he made a ~ at** *or* **for the ball** 他向球猛扑过去 **2** (in fencing) 弓箭步刺
B *vi* 猛冲; **to ~ at sb./sth.** 扑向某人/某物

lungful /ˈlʌŋfʊl/ *n* 一大口; **to take a ~ of fresh air** 深深地吸一口新鲜空气

lung power *n* [u] 发声力

lunk /lʌŋk/, **lunkhead** /ˈlʌŋkhed/ *ns* colloq 呆子

lupin /ˈluːpɪn/ *n* 羽扇豆

lurch¹ /lɜːtʃ/
A *vi* **1** (make a sudden movement) 突然倾斜; **to ~ from side to side** 东倒西歪; **to ~ to one's feet** 一下子站起来 **2** fig (change suddenly) «*opinion, emotion*» 突然改变; **to ~ to the left** Pol 突然倒向左派
B *n* **1** (sudden movement) 突然倾斜; **to give a ~** 猛地一跳 **2** fig (of opinion, emotion) 突然改变

lurch² *n* **to leave sb. in the ~** 弃某人于危难之中

lure /lʊə(r)/
A *vt* 引诱; **to ~ sb. into doing sth.** 引诱某人做某事; **to ~ sb. into a trap** 把某人骗入圈套
B *n* **1** (temptation) 诱惑力; (tempting object) 诱惑物 **2** (in hunting) 诱饵; (in fishing) 鱼饵 **3** (in falconry) 诱回猎鹰的一束羽毛

lurex® /ˈlʊəreks/ *n* [u] (fabric) 卢勒克斯金属丝织物; (thread) 卢勒克斯金属细线

lurgy /ˈlɜːgi/ *n* Brit colloq hum 小病; **the dreaded ~** 吓人的小病

lurid /ˈlʊərɪd/ *adj* **1** (shocking) 骇人听闻的 ‹*description*›; 令人毛骨悚然的 ‹*past, details*› **2** (gaudy) 俗艳的 ‹*colours, green*›

lurk /lɜːk/
A *vi* **1** (lie in wait) 潜伏; **to ~ somewhere** 潜伏在某处 **2** (loiter) 闲逛; **to ~ somewhere** 在某处闲逛 **3** (linger) 潜藏 **4** (in a chatroom or forum) 潜水
B **lurking** *adj* 潜藏的; **a ~ing suspicion** 隐藏在心里的猜疑

lurker /ˈlɜːkə(r)/ *n* 潜水者 [网络上只看帖而不发言的人]

Lusaka /luːˈsɑːkə/ *pr n* 卢萨卡

luscious /ˈlʌʃəs/ *adj* 美味的 ‹*taste, food*›; 性感的 ‹*woman, man*›; 赏心悦目的 ‹*garden, colour, flower*›

lush /lʌʃ/
A *adj* **1** (exuberant) 茂盛的 ‹*vegetation*›; (verdant) 葱翠的 ‹*grass*› **2** (luxurious) 豪华的 ‹*hotel, furnishings*› **3** Brit colloq (sexually attractive) 性感的 **4** colloq (fabulous) 很棒的 ‹*gift, music*›
B *n* colloq 酒鬼

lust /lʌst/
A *n* **1** [u] (sexual desire) 强烈的性欲 **2** [c] (for power, gold) 强烈的欲望; **to have a ~ for sth.** 渴望得到某物
B *vi* 有强烈的欲望; **to ~ for** *or* **after women** 贪恋女色; **to ~ for power/riches** 有极强的权力欲/财富欲

luster *n* Amer = **lustre**

lustful /ˈlʌstfl/ *adj* 好色的

lustily /ˈlʌstɪli/ *adv* 强有力地; **to cry ~** 响亮地哭

lustre /ˈlʌstə(r)/ *n* [u and c] Brit **1** (sheen, glow) 光泽 **2** (glory, distinction) 荣光; **to add ~ to sth.** 给某物增添光彩

lusty /ˈlʌsti/ *adj* 雄壮有力的; **to give a ~ cheer** 高声欢呼

lute /luːt/ ▸p. 395 *n* 琉特琴

lutenist /ˈluːtənɪst/ ▸p. 395, p. 409 *n* 琉特琴弹奏者

lutetium /luːˈtiːʃɪəm/ *n* [u] 镥

Lutheran /ˈluːθərən/
A *n* (follower of Martin Luther) 马丁・路德的信徒; (church member) 路德教派成员
B *adj* 路德教派的 ‹*teachings, doctrine*›; 路德教会的 ‹*churches*›

Lutheranism /ˈluːθərənɪzəm/ *n* [u] 路德主义

luv /lʌv, lʊv/ *n* Brit colloq 亲爱的

luvvy /ˈlʌvɪ/ *n* Brit colloq [尤指表演做作的] 演员

Luxembourg /ˈlʌksəmbɜːg/ *pr n* (country) 卢森堡; (city) 卢森堡市

luxuriance /lʌkˈʒʊərɪəns/ *n* [u] **1** (of growth) 茂盛; **the ~ of the vegetation** 植被的繁茂 **2** (of hair) 浓密

luxuriant /lʌgˈzjʊərɪənt/ *adj* **1** (rich) 茂盛的 ‹*vegetation*›; 草木茂盛的 ‹*garden, valley*› **2** (healthy) 浓密的 ‹*hair, beard*›

luxuriate /lʌgˈzjʊərɪeɪt/ *vi* 尽情享受; **to ~ in sth.** 尽情享受某物

luxurious /lʌɡˈzjʊərɪəs/ *adj* 豪华的 ‹*surroundings, hotel*›; 十分舒适的 ‹*lifestyle*›; 奢侈的 ‹*tastes*›

luxuriously /lʌɡˈzjʊərɪəsli/ *adv* 奢华地 ‹*decorate, fit out*›; 十分舒适地 ‹*stretch, live*›

luxury /ˈlʌkʃəri/
A *n* **1** [u] (comfort, elegance) 奢华; **a life of ~** 奢侈的生活; **in (the lap of) ~** 生活优裕 **2** [c] (rare pleasure) 难得的享受 **3** [c] (expensive item) 奢侈品
B *modif* 奢侈的; **a ~ yacht** 豪华游艇; **~ goods** *or* **items** 奢侈品

LV *abbr* Brit **= luncheon voucher**

LW *abbr* **= long wave**

lychee /ˈlaɪtʃiː, ˌlaɪˈtʃiː/ *n* **1** [c and u] (fruit) 荔枝 **2** [c] (tree) 荔枝树

lychgate /ˈlɪtʃɡeɪt/ *n* 停柩门

Lycra® /ˈlaɪkrə/ *n* [u] 莱卡; **~ shorts** 莱卡短裤

lying /ˈlaɪɪŋ/
A *pres p* ▸**lie¹ A, lie² B, C**
B *n* [u] 说谎
C *adj attrib* 说谎的

lymph /lɪmf/ *n* [u] 淋巴

lymphatic system /lɪmˈfætɪk ˌsɪstəm/ *n* 淋巴系统

lymph: ~ gland *n* 淋巴腺; **~ node** *n* 淋巴结

lymphoma /lɪmˈfəʊmə/ *n* (*pl* **~s** *or* **lymphomata** /lɪmˈfəʊmətə/) 淋巴瘤

lynch /lɪntʃ/ *vt* 用私刑处死

lynching /ˈlɪntʃɪŋ/ *n* [c and u] 用私刑处死

lynch: ~ law *n* [u] 私刑; **~ mob** *n* 动用私刑的暴民; **~pin** *n* **= linchpin**

lynx /lɪŋks/ *n* 猞猁

lynx-eyed *adj* 目光犀利的

lyre /ˈlaɪə(r)/ ▸**p. 395** *n* 里尔琴

lyric /ˈlɪrɪk/
A *n* 抒情诗
B **lyrics** *npl* 歌词
C *adj* 抒情的; **a ~ poem/poet** 抒情诗/抒情诗人

lyrical /ˈlɪrɪkl/ *adj* **1** (poetic, musical) 抒情诗般的 **2** (expressing emotions) 抒情的 ‹*poem*› **3** (effusive) 热情奔放的; **to wax ~ on** *or* **about** *or* **over sth.** 兴高采烈地谈论某事

lyrically /ˈlɪrɪkli/ *adv* **1** (poetically) 抒情诗般地 **2** (emotionally) 抒情地 **3** (effusively) 热情奔放地

lyricism /ˈlɪrɪsɪzəm/ *n* [u] **1** (quality of poetry) 抒情性; (style of poetry) 抒情体 **2** (lyrical quality) 抒情 **3** (enthusiasm) 奔放的热情

lyricist /ˈlɪrɪsɪst/ ▸**p. 409** *n* 歌词作者

lyric writer ▸**p. 409** *n* 歌词作者

l

Mm

M, m /em/

A *n* (*pl* **Ms** *or* **M's**) **1** (letter) [英语字母表的第13个字母] **2** **M** (numeral) [罗马数字] 1000

B *abbr* **1** **m = metre(s)** 米 **2** **m = million A, B** **3** **M = motorway** 高速公路; **on the M1** 在 1 号高速公路上 **4** **M** Clothg **= medium** 中号 **5** **m = mile(s)** 英里

MA *abbr* **1** **= Master of Arts; to have/do an ~** 持有/攻读文科硕士学位 **2** Amer **= Massachusetts**

ma /mɑː/ *n* colloq 妈

ma'am /mæm, mɑːm/ *n* **1** **= madam 1** **2** Brit (when addressing queen, princess) [对王室女性的尊称] …阁下

mac /mæk/ *n* Brit colloq **= mackintosh**

macabre /mə'kɑːbrə/ *adj* 令人毛骨悚然的

macadam /mə'kædəm/ *n* [u] 柏油碎石

Macao /mə'kaʊ/ *pr n* 澳门; **~ Special Administrative Region** 澳门特别行政区

macaroni /ˌmækə'rəʊni/ *n* [u] 通心粉

macaroni cheese *n* [u] 干酪酱通心粉

macaroon /ˌmækə'ruːn/ *n* (with coconut) 蛋白椰子饼干; (with almond) 蛋白杏仁饼干

macaw /mə'kɔː/ *n* 金刚鹦鹉

mace[1] /meɪs/ *n* **1** (ceremonial staff) 权杖 **2** (weapon) 狼牙棒

mace[2] *n* [u] (spice) 肉豆蔻干皮

Macedonia /ˌmæsɪ'dəʊnɪə/ *pr n* **1** (in the Balkans) 马其顿共和国 **2** (in modern Greece) 马其顿区 **3** (ancient country) 马其顿王国

Macedonian /ˌmæsɪ'dəʊnɪən/

A *adj* **1** (of the Balkan republic) 马其顿共和国的 **2** (of the region in modern Greece) 马其顿区的 **3** (of ancient country) 马其顿王国的

B *n* **1** [c] (person) 马其顿人 **2** [u] (language) 马其顿语

macerate /'mæsəreɪt/

A *vt* 把…浸软

B *vi* 浸软

Mach /mɑːk, mæk/ *n* [u] 马赫; **to fly at ~ one** 以1马赫的速度飞行; **~ number** 马赫数

machete /mə'tʃeti, mə'ʃeti/ *n* 大砍刀

Machiavellian /ˌmækɪə'velɪən/ *adj* 阴险狡诈的

machination /ˌmækɪ'neɪʃn/ *n* 阴谋诡计

machine /mə'ʃiːn/

A *n* **1** (piece of equipment) 机器; **to operate** *or* **work a ~** 开动机器 **2** (organization) 机构; (group of powerful people) 核心集团; **the government's propaganda ~** 政府的宣传机器

B *vt* 用机器制作

machine: ~ age *n* **the ~ age** 机器时代; **~-assisted translation** *n* **1** [u] (process) 机器辅助翻译; **2** [c] (text) 由机器辅助翻译的译本; **~ code** *n* [u] 机器语言

machine gun

A *n* 机关枪; **machine-gun fire** 机关枪火力

B **machine-gun** *vt* (*pres p etc.* **-nn-**) 用机关枪射击

machine: ~ intelligence *n* [u] 机器智能; **~ language** *n* [u] 机器语言; **~-made** *adj* 机器制造的; **~ operator** *n* 机器操作工; **~-readable** *adj* 机器可读的

machinery /mə'ʃiːnəri/ *n* [u] **1** (equipment) 机器; **farm/heavy ~** 农用/重型机械; **a piece of ~** 一部机器 **2** (working parts) 机件 **3** fig (system, structure) 机构; **the propaganda ~ of the government** 政府的宣传机器

machine: ~ shop *n* 机械加工车间; **~-stitch** *vt* 用缝纫机缝

machine tool *n* 机床

machine tool operator ▸**p. 409** *n* 机床操作工

machine translation *n* **1** [u] (translation by computer) 机器翻译 **2** [c] (text translated by computer) 由机器翻译的译本 **3** [u and c] **= machine-assisted translation**

machine-washable *adj* 可机洗的

machinist /mə'ʃiːnɪst/ ▸**p. 409** *n* 机工

machismo /mə'tʃɪzməʊ, -'kɪzməʊ/ *n* [u] usu pej 大男子主义

macho /'mætʃəʊ/ *adj* usu pej 大男子气的; **too ~ to ever admit one's wrong** 太大男子主义了，从不认错

macintosh /'mækɪntɒʃ/ *n* **= mackintosh**

mackerel /'mækrəl/ *n* (*pl* **~** *or* **~s**) 鲭鱼

mackerel sky *n* 鱼鳞天

mackintosh /'mækɪntɒʃ/ *n* Brit 雨衣

macramé /mə'krɑːmi/ *n* [u] (craft) 装饰编结术; (products) 装饰结; **a ~ belt** 编结腰带

macro /'mækrəʊ/ *n* 宏指令

macro- /'mækrəʊ/ *combining form* (large) 巨大的; (large-scale) 宏观的; **~molecules** 大分子; **~sociology** 宏观社会学

macrobiotic /ˌmækrəʊbaɪ'ɒtɪk/ *adj* 延年益寿的; **a ~ diet** 养生饮食

macrobiotics /ˌmækrəʊbaɪ'ɒtɪks/ *npl + v sing* 长寿饮食法

macrocosm /'mækrəʊkɒzəm/ *n* **1** (large scale system) 大系统 **2** (universe) **the ~** 宇宙

macroeconomic /ˌmækrəʊiːkə'nɒmɪk, -ekə-/ *adj* 宏观经济的

macroeconomics /ˌmækrəʊiːkə'nɒmɪks, -ekə-/ *npl + v sing* 宏观经济学

macron /'mækrɒn/ *n* 长音符

macrophage /'mækrəʊfeɪdʒ/ *n* 巨噬细胞

macrophotography /ˌmækrəʊfə'tɒgrəfi/ *n* [u] 微距摄影术

macroscopic /ˌmækrəʊ'skɒpɪk/ *adj* **1** (visible to the naked eye) 肉眼可见的 **2** (large-scale) 宏观的

> **Macy's**
>
> 梅西百货。1858 年由罗兰·H·梅西（Rowland H. Macy）创立，总部位于纽约，在美国各地都有分店，号称“世界上最大的商店”。旗舰店位于纽约市先驱广场（Herald Square）。自 1924 年起，几乎每年感恩节都要举行盛大的游行活动，以众多巨大的卡通造型气球为特色，称 Macy's Thanksgiving Day Parade，由全国广播公司（▸**NBC**）直播。

mad /mæd/

A *adj* **1** esp Brit (insane) 疯的; **to drive sb. ~** 使某人发疯; **to go ~** 发疯; **to go ~ with ...** 因…而丧失理智 ‹*grief, rage*›; **to be sth. gone ~** fig 是疯狂的某物; **it's nationalism gone ~** 这是疯狂的民族主义; **sb. must be ~ to do sth.** 某人一定是疯了，居然做某事; **to be as ~ as a hatter** 疯疯癫癫 **2** colloq (foolish) 愚蠢的; **to be ~ to do sth.** 做某事是愚蠢的; **you'd have to be ~ to go out in weather like this** 在这种天气还要出去，你一定是犯傻了; **in a ~ moment, I asked her to come too** 我一时糊涂把她也叫来了 **3** *pred* colloq (angry) 气愤的; **was I (ever) ~!** 真是气死我了！; **to make** *or* **drive sb. ~** 使某人生气; **to be** *or* **get ~ about sth.** 因某事而生气; **to be ~ at** *or* **with sb. for doing sth.** 因某人做某事而对其发火 **4** *pred* (enthusiastic) 狂热的; **to be ~ about** *or* **on sth./sb.** 对某事/某人很着迷; **...-~** 对…着迷的; **to be car-/football-~** 对汽车/足球着迷 **5** (frantic) 狂乱的 ‹*dash, round*›; **to be in a ~ rush/panic** 忙得团团转/恐慌不堪; **to go ~** 忙乱地做事; **to be ~ with ...** 因…而狂乱 ‹*anxiety, joy*›; **to go ~ with sth.** colloq 用太多的 ‹*chilli, perfume*›; **like ~** colloq 拼命地; **to run like ~** 狂奔 **6** (rabid) 患狂犬病的 ‹*dog*› **7** (enraged) 狂暴的 ‹*bull*›

B *adv* Brit colloq 非常; **to be ~ keen on sth./sb.** 非常迷恋某物/某人

Madagascan /ˌmædə'gæskən/

A *adj* (of Madagascar) 马达加斯加的; (of the people) 马达加斯加人的

B *n* 马达加斯加人

Madagascar /ˌmædə'gæskə(r)/ *pr n* 马达加斯加

madam /'mædəm/ *n* **1** (*also* **Madam**) (formal) 夫人; **Dear M~** 尊敬的女士 **2** Brit pej (bossy young woman) 爱支使别人的女子; **you little ~!** 你这个小姑奶奶! **3** (in brothel) 鸨母

madcap /'mædkæp/ *adj* **1** *attrib* (eccentric) 离奇的 **2** colloq (reckless) 鲁莽的

mad cow disease ▸**p. 377** *n* [u] colloq 疯牛病

madden /'mædn/ *vt* (make angry) 使发怒; (make wild) 使疯狂; **be ~ed by pain** 痛得发狂

maddening /'mædnɪŋ/ *adj* 令人发怒的

maddeningly /'mædnɪŋli/ *adv* 令人发怒地; **~ late** 迟得令人恼火

made /meɪd/ *pt, pp* ▸**make A, B, C**

-made /meɪd/ *combining form* (at a particular place) …制造的; (in a particular way) 制作…的; **Italian ~** 意大利制造的; **precision~ instruments** 制作精密的仪器

Madeira /mə'dɪərə/

A *pr n* Geog 马德拉岛

B *n* [u] (wine) 马德拉白葡萄酒

Madeira cake *n* [u] Brit 马德拉蛋糕

made: ~-to-measure *adj* 量身订制的; **~-to-order** *adj* 订做的

made-up *adj* **1** (fictional) 虚构的 **2** (wearing make-up) 化妆的; **heavily ~** 浓妆的 **3** (surfaced) 铺好路面的 ‹*road*›

madhouse /ˈmædhaʊs/ *n* **1** dated (asylum) 精神病院 **2** colloq (mayhem) 喧闹的地方; **this place is a ~!** 这个地方乱哄哄的!

Madison Avenue /ˌmædɪsn ˈævənjuː, Amer -nuː/ *pr n* 麦迪逊大街 [指美国广告业]

madly /ˈmædli/ *adv* **1** (frantically) 发狂地; **to write ~** 拼命地写 **2** (intensely) 非常 ‹*exciting, envious, keen, interested*›; **to be ~ in love with sb.** 疯狂地爱着某人

madman /ˈmædmən/ *n* (*pl* **madmen**) **1** dated (mentally ill man) 疯子 **2** colloq (reckless man) 狂人; **to drive like a ~** 像疯了似地驾车飞驰

madness /ˈmædnɪs/ *n* [u] **1** (insanity) 精神失常; **to be completely overcome by ~** 完全疯了 **2** (foolishness) 极度的愚蠢; **it's sheer ~!** 真是愚蠢至极!

Madonna /məˈdɒnə/ *n* **1** (Virgin Mary) **the ~** 圣母玛利亚 **2** **madonna** (statue) 圣母雕像; (picture) 圣母画像

madras /məˈdræs/ *n* [u] **1** (cotton fabric) 马德拉斯布; (silk fabric) 马德拉斯绸; **a ~ shirt/scarf** 马德拉斯衬衫/围巾 **2** Brit Culin 马德拉斯咖喱菜; **chicken ~** 马德拉斯咖喱鸡

Madrid /məˈdrɪd/ *pr n* 马德里

madrigal /ˈmædrɪgl/ *n* 牧歌

madwoman /ˈmædwʊmən/ *n* (*pl* **madwomen**) dated 女疯子

maelstrom /ˈmeɪlstrəm/ *n* **1** liter (turbulence) 混乱; **the ~ of war** 战乱; **a political ~** 政治动乱 **2** (whirlpool) 大漩涡

maestro /ˈmaɪstrəʊ/ *n* (*pl* **maestri** /ˈmaɪstri/ *or* **~s**) 大师

Mae West /ˌmeɪ ˈwest/ *n* colloq dated 救生背心

Mafia /ˈmæfɪə, Amer ˈmɑːf-/ *n* + *v sing or pl* **1** (criminal organization) **the ~** 黑手党; **under ~ control** 处于黑手党的控制之下 **2** **mafia** (group exerting influence) 小集团; **the middle-class m~** 中产阶级集团

> **the Mafia**
>
> 黑手党，亦称 Cosa Nostra。源于意大利西西里地区的秘密犯罪组织，由若干家族控制。19 世纪末期始现于美国，首领称教父（godfather）。20 世纪 80 年代，美国的黑手党在联邦政府的强力打击下势力衰微。mafia 现亦用于指排外或通过施加影响攫取不当利益的小集团。

Mafioso /ˌmæfɪˈəʊsəʊ/ *n* (*pl* **Mafiosi** /ˌmæfɪˈəʊsi/) 黑手党成员

mag /mæg/ *n* colloq = **magazine 1**

magazine /ˌmægəˈziːn/ *n* **1** (publication) 杂志; **a literary ~** 文学期刊 **2** (on radio, TV) **~ (programme)** 专题节目 **3** (of gun) 弹仓 **4** (store for arms, ammunition) 弹药库

Magellan Strait /məˌgelən ˈstreɪt/ *pr n* **the ~(s)** 麦哲伦海峡

magenta /məˈdʒentə/ ▸**p. 134**

A *adj* 洋红色的

B *n* [u] 洋红色

maggot /ˈmægət/ *n* 蛆

Magi /ˈmeɪdʒaɪ/ *npl* **the ~** 东方三贤士

magic /ˈmædʒɪk/

A *n* [u] **1** (supernatural power) 魔法; **to suddenly disappear as if by ~** 突然神奇地消失; **to practise ~** 施法术; **to work ~** 产生奇迹; **to work like ~** 功效神奇 **2** (conjuring tricks) 魔术; **to do (some) ~** 变戏法 **3** (enchantment) 魔力; **the ~ of music** 音乐的魅力 **4** colloq (skill of person, performance) 卓越的才能

B *adj* **1** (supernatural) 有魔力的 **2** (special) 神奇的 **3** Brit colloq (wonderful) 好极了的; **it's ~!** 棒极了!

C *vt* (*pres p etc.* **-ck-**) **to ~ sth. away** (似)用魔法使某物消失; **the paintings had been ~ked away** 那些画已经不翼而飞; **to ~ sth. out of sth.** (似)用魔法使某物从某物中出来

magical /ˈmædʒɪkl/ *adj* **1** (supernatural, having magic powers) 有魔力的; (using magic powers) 用魔法的 **2** (enchanting) 奇妙的; **the landscape has a ~ quality** 风景非常迷人

magically /ˈmædʒɪkli/ *adv* 神奇地 ‹*disappear, recovered, cured*›

magic: ~ bullet *n* lit, fig 灵丹妙药; **~ carpet** *n* 魔毯; **~ circle** *n* 特权圈子; **~ eye** *n* 电眼

magician /məˈdʒɪʃn/ *n* **1** (sorcerer) 巫师 **2** (entertainer) 魔术师 **3** colloq (expert) 高手

magic: ~ lantern *n* Hist 幻灯机; **~ mushroom** *n* 致幻蘑菇; **~ potion** *n* 魔力药水; **~ spell** *n* 魔咒; **~ square** *n* 纵横图; **~ wand** *n* 魔杖

magisterial /ˌmædʒɪˈstɪərɪəl/ *adj* **1** (authoritative) 权威的; **a ~ pronouncement** 权威性的声明; **to raise a ~ hand** 庄严地举起一只手 **2** (domineering) 专横的

magistrate /ˈmædʒɪstreɪt/ ▸**p. 409** *n* 地方执法官; **to go** *or* **appear** *or* **come up before (the) ~s** 在地方法院出庭

magistrates' court *n* (*also* **Magistrates' Court**) 地方治安法庭

maglev /ˈmæglev/ *n* 磁悬浮列车系统; **a ~ train** 磁悬浮列车

magma /ˈmægmə/ *n* [u] 岩浆

Magna Carta /ˌmægnə ˈkɑːtə/ *n* Hist **the ~** 大宪章

magnanimity /ˌmægnəˈnɪməti/ *n* [u] formal 宽宏大量

magnanimous /mægˈnænɪməs/ *adj* formal 宽宏大量的

magnanimously /mægˈnænɪməsli/ *adv* formal 宽宏大量地

magnate /ˈmægneɪt/ *n* 巨头; **an oil ~** 石油大亨

magnesia /mægˈniːʃə/ *n* [u] 氧化镁

magnesium /mægˈniːzɪəm/ *n* [u] 镁

magnet /ˈmægnɪt/ *n* **1** lit 磁铁 **2** fig (person) 有吸引力的人; (thing) 有吸引力的事物; **the valley acts as a ~ for tourists** 山谷让游客们流连忘返

magnetic /mægˈnetɪk/ *adj* **1** lit 有磁性的 **2** fig 有吸引力的; **a ~ personality** 富有魅力的个性

magnetically /mægˈnetɪkli/ *adv* **1** lit 靠磁性地 **2** fig 有吸引力地; **young people attracted ~ to the big cities** 被大城市的魅力迷住的年轻人

magnetic: ~ compass *n* = **compass A1**; **~ disk** *n* 磁盘; **~ field** *n* 磁场; **~ north** *n* [u] 磁北; **~ resonance** *n* 磁共振; **~ resonance imaging** *n* [u] 磁共振成像; **~ storm** *n* 磁暴; **~ tape** *n* [u] 磁带

magnetism /ˈmægnɪtɪzəm/ *n* [u] **1** lit 磁性 **2** fig 吸引力; **personal ~** 个人魅力

magnetize /ˈmægnɪtaɪz/ *vt* 使磁化

magneto /mægˈniːtəʊ/ *n* 永磁电机

magnetron /ˈmægnɪtrɒn/ *n* 磁控管

magnet school *n* Amer 磁石学校 [大城市中提供基础课以外课程以吸引不同学区和阶层学生的公立学校]

magnification /ˌmægnɪfɪˈkeɪʃn/ *n* **1** [u] (act of magnifying) 放大 **2** [c] (degree of enlargement, magnifying power) 放大倍数

magnificence /mægˈnɪfɪsns/ *n* [u] (of scenery, view) 壮丽; (of ceremony) 盛大; (of parade) 壮观; (of clothes) 华丽; (of building) 宏伟

magnificent /mægˈnɪfɪsnt/ *adj* **1** (spectacular, impressive) 壮丽的 ‹*scenery, view*›; 壮观的 ‹*parade*›; 盛大的 ‹*ceremony*›; 宏伟的 ‹*building*›; 华丽的 ‹*dress, plumage*›; **to look ~ in a wedding dress** 穿着婚纱看上去非常华丽 **2** (excellent) 极好的; **a ~ act of heroism** 英雄壮举; **this book is quite ~** 这本书非常出色

magnificently /mægˈnɪfɪsntli/ *adv* **1** (spectacularly, impressively) 壮观地; (sumptuously) 华丽地 **2** (excellently) 极好地

magnify /ˈmægnɪfaɪ/ *vt* **1** (make appear larger) 放大; **to ~ sth. to 10 times its size** 把某物放大 10 倍 **2** (increase) 扩大; (intensify) 增强; (exaggerate) 夸大; **his problems have been magnified by the deterioration in his health** 健康状况恶化使他的问题雪上加霜

magnifying glass *n* 放大镜

magnitude /ˈmægnɪtjuːd, Amer -tuːd/ *n* **1** [c] (largeness) 巨大; (vastness) 广大; **the ~ of this epidemic is frightening** 这种流行病传播范围之广令人惶惶不安 **2** [u] (importance) 重大; **of the first ~** 最重要的; **the ~ of a problem** 问题的重要性 **3** [u] (size) 大小; **an order of ~** 数量级 **4** [c] Astron 星等

magnolia /mægˈnəʊlɪə/ ▸**p. 134**

A *n* **1** [c] Bot **~ (tree)** 木兰 **2** [u] (colour) 浅乳白色

B *adj* 浅乳白色的

magnum /ˈmægnəm/ *n* [容量为1.5升的] 大酒瓶

magnum opus /ˌmægnəm ˈəʊpəs/ *n* formal 杰作

magpie /ˈmægpaɪ/ *n* 喜鹊

mag tape *n* [u] colloq = **magnetic tape**

maharaja, maharajah /ˌmɑːhəˈrɑːdʒə/ *n* [印度的] 土邦主

mah-jong, mah-jongg /ˌmɑːˈdʒɒŋ/ ▸**p. 307** *n* [u] 麻将; **a ~ set** 一副麻将牌

mahogany /məˈhɒgəni/

A *n* **1** [u] (wood) 红木; **a ~ table** 红木桌子 **2** [c] (tree) 桃花心木属的树 **3** [u] (colour) 红褐色

B *adj* 红褐色的

mahout /məˈhaʊt/ *n* 象夫

maid /meɪd/ *n* (in house) 女仆; (in hotel) 女服务员; **~ of all work** (servant) 家庭女仆; fig (person doing many jobs) 多面手; (thing performing many tasks) 多用途的东西

maiden /ˈmeɪdn/

A *n* **1** archaic or liter (girl, young woman) 少女 **2** (in cricket) = **maiden over**

B *adj attrib* 首次的 ‹*voyage, flight*›

maiden aunt *n* dated (sister of father) 未婚的姑妈; (sister of mother) 未婚的姨妈

maidenhead /ˈmeɪdnhed/ *n* dated **1** (virginity) 童贞 **2** (hymen) 处女膜

maidenhood /ˈmeɪdnhʊd/ *n* **1** [u] archaic or liter (period) 处女时期 **2** [c] dated (virginity) 童贞

maiden: ~ name *n* 娘家姓; **~ over** *n* 未得分的一轮投球; **~ speech** *n* [新当选议员的] 首次演说

> **maiden name**
>
> 娘家姓。西方国家的许多女子结婚后常改随夫姓，结婚以前的姓就称为maiden name，亦称 birth name。娘家姓可在其前用 *née* 标明，如 Jennifer Spencer *née* Lowther，表示这名女子的夫家姓为 Spencer，娘家姓为 Lowther。女子在离婚后可改回娘家姓。

maid of honor *n* Amer (*pl* **maids of honor**) 首席女傧相

mail /meɪl/

A *n* [u] **1** (postal service) 邮递; **to send a parcel by ~** 邮寄包裹 **2** (letters, parcels) 邮件 **3** Comput 电子邮件 **4** Mil, Hist 锁子甲

B *vt* **1** esp Amer (send by post) 邮寄; **to ~ sth. to sb., to ~ sb. sth.** 把某物寄给某人 **2** Comput **to ~ sb. (with sth.)** 给某人发送(有关某物的)电子邮件

mail: ~bag *n* **1** [c] (bag for mail) 邮袋; **2** [u] (correspondence) 公众来函; **to receive a huge ~bag on the subject from readers** 收到读者关于这个题目的大量来函; **~ bomb** *n* **1** Amer (device) 邮包炸弹; **2** Comput 电邮轰炸; **~box** *n* **1** Amer (for posting) 邮箱; (for delivery) 信箱; **2** (for email) 电子邮箱; ~ **car** *n* Amer 邮政车; ~ **carrier** *n* Amer 邮递员; ~ **coach** *n* **1** Rail 邮政车; **2** Hist 邮政马车; ~ **delivery** *n* [u and c] 邮件投递

mailer /ˈmeɪlə(r)/ *n* **1** Amer (person) 发件人 **2** Amer (envelope, container) 邮件封套 **3** Comput 电邮发送程序

mailing /ˈmeɪlɪŋ/ *n* **1** [u] (dispatch) 邮寄 **2** [c] (piece of mass advertising) 广告邮件

mailing: ~ **address** *n* 邮寄地址; ~ **house** *n* 邮件分拣处; ~ **list** *n* 邮寄名单

mail: ~**man** /-mæn/ ▸p. 409 *n* Amer 邮递员; ~ **merge** *n* [u] 邮件合并程序; ~ **order** *n* [u] 邮购; ~ **order catalogue** 邮购商品目录; ~ **room** *n* 邮件收发室; ~ **shot** *n* **1** (despatch) 广告邮件统一寄发; **2** (single item) 广告邮件; ~ **slot** *n* Amer 信箱; ~ **train** *n* 邮政列车; ~ **van** *n* **1** (delivery vehicle) 邮政车; **2** (railway carriage) 邮政车厢

maim /meɪm/
A *vt* 使残废; **to be ~ed for life** 终身残废
B *vi* 致伤

main /meɪn/
A *adj* 主要的; **the ~ points of the speech** 演说的要点; **the ~ meal of the day** 一天中的正餐; **the ~ clause** 主句; **at least you're safe; that's the ~ thing!** 至少你平安无事; 那才是最重要的! ; **in the ~** 基本上
B *n* **1** (pipe, conduit) 总管 **2** (cable) 干线 **3** archaic or liter (sea) **the ~** 大海
C **mains** *npl* **1** (network) (for water, gas, sewers) 管网系统; (for electricity) 电力网; **is the house connected to the ~s?** 这幢房子通水电气了吗? **2** (starting place of supply) (of water) 水源; (of gas) 燃气源; (of electricity) 电源; **to turn off the water at the ~s** 把水的总阀关掉
D **mains** *modif* 主干线的; **is the house on the ~s supply?** 这幢房子通水电气了吗? ; **a ~s plug** 电源插头; **a ~s radio** 交流电收音机

main: ~ **beam** *n* **1** Brit Aut 大灯; **2** Constr 主梁; ~ **bearing** *n* 主轴承; ~ **board** *n* 主板; ~ **course** *n* 主菜; ~ **deck** *n* 主甲板; ~ **drag** *n* Amer colloq 主要街道

Maine /meɪn/ *pr n* 缅因州

mainframe /ˈmeɪnfreɪm/ *n* ~ **(computer)** 主机

mainland /ˈmeɪnlənd/
A *n* 大陆; **the Chinese ~, the ~ of China** 中国大陆地区
B *modif* 大陆的; ~ **Greece** 希腊大陆; ~ **tourists** 大陆游客

mainlander /ˈmeɪnləndə(r)/ *n* 大陆人

main line
A *n* 干线; **main-line stations** 干线车站
B **mainline** *vt* sl 静脉注射 ‹*cocaine, heroin*›

mainly /ˈmeɪnli/ *adv* 主要地; **the people who go there are ~ tourists** 去那儿的人大部分是游客

main: ~ **man** *n* colloq **1** (romantic partner) 密友; **2** (most important person) 最重要的人; ~**mast** *n* 主桅; ~ **memory** *n* [u] 主存储器; ~ **office** *n* 总部; ~ **road** *n* 主干道; ~**sail** *n* 主帆; ~ **sheet** *n* 主帆索; ~**spring** *n* **1** (of clock, watch) 主发条; **2** fig (motive) 主要动力; (reason, cause) 主要原因; ~**stay** *n* **1** Naut 主桅支索; **2** fig (chief support) 支柱; (central component) 主要部分; **the country's economic ~** 该国的经济支柱

mainstream /ˈmeɪnstriːm/
A *n* 主流; **in/outside the ~** 处于主流之内/之外
B *adj* **1** Sch (conventional) 主流的 ‹*ideas, politics, school, education*› **2** Mus 主流派的
C *vt* 使为多数人接受

main street *n* Amer 大街

maintain /meɪnˈteɪn/ *vt* **1** (keep steady) 维持; **to ~ good relations** 保持友好关系; **to ~ world peace** 维护世界和平; **we must ~ our position in the market** 我们必须保持我们的市场地位 **2** (support) 供养; **to ~ a family of 6** 养活一个六口之家; **a children's home ~ed by the local authority** 由地方当局资助的儿童收养所 **3** (assert) 坚称; **to ~ that ...** 坚持说… **4** (look after) 保养 ‹*vehicle, machine, building*›; **to ~ a road** 养护道路

maintained school *n* Brit 公立学校

maintenance /ˈmeɪntənəns/ *n* [u] **1** (of vehicle, machine, road, building) 保养; **road ~** 道路养护 **2** (of morale, standards etc.) 维持; **the ~ of international peace** 世界和平的维护; **the company's main objective is the ~ of its leading position in the market** 公司的主要目标是保持在市场上的领先地位 **3** Brit (alimony) 生活费

maintenance: ~ **contract** *n* 维修合同; ~ **crew** *n* 维修人员; ~ **fees** *npl* 维修费; ~ **grant** *n* 生活补助金; ~ **man** *n* 维修工; ~ **order** *n* Brit 生活费支付令

maisonette /ˌmeɪzəˈnet/ *n* 复式住宅

maize /meɪz/ *n* [u] 玉米

Maj. *abbr* = **major B1**

majestic /məˈdʒestɪk/ *adj* 雄伟的 ‹*building, mountain*›; 壮观的 ‹*scenery*›; 庄严的 ‹*occasion, ceremony*›; 威严的 ‹*person, appearance*›

majestically /məˈdʒestɪkli/ *adv* 雄伟地 ‹*rise, tower*›; 庄严地 ‹*move*›

majesty /ˈmædʒəsti/ *n* **1** **Majesty** [c] (title) 陛下; **Her/His ~** 女王陛下/国王陛下; **to be detained at Her/His ~'s pleasure** 坐牢 **2** [u] (splendour) (of building, mountain) 雄伟; (of scenery) 壮观; (of occasion, ceremony) 庄严; (of person, appearance) 威严

major /ˈmeɪdʒə(r)/
A *adj* **1** (important) 重要的; ~ **changes** 重大变化; **a ~ road** 干道 **2** (serious) 严重的; **a ~ problem** 难题 **3** (main) 主要的 ‹*part, share*› **4** Mus 大音阶的 ‹*scale*›; 大调的 ‹*key*›; **the key of D ~** D 大调
B *n* **1** Mil 少校 **2** Amer (subject) 主修课程 **3** Amer (student) 主修学生; **an English ~** 英语专业的学生 **4** Mus 大调
C *vi* Amer 主修; **to ~ in Chemistry** 主修化学

Majorca /məˈjɔːkə, məˈdʒɔːkə/ *pr n* 马略卡岛

majorette /ˌmeɪdʒəˈret/ *n* = **drum majorette**

major general *n* (in the army) 陆军少将; (in the US air force) 空军少将

majority /məˈdʒɒrəti, Amer -ˈdʒɔːr-/
A *n* **1** [c] + *v sing or pl* Brit (greater part) 大多数; **the ~ of the voters/population** 大多数投票者/人口; **to be in a** *or* **the ~** 占多数 **2** [c] Pol 多数票; **by a ~ of 50** 以 50 票的多数; **Labour had a large ~ over the Conservatives in this constituency** 在该选区工党得票数远远超过保守党 **3** [u] Jur 法定成年年龄; **to reach one's ~** 达到法定成年年龄; **the age of ~** 法定成年年龄
B *modif* 多数的; ~ **rule** 多数裁定原则; **a ~ verdict** 多数裁决

make /meɪk/
A *vt* (*pt, pp* **made**) **1** (create from parts) 制造 ‹*paper, pottery, vehicle*›; 做 ‹*food, garment*›; **to ~ wine/tea/coffee** 酿酒/沏茶/泡咖啡; **to ~ sth. from sth.** 用某物制造某物; **to ~ sth. (out) of sth.** 用某物做成某物; **to ~ sth. for sb., to ~ sb. sth.** 为某人做某物; **to be made by sb./sth.** 由某人/某厂家生产; **show them what you're made of!** 让他们瞧瞧你的本事! ; **a man made for action** 敏于行动的人; **I'm not made for running** 我不是天生就会跑步; **they are made for each other** 他们是天生的一对; **the lift is only made to carry eight passengers** 这台电梯的设计仅能载 8 位乘客; **made in England** 英国制造; **to ~ sth. into sth.** 将某物做成某物; **to ~ fruit into jam** 把水果做成果酱; **the book has been made into a film** 这本书被改编成了电影; **to be as clever/sharp as they ~ them** *or* **they're made** colloq 非常聪明/精明 **2** (cause to exist) 形成 ‹*hole, puddle*›; 留下 ‹*stain*›; **made by sb./sth.** 由某人/某物造成; **the stone made a dent in the car** 石块把汽车砸出了一个坑; **to ~ a mark** lit 留下污渍; fig 留下影响; **to ~ room for sb.** 给某人腾出地方; **to ~ time for sth./to do sth.** 抽空做某事 **3** (establish, draw up) 制定 ‹*rule, law, legislation*›; 拟订 ‹*will, plan, agreement*›; **to ~ sth. for sb./sth.** 为了某人/某事而设立某事; **the two countries have made a non-aggression pact with each other** 两国签定了互不侵犯条约; **to ~ a list/a note of ...** 列出…的清单/记下… **4** (compose) 创作; **to ~ a drawing/sketch of sth./sb.** 画一幅某物/某人的图画/素描 **5** (produce, bring about) 发出 ‹*noise, smell*›; **to ~ a mess** 弄得一团糟; **to ~ trouble/difficulties (for sb.)** (给某人) 带来麻烦/困难; **to ~ some improvement** 有所改进 **6** (cause to become, render) 使变成; **to ~ sb. happy/popular** 使某人快乐/受欢迎; **to ~ sb./sth. better/worse** 使某人/某事更好/更糟; **she made it clear we were not welcome** 她明确表示我们不受欢迎; **to ~ sth. possible** 使某事成为可能; **to ~ it possible to do sth.** 使做某事成为可能; **we'll ~ London our base** 我们要把伦敦作为大本营; **to ~ sth. (out) of sb./sth.** 使某人/某物成为某种人/某物; **we'll ~ a soldier of you yet!** 我们会把你锻造成为一名战士! ; **to ~ a good/bad job of sth.** 把某事做得很好/很差; **to ~ little of sth.** 不很明白某事; **to ~ nothing of sth.** (not understand) 不理解某事; (treat lightly) 不把某事当回事; **to ~ it £5/7 o'clock** 定为 5 英镑/定在 7 点钟; **to ~ it later/earlier** 安排得晚些/早些 **7** (represent as) 使显得; **it ~s me look fat/ill** 它让我显胖/看上去像生病了; **the recording/tape made her voice sound strange/funny** 录音/录音带使她的声音听起来很怪/滑稽; **you've made his nose too big!** 你把他的鼻子画得太大了! **8** (cause to do) 使; **to ~ sb./sth. do sth.** 使某人/某物做某事; **to ~ the car start** 发动汽车; **you must ~ her see a doctor** 你一定要让她去看医生 **9** (force, compel) 迫使; **to ~ sb. do sth.** 迫使某人做某事; **to be made to do sth.** 被迫做某事; **we have ways of making you talk** (in interrogation) 我们有办法让你开口; **they made me (do it)** 他们强迫我(这么做) ; **he must be made to cooperate** 必须逼他合作 **10** **to ~ sb. sth.** (appoint) 任命某人担任某职务; (elect) 选举某人担任某职务; **the people made him their leader** 人民推举他为领袖; **she made him her assistant** 她选他做助手 **11** (be, become) 成为; **that would ~ a good present** 这会是很好的礼物; **these apples ~ good eating** 这些苹果很好吃; **to ~ interesting reading/listening** 读起来/听起来有趣; **to ~ a good husband/wife** 成为好丈夫/好妻子 **12** (function as) 作为; **to ~ a substitute for sth.** 作为某事物的替代; **the cave made an excellent shelter** 山洞成了极好的隐蔽处 **13** (add up to, amount to) 总计; **2 and 2 ~ 4** 2 加 2 等于 4; **that ~s £90 all together** *or* **in total** 总共 90 英镑; **to ~ a pair/set** 成对/成套; **the bride and groom made a handsome couple** 新娘和新郎是完美的一对; **to ~ a fourth** (in game) 凑齐4人; **that ~s the third time I've asked you not to do that!** 这已经是我第三次叫你不要做这事了! **14** (earn) 赚得; **to ~ £100 a week** 每周赚 100 英镑; **how much** *or* **what do you think he ~s?** 你认为他挣多少钱? ; **to ~ sb. sth.** 为某人得到某物; **the deal should ~ him £500, he should ~ £500 on the deal** 这笔交易能让他赚 500 英镑; **to ~ a profit/loss** 获利/亏损 **15** Sport (score) 得到; **England made 295** (in cricket) 英格兰队得了 295 分 **16** (in cards) 赢 ‹*trick, contract*›; **she made her ten of hearts** 她以一个红桃 10 赢了一墩牌 **17** **to ~ sth. of sb./sth.** (estimate, assess) 对某人/某事有某种看法;

what do you ~ of this/him? 你对这这个/他有什么看法?; what time do you ~ it?, what do you ~ the time? 你估计现在是几点钟? 18▸ (travel) 走过 ‹distance›; the road was hard going — we made only 5 miles in 3 hours 路很难走, 我们3小时才走了5英里 19▸ (reach) 到达 ‹place›; 达到 ‹speed, level›; to ~ the summit 到达顶峰; to ~ the charts/best-seller list 进入流行唱片排行榜/畅销书单; to ~ the front page/headlines 登上头版/成为头条; to ~ a connection/connecting flight 乘搭转接班机; to ~ 60 活到60岁; to ~ it (in career) 取得成功; (in getting to destination) 赶到; (survive) 幸存; (attend) 出席; to ~ it with sb. colloq 和某人性交; the car can just ~ 100 mph 这辆汽车勉强每小时能开100英里 20▸ (cause success of) 使成功; this is the film or movie that made him 这就是那部让他成名的电影; a good wine can ~ a meal 美酒可抵佳肴; to ~ or break sb./sth. 是某人/某事成败的关键 21▸ (carry through, execute) 进行 ‹enquiry›; 发表 ‹speech›; 作出 ‹judgement, estimate, arrangement, promise›; to ~ an offer/a suggestion 出价/提建议; stop making a fuss! 别闹了!; to ~ a visit/trip 去参观/旅行; to ~ do (with sth.) 将就(用某物); to ~ sth. do 将就着用某物 22▸ Elec 接通 ‹circuit›

B v refl (pt, pp **made**) to ~ oneself heard/understood 让别人听到/明白自己的话; to ~ oneself at home 不拘束; there's no point making yourself miserable about it 没必要为这件事苦恼; to ~ oneself useful 让自己有用

C vi (pt, pp **made**) 1▸ (act) 作出举动; she made as if to kiss him 她假装要亲吻他; he made like he was injured colloq 他装作受伤了; he made like to stab him colloq 他仿佛要刺他 2▸ (move, go) 移动; she made towards the door 她朝门走去 3▸ (succeed) 成功; it's ~ or break for ... 对于…而言, 这事关成败

D n 1▸ [c] (brand, marque) 品牌; what ~ is your new car? 你的新车是什么牌子的? 2▸ [u] (way sth. is made) 款式 3▸ [u] to be on the ~ colloq (making money) 谋利; (out for sexual pleasure) 猎艳

Phrasal verbs

- **make after** vt [~ after sb./sth.] 追赶
- **make away** vi 1▸ (make off) 逃走; to ~ away with sth. 偷走某物 ‹valuables, property› 2▸ to ~ away with sb. (kill) 杀死某人; to ~ away with oneself 自杀
- **make for** vt [~ for sb./sth.] 1▸ (head for) 向…移动; to ~ for the summit/the open sea 向顶峰进发/驶向公海 2▸ (help create) 促成 ‹state, effect›; those red roses ~ for a wonderful display against the yellow background 红玫瑰在黄色背景的衬托下显得非常好看
- **make off** vi 匆忙离去; they made off across the main road 他们连忙穿过主干道
- **make off with** vt [~ off with sth./sb.] 携…而逃; thieves made off with our jewellery 盗贼偷走了我们的珠宝
- **make out**

A vt (claim, assert) 声称; to ~ out that ... 声称…; he ~s himself out to be richer than he really is 他夸口说自己很有钱, 其实没那么富

B [~ sb./sth. out, ~ out sb./sth.] vt 1▸ (understand) 理解; I can't ~ him out 我搞不懂他; to ~ out if or whether ... 搞清楚是否… 2▸ (manage to see, distinguish) 辨别出 ‹object, writing, sign, person›; 听出 ‹sound›

C [~ sth. out, ~ out sth.] vt 1▸ (write out) 填写; to ~ out a cheque to sb. 给某人开支票; to ~ out a prescription 开处方 2▸ (expound) 阐释; he made out a good case for an amnesty 他提出了充分的理由要求大赦

D vi colloq 1▸ (manage, get on) 应付; how are you making out? 你过得怎样?; to ~ out with sb. 与某人相处; how did you ~ out with his family? 你和他的家人相处得怎么样? 2▸ Amer (have sex) 和某人性交; did you ~ out with her? 你和她做过爱吗?

- **make over** vt 1▸ [~ sth./sb. over, ~ over sth./sb.] (transform) 改造 ‹building›; 改变 ‹person, appearance›; the garage has been made over into a study 车库被改成了书房 2▸ [~ sth. over, ~ over sth.] (transfer) 转让 ‹property›; to ~ sth. over to sb. 把某物移交给某人
- **make towards** vt [~ towards sth.] 朝…走去
- **make up**

A [~ up sth.] vt 1▸ (constitute) 组成; to ~ up 10% of ... 占…的10%; the human body is made up of cells 人体是由细胞构成的 2▸ (compensate for) 补偿; to ~ up sth. with sth. 用某物补偿某物; to ~ up the shortfall with a loan 用贷款填补亏空; to ~ up sth. by doing sth. 用做某事来弥补某事; he made up his lost wages by working overtime 他通过加班来补回损失的工资; to ~ it up to sb. 补偿某人; I'll ~ it up to you 我会给你补偿的 3▸ to ~ it up (with sb.) (after quarrel) (和某人) 言归于好; have they made it up yet? 他们和解了吗?

B [~ sth. up, ~ up sth.] vt 1▸ (prepare) 预备; she made up a basket of food 她弄好了一篮子食物 2▸ (apply make-up to) 给…化妆 ‹person, face, eyes› 3▸ Pharm 配制 ‹medicine›; 配 ‹prescription› 4▸ (sew) 缝制; to ~ sth. up into sth. 把某物缝制成某物; to ~ sth. up for sb./sth. 为某人/某事缝制某物; she was making up an outfit for the wedding 她正在缝制一套结婚礼服 5▸ (put sheets, blankets, etc. on) 铺 ‹bed› 6▸ (stoke up) 给…添加燃料 ‹fire› 7▸ Print 给…排版 ‹type, text, illustrations› 8▸ (invent) 编造 ‹excuse, story›; I was just making it up as I went along 我只是在顺口编造 9▸ (complete) 凑够; to ~ up the number/weight 凑够数量/重量; to ~ up a four (in game) 凑齐4个人

C vi 1▸ to ~ up for sth. (compensate) 补偿某物; hard work can ~ up for lack of intelligence 勤能补拙; to ~ up in full for sth. 彻底补偿某事 2▸ to ~ up to sb. Brit colloq (try to please) 讨好某人 3▸ (after quarrel) 和好; to kiss and ~ up 握手言和 4▸ (apply make-up) 化妆

D v refl to ~ oneself up 化妆

- **make with** vt [~ with sth.] Amer colloq 马上提供; ~ with the money! 快给钱!

make-believe

A /ˈmeɪkbɪliːv/ n [u] 1▸ (pretence) 假装; to play at ~ 玩假扮游戏 2▸ (fantasy) 幻想; a world of ~ 虚幻的世界

B **make believe** /ˌmeɪkbɪˈliːv/ vi (pretend) 假装; (fantasize) 幻想

C modif 虚构的; a ~ world/house 虚幻的世界/假想的房子

make-do-and-mend vi, n [u] 修补将就

make-or-break adj 成败攸关的; a ~ decision 关乎成败的决定

makeover /ˈmeɪkəʊvə(r)/ n (beauty treatment) 美容; (transformation) 改观; to give sb./sth. a ~ 给某人美容/使某物改观

maker /ˈmeɪkə(r)/

A n 1▸ (manufacturer) 制造商 2▸ (creator) 制造者; (of clothes, films) 制作者

B **Maker** n Relig the/his/her/our etc. M~ 上帝; to go to meet one's M~ 去见上帝

makeshift /ˈmeɪkʃɪft/ adj 临时替代的; a ~ bed 临时的床

make-up n [u] 1▸ (cosmetics) 化妆品; to put on one's ~ 上妆; she never wears ~ 她从来不化妆 2▸ (character) 性格; jealousy is not in his or not part of his ~ 嫉妒不是他的品性 3▸ (composition) 组成; to alter the ~ of the committee 改组委员会; the ~ of a compound 化合物的构成

make-up: ~ **artist** ▸p. 409 n 化妆师; ~ **bag** n 化妆包; ~ **base** n 粉底; ~ **girl** ▸p. 409 n 女化妆师; ~ **man** ▸p. 409 n 男化妆师; ~ **remover** n 卸妆液

makeweight /ˈmeɪkweɪt/ n (extra person) 充数的人; (extra thing) 充数的东西

making /ˈmeɪkɪŋ/

A n [u] (creation, manufacture) 制造; to be in the ~ (being made) 在生产过程中; (developing) 在发展中; a social reform in the ~ 酝酿之中的社会变革; these events are history in the ~ 这些事件将载入史册; the ~ of a film 电影制作; problems of sb.'s own ~ 某人自己造成的问题; his four years in university were the ~ of him 四年大学生活造就了他

B **makings** npl 1▸ (essential qualities or ingredients) 必要条件; to have (all) the ~s of sth. 具备成为某事物的(所有)必要条件; her first novel has all the ~s of a classic 她的第一部小说堪称经典之作; she had the ~s of a great teacher 她具备成为一名优秀教师的素质 2▸ colloq dated (earnings) 赚头

malachite /ˈmæləkaɪt/ n [u] 孔雀石

maladjusted /ˌmæləˈdʒʌstɪd/ adj 适应不良的 ‹person, behaviour›

maladministration /ˌmælədˌmɪnɪˈstreɪʃn/ n [u] 1▸ formal (inefficient management) 管理不善 2▸ Jur 腐败

maladroit /ˌmæləˈdrɔɪt/ adj formal (clumsy) 笨拙的; (tactless) 不圆通的

maladroitly /ˌmæləˈdrɔɪtli/ adv formal (clumsily) 笨拙地; (tactlessly) 不圆通地

malady /ˈmælədi/ n liter (illness) 疾病; fig (problem) 弊病; an incurable ~ 不治之症; the ~ facing the education system 教育制度面临的痼疾

Malagasy /ˌmæləˈgæsi/ ▸p. 503, p. 426

A adj (of Madagascar) 马达加斯加的; (of the people) 马达加斯加人的; (of the language) 马达加斯加语的

B n 1▸ [c] (person) 马达加斯加人 2▸ [u] (language) 马达加斯加语

malaise /mæˈleɪz/ n [u] formal (feeling) 莫名的不安; (in society, organization) 难以描述的问题; a general air of ~ 普遍的不安气氛

malapropism /ˈmæləprɒpɪzəm/ n 可笑的近音词误用

malaria /məˈleərɪə/ ▸p. 377 n [u] 疟疾

malarial /məˈleərɪəl/ adj 疟疾的 ‹symptoms, infection›; 传播疟疾的 ‹mosquito, parasite›; 患疟疾的 ‹patient›; 疟疾流行的 ‹region›

Malawi /məˈlɑːwɪ/ pr n 马拉维

Malawian /məˈlɑːwɪən/ ▸p. 503

A adj (of Malawi) 马拉维的; (of the people) 马拉维人的

B n 马拉维人

Malay /məˈleɪ/ ▸p. 503, p. 426

A adj (of the people) 马来人的; (of the language) 马来语的

B n 1▸ [c] (person) 马来人 2▸ [u] (language) 马来语

Malaya /məˈleɪə/ pr n 马来亚 [马来西亚西部的旧称]

Malayan /məˈleɪən/ adj, n = **Malay**

Malaysia /məˈleɪzɪə/ pr n 马来西亚

Malaysian /məˈleɪzɪən/ ▸p. 503, p. 426

A adj (of Malaysia) 马来西亚的; (of the people) 马来西亚人的

B n 马来西亚人

malcontent /ˈmælkəntent/ n formal 不满者

Maldives /ˈmɔːldɪvz/, **Maldive Islands** pr npl the ~ 马尔代夫

male /meɪl/

A adj 1▸ Biol, Zool, Bot 雄性的; (relating to men) 男性的; a ~ student 男生; ~ attitudes 男人的看法 2▸ Tech, Elec 阳的; ~ plug or connector 插头

B n Biol, Zool, Bot 雄性; (man, boy) 男性; the average British ~ 普通英国男子

m

male chauvinism *n* [u] pej 大男子主义

male chauvinist pej
A *n* 大男子主义者
B *adj* 大男子主义的; **a ~ pig** 大男子主义蠢猪

male-dominated /ˌmeɪl'dɒmɪneɪtɪd/ *adj* (run by men) 由男性控制的 ‹*culture, society*›; (predominantly masculine) 以男性为主的 ‹*industry, profession*›

malefactor /'mælɪfæktə(r)/ *n* formal (wrongdoer) 作恶者; (criminal) 罪犯

male: ~ menopause *n* **the ~ menopause** 男性更年期; **~ model** *n* 男模特; **~ voice choir** *n* 男声合唱团

malevolence /mə'levələns/ *n* [u] 恶意; **a look of ~** 歹毒的表情

malevolent /mə'levələnt/ *adj* 有恶意的; **a ~ smile** 恶毒的微笑

malevolently /mə'levələntli/ *adv* 有恶意地

malformation /ˌmælfɔː'meɪʃn/ *n* **1** [c] (abnormally formed part of body) 畸形部位 **2** [u] (condition) 畸形

malformed /ˌmæl'fɔːmd/ *adj* 畸形的 ‹*foetus, spine*›

malfunction /ˌmæl'fʌŋkʃn/
A *vi* «*machine, engine, computer*» 发生故障; «*bodily organ*» 机能失常
B *n* (of machine, engine, computer) 故障; (of bodily organ) 机能失常

Mali /'mɑːli/ *pr n* 马里

Malian /'mɑːlɪən/ ▸p. 503
A *adj* (of Mali) 马里的; (of the people) 马里人的
B *n* 马里人

malice /'mælɪs/ *n* [u] 恶意; **out of ~** 出于恶意; **I bear him no ~** 我对他没有恶意; **with ~ aforethought** Jur 蓄意犯罪

malicious /mə'lɪʃəs/ *adj* 怀有恶意的; **~ rumours** 恶毒的谣言

malicious damage *n* [u] Jur 恶意损害

maliciously /mə'lɪʃəsli/ *adv* 怀有恶意地 ‹*behave, say*›

malicious: ~ prosecution *n* 恶意诉讼; **~ wounding** *n* 故意伤害

malign /mə'laɪn/
A *adj* 恶意的 ‹*intention, person*›; 有害的 ‹*influence, effect*›
B *vt* 诽谤; **to ~ innocent people** 诬蔑清白的人; **to be much ~ed** 遭到大肆诽谤

malignancy /mə'lɪgnənsi/ *n* **1** [u] (desire to harm) 恶意 **2** [u] Med (of cancer, tumour) 恶性 **3** [c] Med (tumour) 恶性肿瘤

malignant /mə'lɪgnənt/ *adj* **1** (cruel) 恶意的 ‹*criticism, intention*›; 恶毒的 ‹*attack, enemy*› **2** Med 恶性的 ‹*cancer, tumour*›; **~ cells** 恶性癌细胞

malinger /mə'lɪŋgə(r)/ *vi* pej 装病

malingerer /mə'lɪŋgərə(r)/ *n* pej 装病的人

mall /mæl, mɔːl/ *n* esp Amer 购物中心

mallard /'mælɑːd, Amer 'mælərd/ *n* (*pl* **~** *or* **~s**) 绿头鸭

malleability /ˌmælɪə'bɪləti/ *n* [u] **1** (of material) 延展性 **2** (of person) 易受影响

malleable /'mælɪəbl/ *adj* **1** (mouldable) 有延展性的 **2** (easily influenced) 易受影响的

mallet /'mælɪt/ *n* **1** (tool) 木槌 **2** Sport 球棒

mallow /'mæləʊ/ *n* 锦葵

malnourished /ˌmæl'nʌrɪʃt/ *adj* 营养不良的

malnutrition /ˌmælnjuː'trɪʃn, Amer -nuː-/ *n* [u] 营养不良

malodorous /ˌmæl'əʊdərəs/ *adj* formal or liter 难闻的

malpractice /ˌmæl'præktɪs/ *n* [u and c] 渎职; **medical ~** 医疗事故

malt /mɔːlt/ *n* **1** [u] (grain) 麦芽 **2** [c and u] (whisky) 麦芽威士忌

Malta /'mɔːltə/ *pr n* 马耳他

malted /'mɔːltɪd/ *adj* 含麦芽的 ‹*biscuit, drink*›

malted milk *n* **1** [c and u] (drink) 麦乳精饮料 **2** [u] (powder) 麦乳精

Maltese /mɔːl'tiːz/ ▸p. 503, p. 426
A *adj* (of Malta) 马耳他的; (of the people) 马耳他人的; (of the language) 马耳他语的
B *n* **1** [c] (person) 马耳他人 **2** [u] (language) 马耳他语
C *npl* **the ~ (people)** 马耳他人

Maltese cross *n* 马耳他十字

malt extract *n* [u] 麦芽汁

maltreat /ˌmæl'triːt/ *vt* 虐待

maltreatment /ˌmæl'triːtmənt/ *n* [u] 虐待

malt: ~ vinegar *n* [u] 麦芽醋; **~ whisky** *n* [u and c] 麦芽威士忌

malware /'mælweə(r)/ *n* [u] 恶意软件

mam /mæm/ *n* Brit, N Eng colloq 妈

mama, mamma *n* **1** /'mæmə, mə'mɑː/ Amer or dated child lang (mother) 妈妈 **2** /'mæmə/ Amer colloq (mature woman) 女人; **she's a real hot ~** 她是个十足的性感女人

mammal /'mæml/ *n* 哺乳动物

mammalian /mə'meɪlɪən/ *adj* 哺乳动物的

mammary /'mæməri/ *adj* 乳房的; **~ glands** 乳腺

mammograph /'mæməgrɑːf, Amer -græf/ *n* 乳腺影像

mammography /mæ'mɒgrəfi/ *n* [u] 乳腺摄影

Mammon /'mæmən/ *pr n* [u] pej 玛门 [指被看作对人有不良影响的财富]; **to worship ~** 拜金

mammoth /'mæməθ/
A *n* 猛犸
B *adj* 巨大的; **a ~ corporation** 庞大的公司; **a ~ task** 重大的任务

mammy /'mæmi/ *n* child lang 妈妈

man /mæn/
A *n* (*pl* **men**) **1** [c] (adult male) 男人; **an old ~** 老人; **a single/married ~** 一位单身/已婚男子; **a ~ of God** 神职人员; **a ~ of the people** 体恤民情者; **(the) ~ of the match** Brit 全场最佳球员; **the ~ of the moment** 时下最受瞩目的人; **~ and boy** 从小到大; **I'm sure the police have arrested the right/wrong ~** 我肯定警察抓对/抓错人了; **the (right) ~ for sth.** 某事的合适人选; **he's not the right ~ for the job** 他不适合做这个工作; **he's your ~** 他就是你要的人; **our ~ in Cairo/Havana** 我们驻开罗/哈瓦那的代表; **the manager/foreman gave the men their instructions** 经理/监工对手下下达了指令; **the television ~ is coming tomorrow to look at it** 电视维修工明天来检修; **(not) the** *or* **a ~ to do sth.** （不是）做某事的那种人; **a ladies' ~** 喜欢在女人堆里厮混的男人; **a ~'s ~** 喜欢和男人在一起的男人; **it's a ~'s world** 这是个男人的世界; **a ~'s gotta do what a ~'s gotta do** colloq 男人就要做男人该做的事情; **a wine/whisky ~** 喜欢喝葡萄酒/威士忌的男人; **a one-pint ~** colloq 能喝1品脱啤酒的男人; **a ~ about town** 喜好社交者; **a fighting ~** Mil 战士; **to be one's own ~** 能自己做主; **when it comes to politics, he's very much his own ~** 在政治方面, 他颇有主见; **to be twice the ~** 大有起色; **a ~ of (many) parts** 多才多艺的男人; **a ~ of his word** 说话算数的男人; **a ~ of the world** 见过世面的男人; **clothes for men** 男装 **2** [c] (person) 人; **as one ~** 一致地; **to a ~** *or* **to the last ~** 无例外地; **the ~ in** *or* **on the street** 普通人; **the common ~** 普通人; **the poor ~'s ...** 穷人的…; **corduroy has always been the poor ~'s velvet** 灯芯绒一向是穷人的天鹅绒; **as good/honest as the next ~** 像别人一样好/诚实; **to hit** *or* **kick a ~ when he's down** 落井下石; **the odd ~ out** 不合群的人; **a ~ after one's own heart** 合意的人 **3** [u] (*also* **Man**) (humankind) 人类; **primitive/modern ~** 原始人/现代人; **the origins/development of ~** 人类的起源/发展; **the rights of ~** 人权; **~ proposes, God disposes** 谋事在人, 成事在天 **4** [c] (husband) 丈夫; (male lover) 情郎; (boyfriend) 男朋友; **to be made ~ and wife** 结为夫妻; **to live as ~ and wife** 以夫妻身份同居 **5** [c] Sport 男队员 **6** [c] dated (manservant) 男仆; (valet) 侍从 **7** [c] (having affiliations) [某地、某机构、从事某活动等的] 男子; **a Birmingham ~** 一位伯明翰男子; **a solid Labour ~** 工党的坚定支持者; **an Oxford ~** 牛津人 [指牛津大学的（男）学生或校友] **8** [c] colloq (as form of address) 老兄; **hurry up, ~!** 快点, 哥儿们! ; **~, it was awful!** 伙计, 真是太糟糕了! ; **my (good) ~** Brit dated 老弟 [屈尊俯就的称呼]; **good ~!** 好样的! ; **young ~** 年轻人 [屈尊俯就的称呼]; **my little ~** 小宝贝 **9** [c] (person of courage) 男子汉; **be a ~! don't cry!** 要像个男人! 不要哭! ; **to be ~ enough to do sth.** 有足够的勇气和能力做某事; **the ~ in him** 他的大丈夫气概; **to sort out the men from the boys** 选出强者; **to make a ~ (out) of sb.** 使某人成为男子汉; **to take it like a ~** 坚韧地承受; **he took the bad news like a ~** 他勇敢地接受了坏消息 **10** [c] (in chess, draughts) 棋子; **to move a ~** 走棋; **to capture** *or* **take a ~** 吃掉一颗棋子
B **men** *npl* Mil （男）士兵
C *vt* (*pres p etc.* **-nn-**) 给…配备人员 ‹*ship, office*›; **fully ~ned** 满员的

manacle /'mænəkl/
A *n* 镣铐
B *vt* 给…戴上镣铐; **to ~ sb. to sth.** 将某人铐在某物上; **a ~d prisoner** 戴着镣铐的囚犯

manage /'mænɪdʒ/
A *vt* **1** (succeed) 完成; **to ~ to do sth.** 做成某事; **I ~d to find us a hotel** 我为大家找到了旅馆; **she ~d to offend everyone** 她居然把大伙都得罪了 **2** (find possible) 做得到; **can you ~ six o'clock?** 6 点钟你行吗? ; **I can't ~ the meeting** 我没法去开会; **could you ~ lunch on Friday?** 星期五你能来吃午饭吗? ; **I couldn't ~ another thing!** 我再也吃不下了! ; **I can ~ sixty words per minute** 我每分钟可以打 60 个字; **he's not very good at French, but he can ~ a few words** 他法语不太好, 但是勉强能说几句 **3** (administer) 管理 ‹*finances, organization, department, project*›; 经营 ‹*business, hotel*›; **a company director must know how to ~ risk/debt** 公司董事必须懂得如何进行风险/债务管理 **4** (control, supervise) 掌管 ‹*team, staff, performer*›; **he ~d Manchester United in the 1960s** 他曾于 20 世纪 60 年代掌管曼联队; **he once ~d the Beatles** 他曾是甲壳虫乐队的经理人 **5** Agric 开发利用 ‹*land, forest*› **6** (deal with, cope with) 能对付 ‹*crisis, stress*›; **parents who have difficulty managing their children** 管不住孩子的父母; **he knows how to ~ her** 他知道如何对付她; **he gets short of breath and can't ~ the stairs** 他气喘吁吁, 楼梯都上不去了; **we could ~ one more in the back (of the car)** 我们（车）后面还能挤下一个人 **7** (organize, use well) 打理 ‹*time, resources*›; **to ~ money** 理财
B *vi* **1** (cope) 应付过去; **I can ~ by myself** 我自己能行; **to ~ without ...** 没有…也能行; **we haven't got any more cheese, so I'll have to ~ without** 我们没有奶酪了, 所以我只能将就一下了; **to just about ~** 勉强能应付; **to ~ on sth.** 靠…勉强过活 ‹*income, amount*› **2** (be manager) 经营

manageable /'mænɪdʒəbl/ *adj* 可处理的 ‹*task, situation, size*›; 易操纵的 ‹*boat, vehicle, machine*›; **~ hair** 易梳理的头发

managed /'mænɪdʒd/ *adj* 受监管的 ‹*reserve, forest*›; **a ~ environment** 受控环境

managed: ~ care *n* [u] Amer 管理医疗保健制度; **~ currency** *n* 管理通货;

m

~ **economy** *n* 管制经济; ~ **fund** *n* 管理基金

management /ˈmænɪdʒmənt/
A *n* [u] 1 (administration) (of finances, organization, department, project, risk, debt) 管理; (of business, hotel) 经营; **the industry has suffered from poor ~ in the past** 该行业过去管理不善 2 + *v sing or pl* (managers collectively) 资方; (management team) 管理人员; **a new agreement between ~ and unions** 资方与工会达成的新协议; **junior/lower/middle/senior/top ~** 初级/低层/中层/高层/顶层管理人员 3 (control, handling) (of animal, person) 控制; (of situation, feeling) 应对; **the ~ of stress** 压力调适
B *modif* 管理的 ‹*job, service, staff*›; 管理层的 ‹*decision*›

management: ~ **accounting** *n* [u] 管理会计; ~ **buyout** *n* 管理层收购; ~ **committee** *n* 管理委员会; ~ **company** *n* 资产管理公司; ~ **consultancy** *n* 管理咨询公司; ~ **consultant** ▸**p. 409** *n* 管理顾问; ~ **fees** *npl* 管理费; ~ **information system** *n* 管理信息系统; ~ **studies** *npl* 管理研究; ~ **style** *n* 管理风格; ~ **trainee** *n* 见习经理

manager /ˈmænɪdʒə(r)/ *n* 1 (of business, farm, project, etc.) 经理 2 (of entertainer, actor, sportsman) 经纪人 3 (of sports team) [运动队的] 经理 4 (of household) 当家人; (of money) 管理人; **he's not a good ~ of money** 他不善于理财

manageress /ˌmænɪdʒəˈres/ *n* Brit 女经理

managerial /ˌmænɪˈdʒɪərɪəl/ *adj* (of management) 管理的; (of managers) 管理人员的

managing: ~ **director** *n* 总裁; ~ **editor** *n* 总编辑; ~ **partner** *n* 任事股东

Managua /məˈnɑːgwə/ *pr n* 马那瓜

Manama /məˈnɑːmə/ *pr n* 麦纳麦

manatee /ˌmænəˈtiː/ *n* 海牛

Manchu /ˌmænˈtʃuː/ ▸**p. 503, p. 426**
A *adj* 1 (of the people) 满族的 ‹*dynasty, emperor, empire*› 2 (of the language) 满语的
B *n* 1 [c] (*pl* ~ *or* ~**s**) (person) 满族人 2 [u] (language) 满语

Manchuria /ˌmæntˈʃʊərɪə/ *pr n* 满洲

Manchurian /ˌmænˈtʃʊərɪən/
A *adj* 满洲的
B *n* 满洲人

Mancunian /ˌmæŋˈkjuːnɪən/
A *adj* 曼彻斯特的 ‹*accent, band*›
B *n* 曼彻斯特人

mandala /ˈmændələ/ *n* 曼荼罗 [印度教和佛教中象征宇宙的圆形图]

mandarin /ˈmændərɪn/ *n* 1 [c] (fruit) 柑橘 2 [c] (tree) 柑橘树 3 **Mandarin (Chinese)** [u] 普通话 4 [c] Pol, Admin 官僚 5 [c] Hist [旧时中国政府的] 高级官吏

mandarin duck *n* 鸳鸯

mandate /ˈmændeɪt/
A *n* 1 (authority) 授权; **to have a ~ to do sth.** 获得做某事的权力; **to give sb. a ~ to do sth.** 授权某人做某事 2 (order) 命令 3 Fin, Jur (document) 委托书
B *vt* 授权给; **to ~ sb. to do sth.** 授权某人做某事

mandatory /ˈmændətəri, Amer -tɔːri/ *adj* 1 (compulsory) 强制的 ‹*attendance, payment*› 2 (required by law) 法定的 ‹*detention, penalty*›; **wearing helmets was made ~ for cyclists** 法律规定骑自行车时必须戴头盔

man-day *n* 工日 [一个人一天可完成的工作量]

mandible /ˈmændɪbl/ *n* 1 (of vertebrate) (jaw) 下颌; (jawbone) 下颌骨 2 (of insect) 颚 3 (of bird) (upper) 鸟喙上部; (lower) 鸟喙下部

mandolin /ˌmændəˈlɪn/ ▸**p. 395** *n* 曼陀林

mane /meɪn/ *n* 1 (of horse) 鬃; (of lion) 鬣 2 fig (of person) 浓密的长发

man-eater *n* 1 (animal) 吃人的动物 2 colloq (woman) [有多个性伴侣的] 男性杀手

man-eating *adj attrib* 吃人的

maneuver /məˈnuːvə(r)/ *vt, vi, n* Amer = **manoeuvre**

man Friday *n* (male servant) 男忠仆; (male assistant) 得力男助手

manful /ˈmænfl/ *adj* 有男子气概的; ~ **resistance** 勇敢的抵抗

manfully /ˈmænfəli/ *adv* 有男子气概地; **to struggle ~** 勇敢地斗争

manga /ˈmæŋgə/ *n* [u] 日本动漫

manganese /ˈmæŋgəniːz/ *n* [u] 锰

mange /meɪndʒ/ *n* [u] 兽疥癣

mangel-wurzel /ˈmæŋglwɜːzl/ *n* 饲料甜菜

manger /ˈmeɪndʒə(r)/ *n* 食槽

mangetout /ˌmɑːnʒˈtuː/ *n* (*pl* ~ *or* ~**s**) esp Brit 荷兰豆

mangle /ˈmæŋgl/
A *vt* 1 (crush, mutilate) 压碎; **his hand was ~d in the machine** 他的手被机器轧烂了; **a ~d wreck** 面目全非的残骸 2 fig (ruin) 糟蹋; **he was mangling Bach on the piano** 他在乱弹巴赫的钢琴曲
B *n* 轧布机

mango /ˈmæŋgəʊ/ *n* (*pl* ~**s** *or* ~**es**) 1 [c and u] (fruit) 芒果 2 [c] (tree) 芒果树

mangold /ˈmæŋgəʊld/ *n* = **mangel-wurzel**

mangrove /ˈmæŋgrəʊv/ *n* 1 [c] (tree) 红树 2 [u and c] ~ **(swamp)** 红树沼泽地

mangy /ˈmeɪndʒi/ *adj* 1 Vet 患疥癣的 ‹*dog, animal*› 2 pej (shabby) 破旧的 ‹*coat, carpet, hotel*›

manhandle /ˈmænhændl/ *vt* 1 (treat roughly) 粗暴地推搡; **he claimed that the police had ~d him** 他声称受到了警察的粗暴对待 2 (move by manpower) 用人力搬动 ‹*cargo, luggage*›

Manhattan /ˌmænˈhætn/ *pr n* 曼哈顿岛

manhole *n* 人孔; ~ **cover** 人孔盖

manhood /ˈmænhʊd/ *n* 1 [u] (adulthood) (period) 成年期; (state) 成年 2 [u] (masculinity) 男子汉气概 3 [u] liter (men collectively) 男子 4 [c] colloq euph (penis) 阴茎

man: ~**-hour** *n* 工时 [一人在一小时内完成的工作量]; ~**hunt** *n* 搜捕

mania /ˈmeɪnɪə/ *n* 1 [u] Psych 躁狂 2 [c] colloq (obsession) 狂热; **to have a ~ for sth./doing sth.** 痴迷于某事/做某事

maniac /ˈmeɪnɪæk/
A *n* 1 (violent or wild person) 狂人; **to drive like a ~** 发了疯似地开车 2 colloq (enthusiast) 狂热分子; **a computer ~** 电脑发烧友
B *adj attrib* colloq 疯狂的 ‹*scheme, driver*›

maniacal /məˈnaɪəkl/ *adj* 疯狂的 ‹*behaviour, laughter, grin*›; **a ~ killer** 杀人狂

manic /ˈmænɪk/ *adj* 1 Psych 躁狂的 2 (hectic) 忙乱的 ‹*activity*› 3 (wild) 癫狂的 ‹*grin, energy*›

manic depression *n* [u] ▸**p. 377** 躁狂抑郁症

manic-depressive ▸**p. 377**
A *adj* 躁狂抑郁症的 ‹*personality, symptom, illness*›; 患躁狂抑郁症的 ‹*person*›
B *n* 躁狂抑郁症患者

manicure /ˈmænɪkjʊə(r)/
A *n* 手部护理
B *vt* 护理 ‹*hands*›; 修剪 ‹*nails*›

manicure: ~ **case** *n* 指甲修护套装; ~ **scissors** *npl* 指甲刀; ~ **set** *n* 一套修指甲用具

manicurist /ˈmænɪkjʊərɪst/ ▸**p. 409** *n* 护手师

manifest /ˈmænɪfest/ formal
A *adj* 明显的; **his nervousness was ~ to us** 我们都看出他很紧张
B *vt* 1 清楚显示; **she ~ed signs of severe depression** 她出现了严重抑郁症的症状 2 (be evidence of) 证明; **bad industrial relations are often ~ed in strikes** 罢工常常是劳资关系恶劣的证明
C *v refl* **to ~ itself** 显现; **fear ~s itself in many different forms** 恐惧有多种不同的表现形式; **the disease may never ~ itself** 该病可能永远都不会发作
D *n* 1 Naut 船货清单 2 Aviat (of passengers) 乘客名单; (of cargo) 货单

manifestation /ˌmænɪfeˈsteɪʃn/ *n* 1 [c] (sign, symptom) 表现形式; **the early ~s of the disease** 该病的早期症状 2 [u] (appearance) 表现

manifestly /ˈmænɪfestli/ *adv* 明显地; **their research findings are ~ flawed** 他们的研究结果显然存在瑕疵

manifesto /ˌmænɪˈfestəʊ/ *n* 宣言; **an election ~** 竞选宣言

manifold /ˈmænɪfəʊld/
A *adj* 多种多样的 ‹*uses, possibilities, responsibilities*›
B *n* Aut 歧管

manikin /ˈmænɪkɪn/ *n* 1 Art, Med 人体模型 2 (very small person) 侏儒

Manila[1] /məˈnɪlə/ *pr n* 马尼拉

Manila[2] *n* 1 [u] ~ **(hemp)** 马尼拉麻 2 [u] ~ **(paper)** 马尼拉纸 3 [c] (cigar) 吕宋烟

man: ~ **in the moon** *n* 月中人; ~ **in the street** *n* 普通人

manioc /ˈmænɪɒk/ *n* = **cassava 1**

manipulate /məˈnɪpjʊleɪt/ *vt* 1 (operate) 操作; **to ~ the control levers** 操纵控制杆 2 pej (influence) 操纵; **she ~d him into accepting the offer** 她巧妙地促使他接受了那项提议; **to ~ public opinion** 左右公众舆论 3 (affect, control) 控制 ‹*weather patterns, development*› 4 (alter) 篡改 ‹*data, statistics*› 5 (in physiotherapy) 对…推拿 ‹*joint, muscle*›

manipulation /məˌnɪpjʊˈleɪʃn/ *n* [u] 1 (operation) 操作 2 pej (influencing) 操纵 3 (control of nature, development) 控制; **genetic ~** 基因操控 4 (alteration) 篡改; **digital image ~** 数字图像处理; **data ~** 数据篡改 5 (in physiotherapy) 推拿

manipulative /məˈnɪpjʊlətɪv/ *adj* 操纵的; **he is very ~** 他很会摆布人

manipulator /məˈnɪpjʊleɪtə(r)/ *n* 操纵者

Manitoba /ˌmænɪˈtəʊbə/ *pr n* 马尼托巴省

mankind /ˌmænˈkaɪnd/ *n* [u] 人类

manky /ˈmæŋki/ *adj* colloq 1 (dirty) 肮脏的 2 (inferior) 次的; (worthless) 无用的

manliness /ˈmænlɪnɪs/ *n* [u] 1 (masculinity) 男子汉气概 2 (bravery) 果敢

manly /ˈmænli/ *adj* 1 (masculine) 有男子汉气概的; **he looks ~ in that uniform!** 他穿那套制服显得英姿焕发!; **his ~ physique** 他强壮的体格 2 (brave) 果敢的 ‹*feat, deed*›

man-made *adj* 人造的 ‹*lake, fibre, substance*›; **(the explosion was) a ~ disaster** (爆炸事件是) 人为灾难

manna /ˈmænə/ *n* [u] 吗哪 [古以色列人过荒野时所得的天赐食物]; **like ~ from heaven** 犹如天赐之物

mannequin /ˈmænɪkɪn/ *n* 人体模型

manner /ˈmænə(r)/
A *n* 1 (way) 方式; **in a ... ~** 以…方式; **the piece was played in a rather sloppy ~** 这首曲子演奏得相当马虎; **the ~ in which ...** …的方式; **in such a ~ that** *or* **as to ...** 以如此的方式以致于…; **in like** *or* **the same ~** 同样地; **the ~ of sth./doing sth.** 某事物/做某事的方式; **an adverb/adverbial of ~** 方式副词/状语 2 (way of behaving) 举止; (attitude) 态度; **sb.'s ~ toward(s) sb.** 某人对某人的态度; **she has a good telephone ~** 她有良好的电话沟通技巧 3 Art, Mus, Literat (style) 风格; **in** *or* **after the ~ of sb.** 以某人的风格 4 (sort, kind) 种类; **in a ~ of speaking** 可以

m

说; **all ~ of X(s)** 各种各样的某物; **by no** *or* **not by any ~ of means** 决不; **(as if) to the ~ born** (似乎)天生就适合

B **manners** *npl* **1** (social behaviour) 礼仪; **good/bad ~s** 有礼貌/无礼的行为; **it's good/bad ~s to do sth.** 做某事是有礼貌/不礼貌的; **to learn (some) ~s** 学(一些)礼貌; **where on earth did she learn her ~s?** 她究竟从哪里学来的那套举止?; **to have no ~s** 没礼貌; **to forget one's ~s** 失礼; **road ~s** 行车礼貌; **~s maketh man** Prov 举止见人品 **2** formal (social habits, customs) 风俗; **a comedy of ~s** 风尚喜剧

mannered /ˈmænəd/ *adj* pej 矫揉造作的 ‹*speech, style, person*›

mannerism /ˈmænərɪzəm/ *n* 习性; **odd ~s** 古怪的习惯

mannerly /ˈmænəli/ *adj* 有礼貌的

manning /ˈmænɪŋ/ *n* [u] 人员配备

manning levels *npl* 人员配备数

mannish /ˈmænɪʃ/ *adj* **1** pej (unfeminine) 像男人的 ‹*woman, appearance*› **2** (suitable for a man) 适合男人的; **~ clothes** 男式服装

manoeuvrability /məˌnuːvrəˈbɪləti/ *n* [u] 易于移动性; **this wheelchair has excellent ~** 这辆轮椅非常灵活

manoeuvrable /məˈnuːvrəbl/ *adj* 易于移动的; **a ~ pushchair** 灵活的幼儿推车

manoeuvre /məˈnuːvə(r)/ Brit

A *vt* **1** (move) 熟练谨慎地移动; **she ~d the car into the garage** 她小心翼翼地把车开进车库 **2** (manipulate) 操纵; **to ~ the conversation round to the subject of money** 巧妙地把谈话引到金钱问题上; **she ~d her way to the top of the company** 她施展手腕进入了公司的高层

B *vi* **1** (move skilfully) 熟练地移动; (move carefully) 谨慎地移动 **2** (plot, scheme) 用策略; **to ~ for power** 施展策略谋取权力; **the new laws have left us little room to ~** 新法律没给我们留下多少回旋的余地

C *n* **1** [c] (movement) 机动动作; **a skilful ~** 熟练的移动 **2** [c] (plan, scheme) 策略 **3** [u] **room for ~** 回旋余地

D **manoeuvres** *npl* Mil 演习; **to be on ~s** 进行演习

manoeuvring /məˈnuːvərɪŋ/ *n* Brit 谨慎灵活的操纵; **after a lot of ~ we got the cars through** 一番巧妙的操作之后我们使车辆通过了; **political/diplomatic ~s** 政治/外交手段

man-of-war *n* (*pl* **men-of-war**) 军舰

manometer /mæˈnɒmɪtə(r)/ *n* (流体)压力计

manor /ˈmænə(r)/ *n* **1** esp Hist (estate) 庄园; **Lord/Lady of the ~** 领主/女领主 **2** ~ (house) 庄园宅第

manorial /məˈnɔːrɪəl/ *adj* 庄园的

manpower /ˈmænpaʊə(r)/ *n* [u] **1** (available workers) (industrial, manufacturing) 劳动力; (military) 兵力; **to cut** *or* **reduce ~** 减少人手; **a ~ shortage** 劳动力短缺 **2** (physical force) 人力; **driven by ~** 靠人力驱动的

manse /mæns/ *n* 牧师住宅

manservant /ˈmænsɜːvənt/ *n* dated 男仆

mansion /ˈmænʃn/ *n* **1** (large, impressive house) 公馆 **2** ~ **(block)** Brit (block of flats) 公寓 [用于公寓楼名]; **she lives in Aldberry M~s** 她住在奥尔德贝里公寓

man-sized /ˈmænsaɪzd/ *adj* 适合成年男子的 ‹*bed, steak, portion*›; **a ~ helping of potatoes** 够一个大男人吃的一份土豆

manslaughter /ˈmænslɔːtə(r)/ *n* [u] 过失杀人; **to commit ~** 犯过失杀人罪

mantel /ˈmæntl/ *n* = **mantelpiece**

mantelpiece /ˈmæntlpiːs/, **mantelshelf** /ˈmæntlʃelf/ *ns* 壁炉台

mantis /ˈmæntɪs/ *n* = **praying mantis**

mantle /ˈmæntl/ *n* **1** liter (covering) 覆盖层; **a ~ of snow** 一层雪 **2** liter (responsibility) 职责; **to lay down the ~ of office** 辞职; **the son has assumed his father's ~** 儿子继承了父亲的衣钵 **3** (of gas lamp) **(gas) ~** 白炽罩 **4** Geol 地幔 **5** archaic (cloak) 披风

man: ~-to-~ *adj* 一对一的; **~-to-~ defence** 人盯人的防守; **~trap** *n* 捕人陷阱

manual /ˈmænjʊəl/

A *adj* **1** (physical) 体力的 ‹*work*›; **a ~ labourer** 体力劳动者 **2** (involving the hands) 手的 ‹*dexterity*› **3** (operated by hand) 用手操作的; **a ~ gearbox** 手动变速箱

B *n* 使用手册; **a training/instruction ~** 培训手册/用法指南

manually /ˈmænjʊəli/ *adv* 用手工; **~ operated** 手工操作的

manufacture /ˌmænjʊˈfæktʃə(r)/

A *vt* **1** Ind 大量生产; **~d goods** 工业品 **2** (produce naturally) 生成; **vitamins cannot be ~d by our bodies** 维生素无法由人体生成 **3** pej (produce in a mechanical way) 粗制滥造 ‹*song, book*› **4** pej (invent) 编造; **to ~ evidence** 捏造证据

B *n* [u] 大量生产

C **manufactures** *npl* 工业品

manufacturer /ˌmænjʊˈfæktʃərə(r)/ *n* 生产者; **an aircraft/a car/clothing ~** 飞机/汽车/成衣制造商

manufacturing /ˌmænjʊˈfæktʃərɪŋ/ *n* [u] 制造业; **a ~ town** 工业城市

manufacturing base *n* **1** (place) 生产基地 **2** (share of country's total output) 制造业比重

manure /məˈnjʊə(r)/

A *n* [u] **1** (dung) 粪肥 **2** (fertilizer) 肥料

B *vt* 给…施肥 ‹*field, crop*›

manure heap *n* 粪肥堆

manuscript /ˈmænjʊskrɪpt/ *n* **1** (old book) 手抄本 **2** (original copy) 手稿; **a ~ of a novel** 小说手稿; *modif* **a ~ letter** 一封手写的信

Manx /mæŋks/ ▸**p. 426** *adj* 马恩岛的; **a ~ cat** 马恩岛猫

Manx: ~man /-mən/ *n* 马恩岛男人; **~woman** *n* 马恩岛女人

many /ˈmeni/

A *adj* (*comp* **more**, *superl* **most**) 许多的; **~ books/people** 很多书/人; **too ~ people/times** 太多人/回; **people of ~ kinds** 形形色色的人; **there are two too ~ chairs** *or* **two chairs too ~** 多两把椅子; **five exams in as ~ days** 5天里5场考试; **a good/great ~ things** 许许多多的事情; **the temptations are ~** 诱惑很多; **to have one too ~** colloq 喝多了

B *pron* 许多; **how ~?** 多少?; **too ~** 太多; **a good/great ~ of those books** 许多那样的书; **~ a man/woman** 许多男人/女人; **four times as ~** 4倍之多; **as ~ stayed as left** 留下的和离去的一样多; **~'s the day/time that ...** 许多天/次…

C *adv* 更加; **there were ~ more/fewer than last time** 比上一次更多/更少

D *n* **1** (the masses) **the ~** 群众; **music for the ~** 通俗音乐; **to sacrifice the interests of the few in favour of the ~** 为了大多数人而牺牲少数人的利益 **2** (large number) 很多人; **the ~ who loved him** 曾经爱他的那许多人

many: ~-coloured, liter **~-hued** *adjs* 色彩斑斓的; **~-sided** *adj* **1** (in shape) 多边的; **2** (multi-talented) 多才多艺的 ‹*person*›; **3** (complex) 多方面的 ‹*analysis*›; **a ~-sided problem** 涉及多方面的问题

mao /maʊ/ ▸**p. 174** *n* (*pl* **mao**) colloq = **jiao**

Maoism /ˈmaʊɪzəm/ *n* [u] 毛泽东主义

Maoist /ˈmaʊɪst/

A *n* 毛泽东主义者

B *adj* 毛泽东主义的

Maori /ˈmaʊri/ ▸**p. 503, p. 426**

A *adj* (of the people) 毛利人的; (of the language) 毛利语的

B *n* **1** [c] (person) 毛利人 **2** [u] (language) 毛利语

Mao Zedong /ˌmaʊ dziːˈdʊŋ/, **Mao Tse-tung** /ˌmaʊ tseɪˈtʊŋ/ *pr ns* 毛泽东 [中国政治家]

map /mæp/

A *n* 地图; **a street ~** 街区图; **to draw/read a ~** 画/看地图; **to put sth./sb. on the ~** fig colloq 使某物/某人出名; **to be wiped off the ~** fig colloq 被彻底消除

B *vt* **1** (make map of) 绘制…的地图 ‹*area*› **2** (show on map) 在地图上标出 ‹*route*›

Phrasal verb

• **map out** *vt* [**~ out sth., ~ sth. out**] 详细安排 ‹*future, career*›; **to ~ out one's plans for the holiday** 详细制订度假计划

maple /ˈmeɪpl/ *n* **1** [c] (tree) 槭树; **a ~ leaf** 槭树叶子 **2** [u] **~ (wood)** 槭木; **a ~ desk** 槭木书桌

maple: ~ sugar *n* [u] Amer 槭糖; **~ syrup** *n* [u] 槭糖浆

map: ~ maker ▸**p. 409** *n* 地图绘制员; **~ reader** *n* 阅图者; **a good ~ reader** 擅长阅图的人; **~ reading** *n* [u] 阅图

Maputo /məˈpuːtəʊ/ *pr n* 马普托

Mar *abbr* = **March**

mar /mɑː(r)/ *vt* (*pres p etc.* **-rr-**) lit, fig 破坏 ‹*appearance, happiness*›; **to ~ one's career** 毁掉自己的事业; **to make or ~ sth./sb.** 使某事/某人成功或失败

maraschino /ˌmærəˈskiːnəʊ/ *n* [u] 黑樱桃酒

maraschino cherry *n* 酒浸樱桃

marathon /ˈmærəθən, Amer -θɒn/

A *n* **1** Sport 马拉松赛跑; **to run (in) a ~** 参加马拉松赛跑 **2** fig 马拉松式的活动; **to be a real ~** «*activity*» 真是一场马拉松; **a TV ~** 马拉松式的电视节目

B *modif* **1** Sport 马拉松赛跑的 ‹*route*›; **~ runners** 马拉松运动员 **2** fig 马拉松式的 ‹*battle, effort*›

marauder /məˈrɔːdə(r)/ *n* (person) 抢劫者; (animal) 猎食的动物

marauding /məˈrɔːdɪŋ/ *adj attrib* 抢劫的 ‹*army, mob*›; 猎食的 ‹*animals*›

marble /ˈmɑːbl/

A *n* **1** [u] (rock) 大理石; **a ~ statue/floor** 大理石雕像/地面 **2** [c] (small glass ball) 弹子; **to have all one's ~s** fig colloq 有理智; **to lose one's ~s** fig colloq 丧失理智

B **marbles** ▸**p. 307** *npl* + *v sing* Game 弹子游戏

marble cake *n* 大理石蛋糕

marbled /ˈmɑːbld/ *adj* 有大理石花纹的 ‹*paper, look*›

marbling /ˈmɑːblɪŋ/ *n* [u] 大理石花纹

March /mɑːtʃ/ ▸**p. 490** *n* 三月; **last/this/next ~** 上个/本年/下个三月份; **in early/late ~** 三月上旬/下旬; **~ weather/morning** 三月的天气/早晨

march /mɑːtʃ/

A *vi* **1** (walk in military manner) 齐步走; **to ~ in time to the music** 踏着音乐节拍齐步走; **to ~ on** 向…进军 ‹*place*›; **forward ~!** Mil 齐步走!; **to ~ (for) forty miles in one day** 在1天内行军40英里; **time/progress ~es on** 时间流逝/不断进步 **2** (walk in protest) 游行示威; **to ~ in protest at/in support of sth.** 游行抗议/支持某事; **to ~ against/for sth.** 游行反对/拥护某事 **3** (walk briskly) 快步行走

B *vt* 使行进; **she grabbed his arm and ~ed him into/out of the office** 她揪住他的胳膊把他推进/推出了办公室; **the officer ~ed the prisoners around the yard** 军官命令囚犯们在院子里来回齐步走; **they ~ed him off to prison** 他们把他押送入狱

C *n* **1** Mil 行军; **a quick/slow ~** 快/慢步走;

m

a forced ~ 急行军; **on the ~** (attack) 行军中; (move) 在行进中 **2** (demonstration) 游行示威; **to go on/take part in a ~** 进行/参加游行示威; **a ~ against/for/in protest at/in support of sth.** 反对/拥护/抗议/支持某事物的游行示威; **a ~ on the White House** 走向白宫的游行示威; **a peace/protest ~** 和平请愿/抗议游行 **3** Mus 进行曲; **a funeral** *or* **dead ~** 哀乐; **a wedding** *or* **bridal ~** 婚礼进行曲 **4** fig (progress) 进展; **the ~ of sth.** 某事的推进; **the steady ~ of time** 时间的不断推移; **the ~ to** *or* **towards sth.** 通向某事的发展过程

marcher /ˈmɑːtʃə(r)/ *n* **1** (in parade, band) 行进者 **2** (in demonstration) 游行示威者; **a peace ~** 为和平而请愿的人

marching /ˈmɑːtʃɪŋ/
A *n* [u] 齐步行进
B *adj attrib* 齐步行进的 ‹*troops*›; **~ demonstrators** 游行示威者

marching: ~ band *n* 行进乐队; **~ orders** *npl* colloq **to give sb. their ~ orders** 辞退某人; **to get one's ~ orders** 被辞退; **~ song** *n* 进行曲

marchioness /ˌmɑːʃəˈnes/ *n* **1** (wife of marquess) 侯爵夫人 **2** (woman with rank of marquess) 女侯爵

march-past *n* 分列式

Mardi Gras /ˌmɑːdi ˈɡrɑː/ *n* [大斋期前的] 狂欢节

mare /meə(r)/ *n* (horse) 母马; (donkey) 母驴

mare's nest *n* colloq **1** (muddle) 杂乱无章 **2** (illusory discovery) 虚幻的发现

margarine /ˌmɑːdʒəˈriːn/ *n* [u] 人造黄油

marge /mɑːdʒ/ *n* [u] Brit colloq = **margarine**

margin /ˈmɑːdʒɪn/ *n* **1** (on paper) 页边空白; **left/right ~** 左/右页边; **in the ~** 在页边空白处 **2** (edge of area, lake) 边缘; **at** *or* **on the ~(s) of the pool** 在池塘边; **the eastern ~ of the Indian Ocean** 印度洋的东岸 **3** *usu pl* fig (fringe) 边缘部分; **people living at** *or* **on the ~(s) of society** 生活在社会边缘的人 **4** Pol 幅度; **to lose by a small ~** 以微弱差距失利; **to win by a ~ of 100 votes** 以 100 票的优势获胜; **to increase one's ~** 扩大领先幅度 **5** (leeway) 余地; **a safety ~** 安全距离; **there is no ~ for error** 不能出任何差错 **6** Comm = **profit margin 7** (furthest limit) 极限; **to be at the ~s of acceptability** 在可接受的最低限度

marginal /ˈmɑːdʒɪnl/
A *adj* **1** (slight) 微不足道的 ‹*effect, difference*› **2** (minor) 非主流的 ‹*political figure, party*›; (peripheral) 边缘的 ‹*role, existence*› **3** Agric 贫瘠的 ‹*land*› **4** Brit Pol 以微弱多数获胜的; **a ~ seat/constituency** 边缘席位/选区 **5** *attrib* (in margin) 页边空白处的 ‹*comment*›
B *n* Brit Pol (seat) 边缘席位; (constituency) 边缘选区

marginalization /ˌmɑːdʒɪnəlaɪˈzeɪʃn, Amer -lɪˈz-/ *n* [u] 边缘化

marginalize /ˈmɑːdʒɪnəlaɪz/ *vt* 使…边缘化 ‹*activity, group, issue*›

marginally /ˈmɑːdʒɪnəli/ *adv* 些微地 ‹*more effective, different*›; **~ bigger** 稍微大一点的

marigold /ˈmærɪɡəʊld/ *n* 万寿菊

marijuana /ˌmærɪˈwɑːnə/ *n* [u] 大麻

marimba /məˈrɪmbə/ *n* 马林巴琴

marina /məˈriːnə/ *n* (moorings) 小船坞; (area) 游艇停靠区

marinade /ˌmærɪˈneɪd/
A *n* 腌泡汁
B *vt, vi* = **marinate**

marinate /ˈmærɪneɪt/
A *vt* 腌泡 ‹*food*›
B *vi* «*food*» 腌泡; **to leave to ~ overnight** 将其腌一晚上

marine /məˈriːn/
A *adj* **1** (of ocean) 海洋的 ‹*creature, ecosystem*›; **a ~ plant** 海生植物 **2** Naut (maritime) 航海的; (naval) 海军的; **a ~ bureau** 海事局; **~ law** 海事法
B *n* 海军陆战队士兵; **the M~s** 海军陆战队

marine: ~ biology *n* [u] 海洋生物学; **~ biologist** ▸p. 409 *n* 海洋生物学家; **M~ Corps** *n* **the M~ Corps** Amer 海军陆战队; **~ engineer** ▸p. 409 *n* 轮机员; **~ engineering** *n* [u] 船舶工程; **~ life** *n* [u] 海洋生物

mariner /ˈmærɪnə(r)/ *n* dated 水手

marine: ~ reserve *n* 海洋保护区; **~ science** *n* [u] 海洋科学

marionette /ˌmærɪəˈnet/ *n* 牵线木偶

marital /ˈmærɪtl/ *adj* 婚姻的 ‹*vows, bliss, problems, relations*›; **~ status** 婚姻状况

marital rape *n* [u] 婚内强奸

maritime /ˈmærɪtaɪm/ *adj* **1** Naut (of trade) 海运的 ‹*history*›; (naval) 海军的; **~ trade** 海上贸易; **the great ~ nations** *or* **powers** 海上列强 **2** (of the sea) 海洋的; (near the sea) 近海的 ‹*provinces*›; **~ mammals** 海生哺乳动物; **the ~ Antarctic** 南极近海地区 **3** Meteorol 海洋性的 ‹*climate*›

maritime law *n* [u] 海事法

marjoram /ˈmɑːdʒərəm/ *n* [u] **1** **(sweet) ~** Culin 墨角兰叶 **2** Bot 墨角兰

mark[1] /mɑːk/
A *n* **1** (visible patch) (on leaf, vegetable, fruit, etc.) 斑点; (on skin) 斑痕; (on fabric, clothing) 污点; **a grease ~** 油迹; **a stubborn ~** 顽渍 **2** (written or printed symbol) 符号; **a proofreading ~** 校对符号; **to put** *or* **make a ~ on** *or* **in sth.** 在某物上做记号; **to put** *or* **make one's ~ (on sth.)** (在某物上) 画押 **3** (point on vertical or horizontal scale) 刻度; (point on graph or curve) 标线; **the high-water ~** 高水位线; **the runners have passed the 3,000-metre ~** 长跑运动员已经通过了 3000 米标志处; **up to the ~** fig 符合标准的; **(not) to be** *or* **feel up to the ~** 感觉 (不) 舒服 **4** (identifying symbol) (on clothing) 标签; (on object) 商标; **a laundry ~** 洗衣店标签; **a printer's ~** 印刷社商标 **5** (sign, symbol) 标志; **as a ~ of sth.** 作为某物的标志; **the ~ of a gentleman** 绅士的特征 **6** (lasting impression) 印记; **to leave** *or* **make its/one's ~ (on sb./sth.)** (给某人/某事物) 留下影响; **to make one's ~ (in sth./as sth.)** (在某方面/从事某事) 成名; **to bear the ~(s) of sth.** 带有某物的印记 **7** esp Brit (score) (for school work) 得分; (for behaviour) 等第; **a ~ in** *or* **for maths/geography** 数学/地理分数; **to get a good/bad/high/low ~** 得到好/差/高/低分; **to give** *or* **award sb. a ~** 给某人打分; **to get no ~s (as sth./for sth./for doing sth.)** (从事某职业/在某方面/做某事) 做得不好 **8** **Mark** (model in series) 型号 **9** **Mark** Brit (oven temperature) 档; **at gas ~ 4** 以4档烤箱温度 **10** (target) 靶子; **to hit** *or* **strike** *or* **find its** *or* **the ~** «*arrow, bullet*» 击中目标; fig «*guess*» 猜对; «*criticism*» 切中要害; **he made a great effort, and hit the ~** 他经过艰苦努力达到了目的; **to miss its** *or* **the ~** lit «*arrow, bullet*» 没击中目标; fig «*guess*» 猜错; **he tried, but completely missed the ~** 他努力了, 但完全失败了; **to be** *or* **fall wide of the ~** lit 远离目标; fig 毫不相关; **on the ~** 准确; **off the ~** 不准确 **11** Sport (starting line) 起跑线; **to be quick/slow off the ~** lit 起跑快/慢; fig 理解快/慢; **to be quick/slow off the ~ to do** *or* **in doing sth.** 不失时机地/慢吞吞地做某事; **to overstep the ~** 做得过分; **on your ~s, (get) set, go!** 各就各位, 预备, 跑! ; **to get off the ~** lit 起跑; fig 出发
B *vt* **1** (stain, disfigure) 留痕迹于; **the apples had all been ~ed** 所有的苹果上都有斑点; **to ~ sb. for life** fig 给某人留下终生影响 **2** (write on) 作记号于 ‹*object, clothing*›; (indicate the position of) 标示 ‹*place, route*›; **to ~ sth. with sth.** 用某物在某物上做记号; **to ~ sth. on sth.** 把某记号标在某物上; **can you ~ the hospital on the map?** 你能在地图上标出医院的位置吗? ; **to ~ one's place (in a book)** 标明 (读书的) 进度; **~ where we have to turn left** 在我们要左转弯的地方做上记号 **3** (identify, indicate) 标志 ‹*end, stage*›; **to ~ sth. as sth.** *or* **as being sth.** 赋予某物某特点; **he is ~ed as a future champion** 他被看成未来的冠军; **to ~ time** lit 原地踏步; fig 等待时机 **4** (celebrate, acknowledge) 庆祝 ‹*occasion, anniversary*›; **to be ~ed by sth.** 以某活动作为庆祝 **5** *usu passive* (characterize) 是…的特征 ‹*period of time, style*›; **to be ~ed by sth.** 以某物为特征; **an age ~ed by unrest and violence** 充满动荡和暴力的时代 **6** esp Brit (award marks to) 给…打分 ‹*student, performance*› **7** (record, tick) 记下 ‹*person, homework*›; **to ~ sb. absent/present** 给某人记缺勤/出勤; **to ~ sth. right/wrong** 把某事物判为正确/错误 **8** *usu imperative* (note) **~ my words** 留心听我的话; **~ you** 你听着 [表示转折]; **~ you, it may not be true** 不过, 这事不一定是真的 **9** Brit Sport 盯防 ‹*opponent*›; **to ~ sb. closely** *or* **tightly** 严密盯防某人
C *vi* **1** Brit Sch, Univ 评分 **2** (become marked) 留下痕迹; **this dress ~s easily** 这件连衣裙容易弄脏

Phrasal verbs

- **mark down** *vt* [**~ sb./sth. down, ~ down sb./sth.**]
1 esp Brit (reduce mark of) 降低…的分数 **2** (adjudge) **to ~ sb. down as sth./as being sth.** 把某人看成是某样的人; **to ~ sb. down as a future star/a no-hoper** 将某人看作是明日之星/无能之人 **3** (record) 记下 ‹*person's name, answer*›; **to ~ sb. down as present/absent** 把某人记为出勤/缺勤 **4** (decrease price of) 给…降价 ‹*item*›; **all goods in the sale have been ~ed down by 10%** 所有特卖商品都削价 10%
- **mark off** *vt* [**~ sth. off, ~ off sth.**]
1 (separate off) 划出 ‹*area*› **2** (tick off) 在…上做记号 ‹*item in list, name*›
- **mark out** *vt* **1** [**~ sb. out, ~ out sb.**] (distinguish, identify) 使与众不同; **to ~ sb. out as sth./as being sth.** 区分某人为某样的人; **his sword ~ed him out as an officer** 从他的佩剑可以看出他是个军官 **2** [**~ sth. out, ~ out sth.**] (delimit) 划出…的界限 ‹*area*›
- **mark up**
A [**~ sb./sth. up, ~ up sb./sth.**] *vt* esp Brit (increase mark of) 提高…的分数
B [**~ sth. up, ~ up sth.**] *vt*
1 Comm (increase price of) 给…加价 ‹*item*› **2** (for keying or typesetting) 为…标注排版说明; (correct text of) 审校

mark[2] *n* Fin, Hist 马克

mark-down *n* 减价

marked /mɑːkt/ *adj* **1** (clear) 明显的 ‹*improvement, contrast*›; **a ~ increase in profits** 利润的显著增加 **2** (in danger) **a ~ man** 目标人物 **3** Ling 有标记的 ‹*form*›; **'drake' is the ~ form, referring to a male duck. 'duck' is the unmarked form** drake 意为公鸭, 是有标记形式, 而 duck 为无标记形式

markedly /ˈmɑːkɪdli/ *adv* 明显地 ‹*better, different, worse, abnormal*›; **to slow down/accelerate ~** 明显减速/加速

marker /ˈmɑːkə(r)/ *n* **1** **~ (pen)** 记号笔 **2** (score keeper) 记分员 **3** (examiner) 阅卷人 **4** (sign, post) 标记 **5** Sport 盯人的防守队员

market /ˈmɑːkɪt/
A *n* **1** (place to buy goods) 市场; **an antique(s) ~** 古玩市场 **2** (gathering for buying/selling) 集市; **a monthly ~** 每月一度的集市 **3** (stock market) 股票市场; **to play the ~** 炒股票 **4** (area of trade) 销售地; **the tea ~, the ~ in tea** 茶叶市场; **the job/property ~** 就业/房地产市场; **to put sth. on the ~** 在市场上出售某物; **to be in the ~ for sth.** 有意购买某物; **a rising ~ in shares** 上涨的股票行情; **to come on**

to the ～ 上市; **to price sth. out of the ～** 对某物漫天要价致使无人问津 5 (customers) 消费群体; **the French ～** 法国市场; **the teenage ～** 青少年为主的市场; *modif* **～ conditions/trends** 市场情况/走向 6 (demand) 销路; **a good ～ for cars** 良好的汽车销路; **there is no ～ for sth.** 某物没有销路
B *vt* 1 (sell) 销售 2 (promote) 推销; **to ～ sth. (to sb.)** （向某人）推销某物

marketability /ˌmɑːkɪtəˈbɪləti/ *n* [u] (of product, asset) 畅销性; (of skills) 有需求

marketable /ˈmɑːkɪtəbl/ *adj* 畅销的 ‹*product, asset*›; 有销路的 ‹*skills*›; **～ qualifications** 大受欢迎的资质

market: ～ analysis *n* [u and c] 市场分析; **～ analyst** ▸**p. 409** *n* 市场分析师; **～ capitalization** *n* [u] 市值; **～ cross** *n* Brit 市场十字架; **～ day** *n* 集日; **～ economy** *n* 市场经济

marketeer /ˌmɑːkɪˈtɪə(r)/ *n* 市场商人

marketer /ˈmɑːkɪtə(r)/ *n* 经销商

market: ～ forces *npl* 市场力量; **～ garden** *n* Brit 果蔬农场; **～ gardener** ▸**p. 409** *n* Brit 果蔬农场经营者; **～ gardening** *n* [u] Brit 果蔬栽培

marketing /ˈmɑːkɪtɪŋ/ *n* [u] 1 (process) 销售 2 (theory) 营销学 3 (branch) 销售部门

marketing: ～ agreement *n* 销售协议; **～ campaign** *n* 促销活动; **～ company** *n* 销售公司; **～ exercise** *n* 促销活动; **～ man** *n* 销售人员; **～ manager** ▸**p. 409** *n* 销售经理; **～ mix** *n* 营销组合; **～ process** *n* 销售过程; **～ research** *n* [u] 营销调研; **～ strategy** *n* 销售策略

market: ～ leader *n* (company) 龙头企业; (product) 最畅销产品; **this operating system is the ～ leader** 这个操作系统市场销量第一; **～-led** *adj* 市场主导的 ‹*approach, growth*›; **a ～-led economy** 市场经济; **～-maker** *n* 做市商; **～-making** *n* [u] 造市; **～ opportunity** *n* 市场机会; **～ penetration** *n* [u] 市场渗透; **～place** *n* 1 (square) 集市; 2 (forum) 交流场所; 3 Comm 商界; **～ potential** *n* [u] 市场潜力; **～ power** *n* [u] 市场影响力; **～ price** *n* 市场价格; **at ～ price** 按市价; **～-ready** *adj* 可以上市的 ‹*product*›; **～ rent** *n* Brit 市场租金; **～ report** *n* 市况报告; **～ research** *n* [u] 市场调研; **～ research agency** *n* 市场调研机构; **～ researcher** ▸**p. 409** *n* 市场调研员; **～ resistance** *n* [u] 市场阻力; **～ share** *n* [c and u] 市场份额; **～ square** *n* 露天集市; **～ stall** *n* 集市摊位; **～ study** *n* 市场研究; **～ survey** *n* 市场调查; **～ town** *n* 集镇; **～ trader** ▸**p. 409** *n* 集市摊贩; **～ value** *n* 市场价值

marking /ˈmɑːkɪŋ/ *n* 1 [u and c] *usu pl* (pattern on animal, plant) 斑点; (line on animal, plant) 斑纹; (symbol on aircraft, vehicle, road) 标志; **a bird with blue ～s** 有蓝色斑纹的鸟; **road ～s** 道路标志 2 [u] Brit Sch (assessment) 评分 3 [u] Sport 盯人防守

marking: ～ ink *n* [u] 标记墨水; **～ pen** *n* 记号笔; **～ scheme, ～ system** *ns* Brit 评分方案

marksman /ˈmɑːksmən/ *n* (*pl* **marksmen**) 1 Sport 射击运动员 2 Mil 神枪手

marksmanship /ˈmɑːksmənʃɪp/ *n* [u] 射击术

markswoman /ˈmɑːkswʊmən/ *n* (*pl* **markswomen**) 1 Sport 女射击运动员 2 Mil 女神枪手

mark-up *n* 1 (retailer's margin) 加成; **a ～-up of 15% (on sth.)** （对某物）15% 的加成 2 (increase) 涨价; **a ～-up on sth.** 对某物的涨价

marl /mɑːl/ *n* [u] 泥灰

marlin /ˈmɑːlɪn/ *n* (*pl* **～** *or* **～s**) 枪鱼

marlinspike /ˈmɑːlɪnspaɪk/ *n* 索针

marmalade /ˈmɑːməleɪd/ *n* [u] 橘子酱

marmalade cat *n* 橙色斑猫

Marmite® /ˈmɑːmaɪt/ *n* [u] Brit 马麦酱

marmoset /ˈmɑːməzet/ *n* 狨

marmot /ˈmɑːmət/ *n* 旱獭

Maronite /ˈmærənaɪt/ *n* 马龙派教徒; **～ Christians/leaders** 马龙派基督教徒/领袖

maroon¹ /məˈruːn/ ▸**p. 134**
A *n* [u] (colour) 褐红色
B *adj* 褐红色的

maroon² *vt* 1 (strand) 使无处可逃; **to be ～ed on a desert island** 被放逐到荒岛上; **a ～ed whale** 搁浅的鲸 2 fig (isolate, abandon) 困住; **to be ～ed at home** 被困在家中

maroon³ *n* Brit (rocket) 报警鞭炮

marque /mɑːk/ *n* [汽车的] 品牌

marquee /mɑːˈkiː/ *n* 1 Brit (tent) 大帐篷 2 Amer (canopy) 遮篷

marquess /ˈmɑːkwɪs/ *n* Brit 侯爵

marquetry /ˈmɑːkɪtri/ *n* [u] 1 (work) 镶嵌细工 2 (art) 镶嵌艺术

marquis /ˈmɑːkwɪs/ *n* (*pl* **～es**) 侯爵

marquise /mɑːˈkiːz/ *n* 1 (wife of marquis) 侯爵夫人 2 (woman with rank of marquis) 女侯爵

marriage /ˈmærɪdʒ/ *n* 1 [u] (state of being married) 婚姻; [c] (legal union) 结婚; **a proposal of ～** 求婚; **～ to sb.** 和某人的婚姻; **her ～ to the doctor was not a success** 她和那位医生的婚姻并不美满; **a mixed** *or* **interracial ～** 异族通婚; **by ～** 通过姻亲关系; **to be related by ～** 有姻亲关系; **to take sb. in ～** «*man*» 娶某人; «*woman*» 嫁给某人; **to give sb. in ～** 把某人嫁出去 2 [c] (ceremony) 婚礼 3 [u] fig (alliance) 紧密结合; **the ～ of poetry and art** 绘画和诗歌的密切结合

marriageable /ˈmærɪdʒəbl/ *adj* 适婚的; **to reach ～ age** 到达适婚年龄

marriage: ～ bed *n* 婚床; **～ bureau** *n* Brit dated 婚姻介绍所; **～ ceremony** *n* 婚礼; **～ certificate** *n* 结婚证书; **～ contract** *n* 婚前协议; **～ guidance** *n* [u] 婚姻咨询; **～ guidance counsellor** ▸**p. 409** *n* 婚姻咨询师; **～ licence** *n* 1 Brit (to allow ～) 结婚许可证; 2 Amer **= ～ certificate**; **～ of convenience** *n* 权宜婚姻; **～ proposal** *n* 求婚; **～ rate** *n* 结婚率; **～ vows** *npl* 结婚誓言

married /ˈmærɪd/ *adj* 1 (wedded) 已婚的; **to get ～** 结婚; **a ～ man/woman** 已婚男子/女子; **to be ～ to sb.** «*woman*» 嫁给某人; «*man*» 和某人结婚; **the newly ～ couple** 新婚夫妇; **to be ～ to one's work** fig 一心扑在工作上 2 (marital) 婚姻的; **～ life** 婚姻生活

married: ～ name *n* 婚后姓名; **～ quarters** *npl* 已婚人员宿舍

marrieds /ˈmærɪdz/ *npl* 已婚者; **(the) newly ～** 新婚夫妇

marrow /ˈmærəʊ/ *n* 1 [u] Anat **(bone) ～** 骨髓; **to the ～** 入骨的; **to be chilled** *or* **frozen to the ～** 感到寒冷刺骨; **to be shocked to the ～** 惊得目瞪口呆 2 [c and u] Brit **(vegetable) ～** 西葫芦

marrowbone /ˈmærəʊbəʊn/ *n* [烹饪用的] 髓骨

marrowfat pea /ˌmærəʊfæt ˈpiː/ *n* 大豌豆

marry /ˈmæri/
A *vi* 1 lit 结婚; **to ～ young** 早婚; **to ～ again** 再婚; **he's not the ～ing kind** 他不是那种想结婚的人 2 fig (blend) 结合; **to ～ with sth.** 与某事物相结合
B *vt* 1 (wed) 与…结婚; **to ～ money** fig colloq «*woman*» 嫁给有钱人; «*man*» 娶个有钱女人 2 (join in marriage) «*minister*» 为…主持婚礼 ‹*couple*›; **to ～ one's daughter/son to sb.** 把女儿嫁给某人/为儿子娶某人 3 fig (combine) 使…相结合 ‹*styles, ideas*›; **to ～ sth. with sth., to ～ sth. and sth.** 使某事物与某事物紧密结合

Phrasal verbs

- **marry into** *vt* [**～ into sth.**] 结婚后成为…的一员 ‹*family, aristocracy*›; 靠结婚获得 ‹*fortune, money*›; **to ～ into a rich family** «*woman*» 嫁到有钱人家; «*man*» 入赘有钱人家
- **marry off** *vt* [**to ～ sb. off, to ～ off sb.**] 为…找结婚对象; **at last we managed to ～ her off!** 我们终于把她嫁出去了!; **to ～ sb. off to sb.** 给…娶某人 ‹*man*›; 把…嫁给某人 ‹*woman*›
- **marry up**
A *vt* 1 (join up) 连结 ‹*parts, pieces*›; **to ～ up the two halves of the poster** 将两半海报拼接起来 2 (combine) 将…紧密结合 ‹*stories, accounts*›; **to ～ up sth. with sth.** 使某物与某物紧密结合
B *vi* 1 (join up) «*parts, pieces*» 连结 2 (agree) «*facts, accounts*» 匹配

Mars /mɑːz/ *pr n* 1 Astron 火星 2 Mythol 马耳斯 [战神]

marsh /mɑːʃ/ *n* [u and c] 沼泽

marshal /ˈmɑːʃl/
A *n* 1 Mil 元帅 2 (at public event) 司仪 3 Amer Jur 执法官
B *vt* (*pres p etc.* **-ll-** Brit, **-l-** Amer) 1 (muster) 召集 ‹*troops, support*› 2 (assemble) 组织安排 ‹*vehicles, railway wagons*›; fig 整理 ‹*facts, arguments*› 3 (usher) 引领; **to be ～led out of the room** 被领出房间; **to ～ the crowd** «*police*» 维持人群的秩序

marshalling yard /ˈmɑːʃlɪŋ jɑːd/ *n* Brit 编组场

Marshall Islands /ˈmɑːʃl ˌaɪləndz/ *pr npl* **the ～** 马绍尔群岛

marsh: ～ gas *n* [u] 沼气; **～land** /-lænd/ *n* [u and c] 沼泽地; **～mallow** *n* [u and c] 棉花软糖

marshy /ˈmɑːʃi/ *adj* (of a marsh) 沼泽的; (like a marsh) 沼泽般的; **～ ground** *or* **land** 沼泽地

marsupial /mɑːˈsuːpiəl/ *n* 有袋目动物; **a ～ animal** 有袋目动物

mart /mɑːt/ *n* (market) 集市; (trade centre) 贸易场所; **a used car ～** 旧车市场

marten /ˈmɑːtɪn, Amer -tn/ *n* 1 [c] Zool 貂 2 [u] (fur) 貂皮

martial /ˈmɑːʃl/ *adj* 军事的 ‹*training, technique*›; **～ music** 军乐; **a ～ tradition** 尚武的传统; **his ～ exploits** 他的战功

martial: ～ arts *npl* 武术; **～ arts classes** 武术班; **～ law** *n* [u] 军事管制

Martian /ˈmɑːʃn/
A *n* 火星人
B *adj* 火星的 ‹*atmosphere, rock, landscape*›; **～ landings/exploration** 火星着陆/探测

martin /ˈmɑːtɪn/ *n* 燕科小鸟; **house ～** 毛脚燕; **sand ～** 崖沙燕

martinet /ˌmɑːtɪˈnet, Amer -tnˈet/ *n* formal 严格执行纪律的人

martini /mɑːˈtiːni/ *n* 1 **Martini®** [u] (brand) 马提尼 [一种味美思酒品牌] 2 [u and c] (cocktail) 马提尼酒

martyr /ˈmɑːtə(r)/
A *n* 1 Relig 殉道者; **to make a ～ of sb., to make sb. a ～** 使某人殉难 2 (for a cause) 烈士; **to be a ～ to the cause of freedom** 是为了自由事业而献身的烈士 3 colloq (sufferer) **to be ～ to sth.** 长期受某苦难的人; **she's a ～ to her rheumatism** 她长期受风湿病的折磨 4 pej or hum (person looking for sympathy) 乞怜者; **stop playing the ～!** 别做出一副可怜兮兮的样子!
B *vt* 1 Relig 使殉难; **to be ～ed for one's faith** 为自己的信仰而殉难 2 fig 折磨

martyrdom /ˈmɑːtədəm/ *n* [u] 1 Relig 殉难 2 (great suffering) 折磨 3 pej (display of suffering) 夸张的痛苦表现; **with a look of ～ he agreed to go** 他带着一副很受罪的样子同意去了

martyred /ˈmɑːtəd/ *adj* 故作痛苦状的 ‹*air, sigh, look*›; **to give sb. a ~ look** 对某人做出痛苦的样子

marvel /ˈmɑːvl/
A *vi* (*pres p etc.* **-ll-** Brit, **-l-** Amer) 感到惊讶; **to ~ at sb./sth.** 对某人/某事感到惊讶; **everyone ~led at his courage** 人人都对他的勇气惊叹不已
B *vt* (*pres p etc.* **-ll-** Brit, **-l-** Amer) 对…感到惊讶; **to ~ that ...** 感到惊讶的是…
C *n* **1** (wonderful thing) 奇迹; (wonderful person) 令人惊奇的人; **to perform** *or* **work ~s** 创造奇迹; **to be a ~ with children** 极善于跟孩子们相处; **to do ~s in the kitchen** 奇迹般地烹调出美味佳肴; **it's a ~ to me that ...** 我感到神奇的是… **2** (fine example) **a ~ of sth.** 奇特的某物; **she's a ~ of patience** 她出奇地有耐心

marvellous Brit, **marvelous** Amer /ˈmɑːvələs/ *adj* **1** (causing wonder) 令人惊奇的 **2** (excellent) 极好的 ‹*idea, time, job*›; **to have a ~ way with animals** 对付动物很有一套; **it's ~ that he can come** 他能来真是太棒了

marvellously Brit, **marvelously** Amer /ˈmɑːvələsli/ *adv* **1** (wonderfully) 令人惊奇地 ‹*successful, skilled*›; **to sleep ~ well** 睡得出奇地好 **2** (excellently) 极好地 ‹*work, sing*›; **to get on ~** 相处极好

Marxism /ˈmɑːksɪzəm/ *n* [u] 马克思主义

Marxism-Leninism /ˌmɑːksɪzəmˈlenɪnɪzəm/ *n* [u] 马克思列宁主义

Marxist /ˈmɑːksɪst/
A *adj* **1** (based on Marxism) 奉行马克思主义的 ‹*government*› **2** (relating to Marxism) 马克思主义的 ‹*theory, revolution*›
B *n* 马克思主义者

Marxist: ~-Leninism *n* [u] 马列主义; **~-Leninist** *n* 马列主义的

Mary /ˈmeəri/ *pr n* 玛丽; **the Virgin ~** 圣母马利亚

Maryland /ˈmeərɪlænd/ *pr n* 马里兰州

marzipan /ˈmɑːzɪpæn, ˌmɑːzɪˈpæn/
A *n* [u] 杏仁蛋白糊; **~ topping/filling** 杏仁蛋白浇汁/馅
B *vt* 在…上抹杏仁蛋白糊 ‹*cake*›

mascara /mæˈskɑːrə, Amer -ˈskærə/ *n* [u and c] 睫毛膏

mascaraed /mæˈskɑːrəd, Amer -ˈskærəd/ *adj* 涂有睫毛膏的 ‹*eyes*›

mascot /ˈmæskət, -skɒt/ *n* 吉祥物

masculine /ˈmæskjʊlɪn/
A *adj* **1** (male) 男性的 ‹*pride, sex*›; (manly) 男子气概的 ‹*voice, physique*› **2** (unfeminine) 像男人的 ‹*build, voice*›; **that suit makes her look very ~** 她穿那套衣服看起来很男性化 **3** Ling 阳性的 ‹*gender, noun, form*›
B *n* Ling 阳性; (word) 阳性词; (form) 阳性形式; **an adjective in the ~** 阳性形容词

masculinity /ˌmæskjʊˈlɪnəti/ *n* [u] **1** (virility) 男子气概 **2** (gender) 男性

maser /ˈmeɪzə(r)/ *n* 微波激射器

mash /mæʃ/
A *n* **1** [c] (mixture) 糊状物 **2** [u] Brit colloq (potatoes) 土豆泥 **3** [u and c] Agric (feed) 谷物饲料
B *vt* 把…捣烂 ‹*food*›; **~ed potatoes** 土豆泥

Phrasal verb
• **mash up** *vt* [**~ up sth., ~ sth. up**] 把…捣烂 ‹*food*›

masher /ˈmæʃə(r)/ *n* 捣碎器

mask /mɑːsk, Amer mæsk/
A *n* **1** (for face) 面罩; **surgical ~** 医用口罩; **Hallowe'en ~** 万圣节面具 **2** fig (front) 伪装; **a ~ for sth.** 某物的伪装; **to hide one's worries behind a ~ of indifference** 装作漠不关心，借以掩饰不安 **3** fig (expression) 固定表情; **his face was a ~ of rage** 他一副怒气冲冲的样子 **4** (sculpture) 面模 **5** Theat 面具 **6** Cosmet 面膜
B *vt* **1** (cover with mask) 用面具遮住 ‹*face, features*› **2** (hide from view) «*facade, cloth*» 遮盖 ‹*sth. unsightly, scar*› **3** fig (conceal, disguise) 掩盖 ‹*emotion, truth, taste*›; **to ~ one's disappointment** 掩饰自己的失望; **to ~ a bad smell** 掩盖难闻的气味

masked /mɑːskt, Amer mæskt/ *adj* (wearing mask) 戴面具的; (disguised) 伪装的

masked ball *n* 假面舞会

masking tape *n* [u] 遮盖胶带

masochism /ˈmæsəkɪzəm/ *n* [u] also fig colloq 受虐狂

masochist /ˈmæsəkɪst/
A *n* also fig colloq 受虐狂者
B *adj attrib* 受虐狂的 ‹*tendencies*›

masochistic /ˌmæsəˈkɪstɪk/ *adj* 受虐狂的 ‹*tendencies, streak, delight, pleasure*›

mason /ˈmeɪsn/ ▸**p. 409** *n* **1** (worker in stone) 石匠 **2** **Mason = Freemason**

Mason-Dixon Line /ˌmeɪsnˈdɪksn laɪn/ *pr n* Amer **the ~** 梅森－狄克森线 [马里兰州和宾夕法尼亚州的分界线，通常视为美国的南北分界线]

Masonic /məˈsɒnɪk/ *adj* 共济会会员的

Masonite® /ˈmeɪsənaɪt/ *n* [u] Amer 梅森奈特纤维板

masonry /ˈmeɪsənri/ *n* [u] **1** (stonework) 砖石结构; **~ course** 圬工砌层 **2** (occupation) 石工行业; **~ tools** 水泥工具

masquerade /ˌmɑːskəˈreɪd, Amer ˌmæsk-/
A *n* **1** [c] (ball) 化装舞会 **2** [u] (wearing of disguise) 化装 **3** [c] fig (pretence) 伪装
B *vi* 假扮; **to ~ as sb./sth.** 乔装成某人/某物; **to ~ under a false name** 以假名冒充; **gossip that ~s as news** 以新闻为幌子的流言

masquerader /ˌmɑːskəˈreɪdə(r), Amer ˌmæsk-/ *n* **1** (at party) 假面舞者 **2** (impostor) 假冒者

Mass /mæs/ **1** [c and u] Relig 弥撒; **to go to** *or* **attend ~** 望弥撒 **2** [c] (*also* **mass**) Mus 弥撒曲

mass /mæs/
A *n* **1** [c] (voluminous body) 堆; (dense aggregation) 团; **a ~ of sth.** (of colour, hair, clouds) 一团某物; (of rubber, metal, rock) 一堆某物; (of trees, flowers) 一丛某物 **2** [c] (cluster, collection) 大量; (large number) 大群; **a ~ of sth.** 大量某物; **a (great) ~ of evidence** 大量证据; **a (great) ~ of examples** 大批例证; **to be a ~ of sth.** 满是某物; **he was just** *or* **simply a ~ of nerves** 他非常紧张 **3** [c] (majority) 大多数; (the main part) 主体; **the ~ of people/voters** 多数人/选民 **4** [u] Phys 质量 **5** [u] (bulk) 体积
B **masses** *npl* **1** **the ~es** (ordinary people) 民众; **the working** *or* **labouring ~es** 劳动大众 **2** esp Brit colloq (large quantity) 大量; **~es of sth.** 大量的某物
C *modif* **1** (large-scale) 大量的 ‹*audience*›; 群众性的 ‹*protest*›; 大规模的 ‹*destruction*›; **on a ~ scale** 大规模 **2** (of or for the people) 大众的 ‹*psychology, education*› **3** (simultaneous) 大批的 ‹*resignations, desertions*›
D *vt* 集中
E *vi* 聚集

Massachusetts /ˌmæsəˈtʃuːsɪts/ *pr n* 马萨诸塞州

massacre /ˈmæsəkə(r)/
A *n* **1** (slaughter) 大屠杀 **2** colloq (defeat) 惨败
B *vt* **1** (slaughter) 大屠杀 **2** colloq (defeat) 彻底击败 **3** colloq (perform badly) 把…搞砸 ‹*lines, part*›; **words were misspelled and syntax ~d** 单词都拼错，句法也一团糟

massage /ˈmæsɑːʒ, Amer məˈsɑːʒ/
A *n* [u and c] 按摩
B *vt* **1** (rub and knead) 按摩; **to ~ sb.'s ego** 奉承某人 **2** (rub in) 用…揉擦; **to ~ sth. in sth.** 把某物揉擦到某物上; **~ the cream into your skin** 把护肤霜抹到皮肤上 **3** fig (manipulate) 粉饰 ‹*data, evidence*›; **to ~ the unemployment figures** 篡改失业人数

massage: ~ oil *n* [u] 按摩油; **~ parlour** *n* **1** (for massage) 按摩院; **2** euph (brothel) 妓院

mass: ~ communications *npl* 大众传播; **~ consumption** *n* [u] 大众消费; **~-energy equation** *n* 质能方程

massed /mæst/ *adj attrib* 成堆的 ‹*ranks, bands, artillery, journalists, photographers*›

masseur /mæˈsɜː(r)/ ▸**p. 409** *n* 按摩师

masseuse /mæˈsɜːz/ ▸**p. 409** *n* 女按摩师

mass grave *n* 万人坑

massif /ˈmæsiːf, mæˈsiːf/ *n* 山峦

massive /ˈmæsɪv/ *adj* **1** (large and solid or heavy) 厚实的 ‹*building, walls*›; 粗大的 ‹*tree*› **2** (very large) 巨大的 ‹*victory*›; 大量的 ‹*increase, crowd*›; 大规模的 ‹*shift, attack*›; 大额的 ‹*bill*› **3** (very serious) 非常严重的 ‹*heart attack*›; **a ~ haemorrhage/stroke** 大出血/严重中风 **4** colloq (successful) 极为成功的; **the band are going to be ~** 该乐队会大获成功

massively /ˈmæsɪvli/ *adv* 大规模地 ‹*oversubscribed, understaffed, underfunded*›; 极度地 ‹*overloaded, expensive, overrated*›

mass market *n* 大宗商品市场

mass-market
A *adj* 面向大众的 ‹*product, promotion*›
B *vt* 大宗生产和销售

mass: ~ marketing *n* [u] 大规模销售; **~ media** *npl* + *v sing or pl* 大众传媒; **~ murder** *n* 大屠杀; **~ murderer** *n* 大屠杀者; **~ noun** *n* 物质名词; **~ number** *n* [原子的] 质量数; **~-produce** *vt* 批量生产; **~-produced** *adj* 批量生产的; **~-producer** *n* 批量生产商; **~ production** *n* [u] 批量生产; **~ screening** *n* [u] 大规模检查; **~ spectrograph** *n* 质谱仪; **~ spectrometer** *n* 质谱测定计; **~ transit** *n* [u] esp Amer （城市）公共交通

mast[1] /mɑːst, Amer mæst/ *n* **1** Naut 桅杆; **to sail before the ~** 当船员; ▸**nail B1** **2** (flagpole) 旗杆 **3** Radio, TV 天线杆

mast[2] *n* [u] (from forest trees) [喂猪的] 饲料坚果

mastectomy /məsˈtektəmi/ *n* 乳房切除术

-masted /ˈmɑːstɪd, Amer ˈmæstɪd/ *combining form* 有…桅杆的; **three~** 三桅的

master /ˈmɑːstə(r), Amer ˈmæs-/
A *n* **1** (person in control) 有控制权的人; **to be ~ of the situation** 是局势的控制者; **to be ~ of oneself** 自控; **to be (the) ~ of one's fate** *or* **destiny** 掌握自己的命运 **2** (skilled practitioner) 能手; **a ~ of sth.** 某方面的能手; **a ~ at doing sth.** 做某事的能手 **3** (owner of animal, slave) 主人; **to be one's own ~** 自己作主; **to meet one's ~** fig 变得驯服 **4** **Master** Univ (holder of Master's degree) 硕士; **to have** *or* **hold a M~'s (degree)** 持有硕士学位; **to be working for** *or* **towards one's M~'s (degree)** 正在攻读硕士学位 **5** Brit Sch (teacher) 男教师 **6** **Master** Brit (college head) （男）院长; (school head) （男）校长 **7** **Master** (title of young man) 少爷 **8** dated (head of household) （男）户主; **to be ~ in one's own house** 自己当家作主 **9** (great artist, player) 大师 **10** Naut 船长 **11** (original copy) 原版
B *modif* **1** (main) 主的 ‹*suite*›; 总的 ‹*control, switch*›; **to play one's ~ card** 打出王牌 **2** (original) 原版的 ‹*print*›; **~ tape** 母带 **3** (skilled) 技艺精湛的 ‹*craftsman, chef, musician*›; 老练的 ‹*smuggler, spy*›
C *vt* **1** (become proficient in) 精通 ‹*subject, language*›; **to ~ the art of doing sth.** 掌握做某事的技巧 **2** (overcome) 控制 ‹*person, animal, situation, emotion*›; 克服 ‹*problem*›

master: ~-at-arms *n* (*pl* **~s-at-arms**) Brit 舰艇纠察长; **~ bedroom** *n* 主卧室; **~ builder** ▸**p. 409** *n* 主建造师; **~ class** *n* 大师班; **~ copy** *n* 底本; **~ cylinder** *n*

主缸；～ **disk** *n* 原始磁盘；～ **file** *n* 主文件

masterful /ˈmɑːstəfl, Amer ˈmæs-/ *adj* 1 (commanding) 有支配力的 ‹*behaviour, voice*›; **to be ～ with sb./sth.** 对某人/某物有驾驭力 2 (skilful) 娴熟的; **a ～ performance/defence** 精湛的表演/巧妙的辩护

masterfully /ˈmɑːstəfəli, Amer ˈmæs-/ *adv* 1 (commandingly) 有支配力地 ‹*behave, speak*› 2 (skilfully) 娴熟地 ‹*perform, play*›

masterfulness /ˈmɑːstəflnɪs, Amer ˈmæs-/ *n* [u] 1 (imperiousness) 专横 2 (skilfulness) 娴熟

master key *n* 万能钥匙

masterly /ˈmɑːstəli, Amer ˈmæs-/ *adj* 娴熟的 ‹*performance, handling*›; **to be ～ in doing sth.** 做某事极为熟练; **in a ～ way** 熟练地

master mariner *n* [尤指有资格当商船船长的] 资深海员

mastermind /ˈmɑːstəmaɪnd, Amer ˈmæs-/
A *n* 智囊; **the ～ of the expedition** 探险的策划人; **the ～ behind sth.** 某事的幕后策划人
B *vt* 策划 ‹*robbery, attack, plot*›

master: M～ of Arts *n* 文科硕士学位; **M～ of Ceremonies** *n* (at formal occasion) 司仪; (presenting entertainment) 主持人; **M～ of Science** *n* 理科硕士学位; **M～ of the Rolls** *n* Brit [上诉法院民事庭的] 主事法官; **～piece** *n* 1 (outstanding work) 杰作; 2 (outstanding example) 典范; 3 (finest work) 代表作; **～ plan** *n* 总体规划; **～ sergeant** *n* Amer 军士长; **～ spy** *n* 王牌间谍; **～stroke** *n* 1 (skilful and opportune act) 高招; 2 (idea, stroke of genius) 绝妙之举; **～ tape** *n* 母带; **～work** *n* = **～piece**

mastery /ˈmɑːstəri, Amer ˈmæs-/ *n* [u] 1 (skill) 精湛技艺; **sb.'s ～ in** *or* **with sth.** 某人在某方面的高超技艺 2 (command of subject) 精通; **to have complete ～ of one's subject** 对自己的研究领域精通的 3 (action of mastering subject) 掌握; (control, superiority) 控制; **to have ～ over sb./sth.** 驾驭某人/某事物; **human ～ of the natural world** 人类对自然界的掌控

masthead /ˈmɑːsthed, Amer ˈmæst-/ *n* 1 Naut 桅顶 2 (of newspaper) 报头; (of magazine) 刊头

masticate /ˈmæstɪkeɪt/
A *vi* 咀嚼; **to have difficulty masticating** 咀嚼困难
B *vt* 咀嚼

mastication /ˌmæstɪˈkeɪʃn/ *n* [u] 咀嚼

mastiff /ˈmæstɪf/ *n* 大驯犬

mastitis /mæˈstaɪtɪs/ ▸ **p. 377** *n* [u] 乳腺炎

mastodon /ˈmæstədɒn/ *n* 乳齿象

masturbate /ˈmæstəbeɪt/
A *vi* 手淫
B *vt* 对…行手淫

masturbation /ˌmæstəˈbeɪʃn/ *n* [u] 手淫

masturbatory /ˌmæstəˈbeɪtəri, Amer -bəˈtɔːri/ *adj* 手淫的

mat¹ /mæt/
A *n* 1 (on floor, table) 垫子; **a heatproof/an ornamental ～** 隔热垫/装饰垫; **an exercise/a door/a prayer ～** 运动垫/门垫/祷告跪垫; **to be on the ～** colloq 受上级训斥 2 (mass) 团; **a ～ of hair/grass** 一团毛发/一墩草
B *vi* (*pres p etc.* **-tt-**) 结团
C *vt* (*pres p etc.* **-tt-**) 使结团; **～ted hair/wool** 结团的毛发/缩绒毛

mat² *adj, n* Amer = **matt**

matador /ˈmætədɔː(r)/ ▸ **p. 409** *n* 斗牛士

match¹ /mætʃ/
A *n* 1 (Sport) esp Brit 比赛; **an away/a home ～** 客场/主场比赛; **a shouting/slanging ～** 大声争吵/互相谩骂 2 (equal, challenger) 对手; **a good/poor ～** 实力相当/实力不济的对手; **to meet one's ～** 棋逢对手; **to be a/no ～ for sb.** 是/不是某人的对手; **to be more than sb.'s ～** 胜过某人 3 (pairing) 相配之物; **a good/poor/perfect ～** 很/不/完全般配的东西; **to form a ～** 匹配; **the blood sample is a perfect ～ with** *or* **for that found at the scene of the crime** 血样与犯罪现场发现的血迹完全一致 4 (partner) 搭档; **to make a good ～ (for sb.)** 是（某人）很好的搭档; **don't you think they're a good ～?** 你不觉得他们是很好的一对吗？ 5 (marriage) 婚姻; (arrangement of marriage) 婚配; **a good/an unfortunate ～** 美满/不幸的婚姻; **to make a ～** 结婚
B *vt* 1 (put together appropriately) 使相配; **to ～ A and B** *or* **A with B** *or* **A to B** 把A和B配对; **can you ～ the names to the photos?** 你能把姓名和照片对上号吗？ 2 (harmonize with) 和…相配 ‹*colour, furnishings*›; Med 和…匹配 ‹*blood type, bone marrow*› 3 (correspond to) 与…一致 ‹*ability, quality, description*›; **which word ～es the definition given?** 哪个词符合给出的定义？ 4 (compete with, equal) 比得上 ‹*standard*›; **to ～ sb. at tennis** 在打网球上和某人旗鼓相当; **～ that if you can!** 有本事你来试一试！; **the government will ～ your contribution dollar for dollar** 你捐出多少钱，政府就会拿出多少钱; **to be ～ed (by sth.)** （与某物）旗鼓相当; **his wit cannot be ～ed** 他的机智无与伦比 5 (put in competition, pit) 使…较量 ‹*person, team*›; 比试 ‹*ability, quality*›; **they ～ed wits** 他们展开了斗智; **to ～ one's skill against sb. else's** 和某人比技巧
C *vi* 《*parts, garments, colours*》 相配; Med 《*blood types, samples*》 匹配; **I can't get the two sides to ～** 我不能使双方达成一致; **shoes with handbag to ～** 有手提包搭配的鞋

Phrasal verb

• **match up**
A *vi* 1 (fit together) 《*parts, designs*》 相配 2 **to ～ up to sth.** (be as good as, equal) 比得上 ‹*standard, quality*›; 与…相适应 ‹*reputation, hopes*›; **somehow it doesn't quite ～ up to my expectations** 不知为什么事情总不如我所料想的
B *vt* [**～ sth. up, ～ up sth.**] 使…相配 ‹*garments, colours*›

match² *n* (for lighting fire) 火柴; **to put** *or* **set a ～ to sth.** 用火柴点燃某物; **a box of ～es** 一盒火柴; **to strike** *or* **light a ～** 划火柴

matchbox /ˈmætʃbɒks/
A *n* 火柴盒
B *modif* 火柴盒般的 ‹*apartment*›

match day *n* [尤指足球的] 比赛日

matched /mætʃt/ *adj* **to be well/badly ～** 很/很不般配; **to be evenly ～** 实力相当; **the two teams were evenly ～** 这两支队伍势均力敌

matching /ˈmætʃɪŋ/ *adj attrib* 匹配的 ‹*handbag, skirt, top*›

matchless /ˈmætʃlɪs/ *adj* 无与伦比的

match: ～maker *n* 媒人; **～making** *n* [u] 做媒; **～ point** *n* [c and u] 赛点; **to have/win/lose ～ point** 得到/赢得/失去赛点; **at ～ point** 处于赛点

matchstick /ˈmætʃstɪk/
A *n* 1 (gen) 火柴杆 2 Culin 细条; **to cut the vegetables into ～s** 将蔬菜切成丝
B *modif* 火柴杆似的 ‹*figure, drawing*›

matchwood /ˈmætʃwʊd/ *n* [u] 碎木片; **to reduce sth. to ～** 将某物弄成碎片

mate¹ /meɪt/
A *n* 1 (sexual partner) 配偶 2 Brit colloq (friend) 伙伴 3 Brit colloq (as form of address) 伙计 4 Brit (assistant) 下手 5 Brit (in merchant navy) 大副
B *vi* 交配
C *vt* 使…交配 ‹*animals, birds*›

mate²
A *n* [u] = **checkmate A1**
B *vt* = **checkmate B1**

material /məˈtɪərɪəl/
A *n* 1 [c and u] (substance) 材料; **waste ～** 废料; **explosive/radioactive ～** 爆炸物/放射性物质; **natural ～s** 天然原料; **clothes made out of natural ～s** 天然材料制成的衣服 2 [c and u] (fabric) 布料; **dress ～** 衣料; **cotton ～** 棉布 3 [c and u] (information, data) 资料; **promotional/publicity/reference ～** 促销/宣传/参考资料; **teaching** *or* **course ～** 教材; **reading ～** 阅读材料; **to collect** *or* **gather ～** 搜集资料; **～ about** *or* **on sth./sb.** 有关某事物/某人的资料; **～ for sth.** 某物的素材 4 [u] (subject matter) 内容; **the ～ in the magazine is controversial** 杂志内容有争议; **to write one's own ～** 自己创作 5 [u] fig (suitable person or people) 人才; **manager/executive ～** 经理/管理人才; **he is (not) university ～** 他（不）是上大学的料
B **materials** *npl* (equipment) 用具; **writing ～s** 书写用具
C *adj* 1 *attrib* (physical, concrete) 物质的 ‹*world, support, damage*›; 有形的 ‹*object, substance*›; (bodily) 肉体的 ‹*need*›; **～ comforts** 物质享受; **to do sth. for ～ gain** 为了物质利益做某事; **in ～ terms** 从物质意义上讲 2 (significant) 重要的 ‹*assistance, change*›; **of ～ benefit to the workers** 对工人有实质利益的 3 (relevant) 有关的 ‹*fact, question*›; Jur 决定性的 ‹*evidence, witness*›; **to be ～ to sth.** 与…相关 ‹*argument, case*›

materialism /məˈtɪərɪəlɪzəm/ *n* [u] 1 (desire for material possessions) 实利主义 2 Philos 唯物主义; **dialectal/historical ～** 辩证/历史唯物主义

materialist /məˈtɪərɪəlɪst/
A *n* 1 (person who desires material possessions) 实利主义者; **you're too much of a ～ for my liking** 我不喜欢你这种信奉物质至上的人 2 Philos 唯物主义者
B *adj* 1 = **materialistic** 2 Philos 唯物主义的 ‹*theory, philosophy*›

materialistic /məˌtɪərɪəˈlɪstɪk/ *adj* 实利主义的

materialize /məˈtɪərɪəlaɪz/ *vi* 1 (happen) 实现; **the threat/strike failed to ～** 恐吓没有兑现/罢工没有进行 2 (appear) 《*spirit*》 显现; 《*object from thin air, idea*》 冒出来 3 colloq (be present) 出现

materially /məˈtɪərɪəli/ *adv* 1 (significantly) 相当大地 ‹*damage, alter*›; **not ～ faster/lower** 快/慢得不多; **to be ～ different from sth.** 与某物有很大不同 2 (regarding worldly goods) 物质上; **a ～ and culturally rich area** 一个物质富足、文化深厚的地区

maternal /məˈtɜːnl/ *adj* 1 (motherly) 母亲般的; **to be ～ to** *or* **towards sb.** 对某人像母亲般慈爱 2 (of a mother) 母亲的 ‹*care, deprivation, bond*› 3 (on mother's side) 母系的 ‹*ancestor, line, genes*›

maternally /məˈtɜːnəli/ *adv* 1 (in a maternal manner) 母亲般地 2 (through or by the mother) 母亲方面

maternity /məˈtɜːnəti/
A *n* [u] 1 (motherhood) 母亲身份 2 (ward) 产科病房 3 (department of shop) 孕产妇部
B *modif* 孕妇的; **～ clothes** *or* **wear** 孕妇服; **～ staff** 产科员工

maternity: ～ benefit *n* [u] Brit 产妇津贴; **～ department** *n* 产科; **～ hospital** *n* 产科医院; **～ leave** *n* [u] 产假; **～ unit** *n* 产科; **～ ward** *n* 产科病房

matey /ˈmeɪti/ *adj* Brit colloq 友好的; **to be ～ with sb.** 对某人很友好

math /mæθ/ *n* Amer colloq = **maths**

mathematical /ˌmæθəˈmætɪkl/ *adj* 1 (relating to mathematics) 数学的 ‹*formula, equation, genius*› 2 (precise) 精确的; **with ～ precision** 极为精确地 3 (good at mathematics) 擅长数学的; **to have a ～ mind** 有一个数学般精确的头脑 4 (possible but improbable) 微乎其微的 ‹*chance*›

mathematically /ˌmæθəˈmætɪkli/ *adv* 以数学方式 ‹*prove, demonstrate*›; **to be ～ inclined** 对数学感兴趣; **to be ～ precise** 极

为精确; **to be ～ possible/impossible** 理论上可能/不可能

mathematician /ˌmæθəˈtɪʃn/ ▸**p. 409** *n* 数学家

mathematics /ˌmæθəˈmætɪks/ *npl* [1] + *v sing* (subject) 数学 [2] + *v sing or pl* (mathematical operations) 运算; **the ～ of sth.** 某物的运算

maths /mæθs/ Brit colloq

A *npl* + *v sing* 数学; **he's a genius at ～** 他是个数学天才

B *modif* 数学的; **a ～ class/teacher** 数学班/老师

matinee, matinée /ˈmætɪneɪ, ˈmætneɪ, Amer ˌmætnˈeɪ/ *n* 午后场; **to go to a** *or* **the ～** 去看下午场演出; **a ～ performance** *or* **show** 下午场的表演

matinee: ～ coat, ～ jacket *ns* Brit 婴儿短外套; **～ idol** *n* colloq dated [女观众喜欢的] 偶像派男演员

matiness /ˈmeɪtɪnɪs/ *n* [u] Brit colloq 友好

mating /ˈmeɪtɪŋ/ *n* [u] 交配

mating: ～ call *n* 交配鸣叫; **～ season** *n* 交配季节

matriarch /ˈmeɪtrɪɑːk/ *n* [1] (head of tribe or family) 女族长 [2] (female leader) 女领导人 [3] (older woman) 有权威的女长者

matriarchal /ˌmeɪtrɪˈɑːkl/ *adj* 母权的 ‹*system*›; 母系的 ‹*society, tribe*›

matriarchy /ˈmeɪtrɪɑːki/ *n* [1] [u] (system) 母权制 [2] (society, country) 母系社会

matrices /ˈmeɪtrɪsiːz/ *pl* ▸**matrix**

matricide /ˈmeɪtrɪsaɪd/ *n* formal [1] [c and u] (crime) 弑母 [2] [c] (perpetrator) 弑母者

matriculate /məˈtrɪkjʊleɪt/

A *vi* [1] (enrol) 注册入大学 [2] S Afr (pass final exam) 通过高中毕业考试

B *vt* 录取…入大学

matriculation /məˌtrɪkjʊˈleɪʃn/ *n* [1] [c and u] (enrolment) 录取入学; **～ fee/requirements** 录取入学费/条件 [2] [c] **～ (examination)** S Afr 高中毕业考试

matrilineal /ˌmætrɪˈlɪnɪəl/ *adj* formal 母系的

matrimonial /ˌmætrɪˈməʊnɪəl/ *adj* formal 婚姻的

matrimony /ˈmætrɪməni, Amer -məʊni/ *n* [u] formal 婚姻; **to be united in holy ～** 共同步入神圣的婚姻殿堂

matrix /ˈmeɪtrɪks/ *n* (*pl* **matrices** *or* **～es**) [1] (mould for metal, liquid etc.) 模型 [2] Math 矩阵 [3] (medium, material) 基体 [4] Geol 基岩 [5] (environment) 环境

matron /ˈmeɪtrən/ *n* [1] (*also* **Matron**) Brit (in boarding school, orphanage, nursing home) 女舍监 [2] Brit dated (in hospital) 女护士长 [3] dated (older married woman) [端庄而有身份的] 中年已婚妇女

matronly /ˈmeɪtrənli/ *adj* [1] (rather fat) 发福的 ‹*woman, figure*› [2] (staid) 端庄的 ‹*woman, smile*›

matron of honour *n* (*pl* **matrons of honour**) [已婚的] 首席女傧相

matt, matte /mæt/

A *adj* 无光泽的 ‹*paint, surface, photograph*›; 暗淡的 ‹*colour*›; **a ～ finish** 亚光罩面漆

B *n* [u] 亚光漆

matted /ˈmætɪd/ *adj* 缠结的 ‹*hair, undergrowth, roots*›

matter /ˈmætə(r)/

A *n* [1] [c] (subject, situation) 事情; **the heart/crux/root of the ～** 问题的本质/关键/根本; **the ～ in hand/under discussion** 手头的/讨论的问题; **business ～s** 商务; **financial ～s** 财务; **the ～ is closed** 事情到此为止; **to let the ～ drop** *or* **rest** (leave alone) 搁置某事; (stop mentioning) 不再提某事; **that is the end of** *or* **an end to the ～** 这事儿就到此为止; **in the ～ of Smith versus Jones** Jur 在史密斯诉琼斯一案中; **there's the small ～ of the £3,000 you owe me!** iron 有件小事：你欠我3000英镑还没还！; **a personal** *or* **private ～** 私事; **that's another** *or* **a different ～ (entirely)** 这（完全）是另一回事; **for that ～** (in that regard) 就此而言; (furthermore) 而且; **no ～** 不要紧; **no ～ who/what/how/why/when/where** 不管谁/什么/怎样/为何/何时/何地; **to be** *or* **make no ～ (to sb.)** （对某人来说）无所谓; **no small/great/easy ～** 不是什么小事/大事/容易的事; **to be no laughing** *or* **joking ～** 是正经事; **a hanging ～** lit 该处以绞刑的事情; fig 严重事件; **not to mince ～s** 坦率地说; **a ～ of principle/taste** 原则/品位问题; **that's a ～ of opinion** 这是个见仁见智的问题; **a life-and-death** *or* **life-or-death ～** 生死攸关的事情; **a ～ of record** 有案可查的事; **a ～ of time** 时间问题; **in just a ～ of hours** 在区区几小时之内; **a (plain) ～ of fact** （简单的）事实问题; **as a ～ of fact** 其实; **as a ～ of course** 照例; **a ～ for sb./sth.** 应该由某人/某物处理的事情 [2] [u] (problem, trouble) 问题; **what's the ～, John?** 怎么啦，约翰？; **what's the ～ with you/your eye?** 你/你的眼睛怎么了？; **there's nothing the ～ with me** 我没事; **what's the ～ with dreaming of a better life?** 向往更好的生活有什么错吗？; **there's nothing the ～ with looking!** 看一看又有什么关系！; **something is the ～** 有问题 [3] [u] Phys (physical substance) 物质; **a particle of ～** 物质微粒; **inert/organic/inorganic ～** 惰性/有机/无机物质; **colouring ～** 染料 [4] [u] Print (written or printed material) **reading ～** 阅读材料; **printed ～** 印刷品 [5] [u] Med (pus) 脓; (discharge from the body) 排出物

B **matters** *npl* (state of affairs) 事态; **to make ～s worse** 使情况更糟; **there's nothing we can do to change ～s** 我们无力改变现状; **to take ～s into one's own hands** 亲自掌控事态的发展

C *vi* 要紧; **punctuality ～s** 准时很重要; **to ～ to sb.** 对某人来说很重要; **it ～s what/how/when/whether ...** 什么/怎样/何时/是否…很重要; **it doesn't ～ (in the least** *or* **slightest)** （一点也）不要紧; **it ～s/doesn't ～ about sb./sth.** 某人/某物很重要/无关紧要

matter-of-fact /ˌmætərəvˈfækt/ *adj* 不带感情的 ‹*person, tone*›; 就事论事的 ‹*attitude, account, assessment*›; **to be ～ about sth./doing sth.** 对某事/做某事实事求是; **in a very ～ way** 实事求是地

matter-of-factly /ˌmætərəvˈfæktli/ *adv* 不带感情地

matting /ˈmætɪŋ/ *n* [u] 编垫子材料; **rush/coconut ～** 灯芯草垫/椰衣垫

mattock /ˈmætək/ *n* 鹤嘴锄

mattress /ˈmætrɪs/ *n* 床垫

mattress cover *n* 床垫套

maturation /ˌmætjʊˈreɪʃn/ *n* [u] (physically, psychologically) 成熟; (of wine, whisky, cheese) 发酵成熟; **sexual ～** 性成熟

mature /məˈtjʊə(r), Amer -ˈtʊər/

A *adj* [1] (fully grown, developed) 成熟的 ‹*animal, plant, tree, market, piece of work*›; **she was now physically ～** 她如今身体已发育成熟 [2] (sensible) 明智的 ‹*attitude*›; 懂事的 ‹*child*›; **a ～ and sensible attitude** 一副深谙世事的态度 [3] euph (middle-aged, old) 中年的; **a person of ～ years** *or* **a ～ age** 中年人 [4] (adult) 成年的 [5] formal (careful, thorough) 深思熟虑的; **after** *or* **upon ～ reflection/consideration** 经过深思熟虑/慎重考虑 [6] Culin 发酵成熟的 ‹*cheese, wine, whisky*›

B *vi* [1] (physically, psychologically) 成熟 [2] Culin «*wine, whisky, cheese*» 发酵成熟 [3] Fin «*bill, loan, policy*» 到期

C *vt* 使…发酵成熟 ‹*cheese, whisky, wine*›

maturely /məˈtjʊəli, Amer -ˈtʊərli/ *adv* 成熟地

mature student *n* Brit 成年学生

maturity /məˈtjʊərəti, Amer -ˈtʊə-/ *n* [u] [1] (full development) 成熟; **to reach ～** 达到成熟状态; **at full ～** 处于完全成熟状态; **artistic ～** 艺术上的成熟 [2] (adultness, sensibleness) 老成; **he has a ～ beyond his years** 他过于老成 [3] (of wine, whisky, cheese) 发酵成熟

matzo, matzoh /ˈmɑːtsəʊ/, **matzah** /ˈmætsə/ *n* [犹太人过逾越节时吃的] 无酵饼

maudlin /ˈmɔːdlɪn/ *adj* [尤指饮酒后] 伤感的

maul /mɔːl/

A *vt* [1] (maim by scratching) 抓伤; (maim by tearing) 撕咬; **to be ～ed to death** 被咬死 [2] (manhandle) 粗暴地对待 ‹*person*›; 笨手笨脚地摆弄 ‹*object*›; **to ～ sb./sth. about** *or* **around** 粗暴地对待某人/摆弄某物 [3] (for sexual gratification) 乱摸 [4] fig (criticize severely) 抨击 [5] colloq (defeat) 击败

B *n* 围挤争球

mauling /ˈmɔːlɪŋ/ *n* [u] [1] (maiming) 伤害 [2] (criticizing) 抨击; **to get a ～ from the critics** 受到评论家们的抨击 [3] colloq (defeat) 击败

Maundy /ˈmɔːndi/: **～ money** *n* [u] Brit 濯足节救济金 [英国君王在濯足节散发的特制银币]; **～ Thursday** *n* Brit 濯足节 [复活节前的星期四，基督教在此日纪念最后的晚餐]

Mauritania /ˌmɒrɪˈteɪnɪə/ *pr n* 毛里塔尼亚

Mauritanian /ˌmɒrɪˈteɪnɪən/ ▸**p. 503**

A *adj* (of Mauritania) 毛里塔尼亚的; (of the people) 毛里塔尼亚人的

B *n* 毛里塔尼亚人

Mauritian /məˈrɪʃn/ ▸**p. 503**

A *adj* (of Mauritius) 毛里求斯的; (of the people) 毛里求斯人的

B *n* 毛里求斯人

Mauritius /məˈrɪʃəs/ *pr n* 毛里求斯

mausoleum /ˌmɔːsəˈliːəm/ *n* (*pl* **～s** *or* **mausolea** /ˌmɔːsəˈliːə/) 陵墓

mauve /məʊv/ ▸**p. 134**

A *adj* 淡紫色的

B *n* [c and u] 淡紫色

maverick /ˈmævərɪk/

A *n* [1] (person) 持不同见解者 [2] Amer (calf) 未打烙印的小牛

B *adj* 不合常规的 ‹*behaviour*›; 自行其事的 ‹*politician*›

maw /mɔː/ *n* [1] (of voracious animal) (mouth) 大口; (throat) 咽喉; (of bird) (crop) 嗉囊 [2] (of greedy person) (mouth) 大嘴; (gullet) 咽喉 [3] fig (abyss) 无底洞

mawkish /ˈmɔːkɪʃ/ *adj* pej 多愁善感的 ‹*person, behaviour*›; 自怜的 ‹*pride, sentimentality*›; **～ verses** 无病呻吟的诗句

mawkishness /ˈmɔːkɪʃnɪs/ *n* [u] pej 多愁善感

max /mæks/ *abbr* colloq = **maximum**

maxi /ˈmæksi/ *n* (coat) 长大衣; (dress) 长连衣裙; *modif* **～ skirt** 长裙

maxilla /mækˈsɪlə/ *n* (*pl* **maxillae** /mækˈsɪli/) 上颌骨

maxillary /mækˈsɪleri/ *adj* (of jaw) 上颌的; (of jawbone) 上颌骨的

maxim /ˈmæksɪm/ *n* 格言; **a ～ for life** 人生格言

maxima /ˈmæksɪmə/ *pl* ▸**maximum B**

maximal /ˈmæksɪml/ *adj attrib* 最大的 ‹*value, sales, efficiency, results, benefit*›

maximization /ˌmæksɪmaɪˈzeɪʃn/ *n* [u] 最大化; **profit/sales/revenue ～** 利润/销售额/税收最大化

maximize /ˈmæksɪmaɪz/ *vt* [1] (make as large as possible) 使…达到最大限度 ‹*output, profit, efficiency, results*›; **to ～ one's potential** 充分挖掘自己的潜力 [2] Comput 使…最大化 ‹*window*› [3] (make best use of) 充分利用 ‹*opportunities, resources*›

maximum /ˈmæksɪməm/

A *adj* 最大的 ‹*dosage, quantity, width, height, capacity*›; 最高的 ‹*speed, temperature, prison sentence, load*›; 最多的 ‹*yield, benefit*›

a ~ **genius** 机械天才 [3] (without thinking) 呆板的; **a ~ gesture/music** 机械的手势/呆板的音乐

mechanical: ~ drawing *n* [c and u] 机械制图; **~ engineer** ▸**p. 409** *n* 机械工程师; **~ engineering** *n* [u] 机械工程学

mechanically /mɪ'kænɪkli/ *adv* [1] (by mechanical means) 机械地 [2] (without thinking) 呆板地

mechanics /mɪ'kænɪks/ *npl* [1] + *v sing* (subject) 力学; **quantum/statistical/fluid ~** 量子/统计/流体力学 [2] + *v pl* (working parts) 机械部件 [3] + *v pl* (workings) 操作方法; **the ~ of the law/management** 法律/管理运作方式

mechanism /'mekənɪzəm/ *n* [1] [c] (working parts) 机械装置 [2] [c] (device, apparatus) 机件 [3] [c] Biol, Physiol 机制; **the ~ of the ear/brain** 耳朵/大脑的机制 [4] [c] (procedure) 途径; (technique) 技巧; **a ~ for doing sth.** *or* **to do sth.** 做某事的方法 [5] [u] Philos 机械论

mechanistic /ˌmekə'nɪstɪk/ *adj* 机械论的 ‹*interpretation, view, science*›

mechanization /ˌmekənaɪ'zeɪʃn, Amer -nɪ'z-/ *n* [u] 机械化

mechanize /'mekənaɪz/
A *vt* 使机械化
B *vi* 机械化

mechatronics /ˈmekəˈtrɒnɪks/ *npl* + *v sing* 机械电子学

Med /med/ *pr n* esp Brit colloq **the ~** 地中海

medal /'medl/ *n* Mil 勋章; Sport 奖牌; **a ~ for bravery/heroism/courage** 英勇/英雄/勇敢勋章; **a gold/silver/bronze ~** 金牌/银牌/铜牌

medallion /mə'dæliən/ *n* [1] (piece of jewellery) 奖章形垂饰 [2] Archit 圆雕饰; Tex 圆形图案 [3] Culin **~s** (meat) 圆形薄肉片; (fish) 圆形薄鱼片

medallist Brit, **medalist** Amer /'medəlɪst/ *n* 奖牌获得者; **the gold/silver/bronze ~** 金牌/银牌/铜牌得主

Medal of Honor *n* Amer 荣誉勋章

meddle /'medl/ *vi* pej [1] (interfere) 管闲事; **to ~ in sb.'s private affairs** 干涉某人的私事 [2] (touch, handle) 瞎搞; **to ~ with sth.** 擅自摆弄某物

meddler /'medlə(r)/ *n* pej 爱管闲事者

meddlesome /'medlsəm/ *adj* pej 爱管闲事的 ‹*person, behaviour*›

meddling /'medlɪŋ/ pej
A *adj attrib* 爱管闲事的
B *n* [u] 干涉

medevac /'medəvæk/ Amer
A *n* [u] 空运后送; **a ~ helicopter/operation** 救伤直升机/行动
B *vt* 空运后送

media /'miːdɪə/ *n* [1] *pl* ▸**medium B** [2] + *v sing or pl* Journ, Radio, TV 大众传媒; **the ~** 媒体; **~ advertising/sales/services** 媒体广告/销售/服务; **(to receive) widespread ~ attention/coverage** （受到）媒体的广泛关注/报道

media: ~ blitz *n* 媒体轰炸; **~ circus** *n* 乱哄哄的媒体群; **~ company** *n* 传媒公司; **~-conscious** *adj* 注意媒体形象的; **~-enabled** *adj* 多媒体的; **a ~-enabled phone/device/product** 多媒体电话/设备/产品; **~ event** *n* 媒体事件

mediaeval /ˌmedɪ'iːvl/ *adj* Brit **= medieval**

media fatigue *n* [u] 媒体疲劳 [因过多接触媒体报道产生的厌倦感]

medial /'miːdɪəl/ *adj* [1] esp Med 近中的 ‹*position, location*›; **~ cortex** 内侧皮层 [2] Phon 中间的; **a ~ vowel** 中元音; **a ~ consonant/syllable** 中间辅音/音节

median /'miːdɪən/
A *adj* [1] (average) 中等的 ‹*income, wage*›; 中间的 ‹*age group, score*› [2] Math 中位数的 ‹*value, sum*›
B *n* 中位数

median strip *n* Amer **= central reservation**

media: ~-shy *adj* 不愿被媒体采访的; **~ star** *n* 媒体明星; **~ student** *n* 大众传媒专业的学生; **~ studies** *npl* + *v sing* 大众传媒学

mediate /'miːdɪeɪt/
A *vi* 调解; **to ~ in sth.** 在某事中进行调解; **to ~ between A and B** 在A和B之间进行调解; **to ~ between two warring nations** 在两个交战国之间进行斡旋
B *vt* 调停解决 ‹*differences, dispute*›; 经调解达成 ‹*agreement, solution, peace*›

mediation /ˌmiːdɪ'eɪʃn/ *n* [u] 调解; **to go to ~** 走调停之路

mediator /'miːdɪeɪtə(r)/ *n* 调解人; **to act as ~** 充当调解人

medic /'medɪk/ *n* [1] colloq (doctor) 医生 [2] Brit colloq (medical student) 医科学生 [3] Amer (medical orderly) 卫生员

Medicaid /'medɪkeɪd/ *n* [u] Amer 医疗救助制度

medical /'medɪkl/
A *adj* [1] (relating to health, medical treatment, etc.) 医疗的; **~ condition/equipment** 病理状况/医疗设备; **to retire on ~ grounds** 由于健康原因退休 [2] (relating to science or practice of medicine) 医学的; **a ~ professional/journal** 医学专业人士/期刊; **~ research** 医学研究; **~ background** (education, experience, etc.) 医学背景; (health) 健康状况 [3] (relating to profession) 医疗职业的; **a ~ correspondent/receptionist/secretary** 医疗记者/接待员/秘书
B *n* **= medical examination**

medical: ~ advice *n* [u] 医疗建议; **~ appointment** *n* 诊病预约; **~ board** *n* esp Amer 医疗卫生管理委员会; **~ care** *n* [u] 医疗保健; **~ certificate** *n* [1] (attesting person's health) 健康证明; [2] (stating unfitness for work) 诊断书; **~ check-up** *n* 体格检查; **~ doctor** ▸**p. 409** *n* （内科）医生; **~ emergency** *n* 急诊; **~ ethics** *npl* 医德; **~ examination** *n* 体格检查; **~ examiner** ▸**p. 409** *n* Amer 法医; **~ expert** *n* 医学专家; **~ history** *n* 病史; **~ insurance** *n* [u] 医疗保险

medicalization /ˌmedɪklaɪ'zeɪʃn, Amer -lɪ'z-/ *n* [u] 医疗化

medicalize /'medɪklaɪz/ *vt* 以医学方法处理

medically /'medɪkli/ *adv* 医学上 ‹*qualified*›; **to examine** *or* **test sb. ~** 给某人体检; **~ fit** *or* **sound** 身体健康的

medical: ~ man *n* colloq 医生; **~ officer** ▸**p. 409** *n* 卫生干事; **~ opinion** *n* [1] [u] (view of the profession) 医学观点; [2] [c] (view of one doctor) 医生的看法; **~ orderly** ▸**p. 409** *n* (in hospital) 护理员; (in army) 卫生员; **~ practitioner** ▸**p. 409** *n* 开业医生; **~ profession** *n* **the ~ profession** 医生职业; **M~ Research Council** *n* Brit 医学研究委员会; **~ school** *n* 医学院; **~ science** *n* [u] 医学; **~ social worker** ▸**p. 409** *n* Brit 医学社会工作者; **~ student** *n* 医科学生; **~ studies** *npl* 医学研究; **~ unit** *n* 医疗室; **~ ward** *n* 病房

medicament /mə'dɪkəmənt/ *n* dated 药物

Medicare /'medɪkeə(r)/ *n* [u] [1] Amer 老年医疗保健制度 [2] Austral, Can 国家医疗保险制度

medicate /'medɪkeɪt/ *vt* [1] (treat) 用药物治疗 ‹*patient, wound*› [2] (add medication to) 给…加药物 ‹*bandage, shampoo*›

medicated /'medɪkeɪtɪd/ *adj* 含药物的; **~ bandage/shampoo** 药物绷带/洗发液

medication /ˌmedɪ'keɪʃn/ *n* [1] [u] (drug treatment) 药物治疗; **to be on ~** 正在接受药物治疗; **to give sb. ~** 对某人进行药物治疗; **to put sb. on/take sb. off ~** 让某人接受/停止药物治疗 [2] [c and u] (medicine) 药物

medicinal /mə'dɪsɪnl/ *adj* 药用的 ‹*compound, purposes, substance*›; **a ~ drug/herb** 药物/药草; **~ properties/use** 药性/药用

medicine /'medsn, Amer 'medɪsn/ *n* [1] [u] (science, profession) 医学; **to practise/study ~** 行医/学医 [2] [c and u] (drug) 药; **a dose of ~** 一剂药; **laughter is the best ~** 笑是最好的药; **to take one's ~** fig 甘愿受罚; **to give sb. a taste** *or* **dose of their own ~** fig 以其人之道还治其人之身

medicine: ~ ball *n* 健身实心球; **~ bottle** *n* 药瓶; **~ box** *n* 药箱; **~ cabinet, ~ chest, ~ cupboard** *ns* 药品柜; **~ man** *n* 巫医

medico /'medɪkəʊ/ *n* (*pl* **~s**) colloq **= medic 1**

medieval /ˌmedɪ'iːvl, Amer ˌmiːd-, *also* mɪ'diːvl/ *adj* [1] (of the Middle Ages) 中世纪的 ‹*church, castle, manuscript, period, times*› [2] fig (primitive) 原始的; **isn't your kitchen a bit ~?** 你的厨房是不是有点落后了？

medievalist /ˌmedɪ'iːvəlɪst, Amer ˌmiːd-, *also* mɪ'd-/ ▸**p. 409** *n* (student) 中世纪史研究者; (specialist) 中世纪史专家

mediocre /ˌmiːdɪ'əʊkə(r)/ *adj* 普通的 ‹*talent, worker*›; 平庸的 ‹*work, performance, novel*›

mediocrity /ˌmiːdɪ'ɒkrəti/ *n* [1] [u] (state) 平庸 [2] [c] (person) 平庸之人

meditate /'medɪteɪt/
A *vi* [1] esp Relig (practise meditation) 冥想 [2] (think, ponder) 沉思; **to ~ on** *or* **upon** *or* **about sth.** 考虑某事
B *vt* 谋划 ‹*revenge, murder*›; **to ~ doing sth.** 考虑要做某事

meditation /ˌmedɪ'teɪʃn/
A *n* [u] [1] esp Relig 冥想 [2] (reflection) 沉思; **to be lost in ~** 陷入沉思
B meditations *npl* 沉思录; **~s on** *or* **upon sth.** 对某事物的沉思录

meditative /'medɪtətɪv, Amer -teɪt-/ *adj* [1] (thoughtful) 深思的; **to be in a ~ mood** 在沉思中 [2] (involving meditation) 陷入沉思的; **a ~ silence/atmosphere** 默默的沉思/冥思的氛围

meditatively /'medɪtətɪvli/ *adv* 沉思地

Mediterranean /ˌmedɪtə'reɪnɪən/
A *adj* [1] (on or in the Mediterranean) 地中海的 ‹*resort, island, coast*› [2] Anthrop 地中海人种的 ‹*type, looks, race*› [3] Meteorol 地中海式的 ‹*temperatures*›; **a ~ climate** 地中海气候
B *pr n* [1] **the ~ (Sea)** 地中海 [2] **the ~** (region) 地中海地区; **in the ~** 在地中海地区 [3] (native) 地中海地区居民

medium /'miːdɪəm/
A *adj* 中等的 ‹*size, weight*›; 适中的 ‹*shade of colour, temperature*›; **of ~ build** *or* **height** 中等身材的
B *n* (*pl* **media** *or* **~s**) [1] (means of communication) 媒介; (agency, means) 途径; **through** *or* **via the ~ of sth.** 通过某种方法; **an advertising/a teaching ~** 广告媒体/教学手段; **a ~ for management/job creation** 管理的方法/创造就业的手段; **a ~ of exchange** 交换的媒介 [2] (art form) 形式; (art material) 材料 [3] (solvent) 溶剂 [4] (mid-point) 中间; **to find** *or* **strike a happy ~** 找到折中办法 [5] Biol 媒质; Phys 培养基; **air is a ~ for sound** 空气是传播声音的媒质 [6] (*pl* **~s**) (spiritualist) 灵媒

medium: ~-dry *adj* 甜度适中的 ‹*wine, champagne*›; **~-length** *adj* 长度适中的; **~-level** *adj* 适中的; **~-range** *adj* 中程的 ‹*aircraft, missile*›; **~-rare** *adj* 半熟的 ‹*steak*›; **~-sized** *adj* 中型的 ‹*company, town*›; **~-term** *adj* 中期的 ‹*plan, goal*›; **~ wave** *n* [u] esp Brit 中波; **on ~ wave** 用中波; **a ~-wave broadcast/signal** 中波广播/信号

medivac /'medɪvæk/ *n* [u], *vt* Amer **= medevac**

medley /ˈmedli/ *n* **1** Mus 混成曲 **2** (mixture) 混杂物; **a ~ of races** 不同民族的混合 **3** (in swimming) 混合泳接力

meek /miːk/
A *adj* 温顺的; **as ~ as a lamb** 如羔羊一般温顺的; **~ and mild** 温顺谦和
B *npl* **the ~** 温顺的人

meekly /ˈmiːkli/ *adv* 温顺地

meet /miːt/
A *vt* (*pt, pp* **met**) **1** (encounter) (by chance) 遇见; (by arrangement) 和…会面; Sport 与…比赛; Mil 与…交战; **~ me on the corner in an hour** 一小时后和我在街角见面; **a terrible scene met their eyes as they entered the room** 他们进屋时看到了一幅可怕的景象; **to ~ sb. halfway** 和某人妥协; **East ~s West in this fascinating city** 东西方文化在这座迷人的城市里交汇 **2** (experience, encounter) 经历 ‹*difficulty, disaster*›; **to ~ one's death/fate** 死去/送命; **to ~ one's Waterloo** 遭到惨败 **3** (make the acquaintance of) 与…相识; **pleased to ~ you!** 很高兴认识你! ; **nice to ~ you** 认识你真高兴 [用于相见时]; **nice to have met you** 能认识你很高兴 [用于告别时]; **she took him to ~ her parents** 她带他去见父母; **Jay, ~ Pete** Amer 杰伊, 这是皮特; **to ~ one's Maker** 见上帝 **4** (greet, await) 接 ‹*person, means of transport*›; **she met her guests at the door** 她在门口迎接客人; **I'll be there to ~ you off** Brit *or* **at** Amer **the bus** 我会到汽车站去接你; **a courtesy bus ~s all incoming flights** 所有进港航班的乘客都有免费班车来接 **5** (come into contact with) 与…相碰 ‹*hand, vehicle*›; **the track ~s the road by a derelict cottage** 小径与公路交接之处有一间破旧的小屋; **they met an oncoming car head-on** 他们与一辆汽车迎头相撞; **his eyes/lips met hers** 他和她的目光/两唇相接; **to ~ sb.'s eye** *or* **gaze** 直视某人; **more than ~s the eye** 并不像看到的那么简单 **6** (fulfil) 满足 ‹*demand, need, order*›; 满足…的需求 ‹*person*›; 达到 ‹*goal, wish, criterion*›; 应对 ‹*challenge*›; **to ~ the case** Brit 符合要求 **7** (pay) 支付 ‹*cost, bill*› **8** Comm (match) 和…意见一致 ‹*person, company*›; 和…一致 ‹*offer*›; **the product is fine, but can we ~ him on price?** 产品很不错, 但是我们能接受他开出的价格吗?
B *vi* (*pt, pp* **met**) **1** (come together) (from opposite directions) «*people, vehicles*» 相遇; (by arrangement) 见面; Sport «*teams, opponents*» 比赛; Mil «*armies, enemies*» 交战 **2** (assemble) «*committee, parliament*» 开会; «*individuals, group*» 集合 **3** (make acquaintance) 相识; **I've a feeling we have met somewhere before** 我觉得我们以前在什么地方见过 **4** (come into contact) «*lines, roads*» 相汇; «*vehicles*» 相撞; «*eyes*» 相遇; «*belt*» 扣上; **their hands/lips met** 他们拉了手/接了吻; **this skirt/these trousers won't ~ (round the middle)!** 这条裙子/裤子系不上 (腰) ! ; **to ~ head on** 迎头相撞; **to make (both) ends ~** (live within one's means) 量入为出; (make just enough money to live on) 勉强维持生计
C *n* **1** Sport 运动会; **a track/track-and-field ~** 田赛/田径运动会; **a swim** *or* **swimming ~** 游泳比赛 **2** Brit (hunt) [打猎前猎人和猎犬的] 集合

Phrasal verbs

- **meet up** *vi* **1** (get together) 见面; **to ~ up with sb.** 与某人见面 **2** (join, intersect) «*roads*» 交汇; **to ~ up with sth.** 与…交汇 ‹*road*›
- **meet with** *vt* **1** [**~ with sb.**] (have meeting with) 和…会晤 ‹*person, delegation*› **2** [**~ with sth.**] (encounter) 遭遇 ‹*opposition, criticism, obstacle, difficulty*›; 受到 ‹*praise*›; **she met with much suspicion at first** 起初她受到了很大怀疑; **his ideas/comments met with no response** 他的想法/评论没有得到回应; **his speech was met with cries of outrage** 他的讲话招来了愤怒的喊声; **to ~ with success/failure** 获得成功/遭到失败

meet-and-greet *n* [名人与追随者的] 见面会

meeting /ˈmiːtɪŋ/ *n* **1** [c] (assembly) 会议; **to call a ~** 召开会议; **to be in a ~** 在开会; **a board/cabinet/prayer ~** 董事会/内阁会/祷告会 **2** [c] (gathering) 会面; **a chance ~** 邂逅 **3** [u] fig (union) 会合; **a ~ of kindred spirits** 志趣相投者的聚会; **a ~ of minds** 意见一致 **4** Sport 运动会

meeting: ~ place *n* 会面地点; **~ point** *n* [游客和导游等的] 会合点

mega /ˈmegə/ *adj* colloq **1** (huge) 巨大的 **2** (excellent) 极佳的

megabit /ˈmegəbɪt/ *n* 兆位

megabucks /ˈmegəbʌks/ *npl* colloq 一大笔钱; **to be making** *or* **earning ~** 大把赚钱

megabyte /ˈmegəbaɪt/ *n* 兆字节

megadeath /ˈmegədeθ/ *n* [u] 百万人的死亡 [核战争死亡人数的计算单位]

megahertz /ˈmegəhɜːts/ *n* (*pl* **megahertz**) 兆赫

megalith /ˈmegəlɪθ/ *n* [古代的] 巨石

megalithic /ˌmegəˈlɪθɪk/ *adj attrib* **1** (made of megaliths) 巨石建造的; **a ~ circle/tomb** 巨石圈/巨石墓 **2** (*usu* **Megalithic**) (era) 巨石时期的; **the ~ era/culture** 史前巨石时期/文化

megalomania /ˌmegələˈmeɪnɪə/ *n* [u] **1** (obsession) 权欲熏心 **2** (delusion) 夸大狂; **to suffer from ~** 患有夸大狂

megalomaniac /ˌmegələˈmeɪnɪæk/
A *n* 夸大狂患者
B *adj attrib* **1** (obsessive) 权欲熏心的 ‹*ruler*› **2** (delusive) 夸大狂的 ‹*tendencies*›

megalopolis /ˌmegəˈlɒpəlɪs/ *n* 特大都市

megamall /ˈmegəmæl, -mɔːl/ *n* 巨型购物中心

megaphone /ˈmegəfəʊn/ *n* 扩音器

megapixel /ˈmegəpɪksl/ *n* 百万像素

megastar /ˈmegəstɑː(r)/ *n* colloq 演艺巨星

megastore /ˈmegəstɔː(r)/ *n* 大型专卖店

megaton, megatonne /ˈmegətʌn/ *n* 百万吨级 [核武器爆炸力的计量单位]

megavolt /ˈmegəvəʊlt/ *n* 兆伏

megawatt /ˈmegəwɒt/ *n* 百万瓦特

meiosis /maɪˈəʊsɪs/ *n* (*pl* **meioses** /maɪˈəʊsiːz/) 减数分裂

Mekong /miːˈkɒŋ/ ▸p. 663 *pr n* **the ~** 湄公河; **the ~ Delta** 湄公河三角洲

melamine /ˈmeləmiːn/ *n* [u] **1** Chem 三聚氰胺; **~ resin** 三聚氰胺树脂 **2** (plastic) 密胺塑料

melancholia /ˌmelənˈkəʊlɪə/ *n* [u] formal 抑郁症

melancholic /ˌmelənˈkɒlɪk/ *adj* 抑郁的 ‹*nature, person*›

melancholy /ˈmelənkəli/
A *adj* **1** (very sad) 忧郁的 ‹*person, mood*› **2** (causing sadness) 令人悲伤的 ‹*music, news*›
B *n* [u] 忧郁

Melanesia /ˌmeləˈniːzɪə/ *pr n* 美拉尼西亚

Melanesian /ˌmeləˈniːzɪən/ ▸p. 503, p. 426
A *adj* (of Melanesia) 美拉尼西亚的; (of the people) 美拉尼西亚人的; (of the languages) 美拉尼西亚语的
B *n* **1** [c] (person) 美拉尼西亚人 **2** [u] (languages) 美拉尼西亚语

melange /ˈmeɪlɑːnʒ, Amer meɪˈlɑːnʒ/ *n* liter 混合物; **a ~ of smells/people/visions** 各种各样的气味/人/景象

melanin /ˈmelənɪn/ *n* [u] 黑色素

melanoma /ˌmeləˈnəʊmə/ *n* [c and u] 黑色素瘤

melatonin /ˌmeləˈtəʊnɪn/ *n* [u] 褪黑素

meld /meld/
A *vt* 使融合; **to ~ sth. and** *or* **with sth.** 将某物与某物合并
B *vi* 融合
C *n* 融合

melee /ˈmeleɪ, Amer meɪˈleɪ/ *n* **1** (brawl, fight) 混战; **in the ~ that ensued** *or* **followed** 在随后发生的混战中 **2** (crowd) 混乱的人群

mellifluous /meˈlɪflʊəs/, **mellifluent** /məˈlɪfluənt/ *adjs* liter 悦耳动听的 ‹*voice, music*›

mellow /ˈmeləʊ/
A *adj* **1** (smooth) 甘美的 ‹*taste, flavour*›; 甜美的 ‹*voice, tone*› **2** (soft) 柔和的 ‹*colour, light, sound*› **3** (well-matured) 醇香的 ‹*wine, whisky*› **4** (calm, relaxed) 成熟老练的 ‹*person, manner*›; **to get** *or* **grow ~ with age** 随着年龄的增长变得老练; **to be in a ~ mood** 心境轻松平和 **5** colloq (slightly drunk) 飘飘然的
B *vi* «*person*» 变得老成; «*colour, light, sound*» 变得柔和; «*wine, whisky*» 变得醇香
C *vt* **1** (calm, relax) 使…变得老成 ‹*person*› **2** (mature) 使…变得醇香 ‹*wine, whisky*›

mellowing /ˈmeləʊɪŋ/ *adj attrib* 使柔和的; **to have a ~ effect on sb.** 让某人感到放松; **fatherhood has had a ~ influence on him** 他做了父亲后变稳重了

mellowness /ˈmeləʊnɪs/ *n* [u] **1** (of taste, flavour) 甘美; (of voice, tone) 甜美 **2** (of colour, light, sound) 柔和 **3** (of wine, whisky) 醇香 **4** (of person, manner) 老练

melodeon /mɪˈləʊdɪən/ ▸p. 395 *n* 德国式手风琴

melodic /mɪˈlɒdɪk/ *adj* **1** *attrib* (relating to melody) 旋律的 ‹*harmony, phrasing*› **2** (tuneful) 音调优美的 ‹*song, ballad*›; 悦耳的 ‹*music, sound, voice*›

melodion /mɪˈləʊdɪən/ *n* = **melodeon**

melodious /mɪˈləʊdɪəs/ *adj* 悦耳的

melodrama /ˈmelədrɑːmə/ *n* **1** [u] (genre) 情节剧 **2** [c] (dramatic piece) 情节剧作品 **3** [u] (overdramatic behaviour) 戏剧性行为 **4** [c] fig (instance of overdramatization) 过分夸大的事件; **to make a ~ out of sth.** 将某事戏剧化地夸大

melodramatic /ˌmelədrəˈmætɪk/ *adj* 夸张的 ‹*behaviour, gesture, language*›; 情绪化的 ‹*person, reaction*›

melodramatically /ˌmelədrəˈmætɪkli/ *adv* 夸张地

melodramatics /ˌmelədrəˈmætɪks/ *npl* (conduct) 夸张的行为; (writing) 夸张的作品

melody /ˈmelədi/ *n* **1** [c] (tune) 曲调; **old Irish/Scottish melodies** 古老的爱尔兰/苏格兰旋律 **2** [c] (principal musical part) 主旋律 **3** [u] (tunefulness) 悦耳

melon /ˈmelən/ *n* **1** [c] (fruit) 瓜 **2** [c] (plant) 瓜类植物 **3** [u] (flesh of this fruit) 瓜肉

melt /melt/
A *vi* **1** (thaw) 融化 **2** (soften, become liquefied) «*food*» 变软; **I'm ~ing!** fig 我要热死了! ; **butter wouldn't ~ in sb.'s mouth** fig 某人装出天真无邪的样子 **3** fig (become tender) «*person*» 变得温柔; «*heart*» 变软 **4** fig (blend, merge) 融合; **to ~ into the crowd/darkness** 融入人群/黑暗之中; **to ~ into sb.'s arms** 投入某人的怀抱中; **red ~s into orange** 红色渐渐变成橙色
B *vt* **1** (cause to thaw) 使融化 **2** (soften, liquefy) 使变软 **3** fig (make more amenable, loving) 软化; **to ~ sb.'s heart** 使某人的心变软
C *n* **1** (thaw) 融化 **2** (sandwich) 奶酪三明治; (hamburger) 奶酪汉堡包

Phrasal verbs

- **melt away** *vi* **1** lit «*snow, ice*» 逐渐融化; «*fog, mist*» 逐渐消散 **2** fig «*anger, confidence*» 逐渐消失; «*crowd*» 逐渐散去
- **melt down** *vt* [**~ down sth., ~ sth. down**] 将…熔化

meltdown /'meltdaʊn/ *n* 1 [c and u] (in nuclear reactor) 熔毁 2 [u] fig (disaster) 崩溃 [尤指股价暴跌]

melting /'meltɪŋ/ *adj attrib* 温柔的 ‹*voice, look*›

melting: ~ **point** *n* 熔点; ~ **pot** *n* 1 lit 坩锅; 2 fig (of people, nationalities) 熔炉 [指多种民族、文化等的融合地]; **to be in the ~ pot** Brit 处于变化之中

melt: ~**-in-the-mouth** *adj attrib* 入口即化的; ~**water** *n* [u] [尤指来自冰川的] 融水

member /'membə(r)/ *n* 1 (of group, family, committee, organization) 成员; **a ~ of the audience/public** 观众/大众的一员; **'~s only'** "仅对会员开放" 2 (part of structure) 构件 3 (of group of figures) 项; (of mathematical set) 元 4 euph (penis) 阴茎

Member: ~ **of Congress** *n* Amer 众议院议员; ~ **of Parliament** *n* Brit, Can, Austral, NZ 下院议员; ~ **of the European Parliament** *n* 欧洲议会议员; ~ **of the House of Representatives** *n* Amer 众议院议员; ~ **of the Scottish Parliament** *n* 苏格兰议会议员; ~ **of the Welsh Assembly** *n* 威尔士议会议员

membership /'membəʃɪp/ *n* 1 [u] (state of belonging) 会员资格; **to resign/renew one's ~** 放弃/延长会员资格; **full/associate/individual/joint ~** 正式/非正式/个人/联合会员身份; **open/closed ~** 向/不向公众开放的会员资格; ~ **committee** 会员资格审查委员会 2 [c] (fee) 会费 3 [c] (number of members) 会员人数; **a society with a large/small ~** 拥有很多/较少会员的社团

membrane /'membreɪn/ *n* 1 (tissue) 膜 2 (barrier) 膜状物; **a damp-proof ~** 防潮薄膜

meme /mi:m/ *n* 模因 [通过模仿等方式传递的文化或行为因子]

memento /mə'mentəʊ/ *n* (*pl* **~s** *or* **~es**) 纪念品

memo /'meməʊ/ *n* = **memorandum**

memo board *n* 记事板

memoir /'memwɑ:(r)/ *n* 1 (account, biography) 回忆录 2 (learned essay) 专题论文

memoirs /'memwɑ:z/ *npl* 自传

memo pad *n* 记事簿

memorabilia /ˌmemərə'bɪlɪə/ *npl* 纪念品

memorable /'memərəbl/ *adj* (easily recalled) 难忘的 ‹*experience, concert, speech*›; (worth remembering) 值得纪念的 ‹*occasion, event*›

memorably /'memərəbli/ *adv* 值得纪念地

memorandum /ˌmemə'rændəm/ *n* (*pl* **memoranda** /ˌmemə'rændə/ *or* **~s**) 1 (written communication) 备忘录; **to prepare** *or* **draw up a ~** 拟订一份备忘录 2 (note, record) 备忘便条; **a ~ to/from sb. to sb.** 一份给某人/某人给某人的备忘便条

memorandum: ~ **of agreement** *n* 协议备忘录; ~ **of association** *n* 公司章程

memorial /mə'mɔ:rɪəl/

A *n* 1 (monument) 纪念碑; **a ~ to sb./sth.** 某人/某事的纪念碑 2 (reminder) 纪念物; **as a ~ to sb./sth.** 作为对某人/某事的纪念

B *modif* 用于纪念的 ‹*chapel*›; **a ~ ceremony/prize/stone** 纪念仪式/纪念奖/纪念碑

memorial: **M~ Day** *n* Amer 阵亡将士纪念日; ~ **service** *n* 悼念仪式

memorize /'meməraɪz/ *vt* 记住

memory /'memәri/ *n* 1 [u] (faculty) 记忆力; **to have a good/bad ~** 记性好/差; **to lose one's ~** 丧失记忆力; **to have an excellent ~ for names/faces** 善于记名字/长相; **from ~** 凭记忆; **to jog** *or* **refresh sb.'s ~** 唤起某人的记忆; **if (my) ~ serves me right** 如果我没记错的话; **to have a lapse** *or* **loss of ~** 记错; **to slip** *or* **escape sb.'s ~** 某人一时记不起来了; **to the best of my ~** 就我的记忆所及; **to have a ~ like a sieve** colloq 记性很差 2 [c] (recollection) 回忆; **to evoke** *or* **awaken a ~** 唤起回忆; **to stir up/blot out a ~** 勾起/抹去回忆; **to take a trip down ~ lane** 回忆往事 3 [u] (period of time) 记忆范围; **in** *or* **within living ~** 在现今人的记忆中 4 [u] (posthumous fame) [对死者的] 怀念; **their ~ lives on** 他们的荣耀永存; **to keep sb.'s ~ alive** *or* **green** 永远怀念某人 5 [u] (commemoration) 纪念; **in (loving) ~ of sb.** (深情地) 纪念某人; **to the ~ of sb./sth.** 作为对某人/某事的纪念; **of blessed ~** 已故的 6 [u] Comput 内存

memory: ~ **bank** *n* 存储体; ~ **board** *n* 存储板; ~ **card** *n* 记忆卡; ~ **chip** *n* 内存芯片; ~ **loss** *n* [u] 记忆丧失; ~ **span** *n* [u] 记忆广度; ~ **stick** *n* 记忆棒

men /men/ *pl* ▸ **man A**

menace /'menəs/

A *n* 1 [u] (threatening quality) 威胁; **a sense of ~ in sb.'s voice** 某人话音里威胁的语气; **an atmosphere of ~ in the film** 电影里的恐怖气氛 2 [c] (threat) 恐吓; **to demand money with ~s** 勒索钱财 3 [c] (danger) (person) 危险的人; (thing) 危险的事物; **to be** *or* **constitute a ~ to sb./sth.** 对某人/某事物构成危险 4 [c] colloq (nuisance) (person) 讨厌的人; (thing) 讨厌的东西

B *vt* 对…构成威胁 ‹*country, society, environment*›; 危及 ‹*wildlife, safety, health*›; **to ~ sb./sth. with sth.** 以某物威胁某人/某物

menacing /'menəsɪŋ/ *adj* 威胁性的 ‹*behaviour, tone*›; 险恶的 ‹*person, weather, cloud, wild animal*›

menacingly /'menəsɪŋli/ *adv* 威胁性地

ménage /meɪ'nɑ:ʒ/ *n* 家庭; ~ **à trois** 三人同居

menagerie /mə'nædʒəri/ *n* 1 (collection of wild animals) [兽笼中供展览的] 野生动物 2 (enclosure) 兽栏

mend /mend/

A *vt* 1 lit (repair) 缝补 ‹*clothes, socks*›; 修补 ‹*shoes, fence, puncture*›; 修理 ‹*watch, car, radio*›; **to ~ the road** 修路; **to ~ a hole in sth.** 修补某物上的破洞 2 fig (improve) 改进 ‹*attitude*›; 使…好转 ‹*matters, situation*›; **to ~ a rift** 弥合嫌隙; **to ~ one's ways/manners** 改过/改变作风; **to ~ relations with sb.** 改善与某人的关系

B *vi* 痊愈

C *n* 修补处; **to be on the ~** 正在康复

mendacious /men'deɪʃəs/ *adj* formal 撒谎的 ‹*person*›; 虚假的 ‹*statement, document*›

mendacity /men'dæsəti/ *n* [u] formal (of person) 不诚实; (of statement, document) 虚假

Mendelian /men'di:lɪən/ *adj* 孟德尔学说的; ~ **genetics/inheritance** 孟德尔遗传学/孟德尔式遗传

mendicant /'mendɪkənt/

A *adj attrib* formal 行乞的 ‹*person, way of life*›

B *n* 乞丐

mending /'mendɪŋ/ *n* [u] 1 (repairing by sewing) 缝补; **to do some ~** 做点缝缝补补的活儿 2 (things to be mended) 需缝补之物

menfolk /'menfəʊk/ *npl* [家庭或社群中的] 男人们

menhir /'menhɪə(r)/ *n* [西欧史前的] 巨石柱

menial /'mi:nɪəl/

A *adj* 技术含量低的 ‹*job, work*›; 地位不高的 ‹*occupation*›

B *n* 干粗活者

meningitis /ˌmenɪn'dʒaɪtɪs/ ▸**p. 377** *n* [u] 脑膜炎

meniscus /mə'nɪskəs/ *n* (*pl* **menisci** /mə'nɪski/) 1 Phys 弯液面 2 (lens) 凹凸透镜 3 Anat 半月板

menopausal /ˌmenə'pɔ:zl/ *adj* 更年期的 ‹*symptom, trouble*›; 处于更年期的 ‹*woman*›

menopause /'menəpɔ:z/ *n* [u] (cessation of menstruation) 绝经; (time of cessation of menstrual cycle) 更年期

menses /'mensi:z/ *npl* 1 (menstruation) 月经 2 + *v sing* (menstruation period) 月经期

men's room *n* esp Amer 男厕所

menstrual /'menstrʊəl/ *adj* 月经的; ~ **blood/pain** 经血/痛经

menstrual: ~ **cycle** *n* 月经周期; ~ **period** *n* 经期

menstruate /'menstrʊeɪt/ *vi* 行经

menstruation /ˌmenstrʊ'eɪʃn/ *n* [u] 行经

menswear /'menzweə(r)/ *n* 男装; ~ **(department)** 男装部

mental /'mentl/ *adj* 1 (of the mind) 智力的 ‹*impairment, ability*›; ~ **faculties** *or* **powers** 智力 2 (in one's head) 内心的 ‹*prayer, calculation*›; ~ **arithmetic** 心算; **a ~ picture of sth.** 某物在脑海里的形象; **to make a ~ note of sth./to do sth.** 记着某事物/要做某事 3 (relating to the health of the mind) 精神健康的; **a ~ illness/disorder/case/hospital** 精神病/精神紊乱/精神病患者/精神病院 4 colloq (insane) 疯的; **to go ~ (about sth.)** (因某事) 发疯

mental: ~ **age** *n* 心理年龄; ~ **block** *n* 思维阻隔; ~ **cruelty** *n* [u] 精神虐待; ~ **handicap** *n* 智力障碍; ~ **health** *n* [u] 心理健康; ~ **home** *n* dated 精神病院

mentality /men'tæləti/ *n* 心态

mentally /'mentəli/ *adv* 在心里 ‹*calculate, estimate, resolve*›; 智力上 ‹*active, exhausted*›; 精神上 ‹*disturbed, unstable*›; ~ **quick/alert** 头脑反应快/机灵; **the ~ ill** 精神病患者; **to be ~ deranged** 精神错乱

mentally handicapped *adj* dated 智障的

menthol /'menθɒl/ *n* [u] 薄荷醇

mentholated /'menθəleɪtɪd/ *adj* 含薄荷醇的

mention /'menʃn/

A *vt* 1 (allude to) 提到; **to ~ sth./sb. to sb.** 对某人提起某事物/某人; **to ~ (to sb.) that ...** (和某人) 提到…; **it must be ~ed that ...** 必须要提的是…; **(please) don't ~ it** (请) 不要客气; **please ~ me to your parents** 请代我问候你父母; **to ~ sb. in one's will** 赠予某人遗产; **without ~ing (any) names** 不点名; **too numerous to ~** 多得无法一一提及; **it is not worth ~ing sth., sth. is not worth ~ing** 某事物不值一提; **not to ~ sth., without ~ing sth.** 更不必说某事物; **as ~ed above** 如上所述; **the countries ~ed above** 上面提到的几个国家 2 (acknowledge) 提名表扬; Mil 传令嘉奖; **to be ~ed in dispatches** 在战报中受到表彰

B *n* 1 [c and u] (reference) 提及; **their eyes light up at the ~ of food** 提到食物时他们眼睛一亮; **to make ~ of sth.** 提及某物; **to get a media/promotional ~** 出现于媒体/广告中 2 [c] (acknowledgement) 提名表扬; Mil 传令嘉奖; **an honourable ~** 荣誉奖

mentor /'mentɔ:(r)/

A *n* 导师

B *vt* 指导

menu /'menju:/ *n* 1 (list of dishes) 菜单; **sth. is on/off the ~** 菜单上有/没有某物; **to put** *or* **take sth. on/off the ~** 将某物加入/撤出菜单 2 Comput 功能菜单

menu: ~ **bar** *n* 菜单栏; ~**-driven** *adj* 菜单驱动的; ~ **item** *n* 1 Comput 菜单选项; 2 (dish) 菜单上的菜

meow /mɪ'aʊ/ *vi, n* = **miaow**

MEP *abbr* = **Member of the European Parliament**

Mephistopheles /ˌmefɪ'stɒfɪli:z/ *pr n* 恶魔 [传说中的恶魔靡菲斯特, 浮士德将自己的灵魂出卖给了它]

mercantile /'mɜ:kəntaɪl, Amer -ti:l, -tɪl/ *adj* 商业的 ‹*monopoly*›; **a ~ person/company** 商人/贸易公司

mercantile: ~ agency *n* 商业征信所; **~ marine** *n* 商船队

mercenary /ˈmɜːsməri, Amer -neri/
A *adj* **1** (interested in money) 唯利是图的 ‹*person*›; 贪财的 ‹*action*› **2** *attrib* (hired by foreign army) 受雇于外国军队的; **a ~ soldier/commander** 雇佣兵/指挥官
B *n* 外国雇佣兵

merchandise /ˈmɜːtʃəndaɪz/
A *n* [u] 商品
B *vt* (*also* **merchandize**) **1** (buy and sell) 买卖 **2** (promote) 推销

merchandiser, merchandizer /ˈmɜːtʃəndaɪzə(r)/ *n* 商人

merchandising /ˈmɜːtʃəndaɪzɪŋ/ *n* [u] **1** (*also* **merchandizing**) (promoting goods) 推销 **2** (products used to promote) 促销品

merchant /ˈmɜːtʃənt/
A *n* **1** (trader) [尤指外贸] 商人 **2** colloq pej **a speed ~** 好飙车的人; **a rip-off ~** 骗子; **a ~ of death** 军火商
B *adj attrib* **1** (of traders) 商人的; (of trade) 贸易的 **2** Naut 货运的; **a ~ vessel/fleet** 商船/商船队; **~ shipping** 海上商运

merchant: ~ bank *n* Brit 商人银行; **~ banker** ▸**p. 409** *n* Brit 商人银行职员; **~ banking** *n* [u] Brit 商人银行业务; **~man** /-mən/ *n* 商船; **~ navy** Brit, **~ marine** Amer *ns* 商船队

merciful /ˈmɜːsɪfl/ *adj* **1** (showing mercy) 仁慈的 ‹*person, action*›; 宽大的 ‹*punishment, sentence*›; **to be ~ to** *or* **towards sb.** 对某人仁慈 **2** (fortunate) 幸运的 ‹*event, escape*›

mercifully /ˈmɜːsɪfəli/ *adv* **1** (compassionately) 仁慈地 ‹*behave, treat*› **2** (fortunately) **to be ~ free of sth.** 幸好没有某物; **the article was ~ free of jargon** 还好这篇文章没有术语; **the area is ~ free of mosquitoes** 幸运的是这个地区没有蚊子

merciless /ˈmɜːsɪlɪs/ *adj* **1** (pitiless) 冷酷的; **to be ~ to** *or* **towards sb./sth.** 毫不怜悯地对待某人/某事物 **2** (relentless) 无情的 ‹*rain, heat*›

mercilessly /ˈmɜːsɪlɪsli/ *adv* **1** (pitilessly) 冷酷地 ‹*treat, beat*›; 毫不怜悯地 ‹*tease, bully, mock*› **2** (relentlessly) 无情地 ‹*rain, snow*›

mercurial /mɜːˈkjʊəriəl/ *adj* 反复无常的

Mercury *pr n* 水星

mercury *n* [u] 汞

mercy /ˈmɜːsi/ *n* **1** [u] (clemency) 仁慈; **to show ~ to** *or* **towards sb.** 对某人表示怜悯; **to have ~ on sb.** 宽待某人; **to beg for ~** 乞求怜悯; **in one's ~** 出于恻隐之心; **for ~'s sake!** colloq dated 看在上帝的份上! **2** [u and c] (power to show mercy) 宽容力; **to be at the ~ of sb./sth.** 任凭某人/某事摆布; **to leave sb. to the ~** *or* **mercies of sb.** 听任某人受某人的摆布; **to throw oneself on sb.'s ~** 指望得到某人的宽恕 **3** [c] (fortunate event) 幸运的事; (relief) 解脱; **to be thankful** *or* **grateful for small mercies** 庆幸不利情况略有改善

mercy: ~ dash *n* 快速救援行动; **~ flight** *n* 急救飞行; **~ killing** *n* 安乐死

mere /mɪə(r)/ *adj attrib* **1** (common, simple) 仅仅的; **a ~ nothing/nobody** 不过是区区小事/无名小卒; **a ~ child/commoner** 只是个孩子/只不过一介平民 **2** (smallest, slightest) 最少的; **the ~ idea/mention/sight/smell of ...** 一想到/提起/看见/闻到… **3** (no more than) 只有的; **the theatre is a ~ mile from here** 剧院离这儿只有一英里; **I spent a ~ hour in the museum** 我只在博物馆待了一个小时

merely /ˈmɪəli/ *adv* 只不过 ‹*ask, mention*›; 仅仅 ‹*weigh*›; 只是 ‹*nod, stare, repeat, copy*›; **I am not ~ requesting, I am ordering** 我不只是要求, 我是命令; **this ~ seemed to make him angrier** 看上去这只不过是让他更气愤罢了; **instead of replying, he ~ shrugged/grinned** 他没有回答, 只是耸了耸肩/咧嘴笑了笑

meretricious /ˌmerɪˈtrɪʃəs/ *adj* formal 华而不实的 ‹*style*›; 虚有其表的 ‹*impression, charm*›

merge /mɜːdʒ/
A *vi* **1** (join) «*company, school*» 合并; «*road, river*» 汇合; **to ~ with/into ...** 与…合并/合并成 ‹*company, department, state*›; **to ~ together** 合并 **2** (blend) «*colour, shape, sound*» 融合; **to ~ into each** *or* **one another** 相互融合
B *vt* **1** (join) 使…合并 ‹*routes, companies, institutions*›; **to ~ sth. and** *or* **with sth.** 将某物与某物合并; **to ~ sth. into sth.** 将某物合并到某物中 **2** (blend) 使…融合 ‹*colours, sounds, designs*›

merger /ˈmɜːdʒə(r)/ *n* 合并; **a ~ between sth. and sth.** 某物与某物的合并; **a ~ with sth.** 与某物的合并

meridian /məˈrɪdɪən/ *n* 子午线

meringue /məˈræŋ/ *n* **1** [u] (mixture) 调合蛋白 **2** [c] (cake) 蛋白酥

merino /məˈriːnəʊ/ *n* **1** [c] (sheep) 美利奴羊 **2** [u] (wool) 美利奴羊毛; (yarn) 美利奴精纺毛纱; (cloth) 美利奴羊毛织物

merit /ˈmerɪt/
A *n* **1** [u] (of idea, philosophy, plan, behaviour) 价值; **to see ~ in sth./sb.** 看到某物/某人的价值; **to have/lack ~** 有/没有价值; **a person of ~** 有美德的人 **2** [u] (worth) 荣誉; **to give (due) ~ to sb. for sth.** 因某事归功于某人; **certificate of ~** 奖状 **3** [c] (grade) 良好
B **merits** *npl* (good points) 长处; **to judge sb./sth. on their's own ~s** 根据某人/某事本身的情况进行评判
C *vt* 值得 ‹*mention, investigation, consideration*›; 应得到 ‹*reward, promotion*›

merit: ~ award *n* 优秀奖; **~ list** *n* 优秀名单 [尤指学生]; **~ mark, ~ point** *ns* 奖励加分

meritocracy /ˌmerɪˈtɒkrəsi/ *n* **1** [u] (rule, government) 精英领导 **2** [c] (ruling class) 精英领导阶层 **3** [c] (social system) 精英管理体制

meritocratic /ˌmerɪtəˈkrætɪk/ *adj* 精英领导的

meritorious /ˌmerɪˈtɔːrɪəs/ *adj* formal 值得称赞的 ‹*conduct, deed, service*›

merit system *n* Amer 考绩制度

merlin /ˈmɜːlɪn/ *n* 灰背隼

mermaid /ˈmɜːmeɪd/ *n* 美人鱼

merman /ˈmɜːmæn/ *n* (*pl* **mermen**) 人鱼

merrily /ˈmerɪli/ *adv* **1** (joyfully) 愉快地 **2** (without thinking) 自顾自地

merriment /ˈmerɪmənt/ *n* [u] 欢乐

merry /ˈmeri/ *adj* **1** (happy) 欢乐的 ‹*occasion, party*›; 愉快的 ‹*look, mood*›; **~ Christmas!** 圣诞快乐! ; **to make ~** 行乐; **the more the merrier!** 人越多越热闹! ; **to give sb. ~ hell** colloq 申斥某人; **to play ~ hell (with sth.)** colloq 严重损坏 (某物) **2** Brit colloq (tipsy) 微醉的

merry-go-round *n* (*pl* **~s**) esp Brit (carousel) 旋转木马; (succession of events) 一连串的事件; **a real ~ of parties** 一个接一个的聚会

merry: ~maker *n* 寻欢作乐者; **~making** *n* [u] 尽情欢乐

Merseyside /ˈmɜːzɪsaɪd/ *pr n* 默西塞德郡

mescaline /ˈmeskəliːn/ *n* [u] 墨斯卡灵 [从仙人球中提取的致幻剂]

mesh /meʃ/
A *n* **1** [u] (netting) 网; **wire/nylon ~** 铁丝网/尼龙网 **2** [c] (spaces in net) 网孔 **3** [u] Mech **to be in ~** 相互啮合
B *vi* **1** (to interlock) «*wheels, gears, teeth*» 相互啮合 **2** **~ (together)** (be in harmony) «*plans, ideas, policies*» 相互协调; **to ~ with sth.** 与某事物吻合

mesh size *n* 网格尺寸

mesmeric /mezˈmerɪk/ *adj* 入迷的 ‹*effect, state*›; 迷人的 ‹*performance, charm*›

mesmerize /ˈmezməraɪz/ *vt* 迷惑 ‹*victim, prey*›

mesomorph /ˈmesəʊmɔːf/ *n* 中胚层体型者

meson /ˈmezɒn, ˈmiːzɒn/ *n* 介子

Mesozoic /ˌmesəʊˈzəʊɪk/
A *adj* (of the period) 中生代的; (of the rock system) 中生界的
B *n* **the ~** (period) 中生代; (rock system) 中生界

mess /mes/
A *n* **1** [c and u] (dirtiness) 脏乱; (untidy state) 混乱; (troublesome state) 困境; **what a ~!** 真乱! ; **to make a ~** 弄得一团糟; **to make a ~ of sth.** lit 把某物弄乱; fig 把某事物搞糟; **to be (in) a ~** 乱七八糟; **his marriage/life was (in) a ~** 他的婚姻/生活一团糟; **to leave sth. in a ~** 把某事物弄得乱七八糟; **to clear up a ~** 清理烂摊子; **to get into a ~ (with sb.)** (与某人的关系) 陷入困境; **to get sb. into a ~** 使某人陷入困境; **his face was a ~ after the accident** 他因为事故毁容了; **you look like a ~** 你看上去很邋遢 **2** [c] (untidy person) 没条理的人; (untidy thing) 乱七八糟的东西; (dirty person) 邋遢的人; (dirty thing) 肮脏的东西; (psychologically) 心理失常的人; **to make a ~ of oneself** 把自己弄得脏兮兮的; **to make a ~ of sth.** 把某物弄脏 **3** [c and u] (spill) 溢出物; (stain) 污渍; **to make a ~ on the tablecloth/carpet** 在台布/地毯上留下污渍; **the dog/cat made a ~ in the corner of the room** euph 狗/猫在房间的角落里拉屎了 **4** [c] Mil (eating place) 食堂; **the officers' ~** 军官食堂 **5** [c] + *v sing or pl* Mil (group) 集体用餐人员 **6** [c] Amer colloq (a lot) **a (whole) ~ of sth.** 大量某物; **I took a (whole) ~ of pictures and chose the best six** 我拍了很多照片, 然后从中选出了6张最好的
B *vt* **1** (make untidy) 把…弄乱; (make dirty) 把…弄脏 **2** euph (defecate in) 在…上排便 ‹*bed, pants*›
C *vi* **1** (potter) 瞎闹; **no ~ing** colloq 不要胡闹; **give me a straight answer, no ~ing** 直接答复我, 不要瞎扯; **to ~ with sth.** 摆弄某物 **2** (interfere, be involved) 打扰; **to ~ with sb.** 惹某人; **to ~ with drugs/firearms** 沾毒/摆弄枪支 **3** euph (defecate) 排便 **4** Mil (eat meals) 集体用膳; **to ~ with sb.** 与某人一起用餐; **to ~ together** 集体用餐

Phrasal verbs

• **mess about, mess around**
A *vi* **1** (act the fool) 胡闹; (waste time) 浪费时间 **2** (potter) **to ~ about in boats** 坐船四处游荡; **to ~ about with friends** 和朋友混在一起 **3** (interfere) 干预; **to ~ about with sth.** 摆弄某物 **to ~ about with sb.** colloq 勾搭某人
B *vt* **1** [**~ sb. about**] Brit colloq (treat badly) 粗鲁地对待 **2** [**~ sth. about**] (leave in a mess) 把…弄乱 ‹*papers, equipment*›

• **mess up**
A [**~ sth. up, ~ up sth.**] *vt*
1 (make untidy) 把…弄乱; (make dirty) 把…弄脏 **2** (spoil) 把…搞砸 ‹*work, chance, exam*›
B [**~ sb. up, ~ up sb.**] *vt*
1 (upset) 使烦恼; **losing his job has really ~ed him up** 失业着实让他苦恼 **2** Amer colloq (beat up) 殴打
C *vi* colloq 搞砸

message /ˈmesɪdʒ/ *n* **1** (communication) 信息; **to take** *or* **deliver a ~** 带个信; **to give/leave sb. a ~** 给某人带/留个信; **a ~ from sb. (for sb.)** 某人 (给某人) 的留言; **the ~ comes over loud and clear** 信息传达得清清楚楚 **2** (meaning) 寓意; **a film with a ~** 一部有寓意的影片; **to get one's ~ across** 把意思讲清楚; **to get the ~** colloq 明白要传达的意思 **3** (significant point) 要旨; **to spread/preach the ~** 传播/宣传这个观点

message box *n* 信息框

m

messaging /ˈmesɪdʒɪŋ/ n [u] 信息传送

messenger /ˈmesɪndʒə(r)/ n 1 (person carrying message) 送信人; **to act as ～ for sb.** 为某人送信 2 (in hotel, office) 收发员; **to dispatch a ～** 派一名收发员 3 (official) 信使

messenger RNA n [u] 信使核糖核酸

mess hall n 食堂

messiah /mɪˈsaɪə/ n 1 (in Judaism) 弥赛亚 [《圣经》预言的犹太民族拯救者] 2 (Jesus Christ) **the Messiah** 救世主基督 3 (leader, saviour) 救星

messianic /ˌmesɪˈænɪk/ adj 弥赛亚降临的 ‹*hopes, expectations, prophecies*›; 信奉救世主的 ‹*cult*›; 救世主的 ‹*mission, zeal*›; 救星似的 ‹*leader, figure*›

mess: ～ kit n 1 (uniform) 晚礼服; 2 (eating utensils) 野战餐具; **～mate** n 共餐伙伴; **～ room** n 食堂

Messrs /ˈmesəz/ npl **= Messieurs** 先生们

mess tin n Brit 军用饭盒

messy /ˈmesi/ adj 1 (untidy) 凌乱的 ‹*hair, room*›; 杂乱的 ‹*heap, pile*›; 邋遢的 ‹*person*› 2 (confused) 混乱的 ‹*situation, business*› 3 (complicated) 棘手的 ‹*job, lawsuit*›; 纠缠不清的 ‹*compromise, divorce*›

Met /met/ abbr colloq **the ～** 1 Brit ▸**Metropolitan Police** 2 Brit ▸**Meteorological Office** 3 Amer **= the Metropolitan Museum of Art** 大都会博物馆 4 Amer **= the Metropolitan Opera House** 大都会歌剧院

met /met/ pt, pp ▸**meet A, B**

metabolic /ˌmetəˈbɒlɪk/ adj 新陈代谢的

metabolically /ˌmetəˈbɒlɪkli/ adv 新陈代谢地

metabolism /məˈtæbəlɪzəm/ n 新陈代谢

metabolize /məˈtæbəlaɪz/ vt 使新陈代谢

metacarpal /ˌmetəˈkɑːpl/
A n 掌骨
B adj 掌骨的

metadata /ˈmetədeɪtə/ npl 元数据

metal /ˈmetl/
A n [c and u] 金属
B adj 金属制的
C vt (pres p etc. **-ll-** Brit, **-l-** Amer) 1 (cover with metal) 用金属包 ‹*plate, surface*› 2 (make, mend) 用碎石修筑 ‹*road*›

metal: ～ detector n 金属探测器; **～ fatigue** n [u] 金属疲劳

metallic /mɪˈtælɪk/ adj 1 (relating to metal) 金属的 ‹*property, substance*› 2 (resembling metal) 有金属光泽的 ‹*paint, appearance*›; 似金属撞击的 ‹*click, clunk*›; **～ taste** 有金属味

metallurgic /ˌmetəˈlɜːdʒɪk/, **metallurgical** /ˌmetəˈlɜːdʒɪkl/ adj 冶金的; **a ～ expert/company** 冶金专家/公司; **the ～ industry** 冶金业

metallurgist /məˈtælədʒɪst, Amer ˈmetəlɜːrdʒɪst/ ▸**p. 409** n 冶金学家

metallurgy /məˈtælədʒi, Amer ˈmetəlɜːrdʒi/ n [u] 冶金学

metal: ～ polish n [u] 金属抛光剂; **～work** n [u] 1 (craft) 金属加工; 2 (objects) 金属制品; **～worker** ▸**p. 409** n 金属加工工人; **～working** n [u] 金属加工工艺

metamorphic /ˌmetəˈmɔːfɪk/ adj 变质的

metamorphism /ˌmetəˈmɔːfɪzəm/ n [u] 变质作用

metamorphose /ˌmetəˈmɔːfəʊz/
A vi 1 Zool «*tadpole, grub, chrysalis*» 变形; **to ～ into sth.** 变成某物 2 (change) «*society, person, organization*» 发生变化; **to ～ into sth.** 成为某物 3 Geol «*rocks*» 变质
B vt 1 (transform) 使…变形 ‹*person, animal, house*›; **to ～ sb. into sth.** 将某人变成某物 2 Geol «*pressure, heat*» 使…变质 ‹*rock, mass*›

metamorphosis /ˌmetəˈmɔːfəsɪs/ n (pl **metamorphoses** /ˌmetəˈmɔːfəsiːz/) 1 [u] Zool 变态; **～ from sth. to sth.** 从某物到某物的蜕变 2 [c] (change) 质变; **a ～ from sth. into sth.** 从某物到某物的质变

metamorphous /ˌmetəˈmɔːfəs/ adj **= metamorphic**

metaphor /ˈmetəfɔː(r)/ n 1 [c] (figure of speech) 隐喻; **to mix one's ～s** 混用隐喻 2 [u] (use of figures of speech) 比喻说法 3 [c] (symbol) 象征; **a ～ for sth.** 某事物的象征; **a ～ for the competitive struggles** 生活中的激烈竞争的喻指

metaphoric /ˌmetəˈfɒrɪk/, **metaphorical** /ˌmetəˈfɒrɪkl/ adj 隐喻的 ‹*use, sense, representation*›; 含比喻的 ‹*phrase*›; **～ language/expressions** 比喻的语言/表达方式

metaphorically /ˌmetəˈfɒrɪkli/ adv 从比喻意义上; **speaking ～** 打个比方

metaphysical /ˌmetəˈfɪzɪkl/ adj 1 (relating to metaphysics) 形而上学的 ‹*theory, argument*› 2 (abstract) 抽象的 ‹*idea, theory*› 3 (supernatural) 超自然的 ‹*realm, being*› 4 Literat 玄学派诗歌的 ‹*period, imagery, notion*›; **～ poet/poetry** 玄学派诗人/诗歌

metaphysics /ˌmetəˈfɪzɪks/ npl + v sing 1 (branch of philosophy) 形而上学 2 (abstract theory or talk) 深奥莫测的推论

metastasis /meˈtæstəsɪs/ n 1 [c] (pl **metastases** /meˈtæstəsiːz/) (tumour) 转移瘤 2 [u] (development of tumours) 转移

metatarsal /ˌmetəˈtɑːsl/
A n 跖骨
B adj 跖骨的

mete /miːt/

Phrasal verb

• **mete out** vt [**～ sth. out, ～ out sth.**] 给予 ‹*punishment, reward*›; **the savage treatment ～d out by the occupying army** 占领军施加的暴行

meteor /ˈmiːtɪə(r)/
A n 流星
B modif 流星的 ‹*impact*›; **a ～ shower/crater** 流星雨/陨石坑

meteoric /ˌmiːtɪˈɒrɪk, Amer -ˈɔːr-/ adj 1 (relating to meteor) 流星的 ‹*impact*›; **～ dust** 流星尘 2 fig (rapid) 迅疾的 ‹*rise, progress, success*›

meteorite /ˈmiːtɪəraɪt/ n 陨石

meteoroid /ˈmiːtɪərɔɪd/ n 流星体

meteorological /ˌmiːtɪərəˈlɒdʒɪkl/ adj 气象的; **a ～ chart/forecast/station** 气象图/气象预报/气象站

meteorologically /ˌmiːtɪərəˈlɒdʒɪkli, Amer ˌmiːtɪɔːr-/ adv 在气象上

Meteorological Office n Brit **the ～** 国家气象局

meteorologist /ˌmiːtɪəˈrɒlədʒɪst/ ▸**p. 409** n 气象学家

meteorology /ˌmiːtɪəˈrɒlədʒi/ n [u] 1 (science) 气象学 2 (climate) 气象

meter /ˈmiːtə(r)/
A n 1 (measuring instrument) 表; **an electricity/a gas/water ～** 电表/煤气表/水表; **to read the ～** 抄表 2 (parking) **～** 停车场收费器; **to set the ～** 设置停车收费器 3 Amer **= metre**
B vt 用仪表计量

meter: ～ reader ▸**p. 409** n 抄表员; **～ reading** n 仪表读数

methadone /ˈmeθədəʊn/ n [u] 美沙酮

methane /ˈmiːθeɪn/ n [u] 甲烷

methanol /ˈmeθənɒl/ n [u] 甲醇

method /ˈmeθəd/ n 1 [c] (system, technique, manner) 方法; **a ～ for doing sth.** 做某事的方法 2 [c] (body of skills) 系列技能 3 [u] (orderliness, orderly processes) 条理; **there is ～ in his madness** 他癫狂的行为中有其道理

method: ～ acting n [u] 体验派表演; **～ actor** n 体验派演员

methodical /məˈθɒdɪkl/ adj 有条理的 ‹*approach, style, mind, arrangement*›; 做事有条不紊的 ‹*person*›

methodically /məˈθɒdɪkli/ adv 有条不紊地

Methodism /ˈmeθədɪzəm/ n [u] 循道宗教义

Methodist /ˈmeθədɪst/ n 循道宗信徒

methodological /ˌmeθədəˈlɒdʒɪkl/ adj 方法的 ‹*problem, flaw, weakness*›; 方法论的 ‹*study, analysis, issue*›

methodologically /ˌmeθədəˈlɒdʒɪkli/ adv 方法上

methodology /ˌmeθəˈdɒlədʒi/ n [从事某一活动的] 方法

meths /meθs/ npl + v sing Brit 甲基化酒精; **a ～ drinker** 喝甲基化酒精上瘾的人

methyl alcohol /ˌmeθɪl ˈælkəhɒl/ n [u] **= methanol**

methylated spirit /ˌmɛθəleɪtɪd ˈspɪrɪt/ n [u] **～(s)** + v sing 甲基化酒精

meticulous /mɪˈtɪkjʊləs/ adj 非常仔细的 ‹*observation*›; 非常注意细节的 ‹*methods*›; 周密的 ‹*arrangements*›; 一丝不苟的 ‹*worker*›; **to be ～ about sth.** 对某事一丝不苟

meticulously /mɪˈtɪkjʊləsli/ adv 周密地 ‹*arrange, plan*›; 非常仔细地 ‹*fold, stack*›

meticulousness /mɪˈtɪkjʊləsnɪs/ n [u] 注重细节

métier /ˈmetɪeɪ/ n 1 (profession, trade) 职业 2 (field of expertise) 专长 3 (characteristic) 特点

Met Office pr n Brit **the ～ = Meteorological Office**

metonymy /məˈtɒnɪmi/ n [u] 转喻

metre /ˈmiːtə(r)/ ▸**p. 436** n 1 (unit of length) 米 2 (in poetry) 格律 3 (in music) 节拍

metric /ˈmetrɪk/ adj 公制的 ‹*measurement, scale, units*›; 用公制计量的 ‹*dimensions, container*›; **the ～ system** 公制; **to go ～** colloq 实行公制

metrical /ˈmetrɪkl/ adj 格律的

metricate /ˈmetrɪkeɪt/ vt 将…改为公制

metrication /ˌmetrɪˈkeɪʃn/ n (adoption) 采用公制; (conversion) 转换为公制

metric ton n 公吨

metro /ˈmetrəʊ/ n [尤指巴黎的] 地铁

metrology /mɪˈtrɒlədʒi/ n [u] 度量衡学

metronome /ˈmetrənəʊm/ n 节拍器

metropolis /məˈtrɒpəlɪs/ n 1 (capital) 首都; (chief city) 大城市 2 (centre of commercial and industrial activity) 中心

metropolitan /ˌmetrəˈpɒlɪtən/
A adj 1 (of city) (within administration) 大都市的 ‹*buildings, amusements, museum, population*›; **～ New York** 大都会纽约 2 (of home territory) 本土的; **～ France** 法国本土
B n 大都市人

metropolitan: ～ authority n Brit 都市管理局; **M～ Police** n Brit **the M～ Police** 伦敦警察局

metrosexual /ˌmetrəʊˈsekʃʊəl/ n 都市丽男

mettle /ˈmetl/ n [u] 奋斗精神; **to be on one's ～** 奋发起来; **to put sb. on his ～** 激励某人尽最大努力; **to show/prove one's ～** 显示/证明奋斗精神

mew /mjuː/
A vi 喵喵叫
B n 喵 [猫叫声或类似猫叫的声音]

mews /mjuːz/ npl Brit 1 + v sing (street) 马厩街 2 + v pl (stables) [小巷两侧或庭院四周的] 马厩; **a ～ house** 马厩改建的漂亮房子

Mexican /ˈmeksɪkən/ ▸**p. 503**
A adj (of Mexico) 墨西哥的; (of the people) 墨西哥人的
B n 墨西哥人

Mexican wave *n* 墨西哥人浪; **to do a ～** 形成墨西哥人浪

Mexico /'meksɪkəʊ/ *pr n* 墨西哥

Mexico City *pr n* 墨西哥城

mezzanine /'mezəniːn/ *n* **1** (storey) 夹楼层; **a ～ floor** 夹楼层 **2** Amer (lowest balcony) 底层楼厅; (front rows of lowest balcony) 底层楼厅前座 **3** Brit (room beneath stage) 舞台下的房间; (floor beneath stage) 舞台下的楼层

mezzo /'metsəʊ/, **mezzo-soprano** *ns* **1** (voice) 女中音; **～ voice** 女中音 **2** (singer) 女中音歌手

MF *abbr* **= medium frequency** 中频

mg *abbr* **= milligram(s)** 毫克

MHz *abbr* **= megahertz**

MI *abbr* Amer **= Michigan**

mi /miː/ *n* **= me²**

MI5 *abbr* Brit **= Military Intelligence Section Five** 军情五处

MI6 *abbr* Brit **= Military Intelligence Section Six** 军情六处

MIA *abbr* **= missing in action**

miaow /mɪ'aʊ/
A *vi* 喵喵叫
B *n* 喵 [猫叫声或类似猫叫的声音]

miasma /mɪ'æzmə/ *n* liter 瘴气

mica /'maɪkə/ *n* [u] 云母

mice /maɪs/ *pl* ▸**mouse**

Michaelmas /'mɪklməs/ *pr n* 米迦勒节 [基督教节日, 每年9月29日]

Michaelmas daisy *n* Brit 紫菀

Michigan /'mɪʃɪgən/ *pr n* 密歇根州

mickey /'mɪki/ *n* Brit colloq **to take the ～ (out of sb.)** 戏弄（某人）

Mickey Mouse
A *pr n* 米老鼠
B *modif* colloq 差劲的 ‹*job, firm*›; **a set of ～ tools** 一套蹩脚的工具

micro /'maɪkrəʊ/ *n* **1** **= microcomputer** **2** **= microprocessor**

micro- *combining form* 微小的

microanalysis /,maɪkrəʊə'nælɪsɪs/ *n* (*pl* **microanalyses** /,maɪkrəʊə'nælɪsiːz/) 微量分析

microbe /'maɪkrəʊb/ *n* 微生物

microbial /maɪ'krəʊbɪəl/ *adj* 微生物的 ‹*population, action*›; 细菌引起的 ‹*infection*›

microbiological /,maɪkrəʊbaɪəʊ'lɒdʒɪkəl/ *adj* 微生物学的

microbiologist /,maɪkrəʊbaɪ'ɒlədʒɪst/ ▸**p. 409** *n* 微生物学家

microbiology /,maɪkrəʊbaɪ'ɒlədʒi/ *n* [u] 微生物学

microblog /'maɪkrəʊblɒg/ *n* 微型博客

microblogging /'maɪkrəʊ,blɒgɪŋ/ *n* [u] 微博维护

microbrewery /'maɪkrəʊbruːəri/ *n* 微酿啤酒作坊

microchip /'maɪkrəʊtʃɪp/ *n* 微芯片

microcircuit /'maɪkrəʊsɜːkɪt/ *n* 微型电路

microcircuitry /,maɪkrəʊ'sɜːkɪtri/ *n* [u] 微型电路系统

microclimate /'maɪkrəʊklaɪmɪt/ *n* [局部地区的] 小气候

microcomputer /,maɪkrəʊkəm'pjuːtə(r)/ *n* 微型计算机

microcomputing /,maɪkrəʊkəm'pjuːtɪŋ/ *n* [u] 微型计算机使用

microcopy /'maɪkrəʊkɒpi/
A *n* 微缩复制品
B *vt* 将…复制成微缩本

microcosm /'maɪkrəkɒzəm/ *n* 缩影; **in ～** 以缩微形式

microcredit /'maɪkrəʊ,kredɪt/ *n* [u] 低息小额贷款

microdot /'maɪkrəʊdɒt/ *n* **1** Phot 微点照片 **2** (LSD tablet) 微型迷幻药

microeconomic /,maɪkrəʊ,ekə'nɒmɪk, -,iːkə'n-/ *adj* 微观经济学的

microeconomics /,maɪkrəʊ,ekə'nɒmɪks, -,iːkə'n-/ *npl + v sing* 微观经济学

microelectronic /,maɪkrəʊɪlek'trɒnɪk/ *adj* 微电子学的

microelectronics /,maɪkrəʊɪlek'trɒnɪks/ *npl* **1** + *v sing* (design, manufacture, use) 微电子学 **2** + *v pl* (devices, circuitry) 微电子设备

microenvironment /,maɪkrəʊɪn'vaɪərənmənt/ *n* 微环境

microfauna /'maɪkrəʊfɔːnə/ *npl* 微动物群

microfibre /'maɪkrəʊfaɪbə(r)/ *n* 超细纤维

microfiche /'maɪkrəʊfiːʃ/ *n* 缩微胶片

microfiche reader *n* 缩微胶片阅读器

microfilm /'maɪkrəʊfɪlm/
A *n* [u] 缩微胶卷
B *vt* 用缩微胶卷拍摄

microfilm reader *n* 缩微胶卷阅读器

microflora /'maɪkrəʊflɔːrə/ *npl* 微生物群

microgram, Brit also **microgramme** /'maɪkrəʊgræm/ ▸**p. 909** *n* 微克

micrograph /'maɪkrəʊgrɑːf, Amer -græf/ *n* 显微照片

micrography /maɪ'krɒgrəfi/ *n* [u] **1** (description, study) 微写术 **2** (technique) 显微镜使用术

microgravity /,maɪkrəʊ'grævəti/ *n* [u] 微重力

microhabitat /,maɪkrəʊ'hæbɪtæt/ *n* 微环境

microinjection /'maɪkrəʊɪn,dʒekʃn/ *n* [u] 显微注射

microlight /'maɪkrəʊlaɪt/ *n* 微型飞机

microlighting /'maɪkrəlaɪtɪŋ/ ▸**p. 307** *n* [u] 乘坐微型飞机

microlitre /'maɪkrəʊliːtə(r)/ *n* 微升

micromanage /'maɪkrəʊ,mænɪdʒ/ *vt* 微观管理

micromesh /'maɪkrəʊmeʃ/ *adj* 微网眼料子

micrometeorite /,maɪkrəʊ'miːtɪəraɪt/ *n* 微陨星

micrometeoroid /,maɪkrəʊ'miːtɪərɔɪd/ *n* 微流星体

micrometre Brit, **micrometer** Amer /maɪ'krɒmɪtə(r)/ *n* 测微计

microminiature /,maɪkrəʊ'mɪnətʃə(r), Amer -tʃʊər/ *adj* 微型的

microminiaturization /,maɪkrəʊ,mɪnɪtʃəraɪ'zeɪʃn, Amer -tʃʊərɪ'z-/ *n* [u] 微型化

microminiaturize /,maɪkrəʊ'mɪnɪtʃəraɪz, Amer -tʃʊər-/ *vt* 使微型化

micron /'maɪkrɒn/ *n* 微米

Micronesia /,maɪkrəʊ'niːzɪə/ *pr n* 密克罗尼西亚

Micronesian /,maɪkrəʊ'niːzɪən/
A *adj* (of Micronesia) 密克罗尼西亚的; (of the people) 密克罗尼西亚人的; (of the languages) 密克罗尼西亚语的
B *n* **1** [c] (person) 密克罗尼西亚人 **2** [u] (languages) 密克罗尼西亚语

microorganism /,maɪkrəʊ'ɔːgənɪzəm/ *n* 微生物

microphone /'maɪkrəfəʊn/ *n* 麦克风; **to sing/speak into the ～** 对着话筒唱/讲话

microphotograph /,maɪkrəʊ'fəʊtəgrɑːf, Amer -græf/
A *n* 微型照片
B *vt* 将…摄成微型照片

microphotography /,maɪkrəʊfə'tɒgrəfi/ *n* [u] (art) 微型照相术; (process) 微型照相

microphysical /,maɪkrəʊ'fɪzɪkl/ *adj* 微观物理学的

microphysicist /,maɪkrəʊ'fɪzɪsɪst/ *n* 微观物理学家

microphysics /'maɪkrəʊfɪzɪks/ *npl + v sing* 微观物理学

microprocessing /,maɪkrəʊ'prəʊsesɪŋ/ *n* [u] 微处理

microprocessor /'maɪkrəʊprəʊsesə(r)/ *n* 微处理器

microprogram /'maɪkrəʊprəʊgræm/ *n* 微程序

microprogramming, microprograming /,maɪkrəʊ'prəʊgræmɪŋ/ *n* [u] 微程序设计

microscope /'maɪkrəskəʊp/ *n* 显微镜; **under the ～** 在显微镜下; fig 经受缜密检查

microscopic /,maɪkrə'skɒpɪk/ *adj* **1** (minute) 微小的; **a ～ organism/particle** 微生物/微粒 **2** colloq (extremely small) 极细小的 ‹*writing, section*› **3** (using a microscope) 用显微镜进行的 ‹*examination, test, analysis*›

microscopical /,maɪkrə'skɒpɪkl/ *adj* **= microscopic 3**

microscopically /,maɪkrə'skɒpɪkli/ *adv* **1** (minutely) 极细小地; **～ small/fine** 极小的/极精细的 **2** (with attention to detail) 极仔细地 ‹*examine, investigate*› **3** (using microscope) 用显微镜 ‹*test, view*›

microscopic section *n* 显微镜切片

microscopy /maɪ'krɒskəpi/ *n* [u] 显微镜观察

microsecond /'maɪkrəʊsekənd/ *n* 微秒

microsite /'maɪkrəʊsaɪt/ *n* **1** Ecol 微环境 **2** Comput 微型网站

microstructural /,maɪkrəʊ'strʌktʃərəl/ *adj* 微观结构的

microstructure /'maɪkrəʊstrʌktʃə(r)/ *n* 微观结构

microsurgery /'maɪkrəʊsɜːdʒəri/ *n* [u] 显微外科手术; **to carry out** *or* **perform ～ on sb.** 为某人施行显微外科手术

microsurgical /,maɪkrəʊ'sɜːdʒɪkl/ *adj* 显微外科的 ‹*expert, operation*›; 显微外科手术的 ‹*equipment, techniques, procedure*›

microtechnique /'maɪkrəʊtekniːk/ *n* 显微技术

microtechnology /'maɪkrəʊteknɒlədʒi/ *n* [u] 微电子技术

microtransmitter /'maɪkrəʊtrænsmɪtə(r)/ *n* 微型发射机

microvolt /'maɪkrəʊvəʊlt/ *n* 微伏

microwatt /'maɪkrəʊwɒt/ *n* 微瓦

microwave /'maɪkrəweɪv/ *n* **1** Phys 微波; **～ generator** 微波发生器 **2** **= microwave oven**

microwaveable /'maɪkrəweɪvəbl/ *adj* 可用微波炉烹调的 ‹*food, meal, dish*›

microwave oven *n* 微波炉

micturate /'mɪktjʊəreɪt/ *vi* formal 排尿

micturition /,mɪktjʊə'rɪʃn/ *n* [u] formal 排尿

mid- /mɪd/ *combining form* 中间 ‹*career, summer*›; 中部 ‹*reign, ocean*›; **in the ～1990's/20th century** 在20世纪90年代中期/在20世纪中叶; **～afternoon** 半下午; **in ～sentence/May** 在句子中间/5月中旬; **in one's ～forties** 在四十五六岁

mid-air /mɪ'deə(r)/
A *adj* 半空中的 ‹*collision, explosion*›; **some planes are capable of ～ refuelling** 有些飞机能在空中加油
B *adv* 在半空中 ‹*collide, refuel, hover*›
C *n* [u] 半空中; **in ～** 在半空中

Midas /'maɪdəs/ *pr n* 迈达斯 [弗里吉亚国王, 被赋予点石成金的法力]; **to have the ～ touch** 有赚大钱的本领

mid-Atlantic *adj* 大西洋中部的

midday /,mɪd'deɪ/ ▸**p. 831** *n* **1** (noon) 正午 **2** (around noon) 中午; **a ～ break** 午休

middle /'mɪdl/
A *n* **1** (centre) 中间; **in the ～ of the room/**

front page 在屋子的中间/在头版的正中; the ~ of a city/region 城市/地区的中心; the ~ of May 5月中旬; in the ~ of the night 在半夜时分; in the ~ of the nineteenth century 在19世纪中叶; not cooked in the ~ 没有熟透; in the ~ of the class 位居班级的中游; to be caught in the ~ of sth. 被卡在某物中间; fig 被卷入某事中; to be in the ~ of sth./doing sth. 正忙于某事/做某事; to be in the ~ of a crisis 正处于危机中; in the ~ of nowhere colloq 在偏远的地方; to split sth. down the ~ 从中间切开 ‹object›; fig 平分 ‹bill, sum of money›; 分担 ‹work›; to split the party down the ~ «issue, policy» 使政党分裂为两派; to knock sb. into the ~ of next week colloq 把某人打得不省人事 2▸ colloq (waist) 腰部; to grab sb. round the ~ 拦腰抱住某人; we were up to our ~s in water 我们站在齐腰深的水中

B adj attrib 1▸ (central) 中间的 ‹part, road›; to stare into ~ space 凝视半空; ~ and eastern Europe 中东欧; to be in one's ~ fifties 在55岁左右; a ~ child 排行居中的孩子; a ~ way between two extremes 折中的办法; to steer or take a ~ course 取中庸之道 2▸ (average) 中等的 ‹price, size, quality›

middle: ~ age ▸p. 15 n 中年; in early/late ~ age 刚到中年/接近老年; to reach ~ age 人到中年; **~-aged** /-'eɪdʒd/ ▸p. 15 adj 中年的 ‹person›; 具有中年人特点的 ‹outlook, views›; ~-aged spread 中年发福; **M~ Ages** npl the M~ Ages 中世纪; the early/late M~ Ages 中世纪早期/晚期; **M~ America** n 1▸ (Midwest of the US) 美国中西部; 2▸ (region of southern North America) 中部美洲; 3▸ (social group) 美国中产阶级

Middle America

1. 美国中产阶级。自认为是美国社会中"沉默的大多数"(silent majority),成员称Middle American。价值观念传统,政治上偏保守,多住在美国中西部地区。

2. 中部美洲。Middle America 比 Central America的范围要大。汉语中的中美洲通常指Central America,即位于墨西哥以南和哥伦比亚以北的狭长陆地,包括伯利兹、危地马拉、萨尔瓦多、洪都拉斯、尼加拉瓜、哥斯达黎加和巴拿马7个国家。汉语中广义的中部美洲除Central America外还包括墨西哥,有时还包括西印度群岛(the West Indies)。

middlebrow /'mɪdlbraʊ/
A adj 品位一般的 ‹book, drama, film, audience›; 平庸的 ‹writer, culture›
B n 品位一般的人

middle C n 中央C音

middle class
A n + v sing or pl 中产阶级
B middle-class adj 中产阶级的

middle: ~ distance n the ~ distance 中景; in the ~ distance 在不远处; 中距离的; a ~-distance runner 中距离赛跑选手; **~ ear** n the ~ ear 中耳; **M~ East** pr n the M~ East 中东; **~-eastern** adj 中东地区的; **M~ England** n 英国中产阶级; **M~ English** n [u] 中古英语 [约公元1150-1470年间的英语]; **~ finger** ▸p. 71 n 中指; to give sb. the ~ finger 朝某人竖起中指 [表示愤怒或挑衅]; **~ ground** n 中间立场; **~-income** adj 中等收入的 ‹family, earner›; **~man** /-mæn/ n 1▸ Comm 中间商; to cut out the ~man 绕过中间商; 2▸ (go-between) 中间人; **~ management** n [u] 中层管理人员; **~ manager** n 中层经理; **~ name** n 中名; trouble/reliability is his ~ name 他的最大特点就是爱惹事/值得信赖; **~-of-the-road** adj 1▸ (moderate) 中立的 ‹views›; 走温和路线的 ‹party, politician›; 2▸ (tuneful but bland) 大众化的 ‹music, band, singer›; **~-of-the-roader** n Amer 持中立观点的人; **~-ranking** adj 中层的; **~ school** n 1▸ Brit [为9到13岁儿童所设的] 中间学校; 2▸ Amer 初中 [相当于6到9年级]; **~-size, ~-sized** adj 中等大小的 ‹city, hotel, nation›; 中等身材的 ‹person›; 中等规模的 ‹school, business›; **~ware** n [u] 中间件; **~ way** n 折中政策; to find the ~ way 找到折中方法; **~weight** n 1▸ [u] (boxing) 中量级; the ~weight champion 中量级拳击冠军; 2▸ [c] (competitor) 中量级拳击选手; **M~ West** n = Midwest

Middle England

英国中产阶级,尤指英格兰南部的中产阶级。政治上偏于保守,社会道德观念更趋传统。不要把 Middle England 和 the Midlands 混淆,the Midlands 是地理概念,指英格兰中部地区。

Middlesex /'mɪdlseks/ pr n Hist 米德尔塞克斯郡

middling /'mɪdlɪŋ/
A adj 中等的; a golfer of ~ talent 能力一般的高尔夫球选手; a ~ chance of success 一半的成功机会; how are you feeling? — (fair to) ~ 你感觉如何? ——还算过得去吧
B adv colloq 中间程度地; ~ good/rich 还算好/富有

midfield /ˌmɪd'fiːld/ n 1▸ (area) 中场; ~ player/area 中场队员/中场; in ~ 在中场; to play ~ 踢中场 2▸ (players) 中场队员

midfielder /ˌmɪd'fiːldə(r)/ n 中场队员

mid-flight adj 飞行中途的

midge /mɪdʒ/ n 蠓

midget /'mɪdʒɪt/
A n 1▸ offensive (dwarf) 侏儒 2▸ colloq (small person) 矮子
B adj attrib 极小的

Midland /'mɪdlənd/
A Midlands pr n + v sing the M~s 英格兰中部地区
B modif 中部的; the ~ region/dialect/accent/economy 英格兰中部地区/方言/口音/经济

midland /'mɪdlənd/ adj attrib 中部的; a ~ region/dialect/accent 中部地区/方言/口音

midlife /'mɪdlaɪf/ n 中年; in ~ 在中年; ~ years/problems 中年时期/问题

midlife crisis n 中年危机

mid-morning n 半上午

midnight /'mɪdnaɪt/ ▸p. 831
A n 午夜; at ~ 在午夜; it's past ~ 午夜已过
B modif 午夜的; to burn the ~ oil 开夜车

midnight: ~ feast n 夜宵; **~ Mass** n 午夜弥撒; **~ sun** n the ~ sun [南北极地区夏季见到的] 子夜太阳

midpoint /'mɪdpɔɪnt/ n 中点

mid-price modif 中等价格的

mid-range modif 中档的 ‹hotel, camera›

midriff /'mɪdrɪf/ n 腹部

mid-season adv 季节中期; in ~ 在季节中期

midshipman /'mɪdʃɪpmən/ n (pl midshipmen) 1▸ Brit (officer) 海军军官候补生 2▸ Amer (trainee) 海军学校学员

midships /'mɪdʃɪps/ adv = amidships

midst /mɪdst/ n 中间; in our ~ 在我们当中; in the ~ of change/war 处于变化/战争中

midstream /ˌmɪd'striːm/ n 1▸ (in river) 中流; in ~ 处于中流 2▸ (part-way through) 中途; in ~ 在中途; to change or swap horses in ~ 中途改变计划

midsummer /ˌmɪd'sʌmə(r)/ n 1▸ (high summer) 仲夏; ~ sun 仲夏的太阳 2▸ (solstice) = summer solstice

Midsummer Day, Midsummer's Day n 施洗约翰节 [6月24日]

midsummer madness n [u] 愚蠢至极的行为

midterm /ˌmɪd'tɜːm/ n 1▸ (in school) 期中; ~ exams 期中考试 2▸ (in office) 中期; ~ elections 中期选举; to resign in ~ 在任职中期辞职

mid-terrace
A n 位于中间的连排房屋
B adj 连排房屋中间的

midtown /'mɪdtaʊn/ n Amer 市中心区

midway /ˌmɪd'weɪ/
A adj 中途的 ‹stop›; 中间的 ‹position, point, mark›
B adv 在中途 ‹lie, stop›; 在中间 ‹start, position›; ~ between/along ... 在/沿…的中间; ~ through sth. 某事过半; ~ up or down sth. 沿某物行进的途中

midweek /ˌmɪd'wiːk/
A n 周中; in ~ 在周中; ~ travel/break 周中旅行/休息
B adv 在周中

Midwest /ˌmɪd'west/ pr n Amer the ~ 中西部

Midwestern /ˌmɪd'westən/ adj Amer 中西部的

Midwesterner /ˌmɪd'westənə(r)/ n Amer 中西部人

midwife /'mɪdwaɪf/ ▸p. 409 n (pl midwives /'mɪdwaɪvs/) 助产士

midwifery /'mɪdwɪfəri, Amer -waɪf-/ n [u] 助产; to study ~ 学习接生

midwinter /ˌmɪd'wɪntə(r)/ n 1▸ (middle of winter) 仲冬; ~ snow 仲冬的雪; in ~ 在仲冬 2▸ (solstice) = winter solstice

mien /miːn/ n formal 风度; a cheerful/gentle ~ 高高兴兴的样子/温文尔雅的风度

miffed /mɪft/ adj colloq 有些生气的; to be/get ~ (about or over sth.) (因某事)有点生气

might¹ /maɪt/ modal aux (negative ~ not or colloq mightn't) 1▸ pt ▸may¹ 2▸ (in sequence of tenses, in reported speech, indicating possibility or unrealized possibility) 可能; I said I ~ go to town 我说过我可能去城里; I thought it ~ rain 我以为会下雨; we ~ be misjudging his motives 我们也许错误地判断了他的动机; you ~ find that ... 你也许会发现…; however unlikely that ~ be 不管那是多么的不可能; I ~ well lose my job 我多半会失业; as you ~ imagine 正如你能想象到的; he looked ashamed, as well he ~ 他显得很羞愧,这也不出所料; whatever the problem ~ be 不管是什么样的问题; ~ not his friends know where he is? Brit 他的朋友会不会知道他在哪里?; I ~ have been killed 我差点送了命; if I had been there, it mightn't have happened 如果我在那儿,这件事也许不会发生 3▸ (asking for permission or information) 可以; ~ I make a suggestion? 我可以提个建议吗?; ~ I ask who's calling? (on telephone) 请问是哪位?; and who, ~ I ask, are you?, and who ~ you be? formal 那么请问你是哪位?; I should like to invite them, if I ~ 如果可以的话,我想邀请他们; how long ~ it take to mend the puncture? 修补这个破洞要花多长时间呢? 4▸ (making suggestions, expressing reproach or irritation) 应该; it ~ be a good idea to leave early 早点离开也许是个好主意; you ~ try making some more enquiries 你不妨试着多打听打听; they ~ do well to consult an expert 他们最好找专家咨询; we ~ as well not have come 我们本不该来的; I ~ as well tell you now 我现在只好告诉你啦; he ~ at least apologize 他至少应该道歉; you ~ try helping iron 你可以试着帮个忙啊; they ~ have consulted us first 他们可以先问问我们嘛 5▸ (making statement or argument in concessive constructions) 也许; one ~ argue or it ~ be argued that ... 我们也许会认为…; he ~ be brilliant, but he lacks common sense 他也许很聪明,可是他缺乏常识 6▸ liter (indicating purpose) 以便; he died that others ~ live 他死了从而别的人能活下来

[7] liter (in wishes) 但愿; **let us pray, that our voices ～ be heard** 让我们祈祷吧，愿我们的声音得到垂听

might² *n* [u] [1] (great power) 威力; **military ～** 武装力量; **～ is right** 强权就是公理 [2] (personal strength) 力气; **with all one's ～** 竭尽全力; **with ～ and main** 用尽全力; **our combined ～ was not sufficient to shift the boulder** 我们齐心协力也搬不动这块巨石

mightily /ˈmaɪtɪli/ *adv* [1] colloq (greatly) 非常 ‹*rejoice, depressed, cheerful*› [2] (vigorously) 强有力地 ‹*push, hit*›; 极力地 ‹*oppose*›

mightn't /ˈmaɪtnt/ colloq = **might not** ▸**might¹**

might've /ˈmaɪtəv/ colloq = **might have** ▸**might¹**

mighty /ˈmaɪti/

[A] *adj* [1] (powerful) 强大的 ‹*nation, ruler, army*›; **high and ～** 盛气凌人的; **the pen is mightier than the sword** Prov 笔比剑更锋利 [2] (vast) 巨大的 ‹*mountain, ship*›; 浩瀚的 ‹*ocean*›; **from little acorns ～ oak trees grow** Prov 参天大树，生于毫末 [3] (performed with strength) 强有力的 ‹*thrust, swing*›; **a ～ punch/rage** 狠狠的一拳/极为愤怒 [4] colloq (huge, terrific) 极大的; **a ～ blow against racism** 对种族主义的一次重创

[B] *npl* **the ～** 强有力的人

[C] *adv* Amer colloq 非常

migraine /ˈmiːɡreɪn, Amer ˈmaɪ-/ ▸**p. 377** *n* [c and u] 偏头痛; **to get a ～** 患偏头痛; **to give sb. (a) ～** 令某人偏头疼

migraine: ～ attack *n* 偏头痛发作; **～ sufferer** *n* 偏头痛患者

migrant /ˈmaɪɡrənt/

[A] *n* [1] (person) 移民 [2] (bird) 候鸟; (animal) 迁徙动物; (fish) 洄游鱼类

[B] *adj* [1] (seasonal) 流动的 ‹*worker, tribe*›; (foreign) 移民的 ‹*worker, labour*› [2] Zool 迁徙的; **～ birds/animals/fish** 候鸟/迁徙动物/洄游鱼类

migrate /maɪˈɡreɪt, Amer ˈmaɪɡreɪt/

[A] *vi* [1] (of people) 移居; **to ～ to a country/city** 移居到一个国家/城市 [2] Zool «*bird, animal*» 迁徙; «*fish*» 洄游 [3] Comput 转移

[B] *vt* 将…转移到另一计算机系统 ‹*programs, hardware*›

migration /maɪˈɡreɪʃn/ *n* [c and u] [1] (of people) 移居 [2] (of birds, animals) 迁徙; (of fish) 洄游 [3] Comput 转移

migratory /ˈmaɪɡrətri, maɪˈɡreɪtəri, Amer ˈmaɪɡrətɔːri/ *adj* 迁徙的 ‹*route*›; 洄游的 ‹*journey*›; **～ birds/animals/fish/species** 候鸟/迁徙动物/洄游鱼类/洄游物种

mike /maɪk/ colloq

[A] *n* 麦克风

[B] *vt* 给…配麦克风

mild /maɪld/

[A] *adj* [1] (gentle) 温和的 ‹*person, temper, voice*› [2] (not cold) 暖和的 ‹*climate, zone, winter*›; **a ～ spell** 一段暖和的日子 [3] (moderate) 不严厉的 ‹*rebuke, reproach, punishment*› [4] (in taste, flavour) 味淡的 ‹*sauce, cigar, cheese*› [5] (gentle in action) 不刺激的 ‹*soap, detergent, medicine*› [6] (not serious) 不严重的 ‹*disease, symptoms, case*› [7] (slight) 轻微的 ‹*astonishment, protest, reaction*›

[B] *n* [u and c] **～ (ale)** Brit 淡味啤酒

mildew /ˈmɪldjuː, Amer -duː/

[A] *n* [u] [1] (mould) 霉菌 [2] (disease) 霉病

[B] *vi* 长霉

mildewed /ˈmɪldjuːd, Amer -duːd/ *adj* 发霉的

mildly /ˈmaɪldli/ *adv* [1] (gently) 和善地 ‹*speak, reply, rebuke*›; **to put it ～** 婉转地说 [2] (moderately) 不严重地 ‹*bleed, suffer*›; **～ ill/overweight** 身体略有不适/略微偏重 [3] (slightly) 微微地 ‹*laugh*›; 温和地 ‹*protest*›; **～ amusing/annoying** 有点有趣的/烦人的; **～ acidic/spiced** 略有些酸的/稍加了香料的

mild-mannered *adj* 温和的

mildness /ˈmaɪldnɪs/ *n* [u] [1] (of person, temper, voice) 温和 [2] (of weather, climate) 暖和 [3] (of taste, flavour) 淡味 [4] (of sauce, cigar, cheese) 无刺激性 [5] (of punishment, reproach, treatment) 宽大 [6] (of disease, illness) 轻微 [7] (of reaction, protest) 不激烈

mild steel *n* [u] 软钢

mile /maɪl/ ▸**p. 436**

[A] *n* [1] (unit of measurement) 英里; **a 10-～ journey** 10英里的旅程; **a miss is as good as a ～** 毫末之错仍为错; **give sb. an inch and they will take a ～** 某人得寸进尺 [2] (considerable distance) 很长距离; **～s from anywhere** 处于偏僻之地; **not a million ～s from here/the truth** 离这儿/真相不远; **to see/recognize sth. a ～ off** 一眼就能看见/认出某物; **to stick** *or* **stand out a ～** 显而易见; **to go the extra ～** 加倍努力; **to be ～s away** 出神; **sorry, I was ～s away** 抱歉，我刚才走神了; **to talk a ～ a minute** colloq 滔滔不绝地说话 [3] (race) **the ～** 一英里赛跑

[B] **miles** *npl* colloq 在很大程度上; **～s better** 好得多; **to be ～s out** 相去甚远

mileage /ˈmaɪlɪdʒ/ *n* [1] [c] (distance) 英里里程 [2] [c] (total travelled by car) 英里数; **to have a low/high ～** 行车里程低/高; **to do a ～ of ...** 开…英里数 [3] [u] (use) 用处; **to get some ～ out of sth.** 从某事中捞到好处; **to have plenty of ～ out of sth.** 充分利用某物 [4] [c] = **mileage allowance** [5] [u] fig (potential) 潜力; **there is plenty of ～ in this idea** 这个想法大有潜力

mileage allowance *n* 里程补贴

mileometer /maɪˈlɒmɪtə(r)/ *n* Brit = **milometer**

milepost /ˈmaɪlpəʊst/ *n* 里程标

milestone /ˈmaɪlstəʊn/ *n* [1] (marker) 里程碑 [2] fig (significant event) 转折点; **to be a ～ in sb.'s life** 是某人一生中的一个转折点

milieu /ˈmiːljɜː, Amer ˌmiːˈljɜː/ *n* (*pl* **milieux** *or* **～s** /ˈmiːljɜːz, Amer ˌmiːˈljɜːz/) formal 社会环境

militant /ˈmɪlɪtənt/

[A] *adj* [1] (aggressive) 好斗的 ‹*feminist, mood, group, faction*›; 激进的 ‹*supporter, method, attitude*› [2] (fighting, warring) 好战的 ‹*tribes, generals*›; 交战的 ‹*countries, nations*›; **the ～ states** 交战国

[B] *n* [1] (activist) 激进分子 [2] (fighter) 好战分子

militarism /ˈmɪlɪtərɪzəm/ *n* [u] 军国主义

militarist /ˈmɪlɪtərɪst/

[A] *n* 军国主义者

[B] *adj* 军国主义的

militaristic /ˌmɪlɪtəˈrɪstɪk/ *adj* 军国主义的

militarize /ˈmɪlɪtəraɪz/ *vt* [1] (equip with military forces) 向…派遣武装力量 ‹*region, frontier*› [2] (adapt for military use) 将…改为军用 ‹*region, area*› [3] (give military character to) 使…军事化 ‹*place, town*›

militarized zone *n* 军事区

military /ˈmɪlɪtri, Amer -teri/

[A] *adj* 军事的 ‹*training, dictatorship, coup*›; 军用的 ‹*equipment, barracks*›; **～ manoeuvres/insurrection** 军事演习/武装起义; **with ～ precision** 如军人般一丝不苟地; **to do ～ service** 服兵役

[B] *n* **the ～** [1] + *v sing* (armed forces) 军队 [2] + *v pl* (soldiers, sailors, etc.) 军人

military: ～ academy *n* 军事学院; **～ attaché** *n* 武官; **～ band** *n* 军乐队; **～ cross** *n* 军功十字勋章; **～ honours** *npl* 军葬礼; **～-industrial complex** *n* 军工联合体; **～ junta** *n* 军政府; **～ law** *n* [u] 军法; **～ police** *n* + *v pl* 宪兵队; **～ policeman** /-mən/ ▸**p. 409** *n* 宪兵; **～ service** *n* 兵役

militate /ˈmɪlɪteɪt/ *vi* 产生影响; **to ～ against sb./sth.** 对某人/某事物产生不利影响

militia /mɪˈlɪʃə/ *n* [1] (citizen army) 民兵组织; **to call out the ～** 出动民兵 [2] Amer (citizens liable for draft) 可征召的所有男性公民

militiaman /mɪˈlɪʃəmən/ *n* (*pl* **militiamen**) 民兵

milk /mɪlk/

[A] *n* [1] [u] (gen) 奶; **a glass of ～** 一杯牛奶; **to produce ～** 泌乳; **to be in ～** «*animal*» 在授乳期; **a land flowing with ～ and honey** 富饶之地; **the ～ of human kindness** 人的善良天性; **to be like ～ and water** 平淡无味; **it's no use** *or* **good crying over spilt ～** Prov 覆水难收，后悔也无济于事 [2] [u] Bot 白色汁液; **the ～ of a coconut** 椰汁 [3] [u and c] Cosmet 乳剂; **cleansing ～** 洗面奶

[B] *vt* [1] Agric 挤…的奶 ‹*cow*› [2] (extract) 抽取 ‹*sap, venom*› [3] fig (draw on) 消耗 ‹*resources*›; **to ～ the fund** 动用资金 [4] fig (exploit) 榨取 ‹*money*›; 套取 ‹*ideas*›; **to ～ sth./sb. of sth., to ～ sth. from** *or* **out of sth./sb.** 从某事物/某人处榨取某物; **to ～ sth./sb. dry** 榨干某物/某人; **to ～ the situation** 趁机牟利自肥; **to ～ sb.'s strength/enthusiasm** 利用某人的体力/热情; **to ～ the audience for applause** 卖力地想博得观众的掌声

milk: ～ bar *n* [出售点心、奶品等的] 奶吧; **～ bottle** *n* 奶瓶; **～ chocolate** *n* [u] 牛奶巧克力; **～ churn** *n* 奶桶; **～ diet** *n* 以牛奶为主的饮食; **～ duct** *n* 乳管; **～ float** *n* Brit 送奶车; **～ gland** *n* 乳腺

milking /ˈmɪlkɪŋ/ *n* [u] 挤奶

milking: ～ herd *n* 奶牛群; **～ machine** *n* 挤奶机; **～ pail** *n* 挤奶桶; **～ parlour** *n* 挤奶间; **～ stool** *n* 挤奶凳; **～ time** *n* 挤奶时间

milk: ～ jug *n* 奶壶; **～ loaf** *n* Brit 牛奶面包; **～maid** *n* archaic 挤奶女工; **～man** /-mən/ ▸**p. 409** *n* 送奶工; **～ of magnesia** *n* [u] 镁乳; **～ pan** *n* 奶锅; **～ powder** *n* [u] 奶粉; **～ products** *npl* 奶制品; **～ pudding** *n* [c and u] 牛奶布丁; **～ round** *n* Brit [1] (delivery) 固定路线的送奶; **to go on** *or* **do a ～ round** 沿固定路线送奶; [2] (visits by recruiting staff) 巡回招聘; **～ run** *n* 例行飞行; **～ saucepan** *n* = **～ pan**; **～ shake** *n* 奶昔; **～ tooth** *n* 乳齿; **～ train** *n* [清晨运送牛奶、亦可载客的] 运奶火车; **～-white** *adj* 乳白色的

milky /ˈmɪlki/ *adj* [1] (containing milk) 含奶的; **a ～ product** 奶制品; **～ tea/coffee** 奶茶/奶咖啡 [2] (resembling milk) 似乳的; **～ white** 乳白色 [3] (cloudy) 混浊的 ‹*liquid, gem*›; **to go** *or* **turn ～** 变得混浊

milky: M～ Way *pr n* **the M～ Way** 银河; **～ white** *adj* 乳白色的

mill /mɪl/

[A] *n* [1] (for corn, grain) 磨坊; **to go through the ～** fig 饱经辛酸; **to put sb. through the ～** fig 使某人经受磨难 [2] (factory) 制造厂; **a ～ town** 多作坊的小镇 [3] (kitchen appliance) 碾磨机 [4] (laborious process or routine) 烦琐程序; **to go through the ～ of ...** 经过…的烦琐程序; **run of the ～** 日常活动

[B] *vt* [1] (grind, crush) 磨 ‹*flour, coffee*› [2] (process, produce) 制造 ‹*steel, textiles*› [3] (in coin manufacturing) 将…轧出凸缘 ‹*coin*›; **a ～ed edge** 轧出的凸缘 [4] (cut, shape) 铣削 ‹*screw, nut, wheel*›

Phrasal verb

- **mill around, mill about** *vi* «*animals, flock*» 兜圈子; «*people, crowd*» 不耐烦地走动

millennial /mɪˈleniəl/ *adj* 一千年的

millennium /mɪˈleniəm/ *n* (*pl* **～s** *or* **millennia** /mɪˈleniə/) (cycle) 一千年; (anniversary) 千周年纪念日

millennium bug *n* 千年虫

millepede /ˈmɪlɪpiːd/ *n* = **millipede**

miller /ˈmɪlə(r)/ *n* ▸**p. 409** (owner) 磨坊主; (worker) 磨坊工人

millet /ˈmɪlɪt/ *n* [u] [1] (cereal) 黍 [2] (seed) 黍的子实

millibar /ˈmɪlɪbɑː(r)/ *n* 毫巴 [大气压强单位]

milligram, Brit also **milligramme** /ˈmɪlɪɡræm/ ▸**p. 909** *n* 毫克

millilitre Brit, **milliliter** Amer /ˈmɪlɪliːtə(r)/ *n* 毫升

millimetre Brit, **millimeter** Amer /ˈmɪlɪmiːtə(r)/ ▸**p. 436** *n* 毫米

milliner /ˈmɪlɪnə(r)/ ▸**p. 409** *n* 女帽制造商

millinery /ˈmɪlɪnəri, Amer -neri/ *n* [u] [1] (women's hats) 女帽; **the ~ department** 女帽部 [2] (business) 女帽业; **a ~ business** 女帽公司

milling /ˈmɪlɪŋ/ *n* [u] [1] (of corn, grain) 碾磨 [2] (of metal) 轧制 [3] (on coin) 凸缘

milling machine *n* 铣床

million /ˈmɪljən/ ▸**p. 521**

A *n* 一百万; **the odds are a ~ to one** 这种可能性极小; **a chance in a ~** 极小的可能性; **to be one in a ~** 万里挑一; **thanks a ~!** colloq iron 真是万分感谢啊!

B **millions** *npl* [1] (numbers from a million to a billion) 数百万 [2] (large amount, quantity) 许多; **the starving ~s** 成千上万挨饿的人; **to have ~s** 非常富有; **in ~s** 数以百万计的

C *pos* colloq (a very large number) 大量; **I've got ~s of empty beer bottles in my cellar** 我地窖里有许多空啤酒瓶

D *adj* [1] (a thousand thousand) 百万的 ‹*cars, miles, pounds*› [2] colloq (lots of) 许多的 ‹*attempts, hours*›; **to be a ~ years old** fig 非常古老; **I've told you a ~ times!** 我告诉过你无数次了! ; **to feel like a ~ dollars** 感觉好极了

millionaire /ˌmɪljəˈneə(r)/ *n* 百万富翁

millionth /ˈmɪljənθ/ ▸**p. 521**

A *n* [1] (ordinal number) 第一百万 [2] (fraction) 百万分之一; **a ~ (of sth.)** (某物的) 百万分之一; **~s (of sth.)** (某物的) 百万分之几

B *adj* [1] (in sequence) 第一百万的 [2] (relating to fraction) 百万分之一的; **a ~ part (of sth.)** (某物的) 百万分之一

millipede /ˈmɪlɪpiːd/ *n* 千足虫

millisecond /ˈmɪlɪsekənd/ *n* 毫秒

millivolt /ˈmɪlɪvəʊlt/ *n* 毫伏

milliwatt /ˈmɪlɪwɒt/ *n* 毫瓦特

mill: **~ pond** *n* 磨坊水池; **to be like a ~ pond** 风平浪静; **~ race** *n* 磨坊引水槽; **~stone** *n* 磨石; **a ~stone round one's neck** fig 套在脖子上的沉重负担; **~stream** *n* 水磨动力水流; **~wheel** *n* [磨坊的] 水车轮; **~ worker** ▸**p. 409** *n* 工厂工人; **~ wright** ▸**p. 409** *n* 碾磨机械技工

> **Mills & Boon**
>
> 米尔斯－布恩公司。英国最知名的言情小说出版公司。1908 年由杰拉尔德·米尔斯 (Gerald Mills) 和查尔斯·布恩 (Charles Boon) 创立。出版的小说人物和情节往往相似，多为女子历经曲折后终于嫁给如意郎君，虽为人诟病，但却极受欢迎，号称每 3 秒钟就售出一册。小说分历史言情和现代言情等类型，上架时间仅限一个月。现隶属于加拿大言情小说出版公司禾林企业 (Harlequin Enterprises)。

milo /ˈmaɪləʊ/ *n* [u] 蜀黍

milometer /maɪˈlɒmɪtə(r)/ *n* Brit 里程计

milord /mɪˈlɔːd/ *n* archaic or hum 老爷

mime /maɪm/

A *n* [1] [u] (art) 哑剧艺术; **to be good at ~** 擅长哑剧表演 [2] [c] (performance) 哑剧表演

B *vt* 用哑剧动作表演 ‹*action, sleeping*›; **to ~ sth. to sb.** 对某人做某手势

C *vi* 做模拟动作; **to ~ to** 配合…做模拟动作 ‹*music, text*›

mime artist ▸**p. 409** *n* 哑剧表演艺术家

mimeograph /ˈmɪmɪəɡrɑːf, Amer -ɡræf/ dated

A *n* [1] (machine) 蜡纸油印机 [2] (copy) 蜡纸油印件; **to roll off ~s** 印出蜡纸油印件

B *vt* 油印 ‹*copies, instructions*›

mimesis /mɪˈmiːsɪs, maɪ-/ *n* [u] 模仿

mimetic /mɪˈmetɪk/ *adj* 模仿的

mimic /ˈmɪmɪk/

A *n* [1] (person) 善于模仿的人; (bird) 会模仿人声的鸟 [2] (professional) 模拟剧演员

B *vt* (*pres p etc.* **-ck-**) [1] (imitate) 模仿 ‹*person, mannerisms, gestures, voice*› [2] (resemble) 和…相似 ‹*surroundings, antique, marble, diamond*› [3] (emulate, simulate) 效仿 ‹*celebrity, lifestyle*›

mimicry /ˈmɪmɪkri/ *n* [u] 模仿

mimosa /mɪˈməʊzə, Amer -məʊsə/

A *n* [1] [c] (tree) 含羞草 [2] [u] (colour) 含羞草花的黄色

B *adj* 含羞草花黄色的

min *abbr* [1] = **minute**[1] **A1** [2] = **minimum**

Min. *abbr* Brit = **ministry 1**

minaret /ˌmɪnəˈret/ *n* [1] (of mosque) 宣礼塔 [清真寺的一部分] [2] (any similar structure) 宣礼塔形建筑

mince /mɪns/

A *n* [u] Brit 碎肉; **beef/pork ~** 牛肉末/猪肉末

B *vt* 绞碎 ‹*meat*›; **not to ~ one's words, not to ~ matters** 直言不讳

C *vi* pej 装腔作势地小步快走; **to ~ into/out of the room** 迈着碎步走进/走出房间

mincemeat /ˈmɪnsmiːt/ *n* [u] [1] (dried fruit and spice mixture) 百果馅; **to make ~ of sb./sth.** colloq 将某人/某事驳得体无完肤 [2] Brit (meat) 碎肉

mince pie *n* 百果馅饼

mincer /ˈmɪnsə(r)/ *n* esp Brit 绞肉机; **to put sth. through the ~** 将某物放入绞肉机; **to put sb. through the ~** fig colloq 彻底击败某人

mincing /ˈmɪnsɪŋ/ *adj attrib* pej 矫揉造作的

mincing machine *n* 绞肉机

mind /maɪnd/

A *n* [1] [u and c] (centre of thought and feelings) 头脑; **the ~/body duality** 精神－肉体的二元性; **the conscious/unconscious/subconscious ~** 意识/无意识/潜意识; **peace of ~** 内心的宁静; **in sb.'s ~** (thoughts) 在某人心里; (imagination) 在某人的想象中; **to cross sb.'s ~** 浮现在某人的脑海中; **sb.'s ~ is in turmoil** 某人心乱如麻; **it's all in the ~** 那纯属想象; **strange thoughts went through my ~** 我的心里产生了奇怪的想法; **to see sth. in one's ~'s eye** 想象出某物; **to build up an image in one's ~ of sb./sth.** 心中形成对某人/某物的印象; **to come to ~** or **come into one's ~** 浮上心头; **if anything comes to ~, let me know** 如果你想起了什么，就告诉我; **I can't get it/her out of my ~** 我心里老想着这件事/她; **to have sth. at the back of one's ~** 隐约意识到某事; **to have sth. on one's ~** 有某事压在心头; **to have a lot on one's ~** 有很多牵挂; **what's on your ~?** 你有什么心事? ; **that's a load** or **weight off my ~** 我如释重负; **to read sb.'s ~** 看出某人的心思; **to set sb.'s ~ at rest** 让某人放心; **to be** or **feel easy in one's ~ (about sth.)** (对某事) 很安心; **to prey** or **weigh on sb.'s ~** 压在某人心头; **with sb./sth. in ~** 考虑到某人/某事物; **designed with women in ~** 专为女性设计的 [2] [u and c] (brain) 智力; **to have the ~ of a two-year-old child** 智力相当于两岁的孩子; **to have a very good** or **keen ~** 非常聪明 [3] [u and c] (way of thinking) 思维; **the human/criminal ~** 人类/罪犯的思维; **sb.'s frame** or **state of ~** 某人的心境; **to be in a calm/confused state of ~** 心里很平静/很乱; **you've got a dirty** or **filthy ~** colloq 你真下流; **travel broadens the ~** 旅行可以开阔心胸 [4] [c] (opinion) 意见; **to be of one/a different ~** 持一致/不同意见; **to be in** Brit or **of** Amer **two ~s** 犹豫不决; **to my ~** 在我看来; **to speak one's ~** 说心里话; **to know one's own ~** 有主见; **to have a ~ of one's own** 有主见; **to be clear in one's ~ about sth.** 心中明白某事; **to make up one's ~** 打定主意; **to change one's ~ (about sth./sb.)** 改变 (对某物/某人的) 看法; **to have** or **keep an open ~ about sth.** 对某事没有成见; **to close one's ~ to sth., to have a closed ~ about sth.** 对某事物不予考虑/对某事物未作考虑 [5] [c] (attention) 注意力; **to turn one's ~ to sth.** 把注意力转向某物; **to take sb.'s ~ off sth.** 使某人的注意力从某物上移开; **the holiday will force you to take your ~ off work** 休假可以迫使你暂时忘掉工作; **to put** or **set one's ~ to sth.** 专心于某事物; **to keep one's ~ on sth.** 专心于某事物; **to let one's ~ wander** 出神; **my ~ was elsewhere** 我走神了; **her ~ isn't on her work** 她的心思不在工作上 [6] [u and c] (memory) 记忆; **to put sth./sb. out of one's ~** 把某事物/某人置之脑后; **it went right** or **clean** or **completely out of my ~** 我把那件事全忘了; **his name slipped my ~** 我想不起他的名字了; **to bring** or **call sth./sb. to ~** 回忆起某事物/某人; **to bear sth./sb. in ~** 记住某事物/某人; **my ~'s a blank** 我的记忆一片空白 [7] [u and c] (sanity) **to be in one's right ~** 头脑正常; **to be of sound/unsound ~** Jur 心智健全/不健全; **to go out of** or **lose one's ~** 发疯; **to drive sb. out of his/her ~** 使某人发疯; **her ~ is going** colloq 她要疯了; **to be bored out of one's ~** colloq 厌烦透顶 [8] [c] *sing* (intention) 意愿; **to have sth./sb. in ~** 考虑某事物/某人; **to have (it) in ~ to do sth.** 打算做某事; **to have (half) a ~** or **a good ~ to do sth.** colloq 可能会做某事; **to have no ~ to do sth.** colloq 不想做某事; **to set one's ~ on sth./doing sth.** 一心想得到某物/做某事 [9] [c] (person) 有才智的人; **the great ~s of the 18th century** 18 世纪的杰出人物; **great ~s think alike** Prov 英雄所见略同

B *vt* [1] (pay attention to) 留意 ‹*person*›; **to ~ one's language/manners** 注意言辞/礼貌; **to ~ one's Ps and Qs** 注意做到举止得体; **don't ~ him** 别理他; **to ~ one's own business** 少管闲事 [2] (care) 在意; **never ~ sth./sb.** (don't worry about sth./sb.) 不用在意某事物/某人; (let alone) 更不用说某事物/某人; **never ~ who/what/why** *etc.* 谁/什么/何种原因等都无所谓; **never ~ doing that** colloq 先别那么做; **he doesn't ~ what you think of him** 他并不在意你怎么看他 [3] (bear in mind) 记住; **it's a secret, ~ you don't tell a soul** 这是秘密，记住不要告诉任何人 [4] (be careful of) 当心 ‹*hazard*›; **~ your head/the step/the gap** 小心碰头/台阶/缝隙; **~ your backs!** Brit 请让一下! ; **~ how you go** Brit 路上小心; **~ you get home early** 注意早点回家; **~ yourself, there's a car coming** 闪开，有车过来了 [5] (object to) 介意 ‹*person, thing*›; **do you ~ coffee?** 你介意喝咖啡吗? ; **I wouldn't ~ a drink/a short break** colloq 我很想喝点什么/休息一会儿; **if you don't ~ my** or **me saying so …** 如果你不介意我这样说的话…; **I don't ~ if I do** 好的 [6] (look after) 照看 ‹*child, animal*›; 看管 ‹*valuables*›

C *vi* [1] (object) 介意; **I don't ~** 我无所谓; **do you ~!** iron 你别这样好不好! ; **if you don't ~, I'd rather not …** 不好意思，我不想… [2] (worry) 担心; **never ~** (it's unimportant) 不要紧; (forget it) 算了; **never ~ about that …** 不用担心…; **never you ~** colloq 不关你的事 [3] **~ you** (conceding) 说真的; (explaining) 请注意; **the firm's gone bust, ~ you, I'm not surprised** 公司已经破产，说真的，我并不感到惊讶; **he claims, ~ you, that he is the owner** 请注意，他声称自己是所有人

Phrasal verb

- **mind out** *vi* Brit colloq **~ out!** 小心! ; **~ out, you're in my way** 请让一让，你挡住

m

我的路了; **to ~ out for sth./sb.** 当心某事物/某人

mind: ~-altering *adj* 致幻的 ‹*drug, substance*›; **~-bender** *adj* Amer 改变想法的事物; **~bending** *adj* colloq 1 (affecting the mind) 致幻的 ‹*drug, effect*›; 2 (difficult, complex) 复杂难懂的 ‹*problem*›; **~-blowing** *adj* colloq 给人印象极深刻的; **~-boggling** *adj* colloq 令人大吃一惊的

minded /ˈmaɪndɪd/ *adj* formal 有意的; **to be ~ to do sth.** 有意做某事; **if you're so ~** 如果你愿意这样的话

minder /ˈmaɪndə(r)/ *n* 1 colloq (bodyguard) 保镖 2 (childminder) 保姆

mind-expanding *adj* 致幻的

mindful /ˈmaɪndfl/ *adj* **to be ~ of sb./sth.** 记着某人/某事物

mind game *n* 心理战术

mindless /ˈmaɪndlɪs/ *adj* 1 (thoughtless, inconsiderate) 欠考虑的 ‹*person, vandal, thug*› 2 (done for no particular reason) 盲目的 ‹*violence, attack*› 3 **~ of sth.** (not thinking of sth.) 不顾某事物 4 (requiring little thought) 无需动脑筋的 ‹*task, routine*› 5 (stupid) 愚蠢的 ‹*idiot, moron*›

mindlessly /ˈmaɪndlɪsli/ *adv* 1 (regardless of others) 不顾他人地 2 (without much thought) 无需动脑地 3 (stupidly) 愚蠢地

mind: ~-numbing *adj* (extreme) 极端到令人无法正常思维的; (intense) 强烈到令人无法正常思维的; **~reader** *n* 洞悉他人心思的人; **~reading** *n* [u] 看透他人心思; **~-set** *n* 观念模式

mine[1] /maɪn/ ▸**p. 487** *pron* 我的; **this book is ~** 这本书是我的; **a friend of ~** 我的一个朋友; **~'s a whisky** 我要的是威士忌; **the book isn't ~ to lend you** 我没有权力把这本书借给你; **will you be ~?** dated 你愿意做我的爱人吗?

mine[2]

A *n* 1 Mining 矿; **to work in** *or* **down the ~s** 在矿井工作; **to go down the ~** 下矿井当矿工 2 (lucrative source) 宝库; **a ~ of information/experience** 丰富的信息/经验 3 (bomb) (on land) 地雷; (in sea) 水雷; **to hit** *or* **strike/lay a ~** 触雷/布雷; **to set off** *or* **detonate a ~** 引爆地雷; **to clear (an area of) ~s** (在一个地区) 排雷

B *vt* 1 (extract) 开采 ‹*coal, gold, diamonds*› 2 (dig, excavate) 在…采矿 ‹*area, earth*›; **to ~ (an area) for (sth.)** (在某地区) 采挖 (某物) 3 (lay mines in) 在…布雷 ‹*area, harbour*› 4 (destroy) 用雷炸毁 ‹*ship, tank, bridge*›

C *vi* 采矿; **to ~ for** 开采 ‹*gems, minerals*›

Phrasal verb

• **mine out** *vt* [**~ out sth., ~ sth. out**] 把…的矿产采尽

mine: ~ clearing *n* [u] 排雷; **~ detector** *n* 探雷器; **~ disposal** *n* [u] 排雷; **~field** *n* 1 lit 雷区; 2 fig (difficult situation) 危机四伏的局面; **a political/legal ~field** 政治/法律上困难重重的局面; **~hunter** *n* 扫雷艇; **~layer** *n* (ship) 布雷艇; (aircraft) 布雷飞机; **~laying** *n* [u] 布雷

miner /ˈmaɪnə(r)/ ▸**p. 409** *n* 矿工

mineral /ˈmɪnərəl/

A *n* 1 [c] (substance, class) 矿物; **a metallic/non-metallic ~** 金属矿/非金属矿 2 [u] (inorganic solid) 无机物; **to class** *or* **classify sth. as ~** 将某物归入无机物类 3 [c] (substance extracted by mining) 开采物 4 [c] Brit (drink) 汽水

B *adj* 矿物的; **~ salts** 矿物盐; **~ deposits** 矿藏

mineral kingdom *n* **the ~** 矿物界

mineralogical /ˌmɪnərəˈlɒdʒɪkl/ *adj* 矿物学的

mineralogist /ˌmɪnəˈrælədʒɪst/ ▸**p. 409** *n* 矿物学家

mineralogy /ˌmɪnəˈrælədʒi/ *n* [u] 矿物学

mineral: ~ oil *n* [u and c] 石油; **~ rights** *npl* 开采权; **~ spring** *n* 矿泉; **~ water** *n* [u] 矿泉水

miner: ~'s lamp *n* 矿灯; **~s' strike** *n* 矿工罢工

mineshaft /ˈmaɪnʃɑːft, Amer -ʃæft/ *n* 竖井; **to sink a ~ into sth.** 往某处挖一条竖井

minestrone /ˌmɪnɪˈstrəʊni/ *n* [u] (意大利) 蔬菜浓汤

mine: ~sweeper *n* 扫雷艇; **~sweeping** *n* [u] 扫雷; **~worker** ▸**p. 409** *n* 矿工; **~ workings** *npl* 矿山作业区

Ming /mɪŋ/ *n* [u] 1 (dynasty) 明代; **the ~ tombs** 明皇陵 2 (porcelain) 明代瓷器; **a ~ vase** 明瓷花瓶

mingle /ˈmɪŋgl/

A *vt* 使混合; **to ~ sth. and** *or* **with sth.** 将某物与某物混合

B *vi* 1 (mix) 混合; **to ~ with ...** 与…混合 2 (socialize) 交往; **to ~ with the crowd/the guests** 混在人群中/和客人交谈

mingy /ˈmɪndʒi/ *adj* colloq 1 (mean) 吝啬的 2 (small) 极少的 ‹*share, portion*›; 极小的 ‹*slice*›

mini /ˈmɪni/

A *combining form* 微型

B *adj* 小型的

C *n* 1 **Mini**® Brit (car) "迷你"牌汽车 2 (skirt) 超短裙

miniature /ˈmɪnətʃə(r), Amer ˈmɪnɪətʃʊər/

A *n* 1 (small version) 缩微模型; **in ~** 小型的 2 (small thing) 小型物 3 (picture, painting) 小画像 4 (bottle) 小瓶酒

B *adj* (very small) 小型的 ‹*camera, radio*›; 小种的 ‹*dog, horse*›

miniature: ~ golf ▸**p. 307** *n* 小型高尔夫球; **~ railway** *n* 小型观光列车; **~ village** *n* 微缩村庄模型

miniaturist /ˈmɪnɪtʃərɪst/ ▸**p. 409** *n* 细密画画家

miniaturization /ˌmɪnɪtʃəraɪˈzeɪʃn, Amer -rɪˈz-/ *n* [u] 微型化

miniaturize /ˈmɪnɪtʃəraɪz/ *vt* 使微型化

minibar /ˈmɪnɪbɑː(r)/ *n* 迷你吧 [宾馆房间内放饮料的小冰箱]

minibike /ˈmɪnɪbaɪk/ *n* 微型摩托车

miniboom /ˈmɪnɪbuːm/ *n* 短暂的繁荣

mini-break *n* 短暂假期

minibudget /ˌmɪnɪˈbʌdʒɪt/ *n* [用于调整经济的] 小预算

minibus /ˈmɪnɪbʌs/ *n* 小型公共汽车

minicab /ˈmɪnɪkæb/ *n* Brit [须电话预订而不能揽客的] 出租汽车

minicomputer /ˌmɪnɪkəmˈpjuːtə(r)/ *n* 小型计算机

minicourse /ˈmɪnɪkɔːs/ *n* Amer 简易课程

minidisc /ˈmɪnɪdɪsk/ *n* 迷你光盘

minidress /ˈmɪnɪdres/ *n* 迷你裙

minigolf /ˈmɪnɪgɒlf/ *n* [u] 小型高尔夫球

minim /ˈmɪnɪm/ *n* Brit 二分音符; **a ~ rest** 二分休止符

minima /ˈmɪnɪmə/ *pl* ▸**minimum A**

minimal /ˈmɪnɪml/ *adj* 1 (very small) 最小的; **to be ~** 是最小的 2 (in art) 极简抽象艺术的

minimal art *n* [u] = **minimalism**

minimalism /ˈmɪnɪməlɪzəm/ *n* [u] 极简抽象艺术

minimalist /ˈmɪnɪməlɪst/ *n* 极简抽象派艺术家

minimalize /ˈmɪnɪməlaɪz/ *vt* 使减少到最低限度

minimally /ˈmɪnɪməli/ *adv* 最小地 ‹*differ, change, increase, decrease*›; 最低程度地 ‹*invasive, disruptive*›

minimal pair *n* 最小对立体

minimarket /ˈmɪnɪmɑːkɪt/ *n* 小型超市

minimart /ˈmɪnɪmɑːt/ *n* Amer 便利店

minimize /ˈmɪnɪmaɪz/ *vt* 1 (reduce) 将…减少到最低限度 ‹*risk, cost, loss*› 2 (play down) 降低 ‹*seriousness*›; 减轻 ‹*pain*›; 贬低 ‹*contribution, achievement*›

minimum /ˈmɪnɪməm/

A *n* (*pl* **minima** *or* **~s**) 1 (least possible or allowed) 最低限度; **to keep sth. to a** *or* **the ~** 把某物保持在最低限度; **to reduce sth. to a** *or* **the ~** 把某物降到最低; **the bare** *or* **absolute ~** 最低值; **to do the ~** 做最少的工作; **at the ~** 以最小值 2 (lowest or smallest quantity or value possible or recorded) 最少量

B *adj* 1 (least) 最少的 ‹*quantity, requirement, interruption, delay*› 2 (lowest) 最低的 ‹*temperature, price, standard, age, level*›

minimum: ~-iron *adj* 最低熨烫限度; **~ wage** *n* 法定最低工资

mining /ˈmaɪnɪŋ/ *n* [u] 1 (extraction from earth) 采矿 2 (laying mines) 布雷

mining: ~ engineer ▸**p. 409** *n* 采矿工程师; **~ engineering** *n* [u] 采矿工程学; **~ rights** *npl* 采矿权

minion /ˈmɪnɪən/ *n* 1 (subordinate) 下属 2 (follower, sycophant) 谄媚者

mini-pill *n* 迷你避孕丸

mini roundabout *n* Brit 微型环交 [道路交叉口以白圈表示的小环形路]

miniskirt *n* 超短裙

minister /ˈmɪnɪstə(r)/

A *n* 1 Brit (head of government department) 部长 2 (diplomat) 外交使节 3 Relig (member of clergy) 牧师; **a ~ of religion** 牧师

B *vi* **to ~ to sb./sb.'s needs** formal 照料某人/照顾某人的需要

ministerial /ˌmɪnɪˈstɪərɪəl/ *adj* 1 Brit (of a ministry) 部长的 ‹*rank, position, duties*›; **to hold ~ office** 担任部长职务 2 (of a religious minister) 牧师的 ‹*responsibilities, training*›

ministering angel /ˌmɪnɪstərɪŋ ˈeɪndʒl/ *n* 救死扶伤的天使

Minister: ~ of State *n* Brit 国务大臣; **~ of the Crown** *n* Brit 内阁阁员; **~ without portfolio** *n* Brit 不管部部长

ministration /ˌmɪnɪˈstreɪʃnz/ *n* 1 **ministrations** formal *or* hum (provision of aid, care) 帮助 2 **ministrations** formal (of priest, clergy) 牧师执职 3 [u] (of sacrament) 宗教仪式的举行

ministry /ˈmɪnɪstri/ *n* 1 [c] Brit (department, building) [政府的] 部; **the M~ of Defence** 国防部 2 [c] (group of ministers) 全体部长; **to form a ~** 组成内阁 3 [c] Brit (tenure) 部长任期 4 [u] (of a religious minister) (profession) 牧师职业; (duties) 牧师职责; **to perform** *or* **carry out one's ~** 履行牧师职责; **to join the ~** 成为牧师; **to serve in the ~** 从事牧师职业 5 [c] (tenure of a religious minister) 神职任期

mink /mɪŋk/ *n* (*pl* **~** *or* **~s**) 1 [c] (animal) 水貂; **a ~ farm** 水貂饲养场 2 [u] (fur) 貂皮; **a ~ coat/hat** 貂皮大衣/帽子 3 [c] (coat) 貂皮大衣

Minnesota /ˌmɪnɪˈsəʊtə/ *pr n* 明尼苏达州

minnow /ˈmɪnəʊ/ *n* 1 (fish) 米诺鱼 2 (small person) 无足轻重的人; (small organization) 无足轻重的小机构

Minoan /mɪˈnəʊən/ Hist

A *adj* 弥诺斯文明的

B *n* 弥诺斯人

minor /ˈmaɪnə(r)/

A *adj* 1 (small) 较小的 ‹*detail, difference, problem*›; 较少的 ‹*concern, interest, expenses*›; **~ royalty** 皇室中的小人物 2 (lesser) 次要的 ‹*position, role, part*›; **a ~ author** 不太重要的作家; **to be of ~ importance** 不太重要 3 (not serious) 轻微的 ‹*burns, fracture, injury*› 4 Mus 小音阶的 ‹*scale*›; 小调的 ‹*key*›; **in a ~ key** 采用小调

B *n* 1 (under-age person) 未成年人 2 Amer (subsidiary subject in university) 辅修科目

m

C *vi* Amer (study a subsidiary subject) 辅修; **to ~ in ...** 辅修…

Minorca /mɪ'nɔːkə/ *pr n* 米诺卡岛

minority /maɪ'nɒrəti, Amer -'nɔːr-/

A *n* **1** [c] (small number or part) 少数; **to be in the ~** 占少数; **a religious ~** 宗教上的少数派; **to be in a ~ of one** 是唯一持不同意见者; **a ~ of people/businesses/countries** 少数人/企业/国家 **2** [c] (race, ethnic group) 少数民族 **3** [u] (state of being underage) 未成年

B *modif* 少数人的 ‹*interest, rights, language*›

minority: ~ government *n* 少数党政府; **~ leader** *n* 少数党领袖; **~ president** *n* Amer 以少数票当选的总统; **~ programme** *n* **1** (broadcast) 少数民族节目; **2** (course) 少数民族科目; **~ report** *n* 少数派报告; **~ rule** *n* [u] 少数派统治; **~ sport** *n* 少数人参加的运动

minor: ~ league *n* 职业球队小联盟; **~ offence** *n* 轻微违法; **~ planet** *n* 小行星; **~ suit** *n* 低级花色

Minsk /mɪnsk/ *pr n* 明斯克

minster /'mɪnstə(r)/ *n* Brit 大教堂

minstrel /'mɪnstrəl/ *n* [中世纪的] 游方艺人

mint[1] /mɪnt/

A *n* **1** (place for coining) 铸币厂; **the Royal M~** Brit 皇家铸币厂 **2** colloq (vast sum) 大量的钱; **to make a ~** 赚大钱; **to cost a ~** 耗费一大笔钱

B *adj* (pristine) 簇新的; **in ~ condition** 崭新的

C *vt* **1** (make) 铸造 ‹*coin, medal*› **2** (invent) 创造 ‹*word, expression*›

mint[2] *n* **1** [c] (plant) 薄荷 **2** [u] (leaves used in cooking) 薄荷叶; **~ sauce/sweet** 薄荷沙司/糖 **3** [c] (sweet) 薄荷糖 **4** [u] (flavour) 薄荷味; **~ chocolate/toothpaste** 薄荷味巧克力/牙膏

mint julep *n* Amer 薄荷冰酒

minuet /,mɪnjʊ'et/ *n* **1** (dance) 小步舞 **2** (music) 小步舞曲

minus /'maɪnəs/

A *prep* **1** (less, reduced by) 减去; **six ~ two equals four** 六减二得四; **it is ~ 15 (degrees)** 气温是零下15度 **2** colloq (without) 缺少

B *adj* **1** (involving subtraction) 表示减的; **~ symbol/key** 减号/减号键 **2** (less than zero) 负的; **a ~ number/value** 负数/负值 **3** (negative) 不利的 ‹*factor, side*› **4** (below grade in school) 略差的; **he got two A ~es** 他得了两个 A- **5** Elec 负电的; **~ pole/terminal** 负极/负极端子

C *n* (*pl* **~es**) **1** (sign) 减号; **two ~es make a plus** 负负得正 **2** (drawback) 缺点

minuscule /'mɪnəskjuːl/

A *adj* **1** (tiny) 非常小的 ‹*fragment, writing, amount*› **2** (lower-case) 小写的 ‹*letter, writing, print*›

B *n* **1** [c] (letter) 小写字母 **2** [u] (writing) 小书写体; **in ~** 用小书写体

minus sign *n* 减号

minute[1] /'mɪnɪt/ ▸ **p. 831**

A *n* **1** (unit of time or measurement) 分; **a few ~s earlier/later** 几分钟之前/之后; **8 degrees 35 ~s (8° 35')** 8 度 35 分; **five ~s past three** 3 点零 5 分; **with 5 ~s to spare** 还剩 5 分钟; **to the ~** 准时地; **to arrive at eight o'clock to the ~** 8 点整到达; **to be accurate to the ~** 《*clock*》 精确到分; **to be ten ~s by car from sth.** 距某地开车有 10 分钟的路程; **the river is five ~s away** 河离这儿有 5 分钟的路程 **2** *sing* colloq (short time) 片刻; **I'll only be a ~** 我一会儿就好; **I'll only be a ~, I won't be a ~** 我马上就好; **just a ~!** (wait) 稍等一下!; (say) 且慢!; **in half a ~** 马上; **within ~s** 在几分钟内; **with only ~s to go** 只剩几分钟时; **not for a** *or* **one ~** 从不; **they're getting richer by the ~** 他们正在迅速致富; **have you got a ~?** colloq 你能抽出一点时间来吗?; **he never gives me a** *or* **one ~'s peace** 他一分钟都没有让我安宁过 **3** colloq (instant) 瞬间; **the ~ I heard the news, I called** 我一听到消息就打电话了; **this ~** (at once) 马上; Brit (just) 刚刚; **just this ~** Brit (right now) 此时此刻; (only just) 就在刚才; **at this ~** 此时此刻; **at any ~ (now)** 随时; **at the last ~** 在最后一刻; **to leave things until the last ~** 把事情拖到最后才做完; **one ~ ... the next ...** 一会儿…一会儿…; **to be up to the ~** 保持最新; **there's a sucker born every ~** colloq 什么时候都不缺傻子 **4** Admin 备忘录; **a Treasury ~** 一份财政部备忘录

B **minutes** *npl* Admin 会议记录; **to take the ~s** 做会议记录

C *vt* **1** (record) 记录…的要点 ‹*meeting*›; 把…记入议事录 ‹*decision*› **2** (inform) 用备忘录通知; **to ~ sb. about sth.** 用备忘录告知某人某事

minute[2] /maɪ'njuːt, Amer -'nuːt/ *adj* **1** (tiny) 微小的 ‹*object, design*›; **a ~ quantity of sth.** 微量的某物; **the stitches were ~** 针脚很小 **2** *usu attrib* (meticulous) 细致的 ‹*description, examination*›; **in ~ detail** 非常仔细地 **3** (insignificant) 微不足道的 ‹*risk, change*›

minute /'mɪnɪt/: **~ book** *n* 会议纪要簿; **~ hand** *n* 分针

minutely /maɪ'njuːtli, Amer -'nuːt-/ *adv* **1** (meticulously) 仔细地 ‹*describe, examine*› **2** (slightly) 微小地 ‹*differ, change*›

minute steak /,mɪnɪt 'steɪk/ *n* 快熟薄牛排

minutiae /maɪ'njuːʃiiː, Amer mɪ'nuːʃiː/ *npl* 细枝末节

minx /mɪŋks/ *n* hum 狡猾轻佻的女子

Miocene /'maɪəsiːn/

A *adj* (of the period) 中新世的; (of the rock system) 中新统的

B *n* **the ~** (period) 中新世; (rock system) 中新统

MIPS, mips /mɪps/ *abbr* = **millions of instructions per second** 每秒百万条指令

miracle /'mɪrəkl/

A *n* 奇迹; **to perform** *or* **work ~s** 创造奇迹; **a ~ of science/technology** 科学/技术上的奇迹; **by some ~** 奇迹般地; **a minor ~** 令人吃一惊的事; **to be nothing short of a ~** 是一个不折不扣的奇迹; **to do ~s with sb.** 对某人创造奇迹; **he can do ~s with a class of children** 他能让一个班的孩子取得出色的成绩

B *modif* 有奇效的 ‹*cure, drug*›; 奇迹般的 ‹*recovery*›

miracle worker *n* lit, fig 奇迹创造者

miraculous /mɪ'rækjʊləs/ *adj* lit, fig 奇迹般的; **to be nothing short of ~** 非常不可思议; **it is ~ that ...** …真是奇迹

miraculously /mɪ'rækjʊləsli/ *adv* lit, fig 奇迹般地

mirage /'mɪrɑːʒ, mɪ'rɑːʒ/ *n* **1** (optical illusion) 海市蜃楼; **a ~ of sth.** 某事物的幻景 **2** (impossibility) 妄想

Miranda warning /mə'rændə ,wɔːnɪŋ/ *n* Amer 米兰达原则 [警方逮捕疑犯时必须告知其有沉默权]

mire /'maɪə(r)/ *n* **1** [c] (boggy area) 泥潭; (marshy area) 沼泽 **2** [u] (mud) 烂泥 **3** [u] fig (bad situation) 困境; **the ~ of poverty/conflict** 贫穷/冲突的困境; **to drag sb.** *or* **sb.'s name through the ~** 使某人声名蒙羞

mired /'maɪəd/ *adj* **to be ~ in sth.** 陷入某种困境

mirror /'mɪrə(r)/

A *n* **1** (looking glass) 镜子; **to look (at oneself) in the ~** 照镜子; **to glance in the ~** 匆匆照一下镜子 **2** (reflecting surface) 反射面 **3** fig (depiction, representation) 写照; **a ~ of sth.** 某事的写照; **to hold a ~ up to sth.** 真实地反映某事物

B *vt* **1** (reflect) 映现出 ‹*image, shape, reflection*›; **the moon was ~ed in the lake** 月亮映照在湖中 **2** fig (correspond to) 反映 ‹*society, life, opinion*› **3** Comput 把…保存到镜像站点

mirrored /'mɪrəd/ *adj* 装有镜子的 ‹*wall, ceiling*›

mirror: ~ image *n* **1** (identical image) 镜像; **2** (close resemblance) (of person) 完全一样的人; (of thing) 完全一样的事物; **to be the ~ image of sb./sth.** 与某人/某事物完全一样; **~ site** *n* 镜像站点; **~ writing** *n* [u] 左右反写

mirth /mɜːθ/ *n* [u] 欢笑; **to provoke** *or* **cause ~** 引起欢笑; **the room resounded with ~** 房间里回荡着欢笑声

mirthful /'mɜːθfl/ *adj attrib* 欢乐的; **a ~ gathering** 欢聚; **~ gaiety** 欢快

mirthless /'mɜːθlɪs/ *adj* 忧郁的 ‹*expression*›; **he gave a ~ laugh** 他苦笑一声

miry /'maɪəri/ *adj* 泥泞的

MIS *abbr* = **management information system**

misadventure /,mɪsəd'ventʃə(r)/ *n* **1** [c] (accident) 不幸遭遇; **we had one or two ~s, but they did not spoil the holiday** 我们遇到了一两次不愉快的事，但没有影响到整个假期 **2** [u] Jur 意外致死; **death by ~** 意外死亡

misadvise /,mɪsəd'vaɪz/ *vt* 误导

misalliance /,mɪsə'laɪəns/ *n* (unsuitable relationship) 不适当的联合; (unsuitable marriage) 不匹配的婚姻

misanthrope /'mɪsənθrəʊp/ *n* 厌恶人类者

misanthropic /,mɪsən'θrɒpɪk/ *adj* 厌恶人类的

misanthropist /mɪ'sænθrəpɪst/ *n* = **misanthrope**

misanthropy /mɪ'sænθrəpi/ *n* [u] 厌恶人类

misapplication /,mɪsæplɪ'keɪʃn/ *n* 误用

misapply /,mɪsə'plaɪ/ *vt* **1** (apply or use wrongly) 误用 ‹*term, information, knowledge*›; 非法使用 ‹*funds, resources*› **2** (waste, misuse) 不当地使用 ‹*talent, ability*›

misapprehend /,mɪsæprɪ'hend/ *vt* 误解 ‹*concept, meaning*›

misapprehension /,mɪsæprɪ'henʃn/ *n* 误解; **to be (labouring) under the ~ that ...** 误以为…

misappropriate /,mɪsə'prəʊprɪeɪt/ *vt* 挪用 ‹*money, funds, revenue*›

misappropriation /,mɪsə,prəʊprɪ'eɪʃn/ *n* [u] 挪用

misbegotten /,mɪsbɪ'gɒtn/ *adj* 拙劣的 ‹*idea, scheme, policy*›

misbehave /,mɪsbɪ'heɪv/ *vi* **1** (behave badly) 行为不端; **stop misbehaving!** 别胡来! **2** (malfunction) 发生故障

misbehaviour Brit, **misbehavior** Amer /,mɪsbɪ'heɪvjə(r)/ *n* [u] 不端行为

misbelief /,mɪsbɪ'liːf/ *n* **1** (false belief) 错误信念 **2** = **disbelief**

miscalculate /,mɪs'kælkjʊleɪt/

A *vi* **1** (calculate wrongly) 算错 **2** (assess situation wrongly) 估计错误; **he admitted that he had ~d over Iraq** 他承认对伊拉克的情况判断错误

B *vt* **1** (calculate wrongly) 算错 ‹*sum, distance*› **2** (assess wrongly) 错误估计 ‹*outcome, reaction, strength of feeling*›

miscalculation /,mɪskælkjʊ'leɪʃn/ *n* **1** (error) 误算 **2** (wrong assessment) 错误的估计

miscarriage /'mɪskærɪdʒ, ,mɪs'kærɪdʒ/ *n* **1** Med 流产; **to have** *or* **suffer a ~** 流产 **2** (unsuccessful outcome) 失败; **the ~ of the project** 该项目的流产

miscarriage of justice *n* 错判

miscarry /,mɪs'kæri/

A *vi* **1** Med 流产 **2** (fail) «*project, attempt, negotiations*» 失败

B vt Med 使流产; **she has miscarried her baby** 她怀的孩子流产了

miscast /ˌmɪsˈkɑːst, Amer -ˈkæst/ vt (pt, pp **miscast**) **1** (referring to actor) 使…扮演不适当的角色 ‹actor, actress›; **to ~ sb. as** or **in the role of sth.** 让某人扮演不合适的某角色 **2** (referring to roles) «director, producer» 使…的角色选择不当 ‹play, film, production›

miscellaneous /ˌmɪsəˈleɪnɪəs/ adj 混杂的 ‹objects, people, assortment, remarks›; 各色各样的 ‹collection, selection›; **~ expenses** 杂费

miscellany /mɪˈseləni, Amer ˈmɪsəlemi/ n **1** (mixture) 混合; **our street is a ~ of architectural styles** 我们的街道汇集了各种建筑风格 **2** (anthology) 杂集 **3** (show, entertainment) 综艺节目

mischance /ˌmɪsˈtʃɑːns, Amer -ˈtʃæns/ n **1** [u] (bad luck) 厄运; **we missed him at the station by pure** or **sheer ~** 我们运气真不好，在车站没碰到他 **2** [c] (misadventure) 倒霉事; **a series of ~s** 一连串的倒霉事

mischief /ˈmɪstʃɪf/ n [u] **1** (playfulness) 顽皮; **to do sth. out of ~** 顽皮地做某事; **to get into ~** 淘气; **to keep sb. out of ~** 让某人安分; **keep out of ~!** 别胡闹！; **to be up to ~** 搞恶作剧; **to be full of ~** 尽是坏点子; **her eyes twinkled with ~** 她的双眼透着顽皮 **2** (harm) 伤害; **to make** or **create ~** 搬弄是非; **to do sb./oneself a ~** 伤害某人/自己; **she wrote those letters out of sheer ~** 她写这些信完全是为了伤害别人; **their son is up to his old ~ again** 他们的儿子又开始祸害人了; **he didn't keep out of ~ for long after he came out of prison** 他出狱后没能安分多久 **3** dated (rascal) 淘气鬼

mischief: ~-maker n 搬弄是非者; **~-making** n [u] 搬弄是非

mischievous /ˈmɪstʃɪvəs/ adj **1** (playful, naughty) 淘气的 ‹grin, puppy› **2** (malicious) 恶意的 ‹lie, allegation, rumour›

mischievously /ˈmɪstʃɪvəsli/ adv **1** (playfully, naughtily) 淘气地 ‹grin, play› **2** (maliciously) 恶意地 ‹gossip, insinuate, allege›

mischievousness /ˈmɪstʃɪvəsnɪs/ n [u] **1** (playful misbehaviour) 淘气 **2** (malicious behaviour) 恶意行为

misconceive /ˌmɪskənˈsiːv/ vt 误解 ‹problem, argument, meaning, poem›

misconceived /ˌmɪskənˈsiːvd/ adj 理解错误的 ‹problem, argument, meaning, poem›; 计划不周的 ‹project›; **~ notions about Islam** 关于伊斯兰教的错误观念

misconception /ˌmɪskənˈsepʃn/ n 错误观念; **a ~ about sth.** 对某事的错误认识; **it's a popular ~** 这种错误观念很普遍

misconduct /ˌmɪsˈkɒndʌkt/ n [u] **1** (improper behaviour) 不端行为; **he is guilty of professional/sexual ~** 他因玩忽职守/性行为不端而被定罪; **gross ~** 严重失职 **2** (mismanagement) 管理不善; **~ of sth.** 对某事的管理不善

misconstruction /ˌmɪskənˈstrʌkʃn/ n [c and u] 误解; **to be open to ~** 容易引起误解; **to put** or **place a ~ on sb.'s words** 误解某人的话

misconstrue /ˌmɪskənˈstruː/ vt 误解 ‹words, intentions, actions›; **to ~ sth. as sth.** 将某事误解为某事

miscount
A /ˌmɪsˈkaʊnt/ vt 数错 ‹money, votes›
B /ˌmɪsˈkaʊnt/ vi 数错
C /ˈmɪskaʊnt/ n 数错; **to make a ~** 数错一处

miscreant /ˈmɪskrɪənt/ n formal 不法之徒

miscue /ˌmɪsˈkjuː/
A vt (in snooker, billiards, pool) 未击中 ‹ball›; (in football) 未踢中 ‹ball›; **a ~d shot** 未射中的球
B vi (in snooker, billiards, pool) 未击中球; (in football) 未踢中球

misdeal /ˌmɪsˈdiːl/
A vt (pt, pp **misdealt** /ˌmɪsˈdelt/) 发错 ‹cards›; **they replayed the misdealt hand** 他们重发了手里发错的牌
B vi (pt, pp **misdealt** /ˌmɪsˈdelt/) 发错牌
C n 发错牌

misdeed /ˌmɪsˈdiːd/ n (wicked act) 恶行; (illegal act) 不法行为

misdemeanour Brit, **misdemeanor** Amer /ˌmɪsdɪˈmiːnə(r)/ n **1** (minor wrongdoing) 不正当的行为 **2** Jur (offence) 轻罪; **to commit/to be found guilty of a ~** 犯轻罪/被定犯轻罪

misdiagnose /ˌmɪsdaɪəgˈnəʊz, Amer ˌmɪsdaɪəgˈnəʊs/ vt 误诊

misdiagnosis /ˌmɪsdaɪəgˈnəʊsɪs/ n 误诊

misdial /ˌmɪsˈdaɪəl/ vi (pres p etc. **-ll-** Brit, **-l-** Amer) 拨错电话号码

misdirect /ˌmɪsdaɪˈrekt, -dɪˈrekt/ vt **1** (send in wrong direction) 给…指错方向; **to ~ sb. somewhere** 把某人错引到某处 **2** (address wrongly) **to ~ sth. to somewhere** 将…错寄到某处 ‹mail, letter, parcel› **3** (misuse) 错用 ‹abilities, talents, efforts›; **I fear that your compliments are ~ed** 恐怕您谬赞了 **4** Jur 错误指示 ‹jury, jurors›

misdirection /ˌmɪsdaɪˈrekʃn, -dɪˈrek-/ n **1** (of letter, parcel) 寄错 **2** (of talents, efforts) 错用 **3** Jur [对陪审团的] 错误指示

miser /ˈmaɪzə(r)/ n 守财奴

miserable /ˈmɪzrəbl/ adj **1** (sad, depressed) 痛苦的 ‹person, mood›; **to feel ~** 感到很痛苦; **to make sb.'s life ~** 使某人生活痛苦; **he's a ~ old devil!** 他是个令人讨厌的老家伙！; **don't be so ~** 别这么闷闷不乐的; **to be as ~ as sin** colloq (morose) 脸色阴沉; (bad-tempered) 脾气很坏 **2** (wretched) 不幸的 ‹failure, defeat›; 悲惨的 ‹poverty, existence›; 糟糕的 ‹performance, dwellings›; 阴沉的 ‹sky, weather, afternoon› **3** pej (small, inadequate) 少得可怜的 ‹quantity, meal, wage›; 差得可怜的 ‹quality›

miserably /ˈmɪzrəbli/ adv **1** (unhappily) 痛苦地 **2** (wretchedly) 悲惨地 ‹live›; 不幸地 ‹fail›; 糟糕地 ‹perform›; **the family is ~ poor** 这家人极为贫困; **it was ~ cold** 天冷得叫人难受; **their marriage has failed ~** 他们的婚姻不幸破裂了; **the prisoners were ~ dressed** 囚犯们穿着灰暗的衣服 **3** (insufficiently) 极少地 ‹paid, fed›; 非常 ‹low, insufficient, small›

miserliness /ˈmaɪzəlɪnɪs/ n [u] **1** (meanness) 吝啬 **2** (smallness) (in quantity) 少; (in size) 小

miserly /ˈmaɪzəlɪ/ adj **1** (mean) 吝啬的 **2** (meagre) 极少的 ‹amount, portion, allowance›

misery /ˈmɪzəri/ n **1** [u] (mental, physical distress) 痛苦; **to lead** or **live a life of ~** 过着悲惨的生活; **to make sb.'s life a ~, to make life a ~ for sb.** 使某人痛苦; **to put sb. out of his/her ~** euph 杀死某人以释其痛苦; **to put an animal out of its ~** euph 杀死动物以释其痛苦; **tell her the answer, put her out of her ~!** hum 把答案告诉她，让她别再烦恼了！ **2** [c] (misfortune) 苦难 **3** [c] (gloomy person) 发牢骚的人

misery guts n colloq 发牢骚的人

misfire /ˌmɪsˈfaɪə(r)/ vi **1** (fail to fire properly) «rocket, engine» 打不着火; **the gun/grenade ~d** 炮/手榴弹哑了 **2** fig (fail to have desired effect) «policy, joke, compliment» 不奏效

misfit /ˈmɪsfɪt/ n 与别人合不来的人; **he's a social ~** 他与社会格格不入

misfortune /ˌmɪsˈfɔːtʃuːn/ n **1** [u] (bad luck) 厄运; **we had the ~ to break down halfway** 我们真倒霉，半路车抛锚了; **that's your ~** 你自认倒霉吧 **2** [c] (unfortunate event) 不幸的事; **she had the ~ to lose the sight of one eye** 她不幸一只眼失明了

misgivings /ˌmɪsˈgɪvɪŋz/ npl **1** (worries) 担忧; **to have ~ about sth./sb.** 为某事/某人担忧 **2** (doubts) 疑虑; **to have ~ about sth./sb.** 对某事/某人存疑; **I signed the contract with serious ~** 我满怀疑虑地签了合同

misgovern /ˌmɪsˈgʌvn/ vt 对…治理不当

misgovernment /ˌmɪsˈgʌvnmənt/ n [u] 治理不当

misguided /ˌmɪsˈgaɪdɪd/ adj 受误导的 ‹youth, ambition, action›

misguidedly /ˌmɪsˈgaɪdɪdli/ adv 受误导地

mishandle /ˌmɪsˈhændl/ vt **1** (handle inefficiently) 不当地处理 ‹issue, relationship, case›; 不当地进行 ‹investigation› **2** (handle roughly) 对…粗手粗脚 ‹parcel›; 胡乱操作 ‹tool›; 虐待 ‹animal›

mishap /ˈmɪshæp/ n 不幸的事; **a slight ~** 小事故; **without ~** 平安地

mishear /ˌmɪsˈhɪə(r)/ vt (pt, pp **misheard** /ˌmɪsˈhɜːd/) 听错; **to ~ sth. as sth.** 把某事错听成某事

mishit
A /ˌmɪsˈhɪt/ vt (pt, pp **mishit**) 误击 ‹ball›
B /ˈmɪshɪt/ n 误击

mishmash /ˈmɪʃmæʃ/ n 混杂物; **a ~ of ...** …的大杂烩 ‹styles, conventions, ideas›

misinform /ˌmɪsɪnˈfɔːm/ vt 向…提供错误信息; **to ~ sb. (about sth.)** 向某人误报（某事）; **to be ~ed (about sth.)** 得到（关于某事的）错误信息

misinformation /ˌmɪsɪnfəˈmeɪʃn/ n [u] 错误信息

misinterpret /ˌmɪsɪnˈtɜːprɪt/ vt 错误地阐释; **to ~ sth. as sth.** 将某事误释为某事

misinterpretation /ˌmɪsɪntɜːprɪˈteɪʃn/ n [u and c] 错误的阐释; **~ of sth. as sth.** 将某事误解为某事; **to be open to ~** 易被误解

misjudge /ˌmɪsˈdʒʌdʒ/ vt **1** (form wrong opinion of) 误判; **I ~d him completely** 我完全看错了他 **2** (estimate wrongly) 错误地估计; **I ~d how wide the stream was** 我对溪流的宽度估计错误

misjudgement, misjudgment /ˌmɪsˈdʒʌdʒmənt/ n **1** (wrong opinion) 误判 **2** (wrong estimate) 错误估计

miskick
A /ˌmɪsˈkɪk/ vt 把…踢偏 ‹ball, shot, penalty›
B /ˌmɪsˈkɪk/ vi 踢出坏球
C /ˈmɪskɪk/ n 踢出坏球

mislay /ˌmɪsˈleɪ/ vt (pt, pp **mislaid** /ˌmɪsˈleɪd/) 乱放 ‹pen, keys, book›

mislead /ˌmɪsˈliːd/ vt (pt, pp **misled**) 误导; **to ~ sb. about** or **as to sth.** 在某事上误导某人; **to ~ sb. into doing sth.** 误导某人做某事

misleading /ˌmɪsˈliːdɪŋ/ adj 误导的 ‹information, impression, statement, claim›; **it would be ~ to say that ...** 说…会使人产生误解

misleadingly /ˌmɪsˈliːdɪŋli/ adv 误导地 ‹worded, imply, ambiguous, assert›; **the puzzle is ~ simple** 这个谜题乍看上去让人误以为简单

misled /mɪsˈled/ pt, pp ▸ **mislead**

mismanage /ˌmɪsˈmænɪdʒ/ vt 对…管理不善 ‹company, project, finances, economy›; 对…处理不当 ‹affairs, relationship›

mismanagement /ˌmɪsˈmænɪdʒmənt/ n [u] (of economy, company, project, finances) 管理不善; (of affairs, relationship) 处理不当

mismatch /ˈmɪsmætʃ/ n (of components, devices) 不匹配; (of clothes, colours, styles) 不协调; (in marriage) 不般配; **a ~ between ...** …之间的不匹配; **the marriage is a ~** 这桩婚事门不当户不对

mismatched /ˌmɪsˈmætʃt/ adj 不匹配的 ‹components, devices›; 不协调的 ‹clothes, colours, styles›; 差距悬殊的 ‹opponents›; 不般配的 ‹partners›

misname /ˌmɪsˈneɪm/ vt 错误命名

misnomer /ˌmɪsˈnəʊmə(r)/ *n* 不恰当的用词; **a ～ for sth.** 对某事物的用词不当; **it's a bit** *or* **something of a ～** 这有点用词不妥

misogynist /mɪˈsɒdʒɪnɪst/ *n* 厌恶女性的男人

misogyny /mɪˈsɒdʒɪni/ *n* [u] 厌恶女性

misplace /ˌmɪsˈpleɪs/ *vt* **1** (mislay) 随意搁置 **2** Sport (aim incorrectly) 《*footballer*》将…踢错位置〈*ball, shot*〉; 《*rugby player*》将…扔错位置〈*ball*〉; 《*tennis player*》将…击错位置; **to ～ a pass** 误传

misplaced /ˌmɪsˈpleɪst/ *adj* 不合时宜的〈*comment, familiarity, humour*〉

misprint

A /ˈmɪsprɪnt/ *n* 印刷错误; **a ～ for sth.** 某词的印刷错误

B /ˌmɪsˈprɪnt/ *vt* 印错; **to ～ sth. as sth.** 将某词错印成某词

mispronounce /ˌmɪsprəˈnaʊns/ *vt* 发错…的音〈*word*〉; **to ～ sth. as sth.** 将某词错读成某词

mispronunciation /ˌmɪsprəˌnʌnsɪˈeɪʃn/ *n* [c and u] 发音错误

misquotation /ˌmɪskwəʊˈteɪʃn/ *n* 错误引用; **～s of** *or* **from Shakespeare** 对莎士比亚的误引

misquote /ˌmɪsˈkwəʊt/ *vt* 错误地引用; **she was ～d as demanding his resignation** 有人引错了她的话，说她要求他辞职

misread /ˌmɪsˈriːd/ *vt* (*pt, pp* **misread** /ˌmɪsˈred/) **1** (read wrongly) 读错; **to ～ sth. as sth.** 将某物错读成某物 **2** (misinterpret) 《*person*》误解〈*situation, action*〉; **to ～ sth. as sth.** 将某事误解成某事

misreading /ˌmɪsˈriːdɪŋ/ *n* **1** (false reading) 读错; **the ～ of a map** 看错地图 **2** (false interpretation) 误解

misrepresent /ˌmɪsreprɪˈzent/ *vt* 歪曲〈*facts, opinions, intentions*〉; **she was ～ed in the press as (being) a racist** 她在报上被歪曲成种族主义者

misrepresentation /ˌmɪsreprɪzenˈteɪʃn/ *n* [c and u] 歪曲; **a gross ～ of the facts** 对事实的极大歪曲

misrule /ˌmɪsˈruːl/

A *n* [u] **1** (bad government) 失政 **2** (disorder) 混乱; **to sow ～ among ...** 在…中煽动骚乱

B *vt* 对…治理不当〈*country, subjects*〉

miss¹ /mɪs/

A *vt* **1** (fail to hit) 未击中〈*target*〉; (fail to receive) 未接住〈*cross, ball*〉; **to ～ a penalty** 罚失点球; **the ball ～ed the goal** 球没有进球网; **you ～ed me by miles** 你扔得离我太远了; **he ～ed the rope and fell** 他没抓住绳子，结果摔了下去 **2** (avoid, escape) 避开〈*object, bad conditions*〉; **to just ～ the other car/having an accident** 差点儿撞上另一辆车/出事故; **to ～ death by inches** 险些丧命 **3** (fail to catch, take, attend) 错过〈*bus, train, person, offer, meeting*〉; **is Lee here? — you just ～ed him** 李在这里吗？——他刚走; **to ～ one's cue** 未听到出场提示; **to ～ an appointment** 未能履约; **to ～ the second act** 未看到第二幕演出; **to ～ the boat** *or* **bus** fig colloq 错失良机; **the chance is too good to ～** 机会太好了，不可错过; **you don't know what you're ～ing!** colloq 你不知道你错过了什么！; **to ～ one's vocation** often iron 入错行; **to ～ one's footing** 失足踏空; **it's an experience I wouldn't have ～ed for anything** 那种经历我是说什么都不会错过的 **4** (fail to see) 未看见〈*landmark*〉; (fail to hear) 未听见; (fail to understand) 未听懂; **you can't ～ it** 你不会看不见的; **he doesn't ～ a trick** colloq 他十分机敏; **sorry I ～ed that, can you repeat it?** 对不起，我没听见，你能再说一遍吗？; **to ～ the joke** 没听懂笑话 **5** (fail to do) 未做到; **to ～ doing sth.** 未能做某事; **to ～ getting an A by 2 marks** 差两分没得到A **6** (skip) 未出席〈*class, lecture*〉; 遗漏〈*line, detail*〉; **to ～ the middle paragraph** 跳过中间的那个段落; **I ～ed lunch** 我没吃午饭; **he never ～es my birthday** 他从来都记得我的生日; **she ～ed her pill** 她忘了服用避孕药 **7** (notice absence of) 发觉遗失〈*object, money*〉; 发觉…不在身边〈*person*〉; **I didn't ～ my purse till I got back to the hotel** 我回到宾馆才发现钱包丢了 **8** (regret absence of) 想念〈*place, activity*〉; **to ～ sb./sth. (very badly** *or* **much)** （非常）想念某人/某物; **keep it, I shan't ～ it** 你留着吧，我不需要它了; **to ～ doing sth.** 惦念做某事; **I don't ～ staying up late!** 我才不想熬夜呢！

B *vi* **1** (fail to hit target) 《*player, blow, bullet*》没打中; **he had an open goal, but he ～ed** 他面对空门却没射进; **you can't ～** lit 你不会打不中的; fig 你肯定能成功 **2** (fail to do sth.) 不做; **I always hear from her at New Year; she never ～es** 我每个新年都会收到她的来信，她一次不落 **3** Aut 《*engine, vehicle*》不点火

C *n* **1** Sport 击不中; **he scored ten hits and two ～es** 他十次击中，两次未中; **a ～ is as good as a mile** Prov (negative) 错误再小也是错; (positive) 死里逃生总是生 **2** Brit colloq **to give sth. a ～** (not visit, try, use, etc.) 避开某事; **to give Rome a ～** 不去罗马; **I'll give the soup a ～** 我不喝汤了 **3** (musical flop) 销量很差的唱片; (cinematic flop) 票房很差的电影

Phrasal verb

- **miss out**

A *vt* [**～ sth./sb. out, ～ out sth./sb.**] Brit **1** (accidentally omit) 遗漏〈*detail, person*〉; **to ～ out the comma** 漏掉逗号; **to ～ sth./sb. out from sth.** 把某物/某人从某物中漏掉 **2** (deliberately omit) 略去〈*section, point*〉; 不考虑〈*person*〉; **to ～ out the middle verse** 跳过中间的那行诗

B *vi* colloq 错过机会; **if you don't go, you'll ～ out** 如果你不去，就会错过机会; **to ～ out on sth.** 错失〈*meal, experience*〉; **to ～ out on a deal** (not join) 错失一笔交易; (not benefit from) 未获收益

miss² *n* **1** (general title) 小姐; **～ Anne Brown** 安·布朗小姐; **～ Oxford/England/World** (title of winner) 牛津/英格兰/世界小姐; **can I help you, ～?** 需要帮忙吗，小姐? **2** colloq pej (silly or headstrong girl) 冒失女孩

mis-sell *vt* 误导销售

mis-selling *n* [u] 误导性销售

misshapen /ˌmɪsˈʃeɪpən/ *adj* 畸形的〈*body, head, limb*〉; 奇形怪状的〈*rock, vegetable, fruit*〉

missile /ˈmɪsaɪl, Amer ˈmɪsl/ *n* **1** (weapon) 导弹; **a nuclear/short-range ～** 核导弹/短程导弹; **a ～ site** 导弹发射场 **2** (thrown object) 投掷物

missing /ˈmɪsɪŋ/ *adj* **1** (lost) 丢失的〈*object*〉; **there's money ～ from the till** 钱柜里有些钱不见了; **to be ～ from its usual place** 不在通常放的地方; **to go ～** colloq 不见了; **to report sth. (as) ～** 报失某物 **2** (untraced) 失踪的〈*person, ship*〉; **to report sb./sth. (as) ～** 报称某人/某物失踪 **3** (lacking) 缺少的〈*information, detail*〉; **to fill in the ～ letters** 填入所缺的字母; **to be ～ from sth.** 为某物所缺少; **there's a part ～ from the machine** 机器缺了一个零件; **the violin has two strings ～** 这把小提琴缺两根弦; **a set of Dickens's novels with two volumes ～** 一套缺了两册的狄更斯小说; **a man with a finger ～** *or* **a ～ finger** 一个少了一根手指的男人

missing: ～ in action *adj* 作战失踪的; **～ link** *n* **1** (in series, knowledge) 缺少的一环; **2** (fossil form) 缺环 [尤指推想中从类人猿发展到人类之间的过渡生物]

mission /ˈmɪʃn/ *n* **1** Mil (planned operation) 军事任务; **to be on a ～** 在执行一项任务; **to be sent on a ～ (to do ...)** 被派遣执行（…的）任务; **～ accomplished!** 任务已完成！; **to fly 30 ～s** 执行30次飞行任务 **2** (important assignment) 重要任务; **a fact-finding/diplomatic ～** 核查事实/外交任务 **3** (group of people) 代表团; **a large UK trade ～ to China** 派往中国的大型英国贸易代表团 **4** Relig (group) 传教团; (church, headquarters) 传教团总部; **a ～ school/hospital** 教会学校/医院 **5** (personal quest) 使命; **a ～ to do sth.** 做某事的使命; **a sense of ～** 使命感 **6** (into space) 太空飞行任务

missionary /ˈmɪʃənri, Amer -neri/ ▸**p. 409** *n* 传教士; **～ work/zeal** 传教/传教士般的极大热忱

missionary position *n* 传教士体位 [男上女下的性交姿势]

mission: ～ control *n* [u] 航天地面指挥中心; **～ creep** *n* [u] 任务蠕变 [指军事任务在执行过程中逐渐发生变化的现象]; **～ statement** *n* 任务说明

missis /ˈmɪsɪz/ *n* colloq hum **= missus**

Mississippi /ˌmɪsɪˈsɪpi/ ▸**p. 663** *pr n* **1** (river) 密西西比河 **2** (state) 密西西比州

missive /ˈmɪsɪv/ *n* esp hum 信函 [尤指官方长信]

Missouri /mɪˈzʊəri/ ▸**p. 663** *pr n* **1** (river) 密苏里河 **2** (state) 密苏里州

misspell /ˌmɪsˈspel/ *vt* (*pt, pp* **～ed** *or* esp Brit **misspelt** /ˌmɪsˈspelt/) 拼写错

misspelling /ˌmɪsˈspelɪŋ/ *n* 拼写错误; **a ～ for sth.** 某词的错误拼写

misspend /ˌmɪsˈspend/ *vt* (*pt, pp* **misspent** /ˌmɪsˈspent/) (spend wastefully) 浪费; (spend wrongly) 误用; **to ～ sth. on sth.** 将…浪费在某事上〈*time, money, energy*〉; **a misspent youth** hum 虚度的青春

misstate /ˌmɪsˈsteɪt/ *vt* 错误陈述

misstatement /ˌmɪsˈsteɪtmənt/ *n* 错误的陈述

missus /ˈmɪsɪz/ colloq hum *n* **1** (wife) 老婆; **the/my ～** 你的/我的老婆 **2** (as term of address) 大姐

missy /ˈmɪsi/ *n* colloq 姑娘 [用作称呼]

mist /mɪst/

A *n* **1** (thin fog) 薄雾 **2** (of perfume, spray) 喷雾 **3** (vapour) 水汽 **4** fig (haze, film) 视线模糊; **to see sb. through a ～ of tears** 泪眼模糊地看某人 **5** fig (of perception, memory) 迷雾; **to be lost in the ～s of time** 湮没在时间的迷雾之中

B *vt* 对…喷雾〈*plant*〉

C *vi* 《*eyes*》模糊不清

Phrasal verbs

- **mist over**

A *vi* **1** (become covered) 《*glasses, window, mirror, windscreen*》蒙上水汽 **2** (become blurred) 《*eyes, vision, TV picture*》模糊不清; **his eyes ～ed over with tears** 他泪眼模糊

B *vt* [**～ over sth., ～ sth. over**] 使…模糊〈*glasses, window, mirror, windscreen*〉; **to be ～ed over (with sth.)** （因某物）变模糊

- **mist up**

A *vi* 《*glasses, mirror, window, windscreen*》蒙上水汽

B *vt* [**～ up sth., ～ sth. up**] 使…模糊〈*glasses, mirror, window, windscreen*〉

mistakable, mistakeable /mɪˈsteɪkəbl/ *adj* 易认错的; **to be ～ for sth./sb.** 易被误认为某事物/某人

mistake /mɪˈsteɪk/

A *n* (misjudgement, error in action or calculation or of fact) 错误; (misunderstanding) 误解; **it is a ～ to do sth.** 做某事是个错误; **by ～** 错误地; **I left the door open by ～** 我不小心忘了关门; **to make a ～/the same ～ again** 犯错误/又犯同样的错误; **we all make ～s** 谁都会犯错误的; **to make a ～ about sth./sb.** 弄错某事/看错某人; **to make a ～ about the weather** 报错天气; **to make a ～ in doing sth.** 做某事犯下错误; **to make a ～ in adding up the total** 把总数加错; **to make the ～ of doing sth.** 错误地做某事; **to make a ～ over sth.** 把某事物弄错; **to learn by** *or* **from one's ～s** 从所犯错误中汲取教训; **the fourth child**

was a ～ 第4个孩子是意外怀孕所生; **that cake was a ～; I feel ill** 那个蛋糕真不该吃，我觉得很难受; **the figure/date/answer was a ～** 数字/日期/答案不正确; **my ～** 我的错; **make no ～ (about it)** colloq （这点）别搞错; **..., and no ～!** …毫无疑问!

B vt (pt **mistook,** pp **mistaken**) **1** (confuse) 误认 ‹*person, identity*›; 弄错 ‹*name, address, fact*›; **you can't ～ it** 你不会弄错的; **I mistook her for Susan** 我误以为她是苏珊; **it's impossible to ～ her style** 她的风格不可能和他人混淆; **there's no mistaking sth./sb.** 某物/某人不会被认错; **that dog's got rabies, there's no mistaking it** 那条狗明显患有狂犬病; **there's no mistaking who/what/why/that ...** 谁/什么/为什么/…不会被弄错 **2** (misinterpret) 误解 ‹*person, meaning, mood*›; **to ～ A for B** 把A误解为B; **to ～ sb.'s silence for consent** 把某人的沉默错当成赞同

mistaken /mɪˈsteɪkən/ adj **1** pred (wrong) 弄错的; **to be ～ about sth./sb.** 弄错某事物/认错某人; **to be ～ in doing sth.** 在做某事上是错的; **unless I'm very much ～, if I am not ～** 如果我没弄错的话 **2** (erroneous) 错误的 ‹*idea, opinion, conclusion*›; **a case of ～ identity** 认错人的例子; **to do sth. in the ～ belief that ...** 因错误地相信…而去做某事 **3** (applied unwisely) 施错对象的 ‹*kindness, enthusiasm, loyalty*›

mistakenly /mɪˈsteɪkənli/ adv 错误地; **whether ～ or not, they remain optimistic** 他们保持着乐观的态度，不管这种乐观是对是错

mister /ˈmɪstə(r)/ n **1** colloq (as form of address) 先生; **hey, ～!** 嗨，先生! **2** = **Mr**

mistime /ˌmɪsˈtaɪm/ vt 在不适当的时候做; **to ～ one's resignation** 在不恰当的时候辞职; **I ～d the announcement** 我宣布得不是时候

mistiming /ˌmɪsˈtaɪmɪŋ/ n 时机不适合

mistiness /ˈmɪstɪnɪs/ n [u] 雾蒙蒙

mistletoe /ˈmɪsltəʊ/ n [u] 槲寄生; **to kiss sb. under the ～** 在槲寄生枝下吻某人 [基督教习俗]

mistook /mɪˈstʊk/ pt ▸**mistake B**

mistranslate /ˌmɪstrænsˈleɪt/ vt 译错

mistranslation /ˌmɪstrænsˈleɪʃn/ n **1** [u] (act of mistranslating) 误译 **2** [c] (instance of mistranslating) 误译之处

mistreat /ˌmɪsˈtriːt/ vt 虐待 ‹*person, animal*›; 粗手粗脚地摆弄 ‹*object*›

mistreatment /ˌmɪsˈtriːtmənt/ n [u] (of person, animal) 虐待; (of object) 粗手粗脚的摆弄

mistress /ˈmɪstrɪs/ n **1** (woman in charge) 女管事; (of servant, animal) 女主人; **the ～ of the house** 房子的女主人; **to be ～ of the situation** 是掌控局面的女子; **she is her own ～** 她凡事自己做主; **to be ～ in one's own home** 是在家中做主的女人 **2** Brit Sch dated 女教师 **3** (sexual partner) 情妇; **to keep** or **have a ～** 养情妇

mistrial /ˌmɪsˈtraɪəl/ n 无效审判

mistrust /ˌmɪsˈtrʌst/

A vt 不信任 ‹*person*›; 怀疑 ‹*motives, promises, abilities*›

B n [u] **1** (lack of trust) 不信任 **2** (suspicion) 怀疑

mistrustful /ˌmɪsˈtrʌstfl/ adj **1** (lacking in trust) 不信任的; **he was ～ of his ability to make the right decision** 他不相信自己有能力作出正确的决定 **2** (suspicious) 多疑的; **am I being unduly ～?** 我是不是太多疑了?

mistrustfully /ˌmɪsˈtrʌstfəli/ adv **1** (without trust) 不信任地 **2** (suspiciously) 怀疑地

misty /ˈmɪsti/ adj **1** Meteorol 有雾的 ‹*weather, morning*›; **～ drizzle** 蒙蒙细雨; **a ～ valley/view** 薄雾笼罩的峡谷/景致 **2** (misted-up) 蒙上水汽的 ‹*lens, window, mirror*› **3** (blurred) 模糊的 ‹*vision, TV picture, photograph*›; **～ blue/grey** 浅蓝色/烟灰色 **4** (tearful, wistful) 泪水模糊的 ‹*eyes*›; 悲伤的 ‹*look*› **5** fig (vague) 模糊的 ‹*past*›; 蒙眬的 ‹*memories*›

misty-eyed adj 泪眼蒙眬的; **to be ～ (about sth.)** （因某事物）感伤

misunderstand /ˌmɪsʌndəˈstænd/ vt (pt, pp **misunderstood**) 误解; **don't ～ me** 别误会我的意思; **young people often feel misunderstood** 年轻人往往觉得被人误解

misunderstanding /ˌmɪsʌndəˈstændɪŋ/ n **1** (error of comprehension) 误解 **2** (minor disagreement) 争执; **a ～ between A and B** A与B之间的争执

misunderstood /ˌmɪsʌndəˈstʊd/ pt, pp ▸**misunderstand**

misuse

A /ˌmɪsˈjuːz/ vt **1** 错用 ‹*equipment, talents*›; 误用 ‹*word, expression*›; 滥用 ‹*power, resources, funds*›; **to ～ sth. as sth.** 将某物错用作某物 **2** (exploit) 虐待 ‹*person, child*›

B /ˌmɪsˈjuːs/ n [c and u] (of equipment, talents) 错用; (of word, expression) 误用; (of funds, power, resources) 滥用; **the ～ of sth. as sth.** 将某物错当作某物用

MIT abbr = **Massachusetts Institute of Technology** 麻省理工学院

mite[1] /maɪt/

A n **1** colloq (small amount) 少量 **2** (small child) 小孩; (small animal) 小动物; **poor little ～!** 可怜的小家伙!

B **a mite** adv colloq 稍许; **a ～ ridiculous** 有点荒唐的; **this curry is a ～ too hot for me** 我觉得这道咖喱菜太辣了点

mite[2] n Zool 螨; **harvest ～** 秋螨; **cheese ～** 干酪蛆; **ear ～** 耳螨

miter /ˈmaɪtə(r)/ n, vt Amer = **mitre**

mitigate /ˈmɪtɪɡeɪt/ vt 缓和 ‹*suffering, anxiety, crisis*›; 减轻 ‹*punishment, effects, sentence*›

mitigating /ˈmɪtɪɡeɪtɪŋ/ adj attrib 起缓和作用的 ‹*effects, measures, excuse*›

mitigating circumstances npl 可减轻处罚的情节

mitigation /ˌmɪtɪˈɡeɪʃn/ n [u] 减轻罪行; **in ～ of ...** 为减轻…的罪行

mitochondrial /ˌmaɪtəʊˈkɒndrɪəl/ adj 线粒体的; **～ DNA/genome/gene** 线粒体DNA/基因组/基因

mitochondrion /ˌmaɪtəʊˈkɒndrɪən/ n (pl **mitochondria** /ˌmaɪtəʊˈkɒndrɪə/) 线粒体

mitosis /mɪˈtəʊsɪs, maɪ-/ n (pl **mitoses** /maɪˈtəʊsiːz/) 有丝分裂

mitral valve /ˈmaɪtrəl vælv/ n 二尖瓣

mitre /ˈmaɪtə(r)/ Brit

A n **1** (headdress) 主教冠 **2** **a ～ (joint)** 斜接头

B vt 使斜接

mitre box 辅锯箱

mitt /mɪt/ n **1** (mitten) 连指手套 **2** colloq (hand) 手; **take** or **get your ～s off me!** 别碰我! **3** (in baseball) 棒球手套

mitten /ˈmɪtn/ n 连指手套

mix /mɪks/

A vt **1** (combine) 使…混合 ‹*object(s), style(s)*›; **to ～ A and B together, to ～ A with** or **and B** 把A和B混合在一起; **to ～ business and** or **with pleasure** 把社交活动和做生意结合起来; **to ～ marriage and a career** 把婚姻和事业结合成一体; **to ～ sth. into sth.** 把某物掺入某物; **to ～ one's drinks** 喝混酒; **to ～ and match** 混合搭配 ‹*garments, colours*› **2** (make up) 调制 ‹*cocktail*›; 配制 ‹*medicine*›; 拌 ‹*concrete*›; **to ～ sb. sth., to ～ sth. for sb.** 为某人调制 ‹*drink*›; **to ～ it (with sb.)** colloq (cause trouble) 找（某人的）茬; (fight) （和某人）打架 **3** Mus, Cin, TV (combine) 混合 ‹*sounds, lighting effects*› **4** Mus (put together) 混录 ‹*album*›

B vi **1** (be combined) «*ingredient(s), style(s)*» 相混合; **to ～ with sth.** 与某物相混合; **to ～ together** 混合在一起; **oil and water don't ～** 油和水不相溶; fig 水火不相容 **2** (socialize) 交往; **to ～ with sb.** 和某人交往

C n **1** [c] (mixture) (of things) 混合物; (of people) 混杂的一群人; **a cotton and polyester ～** 棉涤; **the correct ～ of full-time to part-time staff** 专职和兼职员工的恰当比例 **2** [u and c] Culin 混合料; **cake ～** 蛋糕粉; **egg ～** 鸡蛋糊 **3** [u and c] Constr 配料 **4** [c] Mus 混录; **in the ～** 在混录中

Phrasal verbs

- **mix around** vt [**～ sth. around, ～ around sth.**] 使…混杂 ‹*names, objects*›
- **mix in** vt [**～ sth. in, ～ in sth.**] 掺入 ‹*ingredient, substance*›
- **mix up** vt [**～ sth./sb. up, ～ up sth./sb.**] **1** (get confused over) 把…弄混 ‹*people, names, dates*›; **to ～ up A and** or **with B** 把A和B弄混; **to get sth./sb. ～ed up with sth./sb.** 把…和…弄混 **2** (make confused) 把…弄糊涂 ‹*person*›; **to be/get ～ed up** 被弄糊涂; **to be/get ～ed up over** or **about sth.** 弄不清某事 **3** (jumble up) 弄乱 ‹*objects*› **4** usu passive (involve) **to be/get ～ed up in sth.** 与…有牵连 ‹*crime, drugs*›; **to be/get ～ed up with sb.** 与某人混在一起

mixed /mɪkst/ adj **1** (varied) 混杂的; **the students are a very ～ bunch** 这些学生互相间有很大的不同; **last month, the weather was very ～** 上个月天气变化不定 **2** (contrasting) 互相矛盾的 ‹*response, reaction*›; **to have ～ fortunes** 祸福齐临 **3** (for both sexes) 男女兼收的 ‹*school*›; 男女同住的 ‹*dormitory*›; 男女共用的 ‹*changing rooms*› **4** (multiracial) 种族混杂的 ‹*society, community, neighbourhood*›; **of ～ race/blood** 不同种族/混血的; **of** or **from ～ backgrounds** 不同背景的

mixed: ～ ability adj 不同能力的; **a ～ ability class/group/school** 学生水平不一的班级/群体/学校; **～ bag** n fig colloq 大杂烩; **the applicants for the post make a ～ bag** 应聘该职位的人形形色色; **～ bag** n 福祸参半之事; **～ company** n [u] 男女混合的群体; **in ～ company** 男女都在场时; **～ doubles** npl 混合双打; **～-doubles tournament/partners** 混合双打锦标赛/参赛者; **～ economy** n 混合经济; **～ farming** n [u] 混合农作; **～ feelings** npl 复杂感情; **to have ～ feelings (about sb./sth.)** （对某人/某事物）怀有复杂的感情; **with ～ feelings** 怀着复杂感情; **～ grill** n 烤杂排; **～ herbs** npl 什锦菜 [由欧芹、牛至和百里香等混合制成]; **～ marriage** n (between different races) 异族通婚; (between different religions) 异教通婚; **～ media** npl 混合媒体; **～ metaphor** n 混合隐喻

mixed race

A n **to be of ～** 是混血儿

B **mixed-race** adj 混血的 ‹*child, ancestry*›

mixed salad n 什锦色拉

mixed-up adj colloq 迷茫的 ‹*person*›; 混杂的 ‹*personality, emotions*›; **to be ～ about sth.** 对某事物感到迷惑

mixer /ˈmɪksə(r)/ n **1** Culin (device) 搅拌器 **2** Constr (for concrete) 搅拌机 **3** (person) 擅长交际的人; **to be a good/bad ～** 善于/不擅交际 **4** (drink) 调酒用的饮料 **5** Electron 混音器

mixer tap, Amer **mixer faucet** ns 冷热水混合龙头

mixing: ～ board n = **～ desk**; **～ bowl** n 拌菜碗; **～ desk** n 混录台

mixture /ˈmɪkstʃə(r)/ n **1** [c] (of substances, people, elements) 混合体; **a ～ of A and B** A和B的混合体; **a lethal ～** 致命的组合 **2** [u] (of different qualities, emotions, etc.) 混合; **the commander was regarded with a ～ of admiration and fear** 人们对这位指挥官又敬又怕

mix-up n colloq 混乱; **a ～ over sth.** 对某事的搅乱; **to get into a ～** 陷入混乱

mizzen, mizen /ˈmɪzn/ n **1** **～ (mast)** 后桅 **2** **～(sail)** 后桅纵帆

Mk *abbr* = **Mark** 型号; **a ~ II Jaguar** 捷豹2型

MLitt /ˌemˈlɪt/ *abbr* = **Master of Letters** (degree) 文学硕士学位; (scholar) 文学硕士; **to have/do an ~** 持有/攻读文学硕士学位; **an ~ in philosophy** (degree) 哲学硕士学位; (scholar) 哲学硕士

mm *abbr* = **millimetre(s)** 毫米

MMR *abbr* = **measles, mumps, and rubella** 麻疹－腮腺炎－风疹三联疫苗

MMS *abbr* = **Multimedia Messaging Service** （手机）多媒体信息服务

MN *abbr* Amer = **Minnesota**

mnemonic /nɪˈmɒnɪk/
A *n* 帮助记忆的词句
B *adj* 帮助记忆的 ‹*device, verses*›; **~ techniques** 记忆技巧

MO *abbr* **1** = **Medical Officer** 卫生官员 **2** = **money order** **3** Amer = **Missouri 2**

mo /məʊ/ *n* esp Brit colloq 瞬间; **just a ~!** 稍等一会儿！; **half a ~ and I'll have finished** 就一会儿，我马上就干完了

moan /məʊn/
A *vi* **1** (cry, groan) 呻吟; **to ~ in agony/with pleasure** 痛苦地/快乐地呻吟 **2** pej (complain) 抱怨; **to ~ about sth./sb.** 抱怨某事物/某人; **the children ~ed and groaned the entire journey** 整个旅途中孩子们都在抱怨 **3** (make moaning sound) «*wind*» 呼啸; **the door ~ed on its hinges** 门在铰链上吱吱嘎嘎地响
B *vt* **1** (wail) 呻吟; **'help me,' he ~ed** "救命啊，" 他呻吟道 **2** (complain) 抱怨 ‹*dislike, dissatisfaction*›; **to ~ that ...** 抱怨道…
C *n* **1** (wail, groan) 呻吟 **2** often pej (complaint) 抱怨; **to have a ~ about sth./sb.** 抱怨某事物/某人 **3** (moaning sound) 呜咽; **the ~ of the wind through the trees** 风掠过树丛的萧萧声

moaner /ˈməʊnə(r)/ *n* colloq 发牢骚者

moaning /ˈməʊnɪŋ/ *n* [u] **1** (groaning) 呻吟 **2** (complaining) 抱怨 **3** (sound of wind etc.) 呜咽

moat /məʊt/ *n* 护城河

moated /ˈməʊtɪd/ *adj* 有护城河的 ‹*castle, town*›

mob /mɒb/
A *n + v sing or pl* **1** (crowd) 暴民; **an angry ~ of protestors** 一群激愤的抗议者 **2** (criminal gang) 犯罪团伙; **the Mob** Amer 犯罪集团 **3** colloq (associated group of friends) 一帮; **Byron, Keats, and all that ~** 拜伦、济慈一类的诗人 **4** pej (ordinary people) **the ~** 乌合之众
B *vt* (*pres p etc.* **-bb-**) 围攻 ‹*prey, intruder*›; 成群涌入 ‹*shop*›; 把…团团围住 ‹*pop star*›

mobbing /ˈmɒbɪŋ/ *n* [u] [鸟类的] 聚扰

mobile /ˈməʊbaɪl, Amer -bl, *also* -biːl/
A *adj* **1** (movable) 可移动的 ‹*machine, exhibition, building, device*› **2** Mil, Police 机动的 ‹*artillery, troops, police unit*› **3** (able to walk around) 能走动的; (able to move quickly) 跑动灵活的; (able to travel) 有交通工具的; **he's not as ~ as he was** 他不如从前腿脚灵便了 **4** (adaptable) 适应性强的 ‹*person, population, workforce*›
B *n* 悬挂饰物

mobile: ~ canteen *n* 移动食堂; **~ communications** *npl* 移动通信; **~ home** *n* 活动住房; **~ Internet** *n* [u] 移动互联网; 移动互联网的 ‹*access, market, service*›; **~ library** *n* 流动图书馆; **~ phone** *n* 手机; **~ shop** *n* 流动商店; **~ studio** *n* 移动演播室; **~ telephony** *n* [u] (use) 移动电话使用; (operation) 移动电话操作

mobility /məʊˈbɪləti/ *n* [u] **1** (ability to be moved) 便携性 **2** (agility) 灵活性; (ability to travel) 移动能力 **3** Sociol 流动性

mobility allowance *n* Brit 残疾人交通津贴

mobilization /ˌməʊbɪlaɪˈzeɪʃn, Amer -lɪˈz-/ *n* **1** [u and c] Mil 动员; **~ against sb./sth.** 反对某人/某事物的动员; **to order a ~ of forces** 发出军队动员令 **2** [u] (rallying) 鼓动; **~ of public opinion/the oppressed** 对公众舆论/受压迫者的鼓动 **3** [u] (organization) 组织; **the mayor organized the ~ of the villagers into search parties** 市长把村民组成了几个搜索队 **4** [u] (utilization) 动用; **the full ~ of resources** 对资源的全面调用

mobilize /ˈməʊbɪlaɪz/
A *vt* **1** Mil 动员 ‹*nation, population*›; 调集 ‹*troops, tanks*›; **to ~ sb./sth. against sb./sth.** 动员某人/调动某物抗击某人/某事物 **2** (rally, motivate) 鼓动 ‹*supporters*›; **to ~ one's energies** 鼓足干劲 **3** (organize) 组织 ‹*supporters, volunteers*›; **to ~ sb./sth. to do sth.** 组织某人/某团体做某事; **to ~ sb./sth. for sth.** 为某事组织某人/某团体; **the villagers were ~d into search parties** 村民被组织成儿支搜索队 **4** (utilize) 动用 ‹*resources*›
B *vi* Mil 接受动员; **to ~ against sb./sth.** 动员起来对抗某人/某事物

mob rule *n* [u] 暴民统治

mobster /ˈmɒbstə(r)/ *n* colloq 暴徒

moccasin /ˈmɒkəsɪn/ *n* 莫卡辛软皮鞋

mocha /ˈmɒkə, Amer ˈməʊkə/ *n* **1** [u] (coffee) 摩卡咖啡 **2** [u and c] (flavouring) 摩卡味饮料; **~ flavour/ice-cream/yogurt** 摩卡口味/冰激凌/酸奶

mock /mɒk/
A *vt* **1** (laugh at) 嘲笑 **2** (parody) 戏谑地模仿 ‹*person, style, accent*› **3** fig liter (frustrate) 挫败 ‹*efforts, attempts*›; 使…落空 ‹*hopes*›
B *vi* 嘲笑; **you may ~! one day I'll prove you all wrong** 你们笑吧！总有一天我会证明你们都错了
C *adj attrib* **1** (imitation) 仿制的 ‹*leather, ivory, caviar*›; **~-Gothic architecture** 仿哥特式建筑 **2** (feigned) 假装的 ‹*modesty, solemnity, ignorance, humility*›; **in ~ terror/innocence** 假装恐惧/天真 **3** (for training or practice) 模拟的 ‹*battle, examination, auction, interview*›
D *n* **to make (a) ~ of sth./sb.** 拿某事物/某人开玩笑
E **mocks** *npl* Brit Sch colloq 模拟考试

Phrasal verb
- **mock up** *vt* [**~ sth. up, ~ up sth.**] 仿制 ‹*vehicle, ship, engine*›

mocker /ˈmɒkə(r)/ *n* 嘲笑者; **a ~ of authority** 蔑视权势的人; **to put the ~s on sth.** Brit colloq (thwart) 使某事受挫; (bring bad luck to) 给某事带来厄运

mockery /ˈmɒkəri/ *n* **1** [u] (ridicule) 嘲笑; **the trial was a ~ of justice** 这次审判是对正义的嘲弄 **2** [c] pej (travesty) 歪曲; **to make a ~ of sth.** 歪曲某事 **3** [c] (object of ridicule) 笑柄

mock-heroic *adj* **1** (pretending to be heroic) 模仿英雄气概的 ‹*words, pose*›; **~ defiance** 假装的大无畏 **2** Literat 模仿英雄诗体的; **a ~ poem** 仿英雄体讽刺诗

mocking /ˈmɒkɪŋ/
A *adj* 嘲笑的 ‹*tone, voice*›; 嘲弄的 ‹*laughter, smile*›
B *n* [u] 嘲笑

mockingbird /ˈmɒkɪŋbɜːd/ *n* 嘲鸫

mockingly /ˈmɒkɪŋli/ *adv* 嘲弄地; **to laugh ~** 嘲笑

mock: ~ orange *n* 山梅花; **~ turtle soup** *n* [u] 仿甲鱼汤 [用小牛头或其他肉制成]; **~-up** *n* **1** Tech (model) 实体模型; **2** Print 版面设计

MOD *abbr* = **Ministry of Defence** Brit 国防部

mod /mɒd/ *n* Brit Hist 摩登派 [20世纪60年代穿戴整洁时髦、骑小轮摩托车的青年]; 摩登派的 ‹*hairstyle, band, fashions*›

modal /ˈməʊdl/
A *n* **~ (auxiliary** *or* **verb)** 情态动词 (construction) 情态动词结构
B *adj* **1** 情态动词的 ‹*clause, use*› **2** Mus 调式的 ‹*scale, plainsong, harmony*›

modality /məˈdæləti/ *n* formal 方式

mod cons /ˌmɒdˈkɒnz/ *npl* = **modern conveniences** Brit colloq 现代化生活设备

mode /məʊd/ *n* **1** (way) 方式; (style of speech, behaviour, dress) 风格; (method) 方法; **~ of transport** 运输模式 **2** Comput, Tech 工作状态; **in printing/playback ~** 处于打印/回放状态的 **3** (of person) (way of behaving) 行为方式; (way of feeling) 心情; **I'm still in work ~** 我还是惦念着工作; **when I am at home, I am in wife-and-mother ~** 我在家就做贤妻良母 **4** (fashion) 风尚; **she wears her hair in the latest ~** 她梳着最时髦的发式

model /ˈmɒdl/
A *n* **1** (scale representation) 模型; **a ~ of sth.** 某物的模型; **a ~ of the airport** 机场的模型; **a statistical/mathematical/economic ~** 统计学/数学/经济模型 **2** (type of car, appliance) 型号; **the new/latest ~** 新型号/最新型号; **a 1956 ~** (car) 1956 年款汽车 **3** (example) 样板; **a ~ for sth.** 某物的样板; **to serve as the ~ for a character** 充当人物的原型; **a ~ of ...** …的典型 ‹*good quality, calm*›; **on the ~ of sth.** 仿照某物; **to take sth./sb. as one's** *or* **a ~** 把某事物/某人作为榜样; **to hold sth./sb. up as a ~** 以某事物/某人为榜样 **4** Art, Phot, Fashn 模特儿; **a glamour/photographic ~** 性感/摄影模特儿; **a male ~** 男模特儿
B *adj* **1** (small-scale) 用作模型的; **a ~ aeroplane** 飞机模型 **2** (exemplary) 模范的 ‹*husband, employee*›; 示范的 ‹*farm, prison*›; **a ~ answer to an exam question** 一道考试题的标准答案
C *vt* (*pres p etc.* **-ll-** Brit, **-l-** Amer) **1** (base) **to ~ sth. on** *or* **after sth.** 仿某物塑造 ‹*character*›; 仿某物建造 ‹*building*›; 仿某物制定 ‹*law*›; **to be ~led on previous work** 仿照以前的工作而成; **to ~ oneself on sb.** 效仿某人 **2** (shape) 做…的模型 ‹*figure*›; 用…塑造 ‹*clay*›; **to ~ sth. in clay** 用陶土塑造某物; **to ~ sth. into sth.** 把某物做成某物 **3** Fashn 当模特展示 ‹*garment*›; **to ~ clothes for a living** 做服装模特谋生 **4** Math, Comput 设计…的模型 ‹*economy, climate, process*›
D *vi* (*pres p etc.* **-ll-** Brit, **-l-** Amer) **1** Art, Fashn, Phot 当模特儿; **to ~ for sb./sth.** 为某人/某物当模特儿 **2** (make model) **to ~ in clay** 用陶土做模型

model answer *n* 标准答案

modeller Brit, **modeler** Amer /ˈmɒdələ(r)/ *n* 模型制作者

modelling Brit, **modeling** Amer /ˈmɒdəlɪŋ/ *n* [u] **1** (for photographer, artist, displaying clothes) 当模特儿; **to do ~ for sb./sth.** 为某人/某机构当模特儿 **2** Art (with clay etc.) 模型制作; **clay/wax ~** 泥模/蜡模制作 **3** Comput, Math 模型设计; **~ software** 模型设计软件

modelling clay *n* [u] 制模陶土

modem /ˈməʊdem/ *n* 调制解调器

moderate
A /ˈmɒdərət/ *adj* **1** (not extreme) 中等的 ‹*size, amount, speed*›; 温和的 ‹*temperature, climate*›; 中等强度的 ‹*rainfall*› **2** (mediocre) 一般的 ‹*abilities, intelligence, visibility, performance*› **3** (restrained) 有节制的 ‹*person, temperament, drinker, appetite*›; 适度的 ‹*demands, language, consumption*›; **to be ~ in sth.** 在某事上有节制; **she was ~ in her criticism** 她的批评不过分 **4** esp Pol 温和的 ‹*policies, leadership, politician*›
B /ˈmɒdərət/ *n* esp Pol 温和派
C /ˈmɒdəreɪt/ *vt* **1** (restrain) 节制 ‹*language, appetite, demands*› **2** Brit Sch, Univ (standardize) 使…符合标准 ‹*examinations, examination papers*› **3** (preside over) 主持 ‹*debate, discussion, deliberative body*›
D /ˈmɒdəreɪt/ *vi* «*weather*» 转好; «*storm, wind*» 减弱; «*opinions*» 变得温和; «*drinking*» 有节制; «*hostility*» 减弱

moderate: ~ breeze *n* 和风 [4级风]; **~ gale** *n* 疾风 [7级风]

moderately /'mɒdərətli/ *adv* **1** (quite, fairly) 适度地 ‹*warm, rich, expensive*›; **how hungry are you? — oh, ~** 你饿了吗？——哦，还好; **~ priced/sized** 价格/尺寸适中的 **2** (to a limited degree) 一般地 ‹*good, well, severe, steep, successful, talented*›; **~ satisfactory** 差强人意的 **3** (with restraint) 有节制地 ‹*criticize, exercise, express, drink*›

moderating /'mɒdəreɪtɪŋ/ *adj attrib* 起缓和作用的 ‹*influence, force, factor*›; **a ~ effect** 缓和作用

moderation /ˌmɒdə'reɪʃn/ *n* **1** [u] (self-restraint) 节制; **~ in ...** 在…方面的节制 ‹*appetite, ambition, habit*›; **to act/behave with ~** 行动/行为有节制; **to eat/drink/exercise in ~** 适量进食/饮酒/锻炼 **2** [u and c] (relaxation) 缓和; **he called for a ~ of the government's confrontational style** 他呼吁政府缓和其对抗风格

moderator /'mɒdəreɪtə(r)/ *n* **1** (chairperson) 会议主席 **2** Brit Sch, Univ 评分监督 **3** **Moderator** Relig 长老会会议主席; **M~ of the Church of Scotland** 苏格兰长老会会议主席 **4** Nucl 减速剂

modern /'mɒdn/ *adj* **1** (present-day) 当今的 ‹*world, society, life*› **2** (recent) 近代的 ‹*history*›; **the ~ era** *or* **period** 近代; **in ~ times** 在近代 **3** (up-to-date) 最新的 ‹*technology, computer, method*› **4** (contemporary) 现代的 ‹*person, country*›; 现代派的 ‹*author, literature*›; 新潮的 ‹*outlook, idea*› **5** Ling 现代的 ‹*Greek, Spanish, French*›

modern: ~ art *n* [u] 现代艺术; **~-day** *adj* 现代的

modern dress
A *n* [u] 现代服装
B **modern-dress** *modif* Theat 穿现代服装的 ‹*production, performance*›

modern: ~ English *n* [u] 现代英语 [约公元1500年迄今的英语]; **~ Greek** *n* [u] 现代希腊语; **~ history** *n* [u] 近代史

modernism, Modernism /'mɒdənɪzəm/ *n* **1** [u] Art, Literat, Relig 现代主义 **2** [u] (modern character) 现代风格; **a strange mix of nostalgia and ~** 怀旧与现代风格的奇异混合 **3** [c] usu pej (custom) 现代习俗; (word, expression) 现代词语; (innovation) 现代发明

modernist, Modernist /'mɒdənɪst/
A *adj* 现代派的 ‹*literature, writer*›
B *n* 现代主义者

modernistic /ˌmɒdə'nɪstɪk/ *adj* 现代派的

modernity /mɒ'dɜːnəti/ *n* [u] 现代性

modernization /ˌmɒdɜːnaɪ'zeɪʃn, Amer -nɪ'z-/ *n* [u and c] 现代化; **a ~ programme** 现代化计划

modernize /'mɒdənaɪz/
A *vt* 使现代化; **a fully ~d office/transport system** 完全现代化的办公室/交通体系
B *vi* 现代化

modernizer /'mɒdənaɪzə(r)/ *n* 现代化主义者

modern language *n* 现代语言; **~s** 现代语言学; **a ~s student/teacher** 现代语言专业的学生/教师; **a ~s department** 现代语言学系

modest /'mɒdɪst/ *adj* **1** (unassuming) 谦虚的; **he's just being ~!** 他只是谦虚而已！; **to be ~ about one's achievements** 对自己的成就很谦虚; **may I make a ~ suggestion?** 能否容我谏上一言？ **2** (moderate) 适中的 ‹*results*›; 不多的 ‹*amount, income, profit, insurance*›; 有限的 ‹*improvement*›; **his book was a ~ success** 他的书取得了一定的成功; **her achievements have been ~ in comparison with her predecessor's** 和前任相比，她的成就不算大; **to be ~ in sth.** 在…方面不过分 ‹*ambitions, demands, requirements*› **3** (humble) 简朴的 ‹*house, appearance*›; 卑微的 ‹*background*› **4** (demure) 端庄的 ‹*dress, woman*›

modestly /'mɒdɪstli/ *adv* **1** (unassumingly) 谦虚地 ‹*speak, suggest, deny*› **2** (moderately) 适度地 ‹*priced*›; **he has been ~ successful/satisfied** 他还算成功/满意 **3** (humbly) 简朴地 ‹*live, celebrate*›; **a ~ furnished apartment** 陈设朴素的公寓房 **4** (demurely) 端庄地 ‹*dress, undress*›

modesty /'mɒdɪsti/ *n* [u] **1** (humility) 谦虚; **false ~** 虚伪的谦虚; **in all ~** 毫不自夸地 **2** (smallness) (of result) 适中; (of amount, income, profit, increase) 不多; (of improvement, success, achievements) 有限; (of demands, ambitions, requirements) 不过分 **3** (humbleness) (of surroundings, furnishings) 简朴; (of origins) 卑微 **4** (demureness) 端庄

modicum /'mɒdɪkəm/ *n* formal 少量; **a ~ of sth.** 少量的某物; **a ~ of effort/common sense/truth** 些许努力/常识/真相

modifiable /'mɒdɪfaɪəbl/ *adj* 可修改的 ‹*design, policy, contract*›; 可改变的 ‹*factor*›

modification /ˌmɒdɪfɪ'keɪʃn/ *n* [u and c] 修改; **to make ~s to** *or* **in sth.** 修改 ‹*policy, statement, plan*›; **the machine needs ~** 这台机器需要改装

modifier /'mɒdɪfaɪə(r)/ *n* 修饰语

modify /'mɒdɪfaɪ/ *vt* **1** (alter, change) 修改 ‹*plan, timetable, computer program*›; 改变 ‹*belief, procedure, religion, tradition, form*›; 改装 ‹*engine, weapon*› **2** (moderate) 缓和…的措词 ‹*statement, policy*›; 降低 ‹*demands*›; 减轻 ‹*penalty*›; **the wording was modified to 'notes with concern'** 措词改成了语气较缓和的"关切地注意到" **3** Ling 修饰

modifying /'mɒdɪfaɪɪŋ/ *adj attrib* **1** (gen) 修正的 ‹*statement, note, clause*› **2** Ling 修饰的

modish /'məʊdɪʃ/ *adj* usu pej 时髦的 ‹*style, jargon, design, pessimism*›

modishly /'məʊdɪʃli/ *adv* usu pej 时髦地 ‹*dressed, furnished, decorated*›

modular /'mɒdjʊlə(r), Amer -dʒʊ-/ *adj* **1** Aerosp, Constr, Electron 多部件组成的 ‹*circuits, spacecraft*›; 组合式的 ‹*furniture, house*›; 模块化的 ‹*program*›; 积木式的 ‹*construction*› **2** Sch, Univ 分单元的 ‹*degree course, tuition, method*›

modulate /'mɒdjʊleɪt, Amer -dʒʊ-/
A *vt* **1** (adjust, vary) 变换 ‹*voice, tone, pitch*› **2** formal (regulate, control) 调节 ‹*speed, flow, process, response*› **3** Electron, Radio 调制 ‹*signal, wave, amplitude, frequency*›
B *vi* 转调; **to ~ (from sth.) to sth.** «*music, key*» (从某调) 转至某调

modulation /ˌmɒdjʊ'leɪʃn, Amer -dʒʊ-/ *n* **1** [u and c] (inflection of sound or voice) 调整 **2** [u] formal (control) 控制 **3** [u and c] Electron, Radio 调制; **amplitude/frequency ~** 调幅/调频 **4** [u and c] Mus 转调; **~s from one key to another** 从一音调转为另一音调

module /'mɒdjuːl, Amer -dʒʊ-/ *n* **1** Constr, Electron 标准部件 **2** Comput 模块 **3** Aerosp 独立舱 **4** Sch, Univ 单元

modulus /'mɒdjʊləs, Amer -dʒʊ-/ *n* (*pl* **moduli** /'mɒdjʊli/) **1** Math 模数; **~ of logarithm** 对数模 **2** Phys 模量; **~ of elasticity/rigidity** 弹性/刚性模量

modus operandi /ˌməʊdəs ˌɒpə'rændi/ *n* formal 一贯做法

modus vivendi /ˌməʊdəs vɪ'vendi/ *n* formal [尤指使冲突各方可以和平共处的] 暂行协定

Mogadishu /ˌmɒgə'dɪʃuː/ *pr n* 摩加迪沙

moggie, moggy /'mɒgi/ *ns* Brit colloq pej 猫

mogul¹ /'məʊgl/
A *n* **1** **Mogul** Hist 莫卧儿大帝 **2** colloq (magnate) 大亨; **a newspaper ~** 报业巨头; **a media ~** 媒体巨子
B **Mogul** *adj* Hist 莫卧儿帝国的 ‹*emperor, rule*›; **the M~ dynasty** 莫卧儿王朝

mogul² *n* (in skiing) 猫跳 [滑雪道的隆起处]

MOH *abbr* = **Medical Officer of Health** 健康检查官

mohair /'məʊheə(r)/ *n* [u] (cloth) 马海毛织物; (wool) 马海毛毛线; 马海毛的 ‹*sweater, scarf*›; **~ wool** 马海毛毛线

Mohammed /məʊ'hæmed/ *pr n* 穆罕默德; **if the mountain will not come to ~, then ~ must go to the mountain** 如果事不迁就人，那么人就得迁就事

Mohammedan /məʊ'hæmɪdən/ archaic
A *adj* 伊斯兰教的
B *n* 伊斯兰教徒

Mohammedanism /məʊ'hæmɪdənɪzəm/ *n* [u] archaic 伊斯兰教

mohican /məʊ'hiːkən/ *n* 莫希干发型 [一种朋克发型，只在头的中部留一窄条直立短发]; **a ~ hairstyle** *or* **haircut** 莫希干发式

Mohs scale /'məʊz skeɪl, 'mɔːs-/ *n* 莫式硬度标

moist /mɔɪst/ *adj* **1** (damp) 微湿的 ‹*air*›; 湿润的 ‹*surface, skin, soil*›; **his eyes were ~ with tears** 他眼含泪水 **2** (succulent) 多汁的 ‹*meat*›; 松软的 ‹*cake, dough*›

moisten /'mɔɪsn/
A *vt* 弄湿; **to ~ sth. with sth.** 用某物弄湿某物
B *vi* «*eyes*» 变得湿润

moistness /'mɔɪstnɪs/ *n* [u] **1** (dampness) (of air) 潮湿; (of surface, skin, soil) 湿润 **2** (succulence) (of meat) 多汁; (of cake, dough) 松软

moisture /'mɔɪstʃə(r)/ *n* [u] (in air) 水汽; (in or on soil, surface) 潮气; (sweat) 汗湿

moisturize /'mɔɪstʃəraɪz/ *vt* 滋润 ‹*skin*›

moisturizer /'mɔɪstʃəraɪzə(r)/ *n* [u and c] (lotion) 润肤露; (cream) 润肤霜

moisturizing /'mɔɪstʃəraɪzɪŋ/ *adj attrib* 润肤的 ‹*cream, lotion*›; 滋润的 ‹*agent, shampoo*›

molar /'məʊlə(r)/ *n* 臼齿

molasses /mə'læsɪz/ *n* [u] **1** 糖蜜 **2** Amer (golden syrup) 糖浆

mold /məʊld/ *n, vt* Amer = **mould¹**, **mould²**

molder /'məʊldə(r)/ *vi* Amer = **moulder**

molding /'məʊldɪŋ/ *n* Amer = **moulding**

Moldova /mɒl'dəʊvə/ *pr n* 摩尔多瓦

Moldovan /mɒl'dəʊvən/ ▸p. 503, p. 426
A *adj* (of Moldova) 摩尔多瓦的; (of the people) 摩尔多瓦人的; (of the language) 摩尔多瓦语的
B *n* **1** [c] (person) 摩尔多瓦人 **2** [u] (language) 摩尔多瓦语

moldy /'məʊldi/ *adj* Amer = **mouldy**

mole¹ /məʊl/ *n* **1** Zool 鼹鼠 **2** (spy) 内奸

mole² *n* Med 痣

mole³ *n* (breakwater) 防波堤

mole⁴ *n* Chem, Phys 摩尔; **a ~ of sth.** 一摩尔的某物质

molecular /mə'lekjʊlə(r)/ *adj* 分子的 ‹*structure, chemistry*›; **~ weight/diagram/physics** 分子量/分子模型图/分子物理

molecular biology *n* [u] 分子生物学

molecule /'mɒlɪkjuːl/ *n* 分子

molehill /'məʊlhɪl/ *n* 鼹丘; **to make a mountain out of a ~** 小题大做

moleskin /'məʊlskɪn/ *n* **1** [u and c] (fur) 鼹鼠皮; **~ gloves** 鼹鼠皮手套 **2** [u] Tex (cotton) 厚毛头斜纹棉布; **~ trousers/waistcoat** 厚毛头斜纹布裤子/背心

molest /mə'lest/ *vt* **1** (pester, harass) 骚扰 **2** (sexually assault) 对…进行性骚扰

molestation /ˌməʊle'steɪʃn/ *n* **1** [u] (harassment) 骚扰; **without ~** 不受干扰地 **2** [u and c] (sexual assault) 性骚扰

molester /mə'lestə(r)/ *n* = **child molester**

moll /mɒl/ *n* colloq **(gangster's) ~** 恶棍情妇

mollify /'mɒlɪfaɪ/ *vt* 抚慰 ‹*person*›

m

Modifiers

■ When there is more than one modifier in a sentence, the modifiers must follow a certain sequence in both English and Chinese.

■ In Chinese, all modifiers precede the word they describe. This contrasts with English where modifiers such as attributive clauses, prepositional phrases, etc. follow the noun.

■ Chinese modifiers include adjectives, demonstrative pronouns, possessive adjectives, numeral phrases, nouns, verbal phrases/verbal clauses, etc. Generally speaking, the order is:

pronoun/possessive adjective/ possessive case of noun
↓
place/time noun
↓
demonstrative pronoun
↓
numeral phrase
↓
verbal phrase/verbal clause (usually with the particle 的)
↓
adjective of quality, such as adjective of size, of general description, colour, etc.
↓
noun indicating category, material, origin, etc.

Xiao Zhang's strict father
= 小张严格的父亲

an old friend of his from his hometown
= 他家乡的一位老朋友

two old 1855 copies
or ***two old copies from 1855***
= 1855 年的两本旧版本

that small handbag of yours
= 你那个小手袋

that brand new brown leather handbag of hers
= 她那个簇新的棕色皮革手提包

■ The order of the last two types of modifiers, ie adjectives of quality and nouns, is flexible in Chinese and depends on emphasis:

a small round wooden table
= 一张小圆木桌
or 一张木制小圆桌 (the material is emphasized)

a black leather jacket
= 一件黑色皮夹克
or 一件真皮黑夹克 (the material is emphasized)

delicious French wine
= 美味的法国酒
or 法国美酒 ('French' is emphasized)

beautiful baby clothes
= 漂亮的婴儿服装
or 婴儿的漂亮服装 ('baby' is emphasized)

■ When several adjectives of quality are used to describe a noun in Chinese, there is no fixed order for these multiple modifiers. However, there are two general rules to follow. Firstly, the closer the relationship is between the noun and the adjective, the nearer the adjective is placed to the noun. Secondly, a monosyllabic adjective is usually placed after a polysyllabic adjective if all the modifiers are of equal importance to the noun. Note the use of the punctuation '、' in the Chinese translations below:

a new purple coat
= 一件紫色的新大衣
or 一件崭新的紫色大衣

comfortable, red, cotton shoes
= 舒服的红色棉鞋
or 红色的、舒服的棉鞋

a slim, pretty, blonde girl
= 一位苗条、漂亮的金发女孩
or 一位漂亮、苗条的金发女孩

an elegant, well-made, comfortable bed
= 一张典雅、精制、舒服的床
or 一张精制、舒服、典雅的床
or 一张舒服、精制、典雅的床

■ In Chinese, polysyllabic and monosyllabic adjectives preceded by an adverb of degree often require the particle 的. A modifier with 的 always precedes a modifier without 的:

a big soft pillow
= 软绵绵的大枕头

a very big black box
= 很大的黑箱子

a very tall handsome white man
= 一位个子很高的英俊白种男人

■ Where post-modifiers are used in English, such modifiers in Chinese usually precede the noun they describe and require the particle 的:

in every way possible
= 用各种可能的方法

books available
= 可使用的书

everything necessary
= 一切必要的事物

a stream 200 metres wide
= 200 米宽的溪流

the shop which sells fruits
= 卖水果的商店

the male teacher with glasses
= 那位戴眼镜的男老师

the particle 的

■ 的 is a structural particle in Chinese. It is so called because it cannot be used on its own and it is always added to other words or phrases to indicate grammatical relations. 的 normally occurs after an attributive modifier. In Chinese, various words or phrases can function as attributive modifiers. As a result, 的 does not or cannot always correspond to 'of' in English.

■ Where English uses the possessive case of a noun (eg 'Mary's'), the preposition 'of' to indicate possession (eg 'of Mary' and 'of the school'), possessive pronouns ('hers', 'ours', etc.), or attributive pronouns ('his', 'our', etc.), the particle 的 is often used in Chinese:

the Johnsons' car
= 约翰逊家的车

the son of the guitarist
= 吉他手的儿子

that pretty daughter of hers
= 她那个漂亮的女儿

his mobile phone
= 他的手机

■ 的 is generally omitted to form idiomatic expressions when the modifier is a noun indicating nationality, or when a Chinese pronoun modifies a noun referring to a country, a relationship, an organization, etc.:

the President of France
= 法国总统

my mother
= 我母亲
or 我妈

her home
= 她家

my country
= 我国
but not
我国家

our country
= 我们国家

their company
= 他们公司

■ 的 is not required in some idiomatic expressions as shown in the examples below:

children's clothes
= 儿童服装

a boys' school
= 男校

traveller's cheques
= 旅行支票

the plays of Shakespeare
= 莎士比亚剧作

the members of the union
= 工会会员

■ Note that when 'of' means 'containing', 的 is not required, as in the following examples:

a bag of cereal
= 一袋麦片

a bottle of water
= 一瓶水

■ In English, various prepositions are used in combination with the nouns they modify. In these cases in Chinese, the particle 的 is normally used:

the entrance to the garden
= 花园的入口

our trip to London
= 我们的伦敦之行

the girl in red
= 穿红色衣服的女孩

a student of average intelligence
= 智力一般的学生

a paper on English grammar
= 关于英语语法的论文

a film about World War II
= 关于第二次世界大战的电影

children at play
= 玩耍中的孩子

money for the party
= 聚会用的钱

bills for next month
= 下个月的账单

trees beside the lake
= 湖边的树

mollifying /ˈmɒlɪfaɪɪŋ/ *adj* 抚慰性的 ‹*words, promises, reassurances*›

mollusc Brit, **mollusk** Amer /ˈmɒləsk/ *n* 软体动物

mollycoddle /ˈmɒlɪkɒdl/ *vt* pej 溺爱 ‹*child, pet*›; 纵容 ‹*invalid*›

Molotov cocktail /ˌmɒlətɒf ˈkɒkteɪl/ *n* 莫洛托夫燃烧瓶

molt /məʊlt/ *vi, vt, n* Amer = **moult**

molten /ˈməʊltən/ *adj attrib* 熔化的 ‹*metal, glass, wax*›; ～ **lava** 熔岩

molybdenum /məˈlɪbdənəm/ *n* [u] 钼

mom /mɒm/ *n* Amer colloq 妈妈

mom-and-pop *adj* Amer 夫妻经营的 ‹*business, restaurant*›; **a ～ store** 夫妻店

moment /ˈməʊmənt/ *n* **1** [c] (instant) 片刻; **in a ～** 很快; **for a ～** 一会儿; **not for a** *or* **one ～** 从不; **a few ～s** 一会儿; **I saw her a few ～s ago** 我刚才还看到她了; **just a ～!** 等一下！; **one ～, please** 请等一下; **... and not a ～ too soon!** colloq …差点晚了！; **in ～s of optimism/weakness** 一时乐观/软弱; **without a ～'s hesitation** 毫不犹豫地; **I haven't had a ～ to myself all day** 我一整天忙得一刻也没得闲; **the car hasn't given me a ～'s trouble** 我这辆车从来没出过毛病 **2** [c] (point in time) 时刻; (occasion) 时机; **an important ～ in history** 重要历史关头; **the ～ of birth/death** 出生/死亡的那一刻; **at that ～** 在那时; **at the same ～** 同时; **the ～ that ...** 一…（就…）; **at the ～** 目前; **at this ～ in time** 此时此刻; **at any ～** 随时; **for the ～** (for now) 暂时; (at present) 目前; **of the ～** 当前最重要的; **the ～ of truth** 关键时刻; **on the spur of the ～** 一时冲动地; **in the heat of the ～** 一时激动之下; **never a dull ～** colloq 从不感到乏味; **to have one's** *or* **its ～s** colloq 也有走红的时候; **to change from one ～ to the next** 一会儿一变; **to live for the ～** colloq 过一天算一天; **to leave everything to the last ～** 什么事情都拖到最后一刻 **3** [u] liter (importance) 重要; **of (great) ～** （非常）重要的; **of little/some ～** 无足轻重的/有点儿重要的

momentarily /ˈməʊməntrəli, Amer ˌməʊmənˈterəli/ *adv* **1** (for a moment) 短暂地; **I lost my concentration ～** 我一时走神了 **2** Amer (very soon) 马上

momentary /ˈməʊməntri, Amer -teri/ *adj* 短暂的 ‹*hesitation, doubt, glance, lapse*›; 片刻的 ‹*pause, respite*›; **her panic was only ～** 她只是一时恐慌

momentous /məˈmentəs, məʊˈm-/ *adj* 重大的 ‹*decision, event, occasion, change, step*›

momentousness /məˈmentəsnɪs, məʊˈm-/ *n* [u] 重要性

momentum /məˈmentəm, məʊˈm-/ *n* [u] **1** Phys, Mech 动量; **to gain** *or* **gather/lose ～** 增加/减少动量 **2** fig (impetus) 动力; **to gain** *or* **gather/lose ～** 势头增强/减弱

Mon. ▸**p. 182** *abbr* = **Monday**

Monaco /ˈmɒnəkəʊ/ *pr n* 摩纳哥

monarch /ˈmɒnək/ *n* 君主; **the reigning ～** 在位的君主

monarchic /məˈnɑːkɪk/, **monarchical** /məˈnɑːkɪkl/ *adj* 君主的 ‹*regime, government*›; 君主制的 ‹*state*›; **～ constitution** 君主立宪制

monarchism /ˈmɒnəkɪzəm/ *n* [u] 君主主义

monarchist /ˈmɒnəkɪst/
A *n* 君主主义者
B *adj* 支持君主制的

monarchy /ˈmɒnəki/ *n* **1** [u] (system of government) 君主政体 **2** [c] (country, regime) 君主国

monastery /ˈmɒnəstri, Amer -teri/ *n* 修道院; **a Buddhist ～** 佛教寺院

monastic /məˈnæstɪk/ *adj* **1** Relig 修道院的; **a ～ order** 隐修会 **2** (ascetic) 禁欲的 ‹*lifestyle, pursuits*›; 宁静简朴的 ‹*seclusion*›

monasticism /məˈnæstɪsɪzəm/ *n* [u] 修道院生活

Monday /ˈmʌndeɪ, -di/ ▸**p. 182** *n* 星期一; **on ～** 在星期一; **on ～s/every ～** 每周星期一; **～ morning/afternoon/night** 星期一早晨/下午/晚上; **this/last/next ～** 本周一/上周一/下周一

monetarism /ˈmʌnɪtərɪzəm/ *n* [u] 货币主义

monetarist /ˈmʌnɪtərɪst/
A *adj* 货币主义的
B *n* 货币主义者

monetary /ˈmʌnɪtri, Amer -teri/ *adj* 货币的 ‹*unit, system*›

monetary policy *n* [u and c] 货币政策

money /ˈmʌni/ ▸**p. 174**
A *n* [u] **1** (notes, coins) 钱; **a lot of** *or* **big ～** 一大笔钱; **good ～** (large sum) 大笔的钱; (hard-earned) 辛苦挣来的钱; **spending ～** 零用钱; **to be short of ～** 缺钱; **to spend ～** 花钱; **to lose/make ～** 赔/赚钱; **to make ～ hand over fist** colloq 挣大钱; **is there (any) ～ in it?** 这个生意能赚钱吗？; **to cost ～** 价钱不菲; **to put ～ into sth.** 投资于某生意; **to put ～ on sth.** 把钱押在某事物上; fig 对某事物信心十足; **the smart ～ is on X** 知情者都看好 X; **for my ～** colloq 在我看来; **it is ～ well spent** 这钱花得值; **to get one's ～'s worth** 钱花得值; **it's a bargain, for the ～** 价钱倒是很便宜; **satisfaction guaranteed or your ～ back** 包您满意，否则退款; **to throw** *or* **send good ～ after bad** 继续花钱打水漂; **～ goes** *or* **runs through his hands like water** colloq 他花钱如流水; **～ burns a hole in her pocket** colloq 她一有钱就花光; **to have ～ to burn** colloq 有花不完的钱; **your ～ or your life!** 要钱还是要命！; **～ doesn't grow on trees** colloq 钱不是树上长的; fig 钱来之不易; **to put one's ～ where one's mouth is** colloq 兑现说过的话; **to give sb. a (good) run for his/her ～** 让某人觉得钱花得值; fig 使某人激烈竞争; **to get** *or* **have a (good) run for one's ～** 钱花得值; fig 激烈竞争; **it's ～ for jam** *or* **old rope** Brit colloq 这钱赚得太容易了; **it's ～ from home** Amer 这是轻而易举之事; **time is ～** 时间就是金钱 **2** (currency) 货币; **Chinese/English ～** 中国/英国货币 **3** (salary) 工资; **to earn good ～** 挣高薪 **4** (wealth) 财产; **to have ～** 富有; **to be made of ～** colloq 很有钱; **to inherit** *or* **come into ～** 继承财产; **～ isn't everything** 金钱不是一切; **～ talks** 金钱万能; **not for love nor ～** 决不; **(the love of) ～ is the root of all evil** （贪图）金钱是万恶之首
B **moneys** *npl* formal 款项; **～s paid into an account** 入账金额
C *modif* 钱的 ‹*problems, matters*›

money: ～-back guarantee *n* 退款保证; **～bag** *n* 钱袋; **(old) ～bags** colloq 阔佬; **～ belt** *n* 带钱包的腰带; **～box** *n* 储钱罐; **～-changer** *n* **1** ▸**p. 409** (person) 钱币兑换商; **2** (machine) 零钱兑换机

moneyed /ˈmʌnɪd/ *adj* 富有的; **the ～ classes** 富有阶层

money: ～-grubber /ˈmʌnɪˌɡrʌbə(r)/ *n* pej 敛财者; **～-grubbing** *adj* pej 敛财的 ‹*person, scheme*›; **～lender** ▸**p. 409** *n* 放贷人; **～-loser** *n* (person) 造成亏损者; (product) 赔钱的产品; **～maker** *n* (product) 赚钱的产品; (activity) 赚钱的买卖; **～making** *adj* 赚钱的 ‹*scheme*›; **～man** /-mæn/ *n* colloq 金融家; **～ manager** ▸**p. 409** *n* 基金经理

money market *n* 货币市场

money market fund *n* 货币市场基金

money: ～ order *n* 汇票; **～ spider** *n* 华盖蛛; **～ spinner** *n* esp Brit colloq (product) 摇钱树; (business) 赚大钱的企业; **～ supply** *n* the **～ supply** 货币供应量; **～ purchase pension plan** *n* 货币购买型退休金计划

-monger /ˈmʌŋɡə(r)/ *combining form* **1** (seller) 贩子; **a fish～** 鱼贩 **2** usu pej (promoter or spreader) 散布者; **a gossip～** 散布流言蜚语的人

Mongol /ˈmɒŋɡl/ ▸**p. 503, p. 426**
A *adj* **1** (of the people) 蒙古人的; (of the language) 蒙古语的 **2** **mongol** Med dated or offensive 先天愚型的 ‹*baby, features*›
B *n* **1** [c] (person) 蒙古人 **2** [u] (language) = **Mongolian B2** **3** **mongol** Med dated or offensive 先天愚型患者

Mongolia /mɒŋˈɡəʊlɪə/ *pr n* 蒙古; **Inner/Outer ～** 内蒙古/外蒙古; **it's just around the corner, not Outer ～!** fig hum 就在附近，并非遥不可及！

Mongolian /mɒŋˈɡəʊlɪən/ ▸**p. 503, p. 426**
A *adj* (of Mongolia) 蒙古的; (of the people) 蒙古人的; (of the language) 蒙古语的
B *n* **1** [c] (person) 蒙古人 **2** [u] (language) 蒙古语

mongolism /ˈmɒŋɡəlɪzəm/ *n* [u] Med dated or offensive 先天愚型

mongoloid /ˈmɒŋɡəlɔɪd/ *n, adj* **1** (race) 蒙古人种的 ‹*features*› **2** Med dated or offensive 先天愚型的

mongoose /ˈmɒŋɡuːs/ *n* (*pl* **～s**) 獴

mongrel /ˈmʌŋɡrəl/ *n* 杂种狗; **a ～ breed/puppy** 杂种/杂种狗

monicker /ˈmɒnɪkə(r)/ *n* colloq = **moniker**

monies /ˈmʌnɪz/ *npl* formal = **money B**

moniker /ˈmɒnɪkə(r)/ *n* colloq 名字

monitor /ˈmɒnɪtə(r)/
A *n* **1** (TV screen) 电视监视屏; (computer screen) 显示器 **2** Med 监测器 **3** (measuring device) 监视器 **4** Sch [尤指小学的] 班长; **the homework/blackboard ～** 课代表/擦黑板值日生 **5** (listener) 监听员 **6** (observer) 观察员
B *vt* **1** (measure, observe) 观察 ‹*speed, process, progress*›; 监测 ‹*radioactivity, weather, air quality*›; 监视 ‹*employee, situation*›; **to ～ sth./sb. for sth.** 为某事物监督某人/某事; **the factory's output is ～ed for defective items** 工厂的出厂产品进行了次品检查 **2** Med 监测 ‹*heartbeat, pulse, breathing, temperature*›; 观察 ‹*patient*›; **to ～ sb. for heart problems/neurological changes** 密切注意某人的心脏病/神经病变 **3** (listen in on) 监听 ‹*radio stations, telephone calls*›; **to ～ sth. for sth.** 为了某事对某事物进行监听

monitoring /ˈmɒnɪtərɪŋ/ *n* [u] **1** (measuring, observing) (of process, pulse, breathing) (by person) 监视; (of speed, heartbeat, temperature, radioactivity) (by device, machine) 监测; 监测的 ‹*device, process, techniques*›; **～ for sth.** 对某物的监测; **～ of students/students' progress** 对学生/学生进步的关注 **2** (of radio stations, telephone calls) 监听

monitor lizard *n* 巨蜥

monk /mʌŋk/ *n* 修道士; **a Buddhist ～** 和尚; **to live like a ～** 过禁欲生活

monkey /ˈmʌŋki/ *n* (*pl* **～s**) **1** Zool 猴子; **to make a ～ out of sb.** 愚弄某人; **as artful** *or* **clever as a cartload** *or* **wagonload of ～s** colloq 非常机灵的; **not give a ～'s about sth.** Brit colloq 对某事物毫不在乎 **2** Brit colloq (rascal) 淘气鬼; **you little/cheeky ～!** 你这个小/厚脸皮的捣蛋鬼！

Phrasal verb

- **monkey about, monkey around** *vi* colloq 胡闹; **they ～ about all day instead of working** 他们整天闲荡不做事; **stop ～ing about** *or* **around with the fire extinguisher!** 别瞎鼓捣那只灭火器了！

monkey: ～ bars *npl* [供孩童悬荡玩耍的] 猴架; **～ business** *n* [u] **1** colloq (mischief) 胡闹; **2** (unlawful or unfair activities) 欺骗; **there's some ～ business going on here!** 这里头

m

有鬼名堂！；~ **house** *n* [动物园内的] 猴舍；~ **nut** *n* Brit 落花生；~ **puzzle** *n* ~ **puzzle (tree)** 智利南美杉；~ **tricks** *npl* Brit colloq 恶作剧；~ **wrench** *n* 螺丝扳手；**to throw a ~ wrench in the works** Amer colloq 破坏

monkfish /'mʌŋkfɪʃ/ *n* (*pl* ~ *or* ~**es**) 鮟鱇

monkish /'mʌŋkɪʃ/ *adj* 修士般的

Monmouthshire /'mɒnməθʃɪə(r)/ *pr n* 蒙茅斯郡

mono /'mɒnəʊ/ *n* [u] 单声道放音；**to play/record in** ~ 用单声道播放/录音；**the ~ switch/button** 单声道开关/按钮

monochromatic /,mɒnəkrə'mætɪk/ *adj* 单色的；**a ~ colour scheme** 单色调配

monochrome /'mɒnəkrəʊm/

A *adj* **1** Phot, TV 黑白的 **2** Art 单色的

B *n* [u] Phot, TV 黑白重现；**in** ~ 以黑白重现方式

monocle /'mɒnəkl/ *n* 单片眼镜

monocoque /'mɒnəkɒk/ *n* 单壳体车身；~ **construction/chassis** 单壳体构造/机身

monocular /mə'nɒkjʊlə(r)/

A *adj* 单眼的 ‹*vision, organism*›；单筒的 ‹*microscope*›

B *n* 单目望远镜

monoculture /'mɒnəʊkʌltʃə(r)/ *n* [u] 单一栽培

monocycle /'mɒnəʊsaɪkl/ *n* = **unicycle**

monogamist /mə'nɒgəmɪst/ *n* (in marriage) 单配偶者；(in sexual relationship) 性伴侣单一者

monogamous /mə'nɒgəməs/ *adj* (in marriage) 一夫一妻制的 ‹*tribe*›；单配性的 ‹*animal*›；(in sexual relationship) 性伴侣单一的

monogamy /mə'nɒgəmi/ *n* [u] (marriage) 一夫一妻制；(sexual relationship) 单一性伴侣制

monogram /'mɒnəgræm/ *n* [绣印于物品上的] 字母组合图案

monogrammed /'mɒnəgræmd/ *adj* 带字母组合图案的

monograph /'mɒnəgrɑːf, Amer -græf/ *n* 专著

monohull /'mɒnəʊhʌl/ *n* 单体船

monokini /,mɒnəʊ'kiːni/ *n* 无上装女泳装

monolingual /,mɒnəʊ'lɪŋgwəl/ *adj* 只用一种语言的 ‹*person, country*›；单语的 ‹*dictionary*›

monolith /'mɒnəlɪθ/ *n* **1** (stone) 单块巨石 **2** usu pej (organization) 单一庞大组织

monolithic /,mɒnə'lɪθɪk/ *adj* **1** (formed of a single stone) 巨大的 ‹*rock*›；整块巨石制成的 ‹*monument*› **2** (large and indivisible) 单一庞大的 ‹*organization, state, system*›

monologue, Amer **monolog** /'mɒnəlɒg/ *n* **1** Theat (speech) 独白；(play, story) 独角戏 **2** pej (long tedious speech) 冗长的讲话

monomania /,mɒnəʊ'meɪnɪə/ *n* [u] 单狂 [指对一种事物极度狂热]

monomaniac /,mɒnəʊ'meɪnɪæk/

A *n* 单狂者

B *adj* 单狂的 ‹*patient, personality, obsession*›；狂热的 ‹*zeal*›

monomaniacal /,mɒnəʊmeɪnɪ'ækl/ *adj* 单狂的 ‹*patient, personality, obsession*›；狂热的 ‹*zeal*›

monophonic /,mɒnə'fɒnɪk/ *adj* 单声道的

monophthong /'mɒnəfθɒŋ/ *n* 单元音

monoplane /'mɒnəpleɪn/ *n* 单翼飞机

monopolist /mə'nɒpəlɪst/ *n* 垄断者

monopolistic /mə,nɒpə'lɪstɪk/ *adj* 垄断的 ‹*company*›；垄断性的 ‹*economy, market*›

monopolization /mə,nɒpəlaɪ'zeɪʃn, Amer -lɪ'z-/ *n* [u] **1** Econ 垄断；~ **of sth.** 对某事物的垄断 **2** fig (domination) 独占；**her ~ of all the media attention** 她对媒体注意力的完全吸引

monopolize /mə'nɒpəlaɪz/ *vt* **1** Econ 垄断 **2** fig (dominate, keep to oneself) 完全占据 ‹*time*›；完全吸引 ‹*attention, thoughts*›；独占 ‹*bathroom, job*›；**to ~ a conversation** 垄断谈话；**don't ~ him** 不要缠住他不放

monopoly /mə'nɒpəli/

A *n* **1** Econ 垄断；**to have a ~ on** *or* **of sth.** 垄断某事物；**to break sb.'s ~ on sth.** 打破某人对某事物的垄断 **2** fig (exclusive possession, control) 独占；~ **on sth.** 对某事物的独占；**to have a ~ on** *or* **of sth.** 独占某事物；**a good education should not be the ~ of the rich** 良好的教育不应该成为富人的专利

B **Monopoly®** *n* [u] (board game) 大富翁游戏

monopoly: ~ **capitalism** *n* [u] 垄断资本主义；**M~ money** *n* [u] fig colloq 大富翁钞票 [喻指无实际价值的钱]

monorail /'mɒnəʊreɪl/ *n* (system) 单轨铁路；(train) 单轨列车

monoski /'mɒnəʊskiː/ *n* 单板式滑雪板

monoskiing /'mɒnəʊskiːɪŋ/ ▸**p. 307** *n* [u] 单板滑雪

monosodium glutamate /,mɒnə,səʊdɪəm 'gluːtəmeɪt/ *n* [u] 谷氨酸钠 [味精的主要成分]

monosyllabic /,mɒnəsɪ'læbɪk/ *adj* **1** Ling 单音节的 **2** (untalkative) 简短的 ‹*answer*›；寡言少语的 ‹*person*›

monosyllable /'mɒnəsɪləbl/ *n* 单音节词；**to reply in ~s** 不情愿地回答

monotheism /'mɒnəθiːɪzəm/ *n* [u] 一神论

monotheist /'mɒnəθiːɪst/ *n* 一神论者

monotheistic /,mɒnəθiː'ɪstɪk/ *adj* 一神论的 ‹*doctrine, belief*›；主张一神论的 ‹*religion*›

monotone /'mɒnətəʊn/ *n* 单调的声音；**to speak in a ~** 单调低沉地说话

monotonous /mə'nɒtənəs/ *adj* **1** (tedious) 乏味的 ‹*task, journey*› **2** (unvarying) 单调的 ‹*voice, hum*›；声音单调的 ‹*speech*›

monotonously /mə'nɒtənəsli/ *adv* **1** (tediously) 乏味地 **2** (without variation in tone, pitch) 声音单调地

monotony /mə'nɒtəni/ *n* [u] **1** (tediousness) 乏味 **2** (tonelessness) 音色单调

monoxide /mə'nɒksaɪd/ *n* 一氧化物

Monrovia /mɒn'rəʊvɪə/ *pr n* 蒙罗维亚

monsoon /mɒn'suːn/ *n* **1** (rainy season) 雨季 colloq (downpour) 倾盆大雨；**the ~ season** 雨季 **2** (wind) 季风

monsoon rains *npl* 季风雨

monster /'mɒnstə(r)/

A *n* **1** (imaginary creature) 怪物；**a sea ~** 海怪 **2** (cruel, wicked person) 恶魔 **3** hum (naughty child) 小捣蛋 **4** (giant) (person) 巨人；(object) 庞然大物；**a ~ of a man/a book** 巨人/大部头的书

B *modif* colloq 巨大的；**a ~ hit** 极受欢迎的作品

monstrosity /mɒn'strɒsɪti/ *n* **1** [c] (eyesore) 巨大丑陋之物 **2** [c] (mutant) (animal) 畸形动物；(plant) 畸形植物；(person) 畸形人 **3** [c] (act, behaviour) 恶行 **4** [u] (evil) 邪恶

monstrous /'mɒnstrəs/ *adj* **1** (horrifying) 巨大而可怕的 **2** pej (gigantic) 巨大的 ‹*battleship*›；庞大的 ‹*city, bureaucracy*› **3** (outrageous) 骇人的 ‹*crime, cruelty*›；令人无法容忍的 ‹*lie, waste*›；**it is ~ that .../to say that** …/说那种话是无法容忍的

monstrously /'mɒnstrəsli/ *adv* **1** (extremely) 极度地 ‹*expensive, fat*› **2** (badly) 严重地 ‹*deformed*›；非常 ‹*cruel*›

montage /mɒn'tɑːʒ/ *n* **1** [c] (picture, film) 蒙太奇作品 **2** [u] (technique) 蒙太奇

Montana /mɒn'tænə/ *pr n* 蒙大拿州

Montenegro /,mɒntɪ'niːgrəʊ/ *pr n* 黑山

Montevideo /,mɒntɪvɪ'deɪəʊ/ *pr n* 蒙得维的亚

month /mʌnθ/ ▸**p. 490** *n* **1** (division of year) 月；**next/last ~** 下个/上个月；**in a ~** 一个月之后；~ **by ~** 逐月；~ **in ~ out** 一月又一月；**in the ~ of June** 在 6 月份；**at the end of the (current) ~** 于（本）月底；**what day of the ~ is today?** 今天是几号？；~ **after ~ he forgets to pay** (regular payment) 他每个月都忘记付钱；(single payment) 一个月又一个月过去，他总是忘记付钱；**her** *or* **that time of the ~** euph colloq 月事；**(never in) a ~ of Sundays** colloq 很长时间 **2** (period of 4 weeks or 30 days) 一个月时间；**in the ~ from March 9th to April 8th/9th** 在 3 月 9 日至 4 月 8 日/9 日的那一个月里；**your salary for the ~ beginning May 1** 你从 5 月 1 日开始的那个月的工资；**she was in hospital for ~s** 她住院住了好几个月；**a seven-~-old baby** 7 个月大的婴儿

monthly /'mʌnθli/

A *adj* **1** (happening every month) 每月一次的；~ **instalments** 按月支付的分期付款 **2** (for one month) 有效期为一个月的 ‹*travel pass*›；按月计的 ‹*rent, profit*›；**a ~ income/budget** 月收入/月度预算

B *adv* 每月一次地；**it is £200 ~** 每月 200 英镑

C *n* 月刊

Montreal /,mɒntrɪ'ɔːl/ *pr n* 蒙特利尔

monty /'mɒnti/ *n* **the full ~** Brit colloq 全部；**he cooked me breakfast one morning — it was the full ~** 一天早晨他给我做了早饭——那是全套的早餐；**to do** *or* **go the full ~** 脱得一丝不挂

monument /'mɒnjʊmənt/ *n* **1** (memorial) (building) 纪念馆；(column) 纪念碑；(statue) 纪念像 **2** (historical building) 历史遗迹 **3** fig (memorable example) 典范；(testament) 证明；**to be a ~ to sth.** 是某事的典范；**the pagoda is a ~ to his art/ambition** 这座佛塔是他艺术成就/雄心壮志的明证

monumental /,mɒnjʊ'mentl/ *adj* **1** (commemorative) 纪念性的 ‹*construction*›；**a ~ sculpture/inscription** 纪念雕塑/碑文 **2** (large and impressive) 巨大的 ‹*cathedral*› **3** (major, important) 伟大的 ‹*novel*›；重大的 ‹*success*›；**a ~ work** 煌煌巨作；~ **prestige** 盛名 **4** (massive) 极大的 ‹*blunder, achievement*›；极度的 ‹*ignorance*›；**a ~ task** 极其繁重的工作

monumentally /,mɒnjʊ'mentəli/ *adv* 极度的；~ **ignorant** 极端无知的

monumental mason ▸**p. 409** *n* Brit 墓碑匠

moo /muː/

A *vi* 哞哞叫

B *n* **1** (sound) 哞 **2** Brit colloq pej (woman) 蠢女人

mooch /muːtʃ/ colloq

A *vi* Brit 溜达；**to ~ along** *or* **about** 到处溜达

B *vt* Amer 乞讨；**to ~ sth. from** *or* **off sb.** 向某人讨要某物

mood /muːd/ *n* **1** (frame of mind) 心情；**to be in a good/bad ~** 情绪好/坏；**to be in the/no ~ for doing** *or* **to do sth.** 想/根本不想做某事；**to be in the ~ for work/jokes** 想工作/想开玩笑；**when he's in/not in the ~** 他心情好/不好的时候；**when the ~ takes her** 她心情好的时候 **2** (bad temper) 坏心情；**to be in a ~** 心情不好；**he's in one of his ~s today** 今天他闹情绪了 **3** (atmosphere) 气氛；**the prevailing ~ of the times** 世风；**the general ~ was one of despair** 大家都很绝望；**the crowd was in an ugly ~** 这群人怒气冲天 **4** Ling 语气；**the indicative/subjunctive/imperative ~** 陈述/虚拟/祈使语气

mood-altering /'muːdɔːltərɪŋ/ *adj attrib* 改变情绪的 ‹*drug*›

moodily /'muːdɪli/ *adv* (in a moody manner) 喜怒无常地；(in a gloomy manner) 闷闷不乐地

moodiness /'muːdɪnɪs/ *n* [u] (given to changes of mood) 喜怒无常；(gloominess) 闷闷不乐

mood: ~ **music** *n* [u] 气氛音乐；~ **swing** *n* 情绪波动

moody /'muːdi/ *adj* **1** (unpredictable) 喜怒无常的；(gloomy) 闷闷不乐的 **2** (atmospheric) 有特殊气氛的；**a ~ silence** 忧郁的沉默

mooing /'muːɪŋ/ *n* [u] 哞

moola, moolah /ˈmuːlə/ *n* [u] Amer colloq 钞票

moon /muːn/

A *n* **1** (satellite of the earth) 月球; **there is no ～ tonight** 今晚没有月亮; **by the light of the ～** 凭借月光; **to be over the ～ (about sth./at doing sth.)** esp Brit colloq （因某事物/做某事）非常高兴; **many ～s ago** liter or hum 很久以前 **2** (satellite of any planet) 卫星; **the fourth ～ of Saturn** 土卫四

B *vi* **1** Brit (mope, idle) 懒散 **2** (daydream) 出神地想; **to ～ over sb./sth.** 痴痴地思念某人/想某事 **3** colloq (display buttocks) 露臀; **to ～ at sb.** 冲某人露臀

Phrasal verb

• **moon about, moon around** *vi* colloq 虚度时光

moon: ～beam *n* （一道）月光; **～ boots** *npl* 雪地靴; **～ buggy** *n* colloq 月球车; **～ cake** *n* 月饼; **～-faced** *adj* 圆脸的; **M～ Festival** *n* 中秋节; **～ landing** *n* 登月

Moonie /ˈmuːni/ *n* colloq usu pej [韩国的] 文鲜明统一教团信徒

moonless /ˈmuːnlɪs/ *adj* 没有月亮的 ‹*night, sky*›

moonlight /ˈmuːnlaɪt/

A *n* [u] 月光; **in the** *or* **by ～** 在月光下; **a ～ tryst/picnic** 月光下的幽会/野餐

B *vi* (*pt, pp* **moonlighted**) colloq 赚外快; **he ～s as a taxi driver** 他兼职开出租车

moonlighter /ˈmuːnlaɪtə(r)/ *n* colloq 赚外快者

moonlight flit *n* Brit colloq 夜间潜逃

moonlighting /ˈmuːnlaɪtɪŋ/ *n* [u] colloq 赚外快

moonlit /ˈmuːnlɪt/ *adj* 月光照耀的; **a ～ night** 月夜

moon: ～rise *n* (action) 月出; (time) 月出时刻; **～ rock** *n* [c and u] 月球岩石; **～shine** *n* [u] esp Amer colloq **1** (nonsense) 胡言乱语; **2** (whisky) 私酿的威士忌; (spirits) 私酿酒; **～shiner** *n* Amer colloq (maker) 酿私酒者; (seller) 私酒贩子; **～ shot** *n* [火箭的] 向月球发射; **～stone** *n* 月长石; **～struck** *adj* 发痴的; **～walk** *n* **1** Astron 月球行走; **2** (dance move) 走太空步

Moor /mɔː(r), Amer mʊər/ *n* Hist 摩尔人

moor¹ /mɔː(r), Amer mʊər/ *n* Geog 高沼; **on a/the ～** 在高沼上

moor²

A *vt* Naut 停泊; **to ～ sth. to sth.** 将某船停泊到某处; **the boat is ～ed to the river bank** 小船停泊在河岸边

B *vi* 停泊

moorhen /ˈmɔːhen, Amer ˈmʊər-/ *n* (*pl* **～** *or* **～s**) 黑水鸡

mooring /ˈmɔːrɪŋ, Amer ˈmʊər-/

A *n* (place) 停泊处; **a boat at its ～(s)** 停在泊位的船; *modif* **～ ropes/chains/hooks/buoy** 系泊绳索/链/钩/浮标

B moorings *npl* (ropes, chains) 系泊索具

Moorish /ˈmɔːrɪʃ, Amer ˈmʊərɪʃ/ *adj* Hist 摩尔人的; **～ architecture** 摩尔式建筑

moorland /ˈmɔːlənd, Amer ˈmʊər-/ *n* [u] 高沼地; **～ vegetation/stream** 高沼地植被/溪流

moose /muːs/ *n* (*pl* **moose**) Amer 驼鹿

moot /muːt/ *vt* formal 提出…供讨论; **it has been ～ed that ...** …已被提出进行讨论

moot point, moot question *ns* 悬而未决的问题

mop /mɒp/

A *n* **1** (for floors) 拖把 **2** (for dishes) 洗碗刷 **3** (mass of hair) 蓬乱的头发; **a ～ of red/curly hair** 一头蓬乱的红发/卷发

B *vt* (*pres p etc.* **-pp-**) **1** (wash) 用拖把擦; **to ～ the floor/deck** 拖地板/甲板 **2** (wipe) 擦拭;

Months of the year

■ The Chinese names of the months of the year are formed by adding Arabic numerals or Chinese cardinal numbers to 月 (month). Thus 'January' is 1 月 or 一月. If the year and/or the date are included in one or other of these forms, the month must follow the same form. (see how to express dates in Chinese at note 'Dates' at entry 'date'.) 月 can also be expressed as 月份 if a month is used on its own or with a year.

January	1 月 / 一月
February	2 月 / 二月
March	3 月 / 三月
April	4 月 / 四月
May	5 月 / 五月
June	6 月 / 六月
July	7 月 / 七月
August	8 月 / 八月
September	9 月 / 九月
October	10 月 / 十月
November	11 月 / 十一月
December	12 月 / 十二月

■ 'August' is used in the notes below to represent any month.

Which month?

What month is it? — It is August
= 现在是几月（份）？ —— 8 月（份）

What month did you go on holiday? — In August
= 你哪个月去度假的？ —— 8 月（份）

When?

■ Prepositions such as 'in', 'at', etc. are usually omitted in Chinese, as in these examples:

I will visit you in August
= 我 8 月（份）去拜访你

She was in Edinburgh in August last year
= 她去年 8 月（份）在爱丁堡

She will be 18 in August next year
= 她明年 8 月（份）就 18 岁了

New York is extremely hot in August
= 纽约 8 月（份）非常热

I was on annual leave throughout August or ***I was on annual leave for the whole of August***
= 我整个 8 月（份）都在休年假

It happened in August 2007
= 这件事发生在 2007 年 8 月（份）

We are going to London on the first of August
= 我们 8 月 1 号去伦敦

She was born on 16th August 1995
= 她 1995 年 8 月 16 日出生
or 她出生于 1995 年 8 月 16 日 (rather formal)

■ 8 月 is normally used instead of 8 月份 in these examples:

at the beginning of August
= 8 月初

in the middle of August
= 8 月中旬

at the end of August
= 8 月底

in early August
= 8 月上旬

in mid-August
= 8 月中旬

in late August
= 8 月下旬

■ However, note the use of 月份 in the following examples:

this August
= 今年 8 月（份）

next August
= 明年 8 月（份）

last August
= 去年 8 月（份）

every August
= 每年 8 月（份）

every other August
= 每隔一年的 8 月（份）

last month
= 上个月

the month before last
= 上上个月

per month
= 每个月

Mike earns £2,000 a month
= 迈克每月挣 2,000 镑

Combinations

one August afternoon
= 一个 8 月的下午
or 8 月的一个下午

one August day
= 8 月的一天

the August Moon festival (in Lunar August)
= 8 月中秋节

the warmest August on record
= 记录中最热的 8 月

a rainy/wet August
= 多雨的 8 月

a sunny August
= 阳光灿烂的 8 月

the August sales
= 8 月（份）大减价

August training courses
= 8 月（份）培训课

lunar month
= 农历月份

Lunar January
= 正月
or 农历 1 月
or 阴历 1 月

Lunar December
= 腊月
or 农历 12 月
or 阴历 12 月

to ～ sth. from *or* **off sth.** 将某物从某物上擦掉; **to ～ sb.'s brow** 擦去某人额头的汗水

C *vi* (*pres p etc.* **-pp-**) 用拖把擦干净; **just keep ～ping until the floor is dry** 一直拖到地板干了为止

Phrasal verbs

• **mop down** *vt* [**～ sth. down, ～ down sth.**] 用拖把擦干净; **to ～ down the floor/deck** 拖地板/甲板

• **mop up**

A *vt* [**～ sth. up, ～ up sth.**]
1 (clean up) 把…擦干净 ‹*spillage*› **2** Mil (get rid of) 肃清 ‹*remaining resistance, remaining troops*› **3** (complete) 完成 ‹*remaining work*› **4** (absorb) 获取 ‹*profits, surplus*›

B *vi* 用拖把擦干净; **I'll ～ up** 我来拖

mopboard /ˈmɒpbɔːd/ *n* Amer 踢脚板

mope /məʊp/ *vi* 闷闷不乐; **to ～ about sth.** 为某事物闷闷不乐

Phrasal verb

• **mope about, mope around** *vi* 无聊闲荡

moped /ˈməʊped/ *n* 机动自行车

mophead /ˈmɒphed/ *n* colloq 头发蓬乱的人

moppet /ˈmɒpɪt/ *n* colloq 心肝宝贝

mopping-up operation /ˌmɒpɪŋˈʌp ˌɒpəreɪʃn/ *n* 肃清残敌行动

moquette /mɒˈket, Amer məʊˈket/ *n* [u] 绒头织物; **a ～ carpet/sofa** 割绒地毯/沙发

moraine /məˈreɪn, mɒˈreɪn/ *n* 冰碛

moral /ˈmɒrəl, Amer ˈmɔːrəl/

A *adj* **1** (ethical) 道德的; **on ～ grounds** 基于道德原因; **to take the ～ high ground** 在道义上占优势; **human beings are ～ animals** 人类是有道德感的动物 **2** (virtuous) 品行端正的; **to lead a ～ life** 为人正派 **3** (morally instructive) 有教益的 ‹*tale*›

B *n* (practical lesson) 寓意; **to draw a ～ from sth.** 从某事物中得到教益; **to point a ～** 指明寓意

C **morals** *npl* (standards and principles of behaviour) 道德; **public ～s** 公德; **to have no ～s** 不道德; **a woman of loose ～s** 荡妇

morale /məˈrɑːl, Amer -ˈræl/ *n* [u] (of person) 精神面貌; (of troops, team) 士气; **to raise** *or* **boost ～** 提高士气; **to lower sb.'s ～** 使某人精神不振

morale-booster *n* 振奋精神的事物; **his comment was a ～** 他的讲话振奋人心

moral: ～ fibre *n* 道德力量; **～ hazard** *n* [u] 道德风险

moralist /ˈmɒrəlɪst, Amer ˈmɔːrəl-/ *n* 道德说教者

moralistic /ˌmɒrəˈlɪstɪk, Amer ˌmɔːr-/ *adj* 说教的 ‹*tone, stance*›

morality /məˈræləti/ *n* [u] **1** (moral principles) 道德规范; (particular system) 道德体系; **sexual/public ～** 性道德/公德 **2** (goodness or badness) 道德性; **they discussed the ～ of abortion** 他们讨论了堕胎的道德问题

morality: ～ play *n* 道德剧; **～ tale** *n* 道德故事

moralize /ˈmɒrəlaɪz, Amer ˈmɔːr-/ *vi* 道德说教; **to ～ about sth.** 就某事进行说教

moralizing /ˈmɒrəlaɪzɪŋ, Amer ˈmɔːr-/

A *adj* 爱说教的 ‹*politician, attitude*›; 说教的 ‹*tone*›

B *n* [u] 说教

morally /ˈmɒrəli, Amer ˈmɔːr-/ *adv* **1** (ethically) 道德上 ‹*wrong, repugnant*›; **～ speaking** 从道德上讲 **2** (virtuously) 品行端正地 ‹*behave*›

moral: ～ majority *n + v sing or pl* 持传统道德观的大多数; **～ philosopher** ▸**p. 409** *n* 伦理学家; **～ philosophy** *n* [u] 伦理学; **～ support** *n* [u] 道义上的支持; **～ victory** *n* 道义上的胜利

morass /məˈræs/ *n* **1** (complicated or confused situation) 混乱; **to be bogged down in a ～ of details** 纠缠于细节 **2** (marsh) 沼泽

moratorium /ˌmɒrəˈtɔːrɪəm/ *n* (*pl* **moratoria** /ˌmɒrəˈtɔːrɪə/) formal 暂停; **to declare a ～ on arms sales** 宣布暂停军火销售

morbid /ˈmɔːbɪd/ *adj* **1** (gen) 消极的 ‹*person, imagination, music*› **2** Psych 病态的 ‹*fear, interest, curiosity*›; **to have a ～ fear of/fascination for sth.** 对某事物有种病态的恐惧/迷恋 **3** Med 病变的 ‹*tumour, symptoms*›

morbid anatomy *n* [u] 病理解剖学

morbidity /mɔːˈbɪdəti/ *n* [u] **1** (of imagination, interests) 消极情绪 **2** Psych 病态 **3** Med 发病 **4** (rate of disease) 发病率; **～ rates/statistics** 发病率/发病率统计

morbidly /ˈmɔːbɪdli/ *adv* **1** (gen) 消极地 ‹*remark, reply*›; 不正常地 ‹*curious*›; **to dwell ～ on sth.** 不正常地老是想着某事物 **2** Psych 病态地 ‹*interested, jealous*›

mordant /ˈmɔːdnt/ *adj* formal 尖刻的

mordantly /ˈmɔːdəntli/ *adv* formal 尖酸地 ‹*sarcastic*›; **a ～ funny book** 尖刻滑稽的书

more /mɔː(r)/ ▸**p. 140**

A *det* **1** (greater quantity or number of) 更多的; **～ ... than ...** 比…更多的…; **we have ～ eggs than milk** 我们的鸡蛋比牛奶多; **～ cars than before** *or* **than there used to be** 比以前多的汽车; **some/many ～ books** 稍多/多得多的书籍; **three times ～ money** 三倍多的钱; **(the) ～ fool you!** 你真笨! **2** (additional) 另外的; **I need a few ～ books/days** 我还需要几本书/几天; **have you any ～ questions/problems?** 你们还有什么问题吗?; **there's no ～ time** 没有时间了; **one ～ word and I'll ...** 你敢再说一个字, 我就…; **～ and ～ work** 越来越多的工作

B *adv* **1** (comparative) 更加; **～ ... than ...** 比…更加…; **～ and ～ difficult/beautiful** 越来越难/美; **he looked ～ dead than alive** 他看上去半死不活; **the ～ intelligent (child) of the two** 两个（孩子）中较聪明的一个; **the ～ developed countries** 更加发达的国家; **he is (all) the ～ determined because ...** 他因为…而更坚定了; **you couldn't be ～ mistaken** 你完全错了; **it's ～ or less finished** 这件事差不多做完了; **～ than ever** 比以往任何时候更 **2** (to greater extent) 更多地; **～ and ～ ...** 越来越…; **he talks ～ than I do** 他说得比我多; **you must eat/rest ～** 你必须多吃/多休息; **I couldn't agree ～** 我完全赞成; **he can't sing any ～ than I can, he can no ～ sing than I can** 他并非比我更会唱歌; **he's no ～ a duke than I am** 他和我都不是公爵; **to be ～ than a little surprised** 非常吃惊; **I admired his courage the ～** 我越发敬佩他的勇气了; **the ～ ... the ...** 越…, 越…; **the ～ you rest, the quicker you'll get better** 你休息越多, 康复得就越快; **～ than** 非常; **a ～ than generous offer** 极其慷慨的出价; **it will ～ than cover the cost** 这完全可以支付这笔费用; **he can't understand it, and no ～ can I** 他不明白这件事, 我也不明白; **in York, and even ～ so in Oxford** 在纽约是这样, 在牛津更是如此; **no ～ so than usual/the others** 并非不同凡响 **3** (rather) 更确切些; **he's ～ a babysitter than a teacher** 他更像个保姆, 而不是老师; **～ often than not** 时常; **～ or less** (nearly) 几乎; (about, roughly) 大约; **he's ～ or less an invalid** 他基本上是个病人; **that's ～ or less what he said** 这差不多就是他说的话 **4** (again, further, longer) 再; **once/twice ～** 再一次/两次; **we shall see him no ～** 我们再也见不到他了; **I don't travel any ～** 我不再旅游了; **the factories and mines are no ～** 工厂和矿山都已不复存在 **5** colloq (moreover) 而且; **he was rich, and ～, he was handsome** 他有钱, 而且很英俊

C *pron* **1** (larger amount or number) 更多; **～ of ...** 更多的…; **～ of an X than a Y** 更多的是 X 而不是 Y; **the ～ ... the ...** 越…, 越…; **it costs ～ than I expected** 它的价格超出了我的预料; **he earns much** *or* **far** *or* **a lot ～ than I do** 他比我挣的钱多多了; **we can't afford ～ than a short holiday** 我们只能负担得起短假; **one helping is ～ than enough** 一客就足够了; **it proved ～ of a hindrance than a help** 这证明有碍而无助; **the ～ you earn, the ～ tax you have to pay** 收入越多, 须缴的税就越多; **～ means worse** 多了反而更糟; **we must see ～ of her** 我们必须和她多见面; **(the) ～'s the pity!** 真倒霉!; **they could hardly do ～** 他们尽力了 **2** (additional amount or number) 额外的量; **～ and ～** 越来越多; **tell me ～** 再告诉我一些; **～ remain(s) to be discovered** 还有待更多发现; **many ～ are needed** 还需要更多; **there isn't much ～ to say** 没什么更多的话可说了; **have you heard any ～ from him?** 你还收到过他的信吗?; **let's say no ～ about it** formal 我们别再谈论这件事了; **during our holiday, of which ～ later, ...** 在我们度假期间, 关于这个问题后面还要谈到更多; **～ than meets the eye** 并非如看到的那样; **they have ～ and ～ to do** 他们有越来越多的事情要做; **you're late, and what's ～, you're drunk** 你迟到了, 更过分的是, 你还喝醉了; **neither/nothing ～ nor less (than)** 简直; **he's a thief, neither ～ nor less** 他完全就是一个贼; **no/nothing/not much ～ than ...** 仅仅是…; **it's not much ～ than a formality** 这只不过是一种形式 **3** (higher number) 更大的数目; **～ or less** 大约; **～ than** 多于; **she weighs a kilo ～ than I do** 她的体重比我重 1 公斤; **children aged 7 or ～** 7 岁或 7 岁以上的儿童; **～ than 5 people/£10/half** 5 人/10 英镑/一半以上; **～ than once** 不止一次地

moreish /ˈmɔːrɪʃ/ *adj* colloq 让人想再吃的

morello /mɒˈreləʊ/ *n* **～ (cherry)** 欧洲黑樱桃

moreover /mɔːˈrəʊvə(r)/ *adv* 此外; **it's too expensive and, ～, I don't like the colour** 太贵了, 而且这个颜色我也不喜欢

mores /ˈmɔːreɪz, -riːz/ *npl* formal (of society) 习俗; (of particular group) 规矩

morgue /mɔːg/ *n* (mortuary) 停尸房; (in hospital) 太平间; **this place is like a ～** colloq 这地方死气沉沉的

> **MORI**
>
> 莫里调查公司, 全称 Market and Opinion Research International。英国知名市场调查公司。成立于 1969 年, 总部设在伦敦。2005 年和益普索（Ipsos）公司合并, 名称改为 Ipsos MORI。以社会、政治研究和民意测验知名。通过多种调查方式对广告投放、忠诚度以及民意等进行调查。

moribund /ˈmɒrɪbʌnd/ *adj* formal 缺乏活力的

Mormon /ˈmɔːmən/

A *n* 摩门教徒

B *adj* 摩门教的

morning /ˈmɔːnɪŋ/ ▸**p. 831**

A *n* (before noon) 上午; (first hours of the day) 早晨; **a beautiful ～** 一个美丽的早晨; **at three/ten o'clock in the ～** 凌晨 3 点钟/上午 10 点钟; **this ～** 今天上午; **to take a** *or* **the ～ off** 上午休息; **the following ～, the ～ after** 第二天上午; **in the ～** 在早上; **early/first thing in the ～** 大清早/一大早第一件事; **I'll call her in the ～** 我明天一早给她打电话; **I usually play football on Saturday ～(s)** 我通常在星期六上午去踢足球; **the early hours of Sunday ～** 星期日凌晨; **from ～ to night** 从早到晚; **～, noon, and night** 从早到晚; **the ～ after (the night before)** hum 宿醉; **to do a good ～'s work** 干整整一上午的工作; **to work ～s** 上早班

B *adj attrib* 上午的 ‹*coffee, flight*›; **the ～ papers** 晨报; **the fresh ～ air** 早晨清新的空气

m

C ▸p. 333 *excl* colloq 早上好
D **mornings** *adv* colloq 每天早晨
morning: ～-after pill *n* colloq 事后避孕丸; **～ coat** *n* 男式晨燕尾服; **～ coffee** *n* [u] 晨咖啡; **～ dress** *n* [u] 男式常礼服; **～ paper** *n* 晨报; **～ sickness** *n* [u] 晨吐; **～ star** *n* 启明星; **～ watch** *n* 早班 [清晨4点至8点的值班时间]; **to be on ～ watch** 上早班
Moroccan /mə'rɒkən/ ▸**p. 503**
A *adj* (of Morocco) 摩洛哥的; (of the people) 摩洛哥人的
B *n* 摩洛哥人
Morocco /mə'rɒkəʊ/ *pr n* 摩洛哥
morocco /mə'rɒkəʊ/ *n* [u] **～ (leather)** 摩洛哥羊皮革; **～ shoes/slippers/binding** 摩洛哥羊皮革皮鞋/拖鞋/封皮
morocco-bound *adj* 用摩洛哥羊皮革装帧的 ‹*book*›
moron /'mɔːrɒn/ *n* colloq pej 笨蛋
moronic /mə'rɒnɪk/ *adj* colloq pej 愚蠢的
moronically /mə'rɒnɪkli/ *adv* colloq pej 愚蠢地; **～ stupid** 愚笨的
morose /mə'rəʊs/ *adj* 阴郁的; **to be ～ about sth.** 因某事物而郁闷
morosely /mə'rəʊsli/ *adv* 阴郁地
morph /mɔːf/
A *vi* 渐变; **to ～ into sth./sb.** 渐变成某物/某人
B *vt* 使变形; **to ～ sth. into sth.** 将某物变形为某物
morpheme /'mɔːfiːm/ *n* 词素
morphine /'mɔːfiːn/ *n* [u] 吗啡
morphine: ～ addict *n* 吗啡成瘾者; **～ addiction** *n* [u] 吗啡瘾
morphing /'mɔːfɪŋ/ *n* [u] 变形
morphological /ˌmɔːfə'lɒdʒɪkl/ *adj* **1** Biol 形态的 **2** Ling 词法的
morphologically /ˌmɔːfə'lɒdʒɪkli/ *adv* **1** Biol 在形态上 **2** Ling 在词法上
morphology /mɔː'fɒlədʒi/ *n* [u] **1** Biol 形态学 **2** Ling 词法学
morris /'mɒrɪs/: **～ dance** *n* 莫里斯舞 [英国传统民间舞]; **～ dancer** *n* 跳莫里斯舞的人; **～ dancing** *n* [u] 跳莫里斯舞; **～ man** *n* 跳莫里斯舞的男子
Morse /mɔːs/, **Morse code** *ns* [u] 莫尔斯电码; **to send a message in ～ (code)** 用莫尔斯电码发送消息; **～ (code) signals/messages/alphabet** 莫尔斯电码信号/电报/字母表
morsel /'mɔːsl/ *n* **1** (mouthful) 一小口; **a tasty ～** 美味小吃; **the dog ate every last ～** 狗把食物吃了个精光 **2** fig (small amount) 少量; **a ～ of sth.** 些许 ‹*gossip, common sense*›
mortal /'mɔːtl/
A *adj* **1** (subject to death) 终将死亡的 ‹*being*›; **all human beings are ～** 人总是要死的 **2** liter (fatal) 致命的 ‹*wound, illness, blow*› **3** attrib formal (intense, extreme) 极大的 ‹*insult, offence, error, danger*›; 极度的 ‹*fear, enmity*›
B *n* liter 凡人; **she doesn't talk to ordinary ～s** hum 她是不同凡夫俗子说话的
mortal: ～ combat *n* [u] 殊死搏斗; **～ enemy** *n* 不共戴天的敌人
mortality /mɔː'tæləti/ *n* [u] **1** (state of being mortal) 生命的有限; **to face one's own ～** 面对自己的有限生命 **2** formal (death) 死亡; **the cause/rate of ～** 死因/死亡率 **3** Stat (death rate) 死亡率
mortality rate *n* 死亡率
mortally /'mɔːtəli/ *adv* **1** liter (fatally) 致命地 ‹*wounded, ill*› **2** formal (intensely) 极度地 ‹*offended, afraid*›
mortal: ～ remains *npl* formal 遗体; **～ sin** *n* 死罪
mortar¹ /'mɔːtə(r)/ *n* **1** Mil 迫击炮; **～ fire/attack** 迫击炮的火力/攻击 **2** Culin, Pharm 研钵; **a ～ and pestle** 研钵和杵把

mortar² *n* [u] Constr 砂浆
mortarboard /'mɔːtəbɔːd/ *n* Brit 学位帽
mortgage /'mɔːgɪdʒ/
A *n* Fin (agreement, money loaned) 抵押贷款; **to apply for/take out/raise a ～** 申请/获得/筹集抵押贷款; **a ～ on** …的抵押贷款 ‹*house, property*›; **a ～ of £50,000, a £50,000 ～** 一笔5万英镑的抵押贷款; **pay off** *or* **clear a ～** 偿清抵押贷款
B *vt* 抵押 ‹*house, land*›; **to ～ sth. to sb.** 将某物抵押给某人; **to be ～d up to the hilt** *or* **eyeballs** colloq 债台高筑; **to ～ one's future** fig 赌上自己的前途
mortgage: ～ agreement *n* 抵押贷款协议; **～ broker** ▸**p. 409** *n* 抵押贷款经纪人; **～ deed** *n* 抵押贷款契据
mortgagee /ˌmɔːgɪ'dʒiː/ *n* 受抵押人
mortgage payment *n* 抵押贷款偿付
mortgager, mortgagor /'mɔːgɪdʒə(r)/ *n* 抵押人
mortgage: ～ rate *n* 抵押贷款利率; **～ repayment** *n* **= mortgage payment**
mortice *n* **= mortise**
mortician /mɔː'tɪʃn/ ▸**p. 409** *n* Amer 殡葬业者
mortification /ˌmɔːtɪfɪ'keɪʃn/ *n* [u] **1** (embarrassment) 窘迫; (shame) 羞愧; **to his ～, ...** (embarrassment) 让他窘迫的是, …; (shame) 让他羞愧的是, … **2** Relig 禁欲
mortify /'mɔːtɪfaɪ/
A *vt* **1** (embarrass) 使窘迫; (shame) 使羞愧 **2** Relig 克制; **to ～ the flesh** 禁欲
B **mortifying** *adj* (embarrassing) 令人窘迫的; (shaming) 令人羞愧的; **it is mortifying to discover that ...** (embarrassing) 发现…令人窘迫; (shaming) 发现…令人羞愧
mortifying /'mɔːtɪfaɪɪŋ/ *adj* (embarrassing) 令人窘迫的; (humiliating) 令人羞愧的; **it is ～ to + *inf.*** (embarrassing) 做…令人窘迫; (humiliating) 做…令人羞愧
mortise /'mɔːtɪs/ *n* 榫眼
mortise: ～ and tenon joint *n* 榫卯; **～ lock** *n* 插锁
mortuary /'mɔːtʃəri, Amer -tʃʊeri/ *n* **= morgue**
mosaic /məʊ'zeɪɪk/ *n* **1** (picture) 镶嵌画; (pattern) 镶嵌图案; **a portrait of Christ in ～** 耶稣的镶嵌肖像; **a ～ design** 镶嵌图案 **2** fig (pattern) 多种图案交织的图案; (combination) 融合多种成分的组合体; **the film is a ～ of startling images** 这部电影融合了各种令人惊叹的画面
Moscow /'mɒskəʊ/ *pr n* 莫斯科
Moselle, Mosel /məʊ'zel/ ▸**p. 663**
A *pr n* Geog 摩泽尔河
B *n* [u] **～ (wine)** 摩泽尔白葡萄酒
Moses /'məʊzɪz/ *pr n* 摩西; **Holy ～!** colloq dated 天哪!
Moses basket *n* 婴儿睡篮
mosey /'məʊzi/ colloq
A *vi* 溜达; **I'd better be ～ing along** 我还是去溜达溜达
B *n* esp Brit 溜达
mosh /mɒʃ/ *vi* colloq [随摇滚音乐] 狂舞
mosh pit *n* colloq [音乐会舞台前的] 狂舞区
Moslem /'mɒzləm/ *n, adj* **= Muslim**
mosque /mɒsk/ *n* 清真寺
mosquito /məs'kiːtəʊ, mɒs-/ *n* (*pl* **～es**) 蚊子
mosquito: ～ bite *n* 蚊叮; **～ net** *n* 蚊帐; **～ repellent** *n* [c and u] 驱蚊剂
moss /mɒs, Amer mɔːs/ *n* [u] 苔藓; **a carpet** *or* **bed of ～** 一层厚厚的苔藓
moss: ～-covered *adj* 苔藓覆盖的; **～ green** *n* [u] 苔藓绿; **～-grown** *adj* 长满苔藓的
mossy /'mɒsi, Amer 'mɔːsi/ *adj* 苔藓覆盖的

most /məʊst/
A *det* **1** (majority of, nearly all) 大多数的; **～ people/computers** 大多数人/电脑 **2** (more than all others) 最大量的; **she earns (the) ～ votes/money** 她得到了最多的选票/赚钱最多; **the area where we have had (the) ～ success** 我们取得了最大成功的领域; **for the ～ part** 大部分地; **she agreed with my suggestions for the ～ part** 她基本同意我的建议
B *pron* **1** (the maximum) **the ～** 最大量; **the ～ you can expect is ...** 你所能期待的至多是…; **what's the ～ we'll have to pay?** 我们必须支付的上限是多少? ; **he certainly made the ～ of the story** 他把这个故事讲得真是精彩极了; **to make the ～ of oneself** 充分展现自己 **2** (the majority) 大多数; **～ of his friends/the people** 他的大多数朋友/大多数人; **～ of the money/wine** 大部分钱/葡萄酒; **～ of the day** 白天的大部分时间 **3** (more than all others) 最多; **Nick has got (the) ～** 尼克得到的最多; **at (the) ～** 至多
C *adv* **1** (more than all the rest) 最多地; **what she wants ～ (of all) is ...** 她特别想要的是…; **those who will benefit/suffer ～ from ...** 从…中获益/受苦最多的人 **2** (to the greatest extent) 最; **the ～ comfortable hotel in Cairo** 开罗最舒适的旅馆; **she did it ～ easily of all** 她做这件事最轻松; **the ～ beautifully written prose** 写得最优美的散文 **3** (very) 非常; **～ encouraging/annoying** 非常鼓舞人心/令人恼火; **～ certainly/probably** 非常肯定/极有可能 **4** Amer colloq (almost) 几乎; **～ everyone** 几乎每个人
mostly /'məʊstli/ *adv* **1** (chiefly, typically) 主要地; **he composes, ～ for the piano** 他主要谱写钢琴曲; **coachloads of people, ～ Japanese** 一客车一客车的人, 大部分是日本人 **2** (usually) 通常; **～ he sits by the fire** 他通常坐在炉火边
MOT /ˌeməʊ'tiː/ Brit
A *n* **1** **～ (test** *or* **inspection)** 车辆年检; **to take one's car in for its ～** 将车送检; **to pass/fail the ～** 通过/未通过车检; **an ～ (test) centre** 车辆年检中心 **2** **～ (certificate)** 验车合格证
B *vt* 把…送检 ‹*vehicle*›
motel /məʊ'tel/ *n* 汽车旅馆
motet /məʊ'tet/ *n* 经文歌 [在天主教等教堂中清唱]
moth /mɒθ, Amer mɔːθ/ *n* 蛾
mothball /'mɒθbɔːl, Amer 'mɔːθ-/
A *n* 樟脑丸; **to put sth. in/keep sth. in/take sth. out of ～s** fig 封存/保持封存/重新启用某物
B *vt* **1** 在…内放樟脑丸 ‹*clothes*› **2** fig (stop using) 将…封存 ‹*ship, aircraft*›; (postpone) 推迟 ‹*plan*›
moth-eaten *adj* **1** (damaged by moths) 蛀坏的 ‹*clothes*› **2** colloq (shabby) 破旧的 ‹*armchair*› **3** (antiquated) 过时的 ‹*idea, phrase*›
mother /'mʌðə(r)/
A *n* **1** ▸**p. 419** (parent) 母亲; **a ～ of two** 两个孩子的母亲; **an expectant/a nursing ～** 准妈妈/喂奶的妈妈; **every ～'s son (of them)** (他们中的) 每个人; **at one's ～'s knee** 年少时 **2** **Mother** Relig 嬷嬷; **Reverend M～** 院长嬷嬷 **3** (motherly qualities) **the ～ in her** 她身上的母性 **4** colloq (extreme example) 极端情况; **a** *or* **the ～ of a fight/all traffic jams** 极其激烈的搏斗/最糟的交通堵塞
B *modif* 母亲的 ‹*chimpanzee*›; **～ bird** 母鸟; 根源的; **～ company/church** 母公司/教会母堂
C *vt* **1** also pej (fuss over) 溺爱 **2** dated (give birth to) 生育
mother: ～board *n* [计算机的] 主板; **～ country** *n* **1** (native country) 祖国; **2** Pol [殖民地的] 宗主国; **M～ Earth** *n* 大地母亲; **～ figure** *n* 慈母般的人; **～fucker** *n* esp Amer taboo sl 混蛋 offensive; **～fucking** *adj* attrib esp Amer taboo sl 混账的 offensive; **～ hen** *n*

1 lit 哺育小鸡的母鸡; 2 fig colloq 婆婆妈妈爱操心的人

motherhood /'mʌðəhʊd/ n [u] 母亲身份; **the responsibilities of ~** 母亲的责任; **to combine ~ with a career** 将做母亲与职业结合起来

mothering /'mʌðərɪŋ/ n [u] (motherly care) 呵护; (being a mother) 为人母; **the art of ~** 为母之道

Mothering Sunday n Brit 母亲节

mother: ~-in-law ▸p. 419 n (pl **~s-in-law**) (to a woman) 婆婆; (to a man) 岳母; **~land** /-lænd/ n 祖国

motherless /'mʌðəlɪs/ adj 没有母亲的; **it is a terrible thing for a child to be left ~** 没娘的孩子很可悲

mother love n [u] 母爱

motherly /'mʌðəli/ adj 慈母般的

mother: M~ Nature n 大自然; **~-of-pearl** n [u] 珍珠母; **~'s boy** n Brit colloq pej 脆弱的男性; **M~'s Day** n 母亲节; **~'s help** Brit, **~'s helper** Amer n 保姆; **~ship** n 母舰; **~'s ruin** n [u] Brit colloq 杜松子酒; **M~ Superior** n (pl **M~s Superior** or **M~ Superiors**) 女修道院院长; **~-to-be** n (pl **~s-to-be**) 孕妇; **~ tongue** n 本族语; **to speak one's ~ tongue** 说母语

mothproof /'mɒθpru:f, Amer 'mɔ:θ-/
A adj 防蛀的
B vt 对…作防蛀处理

moth repellent n [u] 防蛀剂

motif /məʊ'ti:f/ n 1 (design) 装饰图案 2 (theme) 主题

motion /'məʊʃn/
A n 1 [u] (movement) 运动; **perpetual ~** 永动; **to be in ~** 处于运动中; **to set** or **put sth. in ~** lit 使某物开始运动; fig 使某事开始运作; **to set the wheels in ~** fig 使一切开始运转 2 [c] (gesture) (of hands) 手势; (of head, body) 姿势; **he made a ~ to close the door** 他做了个关门的手势; **to go through the ~s (of doing sth.)** （做某事）走过场 3 [c] (proposal) 动议; **a ~ to do sth.** 做某事的动议; **to table/second the ~** 提出动议/对动议提出附议; **to carry** or **pass/defeat** or **reject the ~ by 10 votes to 8** 以10票对8票通过/否决动议; **a ~ of censure** 不信任动议; **a Commons ~** Brit 下院的提议 4 [c] Brit formal (emptying of bowels) 排便; **to have a ~** 排便 5 [c] Brit formal (faeces) 粪便
B vi 做手势; **to ~ to** or **for sb. (to do sth.)** 示意某人（做某事）; **he ~ed for me to come over** 他招呼我过去
C vt 向…做手势; **to ~ sb. in/out** 示意某人进来/出去

motionless /'məʊʃnlɪs/ adj 静止的; **they sat ~** 他们坐着一动不动

motion: ~ picture n esp Amer 电影; **the ~-picture industry** 电影业; **~ sickness** n [u] 晕动病 [指晕车、晕船等]

motivate /'məʊtɪveɪt/ vt 1 (prompt) 促动; **to be ~d by sth.** 由某事物促动; **they were ~d by greed** 他们是出于贪婪 2 (inspire) 调动…的积极性; **a teacher who can ~ her pupils** 能调动学生积极性的老师

motivated /'məʊtɪveɪtɪd/ adj 1 (prompted) 有动机的 ‹action›; **politically/racially ~** 有政治动机/种族目的 2 (inspired) 有积极性的 ‹person›; **highly** or **well ~** 积极性高的

motivation /,məʊtɪ'veɪʃn/ n 1 [c] (motive) 动机; **the ~ for/behind sth.** 某事/某事背后的动机 2 [u] (enthusiasm, drive) 积极性; **the ~ to do sth.** 做某事的积极性

motivational /,məʊtɪ'veɪʃnl/ adj 有动机的 ‹speech, speaker›; 促进的 ‹skills›

motivator /'məʊtɪveɪtə(r)/ n (person) 促动者; (thing) 促动因素

motive /'məʊtɪv/
A n 1 [c] (reason) 动机; **to have ulterior ~s** 别有意图; **sb.'s ~ in doing sth.** 某人做某事的动机; **the profit ~** 牟利的动机; **a ~ for the murder** 杀人动机 2 **= motif**
B adj 1 引起运动的 ‹energy›; **~ force** or **power** 原动力 2 fig (driving) 作为动因的 ‹principle›; **she was the ~ force behind the decision** 她是这项决定背后的推动力量

motiveless /'məʊtɪvlɪs/ adj 无动机的

motley /'mɒtli/ adj attrib 混杂的 ‹crowd, collection›; **a ~ crew of** 形形色色的 ‹tourists, students›

motocross /'məʊtəkrɒs/ ▸p. 307 n [u] 摩托车越野赛; **to take up/do ~** 参加摩托车越野赛

motor /'məʊtə(r)/
A n 1 Elec 电动机; Mech 发动机 2 Brit colloq (car) 汽车 3 fig 推动力; **to be the ~ for sth.** 是某事的推动力
B modif 1 (driven by a motor) 机动的 ‹vehicle, vessel› 2 (relating to motor vehicles) 机动车的 ‹show, industry›; **~ accident/insurance/racing** 车祸/车险/车赛 3 Physiol 运动的 ‹nerve, muscle›; **~ area** [大脑皮层的] 运动区
C vi 1 Brit dated (drive) 开车 2 colloq (go fast) 进展迅速; **to ~ through the work** 工作进展迅速; **we were really ~ing** 我们进展得很快

Motorail /'məʊtəreɪl/ n [u] esp Brit 汽车搭火车业务 [指铁路运载汽车及其司机、乘客的业务]

motor: ~bike n 1 Brit (motorcycle) 摩托车; 2 Amer (bicycle with small engine) 机动自行车; **~boat** n 摩托艇; **~ car** n Brit 汽车

motorcade /'məʊtəkeɪd/ n 车队

motorcycle /'məʊtəsaɪkl/ n 摩托车

motorcycle: ~ escort n 摩托车护卫队; **~ messenger** n 摩托车邮递员

motor: ~cycling n [u] 摩托车运动; **~cyclist** n 骑摩托车的人; **~home** n esp Amer 房车

motoring /'məʊtərɪŋ/
A n [u] dated 驾驶汽车; **to go ~** 驾车兜风
B modif 驾车的 ‹correspondent›; 汽车的 ‹magazine, organization›; **~ offences** 驾车违章

motorist /'məʊtərɪst/ n 驾车者

motorization /,məʊtəraɪ'zeɪʃn, Amer -rɪ'z-/ n [u] 1 Mech 安装发动机 2 Mil (of troops) 摩托化

motorize /'məʊtəraɪz/ vt 1 Mech 给…安装发动机 2 Mil 使…摩托化 ‹troops›

motor: ~ launch n 摩托艇; **~ lodge** n Amer 汽车旅馆; **~ mechanic** ▸p. 409 n 汽车机修工; **~mouth** n colloq 喋喋不休的人; **~ mower** n 机动割草机; **~ neurone disease** ▸p. 377 n [u] 运动神经元病; **~ oil** n [u and c] 发动机润滑油; **~ racing** ▸p. 307 n [u] 赛车运动; **~ scooter** n 轻型摩托车

motorway /'məʊtəweɪ/ n Brit 高速公路; 高速公路的 ‹services, police›; 高速公路上的 ‹telephone, crash›

motorway: ~ madness n [u] Brit colloq 高速公路上的疯狂 [指汽车排长队等问题]; **~ service area** n Brit 高速公路服务区

mottled /'mɒtld/ adj 杂色斑驳的; **to go ~** 变得杂色斑驳

motto /'mɒtəʊ/ n (pl **~es** or **~s**) 1 (maxim) (of person) 座右铭; (of institution) 格言; **a school ~** 校训 2 esp Brit (joke, riddle, or saying in cracker) [圣诞彩包爆竹中藏的] 笑话; (riddle) 谜语; (saying) 格言

mould[1] /məʊld/ Brit
A n 1 (shape) (for metal, china, plastic) 模具; Culin (for pudding, jelly) 模子 2 fig (type, style) 类型; **to fit (into) the ~ of sth.** 符合某事物的类型; **to be cast in a similar/the same/a different ~** 具有类似/相同/不同的性格; **to break the ~** 打破陈规
B vt 1 (shape) 用模具塑造 ‹clay, liquid metal, plastic›; 用模具制作出 ‹sculpture, model, piece of wax›; **to ~ sth. into sth.** 用模具把某物做成某形状; **seats ~ed to the shape of the average figure** 用模具按中等身材制成的座椅; **a head ~ed out of** or **in** or **from clay** 通过模具用泥巴制成的头像 2 fig (influence) 影响…的形成; **to ~ a child into a mature adult** 把孩子塑造成思想成熟的成年人; **to ~ public opinion** 左右舆论
C vi 紧贴; **the wet clothes ~ed to her body** 湿衣服贴在她身上

mould[2] n Brit 1 [u and c] (fungus) 霉菌 2 [u] (soil) 松软沃土

mould: ~-breaker n (person) 打破陈规的人; (thing) 打破陈规的事物; **~-breaking** adj 打破陈规的

moulder /'məʊldə(r)/ vi Brit **~ (away)** 1 (decay) «building» 坍塌; «corpse» 腐烂 2 fig (waste away) «person» 虚费光阴; «plans» 搁浅

moulding /'məʊldɪŋ/ n Brit 1 [u] (shaping) 模制 2 [u] fig (forming, influencing) 成形 3 [c] Archit 线脚

mouldy /'məʊldi/ adj Brit 1 (covered with mould) 发霉的 ‹food›; **to go ~** 发霉; **a ~ smell** 霉味 2 Brit fig colloq (dull) 无聊的 ‹person, object› 3 fig (stale) 陈腐的; **~ old stereotypes** 陈规旧套

moult /məʊlt/ Brit
A vi «mammal» 换毛; «bird» 换羽; «reptile» 蜕皮
B vt 换 ‹hair, feathers›; 蜕 ‹skin›
C n 1 [u] (moulting) (of mammals) 脱毛; (of birds) 换羽; (of reptiles) 蜕皮 2 [c] (time of moulting) (of mammals) 脱毛期; (of birds) 换羽期; (of reptiles) 蜕皮期

mound /maʊnd/ n 1 (man-made) (of earth) 土堆; (of stones) 石堆 2 (hillock) 小丘 3 (heap) 堆; **a ~ of sth.** 一堆某物 4 Amer (in baseball) 投手站立的土墩

mount /maʊnt/
A vt 1 (ascend) 登上 ‹stairs, hill, stage›; 骑上 ‹horse, bicycle›; **to ~ the throne** 登上王位; **to ~ the pavement** «car» 驶上人行道 2 (fix in place) 把…装框 ‹picture›; 镶嵌 ‹gem›; 把…固定于载片 ‹specimen›; **to ~ sth. on** or **on to/in sth.** 把某物镶嵌到某物上/内 3 (support) 安装 ‹machine›; **to ~ sth. with sth.** 把某物安装在某物上 4 fig (set up, hold) 发起 ‹campaign, challenge, attack›; 举行 ‹exhibition, performance, raid›; **to ~ checkpoints** 设立检查站; **to ~ guard (at** or **over sb./sth.)** 设岗（守卫某人/某物） 5 Zool 趴到…身上交配 ‹female animal, female bird›
B vi 1 (rise) «blush, blood» 上涌; **a blush/the blood ~ed to her cheeks** 她的脸颊上浮起一片红晕/血涌上她的脸颊 2 Equit 上马 3 (increase in size) «number, debt, costs» 增加; «temperature, prices, unemployment» 上升; **to ~ to sth.** 增加到某一数目 4 (increase in intensity) «concern, tension, excitement» 加剧; «interest» 增强 5 Zool «male mammal, male bird» 趴到身上交配
C n 1 (mountain) 山; **M~ Etna/Everest** 埃特纳山/珠穆朗玛峰 2 (backing) (for picture) 框; (for gem, coin) 托板; (for stamp) 护邮袋; (for transparency, specimen) 载片 3 (support) (for machine, engine, camera) 底座; (for gun) 炮架 4 (horse) 坐骑

Phrasal verb
• **mount up** vi «costs, savings, debts» 增加

mountain /'maʊntɪn, Amer -ntn/
A n 1 lit 山; **the top of the ~** 山顶 2 fig (pile) 大量; **a ~ of sth., ~s of sth.** 大量的 ‹rubble, debts, work› 3 (surplus) 剩余; **the meat ~** 囤积如山的肉
B modif 山中的 ‹path, scenery, guide, air›; **~ people** 山民; **~ rescue** 登山遇难营救

mountain: ~ ash n 花楸; **~ bike** n 山地自行车; **~ biker** n 山地自行车手; **~ biking** ▸p. 307 n [u] 骑山地自行车; **~ climbing** ▸p. 307 n [u] 登山; **M~ Daylight Time** n [u] 山区夏令时间

m

mountaineer /ˌmaʊntɪˈnɪə(r), Amer -ntnˈɪər/ ▸**p. 409** *n* 登山运动员

mountaineering /ˌmaʊntɪˈnɪərɪŋ, Amer -ntnˈɪərɪŋ/ ▸**p. 307** *n* [u] 登山

mountain: ~ goat *n* 石山羊; **~ lion** *n* 美洲狮

mountainous /ˈmaʊntɪnəs, Amer -ntənəs/ *adj* **1** (with many mountains) 多山的 **2** fig (huge) 巨大的 ‹*waves, task*›; **~ seas** 汹涌的波涛

mountain: ~ range *n* 山脉; **~ sickness** *n* [u] 高山病; **~side** *n* (slope) 山坡; (side) 山腰; **M~ Standard Time** *n* [u] Amer 山区冬季时间; **M~ Time** *n* [u] Amer 山区标准时间; **~ top** *n* 山顶

mounted /ˈmaʊntɪd/ *adj* 骑马的 ‹*soldier, troops*›; 骑警的 ‹*patrol*›

mounted: ~ police *n + v pl* 骑警队; **~ policeman** ▸**p. 409** *n* 骑警

Mountie /ˈmaʊnti/ *n* colloq 加拿大皇家骑警队员

mounting /ˈmaʊntɪŋ/
A *adj attrib* 增长的 ‹*excitement, costs, unemployment*›; 加剧的 ‹*tension*›
B *n* 托架

> **Mount Rushmore**
>
> 拉什莫尔山。位于美国南达科他州的黑山地区（Black Hills），海拔 1800 米。山名源自纽约律师查尔斯·E·拉什莫尔（Charles E. Rushmore）。山上刻有乔治·华盛顿（George Washington）、托马斯·杰斐逊（Thomas Jefferson）、亚伯拉罕·林肯（Abraham Lincoln）和西奥多·罗斯福（Theodore Roosevelt）四位总统的大理石头像，分别代表美国的独立、民主、平等与国家统一以及美国在 20 世纪的国际地位。石像高约 18 米。工程开始于 1927 年，1941 年竣工，由雕塑家格曾·博格勒姆（Gutzon Borglum）设计并雕刻。现由国家公园管理局（National Park Service）管理，称为拉什莫尔山国家纪念公园（Mount Rushmore National Memorial）。

mourn /mɔːn/
A *vt* 哀悼
B *vi* 表示哀悼; **to ~ for** *or* **over sb./sth.** 哀悼某人的死/为某事物伤感

mourner /ˈmɔːnə(r)/ *n* 哀悼者; **chief ~** 主殡礼人

mournful /ˈmɔːnfl/ *adj* 悲伤的

mournfully /ˈmɔːnfəli/ *adv* 悲伤地

mourning /ˈmɔːnɪŋ/ *n* [u] **1** (grieving) 哀悼; **a time/day of ~** 服丧期/举丧日; **national ~** 国丧; **to be in ~ (for sb.)** （为某人）服丧; **to go into ~ (for sb.)** 开始（为某人）服丧; **to come out of ~** 结束服丧 **2** (wailing) 恸哭 **3** (clothes) 丧服; **to wear deep ~** 穿深色丧服

mourning: ~ band *n* 黑纱; **~ clothes** *npl* 丧服

mouse /maʊs/ *n* **1** (*pl* **mice**) Zool 鼠; **a house/field/harvest/white ~** 家鼠/田鼠/巢鼠/白鼠; **like a ~** *or* **as quiet as a ~** 悄无声息地; **~ droppings** 老鼠屎 **2** (*pl* **mice** *or* **~s**) Comput 鼠标 **3** (*pl* **mice**) fig (quiet, shy person) 胆小鬼

Phrasal verb
- **mouse over** *vt* [**~ over sth.**] 用鼠标将光标滑到

mouse: ~-driven *adj* 鼠标控制的; **~hole** *n* 鼠洞; **~ mat** *n* 鼠标垫

mouser /ˈmaʊsə(r)/ *n* 捕鼠猫

mousetrap /ˈmaʊstræp/ *n* 捕鼠器; **to set** *or* **lay/spring a ~** 设置/突然合上捕鼠器

mousey /ˈmaʊsi/ *adj* = **mousy**

moussaka /muːˈsɑːkə/ *n* [u] 肉末茄子饼

mousse /muːs/ *n* **1** [c and u] Culin 奶油冻 **2** [u] (for hair) 摩丝

moustache /məˈstɑːʃ/ *n* 小胡子; **to grow a ~** 留小胡子; **~s** 长髯; **a ~ of orange juice around his mouth** 他嘴边挂着的一抹橙汁

moustached /məˈstɑːʃt, Amer ˈmʌstæʃt/, **moustachioed** /məˈstɑːʃɪəʊd, Amer -ˈstæʃ-/ *adjs* 有胡子的 ‹*man, face*›

mousy /ˈmaʊsi/ *adj* **1** (in colour) 暗灰褐色的 **2** pej (timid) 胆小的

mouth
A /maʊθ/ *n* **1** ▸**p. 71** [c] (of human, animal) 嘴; **to open/shut** *or* **close one's ~** lit 张/闭嘴; fig 开口说话/闭嘴; **with one's ~ (wide) open** （大）张着嘴; **to keep one's ~ shut (about sth.)** colloq （对某事）守口如瓶; **to kiss sb. on/hit sb. in the ~** 亲某人的嘴/打某人的嘴巴; **to have something in one's ~** 嘴里含着东西; **to be taken by ~** 口服; **nil by ~** 不得口服; **my ~ is dry** 我口干; **to make sb.'s ~ water** «*food*» 使某人馋得流口水; **to have four ~s to feed** 有 4 口人要养活; **out of sb.'s own ~** 某人亲口说的; **by word of ~** 口头上; **to put words in** *or* **into sb.'s ~** 硬说某人说过某些话; **to take the words (right) out of sb.'s ~** 说出某人（正）想说的话; **to have a big ~** colloq (talk too much) 喋喋不休; (reveal secret) 口风不紧; **to shoot one's ~ off** colloq (boastfully) 胡吹; (indiscreetly) 随便乱说; **to put one's foot in one's ~** 说话不得体; **to watch one's ~** colloq 说话当心; **I'll wash your ~ out with soap!** colloq 再说脏话，我就用肥皂给你洗洗嘴！; **his heart was in his ~** 他的心提到了嗓子眼; **to be down in the ~** 闷闷不乐; **out of the ~s of babes** Prov 童言有道; ▸**lion 1, taste A1** **2** [c] (opening of bag, jar, cave, tunnel, volcano) 口; (of harbour, river) 出口 **3** [u] colloq (talk) 空话; **he's all ~ and no action** 他只说不干 **4** [u] colloq (impudence) 无礼的话; **watch your ~!** 说话注意点！
B /maʊð/ *vt* **1** (say silently) 只嘴动而不出声地说 ‹*word, answer*›; **to ~ sth. to oneself** 不出声地自言自语某事 **2** pej (say insincerely, recite) 言不由衷地说 ‹*promises, apologies*›; 机械地说 ‹*prayers*›

Phrasal verb
- **mouth off** *vi* colloq pej **1** (boast) 高谈阔论; **to ~ off about sth.** 大谈特谈某事物; **to ~ off at sb.** 大声责骂某人 **2** Amer (be indiscreet) 随便乱讲; **to ~ off about sth.** 乱讲某事物

mouthful /ˈmaʊθfʊl/ *n* **1** (of food or drink) 一满口; **a ~/~s of sth.** 一大口/几大口某物; **to eat/swallow sth. in a** *or* **one ~** 一口吃下/吞下某物 **2** colloq (abuse) 指责; **to give sb. a ~** 大骂某人; **to get** *or* **take** *or* **receive a ~** 被骂了一顿; **a ~ of obscenities/curses** 一连串的脏话/咒骂 **3** colloq (word that is difficult to pronounce) 长而拗口的词; (name that is difficult to pronounce) 长而难念的名字

mouth: ~ organ ▸**p. 395** *n* 口琴; **~piece** *n* **1** (of musical instrument) 吹口; (of telephone, headset) 送话口; (of pipe, snorkel) 咬嘴; **2** often pej (spokesperson) 喉舌; **to act** *or* **serve as the ~piece of** *or* **for sb./sth.** 为某人/某事物代言; **~-to-~ resuscitation** *n* [u] 口对口人工呼吸; **to give sb. ~-to-~ resuscitation** 为某人做人工呼吸; **~ ulcer** *n* 口腔溃疡; **~wash** *n* [c and u] 漱口液; **~-watering** *adj* 令人垂涎的

mouthy /ˈmaʊði/ *adj* colloq 唠叨的

movable /ˈmuːvəbl/
A *adj* **1** (able to be moved) 可移动的 ‹*screen, object*›; 活动的 ‹*arm, leg*› **2** Jur 可动的 ‹*furniture, goods*›; **~ property** 动产 **3** (variable in date) 日期不定的 ‹*holiday, feast*›
B **movables** *npl* Jur 动产

move /muːv/
A *vi* **1** (shift position) «*vehicle, equipment, person, animal, body part*» 移动; «*wheel, machine*» 转动; «*current, fluid, gas*» 流动; «*tree, branch*» 摇动; **to ~ up and down** «*lever, handle*» 上下移动; **to ~ on wheels/rails** 靠轮子/滑轨移动; **his fingers ~d over the keys** 他的手指在键盘上移动; **don't ~!** 不许动！; **you'll have to ~, I need this chair** 你得起来，我要用这把椅子 **2** (go forward) «*person, animal, traffic, troops*» 行进; **to keep sb./sth. moving** 使某人/某物继续前进; **~ aside!** 让开！; **it's time we were moving** colloq 我们该走了; **that horse/car can ~!** colloq 那匹马/那辆车速度真快！; **to ~ into third place** 上升到第三位; **to ~ into the lead** 开始领先 **3** (carry oneself) «*person, animal*» 走动; **how gracefully she ~s** 她走起路来真优雅; **to ~ in high society** fig 出入上流社会 **4** (change residence) «*person, family*» 搬家; «*business*» 迁移; **to ~ away** 搬走; **to ~ to** *or* **into/out of sth.** 搬进/搬出某处; **when the firm ~d, I ~d too** 公司迁址的时候我也随迁了 **5** (make progress) «*work*» 进展; **things are starting to ~ on the job front** 找工作的情况开始有进展; **to get sth./things moving** 使某事/情况有进展; **to ~ ahead in the opinion polls** 在民意测验中领先 **6** (change job) 调动工作; **to ~ to head office** 调到总部工作; **to ~ sideways** 平级调动 **7** (change, develop) «*person, society, views*» 转变; **to ~ to the right/left** «*opinion*» 变得右倾/左倾; **to ~ into the final stage** «*project*» 进入最后阶段; **to ~ into a new era** 进入新时代; **to ~ over to** 转而采用 ‹*new method, system*›; **events ~d rapidly** 事情变化很快; **she won't ~ once she's made up her mind** 她一旦拿定主意就不会改变; **to ~ away from one's original position** 偏离最初的立场; **to ~ with the times** 与时俱进; **to ~ apart** fig «*friends*» 分手 **8** (act) «*person, organization, government*» 采取行动; **to ~ on sth.** 针对某事采取措施; **to ~ on the issue** 采取措施应对这一问题; **to ~ to do sth.** 着手做某事; **to ~ against sb./sth.** 采取对付某人/某事物的措施 **9** Games «*player, piece*» 走; **to ~ diagonally** 走对角; **have you ~d? — I ~d there** 你走棋了吗？——我走到那里了 **10** (propose) **to ~ for sth.** 提出 ‹*amendment, adjournment*› **11** (sell) «*goods*» 售出; **to ~ fast** «*product*» 卖得快
B *vt* **1** (set in motion) «*person, force*» 移动 ‹*body part, object*›; **to ~ one's toes** 动一下脚趾; **I can't ~ my leg/the screw** 我动不了腿/拧不动螺丝; **to ~ one's arms/neck around** 活动胳膊/脖子; **to ~ one's head from side to side** 左右摆动头部; **the force that ~s that wheel/the solar system** 驱动那个轮子/太阳系的力量; **to ~ one's bowels** 排便 **2** (change location of) 搬走 ‹*object*›; **who ~d my books?** 谁动了我的书？; **someone ~d my marker** 有人动了我的记号笔; **he's too ill to be ~d** 他病得太重，不能动地方; **to ~ sb. to another hospital** 把某人转到另一个医院; **to ~ sth. off the table/chair** 把某物从桌子/椅子上拿下来; **to ~ sth. into the room/closer to the window** 把某物搬进屋子/搬得离窗户近一些; **to ~ sth. upstairs/downstairs** 把某物搬上楼/搬下楼; **to ~ the tables together** 把桌子拼起来; **to ~ the decimal point** 移动小数点 **3** (shift to one side, budge) 挪走 ‹*object, body part*›; **to ~ sth. to one side** 把某物挪到一边; **to ~ sth. out of the way** 挪开某物; **to ~ the curtain aside** 拉开窗帘; **~ your legs out of the way** 把你的腿挪开; **to ~ sth. further down/up the list** 把某物挪到名单更靠下/更靠上的位置 **4** (transport) 运送 ‹*goods, freight*›; Mil (send) 调集 ‹*troops*›; **to ~ equipment to a new site** 把设备运到新工地; **to ~ artillery across the river** 把炮兵调到河对岸 **5** (to new job, location) 调换 ‹*staff, job*›; «*firm*» 迁移 ‹*office*›; **to be ~d to a new job** 被调去做新工作; **to ~ jobs** Brit 调换工作; **to ~ headquarters to New York** 把总部迁到纽约 **6** (to new residence) 搬 ‹*home, furniture*›; **to ~ house** «*person, family*» 搬家; **a local firm ~d us** 一家本地公司为我们搬了家 **7** (affect)

«*words, appearance, plight*» 打动 ‹*person, crowd*›; **to ~ sb. to tears** 使某人感动得流泪; **to be ~d by sth./sb.** 被某事物/某人打动; **to be (deeply) ~d by the experience** 被这次经历（深深）感动; **to be ~d to anger** 被激怒; **to be ~d to pity by sb.'s plea** 被某人的恳求感动而产生恻隐之心; **to be ~d to laughter** 被逗得大笑起来 **8** (motivate) 驱使; **to ~ sb. to do sth.** 促使某人做某事; **I was ~d to act by her letter** 她的来信促使我采取了行动; **to feel ~d to speak out/protest** 不由得想站出来反对/抗议; **when the spirit ~s me** hum 我有兴致时 **9** Games 走 ‹*piece*› **10** (propose) 提出 ‹*resolution, adjournment*›; **to ~ that ...** 提议…; **I ~ that the matter be put to the vote** 我提议将此事付诸表决 **11** (sell) 售出 ‹*product*›; **stock that we haven't been able to ~** 我们卖不掉的存货

C *n* **1** (movement) 动作; **to watch sb.'s every ~** 观察某人的一举一动; **one false ~ and you're dead!** 别乱动，不然要你的命！; **to make a ~ (towards sth.)** （向某处）走去; **to make no ~** 不采取行动 **2** (shift in location, line of business) 移动; **it's time we were making a ~** Brit 我们该走了; **a company's ~ into electronics** 公司向电子业的转移; **to get a ~ on** colloq 赶快 **3** (change) (of residence) 搬家; (of business premises) 迁移; (of job) 调动; **they are here to help with the ~** 他们来帮忙搬家; **to make the ~ from A to B** 从A迁到B; **she's due for a ~** 她该调换工作了 **4** (state of moving) **to be on the ~** 在行进; **to be always on the ~** 不停奔波; **the circus is on the ~ again** 马戏团又开始四处演出了; **a society on the ~** fig 不断发展的社会 **5** Games 一步棋; **a clever/silly ~** 一步妙棋/蠢棋; **it's your ~** 该你走棋了; **white has the first ~** 白棋先走 **6** (step, act) 行动; **a good/bad/clever ~** 好的/坏的/聪明的举措; **to make a ~** 采取行动; **to make the first/the next ~** 抢先行动/采取下一步行动; **a ~ to do sth.** 做某事的措施; **in a ~ to cut off the enemy's retreat ...** 在切断敌人退路的行动中…

D *v refl* colloq **1** (hurry up) **~ yourself!** 快一点！; **tell them to ~ themselves** 告诉他们快点 **2** (move aside) **~ yourself — I can't get through!** 让开——我过不去了！

Phrasal verbs

- **move about, move around**

A *vi* **1** (shift position) 走动; **to keep moving about** 不停地四处走动; **there's someone moving about upstairs** 楼上有人在走动; **to have plenty of space** *or* **room to ~ about in** 有足够的活动空间; **to ~ about in the socket** «*plug*» 松动 **2** (change residence) «*person, family*» 搬家; **to ~ about a lot** 经常搬家

B [**~ sth. about**] *vt*
1 (change position of) 移动; **to ~ the furniture/pictures about** 重新摆放家具/这些画; **to ~ the cursor about with the mouse** 用鼠标把光标移来移去; **to ~ the aerial about** 转动天线 **2** (assign to different job) 调动 ‹*employee, staff*›; **to get ~d about quite a bit** 经常调动工作

C [**~ about sth.**] *vt*
1 (change position in or on) 在…周围来回走动 ‹*floor, space*›; **to ~ freely about the stage** 随意地在舞台上四处走动 **2** (change residence in) 在…内搬来搬去 ‹*country, region*›

- **move along**

A *vi* **1** (not loiter) 不停留; **the police officer told us to ~ along** 警官告诉我们不要停留 **2** (squeeze up) 挤紧; **~ along!** 挤一挤！; **to ~ along a couple of places** 往里挤几个位置 **3** (keep going) «*person, traffic, parade*» 继续前行 **4** fig (progress) «*work, process*» 进行; **things are moving along nicely** 事情进展顺利

B [**~ sb./sth. along**] *vt*
1 (prevent from loitering) 使不逗留; **the police ~d the crowd along** 警察命令人群不得逗留; **to ~ the traffic along** 让车辆往前走 **2** (change position of) 移动; **to ~ sth. along to the right** 把某物往右边移; **to ~ the pile along the shelf** 把那堆东西沿着搁板推过去

C [**~ along sth.**] *vt* 沿着…移动; **to ~ along a track** «*train*» 沿着轨道前进; **his fingers ~d along the line/keys** 他的手指沿着线条/键盘滑动

- **move around**

A *vi* **= move about A**

B *vt* **1** **= move about B, C** **2** [**~ around sth.**] (circle) 绕着…环行; **to ~ around the sun** 绕着太阳旋转

- **move away**

A *vi* **1** (change residence) «*family, shop*» 搬走; **to ~ away from ...** 从…搬走 ‹*area, city*› **2** (leave scene) 离开; **to ~ away from ...** 从…离开 ‹*place*›

B *vt* [**~ sb./sth. away, ~ away sb./sth.**] 移开

- **move back**

A *vi* **1** (go backwards) 后退; «*troops*» 撤退; **~ back to let me pass** 后退一步让我过去; **to ~ back a space** 后退一个空格 **2** (return) «*person*» 回来; «*mechanism*» 复位; (to old residence, office) 搬回来; **to ~ back to the window** 回到窗前; **to ~ back to London** 把家搬回伦敦 **3** (be postponed) «*date, meeting*» 推迟

B *vt* [**~ sth./sb. back, ~ back sth./sb.**]
1 (shift backwards) 后移 ‹*object*›; 让…后退 ‹*crowd, line*›; **to ~ sth. back a bit/a metre** 把某物向后移一点/移动一米; **~ your troops back behind the ridge** 让你的部队退到山脊后面 **2** (return) 把…搬回来 ‹*object*›; 把…调回 ‹*person*›; **to ~ sth. back (to) where it was (before)** 把某物搬回原处; **to be ~d back to headquarters/London** 被调回总部/伦敦 **3** (postpone) 推迟 ‹*date, meeting*›; **to be ~d back to April** 被推迟到4月

- **move down**

A *vi* **1** (in list, hierarchy) «*person*» 排到底下; Sport «*team, player*» 成绩下滑; **to ~ down a class** Brit «*pupil*» 降一年级; **to ~ down to number 5 in the charts** «*CD, DVD, performer*» 下降到排行榜第5位; **to ~ down three places/to rank number 9** 排名下降3位/到第9位; **to ~ down to the second division** 降为乙级 **2** Fin (decrease) «*stocks, index*» 下跌; **to ~ down two points** 下跌两点 **3** (squeeze up) «*person*» 挤紧; **to ~ down a couple of places** 往里挤几个位置; **~ down, please** 请往里面走

B *vt* [**~ sb./sth. down**] (demote) 使…降职 ‹*employee*›; Sport 使…排名下降 ‹*team, player*›; **to ~ sb. down (a class)** Brit 让…降（一年）级 ‹*pupil*›

- **move forward**

A *vi* **1** (advance) «*person, vehicle*» 前行; «*army, troops*» 前进; **to ~ forward to get a better view** 走到前面以便看得更清楚; **to ~ forward to attack** 冲上前去攻击 **2** (develop) «*person, society, thinking, events*» 进步 **3** (be brought forward) «*date, meeting*» 提前

B *vt* [**~ sb./sth. forward, ~ forward sb./sth.**]
1 (bring or send to front) 使…前进 ‹*players, troops*›; **to ~ forward three infantry divisions** 让3个步兵师向前开进; **United need to ~ their men forward more** 曼联队需要让球员再往前压 **2** (bring forward) 把…提前 ‹*date, meeting*›; **to be ~d forward to July** 被提前到7月

- **move in**

A *vi* **1** (to house, flat, etc.) 入住; **he helped me ~ in** 他帮我搬入新居; **to ~ in on sb.** colloq 擅自搬进来和…同住 ‹*friend(s), family*›; **the whole family ~d in on me for Christmas** 全家人都赶来和我一起过圣诞节; **to ~ in with sb.** 搬来和某人同住; **he's ~d in with me temporarily** 他暂时搬来和我同住; **to ~ in together** (live together) 同居; (share bedroom) 共用一室 **2** (advance) «*police, army*» 冲进来; **to ~ in and surround** 冲进来包围 ‹*building*›; **to ~ in and clear the site** «*crew, bulldozer*» 进来清理场地; **to ~ in on sb./sth.;** «*army, police*» 逼近 ‹*crowd, site*›; **the troops are moving in on their objective** 部队正在逼近目标 **3** (intervene) «*person, government, firm*» 插手; «*referee, police*» 干预; **to ~ in and buy up shares** 介入并买下全部股份; **to ~ in on sth.** «*gang, company*» 插手控制 ‹*racket, market*›; **to ~ in on a deal** 争抢一笔生意

B *vt* [**~ sb./sth. in, ~ in sb./sth.**] (into house, flat, etc.) 使…迁入新居 ‹*person, family*›; 把…搬进去 ‹*furniture*›; **he helped to ~ me in** 他帮我搬入新居

- **move off** *vi* «*parade, vehicle, troops*» 出发

- **move on**

A *vi* **1** (proceed) «*person, vehicle*» 继续前进; «*traveller, nomadic tribe*» 继续迁移; «*time*» 流逝; **I'd better be moving on** 我该走了; **time is moving on quickly** 时间过得真快; **we've already discussed that item, so let's ~ on** 那一项已经讨论过了，我们谈下一个问题吧; **to ~ on to** 转换到 ‹*topic*›; 向…进发 ‹*new place*›; **to ~ on to a new job** 换一个新的工作; **to ~ on to the next topic/another question** 谈下一个话题/另一个问题; **let's ~ on to deal with the next item** 我们接着处理下一项吧 **2** (not loiter) **= move along A1** **3** (develop) «*place, art form, society*» 取得进步; **ballet has ~d on** 芭蕾舞艺术有了发展; **to deal with a trauma and ~ on** 抚平创伤向前看

B *vt* [**~ sb./sth. on**]
1 (prevent from loitering) **= move along B1** **2** (move forward) 加快…的进度 ‹*discussion, work*›; **let's try and ~ things on a bit** 我们想办法抓紧一点吧

- **move out**

A *vi* **1** (leave house, flat, etc.) 搬出; **his wife ~d out** 他妻子搬出去住了; **~ out of** 搬出 ‹*house, flat, office*› **2** Amer colloq (depart) 出发; **let's ~ out!** 出发！

B *vt* [**~ sb./sth. out, ~ out sb./sth.**] «*authorities*» 使…迁出 ‹*tenant*›; «*person*» 把…搬出去 ‹*furniture*›; **to ~ sb./sth. out of sth.** 把某人迁出/把某物搬出 ‹*building, area*›; **to ~ residents out of the tenements** 把住户从公寓迁出; **the troops are being ~d out of the border area** 部队正在撤出边境地区

- **move over**

A *vi* **1** (move aside) 挪开; fig 让位; **to ~ over a bit** 挪过去一点; **to ~ over and let someone else take the responsibility** 让位给别人来当负责人; **to ~ over and make way for a new generation** 给新一代让路 **2** **to ~ over to sth.** (change to) 转变到 ‹*alternative*›; **to ~ over to digital/gas** 改用数字设备/煤气; **to ~ over to another supplier** «*company*» 换一家供应商

B *vt* [**~ sth./sb. over**] 挪动 ‹*object, person*›; **to ~ sth. over to the left** 把某物向左挪

- **move up**

A *vi* **1** (shift forward) 向前挪动; **~ up and make room for me** 挪动一下给我腾出地方; **to ~ up a bit nearer to the front** 往前面挪一点; **to ~ up a few places** 向前挪几个位置 **2** (in list, hierarchy) «*person*» 升级; Sport «*team, player*» 成绩提高; Brit «*pupil*» 升高一年级; **to ~ up to second in the charts** «*CD, DVD, performer*» 上升到排行榜第2位; **to be ~d up to a managerial post/the position of director** 被提升到管理岗位/经理职位; **he ~d up three places/into second place** 他的排名上升了3位/上升到第2位; **to ~ up into the first division** 升到甲级; **to ~ up in the world** colloq 飞黄腾达 **3** Fin (increase) «*stocks, index*» 上升; **to ~ up two points** 升高两点

B *vt* [**~ sb. up**] (promote) 使…晋升 ‹*employee*›; Sport 使…排名提高 ‹*team, player*›; **to ~ sb. up (a class)** Brit 让…升（高一年）级 ‹*pupil*›

moveable /'muːvəbl/ *adj* **= movable A**

movement /ˈmuːvmənt/
A *n* **1** [u and c] (of person, animal, body part) 动作; (of nomad, herd, army, vehicle, traffic) 移动; (of wheel, machine) 转动; (of current, fluid, gas) 流动; (of tree, branch) 摇动; **a graceful/sudden ~** 优雅的/突然的动作; **a dance ~** 舞蹈动作; **an upward/a downward ~** 向上/向下的移动; **the ~ of labour/goods** 劳动力/商品的流动; **troop ~s** 部队的调动 **2** [u and c] fig (trend) 动向; (change) 变动; **an upward/a downward ~ in prices** 价格的上浮/下降 **3** [c] Pol, Sociol, Art, Relig 运动; **the labour/trade union ~** 劳工/工会运动; **the woman's (liberation) ~** 妇女（解放）运动; **a mass ~** 群众运动 **4** [u] Transp 运输; **the ~ of goods by rail/road** 铁路/公路货运 **5** [u] (activity) 动静; **there seems to be some ~ upstairs** 楼上好像有点动静 **6** [c] Mus 乐章; **to be in three ~s** 由 3 个乐章组成 **7** [c] (of clock, watch) 机芯 **8** [c] (of bowels) 大便; **to have a ~** 大便
B **movements** *npl* (activities and whereabouts) 活动; **to study sb.'s ~s** 研究某人的行踪

mover /ˈmuːvə(r)/ *n* **1** (organizer, instigator) 鼓动者; **~s and shakers** colloq 有权势的人 **2** (proposer) 动议人 **3** esp Amer (removal worker) 搬家工人 **4** colloq (dancer) 跳舞的人; **to be a lovely** *or* **great little ~** 舞跳得好

movie /ˈmuːvi/ esp Amer
A *n* (film) 电影; **to go to (see) a ~** 去看电影; **a drive-in ~** 免下车电影; **the ~ industry** 电影业
B **movies** *npl* **the ~s** (cinema) 电影院; (film industry) 电影界; **to go to the ~s** 去看电影; **to be** *or* **work in the ~s** 在电影行业工作

movie: ~ camera *n* esp Amer 电影摄影机; **~ director** ▸ **p. 409** *n* esp Amer 电影导演; **~ film** *n* [u] esp Amer 电影胶片; **~goer** *n* esp Amer 电影观众; **~ house** *n* Amer 电影院; **~ maker** ▸ **p. 409** *n* esp Amer 电影制作人; **~ mogul** *n* esp Amer 电影业巨头; **~ producer** ▸ **p. 409** *n* esp Amer 电影制片人; **~s-on-demand** *n* [u] 电影点播服务; **~ star** *n* esp Amer 电影明星; **~ theater** *n* Amer = **~ house**

moving /ˈmuːvɪŋ/ *adj* **1** (in motion) 运动的 ‹*vehicle, train*›; **a ~ target** 移动靶子 **2** (motivating) 促动的 ‹*power*›; **to be the ~ force** *or* **spirit behind sth.** 是某事物发展的推动力量 **3** (arousing emotions) 感人的 ‹*story, moment, speech*›; **the funeral procession was a ~ sight** 送葬场面很感人

moving box *n* Amer = **packing case**

movingly /ˈmuːvɪŋli/ *adv* 感人地

moving staircase *n* Brit = **escalator**

mow /məʊ/
A *vt* (*pp* **~ed** *or* **mown**) 割 ‹*grass, hay*›; 修剪 ‹*lawn*›
B *vi* 割草
C *n* 割草; **to give the lawn a ~** 修剪草坪

Phrasal verb
• **mow down** *vt* colloq [**~ down sb., ~ sb. down**]
1 (kill) 射杀 **2** (knock down) 撞倒

mower /ˈməʊə(r)/ *n* 割草机

mown /məʊn/ *pp* ▸ **mow A, B**

Mozambican /ˌməʊzæmˈbiːkən/ ▸ **p. 503**
A *adj* (of Mozambique) 莫桑比克的; (of the people) 莫桑比克人的
B *n* 莫桑比克人

Mozambique /ˌməʊzæmˈbiːk/ *pr n* 莫桑比克

mozzarella /ˌmɒtsəˈrelə/ *n* [u] 莫泽雷勒干酪

mozzie /ˈmɒzi/ *n* colloq 蚊子

MP *n* **1** Brit = **Member of Parliament** **2** = **military police** **3** = **military policeman**

mp3 *n* **1** [u] (method) mp3 技术 **2** [c] (file) mp3 文件

mp3 player *n* mp3 播放器

mpg *abbr* = **miles per gallon** 每加仑燃料所行英里数; **to do X ~** 每加仑可跑 X 英里

mph *abbr* = **miles per hour** 每小时所行英里数; **to travel at 50 ~** 以每小时 50 英里的速度行进

MPhil /ˌemˈfɪl/ *abbr* = **Master of Philosophy** 哲学硕士; **to have/do an ~** 持有/攻读哲学硕士学位

MPV *abbr* = **multipurpose vehicle**

Mr /ˈmɪstə(r)/ *abbr* (*pl* **Messrs**) (title for man or position) 先生; **~ (Gwyn) Jones** （格温·）琼斯先生; **~ President** esp Amer 总统先生; **~ Football** 足球先生; **~ Big** 要人; **~ Right** 如意郎君

MRC *abbr* Brit = **Medical Research Council**

MRCP *abbr* Brit = **Member of the Royal College of Physicians** 皇家内科医师学会会员

MRI *abbr* **1** [u] (technique) = **magnetic resonance imaging** **2** [c] (scan) 磁共振扫描

Mrs /ˈmɪsɪz/ *abbr* 夫人; **~ (Sue) Clark** （苏·）克拉克夫人

MRSA *abbr* = **methicillin-resistant Staphylococcus aureus** 耐甲氧西林金黄色葡萄球菌

MS *abbr* **1** (*pl* **MSS**) = **manuscript** **2** Med = **multiple sclerosis** **3** Amer = **Master of Science** **4** Amer = **Mississippi 2**

Ms /mɪz, məz/ *abbr* 女士; **~ (Mary) Green** （玛丽·）格林女士

MSc *abbr* = **Master of Science; to have/do an ~** 持有/攻读理科硕士学位

MST *abbr* Amer = **Mountain Standard Time**

MT *abbr* **1** = **machine translation** **2** Amer = **Mountain Time** **3** Amer = **Montana**

Mt *abbr* = **Mount** 山 [用于地理名称]; **~ Etna/Everest** 埃特纳山/珠穆朗玛峰; **the Rocky ~s** 落基山脉

mth *abbr* = **month** 月

MTR *abbr* = **Mass Transit Railway** 香港地铁

much /mʌtʃ/
A *adj* (*comp* **more**, *superl* **most**) 很多的; **I don't have ~ money/time** 我的钱/时间不多; **she didn't speak ~ English** 她英语会得不多; **it doesn't make ~ sense** 这没有多大意义; **with ~ love from ...** (at end of letter) 深爱你的…; **how ~ liquid does it contain?** 这里面装了多少液体？; **twice as ~ money as ...** 两倍于…的钱; **to have ~ pleasure in introducing sb.** formal 有幸介绍某人; **~ good it did them!** iron 这真让他们受益良多啊！
B *pron* **1** (a great deal) 大量; **~ of (the) ...** …的大部分; **there isn't ~ left** 没有剩下多少; **I don't have ~ to do today** 我今天事情不多; **does it cost ~?** 这很贵吗?; **there isn't ~ to choose between ...** …之间没有什么可选择的; **there isn't ~ in** Brit *or* **to** Amer **it** 不相上下; **there isn't ~ in it for us** 这对我们没什么好处; **we danced for ~ of the night** 我们跳舞跳了大半夜; **~ has been gained from the experience** formal 从这次经历中收获很多; **~ you know about it!** iron 你知道的真多啊！; **to make ~ of sth.** (treat as important) 重视某事物; **I couldn't make ~ of her last book** 她的上一本书我看不太懂; **to make ~ of sb.** 悉心照料某人 **2** (expressing relative amount, degree) 许多; **how ~?** 多少？; **so ~** 那么多; **they are willing to pay so ~ per vehicle** 每辆汽车他们都愿意支付那么多钱; **he'd shouted so ~ that he was hoarse** 他大喊大叫，把嗓子都喊哑了; **she left without so ~ as a word** 她一句话也没说就走了; **they can be imprisoned for so ~ as criticizing the regime** 他们可能仅仅因为批评政权便遭到关押; **so ~ of the earth is polluted** 地球上那么多地方都受到了污染; **so ~ for press freedom/feminine intuition!** 出版自由/女性的直觉不过如此！; **so ~ for that!** 这件事到此为止！; **I've read this/that ~ already** 我已经读了这么/那么多了; **it's that ~ too short** 它短了那么多; **this ~ is certain, we have no choice** 这一点是肯定的，我们没有选择; **do you know how ~ this means to me?** 你知道这对我有多重要吗？; **I've eaten/drunk too ~** 我吃得/喝得太多了; **it's too ~!** 太过分了！; **the heat's too ~ for them** 他们难以忍受这种酷热; **he was too ~ for his opponent** 对于他的对手来说，他太强大了; **twice as ~** 两倍之多; **I'll need half as ~ again** 再给我来一半; **as ~ as possible** 尽可能多; **I enjoy nature as ~ as the next person** 我和大家一样喜爱自然; **it was as ~ as he could do to keep a straight face/not to laugh** 他尽量克制才没有笑出来; **as ~ as to say ...** 就等于说… **3** (focusing on limitations, inadequacy) 不过如此; **he's not ~ to look at** 他看上去很一般; **I don't think ~ of that film** 我认为那部电影不怎么样; **it isn't up to ~** Brit 这没什么了不起; **she isn't ~ of a cook/letter-writer** 她不太会做饭/写信; **that's not ~ of a consolation!** 这算不上什么安慰！; **I'm not ~ of a one for television** 我不大适合上电视
C *adv* **1** (considerably, greatly) 非常; **~ bigger/smaller** 大/小得多; **the film was ~ better than I expected** 这部电影比我预期的好多了; **the shoes are ~ too expensive** 这双鞋太贵了; **does it hurt ~?** 疼得厉害吗？; **~ as** *or* **though I'd like to** 尽管我很愿意; **~ to our annoyance, they didn't phone back** 令我们非常恼火的是，他们没回电话; **we ~ regret having to decline the invitation** formal 我们不能赴约，深感遗憾; **to be not ~ good at sth./doing sth.** 不太擅长某事/做某事; **your comments would be ~ appreciated** 非常欢迎提意见; **the meeting has been ~ criticized** 这次会面遭到了广泛指责; **she was ~ loved by her friends** 她的朋友都很喜欢她 **2** (by far) 极大地; **~ the ...** (with comparative) …得多; (with superlative) 最…; **~ too ...** 过于; **it's ~ the more interesting of the two studies** 在这两项研究中，这个要有趣得多; **she is ~ the best student here** 她是这里最好的学生; **~ rather** 宁愿; **I'd ~ rather not** 我宁可不; **he eats ~ too much** 他吃得实在太多 **3** (often) 经常; **we don't go out ~** 我们不怎么出门; **do you go to concerts ~?** 你经常去听音乐会吗？ **4** (approximately, nearly) 几乎; **his condition is (very) ~ the same as yesterday** 他的情况和昨天几乎（完全）一样; **it's pretty ~ like driving a car** 这和开汽车很相似; **he behaved ~ the way the others did** 他的表现和其他人差不多; **in ~ the same way** 几乎同样地 **5** (indicating degree) 很大程度上; **too ~** 太多; **so** *or* **very ~** 非常; **it's so ~ better** 这好多了; **we enjoyed ourselves very ~** 我们玩得很开心; **not so ~ ... as ...** 与其说…不如说…; **it wasn't so ~ a warning as a threat** 与其说是警告不如说是威胁; **as ~ (...) as** 和…一样; **she doesn't worry as ~ as before** 她不像以前那样担忧了; **I don't want to go as ~ as all that** colloq 我不太想去; **she is as ~ entitled to a visa as you** 她和你一样应该得到签证; **however ~** 无论怎样; **you talk/worry too ~** 你说话太多/多虑了; **I felt very ~ the foreigner** 我感觉完全像个外人; **he hates flying so ~ that he prefers to go by ship** 他很讨厌坐飞机，所以他宁愿乘船; **so ~ the better** 那就更好了; **he said as ~ later** 他后来也这么说; **I thought as ~!** 果然不出我所料！
D **much-** *combining form* 非常; **~admired/loved** 倍受赞赏/喜爱的; **~needed** 迫切需要的

muchness /ˈmʌtʃnɪs/ *n* **to be much of a ～** colloq 非常相似; **they're much of a ～** 他们不相上下

muck /mʌk/ *n* [u] **1** (manure) 堆肥; (excrement) 粪便; **a ～ heap** 肥堆; **cat/bird ～** 猫屎/鸟粪 **2** esp Brit colloq (filth) 污物; (rubbish) 垃圾; **where there's ～ there's brass** 要致富就别怕脏 **3** Brit colloq (unpleasant food) 难吃的饭菜 **4** (defamatory remarks) 诽谤 **5** (mess) **to make a ～ of sth./doing sth.** Brit 搞砸某事/做某事一塌糊涂; **I made a real ～ of that interview/opportunity** 我面试失败了/我没把握住机会

Phrasal verbs

- **muck about, muck around** Brit colloq

A *vi* **1** (play around) 闲荡 **2** **to ～ about with sth.** (interfere with) 胡乱摆弄某物

B *vt* [**～ sb. about**] 敷衍

- **muck in** *vi* **to ～ in (with sb.)** Brit colloq (share task) （与某人）平分任务; (share accommodation) （与某人）合住; (contribute money) （与某人）等额捐款; **we all ～ in here, mate!** 我们这里是人人平等的，伙计！
- **muck out**

A *vt* [**～ sth. out, ～ out sth.**] 打扫 ‹*building*›; 清除…的粪便 ‹*horses, cows*›

B *vi* 打扫牲畜栏

- **muck up** *vt* [**～ sth. up, ～ up sth.**] esp Brit colloq **1** (do badly) 搞砸; **I ～ed up that exam** 我考得很糟 **2** (spoil) 打乱 ‹*plan*›

muck: ～raker /-reɪkə(r)/ *n* pej 揭发丑闻者; **～raking** /-reɪkɪŋ/ *n* [u] pej 揭发丑闻; **a ～raking newspaper** 揭发丑闻的报纸; **～ spreader** *n* Brit 撒粪机; **～-up** *n* esp Brit colloq 一团糟; **to make a ～-up of sth.** 把某事搞得一团糟

mucky /ˈmʌki/ *adj* **1** (dirty) 肮脏的; **～ pup** Brit colloq hum 脏兮兮的家伙 **2** (rude, obscene) 淫秽的 ‹*book, story*›; **～ jokes** 下流的笑话

mucous /ˈmjuːkəs/ *adj* (of mucus) 黏液的; (covered with mucus) 附着黏液的

mucous membrane *n* [c and u] 黏膜

mucus /ˈmjuːkəs/ *n* [u] 黏液; **nasal ～** 鼻涕

mud /mʌd/ *n* [u] 淤泥; **as clear as ～** colloq hum 模糊难懂; **to throw** *or* **sling ～ at sb.** fig 诬蔑某人; **to drag sb. through the ～** fig 公开诋毁某人; **sb.'s name is ～** colloq 某人不受欢迎; **here's ～ in your eye!** colloq 干杯！

mud: ～bank *n* 泥滩; **～bath** *n* 泥浴; fig 泥泞地

muddle /ˈmʌdl/

A *n* **1** (mess) 混乱; **to be in a ～** 乱七八糟; **the string was in a ～** 绳子乱作一团; **their finances are in a terrible ～** 他们的财务状况糟透了; **to get into a ～** 陷入混乱; **to tidy up/clear up a ～** 收拾/清理乱糟糟的场面; **a ～ about** *or* **over sth.** 某事的混乱局面; **there's a bit of a ～ over my booking** 我的预订出了点问题 **2** (mental confusion) 糊涂; **to get in** *or* **into a ～** 犯糊涂; **to be in a ～** 糊涂; **to get sb. out of a ～** 使某人变得清醒

B *vt* **= muddle up**

Phrasal verbs

- **muddle along** *vi* esp Brit 混日子; **to ～ along from day to day** 一天一天混日子
- **muddle through** *vi* 胡乱应付过去
- **muddle up** *vt* [**～ sth./sb. up, ～ up sth./sb.**]

1 (mess up) 把…弄乱 ‹*objects, arrangement*›; **to be ～d up** 被弄乱 **2** (confuse) 把…弄糊涂 ‹*person*›; **to be ～d up** 被弄糊涂; **to get ～d up** 被弄糊涂; **you've got me (all) ～d up!** 你彻底把我弄晕了！ **3** (mistake) 把…弄错; **to ～ A and B up, to ～ A up with B** 分不清A和B

muddled /ˈmʌdld/ *adj* **1** (confused) 糊涂的 **2** (unclear) 含糊的 ‹*account*›; 混乱的 ‹*thinking*›

muddle-headed /ˌmʌdlˈhedɪd/ *adj* 头脑糊涂的

muddy /ˈmʌdi/

A *adj* **1** (covered with or full of mud) 泥泞的 ‹*road*›; 多淤泥的 ‹*river, stream*›; 沾满泥的 ‹*shoes, hands*›; **to make sb./sth. ～** 使某人/某物沾满泥 **2** (murky) 混浊的 ‹*coffee, brew*›; 灰暗的 ‹*complexion*›; **～ green/colour** 暗绿色/暗色

B *vt* 使…沾满泥 ‹*hands, shoes*›; 使…泥泞 ‹*road, field*›; **to ～ the waters** fig 搅浑水

mud: ～ flap *n* 挡泥板; **～ flats** *npl* 潮泥滩; **～guard** *n* Brit 挡泥板; **～ hut** *n* 土屋; **～pack** *n* 泥面膜; **～ pie** *n* [儿童玩耍时做的]泥饼; **～slide** *n* 泥流; **～-slinging** *n* [u] pej 恶意中伤

muesli /ˈmjuːzli/ *n* [u] esp Brit 牛奶什锦早餐

muezzin /muːˈezɪn, Amer mjuː-/ *n* 宣礼员 [通常在清真寺宣礼塔上召集伊斯兰教徒祈祷]

muff /mʌf/

A *n* **1** (mitten) 暖手筒 **2** taboo sl (female genitals) 阴部

B *vt* colloq (bungle) 错失 ‹*shot, catch*›; 失去 ‹*opportunity, action*›; **I ～ed my lines over and over** Theat 我一再忘记台词

muffin /ˈmʌfɪn/ *n* **1** Brit (bun) 松饼 **2** Amer (cake) 小松糕

muffle /ˈmʌfl/ *vt* **1** (wrap up) 裹住; **everyone was ～d up in coats and scarves** 大家都穿着大衣，戴着围巾，裹得严严实实 **2** (quieten) 减弱 ‹*voice, noise*›; **to ～ (the sound of) a bell** 压低铃声 **3** fig (suppress) 镇压 ‹*opposition, protest*›; 抑制 ‹*anger, effect*›

muffler /ˈmʌflə(r)/ *n* **1** dated (scarf) 围巾 **2** Amer Aut (silencer) 消音器

mufti /ˈmʌfti/ *n* [u] esp Mil 便装; **in ～** 穿便服

mug /mʌg/

A *n* **1** (for drink) 有柄大杯 **2** (as measure) 一大杯; **a ～ of sth.** 一大杯某物 **3** colloq usu pej (face) 脸; **get your ugly ～ out of here!** 滚出去！ **4** Brit colloq (gullible person) 傻瓜; **a ～'s game** esp Brit colloq 吃力不讨好的事

B *vt* (*pres p etc.* **-gg-**) colloq 行凶抢劫

Phrasal verb

- **mug up** Brit colloq

A *vt* [**～ up sth., ～ sth. up**] (learn) 突击学习; (revise) 突击复习

B *vi* **to ～ up on sth.** (learn) 突击学习; (revise) 突击复习

mugful /ˈmʌgfʊl/ *n* 一大杯的容量

mugger /ˈmʌgə(r)/ *n* 抢劫犯

mugging /ˈmʌgɪŋ/ *n* **1** [u] (crime) 行凶抢劫罪 **2** [c] (attack) 行凶抢劫

muggins /ˈmʌgɪnz/ *n* (*pl* **～** *or* **～es**) Brit colloq hum 傻瓜; **～ here will pay the bill** 让我这个傻瓜来付账吧

muggy /ˈmʌgi/ *adj* 闷热潮湿的; **it's ～ in here** 这里头又热又潮湿

mugshot /ˈmʌgʃɒt/ *n* colloq [警方存档识别罪犯的]面部照片

Muhammad /məˈhæmɪd/ *pr n* **= Mohammed**

mujaheddin, mujahidin, mujaheddin, mujahideen /ˌmuːdʒəhɪˈdiːn/ *npl* 穆斯林游击队

mulatto /mjuːˈlætəʊ, Amer məˈl-/ dated or offensive

A *n* 黑白混血儿

B *adj* 黑白混血的

mulberry /ˈmʌlbri, Amer -beri/ ▸**p. 134** *n* **1** [c] (tree) 桑树; **～ tree/bush** 桑树/桑树丛 **2** [c] (fruit) 桑椹 **3** [u] (colour) 深紫红色

mulch /mʌltʃ/

A *n* [c and u] 护根 [用以覆盖植物根基、改善土质或防止杂草生长]

B *vt* 用护根覆盖

mule[1] /mjuːl/ *n* **1** (animal) 骡子; **as stubborn** *or* **obstinate as a ～** 十分固执; **a ～ train/track** *or* **path** 骡队/骡道 **2** colloq (stubborn person) 固执的人 **3** colloq **(drug) ～** 骡子 [毒品交货人]

mule[2] *n* (shoe, slipper) 拖鞋

muleteer /ˌmjuːlɪˈtɪə(r)/ ▸**p. 409** *n* dated 赶骡人

mulish /ˈmjuːlɪʃ/ *adj* 执拗的

mull /mʌl/ *vt* [用糖和香料] 将…制成热饮 ‹*ale, cider, wine*›; **～ed wine** 香甜的热酒

Phrasal verb

- **mull over** *vt* [**～ sth. over, ～ over sth.**] 仔细考虑

mullah /ˈmʌlə/ *n* 毛拉 [讲授伊斯兰教神学和宗教法律的教师]

mullet /ˈmʌlɪt/ *n* (*pl* **～** *or* **～s**) **red/grey ～** 鲱鲤/鲻鱼

mulligatawny /ˌmʌlɪgəˈtɔːni/ *n* [u] **～ (soup)** (with meat) 咖喱肉汤; (with chicken) 咖喱鸡汤

mullion /ˈmʌlɪən/ *n* [窗上的] 直棂

mullioned /ˈmʌlɪənd/ *adj* 有直棂的

multi- /ˈmʌlti/ *combining form* 多个; **a ～journey ticket** 多程票

multi-access

A *adj* 多路接入的

B *n* [u] 多路接入

multicellular /ˌmʌltɪˈseljʊlə(r)/ *adj* 多细胞的

multichannel /ˌmʌltɪˈtʃænl/ *adj* 多频道的

multicoloured /ˌmʌltɪˈkʌləd/ *adj* 五彩斑斓的

multicultural /ˌmʌltɪˈkʌltʃərəl/ *adj* 多元文化的

multiculturalism /ˌmʌltɪˈkʌltʃərɪzəm/ *n* [u] 多元文化主义

multidimensional /ˌmʌltɪdaɪˈmenʃənl/ *adj* **1** Phys, Astron 多维的 ‹*space, model*› **2** (having many aspects) 涵盖多方面的 ‹*study, concept*›; 涉及多方面的 ‹*approach, problem*›

multidirectional /ˌmʌltɪdaɪˈrekʃənl, -dɪˈrek-/ *adj* 多向的 ‹*aerial*›

multidisciplinary /ˌmʌltɪdɪsɪˈplɪnəri, Amer -neri/ *adj* 多学科的

multi-ethnic *adj* 多种族的

multi-faceted /ˌmʌltɪˈfæsɪtɪd/ *adj* **1** lit 多面的 ‹*gemstone*› **2** fig (varied) 经历丰富的 ‹*career*›; 复杂的 ‹*personality*›; 涉及多方面的 ‹*problem*›

multifarious /ˌmʌltɪˈfeərɪəs/ *adj* 多样的 ‹*activities, demands*›; 多部分组成的 ‹*rules, regulations*›

multifunction /ˌmʌltɪˈfʌŋkʃn/ *adj attrib* 多功能的

multifunctional /ˌmʌltɪˈfʌŋkʃnl/ *adj* 多功能的

multigym /ˈmʌltɪdʒɪm/ *n* **1** (apparatus) 多功能健身器 **2** (gym) 多功能健身房

multihull /ˈmʌltɪhʌl/ *n* 多船体船

multilateral /ˌmʌltɪˈlætərəl/ *adj* **1** esp Pol 多边的 ‹*agreement, talks*› **2** (with several contributors) 多方的 ‹*force*›; 多方参与的 ‹*trade, action*›

multilevel /ˌmʌltɪˈlevl/ *adj* **1** 多层的 ‹*structure*›; **a building with ～ access** 有多层通道的建筑物; **～ parking** 立体停车 **2** fig (operating on several levels) 多层次的 ‹*analysis*›; 多级的 ‹*marketing*› **3** Comput 多层的 ‹*memory*›

multilingual /ˌmʌltɪˈlɪŋgwəl/ *adj* **1** (using several languages) 说多种语言的 ‹*person, country*›; 使用多种语言的 ‹*organization*› **2** (written in several languages) 多语的 ‹*dictionary, instructions*›

multilingualism /ˌmʌltɪˈlɪŋgwəlɪzəm/ *n* [u] (ability) 使用多种语言的能力; (state) 多种语言的使用; **to encourage/promote ～** 鼓励/提倡使用多种语言

multi-manager fund *n* 多元经理人基金

m

multimedia /ˌmʌltɪˈmiːdɪə/
A n [u] 多媒体
B adj 多媒体的

multi-million *adj attrib* 数百万的; **a ~ pound deal** 数百万英镑的生意

multimillionaire /ˌmʌltɪˌmɪljəˈneə(r)/ *n* 拥有数百万资产的富翁; **a dollar ~** 拥有数百万美元资产的富翁

multi-million-pound *adj attrib* 价值数百万英镑的 ‹*building*›; 耗资数百万英镑的 ‹*campaign*›; 数百万英镑的 ‹*bid, deal*›

multi-nation *adj attrib* 多国的 ‹*talks, treaty*›

multinational /ˌmʌltɪˈnæʃənl/
A *adj* 多国的 ‹*talks, alliance*›; 跨国的 ‹*company, organization*›; 多民族的 ‹*country*›
B *n* 跨国公司

multipack /ˈmʌltɪpæk/ *n* 合装包 [相对于单件购买较便宜的商品包装]

multipartite /ˌmʌltɪˈpɑːtaɪt/ *adj* **1** Pol (multilateral) 多边的 **2** formal (divided into many parts) 由多部分组成的 ‹*document, structure*›; 分多部分进行的 ‹*discussion*›

multi-party *adj attrib* 多党派的; **the ~ system** 多党制

multiple /ˈmʌltɪpl/
A *n* **1** Math 倍数; **a ~ of sth.** 某数的倍数; **to be sold in ~s of six** 按6的倍数出售 **2** Brit (chain of shops) 连锁店
B *adj* **1** (manifold) 多个部分组成的; **a ~ crash** 连环撞车事故; **~ choices** 多项选择; **~ share applications** 多重认股申请 **2** (many and various) 多处的 ‹*injuries*›; 多种的 ‹*functions*›; 多重的 ‹*meanings*›

multiple: ~ birth *n* 多胎产; **~-choice** *adj* 多项选择的 ‹*question, exam*›; **~ entry visa** *n* 多次入境签证; **~ fractures** *npl* 多发性骨折; **~ fruit** *n* 复果; **~ injuries** *npl* 多处受伤; **~ occupancy** *n* [u] 多户合住; **~ ownership** *n* [u] 多重所有制; **~ personality** *n* 多重人格; **~ pile-up** *n* 连环车祸; **~ risk** *adj attrib* Insur 多险种的; **~ sclerosis** ▸p. 377 *n* [u] 多发性硬化; **~ store** *n* Brit 连锁店

multiplex /ˈmʌltɪpleks/
A *n* **1** [c] (cinema) 多厅电影院 **2** [u] Telecom 多路传输
B *adj* formal 多种多样的
C *vt* Telecom 多路传输

multiplexer /ˈmʌltɪpleksə(r)/ *n* Telecom 多路器

multipliable /ˈmʌltɪplaɪəbl/, **multiplicable** /ˈmʌltɪplɪkəbl/ *adjs* 可乘的; **to be ~ by sth.** 可乘以某数字

multiplicand /ˌmʌltɪplɪˈkænd/ *n* 被乘数

multiplication /ˌmʌltɪplɪˈkeɪʃn/ *n* **1** [u] Math 乘法; **to do ~** 做乘法 **2** [c] (instance) 乘法运算题; **an easy/difficult ~** 简单的/难做的乘法题 **3** [u and c] (increase) 成倍增长; **a huge ~ in the number of people seeking treatment** 求医者人数的成倍增加

multiplication: ~ sign *n* 乘号; **~ table** *n* 乘法表

multiplicity /ˌmʌltɪˈplɪsəti/ *n* formal **1** [c] (wide variety) 多样性; **a ~ of sth.** 某事物的多样性; **a computer with a ~ of uses** 多用途计算机 **2** [u] (numerousness) 众多; **the stars in all their ~** 璀璨繁星

multiplier /ˈmʌltɪplaɪə(r)/ *n* 乘数

multiplier effect *n* 倍数效应

multiply[1] /ˈmʌltɪplaɪ/
A *vt* **1** (Math) 乘; **to ~ A by B** A乘以B; **to ~ A and B (together)** 将A与B相乘 **2** (increase) 使成倍增加
B *vi* **1** Math 做乘法 **2** (increase) 成倍增长 **3** Biol 繁殖

multiply[2] /ˈmʌltɪpli/ *adv* 多样地; **a ~ gifted artist** 多才多艺的艺术家; **a ~ injured patient** 多处受伤的病人

multiprocessing /ˌmʌltɪˈprəʊsesɪŋ, Amer -ˈprɒs-/ *n* [u] 多重处理

multiprocessor /ˌmʌltɪˈprəʊsesə(r), Amer -ˈprɒs-/ *n* 多处理器

multiprogramming /ˌmʌltɪˈprəʊgræmɪŋ/ *n* [u] 多道程序设计

multipurpose /ˌmʌltɪˈpɜːpəs/ *adj* 多用途的 ‹*tool, machine*›; 多功能的 ‹*building, facility*›

multipurpose vehicle *n* 多用途车

multiracial /ˌmʌltɪˈreɪʃl/ *adj* 多种族的 ‹*society, school*›

multiracialism /ˌmʌltɪˈreɪʃlɪzm/ *n* [u] 多种族主义

multirole /ˈmʌltɪrəʊl/ *adj attrib* 多作用的 ‹*aircraft*›

multi-screen /ˈmʌltɪskriːn/ *adj* 多银幕放映的 ‹*cinema*›

multisensory /ˌmʌltɪˈsensəri/ *adj* 多种感觉的 ‹*experience*›; 多种感觉并用的 ‹*teaching methods*›

multi-skilled *adj* 多才多艺的

multistage /ˈmʌltɪsteɪdʒ/ *adj* **1** Aerosp 多级的 ‹*rocket*› **2** (gen) 多阶段的 ‹*process*›

multistandard /ˌmʌltɪˈstændəd/ *adj* 多制式的

multi-storey
A *adj* 多层的 ‹*car park, building*›
B *n* Brit 多层停车场

multi-talented *adj* 多才多艺的

multitask /ˌmʌltɪˈtɑːsk/ *vi* «*computer*» 处理多个任务; fig «*person*» 同时做多件事情

multitasking /ˌmʌltɪˈtɑːskɪŋ/ *n* [u] **1** Comput 多任务处理 **2** fig (by person) 同时做多件事

multi-tool *n* 多用刀具

multitrack /ˈmʌltɪtræk/ *adj attrib* 多声道的 ‹*recorder, recording, audio*›

multitude /ˈmʌltɪtjuːd, Amer -tuːd/ *n* formal 大量; **a** *or* **the ~ (of ...)** 大量（的…）; **for a ~ of reasons** 由于种种原因; **to cover** *or* **hide a ~ of sins** often hum 掩藏各种过错

multitudinous /ˌmʌltɪˈtjuːdɪnəs, Amer -ˈtuːd-/ *adj* formal (numerous) 众多的; (comprising many individuals) 形形色色的; **~ relatives** 七大姑八大姨

multiuser /ˌmʌltɪˈjuːzə(r)/ *adj attrib* 多用户的; **~ computer game** 多人电脑游戏

multivitamin /ˌmʌltɪˈvɪtəmɪn, Amer -ˈvaɪtə-/ *n* 复合维生素

mum[1] /mʌm/ *n* Brit colloq 妈妈

mum[2] *adj pred* **to keep** *or* **stay ~** 保持安静; **~'s the word!** Brit colloq (asking sb. to keep a secret) 千万别说出去!; (promising to keep a secret) 我保证不说出去!

mumble /ˈmʌmbl/
A *vi* 咕哝; **he ~d his thanks/apology/question** 他含含糊糊地道谢/道歉/提问
B *vt* 咕哝着说; **to ~ that ...** 咕哝道…
C *n* 咕哝; **to speak in a ~** 咕哝着说话; **a ~ of voices/conversation** 含糊的话音/交谈

mumbo jumbo /ˌmʌmbəʊˈdʒʌmbəʊ/ *n* [u] colloq pej **1** (speech, writing) 不知所云的言辞; **a maze of legal ~** 云山雾罩的法律条文 **2** (ritual) 繁文缛节

mummification /ˌmʌmɪfɪˈkeɪʃn/ *n* [u] 木乃伊制作

mummify /ˈmʌmɪfaɪ/
A *vt* 将…制成木乃伊
B *vi* 变成木乃伊

mummy[1] /ˈmʌmi/ *n* Brit colloq (mother) 妈咪

mummy[2] *n* (embalmed body) 木乃伊

mummy's boy *n* pej (boy) 离不开妈妈的男孩; (man) 离不开妈妈的男子

mumps /mʌmps/ ▸p. 377 *npl + v sing* 流行性腮腺炎; **to have (the) ~** 患流行性腮腺炎

munch /mʌntʃ/
A *vt* 大声咀嚼
B *vi* 大声咀嚼; **to ~ away at sth.** 大嚼某食物

munchies /ˈmʌntʃiːz/ *npl* colloq **1** (snacks) 快餐 **2** (craving) 饥饿感; **to have the ~** 突然觉得饿

munchkin /ˈmʌntʃkɪn/ *n* Amer colloq 小孩

mundane /mʌnˈdeɪn/ *adj* **1** often pej (ordinary) 平凡的 ‹*existence, task*›; (unexciting) 乏味的 ‹*film, activity*› **2** (earthly) 世俗的 ‹*matter*›; **~ concerns** 俗务

mung bean /ˈmʌŋ biːn/ *n* 绿豆

municipal /mjuːˈnɪsɪpl/ *adj attrib* 市政的; **the ~ government** 市政府

municipal court *n* Amer 初审法院

municipality /mjuːˌnɪsɪˈpæləti/ *n* **1** (city) 自治市; (town) 自治镇; (district) 自治区 **2** + *v sing or pl* (governing body) 市政当局

munificence /mjuːˈnɪfɪsns/ *n* [u] formal 慷慨

munificent /mjuːˈnɪfɪsnt/ *adj* formal 慷慨的

munitions /mjuːˈnɪʃnz/ *npl* 军需品; 军需品的 ‹*manufacturer*›; **a ~ factory** 兵工厂

munitions dump *n* 军火库

mural /ˈmjʊərəl/ *n* 壁画

murder /ˈmɜːdə(r)/
A *n* **1** [u] Jur (crime) 谋杀罪; **mass/serial ~** 大屠杀/连环谋杀; **to get away with ~** colloq hum 逍遥法外; **to cry** *or* **scream blue** Brit *or* **bloody** Amer **~** colloq 没命似地叫喊; **~ will out** Prov 恶事终必败露 **2** [c] Jur (act of killing) 谋杀; **the ~ weapon** 凶器 **3** [u] fig colloq (hell) 遭罪的经历; **to be ~** 难得要命; **it's ~ doing sth./trying to do sth.** 做某事/尝试做某事简直要命; **museums can be ~ on the feet** 参观博物馆会让脚累得要命; **did you have fun? — no, it was ~!** 你玩得高兴吗？——哪有，简直是遭罪!; **the winds were ~** 风刮得非常厉害
B *vt* **1** Jur 谋杀; **to ~ sb. with sth.** 用某物谋杀某人 **2** colloq (castigate or punish) 对…不客气 ‹*person*›; **I'll ~ those kids!** 我要宰了那帮孩子! **3** colloq (ruin) 糟蹋 ‹*music, language*› **4** Sport colloq (defeat) 彻底击败 ‹*opponent*› **5** esp Brit colloq (devour) 猛吃 ‹*food*›; 猛喝 ‹*drink*›
C *vi* 杀人

murder: ~ case *n* 谋杀案; **~ charge** *n* 谋杀罪指控

murderer /ˈmɜːdərə(r)/ *n* 杀人犯; **a convicted/serial ~** 被判有罪的杀人凶手/连环杀手

murderess /ˈmɜːdərɪs/ *n* 女杀人犯

murderous /ˈmɜːdərəs/ *adj* **1** (homicidal) 杀人的 ‹*tendencies, intent*›; 杀气腾腾的 ‹*villain*›; **he had a ~ expression on his face** 他满脸杀气; **a ~ attack** 欲置人于死地的攻击 **2** colloq (arduous) 极讨厌的 ‹*heat, traffic, schedule*›

murderous-looking *adj* 杀气腾腾的 ‹*individual*›; 寒气逼人的 ‹*weapon*›

murderously /ˈmɜːdərəsli/ *adv* 恶狠狠地 ‹*glare, stare*›

murder victim *n* 被谋杀者

murk /mɜːk/ *n* [u] (of night) 黑暗; (of smoke, fog, rain) 朦胧

murkiness /ˈmɜːkɪnɪs/ *n* [u] **1** (of night) 黑暗; (of smoke, fog, rain) 朦胧 **2** (of water) 混浊 **3** fig (dubiousness) 隐晦

murky /ˈmɜːki/ *adj* **1** (gloomy) 黑暗的 ‹*night*›; 昏暗的 ‹*light*›; **streets ~ with fog** 因浓雾而显得昏暗的街道 **2** (unclear) 浑浊的 ‹*water*› **3** fig (dubious) 不可告人的 ‹*secret, goings-on*›; 不清白的 ‹*past*›

murmur /ˈmɜːmə(r)/
A *n* **1** (low continuous sound) 连续低沉的声音; **a low ~ of voices** 低声细语; **the ~ of the wind/stream** 飒飒风声/潺潺溪声 **2** (utterance) 咕哝; **(to speak) in a ~** 小声地（说）;

m

a quiet ~ of thanks 小声道谢 **3** Med 杂音 **4** (expressing reaction) 轻声表示; **a ~ of discontent/agreement** 不满/同意的表示; **to obey without a ~** 毫无怨言地服从

B *vt* 低声说; **to ~ (to sb.) that ...** (对某人)低语道…

C *vi* **1** (mutter) 咕哝; **he ~ed in his sleep** 他轻声说着梦话 **2** (make gentle sound) 发出细微声响; **the wind ~ed in the trees** 风在林中沙沙作响; **a stream ~ed in the distance** 小溪在远处潺潺流淌

murmuring /ˈmɜːmərɪŋ/

A *n* [u] (gentle sound) 连续低沉的声音; **the ~ of the wind/the stream** 飒飒风声/潺潺溪声

B **murmurings** *npl* (complaints) 低声抱怨; **~s about sb./sth.** 对某人/某事物的低声抱怨

Murphy's Law /ˈmɜːfɪz lɔː/ *n* [u] 墨菲法则 [凡要出错的事必将出错]

> **Murphy's Law**
>
> 墨菲法则，亦称索德定律（Sod's Law）。指"凡是可能会出错的事终将会出错"（if anything can go wrong it will）。该说法出现于20世纪中叶，通常认为源自美国空军科学家爱德华·墨菲（Edward Murphy）。通常用于调侃，指事情的发展变化总爱和人作对，比如天总是在没有带伞的时候下雨。也有人认为墨菲定律可以利用，即做一件事的时候可以事先考虑可能会出哪些问题，并采取相应的预防措施。

MusB *abbr* = **Bachelor of Music** 音乐学士; **to have/do a ~** 持有/攻读音乐学士学位

Muscat /ˈmʌskæt/ *pr n* 马斯喀特

muscat /ˈmʌskæt/ *n* [u] **~ (grape)** 麝香葡萄

muscatel /ˌmʌskəˈtel/ *n* **1** [u] (wine) 麝香葡萄酒 **2** [c] (raisin) 麝香葡萄干

muscle /ˈmʌsl/

A *n* **1** [c] (in body) 肌肉; **calf/stomach ~s** 小腿/胃部肌肉; **~ relaxant/toner** 肌肉弛缓剂/强健剂; **don't move a ~!** 别动! **2** [u] (tissue) 肌肉组织; **~ fibres/tissues** 肌肉纤维/组织 **3** [u] (strength) 体力 **4** [u] fig (power) 权力; (influence) 影响; **financial/military ~** 金融界/军队的影响力; **to have the ~ to do sth.** 有实力做某事; **to give ~ to sb./sth.** 支持某人/某事

B *vt* esp Amer **1** 用力推挤 ‹*player, rival*›; 用力塞 ‹*baggage*›; **to ~ one's way in/out** 使劲挤进去/出来 **2** (coerce) 强迫; **to be ~d out of the market** 被挤出市场

Phrasal verb

• **muscle in** *vi* colloq **to ~ in on sth./sb.** 强行干涉某事/某人; **to ~ in on sb.'s territory** 侵占某人的地盘

muscle: ~-bound *adj* 肌肉强健的; **~man** /-mæn/ *n* 打手; **~ strain** *n* [c and u] 肌肉拉伤

Muscovite /ˈmʌskəvaɪt/

A *adj* 莫斯科的

B *n* 莫斯科人

muscular /ˈmʌskjʊlə(r)/ *adj* **1** Anat 肌肉的 **2** (strong) 肌肉发达的 ‹*body, person*›; **to have a ~ build** 体格强壮 **3** fig (vigorous) 强有力的 ‹*voice, economy, music*›

muscular dystrophy ▸p. 377 *n* [u] 肌肉萎缩

musculature /ˈmʌskjʊlətʃə(r)/ *n* [u] **1** (muscles) 肌肉系统 **2** (arrangement of muscles) 肌肉组织

muse /mjuːz/

A *vi* 沉思; **to ~ about** *or* **over sth.** 沉思某事

B *vt* 若有所思地说

C *n* **1** Mythol **the M~s** 缪斯女神 **2** fig (source of inspiration) 灵感源泉; **the ~ of music** 音乐灵感; **his ~ had deserted him, and he could no longer write** 他江郎才尽，再也写不出东西了

museum /mjuːˈzɪəm/ *n* 博物馆

museum piece *n* **1** (artefact) 有馆藏价值的物品 **2** fig pej or hum (person, thing) 老古董

mush[1] /mʌʃ/ *n* **1** [c and u] (pulpy mass) 烂糊状物; **boiled to a ~** 煮得很烂的; **the ground was covered in a ~ of rotting vegetation** 地上覆盖着一层腐烂的植被 **2** [u] Amer Culin 玉米粥 **3** [u] colloq (sentimentality) 伤感; (sentimental speech or writing) 伤感作品

mush[2] *n* Brit colloq **1** (face) 脸 **2** (form of address) 老兄

mush[3] *excl* (order to dogs) [赶拉雪橇的狗] 快走

mushroom /ˈmʌʃrʊm, -ruːm/

A *n* **1** Bot, Culin 蘑菇; **a button ~** 未张开的蘑菇; **grow/spring up like a ~** 迅速生长/冒出 **2** (thing resembling a mushroom) 蘑菇状的东西

B *vi* **1** (gather mushrooms) 采蘑菇 **2** (spread) «*demand*» 迅速增长; «*shops*» 迅速增加; «*business*» 迅速发展; **to ~ into sth.** 迅速壮大成某事物

mushroom: ~ cloud *n* 蘑菇云; **~ growth** *n* [u] 迅速发展

mushy /ˈmʌʃi/ *adj* colloq **1** (pulpy) 糊状的; **to get** *or* **become** *or* **go ~** 变成糊状 **2** colloq (sentimental) 伤感的 ‹*film, poem*›; **to go** *or* **get (all) ~** 变得多愁善感

mushy peas *npl* 豌豆糊

music /ˈmjuːzɪk/

A *n* [u] **1** (as art, composition) 音乐; **to write ~** 作曲; **to put** *or* **set sth. to ~** 为…谱曲; **to be ~ to sb.'s ears** 对某人来说是好消息; **to face the ~** 承担自己行为的后果 **2** (in printed form) 乐谱; **to read ~** 识谱

B *modif* 音乐的; **a ~ critic** 乐评人

musical /ˈmjuːzɪkl/

A *adj* **1** (relating to music) 音乐的 **2** (gifted) 有音乐天赋的; (interested) 喜爱音乐的 **3** (melodious) 悦耳的 **4** (accompanied by music) 配乐的

B *n* (play) 音乐剧; (film) 音乐电影

musical: ~ box *n* Brit 八音盒; **~ chairs** *n* [u] **1** ▸p. 307 (game) 闻乐抢座位游戏; **2** fig (situation) 频繁的人事变动; **the management played ~ chairs with the design team** 管理层频繁更换设计团队的成员; **~ evening** *n* 音乐晚会; **~ instrument** ▸p. 395 *n* 乐器

musically /ˈmjuːzɪkli/ *adv* **1** (with regard to music) 在音乐方面 **2** (melodiously) 悦耳地

music: ~ box *n* 八音盒; **~ case** *n* 乐谱夹; **~ centre** *n* Brit 组合音响; **~ college** *n* 音乐专修学校; **~ hall** *n* Brit **1** [c] (theatre) 歌舞杂耍剧场; **2** [u] (entertainment) 歌舞杂耍表演; **~-hall** *modif* Brit 在音乐厅表演的 ‹*song, artist*›; 表演歌舞杂耍的 ‹*entertainer*›

musician /mjuːˈzɪʃn/ ▸p. 409 *n* 音乐家

musicianship /mjuːˈzɪʃnʃɪp/ *n* [u] 音乐才能

music lover *n* 音乐爱好者

musicologist /ˌmjuːzɪˈkɒlədʒɪst/ ▸p. 409 *n* 音乐学家

musicology /ˌmjuːzɪˈkɒlədʒi/ *n* [u] 音乐学

music: ~ stand *n* 乐谱架; **~ stool** *n* 琴凳; **~ video** *n* 音乐录像

musing /ˈmjuːzɪŋ/

A *n* **~s** 沉思

B *adj attrib* 若有所思的 ‹*tone, stare*›

musk /mʌsk/ *n* [u] 麝香

musk deer *n* 麝

musket /ˈmʌskɪt/ *n* Hist 火枪

musketeer /ˌmʌskɪˈtɪə(r)/ *n* Hist 火枪手

musketry /ˈmʌskɪtri/ *n* [u] Hist **1** (skill) 火枪射击术 **2** (musketeers) 火枪队

musk: ~ ox *n* 麝牛; **~rat** *n* **1** [c] (animal) 麝鼠; **2** [u] (fur) 麝鼠皮

musky /ˈmʌski/ *adj* 麝香的 ‹*smell*›; 麝香味的 ‹*perfume*›

Muslim /ˈmʊzlɪm, Amer ˈmʌzləm/

A *n* 穆斯林

B *adj* 穆斯林的

muslin /ˈmʌzlɪn/ *n* [u] 平纹细布; **~ bag** 平纹细布包

musquash /ˈmʌskwɒʃ/ *n* **1** [c] (animal) 麝鼠 **2** [u] (fur) 麝鼠皮

muss /mʌs/ *vt* esp Amer colloq 弄乱; **to ~ sth. (up)** 把某物弄得乱七八糟

mussel /ˈmʌsl/ *n* 蚌

mussel bed *n* 河蚌繁殖地

must[1] /mʌst, məst/

A *modal aux* (*negative* **~ not** *or* colloq **mustn't**) **1** (indicating obligation, prohibition; stressing importance, necessity) 必须; **you ~ be patient** 你必须要有耐心; **we ~ never forget** 我们绝对不能忘记; **withdrawals ~ not exceed £300** 提款不得超过300英镑; **you mustn't mention this to anyone** 你千万不要向任何人提起这件事; **~ we really be up by 7 a.m.?** 我们真的必须早晨7点钟起床吗?; **in order to qualify, candidates ~ have attended all the lectures** 候选者必须听过所有的讲座才能取得资格; **it's very odd, I ~ admit** 我得承认这很怪; **it ~ be said that ...** 必须说明的是…; **very nice, I ~ say** iron 我得说好极了; **you ~ know that ...** 你应该知道…; **we ~ ask you to send us ...** formal (in letters) 请贵方务必给我们寄… **2** (expressing intention) 得; **I ~ check the reference** 我得核对一下出处; **we mustn't forget to put the cat out** 我们可别忘了把猫放出去 **3** (expressing irritation, desire, assumption or probability) 一定; **well, come in if you ~** 好吧，如果你非要进来就进来吧; **he's ill, if you ~ know** 如果你非得知道的话，他病了; **why ~ he always argue?** 他为什么非得争论不休?; **this I ~ see!** 我一定要看这个!; **we simply ~ get away from here!** 我们就是要离开这儿!; **we really ~ get together soon** 我们真的应该马上聚一聚; **he ~ have got lost** 他一定已经迷路了; **what ~ people think?** 人们会怎么想呢?; **they ~ be wondering what happened to us** 他们肯定想知道我们出了什么事

B *n* colloq 必不可少的东西; **this book is a ~ for all gardeners** 这本书是所有花匠的必读书; **this film is a ~** 这部电影不可不看; **a visit to the National Gallery is a ~** 一定要去参观国家美术馆

must[2] /mʌst/ *n* [u] (in wine-making) [发酵前的]葡萄汁

mustache /ˈmʌstæʃ/ *n* Amer = **moustache**

mustang /ˈmʌstæŋ/ *n* 北美野马

mustard /ˈmʌstəd/ ▸p. 134

A *n* [u] **1** (plant) 芥菜 **2** (condiment) 芥末; **~ and cress** 白芥末拌水芹; **to be as keen as ~** 极为热心的 **3** (colour) **~ (yellow)** 褐黄色

B *modif* 芥末的; **~ powder/seeds** 芥末粉/芥子

C *adj* **~(-yellow)** 褐黄色的

mustard: ~ bath *n* 芥末浴; **~ gas** *n* [u] 芥子气; **~ plaster** *n* 芥子膏

muster /ˈmʌstə(r)/

A *n* 集合; **a ~ of troops** 队伍的集结; **to pass ~** 合格

B *vt* **1** Mil 集结 ‹*troops*› **2** (gather) 集合 ‹*teams, people*›; **to ~ the necessary numbers to do sth.** 凑齐人数做某事 **3** **~ (up)** (summon up) 鼓起 ‹*courage*›; 激起 ‹*enthusiasm*›; 赢得 ‹*support*›; **she replied with as much dignity as she could ~ (up)** 她尽量庄重体面地回答

C *vi* **1** Mil «*troops*» 集结 **2** (gather) «*people*» 聚集

muster station *n* 集结站

must-have *adj* colloq 必不可少的; **the ~ blouse of the season** 本季必穿的衬衫

mustiness /ˈmʌstɪnɪs/ *n* [u] **1** (staleness) 霉味 **2** fig (outmodedness) 陈腐

mustn't /ˈmʌsnt/ *abbr* colloq **= must not** ▸**must¹**

must've /ˈmʌstəv/ *abbr* colloq **= must have** ▸**must¹**

musty /ˈmʌsti/ *adj* 1 (stale) 有霉味的; **to go ~** 发霉; **a ~ smell** 霉味 2 fig (old-fashioned) 陈腐的 ‹*thinking*›; **~ old ideas** 陈腐过时的想法

mutable /ˈmjuːtəbl/ *adj* formal 可变的

mutagen /ˈmjuːtədʒən/ *n* 诱变剂

mutagenic /ˌmjuːtəˈdʒenɪk/ *adj* 诱变的 ‹*process, action*›; 致突变的 ‹*substance, radiation*›

mutant /ˈmjuːtənt/

A *adj attrib* （基因）突变的

B *n* 1 Biol （基因）突变体 2 (in science fiction) 突变异体怪物

mutate /mjuːˈteɪt, Amer ˈmjuːteɪt/ *vi* 1 Biol 突变; **to ~ into sth.** 突变成某物 2 (change) 转变; **to ~ into sth.** 变成某事物

mutation /mjuːˈteɪʃn/ *n* 1 [u] Biol (process) 突变; **genetic ~** 基因突变 2 [c] Biol (form) 突变体; **a ~ (from sth.)** （某物的）突变体 3 [c and u] (change) 转变

mutatis mutandis /muːˌtɑːtɪs muːˈtændɪs/ *adv* formal 经必要修正后

mute /mjuːt/

A *adj* 1 (silent) 缄默的 ‹*person*›; 无声的 ‹*bow, sympathy, reproach*›; **to be ~ with fear** 吓得默不作声; **in ~ surprise/admiration** 带着无语的惊讶/敬意 2 dated or offensive (unable to speak) 哑的 ‹*person*› 3 Ling 哑音的 ‹*letter*›

B *n* 1 Mus 弱音器 2 dated or offensive (person unable to speak) 哑巴; **a deaf ~** 聋哑人

C *vt* 1 Mus 用弱音器减弱…的音 2 (weaken) 降低 ‹*enthusiasm*›; 缓和 ‹*criticism*›; 削弱 ‹*opposition*›; 减弱 ‹*effect*›

mute button *n* 1 (on TV) 静音按钮 2 (on telephone) 静音键

muted /ˈmjuːtɪd/ *adj* 1 (quiet) 轻的 ‹*sound*› 2 (subdued) 温和的 ‹*reaction, criticism*›; 被抑制的 ‹*excitement, anger*›; 不热烈的 ‹*applause, celebration*› 3 (not strong or bright) 柔和的 ‹*lighting, tones*› 4 Mus 配弱音器的 ‹*strings, trumpets*›

mutely /ˈmjuːtli/ *adv* 默默无声地

mute swan *n* 疣鼻天鹅

mutilate /ˈmjuːtɪleɪt/ *vt* 伤害 ‹*person, body*›; 截 ‹*limbs*›; 损坏 ‹*book, work of art*›; **the editor ~d my text** fig 编辑把我的文章搞得支离破碎

mutilation /ˌmjuːtɪˈleɪʃn/ *n* 1 [u] (of person, body) 伤害; (of limb) 截除; (of book, work of art) 损坏 2 [c] (injury) 损伤

mutineer /ˌmjuːtɪˈnɪə(r)/ *n* 叛乱者

mutinous /ˈmjuːtɪnəs/ *adj* 1 Mil, Naut 参与叛乱的 2 (rebellious) 不驯服的 ‹*workers, students*›; 反抗的 ‹*look, behaviour*›; **a ~ boy** 顽童; **to turn ~** 变得桀骜不驯

mutiny /ˈmjuːtɪni/

A *n* [c and u] 1 Mil, Naut 叛乱 2 (rebellion by workers, students, etc.) 反抗

B *vi* 1 Mil, Naut 叛乱; **to ~ over sth.** 因某事而叛乱 2 (rebel) «*workers, students*» 反抗; **to ~ against sb.** 反抗某人

mutt /mʌt/ *n* colloq pej 1 (mongrel dog) 杂种狗 2 (stupid person) 笨蛋

mutter /ˈmʌtə(r)/

A *vi* 1 嘟哝; **to ~ to oneself** 喃喃自语 2 (grumble) 轻声抱怨; **to ~ about sb./sth.** 抱怨某人/某事物

B *vt* 嘟哝; **to ~ thanks/complaints/words** 轻声道谢/抱怨/说话; **he ~ed sth. under his breath** 他嘀咕着某事

C *n* **a ~ of sth.** 轻声的 ‹*disgust, dissatisfaction*›; **the soft ~ of voices** 柔和的低语声

muttering /ˈmʌtərɪŋ/ *n* [u] 1 (complaints) 轻声抱怨; **~(s) (about sb./sth.)** （对某人/某事物的）轻声抱怨 2 (quietly spoken words) 喃喃自语

mutton /ˈmʌtn/ *n* 羊肉; **a ~ chop** 羊排; **~ dressed as lamb** Brit colloq pej 扮俏

mutton: ~ chops, ~ chop whiskers *npl* 羊排络腮胡; **~head** *n* colloq 傻瓜

mutual /ˈmjuːtʃʊəl/ *adj* 1 (reciprocal) 相互的 ‹*action*›; **I don't like her, and I think the feeling is ~** 我不喜欢她，我想她也不喜欢我; **a ~ admiration society** pej 相互吹捧俱乐部 2 *attrib* (having the same relationship to each other) 关系对等的; **they are ~ friends/enemies** 他们彼此为友/为敌 3 *attrib* (common) 共同的 ‹*friend, acquaintance, interest*›; 共用的 ‹*entrance, staircase*›; **by ~ agreement** 根据达成的共识 4 *attrib* Fin 互助的 ‹*organization, building society*›; **~ insurance** 互助保险

mutual: ~ consent *n* [u] (of both parties) 双方同意; (of all parties) 各方同意; **by ~ consent** 经双方同意; **~ fund** *n* Amer **= unit trust**

mutually /ˈmjuːtʃʊəli/ *adv* 1 (reciprocally) 互相 ‹*respectful, dependent, exclusive*› 2 (to both parties) 对于双方 ‹*acceptable, agreed*›; (to all parties) 对于各方

muzak® /ˈmjuːzæk/ *n* [u] usu pej 米尤扎克背景音乐［在商店、餐馆、工厂、电梯等地连续播放的预录轻音乐］

muzzle /ˈmʌzl/

A *n* 1 (snout) [动物的] 口鼻 2 (guard worn by animal) 口套 3 (open end of gun) 枪口; (of cannon) 炮口 4 fig (gag) 钳制工具; **censorship is a ~ on free speech** 审查制度是钳制言论自由的工具

B *vt* 1 (put muzzle on) 给…戴口套 ‹*animal*› 2 fig (gag) 钳制…的言论 ‹*person, the press*›; **to ~ freedom of speech** 压制言论自由

muzzle: ~-loader *n* Hist 前装枪; **~ velocity** *n* [子弹、炮弹的] 初速

muzzy /ˈmʌzi/ *adj* colloq 1 (confused) 糊涂的 ‹*person*›; 模糊的 ‹*memory*› 2 (blurred) 模糊不清的 ‹*image*›

MV *abbr* 1 Naut **= motor vessel** 内燃机船 2 Elec **= megavolt(s)** 兆伏

MW *abbr* 1 Radio **= medium wave** 2 Elec **= megawatt(s)** 兆瓦特

my /maɪ/

A ▸**p. 487** *det* 我的; **~ name is John** 我名叫约翰; **~ head hurts** 我头疼; **that's ~ bag you've picked up** 你捡到的那个包是我的

B *excl* **oh ~!** 噢，天哪！

myalgia /maɪˈældʒə/ *n* [u] 肌痛

myalgic encephalomyelitis ▸**p. 377** *n* [u] 肌痛性脑脊髓炎

Myanmar /mjænˈmɑː(r)/ *pr n* 缅甸

mycology /maɪˈkɒlədʒi/ *n* [u] 真菌学

mynah /ˈmaɪnə/ *n* **~ (bird)** 八哥

myopia /maɪˈəʊpɪə/ *n* [u] 1 Med 近视 2 fig (lack of foresight) 目光短浅

myopic /maɪˈɒpɪk/ *adj* 1 Med 近视的 2 fig 目光短浅的

myriad /ˈmɪrɪəd/ liter

A *n* 无数; **a ~ of sth., ~s of sth.** 无数的某物; **a ~ of choices** 数不清的选择

B *adj attrib* 无数的; **~ stars/colours** 繁星/色彩斑斓

myrrh /mɜː(r)/ *n* [u] 没药

myrtle /ˈmɜːtl/ *n* [u] 香桃木

myself /maɪˈself, məˈself/ *pron* 1 (reflexive) 我自己; **I said to ~ ...** 我对自己说…; **I want to find out for ~** 我想自己去弄清楚; **I was (all) by ~** 我独自一人 2 (emphatic) 我本人; **I saw it ~** 我亲眼看到它的; **I'm not much of a dog-lover ~** 我本人不怎么喜欢狗 3 (normal self) 我的正常情况; **I'm not (feeling) ~ today** 我今天感觉不舒服

mysterious /mɪˈstɪərɪəs/ *adj* 1 (puzzling) 神秘的 2 (enigmatic) 故弄玄虚的 ‹*person*›; 诡异的 ‹*look*›; **to be ~ about sth.** 对某事表现得神秘兮兮的

mysteriously /mɪˈstɪərɪəsli/ *adv* 神秘地; **~, there was no answer when I rang** 奇怪的是，我打电话时无人接听

mystery /ˈmɪstəri/ *n* 1 [c] (puzzle) 神秘事物; **an unsolved ~** 未解之谜; **to solve** *or* **clear up** *or* **unravel a ~** 解开谜团; **to remain a ~ to sb.** 对某人来说仍是个谜; **it's a ~ to me why ...** 我怎么样也搞不懂为什么…; **to make a great ~ of sth.** 对某事物故弄玄虚 2 [c] (unknown person) 神秘人物; (unknown thing) 陌生的事物; *modif* **a ~ guest/visitor/woman** 神秘嘉宾/访客/女子 3 [u] (mysteriousness) 神秘; **~ surrounds sth.** 神秘气氛围绕着某事物; **to be shrouded** *or* **cloaked in ~** 笼罩在神秘气氛中; **to be full of ~** 充满神秘感; **there is no ~ about her success** *or* **about why she is successful** 她的成功不是什么谜 4 [c] (book) 疑案作品; (film) 疑案电影; *modif* **a ~ thriller** 惊险疑案小说 5 [c] Relig 奥秘

mystery: ~ play *n* [中世纪以描写耶稣本生为主题的] 神秘剧; **~ tour** *n* 神秘之旅

mystic /ˈmɪstɪk/

A *n* 神秘主义者

B *adj* **= mystical**

mystical /ˈmɪstɪkl/ *adj* 1 (relating to mysticism) 神秘主义的 ‹*religion, writings, cult*›; 神秘的 ‹*power, rites*› 2 (spiritual) 超凡的 ‹*significance, experience*› 3 (awe-inspiring) 令人敬畏的 ‹*beauty, effect*›

mysticism /ˈmɪstɪsɪzəm/ *n* [u] 神秘主义

mystification /ˌmɪstɪfɪˈkeɪʃn/ *n* [u] 1 (bewilderment) 困惑不解; **in some ~, he ...** 带着些许困惑，他… 2 pej (obfuscation) 神秘化

mystify /ˈmɪstɪfaɪ/ *vt* 1 (bewilder) 使困惑; **to be mystified to find** *or* **discover that ...** 困惑地发现… 2 pej (obfuscate) 将…神秘化

mystifying /ˈmɪstɪfaɪɪŋ/ *adj* 使人困惑的; **it is ~ that ...** 令人困惑的是…

mystifyingly /ˈmɪstɪfaɪɪŋli/ *adv* 使人困惑地

mystique /mɪˈstiːk/ *n* [u] 1 (aura, charisma) 神秘色彩; **full of/clothed in ~** 充满神秘色彩/笼罩在神秘色彩中 2 (mystery surrounding activity, subject) 神秘气氛

myth /mɪθ/ *n* 1 [c] (story) 神话故事; **the Creation ~** 创世神话 2 [u] (mythology) 神话 3 [c] (fallacy) [普遍的] 错误观念; **to create/explode** *or* **dispel a ~** 制造/破除错误观念; **the prevailing ~ that ...** 人们普遍认同的…的错误观念; **the popular ~ that life begins at forty** 生活始于四十岁这种广泛流行的错误观念; **the ~ of racial superiority** 种族优越性的鬼话 4 [c] (fabrication) (person) 虚构的人; (thing) 虚构的事物; **to be a complete ~** 纯属虚构

mythic /ˈmɪθɪk/ *adj* 1 (of or relating to myth) 神话的 ‹*significance, story*›; (resembling myth) 类似神话的 ‹*status, quality*› 2 fig (legendary) 神话般的 ‹*hero, quest*›

mythical /ˈmɪθɪkl/ *adj* 1 (of or relating to myth) 神话的 ‹*times*›; (occurring in myth) 神话中的 ‹*kingdom, creature*›; (resembling myth) 类似神话的 ‹*status, quality*› 2 (fictitious) 虚构的 ‹*wealth, relation*›

mythological /ˌmɪθəˈlɒdʒɪkl/ *adj* (occurring in myth) 神话中的 ‹*creature, hero, scene*›; (of or relating to myth) 神话的 ‹*theme, story*›

mythologize /mɪˈθɒlədʒaɪz/ *vt* usu pej 使成为神话

mythology /mɪˈθɒlədʒi/ *n* 1 [c and u] (mythical stories) 神话; **Greek/Roman ~** 希腊/罗马神话 2 [c and u] fig (stories, beliefs) 虚幻的想法 3 [u] (study of myths) 神话学

myxomatosis /ˌmɪksəməˈtəʊsɪs/ *n* [u] 多发黏液瘤病

Nn

N, n /en/
A *n* (*pl* **Ns** *or* **N's**) **1** (letter) [英语字母表的第14个字母] **2** **n** Math [表示任意数]; **... to the power of ~** ⋯的 n 次方
B *abbr* **1** **N** Geog **= north, northern** **2** **N = neutral (gear)** 空挡 **3** **N = nuclear** **4** **n = noun**
C **'n'** *conj* [and的缩略形式，用于连接两个联系紧密的成分]; **rock 'n' roll** 摇滚乐; **fish 'n' chips** 炸鱼和薯条

n/a, N/A *abbr* **1** **= not applicable** 不适用的 **2** **= not available** 得不到的

NAACP *abbr* Amer **= National Association for the Advancement of Colored People** 全国有色人种协进会

NAAFI /ˈnæfi/ *abbr* Brit **1** **= Navy Army and Air Force Institutes** 海陆空军协会 **2** (canteen) 海陆空军小吃部; (shop) 海陆空军小卖部

naan /nɑːn/ *n* ▸**nan²**

nab /næb/ *vt* (*pres p etc.* **-bb-**) colloq **1** (catch) 捉住 ‹*culprit*› **2** (grab) 拿取 ‹*object*›; (take) 抢占 ‹*seat*› **3** (steal) 偷; **to ~ sb.'s pencil** 偷拿某人的铅笔

nacelle /nəˈsel/ *n* 短舱

nacho /ˈnætʃəʊ/ *n* (*pl* **~s**) *usu pl* 墨西哥玉米片

nadir /ˈneɪdɪə(r)/ *n* **1** Astron 最低点 **2** fig 最糟糕的时刻; **to reach a ~** 恶化到极点; **(at) the ~ (of sth.)** (处于)（某事物的）最坏情况; **the party's fortunes are at a ~** 该党的运势差到极点

naff /næf/ *adj* Brit colloq 蹩脚的 ‹*clothes, music, ideas*›; **that suit is pretty ~** 那套西装很土

Phrasal verb
• **naff off** *vi* Brit sl 滚开 offensive

nag¹ /næɡ/
A *vt* (*pres p etc.* **-gg-**) **1** (pester) 唠叨; **to ~ sb. (for sth.)** 缠着某人（要某物）; **he's been ~ging me for a new bike** 他一直在缠着我给他买辆新自行车; **to ~ sb. into doing sth.** 不停唠叨使某人做某事 **2** (niggle) ‹*pain, problem, conscience*› 不断烦扰
B *vi* (*pres p etc.* **-gg-**) 抱怨不停; **to ~ at sb.** 不停地责备某人; **to ~ at sb. to do sth.** 不停地唠叨让某人做某事

nag² *n* colloq pej 马

nagging /ˈnæɡɪŋ/ *adj attrib* **1** (scolding) 一味抱怨的; **her ~ husband** 她那位唠唠叨叨的丈夫 **2** (niggling) 纠缠不休的 ‹*feeling, question*›; **I still have a ~ doubt** 疑虑依然困扰着我

nail /neɪl/
A *n* **1** (metal spike) 钉子; **to hit the ~ on the head** fig 一针见血; **cash on the ~** colloq 现金; **to pay on the ~** colloq 立即支付; **the first/last ~ in sb.'s/sth.'s coffin** fig 给某人/某事物以开始/最后的致命一击 **2** Anat 指甲; **to bite/paint one's ~s** 咬/涂指甲
B *vt* **1** (fasten) 钉住; **to ~ sth. (to** *or* **on to** *or* **on sth.)** 把某物钉（到某物）上; **we ~ed planks over the doors** 我们在门上钉了木板; **to ~ one's colours to the mast** fig 公开表态 **2** fig (fix) 固定 ‹*person*›; 集中 ‹*attention*›; **to ~ one's eye(s) on sth.** 死死盯住某物; **to be ~ed to the ground** *or* **to the spot** 在原地动弹不得 **3** fig (expose) 揭穿 ‹*myth, rumour*› **4** colloq (catch, arrest) 抓住 ‹*debtor, criminal, culprit*› **5** colloq (bring down) 打中 ‹*prey*› **6** Sport colloq 扣杀 ‹*ball, smash, drive*›

Phrasal verbs
• **nail down** *vt* **1** [**~ sth. down, ~ down sth.**] (fasten securely) 钉牢; fig (define precisely) 确定 ‹*origin, agreement*› **2** **to ~ sb. down (to sth.)** (make sb. say precisely) 让某人（对某事）明确表态
• **nail on** *vt* **1** [**~ sth. on, ~ on sth.**] (fasten with nails) 钉上 **2** **to ~ sth. on sb.** fig colloq 指控某人犯有 ‹*murder, arson*›
• **nail up** *vt* [**~ sth. up, ~ up sth.**] **1** (fasten) 钉住 ‹*poster, sign*›; **to be ~ed up (somewhere)** fig colloq 被限制（在某处） **2** (make secure) 钉死 ‹*door, window*›

nail-biting
A *n* [u] **1** (as habit) 咬指甲 **2** (anxiety) 焦虑
B *adj attrib* 令人焦虑的 ‹*finish, wait, suspense*›

nail: **~ bomb** *n* 长钉炸弹; **~ brush** *n* 指甲刷; **~ clippers** *npl* 指甲刀; **~ enamel** *n* Amer **= ~ polish**; **~ file** *n* 指甲锉刀; **~ polish** *n* [u and c] 指甲油; **~ scissors** *npl* 指甲刀; **~ varnish** *n* Brit **= ~ polish**

Nairobi /naɪˈrəʊbi/ *pr n* 内罗毕

naive, naïve /naɪˈiːv/ *adj* **1** (credulous, lacking experience) 幼稚的 ‹*person, argument, remark*›; **to be ~ of sb. to do sth.** 某人做某事很幼稚; **in the ~ hope/belief of doing sth.** 抱着做某事的幼稚希望/信念 **2** (innocent) 天真的 ‹*person, expression, manner*›; **to have a ~ look** 看上去天真无邪 **3** Art 稚拙的 ‹*painter, art*›

naively, naïvely /naɪˈiːvli/ *adv* **1** (credulously) 幼稚地 ‹*hope, believe, assume*› **2** (innocently) 天真地; **his questions were ~ direct** 他的问题单纯直白

naivety, naïveté /naɪˈiːvti/ *n* [u] **1** (credulity) 幼稚; **in my ~ I thought ...** 我幼稚地以为… **2** (innocence) 天真

naked /ˈneɪkɪd/ *adj* **1** (bare) 裸体的 ‹*person*›; 裸露的 ‹*body*›; **to go ~** 赤身裸体; **~ to the waist** 赤膊的 **2** (exposed) 无遮盖的 ‹*object*›; **a ~ sword** 出鞘的剑; **~ fists** 赤手空拳; **a ~ flame** 明火; **a ~ light** 无罩灯 **3** *attrib* (blatant) 赤裸裸的 ‹*aggression, facts, truth*›; 不加掩饰的 ‹*contempt, attempt*› **4** *attrib* (unaided) 无保护的; **the ~ eye** 肉眼; **to fight with ~ strength** 徒手搏斗

nakedness /ˈneɪkɪdnɪs/ *n* [u] 裸体

namby-pamby /ˌnæmbiˈpæmbi/ colloq pej
A *adj* 软弱的 ‹*person, ways, talk*›
B *n* 软弱的人; **don't be such a ~!** 不要婆婆妈妈的！

name /neɪm/
A *n* **1** (of person, place, object) 名字; **what is your ~?** 你叫什么名字？; **my ~ is Anne (Jones)** 我叫安妮（·琼斯）; **to know sb. by ~** 知道某人的名字; **a list of ~s** 名单; **to choose a ~ for sb.** 为某人起名; **what ~ shall I say?** (for announcement) 您怎么称呼？; **my full ~** 我的全名; **a false/assumed ~** 假名/化名; **the common/Latin ~ for this plant** 这种植物的俗名/拉丁学名; **to give** *or* **lend one's ~ to sth.** 以自己的名字命名某物; **to take** *or* **get one's ~ from sb./sth.** 自己的名字来自某人/某物; **it's the ~ that sells the product** 卖产品靠的是牌子; **a girl by the ~ of Viviane Tan** 一个名叫谭维维的女孩; **it's known by another ~ here** 它在这里有另一种叫法; **to mention** *or* **refer to sb. by ~** 提到某人的名字; **it is a marriage in ~ only** 这是有名无实的婚姻; **to be manager in all but ~** 是事实上的经理; **I booked the seats in my ~** 我用我的名字订了座; **in the ~ of** 以⋯的名义 ‹*the law, religion, freedom*›; **what in God's ~ do you think you're doing?** 你究竟在做什么呀？; **she hasn't a penny to her ~** 她一文不名; **he has any number of sporting titles/academic qualifications to his ~** 他获得过许多体育赛事冠军/他有许多学历; **under the ~ of ...** 用⋯的名字; **to give one's ~ (as ...)** 报出自己的名字（是⋯）; **to put one's ~ down (for sth.)** (enrol for) 报名参加（某事）; (apply for) 报名申请（某事）; **to put one's ~ to** 声援 ‹*petition*›; **to take sb.'s ~** 记下某人的名字; **the bullet had his ~ on it** fig 那颗子弹注定是冲着他来的; **(to be) the ~ of the game** colloq (main feature) （是）关键; (the way it is) （是）常规; **no ~s, no pack drill** colloq 不知其名，无从惩罚 **2** (insult, rude term) 辱骂; **to call sb. ~s** 辱骂某人; **he called her some terrible/all sorts of ~s** 他对她大加/肆意辱骂; **~s cannot hurt me** 我不怕被人骂 **3** (reputation) 名声; **a good/bad ~** 好/坏名声; **his ~ stinks in literary circles** 他在文坛臭名昭著; **to have** *or* **get a ~ for sth.** 在某方面出名; **to make sb.'s ~** 使某人出名; **to make one's ~** *or* **make a ~ for oneself as a writer** 成为著名作家; **his ~ is mud** colloq 他名誉扫地; ▸**dog A1** **4** (celebrity) 名人; **a big/famous/top ~ in sth.** 某领域内的头面/著名/顶级人物
B *vt* **1** (give a name to) 为⋯取名; **they ~d the baby Andrew** 他们为婴儿取名叫安德鲁; **a baby ~d Andrew** 一个名叫安德鲁的婴儿; **to ~ sb./sth. after** Brit *or* **for** Amer **sb./sth.** 以某人/某物的名字来命名某人/某物 **2** (cite by name) 说出⋯的名字; **to ~ all the emperors of China** 说出中国历代皇帝的名字; **she can quote from any author you care to ~** 你随便提一位作家，她都能引用他的话; **France, Italy and Spain, to ~ but a few** 法国、意大利、西班牙等等，不一而足; **problems? you ~ it, we've had it** colloq 问题？凡是你想得到的，我们都有 **3** (identify by name) 确定⋯的姓名 ‹*suspect, victim*›; **he's been ~d as a suspect in the robbery** 他被定为这起抢劫案的嫌疑人; **the journalist refused to ~ his sources** 记者拒绝说出其消息来源; **to ~ names** 指名道姓; **naming no names, there is a conspiracy in this club** 我不指名道姓了，但是俱乐部里有人在搞鬼 **4** (nominate) 提名; **to ~ sb. (as) sth.** 提名某人作为 ‹*director, heir*›; **to ~ sb. for sth.** 提名某人获得 ‹*post, award*› **5** (specify)

n

说定 ‹*time, place, terms*›; ～ **your price** 你开个价吧; **to ～ the day** 确定婚期
C -named *combining form* …提到的; **the first ～** 第一个提到的
name-calling *n* [u] 辱骂
namecheck /ˈneɪmtʃek/
A *n* 公开提名
B *vt* 公开提到…的姓名 ‹*person*›
name: ～ day *n* 命名日 [和本人同名的圣徒纪念日]; **～-drop** *vi* (*pres p etc.* **-pp-**) 提到名人以抬高身价; **～-dropper** *n* 提到名人以抬高身价之人; **～-dropping** *n* [u] 提到名人借以自抬身价
nameless /ˈneɪmlɪs/ *adj* **1** (anonymous) 无名的 ‹*person, grave*›; 不知其名的 ‹*organization, company*›; **a certain person, who shall remain** *or* **be ～** 一位不便公开其姓名的人; **to get information from a ～ source** 从一名未透露姓名者那里得到消息 **2** *attrib* (indefinable) 不可名状的 ‹*feeling, sense, foreboding*› **3** *attrib* (horrible) 难以形容的 ‹*horror*›; **～ atrocities/crimes** 难以名状的暴行/罪行
namely /ˈneɪmli/ *adv* 即; **two countries, ～ France and Spain** 两个国家, 即法国和西班牙
name: ～ plate *n* [标有建筑物住户、制造商等的] 名牌; **～sake** *n* 同名人; **～ tag** *n* 名牌; **～ tape** *n* [缝在衣服上的] 姓名标签
Namibia /nəˈmɪbiə/ *pr n* 纳米比亚
Namibian /nəˈmɪbɪən/
A *adj* (of Namibia) 纳米比亚的; (of the people) 纳米比亚人的
B *n* 纳米比亚人
nan[1] /næn/, **nana** /ˈnænə/ *ns* Brit colloq (on father's side) 奶奶; (on mother's side) 外婆
nan[2] /nɑːn/ *n* (bread) 馕 [印度发面烤饼]
nancy /ˈnænsi/, **nancy-boy** *ns* colloq pej (effeminate man) 娘娘腔的男子; (homosexual man) 同性恋男子
nandrolone /ˈnændrələʊn/ *n* [u] 诺龙 [一种类固醇]
Nanking /ˌnænˈkɪŋ/ *pr n* dated 南京
nanny /ˈnæni/ *n* **1** (nurse maid) 保姆 **2** colloq (grandma) (on father's side) 奶奶; (on mother's side) 外婆
nanny: ～ goat *n* 母山羊; **～ state** *n* pej 保姆式国家 [对民众管制过多的国家]
nano- /ˈnænəʊ/ *combining form* 毫微 [十亿分之一]
nanobot /ˈnænəʊbɒt/ *n* 纳米机器人
nanoparticle /ˈnænəʊˌpɑːtɪkl/ *n* 纳米粒子
nanopublishing /ˈnænəʊˌpʌblɪʃɪŋ/ *n* [u] 纳米出版 [指小范围、低成本的网络出版模式]
nanosecond /ˈnænəʊˌsekənd/ *n* 毫微秒
nanotechnology /ˌnænəʊtekˈnɒlədʒi/ *n* [u] 纳米技术
nap[1] /næp/
A *n* (sleep) [尤指白天的] 小睡; **afternoon ～** 午休; **to have** *or* **take a ～** 打个盹
B *vi* (*pres p etc.* **-pp-**) 打盹; **to catch sb. ～ping** lit 发现某人在打瞌睡; fig 使某人措手不及
nap[2] *n* Tex [织物等表面的] 短绒毛; **to brush with/against the ～** 顺毛/逆毛刷
nap[3] *n* Games 纳普牌戏; **to go ～ (on sth.)** (在某物上) 孤注一掷
napalm /ˈneɪpɑːm/
A *n* [u] 凝固汽油; **～ bomb/burns** 凝固汽油弹/凝固汽油烧伤
B *vt* 用凝固汽油弹攻击 ‹*area, village*›
nape /neɪp/ *n* 脖颈; **the ～ of the/one's neck** 后颈
naphtha /ˈnæfθə/ *n* [u] 石脑油
naphthalene /ˈnæfθəliːn/ *n* [u] 萘
napkin /ˈnæpkɪn/ *n* 餐巾; **a paper ～** 纸餐巾
nappy /ˈnæpi/ *n* Brit 尿布; **a disposable ～** 一次性尿布; **to change a baby's ～** 给婴儿换尿布
nappy: ～ liner *n* Brit 尿布衬里; **～ rash** *n* [u] Brit 尿布疹
narcissi /nɑːˈsɪsaɪ/ *pl* ▸ **narcissus**
narcissism /ˈnɑːsɪsɪzəm/ *n* [u] 孤芳自赏
narcissist /ˈnɑːsɪsɪst/ *n* 孤芳自赏者
narcissistic /ˌnɑːsɪˈsɪstɪk/ *adj* 孤芳自赏的 ‹*person, behaviour*›
narcissus /nɑːˈsɪsəs/ *n* (*pl* **narcissi** *or* **～es**) 水仙
narcolepsy /ˈnɑːkəlepsi/ *n* [u] 发作性睡病
narcosis /nɑːˈkəʊsɪs/ *n* [u] 昏迷状态
narcoterrorism /ˈnɑːkəʊˌterərɪzəm/ *n* [u] 毒品恐怖主义
narcotic /nɑːˈkɒtɪk/
A *n* **1** (illegal drug) 致幻毒品; **to be arrested on a ～s charge** 因贩毒指控被逮捕; **～s racket** 毒品非法交易 **2** Med 麻醉剂
B *adj* **1** (relating to illegal drug) 毒品引起的 ‹*addiction, stupor*›; **～ addict** 吸毒成瘾者 **2** Med 麻醉的 ‹*drug, effect*›
narcotic: ～s agent *n* Amer 缉毒警察; **～s squad** *n* Amer 缉毒队
narcotourist /ˈnɑːkəʊˌtʊərɪst, -tɔːr-/ *n* 毒品游客 [去国外买毒品吸食者]
nark[1] /nɑːk/ Brit colloq
A *vt* (annoy) «*person, comments*» 使发火; **it really ～s me to see food wasted** 看到食物被浪费, 我很生气
B *vi* (complain) 抱怨; **to ～ about sth./sb.** 抱怨某事/某人
nark[2] *n* sl 线人
narked /nɑːkt/ *adj* Brit colloq 恼火的 ‹*person, tone, expression*›; **to get ～** 发怒; **to be ～ about** *or* **by sth.** 因某事而发怒
narky /ˈnɑːki/ *adj* Brit colloq 易怒的 ‹*person, mood*›; 恼怒的 ‹*tone, expression*›; **to be/get ～ about** *or* **by sth.** 对某事气恼/因某事发怒
narrate /nəˈreɪt/ *vt* **1** (relate) 讲 ‹*story*›; 叙述 ‹*journey*› **2** Cin, TV, Theat «*narrator*» 为…作解说 ‹*film, documentary*›; **to be ～d by sb.** 由某人解说
narration /nəˈreɪʃn/ *n* **1** (account) 叙述 **2** Cin, TV, Theat 解说
narrative /ˈnærətɪv/
A *adj* 叙述的; **～ poem** 叙事诗; **～ skill** 叙述技巧; **～ line** 叙事线索
B *n* **1** [u and c] (account) 叙述; **a first-person ～** 第一人称叙述; **a ～ of** *or* **about sth.** 关于某事的叙述 **2** [u] (story-telling) 讲故事; **a master of ～** 一个故事大王
narrator /nəˈreɪtə(r)/ *n* **1** Literat 叙述者; **an impersonal ～** 非人格化的叙事者 **2** Cin, TV, Theat 解说员
narrow /ˈnærəʊ/
A *adj* **1** (in width) 狭窄的; **to grow** *or* **become ～** «*road, river*» 变窄; «*eyes*» 眯起; **he has ～ shoulders** *or* **is ～ across the shoulders** 他肩很窄 **2** (limited in scope) 有限的 ‹*range, choice, experience*›; (precise in meaning) 狭义的 ‹*definition, sense*›; pej (too restricted) 狭隘的 ‹*mind*›; **to lead a ～ existence** 过单调的生活; **she's very ～ in her views** 她的观点非常狭隘 **3** (with only a small margin) 差距小的 ‹*result*›; 微小的 ‹*margin*›; 微弱的 ‹*majority, advantage*›; **to win a ～ victory** *or* **a victory by a ～ margin** 险胜; **to suffer a ～ defeat** 惜败; **to have a ～ escape** 侥幸脱逃 **4** (tight-fitting) 紧身的 ‹*jacket, fit*› **5** (barely adequate) 紧缺的 ‹*means, resources*› **6** Phon 窄的 ‹*vowel*›
B *vi* **1** (become less wide) «*road, river*» 变窄 **2** (become closer or more limited) «*range, scope, role, margin*» 缩小; «*choices, surplus*» 减少; **the gap between the two parties has ～ed to 5%** 两党的差距缩小到 5% **3** (become less open-minded) «*outlook, opinions*» 变得狭隘 **4** (almost close) 眯起; **his eyes ～ed to ominous slits** 他的双眼邪恶地眯成了缝
C *vt* **1** (make less wide) 使…变窄 ‹*road, river*›; **to ～ sth. to sth.** 把某物变窄为某物 **2** (restrict, limit, make closer) 缩小 ‹*scope, role, margin*›; 减少 ‹*choice*›; 限定 ‹*meaning, definition*›; **they ～ed the focus of their investigation to two individuals** 他们把调查的重点集中到两个人身上; **the police have ～ed the search to these three towns** 警方把搜查范围缩小到了这三个镇; **the MP's majority has been ～ed to a mere hundred votes** 下院议员的多数优势已经缩小到仅 100 票 **3** (make less open-minded) 使…变得狭隘 ‹*mind, outlook*›; **bad experiences have ～ed her trust in other people** 不愉快的经历使她不大相信别人了 **4** (cause to close) 眯起 ‹*one's eyes*› **5** (make tighter) 收紧 ‹*dress, sleeves*›
D narrows *npl* (of sea) 海峡; (of river) 峡谷
Phrasal verb
• **narrow down**
A *vi* **to ～ down to sth.** «*investigation, search*» 缩小到某范围
B *vt* [**～ sth. down, ～ down sth.**] 缩小 ‹*investigation, search*›; 缩减 ‹*applicants, number of suspects*›; **to ～ down the possibilities to a short list** 把可能性缩小到几种
narrowboat /ˈnærəʊbəʊt/ *n* Brit 运河船
narrow gauge *n* 窄轨距
narrow-gauge: ～ engine *n* 窄轨机车; **～ line** *n* 窄轨铁路; **～ railway** *n* 窄轨铁路
narrowly /ˈnærəʊli/ *adv* **1** (barely) 勉强地 ‹*escape, win, pass*›; 差一点 ‹*miss*›; 以微弱之差 ‹*fail*›; **to ～ escape drowning** 险些淹死 **2** (strictly) 严格地 ‹*define, specify*›; **the law has been interpreted too ～ in this case** 在这个案子里, 对法律的解释过于拘谨
narrow-minded /ˌnærəʊˈmaɪndɪd/ *adj* 心胸狭窄地; **to be ～ about sth.** 对某事物气量狭小
narrow-mindedness /ˌnærəʊˈmaɪndɪdnɪs/ *n* [u] 心胸狭窄
narrowness /ˈnærəʊnɪs/ *n* [u] **1** (of width) 狭窄; (of scope, view) 狭隘; **the ～ of her waist** 她的细腰; **the ～ of the definition/one's vision** 定义的严格/眼光的狭隘 **2** (of victory, defeat, escape) 勉强; **the ～ of one's escape** 九死一生; **the ～ of the majority** 微弱的多数
narwhal /ˈnɑːwəl/ *n* 一角鲸
NASA /ˈnæsə/ *abbr* Amer **= National Aeronautics and Space Administration**

NASA

美国国家航空航天局, 全称 National Aeronautics and Space Administration。成立于 1958 年。负责美国航空航天的研究工作。总部位于华盛顿。下辖多个实验室和研究中心, 如佛罗里达的肯尼迪航天中心 (Kennedy Space Center)、喷气推进实验室 (Jet Propulsion Laboratory) 等。主持实施的重要航天项目包括阿波罗计划 (Apollo Program)、研制航天飞机、建立国际空间站和火星探索等。其中阿波罗计划使人类于 1969 年首次登上月球。

nasal /ˈneɪzl/
A *adj* **1** Anat 鼻的; **the ～ passages** 鼻道; **～ congestion** 鼻阻塞 **2** (of voice, sound) 带鼻音的 ‹*accent, speech, singing*›; **a ～ voice** 鼻音; **～ consonants/vowels** 鼻辅音/元音
B *n* 鼻音
nasalization /ˌneɪzəlaɪˈzeɪʃn, Amer -lɪ-ˈz-/ *n* [u] 鼻音化
nasalize /ˈneɪzəlaɪz/ *vt* 使…鼻音化 ‹*sound, consonant*›; **to be/become ～d** «*vowel, pronunciation*» 鼻化
nascent /ˈnæsnt/ *adj* 刚出现的 ‹*feeling, talent, tumour, career*›; **the ～ space industry** 新兴的航天工业
NASDAQ /ˈnæzdæk/ *abbr* **= National Association of Securities Dealers**

Automated Quotations 纳斯达克; **the ~ Index** 纳斯达克指数

Nassau /ˈnæsaʊ/ *pr n* 拿骚

nastily /ˈnɑːstɪlɪ/ *adv* **1** (unkindly) 恶意地 ‹*behave, say*› **2** (severely) 重重地 ‹*fall*›; 严重地 ‹*cut oneself, bleed*›; 剧烈地 ‹*cough*› **3** (threateningly) 恶狠狠地 ‹*glare, gesture*›

nastiness /ˈnɑːstɪnɪs/ *n* [u] **1** (of food, sight, smell, weather) 恶劣 **2** (of person, tone) 凶狠; (of insult) 恶意; (of look) 无礼 **3** (of fall, injury) 严重 **4** (obscenity) 下流

nasturtium /nəˈstɜːʃəm/ *n* 旱金莲

nasty /ˈnɑːsti/ *adj* **1** (unpleasant) 令人难受的 ‹*food, sight, colour*›; **to smell/taste ~** 气味难闻/味道恶心; **~ weather** 恶劣的天气; **I got a ~ fright** colloq 我大吃一惊; **things could get ~** colloq 事情可能变糟 **2** (threatening) 恶狠狠的 ‹*person, mood, tone*›; 恶意的 ‹*insult, rumour*›; (hateful) 凶恶的 ‹*look, threat*›; **to get/turn ~** 翻脸/变凶; **to be ~ to sb.** 对某人很凶; **to be ~ of sb. (to do sth.)** 某人（做某事）居心叵测; **to say ~ things about sb.** 恶语中伤某人; **a ~ piece of work** 恶棍 **3** (serious) 严重的 ‹*fall, injury, disease*› **4** (indecent) 下流的 ‹*mind, thoughts, joke*›; **that word is ~!** 那个词很下流！ **5** (tricky) 麻烦的; **the situation has turned ~** 情况变得严峻起来

Nat. /næt/ *abbr* **1** = **national A 2** = **nationalist**

natal /ˈneɪtl/ *adj* **1** (of birth) 新生儿的 ‹*injury, care*› **2** (of birthplace, time) 出生的 ‹*day, town*›

natch /nætʃ/ *excl* colloq 当然; **would you like another drink? — ~!** 你想再来一杯？——当然！

nation /ˈneɪʃn/ *n* **1** Pol 国家; **throughout** *or* **across the ~** 在全国 **2** (ethnic group) 民族; **the Scottish ~** 苏格兰民族 **3** (people) 国民; **to address the ~** 向国民发表演说

national /ˈnæʃənl/

A *adj* **1** *attrib* (particular to a nation) 国家的 ‹*unity, interest*›; 民族的 ‹*pride, tradition, dress*›; **~ team** 国家队; **~ flag** 国旗 **2** (relating to whole country) 全国性的 ‹*organization, event*›; **~ affairs** 国家大事; **a ~ strike** 全国罢工 **3** *attrib* (state-run) 国有的 ‹*bank*›; **~ museum/theatre** 国家博物馆/剧院

B *n* **1** (citizen) 国民; **foreign ~s** 外国人 **2** colloq (newspaper) **the ~s** 全国性报纸

national: N~ Aeronautics and Space Administration *n* Amer 国家航空航天局; **~ anthem** *n* 国歌; **N~ Assembly** *n* 国民议会; **~ bank** *n* = **central bank**; **~ curriculum** *n* Brit 全国统一课程; **~ debt** *n* 国债; **N~ Front** *n* Brit **the N~ Front** 民族阵线; **~ grid** *n* Brit 全国高压输电线网; **N~ Guard** *n* Amer **the N~ Guard** 国民警卫队; **N~ Health Service** *n* [u] Brit 国民保健体系; **~ holiday** *n* 全国假日; **~ income** *n* 国民收入; **N~ Insurance** *n* [u] Brit 国民保险制度; **N~ Insurance number/contributions** 国民保险号/国民保险费

> **the National Health Service**
>
> 国民保健体系，简称 NHS。英国公共医疗卫生体系于 1946 年由工党提出，1948 年开始实施。费用主要由政府承担，经费来源主要依靠税收。看病时除处方费、牙科诊疗费和验光配镜费之外免费。分为初级保健（primary care）和二级保健（secondary care）。负责初级保健的医生称全科医生（▸**GP**），是医疗服务的第一站。除急诊外，病人需要专家门诊或住院时，须由全科医生开转诊单和医院预约。NHS 是英国最大的雇主，雇员现有 150 多万人。病人根据自身需要，也可自费前往私人诊所或医院就诊。

nationalism /ˈnæʃnəlɪzəm/ *n* [u] **1** (national pride) 民族主义 **2** (advocating of political independence) 国家主义

nationalist /ˈnæʃnəlɪst/

A *n* 国家主义者

B *adj* 国家主义的 ‹*party, politician, movement*›

nationalistic /ˌnæʃnəˈlɪstɪk/ *adj* **1** often pej (patriotic) 民族主义的 ‹*rhetoric, fervour*› **2** (advocating political independence) 国家主义的 ‹*party*›

Nationalist Party *n* 国民党

nationality /ˌnæʃəˈnæləti/ *n* **1** (citizenship) 国籍; **what ~ is he?** 他是哪国人？ **2** Pol (ethnic group) 民族

nationalization /ˌnæʃnəlaɪˈzeɪʃn, Amer -lɪˈz-/ *n* [u] 国有化

nationalize /ˈnæʃnəlaɪz/ *vt* **1** Pol 使…国有化 ‹*railway, industry*› **2** (give national character to) 使…有民族特点 ‹*architecture, design*›

nationally /ˈnæʃnəli/ *adv* **1** (at national level) 全国性地 ‹*decide, negotiate*› **2** (nationwide) 在全国范围内 ‹*broadcast, enforce*›; **to be ~ known/celebrated** 举国皆知/庆祝

national: N~ Minimum Wage *n* Brit 全国最低工资标准; **~ monument** *n* 名胜古迹区; **~ park** *n* 国家公园; **N~ Rifle Association** *n* Amer 全国步枪协会; **N~ Savings Bank** *n* Brit 国家储蓄银行; **~ security** *n* [u] 国家安全; **N~ Security Council** *n* Amer **the N~ Security Council** 国家安全委员会; **~ service** *n* [u] Brit 兵役; **to do one's ~ service** 服兵役; **N~ Socialism** *n* [u] [希特勒鼓吹的] 国家社会主义; **N~ Trust** *n* Brit **the N~ Trust** 全国托管协会

nationhood /ˈneɪʃnhʊd/ *n* [u] 独立国地位; **to struggle to achieve ~** 争取国家独立

nation state *n* 单一民族的独立国家

nationwide /ˌneɪʃnˈwaɪd/

A *adj* 全国性的 ‹*campaign, shortage, strike, survey*›

B *adv* 在全国 ‹*distribute, broadcast, travel*›; **to have 20 dealers ~** 全国共有20位经销商

native /ˈneɪtɪv/

A *adj* **1** (natal) 出生的 ‹*land, village*›; **his ~ language/country** 他的母语/祖国; **a ~ New Yorker** 土生土长的纽约人; **a ~ French speaker** 法语是母语的人 **2** (indigenous) 原住民的 ‹*tribe, custom, language*›; **to go ~** colloq hum 入乡随俗 **3** Zool, Bot 当地的 ‹*flora, fauna*›; **to be ~ to somewhere** 原产于某地 **4** (innate) 天生的 ‹*instincts, abilities, intelligence*›

B *n* **1** (person born in a certain place) 本地人; **a ~ of London/Canada** 伦敦/加拿大人 **2** (indigenous person) 原住民 **3** *usu pl* (local) 当地人 **4** Zool 土生动物; Bot 土生植物; **to be a ~ of somewhere** 原产于某地

Native American

A *adj* 美洲原住民的 ‹*ancestry, language, culture*›; **a ~ woman/warrior** 美洲原住民妇女/勇士

B *n* 美洲原住民

> **Native American**
>
> 美洲原住民，指美国的原住民时亦称 American Indian。但 American Indian 还可以指南、北美洲的原住民。以前称印第安人（Indian），因为哥伦布到达美洲时，以为自己发现的是印度。这一称呼在政治上已不够正确，因而被取代。目前，美国的原住民分为 500 多个部落，人口约 200 万。亦称 Red Indian，但这一说法有贬义。

ℹ Nationalities

■ In Chinese, 'the name of the country + 人' is used to refer to a person or the people of a specific nationality. 人 can be either singular or plural depending on context:

He is Chinese
= 他是中国人

They are Chinese
= 他们是中国人

He is American
or ***He is an American***
= 他是美国人

She is a Pole
= 她是波兰人

Carla is an Icelander
= 卡拉是冰岛人

Alastair is a Scotsman
= 阿拉斯泰尔是苏格兰人

■ Whether noun or adjective, words such as 'American' and 'British' are always translated as 'name of the country + 人' in Chinese:

She is British
= 她是英国人

The British are famous for their politeness
= 英国人以彬彬有礼著称

They are French
= 他们是法国人

The French are hospitable
= 法国人好客

■ In Chinese, the name of the country may be used to qualify a noun such as 'people', 'woman' etc.:

a British man
=（一个）英国人
or（一个）英国男人

a British woman
=（一个）英国人
or（一个）英国女人

a British diplomat
=（一名）英国外交官

a Chinese businessman
=（一个）中国商人

Italian people
= 意大利人
or 意大利人民

French tourists
= 法国旅客

■ Other expressions:

She is of Chinese extraction
= 她是中国血统

He was born in Pakistan
= 他出生在巴基斯坦

They come from Slovakia
= 他们来自斯洛伐克

He is a Portuguese national
or ***He is a Portuguese citizen***
= 他是葡萄牙公民

Miss Li is a Chinese American
= 李小姐是美籍华人

Eric is a German Italian
= 埃里克是德裔意大利人

native speaker *n* 说本族语的人

Nativity /nəˈtɪvəti/ *n* **the ~** 耶稣的诞生

nativity: ~ play *n* 圣诞剧; **~ scene** *n* 耶稣诞生造型

NATO /ˈneɪtəʊ/ *abbr* **= North Atlantic Treaty Organization**

natter /ˈnætə(r)/ Brit colloq
A *vi* 闲聊; **to ~ (on) to** *or* **with sb.** 与某人闲聊
B *n* 闲聊; **to have a ~** 闲聊

natterer /ˈnætərə(r)/ *n* Brit colloq 闲谈者

natterjack /ˈnætədʒæk/ *n* **~ (toad)** 黄条背蟾蜍

natty /ˈnæti/ *adj* colloq [1] (fashionable) 整洁时髦的 ‹*person, clothes, hairstyle*› [2] (clever) 设计精巧的 ‹*gadget, watch*›; 巧妙的 ‹*idea, solution*›

natural /ˈnætʃrəl/
A *adj* [1] (usual, normal) 正常的 ‹*reaction, consequence*›; **it is ~ (for sb.) to do sth.** （某人）做某事是很正常的; **it is ~ that ...** …是很正常的; **it is ~ that he should want to see his daughter** 他想见女儿是很自然的; **the ~ thing to do would be to protest** 抗议是理所当然的; **it's only ~** 这很正常 [2] (in accordance with nature) 本能的 ‹*urge, behaviour, aversion*›; (innate) 天生的 ‹*ability, orator, linguist*›; **it is ~ (for sb./sth.) to do sth.** （某人/某物）天生会做某事; **it's not ~!** 这有悖天性！; **sb.'s ~ inclinations** 某人与生俱来的爱好; **a ~ gift for singing** 歌唱的天赋 [3] (unaffected) 自然的; **to be ~ with sb.** 与某人在一起时轻松自如; **try and look more ~** 尽量表现得再自然一些 [4] (not man-made) 自然的 ‹*phenomenon, disaster, immunity*›; 天然的 ‹*substance, harbour*›; 天生的 ‹*blonde, curls, beauty*›; **the ~ world** 自然界; **superb ~ advantages/features** 得天独厚的优势/特色; **land in its ~ state** 未开垦的土地; **to die of** *or* **from ~ causes** 自然死亡 [5] (wild) 野生的 ‹*food, state*›; **~ habitat** 自然栖息地; **the elephant has no ~ predators** 象没有天敌 [6] *attrib* (related by blood) 亲生的 ‹*parents, child*› [7] dated (illegitimate) 私生的 ‹*child*› [8] (unprocessed) 纯天然的 ‹*foods, ingredients, medicines*› [9] Mus 本位音的 ‹*key, scale*›; **B ~** B本位音; **a ~ note** 本位音
B *n* [1] colloq (person suited to sth.) 天才; **to be a ~ for** *or* **at sth.** 是天生做某事的料 [2] esp Amer colloq (thing suited to sth.) 合适的事物; **to be a ~ for sth./doing sth.** 与某物般配/适合做某事 [3] Mus (sign) 本位号; (note) 本位音

natural: ~-born *adj attrib* 天生的 ‹*leader, athlete, cynic*›; **~ childbirth** *n* [u] 自然分娩法; **~ gas** *n* [u] 天然气; **~ history** *n* [u] 博物学

naturalism /ˈnætʃrəlɪzəm/ *n* [u] 自然主义

naturalist /ˈnætʃrəlɪst/
A *n* [1] (expert) 博物学家 [2] Literat 自然主义作家; Art 自然主义艺术家
B *adj* **= naturalistic**

naturalistic /ˌnætʃrəˈlɪstɪk/ *adj* [1] (lifelike) 写实的 ‹*account*›; 自然的 ‹*features, setting*› [2] Art, Literat, Philos 自然主义的 ‹*style, painting*›

naturalization /ˌnætrəlaɪˈzeɪʃn, Amer -lɪˈz-/ *n* [u] [1] Admin 加入国籍; **~ papers** 入籍文件 [2] Bot, Zool 顺化

naturalize /ˈnætʃrəlaɪz/
A *vt usu passive* [1] Admin 使加入国籍; **to be ~d** 被归化 [2] Bot, Zool 引进 ‹*animal, plant, species*›; **to be** *or* **become ~d** 顺化 [3] Ling 吸收 ‹*word, expression*›
B *vi* «*plant, animal, species*» 被成功引进

natural justice *n* [u] 自然正义

natural language *n* 自然语言

natural language processing *n* [u] 自然语言处理

natural logarithm *n* 自然对数

naturally /ˈnætʃrəli/ *adv* [1] (obviously) 当然地 ‹*cautious, angry*›; (normally) 自然地 ‹*develop, behave, smile*›; **~ enough, she refused** 她当然拒绝了; **I ~ assumed that ...** 我自然而然地以为…; **to do what comes ~** 顺其自然; **just try and act ~** 尽量自然些 [2] (innately) 天生地 ‹*conservative, athletic*›; **~ talented** 有天赋的; **her hair is ~ curly** 她的头发是自然卷; **to come ~ to sb.** 对某人来说轻而易举 [3] (in nature) 天然地 ‹*grow, decompose, present*›; **~ occurring radioactive isotopes** 天然的放射性同位素

naturalness /ˈnætʃrəlnɪs/ *n* [u] 自然

natural: ~ number *n* 自然数; **~ park** 自然公园; **~ resources** *npl* 自然资源; **~ science** *n* [u and c] 自然科学; **~ sciences** *npl* 自然科学; **~ selection** *n* [u] 自然选择; **~ wastage** *n* [u] 自然减员

nature /ˈneɪtʃə(r)/ *n* [1] [u] (essential quality) 本质; **of this/that ~** 这/那一类的; **of a serious/personal/professional ~** 性质严重的/个人性质的/职业性质的; **to be in the ~ of sth.** formal 与某物类似; **fire is by (its very) ~ dangerous** 火就（其）本质而言是危险的; **it is in the ~ of things that ...** …是理所当然的; **it is in the ~ of living things to die** 生物本质上是要死亡的 [2] [c and u] (fundamental character) 本性; **sb.'s true ~** 某人的本性; **to have a vengeful/artistic/good ~** 生性爱报复/有艺术细胞/脾气好; **by ~** 天生地; **strong by name, strong by ~** 人如其名一样强壮; **it is (not) in his ~ to be kind to people** 他生性对人（不）和善; **to be different/eccentric in ~** 性格不同/怪异; **sb.'s better ~** 某人的良心; **against my better ~, I ...** 我狠心地…; **second ~ (to sb.** *or* **for sb. to do sth.)** （某人的/某人做某事的）第二天性 [3] [u] (the natural world) 自然界; (natural processes) 自然; **to teach sb. about ~** 向某人讲授自然常识; **to paint from ~** 写生; **contrary to** *or* **against ~** 违背自然的; **a law of ~** 自然规律; **to let ~ take its course** 顺其自然; **a call of ~** euph 内急 euph; **~ versus nurture** 先天对后天; **a ~ lover** 热爱大自然的人 [4] [u] (simple life) 原始生活; **to get back** *or* **go back to ~** 返璞归真; **to be in a state of ~** Philos (primitive) 处于原始状态; euph hum (naked) 赤身裸体

nature: ~ conservancy *n* [u] 自然保护; **~ reserve** *n* 自然保护区; **~ trail** *n* 通往自然景观的小道

naturism /ˈneɪtʃərɪzəm/ *n* [u] 裸体主义

naturist /ˈneɪtʃərɪst/
A *n* 裸体主义者
B *adj* 裸体主义者的 ‹*beach, activity*›

naught /nɔːt/ *n* [u] Amer 无; **to come to ~** 毫无结果

naughtily /ˈnɔːtɪli/ *adv* [1] (disobediently) 顽皮地 ‹*giggle, refuse*›; **to behave ~** 调皮 [2] (suggestively) 挑逗地 ‹*say, smile, act*›; **to wink at sb. ~** hum 向某人抛媚眼

naughtiness /ˈnɔːtɪnɪs/ *n* [u] [1] (disobedience) 调皮; **a piece of ~** 一件淘气的事 [2] (of smile, joke, picture) 下流

naughty /ˈnɔːti/ *adj* [1] (disobedient) 顽皮的 ‹*child, pet, trick*›; **to be ~ (of sb.) to do sth.** （某人）做某事真淘气; **you ~ boy!** 你这个淘气的孩子！ [2] (suggestive) 挑逗的 ‹*gesture, picture*›; 撩人的 ‹*underwear*›; **a ~ joke/word** 下流的笑话/脏话

naughty: ~ bits *npl* Brit colloq hum 性器官; **~ nineties** *npl* colloq **the ~ nineties** 弛靡90年代 ［尤指英法两国道德失范的19世纪90年代］

nausea /ˈnɔːsɪə, Amer ˈnɔːʒə/ *n* [u] [1] Med 恶心; **to be overcome by ~** 恶心得受不了 [2] fig (disgust) 极度厌恶; **the idea filled her with ~** 这个想法使她满心厌恶

nauseate /ˈnɔːsɪeɪt, Amer ˈnɔːz-/ *vt* [1] Med 使恶心 [2] fig (disgust) 使感到厌恶

nauseating /ˈnɔːsɪeɪtɪŋ, Amer ˈnɔːz-/ *adj* [1] lit 令人恶心的 ‹*food, smell, sight*› [2] fig 令人厌恶的 ‹*person, attitude*›

nauseatingly /ˈnɔːsɪeɪtɪŋli, Amer ˈnɔːz-/ *adv* [1] lit 令人恶心地 ‹*pungent*›; **~ sweet/rich** 甜/油腻得让人恶心的 [2] fig (disgustingly) 令人厌恶地 ‹*hypocritical, sentimental, violent*›

nauseous /ˈnɔːsɪəs, Amer ˈnɔːʃəs/ *adj* [1] (affected with nausea) 想呕吐的 ‹*feeling, person*›; **to feel ~** 感到恶心 [2] (causing nausea) 令人恶心的 ‹*gas, smell, taste, food*›

nautical /ˈnɔːtɪkl/ *adj* 航海的 ‹*person, career, compass*›; 海员的 ‹*uniform*›; **a ~ term** 航海术语

nautical: ~ almanac *n* 航海（天文）历; **~ mile** *n* 海里

naval /ˈneɪvl/ *adj* 海军的 ‹*vessel, officer, uniform*›; **a ~ power** 海上强国

naval: ~ academy *n* 海军军官学校; **~ architect** ▸**p. 409** *n* 造船工程师; **~ architecture** *n* [u] 造船学; **~ attaché** *n* 海军武官; **~ base** *n* 海军基地; **~ battle** *n* 海战; **~ dockyard** *n* 海军船坞; **~ forces** *npl* 海军; **~ station** *n* 海军港; **~ warfare** *n* [u] 海战

nave /neɪv/ *n* ［教堂的］正厅

navel /ˈneɪvl/ *n* 肚脐; **to contemplate one's ~** fig 埋头沉思

navel: ~-gazing *n* [u] pej (about oneself) 目光如豆; (about issue) 钻牛角尖; **~ ring** *n* 肚脐饰圈

navigable /ˈnævɪgəbl/ *adj* 可通航的 ‹*river, waterway, sea*›

navigate /ˈnævɪgeɪt/
A *vi* [1] Naut, Aviat 导航; **to ~ by the stars** 根据星辰确定航向 [2] Aut «*car passenger*» 指路; **I'll drive, you ~** 我开车，你指路 [3] Zool «*bees, birds*» 辨识方向 [4] (find a way) 顺利通过; **to ~ across/through sth.** 穿越/穿过某处
B *vt* [1] (plot the course of) «*navigator, co-pilot*» 为…领航 ‹*ship, aircraft*› [2] (steer, pilot) 驾驶 ‹*yacht, ship, aeroplane*› [3] (sail) 横渡 ‹*ocean, sea, river*›; 航行于 ‹*passage, course*› [4] fig (find one's way through) 顺利通过 ‹*streets*›; 顺利答出 ‹*questions*›; **the admissions procedure has been ~d by thousands of successful applicants** 几千名申请者顺利通过了录取程序; **he ~d his way through the crowd** 他从人群中穿过 [5] (guide) 为…导航 ‹*ship, aircraft*›; fig (through process) «*guide, map*» 指引; **the handbook will ~ you through the procedure** 这本手册能帮助你了解程序

navigation /ˌnævɪˈgeɪʃn/ *n* [u] [1] (plotting of course) 导航 [2] (steering, piloting) 驾驶 [3] (passage) 航行; **there has been an increase in ~ along this canal** 这条运河的来往船只有所增多

navigational /ˌnævɪˈgeɪʃənl/ *adj* 导航的

navigation: ~ channel *n* 航道; **~ laws** *npl* 航海法规; **~ lights** *npl* 航行灯; **~ satellite** *n* 导航卫星; **~ system** *n* 导航系统

navigator /ˈnævɪgeɪtə(r)/ *n* [1] Naut, Aviat 领航员 [2] Aut 指路的乘客 [3] Comput 浏览器

navvy /ˈnævi/ *n* Brit dated ［修筑道路或运河的］挖土工

navy /ˈneɪvi/
A *n* [1] [c] (fighting force) 海军; **to join the ~** 加入海军; **to be** *or* **serve in the ~** 在海军服役 [2] [c] (fleet) 舰队; **a ~ of six hundred ships** 一支由600艘船只组成的舰队 [3] [u] (colour) 藏青色
B *adj* ▸**p. 134** [1] *attrib* (naval) 海军的 ‹*life, uniform*›; **a ~ wife** 海军军人的妻子 [2] (colour) 藏青色的 ‹*clothes, wool*›

navy bean *n* Amer 菜豆

navy blue ▸**p. 134**
A *n* [u] 藏青色
B **navy-blue** *adj* 藏青色的

navy: N~ Department *n* Amer 海军部; **N~ List** *n* Brit 海军军官花名册; **~ yard** *n* Amer 海军造船厂

nay /neɪ/
A *n* 1 (negative answer) 否定的回答; **to say yea or ～** 肯定或否定 2 Brit (negative vote) 否决票; **the ～s have it** 投反对票者占多数
B *adv* archaic or liter 不仅如此; **she is pretty, ～ beautiful!** 她长得好看, 不, 应该说是美丽!

Nazi /ˈnɑːtsi/
A *n* 1 Hist 纳粹党人 2 colloq pej (fascist) 法西斯分子
B *adj* 1 Hist 纳粹的 2 colloq pej (fascist) 法西斯的

Nazism /ˈnɑːtsɪzəm/, **Naziism** /ˈnɑːtsiːɪzəm/ *ns* [u] 纳粹主义

NB = nota bene /ˌnəʊtə ˈbeneɪ/ 注意

NBA *abbr* Amer **= National Basketball Association** 全国篮球协会

NBC *abbr* Amer **= National Broadcasting Company** 全国广播公司

> **NBC**
> 全国广播公司，全称 National Broadcasting Company，美国三大全国性商业广播电视公司之一。总部位于纽约洛克菲勒中心（Rockefeller Center）。成立于 1926 年，为美国第一个全国性广播网。1940 年开始电视广播。现属于通用电气公司（General Electric Company）。台标为孔雀。

NC *abbr* Amer **= North Carolina**

NCO *abbr* **= non-commissioned officer**

ND *abbr* Amer **= North Dakota**

NE ▸**p. 142** *abbr* 1 **= north-east** 2 **= north-eastern**

Neanderthal /nɪˈændətɑːl/
A *n* 1 lit (prehistoric human) 尼安德特人 2 fig (uncivilized person) 粗鲁的人
B *adj* 1 lit (of prehistoric human) 尼安德特人的; **～ man** 尼安德特人 2 fig (uncivilized) 粗鲁的 ‹*features, thug*›

neap /niːp/ *n* **～ (tide)** 小潮

Neapolitan ice cream /ˌniːəˈpɒlɪtən/ *n* [u] 多色分层冰淇淋

near /nɪə(r)/
A *adv* 1 (nearby) 附近; **to draw sb./sth. ～** 把某人/某物拉近; **to draw/come/move ～** 靠近; **she took a step ～er** 她走近了一步; **help was ～ at hand** 得到帮助轻而易举; **from ～ and far** 来自四面八方; **to be ～ at hand** 近在咫尺 2 (close in time, degree) 接近; **the exams are drawing ～** 考试越来越近了; **as ～ as I can tell** 据我所知; **so ～ and yet so far** 功亏一篑 3 (almost) 几乎; **a ～ perfect performance** 近乎完美的表演; **nowhere ～ finished/ready** 远没有完成/准备好; **he's not anywhere ～ as bright as her** 他远没有她聪明
B *prep* 1 (in space) 靠近; **to move/draw ～ sb./sth.** 向某人/某物靠近; **our house is ～ the park** 我们家在公园附近; **the table ～est the door** 最靠近门的桌子 2 (in time, in degree, close to) 接近; **to get ～ sth.** 临近某事; **to be/come ～ doing sth.** 接近于做某事; **～ the end of the war** 临近战争结束; **～er the time** *or* **date** 日子更近的时候; **to be ～ tears** 几乎要哭; **it's getting ～ Christmas** 圣诞节快到了; **we came ～ (to) being killed** 我们差点丢了性命
C *adj* 1 (close in distance, order) 靠近的; **my house is quite ～** 我家就在附近; **we are ～ neighbours** 我们是近邻; **she has a 12-point lead over her ～est rival** 她领先紧随其后的对手 12 分 2 (close in time, in degree) 接近的; **in the ～ future** 在不远的将来; **the time is ～ when ...** …的时候临近了; **in the ～ darkness** 几乎在黑暗之中; **he's the ～est thing to a great scientist that we've got** 他是我们当中最可能成为伟大科学家的人 3 *attrib* (virtual) 近似于的; **to be a ～ tragedy/disaster** 近乎悲剧/灾难; **his state of ～ despair** 他近乎绝望的状态 4 *attrib* (in relationship) 亲近的; **the ～est relatives** 至亲 5 *attrib* (nearside) 副驾驶一侧的; **the ～ front wheel of the car** 汽车副驾驶一侧的前车轮 6 *attrib* (closer of two) 这一侧的; **the ～ side/bank** 靠这边的一侧/岸 7 *attrib* (short) 短的; **the ～est route** 最短的路线
D *vt* 1 (in space) 靠近; **we ～ed the top of the hill** 我们接近了山顶 2 (in time, degree) 接近; **to ～ the end of sth.** 临近…的结尾 ‹*season, career, tour*›; **she was ～ing the end of her life** 她正在走向她生命的终点; **to ～ completion** ‹*project, book*› 即将完成
E *vi* (in time) 来临; **lunchtime ～ed** 午饭时间就要到了; **as the time ～ed for the exam ...** 当临近考试时…
F **near enough** *adv phr* 1 (close in distance) 足够靠近; **he was ～ enough to hear everything** 他离得很近, 足以听到每一句话 2 (close in degree) 非常接近; **I can only give you £20 — that's ～ enough** 我只能给你 20 英镑——那就差不多够了 3 Brit colloq (approximately) 差不多; **there were 30 yachts, ～ enough** 大约有 30 艘游艇吧
G **near to** *prep phr* 1 (in space) 靠近; **to move/draw ～ to sb./sth.** 走近某人/某物; **the car park ～ to the sawmill** 锯木厂旁的停车场; **how ～ are we to London?** 我们距离伦敦有多近? 2 (in time, degree) 接近; **～er to the time** *or* **date** 日子更近的时候; **it's getting ～ to Christmas** 圣诞节快到了; **she's ～er to 50 than 40** 她快 50 岁了; **to be/come ～ to doing sth.** 接近于做某事; **they were still no ～er to solving the case** 他们的破案工作仍没有进展; **she came ～ to crying** *or* **to tears** 她几乎要哭了

nearby /nɪəˈbaɪ/
A *adv* 在附近; **～, there's a village** 附近有一个村庄
B *adj* 附近的; **a ～ garage** 附近的车库

near-death experience *n* 濒死经历

Near East *pr n* **the ～** 近东

nearest and dearest *npl* 亲朋好友

nearly /ˈnɪəli/ *adv* 1 (almost) 几乎; **it's ～ 9 o'clock** 快到 9 点钟了; **your coffee's ～ cold** 你的咖啡快凉了; **she very ～ died** 她差点死去; **not ～** 远非; **it's not ～ as hot as last year** 天气远远没有去年那么热 2 (closely) 接近地; **the more you look at this portrait, the more ～ it seems to resemble him** 这张肖像越看就越觉得像他

nearly new
A *adj* 二手的 ‹*car, furniture, clothes*›
B *adv* 作为旧货 ‹*buy*›

near miss *n* 1 (narrow escape) 侥幸脱险 2 Aut, Aviat 几乎相撞; **to have a ～** 差点相撞 3 (something almost achieved) 功败垂成; **he only just failed the exam, it was a ～** 他考试刚好不及格, 分数就差一点点 4 (by ball, bomb, bullet) 近距脱靶

nearness /ˈnɪənɪs/ *n* [u] 1 (of place, object) 靠近; (of person) 亲近; **its ～ to his place of work was a distinct advantage** 距离他的工作地点近是个显著的优势; **he longed for her ～** 他渴望与她亲近 2 (in time) 接近; **the ～ of her departure date** 她动身日期的临近

nearside /ˈnɪəsaɪd/ *n* esp Brit **the ～** 左边; **on the ～** 在左边; **the ～ lane** 慢车道; **the ～ rear door** 左后门

near: ～-sighted *adj* esp Amer 近视的; **～-sightedness** *n* [u] esp Amer 近视; **～ thing** *n* 1 (narrow escape) 侥幸的脱险; 2 (near failure) 勉强做成之事

neat /niːt/ *adj* 1 (tidy) 整齐的 ‹*row, pile*›; 整洁的 ‹*appearance, hair, kitchen*›; **their house is always ～ and tidy** 他们的房子总是干净整洁; **to be as ～ as a new pin** 非常整洁 2 (well presented) 工整的 ‹*handwriting, stitching*›; 干净利索的 ‹*person*› 3 (slick, efficient) 简洁的 ‹*phrase, explanation*›; **a ～ solution** 干净利落的解决; **a ～ little argument** 巧妙的论点 4 (ingenious) 灵巧的 ‹*idea, gadget*› 5 Amer colloq (very good) 极好的 ‹*person, thing, idea*› 6 (well formed) 匀称的 ‹*legs, form*›; **she has a ～ little figure** 她体形匀称, 小巧玲珑 7 Brit (unmixed) 纯的 ‹*spirit, liquor, brandy*›; **to drink one's whisky ～** 喝纯威士忌酒

neaten /ˈniːtn/ *vt* 使整洁

neatly /ˈniːtli/ *adv* 1 (tidily, smartly) 整齐地 ‹*arrange, fold, cut, dress*›; **his hair was ～ combed** 他的头发梳得整整齐齐 2 (ingeniously) 巧妙地 ‹*avoid, manoeuvre, construct*›; **～ put!** 说得好!; **the case is designed to fit ～ into your pocket** 盒子设计得正好能装进口袋里

neatness /ˈniːtnɪs/ *n* [u] 1 (tidiness) 整齐 2 (of presentation) 整洁 3 (ingenuity) 灵巧

Nebraska /nɪˈbræskə/ *pr n* 内布拉斯加州

nebula /ˈnebjʊlə/ *n* (*pl* **nebulae** /ˈnebjʊliː/) 星云

nebular /ˈnebjʊlə(r)/ *adj* 星云的

nebulizer /ˈnebjʊlaɪzə(r)/ *n* 喷雾器

nebulous /ˈnebjʊləs/ *adj* 模糊的

NEC *abbr* 1 **= National Executive Committee** 全国执行委员会 2 Brit **= National Exhibition Centre** 国家展览中心

necessarily /ˌnesəˈserəli, Brit also ˈnesəsərəli/ *adv* 1 (definitely) 必定; **not ～!** 不一定!; **all creatures must ～ die** 所有生物都必定会死 2 (of necessity) 必要地 ‹*slow, involve*›; **a ～ cautious statement** 必须谨慎小心的声明

necessary /ˈnesəsəri, Amer -serɪ/
A *adj* 1 (required) (important, desirable) 必要的 ‹*discussion, qualifications, precaution*›; 必需的 ‹*ingredients*›; **if ～** 如果必要的话; **it is ～ for (sb./sth.) to do sth.** 某人/某物必须做某事; **a ～ evil** (thing) 必要的弊害; (event) 不得已的事; (person) 不好但又必不可少的人; **to find it ～ to do sth.** 发现有必要做某事; **when ～** 必要时; **circumstances make it ～ for me to ...** 情势迫使我… 2 (inevitable) 必然的 ‹*consequence, conclusion*›
B *n* 1 **the ～** Brit colloq (money) 钱; **do you have the ～?** 你有钱吗? 2 **the ～** (action) 必须做的事; **to do the ～** 采取必要的行动
C **necessaries** *npl* (food, clothes) 生活必需品

necessitate /nɪˈsesɪteɪt/ *vt* 使成为必要; **the job would ～ your** *or* **you moving** 工作需要你搬家

necessity /nɪˈsesəti/ *n* 1 [u] (need) 必要; **from** *or* **out of ～** 出于需要; **the ～ of sth./doing sth.** 某事/做某事的必要性; **the ～ for sth.** 某事的必要性; **there is no ～ for sth./to do sth.** 某事/做某事没必要; **there is no ～ for sb. to do sth.** 某人做某事没必要; **if the ～ arises** 必要时; **of ～** 势必; **to bow to ～** 迫不得已而为之 2 [c] (essential need, item) 必需品; **the necessities of life** 生活必需品; **to be a ～** 是必不可少的东西; **the bare necessities** 基本的必需品; **～ is the mother of invention** Prov 需要是发明之母 3 [c] (required action) 必要的措施; **a political ～** 政治需要; **to be an absolute ～** 是绝对必须做的事

neck /nek/
A *n* 1 ▸**p. 71** (of person, animal) 脖子; **the back of the** *or* **one's ～** 后脖颈; **to wear sth. around one's ～** 脖子上挂着某物; **to throw one's arms around sb.'s ～** 搂着某人的脖子; **to break one's/sb.'s ～** 折断自己的/某人的脖子; **to have a stiff/sore ～** 脖子僵硬/酸; **to have sth./sb. (hanging) around one's ～** 被某事/某人烦扰; **to be up to one's ～ in sth.** (be overwhelmed by sth.) 埋头于某事; (be deeply involved in sth.) 深陷于某事; **to break one's ～ (doing** *or* **to do sth.)** colloq 拼命（做某事）; **to get** *or* **catch it in the ～ (from sb.)** colloq 遭受（某人的）严厉斥责; **to risk one's ～** 冒生命危险; **to save one's ～** (save one's life) 保住脑袋; (get out of difficult situation) 免受危难; **to stick one's ～ out** (risk

incurring criticism) 奋不顾身; (make a risky guess) 大胆猜测; **to win/lose by a ~** Horse racing 以一颈之差获胜/失败; fig 以微弱之差获胜/失败; **to be ~ and ~ (with sb.)** (与某人) 不相上下 **2** [c] (collar, neckline) 领口; **a top with a high/low/square/round ~** 高领/低领/方领/圆领上衣; **to be open at the ~** 领口开着; **my shirt is rather tight around** *or* **in the ~** 我的衬衫领口很紧 **3** [u] (cut of meat) 颈肉 **4** [c] (of bottle, vase) 瓶颈; (of violin, guitar) 琴颈 **5** [c] (narrow strip) 狭长地带; **a ~ of land** 地峡; **(in) this/our/your** *etc.* **~ of the woods** colloq (在) 这/我们/你们等那一带 **6** [u] Brit dated colloq (cheek, impudence) 厚脸皮; **to have the ~ to do sth.** 有脸做某事 **7** [c] Anat 颈; **the ~ of the womb** 子宫颈 **8** [c] (of a screw) 颈

B *vi* colloq 搂脖子亲嘴; **to ~ with sb.** 和某人拥吻

neckband /ˈnekbænd/ *n* 领圈

neckerchief /ˈnekətʃɪf/ *n* 围巾

necking /ˈnekɪŋ/ *n* [u] colloq 搂脖子亲嘴

necklace /ˈneklɪs/

A *n* **1** (jewellery) 项链 **2** esp S Afr (burning tyre) 火项圈 [套在受害者脖子上的燃烧的轮胎]

B *vt* 套上火项圈烧死 ‹person›

necklacing /ˈneklɪsɪŋ/ *n* [u] esp S Afr 套火项圈烧死

necklet /ˈŋeklɪt/ *n* 项圈

neckline /ˈneklaɪn/ *n* 领口; **a plunging ~** 深V字领

neck: ~ scarf *n* 围巾; **~tie** *n* Amer 领带

necromancer /ˈnekrəʊmænsə(r)/ *n* **1** (medium) 通灵者 **2** (witch doctor) 巫师

necromancy /ˈnekrəʊmænsi/ *n* [u] **1** (divination) 通灵术 **2** (black magic) 巫术

necrophilia /ˌnekrəˈfɪlɪə/ *n* [u] 恋尸癖

necrophiliac /ˌnekrəˈfɪlɪæk/

A *adj* 恋尸的 ‹practice, fantasy, tendency›

B *n* 恋尸者

necropolis /neˈkrɒpəlɪs/ *n* 墓地 [尤指古代城市的大墓地]

necrosis /neˈkrəʊsɪs/ *n* [u] 坏死

nectar /ˈnektə(r)/ *n* [u] **1** Bot 花蜜 **2** Mythol 众神饮的酒 **3** fig (delicious drink) 甘美的饮料

nectarine /ˈnektərɪn/ *n* **1** (fruit) 油桃 **2** (tree) 油桃树

neddy /ˈnedi/ *n* Brit dated child lang 驴

née /neɪ/ *adj* 娘家姓…的; **Gemma Jay, ~ Hayes** 杰玛·杰伊, 原姓海斯

need /niːd/

A *modal aux* (must, have to) 必须; **you ~n't have hurried** 你本没有必要匆匆忙忙的; **it ~ only be said that …** 只需要说…; **~ he reply?** 他必须回复吗?; **it ~n't be the case** 情况不一定如此

B *vt* **1** (require, want) 需要; **I ~ a drink** 我想要一杯饮料; **that's all I ~!** 我受够了! **2** (have to) 定要; **all you ~ to do is to complete this form** 你要做的就是填写这张表; **you ~ to learn some manners** 你要学会一些礼貌; **why do you always ~ to complain?** 你为什么总是要抱怨?

C *n* **1** [u and c] (necessity, want) 需要; **to answer a ~** 满足需要; **I'll carry the box — no ~** 我来拿这个盒子——不用了; **there's no ~ for panic/anger** 没必要恐慌/发脾气; **to be in ~ of sth.** 需要某物; **I'm in ~ of some fresh air** 我想呼吸一点新鲜空气; **when/as/if the ~ arises** 必要时; **if ~ be** 如果有必要的话 **2** [u] (adversity, distress) 困窘; **assistance in time of ~** 在不幸之时的帮助; **in sb.'s hour of ~** 在某人困难的时候 **3** [u] (poverty) 贫困; **to be in ~** 处于贫困之中; **families/children in ~** 贫穷的家庭/儿童 **4** [c] (requirement) 必需品; **day-to-day ~s** 每日必需品; **manpower/energy ~s** 人力/能源需求

needful /ˈniːdfl/

A *adj* formal 必要的

B *n* [u] 必要的事; **to do the ~** 做需要做的事

neediness /ˈniːdɪnɪs/ *n* [u] 贫困

needle /ˈniːdl/

A *n* **1** [c] (for sewing) 针; **to thread a ~** 穿针; **as sharp as a ~** 非常机敏; **like searching for** *or* **trying to find a ~ in a haystack** 犹如大海捞针般困难 **2** [c] (for knitting, crochet, lacemaking) 钩针 **3** [c] Med 注射针; **to be on the ~** Amer 打毒针成瘾 **4** [c] (for acupuncture) 毫针 **5** [c] (on dial, compass) 指针 **6** [c] Bot 针叶 **7** [c] (on record player) 唱针 **8** [u] Brit colloq (hostility) 敌意 **9** [u] Brit colloq (annoyance) **to get the ~** 被惹恼; **to give sb. the ~** 惹恼某人

B *vt* 惹恼; **to ~ sb. about sth.** 用某事激怒某人; **to ~ sb. into sth./doing sth.** 刺激某人做某事

needle: ~craft *n* [u] (sewing) 缝纫手艺; (embroidery) 刺绣技巧; **~ exchange** *n* **1** [u] (action) 针头交换服务 [为吸毒者提供消毒针头的服务]; **2** [c] (place) 针头交换处; **~ game, ~ match** *ns* colloq 死对头间的比赛; **~point** *n* [u] 帆布刺绣

needless /ˈniːdlɪs/ *adj* 不必要的; **~ to say** 不用说

needlessly /ˈniːdlɪsli/ *adv* 不必要地

needlework /ˈniːdlwɜːk/ *n* [u] **1** (items) (of sewing) 缝制品; (of embroidery) 刺绣品 **2** (activity) (of sewing) 缝纫; (of embroidery) 刺绣

need-to-know *adj attrib* 需要知晓的; **on a ~ basis** 按照需要知晓的准则

needy /ˈniːdi/

A *adj* 贫穷的

B *npl* **the ~** 穷人

ne'er /neə(r)/ *adv* archaic 永远不

ne'er-do-well /ˈneəduːwel/

A *n* pej 没出息的人

B *adj* pej 游手好闲的 ‹person, rascal›

nefarious /nɪˈfeərɪəs/ *adj* formal 恶毒的 ‹deed, scheme, crime›

negate /nɪˈgeɪt/ *vt* **1** (cancel out) 取消 ‹effect, influence›; 使…无效 ‹achievement, efforts›; **this change of policy completely ~s everything we have achieved** 政策的变化使我们所取得的一切化为泡影 **2** (deny, invalidate) 否定 ‹importance, existence, theory› **3** Ling, Philos 使…变成否定 ‹sentence, meaning›; 使…变为否定命题 ‹proposition›

negation /nɪˈgeɪʃn/ *n* [u] **1** (contradiction, opposite) 对立面 **2** (denial) 否定 **3** Ling 否定式; Philos 否定命题

negative /ˈnegətɪv/

A *adj* **1** (saying no) 否定的 ‹statement, reply›; **to give a ~ answer** 给予否定的答复 **2** (pessimistic, unhelpful, unfavourable) 消极的 ‹response, attitude, criticism›; **to be ~ about sth.** 对某事持消极态度; **don't be so ~!** 不要太悲观! **3** (harmful) 负面的 ‹feelings, experience, influence› **4** Phys, Electron 负的 ‹charge, particle, ion›; **~ terminal/wire** 负极端子/负极引线 **5** Med 阴性的 ‹result, test› **6** Math 负的 ‹number, quantity› **7** Phot 负的 ‹photograph, image›

B *n* **1** (refusal) 否定; **to answer** *or* **reply in the ~** 作出否定回答 **2** Ling (word) 否定词; (grammatical construction) 否定式; **in the ~** 否定的 **3** Phot 底片 **4** Phys, Electron 负电 **5** (disadvantage, down side) 负面因素; **the ~s outweigh the positives** 负面因素超过了正面因素

negative equity *n* [u] 负资产

negatively /ˈnegətɪvli/ *adv* **1** (pessimistically, unhelpfully, unfavourably) 消极地 ‹react, view, comment› **2** (harmfully) 负面地 ‹affect, influence› **3** Phys, Electron 负极地; **~ charged ions** 负离子

negative sign *n* = **minus sign**

neglect /nɪˈglekt/

A *vt* **1** (fail to care for) 疏于照管 ‹child, building, health, appearance›; **to ~ oneself** (one's health) 不注意自己的健康; (one's appearance) 不修边幅 **2** (ignore) 忽视 ‹friendship, problem, needs›; **to ~ one's duty** 玩忽职守; **to ~ work** 旷工 **3** (underestimate) 不重视 ‹factor, artist, work› **4** (fail) 遗漏; **to ~ to do sth.** 漏做某事; **the police ~ed to inform the child's parents** 警方忘记通知孩子的父母了 **5** (overlook) 不抓住 ‹offer, opportunity›

B *n* [u] **1** (lack of care) 忽视; **to fall into ~** 被忽视; **to be in a state of ~** 处于无人照管的状态; **~ of one's health/appearance** 对自己健康的忽视/不修边幅 **2** (failure to carry out) 疏忽; **~ of sth.** 对某事的疏忽; **~ of duty** 玩忽职守

neglected /nɪˈglektɪd/ *adj* **1** (uncared for) 未被妥善照管的 ‹child, animal, building› **2** (ignored) 被忽视的 ‹child, friendship, family›; **to feel ~** 感觉被忽视 **3** (overlooked) 不受重视的 ‹factor, artist, work›

neglectful /nɪˈglektfl/ *adj* 疏忽的; **to be ~ of sth./sb.** 疏忽某物/某人

neglectfully /nɪˈglektfʊli/ *adv* 疏忽地 ‹behave, forget›

negligee, négligée /ˈneglɪʒeɪ, Amer ˌneglɪˈʒeɪ/ *n* 女式晨衣

negligence /ˈneglɪdʒəns/ *n* [u] **1** (carelessness) 疏忽 **2** Jur 不作为; **medical ~** 医疗事故

negligent /ˈneglɪdʒənt/ *adj* **1** (failing in one's duty, responsibility) 疏忽的 ‹official, doctor, parents›; **to be ~ of sth.** 忽视某事; **to be ~ in one's duties** formal 玩忽职守 **2** (careless) 粗心大意的 ‹person, driving›; **to be ~ in one's work** 工作粗心

negligently /ˈneglɪdʒəntlɪ/ *adv* 马虎地

negligible /ˈneglɪdʒəbl/ *adj* 可忽略不计的 ‹amount, difference›

negotiable /nɪˈgəʊʃəbl/ *adj* **1** (to be agreed) 可协商的 ‹price, demand, term›; **the offer is not ~** 报价不可协商; **'salary ~'** "薪水面谈" **2** Comm 可转让的 ‹cheque, asset, contract› **3** (passable) 可通行的 ‹road, river›

negotiable instrument, negotiable security *ns* 流通票据

negotiate /nɪˈgəʊʃɪeɪt/

A *vi* 谈判; **to ~ about** *or* **over sth.** 协商某事; **to ~ for sth.** 谈判谋求某物; **to ~ with sb.** 与某人谈判

B *vt* **1** (discuss) 商定 ‹sale, loan, salary›; 谈成 ‹agreement› **2** (manoeuvre around) 顺利通过 ‹bend, narrow street›; 成功越过 ‹obstacle, hill› **3** (deal with) 解决 ‹problem, difficulty›; 通过 ‹interview, test› **4** Fin 转让 ‹cheque, bond, securities›

negotiating /nɪˈgəʊʃɪeɪtɪŋ/ *adj attrib* 谈判的 ‹team, skill, strategy›; **to get round the ~ table** 坐到谈判桌前; **a ~ position** 谈判立场

negotiation /nɪˌgəʊʃɪˈeɪʃn/ *n* 谈判; **to enter into ~(s) with sb.** 开始和某人谈判; **by ~** 通过谈判; **to be under ~** 在协商中

negotiator /nɪˈgəʊʃɪeɪtə(r)/ *n* 谈判者; **the chief union ~** 工会首席谈判代表

Negress /ˈniːgrɪs/ *n* dated or offensive 女黑人

Negro /ˈniːgrəʊ/ dated or offensive

A *n* (pl **~es**) 黑人

B *adj* 黑人的 ‹race, origin›; **~ slaves** 黑奴

Negroid /ˈniːgrɔɪd/ *adj* dated or offensive 黑人的 ‹features, races›

Negro spiritual *n* 黑人灵歌

neigh /neɪ/

A *vi* 嘶鸣

B *n* 马嘶声

neighbour Brit, **neighbor** Amer /ˈneɪbə(r)/

A *n* **1** (person living close by) 邻居; **she's our next-door ~** 她是我们的隔壁邻居; **an upstairs/a downstairs ~** 楼上/楼下邻居 **2** (adjacent person) 邻近的人; (object) 邻近的物;

Negation

■ In Chinese, although 不 and 没／没有 are both adverbs of negation, they are used in different ways.

The use of 不

In declarative sentences

■ To express an habitual action either in the past or in the present:

I did not smoke before
= 我以前不抽烟

I never go to the pub
= 我从不去酒吧

The shop doesn't sell fruit
= 那家商店不卖水果

■ To express what is not happening now or is not going to happen in the future:

The tickets are not being sold now
= 现在不卖票

He is not going abroad this year
= 他今年不出国

I will never get married
= 我永远不结婚

■ To negate verbs expressing mental activities such as 认识／知道 (know), 了解／明白 (understand), etc.:

He did not understand what I said
= 他不明白我说的（话）

I have no idea of what is going on
= 我不知道出了什么事

She does not know me
= 她不认识我

They don't like vegetables
= 他们不喜欢（吃）蔬菜

■ In verb-complement phrases such as 拿不动, 做不好／来, 装不下, 看不见, etc. to indicate inability to achieve the action:

I am unable to move the box
= 我搬不动这箱子

I can't do it
= 我做不来

I don't understand his accent
= 我听不懂他的口音

■ Before auxiliary verbs:

They shouldn't have done this
= 他们本不应该做这件事

I can't swim
= 我不会游泳

She dare not go out at night
= 她不敢晚上出去

■ In constructions such as 不是…, 不像…, 不在…, 不存在…, etc.:

She is not an actress
= 她不是演员

Colin doesn't look like his father
= 科林长得不像他父亲

Ghosts do not exist
= 鬼并不存在

■ Before adjectives of general description such as 高兴 (happy), 大 (big), 整齐 (tidy), 漂亮 (beautiful), etc.:

The room is not big
= 房间不大

Your answer is not right
= 你的回答不对

He is not thin
= 他不瘦

■ Before adverbs of degree like 太, 很, 完全, 十分, etc.:

The hotel is not very clean
= 这家旅馆不太干净

I'm not a hundred per cent sure about it
= 我对这事不十分有把握

I don't agree with you completely
= 我不完全同意你

In response to a question

■ When questions are posed in the affirmative and also fall into one of the above-mentioned situations:

Do you smoke? — No, I don't
= 你抽烟吗？—— 不，我不抽

Is she watching TV? — No, she isn't
= 她在看电视吗？—— 不，她没在看

Are you going to buy these books? — No, we aren't
= 你们要买这些书吗？—— 不，我们不买

Can you ride a bicycle? — No, I can't
= 你会骑自行车吗？—— 不，我不会

Is the house beautiful? — No, it isn't
= 房子漂亮吗？—— 不，不漂亮

■ When questions are posed in the negative, 不 is used to deny the negative and 是（的）is used to affirm the negative. This is the opposite to the English convention in which 'yes' is used to deny the negative and 'no' to affirm the negative:

Aren't you hungry? — Yes, I'm hungry
= 你不饿吗？—— 不，我饿

Isn't she coming to the party tonight? — Yes, she is
= 她今晚不来参加聚会吗？—— 不，她来

Haven't you seen her? — No, I haven't
= 你没见过她吗？—— 是的，我没见过

Didn't he see the film yesterday? — No, he didn't
= 他昨天没看电影吗？—— 是，他没看

■ In tag questions, when the statement is in the affirmative, 是（的）is used to affirm the statement and 不 is used to negate the statement. This is consistent with English 'yes' and 'no' answers.

However, if the statement is in the negative, 是（的）is used to affirm the statement and 不 is used to negate the statement. This is opposite to the English convention in which 'yes' negates the statement and 'no' affirms the statement:

He likes playing basketball, doesn't he? — No, he doesn't
= 他喜欢打篮球，不是吗？
—— 不，他不喜欢

The TV is new, isn't it? — Yes, it is
= 这个电视是新的，不是吗？
—— 是的，它是新的

She didn't attend the lecture, did she? — Yes, she did
= 她没有听演讲，是吗？—— 不，她听了

The use of 没／没有

■ 没 is used as the negative form of 有 (equivalent to 'to have' or 'there is/are'). When 有 takes an object in Chinese, 没 on its own can denote negation (有 can be omitted in such sentences):

I don't have a black skirt
= 我没（有）黑裙子

There is nobody in the office
= 办公室里没（有）人

They don't have English dictionaries
= 他们没（有）英语词典

■ Certain English adjectives (eg 'rich', 'polite') are translated idiomatically as '有 + abstract noun' (eg 有钱, 有礼貌). The negative form of this is '没 or 没有 + abstract noun':

The lady is not rich
= 这位女士没（有）钱

The film is not interesting
= 这部电影没（有）意思

The actor is not famous
= 这个男演员没（有）名气

■ 没 or 没有 (equivalent to 'not') is used to express what did not happen in the past or what has not yet happened:

I did not attend the lecture yesterday
= 我昨天没（有）听演讲

The concert has not started
= 音乐会还没开始

They did not come to see me
= 他们没（有）来看我

They have not finished their homework
= 他们还没（有）完成作业

■ 没有 is used in responses to questions where a completed action or past experience is indicated, or where the verb 'to have' or the construction 'there is/are' are used. Note that in this case the question must be in the affirmative:

Did you go to the party last night? — No
= 你昨晚参加聚会了吗？—— 没有

Have you ever been to Shanghai? — No
= 你去过上海吗？—— 没有

Have you got a younger sister? — No
= 你有妹妹吗？—— 没有

■ However, if the questions in the above examples are posed in the negative, 是的 is used in the answer to affirm the negative, unlike in English when 'no' would be used:

Didn't you go to the party last night? — No, I didn't
= 你昨晚没参加聚会吗？
—— 是的，没有参加

Haven't you been to Shanghai? — No, I haven't
= 你没去过上海吗？—— 是的，没有去过

Haven't you got a younger sister? — No, I haven't
= 你没有妹妹吗？—— 是的，没有

(country) 邻国; **Spain's nearest ～s are France and Portugal** 西班牙最邻近的国家是法国和葡萄牙 **3** (esp Relig) 他人; **love thy ～ as thyself** 当爱人如己; **(to be) a good ～ (做)** 一个好人

B *vt* «*house, place*» 与…为邻

neighbourhood Brit, **neighborhood** Amer /ˈneɪbəhʊd/

A *n* **1** [c] (district) 社区; **the theatre in our ～** 在我们地段的戏院 **2** [u] (vicinity) 邻近地区; **in the ～ of the station** 在车站附近

B *modif* 近邻的 ‹*school, clinic*›

neighbourhood watch *n* 居民联防

neighbouring Brit, **neighboring** Amer /ˈneɪbərɪŋ/ *adj* 邻近的

neighbourliness Brit, **neighborliness** Amer /ˈneɪbəlɪnɪs/ *n* [u] 睦邻友好

neighbourly Brit, **neighborly** Amer /ˈneɪbəli/ *adj* 友好的 ‹*action, gesture*›; **～ relations between two countries** 两国间的睦邻友好关系; **it was very ～ of her (to do that)** 她(那样做)很友好

neighing /ˈneɪɪŋ/ *n* [u] 马嘶声

neither /ˈnaɪðə(r), ˈniːð-/

A *conj* 都不; **～ ... nor ...** 既不…也不…; **～ tea, coffee, nor milk** 既不是茶或咖啡，也不是牛奶; **～ Peter nor I was there** 彼得和我都不在那里; ▸**here A1**

B *adv* 也不; **I don't like him — ～ do I** 我不喜欢他——我也不喜欢他; **I don't know — me ～** colloq 我不知道——我也不知道

C *det* 两者都不; **～ answer is correct** 两个答案都不对; **in ～ case** 两种情况都不

D *pron* 两者都不; **～ is suitable** 两个都不合适; **～ of them can drive** 他们两个都不会开车

Nelly, Nellie /ˈneli/ *n* colloq **1** (silly person) 傻瓜 **2** Brit **not on your ～!** (certainly not) 绝对不行!

nelson /ˈnelsn/ *n* 肩下握颈; **a full/half ～** 双/单肩下握颈

nem con /ˌnemˈkɒn/ *adv* 全体一致地 ‹*pass, elect*›

nemesis /ˈneməsɪs/ *n* (*pl* **nemeses** /ˈneməsiːz/) formal or liter 克星; **to be sb.'s ～** 是某人的克星; **to meet one's ～** 遇到劲敌

neoclassical /ˌniːəʊˈklæsɪkl/ *adj* 新古典主义的

neoclassicism /ˌniːəʊˈklæsɪsɪzəm/ *n* [u] 新古典主义

neocolonial /ˌniːəʊkəˈləʊnɪəl/ *adj* 新殖民主义的

neocolonialism /ˌniːəʊkəˈləʊnɪəlɪzəm/ *n* [u] 新殖民主义

neocon /ˈniːəʊkɒn/ *adj, n* colloq = **neoconservative**

neoconservative /ˌniːəʊkənˈsɜːvətɪv/

A *n* 新保守主义者

B *adj* 新保守主义者的 ‹*policy, philosophy*›

> **neoconservative**
>
> 新保守主义者，非正式语境中亦简称neocon，多含贬义。新保守主义是美国的一种政治思潮，兴起于20世纪70年代，9·11事件(▸**9/11**)后影响骤增。和传统的保守主义相比，较少关注社会问题。新保守主义者认为美国是世界超级大国，应在全世界推行自己的价值观，必要时不惜使用武力，这样才能确保美国自身的安全。新保守主义者外交上多推行单边主义(unilateralism)，不注重国际合作。对伊拉克发动的战争即是新保守主义思想的产物之一。

neodymium /ˌniːəʊˈdɪmɪəm/ *n* [u] 钕

neofascism /ˌniːəʊˈfæʃɪzəm/ *n* [u] 新法西斯主义

neofascist /ˌniːəʊˈfæʃɪst/

A *n* 新法西斯主义者

B *adj* 新法西斯主义的 ‹*party, government, ideology*›

Neolithic /ˌniːəˈlɪθɪk/

A *adj* 新石器时代的 ‹*man, settlement, tool*›

B *n* **the ～** 新石器时代

neologism /niːˈɒlədʒɪzəm/ *n* 新词

neon /ˈniːɒn/

A *n* [u] 氖

B *adj* **1** Chem 氖的 ‹*gas, atom*› **2** (in lighting) 霓虹的; **a ～ sign/light** 霓虹灯广告牌/霓虹灯

neonatal /ˌniːəʊˈneɪtl/ *adj* (human) 新生儿的 ‹*ward, care*›; (mammal) 初生哺乳动物的 ‹*survival*›

neonate /ˈniːəʊneɪt/ *n* formal **1** (newborn baby) 新生儿; (mammal) 初生哺乳动物 **2** Med (baby up to one month) 未满月的婴儿

neo-Nazi /ˌniːəʊˈnɑːtsi/

A *n* 新纳粹分子

B *adj* 新纳粹分子的 ‹*group*›; 新纳粹主义的 ‹*slogan*›

neo-Nazism /ˌniːəʊˈnɑːtsɪzəm/, **neo-Naziism** /ˌniːəʊˈnɑːtsɪɪzəm/ *ns* [u] 新纳粹主义

neophyte /ˈniːəfaɪt/ *n* **1** (newcomer) 新手; **a ～ director** 新导演 **2** Relig 新入教者

neoprene /ˈniːəpriːn/ *n* [u] 氯丁橡胶; **a ～ wetsuit** 氯丁橡胶潜水服

Nepal /nɪˈpɔːl/ *pr n* 尼泊尔

Nepalese /ˌnepəˈliːz/ ▸**p. 503, p. 426**

A *adj* (of Nepal) 尼泊尔的; (of the people) 尼泊尔人的; (of the language) 尼泊尔语的

B *n* **1** [c] (person) 尼泊尔人 **2** [u] (language) 尼泊尔语

Nepali /nɪˈpɔːli/ ▸**p. 503, p. 426**

A *adj* (of Nepal) 尼泊尔的; (of the people) 尼泊尔人的; (of the language) 尼泊尔语的

B *n* **1** [c] (*pl* **～** *or* **～s**) (person) 尼泊尔人 **2** [u] (language) 尼泊尔语

nephew /ˈnevjuː, ˈnef-/ ▸**p. 419** *n* (son of brother) 侄子; (son of sister) 外甥

nephritis /nɪˈfraɪtɪs/ ▸**p. 377** *n* [u] 肾炎; **acute/chronic ～** 急性/慢性肾炎

nepotism /ˈnepətɪzəm/ *n* [u] 任人唯亲

Neptune /ˈneptjuːn/ *pr n* 海王星

neptunium /nepˈtjuːnɪəm/ *n* [u] 镎

NERC *abbr* Brit = **Natural Environment Research Council** 自然环境研究委员会

nerd /nɜːd/ *n* colloq pej 书呆子; **a computer ～** 电脑迷

nerdy /ˈnɜːdi/ *adj* colloq pej 书呆子似的

nerve /nɜːv/

A *n* **1** [c] Anat 神经; **to touch** *or* **hit a (raw) ～** 触及要害; **to strain every ～ (to do sth.)** 竭尽全力(做某事); **～ fibres** 神经纤维 **2** [u] (courage) 勇气; **to have the ～ to do sth.** 有勇气做某事; **to keep one's ～** 保持镇定; **to lose/regain one's ～** 失去/恢复勇气; **to get up enough ～ to do sth.** 鼓足勇气做某事; **a test of ～** 对意志力的考验 **3** [u] colloq (impudence) 厚脸皮; **to have the ～ to do sth.** 竟有脸做某事; **of all the ～!** 厚颜无耻!

B **nerves** *npl* 神经质; **to suffer from ～s** 神经紧张; **(to have) an attack** *or* **a fit of ～s** 神经紧张; **to be a bag** *or* **bundle of ～s** 十分紧张; **it's only ～s!** 只是过于紧张!; **my ～s are on edge** 我神经紧张; **to calm sb.'s ～s** 使某人镇定; **to get on sb.'s ～s** 惹某人心烦; **that noise is getting on my ～s** colloq 那噪音使我心绪烦躁; **a war** *or* **battle of ～s** 神经战; **～s of steel** 钢铁般的意志

C *vt* 激励; **to ～ oneself to do sth./for sth.** 鼓起勇气做某事

nerve: ～ cell *n* 神经元; **～ centre** *n* Anat 神经中枢; fig 核心; **～ ending** *n* 神经末梢; **～ gas** *n* [u and c] 神经性毒气; **～ impulse** *n* 神经冲动

nerveless /ˈnɜːvlɪs/ *adj* **1** (from cold) 麻木的 ‹*fingers, limbs*›; (from fear, fatigue) 无力的 ‹*grasp*› **2** (brave) 无畏的 ‹*person, defiance, performance*›; 镇定的 ‹*gaze*›

nerve-racking, nerve-wracking *adj* 使人心烦的 ‹*experience, wait*›

nerviness /ˈnɜːvɪnɪs/ *n* [u] Brit 紧张

nervous /ˈnɜːvəs/ *adj* **1** (anxious) 局促不安的 ‹*person, feeling*›; **to be ～ about sth./doing sth.** 对某事/做某事感到紧张; **to make sb. (feel) ～** «*wait, height*» 使某人(感到)提心吊胆; **to be in a ～ state** 紧张不安 **2** (easily alarmed) 神经质的 ‹*person, animal, disposition, smile*› **3** (tense) 绷紧的 ‹*manner, movement*›; **a ～ handshake** 紧张的握手; **～ handwriting** 僵硬的笔迹 **4** *attrib* Anat, Med 神经的 ‹*disease, disorder*›; **～ exhaustion** 神经疲惫; **～ tension** 神经紧张

nervous: ～ breakdown *n* 神经衰弱; **～ energy** *n* [u] 紧张的精力

nervously /ˈnɜːvəsli/ *adv* 紧张不安地 ‹*smoke, pace, smile*›

nervousness /ˈnɜːvəsnɪs/ *n* [u] **1** (anxiety) 紧张 **2** (misgivings) 担心 **3** (tenseness) 绷紧; (excitability) 神经质; **the ～ of his movements/handwriting** 他的动作/笔迹的僵硬 **4** Fin (instability) 波动; (decline) 下行

nervous: ～ system *n* 神经系统; **～ wreck** *n* colloq 精神脆弱的人

nervy /ˈnɜːvi/ *adj* **1** Brit (anxious) 紧张不安的 ‹*person, animal*›; **to be ～ about sth.** 对某事感到紧张不安 **2** Amer colloq (brazen) 脸皮厚的 ‹*person, action*›

nest /nest/

A *n* **1** (of bird, animal) 窝; **to build** *or* **make a ～** 筑巢; **a wasps'/an ants' ～** 黄蜂/蚂蚁窝; **to leave** *or* **fly the ～** 离家独立生活; **to feather one's (own) ～** 营私自肥 **2** (group) **a ～ of sth.** 一窝 ‹*mice, birds, kittens*› **3** fig (comfortable place) 安乐窝; **a ～ of cushions** 一堆舒适的靠垫 **4** (set) **a ～ of sth.** [可套叠的] 一套 ‹*tables, boxes, bowls*› **5** (gun site) 掩体; **a machine-gun ～** 机枪掩体

B *vi* **1** Zool 筑巢 **2** (fit together) 使套叠; **to ～ into one another** «*tables, boxes*» 互相叠套

nest box *n* 鸟巢箱

nested /ˈnestɪd/ *adj* **1** (fitting together) 套叠的 ‹*tables, boxes, set*› **2** Comput, Math, Ling 嵌套的 ‹*loop, function, construction*›

nest egg *n* 储备金

nesting /ˈnestɪŋ/ *n* [u] 筑巢; **the ～ season/habits** 筑巢期/习性

nesting: ～ box *n* 鸟巢箱; **～ site** *n* 筑巢地

nestle /ˈnesl/

A *vi* **1** (settle) «*person, cat*» 安卧; **to ～ into an armchair** 舒适地躺在单人沙发里 **2** (lie) «*village, object*» 半隐半现; **the house ～s** *or* **is ～d among the trees** 房屋掩隐在树林之中

B *vt* 使…紧贴 ‹*head, body*›; **to ～ a baby in one's arms** 怀里抱个婴儿; **to ～ one's head on sb.'s shoulder** 把头偎依在某人肩上

Phrasal verbs

- **nestle down** *vi* 安卧; **to ～ down in bed** 舒适地躺在床上
- **nestle up** *vi* 偎依; **to ～ up against** *or* **to sb./sth.** 偎依着某人/某物

nestling /ˈneslɪŋ/ *n* 雏鸟

net[1] /net/

A *n* **1** (for fishing etc.) 网 **2** Sport 球网; **to hit the ball into the ～** (tennis) 击球落网; **to come in to** *or* **up to the ～** (tennis) 靠近球网; **to put the ball in** *or* **into the back of the ～** (football) 把球打入网 **3** fig (trap) 罗网; **the ～ was closing in around her** 这张罗网正向她罩过来; **to be caught in the ～** 落网; **to slip through** *or* **escape the ～** 漏网 **4** fig (system for selecting) 选拔机制; **to slip through** *or* **escape the ～** 被遗漏; **to cast the** *or* **one's ～ wide** 广泛撒网 **5** Telecom (network) 通信网 **6** (hairnet) 发网 **7** Tex 网眼织物;

a veil of white ~ 白色网状面纱 **8** (Internet) **the Net** 因特网; **to surf the Net** 上网
B *vt* (*pres p etc.* **-tt-**) **1** (catch with net) 用网捕 **2** fig (acquire through skill) 获得 ‹*prize, trophy, fortune*› **3** (gain as profit) 净赚 ‹*profit, sum of money*›; 从…中净赚 ‹*sale, deal*›; **to ~ sth. from sth.** 从某物中净赚某物; **to ~ sb. sth., to ~ sth. for sb.** «*venture, deal*» 使…净赚某物 **4** (trap) 抓获 ‹*criminal*› **5** Agric, Hort 用网罩住 ‹*trees, seedlings*›
C *vi* colloq 进球

net² *adj* **1** (after tax, weight deduction) 净的 ‹*profit, price, weight*›; **~ of tax/packaging** 税后净额/扣除包装材料后净重; **a profit of £100 ~** 100 英镑的净利润; **20 kilograms ~** 净重 20 公斤; **terms strictly ~** [一切包括在内的] 费用总额 **2** *attrib* (overall) 最终的 ‹*result, increase*›

net: ~ asset value *n* 资产净值; **~ball** *n* **1** [u] (sport) 无挡板篮球 [一种女子球类运动]; **~ball player/court** 无挡板篮球运动员/球场; **2** [c] (ball) [无挡板篮球运动用的] 篮球; **~ cord** *n* **1** (shot) 擦网好球; **2** (cord) 球网吊绳; **~ curtain** *n* 网眼帘; **Net generation** *n* colloq 网络一代; **Nethead, nethead** *n* colloq 网民

nether /ˈneðə(r)/ *adj* dated 下面的 ‹*parts, reaches, edges*›

Netherlands /ˈneðələndz/ *pr n* **the ~** + *v sing or pl* 荷兰

nethermost /ˈneðəməʊst/ *adj* dated 最下面的 ‹*depths, point*›

nether: ~ regions *npl* **1** (lower part) 边地; **into the ~ regions of sth.** 进入某处的下部; **2** euph (of body) 下身; **3** (hell) **= ~world**; **~world** *n* liter **the ~world** 阴间

netiquette /ˈnetɪket/ *n* [u] colloq 网络礼仪

netizen /ˈnetɪzn/ *n* colloq 网民

netpreneur /ˌnetprəˈnɜː(r)/, **netrepreneur** /ˌnetrəprəˈnɜː(r)/ *ns* colloq 网络企业家

net present value *n* 净现值

netspeak /ˈnetspiːk/ *n* [u] colloq 网络用语

netsurfer /ˈnetsɜːfə(r)/ *n* 网上冲浪者

netsurfing /ˈnetsɜːfɪŋ/ *n* [u] 网上冲浪

nett /net/ *adj* Brit **= net²**

netting /ˈnetɪŋ/ *n* [u] 网状物

nettle /ˈnetl/
A *n* 荨麻; **to grasp** *or* **seize the ~** fig 快刀斩乱麻
B *vt* «*person, remarks, behaviour*» 惹恼; **to ~ sb. into doing sth.** 激某人做某事

nettlesome /ˈnetlsəm/ *adj* esp Amer **1** (annoying) 恼人的 ‹*comments, children, chore*› **2** (irritable) 易激怒的 ‹*person, mood*›

network /ˈnetwɜːk/
A *n* 网络; **a ~ of paths/tunnels** 纵横交错的小道/隧道; **a large ~ of contacts** 巨大的关系网; **the old-boys ~** 老同学关系网; **a spy/terrorist ~** 间谍网/恐怖分子网络; **a ~ of roads/canals/railways** 公路/运河/铁路网; **the TV ~s** 电视网; **a wireless/broadband ~** 无线网/宽带网
B *vt* **1** Comput, Tech (link) 把…联网 **2** Brit (broadcast) 联播 ‹*programme*›
C *vi* 建立关系网; **to ~ with buyers throughout Europe** 与欧洲各地的买家建立关系网

networkable /ˈnetwɜːkəbl/ *adj* 可联网的 ‹*device, application*›

network cable *n* 网线

networker /ˈnetwɜːkə(r)/ *n* **1** (person who uses contacts) [为促进职业发展] 建立信息交流网的人 **2** (person who works from home) [利用电脑网络] 在家工作的员工

networking /ˈnetwɜːkɪŋ/ *n* [u] **1** (using contacts) 建立关系网; **a ~ event** 联谊活动 **2** (working from home) [利用电脑网络实现的] 在家工作 **3** Comput 联网

network: ~ operator *n* 网络运营商; **~ television** *n* [u] 全国电视联播

neural /ˈnjʊərəl, Amer ˈnʊ-/ *adj attrib* (of nervous system) 神经系统的 ‹*functions, dysfunction*›; (of nerves) 神经的 ‹*pathways*›

neuralgia /ˌnjʊəˈrældʒə, Amer ˌnʊ-/ ▸**p. 377** *n* [u] 神经痛

neuralgic /ˌnjʊəˈrældʒɪk, Amer ˌnʊ-/ *adj* 神经痛的; **the spasms are definitely ~** 这种痉挛绝对是神经痛引起的

neural network *n* 神经网络

neuritis /ˌnjʊəˈraɪtɪs, Amer ˌnʊ-/ ▸**p. 377** *n* [u] 神经炎

neurobiology /ˌnjʊərəʊbaɪˈɒlədʒɪ, Amer ˌnʊ-/ *n* [u] 神经生物学

neurological /ˌnjʊərəˈlɒdʒɪkl, Amer ˌnʊ-/ *adj* (of neurology) 神经病学的 ‹*specialist*›; (of nervous system) 神经系统的 ‹*disease*›

neurologist /ˌnjʊˈrɒlədʒɪst, Amer ˌnʊ-/ ▸**p. 409** *n* (doctor) 神经科医生; (scientist) 神经病学家

neurology /ˌnjʊəˈrɒlədʒɪ, Amer ˌnʊ-/ *n* [u] 神经学

neuromuscular /ˌnjʊərəʊˈmʌskjʊlə(r), Amer ˌnʊ-/ *adj* 神经肌肉的 ‹*cell, disorder*›

neuron /ˈnjʊərɒn, Amer ˈnʊ-/, **neurone** /ˈnjʊərəʊn, Amer ˈnʊ-/ *ns* 神经元

neuropathology /ˌnjʊərəʊpəˈθɒlədʒɪ, Amer ˌnʊ-/ *n* [u] 神经病理学

neuropathy /ˌnjʊəˈrɒpəθɪ, Amer ˌnʊ-/ *n* [u] 神经病

neurophysiological /ˌnjʊərəʊˌfɪzɪəˈlɒdʒɪkl, Amer ˌnʊ-/ *adj* 神经生理学的 ‹*disorder, research*›

neurophysiologist /ˌnjʊərəʊˌfɪzɪˈɒlədʒɪst, Amer ˌnʊ-/ ▸**p. 409** *n* 神经生理学家

neurophysiology /ˌnjʊərəʊˌfɪzɪˈɒlədʒɪ, Amer ˌnʊ-/ *n* [u] 神经生理学

neuropsychiatric /ˌnjʊərəʊˌsaɪkɪˈætrɪk, Amer ˌnʊ-/ *adj* 神经精神病学的 ‹*research, disorder*›

neuropsychiatrist /ˌnjʊərəʊsaɪˈkaɪətrɪst, Amer ˌnʊ-/ ▸**p. 409** *n* 神经精神病学家

neuropsychiatry /ˌnjʊərəʊsaɪˈkaɪətrɪ, Amer ˌnʊ-/ *n* [u] 神经精神病学

neurosis /ˌnjʊəˈrəʊsɪs, Amer nʊ-/ *n* (*pl* **neuroses**) **1** Med 神经症 **2** fig (fear) 过分恐惧; **to have a ~ about sth.** 对某事物极度恐惧

neurosurgeon /ˌnjʊərəʊˈsɜːdʒn, Amer ˌnʊ-/ ▸**p. 409** *n* 神经外科医生

neurosurgery /ˌnjʊərəʊˈsɜːdʒərɪ, Amer ˌnʊ-/ *n* [u] (study) 神经外科学; (operation) 神经外科手术

neurosurgical /ˌnjʊərəʊˈsɜːdʒɪkl, Amer ˌnʊ-/ *adj attrib* 神经外科的 ‹*clinic, techniques*›

neurotic /ˌnjʊəˈrɒtɪk, Amer nʊ-/
A *adj* **1** Med 患神经症的 ‹*patient*›; **~ fear** 恐惧性神经症 **2** fig (anxious) 神经质的 ‹*person, obsession*›; **to be ~ about sth./doing sth.** 对某事/做某事极为焦虑
B *n* Med 神经症患者

neurotically /ˌnjʊəˈrɒtɪklɪ, Amer nʊ-/ *adv* **1** Med 在神经症方面 ‹*fixated*›; **to be ~ afraid of failure** 患神经症般害怕失败 **2** fig (anxiously) 神经质地 ‹*behave, worry*›

neuroticism /ˌnjʊəˈrɒtɪsɪzəm, Amer nʊ-/ *n* [u] 神经过敏症

neurotoxic /ˌnjʊərəʊˈtɒksɪk/ *adj* 毒害神经的 ‹*chemical, effects*›

neurotransmitter /ˌnjʊərəʊtrænzˈmɪtə(r)/ *n* 神经递质

neuter /ˈnjuːtə(r), Amer ˈnuː-/
A *adj* **1** Ling 中性的 ‹*noun, form*› **2** Bot, Zool 无性的 ‹*plant, flower, insect*›
B *vt* **1** Vet 阉割 ‹*animal*›; **I need to get my cat ~ed** 我需要把我家的猫去势 **2** fig (render ineffective) 使…失去作用 ‹*person, organization, policy*›
C *n* **1** Ling 中性形式 **2** (animal) 已阉割的家畜

neutral /ˈnjuːtrəl, Amer ˈnuː-/
A *adj* **1** (impartial) 中立的 ‹*country, observer, attitude*›; 不偏不倚的 ‹*verdict*›; **~ territory** 中立国的国土; **to remain ~** 保持中立 **2** (bland) 平淡的 ‹*tone, expression, character*› **3** (cancelled out) 相互抵消的 ‹*outcome, effect*›; **to have a ~ effect on sth.** 对某事物起中和的效果 **4** (plain, colourless) 素净的 ‹*colour, dress*›; 无色的 ‹*shoe, polish*› **5** Elec, Phys 不带电的 ‹*wire, charge*› **6** Chem 中性的 ‹*substance*› **7** Phon 中性的 ‹*vowel*›
B *n* **1** [u] Aut 空挡; **to be in ~** 挂空挡 **2** [c] Mil, Pol 中立者

neutralism /ˈnjuːtrəlɪzəm, Amer ˈnuː-/ *n* [u] 中立主义

neutralist /ˈnjuːtrəlɪst, Amer ˈnuː-/
A *adj* 中立主义的 ‹*policy, government*›
B *n* 中立主义者

neutrality /njuːˈtrælətɪ, Amer nuː-/ *n* [u] **1** Pol, Mil 中立; **armed ~** 武装中立; **~ towards sth.** 对某事物不偏不倚的态度 **2** Chem 中性

neutralization /ˌnjuːtrəlaɪˈzeɪʃn, Amer ˌnuːtrəlɪˈzeɪʃn/ *n* [u] **1** (cancelling out) 抵消 **2** Mil (destruction) 摧毁 **3** Chem 中和 **4** Pol (making neutral) 中立化

neutralize /ˈnjuːtrəlaɪz, Amer ˈnuː-/ *vt* **1** (cancel out) 抵消 ‹*effect, action*› **2** Mil 摧毁 ‹*enemy, base*› **3** Chem 使…中和 ‹*poison, acid*› **4** Pol 使…中立 ‹*country, zone*›

neutrino /njuːˈtriːnəʊ, Amer nuː-/ *n* (*pl* **~s**) 中微子

neutron /ˈnjuːtrɒn, Amer ˈnuː-/ *n* 中子

neutron: ~ bomb *n* 中子弹; **~ number** *n* 中子数; **~ star** *n* 中子星

Nevada /nəˈvɑːdə/ *pr n* 内华达州

never /ˈnevə(r)/ ▸**p. 507**
A *adv* **1** (not ever) 从不; **he has ~ been abroad** 他从来没有出过国; **I hope ~ to see him again** 我希望再也不要见到他; **~ ever** 绝不; **seldom or ~** 几乎从不; **~ again** 绝不再; **better late than ~** 迟做总比不做好; **you ~ know** colloq 很难说; **~ in all my life** 我一辈子都没有; **~ in all my born days** dated colloq 我一辈子都没有; **you're ~ 40!** Brit 你肯定没有 40 岁! ; **I punched him — you ~ did!** Brit colloq 我揍了他——你不会吧! ; **well I ~ (did)!** dated colloq 我才不相信呢! ; **well I ~! it's not like him to be so rude!** 真想不到! 他竟然会这么粗鲁! **2** (emphatic negative) 根本不; **he ~ said a word** 他就是一言不发; **he ~ so much as apologized** 他竟然不道歉; **Bob, ~ a strong swimmer, tired quickly** 鲍勃水性一点都不好, 很快就累了; **that would ~ do** 这绝对不行 **3** Brit colloq (in denials) 没有; **you stole it! — no, I ~** 你偷了它! ——不, 我没偷
B *excl* colloq 不会吧; **she won the lottery! — ~!** 她彩票中奖了! ——不可能吧!

never: ~-ending *adj* 没完没了的; **a ~-ending week** 极其漫长的一周; **I had a ~-ending stream of visitors** 来拜访我的人络绎不绝; **~-failing** *adj* 永远可靠的; **~-failing support** 永远不变的支持

nevermore /ˌnevəˈmɔː(r)/ *adv* liter 永不再

never-never *n* Brit colloq **on the ~** 以分期付款方式; **to buy sth. on the ~** 分期付款购买某物

never-never land *n* [u] 虚妄的乐土; **to live in ~** 生活在世外桃源

nevertheless /ˌnevəðəˈles/ *adv* 尽管如此; **thanks ~** 尽管如此, 还是多谢了; **he's stupid, but I like him ~** 他很笨, 不过我还是喜欢他; **it is ~ true that ...** 然而…是真实的; **she saw me, but ~ pretended not to recognize me** 她看见我了, 可是却假装不认识

never-to-be-forgotten *adj* 永远忘不了的 ‹*moment*›; **a ~ experience/sight** 刻骨铭心的经历/场景

new /nju:, Amer nu:/ *adj* **1** (not known, seen, owned etc. before) 新的; **to be dressed in the ~est fashion** 穿着最时髦的衣服; **a ~ baby** 新生儿; **as good as ~** lit (of things) 完好如新; fig (of parts of human body) 恢复如初; **child's cot for sale — as ~** 出售童床——几乎全新; **nearly ~** 九成新的; **to start each question on a ~ sheet of paper** 每个问题另起一页; **that's nothing ~** 这没什么新意; **what's ~?** 有什么新情况吗?; **that's a ~ one on me** 这我还是头一回听说; **to be ~ to sb.** ‹*subject, idea*› 对某人来说是陌生的 **2** (recently arrived) 新来的 ‹*member, recruit*›; **a ~ boy/girl** 新来的男生/女生; **the ~ intake** 新进人员; **we're ~ to the area** 我们初来此地 **3** (renewed, changed) 新派的 ‹*man, woman*›; **the ~ Left/rich** 新左翼/新贵; **~ realism/economics** 新现实主义/新经济学 **4** (latest) 新型的 **5** (harvested early) 新鲜的 ‹*potatoes*›

new- *combining form* 新近的; **a ~built house** 新造的房子; **~laid egg** 刚下的蛋

New Age *n* [以崇尚另类生活方式等为标志的] 新时代; **~ ideas/book** 新时代思想/书籍

> **the New Age**
>
> 新时代。新时代思潮萌芽于 19 世纪，20 世纪七八十年代流行于北美和西欧。它吸收了占星术、基督教和东方宗教及哲学的各种思想，试图摆脱西方的文化传统，以另外一种方式解决哲学、宗教、音乐、医学、环境等问题。表现为拒绝西方的物质主义（materialism）和基督教的原罪观念。相信万物归一，人与自然和谐统一。强调个体的自主（individual autonomy）、自我反思、精神的觉醒以及由此带来的个人的转变（transformation）。新时代音乐（New Age Music）节奏柔和舒缓，并融入大自然的声音。在英国，反传统的新时代漂泊者（New Age Traveller）住在房车里，过着漂泊的生活。

New Age: ~ Movement *n* 新时代运动; **~ traveller** *n* 新时代漂泊者 [指居无定所、生活方式另类的一类人]

newbie /ˈnju:bi, Amer ˈnu:-/ *n* colloq [尤指计算机领域的] 新手

new blood *n* [u] fig 新鲜血液; **to recruit ~ into the company** 为公司招募新人

newborn /ˈnju:bɔ:n, Amer ˈnu:-/
A *adj* 新生的; **a ~ baby** *or* **child** *or* **infant** 新生儿
B *n* (baby) 新生儿; (animal) 兽崽

New Brunswick /ˌnju: ˈbrʌnzwɪk, Amer ˌnu:/ *pr n* 新不伦瑞克省

newcomer /ˈnju:kʌmə(r), Amer ˈnu:-/ *n* 新来的人; **to be a ~ to a town/team** 是小镇/队伍的新成员

New Delhi /ˌnju: ˈdeli, Amer ˌnu:/ *pr n* 新德里

new economy *n* 新经济

newel /ˈnju:əl, Amer ˈnu:əl/ *n* **1** (for hand rail) **~ (post)** 楼梯端柱 **2** (for spiral stairs) 螺旋型楼梯中柱

New England *pr n* 新英格兰 [美国东北部一地区]

new-fangled /ˈnju:fæŋgld, Amer ˈnu:-/ *adj* pej 新奇的 ‹*gadget, notion*›

newfound /ˈnju:faʊnd, Amer ˈnu:-/ *adj* 新产生的 ‹*emotion, excitement*›; 新获得的 ‹*power, freedom*›; 新结交的 ‹*friend*›

Newfoundland /nju:ˈfaʊndlənd, Amer nu:-/ *pr n* **1** (island) 纽芬兰岛; **~ and Labrador** 纽芬兰-拉布拉多省 **2** (dog) 纽芬兰犬

Newfoundlander /nju:ˈfaʊndləndə(r), Amer nu:-/ *n* 纽芬兰人

New: ~ Guinea *pr n* 新几内亚岛; **~ Hampshire** *pr n* 新罕布什尔州; **~ Jersey** *pr n* 新泽西州; **~ Labour** *n* + *v sing or pl* Brit 新工党 [英国首相托尼·布莱尔领导组建的现代工党]; **new-look** *adj* 新式样的 ‹*interior, logo*›

newly /ˈnju:li, Amer ˈnu:-/ *adv* **1** (recently) 新近 ‹*appointed, built*›; **a ~(-)wed couple** 新婚夫妇; **a ~(-)decorated house** 新装修的房子; **his ~(-)found self-confidence** 他新近获得的自信 **2** (differently) 重新 ‹*arranged, translated*›

newly-weds /ˈnju:lɪwedz, Amer ˈnu:-/ *npl* 新婚夫妇

new: ~ man *n* Brit 新男人 [指模范丈夫型的新派男子]; **~ maths** *npl* + *v sing* 数学集论教学体系; **New Mexico** *pr n* 新墨西哥州; **~ moon** *n* 新月; **~-mown** *adj attrib* 新割下的 ‹*grass, hay*›; 刚割过的 ‹*lawn*›; **New Orleans** /ˌnju: ɔ:ˈli:nz, Amer ˌnu:/ *pr n* 新奥尔良

newness /ˈnju:nɪs, Amer ˈnu:-/ *n* [u] **1** (of object, idea, feeling) 新 **2** (inexperience) 生疏

news /nju:z, Amer nu:z/ *n* [u] + *v sing* **1** (personal information) 消息; (political or public information) 新闻; **~ about** *or* **of sb./sth.** 关于某人/某事物的消息; **~ from sb./somewhere** 从某人处/某地传来的消息; **a piece** *or* **an item of ~** (gen) 一条消息; Journ 一则新闻; **that's old** *or* **stale ~** 那是过时的消息; **the latest ~ is ...** 最新消息是…; **~ has just come in that ...** 刚刚传来消息说…; **to be bad ~** colloq 是个麻烦; **this is** *or* **spells bad ~ for ...** 这对…来说是坏消息; **to have ~ for sb.** 有让某人吃惊的消息; **that's ~ to me/him** *etc.* 这对我/他等可是新闻啊; **to be in** *or* **to make the ~** 成为新闻; **(good/bad) ~ travels fast** （好/坏）消息传得快; **no ~ is good ~** 没有消息就是好消息; **'heavy rain in Manchester' is not ~!** "曼彻斯特大雨"没啥稀奇的!; **a ~ report/broadcast/channel** 新闻报道/广播/频道 **2** TV, Radio (programme) **the ~** 新闻广播; **to see/hear sth. on the ~** 从新闻中看到/听到某事物 **3** Journ (column title) 新闻栏目; **Financial/Home ~, page 10** 财经/国内新闻，见第10版; **The Boston N~** 波士顿新闻

news: ~ agency *n* 通讯社; **~agent** ▸**p. 409** *n* Brit (person) 报刊经销人; **~('s)** (shop) 报刊经销店; **~ blackout** *n* 新闻封锁; **~ bulletin** *n* Brit 新闻简报; **~cast** *n* Amer 新闻简报; **~caster** ▸**p. 409** *n* Amer 新闻播音员; **~ conference** *n* 记者招待会; **~dealer** ▸**p. 409** *n* Amer = **~agent**; **~ desk** *n* 新闻采编部; **~ editor** ▸**p. 409** *n* 新闻编辑; **~feed** *n* (service) 新闻馈送; (news) 馈送的新闻; **~flash** *n* 简明新闻; **~gathering** *n* [u] 新闻采集; **~group** *n* （因特网）新闻组; **~ headlines** *npl* 要闻; **~ hound** *n* colloq 新闻记者; **~letter** *n* 业务通讯; **~ magazine** *n* 新闻杂志; **~man** /-mæn/ ▸**p. 409** *n* 男记者; **~-on-demand** *n* [u] 新闻点播服务

New South Wales *pr n* 新南威尔士州

newspaper /ˈnju:zpeɪpə(r), Amer ˈnu:z-/ *n* **1** [c] Journ 报纸; **to publish/edit a ~** 出版/编辑报纸; **to work for a ~** 为一家报社工作; **the Sunday ~s** 星期日周报; **a ~ reporter** 报社记者; **a ~ editor/article** 报纸编辑/文章 **2** [u] (paper) 旧报纸; **to be wrapped in ~** 包在报纸里

newspaper: ~man /-mæn/ ▸**p. 409** *n* 报社记者; **~ office** *n* 报社; **~woman** ▸**p. 409** *n* 报社女记者

newspeak /ˈnju:spi:k, Amer ˈnu:-/ *n* [u] pej 新话 [指模棱两可的政治宣传用语]

news: ~ photographer ▸**p. 409** *n* 新闻摄影师; **~ posting** *n* 新闻公告; **~print** *n* [u] 新闻纸; **~reader** ▸**p. 409** *n* **1** Brit Journ 新闻播音员; **2** Comput 新闻阅读器; **~reel** *n* 新闻短片; **~room** *n* 新闻编辑室; **~-sheet** *n* 小报; **~stand** *n* 报摊; **~ vendor** ▸**p. 409** *n* Brit 卖报人; **~wire** *n* [通过互联网提供的] 新闻专线; **~woman** ▸**p. 409** *n* 女记者; **~worthy** *adj* 有新闻价值的 ‹*event, issue*›; **there's nothing in the story that makes it ~worthy** 故事中没有什么值得报道的

newsy /ˈnju:zi, Amer ˈnu:-/ *adj* 多新闻的 ‹*letter, magazine*›

newt /nju:t, Amer nu:t/ *n* 水螈

New Testament *pr n* **the ~** 《新约》

newton /ˈnju:tn, Amer ˈnu:-/ *n* 牛顿 [力的单位]

Newtonian /nju:ˈtəʊnɪən, Amer nu:-/ *adj* 牛顿的 ‹*account, explanation*›; **~ physics/mechanics** 牛顿物理学/牛顿力学

new: ~ wave *pr n* 新浪潮 [尤指起源于法国的电影新流派]; **New World** *n* **the New World** 新大陆

new year, New Year *n* **1** (coming year) 新年; **Happy ~!** 新年快乐!; **at (the) ~** 在新年的第一天; **for** *or* **over (the) ~** 在新年里; **to see in** *or* **bring in the ~** 守岁迎新; **~ card** 贺年片 **2** (early part of year) 一年的开始; **I'll see you in the ~** 我会在新年去看你

New Year: ~'s Day Brit, **~'s** Amer *n* 元旦; **~'s Eve** *n* 除夕; **on ~'s Eve** 在除夕; **~'s Eve party/celebrations** 除夕晚会/庆祝; **~'s resolution** *n* 新年决心

New Year's Honours *npl* Brit 新年勋誉; **~ list** 新年勋誉人员名单

New York *pr n* 纽约

New York City *pr n* 纽约市

New Yorker *n* 纽约人

New Zealand /ˌnju:ˈzi:lənd, Amer ˌnu:-/ *pr n* 新西兰; **~ government/butter** 新西兰政府/黄油

New Zealander /ˌnju: ˈzi:ləndə(r), Amer ˌnu:/ ▸**p. 503** *n* 新西兰人

next /nekst/
A *adj* **1** (in order, in time) 紧接着的; **the ~ page** 下一页; **to get the ~ train** 赶上下一班火车; **Tuesday ~** Brit 下星期二; **this time ~ week** 下星期的这个时候; **in the ~ two/few days** 在随后的两天/几天里; **we're going to the US ~ May** 我们 5 月份要去美国; **'~ (please)!'** "下一个!"; **she's ~ in the queue** Brit 她排在下一个; **~ in line for take-over/for the presidency** 排在下一个接管/下一届担任总统; **the ~ size up/down** 再大/小一号; **the ~ man/woman/person** *etc.* 普通人; **he's as honest as the ~ person** 他和平常人一样诚实; **~ thing I knew ...** 接下来… **2** *attrib* (adjacent) 隔壁的 ‹*room, house*›
B *adv* **1** (after sth.) 随后; **~, we interviewed Peter** 接着我们面试了彼得; **~, I'd like to say ...** 接下来，我想说…; **what happened ~?** 然后发生了什么? **2** (following in order) 下一个; **it's my turn ~** 下一个轮到我 **3** (nearest in order) 紧随其后; **she's ~ in age to Susan** 她比苏珊年轻; **the ~ tallest is Patrick** 个子第二高的人是帕特里克 **4** (referring to future occasion) 下一次; **when she ~ comes to visit** 当她下一次来访的时候; **they ~ met in 1998** 他们于 1998 年再次见面
C *pron* 下一个; **the ~ to speak was Jenny** 下一位发言的是詹妮; **after this bus the ~ is at noon** 这趟公交车过后，下一班在中午; **I hope my ~ will be a boy** 我希望我的下一个孩子是男孩; **from one minute to the ~** 转瞬之间; **the week/month after ~** 下下个星期/月
D **next to** *prep phr* **1** (beside) 紧邻; **a table ~ to the window** 紧靠着窗户的桌子; **to wear silk ~ to the skin** 贴身穿绸衣 **2** (following in order or importance) 仅次于; **~ to Picasso, my favourite painter is Chagall** 除了毕加索以外，我最喜欢的画家是夏加尔 **3** (in comparison) 与…相比; **~ to her I felt like a fraud** 与她相比，我感觉自己像个骗子
E **next to** *adv phr* 几乎; **~ to impossible/useless** 几乎不可能/毫无用处; **~ to last** 倒数第二; **in ~ to no time** 说时迟那时快

next best *adj attrib* 仅次于最好的; **the ~ thing** 居第二位的事物

next door
A *adv* **1** lit 在隔壁; **to live ~ to sth./sb.** 住在某处/某人隔壁; **to go ~** 到隔壁去 **2** fig colloq (close) 几乎; **that's ~ to impossible** 那几乎是不可能的
B *adj* **1** *postpos* 隔壁的; **the girl ~** lit 邻家女孩; fig 普通女孩; **the house/people ~** 隔壁的房子/隔壁邻居 **2** **next-door** *attrib* 隔壁的 ‹*house, garden*›; **my ~ neighbour** 我隔壁的邻居
C *n* (building) 隔壁的房子; (people) 隔壁邻居; **~'s cat** 隔壁邻居家的猫

next of kin *n + v sing or pl* 直系亲属; **to be sb.'s ~** 是某人的直系亲属

nexus /'neksəs/ *n* (*pl* **~** *or* **~es**) formal **1** (link) 联系; **a ~ between sth. and sth.** 某事物和某事物之间的联系 **2** (network) 一连串; **to have a ~ of contacts in the financial world** 在金融界有广泛的人脉关系 **3** (centre) 中心

N/F *abbr* **= no funds** 无存款

NFL *abbr* Amer **= National Football League** 全国橄榄球联盟

NFU *abbr* Brit **= National Farmers' Union** 全国农场主联合会

NGO *abbr* **= non-governmental organization** 非政府组织

NH *abbr* Amer **= New Hampshire**

NHL *abbr* Amer **= National Hockey League** 全国冰球联合会

NHS *abbr* Brit **= National Health Service** *modif* **an ~ doctor** 提供国民保健服务的医生

NI *abbr* **1** Brit **= National Insurance** **2** **= Northern Ireland**

Niagara /naɪ'ægərə/ ▸**p. 663** *pr n* **the ~** 尼亚加拉河

Niagara Falls /nai,ægrə 'fɔːlz/ *pr n* **the ~** 尼亚加拉瀑布

nib /nɪb/ *n* **1** (of pen) 钢笔尖 **2** (of tube, applicator) 尖突

nibble /'nɪbl/
A *vt* **1** (eat in small pieces) 一点一点地吃 ‹*food, grass*› **2** (bite gently) 轻咬 ‹*ear, lip*› **3** fig (erode) 侵蚀; **to ~ the cliffs away** «*waves*» 慢慢侵蚀峭壁
B *vi* **1** (take small bites) «*animal, person*» 小口小口地咬; **to ~ at sth.** 小口小口地咬某物 **2** (bite gently) **to ~ at sth.** 轻轻地咬 ‹*ear, lip*› **3** fig (show interest) **to ~ at sth.** «*company*» 对…谨慎地表现出兴趣 ‹*project, merger*› **4** fig (erode) **to ~ away at sth.** «*sea*» 侵蚀 ‹*cliff*›; fig 削弱 ‹*spending power*›
C *n* **1** (small mouthful) 一小口; **to feel like** *or* **fancy a ~** 想吃一点 **2** (snack) 点心 **3** (small bite) 啃; **to have** *or* **take a ~ at sth.** 小口小口地咬 ‹*lettuce, cake*› **4** fig (interest) 兴趣; **to get** *or* **have a ~** 有兴趣

nibs /nɪbz/ *n + v sing* Brit colloq hum **his ~** 他那位大人 [指他本人]

Nicam, NICAM /'naɪkæm/ *n* [u] 丽音 [一种数字电视伴音系统]

Nicaragua /,nɪkə'rægjʊə/ *pr n* 尼加拉瓜

Nicaraguan /,nɪkə'rægjʊən/ ▸**p. 503**
A *adj* (of Nicaragua) 尼加拉瓜的; (of the people) 尼加拉瓜人的
B *n* 尼加拉瓜人

nice /naɪs/ *adj* **1** (enjoyable, pleasant) 令人愉快的; **it is ~ that ...** …真好; **it would be ~ (for sb.) to do sth.** （某人）做某事会很不错; **did you have a ~ time?** 你玩得开心吗? ; **it is ~ sitting in the garden** 坐在花园里很惬意; **~ to meet/see you** 认识/见到你很高兴 [见面用语]; **~ to have met/seen you** 认识/见到你很高兴 [道别用语]; **how ~** 太好了; **that's ~** 很好 [表示赞许]; **have a ~ day!** 祝你今天过得开心! **2** (attractive, pleasant) 好的 ‹*place, weather, house, car*›; 好看的 ‹*clothes, picture, view*›; 好吃的 ‹*food, meal*›; **to look/taste ~** 好看/好吃; **a ~ day** 晴天 **3** (kind, friendly) 友好的 ‹*voice, gesture*›; **to have a ~ way of doing sth.** 以友好的方式做某事; **what a ~ man** *or* **guy!** 真是个好男人! ; **to be ~ to** *or* **with sb.** 对某人很好; **it was ~ of him to telephone** 他打来了电话，真好; **how ~ of her to invite me** 她邀请我，这真是太好了; **to say ~ things (about sth.)** 赞美（某事物）; **she is such a ~ person to know** 她是个好人，值得认识 **4** (respectable) 正经的 ‹*people, book, film*›; **a ~ girl/family** 正派少女/清白人家; **it is not nice to ...** …不文雅; **to have ~ manners** 风度翩翩 **5** (good, satisfactory) 出色的 ‹*work, attempt*›; **a ~ shot** 妙射; **to make a ~ job of sth.** 把某事做得很好; **~ point!** 说得好! ; **~ work!** colloq 干得好! ; **~ one!** colloq (sth. clever or skilled) 漂亮! ; (sth. clever or funny) 说得好! ; iron 干得好! ; **a ~ mess** iron 一团糟; **that's a ~ way to talk to your father** iron 你可真有本事，能这样对你父亲讲话 **6** (fine, subtle) 微妙的 ‹*point, argument*›; 细微的 ‹*distinction*›; **he has ~ taste in music** 他乐感很强 **7** formal (precise, exact) 细致的 ‹*task, drilling*›; 精细的 ‹*technique, method*›; **~ coordination** 灵巧的协调性 **8** colloq (used for emphasis) 很; **a ~ long talk** 长谈; **~ and cool/easy/friendly** 酷得很的/极容易的/很友好的; **~ and early** 一大早

nice-looking /,naɪs'lʊkɪŋ/ *adj* 好看的

nicely /'naɪsli/ *adv* **1** (kindly) 和蔼地 ‹*speak, smile*› **2** (satisfactorily) 令人满意地 ‹*situated, function*›; **to be coming along ~** «*building, project*» 进展很顺利; **to be ~ chilled** «*drink*» 冰爽怡人; **to be ~ done** «*food*» 做得恰到好处; **to be ~ placed to do sth.** 有很好的条件做某事 **3** (attractively) 吸引人地 ‹*decorated, presented*›; **to sing/dress very ~** 歌唱得很好/打扮得很好看 **4** (politely) 有礼貌地 ‹*behave, ask*›

niceness /'naɪsnɪs/ *n* [u] (kindness) 善良; (pleasantness) 和蔼可亲; **out of ~** 出于好心

nicety /'naɪsəti/ *n* **1** [u] (precision) 精确; **~ of judgement** 判断之精确; **a point of (great) ~** 需仔细考虑的事; **to a ~** 恰到好处地 **2** [c] *usu pl* (detail) 细节; **the niceties of etiquette** 繁文缛节 **3** [c] *usu pl* (refinement) 优雅; **the niceties of life** 人生的各种享受; **social niceties** 社交中的繁文缛节

niche /nɪtʃ, niːʃ/ *n* **1** lit (recess) 壁龛 **2** fig (position, job) 适合的职业; **to find one's ~** 谋得合适的工作; **to carve out one's** *or* **a ~** 闯出一片天地 **3** Ecol 生态龛 [指动植物物种在生物种群中的地位]

niche: ~ market *n* 利基市场 [指有利可图的专业化小众市场]; **~ marketing** *n* [u] 利基营销

nick /nɪk/
A *n* **1** [c] (notch) 凹痕; **to make a ~ in sth.** 在某物上刻出凹痕; **to take a ~ out of sth.** 划破某物; **in the ~ of time** fig colloq 刚好 **2** [u] Brit colloq **the ~** (jail) 监狱; (police station) 警察局; **they are both in the ~** 他俩都进了警察局 **3** [u] Brit colloq (condition) 状况; **to be in good/bad ~** 状态良好/糟糕
B *vt* **1** (cut) 割破 ‹*finger*›; 在…上刻出凹痕 ‹*stick*›; 在…留下缺口 ‹*cloth*› **2** Brit colloq (steal) 偷 ‹*money, food*›; **to ~ sth. from sb.** 偷某人的某物 **3** Amer sl (overcharge) 敲…的竹杠; **to ~ sb. for sth.** 敲诈某人索要某物 **4** Brit colloq (arrest) 逮捕 ‹*burglar, rioter*›; **to be** *or* **get ~ed (for sth.)** （因某事）被抓

nickel /'nɪkl/
A *n* **1** [u] (metal) 镍; **~ wire** 镍线 **2** [c] Amer, Can (coin) 5 分镍币; (five cents) 5 分钱
B *vt* (*pres p etc.* **-ll-** Brit, **-l-** Amer) 镀镍于 ‹*wire, cutlery*›

nickel-and-dime Amer colloq
A *vt* 斤斤计较地对待 ‹*customer*›
B *adj* (insignificant) 微不足道的; (cheap) 便宜的; **a ~ manufacturing business** 制造业小企业

nickelodeon /,nɪkə'ləʊdɪən/ *n* Amer dated 投币式自动唱机

nickel: ~-plated *adj* 镀镍的 ‹*spoon, metal*›; **~ silver** *n* [u] 铜镍锌合金

nicker /'nɪkə(r)/
A *vi* «*horse*» 嘶鸣
B *n* (*pl* **nicker**) Brit sl 英镑

nickname /'nɪkneɪm/
A *n* 绰号
B *vt* 给…起绰号 ‹*person*›

Nicosia /,nɪkə'sɪə/ *pr n* 尼科西亚

nicotine /'nɪkətiːn/
A *n* [u] 尼古丁
B *modif* 含尼古丁的 ‹*fumes, content*›; 尼古丁的 ‹*addiction, pollution*›

nicotine patch *n* [戒烟用的] 尼古丁贴片

niece /niːs/ ▸**p. 419** *n* (daughter of brother) 侄女; (daughter of sister) 外甥女

Nietzschean /'niːtʃɪən/ *adj* 尼采的 ‹*philosophy*›; 尼采思想的 ‹*scholar*›

niff /nɪf/ Brit colloq
A *n* 难闻的气味; **what a ~!** 真臭!
B *vi* 发出难闻的气味

niffy /'nɪfi/ *adj* Brit colloq 发出难闻气味的 ‹*person, animal, room*›

nifty /'nɪfti/ *adj* colloq **1** (attractive) 漂亮的 ‹*suit, car*›; **a ~ dresser** 衣着入时的人 **2** (skilful) 灵巧的 ‹*work, movement*›; **to be ~ on one's feet** 脚下灵活 **3** (useful) 有用的 ‹*gadget, equipment*›

Niger /'naɪdʒə(r)/ ▸**p. 663** *pr n* **1** (country) 尼日尔 **2** (river) **the ~** 尼日尔河

Nigeria /naɪ'dʒɪərɪə/ *pr n* 尼日利亚

Nigerian /naɪ'dʒɪərɪən/ ▸**p. 503**
A *adj* (of Nigeria) 尼日利亚的; (of the people) 尼日利亚人的
B *n* 尼日利亚人

niggardliness /'nɪgədlmɪs/ *n* [u] 吝啬

niggardly /'nɪgədli/ *adj* **1** (stingy) 吝啬的 ‹*person*› **2** (meagre) 很少的 ‹*quantity, salary*›

nigger /'nɪgə(r)/ *n* sl offensive 黑鬼 offensive

niggle /'nɪgl/
A *vi* **1** (complain) 吹毛求疵; **to ~ about** *or* **over sth.** 挑剔某事物 **2** (fuss) 大惊小怪; **to ~ about** *or* **over sth.** 为某事物烦心; **to ~ over every little detail** 斤斤计较鸡毛蒜皮的小事
B *vt* «*criticism, situation, habit*» 激怒 ‹*person*›
C *n* **1** (complaint) 小牢骚; **to have a small ~ about the book** 对这本书有一个小小的意见 **2** (worry) 小忧虑; **to have a ~ at the back of one's mind** 在内心深处有点小小的不安

niggling /'nɪglɪŋ/
A *adj* **1** (fussy) 吹毛求疵的 ‹*person, manner*› **2** (persistent) 惹人烦恼不已的 ‹*pain, doubt*› **3** (trifling) 琐碎的 ‹*detail, question*›; **a ~ criticism** 婆婆妈妈的批评
B *n* [u] 挑剔

nigh /naɪ/
A *adj pred* archaic 近的; **the end of the world is ~** 世界末日快到了
B *adv* **1** archaic (near) 靠近; **to draw ~** 接近 **2** (almost) **(well) ~** 几乎; **it is ~ (on) impossible to ...** …几乎是不可能的; **to be ~ on forty** 接近四十

night /naɪt/ *n* **1** [c and u] (period of darkness) 夜晚; **at ~** *or* **in the ~** 晚上; **in the middle of/during the ~** 在半夜/夜间; **on the ~ of the gale** 在那个狂风呼啸的晚上; **late at ~** 在深夜; **to travel/hunt by ~** 夜行/夜晚捕猎; **~ and day** 夜以继日地 ‹*work, study*›; **all ~ (long)** 整夜地; **~ after ~** 一夜又一夜地; **in the dead of ~** 在夜深人静时; **last ~** 昨天晚上; **the ~ before (last)** 前一天晚上; **to spend** *or* **pass** *or* **stay a ~** 过夜; **to spend** *or* **stay the ~ with sb.** 与某人一起过夜; **to have a good/bad ~** 晚上睡得好/不好; **to**

n

have a sleepless ~ 彻夜不眠; to have or get an early ~ 睡得早; to retire/settle down for the ~ 晚上上床休息/安顿下来过夜; to be on or work ~s 上夜班; to sit up all ~ (with sb./doing sth.) 熬夜 (陪某人/做某事); far into the ~ (late into the night) 到深夜; (into the early hours of the morning) 到凌晨; throughout the ~ 通宵地; to have a ~ out 晚上出去玩; to take a ~ off 休息一晚上; it's my ~ off/out 今晚我休息/出去玩; to make a ~ of it 痛快地玩一晚上 **2** [c] (of a performance) 夜场演出; (of a special function) 夜晚活动; sb.'s wedding ~ 某人的新婚之夜; he enjoyed his ~ at the opera 他晚上歌剧听得很开心; the play will run for five ~s 该剧将连演 5 个晚上; first or opening ~ 首演之夜; a Shakespeare N~ 莎士比亚之夜 **3** [u] liter (nightfall) 夜幕; ~ fell quickly 天很快黑了下来 **4** [u] (darkness of night) 黑夜; black as ~ 漆黑 **5** [c and u] fig liter (period of gloom) 黑暗时期; in our dark ~ of despair 在我们陷入绝望的黑暗时期

night: ~ **bird** *n* **1** Zool 夜间活动的鸟; **2** ~bird colloq 夜猫子; ~**-blind** *adj* 夜盲的; ~ **blindness** *n* [u] 夜盲; ~**cap** *n* **1** (drink) 夜酒; to have a ~cap 睡前喝些酒; **2** (hat) 睡帽; ~**clothes** *npl* 睡衣; ~**club** *n* 夜总会; a ~club hostess/singer 夜总会女招待/歌手; ~**clubbing** *n* [u] 泡夜总会; to go ~clubbing 去泡夜总会; ~**dress** *n* (女式) 睡衣; ~ **editor** *n* 夜班编辑; ~**fall** *n* [u] 黄昏; at ~fall 在傍晚时刻; before/after ~fall 在黄昏前/后; ~ **fighter** *n* 夜间战斗机; ~**gown** *n* **1** (for sleeping) 睡衣; **2** (dressing gown) 晨衣; ~**hawk** *n* **1** Zool 夜莺 [产于北美]; **2** Amer colloq 夜猫子

nightie /ˈnaɪti/ *n* colloq (女式) 睡衣

nightingale /ˈnaɪtɪŋɡeɪl, Amer -tŋɡ-/ *n* 夜莺; to sing like a ~ 歌声如夜莺般悦耳

night: ~**jar** *n* 夜莺; ~**life** *n* [u] 夜生活; ~ **light** *n* 夜灯; ~**-long** *adj* 通宵的 ‹party, vigil›

nightly /ˈnaɪtli/

A *adj* 每晚的 ‹news, patrol, prayers›

B *adv* 每晚 ‹pray, appear, perform›; twice ~ 每晚两次

nightmare /ˈnaɪtmeə(r)/ *n* **1** (dream) 恶梦; to have a ~ about sth. 做有关某事物的恶梦 **2** fig colloq (event) 可怕的事件; (experience) 可怕的经历; (prospect) 可怕的前景; a living ~ 恶梦般的真实经历; a ~ journey/experience 恶梦般的旅行/经历 **3** (person) 难缠的人; (thing) 难以处理的事物; he is an absolute ~ 他这人实在难对付; the motorway is a ~ 高速公路很可怕

nightmarish /ˈnaɪtmeərɪʃ/ *adj* 恶梦般的 ‹experience, job›

night: ~**-night** *excl* colloq 晚安 [对孩子说话时的用语]; ~ **nurse** *n* 夜班护士; ~ **owl** *n* colloq 夜猫子; ~ **porter** *n* [旅馆总服务台的] 夜班接待员; ~ **safe** *n* 夜间保险柜; ~ **school** *n* 夜校; ~**shade** *n* 茄属植物; ~ **shelter** *n* [为无家可归者提供的] 夜间歇息地; ~ **shift** *n* **1** (period) 夜班时间; to be on or work the ~ shift 上夜班; **2** + v sing or pl (workers) 夜班工人; ~**shirt** *n* 睡衣; ~ **sky** *n* 夜空; ~**spot** *n* colloq 夜总会; ~**stand** *n* Amer 床头柜; ~**stick** *n* Amer 警棍; ~ **table** *n* 床头柜; ~**-time** *n* [u] 夜间; at ~-time 在夜间; ~-time activities 夜间活动; ~ **vision** *n* [u] 夜视力; ~-vision goggles 夜视镜; ~**watchman** ▸p. 409 *n* 守夜人; ~**wear** *n* [u] 睡衣

nihilism /ˈnaɪɪlɪzəm, ˈnɪhɪl-/ *n* [u] 虚无主义

nihilist /ˈnaɪɪlɪst, ˈnɪhɪl-/

A *n* 虚无主义者

B *adj* 虚无主义的 ‹view, philosopher›

nihilistic /ˌnaɪɪˈlɪstɪk, ˌnɪhɪˈl-/ *adj* 虚无主义的 ‹attitude, person›

Nikkei index /ˈnɪkeɪ ˌɪndeks/ *n* 日经指数

nil /nɪl/

A *n* **1** (nothing) 无; our progress is almost ~ 我们差不多毫无进展 **2** Brit Sport (zero) 零; the Welsh won four-~ 威尔士队以4:0获胜

B *adj pred* 不存在的

Nile /naɪl/ ▸p. 663 *pr n* the ~ 尼罗河; the ~ delta 尼罗河三角洲

nimbi /ˈnɪmbaɪ/ *npl* ▸nimbus

nimble /ˈnɪmbl/ *adj* **1** (agile) 灵活的 ‹body›; 敏捷的 ‹movement, athlete›; to be ~ at sth. or at doing sth. 做某事很敏捷; to be ~ on one's feet 腿脚灵活; to be ~ with one's fingers/a screwdriver 手指灵巧/螺丝刀用得灵活; as ~ as a goat 如山羊般敏捷 **2** (clever) 敏锐的 ‹mind›; to be ~ in one's wits 机敏

nimble: ~**-fingered** *adj* 手指灵巧的 ‹surgeon, typist, guitarist›; ~**-footed** *adj* 用脚灵活的 ‹dancer, animal›; a ~-footed player 脚法娴熟的球员

nimbly /ˈnɪmbli/ *adv* 敏捷地 ‹leap, operate›; 灵巧地 ‹sew›

nimbostratus /ˌnɪmbəʊˈstreɪtəs, -ˈstrɑːtəs/ *n* [u and c] 雨层云

nimbus /ˈnɪmbəs/ *n* (*pl* **nimbi** or ~**es**) **1** Meteorol 雨云 **2** (halo) 光环

Nimby /ˈnɪmbi/ *n* (*pl* ~**s**) colloq pej = not in my back yard "宁闭"分子 [反对在自己住宅附近建造危险或不受欢迎设施的人]

nincompoop /ˈnɪŋkəmpuːp/ *n* colloq 笨蛋; to feel like a ~ 感觉像个傻瓜

nine /naɪn/ ▸p. 15, p. 521, p. 831

A *n* **1** (number, quantity) 九; ~ plus two equals eleven 9 加 2 等于 11; in December nineteen hundred and ~ 在 1909 年 12 月; we live at (number) ~, Victoria Road 我们住在维多利亚路 9 号; her phone number is two six double ~ 她的电话号码是 2699; there are ~ of them 他们有 9 个人; to be dressed (up) to the ~s fig colloq 打扮得绝顶漂亮 **2** (in time) 9 点钟; at ~ (o'clock) 在 9 点 **3** (on playing card) 9 点; the ~ of diamonds 方块 9 **4** (age) 9 岁

B *adj* **1** (as quantity) 九的; ~ cats 9 只猫; ~ books 9 本书; ~ weeks 9 周; ~ times out of ten 十之八九; to have ~ lives fig colloq 命大 **2** (in age) 9 岁的; he's nearly ~ 他快 9 岁了; our house is only ~ years old 我们的房子才造了 9 年 **3** (in series) 第九的; number ~ 9 号; page ~ 第 9 页; size ~ 9 号尺码

> **9/11**
>
> 9·11 事件。2001 年 9 月 11 日，恐怖分子劫持民航客机将纽约的标志性建筑世界贸易中心（World Trade Center）撞毁，美国国防部的五角大楼（▸the Pentagon）也遭到袭击，这起事件被称为 9·11 事件。9·11 事件后不久，美国即以保障国家安全为由，在全球范围内发动"反恐战争"。

nine-piece *adj* (people) 9 人组的 ‹band›; (pieces) 9 件的 ‹set, puzzle›

ninepins /ˈnaɪnpɪnz/ ▸p. 307 *npl* + v sing 九柱戏; to go down or fall like ~ fig colloq 横七竖八地倒下

nineteen /ˌnaɪnˈtiːn/ ▸p. 521

A *n* **1** (number, quantity) 十九; to talk ~ to the dozen fig 喋喋不休 **2** (in age) 19 岁

B *adj* **1** (in number) 十九的; ~ metres 19 米; ~ paintings 19 张画 **2** (in age) 19 岁的; to be ~ (years old) 19 岁大; to be over/under ~ 超过/不到 19 岁 **3** (in series) 第十九的; size/number ~ 19 码/号

nineteenth /ˌnaɪnˈtiːnθ/ ▸p. 181, p. 521

A *n* **1** (in sequence) 第十九个 **2** (in date) 19 日 **3** (fraction) 十九分之一

B *adj* **1** (in sequence) 第十九的 **2** (in name, title) 十九; Louis the N~ or Louis XIX 路易十九 **3** (as fraction) 十九分之一的

C *adv* 第十九

ninetieth /ˈnaɪntɪəθ/ ▸p. 521

A *n* **1** (in sequence) 第九十个 **2** (fraction) 九十分之一

B *adj* **1** (in sequence) 第九十的 **2** (as fraction) 九十分之一的

C *adv* 第九十

nine-to-five

A *adj* 朝九晚五的 ‹job, routine›; 正常工作的 ‹attitude›

B *n* 朝九晚五的工作; I've never been keen on the ~ 我对朝九晚五的工作从来不热心

ninety /ˈnaɪnti/ ▸p. 15, p. 521

A *n* **1** (number, quantity) 九十; there are ~ of us 我们有 90 个人 **2** (in age) 90 岁

B *adj* **1** (in number) 九十的; ~ boys 90 个男孩; ~ years 90 年 **2** (in age) 90 岁的; I'm nearly ~ 我快 90 岁了 **3** (in series) 第九十的

ninety-nine *n* Brit 巧克力蛋卷冰激凌

Ningxia /ˌnɪŋˈʃɑː/ ▸p. 604 *pr n* ~ (Hui Autonomous Region) 宁夏 (回族自治区)

ninny /ˈnɪni/ *n* colloq 笨蛋

ninth /naɪnθ/ ▸p. 181, p. 521

A *n* **1** (in sequence) 第九 **2** (in date) 9 日 **3** (fraction) 九分之一 **4** Mus 九度音程

B *adj* **1** (in sequence) 第九的; It's her ~ birthday 这是她 9 岁生日; on the ~ floor 在 10 楼 **2** (in name, title) 九世的; Louis the N~ or Louis IX 路易九世 **3** (as fraction) 九分之一的

C *adv* 第九

niobium /naɪˈəʊbɪəm/ *n* [u] 铌

nip[1] /nɪp/

A *n* **1** (pinch) 夹; to get a ~ on one's finger/toe from sth. 手指/脚趾被某物夹了一下; to take or make a ~ in a dress 把连衣裙改瘦一点 **2** (bite) 咬; to give sb. a ~ (on the leg/ankle) 咬某人 (腿/脚踝) 一口 **3** fig (chill) 寒冷; there was a ~ in the wind 寒风刺骨

B *vt* (*pres p etc.* **-pp-**) **1** (pinch, bite) «dog, bird» 咬住; «hinge, crab» 夹住; to ~ sb. in the arm/leg 掐某人的胳膊/腿; to ~ sb. on the hand/neck 咬住某人的手/脖子 **2** (remove by clipping) 掐断; to ~ sth. off sth. 把某物从某物上掐下来; to ~ sth. in the bud 把某事物扼杀在萌芽状态 **3** (affect with a stinging sensation) «cold, frost» 刺痛 ‹face, hands› **4** Amer colloq (steal) 偷; (snatch) 抓取

C *vi* (*pres p etc.* **-pp-**) **1** (pinch, bite) 轻咬; to ~ at sth. 一点一点地咬某物 **2** Brit colloq (go quickly) 快走; to ~ past sb./sth. 急匆匆地走过某人/某处; to ~ out/in/upstairs/downstairs 匆匆出去/进来/上楼/下楼; to ~ on ahead 赶到前面

Phrasal verbs

- **nip along** *vi* Brit colloq «person» 快步走; «car, train» 快速行驶; to ~ along to sth. 赶往某处
- **nip in** *vt* [~ in sth., ~ sth. in] 把…改小 ‹waist, dress›
- **nip off**

A *vi* Brit colloq 迅速跑开; to ~ off after sth./sb. 追赶某物/某人

B *vt* [~ off sth., ~ sth. off] 掐去

nip[2] *n* colloq **1** (small sip) 一小口酒; a ~ of whisky/brandy 一小口威士忌/白兰地; to take a ~ 喝点酒 **2** esp Brit (small measure) 尼普 [烈酒的度量单位，相当于六分之一吉耳]

nip and tuck

A *n* colloq 势均力敌

B *adj* 势均力敌的 ‹race, competition›

C *adv* 势均力敌地; it was ~ 双方势均力敌

nipper /ˈnɪpə(r)/ *n* **1** Brit colloq (child) 小孩 **2** (insect, animal) 好叮咬的动物 **3** *usu pl* (claw) 螯

nippers /ˈnɪpəz/ *npl* (tool) 钳子; a pair of ~ 一把钳子

nipple /ˈnɪpl/ *n* **1** Anat 乳头 **2** Amer (rubber teat) 奶嘴 **3** Tech 喷嘴; grease ~ 油脂喷嘴

nipple ring *n* 乳环

nippy /ˈnɪpi/ *adj* colloq [1] (cold) 寒冷的 ‹*weather*›; 刺骨的 ‹*wind*› [2] Brit (quick) 敏捷的 ‹*child, footwork*›; **be ~ about it!** 动作快些! [3] (quick to accelerate) 加速快的 ‹*vehicle*›

nirvana /nɪəˈvɑːnə/ *n* [1] [u] Relig 涅槃 [2] [c] (idyllic place) 极乐世界; (state) 无忧无虑的境界

nisi /ˈnaɪsaɪ/ *adj* Jur ▸**decree A2**

nit /nɪt/ *n* [1] (egg) 虱子卵; (larva) 小虱子; **to have ~s** 长虱子 [2] Brit colloq (idiot) 傻瓜

niter *n* [u] Amer = **nitre**

nit: ~-pick *vi* colloq 吹毛求疵; **~-picker** *n* colloq 吹毛求疵的人

nit-picking colloq

[A] *n* [u] 吹毛求疵

[B] *adj* 吹毛求疵的 ‹*attitude, person*›

nitrate /ˈnaɪtreɪt/ *n* (salt) 硝酸盐; (ester) 硝酸酯; **sodium ~** 硝酸钠; **a ~ compound** 硝酸盐化合物

nitre /ˈnaɪtə(r)/ *n* [u] Brit 硝石

nitric: ~ acid *n* [u] 硝酸; **~ oxide** *n* [u] 一氧化氮

nitrogen /ˈnaɪtrədʒən/ *n* [u] 氮; **~ atoms/gas** 氮原子/氮气

nitrogen: ~ dioxide *n* [u] 二氧化氮; **~ monoxide** *n* [u] 一氧化氮

nitrogenous /naɪˈtrɒdʒɪnəs/ *adj attrib* 含氮的 ‹*substance, compound*›

nitroglycerine, nitroglycerin /ˌnaɪtrəʊˈɡlɪsəriːn, Amer -rɪn/ *n* [u] 硝化甘油

nitrous /ˈnaɪtrəs/ *adj attrib* 含氮的 ‹*substance, compound*›

nitrous: ~ acid *n* [u] 亚硝酸; **~ oxide** *n* [u] 一氧化二氮

nitty-gritty /ˌnɪtiˈɡrɪti/ *n* colloq **the ~** 基本事实; **let's get down to the ~** 咱们着手研究关键问题吧

nitwit /ˈnɪtwɪt/ *n* colloq 笨蛋

nix /nɪks/ Amer colloq

[A] *vt* 否决 ‹*plans*›; 拒绝 ‹*idea*›

[B] *pron* 无; **apart from that, ~** 除那之外, 什么也没有

[C] *excl* (refusal) 不行; (denial) 没有

NJ *abbr* Amer = **New Jersey**

NLP *abbr* = **natural language processing**

NM *abbr* Amer = **New Mexico**

NMR *abbr* = **nuclear magnetic resonance**

NNE *abbr* = **north-north-east**

NNW *abbr* = **north-north-west**

no /nəʊ/ ▸**p. 507**

[A] *particle* [1] (giving negative response, expressing disagreement, shock, disappointment) 不; **are you ready? — ~, I'm not** 你准备好了吗? ——没有, 我没准备好; **another drink? — ~ thanks** 再喝一杯? ——不了, 谢谢; **~! don't touch it: it's hot!** 别! 别碰它, 很烫!; **oh ~, look at this!** 哦, 不, 瞧这个!; **to not take ~ for an answer** 非得让人接受; **you're coming and I won't take ~ for an answer** 你一定要来, 你非答应不可 [2] (expressing agreement or affirmation) 没错; **it's not very good, is it? — ~, you're right: it isn't** 它不太好, 对吧? ——没错, 你说得对, 它不好

[B] *det* [1] (not any) 没有; **to have ~ coat/job/money/shoes** 没有外套/工作/钱/鞋子; **he has ~ intention of going** 他毫无走的意思; **there's ~ chocolate like Belgian chocolate** 比利时巧克力无与伦比 [2] (expressing impossibility) 不可能; **there's ~ denying that ...** 不可否认的是…; **there's ~ doing sth.** 没有做某事的可能; **there's ~ telling how he'll react** 谁也不知道他会有何反应 [3] (prohibiting) 禁止; **'~ parking'** 禁止停车; **~ talking!** 不要说话!; **~ surrender!** 绝不投降! [4] (indicating the opposite) 根本不; **she's ~ fool** 她一点儿不傻; **he's ~ expert** 他根本不是专家; **it was ~ easy task** 这任务真不容易; **this is ~ place to stop** 这根本不是停留的地方 [5] (hardly any) 几乎没有; **in ~ time** 立刻; **it was ~ distance to ...** 到…没有多远

[C] *n* (*pl* **noes**) [1] (as an answer) 否定回答; **can't you give me a straight yes or ~?** 你就不能直截了当地回答我是还是否吗? [2] (referring to person) 不赞同的人; **I'll put you down as a ~ for the trip** 我把你算作反对这次旅行的人 [3] (referring to vote) 反对票; **when we took a vote, there were nine yesses and three ~es** 我们进行了投票表决, 有 9 票赞成, 3 票反对; **the ~es have it** (in formal debate) 反对票占多数

[D] *adv* [1] (not any) 一点儿也不; **it's ~ different from driving a car** 这跟开汽车没什么区别; **~ later than Wednesday** 不晚于星期三; **~ fewer than 50 people** 不少于 50 人 [2] formal (not) 不; **tired or ~, you're going to bed** 不管困不困, 你都得上床睡觉; **whether it rains or ~** 不管下不下雨

No., no. *abbr* (*pl* **Nos.**) = **number** 号; **our invoice ~ 3781** 我们的 3781 号发票

Noah /ˈnəʊə/ *pr n* 诺亚; **~'s Ark** 诺亚方舟

nob /nɒb/ *n* Brit colloq 大人物

no-ball

[A] *n* 犯规投球

[B] *vt* «*umpire*» 判…投球犯规 ‹*bowler*›

nobble /ˈnɒbl/ *vt* Brit colloq [1] (drug) 给…下毒阻止获胜 ‹*animal*› [2] (persuade) 缠住…以获取支持 ‹*judge, politician*› [3] (bribe, threaten) 收买 ‹*judge, witness*› [4] (steal) 偷 ‹*object*› [5] (catch) 逮捕 ‹*thief*›

Nobel prize /nəʊˌbel ˈpraɪz/ *n* 诺贝尔奖

Nobel prizewinner *n* 诺贝尔奖获得者

nobility /nəʊˈbɪləti/ *n* [u] [1] (quality) 高贵品质; **~ of purpose** 目的的崇高; **~ of mind** 思想高尚 [2] (social class) **the ~** 贵族阶层

noble /ˈnəʊbl/

[A] *adj* [1] (aristocratic) 贵族的 ‹*family, class*› [2] (in character) 高尚的 ‹*deed, spirit*›; 伟大的 ‹*leader*›; **that was very ~ of you** 你真高尚 [3] (dignified) 高贵的 ‹*appearance, bearing*› [4] (imposing) 宏伟的 ‹*building*›; 壮观的 ‹*sight*› [5] *attrib* (superior) 上等的 ‹*wine*›; 良种的 ‹*pedigree*›; **the ~ art of sth.** 某种上等技艺 [6] *attrib* Chem 惰性的 ‹*element*›; **~ metals** 贵金属

[B] *n* 贵族成员

noble: ~man /-mən/ *n* 贵族成员; **~-minded** *adj* 高尚的 ‹*person, act*›

nobleness /ˈnəʊblnɪs/ *n* [u] [1] (of lineage) 高贵; **~ of birth** 出身的高贵 [2] (of character) 高尚; **~ of spirit** 精神的高尚 [3] (of appearance) 雄伟

noble: ~ savage *n* 高尚的野蛮人; **~woman** *n* 女贵族

nobly /ˈnəʊbli/ *adv* [1] (aristocratically) 贵族化地 ‹*educated*›; **to be ~ born** 出身贵族 [2] (bravely) 勇敢地 ‹*act, fight*› [3] (selflessly) 无私地 ‹*behave, serve, give*› [4] (splendidly) 极好地 ‹*proportioned*›; 华美地 ‹*coloured*›

nobody /ˈnəʊbədi/

[A] *pron* 没有人; **I've told ~** 我谁也没有告诉; **there was ~ at all in the street** 街上空无一人; **~ else can do it** 别人谁也做不了这件事; **~ with any sense would believe ...** 任何稍有头脑的人都不会相信…; **like ~'s business** Brit colloq (very much) 非常; (very fast) 极快; (very well) 很好; **to be ~'s fool** 非常精明

[B] *n* 小人物; **she rose from being a ~ to become a superstar** 她从无名小辈变身为超级明星

no-brainer /nəʊˈbreɪnə(r)/ *n* colloq 不费脑筋的事; **that's a ~** 那事无需动脑

no-claims bonus, no-claims discount *ns* Brit 无索赔保费优惠

nocturnal /nɒkˈtɜːnl/ *adj* (night-time) 夜间的 ‹*activity, habit*›; Zool 夜间活动的 ‹*animal, hunter*›

nocturne /ˈnɒktɜːn/ *n* 夜曲

nod /nɒd/

[A] *n* [1] (movement of head) 点头; **a ~ of the head** 点头; **to give (sb.) a ~ (of greeting/recognition)** (对某人) 点头 (致意/表示认识); **to answer with a ~** 点头作答; **with a ~ to his guests, he left the room** 他向客人点了点头, 离开了房间 [2] fig (agreement, approval) 同意; **to get the ~** Brit colloq (get permission or approval) 得到认可; (be selected) 被选中; **to give sb./sth. the ~** Brit colloq (approve) 许可某人/某事物; (select) 选中某人/某物; **he gave the musician the ~ to start playing** 他对乐手点了点头, 示意可以开始演奏; **a ~ to ...** (acknowledgement) 对…的认可; (concession) 对…的让步; **on the ~** Brit colloq «*approve, pass*» 以点头方式; **a ~ is as good as a wink (to a blind man** *or* **horse)** Prov 一点就通 [3] **the land of Nod** colloq 小睡; **to drift off into the land of Nod** 慢慢入睡; **the land of Nod is calling** 睡意来了

[B] *vi* (*pres p etc.* **-dd-**) [1] (nod the head) 点头; **to ~ at sth.** 点头同意某事; **to ~ to** *or* **at sb. (to do sth.)** 向某人点头示意 (让其做某事); **she ~ded in agreement** 她点头表示同意; **to have a ~ding acquaintance with sb./sth.** 与某人仅是点头之交/对某事物略知一二 [2] (sway) «*flowers, treetops*» 摇摆 [3] colloq (doze) 打盹 [4] colloq (be inattentive) 一时走神

[C] *vt* (*pres p etc.* **-dd-**) [1] (incline) **to ~ one's head** 点头 [2] (signify by nod) 点头表示 ‹*approval, assent, welcome*›

Phrasal verb

• **nod off** *vi* colloq 睡着

noddle /ˈnɒdl/ *n* colloq dated 脑袋

node /nəʊd/ *n* [1] Anat 结; **lymph ~** 淋巴结 [2] Bot 茎节 [3] Comput 节点 [4] Phys 波节

nodular /ˈnɒdjʊlə(r), Amer ˈnɒdʒuːlə(r)/ *adj* 有结节的 ‹*appearance, texture*›

nodule /ˈnɒdjuːl, Amer ˈnɒdʒuːl/ *n* [1] (gen) 小瘤 [2] Bot 根瘤; Anat 瘤 [3] Geol 结核

Noel /nəʊˈel/ *pr n* 圣诞节

noes /nəʊz/ *pl* ▸**no C**

no-fault divorce *n* [u and c] esp Amer 无过失离婚

no-fault insurance *n* [u] esp Amer 不追究责任的保险

no-fly zone *n* 禁飞区

no-frills *adj* 只提供必需品的 ‹*airline, service*›; 只提供起码保险的 ‹*insurance policy*›; 最简朴的 ‹*food, accommodation*›

noggin /ˈnɒɡɪn/ *n* colloq [1] (head) 脑袋 [2] (drink) 少量烈性饮料 [常指四分之一品脱]

no-go *adj* colloq (impossible) 不可能的; (forbidden) 禁止的

no-go area *n* Brit 禁区

no-good *adj attrib* colloq (worthless) 没用的 ‹*layabout*›; (contemptible) 可鄙的 ‹*cheater*›

no-hoper /ˌnəʊˈhəʊpə(r)/ *n* colloq 无成功希望的人

noise /nɔɪz/ *n* [1] [c] (sound) 声音; **a loud/soft ~** 大的/细微的声响; **above the ~ of sth.** 盖过某物声响的; **to make** *or* **produce a ~** 发出声音; **to make ~s about sth.** fig colloq 放出有关某事的风声; **to hear ~s that ...** colloq 听到…的风声; **a big ~** fig 大人物 [2] [u] (din) 噪声; **background ~** 背景噪声; **please make less ~!** 请小点儿声!; **hold your ~** 安静点 [3] [u] Radio, Telecom, Comput 干扰 [4] **noises** *pl* colloq (polite remarks) 议论; **to make polite/sympathetic ~s** 说一些礼貌/同情的话; **to make the right ~s** 随声附和

noise abatement *n* [u] 噪声消减; **~ society** 消减噪声协会

noiseless /ˈnɔɪzlɪs/ *adj* 无声的 ‹*machine, environment*›

noiselessly /ˈnɔɪzlɪslɪ/ *adv* 无声地

noise pollution *n* [u] 噪声污染

noisily /ˈnɔɪzɪli/ *adv* 大声地 ‹*cry, shout*›; 出声地 ‹*eat, work*›

noisiness /ˈnɔɪzɪnɪs/ *n* [u] 吵闹

noisome /ˈnɔɪsəm/ *adj* liter 令人讨厌的 ‹*sight, person*›; 恶臭的 ‹*smell, vapour*›

noisy /ˈnɔɪzi/ *adj* **1** (making, full of noise) 喧闹的 ‹*person, machinery, place*›; **it's too ∼** 太吵了; **a ∼ welcome** 热闹的欢迎 **2** (vociferous) 吵吵嚷嚷的 ‹*opponent, protest*›

nomad /ˈnəʊmæd/ *n* **1** (member of ethnic group) 游牧部落成员 **2** (wanderer) 流浪者

nomadic /nəʊˈmædɪk/ *adj* **1** (of nomads) 游牧的 ‹*peoples, lifestyle*› **2** (wandering) 流浪的 ‹*person, habit*›

nomadism /ˈnəʊmædɪzəm/ *n* [u] 游牧生活

no-man's land *n* [u] **1** Mil 无人区域 **2** fig (indeterminate place) 真空地带; (state) 真空状态

nom de plume /ˌnɒm də ˈpluːm/ *n* (*pl* **noms de plume**) 笔名; **to write under a ∼** 用笔名写作

nomenclature /nəˈmenklətʃə(r), Amer ˈnəʊmənkleɪtʃər/ *n* **1** (system of naming) 命名系统 **2** (names) 术语集

nominal /ˈnɒmɪnl/ *adj* **1** *attrib* (in name only) 名义上的 ‹*leader, rights*› **2** (small) 微不足道的 ‹*charge, sum, amount*› **3** Ling 名词性的 ‹*word, inflection*› **4** colloq (normal) 正常的

nominal damages *npl* 名义上的损害赔偿

nominalization /ˌnɒmɪnəlaɪˈzeɪʃn, Amer -lɪˈz-/ *n* **1** [u] (action) 名词化 **2** [c] (noun) 名词化名词

nominalize /ˈnɒmɪnəlaɪz/ *vt* 使转变为名词

nominally /ˈnɒmɪnəli/ *adv* 在名义上 ‹*rule, head, qualified*›

nominal: ∼ price *n* **1** Fin 虚价; **2** (low price) 低价; **∼ value** *n* 票面价值

nominate /ˈnɒmɪneɪt/ *vt* **1** (propose) 提名 ‹*candidate*›; **to ∼ sb. for a position/for president** 提名某人就任某职位/为总统候选人; **to ∼ sb./sth. for an award** 提名某人/某事获奖 **2** (appoint) 任命 ‹*person*›; **to ∼ sb. as sth.** 任命某人就任某职位; **to ∼ sb. (as) chairman/to a position** 任命某人为主席/就任某职位; **to ∼ sb. to do sth.** 指派某人做某事 **3** (specify) 指定; **to ∼ sth. as** 指定…为 ‹*place, time*›

nomination /ˌnɒmɪˈneɪʃn/ *n* **1** [u] (appointment) 任命; **∼ to sth.** 某职位的任命 **2** [c] (proposal) 提名; **a ∼ for sth.** 做某工作的提名; **his ∼ was approved** 他的提名被批准了 **3** [c] (nominee) 被提名者; **to close the list of ∼s** 结束被提名人员登记

nominative /ˈnɒmɪnətɪv/

A *adj* 主格的 ‹*ending, use*›; **in the ∼ case** 用主格

B *n* 主格; **in the ∼** 用主格

nominator /ˈnɒmɪneɪtə(r)/ *n* 提名者

nominee /ˌnɒmɪˈniː/ *n* (to position) 被任命者; (as candidate) 被提名者

nominee company *n* 托管公司

non- /nɒn-/ *combining form* 非…

non-absorbent *adj* 非吸收性的 ‹*substance, fabric*›

non-academic *adj* 非学术性的 ‹*courses, career*›; **∼ staff** 非教学人员

non-acceptance *n* [u] **1** (rejection) 不接受 **2** Jur 不承兑

non-accountability *n* [u] 无问责性

non-accountable *adj* = **unaccountable 2**

non-addictive *adj* 不致上瘾的 ‹*drug, substance*›

non-affiliated *adj* 非附属的 ‹*business, institution*›

nonagenarian /ˌnɒnədʒɪˈneərɪən/

A *n* 90 多岁的人

B *adj attrib* 90 多岁的 ‹*person*›; 90 多岁人的 ‹*care, memory*›

non-aggression *n* [u] 不侵犯; **a ∼ pact/treaty** 互不侵犯协定/条约

non-alcoholic *adj* 不含酒精的 ‹*beer, beverage*›

non-aligned /ˌnɒnəˈlaɪnd/ *adj* 不结盟的 ‹*state, people*›

non-alignment *n* [u] 不结盟

non-allergenic /ˌnɒnæləˈdʒenɪk/, **non-allergic** /ˌnɒnəˈlɜːdʒɪk/ *adjs* 不引起过敏的 ‹*substance, cloth*›

no-name esp Amer

A *adj attrib* **1** (unbranded) 非名牌的 ‹*clothes, cigarettes*› **2** (unknown) 没名气的 ‹*actor, director*›

B *n* 不知名的人

non-appearance *n* [u] 不到法庭

non-attendance *n* [u] 缺席

non-attributable *adj* 不可归因的

non-availability *n* [u] (of thing) 不可获得; (of person) 不可见到

non-available *adj* 不能获得的 ‹*resources, item*›

non-believer *n* 无信仰的人

non-belligerent

A *adj* (not at war) 非交战的 ‹*nation*›; (peaceable) 不好战的

B *n* 非交战国

non-biodegradable *adj* 不可生物降解的 ‹*substance*›

non-biological *adj* **1** Biol 非生物的 ‹*material*› **2** (enzyme-free) 不含酶的 **3** (not related by blood) 非亲生的 ‹*parent, sibling*›

non-breakable *adj* = **unbreakable**

non-broadcast video *n* 非广播用录像

non-budgetary *adj* 非预算内的 ‹*item, fund*›

nonce /nɒns/ *adj* 临时造的; **a ∼ word/expression/form** 临时造的词/表达方式/形式; **for the ∼** 目前

nonchalance /ˈnɒnʃələns/ *n* 漠不关心; **an air of ∼** 满不在乎的样子

nonchalant /ˈnɒnʃələnt/ *adj* 漠不关心的 ‹*attitude, reply, smile*›

nonchalantly /ˈnɒnʃələntli/ *adv* 满不在乎地 ‹*say, shrug, wave*›

non-Christian

A *n* 非基督教徒

B *adj* 非基督教的 ‹*belief, background, church*›

non-classified *adj* 非保密的 ‹*information, material*›

non-collegiate *adj* **1** (not affiliated to college) 不属于学院的 ‹*student, status*› **2** (not composed of colleges) 不设学院的 ‹*university*›

non-collegiate student *n* 非本院大学生

non-combatant *n* 非战斗人员

non-combustible *adj* 不燃的 ‹*gas, material*›

non-commercial *adj* 非商业性的 ‹*organization, activity, user*›

non-commissioned officer *n* 军士

non-committal /ˌnɒnkəˈmɪtl/ *adj* 不表态的 ‹*politician*›; 含糊的 ‹*statement, answer*›

non-committally /ˌnɒnkəˈmɪtəli/ *adv* 含糊地 ‹*speak, reply*›

non-compliance *n* [u] 不顺从; **∼ with sth.** 不遵守 ‹*ban, order*›

non-conductor *n* 非导体

nonconformism /ˌnɒnkənˈfɔːmɪzəm/ *n* [u] = **nonconformity**

nonconformist /ˌnɒnkənˈfɔːmɪst/

A *n* **1** **Nonconformist** Relig 不信奉英国国教的人 **2** (non-traditional person) 不守成规者

B *adj* **1** **Noncomformist** Relig 不信奉英国国教的 ‹*church, belief*› **2** (non-traditional) 不守成规的 ‹*person, behaviour, idea*›

nonconformity /ˌnɒnkənˈfɔːməti/ *n* [u] **1** **Nonconformity** Relig 不信奉英国国教 **2** (gen) (refusal to conform) 不守成规

non-contentious *adj* 无争议的 ‹*article, discussion, method*›

non-contract *adj attrib* 非签约的 ‹*player, staff*›

non-contributory *adj* 由雇主支付的 ‹*allowance, benefit*›

non-contributory pension scheme *n* [由雇主支付的] 非摊缴退休金制度

non-controversial *adj* 无争议的 ‹*topic, person*›

non-cooperation *n* [u] 不合作 [尤指对政府不合作]; **∼ with sb./sth.** 对某人/某事的不合作

non-cooperative *adj* 不合作的

non-count *adj* 不可数的

non-custodial sentence *n* 监外执行的判决

non-dairy /ˌnɒnˈdeəri/ *adj* 非乳制的 ‹*product, topping*›

non-dazzle *adj* 不耀眼的 ‹*substance, glass*›

non-degradable /ˌnɒndɪˈgreɪdəbl/ *adj* 不可降解的 ‹*plastic, substance*›

non-democratic *adj* 不民主的 ‹*country, action, idea*›

non-denominational *adj* 跨教派的 ‹*school, meeting*›; **a ∼ church** 无特定派别限制的教堂

nondescript /ˈnɒndɪskrɪpt/ *adj* 无特征的 ‹*appearance, building*›; 无个性的 ‹*person*›

non-destructive *adj* 非破坏性的 ‹*method, testing*›

non-detachable *adj* 不可拆卸的 ‹*handle, hood, lining*›

non-directional *adj* 非指令性的 ‹*approach*›

non-disruptive *adj* 不捣乱的 ‹*behaviour, pupil*›

non-distinctive *adj* 无特色的 ‹*appearance, character*›; **his style is on the whole ∼** 总体上他无独特之处

non-dom /ˈnɒndɒm/ *n* Brit colloq 无户籍的人

non-drinker *n* 不喝酒的人

non-driver *n* (sb. who cannot drive) 不会开车的人; (sb. who does not drive) 不开车的人

none /nʌn/

A *pron* **1** (not one) 全无; **we saw several flats, but ∼ we really liked** 我们看了几处公寓，可是没有我们真正喜欢的; **she thought a bad husband was worse than ∼ at all** 她认为一个坏丈夫比没有丈夫还要糟; **∼ of the books was** *or* **were any help** 这些书没一本有用的; **do you have any doubts? — ∼ whatever** 你有什么怀疑吗？——一点都没有 **2** (no part) 什么也没有; **there's ∼ left** 什么也没有留下; **some money is better than ∼** 有点儿钱总比没有好; **he has ∼ of his mother's intelligence** 他根本没有他母亲的智慧; **∼ of your nonsense!** 别尽胡说！; **∼ at all** 根本没有; **to want/have ∼ of sth.** 拒绝接受某事物; **I want ∼ of your nonsense!** 我根本不想听你的废话！ **3** (nobody) 没有人; **as a lawyer, he's second to ∼** 作为律师，他是最棒的; **there's ∼ so clever/old as Jane** 没有人像简那样聪明/老; **∼ but** liter 只有; **she had told ∼ but him** 她只告诉了他; **∼ other than sb.** 竟然是某人; **it was ∼ other than Edward** 那正是爱德华 **4** (on form, questionnaire) 无; **in the box headed 'dependants' he wrote '∼'** 在“供养家属”一栏里，他写上了“无”

B *adv* **1** **∼ too** (not at all) 一点也不; (not very) 不

太; **her sight's ~ too good** 她的视力不太好; **~ too pleased** 不太高兴; **and ~ too soon!** 差点来不及! **2** (in no way) 毫不; **the play is long, but ~ the worse for that** 这部戏虽然很长，但一点也不差

non-edible *adj* 非食用的

non-emergency *adj attrib* 非紧急的 ‹*situation, call*›; 非急诊的 ‹*patient, treatment*›

nonentity /nɒ'nentəti/ *n* **1** (insignificant person) 无足轻重的人; **a complete** *or* **total ~** 一个无名之辈 **2** (non-existent person) 不存在的人; (non-existent thing) 不存在的东西

non-essential *adj* 非必要的 ‹*item, business*›

non-essentials *npl* (objects) 非必需品; (details) 可有可无的细节

nonet /'nəʊnet, 'nɒnet/ *n* 九重奏乐曲

nonetheless /ˌnʌnðə'les/ *adv* = **nevertheless**

non-event *n* 令人失望的事

non-executive director *n* 非执行董事

non-existence *n* [u] 不存在

non-existent *adj* 不存在的 ‹*threat, road*›

non-explosive *adj* 不易爆炸的 ‹*substance*›

non-fat *adj* 脱脂的 ‹*milk*›; **a ~ diet** 无脂肪饮食

non-fattening *adj* 不会使人发胖的 ‹*food*›

non-ferrous *adj* 非铁的 ‹*metal*›

non-fiction *n* [u] 纪实文学; **a work of ~** 纪实文学作品

non-finite *adj* 非限定的 ‹*form, verb*›

non-flammable *adj* 不易燃的 ‹*fabric, substance*›

non-fulfilment *n* [u] (of contract, obligation) 未履行; (of task) 未完成; (hope, aim) 未实现

non-governmental *adj* 非政府的 ‹*agency*›; **~ organization** 非政府组织

non-grammatical *adj* 不合语法的 ‹*sentence*›

non-greasy *adj* 非油性的 ‹*lotion, ointment, skin*›; 低油脂的 ‹*food, liquid*›

non-human
A *adj* 非人类的
B *n* 非人类生物

non-infectious *adj* 非传染性的 ‹*disease, patient*›; 非感染性的 ‹*inflammation*›

non-inflammable *adj* = **non-flammable**

non-inflationary *adj* 非通胀的 ‹*growth, policy*›

non-interference *n* [u] 不干涉

non-intervention *n* [u] 不干涉

non-intoxicating *adj* 不醉人的 ‹*drink*›

non-invasive *adj* **1** Med 无创的 ‹*surgery, treatment*› **2** (not spreading) 非扩散性的 ‹*tumour, tissue*› **3** Hort, Bot 非入侵性的 ‹*plant, species*›

non-involvement *n* [u] 不介入

non-iron *adj* 免熨的 ‹*fabric, clothes*›

non-Jew *n* (by ethnic group) 非犹太人; (by religion) 非犹太教徒

non-Jewish *adj* (by ethnic group) 非犹太人的; (by religion) 非犹太教的

non-judgemental, non-judgemented *adj* 不作道德评判的 ‹*attitude, person*›

non-jury *adj* 无陪审团的 ‹*court, trial*›

non-league *adj* 非联赛的 ‹*team, game*›

non-linear *adj* 非线性的

non-linguistic *adj* 非语言的

non-literate *adj* 不识字的 ‹*person, society*›

non-magnetic *adj* 无磁性的 ‹*material, steel*›

non-malignant /ˌnɒnmə'lɪgnənt/ *adj* 非恶性的 ‹*tumour, cancer*›

non-member *n* 非会员

non-metal *n* (substance) 非金属; (element) 非金属元素

non-metallic *adj* 非金属的 ‹*object, appearance*›; **~ element** 非金属元素

non-militant *adj* 温和的 ‹*person, attitude*›

non-military *adj* 非军事的 ‹*organization*›; **~ personnel** 非军事人员

non-native *adj* **1** Bot, Zool 非本地的 ‹*person, animal, species*› **2** Ling 非母语的; **~ speaker of English** 母语不是英语的操英语者

non-negotiable *adj* **1** (not open to discussion) 无商议余地的 ‹*plan, policy*›; 不可谈判的 ‹*contract, price*›; **a ~ demand** 无法磋商的要求 **2** (not transferable) 禁止转让的 ‹*bond, cheque*›

non-nuclear *adj* 无核武器的 ‹*power, nation*›; 不使用核武器的 ‹*conflict, battle*›

no-no *n* colloq 被禁止的东西; **smoking in bed is a definite ~** 绝对不能在床上吸烟

non-observance *n* [u] formal 不遵守

no-nonsense *adj attrib* (sensible) 明智的; (straightforward) 直截了当的

non-operational duties *npl* 内勤工作

non-organic *adj* 非有机的 ‹*product*›; 未实行有机栽培的 ‹*farm*›

non-partisan *adj* 无党派的 ‹*person*›; 超党派的 ‹*agreement*›; 不偏不倚的 ‹*decision*›

non-party *adj* 超党派的 ‹*vote, issue*›

non-payer *n* 未支付者

non-paying *adj* 不交钱的 ‹*guest*›; 无报酬的 ‹*occupation*›

non-payment *n* [u] 未支付

non-perishable *adj* 不易坏的 ‹*food*›

non-person *n* (*pl* **~s**) **1** pej (insignificant) 无足轻重的人 **2** (ignored) 被忽视的人

nonplus /ˌnɒn'plʌs/ *vt* (*pres p etc.* **-ss-**) «*person, news, event*» 使不知所措

nonplussed /ˌnɒn'plʌst/ *adj* 不知所措的 ‹*person, expression*›

non-political *adj* 非政治性的 ‹*organization, issue*›

non-practising *adj* **1** Relig 不热心的 ‹*Muslim, Jew, Catholic*› **2** Jur 不执业的 ‹*barrister*› **3** (sexually) 不身体力行的 ‹*homosexual*›

non-prescription *adj* 非处方类的 ‹*drug, medication*›

non-productive *adj* 无出产的 ‹*land*›; 非生产性的 ‹*factory*›; 无成效的 ‹*activity, changes*›; **we had a very ~ morning/meeting** 我们今天早上的工作没什么成效/我们的会议没什么结果

non-professional
A *adj* 非专业的 ‹*player, actor*›
B *n* 非专业人员

non-profit *adj* **1** 非营利性的 ‹*business*›; **a ~ organization** 非营利组织; **on a ~ basis** 在非营利的基础上

non-profitmaking /ˌnɒn'prɒfɪtmeɪkɪŋ/ *adj* 非营利性的; **on a ~ basis** 在非营利的基础上

non-proliferation *n* [u] 防止核扩散; **~ treaty** 防止核扩散条约

non-proprietary *adj* **1** (in public domain) 非所有权的 ‹*software*› **2** (generic) 非专利的 ‹*name, drug*›

non-punitive *adj* 非惩罚性的 ‹*action*›; 并非苛刻的 ‹*taxation*›

non-racial *adj* (not racial) 非种族的; (non-discriminatory) 没有种族歧视的

non-receipt *n* [u] 未收到

non-recurring expenses *npl* 临时费用

non-recyclable *adj* 不可回收的 ‹*material, waste*›

non-redeemable *adj* 不可赎回的

non-refillable /ˌnɒnri:'fɪləbl/ *adj* 不可替换笔芯的 ‹*pen*›; 不可再注满的 ‹*bottle, container*›

non-reflective *adj* 不反射的 ‹*surface, properties*›

non-refundable *adj* 不能退款的 ‹*deposit*›; **a ~ ticket** 不可退的票

non-religious *adj* 非宗教的 ‹*group, ceremony, beliefs*›

non-renewable *adj* **1** (not replaceable) 不可再生的 ‹*energy, resources*› **2** (not extendable) 不可延续的 ‹*contract, term*›

non-renewal *n* [u] (of contract, lease) 不延续

non-resident
A *adj* **1** (gen) 不寄宿的 ‹*caretaker*›; 非常住的 ‹*visitor*›; (at hotel) 非住店的 ‹*guest*›; **a ~ student** 走读生 **2** (position) 不提供住宿的 ‹*post, job*›
B *n* (in hotel) 非旅馆住客; (in housing complex) 非常住户

non-residential *adj* **1** (not providing residence) 不提供住宿的 ‹*position, course*› **2** (commercial) 不用于居住的 ‹*building, area*›

nonrestrictive /ˌnɒnrɪ'strɪktɪv/ *adj* **1** (without restriction) 无约束的 ‹*licence*›; **~ growth conditions** 无约束的生长条件 **2** Ling 非限制性的

non-returnable *adj* 不能退还的 ‹*goods, bottle*›

non-run *adj* 不抽丝的 ‹*stockings, material*›

non-runner *n* 未能参赛的马

non-scheduled /ˌnɒn'ʃedju:ld, Amer -'skedʒʊld/ *adj* 不按计划的 ‹*flight, bus*›; **to make several ~ stops** 数次临时停车

non-sectarian *adj* 与任何宗派无关的 ‹*opinion, violence*›

non-segregated *adj* 非隔离的 ‹*area, community*›

nonsense /'nɒnsns, Amer -sens/ *n* [u] **1** (words) 无意义的话; **to talk ~** «*baby*» 咿咿呀呀 **2** (absurd language) 胡说; (behaviour) 荒唐的举动; **the scheme is utter ~** 这个计划愚蠢透顶; **to talk ~** 胡说八道; **to make (a) ~ of sth.** 使某事物变得无意义; **what's all this ~ about ...?** 干吗因为…瞎嚷嚷? ; **(stuff and) ~!** 一派胡言! **3** (unacceptable behaviour) 胡闹; **stop this ~** 别胡闹了; **to stand no ~ from sb.** 不能容忍某人的胡闹; **there is no ~ about sb.** 某人举止稳重严肃; **to knock the ~ out of sb.** 使某人放弃傻念头

nonsense: ~ verse *n* [u] 打油诗; **~ word** *n* 杜撰词

nonsensical /nɒn'sensɪkl/ *adj* 无意义的 ‹*sentence, text*›; 荒谬的 ‹*idea, action*›

nonsensically /nɒn'sensɪkli/ *adv* 荒谬地 ‹*behave, speak, write*›

non sequitur /ˌnɒn 'sekwɪtə(r)/ *n* **1** (statement) 前后不连贯的陈述 **2** Philos 未根据前提的推理

non-sexist *adj* 非性别歧视的 ‹*language, society*›

non-shrink *adj* 不缩水的 ‹*material*›

non-skid *n* 防滑的 ‹*properties*›; **a ~ tyre** 防滑轮胎

non-slip *adj* 防滑的; **a ~ surface** 防滑表面; **~ paint/shoes** 防滑漆/防滑鞋

non-smoker *n* **1** (person) 不抽烟的人 **2** Brit colloq (on train) 禁烟车厢

non-smoking *adj* 禁止吸烟的 ‹*place, area*›; 不吸烟的 ‹*person*›

non-speaking *adj* 无需讲话的 ‹*part, role*›

non-specialist
A *n* 非专家
B *adj* 非专业的 ‹*publication, reader*›

non-specialized *adj* 非专业的 ‹*journal*›; 非专科的 ‹*doctor*›; 非专卖的 ‹*store*›; **a ~ health-care facility** 非专业的医疗保健机构

n

non-specific *adj* 1 (general) 不明确的〈*answer, number*〉2 Med 非特异性的〈*symptoms*〉; ~ **urethritis** 非特异性尿道炎

non-standard *adj* 不规范的〈*usage*〉; ~ **English** 非规范英语

non-starter *n* 1 colloq (hopeless person) 无望成功的人; (hopeless idea) 不切实际的想法 2 (in race) (person) 未能参赛的人; (animal) 未能参赛的动物

non-stick *adj* 不粘食物的〈*coating, surface*〉; **a ~ pan** 不粘底平底煎锅

non-stop
A *adj* 1 Transp 直达的〈*train, flight*〉2 (constant) 不间断的〈*talk, work*〉
B *adv* 不停地〈*work, argue, dig*〉; **to fly ~ from Kuwait to London** 从科威特直飞伦敦

non-stretch *adj* 无伸缩性的〈*fabric, tape*〉

non-student *n* 未获学生身份的人

non-swimmer *n* 不会游泳的人

non-taxable *adj* 免税的〈*income, loan*〉

non-taxpayer *n* 不纳税的人

non-teaching staff *n* [u] 非教学人员

non-technical *adj* 非技术性的〈*term, content, method*〉

non-threatening /ˌnɒnˈθretnɪŋ/ *adj* 非险恶的〈*environment*〉; 友好的〈*way, manner*〉

non-toxic *adj* 无毒的〈*material, waste*〉

non-transferable *adj* 不得转让的〈*membership, ticket, share*〉

non-U /ˌnɒnˈjuː/ *adj* Brit colloq = **non upper class** 非上层阶级所用的〈*language*〉; 不为上层阶级所接受的〈*behaviour*〉

non-union *adj* 未加入工会的〈*worker, labour*〉; 不雇用工会会员的〈*company, organization*〉

non-verbal *adj* 非言语的〈*cues, language*〉; ~ **communication** 非言语交际

non-viable *adj* 1 (unable to live) 不能生长发育的; ~ **fetus/seed** 不能存活的胎儿/不能萌发的种子 2 (not feasible) 不可行的〈*plan, idea*〉

non-vintage *adj* 非特定地区特定年份酿造的〈*wine*〉

non-violence *n* [u] 非暴力

non-violent *adj* 非暴力的; ~ **action/resistance/crimes** 非暴力行动/抵制/罪行; **a ~ protest/offender** 非暴力抗议/罪犯

non-vocational *adj* 非职业培训的〈*class, education*〉

non-volatile *adj* 1 Chem 不挥发的〈*compound, acid*〉2 Comput 非易失性的〈*memory*〉

non-voluntary *adj* 非自愿的〈*group, services*〉; **to do sth. in a ~ capacity** 以非自愿的身份做某事

non-voter *n* (ineligible) 无权投票者; (by choice) 放弃投票者

non-voting share *n* 无表决权股

non-white, non-White
A *n* 非白种人
B *adj* 非白种人的〈*population*〉

non-worker *n* 失业者

non-woven *adj* 无纺的; **a ~ fabric/fibre** 无纺织物/纤维

noodle /ˈnuːdl/ *n* 1 Culin 面条; **egg ~s** 鸡蛋面; **chicken ~ soup** 鸡汤面 2 colloq (head) 脑袋瓜 3 colloq (fool) 傻瓜

nook /nʊk/ *n* 1 (retreat) 隐蔽处 2 (corner) 角落; **every ~ and cranny** 到处

nookie, nooky /ˈnʊki/ *n* [u] sl 性交

noon /nuːn/ ▸ **p. 831** *n* [u] (midday) 中午; (12 pm) 正午; **by/about ~** 到/大约正午时间; **at 12 ~** 在中午 12 点; **at high ~** 在正午; **the ~ sun** 正午的太阳

noonday /ˈnuːndeɪ/ *n* [u] 中午; **the ~ sun** 中午的太阳; **the ~ of his fame** fig 他声望的鼎盛期

no one *pron* = **nobody A**

noontime /ˈnuːntaɪm/ *n* [u] esp Amer 正午; **a ~ rest** 午休

noose /nuːs/
A *n* 1 (loop) 套索 2 (for hanging) 绞索; **to put a ~ around sb.'s neck** 把绞索套在某人颈上; **to put one's head in a ~** fig 自投罗网; **to make a ~ for one's neck** fig 自找苦吃
B *vt* 1 (snare) 用套索捕捉〈*animal*〉; **to ~ sb.** fig 制服某人 2 (make loop) 把…打成活套〈*rope, wire*〉

nope /nəʊp/ *excl* sl 不

nor /nɔː(r), nə(r)/ *conj* 也不; **I have neither the time ~ the money** 我既没有时间也没有钱; **he's not Spanish — ~ is John** 他不是西班牙人——约翰也不是; **not a building ~ a tree was left standing** formal 房屋和树木无一例外全倒了; ▸ **here A1**

nor' /nɔː(r)/ *abbr* = **north** 北 [常用以构成合成词]; **to sail ~-~-east** 向北东北方向航行

NORAD /ˈnɔːræd/ *abbr* = **North American Aerospace Defence Command** 北美空防联合司令部

Nordic /ˈnɔːdɪk/ *adj* 1 (of Scandinavia, Finland and Iceland) 斯堪的纳维亚国家的〈*transport, holiday*〉; **the ~ peoples** 北欧民族; **she has ~ ancestry** 她有斯堪的纳维亚血统 2 (of physical type) 北欧斯堪的纳维亚人的〈*appearance*〉3 Sport **n~ skiing** 北欧两项滑雪赛

Norfolk /ˈnɒːfək/ *pr n* 诺福克郡

norm /nɔːm/ *n* 1 (average) 基准; **above/below the ~** 高于/低于基准水平 2 (standard) 规范; **social ~s, the ~s of society** 社会规范; **to establish** *or* **set a ~** 建立规范 3 Sociol 常态

normal /ˈnɔːml/
A *adj* 1 (usual) 通常的〈*place, method*〉; **to arrive at one's ~ time** 在惯常时间到达; **as ~** 和平常一样; **in the ~ course of events** 在一般情况下 2 (typical, conventional) 正常的〈*behaviour, family, size*〉; **it is ~ for sb. to do sth.** 对于某人来说，做某事是正常的; **it is ~ that ...** …是正常的; **in ~ circumstances** 在正常情况下; **a ~ baby** (free from handicap) 正常的婴儿; **the ~ temperature/length of sth.** (standard) 某物的正常温度/长度; **to take sth. as ~** 把…作为基准〈*height, amount*〉3 Psych 精神正常的〈*person, behaviour*〉; **a ~ response** 正常反应
B *n* [u] 常态; **above/below ~** 高/低于正常值; **to get back** *or* **return to ~** 恢复正常

normalcy /ˈnɔːmlsi/ *n* Amer = **normality**

normality /nɔːˈmæləti/ *n* [u] Brit 正常状态; **to return to ~** 恢复常态

normalization /ˌnɔːməlaɪˈzeɪʃn, Amer -lɪˈz-/ *n* [u] 1 (act, process) 正常化 2 (integration) [不区别对待残疾人和正常人的] 正常化政策

normalize /ˈnɔːməlaɪz/
A *vt* 使…正常化〈*situation, relationship*〉; 使…规范化〈*procedure, typescript*〉
B *vi*《*relations, situation*》正常化

normally /ˈnɔːməli/ *adv* 1 (usually) 通常〈*happy, pale*〉; **I ~ go to work at about 9** 我一般 9 点左右上班 2 (in normal way) 正常地〈*behave, sleep*〉

Norman /ˈnɔːmən/
A *adj* 1 Hist 诺曼人的〈*kings, lineage*〉2 Archit 诺曼式的〈*church*〉
B *n* 1 Hist 诺曼人 2 Ling ~ **(French)** 诺曼语

Norman Conquest *n* **the ~** 诺曼征服 [诺曼底公爵于1066年对英格兰的征服]

Normandy /ˈnɔːməndi/ *pr n* 诺曼底

normative /ˈnɔːmətɪv/ *adj* 规范的〈*regulation, judgement*〉

Norse /nɔːs/
A *n* ▸ **p. 503, p. 426** 1 [u] Ling (Scandinavian) 斯堪的纳维亚语; (Norwegian) 挪威语; **Old ~** 古斯堪的纳维亚语 2 [c] Hist **the ~** + *v pl* (Scandinavians) 斯堪的纳维亚人; (Norwegians) 挪威人
B *adj attrib* Hist (of people) 古斯堪的纳维亚人的〈*legends*〉; (of place) 古斯堪的纳维亚的〈*churches*〉

Norseman /ˈnɔːsmən/ *n* (*pl* **Norsemen**) 古斯堪的纳维亚人

north /nɔːθ/ ▸ **p. 142**
A *n* [u] (direction) 北; (position or location) 北方; (northern part) 北部; **to the ~** (position) 在北面; (movement) 向北面; **from** *or* **in the ~** 来自北面; **when the wind is in the ~** 在刮北风的时候; **up ~** colloq 在北方; **the N~** Amer 美国北方地区 [尤指美国内战期间的北部诸州]; Brit 英格兰北部; **a town in the ~ of Spain** 西班牙北部的一个城镇
B *adj* 1 (northern) 北边的; **on the ~ side of the island** 在岛屿的北侧; ~ **Asia** 北亚 2 *attrib* (from the north) 来自北边的; **a ~ wind** 北风
C *adv* 1 (to the north, on the northern side) 在北边〈*situated*〉; ~ **of sth.** 在某物的北边; **to lie due ~ of London** 位于伦敦正北面 2 (towards the north) 向北; **due ~** 向正北

North Africa *pr n* 北非

North African ▸ **p. 503**
A *adj* 北非的〈*food, climate*〉; ~ **people** 北非人
B *n* (inhabitant) 北非居民; (native, descendant) 北非人

North America *pr n* 北美洲

North American ▸ **p. 503**
A *adj* 北美洲的〈*landscape, culture*〉; ~ **people** 北美洲人
B *n* (inhabitant) 北美洲居民; (native) 北美洲人

Northamptonshire /nɔːˈθæmptənʃɪə(r)/ *pr n* 北安普顿郡

Northants. /nɔːˈθænts/ *abbr* Brit = **Northamptonshire**

north: N~ Atlantic Drift *n* 北大西洋洋流; = **Gulf Stream**; **N~ Atlantic Treaty Organization** *n* 北大西洋公约组织; **~bound** *adj* 1 (travelling north) 北行的〈*traffic, train, passenger*〉; 2 (leading north) 向北的〈*road, line, platform*〉; **N~ Carolina** *pr n* 北卡罗来纳州; ~ **country** *n* 北国 [指一国的北部]; **N~ Dakota** *pr n* 北达科他州

north-east ▸ **p. 142**
A *n* [u] 1 (direction) 东北; (position or location) 东北方; (north-eastern part) 东北部; **to the ~** 朝东北方向; **from** *or* **in the ~** 来自东北方向; **the sun/wind is in the ~** 太阳在东北方/吹的是东北风; **when the wind is in the ~** 在刮东北风的时候 2 (compass point) 东北方 3 (of country, region, town) 东北部
B *adj* 1 (north-eastern) 东北边的; **on the ~ side of the island** 在岛屿的东北侧; ~ **France** 法国东北部 2 *attrib* (from the north-east) 来自东北边的; **a ~ wind** 东北风
C *adv* 1 (to the north-east, on the north-eastern side) 在东北边; ~ **of sth.** 在某物的东北边; **to be** *or* **lie ~ of sth.** 位于某处的东北 2 (towards the north-east) 向东北; **due ~** 向正东北; **to go** *or* **head ~** 向东北方走

northeaster /ˌnɔːθˈiːstə(r)/ *n* 东北风

north-easterly ▸ **p. 142**
A *adj* 1 (in north-eastward position) 东北的〈*point, area*〉2 (in a north-eastward direction) 向东北的〈*aspect, course, journey*〉3 (from a north-eastward direction) 从东北方来的; **a ~ wind** 东北风; **a ~ breeze** 东北微风
B *adv* (from north-east) 从东北方; (towards north-east) 向东北方
C *n* 东北风

north-eastern ▸ **p. 142** *adj attrib* 1 (of or in the north-east) 东北方的; ~ **France** 法国东北部 2 (facing north-east) 向东北的; (going towards north-east) 东北行的

north-eastward
A *adj* 向东北的; ~ **direction** 东北方向
B *adv* (*also* **north-eastwards**) 向东北

northerly /'nɔːðəli/ ▸**p. 142**
A *adj* 1 (in a northward position) 北方的 ‹*point, area*›; ～ **latitude** 北纬 2 (in a northward direction) 向北的 ‹*aspect, course, journey*› 3 (from northward direction) 从北方吹来的; **a ～ wind** 北风
B *n* 北风

northern /'nɔːðən/ ▸**p. 142** *adj attrib* 1 (of or in the north) 北方的; ～ **France** 法国北部; **the ～ wall of the city** 北城墙 2 (facing north) 向北的 ‹*window, wall*›; (going towards north) 北行的 ‹*journey, route*› 3 (*also* **Northern**) Pol, Geog 北方的

northerner, Northerner /'nɔːðənə(r)/ *n* (native) 北方人; (inhabitant) 北方居民

northern hemisphere *n* 北半球

Northern Ireland *pr n* 北爱尔兰

Northern Ireland: ～ Assembly *n* 北爱尔兰议会; ～ **Office** *n* Brit 北爱尔兰办事处

Northern: ～ Irish *adj* 北爱尔兰的 ‹*politics*›; ～ **Irish people** 北爱尔兰人; ～ **Lights** *npl* **the ～ Lights** 北极光

northernmost /'nɔːðənməʊst/ *adj* 最北的

Northern Territory *pr n* **the ～** [澳大利亚的] 澳北区

north-facing *adj* 朝北的 ‹*window*›; **a ～ wall/exit** 北墙/北出口

North Island *n* [新西兰的] 北岛

North Korea *pr n* 朝鲜

North Korean ▸**p. 503**
A *adj* (of North Korea) 朝鲜的; (of the people) 朝鲜人的
B *n* 朝鲜人

north-north-east
A *n* [u] 北东北
B *adj* 1 (in direction) 北东北的 ‹*position*› 2 (from direction) 从北东北吹来的 ‹*wind*›
C *adv* (to direction) 向北东北; (in direction) 在北东北

north-north-west
A *n* [u] 北西北
B *adj* 1 (in direction) 北西北的 ‹*position*› 2 (from direction) 从北西北吹来的 ‹*wind*›
C *adv* (to direction) 向北西北; (in direction) 在北西北

North Pole *n* 1 (of Earth) **the ～** 北极 2 Astron 北天极 3 **north pole** (of magnet) [磁体的] 北极

North Sea *pr n* **the ～** 北海

North: ～ Sea gas *n* 北海天然气; ～ **Sea oil** *n* 北海原油; ～ **Star** *n* **the ～ Star** 北极星

north-south *adj attrib* 南北向的 ‹*road*›; **in a ～ direction** 南北朝向; **the ～ rail route** 纵贯铁路线

North-South divide *n* 1 (global) 南北分歧 2 (in UK) 南北差距

Northumberland /nɒː'θʌmbələnd/ *pr n* 诺森伯兰郡

Northumbria /nɔː'θʌmbrɪə/ *pr n* 1 Geog 诺森布里亚 [英格兰一地区] 2 Hist 诺森布里亚王国

Northumbrian /nɔː'θʌmbrɪən/
A *adj* 1 (of Northumbria) 诺森布里亚的; (of the people) 诺森布里亚人的 2 [u] (of the dialect, accent) 诺森布里亚方言的 3 Hist (of Northumbria) 诺森布里亚王国的; (of the people) 诺森布里亚王国人的
B *n* 1 [c] (native) 诺森布里亚人 2 [u] (ancient language) 中古诺森布里亚方言; (modern dialect) 现代诺森布里亚方言

northward /'nɔːθwəd/ ▸**p. 142**
A *adj* 向北的
B *adv* (*also* **northwards**) 向北

north-west ▸**p. 142**
A *n* [u] 1 (direction) 西北; (position or location) 西北方; (north-western part) 西北部; **to the ～** 向西北方向; **from** *or* **in the ～** 来自西北方向; **the sun/wind is in the ～** 太阳在西北方/吹的是西北风 2 (compass point) 西北方 3 (of country, region, town) 西北部
B *adj* 1 (north-western) 西北边的; **on the ～ side of the island** 在岛屿的西北侧; ～ **France** 法国西北部 2 *attrib* (from the north-west) 来自西北边的; **a ～ wind** 西北风
C *adv* 1 (to the north-west, on the north-western side) 在西北边; **to be** *or* **lie ～ of sth.** 位于某处的西北; ～ **of sth.** 在某物的西北边 2 (towards the north-west) 向西北; **to go** *or* **head ～** 向西北方走; **due ～** 向正西北

northwester /ˌnɔː'θwestə(r)/ *n* 西北风

north-westerly ▸**p. 142**
A *adj* 1 (in a north-westward position) 西北的 ‹*point, area*› 2 (in a north-westward direction) 向西北的 ‹*aspect, course, journey*› 3 (from a north-westward direction) 从西北方来的; **a ～ wind** 西北风; **a ～ breeze** 西北微风
B *adv* (from north-west) 从西北方; (towards north-west) 向西北方
C *n* 西北风

north-western ▸**p. 142** *adj attrib* 1 (of or in the north-west) 西北方的; ～ **France** 法国西北部 2 (facing north-west) 向西北的; (going towards north-west) 西北行的

north: N～-West Passage *pr n* 西北航道 [从大西洋经北美洲海岸到太平洋的航道]; **N～west Territories** *npl* [加拿大的] 西北地区; **N～west Territory** *n* [美国的] 西北地区

north-westward
A *adj* 向西北的
B *adv* (*also* **north-westwards**) 向西北

North Yorkshire /ˌnɔːθ 'jɔːkʃɪə(r)/ *pr n* 北约克郡

Norway /'nɔːweɪ/ *pr n* 挪威

Norwegian /nɔː'wiːdʒən/ ▸**p. 503, p. 426**
A *adj* (of Norway) 挪威的; (of the people) 挪威人的; (of the language) 挪威语的
B *n* 1 [c] (person) 挪威人 2 [u] (language) 挪威语

no-sale *n* 未出售

nose /nəʊz/
A *n* 1 ▸**p. 71** Anat 鼻子; **a roman** *or* **hooked/pug/snub/turned-up/broken ～** 鹰钩鼻/狮子鼻/扁平鼻/翘鼻/豁鼻; **to breathe/speak through one's ～** 用鼻子呼吸/鼻音很重地讲话; **to give sb. a punch on the ～** 打某人鼻子一拳; **to have a bleeding** *or* **bloody ～** 流鼻血; **to have a running** *or* **runny ～** 流鼻涕; **to give sb./get a bloody ～** 把某人打得/被打得流鼻血; **to blow/pick one's ～** 擤鼻涕/挖鼻子; **to see no further than (the end of) one's ～** fig 目光短浅; **(to be) as plain as the ～ on one's face** 显而易见; **to bury one's ～ in a book** 专心看书; **to cut off one's ～ to spite one's face** 损人不利己; **to get up sb.'s ～** colloq 惹恼某人; **to keep one's ～ clean** fig colloq 安分守己; **to lead sb. by the ～** colloq 牵着某人的鼻子走; **to look down one's ～ at sb./sth.** 对某人/某事物不屑一顾; **on the ～** Amer colloq 准确地; **to hit it** *or* **be right on the nose** Amer colloq 丝毫不差; **to pay through the ～ for sth.** colloq 花大价钱购买某物; **to poke** *or* **stick one's ～ into sth.** colloq 管闲事; **to keep one's ～ out of sth.** colloq 不过问某事; **to put sb.'s ～ out of joint** colloq 使某人心烦意乱; **to rub sb.'s ～ in it** colloq 揭某人的短; **to turn one's ～ up at sth./at the idea of doing sth.** colloq 对某事物/做某事的想法嗤之以鼻; **(right) under sb.'s (very) ～** colloq （就）在某人眼皮底下; **with one's ～ in the air** colloq 傲慢地 2 (sense of smell) 嗅觉; **a dog with a good ～** 嗅觉灵敏的狗 3 (of wine) 醇香 4 fig (instinctive talent) 觉察力; **to have a ～ for sth.** 善于发现某物; **to follow one's ～** 凭直觉行事 5 (projecting part) 突出部; **the ～ of a hosepipe** 软管喷嘴 6 (front end) 前端; **the ～ of the aeroplane/car/boat** 机头/车头/船头; ～ **to tail** 首尾相连的 7 (narrow margin) **a ～** 些微差距; **to win by a ～** 险胜
B *vt* 1 (sniff) 嗅; (touch with nose) 用鼻子碰; (rub with nose) 用鼻子拱 2 (manoeuvre) 小心翼翼地驾驶; **to ～ sth. into/out of sth.** 小心翼翼地把…驶入/驶出某处 ‹*ship, car*›
C *vi* 1 (move cautiously) 徐徐行驶; **to ～ into/out of sth.** «*ship, car*» 徐徐驶入/驶出某处 2 colloq (search, pry) 搜寻; **to ～ around (a place)** 搜索（某个地方）; **to ～ into sb.'s affairs** *or* **business** 探听某人的私事; **stop nosing, don't ～** 别多管闲事

Phrasal verbs

- **nose about, nose around** *vi* 搜寻; **the fox was nosing about in the dustbin** 狐狸在垃圾箱里到处乱翻; **to ～ about in other people's affairs** *or* **business** 探听别人的私事
- **nose at** *vt* [**～ at sth.**] (sniff) 嗅; (touch with nose) 用鼻子碰
- **nose out** *vt* [**～ out sth., ～ sth. out**] 1 (smell out) 嗅出 ‹*scent, prey*› 2 fig (detect) 发现 ‹*secret, truth*› 3 (beat by small margin) 以些微之差险胜

nose: ～bag *n* [挂在牲口头上的] 饲料袋; **～band** *n* [马的] 鼻羁; **～bleed** *n* 鼻出血; **～-cone** *n* 头锥

nose-dive
A *n* 1 lit 俯冲; **to go into a ～** 俯冲 2 fig 猛跌; **to go into** *or* **take a ～** «*prices*» 暴跌
B *vi* 1 lit «*plane*» 俯冲 2 fig «*prices, market*» 暴跌

nose: ～ drops *npl* 滴鼻剂; **～ job** *n* colloq 鼻子整形手术; **to have a ～ job** 做鼻子整形手术; **～piece** *n* 1 (on glasses) 鼻梁架; 2 (on helmet) 护鼻; 3 esp Amer [马的] 鼻羁; **～ ring** *n* (of animal) 鼻圈; (of person) 鼻环; **～ stud** *n* 鼻钉; **～ wheel** *n* 前轮

nosey /'nəʊzi/ *adj* = **nosy**

nosh /nɒʃ/ colloq
A *n* 1 [u] Brit (food) 食物 2 [c] esp Amer (meal) 快餐; (snack) 小吃
B *vi* 1 Brit (eat) 吃 2 esp Amer (have a meal) 吃快餐; (have a snack) 吃小吃

no-show *n* 1 (person who does not turn up) 爽约者 2 (person who cancels) 取消预约的人

nosh-up *n* Brit colloq 大餐

nosily /'nəʊzɪli/ *adv* 过分好奇地

nostalgia /nɒ'stældʒə/ *n* [u] 1 (longing for past) 怀旧; **～ for sth.** 对某事物的怀念 2 (in book, on TV) 怀旧之情

nostalgic /nɒ'stældʒɪk/ *adj* 1 (sentimental) 怀旧的 ‹*person, yearning*›; 伤感的 ‹*look, mood*›; **to feel ～** 觉得伤感; **to be ～ for sth.** 怀念某事物 2 (evocative) 引起怀旧情感的 ‹*music, experience, trip*›

nostalgically /nɒ'stældʒɪkli/ *adv* 怀旧地

nostril /'nɒstrɪl/ *n* 鼻孔

nostrum /'nɒstrəm/ *n* 1 (ineffective remedy) 江湖药 2 (over-simple measure) 万灵药

nosy /'nəʊzi/ *adj* (curious) 过于好奇的; (prying) 爱管闲事的; **to be ～** 好打听

nosy parker /ˌnəʊzi 'pɑːkə(r)/ *n* Brit colloq 爱管闲事的人

not /nɒt/ ▸**p. 507**
A *adv* 1 (negating verb, word, phrase) 不; **he told me ～ to come** 他叫我不要来; **they didn't like it** 他们不喜欢它; **please don't go** 请别走; **has he ～/hasn't he seen it?** 他没有见过它吗？; **～ always** 并不总是 2 (contrasting) 而不是; **they live in caves, ～ in houses** 他们住在洞穴里，而不是在房子里; **he's ～ so much aggressive as assertive** 他与其说是好斗，还不如说是很自信 3 (in contrasts) 不只是; **～ only** *or* **just** *or* **simply** *or* **merely ... but (also) ...** 不仅…而且…; **～ merely in Africa, but everywhere** 不仅在非洲，而且在任何地方; **～ all the poems are serious** 并非所有的诗都是严肃的 4 (in tag questions) **it's cold, isn't it?** 天很冷，是吧？ 5 (replacing word, clause, sentence, etc.) 没有; **I'm afraid ～** 恐怕没有; **I hope ～** 我希望不是;

n

why ~? 为什么不？; **if ~** 如果不的话; **certainly/probably ~** 当然不/也许不; **whether it rains or ~** 不管下不下雨; **I believe** *or* **think ~** formal 我不这么认为 6 (less than) 不到; **~ three miles/hours from here** 距离这里不到 3 英里/3 小时路程; **~ five minutes ago** 不到 5 分钟以前 7 (none at all) 根本没有; **~ a** *or* **one ...** 一个…也没有; **~ a sound was heard** 一点声音都听不到; **~ one** *or* **a single person knew** 没有一个人知道 8 (in suggestions) **why ~ do it now?** 为什么不现在做呢？; **hadn't we better go?** 我们该走了吧？; **couldn't we tell them later?** 我们不能晚些告诉他们吗？

B **not at all** *adv phr* 1 (in no way) 一点也不; **I was ~ at all surprised by his reaction** 我对他的反应一点也不觉得吃惊 2 (accepting thanks, agreeing) 没关系; **thanks a lot — ~ at all** 多谢了——不客气; **will it bother you if I smoke? — ~ at all!** 我抽烟你介意吗？——没关系！

C **not but what** *adv phr* archaic 然而; **~ but what the picture has its darker side** 不过美丽的东西也有黑暗的一面

D **not that** *conj phr* 1 (excluding a reason, not as far as) 倒不是; **it's ~ that he hasn't been friendly** 倒不是说他不友好; **is anyone else coming? — ~ that I know of** 还有谁来吗？——这我倒不知道 2 (not suggesting sth.) 并不是说; **she hasn't written, ~ that she said she would** 她还没有写信来，这并不是说她说过她会写

notability /ˌnəʊtəˈbɪləti/ *n* 1 [u] (state, quality) 显要 2 [c] (person) 要人

notable /ˈnəʊtəbl/

A *adj* 著名的 ‹*writer, scientist*›; 重大的 ‹*discovery, achievement*›; 值得关注的 ‹*policy*›

B *n* 要人

notably /ˈnəʊtəbli/ *adv* 1 (in particular) 尤其; **it is very popular, most ~ among young girls** 这个非常受欢迎，特别是在年轻女孩子中间 2 (remarkably) 极其 ‹*rich, talented*›; 显眼地 ‹*absent*›

notarial /nəʊˈteərɪəl/ *adj attrib* formal 由公证人经办的 ‹*seal, matter, deed*›; 公证人的 ‹*profession, status, authority*›

notarize /ˈnəʊtəraɪz/ *vt* formal 公证 ‹*document, contract*›

notary /ˈnəʊtəri/ ▸**p. 409** *n* **~ (public)** 公证人

notate /nəʊˈteɪt/ *vt* 为…谱曲

notation /nəʊˈteɪʃn/ *n* 1 [c] (symbols) 谱号 2 [u] (act, process) 标记 3 [c] (note) 注解

notch /nɒtʃ/

A *n* 1 (indentation) 凹口 2 (nick) 刻痕 3 (of belt) 孔 4 (degree) 等级; **to go up a ~** 提高一个档次; **to be several ~es above sb.** 比某人强好几级

B *vt* 1 (score) 赢得 ‹*goal, point*› 2 (cut) 在…上刻痕 ‹*stick*›; 在…上开凹口 ‹*blade, edge*›

Phrasal verb

• **notch up** *vt* [**~ up sth.**] 获得 ‹*point, win, record*›

notchback /ˈnɒtʃbæk/ *n* esp Amer 凹背式小车

note /nəʊt/

A *n* 1 (written record) 笔记; **to take** *or* **make a ~ of sth.** 记下某事物; **to make a ~ to do sth.** 记下要做某事; **to take** *or* **make ~s in class** 作课堂笔记; **to speak from/without ~s** 照着稿子/脱稿发言; **to make a written ~ (in sth.)** （在某物上）作书面记录; **to make a mental ~ of sth./to do sth.** 记住某事/要做某事; **to compare ~s with sb.** (about ideas, opinions) 与某人交换看法; (about experiences) 与某人交流经验 2 (short letter) 短信; **a ~ of thanks/condolence** 感谢信/吊唁函; **to write** *or* **drop sb. a ~** 给某人写便条; **a ~ to ask/inform/request ...** *or* **asking/informing/requesting ...** 询问/通知/请求…的短信; **to enclose a ~** 附上留言 3 (annotation, footnote) 注释; **see ~ below** 注释见下; **author's/editor's ~** 作者注/编者注; **a ~ on sth.** 关于某事物的注释; **to put** *or* **add ~s into a text** 为文本加注 4 ▸**p. 174** esp Brit (banknote) 钞票; **two £10 ~s** 两张 10 英镑的钞票; **£500 in ~s** 500 英镑的钞票 5 Mus (single tone) 单音; **the closing** *or* **last ~s of the anthem** 圣歌的尾音; **to hold a ~** 保持音高; **a high/low/wrong** *or* **false ~** 高音/低音/错音 6 Mus (written sign) 音符 7 Mus (key on piano etc.) 音键 8 fig (tone) 声调; (tone of voice) 口气; (mood) 情绪; (atmosphere) 气氛; **to sound a ~ of warning** 发出警告; **to hit** *or* **strike the right/wrong ~** (say) 说话得体/不得体; (do) 做事得体/不得体; **to strike a false ~** (insincere) 显得不真诚; (inappropriate) 显得不合适; **on a more serious ~** 更严肃地说; **now on a less serious ~, let's ...** 现在换个轻松一点的话题，咱们来…; **to hold a ~ of ...** 带有…的口吻 ‹*fear, despair, hope*›; **there was a ~ of scorn in her voice** 她语气中带着轻蔑; **his comment struck a discordant/sour ~** 他的评论带着分歧/刻薄的口吻; **to end on a high ~** 在欢乐的气氛中结束 9 (official document) 证明书; **a sick ~** 病假条; **a delivery/dispatch ~** 交货单/发送单 10 (diplomatic memo) 照会 11 Comm 票据 12 **of ~** (notable) 显要的; (important) 重要的; **a man of ~** (famous) 名人; (important) 要人; **a development/contribution of ~** 重大的发展/贡献 13 (attention) 注意; **to take ~ (of sth.)** 注意（到某事物）; **to be worthy of ~** 值得关注 14 (sound of machine or animal) 声音; **a high/low ~** 尖厉/低沉的声音; **to give out a growling ~** 发出一声咆哮

B *vt* 1 (notice, observe) 注意到; (pay attention to) 注意; **to ~ that ...** 注意到…; **it is interesting to ~ that ...** 有意思的是，…; **it should be ~d that ...** 应当注意的是…; **I ~d how tired she was/what she was carrying** 我注意到她很累/她拿的东西; **to ~ sb.'s remarks/comments** 关注某人的话/评论 2 (write down) 记下; **'no change' he ~d** "无变化，"他记道 3 (mention) 提及; **to ~ that ...** 指出…; **as already ~d** 如早已指出的那样

Phrasal verb

• **note down** *vt* [**~ down sth., ~ sth. down**] 记下

note: ~book *n* 1 (small book) 笔记本; 2 (computer) 笔记本电脑; **a ~book computer** *or* **PC** 一台笔记本电脑; **~case** *n* 钱夹

noted /ˈnəʊtɪd/ *adj* 著名的; **to be ~ for sth.** 以某事物见称; **to be ~ as sth.** 以作为某事物闻名

notelet /ˈnəʊtlɪt/ *n* Brit 便笺

note: ~pad *n* 1 (of paper) 笔记本; 2 Comput **~pad (computer)** 袖珍笔触式电脑; **~paper** *n* [u] 信纸

noteworthiness /ˈnəʊtwɜːðɪnɪs/ *n* [u] 显著

noteworthy /ˈnəʊtwɜːði/ *adj* 明显的 ‹*feature, difference*›; 显著的 ‹*achievement*›; 重要的 ‹*moment, day*›; 值得关注的 ‹*composition, book*›

nothing /ˈnʌθɪŋ/

A *pron* 1 (indicating absence of sth.) 没有什么; **~ interesting's happened** 没发生什么有趣的事情; **you'll do ~ of the kind** *or* **sort!** 你绝对不要做这种事！; **she's just a friend, ~ more or less** 她只是一个朋友而已; **she thinks about ~ else** 她别的什么也不考虑; **next to ~** 几乎没有; **to have ~ against sb./sth.** 对某人/某事没有意见; **to be** *or* **have ~ to do with sb./sth.** 与某人/某事毫不相干; **she will have** *or* **she wants ~ to do with us** 她不想与我们有任何瓜葛; **to come to ~** 一事无成; **to stop at ~ (to do sth.)** （为做某事）不择手段; **to have ~ to say for oneself** 没什么要说; **to have ~ on** (no clothes) 没有穿衣服; (no plans) 没有安排; **I've got ~ on this weekend** 我这个周末没有应酬; **to have ~ on sb./sth.** colloq (fall short) 远不及某人/某事; (have no incriminating information) 没有某人/某机构的罪证; **he's got ~ on you!** 他远远比不上你！; **the police have ~ on you** 警方没有证据指控你; **she's five foot ~** colloq 她充其量只有5英尺高; **~ doing** colloq (no activity) 没什么事情发生; (no chance of success) 没什么希望; (expressing refusal) 不行; **he wants to marry her, but ~ doing!** colloq 他想要娶她，但不可能！; **~ (else) for it** Brit 没有选择的余地; **there was ~ for it but to resign** 除了辞职，别无他法; **~ short of sth.** (only) 只有某事; (equal to) 无异于某事; **~ short of a miracle can save them** 只有奇迹能够挽救他们; **it's ~ short of blackmail** 这完全是敲诈; **to be ~ if not ...** 极其…; **you're ~ if not persistent!** 你简直顽固透顶！ 2 (emphasizing insignificance) 琐碎之事; **a fuss about ~** 大惊小怪; **you've cut yourself! — it's ~** 你割伤自己了！——没事儿; **it's ~ more than a cold** 只不过是感冒而已; **to think ~ of sth./doing sth.** 认为某事/做某事算不了什么; **I thought ~ of it** 我没把它当回事儿; **think ~ of it!** formal 没关系！; **it's** *or* **it was ~!** formal 这算不了什么！; **to be ~ without sb./sth.** 没有了某人/某事物就什么也不是; **he's ~ without his career** 没有了事业他就什么也不是; **it is ~ to sb. (to do sth.)** 对于某人来说（做某事）不算什么; **$200 is ~ to you** 200 美元对于你来说无所谓; **there's ~ to it!** 轻而易举！; **there's ~ to doing sth.** 做某事轻而易举; **there's ~ in** *or* **to sth.** 某事是无稽之谈; **there's ~ in it for sb.** 这对某人毫无益处; **to get ~ out of sth.** 从某事中无利可图; ▸**home C1** 3 (for emphasis) [用以强调对比]; **there's ~ more ridiculous than ...** 没有什么比…更荒谬可笑; **there's ~ like sth./doing sth.** 没什么比得了某事物/做某事; **there's ~ like seeing old friends** 没什么比得上和老朋友见面; **it was ~ less than sexual harassment** 这是地地道道的性骚扰; **it was ~ less than tragic** 这简直就是一场悲剧; **to say ~ of sb./sth.** 更不用说某人/某事

B *adv* 一点也不; **to care ~ for sb./sth.** 根本不关心某人/某事; **~ like sb./sth.** (not at all like) 一点也不像某人/某物; (not nearly) 根本不; **the city is ~ like what it was** 这座城市已经面目全非; **it's ~ like enough!** 这根本不够！

C *n* 1 [u] (nothingness) 虚无; **an explanation of how the universe came out of ~** 关于宇宙如何产生于虚无的一种解释 2 [c] (trivial matter) 琐事; **it's a mere ~** 这简直微不足道 3 [c] (unimportant person) 小人物; **she's a ~ and a nobody** 她只是个无名小卒 4 [u] (zero) 零; **we lost four ~** 我们 0 比 4 输了

D **for nothing** *adv phr* 1 (without payment) 不花钱; (without effort) 毫不费力; **he gave it to me for ~** 他把它白白送给了我; **to get something for ~** 不劳而获; **it's money for ~** 这钱来得容易; **you get ~ for ~** 没有付出就没有所得 2 (to no purpose) 徒劳; **all that trouble for ~!** 所有的辛苦都白费了！ 3 (for no reason) 平白无故地; **they aren't called skyscrapers for ~** 它们被称作摩天大楼并非毫无道理; **I'm not English for ~!** hum 我这英国人可不是白当的！

E **nothing but** *adv phr* 只不过; **he's ~ but a coward** 他只是个胆小鬼; **~ but the best for me!** 我只要最好的！

nothingness /ˈnʌθɪŋnɪs/ *n* [u] 虚无; **night had reduced everything to black ~** 夜色使一切消匿于黑暗之中

notice /ˈnəʊtɪs/

A *n* 1 [c] (written sign) 布告 2 [c] (announcement in press) 启事; **a ~ to the public** *or* **a public ~ (about** *or* **of sth.)** （关于某事物的）公告; **a death** *or* **an obituary ~** 讣告 3 [u] (attention) 注意; **to attract ~** 引起注意; **to be beneath one's ~** 不值得理会; **to bring sth.**

to sb.'s ~ 使某人注意某事物; **it has come to my ~ that ...** 我已注意到⋯; **to escape (one's/sb.'s) ~** 未被（自己/某人）注意; **to take ~ of sth./sb.** 注意某事物/某人; **to take no ~** (ignore) 不理会; (not see) 没看到; (not hear) 没听到; **fat lot of ~ he takes of me!** colloq iron 他才不理我呢! **4** [u] (notification, warning) 通知; **~ of sth.** 某事的通知; **advance ~, ~ in advance** 提前通知; **three days'/six weeks' ~** 提前3天/6周的通知; **I'm sorry it's such short ~** 真抱歉，事出如此仓促; **to do sth. at short/a moment's/an hour's ~** 没有时间准备就/一经通知就/提前1小时得到通知后就做某事; **until further ~** 直到再次接到通知; **without ~** 不事先通知地 ‹*dismiss, change, turn up*›; **to give (sb.) ~ of sth./that ...** 通知（某人）某事/说⋯; **you'll get no ~ of an inspection** 你事先不会得到检查的任何通知; **if I want to quit, how much ~ do I have to give?** 如果我想离职的话，得提前多久通知呢? ; **to get** *or* **be given three weeks' ~** 被要求三周后离职; **~ is hereby given that ...** formal 兹通知⋯ **5** [u] (to employer) 辞职信; (to employee) 辞退信; **to hand in one's** *or* **give ~** Brit 递交辞职信; **to give (in) one's ~** Amer 递交辞职信; **to get (one's) ~** 收到辞退信; **to give sb. ~, to give ~ to sb.** (resign) 向某人递交辞职信; (dismiss) 向某人下发辞退信 **6** [u] (to vacate premises) 搬迁通知; **one month's ~** 限期一月的搬迁通知; **to give ~ to sb.** 对某人发出搬迁通知; **to give sb. ~ to quit** 通知某人搬走; **to give the landlord ~** 通知房东要搬走 **7** [u] Admin, Comm 通知书; **a reminder ~** 催单; **~ of receipt** 收到通知; **~ of termination/to appear** Jur 终止/出庭通知书; **to serve ~ on sb. that ...** 正式通知某人⋯; **to give sb. ~ that ...** 通知某人⋯ **8** [c] Theat (review) 短评; **mixed ~s** 褒贬参半的评论

B *vt* **1** (happen to see) 注意到; **to ~ sb./sth. doing sth.** 注意到某人/某物在做某事; **nobody'll ~ (it)** 没人会注意到（它）的; **not (so) as you'd ~** colloq 不太明显 **2** (treat with recognition) 关注; **to be** *or* **get ~d** 受到关注; **to get oneself ~d** 引人注目

noticeable /'nəʊtɪsəbl/ *adj* **1** (perceptible) 明显的; **barely ~** 几乎无法察觉的; **it wasn't ~ to most people** 大多数人都未能发现; **it is ~ that ...** 显而易见，⋯ **2** (noteworthy) 值得注意的

noticeably /'nəʊtɪsəbli/ *adv* 明显地

noticeboard /'nəʊtɪsbɔːd/ *n* Brit 布告牌

notifiable /'nəʊtɪfaɪəbl/ *adj* 依法须上报的 ‹*crime, incident*›; **a ~ disease** 依法须报告的疾病

notification /ˌnəʊtɪfɪ'keɪʃn/ *n* **1** [u] (communication) 通知; **to receive/send ~ of sth.** 接到/发出某通知 **2** [c] (formal announcement) [报纸上登的] 告示; **a ~ of sth.** 有关某事的告示 **3** [c] (written communication) 书面通知; **a ~ of sth.** 有关某事的书面通知

notify /'nəʊtɪfaɪ/ *vt* **1** (inform) 通知 ‹*police, authorities*›; **to ~ sb. of** *or* **about sth.** 通知某人某事; **to ~ sb. that ...** 通知某人⋯ **2** (report) 报告 ‹*theft, crime, result*›; **to ~ sth. to sb.** 向某人报告某事 **3** (give formal notice to) 正式通知 ‹*family, nation*›; **to ~ sb. of sth.** 通知某人 ‹*accident, result*›

notion /'nəʊʃn/

A *n* **1** [c] (idea, opinion, belief) 观念; (concept) 概念; (odd idea) 念头; **to have the** *or* **a ~ that ...** 认为⋯; **to have the ~ of doing sth.** *or* **to do sth.** 想要做某事; **to dispel a ~** 打消念头; **preconceived ~s** 先入为主的观念; **there is a widespread ~ that ...** 人们普遍认为⋯; **cannot bear the ~ of sth./doing sth.** 一想到某事物/做某事就受不了; **to hit on** *or* **upon the ~ of doing sth.** 突然想出做某事的主意; **what gave you the ~ that ...?** 你怎么会认为⋯呢? ; **to put a ~** *or* **put ~s into sb.'s head** 使某人产生某想法; **what a (strange) ~!** 这想法真怪! **2** [c and u] (understanding) 了解; (vague knowledge) 粗识; **a ~ about sth.** 对某事物的见解; **to have some ~ of sth.** 对某事物略知一二; **I had a ~ (that) ...** 我印象中⋯; **she has no ~ of time** 她毫无时间观念; **I had no ~ you were his sister** 我根本不知道你是他姐姐; **to give sb. a rough ~ of sth.** 使某人对某物有大概的了解; **to have no/little/a good ~ of sth.** 一点不懂/几乎不懂/熟知某事物; **I don't have the least** *or* **slightest** *or* **foggiest ~** 我一无所知

B **notions** *npl* Amer (sewing items) 针头线脑

notional /'nəʊʃənl/ *adj* 猜测的

notoriety /ˌnəʊtə'raɪəti/ *n* [u] 恶名

notorious /nəʊ'tɔːrɪəs/ *adj* 臭名昭著的 ‹*criminal, rapist*›; 声名狼藉的 ‹*place, neighbourhood*›; 众人皆知的 ‹*arrogance, temper*›; **to be ~ for sth.** 因某事而臭名昭著

notoriously /nəʊ'tɔːrɪəsli/ *adv* 众所周知地 ‹*inefficient, lazy, bad*›; **to be ~ difficult to do sth.** 做某事众所周知地困难

no trumps *n* + *v sing or pl* 无将牌

Nottinghamshire /'nɒtɪŋəmʃɪə(r)/ *pr n* 诺丁汉郡

Notts. /'nɒts/ *abbr* Brit = **Nottinghamshire**

notwithstanding /ˌnɒtwɪθ'stændɪŋ/

A *prep* 尽管; **~ the poor weather, we enjoyed the holiday** 虽然天气恶劣，但我们假期过得很愉快

B *adv* 然而; **she knew she couldn't win, but she entered ~** 她知道自己不可能赢，但还是参加了

C *conj* (although) 虽然; (in spite of the fact that) 尽管如此

nougat /'nuːɡɑː, 'nʌɡət, Amer 'nuːɡət/ *n* [u] 牛轧糖 [用果仁、糖或蜂蜜以及蛋清做成]

nought /nɔːt/ *n* Brit 零

noughts and crosses ▸ **p. 307** *npl* + *v sing* Brit 圈叉游戏 [两人轮流在井字形九格中画圈或叉，先将三个圈或叉连成一线者获胜]

noun /naʊn/ *n* 名词

noun: ~ clause *n* 名词从句; **~ phrase** *n* 名词词组

nourish /'nʌrɪʃ/ *vt* **1** (feed) 养育 ‹*offspring*›; 喂养 ‹*animal*›; 为⋯提供养分 ‹*plant, seedling*›; **to be well ~ed** 营养良好 **2** (encourage, support) 助长 ‹*illusion, hatred, passion*›

nourishing /'nʌrɪʃɪŋ/ *adj* 营养丰富的

nourishment /'nʌrɪʃmənt/ *n* [u] **1** (food, drink) 营养食物 **2** (action, process) 营养提供

nous /naʊs/ *n* [u] Brit colloq (intelligence) 智力; (common sense) 常识; **use your ~!** 动动你的脑子!

nouvelle cuisine /nuːˌvel kwɪ'ziːn/ *n* [u] 新式烹饪 [讲求食物清淡、量少而精美]

Nov *abbr* = **November**

nova /'nəʊvə/ *n* (*pl* **novae** /'nəʊviː/ *or* **~s**) 新星

Nova Scotia /ˌnəʊvə 'skəʊʃə/ *pr n* **1** (province) 新斯科舍省 **2** (peninsula) 新斯科舍半岛

Nova Scotian /ˌnəʊvə 'skəʊʃn/

A *adj* (province) 新斯科舍省的; (peninsula) 新斯科舍半岛的

B *n* 新斯科舍人

novel /'nɒvl/

A *n* **1** (genre) 小说体 **2** (book) 小说

B *adj* 新颖的 ‹*idea*›; 与众不同的 ‹*method*›; 新奇的 ‹*fashion, device*›

novelette /ˌnɒvə'let/ *n* 矫情小说

novelist /'nɒvəlɪst/ ▸ **p. 409** *n* 小说家

novella /nə'velə/ *n* (long short story) 中篇小说; (short novel) 短篇小说

novelty /'nɒvəlti/ *n* **1** [u] (newness) 新奇; **~ value** 新意 **2** [c] (new experience) 新鲜体验 **3** [c] (toy, ornament, trinket) 小巧廉价的小玩意儿; **a ~ key ring/pencil case** 廉价的小钥匙链/铅笔盒

November /nə'vembə(r)/ ▸ **p. 490** *n* 十一月; **last/this/next ~** 上个/本年/下个十一月份; **in early/late ~** 十一月上旬/下旬; **~ weather/morning** 十一月的天气/早晨

novice /'nɒvɪs/ *n* **1** (beginner) 新手 **2** (monk) 见习修士; (nun) 见习修女 **3** Sport (person) 未获过奖的运动员; (racehorse) 未获过奖的赛马

novitiate /nə'vɪʃɪət/ *n* [u] **1** (state of being a novice) (monk) 见习修士; (nun) 见习修女 **2** (period) 修生见习期

no vote *n* 反对投票

now /naʊ/

A *adv* **1** (at the present moment, time, stage) 现在; **it is ~ just after 4 o'clock** 现在 4 点钟刚过; **they ~ have 5 children** 他们目前有 5 个孩子; **the ~ celebrated court case** 目前倍受关注的庭审案件; **right/just ~** (at this moment) 此刻; (these days) 目前; **before ~** 此前; **up to** *or* **until** *or* **till ~** 直到现在; **I've lived at home up till ~** 我一直在家里住到现在; **by ~** 到现在; **he'll be home by ~** 他现在该到家了; **from ~** 从现在起; **from ~ on** *or* **onwards** 从此以后; **that's all for ~** 暂时就这些; **goodbye for ~** 后会有期; **even ~** 即便如此 **2** (at once) 马上; **you must go ~** 你得马上就走; **right ~** 立即; **it's ~ or never** 机不可失 **3** (then) 当时; **~ the troops attacked** 接着部队发动了攻击; **she was 19 ~** 她当时是 19 岁; **just ~** 刚才 **4** (at that point in time) 那时; **by ~** 到那时; **before ~** 在那以前; **the idea had occurred to her before ~** 以前她有过那个念头; **from ~ on** *or* **onwards** 从那以后; **from ~ on he would earn his living as a painter** 从那以后他就以绘画为生 **5** (in view of events) 如此看来; **I'll never get a job ~** 看来我再也找不到工作了; **how can you trust them ~?** 这样一来你怎么能信任他们呢? **6** (sometimes) 有时; **~ ..., ~ ...** 有时⋯有时⋯; **~ fast, ~ slowly** 时快时慢; **(every) ~ and then** *or* **again** 不时地; **every ~ and again she checked to see if he was still asleep** 她隔一会儿就去看看他是否还在睡 **7** (calculating up to present) 迄今; (calculating to point in past) 到那时; **it has been six months ~** 至今已有 6 个月了; **they've been married four years ~** 到现在他们已经结婚 4 年了; **they had ~ lived there for 10 years** 那时他们已经在那儿住了 10 年 **8** (calculating from present) 从此; **she won't be long ~** 她随后就到; **he could arrive any time** *or* **moment ~** 他随时都有可能到达; **the results will be announced any day ~** 这几天随时会公布结果 **9** (introducing transition, information, opinion) 然后; **~ for the next question** 现在讨论下一个问题; **~ for a drink** 我们来喝一杯吧; **if we ~ compare ...** 如果我们来比较⋯; **~ my first impulse was to run away** 然后我的第一反应就是逃跑 **10** (when pausing in speech) 嗯; **let me see, ~, oh yes, I remember** 让我想想，嗯，噢，对了，我想起来了 **11** (expressing annoyance) 到底; **~ they want to tax food!** 他们居然要征收食物税! ; **what do you want ~?** 你到底想要什么呀? ; **Jane? — what is it ~?** 简? ——又怎么啦? ; **~ what?** (when pestered, interrupted) 又怎么了? ; (when confused) 现在该怎么办? **12** (in requests, warnings, reprimands) 喂; **careful ~!** 喂，小心! ; **run along ~** 走开; **there ~** (satisfaction) 没错吧; (sth. that annoys you) 又来了; **there ~, what did I tell you?** 没错吧，我告诉你什么来着? ; **~, ~!** 行了! ; **~ then** (expressing disapproval) 得啦; (making suggestion, offer) 那么; **~ then, let's get down to work** 得啦，我们开始干吧; **~ then, who's for a coffee?** 那么，谁想喝咖啡? ; **come ~!** dated 得啦!

B *conj* 既然; **~ (that) I've met her, I understand** 我和她见过面了，也就明白了; **he lives in Blackpool ~ he's retired** 由于他

已退休，他住到了布莱克浦
C *adj colloq* 时髦的〈*clothes, fashions*〉

nowadays /ˈnaʊədeɪz/ *adv* 现今

nowhere /ˈnəʊweə(r)/
A *adv* **1** (in, at, to no place) 哪里都不; **she goes almost ~** 她几乎哪儿也不去; **this animal is found in Australia and ~ else** 这种动物只在澳大利亚才有; **to be ~ to be seen/found** 无处可见/可寻; **to be ~ in sight** lit 无处可见; fig 渺茫; **a peace settlement is ~ in sight** 和平协议仍遥遥无期 **2** (in difficult situation) 毫无进展; **I'd be ~ without my laptop** 没有笔记本电脑，我什么也做不了; **to go ~** (make no progress) 停滞不前; (enough to buy little) 买不了什么; **these negotiations are going ~** 这些谈判没有取得任何进展; **£10 goes ~ these days** 如今 10 英镑买不了什么东西; **to get ~ (with sb./sth.)** （与某人/在某事上）没有任何进展; **he'll get ~ with her** 他跟她不会有什么结果的; **we're getting ~ fast** colloq 我们毫无进展; **to get sb. ~** 让某人一无所获; **flattery will get you ~!** 奉承不会给你带来任何好处!
B *pron* 没有地方; **miles from ~** 非常偏僻; **to appear** *or* **come from** *or* **out of ~** 突然冒出来; **she came out of ~ to win the race** 她不知从哪里冒了出来，赢得了赛跑比赛
C **nowhere near** *adv and prep phr* **1** (in distance, degree) 远离; **~ near sth.** 距离某物很遥远; **to be ~ near doing sth.** 离做某事差很远; **the village was still ~ near** 那个村庄仍然很远 **2** (not nearly) 远非; **their performance was ~ near satisfactory** 他们的表现远未达到满意的程度; **the house is ~ near big enough** 房子太小了

no-win *adj attrib* 无望获胜的; **to be in a ~ situation** 处于取胜无望的境地

nowt /naʊt/ *n* N English colloq = **nothing A, B**

noxious /ˈnɒkʃəs/ *adj* **1** lit 有毒的〈*substance, gas*〉; 有害的〈*influence, effect*〉 **2** fig (unpleasant) 令人讨厌的〈*smell, habit*〉

nozzle /ˈnɒzl/ *n* 喷嘴

NPV *n* = **net present value**

nr *abbr* = **near B**

NSPCC *abbr* Brit = **National Society for the Prevention of Cruelty to Children** 全国防止虐待儿童协会

NT *abbr* **1** = **New Testament** **2** Brit = **National Trust**

nth /enθ/ *adj* **1** Math 第n个的 **2** fig 第n次的; **to the ~ degree** 极端地

NTSC *abbr* = **National Television System Committee** [北美和日本电视广播系统的] 全国电视系统委员会制式

nuance /ˈnjuːɑːns, Amer ˈnuː-/ *n* [声音、色彩、感情、外貌或意义方面的] 细微差别

nub /nʌb/ *n* **1** (crux) 实质; **to be the ~ of sth.** 是…的实质〈*problem, issue*〉 **2** (lump) 小突起

nubile /ˈnjuːbaɪl, Amer ˈnuːbl/ *adj* **1** (sexually mature) 性发育成熟的〈*female, woman*〉 **2** (suitable for marriage) 适婚的〈*girl, daughter*〉 **3** (sexually attractive) 性感的〈*female, woman*〉

nuclear /ˈnjuːklɪə(r), Amer ˈnuː-/ *adj* **1** Phys 原子核的; **a ~ particle** 核粒子 **2** (using atomic energy) 核能的

nuclear: **~ bomb** *n* 核弹; **~ capability** *n* 核力量; **~ deterrence** *n* [u] 核威慑战略; **~ deterrent** *n* 核威慑; **~ device** *n* 核装置; **~ disarmament** *n* [u] 核裁军; **~ energy** *n* [u] 核能; **~ facility** *n* 核设备; **~ family** *n* [由父母和子女组成的] 核心家庭; **~ fission** *n* [u] 核裂变; **~-free** *adj* 无核的; **~ fuel** *n* [c and u] 核燃料; **~ magnetic resonance** *n* [u] 核磁共振; **~ physicist** ▸p. 409 *n* 核物理学家; **~ physics** *npl + v sing* 核物理学; **~ power** *n* **1** [u] (energy) 核能; **2** [c] (country) 有核国家; **~-powered** *adj* 核能的; **a ~-powered submarine** 核潜艇; **~ power station** *n* 核电站; **~ reactor** *n* 核反应堆; **N~ Regulatory Commission** *n* Amer 核管理委员会; **~ reprocessing plant** *n* 核燃料后处理工厂; **~ scientist** *n* = **~ physicist**; **~ shelter** *n* 核掩体; **~ submarine** *n* 核潜艇; **~ test** *n* 核试验; **~ testing** *n* [u] 核试验; **~ umbrella** *n* 核保护伞; **~ warhead** *n* 核弹头; **~ waste** *n* [u] 核废料; **~ weapon** *n* 核武器; **~ winter** *n* [u] 核冬季 [科学家预测的核战争之后会出现的一段昏暗、寒冷的时间]

nuclei /ˈnjuːklɪaɪ, Amer ˈnuː-/ *pl* ▸**nucleus**

nucleic acid /njuːˌkliːɪk ˈæsɪd, Amer nuː-/ *n* [u] 核酸

nucleus /ˈnjuːklɪəs, Amer ˈnuː-/ *n* (*pl* **nuclei**) **1** (central part) 核心 **2** (of atom) 原子核 **3** Biol 细胞核 **4** Astron 慧核

nude /njuːd, Amer nuːd/
A *adj* **1** (naked) 裸体的 **2** (depicting naked people) 描写裸体的; **to do ~ scenes** 出演裸妆镜头
B *n* **1** (naked) **in the ~** 赤裸地 **2** (picture) 裸体画; (statue) 裸体塑像 **3** (art form) **the ~** 裸体艺术

nudge /nʌdʒ/
A *vt* **1** (prod) «*person*» [用肘] 轻推; «*animal*» 拱 **2** (push) 轻轻推动〈*gatepost, vehicle*〉 **3** (approach closely) 接近〈*speed, rate, age*〉; **her father's nudging 90** 她父亲快 90 岁了 **4** fig (coax) 哄劝; **to ~ sb. to do sth.** 哄某人做某事
B *n* [肘部的] 轻推; **to give sb. a ~** 轻轻推某人一下; **~ ~ (wink wink)** 眉来眼去

nudism /ˈnjuːdɪzəm, Amer ˈnuː-/ *n* [u] 裸体主义

nudist /ˈnjuːdɪst, Amer ˈnuː-/ *n* 裸体主义者; **a ~ beach/camp** 裸泳海滩/裸体营

nudity /ˈnjuːdəti, Amer ˈnuː-/ *n* [u] 裸体

nugatory /ˈnjuːgətəri, Amer ˈnuːgətɔːri/ *adj* formal **1** (valueless) 无价值的〈*arguments, proposals*〉 **2** (useless) 无用的; (trivial) 琐碎的; **~ trifles** 琐事

nugget /ˈnʌgɪt/ *n* **1** (of gold, silver) 天然贵重金属块 **2** (small lump) 小块; **a ~ of bread** 一小块面包 **3** fig (idea) 宝贵的想法; (fact) 有用的事实; **a ~ of news** 一条宝贵的新闻

nuisance /ˈnjuːsns, Amer ˈnuː-/ *n* **1** (annoyance) 麻烦事; **it's a ~ that ...** 恼人的是… **2** (person) 讨厌的人; **to be a ~ (to sb.)** 令（某）人讨厌; **to make a ~ of oneself** 讨人嫌 **3** Jur 滋扰行为

nuisance: **~ call** *n* 骚扰电话; **~ caller** *n* 打骚扰电话的人; **~ value** *n* [u] 阻扰价值

NUJ *abbr* Brit = **National Union of Journalists** 全国记者协会

nuke /njuːk, Amer nuːk/ colloq
A *vt* **1** (bomb) 用核武器攻击 **2** Amer (microwave) 用微波炉烹饪
B *n* **1** (weapon) 核武器 **2** (power station) 核电站; **a ~ station** *or* **plant** 核电站

null /nʌl/ *adj* 无法律效力的〈*contract, legacy, agreement*〉; **~ and void** 无效的; **to render ~ and void** 使失效

null: **~ character** *n* 空字符; **~ hypothesis** *n* 零假设

nullify /ˈnʌlɪfaɪ/ *vt* **1** (render legally void) 使…失去法律效力〈*contract, legacy*〉 **2** (render ineffective) 抵消〈*value*〉; 使…徒劳〈*intention*〉

nullity /ˈnʌləti/ *n* **1** [u] (state) 无效 **2** [c] (act) 无法律效力的行为; (document, agreement) 无法律效力的文件

NUM *abbr* Brit = **National Union of Mineworkers** 全国矿工联盟

numb /nʌm/
A *adj* **1** (from cold, anaesthetic) 失去知觉的; **to be ~ with cold** 冻僵; **to go ~** 失去知觉 **2** (unable to move) 呆滞的; **~ with shock** 惊呆的 **3** fig (emotionally) 麻木的; **~ with grief** 悲伤得麻木了的
B *vt* **1** (deprive of feeling) 使失去感觉; **to ~ the pain** 消除痛感 **2** (deprive of responsiveness) 使麻木; **my mind/emotions were totally ~ed** 我的头脑/感情彻底麻木了

number /ˈnʌmbə(r)/
A *n* **1** [c] (figure) 数字; **a six-figure ~** 6 位数; **odd/even/whole/cardinal/ordinal ~** 奇数/偶数/整数/基数/序数; **a ~ greater/less than ...** 大于/小于…的数; **the ~ eleven** 11 这个数; **to be good at ~s** colloq 擅长算术 **2** [c] (of bus, house, telephone) 号码; (on list, in queue, in hierarchy) 编号; **page/volume ~** 页码/卷次; **identification/passport ~** 身份证/护照号码; **account/credit card/registration ~** 账号/信用卡号/登记号; **~ 28 in the charts** 排行榜第 28 位; **to live at ~ 220 (Acacia Avenue)** 住在（阿卡西亚大街）220 号; **to wear ~ 10** Sport 穿 10 号球衣; **the French ~ 2** Sport 法国队的 2 号选手; **to colour** *or* **paint by ~s** 执行简单的指令; **to do sth. by ~s** 一板一眼做某事; **to have sb.'s ~** colloq 了解某人的底细; **to have sb.'s ~ on it** colloq «*bullet, bomb*» 注定要击中某人; **sb.'s ~ is up** colloq 某人在劫难逃 **3** [c and u] (amount, quantity) 数量; **a ~ of people/times** 一些人/几次; **the (exact) ~ of ...** …的（准确）数目; **vast** *or* **large ~s of ...** 大量的…; **a certain/small ~ of ...** 有些/少数…; **a large** *or* **great/fair ~ (of ...)** 大量/相当多（的…）; **the ~s were equal on both sides** 双方人数相同; **any ~ of times/people** (very large) 许多次/人; (limitless) 无论多少次/人; **any ~ can play** 随便多少人都可以玩; **we were 12 in ~** 我们有 12 个人; **few/many in ~** 数量很少/很多; **they came in (their) ~s** 他们来的人很多; **in small/large/equal ~s** 少量/大量/数量相同的; **birds in such ~s** 这么多鸟; **beyond** *or* **without ~** liter 无数的; **to do sth. by weight** *or* **force of ~s** 靠人多做某事 **4** liter (group) 一伙; **one of our ~** 我们中的一员; **among their ~, two spoke English** 他们中有两人说英语; **to be of their ~** (one of them) 是他们中的一员; (with them) 和他们是一起的 **5** [c] Journ 一期; **the July ~** 7 月号 **6** [c] Mus, Theat (song) 一首歌; (dance) 一支舞; (piece of music) 一段音乐; **and for my next ~ ...** 我下一首歌曲…; **a couple of jazz/dance ~s** 几段爵士舞/几支舞曲; **my big ~** 我的压轴演出 **7** [c] colloq (object of admiration) (person) 令人艳羡的人; (thing) 令人羡慕的东西; **a low-cut little ~** 时髦的低胸装; **she's a sexy little ~** 她是个性感的小美人儿; **a nice little ~** (job) 肥差; (car etc.) 好东西; (girl) 靓妞儿 **8** [u] Ling 数; **singular/plural ~** 单数/复数
B *vt* **1** (allocate number to) 给…编号; **I ~ed the boxes from 1 to 20** 我给这些盒子从 1 到 20 编上号 **2** (amount to) **to ~ X** 共计 X **3** (include) 把…归入; **to ~ sb./sth. among** *or* **with sth.** 把某人/某物归入某类 **4** (be limited) **to be ~ed** 为数有限; **sb.'s days are ~ed** 某人已时日无多
C *vi* **1** (comprise in number) 计数; **a crowd ~ing in the thousands** 数以千计的一群人 **2** (be included) 归入; **to ~ among sth.** 属于某类

number: **~ cruncher** *n* colloq **1** (computer) 超级计算机; (software) 超级软件; **2** (person) 捣弄数字者 [如统计师、会计等]; **~ crunching** *n* [u] colloq 数字密集运算

numbering /ˈnʌmbərɪŋ/ *n* **1** [u] (action) 编号 **2** [c] (sequence of numbers) 编号方式

numberless /ˈnʌmbəlɪs/ *adj* 数不清的

number one
A *n* colloq **1** (most important person) 头号人物; (most important thing) 头等大事 **2** (record) 最畅销唱片; (book) 最畅销书 **3** (oneself) 自己; **to look after** *or* **look out for** *or* **take care of ~** 替自己打算 **4** child lang (act of urinating) 尿尿; **mummy, I need/did a ~** 妈妈，我要尿尿/尿尿了
B *adj* 头号的; **reducing unemployment is our ~ priority** 降低失业率是我们的头等大事

Numbers

Cardinal numbers in Chinese

■ The numbers in Chinese from one to ten are:

1	一	6	六
2	二 / 两	7	七
3	三	8	八
4	四	9	九
5	五	10	十

■ Note that there are two ways of expressing 2 in Chinese: 二 or 两. 二 is used in counting, telephone numbers, floor numbers, bus numbers, etc. 两 and not 二 is used with measure words such as 个, 本, etc. Note that 'first floor' in British English is 二楼 in Chinese. The Chinese convention is to number floors 1, 2, 3, etc. instead of ground floor, first floor, second floor, etc.

Also note that 1 can be read as 一 (yi) or 幺 (yao) in telephone numbers. in telephone numbers:

bus No. 2/No.2 bus
= 2 路车

two students
= 两个学生

I live on the second floor
= 我住在 3 楼

Tel: 125 0856
= 电话：一二五 零八五六

■ Chinese numbers from eleven to ninety-nine are formed using numbers from one to ten:

11	十一	22	二十二
12	十二	29	二十九
13	十三	30	三十
14	十四	40	四十
15	十五	50	五十
16	十六	60	六十
17	十七	70	七十
18	十八	80	八十
19	十九	90	九十
20	二十	99	九十九

■ Numbers over ninety-nine are formed by combining the following with numbers from one to ninety:

100	百
1,000	千
10,000	万
100,000,000	亿

Note that 两 can be used with 百, 千, 万, and 亿.

■ 零 (zero) must be inserted if there are noughts in the number. If there is more than one zero in a number, only one 零 is inserted in both spoken and written forms:

100	一百
101	一百零一
109	一百零九
110	一百一十 but not 一百十
119	一百一十九
120	一百二十
199	一百九十九
200	二百 or 两百
300	三百
900	九百
999	九百九十九
1,000	一千
1,001	一千零一
1,090	一千零九十
1,900	一千九百
2,000	二千 or 两千
9,000	九千
10,000	一万
10,001	一万零一
10,010	一万零一十
10,100	一万零一百
11,000	一万一千
20,000	二万 or 两万
100,000	十万
200,000	二十万
1,000,000	一百万
2,000,000	二百万 or 两百万
10,000,000	一千万
20,000,000	二千万 or 两千万
100,000,000	一亿
900,000,000	九亿
1,000,000,000	十亿

Ordinal numbers

■ 第 is placed before the cardinal number to create the ordinal number:

1st	第一	19th	第十九
2nd	第二	20th	第二十
3rd	第三	30th	第三十
4th	第四	90th	第九十
5th	第五	100th	第一百
6th	第六	101st	第一百零一
7th	第七	110th	第一百一十
8th	第八	199th	第一百九十九
9th	第九	999th	第九百九十九
10th	第十	1000th	第一千
11th	第十一		

Fractions

■ Both numbers in a fraction (the numerator and denominator) are read as cardinal numbers. The denominator is read first, followed by 分之 (meaning 'part'), followed by the numerator:

	Spoken
1/2	二分之一
3/4	四分之三
3/8	八分之三

Decimals and percentages

■ The numbers before the decimal point are read as whole numbers, and the numbers after are read individually:

	Spoken
0.003	零点零零三
0.33	零点三三
3.58	三点五八
88.66	八十八点六六
266.99	二百六十六点九九

■ 百分之 (%) comes before the numbers in a percentage (numbers after the decimal point are read individually):

	Spoken
0.01%	百分之零点零一
0.22%	百分之零点二二
19%	百分之十九
99%	百分之九十九

Telephone numbers

■ Telephone numbers are often read individually in Chinese. 两个 (double), 三个 (triple), 四个 (quadruple), etc. are also occasionally used:

	Spoken
001 5122 2888	零零一 / 零零幺 五一二二 / 五幺二二 二八八八 or 零零 幺五幺 三个二 三个八
020 8711 5526	零二零 八七一一 五五二六 or 零二零 八七幺幺 五五二六
0044 131 555 6666	零零四四 一三一 / 幺三幺 五五五 六六六六 or 零零四四 幺三幺 三个五 四个六

How many?

How many people are there in the hall? — There are a hundred and fifty people
= 大厅里有多少人？ —— 有 150 人

How many of you are going on the school trip? — Twenty-two of us are going
= 你们中有多少人会参加学校的出游？
—— 我们中 22 人会去

How many tables have been booked? — Five
= 订了多少张桌子？ —— 5 张

■ Note the use of 零 in Chinese:

101 students
= 101 个学生 (written)
= 一百零一个学生 (spoken or written)

120 participants
= 120 个参加者 (written)
= 一百二十个参加者 (spoken or written)

1,005 books
= 1,005 本书 (written)
= 一千零五本书 (spoken or written)

1,020 votes
= 1,020 张选票 (written)
= 一千零二十张选票 (spoken or written)

an audience of 1,300
= 1,300 个听众 (written)
= 一千三百个听众 (spoken or written)

■ For approximate numbers, see note 'Approximation' (at entry 'approximation').

n

number: ～ plate *n* Brit 车牌; **～s game** *n* 1 (manipulation of figures) 数字游戏; 2 Amer (lottery) 数字赌博; **N～ Ten** *n* Brit 唐宁街10号 [英国首相官邸]; **～ theory** *n* [u] 数论

number two *n* 1 (deputy) 二把手; **to be sb.'s ～** 是某人的副手 2 child lang (act of defecating) 拉屉屉; **mummy, I need/did a ～** 妈妈，我要拉屉屉/拉了屉屉

numbly /'nʌmli/ *adv* 呆呆地

numbness /'nʌmnɪs/ *n* [u] 1 (physical) 失去知觉 2 (emotional) 麻木

numbskull /'nʌmskʌl/ *n* colloq 笨脑壳

numeracy /'nju:mərəsi, Amer 'nu:-/ *n* [u] 计算能力

numeracy hour *n* Brit 计算课 [英国政府1999年倡导的课程，旨在提高小学生的口笔算能力]

numeral /'nju:mərəl, Amer 'nu:-/ *n* 1 (figure, symbol) 数字; **Roman/Arabic ～s** 罗马/阿拉伯数字 2 (word) 数词; **the ～ four** 数词四

numerate /'nju:mərət, Amer 'nu:-/ *adj* 算术好的 ‹*child, pupil*›; 计算能力强的 ‹*employee, applicant*›

numeration /,nju:mə'reɪʃn, Amer 'nu:-/ *n* 1 [u] (calculating) 计算; (assigning number) 命数 2 [c] (system) (of numbering) 编号（法）; (of counting or computing) 计算（法）

numerator /'nju:məreɪtə(r), Amer 'nu:-/ *n* 分子

numerical /nju:'merɪkl, Amer 'nu:-/ *adj* 数字的; **in ～ order** 按数字顺序; **the ～ value of sth.** 某物的数值

numerically /nju:'merɪkli, Amer nu:-/ *adv* 在数字上

numerous /'nju:mərəs, Amer 'nu:-/ *adj* 1 (very many) 许多的 ‹*accidents, reports, people*›; **on ～ occasions** 在诸多场合 2 (having many members) 有许多成员组成的; **a ～ family** 大家庭

numinous /'nju:mɪnəs, Amer 'nu:-/ *adj* formal 神圣的 ‹*presence, power, quality*›

numismatic /,nju:mɪz'mætɪk, Amer ,nu:-/ *adj* 1 (relating to coins) 钱币的 2 (relating to medals) 奖章的

numismatics /,nju:mɪz'mætɪks, Amer ,nu:-/ *npl + v sing* 1 (study of coins) 钱币学; (collecting of coins) 钱币收藏 2 (study of medals) 奖章学; (collecting of medals) 奖章收藏

numismatist /nju:'mɪzmətɪst, Amer nu:-/ ▸**p. 409** *n* 1 (coin expert) 钱币学家; (medals expert) 奖章研究专家 2 (coin collector) 钱币收藏家; (medal collector) 奖章收藏家

numskull /'nʌmskʌl/ *n* colloq = **numbskull**

nun /nʌn/ *n* 修女

nuncio /'nʌnʃɪəʊ/ *n* (*pl* **～s**) 罗马教廷大使

nunnery /'nʌnəri/ *n* 女修道院

nuptial /'nʌpʃl/

A *adj* 婚姻的; **～ bliss** 婚姻美满; **the ～ ceremony** 婚礼

B nuptials *npl* 婚礼

nurd /nɜ:d/ *n* colloq pej = **nerd**

nurse /nɜ:s/ ▸**p. 409**

A *n* 1 Med 护士; **a psychiatric/qualified ～** 精神科/合格护士; **N～ Jones** 琼斯护士 2 dated (nanny) 保姆

B *vt* 1 (tend, care for) 护理 ‹*patient*› 2 (try to cure) 调治 ‹*flu*›; **he went to bed to ～ his cold** 他上床休息治疗感冒 3 (hold fondly) 搂抱 ‹*child, animal*› 4 (hold carefully) 小心地抱着 ‹*object*› 5 (breastfeed) 给…喂奶 6 (pay attention to) 养护 ‹*plant*›; 悉心打理 ‹*business*›; **to ～ one's drink** 慢慢地品酒 7 (foster) 心怀 ‹*grudge, desire*›

C *vi* 1 (tend to the sick) 护理 2 (suckle) 吃奶

nurse: ～maid *n* dated 保姆; **～ practitioner** ▸**p. 409** *n* 从业护士

nursery /'nɜ:səri/ *n* 1 (crèche) **(day) ～** 日间托儿所 2 dated (children's room) 儿童室 3 (for plants) 育苗床 4 fig (for ideas, talent) 温床

nursery: ～ education *n* [u] 幼儿教育; **～man** /-mən/ ▸**p. 409** *n* 苗圃工人; **～ nurse** ▸**p. 409** *n* 托儿所保育员; **～ rhyme** *n* 童谣; **～ school** *n* 幼儿园; **～ slopes** *npl* Brit [学滑雪的] 平缓坡地; **～ teacher** ▸**p. 409** *n* **～ (school) teacher** 幼儿园教师

> **nursery rhymes**
>
> 童谣，是一些写给小孩唱诵的简单歌曲或诗歌，不少已有数百年历史。影响最深远的童谣集有1781年在英国出版的*Mother Goose's Melody*，其后于1785年在美国重印。今天一般称为《鹅大妈童谣》（*Mother Goose's Rhymes*）。其中*Baa, Baa, Black Sheep*《咩咩小黑羊》和*London Bridge Is Falling Down*《伦敦桥，快塌了》等都是著名的童谣。

nursing /'nɜ:sɪŋ/ ▸**p. 409**

A *adj attrib* 1 (tending to the sick) 护理病人的; **～ staff/methods** 护理人员/方式 2 (breastfeeding) 母乳喂养的

B *n* [u] 1 (career) 护理行业; (practice) 护理 2 (breastfeeding) 母乳喂养

nursing: ～ bra *n* 哺乳期乳罩; **～ home** *n* 1 (for old people) 养老院; 2 (for convalescing) 疗养院; **～ officer** *n* Brit 护士长; **～ school** *n* 护士学校

nurture /'nɜ:tʃə(r)/

A *vt* 1 (care for and educate) 培养教育 ‹*child*› 2 fig (help to develop) 扶持 ‹*project*›; 培养 ‹*talent*›

B *n* [u] 培养

NUS *abbr* Brit = **National Union of Students** 全国学生联合会

NUT *abbr* Brit = **National Union of Teachers** 全国教师联合会

nut /nʌt/

A *n* 1 (hard fruit) 坚果; **chocolate with ～s in it** 果仁巧克力; **to be a hard** *or* **tough ～** colloq ‹*person*› 很难对付; **a hard ～ to crack** 难题; **～ rissole** 果仁炸肉饼 2 Tech 螺母 3 colloq (eccentric) 怪人; (crazy person) 疯子; **he's a bit of a ～** 他疯疯癫癫的 4 colloq (enthusiast) 入迷者; **a fitness/health food ～** 健身迷/保健食品迷 5 colloq (head) 脑袋; **watch your ～!** 当心碰头！; **use your ～!** 用用脑子！; **to go** *or* **be off one's ～** 发疯; **to do one's ～** Brit 大发雷霆 6 **nuts** *pl* sl (testicles) 睾丸 7 (in climbing) 岩石塞

B *excl* **～s!** 我不在乎！; **～s to you!** 去你的！

C *vt* (*pres p etc.* **-tt-**) Brit colloq 用头撞

nut: ～-brown ▸**p. 134** *adj* 深棕色的; **～case** *n* colloq pej 疯子; **～cracker** *n*, **～crackers** *npl* 坚果钳; **～ cutlet** *n* Brit 果仁炸饼; **～hatch** *n* 鳾; **～house** *n* Brit colloq pej 疯人院; **～loaf** *n* 咸味果仁烘饼

nutmeg /'nʌtmeg/ *n* 1 [u] (spice) 肉豆蔻籽粉末 2 [c] (seed) 肉豆蔻籽 3 [c] (tree) 肉豆蔻树

nutrient /'nju:trɪənt, Amer 'nu:-/ *n* 营养物

nutrition /nju:'trɪʃn, Amer nu:-/ *n* [u] 1 (process) 营养的供给 2 (food) 营养品 3 (science) 营养学

nutritional /nju:'trɪʃənl, Amer nu:-/ *adj* 营养的 ‹*supplement*›; **～ value** 营养价值

nutritionist /nju:'trɪʃənɪst, Amer nu:-/ *n* 营养学家

nutritious /nju:'trɪʃəs, Amer nu:-/ *adj* 有营养的

nutritiousness /nju:'trɪʃəsnɪs, Amer nu:-/ *n* [u] 有营养

nutritive /'nju:trɪtɪv, Amer 'nu:-/ *adj* = **nutritional**

nut roast *n* [c and u] 干果蔬菜烘饼

nuts /nʌts/ *adj* colloq 1 (crazy) 疯狂的; **to go ～** 发疯 2 (enthusiastic) 执著; **to be ～ about sb./sth.** 迷恋某人/某事物

nuts and bolts

A *npl* 基础部分 fig **the ～ of sth.** 某事的基本要点

B nuts-and-bolts *adj* 有关具体细节的 ‹*issues*›; 从具体细节出发的 ‹*approach*›

nutshell /'nʌtʃel/ *n* 1 lit 坚果壳 2 fig **in a ～** 简而言之; **to put sth. in a ～** 对某事简而言之

nutter /'nʌtə(r)/ *n* Brit colloq pej 怪人

nutty /'nʌti/ *adj* 1 (containing nuts) 含果仁的; **～ chocolate/biscuits** 果仁巧克力/饼干 2 (in flavour) 坚果味的 3 colloq (mad) 疯狂的 ‹*person, action, idea*›; **～ as a fruitcake** 疯狂到极点

nuzzle /'nʌzl/

A *vi* 依偎; **to ～ up to sb./sth.** 依偎着某人/某物

B *vt* (push) 拱; (rub) 擦

NV *abbr* Amer = **Nevada**

NVQ *abbr* Brit = **National Vocational Qualification** 国家职业资格证书

NW ▸**p. 142** *abbr* = **north-west, North-West Passage**

NY *abbr* Amer = **New York**

nylon /'naɪlɒn/ *n* [u] 尼龙; **～ stocking** 尼龙长袜

nylons /'naɪlɒnz/ *npl* dated (stockings) 尼龙长袜; (tights) 尼龙紧身裤

nymph /nɪmf/ *n* 1 Mythol [古希腊罗马神话中住在山林水泽的] 仙女 2 (insect) 若虫

nymphet /nɪm'fet/ *n* colloq 性感少女

nympho /'nɪmfəʊ/ *n* colloq 女色情狂

nymphomania /,nɪmfə'meɪnɪə/ *n* [u] 女色情狂

nymphomaniac /,nɪmfə'meɪnɪæk/

A *adj* 女色情狂的

B *n* 女色情狂

NYSE *abbr* = **New York Stock Exchange** 纽约证券交易所

NZ *abbr* = **New Zealand**

NZD *abbr* = **New Zealand dollar** 新西兰元

Oo

O¹, o /əʊ/ *n* (*pl* **Os** *or* **O's**) 1▸ (letter) [英语字母表的第15个字母] 2▸ (number) 零 3▸ (circle) 圆

O², o *excl* archaic or liter = **oh**

o' /ə/ *prep* colloq [of的简写形式]; **a cup ~ tea** 一杯茶

OA *abbr* = **office automation** 办公自动化

oaf /əʊf/ *n* 1▸ (stupid person) 笨蛋 2▸ (ill-mannered person) 没教养的人

oafish /'əʊfɪʃ/ *adj* 1▸ (stupid) 愚笨的; **~ clumsiness** 笨手笨脚 2▸ (ill-mannered) 没教养的

oak /əʊk/ *n* 1▸ [c] (tree) 栎树; **great ~s from little acorns grow** Prov 合抱之树，生于毫末 2▸ [u] (wood) 栎木

oak apple *n* 栎瘿

oaken /'əʊkən/ *adj* liter 栎木制的

OAP *abbr* Brit = **old-age pensioner**

oar /ɔ:(r)/ *n* 1▸ (pole with flat blade) 桨; **to put** *or* **shove** *or* **stick one's ~ in** colloq 横插一杠子 2▸ (rower) 桨手

oarlock /'ɔ:lɒk/ *n* Amer 桨架

oarsman /'ɔ:zmən/ *n* (*pl* **oarsmen**) (rower) 男桨手; (in racing team) 男划艇队员

oarsmanship /'ɔ:zmənʃɪp/ *n* [u] (art of rowing) 划桨技术; (skill as a rower) 划桨技能

oarswoman /'ɔ:zwʊmən/ *n* (*pl* **oarswomen**) (rower) 女桨手; (in racing team) 女划艇队员

oasis /əʊ'eɪsɪs/ *n* (*pl* **oases** /əʊ'eɪsi:z/) 1▸ (in desert) 绿洲 2▸ fig (of peace) 乐土; **an ~ of prosperity in a desert of poverty** 贫穷荒漠中的繁荣乐土

oast /əʊst/ *n* 啤酒花烘炉

oast house *n* 啤酒花烘干房

oat /əʊt/

A *n* (plant) 燕麦

B **oats** *npl* (as food) 燕麦; **to get one's ~s** Brit colloq 性交; **to sow one's wild ~s** [年轻时]沉溺于放荡生活

oatcake /'əʊtkeɪk/ *n* 燕麦饼

oath /əʊθ/ *n* 1▸ Jur 宣誓; **to swear** *or* **take an ~** 宣誓; **to take an ~ to do sth.** 发誓做某事; **to take the ~ (in court)** （在法庭上）宣誓据实作证; **to swear/lie on ~** 发誓/宣誓后说谎 2▸ (swear word) 咒骂

oatmeal /'əʊtmi:l/ *n* [u] 1▸ (crushed oats) 燕麦片 2▸ (porridge) 燕麦片粥 3▸ (colour) 浅褐色

OAU *abbr* = **Organization of African Unity**

obbligato /,ɒblɪ'gɑ:təʊ/ *n* (*pl* **~s** *or* **obbligati** /,ɒblɪ'gɑ:ti/) 助奏; **with piano ~** 钢琴伴奏

obduracy /'ɒbdjʊrəsi, Amer -dər-/ *n* [u] 固执

obdurate /'ɒbdjʊrət, Amer -dər-/ *adj* 固执的 ‹*person, behaviour, refusal, firmness*›

OBE *abbr* Brit = **Officer of the Order of the British Empire** 英帝国官佐勋位

obedience /ə'bi:dɪəns/ *n* [u] 1▸ (compliance) 服从; **to demand/expect ~ of** *or* **from sb.** 要求/期望某人服从; **to pledge** *or* **swear ~ to sb.** 保证服从某人 2▸ Relig 遵守戒律; **to take a vow of ~** 发誓遵守戒律

> **OBE**
>
> 英帝国官佐勋位，全称 Officer of the Order of the British Empire。为英王乔治五世（King George V）1917 年设立的英帝国勋位（Order of the British Empire）的第四等（▸**the honours system**），故亦译作英帝国四等勋位。主要授予政界、商界、娱乐界和体育界取得突出成就的人士。获此勋位者可在名字后加 OBE。

obedient /ə'bi:dɪənt/ *adj* 顺从的 ‹*person, dog, behaviour*›; **to be ~ to sb./sth.** 服从某人/某事; **your ~ servant** dated 您忠实的仆人 [用在正规信件的结尾署名]

obediently /ə'bi:dɪəntli/ *adv* 顺从地

obelisk /'ɒbəlɪsk/ *n* 方尖纪念碑

obese /əʊ'bi:s/ *adj* 肥胖的 ‹*person*›; 过重的 ‹*animal*›

obesity /əʊ'bi:səti/ *n* [u] 肥胖

obey /ə'beɪ/

A *vt* 服从 ‹*parent, superior, order*›; 遵守 ‹*law, instruction*›; 受…支配 ‹*conscience, instinct*›

B *vi* 服从

obfuscate /'ɒbfəskeɪt/ *vt* formal 混淆 ‹*issue, truth, facts*›; 使…模糊不清 ‹*meaning, point*›

obituary /ə'bɪtʃʊəri, Amer -tʃʊeri/ *n* **~ (notice)** 讣告

object

A /'ɒbdʒɪkt/ *n* 1▸ (item) 物品; **everyday ~s** 日常用品; **plastic ~s** 塑料制品 2▸ (focus) 对象; **to be the ~ of sth.** 是…的对象 ‹*ridicule, investigation*›; **to become the ~ of sb.'s affection/hatred** 成为某人钟爱/憎恨的对象; **to be the ~ of one's desires** (thing) 是渴望得到的东西; (person) 是依恋的人 3▸ (goal) 目的; **to have no ~ in life** 没有人生目标; **with the ~ of doing sth.** 抱着做某事的目的; **the ~ of the exercise** 活动的目的 4▸ (hindrance) 障碍; **no ~** 不在话下; **expense/money is no ~** 费用/钱不是问题 5▸ Philos 客体 6▸ Ling 宾语; **direct/indirect ~** 直接/间接宾语; **the ~ of a preposition** 介词的宾语 7▸ Comput 目标

B /əb'dʒekt/ *vi* 反对; **to ~ to sth./sb.** 反对某事/某人; **she ~s to his drinking** 她反对他喝酒; **do you ~ to me** *or* **my smoking?** 你介意我抽烟吗？; **I wouldn't ~ to a rest** colloq 休息一会儿我没意见; **to ~ to doing sth.** 反对做某事; **I don't ~ to putting in a good word for you** 我不在乎为你美言几句; **to ~ to sb. as leader** 反对某人当领导; **to ~ to a witness** Jur 质疑证人

C /əb'dʒekt/ *vt* 反对; **to ~ that ...** 反对…; **'you can't do that', he ~ed** "你不能那样做"，他反对道

object clause *n* 宾语从句

objection /əb'dʒekʃn/ *n* [u and c] 反对; **to raise** *or* **lodge** *or* **voice an ~** 提出异议; **I've no ~ to them coming** 我不反对他们来; **~!** (in court) 反对!; **~ sustained/overruled** (in court) 反对有效/无效

objectionable /əb'dʒekʃənəbl/ *adj* 令人反感的 ‹*language, manner*›; 讨厌的 ‹*smell*›; 难以接受的 ‹*view, proposal*›

objectionably /əb'dʒekʃənəbli/ *adv* 令人反感地 ‹*behave, act*›

objective /əb'dʒektɪv/

A *adj* 1▸ (unbiased) 公正的 ‹*person, view*›; 客观的 ‹*report, assessment, data*›; **he's quite ~ in his reporting** 他的报道很客观 2▸ Philos 客观存在的; **~ fact/existence/values** 客观事实/存在/价值 3▸ Ling 宾语的; **the ~ case** 宾格; **an ~ pronoun** 宾语代词

B *n* 1▸ (aim, goal) 目标; **to achieve/reach one's ~** 实现/达到目标 2▸ Mil 打击目标 3▸ (of telescope, microscope) 物镜

objective lens *n* 物镜

objectively /əb'dʒektɪvli/ *adv* 1▸ (fairly) 公正地 ‹*view, consider*› 2▸ Philos 客观地 ‹*exist*›

objectivity /,ɒbdʒek'tɪvəti/ *n* [u] 客观性

object lesson *n* 借鉴

objector /əb'dʒektə(r)/ *n* 反对者

object-oriented programming *n* [u] 面向对象的程序设计

objet d'art /,ɒbʒeɪ 'dɑ:/ *n* (decorative) 小饰品; (artistic) 小工艺品

obligate /'ɒblɪgeɪt/ *vt* (legally) 使负有法律义务; (morally) 使负有道义义务; **to ~ sb. to do sth.** 迫使某人做某事; **to be ~d to do sth.** 有义务做某事

obligation /,ɒblɪ'geɪʃn/ *n* 1▸ [c] (duty) 义务; **to have an ~ to do sth.** 有义务做某事; **a legal/moral/social ~** 法律/道德/社会义务; **to fulfil** *or* **meet one's ~s** 尽义务 2▸ [u] (commitment) 责任; **a sense of ~** 责任感; **to be under an/no ~ to do sth.** 有责任/无责任做某事 3▸ [c] (financial debt) 债务; (debt of gratitude) 人情债; **to meet one's ~s** 还债; **to repay an ~** 还债; **to be under an ~ to sb. for sth.** 因某事欠某人的债

obligato = **obbligato**

obligatory /ə'blɪgətri, Amer -tɔ:ri/ *adj* 1▸ (compulsory) 强制性的; **seatbelts are now ~** 现在必须系安全带 2▸ (customary) 习惯性的

oblige /ə'blaɪdʒ/

A *vt* 1▸ (compel) 强迫; **to be ~d to do sth.** 被迫做某事; **to feel ~d to do sth.** 觉得有义务做某事; **you are not ~d/they cannot ~ you to answer** 你不一定要回答/他们不能强迫你回答 2▸ (be helpful to) 帮助; **she did it to ~ them** 她做这事来帮助他们

B *vi* 有帮助; **anything to ~!** 乐于效劳!

obliged /ə'blaɪdʒd/ *adj* 感激的; **to be ~ to sb.** 感激某人; **much ~!** 不胜感激!

obliging /ə'blaɪdʒɪŋ/ *adj* 乐于助人的

obligingly /ə'blaɪdʒɪŋli/ *adv* 乐意地

oblique /ə'bli:k/

A *adj* 1▸ (slanting) 倾斜的; **~ lines/strokes/angle** 斜线/斜线号/斜角 2▸ fig (indirect) 间接的 ‹*allusion, compliment*›; **she gave me an ~ look** 她斜眼瞅了我一下

B *n* Brit 斜线号

obliquely /ə'bli:kli/ *adj* 1▸ (at an angle) 倾斜地 ‹*fall, strike*› 2▸ fig (indirectly) 间接地 ‹*refer, allude*›

obliterate /ə'blɪtəreɪt/ *vt* 1▸ (rub out, remove) 清除 ‹*inscription, print*› 2▸ (erase from mind)

忘却 ‹*impression, experience*›; **to ~ sth. from the mind/memory** 从心中/记忆中将某事物抹掉 **3** (destroy) 摧毁 ‹*town, building*› **4** fig (conceal) 掩盖

obliteration /əˌblɪtəˈreɪʃn/ *n* [u] **1** (of mark) 消除 **2** (of memory, impression) 忘却 **3** (destruction) 毁灭

oblivion /əˈblɪvɪən/ *n* [u] **1** (unconsciousness) 无意识状态; **to drink oneself into ~** 喝得不省人事; **to long for ~** 渴望长眠不醒 **2** (state of being forgotten) 被遗忘; **to fall** *or* **sink into ~** 被忘却

oblivious /əˈblɪvɪəs/ *adj* 未察觉的; **to be ~ of** *or* **to sth.** 未察觉某事

oblong /ˈɒblɒŋ, Amer -lɔːŋ/
A *adj* 长方形的 ‹*shape, figure*›
B *n* 长方形

obloquy /ˈɒbləkwi/ *n* [u] formal **1** (condemnation) 公开谴责 **2** (disgrace) 耻辱

obnoxious /əbˈnɒkʃəs/ *adj* 讨厌的 ‹*person, behaviour*›; 难闻的 ‹*smell, stench*›

obnoxiously /əbˈnɒkʃəsli/ *adv* 讨厌地 ‹*behave, arrogant*›

oboe /ˈəʊbəʊ/ ▸**p. 395** *n* **1** (instrument) 双簧管 **2** (player) 双簧管吹奏者

oboist /ˈəʊbəʊɪst/ ▸**p. 395, p. 409** *n* 双簧管吹奏者

obscene /əbˈsiːn/ *adj* **1** (offensive) 淫秽的 ‹*publication, remark*›; **~ phone calls** 色情骚扰电话; **~ jokes/gestures** 下流的笑话/手势 **2** (monstrous) 骇人听闻的 ‹*war, pollution*›; 大得骇人的 ‹*wealth, profit*›

obscenely /əbˈsiːnli/ *adv* **1** (offensively) 淫秽地 ‹*behave, talk*› **2** (monstrously) 令人厌恶地极其 ‹*talented*›; **to be ~ wealthy/rich** 富得流油

obscenity /əbˈsenəti/ *n* **1** [u] (obscene nature) 淫秽; **the ~ laws** 反淫秽法规 **2** [c] (obscene remark) 下流话 **3** [c] (monstrosity) 骇人听闻; **this war is an ~** 这场战争令人发指

obscurantism /ˌɒbskjʊəˈræntɪzəm/ *n* [u] 蒙昧主义

obscurantist /ˌɒbskjʊəˈræntɪst/
A *adj* 蒙昧主义的
B *n* 蒙昧主义者

obscure /əbˈskjʊə(r)/
A *adj* **1** (hard to understand) 费解的 ‹*point, argument, theory, law*›; 复杂的 ‹*relationship*›; 晦涩的 ‹*style, meaning*› **2** (little-known) 鲜为人知的 ‹*novel*›; 无名的 ‹*writer*›; 偏僻的 ‹*village*›; 卑微的 ‹*life, birth*› **3** (indistinct) 模糊的 ‹*outline, sound, memory*›; 难以捉摸的 ‹*feeling*› **4** (dark) 阴森黑暗的 ‹*corner, cave*›
B *vt* **1** (make unclear) 使…费解 ‹*meaning*›; 掩盖 ‹*issues, truth*› **2** (conceal) «*cloud*» 遮挡 ‹*moon, view*›; «*mist*» 笼罩 ‹*view*›; «*noise*» 淹没 ‹*sound*›

obscurely /əbˈskjʊəli/ *adv* 令人费解地 ‹*write, talk*›

obscurity /əbˈskjʊərəti/ *n* [u and c] **1** (of argument, theory, law) 晦涩 **2** (being little known) 默默无闻; **to live** *or* **remain in ~** 默默无闻地活着; **the ~ of his birth** *or* **origins** 他卑微的身世

obsequies /ˈɒbsɪkwɪz/ *npl* formal 葬礼

obsequious /əbˈsiːkwɪəs/ *adj* 巴结奉迎的 ‹*manner, clerk, waiter*›

obsequiously /əbˈsiːkwɪəsli/ *adv* 谄媚地

obsequiousness /əbˈsiːkwɪəsnɪs/ *n* [u] 谄媚

observable /əbˈzɜːvəbl/ *adj* 能看到的 ‹*phenomenon, galaxy*›; 显著的 ‹*feature, improvement*›; 明显的 ‹*difference, effect*›

observably /əbˈzɜːvəbli/ *adv* 显而易见地 ‹*larger, thinner*›

observance /əbˈzɜːvəns/ *n* **1** [u] (of law, rule) 遵守; (of religious event) 纪念; (of anniversary) 庆祝 **2** [c] (religious rite) 宗教仪式

observant /əbˈzɜːvənt/ *adj* **1** (perceptive) 善于观察的 ‹*person*›; 敏锐的 ‹*mind, eye*›; **it's very ~ of you to notice that** 你真有眼力，注意到了这个 **2** formal (of law, custom) 严格遵守的; **to be ~ of sth.** 严格遵守某事

observation /ˌɒbzəˈveɪʃn/ *n* **1** [u] (monitoring) 观测; (medical surveillance) 观察; **to keep sb./sth. under ~** 监视某人/某事物 **2** [u] (ability) 观察力; **powers of ~** 观察力 **3** [c] (finding, result) 观测结果; **clinical/laboratory ~s** 诊室/实验室观测结果 **4** [c] (remark) 评论; **to make an ~ about** *or* **on sb./sth.** 对某人/某事物作出评论

observation: ~ car *n* Amer [火车上有大窗户的] 观景车厢; **~ deck** *n* [机场、野生动物保护区等的] 瞭望台; **~ post** *n* 观察哨; **~ satellite** *n* 观测卫星; **~ tower** *n* 瞭望塔; **~ ward** *n* 观察病房

observatory /əbˈzɜːvətri, Amer -tɔːri/ *n* (astronomical) 天文台; (meteorological) 气象台

observe /əbˈzɜːv/ *vt* **1** (see, notice) 注意到; **to ~ sb. doing sth.** 注意到某人做某事; **did you ~ what she did next?** 你看到她接下来做什么了吗？ **2** (watch carefully) 观察 ‹*patient, phenomenon, development*›; 监视 ‹*suspect*› **3** (remark) 说; (comment) 评论 **4** (adhere to) 遵守 ‹*law, custom, ceasefire*›; **we ~d a one-minute silence** 我们默哀了一分钟 **5** (celebrate) 庆祝 ‹*religious festival*›

observer /əbˈzɜːvə(r)/ *n* **1** (watcher) 观察者; **to a casual ~, he was at peace** 乍看起来，他很平和 **2** (at conference, election) 观察员; **to attend as an ~** 以观察员身份出席; **a military/an international ~** 军事观察家/国际观察员 **3** (commentator) 评论员

obsess /əbˈses/
A *vt* «*worries, fears*» 困扰; «*girl, boy*» 使痴迷; **she was totally ~ed with him** 她被他迷得神魂颠倒; **he was ~ed by** *or* **with thoughts of suicide** 他总想着自杀; **these anxieties ~ed her** 她忧心忡忡
B *vi* 念念不忘; **she ~es over her shoes** 她总唠叨她的鞋

obsession /əbˈseʃn/ *n* **1** [u] (state) 着迷; **his ~ with fishing is quite recent** 他迷上钓鱼是最近的事 **2** [c] (object of attention) 让人着迷的对象; (fixed idea) 执念; **to have an ~ with** *or* **about sth.** 对某事着迷; **she has an ~ with hygiene** 她有洁癖

obsessional /əbˈseʃənl/ *adj* 痴迷的 ‹*thoughts, behaviour, personality*›; **to be ~ about doing sth.** 痴迷于做某事; **~ neurosis** 强迫性神经官能症

obsessive /əbˈsesɪv/ *adj* 痴迷的 ‹*fan, collector, love*›; 执着的 ‹*pursuit, behaviour*›; 萦绕在心头的 ‹*concern, secrecy*›; 难以释怀的 ‹*hatred*›; **~ neatness** *or* **tidiness** 洁癖

obsessive-compulsive disorder *n* [u] 强迫症

obsessively /əbˈsesɪvli/ *adv* 过分地 ‹*concerned, anxious*›; 着魔般地 ‹*work, worry*›

obsidian /əbˈsɪdɪən/ *n* [u] 黑曜岩

obsolescence /ˌɒbsəˈlesns/ *n* [u] 淘汰; **built-in/planned ~** 内在的/计划的陈旧

obsolescent /ˌɒbsəˈlesnt/ *adj* 淘汰的 ‹*machinery, technology*›; 过时的 ‹*system, word*›

obsolete /ˈɒbsəliːt/ *adj* **1** (no longer used) 淘汰的 ‹*machine, technology*›; 过期的 ‹*passport, ticket*›; 过时的 ‹*expression, law, practice*› **2** Biol 退化的 ‹*limb, organ*›

obstacle /ˈɒbstəkl/ *n* lit, fig 障碍; **to clear/overcome an ~** 清除/逾越障碍; **an ~ to progress/peace** 进步/和平的绊脚石; **to place** *or* **put an ~ in sb.'s way** 妨碍某人前进

obstacle: ~ course *n* **1** Mil 障碍训练场; **2** fig 重重困难; **~ race** *n* 障碍赛跑

obstetric /əbˈstetrɪk/ *adj* 产科的; **an ~ unit/clinic** 妇产科/诊所; **~ complications** 产科并发症

obstetrician /ˌɒbstəˈtrɪʃn/ ▸**p. 409** *n* 产科医生

obstetrics /əbˈstetrɪks/ *npl* + *v sing* 产科学

obstinacy /ˈɒbstənəsi/ *n* [u] **1** (stubbornness) 固执 **2** (of illness) 难治; (of resistance) 顽强

obstinate /ˈɒbstənət/ *adj* **1** (stubborn) 执拗的 ‹*person*›; 顽固的 ‹*institution, behaviour*›; **she maintained an ~ silence** 她一味地保持沉默 **2** (difficult to overcome) 棘手的 ‹*problem*›; 难以除掉的 ‹*weeds, stain*›; 难治愈的 ‹*illness, rash*›; 顽强的 ‹*resistance, fight*›

obstinately /ˈɒbstənətli/ *adv* 顽固地 ‹*insist, repeat, refuse*›; 顽强地 ‹*fight, resist*›

obstreperous /əbˈstrepərəs/ *adj* 任性的 ‹*person, behaviour*›; 喧闹的 ‹*party, crowd*›

obstreperously /əbˈstrepərəsli/ *adv* 嘈杂地 ‹*shout, argue*›; 桀骜不驯地 ‹*rebellious*›

obstruct /əbˈstrʌkt/ *vt* **1** (block) 阻挡 ‹*opening, road*›; 阻塞 ‹*pipe, gutter*›; 遮挡 ‹*view*› **2** (hinder) 堵塞 ‹*flow, traffic*›; 阻碍 ‹*progress, movement*›; **to ~ the passage of a bill** Pol 阻挠法案通过 **3** Jur 妨碍 ‹*police, justice*› **4** Sport 犯规性阻挡 ‹*player*›

obstruction /əbˈstrʌkʃn/ *n* **1** [u] (of a road) 堵塞; (of a pipe) 阻塞 **2** [c] (blockage) 堵塞物; **an ~ of the bowel** 肠梗阻 **3** [u] Jur 妨碍 **4** [u and c] Sport 阻挡犯规; **to commit an ~** 阻挡犯规

obstructionism /əbˈstrʌkʃənɪzəm/ *n* [u] 蓄意阻挠

obstructionist /əbˈstrʌkʃənɪst/
A *adj* 蓄意阻挠的 ‹*tactics, intervention*›
B *n* 蓄意阻挠者

obstructive /əbˈstrʌktɪv/ *adj* 阻挠的 ‹*behaviour, policy*›

obstructiveness /əbˈstrʌktɪvnɪs/ *n* [u] 阻挠

obtain /əbˈteɪn/
A *vt* 获得 ‹*information, permission, job, money, shares*›; 赢得 ‹*prize, votes*›; 取得 ‹*degree*›; **the goods were ~ed illegally** 这些财产是非法所得
B *vi* formal «*custom, practice*» 存在; «*fashion*» 流行; «*method*» 适用

obtainable /əbˈteɪnəbl/ *adj* 能买到的 ‹*goods*›; 可获得的 ‹*saving*›; 可达到的 ‹*goal*›

obtrude /əbˈtruːd/ formal
A *vt* 强加 ‹*oneself, opinions, grief*›; **she didn't want to ~ herself on the grief-stricken family** 她不想打扰这个悲痛的家庭
B *vi* «*person*» 惹眼; «*opinions, noise*» 打扰; **to ~ on sb./sth.** 打扰某人/某事

obtrusive /əbˈtruːsɪv/ *adj* 惹眼的 ‹*graffiti, building, decor*›; 刺耳的 ‹*music, noise*›; 刺鼻的 ‹*smell*›

obtrusively /əbˈtruːsɪvli/ *adv* 惹眼地 ‹*behave*›; 炫耀地 ‹*comment*›; 强行地 ‹*intervene*›

obtrusiveness /əbˈtruːsɪvnɪs/ *n* [u] 显眼

obtuse /əbˈtjuːs, Amer -ˈtuːs-/ *adj* **1** Geom 钝角的; **an ~ angle** 钝角 **2** (stupid) 愚蠢的 ‹*person, comment*› **3** (obscure) 晦涩难懂的 ‹*reference, language*›

obtuseness /əbˈtjuːsnɪs, Amer -ˈtuːs-/ *n* [u] 愚蠢

obverse /ˈɒbvɜːs/
A *n* [u] **1** (of coin, medal) [硬币或奖章的] 正面 **2** (opposite) 对立面
B *adj attrib* **1 the ~ side** (of coin or medal) 正面 **2** (contrary) 对立的 ‹*argument, proposition*›

obviate /ˈɒbvɪeɪt/ *vt* 取消 ‹*need, requirement*›; 排除 ‹*difficulty, danger*›; 避免 ‹*delay*›

obvious /ˈɒbvɪəs/
A *adj* **1** (evident) 明确的 ‹*answer, choice*›; 明显的 ‹*mistake, requirement, danger*›; **for ~**

reasons, I do not wish to discuss this 由于显而易见的原因，我不想谈论这件事; **her disappointment was ～ to all** 大家都看得出她很失望; **it was ～ that she didn't know** 显然她原本不知道 **2** pej (unsubtle) 了无新意的 ‹*remark, question*›; 平淡无奇的 ‹*plot, story*›; 太明显的 ‹*lie*›

B *n* [u] **the ～** 显而易见的事; **to state the ～** 说大白话

obviously /'ɒbvɪəsli/ *adv* 明显地; **～, we can't achieve all of these goals immediately** 我们显然无法立刻实现所有的目标; **hasn't he heard of them? — ～ not!** 难道他没有听说过他们? ——当然没有!

obviousness /'ɒbvɪəsnɪs/ *n* [u] **1** (of mistake, change, reason) 明显 **2** (of plot, question) 平淡无奇

ocarina /,ɒkə'ri:nə/ ▸**p. 395** *n* 奥卡里纳笛

occasion /ə'keɪʒn/

A *n* **1** (particular time) 某次; **on one ～** 有一回; **on several ～s** 好几次; **there are ～s when ...** 有时候…; **on ～** 偶尔; **on the ～ of my retirement** 在我退休时; **to rise to the ～** 随机应变; **should the ～ so demand** formal 如有必要 **2** (opportunity) 时机; **a propitious ～** 有利的时机; **at the first possible ～** 一有机会; **if the ～ arises ..., should the ～ arise ...** 如果有机会的话… **3** (event) 特别时刻; (celebration) 庆典; **to celebrate** *or* **mark** *or* **observe an ～** 庆祝一个特别的时刻; **a festive/memorable/special ～** 喜庆的/值得纪念的/特殊的时刻; **ceremonial/social ～s** 庆典/社交聚会; **the wedding was quite an ～** 婚礼非常隆重 **4** formal (reason) 理由; **an ～ to do sth.** 做某事的缘由; **there has been no ～ to use it** 没有机会用到它; **an ～ for sth.** 某事的根据; **there is no ～ for complaint/alarm** 没有什么好抱怨/惊慌的

B *vt* formal «*circumstances*» 引起 ‹*response, event*›; **to ～ sb. much grief** 使某人悲伤不已

occasional /ə'keɪʒənl/ *adj* **1** 偶尔造访的 ‹*visitor*›; 偶尔的 ‹*visit, drink, shower*›; **～ events** 偶发事件; **we passed the** *or* **an ～ hiker on the path** 我们在小路上偶尔会碰上一位不常见的远足者 **2** (for special occasion) 应景的 ‹*poem, music*›

occasionally /ə'keɪʒənəli/ *adv* 偶尔 ‹*occur, use*›; **only very ～** 只是极个别地

occasional table *n* 休闲小桌

Occident /'ɒksɪdənt/ *n* liter **the ～** 西方世界 [尤指欧美]

occidental /,ɒksɪ'dentl/ *adj* liter 西方国家的

occult /ɒ'kʌlt, Amer ə'kʌlt/

A *adj* 超自然的 ‹*powers*›; 神秘的 ‹*arts, ceremony, literature*›; **she exercised some ～ influence over him** 她对他有一种不可思议的影响

B *n* [u] **the ～** (supernatural) 神秘学; (magical) 魔法

occultism /ɒ'kʌltɪzəm, Amer ə'-/ *n* [u] (belief) 神秘论; (study) 神秘学; (practice) 玄术

occupancy /'ɒkjʊpənsi/ *n* [u] **1** (act of occupying) (房屋、土地等的) 占有; (proportion occupied) 入住率; **we have sole ～ of the house** 这房子完全归我们所有; **available for immediate ～** 可随时入住 **2** (period) 占用期

occupant /'ɒkjʊpənt/ *n* **1** (of building) 居住者; **the previous ～s of the house** 房子的前住户 **2** (of vehicle) 乘坐者; (of seat, bed) 占用者 **3** (of post) 任职者; **the previous/new/current ～ of the post** 这个职位的前任/新任/现任

occupation /,ɒkjʊ'peɪʃn/ *n* **1** [u] (of house) 居住; **the rooms are unfit for ～** 这些房间不适合居住; **to be in ～** 被居住 **2** [u] Mil, Pol (action, state) 占领; (period) 占领期; **to be** *or* **come under ～** 被占领; **the ～** Hist [二战期间德国对法国的] 占领; **the workers' ～ of the factory** 工人对工厂的占领; **the ～ forces** *or* **troops** 占领军 **3** [c] (job) 职业; **he's a plumber/doctor by ～** 他的职业是管道工/医生 **4** [c] (leisure activity) 消遣; **gardening is my favourite ～** 园艺是我最喜欢的业余活动

occupational /,ɒkjʊ'peɪʃənl/ *adj* 职业的; **～ disease** 职业病

occupational: ～ hazard *n* 职业性危害; **～ health** *n* [u] 职业卫生保健

occupational pension *n* Brit 职业退休金

occupational pension scheme *n* Brit 职业退休金计划

occupational: ～ psychologist ▸**p. 409** *n* 职业心理学家; **～ psychology** *n* [u] 职业心理学; **～ therapist** ▸**p. 409** *n* 职业治疗师; **～ therapy** *n* [u] 职业疗法

occupier /'ɒkjʊpaɪə(r)/ *n* **1** Brit (of house, building) [房屋或土地的] 占有者 **2** Mil 占领者

occupy /'ɒkjʊpaɪ/ *vt* **1** (inhabit, use) 居住 ‹*house, flat*›; 使用 ‹*office*›; 拥有 ‹*premises*› **2** (take, use) 占用 ‹*room, chair*›; **is this place occupied?** 这位置有人吗? ; **the toilet is occupied** 厕所里有人 **3** (hold) 担任 ‹*position, post*› **4** Mil (take over) 占领 ‹*country, town*›; **occupied territory** 被占领土 **5** (take up) 占据 ‹*space, room, time*›; **the speeches/celebrations occupied the whole day** 演讲/庆祝活动持续了一整天 **6** (keep busy) 使…忙碌 ‹*person*›; 占据 ‹*mind*›; 吸引 ‹*attention*›; **to ～ oneself/sb. with sth.** 使自己/某人忙于做某事; **I kept the kids occupied by reading them a book** 我靠给孩子们读书吸引他们的注意力

occur /ə'kɜ:(r)/ *vi* (*pres p etc.* **-rr-**) **1** (happen) «*accident, event*» 发生; «*death*» 来临; «*epidemic*» 爆发 **2** (be present) «*expression, misprint*» 出现; «*plant, tree*» 存在 **3** (suggest itself) «*idea*» 被想到; **to ～ to sb.** 被某人想到; **it only ～red to me later** 我只是后来才想到; **did it never ～ to you that something was wrong?** 你从未想过出错了吗?

occurrence /ə'kʌrəns/ *n* **1** [c] (event) 发生的事; **a regular/an unusual ～** 定期发生的/不寻常的事 **2** [u] (incidence) 发生; **the frequent ～ of this disease** 这种疾病的频繁出现; **the ～ of cancer increases with age** 癌症发病率随年龄的增长而增长 **3** [u and c] (presence) 存在; (instance) 存在情况

ocean /'əʊʃn/ *n* **1** lit 海洋; **an ～ climate** 海洋性气候; **～ waves** 海浪; **the ～ bed** 海底 **2** fig colloq (large expanse) 大片; (large quantity) 大量; **she wept an ～ of tears** 她泪流成河

oceanarium /,əʊʃə'neərɪəm/ *n* (*pl* **～s** *or* **oceanaria** /,əʊʃə'neərɪə/) 大型海洋水族馆

ocean-going *adj* 远洋的 ‹*vessel, liner*›

Oceania /,əʊʃɪ'eɪnɪə/ *pr n* 大洋洲

oceanic /,əʊʃɪ'ænɪk/ *adj* 海洋的; **a study of ～ plant life** 海洋植物研究; **the ～ crust/coast/current** 海洋地壳/海岸/洋流

ocean liner *n* 远洋班轮

oceanographer /,əʊʃə'nɒgrəfə(r)/ ▸**p. 409** *n* 海洋学家

oceanographic /,əʊʃənə'græfɪk/ *adj* 海洋学的; **an ～ institute** 海洋研究所; **an ～ ship** 海洋调查船

oceanography /,əʊʃə'nɒgrəfi/ *n* [u] 海洋学

ocelot /'əʊsɪlɒt, Amer 'ɒsələt/ *n* 豹猫

och /ɒx/ *excl* Scot 啊 [表示吃惊、蔑视、烦恼、不耐烦或不同意]; **'och, he's only kidding!' she said** "哎呀，他只是在开玩笑!" 她说道

ochre Brit, **ocher** Amer /'əʊkə(r)/ ▸**p. 134**

A *n* [u] **1** (pigment) 赭石 **2** (colour) 赭色

B *adj* 赭色的

o'clock /ə'klɒk/ ▸**p. 831** *adv* …点钟; **it is two ～** 现在是两点钟; **at 7 ～ exactly** *or* **precisely** 在 7 点整

OCR *abbr* **= optical character recognition**

Oct *abbr* **= October**

octagon /'ɒktəgən, Amer -gɒn/ *n* 八边形

octagonal /ɒk'tægənl/ *adj* 八边形的

octahedron /,ɒktə'hi:drən, -'hedrən, Amer -drɒn/ *n* 八面体

octal /'ɒktl/

A *n* [u] 八进制

B *adj* 八进制的

octane /'ɒkteɪn/ *n* [u] 辛烷

octane number, octane rating *ns* 辛烷值

octave /'ɒktɪv/ *n* (series of notes) 八度; (one note) 八度音阶

octavo /ɒk'teɪvəʊ/ *n* (*pl* **～s**) 八开本; **an ～ volume** 八开本卷

octet /ɒk'tet/ *n* **1** (of singers) 八重唱组合; (of instrumentalists) 八重奏乐团 **2** (for singers) 八重唱曲; (for instrumentalists) 八重奏曲

October /ɒk'təʊbə(r)/ ▸**p. 490** *n* 十月; **last/this/next ～** 上个/本年/下个十月份; **in early/late ～** 十月上旬/下旬; **～ weather/morning** 十月的天气/早晨; **the ～ Revolution** [1917年俄国的] 十月革命

octogenarian /,ɒktədʒɪ'neərɪən/

A *n* 八旬老人

B *adj* 八十多岁的

octopus /'ɒktəpəs/ *n* (*pl* **～es**) 章鱼

ocular /'ɒkjʊlə(r)/

A *adj* 眼睛的; **～ lens/tissue** 眼晶状体/组织; **～ disease/trauma** 眼疾/眼损伤

B *n* 目镜

OD

A *n* colloq 过量吸毒

B *vi* colloq (*pres p* **OD'ing**; *pt, pp* **OD'd**, **OD'ed**) 过量服用; **to ～ on chocolate cake** fig hum 大吃巧克力蛋糕

odd /ɒd/

A *adj* **1** (strange) 奇怪的 ‹*thing, appearance, clothes*›; 古怪的 ‹*person, behaviour*›; **it's ～ that he hasn't come** 奇怪的是他没来; **how ～ that ...** 真奇怪…; **that's ～** 这有点怪; **the ～ thing about it is ...** 怪就怪在…; **she's a bit ～** colloq 她有点怪怪的 **2** *attrib* (not matching) 不成对的 ‹*item*›; **he was wearing (two) ～ socks** 他穿着 (两只) 不成双的袜子; **the ～ man** *or* **one out** (left over) 落单者; (different) 异类; **to feel the ～ one out** colloq 感到格格不入; **to lose by the ～ goal** Sport 一球之差输了 **3** *attrib* (miscellaneous, extra) 零散的; **～ scraps** *or* **bits of material** 边角料; **to have a few ～ coins left** 还剩几枚硬币; **do you have the ～ 3p?** 你有 3 便士零钱吗? ; **do you have an ～ minute to spare?** 你能抽出片刻时间吗? **4** *attrib* (occasional) 偶尔的 ‹*occurrence*›; 零星的 ‹*object*›; 临时的 ‹*job*›; **to write the ～ article** 偶尔写写文章; **to have the ～ drink** 难得喝一杯; **the ～ moment of melancholy/despair** 偶尔郁闷/绝望的时候; **at ～ moments/times** 偶尔/不时地; **in ～ corners** 在偏僻的角落 **5** Math 奇数的; **3 is an ～ number** 3 是奇数

B -odd *combining form* (approximately) 略多的; **50～ pounds** 50 多英镑; **twenty～ years** 二十来年

oddball /'ɒdbɔ:l/ colloq

A *n* 怪人

B *adj* 古怪的 ‹*character, type*›

oddity /'ɒdɪti/ *n* **1** [u] (oddness) 古怪 **2** [c] (unusual person) 怪人; (unusual thing) 怪异的事物 **3** [c] (characteristic) 怪异

odd job *n* 零活儿; **to do ～s around the house** 在家里干杂活儿

odd-job man *n* 打零工的人

odd-looking *adj* 长相奇特的 ‹*person*›; 怪模怪样的 ‹*house, object, design*›

oddly /'ɒdli/ *adv* 怪异地 ‹*dressed, shaped*›; 奇特地 ‹*attractive*›; **～ enough, she ignored me** 很奇怪，她没理我

O

oddment /ˈɒdmənt/ *n* (remaining from a large piece) 边角料; (remnant) 零碎

oddness /ˈɒdnɪs/ *n* [u] 古怪

odds /ɒdz/ *npl* **1** (in betting) 投注赔率; **the ~ for/against sth.** 赌赢/赌输某物的赔率; **the ~ are 8 to 1 on/against sth.** 赌赢/赌输某物的赔率是八赔一; **to give** *or* **offer** *or* **quote** *or* **lay ~ of 10 to 1** 设定赔率为 10 赔 1; **short/long ~** 低/高赔率; **the ~ are even that he'll resign** fig 他有一半的可能会辞职; **I'll lay ~ on him getting the job** fig 我打赌他能得到这份工作; **over the ~** Brit colloq 超出预期的 **2** (chance, probability) **the ~** 可能性; **the ~ are that she will be late** 她可能会迟到; **the ~ are very much** *or* **heavily in our favour** 我们胜的几率很大; **by all the ~** (definitely) 毫无疑问; (judging from the past) 按惯例; **to win in the face of overwhelming ~** 在非常不利的情况下取胜 **3** (conflict) 不和; **to be at ~ (over sth.)** (in disagreement) (在某事上) 意见不一致; (fighting) (在某事上) 争吵; **to be at ~ with sth.** 与…不相符 ‹*statement, document*›; **to set two people at ~** 使两个人发生冲突

odds and ends *npl* 零碎

odds and sods *npl* esp Brit colloq 零碎

odds-on *adj* **1** (likely) 很可能的; **it's ~ that he'll lose** 他多半要输 **2** (in betting) 很可能赢的; **this horse/dog is ~ to win** 这匹马/这条狗会赢; **to be the ~ favourite** 被看好要赢

ode /əʊd/ *n* 颂诗; **an ~ to sb./sth.** 对某人/某事的颂歌

odious /ˈəʊdɪəs/ *adj* 讨厌的 ‹*person, behaviour, remark*›; 龌龊的 ‹*regime*›

odiously /ˈəʊdɪəslɪ/ *adv* 讨厌地 ‹*behave, rude*›; **she treated me ~** 她待我很恶劣

odiousness /ˈəʊdɪəsnɪs/ *n* [u] 可憎

odium /ˈəʊdɪəm/ *n* [u] formal 憎恶

odometer /ɒˈdɒmɪtə(r)/ *n* esp Amer 里程表

odor /ˈəʊdə(r)/ *n* Amer = **odour**

odorless /ˈəʊdəlɪs/ *adj* Amer = **odourless**

odorous /ˈəʊdərəs/ *adj* liter 有气味的 ‹*room, clothing*›; **~ breath** 口臭

odour /ˈəʊdə(r)/ *n* Brit **1** (smell) 气味; **a delicious/an unpleasant ~** 香味/臭味; **to emit** *or* **exude** *or* **give off an ~** 发出气味 **2** fig (pervasive quality) 意味; **an ~ of corruption** 堕落腐化的风气; **to be in bad ~ with sb.** 惹某人反感

odourless /ˈəʊdəlɪs/ *adj* Brit 无气味的; **an ~ gas** 无臭气体

odyssey /ˈɒdɪsɪ/ *n* **1** [u] Literat **the O~** 奥德赛 [古希腊史诗] **2** [c] (journey) 艰苦跋涉

OE *abbr* = **Old English**

OECD *abbr* = **Organization for Economic Cooperation and Development**

oedema /ɪˈdiːmə/ *n* [u] Brit 水肿

Oedipal /ˈiːdɪpl/ *adj* 恋母情结的 ‹*desire, fantasy*›

Oedipus complex /ˈiːdɪpəs ˌkɒmpleks/ *n* 恋母情结

oenology /iːˈnɒlədʒɪ/ *n* [u] Brit 葡萄酿酒学

o'er /ɔː(r)/ *adv, prep* liter or archaic = **over**[1]

oesophagus /ɪˈsɒfəgəs/ *n* (*pl* **oesophagi** /ɪˈsɒfəgaɪ/ *or* **~es**) Brit 食管

oestrogen /ˈiːstrədʒən/ *n* Brit 雌激素

oestrus /ˈiːstrəs/ *n* [u] Brit [雌性哺乳动物的] 发情期

of /ɒv, Amer ɔːv/ *prep* **1** (indicating possession, inclusion, qualities) …的; **the crew ~ the aircraft** 全体机务人员; **the legs ~ the table** 桌子腿; **there were five ~ us** 我们有 5 个人; **a man ~ courage** 勇敢的男人; **the work is ~ great interest** 这工作很有趣; **a map ~ Oxford** 牛津地图 **2** (indicating source) [表示来源]; **the symphonies ~ Beethoven** 贝多芬的交响乐; **a family ~ royal origin** 有王室血统的家庭; **a problem ~ his own making** 他自己搞出来的问题 **3** (indicating identity) [表示同一所指]; **the city ~ Rome** 罗马城; **the art ~ photography** 摄影艺术; **the day ~ the earthquake** 地震那天; **that idiot ~ a plumber** 那个白痴管子工 **4** (indicating category) [表示类型]; **various types ~ sth.** 各类某事物 **5** (indicating age) …岁的; **a girl ~ 10** 10 岁大的女孩 **6** (indicating extent) [表示程度]; **an increase ~ 6%** 6% 的增长; **at a speed ~ 5 mph** 以每小时 5 英里的速度 **7** (from among) …中的; **~ the ten, only one came** 10 个人只来了 1 个; **you ~ all people ought to know** 最应该知道的就是你 **8** (made up of) 由…组成的; (made from) 由…制成的; **areas ~ marshland** 沼泽区; **a door ~ mahogany** 桃花心木门; **what is it made ~?** 它是用什么材料做的? **9** (containing) 装有…的; **a glass ~ beer** 一杯啤酒 **10** (in charge of) 掌管…的; **the Lord Mayor ~ London** 伦敦市长阁下 **11** (in, at) 在…的; **the streets ~ Glasgow** 格拉斯哥的街道 **12** (referring to position) 相对于; (referring to quality, time) 在…方面; **for fear ~ sth.** 因为害怕某事; **to be fond ~ sb./sth.** 喜欢某人/某物; **south ~ Birmingham** 伯明翰以南; **slow ~ speech** 口齿不伶俐; **20 years ~ age** 20 岁 **13** (directed toward) 对于…的; **love ~ family** 对家庭的爱; **teachers ~ history** 历史老师 **14** (done by) 由…做的; **the decision ~ the court** 法庭的决定; **to happen ~ itself** 自行发生 **15** (on one's part) 在…一方; **how kind ~ you** 你真好; **it was horrid ~ him to do that** 他做那事真是太可怕了 **16** (indicating removal) [表示去除]; **loss ~ appetite** 没胃口; **to cure sb. ~ Aids** 治愈某人的艾滋病; **to be robbed ~ sth.** 被抢去某物 **17** (in comparisons) 如…般的; **sunsets the colour ~ blood** 血色黄昏 **18** (in dates) [表示日期]; **the 24th ~ June** 6 月 24 日 **19** (on, during) [表示在某个时间]; **your letter ~ the 17th** 你 17 日的来信; **it was often fine ~ a morning** Brit 早晨天气往往挺好 **20** Amer (before) 在…之前; **a quarter ~ six** 六点差一刻

Ofcom /ˈɒfkɒm, Amer ˈɔːf-/ *abbr* Brit = **Office of Communications** 通信管理局

off /ɒf, Amer ɔːf/

A *adv* **1** (leaving) 离开; **to run ~** 跑开; **to roll ~** 滚落; **it's time we were ~** 我们该走了; **I'm ~ to Scotland** 我要去苏格兰了; **he's ~ fishing** 他去钓鱼了; **to get ~ of sth./sb.** 离开某物/某人; **to let sb. ~ at the next stop** 让某人在下一站下车; **~ with you!** 走开!; **and they're ~!** Sport 他们开跑了!; **to get/be ~ to a good start** colloq 头开得不错; **right/straight ~** colloq 马上 **2** (detached, removed) 脱离; **the handle has come/is ~** 手柄脱落了; **with one's jacket/make-up ~** 脱了夹克衫/已卸妆; **to have one's leg ~** 被截掉腿; **to blow the roof ~** ‹*wind*› 掀掉屋顶 **3** (aside) 在旁边; **somewhere ~ to the left** 在左边某处 **4** (adjacent) 邻接着; **bedrooms with bathroom ~** 紧挨着卫生间的卧室 **5** (at a distance, ahead in time) 距; **to be a yard ~** 在一码开外; **some way/not far ~** 一段距离外/不远处; **Easter is a month ~/isn't far ~** 离复活节还有1个月/复活节快到了 **6** (from work) 休息; **to have** *or* **take a week ~** 休假一周; **to ask for time ~** 请假; **to be ~ sick** 因病不上班 **7** (as separation) 分隔; **marked ~ into sections** 被划分为几部分; **fenced/curtained ~** 被栅栏/帘子隔开 **8** (turned off) 关掉; **to be ~** ‹*light*› 关了; **the gas/electricity is ~** 煤气断了/停电了 **9** (cancelled) 取消; **to be ~** 被取消; **their engagement is ~** 他们的婚约取消了; **the meeting is ~** 会议延期了 **10** (deducted) 减掉; **I'll give you 10% ~** 我给你打 9 折 **11** (positioned) 处于…境况; **to be badly/well ~** 贫穷/富裕; **to be better ~ than sb.** 经济比某人宽裕; **how are you ~ for money/time?** 你还有多少钱/时间? **12** (not fresh) 不新鲜; **to be ~** 变质; **the meat's gone ~** 肉坏了 **13** (asleep) 睡着; **I just got the baby ~** 我刚把宝宝哄睡 **14** (by heart) 流利地; **he got it ~ pat** 他都背熟了 **15** Brit colloq (unwell) 不对头; **to feel a bit ~** 感觉不太舒服; **a bit ~** (unwise) 不妥当; (unfair) 不公平; **her behaviour was a bit ~** 她的行为有点怪 **16** Brit colloq (unavailable) 不供应; **the roast beef is ~** 烤牛肉没有了 **17** Theat 在幕后; **voices/noises ~** 幕后声音/噪声

B *prep* **1** (leaving, detaching from) 从…离开; **to fall/jump ~ a wall** 从墙上摔下来/跳下来; **to get ~ a train** 下火车; **to get the car ~ the road** 把车开下公路; **to tear the door ~ its hinges** 把门从铰链上拽下来; **the light reflected ~ the glass** 玻璃的反光; **it's a huge burden ~ my shoulders** fig 我如释重负 **2** (from place, date, event) 离; **3 km ~ the motorway** 距离高速公路 3 公里; **islands ~ the coast** 海岸附近的岛屿; **the lid was ~ the jar** 罐子的盖子被打开了; **to be a long way/not far ~ doing sth.** 离做某事还很远/很近; **only a year ~ retirement** 只有一年就退休了 **3** (deviating from) 偏离; **to be ~ balance** 失去平衡; **to be blown ~ course** ‹*ship*› 被吹离航线; **to take his mind ~ his troubles** 使他忘却烦恼 **4** (accessed from) 在…旁边; **the kitchen is ~ the dining room** 厨房与餐厅相连 **5** colloq (from) 来自; **to get sth. ~ (of) a friend** 从朋友那里得到某物; **to borrow sth. ~ (of) a neighbour** 向邻居借某物; **to eat ~ (of) a plate** 用盘子吃东西; **to work ~ a battery** 靠电池驱动; **a wind blowing ~ the sea** 从海上吹来的风 **6** (disengaged from) 不参与; **to take a week ~ work** 休息一周; **to stay ~ alcohol** colloq 戒酒; **to be ~ drugs** 戒毒 **7** colloq (no longer keen on) 不热衷; **to be ~ sth./sb.** 对某事物/某人不再感兴趣; **to be ~ one's food** 没有胃口 **8** (deducted from) 从…减去; **I'll take a pound ~ the price for you** 我给你便宜1英镑 **9** (deleted from) 从…删去; **to be ~ the menu** 被撤出了菜单; **take my name ~ the list** 把我从名单里删掉

C *adj attrib* **1** (not functioning) 关着的; **the ~ position** 关闭位置 **2** (substandard) 不如意的 ‹*day, period*›; **we both had an ~ day** 那天我俩都挺倒霉的 **3** Brit Aut 右侧的; **the ~ front wheel** 右前轮 **4** (in cricket) 斜前方的 ‹*spin*›; 击球手面向的 ‹*side*›; 向击球手对面的 ‹*drive*›

D *excl* **~ with ...** 把…除掉; **~ with his head!** 把他的头砍了!; **(get) ~!** 走开!

E **off and on** *adv phr* ▸ **on E**

F *n* Brit colloq **1** (start of race) **the ~** 起跑 **2** (outset) **the ~** 开始; **from the ~** 从一开始

G *vi* colloq 离开; **to up and ~** 突然离去

H *vt* Amer colloq 杀死 ‹*person*›

offal /ˈɒfl, Amer ˈɔːfl/ *n* [u] **1** Culin 动物内脏 **2** (waste) 垃圾

offbeat

A *adj* /ˌɒfˈbiːt, Amer ˌɔːf-/ **1** Mus 不合拍的 ‹*rhythm, music*› **2** (unconventional) 另类的 ‹*humour*›; 标新立异的 ‹*person, style, play*›; 不落俗套的 ‹*account*›

B *n* /ˈɒfbiːt, Amer ˈɔːf-/ 弱拍

off: ~-centre *adj, adv* 不居中的 (地); **~chance** *n* **on the ~ chance** 碰运气; **I did it on the ~ chance that ...** 我做这个想看看…; **~ colour** *adj* Brit colloq **1** (unwell) 轻微不适的; **2** (indecent) 粗俗的 ‹*story, remark*›; **~cut** *n* (of fabric, wood, paper) 边角料; (of meat, fish) 残渣; **~-duty** *adj attrib* 休班的

offence /əˈfens/ *n* Brit **1** [c] (illegal act) 犯罪; **to commit an ~** 犯罪; **a first ~** 初犯; **further ~s** 再犯 **2** [c] (violation) 罪过 **3** [u] (annoyance) 冒犯; **to cause** *or* **give ~ to sb.** 冒犯某人; **an ~ against sb./sth.** 对某人/某事物的冒犯; **an ~ to the eye** 不顺眼; **to take ~ (at sth.)** (对某事) 介意 **4** [u] (attack) 进攻; **~ is the best form of defence** 进攻是最好的防守

offend /əˈfend/
A *vt* 1 (hurt) 冒犯; **the article/remark deeply ~ed her** 那篇文章/那句话深深地伤害了她; **to be ~ed (at sth.)** （对某事）恼火 2 (displease) 令人不适; **to ~ the eye/ear** 刺眼/刺耳
B *vi* Jur 犯罪
Phrasal verb
• **offend against** *vt* [~ **against sth.**] 违反〈*law, rule*〉; 有失〈*manners, good taste*〉; 有悖于〈*convention, common sense*〉

offender /əˈfendə(r)/ *n* 1 (law-breaker) 罪犯; **first ~** 初犯; **a habitual** *or* **persistent ~** 惯犯 2 (culprit) 祸害; **the worst ~s** 罪魁祸首

offending /əˈfendɪŋ/ *adj attrib* 1 (responsible) 惹麻烦的〈*object, item, article*〉 2 (offensive) 冒犯的〈*word*〉

offense /əˈfens/ *n* Amer 1 = **offence** 2 Sport **the ~** 前锋

offensive /əˈfensɪv/
A *adj* 1 (insulting) 无礼的〈*remark, behaviour*〉; **to be ~ to sb.** 冒犯某人 2 (vulgar) 粗俗的〈*language*〉; 淫秽的〈*scene*〉 3 (revolting) 极其讨厌的〈*smell*〉 4 *attrib* Mil, Sport 进攻的〈*tactics, capability, player*〉
B *n* 1 esp Mil, Sport 进攻; **to launch** *or* **mount an ~** 发动进攻; **to be** *or* **go on the ~** 主动出击; **to go over to** *or* **take the ~** 先发制人 2 Pol, Advertg 攻势; **a sales/advertising ~** 销售/广告攻势

offensively /əˈfensɪvli/ *adv* 1 (insultingly) 无礼地〈*behave, swear*〉; **~ bad** 糟糕透了 2 Sport 采取攻势地

offensive weapon *n* 攻击性武器

offer /ˈɒfə(r), Amer ˈɔːf-/
A *vt* 1 (propose) 提出〈*suggestion, opinion, resignation*〉; **to ~ (sb.) advice** （给某人）提出劝告; **to have something/nothing to ~** 有/无话要说; **I have nothing to ~** 我无可奉告; **to ~ to do sth.** 主动提出做某事; **to ~ to cook dinner** 主动提出做正餐; **'I'll do it,' she ~ed** "这个我来做吧，"她提议道 2 (proffer) 主动提供〈*job, place, help*〉; 给予〈*friendship, affection*〉; **to ~ sb. a drink** 请某人喝一杯; **to ~ sb. a big salary** 给某人高薪; **to ~ a reward (for sth.)** （为某事物）提供奖赏; **to ~ one's seat to sb.** 给某人让座; **to ~ a big reduction** 开展大降价; **to be ~ed a post at Oxford** 得到在牛津大学的一个职位 3 (provide) 提供〈*idea, job*〉提供〈*advantage, prospects*〉; **to ~ protection from the rain** «*place*» 挡雨; **to ~ shade** «*tree*» 遮荫; **this vest ~s protection against bullets** 这件背心有防弹功能; **to ~ easy access to the beach** «*house, location*» 去海滩很方便; **a hotel ~ing excellent facilities** 设施一流的酒店; **a town with a lot to ~ (to) visitors** 让游客流连忘返的城镇 4 formal (possess) 具备〈*qualification, experience*〉; **to ~ at least one foreign language** «*candidate*» 至少懂一门外语 5 (present) 作出〈*resistance, defence*〉 6 (sell) 出售〈*merchandise*〉; **to ~ sth. for sale** 出售某物 7 Fin 开出; **to ~ £50 for sth.** 出价 50 英镑买某物 8 Relig = **offer up**
B *vi* 自愿提出
C *v refl* 1 (volunteer) **to ~ oneself** 自告奋勇 2 (present) **to ~ itself** 出现; **if the opportunity/occasion ~s itself ...** 如果机会来了/时机到了…
D *n* 1 [c] (proposal) 提议; **a peace ~** 和平倡议; **to make (sb.) an ~** （向某人）提出建议; **to agree to/accept an ~** 同意/接受提议; **to decline** *or* **refuse** *or* **reject an ~** 拒绝提议 2 [c] (act of proffering) 提供; **to accept/reject an ~ of sth.** 接受/拒绝某物的主动提供; **an ~ of marriage** 求婚; **an ~ of a job, a job ~** 工作机会的提供; **~s of help/mediation** 主动提出的帮助/调解; **an ~ to do sth.** 主动提出做某事 3 [c] Fin 出价; **a firm ~** 实盘; **a reasonable/tempting ~** 合理的/诱人的报价; **to make (sb.) an ~** （给某人）出价; **to agree to** *or* **accept an ~** 同意/接受出价; **to decline** *or* **refuse** *or* **reject an ~** 不接受出价; **to be open to ~s** 开价可以商量; **under ~** 已有买主出价 4 [u and c] (promotion) 优惠价; **special ~** 特价; **on (special) ~** 特价出售; **there's a special ~ on sth., sth. is on special ~** 某物在特价销售; **this month's special ~ is ...** 本月的特价商品是…; **a free ~** 免费赠品 5 [u] **on ~** (available) 供出售; **what do you have on ~?** 你有什么可卖的？
Phrasal verb
• **offer up** *vt* [~ **sth. up,** ~ **up sth.**] 1 esp Relig (present) 奉献〈*sacrifice, gift*〉; **to ~ up one's life for a cause** 为事业献身 2 Relig (utter) 虔诚地表达〈*thanks*〉; **prayers were ~ed up for his safety** 为他的平安做了祈祷

offeree /ˌɒfəˈriː, Amer ˌɔːf-/ *n* 受要约人

offerer /ˈɒfərə(r), Amer ˈɔːf-/ *n* = **offeror**

offering /ˈɒfərɪŋ, Amer ˈɔːf-/ *n* 1 [u] (act of giving) 给予; **the ~ of bribes** 行贿 2 [c] (thing offered) 提供的东西; (thing for entertainment or sale) 作品; **I heard her latest ~ on CD the other day** 我前些天听了她最新推出的 CD 歌曲 3 [c] Relig 捐款 4 [c] (sacrifice) 祭品

offeror /ˈɒfərə(r), Amer ˈɔːf-/ *n* 要约人

offer price *n* 要约价

offhand /ˌɒfˈhænd, Amer ˌɔːf-/
A *adj* (*also* **offhanded** /ˌɒfˈhændɪd, Amer ˌɔːf-/) 1 (casual) 漫不经心的〈*comment, tone*〉; **in an ~ manner** 随随便便地 2 (impolite) 冷淡的〈*remark*〉
B *adv* 不假思索地〈*say, tell*〉

offhandedly /ˌɒfˈhændɪdli, Amer ˌɔːf-/ *adv* 1 (casually) 漫不经心地 2 (impolitely) 冷淡地

office /ˈɒfɪs, Amer ˈɔːf-/
A *n* 1 [c] (for clerical work) (room) 办公室; (building) 办公楼; **to go to the ~** 上班 2 [c] (place of business) 营业处; **a lawyer's ~** 律师事务所; **a doctor's/dentist's ~** Amer 诊所/牙医诊所 3 [c] (branch of company) 办事处; **a company with an ~ in London** 在伦敦有办事处的公司 4 [c] (staff) 办公室职员; **our sales ~ will deal with it** 我们销售部的人员会处理此事; **a letter from our London ~** 来自伦敦同事的信 5 [c] Admin, Pol 政府部门; **a local tax ~** 地税局 6 [c] (for service, queries) 服务处; **a booking** *or* **ticket ~** 售票处; **an enquiry ~** 问询处; **the local tourist ~** 当地旅游办事处 7 [u and c] (position) [尤指政府或机构的] 职位; **the ~ of mayor** 市长职位; **to perform the ~ of ...** 行使…的职责; **a term** *or* **period of ~** 任期; **to seek ~** 谋求官职; **to take ~** 就职; **to be in** *or* **hold ~** 在职; **to leave ~** 离职; **to be out of ~** «*party, politician*» 在野; **to stand** Brit *or* **run** Amer **for ~** 竞选职位; **to rise to high ~** 升任高官 8 **Office** [c] Relig 仪式; **the (divine) O~** 日课; **the noon O~** 午间祷告; **the O~ for the dead** 超度亡灵的法事; **to say the O~** 念祷文
B **offices** *npl* formal (services) 相助; **through his/your good ~s** 在他/你的帮助下; **to count on sb.'s good ~s** 指望某人的协助
C *modif* 办公室的〈*work, staff*〉; 办公室职员的〈*outing*〉; **~ equipment/furniture** 办公设备/家具; **to have an ~ job/be an ~ worker** 有一份办公室工作/是上班族; **training in ~ skills** 办公技能培训

office: **~ automation** *n* [u] 办公自动化; **~ block** *n* Brit 办公大楼; **~ boy** ▸ **p. 409** *n* dated 办公室勤杂工; **~ building** *n* 办公大楼; **~holder** *n* 公务员; **~ hours** *npl* 办公时间; **~ junior** ▸ **p. 409** *n* 办公室低级工作人员; **~ manager** ▸ **p. 409** *n* 办公室主任; **~ party** *n* 办公室聚会; **~ politics** *npl* 办公室政治

officer /ˈɒfɪsə(r), Amer ˈɔːf-/ *n* 1 Aviat, Mil, Naut 军官; **~s and ratings** Brit 海军官兵 2 (official) 官员; **~s of state** 政府各部部长 3 (police) 警察; **an ~ of the law** formal 警察; **O~ Smith** 史密斯警官

officer: **O~ Commanding** *n* Brit 指挥官; **~ of the day** *n* 值日军官; **~ of the watch** *n* 舰上值班军官; **~s' mess** *n* 军官餐厅; **O~s' Training Corps** *n* Brit 军官培训团

office: **~ space** *n* [u] 办公场所; **~ technology** *n* 办公设施; **e-mail, word processors, and other modern ~ technologies** 电子邮件、文字处理器以及其他现代化办公设施; **~ worker** ▸ **p. 409** *n* 公司职员

official /əˈfɪʃl/
A *adj* 1 (relating to public office) 官员的〈*duties*〉; **an ~ residence** 官邸; **~ engagements** 公务; **(the) ~ channels** 官方渠道; **in an ~ capacity** 以官方身份 2 (authorized) 官方认可的〈*version, candidate*〉; 得到批准的〈*strike, company policy*〉; 正规的〈*record*〉; **the ~ language** 官方语言; **an ~ biography** 正传; **it's ~!** 已经官方证实！; **not yet ~** 尚未经官方证实 3 *attrib* (formal) 正式的〈*inquiry, opening, reception, visit*〉
B *n* 官员

Official Birthday *n* Brit 官方寿辰 [指英王生日，定在六月份]

officialdom /əˈfɪʃldəm/ *n* [u] 1 pej (officials) 当官的人 2 (bureaucracy) 官僚

officialese /əˌfɪʃəˈliːz/ *n* [u] pej 官样文章

officially /əˈfɪʃəli/ *adv* 1 (formally) 官方地〈*announce, recognize*〉; 正式地〈*invite, engaged, open*〉 2 (theoretically) 理论上; **~ I'm Church of England, but I'm an atheist really** 理论上我信奉英国国教，但事实上我是无神论者

Official: **~ Receiver** *n* Brit 官方接管人; **in the hands of the ~ Receiver** 已破产; **~ Secrets Act** *n* Brit 国家机密法案; **under the ~ Secrets Act** 根据国家机密法案

officiate /əˈfɪʃieɪt/ *vi* «*official*» 履行职务; «*umpire, referee*» 担任裁判; «*priest*» 主持; **to ~ at an event** 主持活动

officious /əˈfɪʃəs/ *adj* pej 指手画脚的〈*person, official*〉; 装腔作势的〈*gesture, manner*〉

officiously /əˈfɪʃəsli/ *adv* 装腔作势地〈*speak, treat, command*〉

officiousness /əˈfɪʃəsnɪs/ *n* [u] pej 装腔作势

offing /ˈɒfɪŋ, Amer ˈɔːf-/ *n* [u] **in the ~** (imminent) 迫在眉睫; (forthcoming) 即将来临

offish /ˈɒfɪʃ, Amer ˈɔːf-/ *adj* colloq 冷漠的; **to be ~ with sb.** 对某人冷淡

off-key
A *adj* 1 Mus 走调的 2 fig (not in keeping) 不和谐的
B *adv* 走调地

off: **~-licence** *n* Brit 外卖酒店; **~-limits** *adj* 1 (out of bounds) 禁止入内的〈*place*〉; 2 (not to be discussed) 禁止谈论的〈*subject*〉

off-line
A *adj* 1 (not connected to the Internet) 离线的〈*access, service*〉; 未联网的〈*mode, storage*〉 2 (not relating to the Internet) 现实世界的〈*media, world, activity*〉
B *adv* 离线地〈*write, work, read*〉

offload /ˌɒfˈləʊd, Amer ˌɔːf-/ *vt* 1 (unload) 卸〈*cargo, goods, passengers*〉 2 (get rid of) 转卖〈*goods, stock*〉; 转让〈*player*〉 3 (unburden oneself of) 排解〈*problem, worry*〉; **to ~ the blame on to sb.** 把过错转嫁到某人身上 4 Comput 卸载〈*data, task*〉

off-message
A *adj* 偏离政党路线的〈*person, statement*〉
B *adv* 偏离政党路线地

off-peak /ˌɒfˈpiːk, Amer ˌɔːf-/
A *adj* 非高峰期的〈*electricity, rate*〉; 淡季的〈*ticket, travel*〉
B *adv* 在淡季〈*travel*〉; 在非高峰期〈*use electricity*〉

off-piste
A *adj* 在滑雪道外的
B *adv* 在滑雪道外

off: **~print** *n* (出版物的) 单行本; **~-putting** *adj* 令人讨厌的 ‹*manner, smell, appearance*›

off-road
A *adv* 越野 ‹*drive, go*›
B *adj* 越野的 ‹*vehicle, driving*›

off: **~-roader** /ˌɒfˈrəʊdə(r)/ *n* **1** (vehicle) 越野赛车; **2** (person) 越野赛车手; **~-roading** *n* [u] 越野赛车; **~-road vehicle** *n* 越野车; **~-sale** *n* 酒类外卖

off-screen
A *adj* **1** (unseen by audience) 画外的 ‹*action, voice*›; 非屏幕上的 ‹*relationship*› **2** (in real life) 现实生活中的 ‹*persona*›
B *adv* **1** (unseen by audience) 在画外 **2** (in real life) 在现实生活中

off season *n* 淡季; **~ training/tariff** 淡季培训/关税

offset /ˈɒfset, Amer ˈɔːf-/
A *vt* (*pres p* **-tt-**; *pt, pp* **offset**) **1** 抵消 ‹*loss, change, donation*›; **to ~ sth. against sth.** 用一事抵消另一事 **2** Print 胶印 ‹*text, picture, article*›
B *n* **1** (counterbalancing factor) 抵消; **as an ~ to sth.** 作为对某事的补偿 **2** (in pipe) 弯管

offset: **~ press** *n* 胶印机; **~ printing** *n* [u] 胶印

offshoot /ˈɒfʃuːt, Amer ˈɔːf-/ *n* **1** (of plant) 分枝 **2** fig (of family) 旁系; (of organization) 分支

offshore /ˌɒfˈʃɔː(r), Amer ˌɔːf-/
A *adj* **1** (away from the coast) 近海的 ‹*island, anchorage*›; 向海的 ‹*wind*› **2** (in oil industry) 海上的 ‹*drilling, oilfield, platform*› **3** Fin 境外的 ‹*banking*›; **an ~ fund/tax haven** 境外基金/避税港
B *adv* **1** (away from the coast) 离岸地 **2** (in oil industry) 在海上 ‹*drill, prospect*› **3** Fin 在境外; **to invest/bank ~** 在海外投资/存钱

offside /ˌɒfˈsaɪd, Amer ˌɔːf-/
A *n* [u] **1** (of vehicle) 外侧 [在英国为右侧]; **on the ~** 在外侧 **2** Sport 越位
B *adj* **1** (of vehicle) 外侧的 ‹*door, wheel, passenger*› **2** Sport 越位的 ‹*position*›; **the ~ rule** 越位规则
C *adv* 越位地 ‹*move, stray*›

off-site
A *adj attrib* 工作场地外的 ‹*meeting, training, storage*›
B *adv* 在工作场地以外 ‹*work, store, manufacture*›

offspring /ˈɒfsprɪŋ, Amer ˈɔːf-/ *n* (*pl* **offspring**) (of animal) 幼仔; (of human) 子女

offstage /ˌɒfˈsteɪdʒ, Amer ˌɔːf-/
A *adv* 在舞台下 ‹*wait, speak, sing*›
B *adj* 幕后的 ‹*voice*›; 现实生活的 ‹*manner*›

off-street parking *n* [u] 私人停车场

off-the-cuff
A *adj* 即兴的 ‹*remark, speech*›
B **off the cuff** *adv* 即兴

off-the-peg
A *adj* Brit 现成的; **~ clothes** 成衣
B **off the peg** *adv* 现成地; **I bought it off the peg** 我买了件成品

off-the-shelf
A *adj* 现成的 ‹*part, product*›
B **off the shelf** *adv* 在商店

off: **~-the-shoulder** *adj* 露肩的 ‹*dress, shirt*›; **~-the-wall** *adj* colloq (eccentric) 古怪的; (unconventional) 新奇的

off-white
A *adj* 米色的
B *n* 米色

off year *n* Amer 非大选年

Ofgas /ˈɒfgæs/ *abbr* Brit = **Office of Gas Supply** 天然气供应局

Ofsted /ˈɒfsted/ *abbr* Brit = **Office for Standards in Education** 教育标准办公室

oft /ɒft, Amer ɔːft/ *adv* liter or archaic 经常

Oftel /ˈɒftel/ *abbr* Brit = **Office of Telecommunications** 电信局

often /ˈɒfn, ˈɒftən, Amer ˈɔːfn/ *adv* **1** (frequently) 经常; **very/so ~** 常常; **to do sth. less ~** 做某事不如以前经常; **more and more ~** 越来越频繁; **as ~ as possible** 尽可能经常地; **how ~ do the boats leave?** 船多长时间发出一班？; **who's done it most ~?** 这事谁做得次数最多？; **it's not ~ (that) you find such a big one** 碰上这么大一个可不是常有的事; **it cannot be said too ~ that ...** …说得再多也不过分; **an ~-repeated remark** 老生常谈 **2** (in many cases) 往往; **they ~ have horns** 它们大多都有角; **more ~ than not, as ~ as not** 通常; **every so ~** 偶尔

oft: **~-heard** *adj attrib* 常听到的 ‹*music, tale*›; **~-quoted** *adj attrib* 常被引用的 ‹*poem, words*›; **~-repeated** *adj attrib* 常重复的; **an ~-repeated truth** 一再重复的真理

Ofwat /ˈɒfwɒt/ *abbr* Brit = **Office of Water Services** 水务办公室

ogle /ˈəʊgl/ *vt* 色迷迷地盯着

ogre /ˈəʊgə(r)/ *n* **1** (giant) [传说中的] 食人巨妖 **2** fig (fearsome person) 可怕的人

OH *abbr* Amer = **Ohio**

oh /əʊ/ *excl* 啊; **~ dear!** (sympathetic) 哎，可怜的人！; (dismayed, cross) 啊，天哪！; **~ damn!** colloq 哎哟，该死！; **~ (really)?** (interested) 啊（真的吗）？; (sceptical) 哦（真的吗）？; **~ really!** 嗨，真是的！; **~ no!** 噢，不！; **~ yes?** (pleased) 啊，是吗？; (sceptical) 噢，是吗？; **~ to be in Paris!** 在巴黎真妙啊！

Ohio /əʊˈhaɪəʊ/ *n* 俄亥俄州

ohm /əʊm/ *n* 欧姆

OHMS *abbr* Brit = **On Her/His Majesty's Service** [英国公函免付邮费的戳记] 为女王/国王陛下效劳

OHP *abbr* = **overhead projector**

oik /ɔɪk/ *n* Brit colloq pej (uncouth) 大老粗; (ignorant) 蠢货

oil /ɔɪl/
A *n* **1** [u] (petroleum) 石油; **crude ~** 原油; **to drill for ~** 钻探石油; **to strike ~** lit 发现油矿; fig (get rich) 发横财; (succeed in business) 生意兴隆; **the ~ industry** 石油业; **an ~ magnate** 石油巨头 **2** [u and c] (for lubrication) 润滑油; (for engine) 机油; (for heat, light) 燃油; **paraffin ~** esp Brit 石蜡油; **~ and water don't mix** colloq 水火不相容 **3** [u and c] Culin, Pharm (from plants) 植物油; (from animals) 动物油; **olive/peanut ~** 橄榄/花生油; **cooking/salad ~** 烹调用油/色拉油; **fried in ~** 油炸的; **to cook with ~** 用油做菜; **an ~ and vinegar dressing** 油醋调味品; **~ of cloves/lemon** 丁香/柠檬油; **sperm** *or* **whale ~** 鲸油 **4** [u and c] Cosmet 防护油; **hair/suntan ~** 发油/防晒油; **essential ~s** 精油; **bath ~** 沐浴油 **5** [u and c] Art (medium) 油画颜料; **to paint in ~s** 作油画; **a landscape in ~(s)** 风景油画 **6** [c] Art (painting) 油画; **an ~ by Rembrandt** 一幅伦勃朗的油画作品 **7** [c] Chem 油类
B *vt* 给…上油 ‹*machine, hinge, bike, wood*›; 在…里放油 ‹*frying pan*›; 在…上抹油 ‹*skin, hair*›; **to need ~ing** «*mechanism, surface*» 需要上油; **to ~ the wheels** *or* **works** fig 进行疏通

oil: **~-based** *adj* 油基的 ‹*product*›; 基于石油的 ‹*economy*›; **an ~-based paint** 油性漆; **~-based fuel** 油基燃料; **~-bearing** *adj* 含油的 ‹*rock, shale*›; **~-burning** *adj* 燃油的 ‹*stove, heater*›; **~ cake** *n* [u] 油渣饼; **~can** *n* (applicator) 油壶; (container) 油罐; **~ change** *n* 换机油; **~cloth** *n* [u and c] **1** (fabric) 油布; **2** dated (linoleum) 油地毡; **~ colour** Amer *n* = **~ paint**; **~-cooled** *adj* 油冷却的 ‹*engine, apparatus, plant*›; **~ drum** *n* 金属油桶

oiled /ɔɪld/ *adj* **1** (lubricated) 上油的; **well-~** 润滑良好的 ‹*lock, mechanism*› **2** (covered in oil) 涂油的 ‹*surface, wood, pan*›; **a lightly ~ baking tray** 涂了少量油的焙烤盘; **an ~ seabird** 沾满油污的海鸟 **3** colloq (drunk) 喝醉酒的

oiler /ˈɔɪlə(r)/ *n* **1** (ship) 油轮 **2** (can) 油壶 **3** Amer (on oil rig) 石油工人; (on ship) 上油工

oil: **~field** *n* 油田; **~ filter** *n* 机油滤清器; **~-fired** *adj* 燃油的 ‹*boiler, furnace, power station*›; **~ gauge** *n* 油压表; **~ heater** *n* 燃油加热器

oiliness /ˈɔɪlɪnɪs/ *n* [u] **1** (of food) 油腻 **2** (of cloth) 油污; (of skin) 油性 **3** (unctuousness) 油滑

oil: **~ lamp** *n* 油灯; **~ level** *n* 油位; **~man** /-mæn/ *n* (owner) 石油商; (worker) 石油工人; **~ paint** *n* [u and c] 油画颜料; **~ painting** *n* **1** [c] (picture) 油画; **to be no ~ painting** Brit colloq 其貌不扬; **2** [u] (activity) 作油画; **~ pan** *n* Amer 集油槽; **~ pipeline** *n* 输油管; **~ platform** *n* 钻井平台; **~-producing** *adj attrib* 产石油的 ‹*country, region*›; **~ refinery** *n* 石油冶炼厂; **~ rig** *n* 石油钻塔; **~seed rape** *n* [u] 油菜

oilskin /ˈɔɪlskɪn/
A *n* **1** [u] (fabric) 防水油布; **~ jacket/trousers/sou'wester** 防雨外衣/裤/帽 **2** [c] (garment) 雨衣
B **oilskins** *npl* 防水服装

oil: **~ slick** *n* 浮油; **~ spill** *n* (event) 漏油; (resulting slick) 浮油; **~stone** *n* 油石; **~ tank** *n* 油罐; **~ tanker** *n* 油轮; **~ technology** *n* [u] 炼油技术; **~ terminal** 油库; **~ well** *n* 油井

oily /ˈɔɪli/ *adj* **1** (covered in oil) 油腻的 ‹*food*›; 油污的 ‹*cloth*›; 油性的 ‹*skin*›; **an ~ complexion** 油光的面色 **2** (in consistency) 涂油的 ‹*margarine, salad dressing*›; 滑腻的 ‹*shampoo, lotion*› **3** (unctuous) 油滑的 ‹*manner*›

oily fish *n* [u and c] 富含油的鱼类

oink /ɔɪŋk/
A *n* [猪的] 哼哼声
B *vi* «*pig*» 哼哼

ointment /ˈɔɪntmənt/ *n* [u and c] 药膏

OIRO *abbr* Brit = **offers in the region of** 售价大约 [广告用语]

OK[1] /əʊˈkeɪ/ colloq
A *excl* **1** (in agreement) [表示同意或接受]; **let's go! — ~** 我们走吧！——好的; **~, ~, I give in** 好，好，我让步 **2** (seeking consensus) [表示征求同意]; **I'm going now, ~?** 我要走了，好吗？ **3** (seeking information) [用于了解情况]; **~, what's going on here?** 那么，这里出什么事了？ **4** (introducing topic) [用于引出话题]; **~, turn to page 26** 好，翻到第 26 页
B *adj* **1** (all right) 尚可的 ‹*job, party, food, behaviour*›; **the music was ~** 音乐还可以; **lunch was ~** 午饭还行; **he's ~ as a plumber** 他是个不错的水管工; **is my hair ~?** 我的发型可以吗？; **the fit's ~, but ...** 衣服还算合身，但是…; **he's an ~ guy** 他这个人不错 **2** *pred* (fine) 良好的; **everything's ~** 一切都好; **are you ~ for money?** 你的钱够吗？; **I'm ~ for time: let's have a coffee** 我有时间：我们喝杯咖啡吧 **3** *pred* (well) 身体好的; **are you ~?** 你没事吧？; **how are you? — ~** 你好吗？——很好; **to feel ~ after a rest** 休息过后感觉好起来了 **4** *pred* (permissible) 可行的; **it's ~/not ~ to do sth.** 可以/不可以做某事; **to be ~ by** *or* **with sb.** 对某人而言是可以的; **it's ~ by me if you want to go** 如果你想走，我没意见; **is it ~ if I go?** 我走可以吗？
C *adv* 不错地; **to manage perfectly ~** 做得非常出色; **to work ~** «*computer, appliance*» 工作正常
D *vt* (*pres p* **OK'ing**; *pt, pp* **OK'd**) 批准 ‹*request, document*›

E *n sing* **the/one's ～** 许可; **to get the/sb.'s ～ for sth.** 获得某事的许可/某人对某事的许可; **to give the** *or* **one's ～ (to sth./to do sth.)** 同意（某事/做某事）

OK² *abbr* Amer = **Oklahoma**

okapi /əʊ'kɑːpi/ *n* (*pl* **～** *or* **～s**) 霍加狓

okay /əʊ'keɪ/ *excl, adj, adv, vt, n* = **OK¹**

okey-doke, okey-dokey /ˌəʊkɪ'dəʊk, ˌəʊkɪ'dəʊki/ *excl, adj, adv* = **OK¹ A, B, C**

Oklahoma /ˌəʊklə'həʊmə/ *pr n* 俄克拉何马州

old /əʊld/ ▸**p. 15**

A *adj* **1** (elderly) 老的; **an ～ man** 老头; **～ Mr Jones** 老琼斯先生; **～ people** 老年人; **～er people** 上了年纪的人; **to get** *or* **grow ～** 变老; **～ and infirm** 年老体弱; **to be ～ before one's time** 未老先衰 **2** (of a certain age) …岁的 ‹*person, animal*›; …久的 ‹*institution, building, geological feature*›; **how ～ are you?** 你几岁了? ; **how ～ is this tree/building?** 这棵树/这幢楼有多少年了? ; **a centuries-～ tradition** 几世纪之久的传统; **I'm ～er than you (are)** 我比你年龄大; **～er sister/daughter** 姐姐/大女儿; **to be ～ for one's age** 比实际年龄显大; **that dress is too ～ for you** 那条连衣裙你穿上太显老了 **3** (not new) 旧的 ‹*object, building*›; (not fresh) 不新鲜的 ‹*vegetables*›; **an ～ rag** 一块破布; **this bread is a week ～** 面包放了一个星期了 **4** (dating far back) 古老的 ‹*building, institution, family, tradition*›; 老掉牙的 ‹*story, song*›; **an ～ custom** 由来已久的风俗; **an ～ enemy/friend/rival** 夙敌/老友/老对手; **an ～ firm** 老牌公司; **the ～ part of Edinburgh** 爱丁堡的老城区; **to be as ～ as the hills** 很古老 **5** *attrib* (former) 以前的 ‹*job, house, admirer*›; **(in) the ～ days** （在）往昔; **it was like ～ times** 就像过去的好时光; **an ～ school mate** 一位老校友; **to put sth. back in its ～ place** 把某物放回原处 **6** *attrib* colloq dated (as term of affection) [表示亲昵或熟悉]; **dear ～ Sally** 亲爱的老萨利; **hello, ～ chap!** dated 喂, 老伙计! ; **my ～ car** 我的老爷车 **7** colloq (as intensifier) [用作强调]; **any ～ time/place** 随时/随地; **any ～ shirt will do** 随便哪件衬衫都行; **I don't want just any ～ doctor** 我不想随便找个医生; **it's a funny ～ world** 这真是可笑的世道

B *n* **1** [c] (elderly people) **the ～** *pl* 老年人; **young and ～** 老老少少; **enjoyed by young and ～ alike** 老少皆宜的 **2** [u] (earlier era) **of ～** 以前; **in days of ～** 从前; **men of ～** 古人; **I know him of ～** 我认识他很久了

old age *n* [u] **1** (later part of one's life) 暮年; **in (one's) ～** 在晚年 **2** (condition of being old) 年老

old-age: ～ pension *n* Brit 养老金; **～ pensioner** *n* 领养老金者

old: Old Bailey *pr n* Brit **the Old Bailey** 老贝利 [指伦敦中央刑事法院]; **Old Bill** *n* Brit colloq **the Old Bill** 老警 [指警方]

> **the Old Bailey**
>
> 老贝利，英国伦敦中央刑事法院（Central Criminal Court）的俗称。名称源自伦敦金融城（City of London）的古城墙（bailey）而建的Old Bailey街。现址历史上曾为英国著名的纽盖特（Newgate）监狱。老贝利数世纪以来一直是伦敦重要的刑事法院，现负责审理大伦敦（Greater London）地区的重要刑事案件，也审理英格兰其他地区和威尔士转来的重大案件。法院大楼的穹顶有司法女神像（Lady Justice）。女神右手握剑，象征惩罚；左手持天平，象征公正。老贝利的法官称为法官大人（My Lord 或 My Lady）。

old boy *n* **1** Brit (ex-pupil) 男校友 **2** colloq (old man) 老头 **3** esp Brit colloq dated (as form of address) 老伙计

old boy network, old boy's network *n* Brit **the ～** 校友关系网

old country *n* **the ～** 故国

olden /'əʊldən/ *adj* archaic 旧时的; **in ～ times** *or* **the ～ days** 从前

Old English *n* [u] 古英语

Old English sheepdog *n* 英国牧羊犬

old-established /ˌəʊldɪ'stæblɪʃt/ *adj* 历史悠久的 ‹*company*›; **an ～ tradition** 古老的传统

olde-worlde /ˌəʊldi 'wɜːldi/ *adj* 古香古色的 ‹*tea shop*›; 古朴的 ‹*village, cottage*›

old-fashioned /ˌəʊld'fæʃnd/ *adj* 老式的 ‹*clothes, furniture*›; 守旧的 ‹*person, attitude*›; 过时的 ‹*idea, custom*›

old-fashioned look *n* 责备的目光; **to give sb. an ～** 责备地看某人一眼

old: ～ favourite *n* (song) 经典老歌; (film) 经典老电影; (book) 经典著作; (TV programme) 经典老节目; (play) 经典老剧; **～ flame** *n* 旧情人; **～ fogey, ～ fogy** *n* colloq 老古板; **～ folks' home** *n* colloq 养老院; **～ girl** *n* **1** Brit (ex-pupil) 女校友; **2** esp Brit colloq (old lady) 老太太; **3** esp Brit colloq dated (as form of address) 大姐; **Old Glory** *pr n* Amer colloq 星条光荣 [指美国国旗]

old gold

A *adj* 浅棕黄色的

B *n* [u] 浅棕黄色

old: ～ guard *n* (保守的) 元老派; **～ hand** *n* 经验丰富的人; **to be an ～ hand at sth.** 是某方面的老手; **～ hat** *adj* colloq **1** (old news) 老生常谈的; **2** (out-dated) 过时的

oldie /'əʊldi/ *n* colloq **1** (film) 经典老电影; (song) 经典老歌; (TV programme) 经典老节目 **2** (old person) 老人

oldish /'əʊldɪʃ/ *adj* 相当老的 ‹*person*›; 相当旧的 ‹*house, establishment, design*›

old: ～ lady *n* **1** (elderly woman) 老妈妈; **2** colloq (wife) 老婆; (girlfriend) 女友; **3** colloq (mother) 老妈; **～ lag** *n* Brit colloq (long-term inmate) 长期蹲监狱的人; (recidivist) 多次蹲监狱的人; **～-line** *adj* (conservative) 守旧的 ‹*politician*›; (well-established) 地位稳固的 ‹*business*›; **～ maid** *n* 老姑娘; **～ man** *n* **1** (elderly man) 老头; **2** colloq (husband) 老公; (boyfriend) 男友; **3** colloq (father) 老爸; **4** colloq (boss) **the ～ man** 老板; **5** Brit colloq dated (as form of address) 老伙计; **～ master** *n* **1** (artist) 早期绘画大师; **2** (painting) 早期的名画; **～ moon** *n* 下弦月; **～ people's home** *n* 养老院

old school *n* 守旧派; **a doctor of the ～** 老派医生

old school tie *n* **1** lit (尤指英国公学的) 母校领带 **2** fig 校友裙带关系

old: ～ soldier *n* **1** (former soldier) 老兵; **2** (old hand) 老手; **to come** *or* **play the ～ soldier with sb.** colloq 摆老资格忽悠某人; **Old South** *n* **the Old South** 旧南方 [美国内战以前的南部诸州]; **～ stager** /əʊld 'steɪdʒə(r)/ *n* 老手

oldster /'əʊldstə(r)/ *n* esp Amer colloq 老人

old: ～-style *adj* 老式的; **Old Testament** *n* **the Old Testament** 《圣经·旧约》; **an Old Testament prophet** 一位《旧约》先知

old-time *adj attrib* 昔日的

old-time dancing *n* [u] 旧式舞蹈

old: ～-timer *n* colloq **1** (in company, club, organization) 老成员; **2** Amer (old man) 老先生; **～ wives' tale** *n* 迷信; **～ woman** *n* **1** (elderly woman) 老妇人; **2** colloq (wife) 老婆; (girlfriend) 女友; **3** colloq (mother) 老妈; **4** colloq (fussy man) 婆婆妈妈的男人; (nervous man) 缩头缩尾的男人; **don't be such an ～ woman** 别这么大惊小怪; **Old World** *n* **the Old World** 旧世界 [指欧洲、亚洲和非洲]; **～-world** *adj* 古代的 ‹*species, flora*›; 老派的 ‹*charm, courtesy*›; **～ year** *n* [刚结束或将结束的] 旧年

ole /əʊl/ *adj attrib* esp Amer colloq 老的

oleaginous /ˌəʊlɪ'ædʒɪnəs/ *adj* **1** (oily) 含油的 ‹*seeds, nuts, plant*› **2** (obsequious) 巴结奉迎的

oleander /ˌəʊlɪ'ændə(r)/ *n* 夹竹桃

O level *n* Brit Hist = **ordinary level**

olfactory /ɒl'fæktəri/ *adj* 嗅觉的 ‹*organ, tract*›; **～ nerve/sense** 嗅神经/嗅觉

oligarch /'ɒlɪgɑːk/ *n* **1** (ruler) 寡头统治集团成员 **2** (magnate) **(business) ～** 商业大亨

oligarchic /ˌɒlɪ'gɑːkɪk/, **oligarchical** /ˌɒlɪ'gɑːkɪkl/ *adj* 寡头的 ‹*system, organization*›; **～ government** 寡头政府

oligarchy /'ɒlɪgɑːki/ *n* **1** [u] (form of government) 寡头政治 **2** [c] (state) 寡头统治的国家; (organization) 寡头掌管的组织 **3** [c] (ruling group) 寡头统治集团

Oligocene /'ɒlɪgəsiːn/

A *adj* (of the period) 渐新世的; (of the rock system) 渐新统的

B *n* **the ～** (period) 渐新世; (rock system) 渐新统

oligopoly /ˌɒlɪ'gɒpəli/ *n* 寡头垄断

olive /'ɒlɪv/

A *n* **1** [c] (fruit) 油橄榄 **2** [c] (tree) 橄榄树 **3** [u] (wood) 橄榄木 **4** [u] (colour) 橄榄绿

B *adj* 橄榄绿的 ‹*paint*›; 浅褐色的 ‹*complexion*›

olive branch *n* 橄榄枝 [和平的象征]; **to hold out** *or* **offer** *or* **extend an ～ (to sb.)** （向某人）伸出橄榄枝

olive drab

A *n* [u] 草绿色 [尤见于美军军服]

B **olive-drab** *adj* 草绿色的

olive green ▸**p. 134**

A *n* 橄榄绿

B **olive-green** *adj* 橄榄绿的

olive: ～ grove *n* 橄榄园; **～ oil** *n* [u] 橄榄油; **～ press** *n* **1** (device) 橄榄油压榨机; **2** (building) 橄榄油压榨房; **～-skinned** *adj* 黄棕色皮肤的 ‹*person*›

Olympiad /ə'lɪmpɪæd/ *pr n* **1** Sport 奥林匹克运动会 **2** (competition) 奥林匹克大赛; **the International Physics ～** 国际奥林匹克物理竞赛

Olympian /ə'lɪmpɪən/

A *adj* 超凡的 ‹*calm, silence*›

B *pr n* 奥林匹克运动员

Olympic /ə'lɪmpɪk/ ▸**p. 307**

A *adj* 奥林匹克运动会的 ‹*medal, athlete, stadium, event*›; **to hold the ～ 5,000m record** 保持奥运会 5,000 米记录

B *npl* **the ～s** 奥林匹克运动会; **the Beijing ～s** 北京奥运会

Olympic: ～ flame *n* 奥运圣火; **～ Games** ▸**p. 307** *npl* **the ～ Games** 奥林匹克运动会; **the London ～ Games** 伦敦奥运会; **～ torch** *n* 奥运火炬

Oman /əʊ'mɑːn/ *pr n* 阿曼

Omani /əʊ'mɑːni/ ▸**p. 503**

A *adj* (of Oman) 阿曼的; (of the people) 阿曼人的

B *n* (*pl* **～s**) 阿曼人

ombudsman /'ɒmbʊdzmən/ *n* (*pl* **ombudsmen**) **1** Admin 申诉专员 **2** Brit = **Parliamentary Commissioner for Administration**

ombudswoman /'ɒmbʊdzwʊmən/ *n* (*pl* **ombudswomen**) 女申诉专员

omega /'əʊmɪgə/ *n* 欧米加 [ω, 希腊语字母表的最后一个字母]; ▸**alpha A1**

omelette Brit, **omelet** Amer /'ɒmlɪt/ *n* (plain) 煎蛋; (with filling) 煎蛋卷; **you can't make an ～ without breaking eggs** Prov 有得必有失

omen /'əʊmən/ *n* 征兆; **to consider** *or* **take sth. as an ～** 将某事物视为预兆; **a black cat is usually taken as a lucky ～** 黑猫通常被视为吉祥之兆

ominous /'ɒmɪnəs/ *adj* 不祥的 ‹*event, noise, silence*›; 威胁的 ‹*look, gesture, tone*›

ominously /'ɒmɪnəsli/ *adv* 威胁地 ‹*gesture, say*›; 不祥地 ‹*change, darken*›; 危险地 ‹*quiet,*

O

low, close〉; **to look ～ like sb./sth.** colloq 看上去可怕地像某人/某物; **it looks ～ like rain** 天气阴沉沉地像要下雨

omission /əˈmɪʃn/ *n* **1** [c] (from list, team) 疏漏; **to correct** *or* **rectify an ～** 纠正疏漏处 **2** [u] (action) 排除 **3** [c] esp Jur (failure) 未履行

omit /əˈmɪt/ *vt* (*pres p etc.* **-tt-**) **1** (intentionally) 删除〈*name, reference, word*〉; (by mistake) 漏掉〈*name, reference, word*〉 **2** (fail) 疏忽; **to ～ to do sth.** 未能做某事

omnibus /ˈɒmnɪbəs/

A *n* (*pl* **～es**) **1** (TV programme) 综合节目 **2** (book) 选集 **3** dated (bus) 公共汽车; **the man on the Clapham ～** Brit 平常人

B *adj attrib* 综合的〈*programme*〉; 汇编的〈*edition*〉; 总括的〈*agreement*〉

omnibus spending bill *n* Amer 综合开支议案

omnidirectional /ˌɒmnɪdɪˈrekʃənl, -daɪ-/ *adj* 全向的〈*microphone, antenna*〉

omnipotence /ɒmˈnɪpətəns/ *n* [u] 全能

omnipotent /ɒmˈnɪpətənt/ *adj* 无所不能的〈*authority, minister*〉; 全能的〈*deity, regime*〉

omnipresence /ˌɒmnɪˈprezns/ *n* [u] formal 遍在

omnipresent /ˌɒmnɪˈpreznt/ *adj* formal 无处不在的〈*deity, authority, secret police*〉; 普遍存在的〈*danger, fear, sadness*〉

omniscience /ɒmˈnɪsɪəns/ *n* [u] 全知; **the ～ of God** 上帝的全知

omniscient /ɒmˈnɪsɪənt/ *adj* 无所不知的〈*deity*〉; 知识渊博的〈*narrator, expert*〉

omnivore /ˈɒmnɪvɔː(r)/ *n* (animal) 杂食动物; (person) 杂食的人

omnivorous /ɒmˈnɪvərəs/ *adj* **1** lit 杂食的〈*person, animal*〉 **2** fig 兴趣广泛的〈*reader, mind, curiosity*〉

on /ɒn/

A *prep* **1** (at location of, in contact with) 在…上; **to sit ～ the floor** 坐在地板上; **～ an island/the coast** 在岛上/海岸上; **a ball ～ a string** 拴在细绳上的球; **～ page 5** 在第5页; **to live ～ 6th Street** 住在第6大街; **accidents ～ and off the piste** 滑雪道内外的事故; **sth. ～ a black background** 黑色背景前的某物; **shrimp is ～ the menu** 菜单上有虾 **2** (towards location of, making contact with) 到…上; **he put a hand ～ my shoulder** 他把一只手搭在我肩上; **to punch sb. ～ the nose** 一拳击中某人的鼻子; **to choke ～ a fish bone** 被一根鱼刺卡住 **3** (in direction of) 向; **～ the right** 在右边; **to creep up ～ sb.** lit 蹑手蹑脚地靠近某人; fig 不知不觉地影响某人 **4** (indicating physical support) 由…支撑着; **to stand ～ one leg** 单腿站立; **to lie ～ one's back** 仰卧; **to put sth. ～ its side** 把某物侧翻过来 **5** (next to) 紧邻着; **a city (right) ～ the frontier** 边境城市; **houses ～ each side of the road** 公路两边的房屋 **6** (with one) 带在…身上; **I've no money ～ me** 我没带钱 **7** (wearing) 穿戴着; **the finger with the ring ～ it** 戴戒指的那个手指 **8** (engaged in) 从事于; **to be ～ duty/strike** 值班/罢工; **to be ～ a team/committee** 是团队/委员会的成员; **five staff work ～ the project** 这个项目有5名工作人员 **9** (on the subject of) 关于; **to lecture ～ sth.** 讲授某题目; **a book ～ grammar** 一本语法书; **Freud ～ dreams** 弗洛伊德有关梦的著作; **we're ～ irregular verbs** 我们在学习不规则动词 **10** (through medium of) 通过; **～ the radio/TV** 在广播中/在电视上; **to hear sth. ～ the news** 从新闻中听到某事; **～ disk** 存在磁盘上; **to play ... ～ the violin** 用小提琴演奏…; **with sb. ～ drums** 由某人担任鼓手 **11** (by means of) 以…的方式; **to be ～ foot/horseback** 步行/骑马; **to travel ～ the train/a return ticket** 乘火车/持来回票旅行; **to run ～ diesel** 用柴油驱动 **12** (earning) 挣得; **he's ～ £49,000 a year** 他的年薪有49,000英镑; **I'm not ～ much** 我挣得不多 **13** (paid for by) 由…支付; **have the meal ～ me** 这顿饭我请客 **14** (derived from) 源于; **profit ～ sales** 销售利润; **a tax ～ sth.** 对某物的税收 **15** (as regards) 在…方面; **to be economical ～ petrol** 很省油 **16** (going by) 根据; **～ past experience** 凭以往的经验; **～ one's (own) terms** 按照自己的条件 **17** (taking, using) 使用; **to be/put sb. ～ tranquillizers** 服用/让某人服用镇静剂; **to be ～ drugs** 吸毒; **to be ～ the computer/the phone** 在用电脑/打电话 **18** ▸**p. 181, p. 182** (in expressions of time) 在; **～ Wednesdays/Tuesday night** 在每周三/周二晚上; **～ and after the 20th** 从20号起; **to leave ～ the hour** 准点走 **19** (immediately after) 一…就; **～ hearing this, he ...** 一听说这个，他马上…; **～ the death of his wife, he ...** 妻子刚死，他就… **20** (during) 在…期间; **～ the tour, we visited ...** 在旅途中我们参观了… **21** (repeated events) …又…; **disaster ～ disaster** 接二连三的灾难; **defeat ～ defeat** 一次又一次失败 **22** (in agreement about) [表示达成协议]; **to shake hands/drink ～ it** 握手/举杯庆贺成交 **23** (added to) 附加于; **to pay/put a tax ～ sth.** 对某物征税; **to pay interest ～ a loan** 付贷款利息 **24** (compared to) 与…相比; **inflation is up ～ last month** 通货膨胀比上月加剧了 **25** (in relation to) 对于; **to have an effect ～ sth.** 对某事起作用; **it's unfair ～ her** 这对她不公平 **26** (in state of) 处于; **to be ～ the decrease/increase** 正在消减/增长 **27** (in betting) 为…下赌注〈*horse*〉; **I put a fiver ～ that dog** 我对那只狗下注5英镑 **28** Jur, Fin [表示法律或财务安排]; **a house ～ a long lease** 长期出租房 **29** (in scoring) 以…的得分; **to be top ～ 23 points** 以23分夺冠

B *adv* **1** (being worn) 穿戴着; **to have a coat/glasses ～** 穿着外套/戴着眼镜; **to have nothing ～** 一丝不挂; **to have make-up ～** 脸上化着妆 **2** (in or into place) 就位; **the top was not ～ properly** 盖子没盖好; **to put the wheel ～** 把车轮装上去 **3** (on surface) 在表面; **a T-shirt with Superman ～** 印着超人的T恤衫 **4** (on to bus or train) 登上; **the conductor/guard helped the old lady to get ～** 售票员/警卫帮助那老婆婆上了车; **the children ran up to the bus and jumped ～** 那些小孩跑到公交车那里，跳了上去; **are we all ～?** 大家是不是全都上了车? **5** (functioning, going) 处于工作状态; **to be ～**《*TV, gas*》开着; **the power is (back) ～** 电（又）通了; **to put the roast ～** Culin 开始做烤肉 **6** (taking place) 在进行中; **their wedding is back ～ again** 他们的婚礼又提上日程了 **7** (arranged) 有安排; **to have a lot/nothing ～** 很忙/闲着 **8** (working) 工作中; **to be ～** 在工作; **to be ～ every Saturday** 每周六值班; **to be ～ for most of the game** Sport 参加大半场比赛 **9** Cin, Radio, Theat, TV **to be ～**《*play*》上演;《*film*》上映;《*concert, exhibition*》举办;《*TV show*》播出; **there's nothing ～** Theat 没有演出; TV, Radio 没有节目; **he's not ～ until Act II** 他到第二幕才出场 **10** (being served) **to be ～** 有供应; **shrimps are ～ today** 今天有虾 **11** colloq (accepting challenge, invitation) 已接受; **to be ～** 接受挑战; **you're ～!** 赌就赌吧!; **are you still ～ for tomorrow's party?** 明天的聚会你还去吗? **12** colloq (at length) 详细地; **to be/go ～ about sth.** 喋喋不休地说某事; **to be/get ～ at sb.** Brit 对某人唠唠叨叨; **～ and ～** 连续不断地; **to talk ～ and ～** 说个不停 **13** Brit colloq (acceptable) 行; **not ～** 不行; **it's just** *or* **simply not ～** 没门儿 **14** (ahead in time) 以后; **a few years ～ from now** 今后的几年; **20 years ～** 20年后; **later ～** 后来; **to be well ～ in the season** 这个季度已过去大半 **15** (forward) 向前; **a little further ～** 再往前一点; **to go ～ to Blackpool** 接着前往布莱克浦; **to crash head ～** 迎面相撞 **16** (continuing) 继续着; **to last well ～ into the night** 一直持续到深夜; **to work ～ till ...** 一直工作到… **17** (in betting) 下注; **the odds were 3 to 1 ～** 投注赔率是3赔1

C *adj attrib* **1** (functioning) 开启的〈*switch*〉; **to be in the ～ position** 在"开启"位置 **2** (in cricket) 腿侧区的〈*side, drive*〉

D **on to** *prep* **1** (into position) 到…上; **to throw sth. ～ to the ground** 把它扔到地上 **2** Transp 登上; **to get ～ to the bus/train** 登上公共汽车/火车 **3** (into group, condition of) 进入; **to be elected ～ to a committee** 入选委员会; **to be ～ to a good thing** 过上舒心的日子 **4** (to apply) 适用于; **to put a tax ～ to sth.** 对某物征税 **5** colloq (aware of) 注意到; **to be ～ to sth./sb.** 注意某物/某人; **the police are ～ to him** 警方盯上了他; **to be ～ to it at last** 终于明白了 **6** colloq (after) 跟着; **to be ～ to sb. (about sth.)** （因某事）找某人; **to be always getting ～ to sb. to do sth.** 老催着某人做某事

E **on and off** *adv phr* 断断续续地; **to live here ～ and off** 断断续续在这里居住; **to be flashing ～ and off**《*light*》在闪烁

on-air

A *adj attrib* **1** (while broadcasting) 直播的; **～ technical problems** 直播技术问题 **2** (broadcasting) 广播的〈*station*〉

B *adv* 在广播期间; **Radio 1 is giving away tickets ～** 第一广播电台正在通过广播赠票

on-board *adj attrib* **1** Aviat 在飞机上的; Naut 在船上的; Aut 在车上的; **～ computer/entertainment** 机载计算器/车内娱乐 **2** Comput 主板的; **～ sound** 板上声卡

ONC *abbr* Brit = **Ordinary National Certificate**

once /wʌns/

A *adv* **1** (one time) 一次; **to hit sth. ～** 击打某物一下; **～ only** *or* **only ～** 只有一次; **just this ～** 仅此一次; **more than ～** 不止一次; **～ again** *or* **more** 再一次; **～ a week/year** 一周/一年一次; **～ in a lifetime** 一生一次; **～ or twice** 一两次; **not** *or* **never ～** 从不; **(every) ～ in a while** 偶尔; **～ too often** 侥幸难再; **～ and for all** 最终; **to try anything ～** 任何事都尝试一下; **if I've told you ～, I've told you 100 times** colloq 我已经跟你说过一百遍了; **～ in a blue moon** 千载难逢 **2** (previously) 以前; (at one time) 曾经; **to have ～ done sth.** 曾经做过某事; **to have ～ been beautiful** 从前很漂亮; **～ upon a time** (in stories) 从前; **～, long ago, ...** 很久以前…; **～ a thief, always a thief** 一朝做贼，永世为贼; **～ bitten, twice shy** Prov 一朝被蛇咬，十年怕井绳 **3** (in family relations) **to be ～ removed** 是隔一代的亲戚 **4** Math 乘以一; **～ two is two** 一二得二

B *n* 一次; **～ is enough** 一次就够了; **the** *or* **this ～** 就这一次; **he only came the ～** 他只来过一次; **I'll let you off this ～** 就这一次我放过你

C **at once** *adv phr* **1** (immediately) 立即; **come at ～!** 马上过来! **2** (simultaneously) 同时; **don't all/both talk at ～** 别全都/两人同时说; **to do several things at ～** 同时做几件事情; **to be at ～ funny and instructive** 寓教于乐 **3** (suddenly) 突然; **all at ～** 突然 **4** (in one go) 一下子; **don't eat it all at ～** 别一下子吃光

D *conj* 一旦; **～ it is dark ...** 一到天黑…; **～ out of prison ...** 一旦从监狱里出来…

once-over *n* colloq **1** (quick look) 扫一眼; **to give sb./sth. a** *or* **the ～** 匆匆看某人/某物 **2** (quick clean or trim) 匆匆收拾; **to give sth. a** *or* **the ～ with the mop** 用拖把匆匆拖一拖某处

oncologist /ɒŋˈkɒlədʒɪst/ ▸**p. 409** *n* 肿瘤学家

oncology /ɒŋˈkɒlədʒi/ *n* [u] 肿瘤学

oncoming /ˈɒnkʌmɪŋ/ *adj* **1** (approaching) 迎面而来的〈*vehicle, traffic*〉; 面临的〈*danger, hurricane*〉 **2** (imminent) 即将到来的〈*election, season*〉

oncost /ˈɒnkɒst/ *n* Brit 间接成本

O

OND *abbr* Brit = Ordinary National Diploma

on-demand *adj* 按需的〈*service*〉; 随选的〈*channel, film*〉; ~ access/computing 按需多址接入/计算; ~ application 随选应用

one /wʌn/ ▸p. 2, p. 15, p. 521, p. 831

A *det* 1 (single) 一; ~ man ~ vote 一人一票; forty-~ dogs 四十一条狗; ~ more time 再一次; ~ or two times 一两次; I don't like it ~ (little) bit 我一点都不喜欢它; to have a thousand *or* million and ~ things to do colloq 忙得不可开交 2 (sole) 唯一的; the ~ person who can help 唯一可以帮忙的人; the ~ thing I can't stand 我唯一不能容忍的事情; the ~ and only ... 绝无仅有的…; she's ~ (hell of a) fine artist Amer colloq 她是一位高超的艺术家 3 (same) 同样的; in ~ direction 朝同一方向; at ~ and the same time 与此同时; to be ~ and the same person/thing 是同一个人/同一件事; to be of ~ mind 看法一致; we are ~ in our opinion that ... 我们一致认为…; it's all ~ to me 对我来说都一样 4 (for identification, emphasis) 某一; ~ day (in stories) 有一天; ~ of these days 日后; at ~ time or another (past) 曾经; for ~ thing, he's old; for another, he's ugly 首先，他老了；其次，他很丑; for ~ reason or another 因种种理由; ~ thing and another colloq 这样那样的事; ~ Simon Richard 一个叫西蒙·理查德的

B *n* 1 (number, quantity) 一; ~ plus two equals three 1 加 2 等于 3; in December nineteen hundred and ~ 在1901 年 12 月; we live at (number) ~, Victoria Road 我们住在维多利亚路 1 号; her phone number is two six double ~ 她的电话号码是 2611; ~ at a time 一次一个; ~ by ~ 逐个地; in ~s and twos 三三两两地; ~ or two fig 一两个; from day ~ 从一开始; in more ways than ~ 在很多方面; all for ~ and ~ for all 人人为我，我为人人; when you've read ~ you've read them all 它们千篇一律，读起来都一样; to have had ~ too many colloq 酒喝多了; to go ~ better than sb. 胜人一筹 2 fig (single entity) 一体; to be ~ 统一; as ~ 一齐; to be at ~ with sb./sth. 与某人/某物和谐一致; to become/be made ~ 结婚; in ~ 集于一体; a TV and DVD-player in ~ 电视和 DVD 一体机; to be sth. and sth. all in ~ *or* rolled into ~ 某物和某物集于一身 3 (age) 1岁; when he was ~ 他一岁大的时候 4 (in time) 1 点钟; at ~ (o'clock) 在 1 点 5 (dominoes, dice) 一点; to throw a ~ 掷出一点 6 (stitch) 一针; knit ~, purl ~ 一平针，一反针 7 colloq (one try) 一下子; to get sth. in ~ 立即明白某事; to drink it down in ~ 一口气喝下去

C *adj* 1 (as quantity) 一的; ~ cat 1 只猫; ~ book 1 本书; ~ week 1 周 2 (in age) 1 岁的; he's nearly ~ 他快 1 岁了; our house is only ~ year old 我们的房子才造了 1 年 3 (in series) 第一的; number ~ 1 号; page ~ 第 1 页

D *pron* 1 (indefinite, part of group) 之一; to be ~ of ... 是…之一; every ~ of ... …中的每一个; she's ~ of my best customers 她是我最好的顾客之一; ~ or another *or* the other 其中的某一个; ~ and all 全体; ~ was grey, and the other was pink 一个是灰色，另一个是粉红色; ~ after another *or* the other 一个接一个地 2 (identifying) [特指的] 一个; which ~? 哪一个？; the pink ~ 粉红色的那个; the ~s on the table 桌上的那些 3 (replacing noun) [用于代替名词]; my new car is faster than the old ~ 我的新车比旧车跑得快; her mood changed to ~ of joy 她的情绪变得喜悦 4 (specific person) …的人; her loved ~s 她所爱的人; the ~ on the left 左边那个人; the little ~s 孩子们; to be ~ to do sth. 是做某事的人; she was never ~ to criticize 她从不批评别人; to be ~ for sth./for doing sth. 是乐于做某事的人; to do sth. like ~ possessed 拼命做某事; I for ~ think that ... 我个人认为…; who disagrees? — I for ~! 谁不同意？——我就是一个！ 5 formal (a person) 任何人; it does make ~ think 这的确发人深省; ~ would like to think that ... 大家会认为…; ~ must try ~'s best 我们要尽力而为 6 colloq (drink) 一杯; to have a quick ~ 小饮一杯; make mine a large ~ 给我来一大杯 7 colloq (joke) 玩笑; did you hear the ~ about ...? 你听过那个关于…的笑话吗？ 8 colloq (blow) 一拳; to land *or* sock sb. ~ 打某人一拳 9 colloq (problem) 问题; that's a tough/tricky ~ 那是个很难/很棘手的问题 10 colloq (advantage) 优势; to get ~ over (on) sb. 胜某人一筹

one-act play *n* 独幕剧

one-armed *adj* 1 (having one arm) 独臂的〈*person*〉 2 (done with one arm) 单臂的〈*hug, swipe*〉

one-armed bandit *n* colloq 吃角子老虎机

one: ~-dimensional *adj* 1 Math 一维的; 2 fig (lacking depth) 肤浅的〈*view, character*〉; **~-eyed** *adj* 独眼的

one-handed

A *adj* 1 (done with one hand) 用单手的 2 (for use with one hand) 为单手使用设计的〈*weapon, tool*〉 3 (having one hand) 一只手的〈*person*〉

B *adv* 单手地

one: ~-horse town *n* colloq 设施简陋的小镇; **~-legged** *adj* 一条腿的; **~-line** *adj* 一句话的〈*message, summary, apology*〉; 一行的〈*part*〉; **~-liner** *n* 俏皮话

one-man *adj* 单人的〈*performance, canoe, operation*〉; 单人操作的〈*machine*〉; 个人的〈*exhibition*〉

one-man band *n* 1 Mus 单人乐队 [常指能同时演奏多种乐器的街头艺人] 2 fig (business) 一人经营的公司; (person) 个体户

one man one vote *n* [u] Brit 一人一票制

one-man show *n* 1 Theat 独角戏 2 Art 个人作品展 3 fig (business) 个体经营的公司

one-nation *adj attrib* Brit [英国保守党旨在消除社会不平等的] 一国保守主义的〈*agenda, party, society*〉; ~ inclusive social policies 一国包容的社会政策

oneness /ˈwʌnnɪs/ *n* [u] (uniformity) 一体; (harmony) 和谐; ~ with God 与上帝的合而为一

one-night stand *n* 1 colloq (sexual encounter) 一夜情; (person) 一夜情对象 2 Theat, Mus 单场演出

one-off

A *n* colloq (thing) 绝无仅有的事物; (person) 卓尔不群的人

B *adj* esp Brit colloq 一次性的〈*object, payment, order*〉; 独特的〈*design, event, achievement, job*〉; a ~ example 绝无仅有的例子

one: ~-on-one *adj, adv* esp Amer = one-to-one; **~-parent family** *n* 单亲家庭; **~-party system** *n* 一党制

one-piece

A *adj* 一件式的〈*dress, swimsuit*〉

B *n* 连身衣

one: ~-price store *n* Amer 一口价商店; **~-room flat** Brit, **~-room apartment** esp Amer *ns* 单间公寓

onerous /ˈɒnərəs/ *adj* 1 (hard) 沉重的〈*workload*〉; 繁重的〈*task, responsibility*〉 2 Jur 有偿的〈*contract*〉; 义务过重的〈*terms*〉

one's /wʌnz/ *det* formal 本人的; one tries (to do) ~ best 尽自己的最大努力; a car of ~ own 自己的汽车; to wash ~ hands 洗手; it limits ~ options 它限制人们的选择

oneself /ˌwʌnˈself/ *pron* 1 (reflexive and after prep) 自己; to hurt ~ 伤着自己; to talk to ~ 自言自语; to make the most of ~ 非常注意仪表; all by ~ 独自 2 by ~ (unaided) 独自; to do sth. by ~ 亲自做某事 3 to feel ~ (normal, healthy) 怡然自得

one-sided *adj* 1 (biased) 片面的〈*reporting, account*〉 2 (ill-matched, uneven) 实力悬殊的〈*contest, game*〉 3 (unequal, unfair) 一方支配的〈*relationship*〉; 一边倒的〈*conversation*〉; 不公平的〈*bargain, deal*〉 4 (with or on one side) 单边的; ~ documents 单方面文件; a ~ headache 偏头痛

one-size *adj* 均码的〈*garment*〉

one-size-fits-all *adj* 1 (designed to fit all sizes) 均码的〈*garment*〉 2 (used in all circumstances) 一刀切的〈*policy*〉; 通用的〈*answer*〉

one: ~-stop shopping *n* [u] 一站式购物; **~-time** *adj attrib* 1 (former) 从前的〈*actor, colleague*〉; 2 (one-off) 一次性的〈*payment, charge*〉

one-to-one

A *adj* 1 (individual) 一对一的〈*contest, basis, comparison*〉; 面对面的〈*session, discussion, fight*〉; ~ tuition 单独辅导; ~ encounter 面对面的交锋 2 Math 完全对应的〈*equivalence, mapping*〉

B *adv* 一一对应地〈*compare*〉; 面对面地〈*discuss, fight*〉

one: ~-touch *adj* 单触式的〈*device, access*〉; ~-touch push-to-talk capability 一键通话功能; **~-track** *adj attrib* 偏狭的〈*thinking*〉; 话题单一的〈*conversation*〉; to have a ~-track mind 满脑子只想一件事 [常指性爱]; **~-trick pony** *n* colloq (person) 单一特长的人; (thing) 单一特色的事物; **~-two** *n* 1 (in boxing) 左右猛击; to give sb. the old ~-two Brit colloq 左右开弓揍某人; 2 (in soccer) 踢墙式二过一; to play a ~ with sb. 和某人配合二过一传球

one-up

A *adv* to be/go ~ on *or* over sb. Sport (by one point) 以/得到一分领先某人; (by one game, match) 以/胜一局领先某人; (have an advantage) 占某人的上风/胜过某人

B *vt* colloq 占…的上风; why do we have to ~ each other 我们为什么一定要相互比个高低

one-upmanship /ˌwʌnˈʌpmənʃɪp/ *n* [u] (practice) 占上风; (technique) 占上风的本事

one-way

A *adj* 1 Transp 单行的〈*tunnel, system*〉; 单向的〈*traffic, valve*〉; a ~ street system 单行道制 2 (single) 单程的; a ~ ticket/trip 单程票/旅行 3 (not reciprocal) 单向进行的〈*process, conversation*〉; 单方面的〈*friendship*〉; 单边的〈*transaction*〉 4 Elec 单路的〈*switch*〉 5 (non-refundable, non-returnable) 不能退的〈*bottle, glass*〉 6 (opaque on one side) 单面的〈*glass, mirror*〉

B *adv* 单向地; it costs £10 ~ 单程票要 10 英镑

one-woman *adj* 一个女人做的〈*job, business*〉; he's a ~ man 他是个对女人专一的人

one-woman show *n* 1 Theat 女独角戏 2 Art 女艺术家个人作品展 3 fig (business) 女子个体经营的公司

one-world *adj* 世界大同的〈*vision, approach*〉; 持世界大同思想的〈*government*〉

ongoing /ˈɒngəʊɪŋ/ *adj* 持续的〈*dispute, negotiations, investigation*〉; 持续存在的〈*problem*〉; 发展中的〈*relationship*〉

onion /ˈʌnɪən/ *n* 洋葱; ~ soup/skin 洋葱汤/皮; to know one's ~s colloq 很在行

onion: ~ gravy *n* [u] 洋葱肉汁; **~ rings** *npl* 炸洋葱圈; **~ set** *n* 洋葱栽子

online /ˌɒnˈlaɪn/

A *adj* 1 (on the Internet) 网上的〈*bookshop, journal, service*〉; ~ chat 网聊 2 Comput 在线的〈*access, data processing*〉

B *adv* 1 (by means of the Internet) 在网上〈*bank, search, shop*〉; to be/go ~ 在网上/在线 2 Comput 在线地〈*work*〉 3 (in or into operation) 启动〈*system, server, site*〉; to be/go ~ 已/开始启动

online: ~ **bank** *n* 网上银行; ~ **banking** *n* [u] 网上银行服务系统; ~ **gamer** *n* 网上游戏玩家; ~ **gaming** *n* [u] 网上游戏; ~ **shop** *n* 网上商店; ~ **shopping** *n* [u] 网上购物

onlooker /ˈɒnlʊkə(r)/ *n* 旁观者

only /ˈəʊnli/

A *adv* 1 (solely) 仅仅; **to be ~ interested in sth.** 只对某事物感兴趣; **we're ~ here for the beer** 我们来这儿就是为了喝啤酒; **God/goodness/heaven ~ knows!** 天晓得!; **'members ~'** "只对会员开放"; **I'll ~ go if you go too** 你去我才去; **not ~ ... but (also) ...** 不但…而且…; **she's not ~ charming but also intelligent** 她不仅迷人，而且很聪慧; **~ (...) if ...** 如果…就…; **it's ~ dangerous if ...** 如果…就很危险 2 (merely) 只; **to be ~ sixteen** 只有 16 岁; **it's ~ that I wanted to ...** 我只是想…; **you can ~ do your best** 你只能尽力而为; **to be the boss in name ~** 只是名义上的老板; **I was ~ joking** 我只不过是开玩笑而已; **you ~ have to ask** 你只要开口; **it's ~ 3 o'clock** 才 3 点钟呢; **~ think of the mess!** colloq 想想看有多乱! 3 (as recently as) 仅在; **~ last week** 就在上周; **it seems like ~ yesterday (that ...)** 仿佛就在昨天 (…) 4 (in immediate past) 才; **to do sth. ~ recently** 最近才做过某事; **~ just** (recently) 刚才; (barely) 差点没; **to have ~ just arrived** 刚刚到达; **it's ~ just tolerable** 勉强过得去 5 (not until) 直到; **to conclude ~ on 10 May** 直到 5 月 10 日才作出决定 6 (in final outcome) 只会; **he'll ~ waste it** 他只会把它浪费掉; **that ~ makes matters worse** 那只会把事情弄得更糟 7 (in wishes) **I ~ wish/hope ...** 但愿/我唯有希望… 8 (surprisingly) 不料; **~ to find/discover that ...** 不料却发现…; **I enquired, ~ to be told ...** 我询问了一下，结果竟被告知… 9 (at the very least) 十分; **it's ~ fair to let him explain** 让他解释一下很公平; **it's ~ natural for her to be curious** 她好奇是很自然的; **~ too** 非常; **it's ~ too obvious that ...** 显而易见的是…; **he was ~ too pleased to help** 他很乐于帮忙

B *adj attrib* 1 (sole) 唯一的; **one and ~** 独一无二的; **the ~ one left** 仅存的一个; **an ~ child** (boy) 独子; (girl) 独女; **the ~ thing is, I'm broke** colloq 问题是，我破产了 2 (best) 最佳的; **skiing is the ~ sport for me** 滑雪是我最喜欢的运动; **whisky is the ~ drink** 威士忌酒是首选

C *conj* 可是; **you may carry it, ~ don't drop it** 你拿着它吧，可别摔了; **it's like skiing, ~ safer/more fun** 这就像滑雪一样，不过更安全/更有趣

on-message

A *adj* Brit 阐明执政党路线的 ‹*person, statement*›; **to be ~** 明确政党路线

B *adv* 与计划路线一致地; **to stay ~** 坚持既定方针

o.n.o. *abbr* Brit = **or nearest offer** 或接近出价 [尤用于分类广告]

on-off *adj* 1 lit 开一关的; **an ~ switch** 双位开关 2 fig 分分合合的 ‹*boyfriend, girlfriend*›; 时断时续的 ‹*affair, relationship*›

onomatopoeia /ˌɒnəˌmætəˈpɪə/ *n* [u] (formation) 拟声

onomatopoeic /ˌɒnəˌmætəˈpiːɪk/ *adj* 拟声的; **an ~ word** 拟声词

onrush /ˈɒnrʌʃ/ *n* [u] (of water) 奔流; (of tears) 涌出; (of emotion, pain) 突如其来; **the sudden ~ of people** 人群的突然涌来

on-screen

A *adj* 1 Comput 屏幕上的 2 TV, Cin 影视上的 ‹*action, sex, persona*›; **~ violence** 影视暴力

B *adv* 1 Comput 在屏幕上 ‹*edit, display*› 2 TV, Cin 在影视上

onset /ˈɒnset/ *n* [u] [常指不快、持久事件的] 开始; **the ~ of sth.** 某事的来临

onshore /ˈɒnʃɔː(r)/

A *adj* 1 (land-based) 陆上的 ‹*operation, drilling*› 2 (towards land) 吹向陆地的 ‹*wind, breeze, current*›

B *adv* 1 (on land) 在陆地 ‹*drill, prospect*› 2 (towards land) 向陆地 ‹*blow*›

onside /ˌɒnˈsaɪd/ *adv* 1 Sport 未越位 2 colloq (in agreement) 一致地; **to bring sb. ~** 取得某人的同意; **to be/come ~** 保持/变得一致

on-site

A *adj attrib* 就地的 ‹*parking, storage*›; 现场的 ‹*facilities, services, meeting, training*›

B *adv* 就地 ‹*store*›; 在现场 ‹*work*›; 实地 ‹*manufacture*›; **he lives ~** 他住在工地

onslaught /ˈɒnslɔːt/ *n* (physical) 猛烈打击; (verbal) 猛烈抨击; **to make an ~ on sth./sb.** 猛烈攻击某事物/某人; **to withstand/repel an ~** 顶住/击退进攻

onstage /ˌɒnˈsteɪdʒ/

A *adj attrib* 舞台上的 ‹*antics, banter, violence*›

B *adv* 在舞台上; **to come ~** 登台; **to take place ~** 发生在舞台上

on-street *adj* 路边的 ‹*parking*›

on-target earnings *npl* [尤指销售业的] 目标收入

Ontario /ɒnˈteərɪəʊ/ *pr n* 安大略省

on-the-job

A *adj attrib* 在职的; **~ training/learning** 在职培训/学习

B on the job *adv* 在职地; **to get one's training on the job** 得到在职培训

on-the-spot *adj attrib* 现场的 ‹*reporting, investigation*›; 当场的 ‹*fine*›; **~ fieldwork** 现场调查工作

onto /ˈɒntuː/ *prep* = **on to** ▸**on D**

ontological /ˌɒntəˈlɒdʒɪkl/ *adj* 本体论的

ontology /ɒnˈtɒlədʒi/ *n* [u] 本体论

onus /ˈəʊnəs/ *n* [u] 职责; **the ~ lies** *or* **rests on** *or* **with sb.** 责任在于某人; **the ~ is on sb. to do sth.** 某人有责任做某事; **the ~ of proof** 举证责任

onward /ˈɒnwəd/

A *adj attrib* 1 Transp 继续的; **an ~ flight to Tokyo** 继续飞往东京的航班; **to make the ~ journey to Cairo** 接着前往开罗旅行 2 (moving forward) 向前的 ‹*movement*›; **the ~ transmission of calls** Telecom 电话的转接; **the ~ sale of goods** Comm 货物的转销; **the ~ march of history** fig 历史的向前发展

B *adv* 1 (ahead) 向前; **to move ~ into the forest** 向前进入森林; **to go ~ and upward** fig 步步高升 2 Transp 继续 ‹*fly, travel*› 3 (in time phrases) **from ... ~** 从…起; **from now/next year ~** 从现在/明年起; **the period from 1969 ~** 从 1969 年开始的这段时期

onwards /ˈɒnwədz/ *adv* = **onward B**

onyx /ˈɒnɪks/ *n* [u] 缟玛瑙

oodles /ˈuːdlz/ *npl* colloq 大量; **he has ~ of charm!** 他太有魅力了!; **it would be fine if I had ~ of cash** 如果我有大把钞票该多好

ooh /uː/

A *excl* 噢 [用于表示惊奇、高兴、期盼、疼痛等]

B *n* "噢"的一声喊叫; **~s and aahs** 哎哟喂啊

C *vi* 发出"噢"声; **to ~ and aah** 惊呼

oolong /ˈuːlɒŋ/ *n* [u] 乌龙 (茶)

oompah /ˈʊmpɑː/ *n* [u] colloq 嗡姆吧声 [铜管乐队吹出的低沉的乐声]; **~ music** 铜管乐

oomph /ʊmf/ *n* [u] colloq 1 (energy) 精力; (verve) 气魄 2 (power) 力量

oops /uːps, ʊps/ *excl* colloq 哎哟 [常表示道歉]

ooze /uːz/

A *n* [u] (mud, slime) 泥浆

B *vi* 1 «*liquid, blood*» 慢慢流出; «*pus, sap*» 渗出 2 **to ~ with sth.** «*bandage, shoes, walls*» 渗出某种黏液; **to ~ with charm** 散发着魅力

C *vt* 1 lit 渗出 ‹*blood, pus*› 2 fig 散发 ‹*charm, confidence, sex appeal*›

Phrasal verb

• **ooze out** *vi* 慢慢流出; **~ out of sth.** 从某处慢慢流出

op /ɒp/ *n* colloq 1 Med 手术 2 Mil 军事行动; **to be/go on ~s** 正在进行/发动军事行动

opacity /əʊˈpæsəti/ *n* [u] 1 lit (of glass, screen) 不透明; (of liquid) 浑浊 2 fig (of language, article) 难懂; (of intentions) 无法理解

opal /ˈəʊpl/ *n* [c and u] 蛋白石

opalescence /ˌəʊpəˈlesns/ *n* [u] (of light) 变幻的乳白色光; (of colours) 变幻的乳色

opalescent /ˌəʊpəˈlesnt/ *adj* 乳白的 ‹*mist*›; 发乳白色光的 ‹*glassware*›; **~ light/colour** 乳白色光/乳白色

opaque /əʊˈpeɪk/ *adj* 1 lit 不透明的 ‹*glass, screen*›; 浑浊的 ‹*liquid*›; 不透光的 ‹*curtain, envelope*› 2 fig 难懂的 ‹*language, article, textbook*›; 摸不着头脑的 ‹*comments*›; 无法理解的 ‹*intentions*›

opaqueness /əʊˈpeɪknɪs/ *n* [u] = **opacity**

op art *n* [u] 光效应艺术

op artist *n* 光效应艺术家

OPEC /ˈəʊpek/ *abbr* = **Organization of Petroleum Exporting Countries**; **~ members** 欧佩克成员国

op-ed /ˌɒpˈed/ *n* Amer 专栏版; **an ~ piece/section** 专栏文章/部分

open /ˈəʊpən/

A *adj* 1 (not closed) 开着的 ‹*window, drawer, tin*›; 翻开的 ‹*book, newspaper*›; 张开的 ‹*mouth, wings*›; 敞开的 ‹*collar, jacket, container, envelope*›; **to leave the door ~ a crack** 把门留一条缝; **I can't get the door ~** 我打不开门; **the door flew ~** 门突然开了; **the bag burst ~** 袋子一下子破了; **his eyes are ~** 他的眼睛睁着; **with one's eyes ~, with ~ eyes** fig 心知肚明地; **the flowers aren't ~ yet** 花还未开; **your fly is** *or* **flies are ~** 你的裤子拉链开了; **to welcome sb. with ~ arms** fig 热情欢迎某人; **with an ~ hand** fig 慷慨大方地 2 *pred* (admitting customers) 开门的 ‹*shop*›; (admitting visitors) 开放的 ‹*museum*›; **the bank won't be ~ until 9** 银行 9 点才开门; **to be ~ to the public** 向公众开放; **the new road won't be ~ until 2018** 这条新建的道路要到 2018 年才通车; **the meeting is now ~** 会议现在向公众开放 3 *usu pred* (not blocked) 畅通的; **to be ~** «*channel, pass*» 畅通无阻; «*bowels, pores*» 通畅; **~ water** 无障碍水域; **to keep the lines of communication ~** 保持通信线路畅通; **an ~ goal** Sport 空门进球; **to be ~ to sth./sb.** 某物/某人可通行; **to be ~ to traffic/boats** 车辆/船只可通行; **the road to riches lay ~ before him** 他面前通往财富的道路畅通无阻 4 (not covered) 敞篷的 ‹*vehicle, carriage*›; 无遮盖的 ‹*sewer, tomb*›; **an ~ boat** 敞舱船; **an ~ fire/drain** 明火/排水明沟 5 (not enclosed) 开阔的 ‹*sky, view*›; **the ~ air** 户外; **~ country** 空旷的田野; **the ~ sea** 开阔的海域; **(wide) ~ spaces** (开阔的) 空旷地带 6 (exposed) 暴露的 ‹*place, coastline*›; (conspicuous) 显眼的 ‹*place*›; **an ~ field** 无遮挡的田地; **to be ~ to sth.** 易受某物影响; **the room is ~ to the air** 房间透气性很好; **~ to the elements** 易受风霜雪雨侵袭的; **to lay** *or* **leave oneself ~ to attack/criticism** 使自己处于易受攻击/批评的地位; **this incident has left his honesty ~ to doubt** *or* **question** 这件事情使大家开始怀疑他的诚信 7 (receptive) 开明的; **to have an ~ mind** 思想开明; **to keep an ~ mind (about sth.)** (对某事) 不怀成见; **to be ~ to sth.** 愿意考虑 ‹*offers, suggestions*›; **to be ~ to persuasion** 愿意听从劝说; **to be ~ to new/good ideas** 能接受新观念/好主意 8 *pred* (available) 空缺的 ‹*position*›; **there's a slot ~ in July** 七月有一个空档; **to keep a job ~ for sb.** 给某人留着一份工作; **to be**

~ to sb. «job, membership» 对某人开放; the competition is ~ to everybody 人人都可参赛; these are the classes that are ~ to you 这些是你可以选择的课程 [9] (unrestricted) 无限制的 ‹access, session, invitation›; an ~ contest or competition 公开赛 [10] (candid) 坦率的 ‹person, attitude, expression›; 坦诚的 ‹discussion, debate›; to be ~ with sb. (about sth.) （在某事上）对某人坦诚; with an ~ heart (frankly) 坦诚地; (kindly) 和善地 [11] (undecided) 待定的 ‹decision, date›; an ~ question 悬而未决的问题; the race is still wide ~ 竞赛仍然胜负未定; ~ ticket/return 不定期机票/回程不定的往返票 [12] (blatant) 公然的 ‹hostility, contempt›; ~ revolt or rebellion 公然的反叛; an ~ scandal 人尽皆知的丑闻 [13] (with spaces) 稀疏的 ‹material, mesh› [14] Ling an ~ vowel 开元音; an ~ syllable 开音节 [15] Mus an ~ string 空弦

B vt [1] (cause not to be closed) 打开 ‹door, safe, book, box, jar›; to ~ one's mouth/eyes 张开嘴巴/睁开眼睛; to ~ an envelope/a parcel 拆开信封/包裹; to ~ a vein/wound 切开静脉/伤口; to ~ a border 开放边境; the wind ~ed the gate 风把大门吹开了; to ~ sb.'s eyes to sth. fig 使某人认清某事; to ~ the door to sth. fig 为某事敞开大门; to ~ one's mind to sth. 愿意考虑某事; to ~ one's heart to sb. 向某人倾诉心声 [2] (spread out) 伸开 ‹legs, hand›; 展开 ‹map, wings, fan›; to ~ a newspaper/an umbrella 翻开报纸/撑开雨伞; ~ the book at page 2 把书翻到第2页 [3] (cut, create) 开出 ‹hole, passage›; fig 开辟 ‹route, path, market› [4] (begin) 开始; to ~ a meeting/show 开始开会/演出; to ~ a case Jur 开始审案; who'll ~ the bidding? 谁首先出价？; to ~ the score or scoring Sport 开局得分; to ~ the batting (in cricket) 开球 [5] (inaugurate) 为…揭幕 ‹fête, exhibition›; 宣布启用 ‹factory, road›; to ~ a new session of parliament 宣布新一届议会召开 [6] (set up) 开办 ‹business, factory›; 开设 ‹branch, office› [7] Fin 开立 ‹account› [8] Comput 打开 ‹file, document›

C vi [1] (become open) «door, container, lid» 打开; «eyes» 睁开; «mouth, wings» 张开; when the flowers ~ in spring 春天花开时; to ~ wide 大开着; the skies or heavens ~ed fig 大雨突降 [2] to ~ into sth. (give access to) «door, window» 通往 ‹passage, yard›; my bedroom ~s into the sitting room 我的卧室通起居室; to ~ on to sth. «door, room» 朝向 ‹road, area›; a window ~ing on to the garden 朝向花园的窗户 [3] lit, fig (appear) «gap, breach» 出现; cracks ~ed in the ice 冰面上出现了裂缝; a split has ~ed in the party 党内出现了分裂 [4] (admit customers, visitors) «shop, museum» 开门; (for first time) «business, branch» 开业; «fête» 开幕; to ~ at nine o'clock every day 每天9点开始营业; there's a new supermarket ~ing in the High Street 商业大街上一家新超市开业了; the exhibition ~s on 6 January 展览会1月6日开幕 [5] Theat, Cin «play» 上演; «film» 上映 [6] (begin) «conference, trial» 开始; to ~ with sth. 以某事开始; shares ~ed at 123p 股票以123便士开盘; we always ~ with a prayer 我们总是先祈祷 [7] (speak, play first) 起头; to ~ for sth./sb. 代表某事物/某人率先开始; to ~ for the defence Jur 由被告方开始发言; to ~ for the government Pol 率先代表政府发言; to ~ for England Sport 为英格兰队开球

D n [1] the ~ (outside) 户外; to spend the night in the ~ 露天过夜 [2] the ~ (exposed position) 明处; to come out into the ~ «animal» 从暗处出来; to be out in the ~ fig 公开; to bring sth. out into the ~ fig 揭开某事物的真面目

Phrasal verbs

• **open out**

A vi [1] (widen) «path, land» 变开阔; «passage, tunnel» 变宽; to ~ out into sth. 变宽成为某物; the stream ~ed out into a pool 小溪逐渐变宽，汇入一个池塘 [2] (unfold) «fan, flower, wings» 展开; the scroll ~s out into a painting 卷轴展开成一幅画

B vt [~ sth. out, ~ out sth.] 展开 ‹fan, wings, map›

• **open up**

A vi [1] (unlock door) 开门; to ~ up for sb. 给某人开门 [2] (flower) «flower, bud» 开放 [3] (get wider) «crack, crevice» 变宽; a gap has ~ed up between A and B Sport A和B之间的距离拉开了; a split has ~ed up in the opposition ranks 对立派别之间的分歧变大了 [4] (start up) «shop» 开门; «business, branch» 营业; «gallery, museum» 开放 [5] (develop) «business, market» 发展; «opportunities, possibilities» 出现; a new phase was ~ing up 一个新阶段正在呈现 [6] Mil «soldier, army» 开火; to ~ up with sth. 用…开火 ‹rifles, machine guns› [7] (speak freely) «person» 畅所欲言

B vt [~ sth. up, ~ up sth.] [1] (make open) 拆开 ‹envelope›; 打开 ‹box, book›; 疏通 ‹blocked pipe›; to ~ up a wound 使伤口裂开 [2] (make wider) 使…变宽 ‹channel, gap, crack, crevice›; to ~ up a lead «athlete, team» 拉开一段距离而领先 [3] (unlock) 开…的门 ‹shop, building›; 打开 ‹safe› [4] (start up) 开办 ‹business›; 开设 ‹branch›; to ~ up an office in ... 在…设立办事处 [5] (make accessible) 开放 ‹area, country›; 开辟 ‹route›; 开拓 ‹opportunities›; to ~ up the hinterland to trade 开放内陆地区的贸易; to ~ up new horizons for sb. 为某人开拓新视野 [6] Aut colloq 使…加速 ‹engine›

C v refl to ~ oneself up 放开; to ~ oneself up to sb./sth. 愿意接纳某人/某事物; the country has recently ~ed itself up to foreign investment 该国最近开放了外国投资; to ~ oneself up to new ideas 愿意考虑新观念

open access

A n [u] [1] (availability to all) 开放使用 [2] (unrestricted admission) 开放

B **open-access** adj [1] (available to all) 开放阅读的 ‹publishing, journal› [2] (accessible to all) 开放的 ‹land, site, area›

open admissions policy n Amer 开放招生制

open-air adj 露天的 ‹swimming pool, market, performance›; 户外的 ‹meeting›

open: **~-and-shut** adj 一目了然的; an ~-and-shut case 证据确凿的案件; **~cast mining** n [u] Brit 露天开采; **~ competition** n [c and u] 公开竞争; **~ court** n 公开法庭; in ~ court 在公开法庭; to bring sth. into ~ court 将某事提交公开法庭; **~ day** n Brit [机关、学校等的] 开放日

open door

A n fig 门户开放

B **open-door** adj 开放的 ‹policy, access›

open-ended adj [1] lit 两头开口的 ‹tube, pipe› [2] fig 灵活的 ‹policy, strategy›; 无限期的 ‹contract, agreement›; 无限制的 ‹discussion, commitment›

opener /ˈəʊpnə(r)/ n [1] (for bottles, cans, envelopes) 开启工具 [2] (first event or item) 开场戏; (first episode) 第一集; (first song) 起首曲; for ~s colloq 首先

open: **~-faced sandwich** n Amer 露馅三明治; **~ government** n [u] 开放式政府; **~-handed** adj 慷慨的; **~ heart surgery** n [u] 心脏直视手术; **~ house** n [c and u] (place) 开放场所; (situation) 开放; to keep ~ house 随时欢迎来访

opening /ˈəʊpnɪŋ/

A n [1] [u] (of building) 落成典礼; (of event) 开幕式; (of play) 首映式; (of negotiations, debate, season) 开始 [2] [c] (in wall) 洞; (in fence) 豁口 [3] [c] (of poem, piece of music) 开头 [4] [c] (available job) 空缺职位 [5] [c] (opportunity) 机遇

B adj 首映的 ‹scene, act, night›; 开盘的 ‹price, offer›; 开局的 ‹move›; 首发的 ‹shots›; ~ remarks 开场白

opening: **~ balance** n 期初盈余; **~ ceremony** n (of building) 落成典礼; (of event) 开幕式; **~ gambit** n [1] (introductory remark) 开场白; (to gain advantage) 抢占先机; [2] (in chess) 弃兵开局; **~ hours** npl 营业时间; **~ night** n 首映之夜; **~ time** n [1] [c] (of shop, bank) 开门时间; [2] [u] Brit (of pub) 合法开门时间

open: **~ learning** n [u] 自主学习; **~ letter** n 公开信

openly /ˈəʊpənli/ adv 公开地 ‹declare, admit, criticize›; 不加掩饰地 ‹partisan, critical›

open: **~ market** n 自由市场; **~ marriage** n [允许婚外关系的] 开放婚姻; **~ mike** n 自愿者即兴表演时间; an ~-mike night 即兴表演之夜; **~-minded** adj 思想开明的; to be ~-minded about sth. 对某事开明; **~-mouthed** adj 目瞪口呆的; **~-necked** adj 开领的; an ~-necked shirt/blouse 开领衬衫/女衬衫

openness /ˈəʊpənnɪs/ n [u] [1] (of person, attitude) 坦诚; (of campaign, government, debate) 开放 [2] (of countryside, view) 开阔

open: **~-plan** adj 敞开式的 ‹office, design›; **~ primary** n Amer 开放初选; **~ prison** n 开放式监狱; **~ road** n 公路; on the ~ road 在公路上; **~ sandwich** n 单片三明治; **~ scholarship** n 开放奖学金; **~ season** n [法定的] 渔猎开放季节; fig [针对某团体的] 言论开放期; **~ secret** n 公开的秘密; **~ sesame** excl 敲门砖; **~ shop** n [1] (system) [可雇用非工会会员的] 自由雇佣制度; [2] (place of work) 自由雇佣企业; **~-source** adj 公开源代码的 ‹software, game›; **~-toed** adj 露趾的 ‹shoes, sandals›; **~-top** adj attrib 敞篷的 ‹bus›; **O~ University** n Brit the O~ University 开放大学; an O~ University course/programme 开放大学科目/课程; **~ verdict** n 死因未详的裁决; **~work** n [u] [1] Sewing 透孔编织; [2] Archit 透雕细工

opera /ˈɒprə/ n [1] [u] (genre) 歌剧艺术 [2] [c] (production) 歌剧; to stage or perform or put on an ~ 上演歌剧

operable /ˈɒprəbl/ adj [1] Med 可动手术的 ‹case, condition›; an ~ tumour 可摘除的肿瘤 [2] (functioning, workable) 可行的 ‹plan, system›; 可运转的 ‹machine, plant›

opera: **~ company** n 歌剧团; **~ glasses** npl 观剧小望远镜; **~-goer** n 经常看歌剧的人; **~ house** n 歌剧院; **~ lover** n 歌剧爱好者

operand /ˈɒpərænd/ n [1] Math 运算元 [2] Comput 操作数

opera singer ▸p. 409 n 歌剧独唱演员

operate /ˈɒpəreɪt/

A vi [1] (function) 运转; to ~ at maximum efficiency 以最大效率运转 [2] (be in effect, work) «factor, law» 起作用; «mind, language» 运作; to ~ against/in favour of (sth.) （对某事）起阻碍/推进作用 [3] (perform surgery) 动手术; to ~ on sb. 给某人动手术 [4] (run) «public transport, company, service» 营业 [5] (engage in activity) «organization» 运营; «criminal, thief, gang» 从事不法活动 [6] (conduct military activities) 采取军事行动

B vt [1] (control) 操作 ‹machine, apparatus›; 开动 ‹vehicle› [2] (administer) 施行 ‹policy, strategy›; 启用 ‹ban›; 经营 ‹mine, factory›; 实行 ‹pension plan, savings scheme›

operatic /ˌɒpəˈrætɪk/ adj 歌剧的; an ~ performance/society 歌剧表演/团

operatics /ˌɒpəˈrætɪks/ npl 歌剧演出; amateur ~ 业余歌剧演出

operating /ˈɒpəreɪtɪŋ/ *adj attrib* 营业的; **~ costs/profit/margin** 营业成本/利润/利润率

operating: ~ budget *n* 营业预算; **~ instructions** *npl* 使用说明; **~ manual** *n* 操作手册; **~ room** *n* Amer **= ~ theatre**; **~ system** *n* 操作系统; **~ table** *n* 手术台; **~ theatre** *n* Brit 手术室

operation /ˌɒpəˈreɪʃn/ *n* 1 [u] (of machine) 运行; (of plant, mine) 经营; **to be in/out of ~** 运转/不运转; **to take out of ~** 停止使用; **his broken leg put him out of ~ for several weeks** 他腿断了几个星期无法走动 2 [u] (administration of scheme, regulations, law) 实施; **to put into ~** 开始实施 3 [c] Med 手术; **to have an ~** 动手术; **to perform an ~ (on sb.)** (给某人) 动手术; **a bowel/shoulder ~** 肠道/肩部手术 4 [c] Mil, Naut, Tech 行动; **to launch** *or* **mount** *or* **stage an ~** 展开行动; **a relief** *or* **salvage** *or* **rescue ~** 解救行动 5 [c] (undertaking) 业务; (organization) 企业 6 Comput 运作 7 Math 运算

operational /ˌɒpəˈreɪʃənl/ *adj* 1 (working) 运转的; **the ship/plant is fully ~** 轮船全面投入使用/工厂全面投入运营 2 *attrib* Comm 业务的 ‹*capability, requirement*›; 经营的 ‹*costs, difficulty*› 3 *attrib* Mil 军事行动的 ‹*forces*›; **~ duty/aircraft/command** 作战任务/飞机/指挥

operational: ~ manager ▸**p. 409** *n* 业务经理; **~ research** *n* [u] 运筹学

operation code *n* 操作码

operations: ~ manager ▸**p. 409** *n* 业务部经理; **~ research** *n* [u] 运筹学; **~ room** *n* 1 Mil 作战指挥室; 2 (police) 行动指挥室

operative /ˈɒpərətɪv, Amer -reɪt-/

A *adj* 1 (effective, in use) 在施行的 ‹*system, law, measure*›; 在运转的 ‹*plant, mine, oil-rig*›; **to become ~** 开始实施 2 (significant) 关键的 ‹*word, phrase, force*› 3 Med 手术的

B *n* 1 (worker) 工人; **a machine/factory ~** 机器操作工/工厂工人 2 (secret agent) 特工人员

operator /ˈɒpəreɪtə(r)/ ▸**p. 409** *n* 1 Telecom 接线员 2 (of machine, equipment) 操作者; **a radio/camera ~** 报务员/摄影师 3 Comm 经营者; **telecoms/tour ~** 电信公司/旅游业从业者 4 (person) 善于钻营的人; **he's a smooth/shrewd ~** 他这人很圆滑/工于心计 5 Math 算子; **a positive integral ~** 正积分算子

operetta /ˌɒpəˈretə/ *n* 1 [u] (genre) 轻歌剧艺术 2 [c] (production) 轻歌剧

ophthalmic /ɒfˈθælmɪk/ *adj attrib* 眼科的 ‹*surgeon, clinic*›; 眼用的 ‹*ointment*›

ophthalmic optician ▸**p. 409** *n* Brit 验光师

ophthalmologist /ˌɒfθælˈmɒlədʒɪst/ ▸**p. 409** *n* 眼科医生

ophthalmology /ˌɒfθælˈmɒlədʒi/ *n* [u] 眼科学

ophthalmoscope /ɒfˈθælməskəʊp/ *n* 检眼镜

opiate /ˈəʊpɪət/ *n* 1 lit 鸦片制剂; **~ drug/addiction/overdose** 鸦片毒品/瘾/服用过量 2 fig 慰藉物

opine /əʊˈpaɪn/ formal

A *vt* 认为

B *vi* 发表意见

opinion /əˈpɪnɪən/ *n* 1 [c] (belief, view) 看法; **an ~ on** *or* **about sth.** 对某事的看法; **to be of the ~ that ...** 认为…; **of the same ~** 看法一致的; **in my/his ~** 依我看/照他看来 2 [u] (general view) 观点; **public/popular ~** 公众/大众舆论; **local/national/international ~** 当地/全国/国际舆论; **legal/medical/political ~** 法学界/医学界/政界的观点; **expert** *or* **professional ~** 专家的观点; **informed ~ has it that ...** 据可靠消息… 3 [c] (evaluation) 评价; **to have a high/low ~ of sth./sb.** 对某事物/某人评价高/低; **sb.'s ~ of sth./sb.** 某人对某事物/某人的评价; **what's your ~ of the play?** 你认为这部剧如何? 4 [c] (professional advice) 专家意见; **a second ~** Med 另一位医生的意见; **to take counsel's ~** Jur 接受律师意见; **to hand down an ~** Jur 宣布判案依据; **an ~ on sth.** 对某事的专家意见 5 [u] (beliefs) 观念; **a difference of ~** 观念的分歧; **shades of ~** 形形色色的观念; **that's a matter of ~** 那只是看法问题; **a programme of news and ~** 新闻和评论节目

opinionated /əˈpɪnɪəneɪtɪd/ *adj* 固执己见的 ‹*person*›; 武断的 ‹*view, style*›

opinion poll *n* 民意测验; **to carry out an ~** 进行民意测验

opium /ˈəʊpɪəm/ *n* lit 鸦片; fig 慰藉物; **the ~ of the people** *or* **masses** 精神鸦片; **an ~ addict** 鸦片瘾君子

opium: ~ den *n* 鸦片烟馆; **~ poppy** *n* 罂粟

opossum /əˈpɒsəm/ *n* 1 (American) 负鼠 2 (Australian) 袋貂

opponent /əˈpəʊnənt/ *n* 1 (in sport, contest) 对手 2 (of project, government) 反对者

opportune /ˈɒpətjuːn, Amer -tuːn/ *adj* 恰当的 ‹*moment*›; 适宜的 ‹*place*›; 适时的 ‹*event*›

opportunely /ˈɒpətjuːnli, Amer -tuːn-/ *adv* 适时地 ‹*occur, arrive, intervene*›

opportunism /ˌɒpəˈtjuːnɪzəm, Amer -ˈtuːn-/ *n* [u] 机会主义; **political ~** 政治机会主义

opportunist /ˌɒpəˈtjuːnɪst, Amer -ˈtuːn-/ pej

A *n* 机会主义者

B *adj* 机会主义的 ‹*policy, attitude*›; **an ~ criminal** 临时起意的犯罪

opportunistic /ˌɒpətjuːˈnɪstɪk, Amer -tuːˈn-/ *adj* 1 pej (gen) 机会主义的 ‹*politician*›; 临时起意的 ‹*thief, theft, crime*›; 趁虚而入的 ‹*attempt*› 2 Ecol 机会性的 ‹*plant, animal*›; **~ species** 机会物种 3 Med 机会性的 ‹*infection, disease, microbe*›

opportunistically /ˌɒpətjuːˈnɪstɪkli, Amer -tuːˈn-/ *adv* 机会主义地

opportunity /ˌɒpəˈtjuːnəti, Amer -ˈtuːn-/ *n* 1 (appropriate time or occasion) 机遇; **to take** *or* **seize** *or* **grab an ~** 抓住机遇; **to miss an ~** 失去机会 2 (possibility, job prospect) [就业、升职的] 机会; **~ knocks** 机会来了; **~ only knocks (but) once!** 机会不等人!

opportunity cost *n* [u] 机会成本

oppose /əˈpəʊz/ *vt* 反对 ‹*war, legislation, plan*›; 抵制 ‹*action, decision*›

opposed /əˈpəʊzd/ *adj* 1 (against) 强烈反对的; **to be ~ to sth.** 强烈反对某事; **to be ~ to (sb.) doing sth.** 强烈反对 (某人) 做某事 2 (conflicting, very different) 截然不同的 ‹*ideas, theories, natures*›

opposing /əˈpəʊzɪŋ/ *adj attrib* 1 (in conflict) 对立的 ‹*army, party*› 2 (in competition) 相竞争的 ‹*team, player*› 3 (very different) 极不相同的 ‹*view, argument*›

opposite /ˈɒpəzɪt/

A *n* 1 (reverse) 对立面; **the very** *or* **exact ~ (of sth.)** (某事物的) 截然对立面; **quite** *or* **just the ~** 恰恰相反 2 (sb. different) 相对立的人; (sth. different) 相反的事物; **black and white are ~s** 黑与白是对立的; **~s attract** 相异相吸

B *adj* 1 *attrib* (facing) 对面的 ‹*bank, wall*›; **the ~ side of the road** 道路的对面; **see illustration on the ~ page** 见对面页上的插图; **~ angles** Math 对角 2 *attrib* (most distant) 另一边的 ‹*way, pole*›; **to sit at ~ ends of the table** 坐在桌子的两端; **the ~ extreme** 另一个极端 3 (reverse) 相反的 ‹*meaning, direction*›; (opposing) 对立的 ‹*attitude, camp*›; **to adopt** *or* **take up the ~ stance** 采取相反的立场; **to take the ~ view** 持相反的观点; **to have** *or* **produce the ~ effect** 效果适得其反; **the ~ sex** 异性; **of the ~ sex** 异性的

C *adv* 在对面 ‹*stand, be*›; **to live directly ~** 住在正对面; **to go into the shop ~** 进入对面的商店; **see ~ for details** 详情见对页

D *prep* 1 (facing) 在…对面 ‹*building, park*›; **to sit down ~ sb.** 在某人对面坐下来 2 Cin, Theat 与…合演; **to play** *or* **appear ~ sb.** 与某人联袂演出; **to play ~ sb.** Sport 与某人联手比赛; **to play ~ one another in a match** 联手比赛

opposite number *n* (in government, company) 职位对等的人; Sport 竞技对手

opposition /ˌɒpəˈzɪʃn/ *n* [u] 1 (resistance) 抵制; (dissent) 反对; **to encounter** *or* **meet with ~** 遭遇抵制; **to put up** *or* **offer ~ against ...** 对…进行抵抗; **to run into** *or* **up against ~ ...** 与…发生冲突 2 **Opposition** Brit Pol **the O~** 反对党 3 Sport 对手 4 (contrast) 对立面

Opposition benches *npl* Brit **the ~** 反对党议席

oppress /əˈpres/ *vt* 1 (subjugate) 压迫 ‹*population, minority*›; 压制 ‹*nation*› 2 (afflict) 压抑

oppressed /əˈprest/

A *adj* 1 (subjugated) 被压迫的 2 (afflicted) 压抑的

B *npl* **the ~** 被压迫者

oppression /əˈpreʃn/ *n* [u] 1 (subjugation) 压迫; **to live under ~** 生活在压迫下 2 (affliction) 压抑; **a sense** *or* **feeling of ~** 压抑感

oppressive /əˈpresɪv/ *adj* 1 (harsh) 残酷的; (tyrannical) 暴虐的 2 (stifling) 令人窒息的 ‹*atmosphere, weather, heat*›

oppressively /əˈpresɪvli/ *adv* 1 (harshly) 残酷地 ‹*severe, unjust, parochial*›; (tyrannically) 暴虐地 ‹*govern, act, dominate*› 2 (stiflingly) 令人窒息地 ‹*close, airless*›; **it's ~ hot** 天气热得令人窒息

oppressor /əˈpresə(r)/ *n* 压迫者

opprobrium /əˈprəʊbrɪəm/ *n* [u] formal 1 (censure) 谴责; **an object of ~** 抨击的对象 2 (disgrace) 耻辱; **to suffer ~** 受辱

opt /ɒpt/ *vi* 选择; **to ~ for sth.** 选择某物; **to ~ to do/not to do sth.** 选择做/不做某事

Phrasal verbs

- **opt in** *vi* 选择参加
- **opt into** *vt* 选择参与
- **opt out** *vi* 选择不参加; **to ~ out of sth.** 决定退出某事

optic /ˈɒptɪk/

A *adj* (of the eye) 眼睛的; (relating to vision) 视觉的; **the ~ disc/nerve** 视盘/视神经

B **Optic®** *n* Brit 奥普蒂克量杯 [一种系在瓶颈上的烈酒量杯]

optical /ˈɒptɪkl/ *adj* 1 (relating to sight) 视觉的; **~ aids/effects** 助视器/视觉效果 2 Phys 光学的; **~ microscope/lens** 光学显微镜/透镜 3 Electron 光电的; **~ drive/scanner/mouse** 光驱/光电扫描仪/光电鼠标

optical: ~ character recognition *n* [u] 光符识别; **~ disk** *n* 光盘; **~ fibre** *n* 光纤; **~ illusion** *n* 视错觉

optician /ɒpˈtɪʃn/ ▸**p. 409** *n* esp Brit (practitioner) 配镜师; (shop) **the ~'s** 眼镜商店

optics /ˈɒptɪks/ *npl* 1 + *v sing* (study) 光学 2 + *v pl* (optical equipment) 光学设备

optima /ˈɒptɪmə/ *pl* ▸**optimum B**

optimal /ˈɒptɪml/ *adj* **= optimum A**

optimism /ˈɒptɪmɪzəm/ *n* [u] 乐观; **cautious/false ~ (about sth.)** (对某事) 谨慎/错误的乐观

optimist /ˈɒptɪmɪst/ *n* 乐观主义者

optimistic /ˌɒptɪˈmɪstɪk/ *adj* 乐观的; **to be ~ about sth.** 对某事乐观; **to be ~ that sth. will happen** 乐观地认为某事将发生

optimistically /ˌɒptɪˈmɪstɪkli/ *adv* 乐观地

optimization /ˌɒptɪmaɪˈzeɪʃn/ *n* [u and c] 1 (of computer program) 优化 2 (of conditions, results) 最佳化

optimize /ˈɒptɪmaɪz/ *vt* 充分利用 ‹*resource*›; 优化 ‹*software*›; 使…最优化 ‹*efficiency, design*›

optimum /ˈɒptɪməm/

A *adj* 最适宜的 ‹*conditions, temperature*›; 最佳的 ‹*time, age*›; 最理想的 ‹*growth, result, solution*›

B *n* (*pl* **optima** *or* **~s**) 最佳条件; **at its ~** 处于最佳条件

option /ˈɒpʃn/ *n* **1** [u] (possibility of choosing) 选择权; **to have the ~ to do** *or* **of doing sth.** 可选择做某事; **to give sb. the ~ of doing sth.** 允许某人做某事; **to have little** *or* **no ~ but to do sth.** 除了做某事外别无选择; **with the ~ of doing sth.** 有做某事的选择权; **to leave** *or* **keep one's ~s open** 暂时不作出选择 **2** [c] (sth. chosen, a choice) 选择; **the easy** *or* **soft ~** 轻松的选择; **to go for an ~** 作出选择 **3** [c] Comm 买卖权; Fin 期权; **to exercise/take up an ~** 履行/行使期权; **to have first ~ on sth.** 有对某物的优先买卖权; **to cancel one's ~s** 取消买卖权; **a call/put ~** 买进/卖出期权; **an exclusive ~** 独家买卖权 **4** [c] Brit Sch, Univ 选修课

optional /ˈɒpʃənl/ *adj* 可选择的; **~ extras/activities/subject** 可选附件/非强制性活动/选修科目; **evening dress ~** 晚装随意

option: ~ trader, ~s trader ▸**p. 409** *n* 期权交易者; **~ trading, ~s trading** *n* [u] 期权交易

optoelectronic /ˌɒptəʊɪlekˈtrɒnɪk/ *adj* 光电子的

optoelectronics /ˌɒptəʊɪlekˈtrɒnɪks/ *npl* + *v sing* 光电子学

optometrist /ˌɒptəˈmetrɪst/ ▸**p. 409** *n* 配镜师

optometry /ɒpˈtɒmətri/ *n* [u] 验光

opt-out clause *n* 退出条款

opulence /ˈɒpjʊləns/ *n* [u] (of lifestyle) 奢侈; (of architecture) 富丽堂皇; (of costume) 华丽; (of surroundings) 豪华

opulent /ˈɒpjʊlənt/ *adj* 奢侈的 ‹*lifestyle*›; 富丽堂皇的 ‹*architecture*›; 华丽的 ‹*costume*›; 豪华的 ‹*surroundings*›

opulently /ˈɒpjʊləntli/ *adv* 奢侈地 ‹*live*›; 华丽地 ‹*dress*›; 豪华地 ‹*decorated*›

opus /ˈəʊpəs/ *n* (*pl* **~es** *or* **opera**) (artistic or musical composition) 作品; (set of artistic or musical compositions) 作品集

OR *abbr* Amer = **Oregon**

or /ɔː(r)/ *conj* **1** (linking alternatives, adding afterthought) 或者; **roasted, grilled, ~ fried** 焙、烧烤或油煎的; **do you have any brothers ~ sisters?** 你有兄弟或姐妹吗？; **with ~ without sugar?** 要不要加糖？; **I can't come today ~ tomorrow** 我今明两天都不能来; **I knew her, ~ at least I thought I did!** 我认识她，或者至少我是这么认为的！; **~ rather** 更确切地说; **my car, ~ rather our car** 我的汽车，确切说是我们的汽车; **it's all over, ~ is it?** 都过去了吧，还是说没完？ **2** (linking opposing alternatives) 还是; **will you ~ won't you come?** 你来还是不来？; **either ... ~ ...** 要么…要么…; **essays may be either handwritten ~ typed** 文章可以手写，也可以打印; **whether ... ~ ...** 是…还是…; **I didn't know whether to laugh ~ cry** 我哭笑不得; **whether (...) ~ not** 不管是否 (…); **whether you like it ~ not, whether ~ not you like it** 不管你愿不愿意; **sth. ~ no sth.** 无论是否有某物; **car ~ no car, I've got to get to work** 不管有没有汽车开，我都得去上班 **3** (indicating approximation) 或许; **once ~ twice a week** 每周一两次; **buy him a tie ~ something** 给他买条领带之类的东西; **~ so** 大约; **in a week ~ so** 大约一周后 **4** (otherwise) 否则; **hurry up, ~ you'll be late** 快点，要不然你就要迟到了; **do as you're told, ~ else!** colloq 按吩咐的去做，否则的话，哼！; **it can't have been serious, ~ she'd have called us** 不会很严重，不然她就会给我们打电话了 **5** (in other words) 或者说; **geology, ~ the science of the earth's crust** 地质学，即研究地壳的科学

oracle /ˈɒrəkl, Amer ˈɔːr-/ *n* lit 传神谕者; fig 权威; **to consult the ~** 向神请示

oracular /əˈrækjʊlə(r)/ *adj* **1** (of oracle) 神谕的 ‹*guidance*›; 神谕似的 ‹*powers*› **2** fig (wise) 睿智的 ‹*utterance, advice*›; 哲人的 ‹*wisdom*› **3** fig (mysterious) 玄妙深奥的

oral /ˈɔːrəl/

A *adj* **1** (spoken, verbal) 口述的 ‹*story*›; 口头的 ‹*account, testimony*›; 口语的 ‹*test, examination*› **2** (relating to the mouth) 口服的 ‹*medicine*›; 口腔的 ‹*hygiene*›; 口用的 ‹*thermometer*›

B *n* 口试; **he failed his ~** 他没有通过口试

oral history *n* **1** [u] (study) 口述历史 **2** [c] (record) 口述历史记录

orally /ˈɔːrəli/ *adv* **1** (by word of mouth) 口头地 ‹*communicate, testify*› **2** (by mouth) 用口地; **this drug can be administered by injection or ~** 这种药可注射可口服; **not to be taken ~** 不得口服

oral: ~ sex *n* [u] 口交; **~ skills** *npl* 口语能力; **~ tradition** *n* [c and u] 口述的传统

orange /ˈɒrɪndʒ, Amer ˈɔːr-/ ▸**p. 134**

A *n* **1** [c] (fruit) 橙子; **~ drink/marmalade** 橙汁/橙子果酱 **2** [c and u] (colour) 橘黄色 **3** [c and u] esp Brit (drink) 橙汁

B *adj* 橘黄色的

orangeade /ˌɒrɪndʒˈeɪd, Amer ˌɔːr-/ *n* [u and c] 橙汁饮料

orange: ~ blossom *n* [c and u] 香橙花; **~ grove** *n* 柑橘园; **~ juice** *n* [u and c] 橙汁; **O~man** /-mən/ *n* 奥兰治党员; **~ peel** *n* [u] 橙皮; **~ revolution** *n* **the ~ revolution** 橙色革命

orangery /ˈɒrɪndʒəri, Amer ˈɔːr-/ *n* 柑橘温室

orange: ~ squash *n* [u and c] Brit 橙汁饮料; **~ tree** *n* 橙树

orang-utan, orang-utang, orang-outang /ɔːˌræŋuːˈtæn, Amer əˌræŋəˈtæn/ *n* 猩猩

orate /ɔːˈreɪt/ *vi* formal [尤指长篇大论地] 演讲

oration /ɔːˈreɪʃn/ *n* formal 演说; **to give** *or* **deliver an ~** 发表演说

orator /ˈɒrətə(r), Amer ˈɔːr-/ *n* 演说者

oratorical /ˌɒrəˈtɒrɪkl, Amer ˌɔːrəˈtɔːr-/ *adj* 演说的 ‹*skill, style, gift*›

oratorio /ˌɒrəˈtɔːrɪəʊ, Amer ˌɔːr-/ *n* (*pl* **~s**) 神剧

oratory /ˈɒrətri, Amer ˈɔːrətɔːri/ *n* [u] formal **1** (art of public speaking) 演讲术 **2** (eloquent language) 雄辩的言辞; (rhetorical language) 华丽的词藻

orb /ɔːb/ *n* 球状物; (in regalia) 王权宝球

orbit /ˈɔːbɪt/

A *n* **1** (about a star or planet) 轨道; **to make an ~ round sth.** 绕某物运行; **to be in ~ round sth.** 在绕某物运行的轨道上; **to go into ~** 进入轨道; **to put sth. into ~** 把某物送入轨道 **2** fig (of person, group) 势力范围; **within/outside sb.'s ~** 在/不在某人的势力范围内

B *vt* 绕…运行

C *vi* 绕轨道运行; **to ~ around sth.** 绕某物运行

orbital /ˈɔːbɪtl/ *adj* **1** (relating to orbit) 轨道的; **an ~ plane/space station** 轨道飞机/航天站 **2** Brit 环城的; **an ~ motorway** 环城高速公路

orbiter /ˈɔːbɪtə(r)/ *n* [尤指不再回收的] 轨道飞行器

orchard /ˈɔːtʃəd/ *n* 果园

orchestra /ˈɔːkɪstrə/ *n* 管弦乐队; **to conduct** *or* **direct** *or* **lead an ~** 指挥管弦乐队; **a chamber/symphony/string ~** 室内乐队/交响乐团/弦乐队

orchestral /ɔːˈkestrəl/ *adj* 管弦乐的 ‹*theme*›; 管弦乐队的 ‹*performance, instrument*›; **an ~ concert/score** 管弦乐音乐会/总谱

orchestra: ~ pit *n* 乐池; **~ seats** Amer, **~ stalls** Brit *npl* 剧院正厅前座

orchestrate /ˈɔːkɪstreɪt/ *vt* **1** lit 把…谱成管弦乐曲; **to ~ sth. for strings** 为弦乐器谱写 ‹*piece of music, melody*› **2** fig (organize) 密谋 ‹*coup, strike*›; 精心策划 ‹*event, campaign*›

orchestration /ˌɔːkɪˈstreɪʃn/ *n* **1** [u and c] lit (of melody, piece of music) 编配管弦乐曲 **2** [u] fig (of event) 精心策划; (of coup, violence) 密谋

orchid /ˈɔːkɪd/ *n* 兰花

ordain /ɔːˈdeɪn/ *vt* **1** (decree) «*monarch, nature*» 主宰; «*God, fate*» 注定; «*law*» 规定 **2** Relig 授…以圣职; **to be ~ed a priest** *or* **minister** 被任命为牧师

ordeal /ɔːˈdiːl, ˈɔːdiːl/ *n* 磨难; **to go through** *or* **undergo an ~** 经历磨难; **to come through** *or* **recover from an ~** 从苦难中解脱出来

order /ˈɔːdə(r)/

A *n* **1** [u] (arrangement) 条理; **a sense of ~** 条理性; **the natural ~ of things** 事物的常态; **to produce ~ out of chaos** 变紊乱为有序; **in (good) ~** (tidy) 井井有条; **to put one's room/affairs in ~** 把房间整理好/把事情安排好; **to put one's (own) house in ~** 管好自己的事情 **2** [u] (working state) 状况; **in good/poor ~** 处于良好/不良状态; **to be kept in good ~** «*house, car*» 维护得很好; **to be in working** *or* **running ~** 运转良好; **to be out of ~** «*phone, line*» 出故障 **3** [u and c] (sequence) 顺序; **alphabetical/numerical/chronological ~** 字母/数字/时间顺序; **ascending/descending ~** 递升的/递降的顺序; **in ~** 按顺序; **out of ~** 乱序的; **these dates are all out of ~** 这些日期顺序都乱了; **in the right/wrong ~** 顺序正确/错误的; **in ~ of priority** 按优先顺序; **in short ~** 立刻 **4** [u] (discipline, control) 秩序; **~ reigned in the streets** 街上秩序井然; **to keep** *or* **maintain ~** 维持治安 **5** [c] (established state) 体制; **the old/new/existing ~** 旧/新/现有体制 **6** [c] Comm 订货; **unfilled/back ~s** 未交货/到期未发货的订单; **a telephone ~** 电话订购; **to place an ~** 下订单; **to put in** *or* **place an ~ (with sb.) for sth.** (向某人) 订购某物; **to supply** *or* **fill an ~** 交付订货; **to take ~s for sth.** 接受某物的订货; **on ~** 在订购中; **the books are on ~** 这批书尚未到货; **to have sth. made to ~** 订做某物; **to be designed to ~** 按用户要求设计; **a tall ~** fig 离谱的要求; **may I take your ~?** (in restaurant) 现在可以点菜了吗？; **an ~ of steak and fries** 一客牛排配炸薯条 **7** [c] esp Mil (command) 命令; **the ~ to retreat** 撤退令; **to give an ~ for the men to disperse** 命令战士们散开; **I left ~s that ...** 我发了话…; **to take** *or* **receive an ~ (to do sth.)** 接受命令 (做某事); **to execute** *or* **obey** *or* **carry out an ~** formal 执行命令; **to be under the ~s of sb.** 受某人的指挥; **to be under** *or* **to have ~s to do sth.** 奉命做某事; **on the ~s of sb., on sb.'s ~s** 奉某人之命; **I did it on your explicit ~s** 我是在你的明确授意下做的; **~s are ~s** colloq 军令如山; **doctor's ~s** hum 医嘱; **to get one's marching ~s** fig 被辞退 **8** [u and c] Jur, Admin (decree) 指令; **an ~ of the court, a court ~** 法院指令; **a deportation/restraining ~** 驱逐/限制令; **by ~ of the Minister/Crown** 经大臣/女王批示; **a buying/selling ~** Fin 买入/卖出指令; **a stop ~** Fin 止损指令 **9** [c] Fin 汇票 **10** [u and c] (correct procedure) 规程; **to call a meeting/class to ~** 宣布会议开始/让全班遵守课堂纪律; **~! ~!** Brit 安静！安静！; **to be in/out of ~** 符合/不符合规程; **the Honourable Member is out of ~** Brit 这位尊敬的议员阁下违反了议事程序; **would it be in ~ if I took her flowers?** 我送花给她合适吗？; **a toast is in ~** 敬杯酒是应该的; **congratulations are in ~** 应该表示祝贺; **your remark**

was way out of ～ 你的话非常不妥当 11 [c] *sing* (rank) 等级; (scale) 级别; **to be of a very high ～** ‹*work, scholarship*› 水平非常高; **artists/goods of the highest ～** 一流艺术家/一等商品; **investment/talent of this ～** 这种级别的投资/人才; **of the ～** Brit /**in the ～** Amer **of sth.** 大约有 ‹*number, sum*›; **his income must be of the ～ of ...** 他的收入肯定差不多有…; **～ of magnitude** (in classification) 数量级; (scale, scope) 规模 12 [u] Mil (formation) 编队; (clothing) 制服; **battle ～** 战斗序列; **drill ～** 操练队形 13 [c] Biol 目; **the ～ of primates** 灵长目 14 **Order** [c] Relig 修道会; **the Dominican O～** 多明我会 15 **Order** [c] Brit (association) 勋爵士团; (title) 勋位; **the O～ of the Garter** 嘉德勋位 16 Archit (style of column) 柱式; (style of architecture) 建筑风格; **columnar ～** 柱型; **the Georgian ～** 乔治王朝建筑风格 17 (expressing purpose) [表示目的]; **in ～ that ...** 为了…; **I did all I could in ～ that ...** 我尽了最大努力以便…; **I came here in ～ that I might talk to you** 我来这里是为了可以跟你谈一下; **in ～ to do sth.** 为了做某事; **in ～ to help sb.** 为了帮助某人; **in ～ to stay healthy/keep sb. safe** 目的是保持健康/使某人安全

B orders *npl* 1 Relig 神品; **major/minor ～s** 高级/低级神品; **holy ～s** 神职; **to take/be in holy ～s** 成为神职人员/担任神职 2 (class) 阶层; **the upper/lower social ～s** 上层/下层社会

C *vt* 1 (give command for or to) 命令 ‹*action, inquiry, person*›; **to ～ the closure of the nightclub** 下令关闭这家夜总会; **to ～ a retrial** 指令再审; **to ～ complete rest** Med 嘱咐卧床静养; **just what the doctor ～ed** fig 正是想要得到的; **to ～ the children to bed** 命令孩子们上床睡觉; **to ～ sth. (to be) done** 命令执行某事; **to ～ the house to be demolished** 下令拆除房屋; **to ～ the talks suspended** 命令会谈暂停; **to ～ that ...** 下令…; **to be ～ed to do sth.** esp Mil 奉命 ‹*shoot, land*› 2 (request) «*company, customer*» 订购 ‹*goods, book, pizza*›; 预订 ‹*service, tickets*›; **to ～ (sth.) online** 网上订购（某物）; **to ～ a meal/coffee** 点饭菜/咖啡; **to ～ a taxi** 叫出租车 3 (arrange) 安排 ‹*life*›; 整理 ‹*room, items*›; **to ～ entries alphabetically** 按字母顺序排列词条

D *vi* 点菜; **are you ready to ～?** 可以点菜了吗？

Phrasal verbs

- **order about, order around** *vt* [**～ sb. about**] 支使; **he likes ～ing people about** 他喜欢支使别人; **don't ～ me about!** 别使唤我！
- **order off** *vt* [**～ sb. off**] 命令…离开; **to ～ sb. off sth.** 命令某人离开某处; **to ～ sb. off the grass** 命令某人退出草坪; **to ～ a player off (the field)** 把运动员罚下场
- **order out** *vt* [**～ sb. out**] 命令…出去; **to ～ sb. out of sth.** 命令某人离开某处; **to ～ a pupil out of the classroom** 把学生赶出教室

order book *n* esp Brit 订货簿

ordered /ˈɔːdəd/ *adj* 整齐的 ‹*ranks*›; 井然有序的 ‹*landscape, society, universe*›; **an ～ whole** 组织有序的整体

order: ～ form *n* 订单; **O～ in Council** Brit 枢密令

orderliness /ˈɔːdəlɪnɪs/ *n* [u] 1 (of pattern, society) 有序; (of room, office) 整洁 2 (of behaviour) 守秩序; (of evacuation, retreat) 井然有序

orderly /ˈɔːdəli/

A *adj* 1 (well-ordered) 有序的 ‹*pattern, arrangement, society*›; 整洁的 ‹*environment, room*› 2 (well-regulated) 守秩序的 ‹*behaviour, conduct*›; 井然有序的 ‹*evacuation, retreat*›; **in an ～ fashion** *or* **manner** 按部就班地

B *n* 1 Med 护理员 2 Mil 勤务兵

orderly: ～ officer *n* Brit 值班军官; **～ room** *n* (regimental) 营部办公室; (company) 连部办公室

order: ～ number *n* 订单号; **～ of business** *n* [u] (meeting) 议程; (issue, topic) 课题; **～ of service** *n* (*pl* **～s of service**) 祭礼仪文; **～ of the day** *n* [u] (for debate, meeting) 议程; (to troops) 特别命令; (prevailing situation) fig 风气; **～ paper** *n* Brit, Can [议会的] 议事日程表

ordinal /ˈɔːdɪnl, Amer -dənl/

A *n* 序数词

B *adj* 序数的; **～ number** 序数

ordinance /ˈɔːdɪnəns/ *n* [c and u] 1 (gen) 惯例 2 Amer Jur 法令; Admin 训令

ordinand /ˈɔːdɪnənd/ *n* 圣职候选人

ordinarily /ˈɔːdənrəli, Amer ˌɔːrdnˈerəli/ *adv* 通常地; **more than ～ quiet/cautious** 异常平静/谨慎

ordinariness /ˈɔːdənrɪnɪs, Amer ˈɔːrdənerɪnɪs/ *n* [u] 平常

ordinary /ˈɔːdənri, Amer ˈɔːrdəneri/

A *adj* 1 (normal) 普通的 ‹*person, object*›; 一般的 ‹*family, life, citizen*›; (everyday) 日常的 ‹*experience, clothes*›; **～ mortals** 凡人; **in the ～ way** 通常地 2 (average) 普通的 ‹*intelligence, consumer, family*›; **the ～ man in the street** 平民百姓 3 (uninspiring) 平庸的 ‹*person*›; 随便的 ‹*meal*›; 平淡无奇的 ‹*performance*›; **my steak was very ～** 我的牛排做得不怎么样

B *n* [u] **the ～** 寻常; **to be out of/above the ～** 不寻常/超乎寻常

ordinary: ～ degree *n* Brit [低于荣誉学位的] 普通学位; **～ grade** *n* [c and u] Scot 普通等级考试; **～ level** *n* [c and u] Brit Hist 普通证书考试; **O～ National Certificate** *n* Brit 国家普通证书; **O～ National Diploma** *n* Brit 国家普通文凭; **～ seaman** *n* Brit 二等水兵; **～ share** *n* Brit 普通股

ordination /ˌɔːdɪˈneɪʃn, Amer -dnˈeɪʃn/ *n* 1 [u] (action) 授圣职 2 [c] (ceremony) 授圣职仪式

ordnance /ˈɔːdnəns/ *n* [u] 1 (munitions) 大炮 2 (department) 军械署

ordnance depot *n* 军械库

Ordnance Survey *n* Brit 全国地形测量局

Ordnance Survey map *n* Brit 全国地形测绘图

Ordovician /ˌɔːdəˈvɪsɪən, ˌɔːdəʊˈvɪʃɪən/

A *adj* (of the period) 奥陶纪的; (of the rock system) 奥陶系的

B *n* **the ～** (period) 奥陶纪; (rock system) 奥陶系

ordure /ˈɔːdjʊə(r), Amer -dʒər/ *n* [u] 1 formal (excrement, dung) 大便 2 euph 秽物

ore /ɔː(r)/ *n* [u and c] 矿石

oregano /ˌɒrɪˈgɑːnəʊ/ *n* [u] 牛至

Oregon /ˈɒrɪgən, Amer ˈɔːr-/ *pr n* 俄勒冈州

organ /ˈɔːgən/ *n* 1 ▸**p. 395** (instrument) 管风琴; **to play the ～** 演奏管风琴; **electric** *or* **electronic ～** 电子琴; **～ pipe/music** 管风琴管/曲 2 (of person, animal, plant) 器官; **the reproductive/sexual ～s** 生殖/性器官; **the ～s of speech, the vocal ～s** 发音器官 3 (official organization) 机关 4 (publication) 机关报刊; **party/government ～** 党/政府的喉舌

organ bank *n* 移植器官库

organdie /ˈɔːgəndi/ *n* 蝉翼纱; **an ～ dress** 蝉翼纱连衣裙

organ: ～ donor *n* 器官捐赠者; **～-grinder** ▸**p. 409** *n* 手摇风琴演奏者

organdy /ˈɔːgəndi/ *n* Amer **= organdie**

organic /ɔːˈgænɪk/ *adj* 1 (without chemicals) 有机的 ‹*produce*›; 不施化肥的 ‹*farming methods, crops*›; **～ food/fertilizer** 有机食物/肥料; **an ～ gardener/restaurant** 实行有机栽培的园艺师/使用有机食品的餐馆 2 (of organ) 器官的; **an ～ disease/disorder** 器官疾病/器质性失调 3 Chem, Biol 有机物的; **～ compounds/remains/material** 有机化合物/有机物残余/有机材料 4 (integral) 统一的; **～ law** 基本法; **～ whole/part/unity** 有机的整体/组成部分/统一; **to be ～ to sth.** 是某事所必不可少的

organically /ɔːˈgænɪkli/ *adv* 1 (without chemicals) 不使用化肥地; **～ grown/reared** 用有机肥料栽种的/用有机饲料饲养的 2 (physiologically) 器官性地; **～ sound/diseased** 器官健康/有病的 3 (naturally) 天然地 ‹*arise, grow, develop, emerge*›

organic: ～ chemist ▸**p. 409** *n* 有机化学家; **～ chemistry** *n* [u] 有机化学; **～ farmer** *n* 使用有机肥的农民

organism /ˈɔːgənɪzəm/ *n* 1 (living thing) 有机体 2 fig (system) 有机组织

organist /ˈɔːgənɪst/ ▸**p. 395, p. 409** *n* 风琴演奏者

organization /ˌɔːgənaɪˈzeɪʃn, Amer -nɪˈz-/ *n* 1 [c] (group, body) 机构 2 [c] (arrangement) 结构 3 [u] (of an event) 组织工作 4 [u] (quality of being systematic) 系统性 5 [u] (unionization) 组织工会

organizational /ˌɔːgənaɪˈzeɪʃənl, Amer -nɪˈz-/ *adj attrib* 1 (managerial) 组织的 ‹*ability, role, method*› 2 (structural) 组织上的 ‹*change, framework*› 3 (institutional) 机构的 ‹*link, connection, affiliation*›

organizationally /ˌɔːgənaɪˈzeɪʃənəli, Amer -nɪˈz-/ *adv* 在组织上

Organization: ～ for Economic Cooperation and Development *n* 经济合作与发展组织; **～ of African Unity** *n* 非洲统一组织; **～ of Petroleum Exporting Countries** *n* 欧佩克 [即石油输出国组织]

organize /ˈɔːgənaɪz/ *vt* 1 (arrange) 安排 ‹*course, meeting*›; 组织 ‹*visit, expedition*›; 使…有条理 ‹*facts, thoughts*›; **to ～ sth. into groups/chapters** 把某物编成小组/章节; **to ～ oneself to do sth.** 有条理地做某事; **to ～ sth. for sb.** 为某人安排某事; **I have to ～ the children for school** 我必须照顾孩子们上学 2 (unionize) 把…组成工会 ‹*group, workforce*›

organized /ˈɔːgənaɪzd/ *adj* 1 (methodical) 安排有序的 ‹*life*›; 井井有条的 ‹*desk*›; 有条理的 ‹*person, thoughts*›; **well/badly ～** 井然有序的/紊乱的 2 *attrib* (large-scale) 有组织的 ‹*tour, resistance*›; **～ games/society** 团体比赛项目/组织严密的社团 3 (unionized) 参加工会的 ‹*workers*›

organized: ～ crime *n* [u] 有组织的犯罪; **～ labour** *n* [u] 工会会员; **～ religion** *n* [u and c] 宗教组织

organizer /ˈɔːgənaɪzə(r)/ *n* 1 (person) 组织者 2 (container) 分类物品箱; **desk/shoe ～** 办公用品整理箱/鞋柜 3 **= personal organizer** 4 **= organizer bag**

organizer bag *n* 多用包 [内有多个口袋的手提包或肩挎包]

organizing /ˈɔːgənaɪzɪŋ/

A *n* [u] 组织; **to be good at ～** 有组织才能

B *adj attrib* 负责组织工作的 ‹*group, committee*›

organ loft *n* 管风琴台

organophosphate /ɔːˌgænəʊˈfɒsfeɪt/ *n* 有机磷酸酯; **～ pesticides** 有机磷酸酯杀虫剂

organ stop *n* 1 (register) 一组音管 2 (knob) 音栓

organ transplant *n* 器官移植

organza /ɔːˈgænzə/ *n* [u] 透明硬纱 [女装面料]

orgasm /ˈɔːgæzəm/

A *n* [u and c] 性高潮

B *vi* 达到性高潮

orgasmic /ɔːˈgæzmɪk/ *adj* 1 lit 性高潮的 2 fig colloq (enjoyable, exciting) 极度兴奋的

orgiastic /ˌɔːdʒɪˈæstɪk/ *adj* 纵欲的 ‹*scene*›; 狂欢的 ‹*dancing*›

orgy /ˈɔːdʒi/ *n* 1 (wild party) 纵酒狂欢会 2 fig (of spending) 放纵; (of violence, killing) 肆意

Orient /ˈɔːrɪənt/ *pr n liter* **the ~** 东方国家

orient /ˈɔːrɪənt/

A *vt* **1** lit (position, align) 使朝向; **the greenhouses are ~ed east-west** 温室是东西向延长的 **2** fig (tailor) 使适应; **magazines ~ed to the business community** 面向商界的杂志

B *v refl* **to ~ oneself** (get one's bearings) 确定方位; fig 熟悉环境; **to ~ oneself in one's new school** 熟悉新学校的环境

oriental, Oriental /ˌɔːrɪˈentl/

A *adj* 东方的 ‹*art, country, cookery*›; 东方人的 ‹*customs, features, ancestry*›

B *n dated* 东方人

orientalist /ˌɔːrɪˈentəlɪst/ ▸**p. 409** *n* 东方学专家

orientate /ˈɔːrɪənteɪt/ *vt, v refl* **= orient**

-orientated /-ˈɔːrɪenteɪtɪd/ *combining form* **= -oriented**

orientation /ˌɔːrɪənˈteɪʃn/ *n* **1** [u] (of student, employee) 培训 **2** [c] (of church, vessel) 定向 **3** [c] (political) 态度; (sexual) 取向

orientation: **~ course** *n* (for new employees) 上岗培训课; (for new students) 迎新情况介绍课; **~ week** *n* esp Amer, Austral 新生熟悉学校情况周

-oriented /-ˈɔːrɪentɪd/ *combining form* 以…为方向的; **customer/family/user~** 面向顾客/家庭/用户的; **defence/profit~** 以防御/营利为目的的

orienteering /ˌɔːrɪənˈtɪərɪŋ/ *n* [u] 定向越野赛

orifice /ˈɒrɪfɪs/ *n* [尤指身体上的] 孔

origami /ˌɒrɪˈɡɑːmi/ *n* [u] 日本折纸艺术

origin /ˈɒrɪdʒɪn/ *n* **1** (of goods) 产地; (of custom, word) 起源; **the problem has its ~(s) in ...** 问题的根源在于…; **of unknown ~** 产地不明的; **in ~** 在起源上; **the gun is French in ~** 这种枪原产于法国 **2** **origins** *pl* (parentage) 出身; **his family has its ~s in Scotland** 他的家族原籍苏格兰; **humble/noble ~s** 卑微/高贵的出身

original /əˈrɪdʒənl/

A *adj* **1** (initial) 最早的 ‹*inhabitant*›; 原来的 ‹*plan, site*›; **the film in the ~ version** 这部电影的原版 **2** (not copied) 非复制的; **~ receipt/manuscript** 原始收据/原稿 **3** (innovative) 有独创性的; **an ~ thinker/design** 有独到见解的思想家/有创意的设计

B *n* **1** (painting, letter) 原件; **to read sth. in the ~** 读某物的原文 **2** (eccentric person) 怪人

originality /əˌrɪdʒəˈnæləti/ *n* [u] 独创性

originally /əˈrɪdʒənəli/ *adv* **1** (initially) 起初 **2** (innovatively) 独创地

original sin *n* [u] 原罪

originate /əˈrɪdʒɪneɪt/

A *vi* 起源; **to ~ in** *or* **from sth.** 源于某事物; **to ~ with sb.** 始自某人

B *vt* 创作 ‹*character, artwork*›; 引发 ‹*craze, idea*›; 发明 ‹*invention, system*›; 编造 ‹*rumour*›

originator /əˈrɪdʒɪneɪtə(r)/ *n* (of character, artwork) 创作人; (of craze, idea) 创始人; (of invention, system) 发明者; (of rumour) 编造者

Orion /əˈraɪən/ *pr n* 猎户星座

Orkney /ˈɔːkni/ *n* (*also* **the ~s, the ~ Islands**) 奥克尼群岛 [苏格兰东北海岸以外的群岛]

ornament

A /ˈɔːnəmənt/ *n* **1** [u] (decoration) 装饰; **(only) for ~** （只是）装饰性的 **2** [c] (trinket) 小饰物

B /ˈɔːnəment/ *vt* 装饰; **to ~ sth. with sth.** 用某物装饰某物

ornamental /ˌɔːnəˈmentl/ *adj* 观赏性的 ‹*tree, plant*›; 装饰性的 ‹*button, design*›

ornamentation /ˌɔːnəmenˈteɪʃn/ *n* [u] 装饰

ornate /ɔːˈneɪt/ *adj* **1** (elaborately decorated) 华美的 ‹*carvings, vase*›; 华丽的 ‹*chandelier, tapestry*›; 豪华的 ‹*furniture, building*› **2** (complicated) 词藻华丽的 ‹*prose, verse, style*›

ornately /ɔːˈneɪtli/ *adv* 华丽地 ‹*decorated*›; 豪华地 ‹*designed*›; **~ carved furniture** 精雕细刻的家具

ornery /ˈɔːnəri/ *adj* Amer colloq 脾气坏的 ‹*person*›; 野性十足的 ‹*animal*›

ornithological /ˌɔːnɪθəˈlɒdʒɪkl/ *adj* 鸟类学的

ornithologist /ˌɔːnɪˈθɒlədʒɪst/ ▸**p. 409** *n* (scientist) 鸟类学家; (enthusiast) 鸟类爱好者

ornithology /ˌɔːnɪˈθɒlədʒi/ *n* [u] 鸟类学

orphan /ˈɔːfn/

A *n* 孤儿; **a little ~ boy/girl** 父母双亡的小男孩/小女孩

B *vt* 使…成为孤儿 ‹*child*›; 使…失去母兽 ‹*animal*›

orphanage /ˈɔːfənɪdʒ/ *n* 孤儿院

orrery /ˈɒrəri/ *n* 太阳系仪

orthodontic /ˌɔːθəˈdɒntɪk/ *adj attrib* 正牙术的; **~ treatment/clinic** 矫牙治疗/诊所

orthodontics /ˌɔːθəˈdɒntɪks/ *npl + v sing* 正牙术

orthodontist /ˌɔːθəˈdɒntɪst/ ▸**p. 409** *n* 正牙医生

orthodox /ˈɔːθədɒks/ *adj* **1** (gen) 传统的 ‹*medicine*›; 普遍接受的 ‹*view, theory*›; 规范的 ‹*behaviour*› **2** **Orthodox** Relig 正统信仰的; **O~ Jews/Christians/Muslims** 正统的犹太/基督/伊斯兰教徒

Orthodox Church *n* **the ~** 正教; **the Greek/Russian ~** 希腊/俄罗斯正教

orthodoxy /ˈɔːθədɒksi/ *n* **1** [c] (belief) 正统信仰; (theory) 正统理论 **2** [u] (state, quality) 正统性

orthographic /ˌɔːθəˈɡræfɪk/, **orthographical** /ˌɔːθəˈɡræfɪkl/ *adj* 拼写的; **an ~ error/system** 拼写错误/拼写法

orthographically /ˌɔːθəˈɡræfɪkli/ *adv* 在拼写上; **~ correct** 拼写正确

orthography /ɔːˈθɒɡrəfi/ *n* [u] **1** (spelling system) 拼写体系 **2** (study of spelling) 拼写学

orthopaedic /ˌɔːθəˈpiːdɪk/ *adj attrib* Brit 整形外科的; **~ surgeon/hospital** 整形外科医生/医院

orthopaedics /ˌɔːθəˈpiːdɪks/ *npl + v sing* Brit 整形外科; **the ~ department** 整形外科

orthopaedist /ˌɔːθəˈpiːdɪst/ ▸**p. 409** *n* Brit 整形外科医师

orthopedic /ˌɔːθəˈpiːdɪk/ *adj attrib* Amer **= orthopaedic**

orthopedics /ˌɔːθəˈpiːdɪks/ *npl + v sing* Amer **= orthopaedics**

orthopedist /ˌɔːθəˈpiːdɪst/ *n* Amer **= orthopaedist**

Orwellian /ɔːˈwelɪən/ *adj* 奥威尔式的 ‹*language, prediction*›; 极权的 ‹*world*›

oryx /ˈɒrɪks, Amer ˈɔːr-/ *n* (*pl* **oryx**) [非洲的] 大羚羊

OS *abbr* **1** Brit Geog **= Ordnance Survey** **2** Fashn **= outsize** **3** Comput **= operating system**

Oscar /ˈɒskə(r)/ *n* 奥斯卡金像奖; ▸**Academy Award**

Oscar-winning *adj attrib* 获奥斯卡金像奖的 ‹*role, film, actress*›

oscillate /ˈɒsɪleɪt/ *vi* **1** Tech, Phys «*pendulum, pointer*» 摆动; «*current, radio wave*» 振荡 **2** fig (fluctuate) «*person, feelings*» 摇摆; **to ~ between sth. and sth.** 在某事和某事之间摇摆

oscillation /ˌɒsɪˈleɪʃn/ *n* **1** [u] (of pendulum, pointer) 摆动 **2** [u] (of radio wave) 振荡 **3** [c] (single movement) 振幅

oscillator /ˈɒsɪleɪtə(r)/ *n* 振荡器

oscillograph /əˈsɪləɡrɑːf, Amer -ɡræf/ *n* [记录用] 示波器

oscilloscope /əˈsɪləskəʊp/ *n* [显示用] 示波器

OSHA *abbr* Amer **= Occupational Safety and Health Administration** 职业安全和健康署

osier /ˈəʊzɪə(r), Amer ˈəʊʒər/ *n* 青刚柳; **an ~ basket/chair** 柳条篮/椅

Oslo /ˈɒzləʊ/ *pr n* 奥斯陆

osmium /ˈɒzmɪəm/ *n* [u] 锇

osmosis /ɒzˈməʊsɪs/ *n* [u] **1** Biol, Chem 渗透; **by ~** 经透析 **2** fig (gradual acceptance of ideas etc.) 潜移默化; **by ~** 通过潜移默化

osmotic /ɒzˈmɒtɪk/ *adj* 渗透的; **~ pressure/action** 渗透压力/作用

osprey /ˈɒspreɪ/ *n* 鹗

Ossetia /ɒˈsiːʃə/ *pr n* [高加索中部的] 奥塞梯

ossicle /ˈɒsɪkl/ *n* 小骨 [尤指听小骨]

ossification /ˌɒsɪfɪˈkeɪʃn/ *n* **1** [u] (transformation into bone) 骨化 **2** [c] (bony formation) 成骨 **3** [u] fig (of attitudes, system) 僵化

ossify /ˈɒsɪfaɪ/

A *vi* **1** Anat «*cartilage, tendon*» 骨化 **2** fig «*attitudes, system*» 僵化

B *vt* **1** Anat 使…骨化 ‹*cartilage*› **2** fig 使…僵化 ‹*system, tradition*›; **to be/become ossified** 僵化/变得僵化

ostensible /ɒˈstensəbl/ *adj attrib* 表面的 ‹*purpose*›; 假托的 ‹*reason*›; 貌似真实的 ‹*intention*›

ostensibly /ɒˈstensəbli/ *adv* 表面上

ostentation /ˌɒstenˈteɪʃn/ *n* [u] [对财富等的] 炫耀

ostentatious /ˌɒstenˈteɪʃəs/ *adj* 炫耀的 ‹*person*›; 卖弄的 ‹*display*›; 浮华的 ‹*lifestyle*›

ostentatiously /ˌɒstenˈteɪʃəsli/ *adv* 炫耀地

osteoarthritis /ˌɒstɪəʊɑːˈθraɪtɪs/ *n* [u] 骨关节炎

osteomyelitis /ˌɒstɪəʊmaɪˈlaɪtɪs/ *n* [u] 骨髓炎

osteopath /ˈɒstɪəpæθ/ ▸**p. 409** *n* 整骨医生

osteopathy /ˌɒstɪˈɒpəθi/ *n* [u] 整骨术

osteoporosis /ˌɒstɪəʊpəˈrəʊsɪs/ ▸**p. 377** *n* [u] 骨质疏松症

ostler /ˈɒslə(r)/ ▸**p. 409** *n* archaic [旧时客栈的] 马夫

ostracism /ˈɒstrəsɪzəm/ *n* [u] 排斥

ostracize /ˈɒstrəsaɪz/ *vt* 排斥 ‹*person, colleague*›; **to be ~d from sth.** 被排斥于某事之外

ostrich /ˈɒstrɪtʃ/ *n* **1** (bird) 鸵鸟; **~ feather/egg** 鸵鸟羽毛/蛋 **2** fig (person) 逃避现实的人

OT *abbr* **= Old Testament**

OTE *abbr* **= on-target earnings**

other /ˈʌðə(r)/

A *adj attrib* **1** (remaining, additional) 其他的; **the ~ one** 另一个; **the ~ children** 其他孩子; **~ possibilities** 其他的可能; **my ~ sister** 我另一个姐姐; **at all ~ times** 在其他任何时间; **both his ~ brothers** 他的另外两个兄弟; **to make one ~ suggestion** 再提一个建议; **to have only one ~ shirt** 只有一件多余的衬衫; **a plant found in, among ~ places, Japan** 一种生长在日本等地的植物; **the ~ world** 来世 **2** (different) 别的; **some ~ child** 某个别的孩子; **~ people** 别人; **to go some ~ time/day** 另找时间去/改天去; **in ~ words** 换句话说; **the ~ woman** (mistress) 别的女人 **3** (opposite) 另一边的; **on the ~ side of the street** 在街对面; **at the ~ end of ...** 在…的另一端 **4** (alternative) **the ~ ...** 另一种…; **he found me, not the ~ way around** 他找到了我，而不是我找到了他 **5** (recent) **the ~ day/week** 那天/那周 **6** (alternate) **every ~ ...** 每隔一…; **every ~ week/year** 每隔一周/一年; **every ~ word was a swear word** 动辄张口骂人

B *pron* **1** **(the) ~s** *pl* (the rest, different ones) 其他

的; **to be quicker than (any of) the ~s** 比（任何）其他的都快; **he doesn't like upsetting ~s** 他不喜欢烦扰别人; **a family like many ~s** 一个很平常的家庭; **X, Y, and ~s** X、Y 等等; **Anna, among ~s, has been chosen** 安娜等人入选了; **show me some ~s** 再给我看几个 [2] (alternate, additional one) **the ~** 另一个; **to raise first one hand and then the ~** 先举起一只手，然后再举起另一只; **both of them distrust the ~** 他俩相互不信任; **one after the ~** 交替地; **I love you and no ~** 我只爱你一个人; **one or ~** 其中一个; **one or ~ of them will phone** 他们中有人会打电话的; **a bit of the ~** Brit colloq 男女之事 [3] (expressing uncertainty) **or ~** 或其他; **somebody or ~ from head office** 总部来的某个人; **for some reason or ~** 由于某种原因; **he's called Bob something or ~** 他名叫鲍勃什么的 [4] (opposite) **the ~** (side) 对面; (end) 另一端; (direction) 反方向; **I went one way, and they went the ~** 我走一条路，他们走另一条路

[C] **other than** *prep phr* [1] (except) 除…之外; **to have no choice ~ than to ...** 别无选择，只能… [2] (anything/anyone but) **he could scarcely be ~ than relieved** 他不能不放心了; **it's none ~ than the Pope!** 正是教皇本人!

otherness /ˈʌðənɪs/ *n* [u] 相异

otherwise /ˈʌðəwaɪz/

[A] *adv* [1] (in other respects) 在其他方面; (in other circumstances) 在其他情况下; **a lonely but ~ happy childhood** 孤单但除此之外还算幸福的童年; **to say what one ~ would keep to oneself** 说出原本会憋在心里的话 [2] (in another way) 以其他方式; **tell him I'm ~ engaged** 告诉他我在忙别的事; **to improve or ~ change the design** 改进或者改变设计; **William, ~ known as Bill** 威廉，也叫比尔 [3] (to the contrary) 与此不同; **no woman, married or ~** 没有女性，无论已婚还是未婚; **he says ..., but I know ~** 他说…，但我知道并非如此; **~ than** 除了

[B] *conj* 否则; **it's quite safe, ~ I wouldn't do it** 这相当安全，不然我不会做这事的

[C] *adj pred* formal 不同的; **I would that it were ~** 我真希望事情不是这个样子

otherworldly /ˌʌðəˈwɜːldlɪ/ *adj* [1] 超脱世俗的 ‹*creature*›; 超自然的 ‹*quality, beauty*› [2] = **unworldly**

otiose /ˈəʊtɪəʊs, Amer ˈəʊʃɪ-/ *adj* 无用的

OTT *abbr* Brit colloq = **over-the-top**

Ottawa /ˈɒtəwə/ *pr n* 渥太华

otter /ˈɒtə(r)/ *n* 水獭

Ottoman /ˈɒtəmən/

[A] *adj* (of the dynasty) 奥斯曼王朝的; (of the empire) 奥斯曼帝国的; **the ~ Empire** 奥斯曼帝国

[B] *n* (*pl* **~s**) 奥斯曼土耳其人

ottoman /ˈɒtəmən/ *n* 软垫凳

OU *abbr* Brit = **Open University**

ouch /aʊtʃ/ *excl* 哎呦 [表示突然的剧痛]

ought /ɔːt/ *modal aux* [1] (indicating obligation, advice) 应该; **I ~ not to have been so direct** 我本不该这么直截了当; **should I apologize? — yes, you ~ to** 我该道歉吗？——对，你应当道歉; **you ~ to see a doctor** 你得去看医生; **~n't we to consult them first?** 我们不应该先和他们商量一下吗? [2] (indicating probability) 应该会; **sb. ~ to do sth.** 某人应该会做某事; **that ~ to fix it** 那样应该能搞定; **things ~ to improve by next week** 到下周情况应该有所改善; **the train ~ not to have left yet** 火车应该还没发车 [3] (prefacing important point) 应当; **sb. ~ to do sth.** 某人应当做某事; **I ~ to say perhaps that ...** 也许我应当说…; **I think you ~ to know that ...** 我想你应当知道…

Ouija board® /ˈwiːdʒə bɔːd/ *n* 灵应牌 [用于降灵会中接受亡魂传递的信息]

ounce /aʊns/ ▸**p. 909** *n* [1] (weight) 盎司 [2] (fluid) 液盎司 [3] fig (small amount) 一点点; **there's not an ~ of truth in what he says** 他的话一点都不真实

our /ˈaʊə(r), ɑː(r)/ ▸**p. 487** *det* [1] (belonging to us or to people in general) 我们的; **~ parents** 我们的父母; **~ modern world** 我们的现代世界; **~ brains** 我们的大脑; **Our Father** Relig 上帝 [2] (royal use) 朕的; (editorial use) 本报刊的; **~ journal** 本刊

ours /ˈaʊəz, ɑːz/ ▸**p. 487** *pron* 我们的; **which tickets are ~?** 哪些票是我们的？; **she's a friend of ~** 她是我们的朋友; **~ is not an easy task** 我们的任务不容易

ourself /aʊəˈself, ɑːˈself/ *pron* 我们自己 [在we泛指人们时用以代替ourselves]

ourselves /aʊəˈselvz, ɑːˈselvz/ *pron* [1] (reflexive) 我们自己; **to see ~ as others see us** 以别人的眼光看我们自己; **(all) by ~** (alone) 单独地; (without help) 独立地 [2] (emphatic) 我们亲自; **we decorated the house ~** 我们亲手粉刷了房屋 [3] (normal selves) 我们的正常情况; **we aren't (feeling) ~ today** 我们今天（感觉）有点不舒服; **we can't be ~ when our parents are around** 在父母身边我们就不能无拘无束了

oust /aʊst/ *vt* 把…赶下台 ‹*dictator, chairman*›; 推翻 ‹*government, regime*›

out /aʊt/

[A] *adv* [1] (outside) 在外面; **standing ~ in the rain** 站在外面的雨中; **~ there/here** 在外面那边/这边; **to be ~ and about** 外出走动; **to be ~ on bail** 被保释出狱 [2] (for social activity) 外出; **to invite sb. ~** 邀请某人外出; **a night ~** 外出的一晚上; **a day ~ at the seaside** 去海边的一天 [3] (from within, from source, into view) 出来; **to go or walk ~** 走出去; **to find one's way ~** 找到出去的路; **get ~!** 滚出去!; **'Out'** "出口"; **I want ~!** colloq 我要解脱!; **to stare ~ at sth.** 向外凝视某物; **~ from under sth.** 从某物下面出来; **to take a cushion ~ from under sb.'s head** 从某人的头下抽出垫子; **to draw ~ £500 from the bank** 从银行取出 500 英镑; **to be/come ~** ‹*sun, stars*› 出现; **to stick one's tongue ~** 伸出舌头 [4] (away, at a distance) 离开; **two days ~ from port/camp** 离开港口/营地的两天; **to live ~ in the country** 住到乡下; **to be ~ at sea** 出海; **when he was ~ in the Middle East** 当他远在中东时; **a cold front ~ in the Atlantic** 大西洋上的一股冷锋; **to score from 70 metres ~** Sport 在距球门 70 米远处射门得分 [5] (not present) **to be ~** 不在; **to be/go ~ shopping** 外出/出门购物; **to be ~ (on loan)** 借出去; **to be/come ~ (on strike)** Ind 罢工; **the jury was still ~** 陪审团还在商议 [6] (published, made public) 公开; **to be ~** ‹*book*› 出版; ‹*film, CD*› 发行; ‹*results, news*› 公布; Jur ‹*warrant*› 发出; **his secret is ~** 他的秘密已经泄露; **truth will ~** Prov 真相会水落石出的 [7] (in bloom) **to be ~** ‹*flower*› 开放; **the trees were ~** (in leaf) 树发芽了; (in blossom) 树开花了 [8] (openly homosexual) **to be ~** 出柜 [指公开同性恋身份] [9] (removed) 除掉; **to get the marks ~** 除掉痕迹; **to have one's stitches ~** 拆线 [10] (extinguished) **to be ~** ‹*fire*› 熄灭; **lights ~ at 10.30 p.m.** 晚上 10 点半熄灯 [11] (over) 结束; **to be ~** ‹*year, season*› 结束; ‹*school*› 放假; **before the week's ~** 在本周内 [12] colloq (unfashionable) **to be ~** ‹*style, garment*› 过时 [13] colloq (not possible) **to be ~** ‹*option, idea*› 不可取 [14] Games, Sport **to be ~** ‹*ball, shot*› 出界; ‹*player*› 出局 [15] Pol **to be ~** ‹*party, person*› 下台; **Tories ~!** 保守党下台! [16] dated (into society) **to be/come ~** ‹*debutante*› 初次参加社交活动 [17] (so as to displace) 脱离; **to pull a tooth ~** 拔牙; **to put one's shoulder ~** 肩关节脱臼 [18] (aloud) 大声地; **to cry/scream ~** 大声呼喊/尖叫; **to speak ~ (about sth.)** 大声说（某事物）; **to say sth. right or straight ~** 直截了当地说某事物; **~ with it!** colloq 说出来啊! [19] (completely) 完全地; **to wipe ~ the bath** 擦干净浴缸 [20] colloq (in search of) **to be ~ to do sth./for sth.** 试图做某事/得到某物; **to be ~ for revenge** 想要报复 [21] = **over**[1] **B 12** [22] Brit (incorrect) **to be ~** 出错; **to be ~ in one's calculations** 计算有误; **to be 3 degrees ~, to be ~ by 3 degrees** 有3度的偏差; **my watch is two minutes ~** 我的手表差了两分钟 [23] Brit colloq (ever) **he's the kindest/stupidest person ~** 他是个极其善良/愚蠢透顶的人 [24] colloq (worn through) **to be ~ at the elbows/knees** ‹*garment*› 肘部/膝盖穿破了

[B] *prep* colloq 从…里出来; **to run ~ the door** 跑出门外

[C] **an out** *n* colloq 出路; **to leave sb. an ~** 给某人留退路; **to look for an ~** 找借口

[D] *vt* colloq 使…出柜 ‹*person*›

[E] **out of** *prep phr* [1] (outwards from) 从…里出来; **to go ~ of the house** 走出房子; **to come ~ of hospital/prison** 出院/出狱; **to look ~ of the window** 向窗外看; **I'm ~ of here!** colloq 我走了!; **get ~ of my/the way!** 让开! [2] (removed from) 从…里拿出来; **to tear a page ~ of a book** 从书上撕下一页; **to take money ~ of the bank** 从银行取钱 [3] (obtained from, part of) 出自; **to drink beer ~ of the bottle** 对着瓶口喝啤酒; **to pay for sth. ~ of one's savings** 用积蓄支付某物; **what do I get ~ of it?** colloq 我从中能得到什么?; **one chapter ~ of a novel** 小说中的一章; **like something ~ of a nightmare** 犹如一场恶梦 [4] (beyond limit of) 超出; **~ of reach/sight** 在手够不到的地方/在视线范围之外; **several miles ~ of London** 离伦敦几英里远; **to live ~ of town** 住在城外 [5] (sheltering from) 避开 ‹*weather, heat*›; **to come in ~ of the rain/sun** 进来躲雨/躲阴凉 [6] (not in condition of) 不在…状态; **to be ~ of control/danger** 失去控制/脱离危险; **it's ~ of the question** 这不可能; **to be ~ of it** colloq (unconscious) 不省人事; (muddled) 昏头昏脑; **to feel/look ~ of it** colloq 感到格格不入/看上去像局外人; **to grow ~ of it** 慢慢放弃习惯; **get ~ (of it)!** colloq 胡说! [7] (made from) **to be made ~ of sth.** 由…制成 ‹*wood, metal*›; **a statue made ~ of bronze** 青铜雕像 [8] (due to) 由于 ‹*malice, respect*› [9] (lacking) 缺乏; **to be ~ of work/luck** 失业/不走运 [10] (excluded from) **to be ~ of sth.** 被排除在…之外 ‹*market, organization*› [11] (expressing ratio) **one ~ of (every) five students** （每）五个学生中的一个 [12] Equit (foaled by) …所生; **Rapido ~ of Lightning** "闪电"所生的"飞驰"

outage /ˈaʊtɪdʒ/ *n* 运行中断; **a power/network ~** 停电/网络中断

out and away *adv* 远远超过地; **he's ~ the best athlete** 他绝对是最好的运动员

out-and-out *adj attrib* 彻头彻尾的 ‹*liar, reactionary*›; 十足的 ‹*fool, crook*›; 完全的 ‹*defeat, success*›

outback /ˈaʊtbæk/ *n* **the ~** [尤指澳大利亚的]内陆地区

outbalance /ˌaʊtˈbæləns/ *vt* [在价值、重要性或影响上] 超过

outbid /ˌaʊtˈbɪd/ *vt* (*pres p* **-dd-**; *pt, pp* **outbid**) 出价高于

outboard /ˈaʊtbɔːd/

[A] *n* (engine) 舷外发动机; (boat) 尾挂机船

[B] *adj* [1] (removable) 舷外的 ‹*motor*› [2] (away from centre) 外侧的 ‹*engine, wing panels*›

outbound /ˈaʊtbaʊnd/ *adj* 往外地的 ‹*traffic, travel*›; 出港的 ‹*passenger, flight*›

out-box *n* 发件箱

outbreak /ˈaʊtbreɪk/ *n* 爆发; **an ~ of rain** 突降大雨; **an ~ of disease** 疾病的爆发; **at the ~ of war** 战争爆发的时候

outbuilding /ˈaʊtbɪldɪŋ/ *n* 附属建筑物

outburst /ˈaʊtbɜːst/ *n* (of laughter) 突然发出; (of energy, anger) 爆发; (of vandalism, trouble) 突然发生; **please refrain from further ~s** 请不要再情绪冲动

outcast /ˈaʊtkɑːst, Amer -kæst/ *n* 被抛弃者; **a social ~** 社会弃儿

outclass /ˌaʊtˈklɑːs, Amer -ˈklæs/ *vt* 远远超过

outcome /ˈaʊtkʌm/ *n* 结果

outcrop /ˈaʊtkrɒp/ *n* [岩石等的] 露出地面部分

outcry /ˈaʊtkraɪ/ *n* 强烈的抗议; **there was an ~ against the new airport** 新机场引发了强烈的抗议

outdated /ˌaʊtˈdeɪtɪd/ *adj* 陈旧的 ‹*idea, concept*›; 过时的 ‹*design, technology*›

outdistance /ˌaʊtˈdɪstəns/ *vt* lit 把…抛在后面; fig 远远超过

outdo /ˌaʊtˈduː/ *vt* (*pt* **outdid**, *pp* **outdone**) 胜过; **to ~ oneself** 超过自己原有水平; **not to be outdone, she redoubled her efforts** 为了不被人超过，她付出了加倍的努力

outdoor /ˈaʊtdɔː(r)/ *adj attrib* 户外的 ‹*activity, life*›; 户外穿的 ‹*clothes, shoes*›; 喜欢户外活动的 ‹*person*›; 露天的 ‹*swimming pool*›

outdoors /ˌaʊtˈdɔːz/

A *adv* 在露天 ‹*sleep*›; 在户外 ‹*play*›; 在野外 ‹*work*›; **to go ~** 出门

B *n* [u] 户外; **the great ~** 旷野

outer /ˈaʊtə(r)/ *adj attrib* **1** (further from the inside) 外围的; (further from the centre) 远离中心的; **~ planets** 带外行星 **2** (outside) 外边的; **~ walls/garments/surface** 外墙/外衣/外表

outermost /ˈaʊtəməʊst/ *adj* **1** (furthest) 最远的 ‹*planet*›; 离中心最远的 ‹*district*› **2** (outside) 最外面的 ‹*layer*›

outer: ~ space *n* [u] 外层空间; **~ suburbs** *npl* 远郊

outerwear /ˈaʊtəweə(r)/ *n* [u] Amer 外衣

outface /ˌaʊtˈfeɪs/ *vt* 凛然面对; **to try to ~ each other** 试图吓退对方

outfall /ˈaʊtfɔːl/ *n* 排放口

outfield /ˈaʊtfiːld/ *n* 外场; **an ~ player/position** 外场手/位置

outfit /ˈaʊtfɪt/

A *n* **1** (set of clothes) 全套服装; **a wedding/tennis ~** 一套结婚礼服/网球服 **2** colloq (company) 公司; (group) 团队

B *vt* (*pres p etc.* **-tt-**) 装备

outfitter /ˈaʊtfɪtə(r)/ ▸**p. 409** *n* **1** esp Brit dated (clothes vendor) 服装零售商; **ladies'/men's ~** 女装/男装供应商; **an ~'s** 服装店 **2** esp Amer (supplier) 提供装备者

outflank /ˌaʊtˈflæŋk/ *vt* **1** Mil 侧翼包抄 **2** fig (gain advantage over) [尤指出其不意地] 胜过

outflow /ˈaʊtfləʊ/ *n* [u and c] 外流

outfox /ˌaʊtˈfɒks/ *vt* colloq 智胜

outgoing /ˈaʊtgəʊɪŋ/ *adj* **1** (sociable) 友好的 ‹*nature, person*›; 外向的 ‹*type, personality*› **2** *attrib* (departing) 离开的 ‹*ship*›; 离任的 ‹*chairman*›; 外发的 ‹*mail*›; **the ~ tide** 退潮; **an ~ call** 打出去的电话

outgoings /ˈaʊtgəʊɪŋz/ *npl* Brit 开支

outgrow /ˌaʊtˈgrəʊ/ *vt* (*pt* **outgrew**, *pp* **outgrown**) **1** (grow too big for) 长得穿不下 ‹*clothes*›; 增长得容不进 ‹*room*›; **to ~ one's resources** 发展得太快而资源不够用 **2** (grow too old for) 因长大而放弃 ‹*activity, way of life*›; 因长大而不再有 ‹*interest, habit*›; **don't worry, he'll ~ it** 别担心，随着年龄的增长，他会改掉的 **3** (grow taller than) 长得比…高

outgrowth /ˈaʊtgrəʊθ/ *n* **1** Bot, Anat 长出物 **2** fig (development) 发展结果

outguess /ˌaʊtˈges/ *vt* 猜透…的意图

outgun /ˌaʊtˈgʌn/ *vt* (*pres p etc.* **-nn-**) **1** Mil (surpass in firepower) 在火力上压过 **2** (shoot better than) 枪打得比…更准 **3** fig (surpass) 胜过

outhouse /ˈaʊthaʊs/ *n* 外围建筑

outing /ˈaʊtɪŋ/ *n* **1** [u] (excursion) 短途旅游; **to go on an ~** 去远足 **2** [u] (revealing homosexuality) 同性恋身份的曝光

outlandish /ˌaʊtˈlændɪʃ/ *adj* 稀奇古怪的 ‹*habit, views, tale, affair*›; **~ clothes/theory** 奇装异服/离奇的理论

outlast /ˌaʊtˈlɑːst, Amer -læst/ *vt* 比…更长久

outlaw /ˈaʊtlɔː/

A *n* 被剥夺法律权益者; **a band of ~s** 一伙亡命之徒

B *vt* 宣布…为非法 ‹*activity, organization, drug*›

outlay /ˈaʊtleɪ/ *n* 开支; **an initial ~ of £200** 200 英镑的初始费用

outlet /ˈaʊtlet/ *n* **1** (for gas, air, water) 出口; **an ~ pipe** 排放管 **2** Comm (market) 市场; (shop) 商店 **3** fig (for energy, emotion, talent) 出路; **an ~ for one's energies/talents** 发泄精力/施展才能的方法 **4** Elec 电源插座

outlet valve *n* 排放阀

outline /ˈaʊtlaɪn/

A *n* **1** (of object) (of mountain, tree, face) 轮廓; (sketch) 略图; **to draw sth. in ~** 画某物的轮廓; **an ~ drawing/plan** 轮廓画/略图 **2** (general description, synopsis) 提纲; (main facts or points) 梗概; **in ~** 扼要地; **to give a broad** *or* **general ~ of sth.** 概要地说明某事物; **An O~ of World History** 《世界史大纲》

B *vt* **1** (delineate) 画…的轮廓 ‹*shape, figure*›; **to be ~d against the sky** 显示出在天空映衬下的轮廓 **2** (give general summary of) 概述 ‹*situation, aims*›

outline: ~ agreement *n* 协议纲要; **~ map** *n* 轮廓图; **~ planning permission** *n* [u] Brit 初步规划许可

outlive /ˌaʊtˈlɪv/ *vt* (live longer than) 比…活得长 ‹*person*›; 活过 ‹*period*›; **to ~ one's/its usefulness** 已失去作用

outlook /ˈaʊtlʊk/ *n* **1** (attitude) 观点; **to have a narrow/positive/healthy ~ on sth.** 对某事的看法狭隘/积极/健康; **to change one's ~ on life** 改变人生观 **2** (future prospects) 前景; Meteorol 天气形势; **the ~ for trade/the weekend** 贸易前景/周末的天气形势 **3** (view) 景色

outlying /ˈaʊtlaɪɪŋ/ *adj attrib* (away from centre) 远离市中心的 ‹*suburbs, areas*›; (remote) 偏远的 ‹*territory, island*›

outmanoeuvre Brit, **outmaneuver** Amer /ˌaʊtməˈnuːvə(r)/ *vt* 在谋略上胜过 ‹*opponent, army*›; **to ~ one's critics** fig 对批评者应付自如

outmoded /ˌaʊtˈməʊdɪd/ *adj* pej 过时的 ‹*idea, system*›; 陈旧的 ‹*technique, equipment*›

outnumber /ˌaʊtˈnʌmbə(r)/ *vt* 在数量上超过; **they were ~ed by two to one** 他们在人数上被超过了一倍

out of bounds *adv* **1** (off limits) 不可进入的; **to be ~ to sb.** 某人不得进入 **2** (in golf) 界外的

out-of-court settlement *n* 庭外和解

out-of-date *adj* 过时的 ‹*clothes, ticket*›; 过期的 ‹*passport, timetable*›; 陈旧的 ‹*technology, facilities*›

out of doors *adv* = **outdoors A**

out-of-pocket *adj attrib* 需现金支付的; **~ expenses** 实付费用

out-of-the-ordinary *adj* 不同寻常的 ‹*idea, book*›; **nothing ~ ever happens here** 这里从未发生离奇的事情

out-of-the-way *adj* 偏僻的 ‹*location, corner, cafe, village*›

outpace /ˌaʊtˈpeɪs/ *vt* lit 在速度上超过; fig 超过

outpatient /ˈaʊtpeɪʃnt/ *n* 门诊病人; **the ~ department** 门诊部

outplacement /ˈaʊtpleɪsmənt/ *n* [u] [为被解雇员工实施的] 再就业安置

outplay /ˌaʊtˈpleɪ/ *vt* 打得比…好; **the Australian team was ~ed by the opposition** 澳大利亚队被对手击败

outpoint /ˌaʊtˈpɔɪnt/ *vt* «*boxer*» 以点数击败

outpost /ˈaʊtpəʊst/ *n* Mil 前哨基地; (gen) 边远居民点; **the last ~ of imperialism** 帝国主义的最后一个堡垒

outpouring /ˈaʊtpɔːrɪŋ/ *n* **1** (flood) 喷涌; **a massive ~ of gamma rays** 伽马射线的大规模喷发 **2** (of emotion) 迸发; **an ~ of grief** 悲伤情绪的宣泄

output /ˈaʊtpʊt/

A *n* **1** [u and c] Comm, Ind 产量 **2** [u] Electron, Mech 输出功率; **an ~ signal** 输出信号 **3** [u] Comput 输出 **4** [u] (of composer, writer) 作品

B *vt* (*pres p* **-tt-**; *pt, pp* **output**) Comput 输出 ‹*data, results*›

outrage /ˈaʊtreɪdʒ/

A *n* **1** [u] (anger) 愤慨; **to express/feel/spark ~** 表示/感到/引发愤恨 **2** [c] (horrifying act) 暴行; **to commit ~s against the people** 对人民犯下暴行 **3** [c] (scandal) 侮辱; **an ~ against decency/dignity/justice** 对体面/尊严/正义的粗暴践踏

B *vt* 激怒 ‹*people, public opinion*›; 冒犯 ‹*sb.'s feelings, decency, dignity*›; **to be ~d at** *or* **by sth.** 因某事物感到愤慨

outrageous /ˌaʊtˈreɪdʒəs/ *adj* **1** (disgraceful) 可耻的 ‹*behaviour, language, demand*›; 骇人的 ‹*incident, lie, price*›; **it is ~ to do sth.** 做某事是可耻的 **2** (unconventional) 怪里怪气的 ‹*dress*›; 荒诞的 ‹*remark*› **3** (exaggerated) 肆无忌惮的 ‹*claim*›

outrageously /ˌaʊtˈreɪdʒəsli/ *adv* 怪里怪气地 ‹*dress*›; 骇人听闻地 ‹*suffer*›; 极端无礼地 ‹*behave*›; **~ expensive** 贵得吓人

outran /ˌaʊtˈræn/ *pt* ▸**outrun**

outrank /ˌaʊtˈræŋk/ *vt* 级别比…高

outré /ˈuːtreɪ, Amer uːˈtreɪ/ *adj* 反常的 ‹*behaviour, ideas*›; 怪异的 ‹*style, remarks*›

outreach /ˌaʊtˈriːtʃ/ *vt* **1** (reach further than) 超过 **2** (extend) 伸出 ‹*arms*›

outrider /ˈaʊtraɪdə(r)/ *n* (on motorcycle) 摩托护卫; (on horseback) 骑士护卫

outrigger /ˈaʊtrɪgə(r)/ *n* Naut **1** (structure) 舷外托架 **2** (boat) 有舷外托架的小船

outright /ˈaʊtraɪt/

A *adv* **1** (completely) 完全 ‹*win, deny, own*› **2** (openly) 直率地 ‹*say*›; **to laugh ~ at sb.** 公然嘲笑某人 **3** (instantly) 立刻 ‹*kill*›

B *adj attrib* **1** (absolute) 完全的 ‹*denial, ownership*›; 绝对的 ‹*control, majority*›; **~ sale/grant** 卖断/赠款 **2** (open) 公然的 ‹*lie, arrogance, opposition*›; (obvious) 毋庸置疑的 ‹*victory, winner*›

outrun /ˌaʊtˈrʌn/ *vt* (*pres p* **-nn-**; *pt* **outran** /ˌaʊtˈræn/; *pp* **outrun**) **1** lit (run faster than) 跑得比…快 **2** fig (exceed) 超出; **his ambition outran his ability** 他志大才疏

outsell /ˌaʊtˈsel/ *vt* (*pt, pp* **outsold**) 卖得比…多

outset /ˈaʊtset/ *n* [u] 开始; **at the ~** 起初; **from the ~** 从一开始

outshine /ˌaʊtˈʃaɪn/ *vt* (*pt, pp* **outshone** /ˌaʊtˈʃɒn/) 比…更出色

outside /ˌaʊtˈsaɪd, ˈaʊtsaɪd/

A *n* **1** (external space) 外面; **the ~ (of sth.)** (某物的) 外面; **to open from the ~** 从外面打开; **on the ~ (of sth.)** 在 (某物的) 外面; **to be on the ~ looking in** fig 被排除在外; **from the ~** fig 客观地看; **from the ~, I'd say ...** 客观地说，我认为… **2** (external surface) 外表; **the ~s of the windows** 窗户的外部; **a coat with fur on the ~** 翻毛外套; **on the ~** (appearance) 外表上; **on the ~ she looked calm** 她貌似镇定 **3** (outer world) 外界; **to bring in an expert from (the) ~** 外聘一名专家; **to smuggle sth. in from (the) ~** 将某物从外面私带进来 **4** Aut (of road) 外侧;

on the ~ (of sth.) 在（某物的）外侧; **to pass a car on the ~** 从外侧超车 **5** Sport (of curve) **the ~** 外圈; **to overtake sb. on the ~ (of the bend)** 在（弯道）外圈超过某人 **6** (maximum) **at the ~** 至多; **to cost £50 at the ~** 顶多要花 50 英镑

B *adj attrib* **1** (outdoor) 户外的〈*temperature, work*〉 **2** (exterior) 外部的; **the ~ wrapping/measurements** 外包装/外部尺寸 **3** (outer) 外侧的〈*track*〉; 靠走道的〈*seat*〉; **the ~ lane/rear wheel** Aut 外车道/外侧后轮; **the ~ edge of sth.** 某物的外侧边 **4** Telecom **an ~ line/call** 外线/外线电话 **5** Brit Radio, TV **an ~ broadcasting van/unit** 实况转播车/组 **6** (maximum) 最大的〈*amount*〉; 最高的〈*price*〉 **7** (beyond usual sphere) 通常领域以外的; **~ interest** 业余爱好; **the ~ world** 外界 **8** (from elsewhere) 来自外部的; **an ~ opinion** 局外人的意见; **~ help/contractors** 外援/外部承包商 **9** (slight) 微不足道的; **an ~ chance of winning** 微乎其微的获胜机会

C *prep* **1** (not within) 在…外面〈*door, boundary*〉; 在…之外〈*place, time, institution*〉; **to land ~ the line** 《*ball*》落在界外; **sex ~ marriage** 婚外性行为; **to go ~ the garden** 出花园; **to wear a shirt ~ one's trousers** 把衬衫穿在裤子外面 **2** (in front of) 在…前面〈*building*〉 **3** (near) 靠近〈*place*〉; **just ~ Sheffield** 就在设菲尔德附近 **4** (not included in) 不属于〈*organization, profession*〉; **public opinion ~ Parliament** 议会之外的舆论 **5** (beyond) 超过〈*limit, jurisdiction*〉; **to be ~ the range** 超出范围; **it's ~ her experience** fig 她没有这方面的经验 **6** (apart from) 除…以外〈*person, activity*〉; **she doesn't see anyone ~ her family** 除了自己的家人，她谁也不见

D *adv* **1** (position) 在外面; (movement toward) 朝外面; **the world ~** 外面的世界; **scenes shot ~** 在室外拍摄的场景; **a coat with fur ~** 翻毛外套; **if you'd like to step ~ ...** (in order to fight) 如果你想出去较量一下… **2** esp Amer **~ of ...** (not within) 在…的外面; (apart from) 除了…; **~ of the law** 超出法律范围

outside: ~ examiner *n* Brit 校外考官; **~ lane** *n* 外车道; **~ left** *n* 左边锋; **~ right** *n* 右边锋

outsider /ˌaʊtˈsaɪdə(r)/ *n* **1** (in community, organization) 外来者 **2** Sport (person) 不被看好的人; (horse) 不被看好的赛马; **he started as a rank ~** 他起步时完全不被看好

outsize /ˈaʊtsaɪz/ *adj attrib* 特大号的〈*clothing, packet*〉; 穿特大号服装的〈*people*〉; 经营特大号服装的〈*shop, department*〉

outsize load *n* 超载

outskirts /ˈaʊtskɜːts/ *npl* **1** (of town, city) 市郊; **on the ~ of London** 在伦敦市郊 **2** (of group) 边缘; **she hovered shyly on the ~ of the group** 她在人群外围胆怯地徘徊

outsmart /ˌaʊtˈsmɑːt/ *vt* 智胜

outsold /ˌaʊtˈsəʊld/ *pt, pp* ▸**outsell**

outsource /ˈaʊtsɔːs/ *vt* **1** (buy from outside suppliers) 外购 **2** (contract out) 将…外包; **we ~ all our computing work** 我们把所有的计算机技术工作都包给外边去做

outsourcing /ˈaʊtsɔːsɪŋ/ *n* [u] **1** (buying from outside suppliers) 外购 **2** (contracting out) 外包

outspoken /ˌaʊtˈspəʊkən/ *adj* 直言不讳的〈*person, critic, remark, criticism*〉; 公开的〈*opponent, supporter*〉; **to be ~ in one's remarks/in criticizing the government** 坦率地发表意见/对政府提出批评

outspokenly /ˌaʊtˈspəʊkənli/ *adv* 坦率地〈*defend, support, critical, supportive*〉

outspokenness /aʊtˈspəʊkənnɪs/ *n* [u] 坦率

outspread /ˌaʊtˈspred/ *adj* 张开的〈*arms, fingers, wings*〉; 铺开的〈*newspaper*〉

outstanding /ˌaʊtˈstændɪŋ/ *adj* **1** (excellent) 杰出的〈*achievement*〉; 优异的〈*performance*〉; 出色的〈*talent*〉; **an ~ beauty** 绝色美人 **2** (prominent) 显著的〈*landmark, characteristic*〉; 突出的〈*feature, example*〉 **3** (unresolved) 未偿还的〈*loan, debt*〉; 未付的〈*interest, bill*〉; 未完成的〈*work*〉; 未解决的〈*problem*〉; **~ shares** 已发行的股票

outstandingly /ˌaʊtˈstændɪŋli/ *adv* 特别地〈*professional, beautiful*〉

outstay /ˌaʊtˈsteɪ/ *vt* 逗留得比…更久〈*person*〉; 逗留时间超过〈*period*〉; **to ~ one's welcome** 作客太久而不受欢迎

outstretched /ˌaʊtˈstretʃt/ *adj* 伸出的〈*legs, fingers*〉; 展开的〈*wings*〉; **to welcome sb. with ~ arms** 张开双臂欢迎某人

outstrip /ˌaʊtˈstrɪp/ *vt* (*pres p etc.* **-pp-**) **1** (overtake) 比…跑得快〈*competitor*〉; **they ~ rival newspapers in circulation** fig 他们报纸的发行量超过了竞争对手 **2** (exceed) 《*demand*》超过〈*supply*〉

out-take *n* 被剪掉的镜头

out tray *n* [办公桌上的] 待发信件盘

out-turn *n* 产量

outvote /ˌaʊtˈvəʊt/ *vt* 以多数票击败

outward /ˈaʊtwəd/

A *adj attrib* **1** (external) 表面的〈*calm, symptom*〉; **to all ~ appearances** 从外表看 **2** (from port, base) 向外的〈*migration, expansion*〉; 外出的〈*journey*〉

B *adv* 向外

outward: ~ bound *adj* **1** (from port, base) 外出的〈*passenger*〉; 离港的〈*ship*〉; **2** (involving outdoor activities) 户外训练的〈*course, centre, instructor*〉; **~ investment** *n* [u] 对外投资

outwardly /ˈaʊtwədli/ *adv* **1** (seen from outside) 从外表看 **2** (apparently) 表面上〈*calm, friendly*〉

outwards /ˈaʊtwədz/ *adv* 向外

outweigh /ˌaʊtˈweɪ/ *vt* 超过; **the advantages ~ the disadvantages** 利大于弊

outwit /ˌaʊtˈwɪt/ *vt* (*pres p etc.* **-tt-**) 智胜〈*enemy, rival*〉; 骗过〈*police*〉

outwith /ˌaʊtˈwɪθ/ *prep* Scot **= outside C**

outwork /ˈaʊtwɜːk/ *n* [u] Brit 外包活儿

outworker /ˈaʊtwɜːkə(r)/ *n* Brit [在家承接缝纫、装配等工作的] 外包工

outworn /ˌaʊtˈwɔːn/ *adj* **1** (worn out) 穿旧的〈*clothes, shoes*〉 **2** (outdated) 过时的〈*theory, expression*〉

ouzo /ˈuːzəʊ/ *n* [u and c] [希腊产的] 茴香烈酒

ova /ˈəʊvə/ *pl* ▸**ovum**

oval /ˈəʊvl/

A *adj* 椭圆形的〈*brooch, mirror*〉; **an ~** *or* **~-shaped face** 鹅蛋脸; **the O~ Office** Amer Pol [美国白宫的] 椭圆形办公室

B *n* 椭圆形物

ovarian /əʊˈveərɪən/ *adj* 卵巢的; **~ cancer/cyst** 卵巢癌/囊肿

ovary /ˈəʊvəri/ *n* **1** Anat 卵巢 **2** Bot 子房

ovation /əʊˈveɪʃn/ *n* 热烈鼓掌; **to give sb. a standing ~** 起立为某人热烈鼓掌

oven /ˈʌvn/ *n* 烤箱; **to cook in a hot/moderate/slow ~** 在烤箱内以高温/中温/低温烹饪; **it's like an ~ in here!** 这里热得像个火炉!

oven: ~ chip *n* 烤薯条; **~ cleaner** *n* [c and u] 烤箱清洗剂; **~ dish** *n* 烤盘; **~ glove** *n* 烤箱手套; **~proof** *adj* 耐热的; **~ rack** *n* Amer **= ~ shelf**; **~-ready** *adj* 可直接入炉的; **~ shelf** *n* Brit 烤架; **~-to-tableware** *n* [u] 烘烤上菜两用盘; **~ware** *n* [u] 烤盘

over¹ /ˈəʊvə(r)/

A *prep* **1** (above) 在…上方; **clouds ~ the valley** 峡谷上空的云; **a bridge ~ the river** 河上的一座桥 **2** (across top, surface of) 穿越…上方; **to jump/look ~ a wall** 从墙头跳过去/望过去; **to walk ~ a bridge** 从桥上走过去 **3** (upon, to cover) 在…上面; **she carried her coat ~ her arm** 她把外套搭在手臂上; **I spilled coffee ~ my dress** 我把咖啡洒在了连衣裙上; **shutters ~ the windows** 窗户上的百叶窗 **4** (beyond) 在…对面; **just ~ the river** 就在河对岸; **the noise came from ~ the wall** 响声从墙那头传来; **to escape ~ the border** 越境逃跑 **5** (across and down) 从…向下〈*edge*〉; **to fall ~ a cliff** 从悬崖上跌落 **6** (down upon) 落到…上; **to hit sb. ~ the head** 打某人的头; **to fall ~ the cat** 被猫绊倒 **7** (higher, louder than) 比…高〈*person, structure*〉; **the water was/came ~ my ankles** 水没过了我的脚踝; **I couldn't hear his voice ~ the noise of the storm** 他的声音被暴风雨的咆哮盖住了，我听不到 **8** (more than) 比…多; **temperatures of ~ 40°** 40 度以上的温度; **well ~ 500 people** 远远多于 500 人; **children of/aged ~ seven** 7 岁以上的儿童; **to take ~ a year** 耗费一年多时间; **~ and above** 除…之外 **9** (above in power) 高于; **the officers ~ him** 他的上级军官; **to rule ~ a kingdom/the French** 统治王国/法国人 **10** (above in degree) 优于; (above in quantity) 多于; **to have an advantage ~ one's enemy** 比敌人更有优势; **to choose that one ~ the other** 选择那个而不是另一个; **an increase of 5% ~ last year's total** 超过去年总量 5% 的增长 **11** (transferring) **to sign/hand ~** 签字转让/移交〈*property, right*〉 **12** (during) 在…期间; **~ the weekend/summer** 在周末/夏季; **~ the last decade** 在过去的十年中; **to discuss sth. ~ lunch** 边吃午餐边商量某事; **to go away ~ Christmas** 圣诞节期间外出 **13** (recovered from) 从…中恢复〈*illness, setback*〉; **to be ~ the worst** 熬过最艰难的时期; **I'll be ~ it soon** 我很快就能熬过去的; **to be/get ~ sb.** (lover) 和某人分手后恢复过来 **14** (by means of) 通过〈*phone, radio, Internet*〉 **15** (everywhere in) 遍及; **to travel all ~ Asia** 游遍亚洲; **to travel the world ~** liter 周游世界; **to show sb. ~ the house** 带某人参观房子各处 **16** (about) 关于; **to laugh ~ sth.** 为某事发笑; **to pause ~ a difficulty** 因一个难题中止 **17** (while engaged with) **to fall asleep ~ one's work** 工作时睡着; **to go ~ the details with sb.** 和某人一起检查细节 **18** (so as to affect) 影响; **a change that came ~ her** 影响她的变化; **what has come ~ her?** 她怎么啦? **19** Math colloq (divided by) 除以〈*numeral*〉; **12 ~ 4 is 3** 12 除以 4 等于 3

B *adv* **1** (up and across) 翻过; **to climb/jump ~** 爬/跳过去; **~ you go!** 翻过去! **2** (across space) 穿过; **to throw/move sth. ~** 把某物扔/搬过去; **to come ~ here** 过来; **to go ~ there** 过去; **to go ~ to Italy** 去意大利; **~ against** lit 在…对面; fig 与…相反; **to put sth. ~ against the wall** 把某物面朝墙放 **3** (at location of) 在; **where? — ~ here/there** 在哪里? ——在这里/那里; **the view ~ in France** 法国那边的风景 **4** (throughout area) 遍及; **to wander all ~** 到处转悠 **5** (to one's place) **to invite** *or* **ask** *or* colloq **have sb. ~** 请某人来家里; **I'll be ~ at 8 o'clock** 我 8 点钟过来; **to come ~ for lunch** 过来吃午饭 **6** (from upright) 往下; **to fall/trip ~** 倒下/绊倒; **to push sth. ~** 把某物推倒 **7** (over edge) 溢出; **the milk boiled ~** 牛奶煮溢了; **sth. spilled ~** 某物溢出来了 **8** (covering) 覆盖; **to paint/board sth. ~** 把某物全部油漆/用木板封住; **the river froze ~** 河面被冰封住了 **9** (on top) 在顶部; **this one goes ~ and that one under** 这个在顶上，那个在下面 **10** (more) 以上; **or/and ~** 及以上; **children of seven and/or ~** 7 岁及 7 岁以上的儿童; **temperatures of 40° and ~** 40° 及 40° 以上的温度 **11** (showing change, transfer) 转移; **to win sb. ~** 将某人争取过来; **hand it ~!** 把它交过来! ; **and now ~ to ...** TV, Radio 现在转到…; **~ to you** 请讲; **~ to Tim for the weather** 下面请蒂姆播送天气预报 **12** Radio 完毕; **~ and out** 通话完毕 **13** (finished) **to be ~** 结束; **the rain is ~** 雨停了; **to get sth. ~ (with)** 做完某事; **to be ~ and done with** 终告结束 **14** (reversed, inverted) **to turn**

~ in bed 在床上翻身; the dog rolled ~ 狗打了个滚; to bend sth./double oneself ~ 折起某物/弯腰; to change the two photos ~ 把两张照片掉换 15 (repeated) 重复地; several/many times ~ 重复几次/多次; ~ and ~ (again) 反复地; do it/start ~ (again) esp Amer 重做这事/重新开始 16 (remaining) to be ~ «number, amount» 剩余; 2 into 5 goes twice and one ~ 5 除以 2 商 2 余 1; there's nothing ~ 什么都不剩了 17 Brit (excessively) 过分; he was not ~ pleased 他没有高兴过了头

over² *n* Sport 一轮投球

overachieve /ˌəʊvərəˈtʃiːv/ *vi* 取得比预期好的成绩

overachiever /ˌəʊvərəˈtʃiːvə(r)/ *n* 成绩超出预期水平者

overact /ˌəʊvərˈækt/
A *vi* «actor» 演得过火
B *vt* 过火地表演 ‹part, role›

overactive /ˌəʊvərˈæktɪv/ *adj* 过于活跃的 ‹child, imagination›; to have an ~ thyroid 患甲状腺机能亢进

overage /ˈəʊvərɪdʒ/ *adj* 超龄的

overall
A /ˌəʊvərˈɔːl/ *adj attrib* 总体的 ‹effect, performance, impression›; 综合的 ‹winner, position›; the ~ length/width 全长/全宽; there has been an ~ improvement 情况有了全面的改善
B /ˌəʊvərˈɔːl/ *adv* 总体上; to come first ~ Sport 综合排名第一
C /ˈəʊvərɔːl/ *n* Brit (garment) 罩衣
D **overalls** *npl* Brit (boiler suit) 工作服; Amer (dungarees) 工装裤

overalled /ˈəʊvərɔːld/ *adj* Brit (in overall) 穿罩衣的; Brit (in boiler suit) 穿工作服的; Amer (in dungarees) 穿工装裤的

overanxious /ˌəʊvərˈæŋkʃəs/ *adj* 过分焦虑的; I'm not ~ to go 我并不急着想去

overarm /ˈəʊvərɑːm/
A *adj* 肩上的 ‹throw›; 上手的 ‹serve›; 单臂出水的 ‹stroke›
B *adv* 肩上 ‹throw›; 上手 ‹serve›

overawe /ˌəʊvərˈɔː/ *vt* 吓倒; to be ~d by the occasion 被这个场面吓坏了

overbalance /ˌəʊvəˈbæləns/
A *vi* 失去平衡
B *vt* 使…失去平衡 ‹boat›

overbearing /ˌəʊvəˈbeərɪŋ/ *adj* 专横的 ‹manner, personality›

overbid /ˌəʊvəˈbɪd/ (*pres p* **-dd-**; *pt, pp* **overbid**)
A *vi* 出价过高
B *vt* 出价高于

overblown /ˌəʊvəˈbləʊn/ *adj* 浮夸的 ‹style, prose›; 过分的 ‹compliments, fears›

overboard /ˈəʊvəbɔːd/ *adv* 向船外; to fall/jump ~ 从船上落入/跳入水中; to push *or* throw sb./sth. ~ lit, fig 抛弃某人/某物; to go ~ (for *or* about sb./sth.) fig 非常热衷（某人/某事物）

overbook /ˌəʊvəˈbʊk/
A *vi* 超额预订
B *vt* 超额订出

overbooking /ˌəʊvəˈbʊkɪŋ/ *n* [u] 超额预订

overburden /ˌəʊvəˈbɜːdn/ *vt* 使…负载过多 ‹mule›; fig 使…负担过重 ‹person›

overcame /ˌəʊvəˈkeɪm/ *pt* ▸**overcome**

overcapacity /ˌəʊvəkəˈpæsəti/ *n* [u] 生产能力过剩

overcapitalize /ˌəʊvəˈkæpɪtəlaɪz/ *vt* 对…投资过多

overcast /ˌəʊvəˈkɑːst, Amer -ˈkæst/ *adj* 多云的

overcautious /ˌəʊvəˈkɔːʃəs/ *adj* 过分谨慎的

overcharge /ˌəʊvəˈtʃɑːdʒ/
A *vt* 1 (financially) 对…要价过高 ‹person›; she ~d me by £5 她多收了我 5 英镑 2 Elec 为…充电过量 ‹battery›
B *vi* 要价过高; they've ~d for that 那东西他们要价过高

overcoat /ˈəʊvəkəʊt/ *n* 长大衣

overcome /ˌəʊvəˈkʌm/ (*pt* **overcame**, *pp* **overcome**)
A *vt* 1 (defeat) 战胜 ‹opponent›; 克服 ‹habit›; 解决 ‹problem, difficulty›; 抑制 ‹rage, nerves› 2 (overwhelm) 压倒; to be ~ by smoke 被烟熏倒; to be ~ with jealousy/fear 嫉妒得不得了/恐惧得要死; I was ~ when I heard the news 我听到这个消息后崩溃了
B *vi* 取胜

overcompensate /ˌəʊvəˈkɒmpenseɪt/ *vi* 过度补偿; to ~ for one's shyness by talking too much 为克服羞怯却说话太多

overconfidence /ˌəʊvəˈkɒnfɪdəns/ *n* [u] 过于自信

overconfident /ˌəʊvəˈkɒnfɪdənt/ *adj* 过于自信的

overconsumption /ˌəʊvəkənˈsʌmpʃn/ *n* [u] 过度消费

overcook /ˌəʊvəˈkʊk/ *vt* 将…煮过头

overcrowded /ˌəʊvəˈkraʊdɪd/ *adj* 过于拥挤的

overcrowding /ˌəʊvəˈkraʊdɪŋ/ *n* [u] 过度拥挤

overdeveloped /ˌəʊvədɪˈveləpt/ *adj* 1 (physically) 过于发达的 ‹muscles› 2 (exaggerated) 极端的 ‹ego›; 过分的 ‹sense of humour› 3 (overbuilt) 过度开发的

overdo /ˌəʊvəˈduː/ *vt* (*pt* **overdid**, *pp* **overdone**) 1 (overwork, overact) 把…做得过分; to ~ the scene/the concern 把这场戏表演得过火/过分关心; to ~ things *or* it 做事过头 2 (use too much of) 过多使用 ‹flavouring, perfume› 3 (overcook) 把…煮过头 ‹food›

overdone /ˌəʊvəˈdʌn/ *adj* 1 (exaggerated) 夸张的 2 (overcooked) 煮过头的

overdose /ˈəʊvədəʊs/
A *n* 服药过量; to take an ~ of vitamins 服用过量的维生素; to die of a heroin ~ 死于过量吸食海洛因; I've had rather an ~ of the classics recently fig 我最近读的名著有点太多了
B *vt* 给…过量服药; to ~ sb. (with sth.) 使某人服用（某）药物过量
C *vi* 用药过量; to ~ on lit 过量服用 ‹tablets, drugs›; fig colloq 过多食用 ‹chocolate›; 过分沉溺于 ‹television›

overdraft /ˈəʊvədrɑːft, Amer -dræft/ *n* (deficit) 透支; (amount) 透支额; to have an ~ 透支; to take out/run up/pay off an ~ 透支/透支严重/还清透支

overdraw /ˌəʊvəˈdrɔː/ (*pt* **overdrew** /ˌəʊvəˈdruː/, *pp* **overdrawn** /ˌəʊvəˈdrɔːn/)
A *vt* 透支; your account is £100 overdrawn 你的账户透支了 100 英镑
B *vi* 透支; to ~ by £50 透支 50 英镑

overdrawn /ˌəʊvəˈdrɔːn/ *adj* 透支的; to be ~ (by £50) «person, account» 透支（50 英镑）

overdress /ˌəʊvəˈdres/
A *vi* 穿得过于讲究
B *vt* 使穿得过于讲究

overdrew /ˌəʊvəˈdruː/ *pt* ▸**overdraw**

overdrive /ˈəʊvədraɪv/ *n* [u] Aut 超速挡; to go into ~ 换到超速挡; fig 加倍努力

overdue /ˌəʊvəˈdjuː, Amer -ˈduː/ *adj* 到期未付的 ‹bill›; 逾期未还的 ‹library book›; 迟来的 ‹period›; 过了预产期的 ‹baby, woman›; the car is ~ for a service 这辆车早就该维修了; the train/your essay is ~ 火车晚点了/你的文章迟交了; this measure is long ~ 这项措施早该采取了

overeager /ˌəʊvərˈiːɡə(r)/ *adj* 过于热切的; to be ~ to do sth. 太急于做某事

over easy *adj* Amer 煎得一面老一面嫩的 ‹egg›

overeat /ˌəʊvərˈiːt/ *vi* (*pt* **overate**, *pp* **overeaten**) 吃得过量

overeating /ˌəʊvərˈiːtɪŋ/ *n* [u] 进食过量

overemphasis /ˌəʊvərˈemfəsɪs/ *n* [u] 过分强调

overemphasize /ˌəʊvərˈemfəsaɪz/ *vt* 过分强调 ‹point›; the importance of this cannot be ~d 此事的重要性无论怎么强调也不过分

overenthusiastic /ˌəʊvərɪnˌθjuːzɪˈæstɪk, Amer -ˌθuː-/ *adj* 过分热心的; to be ~ in doing sth. 在做某事方面过分热心

overestimate
A /ˌəʊvərˈestɪmeɪt/ *vt* 高估
B /ˌəʊvərˈestɪmət/ *n* 过高的估计

overexcited /ˌəʊvərɪkˈsaɪtɪd/ *adj* 过于兴奋的 ‹child, animal›

overexcitement /ˌəʊvərɪkˈsaɪtmənt/ *n* [u] 过于兴奋

overexert /ˌəʊvərɪɡˈzɜːt/ *vt* 使…负荷过度 ‹heart›; to ~ oneself 过分卖力

overexertion /ˌəʊvərɪɡˈzɜːʃn/ *n* [u] 用力过度

overexpose /ˌəʊvərɪkˈspəʊz/ *vt* 使曝光过度

overexposure /ˌəʊvərɪkˈspəʊʒə(r)/ *n* [u] 1 Phot 过度曝光 2 fig (to media attention) 过度报道; (to risk) 过度接触

overfeed /ˌəʊvəˈfiːd/ *vt* (*pt, pp* **overfed** /ˌəʊvəˈfed/) 给…喂食过多 ‹baby, animal›; 给…施肥过多 ‹plant›

overfeeding /ˌəʊvəˈfiːdɪŋ/ *n* [u] (of baby, animal) 喂食过多; (of plant) 施肥过多

overfill /ˌəʊvəˈfɪl/ *vt* 把…装得太满

overfish /ˌəʊvəˈfɪʃ/ *vt* 对…捕捞过度 ‹sea, cod›

overfishing /ˌəʊvəˈfɪʃɪŋ/ *n* [u] 捕捞过度

overflow
A /ˌəʊvəˈfləʊ/ *vi* «liquid, rubbish» 溢出; fig «people» 涌出; to ~ into the streets 涌到大街上; to be full *or* filled to ~ing 满得溢出来了; to ~ with gratitude/love fig 充满感激/爱
B /ˌəʊvəˈfləʊ/ *vt* «water» 溢出 ‹bank›; fig «audience» 挤满 ‹room›
C /ˈəʊvəfləʊ/ *n* 1 [u] (surplus) (of things) 容纳不下的东西; (of people) 容纳不下的人; the ~ of students/passengers 超额的学生/超员的旅客 2 [u] (spillage) 溢出 3 [c] (liquid spilt) 溢出的液体 4 [c] (from bath, sink) 溢流管; (from dam) 溢出口

overflow car park Brit, **overflow parking lot** Amer *ns* 备用停车场

overflowing /ˌəʊvəˈfləʊɪŋ/ *adj* 满得溢出来的 ‹dustbin, bath›; 挤满人的 ‹school, prison›

overfly /ˌəʊvəˈflaɪ/ *vt* (*pt* **overflew**, *pp* **overflown**) 飞越

overgenerous /ˌəʊvəˈdʒenərəs/ *adj* 过于慷慨的; to be ~ with one's praise 过度赞扬; the portions are not ~ 这几客分量不是太大方啊

overgrown /ˌəʊvəˈɡrəʊn/ *adj* 1 (covered in weeds) 杂草蔓生的; ~ with weeds/ivy 长满杂草/常春藤的 2 often hum (grown too big) 长得过大的 ‹animal, plant, child›; they were behaving like a pair of ~ schoolboys 他们虽已成年，但举止就像一对小男生

overhand /ˈəʊvəhænd/ *adj, adv* Amer = **overarm**

overhang
A /ˈəʊvəhæŋ/ *n* 1 (of cliff) 伸出物; (of roof) 悬挑部分; (of tablecloth, bedcover etc.) 悬垂部分 2 Fin (securities) 待沽售的股票; (commodities) 待抛售的商品
B /ˌəʊvəˈhæŋ/ *vi* (*pt, pp* **overhung**) «cliff, branch» 悬垂; «balcony» 突出
C /ˌəʊvəˈhæŋ/ *vt* (*pt, pp* **overhung**) «cliff, branch» 悬垂于…之上; «balcony» 突出于…之上 ‹beach, house›

O

overhanging /ˌəʊvəˈhæŋɪŋ/ *adj* 悬垂的〈*branch, ledge*〉; 突出的〈*balcony*〉; **~ cliff/eaves** 悬崖/飞檐

overhaul
A /ˌəʊvəˈhɔːl/ *vt* **1** (repair) 彻底检修〈*engine, car*〉; fig 全面修订〈*syllabus, procedure*〉 **2** Brit (overtake) 超过〈*vehicle, person*〉
B /ˈəʊvəhɔːl/ *n* 彻底检修; **to give (sth.) an ~** (对某物) 进行大修; **a complete/thorough/major ~** 全面/彻底/大检修

overhead
A /ˌəʊvəˈhed/ *adv* **1** (in the sky) 在空中 **2** (above one's head) 在头顶上〈*fly*〉; **to hold sth. ~** 将某物举过头顶
B /ˈəʊvəhed/ *adj attrib* **1** (above one's head) 头顶上的〈*lighting, compartment*〉; **~ cables/railway** 高架电缆/铁路; **an ~ light** 吊灯 **2** Sport 上手的〈*stroke, kick*〉; **an ~ smash** 高手扣杀 **3** Fin 经常性的〈*costs*〉
C /ˈəʊvəhed/ *n* 经常性开支; **to reduce one's ~s** 减少经常性开支

overhead: ~ camshaft *n* 顶置凸轮轴; **~ locker** *n* 头顶行李柜; **~ luggage rack** *n* 头顶行李架; **~ projector** *n* 投影仪

overhear /ˌəʊvəˈhɪə(r)/ *vt* (*pt, pp* **overheard** /ˌəʊveˈhɜːd/) 无意中听到〈*person, remark, discussion*〉; **to ~ sb. say/saying sth.** 无意中听到某人说/在说某事

overheat /ˌəʊvəˈhiːt/
A *vt* **1** lit 使…过热〈*room, engine*〉; 把…加热过度〈*sauce*〉 **2** fig 使…发展过热〈*market, economy*〉
B *vi* **1** lit《*room, engine*》变得过热 **2** fig《*economy, market*》过热

overheated /ˌəʊvəˈhiːtɪd/ *adj* **1** lit 热得难受的〈*person*〉; 太热的〈*room, car*〉 **2** fig 过热的〈*economy, market*〉

overheating /ˌəʊvəˈhiːtɪŋ/ *n* [u] **1** Med lit 中暑 **2** Econ fig 过热

overhung /ˌəʊvəˈhʌŋ/ *pt, pp* ▸**overhang B, C**

overindulge /ˌəʊvərɪnˈdʌldʒ/
A *vi* 过分沉溺; **to ~ in sth.** 过分沉溺于某事
B *vt* 过分纵容〈*child*〉

overindulgence /ˌəʊvərɪnˈdʌldʒəns/ *n* [u] **1** (excess) 过分沉溺; **~ in sth.** 对某事的过分沉溺 **2** (of child, pet) 过分纵容; **~ of** *or* **towards sb.** 对某人的过分纵容

overindulgent /ˌəʊvərɪnˈdʌldʒənt/ *adj* 过分纵容的〈*parent, attitude*〉

overinvest /ˌəʊvərɪnˈvest/ *vi* 过度投资

overjoyed /ˌəʊvəˈdʒɔɪd/ *adj* 欣喜若狂的; **to be ~ at sth.** 对某事欣喜若狂; **I was ~ that ...** …使我大喜过望

overkill /ˈəʊvəkɪl/ *n* [u] **1** Mil 超量毁伤 **2** fig 过分行为; **advertising/media ~** 铺天盖地的广告/媒体宣传

overlaid /ˌəʊvəˈleɪd/ *pt, pp* ▸**overlay[1] A**

overlain /ˌəʊvəˈleɪn/ *pp* ▸**overlie**

overland /ˈəʊvəlænd/
A *adj* (across land) 横跨陆地的〈*march, trek, cables*〉; (by land) 经由陆路的〈*journey*〉; **the ~ route to ...** 到…的陆上路线
B *adv* 经由陆路〈*travel, go*〉

overlap
A /ˌəʊvəˈlæp/ *vi* (*pres p etc.* **-pp-**)《*tiles, edges*》部分重叠; fig《*duties, activities, sectors*》有相同之处; **his interests ~ with mine to a large extent** 他与我的兴趣在很大程度上是相同的
B /ˌəʊvəˈlæp/ *vt* (*pres p etc.* **-pp-**) 使部分重叠; **the tiles ~ each other** 瓦片互相搭接
C /ˈəʊvəlæp/ *n* **1** Tech 重叠部分; **an ~ of 50 cm** 50 厘米的重叠 **2** fig (common ground) 共同之处; **an ~ between the two systems** 两种系统的共同之处

overlapping /ˌəʊvəˈlæpɪŋ/ *adj* 部分重叠的〈*edges, tiles*〉; fig 有相同之处的〈*services, systems*〉

overlay[1]
A /ˌəʊvəˈleɪ/ *vt* (*pt, pp* **overlaid**) 覆盖; **wood overlaid with gold** 包金木
B /ˈəʊvəleɪ/ *n* **1** (layer) 覆盖物; (decoration) 饰面 **2** (transparent sheet) 透明膜

overlay[2] /ˌəʊvəˈleɪ/ *pt* ▸**overlie**

overleaf /ˌəʊvəˈliːf/ *adv* 在背面; **see ~** 见背面

overlie /ˌəʊvəˈlaɪ/ *vt* (*pt* **overlay,** *pp* **overlain**) 覆在…的上面

overload
A /ˌəʊvəˈləʊd/ *vt* **1** lit 使…超载〈*vehicle*〉; fig (with work, worries) 使…负担过重〈*person*〉; **buses ~ed with passengers** 超载的公共汽车 **2** Elec 使…超负荷〈*circuit*〉
B /ˈəʊvələʊd/ *n* **1** Elec 超负荷 **2** fig 过重的负担

overlong /ˌəʊvəˈlɒŋ/ *adj* 过长的〈*lecture, book*〉

overlook /ˌəʊvəˈlʊk/ *vt* **1** (have a view of) 俯瞰; **we ~ the sea from the balcony** 我们可以从阳台眺望大海 **2** (fail to spot) 看漏〈*spelling mistake, detail*〉; 忽略〈*risk, difficulty*〉 **3** (deliberately ignore) 不理会〈*offence, faults*〉

overlord /ˈəʊvəlɔːd/ *n* 领主

overly /ˈəʊvəlɪ/ *adv* 过于〈*cautious, interested*〉

overmanned /ˌəʊvəˈmænd/ *adj* 人员过多的〈*department, factory*〉

overmanning /ˌəʊvəˈmænɪŋ/ *n* [u] 人员过多

overmuch /ˌəʊvəˈmʌtʃ/
A *adv* (too much) 过多; (very much) 很多; **I do not like him ~** 我不太喜欢他
B *adj attrib* (too much) 过多的; (very much) 很多的

overnight
A /ˌəʊvəˈnaɪt/ *adv* **1** (for the night) 一晚上〈*stop*〉; (through the night) 整晚〈*drive*〉; **to stay ~ at a friend's house** 在朋友家住一晚 **2** fig (suddenly) 一夜之间〈*change*〉
B /ˈəʊvənaɪt/ *adj* **1** (night-time) 夜间的〈*journey, train*〉; 过夜的〈*guest*〉; 持续一晚的〈*stay, party, rain*〉 **2** *attrib* fig (sudden) 一夜之间的〈*success, change*〉

overnight bag *n* 过夜小提包 [内装外宿一夜所用物品的轻便旅行包]

over-optimistic *adj* 过于乐观的〈*person, view*〉

overpaid /ˌəʊvəˈpeɪd/ *pt, pp* ▸**overpay**

over-particular /ˌəʊvəpəˈtɪkjʊlə(r)/ *adj* 过于挑剔的〈*person, examination*〉; **he's not ~ about his reputation** 他对自己的名声不十分在意

overpass /ˈəʊvəpɑːs, Amer -pæs/ *n* esp Amer (for cars) 立交桥; (footbridge) 人行天桥; **a highway/freeway/pedestrian ~** 公路立交桥/高速公路立交桥/人行天桥

overpay /ˌəʊvəˈpeɪ/ *vt* (*pt, pp* **overpaid**) 多支付; **to ~ sb. (for sth.)** (为某事物) 付给某人过多的报酬; **I was overpaid by £500** 我多得了 500 英镑的报酬

overpayment /ˌəʊvəˈpeɪmənt/ *n* 支付过多; **~s will be credited to your account** 多付的款项将存入你的账户

overplay /ˌəʊvəˈpleɪ/ *vt* (exaggerate) 夸大〈*benefits*〉; 夸大…的重要性〈*problem*〉; (overemphasize) 过分强调〈*role, factor*〉; **to ~ one's hand** 不自量力

overpopulated /ˌəʊvəˈpɒpjʊleɪtɪd/ *adj* 人口过多的

overpopulation /ˌəʊvəpɒpjʊˈleɪʃn/ *n* [u] 人口过多

overpower /ˌəʊvəˈpaʊə(r)/ *vt* **1** (by force) 制服〈*burglar, opponent*〉; 征服〈*army, nation*〉 **2** (overwhelm)《*heat, smell, feelings*》压倒

overpowering /ˌəʊvəˈpaʊərɪŋ/ *adj* 难以忍受的〈*smell, heat*〉; 难以抑制的〈*grief, desire*〉; 不可抗拒的〈*person*〉

overpraise /ˌəʊvəˈpreɪz/ *vt* 过分赞扬

overprescribe /ˌəʊvəprɪˈskraɪb/
A *vt*《*doctor*》过量…开〈*drug*〉
B *vi*《*doctor*》过量开药

overprice /ˌəʊvəˈpraɪs/ *vt* 对…定价过高

overpriced /ˌəʊvəˈpraɪst/ *adj* 价格过高的

overprint /ˌəʊvəˈprɪnt/ *vt* 套印; **to ~ a grid on a map** 在地图上套印格子; **to ~ stamps with a new price** 在邮票上加印新的价格

overproduce /ˌəʊvəprəˈdjuːs, Amer -duːs/ *vt* 过度生产

overproduction /ˌəʊvəprəˈdʌkʃn/ *n* [u] 过度生产

overprotect /ˌəʊvəprəˈtekt/ *vt* 溺爱〈*child*〉; 过分保护〈*economy, business interests*〉

overprotective /ˌəʊvəprəˈtektɪv/ *adj* 溺爱子女的〈*parent*〉; 袒护的〈*attitude*〉

overqualified /ˌəʊvəˈkwɒlɪfaɪd/ *adj* 资历过高的; **to be ~ for a job** 资历超过工作的要求

overran /ˌəʊvəˈræn/ *pt* ▸**overrun A, B**

overrate /ˌəʊvəˈreɪt/ *vt* 对…估计过高

overrated /ˌəʊvəˈreɪtɪd/ *adj* 评价过高的

overreach /ˌəʊvəˈriːtʃ/
A *v refl* 贪功致败; **to ~ oneself** 不自量力
B *vi* 伸得过远

overreact /ˌəʊvərɪˈækt/ *vi* 反应过火; **to ~ to sth.** 对某事物反应过激

overreaction /ˌəʊvərɪˈækʃn/ *n* 过火的反应; **a hysterical ~ to the threat** 对威胁的歇斯底里式过激反应

overregulation /ˌəʊvəregjʊˈleɪʃn/ *n* [u] 过度管制

overreliance /ˌəʊvərɪˈlaɪəns/ *n* 过分依赖

override
A /ˌəʊvəˈraɪd/ *vt* (*pt* **overrode** /ˌəʊvəˈrəʊd/; *pp* **overridden** /ˌəʊvəˈrɪdn/) **1** (overrule) 否决〈*opinion, decision*〉; 使…无效〈*order, veto*〉 **2** (take precedence) 优先于〈*consideration, rule*〉; **this order ~s all previous instructions** 这个命令高于所有先前的指示 **3** (control) 手动控制〈*machine*〉; 手控消除〈*automatic system, settings*〉
B /ˈəʊvəraɪd/ *n* 超驰控制装置; **on ~** 处于超驰模式
C *modif* 超驰的〈*mechanism, facility*〉

overriding /ˌəʊvəˈraɪdɪŋ/ *adj attrib* 首要的〈*consideration, factor, goal*〉; 压倒一切的〈*principle, reason, emotion*〉; **this is a matter of ~ importance** *or* **concern** 这是至关重要的一件事

overripe /ˌəʊvəˈraɪp/ *adj* 过熟的〈*fruit, cheese*〉

overrode /ˌəʊvəˈrəʊd/ *pt* ▸**override A**

overrule /ˌəʊvəˈruːl/ *vt* 否决〈*decision, judgement*〉; 驳回〈*argument, claim*〉; **objection ~d!** Jur 反对无效!

overrun
A /ˌəʊvəˈrʌn/ *vt* (*pres p* **-nn-**; *pt* **overran**, *pp* **overrun**) **1** (invade)《*enemy*》横行于〈*country*〉;《*rats*》大批出没于〈*area*〉;《*weeds*》蔓延于〈*garden*〉; **to be ~ with sth.** 被某物肆虐 **2** (exceed) 超出〈*time, budget, edge*〉
B /ˌəʊvəˈrʌn/ *vi* 超越限度; **the lecture overran by an hour** 演讲超过规定时间 1 小时
C /ˈəʊvərʌn/ *n* esp Fin (time) 超时; (cost) 超支; **an ~ on the allotted time** 超出规定时间

oversaw /ˌəʊvəˈsɔː/ *pt* ▸**oversee**

overseas /ˌəʊvəˈsiːz/
A *adv* 在国外〈*work, retire*〉; **from ~** 来自海外
B *adj attrib* **1** (from abroad) 外国的〈*visitor, investor, company*〉 **2** (in other countries) 在国外的〈*investment*〉; (to other countries) 去国外的〈*travel*〉; **to get an ~ posting** 得到一个去海外工作的职务

oversee /ˌəʊvəˈsiː/ *vt* (*pt* **oversaw,** *pp* **overseen** /ˌəʊvəˈsiːn/) 监视〈*prisoners*〉; 监督〈*workers, project*〉

overseer /ˈəʊvəsiːə(r)/ *n* (of workers, convicts) 监督者; (of project) 监工

oversell /ˌəʊvəˈsel/ *vt* (*pt, pp* **oversold**) **1** Fin, Comm 卖空 ‹*commodity, shares*›; 过多出售 ‹*goods*› **2** (exaggerate the merits of) 吹嘘 ‹*idea, plan*›

oversensitive /ˌəʊvəˈsensɪtɪv/ *adj* 过于敏感的; **to be ~ about** *or* **to sth.** 对某事物过于敏感

oversew /ˈəʊvəsəʊ/ *vt* (*pt* **oversewed,** *pp* **oversewn** /ˈəʊvəsəʊn/) 平式缝接

oversexed /ˌəʊvəˈsekst/ *adj* colloq pej 性欲过强的

overshadow /ˌəʊvəˈʃædəʊ/ *vt* **1** lit «*trees, mountains*» 使…浓阴密布 ‹*area*› **2** fig (spoil) «*event, death*» 给…蒙上阴影 ‹*celebration*› **3** fig (eclipse) 使…黯然失色 ‹*reputation, achievement*›

overshoe /ˈəʊvəʃuː/ *n* 罩靴

overshoot /ˌəʊvəˈʃuːt/ *vt* (*pt, pp* **overshot** /ˌəʊvəˈʃɒt/) «*plane*» 冲出 ‹*runway*›; «*train, car*» 冲过 ‹*platform, junction*›; **to ~ the mark** 做得过头

oversight /ˈəʊvəsaɪt/ *n* **1** [c and u] (omission) 疏忽; **due to** *or* **through an ~** 由于疏忽 **2** [u] (supervision) 监管; **under the ~ of sb.** 在某人的监管下

oversimplification /ˌəʊvəˌsɪmplɪfɪˈkeɪʃn/ *n* [c and u] 过于简单化

oversimplify /ˌəʊvəˈsɪmplɪfaɪ/ *vt* 把…过于简单化

oversize /ˈəʊvəsaɪz/, **oversized** /ˈəʊvəsaɪzd/ *adjs* (very big) 过大的 ‹*model, coat, clothes*›; (too big) 超大的 ‹*ears*›

oversleep /ˌəʊvəˈsliːp/ *vi* (*pt, pp* **overslept** /ˌəʊvəˈslept/) 睡过头

oversold /ˌəʊvəˈsəʊld/ *adj* (of commodity, shares) 卖空的; (of goods) 过多出售的

overspend

A /ˌəʊvəˈspend/ *vi* (*pt, pp* **overspent**) 超支; **to ~ on sth.** 在某方面超支; **to ~ by £500** 超支 500 英镑

B *vt* (*pt, pp* **overspent**) 支出超过 ‹*allowance, budget*›

C /ˈəʊvəspend/ *n* 超支

overspending /ˌəʊvəˈspendɪŋ/ *n* [u] 超支

overspent /ˌəʊvəˈspent/ *pt, pp* ▸ **overspend A, B**

overspill /ˈəʊvəspɪl/

A *n* [u] Brit 迁出城市的过剩人口

B *modif* 为迁出人口而提供的 ‹*housing*›; 为迁出人口制定的 ‹*policy*›; **~ town** 卫星城镇; **~ population** 迁出城市的过剩人口

overstaffed /ˌəʊvəˈstɑːft, Amer -ˈstæft/ *adj* 人手过多的; **the section was ~** 这个部门人浮于事

overstate /ˌəʊvəˈsteɪt/ *vt* 夸大 ‹*importance, problem, value, costs*›; **to ~ one's** *or* **the case** 夸大情况; **it cannot be ~d that ...** …怎么说也不为过

overstatement /ˌəʊvəˈsteɪtmənt/ *n* [c and u] 夸大; **~ of sth.** 对某事的夸大

overstay /ˌəʊvəˈsteɪ/ *vt* 逗留时间超过 ‹*visit, time allowed*›; **to ~ one's visa** 居留超过签证期限; **to ~ one's welcome** 作客太久而不受欢迎

oversteer /ˈəʊvəstɪə(r)/ *vi* «*vehicle, driver*» 转向过度

overstep /ˌəʊvəˈstep/ *vt* (*pres p etc.* **-pp-**) 超越 ‹*authority, limit*›; **to ~ the mark** *or* **line** 越轨

overstock /ˌəʊvəˈstɒk/ *vt* **1** (oversupply) 使存货过多; **to ~ sth. with sth.** 使…库存过多的某物 ‹*shop, factory*› **2** (with animals, fish) 在…放养过多的动物 ‹*enclosure, farm, lake*›

overstocked /ˌəʊvəˈstɒkt/ *adj* 存货过多的 ‹*shop*›; 畜禽饲养量过多的 ‹*farm*›; 养殖密度过大的 ‹*pond*›

overstrain /ˌəʊvəˈstreɪn/ *vt* 使…劳累过度 ‹*person*›; 过度开采 ‹*resources*›; **to ~ oneself** 操劳过度; **to ~ one's heart** 使心脏不堪重负

overstress /ˌəʊvəˈstres/ *vt* **1** (overemphasize) 过分强调 ‹*importance, fact*› **2** (subject to excessive stress) 使…压力过重 ‹*person*›

overstressed /ˌəʊvəˈstrest/ *adj* 压力过重的 ‹*teacher, parent*›

overstretched /ˌəʊvəˈstretʃt/ *adj* 过度消耗的 ‹*resources*›; 负荷过重的 ‹*services*›; 过度紧张的 ‹*staff, budget*›; **to be ~ doing sth.** 超负荷做某事

overstuffed /ˌəʊvəˈstʌft/ *adj* **1** (with upholstery) 又厚又软的 ‹*sofa, pillow*› **2** (overfull) 塞得满满的 ‹*case, bag*›

oversubscribed /ˌəʊvəsəbˈskraɪbd/ *adj* 超额认购的 ‹*shares*›; 申请人数过多的 ‹*school*›; 过量预订的 ‹*tickets*›

overt /ˈəʊvɜːt, əʊˈvɜːt/ *adj* 公开的 ‹*criticism, racism*›

overtake /ˌəʊvəˈteɪk/ (*pt* **overtook,** *pp* **overtaken** /ˌəʊvəˈteɪkn/)

A *vt* **1** (pass) 赶超 ‹*person, vehicle*› **2** fig (exceed, do better than) «*supply*» 超过 ‹*demand*›; **we have overtaken the Germans in car production** 我国的小汽车产量已超过了德国; **his fear was overtaken by embarrassment** 他的恐惧变成了窘迫 **3** fig (affect unexpectedly) «*misfortune, storm, change*» 突然侵袭 ‹*person, place*›; «*fear, surprise*» 压倒 ‹*person*›; **he was overtaken by** *or* **with fear** 他恐惧万分; **utter weariness overtook me** liter 我感到疲倦极了; **to be overtaken by events** 计划未赶上情况突变

B *vi* esp Brit 超车

overtax /ˌəʊvəˈtæks/ *vt* **1** Fin 对…征税过重 ‹*person, goods*› **2** (strain) 使…劳累过度 ‹*person, oneself*›; 使…负担过重 ‹*heart*›; 使…超负荷运转 ‹*system*›; **to ~ one's strength** 用力过度; **to ~ sb.'s patience** 使某人不耐烦

over-the-counter

A *adj* 非处方的 ‹*medicine, drug*›

B **over the counter** *adv* 无需处方地; **to sell medicines over the counter** 销售非处方药

over-the-top *adj* esp Brit colloq 怪里怪气的 ‹*person*›; 过分的 ‹*reaction, behaviour*›; 夸张的 ‹*film*›

overthrow

A /ˌəʊvəˈθrəʊ/ *vt* (*pt* **overthrew** /ˌəʊvəˈθruː/; *pp* **overthrown** /ˌəʊvəˈθrəʊn/) 推翻 ‹*government, system*›; 废除 ‹*institution*›

B /ˈəʊvəθrəʊ/ *n* 推翻

overtime /ˈəʊvətaɪm/

A *n* [u] **1** (extra hours) 加班时间; **to put in** *or* **be on** *or* **do ~** 加班 **2** (extra pay) 加班费; **to earn ~ (pay)** 挣加班费 **3** Amer Sport 加时赛; **to play ~** 打加时赛

B *modif* 加班的 ‹*work*›

C *adv* 在加班时间内 ‹*work*›; **my mind was working ~ trying to find a solution** fig 我绞尽脑汁想找到解决办法

overtime: ~ ban *n* 加班禁令; **~ rate** *n* 加班费率

overtired /ˌəʊvəˈtaɪəd/ *adj* 过度疲劳的

overtly /ˈəʊvɜːtli, əʊˈvɜːtli/ *adv* 公开地 ‹*challenge, threaten, religious*›; 公然地 ‹*critical, hostile*›

overtone /ˈəʊvətəʊn/ *n* **1** (nuance) 言外之意; **~s of racism** 种族主义暗示 **2** Mus 泛音

overtook /ˌəʊvəˈtʊk/ *pt* ▸ **overtake**

overtrousers /ˈəʊvətraʊzəz/ *npl* 防水外裤

overture /ˈəʊvətjʊə(r)/ *n* **1** Mus 序曲; **an ~ to a long debate** fig 长时间辩论的序幕 **2** *usu pl* (social) 友好姿态; (business) 提议; **to make an ~** *or* **~s to sb.** 主动接触某人; **romantic/peaceful ~s** 求爱/和平的表示; **to spurn** *or* **reject sb.'s ~s** 拒绝接受某人的提议

overturn /ˌəʊvəˈtɜːn/

A *vt* **1** (turn upside down) 掀翻 ‹*furniture, vehicle*› **2** (reverse) 撤销 ‹*ban, decision*›

B *vi* «*furniture, vehicle*» 翻倒; «*boat*» 倾覆

overuse

A /ˌəʊvəˈjuːz/ *vt* 滥用 ‹*drug, word*›; 过度使用 ‹*facility, product*›

B /ˌəʊvəˈjuːs/ *n* [u] (of drug, word) 滥用; (of facility, product) 过度使用; **to be worn out through ~** 因过度使用而破损

overvalue /ˌəʊvəˈvæljuː/ *vt* 对…估价过高; **the pound is ~d against the dollar** 英镑对美元汇价被高估了

overview /ˈəʊvəvjuː/ *n* 概述

overweening /ˌəʊvəˈwiːnɪŋ/ *adj* formal pej 自负的; **~ ambition** 妄自尊大的野心; **~ arrogance** 傲慢自大

overweight /ˌəʊvəˈweɪt/ *adj* **1** (too fat) 肥胖的 **2** (above allowed weight) 超重的 ‹*parcel, suitcase, vehicle*›; **to be ~ by 10 kilos, to be 10 kilos ~** 超重 10 公斤

overwhelm /ˌəʊvəˈwelm, Amer -ˈhwelm/ *vt* **1** (inundate) «*waves, avalanche*» 吞没; «*flood*» 淹没; fig «*praise, work, offers*» 潮水般涌向 **2** fig (affect emotionally) «*feeling, shame, kindness*» 压垮; **to be ~ed with grief/guilt/gratitude** 悲痛不已/愧疚难当/感激不尽 **3** (defeat, overpower) 战胜 ‹*team, army*›; **to be ~ed by the enemy/by an opponent** 被敌人/对手击败

overwhelming /ˌəʊvəˈwelmɪŋ, Amer -hwelm-/ *adj* 压倒性的 ‹*victory, majority, superiority, evidence*›; 难以抑制的 ‹*feeling, sorrow, interest*›; 难以忍受的 ‹*heat, pressure*›; 无法抗拒的 ‹*misfortune*›

overwhelmingly /ˌəʊvəˈwelmɪŋli, Amer -hwelm-/ *adv* 压倒性地 ‹*win, defeat, successful*›; 以压倒多数 ‹*vote, accept, reject*›; **~ beautiful/generous** 美丽至极/极其慷慨; **a country which is ~ Protestant/rural** 新教教徒占多数的/以农业为主的国家

overwinter /ˌəʊvəˈwɪntə(r)/ *vi* 过冬

overwork /ˌəʊvəˈwɜːk/

A *vi* 劳累过度

B *vt* **1** (cause to work too long) 使…劳累过度 ‹*oneself, employee*› **2** (overuse) 过度使用 ‹*muscle, expression, excuse*›

C *n* [u] 劳累过度

overworked /ˌəʊvəˈwɜːkt/ *adj* **1** (worn out) 劳累过度的 ‹*employee, parent*› **2** (overused) 用得过滥的 ‹*excuse, word*›

overwrite /ˌəʊvəˈraɪt/ *vt* (*pt* **overwrote** /ˌəʊvəˈrəʊt/; *pp* **overwritten** /ˌəʊvəˈrɪtn/) **1** 覆盖 ‹*file, data*› **2** (write on top of) 写在…上面

overwrought /ˌəʊvəˈrɔːt/ *adj* **1** (distressed) 过分紧张的 ‹*state, person*›; **to get ~ about sth.** 对某事物过于紧张 **2** (elaborate) 过于细腻的

overzealous /ˌəʊvəˈzeləs/ *adj* 过分热心的 ‹*person, attitude*›; **to be ~ in sth./doing sth.** 过分热衷于某事物/做某事

oviduct /ˈəʊvɪdʌkt/ *n* 输卵管

ovine /ˈəʊvaɪn/ *adj* (of a sheep) 绵羊的; (resembling a sheep) 似绵羊的

oviparous /əʊˈvɪpərəs/ *adj* 卵生的

ovoid /ˈəʊvɔɪd/ *adj* 卵形的

ovulate /ˈɒvjʊleɪt/ *vi* Zool 产卵; Physiol 排卵

ovulation /ˌɒvjʊˈleɪʃn/ *n* [u and c] Zool 产卵; Physiol 排卵

ovule /ˈəʊvjuːl/ *n* 胚珠

ovum /ˈəʊvəm/ *n* (*pl* **ova**) 卵

ow /aʊ/ *excl* 啊唷 [表示疼痛]

owe /əʊ/ *vt* **1** (have as debt) 欠 ‹*money*›; **I ~ my father £10 for the ticket** 我欠我父亲 10 镑票钱; **to ~ sb. one, to ~ sb. a favour** 欠某人一份人情 **2** (be indebted for) 把…归因

于 ‹*life, invention*›; **he ∼s his success to luck, not ability** 他把自己的成功归功于运气好，而不是靠能力; **I ∼ my life to my wife** 我妻子救了我的命; **his style ∼s much to the Impressionists** 他的风格深受印象派的影响 3 (be morally bound to give) 应给予 ‹*apology, explanation, thanks*›; **to ∼ it to oneself to do sth.** 认为自己应该做某事; **you ∼ it to your parents to work hard** 你应该努力工作以回报父母

owing /ˈəʊɪŋ/
A *adj* 未付的; **£20 is still ∼** 还欠 20 镑; **the amount** *or* **sum ∼** 欠款额
B **owing to** *prep phr* 由于; **∼ to the rain, the match was cancelled** 因为下雨，比赛取消了

owl /aʊl/ *n* 猫头鹰

owlet /ˈaʊlɪt/ *n* 小猫头鹰

owlish /ˈaʊlɪʃ/ *adj* 猫头鹰般的 ‹*stare, eyes*›; 儒雅的 ‹*glasses*›

own /əʊn/
A *adj attrib* 1 (belonging to person, group) 自己的; **his ∼ car** 他自己的车; **the company has its ∼ lawyer** 公司有自己的律师; **to start one's ∼ business** 创办自己的企业; **in his ∼ words ...** 用他自己的话说…; **to be one's ∼ man/woman** 独立自主; **to do one's ∼ thing** colloq 做自己喜欢的事; **virtue is its ∼ reward** Prov 行善本身就是回报 2 (done by self) 自己做的; **to do one's ∼ cooking** 自己做饭; **to make one's ∼ decisions** 自己做决定 3 (emphatic) 本人的; **of my ∼ making** 我亲手做的; **my ∼ daughter** 我的亲生女儿; **to see sth. with one's ∼ eyes** 亲眼看见某物; **my ∼ view is that ...** 我本人的看法是…
B *pron* (*pl* **own**) **one's/its ∼** 自己的/它自己的; **I don't have a company car, I use my ∼** 我没有公车，我开自己的; **of one's ∼** 属于自己的; **a house of my (very) ∼** 我自己的房子; **I have a suggestion of my ∼ to make** 我自己有一个建议想提出来; **a style all her ∼** 一种完全属于她自己的风格; **nothing to call one's ∼** 一无所有; **each to his/her/their ∼** 人各有所好; **on one's ∼** (solitary) 独自地; (without help) 独立地; **to get sb. on his/her/their ∼** 找某人单独说话; **on its ∼** 单独地; **whisky on its ∼** (undiluted) 纯威士忌酒; **to come into one's ∼** 得到充分发挥; **he came into his ∼ once he got to university** 他一进大学就崭露头角; **to get one's ∼ back (on sb.)** colloq 报复（某人）; **to hold one's ∼** 坚持自己的立场
C *vt* 1 (possess) 拥有; **who ∼s this pen?** 这支笔是谁的?; **I ∼ a cat** 我养了一只猫; **to act as if one ∼s the place** colloq pej 举止好像那地方是自己家似的 2 formal (admit) 承认; **to ∼ that ...** 承认…; **he ∼ed himself defeated** 他认输了
D *vi* formal **= own up**

Phrasal verb

- **own up** *vi*; **to ∼ up to sth.** 承认 ‹*mistake, crime*›; **to ∼ up to having done sth./doing sth.** 承认做过某事; **she ∼ed up to having lied/forgotten** 她承认说谎了/忘了

own-brand, own-label *adjs* 自家品牌的

owner /ˈəʊnə(r)/ *n* 物主; **dog ∼** 狗主人; **car ∼** 车主; **restaurant ∼** 餐馆老板

owner-driver *n* 车主驾驶员

ownerless /ˈəʊnəlɪs/ *adj* 无主的 ‹*animal*›

owner: ∼-manager *n* 物主兼经理人; **∼-occupied** *adj* 业主自住的; **∼-occupier** *n* 住自家房屋者

ownership /ˈəʊnəʃɪp/ *n* [u] 所有权; **to be in** *or* **under private/public ∼** 属于私有/公有; **home-/share-∼** 房屋/股份所有权

own goal *n* 1 Sport 乌龙球 2 Brit fig colloq 无意中的损己行为; **the government's attempt to shift the blame was a real ∼** 政府试图推卸责任，结果却引火烧身

owt /aʊt/ *pron* N Eng colloq 任何东西; **I can't see ∼ without my glasses** 不戴眼镜我啥也看不见

ox /ɒks/ *n* (*pl* **oxen**) (animal) 去势公牛; fig (person) 壮汉; **as strong as an ∼** 非常强壮; **a blow that would have felled an ∼** 非常有力的一击

oxalic acid /ˌɒksælɪk ˈæsɪd/ *n* [u] 草酸

oxbow /ˈɒksbəʊ/ *n* [河道的] U 形河曲

oxbow lake *n* 牛轭湖

Oxbridge /ˈɒksbrɪdʒ/ *pr n* 牛津剑桥大学

oxen /ˈɒksn/ *pl* ▸ **ox**

Oxfam /ˈɒksfæm/ *pr n* **= Oxford Committee for Famine Relief** 牛津饥荒救济委员会

Oxford /ˈɒksfəd/ *pr n* 牛津

Oxford: ∼ blue ▸ **p. 134** *n* [u] 牛津蓝 [即深蓝色]; **∼ comma** *n* 连续逗号

Oxfordshire /ˈɒksfədʃə(r)/ *pr n* 牛津郡

oxidation /ˌɒksɪˈdeɪʃn/ *n* [u] 氧化（作用）

oxide /ˈɒksaɪd/ *n* 氧化物

oxidize /ˈɒksɪdaɪz/
A *vi* 氧化
B *vt* 使氧化

Oxon /ˈɒksən, -sɒn/ *abbr* Brit **= Oxfordshire**

oxtail /ˈɒksteɪl/ *n* [c and u] 牛尾

> **Oxbridge**
>
> 牛津剑桥大学。是 Oxford 和 Cambridge 的合称，常与红砖大学（redbrick，19 世纪末、20 世纪初以红砖为材料建成的大学）等其他大学相对而言。两所大学都是学院制大学（collegiate university），没有统一的校园，而是由 30 所左右独立的学院（college）组成。教学采取导师制（tutorial system），导师每次为 1 到 3 名学生授课，称为辅导（牛津称tutorial，剑桥称supervision）。获得两所大学学位者常在学位名称后加 Oxon 或 Cantab——如硕士学位 MA (Oxon) 和 MA (Cantab)——分别表示从牛津或剑桥毕业。牛津和剑桥在学术上是竞争对手，在体育方面也是如此。两校每年复活节前后举行的划船比赛（Boat Race）始于 1829 年，现已成为全国性赛事。

oxtail soup *n* [u] 牛尾汤

ox: ∼ tongue *n* [u and c] 1 (meat) 牛舌; 2 Bot 毛莲菜; **∼ wagon** *n* 牛车

oxyacetylene /ˌɒksɪəˈsetɪliːn/ *adj* 氧乙炔的

oxyacetylene burner, oxyacetylene lamp, oxyacetylene torch *ns* 氧乙炔炬

oxyfuel /ˈɒksɪfjuːəl/ *n* [u] 含氧燃料

oxygen /ˈɒksɪdʒən/ *n* [u] 氧气; **to be on ∼** 输氧; **an ∼ cylinder** *or* **bottle** 氧气瓶

oxygenate /ˈɒksɪdʒəneɪt/ *vt* 为…供氧

oxygenator /ˈɒksɪdʒəneɪtə(r)/ *n* 氧合器

oxygen: ∼ bar *n* 氧吧; **∼ debt** *n* [u and c] 氧债; **∼ mask** *n* 氧气面罩; **∼ tent** *n* 氧气帐

oxymoron /ˌɒksɪˈmɔːrɒn/ *n* 矛盾修辞法

oyster /ˈɔɪstə(r)/ *n* 牡蛎; **the world is your ∼** 你可以随心所欲

oyster: ∼ bed *n* [海底的] 牡蛎养殖床; **∼catcher** *n* 砺鹬; **∼ cracker** *n* Amer 牡蛎苏打饼干; **∼ farm** *n* 牡蛎养殖场

Oz /ɒz/ *pr n* colloq 澳大利亚

oz *abbr* **= ounce(s)** 盎司

ozone /ˈəʊzəʊn/ *n* 1 Chem 臭氧; **∼ molecule/pollution/distribution** 臭氧分子/污染/分布 2 colloq (pure, fresh air) [尤指来自大海的] 清新空气

ozone: ∼-depleting *adj* 损耗臭氧的; **∼ depletion** *n* [u] 臭氧损耗; **∼-friendly** *adj* 对臭氧层无害的 ‹*product, technology, gas*›; **∼ hole** *n* 臭氧洞; **∼ killer** *n* 臭氧杀手; **∼ layer** *n* 臭氧层

Pp

P, p /piː/
A *n* (*pl* **Ps** *or* **P's**) [英语字母表的第16个字母]; **to mind one's P's and Q's** colloq 谨言慎行
B **p** *abbr* **1** Brit **= penny, pence** **2** **= page¹ A; pp 2-9** 第 2 至 9 页

PA *abbr* **1** **= personal assistant** **2** **= public address system; to announce sth. over the ~** 在广播上宣布某事; **a ~ system** 扩音系统 **3** Amer **= Pennsylvania**

pa /pɑː/ *n* dated colloq 爸

p.a. *abbr* **= per annum**

pace /peɪs/
A *n* **1** (step) 一步; **to take a ~ forward/back** 向前迈/后退一步 **2** (distance) 步幅; **twenty ~s (away) from ...** 离…二十步远; **at (a distance of) thirty ~s** 在（相距）三十步远处 **3** (speed) 速度; **at a fast ~** 快速地; **at a brisk** *or* **cracking ~** 迅速地; **at a slow/steady ~** 以缓慢/平稳的速度; **to keep ~ with sb./sth.** 与某人/某物并驾齐驱; **to set the ~** (fix the speed) 确定速度; (establish the standard) 确立标准; (be the leader) 领先 **4** (rate) 节奏; **at a steady ~** 以平稳的步速; **at one's own ~** 按自己的节奏; **the leisurely ~ of life in the country** 乡间悠闲的生活节奏
B **paces** *npl* (routine) 步态; **to put a horse through its ~s** 让马展示步态; **to put sb. through their ~s** 考查某人的能力; **to show one's ~s** «*horse*» 展示步态; «*person*» 展示才能
C *vi* 踱步; **to ~ up and down** 走来走去
D *vt* **1** (walk up and down) 在…上走来走去 ‹*floor*›; 在…里走来走去 ‹*corridor, room*›; **I spent hours pacing the carpet in the waiting room** 我在等候室的地毯上来回走了好几个小时 **2** (set the pace for) 为…确定速度 ‹*runner, cyclist, competitor*›; **he ~d himself perfectly in the run-up to the competition** 他在比赛助跑阶段的速度控制得很完美; **he didn't ~ the lecture properly** 他没把握好演讲的节奏

Phrasal verb
- **pace out** *vt* [**~ out sth., ~ sth. out**] 以步丈量 ‹*distance*›

pacemaker /ˈpeɪsmeɪkə(r)/ *n* **1** Med 心脏起搏器 **2** Sport 领跑者 **3** fig (trendsetter) 先驱

pacer /ˈpeɪsə(r)/ *n* **1** esp Amer Equit 走对侧步的马 **2** **= pacemaker 2**

pacesetter /ˈpeɪssetə(r)/ *n* Amer **1** Sport 领跑者 **2** fig (trendsetter) 先驱

pacey /ˈpeɪsi/ *adj* **= pacy**

pachyderm /ˈpækɪdɜːm/ *n* 厚皮动物

Pacific /pəˈsɪfɪk/ *pr n* **the ~** 太平洋

pacific /pəˈsɪfɪk/ *adj* formal 平静的 ‹*nature, attitude*›; **~ intentions/overtures/policies** 息事宁人的意图/平和的提议/温和的政策

pacification /ˌpæsɪfɪˈkeɪʃn/ *n* [u] formal **1** (of person) 安抚 **2** (of country) 平定

Pacific: ~ Daylight Time *n* [u] Amer 太平洋夏令时间; **~ Islands** *npl* **the ~ Islands** 南太平洋各岛; **~ Ocean** *pr n* **the ~ Ocean** 太平洋; **~ Rim** *pr n* **the ~ Rim** 太平洋周边地区 [尤指东亚诸国]; **~ Standard Time** *n* [u] Amer 太平洋标准时间; **~ Time** *n* [u] Amer 太平洋时间

pacifier /ˈpæsɪfaɪə(r)/ *n* Amer 安抚奶嘴

pacifism /ˈpæsɪfɪzəm/ *n* [u] 和平主义

pacifist /ˈpæsɪfɪst/
A *n* 和平主义者
B *adj* 和平主义者的 ‹*views, aims*›

pacify /ˈpæsɪfaɪ/ *vt* **1** (calm) 安抚 ‹*person, baby*›; 平定 ‹*mob*› **2** (bring peace to) 使…实现和平 ‹*country, tribe*›

pack /pæk/
A *n* **1** (packet) 盒; **a ~ of cigarettes/paper hankies** 一盒香烟/纸巾; **a giant/economy-size ~** 大包装/经济装 **2** Brit (of cards) 一副 **3** (backpack) 背包; (carried by animal) 驮包 **4** (of wolves, hounds) 一群; (of bikers, motorcyclists) 一批; (of thieves) 一伙; **leader of the ~** 领先者; **to hunt in ~s** 集体出击; **a ~ of fools** 一群蠢材; **the young people go around in ~s terrorizing the neighbourhood** 这群年轻人拉帮结伙恐吓四邻 **5** + *v sing or pl* (in rugby) 全体前卫 **6** Sport **the ~** (runners) 跟跑队伍; (riders) 跟骑队伍 **7** Med, Cosmet 敷料
B *vt* **1** (stow) 收好 ‹*clothes, shoes*›; 包裹 ‹*meat, foodstuffs*›; 包装 ‹*appliances, goods*›; **to ~ sth. in sth.** 把某物装进某物 **2** (put things into) 装 ‹*suitcase, box*›; 打 ‹*parcel*›; **to ~ sth. with sth.** 把某物装到某物里; **we're ~ing a box with emergency supplies to send to refugees** 我们正把送给难民的紧急救援物资装箱; **to ~ one's bags** lit 收拾行装; fig 准备离开; **what made you decide to ~ your bags and move to another company?** 是什么让你决定离开，跳槽到另一家公司? **3** (package commercially) «*company, machine*» 加工包装 ‹*produce, goods*› **4** (cram into) «*crowd*» 挤满 ‹*hall, church, theatre*›; **to be ~ed with people** 挤满了人; **you can ~ a lot of reading into a two-week vacation** 两周的假期可以读很多书 **5** Med 包扎; **if you have a nosebleed, ~ the nostrils with cotton wool** 流鼻血时，用药棉塞住鼻孔 **6** (press firmly) 压实; **the wind ~ed the snow against the wall** 风把雪吹得紧贴在墙上; **to ~ the earth around the base of the plant** 把植物根部周围的土拍结实 **7** (fill with supporters) 在…中安插支持者 ‹*jury, committee, audience*› **8** **to ~ a punch** colloq (hit with force) «*fighter, boxer*» 能重拳出击; fig «*speaker, politician*» 很大影响力; «*drink*» 酒劲很大; **she ~ed quite a punch in the committee meeting** 她在委员会会议上的发言掷地有声; **that home-made cherry brandy ~s a tremendous punch** 那种家酿樱桃白兰地酒劲很大 **9** colloq (carry) 携带 ‹*gun*› **10** (store) 储藏; **they used to preserve fish by ~ing it in salt** 他们过去常用盐把鱼腌上储藏
C *vi* **1** (get one's things together) 打点行装 **2** (go, fit) 适合包装; **these little boxes will ~ very easily in the corner of a suitcase** 这些小盒子很容易塞到手提箱的角落 **3** (crowd) 挤满; **to ~ into sth.** 挤满某处

Phrasal verbs
- **pack away** *vt* [**~ sth. away, ~ away sth.**] **1** (put away) 收拾好 ‹*objects, toys, clothes*› **2** (for long-term storage) 保存; **those old photo albums are all ~ed away in the loft** 那些旧影集都存放在阁楼上
- **pack in** colloq
A *vt* **1** [**~ sth. in, ~ in sth.**] (give up, stop doing) 放弃; **to ~ one's job in** 辞掉工作; **to ~ in smoking/drinking** 戒烟/戒酒; **to ~ it (all) in** （彻底）结束; **she ~ed it all in and went off to live in America** 她放弃了一切去美国定居了; **if you don't ~ it in, you won't get any supper** 如果你再不听话，就别想吃晚饭了 **2** [**~ sb./sth. in**] (cram in) 把…塞进; **to be ~ing them in** Theat 场场爆满; **Cats ~ed them in for over twenty years** 《猫》上演二十多年来一直吸引着大批观众
B *vi* (break down) «*machine, car*» 出故障; «*heart, kidneys, liver*» 出毛病
- **pack off** *vt* [**~ sb. off**] colloq 打发; **to ~ sb. off (somewhere)** 打发某人（去某地）; **I was ~ed off to hospital for surgery** 我被送到医院做手术
- **pack up**
A *vi* **1** (get one's things together) 打点行装; **I'm all ~ed up and ready to go** 我整装待发 **2** colloq (finish) 停止; **let's ~ up now and finish the job tomorrow** 我们现在收工吧，明天再把活干完; **school ~s up in about a week's time** 学校大约一周之后放假 **3** colloq (break down) «*machine, engine*» 出故障; «*heart, kidneys, liver*» 出毛病
B *vt* **1** (put away) [**~ sth. up, ~ up sth.**] 收拾好 ‹*tools, belongings*› **2** colloq (stop) 结束 ‹*work, task*›

package /ˈpækɪdʒ/
A *n* **1** (parcel) 包裹 **2** (set, offer) 一组事物; **a ~ of reforms/proposals** 一整套改革/一揽子建议; **an insurance ~** 综合保险; **a pay** *or* **salary ~** 薪酬待遇; **to be part of the ~** 被包括在内 **3** Amer (pack) 包; **a ~ of cigarettes/peanuts** 一包香烟/花生 **4** colloq (tour) 包价旅游 **5** Comput 软件包
B *vt* **1** (put in packaging) 把…打包 ‹*product*› **2** (create image for) 包装 ‹*programme, singer*›; **to ~ news as entertainment** 把新闻包装成娱乐节目 **3** (combine for sale) 捆绑销售 ‹*holidays, services*›

package: ~ deal *n* 一揽子交易; **~ holiday** *n* Brit 包价旅游; **~ store** *n* Amer 瓶装酒销售店; **~ tour** *n* 包价旅游; **~ tourist** *n* 包价旅游者; **~ vacation** *n* Amer 包价旅游

packaging /ˈpækɪdʒɪŋ/ *n* [u] **1** (material) 包装材料 **2** (process of wrapping) 包装 **3** (presentation) 形象包装

pack: ~ animal *n* **1** (used for transport) 驮畜; **2** (living in pack) 群兽; **~ drill** *n* 负重操练; **no names, no ~ drill** 不知其名，无从惩罚

packed /pækt/
A *adj* **1** (crowded) 拥挤的 ‹*hall, house*›; **~ out** Brit colloq 挤得水泄不通的; **to be ~ with people** 挤满人 **2** (full) 满的; **to be ~ with ...** 充满 ‹*information, objects*› **3** (having done one's packing) 收拾好行李的; **are you ~?** 你打点好行李了吗?

B **-packed** *combining form* 装满的; **fun~ holidays** 充满乐趣的假期; **a thrill~ journey** 令人兴奋不已的旅行

packed lunch *n* 自备的午餐

packer /ˈpækə(r)/ *n* **1** (person) 包装工 **2** (machine) 包装机

packet /ˈpækɪt/ *n* **1** Brit (box) 盒; (bag) 包; **a ~ of cigarettes/cornflakes/biscuits** 一盒香烟/一袋脆玉米片/一包饼干 **2** (parcel) 小件包裹 **3** Comput 数据包 **4** esp Brit colloq (large sum of money) 一大笔钱; **to cost/earn a ~** 花/挣一大笔钱

packet switching *n* [u] 分组交换

pack: ~ **horse** *n* 驮马; ~ **ice** *n* [u] 浮冰群

packing /ˈpækɪŋ/ *n* [u] **1** (of possessions) 收拾行囊; **to do one's ~** 收拾行李 **2** (of products) 包装 **3** (material) 包装材料 **4** Tech (filling) 填料

packing: ~ **case** *n* Brit [尤指木制的] 装货箱; ~ **density** *n* 存储密度; ~ **slip** *n* 装箱单

pack: **~sack** *n* Amer 旅行背包; **~saddle** *n* esp Amer 驮鞍; **~thread** *n* [u] 打包绳

pact /pækt/ *n* 协定; **a non-aggression ~** 互不侵犯条约; **to make a ~ with sb.** 与某人签署条约; **to make a ~ to do sth.** 达成协议做某事; **to make a ~ with the devil** colloq 与魔鬼勾结

pacy /ˈpeɪsi/ *adj* **1** (developing quickly) 进展快的 ‹*film, novel*› **2** (fast) 能快跑的 ‹*player*›

pad /pæd/

A *n* **1** (cushioning material) 软垫; **a foam/rubber/felt ~** 泡沫垫/橡胶垫/毡垫; **a scouring ~** 百洁布 **2** Sport (in cricket, hockey) 防护垫; **to wear ~s** 戴护垫 **3** (block of paper) 便笺簿; **a desk ~** 台笺簿; **a ~ of notepaper** 记事簿; **a telephone note ~** 电话留言簿 **4** (of animal's foot) 爪垫; (of human finger) 指肚 **5** (for space launch) 发射台 **6** Bot 睡莲浮叶 **7** (sanitary towel) 卫生巾 **8** colloq (house, flat, room) 住所; **a bachelor ~** 单身公寓

B *vi* (*pres p etc.* **-dd-**) 蹑手蹑脚地走; **he ~ded into the room quietly** 他悄悄地走进房间

C *vt* (*pres p etc.* **-dd-**) **1** (put padding in or on) 给…加衬垫 ‹*jacket, dress, shoulders*›; **to ~ sth. with sth.** 用某物填充某物; **I ~ded the wound with cotton wool** 我在伤口上敷了块药棉 **2** = **pad out 1**

Phrasal verb

- **pad out** *vt* [**~ out sth., ~ sth. out**] **1** (expand unnecessarily) 拉长…的篇幅 ‹*essay*›; 拉长 ‹*speech*› **2** (add items to) 使…丰富 ‹*meal, course*›; 虚报 ‹*bill, expense account*›; **to ~ sth. out with sth.** 给某物添加某物

padded /ˈpædɪd/ *adj* 有衬垫的 ‹*seat, armrest*›; 有垫肩的 ‹*jacket, dress*›; 加垫的 ‹*bra*›; **~ shoulders** 垫肩

padded: ~ **cell** *n* [精神病院的] 软壁病房; ~ **envelope** *n* 夹衬垫的信封

padding /ˈpædɪŋ/ *n* [u] **1** (foam) 垫料; (stuffing) 填料; **protective ~** 防护衬垫 **2** (in book, speech) 赘语

paddle /ˈpædl/

A *n* **1** (oar) 短桨 **2** (on waterwheel) 桨叶 **3** Brit (in sea) 涉水; **to go for** *or* **have a ~** 去趟水

B *vt* **1** (row) 用桨划 ‹*boat*›; **to ~ one's own canoe** fig colloq 自力更生 **2** (dip) 在水中摆动 ‹*feet, fingers*› **3** Amer colloq (spank) 掌掴

C *vi* **1** (row) 划桨 **2** (swim) «*water bird*» 蹼游 **3** Brit (in sea) 涉水

paddle: ~ **boat** *n* 明轮船; ~ **steamer** *n* 明轮船; ~ **wheel** *n* 明轮

paddling pool *n* Brit (at swimming baths) 戏水池; (at home) 浅水池

paddock /ˈpædək/ *n* **1** (field) [牧马或驯马的] 小围场 **2** Horse racing 集中场 **3** (in motor racing) 装备区

Paddy /ˈpædi/ *n* colloq offensive 帕迪 [指爱尔兰人]

paddy[1] /ˈpædi/ *n* **1** [c] (field) 稻田 **2** [u] (rice) 稻谷

paddy[2] *n* Brit colloq (temper fit) 发脾气 [尤指孩子气]; **to be in** *or* **get into a ~** 发怒

paddy: **~field** *n* 稻田; ~ **wagon** *n* Amer colloq 囚车

padlock /ˈpædlɒk/

A *n* 挂锁

B *vt* 用挂锁锁住 ‹*gate, bike*›

padre /ˈpɑːdreɪ/ *n* 随军牧师

paean /ˈpiːən/ *n* liter (of praise) 赞歌; (of triumph) 凯歌

paederast /ˈpedəræst/ *n* = **pederast**

paederasty /ˈpedəræsti/ *n* = **pederasty**

paediatric /ˌpiːdɪˈætrɪk/ *adj* Brit 儿科的; **a ~ ward/nurse** 儿科病房/护士

paediatrician /ˌpiːdɪəˈtrɪʃn/ *n* Brit 儿科医生

paediatrics /ˌpiːdɪˈætrɪks/ *npl + v sing* Brit 儿科学

paedophile /ˈpiːdəfaɪl/ *n* Brit 恋童癖者

paedophilia /ˌpiːdəˈfɪlɪə/ *n* [u] Brit 恋童癖

paella /paɪˈelə/ *n* [u and c] 西班牙什锦饭

pagan /ˈpeɪgən/

A *adj* 异教徒的 ‹*ritual, festival*›

B *n* 异教徒

paganism /ˈpeɪgənɪzəm/ *n* [u] 异教

page[1] /peɪdʒ/

A *n* **1** (in book, newspaper) 页; **at the top** *or* **head of the ~** 在页眉; **at the foot** *or* **bottom of the ~** 在页脚; **the sports/women's ~** 体育/女性版 **2** Comput 页面 **3** fig (episode) 一段历史; **a ~ in the history of the world** 世界史上的一页

B *vt* **1** (over loudspeaker) 通过广播呼叫; **paging Mr Jones** 呼叫琼斯先生 **2** (on pager) 用寻呼机呼叫 **3** (paginate) 为…标页码 ‹*book*›

C *vi* **1** (turn pages) **to ~ backwards and forwards** 前后翻阅; **to ~ through a magazine** 翻阅杂志 **2** Comput **to ~ up/down** 向上/向下翻页

page[2] *n* **1** (in hotel) 男服务生 **2** Amer (in Congress) 青年助理 **3** (at wedding) 小男傧相 **4** Hist (servant) 青年侍从; (knight's attendant) 学习骑士

pageant /ˈpædʒənt/ *n* **1** (entertainment) 露天历史剧; (carnival) [历史事件的] 庆典 **2** (exhibition) 选美比赛; **a beauty ~** 选美比赛 **3** fig (series of events) 繁杂有趣的场面; **part of life's rich ~** 丰富的人生画卷的一部分

pageantry /ˈpædʒəntri/ *n* [u] 盛典

page: **~boy** *n* **1** (at wedding) 小男傧相; **2** (hairstyle) 女子齐肩内卷发; ~ **break** *n* (in text) 分页处; Comput 分页符; ~ **number** *n* 页码; ~ **proof** *n* 拼版样

pager /ˈpeɪdʒə(r)/ *n* 寻呼机

page: ~ **reference** *n* 页码索引; ~ **set-up** *n* 页面设置; **P~ Three®** *n* Brit 第三版 [《太阳报》刊登在第三版的半裸女子特写]; **a P~ Three girl/model** 三版女郎/模特

paginate /ˈpædʒɪneɪt/ *vt* 为…标页码 ‹*book, manuscript*›

pagination /ˌpædʒɪˈneɪʃn/ *n* [u] 标页码

paging /ˈpeɪdʒɪŋ/ *n* [u] **1** Print 标页码 **2** (on pager) 用寻呼机呼叫

paging device *n* 寻呼器

pagoda /pəˈgəʊdə/ *n* (temple) 佛塔; (ornamental structure) 宝塔式建筑

paid /peɪd/

A *pt, pp* ▸ **pay A, B**

B *adj* 有偿的 ‹*work*›; 带薪的 ‹*holiday*›; 领薪金的 ‹*worker*›; 受雇的 ‹*informer, assassin*›; **to put ~ to sth.** Brit colloq 使…成为泡影 ‹*chance*›; 使…破灭 ‹*hope*›

paid-up *adj* **1** (fully-paid) 已付清会费的 ‹*member*› **2** Brit fig colloq (committed) 忠实的 **3** Fin 到账的 ‹*shares, capital*›

pail /peɪl/ *n* (bucket) 桶; (bucketful) 一桶; **a ~ of water** 一桶水

pain /peɪn/

A *n* **1** [u] (physical or mental suffering) 痛苦; **to scream/yell with ~** 痛苦地尖叫/大叫; **a cry of ~** 痛苦的喊叫; **the ~ of separation/loss** 分离/死别之苦 **2** [c] (localized discomfort) 疼痛; **a ~ in the shoulder/leg** 肩疼/腿疼; **whereabouts is the ~?** 哪里疼？; **stomach/abdominal/period/labour ~s** 胃痛/腹痛/经痛/分娩阵痛 **3** [c] colloq pej (nuisance) (person) 讨厌的人; (thing) 烦心事; **a ~ in the neck** (person) 讨厌的人; (thing) 烦心事; **my father/this typewriter is a ~ in the neck** 我父亲/这台打字机真烦人; **a ~ in the arse** Brit *or* **ass** Amer sl pej (person) 极讨厌的人; (thing) 极烦心的事 **4** [u] **on ~ of sth./doing sth.** 违反则以某事/做某事论处; **you are forbidden on ~ of death to take messages to the prisoners** 不得向犯人传信，违者处死

B **pains** *npl* 辛苦; **to take** *or* **go to ~s over** *or* **with sth.** 小心翼翼地做某事; **to take ~s to do sth.** 费力做某事; **to be at ~s to do sth.** 下苦功做某事; **to spare no ~s (to do sth.)** 不遗余力（做某事）; **for my/his/her ~s** iron 作为我/他/她辛苦的报酬; **he got a black eye for his ~s** 辛苦一番，他却被揍得眼圈青肿

C *vt* **1** (give pain to) «*part of body*» 使疼痛; **my leg still ~s me a little** 我的腿仍然有点疼 **2** (grieve, distress) **it ~s me to do this** formal 做这事让我心痛; **it ~s me to see how thin she has become** 看到她变得这么瘦，我很心痛

pain: ~ **barrier** *n* 痛障; ~ **clinic** *n* 疼痛门诊

pained /peɪnd/ *adj* 痛苦的 ‹*expression*›; 凄惨的 ‹*voice*›; **to look ~** 表情痛苦

painful /ˈpeɪnfl/ *adj* **1** (causing pain) 引起疼痛的 ‹*fall, injury*›; (full of pain) 疼痛的 ‹*arm, toe*› **2** (upsetting) 令人痛苦的 ‹*experience, process*› **3** (laborious) 艰苦的 ‹*effort, task*› **4** colloq (bad) 糟糕的 ‹*performance*›

painfully /ˈpeɪnfəli/ *adv* **1** (excruciatingly) 疼痛地 ‹*bruised, swollen*› **2** (with difficulty) 艰难地 ‹*walk, get up*› **3** (extremely) 极其 ‹*obvious*›; 强烈地 ‹*conscious*›; **to be ~ shy** 极其羞涩; **I am ~ aware that ...** 我强烈地意识到…

pain: **~killer** *n* 止痛药; **~killing** *adj attrib* 止痛的 ‹*drug, injection*›

painless /ˈpeɪnlɪs/ *adj* **1** (without pain) 无痛的 ‹*operation, death*› **2** (easy) 轻松的 ‹*way, experience*›

painlessly /ˈpeɪnlɪsli/ *adv* **1** (without pain) 无痛地 ‹*inject, die*› **2** (easily) 轻松地 ‹*achieved, completed*›

pain relief *n* [u] 止痛

painstaking /ˈpeɪnzteɪkɪŋ/ *adj* 艰苦的 ‹*work*›; 细心的 ‹*research*›; 勤勉的 ‹*person*›

painstakingly /ˈpeɪnzteɪkɪŋli/ *adv* 细心地 ‹*researched, planned*›

paint /peɪnt/

A *n* **1** [u] (for decorating) 油漆; **a can** *or* **tin** *or* **pot of ~** 一罐油漆; **be careful, the ~'s still wet on that door** 当心，门上的油漆未干; **it's like watching ~ dry** 这真无聊透顶 **2** [u] (used by artist) 颜料; **acrylic ~** 丙烯酸颜料 **3** [c] **~s** Art 绘画颜料; **a box of ~s** 一盒水彩颜料; **a set of oil ~s** 一套油画颜料 **4** [u] hum (make-up) 化妆品; **she always puts too much ~ on** 她总是浓妆艳抹

B *vt* **1** (apply paint to) 为…刷漆 ‹*room, house*›; **I'm ~ing the walls (in) pink** 我在把墙漆成粉红色; **to ~ one's nails** 涂指甲油; **to ~ the town (red)** 狂欢 **2** (draw) «*painter, artist*» 用颜料画 ‹*portrait, landscape*›; **to ~ a picture on canvas/board/paper** 在画布/木板/纸上作画 **3** (portray) 描绘; **their diaries ~ a vivid picture of country life** 他们的日记生动地描绘了乡村生活; **not as black as he/she/it is ~ed** 他/她/它不像人们说得那么坏

4 (apply with a brush) 涂抹; **to ~ varnish on sth.** 在某处涂抹清漆 5 (apply make-up to) 在…上涂化妆品 ‹*face*›; **to ~ one's nails** 涂指甲; **she ~s her lips bright red** 她把嘴唇涂得鲜红
C *vi* 1 Art ‹*artist*› 绘画; **to ~ in oils/watercolours** 用油画颜料/水彩作画; **I prefer to ~ outdoors** 我更喜欢在户外作画; **to ~ on canvas/wood** 在画布/木头上画画 2 (decorate) 刷油漆

Phrasal verbs

• **paint in** *vt* [**~ sth. in, ~ in sth.**] 补画 ‹*figure, detail*›
• **paint out** *vt* [**~ sth. out, ~ out sth.**] 用颜料涂掉

paintball /ˈpeɪntbɔːl/ ▸**p. 307** *n* [u] 彩弹游戏
paintball gun *n* 彩弹枪
paint: ~box *n* 颜料盒; **~brush** *n* (used by artist) 画笔; (used by decorator) 漆刷
painted lady *n* 小芒麻赤蛱蝶
painter¹ /ˈpeɪntə(r)/ ▸**p. 409** *n* 1 Art 画家; **an abstract/a portrait ~** 抽象/肖像画家 2 (decorator) 油漆匠; **~ and decorator** 油漆装饰工
painter² *n* Naut 缆绳
pain threshold *n* 痛阈; **to have a high/low ~** 痛阈高/低
painting /ˈpeɪntɪŋ/ *n* 1 [u] Art (activity) 绘画; **~ in oils/watercolour** 油画/水彩画绘画 2 [c] (picture) 画; **a ~ of sth.** 画着某物的画 3 [u] (decorating) 上漆
painting book *n* 绘画着色本
paint: ~pot *n* 油漆罐; **~ remover** *n* [u] 1 (for stains) 除漆剂; 2 (before repainting) 脱漆剂; **~ roller** *n* 滚筒油漆刷; **~ spray** *n* 喷漆器; **~ stripper** *n* 1 [u] (solvent) 脱漆剂; 2 [c] (tool) 除漆刮刀; **~ tray** *n* 调漆皿; **~work** *n* [u] (in house) 漆层; (on car, ship) 漆面
pair /peə(r)/
A *n* 1 (of gloves, socks, shoes) 一双; (of cards, ornaments) 一对; **to be one of a ~** 是一对中的一个; **a matching ~** 相匹配的一对; **these gloves aren't a ~** 这两只手套不是一副; **I've only got one ~ of hands!** 我只有一双手!; **she's got a nice ~ of legs** 她有一双美腿; **in ~s** 成对地 2 (of trousers, pants) 一条; (of pyjamas) 一套; (of scissors, shears) 一把; **a ~ of glasses** 一副眼镜 3 (two people) 俩人; **you're a right ~ of fools/layabouts** colloq 你们是一对十足的傻瓜/懒汉 4 (married couple) 夫妻俩 5 (of animals) 一对动物; **a coach and ~** 双驾四轮马车 6 (matching item) 配对的另一个; **I'm looking for a ~ to this china figure** 我正在寻找与这个瓷人配对的另一只
B *vt* 1 (organize in pairs) 把…配对; **I'll ~ the socks and put them in the drawer** 我来把这些短袜配成双放在抽屉里 2 (put together as a pair) 与…搭配 ‹*clothes*›; 为…配搭档 ‹*people*›; 使…交配 ‹*animals*›; **to ~ the jeans with a T-shirt** 用T恤和牛仔裤搭配; **to ~ each name with a photograph** 把每个名字与相应的照片放在一起; **to ~ sb. with sb.** 让某人和某人结对; **I've been ~ed with Jonathan for the mixed doubles** 我被指派与乔纳森组成一对参加混合双打
C *vi* ‹*animals, birds*› 交配; ‹*people*› 结婚; **I'll ~ with Timothy** 我将与蒂莫西结成夫妻

Phrasal verbs

• **pair off**
A *vt* [**~ sb. off, ~ off sb.**] 撮合; **my mother keeps trying to ~ David and me off** 我妈妈一直想撮合我和戴维; **to ~ sb. off with sb.** 撮合某人和某人
B *vi* 结对; **to ~ off with sb.** 与某人配对; **I ~ed off with Charles** 我和查尔斯成了搭档
• **pair up**
A *vi* 结对; **to ~ up with sb.** 与某人结成对; **I ~ed up with Jean to do the experiment** 我与吉恩联手做实验
B *vt* = **pair B**

pair: ~ bond *n* [动物间的] 配偶关系; **~ bonding** *n* [u] 配偶键
paisley /ˈpeɪzli/ *n* [u] 1 (pattern) 佩斯利图案; **a ~ skirt/tie** 佩斯利花纹裙子/领带 2 (fabric) 佩斯利花纹织物
pajamas /pəˈdʒɑːməz/ *npl* Amer = **pyjamas A**
pak choi /ˌpæk ˈtʃɔɪ/ *n* [u] 小白菜
Paki /ˈpæki/ *n* (*pl* **~s**) Brit colloq offensive 巴基佬 [指巴基斯坦人] offensive
Paki: ~-basher /ˈpækɪbæʃə(r)/ *n* Brit colloq pej 殴打巴基佬的人; **~-bashing** *n* [u] Brit colloq pej 对巴基佬施暴
Pakistan /ˌpɑːkɪˈstɑːn, ˌpækɪ-/ *pr n* 巴基斯坦
Pakistani /ˌpɑːkɪˈstɑːni, ˌpækɪ-/ ▸**p. 503**
A *adj* (of Pakistan) 巴基斯坦的; (of the people) 巴基斯坦人的
B *n* 巴基斯坦人
pal /pæl/ *n* colloq 1 (friend) 好友; **to be ~s with sb.** 与某人是哥们儿 2 (form of address) 小子; **listen to me, ~ ...** 听我说, 小子…

Phrasal verb

• **pal up** *vi* colloq 成为朋友; **to ~ up with sb.** 与某人成为哥们儿

palace /ˈpælɪs/ *n* 1 (of ruler) 宫; (of bishop) 府 2 **the P~** + *v sing or pl* (royal family) 王室 3 colloq (mansion) 豪宅
palace revolution *n* 宫廷政变
Palaeocene /ˈpæliəsiːn/ Brit
A *adj* (of the period) 古新世的; (of the rock system) 古新统的
B *n* **the ~** (period) 古新世; (rock system) 古新统
palaeography /ˌpælɪˈɒɡrəfi/ *n* [u] Brit 古文字学
Palaeolithic /ˌpælɪəˈlɪθɪk/ Brit
A *adj* 旧石器时代的 ‹*man*›; **the ~ age/era** 旧石器时代/纪元
B *n* **the ~** 旧石器时代
palaeontology /ˌpælɪɒnˈtɒlədʒi/ [u] Brit 古生物学
Palaeozoic /ˌpeɪlɪəˈzəʊɪk/
A *adj* Brit (of the period) 古生代的; (of the rock system) 古生界的
B *n* **the ~** (period) 古生代; (rock system) 古生界
palatable /ˈpælətəbl/ *adj* 1 (tasty) 可口的 ‹*food, meal*› 2 (acceptable) 可接受的 ‹*proposal, solution*›
palatal /ˈpælətl/
A *adj* 1 Phon 腭音的; **~ sound/consonant** 腭音/腭辅音 2 Anat 腭的; **~ bone** 腭骨
B *n* 腭音
palatalize /ˈpælətəlaɪz/ *vt* 使…腭化 ‹*consonant*›
palate /ˈpælət/ *n* 1 Anat 腭; **the hard/soft ~** 硬腭/软腭 2 (sense of taste) 味觉; **to have a discriminating ~** 善于品味
palatial /pəˈleɪʃl/ *adj* 富丽堂皇的 ‹*bedroom, suite, apartment, hotel, house*›
palaver /pəˈlɑːvə(r), Amer -ˈlæv-/ *n* [u] Brit colloq 忙乱; **what a ~!** 真是烦死人!
pale¹ /peɪl/ ▸**p. 134**
A *adj* 1 (white) 苍白的 ‹*face, complexion*›; 白皙的 ‹*skin*›; **to turn *or* go ~** 变得苍白; **~ with fright** 吓得面无人色的 2 (light) 浅的 ‹*yellow, blue*›; 微弱的 ‹*shade, tint*›; 暗淡的 ‹*light, reflection*›
B *vi* 1 (turn pale) 变得苍白 2 fig (diminish) 相形失色; **to ~ beside *or* next to *or* in comparison with sth.** 与某物相比显得逊色; **to ~ into insignificance** 变得微不足道
pale² *n* **to be beyond the ~** ‹*behaviour, person*› 越轨; ‹*remark*› 出格
pale: ~ ale *n* [u and c] 淡色苦麦芽啤酒; **~face** *n* pej hum 白脸人 [北美印第安人对白种人的称呼]; **~-faced** *adj* 脸色苍白的 ‹*person*›
paleness /ˈpeɪlnɪs/ *n* [u] 1 (of face, complexion) 苍白; (of skin) 白皙 2 (of colour) 浅淡
Paleocene /ˈpælɪəsiːn/ *adj, n* Amer = **Palaeocene**
paleography /ˌpælɪˈɒɡrəfi/ *n* [u] Amer = **palaeography**
Paleolithic /ˌpælɪəˈlɪθɪk/ *adj, n* Amer = **Palaeolithic**
paleontology /ˌpælɪɒnˈtɒlədʒi/ *n* [u] Amer = **palaeontology**
Paleozoic /ˌpælɪəˈzəʊɪk/ *adj, n* Amer = **Palaeozoic**
Palestine /ˈpæləstaɪn/ *pr n* 巴勒斯坦
Palestine Liberation Organization *n* 巴勒斯坦解放组织
Palestinian /ˌpælɪˈstɪnɪən/ ▸**p. 503**
A *adj* (of Palestine) 巴勒斯坦的; (of the people) 巴勒斯坦人的
B *n* 巴勒斯坦人
palette /ˈpælɪt/ *n* 1 (board) 调色板 2 (colours) 一组颜色
palette knife *n* 1 Art 调色刀 2 Brit Culin 铲刀
palimony /ˈpælɪməni/ *n* [u] esp Amer colloq [法院判给前未婚同居对象的] 生活费
palindrome /ˈpælɪndrəʊm/ *n* 回文
paling /ˈpeɪlɪŋ/
A *n* (stake) 尖板条
B **palings** *npl* (fence) 栅栏
palisade /ˌpælɪˈseɪd/
A *n* (of wood) 木栅栏; (of iron) 铁栅栏
B **palisades** *npl* Amer [河边或海边的] 绝壁
pall¹ /pɔːl/ *n* 1 (for coffin) 棺罩 2 (cloud) 尘烟; **a ~ of smoke/dust** 一团烟雾/沙尘 3 fig (atmosphere) 阴郁的气氛; **to cast a ~ of gloom/depression/terror over sth.** 使某事物笼罩上阴郁/沮丧/恐怖的气氛
pall² *vi* (become boring) 变得乏味; **to ~ on sb.** ‹*repeated activity*› 对某人失去吸引力
palladium /pəˈleɪdɪəm/ *n* [u] 钯
pallbearer /ˈpɔːlbeərə(r)/ *n* 抬棺人
pallet /ˈpælɪt/ *n* 托盘
palletize /ˈpælɪtaɪz/ *vt* 用托盘装运 ‹*product*›
pallet truck *n* 叉式装卸车
palliate /ˈpælɪeɪt/ *vt* 1 Med 减轻 ‹*disease, symptom*› 2 fig formal (mitigate) 掩饰 ‹*offence, crime*›
palliative /ˈpælɪətɪv/
A *adj* 1 Med 治标的 ‹*drug, effect*›; **~ care/treatment** 缓和疗护/保守疗法 2 formal (mitigating) 权宜的; **a ~ measure** 权宜之计
B *n* 1 Med 治标药物 2 formal (measure) 权宜之计
pallid /ˈpælɪd/ *adj* 1 (pale) 苍白的 ‹*complexion, face*›; 暗淡的 ‹*light*›; **a ~ ray of winter sun** 一缕惨淡的冬日阳光 2 (insipid) 乏味的 ‹*performance, presentation*›
pallor /ˈpælə(r)/ *n* [u] 苍白的脸色
pally /ˈpæli/ *adj pred* Brit colloq 亲密友好的; **to be ~ with sb.** 与某人很亲密
palm¹ /pɑːm/
A *n* 手掌; **to read sb.'s ~** 为某人看手相; **to grease *or* oil sb.'s ~** fig colloq 向某人行贿; **to have *or* hold sb./sth. in the hand of one's hand** fig colloq 完全控制某人/某事
B *vt* 1 (conceal) ‹*conjuror, dealer*› 把…藏在手中 ‹*card, coin*› 2 (steal) 顺手偷走 ‹*money*› 3 ‹*goalkeeper*› 用手掌挡 ‹*ball*›

Phrasal verb

• **palm off** *vt* colloq 1 [**~ sth. off, ~ off sth.**] (sell, dispose of) 骗卖; **to ~ sth. off as sth.** 把某物作为某物推销出去; **to ~ sth. off on/onto sb.** 骗某人接受某人/某物 2 **to ~ sb. off with sth.** (persuade to accept) 以某事物搪塞某人

P

P

palm² *n* **1** (tree) 棕榈树 **2** (leaf) 棕榈叶; (as mark of honour) 荣誉标志

palmcorder /ˈpɑːmkɔːdə(r)/ *n* 掌上摄像机

palmist /ˈpɑːmɪst/ ▸**p. 409** *n* 看手相的人

palmistry /ˈpɑːmɪstri/ *n* [u] 手相术

palm: P~ Sunday *n* 棕枝主日 [复活节前的星期日]; **~top computer** *n* 掌上电脑; **~ tree** *n* 棕榈树

palpable /ˈpælpəbl/ *adj* **1** (tangible) 可触摸到的 ‹*lump*› **2** fig (obvious) 明显的 ‹*lie, difference*›; (intense) 易觉察的 ‹*tension*›; **a ~ sense of relief** 明显的如释重负感

palpably /ˈpælpəbli/ *adv* 明显地 ‹*false, clear*›

palpitate /ˈpælpɪteɪt/ *vi* **1** Med «*heart*» 悸动 **2** (tremble) «*person*» 发抖; **to ~ with fear/excitement/terror** 害怕/激动/恐惧得发抖

palpitation /ˌpælpɪˈteɪʃn/ *n* Med 心悸; **to have ~s** 心悸

paltry /ˈpɔːltri/ *adj* **1** (small) 可忽略不计的 ‹*sum, amount*› **2** (trivial) 微不足道的 ‹*effort*›; 无意义的 ‹*excuse, gesture*›

pampas /ˈpæmpəs, Amer -əz/ *n + v sing or pl* **the ~** 南美大草原

pampas grass *n* [u] 蒲苇

pamper /ˈpæmpə(r)/ *vt* 纵容 ‹*child, pet*›; **to ~ oneself** 放纵自己

pamphlet /ˈpæmflɪt/ *n* **1** (leaflet) 小册子 **2** (political) 传单; (satirical) 抨击文章

pamphleteer /ˌpæmflɪˈtɪə(r)/ *n* 小册子作者

pan¹ /pæn/

A *n* **1** Culin 有柄平底锅; **pots and ~s** 锅壶瓢盆; **a ~ of water** 一锅水 **2** (on scales) 秤盘 **3** Brit (toilet) 马桶; **to go down the ~** fig (fail) 失败; «*economy*» 萧条; «*scheme*» 作废 **4** Mining 淘盘

B *vt* (*pres p etc.* **-nn-**) **1** Mining 淘洗 ‹*gravel*›; 淘 ‹*gold*›; 在…淘金 ‹*river*› **2** colloq (criticize) 抨击 ‹*film, book, actor*›

C *vi* (*pres p etc.* **-nn-**) Mining 淘金; **to ~ for** 淘 ‹*gold*›

Phrasal verb

- **pan out** *vi* colloq **1** (turn out) 结果是; **things didn't ~ out as I'd expected** 事情的结果并不如我所料; **it ~ned out well in the end** 最终结果不错 **2** (turn out well) 结果令人满意

pan² (*pres p etc.* **-nn-**) Cin, Phot, TV

A *vi* «*camera, person*» 摇摄; **the camera ~ned back to the audience** 摄影机摇回拍摄观众

B *vt* 使摇摄; **to ~ the camera** 摇镜头拍摄全景

panacea /ˌpænəˈsiːə/ *n* 万应药

panache /pæˈnæʃ, Amer pə-/ *n* [u] 神气十足

pan-African *adj* 泛非的 ‹*policy, unity*›; **a ~ conference** 泛非大会

pan-Africanism /ˌpænˈæfrɪkənɪzəm/ *n* [u] 泛非主义

Panama /ˈpænəmɑː/

A *pr n* 巴拿马; **~ City** 巴拿马城

B (*also* **panama**) *n* (hat) 巴拿马草帽

Panama: ~ Canal *pr n* 巴拿马运河; **~ hat** *n* 巴拿马草帽

Panamanian /ˌpænəˈmeɪmɪən/ ▸**p. 503**

A *adj* (of Panama) 巴拿马的; (of the people) 巴拿马人的

B *n* 巴拿马人

pan-American *adj* 泛美的 ‹*unity, conference*›; **the ~ Highway/Union** 泛美高速公路/联盟

pan-Americanism /ˌpænəˈmerɪkənɪzəm/ *n* [u] 泛美主义

pancake /ˈpæŋkeɪk/

A *n* 薄煎饼; **as flat as a ~** fig colloq 非常平的

B *vi* «*plane*» 平坠降落; «*pilot*» 驾机平坠降落

pancake: P~ Day *n* 薄饼日 [封斋期的前一天，按传统习惯吃薄饼]; **~ landing** *n* 平坠着陆; **to make a ~ landing** 进行平降; **~ race** *n* 薄饼赛跑 [参赛者边跑边将平底锅中的薄煎饼抛向空中]

pancreas /ˈpæŋkrɪəs/ *n* (*pl* **~es**) 胰腺

pancreatic /ˌpæŋkrɪˈætɪk/ *adj* 胰腺的; **~ cancer/tissue/enzyme** 胰腺癌/胰腺组织/胰酶

panda /ˈpændə/ *n* **(giant) ~** 大熊猫

panda car *n* Brit colloq 巡逻警车

pandemic /pænˈdemɪk/

A *adj* 大范围流行的 ‹*disease, flu*›

B *n* 大流行病

pandemonium /ˌpændɪˈməʊnɪəm/ *n* [u] 混乱; **it's sheer** *or* **absolute ~** 简直是一片混乱

pander /ˈpændə(r)/ *vi* 迎合; **to ~ to sb./sth.** 迎合 ‹*person*›; 满足 ‹*whim, market*›

Pandora's box /pænˌdɔːrəz ˈbɒks/ *n* 潘多拉魔盒 [指邪恶之源]; **this court case could open up a ~ of similar claims** 这宗诉讼案可能会为类似的申诉开启潘多拉魔盒

pane /peɪn/ *n* 窗玻璃; **a ~ of glass** 一片窗玻璃

panegyric /ˌpænɪˈdʒɪrɪk/ *n* formal (speech) 颂词; (writing) 颂文; **a ~ on sb./sth.** 对某人/某物的颂扬

panel /ˈpænl/

A *n* **1** Archit 嵌板; **glass/wooden ~** 玻璃板/木壁板 **2** Aut, Tech (section) 金属板 **3** (control panel) 控制板; **an instrument/display ~** 仪表/显示盘 **4** (in sewing) 镶饰片 **5** (of judges, advisers) 专家咨询组; **a ~ of experts** 专家组; **to be on a ~** 出席顾问小组 **6** Radio, TV (on quiz show) 评委小组; (on talk show) 讨论小组; **on our ~ tonight we have ...** 今晚出席座谈会的有…

B *vt* (*pres p etc.* **-ll-** Brit, **-l-** Amer) 用镶板镶 ‹*surface, room*›; **to ~ a wall in** *or* **with oak** 用橡木板装饰墙壁; **a ~led door/ceiling** 镶板门/天花板; **oak-/wood-~led** 镶橡木/木板的

panel: ~-beater *n* Brit 板金工; **~-beating** *n* [u] Brit 板金加工; **~ game** *n* Brit 分组智力竞赛

panelling Brit, **paneling** Amer /ˈpænəlɪŋ/ *n* [u] 镶板

panellist Brit, **panelist** Amer /ˈpænəlɪst/ *n* 讨论会成员

panel: ~ pin *n* Brit 镶板钉; **~ truck** *n* Amer 厢式小货车; **~ van** *n* Austral, NZ, S Afr [无窗和乘客座位的] 小货车

pan-fry *vt* 用平底锅煎

pang /pæŋ/ *n* **1** (physical) 剧痛; **~s of hunger** *or* **hunger ~s** 饥饿之苦; **birth ~s** lit 分娩的阵痛; fig (of nation, movement) 初期的困难 **2** (emotional) 痛苦; **a ~ of jealousy/regret/guilt** 一阵嫉妒/悔恨/内疚

panhandle /ˈpænhændl/ Amer

A *n* [从一州突入另一州的] 锅柄状地区; **the Texas P~** 得克萨斯州的锅柄状地区

B *vi* colloq «*person*» 沿街乞讨

C *vt* colloq 向…乞讨 ‹*person*›

panhandler /ˈpænhændlə(r)/ *n* Amer colloq 乞丐

panic /ˈpænɪk/

A *n* **1** [u and c] (state of fear) 恐慌; **to be in a ~** 处于惊恐之中; **to get into a ~ (about sth.)** (对某事) 惊慌失措; **a ~ decision** 慌乱中作出的决定 **2** [c] colloq (hurry) 极度匆忙; **to leave in a ~** 匆忙离开 **3** [c] (financial alarm) 经济恐慌; **to throw Wall Street into a ~** 使华尔街陷入恐慌

B *vi* (*pres p etc.* **-ck-**) 感到惊慌; **to ~ at the idea/sight of ...** 想到/看到…惊慌失措

C *vt* (*pres p etc.* **-ck-**) 使恐慌; **to ~ sb. into doing sth.** 使某人仓皇做某事

panic: ~ attack *n* 一阵心慌意乱; **~ button** *n* 紧急呼救按钮; **to hit** *or* **push the ~ button** fig colloq (panic) 仓促行事; (take emergency measures) 采取紧急措施; **~ buying** *n* [u] 恐慌抢购

panicky /ˈpænɪki/ *adj* colloq 惊恐的 ‹*reaction, voice*›; 惊慌失措的 ‹*person*›

panic: ~ measure *n* 紧急措施; **~ selling** *n* [u] 恐慌抛售; **~ stations** *npl* Brit colloq 慌乱的状态; **~-stricken** *adj* 惊慌失措的 ‹*crowd, behaviour*›; 受惊的 ‹*animal*›

panjandrum /pænˈdʒændrəm/ *n* 达官贵人

pannier /ˈpænɪə(r)/ *n* **1** (on bike, motorcycle) 挂篮 **2** (on pack animal) 驮篓

panoply /ˈpænəpli/ *n* formal **1** (array) 全套; **a ~ of insults** fig 一连串的辱骂 **2** (display) 华丽的炫耀

panorama /ˌpænəˈrɑːmə/ *n* **1** lit (view) 全景 **2** fig (of situation) 概述

panoramic /ˌpænəˈræmɪk/ *adj* **1** lit 全景的 ‹*view, shot*› **2** fig 概括的 ‹*study, overview*›

pan: ~pipes *npl* 排箫; **~ scourer, ~ scrubber** *ns* 抹锅刷

pansy /ˈpænzi/ *n* **1** Bot 三色堇 **2** colloq pej (homosexual) 同性恋男子; (effeminate man) 娘娘腔的男人

pant /pænt/

A *vi* **1** (breathe rapidly) 气喘; **to be ~ing for breath** 上气不接下气; **to come ~ing up the stairs** 气喘吁吁地上楼梯 **2** (long for) 渴望; **to be ~ing for sth./to do sth.** 渴望得到某物/做某事

B *vt* 气喘吁吁地说 ‹*message, words*›

C *n* 气喘; **to breathe in shallow ~s** 呼吸急促

Phrasal verb

- **pant out** *vt* [**~ out sth., ~ sth. out**] 气喘吁吁地说 ‹*message, words*›

pantaloons /ˌpæntəˈluːnz/ *npl* **1** (baggy trousers) 女式灯笼裤 **2** Hist (breeches) 马裤

pantechnicon /pænˈteknɪkən/ *n* Brit dated 厢式家具搬运车

pantheism /ˈpænθiːɪzəm/ *n* [u] Philos 泛神论; Relig 泛神崇拜

pantheist /ˈpænθiːɪst/ *n* Philos 泛神论者; Relig 泛神论崇拜者

pantheistic /ˌpænθiːˈɪstɪk/ *adj* 泛神论的 ‹*view*›; 泛神崇拜的 ‹*religion*›

pantheon /ˈpænθɪən, Amer -θɪɒn/ *n* **1** (temple) 万神庙; (monument to heroes) 伟人祠 **2** (gods) 众神 **3** formal (famous people) 名人

panther /ˈpænθə(r)/ *n* **1** (leopard) 黑豹 **2** Amer (puma) 美洲狮

panties /ˈpæntɪz/ *npl* 女式短衬裤

panting /ˈpæntɪŋ/

A *n* [u] 气喘

B *adj attrib* 气喘吁吁的 ‹*person, animal*›

panto /ˈpæntəʊ/ *n* Brit colloq = **pantomime 1**

pantograph /ˈpæntəgrɑːf, Amer -græf/ *n* **1** Rail 导电弓 **2** (for copying) 缩放仪

pantomime /ˈpæntəmaɪm/ *n* **1** [u and c] Brit (play for children) **a (Christmas) ~** 圣诞童话剧; **a ~ character** 圣诞童话剧中的人物 **2** [u] (mute acting) 哑剧; **to do ~** 表演哑剧 **3** [u and c] (mime) 荒唐的夸张动作; **to explain/describe sth. in ~** 用夸张动作解释/描述某事物 **4** [c] (absurd situation) 滑稽可笑的局面

pantomime

圣诞童话剧，简称 panto。于圣诞节前后几个星期上演，观众主要为儿童和家长。剧目改编自童话，并融入喜剧成分、音乐、歌唱和杂技动作等。常见剧目有《阿拉丁》（*Aladdin*）、《灰姑娘》（*Cinderella*）、《杰克和豆蔓》（*Jack and the Beanstalk*）等。演员和观众之间通常有互动，这也是其一大特色。传统上由年轻女演员扮演男主人公（hero 或 principal boy），男喜剧演员扮演滑稽老太婆（dame）。亦有演员扮成动物。pantomime 在美国英语中是“哑剧”的意思。

pantry /ˈpæntri/ *n* **1** (room) 食品储藏室; (cupboard) 食品储藏柜 **2** (for tableware) 餐具间

pants /pænts/ *npl* 1 Amer (trousers) 裤子; **to beat/bore/charm/scare the ~ off sb.** colloq 把某人揍得屁滚尿流/使某人厌烦透顶/使某人完全陶醉/把某人吓得魂不附体; **to catch sb. with their ~ down** colloq 趁某人不备逮个正着; **to wear the ~** colloq 掌权 2 Brit (underwear) 内裤 3 Brit colloq (rubbish) 废物; **I thought that the band were ~** 我觉得这支乐队很烂

pantsuit /ˈpæntsu:t, -sju:t/ *n* Amer 女式衣裤套装

panty /ˈpænti/: **~ girdle** *n* 束腹紧身短裤; **~ hose** *npl* Amer 尼龙连裤袜; **~ liner** *n* 卫生护垫

pap /pæp/ *n* [u] 1 Culin 流食 2 fig pej (rubbish) 消遣物

papa /pəˈpɑ:, Amer ˈpɑ:pə/ *n* dated 爸爸

papacy /ˈpeɪpəsi/ *n* (office) 教皇职位; (term) 教皇任期; (institution) 教皇体制

papal /ˈpeɪpl/ *adj* 教皇的 ‹*authority, visit*›

papal bull *n* 教皇诏书

paparazzi /ˌpæpəˈrætsi/ *npl* 狗仔队

papaya /pəˈpaɪə/ *n* 1 [c and u] (fruit) 番木瓜 2 [c] **~ (tree)** 番木瓜树

paper /ˈpeɪpə(r)/
A *n* 1 [u] (material) 纸; **a piece** *or* **sheet of ~** 一张纸; **to commit to ~** 写在纸上; **to get** *or* **put sth. down on ~** 把某事记在纸上; **on ~** (in writing) 在字面上; (in theory) 理论上; **not worth the ~ it's written on** 毫无价值; **all these assurances are just so much ~** 所有这些保证都不过是一纸空文; **I need some ~ to wrap this present** 我需要一些纸包这件礼物 2 [c] (for sweet) 糖纸; (for cigarette) 卷烟纸 3 [c] (newspaper) 报纸; **a daily/weekly ~** 日报/周报; **a local/national ~** 地方性/全国性报纸 4 [c] (written or printed document) 文件; **to sign a ~** 签署一份文件 5 [c] (in examination) 试卷; **a history/chemistry ~** 历史科/化学科试卷; **she did a very good ~ on medieval history** 她中世纪历史的试卷答得很好 6 [c] (scholarly essay) 论文; **to give/read a ~** 提交/宣读一篇论文 7 [u and c] (wallpaper) 壁纸 8 [c] Amer Comm 票据; **bond ~** 债券 9 [c] Pol 官方文件
B **papers** *npl* (documents) 文件; **identity ~s** 身份证件
C *modif* 1 (made of paper) 纸制的 ‹*doll, aeroplane, hat*›; **a ~ cup/plate** 纸杯/纸盘; **a ~ handkerchief/towel** 纸巾/擦手纸; **~ currency** *or* **money** 纸币; **a ~ tiger** 纸老虎; **~ tape** 纸带 2 (existing only on paper) 书面的 ‹*agreement, promise, qualifications*›; 账面的 ‹*profits*›
D *vt* 1 (cover with paper) 为…贴壁纸 ‹*room, wall*› 2 **to ~ the house** Amer 让持免费票的观众坐满影院

Phrasal verb
- **paper over** *vt* [**~ over sth.**] 盖住 ‹*bump, crack*›; fig 掩盖 ‹*disagreement, differences, flaws*›; **to ~ over the cracks** fig 粉饰太平

paperback /ˈpeɪpəbæk/ *n* 平装本; **in ~** 以平装出版; **a ~ book/version** 平装书/版

paperback rights *npl* 平装本出版权

paper: ~ bank *n* (place) 废纸回收站; (container) 废纸回收箱; **~board** *n* [u] 纸板; **~ boy** *n* 男报童; **~ chain** *n* 纸彩带; **~ chase** *n* 1 Brit Sport 撒纸追逐赛; 2 colloq (paperwork) 过多的书面工作; **~clip, ~ fastener** *ns* 回形针; **~ feed tray** *n* 送纸盘; **~ girl** *n* 女报童; **~hanger** *n* Brit 裱糊工; **~ industry** *n* [u] 造纸业; **~ jam** *n* 卡纸; **~ knife** *n* 裁纸刀

paperless /ˈpeɪpəlɪs/ *adj* 无纸化的 ‹*office*›; 无纸的 ‹*system*›

paper: ~ mill *n* 造纸厂; **~-pusher** *n* Amer colloq pej (bureaucrat) 官僚; (clerk) 办公室小职员; **~ qualifications** *npl* 文凭; **~ round** *n* 送报; **to do a ~** 送报纸; **~-seller** ▸**p. 409** *n* 卖报人; **~ shop** *n* 报刊经销店; **~-thin** *adj* 1 lit 极薄的 ‹*partition, wall*›; 2 fig 脆弱的 ‹*character*›; 单薄的 ‹*storyline*›; **~ trail** *n* esp Amer [揭示来龙去脉的] 系列文件; **~weight** *n* 镇纸; **~work** *n* [u] 1 (clerical work) 文书工作; 2 (documents) 全部文件

papery /ˈpeɪpəri/ *adj* 薄如纸的 ‹*texture, leaf*›; 干而薄的 ‹*skin*›

papist /ˈpeɪpɪst/ pej
A *n* 天主教徒
B *adj* 天主教的 ‹*plot, oppression*›

papoose /pəˈpu:s/ *n* 1 (carrier) 婴儿背囊 2 (baby) [北美印第安人的] 婴儿

pappy /ˈpæpi/ *adj* colloq 糊状的 ‹*food*›; 黏稠的 ‹*consistency*›

paprika /ˈpæprɪkə, pəˈpri:kə/ *n* [u] 红辣椒粉

Papua New Guinea /ˌpɑ:puə nju: ˈgɪni:, Amer nu:-/ *pr n* 巴布亚新几内亚

papyrus /pəˈpaɪərəs/ *n* 1 [u] (paper) [古埃及用的] 纸莎草纸 2 [c] (*pl* **papyri** /pəˈpaɪəraɪ, -ri:/ *or* **~es**) (document) [写在纸莎草纸上的] 文献

par /pɑ:(r)/ *n* 1 Fin, Comm (face value) 票面价值; (of exchange rate) 外汇比值; **at ~** 照票面价; **to be above/below ~** 高于/低于票面价 2 (equal) **to be on a ~ with sb./sth.** 与某人/某事物不相上下 3 (standard) **to be up to ~** 达到通常水准; **to be below** *or* **under ~** (of person) 感觉不太好; (of work) 不及平常好; **to be ~ for the course** fig 不出所料 4 (in golf) 标准杆数; **two under ~** 低于标准杆两杆; **the sixth hole is a ~ 5** 第六穴的标准杆数为 5 杆

par. *abbr* = **paragraph A**

para[1] /ˈpærə/ *abbr* = **paragraph A**

para[2] *abbr* Brit colloq **the ~s** 伞兵

parable /ˈpærəbl/ *n* 寓言故事

parabola /pəˈræbələ/ *n* 抛物线

parabolic /ˌpærəˈbɒlɪk/ *adj* 抛物线的 ‹*curve, flight*›

parabolic reflector *n* 抛物面反射镜

paracetamol /ˌpærəˈsetəmɒl, -ˈsi:təmɒl/ *n* [u and c] Brit 扑热息痛

parachute /ˈpærəʃu:t/
A *n* 降落伞
B *vi* 跳伞
C *vt* 伞投 ‹*troops, supplies*›

parachute: ~ drop *n* 伞投; **~ jump** *n* 跳伞; **~ regiment** *n* 空降兵团; **~ silk** *n* [u] 降落伞绸

parachuting /ˈpærəʃu:tɪŋ/ ▸**p. 307** *n* [u] 跳伞; **to go ~** 去跳伞

parachutist /ˈpærəʃu:tɪst/ *n* (gen) 跳伞者; Mil 伞兵; Sport 跳伞运动员

parade /pəˈreɪd/
A *n* 1 [c] (procession) 游行行列; **a ~ of floats** 游行彩车队伍 2 [u and c] Mil 阅兵; **to be on ~** 在接受检阅 3 [c] (exhibition of models) 展示 4 [u and c] fig pej (display) 炫耀; **to make a ~ of sth.** 暴露 ‹*emotion*›; 夸耀 ‹*knowledge*›; **to be on ~** 在炫耀自己 5 [c] Brit (row of shops) 一排商店; (street) 有一排商店的街; **South P~** 南商业街
B *vt* 1 (assemble) 使…列队 ‹*soldiers*› 2 (walk through) 在…招摇而行 ‹*street, corridor*› 3 (display) 巡行展示 ‹*flags, signs*› 4 esp pej (flaunt) 炫耀 ‹*knowledge, success, wealth*› 5 (advertise) **to ~ sth./sb. as sth.** 把某物/某人标榜为某物; **to ~ oneself as a supporter of the party** 宣称自己为该党的支持者
C *vi* 1 Mil «*soldiers*» 列队集合 2 (march in procession) 游行 3 esp pej (strut) 招摇过市; **to ~ up and down the street** 在街上招摇地走来走去 4 (masquerade) **to ~ as sth.** 冒充某物; **myth parading as fact** 外表看似真实的神话

Phrasal verb
- **parade about, parade around** *vi* 四处招摇

parade ground *n* (for drills) 练兵场; (for parade) 阅兵场

paradigm /ˈpærədaɪm/ *n* 1 (model) 范例; **a ~ for students to copy** 供学生效仿的榜样 2 Ling 词形变化表

paradigmatic /ˌpærədɪgˈmætɪk/ *adj* 典型的 ‹*example, case*›

paradigm shift *n* 范式转移

paradise /ˈpærədaɪs/ *n* 1 [u] Relig (heaven) 天堂; (Garden of Eden) 伊甸园 2 [c] (idyllic place) 乐园; **a mountain/tropical ~** 山上/热带的人间乐园; **an artist's/a shopper's ~** 艺术家/购物者的天堂 3 [u] (bliss) 极乐

paradox /ˈpærədɒks/ *n* 1 [u and c] (premise, statement) 悖论 2 [c] (person) 矛盾的人; (fact, situation) 矛盾的事物

paradoxical /ˌpærəˈdɒksɪkl/ *adj* 自相矛盾的 ‹*statement, position*›

paradoxically /ˌpærəˈdɒksɪkli/ *adv* 自相矛盾地 ‹*argue, state*›

paraffin /ˈpærəfɪn/ *n* [u] 1 Brit (fuel) 煤油; **a ~ lamp/stove** 煤油灯/炉 2 (wax) 石蜡

paraglide /ˈpærəglaɪd/ *vi* 进行滑翔伞运动

paraglider /ˈpærəglaɪdə(r)/ *n* 1 (canopy) 滑翔伞 2 (person) 滑翔伞运动员

paragliding /ˈpærəglaɪdɪŋ/ ▸**p. 307** *n* [u] 滑翔伞运动

paragon /ˈpærəgən, Amer -gɒn/ *n* 1 (perfect example) 典范; **a ~ of virtue/honesty/politeness** 美德/诚实/儒雅的典范 2 (model of excellence) 完人

paragraph /ˈpærəgrɑ:f, Amer -græf/
A *n* 1 (section of text) 段落; **new ~!** (in dictation) 另起一段! 2 (article) 短文 3 Print **~ (mark)** 段落号
B *vt* 将…分成段落 ‹*page, essay*›

Paraguay /ˈpærəgwaɪ/ *pr n* 巴拉圭

Paraguayan /ˈpærəgwaɪən/ ▸**p. 503**
A *adj* (of Paraguay) 巴拉圭的; (of the people) 巴拉圭人的
B *n* 巴拉圭人

parakeet /ˈpærəki:t/ *n* 长尾小鹦鹉

parallax /ˈpærəlæks/ *n* [u and c] 视差

parallel /ˈpærəlel/
A *adj* 1 Math 平行的 ‹*lines, rows*›; **~ to** *or* **with sth.** 与某物平行的 2 (similar) 极相似的 ‹*feature, case*›; **to develop along ~ lines** 并行发展 3 (concurrent) 同时存在的; **a ~ universe** 平行宇宙 4 Elec 并联的 ‹*circuit*›
B *adv* 1 (side by side) 平行地; **~ to** *or* **with sth.** 与某物平行地; **to swim ~ to the shore** 沿着海岸游泳; **to run ~ to** *or* **with the road** «*river*» 和道路平行; **to run ~** fig «*careers*» 齐头并进 2 (concurrently) 同时地; **~ to** *or* **with sth.** 与某物同时地; **to evolve/develop ~ to one another** 彼此一同进化/发展
C *n* 1 Math 平行线 2 Geog 纬线 3 (similarity) 相似处; (comparison) 比拟; **to be on a ~ with sth.** 与某物类似; **to draw** *or* **establish a ~ between ...** 在…之间找到相似点 ‹*two situations, countries*›; **to develop/proceed in ~** (side by side) 并行发展/齐头并进; (concurrently) 同时发展/进行; **without ~** 无与伦比的 4 Elec **to be connected in ~** 并联
D *vt* (*pres p* **-ll-** Brit, **-l-** Amer) 1 (be side by side with) 与…平行 ‹*road, line*› 2 (be similar to) 与…相似 ‹*event, experience*› 3 (equal) 与…媲美 ‹*achievement, beauty*› 4 (find analogy in) 将…作比拟 ‹*history, culture*›

parallel bars *npl* 双杠

parallelism /ˈpærəlelɪzəm/ *n* [u] 相似

parallelogram /ˌpærəˈleləgræm/ *n* 平行四边形

parallel park
A *vi* 并排停车
B *vt* 使…并排停车 ‹*vehicle*›

parallel: ~ port *n* 并行端口; **~ processing** *n* [u] 并行处理

p

P

Paralympian /ˌpærəˈlɪmpɪən/
A *adj* 残奥会的 ‹*sport, medallist*›
B *n* 残奥会选手

Paralympic Games /ˌpærəlɪmpɪk ˈɡeɪmz/ *npl* = **Paralympics**

Paralympics /ˌpærəˈlɪmpɪks/ *npl* 残疾人奥运会

paralysation /ˌpærəlaɪˈzeɪʃn, Amer -lɪˈz-/ *n* [u] Brit 瘫痪

paralyse /ˈpærəlaɪz/ *vt* Brit 使…瘫痪 ‹*person, industry*›; 使…麻痹 ‹*part of body*›

paralysed /ˈpærəlaɪzd/ *adj* Brit 瘫痪的 ‹*person, market, traffic*›; **to be ∼ from the waist down** 腰部以下瘫痪; **my arm/leg is ∼** 我的手臂/腿瘫痪了; **he was ∼ with fear** fig 他吓得动弹不得

paralysis /pəˈræləsɪs/ *n* [u and c] (*pl* **paralyses** /pəˈræləsiːz/) 瘫痪; **∼ of the arm** 胳膊的麻痹; **∼ of the railway network** 铁路网的瘫痪

paralytic /ˌpærəˈlɪtɪk/ *adj* **1** Med 瘫痪的 ‹*person*›; 麻痹的 ‹*arm, leg*›; **the incidence of ∼ disease** 麻痹症的发病率 **2** *pred* Brit colloq (drunk) 烂醉如泥的

paralyzation /ˌpærəlaɪˈzeɪʃn, Amer -lɪˈz-/ *n* [u] esp Amer = **paralysation**

paralyze /ˈpærəlaɪz/ *vt* esp Amer = **paralyse**

paralyzed /ˈpærəlaɪzd/ *adj* esp Amer = **paralysed**

paramedic /ˌpærəˈmedɪk/ ▸**p. 409** *n* 急救护理人员

paramedical /ˌpærəˈmedɪkl/ *adj* 辅助医疗的 ‹*services, staff*›

parameter /pəˈræmɪtə(r)/ *n* **1** Math 参数 **2** *usu pl* (limiting factor) 界限; **to set/define the ∼s of sth.** 制定/设定…的规范 ‹*plan, job*›; **within the ∼s of sth.** 在…的限度内 ‹*budget*›

paramilitary /ˌpærəˈmɪlɪtri, Amer -teri/
A *adj* 准军事的 ‹*group, police*›
B *n* 准军事组织成员

paramount /ˈpærəmaʊnt/ *adj* **1** (most important) 首要的 ‹*consideration, goal*›; **to be ∼** *or* **to be of ∼ importance** 是至关重要的 **2** *attrib* (supreme) 至高无上的; **a ∼ chief** 最高首领; **China's ∼ leader** 中国的最高领导人

paranoia /ˌpærəˈnɔɪə/ ▸**p. 377** *n* [u] **1** Psych 妄想症 **2** (suspicion) 多疑

paranoiac /ˌpærəˈnɔɪæk. -æk/, **paranoic** /ˌpærəˈnɔɪk/ *adjs* = **paranoid**

paranoid /ˈpærənɔɪd/ *adj* **1** Psych 患妄想症的 ‹*person, state*›; **∼ delusion** 偏执妄想 **2** (suspicious) 多疑的 ‹*person, reaction*›; **to be ∼ about sth.** 对某事猜疑

paranoid schizophrenia *n* [u] 妄想型精神分裂症

paranormal /ˌpærəˈnɔːml/
A *adj* 超自然的 ‹*phenomenon, power*›; 超常的 ‹*researcher, experience, activity*›
B *n* **the ∼** 超常事件

parapet /ˈpærəpɪt/ *n* **1** Archit 女儿墙 **2** Mil 胸墙; **to put** *or* **stick one's head above the ∼** fig 贸然出头

paraphernalia /ˌpærəfəˈneɪlɪə/ *n* + *v sing or pl* **1** (items) 各种物件; (equipment) 各种配件 **2** Brit (trappings) 烦琐的手续

paraphrase /ˈpærəfreɪz/
A *n* 释义
B *vt* 解释 ‹*poem, passage*›

paraplegia /ˌpærəˈpliːdʒə/ *n* [u] 截瘫

paraplegic /ˌpærəˈpliːdʒɪk/
A *adj* 患截瘫的 ‹*patient, athlete*›; 截瘫患者的 ‹*sports, games*›
B *n* 截瘫患者

parapsychological /ˌpærəsaɪkəˈlɒdʒɪkl/ *adj* 心灵学的 ‹*phenomenon, study*›

parapsychology /ˌpærəsaɪˈkɒlədʒi/ *n* [u] 心灵学

paraquat /ˈpærəkwɒt/ *n* [u] 百草枯

parasail /ˈpærəseɪl/
A *vi* 滑帆伞
B *n* 帆伞

parasailing /ˈpærəseɪlɪŋ/ *n* [u] 帆伞运动; **to go ∼** 滑帆伞

parascending /ˈpærəsendɪŋ/ *n* [u] Brit = **parasailing**

parasite /ˈpærəsaɪt/ *n* **1** Bot, Zool 寄生生物 **2** fig pej (person) 寄生虫

parasitic /ˌpærəˈsɪtɪk/, **parasitical** /ˌpærəˈsɪtɪkl/ *adj* **1** Bot, Zool 寄生的 ‹*plant, animal, species*› **2** fig pej (exploitative) 寄生虫似的 ‹*person, behaviour, existence*›; **to be ∼ on sb./sth.** 依赖某人/某事物生活

parasitism /ˈpærəsɪtɪzəm/ *n* [u] **1** Bot, Zool 寄生现象 **2** fig pej (exploitation) 寄生行为

parasitology /ˌpærəsɪˈtɒlədʒi/ *n* [u] 寄生生物学

parasol /ˈpærəsɒl, Amer -sɔːl/ *n* **1** (for beach, table) 大遮阳伞 **2** (hand-held) 阳伞

paratrooper /ˈpærətruːpə(r)/ ▸**p. 409** *n* 伞兵

paratroops /ˈpærətruːps/ *npl* 伞兵部队

parboil /ˈpɑːbɔɪl/ *vt* 把…煮成半熟 ‹*vegetables, potatoes*›

parcel /ˈpɑːsl/
A *n* **1** esp Brit (package) 包裹; **a ∼ of sth.** 一包 ‹*books, letters*› **2** (piece of land) 一块地
B *vt* (**-ll-** Brit, **-l-** Amer) = **parcel up**

Phrasal verbs
- **parcel out** *vt* [∼ out sth., ∼ sth. out] 分配 ‹*land, supplies, work*›
- **parcel up** *vt* [∼ up sth., ∼ sth. up] 把…打成包 ‹*objects, goods*›

parcel: ∼ bomb *n* 邮包炸弹; **∼ office** *n* 包裹房; **∼ post** *n* [u] 包裹邮递; **to send sth. (by) ∼ post** 把某物用包裹寄出

parch /pɑːtʃ/ *vt* «*sun, heat*» 使…干枯 ‹*crops, land*›; 使…极干燥 ‹*skin, lips*›

parched /pɑːtʃt/ *adj* **1** 干枯的 ‹*soil, skin, lips*›; 干渴的 ‹*tongue, mouth*› **2** *pred* colloq (thirsty) 口渴的; **to be ∼** 口干舌燥

parchment /ˈpɑːtʃmənt/ *n* **1** [u] Hist (material) 羊皮纸 **2** [c] Hist (document) 羊皮纸文稿 **3** [u] (high-quality paper) 仿羊皮纸

pardon /ˈpɑːdn/ ▸**p. 29**
A *n* **1** [u] (forgiveness) 原谅; **to ask sb.'s ∼** 请求某人的原谅 **2** [c] Jur 赦免; **royal/presidential ∼** 皇家/总统特赦
B *excl* **1** **∼?** (excuse me?) 你说什么? **2** **∼!** (sorry!) 对不起!
C *vt* **1** (forgive) 原谅 ‹*mistake, rudeness*›; **to ∼ sb. for sth./doing sth.** 原谅某人某事/做某事; **∼ me!** 对不起!; **∼ me for breathing** *or* **living** colloq iron 请原谅，我活着让你受罪了 **2** Jur 赦免 ‹*criminal*›

pardonable /ˈpɑːdnəbl/ *adj* 可原谅的 ‹*mistake, offence, lapse*›

pardonably /ˈpɑːdnəbli/ *adv* 情有可原地 ‹*proud, upset*›

pare /peə(r)/ *vt* **1** (peel) 削去…的皮 ‹*fruit*› **2** (trim) 修剪 ‹*nails*› **3** (reduce) 逐渐削减 ‹*costs, outlay*›; **to ∼ sth. to the bone** 把某物减到最低

Phrasal verb
- **pare down** *vt* [∼ sth. down, ∼ down sth.] 逐渐削减 ‹*budget, costs*›

pared-down *adj attrib* 削减了的 ‹*budget*›; 删减了的 ‹*version, prose*›

parent /ˈpeərənt/
A *n* **1** (father) 父亲; (mother) 母亲; **my/our ∼s** 我的/我们的父母 **2** (animal, plant) 亲本
B *adj attrib* **1** (parental) 父母的 ‹*involvement, concern*› **2** Zool, Bot 亲本的 ‹*animal, plant*› **3** Comm 母公司的; **a ∼ bank/organization** 总行/机构总部

parentage /ˈpeərəntɪdʒ/ *n* [u] 出身; **to be of humble/unknown ∼** 出身卑微/不明的

parental /pəˈrentl/ *adj* 父母的 ‹*love, authority, duties*›; **∼ contribution** 家长教育金

parental guidance *n* [u] 家长指导级

parent: ∼ company *n* 母公司; **∼craft** *n* [u] 育儿知识; **∼-governor** *n* Brit [有子女在学校就读的] 家长董事

parenthesis /pəˈrenθəsɪs/ *n* (*pl* **parentheses** /pəˈrenθəsiːz/) **1** *usu pl* Print 圆括号 **2** (interpolation) 插入语; **in ∼** 作为插入语

parenthood /ˈpeərənthʊd/ *n* [u] 父母身份

parenting /ˈpeərəntɪŋ/ *n* [u] 养儿育女; **∼ skills** 育儿技巧

parent: ∼ power *n* [u] colloq 家长决定教育权; **∼s' evening** *n* 家长会; **∼-teacher association** *n* 家长教师联谊会

parer /ˈpeərə(r)/ *n* 削皮刀

pariah /pəˈraɪə, ˈpærɪə/ *n* 被社会遗弃者; **a ∼ state** 被遗弃的国家

parietal /pəˈraɪətl/
A *adj* **1** Anat, Biol 顶骨的; **∼ bone/lobe** 顶骨/顶叶 **2** Amer Univ 学生宿舍的 ‹*rules, board*›
B *n* Anat, Zool 顶骨
C **parietals** *npl* Amer Univ (rules) 异性访客规定

paring /ˈpeərɪŋ/
A *n* [u] **1** lit (of fruit) 削皮 **2** fig (of budget, economy) 逐渐削减
B **parings** *npl* (of fruit, vegetables) 削下的皮; (of nails) 剪下的指甲

paring knife *n* 水果刀

Paris /ˈpærɪs/ *pr n* 巴黎

parish /ˈpærɪʃ/ *n* **1** Relig (area) 堂区; (parishioners) 教区居民 **2** Brit Pol, Admin 乡村行政小区

parish: ∼ church *n* 堂区教堂; **∼ council** *n* Brit Relig 堂区委员会; Pol 行政区议会

parishioner /pəˈrɪʃənə(r)/ *n* 堂区居民

parish: ∼ priest *n* 堂区司铎; **∼-pump** *adj attrib* Brit pej 小地方的 ‹*gossip, rivalry*›; **∼-pump politics** 区域性政治; **∼ register** *n* 堂区记事簿

Parisian /pəˈrɪzɪən/
A *adj* 巴黎的
B *n* 巴黎人

parity /ˈpærəti/ *n* [u] 平等; **∼ of sth.** 某物的同等; **∼ of powers/pay** 权力的均衡/同酬; **∼ between ...** …之间的平等; **∼ with ...** 与…的平等; **the pound was at ∼ with the euro** 英镑曾和欧元平价

park /pɑːk/
A *n* **1** (public garden) 公园 **2** Comm, Ind 园区; **a business/industrial ∼** 商业/工业园区 **3** (estate) 庄园 **4** Brit colloq (pitch) 运动场
B *vt* **1** (station) 停放 ‹*vehicle*› **2** colloq (deposit) 寄放 ‹*belongings, things*›; **I ∼ed the children at my mother's** 我把孩子托放在母亲家里
C *vi* 停车
D *v refl* colloq **to ∼ oneself** 坐下

parka /ˈpɑːkə/ *n* [带兜帽的] 派克大衣

parkade /pɑːˈkeɪd/ *n* Can 多层停车场

park: ∼-and-ride *n* Brit 停车换乘体系; **∼ bench** *n* 公园里的长椅

parking /ˈpɑːkɪŋ/ *n* [u] **1** (action) 停车; **'no ∼'** "禁止停车" **2** (space for cars) 停车场

parking: ∼ attendant ▸**p. 409** *n* 看车人; **∼ bay** *n* 停车位; **∼ brake** *n* Amer 手刹车; **∼ garage** *n* Amer 多层停车库; **∼ light** *n* 停车灯; **∼ lot** *n* Amer 停车场; **∼ meter** *n* 停车收费器; **∼ offence** *n* 违章停车; **∼ permit** *n* 停车许可证; **∼ place, ∼ space** *ns* 停车位; **∼ ticket,** Amer **∼ violation** *ns* (offence) 违章停车; (notice) 违章停车罚单

Parkinson /'pɑːkɪnsən/: **~'s disease** ▸p. 377 *n* [u] 帕金森病; **~'s law** *n* hum 帕金森定律 [工作总是到最后一刻才会完成]

park: ~ keeper ▸p. 409 *n* 公园管理员; **~land** /-lænd/ *n* [u] 稀树草原; **~ ranger, ~ warden** ▸p. 409 *ns* 公园管理员; **~way** *n* Amer 林荫大道

parky /'pɑːki/ *adj* Brit colloq 寒冷的

parlance /'pɑːləns/ *n* [u] formal 说法; **in legal/medical ~** 用法律/医学用语; **in common ~** 用普通的说法

parlay /'pɑːleɪ/ Amer

A *n* [赌本加彩头的] 连续赌

B *vt* 将…再押上 ‹*sum, stake*›; **to ~ a small bankroll into big winnings** 以小赌本赢大钱

parley /'pɑːli/

A *n* 和谈

B *vi* 和谈; **to ~ with sb.** 与某人和谈

parliament /'pɑːləmənt/

A **Parliament** *pr n* Brit (institution) 英国议会; (members) 一届议会

B *n* (in other countries) (institution) 议会; (members) [一届议会的] 全体议员; **in ~** 在议会上

parliamentarian /ˌpɑːləmen'teərɪən/

A *n* **1** Pol (member) [尤指老道的] 议员 **2** **Parliamentarian** Brit Hist [英国内战时期支持议会的] 议会党人

B **Parliamentarian** *adj* Brit Hist 议会党人的

parliamentary /ˌpɑːlə'mentri, Amer -teri/ *adj* 议会的 ‹*debate, democracy*›; 设有议会的 ‹*government*›

parliamentary: P~ Commissioner for Administration *n* Brit 行政管理专员; **~ election** *n* 议会选举; **~ government** *n* [u] 议会政体; **~ private secretary** *n* Brit 议会私人秘书; **~ privilege** *n* [u] 议员言论免责权; **~ secretary** *n* Brit 政务次官; **~ undersecretary** *n* Brit 政务次长

parlour Brit, **parlor** Amer /'pɑːlə(r)/ *n* dated 起居室

parlour car *n* Amer 特等车厢

parlour game *n* 室内游戏

parlous /'pɑːləs/ *adj* archaic or hum 充满危险的 ‹*condition*›; **in view of the ~ state of my finances** 考虑到我不稳定的财务状况

Parmesan /'pɑːmɪzæn, Amer ˌpɑːrmɪ'zæn/ *n* [u] **~ (cheese)** 帕尔马干酪

parochial /pə'rəʊkɪəl/ *adj* **1** (of parish) 教区的 ‹*business, level*› **2** pej (narrow-minded) 偏狭的 ‹*attitude, view*›; 地方观念的 ‹*person*›

parochialism /pə'rəʊkɪəlɪzəm/ *n* [u] pej 狭隘观念

parochial school *n* Amer 教区学校

parodist /'pærədɪst/ *n* 滑稽模仿作品作者

parody /'pærədi/

A *n* **1** [u and c] (satire) 滑稽模仿作品 **2** [c] (travesty) 拙劣的模仿

B *vt* 滑稽地模仿 ‹*person, work, style*›

parole /pə'rəʊl/

A *n* [u] 假释; **to be on ~** 获假释; **to release sb. on ~** 假释某人; **to break (one's) ~** 违反假释条件

B *vt* 假释 ‹*prisoner*›

parole: ~ board *n* 假释裁决委员会; **~ officer** *n* Amer 假释官

paroxysm /'pærəksɪzəm/ *n* **1** Med 阵发 **2** (outburst) 突发; **a ~ of rage/laughter** 一阵狂怒/大笑

parquet /'pɑːkeɪ, Amer pɑːr'keɪ/

A *n* **1** [u] (flooring) 镶木地板; **to lay ~** 铺拼花地板 **2** [c] Amer Theat 正厅前排座位

B *vt* 为…铺镶木地板 ‹*hall, room*›; **to ~ the floor** 铺镶木地板

parquet floor *n* 镶木地板

parquetry /'pɑːkɪtri/ *n* [u] 镶木细工

parricide /'pærɪsaɪd/ *n* **1** [u] (crime) 杀亲罪 **2** [c] (person) 杀亲犯

parrot /'pærət/

A *n* **1** Zool 鹦鹉; **as sick as a ~** Brit colloq hum 非常失望的 **2** colloq pej (person) 学舌者

B *vt* pej 机械地重复 ‹*words, slogan*›

parrot-fashion, parrot-like *advs* 鹦鹉学舌般地 ‹*repeat, learn*›

parry /'pæri/

A *vt* **1** lit «*fencer, boxer*» 挡开 ‹*thrust, blow*› **2** fig (deflect) 回避 ‹*question*›

B *vi* «*fencer, boxer*» 挡开进攻

C *n* **1** (in fencing, boxing) 挡开 **2** fig (argument) 反驳

parse /pɑːz/ *vt* **1** Ling 从句法上分析 ‹*sentence, text*› **2** Comput 对…进行语法分析 ‹*data, file*›

parsec /'pɑːsek/ *n* 秒差距 [天体距离单位, 约等于3.25光年]

parser /'pɑːzə(r)/ *n* 语法分析程序

parsimonious /ˌpɑːsɪ'məʊnɪəs/ *adj* formal 吝啬的 ‹*person*›

parsimoniously /ˌpɑːsɪ'məʊnɪəsli/ *adv* formal 吝啬地 ‹*dole out, distribute*›

parsimony /'pɑːsɪməni, Amer -məʊni/ *n* [u] formal 吝啬

parsley /'pɑːsli/ *n* [u] 欧芹

parsley sauce *n* [u] 欧芹沙司

parsnip /'pɑːsnɪp/ *n* 欧洲防风; **fine words butter no ~s** colloq 好话中听不中用

parson /'pɑːsn/ *n* dated 教区牧师

parsonage /'pɑːsənɪdʒ/ *n* 教区牧师住宅

parson's nose *n* [u] colloq [煮熟家禽的] 尾部肉

part /pɑːt/

A *n* **1** (piece, section) 部分; **the eastern/northern ~** 东部/北部; **I'm only here ~ of the time** 我只是部分时间在这里; **Gaul was divided into three ~s** 高卢划分为三个部分; **the latter ~ of the twentieth century** 20 世纪后半期; **a hundredth ~ of a second** 百分之一秒; **~ of me hates him** 我有点恨他; **~s of the broadcast** 广播的片段; **to feel ~ of the family/team** 感到是家庭/团队的一员; **for the most ~** 多半; **in ~** 部分地; **in ~s** 有些部分; **to be ~ and parcel of ...** 是…的重要部分 **2** Aut, Tech 部件; **~s and labour** 零件带人工费 **3** (of book, play) 部; (of radio/TV programme) 集; **a four-~ series** 四集连续剧 **4** (measure) 等份; **to mix one ~ flour and three ~s water** 把一份面粉和三份水混合; **the human body is five ~s water** 人体六分之五是水 **5** (share, role) 职责; **to do one's ~ (in doing sth.)** 尽 (做某事的) 本分; **to play a key ~** 发挥关键作用; **to have a ~ in sth.** (contribute to) 在某事中起作用; (participate in) 参与某事; **to take ~ (in ...)** 参与 (…); **Russia took no further ~ in the war** 俄罗斯没有进一步卷入战争; **I want no ~ in it, I don't want any ~ of it** 我不想牵涉进去 **6** Theat, Cin 角色; **have you learned your ~ yet?** 你记住台词没有? ; **she played a lot of leading ~s** 她多次扮演主角 **7** Mus (for instrument) 音部; (for voice) 声部; **the viola/horn ~** 中提琴/圆号部; **the soprano/tenor ~** 女高音/男高音声部 **8** (side, behalf) 方面; **for my/his ~** 就我/他而言; **a mistake on the ~ of the bank** 银行方面的错误; **to take sb.'s ~** 支持某人; **to take sth. in good ~** 从容面对某事 **9** (region) 地区; **in this ~ of the world** 在这里; **one's ~ of the world** 自己的家乡; **foreign ~s** 外国 **10** (skill) **a man of (many) ~s** 多才多艺的人 **11** Amer (parting in hair) 分缝

B *adv* 部分地; **my mother was ~ Irish, ~ French** 我的母亲一半是爱尔兰血统, 一半是法国血统

C *vt* **1** (separate physically) 分开 ‹*boxers, friends*›; 拉开 ‹*curtains*›; 张开 ‹*lips*›; **nothing will ever ~ us** 什么也不能把我们分开; **the war ~ed many couples/families** 战争拆散了许多夫妻/家庭; **a fool and his money are soon ~ed** Prov 愚人有钱留不住; **to ~ the crowds** 驱散人群; **to be ~ed from sb.** 与某人分开; **to ~ company** 公开分手; **John and Linda have decided to ~ company** 约翰和琳达已经决定分道扬镳; **the horse and rider ~ed company** hum 马把骑手甩了下去; **to ~ company with sb.** (separate from) 与某人分手; (differ with) 与某人有分歧 **2** (make parting in) 给…分缝 ‹*hair*›

D *vi* **1** (take leave) «*friends*» 分别; (split up) «*married couple, lovers*» 分手; **we ~ed good friends** *or* **on good terms** 我们友好地分手了 **2** (divide) «*crowd*» 散去; «*lips*» 张开; «*curtains*» 拉开; **the clouds ~ed, and the sun shone through** 云开日见 **3** (break) «*rope, cable, line*» 断裂

Phrasal verb

- **part with** *vt* [**~ with sth.**] 割舍 ‹*cherished object*›

partake /pɑː'teɪk/ *vi* (*pt* **partook,** *pp* **partaken** /pɑː'teɪkən/) formal **1** **to ~ in sth.** (participate, share) 参与 ‹*activity, decision-making*›; 分享 ‹*profit, happiness*› **2** **to ~ of sth.** (receive) 享用 ‹*food, drink*›

part exchange

A *n* [u and c] Brit 部分抵价交易; **to take/sell sth. in ~ (for sth.)** 收下/卖掉某物抵付 (购买某物的) 部分款额

B **part-exchange** *vt* 以…作部分抵价交易 ‹*car, article*›; **to ~ sth. for sth.** 以某物作部分抵价购买某物

partial /'pɑːʃl/ *adj* **1** (part) 部分的 ‹*success, failure, knowledge*›; **to make a ~ recovery** 部分恢复 **2** (biased) 偏袒的 ‹*judgement, attitude*›; **to be ~ towards sb./sth.** 偏袒某人/某物 **3** *pred* colloq (fond) 钟爱; **to be ~ towards** *or* **to sb./sth.** 钟爱某人/某物

partial: ~ disability *n* [u and c] 局部残疾; **~ eclipse** *n* 偏食

partiality /ˌpɑːʃɪ'æləti/ *n* [u] formal **1** (bias) 偏袒 **2** (fondness) 酷爱; **a ~ for sth./sb.** 对某物/某人的酷爱

partially /'pɑːʃəli/ *adv* 部分地 ‹*successful, recovered, hidden*›; **to be ~ aware/to blame** 有一点察觉/负有部分责任

partially sighted

A *adj* 弱视的 ‹*person*›

B *n* + *v pl* **the ~** 弱视者

participant /pɑː'tɪsɪpənt/ *n* 参与者; **a ~ in sth.** 某事的参与者

participate /pɑː'tɪsɪpeɪt/ *vi* 参加; **to ~ in sth.** 参与某事

participation /pɑːˌtɪsɪ'peɪʃn/ *n* [u] 参加; **~ in sth.** 对某事的参与

participatory /pɑːˌtɪsɪ'peɪtəri, Amer -tɔːri/ *adj* 参与的 ‹*role, audience*›; **~ play** 观众参与式戏剧; **~ democracy** 参与式民主制

participle /'pɑːtɪsɪpl/ *n* 分词; **past/present ~** 过去/现在分词

particle /'pɑːtɪkl/ *n* **1** (tiny piece) 颗粒; **not a ~ of truth/evidence** fig 没有丝毫真实性/证据 **2** Phys 粒子 **3** Ling 小品词

particle: ~ accelerator *n* 粒子加速器; **~ board** *n* [u] Amer 写字夹板; **~ physics** *npl* + *v sing* 粒子物理学

particoloured Brit, **particolored** Amer /'pɑːtɪkʌləd/ *adj* 色彩斑驳的 ‹*plumage, costume*›

particular /pə'tɪkjʊlə(r)/

A *adj* **1** (specific) 特指的; **her ~ brand of humour isn't much to my taste** 她那种幽默不太对我的口味; **is there any ~ colour you would prefer?** 有没有你喜欢的那种颜色? ; **nothing (in) ~** 没什么特别的; **in ~** 尤其; **why me in ~?** 为什么偏偏是我? **2** (special, exceptional) 特别的 ‹*attention, significance*›; **we view these developments with ~ concern** 我们特别关注这些进展; **a**

P

matter of ~ importance 格外重要的事情; a ~ friend 好朋友; this painting is a ~ favourite of mine 这是我最喜欢的一幅画 3 (fussy) 挑剔的; to be ~ about sth./doing sth. 对某事/做某事挑剔; to be ~ about cleanliness/punctuality 非常讲究整洁/守时

B *n* 1 (detail) 细节; (to be accurate/exact/correct) in every ~ 在每个细节上（都准确/精确/正确）; I don't think we need to go into ~s at this stage 我认为这个阶段我们没有必要谈论细节 2 particulars *pl* (personal information) 详细资料; get her ~s down in your notebook 在你的笔记本上记下她的详细信息

particularly /pəˈtɪkjʊləli/ *adv* 1 (in particular) 专门 ‹*choose, remember*›; to be ~ selected for sth. 专门为了某事选出来 2 (very) 特别 ‹*clever, awful*› 3 (specifically) 具体地 ‹*ask, instruct*›

parting /ˈpɑːtɪŋ/

A *n* 1 [u and c] (separation) 离别 2 [u] (dividing) 分开; the ~ of the ways fig 分道扬镳处 3 [c] Brit (in hair) 分缝

B *adj* 离别的 ‹*gift, kiss, vow*›

parting shot *n* 临别时的尖酸话

partisan /ˈpɑːtɪzæn, ˌpɑːtɪˈzæn, Amer ˈpɑːrtɪzn/

A *n* 1 (adherent) 坚定的支持者 2 Mil 游击队员

B *adj* 1 (biased) 偏袒的 ‹*approach, attitude*›; 盲目拥护的 ‹*person*› 2 Mil 游击队的 ‹*attack, group*›

partisanship /ˈpɑːtɪzænʃɪp, ˌpɑːtɪ-, Amer ˈpɑːrt-/ *n* [u] 党派偏见

partition /pɑːˈtɪʃn/

A *n* 1 [c] (wall) 隔墙; (screen) 隔扇; glass/wooden ~ 玻璃/木头隔断 2 [u] Pol (of country) 分割

B *vt* 1 (divide) 分隔 ‹*room, space*› 2 Pol 分割 ‹*country*›

Phrasal verb

- **partition off** *vt* [~ off sth., ~ sth. off] 隔开 ‹*area, section*›

partition wall *n* 隔墙

partly /ˈpɑːtli/ *adv* 在一定程度上 ‹*true, responsible*›; 部分地 ‹*finished, open*›

partner /ˈpɑːtnə(r)/

A *n* 1 (in a company or law firm) 合伙人; senior/junior ~ 高级/初级合伙人; ~ in crime hum 同谋犯 2 Pol 伙伴; Britain's NATO ~s 英国的北约伙伴 3 (in sport) 搭档; (in dance) 舞伴 4 (lover) 性伴侣; (in long-term relationship) 伴侣; (spouse) 配偶

B *vt* (in sport) 做…的搭档; (in dance) 做…的舞伴

Phrasal verb

- **partner up** *vi* 成为搭档; to ~ up with sb. 与某人搭档

partnership /ˈpɑːtnəʃɪp/ *n* 1 [u and c] (association) 合伙关系; in ~ with sb. 与某人合伙; to go *or* enter into ~ (with sb.) （与某人）结成合作关系 2 [c] Comm, Jur 合伙企业; a limited ~ 有限责任合伙公司 3 [c] (position) 合伙人身份; to take sb. into ~ 让某人成为合伙人

partnership agreement *n* 合伙契约

part: ~ **of speech** *n* (*pl* ~**s of speech**) 词性; ~ **owner** *n* 共有者; ~ **payment** *n* 部分付款

partook /pɑːˈtʊk/ *pt* ▸ **partake**

partridge /ˈpɑːtrɪdʒ/ *n* 山鹑

part song *n* 主调合唱曲

part-time

A *adj* 兼职的 ‹*job, employee*›

B *adv* 兼职地 ‹*work*›

C *n* [u] 兼职工作; to be on *or* to work ~ 做兼职工作

part: ~**-timer** *n* 兼职者; ~**way** *adv* 到半途; ~way down the page 接近页面的底端; to be ~way through doing sth. 某事做到一半; ~ **work** *n* Brit 分辑

party /ˈpɑːti/

A *n* 1 (social event) 聚会; a Christmas/New Year's Eve ~ 圣诞/除夕晚会; a dinner ~ 宴会; to give *or* have a ~ (for sb./sth.) （为某人/某事）举行聚会; a pretty ~ frock 漂亮的女式宴会礼服 2 (organized group) 团体; a ~ of tourists/children 旅游团/儿童团队 3 Pol 党派; a political ~ 政党; a right-wing/left-wing/centre ~ 右翼/左翼/中间党派; the Conservative/Labour P~ 保守党/工党; the P~ (ruling party) 执政党; (Communist Party) 共产党; ~ policy 政党政策 4 Jur (person) 当事人; a ~ to an agreement/a contract 协议/合同的一方; the ~ of the first part 甲方; a ~ to the action *or* suit 诉讼方; the innocent/guilty ~ 无罪/有罪的一方; to be (a) ~ to ... 参与…; to make sb. (a) ~ to sth. 使某人参与某事

B *vi* colloq 狂欢; they partied all night 他们寻欢作乐了一整夜; let's go ~ 咱们去玩玩吧

party: ~ **animal** *n* colloq 聚会迷; ~**goer** *n* 聚会常客; ~ **hat** *n* 聚会帽; ~ **line** *n* 1 Pol 政党路线; to follow the ~ line 追随政党路线; 2 Telecom dated 合用线; ~ **piece** *n* Brit 聚会小节目

party political *adj* esp Brit 党派政治的 ‹*bias, propaganda*›

party political broadcast *n* Brit 党派政治广播节目

party: ~ **politics** *npl* + *v sing or pl* [一切服从党的利益的] 政党政治; ~**-pooper** *n* colloq [社交场合] 令人扫兴之人; ~ **popper** *n* 聚会彩炮; ~ **wall** *n* 隔断墙

par value *n* 票面价值

paschal candle /ˈpæskl ˌkændl, ˈpɑːskl/ *n* 复活节蜡烛

pashmina /pʌʃˈmiːnə/ *n* 羊绒披巾

Pashto /ˈpæʃtəʊ/ *n* [u] 普什图语

pass /pɑːs, Amer pæs/

A *vi* 1 (move forward) 通过; the street was so crowded I could not ~ 街道非常拥挤，我过不去; to let sb. ~ 让某人通过 2 (go past) 经过 3 (move) 行进; he glanced at her and ~ed on without a word 他瞥了她一眼，一言不发继续往前走; ~ right down the bus, please! 上车后请往里走！; to ~ out of sight/into oblivion 消失/被忘却 4 Sport «*player, footballer*» 传球; to ~ back/forward(s) 回传/向前传球 5 (be transferred) «*inheritance, estate*» 遗留; «*responsibility*» 转移; to ~ to sb. 传给某人; the title ~ed to the eldest son 爵位传给了长子 6 (change) «*substance, person*» 转变; his mood ~ed from joy to despair 他的情绪由高兴转为绝望 7 (go by) «*period of time*» 流逝; how time ~es! 时间飞逝！; to ~ slowly/quickly 过得慢/快; the moment had ~ed 时机已过 8 (come to an end) «*crisis, storm*» 结束; «*opportunity*» 丧失; «*emotion*» 消失; «*illness*» 痊愈 9 (succeed in exam) «*candidate*» 及格; she hopes to ~ in all three subjects 她希望三门课全都及格 10 (in vote) «*proposal, motion*» 经表决通过; the bill ~ed with a large majority 议案以绝大多数赞成票获得通过 11 (be tolerated) «*action, behaviour*» 被容忍; (be accepted) «*person, words*» 被接受; to ~ as *or* for sth. 被当作某情况; he speaks French well enough to ~ for a Frenchman 他法语讲得很好，足以被当成法国人 12 (happen, occur) «*event, occurrence*» 发生; I just could not forgive him after all that had ~ed 所有这一切发生后，我真是无法原谅他; to come to ~ formal or liter 发生 13 (be said) 被说出; (be done) 被做出; several sharp comments had ~ed between them 他们对骂了几句; his comment appeared to ~ unnoticed 他的评论好像未引起注意 14 (in cards) (not play a card) 不出牌; (not make a bid) 不叫牌

B *vt* 1 (cross to the other side of) 通过 ‹*barrier, customs, frontier*›; the yacht ~ed the finishing line 快艇冲过了终点线; not a drop of water had ~ed his lips all day 他一整天滴水未沾; not a word ~ed her lips 她没透露过一个字 2 (go past) 经过; she ~ed me in the street without a word 她在大街上一言不发从我身边走过; to ~ this/that way 走这条/那条路 3 (move) 移动; they ~ed the injured man across the stream 他们把受伤的人抬过小河; to ~ the rope round the tree 把绳子绕在树上; she ~ed the thread through the eye of the needle 她引线穿针; he ~ed his hand over his face 他用手抹了一把脸 4 (hand over) 传递; to ~ sth. to sb., to ~ sb. sth. 把某物递给某人; here! ~ it over! 喂！把它递过来！; to ~ stolen goods/forged money 销赃/使用伪钞; to ~ the word 传话; to ~ the parcel Games 传递包裹 5 Sport «*player*» 传 ‹*ball*› 6 (spend) 度过; how did you ~ the time? 你是怎样打发时间的？; to ~ one's time 消磨时光 7 (succeed in) «*candidate, vehicle, machinery*» 通过 ‹*examination, test*› 8 (declare satisfactory) «*examiner, inspector, censor*» 准予…通过 ‹*candidate, work, film*›; to ~ an invoice 核实发票; to ~ the proofs (for press) 核准校样（待印）; to be ~ed fit for service 体检合格可入伍 9 (vote in) «*parliament, committee, board*» 经表决通过 ‹*bill, law, legislation*› 10 (be approved by) «*law, legislation*» 在…得到通过 ‹*parliament, assembly*›; the film was too explicit to ~ the censors 这部影片太露骨，没能通过审查 11 (pronounce) «*judge*» 宣布 ‹*verdict*›; «*critic*» 发表 ‹*comment*›; to ~ sentence *or* judgement (on sb.) Jur 宣布（对某人的）判决; he ~ed some very rude remarks about her! 他对她出言不逊！ 12 (exceed) 超越; to ~ belief/comprehension/all expectations 难以置信/难以理解/出乎意料 13 Med (discharge) 排泄 ‹*urine, faeces*›; if you're ~ing blood, you should see a doctor 如果便血，就应该去看医生; to ~ water colloq 撒尿

C *n* 1 (at school, university, in professional exam) 及格; (in driving test) 通过; a ~ in Maths/English 数学/英语考试的及格; to get a ~ 及格 2 (to enter, leave a place) 通行证; Mil (for leave of absence) 休假证; (of safe conduct) 许可证; a cinema ~ 电影院入场券; a ~ to sth./to do sth. 进入某处的通行证/做某事的许可证; to show one's ~ 出示通行证; on ~ 获得许可; sailors leaving ship on ~ 获准离船的海员 3 (for bus, train) 乘车证; a monthly/an annual ~ 月票/年票 4 Sport (in ball games) 传球; (in fencing) 戳刺; a long/short ~ 长传/短传; a forward/back *or* backward ~ 前传/回传; to intercept a ~ 截球 5 (in mountains) 山隘; (route or road) 山路; the St. Bernhard P~ 圣伯纳德山隘道; to head *or* cut sb./sth. off at the ~ hum 在开始时遏止某人/某事; to sell the ~ 背信弃义 6 (in cards) (skipping a turn) 不出牌; (not making a bid) 不叫牌 7 (by conjuror, hypnotist) 挥动; the conjuror made a ~ with his hand/wand, and out popped a white rabbit! 魔术师挥了挥手/魔杖，一只白兔蹦了出来！ 8 Aviat 俯冲; the bomber made a ~ over the target 轰炸机向目标俯冲; to fly a low ~ over sth. 在某物上低飞掠过 9 (critical position) 难关; to come to a pretty ~/such a ~ that ... 陷入…的困境/田地 10 colloq (amorous advance) 挑逗; to make a ~ at sb. 挑逗某人

Phrasal verbs

- **pass away** ▸ p. 247 *vi* euph 去世
- **pass by**

A *vi* (go past) «*pedestrian, procession, vehicle*» 经过; (by chance) «*person*» 路过

B [~ by sb./sth.] *vt* (go past) «*procession, pedestrian, vehicle*» 经过 ‹*person, place, vehicle*›

C [~ sb./sth. by] *vt*

1 (occur unnoticed) 绕过; life has ~ed me by 我从未享受过人生的机遇欢乐 2 (go past without acknowledging) 忽略; he ~ed me by 他没理睬我

- **pass down** *vt* [~ **sth. down**] 传承; **the sacred rites were ~ed down through the generations** 神圣的礼仪世代相传
- **pass off**

A *vi* 1 (happen, be carried through) «*event, proceedings*» 进行; **the party ~ed off well** 聚会圆满结束 2 (come to an end) «*pain, effects*» 消退

B *vt* **to ~ sb./sth. off as sb./sth.** 将某人/某物伪装成某人/某物; **she ~ed herself off as a well-wisher** 她假惺惺地表示祝愿

- **pass on**

A *vi* 1 (proceed) 接着进行; **to ~ on to sth.** 进入某事 2 euph (die) 去世; **to ~ on to a higher place** *or* **better world** 升上天堂

B *vt* [~ **sth. on,** ~ **on sth.**] 传递 ‹*message, information*›; 传染 ‹*cold*›; **to ~ sth. on to sb.** 把某物传给某人

- **pass out** *vi* 1 (faint) 昏迷 2 Mil 从军校毕业
- **pass over** *vt* 1 [~ **sb. over**] (ignore) 不考虑; **he was hoping for promotion, but he was ~ed over** 他希望得到提升，但是未被考虑 2 [~ **over sth.**] (disregard) 对…置之不理
- **pass through**

A *vi* 路过

B *vt* [~ **through sth.**] 经历 ‹*period of time, phase*›

- **pass up** *vt* [~ **sth. up,** ~ **up sth.**] colloq 放弃 ‹*opportunity, offer*›

passable /ˈpɑːsəbl, Amer ˈpæs-/ *adj* 1 (satisfactory) 尚可的 ‹*quality, meal, French*› 2 (traversable) 能通行的 ‹*road, route*› 3 (crossable) 可渡过的 ‹*river, ford*›

passably /ˈpɑːsəbli, Amer ˈpæs-/ *adv* 尚可地 ‹*sing, perform*›; 相当地 ‹*amused*›

passage /ˈpæsɪdʒ/ *n* 1 [c] (narrow way) (indoors) 走廊; (outdoors) 过道 2 [c] (way through) 通道; **to clear/force/leave a ~** 开/挤/留出一条通道 3 [c] Anat 道; **ear/urinary/nasal ~s** 耳道/尿道/鼻腔 4 [c] (of speech, poetry, book etc.) 段落; (of music) 乐段; **selected ~s** 选段 5 [u] (movement) 通行; **the ~ of vehicles/ships** 车辆/船只的通行 6 [u] Jur formal 通行权; **to deny sb. ~** 拒绝某人通行 7 [u] (passing) 推移; **the ~ of time/years** 时间/岁月的流逝 8 [u] (transition) 过渡; **the ~ from childhood to adolescence** 从童年到少年的过渡 9 [c] dated (journey) 旅程; **to book/work one's ~** 订购船票/在船上打工以支付旅费 10 [u] Pol [法案的] 通过

passageway /ˈpæsɪdʒweɪ/ *n* = **passage 1**

pass degree *n* Brit 普通学士学位

passé /ˈpæseɪ, Amer pæˈseɪ/ *adj pred* pej 过时的 ‹*clothes, songs, style*›

passel /ˈpæsl/ *n* esp Amer colloq 一大批

passenger /ˈpæsɪndʒə(r)/ *n* 1 (traveller) 旅客 2 esp Brit colloq pej (idler) 闲散人员

passenger: ~ **aircraft** *n* 客机; ~ **coach** Brit, ~ **car** Amer *ns* 客车; ~ **compartment** *n* Brit 客厢; ~ **door** *n* (train) 车门; (plane) 舱门; ~ **ferry** *n* 客运渡轮; ~ **inquiries** *npl* 铁路客运问讯处; ~ **jet** *n* 客机; ~ **list** *n* 旅客名单; ~ **mile** *n* 客英里; ~ **plane** *n* 客机; ~ **seat** *n* 副驾驶座; ~ **service** *n* [u and c] 客运服务; ~ **train** *n* 客运列车

passer-by /ˌpɑːsəˈbaɪ/ *n* (*pl* **passers-by**) 路过者

passing /ˈpɑːsɪŋ, Amer ˈpæs-/

A *adj attrib* 1 (going by) 经过的 ‹*pedestrian, car*›; **with each ~ day/year** 随着日子/岁月的流逝 2 (fleeting) 瞬间的 ‹*thought, desire*›; **a ~ glimpse/whim** 匆匆的一瞥/一时的兴致 3 (cursory) 漫不经心的 ‹*glance*›; **a ~ reference/remark** 一笔带过/不经意的话 4 (vague) 粗略的 ‹*resemblance*›

B *n* [u] 1 (passage) 推移; **the ~ of the years/of time** 岁月的流逝/时间的推移; **to mention sth. in ~** 随口提到某事 2 (end) 结束; **the ~ of summer** 夏天的逝去; **the ~ of traditional customs** 传统习俗的消亡 3 euph (death) 逝世

passing: ~**-out parade** *n* 训练结业会操; ~ **place** *n* 会车带; ~ **shot** *n* 超身球

passion /ˈpæʃn/ *n* 1 [u and c] (fervour) 激情; ~**s ran high** 群情激昂 2 [u] (rage) 激愤; **a fit of ~** 一阵愤怒; **to be in a ~ (over sth.)** （对某事）义愤填膺 3 [u] (sexual desire) 情欲; ~ **for sb.** 对某人的情欲 4 [c] (love) 酷爱; **a ~ for nature/art** 对自然/艺术的酷爱 5 [c] (hobby) 爱好 6 [u] Relig **the P~** 耶稣的受难; **the St Matthew P~** 马太福音受难曲

passionate /ˈpæʃənət/ *adj* 1 (fervent) 充满激情的 ‹*speech, defender, plea*› 2 (amorous) 多情的 ‹*affair*›; **a ~ kiss/lover** 深情的一吻/感情热烈的情人 3 (excitable) 暴躁的 ‹*person, temperament*›

passionately /ˈpæʃənətli/ *adv* 1 (fervently) 热切地 ‹*plead*›; 强烈地 ‹*opposed*›; **to be ~ fond of sb./sth.** 酷爱某人/某物 2 (amorously) 深情地 ‹*love, kiss*›; **to be ~ in love (with sb.)** （和某人）在热恋

passion: ~ **flower** *n* 西番莲; ~ **fruit** *n* [u and c] 百香果

passionless /ˈpæʃənlɪs/ *adj* 1 (emotionless) 冷漠的 ‹*relationship*›; 没有激情的 ‹*marriage*› 2 (dull) 平淡的 ‹*account, approach*›

Passion play *n* 耶稣受难剧

passive /ˈpæsɪv/

A *adj* 1 (inactive) 被动的; (submissive) 顺从的; ~ **obedience** 消极的服从 2 (emotionless, unresponsive) 冷漠的 3 Pol 非暴力的 ‹*rejection, opposition*› 4 Ling 被动的 ‹*tense, voice*›

B *n* **the ~** 被动语态

passive disobedience *n* [u] 非暴力不合作

passively /ˈpæsɪvli/ *adv* 1 (in inactive manner) 被动地; (in submissive manner) 顺从地 2 (in emotionless manner) 冷漠地 3 Ling 被动地

passiveness /ˈpæsɪvnɪs/ *n* [u] 被动状态

passive: ~ **resistance** *n* [u] 消极抵抗; ~ **restraint** *n* 乘员消极保护装置; ~ **smoker** *n* 被动吸烟者; ~ **smoking** *n* [u] 被动吸烟

passivity /pæˈsɪvəti/ *n* [u] 被动状态

pass: ~ **key** *n* 1 (to restricted area) 专用钥匙; 2 (master key) 万能钥匙; ~ **mark** *n* 及格分数

Passover /ˈpɑːsəʊvə(r), Amer ˈpæs-/ *n* [u] [犹太人的] 逾越节

passport /ˈpɑːspɔːt, Amer ˈpæs-/ *n* 1 (document) 护照 2 fig 途径; **a ~ to success** 获得成功的途径

passport holder *n* 护照持有者

pass: ~ **the parcel** *n* [u] 击乐传包游戏; ~**-through** *n* Amer 传菜小窗口

password /ˈpɑːswɜːd, Amer ˈpæs-/ *n* 1 (secret word, phrase) 口令 2 Comput 密码

password: ~**-protected** *adj* 有密码保护的; ~ **protection** *n* [u] 密码保护

past /pɑːst, Amer pæst/

A *prep* 1 (beyond in time) 过; **quarter/half ~ 3** 3 点 1 刻/3 点半; **it is ~ 11 o'clock** 已经过了 11 点了; **she is ~ 60** 她 60 出头了 2 (to the other side of) 到…的另一边; (farther than, beyond) 在…的另一边; **he rushed ~ me** 他从我身旁冲过去; **just ~ the post office** 就在邮局的那一头 3 (beyond, above or below a certain level) 超过; **I never got ~ the first chapter** 我一直停留在第一章; **she didn't get ~ the initial interview** 她没能通过最初的面试; **they can't count ~ 3** 他们不会数超过 3 的数; **the temperature went down ~ zero** 温度降到了零下; **to be ~ its best** (of food) 不新鲜了; **the car is ~ its prime** 这辆车已风光不再 4 (no longer capable of) 超出…的能力; **he's ~ playing football** 他不再能踢足球了; **to be ~ it** colloq 年纪大不中用了 5 (beyond scope of) 超出…的范围; **it is ~ all understanding** 这简直匪夷所思; **to be ~ caring** 什么也不在乎了; **to not put it ~ someone (to do sth.)** (to do sth. wrong) 相信某人做得出来（某事）; (to do sth. rash) 相信某人会鲁莽（做某事）

B *n* 1 (time that is over, previous history) 过去; **in the ~** 在过去; **she lives in the ~** 她活在过去的时光中; **a thing of the ~** 过去的事; **a nation with a glorious ~** 有着光辉历史的民族; **a woman with a ~** 有一段不光彩历史的女人 2 Ling (past tense) 过去时; (past form) 过去式

C *adj* 1 *attrib* (preceding) 刚过去的; **for the ~ few years** 近几年来; **the ~ week** 上周 2 *attrib* (earlier, former) 从前的; ~ **generations/president** 先辈/前任总统; **in times ~** 在过去; ~ **achievements** 过去的成就; **he has a ~ history of violence** 他有过使用暴力的历史 3 *pred* (gone by) 结束的; **summer is ~** 夏天过去了; **all that is now ~** 一切已经过去了 4 *attrib* Ling 过去时的; **in the ~ tense** 用过去时

D *adv* 1 (from one side to another) 经过; **to hurry ~** 匆忙经过 2 (ago) 过去; **two years ~** 两年前

pasta /ˈpæstə/ *n* [u] 意大利面食

paste /peɪst/

A *n* 1 [u] (mixture) 面团 2 [c] Culin 酱 3 [u] (glue) 浆糊

B *vt* 1 (stick) 用浆糊粘; **to ~ sth. on sth.** 把某物粘在某物上 2 (coat with glue) 在…上涂浆糊 3 Comput 粘贴; **to cut/copy and ~ sth.** 剪贴/复制贴上某物 4 colloq (defeat) 彻底击败 5 colloq (hit) 痛打

Phrasal verb

- **paste up** *vt* [~ **sth. up,** ~ **up sth.**] 用浆糊张贴

pasteboard /ˈpeɪstbɔːd/ *n* [u] 硬纸板

pastel /ˈpæstl, Amer pæˈstel/ *n* 1 [c] (crayon) 蜡笔 2 [c] (picture) 蜡笔画 3 [c] (colour) 淡雅的色彩; **a ~ tone** 淡雅的色调 4 [u] (medium) 蜡笔画法; ~ **skills** 蜡笔画技法

paste-up *n* 拼版

pasteurization /ˌpɑːstʃəraɪˈzeɪʃn, Amer ˌpæstʃərɪˈzeɪʃn/ *n* [u] 巴氏消毒

pasteurize /ˈpɑːstʃəraɪz, Amer ˈpæst-/ *vt* 对…进行巴氏消毒

pasteurized /ˈpɑːstʃəraɪzd, Amer ˈpæst-/ *adj* 巴氏消毒的 ‹*wine*›; ~ **milk** 巴氏奶

pastiche /pæˈstiːʃ/ *n* Art, Literat, Mus 1 [c] (imitation) 模仿作品 2 [c] (composition of different elements) 混成作品 3 [u] (technique) 混成技艺

pastille /ˈpæstəl, Amer pæˈstiːl/ *n* esp Brit 含片; **a throat ~** 喉片

pastime /ˈpɑːstaɪm, Amer ˈpæs-/ *n* 消遣; **her favourite ~ is golf** 她最喜爱的娱乐活动是打高尔夫球

pasting /ˈpeɪstɪŋ/ *n* colloq 1 (defeat) 惨败 2 (beating) 痛击; **to give sb. a ~** 痛打某人 3 (criticism) 严厉批评; **to get** *or* **take a ~** 挨训

past master *n* 行家; **she's a ~ at getting what she wants** 她精明能干，想要什么就能得到什么

pastor /ˈpɑːstə(r), Amer ˈpæs-/ ▸**p. 409** *n* 牧师

pastoral /ˈpɑːstərəl, Amer ˈpæs-/

A *adj* 1 (agricultural) 畜牧的; **a ~ economy** 畜牧经济; ~ **farms** 牧场 2 (rural) 乡村的 ‹*life*›; 放牧的 ‹*nomad, tribe, race*› 3 Art, Literat, Mus 田园式的; ~ **poetry** 田园诗 4 Relig 牧灵的 ‹*duty, visit*› 5 Brit Sch, Univ 教导的 ‹*role, capacity*›

B *n* 田园式作品; **her pictures include a number of ~s** 她的画作里有许多田园画

pastoral: ~ **care** *n* [u] 1 Relig 牧师的关顾; 2 Brit Sch, Univ 教师的关心; ~ **letter** *n* 牧函

past: ~ **participle** *n* [动词的] 过去分词; ~ **perfect** *n* = **pluperfect B**

pastrami /pæ'strɑːmi/ *n* [u] 五香熏牛肉

pastry /'peɪstri/ *n* 1 [u] (dough) 油酥面团 2 [c] (cake) 油酥糕点

pastry: ~ **board** *n* 擀面板; ~ **brush** *n* 面团刷; ~ **case** *n* 油酥面皮; ~ **cook** *n* 糕点师傅; ~ **cutter** *n* 面团切刀

past tense *n* 过去式

pasturage /'pɑːstʃərɪdʒ, Amer 'pæs-/ *n* [u] 1 (land) 牧场 2 (activity) 放牧

pasture /'pɑːstʃə(r), Amer 'pæs-/

A *n* 1 [u or c] (land, field) 牧场; **to put the cattle out to** ~ 放牛群到牧场; **to put sb. out to** ~ fig 迫使某人退休; ~**s new** fig 新天地; **she left the office for** ~**s new** 她离职换新工作了 2 [u] (grass) 牧草

B *vt* 放牧

pasture land *n* [u] 牧场

pasty[1] /'peɪsti/ *adj* 1 (pale) 苍白的 ‹*face, complexion*›; ~**-faced** 脸色苍白的 2 (of paste) 面团的; (like paste) 面团似的

pasty[2] /'pæsti/ *n* Brit 馅饼

pat[1] /pæt/

A *vt* (*pres p etc.* **-tt-**) 1 (tap) 轻拍 2 (stroke) 轻抚; **to** ~ **sb. on the back** lit 轻拍某人的背; **to** ~ **sb./oneself on the back** fig 称赞某人/自己 3 (put into shape) 轻拍使成形; (put into position) 把…轻拍到位; **to** ~ **one's hair into place** 把头发拍整齐

B *n* 1 (tap) 轻拍; **to give sb. a** ~ **on the back** 轻拍某人的背; **to give oneself/sb. a** ~ **on the back** fig 称赞自己/某人 2 (of butter) 小块

pat[2]

A *adv* 1 (memorized) 熟记地; **to have sth. off** *or* **down** ~ 对某事物了如指掌 2 (opportunely) 恰好地; **he answered** ~ 他回答得恰到好处 3 Amer **to stand** ~ 固执己见

B *adj* pej 简单随便的

pataca /pə'tɑːkə/ ▸**p. 174** *n* 澳门元

Patagonia /ˌpætə'gəʊnɪə/ *pr n* 巴塔哥尼亚

Patagonian /ˌpætə'gəʊnɪən/

A *adj* (of Patagonia) 巴塔哥尼亚的; (of the people) 巴塔哥尼亚人的

B *n* 巴塔哥尼亚人

patch /pætʃ/

A *n* 1 (for repair in clothes, tyre, airbed) 补丁; **he put a** ~ **on the inner tube** 他在内胎打了个补丁 2 (protective cover on eye) 眼罩 3 Hist, Cosmet 饰颜贴片 4 (area) 小片; **a damp** ~ **on the ceiling** 天花板上的一片湿渍; ~**es of ice on the road** 路上的片片冰层; **a small** ~ **of sunlight** 一小片阳光; **in** ~**es** 斑驳陆离地; **he's got a bald** ~ 他有点秃 5 (area of ground) 小片土地; (for planting) 菜地; **a small** ~ **of land used for growing vegetables** 用于种菜的一小块地 6 Brit colloq (area, territory) 地盘; **each social worker has responsibility for a particular** ~ 每位社工负责一个特定区域 7 Brit colloq (period) 时期; **to go through a bad** *or* **sticky** ~ 经历一段艰难时期; **to hit a bad** *or* **sticky** ~ 陷入困境; **the weather was good in** ~**es** 天气时好时坏 8 Comput 补丁 9 **not a** ~ **on** Brit colloq fig 远不如; **she isn't a** ~ **on her sister** 她跟她姐姐没法比

B *vt* 1 (repair) 补 ‹*tear, trousers, tyre*› 2 Comput 为…安装补丁 ‹*routine, program*›

Phrasal verb

• **patch up**

A [~ **up sth.,** ~ **sth. up**] *vt* 1 (mend) 缝补 ‹*clothes*›; 修理 ‹*car*›; 整修 ‹*wall*› 2 fig colloq (restore relations after) 调停 ‹*quarrel, dispute*›; 弥合 ‹*differences*›

B [~ **sb. up,** ~ **sb. up**] *vt* colloq 为…临时包扎

patch: ~ **pocket** *n* 贴袋; ~ **test** *n* 斑贴试验

patchwork /'pætʃwɜːk/ *n* 1 [u] Sewing 杂布拼缝物; **a** ~ **quilt** 百衲被 2 [c] fig 拼凑之物; **from the plane, the landscape was just a** ~ **of fields** 从飞机上俯瞰，满目尽是阡陌交错; **a** ~ **of borrowed theories** 各种借用理论的大杂烩; **a** ~ **theory** 东拼西凑的理论

patchy /'pætʃi/ *adj* 1 (uneven) 分布不匀的; ~ **fog** 团团的雾 2 (inconsistent) 参差不齐的; **my knowledge of the subject is rather** ~ 我对该科目一知半解; **her work was a bit** ~ 她的工作质量时好时差

pâté /'pæteɪ, Amer pɑː'teɪ/ *n* [u] (meat) 肉酱; (fish) 鱼酱

patent /'pætnt, 'peɪtnt, Amer 'pætnt/

A *adj* 1 (obvious) 明显的; **a** ~ **lie** 赤裸裸的谎言; **her honesty was** ~ **to everyone** 她的诚实是有目共睹的 2 (patented) 受专利保护的 3 (proprietary) 专利生产经销的; ~ **drugs** 专利药物

B *n* 1 [u and c] (authority) 专利权; **to take out/hold a** ~ **on sth.** 取得/拥有某物的专利; **the device was protected by** ~ 该设备受专利保护 2 [c] (document) 专利证书 3 [c] (patented invention) 专利发明

C *vt* 获得…的专利权

patentable /'pætntəbl, 'peɪt-, Amer 'pæt-/ *adj* 可以获得专利的

patent agent Brit, **patent attorney** Amer ▸**p. 409** *ns* 专利代理人

patentee /ˌpeɪtn'tiː, Amer ˌpætn-/ *n* 专利权人

patent leather *n* 漆皮; **a pair of** ~ **shoes** 一双漆革皮鞋

patently /'peɪtntli, Amer 'pæt-/ *adv* 明显地; **he was quite** ~ **lying** 他显然在撒谎

patent: ~ **medicine** *n* 专利药品; **P**~ **Office** *n* Brit **the P**~ **Office** 专利局; ~ **right** *n* 专利权

paternal /pə'tɜːnl/ *adj* 1 (fatherly) 父亲般的; **to be** ~ **to** *or* **towards sb.** 对某人像父亲般慈爱 2 (of a father) 父亲的 ‹*care, deprivation, bond*›; ~ **love** 父爱 3 (on father's side) 父系的 ‹*ancestor, line, genes*›

paternalism /pə'tɜːnəlɪzəm/ *n* [u] 家长作风

paternalist /pə'tɜːnəlɪst/ *adj* 家长作风的; **a** ~ **regime** 专制政权

paternalistic /pəˌtɜːnə'lɪstɪk/ *adj* pej 家长作风的; **I find his attitudes a bit** ~ 我发现他的态度有一些专断

paternalistically /pəˌtɜːnə'lɪstɪkli/ *adv* pej 家长式地; **to behave** ~ 专断行事

paternally /pə'tɜːnəli/ *adv* 父亲般地

paternity /pə'tɜːnəti/ *n* [u] 父亲身份; **to deny/acknowledge** ~ **of a child** 否认/承认是孩子的父亲; **a child of unknown** ~ 生父不明的孩子

paternity: ~ **leave** *n* [u] [父亲的] 陪产假; ~ **suit** *n* esp Amer 生父确认诉讼; ~ **test** *n* 亲子鉴定

paternoster /ˌpætə'nɒstə(r)/ *n* ~ **(lift)** 链斗式提升机

path /pɑːθ, Amer pæθ/ *n* 1 (track) 小路; **a mountain** ~ 山路; **to beat a** ~ **to sb.'s door** 争先恐后去某人处; **the whole world seemed to beat a** ~ **to our door** 我们似乎成了整个世界注意的焦点 2 (course) 路线; **the** ~ **of the planets** 行星的轨道; **her** ~ **through life has not been easy** 她的生活不太平顺; **to stand in sb.'s** ~ lit 挡住某人的去路; fig 妨碍某人 3 (course of action, option) 行动路线; **the** ~ **of least resistance** 最简单的做法 4 fig (means) 途径; **the** ~ **to riches/success** 通向富裕/成功的道路 5 Comput 路径

pathetic /pə'θetɪk/ *adj* 1 (pitiable) 可怜的; **the scene was** ~ 场面很凄惨 2 (inadequate) 严重不足的; **her** ~ **rags** 她那褴褛的衣衫; **a** ~ **bonfire** 微弱的篝火 3 colloq pej (worthless, useless) 无用的; **a** ~ **excuse** 牵强的借口; **to make a** ~ **attempt to smile** 勉强地笑笑

pathetically /pə'θetɪkli/ *adv* 1 (pitiably) 可怜地 2 colloq pej (ludicrously) 荒谬乏味地; **a** ~ **feeble joke** 十分无趣的笑话

path: ~**finder** *n* 1 (person) 探路者; 2 fig (trailblazer) 开拓者; 3 (aircraft) 导航器; ~**name** *n* 路径名

pathological /ˌpæθə'lɒdʒɪkl/ *adj* 1 (relating to pathology) 病理学的 2 (of disease) 疾病的; (caused by disease) 疾病引起的 3 (abnormal, excessive) 病态的; **a** ~ **liar** 说谎成性的人

pathologically /ˌpæθə'lɒdʒɪkli/ *adv* 1 (relating to pathology) 在病理学上 ‹*definable, confirmed*› 2 (abnormally, excessively) 病态地; **he's** ~ **mean** 他吝啬得近乎病态

pathologist /pə'θɒlədʒɪst/ ▸**p. 409** *n* 病理学家

pathology /pə'θɒlədʒi/ *n* 1 [u] (study of disease) 病理学 2 [c] (pathological features) 病理

pathos /'peɪθɒs/ *n* [u] 感染力; **the** ~ **of sb.'s situation** 某人处境的令人同情; **to narrate with great** ~ 叙述得极其感人

pathway /'pɑːθweɪ/ *n* 小路; **a mountain** ~ 山路

patience /'peɪʃns/ *n* [u] 1 (forbearance) 耐心; **to have no** ~ **with sth.** 对某事没有耐心; **to lose** ~ **(with sb.)** （对某人）失去耐心; **to try** *or* **test sb.'s** ~ 使某人忍无可忍; **my** ~ **is running out** *or* **wearing thin** 我要忍耐不住了 2 (perseverance) 坚忍; **to display** *or* **show great** ~ 表现出极大的毅力; ~ **is a virtue** 坚忍是美德 3 ▸**p. 307** Brit Games 单人纸牌游戏

patient /'peɪʃnt/

A *adj* 1 (forbearing) 有耐心的; **to be** ~ **with sb.** 对某人有耐心 2 (persevering) 坚忍的

B *n* 病人

patient care *n* [u] 病人照护

patiently /'peɪʃntli/ *adv* 1 (with forbearance) 耐心地 2 (with perseverance) 坚忍地

patient record *n* 病历

patina /'pætɪnə/ *n* 1 (on metal) 绿锈 2 (on wood) 光泽 3 fig (aura) 神态; **he had the** ~ **of success** 他给人成功的印象

patio /'pætɪəʊ/ *n* 露台

patio: ~ **doors** *npl* 露台滑动玻璃门; ~ **furniture** *n* [u] 露台家具; ~ **garden** *n* 庭院

patois /'pætwɑː/ *n* (*pl* **patois**) 1 (regional dialect) 方言 2 (jargon) 行话

patriarch /'peɪtrɪɑːk, Amer 'pæt-/ *n* 1 (head of tribe or family) 族长 2 (senior figure) 元老 3 Relig 宗主教

patriarchal /ˌpeɪtrɪ'ɑːkl, Amer ˌpæt-/ *adj* 1 (of a patriarch) 族长的 2 (old, venerable) 年高德劭的 3 (ruled by men) 男性统治的; **a** ~ **society** 父权社会

patriarchy /'peɪtrɪɑːki, Amer 'pæt-/ *n* 1 [u] (system) 父权制 2 [c] (society, country) 父系社会

patrician /pə'trɪʃn/

A *adj* 贵族的 ‹*figure, family*›; 贵族似的 ‹*arrogance*›; **she comes from a** ~ **background** 她出身名门望族

B *n* 贵族

patricide /'pætrɪsaɪd/ *n* 1 [c and u] (crime) 弑父 2 [c] (perpetrator) 弑父者

patrilineal /ˌpætrɪ'lɪnɪəl/ *adj* formal 父系的; **a** ~ **society** 父系社会; ~ **succession** 父子相传

patrimony /'pætrɪməni, Amer -məʊni/ *n* [u] formal 1 (inheritance) 祖传财产 2 (heritage) 遗产

patriot /'pætrɪət, Amer 'peɪt-/ *n* 爱国者

patriotic /ˌpætrɪ'ɒtɪk, Amer ˌpeɪt-/ *adj* 爱国的; **a** ~ **song** 爱国歌曲

patriotically /ˌpætrɪ'ɒtɪkli, Amer ˌpeɪt-/ *adv* 爱国地

patriotism /'pætrɪətɪzəm, Amer 'peɪt-/ *n* [u] 爱国精神

patrol /pə'trəʊl/

A *n* 1 [u and c] (surveillance, activity) 巡逻; **to carry out** *or* **make a** ~ 去巡逻; **the soldiers on** ~

巡逻的士兵; **a ～ vehicle** 巡逻车 **2** [c] (group) 巡逻队; **a police ～** 警察巡逻队 **3** [c] (of Scouts, Guides) 童子军小队
B vt (*pres p etc.* **-ll-**) 在…巡逻 ‹*border, perimeter, area*›
C vi (*pres p etc.* **-ll-**) 巡逻

patrol: ～ boat n 巡逻艇; **～ car** n 巡逻警车; **～ leader** n 巡逻队长; **～man** /-mən/ ▸**p. 409** n Amer 巡警; **～ vessel** n 巡逻艇; **～ wagon** n Amer 囚车

patron /ˈpeɪtrən/ n **1** (benefactor) 赞助人 **2** (supporter) 名义赞助人 **3** (customer) 顾客

patronage /ˈpætrənɪdʒ/ n [u] **1** (support) 赞助; **under the ～ of sb.** 在某人的赞助下 **2** (custom) 光顾 **3** Pol 任命权; pej 滥用任命权

patronize /ˈpætrənaɪz/ vt **1** pej (treat condescendingly) 屈尊俯就地对待; **don't ～ me!** 别在我面前摆出高人一等的样子! **2** (be customer of) 经常光顾 **3** (support) 赞助

patronizing /ˈpætrənaɪzɪŋ/ adj pej 屈尊俯就的; **he's so ～!** 他自认为高人一等!

patronizingly /ˈpætrənaɪzɪŋli/ adv pej 屈尊俯就地

patron saint n 守护圣人

patronymic /ˌpætrəˈnɪmɪk/ n 源于父系的名字

patsy /ˈpætsi/ n esp Amer colloq pej **1** (dupe) 易吃亏上当的人 **2** (scapegoat) 替罪羊

patter[1] /ˈpætə(r)/
A n [u] **1** colloq (rapid talk) 喋喋不休; **the usual ～ of the comedian** 滑稽演员惯常说的急口词 **2** (jargon) 行话
B vi (talk at length) **to ～ away** *or* **on** 喋喋不休

patter[2]
A n [u] (tapping sound) 啪嗒声; **～ of footsteps** 啪嗒啪嗒的脚步声; **we'll soon be hearing the ～ of tiny feet** 我们的宝宝很快就要出生了
B vi **1** (strike, tap) 嗒嗒拍打; **raindrops ～ed on the window** 雨点啪嗒啪嗒地打在窗户上 **2** (run lightly) 轻盈地跑

pattern /ˈpætn/
A n **1** (decorative design) 图案; **a wavy/stripy ～** 波浪线/条纹图案 **2** (repeated motifs) 式样; **the cards have a ～ of holes on them** 这些卡片上有一串孔状图形; **the ～ on a tyre** 轮胎的纹路 **3** (for sewing, knitting) 图样; **a knitting ～** 编织图样; **a paper ～** 纸样 **4** (model, example) 榜样; **on the ～ of ...** 以…为榜样; **to establish** *or* **set a** *or* **the ～ for sth.** 为某事树立榜样 **5** (regular or standard way) 模式; **～s of behaviour, behaviour ～s** 行为模式; **to follow a set ～** 遵循固定模式; **sentences having a similar grammatical ～** 具有类似语法结构的句子 **6** (sample of cloth, wallpaper etc.) 样品 **7** Tech 模子
B vt **1** (model) 模仿; **to ～ sth. on** *or* **after sth.** 按照某物仿造某物; **his ideas are ～ed on Hayek's** 他的想法仿自海克 **2** (decorate) 装饰 ‹*fabric, wall*›; **rosebud ～ed wallpapers** 玫瑰花蕾图案壁纸

pattern book n 图样簿

patterned /ˈpætnd/ adj 有图案的 ‹*design, blouse, carpet*›

patterning /ˈpætnɪŋ/ n [u] **1** (patterns) 图案结构; **the ～ on the zebra's coat** 斑马皮毛上的花纹 **2** Psych 固有行为模式的形成; **cultural ～** 文化形态的形成

patty /ˈpæti/ n 肉饼

paucity /ˈpɔːsəti/ n formal 不足; **a ～ of water** 缺水; **a ～ of work** 少量工作

paunch /pɔːntʃ/ n 大肚子; **to get a ～** 变得大腹便便

paunchy /ˈpɔːntʃi/ adj 大腹便便的 ‹*person*›; 肥大的 ‹*belly*›

pauper /ˈpɔːpə(r)/ n 穷人; **to die a ～** 死时身无分文

pause /pɔːz/
A n **1** (brief silence, break, stoppage) 暂停; **a ～ in the conversation** 谈话中的停顿; **she spoke for an hour without a ～** 她一直不停地讲了一个小时; **there was a ten-minute ～ in production** 生产停顿了 10 分钟 **2** **to give sb. ～ (for thought)** (make sb. think) 使某人认真考虑; (make sb. hesitate) 使某人犹豫
B vi **1** (stop) 暂停; **she ～d and then went on in a quiet voice** 她停顿了一下，然后平静地继续说; **to ～ in sth.** 暂停做某事; **to ～ for breath** 停下来歇口气 **2** (hesitate, wait) 犹豫; **to ～ over sth.** 在某物前驻足

pause button n 暂停键

pave /peɪv/ vt 铺 ‹*road, path, area*›; **to be ～d with gold** fig 遍地是黄金; **to ～ the way for sb./sth.** fig 为某人/某事铺平道路; ▸**road 1**

pavement /ˈpeɪvmənt/ n **1** [c] Brit (for pedestrians) 人行道 **2** [c] Amer (road surface) 路面 **3** [u] (paving material) 铺路材料 **4** [c] (paved area) 铺面

pavement: ～ artist ▸**p. 409** n Brit 马路画家; **～ cafe** n Brit 路边咖啡馆; **～ stall** n Brit 路边摊位

pavilion /pəˈvɪlɪən/ n **1** Brit (at sports ground) 休息室 **2** (in park, garden) 亭子 **3** (ornamental building) 装饰性建筑 **4** (at exhibition) 临时展馆; **the Canadian ～** 加拿大展馆

paving /ˈpeɪvɪŋ/ n [u] **1** (paved surface) 铺面 **2** (material) 铺料

paving slab, paving stone ns 铺路石板

paw /pɔː/
A n **1** (of animal) 爪 **2** colloq (hand) 手; **get your dirty ～s off me!** 把你的脏手从我身上拿开!
B vt **1** (touch with paw) 用爪子挠 **2** (scrape with hoof) 用蹄子刨 **3** colloq (maul) 猥亵地摩挲; **stop ～ing me!** 别对我动手动脚!

pawl /pɔːl/ n 棘爪

pawn[1] /pɔːn/ n **1** (in chess) 卒 **2** fig (person) 走卒; **he is a ～ in the hands of the boss** 他受老板的摆布

pawn[2]
A vt 典当
B n [u] (being deposited) 典当; **my watch is in ～** 我把表当了; **to get sth. out of ～** 赎回某物

pawn: ～broker ▸**p. 409** n 典当商人; **～shop** n 当铺; **～ ticket** n 当票

pawpaw /ˈpɔːpɔː/ n **1** (fruit) 木瓜 **2** **～ (tree)** 木瓜树

pay /peɪ/
A vi (*pt, pp* **paid**) **1** (hand over money) «*person, company, government*» 付费; **the work ～s poorly** 这份工作收入很低; **to ～ for sth.** 支付某事物的费用; **to ～ for sb.** 为某人付款; **to ～ dearly for sth.** fig 为某事遭受惩罚; **you'll ～ for this!** fig 你要为这事付出代价的!; **there'll be hell** *or* **the devil to ～ (for sth.)** colloq (因为某事) 后果会不堪设想; **～ on entry** (on notice) 上车投币; **～ to the order of ...** (on cheque) 根据…的指令付款; **Paid** (on invoice) 付讫 **2** (be profitable) «*shop, business, venture*» 赢利; «*job, activity*» 赚钱; **to ～ handsomely** *or* **well** 获利丰厚; **to ～ for itself** 赚回成本 **3** (be advantageous) «*activity, quality, state*» 有利; **crime doesn't ～** 犯罪划不来; **in the long run dishonesty doesn't ～** 从长远来看，不诚实得不偿失; **it ～s to tell the truth** 说实话有好处
B vt (*pt, pp* **paid**) **1** (for services, goods, work) 付款给; **to ～ sb. for sth.** 为某事物给某人付钱; **to ～ sb. to do sth.** 付钱让某人做某事; **to ～ sb. in cash/by cheque** 用现金/支票支付某人; **to ～ a cheque into the bank** 把支票存入银行; **～ the money into your bank account** 把钱存入你的银行账户; **to ～ one's own way** 支付自己的费用; **he left without ～ing his account** 他没付账就离开了; **(all) expenses paid** 费用全包; **to be paid weekly/monthly** 按周/按月领薪水 **2** (give what is owed) 交纳 ‹*bill, debt, rent, fine, taxes*›; 支付 ‹*rates, interest*›; **to ～ a subscription to ...** 支付…的订阅费; **he paid £50 out of his own pocket** 他自己掏腰包付了 50 英镑; **to ～ high/low wages** 付高薪/低薪; **to ～ a lot/little** 待遇优厚/很差; **to ～ cash** 付现金; ▸**piper** **3** (benefit) 使受益; **in the long run dishonesty doesn't ～ anybody** 从长远来看，不诚实对谁都没好处; **it ～s/doesn't ～ sb. to do sth.** 做某事对某人有利/不利 **4** (give, bestow) 给予 ‹*attention, respect, compliment*›; **to ～ a visit** *or* **call** colloq euph 去洗手间
C n [u] (to worker) 薪金; (to soldier, sailor) 军饷; **overtime ～** 加班费; **to be in the ～ of sb./sth.** 受雇于某人/某处; **equal ～ for equal work** 同工同酬; **low** *or* **poor/high** *or* **good ～** 低薪/高薪; **a cut** *or* **reduction in ～** 减薪; **basic ～** 基本工资
D modif **1** (regarding salary) 薪酬的 ‹*negotiations, structure, cheque*›; **a ～ rise/cut** 加薪/减薪 **2** (requiring money) 投币的; **a ～ toilet** 投币厕所; **a ～ station** Amer 投币电话亭

Phrasal verbs

• **pay back**
A vt [**～ sth. back**] 还; **she paid me back my $50** 她把我的 50 英镑还给我了
B vt [**～ sb. back**]
1 (return money to) 还钱给 **2** fig (take revenge) 报复; **to ～ sb. back in his/her own kind** 以其人之道还治其人之身; **to ～ sb. back with interest** 变本加厉报复某人

• **pay off**
A vi 成功; **all that hard work paid off handsomely** 所有那些辛苦都很值得
B [**～ sb. off, ～ off sb.**] vt
1 (pay and dismiss sb.) 遣散 **2** colloq (give money to sb.) 买通
C [**～ sth. off, ～ off sth.**] vt (repay) 还清 ‹*debt*›

• **pay out** vt [**～ sth. out**]
1 (pay) 支付 ‹*money*›; **the company is ～ing out £50,000 a year on advertising** 公司每年支出 5 万英镑的广告费用 **2** (let out) 徐徐放出 ‹*rope*›

• **pay up**
A vi 还清欠款
B vt [**～ up sth.**] 还清; **he paid up everything he owed me** 他还清了欠我的所有款项

payable /ˈpeɪəbl/ adj pred **1** (requiring payment) 应付的; **～ on demand** 见票即付 **2** (able to be paid) 可付的; **～ in instalments** 可分期支付的

pay and display Brit
A n [u] 泊车付费系统
B **pay-and-display** modif 泊车付费的 ‹*car park, car parking*›

pay-as-you-earn n [u] Brit 所得税预扣法

pay as you go
A n [u] (paying debts) 到期即付; (meeting costs) 现购现付
B **pay-as-you-go** modif (paying debts) 到期即付的 ‹*service*›; (meeting costs) 现购现付的 ‹*tariff*›; **～ telephones** 预付费电话

pay: ～-as-you-talk adj 通话收费的 ‹*phone, tariff*›; **～back** n [c and u] **1** Fin 投资回收; **2** (advantage, reward) 回报; **3** (revenge) 报复; **it's ～back time** colloq 报应的时候到了; **～bed** n Brit 自费病床; **～ channel** n 收费频道; **～ cheque** n **1** (cheque) 薪金支票; **2** Amer (salary) 薪金; (income) 收入; **～day** n 发薪日; **～desk** n 收银台; **～ dirt** n [u] esp Amer **1** (ground) 含矿土; **2** fig colloq (profit) 财源; (success) 成功; **to hit** *or* **strike ～ dirt** (to make large profit) 暴富; (to be a success) 骤然成功

PAYE abbr esp Brit = **pay-as-you-earn**

payee /peɪˈiː/ n 受款人

payer /ˈpeɪə(r)/ n 付款人; **he's a good ～** 他付款及时

pay freeze n 薪资冻结

paying /ˈpeɪɪŋ/
A *adj attrib* 有利的 ‹*proposition, scheme*›
B *n* [u] 付款

paying: ~ **guest** *n* 房客; **~-in book** *n* Brit 存款簿; **~-in slip** *n* Brit 存款单

payload /ˈpeɪləʊd/ *n* 1 (of ship, aircraft) 装载量 2 (warhead) 弹头 3 (of spacecraft) 有效载荷

paymaster /ˈpeɪmɑːstə(r), Amer -mæstər/ *n* 1 (official who pays wages) 工资出纳员 2 pej (employer) 后台老板

Paymaster General *n* Brit 主计大臣

payment /ˈpeɪmənt/ *n* 1 [u] (act of paying) 付款; **to make ~ by instalments** 分期付款; **they did it for us without ~** 他们无偿地为我们做了这件事; **on ~ of £25** 支付 25 英镑后 2 [c] (amount) 支付的款项; **a cash ~** 现金付款; **in 10 monthly ~s** 分 10 个月付清; **to suspend ~s** 暂停付款; **social security ~s** 社会保险金 3 [u] (reward) 报偿; **I'd like you to accept this gift in ~ for your kindness** 谨以薄礼答谢厚爱, 敬请笑纳

pay-off *n* colloq 1 (bribe) 贿赂; (on leaving job) 遣散金 2 (return) 收益 3 (reward) 回报 4 (outcome, denouement) 结果

payola /peɪˈəʊlə/ *n* [u] esp Amer colloq 贿赂

pay: ~ **packet** *n* Brit 1 lit 薪金袋; 2 fig (salary) 薪金; (income) 收入; **~-per-view** *n* [u] 付费点播; **~phone** *n* 公用电话; **~roll** *n* 1 (list of employees) 工资名单; **to take sb. off the ~roll** 解雇某人; **to be on the ~roll** 在编; **a company with 500 employees on the ~roll** 有 500 名在编员工的公司; 2 (total wages paid) 工资总支出; ~ **round** *n* 年度工资谈判; ~ **scale** *n* 工资级差表; **~slip** *n* esp Brit 工资单; ~ **television** *n* [u] 收费电视

> **PBS**
> 公共电视网, 全称 Public Broadcasting Service。美国公共电视网络, 成员包括 356 家公共电视台。成立于1969年。总部位于弗吉尼亚州的阿灵顿 (Arlington, Virginia)。属非营利性质, 没有广告, 经费主要来自各级政府的拨款和社会捐款。节目以高质量著称, 其中儿童节目《芝麻街》(*Sesame Street*)、系列片《自然》(*Nature*) 和《国家地理特辑》(*National Geographic Special*) 非常有名。

PC *abbr* 1 = **personal computer** 2 Brit = **police constable** 3 = **politically correct**

p.c. *abbr* 1 = **per cent** 2 = **postcard**

PCT *abbr* Brit = **Primary Care Trust**

pd *abbr* = **paid** 付讫

PDA *n* = **personal digital assistant**

PDF *n* [c and u] 可携式文件格式; ~ **files/format** PDF文件/格式

PDT *abbr* Amer = **Pacific Daylight Time**

PE *abbr* = **physical education**

pea /piː/ *n* 豌豆; **like ~s or two ~s in a pod** 一模一样

peabrain /ˈpiːbreɪn/ *n* colloq 笨蛋

peace /piːs/
A *n* [u] 1 (absence of violence or conflict) 和平; **the two countries are at ~** 两国现在和平相处; **to make ~** 议和 2 (period without war) 和平时期; **a lasting ~** 持久和平 3 (treaty) 和约; **a negotiated ~** 谈判达成的和约 4 (tranquillity) 安静; (serenity, calmness) 宁静; **to leave sb. in ~** 不打扰某人; **to give sb. no ~** 不断地打扰某人; **~ of mind** 心境的安宁; **to be** *or* **live at ~ with the world** 与世无争; **to be at ~** euph 安息; **to hold one's ~** 保持沉默 5 (concord, friendliness) 和睦; **to keep the ~ in the family** 保持家庭和睦; **to make (one's) ~ (with sb.)** (与某人) 和解 6 (law and order) 治安; **to keep the ~** (enforce lawful ways) 维持治安; (behave in a lawful way) 遵纪守法

B *modif* 呼吁裁军的 ‹*meeting, campaign*›; **a ~ demonstration/march** 和平示威/游行

peaceable /ˈpiːsəbl/ *adj* 1 (amicable) 温和的 2 (peaceful) 和平的

peaceably /ˈpiːsəbli/ *adv* 1 (amicably) 温和地; **to co-exist ~** 和睦共处 2 (peacefully) 和平地

peace: ~ **camp** *n* 和平营; ~ **campaigner** *n* 倡导和平的人; **P~ Corps** *n* Amer 和平队; ~ **envoy** *n* 和平使者

peaceful /ˈpiːsfl/ *adj* 1 (tranquil) 安静的; (serene, calm) 宁静的; **a ~ look** 安详的神情 2 (without violence or conflict) 和平的; **a ~ reign** 太平盛世 3 (peaceable) 爱好和平的 ‹*nation*›; 温和的 ‹*person, disposition*›

peacefully /ˈpiːsfəli/ *adv* 1 (tranquilly) 安静地; (serenely, calmly) 宁静地; **he was sleeping ~** 他睡得很安稳 2 (without violence or conflict) 和平地 3 (peaceably) 和睦地

peacefulness /ˈpiːsflnɪs/ *n* [u] 1 (tranquillity) 安静; (serenity, calmness) 宁静 2 (absence of violence or conflict) 和平

peace: **~keeper** *n* 1 Mil [尤指多国组成的] 维和部队成员; 2 Pol (nation) 维和国家; 3 (conciliator) 调停者; **~keeping** *n* [u] 维护和平; **~keeping force** *or* **troops** 维和部队; ~ **lobby** *n* 提倡和平的游说团体; **~-loving** *adj* 爱好和平的; **~maker** *n* 调解人; **P~ Movement** *n* 和平运动; ~ **offensive** *n* 和平攻势; ~ **offering** *n* 1 (present) 表示和解的礼物; **he took her some flowers as a ~ offering** 他送花给她表示歉意; 2 Relig 谢恩祭; ~ **pipe** *n* 和平烟斗; ~ **process** *n* 和平进程; ~ **settlement** *n* 和平协议; ~ **studies** *npl* + *v sing or pl* 和平研究; ~ **talks** *npl* 和平谈判; **~time** *n* [u] 和平时期; **in ~time** 在和平时期; **~time use** 平时的使用; ~ **treaty** *n* 和平协定

peach /piːtʃ/ ▸p. 134
A *n* 1 [c] (fruit) 桃子; ~ **stone** 桃核 2 [c] (tree) ~ **(tree)** 桃树; ~ **blossom** 桃花 3 [u] (colour) 桃红色 4 [c] colloq (person) 惹人喜爱的人; (thing) 惹人喜爱的事物; **his girlfriend is a real ~!** 他的女朋友真是个大美人儿; **a ~ of a dress** 特别漂亮的连衣裙
B *adj* 桃红色的

peaches and cream *adj* 白里透红的 ‹*complexion, look*›

peachy /ˈpiːtʃi/ *adj* 1 (like a peach) 桃子似的; ~ **cheeks** 白里透红的脸颊 2 esp Amer colloq (excellent) 极好的

peacock /ˈpiːkɒk/ *n* 雄孔雀

peacock: ~ **blue** ▸p. 134 *n* [u] 孔雀蓝; ~ **butterfly** *n* 孔雀蛱蝶

pea green ▸p. 134
A *adj* 豆绿的
B *n* [u] 豆绿色

peahen /ˈpiːhen/ *n* 雌孔雀

peak /piːk/
A *n* 1 (of mountain) 山顶; **snow-covered ~s** 积雪覆盖的群峰; **a mountain ~** 山巅 2 (mountain) 山峰; **to climb** *or* **scale a ~** 登上顶峰 3 (of cap) 帽舌 4 (pointed edge) 尖顶; **the ~ of a roof** 屋顶尖 5 fig (of fitness, success, power) 巅峰; (of traffic flow, inflation, discontent) 高峰; Telecom 忙时; **at the ~ of one's fame/success/power/career** 处于声望/成功/权力/事业的巅峰; **to be at the ~ of (one's) fitness** 体质处于最佳状态; **to be past its** *or* **one's ~** 过了巅峰期; **during the morning/evening ~** 在早/晚交通高峰期; **50 pence ~** 忙时话费 50 便士
B *modif* 最高的 ‹*level*›; 最大的 ‹*capacity, demand*›; 最佳的 ‹*fitness, form, period*›; ~ **listening audience** Radio 黄金时段的听众; ~ **viewing audience** TV 黄金时段的观众
C *vi* ~ **(out)** ‹*workload, business, demand, sales, traffic*› 达到最高峰

peak demand *n* [u] 高峰需求; **a time of ~ for the product** 对该产品需求最旺的时期

peaked /piːkt/ *adj* 1 (with peak) 有帽舌的 2 (pointed) 有尖顶的 ‹*roof*› 3 *pred* esp Amer = **peaky**

peak: ~ **hours** *npl* 高峰时间; **at** *or* **during ~ hours** 在高峰期; ~ **listening time** *n* 黄金收听时段; ~ **load** *n* 高峰负荷; ~ **period** *n* 高峰期; ~ **production** *n* [u] 最高产量; ~ **rate** *n* 1 (highest rate) 高峰费率; 2 (customs duty) 高峰税率; ~ **season** *n* 旺季

peak time
A *n* [u] 1 TV, Radio 黄金时段 2 (busiest period) 高峰期
B **peak-time** *modif* 1 TV, Radio 黄金时段的 ‹*programming, viewing*› 2 (in busiest period) 高峰期的 ‹*train, service*›

peaky /ˈpiːki/ *adj* colloq 1 (pale) 苍白的 2 (ill) 有病容的

peak year *n* 高峰年

peal /piːl/
A *n* 1 (ringing) 钟声 2 (in bell-ringing) 钟乐 3 (of laughter, thunder, organ) 响亮的声音; **~s of laughter** 阵阵欢笑声; **a ~ of thunder** 一声响雷
B *vi* 1 (ring) 鸣响; **the bells ~ed (out)** 钟声齐鸣 2 (sound loudly) 大声作响; **thunder ~ed in the distance** 远方雷声隆隆
C *vt* 敲响 ‹*bell*›

peanut /ˈpiːnʌt/
A *n* 1 (nut) 花生 2 (plant) 花生植株
B **peanuts** *npl* colloq 很少的钱; **they're paid ~s** 他们的报酬很低

peanut: ~ **butter** *n* [u] 花生酱; ~ **oil** *n* [u] 花生油

pea pod *n* 豌豆荚

pear /peə(r)/ *n* 1 (fruit) 梨 2 (tree) ~ **(tree)** 梨树

pearl /pɜːl/
A *n* 1 [c] (object) 珍珠; **to cast ~s before swine** 明珠暗投; **talking to those kids about opera is casting ~s before swine** 跟那些孩子谈歌剧无异于对牛弹琴; **imitation ~s** 人造珍珠; ~ **earrings** 珍珠耳环 2 [c] fig (of dew, sweat) 似珍珠之物; **~s of dew** 露珠 3 [c] (precious person) 有价值的人; (precious object) 有价值的物品; **a ~ among women** 女中俊杰; **~s of wisdom** 智慧的结晶; **thank you for your ~s of wisdom** 谢谢你的金玉良言 4 [u] (substance) = **mother-of-pearl**
B **~s** *npl* 珍珠项链

pearl: ~ **barley** *n* [u] 珍珠大麦; ~ **diver** ▸p. 409 *n* 潜水采珠人; ~ **diving** *n* [u] 潜水采珠

pearl grey ▸p. 134
A *n* [u] 珠灰色
B *adj* 珠灰色的

pearl: **~-handled** *adj* 有镶嵌珍珠把手的; ~ **necklace** *n* 珍珠项链; ~ **oyster** *n* 珠母贝; **P~ River** ▸p. 663 *pr n* **the P~ River** 珠江; **the P~ River delta** 珠江三角洲

pearly /ˈpɜːli/ *adj* 1 (resembling a pearl) 似珍珠的; ~ **teeth** 珍珠般的皓齿 2 (pearl-coloured) 珍珠色的 3 (decorated with pearls) 饰有珍珠的

Pearly Gates *npl* **the ~** Brit colloq 天堂之门

pear-shaped *adj* (of shape) 梨形的; (of person) 上身窄臀部宽的; **to go ~** fig colloq 出问题

peasant /ˈpeznt/
A *n* 1 (farmer) 小农 2 (country person) 乡下人 3 pej (lout) 乡巴佬
B *adj* 农民的

peasant: ~ **farmer** ▸p. 409 *n* 个体农民; ~ **farming** *n* [u] 个体农业

peasantry /ˈpezntri/ *n* + *v sing or pl* **the ~** (一国的) 农民

pease pudding /ˌpiːz ˈpʊdɪŋ/ *n* [u] Brit 豌豆布丁

pea: ~ shooter *n* 射豆玩具枪; **~ soup** *n* [u] 1 Culin 豌豆汤; 2 Brit colloq (fog) 黄色浓雾; **~-souper** /ˌpiːˈsuːpə(r)/ *n* Brit colloq 黄色浓雾

peat /piːt/ *n* 1 [u] (substance) 泥炭 2 [c] (piece) 泥炭块

peat: ~ bog *n* 泥炭沼; **~ cutter** *n* 1 (person) 挖泥炭工; 2 (tool) 泥炭铲; **~ moss** *n* [u] 泥炭藓

peaty /ˈpiːti/ *adj* 泥炭的; **a ~ malt whisky** 泥炭麦芽威士忌

pebble /ˈpebl/ *n* 卵石; **he/she is not the only ~ on the beach** 他/她这样的人多的是; **~ beach** 遍布卵石的海滩; **~ lenses/glasses** colloq 深度厚镜片/眼镜

pebble-dash
A *n* [u] 小卵石灰浆; **~ walls** 抹小卵石灰浆的墙
B *vt* 用小卵石灰浆涂抹

pebbly /ˈpebli/ *adj* 遍布卵石的 ‹*beach, surface*›

pecan /ˈpiːkən, prˈkæn, Amer prˈkɑːn/ *n* 1 (nut) 美洲山核桃; **a ~ pie** 山核桃馅饼 2 (tree) 美洲山核桃树

peccadillo /ˌpekəˈdɪləʊ/ *n* (*pl* **~s** *or* **~es**) 过失

peccary /ˈpekəri/ *n* 西猯 [一种形如小猪的哺乳动物]

peck¹ /pek/
A *n* 1 (with beak) 啄 2 colloq (kiss) 匆匆轻吻; **to give sb. a ~ on the cheek** 匆匆轻吻某人的面颊
B *vt* 1 (with beak) 啄; (form by pecking) 啄出 ‹*hole*›; **chickens ~ing corn in the yard** 在院子里啄食玉米的小鸡 2 colloq (kiss) 匆忙轻吻
C *vi* 1 (with beak) 啄; **to ~ at sth.** 啄某物; **the hens were ~ing at the corn** 母鸡在啄食玉米 2 fig colloq (eat very little) **to ~ at sth.** 对…浅尝几口 ‹*food*›

Phrasal verb
- **peck out** *vt* [**~ sth. out, ~ out sth.**] 啄出

peck² *n* Meas 配克 [相当于2加仑]

pecker /ˈpekə(r)/ *n* Brit colloq 精神; **to keep one's ~ up** 振作精神

pecking order *n* 1 Zool 啄序 [禽群成员的地位次序] 2 fig (hierarchy) 权势等级; **to have a low position in the ~** 地位低下

peckish /ˈpekɪʃ/ *adj* Brit colloq 有些饿的; **to feel ~** 觉得有点饿

peck order *n* = **pecking order**

pecs /peks/ *npl* colloq 胸肌

pectoral /ˈpektərəl/
A **pectorals** *npl* 胸肌
B *adj* 胸部的; **~ muscles** 胸肌

peculiar /prˈkjuːlɪə(r)/ *adj* 1 (unusual, strange) 奇怪的; **the soup had a ~ taste** *or* **smell** 这汤有股怪味 2 (odd, bizarre) 古怪的; **what a ~ individual!** 真是个怪人! 3 (unwell) 不舒服的; **to feel ~** 感觉有点不舒服 4 (exceptional) 特别的; **a question of ~ interest** 具有特殊意义的问题 5 (exclusive) 特有的; **a species ~ to Asia** 亚洲独有的物种; **he has his own ~ style** 他有自己独特的风格

peculiarity /pɪˌkjuːlɪˈærəti/ *n* 1 [u] (strangeness) 奇怪 2 [u] (bizarreness) 古怪 3 [c] (idiosyncrasy) 怪异的事物; **the peculiarities of the situation** 该情况的种种怪异之处; **it's just one of his peculiarities** 这只是他的怪癖之一 4 [c] (unique feature) 特性; **each city has its own peculiarities** 每座城市都有它自己的特点

peculiarly /prˈkjuːlɪəli/ *adv* 1 (strangely) 奇怪地 2 (particularly) 特别地 3 (uniquely) 独一无二地; **a custom that is ~ English** 英国人独有的习俗

pecuniary /prˈkjuːnɪəri, Amer -ieri/ *adj* formal (of money) 金钱的; (concerning money) 与钱相关的; **~ aid** 资助; **~ advantage** 金钱利益

pedagogic /ˌpedəˈgɒdʒɪk/, **pedagogical** /ˌpedəˈgɒdʒɪkl/ *adj* formal 教学法的; **~ skills** 教学技巧

pedagogue /ˈpedəgɒg/ *n* archaic or hum 教师

pedagogy /ˈpedəgɒdʒi/ *n* [u] formal 教学法

pedal /ˈpedl/
A *n* 1 (on bicycle) 脚蹬子 2 Aut 踏板 3 Mus (on piano, harp) 踏板; (on organ) 脚键盘
B *vt* (*pres p etc.* **-ll-** Brit, **-l-** Amer) 1 (operate by pedalling) 用脚蹬; **to ~ a bicycle** 骑自行车 2 (cycle) 骑车走过 ‹*distance*›; **he ~led 90 miles that day** 他那天骑车走了 90 英里
C *vi* (*pres p etc.* **-ll-** Brit, **-l-** Amer) 1 (use pedal) 踩踏板; **to ~ along** 一直踩踏板; **to ~ hard/furiously** 用力/拼命蹬车 2 (cycle) 骑自行车; **to ~ down the hill** 骑车下山

pedal: ~ bin *n* Brit 脚踏式垃圾桶; **~ boat** *n* 脚踏船; **~ car** *n* 儿童脚踏汽车; **~ cycle** *n* 自行车; **~ cyclist** *n* 骑自行车的人

pedalo /ˈpedələʊ/ *n* (*pl* **~s** *or* **~es**) 脚踏游船

pedal steel guitar *n* 踏板电子吉他

pedant /ˈpednt/ *n* 1 (stickler for detail) 学究 2 (one who overrates learning) 卖弄学问者

pedantic /prˈdæntɪk/ *adj* 1 (detail-oriented) 学究式的; **a ~ clerk** 迂腐的办事员 2 (learned) 卖弄学问的 ‹*teacher, book*›

pedantically /prˈdæntɪkli/ *adv* 1 (in excessive detail) 学究式地 2 (in a learned manner) 卖弄学问地

pedantry /ˈpedntri/ *n* [u] 1 (excessive attention to details) 迂腐 2 (display of learning) 卖弄学问

peddle /ˈpedl/ *vt* 1 (sell) 兜售; (sell illegally) 非法贩卖; **to ~ drugs** 贩毒 2 fig pej (promote) 宣传 ‹*plan, policy*›; 散播 ‹*ideas, gossip*›

peddler /ˈpedlə(r)/ *n* = **pedlar**

pederast /ˈpedəræst/ *n* 恋童癖男子

pederasty /ˈpedəræsti/ *n* [u] 男恋童癖

pedestal /ˈpedɪstl/ *n* 1 (of statue, column) 底座 2 fig (position) 显要地位; **to keep** *or* **put sb. on a ~** 奉某人为偶像; **to knock sb. off their ~** 使某人威信扫地

pedestal: ~ desk *n* 抽屉写字台; **~ table** *n* 独腿桌; **~ washbasin** *n* 支柱式洗脸盆

pedestrian /prˈdestrɪən/
A *n* 行人; **a ~ street** 步行街
B *adj* 乏味的

pedestrian crossing *n* Brit 人行横道

pedestrianization /pɪˌdestrɪənaɪˈzeɪʃn, Amer -nɪˈz-/ *n* [u] 行人专用化

pedestrianize /prˈdestrɪənaɪz/ *vt* 使…为行人专用 ‹*area*›

pedestrian: ~ precinct *n* Brit 步行区; **~ traffic** *n* [u] 行人往来

pediatric /ˌpiːdɪˈætrɪk/ *adj* Amer = **paediatric**

pediatrician /ˌpiːdɪəˈtrɪʃn/ ▸p. 409 *n* Amer = **paediatrician**

pediatrics /ˌpiːdɪˈætrɪks/ *npl* Amer = **paediatrics**

pedicab /ˈpedɪkæb/ *n* 人力三轮车

pedicure /ˈpedɪkjʊə(r)/ *n* 修脚

pedigree /ˈpedɪgriː/
A *n* 1 [c] (ancestral line) 家系 2 [u] (distinguished ancestry) 名门世系; **a family without ~** 非名门望族的家庭 3 [c] (table, chart) 家谱 4 [c] (record of animal's descent) 动物血统记录 5 [c] (animal's line of descent) 动物纯种谱系; **an animal with a superb ~** 纯种的动物 6 [c] (background) 出身; **to have a criminal ~** 有犯罪家史 7 [c] (line of development) 起源; **the scheme has a long ~** 该计划由来已久
B *modif* 纯种的 ‹*animal, dog*›

pediment /ˈpedɪmənt/ *n* 三角楣饰

pedlar /ˈpedlə(r)/ *n* Brit 1 (itinerant trader) 流动小贩 2 (of illegal drugs) 毒品贩子; (of stolen goods) 卖赃物的人; **a drug ~** 毒品贩子 3 fig pej (of lies, gossip) 散播者

pedometer /prˈdɒmɪtə(r)/ *n* 计步器

pedophile /ˈpedəfaɪl/ *n* Amer = **paedophile**

pedophilia /ˌpedəˈfɪlɪə/ *n* [u] Amer = **paedophilia**

pee /piː/ colloq
A *vi* 撒尿
B *vt* 小便失禁尿湿; **to ~ oneself** *or* **one's pants** 小便失禁
C *n* 1 [u] (urine) 尿 2 [c] (act of urinating) 撒尿; **to have** *or* **do a ~** 小便

peek /piːk/
A *n* (quick glance) 一瞥; (furtive glance) 偷偷的一看; **to have** *or* **take a ~ at sth.** 偷看一下某物
B *vi* (glance quickly) 瞥; (glance furtively) 偷看; **to ~ at sth./sb.** 偷看某物/某人

peekaboo /ˌpiːkəˈbuː/
A *n* [u] 藏猫猫; **to play ~** 玩藏猫猫
B *adj* (almost transparent) 近透明织物制的; (patterned with small holes) 孔眼织物制的

peel /piːl/
A *n* [u] 皮
B *vt* 去掉…的皮; **to ~ an apple** 削苹果; **to ~ shrimps** 剥虾; **to keep one's eyes ~ed** colloq 留心
C *vi* 1 (flake, lose outer layer) «*paint, surface*» 剥落; «*wall*» 外层剥落 2 (shed skin) 脱皮; **I was ~ing after a few days in the sun** 我晒了几天太阳，脱皮了; **my arms/legs were ~ing** 我的胳膊/腿脱皮了 3 (be peelable) 可去皮; **oranges that don't ~ easily** 不容易剥皮的橘子

Phrasal verbs
- **peel away**
A *vi* «*skin*» 脱落; «*paint, wallpaper*» 剥落
B *vt* [**~ away sth., ~ sth. away**] 剥掉
- **peel back** [**~ back sth., ~ sth. back**] *vt* 剥掉
- **peel off**
A *vi* 1 «*skin*» 脱落; «*paint, wallpaper*» 剥落 2 (from group) 离队 3 Brit colloq (undress) 脱衣服
B *vt* [**~ off sth., ~ sth. off**] 1 (remove) 揭掉 ‹*stamp, sticker, wallpaper*› 2 (take off) 脱去 ‹*clothes*›

peeler /ˈpiːlə(r)/ *n* 去皮器

peeling /ˈpiːlɪŋ/
A *n* 1 [c] (skin of fruit, vegetable, bark) 去掉的皮 2 [u] (flaking) 脱皮
B *adj* 剥落的 ‹*wall, paint*›; 脱落的 ‹*skin*›

peep¹ /piːp/
A *n* (quick look) 一瞥; (furtive look) 窥视; **to have** *or* **take a ~ at sth./sb.** 瞥一眼某物/某人; **just have a ~!** 就看一下！; **to get a ~ at sb./sth.** 偷偷看某人/某物一眼; **he had a quick ~ at his present** 他匆匆扫了一眼他的礼物
B *vi* 1 (look) 窥视; **to ~ at sb./sth.** 窥视某人/某物; **to ~ through a hole in the wall** 透过墙上的洞偷看 2 (be just visible) «*light, dawn*» 隐约出现; **daylight was ~ing through the curtains** 日光穿过窗帘微微透进来

Phrasal verb
- **peep out** *vi* 1 (take a short look) 瞟一眼 2 (appear partly) 半隐半现; **the sun ~ed out from behind the clouds** 太阳从云层后露了一下脸

peep²
A *n* 1 (of bird) 啾啾声; (of mouse) 吱吱声; (of horn) 嘟嘟声; **~! ~!** 嘟！嘟！ 2 colloq (word, noise) 嘟囔声; **one ~ out of you and there'll be trouble!** 你吭一声就让你好看！; **have you heard from them? — not a ~** 你收到他们的来信了吗？——半个字儿也没有
B *vi* «*bird*» 啾啾叫; «*mouse*» 吱吱叫; «*horn, car*» 嘟嘟响; «*driver*» 嘟嘟鸣喇叭
C *vt* «*driver, car*» 鸣响 ‹*horn*›

peep-bo /ˈpiːpbəʊ/ *n* [u] Amer 藏猫猫; **to play ~** 玩藏猫猫

peeper /ˈpiːpə(r)/ *n* colloq 眼睛

peephole /ˈpiːphəʊl/ *n* 窥视孔; **a door with a ~** 有猫眼的门

Peeping Tom /ˌpiːpɪŋ ˈtɒm/ *n* pej 有窥淫癖者

peep: ~show *n* **1** (sequence of pictures) 西洋镜; **2** dated (film) 窥淫秀 [投币观看的淫秽电影]; **~-toe** *adj* 露脚趾的 ‹*shoe, style*›

peer¹ /pɪə(r)/ *vi* 仔细看; **she ~ed inquiringly at me** 她好奇地注视着我

peer² *n* **1** (equal in rank, status) 同等地位的人 **2** (equal in talent, ability) 相匹敌的人; **to be without ~** *or* **have no ~** 没有对手 **3** (contemporary) 同龄人 **4** Brit Pol **~ (of the realm)** 贵族

peerage /ˈpɪərɪdʒ/ *n* Brit Pol **1** (group) 贵族 **2** (rank) 贵族爵位

peeress /ˈpɪəres/ *n* Brit Pol **1** (female peer) 女贵族 **2** (wife of peer) 贵族夫人; (widow of peer) 贵族遗孀

peer group *n* (of similar status) 同地位群体; (of similar age) 同龄群体; **she gets on well with her ~** 她与同龄人相处融洽

peer group pressure *n* [u] 同侪压力

peerless /ˈpɪəlɪs/ *adj* 无双的; **a woman of ~ beauty** 绝世佳人

peer: ~ pressure *n* [u] 同侪压力; **~ review** *n* [u] 同行评价

peeve /piːv/ colloq

A *vt* 惹恼; **to be ~d by sth.** 为某事生气; **it ~d me that she didn't answer my letters** 她没有回我的信, 真让我生气

B *n* **pet ~** 特别讨厌的东西

peeved /piːvd/ *adj* colloq 恼怒的; **to look/sound ~** 看上去/听上去很不高兴

peevish /ˈpiːvɪʃ/ *adj* **1** (irritable) 易怒的; **a ~ child** 坏脾气的小孩 **2** (showing vexation) 带怒气的; **he gave me a ~ look** 他生气地看了我一眼

peevishly /ˈpiːvɪʃli/ *adv* 恼怒地

peevishness /ˈpiːvɪʃnɪs/ *n* **1** (irritability) 易怒 **2** (bad temper) 恼怒

peewee /ˈpiːwiː/ esp Amer Sport

A *adj* 少年选手的 [在美国为8-9岁, 在加拿大为12-13岁]; **a ~ baseball team/football league** 少年棒球队/足球联赛

B *n* 少年选手

peewit /ˈpiːwɪt/ *n* = **lapwing**

peg /peg/

A *n* **1** (to hold things together) 夹子; (to hang things) 挂物钉; **to use sth. as a ~ (to hang a discussion/a theory on)** fig 以某事物为由头 (展开讨论/理论) **2** (for garments) 衣服钩; **coat/hat ~** 衣钩/帽钩; **to buy sth. off the ~** 买某衣物的成品 **3** (for tent) 帐篷桩子 **4** (for clothes) 晾衣夹子 **5** (marking position) 界桩; (for surveying) 地标; **a surveyor's ~** 测标 **6** (in carpentry) 栓 **7** Mus 琴栓; **a tuning ~** 调音栓 **8** (barrel stop) 塞子 **9** (in mountaineering) 攀岩钉 **10** Brit (of small drink) 少量酒; **a ~ of whisky** 一小杯威士忌酒 **11** (in self-esteem) **to be taken** *or* **brought down a ~ or two** 被煞了几分威风; **to take** *or* **bring sb. down a ~ (or two)** 挫某人的锐气

B *vt* (*pres p etc.* **-gg-**) **1** (fasten) 用夹子夹住 ‹*clothes, washing*›; 用桩固定 ‹*tent*› **2** Econ 限定 ‹*price, deficit, currency*› **3** Amer colloq (characterize) 把…看作; **the policeman probably has us ~ged as criminals** 那名警察很可能把我们当成了罪犯

Phrasal verbs

- **peg away** *vi* colloq 坚持不懈地工作; **to ~ away at sth.** 兢兢业业地做某事
- **peg down** *vt* [**~ down sth./sb., ~ sth./sb. down**]
  1 (fix in place) 用桩固定 ‹*tent, canvas, rope*› **2** fig (force to be specific) 让…说定 ‹*person*›; (force to make a commitment) 让…作出承诺 ‹*person*›; **to ~ sb. down to a price** 让某人定好价
- **peg out**
  A *vt* [**~ out sth., ~ sth. out**]
  1 (mark) 用界桩标出 ‹*area of land*›; **to ~ out a claim** 用界桩标出自己的土地 **2** (fasten) 铺开钉住 ‹*animal skin*›
  B *vi* sl (die) 断气

peg: ~board *n* **1** Games 插孔游戏板; **2** (for hanging up objects) 配挂板; **~ leg** *n* colloq 假腿

pejorative /pɪˈdʒɒrətɪv, Amer -ˈdʒɔːr-/ *adj* 贬义的

peke /piːk/ *n* colloq = **Pekinese**

Pekinese, Pekingese /ˌpiːkɪˈniːz/ *n* (*pl* **~** *or* **~s**) 狮子狗

Peking /piːˈkɪŋ/ *pr n* = **Beijing**

Peking duck *n* [u] 北京烤鸭

pelargonium /ˌpeləˈgəʊnɪəm/ *n* 天竺葵

pelican /ˈpelɪkən/ *n* 鹈鹕

pelican crossing *n* Brit 自控人行横道

pellet /ˈpelɪt/ *n* **1** (small compressed mass) 颗粒状物; **paper/wax ~s** 小纸团/蜡丸; **~s of dung** 粪粒 **2** (of shot) 弹丸 **3** Zool (of certain birds) 颗粒状呕吐物 **4** Chem 胶囊

pell-mell /ˌpelˈmel/ *adv* **1** (headlong) 忙乱地 ‹*run*›; **the children rushed ~ down the stairs** 孩子们一窝蜂地冲下楼梯 **2** (in disorder) 杂乱地 ‹*lie, scattered*›

pellucid /peˈluːsɪd/ *adj* liter **1** (translucent) 清澈的 ‹*water*› **2** (lucid) 清晰的 ‹*style, prose, writing*›

pelmet /ˈpelmɪt/ *n* (of wood) 窗帘盒; (of cloth) 窗帘短帷幔

pelota /pəˈləʊtə/ ▸**p. 307** *n* [u] 回力球运动

pelt¹ /pelt/

A *vt* lit (with missiles) 向…投掷; **to ~ sb. with stones** 向某人扔石头; **to ~ sb. with questions** fig 向某人提出一连串的问题

B *vi* **1** (fall heavily) 下得很大; **it** *or* **the rain was ~ing (down)** 大雨如注; **the ~ing rain** 倾盆大雨 **2** colloq (run) 飞跑; **to go ~ing down the hill** 飞跑下山

C **(at) full pelt** *adv phr* 全速地; **we hurtled (at) full ~ down the hill** 我们飞奔下山

pelt² *n* (animal skin) 毛皮

pelvic /ˈpelvɪk/ *adj* (of the pelvis) 骨盆的; (near the pelvis) 骨盆区的; **~ floor** 盆底

pelvis /ˈpelvɪs/ ▸**p. 71** *n* (*pl* **~es** *or* **pelves**) 骨盆

Pembrokeshire /ˈpembrʊkʃɪə(r)/ *pr n* 彭布鲁克郡

pemmican /ˈpemɪkən/ *n* [u] 干肉饼

pen¹ /pen/

A *n* **1** (writing instrument) 笔; **to put ~ to paper** 动笔; **to put** *or* **run one's ~ through sth.** 划掉某物; **the suggestions that have come from her ~** fig 她起草的建议 **2** fig (writing) 写作; **to live by one's ~** 以写作谋生 **3** fig (the written word) **the ~** 文字; **the ~ is mightier than the sword** Prov 笔墨胜刀剑

B *vt* (*pres p etc.* **-nn-**) 写

pen²

A *n* **1** (enclosure for animals) 畜栏; **a sheep-~** 羊圈 **2** (for children) 围栏

B *vt* (*pres p etc.* **-nn-**) **1** (enclose in pen) 把…圈起来 **2** (confine) 关押

Phrasal verb

- **pen in** *vt* [**~ sb. in, ~ in sb.**]
  1 (confine) 关押 **2** fig (restrict) 禁锢; **she felt ~ned in by her role as housewife** 她觉得做家庭主妇很受束缚

pen³ *n* (swan) 雌天鹅

penal /ˈpiːnl/ *adj* **1** (relating to punishment) 刑罚的 ‹*reform*›; **a ~ law** 刑法; **the ~ system** 刑罚制度; **~ code** 刑法典 **2** (used for punishment) 作处罚场所的; **~ institution** 服刑机构; **a ~ colony** 罪犯流放地 **3** (punishable by law) 当受刑罚的; **a ~ offence** 刑事罪 **4** (exorbitant) 繁重的 ‹*taxation*›; **~ rates of interest** 很重的利率

penalization /ˌpiːnəlaɪˈzeɪʃn, Amer -lɪˈz-/ *n* [u] **1** (punishment, penalty) 处罚 **2** (imposition of penalty for) 给予处罚 **3** (placing at disadvantage) 置于不利地位 **4** Jur 宣布应受处罚

penalize /ˈpiːnəlaɪz/ *vt* **1** (punish, award penalty) 处罚 ‹*person, competitor, team*›; **drunk drivers should be heavily ~d** 醉酒驾车者应予以重罚; **the offending player was ~d with a yellow card** Sport 那位犯规的球员被判罚黄牌; **to be ~d for sth.** 因…受处罚 ‹*crime, misconduct*›; **he was ~d for the offence by removal of privileges** 他因犯规被罚免除特殊待遇 **2** (impose penalty for) 处罚 ‹*offence, rudeness*›; **the referee failed to ~ this foul play** 裁判没有处罚这次犯规 **3** (disadvantage) 使处于不利地位; **a law that ~s the poor** 对穷人不利的法律 **4** Jur ‹*parliament, government, law*› 宣布…可处罚 ‹*act*›

penalty /ˈpenlti/ *n* **1** Jur (punishment) 处罚; **the death ~** 死刑; **a ~ for sth.** 对某事的处罚; **to mete out** *or* **impose a ~ for sth.** 对某事予以惩处; **to fulfil a contract on** *or* **under ~ of fines** 履行合同, 否则受罚款处罚 **2** (sanction, fine) 罚款 **3** (unpleasant result) 不利结果; **I had to pay the ~ for my wrong decisions** 我作了错误的决定, 只好自食其果; **loss of privacy is a ~ of fame** 失去隐私是成名带来的弊端 **4** Sport, Games (disadvantage) 处罚; (free shot at goal) 点球; **to score (from) a ~** 罚点球得分; **there's a ten-point ~ for a wrong answer** 回答错误扣 10 分

penalty: ~ area *n* 罚球区; **~ box** *n* **1** (in football) 罚球区; **2** (in ice hockey) 受罚席; **~ clause** *n* 罚金条款; **~ goal** *n* (in rugby) 罚球得分; **~ kick** *n* (in rugby) 罚球; (in football) 点球; **~ shoot-out** *n* 罚点球决定胜负; **~ spot** *n* (in football) 罚球点; **~-taker** *n* (in football) 主罚点球队员

penance /ˈpenəns/ *n* **1** [u] (atonement) 自我惩罚; **to do ~ for one's sins** 为赎罪而自我惩罚; **to do sth. as a ~ for sth.** 做某事以补赎某事 **2** [c and u] (task, duty) 苦差事

pen-and-ink drawing *n* 钢笔画

pence /pens/ ▸**p. 174** *pl* Brit ▸**penny**

penchant /ˈpɑːnʃɑːn, Amer ˈpentʃənt/ *n* 爱好; **to have a ~ for Chinese food** 酷爱中国食物

pencil /ˈpensl/

A *n* **1** [c] (writing, drawing instrument) 铅笔 **2** [u] (graphite) 铅芯; **to write in ~** 用铅笔写; **~ rubs out easily** 铅笔写的容易擦掉; **a ~ drawing/mark** 铅笔画/记号 **3** [c] (pencil-shaped object) 铅笔状细长物; **an eyebrow ~** 眉笔 **4** [c] fig (beam) 光束; **a ~ of light** 一束光

B *vt* (*pres p etc.* **-ll-** Brit, **-l-** Amer) (write) 用铅笔写; (draw) 用铅笔画; (mark) 用铅笔作记号

Phrasal verb

- **pencil in** *vt* [**~ in sth., ~ sth. in**]
  1 (write down) 用铅笔写 **2** (arrange provisionally) 临时安排; **let's ~ in 3 June for dinner** 我们把吃饭暂定在 6 月 3 号吧; **can you ~ me in for Thursday?** 你把我暂时安排在星期四可以吗?

pencil: ~ box *n* 铅笔盒; **~ case** *n* 铅笔盒; **~ crayon** *n* 彩色铅笔; **~ rubber** *n* 橡皮擦; **~ sharpener** *n* 卷笔刀

pendant /ˈpendənt/ *n* **1** (on necklace, earring) 垂饰 **2** (necklace) 有饰坠的项链 **3** (ceiling light) 吊灯

pending /ˈpendɪŋ/

A *adj* **1** (not yet concluded) 待决的; **a patent ~** 待批专利; **the case is ~** Jur 此案悬而未决 **2** (imminent) 即将发生的; **the results of the investigation were ~** 调查结果就要出来了

B *prep* 在等待…之际; **he was held in custody ~ trial** 他被拘留候审

pending tray *n* 待处理文件盘

pendulous /ˈpendjʊləs, Amer -dʒʊləs/ *adj* formal 悬垂摆动的; ~ **breasts** 松垂的乳房

pendulum /ˈpendjʊləm, Amer -dʒʊləm/ *n* **1** (in clock) 钟摆 **2** (weight) 摆锤 **3** fig (tendency to change) 摇摆不定的趋势; **the ~ of public opinion** 舆论的摇摆不定

penetrable /ˈpenɪtrəbl/ *adj* **1** (passable) 可进入的 ‹*terrain, defence*› **2** (able to be pierced) 可穿透的 ‹*surface, armour, hull*› **3** (able to be seen through) 目光可穿透的 ‹*darkness, fog*› **4** (understandable) 可理解的 ‹*mystery, thoughts, plan*› **5** (discoverable) 可识破的 ‹*disguise*› **6** Comm 可被占领的 ‹*market*›; 可被占领市场的 ‹*country*›

penetrate /ˈpenɪtreɪt/

A *vt* **1** (enter, force a way through) 进入 ‹*terrain, defence*› **2** (pierce) 穿透; **the needle ~d her skin** 针刺进了她的皮肤; **the bullet ~d the skull** 子弹打穿了头骨 **3** (seep through) «*liquid*» 渗入 ‹*material*› **4** fig (permeate) 渗透; **cold horror ~d his whole being** 他吓得浑身发冷; **a scream ~d the silence** 一声尖叫划破了寂静 **5** (illuminate sth. opaque) 透过; (see through sth. opaque) 看透; **the headlamps ~d the fog** 车前灯的光射进雾中; **my eyes could not ~ the darkness** 我在黑暗中什么也看不见 **6** (understand) 洞察; **to ~ a mystery** 揭示奥秘 **7** fig (get through to) 被…理解; **nothing you say will ~ his thick skull** 无论你说什么他那木脑袋都听不进去 **8** (discover, see through) 识破 ‹*disguise*› **9** (infiltrate) «*spy*» 打入…的内部 ‹*organization*› **10** (sexually) 以阴茎插入 **11** Comm 打入 ‹*market*›; 打入…的市场 ‹*country*›

B *vi* **1** (enter) «*person, traveller, army*» 进入 **2** (pierce) «*needle, bullet, claws*» 穿透; **to ~ through sth.** 穿透某物 **3** (seep into) 渗透 **4** (be understood) 被理解; **I kept telling him, but it just didn't ~** 我不断地给他讲, 但他就是听不进去 **5** (be perceived) 被听见; **the noise did not ~ into my secluded retreat** 在我的隐居处没有听见那声音

penetrating /ˈpenɪtreɪtɪŋ/ *adj* **1** (loud, shrill) 刺耳的 **2** (harsh) 刺骨的 ‹*wind, rain, cold*› **3** (intense) 锐利的 ‹*look, eyes*› **4** (perceptive) 有洞察力的; **a ~ mind** 敏锐的头脑; **a ~ question** 尖锐的问题; **a ~ analysis** 精辟的分析

penetratingly /ˈpenɪtreɪtɪŋli/ *adv* **1** (loudly) 刺耳地 **2** (perceptively) 有洞察力地; **to analyse sth. ~** 精辟地分析某事物

penetration /ˌpenɪˈtreɪʃn/ *n* [u] **1** (entering) 进入 **2** (piercing) 穿透 **3** (understanding) 洞察 **4** (infiltration) 打入内部 **5** (sexual intercourse) 阴茎的插入 **6** Comm (of market) 打入市场; (extent) 打入市场的程度; **to achieve a high degree of (market) ~** 实现很高的市场占有率 **7** (of bullets, shells) 穿透力 **8** (insight) 洞察力; **powers of ~** 洞察力

penetrative /ˈpenɪtrətɪv, Amer -treɪtɪv/ *adj* **1** (able to make a way through, into) 有穿透力的 **2** (insightful) 有洞察力的 **3** (of sexual activity) 行房的; **to have ~ sex with sb.** 与某人行房事

penfriend /ˈpenfrend/ *n* esp Brit 笔友

penguin /ˈpeŋgwɪn/ *n* 企鹅

pen holder *n* 笔筒

penicillin /ˌpenɪˈsɪlɪn/ *n* [u] 青霉素

peninsula /pəˈnɪnsjʊlə, Amer -ɪnsələ/ *n* 半岛

peninsular /pɪˈnɪnsjʊlə(r), Amer -ɪnsələr/ *adj* 半岛上的 ‹*region*›; 半岛的 ‹*situation, language*›

penis /ˈpiːnɪs/ *n* (*pl* **~es** *or* **penes**) 阴茎

penitence /ˈpenɪtəns/ *n* [u] 忏悔; **to show ~** 表现出愧疚; **~ for sth.** 因某事的愧疚

penitent /ˈpenɪtənt/

A *adj* 忏悔的; **to be ~ for sth.** 为某事忏悔

B *n* 悔罪者

penitential /ˌpenɪˈtenʃl/ *adj* 悔罪的 ‹*pilgrimage, mood*›

penitentiary /ˌpenɪˈtenʃəri/ *n* Amer 监狱

penitently /ˈpenɪtəntli/ *adv* 悔罪地

penknife /ˈpennaɪf/ *n* 小折刀

penmanship /ˈpenmənʃɪp/ *n* [u] 书法

pen name *n* 笔名

pennant /ˈpenənt/ *n* **1** Naut 三角旗 **2** Amer Sport 锦旗

pen nib *n* 笔尖

penniless /ˈpenɪlɪs/ *adj* 一文不名的; **a ~, destitute family** 穷困潦倒的家庭; **to be left ~** 落得身无分文

Pennines /ˈpenaɪnz/ *pr npl* **the ~** 奔宁山脉

Pennsylvania /ˌpensɪlˈveɪnɪə/ *pr n* 宾夕法尼亚州

Pennsylvanian /ˌpensɪlˈveɪnɪən/

A *adj* 宾夕法尼亚州的

B *n* 宾夕法尼亚州人

penny /ˈpeni/ ▸ **p. 174** *n* (*pl* **pennies** *for separate coins*, **pence** *for sum of money*) **1** Brit (*abbr* **p**, *pl* **pence**) 便士; **a 32 pence** *or* **32p stamp** 一枚32便士的邮票; **a new ~** 新便士 [面值为1/100英镑]; **a 5p piece** 一枚5便士硬币 **2** Brit Hist (*abbr* **d**, *pl* **pence** *or* **pennies**) 便士 [面值为1/12先令]; **it costs 6 pence** *or* **6d** 它值六便士; **an old ~** 旧便士; **a three-~ bit** 一枚3便士的硬币; **a two-~ ice-cream** 两便士冰激凌 (one-cent coin) **3** Amer colloq (one-cent coin) 分 **4** (*pl* **pennies**) (small amount of money) 小笔钱; **it didn't cost him a ~!** 没花他一分钱! ; **to be two** *or* **ten a ~** esp Brit 普通得不值钱; **to earn** *or* **turn an honest ~** 赚正当的钱; **to make** *or* **earn a quick ~** 来钱快; **in for a ~, in for a pound** 一不做, 二不休; **the ~ dropped** esp Brit colloq 茅塞顿开; **a ~ for your thoughts** 你呆呆地想什么呢; **to be ~ wise (and) pound foolish** 小事精明, 大事糊涂; **to spend a ~** Brit colloq euph 去方便; **to turn up like a bad ~** colloq 冤家路窄; **not to be a ~ wiser** 不见得有多高明; **not to have a ~ to one's name** 一文不名; **not to have two pennies to rub together** 穷得叮当响; **not to get a ~** 分文未继承到; **take care of the pennies and the pounds will look after themselves** Prov 省小钱来大钱; **a ~ saved is a ~ gained** *or* **earned** 省一文等于挣一文; **to be worth every ~** 物有所值; **not to cost a ~** 不费毫厘; ▸**pretty A**

penny: ~ arcade *n* esp Amer 便士游乐场 [设有投币启动式游艺机]; **~ dreadful** *n* Brit colloq dated 廉价恐怖小说; **~-farthing** *n* 前轮大后轮小的自行车; **~-pincher** *n* colloq 吝啬鬼

penny-pinching colloq

A *n* [u] 吝啬

B *adj* 吝啬的

penny: ~ whistle *n* 六孔小笛; **~-wise** *adj* 省小钱的 ‹*person*›

pennyworth /ˈpenɪwəθ/ *n* Brit **1** (amount for a penny) 值一便士的量; fig (small amount) 少量; **a ~ of sweets** 一便士的糖果 **2** (opinion) 个人意见; **to put** *or* **get in one's two ~** 发表意见

penology /piːˈnɒlədʒi/ *n* [u] (crime and punishment) 刑罚学; (management of prisons) 监狱管理学

pen: ~ pal *n* esp Amer 笔友; **~ pusher** *n* colloq pej 摇笔杆的人; **~ pushing** *n* [u] colloq pej 笔头工作

pension /ˈpenʃn/ *n* **1** (to old people) 养老金; (to widow, disabled person) 抚恤金; **to draw one's ~** 领取抚恤金; **an old age/a war ~** 养老金/战争抚恤金 **2** (from employer) 退休金; **to retire on a ~** 领取退休金退休; **a private/company ~** 个人/公司退休金

Phrasal verb

• **pension off** *vt* [**~ off sb./sth., ~ sb./sth. off**] **1** (retire) 发退休金使退休 **2** fig colloq (discard) 使报废; **this bus is ~ed off** 这辆公交车报废了

pensionable /ˈpenʃənəbl/ *adj* 可享受养老金的 ‹*job, position*›; **to be of ~ age** 到了领退休金的年龄

pension: ~ book *n* Brit 养老金发放簿; **~ contributions** *npl* 养老金供款

pensioner /ˈpenʃənə(r)/ *n* (old person) 领养老金的人; (widow, disabled person) 领抚恤金的人

pension: ~ fund *n* 养老基金; **~-fund manager** 养老基金经理; **~ plan, ~ scheme** *ns* 养老金计划; **~ rights** *npl* 享受养老金的权利

pensive /ˈpensɪv/ *adj* 沉思的 ‹*mood*›; 令人忧虑的 ‹*expression*›; **he was looking very ~** 他看起来心事重重

pensively /ˈpensɪvli/ *adv* 沉思地

pensiveness /ˈpensɪvnɪs/ *n* [u] 沉思

pentagon /ˈpentəgən, Amer -gɒn/ *n* **1** Math 五边形 **2** Amer (building) **the P~** 五角大楼 **3** Amer (institution) **the P~** 美国国防部; **a P~ spokesperson** 美国国防部发言人

> **the Pentagon**
>
> 五角大楼。位于美国弗吉尼亚州的阿灵顿（Arlington，Virginia），美国国防部所在地。建筑物呈五边形，故名"五角大楼"。1943 年建成，为世界上最大的办公建筑之一。非正式场合亦指美国的军事领导人。

pentagonal /penˈtægənl/ *adj* 五边形的

pentagram /ˈpentəgræm/ *n* 五角星形

pentahedron /ˌpentəˈhiːdrən, Amer -drɒn/ *n* (*pl* **~s** *or* **pentahedra** /ˌpentəˈhiːdrə/) 五面体

pentameter /penˈtæmɪtə(r)/ *n* 五音步诗行

pentathlete /penˈtæθliːt/ *n* 五项全能运动员

pentathlon /penˈtæθlən, -lɒn/ *n* 五项全能运动

pentatonic /ˌpentəˈtɒnɪk/ *adj* 五声音阶的 ‹*scale, melody*›

Pentecost /ˈpentɪkɒst, Amer -kɔːst/ *n* **1** (Christian festival) 圣灵降临节 [复活节后第7个星期日] **2** (Jewish festival) 五旬节 [逾越节后第50天]

Pentecostal /ˌpentɪˈkɒstl, Amer -ˈkɔːstl/ *adj* **1** (relating to Christian Pentecost) 圣灵降临节的 **2** (relating to religious group) 五旬节派的 ‹*church, pastor*›

Pentecostalism /ˌpentɪˈkɒstəlɪzəm, Amer -ˈkɔːst-/ *n* [u] 五旬节派教义

Pentecostalist /ˌpentɪˈkɒstəlɪst, Amer -ˈkɔːst-/

A *n* 五旬节派教徒

B *adj* 五旬节派教义的

penthouse /ˈpenthaʊs/ *n* 顶层豪华公寓; **a ~ suite** 顶层豪华套房

pent-up /ˌpentˈʌp/ *adj* **1** (repressed) 压抑的 ‹*emotion, energy*› **2** (confined) 积压的 ‹*pressure*›

penultimate /pɪˈnʌltɪmət/ *adj* 倒数第二的

penumbra /pɪˈnʌmbrə/ *n* (*pl* **~s** *or* **penumbrae** /pɪˈnʌmbriː/) **1** (shaded region) 半阴影 **2** (in an eclipse) 半影

penury /ˈpenjʊri/ *n* [u] 贫困; **to live in ~** 过贫穷的生活

peony /ˈpiːəni/ *n* (herbaceous) 牡丹; (shrubby) 芍药

people /ˈpiːpl/

A *n* (of nation) 人民; (of race) 民族; (of tribe) 族群; (of community) 民众; **the primitive ~s of the Early Stone Age** 早期石器时代的原始民族; **the English-speaking ~(s)** 说英语的民族; **the chosen ~** 上帝的选民

B *npl* **1** (persons) 人们; **old/young/average ~** 老年人/年轻人/普通人; **important/several/other ~** 要人/几个人/其他人; **you ~** 你们这些人 **2** (inhabitants) 居民; **the British ~** 英国人; **the ~ of Winchester** 温切斯特人;

city/country ～ 城里人/乡下人 **3** (experts) 业界人士; **technical/medical** ～ 技术/医学界人士 **4** (citizens) **the** ～ 公民; **the will of the** ～ 人民的意志; **the** ～ **at large** 公众; **the P～'s (Democratic) Republic** 人民（民主）共和国 **5** (ordinary persons) **the** ～ 百姓; **the common** ～ 普通人; **a man of the** ～ 得民心的人 **6** (subjects of ruler) 臣民; (supporters of ruler) 支持者 **7** dated colloq (parents) 父母; (relatives) 亲人; **my** ～ **come from Yorkshire** 我的家人是约克郡人
C *vt* 居住在 ‹*town, country, planet*›; **weird creatures that** ～**d his nightmares** 他噩梦中的怪物; **a remote area** ～**d with nomadic tribesmen** 游牧部落居住的偏远地区

P

people: ～ **carrier** *n* 三排座小客车; ～ **management** *n* [u] 人事管理; ～ **mover** *n* 旅客捷运系统; ～ **person** *n* colloq 喜欢社交的人; ～ **power** *n* [u] 人民力量; ～**'s army** *n* 人民军队; ～**'s democracy** *n* 人民民主政体; ～**'s front** *n* 人民阵线; **P～'s Liberation Army** *n* 中国人民解放军; ～**'s park** *n* 社区公园; ～**'s republic** *n* 人民共和国; **P～'s Republic of China** *pr n* 中华人民共和国; ～ **trafficker** *n* 蛇头

pep /pep/ *n* [u] colloq 精力; **full of** ～ 精力旺盛的

Phrasal verb

• **pep up** (*pres p etc.* **-pp-**)
A *vt* [～ **sb./sth. up,** ～ **up sb./sth.**] 使活跃; **this good news** ～**ped him up** 这个好消息使他精神振奋; **she** ～**ped up the drink with a dash of gin** 她往饮料里加了少许杜松子酒调味
B *vi* **1** (recover energy) «*person*» 恢复精力 **2** (increase in activity) «*business, economy*» 振兴

peperoni /ˌpepəˈrəʊni/ *n* [u] = **pepperoni**

pepper /ˈpepə(r)/
A *n* **1** (spice) [u] 胡椒粉 **2** [c] (vegetable) 甜椒 **3** [c] (vine) 胡椒
B *vt* **1** Culin 在…上撒胡椒粉 **2** (sprinkle liberally) 使布满; **a conversation** ～**ed with swear words** 满是脏骂的谈话; **her French was heavily** ～**ed with Americanisms** 她的法语带着浓厚的美国腔 **3** (hit repeatedly) 向…不断射击; **the wall had been** ～**ed with bullets** 墙上有密集的弹痕

pepper-and-salt *adj* **1** (flecked) 黑白相间的 ‹*pattern*› **2** (greying) 花白的 ‹*hair*›

peppercorn /ˈpepəkɔːn/ *n* 胡椒粒

pepper: ～**corn rent** *n* Brit 象征性租金; ～**mill** *n* 胡椒磨; ～**mint** *n* **1** [u] (herb) 胡椒薄荷; ～**mint cream/sweet** 薄荷奶油/糖; **2** [c] (sweet) 薄荷糖

pepperoni /ˌpepəˈrəʊni/ *n* [u] 意大利辣肉肠

pepper: ～ **pot** Brit, ～ **shaker** Amer *ns* 胡椒瓶; ～ **spray** *n* 胡椒粉喷雾剂

peppery /ˈpepəri/ *adj* 胡椒味的

pep pill *n* colloq 兴奋丸

peppy /ˈpepi/ *adj* Amer colloq 精力充沛的; **to feel** ～ 感觉精力旺盛

pep rally *n* Amer 动员会

pepsin /ˈpepsɪn/ *n* [u] 胃蛋白酶

pep talk *n* colloq 激励的话; **to give sb. a** ～ 给某人打气

peptic /ˈpeptɪk/ *adj* (of digestion) 消化的; (of the digestive system) 消化系统的; ～ **ulcer** 消化系统溃疡

per /pɜː(r)/ *prep* **1** (for each) 每一; ～ **head** 每人; **80 km** ～ **hour** 每小时80公里 **2** (in accordance with) 按照; **as** ～ **your instructions** 根据你的指示; **as** ～ **usual** colloq 照常; **she was late, as** ～ **usual** 她一如既往地迟到了

perambulator /pəˈræmbjʊleɪtə(r)/ *n* Brit dated formal 手推童车

per annum /ˌpɜːr ˈænəm/ *adv* 每年 ‹*cost, yield, pay*›

per capita /ˌpɜː ˈkæpɪtə/
A *adv* 人均
B *adj* 人均的

perceive /pəˈsiːv/ *vt* **1** (become aware of) 察觉; **he** ～**d a change in her attitude** 他注意到她的态度发生了改变 **2** (interpret) 把…看作; **to** ～ **sth./sb. as sth.** 把某事/某人看作某情况; **it was meant to be a joke, but she** ～**d it as a threat** 这本来是说着玩的, 但她认为是威胁

per cent /pəˈsent/ *adv* 百分之; **interest of five** ～ **a month** 每月5%的利息; **a twenty** ～ **discount** *or* **reduction** 八折

percentage /pəˈsentɪdʒ/ ▸**p. 521** *n* **1** (rate, number, amount) 百分比; **the figure was expressed as a** ～ 这个数字是用百分率表示的; **in** ～ **terms, this represents a real increase** 按百分比来说, 这代表着实实在在的增长 **2** (proportion) 比例; **a high** ～ **are unemployed** 很大一部分人失业 **3** colloq (profit) 利润分成; **I got a** ～ **on the deal** 我从这笔交易中得到一份提成

percentage point *n* 百分点

perceptible /pəˈseptəbl/ *adj* **1** (visible) 可见的; (audible) 可听见的; **these sounds are not** ～ **to the human ear** 这些声音人耳听不见 **2** (noticeable, observable) 可察觉的 ‹*change, increase*›

perceptibly /pəˈseptəbli/ *adv* 可察觉地; ～ **different** 明显不同的

perception /pəˈsepʃn/ *n* **1** [u] (awareness) 感觉; **visual** ～ 视觉; **he did not have any** ～ **of her problems** 他对她的问题毫无觉察 **2** [u] (insight) 洞察; **to say sth. with unusual** ～ 一针见血地说出某话 **3** [u] (ability to perceive) 洞察力 **4** [c] (impression) 看法; **what is your** ～ **of what needs to be done?** 你认为需要做些什么?; **popular** ～**s of old age** 对老龄问题的普遍看法

perceptive /pəˈseptɪv/ *adj* **1** (quick to notice) 反应敏锐的 **2** (insightful) 有洞察力的; **a** ～ **comment** 富有见地的评论

perceptively /pəˈseptɪvli/ *adv* 有洞察力地; **to analyse the economic crisis** ～ 精辟地分析经济危机

perceptiveness /pəˈseptɪvnɪs/ *n* [u] = **perception 2**

perch[1] /pɜːtʃ/ *n* (*pl* **perch** *or* ～**es**) Zool 鲈鱼

perch[2]
A *n* (for bird) 栖息处; (for person, animal) 歇脚处; **the parrot was on its** ～ **in the cage** 鹦鹉站在笼子里的栖木上; **to knock sb. off his/her** ～ colloq 使某人丧失名位; **Liverpool were knocked off their** ～ **at the top of the League** 利物浦队被赶下了联赛冠军的宝座
B *vi* «*bird*» 栖息; «*person, animal*» 坐; «*thing*» 坐落; **the bird** ～**ed on a branch** 鸟儿落在树枝上; **we** ～**ed on the high bar stools** 我们坐在酒吧高脚凳上; **the village** ～**ed on the side of the mountain** 村庄坐落在山坡上
C *vt* 放置; **he** ～**ed the infant on his knee** 他把婴儿放在膝上; **the cottage was** ～**ed above the lake** 小屋位于湖泊上方

percipient /pəˈsɪpiənt/ *adj* formal **1** (quick to notice, understand) 目光敏锐的 **2** (insightful) 有洞察力的; **he made some extremely** ～ **remarks** 他说了一些极其精辟的话

percolate /ˈpɜːkəleɪt/
A *vt* [用渗滤式咖啡壶] 滤煮; ～**d coffee** 滤煮的咖啡
B *vi* **1** lit (filter gradually) «*coffee*» [用渗滤式咖啡壶] 滤煮; «*liquid*» 渗透; **the water** ～**s through the sand** 水渗漏到沙子里了 **2** fig (spread) 扩散; **the news gradually** ～**d through the community** 消息逐渐在社区里传开了

percolator /ˈpɜːkəleɪtə(r)/ *n* 渗滤式咖啡壶

percussion /pəˈkʌʃn/ *n* [u] **1** Mus 打击乐器; **to play** ～ 演奏打击乐; ～ **instruments** 打击乐器 **2** Med 叩诊

percussion: ～ **cap** *n* 雷管; ～ **drill** *n* = **hammer drill**

percussionist /pəˈkʌʃənɪst/ *n* 打击乐器演奏者

percussive /pəˈkʌsɪv/ *adj* 打击乐器的; ～ **instruments** 打击乐器

perdition /pəˈdɪʃn/ *n* [u] **1** Relig 万劫不复 **2** fig 毁灭; **the road to** ～ 毁灭之路

peregrination /ˌperɪgrɪˈneɪʃn/ *n* liter 长途旅行; **our** ～ **through life** 我们漫长的人生旅程

peregrine /ˈperɪgrɪn/ *n* ～ **(falcon)** 游隼

peremptorily /pəˈremptrəli, Amer ˈperəmptɔːrəli/ *adv* 专横地

peremptory /pəˈremptəri, Amer ˈperəmptɔːri/ *adj* 专横的; **to speak in a** ～ **tone of voice** 用咄咄逼人的语气说话

perennial /pəˈrenɪəl/
A *adj* **1** (enduring) 持久的 **2** (recurring) 反复出现的 **3** Bot 多年生的 **4** *attrib* fig 长期的; **he is a** ～ **student** 他一直在上学
B *n* 多年生植物

perennially /pəˈrenɪəli/ *adv* **1** (enduringly) 持久地 **2** (continually) 反复地

perfect
A /ˈpɜːfɪkt/ *adj* **1** (flawless) 完美的; **to be in** ～ **condition** 状况极佳; **nobody's** ～ 人无完人; **he speaks** ～ **English** 他讲一口地道的英语; **a** ～ **crime** 一桩无头案 **2** (totally precise) 精确的; **a** ～ **circle** 正圆; **your timing is** ～ 你的时机掌握得恰到好处 **3** (totally suitable) 理想的; **she's absolutely** ～ **for the job** 她是这项工作的最佳人选; **they make a** ～ **couple** 他们是天造地设的一对 **4** (wonderful) 极好的; ～**!** 太好了! **5** (total) 完全的; **a** ～ **idiot** 十足的白痴; **a** ～ **stranger** 百分之百的陌生人 **6** Ling 完成时的; **the** ～ **tense** 完成时态
B /ˈpɜːfɪkt/ *n* **the** ～ 完成时
C /pəˈfekt/ *vt* 使完美; **to** ～ **one's French** 提高法语水平; **my technique is in need of** ～**ing** 我的技巧还需完善

perfectibility /pəˌfektɪˈbɪləti/ *n* [u] 可完善性

perfectible /pəˈfektəbl/ *adj* 可完善的 ‹*technique, performance*›

perfection /pəˈfekʃn/ *n* [u] **1** (state, quality) 完美; **the beef was roasted to** ～ 牛肉烤得恰到好处; **that dress fits you to** ～ 那条裙子你穿着合身极了 **2** (action, process) 圆满 **3** (faultless) (person) 完美的人; (thing) 完美的事物; **his performance was** ～ **(itself)** 他的演技真是炉火纯青

perfectionism /pəˈfekʃənɪzəm/ *n* [u] 完美主义

perfectionist /pəˈfekʃənɪst/
A *n* 完美主义者
B *adj* 追求完美的

perfective /pəˈfektɪv/ Ling
A *adj* 完成时的
B *n* (aspect) 完成体; (verb) 完成体动词

perfectly /ˈpɜːfɪktli/ *adv* **1** (flawlessly) 完美地; **she speaks French** ～ 她讲一口地道的法语 **2** (precisely) 精确地; **the ring fitted her finger** ～ 那枚戒指她戴着正合适; **to go** ～ **to plan** 完全按照计划进行 **3** (very well) 极好地; **a** ～**-matched couple** 天造地设的一对; **everything ran** ～ 诸事顺利 **4** (totally) 完全地; **she looked** ～ **idiotic** 她看起来十分愚蠢

perfect pitch [u] 绝对音高; **to have** ～ 有绝对音感

perfidious /pəˈfɪdɪəs/ *adj* liter 背信弃义的; **a** ～ **lover** 负心的情人

perfidiously /pəˈfɪdɪəsli/ *adv* liter 背信弃义地

perfidy /ˈpɜːfɪdi/ *n* [u] liter 背信弃义

perforate /ˈpɜːfəreɪt/ *vt* **1** (pierce) 刺穿; **the bullet** ～**d her heart** 子弹打穿了她的心脏 **2** (make small holes in) 在…上打齿孔 ‹*paper*›; **a** ～**d line** 齿孔线

perforated ulcer *n* 穿孔性溃疡

perforation /ˌpɜːfəˈreɪʃn/ *n* 1 [u] (action) 穿孔 2 [c] (small hole) 齿孔

perforce /pəˈfɔːs/ *adv* formal 必定; **much of what is said about the birth of civilization is, ~, guesswork** 关于文明起源的许多说法必然只是猜测

perform /pəˈfɔːm/
A *vt* 1 (carry out) 做; **to ~ an operation** 施行手术; **to ~ an important role** 发挥重要作用; **a saint who ~ed numerous miracles** 创造出无数奇迹的圣人 2 (for entertainment) 表演; **the violinist ~ed a solo** 小提琴手演奏了一首独奏曲; **she ~ed the part of the queen** 她扮演了女王的角色; **to ~ tricks** 要把戏 3 (enact) 主持 ‹*ceremony, ritual*›
B *vi* 1 (in play, film, concert etc.) 表演; **to ~ live** 现场演出; **to ~ on the violin** 演奏小提琴; **she ~ed brilliantly as Viola** 她把维奥拉演得惟妙惟肖 2 (conduct oneself) 表现; **the students ~ed better in their exams than last year** 学生们考得比去年好 3 (work, function) 运行; **how is the machine ~ing?** 机器的性能如何? 4 Comm, Fin 业绩良好; **the economy has been ~ing rather sluggishly** 经济一直都很萧条

performance /pəˈfɔːməns/ *n* 1 [c] (for entertainment) 表演; **to give** *or* **put on a ~** 进行演出; **a live ~** 现场演出; **a benefit/gala ~** 慈善/庆典演出 2 [c] (manner or performing) 表现; **he won a medal for his fine ~ in the Olympics** 他在奥运会上表现良好获得了一枚奖牌; **his ~ of King Lear left me cold** 他演的李尔王没有打动我; **the violinist gave a superb ~** 小提琴家进行了精彩的演奏; **his ~ in the test wasn't up to scratch** 他考得不好 3 [u] (of duties, services) 履行; **he is meticulous in the ~ of his duties** 他履行职责一丝不苟 4 [u] (of vehicle, engine) 性能 5 [u] Comm, Fin 业绩; **the ~ of the economy** 经济状况 6 [u] colloq (exaggerated behaviour) 夸张的行为; (disgraceful behaviour) 丢脸的行为; **what on earth did she mean by that ~ in the cafe?** 她在咖啡馆里那么丢人现眼到底是什么意思? 7 [u] colloq (fuss) 忙乱; **what a ~!** 真够忙乱的!; **starting up this old car is a bit of a ~** 发动这辆旧车真是有些麻烦

performance: ~ appraisal *n* [u and c] 绩效考核; **~ art** *n* [u] 戏剧表演艺术; **~ artist** ▸p. 409 *n* 戏剧表演艺术家; **~-enhancing drug** *n* 兴奋剂; **~ indicator** *n* 绩效指标; **~-related pay** *n* [u] 绩效工资; **~ review** *n* = **~ appraisal**

performer /pəˈfɔːmə(r)/ *n* 1 (artist) 表演者; **a fine ~ on the piano** 优秀的钢琴演奏者; **a theatrical ~** 戏剧演员 2 (achiever) 履行者; **the car is a good ~ on hilly terrain** 这辆车在山区行驶性能很好 3 (exponent) 能手; **a talented ~ on the football field** 足球场上的天才球员

performing /pəˈfɔːmɪŋ/ *adj attrib* 会表演的 ‹*animal*›

performing arts *npl* 表演艺术

perfume /ˈpɜːfjuːm, Amer pərˈfjuːm/
A *n* [c and u] 1 (fragrance) 香水 2 (smell, scent) 芳香; **a sweet ~** 甜香
B *vt* 使香气弥漫; **she ~d herself with delicate dabs of cologne** 她在身上洒了点清淡的古龙香水

perfumery /pəˈfjuːməri/ *n* 1 [c] (shop) 香水商店; (factory) 香水制造厂 2 [u] (science, process) 香水制造

perfunctorily /pəˈfʌŋktrəli, Amer -tɔːrəli/ *adv* 敷衍地; **to carry out a task ~** 例行公事地执行任务

perfunctory /pəˈfʌŋktəri, Amer -tɔːri/ *adj* 敷衍的; **a ~ search** 马虎的搜寻; **a ~ kiss** 漫不经心的一吻; **in a ~ manner** 敷衍了事地

pergola /ˈpɜːgələ/ *n* 藤架

perhaps /pəˈhæps/ *adv* 或许; **~ he will come** 他可能会来; **she's rather young, ~, but she's very able** 她也许还很年轻, 但她非常能干; **~ I might copy this?** 我可以把这个复印一下吗?; **~ I should first explain that ...** 我也许应当先解释一下…; **he seemed cross, or ~ rather disappointed** 他似乎生气了, 或许说有点失望

perianth /ˈperɪænθ/ *n* 花被

pericardium /ˌperɪˈkɑːdɪəm/ *n* (*pl* **pericardia** /ˌperɪˈkɑːdɪə/) 心包

pericarp /ˈperɪkɑːp/ *n* 果皮

perigee /ˈperɪdʒiː/ *n* 近地点

peril /ˈperəl/ *n* 1 [u] (risk of harm) 危险; **to be** *or* **live in ~ of one's life** 有生命危险; **at one's ~** 自冒风险 2 [c] (danger) 危害; **the ~s of smoking** 吸烟的危害

perilous /ˈperələs/ *adj* 危险的 ‹*journey, situation*›; **such an investment seems a ~ undertaking** 那样的投资似乎是十分冒险的事

perilously /ˈperələsli/ *adv* 危险地; **we came ~ close to disaster** 我们险些出了大乱子

perimeter /pəˈrɪmɪtə(r)/ *n* 1 (boundary) 边缘; **to patrol the ~ of the airport** 在机场四周巡逻; **~ wall** 围墙 2 Math 周长

perimeter fence *n* 围栏

perinatal /ˌperɪˈneɪtl/ *adj* 围产期的

period /ˈpɪərɪəd/ *n* 1 (of time) 一段时间; **a ~ of two years** 两年时间; **the incubation ~ of measles** 麻疹的潜伏期; **the post-war ~** 战后时期; **the Victorian ~** 维多利亚时代; **the Jurassic ~** 侏罗纪 2 Art 时期; **Picasso's blue ~** 毕加索的消沉时期 3 (of weather) 一段持续时间; **tomorrow there will be rain and bright ~s** 明天是阵雨间晴 4 (class, lesson) 课时; **the Maths ~** 数学课; **to have a free ~** 上自习课 5 Amer (full stop) 句号 6 (menstruation) 经期; **to have one's ~** 来例假 7 Astron 周期 8 colloq (preventing or cutting off discussion) [用以终止谈话]; **I am the sole owner of the trademark — ~** 我是商标的唯一拥有人——就是这么回事 9 Sport (of match) 局

period: ~ costume, ~ dress *ns* [u] (仿) 古装; **~ furniture** *n* [u] (仿) 古家具

periodic /ˌpɪərɪˈɒdɪk/ *adj* 周期性的; **to have ~ health check-ups** 定期接受体检

periodical /ˌpɪərɪˈɒdɪkl/
A *adj* 周期性的; **~ training** 定期训练
B *n* 期刊

periodically /ˌpɪərɪˈɒdɪkli/ *adv* 周期性地; **we meet ~** 我们不时见面

periodicity /ˌpɪərɪəˈdɪsəti/ *n* [u] 周期性

periodic table *n* 元素周期表

period: ~ of office *n* (*pl* **~s of office**) 任期; **~ pains** *npl* 痛经; **~ piece** *n* (object) 具有时代特征的物品; (artistic work) 具有时代特征的艺术品

peripatetic /ˌperɪpəˈtetɪk/ *adj* 巡回工作的; **a ~ violin teacher** 一位在多所学校任教的小提琴教师

peripheral /pəˈrɪfərəl/
A *adj* 1 (situated on the edge) 外围的; **the ~ provinces of the country** 该国的边缘省份 2 (marginal) 次要的; **this question seems ~ to me** 这个问题对我来说似乎无关紧要 3 *attrib* Comput 外设的; **~ devices** 外围设备
B *n* 外围设备

peripheral vision *n* [u] 周边视觉

periphery /pəˈrɪfəri/ *n* 1 (edge) 外围; **the ~ of the town** 城镇的周边地区 2 fig (marginal position) 次要位置; (marginal part) 次要部分; **to be on the ~ (of sth.)** 处于 (某事的) 边缘; **she remained on the movement's ~** 她仍然留在该运动的外围

periscope /ˈperɪskəʊp/ *n* 潜望镜

perish /ˈperɪʃ/ *vi* 1 (die) 死亡; **to ~ from sth.** 死于某事; **to ~ from disease/the cold** 病逝/冻死; **we shall do it or ~ in the attempt** 我们将拼死一试; **to ~ by the sword** 遭暴力致死; **~ the thought!** colloq 死了心吧! 2 (rot) «*food, organic substance*» 腐烂; «*rubber, leather*» 老化

perishable /ˈperɪʃəbl/
A *adj* 易腐烂的 ‹*food, organic substance*›; 易老化的 ‹*leather, rubber*›
B **perishables** *npl* 易腐烂的东西

perished /ˈperɪʃt/ *adj pred* colloq 冷的; **to be ~ with cold** 冷极了

perisher /ˈperɪʃə(r)/ *n* Brit colloq (person) 讨厌鬼; (thing) 讨厌的事物; **stop that, you little ~s!** 别那样, 你们这些小淘气!

perishing /ˈperɪʃɪŋ/ *adj* Brit colloq 1 (very cold) 极冷的; **I'm ~!** 我冷极了! 2 *attrib* dated pej (wretched) 讨厌的; **what a ~ nuisance!** 真讨厌!

peritoneum /ˌperɪtəˈniːəm/ *n* (*pl* **~s** *or* **peritonea** /ˌperɪtəˈniːə/) 腹膜

peritonitis /ˌperɪtəˈnaɪtɪs/ ▸p. 377 *n* [u] 腹膜炎

periwinkle /ˈperɪwɪŋkl/ *n* 1 Bot 蔓长春花 2 Zool = **winkle**

perjure /ˈpɜːdʒə(r)/ *v refl* **to ~ oneself** 作伪证

perjured /ˈpɜːdʒəd/ *adj* 1 (having committed perjury) 作伪证的 ‹*witness*› 2 (involving lies) 伪证的; **he gave ~ evidence** *or* **testimony** 他作了伪证

perjurer /ˈpɜːdʒərə(r)/ *n* 作伪证者

perjury /ˈpɜːdʒəri/ *n* [u] 伪证罪; **to commit ~** 作伪证; **to be guilty of ~** 犯伪证罪

perk /pɜːk/ *n* colloq 1 (of job, position) 补贴 2 (of situation) 好处

Phrasal verb

• **perk up**
A *vi* colloq «*person, animal*» 振作; «*weather*» 放晴
B *vt* [**~ sb./sth. up, ~ up sb./sth.**] colloq 使…振作/使…充满活力; **a chat with your friends would ~ you up** 和朋友们聊天会让你快活起来

perkily /ˈpɜːkɪli/ *adv* (lively) 精力充沛地; (cheerfully) 快活地

perkiness /ˈpɜːkɪnɪs/ *n* [u] (liveliness) 精力充沛; (cheerfulness) 快活

perky /ˈpɜːki/ *adj* (lively) 精力充沛的; (cheerful) 快活的

perm[1] /pɜːm/
A *n* (permanent wave) 烫出的卷发; **to have a ~** 烫卷发
B *vt* (give a permanent wave to) 烫; **to ~ sb.'s hair** 给某人烫发

perm[2] Brit colloq
A *n* (selection in football pools) 选定组合
B *vt* (select) 选定…组合; **to ~ 8 from 16** 从 16 个数字中选 8 个进行组合

permafrost /ˈpɜːməfrɒst, Amer -frɔːst/ *n* [u] 永冻土层

permanence /ˈpɜːmənəns/, **permanency** /ˈpɜːmənənsi/ *ns* [u] 永久性; **the ~ of marriage** 婚姻的天长地久

permanent /ˈpɜːmənənt/ *adj* 永久的; **a ~ job** 固定工作; **~ staff** 固定职工; **she's in a ~ state of worry** 她一直忧心忡忡

permanently /ˈpɜːmənəntli/ *adv* 永久地; **a ~ high level of unemployment** 居高不下的失业率

permanent: ~ press *n* 免熨; **P~ Secretary** *n* Brit = **Permanent Undersecretary**; **~ tooth** *n* 恒齿; **P~ Undersecretary** *n* Brit 常务次官; **~ wave** *n* dated 烫发; **~ way** *n* 路基

permanganate /pəˈmæŋgəneɪt/ *n* [u] 高锰酸盐

permeability /ˌpɜːmɪəˈbɪləti/ *n* [u] 渗透性

permeable /ˈpɜːmɪəbl/ *adj* 可渗透的

permeate /ˈpɜːmɪeɪt/

A *vt* **1** (penetrate) «*liquid*» 渗透; «*gas, smell*» 弥漫; **the room was ~d with tobacco smoke** 房间里烟雾缭绕 **2** fig (spread through) 散布; **their attitude was ~d by a mood of defeat** 他们的态度掺杂着失败的情绪

B *vi* **1** (penetrate) «*liquid*» 渗透; «*gas, smell*» 弥漫 **2** fig (spread) 散布; **the ideas gradually ~d through the people** 这些思想逐渐深入民心

Permian /ˈpɜːmɪən/

A *adj* (of the period) 二叠纪的; (of the rock system) 二叠系的

B *n* **the ~** (period) 二叠纪; (rock system) 二叠系

permissible /pəˈmɪsɪbl/ *adj* 许可的; **to be ~ to do sth.** 可以做某事; **it is ~ to reserve tables in advance** 可以订位

permission /pəˈmɪʃn/ *n* **1** [u] (consent) 许可; **to give** *or* **grant (sb.) ~ to do sth.** 准许（某人）做某事; **to refuse (sb.) ~ to do sth.** 不允许（某人）做某事; **~ to speak, sir** Mil 请求发言，长官; **with your (kind) ~** 承蒙惠允; **by kind ~ (of sb.)** 承蒙（某人）允许 **2** [c] (official document) 许可证; **~s to reproduce copyright material** 准予复制版权资料的许可文件

permissive /pəˈmɪsɪv/ *adj* 纵容的; **the ~ society** 宽容的社会

permissiveness /pəˈmɪsɪvnɪs/ *n* [u] 纵容

permit

A /ˈpɜːmɪt/ *n* **1** [c] (document) 许可证; **to apply for a ~** 申请许可证; **a gun/fishing ~** 持枪/钓鱼许可证 **2** [u] (official or formal permission) 许可; **by ~ only** 经许可者除外

B /pəˈmɪt/ *vt* (*pres p etc.* **-tt-**) **1** (authorize) 准许; **to ~ sb. to do sth.** 允许某人做某事; **to ~ sb. sth.** 允许某人某事; **are we ~ted to smoke here?** 这里可以抽烟吗? **2** (make possible) 使有可能; **the good weather will ~ people to get out and about** 好天气将使人们能外出活动

C /pəˈmɪt/ *vi* (*pres p etc.* **-tt-**) **1** (make possible) 使有可能; **weather ~ting** 天气好的话; **if time/weather ~s** 如果时间够/天气好的话 **2** formal (allow) **to/to not ~ of sth.** «*passage*» 容许/不容许某事物; **each text ~ted of several interpretations** 每篇文本都可以有几种解释

D /pəˈmɪt/ *v refl* (*pres p etc.* **-tt-**) **to ~ oneself sth.** 允许自己做某事; **she ~ted herself one drink only** 她只准自己喝一杯酒

permutation /ˌpɜːmjʊˈteɪʃn/ *n* **1** [c] (arrangement) 一组排列; **~s and combinations** 各种排列组合 **2** [u] Math 排列 **3** [c] Brit (selection in football pools) 选定组合

permute /pəˈmjuːt/ *vt* 重新排列

pernicious /pəˈnɪʃəs/ *adj* 有害的; **a ~ lie** 恶毒的谎言; **a ~ disease** 恶疾; **to be ~ to sth.** 对某事物有害

pernicious anaemia ▸**p. 377** *n* [u] 恶性贫血

perniciously /pəˈnɪʃəsli/ *adv* 有害地

pernickety /pəˈnɪkəti/ *adj* 吹毛求疵的; **to be ~ about sth.** 对某事物十分挑剔

peroration /ˌperəˈreɪʃn/ *n* formal 结尾

peroxide /pəˈrɒksaɪd/ *n* **1** [c] Chem 过氧化物; **a ~ solution** 过氧化物溶液 **2** [u] (substance for bleaching hair) 过氧化氢

peroxide blonde

A *adj* 漂染为金色的 ‹*hair*›; 漂染金发的 ‹*person*›

B *n* colloq 漂染金发的女子

perpendicular /ˌpɜːpənˈdɪkjʊlə(r)/

A *adj* **1** (at a right angle) 成直角的; **to be ~ to sth.** 与某物垂直 **2** (vertical) 直立的; **a ~ cliff** 峭壁; **a ~ line** 垂线

B *n* 垂直线; **to lean from the ~** 倾斜

perpendicularly /ˌpɜːpənˈdɪkjʊləli/ *adv* 垂直地

perpetrate /ˈpɜːpɪtreɪt/ *vt* 犯 ‹*crime, blunder*›; 进行 ‹*deception, hoax*›; **who ~d this dreadful deed?** 这件可怕的事是谁干的?

perpetrator /ˈpɜːpɪtreɪtə(r)/ *n* (of crime) 犯罪者; (of other wicked deed) 作恶者; **the ~ of a hoax** 诈骗犯

perpetual /pəˈpetʃʊəl/ *adj* **1** (occurring repeatedly) 一再反复的; **to make oneself a ~ nuisance** 弄得自己老是惹人厌 **2** (never ending or changing) 无休止的; **~ noise** 持续不断的噪音; **to live in a state of ~ happiness** 一直生活在幸福之中

perpetual calendar *n* 万年历

perpetually /pəˈpetʃʊəli/ *adv* (permanently) 永久地; (endlessly) 无休止地; **my ~ smiling grandmother** 我那总是面带微笑的祖母

perpetual motion *n* [u] 永恒运动

perpetuate /pəˈpetʃʊeɪt/ *vt* 使永久; **to ~ inequality** 延续不平等; **to ~ the memory of sb.** 长忆某人

perpetuation /pəˌpetʃʊˈeɪʃn/ *n* 永久化; **the ~ of sth.** 某事的持续

perpetuity /ˌpɜːpɪˈtjuːəti, Amer -ˈtuː-/ *n* [u] formal 永久; **in ~** 永远

perplex /pəˈpleks/ *vt* 使困惑

perplexed /pəˈplekst/ *adj* 困惑的

perplexedly /pəˈpleksɪdli/ *adv* 困惑地

perplexing /pəˈpleksɪŋ/ *adj* 使人困惑的; **a ~ problem** 费解的问题

perplexity /pəˈpleksəti/ *n* [u] 困惑

perquisite /ˈpɜːkwɪzɪt/ *n* formal 额外待遇

perry /ˈperi/ *n* [u and c] 梨酒

per se /ˌpɜː ˈseɪ/ *adv* formal 本身; **religion is neither good nor bad ~** 宗教本身没有好坏之分; **money ~ is just a necessity** 金钱在本质上只是一种必需品

persecute /ˈpɜːsɪkjuːt/ *vt* **1** (harass, oppress) 迫害 **2** (bother, annoy) 纠缠

persecution /ˌpɜːsɪˈkjuːʃn/ *n* [u] 迫害; **to be subjected to ~** 遭受迫害

persecution complex, persecution mania *ns* 受迫害妄想症

persecutor /ˈpɜːsɪkjuːtə(r)/ *n* 迫害者

perseverance /ˌpɜːsɪˈvɪərəns/ *n* [u] 坚持不懈; **to show great ~ in the face of difficulties** 面对困难表现出坚强的毅力; **he succeeded by (sheer) ~** 他（完全是）锲而不舍才获得成功

persevere /ˌpɜːsɪˈvɪə(r)/ *vi* 坚持不懈; **to ~ in sth./doing sth.** 在某事方面锲而不舍/锲而不舍地做某事; **to ~ at** *or* **with sth.** 坚持某事

persevering /ˌpɜːsɪˈvɪərɪŋ/ *adj* 坚持不懈的; **to be ~ in sth.** 在某事方面锲而不舍

Persia /ˈpɜːʃə/ *pr n* Hist 波斯

Persian /ˈpɜːʃn/ ▸**p. 503, p. 426**

A *adj* (of Persia) 波斯的; (of the people) 波斯人的; (of the language) 波斯语的

B *n* **1** [c] (person) 波斯人 **2** [u] (language) 波斯语 **3** [c] (cat) **~ (cat)** 波斯猫

Persian: ~ carpet *n* 波斯地毯; **~ Gulf** *pr n* **the ~ Gulf** 波斯湾; **~ rug** *n* 波斯地毯

persimmon /pɜːˈsɪmən/ *n* **1** (fruit) 柿子 **2** (tree) 柿子树

persist /pəˈsɪst/ *vi* **1** (continue to exist) 持续存在; **if symptoms ~, consult your doctor** 如果症状不消除，就去看医生 **2** (continue in action or belief) 坚持不懈; **if you (will) ~, you'll get no help from anyone** 你若固执，就得不到他人的帮助; **'but why did you tell them?' she ~ed** "但你为什么告诉他们?" 她追问道; **to ~ with sth.** 坚持 ‹*policy, idea*›; **to ~ in sth./in doing sth.** 坚持某事/做某事; **the children ~ed in chattering and giggling** 孩子们不停地说说笑笑; **he ~ed in his belief that I was responsible** 他认定该我负责

persistence /pəˈsɪstəns/, **persistency** /pəˈsɪstənsi/ *ns* [u] **1** (continuing in action or belief) 坚持不懈; **to reach one's goals by dogged ~** 不屈不挠地达到目标; **~ in sth./doing sth.** 对某事/做某事的坚持 **2** (continuing to exist) 持续存在; **the ~ of religious beliefs despite persecution** 受迫害时对宗教信仰的坚持

persistent /pəˈsɪstənt/ *adj* **1** (persevering) 坚持不懈的; **to be ~ in sth.** 坚持不懈地做某事; **~ efforts** 执着的努力 **2** (continuing to exist) 持续存在的; (occurring repeatedly) 反复出现的; **a ~ smell** 持续不散的气味; **~ questioning** 无休止的讯问

persistently /pəˈsɪstəntli/ *adv* (continuously) 持续地; (repeatedly) 反复地

persistent: ~ offender *n* 惯犯; **~ organic pollutant** *n* 持久性有机污染物; **~ vegetative state** *n* 永久植物人状态

persnickety /pəˈsnɪkəti/ *adj* Amer = **pernickety**

person /ˈpɜːsn/ *n* **1** (*pl* **people** *or* formal **~s**) (human being) 人; **the average English ~** 普通英国人; **stolen by ~** *or* **~s unknown** Jur 遭身份不明的人偷窃; **the ~** *or* **~s concerned** 当事人; **to do sth. in ~** 亲自做某事; **the company had a great asset in the ~ of the stage manager** 舞台监督是这家剧团的顶梁柱 **2** (type, individual) 有特定爱好的人; **I'm a tea ~ myself** 我本人是个喜欢喝茶的人; **she's a cat ~** 她是个爱猫的人 **3** (body) 身体; **to have** *or* **carry sth. on** *or* **about one's ~** 随身携带某物; **with drugs concealed about his ~** 他身上藏有毒品; **offences against the ~** Jur 人身攻击 **4** Ling 人称; **the first ~ singular** 第一人称单数; **the second ~ plural** 第二人称复数

persona /pɜːˈsəʊnə/ *n* **1** (*pl* **personae** /pɜːˈsəʊniː/) Theat 角色 **2** (*pl* **~s** *or* **personae**) Psych 表象人格

personable /ˈpɜːsənəbl/ *adj* 品貌兼优的; **a ~ young man** 翩翩少年

personage /ˈpɜːsənɪdʒ/ *n* 名人; **an important ~** 要人

personal /ˈpɜːsənl/

A *adj* **1** (individual) 个人的 ‹*belief, income*›; (private) 私人的 ‹*friend, property, possession(s)*›; **~ liberty/insurance** 人身自由/保险; **to have a strong ~ preference for sth.** 本人非常喜欢某事物 **2** (referring to character) 针对个人的 ‹*comment, insult*›; **don't be so ~!** 不要这样搞人身攻击! **3** (for a particular person) 给个人的; **a letter marked '~'** 标有"私人"字样的信件 **4** (relating to the body) 外表的 ‹*beauty*›; 身体的 ‹*cleanliness, freshness*›; **one's ~ appearance** 长相; **~ hygiene** 个人卫生 **5** *attrib* (done in person) 亲自的; **to pay sb. a ~ visit** 亲自拜访某人 **6** *attrib* Ling 人称的; **~ pronouns** 人称代词

B **personals** *npl* Amer **the ~s** 私人广告

personal: ~ accident insurance *n* [u] 人身意外保险; **~ advertisement,** colloq **~ ad** *ns* 个人广告; **~ allowance** *n* Brit 个人免税额; **~ assistant** ▸**p. 409** *n* 私人助理; **~ column** *n* 私人广告栏; **~ computer** *n* 个人计算机; **~ damages** *npl* 人身伤害赔偿; **~ details** *npl* (on application form) 个人信息; (intimate details) 个人隐私; **~ digital assistant** *n* 个人数字助理; **~ equity plan** *n* Brit 个人投资计划; **~ identification number** *n* 个人识别码; **~ injury** *n* [u] Jur 人身伤害

personality /ˌpɜːsəˈnæləti/ *n* **1** [c] (characteristics, qualities) (of person) 个性; (of animal, place) 特性; **their son has a very strong ~** 他们的儿子个性很强 **2** [u] (distinctive character) 气质; **she's a person with a lot of ~** 她是个富有独特

魅力的人 **3** [c] (individual) 名人; **a sporting/television ~** 体育界/电视圈名人

personality: ~ cult *n* 个人崇拜; **~ disorder** *n* 人格障碍; **~ type** *n* 人格类型

personalize /ˈpɜːsənəlaɪz/ *vt* **1** (tailor to individual) 为个人特制; **to ~ a product/service** 个别定制产品/进行个性化服务 **2** (make identifiable) 使成为个人专有; **~d clothes/stationery/number plate** 个人专用的衣服/文具/号牌 **3** (introduce personalities into) 使…针对个人 ‹*argument, debate*›; **there's no need to ~ the issue** 没必要把这个问题个人化

personal loan *n* 个人贷款

personally /ˈpɜːsənəli/ *adv* **1** (in person) 亲自; **I don't know him ~** 我本人并不认识他; **to take sth. ~** 认为某事针对自己 **2** (subjectively) 就本人而言; **~ speaking, speaking ~** 就本人而言

personal organizer *n* **1** (notebook) 私人记事本 **2** (microcomputer) 电子记事簿

personal pension *n* 个人养老金计划

personal pension plan, personal pension scheme *ns* 个人养老金计划

personal: ~ pronoun *n* 人称代词; **~ property** *n* [u] 动产; **~ shopper** *n* 私人购物助理; **~ stereo** *n* 随身听; **~ trainer** *n* 私人健身教练

persona non grata /pɜːˌsəʊnə nɒn ˈɡrɑːtə/ *n* (*pl* **personae non gratae** /pɜːˌsəʊniː nɒn ˈɡrɑːtiː/) 不受欢迎的人; **to declare sb. ~** 宣布某人不受欢迎

person-day *n* 人日 [工作量单位]

personification /pəˌsɒnɪfɪˈkeɪʃn/ *n* 化身; **the ~ of sth./sb.** 某事物的典型/某人的化身

personify /pəˈsɒnɪfaɪ/ *vt* 把…人格化; **beauty is sometimes personified as a naked goddess** 美有时拟人化地表现为一位裸体女神; **she is envy personified** 她是妒忌的化身

personnel /ˌpɜːsəˈnel/ *n* **1** + *v pl* (employees, staff) 员工 **2** + *v sing* (department) 人事部门; **to work in ~** 在人事部工作 **3** + *v pl* Mil 人员

personnel: ~ agency *n* 职业介绍所; **~ carrier** *n* 兵员运输车; **~ department** *n* 人事部; **~ file** *n* 人事档案; **~ manager** ▸**p. 409** *n* 人事部经理; **~ officer** ▸**p. 409** *n* 人事主管

person-to-person

A *adj* **1** Amer Telecom 指定受话人的; **to make a ~ call** 打一个叫人电话 **2** (directly between individuals) 直接通过个人的; **technical support is offered on a ~ basis** 技术支援是向个人直接提供的

B *adv* **1** Amer Telecom 以指定受话人的方式; **to phone** *or* **call (sb.) ~** (给某人)打叫人电话 **2** (directly between individuals) 直接通过个人; **we communicated ~** 我们面对面地进行交流

perspective /pəˈspektɪv/ *n* **1** [u] (in art) 透视法; **to draw sth. in ~** 用透视法画某物; **the castle is out of ~ with the other buildings** 城堡与其他建筑不成比例 **2** [c] (attitude, point of view) 观点; **to see things from a religious ~** 从宗教的角度看待事物 **3** [u] (sense of proportion) 权衡轻重的能力; **to have a sense of ~** 明察事理; **to get** *or* **put sth. in** *or* **into ~** 正确处理某事; **you have to keep things in ~** 处理事情要分轻重缓急; **to see/judge sth. in ~** 合理地看待/评价某事物

Perspex® /ˈpɜːspeks/ *n* [u] 珀斯佩有机玻璃

perspicacious /ˌpɜːspɪˈkeɪʃəs/ *adj* formal 有洞察力的

perspicacity /ˌpɜːspɪˈkæsəti/ *n* [u] formal 洞察力; **to have the ~ to do sth.** 有做某事的洞察力

perspiration /ˌpɜːspɪˈreɪʃn/ *n* [u] **1** (sweat) 汗; **drops** *or* **beads of ~** 汗珠; **to be bathed in ~** 大汗淋漓 **2** (sweating) 出汗

perspire /pəˈspaɪə(r)/ *vi* 出汗

persuadable /pəˈsweɪdəbl/ *adj* 可说服的

persuade /pəˈsweɪd/ *vt* **1** (influence) 说服; **to ~ sb. (not) to do sth.** 说服某人(不)做某事; **to ~ sb. into/out of sth./doing sth.** 说服某人做/不做某事 **2** (convince intellectually) 使相信; **I am not totally ~d of the necessity for that** 我不完全确信那件事的必要性

persuasion /pəˈsweɪʒn/ *n* **1** [u] (act, process) 说服; **they have great powers of ~** 他们的游说能力很强; **no amount of ~ will make her change her mind** 费多少口舌也无法使她改变想法 **2** [c] (belief) 信仰

persuasive /pəˈsweɪsɪv/ *adj* 有说服力的; **~ reasons** 令人信服的理由; **he can be very ~** 他有时很会说服人

persuasively /pəˈsweɪsɪvli/ *adv* 有说服力地; **arguments presented clearly and ~** 既阐述清楚又令人信服的论点

persuasiveness /pəˈsweɪsɪvnɪs/ *n* [u] 说服力

pert /pɜːt/ *adj* **1** (sexually attractive) 活泼诱人的; **a ~ little waitress** 小巧伶俐的女招待 **2** (neat and jaunty) 匀称的 ‹*chin*›; 别致的 ‹*jacket, skirt*›; **a ~ little nose** 小巧笔挺的鼻子 **3** (impudent) 冒失的; **she's always ready with a ~ reply** 她回答时总是冒冒失失

pertain /pəˈteɪn/ *vi* **1** formal (relate, apply to) 有关; **to ~ to sth.** 与某事物相关; **a book ~ing to birds** 有关鸟类的书 **2** Jur (belong to) 从属; **to ~ to sth.** 从属于某事物; **the assets ~ing to the business** 该公司的附属资产

pertinence /ˈpɜːtɪnəns, Amer -tənəns/ *n* [u] formal 相关性; **what is the ~ of these points to the debate?** 这些观点和那个争论有什么关系?

pertinent /ˈpɜːtɪnənt, Amer -tənənt/ *adj* formal 有关的; **to be ~ to sth.** 与某事物有关

pertinently /ˈpɜːtɪnəntli, Amer -tənəntli/ *adv* formal 有关地; **she spoke ~ and to the point** 她说的话中肯切题

pertly /ˈpɜːtli/ *adv* 冒失地

pertness /ˈpɜːtnɪs/ *n* [u] 冒失

perturb /pəˈtɜːb/ *vt* 使不安; **I was ~ed by the look on the doctor's face** 医生脸上的表情让我很担心

perturbation /ˌpɜːtəˈbeɪʃn/ *n* **1** (disquiet) 不安 **2** (disturbance) 搅乱; **~s to the climate** 气候的些微变化

perturbing /pəˈtɜːbɪŋ/ *adj* 令人不安的

Peru /pəˈruː/ *pr n* 秘鲁

perusal /pəˈruːzl/ *n* formal 细读

peruse /pəˈruːz/ *vt* formal 细读

Peruvian /pəˈruːvɪən/ ▸**p. 503**

A *adj* 秘鲁的

B *n* 秘鲁人

pervade /pəˈveɪd/ *vt* **1** (permeate) 弥漫于; **smoke ~d the whole room** 整个房间里烟雾缭绕 **2** (be apparent throughout) 遍及; **to be ~d by sth.** 充满某事物; **her work is ~d by nostalgia for a past age** 她的作品充满怀旧之情; **an all-pervading sense of fear** 普遍的恐惧情绪

pervasive /pəˈveɪsɪv/ *adj* **1** (permeating) 弥漫的 **2** (widespread) 普遍的; **the all-~ influence of the medieval church** 中世纪教会的普遍影响

perverse /pəˈvɜːs/ *adj* **1** (twisted, deviant) 任性的; **they take a ~ pleasure in displeasing the boss** 他们惹老板生气，从违拗中得到快乐; **a ~ judgement** 罔顾事实的裁决 **2** (contrary) 不合常理的

perversely /pəˈvɜːsli/ *adv* 任性地

perverseness /pəˈvɜːsnɪs/ *n* [u] = **perversity**

perversion /pəˈvɜːʃn, Amer -ʒn/ *n* **1** (distortion, corruption) 歪曲; **a ~ of justice** 对正义的歪曲 **2** (deviant behaviour or desire) 变态

perversity /pəˈvɜːsəti/ *n* [u] 任性; **he blamed his misfortune on the ~ of fate** 他认为自己的不幸是命运捉弄

pervert

A /pəˈvɜːt/ *vt* **1** (corrupt, deprave) 使堕落; **books which ~ young minds** 腐蚀年轻人心灵的书 **2** (alter) 歪曲; **to ~ the course of justice** 枉法

B /ˈpɜːvɜːt/ *n* 行为反常者; **sexual ~** 性变态者

perverted /pəˈvɜːtɪd/ *adj* **1** (sexually deviant) 性变态的 **2** (distorted) 歪曲的; **his ~ logic** 他那反常的逻辑

pervious /ˈpɜːvɪəs/ *adj* 能渗透的; **most soils are ~ to gas** 大多数土壤能透气

peseta /pəˈseɪtə/ *n* Hist 比塞塔 [2002年以前的西班牙货币单位]

pesky /ˈpeski/ *adj attrib* Amer colloq 讨厌的

peso /ˈpeɪsəʊ/ ▸**p. 174** *n* 比索 [前西班牙殖民地国家使用的货币单位]

pessary /ˈpesəri/ *n* 阴道栓剂

pessimism /ˈpesɪmɪzəm/ *n* [u] 悲观情绪

pessimist /ˈpesɪmɪst/ *n* 悲观主义者

pessimistic /ˌpesɪˈmɪstɪk/ *adj* 悲观的; **to be** *or* **feel ~ about** *or* **at sth.** 对某事物感到悲观

pessimistically /ˌpesɪˈmɪstɪkli/ *adv* 悲观地

pest /pest/ *n* **1** (animal) 害兽; (insect) 害虫 **2** colloq (person) 讨厌的人; (thing) 讨厌的事物; **he's a real ~!** 他真讨厌!

pest control *n* [u] (of animals) 害兽防治; (of insects) 虫害防治

pest control officer ▸**p. 409** *n* (for animals) 害兽防治员; (for insects) 虫害防治员

pester /ˈpestə(r)/ *vt* 打扰; **to ~ sb. for sth.** 因某事打扰某人; **the beggar ~ed passers-by for money** 那个乞丐缠着行人要钱; **to ~ sb. with questions** 缠住某人不断提问; **to ~ sb. about sth.** 关于某事烦扰某人; **to ~ sb. to do** *or* **into doing sth.** 纠缠着要某人做某事; **she ~ed me to buy a new suit** 她缠着我买一套新西装; **to ~ the life out of sb.** colloq 使某人烦得要死; **to be ~ed over the telephone** 被人电话骚扰

pesticidal /ˌpestɪˈsaɪdl/ *adj* 杀虫的

pesticide /ˈpestɪsaɪd/ *n* [u and c] 杀虫剂; **crops treated with ~** 打过杀虫剂的作物

pestilence /ˈpestɪləns/ *n* **1** archaic (plague) 瘟疫 **2** fig (pernicious influence) 弊害; **these ideas are a ~ affecting our society** 这些思想对我们的社会有害

pestilential /ˌpestɪˈlenʃl/ *adj* **1** (destructive, infectious) 致死的; **a ~ disease** 致命的疾病 **2** *attrib* colloq dated (annoying, troublesome) 讨厌的

pestle /ˈpesl/ *n* 杵; **~ and mortar** 杵臼

pesto /ˈpestəʊ/ *n* [u] 松子青酱

pet /pet/

A *n* **1** (animal) 宠物 **2** (favourite) 宠儿; **to be teacher's ~** 是老师的得意门生 **3** colloq (as term of address) 宝贝

B *vt* (*pres p etc.* **-tt-**) **1** (treat affectionately, spoil) 宠爱 **2** (stroke, pat) 抚摸 **3** (caress) 抚摸调情

C *vi* (*pres p etc.* **-tt-**) 抚摸调情

petal /ˈpetl/ *n* 花瓣

petard /pəˈtɑːd/ *n* 攻城炸药箱; ▸**hoist A1**

pet door *n* Amer 宠物门

Pete /piːt/ *pr n* colloq 皮特; **for ~'s sake!** 看在老天的份上!

Peter /ˈpiːtə(r)/ *pr n* 彼得; **to rob ~ to pay Paul** 借新债还旧账; **this moving of funds between budgets is just robbing ~ to pay Paul** 预算之间资金的转移无异于拆东墙补西墙

peter out *vi* 逐渐消失; **our supplies of petrol have petered out** 我们的石油储备渐

渐用完了; **the conversation petered out** 谈话终止了; **after four miles the road suddenly petered out** 那条路延伸了四英里之后突然断了

Peter principle *n* 彼得原则 [等级制度中成员晋升至与其能力不相称的级别方可止步]

pet: ~ food *n* [u and c] 宠物食品; **the ~ food industry** 宠物食品业; **~ hate** *n* 特别讨厌的事物

petit bourgeois /ˌpetɪ ˈbɔːʒwɑː, Amer -ˈbʊərʒ-/
A *adj* 小资产阶级的
B *n* (*pl* **petits bourgeois** /ˌpetɪˈbɔːʒwɑː, Amer -ˈbʊərʒ-/) 小资产阶级分子

petit bourgeoisie /ˌpetɪ ˌbɔːʒwɑːˈziː, Amer -ˌbʊərʒ-/ *n + v sing or pl* **the ~** 小资产阶级

petite /pəˈtiːt/ *adj* **1** (daintily attractive) 娇小的 **2** (clothing size) 小号的

petit four /ˌpetɪ ˈfɔː(r)/ *n* (*pl* **petits fours** /ˌpetɪ ˈfɔːz/) [杏仁蛋白糖] 花式小点心

petition /pəˈtɪʃn/
A *n* **1** (document) 请愿书; **to get up a ~ (for/against sth.)** 组织请愿（要求/反对某事物）; **to present a ~ (to sb.)** （向某人）递交请愿书 **2** (appeal, request) 祈求 **3** Jur 诉状; **to file a ~ for sth.** 提出申诉要求某事
B *vt* 请求; **to ~ (sb.) for sth.** 请求（某人）做某事; **they ~ed Parliament for a change in the law** 他们向议会请愿，要求修改法律; **to ~ for divorce** 要求离婚; **to ~ sb. to do sth.** 请求某人做某事

petitioner /pəˈtɪʃnə(r)/ *n* **1** (person presenting request) 请愿人 **2** Jur 离婚案原告

petits pois /ˌpətɪˈpwɑː/ *npl* 青豌豆

pet: ~ name *n* 昵称; **~ owner** *n* 宠物主人; **~ project** *n* 特别感兴趣的事情; **the idea is the ~ project of a small but vocal minority** 这个想法是敢于发言的少数人的兴趣所在

petrel /ˈpetrəl/ *n* 海燕

petrifaction /ˌpetrɪˈfækʃn/ *n* [u] = **petrification**

petrification /ˌpetrɪfɪˈkeɪʃn/ *n* [u] 石化

petrified /ˈpetrɪfaɪd/ *adj* **1** (terrified) 吓呆的 **2** Geol 石化的

petrify /ˈpetrɪfaɪ/
A *vt* **1** (terrify) 把…吓呆 **2** Geol 使石化
B *vi* 石化

petrifying /ˈpetrɪfaɪɪŋ/ *adj* 可怕的

petrochemical /ˌpetrəʊˈkemɪkl/ *n* 石油化学产品; **the ~ industry** 石油化学工业

petrochemistry /ˌpetrəʊˈkemɪstri/ *n* [u] **1** (chemistry of rocks) 岩石化学 **2** (chemistry of petroleum or gas) 石油化学

petrodollar /ˈpetrəʊdɒlə(r)/ *n* 石油美元

petrol /ˈpetrəl/ *n* [u] Brit 汽油

petrolatum /ˌpetrəˈleɪtəm/ *n* [u] Amer = **petroleum jelly**

petrol: ~ bomb *n* Brit 汽油弹; **~ can** *n* Brit 汽油罐; **~ cap** *n* Brit 油箱帽; **~-driven** *adj* Brit 以汽油为燃料的; **~ engine** *n* Brit 汽油发动机

petroleum /pəˈtrəʊlɪəm/ *n* [u] 石油; **~ industry** 石油工业

petroleum jelly *n* [u] 凡士林

petrol: ~ gauge *n* Brit 汽油计量表; **~head** *n* Brit colloq 汽车迷

petrology /pəˈtrɒlədʒi/ *n* [u] 岩石学

petrol: ~ pump *n* Brit **1** (device dispensing petrol) 汽油加油泵; **2** (part of engine) 汽油泵; **~ station** *n* Brit 加油站; **~ tank** *n* Brit 汽油箱; **~ tanker** *n* Brit **1** (ship) 汽油油轮; **2** (lorry) 汽油油槽车

pet: ~ shop Brit, **~ store** Amer *ns* 宠物商店; **~ subject** *n* 特别喜爱的话题

petticoat /ˈpetɪkəʊt/ *n* 衬裙

pettifogging /ˈpetɪfɒgɪŋ/ *adj* **1** (petty) 琐碎的 ‹*details*› **2** (quibbling) 吹毛求疵的 ‹*person*›

pettiness /ˈpetɪnɪs/ *n* [u] 小气

petting /ˈpetɪŋ/ *n* [u] 抚摸调情; **heavy ~** 热烈的爱抚

pettish /ˈpetɪʃ/ *adj* 任性的

petty /ˈpeti/ *adj* **1** (trivial) 琐碎的; **~ details** 细枝末节 **2** (small-minded) 小气的; **it was extremely ~ of him to criticize their work publicly** 他公开批评他们的工作，表现得极为心胸狭隘 **3** *attrib* (minor) 次要的; **a ~ official** 小官员 **4** Jur 轻微的 ‹*crime, offence*›; **a ~ criminal** 轻罪犯

petty: ~ cash *n* [u] 小额备用现金; **~ larceny** *n* [u] Amer 轻盗窃罪; **~-minded** *adj* 心胸狭窄的; **~-mindedness** *n* [u] 心胸狭窄; **~ officer** *n* 海军军士; **~ sessions** *npl* Brit 简易法庭; **~ theft** *n* [u and c] 轻微偷窃

petulance /ˈpetjʊləns, Amer -tʃʊ-/ *n* [u] 任性

petulant /ˈpetjʊlənt, Amer -tʃʊ-/ *adj* 任性的

petulantly /ˈpetʊləntli, Amer -tʃʊ-/ *adv* 任性地

petunia /pəˈtjuːnɪə, Amer -ˈtuː-/ *n* 矮牵牛

pew /pjuː/ *n* (seat) 教堂长椅; (box) 教堂包厢; **have** *or* **take a ~!** fig colloq 坐下!

pewter /ˈpjuːtə(r)/ *n* [u] **1** (metal) 白镴; **a ~ tankard** 白镴酒杯 **2** (utensils) 白镴器皿

PFI *abbr* Brit = **private finance initiative**

PFLP *abbr* = **Popular Front for the Liberation of Palestine** 解放巴勒斯坦人民阵线

PG *abbr* Cin = **parental guidance**

PGCE *abbr* Brit = **Postgraduate Certificate of Education** 研究生教育证书

pH *abbr* = **potential of hydrogen** pH值

phalanx /ˈfælæŋks/ *n* (*pl* **~es**) formal **1** (group) (of people) 密集的人; (of things) 密集的事物; **a ~ of bodyguards** 一大群保镖 **2** (group of troops, police) 密集队形; **a ~ of police** 警察人墙

phallic /ˈfælɪk/ *adj* **1** (of phallus) 阴茎的 ‹*symbolism, imagery*› **2** Psych 生殖器期的 ‹*fixation*›

phallus /ˈfæləs/ *n* (*pl* **phalli** /ˈfæliː/ *or* **~es**) [尤指象征男性力量与生殖力的] 阴茎

phantasm /ˈfæntæzəm/ *n* liter 幻觉

phantasmagoria /ˌfæntæzməˈgɒrɪə, Amer -ˈgɔːrɪə/ *n* liter 变幻情景

phantasmagoric, phantasmagorical /ˌfæntæzməˈgɒrɪk(l), Amer -ˈgɔːrɪk(l)/ *adj* liter 幻影似的

phantom /ˈfæntəm/
A *n* **1** (ghost) 幽灵 **2** (illusion) 幻觉
B *modif* 幽灵似的; **a ~ army** 影子部队; **a ~ pain in the leg** 腿部的幻痛

phantom limb *n* [被截肢者的] 幻肢感

pharaoh /ˈfeərəʊ/ *n* 法老

pharm /fɑːm/ *n* 转基因药物农场

pharma /ˈfɑːmə/ *n* 制药业; **a ~ company** 制药公司

pharmaceutical /ˌfɑːməˈsjuːtɪkl, Amer -ˈsuː-/
A *adj* (of medicinal drugs) 药物的; (of their preparation) 制药的; (of their use) 药用的; (of their sale) 卖药的; **~ products** 药品
B *n* 药物; **the ~ industry** 制药业
C **pharmaceuticals** *npl* 药业股份

pharmacist /ˈfɑːməsɪst/ ▸**p. 409** *n* 药剂师; **~'s shop** 药房

pharmacological /ˌfɑːməkəˈlɒdʒɪkl/ *adj* 药物学的

pharmacology /ˌfɑːməˈkɒlədʒi/ *n* [u] 药物学

pharmacopoeia, Amer also **pharmacopeia** /ˌfɑːməkəˈpiːə/ *n* **1** (book) 药典 **2** (stock of drugs) 备用药品

pharmacy /ˈfɑːməsi/ ▸**p. 409** *n* **1** [c] (shop, hospital dispensary) 药房 **2** [u] (science, practice) 药剂学

pharm animal *n* 药用转基因动物

pharming /ˈfɑːmɪŋ/ *n* [u] **1** Agric 药耕 **2** Comput 域欺骗

pharyngitis /ˌfærɪnˈdʒaɪtɪs/ ▸**p. 377** *n* [u] 咽炎

pharynx /ˈfærɪŋks/ *n* (*pl* **pharynges** /fəˈrɪndʒiːz/) 咽

phase /feɪz/
A *n* **1** (period) 阶段; **to go through a difficult ~** 经历困难时期; **it's just a ~ (she's going through)** 这只是（她正经历的）一个阶段; **the rebellious ~** 叛逆期 **2** Astron 相; **the ~s of the moon** 月相 **3** (harmony) **to be in ~/out of ~** 协调/不协调; **her ideas and mine were just not in ~** 她的观念同我的格格不入
B *vt* 分阶段进行; **a ~d withdrawal of troops** 分阶段的撤军; **they ~d their acquisition of the company's shares** 他们逐步取得了该公司的股份

Phrasal verbs
- **phase in** *vt* [**~ in sth., ~ sth. in**] 逐步引入; **we will ~ in the new system over four years** 我们将在四年内逐步实行新制度
- **phase out** *vt* [**~ out sth., ~ sth. out**] 逐步废除; **the old coinage was gradually ~d out** 旧币制逐步废除了

phatic /ˈfætɪk/ *adj* 交际性的; **~ language/communion** *or* **communication** 应酬话/客套话

PhD *abbr* = **Doctor of Philosophy**

pheasant /ˈfeznt/ *n* 野鸡

phenol /ˈfiːnɒl/ *n* 酚

phenomena /fəˈnɒmɪnə/ *pl* ▸**phenomenon**

phenomenal /fəˈnɒmɪnl/ *adj* 不寻常的; **a ~ success** 巨大的成功; **a man of ~ talent** 有杰出才能的人; **at ~ speed** 以惊人的速度

phenomenally /fəˈnɒmɪnəli/ *adv* 不寻常地; **she has had a ~ successful career** 她的事业非常成功; **crime has increased ~** 犯罪率显著上升了

phenomenological /fəˌnɒmɪnəˈlɒdʒɪkl/ *adj* 现象学的

phenomenologist /fəˌnɒmɪˈnɒlədʒɪst/ *n* 现象学学家

phenomenology /fəˌnɒmɪˈnɒlədʒi/ *n* [u] 现象学

phenomenon /fəˈnɒmɪnən/ *n* (*pl* **phenomena**) **1** (occurrence, situation) 现象; **unemployment is a city ~** 失业问题是城市现象; **natural/social/historical/atmospheric phenomena** 自然/社会/历史/大气现象 **2** (odd, unusual fact, circumstance) 不寻常的情况; **an isolated ~** 孤立现象 **3** (remarkable person) 非凡的人; (remarkable thing or event) 非凡的事物; **a ~ at tennis** 网球奇才

pheromone /ˈferəməʊn/ *n* 信息素

phew /fjuː/ *excl* colloq 哦 [表示疲倦、惊讶、厌恶、宽慰等]; **~, it's hot today!** 唷，今天真热呀!; **~, I'm glad that's over!** 哦，那事总算结束了!

phial /ˈfaɪəl/ *n* 管形小瓶; **a ~ of medicine/perfume** 一小瓶药/香水

Phi Beta Kappa /ˌfaɪ biːtə ˈkæpə/ *n* Amer **1** (group) Φ β K 联谊会 [美国大学优秀生组织] **2** (*pl* **~s**) (person) Φ β K 联谊会会员

Philadelphia /ˌfɪləˈdelfɪə/ *pr n* 费城

philander /fɪˈlændə(r)/ *vi* 玩弄女性

philanderer /fɪˈlændərə(r)/ *n* 玩弄女性者; **I'm not a ~, I just like women** 我不是色鬼，我只是喜欢女性

philandering /fɪˈlændərɪŋ/ *n* [u] 玩弄女性

philanthropic /ˌfɪlənˈθrɒpɪk/ *adj* 慈善的; **he's a ~ kind of chap** 他是个乐善好施的人

philanthropist /fɪˈlænθrəpɪst/ *n* 慈善家

philanthropy /fɪˈlænθrəpi/ *n* [u] 慈善

philatelic /ˌfɪləˈtelɪk/ *adj attrib* 集邮的 ‹*club, society*›
philatelist /fɪˈlætəlɪst/ *n* 集邮家
philately /fɪˈlætəli/ *n* [u] 集邮
philharmonic /ˌfɪlɑːˈmɒnɪk/ *adj* 爱好音乐的; **the Berlin P～ (Orchestra)** 柏林爱乐（管弦）乐团
philippic /fɪˈlɪpɪk/ *n* liter 抨击
Philippine /ˈfɪlɪpiːn/ ▸**p. 503** *adj* 菲律宾的
Philippines /ˈfɪlɪpiːnz/ *pr n* **the ～** 菲律宾
philistine /ˈfɪlɪstaɪn/
A *n* 文化艺术修养低的人; **she thought that people who didn't like opera were ～s** 她认为不喜欢歌剧的人都是文化修养低的
B *adj* 庸俗的
philistinism /ˈfɪlɪstɪnɪzəm/ *n* [u] 庸俗; **the ～ of the popular press** 通俗报刊的庸俗
Phillips® /ˈfɪlɪps/ *adj* 十字形的 ‹*screw, screwdriver*›
philological /ˌfɪləˈlɒdʒɪkl/ *adj* 语文学的
philologist /fɪˈlɒlədʒɪst/ *n* 语文学家
philology /fɪˈlɒlədʒi/ *n* [u] 语文学
philosopher /fɪˈlɒsəfə(r)/ *n* **1** (scholar, thinker) 哲学家 **2** fig (stoical person) 达观的人; **to be sth. of a ～** 泰然自若
philosopher's stone *n* 魔法石
philosophical /ˌfɪləˈsɒfɪk/ *adj* **1** (relating to philosophy) 哲学的 **2** (stoical) 达观的; **to be ～ about sth.** 对某事处之泰然
philosophically /ˌfɪləˈsɒfɪkli/ *adv* **1** Philos 在哲学上; **to think ～** 从哲学的角度思考 **2** (stoically) 达观地; **he reacted ～ to the news of the failure** 他镇定地面对失败的消息
philosophize /fɪˈlɒsəfaɪz/ *vi* 高谈阔论; **to ～ about the meaning of life** 大谈人生的意义
philosophy /fɪˈlɒsəfi/ *n* **1** [u] (academic discipline) 哲学; **to study ～** 研究哲学 **2** [c] (philosophical theory) 哲学思想 **3** [c] (personal outlook) 理念; **my ～ of life** 我的人生哲学
phishing /ˈfɪʃɪŋ/ *n* [u] 网络诱骗
phlebitis /flɪˈbaɪtɪs/ ▸**p. 377** *n* [u] 静脉炎
phlegm /flem/ *n* [u] **1** (mucus) 痰 **2** (calm) 冷静
phlegmatic /flegˈmætɪk/ *adj* 冷静的; **to be/remain ～ about sth.** 对某事冷静/保持冷静
phlegmatically /flegˈmætɪkli/ *adv* 冷静地
Phnom Penh /ˌnɒm ˈpen/ *pr n* 金边
phobia /ˈfəʊbɪə/ *n* 恐惧症; **to have a ～ about sth.** 对某事物有恐惧症
phobic /ˈfəʊbɪk/ *adj* 有恐惧症的; **to be ～ about sth.** 惧怕某事物
phoenix /ˈfiːnɪks/ *n* 凤凰; **to rise like a ～ from the ashes** 再生
phone[1] /fəʊn/
A *n* (telephone) 电话; **to be on the ～ (to sb.)** 正在（与某人）通电话; **to talk to sb. over the ～** 与某人通电话; **to tell sb. sth. by ～** 打电话告诉某人某事; **to hear sth. over the ～** 在电话里听到某事
B *vt* 给…打电话 ‹*person, organization*›; 打电话告知 ‹*information, news*›; **to ～ France** 往法国打电话; **try phoning his home number** 试试打他家的电话
C *vi* 打电话; **to ～ for a doctor/taxi** 打电话叫医生/出租车; **he ～d for the clerk to bring in the report** 他打电话让文书把报告带来
Phrasal verbs
• **phone in**
A *vi* 打电话; **to ～ in sick** 打电话请病假
B *vt* [**～ in sth., ～ sth. in**] 打进电话告知 ‹*information, report*›
• **phone up**
A *vi* 打电话
B *vt* [**～ up sb., ～ sb. up**] 给…打电话
phone[2] *n* Ling 音素

phone: ～ bill *n* 电话费账单; **～ book** *n* 电话簿; **～ booth** *n* 电话亭; **～ box** *n* Brit 电话亭; **～ call** *n* 电话通话; **to make a ～ call** 打电话; **～ card** *n* Brit 电话卡; **～ company** *n* 电话公司; **～ directory** *n* **= ～ book**; **～-in** *n* TV 观众来电直播节目; Radio 听众来电直播节目; **～ line** *n* 电话线; **～ link** *n* 电话连接
phoneme /ˈfəʊniːm/ *n* 音位
phonemic /fəˈniːmɪk/ *adj* 音位的
phonemics /fəˈniːmɪks/ *npl + v sing* 音位学
phone: ～ number *n* 电话号码; **～ sex** *n* [u] 电话色情服务; **～ tapping** *n* [u] 电话窃听
phonetic /fəˈnetɪk/ *adj* **1** (of sounds) 语音的 **2** (of the study of sounds) 语音学的
phonetic alphabet *n* 音标
phonetician /ˌfəʊnəˈtɪʃn/ ▸**p. 409** *n* 语音学家
phonetics /fəˈnetɪks/ *npl + v sing* 语音学
phone voucher *n* 手机充值卡
phoney /ˈfəʊni/
A *adj* **1** (not genuine) 虚假的; **his ～ American accent** 他那装出来的美国口音; **a ～ story** 虚构的故事; **a ～ $10 bill** 一张 10 美元的伪钞 **2** (insincere) 虚伪的
B *n* (*pl* **phonies** *or* **～s**) 假冒者; **he's not a real scientist, he's a ～** 他不是真正的科学家，他是个冒牌货; **the necklace is a ～** 那条项链是赝品
phonic /ˈfɒnɪk/ *adj* **1** Ling 语音的 **2** (relating to phonics) 拼读法的
phonics /ˈfɒnɪks/ *npl + v sing* 拼读法
phonograph /ˈfəʊnəgrɑːf, Amer -græf/ *n* **1** Brit (early form of gramophone) 留声机 **2** Amer (record player) 电唱机
phonological /ˌfəʊnəˈlɒdʒɪkl/ *adj* 音系学的
phonologically /ˌfəʊnəˈlɒdʒɪkli/ *adv* 从音系学角度
phonologist /fəˈnɒlədʒɪst/ ▸**p. 409** *n* 音系学家
phonology /fəˈnɒlədʒi/ *n* [u] **1** (study) 音系学 **2** (sound system) 音系
phony /ˈfəʊni/ *adj, n* **= phoney**
phooey /ˈfuːi/
A *excl* 呸 [用于表示轻蔑、不信]; **he says he'll win easily — ～!** 他说他会轻松获胜——呸!
B *n* 胡扯
phosgene /ˈfɒzdʒiːn/ *n* [u] 光气
phosphate /ˈfɒsfeɪt/ *n* [c] **1** (salt) 磷酸盐; (ester) 磷酸酯 **2** [u and c] Agric 磷肥
phosphide /ˈfɒsfaɪd/ *n* 磷化物
phosphine /ˈfɒsfiːn/ *n* [u] 磷化氢
phosphoresce /ˌfɒsfəˈres/ *vi* 发磷光
phosphorescence /ˌfɒsfəˈresns/ *n* [u] **1** (light) 磷光 **2** (process) 发磷光
phosphorescent /ˌfɒsfəˈresnt/ *adj* 发磷光的
phosphoric /fɒsˈfɒrɪk, Amer -ˈfɔːr-/ *adj* (of phosphorus) 磷的; (containing phosphorus) 含磷的
phosphorous /ˈfɒsfərəs/ *adj* (of phosphorus) 磷的; (containing phosphorus) 含磷的
phosphorus /ˈfɒsfərəs/ *n* [u] 磷
photo /ˈfəʊtəʊ/
A *n* **= photograph A**
B **photo-** *combining form* 照片的
photo: ～ album *n* 相册; **～ booth** *n* 自助快照亭; **～call** *n* Brit 媒体拍照时间
photocell /ˈfəʊtəʊsel/ *n* **= photoelectric cell**
photochemical /ˌfəʊtəʊˈkemɪkl/ *adj* (of the chemical action of light) 光化作用的; (of photochemistry) 光化学的
photochemistry /ˌfəʊtəʊˈkemɪstri/ *n* [u] 光化学

photochromic /ˌfəʊtəʊˈkrəʊmɪk/ *adj* 光致色变的
photocompose /ˌfəʊtəʊkəmˈpəʊz/ *vt* 将…照相排版; **a ～d text** 照相排版文本
photocomposition /ˌfəʊtəʊˌkɒmpəˈzɪʃn/ *n* [u] 照相排版
photocopiable /fəʊtəʊˈkɒpɪəbl/ *adj* 可复印的
photocopier /ˈfəʊtəʊkɒpɪə(r)/ *n* 复印机
photocopy /ˈfəʊtəʊkɒpi/
A *n* 复印件; **to make a ～ of sth.** 复印某物
B *vt* 复印
photocopying /ˈfəʊtəʊˌkɒpiːɪŋ/ *n* [u] 复印
photoelectric /ˌfəʊtəʊɪˈlektrɪk/, **photoelectrical** /ˌfəʊtəʊɪˈlektrɪkl/ *adj* 光电的
photoelectric cell *n* 光电池
photoelectricity /ˌfəʊtəʊɪlekˈtrɪsəti/ *n* [u] 光电现象; **the phenomenon of ～** 光电现象
photoelectron /ˌfəʊtəʊɪˈlektrɒn/ *n* 光电子
photoengraving /ˌfəʊtəʊɪnˈgreɪvɪŋ/ *n* **1** [u] (process) 照相凸版制版 **2** [c] (plate) 照相凸版; (print) 照相凸版印刷品
photo: ～ finish *n* Sport (finish) 摄影定名次; (close competition) 难分胜负的竞赛; **～fit** *n* Brit 通缉犯拼像; **～flash** *n* **= flashbulb**; **～flood** *n* 照相泛光灯
photogenic /ˌfəʊtəʊˈdʒenɪk/ *adj* 上镜的; **his wife's very ～** 他的妻子非常上相
photograph /ˈfəʊtəgrɑːf, Amer -græf/
A *n* 照片; **to take a ～ of sb./sth.** 给某人/某物照相; **to be in a ～** 在相片里
B *vt* 给…拍照; **the children refused to be ～ed** 孩子们拒绝照相
C *vi* 在照片上显得; **to ～ well/badly** 上相/不上相
photograph album *n* 相册
photographer /fəˈtɒgrəfə(r)/ ▸**p. 409** *n* 摄影师
photographic /ˌfəʊtəˈgræfɪk/ *adj* 摄影的; **to have a ～ memory** 拥有过目不忘的记忆力
photographically /ˌfəʊtəˈgræfɪkli/ *adv* 在摄影方面; **～ speaking** 从摄影的角度讲
photographic library *n* 照片库
photography /fəˈtɒgrəfi/ *n* [u] (art) 摄影术; (practice) 摄影
photogravure /ˌfəʊtəʊgrəˈvjʊə(r)/ *n* **1** [u] (process) 照相凹版印刷 **2** [c] (image) 照相凹版印刷图像
photojournalism /ˌfəʊtəʊˈdʒɜːnəlɪzəm/ *n* [u] **1** (practice) 摄影新闻报道 **2** (art) 摄影新闻
photojournalist /ˌfəʊtəʊˈdʒɜːnəlɪst/ ▸**p. 409** *n* 摄影新闻记者
photo lab *n* 照相馆
photolithograph /ˌfəʊtəʊˈlɪθəgrɑːf, Amer -græf/ *n* 照相平版印刷图像
photolithography /ˌfəʊtəʊlɪˈθɒgrəfi/ *n* [u] 照相平版印刷
photomap /ˈfəʊtəʊmæp/ *n* 照相地图
photomechanical /ˌfəʊtəʊmɪˈkænɪkl/ *adj* 照相制版的
photometer /fəʊˈtɒmɪtə(r)/ *n* 光度计
photometric /ˌfəʊtəʊˈmetrɪk/ *adj* 光度测量的
photometry /fəʊˈtɒmɪtri/ *n* [u] 光度测量
photomontage /ˌfəʊtəʊmɒnˈtɑːʒ/ *n* **1** [u] (method, process) 照片合成 **2** [c] (image) 合成照片
photomultiplier /ˌfəʊtəʊˈmʌltɪplaɪə(r)/ *n* 光电倍增器
photon /ˈfəʊtɒn/ *n* 光子
photo opportunity *n* [c and u] 为名人拍照的时机
photorealism /ˌfəʊtəʊˈriːəlɪzəm/ *n* [u] **1** (in art) 照相写实主义 **2** (in non-photographic medium) 照相绘图

p

photoreceptor /ˈfəʊtəʊrɪseptə(r)/ *n* 光感受器

photoreconnaissance /ˌfəʊtəʊrɪˈkɒnɪsəns/ *n* [u] 空中照相侦察

photosensitive /ˌfəʊtəʊˈsensətɪv/ *adj* 光敏的; ～ **film** 光敏胶片

photosensitivity /ˌfəʊtəʊsensəˈtɪvɪti/ *n* [u] 光敏性

photo: ～ **session** *n* 媒体预约拍照时间; ～ **shoot** *n* [为名人、时装模特等所作的] 专业摄影

photosetting /ˈfəʊtəʊsetɪŋ/ *n* [u] = **phototypesetting**

photosphere /ˈfəʊtəʊsfɪə(r)/ *n* 光球

Photostat® /ˈfəʊtəstæt/

A *n* 直接影印件; **to make a ～ (of sth.)** 直接影印（某物）

B *vt* (*pres p etc.* **-tt-**) 用直接影印机复印

photosynthesis /ˌfəʊtəʊˈsɪnθəsɪs/ *n* [u] 光合作用

photosynthesize /ˌfəʊtəʊˈsɪnθəsaɪz/ *vi* 进行光合作用

phototype /ˈfəʊtəʊtaɪp/ *n* **1** [u] (process) 照相制版 **2** [c] (printing plate) 照相印版 **3** [c] (print) 照相制版印刷件

phototypesetting /ˌfəʊtəʊˈtaɪpsetɪŋ/ *n* [u] Amer 照相排版

phrasal /ˈfreɪzəl/ *adj attrib* (of phrases) 短语的; (composed of phrases) 词组的

phrasal verb *n* 短语动词

phrase /freɪz/

A *n* **1** (expression) 习语; **a turn of ～** 措词; **she has a neat turn of ～** 她措词巧妙; **to coin a ～** 套用一句老话 **2** (group of words) 词组; **noun ～** 名词短语 **3** Mus 乐句

B *vt* **1** (express) 表达; **a neatly ～d letter** 措词巧妙的信 **2** Mus 将…划分乐句

phrase book *n* 外语常用语手册

phraseology /ˌfreɪzɪˈɒlədʒi/ *n* [u] 措词; **the differences between English and French ～** 英语和法语在遣词造句上的不同; **the local ～** 本地用语; **that's the kind of ～ lawyers use** 那是律师使用的术语

phrase structure *n* [u] 短语结构

phrasing /ˈfreɪzɪŋ/ *n* [u] **1** Ling 措词; **I know what you mean but your ～ is awkward** 我知道你的意思，但是你的说法很别扭; **the rhythmic ～ of the verses** 那首诗抑扬顿挫的节奏 **2** Mus 乐句划分法

phreak /friːk/ *n* esp Amer colloq 电话飞客 [非法闯入通信系统、特别是盗打电话的人]

phreaking /ˈfriːkɪŋ/ *n* [u] esp Amer colloq 非法侵入通信系统

phut /fʌt/ *excl* 啪的一声; **to go ～** colloq (fail to work properly) 坏掉; (fail to work at all) 完蛋; **my hopes and plans — all gone ～!** 我的希望和计划——全告吹了!

phylogenesis /ˌfaɪləʊˈdʒenəsɪs/ *n* [u] 种系发生

phylogenetic /ˌfaɪləʊdʒɪˈnetɪk/, **phylogenic** /ˌfaɪləʊˈdʒenɪk/ *adjs* 种系发生的

phylogeny /faɪˈlɒdʒɪni/ *n* [u] **1** (branch of biology) 种系发生学 **2** = **phylogenesis**

phylum /ˈfaɪləm/ *n* (*pl* **phyla** /ˈfaɪlə/) **1** Zool 门 **2** Ling 语群

physical /ˈfɪzɪkl/

A *adj* **1** (relating to the body) 身体的; ～ **beauty** 形体美; **a ～ check-up** 体检; **to get ～** colloq (become violent) 动武; (become sexually intimate) 动手动脚 **2** (involving bodily contact) 有身体接触的; **a ～ relationship** 性关系 **3** (relating to the concretely existing world) 物质的; **the ～ properties of iron** 铁的物理性质; **the ～ laws that govern the universe** 宇宙中的自然规律; **the ～ environment** 自然环境; ～ **assets** 实物资产; **the ～ size of a computer** 计算机的实际大小

B *n* = **physical examination; to have/go for a ～** 进行/去体检

physical: ～ **anthropology** *n* [u] 体质人类学; ～ **chemistry** *n* [u] 物理化学; ～ **education** *n* [u] 体育; ～ **examination** *n* 体检; ～ **fitness** *n* [u] 身体健康; ～ **geography** *n* [u] 自然地理学; ～ **jerks** *npl* Brit colloq dated 体操

physically /ˈfɪzɪklɪ/ *adv* 身体上; **I felt ～ sick** 我感到身体不适; **he doesn't attract me ～** 我不觉得他长得帅; **it's ～ impossible to get to the airport before 8 am** 上午8点之前赶到机场非人力所及

physical: ～ **sciences** *npl* 自然科学; ～ **therapist** ▸**p. 409** *n* Amer = **physiotherapist**; ～ **therapy** *n* [u] Amer = **physiotherapy**; ～ **training** *n* [u] 体育锻炼

physician /fɪˈzɪʃn/ ▸**p. 409** *n* (doctor) 医生; (specialist in diagnosis and medical treatment) 内科医师

physicist /ˈfɪzɪsɪst/ ▸**p. 409** *n* (expert) 物理学家; (student) 物理专业学生

physics /ˈfɪzɪks/ *npl + v sing* **1** (science) 物理学 **2** (physical properties) 物理特性

physio /ˈfɪzɪəʊ/ *n* Brit esp Sport colloq **1** [c] (*pl* **～s**) = **physiotherapist** **2** [u] = **physiotherapy**

physiognomy /ˌfɪzɪˈɒnəmi, Amer -ˈɒgnəmi/ *n* **1** [c] Anat 容貌; **the ～ of the Australian aborigine** 澳大利亚土著居民的面貌特征 **2** [u] (general form, appearance) 外貌; **the ～ of Europe** 欧洲的地貌

physiological /ˌfɪzɪəˈlɒdʒɪkl/ *adj* 生理学的 ‹*theory, research*›; 生理的 ‹*effect, process, change*›

physiologist /ˌfɪzɪˈɒlədʒɪst/ ▸**p. 409** *n* (expert) 生理学家; (student) 生理学专业学生

physiology /ˌfɪzɪˈɒlədʒi/ *n* [u] **1** (branch of biology) 生理学 **2** (physiological functioning) 生理机能

physiotherapist /ˌfɪzɪəʊˈθerəpɪst/ ▸**p. 409** *n* 理疗师

physiotherapy /ˌfɪzɪəʊˈθerəpi/ *n* [u] 物理疗法

physique /fɪˈziːk/ *n* 体格; **to build up one's ～** 锻炼身体

phytoplankton /ˌfaɪtəʊˈplæŋktən/ *n* [u] + *v sing or pl* 浮游植物

pi /paɪ/ *n* [u] 圆周率

pianist /ˈpɪənɪst/ ▸**p. 395, p. 409** *n* (professional) 钢琴家; (enthusiast) 钢琴演奏者

piano /pɪˈænəʊ/ ▸**p. 395** *n* 钢琴; **to play/learn/tune the ～** 弹/学/调钢琴; **to be accompanied by sb. at** *or* **on the ～** 由某人担任钢琴伴奏

piano accordion ▸**p. 395** *n* 键盘式手风琴

pianoforte /pɪˌænəʊˈfɔːteɪ, -ti/ ▸**p. 395** *n* formal = **piano**

piano: ～ **player** *n* 钢琴演奏者; ～ **stool** *n* 琴凳

pic /pɪk/ *n* colloq (photograph) 照片; (film) 影片

pica /ˈpaɪkə/ *n* 12 点活字

picaresque /ˌpɪkəˈresk/ *adj* 流浪汉小说题材的; **a ～ novel** 一部流浪汉小说

piccalilli /ˌpɪkəˈlɪli/ *n* [u] 酸辣泡菜

piccaninny /ˌpɪkəˈnɪni/ *n* dated offensive (black child) 小黑鬼 offensive; (Australian Aboriginal child) 澳大利亚土著小孩

piccolo /ˈpɪkələʊ/ ▸**p. 395** *n* (*pl* **～s**) **1** (musical instrument) 短笛 **2** (player) 短笛吹奏者

pick /pɪk/

A *vt* **1** (choose, select) 挑选 ‹*object, colour*›; 选择 ‹*candidate, place*›; **have you ～ed a name for the baby yet?** 你给宝宝取名了吗?; **to be ～ed for the Olympic Games** 入选参加奥运会; **to ～ the winner** Horse racing 投注获胜的马; **he certainly** *or* **sure knows how to ～ them!** colloq 他可真会选!; **to ～ a fight (with sb.)** (向某人) 挑衅; **to ～ one's way** 择路而行 **2** (pluck, gather) 采摘 ‹*flowers, vegetables*›; **we ～ed apples from** *or* **off the trees** 我们从树上摘苹果 **3** (grasp and move) 拿起; **to ～ a book off the shelf** 从书架上取下书; **I ～ed all the cherries off the top of the cake** 我拣走了蛋糕顶上所有的樱桃; **a helicopter ～ed him off his boat** 一架直升机把他从船上吊了起来; **she ～ed the baby out of his pram** 她把婴儿从婴儿车里抱了出来 **4** (poke at) 剔; **to ～ one's teeth/nose** 剔牙/挖鼻孔; **don't ～ your spot/scab** 不要抠粉刺/结痂; **to ～ sth. off** 去除某物; **to ～ a hole in sth.** 把某物抠出一个洞; **to ～ holes in sth.** fig 寻找某事的漏洞 **5** (steal from) **to ～ sb.'s pocket** 掏某人的兜儿 **6** (work open) 撬开 ‹*lock*›

B *vi* **1** (choose) 挑选; **to ～ and choose** 精挑细选 **2** (poke) 戳; **the hens were ～ing about** 母鸡到处啄食; **don't ～!** 别抠!

C *n* **1** (tool) (for breaking up hard ground) 鹤嘴锄; (used by climber, geologist) 尖嘴镐 **2** *sing* (choice) 选择; **to take one's ～** 进行挑选; **to have one's ～ of sth.** 有某事物的选择权 **3** colloq (best person) 精英; (best thing) 精品; **the ～ of sth.** 某事物中的极品

Phrasal verbs

- **pick at**

A [～ **at sth.**] *vt*

1 (eat in small amounts) 小口吃 ‹*food, meal*› **2** (poke at) 抠 ‹*scab, sore*›; (pull) 扯 ‹*fabric*›

B [～ **at sb.**] *vt* esp Amer = **pick on 1**

- **pick off** *vt* [～ **sb. off,** ～ **off sb.**] 单独射杀 ‹*person, animal*›

- **pick on** *vt* **1** [～ **on sb.**] (victimize) 欺负; (criticize) 数落; **～ on someone your own size!** 别以大欺小! **2** [～ **on sb./sth.**] (select) 选中 ‹*person, item*›; **to ～ on sb. to do sth.** 选中某人做某事; **to ～ on sb. for sth.** 为某事选中某人

- **pick out** *vt* [～ **sb./sth. out,** ～ **out sb./sth.**]

1 (select) 选中 **2** (make out, distinguish) 分辨出 ‹*distant object, landmark*›; 认出 ‹*person, suspect*›; **you can just ～ out the church tower** 你刚刚能看得见教堂塔楼 **3** Mus 慢慢弹奏出 ‹*tune, melody*› **4** (highlight) 突出显示; **the title was ～ed out in bold type** 标题采用粗体字加以突出; **letters ～ed out in red on a black background** 黑色背景下醒目的红字 **5** (illuminate) «*light, torch*» 照见 ‹*person, object*›

- **pick over** *vt* [～ **sth. over,** ～ **over sth.**] 挑拣 ‹*articles, rubbish*›; 挑选 ‹*lentils, fruit, raisins*›

- **pick up**

A [～ **sb./sth. up,** ～ **up sb./sth.**] *vt*

1 (lift, take hold of) 拿起 ‹*object*›; 抱起 ‹*child*›; 捡起 ‹*litter*›; **if you need me, just ～ up the telephone** 如果需要帮忙，就给我打电话; **to ～ up the pieces** 收拾残局; **to ～ up the tab** *or* **bill** 付账 **2** (take on board) 搭载 ‹*hitchhiker, passenger*›; 装载 ‹*supplies, cargo*› **3** (collect) 取回 ‹*dry-cleaning, ticket, keys*›; 接 ‹*person*›; **my father's ～ing me up at the airport/station** 我父亲要来机场/车站接我 **4** (illuminate) «*person, light*» 照见 ‹*person, animal, object*›; (focus on) «*camera*» 聚焦于 ‹*person, animal, object*›

B [～ **sth. up,** ～ **up sth.**] *vt*

1 (buy) 买到; **to ～ up a casual/hasty purchase** 随便/匆忙买点东西; **she ～ed the trousers up for a fiver** 她花5英镑买了条裤子 **2** (learn, acquire) 学会 ‹*language*›; 掌握 ‹*knowledge, skill*›; 养成 ‹*habit*› **3** Med 患上; **to ～ up a fever/chill** 发烧/着凉 **4** Radio, Telecom 接收 ‹*broadcast, message, signal*›; **the train ～s up current from the live rail** 火车从带电铁轨中取电 **5** (notice, register) «*person, device, sensor*» 发现 ‹*fault, defect, sign*›;

«*person*» 走上 ‹*route*›; **to ~ up a hint** 领悟暗示; **to ~ up the sound of sth.** 听见某物的声音; **to ~ up the road/motorway** 开上公路/高速公路; **to ~ up a scent/trail** 嗅到气味/发现踪迹 6 (resume) 恢复 ‹*career, relationship*›; **I'd like to ~ up the point that Dave made earlier** 我想回到戴夫先前提出的论点 7 (gain, earn) 获得 ‹*award, qualification*› 8 (increase) 加快 ‹*speed*›

C [**~ sb. up, ~ up sb.**] *vt*
1 (rescue) «*person, helicopter, ship*» 解救 ‹*survivor, casualty*› 2 colloq esp pej (strike up relationship with) 与…勾搭; **he ~ed her up in the pub/at a dance** 他在酒吧/舞会上搭上了她 3 colloq (arrest) 抓获 ‹*suspect, wanted person*› 4 (find fault with) 挑…的毛病; **to ~ sb. up on sth.** 在某事上找某人的碴子 5 (make feel better) «*medicine, treatment*» 使好转; «*food*» 使恢复精力; «*drink*» 给…提神

D *vi* 1 (improve) «*trade, business*» 改善; «*invalid, weather*» 好转 2 (increase) «*speed*» 提高; «*activity*» 增加; **the wind has ~ed up** 风大了起来 3 (resume) «*person*» 重新开始; «*machine*» 重新启动; **to ~ up on sth.** 重提 ‹*point, remark*›; 恢复 ‹*attitude, atmosphere*› 4 (take a call) 接听 5 esp Amer colloq (tidy up) 收拾; **to ~ up after sb.** 跟在某人后面收拾

E *v refl* **to ~ oneself up** (get up) [跌倒后] 爬起来; fig (recover) 振作; **she ~ed herself up after the divorce** 她从离婚的打击中恢复过来

pick-and-mix *adj* Brit 组合的; **a ~ programme of study** 综合课程

pickaninny /ˌpɪkəˈnɪni/ *n* Amer dated offensive **= piccaninny**

pickaxe Brit, **pickax** Amer /ˈpɪkæks/ *n* 鹤嘴锄

picker /ˈpɪkə(r)/ *n* (person) 采摘者; (machine) 采摘机; **a mechanical cotton ~** 采棉机

picket /ˈpɪkɪt/
A *n* 1 (in strike) (group of people) 纠察队; (one person) 纠察员 2 (blockade) 纠察; **to form a ~** 设置纠察 3 (soldier on watch) 警戒哨; (detachment on watch) 警戒队 4 (stake) 尖木桩
B *vt* (protest outside) 在…外抗议; (stand outside to persuade others not to enter) 在…外罢工
C *vi* (protest outside) 在外抗议; (stand outside to persuade others not to enter) 在外罢工

picket fence *n* 尖桩篱栅

picketing /ˈpɪkɪtɪŋ/ *n* [u] 罢工纠察的设置

picket line *n* (of striking workers) 纠察线; (of protesters) 抗议的人墙

pickings /ˈpɪkɪŋz/ *npl* 1 (profits, gains) 油水; **there'll be slim ~ for us on this job** 我们干这个工作赚不到什么油水; **easy ~** 横财 2 (leftovers) 残羹剩饭

pickle /ˈpɪkl/
A *n* 1 [c and u] (preserved food) 泡菜; **salad, cold meat and ~(s)** 色拉、冷肉和腌菜 2 [c] colloq (difficult situation) 困境; **to be in/to get into a ~ (over sb./sth.)** （在某人/某事方面）处于/陷入困境
B *vt* 腌渍

pickled /ˈpɪkld/ *adj* 1 Culin 腌渍的; **~ onions** 腌洋葱 2 colloq (drunk) 醉醺醺的; **he is totally ~** 他喝得酩酊大醉

picklock /ˈpɪklɒk/ *n* 1 (instrument) 撬锁工具 2 (burglar) 撬锁贼

pick-me-up *n* colloq 兴奋剂; **a cup of tea is a good ~ after a hard day's work** 劳作一天之后喝杯茶可以很好地提神; **the holiday acted as a wonderful ~** 这次度假让人精神焕发

pick 'n' mix *adj* **= pick-and-mix**

pickpocket /ˈpɪkpɒkɪt/ *n* 扒手

pickup /ˈpɪkʌp/ *n* 1 [c] **= pickup truck** 2 [c] (improvement in trade, profits) 好转; **the recent ~ in orders** 最近订单的增多 3 [u and c] (collection by lorry, bus) (of goods) 提货; (of passenger) 接人 4 [c] (arm of record player) 唱头 5 [c] (transducer) 拾音器 6 [c] (collection by spy, drug runner) 秘密收取物品 7 [c] colloq (sexual partner) 勾搭上的人

pickup: ~ arm *n* 唱臂; **~ point** *n* (for passengers) 搭车处; (for goods) 收取处; **~ truck**, Brit **~ van** *ns* 轻型货车

picky /ˈpɪki/ *adj* colloq 挑剔的; **a ~ eater** 挑食的人; **he's a very ~ sort of person** 他是那种吹毛求疵的人

pick-your-own
A *adj attrib* 自行采摘的 ‹*fruit, vegetables*›; 供人采摘的 ‹*farm*›
B *n* 自行采摘农场

picnic /ˈpɪknɪk/
A *n* 1 (outing, occasion) 野餐; **to go for** *or* **on a ~** 去野餐; **to have a ~** 野餐 2 (meal) 野餐食物; **to make** *or* **pack a ~** 准备野餐食物; **it's no ~!** colloq 这不是件轻松愉快的事!
B *vi* (*pres p etc.* **-ck-**) 去野餐; **to ~ off sth.** 野餐吃某物

picnic: ~ area *n* 野餐区; **~ hamper** *n* [带提手和盖子的] 野餐篮

picnicker /ˈpɪknɪkə(r)/ *n* 野餐者

Pict /pɪkt/ *n* Hist 皮克特人 [罗马人统治时期居住在苏格兰北部]

pictograph /ˈpɪktəgrɑːf, Amer -græf/, **pictogram** /ˈpɪktəgræm/ *ns* 1 (symbol) 象形文字 2 (on chart, graph) 统计图表

pictorial /pɪkˈtɔːrɪəl/
A *adj* 1 (illustrated) 有插图的; **a ~ calendar** 有图片的日历 2 (relating to painting or drawing) 绘画的 3 (graphic) 形象化的; **a ~ description of the fight** 对战斗的生动描述
B *n* dated 画报

pictorially /pɪkˈtɔːrɪəli/ *adv* 用图表示地; **the photos told the whole story ~** 这些照片形象地讲述了整个故事

picture /ˈpɪktʃə(r)/
A *n* 1 (visual depiction) 图画; **to paint** *or* **draw a ~ of sb./sth.** 绘制某人/某物的画像; **family ~s** 亲族画像; **the book is almost all ~s and no text** 这本书里几乎都是插图，没有文字 2 Phot 照片; **to take a ~ of sth./sb.** 给某物/某人拍照 3 TV 图像 4 Cin 电影; **to make a ~** 拍摄电影; **it won several awards, including 'best ~'** 它获得了好几个奖项，包括最佳影片奖 5 (mental image) 印象; **to be the ~ of health** 显得非常健康; **he's the ~ of his father** dated 他长得酷似他父亲 6 fig (description) 描述; **to give** *or* **present a vivid/accurate ~ of sth.** 生动/准确地描述某物; **to paint** *or* **draw a bleak/gloomy/optimistic ~ of sth.** 把某物描绘得一片暗淡/惨淡/光明 7 (overview) 情形; **that's only part of the ~** 那只是部分情况; **to get the ~** colloq 明白; **to be in the ~** 了解情况; **to put** *or* **keep sb. in the ~** 让某人了解情况 8 (beautiful sight) 美景; (unusual sight) 不寻常的景色; **to be** *or* **look a ~** 漂亮; **her face was a ~!** 她显得非常震惊!
B pictures *npl* 1 esp Brit (cinema show) **the ~s** 电影院; **to go to the ~s** 去看电影; **what's on at the ~s?** 电影院在上映什么影片? 2 (film industry) 电影业; **to be in the ~s** 从事电影业
C *vt* 1 (represent in picture) 在照片上显示 ‹*person, scene, place*› 2 (form mental image of) 想象 ‹*person, scene, situation*› 3 (describe) 描写 ‹*person, series of events*›

picture: ~ book *n* 图画书; **~ card** *n* 1 (illustrated card) 画片; 2 (in pack of cards) **= court card**; **~ desk** *n* 图片编辑部; **~ editor** ▸ p. 409 *n* 图片编辑; **~ frame** *n* 画框; **~ framer** ▸ p. 409 *n* 配画框的人; **~ framing** *n* [u] 配画框; **~ gallery** *n* 画廊; **~ hook** *n* 画钩; **~ postcard** *n* 美术明信片; **~ rail** *n* 挂画线

picturesque /ˌpɪktʃəˈresk/ *adj* 1 (visually attractive) 如画的 ‹*scene, village, view*› 2 (vivid, colourful) 生动的 ‹*language, speech*›

picturesquely /ˌpɪktʃəˈreskli/ *adv* 1 (attractively) 如画地 2 (vividly, colourfully) 生动地

picture: ~ window *n* 大观景窗; **~ wire** *n* [u] 挂画用金属线; **~ writing** *n* [u] 1 (mode of recording) 图画记载法; 2 (pictography) 象形文字

piddle /ˈpɪdl/ colloq
A *vi* 撒尿
B *n* 1 [u] (urine) 尿 2 [c] (urinating) 撒尿; **to go for a ~** 去小便

piddling /ˈpɪdlɪŋ/ *adj* colloq (trivial) 琐碎的; (of trifling importance) 微不足道的; **a ~ salary** 微薄的薪水; **a ~ little village** 不起眼的小村庄

pidgin /ˈpɪdʒɪn/ *n* [u] 混杂语; **~ English** 洋泾浜英语

pie /paɪ/ *n* [c and u] 馅饼; **apple ~** 苹果派; **~ in the sky** 空中楼阁; **all these promises are just ~ in the sky** 所有这些承诺都是空头支票; **to want a piece of the ~** 想要得到一份; **all her sisters want a piece of the ~** 她的姐妹都想分一杯羹; **to have a finger in every ~** fig 凡事插手; **to be as easy as ~** 极其容易; **to be as nice as ~** 和颜悦色; **to eat humble ~** 赔礼道歉

piebald /ˈpaɪbɔːld/
A *adj* (having two colours) 双色花斑的; (black and white) 黑白两色的 ‹*horse, pony*›
B *n* (horse) 花斑马; (other animal) 花斑动物

piece /piːs/ *n* 1 (portion, fragment) 块; **a ~ of wood/glass/metal** 一块木头/玻璃/金属; **to give sb. a ~ of one's mind** fig 对某人表示不满 2 (slice) 片; **a ~ of cake/bread** 一片蛋糕/面包 3 (length) 段; **a ~ of rope/string/ribbon** 一根绳子/细绳/丝带 4 (sheet) 张; **a ~ of paper/cardboard** 一张纸/硬纸板 5 (unit, item, instance) 件; **a ~ of poetry/luck/sculpture/history/music** 一首诗/一桩幸事/一件雕塑/一段历史/一支曲子; **a superb ~ of fielding/horsemanship** 一记精彩的接球/一场精彩的骑术表演; **to pay/sell by the ~** 按件付款/销售; **a ~ of work** 一件作品; **to be in one ~** «*object*» 完好如初; «*person*» 安然无恙; **to be (all) of a ~ (with sth.)** «*objects*» （与某物）（完全）相仿; «*attitudes, opinions*» （与某情况）（完全）一致; **to say one's ~** 发表意见; **a nine-~ band** 由 9 件乐器组成的乐队 6 (component, part) 部件; **a jigsaw with 300 ~s** 一副 300 片的拼图玩具; **the ~s were all in place, and he was about to name the guilty person** 线索都已找到，他也即将确定谁是罪犯; **~ by ~** 逐个地; **to come to ~s** 被拆散; **to go to ~s** 精神崩溃; **to take sth. to ~s** 把某物拆开; **to pull** *or* **pick sth. to ~s** lit 把某物撕成碎片; fig 把某事批得体无完肤 7 (broken fragment) 碎片; **in ~s** 破碎了的; **to ~s** 成碎片; **to fall to ~s** lit 破碎; fig 崩溃 8 (coin) 硬币; **a 50p ~** 一枚面值 50 便士的硬币; **30 ~s of silver** Hist 30 枚银币 9 (in chess, draughts) 棋子 10 (gun) 枪; (cannon) 炮; **an artillery ~** esp Amer colloq 大炮 11 colloq (woman) 女人; **who's the sexy ~ in the red frock?** 那个穿红色连衣裙的风骚娘们儿是谁?; **it's some fancy ~ he picked up at a party in London** pej 那是他在伦敦聚会上结识的狐狸精

Phrasal verb

• **piece together** *vt* [**~ sth. together, ~ together sth.**]
1 (assemble) 拼合 ‹*jigsaw, vase, fragments*› 2 fig (make sense of) 厘清 ‹*evidence, facts*›; 把…拼凑完整 ‹*story*›

pièce de résistance /ˌpjes də reˈzɪstɑːns, Amer -ˌreziˈstɑːns/ *n* (*pl* **pièces de résistance** /ˌpjes də reˈzɪstɑːns, Amer -ˌreziˈstɑːns/) (masterpiece) 代表作品; (main course) 主菜

piecemeal /ˈpiːsmiːl/
A *adj* 零碎的; **~ changes** 零星的变化; **a ~ approach** 全无章法的方式

p

B *adv* 一点一点地; **to deal with matters ~** 零敲碎打地处理问题

piece: ~work *n* [u] 计件工作; **~work wages** 计件工资; **~worker** *n* 计件工人

pie: ~ chart *n* 饼形图; **~ crust** *n* 馅饼皮

pied /paɪd/ *adj* (having two colours) 双色的; (having many colours) 杂色的

pied-à-terre /ˌpjeɪd ɑː ˈteə(r)/ *n* (*pl* **pieds-à-terre** /ˌpjeɪd ɑː ˈteə(r)/) 备用房

pie: ~ dish *n* 馅饼盘; **~-eyed** *adj* colloq 喝醉了的

pier /pɪə(r)/ *n* **1** Brit (promenade jutting out into the sea) [通常设有娱乐和餐饮场所的] 突堤 **2** (landing stage) 凸式码头 **3** (pillar) 支柱; **the ~s of a bridge** 桥墩

pierce /pɪəs/ *vt* **1** (make hole in) 穿孔于; **to have one's ears ~d** 打耳洞; **to ~ a hole in** *or* **through sth.** 刺穿某物; **the machine ~s small holes in the plastic sheets** 机器在塑料片上扎出许多小孔 **2** fig (penetrate) «*voice*» 穿透; «*wind*» 穿过; «*light*» 透过; «*eyes, look*» 洞悉; **her screams ~d the night air** 她的尖叫声划破了夜空; **the cold ~d their bones** 他们感到寒冷彻骨; **her heart was ~d by pain** 她心如刀割

piercing /ˈpɪəsɪŋ/ *adj* 尖厉的 ‹*scream, voice*›; 刺骨的 ‹*cold, wind*›; 刺眼的 ‹*light*›; 敏锐的 ‹*eyes, look*›; **a smile of ~ sweetness** 甜美动人的微笑

piercingly /ˈpɪəsɪŋli/ *adv* 尖厉地 ‹*scream*›; 敏锐地 ‹*look*›; 刺骨地 ‹*cold*›

piety /ˈpaɪəti/ *n* [u] 虔诚

piezoelectric /piːˌeɪzəʊɪˈlektrɪk/ *adj* 压电的

piezoelectricity /piːˌeɪzəʊˌɪlekˈtrɪsəti/ *n* [u] 压电

piffle /ˈpɪfl/ *n* [u] colloq 废话; **to talk ~** 胡说八道

piffling /ˈpɪflɪŋ/ *adj* colloq 微不足道的

pig /pɪg/

A *n* **1** [c] (domesticated animal) 猪; **to buy a ~ in a poke** 未看货就买下; **~s might fly!** Brit iron 猪也会飞了! [表示完全不可信]; **to live like ~s** 邋遢地生活; **in a ~'s eye!** esp Amer colloq 鬼才信呢! ; **to make a ~'s ear (out) of sth.** Brit colloq 把某事物弄得一团糟; **~ in the middle** esp Brit ▸**piggy A**; **to be in ~** «*sow*» 怀胎; **the ~ family** 猪科 **2** [c] (wild animal) 野猪; **to bleed like a stuck ~** 血流如注; **to go ~-sticking** 去打野猪 **3** [u] (as meat) 猪肉 **4** [c] colloq pej (objectionable, dirty person) 肮脏的人; (unpleasant, greedy person) 贪婪的人; **to make a ~ of oneself** (eat excessively) 大吃大喝; (overindulge) 过分放纵自己 **5** [c] pej (police officer) **the ~s** 猪猡 [对警察的蔑称] **6** [c] Brit colloq (difficult task) 苦差事; **a ~ of a job** 棘手的工作 **7** [u] **= pig iron** **8** [c] (oblong mass of iron or lead) 铸块

B *vt* colloq **1** (live in squalor) **to ~ it** 过猪一般的邋遢生活 **2** (gorge oneself) **to ~ it** 狼吞虎咽地吃

C *v refl* colloq **to ~ oneself (on sth.)** 狼吞虎咽地吃(某物)

Phrasal verb

• **pig out** *vi* colloq 狼吞虎咽地吃; **to ~ out on sth.** 狼吞虎咽地吃某物

pigeon /ˈpɪdʒɪn/ *n* 鸽子; **to put** *or* **set the cat among the ~s** fig 招惹麻烦

pigeon fancier *n* 鸽子迷

pigeon-hole

A *n* **1** (in desk, office) 文件格; **leave a note for me in my ~** 在我的信件格里给我留张便条 **2** (for pigeon) 鸽巢 **3** (category) 种类; **to find a ~ for sb./sth.** 把某人/某事物归类

B *vt* **1** (categorize) 把…分类; **he ~d the new recruits as 'good' or 'bad'** 他把新招募的人员分为"优"和"劣"两类 **2** (deposit document, letter etc.) 把…放入文件格 **3** (put aside) 搁置; **the boss had ~d his report** 老板将他的报告束之高阁

pigeon: ~ house, ~ loft *ns* (building) 鸽舍; (shed) 鸽棚; **~ post** *n* [u] 信鸽邮政; **~ racing** *n* [u] 赛鸽; **~-toed** /ˈpɪdʒɪnˌtəʊd/ *adj* 足内翻的; **he is ~-toed** 他走路内八字

pig: ~ farm *n* 养猪场; **~ farmer** ▸**p. 409** *n* 猪农; **~ farming** *n* [u] 养猪

piggery /ˈpɪgəri/ *n* 养猪场

piggish /ˈpɪgɪʃ/ *adj* 似猪的; **what a ~ way to behave!** 那样做真贪婪! ; **to be in a ~ mood** 情绪不好

piggy /ˈpɪgi/

A *n* child lang 猪猪; **~ in the middle** esp Brit (game) 夹缝抢球游戏; fig (person) 左右为难的人

B *adj* 似猪的; **to have little ~ eyes** 长着猪眼似的小眼睛

piggyback /ˈpɪgɪbæk/

A *n* **1** **~ (ride)** (on sb. else's back) 背驮; (on sb. else's shoulders) 肩扛; **to give sb. a ~** 背某人 **2** Rail, Aerosp 背负式装运; **a ~ load** 背负式载运

B *adv* **1** (on sb. else's back) 在背上; (on sb. else's shoulders) 在肩上; **to carry sb. ~** 背某人 **2** fig (on truck, vehicle) 背负式地

C *vi* 附带发生; **to ~ on sth.** «*plan, expenditure*» 附带在某物上

piggy bank *n* **1** (money box) [尤指猪形的] 储蓄罐 **2** fig (savings) 储蓄

pig-headed *adj* 固执的

pig-headedly *adv* 固执地

pig-headedness *n* [u] 固执

pig: ~-ignorant *adj* colloq (stupid) 极其愚蠢的; (crude) 非常粗鄙的; **~ iron** *n* [u] 生铁

piglet /ˈpɪglɪt/ *n* 小猪

pigment /ˈpɪgmənt/ *n* **1** (colouring) 色素 **2** (substance) 颜料

pigmentation /ˌpɪgmənˈteɪʃn/ *n* [u] 天然颜色; **variations in human ~** 人类肤色的差异

pigmented /ˈpɪgməntɪd/ *adj* 天然色的; **people with ~ skin** 有色人种; **highly ~** 颜色鲜艳的

pigmy /ˈpɪgmi/ *n* **= pygmy A**

pig: ~-out *n* colloq 一顿大吃; **~pen** *n* Amer **= ~sty**; **~skin** *n* [u] 猪皮革; **a ~skin travelling case** 猪皮旅行箱; **~sty** *n* **1** (pen) 猪圈; **2** colloq (dirty, untidy place) 肮脏的地方; **his room is a ~sty** 他的房间像个猪圈; **~swill** *n* [u] **1** (food for pigs) 泔脚; **2** colloq (unpalatable food) 难吃的食物; **~tail** *n* 辫子; **to wear one's hair in ~tails** 把头发梳成辫子

pike[1] /paɪk/ *n* Hist (weapon) 长矛

pike[2] *n* (*pl* **pike**) (fish) 狗鱼

pike[3] *n* Brit Sport 屈体 [跳水和体操动作]

pikestaff /ˈpaɪkstɑːf, Amer -stæf/ *n* **as plain as a ~** 显而易见的

pilaster /pɪˈlæstə(r)/ *n* 壁柱

pilchard /ˈpɪltʃəd/ *n* 沙丁鱼

pile /paɪl/

A *n* **1** (untidy heap) 堆; **a ~ of stones/dirty clothes/cigarette ash** 一堆石头/脏衣服/烟灰; **to make a ~ of sth., to put sth. in a ~** 把某物堆成一堆; **to be at the top/bottom of the ~** 处于顶层/底层; **to stay (at the) top of the ~** fig 保持长盛不衰 **2** (stack) (of books, magazines, clothes) 摞; (of paper, documents) 沓; (of dishes) 叠; **to sort sth. into ~s** 把某物整理成一摞一摞的; **to put sth. in a ~** 把某物摞起来 **3** colloq (large amount) 大量; **~s** *or* **a ~ of sth.** 大量某物; **to make a** *or* **one's ~ (doing sth./out of sth.)** (做某事/从某事物中) 赚大钱 **4** colloq hum (grand building) 宏伟建筑; **a Georgian ~** 乔治王朝时期的雄伟建筑 **5** Tex (soft surface) 绒面; **a carpet with a deep ~** 厚绒地毯 **6** Constr (part of foundation) (of building) 桩基; (of bridge) 桥墩 **7** Elec (dry battery) 电池组

B *vt* **1** (put into pile) 叠放 ‹*dishes*›; 堆放 ‹*logs, food*›; 把…放成一摞 ‹*books, papers*›; **to ~ sth. on top of sth.** 把某物堆放在某物上面; **to ~ coal on (to) the fire** 给炉火加煤; **to ~ sth. into a stack** 把某物堆成一堆 **2** colloq (heap haphazardly) 胡乱堆放; **to ~ sth. into sth.** 胡乱地把某物塞进某物 **3** (load) 堆满; **to be ~d with sth.** «*desk, floor, room*» 堆满某物

C *vi* **1** colloq (move en masse) 拥挤; **they ~d through the gate/towards the exits** 他们蜂拥穿过大门/挤向出口; **they ~d on to/off the bus** 他们一窝蜂地上了/下了公交车 **2** (crash) **to ~ into sth.** «*vehicle, driver*» 撞上某物

Phrasal verbs

• **pile on** *vt* [**~ on sth., ~ sth. on**]
1 (heap on) 把…堆起来 ‹*objects, clothes, coal*› **2** colloq (intensify for effect) 夸大 ‹*pathos, nostalgia*›; **he really knows how to ~ on the charm** 他对如何展示魅力颇有心得; **to ~ it on** 夸大其词; **to ~ on the agony** 过分渲染悲痛

• **pile up**

A *vt* [**~ sth. up, ~ up sth.**]
1 (put into pile) 堆积 **2** (load) 堆在…上 ‹*table, floor*›; 堆在…里 ‹*room*›; **the yard was ~d up with rubbish** 院子里堆满了垃圾 **3** fig (accumulate) 积压 ‹*work, problems, debts*›; 累积 ‹*losses, profits*›; 积累 ‹*evidence, reasons*›

B *vi* **1** (form into pile) «*papers, rubbish, snow*» 堆积 **2** fig (accumulate) «*work, problems, debts*» 积压; «*losses, profits*» 累积; «*facts, evidence, clues*» 积累; **to ~ up on sb.** 积聚到某人身上 **3** (crash) «*vehicles*» 撞毁

pile: ~ driver *n* **1** (machine) 打桩机; **2** Brit colloq (punch) 重击; **~ dwelling** *n* [史前时期的] 湖上木排屋; **~ fabric** *n* [u] 起绒织物; **~-up** *n* 多车相撞; **the thick fog has caused several bad ~-ups** 大雾造成了几起严重的连环撞车事故

piles /paɪlz/ *npl* **= haemorrhoids**

pilfer /ˈpɪlfə(r)/

A *vt* 偷窃; **to ~ sth. from sth./sb.** 从某处/某人处偷窃某物

B *vi* 小偷小摸

pilferage /ˈpɪlfərɪdʒ/ *n* [u] 失窃量

pilferer /ˈpɪlfərə(r)/ *n* 小偷

pilfering /ˈpɪlfərɪŋ/ *n* [u] 小偷小摸

pilgrim /ˈpɪlgrɪm/ *n* 朝圣者

pilgrimage /ˈpɪlgrɪmɪdʒ/ *n* **1** Relig 朝圣; **to go on** *or* **make a ~ (to somewhere)** (到某处) 去朝圣 **2** fig (journey) 瞻仰之旅; **his grave has become a place of ~** 他的陵墓成了参拜之地

Pilgrim Fathers /ˌpɪlgrɪm ˈfɑːðəz/ *npl* **the ~** [最初为逃避宗教迫害从英国到北美洲拓殖的] 清教徒前辈移民

pill /pɪl/ *n* **1** (round drug) 药丸; (flat drug) 药片; **to take a ~** 吃一粒药; **to sugar** *or* **sweeten the ~** fig 使不愉快的事变得较易接受; **a bitter ~ (for sb. to swallow)** fig (某人不得不承受的) 苦事; **the election defeat came as a bitter ~ for the party** 选举失败是该党难以下咽的苦果 **2** (contraceptive) 口服避孕药; **to be/go on the ~** 服用/开始服用避孕药; **to come off the ~** 停服避孕药

pillage /ˈpɪlɪdʒ/

A *vt* [尤指战争中] 劫掠 ‹*town, land, countryside*›

B *vi* 劫掠

C *n* [u] 劫掠

pillar /ˈpɪlə(r)/ *n* **1** Archit 柱子; **to go** *or* **rush from ~ to post** fig 四处奔走 **2** (tall, narrow thing) 柱状物; **a ~ of smoke** 烟柱 **3** (reliable person) 支柱; **a ~ of society/the church** 社会中坚/教会骨干分子; **to be a ~ of strength to sb.** 是某人的坚强支柱 **4** fig (foundation) 基础; (support) 支柱 **5** Aut [车门或风窗之间的] 立柱

pillar box *n* Brit 邮筒

pillar-box red ▸p. 134 Brit
A *adj* 鲜红的
B *n* [u] 鲜红色

pillbox /ˈpɪlbɒks/ *n* **1** (container) 药盒 **2** Mil 掩体 **3** ~ **(hat)** dated 小圆帽

pillion /ˈpɪlɪən/
A *n* ~ **(seat)** 摩托车后座; **a ~ passenger** 摩托车后座乘客
B *adv* 在摩托车后座上; **to ride ~** 坐在摩托车后座上

pillock /ˈpɪlək/ *n* Brit colloq pej 笨蛋

pillory /ˈpɪləri/
A *n* Hist 颈手枷
B *vt* **1** Hist (punish) 给…戴颈手枷 **2** (criticize) 公开批评; **to be pilloried for sth.** 因某事受到抨击

pillow /ˈpɪləʊ/
A *n* **1** (feather or foam-rubber head rest) 枕头 **2** fig (thing acting as head rest) 垫子; **a ~ of moss/grass/papers** 苔藓/草/报纸垫子
B *vt* 枕着; **soft cushions to ~ your head** 用来枕头的软垫

pillow: ~case *n* 枕套; **~ fight** *n* 枕头打闹; **~slip** *n* 枕套; **~ talk** *n* [u] 枕边悄悄话

pill: ~ popper *n* colloq 嗑药族 [指随意服用大量兴奋剂类药物的人]; **~-popping** *n* [u] 嗑药

pilot /ˈpaɪlət/ ▸p. 409
A *n* **1** (of aircraft) 飞行员; **~ training** 飞行员培训 **2** (of ship) 领航员 **3** (TV or radio programme) 试播节目; **~ radio programme** 试播电台节目
B *vt* **1** (fly) 驾驶 ‹*aircraft*› **2** (navigate) 为…领航 ‹*ship*› **3** (steer) **to ~ a bill/new law through parliament** 使议案/新的法律在议会通过 **4** (test) 试用 ‹*new system, device*› **5** (guide) 引导 ‹*country, person, economy*›; **to ~ the Party through its most difficult years/to an election victory** 领导该党度过最艰难的岁月/取得选举胜利

pilot: ~ boat *n* 领航船; **~ house** *n* = **wheelhouse**; **~ licence, ~'s licence** *n* 飞行执照; **~ light** *n* **1** (flame) 引火火苗; **2** (red light) [显示电器开关状态的] 指示灯; **~ officer** *n* Brit 空军少尉; **~ plant** *n* 试验工厂; **~ programme** *n* **1** (scheme, prototype) 试验方案; **2** (TV programme) 试播节目; **~ scheme** *n* 试验计划; **~ study** *n* 试点研究

pimp /pɪmp/
A *n* 拉皮条的男人
B *vi* **1** (find customers) 拉皮条; **to ~ for a prostitute** 替妓女拉客 **2** (control prostitutes) 操控妓女卖淫

pimping /ˈpɪmpɪŋ/ *n* [u] 拉皮条

pimple /ˈpɪmpl/ *n* 丘疹; **to break out in ~s** 长出许多粉刺

pimply /ˈpɪmpli/ *adj* 有丘疹的

PIN /pɪn/ *abbr* = **personal identification number**

pin /pɪn/
A *n* **1** (for sewing, fastening) 大头针; **(as) bright as a (new) ~** 聪明伶俐的; **like a new ~** (clean) 洁净如新的; (neat, tidy) 非常整洁的; **(as) clean/neat as a new ~** 非常干净/整洁的; **for two ~s I'd/she'd/he'd do it, but ...** Brit 我/她/他巴不得这么做, 可是…; **it was so quiet you could have heard a ~ drop** 安静得连针落在地上的声音都可以听到 **2** (brooch) 饰针; **a diamond/an enamel ~** 一枚钻石/珐琅胸针; **a fraternity/sorority ~** Amer 男生/女生联谊会徽章 **3** Elec 插脚; **a two-/three-~ plug** 双芯/三芯插头 **4** (of grenade) 保险针 **5** Med 钢钉 **6** (of musical instrument) 弦轴 **7** Tech (rod, bolt, peg) (for machine) 销钉; (for coupling) 连接销 **8** (in bowling) 瓶柱 **9** (in golf) 标号旗杆
B **pins** *npl* colloq dated 双腿; **the old man isn't very steady on his ~s** 这位老人走路不太利索
C *vt* (*pres p etc.* **-nn-**) **1** (attach with pin) 固定; **to ~ A and B together** 将A和B钉在一起; **to ~ sth. on** *or* **to** *or* **on to sb./sth.** 把某物别在某人身上/钉在某物上; **she ~ned the brooch to her dress** 她把胸针别在连衣裙上; **to ~ sth. with sth.** 用某物别住某物 **2** (trap, press) 使不能动弹; **to ~ sb./sth. to** *or* **against sth.** 把某人/某物按在某物上; **to be ~ned under the wreckage/a fallen tree** 被困在残骸下无法脱身/被压在倒伏的大树下动弹不得 **3** (attribute) 把…归咎于; **to ~ sth. on sb.** 让某人承担 ‹*blame, responsibility*› **4** **to ~ one's hopes/faith on sb./sth./doing sth.** (rely completely on) 把希望/信任寄托在某人身上/某事物上/做某事上 **5** Mil, Sport **to be ~ned in sth.** 被困在某处

Phrasal verbs

• **pin back** *vt* [**~ sth. back, ~ back sth.**] 夹住 ‹*hair*›; **to ~ one's ears back** fig 聆听

• **pin down**
A [**~ sth. down, ~ down sth.**] *vt*
1 (hold in place with pins) 固定住 ‹*map, cloth, rug*› **2** (define) 确切说明 ‹*concept, truth, difference*›; **I can't quite ~ down his exact meaning** 我说不太清楚他到底是什么意思
B [**~ sb. down, ~ down sb.**] *vt*
1 (hold down) 按住 ‹*opponent, person*› **2** (force to be specific) 使说清楚; **to ~ sb. down to sth.** 使某人明确说出 ‹*time, price, commitment*›; **to ~ sb. down to a promise** 使某人遵守诺言; **the Minister would not be ~ned down** 部长不会明确表态; **have you ~ned her down to naming the day, yet?** 你让她把日期定下来了吗? **3** Mil 火力压制; **the troops were ~ned down on the beach and suffered heavy losses** 部队被火力压制在海滩上, 损失惨重; **we were ~ned down by heavy machine-gun fire** 我们被密集的机枪火力压制住了

• **pin on** *vt* [**~ sth. on, ~ on sth.**] 别上 ‹*badge*›; 钉上 ‹*notice*›

• **pin up** *vt* [**~ sth. up, ~ up sth.**]
1 (put on display) 把…钉起来 ‹*notice*› **2** (turn up and pin) 用别针固定 ‹*hem*› **3** (hold up) 用发卡绾起 ‹*hair*›

pina colada /ˌpiːnə kəˈlɑːdə/ *n* [c and u] 菠萝椰汁朗姆酒

pinafore /ˈpɪnəfɔː(r)/ *n* **1** Brit (apron) 围裙 **2** = **pinafore dress**

pinafore dress *n* Brit 无袖连衣裙

pinball /ˈpɪnbɔːl/ *n* [u] 弹球游戏

pinball machine *n* 弹球机

pince-nez /ˌpænsˈneɪ/ *n* + *v sing or pl* 夹鼻眼镜

pincer /ˈpɪnsə(r)/ *n* **1** **pincers** (tool) 钳子; **a pair of ~s** 一把钳子 **2** (front claw) 螯

pincer movement *n* 钳形攻势

pinch /pɪntʃ/
A *vt* **1** (grip skin of) 捏 ‹*person, cheek*›; **to ~ sb.'s arm/bottom, to ~ sb. on the arm/bottom** 拧某人的胳膊/屁股 **2** colloq (steal) 偷走 ‹*money, food*›; 偷偷勾走 ‹*boyfriend*›; 盗用 ‹*idea, title, example*› **3** (hurt) «*shoes*» 夹痛 ‹*feet*› **4** Brit colloq dated (arrest) 逮住 **5** (close tightly) 紧闭 ‹*lips*› **6** **to ~ out** *or* **off** (remove) 掐掉 ‹*bud, shoot*›
B *vi* **1** (hurt) «*shoes*» 夹脚 **2** (be thrifty) **to ~ and scrape** 省吃俭用
C *n* **1** (nip) 捏; **to give sb. a ~ on the cheek** 捏某人的脸颊; **at a ~** 必要时; **to feel the ~** fig 感到手头拮据 **2** (tiny amount) 少量; **a ~ of snuff** 一撮鼻烟; **to take sth. with a ~ of salt** fig 对某事半信半疑

pinchbeck /ˈpɪntʃbek/ *n* [u] 金色铜 [一种外观似金的铜锌合金]; **~ jewellery** 廉价仿金首饰

pinched /pɪntʃt/ *adj* 苍白清瘦的

pinch: ~-hit *vi* **1** (in baseball) 代击球; **to ~-hit for sb.** 代替某人击球; **2** Amer colloq (stand in) 临时顶替; **to ~-hit for sb.** 顶替某人; **~-hitter** *n* **1** (in baseball) 替补击球员; **2** Amer colloq (stand-in) 替代者

pincushion /ˈpɪnkʊʃn/ *n* [插缝纫针用的] 针垫

pine[1] /paɪn/ *n* **1** [c] **~ (tree)** 松树; **a ~ forest** 松树林 **2** [u] (timber) 松木; **~ furniture** 松木家具 **3** [u] (smell) 松木香味; **~ fragrance** 松木味香水

pine[2] *vi* **1** (miss) 想念; (long for) 渴望; **to ~ for sb./sth.** 思念某人/怀念某事物 **2** (decline mentally, physically) «*person, animal*» 悲痛憔悴

Phrasal verb

• **pine away** *vi* 日渐憔悴

pineapple /ˈpaɪnæpl/ *n* 菠萝; **~ juice/flavour** 菠萝汁/味

pine: ~-clad *adj* 种满松树的; **~ cone** *n* 松果; **~ kernel** *n* 松仁; **~ marten** *n* **1** [c] (animal) 松貂; **2** [u] (fur) 松貂皮; **~ needle** *n* 松针; **~ nut** *n* = **~ kernel**; **~-scented** *adj* 有松木香味的; **~wood** *n* 松树林

ping /pɪŋ/
A *vi* «*bell, timer*» 叮当响; «*metal object, bullet*» 乒乓作响
B *vt* 使…叮当响 ‹*bell*›; 叮当地敲 ‹*metal object*›
C *n* (of bell) 叮当声; (of metal object, bullet) 乒乓声

pinger /ˈpɪŋə(r)/ *n* Brit 响铃定时器

ping-pong /ˈpɪŋpɒŋ/ ▸p. 307 *n* [u] 乒乓球; **~ ball/table** 乒乓球/乒乓球台

pinhead /ˈpɪnhed/ *n* **1** (end of pin) 大头针的针帽 **2** colloq (stupid person) 傻瓜

pinhole /ˈpɪnhəʊl/ *n* (hole made by pin) 针孔; (very small hole) 小孔

pinhole camera *n* 针孔照相机

pinion /ˈpɪnɪən/ *vt* 固定住; **to ~ sb.'s arms** 绑住某人的胳膊; **to ~ sb./sb.'s arms against** *or* **to the wall** 把某人/某人的胳膊按在墙上

pink /pɪŋk/ ▸p. 134
A *adj* **1** (in colour) 粉红色的 **2** (with embarrassment, anger, etc.) 绯红的 ‹*face, cheeks*›; **to go** *or* **turn ~** 面红耳赤; **to look ~** 面色发红 **3** colloq (left-wing) 略为左倾的 **4** colloq (homosexual) 同性恋的; **~ rights/issues** 同性恋权利/问题
B *n* **1** [c and u] (colour) 粉红色; **to be in the ~** 满面红光; fig 非常健康 **2** [c] (plant) 石竹; (flower) 石竹花 **3** [c] (snooker ball) 粉球
C *vt* (sew scallop edge) 把…剪成扇形; (sew zigzag edge) 把…剪成锯齿形
D *vi* Brit «*engine, vehicle*» 敲缸

pink gin *n* [u and c] 红杜松子酒

pinkie /ˈpɪŋki/ *n* colloq 小指

pinking /ˈpɪŋkɪŋ/ *n* [u] Brit 敲缸声

pinking shears, pinking scissors *npl* 齿边布样剪刀

pinkish /ˈpɪŋkɪʃ/ ▸p. 134 *adj* **1** (in colour) 浅粉色的 **2** colloq (left-wing) 略为左倾的

pinko /ˈpɪŋkəʊ/ Amer colloq pej
A *adj* 左倾的 [右翼人士用语]
B *n* (*pl* **~s** *or* **~es**) 左倾分子

pink: ~ pound *n* Brit "粉红英镑" [指同性恋者的购买力]; **~ slip** *n* Amer colloq **1** (job dismissal) 解雇通知; **to get a ~ slip** 被解雇; **to be given** *or* **handed a ~ slip** 被解雇; **2** Amer colloq (vehicle title) 车主证

pin money *n* [u] 小额零用钱

pinnacle /ˈpɪnəkl/ *n* 顶峰

PIN number *n* 个人识别码

pinny /ˈpɪni/ *n* colloq 围裙

pinpoint /ˈpɪnpɔɪnt/
A *n* 小点; **a ~ of light** 一点亮光
B *adj attrib* 精确的; **with ~ accuracy** *or* **precision** 精准地
C *vt* 准确找到 ‹*location, position, target*›; 确定 ‹*moment, reason, cause*›

pinprick /ˈpɪnprɪk/ *n* **1** (slight pain) 刺痛 **2** (unpleasant feeling) 一丝烦恼; **he felt a ~ of remorse/jealousy** 他感到一丝悔恨/妒意;

the ~s of one's conscience 良心的不安 3 (spot, dot) 小点

pins and needles *npl + v sing* 麻木; **to have** *or* **get ~** 感到发麻

pinstripe /ˈpɪnstraɪp/
A *adj attrib* 有细条纹的 ‹*cloth, suit*›
B *n* 1 (stripe in cloth) 细条纹 2 (suit) 细条纹西装

pinstriped /ˈpɪnstraɪpt/ *adj* = **pinstripe A**

pint /paɪnt/ *n* 1 (liquid measure) 品脱; **a two-~ carton of milk** 一盒两品脱装的牛奶 2 Brit colloq (glass, tankard) 品脱杯; (of beer) 一品脱啤酒; **to go for a ~** 去喝杯啤酒; **he's fond of a ~** 他喜欢喝啤酒

pinta /ˈpaɪntə/ *n* Brit colloq 一品脱牛奶 [主要作广告用语]

pint glass *n* 品脱杯

pinto /ˈpɪntəʊ/
A *n* Amer (*pl* **~s**) 花斑马
B *adj* 杂色的; **a little ~ pony** 一匹杂色小矮种马

pinto bean *n* 花豆

pintsize /ˈpaɪntsaɪz/, **pintsized** /ˈpaɪntsaɪzd/ *adj* colloq 个头小的 ‹*person, horse*›; 小型的 ‹*car, apartment*›; 较小的 ‹*portion*›

pin-up *n* 1 (poster) (famous person) 名人招贴画; (attractive woman) 美女招贴画; **a ~ girl/star** 招贴画女郎/明星 2 (famous person) 招贴画名人; (attractive woman) 招贴画女郎; **a ~ calendar** 有招贴画人物的挂历

pinwheel /ˈpɪnwɪəl, Amer -hwɪəl/ *n* 五彩转轮 [一种烟火]

Pinyin /ˈpɪnjɪn/ *n* [u] （汉语）拼音

pioneer /ˌpaɪəˈnɪə(r)/
A *n* 1 (innovator in activity, field of knowledge) 先驱; **a ~ study** 开创性的研究 2 (explorer) 探索者 3 (settler) 拓荒者; **a ~ settler/settlement** 拓荒者/拓荒者居留地 4 (soldier) 轻工兵
B *vt* 1 (develop, use first) 开创 ‹*technique, process, invention*›; **to ~ the use/study of ...** 倡导…的使用/研究 2 (explore, settle) 开辟 ‹*route, settlement*›

pioneering /ˌpaɪəˈnɪərɪŋ/ *adj attrib* 有开拓精神的 ‹*scientist, film maker, socialist*›; 开拓性的 ‹*work, study, invention, thought*›

pioneer settler *n* [新国家或地区的] 先驱开拓者

pious /ˈpaɪəs/ *adj* 1 (devout) 虔诚的 ‹*person, devotion, deed*›; 笃信宗教的 ‹*community*› 2 (sanctimonious) 道貌岸然的 ‹*person, expression*›; 伪善的 ‹*attitude, remark*› 3 (unrealistic) 可望而不可及的 ‹*hope, wish, aim*›

piously /ˈpaɪəsli/ *adv* 1 (devoutly) 虔诚地 ‹*pray, worship, kneel*› 2 (sanctimoniously) 伪善地 ‹*moralize, say, look*›

pip /pɪp/
A *n* 1 esp Brit (seed) [苹果、梨等水果的] 核 2 Brit (sound) **the ~s** [电台报时或电话提醒再次投币的] 嘀嘀声 3 Brit (display of rank on uniform) [军官制服肩章上标示军阶的] 星 4 (spot on card, dice, domino) 点
B *vt* (*pres p etc.* **-pp-**) Brit colloq 险胜; **to ~ sb. for sth.** 险胜某人而赢得某物; **to ~ sb. at** *or* **to the post** 最后一刻以些微优势反超某人取胜

pipe /paɪp/
A *n* 1 (conduit) 管子; **a sewage ~** 污水管; **to have a burst/leaking/blocked ~** 管子爆裂/渗漏/堵塞 2 (for smoking) 烟斗; **to puff on one's ~** 抽烟斗; **to fill/light a ~** 填装/点烟斗; **stick that in your ~ and smoke it!** colloq 这事由不得你! 3 (amount of tobacco) 一斗烟; **I smoke** *or* **have three ~s a day** 我每天抽三斗烟 4 Mus (in organ) [管风琴的] 音管 5 Mus (wind instrument) 管乐器 6 (birdsong) 鸟鸣声 7 Naut [水手长的] 长口哨
B **pipes** *npl* 风笛; **to play the ~s** 吹奏风笛
C *vt* 1 (carry in pipe) 用管子输送 ‹*gas, oil, water, sewage*›; **~d water** 自来水 2 (say) 尖声说 ‹*words*› 3 (sing) 尖声唱 ‹*tune*› 4 (play on pipe(s)) 用管乐器演奏 ‹*tune*›; **he ~d a jig** 他吹奏了一首吉格舞曲 5 (transmit) 播送 ‹*music, radio programme*› 6 (trim, decorate) 为…滚边 ‹*cushion, collar, skirt*›; **to ~ sth. with sth.** 用某物为某物滚边 7 Culin 裱 ‹*cream, pattern*›; **to ~ icing on a cake** 给蛋糕裱糖霜 8 Naut **to ~ sb. aboard** 吹奏管乐欢迎某人登船
D *vi* 1 Mus 吹奏管乐 2 Naut 吹长口哨 3 (sing) «*bird*» 啼鸣; (cry) «*person*» 尖叫

Phrasal verbs

- **pipe down** *vi* colloq 安静下来
- **pipe in** *vt* [**~ sb./sth. in, ~ in sb./sth.**] 吹奏管乐欢迎 ‹*guest*›; 在管乐声中端上 ‹*haggis, plum pudding*›
- **pipe up** *vi* 开始尖声说话; **to ~ up with sth.** 开始尖声说某事

pipe: ~ band *n* 风笛乐队; **~clay** *n* [u] [用于制烟斗或鞋粉的] 白陶土; **~-cleaner** *n* 烟斗通条

piped music *n* [u] [超市等处播放的] 背景音乐

pipe: ~-dream *n* 幻想; **~line** *n* 1 (pipe) 管道; **to lay a gas/an oil ~line** 铺设煤气/石油管线; 2 (channel for goods or information) 渠道; 3 (production process) **to be in the ~line** «*changes, proposals, laws*» 在酝酿中; **~ major** *n* 风笛乐队指挥; **~ of peace** *n* 和平烟斗 [某些美洲原住民为表示互相和解而同吸的烟斗]; **to smoke a ~ of peace with sb.** 与某人和解; **~ organ** *n* 管风琴

piper /ˈpaɪpə(r)/ ▸ **p. 395, p. 409** *n* 1 (bagpipe player) 风笛手; **he who pays the ~ calls the tune** Prov 谁出钱，谁点戏 2 (pipe player) [尤指巡回演出的] 管乐器吹奏者

pipe: ~ rack *n* 烟斗架; **~-smoker** *n* 抽烟斗的人; **~-smoking** *adj attrib* 抽烟斗的; **~s of Pan** /ˌpaɪps əv ˈpæn/ ▸ **p. 395** *npl* 排箫; **~ tobacco** *n* [u] 烟斗丝

pipette /pɪˈpet/ *n* 移液管

pipework /ˈpaɪpwɜːk/ *n* [u] 管道系统

piping /ˈpaɪpɪŋ/
A *n* [u] 1 (pipes) 管道 2 (system of pipes) 管道系统 3 (cloth decoration) 滚边 4 (decoration on cake) 条纹花饰 5 (music) 管乐; (pipe-playing) 管乐器吹奏
B *adj* 尖厉的 ‹*voice, sound*›

piping: ~ bag *n* 挤花袋 [用来挤糖霜、奶油等装饰糕点]; **~ hot** *adj* 滚烫的

pipit /ˈpɪpɪt/ *n* 鹨

pipsqueak /ˈpɪpskwiːk/ *n* colloq 小人物

piquancy /ˈpiːkənsi/ *n* [u] 1 (sharpness) 辛辣适口; (appetizing flavour) 开胃爽口 2 (excitement) 刺激; (interest) 趣味; **to add ~ to sth.** 使某事物变得更有趣

piquant /ˈpiːkənt/ *adj* 1 (pleasantly sharp) 辛辣适口的; (appetizingly tasty) 开胃爽口的 2 (stimulating, exciting) 激动人心的 ‹*memory, plot, ending, sketch*›; 有趣的 ‹*incident, remark, contrast, observation*›

piquantly /ˈpiːkəntli/ *adv* (stimulatingly) 激动人心地; (interestingly) 有趣地; **to describe sth. ~** 把某事物描述得引人入胜; **~ ironic** 令人啼笑皆非的; **~ witty** 诙谐生动的

pique /piːk/
A *vt* 1 (offend) 使恼火 2 (arouse) 激起 ‹*interest, curiosity, imagination*›
B *n* [u] 恼怒; **to do sth. out of ~** 因为生气而做某事; **in a fit of ~** 一气之下

piqued /piːkt/ *adj* 恼火的; **to be ~ at** *or* **by sth.** 为某事物生气

piracy /ˈpaɪərəsi/ *n* [u] 1 (robbing ships) 海盗行为 2 (hijacking) 劫持; **air ~** 劫机 3 (illegal copying) 盗版

piranha /pɪˈrɑːnə/ *n* 水虎鱼

pirate /ˈpaɪərət/
A *n* 1 (at sea) 海盗; **a ~ ship** 海盗船 2 (illegal copier) 盗版者; **a ~ book/video** 盗版书/录像带 3 (illegal operator) 非法从业者; **a ~ firm** 非法营业的公司
B *vt* 1 (copy illegally) 盗印 ‹*book*›; 非法复制 ‹*computer program, CD, game*›; 非法仿制 ‹*design, clothing, furniture*› 2 (steal) 盗用 ‹*idea, design, invention, recipe*›; 非法转播 ‹*TV programme*›

pirated /ˈpaɪərətɪd/ *adj* 盗版的; **a ~ version** *or* **edition** 盗版

pirate: ~ radio ship *n* 非法广播船; **~ radio station** *n* 非法广播电台

piratical /ˌpaɪəˈrætɪkl/ *adj* 海盗式的 ‹*exploits*›; 像海盗的 ‹*laugh, beard*›

pirating /ˈpaɪərətɪŋ/ *n* [u] 盗版行为

pirouette /ˌpɪrʊˈet/
A *n* 单脚尖旋转
B *vi* 单脚尖旋转

Piscean /ˈpaɪsɪən/
A *adj* 双鱼座的
B *n* 双鱼座的人

Pisces /ˈpaɪsiːz/ *n* 1 [u] Astron 双鱼（星）座 2 [u] Astrol (sign) 双鱼宫 [黄道第十二宫] 3 [c] *sing* Astrol (person) 属双鱼（星）座的人

piss /pɪs/ taboo sl
A *vi* 撒尿; **to ~ on the floor/in one's pants/in** *or* **into a chamber pot** 尿在地板上/尿裤子/尿在夜壶里; **it's ~ing with rain** 正下着瓢泼大雨; **it's ~ing in the wind** fig 这是在浪费时间
B *vt* 1 (urinate in) 尿在…上; **to ~ one's pants** 尿裤子 2 (pass in urine) 尿 ‹*blood*›
C *v refl* **to ~ oneself** 尿裤子; **to ~ oneself (laughing)** 大笑不止
D *n* 1 [c] (act of urinating) 撒尿; **to go for a ~** 去撒尿; **to have** Brit *or* **take** Amer **a ~** 去撒尿 2 [u] (urine) 尿; **to be/go on the ~** Brit 暴饮/开始暴饮; **to take the ~ (out of sb./sth.)** 嘲笑（某人/某事物）; **a piece of ~** Brit 轻而易举的事

Phrasal verbs

- **piss about, piss around** taboo sl
A *vi* 1 (dither) 游手好闲 2 (behave childishly) 行为愚蠢幼稚; **stop ~ing about and get on with your work!** 别胡闹了，赶快干正经事去!
B *vt* [**~ sb. about**] 耍弄
- **piss away** *vt* [**~ away sth., ~ sth. away**] taboo sl 挥霍 ‹*fortune, inheritance*›; 浪费 ‹*money*›
- **piss down** *vi* taboo sl 下大雨; **it's ~ing down!** 下大雨啦!
- **piss off** taboo sl
A *vi* 走开
B *vt* [**~ sb. off, ~ off sb.**] 激怒
- **piss on** *vt* [**~ on sb./sth.**] taboo sl 1 (show contempt for) 怠慢 ‹*opponent, rival*›; 亵渎 ‹*place, memory*› 2 Brit (defeat heavily) 战胜 ‹*team, opponent, rival*›

piss artist *n* Brit taboo sl 1 (heavy drinker) 酒鬼 2 (person who behaves stupidly) 混混儿

pissed /pɪst/ *adj* 1 Brit sl 醉醺醺的; **to get ~** 喝得醉醺醺的; **~ out of one's mind** *or* **brain** 烂醉如泥的; **~ as a newt** 烂醉如泥 2 Amer colloq (annoyed) 恼火的; **to be ~ at sb.** 对某人生气

pissed off *adj* colloq 郁闷的; **to be ~ (with** *or* **at ...)** （对…）感到郁闷

piss: ~head *n* Brit taboo sl 酒鬼 offensive; **~-poor** *adj* taboo sl 很差劲的; **~-take** *n* Brit sl 恶搞; **~-up** *n* Brit taboo sl 纵酒狂欢; **he couldn't organize a ~-up in a brewery** 他即使到了酒厂都组织不了大家狂喝痛饮

pistachio /pɪˈstɑːʃɪəʊ, Amer -ˈstæʃ-/ *n* (*pl* **~s**) 1 (nut) 开心果; **~ ice cream** 开心果冰激淩 2 (tree) 开心果树

piste /piːst/ *n* 滑雪道

pistil /ˈpɪstɪl/ *n* 雌蕊

pistol /ˈpɪstl/ *n* 手枪

pistol: ~ **grip** *n* 手枪式握把; ~ **shot** *n* 手枪射击; **~-whip** *vt* 用手枪柄殴打

piston /ˈpɪstən/ *n* 活塞

piston: ~ **engine** *n* 活塞式发动机; **~-engined** *adj* 装有活塞式发动机的; ~ **ring** *n* 活塞环; ~ **rod** *n* 活塞杆

pit /pɪt/

A *n* **1** (large hole) 深坑; **to be at the bottom of a deep** ~ fig 情绪跌入低谷; **a black** ~ **of depression** 灰心沮丧的深渊 **2** (indentation) 凹陷; **the spaceship's hull was covered in tiny** ~**s** 宇宙飞船的船体上布满了坑坑洼洼的小洞 **3** Mining 矿井; (colliery) 煤矿; **to work at the** ~ 在煤矿工作; **to work down the** ~ 在井下工作; **he went down the** ~ **when he was just 16** 他 16 岁时就当了矿工到井下作业; **a chalk/lime/clay** ~ 白垩/石灰/黏土矿坑; **a** ~ **closure/disaster** 煤矿关闭/矿难 **4** (pockmark) 麻子 **5** (hollow) 窝; **the** ~ **of the** *or* **one's stomach** 心窝; **a feeling of fear/anxiety in the** ~ **of one's stomach** 深深的恐惧感/焦虑感 **6** Aut (at garage) **the** ~ 检修坑 **7** Brit Theat dated **the** ~ 正厅后座区 **8** Fin 交易场地; **a wheat** ~ 小麦交易场 **9** Hist (arena for animal fights) 斗兽场; **a bear/cock** ~ 斗熊场/斗鸡场 **10** esp Amer (fruit stone) 果核

B **pits** *npl* **1** **the** ~**s** colloq (the worst) 最坏的东西; **it's the** ~**s!** 这真是糟糕透顶! **2** (in motor racing) **the** ~**s** 检修加油站; ~ **stop** 检修加油停车

C *vt* (*pres p etc.* **-tt-**) **1** (in struggle) 使…竞争 ‹*competitor, team*›; **to be** ~**ted against sb.** 与某人竞争; **to** ~ **one's wits against sb.** 与某人斗智 **2** (mark) 使…有凹陷 ‹*surface, metal, glass*›; 在…上留斑点 ‹*skin*›; **the disease had** ~**ted her face with pockmarks** 这场病弄得她满脸麻子 **3** (remove stone from) 去除…的核 ‹*fruit, cherry, plum*›

D *v refl* (*pres p etc.* **-tt-**) **to** ~ **oneself against sb.** 与某人竞争

pit-a-pat, pitapat /ˌpɪtəˈpæt/

A *adv* 噼噼啪啪地; **my heart goes** ~ **every time I see her** 每次见到她我的心就噗噗直跳

B *n* (of rain, feet) 噼啪声; (of heart) 噗噗声

pit babe *n* colloq 赛车宝贝

pit bull terrier, pit bull *ns* 比特犬

pitch[1] /pɪtʃ/

A *n* **1** [c] Brit Sport (playing area) 场地; **a football/rugby/hockey/cricket** ~ 足球场/橄榄球场/曲棍球场/板球场; **on/off the** ~ 在场上/场下 **2** [u] (sound quality of note or voice) 音高; **to rise in** ~ 提高声调; **a note of a higher/lower** ~ 音调较高/较低的音符 **3** [c] *sing* (degree of intensity) 强度; (high or climactic degree) 顶点; **a** ~ **of tension/anticipation/terror** 紧张/期待/恐惧的程度; **to be at one's (highest)** *or* **at full** ~ 达到极点 **4** [c] Brit (stand) (for street trader) 摊位; (for street entertainer) 表演地点 **5** [c] (sales talk) 宣传用语; **a sales/campaign** ~ 推销用语/竞选口号; **to make one's** ~ 作自我宣传; **to make a** ~ **for sth./sb.** 宣传鼓吹某事物/勾引某人 **6** [u] Naut, Aviat (movement) 颠簸 **7** [c] (in baseball) (act of throwing) 投球; (manner of throwing) 投球方法; **the** ~ **was easily hit** 投出的球被轻易击中了 **8** [c] (in cricket) 弹跳点 **9** [c] (in golf) 下旋高球 **10** [c] (slope of roof) 斜度 **11** [c] (in mountaineering) 斜坡; **to climb the most difficult** ~ 爬最难攀爬的坡段

B *vt* **1** (throw) 投掷 ‹*object, ball, stone*›; **the explosion** ~**ed her into the air** 爆炸把她抛向空中; **the new government has already been** ~**ed into a crisis** 新政府已经陷入危机 **2** (set, aim) 确定…的标准 ‹*price*›; 确定…的目标市场 ‹*campaign, advertising, film, product*›; 使…有针对性 ‹*textbook, lecture*›; **to** ~ **sth. at sb.** 使某事物针对某人; **a newspaper/programme** ~**ed at young people** 面向年轻人的报纸/节目; **the exam was** ~**ed at a high level** 考试标准定得很高; **to** ~ **one's ambitions too high** 把目标定得过高; **to** ~ **sth. a bit strong** *or* **high** 对某事物夸大其词 **3** Mus (set at particular modulation) 为…定音高; **to** ~ **a song in a higher key** 给歌起调高一些; **to be** ~**ed at the right level** ‹*cry, voice*› 音调定得恰到好处 **4** (dislodge) 使重重摔倒; **the rider was** ~**ed off his horse** 骑手从马背上摔了下来 **5** colloq (throw away) 扔 ‹*rubbish*›; **he** ~**ed the cigarette end into the fire** 他把烟蒂扔进了火堆; ~ **it!** Amer 扔掉它! **6** (erect) 搭 ‹*tent*›; **to** ~ **camp** 扎营 **7** (in baseball) 投; **the ball was** ~**ed low/at the batter's head** 球投得很低/对准击球手的头部投出 **8** (in cricket) 使定点落地 ‹*ball*› **9** (in golf) 把…击成下旋高球; **he** ~**ed the ball close to the hole** 他打出的下旋高球落在洞口附近 **10** Constr (cause to slope) 使倾斜; **the roof was** ~**ed at an angle of 75 degrees** 屋顶呈 75 度倾斜

C *vi* **1** (be thrown) «*passenger, cyclist*» 猛然摔出; **the rider** ~**ed over the fence/into the water/off his horse** 骑手摔过了围栏/摔下来落入水中/从马上摔下来 **2** Naut, Aviat «*boat, aircraft*» 颠簸; **to** ~ **from side to side** 左摇右晃 **3** (in baseball) 投球; **to be in there** ~**ing** Amer colloq 兴致勃勃地参与 **4** (in golf) 击下旋高球 **5** Comm 竞标; **to** ~ **for sth.** 投标竞争 ‹*contract, business*›

Phrasal verbs

- **pitch in**

A *vi* colloq **1** (join in to help) 热情参与; **to** ~ **in with sth.** 积极为某事提供帮助 **2** (join in argument) 加入争斗 **3** (eat heartily) 开怀大吃

B *vt* **1** [~ **sth. in,** ~ **in sth.**] (contribute) 出…相助 ‹*sum of money*› **2** [~ **sb. in,** ~ **in sb.**] (land in new situation) 使陷入困境; **the new manager was** ~**ed in at a very difficult time** 新任经理临危被卷了进来

- **pitch into** *vt* [~ **into sb./sth.**] colloq **1** (attack physically) 击打 **2** (attack verbally) 抨击 **3** (engage in) 积极投入 ‹*job, activity, game*›; 开始大吃 ‹*meal*›
- **pitch over** *vi* 摔倒; **he** ~**ed over and fell flat on his face** 他摔了个嘴啃泥
- **pitch up** *vi* Brit colloq 露面

pitch[2]

A *n* [u] (black substance) 沥青; **(as) black as** ~ 漆黑的

B *vt* 给…涂抹沥青 ‹*surface, roof, hull*›

pitch: ~ **and putt** *n* [u] 小场地高尔夫球; **~-black** *adj* **1** (completely black) 漆黑的; **2** = **~-dark**

pitchblende /ˈpɪtʃblend/ *n* [u] 沥青铀矿

pitch: **~-dark** *adj* 漆黑的; **~-darkness** *n* [u] 漆黑

pitched /pɪtʃt/**:** ~ **battle** *n* **1** (static battle) 阵地战; **2** (violent confrontation) 群殴; ~ **roof** *n* 斜屋顶

pitcher[1] /ˈpɪtʃə(r)/ *n* **1** Brit (container) 有耳陶罐 **2** Amer (jug) 壶 **3** (contents) (of earthenware container) 一罐; (of jug) 一壶; **a** ~ **of milk** 一壶牛奶

pitcher[2] *n* (baseball player) 投手

pitchfork /ˈpɪtʃfɔːk/

A *n* 干草叉

B *vt* **1** Agric (lift, turn, toss) 用干草叉叉 ‹*hay, straw, grass*›; **to** ~ **the hay into** *or* **on to the cart** 把干草叉到马车上去 **2** (force sb. into difficult situation) **to** ~ **sb. into sth.** 强行把某人推入某境况

pitch: ~ **invasion** *n* Brit [为了表示庆祝或抗议的] 闯入比赛场地; **~man** /-mæn/ *n* Amer colloq 推销员; ~ **pipe** *n* 定音管

piteous /ˈpɪtɪəs/ *adj* 可怜的

piteously /ˈpɪtɪəsli/ *adv* 可怜地

pitfall /ˈpɪtfɔːl/ *n* **1** (trap) 陷阱 **2** (danger, difficulty) (of action, policy) 隐患; (of language, work) 隐藏的困难

pith /pɪθ/ *n* [u] **1** (of fruit) [柑橘类水果的] 衬皮 **2** (of stem) 木髓 **3** (of argument, matter) 核心

pit head *n* 矿井井口

pith helmet *n* 木髓遮阳帽

pithiness /ˈpɪθɪnɪs/ *n* [u] **1** (of fruit, plant) 多髓 **2** (of remark, style, writing) 简练

pithy /ˈpɪθi/ *adj* **1** (containing pith) 多髓的 ‹*substance, texture*›; 衬皮厚的 ‹*fruit*› **2** (terse) 简练的 ‹*remark, style, writing*›

pitiable /ˈpɪtɪəbl/ *adj* **1** (deserving pity) 可怜的 **2** (contemptibly small) 少得可怜的 ‹*income, amount*›; (poor) 拙劣的 ‹*performance*›

pitiably /ˈpɪtɪəbli/ *adv* 可怜地

pitiful /ˈpɪtɪfl/ *adj* **1** (deserving pity) 可怜的 **2** (arousing contempt) 拙劣的 ‹*excuse, lie, singer, performance*›; 可鄙的 ‹*cowardice, coward, liar*›

pitifully /ˈpɪtɪfəli/ *adv* **1** (arousing pity) 可怜地 **2** (arousing contempt) 可恨地 ‹*slow*›; 差劲地 ‹*sing, perform*›; ~ **bad/small** 差得/小得要命的

pitiless /ˈpɪtɪlɪs/ *adj* **1** (merciless) 无情的 **2** (harsh, severe) 严酷的; **the** ~ **sun** 毒日头; **the** ~ **cold** *or* **chill** 严寒

pitilessly /ˈpɪtɪlɪsli/ *adv* **1** (mercilessly) 无情地 **2** (harshly, severely) 严酷地; ~ **hot** 酷热的; ~ **cold** 严寒的

piton /ˈpiːtɒn/ *n* 岩钉

pit: ~ **pony** *n* Brit 驮煤小马; ~ **prop** *n* 坑木; ~ **stop** *n* **1** (in motor racing) 进站加油维修; **2** colloq (in journey) 停车休息; (in activities) 中途休息

pitta /ˈpɪtə/ *n* ~ **(bread)** [可撕开填入馅料的] 口袋面包

pittance /ˈpɪtns/ *n* (allowance) 微薄的津贴; (wage) 微薄的工资; **she lives on a** ~ 她靠微薄的薪水生活

pitted /ˈpɪtɪd/ *adj* **1** (having indentations in surface) 坑坑洼洼的 ‹*metal, surface*›; 有疤痕的 ‹*face, skin*›; **the car was** ~ **with rust** 这辆车锈迹斑斑 **2** (with the stone removed) 去核的 ‹*fruit*›

pitter-patter /ˈpɪtəpætə(r)/

A *n* 噼啪声

B *adv* 噼噼啪啪地

pituitary /pɪˈtjuːɪtəri, Amer -ˈtuːəteri/

A *n* ~ **(gland** *or* **body)** 垂体

B *adj attrib* 垂体的; ~ **functions/secretions** 垂体功能/分泌物

pit worker ▸**p. 409** *n* 煤矿工人

pity /ˈpɪti/

A *n* [u] **1** (compassion) 同情; ~ **for sb./sth.** 对某人/某事物的同情; **to feel** ~ **for sb.** 同情某人 **2** (regret) 遗憾; **what a** ~**!** 太遗憾了!; **the** ~ **(of it) is that ...** 可惜的是…; **it would be a** ~ **if ...** 如果…那就太可惜了; **I neglected to warn him, more's the** ~ 不幸的是，我没有警告他 **3** (mercy, sympathy) 怜悯; **to have** *or* **take** ~ **on sb.** 可怜某人; **to show** ~ **(towards sb.)** （对某人）表示怜悯

B *vt* **1** (feel compassion for) 同情 **2** (feel contempt for) [含鄙视意味地] 可怜

pitying /ˈpɪtɪɪŋ/ *adj* **1** (showing compassion) 同情的; **to give sb. a** ~ **glance** 同情地看了某人一眼 **2** (showing contempt) 垂怜的 ‹*look, sneer*›

pityingly /ˈpɪtɪɪŋli/ *adv* **1** (showing compassion) 同情地 **2** (showing contempt) 垂怜地

pivot /ˈpɪvət/

A *n* **1** (point) 支点; (pin) 轴销; (shaft) 枢轴 **2** fig (central person or thing) 中枢

B *vi* **1** (turn) «*handle, gate, wheel*» 转动; «*person*» 转身; **to** ~ **on one's heel** 以脚跟为轴转身; **to** ~ **from the hips** 臀部转动 **2** (depend) **to** ~ **on sth.** 取决于某事物

C *vt* 给…装枢轴

pivotal /ˈpɪvətl/ *adj* 关键的

pix /pɪks/ *npl* colloq = **pictures** (photos) 照片; (pictures) 图片

P

pixel /'pɪksl/ *n* 像素

pixelate /'pɪkseleɪt/ *vt* **1** (divide into pixels) 使像素化; **heavily ~d images** 像素颗粒明显的图像 **2** (display disguised image of) 给…加马赛克

pixie, pixy /'pɪksi/ *n* 小精灵

pixie hood *n* 尖兜帽

pizazz *n* colloq = **pizzazz**

pizza /'pi:tsə/ *n* 比萨饼; **~ topping** 比萨饼配料; **a ~ oven** 比萨饼烤炉

pizza parlour *n* 比萨饼店

pizzazz /pɪ'zæz/ *n* [u] colloq 活泼的魅力

pizzeria /ˌpi:tsə'ri:ə/ *n* 比萨饼店

pizzicato /ˌpɪtsɪ'kɑ:təʊ/

A *adv* 用拨奏

B *adj* 拨奏的

C *n* (*pl* **~s** *or* **pizzicati** /ˌpɪtsɪ'kɑ:ti/) **1** [u] (technique) 拨奏 **2** [c] (note, passage) 拨奏乐曲

PLA *abbr* = **People's Liberation Army**

placard /'plækɑ:d/

A *n* (at protest march) 标语牌; (on wall) 海报

B *vt* 张贴 ‹*notice*›; 张贴海报于 ‹*wall, hoarding, town*›

placate /plə'keɪt, Amer 'pleɪkeɪt/ *vt* 使息怒

placatory /plə'keɪtəri, Amer 'pleɪkətɔ:ri/ *adj* 安抚的

place /pleɪs/

A *n* **1** [u and c] (specified location) 地点; (unspecified location) 地方; (geographical location) 地区; **he had no ~ to go** 他无处可去; **at** *or* **in a ~** 在某个地方; **from ~ to ~** 到处; **same time, same ~** 老时间，老地方; **there's no ~ like home** Prov 普天之下家最好; **not here, of all ~s!** 别的什么地方都行，就是不能在这里！; **to be seen in all the right ~s** 在所有的重要场合抛头露面; **a ~ in the sun** fig 有发展前途的职位; **to be all over the ~** colloq (be everywhere) 到处都是; (be disorderly) 乱七八糟; (be disorganized) 杂乱无章; **to go ~s** (travel) 旅行; (go about) 四处走动; **to be going ~s** fig 春风得意; **to take ~** 发生; **the country is hilly in ~s** 该国家的某些地区多丘陵; **in high ~s** fig 处于权势阶层 **2** [c] (site, home) 场所; **a ~ of worship/business/entertainment/execution** 礼拜堂/营业场所/娱乐场所/刑场; **a ~ of learning/refuge** 学府/避难所; **a country/seaside ~** 乡村/海边处所; **a meeting/stopping ~** 聚会地点/中途停留地; **we're having a party at our ~ tonight** 今晚我们要在家里举行聚会; **a ~ of one's own** 自己的居所; **to scream the ~ down** 吵死人; **there are ~s for people like you!** 自有地方收容你这样的人! **3** [c] (suitable location) 适当位置; **a** *or* **the ~ for sb./sth./to do sth.** 适合某人/某事物/做某事的地方; **she put the book back in its ~** 她把书放回了原位; **a ~ for everything, and everything in its ~** 兼容并蓄，各得其所; **in ~** (proper position) 在适当位置; (ready to work) 准备就绪的; (suitable) 合适的; (on the spot) 在现场; **the new manager is not yet in ~** 新经理还未上任; **to put a law/scheme/regime in ~** 施行法律/执行计划/实行制度; **a word of thanks would be in ~** Amer 说声谢谢就可以了; **to fall** *or* **slot** *or* **click into ~** (become organized) 变得有条不紊; (become clear in the mind) 变得明朗; **out of ~** (not in the proper position) 位置不当的; (not suitable for a particular context) 不得体的; **modern furniture would be out of ~ in a Victorian house** 现代家具放在维多利亚式住宅里会显得不伦不类; **to look/feel out of ~** 看上去/感到格格不入 **4** [c] (point reached) (in book, paragraph, speech) 某处; (point reached in time) (in film, play, piece of music) 某时点; **I've lost my ~ in the book** 我忘了书上次读到哪儿了; **the audience laughed in all the wrong ~s** 观众总在不该笑的时候哄堂大笑; **the show was funny/boring/silly in ~s** 演出有时很有趣/无聊/荒唐 **5** [c] (seat, space) 座位; **to show sb. to his** *or* **her ~** 给某人引座; **to keep** *or* **save a ~ for sb.** 为某人留座位; **to take one's ~** (go to necessary physical position) 就座; (take rightful position in society etc.) 得到应有的社会地位; **to be in one's ~** 在位置上; **to lay** *or* **set a ~ for sb. at the table** 在餐桌上为某人摆放餐具; **the ~ of honour** 贵宾席位 **6** [u and c] (social, historical position) 地位; (social, historical role) 身份; **to have a ~ in sth.** 在某事物中占有一席之地; **to take sb.'s ~** *or* **the ~ of sb.** 代替某人; **to put/keep sb. in his** *or* **her ~** 煞某人的威风/让某人明白自己的身份; **violence has no ~ in their political creed** 他们的政治理念排斥使用暴力; **it's not my ~ to tell you what you should do!** 告诉你该干什么不是我该做的事！; **in ~ of sb./sth.** 取代某人/某事物的; **to keep (to) one's ~** 安分守己; **to know/forget one's ~** 有/没有自知之明; **how dare you speak to a lady like that! you're forgetting your ~!** 你怎么敢同一位女士这么说话！你太不知天高地厚了！; **a woman's ~ (is in the home)** 女人的本分（是持家） **7** [c] (personal situation) 位置; **to put oneself in sb. else's** *or* **sb.'s ~** 设身处地替某人着想; **to change** *or* **swap** *or* **trade ~s with sb.** 与某人交换位置; **I'm perfectly happy — I wouldn't change ~s with anyone** 我非常满足——我不愿成为其他任何人 **8** [u and c] (relative position in test, contest) 名次; **to win** *or* **gain first ~** 获得第一名; **to finish in first/second ~** 获得第一/第二名; **to take** *or* **get a ~ in an exam** 在考试中获得好成绩; **to get a low/high ~ in class** 在班级里排名靠后/靠前; **the top/bottom three ~s** 前/后三名; **to take second ~ to sth.** 比不上某事物; **in the first/second/third ~** 处在第一/第二/第三位; **to give ~ to sb./sth.** 让位于某人/某事物 **9** [c] (position of employment or responsibility) 职位; **he has a ~ in publishing** 他在出版行业供职; **a ~ on the committee/board** 委员会/董事会成员的职位; **she has a ~ as a cook** 她是厨师 **10** [c] Brit Sch, Univ 就读机会; **to be offered a ~ (at university)** 被录取（进大学）; **a free/fee-paying ~** 免费的/须支付学费的名额 **11** [c] Sport (position on team) 队员资格; **a ~ in the national Olympic squad** 国家奥林匹克运动队的队员资格; **a ~ as team captain** 队长身份 **12** [c] Math [小数点后的] 位; **three decimal ~s, three ~s of decimals** 小数点后三位 **13** **Place** *sing* esp Brit (in place names) (square) 广场; (street) 街; (large country house) 宅院; **Langham P~, London** 伦敦兰海姆广场 **14** [u] Theat [三一律中的] 地点; **the unities of action, time, and ~** 情节、时间、地点的一致

B *vt* **1** (locate or put carefully) 放置; **the house is badly ~d on a busy main road** 房子位于繁忙的主干道旁，位置很糟糕; **to ~ sth. high up/low down/to one side** 把某物放在高处/低处/一旁; **to ~ sth. in order/in position** 把某物放整齐/放到适当的位置; **to ~ proposals before a committee** 将提案递交给委员会; **to ~ evidence before a court** 向法庭出示证据 **2** (put in situation) 安置 ‹*person*›; **to ~ sb. in sth.** 安排某人某事; **to ~ sb. in a dilemma/a tight corner** 使某人进退两难/陷入困境; **to ~ sb. with sb./sth.** 把某人安排在某人处/某处; **to ~ sb. in charge/command (of sth./sb.)** 让某人负责/指挥（某事/某人）; **to ~ sb. under arrest/surveillance** 逮捕/监视某人; **to ~ sb. at an advantage/a disadvantage/risk** 使某人处于有利位置/处于不利位置/身处险境; **to ~ sb. on a list** 把某人列入名单; **to ~ sb. in care/in the care of sb.** 使某人得到照顾/得到某人的照顾; **you're best ~d to judge** 你是作评判的最佳人选; **I'm very well ~d at the moment** 我现在一切顺利; **he's better ~d than most people think** 他过得比大多数人想的要好; **to be badly/awkwardly/similarly ~d** 处境困难/糟糕/相似 **3** (allocate, assign) 给予; **to ~ limitations/blame/reliance on sb.** 限制/责备/信赖某人; **to ~ emphasis on sth.** 强调某事物; **to ~ pressure on sb.** 向某人施加压力; **to ~ one's faith** *or* **trust in sb.** 信任某人; **to ~ (the) responsibility for sth. in sb.'s hands** 让某人负责某事; **they ~ a high value on punctuality** 他们非常注重守时 **4** (arrange for) 安排; **to ~ an advertisement in a paper** 在报纸上刊登一则广告; **to ~ an order/a contract for sth. (with sb.)** （向某人）发出某物的订单/（与某人）签订某事物的合同; **to ~ a bet on sth. (with sb.)** （与某人）就某事物下赌注 **5** (identify) 认出 ‹*person, locality*›; 辨认 ‹*face*›; **I can't quite ~ his accent** 我不太能辨别他的口音 **6** Brit (rank) 划分; **I would ~ him among the greatest players of all time** 我认为他是史上最伟大的选手之一; **to ~ sb./sth. high/low** 高估/低估某人/某事物; **the judges ~d her second** 评委给她第二; **she (was) ~d fifth in the exam** 这次考试她考了第五名; **to be ~d** Sport (be among the first three) 名列前三; Brit (be among the first four) 名列前四; **my horse has been ~d several times** 我的赛马几次获得名次 **7** Fin 投入; **to ~ money on deposit** 存钱; **she ~d all her savings in gilts/blue chips** 她把自己所有的积蓄都购买了金边债券/蓝筹股

C *v refl* **to ~ oneself (somewhere)** (take up position physically) 处于（某位置）; (put in particular situation) 处于（某境地）; **he ~d himself where he could observe the audience** 他在可以观察所有观众的位置上; **you are not placing yourself under any obligation** 你不会承担任何责任

D *vi* Sport (be among the first three) 名列前三; Brit (be among the first four) 名列前四; **the one I bet on didn't even ~** 我下了赌注的那匹马连名次都没得到

place bet *n* 名次投注 [就前三名或前两名打的赌]

placebo /plə'si:bəʊ/ *n* (*pl* **~s**) **1** (pill, medicine) 安慰剂 **2** (palliative measure) (sth. done or given) 使人宽慰的东西; (sth. said) 安慰的话

placebo effect *n* 安慰剂效应

place: ~ card *n* [标有人名的] 座位卡; **~ kick** *n* 定位球; **to take a ~ kick** 踢定位球; **~man** /-mæn/ *n* Brit pej 官禄虫 [希望获得一官半职的唯唯诺诺之人]; **~ mat** *n* 餐具垫

placement /'pleɪsmənt/ *n* **1** [u] (putting in place) 放置 **2** [c] (period of time in training, work) 实习; **to get a ~ somewhere** 在某处得到实习机会 **3** [u] (finding sb. job or home) 安置

placement test *n* Amer 分班考试

place name *n* 地名

placenta /plə'sentə/ *n* (*pl* **placentae** /plə'senti:/ *or* **~s**) 胎盘

place: ~ setting *n* 餐位餐具 [餐桌上供一个人使用的整套餐具]; **~ value** *n* 位值

placid /'plæsɪd/ *adj* **1** (equable) 平和的 ‹*person, nature, smile*›; 安静的 ‹*baby*›; 温驯的 ‹*animal*› **2** (calm and peaceful) 平静的 ‹*sea, conditions*›

placidity /plə'sɪdəti/ *n* [u] **1** (equability) (of person) 平和; (of baby) 安静; (of animal) 温驯 **2** (calmness) 平静

placidly /'plæsɪdli/ *adv* 平静地

placing /'pleɪsɪŋ/ *n* **1** (position in race, contest) 排名 **2** (positioning) (of ball, ornament) 放置; (of players) 位置安排

plagiarism /'pleɪdʒərɪzəm/ *n* [u] 抄袭

plagiarist /'pleɪdʒərɪst/ *n* 抄袭者

plagiaristic /ˌpleɪdʒə'rɪstɪk/ *adj* 抄袭的

plagiarize /'pleɪdʒəraɪz/

A *vt* 抄袭 ‹*idea, essay, research*›; 抄袭…的成果 ‹*author*›

B *vi* 抄袭

plague /pleɪɡ/

A *n* **1** [u] Med (epidemic) 瘟疫; (bubonic plague) 鼠疫; **a ~ of typhoid/cholera** 伤寒/霍乱瘟疫; **a**

~ epidemic/bacterium/vaccine 瘟疫流行/病菌/疫苗; the Great P~ 大瘟疫 [1665-1666 年主要在英国伦敦流行的黑死病]; to avoid sb./sth. like the ~ colloq 极力回避某人/某事物 2 [c] (large number) 灾祸; a ~ of locusts/rats/muggers 蝗灾/鼠害/抢劫祸患 3 [c] colloq (annoying person) 讨厌的人; (annoying thing) 令人烦恼的事物; the noise is a constant ~ to the residents 噪音一直烦扰着居民; that dog is a real ~! 那只狗实在讨厌!
B vt 1 (beset) 困扰; to be ~d with or by sth. 为某事物所困扰; the computer is ~d with or by technical faults 这台计算机频频出现技术故障; we were ~d with or by wasps 我们为黄蜂所困扰 2 (harass) 纠缠; to ~ sb. with questions/complaints 不断提问题/发牢骚烦扰某人; to ~ sb. for sth. 缠着某人要求某事物; to ~ sb. to do sth. 缠着某人做某事; to ~ the life out of sb. colloq 把某人烦得要死

plague: ~-ridden adj 遭瘟疫的; **~-stricken** adj 罹患瘟疫的 ‹person, animal›; 瘟疫流行的 ‹town, community›

plaice /pleɪs/ n (pl plaice) 鲽

plaid /plæd/
A n 1 [u] (fabric) 格子呢; (pattern) 格子图案 2 [c] (piece of cloth) [苏格兰高地人的] 格子披肩
B modif (of fabric) 格子呢的; (of pattern) 格子的

Plaid Cymru /ˌplaɪd ˈkʌmri:/ n 威尔士民族主义党

plain¹ /pleɪn/
A adj 1 (simple) 简朴的 ‹dress, style, living, building›; 清淡的 ‹cooking, food, diet›; 无糖衣的 ‹cake, biscuit›; 仅加盐的 ‹crisps›; ~ rice/water/yogurt 白饭/白开水/原味酸奶 2 (uniform) 单色的 ‹fabric›; 素色的 ‹garment›; 无格的 ‹paper, envelope›; 单一的 ‹colour› 3 (visible, clear, obvious) 清晰的 ‹line, marking, signal›; 明显的 ‹fact, situation›; it is ~ that ... 显然…; to be ~ to sb. 对某人而言很明显; he kicked him in ~ view of the referee 他当着裁判员的面踢了他; ~ and simple 显而易见; to make it ~ (to sb.) that ... (向某人) 明确表示…; to make oneself ~ 把自己的意思说明白; to be (as) ~ as the nose on your face, to be as ~ as day colloq 一目了然 4 attrib (clearly expressed, direct) 直截了当的 ‹answer›; 简单明了的 ‹language, talk›; 坦诚的 ‹person, speaking›; to be ~ about sth. 在某事物上表现坦诚; to be ~ with you, ... 坦白对你说, …; in ~ words or English, you're fired! 说白了, 你被解雇了!; I killed him, and that's the ~ truth 我杀了他, 这事明明白白的 5 attrib (downright) 纯粹的 ‹ignorance, common sense, luck, idleness› 6 (ordinary, simple, average) 平凡的; I'm not a Dr Brown, I'm ~ Mr Brown 我不是什么布朗博士, 我是普普通通的布朗先生 7 (unattractive) 相貌平平的 ‹woman, girl› 8 (in knitting) 平针的 ‹stitch, knitting›
B adv colloq 1 (completely) 完全 ‹wrong›; 极其 ‹stupid, lucky, absurd› 2 (directly, simply) 直率地 ‹speak, tell›
C n [u and c] (pl plain) (basic type of stitch) 平针; (knitted yarn) 平针针脚; two ~, one purl 两针平, 一针反; a pullover knitted in ~ 平针套衫

plain² n (area of land) 平原; the (Great) P~s 北美大平原

plain: ~chant n [u] = ~song; **~ chocolate** n [u] Brit 纯巧克力

plain clothes
A npl 便衣
B plain-clothes modif 穿便衣的 ‹police officer›

plain: ~ dealing n [u] 光明磊落; **~ flour** n [u] Brit 中筋面粉 [不含发酵粉]; **~ Jane** n colloq 相貌平平的女子

plainly /ˈpleɪnli/ adv 1 (obviously) 显然; he was ~ lying 他明显在撒谎 2 (distinctly, easily) 清晰地 3 (frankly) 简单明了地 4 (simply, not elaborately) 简朴地

plainness /ˈpleɪnnɪs/ n [u] 1 (ordinariness) 简朴 2 (unattractiveness) 相貌平平

plain sailing n [u] 一帆风顺; to be ~ 一帆风顺; the team building was not all ~ 团队建设并非一帆风顺

Plains Indian n [旧时的] 北美大平原印第安人

plainsman /ˈpleɪnzmən/ n (pl plainsmen) [尤指北美大平原的] 平原居民

plain: ~song n [u] 素歌; **~ speaker** n 说话直截了当的人

plain speaking
A n [u] 直言不讳
B adj = plain-spoken

plain: ~-spoken adj 直言不讳的; **~ text** n [u] 纯文本

plaintiff /ˈpleɪntɪf/ n 原告

plaintive /ˈpleɪntɪv/ adj 悲伤的

plaintively /ˈpleɪntɪvli/ adv 悲伤地

plait /plæt/ Brit
A n (of hair) 辫子; (of straw) 草辫; (of rope) 辫绳; (of other material) 辫; she wore her hair in ~s 她把头发扎成了辫子
B vt 1 (twist) 把…编成辫; to ~ one's hair 梳辫子 2 (make by twisting) 编制 ‹rope, necklace, basket›

plaited /ˈplætɪd/ adj 编成辫的

plan /plæn/
A n 1 (scheme, proposal) 计划; Econ 规划; a ~ to do sth. 做某事的计划; a five-year ~ 五年计划; to go according to ~ 按计划进行 2 (regular payment scheme) 投资方式; a pension/a savings/an instalment ~ 养老金/储蓄/分期付款计划 3 (diagram) (of building, geographical area) 平面图; (of installation, machine) 设计图; a seating ~ 座位图; to draw or make a ~ (of sth.) 绘制 (某物的) 平面图 4 (rough outline) 提纲; a ~ of or for an essay 一篇文章的写作提纲
B plans npl 1 (intentions) 打算; (arrangements) 安排; to have ~s for sb. 为某人作出安排; to have ~s to do sth. 计划做某事; to make ~s (for sth./to do sth.) 拟定 (某事物/做某事的) 计划; to change one's ~s 改变计划; to upset/spoil sb.'s ~s 打乱/破坏某人的计划 2 (blueprints) 设计图; to draw up ~s for sth. 为某物绘制设计图
C vt (pres p etc. -nn-) 1 (arrange, decide on) 计划 ‹visit, departure, pregnancy›; 谋划 ‹murder, escape›; 部署 ‹attack, invasion›; 规划 ‹project, career, future›; to ~ to do sth. 打算做某事; to do sth. as ~ned 按计划做某事; I ~ned it so (that) I would be home before her 我的安排是我在她前面到家 2 (design, structure) 设计 ‹building, park›; 构思 ‹book, talk›; a well-~ned kitchen 精心设计的厨房; the essay wasn't very well ~ned 文章的谋篇布局不够理想
D vi (pres p etc. -nn-) 制定计划; to ~ for the future/one's retirement 筹划未来/退休生活; I didn't ~ for this to happen 我没有料到会发生这样的事

Phrasal verbs
- **plan ahead** vi 事先计划; in business, it is important to ~ ahead 在商界, 未雨绸缪很重要
- **plan on** vt [~ on sth.]
1 (intend) 打算 ‹visit, picnic›; we ~ on getting married next year 我们打算明年结婚 2 (expect) 期待; they didn't ~ on such strong opposition 他们没料到会遭到如此强烈的反对
- **plan out** vt [~ sth. out, ~ out sth.] 规划 ‹career, route, policy›

plane¹ /pleɪn/
A n (aircraft) 飞机; to travel by ~ 乘飞机旅行; a ~ crash 飞机坠毁; a ~ ticket 飞机票
B vi 1 (move on water) «motor boat, hovercraft, hydrofoil» 在水面滑行 2 (glide) «bird, glider» 滑翔

plane² n 1 Math 平面; the horizontal/vertical ~ 水平面/垂直面 2 (flat or level surface) 面 3 (level of existence, attainment etc.) 水平; a higher ~ of development 更高的发展阶段

plane³
A n (tool) 刨子
B vt 把…刨平 ‹wood, edges›; to ~ sth. smooth 将某物刨光

Phrasal verb
- **plane down** vt [~ down sth., ~ sth. down] 刨掉

plane⁴ n ~ (tree) 悬铃木; ~ leaf 悬铃木树叶

planet /ˈplænɪt/ n 行星; P~ Earth 地球; to be on another ~ fig 异想天开

planetarium /ˌplænɪˈteərɪəm/ n (pl ~s or planetaria /ˌplænɪˈteərɪə/) 天文馆

planetary /ˈplænɪtri, Amer -teri/ adj 行星的; ~ rings 行星环

planetology /ˌplænɪˈtɒlədʒi/ n [u] 行星学

plank /plæŋk/ n 1 (piece of wood) 木板; to be as thick as two short ~s colloq 笨得要命 2 (main principle) 要点

Phrasal verb
- **plank down** vt colloq = plonk down

planking /ˈplæŋkɪŋ/ n [u] (wood) 板材; (structure of floor) 地板木料; (structure of ship) 船壳板

plankton /ˈplæŋktən/ n [u] 浮游生物

planned /plænd/ adj 1 (following a plan) 有计划的 ‹growth, redundancy, sale› 2 (premeditated) 策划好的 ‹walkout›; 有预谋的 ‹crime, disruption›

planned: ~ economy n 计划经济; **~ obsolescence** n [u] 计划报废 [指为加快消费品更新速度而控制其质量和耐久性的设计理念]; **~ parenthood** n [u] 计划生育

planner /ˈplænə(r)/ n 1 (person who makes plans) 策划人 2 (urban layout designer) 规划师 3 (list, chart) 计划表

planning /ˈplænɪŋ/
A n [u] 1 (of future activities) 计划; the ~ of an essay 文章的构思 2 (of future projects) 策划 3 (of towns, cities, land) 规划
B modif 1 (in local government, with public works) 规划的; ~ department/policy/decisions 规划部门/政策/决策 2 (in industry, by government) 计划的; ~ meeting/decisions 计划会议/决策

planning: ~ application n 规划申请; **~ blight** n [u] 规划病; **~ committee** n 规划委员会; **~ permission** n [u] Brit 规划许可; **~ regulations** npl 规划条例

plant /plɑ:nt, Amer plænt/
A n 1 [c] Bot 植物; ~ genetics/expert/disease 植物遗传学/专家/病害 2 [c] Ind (factory) 工厂; (power station) 发电站 3 [u] Ind (machinery) 大型机器; ~ maintenance/manufacturing/costs 设备保养/生产/成本 4 [c] (spy) 卧底 5 [c] colloq (piece of evidence) 栽赃物品
B vt 1 Agric, Hort (put in ground) 播种 ‹seed›; 栽种 ‹bulb, flower, bush, tree›; 种植 ‹crop› 2 Agric, Hort (put plants in) 在…栽种 ‹orchard, garden, field›; fields ~ed with maize 种植了玉米的田地 3 (put down) 安放 ‹large object›; 竖立 ‹flagpole›; to ~ one's feet firmly 两脚稳稳地站立; to ~ a flag on the summit 在山顶插上旗帜; to ~ a spade in the soil 把铲子插在泥土里 4 (place on body) 给予 ‹punch, kick›; to ~ a kiss on sb.'s cheek 在某人的脸颊上吻一下; to ~ a blow on sb.'s head 对准某人的头打一拳 5 (hide for use) 秘密放置 ‹explosive, listening device› 6 (place to produce result) 将…栽赃 ‹stolen goods, evidence, drugs›; to ~ sth. on sb. 把某物栽赃于某人; to ~ a question 事先策划好问题 7 (place as helper) 安插 ‹spy, informer› 8 (embed) 灌输 ‹idea, rumour›; to ~ sth. in sb.'s mind or head 把某事物灌输进某人的头脑; to ~ the seeds of doubt in sb.'s mind 在某人心中播下疑

虑的种子 9 (found, establish) 建立 ‹*colony, settlement*›

C *v refl* colloq **to ~ oneself** 占据位置; **she ~ed herself at the front of the queue/in an armchair** 她排到队列的前面/坐在扶手椅上

Phrasal verb

• **plant out** *vt* [**~ sth. out, ~ out sth.**] 均匀栽种 ‹*young plant, seedling*›

plantain /ˈplæntɪn/ *n* 1 [c] (tree) 大蕉树 2 [u] (fruit) 大蕉 3 [u] (weed) 车前草

plantation /plænˈteɪʃn/ *n* 1 (land with crops) 种植园; **tea/rubber ~** 茶园/橡胶园 2 (land planted with trees) 林地

plant breeder *n* 植物育种家

planter /ˈplɑːntə(r), Amer ˈplænt-/ *n* 1 (plantation owner) 种植园主; (plantation manager) 种植园经营者 2 (person who plants) 种植者; (machine that plants) 播种机 3 (plant pot) 花盆; (container holding pot) 花架

plant: ~ food *n* [u] 肥料; **~ geneticist** ▸**p. 409** *n* 植物遗传学家; **~ genetics** *npl + v sing* 植物遗传学; **~ hire** *n* [u] Brit 机械租赁; **a ~ hire business/company** 机械租赁行/公司; **~ kingdom** *n* 植物界; **~ life** *n* [u] 植物; **~ louse** *n* 蚜虫; **~ pot** *n* 花盆

plaque /plɑːk, Amer plæk/ *n* 1 [c] (plate, tablet) 匾牌 2 [u] (dental deposit) 齿菌斑

plasma /ˈplæzmə/ *n* 1 [u] (in blood) 血浆 2 [c] (gas) 等离子体

plasma: ~ screen *n* 等离子屏幕; **~ television** *n* 等离子电视

plaster /ˈplɑːstə(r), Amer ˈplæs-/

A *n* 1 [u] Constr 灰泥 2 [u] (for healing limbs) 石膏; **to have an arm in ~** 胳膊打了石膏; **to put sb.'s leg in ~** 给某人的腿打石膏; **a ~ model/figure** 石膏模型/塑像 3 [c and u] Brit (for covering wounds) 创可贴

B *vt* 1 Constr 在…上抹灰泥 ‹*wall, ceiling*› 2 (cover or apply thickly) 厚厚地涂抹; **the artist ~ed paint all over the canvas** 画家在画布上涂满了厚厚的颜料 3 (cause to lie flat) 使紧贴; **the rain had ~ed his clothes to his body** 淋雨使得衣服紧紧贴在他身上 4 (post up) 张贴; **to ~ the wall with posters** 在墙上张贴海报; **to ~ notices on the wall** 在墙上贴通知 5 (display prominently) 醒目地刊登 ‹*article, picture*›; **the story was ~ed all over the front page** 这篇报道醒目地占据了整个头版

C *vi* 抹灰泥

Phrasal verb

• **plaster over**

D *vt* [**~ over sth.**] 用灰泥抹 ‹*crack, hole, surface*›

plasterboard /ˈplɑːstəbɔːd, Amer ˈplæst-/ *n* [u] 石膏板; **~ walls/ceiling** 石膏板墙壁/屋顶

plaster cast *n* 1 (cover protecting broken bone) 石膏绷带 2 (mould) 石膏模型

plastered /ˈplɑːstəd, Amer ˈplæst-/ *adj* colloq 烂醉的; **to get ~** 喝醉

plasterer /ˈplɑːstərə(r), Amer ˈplæst-/ ▸**p. 409** *n* 抹灰工

plastering /ˈplɑːstərɪŋ, Amer ˈplæst-/ *n* [u] 抹灰泥; **to do the ~** 抹灰泥

plaster: ~ of Paris *n* [u] 熟石膏; **~work** *n* [u] 石膏装饰图案

plastic /ˈplæstɪk/

A *n* [u] 1 (substance) 塑料 2 colloq (credit card) 信用卡

B **plastics** *npl* 塑料; **the ~s industry** 塑料工业

C *adj* 1 (made of plastic) 塑料的 2 (malleable) 可塑的 3 (impressionable) 易受影响的 ‹*mind*›; 可塑的 ‹*personality*›; 易变的 ‹*notion, image*› 4 (false, insincere) 做作的 ‹*entertainer, smile*›; 华而不实的 ‹*environment*› 5 colloq (artificial, synthetic) 味同嚼蜡的 ‹*hamburger, coffee, airline food*›

plastic: ~ arts *npl* **the ~ arts** 造型艺术; **~ bag** *n* 塑料袋; **~ bomb** *n* 塑料炸弹; **~ bullet** *n* 塑料子弹; **~ cup** *n* 塑料杯; **~ explosive** *n* [u and c] 塑料炸药

Plasticine® /ˈplæstɪsiːn/ *n* [u] 橡皮泥; **~ model/modelling clay** 橡皮泥模型/雕塑土

plasticity /plæsˈtɪsəti/ *n* [u] 1 (malleability) 可塑性 2 (impressionability) 易受影响

plastic: ~ mac *n* 塑料雨衣; **~ money** *n* [u] colloq 塑料币 [指信用卡、借记卡等]; **~ surgeon** ▸**p. 409** *n* 整形外科医生; **~ surgery** *n* [u] 整形手术; **~ wood** *n* [u] 塑化木; **~ wrap** *n* [u] Amer 保鲜膜

plate /pleɪt/

A *n* 1 [c] (large dish) 盘子; (small dish) 碟子; (serving dish) 托盘; **to hand** *or* **give** *or* **present sth. to sb. on a ~** fig 把某物拱手送给某人; **to clean** *or* **empty one's ~** 把饭菜吃光; **to have a lot/enough/too much on one's ~** fig 要处理的事情很多/足够了/太多 2 [c] (dishful) 一盘; **a ~ of pasta** 一盘意大利面 3 [c] (sheet of metal) 金属板; **a metal ~** 一块金属板 4 [c] (nameplate) [写有名字的] 匾牌 5 [c] (vehicle licence plate) 牌照 6 [u] (dishes, bowls, and cups) (made of gold) 金质餐具; (made of silver) 银质餐具 7 [u] (plated metal) 有镀层的金属; **gold ~** 镀金层 8 [c] (metal sheet for printing) 印版 9 [c] (book or magazine illustration) 插图 10 [c] (covering and protecting animal) 鳞甲 11 [c] Phot 感光板 12 [c] (denture) 假牙托 13 [c] (piece of earth's surface) 板块 14 [c] (competition trophy) (dish) 奖牌; (cup) 奖杯

B *vt* 1 (cover with gold, silver etc.) 电镀 ‹*metal, dish*› 2 (reinforce) 给…装金属护板 ‹*ship, hull*›

plateau /ˈplætəʊ, Amer plæˈtəʊ/ *n pl* (**~s** *or* **plateaux** /ˈplætəʊz, Amer plæˈtəʊz/) 1 (high flat land) 高原 2 (stable level) 稳定期; **to reach a ~** 稳定下来

plateful /ˈpleɪtfʊl/ *n* 一盘; **a ~ of spaghetti** 一盘意大利细面条

plate glass *n* [u] 平板玻璃; **~ window/door/mirror** 平板玻璃窗/门/镜子

platelayer /ˈpleɪtleɪə(r)/ ▸**p. 409** *n* Brit (person laying railway tracks) 铺轨工; (person repairing railway tracks) 养路工

platelet /ˈpleɪtlɪt/ *n* 血小板

platen /ˈplætən/ *n* 1 (in printing press) 压印盘 2 (in computer printer, typewriter) 压纸卷筒

plate: ~ rack *n* 餐具架; **~ tectonics** *npl + v sing* 板块构造学

platform /ˈplætfɔːm/ *n* 1 (stage) (for performance) 舞台; (at public meeting) 讲台; **to share a ~ with sb.** 与某人同台 2 (at railway station) 月台 3 (aims and policies of political party) 政纲; **on a ~ of economic reform** 以经济改革为纲领 4 (flat raised structure) (gen) 平台; (on weighing machine) 秤台; (on oil rig) 钻井平台; (for weapons) 炮台 5 (opportunity for airing one's views) [发表观点的] 论坛 6 Comput (operating system) 计算机平台

platform: ~ scales *npl* 台秤; **~ shoes** *npl* 松糕鞋; **~ ticket** *n* Brit 站台票

plating /ˈpleɪtɪŋ/ *n* 1 (metal coating) 镀层 2 (protective casing) 金属护板

platinum /ˈplætɪnəm/

A *n* [u] 铂; **to go ~** «*CD, album, performer*» 达到白金销量

B *modif* 1 (made of platinum) 铂制的 ‹*jewellery*› 2 (containing platinum) 含铂的 ‹*ore, deposit*›; **a ~ alloy** 铂合金 3 (colour) 银白色的 ‹*hair*›

platinum: ~ blonde *n* 银发女郎; **~-blonde** *adj* 银白色的 ‹*hair, wig*›; **~ disc** *n* 白金唱片

platitude /ˈplætɪtjuːd, Amer -tuːd/ *n* [尤指说教性的] 陈词滥调

Platonic /pləˈtɒnɪk/ *adj* 1 (*also* **platonic**) (affectionate but not sexual) 柏拉图式的 ‹*relationship, love*› 2 (relating to Plato) 柏拉图的 ‹*philosophy, influence*›

platoon /pləˈtuːn/ *n + v sing or pl* 1 (group of soldiers) 排 2 (group of people) 队; **a ~ of firemen** 一队消防员

platoon: ~ commander *n* Brit 排长; **~ sergeant** *n* Amer 副排长

platter /ˈplætə(r)/ *n* 1 (dish) 大盘; **to hand sb. sth. on a ~** fig 把某物拱手送给某人; **don't expect things to be handed to you on a ~** 别指望天上会掉馅饼 2 (plateful) 一大盘; **a ~ of smoked fish** 一大盘熏鱼

platypus /ˈplætɪpəs/ *n* (*pl* **~es**) 鸭嘴兽

plaudits /ˈplɔːdɪts/ *npl* (praise) 称赞; (approval) 赞赏

plausibility /ˌplɔːzəˈbɪləti/ *n* [u] 1 (of argument, theory, excuse, statement) 貌似有理; **the ~ of her alibi** 她的不在犯罪现场证明貌似合理; **a plot that strains ~** 牵强附会的情节 2 (of person) 貌似可信; **the ~ of a witness** 证人的可信度

plausible /ˈplɔːzəbl/ *adj* 1 (seemingly reasonable) 貌似合理的 ‹*statement, theory, excuse, argument*› 2 (skilled at being persuasive) 花言巧语的 ‹*liar, character*›

plausibly /ˈplɔːzəbli/ *adv* 令人信服地 ‹*argue, explain, behave*›; 花言巧语地 ‹*lie*›

play /pleɪ/

A *vi* 1 (enjoy oneself) 玩耍; **to ~ at soldiers/hide-and-seek** 玩当大兵/捉迷藏游戏; **to ~ together** «*children*» 一起玩; **to ~ at being a Buddhist** 把做佛门弟子当儿戏; **to ~ with each other** 一起玩; fig 相互捉弄; **he has no intentions of marrying her — he's just ~ing with her** 他无意娶她——只是和她逢场作戏罢了; **to ~ with a toy/one's food** 玩玩具/摆弄食物; **I'm ~ing with the idea** 我这个想法是闹着玩儿的; **a person who loves to ~ with words/emotions** 爱玩文字游戏/喜欢玩弄感情的人; **to ~ with fire** fig 玩火; **to ~ with oneself** euph 手淫 2 Sport, Games (compete) 参加比赛; **to ~ at chess/tennis** 比赛下国际象棋/打网球; **to ~ with** *or* **against sb.** 与…比赛 ‹*sportsperson, team, country*›; **to ~ for a team/one's country** 代表某运动队/国家参赛; **to ~ in the final** 参加决赛; **Manchester United are ~ing at home to Arsenal** 曼联队将在主场迎战阿森纳队; **to ~ fair/false (with sb.)** (与某人) 进行公平/不公平交易; **to ~ for money** 进行有报酬的比赛; **to ~ for time** 拖延时间; **there's everything to ~ for** 一切都尚未尘埃落定; **he needs financial backing, but the bank won't ~** 他需要财政支持，可是银行却不肯出手相助 3 Sport (take position) 充任位置; **to ~ in defence/the attack/goal** 打后卫/打前锋/担当守门员; **to ~ as** *or* **at left wing/fullback** 担任左边锋/后卫 4 Sport (hit, shoot) «*person*» 击打; **to ~ into the bunker/net** 把球打进沙坑/球网; **the batsman ~ed on to his wicket** 击球手把球打进己方三柱门; **to ~ on one's opponent's backhand** 把球打向对手的反手位; **to ~ to sb.'s strength(s)/weakness(es)** 把球打向某人最擅长/最薄弱的位置; **the government is ~ing to the opposition's weaknesses** 政府正在针对反对党的弱点发起攻击 5 Sport (be fit to play on) **the court/pitch is ~ing well/fast** 这个球场适合比赛/球速较快; **to ~ true** 弹性正常 6 (gamble) 打赌; **to ~ for high stakes** 下大赌注赌博 7 Games (move) 走子; **it's your turn to ~** 轮到你走了 8 Games (submit card) 出牌; **to ~ out of turn** 抢出牌 9 Mus (perform, produce sound) «*musician, orchestra, music*» 演奏; «*song*» 唱出; «*CD, record, cassette tape*» 播放; **to ~ on the clarinet/flute/xylophone** 吹单簧管/吹长笛/敲木琴; **to ~ to** *or* **for sb.** 为某人演奏; **to ~ in/out of tune** 演奏合调/走调; **to ~ in time** 和着节拍演奏 10 (be acted, shown) «*play, opera, film*» 上演; (act) 演出; **the film is ~ing at the Odeon** 影片正在奥登影院上映; **to ~ to audiences all over**

the country 对全国观众演出; to ~ in Macbeth 在《麦克白》中扮演角色; to ~ with/opposite sb. 与某人联袂演出/演对手戏; to ~ dead 装死 11 (move lightly) «light, sunshine» 闪烁; «shadow» 摇曳; «breeze» 轻拂; to ~ over/around sth. 在某物上方/周围摇曳; a smile ~ed on his lips 他的嘴角露出一丝微笑 12 (emit stream or beam) «water, beam» 喷出; «light» 照射; the relaxing sound of a fountain ~ing 喷泉喷涌时令人感觉轻松惬意的声音; a spotlight ~ed on the empty stage 一束聚光灯的灯光打在空荡荡的舞台上

B *vt* 1 (engage in for enjoyment) 玩 ‹*game*›; 假扮…玩游戏 ‹*soldiers, pirates*›; to ~ mummies and daddies 玩过家家游戏; to ~ nurses/keeping shop 玩当护士/开商店的游戏 2 (trick sb. with) 开 ‹*joke*›; 耍 ‹*trick*›; the children ~ed a prank on their teacher 孩子们要恶作剧捉弄老师 3 (compete in) 参加 ‹*game*›; 打 ‹*cricket, tennis, basketball*›; 玩 ‹*bridge*›; to ~ sth. against sb. 与某人比赛某项目; to ~ football for one's university 代表大学参加足球比赛; to ~ sth. as a professional/an amateur 以职业运动员/业余身份参加某比赛; to ~ a game of chess/tennis with sb. 与某人下国际象棋/打网球 4 (compete against) 与…比赛 ‹*competitor, team, country*›; to ~ sb. at his *or* her own game fig 对某人以牙还牙; to ~ sb. false 欺骗某人 5 Sport (take position of) 担任 ‹*back, forward, goal(keeper), wing(er)*›; he ~ed centre forward for Albion 他担任阿尔比恩队的中锋 6 Sport (select) 选中 ‹*player, footballer*›; to ~ sb. as *or* at sth. 选派某人担任 ‹*goalkeeper, midfielder*› 7 Sport (hit, strike) 击; to ~ a forehand/backhand (stroke) 正手/反手击球; he ~ed a drive through the covers 他一记大力击球，把球打出外场防守区; to ~ the ball into *or* on to sth. 把球打至某处; to ~ the ball to sb./sth. 把球击向某人/到某处; she ~ed the ball to her opponent's backhand 她把球打到了对手的反手位 8 (gamble at) 对…下赌注; to ~ the stock market/horses 玩股票/赌马; to ~ sth. for high stakes 以大赌注赌某物 9 Games (put on table) 打出 ‹*card*› 10 Mus (perform) 演奏 ‹*instrument, symphony*›; to ~ the guitar/violin 弹吉他/拉小提琴; to ~ sth. on sth. 用某乐器演奏某乐曲; to ~ a tune to the children 为孩子们演奏一支曲子 11 Audio (put on) 播放 ‹*disc, tape, record*› 12 (represent) 扮演 ‹*character, part*›; to ~ sth. for laughs Theat colloq 扮演某角色搞笑; to ~ it rough/cool/safe 行为粗暴/冷静/稳妥; to ~ it for kicks 寻求刺激 13 Cin, Theat (put on) «*theatre, cinema*» 上演 ‹*play, film, concert*› 14 Mus, Theat (perform at) «*actor, performer, show, band*» 在…演出 ‹*theatre, venue*› 15 (behave like) 装扮; to ~ the politician/diplomat 装扮成政治家/外交官; to ~ the innocent 装成很无辜的样子 16 (direct) 射出 ‹*beam, light*›; 喷 ‹*water*›; to ~ the hoses over the flames 把消防水带对着大火喷水; to ~ the searchlights along the road 用探照灯沿路照射 17 Fishg «*angler*» 拉线使…挣扎得筋疲力尽 ‹*fish*›

C *n* 1 [u] (amusement, recreation) 玩耍; at ~ 在玩耍; to learn through ~ 寓学于乐; child's ~ 易如反掌的事; I only said it in ~! 我只是开开玩笑而已！; all work and no ~ makes Jack a dull boy Prov 只用功，不玩耍，聪明的孩子也变傻; ~ box/clothes/room 玩具箱/游乐服/游戏室 2 [c] Theat 戏剧; the characters in a ~ 剧中人物; a television ~, a ~ for television 电视剧; a one-/five-act ~ 独幕/五幕剧; to present *or* produce *or* put on a ~ 上演戏剧; to write a ~ 写剧本; to act in a ~ 在剧中扮演角色 3 [u and c] Sport (playing of game) 比赛; (manner of playing) 赛风; (move in game) 比赛动作; fair/foul/rough ~ 公平/不公平/粗野的竞赛; a fine defensive/offensive ~ 精彩的防守/进攻动作; the state of ~ (score) [尤指板球比赛的] 比分; (situation) 争执情况 4 [c] (turn) (in cards) 出牌机会; (in chess) 走棋机会; it's your ~ next 下面该你了; to make a ~ for sb./sth. 想方设法吸引某人/得到某物; to make one's ~ (for sth.) （为某事）处心积虑 5 [c] (clever use) 巧妙使用; a ~ on words 双关语 6 [u] Mech 间隙; give the line more/less ~ 放松/拉紧线绳 7 [u] (freedom) (to act) 活动自由; (to operate) 运作自由; to bring *or* call sth. into ~ 使某事物开始起作用; to come into ~ (be active) 开始活动; (have an influence) 开始起作用; luck comes into ~ 开始走运; to give free ~ to sb./sth., to give sb./sth. free ~ 让某人/某事物自由发挥; she gave *or* allowed free ~ to her pent-up emotions 她释放出了压抑的情绪; to make great ~ of *or* with sth. 强调某事物; the ~ of the imagination 想象力的发挥 8 [u] (shifting movement of light, colours, flames, shadows) 摇曳; the ~ of sunlight on the surface of the lake 湖面上的粼粼波光

Phrasal verbs

- **play about** *vi* = play around
- **play along**

A *vi* 1 (pretend to cooperate) 假装合作; to ~ along with sb./sth. 假装与某人合作/认同某事物 2 Mus (accompany) 伴奏; to ~ along with sb./sth. 给某人/某物伴奏; I'll sing, you ~ along on the piano 我唱歌，你用钢琴伴奏

B *vt* [~ sb. along] colloq 欺骗

- **play around** *vi* 1 to ~ around with sth. (fiddle with, handle casually) 胡乱摆弄某物; don't ~ around with that expensive vase — you might drop it 别摆弄那个昂贵的花瓶——你会摔了它的; to ~ around with the idea of doing sth. 琢磨做某事的念头; how much time/money do you have to ~ around with? 你有多少时间/钱可以用来折腾? 2 colloq (be promiscuous) 乱搞; they say her husband ~s around 据说她的丈夫爱拈花惹草; to ~ around with sb. 和某人鬼混
- **play away** *vi* Brit 1 Sport «*team*» 在客场打比赛; Manchester United ~ away to Arsenal 曼联队在客场挑战阿森纳队 2 colloq (have affair) 搞婚外恋
- **play back** *vt* [~ sth. back, ~ back sth.] 播放 ‹*recording, music, film*›; to ~ sth. back to sb. 给某人播放…
- **play down** *vt* [~ sth. down, ~ down sth.] 降低…的重要性 ‹*crisis, defeat*›; 淡化 ‹*situation, effects, seriousness*›
- **play off**

A *vi* «*competitors, teams*» 进行加赛; to ~ off against sb. 与某人打加赛

B *vt* [~ off sth., ~ sth. off]
1 Sport «*competitors, teams*» 参加…以决定胜负 ‹*match*›; the deciding round will be ~ed off tomorrow 明天将进行决胜轮比赛 2 (put in conflict) 挑拨; to ~ sb. off against sb. 挑拨某人使其与某人不和; the government ~ed the rival factions off against each other 政府鼓动两个敌对派相互争斗

- **play on**

A *vi* «*player, team*» 继续比赛; «*musician*» 继续演奏

B *vt* [~ on sth.] 利用 ‹*feeling, prejudice, ignorance*›

- **play out** *vt* 1 [~ out sth., ~ sth. out] (enact) 演出 ‹*scene, fantasy, drama, role*›; their love affair was ~ed out against a background of war 他们的爱情剧以战争为背景，已公开上演 2 [~ out sb., ~ sb. out] Mus 奏乐為…送行; the bagpipes ~ed them out of the dining room 他们在风笛乐曲伴奏下走出宴会大厅
- **play up** Brit

A *vi* 1 colloq (cause problem) 添麻烦; my back/rheumatism is ~ing up again 我的背痛/风湿病又发作了; the computer keeps ~ing up 这台电脑不断出故障 2 Sport «*player, team*» 全力投入比赛; ~ up and ~ the game! 加油比赛！ 3 colloq to ~ up to sb. (flatter) 奉承某人

B *vt* 1 [~ sb. up, ~ up sb.] colloq (cause problem for) 给…添麻烦 ‹*person*› 2 [~ sth. up, ~ up sth.] (exaggerate) 夸大 ‹*danger, benefits, mystery*›

- **play upon** *vt* = play on B

playable /ˈpleɪəbl/ *adj* 1 Sport (able to be played) 可以打的 ‹*shot*›; (fit for playing on) 可用于比赛的 ‹*pitch, course, track*› 2 Audio (able to be played) 可以播放的 ‹*record, CD, track*› 3 (easy to play) 容易玩的 ‹*game*›; 容易演奏的 ‹*piece of music*›

play-act

A *vi* 1 (pretend) «*child*» 假装 2 (behave theatrically) «*person*» 做戏

B *vt* 假装; to ~ their favourite stories 演他们最喜欢的故事

play: **~-acting** *n* [u] 1 (make-believe, pretence) 假装; 2 (melodramatic behaviour) 做戏; **~-actor** *n* 装模作样的人; **~ area** *n* (outside) 儿童游乐场; (inside) 儿童活动区

playback /ˈpleɪbæk/ *n* 1 [u] (reproduction) (of sound) 录音播放; (of pictures) 录像播放 2 [c] (device) 播放装置

playback head *n* 播放头

play: **~bill** *n* 戏剧海报; **~book** *n* Amer [尤指美式橄榄球的] 攻略手册; to take a page out of another's ~book fig 采用别人的战术

playboy /ˈpleɪbɔɪ/ *n* 花花公子; ~ millionaire/lifestyle 花花公子式的富翁/生活方式

play-by-play *n* Amer Sport 现场解说; ~ coverage/results 现场报道/比分

play: **~ centre** *n* 校外游戏场; **~-centred learning** *n* [u] 以游戏为中心的学习

played-out *adj* colloq 精疲力竭的 ‹*person*›; 消退的 ‹*emotion, passion*›; 过时的 ‹*theory, argument*›

player /ˈpleɪə(r)/ *n* 1 (of sport, game) 运动员; (of ball games) 球员; chess ~ 棋手; poker ~ 扑克玩家 2 (musician) 演奏者 3 (actor) 演员 4 (influential entity) 重要参与者; a major ~ in the stock market 股市大炒家 5 (music-playing device) 播放机; a record ~ 电唱机

player-manager *n* [尤指足球队的] 队员兼教练

playfellow /ˈpleɪfeləʊ/ *n* 玩伴

playful /ˈpleɪfl/ *adj* 1 (light-hearted) 开玩笑的 ‹*remark, banter, action, mood*›; 爱开玩笑的 ‹*person*› 2 (lively) 活泼有趣的

playfully /ˈpleɪfəli/ *adv* 开玩笑地 ‹*remark, say, tease, pinch*›; 嘻嘻哈哈地 ‹*joke, banter*›; 快乐地 ‹*frolic, gambol*›

playfulness /ˈpleɪflnɪs/ *n* [u] 1 (light-heartedness) (of remark, action, mood) 开玩笑; (of person) 爱开玩笑 2 (liveliness) 活泼有趣

play: **~goer** *n* 戏迷; **~ground** *n* 游乐场; **~group** *n* Brit [由父母组织定期活动的] 幼儿游戏班; **~house** *n* 1 (for children) 游戏房; 2 (theatre) 剧院

playing: **~ card** *n* 扑克牌; **~ field** *n* 运动场; a level ~ field fig 公平竞争的环境

playlet /ˈpleɪlɪt/ *n* 短剧

play: **~list** *n* 播放曲目; **~maker** *n* 组织进攻的队员; **~mate** *n* 玩伴; **~-off** *n* 1 (at end of match, game) [决定胜负的] 附加赛; to go to a ~-off 进入附加赛; 2 (contest) 决赛; **~ on words** *n* 双关语; **~pen** *n* 游戏护栏; **~ reading** *n* 剧本朗读; **~room** *n* 游戏室; **~scheme** *n* [为儿童假期娱乐提供设施的] 活动计划; **~school** *n* Brit [通常为半日制的] 幼儿游戏班; **~suit** *n* 1 连身衣; 2 (children's costume) 模仿套装; **~thing** *n* 玩物; **~time** *n* [u] [教学日中的] 游戏时间; **~wright** /ˈpleɪraɪt/ *n* 剧作家

plaza /ˈplɑːzə, Amer ˈplæzə/ *n* 1 (public square) 广场 2 Amer (shopping centre) 购物中心

plc, PLC *abbr* = public limited company

plea /pliː/ *n* **1** (appeal for tolerance, mercy) 请求; **to make a ~ for aid/peace** 请求援助 **2** (trial statement) 抗辩; **to make a ~ of not guilty** 提出无罪抗辩; **to enter a guilty ~** 表示认罪; **a ~ in mitigation** 从轻发落的请求

plea: ~ bargain *n* 辩诉交易 [起诉人与被告达成的由被告承认轻罪以减轻处罚的协议]; **~ bargaining** *n* [u] 辩诉交易

plead /pliːd/ (*pt, pp* **~ed**, Amer **pled**)
A *vi* **1** (beg) 乞求; **to ~ with sb. (to do sth.)** 恳求某人(做某事); **to ~ with sb. for mercy** 乞求某人宽恕 **2** (argue) 声援; **to ~ for sb.** 为某人辩护; **to ~ for sth.** 呼吁某事; **to ~ against sb.** 反驳某人 **3** Jur (of defendant) 申辩; (of lawyer, barrister) 为…辩护; **to ~ guilty/not guilty (to a charge)** (对指控)认罪/不认罪; **how do you ~?** 你有何辩护?
B *vt* **1** (beg) 乞求; **she ~ed to be forgiven** 她乞求原谅 **2** (argue) «*lawyer, person*» 为…辩护 ‹*case, cause*›; **to ~ insanity** 提出精神失常的抗辩 **3** (give as excuse) 提出…作为借口 ‹*ignorance, other commitments*›

pleading /ˈpliːdɪŋ/
A *adj* 恳求的
B *n* [u] 恳求

pleadingly /ˈpliːdɪŋli/ *adv* 恳求地

pleasant /ˈpleznt/ *adj* **1** (pleasing, satisfying) 悦耳的 ‹*music, voice*›; 悦目的 ‹*shape, painting*›; 舒适的 ‹*place, building*›; 愉快的 ‹*experience, conversation, journey, atmosphere*›; 宜人的 ‹*climate, summer, breeze, smell*›; 可口的 ‹*wine*›; **a ~ surprise** 一个惊喜; **~ to the ear/taste** 悦耳的/好吃的 **2** (friendly, likeable) 友善的 ‹*person, manner, smile, letter*›

pleasantly /ˈplezntli/ *adv* **1** (pleasingly, satisfyingly) 令人愉快地; **~ surprised** 又惊又喜的; **~ warm/quiet** 温暖舒适/宁静宜人的 **2** (agreeably, politely) 和气地 ‹*behave, say, smile*›

pleasantry /ˈplezntri/ *n* 客套; **to exchange** *or* **swap pleasantries** 相互寒暄

please /pliːz/ ▸**p. 818**
A *excl* **1** (accepting politely, or giving permission) 请; **two coffees, ~** 请来两杯咖啡; **would you like another cup of tea? — yes, ~** 要再来一杯茶吗?——好的,谢谢; **may I smoke? — ~ feel free** 我可以吸烟吗?——请自便 **2** (with request, as question) 请问; **~ could I leave early today?** 请问我今天早点走行吗? **3** (requesting attention) 对不起; **~, I don't understand** 对不起,我不明白 **4** (in protest, entreaty) 请不要; **children, ~** 孩子们,别闹了; **I'll pay — ~, you're my guest!** 我来付钱——请别这样,你是我的客人嘛!
B *vt* **1** (give happiness or satisfaction to) 使高兴; **there's no pleasing some people** 有些人难以取悦; **to ~ the eye/ear** 悦目/悦耳 **2** dated (be the will of) 合…的心意 ‹*person*›; **may it ~ Your Majesty** 希望陛下满意; **~ God he comes!** 但愿他能来!; **if you ~** (in orders, requests) 烦请; (showing indignation) 岂有此理; **then, if you ~, he expects me to pay!** 接下来,你听听,他居然指望我付钱!
C *v refl* **to ~ oneself** 随心所欲; **you must ~ yourself whether you come or not** 来不来随便你; **~ yourself!** 请自便!
D *vi* **1** (give happiness or satisfaction) 使人满意; **she's eager** *or* **anxious to ~** 她急于取悦别人 **2** (like, think fit) 愿意; **I'm going now — as you ~** 我要走了——你想走就走吧; **she walked forward as calm as you ~** 她非常镇定地走上前去; **take as much as you ~** 你想拿多少就拿多少
E *n* 请; **without so much as a ~ or thank you** 连个"请"或"谢谢"都没说

pleased /pliːzd/ *adj* 高兴的; **to look** *or* **seem ~** 似乎很高兴; **to be/look ~ with oneself** 沾沾自喜/显得飘飘然; **I'm none too ~** 我气愤不已; **I am only too ~ to help** 我非常乐意帮忙; **I am ~ to announce that/to inform you that ...** 谨此欣告…; **I'm ~ to hear it!** 听到这消息我真高兴!; **~ to meet you** 很高兴认识你; **you've passed, I'm ~ to say** 我很高兴地告诉你,你及格了; **she is ~ to accept the invitation** formal 她欣然接受邀请

pleasing /ˈpliːzɪŋ/ *adj* 喜人的 ‹*outcome, effect, news*›; 好听的 ‹*voice*›; 好看的 ‹*appearance, shape, colour*›; 令人愉快的 ‹*person, manner, smile, personality*›; **~ to the ear/eye** 悦耳/悦目的

pleasingly /ˈpliːzɪŋli/ *adv* 令人满意地; **~ cool** 凉爽宜人的; **~ simple/colourful** 简单宜人的/缤纷悦目的

pleasurable /ˈpleʒərəbl/ *adj* 愉快的

pleasurably /ˈpleʒərəbli/ *adv* 愉快地; **~ warm/relaxing** 温暖舒适的/轻松愉快的

pleasure /ˈpleʒə(r)/
A *n* **1** [u] (happiness) 快乐; (satisfaction) 满足; (enjoyment) 享乐; **to watch/listen with ~** 开心地观看/聆听; **to take all the ~ out of sth.** 尽情享受某事物的乐趣; **to take ~ in sth./doing sth.** 以某事物/做某事为乐; **to take no ~ in sth./doing sth.** 一点儿也不喜欢某事物/做某事; **to find ~ in sth.** 从某事物中找到乐趣; **to do sth. for ~** 为了取乐而做某事; **a life of ~** 纵情享乐的生活; **sexual ~** 性快感 **2** [c] (enjoyable activity, experience) 乐事 **3** [c] (in polite formulae) **it's been a ~ meeting you** *or* **to meet you — the ~ was all mine** 见到你很高兴——我也是; **my ~** (replying to request for help) 乐意效劳; (replying to thanks) 别客气; **I look forward to the ~ of meeting you** 我期待与你见面; **may I have the ~ (of this dance)?** 可以一起跳(这支舞)吗?; **we request the ~ of your company at our daughter's wedding** (on invitation) 敬请光临小女的婚礼 **4** [u] (leisure, recreation) 玩乐 **5** [u] formal (wish, will, desire) 意愿; **what is your ~?** 你要点儿什么?; **at sb.'s ~** 根据某人的意愿; **to be detained at Her/His Majesty's ~** Brit 被不定期监禁
B *modif* 游览的; **a ~ trip** *or* **tour** 观光旅行; **a ~ steamer** 游轮

pleasure: ~ boat *n* 游艇; **~ craft** *n* (*pl* **~ craft**) 游艇; **~ cruise** *n* 航游; **~-loving** *adj* 喜欢享乐的; **~ principle** *n* 快乐原则; **~-seeker** *n* 寻欢作乐的人

pleat /pliːt/
A *n* 褶
B *vt* 给…打褶

pleb /pleb/ *n* Brit colloq pej 草民; **the ~s** 平头百姓

plebeian /plɪˈbiːən/
A *n* **1** (citizens of ancient Rome) 平民; **the ~s** 平民 **2** formal (lower-class person) 百姓
B *adj* **1** (of the citizens of ancient Rome) 平民的 **2** formal (of the lower social classes) 下层的 ‹*person*›; 平民百姓的 ‹*taste, attitude*› **3** formal pej (lacking in education and culture) 普通的 ‹*origins*›; 粗俗的 ‹*accent, sport, taste, appearance*›

plebiscite /ˈplebɪsaɪt, -sɪt/ *n* 全民公决; **to hold a ~** 举行全民公投

plectrum /ˈplektrəm/ *n* (*pl* **~s** *or* **plectra** /ˈplektrə/) 琴拨

pled /pled/ *pt, pp* Amer ▸**plead**

pledge /pledʒ/
A *n* **1** (promise) 诺言; (guarantee) 保证; **to make** *or* **give a ~ to do sth.** 承诺做某事; **to take** *or* **sign the ~** euph 发誓戒酒; **to be under a ~ of allegiance/secrecy** 宣誓效忠/保密; **to sign a ~** 签署保证书; **to keep** *or* **honour** *or* **fulfil a ~** 履行诺言; **to break a ~** 违背诺言 **2** (promise to donate) 慈善捐赠承诺; **a ~ of £500** 500 英镑的捐助承诺 **3** (thing deposited as security) 抵押品; **to redeem a ~** 赎回抵押物 **4** (token) 信物; **as a ~ of (sb.'s) love/friendship/sincerity** 作为(某人的)爱情信物/友谊信物/诚意保证 **5** Amer Univ 许诺加入联谊会的学生
B *vt* **1** (promise) 承诺; (guarantee) 保证; **to ~ sth. to sb.** 向某人承诺某事; **to ~ to do sth.** 保证做某事; **I ~ you my word that I will never desert you** 我向你保证决不抛弃你; **I'd be willing to ~ anything for his honesty** 我绝对保证他是诚实的 **2** (promise to donate) 承诺捐助 ‹*(sum of) money*›; **to ~ £50 to a charity** 承诺向慈善机构捐款 50 英镑 **3** (commit) 使…保证 ‹*person, followers, government*›; **to ~ sb. to sth./to do sth.** 让某人保证某事/做某事; **the leader has ~d the movement to non-violence** 运动领袖保证该运动不使用暴力; **to ~ sb. to secrecy** 使某人发誓保密 **4** (deposit as security) 抵押 ‹*jewellery, property*› **5** Amer Univ (accept promise to join) 准许…入会 ‹*(new) student*›; **to be ~d to a fraternity/sorority** 获准加入男生/女生联谊会 **6** Amer Univ (agree to join) «*(new) student*» 立誓加入 ‹*fraternity, sorority*›
C *vi* Amer «*(new) student*» 立誓入会
D *v refl* **to ~ oneself to do sth.** 保证做某事; **the government ~d itself to deal with environmental problems** 政府承诺着手解决环境问题

Pledge of Allegiance *n* Amer 效忠誓词

Pleistocene /ˈpleɪstəsiːn/
A *adj* (of the period) 更新世的; (of the rock system) 更新统的
B *n* **the ~** (period) 更新世; (rock system) 更新统

plenary /ˈpliːnəri, Amer -eri/
A *adj* **1** (of assembly, council etc.) 全体出席的 ‹*debate, session*›; **a ~ meeting of the association** 协会全体成员会议 **2** (absolute) 绝对的 ‹*authority*›; **~ power** 全权
B *n* 全体会议

plenipotentiary /ˌplenɪpəˈtenʃəri, Amer -eri/
A *n* 全权代表 [尤指外交人员]
B *adj* 有全权的; **an ambassador ~** 全权大使; **~ powers** 全权

plenitude /ˈplenɪtjuːd, Amer -tuːd/ *n* [u] liter 充足

plenteous /ˈplentɪəs/ *adj* liter 丰富的; **a ~ harvest** 丰收

plentiful /ˈplentɪfl/ *adj* 充足的; **fish were ~ in this river** 这条河中鱼很多; **a ~ supply of food** 充足的食品供应; **in ~ supply** 供应充足的; **a ~ harvest** 丰收

plentifully /ˈplentɪfəli/ *adv* 大量地

plenty /ˈplenti/
A *pron* 大量; **~ of ideas/information** 很多想法/信息; **to get ~ of time/money** 有充裕的时间/充足的金钱; **£50 will be ~** 50 英镑够多的了; **that's ~** (referring to food) 够了
B *adv* **1** (a lot) 很多; **there's ~ more paper** 还有很多纸; **there's ~ more where that came from** euph 钱有的是 **2** colloq (more than sufficiently) 绰绰有余地; **~ big/tall enough** 大/高得绰绰有余; **the rope was ~ long enough to reach the ground** 这根绳子很长,拉到地面仍有富余 **3** Amer colloq (very much) 非常; **to be ~ thirsty** 口渴得很
C *n* [u] 充裕; **days/years of ~** 富足的日子/岁月; **to live in ~** 生活富裕; **a land of ~** 富庶地区

plethora /ˈpleθərə/ *n* formal 过多; **there is a ~ of sth.** 有太多的某物

pleurisy /ˈplʊərəsi/ ▸**p. 377** *n* [u] 胸膜炎

Plexiglas® /ˈpleksɪglɑːs, Amer -glæs/ *n* [u] Amer 普列克斯有机玻璃

pliability /ˌplaɪəˈbɪləti/ *n* [u] **1** (malleability) 易弯; **the ~ of these materials** 这些材料的柔韧性 **2** fig (flexibility) 顺从; **he lacks ~** 他缺乏圆通

pliable /ˈplaɪəbl/ *adj* **1** (malleable) 易弯的 ‹*material*› **2** fig (flexible) 易摆布的 ‹*mind, person*›

pliant /ˈplaɪənt/ *adj* **1** (malleable) 易弯的 ‹*material*› **2** fig (flexible) 易受影响的 ‹*mind*›; 容易摆布的 ‹*person, government*›

pliers /ˈplaɪəz/ *npl* 钳子; **a pair of ~** 一把钳子

plight /plaɪt/ *n* 困境; **what an awful ~ she's in!** 她的处境真糟糕!

plimsoll /ˈplɪmsəl/, **plimsole** /ˈplɪmsəʊl/ *ns* Brit 橡胶底帆布鞋

Plimsoll line /ˈplɪmsəl laɪn/ *n* 载重线标志

plink /plɪŋk/

A *n* 叮当声; **the ~ of the keys on the piano** 钢琴键发出的叮咚声

B *vi* **1** (emit sound) 发出叮当声 **2** (play instrument) 叮叮当当地弹奏

plinth /plɪnθ/ *n* **1** (column base) 柱基 **2** (base for statue, equipment) 底座

Pliocene /ˈplaɪəʊsiːn/

A *adj* (of the period) 上新世的; (of the rock system) 上新统的

B *n* **the ~** (period) 上新世; (rock system) 上新统

PLO *abbr* **= Palestine Liberation Organization**

plod /plɒd/

A *vi* **1** (*pres p etc.* **-dd-**) (walk slowly) 沉重缓慢地行走 **2** fig (work slowly) 埋头苦干; **I ~ded through a huge text book** 我埋头苦读一本大部头的课本

B *n* 沉重缓慢的行进; **it's a long ~ home** 回家的路漫长而艰难; **the slow ~ of hooves** 马匹缓慢沉重的步履

Phrasal verb

• **plod along, plod on** *vi* **1** (walk slowly) 沉重缓慢地行走 **2** fig (work slowly) 埋头苦干

plodder /ˈplɒdə(r)/ *n* pej 老黄牛

plodding /ˈplɒdɪŋ/ *adj* **1** (slow-moving) 缓慢沉重的 ‹*step*› **2** fig (slow and unimaginative) 老黄牛式的 ‹*worker*›; 单调乏味的 ‹*drama*›

plonk /plɒŋk/ colloq

A *n* **1** [c] (sound) 扑通声 **2** [u] Brit (cheap wine) 廉价酒; (poor quality wine) 劣质酒

B *adv* 扑通一声 ‹*drop, fall*›

C *vt* 重重放下; **she ~ed the shopping (down) on the floor** 她嘭地一下把买来的东西扔在地板上

Phrasal verbs

• **plonk away** *vi* colloq 胡乱弹奏 [尤指弹钢琴]

• **plonk down** *vt* [**~ sth. down**] colloq 重重放下; **to ~ oneself down** 重重坐下; **she ~ed herself down in the armchair** 她一屁股坐在扶手椅上

plonker /ˈplɒŋkə(r)/ *n* Brit colloq (fool) 蠢人; (inept person) 无能的人

plop /plɒp/

A *n* 扑通声

B *vi* (*pres p etc.* **-pp-**) «*pebble, fish*» 扑通落下; «*jelly, raindrop*» 啪嗒落下

C *vt* (*pres p etc.* **-pp-**) 使轻声落下; **she ~ped a sugar cube into her tea** 她啪嗒一声往茶里投了一块糖; **to ~ oneself down** 轻轻坐下

plosive /ˈpləʊsɪv/

A *adj* 破裂的

B *n* 破裂音

plot /plɒt/

A *n* **1** (piece of ground) 小块土地; **a ~ of land** 一块地; **a vegetable ~** 一块菜地; **a cemetery ~** 一块墓地 **2** (conspiracy) 密谋; **an assassination ~** 暗杀阴谋 **3** (narrative of novel, film, play) 情节; **I couldn't follow the ~** 我搞不明白故事情节; **the ~ thickens** 情况变得复杂起来

B *vt* (*pres p etc.* **-tt-**) **1** (secretly plan) 密谋; **to ~ to do sth.** 暗中策划做某事 **2** (make plan of) 设计…的方案; (map) 绘制…的平面图; **they have ~ted a way forward for company expansion** 他们为公司设计好了一条扩张之路 **3** (chart) 在图上标绘出 ‹*course, position, progress*› **4** (on graph) 绘制 ‹*curve*›; 标定 ‹*point, figure*›

C *vi* (*pres p etc.* **-tt-**) 密谋; **to ~ against the government** 密谋反政府

plotter /ˈplɒtə(r)/ *n* **1** (schemer) 密谋者 **2** (device) 绘图机

plough /plaʊ/ Brit

A *n* **1** Agric 犁; **a horse and ~** 一套马和犁; **under the ~** 用于耕作的; **to put** *or* **set one's hand to the ~** lit 开始耕作; fig 着手 **2** esp Amer **= snowplough A1** **3** Brit Astron **the P~** 北斗七星

B *vt* **1** Agric (break up with plough) 犁 ‹*field, land*›; (create with plough) 犁出 ‹*furrow*›; **a ~ed field** 犁过的田地; **to ~ a lonely furrow** fig 自耕孤畴; **to ~ one's way through sth.** fig 奋力穿过某物; **to ~ one's way through a pile of legal documents** 埋头苦读大量法律文件 **2** esp Amer (clear with snowplough) 用扫雪机清扫 **3** (invest) **to ~ money into sth.** 将大笔资金投资于某事物 **4** Brit Univ colloq dated «*examinee*» 未通过 ‹*examination*›; «*examiner*» 使…不及格 ‹*examinee*›

C *vi* «*farmer, horse, ox*» 犁地; «*tractor*» 耕地

Phrasal verbs

• **plough back** *vt* [**~ sth. back, ~ back sth.**] 把…再投资 ‹*profit, surplus, income*›; **to ~ sth. back into sth.** 把某物再投资于某事

• **plough in** *vt* [**~ sth. in, ~ in sth.**] 犁埋 ‹*crop, grass*›

• **plough into** *vt* [**~ into sth.**] «*driver, vehicle*» 猛撞 ‹*vehicle, person, tree*›

• **plough on** *vi* «*person, group*» 坚持下去; «*vehicle*» 继续前进

• **plough through** *vt* [**~ through sth.**] 费力地穿越 ‹*wave, obstacle, snow, mud*›; 苦读 ‹*book*›; 费力做 ‹*exercise*›

• **plough up** *vt* [**~ sth. up, ~ up sth.**] **1** Agric 犁耕 ‹*land, field*› **2** (destroy surface of) «*vehicle*» 碾坏 ‹*field, track*›

plough: ~ horse *n* 耕马; **~land** /-lænd/ *n* [u] 耕地

ploughman /ˈplaʊmən/ ▸**p. 409** *n* 犁田者

ploughman's lunch *n* Brit 农夫午餐 [包括面包、乳酪、泡菜与色拉]

ploughshare /ˈplaʊʃeə(r)/ *n* 犁铧

plover /ˈplʌvə(r)/ *n* 鸻

plow /plaʊ/ *n, vt, vi* Amer **= plough**

plowman /ˈplaʊmən/ *n* **= ploughman**

plowshare /ˈplaʊʃeə(r)/ *n* **= ploughshare**

ploy /plɔɪ/ *n* 策略; **a delaying ~** 拖延手段; **to resort to a ~** 耍花招

PLR *abbr* Brit **= public lending right**

pluck /plʌk/

A *vt* **1** (pick) 摘 ‹*flower, fruit*› **2** (pull or tug sharply) 扯 ‹*paper, sleeve*›; **to ~ sth. from sb.'s grasp** 抢走某人紧抓的某物 **3** (pull feathers off) 拔…的毛 ‹*chicken, goose*› **4** (pull out with tweezers) 用镊子拔; **to ~ one's eyebrows** 拔眉毛 **5** Mus 弹奏 ‹*guitar, banjo*› **6** (remove) 解救; **to ~ sb. to safety** 救某人脱险; **to be ~ed from obscurity** 一举成名

B *n* **1** [c] (sharp tug) 拽; **he felt a ~ at his sleeve** 他感到袖子被拉了一下 **2** [u] (courage) 勇气; **he has plenty of ~** 他很有胆量; **to show ~** 表现出勇气; **to have the ~ to do sth.** 有勇气做某事

Phrasal verbs

• **pluck at** *vt* [**~ at sth.**] 拽 ‹*garment*›; **to ~ at sb.'s sleeve** 拉某人的袖子

• **pluck off** *vt* [**~ off sth., ~ sth. off**] 拔掉 ‹*feather, fluff*›

• **pluck out** *vt* [**~ out sth., ~ sth. out**] 挖出 ‹*eye*›; 掏出 ‹*ball, handkerchief*›; 夺走 ‹*purse*›

• **pluck up** *vt* **to ~ up (the) courage (to do sth.)** 鼓起勇气（做某事）

pluckily /ˈplʌkɪli/ *adv* 勇敢地

plucky /ˈplʌki/ *adj* 有勇气的; **to be ~** 有胆量

plug /plʌg/

A *n* **1** Elec (on appliance) 插头; **to fit a ~** 插上插头; **to pull the ~ on sth.** colloq 抽掉用于某事物的资金 **2** Elec (socket) 插座 **3** (in bath, sink) 塞子; **to put in/pull out the ~** 塞上/拔出塞子 **4** (device for blocking or stopping leak or flow) 填塞物; **to use sth. as a ~ for the leak** 用某物堵漏洞; **a cotton-wool/spark/fire/volcanic ~** 棉塞/火花塞/消防栓/火山栓 **5** (cake of tobacco) 口嚼烟草块 **6** colloq (advertisement) (on TV, radio) 插播广告; (in speech) 捧场话; **to give sb./sth. a ~, to put in a ~ for sb./sth.** 吹捧某人/插播某物的广告

B *vt* (*pres p etc.* **-gg-**) **1** (block up) 塞住 ‹*leak, hole, crack*›; **to ~ the gap in a market/drain on resources** 堵住市场/资源消耗的漏洞 **2** (insert) 用…堵塞; **to ~ a rag into the gap/hole** 用破布堵缺口/洞 **3** Elec **to ~ sth. into a socket/the mains** 把某物插入插座/插线板; **to ~ the printer into the computer** 把打印机接入电脑; **to be ~ged into sth.** fig (be knowledgeable about) 对某事物了如指掌; (be involved with) 参与某事 **4** colloq (advertise) 宣传 ‹*show, brand, company*›; 推广 ‹*record, book*›; 吹捧 ‹*singer*› **5** Amer colloq (shoot) 向…射击 ‹*game, person, object*›; (hit) 拳打 ‹*person*›

C *vi* (*pres p etc.* **-gg-**) **to ~ into sth.** **1** (connect to) 与…相连接 ‹*device, appliance, wall*› **2** fig (have access to) 进入 ‹*market, system*›

Phrasal verbs

• **plug away** *vi* colloq 坚持不懈; **to ~ away at sth.** 埋头做某事

• **plug in**

A *vt* [**~ sth. in, ~ in sth.**] 为…接通电源 ‹*device, appliance, lamp*›

B *vi* «*device, appliance, lamp*» 接通电源

• **plug up** *vt* [**~ sth. up, ~ up sth.**] 堵塞 ‹*leak, hole*›

plug: ~ and play *n* 即插即用; **~-and-play technology** 即插即用技术; **~hole** *n* Brit 排水孔; **to go down the ~hole** «*water*» 从排水孔流走; «*object*» 从排水孔冲走; fig colloq (be lost) 失败; (be wasted) 被浪费; **two years' hard work went down the ~hole** 两年的辛苦工作付诸东流了; **the company went down the ~hole** 公司破产了

plug-in

A *adj* 插入式的 ‹*shaver, component, telephone*›

B *n* Comput 插件

plug-ugly esp Amer colloq

A *adj* 极丑陋的

B *n* 恶棍

plum /plʌm/ ▸**p. 134**

A *n* **1** (fruit) 李子; (tree) 李树 **2** (colour) 紫红色 **3** fig colloq (good thing) 好东西; (thing worth having) 值得拥有的东西; **a ~ of a job** 称心如意的工作

B *modif* **1** (of fruit) 李子的 ‹*stone, juice*› **2** colloq (good) 称心的 ‹*assignment*›; **to get** *or* **land a ~ job/part** 得到一份称心的工作/一个梦寐以求的角色

C *adj* 紫红色的

plumage /ˈpluːmɪdʒ/ *n* [u] [鸟的] 全身羽毛; **a bird with superb ~** 羽毛华美的鸟

plumb /plʌm/

A *n* (for wall) 铅锤; (for water) 测深锤; **to be out of** *or* **off ~** 不垂直

B *adj* (vertical) 垂直的 ‹*wall, post*›

C *adv* **1** (precisely) 恰恰; **~ in** *or* **down/through the middle** 在正中央/正好穿过中心 **2** Amer colloq (completely) 完全地 ‹*crazy, stupid*›; **it was ~ idiotic of him to do that** 他做那事真傻透了

D *vt* **1** (measure) 测 ‹*depth*›; (measure depth of) 测…的深度 ‹*waters*› **2** fig (explore fully) 探究 ‹*soul, mystery*›; **to ~ the depths of sth.** 达到…的极限 ‹*despair, misery*›; **this play ~s the depths of bad taste** 这部戏品位极其低下

Phrasal verb

• **plumb in** *vt* [**~ sth. in, ~ in sth.**] 将…与水管连接 ‹*washing machine, dishwasher*›

p

plumber /ˈplʌmə(r)/ ▸p. 409 *n* 管子工

plumbing /ˈplʌmɪŋ/ *n* [u] 1 (system of pipes) [建筑物中的] 管道系统; ～ **system** 水暖系统 2 (installing) 管道施工; (maintaining) 管道维修 3 euph hum (urinary system) 泌尿系统; (excretory system) 排泄系统

plumb line *n* 铅垂线

plum: ～ brandy *n* [u] 李子白兰地; ～ **cake** *n* [u and c] Brit 水果干蛋糕; ～ **duff,** ～ **pudding** *ns* [u and c] 水果干布丁

plume /pluːm/

A *n* 1 (feather) 羽毛 2 (on hat) 羽饰 3 fig (of steam, smoke etc.) 缕; **the chimney was emitting a ～ of smoke** 烟囱里冒出一缕青烟

B *vi* 一缕缕冒出

C *v refl* **to ～ oneself** 扬扬自得; **she ～d herself on her trim waist** 她因为腰细而沾沾自喜

plumed /pluːmd/ *adj* 1 (of bird) 有羽毛的; **a white-～ egret** 白羽鹭鸶 2 (decorated with feathers) 羽毛装饰的 ‹*horse, hat*›

plum jam *n* [u] 李子酱

plummet /ˈplʌmɪt/ *vi* 1 «*bird, aircraft*» 坠落 2 «*price, share*» 暴跌; «*temperature, morale*» 猛降

plummy /ˈplʌmi/ *adj* 1 Brit colloq (upper-class) 上流社会腔调的; **a ～ accent** 上等人的腔调 2 Brit colloq (desirable) 称心合意的; **a ～ job** 美差 3 (plum-like) 像李子的

plump[1] /plʌmp/ *adj* (chubby) 胖乎乎的 ‹*baby, cheek, arm*›; 丰满的 ‹*person*›; 肥硕的 ‹*chicken*›; 胀鼓鼓的 ‹*cushion*›

Phrasal verb

• **plump up**

A *vt* [**～ sth. up, ～ up sth.**] 使蓬松

B *vi* 胀起; **soak the raisins in brandy and they will ～ up** 葡萄干泡在白兰地中就会胀大

plump[2]

A *vt* (drop suddenly) 重重放下; **he ～ed his suitcase (down) on the bed** 他把手提箱摔到了床上

B *adv* (suddenly) 突然; (heavily) 沉重地; **he sat down ～ on the bed** 他一屁股坐在床上

Phrasal verbs

• **plump down** *vt* [**～ sth. down, ～ down sth.**] colloq 重重放下; **to ～ oneself down** 扑通坐下; **he ～ed himself down on the sofa** 他一屁股坐在沙发上

• **plump for** *vt* [**～ for sth.**] colloq 选中; **he ～ed for the grilled plaice instead of the steak** 他要了烤比目鱼而不是牛排

plumpness /ˈplʌmpnɪs/ *n* [u] (of person) 丰满; (of arms, legs, etc.) 圆滚滚

plum: ～ tomato *n* 李形番茄; ～ **tree** *n* 李树

plunder /ˈplʌndə(r)/

A *vt* 1 (loot) 掠夺 ‹*wealth, property*›; 劫掠 ‹*town, shop*› 2 fig (appropriate) 借鉴

B *n* [u] 1 (act of stealing) 劫掠 2 (booty) 劫掠物; (stolen property) 赃物

C *vi* 劫掠

plunderer /ˈplʌndərə(r)/ *n* 劫掠者

plundering /ˈplʌndərɪŋ/

A *n* [u] 劫掠

B *adj* 大肆劫掠的 ‹*mob, troops*›

plunge /plʌndʒ/

A *vi* 1 (move headlong) «*diver*» 纵身一跳; «*bird*» 俯冲; «*submarine*» 突然下沉; **the goalkeeper ～d to his left** 守门员纵身向左侧扑去; **to ～ into the river/lake** 纵身跳进河里/湖里; **he ～d from the rock into the water** 他从岩石上跳入水中; **the country ～d into chaos/a crisis** 该国陷入混乱/危机 2 (drop or fall from height) «*ship*» 下沉; «*vehicle*» 跌落; «*road, waterfall*» 陡然而下; «*neckline*» 开得很低; **she ～d to her death from a fifth-floor balcony** 她从6楼的阳台上跳下来摔死了; **the plane ～d into the sea/to the ground** 飞机坠海/坠地 3 (get involved) 参与; **to ～ into sth.** 投身于 ‹*activity, career, negotiations*› 4 (move uncontrollably) «*vehicle, driver*» 横冲直撞; (rush) «*person, animal*» 猛冲; **to ～ into/out of/across/for/through sth.** 冲进/冲出/冲过/冲向/迅速穿过某物

B *vt* 1 (cause to enter forcibly) 猛地投入; **to ～ sth. into sth.** 把某物猛力插入某物; **he ～d the knife into her side/heart/chest** 他猛地将匕首插入她的肋部/心脏/胸膛 2 (thrust, hurl downwards) 甩下; **he ～d his hands deeper into his pockets** 他双手往口袋里插得更深了; **the sudden tilt of the deck ～d him into the sea** 甲板突然倾斜, 把他甩入海中 3 fig (bring suddenly into particular condition) 使陷入; **to be ～d into war/despair/darkness** 卷入战争/陷入绝望/陷入黑暗

C *n* 1 (downward drop) 突然跌落; **a death ～** 致命的一跌; **a ～ into sth.** 进入某物的下跌; **a ～ into debt/chaos** 陷入负债境地/混乱; **a ～ in confidence** 信心的急速下降 2 (jump or dive into water) 跳水; **a refreshing ～ in the lake** 令人神清气爽的湖中一游; **to take a ～** 下水游泳 3 fig (sudden involvement) 卷入; **a ～ into sth.** 对…的投入 ‹*market, sphere of activity*›; **to take the ～** 冒险一试 4 fig (sharp decline) 猛跌; **a ～ in share** Brit *or* **stock** Amer **prices** 股价的暴跌; **oil/house prices started on a downward ～** 油价/房价开始暴跌

Phrasal verbs

• **plunge forward** *vi* «*person, vehicle*» 向前猛冲; «*horse*» 向前狂奔

• **plunge in**

A *vi* 1 (jump or dive in) «*person, diver*» 跳入水中; «*swimmer*» 潜入水中 2 fig (become involved) 投身

B *vt* [**～ sth. in, ～ in sth.**] 猛插入 ‹*knife, sword*›

plunge: ～ bath *n* 1 (deep bath) 深浴缸; (pool) 大浴池; 2 (bathe in deep bath) 在深浴池中的洗浴; ～ **pool** *n* 冷水池

plunger /ˈplʌndʒə(r)/ *n* 1 (part of device or mechanism) 柱塞 2 (for clearing blockages) 搋子

plunging /ˈplʌndʒɪŋ/ *adj* 深开领的; **a ～ neckline** 低领口

plunk /plʌŋk/ colloq

A *vi* [尤指毫无表现力地] 叮叮咚咚弹奏

B *vt* 1 (put down) 重重放下 2 (strum) 弹拨

Phrasal verb

• **plunk down** *vt* colloq = **plonk down**

pluperfect /pluːˈpɜːfɪkt/

A *adj* 过去完成时的

B *n* **the ～** 过去完成时

plural /ˈplʊərəl/

A *adj* 1 Ling 复数的 ‹*noun, form*› 2 Pol 多元的 ‹*society, system*›

B *n* 复数; **in the ～** 以复数形式

pluralism /ˈplʊərəlɪzəm/ *n* [u] 1 Sociol 多元化 2 (principle of peaceful coexistence) 多元主义 3 Philos 多元论

pluralist /ˈplʊərəlɪst/

A *n* 1 Sociol 多元主义者 2 Philos 多元论者

B *adj* 多元主义的 ‹*policy*›; 多元论的 ‹*view*›; **to live in a ～ society** 生活在多元化社会

plurality /plʊəˈræləti/ *n* 1 (multitude) 众多; **a ～ of sth.** 大量的某物 2 Amer (majority) [未超过半数的] 相对多数 (票)

plus /plʌs/

A *prep* 1 (added to) 加; **15 ～ 12** 15 加 12 2 (as well as) 外加; **don't forget you're taking John — ～ all his animals** 别忘了你要带上约翰——还有他所有的动物; **two adults ～ a baby** 两个大人和一个孩子; **he looked odd, ～ he was a foreigner** 他看上去很古怪, 而且他还是个外国人

B *adj* 1 Math (indicating addition) 加的; (positive) 正的; **a ～ quantity** 正量 2 Elec 阳性的 3 (advantageous) 有利的 ‹*point, factor*›; **(on) the ～ side** (在) 好的方面 4 *postpos* (more than) 略高一些的; **50 ～** 50 多; **A ～** A+; **he got two B ～es** 他得了两个 B+

C *n* 1 Math 加号 2 fig (advantage) 有利因素; **his knowledge of French is a big ～** 他的法语知识是一大优势

plus fours /ˌplʌs ˈfɔːz/ *npl* [射击、高尔夫等运动中穿的] 灯笼裤

plush /plʌʃ/

A *adj* 1 colloq (luxurious) 豪华的 ‹*hotel, interior*› 2 Tex 长毛绒的 ‹*sofa, carpet, curtain*›

B *n* [u] 长毛绒

plushy /ˈplʌʃi/ *adj* colloq 豪华的 ‹*hotel, interior*›

plus: ～ sign *n* (indicating addition) 加号; (indicating positive value) 正号; **～-size** *adj* Amer 特大号的 ‹*garment*›; 高大的 ‹*woman*›

Pluto /ˈpluːtəʊ/ *pr n* 冥王星

plutocracy /pluːˈtɒkrəsi/ *n* 1 [u] (system) 富豪统治 2 [c] (state) 富豪统治的国家; (government) 富豪统治的政府 3 [c] (class) 富豪统治阶级

plutocrat /ˈpluːtəkræt/ *n* 财阀

plutocratic /ˌpluːtəˈkrætɪk/ *adj* 富豪统治的 ‹*government, dynasty*›; 富豪的 ‹*rule, class*›

plutonium /pluːˈtəʊnɪəm/ *n* [u] 钚

ply[1] /plaɪ/

A *vt* 1 (sell) 巡回销售 ‹*wares, goods*› 2 (perform) 从事 ‹*trade, profession*› 3 (use) 辛勤地使用 ‹*tool*›; 猛划 ‹*oar*›; **to ～ one's needle** 飞针走线 4 (travel) 定期航行于 ‹*river, sea*›; **to ～ the route between two ports** 定期往返于两个港口之间 5 (provide continuously) 持续提供; **to ～ sb. with food/drink** 不断为某人提供食物/饮料 6 (repeatedly question) 不断提问; **they plied us with questions about China** 他们一个劲地问我们有关中国的问题

B *vi* «*boat*» 定期航行; «*coach*» 定期行驶

ply[2] *n* [u] (of cloth) 层; (of yarn) 股; **two/three ～ paper** 两/三层纸; **two ～ wool** 两股毛线

plywood /ˈplaɪwʊd/ *n* [u] 胶合板; **～ furniture** 胶合板家具

PM *abbr* 1 **= prime minister** 2 **= post-mortem** 3 **= provost marshal**

p.m. ▸p. 831 *abbr* **= post meridiem** 下午; **2 ～** 下午两点; **9 ～** 晚上九点

PMG *abbr* Brit **= Paymaster General**

PMS *abbr* **= premenstrual syndrome**

PMT *abbr* esp Brit **= premenstrual tension**

pneumatic /njuːˈmætɪk, Amer nuː-/ *adj* 1 Mech 风动的 ‹*system*›; **～ brakes** 气压制动器 2 (filled with air) 充气的 ‹*bag*› 3 Brit colloq (having full bust) 胸部丰满的 ‹*beauty, model*›

pneumatically /njuːˈmætɪkli, Amer nuː-/ *adv* 通过气压 ‹*work, function*›

pneumatic: ～ drill *n* esp Brit 风钻; **～ tyre** *n* 充气轮胎

pneumonia /njuːˈməʊnɪə, Amer nuː-/ ▸p. 377 *n* [u] 肺炎

PO *abbr* 1 **= post office** 2 **= postal order**

poach[1] /pəʊtʃ/

A *vt* 1 (catch illegally) 偷猎 ‹*game, deer*›; 偷捕 ‹*salmon*› 2 fig (lure) 挖 ‹*employee, player*› 3 fig (steal) 窃取; **to ～ sth. from sb.** 从某人处窃取 ‹*idea, policy*›

B *vi* 1 (hunt illegally) 偷猎; **to ～ for sth.** 偷猎某物 2 fig (encroach) 侵犯; **to ～ on sb.'s territory** 侵犯某人的领地

poach[2] *vt* (in boiling water) 水煮; (over boiling water) 清蒸; (in simmering water) 煨炖 ‹*fruit, fish*›; **～ed egg** 水煮荷包蛋; **～ed salmon** 清炖鲑鱼

poacher[1] /ˈpəʊtʃə(r)/ *n* (hunter) 偷猎者

poacher[2] *n* (for eggs) 煮蛋锅; (for fish) 蒸锅

pock /pɒk/ *n* **= pockmark**

pocket /ˈpɒkɪt/

A *n* 1 (in garment) 衣袋; **a coat/jacket/trouser ～** 外衣/夹克衫/裤子口袋; **to have one's hands in one's ～s** 手插在口袋里; **to have very deep ～s** fig 很富有; **to put one's hand**

in one's ~ lit 把手插进口袋; fig 自己掏腰包; **the deal will put a lot of money in your ~** 这笔交易会为你赚一大笔钱; **to fill** or **line one's ~s** fig 中饱私囊; **to have sb. in one's ~** fig 让某人任使唤; **to have a game in one's ~** fig 比赛稳操胜券; **to live in each other's ~s** fig 形影不离 **2** (in car door, suitcase, folder, bag, etc.) 小口袋 **3** fig colloq (financial resources) 财力; **to be beyond sb.'s ~** 超出某人的财力; **easy/hard on the ~** 便宜/昂贵的; **to be a drain on sb.'s ~** 是某人的经济负担; **that's going to hurt his ~** 那东西要让他破费了; **out of one's own ~** 自己掏腰包; **to be in ~** Brit (be financially comfortable) 有钱; (have made a profit) 赚了钱; **to be out of ~** Brit (be short of money) 缺钱; (have made a loss) 赔钱 **4** (small area) [与周围不同的] 小区域; **~s of resistance/unemployment/snow** 孤立的抵抗势力/小批失业者/小片残雪; **a gas/coal ~** 气团/煤仓 **5** Games (in billiards, snooker, pool) 球袋

B *modif* **1** (portable) 袖珍的 ‹*torch, dictionary, edition*› **2** (relatively small) 小型的; **a ~ model** 小模型

C *vt* **1** (put in pocket) 把…装入口袋 ‹*object, change, ticket*›; **to ~ one's pride** fig 收敛傲气 **2** colloq (keep for oneself) 把…据为己有 ‹*profits, sum, takings*› **3** colloq (earn, win) 赚取 ‹*sum*› **4** Games (in billiards, snooker, pool) 把…击入球袋 ‹*ball*›

pocket: ~book *n* **1** Amer (wallet, purse) 钱包; (handbag) 坤包; **2** Amer (small book) 袖珍本; **3** Brit (notebook) 笔记本; **~ calculator** *n* 袖珍计算器

pocketful /ˈpɒkɪtfʊl/ *n* **1** (pocket-sized amount) 一衣袋; **he collected a ~ of shells** 他捡了一口袋贝壳 **2** colloq (large amount) 大量; **he made a ~ of cash** 他挣了一大笔钱

pocket: ~ handkerchief *n* **1** (small handkerchief) 手帕 **2** fig (small area) 小块地; **a ~-handkerchief garden** 小花园; **~ knife** *n* esp Amer 小折刀; **~ money** *n* [u] Brit 零花钱; **~-size, ~-sized** *adj* **1** (compact) 袖珍的 ‹*map, dictionary*›; **2** fig (tiny) 小规模的 ‹*estate*›; **~ watch** *n* 怀表

pock: ~mark *n* 麻点; **his face was covered with ~marks** 他满脸麻子; **~marked** *adj* 有麻点的 ‹*features, skin*›; **his ~marked face** 他的麻子脸

pod /pɒd/

A *n* **1** (of peas, beans) 荚果 **2** Aviat (for engine) 吊舱; (for weapons) 发射架; (for fuel) 油箱 **3** Aerosp 分离舱

B *vt* (pres p etc. **-dd-**) 剥 ‹*bean*›; **a bag of ~ded peas** 一袋剥好的豌豆

pod: ~cast *n* 播客节目; **~caster** *n* 播客; **~casting** *n* [u] 播客节目制作

podgy /ˈpɒdʒi/ *adj* colloq 胖乎乎的 ‹*person, arms*›

podia /ˈpəʊdɪə/ *pl* ▸ **podium**

podiatrist /pəˈdaɪətrɪst/ ▸ **p. 409** *n* esp Amer **= chiropodist**

podiatry /pəˈdaɪətri/ *n* [u] esp Amer **= chiropody**

podium /ˈpəʊdɪəm/ *n* (*pl* **~s** or **podia**) (for speaker) 讲台; (for conductor) 指挥台; (for winner) 领奖台

poem /ˈpəʊɪm/ *n* 诗; **a prose ~** 散文诗

poet /ˈpəʊɪt/ *n* 诗人

poetess /ˈpəʊɪtes/ ▸ **p. 409** *n* 女诗人

poetic /pəʊˈetɪk/ *adj* **1** (expressive) 富有诗意的 ‹*picture, expression*› **2** (relating to poetry) 诗的 ‹*form, metre*›; **~ work/style** 诗作/诗体

poetical /pəʊˈetɪkl/ *adj* 诗的; **beautiful, ~ language** 富有诗意的优美语言

poetically /pəʊˈetɪkli/ *adv* 富有诗意地 ‹*describe, write*›

poetic: ~ justice *n* [u] 报应; **~ licence** Brit, **~ license** Amer *n* [u] 诗的破格

poetics /pəʊˈetɪks/ *npl* + *v sing* [u] **1** (study of poetry, literature) 诗学 **2** Ling 理论范式

Poet Laureate /ˌpəʊɪt ˈlɒrɪət/ *n* (*pl* **~** or **~s**) 桂冠诗人

> **Poet Laureate**
>
> 桂冠诗人。英国授予优秀诗人的称号，为终身制。桂冠指月桂树（laurel）叶编成的帽子，古希腊人将其授予杰出诗人和竞技比赛的优胜者，后成为荣誉的象征。第一位桂冠诗人为本·琼生（Ben Johnson, 1572-1637）。琼生是御前诗人，领取薪俸，在国王生日和重要国事场合赋诗。19 世纪起，桂冠诗人头衔成为对诗人诗歌成就的褒奖。美国自 1986 年起开始设立桂冠诗人头衔，由国会图书馆（Library of Congress）授予，但获此头衔者只能保有此头衔一年或两年。

poetry /ˈpəʊɪtri/ *n* [u] **1** (poems) 诗歌; **a collection of ~** 诗集 **2** (poetic skill) 诗歌创作技巧; (poetic effect) 诗的意境; **the magnificent ~ of this play** 这部剧作非凡的诗意 **3** (quality of beauty) 美好品质; (emotional effect) 诗意; **there was ~ in her every movement** 她举手投足气质优雅

po-faced /ˈpəʊfeɪst/ *adj* Brit colloq 一本正经的; **to look ~** 看上去一本正经

pogey /ˈpəʊgi/ *n* [u] Can colloq 失业救济

pogo /ˈpəʊgəʊ/

A *n* **= pogo stick**

B *vi* (*pres p* **~ing**; *pt, pp* **~ed**) colloq 随朋克摇滚乐上下蹦跳

pogo stick *n* 弹簧单高跷

pogrom /ˈpɒgrəm, Amer pəˈgrɒm/ *n* [尤指因种族或宗教原因对某特定群体的] 集体迫害

poignancy /ˈpɔɪnjənsi/ *n* [u] 辛酸; **a song/moment of great ~** 极其伤感的歌曲/时刻; **to add ~ to sth.** 使某事变得更加惨痛

poignant /ˈpɔɪnjənt/ *adj* (evoking sadness) 酸楚的; **a ~ sight/story/memory** 悲惨的景象/故事/回忆; (evoking regret) 痛悔的 ‹*cry, entreaty*›

poignantly /ˈpɔɪnjəntli/ *adv* 酸楚地 ‹*describe, feel*›

point /pɔɪnt/

A *n* **1** [c] (of blade, knife, pin) 尖; (of tool, pencil, stake) 尖头; **a star with five ~s** 五角星; **the ~ of the jaw** or **chin** 颌尖 **2** [c] (dot) 点; (as punctuation mark) 句点; (in decimals) 小数点; (as diacritic) 变音符; **a ~ of light** 一点光亮; **a full ~** 句点 **3** [c] (position) 地方; (on surface) 地点; (on map) 方位点; (on scale) 标度; **the furthermost ~ of the gallery** 画廊的尽头; **the assembly** or **meeting ~** 集合地点; **the check-in ~** 登机手续办理处; **at the ~ where the path divides** 在岔道口; **all ~s north/south/east/west** 北方/南方/东部/西部各地; **~ of the compass** 罗盘方位; **from all ~s of the compass** 从四面八方; **~ of entry** (into country) 入境处; (of bullet into body) 射入点; (into atmosphere) 进入点 **4** [c] (extent, degree) 点; **boiling/freezing ~** 沸点/冰点; **his nerves were strained to breaking ~** 他的神经紧张到几近崩溃的地步; **up to a ~** 在某种程度上 **5** [c] (moment) 时刻; **a ~ in time** 某一时刻; **at this ~ in time** formal 目前; **at some ~ in the future** 在将来某一时刻; **at this/that ~** 在这时/那时; **to be on the ~ of sth./doing sth.** 正要发生某事/做某事时; **to be on the ~ of bankruptcy/tears** 濒临破产/差点掉泪; **to be on** or **at the ~ of death** 处于死亡的边缘; **there comes a ~ when** or **at which ...** 有时候会…; **when it comes to the ~** 必须作决定时 **6** [c] (unit in sport, game) 得分; (in poll, election, financial index) 点; **they won/lost by 3 ~s** 他们赢了/输了 3 分; **to win on ~s** (in boxing) 以点数获胜; **an average hand is worth 10 ~s** (in bridge) 一手平均牌值 10 点; **~s above/below the line** (in bridge) 线上/线下得分; **the party's share of the vote fell by ten percentage ~s** 该政党的得票率下跌了 10 个百分点; **the Dow-Jones average index is up/down three ~s** 道琼斯平均指数上涨/下降了 3 点; **to evaluate sth. on a five-~ scale** 按五分制标准评估某物 **7** [c] (question) 问题; (matter, idea) 论点; **the committee agreed on all ~s** 委员会在所有问题上达成了一致; **good ~!** 说得好! ; **~ by ~** 逐点地; **~ at issue** 争论点; **a ~ of detail** 细节问题; **in ~ of fact** 事实上; **a ~ of information** 需要说明的一点; **to carry** or **gain** or **win one's ~** 说服别人; **to have a ~** colloq 说到点子上; **to make a ~** 阐明观点; **to make a ~ of doing sth.** 保证做某事; **to prove a** or **the** or **one's ~** 证明看法; **to raise a ~** 提出问题; **to take the/sb.'s ~** 接受这个/某人的观点; **all right, ~ taken!** 好吧, 接受你的观点! **8** [c] (central idea) 要点; **the ~ is that ...** 关键是…; **to be beside the ~** 无关紧要; **off the ~** 离题; **to be** or **come** or **get to the ~** 说正题; **to keep** or **stick to the ~** 不跑题; **to miss the ~** 没听懂; **to see** or **get the ~** 明白 **9** [u and c] 意义; **what's the ~?** 有什么意义? ; **what's the ~ of paying someone to do it?** 为什么要花钱雇人做这事? ; **there's no/not much/little ~ in doing sth.** 做某事毫无/没有多大/没有什么/有一些意义; **to have a/some/no ~** 有/有一些/没有意义; **to see the ~ (of doing sth.)** 明白（做某事的）意义 **10** [c] (feature, characteristic) 特征; **a ~ of difference/similarity** 不同/相似之处; **good/bad ~s** 优点/缺点; **a strong/weak ~** 长处/短处; **it's a ~ in their favour** 这是对他们有利的一点; **to have one's ~s** 有其长处 **11** [c] Brit Elec 插座; **a power/telephone/shaver ~** 电源/电话/剃须刀插座 **12** [u] formal (effectiveness) 合理性; **to give ~ to sth.** 证明某事物的合理性; **to have/lack ~** 具备/缺乏合理性 **13** [c] Geog 岬角; **Cape P~** 开普角 **14** [u] Comput, Print 磅值; **~ size** 磅值大小

B **points** *npl* **1** Aut [发动机分电器的] 接触点 **2** Brit Rail 道岔 **3** Dance [芭蕾舞鞋的] 硬鞋尖; **to dance on ~s** 足尖点地跳舞

C *vt* **1** (direct) 用…指向; **to ~ sth. at sb./sth.** 持…对着某人/某物 ‹*weapon, camera*›; **to ~ one's** or **the finger at sb.** 用手指指着某人; **could you ~ me towards the public library, please?** 请告诉我去公共图书馆怎么走好吗? **2** (show) 指示 ‹*way*›; **to ~ the way (to sth.)** lit 指（通向某处的）路; fig 指引（达到某目的）; **the fans are looking to the new players to ~ the way to victory** 球迷都指望着新球员能够引领球队走向胜利 **3** (taper) 把…削尖 ‹*pencil, stick, stake*›; **to ~ one's toes** 踮起脚尖 **4** Constr 给…勾缝 ‹*wall, brickwork*›

D *vi* **1** (indicate) «*person, finger*» 指; «*signpost, weapon, compass needle*» 指向; Hunt «*dog*» 指示猎物位置; **it's rude to ~** 对人指指画画很不礼貌; **she ~ed in the direction of the exit** 她手指着出口方向; **to ~ at** or **to** or **towards sth./sb.** 指向某物/某人 **2** (suggest) «*evidence, facts, signs*» 表明; **everything ~s in that direction/to the same conclusion** 一切都指向那一个方向/同一结论; **the forensic evidence ~s to it being murder rather than suicide** 法医证据表明这是谋杀而不是自杀 **3** (cite) 援引; **to ~ to sth. as evidence of success** 把某事作为证明成功的证据来引用

Phrasal verbs

- **point out** *vt* [**~ sth./sb. out, ~ out sth./sb.**] (show) 指示 ‹*sight, object, person*›; 指出 ‹*fact, advantage, discrepancy*›; **to ~ sth. out to sb.** 向某人指出某事物; **to ~ out that/where/who/what ...** 指出…/哪里…/谁…/什么…; **she ~ed out the flaws in the argument (to me)** 她（给我）指出了这段论述中的错误
- **point up** *vt* [**~ sth. up, ~ up sth.**] 强调 ‹*contrast, similarity*›; 昭示 ‹*fact, incompetence*›

point: ~-and-click *adj* 可点击的 ‹*interface, menu*›; **~-and-shoot** *adj* 全自动的

p

point-blank
A *adj* 1 (fired from very close range) 近距离的〈*shot*〉; 近距离射出的〈*bullet*〉; **~ range** 近距离射程 2 fig (blunt, direct) 直截了当的〈*refusal, question, statement*〉; **a ~ denial of responsibility** 对责任的断然否认
B *adv* 1 (at very close range) 近距离地〈*shoot*〉 2 fig (bluntly, directly) 直截了当地〈*refuse, demand*〉

point duty *n* [u] Brit [交通警察的] 值勤; **to be on ~** 在指挥交通

pointed /ˈpɔɪntɪd/ *adj* 1 (sharp) 尖的〈*stick, pencil*〉; 有尖顶的〈*window, arch*〉; **a ~ roof/nose/chin** 尖屋顶/尖鼻子/尖下巴 2 fig (direct) 尖锐的〈*question, criticism, rebuke*〉; **her ~ remarks were not lost on me** 我注意到了她咄咄逼人的言辞

pointedly /ˈpɔɪntɪdli/ *adv* 尖锐地〈*say, ask*〉; 刻意地〈*look*〉; **somewhat ~, he remained silent** 他一言不发，多少有几分刻意

pointer /ˈpɔɪntə(r)/ *n* 1 (advice) 忠告; (tip) 提示; **can you give me some ~s on how to proceed?** 能给我指点一下接下来该怎么做吗?; **a ~ to sth.** 对某事的建议 2 (indicator) 指针 3 (rod) 教鞭 4 (dog) 指示犬 [嗅到猎物后会站立不动，并向主人指示猎物方向] 5 Comput = **cursor**

pointing /ˈpɔɪntɪŋ/ *n* [u] 1 (cement) 勾缝水泥; (mortar) 嵌填灰浆 2 (process) 勾缝

pointless /ˈpɔɪntlɪs/ *adj* 1 (senseless) 无意义的〈*criticism, effort*〉; (aimless) 无目的的〈*activity, attempt*〉; **it's ~ to do/for me to do sth.** 做某事/我做某事没有意义; **he made some ~ remark about the weather** 他没头没脑地说了说天气 2 (without scoring a point) 未得分的〈*team*〉

pointlessly /ˈpɔɪntlɪsli/ *adv* (without purpose) 无目的地〈*continue, strive*〉; (without meaning) 无意义地〈*die, obstinate*〉

pointlessness /ˈpɔɪntlɪsnɪs/ *n* [u] 无意义

point: ~ of contact *n* 联系人; **~ of departure** *n* 出发点; **~ of law** *n* 司法解释问题; **~ of no return** *n* lit 不可返回点; fig 欲罢不能的状态; **~ of order** *n* 议事程序问题; **to reject sth. on a ~ of order** 因议事程序问题驳回某事; **~ of principle** *n* 原则问题; **~ of reference** *n* 参照依据

point of sale *n* 销售点

point-of-sale: ~ advertising *n* [u] 零售点广告; **~ bin** *n* 售货柜; **~ terminal** *n* 电子售货终端

point of view *n* 1 (perspective) 观点; **to see sth. from my/her ~** 从我的/她的角度看某事物; **it depends on your ~** 这取决于你的考虑角度 2 (in writing) 叙事角度

point: ~sman /ˈpɔɪntsmən/ ▸p. 409 *n* Brit Rail 扳道工; **~s system, ~ system** *n* 记分制

point-to-point
A *n* Brit 定点越野赛马
B *adj* 1 Brit Equit 定点越野的 2 (direct) 直达的〈*travel, route*〉

pointy /ˈpɔɪnti/ *adj* colloq 有尖头的〈*shoes*〉; **to have ~ ears/nose** 长着尖耳朵/尖鼻子

pointy-headed /ˌpɔɪntɪˈhedɪd/ *adj* colloq pej 尖头的 [指专家或知识分子]

poise /pɔɪz/
A *n* [u] 1 (composure, dignity) 镇定; **her admirable ~ and assurance** 她令人钦佩的沉着与自信 2 (graceful bearing) 仪态; **the ~ and grace of the dancers/models** 舞蹈演员/模特儿的优雅姿态
B *vt* (hold, carry) 平稳握持〈*stick, spear*〉; **she ~d the racket above her head** 她把球拍握稳举过头顶; **he ~d himself on the diving board** 他在跳板上摆好姿势准备跳水
C **poised** *pp* 1 (positioned, hovering) 悬停; **with fingers ~d over the keyboard** 手指停在琴键上方; **~d high in the air, the eagle was little more than a speck** 老鹰盘旋在高空，看上去就一个小黑点; **to be ~d between life and death** fig 徘徊于生死之间; **the world was ~d between peace and war** fig 世界徘徊在战争与和平之间 2 (ready) **to be ~d to do sth./for sth.** 为做某事/为某事作好准备; **the cat was ~d to jump** 这只猫作势要起跳

poised /pɔɪzd/ *adj* 1 (calm, dignified) 泰然自若的〈*person, manner*〉 2 (graceful, elegant) 仪态优雅的〈*dancer, performance*〉

poison /ˈpɔɪzn/
A *n* [u and c] 1 (noxious substance) 毒物; **to take ~** 服毒; **a lethal/slow ~** 致命的/慢性毒药 2 fig (corrupting influence) 有害物; **this racist propaganda is pure ~** 这一种族主义宣传纯属精神毒药
B *vt* 1 (kill) 毒死; (make ill) 使中毒; **he ~ed his wife with cyanide** 他用氰化物毒死了妻子; **to have a ~ed finger/toe** 手指/脚趾受感染发炎 2 (add poison to) 在…上涂毒〈*dart, shirt*〉; 给…下毒〈*food*〉 3 Ecol (contaminate) 污染〈*river, air, environment*〉 4 fig (spoil) 毒化〈*life, outlook*〉; **this quarrel ~ed their relationship** 这次吵架使他们的关系恶化了 5 fig (injure morally) «*person, propaganda*» 毒害〈*mind*〉

poisoner /ˈpɔɪzənə(r)/ *n* 投毒杀人者

poison gas *n* [u and c] 毒气

poisoning /ˈpɔɪzənɪŋ/ *n* [u and c] (giving poison) 下毒; (taking poison) 服毒; (result) 中毒; **alcohol-ic/cyanide ~** 酒精/氰化物中毒

poison: ~ ivy *n* [u] 毒常春藤; **~ oak** *n* [u] 毒栎

poisonous /ˈpɔɪzənəs/ *adj* 1 (noxious) 有毒的〈*chemical, plant*〉; **~ fumes/gas** 毒烟/毒气; **the coffee's absolutely ~!** fig colloq 这咖啡难喝死了! 2 (venomous) 有毒的〈*insect*〉; **a highly ~ snake** 剧毒的毒蛇 3 fig (extremely unpleasant) 极其可恶的〈*allegation, rumour*〉; (vicious) 恶毒的〈*person, ideology*〉; **she tells ~ lies about people** 她恶意诽谤他人

poison-pen letter *n* 匿名诽谤信

poke¹ /pəʊk/
A *vt* 1 (with hand) 戳〈*person, substance, ground, heap*〉; (with poker) 拨〈*fire, embers*〉; **to ~ sb./sth. with sth.** 用某物捅某人/某物; **to ~ sb. in the eye with a stick** 用棍子戳某人的眼睛 2 colloq (punch) 拳打〈*person*〉; **to ~ sb. one** 打某人一拳 3 (create by prodding) 捅出〈*gap, opening*〉; **~ a hole in the sack/fence** 把袋子/篱笆捅出一个洞; **it's easy to ~ holes in their argument** fig 很容易找出他们论点中的漏洞 4 (push, put) 插入〈*stick*〉; 塞入〈*umbrella, piece of paper*〉; **he ~d a rag into the hole** 他把一块破布塞进了洞里; **~ a fork into the meat** 把叉子插进肉里; **to ~ one's finger up one's nose** 用手指捅鼻子; **to ~ one's head out of the window** 把头伸出窗户 5 sl pej (penetrate sexually) «*man*» 跟…性交〈*woman*〉
B *vi* 1 (be visible) «*part of body*» 伸出; «*object, flower*» 露出; **his elbows ~d through the holes in his sweater** 他的胳膊肘从毛衣的破洞中露了出来 2 (prod, jab) «*person*» 戳弄; **to ~ into sth.** 戳弄某物; **he's no right to come round here poking into my business** fig 他无权来这里干涉我的事情
C *n* 1 [c] (prod) 戳; **to give the fire a ~** 拨一下火 2 [c] colloq (punch) 一拳; **to take a ~ at sb.** 打某人一拳; **to give sb. a ~ in the ribs** 打某人肋部一拳; **to get a ~ in the eye** fig 遭受巨大不幸 3 [c] sl pej (sexual penetration) 性交; **to have a ~** 与人性交

Phrasal verbs

• **poke about, poke around** *vi* colloq 翻找; **to ~ about** *or* **around for sth.** 翻找某物; **we've had journalists poking around asking a lot of questions** 我们被记者追问了许多问题

• **poke at** *vt* [**~ at sb./sth.**] 戳〈*person*〉; 捅〈*ground, heap*〉; 拨弄〈*fire*〉; **she kept poking at me with her finger** 她不停地对我指指画画

• **poke out**
A *vi* «*part of body*» 伸出; «*object, flower*» 露出; «*stomach, breasts, bottom*» 凸出; **to ~ out of sth.** 从某处露出; **a few shoots were poking out of the soil** 几根嫩芽破土而出; **to ~ out through sth.** 穿透某物露出; **the first snowdrops were poking out through the snow** 第一批雪花莲从雪中探出头来; **to ~ out from under sth.** 从某物下面露出
B *vt* [**~ sth. out, ~ out sth.**]
1 (make visible) 伸出〈*head, tongue*〉; **I haven't so much as ~d my nose out all day** fig 我一整天连门都没出过 2 (remove) 捅出〈*object*〉; **he nearly ~d my eye out** 他差点把我的眼珠捅出来

• **poke up** *vi* «*flower, shoot, spring*» 露出; **to ~ up through** 钻出〈*surface, ground, grass*〉; **snowdrops were poking up through the snow** 雪花莲破雪而出了

poke² *n* esp Scot (bag) 袋; **a ~ of crisps** 一袋薯片

poker¹ /ˈpəʊkə(r)/ *n* (for fire) 拨火棒

poker² ▸p. 307 *n* [u] (card game) 扑克牌戏; **to play ~** 打扑克

poker: ~ dice *npl* 扑克骰子 [刻有从9到A的扑克牌图形]; **~-face** *n* 毫无表情的脸; **~-faced** *adj* 面无表情的〈*person*〉; 无表情的〈*look*〉

pokey /ˈpəʊki/
A *n* Amer colloq 监狱
B *adj* = **poky**

poky /ˈpəʊki/ *adj* pej 狭小的〈*room*〉

Poland /ˈpəʊlənd/ *pr n* 波兰

polar /ˈpəʊlə(r)/ *adj* 1 Geog 极地的〈*ice cap, regions, expedition*〉 2 fig (directly opposed) 截然对立的〈*extremes*〉; **to be ~ opposites** fig 完全相反

polar bear *n* 北极熊

polarimeter /ˌpəʊləˈrɪmɪtə(r)/ *n* 偏振计

Polaris /pəˈlɑːrɪs/ *pr n* 1 Astron 北极星 2 Mil 北极星导弹

polarity /pəˈlærəti/ *n* 1 Elec, Phys (of magnet) 极性; **reversed ~** 反极性 2 fig (state of being opposite) 对立; **the polarities of good and evil** 善与恶的截然对立

polarization /ˌpəʊlərаɪˈzeɪʃn, Amer -rɪˈz-/ *n* [u and c] 1 Elec, Phys 偏振 2 fig (division) 两极化; **the growing ~ between rich and poor nations** 富国与穷国之间越来越严重的两极分化

polarize /ˈpəʊləraɪz/
A *vt* 1 Phys 使偏振; **~d light** 偏振光; **~d sun glasses** 偏光太阳镜 2 fig (divide) «*event, policy*» 使…两极分化〈*views, people*〉; **an event that has ~d opinion in the party** 使党内意见截然对立的事件
B *vi* «*opinion, party*» 两极化; **to ~ on** *or* **over sth.** 因某事物产生分化

Polaroid® /ˈpəʊlərɔɪd/
A *n* 1 [c] (camera) 宝丽来照相机 2 [c] (photograph) 宝丽来照片 3 [u] (anti-glare material) 偏光薄膜
B *modif* 1 Phot 用宝丽来照相机拍摄的〈*photograph*〉; **to use ~ film** 使用宝丽来胶片 2 (anti-glare) 偏光薄膜的〈*glass, sunglasses*〉
C **Polaroids®** *npl* (sunglasses) 偏光膜太阳镜

Pole /pəʊl/ ▸p. 503 *n* 波兰人

pole¹ /pəʊl/
A *n* 1 (for tent, flag, telegraph lines) 柱; (for curtain, skiing, fishing) 杆; (in athletics event) 撑竿; (for propelling boat) 篙; (for cart, carriage) 辕; (for barber's shop) 转花筒; **to send** *or* **drive sb. up the ~** colloq (cause sb. extreme irritation) 激怒某人; (drive sb. insane) 使某人发疯; **to be up the ~** colloq (be mistaken) 弄错; Brit (be insane) 发疯; **she's up the ~ about those figures** 她把这些数字

弄错了 **2** esp Brit Hist (length) 杆 [相当于5.03米]; (area) 平方杆 [相当于25.29平方米]

B *vt* 用篙撑 ‹*boat, punt, barge*›

pole² *n* **1** **Pole** Geog 地极; **the North/South P~** 北/南极; **the magnetic ~** 磁极; **the news spread from ~ to ~** fig 这一新闻传遍了全世界 **2** Phys (of magnet) 磁极; (of electric battery) 电极; **the negative/positive ~** 负极/正极 **3** **poles** fig (extremes) 对立极端; **to be at opposite ~s** 截然相反; **to be ~s apart** 大相径庭

poleaxe Brit, **poleax** Amer /ˈpəʊlæks/
A *n* **1** (axe) 战斧 **2** (butcher's tool) 屠斧
B *vt* **1** (hit) 用斧头砍; (kill) 用斧头杀死 **2** fig (knock down) «*boxer*» 击倒 **3** fig (shock) «*news, discovery*» 使震惊

polecat /ˈpəʊlkæt/ *n* **1** **(European) ~** 臭貂 **2** Amer (skunk) 臭鼬

pole: ~ dancer *n* 跳钢管舞者; **~ dancing** *n* [u] 钢管舞

polemic /pəˈlemɪk/
A *n* **1** [c] (written, verbal attack) 激烈抨击; **a ~ against sb./sth.** 对某人/某事物的激烈抨击 **2** [u] (activity) 辩论
B *adj* = **polemical**

polemical /pəˈlemɪkl/ *adj* 辩论的 ‹*article, approach*›; 好辩的 ‹*person*›; **I don't think he intended to be ~** 我认为他原先并没打算争辩

polemicist /pəˈlemɪsɪst/ *n* 善辩者

pole: ~ position *n* [u] (in motor racing) 最前排位置; **to be in** *or* **have ~ position** lit 处于首发位置; fig 处于有利地位; **P~ Star** *n* **the P~ Star** 北极星

pole vault /ˈpəʊlvɔːlt/
A *n* **1** [u] (event) 撑竿跳高 **2** [c] (vault) 一次撑竿跳
B *vi* 作撑竿跳高

pole: ~-vaulter *n* 撑竿跳高选手; **~ vaulting** ▸**p. 307** *n* [u] 撑竿跳高

police /pəˈliːs/
A *n* **1** + *v pl* (official body) 警察部门; **the ~** 警方; **to be in the ~** 在警察部门工作; **to assist the ~ with their enquiries** 接受警方的讯问; **~ vehicles** 警车; **~ intervention** 警方介入 **2** (officers) 警察 **3** fig (enforcement organization) 警卫组织
B *vt* **1** (keep in order) «*authorities, stewards, police*» 维持…的治安 ‹*place, gathering*›; **the demonstration was ~d by mounted officers** 游行示威受到了骑警的监控 **2** (control) «*teachers, guards*» 守卫 ‹*building, nightclub, frontier*› **3** (enforce) 监督…的执行 ‹*regulations, treaty*›

police: ~ academy *n* Amer 警察学院; **~ car** *n* 警车; **~ cell** *n* 警察局拘留室; **~ chief** *n* 警察局长; **~ college** *n* 警察学院; **~ constable** *n* = **constable**; **~ court** *n* [审理轻微违法行为的] 治安法庭; **~ custody** *n* [u] 警方的拘留; **~ department** *n* Amer 警察局; **~ dog** *n* 警犬; **~ escort** *n* [尤指护送要员的] 警察卫队; **~ force** *n* 警察部队; **to join the ~ force** 加入警队; **~ headquarters** *npl* + *v sing or pl* 警察总部; **~ informer** *n* 警方线人; **~man** /-mən/ ▸**p. 409** *n* 男警察; **~ officer** *n* 警察; **~ record** *n* 前科; **~ state** *n* pej 警察国家; **~ station** *n* 警察局; **~ van** *n* 囚车; **~woman** ▸**p. 409** *n* 女警察; **~ work** *n* [u] 治安工作

policing /pəˈliːsɪŋ/ *n* [u] **1** (maintaining law and order) 维持治安; **the ~ of our city streets** 我们城市街道的治安; **community ~** 社区治安的维护 **2** (patrolling) 巡逻; **the ~ of the border** 边境巡逻 **3** (staffing with police) 配备警察 **4** (monitoring) 监督; **the ~ of the new regulations** 对新条例执行情况的监管

policy¹ /ˈpɒləsi/
A *n* [c and u] **1** (political line) 政策; **foreign/economic/social ~** 外交/经济/社会政策; **to make ~** 制定政策; **to carry out** *or* **implement a ~** 执行政策; **it is good/bad ~ to ...** …是好/坏政策; **our company has a no-smoking ~** 我们公司规定不准吸烟 **2** (habitual practice) 原则; **it is our ~ to do sth.** 做某事是我们的原则; **it is our ~ that ...** …是我们的原则; **to have** *or* **follow a ~ of doing sth.** 遵循做某事的原则; **it's a matter of ~** 这是原则问题
B *modif* 有关政策的 ‹*discussion, debate, meeting, decision*›

policy² *n* Insur **1** (contract) 保险合同; **to take out a ~** 投保 **2** (document) 保险单

policy: ~holder *n* 投保人; **~ maker** *n* 政策制定者; **~-making** *n* [u] 决策; **~ unit** *n* 政策部门

polio /ˈpəʊliəʊ/ ▸**p. 377** *n* [u] 小儿麻痹症; **~ vaccine** 小儿麻痹疫苗

poliomyelitis /ˌpəʊliəʊmaɪəˈlaɪtɪs/ ▸**p. 377** *n* [u] 小儿麻痹症

Polish /ˈpəʊlɪʃ/ ▸**p. 503, p. 426**
A *adj* (of Poland) 波兰的; (of the people) 波兰人的; (of the language) 波兰语的
B *n* (language) 波兰语
C *npl* (people) **the ~** 波兰人

polish /ˈpɒlɪʃ/
A *n* **1** [u and c] (for shoes, furniture, wood, floor, fingernails, toenails) 上光剂; (for brass, silver, car) 抛光剂; **a tin of ~** 一罐上光剂; **liquid/wax ~** 液体上光剂/亮光蜡 **2** [c] (removing dust, dirt) 擦亮; (applying polish) 上光; **to give sth. a thorough ~** 将某物彻底擦亮 **3** [c] (shine) 光亮表面; **there isn't much of a ~ on these boots** 这双靴子不太光洁; **it has lost its ~** 它已失去了光泽 **4** [u and c] fig (refinement) 优雅; **the performance needs a bit more ~** 表演尚需改进; **a man of integrity but quite without ~** 正直但品位很差的男人
B *vt* **1** (apply polish to) 给…涂亮光剂 ‹*metal, leather*›; **to ~ the shoes/floor** 擦鞋/给地板打蜡 **2** (shine by rubbing) 擦亮 ‹*spectacles, glass*›; 打磨 ‹*stone, jet, marble*› **3** fig (refine) 改进 ‹*performance, image, style, manners*›

Phrasal verbs

• **polish off**
A [**~ sth. off, ~ off sth.**] *vt* **1** (consume quickly) 迅速吃光 ‹*food, meal*›; 迅速喝干 ‹*drink*› **2** (finish) 快速完成 ‹*exam paper, job, task*›
B [**~ sb./sth. off, ~ off sb./sth.**] *vt* (defeat) 打败 ‹*opponent, rebels, forces*›

• **polish up** *vt* [**~ sth. up, ~ up sth.**] **1** (shine) 擦亮 ‹*glass, spectacles, floor*› **2** fig (improve, perfect) 改进; **to ~ up one's French/knowledge/pronunciation** 提高法语水平/完善知识结构/改进发音; **the hotel has ~ed up its act since last year** 这家旅馆自去年以来改善了经营

polished /ˈpɒlɪʃt/ *adj* **1** (shiny) 擦亮的 ‹*leather, shoes*›; 抛光的 ‹*wood, surface*›; **a highly-~ floor** 擦得很亮的地板 **2** fig (refined, sophisticated) 优雅的 ‹*manner, person*› **3** (accomplished) 娴熟的 ‹*performance, performer*›

polisher /ˈpɒlɪʃə(r)/ ▸**p. 409** *n* **1** (for floor) 打蜡机; (for stones, gems) 抛光机; (for shoes) 擦鞋机 **2** (person) 抛光工人

politburo /ˈpɒlɪtbjʊərəʊ/ *n* (*pl* **~s**) [共产党执政国家的] 政治局

polite /pəˈlaɪt/ *adj* **1** (well-mannered) 有礼貌的 ‹*person, refusal*›; **to be ~ to sb.** 对某人有礼貌; **he wasn't very ~ about my appearance** 他对我外表的评价不太客气 **2** (socially correct) 礼节性的 ‹*smile*›; **when I complimented her I was only being ~** 我称赞她只不过是客套; **to make ~ conversation** 说应酬话; **I made ~ noises about his presence** 我对他的到场说了些客套话 **3** (cultured, refined) 有教养的 ‹*company*›; **in ~ society** 在上流社会; **to keep a ~ distance** 保持礼貌距离; **to use the ~ form** Ling 使用尊称

politely /pəˈlaɪtli/ *adv* 礼貌地; **I asked them ~ to leave** 我客气地请他们离开

politeness /pəˈlaɪtnɪs/ *n* [u] 礼貌; **out of ~** 出于礼貌

politic /ˈpɒlɪtɪk/ *adj* formal 明智的 ‹*action, statement*›; **she deemed** *or* **thought it ~ to stay away** 她觉得置身事外是上策

political /pəˈlɪtɪkl/ *adj* **1** (of public affairs in general) 政治的 ‹*grounds*›; (relating to government) 政府的 ‹*rights, power*›; **the ~ system of the country** 这个国家的政治体制 **2** (relating to parties) 政党的 ‹*debate, opinions*›; **he's a ~ animal** 他是个搞政治的人 **3** pej (relating to power or status) 涉及权位利益的 ‹*reason, issue*›

political: ~ act *n* 政治行动; **~ action committee** *n* Amer 政治行动委员会; **~ analyst** ▸**p. 409** *n* 政治分析家; **~ asylum** *n* [u] 政治避难; **~ commentator** ▸**p. 409** *n* 政治评论家; **~ correctness** *n* [u] 政治正确; **~ football** *n* colloq 政治皮球 [指未解决的有争论的政治问题]; **~ geography** *n* [u] 政治地理学

> **political correctness**
>
> 政治正确。形容词形式为 politically correct，简称 PC。指在语言和行为上避免歧视任何人，包括种族、肤色、性别、年龄、性取向和身体残疾等方面的歧视。该用法始见于 20 世纪 80 年代末的美国大学。受此思潮影响，许多语言表达都发生了改变，如将印第安人（Indian）改称美洲原住民（▸**Native American**）。泛指的第三人称代词从 he 改成 he or she 或 he/she，或者为了避免指称性别，改成 they。政治正确现在往往被认为虚伪或是走极端，所以有些政治正确用语常表示讽刺或戏谑，如称个子矮的人为 vertically challenged。

politically /pəˈlɪtɪkli/ *adv* 政治上 ‹*naive, disastrous, stable*›; **~ speaking** 从政治角度讲

politically: ~ correct *adj* 政治上正确的 ‹*language, film*›; **~ incorrect** *adj* 政治上不正确的 ‹*language, opinion*›; **~-minded** *adj* 热衷于政治的; **~-sensitive** *adj* 政治上敏感的 ‹*issue*›

political: ~ offence *n* 政治犯罪; **~ prisoner** *n* 政治犯; **~ refugee** *n* 政治避难者; **~ science** *n* [u] 政治学; **~ scientist** ▸**p. 409** *n* 政治学者

politician /ˌpɒlɪˈtɪʃn/ ▸**p. 409** *n* **1** Pol 政治家 **2** Amer pej (devious person) 政客

politicization /pəˌlɪtɪsaɪˈzeɪʃn/ *n* [u] 政治化

politicize /pəˈlɪtɪsaɪz/ *vt* 使…政治化 ‹*issue, movement*›; **education should not be ~d** 教育不应该被赋予政治色彩; **to ~ sb.** 使某人有政治意识

politicking /ˈpɒlətɪkɪŋ/ *n* [u] colloq pej [尤指为赢得选票或支持而进行的] 政治活动

politico /pəˈlɪtɪkəʊ/ *n* (*pl* **~s**) colloq pej 政客

politico-economic /pəˌlɪtɪkəʊiːkəˈnɒmɪk/ *adj* 政治经济的 ‹*analysis, crisis*›; **a ~ system** 政治经济体制

politics /ˈpɒlətɪks/ *npl* **1** + *v sing* (political life) 政治; (political affairs) 政治事务; **English/local ~** 英国/地方政治; **to talk ~** colloq 谈论政治; **a career in ~** 从政生涯; **to go into ~** 从政 **2** + *v sing* (academic subject) 政治学 **3** + *v pl* (political views) 政治观点 **4** pej + *v sing* (manoeuvring) 勾心斗角; **office ~** 办公室政治; **there's too much ~ in my job** 我的工作中有太多的权势之争

polka /ˈpɒlkə, Amer ˈpəʊlkə/
A *n* **1** Dance 波尔卡舞 **2** Mus 波尔卡舞曲
B *vi* 跳波尔卡舞

polka dot *n* [织物上的] 圆点花纹; **a polka-dot dress** 圆点连衣裙

poll /pəʊl/
A *n* **1** (vote casting) 投票; (vote counting) 记票; **he was successful at the ~** 他当选了; **on the eve of the ~** 在投票日前夜 **2** (number of

votes cast) 投票数; **to head** *or* **top the ～** 得票数领先; **a light/heavy ～** 低/高投票率; **she got 25% of the ～** 她赢得了 25% 的选票 **3** (list of voters) 选民名册; (list of taxpayers) 纳税人名册 **4** (survey) 民意调查; **to conduct** *or* **carry out a ～** 进行民意调查; **to take a ～ on sth.** 就某事进行民意调查; **(public) opinion ～** 民意测验
B **polls** *npl* Pol (vote, election) 投票地点; **the country goes to the ～s tomorrow** 全国明天举行选举投票; **to win at the ～s** 当选
C *vt* **1** (obtain in election) 获得 ‹*votes*› **2** (canvass) 调查 ‹*members of the public, group*›; **to ～ housewives for their opinions** 征求家庭主妇的意见 **3** Agric 截掉…的角尖 ‹*cattle, sheep*› **4** Comput 查询
D *vi* «*party, candidate*» 获得选票; **to ～ heavily/badly** 赢得大量/很少选票

pollard /ˈpɒləd/
A *vt* 修剪…的树冠
B *n* 去顶的树

pollen /ˈpɒlən/ *n* [u] 花粉

pollen: ～ count *n* 花粉计数; **the ～ count is high/low** 花粉计数高/低; **～ sac** *n* 花粉囊

pollinate /ˈpɒləneɪt/ *vt* 给…授粉 ‹*flower*›

pollination /ˌpɒləˈneɪʃn/ *n* [u] 授粉

polling /ˈpəʊlɪŋ/ *n* [u] 投票; **～ was light/heavy** 投票的人不多/很多

polling: ～ booth *n* 投票亭; **～ card** *n* esp Brit 投票卡; **～ day** *n* 投票日; **～ station,** Amer **～ place** *ns* 投票站

pollster /ˈpəʊlstə(r)/ *n* 民意测验主办人; **according to the ～s** 根据民调

poll tax *n* [c and u] **1** (tax on all adults) 人头税 **2** Brit Hist (community charge) 社区收费

pollutant /pəˈluːtənt/ *n* 污染物; **industrial ～s** 工业污染物

pollute /pəˈluːt/ *vt* **1** (contaminate) 污染 ‹*air, environment, river*› **2** fig (sully) 使…堕落 ‹*minds*› **3** fig (desecrate) 玷污 ‹*altar, purity*›

polluter /pəˈluːtə(r)/ *n* 污染者; **major greenhouse ～s** 主要温室污染物

pollution /pəˈluːʃn/ *n* [u] **1** Ecol 污染; **noise/oil ～** 噪声/石油污染 **2** fig (moral corruption) 道德败坏 **3** fig (desecration) 玷污

Pollyanna /ˌpɒlɪˈænə/ *n* esp Amer 盲目乐观的人

polo /ˈpəʊləʊ/ *n* **1** ▸**p. 307** [u] Sport 马球; **a ～ match** 马球比赛 **2** [c] Brit colloq = **polo neck 2**

polonaise /ˌpɒləˈneɪz/ *n* **1** (dance) 波洛奈兹舞 **2** (music) 波洛奈兹舞曲

polo neck *n* **1** Brit (collar) 高圆翻领; **a polo-neck(ed) jumper** 高圆翻领套衫 **2** (garment) 高圆翻领套衫

polo-neck sweater *n* 高圆翻领套衫

polonium /pəˈləʊnɪəm/ *n* [u] 钋

polo: ～ pony *n* 马球比赛用马; **～ shirt** *n* 马球衫; **～ stick** *n* 马球杆

poltergeist /ˈpɒltəgaɪst/ *n* 促狭鬼

poly /ˈpɒli/ *n* Brit colloq = **polytechnic**

polyanthus /ˌpɒlɪˈænθəs/ *n* (*pl* **polyanthus**) 西洋樱草

polyclinic /ˈpɒlɪklɪnɪk/ *n* 综合诊所

polycotton /ˌpɒlɪˈkɒtn/ *n* [u] 涤棉布

polyester /ˌpɒlɪˈestə(r)/ *n* [u] 聚酯纤维; **a ～ shirt** 涤纶衬衫

polyethylene /ˌpɒlɪˈeθəliːn/ *n* [u] esp Amer = **polythene**

polygamist /pəˈlɪgəmɪst/ *n* 多妻的男人

polygamous /pəˈlɪgəməs/ *adj* 一夫多妻的

polygamy /pəˈlɪgəmi/ *n* [u] 一夫多妻

polyglot /ˈpɒlɪglɒt/
A *adj* **1** (knowing many languages) 通晓多种语言的 ‹*person*› **2** (written in many languages) 多种语言的 ‹*edition*›; **a ～ dictionary of engineering** 多语工程词典
B *n* 说多种语言的人

polygon /ˈpɒlɪgən, Amer -gɒn/ *n* 多边形 [常指多于5个边]

polyhedron /ˌpɒlɪˈhiːdrən, Amer -drɒn/ *n* (*pl* **polyhedra** /ˌpɒlɪˈhiːdrə/ *or* **～s**) 多面体 [常指多于6个面]

polymath /ˈpɒlɪmæθ/ *n* 博学家

polymer /ˈpɒlɪmə(r)/ *n* 聚合物

polymerization /ˌpɒlɪməraɪˈzeɪʃn, Amer -rɪˈz-/ *n* [u] 聚合

polymerize /ˈpɒlɪməraɪz/ *vt* 使聚合

Polynesia /ˌpɒlɪˈniːʒə/ *pr n* 波利尼西亚

Polynesian /ˌpɒlɪˈniːʒn/ ▸**p. 503, p. 426**
A *adj* (of Polynesia) 波利尼西亚的; (of the people) 波利尼西亚人的; (of the languages) 波利尼西亚语的
B *n* **1** [c] (person) 波利尼西亚人 **2** [u] (language group) 波利尼西亚语

polyp /ˈpɒlɪp/ *n* **1** Zool 珊瑚虫 **2** Med 息肉

polyphonic /ˌpɒlɪˈfɒnɪk/ *adj* 复调的 ‹*music*›; 复调音乐的 ‹*singing, composition*›

polyphony /pəˈlɪfəni/ *n* [u] (style of composition) 复调风格; (piece of music) 复调乐曲

polypropylene /ˌpɒlɪˈprəʊpɪliːn/ *n* [u] 聚丙烯

polysemous /ˌpɒlɪˈsiːməs, pɒlˈɪsɪməs/, **polysemic** /ˌpɒlɪˈsiːmɪk/ *adj* 多义的

polysemy /ˌpɒlɪˈsiːmi, pəˈlɪsɪmi/ *n* [u] 一词多义

polystyrene /ˌpɒlɪˈstaɪriːn/ *n* [u] 聚苯乙烯

polysyllabic /ˌpɒlɪsɪˈlæbɪk/ *adj* 多音节的

polytechnic /ˌpɒlɪˈteknɪk/ *n* Brit 理工学院 [现均已改称university]

polytheism /ˈpɒlɪθiːɪzəm/ *n* [u] (worship) 多神崇拜; (belief) 多神信仰

polytheistic /ˌpɒlɪθiːˈɪstɪk/ *adj* 多神的 ‹*belief*›; 多神信仰的 ‹*practice, cult*›

polythene /ˈpɒlɪθiːn/ *n* [u] Brit 聚乙烯; **a ～ bag** 聚乙烯塑料袋

polytunnel /ˈpɒlɪtʌnl/ *n* 塑料大棚

polyunsaturated /ˌpɒlɪʌnˈsætʃəreɪtɪd/ *adj* 多不饱和的; **～ fats** 多不饱和脂肪

polyunsaturates /ˌpɒlɪʌnˈsætʃərəts/ *npl* (fats) 多不饱和脂肪; (fatty acids) 多不饱和脂肪酸

polyurethane /ˌpɒlɪˈjʊərəθeɪn/ *n* [u] 聚氨基甲酸乙酯; **～ gloss** 聚氨酯亮光漆

pom /pɒm/ *n* Austral colloq pej 英国佬

pomade /pəˈmɑːd/
A *n* 发油
B *vt* 用发油搽

pomander /pəˈmændə(r)/ *n* (ball) 香球; (container) 香盒

pomegranate /ˈpɒmɪgrænɪt/ *n* **1** (fruit) 石榴 **2** (tree) 石榴树

Pomeranian /ˌpɒməˈreɪmɪən/ *n* 波美犬 [一种小型长毛犬, 毛皮光滑, 尖嘴竖耳]

pommel /ˈpʌml/
A *n* **1** (on saddle) 鞍头 **2** (on weapon) 圆头 **3** (in gymnastics) 鞍马
B *vt* = **pummel**

pommel horse *n* 鞍马

Pommy, Pommie /ˈpɒmi/ Austral colloq pej
A *n* 英国佬
B *adj* 英国的 ‹*bastard*›

pomp /pɒmp/ *n* [u] 盛况; **with great ～** 很排场地; **～ and circumstance** 隆重的仪式

pompadour /ˈpɒmpədʊə(r)/ *n* Amer **1** (for men) 大背头 **2** (for women) 高卷式发型

pompom, pompon /ˈpɒmpɒm/ *n* 小绒球

pomposity /pɒmˈpɒsəti/ *n* [u] (of manner) 虚夸; (of voice) 拿腔作势

pompous /ˈpɒmpəs/ *adj* 自负的 ‹*person*›; 浮夸的 ‹*speech, style, tone*›; **a ～ official** 自命不凡的官员

pompously /ˈpɒmpəsli/ *adv* 自命不凡地 ‹*announce, strut*›; **the headmaster talked ～ about the honour of the school** 校长傲慢自负地大谈学校的荣耀地位

ponce /pɒns/ Brit colloq dated *n* **1** (pimp) 拉皮条的男人 **2** offensive (homosexual) 同性恋男子; (effeminate man) 娘娘腔的男人

Phrasal verb

- **ponce about, ponce around** *vi* Brit colloq [尤指女人气地] 四处招摇

poncho /ˈpɒntʃəʊ/ *n* (*pl* **～s**) 庞乔斗篷 [在大块织物中间开领口制成]

pond /pɒnd/ *n* 池塘; **a garden/village ～** 花园/村子的池塘

ponder /ˈpɒndə(r)/
A *vt* 仔细考虑 ‹*chances, prospects, developments*›; 琢磨 ‹*events*›
B *vi* 仔细考虑; **to ～ on** *or* **over sth.** 仔细考虑某事

ponderous /ˈpɒndərəs/ *adj* **1** (slow, clumsy) 行动迟缓的 ‹*person*›; 笨重的 ‹*footsteps, movement*› **2** (dull, solemn) 乏味的 ‹*speech, humour*›; **his ～ manner of speaking** 他慢条斯理的说话方式

ponderously /ˈpɒndərəsli/ *adv* 笨拙地 ‹*move*›; 乏味地 ‹*write, talk*›

ponderousness /ˈpɒndərəsnɪs/ *n* [u] **1** (of gait, movement) 迟缓 **2** (of style, performance) 乏味

pond: ～ life *n* [u] **1** Zool 池生动物 [尤指无脊椎动物]; **2** fig colloq (lowlife) 可鄙的小人物; **～weed** *n* [u] 水池草

pone /pəʊn/ *n* [u] Amer 玉米面包

pong /pɒŋ/ Brit colloq
A *n* 难闻的气味; **to give off an awful ～** 散发出一股恶臭
B *vi* 散发臭味

pongy /ˈpɒŋi/ *adj* Brit colloq 难闻的

pontiff /ˈpɒntɪf/ *n* 教皇; **the Supreme P～** 罗马教宗

pontifical /pɒnˈtɪfɪkl/ *adj* **1** Relig 教宗的 ‹*decree, visit*› **2** pej (pompous) 自负的 ‹*manner, tone*›

pontificate
A /pɒnˈtɪfɪkət/ *n* **1** (office) 教宗职务 **2** (period of time) 教宗任期
B /pɒnˈtɪfɪkeɪt/ *vi* pej 自负地谈论; **to ～ about sth.** 自以为是地谈论某事物

pontoon /pɒnˈtuːn/ *n* **1** [c] (boat) 浮舟; (barrel, cylinder) 浮筒 **2** [c] (bridge) 浮桥 **3** [c] (landing stage) 浮码头 **4** [c] Aviat (float) 充气浮筒 **5** ▸**p. 307** [u] Brit (card game) 21 点牌戏

pontoon bridge *n* 浮桥

pony /ˈpəʊni/ *n* 小型马

pony: ～tail *n* 马尾辫; **to wear one's hair in a ～tail** 把头发梳成马尾辫; **～-trekking** *n* [u] 骑矮马出游

poo /puː/ *excl, n, vi* esp child lang = **pooh**

pooch /puːtʃ/ *n* colloq 狗

poodle /ˈpuːdl/ *n* **1** (dog) 卷毛狗 **2** fig colloq (servile person) 奴才

poof /pʊf/, **poofter** /ˈpʊftə(r)/ *ns* Brit colloq offensive (homosexual) 假鸳鸯; (effeminate man) 脂粉气的男子

poofy /ˈpʊfi/ *adj* Brit colloq offensive (homosexual) 假鸳鸯的; (effeminate) 脂粉气的

pooh /puː/
A *n* [u] Brit esp child lang **1** [u] (excrement) 屁屁 **2** [c] (action) 拉屁屁; **to have a ～** 拉屁屁
B *excl* (expressing scorn) 哼; (expressing disgust) 呸
C *vi* Brit esp child lang 拉屁屁

pooh-pooh *vt* colloq 对…嗤之以鼻 ‹*suggestion, idea, anxieties*›

pool¹ /puːl/ *n* **1** (pond) 池塘; (still spot in river) 水潭 **2** (for swimming) 游泳池 **3** (puddle) 一摊; **to be lying in a ～ of blood** 躺在血泊之中

pool²
A *n* **1** (of money) 共用资金; (of resources, goods,

services) 共用资源; **a ~ of vehicles** 共用的车辆 **2** (of labour) 备用人员 **3** (of talent, experience) 储备 **4** Amer (monopoly trust) 垄断经营集团

B pools *npl* Brit = **football pools**

C *vt* 集中 ‹*resources, funds*›

pool³ *n* [u] (game) 落袋台球戏; **to shoot ~** Amer 打落袋台球

pool: ~ attendant ▸p. 409 *n* 泳池救生员; **~ party** *n* 泳池聚会; **~room** *n* Amer 台球室; **~side** *n* [u] 泳池边; **~ table** *n* 台球台

poop¹ /puːp/ *n* **~ (deck)** 艉楼甲板

poop² Amer colloq

A *n* [u] (excrement) 粪便

B *vi* 拉屎

pooped /puːpt/ *adj* Amer colloq 筋疲力尽的; **to be ~ (out)** 筋疲力尽

pooper scooper /ˈpuːpəskuːpə(r)/ *n* colloq 狗粪铲

poor /pɔː(r), Amer pʊər/

A *adj* **1** (lacking resources, deficient in sth., insufficient) 贫穷的 ‹*person, country, region*›; 不足的 ‹*pay, output, consolation*›; **she has a very ~ chance of success** 她成功的可能性很小; **a ~ harvest/income/attendance** 歉收/微薄的收入/很差的出席率; **to be ~ in sth.** 缺乏某物; **as ~ as a church mouse** 一贫如洗的; **the ~ man's champagne** 香槟酒的廉价替代品 **2** (deserving pity, pathetic) 可怜的 ‹*creature, idiot, effort, excuse*›; **the ~ things looked so miserable** 这些可怜的家伙看上去真悲惨; **it's a ~ thing** *or* **show when ...** colloq …时真可悲 **3** (inferior) 不良的 ‹*record, education, result*›; 贫瘠的 ‹*soil*›; 差的 ‹*quality, English, visibility*›; 拙劣的 ‹*planning, substitute*›; 糟糕的 ‹*performance, weather, start, work*›; **he made a ~ job of the decorating** 他把装修做得一塌糊涂; **the vehicle is in (a) ~ condition** 这辆车的车况很差; **a comedy in ~ taste** 一部低品位的喜剧; **to have a ~ opinion of sb./sth.** 对某人/某事物评价低; **to take a ~ view of sth.** 不喜欢某事物 **4** (not skilful) 不熟练的 ‹*performer, swimmer*› **5** (ineffectual) 不擅长的; **to be ~ at sth./doing sth., to be a ~ hand at sth./doing sth.** 不擅长某事/做某事; **he's such a ~ loser** 他输不起; **he's a ~ judge of character** 他看不准人 **6** (defective) 差的; **to have ~ eyesight/hearing/memory** 视力/听力/记忆力不好; **to be in ~ health** 身体不好

B *npl* **the ~** 穷人; **the ~ are always with us** Prov 什么时候都有穷人

poor: ~ box *n* [教堂里的] 济贫募捐箱; **~boy** *n* **~ boy (sandwich)** Amer 大号三明治; **~house** *n* Brit Hist = **workhouse**

poorly /ˈpɔːli, Amer ˈpʊərli/

A *adj pred* (not in good health) 健康不佳的; (not feeling well) 身体不舒服的; **she was feeling ~** 她感到有些不适

B *adv* **1** (not richly) 贫穷地; **to be ~ off** 生活贫困; **a ~-dressed man** 穿着破旧的人 **2** (badly) 糟糕地 ‹*perform, plan, act*›; **to do ~** 表现糟糕 **3** (inadequately) 不足地 ‹*maintain, manage*›; **~ designed machines** 设计不周的机器

poorness /ˈpɔːnɪs, Amer ˈpʊərnɪs/ *n* [u] **1** (of land, soil) 贫瘠; (of diet) 低劣 **2** (of education, pay) 低下 **3** (of appetite, hearing, eyesight) 糟糕

poor: ~ relation *n* **1** (impoverished family member) 穷亲戚; **2** fig (inferior person) 逊色的人; (inferior thing) 略逊一筹的事物; **~ white** *n* pej [尤指美国南部的] 穷苦白人

pop¹ /pɒp/

A *n* **1** [c] (sound) 砰; **with a ~** 砰的一声; **to go ~** 发出砰的一声 **2** [u] Amer colloq dated (drink) 汽水 **3** [c] colloq (physical attack) 击打; (verbal attack) 抨击; **to take** *or* **have a ~ at sb./sth.** 攻击某人/某事物; **the book has a ~ at astrology and astrologists** 这本书抨击了占星术和占星家

B *vt* **1** (burst) 使…爆裂 ‹*balloon*›; Amer (open) 啪的一声拉开 ‹*cork, button, opener*›; (close) 啪的一声合上 ‹*fastener, stud*›; **to ~ one's clogs** Brit colloq (die) 蹬腿儿 **2** Culin 加热爆开 ‹*grain*›; **to ~ corn** 做爆米花 **3** esp Brit (put) 突然探出 ‹*head*›; [冷不防地] 放下 ‹*small object, bag, letter*›; **to ~ sth. in(to) sth.** 突然把某物丢进某处; **he ~ped the meat into the oven** 他迅速把肉扔进炉子里; **to ~ pills** colloq 大量服药; **to ~ the question** colloq 开口求婚 **4** Brit colloq (pawn) 典当 ‹*valuables, watch, jewellery*›

C *vi* **1** (go bang) «*balloon*» 爆裂; «*cork*» 啪的一声打开; **my ears were ~ping** (at speed or altitude) 我耳朵里嗡嗡作响 **2** (bulge) 凸出; **to make sb.'s eyes ~** Brit colloq 使某人惊讶得眼睛都要鼓出来了 **3** esp Brit (go, nip) 急忙赶去; **I was just ~ping into town** 我正赶着去城里; **she ~ped round** *or* **over to see us** 她赶来看我们 **4** esp Brit (appear) 突然出现; **a head ~ped round the door/over the wall** 一个脑袋从门后/墙头冷不防探了出来

Phrasal verbs

• **pop back** esp Brit

A *vi* 赶回去

B *vt* [**~ sth. back, ~ back sth.**] 迅速放回 ‹*cover, small object*›; **to ~ the lid back on** 迅速把盖子盖上

• **pop in** esp Brit

A *vi* 短暂拜访; **to ~ in for a chat/to say hello** 进来聊一会儿/问声好

B *vt* [**~ sth. in**] 迅速放进; **I'll ~ my library books in on the way to town** 我进城时会顺便把从图书馆借的书还回去的

• **pop off** *vi* **1** esp Brit (leave) 离开; **to ~ off to town** 去城里 **2** esp Brit colloq (die) 一命呜呼

• **pop on** *vt* [**~ sth. on, ~ on sth.**] Brit 迅速穿上 ‹*coat, sweater*›; 迅速戴上 ‹*ring*›

• **pop out** *vi* **1** (come out) 突然跳出; **to make sb.'s eyes ~ out** colloq 令某人惊得眼睛都要鼓出来了; **to ~ out of sth.** 突然从某处出现; **the cork ~ped out of the bottle** 瓶塞突然从瓶口跳了出来 **2** Brit (go out) 匆忙出去一会儿; **to ~ out to the shop** 匆忙离开去一下商店

• **pop up** *vi* **1** (rise) «*face, head*» 突然抬起; «*rabbit, fish*» 突然跳起 **2** (appear) «*person*» 突然露面; Comput «*menu*» 弹出 **3** (occur) «*name*» 偶然提起; «*memory*» 偶然出现

pop²

A *adj attrib* **1** (commercial) 流行音乐的 ‹*star, group, concert, festival*›; **the ~ music charts** 流行音乐排行榜; **a ~ singer/song** 流行歌手/歌曲 **2** (popularized) 通俗的 ‹*science*›

B *n* [u] 流行音乐; **rock, ~, and soul** 摇滚乐、流行乐和灵乐

C pops *npl* **top of the ~s** 流行音乐排行榜榜首

pop³ *n* esp Amer colloq (dad) 爸爸; **yes, ~(s)** 好的，老爹（们）

pop. *abbr* = **population**

pop: ~ art *n* [u] 波普艺术; **~ artist** *n* 波普艺术家; **~ charts** *npl* 每周流行音乐榜; **~ corn** *n* [u] 爆玉米花

pope /pəʊp/ *n* **the P~** 教皇; **P~ Paul VI** 教皇保罗六世

Popemobile /ˈpəʊpməbiːl/ *n* colloq 教皇专车

pop: ~-eyed /ˈpɒpaɪd/ *adj* **1** (permanently) 眼睛凸出的; **she looks a bit ~-eyed** 她看上去眼睛有点儿向外凸; **2** (with amazement) 睁大眼睛的; **he was ~-eyed with astonishment** 他惊得瞠目而视; **~ gun** *n* 玩具气枪

popish /ˈpəʊpɪʃ/ *adj* pej 天主教的 ‹*ceremonies, doctrines, creed*›

poplar /ˈpɒplə(r)/ *n* 杨树

poplin /ˈpɒplɪn/ *n* [u] 府绸; **a ~ shirt** 府绸衬衫

popover /ˈpɒpəʊvə(r)/ *n* Amer 膨松饼

poppadom, poppadum, poppadam /ˈpɒpədəm/ *n* 印度炸圆面包

popper /ˈpɒpə(r)/ *n* Brit colloq 揿扣

poppet /ˈpɒpɪt/ *n* colloq **1** Brit (form of address) 宝贝儿; **my (little) ~** 我的（小）宝贝儿 **2** (sweet person) 小巧玲珑的人; **she's a real ~** 她真是个小美人

poppy /ˈpɒpi/ *n* **1** [c] Bot 罂粟; **a ~ seed** 罂粟种子 **2** [u] (colour) 深橘红色 **3** [c] Brit (worn in buttonhole) 人造罂粟花 [荣军纪念星期日佩戴]

poppycock /ˈpɒpɪkɒk/ *n* [u] colloq dated 胡说

Poppy Day *n* Brit colloq = **Remembrance Day**

Popsicle® /ˈpɒpsɪkl/ *n* Amer 冰棒

pop: ~sock *n* 尼龙中筒袜; **~-top** *n* Amer **1** (ring pull) 拉环; (can) 易拉罐; **~-top soda can** 苏打汽水易拉罐; **2** Aut (roof) 活动顶棚; (vehicle) 活动顶棚车; **~-top caravans** 活动顶棚旅行拖车

populace /ˈpɒpjʊləs/ *n* + *v sing or pl* formal **1** (inhabitants) 全体居民 **2** (public) 民众

popular /ˈpɒpjʊlə(r)/ *adj* **1** (well-liked) 受欢迎的 ‹*person, teacher*›; 讨人喜欢的 ‹*pupil*›; (widely enjoyed) 广受欢迎的 ‹*activity, product, resort*›; 流行的 ‹*method, colour, design*›; **to be ~ with sb.** 受某人喜爱; **to be ~ as sth.** 作为某角色受欢迎; **to be ~ among ...** 在…中受欢迎; **he was a ~ choice as chairman** 他是受大家欢迎的主席人选; **it was not a ~ decision** 那是个不得人心的决定 **2** (of or for the people) 民众的 ‹*issue, demand, revolt*›; **~ government/democracy** 民选政府/大众民主; **P~ Liberation Front** 人民解放阵线 **3** *attrib* (common) 普遍的 ‹*interest, image*›; 常见的 ‹*mistake, practice, reason*›; **contrary to ~ belief, he is happy to be single** 与大家的想法相反，他乐意单身; **the ~ view/perception of sth.** 对某事物的普遍观点/理解; **a ~ etymology** 流俗词源; **by ~ demand/request** 应大家要求/请求 **4** *attrib* (not highbrow or specialist) 大众化的 ‹*entertainment, TV programme*›; 通俗的 ‹*culture, music, press*›; **to have ~ appeal** 对大众有吸引力

popular front *n* 人民阵线 [指左翼的党派或联盟]

popularist /ˈpɒpjʊlərɪst/ *adj* 迎合大众的 ‹*appeal, approach, view*›

popularity /ˌpɒpjʊˈlærəti/ *n* [u] 受欢迎; **to lose ~** 不再受欢迎; **to acquire** *or* **win** *or* **gain ~** 受到欢迎; **to grow in ~** 日益风行; **~ with sb./sth.** 在某人心目中/在某地受欢迎

popularity rating *n* 支持率

popularization /ˌpɒpjʊlərarˈzeɪʃn, Amer -rɪˈz-/ *n* [u] 普及; **the eighties saw the ~ of personal computers** 个人电脑在 80 年代得到了普及

popularize /ˈpɒpjʊləraɪz/ *vt* **1** (make popular) 使…受欢迎 ‹*style, fashion, sport, product*›; **the fashion was first ~d in the mid-eighties** 这种时尚首先流行于 80 年代中期 **2** (make intelligible) 使…通俗化 ‹*theory, system, science*›; **a writer who did much to ~ the idea of evolution** 为普及进化论作了很大贡献的作家

popularizer /ˈpɒpjʊləraɪzə(r)/ *n* 普及者

popularly /ˈpɒpjʊləli/ *adv* **1** (generally) 一般地 ‹*known, called, said*› **2** (informally, commonly) 普遍地 ‹*believed, thought, held*›

popular music *n* [u] 流行音乐

populate /ˈpɒpjʊleɪt/ *vt* **1** (inhabit) 居住于 ‹*district, area, region*›; **waste land largely ~d by rats** 大量老鼠栖居的荒原; **densely** *or* **heavily/sparsely ~d** 人口密集的/人烟稀少的 **2** (settle in) 向…移民 ‹*area, island, country*› **3** fig (fill with, be present in) 占据 ‹*book, profession, environment*›; **the legal profession is ~d by clever, witty people** 法律界多睿智练达之士

population /ˌpɒpjʊˈleɪʃn/ *n* **1** (inhabitants) 全部居民; **a stable/transient ~** 固定/流动

人口 **2** (specific group, type of people) 一类人; (of animals) 种群; **the local ~** 本地居民; **the civilian ~** 平民; **the working ~** 就业人口 **3** (total number) 人口; **what is the ~ of the province?** 该省有多少人口? ; **areas of dense/sparse ~** 人口稠密/人口稀少的地区; **~ expansion/growth/density** 人口膨胀/增长/密度

population: ~ control *n* [u] 人口控制; **~ explosion** *n* 人口爆炸; **~ figures** *npl* 人口数据

populism /ˈpɒpjʊlɪzəm/ *n* [u] 民粹主义

populist /ˈpɒpjʊlɪst/
A *n* 民粹主义者
B *adj* 民粹主义的 ‹*ideology, theory, propaganda*›

populous /ˈpɒpjʊləs/ *adj* 人口众多的

pop-up: ~ book *n* [有立体活动图的] 立体书; **~ headlight** *n* 弹出式前灯; **~ menu** *n* 弹出式菜单; **~ toaster** *n* 自动弹出式烤面包机; **~ window** *n* 弹出式窗口

porcelain /ˈpɔːsəlɪn/ *n* [u] **1** (substance) 瓷; **a ~ bowl/glaze** 瓷碗/釉 **2** (ware) 瓷器; **a piece of ~** 一件瓷器; **to collect ~** 收藏瓷器

porcelain ware *n* [u] 瓷器

porch /pɔːtʃ/ *n* **1** (of house, church) 入口处; **in the church ~** 在教堂的门廊内 **2** Amer (veranda) [建筑物外侧的] 走廊; **sun ~** 阳光房

porcupine /ˈpɔːkjʊpaɪn/ *n* 豪猪

pore¹ /pɔː(r)/ *n* **1** (in skin) 毛孔; **she was sweating at every ~** 她浑身是汗 **2** (of plants) 气孔 **3** (in soil, rock) 细孔

pore² *vi* **to ~ over sth.** (looking at) 仔细打量某物; (thinking about) 认真研究某事物; **she's always poring over her books** 她总是在埋头看书

pork /pɔːk/ *n* [u] 猪肉

pork: ~ barrel *n* Amer colloq 分肥拨款 [指为取悦选举人或议员而提供的政府拨款]; **~ butcher** ▸**p. 409** *n* Brit 猪肉贩; **~ chop** *n* 猪排

porker /ˈpɔːkə(r)/ *n* **1** (pig) 食用猪 **2** fig colloq pej (person) 胖猪 offensive

pork pie *n* 猪肉馅饼

pork-pie hat *n* 平顶阔边帽

pork: ~ sausage *n* 猪肉香肠; **~ scratchings** *npl* Brit 脆猪皮片

porky /ˈpɔːki/ *adj* colloq 肥胖的

porn /pɔːn/ colloq
A *n* [u] **= pornography**
B *adj* (*also* **porno** /ˈpɔːnəʊ/) **= pornographic**

pornographer /pɔːˈnɒɡrəfə(r)/ *n* (producer) 色情作品制作者; (promoter) 色情作品发行人

pornographic /ˌpɔːnəˈɡræfɪk/ *adj* 色情的 ‹*film, magazine*›

pornography /pɔːˈnɒɡrəfi/ *n* [u] 色情作品

porn shop *n* 色情作品专售店

porosity /pɔːˈrɒsəti/ *n* [u] 多孔性

porous /ˈpɔːrəs/ *adj* 多孔的 ‹*rock, material, layer*›; **sand was added to the soil, making it more ~** 沙子被添加到土壤中，使其渗水性更强

porpoise /ˈpɔːpəs/ *n* 鼠海豚

porridge /ˈpɒrɪdʒ, Amer ˈpɔːr-/ *n* [u] **1** esp Brit Culin 粥 **2** Brit colloq (time in prison) 监禁期; **to do ~** 坐班房

port¹ /pɔːt/ *n* **1** (harbour) 港口; **in ~** 停泊在港的; **to come** *or* **put into ~** 进港; **~ of dispatch/embarkation/entry** Amer 发货口岸/起航港/入境口岸; **~ facilities/security/development** 港口设施/安全/开发 **2** fig (stopping or resting place) 停靠点; **any ~ in a storm** 饥不择食

port² *n* **1** (opening) 舱口 **2** (window) **= porthole** **3** (for guns) 射击孔; **a machine gun ~** 机枪眼 **4** (aperture) 汽门 **5** Comput 端口

port³
A *n* [u] (left side) 左舷; **to ~/on the ~ side** 向/在左侧
B *adj* 左舷的 ‹*bow, guns, lights*›

port⁴ *n* [u and c] (wine) 波尔图葡萄酒

port⁵ *vt* Comput 移植; **the software can be ~ed to your firm's system** 该软件可以移植到你们公司的系统中

portability /ˌpɔːtəˈbɪləti/ *n* [u] **1** (movability) 便携性 **2** Comput 可移植性

portable /ˈpɔːtəbl/
A *adj* **1** (movable) 便于携带的; **a ~ TV/computer** 便携式电视机/计算机 **2** Comput 可移植的
B *n* 便携式设备

portage /ˈpɔːtɪdʒ/ *n* **1** [u] (of boat, cargo) [两条水路间的] 陆上运输 **2** [c] (place) 陆上运输点

Portakabin® /ˈpɔːtəkæbɪn/ *n* Brit 活动房屋

portal /ˈpɔːtl/ *n* **1** (doorway, gateway) 出入口 **2** Comput 门户网站

Port-au-Prince /ˌpɔːtəʊˈprɪns/ *pr n* 太子港

port authorities *npl* 港务局

portcullis /pɔːtˈkʌlɪs/ *n* (*pl* **~es**) 吊门; **to lower/raise the ~** 放下/升起吊门

port dues /ˈpɔːt djuːz, Amer duːz/ *npl* 港口费

portend /pɔːˈtend/ *vt* «*event, dream*» 预示 ‹*change, thing*›

portent /ˈpɔːtent/ *n* [常指不祥的] 征兆; **~ of sth.** 某事的征兆

portentous /pɔːˈtentəs/ *adj* **1** (significant) 有重大影响的 ‹*consequences, events, decision*›; 预示未来的 ‹*sign*› **2** (ominous) 带不祥预兆的 ‹*face, look, gravity*› **3** pej (pompous) 装腔作势的 ‹*essay, way*›

portentously /pɔːˈtentəsli/ *adv* **1** (ominously) 不祥地 **2** pej (pompously) 装腔作势地 ‹*announce, proclaim*›

porter /ˈpɔːtə(r)/ ▸**p. 409** *n* **1** [c] (in station, hotel, market) 行李员 **2** [c] (in hospital) 护工 **3** [u and c] (beer) 黑啤酒

portfolio /pɔːtˈfəʊlɪəʊ/ *n* **1** (for carrying drawings, papers, etc.) 公事包 **2** (set of representative items) 代表作品集; **a fine ~ of drawings/photographs** 优秀的绘画/摄影作品选集 **3** Pol 部长职; **minister without ~** 不管部部长 **4** (of investments) 投资组合

portfolio: ~ career *n* [包括多种短期或兼职工作的] 组合式职业; **~ management** *n* [u] 投资组合管理; **~ manager** ▸**p. 409** *n* 投资组合管理人

porthole /ˈpɔːthəʊl/ *n* 舷窗

portico /ˈpɔːtɪkəʊ/ *n* (*pl* **~s** *or* **~es**) 柱廊

portion /ˈpɔːʃn/ *n* **1** (slice, segment) 一部分; **she divided the cake into six equal ~s** 她把蛋糕分成6等份 **2** (amount of food) [食物的] 一份; **an extra ~** 额外的一客; **two ~s of fried rice** 两份炒饭

Phrasal verb

- **portion out** *vt* [**~ out sth., ~ sth. out**] 把…分成多份

portliness /ˈpɔːtlmɪs/ *n* [u] 发福

portly /ˈpɔːtli/ *adj* 发福的

portmanteau /pɔːtˈmæntəʊ/ *n* (*pl* **~s** *or* **portmanteaux** /pɔːtˈmæntəʊz/) 两格式旅行箱

portmanteau word *n* 合并词

Port Moresby /ˌpɔːt ˈmɔːzbi/ *pr n* 莫尔兹比港

Port-of-Spain /ˌpɔːtəvˈspeɪn/ *pr n* 西班牙港

portrait /ˈpɔːtreɪt, -trɪt/ *n* **1** (of person) 肖像 **2** (in writing, on film) 描绘

portrait gallery *n* 肖像馆

portraitist /ˈpɔːtreɪtɪst, -trɪtɪst/ ▸**p. 409** *n* (artist) 肖像画家; (photographer) 人像摄影师

portrait: ~ painter ▸**p. 409** *n* 肖像画家; **~ photographer** ▸**p. 409** *n* 人像摄影师; **~ photography** *n* [u] 人像摄影

portraiture /ˈpɔːtrɪtʃə(r), -trɪtʃə(r), Amer -treɪtʃʊər/ *n* [u] 画像技法

portray /pɔːˈtreɪ/ *vt* **1** Art 画 ‹*person, group, scene*› **2** (in words, film) 描绘 ‹*background, town, life*›; **her biographer ~ed her as an unhappy woman** 她的传记作者把她描绘成一个不幸的女人 **3** (in play) 扮演 ‹*part, person, animals*›

portrayal /pɔːˈtreɪəl/ *n* **1** (by actor) 表演 **2** (by painter, author, film-maker) 描绘; **his ~ of country life** 他对乡村生活的描述

Portugal /ˈpɔːtʃʊɡl/ *pr n* 葡萄牙

Portuguese /ˌpɔːtʃʊˈɡiːz/ ▸**p. 503, p. 426**
A *adj* (of Portugal) 葡萄牙的; (of the people) 葡萄牙人的; (of the language) 葡萄牙语的
B *n* **1** [c] (person) 葡萄牙人; **the ~** *pl* 葡萄牙人 **2** [u] (language) 葡萄牙语

Portuguese man-of-war *n* 僧帽水母

POS *abbr* **= point of sale**

pose /pəʊz/
A *vi* **1** (for photograph, painting) 摆姿势; **to ~ for one's portrait** 为画像摆好姿势; **to ~ for sb.** (for photograph) 摆好姿势让某人照相; (for painting) 摆好姿势让某人画像 **2** (masquerade) 假装; **to ~ as sb.** 冒充某人 **3** pej (posture) 装腔作势
B *vt* **1** (present) 构成 ‹*problem, challenge, threat*› **2** (ask, put forward) 提出 ‹*question, concept*› **3** Art 使摆好姿势
C *n* **1** (position, manner) 姿势; **to adopt a ~** 摆出一种姿势 **2** pej (affected or deceiving behaviour) 故作姿态; **it's all a ~** colloq 这完全是装腔作势; **to strike a ~** 装模作样

poser /ˈpəʊzə(r)/ *n* **1** colloq (question, problem) 难题 **2** pej (person) 装腔作势的人

poseur /pəʊˈzɜː(r)/ *n* **= poser 2**

posh /pɒʃ/
A *adj* **1** colloq (elegant) 雅致的 ‹*clothes*›; (stylishly luxurious) 豪华的 ‹*restaurant, area, wedding*› **2** Brit (upper class) 上流社会的 ‹*person, voice*›
B *adv* Brit 以上流社会腔调; **to talk ~** 谈吐优雅

Phrasal verb

- **posh up** *vt* [**~ sb./sth. up, ~ up sb./sth**] Brit colloq 使…变得漂亮 ‹*house, clothes, oneself*›; **to be all ~ed up** 打扮得漂漂亮亮

posit /ˈpɒzɪt/ *vt* formal 假设 ‹*features, principle*›

position /pəˈzɪʃn/
A *n* **1** [c] (location) 位置; **to take up a ~** 占据位置; **to take up one's ~** 就位; **what ~ do you play (in)?** Sport 你打什么位置? ; **to be in a good/sunny ~** 处于有利位置/在阳光充足的地方; **~s, everybody, curtain's going up** Theat 请大家就座，演出就要开始了 **2** [u] (correct location) 恰当位置; **to be in ~** 就位; **to be out of ~** 不在原定位置; **to get (sth.) into ~** (使某物) 进入适当位置; **to jostle** *or* **manoeuvre for ~** 争抢有利位置 **3** [u and c] (posture, attitude of body) 姿势; **a sitting/kneeling/lying ~** 坐姿/跪姿/卧姿 **4** [u and c] (of switch, lever) 挡位; **the controls have three ~s** 这套操纵装置有三个挡; **a switch in the on/off ~** 开着/关着的开关 **5** [c] (ranking) 名次; **top/bottom ~** 榜首/垫底的排名; **to move up/down to a new ~** 上升/下降到新的排名 **6** [u and c] (social status) 地位; **~ in society** 社会地位; **a man of ~** 有身份的男子 **7** [c] (job) 职位; **a management/government ~** 管理岗位/政府职位; **to resign one's ~** 辞职; **to take a senior ~** 担任高级职务; **a ~ of power/authority** 有权力/有权威的职务 **8** [c] (state) 状况; **the economic/financial ~** 经济/财务状况; **to be/find oneself in a good/bad ~** 处于/发现自己处于良好/糟糕的境况; **to be in a/no ~ to do sth.** 能够/不能做某事; **you're in a good ~ to judge** 你完全可以作出判断; **if I were in your ~, I'd ...** 如果我碰到你的情况，我就…; **to get oneself/sb. into a difficult ~** 使自己/某人陷入困境; **put yourself in his ~** 设身处地为他想想 **9** [c] (stance,

attitude〉立场; **to declare/reconsider/shift/change one's ~** 宣布/重新考虑/转变/改变立场; **to take up a ~** 持某种态度; **I have made my ~ very clear** 我已经明确给出了自己的立场; **to have a ~ on sth.** 对某事物持有某态度 10 [c] Mil 阵地; **defensive/forward/enemy ~s** 防御/前方/敌方阵地 11 [c] (counter) 柜台; **'~ closed'** 本柜台停止营业

B *vt* 1 (place, station) 摆放〈*object, ornament*〉; 部署〈*army, troops*〉; **to be ~ed** «*building, object*» 被安置; «*artillery, soldiers*» 被部署; **the house is badly ~ed** 这幢房子位置很差 2 Comm 为…打开市场〈*product, service, business*〉 3 (get at correct angle) 调准…的角度〈*telescope, aerial, lamp*〉 4 (ascertain position of) 确定…的位置〈*ship, aircraft*〉

C *v refl* 使位于; **to ~ oneself next to** *or* **by sth.** 站在某物旁; **I ~ed myself next to a pillar and waited** 我站在一根柱子旁边等候

positive /ˈpɒzətɪv/

A *adj* 1 *pred* (certain, sure) 确定的; **to be ~** 有把握; **~!** 绝对肯定! 2 (hopeful) 乐观的; (confident) 有信心的; **to be ~ about sth.** 对…有信心〈*idea, plan*〉 3 (good, useful, constructive) 积极向上的〈*feeling, achievement, contribution*〉; **~ thinking** 积极的思考; **to think ~** 往积极的方面去想 4 (encouraging) 表示赞同的〈*response, statement, sign*〉; **she made some really ~ criticisms** 她提出了一些非常有建设性的批评意见 5 (clear) 明确的〈*instructions, orders, rules*〉 6 (conclusive) 令人信服的〈*identification, proof, evidence*〉 7 (indicating the presence of sth.) 呈阳性的〈*test, result, reaction*〉 8 *attrib* (absolute, extreme) 十足的〈*disgrace, miracle, fool*〉; **she's a ~ genius** colloq 她是个真正的天才; **the fellow's a ~ menace** colloq 那家伙绝对是个威胁 9 (beneficial) 有助益的〈*good, advantage*〉 10 Math 正的〈*number, sign*〉 11 Elec 正电的; **a ~ terminal** 正极 12 Phot 正片的; **a ~ image** 正片图像 13 Ling 原级的

B *n* 1 (good quality or attribute) 优点 2 (affirmative) 肯定; **the answer was in the ~** 答案是肯定的 3 Phot 正片 4 Ling 原级 5 Elec 正极

positive: ~ discrimination *n* [u] Brit 积极性区别对待 [对弱势群体的优惠待遇]; **~ feedback** *n* [u] Electron 正反馈

positively /ˈpɒzətɪvli/ *adv* 1 (constructively) 积极地〈*think, play, contribute*〉 2 (hopefully) 乐观地; (confidently) 有信心地 3 (encouragingly) 赞成地〈*respond, react, worded*〉 4 (conclusively) 令人信服地〈*identify, prove*〉 5 (absolutely, extremely) 非常〈*disgraceful, stupid, rude*〉; **I ~ hated the film** 我非常讨厌那部电影 6 Elec 带正电; **~ charged** 带正电的 7 (actually) 的的确确地〈*approve, refreshed, reinvigorated*〉

positiveness /ˈpɒzətɪvnɪs/ *n* [u] 1 (hopefulness) 积极乐观; (confidence) 自信 2 (encouragement) 建设性 3 (conclusiveness) 令人信服

positive: ~ sign *n* 正号; **~ vetting** *n* [u] Brit [对涉密工作者进行的] 道德审查

positivism /ˈpɒzɪtɪvɪzəm/ *n* [u] 实证主义

positivist /ˈpɒzɪtɪvɪst/ *n* 实证主义者

positron /ˈpɒzɪtrɒn/ *n* 正电子

posse /ˈpɒsi/ *n* 1 colloq (group) 一群; **a ~ of photographers and reporters** 一群摄影师和记者 2 colloq (social group) 社交群 3 Amer Hist [县治安官为维持治安而调集的] 地方武装团队

possess /pəˈzes/ *vt* 1 (own) 拥有〈*property, money, weapons, proof*〉 2 (be endowed with) «*person*» 具有〈*quality, skill, charm*〉; «*place*» 有〈*feature, bridge*〉 3 (take control of) «*fury, demon*» 攫住〈*person*〉; (influence strongly) «*rage, bitterness*» 支配〈*person*〉; **what ~ed him to do that?** 他着了什么魔竟然做那种事?

possession /pəˈzeʃn/

A *n* 1 [u] (state of having) 拥有; **the ~ of a driving licence is a requirement** 规定必须持有驾照; **to be in ~ of sth.** 拥有某物; **to come into sb.'s ~** 为某人所获得; **to have sth. in one's ~** 拥有某物; **to have ~ of sth.** 拥有某物; **to get ~ of sth.** (legally) 得到某物; (by force) 夺得某物 2 [u] Jur (illegal ownership) 私藏; **to be in ~ of** 私藏〈*drugs*〉 3 [u] Jur (ownership of house, land) 占有; **to come into ~ of sth.** 占有某物; **to take ~ of** 占有〈*premises*〉; **~ is nine-tenths of the law** Prov 现实占有, 败一胜九 [指占有者在诉讼中总占上风] 4 [u] Sport (control of the ball) 控球; **to be in** *or* **have ~** 拥有控球权; **to win/lose ~** 赢得/失去控球权 5 [u] (control by evil spirit) 附身 6 [c] (country, territory) 领地

B **possessions** *npl* (personal property) 财产

possession order *n* [法庭关于财产归属的] 占有决议

possessive /pəˈzesɪv/

A *adj* 1 (demanding) 占有欲强的〈*person, behaviour, streak*〉; **to be ~ towards** *or* **with sb.** 对某人有很强的占有欲 2 (unwilling to share) 不愿分享的; **he's ~ about his toys** 他不愿意别人碰他的玩具 3 Ling 表示所属关系的; **a ~ pronoun** 物主代词; **the ~ case** 所有格

B *n* (word) 属有词; (form) 所有格

possessively /pəˈzesɪvli/ *adv* 不愿失去地〈*behave, cling*〉

possessiveness /pəˈzesɪvnɪs/ *n* [u] 1 (towards a person) 占有欲强 2 (with toys, clothes) 不愿分享

possessor /pəˈzesə(r)/ *n* 拥有者

possibility /ˌpɒsəˈbɪləti/

A *n* 1 [u] (likelihood, chance, prospect) 可能性; **he had ruled out the ~ that he might win** *or* **of winning** 他排除了他获胜的可能性; **there is no ~ of him succeeding** 他不可能成功; **there is little/no ~ of a strike** 罢工几乎/根本不可能; **within/beyond the bounds of ~** 在可能的范围内/外 2 [c] (potential option) 可能的选择; (potential occurrence) 可能的事; **the ~ of a refusal/of failure** 拒绝/失败的可能性; **the collapse of the company is now a ~** 公司倒闭现在是有可能的

B **possibilities** *npl* 潜力; **the idea/the market has possibilities** 这个想法有可能实现/该市场有发展前途

possible /ˈpɒsəbl/

A *adj* 1 *usu pred* (achievable) 能做到的; **the experiments are technically ~** 实验从技术上来讲是可行的; **as quickly/soon as ~** 尽快/尽早; **to do everything** *or* **as much as ~** 尽最大努力; **as far as ~** 尽量; **whenever ~** 只要有可能; **if ~, I would like a move** 如果可能的话我想动身了; **we spent every ~ moment on the beach** 我们一有时间就去海滩; **to make sth. ~** 使某事有可能; **the best education ~** 尽可能好的教育 2 (likely) 可能发生的〈*event, consequence*〉; 可能出现的〈*decline, increase*〉; **~ risks/effects/trouble** 可能发生的危险/产生的作用/出现的麻烦; **it is ~ (that ...)** (…) 是可能的; **it is ~ for you to refuse** 你可以拒绝; **with the ~ exception of ...** 可能不包括… 3 *attrib* (potential, acceptable) 合适的〈*candidate, successor*〉; 可接受的〈*answer*〉; 合理的〈*solution, explanation*〉; **a ~ future customer** 潜在的客户 4 (for emphasis) **what ~ interest can she have in him?** 她对他究竟会有什么兴趣?; **there can be no ~ excuse for such behaviour** 这种行为根本没有理由

B *n* 1 (highest achievable score) 可能的事; **Mickey scored the ~** Sport 米奇获得了最高分 2 (suitable candidate) 恰当人选; **a list of ~s for the vacancy** 填补该空缺的合适人选名单

possibly /ˈpɒsəbli/ *adv* 1 (perhaps) 也许 2 (for emphasis) [表示强调]; **how could they ~ understand?** 他们怎么可能会明白呢?; **we can't ~ afford it** 我们根本负担不起 3 (emphasizing effort) 尽全力地; **she'll come as soon as she ~ can** 她会尽快赶来

possum /ˈpɒsəm/ *n* 1 (Australian) 袋貂; **to play ~** fig colloq (feign sleep) 装睡; (feign death) 装死 2 (American) 负鼠

post[1] /pəʊst/

A *n* 1 (as support) 柱 2 (as marker) 标志杆; **starting/finishing** *or* **winning ~** 起点/终点杆; **a corner ~** Sport 角杆 3 Horse racing **the ~** (beginning) 起点柱; (end) 终点柱; **to be beaten at the ~** lit 在接近终点处被超过; fig 在最后一刻被击败; **to be left at the ~** 被远远抛在后面; **to go** *or* **come to ~** «*racehorse*» 开始比赛 4 (goalpost) 球门柱; **the ball bounced back off the ~** 球从门柱上反弹回来

B *vt* 1 (stick up) 张贴〈*poster, notice, rules*〉; **~ no bills** 禁止招贴 2 (announce) 公布〈*results, profit, loss*〉; **to ~ details on the Internet** 在互联网上发布细节; **to be ~ed (as) missing in action** Mil 被宣布在战斗中失踪 3 (put posters on or in) 在…上张贴海报〈*place, wall, building*〉

Phrasal verb

- **post up** *vt* [**~ sth. up, ~ up sth.**] 张贴〈*poster, notice, rules*〉

post[2]

A *n* 1 (job) 职位; **a civil service/management/teaching ~** 公务员/管理/教学职位; **he took up a ~ in government** 他在政府部门担任了职务 2 (place of duty) 岗位; Mil 哨所; **to be at one's ~** 在执勤; **command/customs/lookout ~** 指挥所/海关关卡/监视哨 3 (settlement) 偏远居民点; Mil 要塞; **trading ~** 贸易点; **the frontier ~s were all well-defended** 各边防要塞防守都很严密

B *vt* 1 Admin, Mil (send to take up appointment) 派驻〈*officer, worker, diplomat*〉; **he was ~ed to Washington as military attaché** 他被派驻华盛顿任武官 2 (station) 派…值勤〈*soldier, police officer*〉; 部署〈*guard, sentry*〉; **lookouts were ~ed on the roof** 屋顶上部署了监视哨 3 esp Amer Jur 交付〈*bail, bond*〉; 交〈*collateral*〉

post[3]

A *n* esp Brit 1 [u] (mail system) 邮政; **by ~** 通过邮寄; **the parcel was damaged in the ~** 包裹在邮寄过程中损坏了; **letter/parcel/registered ~** 信函/包裹/挂号邮寄; **to send sth. first-class/second-class ~** 把某物作为一类/二类邮件邮寄 2 [u] (letters) 邮件; **to deal with/answer one's ~** 处理/回复邮件 3 [c] (delivery or collection) 邮班; **there used to be two ~s each day** 过去每天有2个邮班; **has the ~ gone yet?** 邮班走了吗?; **to catch/miss the ~** 赶上/错过邮班; **by return of ~** [信函中] 请即回复 4 [u] (collection point) **the post** 邮筒; **please drop this in the ~ for me** 请替我把这封信投进邮筒 5 [c] Hist (rider) 邮差; (coach) 邮车

B *vt* 1 esp Brit (send) 邮寄〈*letter, card, parcel*〉; (put in the mail) 把…投入邮筒; **to ~ sb. sth., to ~ sth. to sb.** 把某物寄给某人; **to ~ a card for sb.** 帮某人投寄一张卡片; **to keep sb. ~ed (about sth.)** 向某人及时通报 (某事) 2 Accts (enter) 把…入账〈*item, figures*〉; **to ~ an entry to a ledger** 把账目登入分类账 3 Accts (update) 将新账目登入〈*ledger*〉

C *vi* 1 Hist, Post «*courier, messenger*» 乘邮车旅行 2 Post 投寄; **to ~ early for Christmas** 圣诞之前尽早投寄邮件

Phrasal verb

- **post off** *vt* [**~ sth. off, ~ off sth.**] esp Brit 邮寄〈*letter, card, parcel*〉

postage /ˈpəʊstɪdʒ/ *n* [u] 邮费; **~ extra** 邮费另计; **~ free** 免付邮资

postage meter *n* Amer 邮资机

postage paid

A *adv* 邮资已付

B **postage-paid** *adj* 邮资已付的

postage: ~ rates *npl* 邮资费率; **~ stamp** *n* 邮票

P

P

postal /ˈpəʊstl/ *adj* 1 (of or relating to mail) 邮政的 ‹*code, workers*›; **～ districts** 邮区; **the ～ strike lasted three days** 邮政部门罢工持续了3天 2 Brit (by means of mail) 邮递方式的; **～ application/ballot** 邮寄申请/投票

postal: ～ code *n* Brit = **postcode**; **～ order** *n* Brit 邮政汇票; **～ service** *n* 邮政业; **～ vote** *n* Brit 邮寄选票

post: ～bag *n* Brit 1 (sack, bag) 邮袋; 2 (correspondence) 公众来信; **～box** *n* esp Brit 邮箱; **～card** *n* 明信片; **～code** *n* Brit 邮政编码; **～date** *vt* 填迟…的日期 ‹*cheque, letter*›

postdoctoral /ˌpəʊstˈdɒktərəl/ *adj attrib* 博士后的 ‹*research, thesis*›

post-earthquake *adj* 震后的; **～ reconstruction** 震后重建; **～ relief programs** 震后救援计划

poster /ˈpəʊstə(r)/ *n* 海报; **to put up a ～** 张贴海报

poste restante /ˌpəʊst ˈrestɑːnt, Amer reˈstænt/
A *n* Brit 邮件存局候领处
B *adv* 以存局候领方式

posterior /pɒˈstɪərɪə(r)/
A *adj* Anat (behind) 后面的; (back) 背部的
B *n* hum colloq (buttocks) 屁股; **a slap on the ～** 打在屁股蛋儿上的一巴掌

posterity /pɒˈsterəti/ *n* [u] 后代; **to go down to ～ as ...** 被后人视为…; **wildlife should be preserved for the benefit of ～** 为了后代子孙的利益，野生动植物应该受到保护

poster paint *n* [c and u] 广告颜料

post exchange *n* Amer 军人服务社

post-feminist *adj* 后女权运动的

post-free
A *adj* (no charge) 免邮资的; (already paid) 邮资已付的
B *adv* (no charge) 免邮资; (already paid) 邮资已付

postgraduate /ˌpəʊstˈgrædʒʊət/
A *n* 研究生
B *adj* 研究生的 ‹*research, thesis*›

post: ～-haste *adv* Brit liter or dated 急忙 ‹*go, come, return*›; **～ horn** *n* 驿车号

posthumous /ˈpɒstjʊməs, Amer ˈpɒstʃəməs/ *adj* 死后获得的 ‹*fame, award, medal*›; 死后出版的 ‹*novel*›; **～ works** 遗作

posthumously /ˈpɒstjʊməsli, Amer ˈpɒstʃəməsli/ *adv* 于死后 ‹*awarded*›; **her last novel was published ～** 她的最后一部小说是在她去世后出版的

postimpressionism /ˌpəʊstɪmˈpreʃənɪzəm/ *n* [u] [19世纪法国的] 后期印象派

postimpressionist /ˌpəʊstɪmˈpreʃənɪst/
A *n* 后期印象派画家
B *adj* 后期印象派的 ‹*painting, movement, exhibition*›

postindustrial /ˌpəʊstɪnˈdʌstrɪəl/ *adj* 后工业化的 ‹*society, era, economy*›

posting /ˈpəʊstɪŋ/ *n* 1 [c] Brit (assignment to a post) 派驻; **an overseas ～** 派驻海外 2 [u] Brit (sending by post) 邮寄; **proof of ～** 邮寄证明

Post-it® /ˈpəʊstɪt/ *n* 报事贴

postman /ˈpəʊstmən/ ▸p. 409 *n* (*pl* **postmen**) Brit 邮递员

postman's knock *n* [u] Brit 邮差敲门游戏

postmark /ˈpəʊstmɑːk/
A *n* 邮戳; **date as ～** 日期以邮戳为准
B *vt* 盖邮戳于

post: ～master ▸p. 409 *n* 邮政局长; **～mistress** ▸p. 409 *n* 女邮政局长

postmodern /ˌpəʊstˈmɒdn/ *adj* 后现代主义的 ‹*irony, era, theory, culture*›

postmodernism /ˌpəʊstˈmɒdənɪzəm/ *n* [u] 后现代主义

postmodernist /ˌpəʊstˈmɒdənɪst/
A *n* 后现代主义者
B *adj* 后现代主义的 ‹*theory, author, thinking*›

post-mortem /ˌpəʊstˈmɔːtəm/ *n* 1 Med 验尸; **to carry out** *or* **hold a ～ (on sb.)** (对某人) 进行验尸; **～ examination** 尸检 2 fig (discussion) 事后剖析

post-natal /ˌpəʊstˈneɪtl/ *adj* 产后的

post-natal depression *n* [u] 产后抑郁症

post office *n* 邮局

post office box *n* 邮政信箱

post-operative /ˌpəʊstˈɒpərətɪv, Amer -reɪt-/ *adj* 手术后的 ‹*complication*›; **～ care** 术后护理

post-paid
A *adj* 邮资已付的
B *adv* 邮资已付

postpone /pəˈspəʊn/ *vt* 推迟; **the match has been ～d indefinitely** 比赛已被无限期推迟; **to ～ doing sth.** 延缓做某事

postponement /pəˈspəʊnmənt/ *n* [u and c] 延迟; **the ～ of sth.** 某事的延缓; **why not apply for a ～?** 为什么不申请延期?

postpositive /ˌpəʊstˈpɒsɪtɪv/ *adj* 后置的 ‹*adjective*›

postprandial /ˌpəʊstˈprændɪəl/ *adj* formal or hum 饭后的 ‹*speech, coffee, nap*›

post-quake *adj attrib* colloq = **post-earthquake**

postscript /ˈpəʊstskrɪpt/ *n* 1 (to letter) [信末的] 附笔 2 (to book) 跋; (to document) 补充说明; (to film) 结尾片花

post-tax *adj* 税后的 ‹*income, figure, profit*›

post-traumatic *adj* (after injury) 外伤后的; (after psychological shock) 创伤后的; **～ stress disorder** 创伤后精神紧张性障碍

postulate
A /ˈpɒstjʊlət, Amer -tʃʊ-/ *n* 假设
B /ˈpɒstjʊleɪt, Amer -tʃʊ-/ *vt* 假定 ‹*fact, idea*›; **to ～ that ...** 假设…

posture /ˈpɒstʃə(r)/
A *n* 1 [c] (physical position) 姿势 2 [u] (bearing) 仪态; **to have good/bad ～** 有良好的/不良的仪态 3 [c] fig (stance) 立场; (attitude) 态度; **to adopt** *or* **assume a ～** 采取某种态度 4 [c] fig (pose) 故作姿态
B *vi* 1 (strike pose) 摆姿势 2 fig (intend to deceive) 装模作样; **to ～ as sb./sth.** 装成某人/某物

posturing /ˈpɒstʃərɪŋ/ *n* [u] 装腔作势

post-war *adj attrib* 战后的 [尤指第二次世界大战]; **the ～ period/years** 战后期间/年代

postwoman /ˈpəʊstwʊmən/ ▸p. 409 *n* (*pl* **postwomen**) Brit 女邮递员

posy /ˈpəʊzi/ *n* 小花束; **a ～ of flowers** 一小束花

pot[1] /pɒt/
A *n* 1 Culin (container for cooking) 锅; **～s and pans** 锅碗瓢盆; **for the ～** 用于烹饪的; **it's the ～ calling the kettle black** Prov 五十步笑百步; **a watched ～ never boils** Prov 守着水壶水难开; **to keep the ～ boiling** (earn enough money to stay alive) 挣钱糊口; (keep going at a fast pace) 保持快速; **to go to ～** colloq ‹*business, person*› 完蛋; «*plans, hopes*» 泡汤 2 (container) (for jam, fish paste, yogurt, etc.) 罐; (for tea, coffee) 壶; (for paint, glue, ink) 桶 3 (contents) (jam, fish paste, yogurt, etc.) 一罐; (tea, coffee) 一壶; (paint, glue, ink) 一桶 4 (piece of pottery) 陶器; **to make** *or* **throw a ～** 制作陶罐 5 (container for plant) 花盆; **plastic/clay ～s** 塑料/陶土花盆; **a ～ of chrysanthemums** 一盆菊花 6 (potty) 便盆 7 dated (tankard) 大啤酒杯 8 Fishg 捕虾蟹笼 9 Sport colloq (prize) 奖杯 [尤指银质奖杯] 10 colloq (large sum of money) 巨款; **to have/make ～s of money** 有了/挣了一大笔钱 11 (in cards) **the ～** 一局的全部赌注; **Jim raked in the ～** 吉姆把一半的赌注收入囊中 12 (pooled funds) **the ～** 凑集的资金 13 Sport (in billiards, snooker, pool) 击球入袋
B *vt* 1 esp Brit (put in container) 把…装罐 ‹*jam, fish paste*› 2 Hort 把…栽入花盆 ‹*cutting, plant*› 3 Brit (sit on potty) 让…坐便盆 ‹*child*› 4 (in snooker, billiards, pod) 击…入袋 ‹*ball*›; **he needs to ～ the red next** 接下来他该打红球入袋了 5 Hunt colloq 射杀 ‹*bird, animal*›
C *vi* 1 (make pottery) 制作陶器 2 (shoot) 射击; **to ～ at sth.** «*hunter, poacher*» 射击某物

Phrasal verbs
- **pot on** *vt* [**～ sth. on, ～ on sth.**] 把…移栽到大花盆 ‹*plant, cutting*›
- **pot up** *vt* [**～ sth. up, ～ up sth.**] 把…移栽到花盆 ‹*cutting, seedling*›

pot[2] *n* [u] colloq (cannabis) 大麻; **to smoke ～** 吸大麻

potash /ˈpɒtæʃ/ *n* [u] 钾碱

potassium /pəˈtæsɪəm/ *n* [u] 钾

potato /pəˈteɪtəʊ/ *n* (*pl* **～es**) 土豆，马铃薯; **boiled/roast/fried ～es** 煮/烤/炸土豆; **to peel/scrub ～es** 削/刮土豆皮

potato: ～ blight *n* [u] 马铃薯晚疫病; **～ crisp** Brit, **～ chip** Amer *ns* 炸薯片; **～ masher** *n* 马铃薯捣烂器; **～ peeler** *n* 马铃薯削皮器; **～ salad** *n* [u] 土豆色拉

pot: ～bellied *adj* 肚子大的 [因饮食过量或营养不良造成]; **～ belly** *n* 大肚子; **～boiler** *n* colloq pej [迎合大众口味，以赚钱为目的的] 营利文艺; **～-bound** 根满盆的

poteen /pɒˈtiːn/ *n* [u] esp Ir 卜丁酒 [私酿的威士忌]

potency /ˈpəʊtnsi/ *n* [u and c] 1 (strength) 力量; (of drug, drink) 效力 2 (power) 权力; (ability) 能力; **the ～ to do sth.** *or* **for sth./doing sth.** 做某事的能力 3 (virility) [男子的] 性能力

potent /ˈpəʊtnt/ *adj* 1 (strong) 迅速见效的 ‹*drug, charm*›; 浓烈的 ‹*drink*› 2 (powerful, effective) 强大的 ‹*weapon*›; 强有力的 ‹*argument, reasoning*› 3 (virile) 有性能力的 ‹*man*›

potentate /ˈpəʊtnteɪt/ *n* (monarch) 君主; (ruler) 统治者

potential /pəˈtenʃl/
A *adj attrib* 潜在的 ‹*enemy, artist, danger*›; 可能的 ‹*investor, success*›
B *n* 1 [u] (capacity) 潜力; **to have ～** 有潜力; **the ～ to do ...** 做…的潜力; **to fulfil one's ～** 发挥潜能 2 [u] (possibility) 可能性; **to develop/realize one's ～** 开发潜能/实现可能性 3 [u and c] Phys 势; Elec 电势

potential difference *n* 电位差

potentiality /pəˌtenʃɪˈæləti/ *n* 1 [u] (capacity) 潜在可能性; **the ～ for sth.** 某事发生的潜在可能性; **～ as sb./sth.** 成为某人/某物的内在可能 2 [c] (aptitude) 潜力

potentially /pəˈtenʃəli/ *adv* 潜在地

pot: ～head *n* colloq 大麻瘾君子; **～herb** *n* 调味香草; **～hole** *n* 1 (in road) 坑洼; 2 (in river bed) 壶穴; 3 (cave) 锅穴; **～holer** *n* Brit 洞穴探险者; **～holing** ▸p. 307 *n* [u] Brit 洞穴探险

potion /ˈpəʊʃn/ *n* [有某种效力的] 饮剂; **a magic ～** 魔法药水; **a love ～** 春药饮剂

potlatch /ˈpɒtlætʃ/ *n* Amer [某些北美印第安部落的] 炫富宴

pot: ～ luck *n* [u] 运气; **to take ～ luck** 锅里有什么就吃什么; fig 碰运气; **～ pie** *n* Amer 菜肉馅饼; **～ plant** *n* Brit 盆栽植物

pot-pourri /ˌpəʊˈpʊəri, Amer ˌpəʊpəˈriː/ *n* (*pl* **～s**) 1 [u] (perfume mixture) 百花香 [使室内空气清新的花瓣、香草和香料混合物] 2 [c] fig Mus 集锦曲; Literat 杂集

pot roast
A *n* 炖肉块 [尤指牛肉]
B **pot-roast** *vt* 用焖罐炖 ‹*meat*›

pot: ～sherd /ˈpɒtʃɜːd/ *n* Archaeol 陶器碎片; **～shot** *n* 1 (random shot) 盲目射击; **to take a ～shot at sth.** 向某物乱开枪; 2 (critical remark) 胡乱批评; **her new play takes a ～shot at feminism** 她的新剧胡乱批评了一通女权主义

potted /ˈpɒtɪd/ *adj attrib* 1 (sealed in jars) 罐装的 ‹*meat, fish, shrimps*› 2 Hort 盆栽的 ‹*plant,* palm› 3 fig (short, abridged) 简略的 ‹*version, history*›

potter[1] /ˈpɒtə(r)/ Brit
A *vi* (work) 从容做事; (move) 闲逛
B *n* 闲逛; **a ~ around town** 在镇上闲荡

Phrasal verbs
- **potter about** *vi* Brit 闲逛
- **potter along** *vi* Brit «*person, vehicle*» 兜风
- **potter around** *vi* Brit = **potter about**

potter[2] ▸p. 409 *n* (maker of ceramics) 陶工

potter's wheel *n* 陶轮

pottery /ˈpɒtəri/ *n* 1 [u] (craft) 制陶手艺; (profession) 制陶行业; **~ class** 陶艺班 2 [u] (ware) 陶器; **a piece of ~** 一件陶器; **to sell/make ~** 销售/制造陶器; **~ exhibition** 陶器展 3 [c] (factory) 陶器厂; (workshop) 制陶作坊

potting: ~ compost *n* [u] 盆栽用土; **~ shed** *n* 盆栽育秧棚

potty[1] /ˈpɒti/ *n* colloq (child's chamber pot) 幼儿用便盆

potty[2] *adj* Brit colloq 1 (crazy) 癫狂的 ‹*person*›; **to drive sb. ~** 把某人逼疯 2 (silly) 愚蠢的 ‹*suggestion, plan*›; 站不住脚的 ‹*idea*› 3 (enthusiastic) 痴迷的; **to be ~ about sth./sb.** 迷恋某事物/某人

potty-train *vt* 训练…使用便盆 ‹*child*›

pouch /paʊtʃ/ *n* 1 (bag) [随身携带的] 小袋子 2 (contents) 一小袋 3 (of skin) 松垂的眼皮; **the old man had deep ~es under his eyes** 老人的下眼袋下垂很厉害 4 (of marsupials) 育儿袋 5 (of rodents) 颊袋

pouchful /ˈpaʊtʃfʊl/ *n* 一小袋

pouch-shaped *n* 小袋子状的

pouffe, pouf /puːf/ *n* (footstool) 脚凳; (seat) 矮凳

poulterer /ˈpəʊltərə(r)/ ▸p. 409 *n* Brit 禽贩

poultice /ˈpəʊltɪs/
A *n* 泥敷剂; **a ~ of herbs** 药草敷剂
B *vt* 在…上抹泥敷剂 ‹*wound, sore, boil*›

poultry /ˈpəʊltri/ *n* [u] 1 (domestic fowl) 家禽 2 (meat) 家禽肉

poultry: ~ dealer ▸p. 409 *n* 家禽商贩; **~ farm** *n* 家禽饲养场; **~ farmer** ▸p. 409 *n* 家禽饲养场场主; **~ farming** *n* [u] 养禽业

pounce /paʊns/
A *vi* 1 (spring, swoop) «*animal, person*» 猛扑; **to ~ on sth.** 向…猛扑过去 ‹*prey, criminal, victim*› 2 fig (take advantage of, grab or accept eagerly) 一下抓住; **to ~ on** *or* **upon sth./sb.** 抓住某物/某人; **the editor ~d on the keyboarder's errors** 编辑一眼看出了键盘输入员的错误; **my son ~d on my newspaper before I had a chance to open it** 还没等我打开报纸, 我儿子一把就把它抓过去了
B *n* 猛扑

pound[1] /paʊnd/ *n* 1 ▸p. 909 Meas (avoirdupois) 磅 [等于16盎司, 合0.454公斤]; **to be sold by the ~** 按磅卖; **to demand/have/want one's ~ of flesh** 强索欠债; **a ~ weight** 一磅的秤砣; **a two-~ box of chocolates** 一盒两磅装的巧克力 2 ▸p. 909 Meas (troy) 金衡磅 [等于12盎司, 合0.373公斤]; **six ~s of gold** 6 磅黄金 3 ▸p. 174 Fin (UK monetary unit) 英镑; **the ~** 英镑 [指英镑对其他货币的比值]; **the ~ closed slightly down at $1.534** 英镑收于1.534美元, 略微下跌; **the strength/weakness of the ~** 英镑的坚挺/疲软; **to pay 5p in the ~** 每镑付 5 便士佣金; **to be penny wise, ~ foolish** Prov 小事聪明, 大事糊涂; **in for a penny, in for a ~** colloq 一不做二不休; **a two-~ coin** 面值两英镑的硬币 4 ▸p. 174 Fin (in some Middle Eastern countries) 镑; **the Egyptian/Syrian ~** 埃及/叙利亚镑

pound[2]
A *vt* 1 Culin, Pharm (grind, crush) 捣碎 ‹*spice, grain, garlic, drug*›; **to ~ sth. to** *or* **into sth.** 把某物捣成某物; **~ the garlic to a paste** 把蒜捣成泥 2 (hit with fist) 擂 ‹*door, table*›; 拳打 ‹*person, body*› 3 (hit with tool) 夯实 ‹*earth, paving stones*›; 砸 ‹*stake, concrete*›; **he ~ed the post into the ground** 他把柱子砸进地里; **to ~ sth. into sb.** fig 向某人灌输某事物 4 (lash) «*waves, sea*» 拍打 ‹*rocks, shore, boat*› 5 Mil «*army, gunfire*» 轰炸 ‹*enemy, position*› 6 Culin (prepare by beating) 敲打 ‹*meat, dough*›; **to ~ the steaks to make them tender** 敲打肉排使其变嫩 7 (strike noisily) 敲击 ‹*piano, keyboard, typewriter*› 8 (walk) 咚咚地走在…上 ‹*streets, pavements*›; **to ~ the beat** «*police officer*» 在辖区巡逻
B *vi* 1 (knock loudly) 敲打; **to ~ on sth.** 敲打 ‹*door, table, wall*› 2 (lash) «*waves, sea*» 拍打; **to ~ on** *or* **against the rocks/shore/boat** 拍打岩石/水岸/船舷 3 **to ~ on** 敲击 ‹*piano, keyboard, typewriter*› 4 (run noisily) «*person, large animal*» 咚咚地走动; **he ~ed up the stairs** 他咚咚咚地跑上了楼 5 (throb) «*heart*» 怦怦跳; «*head*» 突突作痛 6 (sound noisily) «*drum*» 咚咚作响

Phrasal verbs
- **pound away** *vi* 1 «*pianist*» 埋头弹奏; «*keyboarder, typist*» 埋头敲击键盘; **to ~ away at** *or* **on sth.** 埋头弹奏 ‹*piano*›; 埋头敲击 ‹*keyboard, typewriter*› 2 (work doggedly) «*writer*» 埋头工作; **to ~ away at sth.** 埋头写 ‹*notes, letter, novel*› 3 Mil «*army, gunfire*» 连续轰炸; **to ~ away at sth.** 连续轰炸 ‹*enemy, town*›
- **pound out**
A *vt* [**~ sth. out, ~ out sth.**] 咚咚地弹奏 ‹*tune*›; 噼噼啪啪地打出 ‹*article, novel, report*›
B *vi* «*music, tune*» 嘈杂地播放

pound[3] *n* 1 (for stray dogs, cats) 收容所 2 (for cars) 违章停车车辆扣留场

pound: ~ cake *n* Amer 磅饼 [一种重油重糖蛋糕]; **~ coin** *n* Brit 一英镑硬币

pounding /ˈpaʊndɪŋ/ *n* 1 [u] (of waves) 猛烈的拍打声; (of drums) 猛烈的敲击声; (of heart) 剧烈的心跳声 2 [c] fig (damage) 重创; **to take a ~** 遭受严重破坏 3 [c] colloq (defeat) 惨败; **to give sb./take a ~** 大败某人/遭到惨败

pound: ~ note *n* 一英镑钞票; **~ sign** *n* 英镑符号 [即£]

pour /pɔː(r)/
A *vt* 1 (cause to flow) 倒出 ‹*liquid, sauce, sugar*›; 倾倒 ‹*metal, cement*›; **to ~ sth. into/over/down sth.** 把某物倒进某物/浇到某物上/沿某物浇下; **I was ~ing sweat** 我汗流浃背; **it's ~ing buckets** colloq 正下着瓢泼大雨; **to ~ it on** colloq (praise excessively) 大肆吹捧; Amer (work with energy) 加油干; **to ~ oil on the flames** 火上浇油; **to ~ oil on troubled waters** 调解争端 2 (serve) «*hostess, waiter*» 倒 ‹*cup of sth., drink*›; **to ~ sth. for sb., to ~ sb. sth.** 为某人斟上某饮料 3 fig (supply freely) 不断地大量投入 ‹*money, resources, personnel*›; 倾注 ‹*energy, enthusiasm*›; **they are ~ing more soldiers into the battle zone** 他们正向战区增派大批士兵
B *v refl* colloq hum 费力穿上; **to ~ oneself into a dress** 用力套上连衣裙
C *vi* 1 (flow) «*water, light, sunshine*» 倾泻; «*sweat*» 不断流下; «*smoke, steam*» 滚滚冒出; **blood was ~ing from the wound** 伤口血流如注; **words ~ed from her mouth** 她口若悬河滔滔不绝; **relief ~ed over me** 我收到了大量救济物资 2 «*people*» 纷至沓来; «*vehicles, animals*» 蜂拥而来; **refugees ~ed over the border** 难民大量涌过边境 3 (rain) 下大雨; **it was absolutely ~ing** 简直就是倾盆大雨 4 colloq (serve drink) 倒饮料 5 «*jug, bottle*» 倒起来; **the jug doesn't ~ very well** 这把壶倒起来不太方便

Phrasal verbs
- **pour away** *vt* [**~ sth. away, ~ away sth.**] 倒掉 ‹*water, dregs*›; **he ~ed the dirty water away** 他把脏水倒进了下水管
- **pour down** *vi* «*rain*» 倾盆而下; **it's ~ing down outside** 外面大雨滂沱
- **pour forth** *vi* formal or liter = **pour out A**
- **pour in**
A *vi* 1 (flow in) «*water, smoke*» 大量涌进; «*rain*» 倾泻; «*sunshine, light*» 照射进来 2 «*people, animals, vehicles*» 涌入; «*complaints, reports*» 纷至沓来; «*money*» 大量投入; **visitors were ~ing in from all over the country** 观光者从全国各地涌来
B *vt* [**~ sth. in, ~ in sth.**]
1 (transfer) 倒入 ‹*liquid, molten metal, concrete*›
2 fig (provide) 大量投入 ‹*money, funding*›
- **pour off** *vt* [**~ sth. off, ~ off sth.**] 倒出 ‹*liquid*›; **she ~ed off the cream into a separate jug** 她把奶油单独倒进一个罐子
- **pour out**
A *vi* 1 (flow out) «*liquid*» 流出; «*smoke, steam*» 滚滚冒出 2 fig (be expressed) «*words, troubles*» 被倾吐; «*feelings*» 迸发; «*ideas*» 被和盘托出 3 «*people, animals, vehicles*» 涌出
B *vt* [**~ out sth., ~ sth. out**]
1 (serve) 斟 ‹*tea, wine, glass of water*›; **to ~ sb. out sth.** 给某人斟上某物 2 (emit) 大量排放 ‹*smoke, sewage*› 3 (produce in large amounts) 大量产出 ‹*goods*›; 大批吐出 ‹*exports*› 4 fig (express freely) 倾诉 ‹*feelings, troubles*›; 尽情宣泄 ‹*indignation*›; **to ~ out one's heart/story** 倾吐心声/把事情原委和盘托出; **to ~ out curses/threats** 破口大骂/横加威胁

pouring /ˈpɔːrɪŋ/ *adj* 瓢泼的 ‹*rain*›; **a ~ wet day** 大雨如注的一天

pout /paʊt/
A *vi* [尤指生气时] 撅嘴
B *vt* 撅起; **to ~ one's lips** 撅起嘴
C *n* 撅嘴; **to answer with a ~** 撅着嘴回答

poutine /puːˈtiːn/ *n* [u] 肉汁乳酪薯条

poverty /ˈpɒvəti/ *n* [u] 1 (lack of money) 贫穷; **to live in ~** 生活贫困; **to be reduced to ~** 陷入贫困 2 fig (lack) 贫乏; **the ~ of sth.** 某事物的缺乏; **the ~ of the soil** 土壤的贫瘠

poverty: ~ line, ~ level *ns* 贫困线; **below/near the ~ line** 在贫困线之下/接近贫困线; **~-stricken** *adj* 贫穷的; **~ trap** *n* Brit 贫困的牢笼 [指收入增加后领取的救济相应减少、生活更糟或未改善的状况]

POW *abbr* = **prisoner of war** 战俘; **a ~ camp** 战俘营

powder /ˈpaʊdə(r)/
A *n* [u] 1 (fine dry particles) 粉末; **to crush/grind/turn sth. to ~** 把某物压成/磨成/变成粉末; **in ~ form** 呈粉末状; **stain-removing ~** 去污粉 2 (cosmetic) 美容粉 3 Mil 火药; **to keep one's ~ dry** 做好应急准备
B *vt* 1 (apply to face, body) 在…上搽粉; **to ~ one's nose** euph 补妆 [指上厕所] 2 (dust, sprinkle) 撒粉状物于 ‹*cake*›; «*pollen, snow*» 撒满 ‹*leaves, fields*›; **her face is ~ed with freckles** 她的脸上布满雀斑 3 (pulverize) 把…磨成粉末 ‹*chalk, rocks*›

powder blue ▸p. 134
A *n* [u] 浅蓝色
B **powder-blue** *adj* 浅蓝色的

powder compact *n* 香粉盒

powdered /ˈpaʊdəd/ *adj* 粉状的; **~ milk/coffee** 奶粉/咖啡粉

powdering /ˈpaʊdərɪŋ/ *n* 一层粉状物

powder: ~ keg *n* 1 (for gunpowder) [金属制的] 小型火药桶; 2 fig (dangerous situation) 火药桶; **~ magazine** *n* 火药库; **~ puff** *n* 粉扑; **~ room** *n* euph 女洗手间; **~ snow** *n* [u] 干松雪

powdery /ˈpaʊdəri/ *adj* 1 (resembling powder) 粉状的 ‹*snow, stone, chalk*› 2 (covered with powder) 布满粉的; **the baker's ~ hands** 面包师沾满面粉的双手; **her pale ~ cheeks** 她搽满粉的苍白面颊

power /ˈpaʊə(r)/
A *n* 1 [u] (control) 控制力; **political/economic/military ~** 政治权力/经济实力/军事力量;

the ~ of the press/media/church 报章/媒体/教会的影响力; **to be in ~** 当政; **to come to ~** 上台执政; **to gain/win/take/seize ~** 取得/赢得/掌握/夺取政权; **~ to the people!** 还政于民！; **~ corrupts, and absolute ~ corrupts absolutely** 权力导致腐败，而绝对的权力绝对导致腐败 **2** [u and c] (capability) 能力; **to be in sb.'s ~ (to do sth.)** 某人有能力（做某事）; **an accident which (it) was not in my ~ to prevent** 我没有能力阻止的事故; **the ~ of speech/sight/hearing** 说话能力/视力/听力 **3** [u and c] (authority) 职权; **to have (the) ~ to do sth.** 有权做某事; **we have no ~ to act in this case** 在这种情况下我们无权行动; **this warrant gives me the ~ to search these premises** 这道搜查令授权我搜查这些场所 **4** [u] (force, strength) 力量; **the ~ of the storm/explosion** 暴风雨/爆炸的威力; **it was a shot of tremendous ~** 这一击威力巨大 **5** [u] Phys, Tech 能量 **6** [u] Elec 电; **hydroelectric ~** 水电力; **to generate ~ from waste** 利用垃圾废物发电; **switch the ~ on/off** 接通/关掉电源 **7** [u] Sci (magnification) 放大率; **a high-/low-~ lens** 高倍/低倍放大镜 **8** [c] (person) 有权势的人; (institution) 权力机构; **he's a ~ to be reckoned with** 他是个不容忽视的实权人物 **9** [c] (country) **the big** *or* **great ~s** 大国; **an allied/enemy ~** 结成同盟的大国/敌对强国 **10** [u] Math 乘方; **2 to the ~ (of) 4 equals 16** 2 的 4 次方是 16; **the third/fourth ~ of 10** 10 的 3 次方/4 次方

B *modif* **1** Mech 动力的 ‹*lathe, drill, brakes*›; 电动的 ‹*mower*› **2** Elec 电的; **~ generation/supply/failure** 发电/供电/断电; **a ~ cable/line/grid** 电缆/电线/输电网 **3** (relating to control, authority) 权力的 ‹*struggle*›

C *vt* **1** «*generator, battery, engine*» 驱动 ‹*vehicle, aircraft, boat*›; 为…供电 ‹*factory*› **2** (send powerfully) 使迅猛移动 ‹*ball, shot*›; **she ~ed her way into the lead** 她迅速发力冲到最前面

Phrasal verbs

- **power down** *vt* [**~ sth. down, ~ down sth.**] 关掉 ‹*device, computer, machine*›
- **power up** *vt* [**~ sth. up, ~ up sth.**] 启动 ‹*device, computer, machine*›

power: ~-assisted *adj* 助力的 ‹*brakes, steering*›; **~ base** *n* 权力基础; **~boat** *n* 汽艇; **a ~boat race** 汽艇赛; **~ breakfast** *n* [商界或政界巨头的] 权力早餐会; **~ broker** *n* [能施加影响的] 权力经纪人; **~ cut** *n* 停电; **~ dispute** *n* 电力行业劳资纠纷; **~ dive** *n* 动力俯冲; **~ dressing** *n* [u] 显贵穿着; **~-driven** *adj* 机动的

powerful /'paʊəfl/ *adj* **1** (having great strength) 强有力的 ‹*blow, current*›; 强壮的 ‹*arm*›; 强大的 ‹*force, weapon*›; 大功率的 ‹*telescope, lens, car, engine*›; **the world's most ~ supercomputer** 世界上最强大的超级计算机; **a ~ swimmer** 游泳健将 **2** (having great influence) 有影响力的 ‹*businessman, official, nation*›; 有法力的 ‹*wizard*›; **a ~ country** 强国 **3** (having a strong effect) 强烈的 ‹*emotion*›; 强效的 ‹*drug*›; 鲜明的 ‹*image, imagination*›; 动人的 ‹*performance*› **4** (pungent) 浓烈的 ‹*smell*›

powerfully /'paʊəfəli/ *adv* **1** (with great strength) 强有力地; **to be ~ built** 体格健壮 **2** (with great influence or effect) 有力地 ‹*argue, affect, influence*›; 有感染力地 ‹*portray*›; **he gave a ~ moving speech** 他作了一个极为动人的演讲 **3** (pungently) 浓烈地 ‹*smell*›

power: ~ game *n* **1** Sport 力量竞技; **2** Pol 权力竞争; **~house** *n* **1** (dynamic person) 精力充沛的人; (dynamic organization) 强大的集团; **2** Amer *or* dated **= ~ station**

powerless /'paʊəlɪs/ *adj* **1** (without power) 无权力的; (without influence) 无影响力的 **2** (helpless) 无能为力的; **to be ~ to help** 无力相助

powerlessly /'paʊəlɪsli/ *adv* 无能为力地 ‹*stand by, look on*›

powerlessness /'paʊəlɪsnɪs/ *n* [u] **1** (lack of influence) 无权力 **2** (helplessness) 无能为力

power: ~lifting *n* [u] 力量举重 [参赛者按规定顺序完成后蹲、硬拉、卧推三种动作]; **~ line** *n* 输电线; **~ lunch** *n* [商界或政界巨头的] 权力午餐会; **~ nap** *n* [恢复精力的] 小睡; **~ napping** *n* [u] 小睡; **~ of attorney** *n* [u] 代理权; **~ outage** *n* 停电; **~ pack** *n* 电源组; **~ plant** **1** (for generating electricity) 发电厂; **2** (engine) 动力设备; **~ play** *n* **1** [c] Sport (gen) 力量型打法; (in ice hockey) 以多打少; **2** [c and u] fig (tactical manoeuvre) 权术运用; **~ point** *n* Brit 电源插座; **~ politics** *npl* + *v sing or pl* 强权政治; **~-sharing** *n* [u] 权力分掌; **a ~-sharing agreement** 权力分享协议; **~ shower** *n* 强力淋浴器; **~ station** *n* Brit 发电厂; **~ structure** *n* 权力机构; **~ surge** *n* 电涌; **~ tool** *n* 电动工具; **~ training** *n* [u] 力量训练; **~ user** *n* 计算机高手; **~ worker** *n* 发电厂工人

powwow /'paʊwaʊ/

A *n* **1** (ceremony) [北美印第安人有盛宴和舞蹈等活动的] 帕瓦仪式 **2** fig colloq (meeting) 讨论会; (discussion) 商谈; **to hold a ~** 开讨论会

B *vi* colloq 详细讨论; **to ~ with sb.** 和某人详谈

Powys /'paʊɪs/ *pr n* 波厄斯郡

pox /pɒks/ ▸**p. 377** *n* **1** (disease) 痘; **a ~ on sb./sth.** 降灾祸于某人/某物 **2** colloq (syphilis) **the ~** 梅毒 **3** Hist (smallpox) 天花

poxy /'pɒksi/ *adj* esp Brit colloq (worthless) 无价值的; (of poor quality) 蹩脚的; **they've won one ~ trophy** 他们赢得了一个一文不值的奖杯; **there's one tiny ~ snack bar** 有一家糟透的小点心店

Poyang Lake /pəʊ'jæŋ/ ▸**p. 424** *pr n* 鄱阳湖

pp *abbr* **= per procurationem** 代表 [表示代某人签署信件]

PPI *abbr* **= producer price index**

PPP *abbr* **= private pension plan**

PPS *abbr* **= post postscriptum** 再附言

PPV *abbr* **= pay-per-view**

PR *abbr* **1** **= public relations** **2** **= proportional representation**

practicability /ˌpræktɪkə'bɪləti/ *n* [u] **1** (feasibility) 可行性; **the ~ of sth.** 某事的可行性 **2** (of access) 可通行

practicable /'præktɪkəbl/ *adj* **1** (feasible) 可行的 ‹*solution, plan, idea*›; **a ~ project for saving water** 一项切实可行的节水工程 **2** (passable) 可通行的 ‹*road, route*› **3** (useful) 适用的 ‹*signal, system, method*›; **a ~ infrastructure** 适用的基础设施

practical /'præktɪkl/

A *adj* **1** (concrete) 实际的 ‹*difficulties, application, experience, skills*›; **for all ~ purposes** 实际上; **in ~ terms** 具体来说 **2** (viable) 切实可行的 ‹*idea, plan*› **3** (useful) 实用的 ‹*clothes, shoes, device*› **4** (sensible) 实事求是的 ‹*mind, outlook, approach, attitude*›; **to be ~** 实事求是 **5** (skilled) 动手能力强的 **6** (virtual) **it's a ~ certainty that ...** …实际上已确定无疑

B *n* Brit (examination) 实验考核; (lesson) 实践课

practicality /ˌpræktɪ'kæləti/

A *n* [u] **1** (of task, approach) 可行性; **the ~ of sth.** 某事的可行性 **2** (of clothing, equipment) 实用性 **3** (of person) 实事求是

B **practicalities** *npl* 实际情况; **the practicalities of living in the country** 乡村生活的现实情况

practical: ~ joke *n* 恶作剧; **~ joker** *n* 恶作剧者

practically /'præktɪkli/ *adv* **1** (virtually) 几乎 **2** (rationally, sensibly) 实事求是地

practicalness /'præktɪklnɪs/ *n* **= practicality A**

practical nurse ▸**p. 409** *n* Amer [所受培训不及注册护士的] 经验护士

practice /'præktɪs/

A *n* **1** [u] (action, operation) 实践; **to put sth. into ~** 把某事付诸实践; **in ~** 实际上; **the principles and ~ of teaching** 教学理论与实践 **2** [u] (repetition, exercises) 练习; **to be/keep in ~** 在/保持练习; **to be** *or* **get out of ~** 疏于练习; **two hours' ~ a day** 每天练习两小时; **~ makes perfect** Prov 熟能生巧 **3** [u] (procedure) 常规; **to be good/common/accepted/standard ~ to do sth.** 是做某事的优良/一般/公认/标准做法 **4** [c] (habit, custom) 习惯; **the ~ of doing sth.** 做某事的习惯; **as is my (usual) ~, I got up at 6 a.m.** 我一如既往地在早上 6 点钟起床了 **5** [u and c] (of doctor, lawyer) 工作; **to set up in** *or* **go into ~ (as a doctor/lawyer)** 开始执业（行医/做律师）; **to work in general/private ~** 从事普通诊疗/开设私人诊所行医; **she has a profitable medical/legal ~** 她的诊所/律师事务所很赚钱; **a large/efficiently-run ~** 规模很大的/高效运营的执业机构

B *modif* 训练的 ‹*exam, game, flight, session*›

C *vt, vi* Amer **= practise**

practice: ~ run *n* **1** (trial run) (for task) 试行; (for race) 试跑; (of car) 试驾; (of plane) 试飞; **2** esp Theat (rehearsal) 排练; **~ teacher** *n* [大学生] 实习教师

practise /'præktɪs/ Brit

A *vt* **1** (work at) 练习; **to ~ the piano** 练习弹钢琴; **to ~ doing** *or* **how to do sth.** 练习做某事; **to ~ one's French on sb.** 跟某人练习法语 **2** (use) 实施; **they ~ birth control** 他们实行计划生育; **it is a method of breathing ~d by yogis** 这是瑜伽修炼者采用的呼吸方法; **to ~ what one preaches** 身体力行 **3** (observe) 奉行 ‹*faith, rules, beliefs*›; **she ~s Buddhism** 她信奉佛教 **4** (exercise) 养成…的习惯 ‹*patience, tolerance, self-control*›; **to ~ economy** 厉行节约 **5** (follow a profession) 从事; **to ~ medicine/law** 行医/做律师

B *vi* **1** (work at) 练习; **to ~ for sth.** 为…而练习 ‹*exam, interview*› **2** (follow a profession) 执业; **to ~ as a lawyer/doctor** 从事律师工作/做医生

practised /'præktɪst/ Brit *adj* 老练的 ‹*liar, eye, performance*›; **to be ~ in/in doing sth.** 在某方面/做某事很老练; **she is well ~ in the art of forging cheques** 她伪造支票的手艺娴熟

practising /'præktɪsɪŋ/ Brit *adj attrib* **1** (actively following faith, persuasion) 虔诚的 ‹*Christian, Roman Catholic, Muslim*›; 身体力行的 ‹*pacifist, vegetarian, homosexual*› **2** (actively working) 执业的 ‹*doctor, lawyer*›

practitioner /præk'tɪʃənə(r)/ *n* **1** (of profession) 从业人员 [尤指医师] **2** (of art, belief) 实践者

praesidium /prɪ'sɪdɪəm/ *n* esp Brit **= presidium**

pragmatic /præg'mætɪk/ *adj* 务实的 ‹*ideas, approach, person*›

pragmatically /præg'mætɪkli/ *adv* 务实地; **let's approach the problem ~** 我们还是实事求是地处理问题吧

pragmatism /'prægmətɪzəm/ *n* [u] 实用主义

pragmatist /'prægmətɪst/ *n* 实用主义者

Prague /prɑːg/ *pr n* 布拉格

prairie /'preəri/ *n* 大草原; **~ farmers** 大草原农场主

prairie: ~ chicken *n* 北美草原松鸡; **~ dog** *n* 草原犬鼠; **~ wolf** *n* Amer **= coyote 1**

praise /preɪz/

A *n* [u] **1** (approval, admiration) 称赞; **in ~ of sb./sth.** 赞扬某人/某事物; **beyond ~** 赞美不尽的; **to be loud in one's ~ of sb./sth.** 对某人/某事物大加赞扬; **to heap ~ on sb.** 大肆称赞某人; **faint ~** 轻描淡写的赞扬; **high ~** 高度赞扬 **2** Relig 赞颂; **let us give ~ unto the Lord!** 让我们赞美上帝吧！; **a**

hymn/song of ~ 赞美诗/颂歌; **P~ be to God!** 谢天谢地!
B *vt* **1** (approve, admire) 称赞; **to ~ sb. for sth./for doing** 赞扬某人某事/做某事; **to ~ sb./sth. as sth.** 把某人/某物誉为某事物; **to ~ sb./sth. to the skies** 把某人/某事物捧上天; **to sing sb.'s/sth.'s ~s** 高度赞扬某人/某事物 **2** Relig 赞颂 ‹*God, the Lord, Allah*›; **to ~ God for sth.** 因某事物而赞美上帝; **~ God!** 感谢上帝!

praiseworthiness /ˈpreɪzwɜːðɪnɪs/ *n* [u] 值得赞扬; **the ~ of sth.** 某事之可嘉

praiseworthy /ˈpreɪzwɜːði/ *adj* 值得赞扬的

praline /ˈprɑːliːn/ *n* [u and c] 果仁糖

pram /præm/ *n* Brit 婴儿车

prance /prɑːns, Amer præns/ *vi* **1** (horse) 腾跳 **2** (person) 阔步行走; **to ~ about** *or* **around** 趾高气扬地走来走去; **to ~ in/out** 昂首阔步走进/走出

prank /præŋk/ *n* 恶作剧; **to play a ~ on sb.** 捉弄某人

prankster /ˈpræŋkstə(r)/ *n* 恶作剧者

praseodymium /ˌpreɪzɪəˈdɪmɪəm/ *n* [u] 镨

prat /præt/ *n* Brit colloq 傻瓜

pratfall /ˈprætfɔːl/ *n* colloq **1** (fall) 坐跌; **to take a ~** 一屁股坐在地上 **2** (humiliating action) 丢人现眼

prattle /ˈprætl/
A *vi* 闲扯; **to ~ on about sth.** 没完没了地唠叨某事; **we'd better stop prattling (on)** 我们别胡扯了
B *n* [u] 闲扯; **the ~ of little children** 小孩子的咿咿呀呀的儿语; **I don't want to listen to a lot of ~!** 我不想听这么一大堆废话!

prawn /prɔːn/ *n* 对虾; **a ~ salad** 对虾色拉

prawn: ~ cocktail *n* 大虾冷盘; **~ cracker** *n* 虾片

pray /preɪ/
A *vi* (say prayers) 做祷告; (beseech) 祈求; **to ~ to God for sth.** 为某事物向上帝祈祷; **to ~ for rain/fair weather** 祈求下雨/好天气
B *vt* **1** Relig 祈求 ‹*the Lord, Allah*›; **to ~ God for forgiveness** 祈求上帝原谅 **2** (wish, hope) 祈望

prayer /ˈpreə(r)/
A *n* **1** [u] (action of praying) 祷告; **in ~** 在祈祷的; **to be at ~** *or* **at one's ~s** 做祷告 **2** [c] (request) 祈求; (expression) 祷文; **to say one's ~s** 念祷文; **you are in my ~s** 我为你祝福; **not to have a ~** colloq 没有丝毫成功的机会 **3** fig (wish, hope) 祈望
B **prayers** *npl* 祷告式; **family ~s** 家庭祈祷仪式; **evening/morning ~s** 晚祷/早祷

prayer: ~ beads *npl* 念珠; **~ book** *n* 祈祷书; **the P~ Book** 英国国教祈祷书; **~ mat, ~ rug** *ns* [伊斯兰教徒祷告时用的] 祈祷跪垫; **~ wheel** *n* [藏传佛教信徒祈祷用的] 转经筒

praying mantis *n* (*pl* **~** *or* **~es**) 螳螂

PRC *abbr* **= People's Republic of China**

preach /priːtʃ/
A *vi* **1** Relig 讲道; **to ~ about** *or* **on sth.** 宣讲某事物; **to ~ to the converted** 向教徒宣教 **2** fig pej (give moral advice) 说教; **to ~ at** *or* **to sb.** 对某人说教
B *vt* **1** (proclaim, teach) 宣讲 ‹*religion, doctrine*›; **to ~ sth. to sb.** 向某人宣讲某事物 **2** (deliver) 布 ‹*sermon*› **3** fig (urge) 宣扬 ‹*tolerance, virtues, pacifism*›; **~ing brotherly love is easier than practising it** 兄弟般的友爱说起来容易做起来难

preacher /ˈpriːtʃə(r)/ *n* 传道者

preachify /ˈpriːtʃɪfaɪ/ *vi* colloq 说教

preaching /ˈpriːtʃɪŋ/ *n* [u and c] **1** Relig 布道 **2** (moralizing) 说教

preadolescent /ˌpriːædəˈlesnt/
A *adj* 准青春期的 ‹*child*›; 青春前期的 ‹*prank, games, fantasy*›
B *n* 青春前期的少年

preamble /priːˈæmbl/ *n* [c and u] (preliminary) 序言; (preparatory) 开场白; **the ~ to the book** 书的序言; **without ~** 开门见山地

preamplifier /priːˈæmplɪfaɪə(r)/ colloq **preamp** /priːˈæmp/ *ns* 前置放大器

prearrange /ˌpriːəˈreɪndʒ/ *vt* 预先安排

precancerous /priːˈkænsərəs/ *adj* 癌变前的; **~ lesions** 癌前病变

precarious /prɪˈkeərɪəs/ *adj* **1** (hazardous) 不稳固的 ‹*position, hold, seat*›; 危险的 ‹*crossing, bridge*› **2** (insecure) 不安稳的 ‹*position, career*›

precariously /prɪˈkeərɪəsli/ *adv* **1** (hazardously) 不稳地 ‹*walk, hang, perch*›; 危险地 ‹*move, swing*› **2** (insecurely) 不安稳地 ‹*live*›; **they worked ~ in the acting profession** 他们在演艺行业的工作朝不保夕

precast /ˌpriːˈkɑːst, Amer -ˈkæst/ *adj* 预浇的; **~ concrete blocks** 预制混凝土砌块

precaution /prɪˈkɔːʃn/ *n* 预防措施; **as a ~** 以防万一; **to take ~s** 采取预防措施; **to take the ~ of doing sth.** 做某事以防不测; **they didn't take ~s so now she's pregnant** euph 他们没有采取避孕措施, 所以现在她怀孕了

precautionary /prɪˈkɔːʃənəri, Amer -neri/ *adj* 预防的; **as a ~ measure** 作为预防措施

precede /prɪˈsiːd/ *vt* **1** (go before) 先于; **her death was ~d by a long illness** 她死前病了很长一段时间; **to ~ sb. as president** 在某人之前担任总裁; **the great man was ~d by his little dog** 那位伟人的小狗走在他前面; **to ~ a speech with a few words of thanks** 在演讲之前先说几句感谢的话 **2** (in rank) «*king*» 地位高于 ‹*aristocrat*›

precedence /ˈpresɪdəns/ *n* [u] **1** (in importance) 优先; **to take** *or* **have ~ over sth./sb.** 优先于某事物/某人; **to give ~ to sb./sth.** 首先关注某人/某事物 **2** (in rank) 级别高低; **to have ~ over sb.** 级别高于某人; **in order of ~** 按行辈

precedent /ˈpresɪdənt/ *n* [c and u] **1** (event, action) 先例; **to set** *or* **create** *or* **establish a ~** 开创先例; **to break with ~** 打破常规 **2** Jur 判例

preceding /prɪˈsiːdɪŋ/ *adj* 在前的; **in the ~ year/sentence** 在上一年/上一句; **on the ~ day** 在前一天

precept /ˈpriːsept/ *n* (rule) 准则; (maxim) 格言

prechilled /ˈpriːtʃɪld/ *adj* 预冷的 ‹*food, glass*›

pre-Christian /ˌpriːˈkrɪstʃən/ *adj* 公元前的 ‹*era, society, morals*›

precinct /ˈpriːsɪŋkt/
A *n* **1** Brit (in town, city) 步行区; **a shopping/pedestrian ~** 购物区/步行区 **2** Amer (police district) 警区 **3** Amer (electoral district) 选区
B **precincts** *npl* **1** (surrounding area) 外围; **the airport and its ~s** 机场及其周边 **2** Brit (of cathedral) 教堂地界; (of university) 校园区域

precious /ˈpreʃəs/
A *adj* **1** (valuable) 贵重的 ‹*jewellery, vase*›; 宝贵的 ‹*time, life, resources*› **2** (beloved) 珍贵的 ‹*friendship*›; **~ memories** 宝贵的记忆 **3** colloq (expressing exasperation) 宝贝似的 ‹*stamps, car*›; **you and your ~ books!** 你和你的那些宝贝书! **4** pej (affected) 做作的 ‹*language, style, person*› **5** attrib colloq (as intensifier) [表示强调]; **there is ~ little that can be done** 几乎没什么可做的; **a ~ lot of good that did** 那可是大有帮助
B *n* 宝贝

precious metal *n* 贵重金属

preciousness /ˈpreʃəsnɪs/ *n* [u] **1** (of possessions) 贵重; (of time, friendship) 宝贵 **2** pej (affectedness) 做作

precious stone *n* 宝石

precipice /ˈpresɪpɪs/ *n* **1** (steep drop) 悬崖 **2** fig (dangerous situation) 险境

precipitate
A /prɪˈsɪpɪteɪt/ *vt* **1** (cause) «*events, miscalculation*» 引发 ‹*crisis, disaster*› **2** (hasten) «*events, miscalculation*» 加速 ‹*crisis, disaster*› **3** (hurl downwards) «*force, crash, impact*» 抛下 ‹*victim, occupant*›; (hurl forwards) «*force, crash, impact*» 抛出 ‹*victim, occupant*› **4** (send, throw) **to ~ sb./sth. into crisis/a war** 使某人/某事物突然陷入危机/战争 **5** Chem 沉淀 **6** **to be ~d as rain/snow** «*clouds, water vapour*» 凝结成雨/雪
B /prɪˈsɪpɪteɪt/ *vi* **1** Chem 沉淀 **2** «*clouds, water vapour*» 凝结降雨
C /prɪˈsɪpɪteɪt/ *n* Chem 沉淀物
D /prɪˈsɪpɪtət/ *adj* **1** (rash, hasty) 仓促的 ‹*remark, reaction, decision*› **2** (sudden) 突如其来的 ‹*flood, crash, conflict*›

precipitately /prɪˈsɪpɪtətli/ *adv* 仓促地

precipitation /prɪˌsɪpɪˈteɪʃn/ *n* [u] **1** Chem 沉淀 **2** (rain, snow) 降水

precipitous /prɪˈsɪpɪtəs/ *adj* **1** (high, steep) 陡峭的 ‹*slope, path*› **2** (hasty) 仓促的 ‹*action*›

precipitously /prɪˈsɪpɪtəsli/ *adv* **1** (steeply) 陡峭地 ‹*slope, drop, rise*›; **oil production/share prices fell ~** 石油产量/股价猛跌 **2** (hastily) 仓促地

précis /ˈpreɪsiː, Amer preɪˈsiː/
A *n* (*pl* **précis**) 梗概; **to write/produce a ~ of sth.** 写/写出某事物的摘要
B *vt* «*student*» 写出…的概要 ‹*text, lecture*›

precise /prɪˈsaɪs/ *adj* **1** (clear) 清晰的 ‹*description, images*›; 明确的 ‹*instructions*›; (accurate) 精确的 ‹*measurements, timing*›; **to be ~ ...** 确切地说… **2** (exact) 恰好的 ‹*sum, place*›; **at this ~ moment** 就在这时候 **3** (meticulous) 严谨周密的 ‹*person, mind, manner, method*›; 细微的 ‹*movement*›

precisely /prɪˈsaɪsli/ *adv* **1** (exactly) 恰好; **I saw her ~ four times** 我见过她正好 4 次; **~ because ...** 正因为…; **at ten o'clock ~** 在 10 点整 **2** (accurately) 清晰地 ‹*describe*›; 明确地 ‹*instruct, explain*›; 精确地 ‹*measure, calculate, record*› **3** (meticulously) 严谨地 ‹*write, speak*› **4** (expressing agreement) 的确如此 [用来加强同意语气]

preciseness /prɪˈsaɪsnɪs/ *n* [u] **= precision**

precision /prɪˈsɪʒn/ *n* [u] **1** (of description) 清晰; (of instructions) 明确; (of measurements) 精确; **with ~** 精确地; **~ instruments** 精密仪器 **2** (of sum) 恰好 **3** (of person, manner, method) 严谨周密; (of movement) 细微

precision: ~ bombing *n* [u] 精确轰炸; **~ engineering** *n* [u] 精密工程

preclude /prɪˈkluːd/ *vt* 杜绝 ‹*error*›; 排除 ‹*suspicion*›; 防止 ‹*identification*›; **to ~ sb./sth. from doing sth.** 阻止某人/某物做某事

precocious /prɪˈkəʊʃəs/ *adj* 早熟的 ‹*child, ability, talent*›; 过早出现的 ‹*quality*›

precociously /prɪˈkəʊʃəsli/ *adv* 早熟地

precociousness /prɪˈkəʊʃəsnɪs/, **precocity** /prɪˈkɒsəti/ *ns* [u] 早熟

precognition /ˌpriːkɒɡˈnɪʃn/ *n* [u] 预知 [尤指超感官知觉]

pre-Columbian /ˌpriːkəˈlʌmbɪən/ *adj* 哥伦布到达之前美洲的 ‹*tombs, civilization*›; **~ artefacts** 前哥伦布手工艺品

preconceived /ˌpriːkənˈsiːvd/ *adj* 预先形成的 ‹*idea, belief*›

preconception /ˌpriːkənˈsepʃn/ *n* 先入之见; **a ~ about sb./sth.** 对某人/某事物的成见

precondition /ˌpriːkənˈdɪʃn/
A *n* 先决条件; **to be a ~ of** *or* **for sth.** 是某事的前提
B *vt* «*scientist, media*» 使…预先适应 ‹*person, animal*›; **to ~ sb. to do sth.** 使某人事先有准备做某事

pre-cook /ˌpriːˈkʊk/ *vt* 预煮

precursor /ˌpriːˈkɜːsə(r)/ *n* **1** (person) 前任; (thing, event) 先驱; (sign) 前兆 **2** (earlier form) 前

P

身; a *or* the ～ of the violin/laser printer 小提琴/激光打印机的前身

precursory /ˌpriːˈkɜːsəri/ *adj* 预先的 ‹*glimpse*›; 先兆性的 ‹*activity*›; **a few ～ remarks** 几句开场白

pre-date *vt* **1** (put earlier date on) 倒填…的日期 ‹*document, cheque, letter*› **2** (exist before) 早于 ‹*event, building*›

predator /ˈpredətə(r)/ *n* **1** (animal) 捕食性动物 **2** (person) 掠夺者

predatory /ˈpredətri, Amer -tɔːri/ *adj* **1** (relating to animals) 捕食性的 ‹*insects, behaviour, instincts*› **2** (exploiting or oppressing others) 掠夺成性的 ‹*abuser, boss, criminal*›; 掠夺性的 ‹*raid, campaign*›

predatory: ～ competition *n* [u] [压低价格的] 掠夺性竞争; **～ pricing** *n* [u] 掠夺性定价

predecease /ˌpriːdɪˈsiːs/ *vt* formal 先于…去世

predecessor /ˈpriːdɪsesə(r), Amer ˈpredə-/ *n* **1** (person) 前任 **2** (thing) 被替代的事物

predestination /ˌpriːdestɪˈneɪʃn/ *n* [u] 宿命论

predestine /ˌpriːˈdestɪn/ *vt* 注定; **it is *or* has been ～d that ...** …是命中注定的

predetermine /ˌpriːdɪˈtɜːmɪn/ *vt* 预先决定

predicament /prɪˈdɪkəmənt/ *n* (awkward situation) 尴尬的处境; (difficult situation) 困境; **to help sb. out of his/her ～** 帮助某人摆脱困境

predicate

A /ˈpredɪkeɪt/ *vt* **1** (assert) 断言 ‹*property, condition*›; **to ～ that ...** 断定…; **to ～ sth. to be ...** 肯定某物是… **2** (base) 使基于 ‹*programme, belief, argument*›; **to ～ sth. on sth.** 使某事基于某事

B /ˈpredɪkət/ *n* (part of sentence) 谓语

predicative /prɪˈdɪkətɪv, Amer ˈpredɪkeɪtɪv/ *adj* 作表语的 ‹*noun, adjective*›

predicatively /prɪˈdɪkətɪvli, Amer ˈpredɪkeɪtɪvli/ *adv* 作为谓语

predict /prɪˈdɪkt/ *vt* 预言 ‹*events, actions*›; **to ～ that ...** 预言…

predictability /prɪˌdɪktəˈbɪləti/ *n* [u] **1** (ability to be predicted) 可预测性 **2** pej (tendency to act as expected) 墨守成规

predictable /prɪˈdɪktəbl/ *adj* **1** (able to be predicted) 可预报的 ‹*weather*›; 可预计的 ‹*result*›; **the outcome of the election was ～** 选举的结果可想而知 **2** pej (behaving or occurring as expected) 墨守成规的 ‹*person, behaviour*›; 意料之中的 ‹*ending*›

predictably /prɪˈdɪktəbli/ *adv* 可预料地; **～, nobody came** 不出所料，没一个人来

prediction /prɪˈdɪkʃn/ *n* **1** [c] (forecast) 预言; (sth. that has been predicted) 预言的事; **to make a ～ about sth.** 预测某事 **2** [u] (action of predicting sth.) 预测

predictive /prɪˈdɪktɪv/ *adj* 预测的 ‹*model, accuracy*›; 预言性的 ‹*sayings, writings*›

predictive text messaging *n* [u] 手机短信联想输入法

predigested /ˌpriːdaɪˈdʒestɪd/ *adj* **1** (processed) 预先消化的 **2** (made easier) 简化的

predilection /ˌpriːdɪˈlekʃn, Amer ˌpredlˈek-/ *n* 偏爱; **to have a ～ for sth.** 偏好某事物

predispose /ˌpriːdɪˈspəʊz/ *vt* 使有倾向; **to ～ sb. to sth.** 使某人有某种倾向; **to ～ sb. to do sth.** 使某人倾向于做某事; **she was ～d to like him** 她自然而然地喜欢上了他

predisposition /ˌpriːdɪspəˈzɪʃn/ *n* (to certain behaviour) 倾向; (to disease) 易受感染的体质; **his ～ towards asthma** 他易患哮喘的体质

predominance /prɪˈdɒmɪnəns/ *n* [u] **1** (in power) 主导地位; **to have ～ over sb./sth.** 支配某人/某物 **2** (in number) 优势; **there is a ～ of women on the committee** 委员会中女性占绝大多数

predominant /prɪˈdɒmɪnənt/ *adj* **1** (more powerful) 占优势的 ‹*member, party*›; 主导的 ‹*role*› **2** (more evident) 明显的 ‹*colour, mood, feature*› **3** (more numerous) 占大多数的

predominantly /prɪˈdɒmɪnəntli/ *adv* 主要地; **～ influenced by ...** 主要受…的影响的

predominate /prɪˈdɒmɪneɪt/ *vi* **1** (exert power) «*nation, wish, characteristic*» 占主导地位; **to ～ over sb./sth.** 支配某人/某物 **2** (be main element) 最显著; (be greater in number) 占大多数

pre-eminence /ˌpriːˈemɪnəns/ *n* [u] 卓越

pre-eminent /ˌpriːˈemɪnənt/ *adj* 卓越的

pre-eminently /ˌpriːˈemɪnəntli/ *adv* **1** (to a great extent) 很大程度上 **2** (above all) 主要地

pre-empt /ˌpriːˈempt/ *vt* **1** (thwart, frustrate) 预先制止 ‹*plan, decision, action, statement*› **2** (acquire) 抢先占有 ‹*land, art work, position*›

pre-emptive /ˌpriːˈemptɪv/ *adj* 先发制人的 ‹*attack, measure*›

preen /priːn/

A *vt* «*bird*» 用喙整理 ‹*feathers, tail, itself*›

B *v refl* **1** (devote time to one's appearance) **to ～ oneself** 精心打扮自己 **2** (congratulate oneself) **to ～ oneself on sth.** 为某事物得意洋洋

pre-exist /ˌpriːɪgˈzɪst/

A *vt* 先于…存在

B *vi* 在先存在; **a ～ing medical condition** 宿疾

prefab /ˈpriːfæb, Amer ˌpriːˈfæb/ *n* colloq 预制房屋

prefabricate /ˌpriːˈfæbrɪkeɪt/ *vt* 用预制构件组装; **～d components** 预制构件

prefabrication /ˌpriːfæbrɪˈkeɪʃn/ *n* [u] 预制

preface /ˈprefɪs/

A *n* **1** (to book) 序言 **2** (to speech) 开场白

B *vt* **1** (provide with a preface) 为…写序言 ‹*book, anthology*›; **to ～ sth. with sth.** 为某书写某种序言 **2** (introduce) 为…作开场白 ‹*speech, lecture*›; **to ～ sth. with *or* by sth.** 以某讲话作为某事的开场白

prefaded /ˌpriːˈfeɪdɪd/ *adj* 预褪色的 ‹*jeans*›

prefatory /ˈprefətri, Amer -tɔːri/ *adj* 序言性的 ‹*pages, essay*›; 作为开场白的 ‹*comment, joke*›; **～ note** 卷首语; **～ remarks** 开场白

prefect /ˈpriːfekt/ *n* **1** Brit Sch (senior pupil) 学长 **2** (government official) 地方行政长官

prefer /prɪˈfɜː(r)/ *vt* (*pres p etc.* **-rr-**) **1** (like better) 较喜欢; **to ～ sth. to ...** 比…更喜欢某物; **to ～ doing ...** 宁可做…; **to ～ to do ... rather than to ...** 更愿意做…而不是…; **to ～ sb. to do/not to do sth.** 更希望某人做/不做某事; **to ～ that ...** 宁愿…; **I would ～ it if you didn't smoke** 我觉得你还是不抽烟为好 **2** formal (submit) 提出 ‹*charge*›; **to ～ charges against sb.** 指控某人

preferable /ˈprefrəbl/ *adj* (to be preferred or desirable) 更可取的; (more suitable) 更合适的; **to be ～ (to sth.)** （比某事物）更好; **anything would be ～ to going to his house** 什么都比去他家好

preferably /ˈprefrəbli/ *adv* 更可取地; **keep it hidden, ～ in a locked cupboard** 把它藏起来，最好是锁进橱柜里

preference /ˈprefrəns/ *n* **1** [u] (greater liking) 偏爱; **to have a ～ for sth.** 偏爱某事物; **in ～ to sth./doing sth.** 而不是某事物/做某事; **she came with us in ～ to them** 她跟我们来了，而没有跟他们 **2** [c] (preferred thing) 偏爱的事物; (preferred person) 偏爱的人 **3** [u] (favour) 偏心; **to give ～ to sb. (over sb.)** 优先考虑某人（而不是某人）; **to show ～ to *or* towards sb.** 表现出偏爱某人

preference share Brit, **preference stock** Amer *ns* 优先股

preferential /ˌprefəˈrenʃl/ *adj* **1** (better) 优惠的 ‹*terms, tariff, trade*›; **to give sb./get ～ treatment** 给予某人优待/获得优待 **2** (in election) 选择选举制的 ‹*ballot, voting*›

preferment /prɪˈfɜːmənt/ *n* [u and c] [尤指教会中的] 提升

preferred /prɪˈfɜːd/ *adj attrib* 优先选取的 ‹*route, option, solution, bidder*›; **there is a ～ candidate** 有一位首选的候选人

preferred share Brit, **preferred stock** Amer *ns* 优先股

prefigure /ˌpriːˈfɪgə(r), Amer -gjər/ *vt* 预示

prefix /ˈpriːfɪks/

A *n* **1** (in front of word) 前缀 **2** (word, number, letter) 前置代号; (title before name) [人名前的] 称谓

B *vt* (add sth. as prefix) 加…作前缀 ‹*particle*›; 把…置于前面 ‹*title*›; (add sth. as introduction) 加…作前言 ‹*note, pages, word*›

preflight /ˈpriːflaɪt/ *adj attrib* 起飞前的 ‹*checks*›

pregnancy /ˈpregnənsi/ *n* [c and u] (condition, instance) 怀孕; (duration) 孕期

pregnancy test *n* 妊娠化验

pregnant /ˈpregnənt/ *adj* **1** (carrying young in womb) 怀孕的 ‹*woman, animal*›; **to become ～** 怀孕; **to get ～ by sb.** 怀上某人的孩子; **to get sb. ～** colloq 使某人怀孕; **to be two months ～** 怀孕两个月; **to be ～ with twins** 怀上双胞胎 **2** (suggestive) 意味深长的 ‹*remark, phrase*›; **to be ～ with sth.** 充满某含义; **a ～ pause/silence** 耐人寻味的停顿/沉默

preheat /ˌpriːˈhiːt/ *vt* 预热; **to ～ the oven to 200°** 把烤箱预热到 200 度

prehensile /ˌpriːˈhensaɪl, Amer -sl/ *adj* 能抓住东西的 ‹*foot, tail, claws*›

prehistoric /ˌpriːhɪˈstɒrɪk, Amer -ɔːrɪk/ *adj* **1** (ancient) 史前的 ‹*dwelling, art*›; **in ～ times** 在史前时代 **2** colloq (old-fashioned) 老掉牙的 ‹*idea*›; 落伍的 ‹*person*›

prehistory /ˌpriːˈhɪstri/ *n* [u] **1** Hist 史前时期 **2** (beginnings) 初期; (earliest stage) 开始阶段

prejudge /ˌpriːˈdʒʌdʒ/ *vt* 预先判断

prejudice /ˈpredʒʊdɪs/

A *n* **1** [u] (hostility) 偏见; **racial/political ～** 种族/政治偏见 **2** [c] (prior opinion) 先入之见; **a ～ against/in favour of sb./sth.** 对某人/某事物的成见/偏爱; **to overcome one's ～s** 克服成见 **3** [u] (harm) 侵害; **to the ～ of ...** 有损于…; **without ～ to ...** 无损于…

B *vt* **1** (bias) «*looks, circumstances, events*» 使…产生偏见 ‹*jury*›; **to ～ sb. against/in favour of sb./sth.** 使某人对…有偏见/偏爱… **2** (harm, jeopardize) «*person, circumstances*» 对…不利 ‹*claim, case, expectations, chances*›

prejudiced /ˈpredʒʊdɪst/ *adj* 有偏见的; **to be ～ against/in favour of ...** 对…有偏见/偏爱…

prejudicial /ˌpredʒʊˈdɪʃl/ *adj* formal 有损害的 ‹*action, effect, development*›; **to be ～ to sth.** 对某事物不利; **～ evidence** 不利证据

prelate /ˈprelət/ *n* 教长

preliminary /prɪˈlɪmɪnəri, Amer -neri/

A *adj* **1** (prior) 初步的 ‹*draft, discussion, estimate*›; **～ to ...** 先于…的; **～ remarks** 开场白 **2** (before main sports contest) 预赛的 ‹*round*›; **～ contests** 预赛

B *n* 初步活动

C **preliminaries** *npl* **1** Sport 预赛 **2** (polite talk) 客套

preliminary: ～ hearing *n* Brit 预审; **～ inquiry, ～ investigation** *ns* 初步调查

prelims /ˈpriːlɪmz/ *npl* **1** Sport 预赛 **2** (in book) 前页

prelude /ˈpreljuːd/ *n* **1** (introduction) 前奏; **to be a ～ to sth.** 是某事的前奏 **2** (introductory music in suite, opera etc.) 序曲 **3** (short piano piece) 前奏曲

premarital /ˌpriːˈmærɪtl/ *adj attrib* 婚前的; **~ relations/sex** 婚前性行为; **a ~ pregnancy** 未婚先孕

pre-match /ˈpriːmætʃ/ *adj attrib* 赛前的 ‹*build-up, interview*›

premature /ˈpremətjʊə(r), Amer ˌpriːməˈtʊər/ *adj* **1** (too early) 过早的 ‹*flowering, departure*›; (hasty) 仓促的 ‹*decision, judgement*›; **to be ~ to do sth.** 做某事是草率的; **to be ~ in doing sth.** 仓促做某事 **2** (earlier than usual) 早产的 ‹*baby*›; 早产儿的 ‹*delivery*›; 提前的 ‹*baldness*›; **to be born two weeks ~** 早产两周; **~ ejaculation** 早泄; **~ death** 早逝

prematurely /ˈpremətjʊəli, Amer ˌpriːməˈtʊərli/ *adv* 过早地; **to retire ~** 提前退休

premedication /ˌpriːmedɪˈkeɪʃn/ *n* [u] 前驱给药

premeditated /ˌpriːˈmedɪteɪtɪd/ *adj* 有预谋的 ‹*attack, act*›

premenstrual /ˌpriːˈmenstrʊəl/ *adj* 月经前的

premenstrual: ~ syndrome *n* [u] 经前综合征; **~ tension** *n* [u] 经前紧张

premier /ˈpremɪə(r), Amer ˈpriːmɪər/
A *n* (head of government) 总理; (in UK) 首相; Austral (head of state) 州总理; Can (head of province) 省总理
B *adj* 最重要的 ‹*city, producer*›; **of ~ importance** 头等重要的

première /ˈpremɪeə(r), Amer ˈpriːmɪər/
A *n* 首次公演
B *vt* 首次公演 ‹*film, play*›

premiership /ˈpremɪeəʃɪp, Amer prɪˈmɪərʃɪp/ *n* **1** (position) 总理职位; (in UK) 首相职位; Austral (of state) 州总理职位; Can (of province) 省总理职位 **2** (period of office) 总理任期; (in UK) 首相任期; Austral (of state) 州总理任期; Can (of province) 省总理任期 **3** Brit (in soccer) **the P~** 足球超级联赛

premise /ˈpremɪs/ *n* **1** (basic idea) 假定; **on the ~ that ...** 根据…的假设 **2** (proposition) 前提

premises /ˈpremɪsɪz/ *npl* 房屋建筑及附属场地; **business ~** 营业场所; **embassy/office ~** 大使馆驻地/办公区; **on the ~** 在场区内; **off the ~** 在场区外

premium /ˈpriːmɪəm/
A *n* **1** (on interest rate, for additional service) 附加费; (on wages) 津贴; **to buy/sell at a ~** 支付额外费用购买/高价出售 **2** (on share) 溢价; **to sell shares** *or* **stock at a ~** 以高于面值的价格卖股票 **3** (insurance fee) 保险费 **4** **to be at a ~** (scarce) 非常稀缺; (in demand) 十分需要; **time is at a ~** 时间很紧张; **to set** *or* **put** *or* **place a ~ on sth./sb.** 高度重视某事物/某人
B *adj* (high-priced) 优质高价的 ‹*brand, service, fuel*›; **~ vodka** 优质伏特加酒

premium: P~ Bond *n* Brit 以奖金代息储蓄债券; **~ price** *n* 溢价; **~ product** *n* 质优价高的产品; **~ rate** *n* 最高费率; **~ rent** *n* 高价租金

premonition /ˌpriːməˈnɪʃn, ˌpre-/ *n* [不祥的]预感; **to have a ~ of sth.** 预感到某事

prenatal /ˌpriːˈneɪtl/ *adj* 产前的 ‹*classes, exercises*›

prenup /ˌpriːˈnʌp/ *n* Amer colloq = **prenuptial agreement**

prenuptial /ˌpriːˈnʌpʃl/ *adj* 婚前的

prenuptial agreement *n* 婚前协议; **to sign a ~** 签婚前协议

preoccupation /ˌpriːɒkjʊˈpeɪʃn/ *n* (state) 全神贯注; (subject, problem) 长久思考的事; **to have a ~ with sth.** 专注于某事物

preoccupied /ˌpriːˈɒkjʊpaɪd/ *adj* 全神贯注的; **to be ~ with sth.** 对某事物专心致志

preoccupy /ˌpriːˈɒkjʊpaɪ/ *vt* 使全神贯注

pre-op /ˌpriːˈɒp/ colloq
A *n* 术前治疗
B *adj* 手术前的

preoperative /ˌpriːˈɒpərətɪv, Amer -reɪt-/ *adj attrib* 术前的 ‹*care, examination*›

preordain /ˌpriːɔːˈdeɪn/ *vt* «*leader, authority*» 预先决定 ‹*ceremony, event, circumstance*›; «*God, Fate*» 注定 ‹*event*›

pre-owned /ˌpriːˈəʊnd/ *adj* 二手的

prep /prep/ colloq
A *n* **1** Brit dated (homework) 家庭作业 **2** Brit (study period) 自习时间 **3** Amer (student) 预备学校的学生
B *vi* (*pres p etc.* **-pp-**) Amer colloq 准备; **to ~ for an exam** 为考试作准备
C *vt* (*pres p etc.* **-pp-**) Amer colloq 准备

pre-pack /ˌpriːˈpæk/
A *vt* 预先包装
B *n* Fin, Comm 预打包托管 [将进入破产管理的公司立即出售, 通常由原公司管理层购买, 使其在新公司名义下继续运营, 以减少破产清算给公司运营带来的影响]

pre-package /ˌpriːˈpækɪdʒ/ *vt* = **pre-pack A**

prepaid /ˌpriːˈpaɪd/ *adj* 预付的; **a ~ envelope** 邮资已付的信封

preparation /ˌprepəˈreɪʃn/ *n* **1** [u] (action) (of meal, event, report, lecture) 准备; **in ~ for ...** 在为…作准备; **to be in ~** 在准备中 **2** [c] (arrangement) 准备工作; **~(s) for sth.** 某事的准备工作; **to make ~s to do sth.** 为做某事进行准备; **~ time** 准备时间 **3** [c] (product) 配制品; **a pharmaceutical/herbal ~** 药物/草药制剂

preparatory /prɪˈpærətri, Amer -tɔːri/ *adj* 预备的; **~ to sth./doing sth.** 在某事/做某事前的

preparatory school *n* **1** Brit (for age 7-13) [进入公学前的] 预备小学 **2** Amer (before college) [上大学前的] 预备学校

prepare /prɪˈpeə(r)/
A *vt* **1** (make ready) 准备 ‹*lesson, bed, document, speech*›; 布置 ‹*room*›; **to ~ one's defence** Jur 准备辩护; **to ~ the ground** *or* **way for sth.** 为某事铺平道路 **2** (produce) «*cook*» 做 ‹*meal, dish, food*›; «*chemist*» 配制 ‹*medicine, remedy*› **3** (train) 给…进行预备训练 ‹*person, class*›; **to ~ sb. for sth.** 帮助某人准备 ‹*exam*›; 帮助某人准备面对 ‹*shock*›; **to ~ oneself for sth.** 对某事有心理准备; **to ~ sb. to do sth.** 训练某人做某事
B *vi* (make arrangements, train) 作准备; **to ~ to do sth.** 准备做某事; **to ~ for sth.** 准备某事; **to ~ for action** 准备行动

prepared /prɪˈpeəd/ *adj* **1** (ready-made) 准备好的 ‹*response, speech, lesson*›; 制作好的 ‹*soup, sauce, meal*›; **a carefully ~ reply** 精心准备的回答 **2** (with necessary resources) 有准备的; **to be ~ for sth.** 对…有所准备 ‹*disaster*›; **to be well-/ill-~** 准备得充分/不充分; **to come ~** 有备而来; **be ~!** 作好准备! ; **to be ~ for the worst** 作好最坏的打算 **3** (willing) 乐意的; **to be ~ to do sth.** 愿意做某事

preparedness /prɪˈpeərɪdnɪs/ *n* [u] formal 准备状态 [尤指为战争]; **~ for ...** 对…的准备状态; **a state of ~** 战备状态

prepay /ˌpriːˈpeɪ/
A *vt* 预先支付
B *adj attrib* 预付费的 ‹*mobile*›

prepayment /ˌpriːˈpeɪmənt/ *n* [u] 预先支付

pre-plan /ˌpriːˈplæn/ *vt* (*pres p etc.* **-nn-**) 预先计划

preponderance /prɪˈpɒndərəns/ *n* [u] 优势; **a ~ of sth.** 某方面的优势; **a ~ of sth. over sth.** 某事物对某事物的优势

preponderant /prɪˈpɒndərənt/ *adj* (predominant) 主要的 ‹*role, power*›; (greater) 占多数的 ‹*race, class*›

preponderantly /prɪˈpɒndərəntli/ *adv* (in the majority) 占大多数; (mainly) 主要地; (on the whole) 大体上

preposition /ˌprepəˈzɪʃn/ *n* 介词

prepositional /ˌprepəˈzɪʃənəl/ *adj* 介词的

prepossessing /ˌpriːpəˈzesɪŋ/ *adj* 动人的 ‹*smile, manner, appearance*›

preposterous /prɪˈpɒstərəs/ *adj* 荒谬的; **to be ~ to do sth.** 做某事是荒唐的

preposterously /prɪˈpɒstərəsli/ *adv* 荒唐地

preposterousness /prɪˈpɒstərəsnɪs/ *n* [u] 荒唐

preppy, preppie /ˈprepi/ Amer colloq
A *adj* 衣着笔挺的
B *n* 私立预备学校学生

> **preppy**
>
> 亦作 preppie。美国俚语。指美国私立预备学校 (preparatory school 或 prep school) 的学生。他们家境富裕、衣着光鲜。现也指举止或衣着像私立预备学校学生那样的人。preparatory school 在英国指为进入公学 (▸**public school**) 作准备的私立小学。

preprogrammed /ˌpriːˈprəʊɡræmd, Amer -ɡrəmd/ *adj* 预编程序的; **to be ~ to do sth.** 按预定程序做某事

prep school *n* = **preparatory school**

prepster /ˈprepstə(r)/ *n* Amer colloq 私立预备学校学生

prepubescent /ˌpriːpjuːˈbesnt/
A *adj* 青春期前的 ‹*girl, boy, body*›
B *n* 青春期前的少年

prequel /ˈpriːkwəl/ *n* 前篇

pre-record /ˌpriːrɪˈkɔːd/ *vt* 预先录制

preregister /ˌpriːˈredʒɪstə(r)/ *vi* Amer 预先登记

preregistration /ˌpriːredʒɪˈstreɪʃn/
A *n* [u] Amer 预先登记
B *adj* 预注册期的 [指医生在获得注册前的训练阶段]

prerelease /ˌpriːrɪˈliːs/ *adj* 预映的

prerequisite /ˌpriːˈrekwɪzɪt/
A *n* 先决条件; **to be a ~ for sth.** 是某事的前提
B *adj* 必备的

prerogative /prɪˈrɒɡətɪv/ *n* **1** (right) 特权; **to use** *or* **exercise one's ~** 行使特权; **to be sb.'s ~ to do sth.** 做某事是某人的特权; **the ~ of doing sth.** 做某事的特权 **2** (power of sovereign) 君权; **to exercise the Royal ~** Brit 行使君权

presage liter /ˈpresɪdʒ, prɪˈseɪdʒ/ *vt, n* 预示

Presbyterian /ˌprezbɪˈtɪərɪən/
A *n* [尤指苏格兰国教的] 长老会教友
B *adj* 长老会的; **a ~ church/school** 长老会教会/学校

Presbyterianism /ˌprezbɪˈtɪərɪənɪzəm/ *n* [u] 长老制

preschool /ˈpriːskuːl/
A *n* 幼儿园
B *adj* 学龄前的; **~ children, children of ~ age** 学龄前儿童; **~ education** 学前教育

preschooler /ˌpriːˈskuːlə(r)/ *n* Amer 学龄前儿童

preschool playgroup *n* Brit = **playgroup**

prescience /ˈpresɪəns/ *n* [u] (foreknowledge) 预知; (ability to predict) 预知能力

prescient /ˈpresɪənt/ *adj* 有预知能力的 ‹*person*›; 有先见之明的 ‹*remark, article*›

prescribe /prɪˈskraɪb/ *vt* **1** (authorize or recommend) 嘱咐 ‹*treatment, course of action*›; 开 ‹*medicine, pills*›; **to ~ sth. (for sb.)** (为治疗某疾病) (为某人) 开某药品; **he was ~d aspirin** 给他开了阿司匹林; **what do you ~?** hum 你有什么嘱咐? **2** (ordain)

P

«*authoritative body, regulations*» 规定 〈*duties, rights, punishment*〉; **to ~ sth. for sth.** 为某物规定某物; **heavy penalties are ~d by the authorities for this offence** 当局对这种违法行为规定了严厉的处罚措施

prescription /prɪˈskrɪpʃn/ *n* 1 [u] (prescribing) 开处方; **on ~** 凭处方 2 [c] (written instruction) 处方; **a ~ for sth.** 某药品的处方 3 [c] (medicine) 处方上开的药 4 [u and c] (ordaining) 规定; **the ~ of sth.** 某事的规定

prescription charge *n* Brit 处方药费

prescriptive /prɪˈskrɪptɪv/ *adj* 1 (rigid) 规定的 〈*method, attitude*〉 2 (imposing rules) 规范的; **~ grammar** 规定语法; **a ~ dictionary** 规范词典

prescriptivism /prɪˈskrɪptɪvɪzəm/ *n* [u] 规定主义

presence /ˈprezns/ *n* 1 [u] (at a place) 在场; **in the ~ of sb., in sb.'s ~** 当着某人的面; **to be admitted to sb.'s ~** 被允许来到某人面前; **signed in the ~ of ...** Jur 有…见证签署的; **your ~ is requested at ...** 敬请光临…; **to make one's ~ felt** 突显自己 2 [u] (personal quality) 风度; (appearance) 仪态; **stage ~** 台风; **a man/woman of tremendous ~** 仪表堂堂的男子/仪态不凡的女子 3 [c] (human or ghostly) 感觉中的存在物; **to sense a ~** 感觉到有东西在; **a ghostly ~** 鬼魂 4 [u] (of troops, representatives) 势力; **a military ~** 驻军; **a heavy police ~** 大批警察

presence of mind *n* [u] 沉着冷静; **to show** *or* **display great ~ (by doing sth.)** (通过做某事) 表现出镇定自若

present[1] /ˈpreznt/

A *adj* 1 *pred* (in attendance) 在场的; **to be ~ at sth.** 出席 〈*meeting, ceremony*〉; **all those** *or* **everybody ~** 在场的所有人; **you are ever ~ in my thoughts** 我总是想到你; **~ company excepted** 在座诸位除外; **all ~ and correct** Brit *or* **accounted for** Amer 全体到齐 2 *pred* (found, existing) 存在的; **to be ~ in sth.** 存在于某物中; **oxygen ~ in the atmosphere** 大气中的氧气 3 *attrib* (current) 当前的 〈*situation, problem*〉; 现在的 〈*address, price, owner*〉; 现行的 〈*system*〉; 现任的 〈*president*〉; **in the ~ climate** fig 在目前的情况下; **the ~ government** 现政府; **sb.'s ~ wife** 某人现在的妻子; **on ~ form** Sport 根据目前的表现; **the ~ day** (nowadays) 如今; (modern times) 现代; **up to the ~ day** 迄今; **at the ~ time** *or* **moment** 目前; **(in) the ~ month** (在) 本月 4 *attrib* (under consideration) [表示当下涉及的]; **the ~ case/article/plan** 本案/本文/本计划 5 *attrib* Ling 现在的; **the ~ tense** 现在时

B *n* [u] 1 (now) **the ~** 现在; **at ~** (at this moment) 此刻; (currently) 目前; **for the ~** 暂时; **to live in the ~** (enjoy) 享受眼前的一切; (be free from worry) 只顾今朝; **there is no time like the ~** Prov 机不可失，时不再来 2 Ling **the ~** 现在时; **the verb is in the ~** 这个动词用的是现在式

present[2]

A /ˈpreznt/ *n* 礼物; **a wedding ~** 婚庆贺礼; **to give sb. sth.** *or* **give sth. to sb. as a ~** 把某物作为礼物送给某人; **to make sb. a ~ of sth.** fig 把某物赠送给某人; **don't make them a ~ of the match!** 别把比赛拱手相让!

B /prɪˈzent/ *vt* 1 (formally give) 颁发 〈*prize, medal, degree*〉; **to ~ sth. to sb., to ~ sb. with sth.** 把某物颁发给某人; **we were ~ed with our certificates** 我们领到了证书; **she ~ed her husband with twins** fig 她为丈夫生了双胞胎 2 (show) 出示 〈*passport, ticket*〉 3 (proffer for payment) 支付 〈*cheque, bill*〉; **to ~ sth. for payment** 提交某物兑现 4 formal (express) 表示 〈*respects*〉; **to ~ one's apologies/greetings (to sb.)** (向某人) 致歉/致以问候 5 Mil 持…敬礼 〈*rifle*〉; **~ arms!** 行持枪礼! 6 (submit for consideration) 提交 〈*proposal, report, petition, witness, evidence*〉; 提出 〈*opinion, proof*〉; Pol 递交 〈*bill*〉; **the defence will ~ its case tomorrow** 辩方将在明天提交证据; **to ~ sth. to sb., to ~ sb. with sth.** 向某人提交某物 7 (portray) 描述; **to ~ sb./sth. as sth.** 把某人/某事物描述成某事物; **to ~ sb./sth. in a good/different light** 从好的/不同的角度描述某人/某事物 8 (be cause of, occasion for) 带来 〈*problem, danger, opportunity*〉; 为…带来 〈*person*〉; **to ~ sth. to sb., to ~ sb. with sth.** 给某人带来某物; **chemicals may ~ a fire risk** 化学品可能引起火险 9 (exhibit) 呈现 〈*sight, appearance, image*〉; 表现出 〈*aspect*〉; **to ~ sth. to sb., to ~ sb. with sth.** 向某人展现某物; **the article ~ed these proposals as misguided** 文章称这些提议受了误导; **he always ~s a smiling face to the world** 他总是对所有人都面带微笑; **we were ~ed with a splendid panorama** 壮丽的景色展现在我们眼前; **to be ~ed with a choice/dilemma** 面临选择/两难处境; **he ~ed an easy target** 他很容易受人攻击 10 (put on) 上演 〈*play, film*〉; 展出 〈*exhibition*〉 11 (in production) 让…出演角色; **to have the pleasure of ~ing sb. as ...** 有幸邀请某人出演… 12 TV, Radio 主持 〈*programme*〉 13 (introduce) 介绍 〈*person*〉; **to ~ sb. to sb.** 把某人介绍给某人; **may I ~ Mr X?** 请允许我介绍X先生; **to be ~ed (at court)** Brit Hist 进宫谒见

C *v refl* 1 (appear formally) **to ~ oneself** 到来; **to ~ oneself for interview/at the office** 到场面试/出现在办公室 2 (occur, arise) **to ~ itself** «*thought*» 产生; «*opportunity*» 出现; **if the chance ever ~s itself, ...** 一有机会，… 3 (portray) **to ~ oneself** 展示; **he ~s himself as a radical figure** 他表现出一副激进派人物的样子 4 Med **to ~ itself** «*disease*» 显现; «*symptom*» 出现症状

D *vi* Med 1 **to ~ with a symptom/disease** «*patient*» 出现症状/出现某种疾病的症状 2 (during birth) «*part of body*» 先露

presentable /prɪˈzentəbl/ *adj* 像样的; **I must go and make myself ~** 我得去打扮一下好见人

presentation /ˌprezənˈteɪʃn/ *n* 1 [u] (of gift, cheque) 赠送; (of award) 授予; **to make (sb.) a ~ (of sth.)** 赠送 (某人) (某物); **on ~ of your passport/this voucher** 经出示护照/代币券 2 [c] (speech) 陈述; **to do** *or* **give** *or* **make a ~ on sth.** 作关于…的陈述 3 [u] (appearance) 外观 4 [u] (portrayal) 表演 5 [u] formal (introduction) 引见

presentational skills *npl* = **presentation skills**

presentation: ~ box, ~ case *ns* 礼品盒; **~ copy** *n* 赠阅本; **~ pack** *n* (of promotional items) 礼品包; (stamps) 邮票套册; **~ skills** *npl* 陈述技巧

present-day *adj* 当今的

presenteeism /ˌprezənˈtiːɪzəm/ *n* [u] 超时工作

presenter /prɪˈzentə(r)/ ▸**p. 409** *n* 节目主持人; **television/radio ~** 电视/广播节目主持人

presentiment /prɪˈzentɪmənt/ *n* formal [尤指不祥的] 预感; **to have a ~ that ...** 隐约预感到…

presently /ˈprezəntli/ *adv* 1 (currently) 现在 〈*work, consider*〉 2 (soon) 不久 〈*arrive*〉; **he will be here ~** 他一会儿就到

present perfect *n* 现在完成时

preservation /ˌprezəˈveɪʃn/ *n* [u] 1 (of wildlife, buildings) 保护 2 (of peace, standards, self-respect) 保持 3 (condition) 保存状况; **in a good state of ~, in good ~** 保存完好的 4 (of food) 保藏

preservationist /ˌprezərˈveɪʃənɪst/ *n* [尤指历史建筑的] 保护者

preservation: ~ order *n* 文物及环境保护令; **to put a ~ order on sth.** 明令保护某物; **~ society** *n* 保护组织; **a wildlife/railway ~ society** 野生动物/铁路保护组织

preservative /prɪˈzɜːvətɪv/ *n* 防腐剂

preserve /prɪˈzɜːv/

A *vt* 1 (save) 保护 〈*buildings, manuscripts, traditions, environment*〉; **to ~ sth. for sth.** 为某目的保护某物 2 (maintain, keep) 保养 〈*old furniture, leather*〉; 保持 〈*standards, peace, dignity*〉; 维护 〈*rights, reputation*〉 3 (save life of) 拯救 〈*life, passengers*〉; **God ~ us!** dated 我的天啊!; **heaven** *or* **the saints ~ us from that!** dated 老天保佑我们! 4 Culin 保藏 〈*vegetables, fruit, meat*〉

B *n* 1 [c and u] (fruit) 水果蜜饯; (vegetable) 腌菜; (chutney) 酸辣酱 2 [c and u] (jam) 果酱 3 [c] (for wildlife conservation) 野生动植物保护区; (for private use) 私人渔猎场; **a fishing/hunting ~** 禁渔/禁猎地 4 [c] (sphere of activity) 专门领域; **to be a male ~** 为男性专有

preset /ˌpriːˈset/ *vt* (*pres p* **-tt-**; *pt, pp* **preset**) 预先设置; **to ~ sth. to do sth.** 预先设定某物做某事

preshrunk /ˌpriːˈʃrʌŋk/ *adj* 防缩的 〈*cloth, jeans*〉

preside /prɪˈzaɪd/ *vi* 1 (at meeting) 担任主席; **to ~ at a meeting** 主持会议 2 (over trial, ceremony) 主持; **he ~d over the collapse of the firm** fig 在他的领导下，公司破产倒闭

presidency /ˈprezɪdənsi/ *n* 1 (office) 总统的职位 2 (period) 总统的任期

president /ˈprezɪdənt/ *n* 1 (head of state) 总统; **to run for ~** 竞选总统 2 (of society, organization) 会长 3 Amer (of company) 总裁

> **president**
>
> 总统。美国总统既是国家元首 (head of state)，也是政府首脑 (head of government)，同时还是武装部队总司令 (commander-in-chief)。总统任命政府各部门负责人和联邦法院法官。国会通过的法案通常须经总统批准后才成为正式法律。总统选举先由政党推选出各自的候选人，再参加全国的选举，候选人中也有不属于任何政党的独立候选人 (independent candidate)。美国总统并非由选民直接选出，而是由各州按人口比例委任选举团 (electoral college) 代表选出。任期四年，可连任一次。办公地点为白宫 (▸**the White House**) 内的椭圆形办公室 (Oval Office)。总统的家庭称为第一家庭 (First Family)，夫人称第一夫人 (First Lady)。乘坐的专机通常称为空军一号 (Air Force One)。休假处为戴维营 (Camp David)，位于马里兰州，总统常在此接见外国领导人。

president-elect *n* (*pl* **presidents-elect**) 候任总统

presidential /ˌprezɪˈdenʃl/ *adj* 总统的

presidentially /ˌprezɪˈdenʃəli/ *adv* 作为总统

President's Day *n* Amer 总统日 [每年2月的第3个星期一]

> **President's Day**
>
> 总统日，亦称 Presidents' Day。在每年2月的第3个星期一，是美国多数州的法定假日。为纪念乔治•华盛顿 (George Washington，2月22日) 和亚伯拉罕•林肯 (Abraham Lincoln，2月12日) 的生日而设立。但也有些州将二者分开纪念。

presidium /prɪˈsɪdɪəm/ *n* [尤指共产党执政国家的] 常务委员会

presoak /ˌpriːˈsəʊk/ *vt* 预浸

presort /ˌpriːˈsɔːt/

A *vt* 1 Amer 按邮政编码预先分拣 〈*mail*〉 2 (before washing, processing) 预先对…分类 〈*clothes, documents, rubbish*〉

B *n* 1 Amer (of mail) 按邮政编码预先分拣邮件 2 (of clothes, rubbish) 预先分类

press /pres/

A *vt* **1** (push) 按 ‹*button, switch*›; 扣动 ‹*trigger*›; 踩 ‹*pedal*›; **to ~ sth. in/down/up** 把某物按进/按下/按起来 **2** (apply) 使…贴紧 ‹*hand, arm*›; 用…压紧 ‹*bandage, handkerchief*›; **he ~ed his fingers/knees/lips together** 他捏紧手指/并拢膝盖/抿紧嘴唇; **to ~ sb./sth. against** *or* **on (to) sth.** 使某人/某物紧贴某物; **to ~ sth. to sth.** 使某物紧贴某物; **she ~ed her face to his** 她把脸紧贴着他的脸; **to be ~ed for sth.** 急需某物; **to be (hard) ~ed to do sth.** 急于做某事 **3** (push into place) 塞进 ‹*coin*›; 扣上 ‹*cap, lid*›; 铺平 ‹*cloth*›; **to ~ sth. into/on to** *or* **over sth.** 把某物塞进某物/压到某物上; **to ~ a stamp/label on to sth.** 把邮票/标签贴到某物上; **to ~ sth. home** *or* **into place** *or* **position** 把某物推到位; **he ~ed the bolts home** 他把插销插好; **he ~ed his advantage home** 他充分利用了自己的优势 **4** (squeeze to remove liquid) 榨…的汁 ‹*fruit, vegetables*›; (squeeze out) 榨取 ‹*juice, oil*›; **to ~ the grapes and collect the juice** 榨取葡萄汁; **to ~ sth. dry** 榨干某物 **5** (alter shape of) 把…压平 ‹*soil, clay*›; **to ~ sth. flat/into shape** 把某物压平/压成型; **~ed flowers** 压花 **6** (iron) 熨平 ‹*clothes, fabric*›; **to ~ sth. flat** *or* **down** 把某物熨平 **7** (hold close) 抱紧 ‹*person, animal*›; **to ~ sb./sth. to one** 紧抱某人/某物; **to ~ sb. to one's chest** *or* **bosom** 把某人搂在怀里 **8** (squeeze in affection) 紧握 ‹*hand, arm*›; **to ~ the flesh** colloq 和群众握手致意 **9** (pressurize) 催促; **to ~ sb. to do sth.** 催促某人做某事; **to ~ sb. into doing sth.** 迫使某人做某事; **on being ~ed ...** 被逼问时…; **if ~ed, ...** 如被逼迫, …; **to ~ sb. for sth.** 因某事物催促某人; **to ~ sb. for action** 催促某人行动; **to ~ sb. into a role** 逼迫某人出演某角色; **to ~ sth. on** *or* **upon sb.** 强迫某人接受 ‹*gift, invitation*› **10** (emphasize) 反复强调 ‹*point*›; **to ~ one's case** 抓住事情不放; **to ~ a** *or* **one's claim** 坚持索赔; **to ~ one's suit** dated 坚持起诉 **11** Tech (press from mould) 压制 ‹*disc, car body*›; **~ed metal/steel** 压制金属/钢材 **12** (in weightlifting) 推举; **he ~ed 200 kg** 他推举起了 200 公斤 **13** Mil, Hist 强征…入伍 ‹*man, recruit*›; **to ~ sth. into service** fig 临时征用某物

B *vi* **1** (push) «*hand*» 按; «*foot*» 踩; «*burden, weight*» 压; **~ (here) to open** (在此处) 按下打开; **to ~ against** *or* **on sth.** 压在某物上; **to ~ on the accelerator** 踩油门; **to ~ down on sb./sth.** 重压某人/某物; **her guilt ~ed down on her** fig 她深感内疚; **to ~ (down) hard** 用力 (向下) 压; **to ~ heavily on sb.** fig 使某人感到负担沉重 **2** (in crowd, battle) «*crowd*» 拥挤; **to ~ through/in** *or* **into/out of/around sth.** 挤过/挤入/挤出/围住某物; **their enemies ~ed in on all sides** 敌人从四面八方压来; **a host of unwelcome thoughts were ~ing in on him** 一大堆苦恼的思绪涌上他心头 **3** (agitate) **to ~ for sth.** 不断要求 ‹*action, information, support*›; **local people are ~ing for greater autonomy** 当地的人们强烈要求更大的自治权 **4** (be urgent) «*time, matter*» 紧迫

C *v refl* **to ~ oneself against** *or* **to sth./sb.** 紧贴某物/某人

D *n* **1** [c] (push) 推; **a steady ~** 持续的推压; **with a ~ of sth.** 通过按压某物; **the windows open at the ~ of a button** 那些窗户一摁按钮就开 **2** [c] (for grapes, olives) 榨汁机; (for gluing) 胶合机; (for moulding) 压床; (for racket) 球拍夹; (for clothes) 熨斗; **a hydraulic ~** 水压机; **a power(-assisted)/manual ~** 机动/手动榨汁机; **to put/keep sth. in a ~** 把某物放在/保存在夹具中 **3** [c] (with iron) 熨; **to give the trousers a ~ (with the iron)** (用熨斗) 熨裤子 **4** [c] Print (machine) 印刷机; **to come off the ~** «*book*» 出版; **a story that is hot off the ~** fig 刚见报的新闻报道 **5** [u] (printing) 印刷; **to pass sth. for ~** 准予某物付印; **to go to ~** «*book*» 付印; **to be at** *or* **in (the) ~** «*book*» 在印刷中 **6** + *v sing or pl* (journalists and broadcasters) 新闻工作者; (print media) 印刷媒体; (radio, TV) 广电界; **the ~** 新闻界; **the freedom of the ~** 新闻自由; **to be in the ~** «*story, person*» 见报; **the provincial/sporting ~** 省级/体育报刊; **to censor** *or* **muzzle the ~** 压制新闻自由; **~ coverage of sth.** 对某事的报道; **~ advertising** 报刊广告 **7** [u and c] Journ (coverage) 报道; **(to get** *or* **have) a good/bad ~** (获得) 新闻界的好评/责难 **8** [c] (publishing house) 出版社; **Oxford University P~** 牛津大学出版社 **9** [c] (crowd) 大批 [指人或车辆]; **a ~ of people/cars** 人群/车流 **10** [c] esp Scot, Ir (cupboard) 橱柜 **11** [c] Sport (in weightlifting) 推举; **to do a ~** 推举 **12** [c] Mil, Hist 抓壮丁

Phrasal verbs

- **press ahead** *vi* **to ~ ahead with sth.** 推动 ‹*project, reform, negotiation*›
- **press on** *vi* (continue) 加紧继续进行; (hurry forward) 匆忙前进; **to ~ on regardless** (continue) 不顾一切地加紧进行; (hurry) 不顾一切地前进; **to ~ on through the rain** 冒雨赶路; **to ~ on with sth.** 加紧进行 ‹*project, reform, negotiation*›; **let's ~ on to the next item** 我们抓紧来看下一项
- **press out** *vt* [~ **sth. out,** ~ **out sth.**] 熨平 ‹*crease*›; 榨出 ‹*juice, oil*›; **to ~ the cherry stones out** 挤出樱桃核

press: ~ agency *n* 通讯社; **~ agent** ▸p. 409 *n* [剧院或名人等雇用的] 广告宣传员; **P~ Association** *n* Brit **the P~ Association** 报业协会; **~ attaché** *n* 大使馆官员; **~ baron** *n* colloq 报业巨头; **~ box** *n* 记者席; **~ card** *n* 记者证; **~ clipping** *n* 剪报; **~ conference** *n* 记者招待会; **~ corps** *n* 记者团; **~ cutting** *n* Brit 剪报; **~ gallery** *n* [尤指议会和法庭的] 记者席

press-gang

A *n* + *v sing or pl* 抓丁队

B *vt* **1** Mil, Hist 强征…入伍; **to ~ sb. into the navy** 强征某人加入海军 **2** colloq (compel) 强迫; **to ~ sb. into doing sth.** 强迫某人做某事

pressing /'presɪŋ/

A *n* [c and u] **1** (of olives) (process) 压榨; (oil) 压榨的橄榄油 **2** (of records) (process) 压制唱片; (product) 同一批压制的唱片

B *adj* **1** (urgent) 迫切的 ‹*need*›; 紧迫的 ‹*issue, task, concern*› **2** (insistent) 恳切的 ‹*invitation*›; 急切的 ‹*anxiety, emotion*›

pressman /'presmən/ ▸p. 409 *n* (*pl* **pressmen**) 记者

press: ~ officer ▸p. 409 *n* 新闻发言人; **~-on** *adj* 按压上的 ‹*lettering, label*›; **~ pack** *n* **1** (information) [公司等为记者准备的] 一揽子新闻; **2** colloq (journalists) 记者群 [尤指小报记者]; **~ pass** *n* 采访证; **~ photographer** ▸p. 409 *n* 摄影记者; **~ release** *n* 新闻稿; **~room** *n* 记者室; **~ secretary** ▸p. 409 *n* 新闻秘书; **~ stud** *n* Brit 摁扣; **~-up** *n* Brit 俯卧撑

pressure /'preʃə(r)/

A *n* **1** [u and c] Phys (force, weight) 压力; **to apply ~ to sth., to exert** *or* **put ~ on sth.** 给某物施加压力; **the machine is running at full ~** 这台机器在全速运转; **to be under ~** Tech 在受压状态下; **water/air ~** 水压/气压; **to ease** *or* **relieve/increase the ~** 减压/增压 **2** [u] Meteorol 气压; **a band of low ~** 低压带; **atmospheric ~** 大气压 **3** [u and c] fig (persuasive force) 催促; **~ on/from sb.** 施加给/来自某人的压力; **the ~s of sth./doing sth.** 某事/做某事的压力; **parental/public ~** 父母/公众的压力; **the ~ of public opinion** 舆论的压力; **to put** *or* **place** *or* **exert ~ on sb. (to do sth.)** 强迫某人 (做某事); **to bring ~ to bear (on sb.) (to do sth.)** (对某人) 施加压力 (做某事); **to do sth. under ~** 被迫做某事; **she was kept at her desk by ~ of work** 她忙得无法离开办公桌; **to be under a lot of ~** 承受很大压力 **4** [u] (volume) (of traffic) 堵塞; (of tourists) 拥挤

B *vt* 强迫; **to ~ sb. to do sth.** *or* **into doing sth.** 强迫某人做某事; **stop trying to ~ me!** 别勉强我!

pressure: ~ cabin *n* 增压舱; **~-cook** *vt* 用压力锅煮; **~ cooker** *n* 压力锅; **~ gauge** *n* 压力计; **~ group** *n* + *v sing or pl* 压力集团; **~ point** *n* (on artery) 加压止血点; (on body) 压觉点; **~ sore** *n* 褥疮; **~ suit** *n* 增压服; **~ vessel** *n* 压力容器

> **pressure group**
>
> 压力集团。大体可分为两类，一类代表某个社会群体的利益，称利益集团（interest group），如工会（trade union）。一类就某个特定领域的问题进行游说，称倡导集团（promotional group），如环境保护组织"地球之友"（Friends of the Earth）。压力集团通过多种手段，如请愿、示威、媒体的呼吁等引起人们的关注，从而影响政府决策。有时压力集团会直接游说国会或议会议员，称作院外游说（lobbying）。政府修订法律时也会征求影响较大的游说集团的意见，有时还邀请其加入修订工作小组。

pressurization /,preʃəraɪ'zeɪʃn, Amer -rɪ'z-/ *n* [u] 增压

pressurize /'preʃəraɪz/ *vt* **1** (put pressure into) 使…保持正常气压 ‹*cabin, spacesuit*› **2** (put under pressure) 给…加压 ‹*water, container*›; **~d gas** 压缩气体 **3** (force) 逼迫; **to ~ sb. into doing sth.** 强迫某人做某事

pressurized: ~ cabin *n* 增压舱; **~ water reactor** *n* 压水反应堆

prestige /pre'sti:ʒ/

A *n* [u] 威望

B *adj attrib* 有声望的

prestigious /pre'stɪdʒəs/ *adj* 有声望的

presto /'prestəʊ/

A *adv* Mus 急板地

B *excl* = **hey presto**

prestressed /,pri:'strest/ *adj* 预应力的; **~ concrete** 预应力混凝土

presumably /prɪ'zju:məbli, Amer -'zu:m-/ *adv* 大概; **~ they'll arrive tomorrow** 他们大概明天到达

presume /prɪ'zju:m, Amer -'zu:m/

A *vt* **1** (suppose) 推测; **I ~ he's honest** 我想他是诚实的; **to ~ sb./sth. to be sth.** 推测某人/某物为某物 **2** (in court) «*person, law, court*» 认定 ‹*defendant, accused*›; **he was ~d dead/innocent/guilty** 他被认定死亡/无罪/有罪 **3** (presuppose) 假定 ‹*existence, theory*›; **to ~ that ...** 假定…

B *vi* **1** (dare) 擅自行事; **to ~ to do sth.** 擅自做某事; **I hope I'm not presuming** 我希望我没有擅作主张; **you ~ too much!** 你太放肆了! **2** (take advantage) 利用; **to ~ on** *or* **upon sth./sb.** (take advantage) 利用某事物/某人; (rely) 指望某事物/某人

presumption /prɪ'zʌmpʃn/ *n* **1** [u and c] (supposition) 假定; (in court) 推定; **on the ~ that ...** 根据…的假定; **to make a ~** 作推定; **the ~ of innocence** 无罪推定 **2** (impudence) 冒昧

presumptive /prɪ'zʌmptɪv/ *adj* 推断的; **the heir ~** 假定继承人

presumptuous /prɪ'zʌmptʃʊəs/ *adj* 放肆的; **to be ~ of sb. (to do sth.)** 某人 (做某事) 很放肆

presumptuously /prɪ'zʌmptʃʊəsli/ *adv* 放肆地

presumptuousness /prɪ'zʌmptʃʊəsnɪs/ *n* [u] 放肆

presuppose /,pri:sə'pəʊz/ *vt* 以…为前提 ‹*existence, knowledge*›

presupposition /,pri:sʌpə'zɪʃn/ *n* [c and u] 预设

pre-tax *adj* 税前的 ‹*profit, figure*›

P

pre-teen /ˌpriːˈtiːn/
A *adj* 即将迈入青春期的
B *n* [约10到12岁的] 小少年

pretence /prɪˈtens/ *n* Brit **1** (false show) 假装; **to make a ~ of sth.** 装出某种样子; **to make a ~ of doing sth.** 假装做某事; **to make no ~ of** *or* **at sth.** 真情作某种表露 **2** (false claim) 妄称; **under** *or* **on the ~ that** *or* **of ...** 以…为借口

pretend /prɪˈtend/
A *vt* **1** (feign) 假装 ‹*ignorance, illness, indifference*›; **to ~ that ...** 假装…; **to ~ to do sth.** 假装做某事; **don't ~ to be asleep!** 别装睡了! **2** (claim) 自称; **to ~ to do sth.** 宣称做某事; **I don't ~ to know the answer** 我不会自称知道答案
B *vi* **1** (feign) 假装; **I was only ~ing** 我只是在作戏 **2** (claim) 自称
C *adj* colloq (make-believe) 假想的 ‹*fight, gun, money*›; **it's only ~!** 这只是假想的!

pretended /prɪˈtendɪd/ *adj* 假装的

pretender /prɪˈtendə(r)/ *n* [王位或头衔的] 觊觎者

pretense *n* Amer = **pretence**

pretension /prɪˈtenʃn/ *n* **1** [c and u] (claim) 自命; **to have ~s to sth.** 自诩为某物; **to have ~s to doing ...** 标榜做了… **2** [u] (affectation) 做作

pretentious /prɪˈtenʃəs/ *adj* 做作的 ‹*play, person*›; 自命不凡的 ‹*remark*›; 炫耀的 ‹*style, design*›; 矫饰的 ‹*building*›

pretentiously /prɪˈtenʃəsli/ *adv* 做作地 ‹*behave*›; 自命不凡地 ‹*remark*›; 虚夸地 ‹*designed*›

pretentiousness /prɪˈtenʃəsnɪs/ *n* [u] 做作

preterite /ˈpretərət/ *n* 过去时

preternatural /ˌpriːtəˈnætʃərəl/ *adj* 超自然的 ‹*being*›; 异乎寻常的 ‹*ability, beauty*›

pretext /ˈpriːtekst/ *n* 借口; **under** *or* **on the ~ of sth./of doing sth.** 以某事/做某事为借口

Pretoria /prɪˈtɔːrɪə/ *pr n* 比勒陀利亚

pretrial /ˌpriːˈtraɪl/
A *n* Amer 预审
B *adj* 审判前的 ‹*hearing, deposition*›

prettify /ˈprɪtɪfaɪ/ *vt* 装点

prettily /ˈprɪtɪli/ *adv* **1** (attractively) 漂亮地 ‹*dress, decorate*›; 妩媚地 ‹*smile, blush*› **2** (charmingly) 迷人地 ‹*play, dance, sing*›

pretty /ˈprɪti/
A *adj* (attractive) 漂亮的 ‹*face, woman, garden, colour, view*›; 悦耳的 ‹*tune*›; **not a ~ sight** 有碍观瞻; **as ~ as a picture** 美丽如画; **not just a ~ face** 不只脸蛋漂亮; **this/that is a ~ state of affairs** iron 这/那糟透了; **things have come to a ~ pass** 事情变得很糟; **to cost (sb.) a ~ penny** colloq 花费(某人)一大笔钱
B *adv* colloq (very) 非常; (fairly) 相当; **~ good/bad** 非常好/糟; **~ nearly** *or* **well** *or* **much finished** 几乎完成的; **to be sitting ~** 处境有利

Phrasal verb

• **pretty up** *vt* [**~ sth. up, ~ up sth.**] colloq 装饰 ‹*house*›; 打扮 ‹*child, oneself*›

pretty-pretty *adj* pej 装饰得过分的

pretzel /ˈpretsl/ *n* 椒盐卷饼

prevail /prɪˈveɪl/ *vi* **1** (be current) «*custom, idea, fashion*» 流行 **2** (win) «*virtue, common sense, argument, person*» 占优势; **to ~ over** *or* **against sth.** 胜过某事物

Phrasal verb

• **prevail upon** *vt* [**~ upon sb.**] 劝说; **to ~ upon sb. to do sth.** 说服某人做某事

prevailing /prɪˈveɪlɪŋ/ *adj* 流行的 ‹*style, culture*›; 普遍的 ‹*conditions, view*›; 通行的 ‹*policies*›

prevailing wind *n* 盛行风

prevalence /ˈprevələns/ *n* [u] (widespread nature) 流行; (extent) 流行程度

prevalent /ˈprevələnt/ *adj* 流行的 ‹*fashion, customs, disease*›; 普遍的 ‹*attitude, behaviour, conditions*›

prevaricate /prɪˈværɪkeɪt/ *vi* formal 搪塞

prevarication /prɪˌværɪˈkeɪʃn/ *n* [u and c] formal 搪塞

prevent /prɪˈvent/ *vt* 阻止 ‹*disaster, war, accident*›; **to ~ sb./sth. from doing sth.** 阻止某人/某物做某事; **to ~ the fire from spreading** 阻止火势蔓延

preventable /prɪˈventəbl/ *adj* 可防止的 ‹*accident, death*›; 可预防的 ‹*disease, infection*›

preventative /prɪˈventətɪv/ *adj* = **preventive**

prevention /prɪˈvenʃn/ *n* [u] 防止; **crime ~** 犯罪预防; **fire ~** 防火; **~ is better than cure** 预防胜于补救

preventive /prɪˈventɪv/ *adj* 预防的; **~ detention** 预防性拘留; **~ medicine** 预防医学

preview /ˈpriːvjuː/ *n* **1** (of film) 预映; (of play) 预演; (of exhibition) 预展 **2** (of TV, radio programme) 预告

previous /ˈpriːvɪəs/ *adj* **1** *attrib* (earlier) 先前的; **the ~ page** 上一页; **the ~ day** 前一天; **the ~ week/year** 上一周/年; **in a ~ life** 在前世; **on ~ occasions** 在以前的场合中; **he has no ~ convictions** Jur 他没有前科; **to have a ~ engagement** 有约在先; **~ to ...** 在…以前 **2** *pred* colloq (hasty) **to be ~** «*person, action*» 仓促

previously /ˈpriːvɪəsli/ *adv* **1** (in the past) 以前 ‹*say, work, live*› **2** (before) 之前; **two years/days ~** 两年/两天前; **at a ~ arranged location** 在预定地点

pre-war /ˌpriːˈwɔː(r)/ *adj* 战前的 [常指第二次世界大战前]; **the ~ period** *or* **years** 战前时期

prewash /ˌpriːˈwɒʃ/ *n, vt* 预洗

prexy /ˈpreksi/ *n* Amer colloq 校长

prey /preɪ/ *n* [u] **1** (animal) 被捕食的动物; **a bird of ~** 猛禽 **2** (person, product) 受害者; **to fall ~ to sth./sb.** lit 被某物/某人捕食; fig 成为某事物/某人的牺牲品; **to be easy ~ (for sb.)** (readily deceived) 易受(某人的)欺骗; (easily harmed) 易受(某人的)伤害; **to be ~ to sth.** 易受某事物的影响

Phrasal verb

• **prey on** *vt* [**~ on sb./sth.**] **1** (hunt) «*animal*» 捕食 **2** (worry) «*illness, problem, fear*» 折磨 ‹*person*›; **to ~ on sb.'s mind** 使某人内心不安 **3** (exploit) 利用 ‹*person, weakness, fear*›

prezzie, prezzy /ˈprezi/ *n* Brit colloq 礼物

price /praɪs/ ▸**p. 174**
A *n* **1** [c and u] (cost) 价格; **~ £85** 售价85英镑; **trade-in/factory-gate ~** 置换价/出厂价; **catalogue/cash ~** 商品目录/现付价格; **bargain/discount/going/bottom ~** 廉价/折扣价/现价/最低价; **to pay/give a ~** 支付定价/出价; **to sell off sth. at rock-bottom** *or* **giveaway ~s** 以最低价抛售某物; **the right ~** 公道的价格; **the ~ goes up** *or* **increases/goes down** *or* **decreases** 价格上涨/下跌; **to raise** *or* **increase/lower a ~** 涨价/降价; **to maintain/freeze a ~** 维持/冻结价格; **a rise/fall in ~** 价格的上涨/下跌; **he puts** *or* **sets a high ~ on loyalty** fig 他十分看重忠诚; **to quote a ~ (for sth./doing sth.)** (为某物/为做某事)报价; **to sell sth. at** *or* **for a good ~** 把某物卖个好价钱; **to do sth. for a ~** 以高价做某事; **to give a good/low ~ (for sth./doing sth.)** (为某物/为做某事)开价高/低; **the ~ in sterling/dollars** 英镑/美元定价; **an agreed/fixed ~** 商定/固定的价格; **(at) half/full ~** (以)半价/全价; **the net ~** 净价; **a slump in ~s** 价格的暴跌; **at a ~** 以高价; **at what a ~!** 好贵啊!; **to be cheap at the ~** 物超所值; **everyone** *or* **every man has his ~** Prov 人皆有价 [指人都是可以收买的]; **not at any ~** 无论如何也不; **beyond** *or* **above ~** 无价的; **a pearl beyond ~** 无价珍珠 [常喻指美人]; **to put a ~ on sb.'s head** (for capture) 悬赏缉拿某人; (to kill) 悬赏杀死某人; **to put a ~ on sth.** 为某物定价; **what's your best ~?** colloq 你最低价是多少?; **what ~ X?** colloq X有什么用? **2** [c] fig (condition for achieving sth.) 代价; **to pay a ~** 付出代价; **to pay a (high) ~ for sth.** 为某事付出(巨大)代价; **whatever the ~, at whatever ~** 不惜任何代价; **to seek peace at any ~** 不惜任何代价谋求和平; **no ~ is too high for sth./doing sth.** 为某事物/做某事,花再大的代价也值; **that's a small ~ to pay for sth./doing sth.** 为某事物/做某事付出这点不算什么; **that's the ~ one pays for being famous** 这就是成名的代价 **3** [c] (odds) 投注赔率; **the starting ~** 开跑赔率; **what ~ he'll turn up late?** 他不可能晚到吧?
B *vt* **1** (fix cost of) 给…定价; **he ~d them at £50 each** 他给它们定价每个50英镑; **to ~ sth. (too) high/low** 给某物定价(过)高/低; **to ~ oneself/sth. out of the market** 为自己/某物索价过高而无人问津; **this product is reasonably/competitively ~d** 这个产品定价合理/有竞争力; **a moderately ~d hotel** 价格适中的酒店 **2** (estimate worth of) 给…估价 ‹*house, picture*› **3** (mark cost of) 在…上标价 ‹*goods*› **4** (establish cost of) 比较…的价格 ‹*product, model*›

Phrasal verbs

• **price down** *vt* [**~ sth. down, ~ down sth.**]
1 (reduce cost of) 降低…的价格 **2** (mark down) 在…上标明降价

• **price up** *vt* [**~ sth. up, ~ up sth.**]
1 (increase cost of) 提高…的价格 **2** (mark up) 在…上标明涨价

price: ~ bracket *n* = **~ range**; **~ comparison site** *n* 价格对比网站; **~ control** *n* 物价控制; **~ curve** *n* 价格曲线; **~ cut** *n* 降价; **~ cutting** *n* [u] 削价; **~ difference** *n* 差价; **~ discrimination** *n* [u] 价格歧视; **~-earnings ratio** *n* 市盈率; **~ fixing** *n* [u] 价格垄断; **~ freeze** *n* 价格冻结; **~ increase** *n* 涨价; **~ index** *n* 物价指数; **~ inflation** *n* [u] 物价膨胀; **~ label** *n* 价格标签

priceless /ˈpraɪslɪs/ *adj* **1** (extremely valuable) 无价的 ‹*jewel, treasure*›; **impressionist paintings that have become ~** 变得价值连城的印象派画作 **2** (extremely useful) 宝贵的 ‹*advice, information*› **3** colloq (amusing) 极有趣的 ‹*joke, remark*›; **to look ~** 看上去极为可笑

price: ~ limit *n* 价格上限; **~ list** *n* (in shop, catalogue) 价目表; (in bar, restaurant) 价格单; **~ rally** *n* 股价反弹; **~ range** *n* 价格幅度; **~ restrictions** *npl* 价格限制; **~ rigging** *n* [u] 价格操纵; **~ ring** *n* 价格垄断集团; **~ rise** *n* 价格上涨; **~-sensitive** *adj* **1** (influenced by price) 对价格敏感的 ‹*product, consumer*›; **2** (affecting share prices) 会影响股价的 ‹*information, data*›; **~ support** *n* [u] 价格支持; **~ tag** *n* **1** (label) 价格标签; **2** (cost) 价格; **the ~ tag on sth.** 某事物的代价; **~ ticket** *n* 标价签; **~ war** *n* 价格战

pricey, pricy /ˈpraɪsi/ *adj* Brit colloq 昂贵的

prick /prɪk/
A *vt* **1** (pierce) «*needle, thorn*» 刺穿 ‹*plastic, surface, balloon*›; **to ~ a hole in sth.** 在某物上戳个洞 **2** (cause pain) «*thorn, needle*» 刺痛 ‹*person, skin, oneself*›; **I ~ed myself/my finger on a thorn** 我/我的手指被一根刺刺到了; **to ~ sb.'s conscience** 刺痛某人的良心

B *n* 1 (action) 刺; (pain) 刺痛; (hole) 刺孔; **to give sth. a ~** 扎某物一下; **a ~ of conscience** 良心的刺痛 2 taboo sl (penis) 鸡巴 offensive 3 sl (stupid man) 蠢材 offensive; (contemptible man) 小人

Phrasal verbs

• **prick out** *vt* [**~ out sth., ~ sth. out**] 移栽 ‹*seedlings*›

• **prick up**

A *vt* [**~ up sth.**] «*animal, person*» 竖起 ‹*ears*›

B *vi* «*ears*» 竖起

prickle /ˈprɪkl/

A *n* 1 (small thorn or spine) 刺 2 (feeling) 刺痛感

B *vt* «*clothes, wool*» 刺痛 ‹*skin*›

C *vi* «*skin, body*» 感到刺痛

prickly /ˈprɪkli/ *adj* 1 (containing prickles) 多刺的 ‹*bush, leaves*› 2 (itchy) 刺痛的 ‹*hands, skin*›; 扎人的 ‹*fabric, beard*› 3 colloq (touchy) 易怒的 ‹*person, mood*›; (difficult) 棘手的 ‹*relationship, subject*›

prickly: ~ heat *n* [u] 痱子; **~ pear** *n* 仙人果

pride /praɪd/

A *n* 1 [u] (satisfaction) 骄傲; **a source of ~ to sb.** 某人的骄傲; **to burst** *or* **glow with ~** 满怀自豪; **to fill sb. with ~** 让某人充满自豪; **to take ~ in sth.** 为某事物骄傲 2 [u] (self-respect) 自尊; **to hurt** *or* **wound sb.'s ~** 伤害某人的自尊心; **a blow to sb.'s ~** 对某人自尊心的打击; **~ alone prevented him from resigning** 他只是出于尊严而没有辞职; **a false sense of ~** 妄自尊大; **to swallow one's ~** 收起自尊; **family/national/male ~** 家族/民族/男性自尊心 3 [u] pej (conceit) 自负; **puffed up with ~** 自鸣得意的; **~ goes** *or* **comes before a fall** Prov 骄者必败 4 [u and c] (source of satisfaction) (person) 值得骄傲的人; (thing) 值得骄傲的事物; **to be the ~ of sb./sth.** 是某人/某事物的骄傲; **to be sb.'s ~ and joy** (person) 是某人最引以为豪的人; (thing) 是某人最引以为豪的事物; **to have** *or* **take ~ of place** 处于最荣耀的位置; **to give sb./sth. ~ of place** 突出某人/某事物 5 [c] (of lions) 狮群; **a ~ of lions** 一群狮子

B *v refl* **to ~ oneself on sth./doing sth.** 为某事物/做某事而自豪

priest /priːst/ *n* 祭司

priestess /ˈpriːstes/ *n* 女祭司

priesthood /ˈpriːsthʊd/ *n* [u] 1 (position) 祭司的职位; **to enter the ~** 成为祭司 2 (clergy) 神职人员

priestly /ˈpriːstli/ *adj* 祭司的

prig /prɪɡ/ *n* pej 自命不凡的人

priggish /ˈprɪɡɪʃ/ *adj* pej 自命不凡的

priggishness /ˈprɪɡɪʃnɪs/ *n* [u] pej 自命不凡

prim /prɪm/ *adj* **~ and proper** 一本正经的

prima ballerina /ˌpriːmə ˌbæləˈriːnə/ *n* [芭蕾舞团的] 首席女舞蹈演员

primacy /ˈpraɪməsi/ *n* [u] 1 (pre-eminence) 卓越; (primary role) 第一位; **to have ~** 居首位 2 Relig (office) 总主教职位; (period of office) 总主教任期; (authority) 总主教的权力

prima donna /ˌpriːmə ˈdɒnə/ *n* 1 (difficult person) 自负而喜怒无常的人 2 (lead female singer) [歌剧中的] 首席女歌唱演员

primaeval *adj* **= primeval**

prima facie /ˌpraɪmə ˈfeɪʃiː/

A *adj* 基于初步印象的; **a ~ case** 初步认定的案件; **~ evidence** 初步证据

B *adv* 据初步认定

primal /ˈpraɪml/ *adj* 1 (primitive) 最初的 ‹*feeling, force*›; 原始的 ‹*myth, instinct*› 2 (principal) 主要的

primarily /ˈpraɪmərəli, Amer praɪˈmerəli/ *adv* 主要地

primary /ˈpraɪməri, Amer -meri/

A *adj* 1 (main) 主要的 ‹*reason, aim, producer*›; **of ~ importance** 最重要的 2 (initial) 最初的 3 (elementary) 初等教育的; **a ~ teacher** 小学教师; **~ children** 小学生

B *n* Amer 初选

primary care *n* [u] 初级保健护理

Primary Care Trust *n* Brit 初级保健托管机构

primary: ~ colour *n* 基色; **~ election** *n* 初选; **~ evidence** *n* [u] 基本证据; **~ health care** *n* [u]; **= primary care**; **~ industry** *n* [u] 第一产业; **~ infection** *n* [c and u] 原发感染; **~ school** *n* Brit 小学; *modif* **~ school teacher, ~ teacher** 小学教师; **~ stress** *n* 主重音

primate /ˈpraɪmeɪt/ *n* 1 (mammal) 灵长目动物 2 (bishop or archbishop) 总主教

prime /praɪm/

A *adj attrib* 1 (chief) 首要的; **their ~ concern is ...** 他们最关心的是…; **of ~ importance** 最重要的 2 (most suitable) 最合适的 ‹*candidate, target*› 3 (good quality) 最好的; **a ~ site in the city centre** 市中心的最佳地段; **~ cuts of meat** 上好的肉块; **to be in ~ condition** «*foodstuffs*» 处于最新鲜的状态; «*livestock*» 处于最健壮的时期; «*machine*» 处于最佳的运行状态; **to be of ~ quality** «*product*» 质量上乘 4 (classic) 典型的 ‹*example*› 5 Math 素数的; **~ numbers** 素数

B *n* 1 [c] (peak period) 盛年; **to be in one's ~** (in age) 正值壮年; (in career) 正值巅峰期; **to be in its ~** «*organization, style*» 正值全盛期; «*plants*» 正值鼎盛花期; «*machine*» 处于性能最佳时期; **to be past one's ~** 已过壮年; **to be in the ~ of life** 正值英姿勃发的年华 2 [c] Math 素数 3 [c] Print 上标符号 4 [u] Relig 晨经

C *vt* 1 (brief) 事先指点; **to ~ sb. about sth.** 事先告知某人 ‹*circumstances*›; **to ~ sb. with sth.** 事先向某人提供 ‹*facts, information*›; **to be (well) ~d for sth.** 为某事作好（充分）准备 2 Constr (for painting) 在…上涂底漆 3 Tech 给…注水启动 ‹*pump*›; **the money was intended to ~ the community-care pump** 这笔经费旨在振兴社区保健事业 4 Mil 给…装火药; **the bomb was ~d** 炸弹装有火药 5 **to be well ~d** colloq (with food) 吃得很饱; (with drink) 喝足了饮料

D *v refl* **to ~ oneself with sth.** (food) 吃饱某物; (drink) 喝足某物

prime: ~ cost *n* 主要成本; **~ meridian** *n* 本初子午线; **~ minister, P~ Minister** *n* (of UK) 首相; (of Australia, Canada etc.) 总理; **~-ministerial** *adj* (in UK) 首相的; (in Australia, Canada etc.) 总理的; **~ ministership** *n* 1 (duties, in UK) 首相的职责; (duties, in Australia, Canada etc.) 总理的职责; 2 (term, in UK) 首相任期; (term, in Australia, Canada etc.) 总理任期; **~ mover** *n* 1 (influential force) 推动者; 2 (in physics, technology) 原动力

> **prime minister**
>
> 君主制国家的prime minister通常译为“首相”。英国的首相是英国政府首脑，起初由君主按照自己的意愿任命，现为民选。议会选举后，获得多数议席的政党领袖接受君主召见，被任命为首相。首相任命并领导其他内阁成员，对议会负责。任期每届最高5年，可以连任。5年任期内，首相可提请君主解散议会，提前举行大选。授勋（**▸the honours system**）名单也由首相推荐，经君主批准。英国首相的官邸为唐宁街（**▸Downing Street**）10号。

primer /ˈpraɪmə(r)/ *n* 1 [u and c] (paint) 底漆 2 [c] (textbook) 启蒙读本

prime: ~ rate *n* 优惠利率; **~ time** *n* [u] 黄金时间

primeval /praɪˈmiːvl/ *adj* 1 (ancient) 原始的 ‹*beast, world*› 2 (instinctive) 本能的 ‹*force, urge*›

primeval soup *n* [u] [据信产生了生命的] 原生浆液

priming coat *n* **= primer 1**

primitive /ˈprɪmɪtɪv/ *adj* 1 Anthrop 原始的 ‹*religion*›; **~ tribes/people** 原始部落/原始人 2 (early) 早期的 ‹*form, weapon, structure*› 3 (crude) 简陋的 ‹*living conditions, sanitation, transport system*›

primly /ˈprɪmli/ *adv* 1 (prudishly) 一本正经地 ‹*behave, refuse, dress*› 2 (demurely) 端庄地 ‹*smile, behave, dress*›

primness /ˈprɪmnɪs/ *n* [u] 1 (prudishness) 一本正经 2 (demureness) 端庄

primordial /praɪˈmɔːdɪəl/ *adj* 原始的

primp /prɪmp/

A *vi* 打扮; **to ~ (and preen)** 梳妆打扮

B *vt* 整理 ‹*clothes, hair*›; 修整 ‹*make-up*›; 打扮 ‹*oneself*›

primrose /ˈprɪmrəʊz/ *n* 报春花; **the ~ path** fig 享乐之路

primrose yellow **▸p. 134**

A *adj* 淡黄色的

B *n* 淡黄色

primula /ˈprɪmjʊlə/ *n* 报春花属植物

Primus® /ˈpraɪməs/ *n* **~ (stove)** 普赖默斯便携式燃油炉

prince /prɪns/ *n* 1 (son) 王子; (male relative) 王室的男性成员; (ruler) [小国的] 君主; **P~ Charles** 查尔斯王子; **P~ Charming** 白马王子 2 (most important person) 大王; **the ~ of darkness** 黑暗王子 [指撒旦]; **the ~ of porn** 色情作品大王

Prince Edward Island *pr n* 爱德华王子岛

princeling /ˈprɪnslɪŋ/ *n* 1 (young prince) 幼年王子 2 (insignificant ruler) 小王公

princely /ˈprɪnsli/ *adj* 1 (grand) 巨额的 ‹*sum*›; 丰厚的 ‹*salary, gift*›; 豪华的 ‹*accommodation*› 2 (of a prince) 王子的 ‹*role, life*›

prince regent *n* 摄政王

princess /prɪnˈses/ *n* (daughter) 公主; (female relative) 王室的女性成员; (rule) [小国的] 女王; (wife or widow of a prince) 王妃; **the P~ Royal** 长公主

principal /ˈprɪnsəpl/

A *adj* 最重要的

B *n* 1 (headteacher) 校长 2 (lead actor) 主角 3 (sum of money) 本金 4 (employer) 委托人

principal boy *n* Brit [女演员扮演的] 哑剧男主角

principality /ˌprɪnsəˈpæləti/ *n* 公国

principally /ˈprɪnsəpli/ *adv* 主要地

principle /ˈprɪnsəpl/ *n* 1 [c and u] (basic tenet) 原则; **on the ~ that ...** 按照…的原则; **in ~** 理论上 2 [c and u] (rule of conduct) 行为准则; **to be against sb.'s ~s (to do sth.)** （做某事）违背某人的行为准则; **to have high ~s** 有崇高道德原则; **on ~** 根据行为准则; **a matter of ~** 原则问题; **a woman of ~** 正直的女人; **to make it a ~ to do sth.** 把做某事视为原则 3 [c] (scientific law) 原理

principled /ˈprɪnsəpld/ *adj* 1 (based on principles) 根据原则的; **a ~ decision/position/approach** 根据原则所作的决定/所采取的立场/所用的方法; **to act in a ~ way** 按照原则办事 2 (having principles) 坚持原则的; **to be ~** 原则性强

print /prɪnt/

A *n* 1 [u] (typeface, lettering) 字体; **the title is in roman/italic ~** 标题用的是罗马体/斜体; **large/small ~** 大/小号字体; **to set sth. up in ~** 给…排版 ‹*text*› 2 [u] (printed text) 印刷品; **a page of ~** 一印刷页; **the ~ media** 印刷媒体; **the medium of ~** 印刷媒体; **~ quality/format** 印刷质量/格式 3 [u] (availability in published form) 出版; **in/out of ~** 已出版/绝版的; **to put** *or* **get sth. into ~** 出版某物; **to appear in** *or* **get into ~** «*book*» 出版; **to see sth./oneself in ~** 看到某物/自己的作品出版; **at the time of going to ~** 在付印之际; **to rush sth. into ~** 匆忙发表某物 4 [c] (of finger) 指印; (of hand) 掌印; (of foot, paw) 足迹; (of hoof) 蹄印; (of tyre) 印记; **the ~ of a pattern in a mould** 模具印出的图案 5 [c] Art 版画 6 [c] Phot 照片; **to make a ~ from a negative** 用底片印照片 7 [c and u] Tex 印花布; **light summer ~s** 轻薄的印花夏装; **a ~ dress/curtain** 印花连衣裙/窗帘 8 [u] (writing) 印刷体书写

B **prints** *npl* (fingerprints) 指纹; **a set of ~s** 一组指纹; **to take sb.'s ~s** 提取某人的指纹

C *vt* 1 Print 印刷 ‹*text, image, banknote, book*›; **to ~ sth. in lower case/upper case/italics** 用小写字体/大写字体/斜体印刷某物; **~ed matter** 印刷品; **~ed notepaper** 印有信头的信纸; **~ed in China** 中国印制; **over 1,000 copies of the book have been ~ed** 该书已印了 1,000 多册 2 (publish) 刊登 ‹*article, allegation, interview*›; **the newspaper is going to ~ the story** 该报纸将要刊登这篇报道; **the ~ed word** 已发表的文字 3 (write) 用印刷体写; **~ your name in block capitals/in black ink** 请用印刷体正体大写字母/黑色墨水并用印刷体书写姓名 4 (make impression of) 印上 ‹*letters, design*›; **to ~ sth. on sb.'s memory** fig 让某人铭记某事物 5 (make impression on) 印染; **to ~ fabrics (with …)** (把…) 印上布料; **~ed cotton/wallpaper** 印花棉布/墙纸 6 Phot 洗印 ‹*photograph*›; **how many copies shall I ~?** 我要印多少张呢?

D *vi* 1 (write) 用印刷体写; **to learn to ~** 学写印刷体 2 Print 印刷 3 Comput 打印 4 Phot ‹*plate, negative*› 冲印

Phrasal verbs

- **print off** *vt* [**~ sth. off, ~ off sth.**] 大量印刷
- **print out**

A *vt* [**~ sth. out, ~ out sth.**] 打印出

B *vi* 被打印出; **the report won't ~ out on a single page** 这份报告一张纸印不下

printable /'prɪntəbl/ *adj* 1 (capable of being printed) 可印刷的 2 (publishable) 可发表的 ‹*article, comment, views, remarks*›; **barely** *or* **scarcely ~** 简直不适合出版的

print character *n* 印刷字符

printed /'prɪntɪd/ *adj* 印刷的

printed: ~ circuit *n* 印刷电路; **~ matter** *n* [u] 印刷品

printer /'prɪntə(r)/ *n* 1 (machine) 打印机 2 (person) 印刷工人; (owner) 印刷商; (firm) 印刷公司; **at the ~'s** *or* **~s** 在排印中

printer's ink *n* [u] 油墨

print: ~ format *n* 打印方式; **in ~ format** 以打印的方式; **~head** *n* 打印头

printing /'prɪntɪŋ/ *n* 1 [u] (of book, newspaper) 印刷; (of photograph) 印相; (of fabric) 印花工艺; **a ~ business** 印刷公司 2 [c] (print run) 一次印刷 3 [u] (writing) 印刷字体

printing: ~ frame *n* 晒版架; **~ house** *n* 印刷厂; **~ ink** *n* [u] 油墨; **~ press** *n* 印刷机; **~ works** *npl + v sing or pl* 印刷厂

print: ~ journalism *n* [u] 报刊业新闻工作; **~maker** ▸p. 409 *n* 版画匠; **~making** *n* [u] 版画复制; **~out, ~off** *ns* 打印件; **~-preview** *n* 打印预览; **~ queue** *n* 打印队列; **~ run** *n* 一次印数; **~ shop** *n* 1 (workshop) 印刷所; 2 (art shop) 书画刻印作品店; **~ union** *n* 印刷行业工会

prion /'pri:ɒn/ *n* 朊病毒

prior /'praɪə(r)/

A *adj* 1 (previous) 在先的 ‹*knowledge, experience, engagement, consent*›; **~ notice** 预先通知; **~ to sth.** 在某事以前的 2 (more important) 优先的 ‹*duty, claim*›

B *n* Relig (superior) [小隐修院] 院长; (deputy) [隐修院] 副院长

prioress /ˌpraɪə'res/ *n* (superior) [小女隐修院] 院长; (deputy) [女隐修院] 副院长

prioritization /praɪˌɒrɪtaɪ'zeɪʃn, Amer -'ɔ:r-/ *n* [u] 1 (giving priority) 优先考虑 2 (ordering) 确定优先顺序

prioritize /praɪ'ɒrɪtaɪz, Amer -'ɔ:r-/

A *vt* 1 (give priority to) 优先考虑 2 (put in order of priority) 确定…的优先顺序 ‹*goals, tasks*›

B *vi* 确定优先顺序

priority /praɪ'ɒrəti, Amer -'ɔ:r-/

A *n* 1 [c] (main concern) 优先事项; **the main** *or* **highest ~** 头等大事; **a high/low ~** 重点/非重点项目; **to get one's priorities right/wrong** 分清/分不清轻重缓急 2 [u] (precedence) 优先; **to have** *or* **take ~ over sth.** 比某事优先考虑; **to get ~** 享有优先权 3 [u] Brit (on road) 优先通行权; **~ to the right** 右侧优先通行权

B *adj* 享有优先权的; **the ~ list** 优先事项表

priory /'praɪəri/ *n* (monastery) 小隐修院; (nunnery) 小女隐修院

prise /praɪz/ *vt* 撬开

Phrasal verbs

- **prise apart** *vt* [**~ sth. apart**] 撬开 ‹*layers, planks*›; 强行把…分开 ‹*people*›
- **prise away** *vt* [**~ sth./sb. away**] 把…拉开 ‹*person, object*›; **to ~ sb. away from …** 把某人从…拉开
- **prise off** *vt* [**~ sth. off**] 撬掉 ‹*object, lid*›
- **prise open** *vt* [**~ sth. open, ~ open sth.**] 撬开 ‹*tin, barrel, door*›
- **prise out** *vt* [**~ sth. out**] 撬出 ‹*nail*›; 挖出 ‹*information*›; **to ~ sth. out of sb.** 逼迫某人说出某事

prism /'prɪzəm/ *n* 棱镜

prismatic /prɪz'mætɪk/ *adj* 1 (resembling a prism) 棱镜似的 ‹*shape, layer*›; (containing a prism) 有棱镜的 ‹*compass*› 2 *attrib* (spectral) 五光十色的 ‹*light, colours*›

prismatic: ~ binoculars *npl* 棱镜式双筒望远镜; **~ compass** *n* 棱镜罗盘

prison /'prɪzn/ *n* 监狱; **to be in ~** 在狱中; **to go to ~** 入狱; **to send sb. to ~** 将某人投入监狱; **her house felt like a ~** 她的房子感觉像个牢笼; **a ~ cell** 牢房

prison: ~ authorities *npl* 监狱当局; **~ camp** *n* Mil 战俘营; Pol 拘禁地

prisoner /'prɪznə(r)/ *n* (in jail) 犯人; (in custody) 拘留犯; (captured by enemy) 俘虏; **to hold** *or* **keep sb. ~** 囚禁某人; **they took me ~** 他们俘虏了我; **to take no ~s** 不择手段

prisoner: ~ of conscience *n* (for political belief) 政治犯; (for religious belief) 宗教犯; **~ of war** *n* 战俘

prison: ~ guard ▸p. 409 *n* 监狱看守; **~-issue** *adj* 监狱提供的; **~ officer** ▸p. 409 *n* 狱吏; **~ riot** *n* 监狱暴乱; **~ sentence** *n* 徒刑; **~ service** *n* 监狱部门; **~ term** *n* 服刑期; **~ van** *n* 囚车; **~ visitor** *n* 义务探监者

prissy /'prɪsi/ *adj* 谨小慎微的

pristine /'prɪsti:n, 'prɪstaɪn/ *adj* 崭新的 ‹*copy, car*›; 未触动过的 ‹*layer of snow*›; **to be in ~ condition** 是全新的

privacy /'prɪvəsi, 'praɪ-/ *n* [u] 1 (solitude) 不受干扰; **in the ~ of your own home** 在自己家中不受打扰时 2 (private life) 隐私; **to respect/invade sb.'s ~** 尊重/侵犯某人的隐私; **the right to ~** 隐私权

privacy: ~ laws *npl* 隐私保护法; **~ policy** *n* 隐私政策

private /'praɪvɪt/

A *adj* 1 (not for general public) 私人的; **a ~ viewing of a film/exhibition** 私下观看电影/展览; **~ and personal** *or* **confidential** 私密的; **~ facilities** 独立卫浴; **for sb.'s (own) ~ use** 供某人私人使用; **the wedding/funeral will be ~** 婚礼/葬礼将不公开举行; **~ study** 自学; **a person with ~ means/a ~ income** 有个人财产/收入的人; **in sb.'s ~ life** 在某人的私生活中; **(to act) in a ~ capacity** *or* **as a ~ person** 以私人身份 (行事); **the ~ citizen** 平民 2 (not openly revealed) 秘密的 ‹*agreement, information*›; 私下的 ‹*opinion, conversation, meeting*›; **they came to** *or* **had a ~ understanding** 他们秘密达成了谅解; **a ~ joke** 外人听不懂的笑话; **sb.'s ~ thoughts** 某人私下的想法; **please keep the matter ~** 请对这件事保密; **to have a ~ chat** *or* **talk with sb.** 与某人密谈; **the ~ hearing of a case** 案件的非公开听审 3 (secretive) 内向的 ‹*person*› 4 (free from people) 僻静的 ‹*place, spot, corner*› 5 *pred* (undisturbed) 不受打扰的; **let's go upstairs where we can be a bit more ~** 我们上楼去吧，那里清静些 6 (not state-run) 私立的 ‹*hospital, school*›; 私营的 ‹*company*›; **to be in ~ employment** 受私营企业雇用; **~ ownership/bank** 私有制/私人银行; **she's having ~ maths lessons** 她在请家教学数学; **to go ~** Brit 选择自费医疗 7 Comm 个人之间的 ‹*transaction, sale*›

B *n* 1 [c] Mil 列兵; **he enlisted as a ~** 他参军当了兵; **P~ Taylor** 列兵泰勒 2 [u] **in ~** 私下

C **privates** *npl* colloq euph 私处 euph

private: ~ bar *n* Brit 雅座酒吧; **~ bill** *n* 私法法案; **~ buyer** *n* 私人买家; **~ company** *n* 私营公司; **~ detective** ▸p. 409 *n* 私人侦探; **~ enterprise** *n* [c and u] 私营企业

private equity *n* [u] 私募股权

private equity firm *n* 私人股本公司

private: ~ eye *n* colloq 私人侦探; **~ finance initiative** *n* Brit 私人融资计划; **~ first class** *n* Amer (陆军) 一等兵; **~ health care** *n* [u] 私人医疗保健; **~ health insurance** *n* [u] 私人医疗保险; **~ income** *n* [u] 非劳动收入; **~ investigator** ▸p. 409 *n* 私人侦探; **~ investor** *n* 散户; **~ key** *n* 私有密钥; **~ law** *n* [u] 私法

privately /'praɪvɪtli/ *adv* 1 (not publicly) 私下 ‹*talk, object, admit*›; **the matter was discussed ~** 大家在私底下谈论这件事 2 (secretly) 暗自 ‹*think, feel*›; **~ she was furious** 她内心里十分气愤 3 (as a private individual) 以个人名义 ‹*write, apply, visit*› 4 (out of state sector) 私营地; **~ managed hospitals** 私营医院; **~-owned** 私有的; **a ~ funded** *or* **financed institution of higher education** 私立高等学校; **he educated his children ~** 他让子女们上私立学校 5 Comm 在个人之间 ‹*sell, transact*›

private member *n* 普通议员

private member's bill *n* Brit 普通议员法案

private: ~ parts *npl* euph 私处 euph; **~ patient** *n* Brit 自费病人; **~ pension plan, ~ pension scheme** *ns* 私人养老金计划; **~ practice** *n* 1 [c] (medical practice) 私人医师开业; 2 [u] (professional work) 私人开业; **~ school** *n* 私立学校; **~ secretary** *n* 1 (secretary) 私人秘书; 2 Pol (aide) 高官助理; **~ sector** *n* 私营部分; **~ treaty** *n* [u] 财产出让契约; **~ view** *n* 画作预展

privation /praɪ'veɪʃn/ *n* [u and c] 匮乏

privatization /ˌpraɪvɪtaɪ'zeɪʃn, Amer -tɪ'z-/ *n* [u] 私有化

privatize /'praɪvɪtaɪz/ *vt* 使私有化

privet /'prɪvɪt/ *n* [u] 女贞

privilege /'prɪvəlɪdʒ/ *n* 1 [c and u] (prerogative) 特权 2 [c] (honour) 荣幸

privileged /'prɪvəlɪdʒd/

A *adj* 1 (having privileges) 有特权的 ‹*group, life, position*›; (honoured) 荣幸的; **to be ~ to meet sb./to see sth.** 有幸遇见某人/看到某物; **the ~ few** 享有特权的少数人 2 (legally protected) 特许保密的 ‹*information, document*›

B *npl* **the ~** 特权人士; **the less ~** (economically) 穷人; (in luck) 不幸的人

privy /ˈprɪvi/
A *adj* 知情的; **to be ~ to sth.** 知晓某事
B *n* dated 茅房

Privy: ~ Council *n* Brit **the ~ Council** 枢密院; **~ Councillor** *n* Brit 枢密院官员

prize[1] /praɪz/
A *n* [1] (in competition) 奖品; (in lottery) 奖; **to win a ~** 获奖; **a cash ~** 现金奖励; **first/second ~** 一等奖/二等奖; **to award** *or* **give a ~** 发奖; **there are no ~s for guessing** 这是明摆着的 [2] (reward for effort) 回报; **happiness is a ~ worth striving for** 幸福值得努力追求
B *adj attrib* [1] (victorious) 获奖的 ‹*rose, sheep, exhibit*› [2] (treasured) 珍视的 ‹*possession, glasses, tea set*› [3] fig (perfect) 典型的 ‹*example*›; 十足的 ‹*idiot, fool*› [4] (with prize as a reward) 有奖的 ‹*crossword, draw*›
C *vt* (value) 珍视 ‹*independence, work*›; **a ~d possession** 最珍爱的财物; **to be ~d for sth.** 因某物而受到高度重视

prize[2] *vt* Amer = **prise**

prize: ~ day *n* [学校每年一次的] 颁奖日; **~ draw** *n* 抽奖; **~ fight** *n* 职业拳击赛; **~ fighter** *n* 职业拳击手; **~ fighting** *n* [u] 职业拳击; **~-giving** *n* Brit 颁奖仪式; **~ money** *n* [u] 奖金; **~winner** *n* (in lottery) 中奖者; (in competition) 优胜者; (of academic, literary award) 获奖者; **~-winning** *adj attrib* 获奖的 ‹*entry, novel*›; 中奖的 ‹*ticket*›

pro /prəʊ/
A *n* (*pl* **~s**) [1] colloq (professional) 专业人员; **to turn ~** 成为职业选手 [2] colloq (prostitute) 妓女 [3] (advantage) 益处; (argument) 赞成的观点; **the ~s and cons** 利弊; **to weigh up the ~s and cons (of sth.)** 权衡（某事的）利弊
B *prep* colloq 赞成; **to be ~ sth.** 支持某事

pro- /prəʊ/ *combining form* [1] (favouring) 赞成; **to be ~democracy** 拥护民主; **to be ~American** 亲美 [2] (deputy) 副; (substitute) 代; **the ~consul** 副领事

pro-abortion *adj* 赞成堕胎的

pro-abortionist *n* 赞成堕胎者

proactive /prəʊˈæktɪv/ *adj* 积极主动的

pro-am /ˌprəʊˈæm/ *adj* 包括职业和业余选手的

probability /ˌprɒbəˈbɪləti/ *n* [1] [u] (likelihood) 可能性; **in all ~** 很可能 [2] [c] (likely event) 可能的事; (likely result) 可能的结果; **war is a ~** 战争很可能爆发 [3] [u] (statistic, measure) 概率; **the theory of ~, ~ theory** 概率论

probable /ˈprɒbəbl/
A *adj* 很可能的
B *n* Brit (person) 可能入选者; (thing) 很可能的事; **to be a ~ (for sth.)** 是（某事的）可能人选

probably /ˈprɒbəbli/ *adv* 很可能

probate /ˈprəʊbeɪt/
A *n* [1] [u] (process) 遗嘱检验; **to grant ~ (of a will)** 核准遗嘱验证; **to be in ~** 进行遗嘱验证; **a ~ judge** 遗嘱检验法官 [2] [c] (copy of will) 经验证的遗嘱
B *vt* Amer «*lawyer, court*» 检验 ‹*will*›

Probate Registry *n* Brit 遗嘱检验登记处

probation /prəˈbeɪʃn, Amer prəʊ-/ *n* [u] [1] Jur 缓刑; **to put sb. on ~** 判某人缓刑; **to be on ~** 在服缓刑; **to be out on ~** 被假释 [2] (trial period) 试用期; **to be on academic ~** 在试读

probationary /prəˈbeɪʃnri, Amer prəʊˈbeɪʃəneri/ *adj* [1] Jur 缓刑的; **a ~ period** 缓刑期 [2] (in employment) 见习的 ‹*status*›; **a ~ period** 见习期

probationary teacher *n* Brit 见习教师

probationer /prəˈbeɪʃənə(r), Amer prəʊ-/ *n* [1] Jur (offender) 缓刑犯 [2] (employee) 试用人员

probation: ~ officer ▸p. 409 *n* 缓刑监督官; **~ order** *n* 缓刑令; **~ service** *n* 缓刑监督机构

probe /prəʊb/
A *vt* [1] (investigate) 调查 ‹*scandal, allegation, cause*›; 探究 ‹*mystery, psyche*› [2] (examine) «*doctor, animal, finger*» 探查 ‹*wound, DNA, crack*› [3] (explore) 探测 ‹*sky, darkness, space*›
B *vi* [1] (investigate) 调查; **to ~ for more information** 探求更多的消息; **to ~ into sth.** 调查某事 [2] (search) «*person, animal*» 翻寻; **to ~ for sth.** 翻找某物
C *n* [1] (investigation) 调查; **to carry out a ~ into sth.** 对某事展开调查 [2] (surgical instrument) 探针; (operation, examination) 探查; **to do a ~** 用探针探查 [3] (measuring instrument) 探测仪; **a temperature ~** 温度探测仪 [4] (unmanned spacecraft) 航天探测器

probing /ˈprəʊbɪŋ/
A *adj* 寻根究底的 ‹*question*›; **she gave me an intense, ~ look** 她看了我一眼，目光急切，咄咄逼人
B *n* [1] (examination) 探索 [2] (questions) 追问

probiotic /ˌprəʊbaɪˈɒtɪk/
A *adj* 促进有益微生物生长的; **~ milk/bacteria** 益生菌牛奶/益生菌
B *n* 益生素

probity /ˈprəʊbəti/ *n* [u] formal 诚实

problem /ˈprɒbləm/
A *n* [1] (difficulty) 问题; **to have a weight/housing/marital ~** 有肥胖/住房/婚姻问题; **to cause** *or* **create** *or* **pose** *or* **present a ~** 引发问题; **to bring up** *or* **raise/resolve** *or* **settle/tackle** *or* **address a ~** 提出/解决/处理问题; **it's a real ~** 这确实是个问题; **it's a bit of a ~** 这有点问题; **that's the least of my ~s!** 那不关我的事！; **the ~ is that ...** 问题是…; **what's the ~?** colloq 怎么啦？; **what's your ~?** colloq 你怎么了？; **to be a ~ to sb.** 对某人来说是个难题; **to have ~s with sth.** 在某方面有问题; **health ~s** 健康问题; **it's a ~ to get** *or* **getting him to concentrate** 想让他集中注意力很难; **to have a ~ in doing sth.** 做某事有困难; **I had no ~ in finding the house** 我没费劲儿就找到了那所房子; **no ~!** 没问题！; **to have a ~ with sth.** colloq 反对某事 [2] (question, test) 题目; **to solve a ~** 解答题目; **to do ~s at school** 在学校做题; **a chess ~** 棋题
B *modif* [1] (problematic) 成问题的; **a ~ child/family** 问题儿童/家庭 [2] Literat (social) 有关社会问题的; (moral) 有关道德问题的; **a ~ novel/play** 问题小说/戏剧

problematic /ˌprɒbləˈmætɪk/, **problematical** /ˌprɒbləˈmætɪkl/ *adj* 造成困难的 ‹*situation, relationship, concept*›

problem: ~ case *n* (gen) 难题; (person) 成问题的人; (situation) 成问题的局面; **~ drinker** *n* 问题酗酒者; **~ drinking** *n* [u] 问题酗酒; **~ page** *n* 问题解答专栏

proboscis /prəˈbɒsɪs/ *n* (*pl* **probosces** /prəˈbɒsiːz/ *or* **proboscides** /prəˈbɒsɪdiːz/) (of elephant) 长鼻; (of tapir) 吻; (of insects) 喙; (of some worms) 吮吸器官

procedural /prəˈsiːdʒərəl/ *adj* 程序上的

procedure /prəˈsiːdʒə(r)/ *n* [1] (method) 程序; **to follow a ~** 依照程序; **the normal ~ is to do ...** 正常的步骤是做…; **what's the ~?** colloq 该怎么做? [2] Comput = **subroutine**

proceed /prəˈsiːd, prəʊ-/
A *vi* [1] (continue) 继续; **before we ~ any further** (at meeting) 在我们继续下一议项之前; (in middle of speech) 在我们谈下一点之前; **please ~** formal 请继续; **to ~ to sth.** 接下来处理 ‹*item, problem*›; **to ~ with sth.** 继续 ‹*plan, sale*›; Pol 继续进行 ‹*election*›; Jur 继续审理 ‹*case*›; **to ~ to do sth.** 接下来做某事 [2] (progress) «*action, project*» 进展; «*interview, talk*» 继续; **the trial is ~ing** 审理在进行中 [3] formal (move) 前行; **to ~ towards/along ...** 前往…/沿…前行; **to ~ to ...** 前行到…; **they ~ed on their way** 他们继续行进; **~ with care** *or* **caution!** 一路小心！ [4] formal (lead) «*road, river*» 延伸; **to ~ towards/through sth.** 延伸向/过某处; **to ~ in an easterly direction (towards sth.)** 向东（朝某处）延伸 [5] formal (issue, result) **to ~ from sth.** «*smell*» 来自某物; «*power*» 源自某事物; «*evil*» 由某事物引起 [6] Jur 起诉; **to ~ against sb.** 起诉某人
B *vt* 继续讲; **'well,' she ~ed, 'it was like this ...'** "哦，" 她接着说，"事情是这样的…"

proceedings /prəˈsiːdɪŋz/ *npl* [1] (event) 事件; (meeting, ceremony) 议项 [2] (legal action) 诉讼; **extradition ~** 引渡诉讼; **to take** *or* **institute ~ (against sb.)** （对某人）起诉; **to start divorce ~** 诉请离婚; **to commence criminal ~ (against sb.)** （对某人）提请刑事诉讼 [3] (report) 会议记录

proceeds /ˈprəʊsiːdz/ *npl* 收益

process[1] /ˈprəʊses, Amer ˈprɒses/
A *n* [1] [c] (series of steps) 过程; (natural change) 进程; **mental ~es** 心理历程; **a ~ of elimination** 淘汰过程; **the learning ~** 学习过程; **in the ~ of time** 随着时间的流逝; **to be in/begin the ~ of doing sth.** 正在/开始做某事; **in the ~ of doing this** 做这件事时; **in the ~** 在其间 [2] [c] Ind, Sci 工序; **a manufacturing ~** 制造方法; **a ~ for sth./doing sth.** 某事物/做某事的流程 [3] [c and u] Jur （诉讼）程序; **the ~es of the law** 法律程序 [4] [c] Jur (summons) 传票; **to serve (a) ~ on sb.** 向某人发出传票 [5] [c] Comput 处理 [6] [c] Zool, Bot (projecting part) 突起
B *vt* [1] (treat) 加工 ‹*raw material, chemical, food*›; 处理 ‹*waste product*› [2] Phot 冲洗 ‹*film*› [3] Admin (deal with) 受理 ‹*application, request, complaint*›; 审查 ‹*applicant*› [4] Comput 处理 ‹*data, request*› [5] Amer (straighten) 拉直 ‹*hair*›

process[2] /prəˈses/ *vi* formal (move) 列队行进; **to ~ down** *or* **along sth.** 沿…列队行进 ‹*road*›

process control *n* [u] 过程控制

processed /ˈprəʊsest, Amer ˈprɒs-/ *adj* 加工过的 ‹*food, cheese, steel*›

processing /ˈprəʊsesɪŋ, Amer ˈprɒs-/ *n* [u] [1] (of data, form, application, waste) 处理 [2] (of raw material, food product) 加工; **the food ~ industry** 食品加工业 [3] (of undeveloped film) 冲洗

procession /prəˈseʃn/ *n* (group of people) 队伍; (action) 列队行进; **carnival ~** 狂欢节的巡游队伍; **funeral/wedding ~** 送葬/婚礼队列; **to walk/drive along in ~** 列队行走/行驶

processional /prəˈseʃənl/
A *adj* 列队行进的
B *n* 列队行进礼仪书

processor /ˈprəʊsesə(r), Amer ˈprɒs-/ *n* [1] (machine) 加工机; (person) 加工工人; (company) 加工公司 [2] Comput 处理器

process printing *n* [u] 彩色凸版印刷

pro-choice *adj* 主张堕胎合法的

pro-choicer /ˌprəʊˈtʃɔɪsə(r)/ *n* 主张堕胎合法者

proclaim /prəˈkleɪm/ *vt* [1] (announce) 宣布 ‹*independence, peace*›; **to ~ sb. king/queen** 宣告立某人为国王/女王; **to ~ war** 宣战 [2] (indicate) «*tone, expression*» 表明 ‹*innocence, honesty*›; **this fact ~ed her guilt** 这个事实说明她有罪; **to ~ sb. a liar** 表明某人是个骗子

proclamation /ˌprɒkləˈmeɪʃn/ *n* 宣布; **to issue** *or* **make a ~** 发表声明

proclivity /prəˈklɪvəti/ *n* formal [常指坏的] 倾向; **a ~ for** *or* **towards violence** 暴力倾向

procrastinate /prəʊˈkræstɪneɪt/ *vi* 拖延

procrastination /prəʊˌkræstɪˈneɪʃn/ *n* [u] 拖延; **the opposition accused the Prime Minister of ~** 反对党指责首相行事拖沓

procrastinator /prəʊˈkræstɪneɪtə(r)/ *n* 拖延者

procreate /ˈprəʊkrieɪt/ *vi* formal «*person*» 生育; «*animal*» 繁殖

procreation /ˌprəʊkriˈeɪʃn/ *n* [u] formal (of person) 生育; (of animal) 繁殖

proctor /ˈprɒktə(r)/ *n* [1] Brit Univ (official) 学监 [2] Amer Univ (invigilator) 监考人

procurator fiscal /ˌprɒkjʊreɪtəˈfɪskl/ *n* (*pl* **procurators fiscal**) Scot 地方检察官

procure /prəˈkjʊə(r)/ *vt* [1] 设法获得 ‹*alcohol, weapons, supplies*›; **to ~ sth. for sb.** 替某人弄到某物 [2] Jur 诱使…卖淫 ‹*prostitute, woman*›; **to ~ sb. for sb.** 诱使某人向某人卖淫

procurement /prəˈkjʊəmənt/ *n* [u] 购买; **arms/steel ~** 军火/钢铁采购

prod /prɒd/
A *vt* (*pres p etc.* **-dd-**) [1] (poke) 戳 ‹*person, object, food*›; 捅 ‹*fire*›; **to ~ sb./sth. with sth.** 用某物戳某人/某物; **to ~ sb. in the stomach** (hard) 猛戳某人的肚子; **to ~ sb.'s stomach** (gently) 轻杵某人的肚子 [2] fig (remind) 催促; (encourage) 鼓励; **to ~ sb. into doing sth.** 催某人做某事; **to ~ sb. into action** 催某人采取行动; **he needs to be ~ded occasionally** 他需要别人时不时地催一下
B *vi* (*pres p etc.* **-dd-**) 戳; **to ~ at sb./sth.** 戳某人/某物; **the dog ~ded at the kitten with its nose** 狗用鼻子拱小猫
C *n* [1] (poke) 戳; **to give sb./sth. a ~ (with sth.)** (用某物) 戳某人/某物 [2] fig (reminder) 催促; (encouragement) 鼓励; **to give sb. a ~** 催促某人; **she needs a ~** 她需要点鼓励 [3] Agric (instrument) [赶牲畜用的] 刺棒; **an electric cattle ~** 电动驱牛棒

prodigal /ˈprɒdɪgl/ *adj* liter 挥霍的; **the ~ son** 回头的浪子; **to be ~ in the use of sth.** 在使用某物时大手大脚

prodigally /ˈprɒdɪgəli/ *adv* 挥霍浪费地; **we must not use our resources ~** 我们决不能挥霍资源

prodigious /prəˈdɪdʒəs/ *adj* 庞大的 ‹*amount, cost*›; 惊人的 ‹*talent, achievement*›

prodigiously /prəˈdɪdʒəsli/ *adv* 大量地 ‹*eat, increase*›; 惊人地 ‹*successful*›; **a ~ talented performer** 才华横溢的表演者

prodigy /ˈprɒdɪdʒi/ *n* [1] (exceptional person) 奇才; **a child ~** 神童; **a musical ~** 音乐奇才 [2] (wonder) 奇迹; **the prodigies of nature** 大自然的奇迹

produce
A /prəˈdjuːs, Amer -ˈduːs/ *vt* [1] (manufacture, create) 生产 ‹*car, radio*›; 制造 ‹*ship*›; 制作 ‹*work of art, furniture*›; 制定 ‹*timetable*›; 提出 ‹*idea*›; **to ~ sth. from sth.** 用某物做某物; **to ~ a meal** 做出一顿饭 [2] (supply, yield) 出产 ‹*oil, food*›; 产生 ‹*interest, profit*›; 培养 ‹*scientist, artist*›; **these vineyards ~ excellent wines** 这些葡萄园出产美酒; **the investment can be expected to ~ a return of 12%** 这笔投资预期回报率为 12%; **the country that ~d Li Tai-po** 培育出李太白的国度 [3] (generate) 产生 ‹*heat, energy, gas*›; **to ~ electricity from coal** 用煤炭发电; **a Chinese instrument that ~s a beautiful sound** 奏出优美乐声的中国乐器 [4] (create biologically) 生育 ‹*offspring*›; 产生 ‹*secretion*›; 产出 ‹*nectar, pollen*›; **to encourage people to ~ fewer children** 鼓励人们节育; **to ~ leaves/flowers/fruit** «*plant*» 长叶/开花/结果 [5] (cause) 引起 ‹*change, interest*›; 激起 ‹*reaction, anger*›; 产生 ‹*result, effect*› [6] (present, show) 出示 ‹*letter, passport, ticket*›; 掏出 ‹*money, gun*›; 提出 ‹*evidence, argument*›; **to ~ sth. from ...** 从…中掏出某物 ‹*pocket, bag*›; **to ~ sth. from behind one's back** 从背后拿出某物 [7] Cin, Theat 制作 ‹*film, play, programme, record*›; **well-~d** 制作精良的
B /ˈprɒdjuːs, Amer -duːs/ *n* [u] 农产品; **agricultural/garden/farm ~** 农业/园圃/农产品

producer /prəˈdjuːsə(r), Amer -ˈduːs-/ ▸**p. 409** *n* [1] (company, person) 生产商; 供应商 [2] (of film) 制片人; (of programme, play, record) 监制人

producer: ~ gas *n* [u] 发生炉煤气; **~ goods** *npl* 生产资料; **~ price index** *n* 生产者物价指数

-producing /prəˈdjuːsɪŋ, Amer -ˈduːs-/ *combining form* 生产的; **oil~ companies** 产油公司; **the main tea/coffee~ countries** 主要产茶国/主要咖啡生产国

product /ˈprɒdʌkt/ *n* [1] Ind, Comm 产品; **food ~s** 食品; **consumer ~s** 消费品; **the finished ~** 成品; **children who are the ~s of broken homes** fig 破裂家庭的产儿; **the ~ of sb.'s imagination** fig 某人想象力的产物; **the end ~** 最终结果 [2] Math (乘) 积

product: ~ designer ▸**p. 409** *n* 产品设计师; **~ development** *n* [u] 产品研发

production /prəˈdʌkʃn/ *n* [1] [u] Agric, Ind 生产; **steel/wheat ~** 钢铁/小麦生产; **mass ~** 批量生产; **~ costs/processes/level** 生产成本/过程/水平; **to go into/out of ~** 投入生产/停产 [2] [u] (output) 产量; **~ increases** *or* **rises** 产量增长; **~ falls** *or* **drops** 产量下降 [3] [u] Chem, Biol 产生; **a drug to help blood cell ~** 能帮助血细胞生成的药物 [4] [u] (presentation) 出示; **discounts are available on ~ of a valid student card** 出示有效的学生证即可打折 [5] [u] (of film, programme, play, record) 制作 [6] [c] (film, opera) 上演; (programme, show) 播放; **to put on** *or* **stage a ~ of sth.** 上演某剧

production: ~ company *n* 制作公司; **~ line** *n* 生产线; **to come off the ~ line** 从流水线上下来; **~ manager** ▸**p. 409** *n* [1] (in company, industry) 生产部经理; [2] (in TV, film, theatre) 监制

productive /prəˈdʌktɪv/ *adj* [1] Ind, Agric 高产的 ‹*industry, methods, land*› [2] (constructive) 富有成效的 ‹*meeting, collaboration*›; 有收获的 ‹*experience, life*›

productively /prəˈdʌktɪvli/ *adv* 高效地 ‹*work, farm*›; 有效地 ‹*use, invest*›

productivity /ˌprɒdʌkˈtɪvəti/ *n* [u] [1] Ind, Econ 生产率; **to increase ~** 提高生产率; *modif* **~ bonus/agreements** 增产奖金/协议 [2] Agric 丰产

product: ~ liability *n* [u] 产品责任; **~ licence** *n* [尤指药品的] 产品销售许可证; **~ lifecycle** *n* 产品生命周期; **~ manager** ▸**p. 409** *n* 产品经理; **~ placement** *n* [u] [影视中带有广告性质的] 产品安插; **~ range** *n* 产品系列; **~ recall** *n* 产品召回

pro-European
A *adj* 亲欧盟的
B *n* 亲欧盟者

Prof /prɒf/ *abbr* (as title) = **professor**

prof /prɒf/ *n* colloq 教授

pro-family *adj* 家庭第一的; **a conservative, ~ outlook** 家庭观念强的保守态度

profane /prəˈfeɪn, Amer prəʊˈfeɪn/
A *adj* [1] (blasphemous) 渎神的 ‹*behaviour, language*› [2] *attrib* (secular) 世俗的 ‹*world, literature*›
B *vt* 亵渎

profanity /prəˈfænəti, Amer prəʊ-/ *n* [1] [u] (blasphemous language) 亵渎的语言; (irreverent behaviour) 不敬的行为 [2] [c] (oath) 诅咒; **to utter profanities** 说脏话

profess /prəˈfes/ *vt* [1] (claim) 声称 ‹*ignorance, knowledge*›; **I don't ~ to be a lover of poetry** 我不敢自诩是诗歌爱好者 [2] (declare openly) 公开表明 ‹*love, loyalty*›; 显示出 ‹*relief, dismay*›; **she ~ed herself amazed at his ability** 她表示对他的能力感到惊讶 [3] Relig 宣称相信 ‹*faith, belief*›; 信奉 ‹*Christianity, Buddhism*›

professed /prəˈfest/ *adj attrib* 公开表明的 ‹*aim, concern, belief*›; 自称的 ‹*atheist, supporter*›

professedly /prəˈfesɪdlɪ/ *adv* 自称地 ‹*anarchist, Christian*›; 表面上 ‹*happy, optimistic*›

profession /prəˈfeʃn/ *n* [1] (occupation) 职业; **to enter/choose/leave a ~** 从事/选择/放弃一种职业; **a barrister by ~** 职业为大律师; **the oldest ~** 最古老的职业 [指卖淫] [2] + *v sing or pl* (group) 职业界; **the legal/medical/teaching ~** 法律/医学/教学界 [3] formal (declaration) 宣称; **a ~ of belief/loyalty** 信仰/忠诚的表白

professional /prəˈfeʃənl/
A *adj* [1] (not amateur) 职业性的; **~ rugby/tennis** 职业橄榄球/网球; **~ footballers/dancers** 职业足球运动员/专业舞蹈演员; **to seek/take ~ advice** 寻求/接受专业咨询 [2] (relating to one's occupation) 职业上的; **a ~ qualification/duty** 职业资格/职责; **~ practice** 行业惯例; **~ misconduct** 职业不端 [3] (of high standard) 专业的 ‹*approach, letter*›; **he did a very ~ job** 他的工作干得非常专业 [4] colloq (habitual) 习惯性的; **he's a ~ trouble-maker/gossip** 他老爱捣乱/嚼舌根
B *n* [1] (not amateur) 职业选手; **a golf ~** 高尔夫球职业选手 [2] (member of a profession) 业内人士 [3] (competent person) 内行

professional: ~ fee *n* 专业费用; **~ foul** *n* [尤指足球比赛中的] 故意犯规

professionalism /prəˈfeʃənəlɪzəm/ *n* [u] [1] (professional standards) 专业水准 [2] Sport [体育运动的] 职业化; **the trend towards ~** 职业化的趋势

professionally /prəˈfeʃənəli/ *adv* [1] (expertly) 在专业上; **her voice has been ~ trained** 她的嗓子受过专业训练; **~ qualified** 有专业资格的 [2] (in work situation) 在职业上; **~, he's very successful but his private life is a different matter** 他在职场中相当成功, 但他的私生活却是另外一回事 [3] (as paid job) 专职地 ‹*play, perform*›; **he sings/dances ~** 他是职业歌手/专业舞蹈演员 [4] (to high standard) 娴熟地 ‹*work, act*›

professional school *n* Amer 职业学院

professor /prəˈfesə(r)/ *n* Univ [1] (teacher of the highest rank) 教授; **P~ Jones** 琼斯教授; **an associate ~** 副教授; **an assistant ~** esp Amer 助理教授 [2] Amer (teacher) 大学教师

professorial /ˌprɒfəˈsɔːrɪəl/ *adj* [1] Univ 教授的 ‹*post, salary*› [2] (imposing) 教授似的 ‹*manner, appearance*›

professorship /prəˈfesəʃɪp/ *n* Univ [1] (chair) 教授职衔; **to obtain a ~** 获得教授职位; **the ~ of Physics** 物理教授职位 [2] Amer (teaching post) 教师职位

proffer /ˈprɒfə(r)/ *vt* 提出 ‹*advice, resignation*›; 提供 ‹*evidence, assistance*›; 表示 ‹*thanks, apologies*›; 递上 ‹*pen, handkerchief*›; 伸出 ‹*hand, arm*›

proficiency /prəˈfɪʃnsi/ *n* [u] 熟练; **to show** *or* **demonstrate ~ in mathematics** 表现出在数学方面的精通; **to lack ~** 不熟练

proficiency test *n* 水平测试; **a reading ~** 阅读水平测试

proficient /prəˈfɪʃnt/ *adj* 熟练的 ‹*worker*›; 娴熟的 ‹*swimmer, driver*›; **to be ~ at** *or* **in sth.** 在某方面很娴熟

profile /ˈprəʊfaɪl/
A *n* [1] (of face) 侧面; **photographs taken in ~** 侧面相片 [2] (image) 形象; **to maintain** *or* **keep a high/low ~** 保持高/低姿态; **raising the ~ of women in industry** 提升女性在工业界的形象 [3] (outline) 轮廓; (vertical cross-section) 纵断面 [4] Journ, TV (description) 概述 [5] (analysis) 数据图表; **a DNA/psychological ~** DNA 序列图/心理特征图
B *vt* 简要介绍 ‹*writer, organization*›

profiler /ˈprəʊfaɪlə(r)/ *n* ▸**p. 409** 犯罪心理轮廓分析专家

profit /ˈprɒfɪt/
A *n* [1] [u and c] Fin (financial gain) 利润; **gross/net/**

clear ~ 毛利/纯利润/净利润; ~ **and loss** 盈亏; ~ **growth** 利润的增长 **2** [u] fig (benefit) 益处; **to turn sth. to** ~ 从某物中得益
B *vi* 受益; **I have** ~**ed from your advice** 我从你的忠告中受益

profitability /ˌprɒfɪtəˈbɪləti/ *n* [u] 利润率; **a decline in** ~ 利润率的降低; **to increase** ~ 增加收益

profitable /ˈprɒfɪtəbl/ *adj* **1** Fin 获利的 ‹*deal, investment, sale*›; 赢利的 ‹*company, commodity, product*›; **some farmers claim that it is not** ~ **to grow organic crops** 有些农民声称，种植有机农作物无利可图 **2** fig (useful) 富有成效的 ‹*meeting, visit*›; 有益的 ‹*exercise, use*›; **a most** ~ **afternoon** 非常有收获的一个下午

profitably /ˈprɒfɪtəbli/ *adv* **1** Fin 有赢利地 ‹*trade, deal*›; ~ **invested capital** 有利可图的投资 **2** fig (usefully) 有成效地 ‹*use, spend*›

profit: ~ **and loss account** *n* 损益账; ~ **and loss statement** *n* 损益表; ~ **balance** *n* 赢利额; ~ **centre** *n* 利润中心

profiteer /ˌprɒfɪˈtɪə(r)/
A *n* 牟取暴利的人; **a war** ~ 大发战争横财者
B *vi* 牟取暴利

profiteering /ˌprɒfɪˈtɪərɪŋ/ *n* [u] 牟取暴利

profit forecast *n* 利润预测

profitless /ˈprɒfɪtlɪs/ *adj* 无利可图的 ‹*venture*›; 无益的 ‹*visit*›

profit: ~**-making organization** *n* 营利性组织; ~ **margin** *n* 利润幅度; ~ **motive** *n* 获利动机; ~**-sharing** *n* [u] 利润分成; **a** ~**-sharing scheme** 分红制; ~ **squeeze** *n* 利润紧缩; ~**-taking** *n* [u] 获利回吐; ~ **warning** *n* 赢利预警

profligacy /ˈprɒflɪɡəsi/ *n* [u] 肆意挥霍

profligate /ˈprɒflɪɡət/ *adj* 肆意挥霍的; ~ **use of taxpayers' money** 对纳税人金钱的肆意挥霍

pro forma /ˌprəʊ ˈfɔːmə/
A *adj* **1** (standard) 按惯例的 ‹*report*› **2** Fin 预估的 ‹*earnings, profit, figure*›
B *n* 预估单

pro forma: ~ **invoice** *n* 形式发票; ~ **letter** 例行信函

profound /prəˈfaʊnd/ *adj* **1** (great, deep) 巨大的 ‹*change*›; 强烈的 ‹*emotion, interest*›; 极度的 ‹*ignorance*›; **a** ~ **mystery** 难解的奥秘; **a** ~ **silence** 一片沉寂 **2** (wise) 深邃的 ‹*thinker, insight*›; 深奥的 ‹*book, remark*›

profoundly /prəˈfaʊndli/ *adv* **1** (greatly, deeply) 极大地 ‹*affect, change*›; 极度地 ‹*ignorant, shock*›; 深深地 ‹*yawn, blush*›; ~ **deaf** 全聋; **a** ~ **disturbing experience** 极其令人不安的经历; **I am** ~ **grateful for your assistance** 对你的帮助我深为感激 **2** (wisely) 有深度地 ‹*say, look*›

profundity /prəˈfʌndəti/ *n* **1** [u] (depth of knowledge) 高深 **2** [u] (intensity) 深刻; **the** ~ **of the silence** 沉寂; **the** ~ **of the change in him** 他身上的深刻变化 **3** [c] (wise remark) 高深的话 [常用作反语]

profuse /prəˈfjuːs/ *adj* 大量的 ‹*bleeding, flowering, growth*›; ~ **tears** 泪如雨下; ~ **sweating** 汗流浃背; **to be** ~ **in one's thanks/apologies** 千恩万谢/一再道歉

profusely /prəˈfjuːsli/ *adv* 大量地 ‹*bleed, sweat, bloom*›; 再三地 ‹*praise, thank*›; **to apologize** ~ 一再道歉

profusion /prəˈfjuːʒn/ *n* [u] 大量; **a** ~ **of flowers/colours** 繁花似锦/色彩缤纷; **daffodils growing in** ~ 生长茂盛的水仙花

progenitor /prəʊˈdʒenɪtə(r)/ *n* formal **1** (ancestor) 祖先; (parent) 亲本 **2** (originator) 先驱; **the** ~ **of modern jazz/sculpture** 现代爵士乐/雕刻术的创始人

progeny /ˈprɒdʒəni/ *n* [u] + *v sing or pl* **1** (of person, animal) 后代 **2** fig (successors) 后继物

progesterone /prəˈdʒestərəʊn/ *n* [u] 黄体酮

prognosis /prɒɡˈnəʊsɪs/ *n* (*pl* **prognoses** /prɒɡˈnəʊsiːz/) **1** Med 预后 [医生预测的疾病发展情况]; **a good/poor** ~ 预后很好/不良 **2** (prediction) 预测; **the** ~ **for** *or* **on sth.** 对某事的展望

prognostic /prɒɡˈnɒstɪk/ *adj* 预后的 ‹*information, tool, accuracy*›; 前兆的 ‹*error, factor*›; **a** ~ **indicator** 先行指标

prognosticate /prɒɡˈnɒstɪkeɪt/ formal
A *vt* 预测 ‹*disaster, happiness*›
B *vi* 作出预言

prognostication /prɒɡˌnɒstɪˈkeɪʃn/ *n* formal **1** [c] (prophecy) 预言 **2** [u] (action) 预告

program /ˈprəʊɡræm, Amer -ɡrəm/
A *n* **1** Comput 程序; **to install/uninstall a** ~ 安装/卸载程序; **to run a** ~ 运行程序 **2** esp Amer Sch, Univ (course) 课程; **a graduate/undergraduate/training** ~ 研究生/本科生/培训课程 **3** esp Amer = **programme**
B *vt* (*pres p etc.* **-mm-** Brit, **-m-** Amer) Comput 为…编程

programer /ˈprəʊɡrəmə(r)/ ▸**p. 409** *n* Amer = **programmer**

programing /ˈprəʊɡrəmɪŋ/ *n* Amer = **programming**

programmable /prəʊˈɡræməbl/ *adj* 程控的 ‹*device, thermostat, controller*›

programme /ˈprəʊɡræm/ Brit
A *n* **1** (plan) 计划; (schedule) 日程; **to introduce/launch/carry out a** ~ 引进/启动/施行计划 **2** Mus 曲目 **3** Theat, Mus (booklet) 节目单 **4** TV, Radio (slot) 节目; **a request** ~ 点播节目; **a** ~ **director/schedule** 节目导演/时间表 **5** Radio, TV dated (channel) 频道
B *vt* **1** (set) 设定 ‹*system, microwave*›; **the machine is** ~**d to shut down automatically after six hours** 这台机器设定在6小时后自动关闭; **I've got your number** ~**d into my mobile phone** 我把你的号码设在了我的手机里 **2** (schedule) 安排 ‹*meeting, visit*› **3** Biol (predetermine) 命定

programme: ~ **maker** *n* (person) 节目制作人; (company) 节目制作公司; ~ **music** *n* [u] 标题音乐; ~ **note** *n* 节目简介

programmer /ˈprəʊɡræmə(r)/ ▸**p. 409** *n* Brit 编程人员

programming /ˈprəʊɡræmɪŋ/ *n* [u] Brit **1** Comput 编程; **a** ~ **error** *or* **fault** 程序错误 **2** TV, Radio (scheduling) 节目编排 **3** TV, Radio (programmes) 节目

programming language *n* 程序设计语言; **a high-level** ~ 高级编程语言

progress
A /ˈprəʊɡres, Amer ˈprɒɡres/ *n* [u] **1** (in science, economy, knowledge) 进步; (in project, relationship, negotiations) 进展; **to make** ~ **(in one's work/in physics)** (在工作/物理学上) 取得进步; **to make slow/steady** ~ 进展缓慢/稳定; **to make little/no** ~ 几乎没有/毫无进展; **to make** ~ **with sth.** 在…上取得进展 ‹*project*›; ~ **on economic cooperation** 经济合作的进展; **to make** ~ **towards settling the dispute** 在解决争端方面取得进展; **some/a small amount of** ~ 一些/些许进展; **the patient is making** ~ 病人的情况正在好转 **2** (course, evolution) 发展; **to be in** ~ «*meeting, work*» 在进行中; **'examination in** ~**'** "正在考试" **3** (forward movement) 行进; **I watched his** ~ **up the hill** 我看着他上山坡; **to make slow/steady** ~ 缓慢/稳步行进
B /prəˈɡres/ *vi* **1** (develop, improve) «*society*» 发展; «*technology, studies, student*» 进步; «*work, research*» 进展; «*patient*» 好转; **to** ~ **towards** *or* **to sth.** 向某事物发展; **to** ~ **beyond sth.** 超越某事物 **2** (follow course) «*journey*» 持续; «*game, discussion*» 进行; «*day, holiday*» 流逝; **as the novel** ~**es** 随着小说情节的展开 **3** (move forwards) 前行; **cases can take months to** ~ **through the courts** 有些案件要花上好几个月才可以审结
C /prəˈɡres/ *vt* 使…取得进展 ‹*matter, affair*›

progression /prəˈɡreʃn/ *n* **1** [u and c] (development) 发展; (improvement) 进步; **good opportunities for career** ~ 事业发展的好机遇; **a natural/logical** ~ 自然/必然的过渡 **2** [u and c] (forward movement) 前进; **a steady** ~ **towards your goals** 朝着目标的稳步前进 **3** [c] (series) 系列; **an endless** ~ **of meetings** 没完没了的会议; **a long** ~ **of sunny days** 持续很久的晴天 **4** [u and c] Math 级数; **arithmetic/geometric** ~ 算术/几何级数

progressive /prəˈɡresɪv/
A *adj* **1** (gradual) 逐步的 ‹*change, industrialization*›; **a** ~ **illness** 逐渐恶化的疾病; ~ **taxation** 累进税 **2** (radical) 进步的 ‹*idea, policy, period*›; **a** ~ **school/education** 先进的学校/教育 **3** Ling (continuous) 进行的; **the present** ~ **tense** 现在进行时
B *n* (advocate of social reform) 改革派; (person with forward-thinking ideas) 进步人士

progressively /prəˈɡresɪvli/ *adv* 逐渐地; **the questions get** ~ **harder** 问题变得越来越难

progressiveness /prəˈɡresɪvnɪs/ *n* [u] 进步性

progress report *n* (on project, negotiations) 进度报告; (on patient, pupil) 进展报告

prohibit /prəˈhɪbɪt, Amer prəʊ-/ *vt* **1** (forbid) 禁止 ‹*sale, weapon, drug*›; **to** ~ **sb. from doing sth.** 禁止某人做某事; **smoking is** ~**ed** 禁止吸烟 **2** (make impossible) 阻止 ‹*use, involvement, activity*›; **to** ~ **sb. from doing sth.** 阻止某人做某事; **his poor health** ~**s him from playing sports** 他健康状况不佳，无法参加体育运动

prohibition /ˌprəʊhɪˈbɪʃn, Amer ˌprəʊəˈbɪʃn/
A *n* **1** [c] (ban) 禁令; **a** ~ **on the sale of firearms** 武器销售禁令 **2** [u] (forbidding) 禁止; **a** ~ **notice/order** 禁止通知/禁令
B **Prohibition** *pr n* [1920-1933年美国的] 禁酒时期; **a P**~ **era/law** 禁酒时期/法令

prohibitionism /ˌprəʊhɪˈbɪʃənɪzəm, Amer ˌprəʊə-/ *n* [u] 禁酒主义

prohibitionist /ˌprəʊhɪˈbɪʃənɪst, Amer ˌprəʊə-/ *n* 禁酒主义者

prohibitive /prəˈhɪbətɪv, Amer prəʊ-/ *adj* **1** (exorbitant) 令人望而却步的 ‹*cost, price*›; 高昂的 ‹*tax, level*› **2** (proscriptive) 禁止的; ~ **law** 禁令

prohibitively /prəˈhɪbɪtɪvli, Amer prəʊ-/ *adv* 使人望而却步地; **prices are** ~ **high** 价格高得令人却步

project
A /ˈprɒdʒekt/ *n* **1** (enterprise) 项目; (scheme) 方案; (task) 任务; **a** ~ **manager/sponsor** 项目经理/赞助者; **a third world development** ~ 一项第三世界发展规划; **my next** ~ **is to make a bookcase** 我的下一个工作是做一只书橱 **2** Sch, Univ 研究课题 **3** Amer (housing development) [政府出资兴建、租金较低的] 住宅区
B /prəˈdʒekt/ *vt* **1** (throw, send) 投掷 ‹*object*›; 发射 ‹*missile*›; 传送 ‹*voice, sound, oneself, thoughts*› **2** Phys, Cin 放映 ‹*slide, film*›; 投射 ‹*image, light*› **3** (put across) 展现 ‹*organization, view, oneself, image*›; **she** ~**s an aura of mystery** 她显得神秘兮兮的 **4** (forecast) 预测 ‹*growth, shortfall*› **5** Psych 投射 ‹*guilt, fears, fantasy*›; **to** ~ **sth. on to** *or* **upon sb.** 把某事物投射到某人身上
C /prəˈdʒekt/ *vi* (stick out) «*beam, balcony*» 伸出; «*land mass*» 突出; «*nose*» 凸出

projected /prəˈdʒektɪd/ *adj* **1** (planned) 计划中的 ‹*visit, road, improvement*› **2** (predicted) 预计的 ‹*figures, rate, growth*›

projectile /prəˈdʒektaɪl, Amer -tl/ *n* **1** (missile) 导弹 **2** (stone, bottle, coin) [尤指用作武器的] 投掷物

P

P

projecting /prəˈdʒektɪŋ/ *adj attrib* 伸出的; ～ **rocks** 突岩; ～ **teeth** 龅牙

projection /prəˈdʒekʃn/ *n* 1 [c] (part sticking out) 凸出物 2 [u] Cin (presentation) 放映; [c] (image) 放映的影像 3 [u] (of public image) 公众形象 4 [c] (forecast) 预测 5 [u and c] Psych (transfer) 投射; **monsters can be understood as mental ～s of mankind's fears** 怪物可以理解为人类恐惧的心理表征 6 Geog [u] (method) 投影法; [c] (representation) 投影

projectionist /prəˈdʒekʃənɪst/ ▸p. 409 *n* 电影放映员

projection room *n* 放映室

projector /prəˈdʒektə(r)/ *n* (for slides) 幻灯机; (for film) 放映机

prolapse /ˈprəʊlæps/
A *n* 脱垂; **a mitral valve/vaginal/rectal ～** 二尖瓣/阴道/直肠脱垂
B *vi* 脱垂

prole /prəʊl/ *n* colloq pej 无产者

proletarian /ˌprəʊlɪˈteərɪən/
A *adj* 无产阶级的
B *n* 无产者

proletarianize /ˌprəʊlɪˈteərɪənaɪz/ *vt* (reduce to a proletarian level) 使成为无产者; (treat like the working class) 视…为工人阶级

proletariat /ˌprəʊlɪˈteərɪət/ *n* [u] + *v sing or pl* 无产阶级; **the exploited ～** 被剥削的无产阶级

pro-life *adj* (opposing abortion) 反堕胎的; (opposing euthanasia) 反对安乐死的

pro-lifer /ˌprəʊˈlaɪfə(r)/ *n* (opposing abortion) 反堕胎者; (opposing euthanasia) 安乐死反对者

proliferate /prəˈlɪfəreɪt, Amer prəʊ-/ *vi* 激增; **environmental groups have ～d over the past decade** 在过去 10 年间环保团体数量猛增

proliferation /ˌprəlɪfəˈreɪʃn, Amer ˌprəʊ-/ *n* [u] 激增; **a non-～ treaty** 核武器不扩散条约

prolific /prəˈlɪfɪk/ *adj* 1 (productive) 多产的; (high-scoring) 得分多的; **he's been the side's most ～ goalscorer this season** 他是该队在本赛季进球最多的队员 2 (in growth, reproduction) 丰产的 ‹*tree, vine*›; **a ～ raspberry with good flavour** 高产的美味山莓; **the bird life is fabulously ～ here** 这个地区的鸟类异常繁多

prolix /ˈprəʊlɪks, Amer prəʊˈlɪks/ *adj* formal pej 冗长的 ‹*article, speech*›; 烦琐的 ‹*style*›; 啰唆的 ‹*writer, speaker*›

prolixity /prəʊˈlɪksəti/ *n* [u] formal pej 冗长

prologue /ˈprəʊlɒg, Amer -lɔːg/ *n* 1 Literat 序言 2 (to a race, fight, debate) 开端

prolong /prəˈlɒŋ, Amer -ˈlɔːŋ/ *vt* 延长; **drugs that help to ～ life** 有助于延长生命的药物

prolongation /ˌprəʊlɒŋˈgeɪʃn, Amer -lɔːŋ-/ *n* 1 [u] (lengthening) 延长; **the ～ of human life** 人类寿命的延长 2 [c] (addition, extension) 延伸部分

prolonged /prəˈlɒŋd, Amer -ˈlɔːŋd/ *adj* 持久的 ‹*struggle, silence, drought*›; 长期的 ‹*absence*›

prom /prɒm/ *n* 1 Amer colloq (ball) 正式舞会 2 Brit colloq (at seaside) **the ～** 海滨人行道 3 **Prom** Brit Mus (concert) **the P～s** 逍遥音乐会

promenade /ˌprɒməˈnɑːd, Amer -ˈneɪd/
A *n* 1 (walkway) 步行大道 2 dated (leisurely walk) 漫步; (leisurely ride) 乘车兜风; (leisurely drive) 驾车兜风
B *vi* dated 漫步
C *vt* dated (escort) 带着…兜风 ‹*child, dog*›; (walk along) 沿着…漫步 ‹*street*›

promenade: ～ **concert** *npl* Brit 逍遥音乐会 [部分听众持站票的古典音乐会]; ～ **deck** *n* 上层甲板

promethium /prəˈmiːθɪəm/ *n* [u] 钷

prominence /ˈprɒmɪnəns/ *n* [u] 1 (of person, issue) 显赫; **to gain or acquire ～** 获得声望; **a story that is given ～ in today's newspapers** 在今天的报纸上占据显著位置的一篇报道 2 (of feature, building, object) 显眼; (protuberance) 凸起; **the ～ of her cheek-bones** 她颧骨的高凸

prominent /ˈprɒmɪnənt/ *adj* 1 (important) 重要的 ‹*figure, role*›; 著名的 ‹*writer, company*› 2 (conspicuous) 显眼的 ‹*position*›; 显著的 ‹*feature, markings*› 3 (protuberant) 凸出的 ‹*nose, cheekbones*›; ～ **eyes/teeth** 金鱼眼/龅牙

prominently /ˈprɒmɪnəntli/ *adv* 1 (importantly) 重要地; **she figured ～ in the negotiations** 她在谈判中起着举足轻重的作用 2 (conspicuously) 显眼地 ‹*display, place*›

promiscuity /ˌprɒmɪˈskjuːəti/ *n* [u] 淫乱

promiscuous /prəˈmɪskjʊəs/ *adj* 1 (licentious) 淫乱的 ‹*behaviour, lifestyle*›; **a ～ woman** 荡妇 2 (indiscriminate) 不加选择的 ‹*friendship*›; **a ～ array of values** 五花八门的价值观

promiscuously /prəˈmɪskjʊəsli/ *adv* 1 (licentiously) 放荡地 ‹*flirt, behave*› 2 (indiscriminately) 胡乱地 ‹*use, switch*›

promiscuousness /prəˈmɪskjʊəsnɪs/ *n* [u] 淫乱

promise /ˈprɒmɪs/
A *n* 1 [c] (pledge) 承诺; (content of pledge) 诺言; **a ～ to do sth.** 做某事的承诺; **a ～ of marriage/faithfulness** 婚约/效忠的承诺; **to make or give a ～ (to sb.)** (向某人) 作出承诺; **to keep/fulfil/break one's ～** 遵守/履行/违背诺言; **to keep or hold sb. to their ～** 让某人遵守诺言; **under the ～ of secrecy** 许下保密承诺地; **a hollow or empty ～** 空洞的诺言; **is that a ～?** colloq 此话当真?; **it's a ～!** 就这么定了!; **～s, ～s!** 承诺来, 承诺去! [表示对许诺的怀疑或嘲讽] 2 [u and c] (hope, prospect) 希望; **a ～ of sth.** 某事的希望; **there is some/little ～ of better weather ahead** 今后的天气有望/无望好转 3 [u] (likelihood to succeed) 成功前景; **to show (great) ～** 前景 (很) 好; **a young writer of ～** 有前途的青年作家
B *vt* 1 (pledge) 答应 ‹*person*›; 许诺 ‹*present, money, better conditions*›; **to ～ (sb.) that ...** 答应 (某人) …; **to ～ (sb.) to do sth.** 答应 (某人) 做某事; **I ～ you** 我向你保证; **I'll do it tomorrow, I ～!** 我明天做这事, 我保证!; **he has ～d a thorough investigation** 他答应彻底调查; **to ～ sb. sth., to ～ sth. to sb.** 向某人许诺某事; **I can't ～ anything** 我无法作出任何许诺; **to ～ sb. the earth or moon** 向某人开空头支票 2 (predict with confidence) 预报 ‹*weather*›; 断言 ‹*harvest, outcome*›; **the weathermen have ～d us a sunny day tomorrow** 气象员预报明日晴天; **we're ～d more winter weather tonight** 预报说今晚的天气会更寒冷; **it won't be easy, I ～** 不会容易的, 我敢说 3 (give prospect of) 预示; **the clouds ～d rain** 乌云预示有雨; **it ～s to be a fine day/lively party** 看来将是晴天/欢快的聚会
C *v refl* **to ～ oneself that ...** 期望…; **to ～ oneself to do sth.** 期望做某事; **I've ～d myself a new coat this winter** 我想这个冬天为自己弄件新外套
D *vi* 1 (give pledge) 承诺; **will you ～?** 你答应吗?; **but you ～d!** 但是你答应过的!; **I ～/can't ～** 我保证/没法保证 2 (have good prospects) 前景好; **to ～ well** 前景好

Promised Land /ˌprɒmɪst ˈlænd/ *n* **the ～** (ideal state) 妙境; (ideal place) 乐土; **Italy is the ～ for any musician** 意大利是音乐家的乐土

promising /ˈprɒmɪsɪŋ/ *adj* 前景看好的 ‹*candidate, career*›; **a ～ young artist** 很有前途的年轻艺术家; **a ～ sign** 很好的迹象; **the weather looks a bit more ～ today** 今天天气看起来会好一点

promisingly /ˈprɒmɪsɪŋli/ *adv* 有希望地 ‹*start, open*›

promissory note /ˈprɒmɪsəri nəʊt, Amer -sɔːri/ *n* 本票

promo /ˈprəʊməʊ/ *n* colloq 广告短片

promontory /ˈprɒməntri, Amer -tɔːri/ *n* 岬 (角)

promote /prəˈməʊt/ *vt* 1 (in rank) 晋升 ‹*assistant, sergeant*›; 将…晋级 ‹*football team*› 2 (encourage) 促进 ‹*cause, growth, investment*›; **to ～ friendship between nations** 增进国与国之间的友谊; **to ～ awareness of environmental issues** 提高环境问题意识 3 (advertise) 推销 ‹*book, service*›; 宣传 ‹*venture*›; **to ～ new products** 宣传新产品; **to ～ a bill** 促使议案通过

promoter /prəˈməʊtə(r)/ *n* 1 (of sporting event) 筹办人 2 (of product) 促销员 3 (of cause, integration) 倡导者

promotion /prəˈməʊʃn/ *n* 1 [u and c] (in job) 晋升; (in sport) 晋级; **to get or gain a ～** 得到提拔; **to be in line for ～** 有望获得晋升 2 [u] (of cause, integration, equality) 促进; **to work for the ～ of world peace** 为促进世界和平而努力 3 [u and c] Comm (activity) 广告宣传; (campaign) 促销活动 4 [u] (of sporting event) 晋级

promotional /prəˈməʊʃənl/ *adj* 1 Comm 广告宣传的 ‹*material, literature*›; **a ～ tour by the author** 作者的一次巡回宣传 2 (in job) 晋升的; **a job with good ～ prospects** 有良好晋升前景的工作; **to climb the ～ ladder** 力图得到升迁

promotional video *n* 1 (for product) 广告宣传片 2 Mus 音乐宣传片

promotion: ～ **prospects** *npl* 晋升前景; ～**s manager** ▸p. 409 *n* 推销部经理

prompt /prɒmpt/
A *adj* 及时的; **we would appreciate a ～ reply** 如能及时回复, 我们将不胜感激; **we require ～ payment of this account** 我们要求立即付清这笔账
B *adv* Brit 准时地; **at six o'clock ～** 在6点整
C *vt* 1 (cause) 导致 ‹*protest, reaction, remark*›; **to ～ sb. to do sth.** 促使某人做某事; **the strike was ～ed by the sacking of a worker** 罢工是由一名工人被解雇引起的 2 (remind) 给…提词 ‹*actor*› 3 (encourage to talk) 鼓励…说下去 ‹*speaker*›
D *n* 1 提词; **to give sb. a ～** 给某人提词 2 Comput 提示符

prompter /ˈprɒmptə(r)/ *n* Theat 提词员

prompting /ˈprɒmptɪŋ/ *n* [u and c] 敦促; **he needed no ～ from me** 他不用我催

promptly /ˈprɒmptli/ *adv* 1 (without delay) 及时地 ‹*reply, react, pay*› 2 (punctually) 准时地 ‹*start, arrive*› 3 (immediately) 立即

promptness /ˈprɒmptnɪs/ *n* [u] (speed) 迅速; (punctuality) 准时; **thank you for your ～ in replying to my letter** 谢谢你及时回我的信

promulgate /ˈprɒmlgeɪt/ *vt* formal 1 (promote) 宣传 ‹*doctrine, policy*›; **the author ～s his political beliefs in his latest book** 作者在他的新书里宣扬他的政治信仰 2 (proclaim) 颁布 ‹*decree, law*›

promulgation /ˌprɒmlˈgeɪʃn/ *n* [u] formal 1 (of doctrine, policy) 宣扬; **the ～ of new ideas** 新思想的传播 2 (of decree, law) 颁布

prone /prəʊn/
A *adj* 1 (prostrate) 俯卧的; **to lie ～** 俯卧; **he was lying in a ～ position** 他俯卧着 2 *pred* (liable) 容易…的; **to be ～ to sth.** 容易遭受某事; **～ to injury/illness** 易受伤/易患病的; **to be ～ to lose one's temper** 容易发脾气
B **-prone** *combining form* 有…倾向的; **a strike ～ industry** 易发生罢工的产业

prong /prɒŋ, Amer prɔːŋ/ *n* 1 (of fork) 尖齿; (of other instrument) 尖头; (of antler) 鹿角尖 2 fig (of strategy) 方面; (of business) 分支

-pronged /prɒŋd, Amer prɔːŋd/ *combining form* 1 (with prongs) 有叉的; **two/three～** 两叉/三

叉的 **2** fig (sided) …方面的; **a two～ attack** 两路攻击

pronominal /prəʊˈnɒmɪnl/ *adj* 代词的

pronoun /ˈprəʊnaʊn/ *n* 代词; **a personal/relative/possessive** ～ 人称/关系/物主代词

pronounce /prəˈnaʊns/

A *vt* **1** Ling 发…的音 ‹*word, letter*›; **is the 'h' ～d?** 这里的"h"发音吗? **2** (announce) 宣布 ‹*verdict*›; **the judge ～d sentence** 法官宣布了判决 **3** (declare) 宣告 ‹*defendant, victim*›; **to ～ sb. dead/guilty** 宣告某人死亡/有罪; **I now ～ you man and wife** 现在我宣布你们结为夫妻; **he ～d the wine to be excellent** 他宣称该葡萄酒质量上乘

B *vi* Jur «*judge*» 宣判; «*inquiry*» 断定; **to ～ for/against sb./sth.** 对某人/某事物作出有利的/不利的判决; **the court ～d against the accused** 法庭宣判被告败诉; **to ～ on sth.** 对某事物作出评判

pronounceable /prəˈnaʊnsəbl/ *adj* 读得出的

pronounced /prəˈnaʊnst/ *adj* **1** (noticeable) 明显的 ‹*accent, limp*›; 显著的 ‹*features, change*› **2** (strongly felt) 明确的 ‹*views, ideas*›

pronouncement /prəˈnaʊnsmənt/ *n* 声明; **a ～ on sth.** 关于某事物的声明

pronto /ˈprɒntəʊ/ *adv* colloq 立刻; **tell him I want to see him ～!** 告诉他我想立马见他!

pro-nuclear *adj* 提倡使用核电的

pronunciation /prəˌnʌnsɪˈeɪʃn/ *n* **1** [u] (of language, speaker) 发音; ～ **practice** 发音训练; **her German ～ is excellent** 她的德语发音相当棒 **2** [c] (of word) 读法

proof /pruːf/

A *n* **1** [u] (evidence) 证据; **to have ～ (of sth.)** 掌握(某事的)证据; **to have ～ that ...** 有证据证明…; **to take sth. as ～ that ...** 把某物作为…的证据; **to give ～ of sth.** 为…提供证明 ‹*purchase, credit*›; **he gave ～ of great courage** 他证明了自己无畏的勇气; **written** *or* **documentary ～** 书面证据; **absolute** *or* **conclusive** *or* **incontrovertible ～** 确凿的证据; **to be ～ of sb.'s worth/age/existence/intentions** 是某人价值/年龄/存在/意图的证明; **～ of identity** 身份证明; **to be (a) living ～ of sth.** 是某事物的人证; **through lack of ～** 由于缺乏证据; **to produce sth. as ～** 出示某物作证; **this is ～ that ...** 这可以证明…; **there is no ～ that ...** 无法证明… **2** [u] (corroboration) 验证; **～ of your allegation will not be easy** 很难验证你的说法是否真实; **in ～ of sth.** 以证明某事物; **to be capable of ～** 经得住考验; **to put sb./sth. to the ～** 验检某人/某事物; **the ～ of the pudding is in the eating** Prov 布丁好不好,吃后才知道 [意谓空谈不如实践] **3** [c] Math, Philos 证明 **4** [c] Print 校样; **to pass the ～s for press** 同意清样付印; **to be in ～** «*book*» 尚为校样阶段; **to be at the ～ stage** «*book*» 在校对阶段; **a ～ copy** 校对本 **5** [c] Phot 照相毛片 **6** [u] (alcoholic strength) 标准酒精度; **to be 70° or 70% ～** 酒精度为70度

B *adj* **1** (protection) 防护的; **to be ～ against sth.** 抗 ‹*infection*›; 防 ‹*erosion, wind, bullets*›; 耐 ‹*wear*›; **earthquake-～ buildings/structures** 抗震建筑/结构体; **leak-～ batteries** 防漏电池; **toddler-～ toys** 儿童安全玩具 **2** formal (resistant) 能抵抗的; **to be ～ against sth.** 能克制 ‹*ambition, desire*›; 能抵御 ‹*temptation*›

C *vt* **1** (make waterproof, soundproof) 使…防水 ‹*fabric, tent*›; 使…隔音 ‹*room*› **2** Print 校对 ‹*text, copy*›

proof: ～ of delivery *n* [u] 交货证明; **～ of ownership** *n* [u] 所有权证明; **～ of postage** *n* 邮寄凭证; **～ of purchase** *n* 购买凭证

proofread /ˈpruːfriːd/ (*pt, pp* **proofread** /ˈpruːfred/) *vt, vi* 校对

proof: ～reader ▸**p. 409** *n* 校对员; **～reading** *n* [u] 校对; **～ spirit** *n* [u] 标准烈度的酒 [酒精含量英制为57.1%, 美制为50%]

prop[1] /prɒp/

A *n* **1** Constr, Tech (support) 支柱; **a pit ～** 坑柱 **2** fig (supportive person) 支持者; **she was his ～ in times of trouble** 在艰难时期她是他的后盾 **3** Sport (in rugby) 支柱前锋

B *vt* (*pres p etc.* **-pp-**) **1** (support) 撑住 ‹*tunnel, wall*›; **I ～ped his head on a pillow** 我把他的头靠在枕头上; **he took a chair and ～ped the door open with it** 他拿了把椅子把门撑开 **2** (lean) 支起; **he ～ped the ladder against the wall** 他把梯子靠着墙支住

Phrasal verb

• **prop up** *vt* [～ **sth. up**, ～ **up sth.**] **1** lit 撑起 ‹*wall, roof*› **2** fig 扶持 ‹*regime, business*›; **to ～ up the pound** 扶持英镑

prop[2] *n* Theat 道具

prop[3] *n* colloq (aircraft propeller) 螺旋桨

prop. *abbr* = **proprietor**

propaganda /ˌprɒpəˈɡændə/ *n* [u] 宣传鼓动; **people want to hear the truth, not ～** 人们希望知道真相,而不是宣传; **a ～ campaign/machine/tool** 宣传活动/机器/工具

propagandist /ˌprɒpəˈɡændɪst/ *n* 鼓吹者

propagandize /ˌprɒpəˈɡændaɪz/

A *vi* 宣传鼓动

B *vt* **1** (promote) 鼓吹 ‹*view, cause*› **2** (communicate with) 对…鼓吹 ‹*person, group*›

propagate /ˈprɒpəɡeɪt/

A *vt* **1** Hort 繁殖; **trees ～ themselves by seeds** 树木通过种子繁殖; **he ～s plants from seeds and cuttings** 他用种子和插枝培育植物 **2** (spread) 传播 ‹*belief, idea*› **3** Phys 传送 ‹*wave, signal*›

B *vi* 繁殖; **plants will not ～ in extreme conditions** 植物在极端条件下不会繁殖

propagation /ˌprɒpəˈɡeɪʃn/ *n* [u] **1** (of plants) 繁殖 **2** (of ideas, beliefs) 传播 **3** (of waves, signals) 传送

propagator /ˈprɒpəɡeɪtə(r)/ *n* **1** (of theory, view) 宣传者; **a ～ of the faith** 信仰传播者 **2** Hort 繁殖盒

propane /ˈprəʊpeɪn/ *n* [u] 丙烷

propel /prəˈpel/ *vt* (*pres p etc.* **-ll-**) **1** (move forward) «*motor, steam, jet*» 推进 ‹*vehicle, machine, aircraft, ship*›; «*rower, oar*» 划动 ‹*boat*›; **mechanically ～led** 机动的 **2** (push) 推; **he ～led me in the direction of the exit** 他把我推向出口 **3** fig (spur, drive) «*emotion, event*» 驱使; **all his life he had been ～led by ambition and greed** 他的一生被野心与贪婪驱使

propellant /prəˈpelənt/ *n* [u and c] **1** (in aerosol) 喷射剂 **2** (in missile, rocket) 推进剂 **3** (in gun) 发射用火药

propellent /prəˈpelənt/ *adj* 推进的 ‹*gas, charge*›; **a ～ agent** 推进剂

propeller /prəˈpelə(r)/ *n* 螺旋桨

propeller: ～ blade *n* 螺旋桨叶片; **～-head** *n* colloq 计算机迷

propelling pencil *n* 活动铅笔

propensity /prəˈpensəti/ *n* 习性; **to have a ～ for** *or* **to** *or* **towards sth.** 生性喜好某事物; **to have a ～ to do** *or* **for doing sth.** 有做某事的习性; **a ～ for violence** 暴力倾向

proper /ˈprɒpə(r)/

A *adj* **1** (appropriate) 合适的 ‹*clothes, tool, person*›; 适当的 ‹*respect, choice, response*›; **he lived in a manner ～ to his rank** 他以适合自己身份的方式生活; **to do as one thinks ～** 做自己认为合适的事情; **at the ～ time** *or* **moment** 在适当的时候; **it is only ～ for sb. to do sth.** 某人只能做某事; **right and ～** 天经地义的 **2** *attrib* (correct) 正确的 ‹*time, order*›; **the ～ way to do sth.** 做某事的正确方式; **the ～ sense** *or* **meaning of the word** 这个词的正确意义 **3** (respectably correct) 得体的 ‹*behaviour*›; 体面的 ‹*person, life*›; **to be ～ in one's behaviour** 举止得体; **to do the ～ thing (by sb.)** (对某人)行为得当 **4** (adequate) 足够的 ‹*education, facilities*›; **lack of ～ funding** 资金的缺乏 **5** *attrib* esp Brit colloq (real) 像样的 ‹*job, holiday, food*›; 真正意义上的 ‹*doctor*› **6** (actual) 真正的; (itself) 自身的; **the competition ～** 正式比赛; **outside Shanghai ～** 上海市区以外的; **the town/meal ～** 本城/正餐 **7** *attrib* colloq (complete) 完全的 ‹*mess, disaster*›; 十足的 ‹*fool, idiot*›; **a ～ charlie!** Brit 十足的呆瓜!; **to give sb. a ～ hiding** 狠揍某人一顿; **to make** *or* **do a ～ job of sth.** 把某事做彻底 **8** *pred* (particular) 独具的; **to be ～ to sb./sth.** «*quality, type*» 为某人/某事物所特有

B *adv* Brit colloq or dial **1** (correctly) 得体地 ‹*talk, behave, dress*›; 清楚地 ‹*see*› **2** (thoroughly) 彻底地; **the weather's ～ cruel!** 这鬼天气真让人受不了!; **good and ～** 彻底地

proper fraction *n* 真分数

properly /ˈprɒpəli/ *adv* **1** (correctly) 正确地 ‹*do, use*›; **～ speaking** 确切地说; **to act ～** 行为恰当 **2** (adequately) 充足地 ‹*eat, rest*›; 适当地 ‹*organized, funded*› **3** (suitably) 得体地 ‹*dress, behave*› **4** esp Brit colloq (thoroughly) 完全; **I'm feeling ～ fed up!** 我快烦死了!

proper name, proper noun *ns* 专有名词

propertied /ˈprɒpətɪd/ *adj* 有财产的; **a member of the ～ classes** 有产阶级一员

property /ˈprɒpəti/ *n* **1** [u] (possessions) 财产; **personal/public ～** 私人/公共财产; **to be public** *or* **common ～ that ...** 众所周知… **2** [u] (land and buildings) 房屋及院落; (real estate) 房地产; **a ～ manager/speculator** 房产经理/投机者; **to have ～ abroad** 在国外拥有房产; **to invest in ～** 投资房地产; **the farmer ordered the campers off his ～** 那位农场主命令野营者离开他的地盘 **3** [c] (house) 住宅; **private ～! keep out!** 私人住宅! 勿入!; **many people now own their own properties** 很多人现在都拥有自己的住宅 **4** [u and c] Jur (thing owned) 所有物; (ownership) 所有权; **literary/intellectual ～** 著作权/知识产权 **5** (quality) 特性; **a herb with medicinal properties** 药用植物

property: ～ dealer ▸**p. 409** *n* 房地产商; **～ developer** ▸**p. 409** *n* 房地产开发商; **～ insurance** *n* [u] 财产保险; **～ market** *n* 房产市场; **～ owner** *n* 财产所有人; **～ sales** *npl* 房产销售; **～ speculation** *n* [u] 房产投机; **～ tax** *n* [c and u] 财产税

prophecy /ˈprɒfəsi/ *n* **1** [u] (faculty) 预言能力; **the gift/power of ～** 预言天赋/能力 **2** [c] (prediction) 预言; **a ～ of sth.** 对某事物的预言

prophesy /ˈprɒfəsaɪ/ *vt, vi* 预言

prophet /ˈprɒfɪt/ *n* **1** (soothsayer) 预言者; **a weather ～** 预测天气者; **a ～ of doom** 预言毁灭的人 **2** Relig 先知; **the Old Testament ～, Jeremiah** 《圣经·旧约》中的先知耶利米 **3** **Prophet** Relig **the P～** 穆罕默德 [伊斯兰教的创始人] **4** (visionary) 有远见的人; **～s of socialism** 社会主义先驱

prophetic /prəˈfetɪk/, **prophetical** /prəˈfetɪkl/ *adj* **1** (of a prophet) 预言家的; (prophet-like) 像预言家的 **2** (prescient) 有预见的 ‹*remarks, book*›; **to be ～ of sth.** 是某事的预兆

prophetically /prəˈfetɪkli/ *adv* 预言性地 ‹*speak, state*›; 有预见地 ‹*warn, write*›

prophylactic /ˌprɒfɪˈlæktɪk/

A *adj* 预防的 ‹*measure*›

B *n* **1** (treatment) 预防性药物; (measure) 预防性措施 **2** esp Amer (condom) 避孕套

propitiate /prəˈpɪʃɪeɪt/ *vt* formal 使息怒; **they offered sacrifices to ～ the gods** 他们供奉祭品以求神灵息怒

propitiation /prəˌpɪʃɪˈeɪʃn/ *n* [u] formal 抚慰

propitious /prəˈpɪʃəs/ *adj* formal 吉利的 ‹*circumstances, conditions*›; **a particularly ~ time** 极佳的时机

propitiously /prəˈpɪʃəsli/ *adv* formal 吉利地 ‹*start*›; 有利地 ‹*phrased, worded*›

prop jet *n* colloq (aircraft) 涡轮螺旋桨式飞机; (engine) 涡轮螺旋桨发动机

proponent /prəˈpəʊnənt/ *n* 倡导者; **a ~ of sth.** 某事的倡导者

proportion /prəˈpɔːʃn/
A *n* **1** [c] (part, fraction) 部分; **a ~ of sth.** 某事物的一部分; **a large/small/certain (of ...)** (…的) 大部分/小部分/某一部分; **in equal ~s** 以相同的量 **2** [u] (ratio) 比例; **the ~ of sth. to sth.** 某物对某物的比例; **the ~ of men to women** 男女比例; **by a high ~** 高比例地; **to be rewarded in due ~** 得到相应的奖励; **in (direct/inverse) ~ to sth.** 与某物成 (正/反) 比例地 ‹*increase, decrease*›; **to be in/out of ~ to sth.** 与某物成/不成比例 **3** [c and u] (harmony, symmetry) 均衡; **the classical ~s of the Parthenon** 帕台农神庙的经典比例; **to lack ~** 比例失调; **in/out of ~** 比例协调/失调地; **to be out of ~ (with sth.)** (与某物) 比例失调 **4** [u] fig (perspective) 分寸感; **to have a sense of ~** 有分寸感; **to be in/out of ~** 有/无分寸感; **to get** *or* **blow sth. out of (all) ~** (很) 偏颇地看待某事物 **5** [u] Math 等比关系; **in ~** 成等比的
B **proportions** *npl* 规模; **of huge ~s** 巨大的; **a lady of generous** *or* **ample ~s** 体态丰腴的女士; **a building of magnificent ~s** 恢宏的建筑; **a problem of manageable ~s** 可掌控的问题
C *vt* 使…成比例 ‹*model*›; **well/badly ~ed** 比例匀称的/失调的

proportional /prəˈpɔːʃənl/ *adj* 成比例的; **to be ~ to sth.** 与某物成比例

proportionally /prəˈpɔːʃənəli/ *adv* 相应地; **if your income grows, then the tax you have to pay will increase ~** 如果你的收入上升, 那么你要支付的税也会相应增加

proportional representation *n* [u] 比例代表制

proportionate /prəˈpɔːʃənət/ *adj* 相称的; **price increases and costs are ~** 价格上升与成本增加是成比例的

proportionately /prəˈpɔːʃənətli/ *adv* 相应地

proposal /prəˈpəʊzl/ *n* **1** (action of proposing) 提议 **2** (suggestion) 建议; **to make** *or* **put forward a ~** 提出建议 **3** (of marriage) 求婚; **to accept a/sb.'s ~ (of marriage)** 接受求婚/某人的求婚

propose /prəˈpəʊz/
A *vt* **1** (suggest) 提出 ‹*plan, measure*›; **to ~ that ...** 提议…; **to ~ doing sth.** 提议做某事; **I ~ an early start tomorrow** 我建议明天早点出发; **to ~ a toast (to sb.)** 提议 (为某人) 干杯 **2** (intend) 打算; **to ~ to do sth.** 打算做某事 **3** (offer) 求; **to ~ marriage to sb.** 向某人求婚 **4** (nominate) 提名; **to ~ sb. for sth.** 提名某人做某事; **I was ~d as a candidate for the presidency** 我被提名为主席候选人
B *vi* 求婚

proposer /prəˈpəʊzə(r)/ *n* (of motion) 提议人; (for membership) 推荐人

proposition /ˌprɒpəˈzɪʃn/
A *n* **1** (assertion) 主张 **2** (plan, scheme) 计划; (business proposal) 生意; (suggestion) 提议; **an attractive ~** 有吸引力的建议; **to make sb. a ~** 向某人提出建议; **an economic** *or* **a paying ~** 赚钱的生意 **3** (undertaking) 任务; **running a marathon is a serious ~** 跑马拉松可不是闹着玩的; **he's a tough** *or* **difficult ~** 他是个难对付的家伙 **4** Math, Philos 命题
B *vt* 向…求欢

propound /prəˈpaʊnd/ *vt* 提出…供考虑 ‹*theory, doctrine, argument*›

proprietary /prəˈpraɪətri, Amer -teri/ *adj* **1** Comm 专卖的 ‹*software, detergent*›; 专利的 ‹*technology, information*› **2** (proprietorial) 所有者的; **~ rights** 所有权; **a ~ air** 一副主人的架势

proprietary: ~ brand *n* 专利品牌; **~ medicine** *n* 专卖药品; **~ name, ~ term** *ns* 专利商标名

proprietor /prəˈpraɪətə(r)/ *n* 所有者

proprietorial /prəˌpraɪəˈtɔːrɪəl/ *adj* formal **1** (relating to ownership) 所有者的; **~ rights** 所有权 **2** (possessive) 主人似的; **a ~ attitude** 一副主人的样子

proprietorship /prəˈpraɪətəʃɪp/ *n* [u] 所有权

proprietress /prəˈpraɪətrɪs/ *n* 女所有人

propriety /prəˈpraɪəti/
A *n* [u] **1** (politeness) 得体的举止; **to offend ~** 有失体面 **2** (correctness) 得体; **the ~ of one's dress** 衣着的得体
B **proprieties** *npl* 行为规范; **to observe the proprieties** 恪守规范

props: ~ master ▸p. 409 *n* 男道具管理员; **~ mistress** ▸p. 409 *n* 女道具管理员

propulsion /prəˈpʌlʃn/ *n* [u] 推进; **jet/rocket ~** 喷气/火箭推进; **~ unit** 推进器

propulsive /prəˈpʌlsɪv/ *adj* 推进的; **~ power** 推力

pro rata /ˌprəʊ ˈrɑːtə/
A *adj* 成比例的; **~ increases in prices** 价格的相应增加
B *adv* 成比例地; **to be paid ~** 按比例获得报酬

prorate /ˌprəʊˈreɪt/ *vt* esp Amer 按比例分配

prosaic /prəˈzeɪɪk/ *adj* **1** (prose-like) 散文的 ‹*style*› **2** (lacking originality) 无新意的 ‹*metaphor, decor, description*›; 平庸的 ‹*writer*› **3** (dull) 平淡的 ‹*existence*›

prosaically /prəˈzeɪɪkli/ *adv* 乏味地

proscenium /prəˈsiːnɪəm/ *n* (*pl* **~s** *or* **proscenia** /prəˈsiːnɪə/) 台口; **~ lighting** 台口照明

proscenium arch *n* 台口拱形框架

proscribe /prəˈskraɪb, Amer prəʊ-/ *vt* 严禁

proscription /prəˈskrɪpʃn, Amer prəʊ-/ *n* [u and c] 禁止

prose /prəʊz/ *n* **1** [u] (not verse) 散文 **2** [c] Sch, Univ (passage for translation) 外语翻译练习; **a French ~** 法语翻译练习

prosecute /ˈprɒsɪkjuːt/ *vt* **1** Jur 起诉; **to ~ sb. for sth./doing sth.** 起诉某人犯某罪; **to be ~d for speeding** 被控超速驾驶; **trespassers will be ~d** 闲人莫入, 违者必究 **2** formal (pursue) 继续进行 ‹*war, inquiry, studies*›

prosecuting: ~ attorney *n* Amer (lawyer) 控方律师; (public official) 检察官; **~ counsel, ~ lawyer** *ns* Jur 控方律师

prosecution /ˌprɒsɪˈkjuːʃn/ *n* **1** [u] Jur (bringing of case) 起诉; **liable to ~** 可能被起诉的; **to face/escape ~** 面临/免于起诉; **criminal ~** 刑事起诉; **the Crown P~ Service** Brit 皇家检控署 **2** [c] Jur (court case) 诉讼; **a private ~** 民事诉讼 **3** [u] + *v sing or pl* Jur (prosecution team) 控方; **a ~ witness, a witness for the ~** 控方证人 **4** [u] formal (carrying out) 从事; **he met a great deal of resistance in the ~ of his duties** 他在执行任务时遇到了很多阻力

prosecutor /ˈprɒsɪkjuːtə(r)/ *n* 公诉人

proselytize /ˈprɒsəlɪtaɪz/
A *vi* 宣教
B *vt* 使…归附 ‹*person*›; 主张 ‹*view*›

prose: ~ poem *n* 散文诗; **~ writer** *n* 散文作家

prosodic /prəˈsɒdɪk/ *adj* **1** Literat 诗体学的 **2** Ling 韵律结构的

prosody /ˈprɒsədi/ *n* [u] **1** Literat 韵律 **2** Ling 韵律结构

prospect
A /ˈprɒspekt/ *n* **1** [c and u] (hope, expectation) 希望; **the ~ of sth./doing sth.** 某事/做某事的希望; **there is some/little/no ~ of improvement** 有望/几乎无望/无望改进; **events in ~** 可望发生的事; **to hold out the ~ of sth.** 带来某事的希望; **there is some ~ that ...** 有希望会…; **there is every ~ of sth./doing sth.** 某事物/做某事极有希望; **there is no ~ of the strike ending soon/of him succeeding** 罢工无望很快停止/他无望成功 **2** [c] (view) 景色; **to afford a fine ~** ‹*mountain, building*› 视野开阔 **3** [c] (mental picture) 前景; **a bleak** *or* **gloomy ~** 惨淡的前景; **to view the ~ of an election with enthusiasm** 热切地展望选举的前景 **4** [c] (good option) 有望获胜者; **a ~ for sth.** 某事的上佳人选; **a fine** *or* **good ~** 很好的人选 **5** [c] Comm (possible customer) 潜在客户; **an easy/a good ~** 容易劝动的买主/大买主
B **prospects** *npl* (chance of success) 成功机会; **the ~s for sth.** …的前景 ‹*growth, economy*›; **he has good ~s of promotion** *or* **of being promoted** 他晋升的机会很大; **market ~s** 市场前景; **to have no ~s** ‹*person*› 没前途; **future/career ~s** 前景/事业前程; **an industry with good ~s** 前景看好的产业
C /prəˈspekt, Amer ˈprɒspekt/ *vi* 勘探; **to ~ for sth.** 勘探 ‹*gold, diamonds, oil*›; **to ~ for customers** 挖掘客户
D /prəˈspekt, Amer ˈprɒspekt/ *vt* 勘探 ‹*region*›; **to ~ the area for oil** 在这个地区勘探石油

prospecting /prəˈspektɪŋ, ˈprɒspektɪŋ/ *n* [u] 勘探; **gold/oil ~** 黄金/石油勘探

prospective /prəˈspektɪv/ *adj* 预期的 ‹*yield*›; **a ~ buyer/client** 可能的买主/潜在的客户; **she introduced him as her ~ son-in-law** 她把他作为准女婿来介绍

prospector /prəˈspektə(r), ˈprɒspektər/ *n* 勘探者

prospectus /prəˈspektəs/ *n* (*pl* **~es**) 简介

prosper /ˈprɒspə(r)/ *vi* ‹*person*› 富有; ‹*business*› 兴隆; ‹*economy, country*› 繁荣

prosperity /prɒˈsperəti/ *n* [u] 繁荣; **a time of peace and ~** 和平与繁荣的年代

prosperous /ˈprɒspərəs/ *adj* 富有的 ‹*person, businessman*›; 繁荣的 ‹*town, country*›; 兴旺的 ‹*business, farm*›

prosperously /ˈprɒspərəsli/ *adv* 兴旺地 ‹*develop*›; **to live ~** 过富裕的生活

prostate /ˈprɒsteɪt/ *n* 前列腺

prostate cancer *n* [u] 前列腺癌

prosthesis /prɒsˈθiːsɪs/ *n* (*pl* **prostheses** /prɒsˈθiːsiːz/) 假体; **a dental ~** 假牙; **a retinal ~** 人工视网膜; **a neural ~** 神经假体

prosthetic /prɒsˈθetɪk/ *adj* 假体的; **~ limbs** 假肢

prostitute /ˈprɒstɪtjuːt, Amer -tuːt/
A *n* 娼妓; **a male ~** 男妓
B *v refl* **to ~ oneself** lit 卖淫; fig 滥用才能; **she ~d herself in order to support her children** 她为了养活孩子而出卖肉体
C *vt* 滥用; **to ~ one's talent(s)** 滥用才华

prostitution /ˌprɒstɪˈtjuːʃn, Amer -tuː-/ *n* [u] **1** lit 卖淫; **to be forced into ~** 被迫卖淫 **2** fig (unworthy use) 糟蹋

prostrate
A /ˈprɒstreɪt/ *adj* **1** (face down) 俯卧的; **he was found ~ on the floor** 他被发现脸朝下倒在地板上 **2** (incapacitated) 垮掉的; **the illness left her ~ for several weeks** 这场病让她身体垮了好几个星期; **the country was ~ after years of war** 多年战争后, 这个国家一蹶不振
B /prɒˈstreɪt/ *v refl* **to ~ oneself** 拜倒在地
C /prɒˈstreɪt, Amer ˈprɒstreɪt/ *vt* (incapacitate) ‹*illness*› 使虚弱; ‹*exhaustion, heat*› 使精疲力竭; ‹*news*› 使束手无策; **the runners were**

~d by heat and exhaustion 赛跑者因炎热和疲惫而倒下; **the poor woman was ~d by grief** 那个可怜的女人悲痛欲绝

prostration /prɒˈstreɪʃn/ *n* [u] **1** (in submission, worship) 拜倒 **2** (from illness, overwork) 衰竭

prosy /ˈprəʊzi/ *adj* pej 乏味的

protactinium /ˌprəʊtækˈtɪniəm/ *n* [u] 镤

protagonist /prəˈtægənɪst/ *n* **1** (main character) 主人公 **2** (of a movement, cause) 倡导者; (in a situation, battle, strike) 领导人物; **a leading ~ of the Green Movement** 绿色运动的急先锋

protean /ˈprəʊtiən, -ˈtiːən/ *adj* formal 变化多端的

protect /prəˈtekt/ *vt* **1** (keep safe) 保护 ‹*property, data, habitat, interests*›; 保卫 ‹*country*›; **a bodyguard ~s the minister at all times** 一个保镖时刻护卫着部长 **2** Econ 对…实行保护 ‹*investment, economy*›; **legislation designed to ~ the industry against unfair competition** 旨在保护行业发展、打击不正当竞争的立法

protection /prəˈtekʃn/ *n* [u] **1** (defence, shelter, safety) 保护; **~ against** *or* **from sb./sth.** 对某人/某事物的抵御; **tall trees which provided ~ against the midday sun** 抵御正午烈日的大树; **to afford** *or* **offer** *or* **give (some degree of) ~** 提供(某种程度上的)保护 **2** (safeguard) 防护物; **head/eye ~** 安全帽/护目镜; **to take vitamin C tablets as a ~ against the common cold** 吃维生素C片以防感冒 **3** Econ 贸易保护制度; **trade ~** 贸易保护 **4** (extortion) 保护费

protection factor *n* 日光防护指数

protectionism /prəˈtekʃənɪzəm/ *n* [u] 贸易保护主义

protectionist /prəˈtekʃənɪst/

A *adj* 贸易保护主义的

B *n* 贸易保护主义者

protection: ~ money *n* [u] 保护费; **~ racket** *n* 勒索保护费

protective /prəˈtektɪv/

A *adj* **1** (providing security) 防护性的 ‹*layer, circuit*›; **~ clothing/headgear** 防护服/安全帽 **2** (caring) 关切保护的 ‹*gesture, manner*›; **he was very ~ of his young wife** 他对他年轻的妻子呵护有加 **3** Econ 贸易保护的; **~ tariff** 保护性关税

B *n* **1** Brit (thing that protects) 防护物 **2** dated (condom) 安全套

protective: ~ colouration, ~ colouring *ns* [u] 保护色; **~ custody** *n* [u] 保护性监禁

protectively /prəˈtektɪvli/ *adv* 防护性地

protectiveness /prəˈtektɪvnɪs/ *n* [u] 保护欲

protector /prəˈtektə(r)/ *n* **1** (defender) 保护者 **2** (item of clothing) 保护装置; **arm/ear ~** 护臂/护耳

protectorate /prəˈtektərət/ *n* 受保护国

protégé /ˈprɒtɪʒeɪ/ *n* 门生

protégée /ˈprɒtɪʒeɪ/ *n* 女门生

protein /ˈprəʊtiːn/ *n* [u and c] 蛋白质; **to be high/low in ~** 蛋白质含量高/低; **the ~ content of eggs** 鸡蛋的蛋白质含量

protein deficiency *n* [c and u] 蛋白质缺乏

pro tem /ˌprəʊ ˈtem/

A *adj* 临时的 ‹*arrangement*›; **a ~ committee** 临时委员会

B *adv* 暂时

Proterozoic /ˌprəʊtərəˈzəʊɪk/

A *adj* (of the period) 原生代的; (of the rock system) 原生界的

B *n* **the ~** (period) 原生代; (rock system) 原生界

protest

A /ˈprəʊtest/ *n* **1** [c] (oral complaint) 抗议; (written complaint) 抗议书; **as a ~ about** *or* **at** *or* **against sth.** 作为对某事物的抗议; **to enter** *or* **lodge** *or* **make** *or* **register a ~** 提出抗议; **a letter of ~** 抗议信; **under/without ~** 不情愿地/情愿地 **2** [c] (demonstration) 抗议游行; **a ~ against** *or* **over sb./sth.** 反对某人/某事物的游行; **to stage a ~** 组织游行抗议 **3** [u] (disapproval) 反对; **to do sth. as a token of ~** 做某事以示抗议; **mass demonstrations in ~ at** *or* **over living standards** 因对生活水准不满而进行的大规模抗议游行; **a ~ movement/demonstration** 抗议运动/游行 **4** [c] Jur 拒付证书

B /prəˈtest/ *vi* **1** (complain) 抱怨; **to ~ about** *or* **at sb./sth.** 对某人/某事物表示不满; **to ~ to sb./sth.** 向某人/某机构表示不满; **to ~ too much** 过度抱怨, 适得其反 **2** (demonstrate) 抗议游行; **the demonstrators were ~ing against rising food prices** 示威者在游行抗议食品涨价

C /prəˈtest/ *vt* **1** (complain) 提出异议说; **to ~ that ...** 抱怨说…; **'that's unfair!' they ~ed** "那不公平!"他们抱怨道 **2** Amer (complain about) 对…表示不满 ‹*decision, injustice*›; (demonstrate against) 游行抗议 ‹*policy, decision*› **3** (declare) 声明; **he ~ed the truth** *or* **veracity of what he had stated** formal 他坚持自己说的是真话; **to ~ one's innocence** 坚持说自己是无辜的 **4** Jur, Fin 书面声明拒付 ‹*bill*›

Protestant /ˈprɒtɪstənt/

A *n* 新教教徒

B *adj* 新教的

> **Protestant**
>
> 新教教徒。基督教有三大派别: 天主教、东正教和新教。16 世纪, 许多宗派从罗马天主教分离出来, 不再属于天主教, 统称新教, 中国亦常称之为基督教, 是为狭义的基督教。安立甘宗(Anglican Communion, 即英国国教会, ▸**the Church of England**)、循道宗(Methodist Church)等都属于新教。和天主教相比, 新教否定教皇的绝对权威, 更强调布道(preaching)和《圣经》的权威性, 礼仪上也更为简单。英国和美国的大多数基督徒都是新教徒。

Protestantism /ˈprɒtɪstəntɪzəm/ *n* [u] 新教教义

protestation /ˌprɒtɪˈsteɪʃn/ *n* [c and u] **1** (declaration) 严正声明 **2** (protest) 抗议; **voices in ~** 抗议的呼声

protester /prəˈtestə(r)/ *n* 抗议者

protocol /ˈprəʊtəkɒl, Amer -kɔːl/ *n* **1** [u] (official etiquette) 礼仪; **a breach of ~** 违反外交礼节 **2** [c] Pol (draft) 条约草案; (amendment) 条约修订案 **3** [c] Comput [数据传递的] 协议

proton /ˈprəʊtɒn/ *n* 质子

protoplasm /ˈprəʊtəplæzəm/ *n* [u] 原生质

prototype /ˈprəʊtətaɪp/ *n* (original example) 原型; (first model) 样品; **a ~ of the weapon** 武器样品; **a ~ aircraft/car** 样机/样车

prototype system *n* 原型系统

prototyping /ˈprəʊtəʊtaɪpɪŋ/ *n* [u] 原型设计制作

protozoon /ˌprəʊtəˈzəʊɒn/ *n* (*pl* **protozoa** /ˌprəʊtəˈzəʊə/) 原生动物

protract /prəˈtrækt, Amer prəʊ-/ *vt* 拖延

protracted /prəˈtræktɪd, Amer prəʊ-/ *adj* 拖延的; **a ~ legal battle** 旷日持久的官司

protraction /prəˈtrækʃn, Amer prəʊ-/ *n* [u] **1** (prolongation) 拖延 **2** (extension) 伸展; **the ~ and retraction of the wings** 翅膀的伸展与收缩

protractor /prəˈtræktə(r), Amer prəʊ-/ *n* 量角器

protrude /prəˈtruːd, Amer prəʊ-/ *vi* «*rock, nail*» 突出; «*ears*» 伸出; «*eyes, teeth*» 凸出

protruding /prəˈtruːdɪŋ, Amer prəʊ-/ *adj* 突出的 ‹*rock, spike*›; 伸出的 ‹*ears, jaw*›; **~ teeth/eyes** 龅牙/金鱼眼; **a ~ stomach** 隆起的腹部; **a young man with a ~ chin** 下巴上翘的小伙子

protrusion /prəˈtruːʒn, Amer prəʊ-/ *n* **1** [u] (sticking out) 突出; **the slight ~ of her eyeballs signals a thyroid problem** 她眼珠微凸, 表明她患有甲状腺疾病 **2** [c] (bulge, projection) 突出物; **rocky ~s on a cliff-face** 悬崖表面突起的岩石

protuberance /prəˈtjuːbərəns, Amer prəʊˈtuː-/ *n* **1** [u] (sticking out) 隆起; **the ~ of his stomach** 他的啤酒肚 **2** [c] (bulge) 隆起物; **the diseased trees are marked by ~s on their bark** 树皮上的结节表明这些树木有病

protuberant /prəˈtjuːbərənt, Amer prəʊˈtuː-/ *adj* 凸出的 ‹*eye, teeth*›; 翘起的 ‹*nose*›; 隆起的 ‹*stomach*›

proud /praʊd/ *adj* **1** (satisfied) 自豪的 ‹*parent, owner, winner*›; **to be ~ of sb./sth.** 为某人/某事物感到骄傲; **I hope you're ~ of yourself!** iron 这下你可光彩了!; **as ~ as a peacock** 非常高傲; **to do sb. ~** Brit colloq (give pride) 替某人增光; (treat well) 盛情款待某人 **2** (self-respecting) 有自尊的 ‹*nation, family*›; **I'm not ~!** 我没架子! **3** *attrib* (valued) 值得骄傲的 ‹*possession*›; (splendid) 辉煌的 ‹*ship*›; **a ~ moment/day (for sb.)** (某人)荣耀的时刻/日子 **4** pej (self-important) 傲慢的; **he's become too ~ to be seen with his old friends** 他变得非常自负, 不愿被人看到和他的老朋友在一起 **5** *pred* Brit (protruding) **to be ~** «*nail, patch*» 突出的; **to be** *or* **stand ~ of sth.** 突出在某物外面

proudly /ˈpraʊdli/ *adv* 自豪地 ‹*display, say*›; 壮观地 ‹*sail, fly*›

Prov. *abbr* Can = **province A1**

provable /ˈpruːvəbl/ *adj* 可证明的 ‹*theory*›; 可证实的 ‹*accusation, case*›

prove /pruːv/ (*pt* **~d,** *pp* **~d** *or* **proven** /ˈprəʊvn/)

A *vt* **1** (show, demonstrate) 证明; **evidence that ~d the innocence of the accused** 证明被告无罪的证据; **it remains to be ~d** 这尚待证实; **events ~d him right/wrong** 后来发生的事证明他是对的/错的 **2** Jur 认证 ‹*will*›

B *vi* **1** (turn out) 证明是; **his prediction ~d (to be) accurate** 他的预测后来证明是准确的; **upon examination his leg ~d to be broken** 检查后发现他的腿折了; **it ~d otherwise** 结果不是那么回事 **2** Culin «*dough*» 发酵

C *v refl* **to ~ oneself** 展示自己; **the new system has already ~d itself** 新系统的价值已经体现

proven /ˈpruːvn/ *adj* 被证实的 ‹*fact, method*›; **not ~** Scot Jur 证据不足

provenance /ˈprɒvənəns/ *n* [u] (origin) 起源; (history) 由来; **the ~ of a word** 词的来源; **antique furniture of doubtful ~** 真伪不明的古董家具

proverb /ˈprɒvɜːb/ *n* 谚语

proverbial /prəˈvɜːbiəl/ *adj* **1** (as in proverb) 谚语的 ‹*wisdom, expression*›; **a ~ saying** 一句谚语; **he's got me over the ~ barrel** colloq 如俗话所说, 他对我可以想怎么着就怎么着 **2** (widely-known) 众所周知的 ‹*generosity, meanness*›; **his bravery was ~** 他的勇敢人人皆知

proverbially /prəˈvɜːbiəli/ *adv* 众所周知地

provide /prəˈvaɪd/

A *vt* **1** (supply, offer) 提供; **to ~ sb. with sth.** 为某人提供某物; **to ~ sth. for** *or* **to sb./sth.** 提供某物给某人/某物; **to ~ (sb. with) the ammunition to do sth.** fig (为某人)提供做某事的论据; **to ~ an answer** 给出答案; **curtains ~ privacy** 窗帘可以保护隐私; **to ~ an incentive for sb. to do sth.** 刺激某人做某事; **to ~ the perfect introduction to ...** 详尽介绍 ‹*subject*›; **to ~ access to ...** «*path, door*» 通向…; **'training ~d'** "提供培训" **2** Jur, Admin (stipulate) «*law, agreement, judge*» 规定; **to ~ that ...** 规定…; **unless**

P

otherwise ~d 除非另行规定; except as ~d (below) 除(下文)规定外

B vi archaic «*God, the state*» 提供生活必需品; the Lord will ~ 上帝会恩赐的

Phrasal verbs

- **provide against** *vt* [~ against sth.] formal 防备 ‹*damage, change, shortage*›
- **provide for** *vt* **1** [~ for sb./sth.] (finance, maintain) 供养 ‹*person, family*›; **I have to ~ for my old age** 我必须为年老时作准备 **2** [~ for sth.] (allow for) 把…考虑在内 ‹*risk, eventuality*›; 规定 ‹*action, compensation*›; **expenses ~d for in the budget** 纳入预算中的开支; **the law ~s for sth. to be done** 法律规定要做某事

provided /prəˈvaɪdɪd/ *conj* 假如; **a picnic will be very pleasant, ~ (that) we get good weather** 如果天气好的话, 出去野餐很不错

providence /ˈprɒvɪdəns/ *n* [u] **1** (*also* **Providence**) (God) 上帝; (nature) 上苍; **to tempt ~** 冒险 **2** (foresight) 远见; **the ~ of those who save for a rainy day** 那些未雨绸缪者的远见卓识

provident /ˈprɒvɪdənt/ *adj* (wise) 未雨绸缪的; (thrifty) 节俭的

provident association *n* Brit 互济会

providential /ˌprɒvɪˈdenʃl/ *adj* formal 适时的 ‹*arrival, intervention*›; 凑巧的 ‹*death*›

providentially /ˌprɒvɪˈdenʃəli/ *adv* formal 恰好地

provident society *n* Brit = **friendly society**

provider /prəˈvaɪdə(r)/ *n* **1** (supplier) 提供者; **an Internet/broadband ~** 互联网/宽带提供商; **an important ~ of employment** 一个重要的雇主 **2** (breadwinner) 供养人

providing /prəˈvaɪdɪŋ/ *conj* = **provided**

province /ˈprɒvɪns/

A *n* **1** (region) 省 **2** fig (field) 领域; **that is not my ~** 那不属于我的专业范畴; **the matter is outside my ~** 这件事不归我管

B *npl* **provinces** Brit **the ~s** 首都以外的地区

provincial /prəˈvɪnʃl/

A *adj* **1** *attrib* (of province) 省的 ‹*taxes, legislation*›; **the ~ government** 省政府 **2** *attrib* (outside the capital) 首都以外的 ‹*theatre, town*› **3** pej (narrow) 狭隘的 ‹*attitude, intolerance*›

B *n* pej 外乡人

provincialism /prəˈvɪnʃəlɪzəm/ *n* [u] pej 狭隘

proving ground /ˈpruːvɪŋ ɡraʊnd/ *n* 试验场

provision /prəˈvɪʒn/

A *n* **1** [u] (supplying) 供给; **the ~ of sth.** 某物的供给; **to be responsible for the ~ of education/transport** 有责任提供教育/交通服务; **health care ~** 医疗服务的提供; **a ~ merchant** 供应商 **2** [c] (amount supplied) 供应量; **an increased** *or* **greater ~** 更大的供应量 **3** [u and c] (arrangements) 准备; **~ for sb./sth.** 为某人/某事物所作的安排; **~ against sth.** 对某事物的预防措施; **~ had been made against flooding** 已制定防洪措施; **to make ~ for sth.** 为某事物作准备; **~s to ensure equal treatment** 为保证待遇平等而采取的措施 **4** [c and u] Jur, Admin (condition, stipulation) 规定; **under the ~s of ...** 按照…的规定; **according to** *or* **within the ~s** 根据条款; **to exclude sb./sth. from its ~s** 将某人/某事物排除在其条款外

B **provisions** *npl* (food and drink) 饮食供应; **a stock of ~s** 食品存储; **to get (in) ~s** 购买食品

C *vt* (supply) 为…提供必需品 ‹*expedition, household*›; **the ship had been ~ed for a long voyage** 这艘船已装备了远航的必需品; **to be well ~ed with food and fuel** 储备好充足的食物和燃料; **to be fully ~ed** 储备充分

provisional /prəˈvɪʒənl/

A *adj* 临时的 ‹*contract, solution*›

B **Provisional** *n* 爱尔兰共和军临时派成员

provisional: ~ driving licence *n* Brit 临时驾照; **P~ IRA** *n* **the P~ IRA** 爱尔兰共和军临时派

provisionally /prəˈvɪʒnəli/ *adv* 临时地

proviso /prəˈvaɪzəʊ/ *n* (*pl* **~s**) 限制性条款; **with the ~ that ...** 附加条件是…

provocation /ˌprɒvəˈkeɪʃn/ *n* [u and c] (by action, speech) 挑衅; (by cause, thing) 激怒; **he will react violently under ~** 他被激怒的话是会暴力相向的; **at the least** *or* **slightest ~** 稍一招惹

provocative /prəˈvɒkətɪv/ *adj* **1** (sexually suggestive) 撩人的 ‹*smile, pose, dress*› **2** (causing controversy) 引起争议的 ‹*book, title*›; (causing offence) 挑衅的 ‹*comment, behaviour*›; **he is being deliberately ~** 他是在蓄意挑衅

provocatively /prəˈvɒkətɪvli/ *adv* **1** (suggestively) 撩人地 ‹*smile, pose, smutty*› **2** (controversially) 引起争议地 ‹*argue, behave*›; (offensively) 挑衅地 ‹*speak, behave*›

provoke /prəˈvəʊk/ *vt* **1** (annoy) 激怒; **the snake is quite harmless, unless ~d** 这种蛇除非被激怒, 否则不会伤人 **2** (incite) «*behaviour, remark*» 挑衅; **to ~ sb./sth. to do sth.** *or* **into doing sth.** 刺激某人/某物做某事 **3** (cause, arouse) 引起 ‹*laughter, criticism*›; 激起 ‹*indignation, riot*›; **his new book has ~d a great deal of controversy** 他的新书引起了很大的争议

provost /ˈprɒvəst/ *n* **1** Brit Univ (head) 院长 **2** Amer Univ (administrator) 教务长 **3** Scot (of council) 镇长; (mayor) 市长

provost: ~ guard *n* Amer 宪兵纠察队; **~ marshal** *n* 宪兵司令

prow /praʊ/ *n* 船首

prowess /ˈpraʊɪs/ *n* [u] **1** (skill, expertise) 高超的技艺; **technical/academic/musical ~** 技术/学术/音乐造诣 **2** (bravery) 英勇无畏

prowl /praʊl/

A *vi* «*lion, tiger*» 潜行; **wild animals ~ing in the forest** 在森林里出没的野兽; **I could hear him ~ing (about** *or* **around) in his bedroom** 我能听见他在卧室里走来走去

B *vt* «*lion, tiger*» 潜行于; **muggers ~ing the streets at night** 夜里在街道上出没的抢劫犯

C *n* (for prey) 悄然潜行; **the soldiers went on the ~, hoping to meet some girls** 那些大兵们四处寻觅, 希望能碰上几个姑娘

prowl car *n* Amer 警车

prowler /ˈpraʊlə(r)/ *n* 潜行者

proximity /prɒkˈsɪməti/ *n* [u] 接近; **the airport is in the immediate ~ of the town** 机场紧挨着城镇

proximity: ~ card *n* 感应卡; **~ card reader** 感应卡读卡器; **~ fuse** *n* 感应引信

proxy /ˈprɒksi/ *n* **1** [c] (person) 代理人; **to act as sb.'s ~** 做某人的代表; **to make sb. one's ~** 让某人做自己的代理人 **2** [u] (authority) 代理权; **to vote by ~** 委托他人投票 **3** [c] (document) 委托书

proxy: ~ battle, ~ fight *ns* 代理权争夺战 [公司内两派为获取股东投票代理权进行的争斗]; **~ vote** *n* 代理投票; **~ war** *n* 代理战争 [指由大国挑起但不直接参与的战争]

Prozac® /ˈprəʊzæk/ *n* [u and c] 百忧解 [一种抗抑郁药]

ℹ Chinese provinces / place names

■ All China's provinces, autonomous regions, and municipalities have full names and abbreviations (given in brackets) as in the following examples:

Guangdong Province	广东省 (粤)
Hunan Province	湖南省 (湘)
Beijing	北京市 (京)
Shanghai	上海市 (沪)
Ningxia Huizu Autonomous Region	宁夏回族自治区 (宁)

■ Some provinces have two abbreviations, for example:

Sichuan Province	四川省 (川 / 蜀)
Gansu Province	甘肃省 (陇 / 甘)

■ The abbreviations are used mostly in set phrases as in the examples below:

the Beijing-Shanghai Railway
= 京沪铁路

Beijing Opera
= 京戏
or 京剧

Guangdong cuisine
= 粤菜

Hunan embroidery
= 湘绣

Sichuan food
= 川菜

Sichuan brocade
= 蜀锦

Gansu opera
= 陇剧

■ Chinese has two ways to say or write the names of places: names alone or names followed by a status noun such as 省 (province), 地区 (district), 市 (city), 县 (county), 镇 (town), 村 (village), etc. The status noun must be used if two places have the same name:

Guangzhou
or ***the City of Guangzhou***
= 广州
or 广州市

Henan
or ***Henan Province***
= 河南
or 河南省

but

Zhoukou District
= 周口地区

the city of Zhoukou
= 周口市

■ When writing addresses in Chinese, the largest entity comes first and the smallest last:

Department of English
School of Foreign Languages
South China University of Technology
Guangzhou
China

= 中国
广州
华南理工大学
外语学院
英语系

prude /pruːd/ *n* 正经过度的人

prudence /ˈpruːdns/ *n* [u] 审慎

prudent /ˈpruːdnt/ *adj* 深谋远虑的 ‹*politician, soldier*›; 审慎的 ‹*decision, policy*›; **it was a ~ choice** 这是一个慎重的选择

prudently /ˈpruːdntli/ *adv* 审慎地 ‹*act, speak*›; 节俭地 ‹*use, spend*›

prudery /ˈpruːdərɪ/ *n* [u] [在性问题上] 故作正经; **her friends were amused by her ~** 她的朋友们对她的一本正经忍俊不禁

prudish /ˈpruːdɪʃ/ *adj* 谈性色变的; **to be ~ about sth./about doing sth.** 在某事上/在做某事上过分拘谨

prudishness /ˈpruːdɪʃnɪs/ *n* [u] = **prudery**

prune[1] /pruːn/ *n* 1 Culin 干梅子 2 colloq (person) 乏味的人

prune[2] *vt* 1 (trim) 修剪 ‹*roses, tree*› 2 (cut off) 剪去 ‹*twig, dead wood*› 3 fig (reduce) 裁减 ‹*workforce*›; 削减 ‹*budget*›; 删减 ‹*novel, essay*›

Phrasal verbs

- **prune back** *vt* 修剪 ‹*roses, tree*›
- **prune off** *vt* 剪去 ‹*twig, dead wood*›

pruning /ˈpruːnɪŋ/ *n* 1 [u] (action) 修剪; **to do the ~** 整枝 2 (branch, twig) **~s** 修剪下的树枝

pruning: ~ hook *n* 整枝钩刀; **~ shears** *npl* 整枝剪

prurience /ˈprʊərɪəns/ *n* [u] 好色

prurient /ˈprʊərɪənt/ *adj* 好色的

prussic acid /ˌprʌsɪk ˈæsɪd/ *n* [u] 氢氰酸

pry[1] /praɪ/ *vi* 刺探; **to ~ into sth.** 打听某事; **he's far too fond of ~ing into other people's affairs** 他太喜欢打探别人的事情了

pry[2] *vt* Amer = **prise**

prying /ˈpraɪɪŋ/ *adj* 刺探的 ‹*eye, question*›

PS *abbr* = **postscriptum** 附言

psalm /sɑːm/ *n* 赞美诗; **(the book of) P~s** 《〈圣经〉诗篇》

psalm book *n* 圣咏集

psalter /ˈsɔːltə(r)/ *n* (Book of Psalms) 《〈圣经〉诗篇》; (collection of psalms) 圣咏集

PSB *abbr* = **Public Security Bureau**

psephologist /seˈfɒlədʒɪst, Amer siː-/ ▸**p. 409** *n* 选举统计学家

psephology /seˈfɒlədʒi, Amer siːˈf-/ *n* [u] 选举统计学

pseud /sjuːd, Amer suːd/ *n* Brit colloq 假装有学识的人

pseudo- /ˈsjuːdəʊ, Amer ˈsuːdəʊ/ *combining form* 假的; **the ~science of astrology** 占星术这种伪科学; **~intellectual** 假知识分子

pseudonym /ˈsjuːdənɪm, Amer ˈsuːd-/ *n* (fictitious name) 假名; (pen-name) 笔名; **under a ~** 用笔名

psi *abbr* = **pounds per square inch** 磅/平方英寸

psittacosis /ˌsɪtəˈkəʊsɪs/ ▸**p. 377** *n* [u] 鹦鹉热 [一种鸟类传染病，传染给人后会引发肺炎]

psoriasis /səˈraɪəsɪs/ ▸**p. 377** *n* [u] 牛皮癣

psst /pst/ *excl* 嘘; **~, I'm over here!** 嘘，我在这里！

PST *abbr* Amer = **Pacific Standard Time**

PSV Brit ▸**public service vehicle**

psych, psyche /saɪk/

Phrasal verbs

- **psych out** *vt* [**~ out sb., ~ sb. out**] 1 colloq (intimidate, unnerve) 震慑 2 esp Amer (outguess) 猜透…的动机
- **psych up** *vt* [**~ sb. up, ~ up sb.**] colloq 使作好心理准备; **he ~ed himself up for the match** 他为比赛作好了心理准备

psyche /ˈsaɪki/ *n* (mind) 心理; (soul) 心灵

psyched /saɪkt/ *adj* colloq **~ (up)** 兴奋的

psychedelia /ˌsaɪkəˈdiːlɪə/ *n* [u] (music) 迷幻音乐; (culture) 迷幻文化; (art) 迷幻艺术

psychedelic /ˌsaɪkˈdelɪk/ *adj* 1 (hallucinogenic) 引起幻觉的 ‹*drug, experience*› 2 Mus 造成迷幻效果的 ‹*rock*› 3 (multicoloured) 色彩炫目的 ‹*imagery, effect*›

psychiatric /ˌsaɪkɪˈætrɪk/ *adj* 精神病的; **a ~ illness/disorder** 精神病/精神紊乱; **~ treatment/research** 精神病治疗/研究; **a ~ case/clinic/nurse** 精神病患者/诊所/护理人员

psychiatrist /saɪˈkaɪətrɪst, Amer sɪ-/ ▸**p. 409** *n* 精神病专家

psychiatry /saɪˈkaɪətri, Amer sɪ-/ *n* [u] (study) 精神病学; (treatment) 精神病治疗

psychic /ˈsaɪkɪk/

A *adj* 超自然的; **to have ~ power/abilities** 有超自然的力量/能力

B *n* 有特异功能的人

psycho /ˈsaɪkəʊ/ *n* (*pl* **~s**) colloq 精神变态者

psychoactive /ˌsaɪkəʊˈæktɪv/ *adj* 作用于精神的

psychoanalysis /ˌsaɪkəʊəˈnæləsɪs/ *n* [u] 精神分析; **to practise/undergo ~** 进行/接受精神分析

psychoanalyst /ˌsaɪkəʊˈænəlɪst/ ▸**p. 409** *n* 精神分析学家

psychoanalytic, psychoanalytical /ˌsaɪkəʊænəˈlɪtɪk, ˌsaɪkəʊænəˈlɪtɪkl/ *adj* 精神分析的

psychoanalyze /ˌsaɪkəʊˈænəlaɪz/ *vt* 对…进行精神分析

psychobabble /ˈsaɪkəʊbæbl/ *n* [u] colloq pej 心理学呓语

psycholinguistic /ˌsaɪkəʊlɪŋˈgwɪstɪk/ *adj* 心理语言学的

psycholinguistics /ˌsaɪkəʊlɪŋˈgwɪstɪks/ *npl* + *v sing* [u] 心理语言学

psychological /ˌsaɪkəˈlɒdʒɪkl/ *adj* 1 (mental) 心理的; **~ disorders/state** 心理紊乱/状态 2 (relating to psychology) 心理学的 ‹*methods*›; **~ research** 心理学研究

psychologically /ˌsaɪkəˈlɒdʒɪkli/ *adv* 心理上; **the experience affected him ~** 这次经历对他造成了心理影响

psychological: ~ moment *n* 最佳心理时刻; **he proposed to her at just the right ~ moment** 他在最恰当的时候向她提出了求婚; **~ profile** *n* 心理特征描述; **~ warfare** *n* [u] 心理战; **to engage in ~ warfare** 打心理战

psychologist /saɪˈkɒlədʒɪst/ ▸**p. 409** *n* 心理学家

psychology /saɪˈkɒlədʒi/ *n* [u] 1 (science) 心理学; **letting him take the decision himself was good ~** 让他自己作决定可以说是摸透了他的心思 2 (mentality) 心理特征

psychometric /ˌsaɪkəʊˈmetrɪk/ *adj* 心理测量的; **~ tests** *or* **testing** 心理测试

psychometrics /ˌsaɪkəʊˈmetrɪks/ *npl* + *v sing* 心理测量学

psychopath /ˈsaɪkəʊpæθ/ *n* 精神变态者

psychopathic /ˌsaɪkəʊˈpæθɪk/ *adj* 精神变态的; **a ~ disorder** 精神错乱; **a ~ serial killer** 精神变态连环杀手

psychosis /saɪˈkəʊsɪs/ (*pl* **psychoses** /saɪˈkəʊsiːz/) *n* [c and u] 精神错乱

psychosomatic /ˌsaɪkəʊsəˈmætɪk/ *adj* 心理压力造成的 ‹*illness, disorder*›

psychotherapist /ˌsaɪkəʊˈθerəpɪst/ ▸**p. 409** *n* 精神治疗师

psychotherapy /ˌsaɪkəʊˈθerəpi/ *n* [u] 精神疗法; **to undergo** *or* **receive ~** 接受精神疗法

psychotic /saɪˈkɒtɪk/

A *adj* 精神错乱的; **a ~ disorder** *or* **illness** 精神错乱

B *n* 精神错乱者

PT *abbr* Brit = **physical training**

pt *abbr* 1 = **pint 1** 2 = **point A6**

PTA *abbr* = **parent-teacher association**

PTO *abbr* Brit = **please turn over** 请见下页

pub /pʌb/ *n* Brit 酒吧; **a traditional/country ~** 老式/乡村酒吧

> **pub**
>
> 酒吧。全称 public house，但较少用。英国共有数万家酒吧，它们在人们的生活中占有重要的地位。可分专营酒吧（tied house）和非专营酒吧（free house），前者主要销售某个酿酒公司的啤酒，后者则可以出售各种品牌的啤酒。酒类以啤酒（beer）、拉格啤酒（lager）和艾尔啤酒（ale）最受欢迎。有些酒吧在傍晚时分会打折，称欢乐时光（happy hour）。营业时间一般到晚上11点。打烊时间将近时，吧台服务员会通知："Last orders（最后一次点单）！"，提醒顾客买最后一杯酒。关门前会喊："Time（时间到）！"。酒吧一般提供简单的小吃和一些娱乐设施。

pub crawl *n* Brit colloq 串酒馆; **to go on a ~** 挨店喝酒

pube /pjuːb/ *n* colloq 阴毛

puberty /ˈpjuːbəti/ *n* [u] 青春期

pubescence /pjuːˈbesns/ *n* [u] 到达青春期

pubescent /pjuːˈbesnt/ *adj* 到达青春期的

pub: ~ food *n* [u] Brit 酒馆小吃; **~ grub** *n* [u] Brit colloq 酒馆食物

pubic /ˈpjuːbɪk/ *adj* 阴部的; **~ bone** 耻骨

pubic hair *n* [c and u] 阴毛

public /ˈpʌblɪk/

A *adj* 1 (involving people in general) 公众的; **in the ~ interest** 为了公众利益; **the ~ good** 公益; **to allay ~ disquiet** 安民; **~ resistance/opposition (to sth.)** 公众（对某事物）的反抗/反对; **to receive ~ acclaim** 受到公众欢迎; **a token of ~ respect** 公信力的标志; **to be in ~ circulation** 公开发行; **it is ~ knowledge that ...** …是众所周知的; **to be in the ~ eye** 被广泛关注; **to go into/be in ~ life** 开始做/做出头露面的工作; **to go ~** ‹*business*› 挂牌上市 2 (relating to the state) 政府的 ‹*funding*›; **at ~ expense** 以公款 3 (for general use) 公用的 ‹*building*›; 公共的 ‹*service*›; **~ property** lit 众所周知的事物; **reporters view these stars as ~ property** fig 记者把这些明星看作是公众人物; **a sense of ~ duty** 公共责任意识; **~ facility/education** 公用设施/公共教育 4 (prominent, known) 人人皆知的; (done in public) 公开的; **a ~ figure/affair** 公众人物/公开事件; **sb.'s ~ image** 某人的公众形象; **to make sth. ~** 公开某事物; **a ~ speaker** 演说家; **a place of ~ execution** 公开的刑场; **to go ~ (with** *or* **about sth.)** （将某事物）公诸于世 5 (not private) 大庭广众的 ‹*place, spot, room*›; **let's go somewhere less ~** 我们去找个稍微僻静的地方

B *n* 1 (populace) 公众; **the (general) ~** 公众; **the Chinese ~** 中国民众; **the great British ~** 大英子民 [多有嘲讽意味]; **a member of the ~** 公众的一员; **to be open/closed to the ~** 对/不对公众开放 2 (group sharing sth.) [有共同特点的] 群体; **the author knows how to satisfy/please his ~** 这位作家懂得如何满足/取悦读者群; **the theatre-going/sporting ~** 爱看戏的民众/体育运动族 3 **in ~** 公开地

public: ~ access channel *n* esp Amer 公共频道; **~ access television** *n* [u] esp Amer [公众可自行制作播放节目的] 公共频道电视; **~ address system, ~ address** *ns* 扩音系统; **~ affairs** *npl* 1 (current affairs) 公共事务; **a ~ affairs department** 公共事务部; 2 (public relations) 公共关系; **~ affairs consultant/manager/office** 公共关系顾问/经理/办公室

publican /ˈpʌblɪkən/ ▸p. 409 *n* Brit 酒馆老板

public: ～ **appearance** *n* [尤指名人、政客等的] 公开露面; ～ **assistance** *n* [u] Amer 政府补助

publication /ˌpʌblɪˈkeɪʃn/ *n* **1** [u] (printing) 出版; **the date of** ～ 出版日期 **2** [c] (book, journal) 出版物 **3** [u] (making public) 公布

public: ～ **bar** *n* Brit [酒店里的] 廉价酒吧; ～ **bill** *n* 公共政策法案; ～ **company** *n* 公开招股公司; ～ **convenience** *n* Brit 公厕; ～ **corporation** *n* Amer 公开招股公司; ～ **debt** *n* [u] esp Amer 公债; ～ **defender** *n* Amer 公设辩护律师; ～ **domain** *n* [u] 公有领域; **in the** ～ **domain** 不受版权保护; ～ **domain software** 无版权软件; ～ **enemy** *n* **1** (criminal) 社会公敌; ～ **enemy number one** 头号公敌; **2** (problem, threat) 头号威胁; ～ **examination** *n* [人人都可参加的] 公开考试; ～ **gallery** *n* **1** (in court, parliament) 公众旁听席; **2** Amer (art gallery) 公共美术馆; ～ **holiday** *n* Brit 公共假日; ～ **house** *n* Brit formal 酒吧

publicist /ˈpʌblɪsɪst/ *n* 推介人员; **a book/music/film** ～ 图书/音乐/电影宣传员

publicity /pʌbˈlɪsəti/ *n* [u] **1** (media attention) 媒体的关注; **to seek/attract** ～ 寻求曝光率/吸引媒体注意; **adverse** ～ 反面报道; **a blaze of** ～ 全面曝光 **2** (advertising) 宣传; ～ **department/manager** 宣传部/经理; **to be great/bad for** ～ 适合大加宣传/不适合宣传 **3** (advertising material) 宣传材料

publicity: ～ **agency** *n* 广告代理; ～ **agent** ▸p. 409 *n* 推介人员; ～ **campaign,** ～ **drive** *ns* (to raise social issue) 宣传运动; (to sell product) 广告促销活动; ～ **machine** *n* 宣传机器; ～ **photograph** *n* 宣传照; ～**-seeking** *adj* 追求曝光率的 ‹*person*›; 期望达到宣传效果的 ‹*stunt, exercise*›; ～ **stunt** *n* 宣传噱头

publicize /ˈpʌblɪsaɪz/ *vt* **1** (make known) 宣传 ‹*case, event, danger*›; 报道 ‹*story*› **2** (advertise) 推介 ‹*concert, product*›

public: ～ **key** *n* 公共密钥; ～ **law** *n* [u] 公法; ～ **lending right** *n* Brit 公共出借报酬权; ～ **limited company** *n* 公开招股公司

publicly /ˈpʌblɪkli/ *adv* **1** (openly) 公开地 ‹*say, do*› **2** (by the state) 由国家; ～ **owned** 国有的; ～**-funded** *or* **-financed** 政府出资的

public nuisance *n* Brit **1** Jur 妨害公共利益的行为 **2** (person) 为公众厌恶的人

public order *n* [u] 公共秩序

public order: ～ **act** *n* Brit 公共秩序法; ～ **offence** *n* Brit 妨害公共秩序罪

public: ～ **ownership** *n* [u] 国家所有制; **to be taken into** ～ **ownership** 被国有化; ～ **prosecutor** *n* Brit 检察官; ～ **purse** *n* **the** ～ **purse** 国库; **P**～ **Record Office** *pr n* Brit 公共档案局

public relations *npl* + *v sing or pl* **1** (maintenance of public image) 公关活动 **2** (relationship with public) 公共关系; **the** ～ **industry** 公关行业

public relations: ～ **exercise** *n* 公关活动; ～ **officer** ▸p. 409 *n* 公关员

public restroom *n* Amer 公共厕所

public school *n* [c and u] **1** Brit (independent school) 公学 [寄宿制的私立付费学校]; **he had a** ～ **education** 他接受的是公学教育 **2** Amer (publicly funded school) 公立学校

public: ～ **schoolboy** *n* Brit 公学男生; ～ **sector** *n* 公营部门

Public Security Bureau *n* (in China) 公安局

public servant *n* 公务员

public service *n* **1** [u] (public administration) 公职; ～ **workers** 公务人员 **2** [c] (service provided for the community) 公共事业

> **public school**
>
> 1.（英国的苏格兰地区和美国）公立学校。
>
> 2.（英国除苏格兰以外的大部分地区）公学。指私立中学和私立小学（preparatory school, ▸**preppy**），都是独立学校（independent school），不由国家提供经费，而收取昂贵的学费。最初称为文法学校（grammar school），入学年龄为13岁，多为寄宿学校（boarding school）。伊顿（Eton）公学和哈罗（Harrow）公学都是英国的著名公学。公学在学术上要求很高，毕业生进入牛津大学和剑桥大学的比例远远高于公立学校。体育课程也占有相当比重，如橄榄球（rugby）运动即源于拉格比（Rugby）公学。和公学相对的公立学校称state school。

public service: ～ **broadcasting** *n* [u] 公共广播; ～ **corporation** *n* Amer 公用事业公司; ～ **vehicle** *n* 公交车

public: ～ **speaking** *n* [u] (act) 演讲; (skill) 演讲术; **the art of** ～ **speaking** 演讲技巧; **a** ～ **speaking engagement** 演讲约定; ～ **spirit** *n* [u] 公益心; ～**-spirited** *adj* 热心公益的 ‹*person, act*›; ～ **television** *n* [u] Amer 大众教育电视; ～ **transport** *n* [u] 公共交通; ～ **utility** *n* **1** (service, supply) 公用事业; **2** (company) 公用事业公司; ～ **works** *npl* 公共工程; ～ **works projects/spending** 公共工程项目/开支

publish /ˈpʌblɪʃ/

A *vt* **1** (issue in print) 出版 ‹*book*›; 发行 ‹*journal, newspaper*›; **to be** ～**ed weekly/monthly** 每周/每月出版一次; **he** ～**ed an article in the Lancet** 他在《柳叶刀》上发表了一篇文章 **2** (on the Internet) 发表 ‹*e-book*› **3** (make public) 公布 ‹*accounts, results*›; **the** ～**ed tariff** 官方关税

B *vi* «*researcher, academic*» 发表

publishable /ˈpʌblɪʃəbl/ *adj* **1** (able to be published) 可发表的 ‹*format, information, version*› **2** (fit for publication) 适合发表的 ‹*novel, story*›

publisher /ˈpʌblɪʃə(r)/ ▸p. 409 *n* **1** (of books) (person) 出版人; (firm) 出版公司 **2** (of newspapers, journals) (person) 发行人; (firm) 发行公司

publishing /ˈpʌblɪʃɪŋ/ *n* [u] 出版业

publishing house *n* 出版社

pub: ～ **lunch** *n* Brit 酒店午餐; **to go for a** ～ **lunch** 到酒店吃午餐; ～ **quiz** *n* Brit 酒吧竞猜

puce /pjuːs/ ▸p. 134

A *adj* (dark red) 暗红色的; (purple-brown) 紫褐色的; **the man's face was** ～ **with rage** 那人气得脸色发紫

B *n* [u] (dark red) 暗红色; (purple-brown) 紫褐色

puck /pʌk/ *n* 冰球

pucker /ˈpʌkə(r)/

A *vi* «*face, brow*» 皱起; «*dress, trousers*» 起褶子

B *vt* 皱起 ‹*brow*›; 撅起 ‹*lips*›; 给…打褶 ‹*dress*›

C *n* (on face) 皱纹; (in garment) 皱褶

Phrasal verb

- **pucker up**

A *vi* (form wrinkles) 起皱纹; (form folds) 起褶子

B *vt* [～ **up sth.,** ～ **sth. up**] (cause to form wrinkles) 使起皱; (cause to form folds) 使起褶子; **she** ～**ed up her lips** 她撅起了嘴

pud /pʊd/ *n* [c and u] Brit colloq = **pudding 1**

pudding /ˈpʊdɪŋ/ *n* **1** [u and c] (cooked sweet dish) 甜食; (dessert) 甜点 **2** [u and c] (cooked savoury dish) 布丁; **the proof of the** ～ **is in the eating** 布丁好不好，吃吃就知道 **3** [c] colloq (fat person) 胖子; (slow person) 呆瓜; **a** ～ **face** 柿饼脸

pudding basin, pudding bowl *ns* Brit 布丁盆; **a** ～ **haircut** 布丁盆式发型

puddle /ˈpʌdl/ *n* 水洼

pudenda /pjuːˈdendə/ *npl* 外阴

pudgy /ˈpʌdʒi/ *adj* colloq 矮胖的 ‹*person*›; 短粗的 ‹*finger, hand*›; 胖乎乎的 ‹*face*›

puerile /ˈpjʊəraɪl, Amer -rəl/ *adj* 幼稚的 ‹*behaviour, attitude*›; 愚蠢的 ‹*question, argument*›

puerility /ˌpjʊəˈrɪləti/ *n* **1** [u] (childishness) 幼稚 **2** [c] (childish act, idea) 幼稚的言行

Puerto Rican /ˌpwɜːtəʊ ˈriːkən/ ▸p. 503

A *adj* (of Puerto Rico) 波多黎各的; (of the people) 波多黎各人的

B *n* 波多黎各人

Puerto Rico /ˌpwɜːtəʊ ˈriːkəʊ/ *pr n* 波多黎各

puff /pʌf/

A *n* **1** [c] (burst of breath) 喘气; (burst of wind) 阵风; **to blow out the candles in one** ～ 一口气吹灭所有蜡烛 **2** [c] (small quantity) 少量; ～**s of cloud** 一缕缕云; **to vanish** *or* **go up in a** ～ **of smoke** lit 在一阵轻烟中消失; fig 转瞬即逝 **3** [c] (action) 吸; **to take a** ～ **(on a cigarette/pipe)** 吸一口（香烟/烟斗） **4** [c] Cosmet = **powder puff** **5** [c] Culin 千层酥; **a cream** ～ 奶油酥 **6** [u] Brit colloq (breath) 呼吸; **to be out of** ～ 上气不接下气 **7** [u and c] colloq (favourable publicity) 吹捧; **the new car got a lot of** ～ 这款新车被吹得天花乱坠; **to give sth. a** ～ 吹捧 ‹*book, film*›; **a** ～ **piece about her performance** 吹捧她演出的一篇文章 **8** [c] Sewing 泡褶

B *vt* **1** (emit) 冒出 ‹*steam*›; 喷出 ‹*powder*›; **to** ～ **smoke into sb.'s face** 把烟吹到某人脸上; **to** ～ **sth. from** *or* **out of sth.** 从某处冒出某物 **2** (inhale) 吸 ‹*cigarette, pipe*› **3** colloq (praise exaggeratedly) 吹捧 ‹*book, film*›

C *vi* **1** 一阵阵冒出; **to** ～ **from** *or* **out of sth.** «*smoke, steam*» 从某处一阵阵冒出来; «*powder*» 从某处一阵阵喷出来 **2** (take a drag) 一口一口地吸; **to** ～ **at** *or* **on sth.** 一口一口地吸 ‹*cigarette, pipe, inhaler*› **3** colloq (breathe) 喘气; **to** ～ **like a grampus** 气喘如牛; **to** ～ **and blow** (breathe noisily) 气喘吁吁; (show annoyance) 吹胡子瞪眼

Phrasal verbs

- **puff away** *vi* 吸; **to** ～ **away at** *or* **on sth.** 吸 ‹*cigarette, pipe, inhaler*›
- **puff out**

A *vt* [～ **sth. out,** ～ **out sth.**] **1** (expel) 冒出 ‹*smoke, steam*›; 喷出 ‹*powder*› **2** (cause to swell) 鼓起 ‹*cheeks, chest, sail*›; 蓬起 ‹*feathers*› **3** colloq (extinguish) 吹灭 ‹*candle, flame*› **4** Brit colloq (make breathless) «*exertion, run*» 使气喘

B *vi* **1** (be emitted) «*smoke, steam*» 冒出; «*powder*» 喷出 **2** (swell) «*cheeks, chest*» 鼓起; «*feathers*» 蓬起

- **puff up**

A *vt* [～ **sth. up,** ～ **up sth.**] 鼓起 ‹*chest*›; 蓬起 ‹*feathers*›; **to be** ～**ed up** fig 自负; **to be** ～**ed up with pride** 自满

B *vi* «*cheeks, chest, eyes*» 鼓起; «*feathers*» 蓬起; **the rice has** ～**ed up nicely** 米饭煮得很松软了

puff: ～ **adder** *n* 鼓腹巨蝰; ～**ball** *n* 马勃（菌）

puffed /pʌft/ *adj* **1** (swollen) 肿胀的 ‹*face, lip*›; 浮肿的 ‹*eye*› **2** Brit colloq (breathless) 气喘吁吁的 **3** Clothg 蓬起的; **a dress with** ～ **sleeves** 带泡泡袖的连衣裙

puffer /ˈpʌfə(r)/ *n* child lang 火车头; **a** ～ **train** 蒸汽火车

puffin /ˈpʌfɪn/ *n* 角嘴海雀

puffiness /ˈpʌfɪnɪs/ *n* [u] 肿胀

puff: ～ **pastry** *n* [u] 油酥面团; ～ **puff** *n* Brit child lang 蒸汽火车

puffy /ˈpʌfi/ *adj* **1** (swollen) 肿胀的 ‹*face*›; 浮肿的 ‹*eyes*›; 鼓胀的 ‹*texture*› **2** (padded) 加衬里的 ‹*jacket, sleeve*› **3** (rounded and light) 蓬松的 ‹*hair, cloud*›

pug /pʌɡ/ *n* ～ **(dog)** 哈巴狗

pugnacious /pʌɡˈneɪʃəs/ *adj* 好斗的 ‹*person, animal*›; 争强好胜的 ‹*nature, attitude*›

pugnaciously /pʌɡˈneɪʃəsli/ *adv* 好斗地

pug: ～ **nose** *n* 狮子鼻; ～**-nosed** *adj* 长着狮子鼻的

puke /pjuːk/ colloq

A *vi* 呕吐; **it's enough to make you (want to)** ～ 这足以令人作呕

B *n* [u] 呕吐物

Phrasal verb

• **puke up** colloq

A *vi* 呕吐

B *vt* [～ **sth. up,** ～ **up sth.**] 呕吐出; **the baby has just** ～**d her milk up** 婴儿刚刚将奶吐了出来

pukka /ˈpʌkə/ *adj* **1** (genuine) 真的; **he's a** ～ **sahib** 他是一位真正的绅士 **2** Brit colloq (excellent) 一流的

> **Pulitzer Prize**
>
> 普利策奖。1917 年设立，奖励在新闻、历史、文学和音乐等领域作出突出贡献的人士，每年 5 月颁发。美国现代报业奠基人约瑟夫·普利策（Joseph Pulitzer）去世前设立遗嘱，将财产赠予哥伦比亚大学（Columbia University），用于创建新闻学院（School of Journalism），并设立普利策奖，由哥伦比亚大学组织评选并颁发。

pull /pʊl/

A *vt* **1** (tug) 拉; **to** ～ **the curtains/blinds** (close) 拉上窗帘/百叶窗; (open) 拉开窗帘/百叶窗; **to** ～ **sb.'s hair, to** ～ **sb. by the hair** 揪某人头发; **to** ～ **a sweater over one's head** (put it on) 从头上套上毛衣; (take it off) 从头上脱下毛衣; **he** ～**ed her to** *or* **towards him** 他把她拉过来; **to** ～ **the door shut** *or* **to** 拉上门; **to** ～ **sb. clear (of sth.)** 把某人（从某处）拉开; **to** ～ **sb./sth. to pieces** 把某人/某事物批得体无完肤; **to** ～ **sb.'s leg** colloq 戏弄某人; ～ **the other one (it's got bells on)** colloq 鬼才信呢; **to** ～ **sth. from sb.'s grasp** 让某事物脱离某人的掌控; **it** ～**ed me back to reality** 它把我拖回到现实中; **to** ～ **the rug** *or* **carpet from under sb.'s feet** colloq 突然拆某人的台; **to** ～ **one's weight** 做好份内的事; **to** ～ **the wool over sb.'s eyes** fig colloq 欺瞒某人 **2** (remove by tugging) 拔出 ‹*cork, tooth*›; 采 ‹*flower*›; **to** ～ **a gun/knife (on sb.)** （对某人）拔枪/拔刀; **to** ～ **a thread on** 把…弄得抽丝 ‹*piece of cloth*›; **to** ～ **the plug on sb./sth.** fig colloq 阻止某人/某事物; **to** ～ **trumps** Games colloq 出主牌 **3** Med 拉伤; **a** ～**ed muscle/ligament** 拉伤的肌肉/韧带 **4** (operate) 扳动 ‹*lever, switch*›; 扣 ‹*trigger*› **5** colloq (complete successfully) 进行…得逞 ‹*raid, burglary*›; **to** ～ **a bank job** 抢银行; **to** ～ **a trick on sb.** 耍花招骗某人; **to** ～ **a fast one** *or* **a flanker (on sb.)** (gain advantage) （把某人）捉弄得团团转; (deceive) 欺骗（某人）; **to** ～ **a stunt** 逞能 **6** (steer) 使…转向 ‹*vehicle, vessel*›; **to** ～ **sth. to the left/right** 把某物向左/向右转; **to** ～ **sth. to** *or* **towards sth.** 把某物转向某处; **he** ～**ed the car into the side of the road** 他把车开到了路边; **to** ～ **a plane out of a dive** 拉升飞机; **to** ～ **a boat into the bank** 让船靠岸 **7** Equit 勒住 ‹*racehorse*› **8** (in boxing) 收回 ‹*blow, hook*›; **to** ～ **one's punches** fig colloq 手下留情 **9** (in golf) 把…击偏; (in cricket) 把…击向相对场地; **to** ～ **the ball to** *or* **into sth.** 把球打偏到某处 **10** colloq (attract) 吸引 ‹*audience, person*›; 赢得 ‹*support, votes, voter*›; 引起 ‹*interest*›; **he can still** ～ **the girls!** 他仍然能让姑娘们着迷! **11** colloq (cancel) 取消 ‹*entertainment, show*›; (withdraw) 撤掉 ‹*advertisement, story, photograph*› **12** Print 印出 ‹*proof*› **13** (make) 扮; **to** ～ **a funny face at sb.** 对某人扮鬼脸; **to** ～ **a strange expression** colloq 表情怪怪的

B *vi* **1** (tug or draw sth. towards oneself) 拉; **to push and** ～ 推拉; **to** ～ **hard** 使劲拉; **to** ～ **at** *or* **on sth.** 拉某物; **he** ～**ed at her sleeve** 他拽了拽她的袖子 **2** (in rowing) 划船; **to** ～ **hard** 拼命划桨 **3** (smoke, drink) **to** ～ **at** *or* **on sth.** 吸 ‹*cigarette, pipe*›; 对着…喝 ‹*bottle*› **4** Mech «*engine, vehicle*» 正常运转; **to** ～ **well** 运转良好 **5** Equit 逆着马嚼子用力拉; **to** ～ **at the bit** 用力拉马嚼子 **6** Aut «*vehicle, wheel*» 转向; **to** ～ **to the left/right** 向左/右转 **7** (in golf) 击偏球; (in cricket) 把球击向相对场地; **to** ～ **into** *or* **to sth.** 把球反打到某处 **8** (move steadily) «*vehicle*» 平稳行驶; «*driver*» 平稳驾驶; **the police car** ～**ed alongside** 警车开了过来 **9** Brit colloq (attract a man, woman) 吸引异性 **10** (move) «*handle, rope, chain*» 拉得动; **it won't** ～ 这东西拉不动

C *v refl* **to** ～ **oneself in/out** 被困住/摆脱; **he** ～**ed himself free and ran off** 他挣脱出来跑掉了

D *n* **1** [c] (tug) 拉; **a** ～ **at** *or* **on sth.** 对某物的一拉; **to give (sth.) a (sharp)** ～ （猛）拽（某物）一把 **2** [c] Phys 引力; **gravitational** ～ 重力; **the** ～ **of the earth** 地球引力 **3** [c] fig (attraction) 吸引力; **to have** *or* **exert a** ～ **over sb.** 吸引某人; **to be on the** ～ Brit colloq 进行性诱惑 **4** [u] colloq (influence) 影响力; **to have a lot of** ～ **with sb.** 对某人有很大影响; **to use one's** ～ 发挥影响力; **social/political** ～ 社会/政治影响 **5** [c] colloq (swig) 大口喝; **to take a long** ～ **at sth.** 大口喝某物 **6** [c] colloq (on cigarette, pipe) 深吸; **to take a** ～ **at** *or* **on sth.** 深吸某物 **7** [c] Brit colloq (prolonged effort) 艰难前行; **a long, hard** ～ 长途跋涉 **8** [c] (handle) 拉手; (cord, rope) 拉绳; **a bell/door** ～ 钟绳/门把手 **9** [c] Print (impression) 印次; (proof) 校样 **10** [c] (in cricket) 向相对场地的一击; (in golf) 击偏了的球; **a** ～ **to the leg boundary** (in cricket) 把球击到相对外场的一击; **a** ～ **into the rough** (in golf) 被打到深草区的击偏了的球 **11** [c] (in rowing) (stroke) 一次划桨动作; (outing) 划船; **a few more** ～**s and ...** 再划几下桨，就…; **to go out for a** ～ 出去划船 **12** [c] (snag in material) 抽丝; **there's a** ～ **in ...** …上有一处抽丝 **13** [c] Med 拉伤

Phrasal verbs

• **pull about, pull around** *vt* [～ **sb./sth. about,** ～ **about sb./sth.**] 粗暴对待 ‹*person*›; 乱扯 ‹*clothing*›

• **pull apart** *vt* [～ **sb./sth. apart,** ～ **apart sb./sth.**]

1 (separate) 拉开 ‹*people, animals*›; 拆开 ‹*pages, sheets of paper*› **2** (dismantle) 拆开 ‹*structure, machine*›; **I don't care if I have to** ～ **the place apart!** 就算把这个地方翻个底朝天，我也无所谓! **3** (dismember) 肢解 ‹*prey, body*› **4** fig (disparage) 抨击 ‹*person, performance*›; 诋毁 ‹*character, reputation*›

• **pull away** *vi* **1** (move away) «*vehicle, driver*» 开走; **the car** ～**ed away from the kerb** 汽车驶离了路缘 **2** (become detached) «*component, piece*» 脱落; **to** ～ **away from sth.** 从某物脱落 **3** (open up lead) «*racing driver, vehicle*» 拉开距离; **to** ～ **away from sb./sth.** 把某人/某物甩在身后; **the leader** ～**ed away on the straight** 领跑的人在直道上拉开了距离

• **pull back**

A *vi* **1** Mil «*troops, army*» 撤退; **the troops** ～**ed back to a safer position/from the front line** 部队撤到了更安全的阵地/撤离了前线 **2** (move backwards) «*person, vehicle*» 后退; **to** ～ **back from the brink** fig 悬崖勒马 **3** fig (not go ahead) 退缩; **to** ～ **back from sth.** 退出 ‹*conflict, course of action*›; 放弃 ‹*decision*› **4** Sport «*runner, racing driver, vehicle*» 缩短距离; **United** ～**ed back to 4-3** 曼联队将比分追回到 4 比 3

B *vt* [～ **sb./sth. back,** ～ **back sb./sth.**]

1 Mil 撤回 ‹*army, unit*›; **the general** ～**ed the troops back from the front line** 将军将部队撤离前线 **2** Sport «*runner, racing driver, vehicle*» 追回 ‹*time, distance*›; 扳回 ‹*goal*› **3** (draw back) 拉回 ‹*rope, cord*›; 拉起 ‹*curtains*›

• **pull down**

A [～ **sth. down,** ～ **down sth.**] *vt*

1 (lower) 放低 ‹*box, book*›; 拉下 ‹*trousers*›; 放下 ‹*blind, curtain*›; **he'll** ～ **you down with him** fig 他会拖累你的 **2** (demolish) 拆毁 ‹*building, structure*› **3** (reduce) 降低 ‹*prices, inflation*›; **the maths paper** ～**ed her overall mark down** 数学科试卷的成绩拉低了她的总分 **4** colloq (earn) 挣 ‹*amount, salary*›

B [～ **sb. down**] *vt* colloq (weaken) «*illness*» 使虚弱

• **pull in**

A [～ **sth. in,** ～ **in sth.**] *vt*

1 (retract) 缩回 ‹*claw, antenna, stomach*› **2** colloq (earn) 挣 ‹*amount, salary*›

B [～ **sb. in,** ～ **in sb.**] *vt*

1 colloq (detain) 拘留; **he was** ～**ed in for questioning** 他被带回警察局审问 **2** (attract) «*performance, event*» 吸引 ‹*spectators, audience, crowd*›; «*candidate, party*» 赢得 ‹*voters*›

C *vi* Brit **1** (arrive) 到站; **the train** ～**ed in to the station** 火车进站了 **2** (leave road) «*vehicle, driver*» 驶到路边停靠; **to** ～ **in at the next service station** 在下一个服务站停车; **to** ～ **in for sth./to do sth.** 为某事物/做某事把车驶到路边停下

• **pull off**

A [～ **sth. off,** ～ **off sth.**] *vt*

1 (take off) 脱下 ‹*garment, shoe*› **2** (remove by tugging) 拆掉 ‹*handle*›; 扯掉 ‹*leaf*›; 取下 ‹*lid*›; 撕下 ‹*wrapping, sticker*›; **to** ～ **sb./sth. off sb./sth.** 把…从…拉开 **3** colloq (succeed in, clinch) 进行…得逞 ‹*robbery, coup*›; 弄到 ‹*scoop*›; 达成 ‹*deal*›; 取得 ‹*success, feat*›; **I never thought you'd** ～ **it off** 我压根没想过你会办成这件事

B [～ **off sth.**] *vt* **to** ～ **off the road/track** 驶向路边/赛道边停车

C *vi* **1** (leave road) «*vehicle, driver*» 驶到路边停靠 **2** (be taken off) «*part, handle*» 可拆卸; «*lid*» 可取下

• **pull on** *vt* [～ **sth. on,** ～ **on sth.**] 穿上 ‹*garment, shoe*›

• **pull out**

A [～ **sth./sb. out,** ～ **out sth./sb.**] *vt*

1 (extract) 拔掉 ‹*splinter, tooth, weeds*›; 拉出 ‹*trapped person*›; **to** ～ **sth. out of ...** 从…中拔出某物 ‹*ground, part of body*›; **to** ～ **sb. out of ...** 从…中拉出某人 ‹*wreckage, river*› **2** (withdraw) 撤出 ‹*army, staff*›; **to** ～ **sb./sth. out of sth.** 将某人/某队伍撤离某处; **to** ～ **one's troops out of the battle zone** 将部队撤离战区

B [～ **sth. out,** ～ **out sth.**] *vt*

1 (take out) 拔出 ‹*knife, gun*›; **to** ～ **sth. out of sth.** 从某处拘出某物 **2** Aviat **to** ～ **an aircraft out of a dive/spin** 使飞机从俯冲/旋冲中拉升起来

C *vi* **1** (move out) «*vehicle, driver*» 驶离; **to** ～ **out into sth.** 驶离到某处; **to** ～ **out in front of sb./sth.** 从某人/某物面前驶离; **to** ～ **out of** 驶离 ‹*drive, parking space, street*› **2** (leave) «*train*» 驶离车站; **to** ～ **out of sth.** 驶离某处; **the express** ～**ed out of the station exactly on time** 特快列车准点从车站开出 **3** (withdraw) «*army*» 撤退; «*candidate, competitor*» 退出; **to** ～ **out of sth.** 退出 ‹*competition, talks, agreement*› **4** (be taken out) «*drawer*» 可拉开; «*component, section*» 可取出 **5** Aviat «*aircraft, pilot*» 恢复水平飞行; **to** ～ **out of sth.** 从…中拉升起来 ‹*dive, spin*›

• **pull over**

A *vt* **1** [～ **sb./sth. over,** ～ **over sb./sth.**] (stop) «*police*» 让…驶到路边 ‹*driver, car*› **2** [～ **sth. over**] (to side of road) 把…开到一边 ‹*vehicle*›

B *vi* «*vehicle, driver*» 开到一边

• **pull round** *vi* esp Brit (regain consciousness) 苏醒; (recover) 痊愈

• **pull through**

A *vi* **1** (from illness) «*patient*» 挺过来 **2** (from difficulty) «*person*» 熬过来

B [～ **sb. through**] *vt* (from illness) 使恢复健康; (from crisis) 使渡过危机; **to** ～ **sb. through sth.** 使某人渡过某事

P

C [~ **through sth.**] *vt* (overcome, survive) 渡过 ‹*difficulty, crisis*›

• **pull together**

A *vi* 齐心合力

B *vt* [~ **sth. together,** ~ **together sth.**] 整合 ‹*summary, report*›; 结成 ‹*alliance*›

C *v refl* ~ **oneself together** 振作精神

• **pull up**

A [~ **sth. up,** ~ **up sth.**] *vt*
1 (lift) 拉高 ‹*garment*›; **to** ~ **sb./sth. up the cliff/out of the well** 把某人/某物拉上悬崖/拉出井; **to** ~ **oneself up out of the water** 从水里爬上来 **2** (uproot) 拔起 ‹*plant*› **3** (move closer) 把…拉近 ‹*chair*›; **he** ~**ed a stool up to the table and sat down** 他把凳子拖到桌边坐下 **4** (stop) 使…停下 ‹*vehicle, horse, athlete*›; **to** ~ **sb. up short** *or* **sharply** 使某人怔住

B [~ **sb. up,** ~ **up sb.**] *vt* Brit colloq (reprimand) 责备; **to** ~ **sb. up for sth./doing sth.** 因某事物/做某事而责骂某人

C *vi* **1** (stop) «*person*» 停车; «*vehicle*» 停下; **to** ~ **up at the traffic lights** 在交通灯前停车 **2** (regain lost ground) «*athlete, pupil*» 追上

pull-down menu *n* 下拉菜单

pulley /ˈpʊli/ *n* **1** (lifting apparatus) 滑车 **2** (wheel, drum) 滑轮

pull-in *n* esp Brit 路边停车带

pulling power *n* [u] **1** (ability to haul) 牵引力 **2** fig colloq (attractiveness) 吸引力

Pullman /ˈpʊlmən/ *n* **1** (carriage) 普尔曼豪华车厢; (train) 普尔曼豪华火车 **2** Amer (suitcase) 普尔曼式大手提箱

pull-off *adj* 可取下的 ‹*lid, top*›; **a** ~ **connector** 一个分离式连接器

pull-out

A *n* **1** (of newspaper, magazine) 活页 **2** (withdrawal) 撤出

B *modif* 可抽出的 ‹*map, supplement*›

pull: ~**over** *n* 套头毛衣; ~ **tab** *n* Amer 易拉环; ~**-up** *n* 引体向上

pulmonary /ˈpʌlmənəri, Amer -neri/ *adj* 肺的; ~ **diseases** 肺病; **the** ~ **arteries and veins** 肺动静脉; ~ **tuberculosis** 肺结核

pulp /pʌlp/

A *n* [u] **1** (of fruit) 果肉 **2** (of tooth) 牙髓; **the** ~ **cavity** 牙腔 **3** (crushed mass) 浆; **wood** ~ 木浆; **to mash to** *or* **into (a)** ~ 捣成浆; **to reduce** *or* **crush sth. to a** ~ 把某物压成浆; **to reduce** *or* **crush the garlic to a** ~ 把大蒜碾成泥; **to beat sb. to a** ~ fig colloq 把某人打得稀巴烂 **4** pej (trashy books) 粗制滥造的书籍

B *vt* (crush) 把…捣成浆 ‹*berries, vegetables*›; (withdraw and recycle) 把…化成纸浆 ‹*books, newspapers*›

pulp fiction *n* [u] 粗制滥造的小说

pulpit /ˈpʊlpɪt/ *n* 布道坛

pulp novel *n* 粗制滥造的小说

pulsar /ˈpʌlsɑː(r)/ *n* 脉冲星

pulsate /pʌlˈseɪt, Amer ˈpʌlseɪt/ *vi* «*heart, vein*» 搏动; «*rhythm, music*» 震颤

pulsating /pʌlˈseɪtɪŋ, Amer ˈpʌlseɪtɪŋ/ *adj* **1** lit (beating) 跳动的 ‹*rhythm, music*›; 闪烁的 ‹*light*› **2** fig (exciting) 激动人心的 ‹*contest*›

pulsation /pʌlˈseɪʃn/ *n* **1** [c] (beat) 一次震动; (heartbeat) 一次心跳; **a rate of 60** ~**s per minute** 每分钟 60 跳的心率 **2** [u] (action) 跳动; **the** ~ **of the heart** 心脏的搏动

pulse[1] /pʌls/

A *n* **1** [u and c] Anat 脉搏; **to take** *or* **feel sb.'s** ~ 为某人把脉; **a low** *or* **weak** ~ 弱脉搏; **a regular/an irregular** ~ 规则/不规则脉搏; **to have** *or* **keep one's finger on the** ~ **of sth.** 对某事物了如指掌 **2** Elec, Phys (short burst) 脉冲; **to emit a** ~ 发出脉冲

B *vi* «*heart*» 跳动; «*star*» 闪烁; **the vibrant life pulsing through a great city** 大城市盎然勃发的生机

pulse[2] *n* Bot, Culin 豆子

pulse: ~ **dialling** *n* [u] 脉冲拨号; ~ **jet** *n* 脉冲式喷气发动机; ~ **rate** *n* 脉搏率

pulverization /ˌpʌlvəraɪˈzeɪʃn, Amer -rɪˈz-/ *n* [u] **1** (of nuts, beans, coal) 粉碎 **2** fig (of opponent) 击败

pulverize /ˈpʌlvəraɪz/ *vt* **1** (turn to powder) 将…弄碎 **2** fig colloq (defeat) 彻底击败 ‹*opposition, enemy*›

puma /ˈpjuːmə/ *n* 美洲狮

pumice /ˈpʌmɪs/ *n* [u] ~ **(stone)** 浮石

pummel /ˈpʌml/ *vt* (*pres p etc.* **-ll-** Brit, **-l-** Amer) 连续击打

pummelling /ˈpʌmlɪŋ/ *n* [u] 连续击打; **we took a real** ~ fig 我们遭到惨败

pump /pʌmp/

A *n* **1** Tech (for air, gas) 泵; (for water, liquid) 抽水机; **a hand/foot** ~ 手摇泵/脚踏泵; **all hands to the** ~**s!** 大家加油呐! **2** (action) 泵送; **the** ~ **of blood to the heart** 血液向心脏的输送; **to give sb.'s hand a** ~ fig 起劲地握某人的手 **3** Brit (plimsoll) 胶底帆布鞋; (dancing shoe) 轻舞鞋; **ballet** ~**s** 芭蕾舞鞋 **4** Amer (court shoe) 半高跟鞋

B *vt* **1** (push) 用泵输送 ‹*liquid, gas, waste*›; **the cyclist** ~**ed air into the back tyre** 骑自行车的人给后胎充了气; **to** ~ **bullets into sb.** colloq 喂某人吃枪子儿; **the firm** ~**ed money into the new product** colloq 公司把钱大量投到新产品上; **to** ~ **sth. into sb.** fig 硬给某人灌输某事物; **the tank will have to be** ~**ed dry** 一定要把水池的水抽干; **to** ~ **iron** colloq (exercise with weights) 练举重; (do bodybuilding exercises) 练健美 **2** (inject, fill) 向…灌注 ‹*person, animal*›; **to** ~ **sb. full of lead** 用子弹打烂某人; **to** ~ **sb. full of drugs** 让某人大量服药 **3** (move) 不停地摇 ‹*hand, handle, lever*›; 不停地踩 ‹*brakes, kickstart*› **4** colloq (question) 盘问 ‹*person*›; (extract) 打探 ‹*information, details, names*›; **to** ~ **sb. for ...** 向某人追问… ‹*information, details, names*›; **to** ~ **sb. about sth.** 向某人盘问某事; **to** ~ **sth. out of sb.** 从某人那里打探出某事 **5** Med 灌洗; **to** ~ **sb.'s stomach** 为某人洗胃

C *vi* **1** (use pump) 用泵输送 **2** (function) «*machine*» 唧筒似地运作; «*piston*» 上下运动; «*legs*» 不停地晃动 **3** (beat) «*heart*» 搏动; «*lungs*» 起伏 **4** (flow) «*oil, water, blood*» 涌流

Phrasal verbs

• **pump in** *vt* [~ **sth. in,** ~ **in sth.**] 注入 ‹*gas, liquid*›; **to** ~ **some air in** 充点儿气进去; **if we don't** ~ **more funds in, ...** 如果我们不再多注入点资金, …

• **pump out**

A *vt* [~ **sth. out,** ~ **out sth.**]
1 (pour out) 用泵抽出 ‹*gas, liquid*›; 射出 ‹*bullets, rounds*›; fig 不停地播放 ‹*music, propaganda*› **2** (drain) 抽干 ‹*tank, container*›; **to** ~ **out sb.'s stomach** 为某人洗胃

B *vi* «*oil, water, blood*» 涌出; fig «*music, propaganda*» 不停地播放

• **pump up** *vt* **1** (inflate) [~ **sth. up,** ~ **up sth.**] 给…充气 ‹*tyre, inflatable*› **2** [~ **sb. up**] fig colloq (enthuse) 为…加油; **to be** ~**ed up** 士气高涨 **3** [~ **sth. up,** ~ **up sth.**] colloq (increase) 提高 ‹*rate*›; 开大 ‹*volume*›

pump: ~**-action** *adj* 压动式的 ‹*shotgun*›; 手按式的 ‹*bottle, spray*›; ~ **attendant** ▸p. 409 *n* 加油站服务员; ~ **dispenser** *n* 手按式喷雾器

pumped up /ˌpʌmpt ˈʌp/ *adj* colloq (enthusiastic) 热情高涨的; (excited) 高度兴奋的

pump house *n* 水泵房

pumpkin /ˈpʌmpkɪn/ *n* [c and u] 南瓜

pumpkin pie *n* [c and u] 南瓜馅饼

pump: ~ **prices** *npl* 加油站油价; ~ **priming** *n* [u] **1** Tech 泵充水; **2** Fin 注资刺激经济; ~ **room** *n* **1** (room housing pumps) 水泵房; **2** (in spa) 矿泉水供应室

pun /pʌn/

A *n* 双关语; **to make a** ~ 用双关语

B *vi* (*pres p etc.* **-nn-**) 用双关语

Punch /pʌntʃ/ *pr n* 潘趣 [英国传统木偶剧中的驼背滑稽人物]; **a** ~ **and Judy show** 《潘趣和朱迪》木偶剧; **as pleased as** ~ 得意洋洋

punch[1] /pʌntʃ/

A *vt* **1** (hit) 拳打; **to** ~ **sb. hard** 用拳头重击某人; **to** ~ **sb. on the jaw/nose** 用拳打某人的颌/鼻子; **to** ~ **sb. in ...** 用拳打某人的 ‹*face, stomach, back*›; **to** ~ **sth. through sth.** 用某物击穿某物; **to** ~ **the ball over the bar** «*goalkeeper*» 将球击过横梁; **to** ~ **the air** 挥舞拳头 **2** Amer Agric 放牧 ‹*cattle*›

B *vi* «*boxer*» 出拳; **to** ~ **low** 出拳击打下身

C *n* **1** [c] (blow) 拳打; **to give sb. a** ~ **(on the chin/jaw/nose)** 用拳猛击某人(下巴/颌/鼻子)一下; **a** ~ **in the face/stomach/back** 打在脸/肚子/后背上的一拳; **a** ~ **to the solar plexus** 当胸的一拳; **to throw a** ~ **at sb.** 向某人挥拳头; **to land a** ~ 打中一拳; **to ride a** ~ 躲闪来拳 **2** [c] (capacity to hit) 出重拳的能力; **a boxer with a tremendous** ~ 出拳狠的拳击手; **to pack a** ~ 重拳出击; **your cocktails certainly pack a** ~**!** 你的鸡尾酒真够劲儿! **3** [u] fig (forcefulness) 力量; **a speech with plenty of** ~ 十分有说服力的演讲; **to have/have no** ~ 有/缺乏力度

Phrasal verbs

• **punch in** *vt* [~ **sth. in,** ~ **in sth.**] 砸开; **I'll** ~ **the door in!** 我会破门而入的! ; **to** ~ **sb.'s face** *or* **head in** colloq 狠揍某人

• **punch out** *vt* [~ **sth. out,** ~ **out sth.**] 打掉 ‹*teeth*›; 砸破 ‹*window*›

punch[2]

A *n* **1** (for piercing paper, leather, metal) 穿孔机; **a** ~ **mark** 冲孔标记 **2** (for nails, bolts) 起压钉器 **3** (for stamping, shaping) 压印器 **4** (die) 凸模

B *vt* **1** (make hole in) 给…打孔 ‹*paper, leather, metal*›; **to** ~ **a ticket** 打孔检票 **2** (create in paper, leather, metal) 钻出 ‹*perforation*›; 打出 ‹*indentation*›; **to** ~ **sth. in sth.** 在某物上钻出某物 **3** (press) 用力摁 ‹*button, key*›

Phrasal verbs

• **punch in**

A *vt* [~ **sth. in,** ~ **in sth.**] 输入 ‹*data, code*›

B *vi* Amer = **clock in**

• **punch out**

A *vt* [~ **sth. out,** ~ **out sth.**]
1 Comput, Telecom 按键输入 ‹*telephone number*›; 键入 ‹*data*› **2** (make with punch) 钻出 ‹*hole*›; 压出 ‹*shape, design*›

B *vi* Amer = **clock out**

punch[3] *n* [u and c] (mixed drink) 潘趣酒

punch: ~**bag** *n* [拳击训练用的] 沙袋; ~ **ball** *n* Brit [拳击训练用的] 梨球; ~ **bowl** *n* 潘趣酒碗; ~ **card** *n* 穿孔卡; ~**-drunk** *adj* (in boxing) 被击晕的; fig (from fatigue etc.) 晕头转向的

punched: ~ **card** 穿孔卡; ~ **tape** *n* 穿孔带

punching bag *n* = **punchbag**

punch: ~**line** *n* 妙语; ~**-up** *n* colloq 斗殴; **to have a** ~**-up (with sb.)** (和某人) 打架

punchy /ˈpʌntʃi/ *adj* 简洁有力的 ‹*rhythm, line, argument*›

punctilious /pʌŋkˈtɪliəs/ *adj* formal 谨小慎微的; **he was** ~ **about his work** 他对工作一丝不苟

punctiliously /pʌŋkˈtɪliəsli/ *adv* formal 谨小慎微地; **to follow instructions** ~ 一丝不苟地遵守指令

punctual /ˈpʌŋktʃʊəl/ *adj* 准时的; **to be** ~ **for sth.** 在某方面很守时; **to be** ~ **in doing sth.** 做某事准时

punctuality /ˌpʌŋktʃʊˈæləti/ *n* [u] (of person) 守时; (of train, bus) 正点

punctually /ˈpʌŋktʃʊəli/ *adv* 准时地; **to arrive** ~ **at 10** 10 点钟准时到达

punctuate /ˈpʌŋktʃueɪt/
A *vt* **1** (insert punctuation in) 给…加标点符号 **2** (interrupt) 不时打断 ‹*speech, remarks*›; 不时中断 ‹*history, development*›
B *vi* 加标点符号

punctuation /ˌpʌŋktʃʊˈeɪʃn/ *n* [u] **1** (punctuation marks) 标点符号 **2** (knowledge, use) 标点符号用法

punctuation mark *n* 标点符号

puncture /ˈpʌŋktʃə(r)/
A *n* (in tyre, airbed) 刺孔; (in lung) 穿孔
B *vt* **1** (perforate) 刺破 ‹*tyre, eardrum*›; **one of his ribs had ~d a lung** 他的一根肋骨在肺上穿了个洞 **2** fig (deflate) 挫伤 ‹*ego*›
C *vi* «*tyre, airbed*» 被刺破

puncture: ~ kit, ~ repair kit *ns* 补车胎工具箱; **~-proof** *adj* 防扎的; **~ wound** *n* 刺伤

pundit /ˈpʌndɪt/ *n* 行家

pungency /ˈpʌndʒənsi/ *n* [u] (of taste, smoke, smell) 刺激; **the ~ of his remarks** fig 他的话语之尖锐

pungent /ˈpʌndʒənt/ *adj* **1** (strong) 刺激的 ‹*taste, sauce*›; **the ~ smell of burning rubber** 烧橡胶的刺鼻气味 **2** fig 尖锐的 ‹*satire, criticism*›

pungently /ˈpʌndʒəntli/ *adv* **1** (strongly) 刺鼻地 ‹*smell*›; **a ~ flavoured sauce** 味道呛人的调味汁 **2** fig 尖锐地 ‹*express, argue*›; **a few ~ phrased remarks** 几句措词激烈的话语

punish /ˈpʌnɪʃ/ *vt* **1** (inflict penalty on) 惩罚; **to ~ sb. for sth.** 因某事惩罚某人; **murder is ~ed by life-imprisonment** 谋杀罪要判无期徒刑; **a crime ~ed by death** 死罪 **2** colloq (treat roughly) 粗暴对待 ‹*opponent, car*›; 大肆利用 ‹*mistake*›; **a rise in prescription charges would ~ the poor** 诊费提高会使穷人遭殃

punishable /ˈpʌnɪʃəbl/ *adj* 可处罚的; **to be ~ by a fine** 应罚款; **to be ~ by law** 应受法律处罚

punishing /ˈpʌnɪʃɪŋ/
A *adj* 令人精疲力竭的 ‹*schedule, pace, climb*›; 严酷的 ‹*test, defeat*›
B *n* [u] (severe defeat) 惨败; (severe damage) 严重损坏; **to take a ~** 遭到惨败

punishment /ˈpʌnɪʃmənt/ *n* **1** [u] (action) 惩罚; **corporal** *or* **physical ~** 体罚; **crime and ~** 罪与罚 **2** [u and c] (penalty) 处罚; **to inflict a ~ on sb.** 对某人施以处罚; **let the ~ fit the crime** 按罪量刑; **to take one's ~ bravely** *or* **like a man** 勇敢地接受处罚 **3** colloq [u] (rough treatment) 粗暴对待; **to withstand** *or* **stand up to ~** 经受折磨

punitive /ˈpjuːnətɪv/ *n* **1** (inflicting punishment) 惩罚性的 ‹*action, measure, restriction*›; **a ~ expedition** 讨伐; **~ damages** Jur 惩罚性损害赔偿 **2** (extremely high) 苛刻的 ‹*tariff, tax*›

Punjab /ˌpʌnˈdʒɑːb/ *pr n* **(the) ~** (region) 旁遮普; (Indian state) 旁遮普邦; (Pakistani province) 旁遮普省

Punjabi /ˌpʌnˈdʒɑːbi/ ▸p. 426
A *adj* (of the Punjab) 旁遮普的; (of the people) 旁遮普人的; (of the language) 旁遮普语的
B *n* **1** [c] (person) 旁遮普人 **2** [u] (language) 旁遮普语

punk /pʌŋk/
A *n* **1** (music) 朋克摇滚乐; (movement) 朋克运动; **a ~ hairstyle** 朋克发型 **2** (person) 朋克摇滚乐迷 **3** Amer colloq (useless person) 小混混; (hoodlum) 小流氓
B *adj* Amer colloq (bad) 糟糕的

punk rock *n* [u] 朋克摇滚乐

punnet /ˈpʌnɪt/ *n* Brit 小果篮

punt¹ /pʌnt/
A *n* (boat) [用篙撑的] 方头平底船
B *vi* 乘方头平底船航行

punt²
A *vi* (kick) 踢悬空球
B *n* 踢出的悬空球; **a 30-yard ~** 一记 30 码的悬空球

punt³ *n* Brit colloq (bet) 打赌

punt⁴ /pʊnt/ *n* Hist (currency) 爱尔兰镑

punter /ˈpʌntə(r)/ *n* esp Brit colloq **1** (gambler) 赌徒 **2** (client) 顾客

puny /ˈpjuːni/ *adj* **1** (small and weak) 弱小的 ‹*person, body*› **2** fig (poor) 微不足道的 ‹*attempt*›

pup /pʌp/
A *n* **1** (young dog) 幼犬; **to be in ~** (母狗) 怀胎; **to sell sb. a ~** Brit fig colloq 卖给某人伪劣货 **2** (young seal, rat etc.) 幼崽 **3** dated (youth) 傲慢的小子
B *vi* (*pres p etc.* **-pp-**) 生崽

pupa /ˈpjuːpə/ *n* (*pl* **pupae** /ˈpjuːpiː/) 蛹

pupate /pjuːˈpeɪt, Amer ˈpjuːpeɪt/ *vi* 化蛹

pupil¹ /ˈpjuːpɪl/ *n* Sch 小学生; **~ numbers** 学生数量; **a private ~** 家教学生

pupil² *n* Anat 瞳孔; **a dilated ~** 放大的瞳孔

puppet /ˈpʌpɪt/ *n* **1** (doll) 木偶; **she was like a ~ on a string** 她很容易被人操纵 **2** fig 傀儡; **a ~ regime/state** 傀儡政权/国家

puppeteer /ˌpʌpɪˈtɪə(r)/ ▸p. 409 *n* 演木偶戏的人

puppetry /ˈpʌpɪtri/ *n* [u] (making puppets) 木偶制作工艺; (handling puppets) 木偶表演艺术

puppet: ~ show *n* 木偶戏; **~ theatre** *n* **1** [c] (stage) [上演木偶戏等的] 微型舞台; **2** [u] (performances, shows) 木偶戏

puppy /ˈpʌpi/ *n* **1** (young dog) 幼犬; **to have puppies** 生小狗 **2** dated (youth) 傲慢的小子

puppy: ~ fat *n* [u] Brit 婴儿肥; **~ love** *n* [u] 少年初恋

pup tent *n* Amer 三角形小帐篷

purblind /ˈpɜːblaɪnd/ *adj* **1** (partly blind) 半盲的 **2** (lacking insight) 迟钝的

purchase /ˈpɜːtʃəs/
A *n* **1** [u and c] (action) 购买; **to make a ~** 采购; **proof of ~** 购货凭证 **2** [c] (thing bought) 购置物 **3** [u and c] (grip) 紧握; **to have** *or* **get a** *or* **some ~ on sth.** 抓住某物
B *vt* 购买; **to ~ sth. on credit** 赊购某物; **to ~ sth. for cash** 用现金购买某物

purchase: ~ ledger *n* 进货分类账; **~ order** *n* 订购单; **~ price** *n* 买价

purchaser /ˈpɜːtʃəsə(r)/ *n* 买主

purchase tax *n* [u] Brit 购买税

purchasing /ˈpɜːtʃəsɪŋ/ *n* [u] 购买; **~ costs** 采购费用

purchasing: ~ department *n* 采购部门; **~ power** *n* [u] 购买力

purdah /ˈpɜːdə/ *n* [u] [伊斯兰和印度教社会的] 深闺制度; **he never required his daughters to observe ~** 他从来没有要求女儿们恪守深闺习俗; **to go into ~** fig colloq 足不出户

pure /pjʊə(r)/ *adj* **1** (unadulterated) 纯的; (uncontaminated) 纯净的 ‹*air, water*›; **~ white** 纯白色; **~ silk** 真丝; **~ cotton/wool/gold** 纯棉/纯毛/纯金; **~ alcohol/oxygen/breed** 纯酒精/纯氧/纯种; **~ joy/bliss/evil** 真正的快乐/极乐/罪恶 **2** (chaste) 纯洁的 ‹*love, motive, person*›; **~ in body and in mind** 身心纯洁的; **to keep oneself ~** 洁身自好 **3** (clear) 纯正的 ‹*note, voice*› **4** *attrib* (sheer) 十足的 ‹*folly, extravagance, hypocrisy*›; **out of ~ curiosity** 完全出于好奇; **~ accident** *or* **chance** 纯属意外; **~ and simple** 不折不扣的 **5** *attrib* (not applied) 纯理论的 ‹*science, research*›; **~ mathematics/art** 纯粹数学/纯艺术

pure-bred
A *adj* 纯种的; **a ~ shire horse** 纯种大挽马
B *n* 纯种动物

purée /ˈpjʊəreɪ, Amer pjʊˈreɪ/
A *n* [用水果或熟蔬菜研成的] 糊; **apple ~** 苹果泥
B *vt* 把…研成糊状; **~d vegetables** 蔬菜泥

purely /ˈpjʊəli/ *adv* 仅仅; **~ by chance** 纯属偶然; **~ and simply** 不折不扣地

pureness /ˈpjʊənɪs/ *n* [u] (of substance, colour) 纯; (of air, water) 纯净; (of sound, motives) 纯正

pure vowel *n* 纯元音

purgative /ˈpɜːgətɪv/
A *n* 泻药; **to administer/prescribe a ~** 用/开泻药
B *adj* 通便的 ‹*effect*›; **~ medicine** 通便药

purgatory /ˈpɜːgətri, Amer -tɔːri/ *n* [u] **1** Relig 炼狱 **2** fig (suffering) 折磨

purge /pɜːdʒ/
A *vt* **1** Med 清除; **~ sth. from sth.** 把某物从某物中清除出去; **~ sb./sth. of sth.** 为某人/某物清除某物; **we had to ~ his system of the poison** 我们不得不清除他体内的毒物 **2** fig (make pure) 净化 ‹*mind, heart*›; **~d of his sins, he died in peace** 获得赎罪后他安详地死去 **3** Pol 清洗; **he ~d the party of extremists** 他清洗了党内的极端分子
B *n* Pol 清洗; **political ~s** 政治清洗

purification /ˌpjʊərɪfɪˈkeɪʃn/ *n* [u] **1** (removal of contaminants) 净化; **a system of water ~** 水净化系统 **2** Relig fig 涤罪

purification plant *n* 净化装置

purifier /ˈpjʊərɪfaɪə(r)/ *n* 净化器

purify /ˈpjʊərɪfaɪ/ *vt* **1** (remove contaminants) 净化 **2** Relig 为…涤罪; **a ritual bath to ~ the soul** 净化灵魂的洗礼

purism /ˈpjʊərɪzəm/ *n* [u] 纯粹主义

purist /ˈpjʊərɪst/ *n* 纯粹主义者

Puritan /ˈpjʊərɪtən/ Hist
A *n* 清教徒
B *adj* 清教徒的 ‹*belief, family*›

puritan /ˈpjʊərɪtən/
A *n* (prudish person) 禁欲者
B *adj* (prudish) 禁欲的

puritanical /ˌpjʊərɪˈtænɪkl/ *adj* pej 清教徒似的; **a ~ attitude toward sex** 禁欲的态度

puritanism /ˈpjʊərɪtənɪzəm/ *n* [u] **1** **Puritanism** Hist 清教主义 **2** (prudishness) 清心寡欲

purity /ˈpjʊərəti/ *n* [u] **1** (of substance) 纯净; (of sound) 纯正; (of language) 纯粹; **a diamond of great ~** 高纯度钻石 **2** fig (innocence) 纯洁

purl /pɜːl/
A *n* [u] 反针; **~ stitches/rows/knitting** 反针/倒行/倒织
B *vt* 用反针编织

purlin /ˈpɜːlɪn/ *n* 檩

purloin /pɜːˈlɔɪn/ *vt* 偷窃; **they ~ed my supper** 他们不请自来, 享用了我的晚餐

purple /ˈpɜːpl/ ▸p. 134
A *adj* 紫色的; **he was ~ with rage** 他气得脸色发青
B *n* [u and c] 紫色; **to be dressed in ~** 穿紫色衣服; **a rich/warm/cool ~** 深/暖/冷紫色

purple: P~ Heart *n* Amer [美国授予阵亡或受伤战士的] 紫心勋章; **~ heart** *n* Brit colloq 紫心片 [心型麻醉药片]; **~ passage** *n* 词藻华丽的章句; **~ patch** *n* Brit colloq (success) 接二连三的成功; (good luck) 接连不断的好运; **to have** *or* **hit a ~ patch** 福星高照; **~ prose** *n* [u] 词句华丽的散文

purplish /ˈpɜːplɪʃ/ ▸p. 134 *adj* 带紫色的

purport
A /pəˈpɔːt/ *vt* 标榜; **to ~ to do sth.** 标榜做某事; **the statue is ~ed to be of pure gold** 这尊塑像据称是纯金的
B /ˈpɜːpət/ *n* [u] formal 意义

purported /pəˈpɔːtɪd/ *adj* 据称的

purportedly /pəˈpɔːtɪdli/ *adv* 据称; **the yeti ~ seen by the mountaineers** 据说被登山者看到的雪人

p

purpose /ˈpɜːpəs/

A n **1** [u and c] (aim) 目的; **his ~ in life** 他的生活目标; **a story with a ~** 有说教寓意的故事; **sb.'s ~ in doing sth.** 某人做某事的目的; **with** *or* **for the ~ of doing sth.** 为了做某事; **on ~** 特意地; **I came here on ~ to see you** 我来这里就是要见你 **2** [u and c] (function, use) 用途; **the building is no longer used for its original ~** 这座建筑物不再用于原来计划的用途了; **to serve a/no (useful) ~** 有用/无用; **~ unknown** 用途不明; **the car is large enough for the ~** 这辆车派此用场够大了; **to good/some/little/no ~** 作用很大/有点作用/作用不大/徒劳; **to be fit/unfit for ~** 能够/无法起作用 **3** [u] (determination) 决心; **to have a sense of ~** 果断; **lack of ~** 优柔寡断

B **purposes** npl 情势需要; **for the ~s of sth.** 出于对某事的考虑; **for sb.'s (own) ~s** 对某人（自己）而言; **to go to Shanghai for business ~s** 去上海出差; **for all practical ~s** 实际上; **earned income for tax ~s** 应税的劳动收入

purpose-built adj Brit 特制的

purposeful /ˈpɜːpəsfl/ adj **1** (determined) 坚定的 ‹*character, manner, stride*› **2** (useful) 有意义的 ‹*activity*› **3** (intentional) 故意的 ‹*use*›

purposefully /ˈpɜːpəsfəli/ adv **1** (determinedly) 坚定地 ‹*move, stride*› **2** (intentionally) 故意地 ‹*ambiguous*›

purposefulness /ˈpɜːpəsflnɪs/ n [u] 坚定

purposeless /ˈpɜːpəslɪs/ adj 无目的的 ‹*person, movement*›; 无意义的 ‹*life*›; 盲目的 ‹*force*›

purposelessness /ˈpɜːpəslɪsnɪs/ n [u] 无目的; **the ~ of life** 生活的无意义

purposely /ˈpɜːpəsli/ adv 故意地

purpose-made adj Brit 特制的

purr /pɜː(r)/

A vi «*cat, lion*» 发出呼噜声; «*engine*» 轰隆作响

B vt fig (utter) 低声柔和地说

C n (of cat) 呼噜声; (of engine) 轰隆声

purse /pɜːs/

A n **1** esp Brit (for money) 手提包; **to hold** *or* **control the ~ strings** fig 掌握财权; **to tighten/loosen the ~ strings** fig 紧缩/放宽支出 **2** Amer (handbag) 坤包 **3** fig (resources) 资金; **beyond sb.'s ~** 对某人来说太昂贵 **4** (prize) [尤指拳击赛的] 奖金

B vt 撅 ‹*lips, mouth*›

C vi «*lips*» 撅起

purser /ˈpɜːsə(r)/ ▸**p. 409** n [商船队的] 事务长

pursuance /pəˈsjuːəns, Amer -ˈsuː-/ n [u] formal **1** (of duty) 执行; **in (the) ~ of sth.** 在执行某职责的过程中 **2** (of objective) 追求

pursuant /pəˈsjuːənt, Amer -ˈsuː-/ adv formal **~ to sth.** 根据某事; **~ to his religious beliefs** 依照宗教信仰

pursue /pəˈsjuː, Amer -ˈsuː/ vt **1** (chase) 追逐 ‹*criminal, prey*›; **he was ~d by misfortune** fig 他厄运连连 **2** (seek) 追求 ‹*success, love*› **3** (engage in) 从事 ‹*studies, profession*› **4** (continue to investigate) 追查 ‹*clue*›; **the police are not pursuing the matter** 警方没在追查此事

pursuer /pəˈsjuːə(r), Amer -ˈsuː-/ n 追逐者

pursuit /pəˈsjuːt, Amer -ˈsuːt/ n **1** [u] (chasing, seeking) 追逐; **in ~ of an escaped prisoner** 正在追捕逃犯; **in hot ~** 紧追不舍; **the ~ of happiness** fig 对幸福的追求 **2** [c] (interest, hobby) 爱好; **literary ~s** 文学爱好

pursuit plane n 驱逐机

purvey /pəˈveɪ/ vt formal **1** (supply) 供应 ‹*foodstuffs, goods*›; **to ~ sth. to sb.** 为某人供应某物 **2** fig (distribute) 提供 ‹*information*›; 散布 ‹*gossip*›

purveyor /pəˈveɪə(r)/ n **1** (of foodstuffs, goods) 供应者 **2** fig (of information) 提供者; (of gossip) 散布者

purview /ˈpɜːvjuː/ n [u] formal 范围; **to be within/outside the ~ of sth.** 在某事的范围内/外

pus /pʌs/ n [u] 脓

push /pʊʃ/

A vt **1** (move, shove) 推; **he walked slowly up the hill, ~ing his bike** 他推着自行车慢慢向山上走去; **to ~ sth. home** lit 把某物推到位; fig (persevere with) 抵挡回 ‹*attack*›; **to ~ the door open/shut** 推开/推上门; **to ~ sth. down the street/hill** 沿街道/小山推某物; **to ~ sb. down the stairs/slide** 把某人推下楼梯/滑梯; **to ~ sth. into sth.** 把某物推入 ‹*river, ditch, house*›; 把某物塞进 ‹*pocket, hand, slot*›; **to ~ one's finger/a stick into sth.** 把手指/棍子插到某物里; **this could ~ the country into recession** 这样可能使国家陷入萧条; **to ~ sb. off sth.** lit 把某人推下 ‹*seat, platform, bridge*›; fig 把某人排挤出 ‹*committee*›; **to ~ sth./sb. out of sth.** 把某物/某人推出某物; **to ~ sth./sb. through sth.** 把某物/某人推进某物; **to ~ a bill through parliament** 促使国会通过法令; **to ~ sth. to new heights** 推动某事使之达到新高度; **to ~ sth. to the back of one's mind** 把某事丢到脑后; **to ~ sth. towards sb.** 把某物推向某人; **to ~ sth. up** 把某物推上 ‹*ladder, hill*›; **to be ~ing 60** 年近花甲; **that's ~ing it a bit!** 这有点儿过分了！; **did she resign or was she ~ed?** 她是辞职还是被迫下台的？ **2** colloq (urge, drive) 催促; **to ~ sb. into doing sth.** 催某人开始做某事; **to ~ sb. into action** 催某人行动起来; **to ~ sb. to do sth.** 催某人做某事; **to ~ sb. hard** 猛催某人; **to ~ sb. to the brink of sth./to breaking point** 把某人逼到某事的边缘/极限; **to ~ sb. to the limits (of sth.)** 把某人逼到（某事的）极限; **to ~ sb. too far** 逼某人太紧; **to ~ one's luck** *or* **it** colloq 继续碰运气 **3** (make) 强行通过 ‹*path*›; **he ~ed his way through the crowd/past the onlookers/to her** 他挤过了人群/从围观者中间挤了过去/挤到了她身边 **4** (operate) 按 ‹*button, bell, switch*› **5** (put under pressure) 逼迫; **to ~ sb. for sth.** 为某事物逼迫某人; **to be ~ed for** colloq 缺 ‹*money, time*›; **I'm a bit ~ed for cash** 我手头有点儿紧; **to be ~ed** colloq 很匆忙; **to be ~ed to do sth.** colloq 勉强做某事 **6** colloq (promote) 推销 ‹*goods, product, model*› **7** colloq (advocate) 推行 ‹*idea, plan, policy*›; **to ~ a point** 强调一个观点 **8** (deal in) 贩卖 ‹*drugs*› **9** (in cricket) 推击 ‹*ball*›

B v refl **1** (move) **to ~ oneself** 撑起身体; **to ~ oneself upright/into a sitting position** 挺直背/坐起来; **she ~ed herself through a gap** 她从空隙间挤了过去 **2** (make effort) 勉强; **to ~ oneself to do sth.** 勉强做某事

C vi **1** (apply force) 推; **to ~ hard** 用力推; **to ~ and shove** 推搡; **to ~ at sth.** 不停地推某物; **he ~ed at the food with obvious distaste** 他把食物拨来拨去，显然没什么胃口; **to ~ on** *or* **against sth.** 撞到某物 **2** (advance) 推进; **to ~ into sth.** 挤进 ‹*queue, space, crowded room*›; **to ~ past** 挤过去; **to ~ past sb.** 挤过某人; **to ~ through sth.** 挤出 ‹*crowd, room*›; **to ~ towards a place/destination** 向某处/某目的地推进 **3** (press to operate sth.) 摁; **'Push'** (on bell) "请按铃"; (on door) "推" **4** (make great efforts) «*runner, athlete*» 奋力; **to ~ hard** 拼命 **5** (demand) 一再要求; **to ~ for sth.** 努力争取 ‹*improvement, information*›; **to ~ for action** 一再要求采取行动

D n **1** [c] (shove) 推; **to give sb./sth. a ~** 推某人/某物一下; **at the ~ of a button** 一摁按钮; **to move sth. with a (hard) ~** 把某物一下子（使劲）推开; **at a ~** Brit colloq 迫不得已时; **to give sb. the ~** Brit colloq (dismiss) 开除某人; (get rid of) 与某人断交; **to get the ~** Brit colloq «*employee*» 被开除; «*boyfriend, girlfriend*» 被抛弃; **when** *or* **if ~ comes to shove** colloq 如果到紧要关头时; **if it comes to the ~** colloq 如果迫不得已 **2** [c] Mil 突围进攻; **the big/autumn ~** 大突围/秋季攻势; **a ~ against sb./sth.** 向某人/某处发动的攻击 **3** [u] fig colloq (determination) 决心; (drive) 动力; **not to have enough ~** 缺乏进取心; **to have plenty of ~ and go** 劲头十足 **4** [c] fig colloq (campaign, drive) 运动; (effort) 努力; **a ~ for/to do sth.** 推动/做某事的努力; **a sales ~ to increase turnover** 增加营业额的促销活动; **a ~ on sth.** 对某事的推行 **5** [c] fig colloq (shift) 变动; **a ~ to** *or* **towards sth.** 向某事的发展 **6** [c] fig colloq (stimulus) 激励; **to give sth. a ~, to give a ~ to sth.** 推动某事; **to give sb./sth. a ~ in the right direction** 把某人/某事推向正确方向 **7** [c] Sport 推击; **a ~ to mid-on** 向投手右侧外场的推球

Phrasal verbs

- **push about** vt [~ sb. about, ~ about sb.] = **push around**
- **push ahead** vi **1** (on journey) 继续前行 **2** (with plans) «*person, organization*» 毅然推行; **to ~ ahead with sth.** 坚定推行 ‹*plan, change*›; 坚定推进 ‹*move, purchase*›
- **push along** vi **1** colloq (leave) 动身出发 **2** (travel fast) «*person, driver, vehicle*» 快速前行
- **push around** vt [~ sb. around, ~ around sb.] colloq 对…发号施令
- **push aside** vt [~ sth./sb. aside, ~ aside sth./sb.]
  1 (move) 推开 **2** fig (ignore) 把…抛到脑后 ‹*feeling, doubt, idea*›
- **push away** vt [~ sth./sb. away, ~ away sth./sb.] 推开
- **push back** vt [~ sth./sb. back, ~ back sth./sb.]
  1 (move back) 往后推 ‹*person, chair*›; 使…后移 ‹*forest*›; **she ~ed her hair back** 她向后理了理头发 **2** Mil 迫使…后退 ‹*troops, front*› **3** (put back) 推迟 ‹*time, date, event*›; **the start was ~ed back from 2 p.m. to 4 p.m.** 出发时间从下午 2 点推迟到 4 点
- **push down** vt [~ sth. down, ~ down sth.] (reduce) 降低; **to ~ the price/number/temperature down to ...** 把价格/数目/温度降低到…
- **push forward**

A vi (advance) «*troops*» 向前推进

B vt [~ sb./sth. forward, ~ forward sb./sth.]
1 (move forward) 向前推 ‹*person, troops, chair*› **2** fig (put forward) 极力坚持 ‹*idea, proposal*›

- **push in**

A vt [~ sb./sth. in, ~ in sb./sth.]
1 (force to go in) 把…推入 ‹*key, peg, bolt*› **2** (press inwards) 踹开 ‹*door, window*›

B vi Brit «*person, vehicle*» 加塞儿

- **push off**

A vi **1** Brit colloq (leave) 离开; **it's time we were ~ing off** 我们该走了; **~ off, will you!** 劳驾你滚开！ **2** (in boat) 划船离去; **to ~ off aft** 向后划船; **to ~ off from the bank/quay** 从岸边/码头划走

B vt [~ sth. off, ~ off sth.]
1 (remove) 揭掉 ‹*lid, covering*›; **to ~ sth. off sth.** 从某处把某物揭掉 **2** Naut 划走 ‹*boat*›

- **push on**

A vi **1** (on journey) 继续前行 **2** (with plans) **= push ahead 2**

B vt [~ sth. on, ~ on sth.] 推上 ‹*lid, covering*›

- **push out**

A [~ sb. out, ~ out sb.] vt (force to leave) 赶走 ‹*person, rival*›

B vt [~ sth. out, ~ out sth.]
1 (replace) 取代 ‹*product, fashion*›; 改变 ‹*attitude*› **2** (move outwards) 使突出; **to ~ out one's chest** 挺起胸膛; **she ~ed her lips out in a pout** 她撅起了嘴 **3** (mass-produce) 批量生产 ‹*product*›; **universities ~ing out graduates with useless degrees** 培养出成批持无用文凭毕业生的大学

- **push over**

A vt [~ sb./sth. over, ~ over sb./sth.] 推倒

B vi colloq 挪开; **~ over!** 挪过去！

- **push through**

A vt [~ sth. through, ~ through sth.] 使…获得批准 ‹*policy, deal*›; **to ~ a bill through**

parliament 促使议会通过一项法案; **he promised to ~ through her visa application** 他答应让她的签证申请尽快办下来
B *vi* «*person, vehicle*» 挤过去
• **push up** *vt* [**~ sth. up, ~ up sth.**] 使持续增长 ‹*price, rate, unemployment, inflation*›; **the shortage of building land is bound to ~ up house prices** 建筑用地短缺肯定会推高房价

pushbike /ˈpʊʃbaɪk/ *n* Brit colloq 自行车

push-button /ˈpʊʃbʌtn/
A **push button** *n* 电钮
B *adj attrib* 电钮控制的; **~ warfare** 按钮战争

push: ~cart *n* 手推车; **~chair** *n* Brit 折叠式婴儿车

pusher /ˈpʊʃə(r)/ *n* colloq 毒品贩子

push-fit *n* 推合座; **~ connector/connection** 推合连接器/接头

pushiness /ˈpʊʃmɪs/ *n* [u] 一意孤行

pushing /ˈpʊʃɪŋ/ *n* [u] 推搡

pushover /ˈpʊʃəʊvə(r)/ *n* colloq **1** (task) 轻而易举的事 **2** (person) 耳根软的人

push: ~pin *n* Amer 图钉; **~rod** *n* 挺杆

push-start
A /ˌpʊʃˈstɑːt/ *vt* 推发动 ‹*vehicle*›
B /ˈpʊʃstɑːt/ *n* 推车起动

push technology *n* [u] 推送技术 [可以通过互联网不断提供用户选定类别的信息]

push-up
A *n* esp Amer 俯卧撑
B *adj attrib* 上托的 ‹*bra*›

pushy /ˈpʊʃi/ *adj* pej 执意强求的; **a ~ salesman** 纠缠不休的推销员

pusillanimous /ˌpjuːsɪˈlænɪməs/ *adj* pej 怯懦的 ‹*person, behaviour*›

puss /pʊs/ *n* colloq **1** esp Brit (cat) 猫咪 **2** Amer, Scot, Ir colloq (mouth) 嘴巴; (face) 脸蛋

pussy /ˈpʊsi/ *n* **1** colloq (cat) 猫咪 **2** taboo sl (female genitals) 屄 offensive **3** taboo sl (intercourse) **to get some ~** 搞女人 **4** Amer colloq (wimp) 懦弱的男子

pussy: ~cat *n* **1** colloq (cat) 猫咪; **2** (person) 随和的人; **~foot** *vi* colloq pej **to ~foot (around)** 瞻前顾后; **~footing** *n* [u] colloq pej 谨小慎微; **~ willow** *n* (tree) 褪色柳; (catkin) 柔荑花序

pustule /ˈpʌstjuːl, Amer -tʃuːl/ *n* 脓疱

put /pʊt/
A *vt* (*pres p* **-tt-**; *pt, pp* **put**) **1** (place) 安置 ‹*person*›; 放 ‹*object, feet*›; **to ~ sth. in/on/under/around sth.** 把某物放到某物里/上/下/周围; **he ~ his arm around her/her waist** 他用胳膊搂着她/她的腰; **to ~ sth. high up/low down** 把某物放到高处/下面; **someone had ~ a ladder against the wall** 有人靠墙放了一把梯子; **I've ~ you in the spare room** 我把你安排到空余的房间里了; **to ~ a ball out (of court)** 把球击到场外; **to ~ an advertisement/announcement in the paper** 在报纸上登广告/声明; **I wouldn't ~ it past him/her (to do sth.)** colloq 我看他/她是干得出(某事)的; **I wouldn't ~ anything past him/her** colloq 我看他/她什么事都做得出来; **to ~ one's trust/confidence in sb.** 信任某人/对某人有信心; **~ your faith in the Lord!** 皈依主吧! **2** (affix) 安装; **to ~ a new lock on a door** 给一扇门装新锁; **to ~ a stamp on a letter** 往信上贴邮票; **to ~ a button on a shirt** 在衬衫上钉纽扣 **3** (cause to be or do) 使处于…状态; **the doctor ~ me on a diet** 医生让我节食; **my brother ~ me on the train** 哥哥把我送上了火车; **to ~ sth. into service/in order** 把某物投入使用/整理好; **to ~ sb. in an awkward** *or* **difficult position** 让某人为难; **to ~ sb. in a good/bad mood** 让某人心情好/差; **she ~ her hair in a ponytail** 她扎起了马尾辫; **to ~ sb. over/under sb.** Mgmt 让某人当某人的上司/下属; **to ~ sb. in goal/defence** 让某人当守门员/防守; **to ~ a clock/watch right** 把钟/表拨准; **to ~ sth. on one side** 把某物放在一旁; **he was ~ to work in the kitchen** 他被派到厨房去干活儿了; **I do hope we're not ~ting you to too much trouble** 我希望我们没有给你带来太多麻烦 **4** (cause to have) 产生 ‹*gloss*›; 留下 ‹*edge, hole*›; **to ~ a shine on sth.** 使某物有光泽; **to ~ a dent in sth.** 在某物上弄出凹痕; **the fresh air ~ some colour into his cheeks** 新鲜空气让他面颊有了血色 **5** (rate) 给…评级; **I ~ him among the great composers** 我认为他是一位伟大的作曲家; **to ~ sb./sth. before** *or* **above sb./sth.** 把某人/某事物看得比某人/某事物重要; **to ~ children/safety first** 优先考虑孩子们/把安全放在首位 **6** (express) 表达 ‹*thoughts, feelings*›; 提出 ‹*argument, proposal*›; **as the poet ~s it, ...** 正像诗人所说的那样, …; **to ~ it bluntly, ...** 直截了当地说, …; **that's one way of ~ting it** 这是一种说法; **to ~ sth. into ...** 用…表达某事物 ‹*words, music*›; 把某物翻译成 ‹*another language*›; **to ~ sth. in a few words** 简述某事; **how would you ~ that in Chinese?** 这个用汉语怎么说?; **nicely ~!** 说得好! **7** (thrust) 塞 ‹*object*›; **he ~ his hands into his pockets** 他把手插进了衣袋; **to ~ sth. through sth.** 把某物塞进 ‹*letter box*›; **to ~ sth. through the books** Accts 以记账方式购买某物; **to ~ sth. through a test/process** 让某物经过检验/工序流程; **to ~ sb. through sth.** (support financially) 供某人上 ‹*school, university, college*›; colloq (force) 让某人经受 ‹*test, suffering*›; **he ~ his family through a great deal of trouble** 他给家人惹了好多麻烦; **to ~ sb. through it** 让某人受苦; **to ~ a bullet in sb./sth.** 开枪打中某人/某物; **to ~ sth. behind one** 把某事抛到脑后; **he ~ his hand up the pipe** 他把手放到管子上; **the guard ~ him out of the building** 保安把他赶出了大楼 **8** (devote, invest) 投入 ‹*money, time, energy*›; **he ~ as much feeling into his voice as he could** 他尽可能让自己的声音充满感情; **to ~ a lot of oneself into sth.** 全身心投入某事; **he ~s £150 in a savings account every month** 他每月存入储蓄账户 150 英镑 **9** (wager) 赌; **to ~ ten pounds/a bet on a horse** 在一匹马上下 10 英镑赌注/下赌注 **10** (assign) 确定; (attribute) 认定; **to ~ a price on sth.** 为某物定价; **I don't ~ any value on it** *or* **I ~ no value on it** 我认为这个毫无价值; **it's difficult to ~ a date on it** 很难确定它的年代; **to ~ a limit on sth.** 限制某事物 **11** (impose) 施加; **commentators ~ some of the blame on Congress** 评论家们把一部分过错归咎于国会 **12** (add) 增加 ‹*money, savings*›; **to ~ sth. towards sth.** 为某事凑钱; **to ~ money towards a holiday** 为休假攒钱; **to ~ sth. on sth.** 将某物增加某数目; **the Chancellor has ~ a penny on income tax** 财政大臣把所得税提高了1便士; **to ~ tax** *or* **duty on sth.** 对某事物征税; **the experience has ~ 10 years on him** 这次经历让他老了 10 岁 **13** (write) 写出 ‹*name, initials, punctuation mark*›; 画出 ‹*cross, mark*›; **to ~ one's signature to a document** 在文件上签名; **I couldn't read what she had ~** 我看不懂她写的字 **14** (offer for consideration) 提出…供考虑 ‹*argument, proposal*›; **to ~ sth. to sb./sth.** 向某人/某机构提出某事; **to ~ sth. to sb.** (express) 给某人说某事; (communicate) 把某事传达给某人; (submit) 向某人提交某物; **I ~ it to you that ...** 我告诉你…; **to ~ a plan/one's complaint before sb.** 向某人提交计划/投诉 **15** (estimate) 估计; **to ~ sth. at sth.** 估计某物为某数值; **I'd ~ its value at around £500** 我估计它大约值 500 英镑; **I'd ~ her (age) at about 35** 我估计她大约 35 岁
B *v refl* (*pres p* **-tt-**; *pt, pp* **put**) **to ~ oneself in an awkward/a strong position** 把自己弄得很尴尬/使自己处于强势地位; **~ yourself in his position** *or* **place** *or* colloq **shoes** 你设身处地为他想想; **I didn't know where to ~ myself** colloq 我尴尬得手足无措
C *vi* (*pres p* **-tt-**; *pt, pp* **put**) Naut 进港; **to ~ into port** 驶入港口
D *n* Sport 推铅球

Phrasal verbs

• **put about**
A *vi* «*vessel, sailor, captain*» 掉转航向
B *vt* [**~ sth. about, ~ about sth.**]
1 Naut 使…掉转航向 ‹*vessel*› **2** Brit (spread) 散布 ‹*rumour, gossip*›; **it's being ~ about that ...** 纷纷传说…

• **put across**
A *vt* [**~ sth. across, ~ across sth.**] (communicate) 表达 ‹*idea, concept, point of view*›; 传达 ‹*message*›
B *v refl* **to ~ oneself across** 表达自己; **to be good at ~ting oneself across** 善于表达自己

• **put aside** *vt* [**~ sth. aside, ~ aside sth.**]
1 (place to one side) 把…放到一边 **2** (save) 存 ‹*money*›; **to ~ something aside for a rainy day** 未雨绸缪 **3** (devote) 留出 ‹*time*›; **I ~ aside half an hour every day to write** *or* **for writing my diary** 我每天抽出半小时写日记 **4** Comm (reserve) 预留; **to ~ aside sth. for sb.** 为某人保留某物 **5** (end) 搁置 ‹*differences, doubts, problems*›

• **put away**
A [**~ sth. away, ~ away sth.**] *vt*
1 (tidy away) 收起 **2** (save) 存 ‹*money*›; **she's got a tidy sum ~ away!** 她攒了不少钱!
3 colloq (consume) 大吃 ‹*food*›; 猛喝 ‹*drink*›
4 Sport colloq 踢进 ‹*goal, shot, penalty, conversion*›
B [**~ sb. away, ~ away sb.**] *vt* colloq (confine) (in prison) 囚禁; (in psychiatric hospital) 收容; **to ~ sb. away for 10 years/life** 把某人关押 10 年/终身监禁; **she went a bit queer in the head and had to be ~ away** 她脑子出了点问题, 不得不被送进精神病院

• **put back**
A *vt* [**~ sth. back, ~ back sth.**]
1 (return, restore) 放回; **to ~ sth. back on/in/under sth.** 把某物放回到某物上/里/下; **to ~ sth. back together again** 重新把某物组装好 **2** (wind backwards) 往后拨 ‹*clock, watch*›; **to ~ the time back to 3 o'clock** 把时间拨回到 3 点; **to ~ the big hand back five minutes** 把时针拨后 5 分钟 **3** (postpone) 推迟 ‹*event, departure, time*›; **to ~ sth. back to** *or* **until ...** 把某事推迟到…; **the meeting has been ~ back to a later date/the 23rd** 会议被推迟到以后的某个日期/23 号
4 (delay) 延误 ‹*production, completion*›; **the strike has ~ deliveries back by two weeks** 罢工使得交货时间延误了两周
5 colloq (knock back) 猛喝 ‹*drink*›
B *vi* 返回; **the ship had to ~ back to port** 船不得不返回港口

• **put by** *vt* [**~ sth. by, ~ by sth.**] esp Brit 积攒 ‹*money*›; **he tries to ~ something by every month** 他尽量每月攒一些钱; **I have a bit ~ by** 我攒了一点钱

• **put down**
A [**~ sth./sb. down, ~ down sth./sb.**] *vt*
1 (on ground, surface) 放下; **it's a great book. I couldn't ~ it down** 这本书太棒了, 我爱不释手; **she ~ the phone down on me** Brit 她挂掉了我的电话 **2** Transp 让…下车 ‹*passengers*› **3** colloq (criticize) 责难; (humiliate) 羞辱 **4** (classify) (mentally) 把…看作; (in writing) 把…归类; **to ~ sb./sth. down as sb./sth.** 把某人/某事物视作某人/某事物 **5** (enter on list) 登记 ‹*person, name*›; **to ~ sb./sth. down for sth.** 为某事给某人/某事物登记; **you can ~ me down for £10** 请给我登记认捐 10 英镑; **they've ~ their son down for Eton** 他们为儿子报名上伊顿公学
B [**~ sth. down, ~ down sth.**] *vt*
1 (write down) 写下; **can you ~ it down in writing?** 你能把它写下来吗? **2** (suppress)

P

镇压 〈*rebellion, opposition*〉; **to ~ sth. down by force** 武力镇压某活动 **3** Aviat 驾驶…着陆 〈*aircraft*〉 **4** (put in storage) 储存 〈*wine, cheese, produce*〉 **5** Vet 弄死 〈*animal*〉; **to ~ an animal down humanely** 人道地杀死动物 **6** Pol 提交 〈*motion*〉 **7** (deposit) 预交 〈*money*〉; **to ~ sth. down on sth.** 为某物交某定金; **we ~ all our savings down on a new house** 我们拿出全部积蓄付了新房子的定金 **8** Transp 让某人下车 〈*passengers*〉 **9** (charge) 以记账方式购买 〈*article*〉; **to ~ sth. down to sth.** 把某物的款项记在某处; **~ these shoes down to my account, please** 请把鞋子的款项记在我的账上 **10** (ascribe) **to ~ sth. down to sth.** 把某事归因于某事物; **I ~ the error down to sheer carelessness/negligence** 我认为这个错误纯粹是马虎/疏忽造成的; **to ~ sth. down to experience** 吸取某事的经验

C *vi* «*aircraft, pilot*» 着陆

D *v refl* [**~ oneself down**] (be self-deprecatory) 自我贬低; (be self-critical) 自责

• **put forth** *vt* [**~ sth. forth, ~ forth sth.**] formal or liter 长出 〈*leaves, roots*〉; 伸出 〈*arm, hand*〉

• **put forward**

A [**~ sb./sth. forward, ~ forward sb./sth.**] *vt* (propose) 提议; **are you going to ~ him/your name forward for the post?** 你会推荐他/自荐担任此职吗?; **can I ~ you forward as a candidate?** 我可以提名你做候选人吗?

B [**~ sth. forward, ~ forward sth.**] *vt*

1 (wind forwards) 往前拨 〈*clock, watch*〉; **to ~ the big hand forward an hour/to 3 o'clock** 把时针拨快 1 小时/拨到 3 点 **2** (advance in time) 把…提前 〈*event, departure, time*〉; **to ~ sth. forward by sth.** 将某事提前某量; **they ~ the wedding forward (by) a month** 他们把婚礼日期提前了一个月; **to ~ sth. forward to** *or* **until sth.** 将某事提前到某时间; **~ the meeting forward to the 21st of the month** 把会议的日期提前到本月21日 **3** (suggest) 提出 〈*suggestion, theory*〉; **to ~ sth. forward for sth.** 为某事提出某事; **he ~ forward radical proposals for reforming the electoral system** 他提交了有关改革选举制度的激进提案; **to ~ forward sth. to do sth.** 提议某事做某事; **the authorities have ~ forward a new plan to combat vandalism** 当局提出了一项防止破坏公物行为的新计划

C *v refl* **to ~ oneself forward** 自荐; **to ~ oneself forward for sth.** 为某事物自荐; **are you going to ~ yourself forward for the post?** 你要自荐担任此职吗?; **to ~ oneself forward as sth.** 自荐担任某角色

• **put in**

A [**~ sth. in, ~ in sth.**] *vt*

1 (add) 加入 〈*ingredient*〉 **2** (install, fit) 安装 〈*appliance, equipment*〉 **3** (insert) 戴上 〈*contact lens*〉; 镶上 〈*false teeth*〉; (in opening, container) 放入 〈*cork, plug*〉 **4** (include) 插入 〈*word, paragraph, punctuation mark*〉; **to ~ in that ...** 插话说… **5** (submit) 提出 〈*request, resignation*〉; **to ~ in an application for sth.** 为某事物提交申请; **to ~ in a claim for sth.** 提出对某事物的要求; **to ~ in an appearance** 露一下面 **6** (devote) 付出 〈*time, effort*〉; **to ~ in time/a lot of work doing sth.** 花时间/费很大工夫做某事; **he has ~ in an honest day's work** 他辛苦工作了一整天 **7** Fin 投入 〈*money, resources*〉 **8** (in boxing) 击出 〈*punch*〉

B [**~ in sth.**] *vt* (interject) 插入 〈*words*〉; **to ~ in a word for sb.** 为某人说几句话; **'but what about us?' he ~ in** "那我们怎么办?" 他插嘴问道

C [**~ sb. in, ~ in sb.**] *vt*

1 Pol (choose) 使…当选 〈*candidate*〉; 选举…执政 〈*party*〉 **2** (enter, recommend) 推荐 〈*candidate*〉; **to ~ sb. in for sth.** 为某事推荐某人/某物; **to be ~ in for promotion/a competition** 被荐举晋升/参加比赛 **3** (begin to employ) 指派; **you need to ~ a member of staff in as a caretaker** 你需要派一名员工代管 **4** (in cricket) 让…先击球 〈*team*〉; **to ~ sb. in to bat** 让某人先击球

D *v refl* **to ~ oneself in for** 报名参加 〈*competition, exam*〉; 报名申请 〈*promotion, award*〉

E *vi* **1** esp Brit (apply) 申请; **to ~ in for sth.** 申请某事; **are you going to ~ in for the post/six months' leave?** 你要申请这个职位/半年休假吗? **2** Naut «*vessel, crew*» 进港; **the ship ~ in at Lagos for repairs** 这艘船停靠在拉各斯港进行维修

• **put off**

A [**~ sth. off, ~ off sth.**] *vt*

1 (postpone) 推迟 〈*task, appointment, decision*〉; **she keeps on ~ting off going to the dentist** 她一直拖着没去看牙医; **the meeting has been ~ off until June/after Christmas** 会议推迟至 6 月/圣诞节后召开 **2** (switch off) 关 〈*light, appliance*〉; 断 〈*electricity*〉

B [**~ sb. off, ~ off sb.**] *vt*

1 (displease, repel) 使反感; **the very thought of eating snails ~s me off!** 一想到吃蜗牛我就恶心!; **to ~ sb. off sth./sb./off doing sth.** 使某人讨厌某事物/某人/做某事; **the accident ~ her off driving for life** 那次车祸让她一辈子不想开车 **2** (allow to get off) (from bus) 让…下车; (from boat) 让…下船 **3** (stall, fob off) 取消与…的会面; **she ~ him off with a vague excuse/promise that ...** 她含含糊糊地找了个借口/用…的承诺把他打发掉了; **to be easily ~ off** (discouraged) 容易泄气; (dissuaded) 容易打发 **4** Brit (distract) 干扰 〈*person, player*〉; **to ~ sb. off sth.** 扰乱某人做某事; **any sudden noise will ~ him off his game** 任何突然的声响都会干扰他比赛

C *vi* «*ship, crew*» 离港; **to ~ off from the quay** 离开码头

• **put on** *vt* [**~ sth. on, ~ on sth.**]

1 (dress oneself in) 穿 〈*clothes, shoes*〉; 戴 〈*hat, gloves*〉 **2** (apply to skin) 涂抹 〈*cream, suntan oil, make-up, lipstick*〉 **3** (put in place) 装 〈*tyre*〉; 铺 〈*bedclothes*〉 **4** (switch on, operate) 打开 〈*appliance*〉; 开 〈*light*〉; 接通 〈*electricity*〉; **to ~ the kettle on** 把水壶烧上; **I'll ~ the dinner on in a minute** 我马上做晚饭 **5** (play) 播放 〈*music, CD, record*〉; **to ~ some jazz/Beethoven on** 放一些爵士乐/贝多芬的乐曲 **6** (gain) 增加 〈*weight*〉; **I ~ on a few kilos over Christmas** 圣诞节期间我重了好几公斤 **7** (add, impose) 征收 〈*excise duty, tax*〉 **8** (stage) 上演 〈*play, film*〉; 举办 〈*display, exhibition*〉 **9** (add to service) 增开 〈*extra train, carriage*〉; 增设 〈*bus service, rail service*〉 **10** (make available) 供应 〈*meal, food*〉 **11** (wind forwards) 往前拨 〈*clock, watch*〉; **~ the big hand on one hour** 把时针拨快一小时 **12** (assume, adopt) 装出 〈*air, expression*〉

• **put out**

A [**~ sth. out, ~ out sth.**] *vt*

1 (take outside) 把…放到屋外 〈*dustbin, rubbish, milk bottle*〉 **2** (make available, arrange) 把…准备好 〈*food, towel, clothes*〉; 摆好 〈*cards, chess pieces*〉 **3** (extend) 伸出 〈*hand, arm, foot, leg*〉; **to ~ out one's tongue** 伸出舌苔让医生检查 **4** (in tennis, badminton) 把…击出场外; (in basketball) 把…投出场外; (in football) 把…踢出场外 **5** Bot 长出 〈*leaves, roots*〉 **6** (issue) 发出 〈*report, appeal, warning*〉; 发布 〈*statement*〉 **7** (extinguish) 扑灭 〈*fire*〉; 吹灭 〈*candle*〉; 掐灭 〈*cigarette*〉 **8** (switch off) 关掉 〈*light, gas*〉 **9** (cause to be wrong) 使…出错 〈*result, calculation*〉; **that has ~ all my plans out** 那使我的计划都泡汤了 **10** Comm (subcontract) 把…承包出去 〈*work, job*〉; **we ~ a lot of our work out to freelancers** 我们把许多活儿都承包给了自由职业者; **to ~ sth. out to tender** 就某事招标 **11** (launch) 生产 〈*product*〉

B *vt* **1** [**~ sb. out, ~ out sb.**] (knock out) (with blow) 打晕; (with drugs) 麻醉; **to ~ sb. out for the count** 把某人击倒在地上, 等待从 1 倒数到 10 **2** (inconvenience) 给…带来不便 **3** (annoy) 惹恼; **to look/feel ~ out** 看上去/感觉很烦

C *v refl* **to ~ oneself out** 特意; **please don't ~ yourself out!** 不用麻烦!; **to ~ oneself out to do sth.** 特意做某事; **to ~ oneself out on sb.'s account** *or* **for sb.** 特意为某人费事

D *vi* **1** Naut «*ship, crew*» 出海; **to ~ out to sea** 出海 **2** Amer colloq (consent to sex) 同意发生性关系

• **put over** *vt* = **put across A**

• **put through**

A [**~ sth. through, ~ through sth.**] *vt* (implement successfully) 完成 〈*scheme, plan, reform*〉; 达成 〈*deal*〉

B [**~ sb./sth. through, ~ through sb./sth.**] *vt* Telecom 为…接通电话; **she ~ through a call from my husband** 她接到我丈夫的一个电话; **to ~ sb. through to sb./sth.** 把某人的电话接通到某人/某处; **I was ~ through to the wrong department** 我的电话被转错了部门

• **put together** *vt* [**~ sth. together, ~ together sth.**]

1 (assemble) 安装 〈*machine, furniture, parts, pieces*〉; **she's smarter than the rest of the family ~ together** 她比家里其他人加起来还要聪明 **2** (place together) 集中 〈*animals, objects, people*〉; **I ~ the DVDs together with the tapes** 我把 DVD 和磁带放在了一起; **to ~ one's hands together (for sb.)** (为某人) 鼓掌 **3** (form) 组成 〈*partnership, team*〉 **4** (compile, write, edit) 编制 〈*file, anthology, leaflet*〉; 撰写 〈*case, essay, application*〉; 制作 〈*programme*〉 **5** (prepare) 烹制出 〈*meal*〉

• **put up**

A [**~ sth. up, ~ up sth.**] *vt*

1 (raise) 升起 〈*flag, sail*〉; **to ~ up one's hair** 把头发盘起来; **to ~ one's hand up** 举手; **~ 'em up!** colloq (to surrender) 举起手来!; (to fight) 握紧拳头!; **she ~ up her collar** 她翻起了领子; **to ~ up an umbrella** 打开伞 **2** (build, erect) 盖起 〈*memorial, shed, building*〉; 砌起 〈*fence*〉; 支起 〈*tent*〉; 架起 〈*aerial, radio mast, barrier*〉 **3** (post up) 张贴; **he had ~ up a notice on the board** 他在板上贴了一个通告 **4** (increase) 提高 〈*price, temperature, level*〉; 增加 〈*pressure, total*〉; **the government has ~ up income tax** 政府调高了所得税 **5** (show, present) 发起 〈*resistance, struggle*〉; **our side ~ up a good performance** 我们这边表现相当不错; **they surrendered without ~ting up much of a fight** 他们没有激烈反抗就投降了 **6** Fin 提供 〈*money*〉 **7** (present) 提出 〈*case, proposal, idea*〉; **to ~ sth. up for discussion/consideration** 提出某事供讨论/考虑 **8** Aerosp 发射 〈*satellite, rocket, space station*〉 **9** (offer) 拿出来 [出售或拍卖]; **to ~ sth. up for sale/auction** 拿某物出来卖/拍卖

B [**~ sb. up, ~ up sb.**] *vt*

1 (provide with accommodation) 为…提供食宿; **to ~ sb. up for the night** 留某人过夜 **2** (as candidate) 提名; **to ~ sb. up for promotion** 提名某人晋升 **3** colloq (incite) **to ~ sb. up to a crime/stealing the money** 怂恿某人犯罪/偷钱 **4** (promote) 让…升级 〈*pupil, team*〉; **she was ~ up from set 2 to set 1** 她被从二级提升到了一级

C *vi* **1** (stay) 过夜; **to ~ up with friends** 住在朋友家里; **to ~ up at a stranger's house** 在陌生人家里过夜 **2** (be candidate) 自荐; **to ~ up for the post of .../for the election** 自荐出任…之职/参加选举; **to ~ up or shut up** colloq 要么澄清自己, 要么闭嘴; **they called for the minister to either ~ up or shut up** 他们要求那位部长要么澄清自己, 要么就闭嘴

D *v refl* **to ~ oneself up** 自荐; **to ~ oneself up for the post of .../for election** 自荐出任…之职/参加选举

• **put up with** *vt* [**~ up with sb./sth.**]

容忍; **how can you ~ up with that noise?** 你怎么能忍受那种噪声?

putative /ˈpjuːtətɪv/ *attrib adj* formal 推定的 ‹*author, father*›

put: ~-down *n* colloq 噎人的话; **he was still smarting from the ~-down** 他仍为那句噎人的话感到难受; **~-in** *n* (in rugby) 把球传进并列争球区

putonghua /puːˈtʊŋhwɑː/ *n* [u] 普通话

put option *n* 看跌期权

put-put /ˈpʌtpʌt/
A *n* 噗噗声
B *vi* (*pres p etc.* **-tt-**) 噗噗作响

putrefaction /ˌpjuːtrɪˈfækʃn/ *n* [u] 腐烂

putrefy /ˈpjuːtrɪfaɪ/ *vi* «*meat, fruit, vegetable*» 腐烂; «*organic matter, corpse*» 腐败

putrescence /pjuːˈtresns/ *n* [u] formal 腐臭

putrescent /pjuːˈtresnt/ *adj* formal 腐臭的

putrid /ˈpjuːtrɪd/ *adj* **1** (decaying) 腐烂的 ‹*meat, fruit*›; 腐臭的 ‹*body, smell, breath*› **2** fig colloq (disgusting) 令人厌恶的 ‹*behaviour, sight*›

putsch /pʊtʃ/ *n* 政变

putt /pʌt/
A *n* 推杆
B *vt* 轻击 ‹*golfball*›
C *vi* 轻击球

putter¹ /ˈpʌtə(r)/ *n* **1** (club) 轻击球杆 **2** (player) 轻击球者

putter²
A *n* (sound) [小型汽油引擎的] 噗噗声
B *vi* 噗噗作响

putting green /ˈpʌtɪŋ ɡriːn/ *n* [高尔夫球的] 轻击区

putty /ˈpʌti/
A *n* [u] 油灰; **to be like ~ in sb.'s hands** 任由某人摆布
B *vt* 抹油灰于

put: ~-up job *n* Brit colloq 骗局; **~-you-up** *n* Brit 沙发床; **~-upon** *adj* 被利用的 ‹*person*›; **to feel ~-upon** 感到被利用

putz /pʊts/ *n* Amer colloq (stupid person) 傻瓜; (worthless person) 饭桶

puzzle /ˈpʌzl/
A *n* **1** (mystery) 谜; **to be a ~ to sb.** 对某人而言是个谜; **to solve** *or* **work out a ~** 破解谜团; **to be in a ~ over** *or* **about sth.** 对某事物感到困惑 **2** (game) 智力游戏; **crossword ~** 纵横字谜; **jigsaw ~** 拼图游戏
B *vt* «*person, event, book, film*» 使困惑
C *vi* 苦思冥想; **to ~ about** *or* **over sth.** 苦苦思索某事

Phrasal verb

- **puzzle out** *vt* [**~ out sth., ~ sth. out**] 弄明白 ‹*problem, meaning*›; 琢磨出 ‹*solution, reason*›

puzzle book *n* 谜题书

puzzled /ˈpʌzld/ *adj* 困惑的; **I was ~ as to how he knew my name** 我弄不明白他怎么会知道我的名字

puzzlement /ˈpʌzlmənt/ *n* [u] 困惑

puzzler /ˈpʌzlə(r)/ *n* **1** (problem) 谜团 **2** (person) 智力游戏玩家

puzzling /ˈpʌzlɪŋ/ *adj* 令人困惑的 ‹*behaviour, action*›; 费解的 ‹*problem, mechanism*›

PVC *abbr* = **polyvinyl chloride** 聚氯乙烯; **a ~ raincoat** 一件塑料雨衣

Pvt *abbr* Amer = **private B1**

p.w. *abbr* = **per week** 每周; **three times ~** 每周三次

PX *abbr* Amer = **post exchange**

pygmy /ˈpɪɡmi/
A *n* **1** **Pygmy** Anthrop 俾格米人 **2** fig pej (insignificant person) 微不足道的人; **he regarded them as intellectual pygmies** 他把他们视为知识上的侏儒
B *modif* 矮小的; **~ owl** 鸺鹠; **~ shrew** 姬鼩鼱; **~ chimpanzee** 倭黑猩猩; **~ seahorse** 豆丁海马; **~ rabbit/elephant** 侏儒兔/象

pyjamas /pəˈdʒɑːməz/ Brit
A *npl* 睡衣裤; **to be in one's ~** 穿着睡衣; **a pair of ~** 一套睡衣
B **pyjama** *modif* 睡衣裤的; **pyjama top/bottoms** 睡衣上衣/睡裤

pylon /ˈpaɪlən, -lɒn/ *n* **1** (for electricity cables) 电缆塔 **2** (on wing) 外挂架

pylorus /paɪˈlɔːrəs/ *n* (*pl* **pylori** /paɪˈlɔːriː/) 幽门

PYO *abbr* = **pick-your-own**

Pyongyang /pjɒŋˈjæŋ/ *pr n* 平壤

pyramid /ˈpɪrəmɪd/ *n* **1** Archit 金字塔; **the ~s of Egypt** 埃及的金字塔 **2** Geom 锥体

pyramid selling *n* [u] 传销

pyre /ˈpaɪə(r)/ *n* 火葬柴堆

Pyrenean /ˌpɪrəˈniːən/ *adj* 比利牛斯山脉的

Pyrenees /ˌpɪrəˈniːz/ *pr npl* **the ~** 比利牛斯山脉

Pyrex® /ˈpaɪreks/ *n* [u] 派莱克斯耐热玻璃

pyrite, pyrites /paɪˈraɪt, -ˈraɪtiːz, Amer pɪ-/ *ns* [u] 硫化矿物

pyromania /ˌpaɪrəʊˈmeɪnɪə/ *n* [u] 纵火狂

pyromaniac /ˌpaɪrəʊˈmeɪnɪæk/ *n* 纵火狂患者

pyrotechnic /ˌpaɪrəˈteknɪk/ *adj* **1** lit 烟火的; **a ~ display** 烟花燃放; **a ~ device** 烟火装置 **2** fig (brilliant) 令人眼花缭乱的 ‹*effect, imagery, technique*›

pyrotechnics /ˌpaɪrəˈteknɪks/ *npl* **1** + *v sing* (making fireworks) 烟火制造; (setting off fireworks) 烟火燃放 **2** + *v pl* fig 出色展示; **musical/intellectual ~** 音乐技巧/智慧的出色展示

pyrrhic /ˈpɪrɪk/ *adj* 付出惨重代价的 ‹*victory*›

Pythagoras' theorem /paɪˌθæɡərəs ˈθɪərəm/ *n* 毕达哥拉斯定理

python /ˈpaɪθn, Amer ˈpaɪθɒn/ *n* 蟒

P

Qq

Q, q /kjuː/ *n* (*pl* **Qs** *or* **Q's**) [英语字母表的第17个字母]

QA *abbr* **= quality assurance**

Qatar /kæˈtɑː(r)/ *pr n* 卡塔尔

Qatari /kæˈtɑːri/ ►**p. 503**

A *adj* (of Qatar) 卡塔尔的; (of the people) 卡塔尔人的

B *n* 卡塔尔人

QC *abbr* Brit **= Queen's Counsel**

qian /tʃɪˈan/ ►**p. 909** *n* (*pl* **qian**) 钱

Qin /tʃɪn/ *pr n* 秦（朝）

Qing /tʃɪŋ/ *pr n* 清（朝）

Qinghai /ˌtʃɪŋˈhaɪ/ ►**p. 604** *pr n* ~ **(Province)** 青海（省）

Qinghai Lake ►**p. 424** *pr n* 青海湖

qty *abbr* **= quantity 1**

quack[1] /kwæk/

A *n* (duck call) 嘎嘎声

B *vi* 1 lit «*duck*» 嘎嘎叫 2 fig colloq «*person*» 聒噪; **to ~ on** *or* **away about sth.** 叽叽呱呱地谈论某事物

quack[2] *n* colloq 1 pej (charlatan) 冒牌医生 2 Brit (doctor) 医生

quackery /ˈkwækəri/ *n* [u] 1 (bogus medicine) 江湖医术 2 (deception) 骗术

quad /kwɒd/ *abbr* 1 **= quadrangle** 2 **= quadruplet** 3 **= quad bike**

quad: ~ **bike** *n* Brit 四轮摩托车; ~ **biking** /ˈkwɒd ˌbaɪkɪŋ/ ►**p. 307** *n* [u] 四轮摩托车运动

quadrangle /ˈkwɒdræŋɡl/ *n* 1 Math 四边形 2 Archit 四方院子

quadrangular /kwɒˈdræŋɡjʊlə(r)/ *adj* 四方形的; **a ~ castle/courtyard** 四方形城堡/庭院

quadrant /ˈkwɒdrənt/ *n* 四分之一圆周

quadraphonic /ˌkwɒdrəˈfɒnɪk/ *adj* 四声道的 ‹*system, recording*›

quadratic /kwɒˈdrætɪk/ *adj* 二次方的; ~ **formula** 二次方程式

quadratic equation *n* 二次方程

quadrilateral /ˌkwɒdrɪˈlætərəl/

A *adj* 四边的 ‹*shape, surface*›

B *n* 四边形

quadrille /kwɒˈdrɪl/ *n* 1 Dance 方阵舞 2 Mus 方阵舞曲

quadrillion /kwɒˈdrɪlɪən/ *n* (*pl* **~s or ~**) 千的五次幂

quadriplegia /ˌkwɒdrɪˈpliːdʒə/ *n* [u] 四肢瘫痪

quadriplegic /ˌkwɒdrɪˈpliːdʒɪk/

A *n* 四肢瘫痪者

B *adj* 四肢瘫痪的 ‹*patient, injuries*›

quadrophonic /ˌkwɒdrəˈfɒnɪk/ *adj* **= quadraphonic**

quad runner *n* Amer **= quad bike**

quadruped /ˈkwɒdrʊped/ *n* 四足动物

quadruple ►**p. 288**

A /ˈkwɒdrʊpl, Amer kwɒˈdruːpl/ *adj* 1 (fourfold) 四倍的 ‹*amount, weight, size*›; **a ~ whisky** 一份四倍的威士忌 2 (having four parts) 四部分组成的; **a ~ alliance** 四方联盟

B /ˈkwɒdrʊpl, Amer kwɒˈdruːpl/ *n* 四倍

C /kwɒˈdruːpl/ *vt* 使…成为四倍 ‹*number*›; **to ~ sales** 使销售量增加三倍

D /kwɒˈdruːpl/ *vi* «*price, number*» 成为四倍

quadruplet /ˈkwɒdrʊplət, Amer kwɒˈdruːplət/ *n* 四胞胎之一; **a set of ~s** 四胞胎; **to give birth to ~s** 生四胞胎

quaff /kwɒf, Amer kwæf/ *vt* dated or hum 痛饮

quagmire /ˈkwɒɡmaɪə(r), ˈkwæɡ-/ *n* 1 lit 沼泽地 2 fig 困境

quail[1] /kweɪl/ *vi* liter «*person, spirit*» 畏缩; **to ~ before sth./sb.** 在某事物/某人面前畏缩

quail[2] (*pl* **~** *or* **~s**) *n* 1 [c] Zool 鹌鹑 2 [u] Culin 鹌鹑肉

quaint /kweɪnt/ *adj* 1 (picturesque) 古色古香的 ‹*house, furniture, name*› 2 (old-fashioned) 老派的 ‹*manners, idea*›; 老式的 ‹*clothes, fashion*›

quaintly /ˈkweɪntli/ *adv* (in curious manner) 别致地 ‹*dress, decorated*›; (in old-fashioned manner) 古色古香地 ‹*furnished*›

quaintness /ˈkweɪntnɪs/ *n* [u] (picturesqueness) 古色古香; (old-fashionedness) 老派

quake /kweɪk/

A *vi* «*earth*» 震动; «*person*» 颤抖; **to ~ with fear** 吓得发抖

B *n* colloq 地震

Quaker /ˈkweɪkə(r)/ *n* 贵格会教徒; 贵格会教徒的 ‹*belief, community*›

quake-resistant *adj* colloq **= earthquake-resistant**

qualification /ˌkwɒlɪfɪˈkeɪʃn/ *n* 1 [c] (diploma, degree) 资格; **to gain/have a ~ in sth.** 取得/拥有某方面的资格 2 [c] (necessary quality) 素质; (necessary skill) 能力 3 [u] (restriction) 限定; **to accept sth. without ~** 毫无保留地接受某事物 4 [c] (proviso) 先决条件

qualified /ˈkwɒlɪfaɪd/ *adj* 1 (certified) 有资格的 ‹*professional*›; **a ~ doctor** 取得执业资格的医生; **to be ~ for sth./to do sth.** 有资格做某事 2 (competent) 胜任的 ‹*person*›; **I am not ~ to comment on that subject** 我对那个话题没有发言权 3 (limited) 有保留的 ‹*approval, praise*›; **the concert was a ~ success** 音乐会还算成功

qualifier /ˈkwɒlɪfaɪə(r)/ *n* 1 Ling 修饰词 2 (contestant) 取得参赛资格的人; (team) 取得参赛资格的运动队 3 (match, round) 资格赛

qualify /ˈkwɒlɪfaɪ/

A *vt* 1 (make fit for) 使具有资格; **this test qualifies you to drive heavy vehicles** 通过这一考试就有资格驾驶重型车辆; **his experience qualifies him for the job** 他的经验使他能胜任这份工作 2 (give right to) 使有权; **paying a fee doesn't automatically ~ you for membership** 交纳会费并不能使你自动成为会员; **that doesn't ~ you to criticize me** 那并不能使你有权批评我 3 (add conditions to) 限定; **she felt obliged to ~ her short answer** 她只得对自己的简短回答作了一下修正 4 Ling «*adjective, adverb*» 修饰 ‹*noun, verb*›

B *vi* 1 (have the necessary credentials) 具备资格; **to ~ as a doctor** 取得医师资格; **he qualifies for the job** 他胜任这份工作 2 (obtain official right) 有权; **to ~, you must have lived in this country for at least three years** 你必须在这个国家至少住满三年才能享有此权利; **if you live in the area, you ~ for a parking permit** 在本地区居住者有权获得停车许可证 3 Sport 获得参赛资格; **our team has qualified for the final** 我们队打进了决赛 4 (have right qualities) 合格; **to ~ as sth.** 配得上某名称; **he hardly qualifies as a poet** 他算不上是个诗人

qualifying /ˈkwɒlɪfaɪɪŋ/ *adj attrib* 1 (making eligible) 获取资格的 ‹*exam*›; **a ~ round** *or* **heat** 资格赛; **~ shares** 资格股; **the ~ period for citizenship** 获得公民身份所需的居住期 2 Ling 修饰的; **a ~ word/phrase** 修饰词/短语

qualitative /ˈkwɒlɪtətɪv, Amer -teɪt-/ *adj* 性质的 ‹*evaluation*›; **~ research/data** 定性研究/数据; **~ differences** 质的区别; **a ~ leap/change** 质的飞跃/改变

qualitatively /ˈkwɒlɪtətɪvli, Amer -teɪt-/ *adv* 在质的方面 ‹*evaluate, important, inferior*›; **to be ~ different (from sth.)** （与某事物）有本质的不同

quality /ˈkwɒləti/

A *n* 1 [u] (standard) 质量; **good/poor ~ of workmanship** 做工好/差; **~ of life** 生活质量 2 [c] (attribute) 性质; **the musical ~ of her voice** 她嗓子的音色 3 [u] (excellence) 优质; **I'm looking for ~ not quantity** 我要的是质而不是量

B *modif* 高质量的 ‹*shop, goods, service*›; **the ~ newspapers** 高品位报纸

quality: ~ assurance *n* [u] 质量保证; **~ control** *n* [u] 质量管理; **~ controller** ►**p. 409** *n* 质量管理员; **~ time** *n* [u] [为与亲人增进感情而全心付出的] 珍贵时光

qualm /kwɑːm/ *n* 不安; **to have** *or* **feel ~s about doing sth.** 对做某事感到不安; **~s of conscience** *or* **guilt** 愧疚感; **without a ~** 心安理得

quandary /ˈkwɒndəri/ *n* 困窘; **to be in a ~ about** *or* **over sth.** 在某事上犹豫不决

quango /ˈkwæŋɡəʊ/ *n* (*pl* **~s**) Brit usu pej 半官方机构

quanta /ˈkwɒntə/ *pl* ►**quantum**

quantifiable /ˌkwɒntɪˈfaɪəbl/ *adj* 可量化的 ‹*evidence, effects*›

quantifier /ˈkwɒntɪfaɪə(r)/ *n* （数）量词

quantify /ˈkwɒntɪfaɪ/ *vt* 量化 ‹*amount, value*›; **it is difficult to ~ the extent of the damage** 损坏程度很难量化

quantitative /ˈkwɒntɪtətɪv, Amer -teɪt-/ *adj* 量化的 ‹*evaluation, measurement, data*›; **~ analysis/research** 定量分析/研究

quantitative easing *n* [u] (practice) 量化宽松; (policy) 量化宽松的货币政策

quantitatively /ˈkwɒntɪtətɪvli, Amer -teɪt-/ *adv* 在数量上 ‹*analyse, describe, equal, different*›; **a result that can/can't be measured ~** 可以/无法量化的结果

quantity /ˈkwɒntəti/ *n* **1** (amount) 数量; **a large/small ~ (of sth.)** 大量/少量（的某物）; **in large/small quantities** 大量地/少量地 **2** (large amount) 大量; **a ~ of sth., quantities of sth.** 大量的某物; **to buy sth. in ~** 批量购买某物

quantity: ~ mark *n* 容量刻度; **~ surveying** *n* [u] 工料估算; **~ surveyor** ▸p. 409 *n* 估算师

quantum /ˈkwɒntəm/ *n* (*pl* **quanta**) 量子; **~ optics/statistics** 量子光学/统计学; **~ state** 量子态

quantum: ~ jump *n* **1** Phys 量子跃迁; **2** = **~ leap**; **leap** *n* 跃进; **~ mechanics** *npl* + *v sing* 量子力学; **~ physics** *npl* + *v sing* 量子物理学; **~ theory** *n* [u] 量子论

quarantine /ˈkwɒrəntiːn, Amer ˈkwɔːr-/
A *n* [u] 检疫隔离; **to put** *or* **place a person/an animal in ~** 隔离某人/某动物; **~ period/laws/kennel/hospital** 隔离期/隔离法/隔离养狗场/隔离医院
B *vt* 将…隔离 ‹*person, animal*›

quark /kwɑːk/ *n* 夸克

quarrel /ˈkwɒrəl, Amer ˈkwɔːrəl/
A *n* **1** (argument) 争吵; **a ~ about** *or* **over sth.** 为某事物的争吵; **to have a ~ (with sb.)** （和某人）吵架; **to pick a ~ (with sb.)** （向某人）寻衅 **2** (difference of opinion) 分歧; **an intellectual ~** 知识方面的分歧 **3** (feud) 长期不和; **a long-standing ~** 夙怨; **to start a ~** 产生不和 **4** (reason for disagreement) **to have no ~ (with sb./sth.)** （对某人/某事物）没有怨言
B *vi* (*pres p etc.* **-ll-**, Amer **-l-**) **1** (argue) 争吵 **2** (disagree) **to ~ with sth.** 不赞成 ‹*idea, approach*›

quarrelling, Amer **quarreling** /ˈkwɒrəlɪŋ, Amer ˈkwɔːr-/
A *n* [u] 争吵; **stop your ~!** 别吵了！
B *adj* 吵吵嚷嚷的 ‹*people, factions*›

quarrelsome /ˈkwɒrəlsəm, Amer ˈkwɔːr-/ *adj* 好口角的 ‹*person, nature*›; 争辩的 ‹*remark, comment*›

quarry¹ /ˈkwɒri, Amer ˈkwɔːri/
A *n* 采石场
B *vt* 采 ‹*rock, marble*›; 在…开采 ‹*hillside, cliff*›
C *vi* **to ~ for sth.** 开采某物; **to ~ into sth.** 在某处开采

Phrasal verb
- **quarry out** *vt* [**~ out sth., ~ sth. out**] 采出 ‹*rock, marble*›

quarry² *n* (prey) 猎物; (person) 被追捕的人

quarry: ~man /-mən/ ▸p. 409 *n* 采石工人; **~ tile** *n* 缸砖; **~ tiled** *adj* 贴缸砖的 ‹*floor, patio*›

quart /kwɔːt/ *n* 夸脱; **a ~ of milk** 一夸脱牛奶; **to put a ~ into a pint pot** Brit colloq 以小容大

quarter /ˈkwɔːtə(r)/
A *n* **1** [c] (one fourth) 四分之一; **a ~ of a mile/pound** 四分之一英里/磅; **to divide the cake into four ~s** 把蛋糕分成四等份; **from all ~s of the globe** fig 来自全球各地; **the box is only a ~ full** 盒子只装了四分之一; **the city is only a ~ the size of London** 该市只有伦敦的四分之一大小 **2** ▸p. 831 [c] (period of 15 minutes) 一刻钟; **(a) ~ of an hour** 一刻钟; **an hour and a ~** 一小时多一刻钟; **it's already (a) ~ to: we should get going** 还差一刻钟: 我们该走了; **we are leaving at a ~ to** esp Brit *or* **of** Amer **seven** 我们将在六点三刻动身; **I'll meet you at a ~ past** esp Brit *or* **after** Amer **ten** 我十点一刻和你见面 **3** [c] (period of three months) 3 个月; **she's ten and a ~** 她 10 岁零 3 个月; **productivity rose 1% in the first ~ of the year** 第一季度的生产力提高了 1% **4** [c] (district of a town) 城区; **the poor ~** 贫民区; **a residential ~** 住宅区 **5** [c] (person) [尤指可能提供帮助、信息或作出反应的] 个人; (group) 群体; **news from the highest ~s** 来自最高层的消息; **the news was greeted with dismay in some** *or* **certain ~s** 有一部分人对这条消息感到泄气; **don't expect any help from that ~!** 别指望从那一方得到帮助! **6** [c] Amer, Can, Austral (25 cents) 25 分; **it only cost me a ~!** 它只花了我两毛五分钱! **7** [c] Astron (of moon) 半圆的月相; **the moon is in its first/last ~** 月亮正处于上/下弦 **8** [c] Sport (time period) 一节 **9** ▸p. 909 [c] (four ounces) 夸特 [合4盎司]; **a ~ of cheese** 一夸特干酪 **10** ▸p. 909 [c] (quarter hundredweight) 夸特 [在英国合28磅, 在美国合25磅] **11** [u] dated or liter (mercy) 慈悲; **his rivals knew that they could expect no ~ from him** 他的对手们知道他决不会手下留情 **12** [c] (direction) 方位; **a wind from a northerly ~** 北风 **13** [c] Naut 船侧后部; **on the port/starboard ~** 在左舷/右舷船尾 **14** [c] Culin (of carcass) 四分之一胴体; **a ~ of beef** 带一条腿的大块牛肉 **15** [c] Herald 盾的四分之一
B **quarters** *npl* (accommodation) 住处; (for military personnel) 营房; **they took up ~s in the farmhouse** 他们住进了农舍; **married ~s** 已婚军人宿舍; **sleeping ~s** 卧室
C *adj attrib* 四分之一的; **it's a ~ century old** 它已有 25 年的历史
D **at close quarters** *adv phr* 在近处; **to fight at close ~s** 近距离作战; **seen at close ~s, he's ugly** 他近看很丑
E *vt* **1** (divide into four) 把…分为四部分; **she peeled the apple and ~ed it** 她把苹果削了皮, 切成四瓣 **2** Hist (as punishment) 肢解; **to be hanged, drawn, and ~ed** 被绞死并开膛分尸 **3** (accommodate) 为…提供食宿; **the airmen are ~ed on local villagers** 飞行员住在当地村民家中; **the soldiers were ~ed in the town** 士兵们在镇上宿营

quarterback /ˈkwɔːtəbæk/
A *n* Amer [美式橄榄球的] 四分卫
B *vt* 担任…的四分卫 ‹*team*›

quarter: ~deck *n* [军官使用的] 上层后甲板区; **~-final** *n* 四分之一决赛; **~-light** *n* Brit [汽车里的] 三角窗

quarterly /ˈkwɔːtəli/
A *adj* 季度的 ‹*bill, subscription, meeting*›
B *adv* 按季度 ‹*pay, receive, issue*›
C *n* 季刊

quartermaster /ˈkwɔːtəmɑːstə(r), Amer -mæs-/ *n* **1** Mil 军需官 **2** Naut 舵工

Quartermaster General *n* 军需主任

quarter: ~ note *n* esp Amer = **crotchet**; **~-pounder** /ˌkwɔːtəˈpaʊndə(r)/ *n* 基本牛肉汉堡 [内中牛排重四分之一磅]

quartet /kwɔːˈtet/ *n* **1** Mus (musicians) 四重奏乐团; (singers) 四重唱组合; (composition) (for musicians) 四重奏曲; (for singers) 四重唱曲 **2** (four people) 四人组; (four things) 四件套

quarto /ˈkwɔːtəʊ/ *n* (*pl* **~s**) **1** [c] (book) 四开本书 **2** [u] (size) 四开; **~ book/volume/size** 四开本的书/四开本卷册/四开

quartz /kwɔːts/ *n* [u] 石英; **~ mine/crystal/dust** 石英矿/晶体/粉尘

quartz: ~ clock *n* 石英钟; **~ glass** *n* [u] 石英玻璃

quartzite /ˈkwɔːtsaɪt/ *n* [u] 石英岩

quartz: ~ lamp *n* 石英灯; **~ watch** *n* 石英手表

quasar /ˈkweɪzɑː(r)/ *n* 类星体

quash /kwɒʃ/ *vt* **1** Jur «*judge*» 撤销 ‹*verdict, appeal*› **2** (reject) 否决 ‹*decision, initiative*› **3** (suppress) 平息 ‹*revolt, uprising*›

quasi- /ˈkweɪzaɪ, ˈkwɑːzi/ *combining form* **1** esp pej (supposedly) 类似的; **a ~scientific explanation** 类似科学的解释 **2** (partly) 准的; **a ~official role/body** 半官方的角色/机构; **a ~feudal system** 半封建制度

quatercentenary /ˌkwætəsenˈtiːnəri, Amer -ˈsentəneri/ *n* 400 周年纪念; **a ~ celebration/commemoration** 400 周年庆祝/纪念活动

Quaternary /kwəˈtɜːnəri/
A *adj* (of the period) 第四纪的; (of the rock system) 第四系的
B *n* **the ~** (period) 第四纪; (rock system) 第四系

quatrain /ˈkwɒtreɪn/ *n* 四行诗

quaver /ˈkweɪvə(r)/
A *n* **1** (tremble) [声音的] 颤抖 **2** esp Brit Mus 八分音符
B *vi* «*voice*» 颤抖; «*person*» 声音颤抖
C *vt* «*person*» 声音颤抖地说 ‹*words, remark*›

quavering /ˈkweɪvərɪŋ/
A *adj* 颤抖的 ‹*voice, words*›
B *n* [声音的] 颤抖

quavery /ˈkweɪvəri/ *adj* = **quavering A**

quay /kiː/ *n* 码头; **at the ~** 靠在码头

quayside /ˈkiːsaɪd/ *n* 码头区; **a ~ boatyard** 位于码头区的造船厂

queasiness /ˈkwiːzɪnɪs/ *n* [u] **1** (nausea) 恶心 **2** fig (uneasiness) 不安

queasy /ˈkwiːzi/ *adj* **1** (nauseous) 恶心的 ‹*feeling*›; **to be** *or* **feel ~** 觉得恶心; **to have a ~ stomach** 有些反胃 **2** fig (uneasy) 心神不定的 ‹*feeling*›; **a ~ sense of guilt/foreboding** 忐忑不安的内疚感/预感; **to have** *or* **get a ~ conscience (about sth.)** （对某事）有些良心不安

Quebec /kwɪˈbek/ *pr n* **1** (city) 魁北克市 **2** (province) 魁北克省

queen /kwiːn/
A *n* **1** (monarch) 女王; (king's wife) 王后 **2** fig (top female) 出众的女子; **a movie ~** 影后 **3** Zool [蜂、蚁等的] 雌性昆虫; **a ~ ant** 蚁后 **4** (in chess) 后; (in cards) 王后（牌） **5** colloq pej (homosexual man) 假娘儿们
B *vt* **to ~ it over (sb.)** （对某人）盛气凌人

queen: ~ bee *n* **1** Zool 蜂王; **2** fig (woman) 大姐大; **~ consort** *n* 王后

queenly /ˈkwiːnli/ *adj* 女王般的 ‹*demeanour, wave*›; **a woman of ~ bearing** 仪态万方的女人

queen: ~ mother *n* 太后; **Q~'s Counsel** *pr n* Brit 王室法律顾问; **Q~'s English** *n* [u] **the Q~'s English** （英国）标准英语; **Q~'s evidence** *n* Brit 对同案犯不利的证据; **to turn Q~'s evidence against sb.** 供出对某同案犯不利的证据; **Q~'s highway** *n* Brit (formal) **the Q~'s highway** [女王保护下的] 国道; **~-size bed** *n* 大号床

> **the Queen's English**
> （英国）标准英语。包括发音和书面语两方面。指发音时亦称标准发音（RP, 即 received pronunciation）或 BBC 英语（▸the BBC）。国王在位时称 King's English。

Queensland /ˈkwiːnzlənd/ *pr n* 昆士兰州

Queen: ~'s Messenger *n* Brit 外交信使; **~'s speech** *n* Brit [英国新一届议会开始时宣读的] 女王施政演说

queer /kwɪə(r)/
A *adj* **1** (odd) 古怪的 ‹*person*›; 反常的 ‹*event*› **2** (suspicious) 可疑的 ‹*noise, behaviour*›; **it's very ~ that ...** 非常可疑的是… **3** Brit colloq dated (unwell) 不舒服的; **to come over/feel ~** 突然感到眩晕/觉得不舒服 **4** colloq pej (homosexual) 同性恋的 ‹*person*›
B *n* colloq pej 同性恋者
C *vt* Brit colloq **to ~ sb.'s pitch** 破坏某人的计划

queer bashing *n* [u] colloq pej 对同性恋者的无端攻击

queerly /ˈkwɪəli/ *adv* 反常地 ‹*act, speak*›; 古怪地 ‹*dressed, decorated*›; **to look at sb. ~** 异样地看着某人

quell /kwel/ *vt* **1** (calm) 减轻 ‹*anger, fears*› **2** (subdue) 震慑 ‹*person*›; **to ~ sb. with a**

q

look 用眼神镇住某人 3 (stop) 平息 ‹revolt, disturbance›

quench /kwentʃ/ vt 1 (slake) 止; **to ~ one's thirst** 止渴 2 formal (put out) 扑灭 ‹fire› 3 fig (stifle) 抑制 ‹desire, anger›

querulous /'kwerʊləs/ adj 抱怨的 ‹person, manner, tone›; 怒气冲冲的 ‹request, response›

querulously /'kwerʊləsli/ adv 怒气冲冲地 ‹speak, complain›

query /'kwɪəri/

A n 1 (request for information) 询问; (expression of doubt) 疑问; **to reply to** or **answer queries from customers** 回答顾客提出的问题; **readers' queries** 读者的疑问; **if you have a ~ about your insurance policy, contact our helpline** 如果对保险单有疑问，请拨打我们的服务热线 2 Comput 查询指令 3 (question mark) 问号

B vt 1 (express doubt about) 对…表示怀疑; **I'm not in a position to ~ their decision** 我无权怀疑他们的决定; **we queried the bill, as it seemed far too high** 我们对账单提出了疑问，因为花费看起来高得离谱; **to ~ sb.'s ability** 怀疑某人的能力 2 (in questions) 提问; **'who will be leading the team?' queried Simon** "谁来当队长呢？" 西蒙问道

query: ~ language n 查询语言; **~ window** n 查询对话框

quest /kwest/ n 追寻; **a ~ for ...** 对…的追求 ‹knowledge, truth›; **a ~ for sb.** 对某人的寻找

question /'kwestʃən/

A n 1 [c] (request for information) 问题; **to ask/answer a ~** 提出/回答问题; **there's sure to be a ~ on energy in the exam** 试卷上肯定有一道关于能量的题目; **the ~ is, how much are they going to pay you?** 问题是他们打算付给你多少钱？; **the ~ arises as to whether or not he knew of the situation** 问题是，他对局势是否了解; **the key ~ of what caused the leak remains unanswered** 泄漏是怎么造成的，这一关键问题仍没有答案; **he put a ~ to the minister about the recent reforms** 他就最近的改革向部长提了一个问题; **(a) good ~!** 问得好！; **an open ~** (to which there is no yes or no) 开放式问题 2 [c] (issue) [待讨论或处理的] 事情; **the Palestinian ~** 巴勒斯坦问题; **it's merely a ~ of time before the business collapses** 这家企业的倒闭只是时间问题; **there is no ~ of my taking the afternoon off work** 我下午不可能不上班; **an open ~** (undecided) 未决的问题; **it's an open ~ as to whether or not he was guilty** 他是否有罪尚无定论; **in ~** 讨论中的; **on the day in ~ we were in London** 在所说的那一天，我们在伦敦; **out of the ~** 不可能的 3 [c and u] (doubt) 疑问; (uncertainty) 不确定; **there is no ~ about his honesty** 他的诚实毋庸置疑; **to call** or **bring** or **throw sth. into ~** (for doubt) 引起对某事物的怀疑; (for discussion) 引起对某事物的讨论; **to come into ~** (for doubt) 被怀疑; (for discussion) 被讨论; **to be open to ~** 不确定; **in ~** (in doubt) 有疑问的; (uncertain) 不确定的; **the future of public transport is not in ~** 公共交通的未来发展是不容置疑的; **beyond** or **without ~** 毫无疑问; **to do sth. without ~** 毫无异议地做某事; **he obeyed without ~** 他二话没说就服从了

B vt 1 (ask, interrogate) 问; **over half of those ~ed said they rarely took any exercise** 被问到的人有一半以上都说他们很少锻炼身体; **she was arrested and ~ed about the fire** 她被拘留讯问有关火灾的事情; **the witness was ~ed about his drinking habits** 证人被问到他的喝酒习惯 2 (be doubtful of) 怀疑; **to ~ sb.'s judgement** 对某人的判断表示怀疑; **I ~ whether he really paid that money into her account** 我怀疑他是否真的把钱划入她的账户了

questionable /'kwestʃənəbl/ adj 1 (debatable) 有问题的 ‹motive, decision› 2 (dubious) 可疑的 ‹sincerity, dealings, excuse›; **a joke in ~ taste** 暧昧的笑话

question-begging

A adj 想当然的 ‹statement, argument›

B n [u] 武断

questioner /'kwestʃənə(r)/ n 提问人

questioning /'kwestʃənɪŋ/

A adj 探究的 ‹look, expression, mind›; **she raised a ~ eyebrow** 她怀疑地挑起眉毛

B n [u] 1 (asking questions) 提问; **a line of ~** 探究思路; **~ by sb.** 某人的质问 2 (challenging) 质疑; **a ~ of sth.** 对…的质疑 ‹authority, values, authenticity›

question: ~ mark n 1 Ling 问号; 2 (doubt) 疑问; **a ~ mark about** or **over sth./sb.** 对某事物/某人的疑问; **there is a ~ mark hanging over his future** 他的前途是个问号; **~ master** n Brit 问答节目主持人

questionnaire /ˌkwestʃə'neə(r)/ n 调查表; **to fill in/answer a ~** 填写/回答问卷

question: ~ tag n 附加疑问成分; **~ time** n Brit [英国下议院议员的] 提问时间

queue /kju:/ esp Brit

A n (of people or vehicles) 行列; **to line up** or **stand in a ~** 排队; **a bus ~** 排队等公共汽车的人; **to jump the ~** 插队

B vi **~ (up)** «person, vehicles» 排队; **to ~ up to do sth.** fig 纷纷等着做某事

queue: ~-jump vi Brit 插队; **~-jumper** n Brit 插队者; **~-jumping** n [u] Brit 插队

quibble /'kwɪbl/

A n 牢骚; **a ~ about** or **over sth.** 对某事物的抱怨

B vi «person, article» 挑刺; **to ~ about** or **over sth.** 对某事物吹毛求疵

quibbler /'kwɪblə(r)/ n 吹毛求疵的人

quibbling /'kwɪblɪŋ/

A adj 吹毛求疵的 ‹debate, detail›

B n [u] 吹毛求疵

quiche /ki:ʃ/ n [u and c] 鸡蛋馅饼

quick /kwɪk/

A adj 1 (speedy) 快的; **be ~ about it!** 快点儿！; **a ~ worker** 手脚快的人; **she's a ~ worker: she only met him last week, and now they are engaged!** 她的动作可真快: 上周才遇见他，现在两人已经订婚了！; **she gave him a ~ look** 她匆匆扫了他一眼; **to make a ~ decision** 立机立断; **he fired three shots in ~ succession** 他瞬间连发3枪; **the company is just out to make a ~ profit** 这家公司只图赚快钱 2 (without delay) 立即的; **he was always ~ to point out her mistakes** 他总是立即指出她的错误; **to be ~ to anger** 动辄发怒; **to have a ~ temper** 脾气暴躁 3 (intelligent) 聪敏的; **~ wits** 急智; **he's a ~ learner** or Amer colloq **study** 他学东西很快; **it was ~ of him to spot the mistake** 他敏锐地发现了这个错误

B adv 快; **come ~!** 快来！; **to get rich ~** 迅速致富; **~ march!** Mil 齐步走！; **~ as a flash** or **as lightning** 飞快地

C n **the ~** [指甲下的] 活肉; **to bite one's nails (down) to the ~** 咬指甲直到肉根; **to cut** or **sting sb. to the ~** 深深伤害某人

D npl archaic or liter **the ~ and the dead** 生者与死者

quick: ~-acting adj 速效的 ‹drug, solvent›; **~ and dirty** adj colloq 仓促应急的 ‹method, estimate›; **a ~ and dirty solution to the problem** 对这一问题仓促出台的临时解决办法; **~-assembly** adj 快速组装的 ‹furniture›; **~ change artist** n 快速变装师; **~-drying** adj 速干的 ‹paint, fabric›

quicken /'kwɪkən/

A vt 1 (speed up) 加快 ‹pace, rhythm› 2 (stimulate) 激起 ‹anger, interest, appetite›

B vi 1 (speed up) «pace, heartbeat, music» 加速 2 (be stimulated) «jealousy, interest» 被激起

quick: ~-fire adj attrib 1 lit 急射的 ‹gun, weapon›; 2 fig 连珠炮似的 ‹question, round›; 一连串的 ‹humour, repartee›; **~-firing** adj 急射的 ‹gun, weapon›; **~ fix** n 速效措施; **there is no ~ fix for weight loss** 减肥没有捷径; **~-freeze** vt (pt **~-froze**, pp **~-frozen**) 将…速冻

quickie /'kwɪki/ n colloq 1 (drink) 两三口喝下的酒 2 (sexual act) 瞬间完事的性交 3 (question) 简短的问题

quickie divorce n colloq 闪电式离婚

quicklime /'kwɪklaɪm/ n [u] 生石灰

quickly /'kwɪkli/ adv 1 (rapidly) 快速地; **as ~ as possible** 尽快地; **to talk too ~** 说话太快; **it ~ became clear that ...** …很快就清楚了 2 (promptly) 立刻 ‹answer, arrive›; **the problem was ~ resolved** 问题立即得到了解决

quick march

A n 快步行进

B excl **(by the left,) ~!** （左看齐，）快步走！

quickness /'kwɪknɪs/ n [u] 1 (speed) 快速; **~ to respond** 反应的迅速; **~ of wit** 反应敏捷; **~ of temper** 脾气暴躁 2 (nimbleness) 敏捷 3 (quick-wittedness) 机敏

quick: ~-release adj 能迅速松开的 ‹lever, mechanism›; **~sand** n [u] 1 lit 流沙; 2 fig 危险的困境; **~sands** npl = **~sand**; **~-setting** adj 速凝的; **~-setting concrete** 快干混凝土; **~silver** n [u] 水银; **like ~silver** 变化多端; **~step** n 1 Dance 快狐步舞; 2 Mus 快狐步舞曲; **~-tempered** adj 火爆脾气的 ‹person›; **~ time** n [u] Mil 疾步走; **~-witted** adj 机敏的

quid[1] /kwɪd/ n (pl **quid**) Brit colloq (pound) 一英镑

quid[2] n (tobacco) 口嚼烟草块

quid pro quo /ˌkwɪd prəʊ 'kwəʊ/ n (pl **quid pro quos**) formal (sth. given in return) 回报物; (sth. given as a substitute) 替代品; **to be a ~ for sth.** 是对某事物的回报

quiescence /kwaɪ'esns, kwɪ'esns/ n [u] formal (inertia) 静止; (dormancy) 休眠; **a state/period of ~** 静止状态/静止期

quiescent /kwaɪ'esnt, kwɪ'esnt/ adj formal 不活跃的 ‹mood, workforce›; 静止的 ‹period, growth›; 沉默的 ‹acceptance›; **to be in a ~ state** «volcano, plant» 处于休眠状态

quiet /'kwaɪət/

A adj 1 (noiseless) 安静的; (not noisy) 轻声的; (not speaking) 沉默的; **could you keep the kids ~ while I'm on the phone?** 我打电话时你让孩子们安静点好吗？; **to speak in a ~ voice** 轻声说话; **her new car is very ~** 她的新车噪音很小; **to keep** or **stay ~** 保持沉默; **~ please!** 请安静！ 2 (tranquil, slow) 寂静的 ‹village, street›; 平静的 ‹life, sea›; **business is very ~** 生意很清淡 3 (sparsely attended) 不事张扬的 ‹dinner, wedding, funeral› 4 (undisturbed) 宁静的; **a ~ evening** 宁静的夜晚; **to have a ~ drink** 悠闲地喝一杯 5 (subdued) 文静的; **he was always very ~ at school** 他在学校总是寡言少语; **a ~ pony** 温顺的矮马 6 (not expressed or done openly) 暗中的; (discreet) 不显眼的; **he has an air of ~ authority** 他的神态威严凝重; **to have a ~ laugh over sth.** 对某事暗自窃笑; **with a ~ smile** (restrained) 带着淡然的微笑; (knowing) 带着会意的微笑; **to have a ~ word (with sb.) (about sth.)** （与某人）（就某事物）进行私下交谈 7 (secret) 秘密的; **to keep sth. ~, to keep ~ about sth.** 将某事保密; **I've decided to resign, but I'd rather you kept ~ about it** 我已决定辞职，但希望你不要声张出去 8 (unobtrusive) 素净的 ‹colour, garment›

B n [u] 1 (silence) 安静; **the ~ of the early morning** 清晨的寂静 2 (freedom from disturbance) 宁静; **I went to the library for a little peace and ~** 我去图书馆清静了一下 3 (peaceful state of affairs) 安定; **a time of ~** 和平时期 4 colloq **to do sth. on the ~** (in secret) 秘密做某事; **to have a drink on the ~** 偷偷喝酒

C vt esp Amer = **quieten**

Phrasal verb

• **quiet down** vi, vt esp Amer = **quieten down**

quieten /ˈkwaɪətn/ vt **1** (silence) 使…安静 ‹child, crowd›; 使…平息 ‹uproar, protests›; 使…闭嘴 ‹critics› **2** (calm) 安抚 ‹child, animal› **3** (allay) 减轻 ‹fears, suspicions, conscience›

Phrasal verb

• **quieten down**

A vt [~ **down sb./sth.**, ~ **sb./sth. down**] **1** (silence) 使…平静 ‹child, crowd› **2** (calm) 安抚 ‹child, animal›

B vi **1** (fall silent) 安静下来 **2** (become calm) 变得平和

quietism /ˈkwaɪətɪzəm/ n [u] **1** Relig [基督教的] 寂静主义 **2** Philos 清静无为

quietist /ˈkwaɪətɪst/

A adj **1** Relig 寂静主义的 ‹belief› **2** Philos 清静无为的 ‹attitude›

B n **1** Relig 寂静主义者 **2** Philos 清静无为者

quietly /ˈkwaɪətli/ adv **1** (not noisily) 轻轻地 ‹move, cough, laugh, sing›; **the music was playing** ~ 音乐在低声演奏; **the engine runs** ~ 这种发动机运转安静 **2** (silently) 静静地 ‹sit, play, read› **3** (discreetly) 悄悄地 ‹talk, smile›; **to be** ~ **optimistic/resentful** 暗自乐观/怨恨 **4** (simply) 清静地 ‹live›; 低调地 ‹get married, be buried› **5** (calmly, without fuss) 平静地 ‹speak, give orders›; **all right, I'll come** ~ 好吧，我不会反抗的 [罪犯被逮捕时所说] **6** (soberly) 素净地; **to be** ~ **dressed/decorated** 穿着/装饰素雅

quietness /ˈkwaɪətnɪs/ n [u] **1** (silence) 寂静 **2** (of voice) 低声 **3** (calmness) 文静 **4** (peacefulness) (of place, time) 宁静; (of life) 平静

quietude /ˈkwaɪɪtjuːd, Amer -tuːd/ n [u] liter 宁静

quiff /kwɪf/ n esp Brit 额发 [男子从额头向后上方梳的一绺头发]

quill /kwɪl/ n **1** (of bird) (feather) 翎; (hollow shaft) 羽毛管 **2** ~ **(pen)** 翎笔 **3** (of spiny animal) 刺

quilt /kwɪlt/ n **1** Brit (duvet) 被子 **2** (quilted coverlet) 加衬芯床罩; (bedspread) 床罩

quilted /ˈkwɪltɪd/ adj 加衬芯的; **a** ~ **jacket/bedspread/lining** 棉衣/絮棉床罩/絮棉衬里

quilting /ˈkwɪltɪŋ/ n [u] **1** (quilt-making) 缝被子 **2** (stitched design) 绗缝图案 **3** (material) 绗缝材料

quilting bee n Amer 缝被子聚会

quin /kwɪn/ abbr Brit colloq = **quintuplet**

quince /kwɪns/ n **1** (tree) 榅桲树 **2** (fruit) 榅桲果; ~ **cheese/jelly/jam** 榅桲奶酪/果冻/果酱

quincentenary /ˌkwɪnsenˈtiːnəri, Amer -ˈsentəneri/ n 五百周年纪念; **a** ~ **celebration** 五百周年庆祝活动

quinine /kwɪˈniːn, Amer ˈkwaɪnaɪn/ n [u] 奎宁

quint /kwɪnt/ n Amer colloq = **quintuplet**

quintessence /kwɪnˈtesns/ n formal **1** (perfect example) 典范; **the** ~ **of tact/diplomacy** 极老练的人/外交手腕极灵活的人 **2** (intrinsic character) 本质; **the** ~ **of humanism** 人文主义的精髓

quintessential /ˌkwɪntɪˈsenʃl/ adj formal 典型的 ‹character, quality, example›

quintet /kwɪnˈtet/ n **1** Mus (musicians) 五重奏乐团; (singers) 五重唱组合; (composition) 五重奏曲 **2** (five people) 五人组; (five things) 五件套

quintillion /kwɪnˈtɪljən/ n (pl ~**s** or ~) 百万的三次幂

quintuple

A /ˈkwɪntjʊpl, Amer kwɪnˈtuːpl/ adj attrib **1** (fivefold) 五倍的 ‹amount, weight, size› **2** (having five parts) 五部分组成的

B /kwɪnˈtjʊpl/ vt 使…成为五倍 ‹number, amount›; **to** ~ **sales** 使销售量增加四倍

C /kwɪnˈtjʊpl/ vi 成为五倍

quintuplet /ˈkwɪntjuːplet, Amer kwɪnˈtuːplɪt/ n 五胞胎之一; **a set of** ~**s** 五胞胎; **to give birth to** ~**s** 生五胞胎

quip /kwɪp/

A n (witticism) 妙语; (wisecrack) 俏皮话

B vi (pres p etc. **-pp-**) (utter witticism) 讲妙语; (make wisecrack) 说俏皮话

C vt (pres p etc. **-pp-**) 俏皮地说

quirk /kwɜːk/ n **1** (idiosyncrasy) 怪癖; **one of his little** ~**s** 他的一个小小的怪癖 **2** (chance) 巧合; **(by) a** ~ **of fate** (由于) 天缘巧合

quirky /ˈkwɜːki/ adj 古怪的 ‹habit, style›; **to have a** ~ **sense of humour** 有怪异的幽默感

quisling /ˈkwɪzlɪŋ/ n pej 卖国贼; **a** ~ **government** 傀儡政府

quit /kwɪt/

A vt (pres p **-tt-**; pt, pp **quit**) **1** esp Amer colloq (stop) **to** ~ **doing sth.** 停止 ‹working, laughing›; **to** ~ **smoking** 戒烟 **2** (resign from) 辞去; **to** ~ **a job/teaching** 辞职/辞去教职; **to** ~ **school/the army** 退学/退伍 **3** (leave) 离开 ‹place, wife, partner, apartment› **4** Comput 退出 ‹program, application›

B vi (pres p **-tt-**; pt, pp **quit**) **1** esp Amer (stop) 停止; **I** ~**!** 我不干了！; **don't offer me cigarettes, I'm trying to** ~ 别给我烟抽，我正在戒烟 **2** (resign) 辞职 **3** (leave) 离去; **to give a tenant notice to** ~ 通知房客搬家 **4** Comput 退出

C adj pred **to be** ~ **of sb./sth.** 摆脱 ‹person, responsibility›

quite /kwaɪt/ adv **1** Brit (rather) 比较; **it's** ~ **cold/warm today** 今天比较冷/暖和; ~ **a lot of money/opposition** 比较多的钱/反对意见; **I** ~ **like Chinese food** 我比较喜欢中餐 **2** Brit (considerably) 相当; ~ **a few/lot of people/things** 相当多的人/东西; **I've thought about it** ~ **a bit** 这件事情我已经考虑了很多; **it's** ~ **a lot colder/warmer today** 今天冷/暖和得多; ~ **some time** 相当长的时间; **they won** ~ **easily** 他们赢得相当轻松 **3** Brit (completely) 完全; **are you** ~ **sure?** 你有十足把握吗？; **you're** ~ **right/wrong** 你完全正确/错了; **it's/that's** ~ **all right** (in reply to apology) 真的没关系; **I** ~ **agree/understand** 我十分赞同/理解; **have you** ~ **finished?** iron 你全部完成了？; ~ **frankly** 很坦率地说; **(and)** ~ **right too!** 的确是这样！; **that's** ~ **enough!** 那完全够了！; **not** ~ **as interesting/expensive** 不那么有趣/贵; **there were not** ~ **as many as last time** 并非像上一次那么多; **that's not** ~ **all** (giving account of sth.) 那可不是全部 **4** (very) 很; **to be** ~ **comfortable/happy** 很舒服/高兴; **he's** ~ **clearly mad** 很显然他是疯了; **our whisky is** ~ **simply the best!** 我们的威士忌当然是最好的！; **it's** ~ **likely that ...** …很有可能 **5** Brit (definitely) 毫无疑问; **it was** ~ **the best answer** 这无疑是最佳答案 **6** (as intensifier) 的确; **that will be** ~ **a change for you** 那对你来说的确会是一个大改变; **she's** ~ **a beauty** 她是个大美人; **that was** ~ **some party!** 那个晚会真棒！; **their house is really** ~ **something** colloq 他们的房子可真是不同凡响; **it was** ~ **a sight** 这可真够壮观的 **7** Brit (expressing agreement) 一点不错; **he could have told us —** ~**!** 他原本可以告诉我们的——没错！; **it's just common sense —** ~ **so!** formal 这只是常识而已——一点不错！

quits /kwɪts/ adj pred **to be** ~ **(with sb.)** (与某人) 互不相欠; **to call it** ~ 扯平

quitter /ˈkwɪtə(r)/ n pej colloq 虎头蛇尾的人; **he's no** ~ 他绝不会轻言放弃

quiver[1] /ˈkwɪvə(r)/

A vi (tremble) «body, lips, heart, voice» 发抖; «flame, eyelids» 跳动; «wings, leaves, note» 颤动; **to** ~ **with rage/fear/cold** 气得/害怕得/冻得发抖

B n 颤抖; **the** ~ **of his lips** 他嘴唇的抖动; **there was a** ~ **in his voice** 他声音发颤

quiver[2] n (arrow case) 箭筒

quixotic /kwɪkˈsɒtɪk/ adj 异想天开的 ‹attitude, plan, person›; 不切实际的 ‹quest, attempt›

quixotically /kwɪkˈsɒtɪkli/ adv 异想天开地 ‹behave, offer›

quiz /kwɪz/

A n (pl **quizzes**) **1** (game) (on TV, radio) 知识竞赛; **a sports/general knowledge** ~ 体育知识/常识问答竞赛 **2** Amer Sch 小测验

B vt (pres p etc. **-zz-**) 盘问; **to** ~ **sb. about sth.** 就某事盘问某人

quiz: ~ **game** n 知识竞赛; ~ **master** n Brit 问答节目主持人; ~ **night** n 知识竞赛晚会; ~ **show** n 问答节目

q

quizzical /ˈkwɪzɪkl/ adj 诧异的 ‹look, smile, tone›

quizzically /ˈkwɪzɪkli/ adv 诧异地 ‹look, smile, ask›

quoit /kɔɪt, Amer kwɔɪt/

A n [套环游戏中用的] 套圈

B **quoits** npl + v sing 套环游戏; **to play** ~**s** 玩套环游戏

Quonset hut® /ˈkwɒnsɪt ˌhʌt/ n Amer [军事人员使用的] 匡西特半圆形铁皮房

quorate /ˈkwɔːrət, -reɪt/ adj Brit 够法定人数的; **the meeting is** ~ 会议出席者达到法定人数

Quorn® /kwɔːn/ n [u] [用菌类制成的] 阔恩素肉

quorum /ˈkwɔːrəm/ n (pl ~**s**) 法定人数; **to have a** ~ 够法定人数

quota /ˈkwəʊtə/ n **1** (fixed share) 定额; **to do one's** ~ 完成分内事 **2** (maximum number) 限额; **to fix/impose a** ~ **(on sth.)** (为某物) 确定/规定配额; **to fill** or **meet a** ~ 达到限额

quotable /ˈkwəʊtəbl/ adj **1** (worth citing) 值得引用的 ‹remark, paper› **2** (allowed to be cited) 可以引用的 ‹comment, writings›

quota system n 配额制

quotation /kwəʊˈteɪʃn/ n **1** (citation) 引文; **a** ~ **from sth.** 来自某处的引文 **2** (estimate) 报价; **to ask for/get a** ~ 要求/得到报价

quotation mark n 引号; **to put quotation marks around sth., to put sth. in quotation marks** 给某物加引号

quote /kwəʊt/

A vt **1** (cite) 引用; **he** ~**d a passage from the minister's speech** 他引用了部长的一段讲话; **to** ~ **Shakespeare** 引用莎士比亚的话; **don't** ~ **me (on this), but she's pregnant** 别说（这话）是我说的——她怀孕了; **to** ~ **sb. as saying that ...** 引用某人的话说… **2** (mention) 援引 ‹reference, fact, law›; **please** ~ **this number in all correspondence** 请在所有函件中标明这个编号; **to** ~ **sb./sth. as an example** 引某人/某事物为例; **can you** ~ **me an instance of this happening?** 你能否给我举例说明这种事件? **3** Comm (give) 报 ‹figure, price›; **they** ~**d us £600 for repairing** or **to repair the car** 修这辆车他们向我们开价 600 英镑 **4** Fin (state price of) 报…的价; **yesterday the pound was** ~**d at $1.8285** 昨天英镑的报价为 1.8285 美元 **5** Fin (list on stock exchange) 给…挂牌; **several football clubs are now** ~**d on the Stock Exchange** 已有好几家足球俱乐部在证券交易所挂牌上市 **6** (in betting) 报出…的投注赔率; **they are** ~**d (at** or **as) 6-1** 它们的投注赔率为 6 赔 1; **to** ~ **odds of 3-1** 开出 3 赔 1 的赔率

B vi **1** (recite from text) 引用; **he often** ~**s from**

the Bible 他经常引用《圣经》中的语句; **~ (... unquote)** (in dictation) 引号起（…引号止）; colloq (in speaking) 原话起（…原话止）; **it was ~ 'the hardest decision of my life' unquote** 那是，引文开始，"我一生中最难作出的决定"，引文结束 **2** Comm (give price) 报价; **to ~ for sth.** 为某物报价

C *n* **1** (from speech, book) 引文; **a ~ from the Bible** 引自《圣经》的语句 **2** (short statement to journalist) 声明 **3** Comm (estimate) 报价; **their ~ for the job was too high** 他们对那单活儿开价太高 **4** Fin (for sale or purchase of stock) 牌价

D quotes *npl* = **quotation marks**

quotient /ˈkwəʊʃnt/ *n* **1** (level) 程度; **the job has a high stress ~** 这项工作压力很大 **2** Math 商

qv *abbr* = **quod vide** 参见该条

QWERTY, qwerty /ˈkwɜːti/ *adj* 标准键盘的 ‹*layout*›; **a ~ keyboard/typewriter** 标准键盘/标准键盘打字机

q

Rr

R, r /ɑː(r)/

A *n* (*pl* **Rs** *or* **R's**) [英语字母表的第18个字母]

B *abbr* **1** **R = Rex, Regina** **2** **R = river 1** **3** **r = radius 1** **4** **r = right A3, C6**

Rabat /rəˈbæt/ *pr n* 拉巴特

rabbet /ˈræbɪt/ *n* Amer 榫眼

rabbi /ˈræbaɪ/ *n* 拉比 [犹太教经师或神职人员]; **the Chief R～** 首席拉比

rabbinic /rəˈbɪnɪk/, **rabbinical** /rəˈbɪnɪkl/ *adj* 拉比的 ‹*teaching, writings*›; **～ traditions recorded in the Talmud** 《塔木德经》中记载的犹太教传统

rabbit /ˈræbɪt/

A *n* **1** [c] Zool 兔 **2** [u] (fur) 兔皮 **3** [u] (meat) 兔肉; **～ stew** 炖兔肉

B *vi* Brit colloq 闲扯; **to ～ on** *or* **away (about sth.)** 没完没了地唠叨（某事）; **to ～ on** *or* **go ～ing on** 喋喋不休

rabbit: ～ burrow, ～ hole *ns* 兔子洞; **～ hutch** *n* 兔笼; **～ punch** *n* 向颈背的掌劈; **～ warren** *n* **1** (network of burrows) 野兔繁殖区; **2** fig (building) 迷宫般的建筑; (district) 曲里拐弯的城区

rabble /ˈræbl/ *n* pej **1** (crowd) 乌合之众; **a ～ of noisy youths and trouble makers** 一帮吵吵嚷嚷的年轻人和闹事者 **2** (populace) **the ～** 下层民众

rabble-rouser /ˈræblraʊzə(r)/ *n* pej 煽动民众者

rabble-rousing /ˈræblraʊzɪŋ/ pej

A *n* [u] 煽动民众

B *adj* 煽动性的 ‹*speech*›; 蛊惑人心的 ‹*speaker*›

rabid /ˈræbɪd, ˈreɪbɪd/ *adj* **1** (suffering from rabies) 患狂犬病的 **2** fig pej (fanatical) 狂热的 ‹*fascist, communist*›; 偏激的 ‹*racist, feminist*›; **～ hatred/greed** 痛恨/极端的贪婪; **the ～ tabloid press** 激进的小报新闻界

rabidly /ˈræbɪdli, Amer ˈreɪ-/ *adv* pej 疯狂地 ‹*attack*›; 狂热地 ‹*campaign*›; **he was ～ throwing insults at her** 他正在疯狂地辱骂她; **a ～ loyal follower** 死忠的追随者

rabies /ˈreɪbiːz/ ▸**p. 377** *n* [u] 狂犬病

RAC *abbr* Brit = **Royal Automobile Club** 皇家汽车俱乐部

raccoon /rəˈkuːn, Amer ræˈk-/ *n* **1** [c] (*pl* **～s** *or* **raccoon**) (animal) 浣熊 **2** [u] (fur) 浣熊毛皮

race¹ /reɪs/

A *n* **1** [c] Sport 速度竞赛; **to win/lose a ～** 跑赢/跑输; **to come first/second** *etc.* **in a ～** 赛跑获得第一/第二名等; **to take part in** *or* **enter a ～** 参加速度竞赛; **a boat/horse/dog/running ～** 赛艇/赛马/赛狗/赛跑; **a road/car/bicycle/swimming ～** 公路赛/赛车/自行车赛/游泳比赛; **a five-kilometre/200-metre ～** 5 公里/200 米速度竞赛; **a ～ between sb./sth. and sb./sth.** …与…之间的速度竞赛; **a ～ against sb./sth.** 与某人的赛跑/与某物的速度竞赛; **to have a ～ with** *or* **against sb./sth.** 与某人赛跑/与某物竞速; **to run a ～ (with sb.)** （和某人）赛跑; **to run in a ～** 参加赛跑; **a ～ against time** *or* **the clock** 计时赛; fig 争分夺秒 **2** [c] fig (rush) 匆忙; **a ～ to do sth.** 对做某事的抓紧; **it will be a ～ to get this job finished before the end of the week** 在周末之前完成这项工作得抓紧时间 **3** [c] fig (contest) 竞争; **the presidential/mayoral ～** 总统/市长竞选; **a ～ for sth.** 为某事物展开的竞争; **to win the ～ for the White House** 竞选美国总统获胜; **a ～ to do sth.** 在做某事方面的竞争; **the ～ to conquer space/reach the moon** 征服太空/登月的竞争; **the ～ is on to do sth.** 做某事的竞争已经开始 **4** [c] (in sea, river) 急流; **a tidal ～** 急潮流

B **races** *npl* **the ～s** (horse races) 赛马会; (dog races) 赛狗会; **to go to the ～s** (horse races) 去看赛马会; (dog races) 去看赛狗会; **a day at the ～s** (horse races) 看赛马会的一天; (dog races) 看赛狗会的一天

C *vt* **1** (compete with) 同…竞速; **come on, I'll ～ you!** 来呀，我要和你比比谁快！; **to ～ sb. to sth.** 与某人竞相奔向某物; **we ～d each other back to the car** 我们争先恐后跑回汽车上 **2** (enter for race) 使…参加速度竞赛 ‹*animal, vehicle, vessel*›; **to ～ pigeons** 赛鸽子 **3** (move fast) 使…疾走 ‹*person*›; 使…快速行驶 ‹*vehicle*›; 使…快速移动 ‹*product*›; **she ～d her car through the town** 她驾车飞驰穿过小镇; **to ～ sb./sth. to sb./sth.** 使某人/某物向某人/某物快速移动; **they ～d her to hospital** 他们火速将她送往医院 **4** (rev up) 使…空转 ‹*engine*›

D *vi* **1** (take part in a race) 参加速度竞赛; **he'll be racing for the senior team next year** 明年他要参加高级组别赛跑; **to ～ against sb./sth. (in the final/semi-final** *etc.***)** 同某人/某物（在决赛/半决赛等中）竞速; **to ～ to sth.** 冲向某物; **they ～d to a thrilling victory in the relay** 他们在接力赛中以令人振奋的成绩获胜; **to ～ with sb./sth.** 同某人/某物竞赛; **to ～ around the track** 环绕跑道竞速 **2** (move fast) **to ～ in** «*person*» 快速走入; «*vehicle, vessel*» 快速驶入; **to ～ out** 冲出; **he ～d out into the street** 他冲到街上; **to ～ along** «*person*» 疾行; «*vehicle, vessel*» 疾驰; **to ～ past** «*person*» 匆匆走过; «*vehicle, vessel*» 匆匆驶过; **to ～ up/down sth.** «*person*» 快速走上/走下某物; «*vehicle, vessel*» 快速驶上/驶下某物; **he ～d up the stairs/down the street** 他冲上楼梯/沿着马路疾行; **to ～ for sth.** «*person*» 向…疾行 ‹*vehicle, vessel*›; **to ～ for the train** 赶火车; **to ～ after sb./sth.** 追赶某人/某物; **to ～ to sth.** 冲向某物 **3** (try to be first) 争先; **to ～ to do sth.** 竞先做某事 **4** (operate quickly) «*mind*» 急速转动; «*heart, pulse*» 急速跳动 **5** Aut «*engine*» 空转 **6** (hurry) 匆忙; **to ～ to do sth.** 匆忙做某事; **we ～d to get the job finished by lunchtime** 我们赶着在午饭前完工; **to ～ through sth.** 匆忙完成 ‹*exercise, task*›; **he ～d through the novel in record time** 他飞快地翻阅完那本小说; **to ～ against time** 争分夺秒

Phrasal verbs

- **race away** *vi* **to ～ away from sb./sth.** 快速超出某人/某物; **the horse ～d away from the rest of the field to a comfortable victory** 那匹马飞快甩开其他参赛马轻松获胜
- **race by** *vi* «*time*» 飞逝; **the weeks seemed to ～ by** 几个星期仿佛一晃而过

race² *n* **1** [u and c] Anthrop 种族; **the Caucasian/Mongolian ～** 白种人/蒙古人种; **～ law/hatred** 种族法/仇恨 **2** [c] Sociol 民族; **the Nordic ～s** 北欧日尔曼民族; **people of an ancient and noble ～** 世家的后裔 **3** [c] Bot, Zool 族 [尤指亚种]; **a new ～ of cattle** 新品种的牛

race: ～ car *n* Amer 赛车; **～card** *n* 赛程表; **～course** *n* Brit (horse) 赛马场; (dog) 赛狗场; **～ discrimination** *n* [u] 种族歧视; **～goer** *n* 赛马会常客; **～horse** *n* 赛马; **～ meeting** *n* Brit 赛马大会

racer /ˈreɪsə(r)/ *n* **1** (person) 赛跑者 **2** (bicycle, motorbike, car) 赛车 **3** (yacht) 赛艇

race: ～ relations *npl* 种族关系; **～ riot** *n* 种族骚乱; **～track** *n* **1** Horse racing 赛马场; **2** (for cars, motorbikes) 赛车道; **3** (for dogs) 赛犬跑道; **～way** *n* Amer (for cars) 赛车道; (for harness racing) 赛马场

racial /ˈreɪʃl/ *adj* **1** (relating to race) 种族的; **～ minority** 少数民族; **～ features/origin** 种族特征/起源 **2** (on the grounds of race) 基于种族的 ‹*barrier*›; 种族之间的 ‹*tension, violence*›; **～ inequality/prejudice/harmony/reconciliation/differences** 种族不平等/偏见/和睦/和解/差异

racial: ～ discrimination *n* [u] 种族歧视; **～ equality** *n* [u] 种族平等; **～ harassment** *n* [u] 种族骚扰

racialism /ˈreɪʃəlɪzəm/ *n* [u] **= racism**

racialist /ˈreɪʃəlɪst/ *adj, n* **= racist**

racially /ˈreɪʃəli/ *adv* 在种族上; **the attack was ～ motivated** 袭击事件是由种族原因引起的; **a ～ diverse community** 一个多种族社区; **the dialogue is ～ offensive** 该对话冒犯种族

racily /ˈreɪsɪli/ *adv* **1** (in a lively manner) 活泼地 ‹*written, told*› **2** (in risqué manner) 近乎淫猥地 ‹*dress, talk*›

raciness /ˈreɪsɪnɪs/ *n* [u] **1** (lively quality) 活泼 **2** (risqué quality) 有伤风化

racing /ˈreɪsɪŋ/ *n* [u] **1** Horse racing 赛马 **2** (with cars, bikes) 赛车; (with boats) 赛艇; (with animals) 动物竞速; **motor** Brit *or* **car** Amer **～** 赛车; **pigeon ～** 赛鸽; **the ～ world** (car) 赛车界; (horse) 赛马界; **a ～ boat/yacht** 赛船/赛艇

racing: ～ bicycle, ～ bike *ns* 比赛自行车; **～ car** *n* Brit 赛车; **～ colours** *npl* 赛马骑手着装的颜色; **～ driver** *n* 赛车手; **～ pigeon** *n* 赛鸽; **～ stable** *n* 赛马饲养训练场

racism /ˈreɪsɪzəm/ *n* [u] **1** (belief) 种族主义 **2** (racist behaviour) 种族歧视

racist /ˈreɪsɪst/

A *adj* 种族主义的 ‹*remark, view, politician*›; **a ～ society** 种族主义社会

B *n* 种族主义分子

rack /ræk/

A *n* **1** (stand) 支架; **a ～ of clothes** 一架子衣服; **a letter ～** 信插 **2** (shelf) 行李架 **3** (torture) 拉肢刑具; **to be on the ～** fig 备受煎熬

4 **to go to ~ and ruin** 变得一团糟; **they let the house go to ~ and ruin** 房子越来越破旧，他们也不管

B *vt* 1 fig (torment) «*fear, guilt, pain*» 使…痛苦不堪 ‹*person, body, mind*›; **to be ~ed with** 深感 ‹*guilt, shame, fear*›; **an industry ~ed by crisis** 受危机打击的产业; **to ~ one's brain(s)** 绞尽脑汁 2 (draw off) 从沉渣中榨取; **to ~ off** 从酒糟中榨取; **the wine is ~ed (off) into large oak casks** 葡萄酒被榨出抽取到大橡木桶里

rack-and-pinion *n* 齿条齿轮装置; **~ steering** 齿条齿轮式转向装置

racket[1] /ˈrækɪt/ *n* Sport 球拍; **~ strings** 球拍线

racket[2] *n* 1 colloq (noise) 吵闹声; **to make a ~** 大吵大闹 2 (swindle) 诈骗; **it's a ~!** 这是个骗局! 3 colloq (illegal activity) 非法勾当; **the drugs ~** 毒品买卖; **he's in on the ~** colloq 他卷入了非法买卖

racket: ~ abuse *n* [u] 摔球拍; **~ball** *n* = **racquetball**

racketeer /ˌrækəˈtɪə(r)/ *n* 诈骗者

racketeering /ˌrækəˈtɪərɪŋ/ *n* [u] 诈骗

racket press *n* 球拍夹

racking /ˈrækɪŋ/ *adj attrib* 剧烈的 ‹*pain*›; 强烈的 ‹*guilt*›; **~ sobs** 恸哭

rack railway *n* 齿轨铁路

raconteur /ˌrækɒnˈtɜː(r)/ *n* 擅长讲故事的人

racoon /rəˈkuːn, Amer ræˈk-/ *n* = **raccoon**

racquet /ˈrækɪt/ *n* = **racket[1]**

racquetball /ˈrækɪtbɔːl/ ▸**p. 307** *n* [u] esp Amer 短网拍墙球

racy /ˈreɪsi/ *adj* 1 (lively) 生动的 ‹*speech*›; 活泼的 ‹*behaviour, character*›; **a ~ description of sth.** 对某事物栩栩如生的描写 2 (risqué) 近乎淫猥的 ‹*story, behaviour*›; **the novel was considered rather ~ at the time** 这部小说在当时被认为有伤风化 3 (in flavour) 辛辣的 ‹*wine*›

RADA /ˈrɑːdə/ *abbr* Brit = **Royal Academy of Dramatic Art** 皇家戏剧艺术学院

radar /ˈreɪdɑː(r)/ *n* [u] 雷达; **by ~** 通过雷达; **they were following the course of the submarine on the ~** 他们当时正在用雷达追踪潜水艇; **a ~ screen/sensor/beacon** 雷达显示屏/传感器/信标

radar: ~ astronomy *n* [u] 雷达天文学; **~ scanner** *n* 旋转雷达天线; **~ trap** *n* 雷达阱 [警察用来监测车速的雷达设备]; **to get caught in a ~ trap** 被雷达阱监测到

radial /ˈreɪdɪəl/

A *adj* 1 (arranged like rays) 辐射状的 ‹*arms, lines, structure*›; **~ walkways** 辐射状走道 2 (running from town centre) 从市中心直通郊区的 ‹*route*› 3 Aut, Aviat 星形的; **a ~ engine** 星形发动机

B *n* **~ (tyre)** 子午线轮胎

radiance /ˈreɪdɪəns/, **radiancy** /ˈreɪdɪənsi/ *ns* [u] 1 (brightness) 光辉; **in the soft ~ of the candlelight** 在柔和的烛光下 2 fig (of beauty, smile) 容光焕发 3 fig (joy) 喜悦

radiant /ˈreɪdɪənt/ *adj* 1 (shining) 灿烂的 ‹*sun, light*›; 闪闪发光的 ‹*petal, sea*› 2 fig (exuberant) 光彩照人的 ‹*beauty, smile*›; **to be ~** «*bride, princess*» 明艳动人 3 fig (joyful) 喜气洋洋的 ‹*person, face*›; **to be ~ with sth.** 因…而容光焕发 ‹*joy, health*› 4 Phys 辐射的; **~ heat/energy** 辐射热/能; **a ~ heater** 辐射式加热器

radiantly /ˈreɪdɪəntli/ *adv* 1 (brightly) 灿烂地 ‹*glow*› 2 fig (exuberantly) 光彩照人地; **~ beautiful** 光艳照人的 3 (joyfully) 喜气洋洋地 ‹*beam, say*›; **~ happy** 幸福洋溢的

radiate /ˈreɪdɪeɪt/

A *vt* 1 Phys 散发 ‹*heat, light*› 2 (emanate, give out) 流露; **she ~s confidence and enthusiasm** 她显得自信热情; **she bounced in, radiating health and vitality** 她冲了进来，浑身散发着健康与活力

B *vi* 1 Phys 辐射; **to ~ from …** «*heat, light*» 从…散发出 2 (emanate) 流露; **to ~ from …** «*warmth, confidence*» 从…流露出 3 (spread out) 呈辐射状散发; **to ~ from …** «*lines, beams*» 从…向四周伸展; **radiating roads/passageways/lines** 辐射状的道路/通道/线条

radiation /ˌreɪdɪˈeɪʃn/ *n* [u] 1 Phys (of heat) 发热; (of energy) 辐射; (of light) 发光; **high solar ~** 强烈的太阳辐射; **~ levels** 辐射强度 2 (radioactivity) 放射线; **to be exposed to ~** 受放射线照射; **a low/high level of ~** 低/高强度辐射

radiation: ~ exposure *n* [u] 放射线照射; **~ processing** *n* [u] 辐照加工; **~ sickness** *n* [u] 辐射病; **~ therapy** *n* [u and c] 放射疗法; **~ treatment** *n* [u and c] 放射治疗; **~ worker** *n* 放射工作人员

radiator /ˈreɪdɪeɪtə(r)/ *n* 1 (for heat) 暖气; **to turn a ~ on/off** 开/关暖气; **to turn a ~ up/down** 把暖气温度调高/低 2 (in engine) 冷却器; **to top up a ~** 加满水箱; **a ~ cap** 散热器盖子

radiator grille *n* 散热器护栅

radical /ˈrædɪkl/

A *adj* 1 Pol 激进的 ‹*campaigner, movement, bookshop*› 2 (fundamental) 根本的 ‹*fault, difference*›; 基本的 ‹*thought*› 3 (thorough) 彻底的 ‹*reform, re-examination*›; **the need for changes in the law** 彻底改革法律的需要 4 Med 根治的 ‹*treatment*›; **he will undergo ~ plastic surgery** 他要做一次彻底的整形手术

B *n* 1 Pol 激进分子 2 Chem 基; **free ~s** 自由基 3 Ling 偏旁

radicalism /ˈrædɪkəlɪzəm/ *n* [u] 激进主义

radicalize /ˈrædɪkəlaɪz/ *vt* 1 Pol 使激进; **to ~ sb. against sth.** 使某人对某事持偏激态度 2 (change fundamentally) 彻底改变

radically /ˈrædɪkli/ *adv* 根本地; **a ~ altered policy** 彻底改变的政策

radicle /ˈrædɪkl/ *n* 胚根

radii /ˈreɪdɪaɪ/ *pl* ▸**radius**

radio /ˈreɪdɪəʊ/

A *n* (*pl* **~s**) 1 [u] (system) 无线电; **to send a message by ~** 通过无线电发送信息 2 [c] (apparatus) 收音机; **to turn the ~ up/down** 把收音机音量开大/关小; **to have the ~ on** 让收音机开着; **an AM/FM ~** 中波/调频收音机; **a portable/stereo ~** 手提式/立体声收音机 3 [u] (broadcasting) 无线电广播; **on the ~** 在广播中; **to listen to the ~** 听广播; **to be** *or* **work in ~** 在电台工作 4 [c] (communication device) 无线电设备; **a ~ receiver/transmitter** 无线电接收器/发送器; **the taxi driver used his ~ to call for help** 出租车司机用无线电求助

B *vt* (*pres* **~es**; *pt, pp* **~ed**) 1 (communicate with) 用无线电联系 ‹*person, ship*› 2 (send) 用无线电发送 ‹*information*›

C *vi* (*pres* **~es**; *pt, pp* **~ed**) 用无线电通讯; **to ~ for help** 用无线电求助

radioactive /ˌreɪdɪəʊˈæktɪv/ *adj* 放射性的 ‹*substance*›; **~ waste/decay** 放射性废物/衰变; **~ fallout** 放射性尘降物

radioactivity /ˌreɪdɪəʊækˈtɪvɪti/ *n* [u] 1 (emission of radiation) 放射性 2 (radiation) 放射线

radio: ~ alarm, ~ alarm clock *ns* 收音机闹钟; **~ announcer** ▸**p. 409** *n* 电台播音员; **~ astronomy** *n* [u] 射电天文学; **~ beacon** *n* 无线电信标; **~biology** *n* [u] 放射生物学; **~ broadcast** *n* (programme) 无线电广播节目; (transmission) 无线电广播; **~ broadcasting** *n* [u] 无线电广播; **~ button** *n* 单选按钮; **~ cab** *n* 有车载无线电通讯设备的出租车; **~ car** *n* 有车载无线电通讯设备的汽车 [尤指警车]

radiocarbon /ˈreɪdɪəʊˌkɑːbən/ *n* [u] 放射性碳

radiocarbon dating *n* [u] 碳定年法

radio: ~ cassette, ~ cassette recorder *ns* 卡式收录机; **~chemistry** *n* [u] 放射化学; **~ communication** *n* [u] 无线电通信; **~ compass** *n* 无线电罗盘; **~-controlled** *adj* 无线电遥控的 ‹*toy*›; 无线电控制的 ‹*taxi*›; **~ documentary** *n* 电台纪实报道; **~-element** *n* 放射性元素; **~ frequency** *n* 无线电频率

radiogram /ˈreɪdɪəʊgræm/ *n* 1 Brit dated (radio and record player) 收音电唱两用机 2 (telegram) 无线电报

radiograph /ˈreɪdɪəʊgrɑːf, Amer -græf/ *n* 射线照片

radiographer /ˌreɪdɪˈɒgrəfə(r)/ ▸**p. 409** *n* 放射技师

radiography /ˌreɪdɪˈɒgrəfi/ *n* [u] 射线摄影

radio: ~ ham *n* colloq 业余无线电爱好者; **~ interview** *n* 电台采访; **~isotope** *n* 放射性同位素; **~ journalist** ▸**p. 409** *n* 电台记者; **~ link** *n* 无线电通信线路

radiological /ˌreɪdɪəˈlɒdʒɪkl/ *adj* 1 Med 放射学的; **a ~ examination** 放射学检查 2 Phys, Tech 辐射的; **a ~ agent** 放射剂; **~ protection/safety** 辐射防护/安全

radiologist /ˌreɪdɪˈɒlədʒɪst/ ▸**p. 409** *n* 放射学家

radiology /ˌreɪdɪˈɒlədʒi/ *n* [u] 放射学

radio mast *n* 无线电杆

radiometer /ˌreɪdɪˈɒmɪtə(r)/ *n* 辐射计

radio: ~ microphone, colloq **~ mike** *ns* 无线话筒; **~ play** *n* 广播剧; **~ presenter** ▸**p. 409** *n* 电台主持人

radioscopy /ˌreɪdɪˈɒskəpi/ *n* [u] 放射检查

radio: ~ set *n* dated 收音机; **~ silence** *n* [u] 无线电寂静; **~ source, ~ star** *ns* 射电源; **~ station** *n* (channel) 广播电台; (installation) 无线电站; **~ taxi** *n* 无线电出租车; **~-telephone** *n* 无线电话; **~-telephony** *n* [u] 无线电话通讯; **~ telescope** *n* 射电望远镜; **~therapist** ▸**p. 409** *n* 放射治疗师; **~therapy** *n* [u and c] 放射疗法; **~ wave** *n* 无线电波

radish /ˈrædɪʃ/ *n* 萝卜

radium /ˈreɪdɪəm/ *n* [u] 镭

radium therapy *n* [u] 镭疗 (法)

radius /ˈreɪdɪəs/ *n* (*pl* **radii** *or* **~es**) 1 Math 半径 2 (distance) 半径范围; **within a 10 km ~ of here** 离这里方圆10公里以内 3 Anat 桡骨

radon /ˈreɪdɒn/ *n* [u] 氡

RAF *abbr* = **Royal Air Force**

raffia /ˈræfɪə/ *n* [u] 酒椰叶纤维; **~ baskets** 酒椰叶编的篮子

raffish /ˈræfɪʃ/ *adj* liter 放荡不羁的 ‹*behaviour, air*›; **a rather ~ group of young men** 一群相当狂放的年轻人

raffle /ˈræfl/

A *n* 抽奖; **to hold a ~** 举行抽奖; **a ~ ticket/prize** 兑奖券/抽彩奖品

B *vt* 在兑奖销售中奖给; **to ~ sth. (off)** 将某物作为抽奖销售的奖品

raft /rɑːft, Amer ræft/ *n* 1 (floating platform) 筏子 2 (small boat) 充气船 3 colloq (large amount) 大量; **a ~ of new proposals** 许多新提议

rafter /ˈrɑːftə(r), Amer ˈræftə(r)/ *n* 1 Constr 椽子 2 Sport 筏夫

rafting /ˈrɑːftɪŋ, Amer ˈræftɪŋ/ *n* [u] 漂筏运动; **to go ~** 去漂流

rag[1] /ræg/ *n* 1 [c and u] (cloth) 破布; **a bit of ~** 一点儿破布; **(to feel) like a wet ~** colloq (感到) 身心疲惫; **to lose one's ~** Brit colloq 发脾气 2 colloq pej (newspaper) 小报; **the local ~** 当地小报

rag[2]

A *n* Brit Univ [学生每年组织的] 慈善募捐活动; **a ~ magazine** 募捐杂志

B *vt* (*pres p etc.* **-gg-**) colloq 捉弄; **to ~ sb. (about/for sth.)** (拿/为某事物) 取笑某人

rag³ *n* Mus 雷格泰姆音乐

raga /ˈrɑːgə/ *n* 拉伽 [印度古典音乐中的基本曲调之一]

ragamuffin /ˈrægəmʌfɪn/ *n* dated 衣衫褴褛肮脏的人

rag: ~-and-bone man *n* Brit colloq dated 挨家挨户收废品的人; **~bag** *n* 1 lit (bag of old cloth) 放碎布头的袋子; 2 fig (jumble) 大杂烩; 3 pej (sloppily dressed woman) 邋遢女人; **~ doll** *n* 碎布娃娃

rage /reɪdʒ/
A *n* 1 [c and u] (anger) 狂怒; **trembling/white/red with ~** 气得发抖/脸色发白/涨红了脸; **to be in** *or* **fly into a ~** 勃然大怒 2 [c] colloq (fashion) 时尚; **to be all the ~** 风靡一时; **it's all the ~ in Paris** 这是巴黎非常流行的东西
B *vi* 1 (be angry) 发怒; **she ~d against the cruelty** 她怒斥这种残酷行为 2 (continue strongly) «*storm*» 肆虐; «*argument, battle*» 激烈进行 3 (spread rapidly) 蔓延; **fire ~d through the building** 大火在楼内蔓延

ragged /ˈrægɪd/ *adj* 1 (torn and shabby) 破烂的 ‹*clothes*› 2 (scruffy) 邋遢的 ‹*person*›; **a ~ little boy** 脏兮兮的小男孩 3 (rough, shaggy) 蓬乱的 ‹*fringe, beard*› 4 (jagged) 参差不齐的 ‹*edge*›; 形状不规则的 ‹*cloud*›; 毛边的 ‹*cuff*› 5 (poor, disorderly) 粗劣的 ‹*performance, music*› 6 (motley) 混杂的 ‹*community*› 7 (tired, worn out) 精疲力竭的; **to run sb./oneself ~** 使某人/自己疲惫不堪

raging /ˈreɪdʒɪŋ/ *adj* 1 (intense) 肆虐的 ‹*storm*›; 汹涌的 ‹*sea, torrent*›; 强烈的 ‹*thirst, hunger, pain*›; 狂暴的 ‹*anti-Semitism, passion*›; **a ~ toothache** 剧烈的牙痛; **a ~ fever** 高烧; **~ hatred** 痛恨; **he's in a ~ temper** 他怒不可遏 2 (tremendous) 极度的; **he had been a ~ success in Spain** 他曾在西班牙红极一时 3 (angry) 盛怒的; **a ~ bull** 狂暴的公牛

raglan /ˈræglən/ *adj* 插肩式的 ‹*coat*›; **a ~ sleeve** 插肩袖

ragout /ræˈguː/ *n* [u and c] 蔬菜炖肉

rag-roll *vt* 用破布滚刷出纹理效果; **the walls have been ~ed in a mid blue** 墙壁用破布滚刷成了淡蓝色条纹

rag-rolling *n* [u] 破布滚刷法

rags /rægz/ *npl* 破衣烂衫; **to be dressed in ~** 穿着破烂衣服; **to be in ~** 处于破烂状态; **(to go) from ~ to riches** 从赤贫到巨富; **a ~-to-riches story** 穷人发迹史

ragtag /ˈrægtæg/ *adj* colloq pej 杂乱的 ‹*organization, group*›; **a ~ bunch of salesmen** 一群散漫的推销员

ragtime /ˈrægtaɪm/ *n* [u] **~ (music)** 雷格泰姆音乐 [1900年左右出现的一种爵士乐]

rag: ~top *n* Amer colloq 敞篷汽车; **~ trade** *n* [u] colloq **the ~ trade** 服装业; **~weed** *n* [u] 豚草; **~ week** *n* Brit Univ 学生募捐周

rah-rah /ˈrɑːrɑː/ *adj* Amer colloq 激情澎湃的 ‹*style*›; 狂热喝彩的 ‹*response*›; **a ~ skirt** 啦啦队裙

raid /reɪd/
A *n* 1 Mil (by soldiers, ships) 突袭; (by aircraft) 空袭; **a cross-border ~ by guerrillas** 游击队的越境突袭; **a ~ on sth.** 对…的突袭 ‹*town, outpost, base*›; **to carry out** *or* **make a ~ (on sth.)** (对某物) 实施袭击 2 (surprise swoop) 突击搜查; **a ~ on sth.** 对…的突击搜查 ‹*house, club, casino*›; **to carry out** *or* **make a ~ (on sth.)** 突然搜查 (某物) 3 (robbery) 抢劫; **a ~ on sth.** 对…的抢劫 ‹*bank, shop, post office*›; **to carry out** *or* **make a ~ (on sth.)** (对某处) 实施抢劫 4 Fin 恶意收购; **a ~ on sth.** 对…的恶意收购 ‹*company, business*›
B *vt* 1 Mil «*soldiers, ships*» 突袭; «*aircraft, pilots*» 空袭 2 (swoop on) «*police, customs officers*» 突击搜查 ‹*premises*› 3 (rob) 抢劫 ‹*bank*› 4 fig (remove items from) 洗劫 ‹*piggy bank, cash box*›; 清空 ‹*fridge, cupboard*› 5 Fin (take illicitly) 侵吞 ‹*fund, reserves*›; (use illicitly) 挪用 ‹*fund, reserves*›

raider /ˈreɪdə(r)/ *n* 1 (soldier) 侵入者 2 (robber, bandit) 劫掠者 3 Fin (corporate raider) 恶意收购者 4 (aircraft) 袭击机; (ship) 武装劫掠船

rail¹ /reɪl/
A *n* 1 [c] (handrail) 栏杆; (on ship) 舷栏 2 [c] (bar for hanging things on) 横杆; **a curtain ~** 窗帘杆 3 [c] (track) 铁轨; **tram ~s** 电车轨道; **to come** *or* **go off the ~s** lit 出轨; **to go off the ~s** fig «*person*» 举止怪异; «*project*» 无法正常运行; **he seems to have gone off the ~s a bit** 他似乎变得有点疯疯癫癫; **our plans have rather gone off the ~s** 我们的计划乱了套 4 [u] (as means of travel) 铁路; **by ~** 乘火车 ‹*travel*›; 由铁路 ‹*send*›; **to go by ~** 乘火车去; **~ transport/journey/network/worker** 铁路运输/旅行/网/工人; **a ~ ticket** 火车票
B **rails** *npl* Horse racing 赛马场围栏

Phrasal verbs

- **rail in** *vt* [**~ sth. in, ~ in sth.**] 用栏杆围住 ‹*animal, area*›; **the sheep were ~ed in** 羊被圈在栅栏里
- **rail off** *vt* [**~ sth. off, ~ off sth.**] 用栏杆隔开 ‹*area*›; **they had ~ed off a section of the field for use as a car park** 他们围出一块地用作停车场

rail² *vi* formal (complain) 怒斥; **to ~ against** *or* **at sth.** 愤怒抗议某事物

rail: ~ accident *n* 铁路事故; **~car** *n* Brit 有轨机动车; **~card** *n* Brit 铁路优惠卡; **~head** *n* (during construction) 铁轨尽头; (terminus) 铁路转运点

railing /ˈreɪlɪŋ/ *n* 栏杆; **iron ~s** 铁栏杆

rail journey *n* 乘火车旅行; **a ~ across America** 乘火车穿越美国的旅行

raillery /ˈreɪləri/ *n* [u] liter 打趣

railroad /ˈreɪlrəʊd/
A *n* Amer 1 (network) 铁路 2 **~ (track)** 铁轨 3 (company) 铁道部门
B *vt* 1 colloq (compel) 逼迫; **to ~ sb. into doing sth.** 迫使某人仓促做某事; **to ~ sth. through** 强使…草率通过 ‹*plan, bill*› 2 Amer (send by rail) 用铁路运输 3 Amer colloq (imprison) 轻率判处

railroad: ~ car *n* Amer 火车车厢; **~ crossing** *n* Amer = **level crossing**; **~ tie** *n* Amer = **sleeper 5**

rail: ~ terminus *n* Brit 火车终点（站）; **~ traffic** *n* [u] 铁路交通

railway /ˈreɪlweɪ/ Brit *n* 1 (network) 铁路; **a ~ ticket/timetable** 火车票/列车时刻表; **a ~ journey/network/bridge** 铁路旅行/网/桥; **to travel around the country on the ~(s)** 坐火车周游全国 2 **~ (track)** 铁轨 3 (company) 铁道部门

railway: ~ carriage *n* Brit 火车车厢; **~ embankment** *n* Brit 铁路路堤; **~ engine** *n* Brit 火车头; **~ junction** *n* Brit 铁路交叉点; **~ line** *n* Brit 1 (route) 铁路线; 2 (track) 铁轨; **~man** /-mən/ ▸**p. 409** *n* Brit 铁路职工; **~ station** *n* Brit 火车站

rain /reɪn/
A *n* 1 [u] Meteorol 雨; **there will be ~ tomorrow** 明日有雨; **~ is forecast for the weekend** 预报说周末有雨; **a drop of ~** 一滴雨; **the ~ was coming down in huge drops** 雨大滴大滴地落下来; **the ~ is pouring down, it's pouring with ~** 大雨倾盆; **don't go out in the ~** 不要冒雨出去; **(a) light/heavy ~** 小雨/大雨; **steady/driving** *or* **pouring** *or* **torrential ~** 淫雨/倾盆大雨; **it looks like ~** 好像要下雨了; **to shelter from the ~** 避雨; **to come in out of the ~** 躲进室内避雨; **(come) ~ or shine** 无论晴雨; **to be (as) right as ~** colloq «*person*» 非常健康; «*object*» 毫无问题; **~ cloud** 雨云 2 [c] fig (large number) **a ~ of sth.** 雨点般的 ‹*arrows, bullets, blows*›
B **rains** *npl* **the ~s** 雨季
C *v impers* 下雨; **it's ~ing** 下雨了; **it ~ed all day/all summer** 整天/整个夏天都在下雨; **to ~ heavily** *or* **hard** 下大雨; **it never ~s but it pours** Brit, **when it ~s it pours** Amer 祸不单行
D *vi* 1 (fall) 雨点般落下; **to ~ on sb./sth.** 雨点般地落在某人身上/某物上; **confetti ~ed on their heads** 五彩纸屑纷纷扬扬掉落在他们头上; **a flurry of blows ~ed on him** 一阵拳头劈头盖脸地打在他身上 2 (be uttered) 连珠炮似地发出; **to ~ on sb.** 接连向某人说出; **more insults/abuse/questions ~ed on him** 更多的侮辱/辱骂/问题连珠炮似地向他袭来
E *vt* 1 (cause to fall) 使大量降落; **to ~ arrows into the path of sb.** 雨点般地向某人通行的道路射箭; **to ~ sth. on sb./sth.** 使某物雨点般地落在某人身上/某物上; **he ~ed blows on the woman** 他连续不断用拳头打那个女人 2 (utter) 连珠炮似地说出; **to ~ compliments/questions on sb.** 一个劲儿地恭维某人/连珠炮似地向某人发问; **he ~ed abuse on her head** 他对她劈头盖脸一顿辱骂

Phrasal verbs

- **rain down**

A *vi* 1 (fall in large quantities) 雨点般落下; **bombs ~ed down** 炸弹雨点般地落下; **to ~ down on sb./sth.** 倾泻在某人身上/某物上; **the blows ~ed down on him** 拳头如雨点般落在他身上 2 (be uttered) 连珠炮似地发出; **the plaudits ~ed down** 人们纷纷表示赞赏; **to ~ down on sb.** 连珠炮似地向某人说出; **abuse/accusations/questions ~ed down continually on him** 辱骂/谴责/问题连珠炮似地向他袭来
B *vt* [**~ down sth., ~ sth. down**] 1 (cause to fall) 使大量降落; **to ~ sth. down on sb./sth.** 使某事物雨点般地落在某人身上/某物上; **the cherry tree ~ed white blossom down on him** 樱桃树上的白花纷纷掉落在他身上 2 (utter) 连珠炮似地说出; **to ~ sth. down on sb.** 连珠炮似地向某人说出某物; **he ~ed down curses on them** 他不停地咒骂他们

- **rain off** *vt* [**~ off sth., ~ sth. off**] Brit 因雨取消; **to be ~ed off** 因雨取消
- **rain out** *vt* Amer = **rain off**

rainbow /ˈreɪnbəʊ/ *n* 1 Meteorol 彩虹; **at the end of the ~** 在可望而不可即的地方; **that is the price you pay for believing in the pot of gold at the end of the ~** 那就是你痴心妄想所付出的代价 2 (display of colours) 五彩缤纷; **a black sweater with a ~ of colour across the front** 前胸五颜六色的黑毛衣

rainbow coalition *n* [尤指在美国由不同党派组成的] 彩虹联盟

rain: ~ chart *n* 雨量统计表; **~ check** *n* Amer 1 Sport [赛事等因雨取消后] 可延期使用的票根; **to take a ~ check (on sth.)** fig (对某事) 改日再说; 2 Comm [商店在减价商品售罄时给顾客的] 货到优先供应券; **~coat** *n* 雨衣; **~drop** *n* 雨点; **~fall** *n* [u] 降雨量; **50 cm of ~fall** 50 厘米的降雨量; **heavy/low ~fall** 强降雨/低雨量; **~forest** *n* 热带雨林; **~ gauge** *n* 雨量器

rainless /ˈreɪnlɪs/ *adj* 无雨的 ‹*area, month*›

rain: ~maker *n* 1 (creator of rain) [尤指印第安人的] 求雨法师; 2 Amer fig colloq (of income) 使公司生意兴隆的人; **~making** *n* [u] 1 (attempting to cause rainfall) 祈雨; **a ~making ceremony** 求雨法事; 2 (cloud seeding) 人工造雨; 3 Amer fig colloq (generating income) 促成生意; **~ shadow** *n* 雨影 [指因山脉遮挡雨量较少的区域]; **~-soaked** *adj* 被雨淋透的 ‹*person, newspaper*›; 浸透雨水的 ‹*ground, street*›; **~storm** *n* 暴风雨; **~water** *n* [u] 雨水; **~wear** *n* [u] 防雨服

rainy /ˈreɪni/ *adj* 阴雨的 ‹*afternoon*›; 多雨的 ‹*weather, place*›; **the ~ season** 多雨季节; **a ~ day** 雨天; **to save** *or* **keep sth. for a ~ day** fig 存储某物以备不时之需

raise /reɪz/

A *vt* **1** (move upwards) 举起 ‹*stick, weight*›; 抬起 ‹*head, leg*›; 拉起 ‹*blind, window, trapdoor, lid*›; 升起 ‹*flag*›; 提升 ‹*level, ceiling*›; **to ~ a** *or* **one's hand** 举手; **to ~ a** *or* **one's hand/fist to sb.** 对某人扬起手/挥拳头; **to ~ sth. to sth.** 将某事物升高到某事物; **he ~d the glass to his lips** 他将杯子举到唇边; **to ~ a** *or* **one's glass (to sb./sth.)** (为某人/某事物) 举杯庆贺; **to ~ sth. from sth.** 从某处抬起某物; **the throne was on a podium, slightly ~d from floor level** 御座位于比地面稍高的平台上; **to ~ sth. up** 举起某物; **to ~ one's hat (to sb.)** (向某人) 挥帽致意; **to ~ the curtain** Theat 启幕; **to ~ sth. above** *or* **over one's head** 将某物举过头顶; **to ~ an eyebrow (at sb./sth.)** lit, fig (对某人/某事物) 扬起眉毛 [表示不赞成或吃惊] **2** (place upright) 竖起 ‹*mast, flagpole*›; 扶起 ‹*person, animal*›; **to ~ sb./sth. from sth.** 从某处扶起某人/竖起某物; **we managed to ~ her to her feet** 我们设法扶她站了起来; **to ~ sb./sth. up** 扶起某人/某物 **3** (increase) 提高 ‹*level, rate, limit*›; **to ~ sb.'s awareness** *or* **consciousness of sth.** 提高某人对某事物的意识; **to ~ the bidding** (in gambling) 增加赌注; **to ~ sth. to sth.** 将某事物提高到某水平; **he ~d his bid to £240** (at auction) 他将出价加到 240 英镑; **to ~ sth. from sth.** 从某处提高某物; **to ~ the speed limit from 70 mph to 80 mph** 将限速从每小时 70 英里提高到每小时 80 英里; **to ~ one's voice (at sb.)** (冲某人) 提高嗓门嚷嚷; **to ~ one's voice against sth.** fig 强烈反对某事物; **to ~ sb.'s expectations** 唤起某人的期望 **4** (bring to surface) 打捞 ‹*treasure*›; **to ~ a ship from the sea floor** 从海底打捞起船只 **5** (promote) 提拔; **to ~ sb. to the rank of captain** 晋升某人为上尉; **to ~ sb. to the title of ...** 提拔某人授予其…的称号 **6** (resurrect) 使复活; **to ~ sb. from the dead** 使某人起死回生 **7** (cause to appear) 使…出现 ‹*suspicion, fears, difficulty*›; 唤起 ‹*memories, spirit*›; 扬起 ‹*dust*›; **her words ~d the shadow of a doubt in his mind** 她的话让他起了一丝疑心; **to ~ a blush** 让人脸红; **to ~ a fuss/commotion** colloq 引发一阵忙乱/引起骚动; **to ~ a storm** *or* **howls of protest** 激起如潮的抗议; **to ~ a cheer (among ...)** «*speech, victory*» (在…中) 引起欢呼; **to ~ a laugh/smile** 引起哄笑/露出笑容; **to ~ the alarm** 发出警报 **8** (improve, lift) 提高; **to ~ the tone** 提高品位; **to ~ sb.'s spirits** 鼓舞某人 **9** (mention) 提出 ‹*point, matter, problem, subject*›; **did he ~ any objections?** 他表示反对了吗? ; **please ~ any queries** *or* **questions now** 现在请大家提问 **10** (obtain) 筹措 ‹*capital, money, funds, loan*›; **to ~ sth. for sth.** 为某事物筹措某物; **to ~ sth. against** *or* **on sth.** 抵押某物以筹措某物; **I ~d £300 against my watch** 我把手表抵押了 300 英镑 **11** (collect) 收 ‹*tax*›; 得到 ‹*support*›; **money ~d from the concert** 音乐会所得款项; **to ~ sth. for sth.** 为某事物筹集某物; **to ~ money for charity** 筹集善款 **12** (form) 组建 ‹*army*›; 召集 ‹*team*› **13** esp Amer (bring up) 抚养大 ‹*child*›; 饲养大 ‹*animal*›; **he was born and ~d in Shanghai** 他生长在上海; **to be ~d (as) sth.** 被培养成为 ‹*atheist, Catholic, city boy*›; **to be ~d to do sth.** 从小被教育要做某事; **to be ~d on sth.** 是靠某事物长大的; **I was ~d on these stories** 我是听着这些故事成长的 **14** Agric (breed, grow) 饲养 ‹*animals, livestock*›; 种植 ‹*crop, corn*› **15** (erect) 竖起 ‹*statue, monument*›; **to ~ sth. to sb.** 为某人建造某物 **16** (end) 解除 ‹*siege, blockade, restriction*›; **to ~ an embargo on sth.** 解除对某物的禁运 **17** Brit colloq (contact) 和…取得联系 ‹*person*›; **to ~ sb. on sth.** 通过某物和某人取得联系; **to ~ sb. on the phone/radio** 和某人通过手机/无线电联系 **18** Math 使自乘; **8 is 2 ~d to the power of 3** 8 是 2 的 3 次方 **19** Games (in poker) 下注超过 ‹*player*›; (at bridge) 对…的叫牌加叫; **I'll ~ you 200 dollars!** 我比你多下 200 元! ; **she ~d her partner to three clubs** 她将同伴的叫牌加叫到三张梅花 **20** Culin 使…发酵 ‹*bread, dough*›

B *v refl* **to ~ oneself (up)** 直起身子; **to ~ oneself up on one's elbow** 用胳膊肘支起身子; **to ~ oneself from sth.** 从…上起身 ‹*sofa*›; **he ~d himself to a sitting position** 他直起身子, 坐了起来; **to ~ oneself to one's full height** 站得笔直

C *n* **1** Amer (pay rise) 加薪; **a three per cent ~** 3% 的加薪; **to ask sb. for a ~** 向某人要求加薪 **2** Games (in poker) 赌注加码; (in bridge) 加叫; **what's your call? — a ~** 你叫多少? ——加注; **a ~ to three hearts** 加叫三张红桃

raised /reɪzd/ *adj* **1** (elevated) 凸起的 ‹*area, platform*›; (lifted up) 扬起的 ‹*eyebrows*›; **to cause ~ eyebrows** 使人惊讶 **2** (higher than normal) 升高的 ‹*level, pressure*›; **~ voices** 提高的嗓音 **3** (in relief) 有浮雕的 ‹*pattern*›; **~ letters** 凸印的字母

raisin /ˈreɪzn/ *n* 葡萄干

raising agent /ˈreɪzɪŋ ˌeɪdʒənt/ *n* 膨松剂

rake[1] /reɪk/

A *n* **1** (tool) 耙 **2** (in casino) 钱耙

B *vt* **1** (gather) 耙 ‹*leaves, weeds, soil*›; **to ~ sth. into a pile** 把某物耙成一堆 **2** (smooth) 耙平 ‹*earth*›; **to ~ sth. over** 把某物耙平 **3** (scratch) 搔 ‹*arm, face*› **4** (drag) 拉拖; **she ~d a comb through her hair** 她用梳子梳了梳头发 **5** (with shots) «*bullets, soldiers*» 向…扫射; (with light, eyes) «*person, searchlight*» 向…扫视 ‹*area, horizon*›; **her eyes ~d the room** 她的眼睛扫过整个房间

Phrasal verbs

- **rake in** *vt* [**~ sth. in, ~ in sth.**] colloq 大量聚敛 ‹*money, profits*›; **he's raking it in!** 他正大把大把地赚钱呢!
- **rake out** *vt* [**~ sth. out, ~ out sth.**] 用灰封 ‹*fire*›; 耙掉 ‹*ashes*›
- **rake over** *vt* [**~ over sth., ~ sth. over**] **1** (make smooth) 用耙耙平 ‹*earth, patch*› **2** fig 不断重复 ‹*memories*›; 一再提及 ‹*worries*›; **let's not ~ over the past** 我们不要翻老账吧
- **rake through** *vt* [**~ through sth.**] 搜遍; **to ~ through old papers** 找遍旧报纸
- **rake up** *vt* [**~ up sth., ~ sth. up**] **1** (collect) 耙拢 ‹*leaves, weeds*› **2** fig (gather) 集拢 ‹*helpers*›; 多方筹集 ‹*funds, support*›; 多方寻求 ‹*equipment*› **3** fig pej (revive the memory of) 重提 ‹*the past, story*›

rake[2] *n* dated (libertine) 浪子

rake[3] *n* (angle) 斜度; **to adjust the ~ of one's seat** 调整椅子的倾斜度

raked /reɪkt/ *adj* 倾斜的 ‹*seat*›; **a ~ stage** 倾斜舞台

rake-off *n* colloq (legal) 佣金; (illicit) 回扣; **to get a ~ of sth.** 得到某数额的回扣

rakish /ˈreɪkɪʃ/ *adj* **1** dated (dissolute) 放浪形骸的 ‹*young man, appearance, life*› **2** (jaunty) 潇洒的 ‹*charm, grin*›; **to wear one's hat at a ~ angle** 潇洒地歪戴着帽子

rakishly /ˈreɪkɪʃli/ *adv* **1** dated (dissolutely) 放荡地 ‹*live, smile, dress*› **2** (jauntily) 潇洒地 ‹*worn, set, perch, tilted*›

rally /ˈræli/

A *n* **1** (meeting) 群众集会; **an electoral/a peace ~** 选举人/和平大会; **to hold** *or* **organize a ~** 组织集会 **2** (open-air motor show) 户外汽车赛会 **3** (car race) 拉力赛; **a ~ car** 拉力赛赛车 **4** (in tennis, badminton etc.) 往返拍击; **a fifteen-stroke ~** 连续 15 击的回合 **5** (in health) 复元; (in share prices) 止跌回升; **prices on the London stock exchange staged a late ~ yesterday** 伦敦股票交易所的股价昨天晚些时候反弹了

B *vt* **1** (gather, encourage) 召集 ‹*members*›; 争取 ‹*support*›; 争取…支持 ‹*public opinion*›; **to ~ one's supporters around** *or* **behind one** 把支持者们召集在自己周围 **2** (muster) 集合 ‹*troops*›; **the commander rallied his men round him** 指挥官把士兵集合起来了

C *vi* **1** (come together) «*supporters*» 集合; **to ~ to the defence of sb.** 团结一致捍卫某人; **to ~ to the cause** 团结起来支持事业 **2** (recover) «*patient, health*» 复元; «*player, team*» 振作精神; «*stock market, currency*» 止跌回升; **her spirits rallied** 她又振作起精神了 **3** Mil «*soldiers*» 集结

Phrasal verb

- **rally round, rally around**

A *vi* 团结在一起; **colleagues rallied round to help Anne** 同事们都站在安一边帮助她

B *vt* [**~ round sb.**] 合力支持

rally: ~ driver ▸p. 409 *n* 拉力赛车手; **~ driving** ▸p. 307 *n* [u] 汽车拉力赛

rallying /ˈrælɪɪŋ/ *n* [u] 汽车拉力赛

rallying: ~ call, ~ cry *ns* lit 战斗口号; fig 呼吁; **~ point** *n* lit 集合地; fig 号召力

RAM /ræm/ *abbr* [u] **= random-access memory** 内存

ram /ræm/

A *n* **1** Zool 公羊 **2** (of pile driver) 夯锤; (plunger) 柱塞; **hydraulic ~** 水锤扬水机

B *vt* (*pres p etc.* **-mm-**) **1** (crash into) 猛撞 ‹*car, boat*› **2** (push) 硬塞; **to ~ sth. into/in/on sth.** 把某物硬塞入某物/硬塞进某物/硬压到某物上; **to ~ sth. down** 把某物猛压下去; **she ~med her hat on her head and stalked out in disgust** 她猛地把帽子往头上一扣, 厌恶地大步走了出去; **to ~ sth. down sb.'s throat** fig 强行向某人灌输某物

C *vi* (*pres p etc.* **-mm-**) 猛撞; **to ~ into/against sth.** 猛地撞入/撞上某物

Phrasal verb

- **ram home** *vt* [**~ sth. home, ~ home sth.**]

1 (force into place) 塞入; **he ~med home the bullet clip** 他把弹匣压进枪里 **2** fig (make clearly understood) 迫使明白 ‹*point, message*›; **seeing those pictures really ~med it home to me just how awful the war had been** 看到那些照片, 确实让我痛感这场战争的可怕

Ramadan /ˌræməˈdæn, -ˈdɑːn/ *pr n* 斋月

ramble /ˈræmbl/

A *n* (乡间) 漫步; **to go for a ~** 去散步

B *vi* **1** (walk) (with itinerary) 漫游; (without itinerary) 闲逛 **2** (talk at length) 漫谈; (write at length) 信笔写 **3** Hort «*plant*» 蔓生; **a beautiful rose ~d over the wall** 一株美丽的蔷薇爬上了墙头

Phrasal verb

- **ramble on** *vi* 东拉西扯; **to ~ on about sth.** 没完没了地说某事

rambler /ˈræmblə(r)/ *n* **1** esp Brit (hiker) (乡间) 漫步者 **2** (plant) 蔓生植物

rambling /ˈræmblɪŋ/

A *adj* **1** (sprawling) 布局零乱的 ‹*building, village*› **2** (long-winded) 杂乱无章的 ‹*speech, letter*› **3** Hort 蔓生的 ‹*rose*›

B *n* [u] (乡间) 漫步; **he goes ~ every weekend** 他每个周末都去漫步

rambunctious /ræmˈbʌŋkʃəs/ *adj* esp Amer colloq 喧闹的 ‹*kid, teen*›

RAM chip *n* 内存芯片

ramification /ˌræmɪfɪˈkeɪʃn/ *n* 后果; **he didn't think through the ~s of what he had said** 他没有想明白自己的话的后果

ramjet /ˈræmdʒet/ *n* **~ (engine)** 冲压式喷气发动机

ramp /ræmp/ *n* **1** (for wheelchair, vehicles) 坡道; (on to boat) 跳板; **Beware R~** (in roadworks) 小心! 道路不平 **2** Amer (on freeway) 匝道; **the**

on *or* **entry/off** *or* **exit** ~ 入口/出口匝道 **3** (for raising vehicle) 升降设备; **a hydraulic** ~ 液压升降台

rampage

A /ræmˈpeɪdʒ/ *vi* 横冲直撞; **to** ~ **through/over/around ...** 在…里/上/周围横冲直撞; **several thousand demonstrators** ~**d through the city** 几千名示威者在市内胡作非为

B /ˈræmpeɪdʒ/ *n* 狂暴行为; **to go** *or* **be on the** ~ 横冲直撞; **football hooligans on the** ~ 寻衅滋事的足球流氓

rampant /ˈræmpənt/ *adj* **1** (uncontrolled) 猖獗的 ‹*violence, corruption, cholera*›; **rumours were** ~ **that ...** …的谣言四起; ~ **inflation** 失控的通货膨胀 **2** (luxuriant) 疯长的 ‹*roses, weeds*›; ~ **vegetation** 繁茂的植被

ramparts /ˈræmpɑːts/ *npl* 壁垒

ram-raid Brit

A *vt* 开车闯入…抢劫

B *n* 开车闯入进行的抢劫

ramrod /ˈræmrɒd/ *n* (for small gun) 推弹杆; (for cannon) 输弹机; **as stiff** *or* **straight as a** ~ 笔直地; **her back was as straight as a** ~ 她的背挺得直直的; **the soldiers were standing** ~ **straight** 士兵们笔直地站着

ramshackle /ˈræmʃækl/ *adj* 东倒西歪的 ‹*building, old bus, caravan*›

ran /ræn/ *pt* ▸ **run A, B**

ranch /rɑːntʃ, Amer ræntʃ/ *n* 牧场; **a cattle** ~ 牧牛场; **a mink** ~ 水貂养殖场

rancher /ˈrɑːntʃə(r), Amer ˈræntʃə(r)/ *n* Amer (owner) 牧场主; (manager) 牧场经理; (employee) 牧场工人

ranch: ~ **hand** *n* 牧场工人; ~ **house** *n* Amer **1** (building on ranch) 牧场住宅; **2** (single-story building) 平房住宅

ranching /ˈrɑːntʃɪŋ, Amer ˈræn-/ *n* [u] 牧场经营

rancid /ˈrænsɪd/ *adj* 变质的 ‹*butter, bacon*›; **to go** ~ 变质

rancorous /ˈræŋkərəs/ *adj* 充满敌意的 ‹*person, debate, tone*›; **to feel** *or* **be** ~ **towards sb.** 对某人充满恶意

rancour Brit, **rancor** Amer /ˈræŋkə(r)/ *n* [u] 怨恨; **he spoke without** ~ 他毫无敌意地说

rand /rænd/ ▸ **p. 174** *n* 兰特 [南非货币]

R & B *abbr* = **rhythm and blues**

R & D *abbr* = **research and development**

random /ˈrændəm/

A *adj* 随机的 ‹*choice, pattern, number*›; **on a** ~ **basis** 随机地; ~ **sampling** 随机抽样; **the** ~ **killing of innocent people** 对无辜者的滥杀

B *n* **at** ~ 随意地; **the winning numbers are selected at** ~ 获奖号码是随机选取的

random access *n* [u] 随机存取

random-access memory *n* [u] = **RAM**

randomize /ˈrændəmaɪz/ *vt* 使…随机化 ‹*order, trial*›

randomly /ˈrændəmli/ *adv* 随机地 ‹*select*›; **the gunman began firing** ~ **into the crowd** 枪手开始向人群胡乱开枪

randy /ˈrændi/ *adj* colloq **1** (sexually excited) 性兴奋的 ‹*person*›; 发情的 ‹*animal*›; **to make sb.** ~ 使某人春心荡漾 **2** (highly-sexed) 好色的 ‹*person*›; 性欲强的 ‹*animal*›

rang /ræŋ/ *pt* ▸ **ring² A, B**

range /reɪndʒ/

A *n* **1** [c] (variety) 种类; **a wide** ~ **of opinions/facilities** 各种各样的看法/设施; **a limited** ~ **of colours** 有限的色彩; **a wide** ~ **of interests** 广泛的兴趣; **a full** ~ **of activities** 全套的活动 **2** [c] Comm (of products, models, designs) 系列; **the latest model in the** ~ 本系列中的最新型号; **to launch a new product** ~ 把新的产品系列投入市场; **a new** ~ **of hair products** 新的洗护发产品系列; **at the upper/lower end of a** ~ 在高/低档次上; **at the top/bottom of the** ~ 在最高/最低档次上 **3** [c] (of prices, salaries) 幅度; (of temperatures, sizes, ages) 范围; (of abilities) 水平; **(an increase) in the 30-40%** ~ 在 30%—40% 之间（的增长）; **the dress is available in a** ~ **of sizes** 这种连衣裙有各种尺寸; **salary/price** ~ 工资/价格幅度; **the students are in the 17-20 age** ~ 这些学生的年龄在 17 至 20 岁之间; **it's difficult to find a house in our price** ~ 很难找到我们买得起的房子; **ability** ~ 能力水平; **the dollar is within its old** ~ 美元的波动又回到了从前的范围 **4** [c] Mus (of voice, instrument) 音域 **5** [c] (of hearing) 听觉范围; **a sound that is out of our** ~ **of hearing** 我们无法听见的声音 **6** [c] (of knowledge) 知识面; (of abilities) 水平 **7** [c] (extent) 范围; **to be outside the** ~ **of sb.'s ...** 超出某人的…范围 ‹*responsibility, ability, experience, research*› **8** [u and c] (maximum distance seen) (by person) 视野; (by telescope, binoculars) 视界; (maximum distance heard) 听觉范围; **to be within/out of sb.'s** ~ **of vision** 在某人的视野内/外; **a telescope with a longer** ~ 视界更大的望远镜; **to be within/out of hearing** ~ **(of sb./sth.)** 在（某人/某物的）听觉范围内/外; **the cat stayed well out of** ~ **of the children** 这只猫离孩子们远远的 **9** [u and c] Radio (of radar, transmitter, listening device) 量程; **to have a very long** ~ 量程很大; **within/out of** ~ **(of sth.)** 在（某物的）量程之内/之外; **planets within radio** ~ **of Earth** 在地球无线电传播范围之内的行星; **we went out of** ~ **of the microphone** 我们走出了麦克风收音的有效距离 **10** [u and c] (maximum distance of weapon) 射程; **the gun has only a limited** ~ 这门炮射程很短; **to have a** ~ **of 600 miles** 有 600 英里远的射程; **out of** *or* **beyond/within (the)** ~ **of sth.** 在某物的射程之外/之内; **at close** *or* **point-blank** ~ 在近距离; **to shoot sb. at close** ~ 近距离射杀某人; **at a** ~ **of 200 yards** 在 200 码的射程; **at/from long** ~ 在/从远距离 **11** [u and c] Phot (of camera) 距离; **scenes containing dialogue are frequently shot at this camera** ~ 对话场景往往从这个距离拍摄 **12** [c] (maximum distance) (of vehicle) 行程; (of aircraft, ship) 航程; **to have a short** ~ 航程短; **a vehicle with a good** ~ 行程很长的汽车; **the vans have a** ~ **of 125 miles** 这些货车的行程是125 英里 **13** [c] Geog **a mountain** ~ 山脉; **a** ~ **of hills** 一片丘陵 **14** [c] Amer (prairie) **the** ~ 牧场; **on the** ~ 在牧场上 **15** [c] (for firing guns, rifles) 射击场; (for testing military equipment) 武器试验场; **on the** ~ 在射击场 **16** [c] (stove) [尤指旧时的] 炉灶 **17** [c] Amer (cooker) (gas) 煤气灶; (electric) 电灶

B *vt* **1** (place) 排列; **to be** ~**d along sth.** ‹*person, thing*› 沿某物排列; **to be** ~**d in rows** 排列成行 **2** (cause to adopt stance) 使…采取某种姿态 ‹*forces, nations*›; **to be** ~**d against sb./sth.** 反对某人/某事物; **to be** ~**d with sb.** 站在某人一边 **3** (move around) 漫游于; **her eyes** ~**d the room** 她的目光在房间里来回扫视

C *v refl* **1** (arrange oneself in particular order) **to** ~ **oneself** 排列; **the children** ~**d themselves neatly in front of the stage** 孩子们整齐地排在舞台前 **2** (adopt stance) **to** ~ **oneself** 采取某种姿态; **to** ~ **oneself against sb./sth.** 反对某人/某事物; **to** ~ **oneself with sb.** 同某人站在一边

D *vi* **1** (extend) 延伸; **to** ~ **from sth. to sth.** «*cost, increase, temperature, age*» 范围在某物与某物之间; **prices** ~ **from £6 to £17** 价格范围在 6 至 17 英镑之间 **2** (vary) [在特定范围内] 变动; **to** ~ **between sth. and sth.** «*price, cost, increase, temperature*» 在某物与某物之间变动; **students' ages** ~ **between 16 and 60** 学生的年龄从 16 岁至 60 岁不等 **3** (cover) 包括; **to** ~ **from sth. to sth.** «*problems, topics, suggestions, opinions*» 涉及从某物到某物的内容 **4** (move around) 漫游; **to** ~ **far and wide** 四处游历; **to** ~ **over the plains** 在平原上漫游

Phrasal verb

- **range over** *vt* [~ **over sth.**] **1** (include) «*conversation, article, lecture*» 涉及 **2** Mil «*gun, missile*» 有…的射程 ‹*distance*›

rangefinder /ˈreɪndʒfaɪndə(r)/ *n* 测距仪

ranger /ˈreɪndʒə(r)/ *n* **1** (warden) 护林员 **2** Amer Mil 巡逻队队员 **3** **Ranger** Brit (in the Guides) **R**~ **(Guide)** 高年级女童子军

rangy /ˈreɪndʒi/ *adj* 四肢修长的 ‹*person, frame*›

rank¹ /ræŋk/

A *n* **1** [u and c] (in hierarchy, politics, society) 地位; (in organization, company) 级别; **to achieve the** ~ **of Cabinet Minister** 获得内阁大臣之职; **he was elevated to ministerial** ~ 他被提升到部级; **of high/low** ~ 地位高/低的; **people of high social** ~ 社会上层人士 **2** [u and c] (in army) 军衔; (in police) 警衔; **to be stripped of one's** ~ 被剥夺军衔; **promotion to a higher** ~ 晋升; **to be promoted to the** ~ **of captain** 晋升到上校军阶; **a high** *or* **senior/low** *or* **junior** ~ Mil 高级/低级军衔; **officers of senior** ~ 高级军官; **officers and other** ~**s** 官兵; **in** ~ 在军阶上; **to pull** ~ **(on sb.)** 运用权势（压服某人） **3** [u] (high social position) 高层社会地位; **persons of** ~ **and breeding** 地位高有教养的人 **4** [c] (degree) 等级; **a painter of the first** ~ 一流的画家; **Britain is no longer in the front** ~ **of world powers** 英国不再是位于前列的世界强国 **5** [c] (line, row) 行列; ~ **upon** ~ **of soldiers/police** 一排一排的士兵/警察; **to break** ~**s** lit «*soldiers, police*» 打乱队形; fig 不再支持所属团体; **15 MPs broke** ~**s and voted with the Opposition** 15 名议员反水投了反对党的票; **to close** ~**s (against sb.)** lit «*soldiers, police*» 集中队列（以防御某人）; fig 紧密团结（以反对某人） **6** [c] (line, row) 排; **massed** ~**s of spectators** 密集的观众; **the trees grew in serried** ~**s** 树木密密麻麻地长在一起; **half-made pots standing in** ~**s on shelves** 摆在架子上的一排排半成品罐子 **7** [c] Brit (for taxis) 出租车站 **8** [u and c] Ling 级 **9** [c] (in chess) [棋盘的] 横排

B **ranks** *npl* **1** Mil 普通士兵; **(to be) in** *or* **among** *or* **within the** ~**s** 当兵; **to serve in the** ~**s** 服兵役; **to be reduced to the** ~**s** 被降为士兵; **to rise** *or* **come up from the** ~**s, to rise through the** ~**s** 从士兵升为军官 **2** (members) 成员; **the** ~**s of the unemployed/the homeless** 失业者/无家可归者的大军; **in** *or* **among** *or* **within the** ~**s of ...** 在…的成员中; **to join the** ~**s of ...** 加入…的行列; **to rise from** *or* **come up from the** ~**s (of sth.), to rise through the** ~**s (of sth.)** 从（某行业的）卑微身份发迹; **he rose through the** ~**s to become managing director** 他级级攀升，当上了常务董事

C *vt* **1** (classify) 把…分等级; **to be** ~**ed in order of difficulty** 被按照难度分类; **the highest** ~**ed player in the world** 世界排名最高的运动员; **the university is** ~**ed number one/second in the country for engineering** 该大学的工程学名列全国之首/第二; **to** ~ **sb./sth. as sb./sth.** 将某人/某事物列为某人/某事物; **this area is** ~**ed as one of the most beautiful places in Britain** 这个地区是英国最美的地方之一; **to** ~ **sb./sth. among sb./sth.** 将某人/某事物列入某人/某事物; **his work must be** ~**ed among the best in Britain** 他的作品一定属于英国最优秀作品之列; **to** ~ **sb./sth. with** *or* **alongside sb./sth.** 使某人/某事物跻身于某人/某事物之列; **historians will** ~ **her alongside Marie Curie** 历史学家将会把她与玛丽·居里比肩而列; **to** ~ **sb./sth. above/below sb./sth.** 将某人/某事物列于某人/某事物之上/之下; **I would** ~ **him below Hemingway** 我觉得他在海明威之下;

r

to ~ sb./sth. highly 对某人/某事物评价高 **2** (arrange in line) 将…排成行; **the tents were ~ed in orderly rows** 帐篷整整齐齐地排成几排 **3** Amer (be senior to) 级别高于; **the Secretary of State ~s all the other members of the cabinet** 国务卿的级别高于任何其他内阁成员

D *vi* **1** (rate) 排位; **how do I ~ compared to her?** 我同她相比，高下如何？; **that doesn't ~ very high on my list of priorities** 那并不是我的当务之急; **at the height of her career she ~ed second in the world** 事业处于顶峰时，她排名世界第二; **to ~ as sb./sth.** 被列为某人/某事物; **this must ~ as one of the worst films I've ever seen** 这肯定是我看过的最烂的电影之一; **to ~ among sb./sth.** 属于某人/某事物之列; **this book must ~ among the top literary classics** 这本书堪称最优秀的经典文学作品之一; **to ~ with** *or* **alongside sb./sth.** 与某人/某事物比肩; **their research ~s with that produced by the most successful laboratories** 他们的研究可与最成功的实验室研究媲美; **to ~ above/below sb./sth.** 位列某人/某事物之上/之下 **2** Amer Mil «*officer, general*» 级别最高; **as captain I must ~ here** 作为上校，我在这里一定是级别最高的

rank² *adj* **1** *attrib* pej (absolute) 绝对的; **it's ~ stupidity!** 愚蠢透顶！; **a ~ beginner** 彻头彻尾的生手 **2** (foul) 难闻的 ‹*smell, taste*› **3** (full) 疯长的; **to be ~ with sth.** «*garden, orchard*» 长满 ‹*weeds, nettles*›

rank and file
A *n + v pl* 普通成员
B **rank-and-file** *modif* 基层的; **~ members/opinion** 普通成员/基层的意见

ranking /ˈræŋkɪŋ/
A *n* **1** [c] (position) 排位; **his world number-one ~** 他世界第一的排名 **2** [u] (grading) 等级评定; **the ~ of students** 学生的名次
B **rankings** *npl* 最佳运动员排名表; **the world ~s** 世界最佳运动员排名表
C **-ranking** *combining form* …级别的; **high/low~** 高/低级别的

rankle /ˈræŋkl/
A *vi* «*insult, failure*» 使人怨恨; **to ~ with sb.** 使某人耿耿于怀
B *vt* «*insult, failure*» 使…怨恨 ‹*person*›; **it ~s me (to think) that ...** (想到)…我耿耿于怀

rankness /ˈræŋknɪs/ *n* [u] **1** (foul smell) 恶臭 **2** (luxuriance) 繁茂

ransack /ˈrænsæk, Amer rænˈsæk/ *vt* **1** (search) 在…中乱翻 ‹*luggage, building, cupboard, files*›; **to ~ a place for sth.** 在一个地方翻找某物 **2** (plunder) 洗劫 ‹*house, shop*›

ransom /ˈrænsəm/
A *n* 赎金; **to demand/pay a ~** 索要/支付赎金; **to hold sb. to ~** 将某人绑票; **the government accused the unions of holding the country to ~** fig 政府谴责工会拿国家作要挟; **the ~ money** 赎金; **a ~ note** 勒索信
B *vt* **1** (obtain release of) 赎回 **2** (demand payment for release of) 绑架…要求赎金

ransom demand *n* 赎金要求

ransomware /ˈrænsəmweə(r)/ *n* [u] 勒索软件

rant /rænt/ *vi* pej 咆哮; **to ~ (at sb.) (about sth.)** (为某事物)大声责骂(某人); **to ~ on (about sth.)** 没完没了地嚷嚷(某事); **to ~ and rave (at sb.) (about sth.)** (为某事物)(对某人)大叫大嚷

ranting /ˈræntɪŋ/
A *n* [u] **~(s** *pl***)** 大叫大嚷; **the ~s of an embittered old man** 一位心怀怨愤的老人的怒吼
B *adj* 怒气冲冲的 ‹*politician, speech*›

rap /ræp/
A *vt* (*pres p etc.* **-pp-**) **1** (tap) 敲 ‹*table, door*›; 敲打 ‹*knuckles, person*› **2** (criticize) 严厉批评
B *vi* (*pres p etc.* **-pp-**) **1** (tap) 敲; **to ~ on the table/at the door** 敲桌子/敲门 **2** Amer colloq (chat) 闲聊
C *n* **1** [c] (sharp knock) 敲击 **2** [c] (severe criticism) 斥责; **a ~ over the knuckles** fig 训斥; **to get the ~ for sth.** 为某事受责备 **3** [c] colloq (blame) 罪责; **to take the ~ (for sth.)** (为某事)受罚 **4** [c] Amer colloq (accusation) 刑罚; **to beat the ~** 逃脱刑罚; **to hang a murder/burglary ~ on sb.** 以谋杀/盗窃罪起诉某人 **5** [c] Amer colloq (prison sentence) 徒刑 **6** [u] Mus **~ (music)** 说唱 **7** [c] Mus (song, words) 说唱乐曲; **a ~ artist** *or* **musician** 说唱艺人 **8** [c] Amer colloq (conversation) 闲聊; **a ~ over a beer** 边喝啤酒边聊天

Phrasal verb

- **rap out** *vt* [**~ out sth., ~ sth. out**] **1** (say sharply) 厉声说出 ‹*order, question*› **2** (tap out) 敲击出 ‹*tune, beat*›

> **rap**
>
> 说唱乐。节奏强劲，歌词为说白。20 世纪 70 年代源于美国纽约的黑人社区。rap 为黑人俚语，意思为“聊天”。乐队由说唱歌手（rapper，亦称 MC，即 master of ceremonies）和乐师（DJ，即disk jockey）组成。乐师负责配乐，常从其他唱片中取样（sampling），糅合成一体。说唱乐有很多流派，对其他流行音乐形式影响巨大。

rapacious /rəˈpeɪʃəs/ *adj* formal pej 贪婪的 ‹*landlord, capitalism*›; **~ western expansion** 强取豪夺的西方扩张; **to levy ~ taxes and fees** 征收掠夺性的税费

rapaciously /rəˈpeɪʃəsli/ *adv* 贪婪地; **a ~ competitive city** 贪婪竞争的城市

rape¹ /reɪp/
A *vt* **1** Jur 强奸 **2** fig (despoil) 蹂躏; **the capitalists have ~d our land and resources** 资本家糟蹋了我们的土地和资源
B *n* **1** [c and u] Jur 强奸; **to commit ~** 犯强奸罪 **2** [u] fig (destruction) 蹂躏; **many people have accused farmers of the ~ of our countryside** 许多人指责农场主糟蹋了我们的乡村

rape² *n* [u] Agric 油菜

rape: ~ alarm *n* 强奸警报器; **~ counselling** *n* [u] [为受害人提供的] 强奸案咨询; **~ counselling advice/group** 强奸案咨询建议/小组; **~ crisis centre** *n* 强奸受害者援助中心; **~ oil** *n* [u] 菜籽油

rapeseed /ˈreɪpsiːd/ *n* [u] 油菜籽

rapeseed oil *n* [u] 菜籽油

rape victim *n* 强奸案受害人

rapid /ˈræpɪd/ *adj* 快速的 ‹*movement, pulse, deterioration*›; 湍急的 ‹*river, current*›; **a ~ increase in unemployment/prices** 失业率/价格的猛升; **we had to take ~ action to prevent a disaster** 我们不得不火速采取行动防止灾难; **in ~ succession** 接连不断地

rapid: ~ deployment force *n* 快速部署部队; **~ eye movement** *n* [u] 快速眼动; **~ fire** *n* [u] 速射; **~-fire** *adj attrib* **1** 连发的 ‹*gunfire*›; 速射的 ‹*gun*›; **2** fig (fast-paced) 连珠炮似的 ‹*dialogue*›

rapidity /rəˈpɪdəti/ *n* [u] (of action, growth etc.) 迅速; (of current) 湍急; **with great ~** 极其迅速地

rapidly /ˈræpɪdli/ *adv* 迅速地; **a ~ changing world** 快速变化的世界; **a ~ growing economy** 迅猛增长的经济

rapid reaction force *n* 快速反应部队

rapids /ˈræpɪdz/ *npl* 急流; **to shoot** *or* **ride the ~** 穿过急流

rapid transit *n* [u] esp Amer 高速交通; **~ system** 高速交通系统

rapier /ˈreɪpɪə(r)/ *n* 双刃长剑; **a ~ thrust** 用长剑的刺戳

rapist /ˈreɪpɪst/ *n* 强奸犯

rapper /ˈræpə(r)/ *n* 说唱歌手

rapping /ˈræpɪŋ/ *n* [u] **1** (knocking) 敲; (knocking sound) 敲击声 **2** Mus 说唱

rapport /ræˈpɔː(r), Amer -ˈpɔːrt/ *n* [c and u] 融洽关系; **to establish a ~** 建立融洽关系; **there is a great ~ between the two performers** 这两个演员之间非常默契; **in ~ with sb.** 与某人关系融洽

rapprochement /ræˈprɒʃmɒŋ, ræˈprəʊʃ-, Amer ˌræprəʊʃˈmɒŋ/ *n* [c and u] formal [尤指两国间的] 和解; **a ~ with/between ...** 与…/…之间友好关系的恢复

rap sheet *n* Amer colloq 犯罪记录

rapt /ræpt/ *adj* 专心致志的 ‹*interest, expression*›; 全神贯注的 ‹*person*›; **to be ~ with wonder** 目瞪口呆; **the children listened in ~ silence** 孩子们屏气静心地听; **to watch with ~ attention** 全神贯注地凝视; **to be ~ in contemplation** *or* **thought** 出神

rapture /ˈræptʃə(r)/ *n* [u] 狂喜; **to go into ~s over** *or* **about sth.** 对某事欣喜若狂; **with** *or* **in ~** 着迷地

rapturous /ˈræptʃərəs/ *adj* 狂热的 ‹*welcome, applause*›; 痴迷的 ‹*gaze*›; **an expression of ~ delight** 狂喜的表情

rapturously /ˈræptʃərəsli/ *adv* 狂热地 ‹*welcome*›; 痴迷地 ‹*gaze*›; **his fans applauded him ~** 他的仰慕者发疯般地给他鼓掌

rare /reə(r)/ *adj* **1** (infrequent) 罕见的 ‹*example, disease, treat, occurrence, sight*›; 珍稀的 ‹*plant, animal, antique*›; **it is ~ (for sb.) to do sth.** (某人)做某事难得; **it's very ~ for him to go to the library on a Saturday!** 他星期六去图书馆是很少有的！; **this first edition is a very ~ book** 第一版是珍本; **on the ~ occasions when ...** 在…的难得场合; **it is ~ to see ...** 很少看见…; **to be ~ for ...** 对…很罕见; **with one or two ~ exceptions, everyone in our family has blonde hair** 除了一两个少有的例外，我们家每个人都是金发 **2** (exceptional) 不寻常的 ‹*degree, beauty*›; **he's a man of ~ talent** 他是个极有天分的人; **he plays with ~ sensitivity** 他的演奏具有非同一般的悟性 **3** (lightly cooked) 半熟的 ‹*steak*› **4** dated (wonderful) 美好的; **to have a ~ old time** 度过非常愉快的时光

rarebit /ˈreəbɪt/ *n* = **Welsh rarebit**

rare earth, rare earth element, rare earth metal *ns* 稀土元素

rarefied /ˈreərɪfaɪd/ *adj* **1** (thin) 稀薄的 ‹*air, atmosphere*› **2** (esoteric, refined) 精致的 ‹*existence, life*›; **to live in the ~ atmosphere of university life** 生活在大学的阳春白雪氛围里

rarefy /ˈreərɪfaɪ/
A *vt* 使…变稀薄 ‹*air, atmosphere*›
B *vi* «*air, atmosphere*» 变稀薄

rarely /ˈreəli/ *adv* 难得 ‹*eat, dance, better, happy*›; **a flower that is ~ grown nowadays** 现在很少栽种的花; **I see her only ~ these days** 我现在只是偶尔看见她; **a ~ performed piece of music** 很少演奏的曲目; **I ~ have time to go to the theatre** 我几乎没有时间看电影

rareness /ˈreənɪs/ *n* [u] (of book, antique etc.) 珍贵; (of plant, animal) 珍奇; (of disease) 罕见; **the ~ of this piece of furniture makes it extremely valuable** 这款家具非常珍稀，因此价值连城; **the very ~ of rail accidents makes them newsworthy** 火车事故很少见，所以有新闻价值

rarified /ˈreərɪfaɪd/ *adj* = **rarefied**

rarify /ˈreərɪfaɪ/ *vt, vi* = **rarefy**

raring /ˈreərɪŋ/ *adj pred* colloq **to be ~ to do sth.** 渴望做某事; **to be ~ to go** 巴不得马上就走

rarity /ˈreərəti/ *n* **1** [c] (rare thing) 稀有物; (collector's item) 珍品; **to be a ~** 是珍品; **tourists are a ~ in this part of the world** 这一带鲜见游客 **2** [u] (uncommonness) 罕见; **the ~ of the disease** 这种病的罕见

rascal /'rɑːskl, Amer 'ræskl/ *n* **1** (mischievous person) 捣蛋鬼; **he's an old ~** 他是个老顽童 **2** dated (scoundrel) 无赖

rascally /'rɑːskəli/ *adj* **1** (mischievous) 捣蛋的 ‹*boy, man, trick, habit*›; **a ~ wink** 调皮的眨眼睛 **2** (untrustworthy) 奸诈的 ‹*lawyer*›; 靠不住的 ‹*reputation*›

rash¹ /ræʃ/ *n* **1** (spots) 皮疹; **to have a ~** 出疹子; **to come** *or* **break out in a ~** 身上出满疹子 **2** fig (spate) 一连串; **a ~ of ...** 接二连三的…; **the country has been affected by a ~ of strikes** 国家受到了一连串罢工的影响

rash² *adj* 草率的 ‹*person, behaviour, promise*›; **it was ~ of you to agree to meet him** 你答应见他太轻率了; **to be ~ enough to do sth.** 做某事太莽撞了; **in a ~ moment** 贸然

rasher /'ræʃə(r)/ *n* 火腿片

rashly /'ræʃli/ *adv* 草率地 ‹*offer, decide*›; **I promised, rather ~, to take him abroad next year** 我非常轻率地答应明年带他出国

rashness /'ræʃnɪs/ *n* [u] 草率

rasp /rɑːsp, Amer ræsp/

A *n* **1** (harsh sound) 刺耳声 **2** (file) 粗锉刀

B *vt* **1** (scrape) 锉 **2** (say in grating voice) 用刺耳的声音说; **to ~ sth. (out)** 厉声说出 ‹*order, question*›

C *vi* 发出刺耳声; **my breath ~ed in my throat** 我呼哧呼哧地喘着

raspberry /'rɑːzbri, Amer 'ræzberi/ *n* **1** (fruit) 山莓; **~ jam/ice-cream** 山莓酱/冰激凌 **2** (plant) 悬钩子属植物; **a ~ cane/bush** 一株山莓/悬钩子灌木 **3** colloq (rude noise) 呸声; **to blow a ~** 呸了一声

Rasta /'ræstə/ *n, adj* colloq **= Rastafarian**

Rastafarian /ˌræstə'feərɪən/

A *n* 拉斯塔法里教徒 [源于牙买加、崇拜前埃塞俄比亚皇帝海尔·塞拉西的教派成员]

B *adj* 拉斯塔法里教徒的 ‹*hairstyle, lifestyle*›

rat /ræt/

A *n* **1** Zool 老鼠; **(to look) like a drowned ~** colloq （看上去）像只落汤鸡; **to smell a ~** fig 起疑心 **2** colloq pej (person) 卑鄙小人

B *vi* (*pres p etc.* **-tt-**) **1** colloq (inform on) **to ~ on sb.** 告发某人 **2** dated (renege on) **to ~ on sth.** 背弃做某事的承诺; **they ~ed on the deal at the last minute** 他们在最后一刻违约了

C rats *excl* colloq 该死; **Rats! I've lost my ticket** 真要命！我的票丢了

ratable /'reɪtəbl/ *adj* **= rateable**

rat: ~-arsed /'rætɑːst/ *adj* Brit taboo sl 烂醉如泥的; **~bag** *n* Brit colloq 讨厌的家伙; **~catcher** *n* [以除鼠害为业的] 捕鼠人

rat-a-tat /'rætətæt/ *n* **= rat-tat**

ratchet /'rætʃɪt/

A *n* (toothed rack) 棘齿条; (wheel) 棘轮; **~ screw-driver/wheel** 棘齿螺丝刀/棘轮

B *vt* **to ~ (up)** 小幅提升 ‹*price*›

rate /reɪt/

A *n* **1** (speed) 速度; **to work at a steady ~** 以平稳的速度工作; **a rapid ~ of change** 变化的迅速; **at a** *or* **the ~ of ...** 以…的速度; **to flow at a ~ of 150 gallons an hour** 以每小时 150 加仑的速度流动; **at this/that ~** (at this speed) 以这一/那一速度; (continuing in same way) 照这种/那种情形; **at the ~ sb. is going** 照某人现在的样子发展下去; **at any ~** (no matter what) 不管怎么说; (more specifically) 确切地说; (more importantly) 总而言之 **2** Stat (number of occurrences) 比率; **the (annual) divorce/birth/crime/unemployment ~** （年）离婚率/出生率/犯罪率/失业率; **a high success/failure ~** 很高的成功/失败率; **the pass/failure ~ for the exam is 60%** 考试的及格/不及格率为 60%; **at a** *or* **the ~ of ...** 以…的比率; **at a ~ of 50 an hour** 以每小时 50 个的速率 **3** (amount) 率; **the ~ of economic growth/inflation/exchange** 经济增长率/通货膨胀率/汇率 **4** (charge) 价格; **advertising ~s** 广告费; **postal** *or* **postage ~s** 邮资; **at a reduced ~** 以优惠价; **to get a reduced ~** 获得优惠价; **telephone calls are charged at several ~s** 打电话按照不同的资费标准收费; **the ~ for sth.** 某物的价格 **5** (wage) 工资; **his hourly ~ is £22** 他每小时酬金 22 英镑; **translator's ~s** 翻译稿酬; **the ~ for sb./sth.** 某人/某事的报酬; **to pay sb. the going ~ for the job** 按当前标准支付给某人工资; **~ of pay** 薪酬 **6** Fin 费率; **the ~ of interest** 利息率; **at a ~ of 4.5%** 按照 4.5% 的费率; **the basic ~ of tax** 基本税率

B rates *npl* Brit Tax (on commercial property) 房地产税; Hist (on private property) 不动产税; **business ~s** 营业财产税; **~ increases/rebates** 房地产税的增加/退还

C *vt* **1** (evaluate) 评估; **how do you ~ this restaurant?** 你认为这家餐馆怎样？; **she is ~d a highly efficient businesswoman** 她被认为是效率极高的女企业家; **to ~ sth. high on one's list of priorities** 将某事物列为优先考虑的大事; **to ~ sb./sth. highly (for sth.)** （因某事物）高度评价某人/某事物; **to ~ sb./sth. as sb./sth.** 认为某人/某事物是某人/某事物; **I ~ her as one of our best modern novelists** 我认为她是最优秀的现代小说家之一; **to ~ sb./sth. among sb./sth.** 将某人/某事物列入某人/某事物; **she is ~d among the best pianists in the world** 她被公认为世界上最优秀的钢琴家之一 **2** (classify) 给…划分等级; **he is currently ~d number two in the world** 他当前的世界排名是第二; **to ~ sb./sth. at sth.** 将某人/某事物定为某等级; **on a scale of good looks from 1 to 10, I'd probably ~ him an 8** 按照从 1 到 10 的美貌等级评定，我大概会把他定在 8 **3** colloq (have high opinion of) 看好 **4** (deserve) 配得上 ‹*medal, round of applause*›; **the incident didn't even ~ a mention in the press** 这件事根本不值得上报纸 **5** (receive as award) «*hotel, restaurant*» 被授予; **this is ~d as a three-star hotel** 这家酒店被评为三星级

D *vi* 被评价; **how did our cheese ~?** 大家怎么看我们的乳酪？; **where do I ~ compared to him?** 我同他相比怎么样？; **it doesn't ~ high on my list of priorities** 我优先考虑的事情中它排不上号; **our needs do not ~ very high with this administration** 我们的需求不怎么受这届政府的重视; **to ~ as sb./sth.** 被认为是某人/某事物; **that ~s as the best wine I've ever tasted** 那是我喝过的最好的酒; **to ~ among sb./sth.** 被列入某人/某事物; **she ~s among the best sopranos in Europe** 她被认为是欧洲最优秀的女高音之一

E *v refl* **to ~ oneself** 自我评价; **how do you ~ yourself as a driver?** 你觉得自己的驾车技术怎么样？; **she doesn't ~ herself very highly** 她自视不高

rateable /'reɪtəbl/ *adj* **1** (for local tax) 应征税的 ‹*property*›; **~ value** Brit [对房屋估定的] 课税价值 **2** (assessable) 可评价的

rate: ~-cap *vt* Brit Hist 为…制定地方税额上限 ‹*local authority*›; **~-capping** *n* [u] Brit Hist 地方税额限定; **~ of climb** *n* 爬升速度; **~ of flow** *n* 流量; **~payer** *n* Brit 地方税纳税人; **~ tart** *n* colloq 免息馅饼吃客 [指利用免息期将欠款在信用卡之间不断倒腾的人]

rather /'rɑːðə(r)/

A *adv* **1** (to some degree) 有点儿; **a ~ hot day, ~ a hot day** 有点儿热的一天; **they won ~ easily** 他们赢得挺轻松; **he's ~ a fool** 他有点傻乎乎的; **it ~ surprised her** 这令她颇为吃惊 **2** (excessively) 相当; **it's ~ expensive** 这东西贵了点儿; **he's ~ young to marry** 他年纪太小，还不能结婚 **3** (expressing preference) 宁愿; **would you ~ she left?** 你愿意她离开吗？; **sb. would ~ do sth. (than do sth.)** 某人宁愿做某事（而不做某事）; **would you ~ walk or take the bus?** 你愿意步行还是坐公交车？; **she'd ~ die than give a speech** 她宁死都不肯发言; **I'm going climbing tomorrow — ~ you than me!** colloq 我明天去爬山——换了我才不去呢！ **4** (instead of) **~ than** 而不是; **you should go ~ than me** 是你该走，而不是我; **I think I'll have a cold drink ~ than coffee** 我想要一杯冷饮，不要咖啡; **he'd die ~ than admit it** 他死也不承认这件事 **5** (making a correction) 更确切地说; **a tree, or ~ a bush** 一棵树，更确切地说，一株灌木; **last night or ~ early this morning** 昨天夜里，准确地说是今天凌晨 **6** (on the contrary) 相反; **it didn't improve, but ~ deteriorated** 情况没有好转，反而恶化了; **the walls were not white, ~ a sort of dirty grey** 墙不是白色的，是灰不溜秋的

B *excl* Brit dated 当然; **you are glad to be home, aren't you? — ~!** 你很高兴回到家，是吧？——当然！; **isn't it lovely! — ~!** 多么可爱啊！——确实如此！

ratification /ˌrætɪfɪ'keɪʃn/ *n* [u] 正式批准

ratify /'rætɪfaɪ/ *vt* 正式批准 ‹*proposal*›

rating /'reɪtɪŋ/

A *n* **1** [c] (on scale) 等级; (in poll) 评分; **popularity ~** 受欢迎程度; **IQ ~** Brit 智商水平; **credit ~** 信用等级 **2** [c and u] Brit (for local tax) 房产税额; **~ assessments** 房产税额估价 **3** [c] Brit (in the navy) 水兵

B ratings *npl* TV 收视率; Radio 收听率; **to be top/bottom of the ~s** 收视率居首/垫底

rating system *n* Brit 分级制度

ratio /'reɪʃɪəʊ/ *n* 比例; **the pupil to teacher ~** 师生比; **the ~ of men to women is two to five** 男女比例是 2 : 5; **in direct/inverse ~ to sth.** 与某物成正比/反比; **in** *or* **by a ~ of 60:40** 以 60 : 40 的比例

ration /'ræʃn/

A *n* **1** (allowance) 配给量; **sugar/meat ~** 糖/肉的定量 **2** (of problems, luck) 正常量; **that family has had more than its ~ of troubles in the past few years** 在过去的几年里，那个家庭遭受了过多的麻烦; **turn it off now: you've had your ~ for today** 现在关掉电视：你今天已经看够了

B rations *npl* Mil 定量口粮; **on short/full ~s** 口粮短缺/充足地

C *vt* **1** 定量供应 ‹*food, clothing, petrol*›; **bread was ~ed to one loaf per family** 面包的配给量是每户一条 **2** (allow an amount of) 对…实行配给; **to ~ sb. to sth.** 对某人定量供应某物; **I'm going to ~ the children to one hour's television a day** 我准备限定孩子们每天看一小时电视

Phrasal verb

- **ration out** *vt* [**~ sth. out, ~ out sth.**] 配给 ‹*food, petrol*›

rational /'ræʃənl/ *adj* **1** (intelligent) 理性的 ‹*thought*›; **a ~ being** Philos 理性动物; **it is ~ to do sth.** 做某事是理智的 **2** (sensible) 合理的 ‹*explanation, behaviour*›; **it seemed the ~ thing to do** 做这件事似乎合情合理 **3** (lucid, coherent) 神智清楚的 ‹*person*›

rationale /ˌræʃə'nɑːl, Amer -'næl/ *n* (basic reasons) 根本原因; (logical basis) 逻辑依据; **the ~ behind** *or* **for sth.** 某事的理据

rationalism /'ræʃnəlɪzəm/ *n* [u] 理性主义

rationalist /'ræʃnəlɪst/

A *n* 理性主义者

B *adj* 理性主义的

rationalistic /ˌræʃnə'lɪstɪk/ *adj* **= rationalist B**

rationality /ˌræʃə'næləti/ *n* [u] **1** (ability to reason) 理性 **2** (of explanation, analysis) 合理性 **3** (lucidity) 神智清醒

rationalization /ˌræʃnəlaɪ'zeɪʃn/ *n* **1** [u] (explaining) 辩解; **no amount of ~ could justify his actions** 无论怎么辩解，他的行为都不能说是正当的 **2** [c] (explanation) 解释; **his main objective was to provide a ~ for this violence** 他的主要目的是为这种暴力行为提供理由 **3** [c and u] Brit Econ 合理化改革; **the industry underwent a ~ during**

r

the 1980's 该行业在20世纪80年代经历了一次合理化改革

rationalize /'ræʃnəlaɪz/ *vt* [1] (justify) 对…作合理解释〈*action, decision, emotion*〉[2] Brit Econ 对…进行合理化改革〈*industry, system*〉[3] (make consistent) 使合乎逻辑

rationally /'ræʃnəli/ *adv* 理性地〈*discuss, think*〉

ration: ～ **book** *n* 配给票证簿; ～ **card** *n* 配给卡

rationing /'ræʃnɪŋ/ *n* [u] 定量配给

rat: ～ **pack** *n* colloq 耗子帮 [指追踪骚扰名人的记者]; ～ **poison** *n* [u and c] 老鼠药; ～ **race** *n* pej 疯狂竞争; ～ **run** *n* Brit colloq [司机为避开拥堵而选择的] 小街

rattan /ræ'tæn/ *n* [1] [c] (palm) 藤 [2] [u] (material) 藤条

rat-tat /'rættæt/, **rat-tat-tat** /ˌrættæt'tæt/ *n* 吧嗒; **there was a sharp ～ on the door** 传来一记急促的敲门声

rattle /'rætl/

A *vi* [1] (shake)《*bottles, cans, window, door, gunfire*》乒乓响;《*chains, coins*》当啷响;《*car*》砰砰响; **I could hear things rattling inside the box** 我听到箱子里的东西哗啦哗啦响; **to shake sb. till** *or* **until their teeth ～** fig 使劲摇晃某人 [2] (move) 咔嚓咔嚓地行驶; **to ～ by** *or* **past**《*car, train, truck*》轰隆隆地驶过; **to ～ over sth.** 在…上咔嚓咔嚓地行进〈*cobblestones*〉; **to ～ along the street** 咔嚓咔嚓地沿街道前进

B *vt* [1] (shake) 使…乒乓响〈*bottle, can, window*〉; 使…当啷响〈*chains, coins*〉; 使…砰砰响〈*car, door, steering wheel*〉; **to ～ sb.'s cage** colloq 惹火某人 [2] colloq (make nervous) 使紧张; (frighten) 使害怕; (worry) 使担忧; **to get ～d** 被激怒

C *n* [1] (of bottles, cans, window, door, gunfire) 乒乓声; (of chains, coins) 当啷声; (of bodywork, engine) 砰砰声 [2] (baby's toy) 拨浪鼓 [3] (of sports fan) [为比赛助阵的] 响板 [4] Zool 角质环

Phrasal verbs

- **rattle around** colloq

A *vi* **to ～ around in sth.** (live) 在空荡的…中居住〈*house, flat*〉; (work) 在空荡的…中工作〈*office*〉; **the house was too big: we just ～d around in it** 房子太大了，我们住着有点空落落的

B *vt* [～ **around sth.**] (live in) 在空荡的…中生活〈*house, flat*〉; (work in) 在空荡的…中工作〈*office*〉

- **rattle away** *vi* colloq = **rattle on**
- **rattle off** *vt* [～ **off sth.,** ～ **sth. off**] 不假思索地说出〈*speech*〉; 一口气写出〈*letter, article*〉
- **rattle on** *vi* colloq 喋喋不休; **to ～ on about sb./sth.** 喋喋不休地谈论某人/某事物
- **rattle through** *vt* [～ **through sth.**] [1] (deal with) 迅速进行〈*work, discussion*〉; **they ～d through the rest of the meeting** 他们匆忙把剩余的会开完 [2] (say) 快速说出; **she ～d through the list of names** 她一口气念完了名单

rattler /'rætlə(r)/ *n* colloq = **rattlesnake**

rattlesnake /'rætlsneɪk/ *n* 响尾蛇

rattletrap /'rætltræp/ *n* dated pej 老爷车

rattling /'rætlɪŋ/

A *n* = **rattle C1**

B *adj attrib* [1] (vibrating) 格格作响的〈*sound, chain*〉; 呼噜呼噜的〈*cough*〉; **a ～ door/window** 嘎吱作响的门/窗户 [2] (quick) 轻快的〈*speed*〉; **at a ～ pace** 快速地

C *adv* colloq dated 非常; **a ～ good book/meal** 极好的一本书/一顿饭

rat trap *n* 捕鼠夹; **his first job was a real ～** fig colloq 他的第一份工作完全是个牢笼

ratty /'ræti/ *adj* Brit colloq 暴躁的〈*person, mood*〉; **she gets rattier as she gets older!** 她年纪越大脾气越坏!

raucous /'rɔːkəs/ *adj* [1] (harsh-sounding) 刺耳的〈*laughter, sound*〉; **the ～ call of crows** 乌鸦的呱呱叫声 [2] (boisterous, rowdy) 喧闹的〈*evening, behaviour, person, party*〉

raucously /'rɔːkəsli/ *adv* [1] (harshly) 刺耳地〈*laugh*〉[2] (boisterously) 喧闹地〈*behave*〉; **they were ～ drunk** 他们喝醉了，吵闹不止

raucousness /'rɔːkəsnɪs/ *n* [u] [1] (of voice, laughter) 刺耳 [2] (of behaviour, person) 喧闹

raunch /rɔːntʃ/ *n* [u] esp Amer colloq 淫秽; **the ～ of his first album** 他第一张专辑的粗俗下流

raunchy /'rɔːntʃi/ *adj* colloq 淫荡的〈*voice, person, song*〉; **a ～ film/joke** 色情电影/下流笑话

ravage /'rævɪdʒ/

A *vt* [1] (devastate)《*war, storm, fire*》毁坏〈*region, forest*〉; **a body ～d by disease** 受疾病摧残的身体 [2] (plunder) 劫掠〈*countryside*〉

B **ravages** *npl* 毁坏; **the ～s of war** 战争的蹂躏; **the ～s of time** 时间的摧残

rave /reɪv/

A *vi* [1] (rant) 咆哮; **to ～ at sb.** 对某人怒吼; **to ～ against/about sth.** 大声反对/叫嚷某事 [2] (talk incoherently)《*patient*》胡言乱语 [3] (enthuse) 热烈赞扬; **to ～ about sth.** 狂热吹捧某事物; **critics are raving about her new novel** 评论家在大肆吹捧她的新小说

B *vt* 热烈地说

C *adj attrib* colloq 热烈赞扬的〈*review, notice*〉

D *n* esp Brit colloq (party) 狂欢聚会; (organized event) 锐舞舞会

raven /'reɪvn/

A *n* 渡鸦

B *adj* 乌亮的; **～ black hair** 乌黑发亮的头发

raven-haired *adj* 头发乌亮的

ravening /'rævənɪŋ/ *adj* 凶猛饥饿的; **they turned on each other like ～ wolves** 他们像饿狼一样扑向对方

ravenous /'rævənəs/ *adj* 极饿的〈*person*〉; 极强的〈*appetite*〉; 十分的〈*hunger*〉; **to be ～** 饿极了

ravenously /'rævənəsli/ *adv* 贪婪地〈*eat, look*〉; **to be ～ hungry** 饿极了

raver /'reɪvə(r)/ *n* colloq [1] Brit (uninhibited person) 寻欢作乐的人 [2] (partygoer) 狂欢聚会的常客 [3] (person talking incoherently) 语无伦次的人

rave-up *n* Brit colloq 狂欢聚会

ravine /rə'viːn/ *n* 沟壑

raving /'reɪvɪŋ/

A *adv* 完全地〈*mad*〉

B *adj* [1] (fanatical) 胡言乱语的; **a ～ idiot** 满口胡言的傻瓜 [2] (tremendous) 绝顶的; **she's a ～ beauty** 她是个绝代佳人

C **ravings** *npl* 胡言乱语; **the ～s of a lunatic** 精神病人的疯话

ravioli /ˌrævɪ'əʊli/ *npl* + *v sing or pl* 意大利小方饺

ravish /'rævɪʃ/ *vt* [1] liter (delight)《*painting, sight, beauty*》使陶醉; **the garden ～ed her eyes** 花园让她看得出了神 [2] dated (rape) 强奸

ravishing /'rævɪʃɪŋ/ *adj* 迷人的〈*sight, smile, woman*〉; **to look ～** 看上去迷人; **a ～ beauty** 绝色美人

ravishingly /'rævɪʃɪŋli/ *adv* 迷人地〈*beautiful, smile*〉

raw /rɔː/

A *adj* [1] (uncooked) 生的〈*fruit, meat*〉; **to eat sth. ～** 生吃某物 [2] (unprocessed) 未经处理的〈*sewage*〉; **～ cotton/wood/sugar** 原棉/原木/原糖; **～ silk/rubber** 生丝/生橡胶; **drinking ～ alcohol would kill you** 喝纯酒精会致命 [3] (not evaluated) 未经分析的〈*facts*〉; **I'm still gathering ～ data** 我还在搜集原始数据 [4] (without skin, sore) 擦破皮的〈*back, hand, blister*〉; ▸**nerve A1** [5] (cold, damp) 阴冷的〈*day*〉[6] (inexperienced) 无经验的〈*reporter, kid*〉; **why did you give the job to a ～ recruit?** 你为什么把工作交给一个新兵? [7] (realistic) 真实的〈*portrayal*〉[8] (undisguised) 不加掩饰的〈*emotion, quality*〉[9] (unpolished) 粗犷的〈*style, characterization*〉; **～ but authentic artistic power** 原始但真实的艺术力量 [10] colloq (unfair) 不公正的; **a ～ deal** 不公的待遇; **to get** *or* **have a ～ deal** 受到不公正待遇; **to give sb. a ～ deal** 对某人苛刻

B *n* **to catch** *or* **touch sb. on the ～** Brit 触及某人痛处; **in the ～** (as sth. really is) 自然状态下的; colloq (naked) 赤身裸体的; **he writes about life in the ～** 他描写真实的生活; **I slept in the ～** 我裸睡

raw: **～-boned** *adj* 骨瘦如柴的; **～-boned farmhands** 瘦骨嶙峋的农夫; **～hide** *n* [u] 生皮; **a ～hide belt/whip** 生皮皮带/鞭子

Rawlplug® /'rɔːlplʌg/ *n* Brit 罗威套管

raw material *n* [1] [c] (substance) 原料 [2] [u] fig (person, thing) 素材

raw material costs *npl* 原料成本

rawness /'rɔːnɪs/ *n* [u] [1] (of food) 生; **we tried to ignore the ～ of the meat** 我们尽量不理会肉的夹生 [2] (soreness) 疼痛; **the ～ of grief** fig 悲伤的痛楚 [3] (of wind, weather) 阴冷 [4] (realism) 真实状态 [5] (inexperience) 无经验; **the ～ of his crew delayed the ship's passage** 由于他的船员缺乏经验，延误了船的航行 [6] (of language, style) 未经润饰; **the ～ of his diary made it unpublishable** 他的日记太粗糙，不能出版

raw score *n* Amer 原始分数

ray¹ /reɪ/ *n* (of light) 光线; (of radiation) 射线; **ultraviolet ～s** 紫外线; **a ～ of hope/comfort** fig 一线希望/一丝安慰; **his daughter was a ～ of sunshine in his life** fig 女儿是他生活中的一线阳光

ray² *n* (fish) 鳐

ray³ *n* Mus [大调音阶的第2音]

ray gun *n* [科幻作品中的] 射线枪

rayon /'reɪɒn/ *n* [u] 人造丝; **a ～ shirt** 人造丝衬衫

raze /reɪz/ *vt* 把…夷为平地〈*building, town*〉; **to ～ sth. to the ground** 把某物夷为平地

razor /'reɪzə(r)/ *n* 剃须刀; **an electric ～** 电动剃须刀

razor: **～back** *n* Amer [美国南部产的] 尖背野猪; **～ blade** *n* 剃须刀刀片; **～ burn** *n* [u] 剃须灼痛; **～ cut** *n* 剃刀削刮; **～ edge, ～'s edge** *n* [1] (sharp edge) 刀锋; [2] **to be on a** *or* **the ～('s) edge** 处于危急关头; **～-sharp** *adj* [1] (very sharp) 极锋利的〈*knife, teeth*〉; [2] (perceptive) 极犀利的〈*wit, mind*〉; **～ shell** *n* Brit 竹蛏; **～ wire** *n* [u] 带刺钢丝

razzle /'ræzl/ *n* Brit colloq **to go on the ～** 外出寻欢作乐

razzledazzle /ˌræzl'dæzl/ *n* [u] = **razzmatazz**

razzmatazz /ˌræzmə'tæz/ *n* [u] colloq 五光十色; **all the ～ of Hollywood** 好莱坞所有令人眼花缭乱的活动

RC *abbr* = **Roman Catholic**

RCMP *abbr* = **Royal Canadian Mounted Police** 加拿大皇家骑警

Rd *abbr* = **road 2**

RDA *abbr* = **recommended daily amount**

RE *abbr* Brit [1] Sch = **religious education** [2] Mil = **Royal Engineers** 皇家工兵部队

re¹ /reɪ/ *n* [大调音阶的第2音]

re² /riː/ *prep* (with reference to) 兹就; (about) 关于; **～ your letter ...** 兹就来函…; **I spoke to the deputy head ～ the incident** 关于这起事件，我跟副校长谈过了

reach /riːtʃ/

A *vt* [1] (arrive at) 到达; **the village is easily ～ed by bus** 乘坐公共汽车很容易到达那个村庄; **I hope this letter ～es you** 我希望你能收到这封信; **the rumours eventually ～ed the President** 传闻最终引起了总统的注意; **the show is due to ～ our screens early next year** 预计明年年初我们就能在电视上看到这个节目; **to ～ land** 到岸

[2] (increase to) 达到 ‹level, peak, speed, temperature›; when people ~ the age of 60 当人到了 60 岁 [3] (progress to) 发展到 ‹stage, position›; matters ~ed a point where ... 事态发展到了…的地步; I've ~ed the point where I can't stand this any longer! 我对此已经忍无可忍了！; the negotiations have ~ed deadlock 谈判陷入了僵局; to ~ the finals 进入决赛; to ~ maturity 成熟 [4] (achieve) 达成 ‹agreement, compromise, consensus›; 作出 ‹decision, verdict›; 得出 ‹conclusion› [5] (contact) 同…取得联系 ‹person, office›; to ~ sb. by phone 与某人电话联系; to ~ sb. on Brit or at 6564 2222 拨打 65642222 同某人取得联系 [6] (extend to) «skirt, hair, trousers» 长及; «arm, ladder» 够到; «water» 漫到; «snow» 积到; his feet can't ~ the pedals 他的双脚踩不到踏板 [7] (touch, get by stretching) «person» 够到; put medicines where children can't ~ them 把药放在儿童够不到的地方 [8] (pass) 递; to ~ sth. for sb., to ~ sb. sth. 将某物递给某人 [9] Radio, TV (make impact on) 打动 ‹audience, public, market›; to ~ sb. with sth. 通过…影响某人 ‹ad campaign›

[B] vi [1] (extend arm) 伸手; to ~ across or over 伸过手去; to ~ down/up 探手下去/抬起手; to ~ under/inside sth. 把手伸到某物下/伸进某物; to ~ for sth. 伸手够某物; I can't ~ that high or as high as that 我手伸不了那么高; the film will have you ~ing for your hanky! hum 这部电影会让你掏手绢的！; ~ for the sky! dated or hum 举手投降! [2] (extend) «clothes, hair, ladder, rope» 足够长; «water» 足够高; the cable won't ~ 电缆不够长; to ~ as far as sth. 长达某处; to ~ to sth. 长及某物; to ~ up/down to sth. 高/低到某处; her hair ~ed down to her waist 她的头发垂及腰部; to ~ across sth. 伸过某物; the carpet only ~ed halfway across the room 地毯只够铺半间屋子

[C] n [u and c] [1] (of arm) 臂展; a long or good ~ gives a boxer a distinct advantage 臂展长是拳击手的明显优势; to be beyond or out of/within (one's or arm's) ~ 在（手臂）够不着/够得着的地方; to be beyond or out of/within the ~ of sb. 在某人够不着/够得着的地方; 'keep out of ~ of children' “勿使儿童接触”; to be within easy ~ (of arm) 在容易够着的地方; (nearby) 在近处; an excellent selection of shops is within easy ~ 附近有一些非常不错的商店; to be within easy ~ of sth. 离…很近 ‹shop, office, town centre› [2] (of tool or device) 长度; shears with a long ~ 长剪 [3] (capability) 智力水平; to be beyond or out of/within sb.'s ~ 为某人不能/所能理解 [4] (power, influence) 影响力; beyond or out of ~ of sb./sth. 在某人/某事物的势力范围之外; he's beyond the ~ of the law 他正逍遥法外; victory is now out of her ~ 胜利现在对她来说遥不可及 [5] (financial means) 财力; to be beyond or out of/within sb.'s ~, to be beyond or out of/within ~ for sb. 让某人负担不起/负担得起; to put sth. beyond or out of/within sb.'s ~ «price» 使某人无力/能够购买 ‹goods›

[D] reaches npl [1] (of river) 河段; the upper/lower ~es (of a river) （河的）上游/下游 [2] (distant areas) 边远地区; the outer/further ~es (of sth.) （某地区的）外部/偏远地带; the outer ~es of space 外太空 [3] (sections of society, organization) 部门; the upper/lower ~es (of government) （政府的）上层/下层机构

Phrasal verbs

- **reach back** vi «memories, records, reviews» 追溯; to ~ back as far as or to sb./sth. 追溯到 ‹era, person›; the origins of the custom ~ back to pre-Qin times 那个风俗的起源可追溯到先秦时期
- **reach down** vt [1] [~ sth. down, ~ down sth.] (get down) 伸手取; to ~ sth. down from sth. 从某物上取下某物; to ~ sth. down for sb. 为某人取下某物 [2] [~ sb. down sth.] (pass) 将…递给…; to ~ sb. down a book from the top shelf 从书架顶层拿下一本书递给某人
- **reach out**

[A] vi [1] (extend hand) 伸手; to ~ out for sth. 伸手够某物 [2] (offer help) 伸出援手; to ~ out to sb./sth. 向某人/某群体伸出援手 [3] to ~ out to sb./sth. (show interest) 争取某人/某群体; we must ~ out to all levels of society and to all ages 我们必须争取社会各阶层和各年龄段的人 [4] (request help) 求助; to ~ out to sb./sth. 向某人/某机构求助

[B] vt [~ out sth., ~ sth. out] 伸出; to ~ out one's hand/arm (to do sth.) 伸出手/胳膊（做某事）

- **reach out for** vt [~ out for sth.] 争取 ‹success, help, peace›

reachable /ˈriːtʃəbl/ adj [1] (accessible) 可到达的 ‹place›; the island is only ~ by plane 该岛只能坐飞机去 [2] (contactable) 可联系上的 ‹person› [3] (achievable) 可实现的 ‹goal, target›

react /rɪˈækt/ vi [1] (respond) 作出反应; to ~ (to sth.) in a positive/negative/childish way （对某事物）作出积极/消极/孩子气的反应; to ~ positively/negatively 积极/消极地应对; to ~ against sth. 对某事物表示反对 [2] Med 有不良反应; to ~ to sth. 对某物产生不良反应 [3] Chem 起化学反应; to ~ with sth. «chemical» 和某物起化学反应; to ~ together 一起发生化学反应

reaction /rɪˈækʃn/

[A] n [1] [c and u] (response) 反应; sb.'s ~ (to sth.) 某人（对某事）的反应; a ~ against sth. 对某事的反对; what would be your ~ if I said she was gay? 如果我说她是同性恋，你会怎么想？ [2] [c] Med 不良反应; adverse ~s 副作用; an allergic ~ 过敏反应 [3] [c] Chem 化学反应; a nuclear ~ 核反应 [4] [u] Pol 反动; the forces of ~ 反动力量

[B] reactions npl 反应能力; you need quick ~s to be a fighter pilot 战斗机飞行员必须反应敏捷

reactionary /rɪˈækʃənri, Amer -neri/

[A] adj pej 反动的 ‹person, policy›; ~ attitudes towards women's rights 对妇女权利的极端保守态度

[B] n 反动分子

reaction time n 反应时间

reactivate /rɪˈæktɪveɪt/ vt 使…恢复活动 ‹idea, market›; measures to ~ the economy 振兴经济的措施

reactive /rɪˈæktɪv/ adj [1] Chem 易起化学反应的; a ~ gas 活性气体; a ~ metal 活性金属 [2] Psych 反应性的; a proactive rather than a ~ approach 积极主动而非消极被动的方法

reactor /rɪˈæktə(r)/ n [1] = nuclear reactor [2] Chem, Tech (container) 反应器

reactor: ~ disaster n 核反应堆事故; **~ safety** n [u] 核反应堆安全

read /riːd/

[A] vt (pt, pp read /red/) [1] (look through) 读 ‹book, newspaper›; 读…的作品 ‹author›; to ~ sth. from sth. 读某物上的某内容; he used to ~ a passage from the Bible every evening 他过去常常每晚读一段《圣经》; to ~ sth. to oneself 默读某物; to ~ sth. silently 默读某物; to take sth. as read 假定大家都读过并认可 ‹minutes, report›; fig 不经讨论即认定某事; to take it as read (that) ... 直接认定… [2] (understand meaning of) 看懂 ‹text, foreign language, writing›; can you ~ music? 你识谱吗？ [3] (give oral rendition of) 朗读; to ~ sth. aloud or out loud 朗读某物; to ~ sth. to sb., to ~ sb. sth. 读某物给某人听; go on: ~ it to us 念吧，念给我们听听; to ~ sth. for sb. 为某人读某物 [4] (discover) 读到; to ~ sth. about sb./sth. 读到有关某人/某事物的 ‹news, details›; to ~ sth. in sth. 在…上读到某事 ‹newspaper›; to ~ (that) ... 读到…; to ~ how ... 查阅到如何… [5] (in telling future) 占卜观察; to ~ the stars 看星象; to ~ sb.'s tea leaves 用某人喝剩的茶叶为其算命 [6] (understand movements of) to ~ sb.'s lips 读某人的唇语; ~ my lips! colloq 听好了！; ~ my lips: no new taxes 听我说，不会征新税 [7] (guess at) 猜测 ‹intention›; to ~ sb.'s thoughts or mind 猜测某人的心思; to ~ sb.'s mood 揣摩某人的脾气 [8] (interpret) 解读; how do you ~ the situation? 你对目前的形势怎么看？; to ~ the signs 识别征兆; this passage can be read in various ways 这段话可以有几种理解; to ~ sth. as sth. 将某事物理解为某事物; don't ~ his comments as proof of his sincerity 别以为他的评论证明了他的诚意; the book can be read as a satire 这本书可以说是一部讽刺作品 [9] (have as wording) «notice» 写着; the sign ~s 'no admittance' 告示牌上写着“禁止入内” [10] (inspect and record) 读取…的读数; I can't ~ what the pressure gauge says 我不会看压力计上的读数; I've come to ~ the gas meter 我是来抄煤气表的 [11] (show) «meter, dial, gauge, instrument» 显示; the thermometer ~s 20 degrees 温度计上显示 20 度 [12] Comput 读 ‹disk, file›; we can ~ the data we need from the disk 我们可以从那张盘上读取所需数据 [13] Radio, Telecom 收听到 ‹person, pilot›; to ~ sb. loud and clear 听到某人的声音了，响亮又清楚 [14] Brit Univ dated 学习 ‹subject›; he's decided to ~ law for his degree 他已决定攻读法学学位 [15] Publg 替换为 ‹word›; for 'cat' in line 12 ~ 'cart' 第 12 行中的cat应为cart

[B] vi (pt, pp read /red/) [1] (understand words) 识字; the baby can ~ pretty well 这个孩子能识好多字了; to ~ and write 看书写字 [2] (go through written text) 阅读; to ~ silently, to ~ to oneself 默读; to ~ between the lines 领悟言外之意 [3] (say text out loud) 朗读; to ~ aloud 朗读; to ~ to sb. 读给某人听; to ~ from sth. 朗读某物上的内容; to ~ to sb. from sth. 给某人读某物上的内容; to ~ for sb. 为某人朗读 [4] (find out) to ~ about sb./sth. 读到某人/某事物 [5] (contain wording) «paragraph, sentence, clause» 行文; the text at this point ~s thus/as follows ... 文章此处行文是这样的/如下… [6] (come across) «story, essay, paragraph» 读起来; how do you think the essay ~s? 你觉得这篇散文读上去怎么样？; to ~ well/badly/smoothly 读起来很好/很糟/很通顺; to ~ like sth. 读起来像某事物; the poem ~s like a translation 这首诗读起来像是翻译过来的 [7] Brit Univ dated to ~ for sth. 攻读某学科; he's ~ing for a degree in physics/an English degree at Oxford 他正在牛津攻读物理学/英语学位

[C] n colloq [1] esp Brit (act of reading) 阅读; I've got a new bestseller: do you want a ~? 我有本新的畅销书：你要看吗？; a long/quiet/little ~ 长时间/安静/少量的阅读; I enjoy a good ~ when I'm on my own 我独自一人时喜欢惬意地读读书; to have a ~ of sth. 读一读 ‹novel, book› [2] (piece of writing) 读物; to be an easy/exciting ~ 读来轻松/激动人心; I always think he's a good ~ 我总觉得他的书很好看

Phrasal verbs

- **read back** vt [~ sth. back, ~ back sth.] 读出; to ~ sth. back to sb. 给某人读出某物; can you ~ that last bit back to me? 把最后那点再给我念一遍好吗？
- **read in** vt [~ sth. in, ~ in sth.] 读入 ‹disk, data, file›
- **read into** vt [~ sth. into sth.] [1] (attribute significance to) to ~ too much into sth. 对…作过多的理解 ‹statement, message, comment›; I wouldn't ~ too much into what she says 对她的话，我不会多想的; was I ~ing too much into his behaviour? 我是不是对他的表现多心了？ [2] Comput

把…读入… ‹*disk, data, file*›; **to be read into a computer** 被读入电脑

• **read off** *vt* [~ off sth., ~ sth. off] **1** (go through) 接连读出 ‹*names, scores*›; **she read a few names off from the list** 她从名单上读了几个名字 **2** (ascertain) 确定 ‹*altitude, temperature, speed, time*›; **the reaction time was read off the timer** 从计时器读取了反应时间

• **read on** *vi* 继续读; **how will our hero escape? ~ on** 我们的主角将如何逃脱呢？下面接着读

• **read out** *vt* [~ sth. out, ~ out sth.] 宣读; **to ~ sth. out to sb.** 给某人朗读某物; **she read out the letter to all of us** 她把信高声读给我们大家听

• **read over, read through** *vt* [~ over sth., ~ sth. over] 认真通读

• **read up** *vt* [~ sb./sth. up, ~ up sb./sth.] 围绕…广泛阅读 ‹*subject, author*›

• **read up on** *vt* [~ up on sb./sth.] 围绕…广泛阅读 ‹*subject, author*›

readability /ˌriːdəˈbɪləti/ *n* [u] **1** (legibility) 清晰可辨 **2** (enjoyability) 可读性; **a fine novel of undoubted ~** 脍炙人口的好小说

readable /ˈriːdəbl/ *adj* **1** (legible) 清晰易辨的 ‹*handwriting, code*› **2** (enjoyable) 可读性强的 ‹*style, book*›; **a highly ~ article on an abstruse topic** 一篇有关深奥话题的通俗易懂的文章

readdress /ˌriːəˈdres/ *vt* **1** Post 更改…的邮寄地址 ‹*letter*›; **could you ~ any mail to my new house please?** 请把邮件改寄到我的新住处好吗？ **2** (take up again) 重新处理 ‹*issue, problem*›

reader /ˈriːdə(r)/ *n* **1** (person who reads) 读者; **an avid ~ of science fiction** 科幻小说迷; **our regular ~s** 我们的忠实读者; **he's a slow ~** 他读书很慢 **2** Sch (book) 读本 **3** Brit Univ (senior lecturer) 准教授; **a ~ in sth.** 某专业的准教授 **4** Publg 审稿人

readership /ˈriːdəʃɪp/ *n* **1** + *v sing or pl* (number of readers) 读者; **the magazine has a ~ of 35,000** 这本杂志有 35,000 名读者 **2** **Readership** Brit Univ 准教授职位; **to have** *or* **hold a R~** 有准教授的头衔

read head *n* 读磁头

readily /ˈredɪli/ *adv* **1** (willingly) 乐意地 ‹*answer, go, agree*›; **~ enough** 很乐意地; **he ~ accepted my proposals** 他欣然接受了我的提议 **2** (easily) 容易地 ‹*forgive*›; **~ available/accessible** 便捷可得的/易接近的; **the sofa can be ~ converted to a bed** 这个沙发可以方便地变成一张床

readiness /ˈredɪnɪs/ *n* [u] **1** (preparedness) 准备就绪; **in ~ for sth.** 为某事物准备就绪; **to be in a state of ~** 处于准备好的状态; **to hold** *or* **keep sb./sth. in ~** 使某人/某事物准备就绪 **2** (willingness) 乐意; **sb.'s ~ to do sth.** 某人做某事的意愿; **her ~ to help** 她的乐于助人 **3** (quickness) 敏捷; **~ of wit/response** 思维/反应的敏捷

reading /ˈriːdɪŋ/ *n* **1** [u] (activity) 阅读; **her ~ is poor** 她的阅读能力很差; **the ~ public** 广大读者; **~ materials** 阅读材料 **2** [c] (act of reading) 读; (period of reading) 阅读时间; **a closer ~ of the text** 对这篇文章更仔细的阅读; **at** *or* **in one ~** *or* **a single ~** 以一次阅读; **she read this book at one ~** 她一口气看完了这本书 **3** [u] (books) 读物; **light ~** 轻松的读物; **the article is not exactly light ~** 这篇文章读起来并不轻松; **heavy** *or* **serious ~** 艰涩的读物; **to make** *or* **be interesting/dull ~** 读起来有趣味/很枯燥; **suggested** *or* **recommended/required ~** 推荐/指定读物; **further ~** 其他阅读参考资料 **4** [u] (knowledge) 书本知识; **a man/woman of immense ~** 博览群书的男子/女子; **~ in sth.** 某方面的学识; **his ~ in Egyptian art is without parallel** 他在埃及艺术方面的学识无人能及 **5** [c] (recorded measurement) 读数; **odometer/thermometer/gas ~** 里程计/温度计/煤气表读数; **to take a ~** 查表; **meter ~s are taken every three months** 每三个月抄一次表 **6** [c] (interpretation) 解读; **a ~ of sth.** 对某事的解读; **a literal ~ of the text** 对这个文本的字面理解; **what's your ~ of ...?** 你怎么理解…？; **my own ~ of events** 我本人对事态的看法; **to give sb. one's ~ (of sth.)** 告诉某人自己（对某事物）的看法 **7** [c] (literary event) 朗诵会; (extract, story) 朗诵的作品; **a poetry ~** 诗歌朗诵会; **a ~ from sth.** 朗诵的某作品选段 **8** [c] Bible [在礼拜仪式上诵读的]《圣经》选段; **a Bible ~** 诵读的《圣经》章节; **a ~ from sth.** 选自某章节的朗读经文 **9** [c] (announcement) 宣读; **the ~ of a will** 遗嘱的宣读 **10** [c] Brit Pol [议案、法案等的] 宣读; **the first/second/third ~ (of sth.)** （某议案的）第一/二/三次宣读; **the third and final ~ of the bill** 该法案的第三次也是最终宣读; **at a bill's first/second ~** 在法案第一/二次宣读时 **11** [c] (wording) 版本; **an alternative** *or* **variant ~ of sth.** 某物的另一版本

reading: ~ **age** *n* 阅读年龄 [指某一年龄段儿童的阅读能力]; **a thirty-year-old man with a ~ age of eight** 阅读能力相当于 8 岁儿童的 30 岁男子; ~ **desk** *n* 斜面书桌; ~ **glasses** *npl* 老花镜; ~ **group** *n* 读书会; ~ **knowledge** *n* 阅读能力; **to have a ~ knowledge of German** 能阅读德语; ~ **lamp** *n* (by bed) 阅读灯; (on desk) 台灯; ~ **list** *n* 阅读书单; ~ **matter** *n* [u] 读物; **it is not suitable ~ matter for children** 这读物不适合儿童阅读; ~ **room** *n* 阅览室; ~ **scheme** *n* Brit 阅读计划; ~ **speed** *n* **1** (of person) 阅读速度; **2** Comput 读出速度

readjust /ˌriːəˈdʒʌst/
A *vt* **1** (rearrange) 整理 ‹*clothes, strap*›; **she ~ed her hat** 她整了整帽子 **2** (reset) 重新调校 ‹*TV, thermostat*›; 重新设置 ‹*machine, instrument*›; **I had to ~ the microscope** 我只好把显微镜重调一下 **3** (alter the amount of) 调整 ‹*salary*›
B *vi* 重新适应; **to ~ to sth.** 重新适应某事物

readjustment /ˌriːəˈdʒʌstmənt/ *n* **1** [c and u] (of TV, machine) 重调; **minor ~s to the controls** 对控制装置的微调 **2** [c and u] (of salary) 调整 **3** [u] (to new situation) 重新适应

readmission /ˌriːədˈmɪʃn/ *n* [c and u] (to organization, place) 重新接纳; (to hospital) 再次住院

readmit /ˌriːədˈmɪt/ *vt* (to organization, place) 重新接纳; (to hospital) 再次接收…住院

readmittance /ˌriːədˈmɪtns/ *n* [u] 重新接纳

read mode *n* 只读模式

read-only *adj* 只读的 ‹*file, disk*›

read-only memory *n* [u] 只读存储器

read-out *n* 读出

readvertise /ˌriːˈædvətaɪz/ *vt* 为…再做广告 ‹*post, job*›

readvertisement /ˌriːədˈvɜːtɪsmənt, Amer ˌriːædvərˈtaɪzmənt/ *n* 再次刊登的广告

read-write *adj* 读写的; **~ mode/drive** 读写模式/驱动器

read-write: ~ **access** *n* [u] 读写访问; ~ **head** *n* 读写磁头; ~ **memory** *n* [u] 读写存储器

ready /ˈredi/
A *adj* **1** *pred* (prepared to act) 准备好的; **are you nearly ~?** 你准备得差不多了吗？; **~ when you are** 都准备好啦，只等你了; **to be ~, willing, and able** 有准备，有意愿，且有能力; **to be ~ and waiting** 准备就绪，正在待命; **to be ~ for sth.** 为某事做好准备; **to be ~ for exams** 做好应试准备; **~ for anything** 做好万全准备的; **to be ~ to do sth.** 准备好做某事; **waiter! we're ~ to order now** 服务员！我们要点菜了; **to get ~** 准备好; **to get ~ for sth.** 为某事做好准备; **to get ~ to do sth.** 准备好做某事; **to get sb. ~ (for sth.)** 让某人（为某事）做好准备; **to get oneself ~** 做好准备; **to make ~** formal 做好准备; **to make ~ to do sth.** formal 准备好做某事; **to make ~ for sth.** formal 为某事做好准备; **~ about!** Naut 准备转向！; **~, steady, go!** Brit Sport 各就各位，预备，跑！; **(get) ~, (get) set, go!** esp Amer Sport 各就各位，预备，跑！ **2** *pred* (available to use) 预备好的; **dinner's ~** 饭好啦; **have your excuses ~!** 找好借口吧！; **~ for sth.** 为某事预备好的; **your suit is ~ for collection** 您的西装可以取了; **~ for use** *or* **to use** 随时可用的; **~ to do sth.** 预备好做某事的; **the contract will be ~ to sign in two weeks** 合同两周之后可以签署; **the fruit is ~ to be picked** 果实可以摘了; **to get sth. ~** 把某物预备好 **3** (easily available) 现成的 ‹*supply, source*›; **we have ~ access to the facilities** 我们可以随时使用那些设备; **a ~ market** 会有销路的市场; **~ to hand** 随手可用的; **to keep sth. ~** 让某物随手可用 **4** *pred* (eager) 急切的; **I was very angry and ~ for a fight** 我很气愤，想打一架; **I'm ~ for what promises to be an interesting contest** 我乐意看看想必会很有趣的比赛; **~ to do sth.** 急切想做某事的; **don't be so ~ to find fault!** 别这么爱挑刺！; **to be more than ~ to do sth.** 非常想做某事 **5** *pred* (quick to give) **~ with sth.** 迅速提供某物的; **he's a bit too ~ with his criticism** 他有点太急于批评了; **she was very ~ with advice/her excuses** 她很会提建议/她总是有借口 **6** *pred* (on the point of) **~ to do sth.** 马上要做某事的; **I was just about ~ to burst into tears** 我都快要哭了; **the house looked** *or* **seemed ~ to collapse** 这房子似乎摇摇欲坠 **7** *pred* (in need of) 需要的; **~ for sth.** 需要某物的; **I really am ~ for bed/a holiday!** 我真的很想睡觉/度假！; **you look ~ for a good meal** 你看起来需要好好吃一顿; **I feel ~ for a rest** 我想休息一下 **8** *attrib* (quick to react) 机敏的 ‹*mind*›; **she has a ~ wit** 她才思敏捷 **9** *attrib* (quickly produced) 立刻的 ‹*response, solution*›; **a young man with a ~ smile** 总是面带微笑的小伙子
B *vt* formal 使做好准备; **to ~ sb./sth. for sth.** 使某人/某事物为某事做好准备; **the ship has been readied for battle** 军舰已进入战备状态; **nothing could have readied him for such a shock** 对这样的打击他完全没有思想准备
C *v refl* formal **to ~ oneself** 做好准备; **to ~ oneself for sth.** 为某事做好准备; **to ~ oneself to do sth.** 准备好做某事
D *n* **1** **to have sth. at the ~** (for immediate use) 把某物准备好 **2** Brit colloq (cash) **the ~** 现钱
E **readies** /ˈredɪz/ *npl* Brit colloq 现钱; **she paid £300 in readies** 她付了 300 英镑现金

ready: ~ **cash** *n* [u] = ~ **money**; **~-cooked** *adj* 即食的 ‹*meal, food*›

ready: **~-made** *adj* **1** (for immediate use) 预制的 ‹*fittings, curtain*›; **a kitchen fitted with ~-made cupboards** 配有整体橱柜的厨房; **2** (ready-to-wear) 成品的; **a ~-made suit** 成品套装; **3** (immediately available) 现成的 ‹*answer*›; (prepared in advance) 预先准备好的 ‹*ideas, phrases*›; **a ~-made solution** 现成的解决方案; **4** Culin 即食的 ‹*food, meal*›; ~ **meal** *n* Brit 即食餐; **~-mix** *n* [u] 预拌混凝土; **~-mixed** *adj* 预先调制的 ‹*cake, soup, feed*›; ~ **money** *n* [u] colloq 现金; **to pay sb. in ~ money** 现款付账给某人; ~ **reckoner** *n* 简便计算表; **~-to-serve** *adj* 即食的 ‹*food*›; **~-to-wear** *adj* 现成的; **a ~-to-wear garment** 成衣

reaffirm /ˌriːəˈfɜːm/ *vt* 重申 ‹*commitment, intention*›; **she ~ed that she would not resign** 她重申自己不会辞职

reafforestation /ˌriːəˌfɒrɪˈsteɪʃn/ *n* [u] Brit = **reforestation**

reagent /riːˈeɪdʒənt/ *n* 试剂

real /rɪəl/
A *adj* 1 *usu attrib* (actual) 实际存在的; **there's no ~ cause for alarm** 实在没有理由惊慌; **there's no ~ possibility of ...** …是绝不可能的; **the threat is very ~** 这种威胁是实实在在的; **we have a ~ chance of success** 我们确实有可能成功; **he has no ~ power** 他没有实权; **to have no ~ understanding of sth.** 根本不理解某事物; **in ~ life** 在现实生活中; **you need to keep in touch with the ~ world** 你不能与现实世界脱节; **get ~!** colloq 现实点吧！ 2 *usu attrib* (not artificial or imitation) 真的 ‹*diamond, champagne, flower*›; **~ leather/silk** 真皮/真丝; **the ~ thing** 真正的东西; **as soon as I met her I knew that I'd found the ~ thing at last** 我一遇到她就知道我终于找到了真爱; **this time it's the ~ thing** 这回是动了真情; **the ~ McCoy** colloq 货真价实的东西 3 *attrib* (true) 真实的 ‹*reason, story, self*›; **the ~ truth** 实情; **the ~ France/you** 真实的法国/你; **a ~ live celebrity** 活生生的名人 4 *attrib* (proper) 名副其实的 ‹*Buddhist, communist, altruism*›; 真正的 ‹*regret*›; **a ~ man/accident/problem** 真正的男子汉/事故/问题; **to have a ~ holiday** 好好度个假; **his first ~ kiss** 他真正的初吻 5 *attrib* (for emphasis) 十足的 ‹*idiot*›; **it's a ~ shame you can't come** 你不能来真是可惜; **it's been a ~ pleasure to meet you** 很高兴见到你; **a ~ laugh** colloq 真好笑; **a ~ stroke of luck/misfortune** 十足的好运/不幸; **this room is a ~ oven** 屋里热得像火炉; **he was making a ~ effort to be nice to her** 他费尽心思地对她好 6 *attrib* Comm, Fin 实际的 ‹*capital, cost, value, income*›; **~ assets** 不动产 7 Math 实（数）的; **~ analysis** 实分析 8 Philos 实在的; **~ entities/phenomena** 实体/实相
B **for real** *adj phr* colloq 1 (genuine) 真实的; **I wonder if he is for ~** 我不知道他是不是冒牌货; **those tears weren't for ~** 那些眼泪不是真心的 2 esp Amer (serious) 认真的; **are those guys for ~?** 那些家伙当真吗？
C *adv* Amer colloq 很; **I'm ~ sorry** 我很抱歉; **that tastes ~ good** 那东西的味道很不错
D *n* **the ~** 现实

real ale *n* [c and u] Brit 传统散装啤酒

real estate *n* [u] esp Amer 1 (property) 房地产; **they own a piece of New York ~** 他们在纽约拥有一处房产 2 (as profession) 房地产业; **to be in ~** 做房地产生意

real estate: ~ agent ▸p. 409 *n* Amer 房地产经纪人; **~ developer** ▸p. 409 *n* Amer 房地产开发商; **~ investment trust** *n* Amer 不动产投资信托公司; **~ office** *n* Amer 房地产公司

realign /ˌriːəˈlaɪn/
A *vt* 1 (change position of) 调整…的位置 ‹*row, paper*›; **several parts of the engine had to be ~ed** 发动机的一些部件必须校准 2 fig (adapt) 调整 ‹*view, policy*›
B *vi* «*parties, forces*» 重新结盟; **to ~ with ...** 与…重结联盟

realignment /ˌriːəˈlaɪnmənt/ *n* [c and u] 1 (of mechanism, parts) 调整位置; **the front wheels are in need of ~** 前轮需要校准 2 (of views, party) 再结盟; **social/political ~** 社会/政治重组

realism /ˈriːəlɪzəm/ *n* [u] 1 (pragmatism) 务实; **there's a lack of ~ in these proposals** 这些提议缺少务实性 2 (authenticity) 真实性; **with some degree of ~** 带点真实性 3 Art, Literat 现实主义; **to lend ~ to sth.** 为某物增添现实感

realist /ˈriːəlɪst/ *n* 1 (practical, realistic person) 务实的人; **she's enough of a ~ not to waste any tears over the situation** 她很实际，不会为了这种情况浪费眼泪 2 (writer) 现实主义作家; (painter) 现实主义画家

realistic /ˌrɪəˈlɪstɪk/ *adj* 1 (sensible, achievable) 切实可行的 ‹*attitude, goal*›; **it is not ~ to expect him to resign** 指望他辞职是不实际的 2 (practical) 注重实际的 ‹*person*›; **to be ~ about sth.** 对某事物实事求是; **be ~: you won't win** 现实点儿，你赢不了 3 (true to life) 逼真的 ‹*portrayal*›; **a ~ account of everyday life in the ghetto** 对贫民窟日常生活的栩栩如生的描写 4 (fair) 合理的 ‹*salary, price, valuation*›

realistically /ˌrɪəˈlɪstɪkli/ *adv* 1 (pragmatically) 切合实际地 ‹*approach, think*›; **~, she can expect ...** 实事求是地说，她可以指望… 2 (authentically) 逼真地 ‹*portray*›

reality /rɪˈæləti/ *n* 1 [u] (the real world) 现实; **to be out of touch with ~** 脱离实际; **to face (up to) ~** 面对现实; **in ~** 实际上; **a knock at the door brought me back to ~** 敲门声把我拉回了现实 2 [c and u] (truth) 真实; **the harsh/grim/sober ~ of the situation** 严峻/严酷/严肃的真实情况; **economic realities** 经济现状 3 [c and u] (fact) 事实; **the ~ is that ...** 事实是…; **to become a ~** 成为现实; **in ~** 其实; **I was, in ~, a little nervous** 其实我有点紧张

reality: ~-based *adj* 1 (non-fictional) 纪实的 ‹*programme*›; 2 (realistic) 基于现实的 ‹*reporting*›; **~ check** *n* colloq [提醒人面对现实的] 实际检验; **~ show** *n* 真人秀; **~ TV** *n* [u] 真实电视

> **reality TV**
>
> 真实电视。通俗译名多作真人秀电视节目。20 世纪 90 年代蔚然兴起的一类电视节目。所谓的"真实"体现在不使用专业演员，没有事先准备好的台词，用摄像机记录普通人的生活。包括多种类型，如警察出警纪实、真人电视比赛等。前者以美国的《警员》（*Cops*）为代表。后者一般都有选手或观众进行投票、逐一淘汰参赛选手的环节，著名的节目包括英国的《老大哥》（*Big Brother*）和美国哥伦比亚公司（▸**CBS**）播放的《幸存者》（*Survivor*）。

realizable /ˈrɪəlaɪzəbl/ *adj* 1 (achievable) 可实现的 ‹*vision, dream*›; **I didn't know how far from being ~ my plan was** 我不知道我的计划离实现有多远 2 Fin 可变现的 ‹*investments*›

realization /ˌrɪəlaɪˈzeɪʃn, Amer -lɪˈz-/ *n* 1 [u] (awareness) 认识; **the (sudden) ~ that ...** （突然）意识到…; **a growing ~ that ...** 越来越认识到…; **to come to the ~ that ...** 逐渐意识到… 2 [u] formal (of design, idea) 体现; **the ~ of this design in stone** 这个设计通过石头的体现 3 [u] (fulfilment) 发挥; **the ~ of his full potential** 他全部潜力的发挥 4 [u] (of fear) 成真; **the ~ of his worst nightmares** 他最可怕的噩梦成真 5 [u and c] (of ambition, hope) 实现; **the ~ of a cherished dream** 夙愿的实现 6 [u] Fin (liquidation) 变现; **the ~ of assets** 资产的变现

realize /ˈrɪəlaɪz/ *vt* 1 (know, be aware of) 认识到 ‹*mistake, truth, significance*›; **I ~ that you feel differently** 我明白你的感受不一样; **to ~ how/why/what** 意识到怎样/为什么/什么; **to come to ~ sth.** 逐渐明白某事; **to make sb. ~ sth.** 使某人了解某事; **do you ~ that I'm waiting for you?** 你明白我在等你吗？ 2 (make concrete, real) 体现 ‹*design, idea*› 3 (fulfil) 发挥 ‹*potential*›; 实现 ‹*possibilities*› 4 (cause to happen) 使成真; **my worst fears were ~d** 我最担心的事情发生了 5 (achieve) 将…变为现实 ‹*dream, hope*› 6 Fin (liquidate) 把…变现 ‹*shares*›; **the company had to ~ its most valuable assets** 公司只好变卖最值钱的资产 7 (be sold for) 售得 ‹*amount*›; **how much do you expect the furniture to ~?** 这家具你想卖多少钱？ 8 Comm (make, earn) 赚得; **to ~ a sum on sth.** 在某物上赚一笔钱

reallocate /ˌriːˈæləkeɪt/ *vt* 重新分配 ‹*funds, time, task*›

reallocation /ˌriːæləˈkeɪʃən/ *n* [c and u] 重新分配; **budget ~s** 预算再分配

really /ˈrɪəli/
A *adv* 1 (in actual fact) 真正地; **what I ~ mean is that ...** 我其实想说的是…; **it didn't ~ matter** 其实没什么关系; **~, there are only three options** 实际上，只有三种选择 2 (for emphasis) 确实; **do you ~ think he'll apologize?** 你真以为他会道歉吗？; **I don't believe it; ~ I don't** 我不相信，我确实不信; **I ~ must go** 我确实得走了; **I ~ and truly am in love this time** 我这一次确确实实是在恋爱 3 (expressing interest, surprise, doubt) **~?** 是吗？; **I've been working hard — ~?** 我一直工作很努力——真的吗？ 4 (very) 十分; **a ~ hot day** 十分炎热的一天; **I'm ~ sorry** 我非常抱歉
B *excl* 真是的; **well, ~! how ridiculous!** 唉，真是的！太荒谬了！

realm /relm/ *n* 1 liter (kingdom) 王国 2 (sphere, area) 领域; **the role of public opinion in the ~ of politics** 公共舆论在政界的作用

real number *n* 实数

realpolitik /reɪˈɑːlpɒlɪtiːk/ *n* [u] 现实政治

real: ~ property *n* [u] 房地产; **~ tennis** *n* [u] 庭院网球; **~ time** *n* [u] 1 (actual time) 即时; **~ time news/reports** 即时新闻/报道; 2 Comput 实时; **in ~ time** 实时地

real-time: ~ computer *n* 实时计算机; **~ computing** *n* [u] 实时计算; **~ processing** *n* [u] 实时处理; **~ system** *n* 实时系统

realtor /ˈriːəltə(r)/ ▸p. 409 *n* Amer 房地产经纪人

ream /riːm/
A *n* (of paper) 令 [纸张的计数单位，等于500张]
B **reams** *npl* colloq (a great deal) 大量; **she always writes ~s** 她总是下笔千言

reanimate /ˌriːˈænɪmeɪt/ *vt* 1 (reinvigorate) 使…重新活跃 ‹*party, scene*›; **his personal dislike of the man was ~d** 他又开始讨厌这个男人了 2 (revive) 救活 ‹*person, body*›

reap /riːp/
A *vt* 1 Agric 收割 ‹*crop*›; **we ~ed a bumper harvest this year** 我们今年获得了大丰收 2 fig (receive) 获得 ‹*fruits, profits*›; **to ~ the rewards of one's efforts** 因努力而获得回报; **to ~ what you sow** 自食其果
B *vi* 收割

reappear /ˌriːəˈpɪə(r)/ *vi* 重新出现; **her symptoms ~ed** 她的病症复发了

reappearance /ˌriːəˈpɪərəns/ *n* 重新出现

reapply /ˌriːəˈplaɪ/
A *vi* «*candidate*» 重新申请; **to ~ for sth.** 重新申请某物
B *vt* 1 (use in different situation) 再应用 ‹*rule, principle*›; **skills that can be reapplied** 可再次应用的技能 2 (apply again) 再敷 ‹*paint*›; **~ the sunscreen hourly** 每小时再抹一次防晒霜

reappoint /ˌriːəˈpɔɪnt/ *vt* 重新任命

reappointment /ˌriːəˈpɔɪntmənt/ *n* [c and u] 重新任命

reapportion /ˌriːəˈpɔːʃn/ *vt* 重新分派

reappraisal /ˌriːəˈpreɪzl/ *n* [c and u] (of question, policy) 重新评估; (of writer, work) 重新评价; **to do** *or* **undertake a ~ of sth.** 对某事物进行再评估

reappraise /ˌriːəˈpreɪz/ *vt* 重新评估 ‹*policy, strategy, role*›; 重新评价 ‹*writer, work*›

rear¹ /rɪə(r)/
A *n* 1 (back part) (of building, car, room) 后部; **at the ~ of the house** 在房子后面; **(viewed) from the ~** 从后面（看）; **from the ~, the car looks a bit square** 这辆车从后面看有点方 2 (of unit, convoy, column) 后尾; (of procession, train) 尾部; **to attack the enemy in the ~** 攻击敌人的后方; **to bring up the ~** 殿后 3 colloq euph (bottom) 臀部

r

B *adj attrib* 后部的; **he got in by the ~ entrance** 他从后门进来了

rear²

A *vt* **1** (bring up) 抚养 ‹*child*›; **she had ~ed a large family** 她供养了一个大家庭; **to be ~ed on classical music** 听古典音乐长大 **2** (care for) «*animal*» 孵育; **they ~ their young in a pouch** 它们在育儿袋里哺育幼兽 **3** (breed) 饲养 ‹*sheep, poultry*› **4** (grow) 栽种 ‹*plant, crop*› **5** (lift up) 抬高; **the snake ~ed its head menacingly** 蛇威胁地抬起头; **civil war was about to ~ its ugly head** fig 内战就要爆发了

B *vi* «*snake*» 直起上半身; **the horse ~ed (up) suddenly** 马突然用后腿直立

rear: ~ access *n* [u] 后门; **~ admiral** *n* 海军少将; **~ bumper** *n* 后保险杠; **~ compartment** *n* 后厢; **~ door** *n* (in house) 后门; (in car) 后厢门; **~-drive** *adj* 后驱的

rear end

A *n* **1** (of vehicle) 后部 **2** colloq euph (of person) 屁股

B **rear-end** *vt* Amer colloq 撞到…的后部 ‹*person*›; **he rear-ended the car in front** 他跟前面的车追尾了

rear-engined /ˌrɪər'endʒɪnd/ *adj* 发动机后置的

rearguard /'rɪəgɑ:d/ *n* **1** Mil 后卫部队 **2** (of party, movement) 顽固保守派

rearguard action *n* **1** (military action) 后卫战斗; **to fight a ~ against sth./sb.** 与某组织/某人打一场后卫战 **2** (final attempt) 最后一搏; **a ~ against the reforms** 对改革的最后抗争

rear gunner *n* [军用飞机的] 机尾射手

rearm /ˌri:'ɑ:m/

A *vt* «*government*» 重新武装 ‹*troops*›; **to ~ our military forces** 重新装备我们的武装力量

B *vi* «*country, nation*» 重新武装; **Germany's plan to ~** 德国的重整军备计划

rearmament /ˌri:'ɑ:məmənt/ *n* [u] 重整军备

rearmost /'rɪəməʊst/ *adj* 最后面的

rear: ~-mounted *adj* 后置的; **~ projection** *n* [u] 背投; **a ~-projection screen/television** 背投屏幕/电视

rearrange /ˌri:ə'reɪndʒ/ *vt* **1** (reposition) 重新布置 ‹*room, furniture*›; 重新整理 ‹*hat, hair, clothes*› **2** (reschedule) 重新安排 ‹*fixture, dinner, match*›

rearrangement /ˌri:ə'reɪndʒmənt/ *n* [c and u] **1** (change in position) 重新布置; **the ~ of the furniture** 家具的重新摆放 **2** (change in time, date) 重新安排; **these dates require some ~** 这些日期需要作一些改动

rear-view mirror *n* 后视镜

rearward /'rɪəwəd/

A *adj* 后面的 ‹*part, seat*›; 向后的 ‹*movement*›; **the detachment took up a ~ position** 分遣队占据了后方阵地

B *adv* (*also* **rearwards**) 向后面 ‹*move*›; **the engine nozzles point ~** 发动机喷嘴是朝后的

rear wheel *n* 后轮

rear-wheel drive *n* [u] 后轮驱动

rear window *n* 后车窗

reason /'ri:zn/

A *n* **1** [c] (cause) 原因; (explanation) 理由; **a ~ for sth.** 某事的原因; **the ~ behind sth.** 某事背后的原因; **for a/no good ~** 有/无正当原因地; **for no ~** 无故; **why did you do it? — for no ~** 你为什么那么做? —— 不为什么; **the man attacked me for no apparent ~** 那名男子莫名其妙地袭击了我; **for some ~ (or other)** 出于某种原因; **for some unknown ~** 出于某种未知的原因; **if you are late for any ~, ...** 不论你为何迟到…; **for ~s best known to himself/herself** 出于唯有他/她自己才知道的原因; **for the very good** *or* **very simple ~ that ...** 就是因为…; **I won't do it, for that very simple ~** 就是因为这个, 我才不会那么做的; **for ~s of sth.** 由于某事物的原因; **for ~s of space/time/security** 由于空间/时间/安全原因; **for health/personal ~s** 由于健康/个人原因; **people who, for whatever ~, are unable to support themselves** 那些无论出于何种原因都没法养活自己的人们; **I have ~ to believe that ...** 我有理由相信…; **by ~ of sth.** formal 因为某事物; **to give sb. a ~** 给某人一个理由; **to have one's ~s (to do sth.)** 有理由 (做某事); **(and that's) the ~ why ...** (那就是) 为什么…; **the ~ why I'm late is that ...** 我迟到是因为…; **a ~ for sth./doing sth.** 某事/做某事的理由; **she gave no ~s for her decision** 她没解释为什么这样决定; **what was his ~ for resigning?** 他为什么辞职? ; **my ~ for going** *or* **the ~ for my going is (that) ...** 我要去的理由是…; **the ~ is (that) ...** 理由是…; **the ~ given is that ...** 给出的理由是… **2** [u] (grounds) 正当理由; **there is good ~ for sth./doing sth.** 某事物/做某事是有道理的; **to have every ~ for doing** *or* **to do sth.** 完全有理由做某事; **I have ~ to believe (that) ...** 我有理由相信…; **to have good/no good ~ to do sth.** 有/无充分理由做某事; **I see no ~ to think so** 我不明白为什么要这么想; **there is ~ (for sb.) to do sth.** (某人) 有理由做某事; **there was no ~ for you to worry** 你没必要担心; **all the more ~ for sth.** 某事更多的理由; **this result gives us all the more ~ for optimism** 这个结果让我们更有理由乐观了; **all the more ~ to do sth.** *or* **for doing sth.** 做某事更多的理由; **with (good) ~, not without ~** 有道理地; **she was angry, and with good** *or* **not without ~** 她很生气, 这是理所当然的; **without good ~** 没道理地 **3** [u] (common sense) 情理; **to be open to ~** 听劝; **she just isn't open to ~** 她就是听不进道理; **there's a good deal of ~ in that** 那样做是合情合理的; **to listen to** *or* **see ~** 明白事理; **to make sb. see ~** 让某人明白道理; **within ~** 合情合理地; **the voice of ~** 理性之声; **sweet ~** hum 美好的理由; **it** *or* **that stands to ~ (that) ...** 这是很显然的; **it stands to ~ (that) ...** …是明摆着的 **4** [u] (ability to think logically) 理性; **only human beings are capable of ~** 唯有人类有理性思考的能力; **the power of ~** 推理能力; **to lose one's ~** dated 丧失理智

B *vt* **1** (conclude) 推断; **to ~ (that) ...** 推断…; **she must have killed him, he ~ed** 肯定是她杀了他, 他推断道 **2** (argue) 争辩; **to ~ (that) ... suppose she killed him, he ~ed** 假如是她杀了他呢, 他争辩道

C *vi* 推理; **mankind's power** *or* **ability to ~** 人类的思考能力; **to ~ from sth.** 根据…进行推理 ‹*facts*›

Phrasal verbs

- **reason out** *vt* [**~ out sth., ~ sth. out**] 对…进行分析推断 ‹*problem, enigma*›; **to ~ out how the thief got in** 推断出贼是如何进来的
- **reason with** *vt* [**~ with sb.**] 劝说; **one can't ~ with him** 他不可理喻

reasonable /'ri:znəbl/ *adj* **1** (sensible) 明智的 ‹*person*›; **be ~!** 讲点道理! ; **to be ~ about sth.** 对某事很理智; **to be ~ in sth.** 在某方面通情达理 **2** (justified) 合乎情理的 ‹*interpretation, conclusion, suspicion, attitude*›; **it is ~ for sb. to do sth.** 某人做某事是合理的; **beyond ~ doubt** 确切无疑 **3** (not too expensive) 合理的 ‹*cost, price*›; (fair) 公道的 ‹*fee, offer*›; **all ~ claims will be considered** 所有公平合理的要求都会考虑 **4** colloq (moderately good) 尚好的 ‹*weather, health, access*›; **the food is ~** 食物还算不错

reasonableness /'ri:znəblnɪs/ *n* [u] **1** (of person) 明智; (of action) 合理 **2** (of price, offer) 公道

reasonably /'ri:znəbli/ *adv* **1** (sensibly) 明智地 ‹*talk, discuss*› **2** (inexpensively) 公道地; **the shoes are quite ~ priced** 这鞋的价格还合理 **3** (moderately) 还算 ‹*attractive, good, happy, satisfied, warm*›; **the train was ~ fast** 火车还算比较快; **she's doing ~ well at school** 她在学校的功课还不错; **how are you getting on? — ~ well** 你过得怎么样? ——还行 **4** (legitimately) 合理地 ‹*believe, suspect, conclude*›; **one might ~ suppose that ...** 人们也许有理由认为…

reasoned /'ri:zənd/ *adj* 合乎逻辑的

reasoning /'ri:znɪŋ/ *n* [u] **1** (thinking) 推理; **powers of ~** 推理能力 **2** (argumentation, reason) 论据; **the ~ behind sth.** 某事物背后的根据

reassemble /ˌri:ə'sembl/

A *vt* **1** (bring together again) 重新召集 ‹*troops, pupils, participants*›; **the chairman ~d the committee members** 主席重新召集委员会成员 **2** (put together again) 重新装配 ‹*parts, machine, engine, wardrobe*›

B *vi* «*troops, members, pupils*» 重新聚集; **school ~s on 7 January** 学校1月7日开学

reassert /ˌri:ə'sɜ:t/

A *vt* **1** (reconfirm) 再次确认 ‹*authority, dominance, control*› **2** (state again) 重申

B *v refl* **1** **to ~ oneself** (assert one's authority) 重申自己的权威 **2** **to ~ itself** (reappear) «*habit, common sense*» 重新起作用; **ambition soon ~ed itself** 雄心很快占了上风

reassess /ˌri:ə'ses/ *vt* **1** (re-examine, reconsider) 重新考虑 ‹*impact, result, problem*›; **to ~ the likelihood of a recession** 重新估量衰退的可能性 **2** (recalculate) 重新计算 ‹*tax, liability*›

reassessment /ˌri:ə'sesmənt/ *n* [c and u] (of situation) 重新估计; (of tax) 重新计算

reassurance /ˌri:ə'ʃɔ:rəns, Amer -'ʃʊər-/ *n* **1** [u] (act of reassuring) 宽慰; **children need ~ and praise** 孩子们需要肯定和表扬 **2** [c] (statement) 保证; **to seek/give ~s that ...** 寻求/给予保证…; **you'll have the ~ of a three-year guarantee** 你会得到三年保修期的保证; **to receive ~s** *or* **a ~ from sb. that ...** 从某人那里得到保证…

reassure /ˌri:ə'ʃɔ:(r), Amer -'ʃʊər-/ *vt* 使安心; **to ~ sb. about sth.** 消除某人对某事的担忧; **to ~ sb. that ...** 向某人保证…; **I was able to ~ him** 我让他放下了心

reassuring /ˌri:ə'ʃɔ:rɪŋ, Amer -'ʃʊər-/ *adj* 令人宽慰的; **his presence is ~** 他在场让人放心了; **it was ~ not to be alone** *or* **that we were not alone** 我们并不孤单, 这就不必担心了

reassuringly /ˌri:ə'ʃɔ:rɪŋli, Amer -'ʃʊər-/ *adv* 令人宽慰地; **she smiled ~ at me** 她对我笑了笑, 这使我感到踏实

reawaken /ˌri:ə'weɪkən/

A *vt* **1** (rekindle) 重新唤起 ‹*interest, enthusiasm, longing*› **2** (wake again) 使…再次苏醒 ‹*person, animal*›

B *vi* **1** (be rekindled) «*feeling, desire, interest*» 被重新唤起 **2** (wake again) «*person, animal*» 再次苏醒

reawakening /ˌri:ə'weɪkənɪŋ/ *n* 重新唤起; **a ~ of religious fervour** 宗教狂热的再度兴起

rebate¹ /'ri:beɪt/ *n* **1** (refund) 返款; **to qualify for a ~** 有资格获得返款; **we get a small ~ on our rent/rates/taxes** 我们得到一小笔房租返款/地方税退款/退税 **2** (discount) 折扣; **buyers are offered a cash ~** 购买者享受现金折扣

rebate² *n* (groove) 槽口

rebel

A /'rebl/ *n* **1** Mil 叛乱者; **armed ~s** 武装叛乱分子; **he joined the ~ forces** 他加入了叛军 **2** (in party, organization) 反对派; **a ~ delegate** 反对派代表 **3** (nonconformist) 反抗者; **he was a real ~ at school** 他以往在学校

里是个叛逆分子；**a ~ against sth.** 某事物的叛逆者；**a ~ streak** 叛逆的性格
B /rɪ'bel/ *vi* (*pres p etc.* **-ll-**) **1** Mil «*subject, province*» 反抗；**to ~ against sth.** 反抗某事物 **2** (against leadership) «*MP, delegate*» 持反对立场 **3** (against authority, parents) «*teenager, tearaway, artist*» 叛逆；**to ~ against sth./sb.** 对某事物/某人叛逆 **4** (protest) 嫌恶；**to ~ at sth.** 对某事物反感 **5** fig (show resistance) «*feet, arms*» 抗拒；**after six hours' walking, my legs began to ~** 走了 6 个小时路以后，我的腿开始不听使唤了；**his stomach ~led at the thought of more food** 一想到要吃更多的食物他就反胃

rebellion /rɪ'belɪən/ *n* [c and u] **1** Mil 叛乱；**a ~ against sth.** 对某事物的反叛；**to foment** *or* **stir up a ~** 煽动叛乱；**to crush** *or* **put down** *or* **quash a ~** 平定叛乱；**the spirit of ~** 反叛精神；**to rise in ~** 起来造反 **2** (against leader, party) 反对；**signs of incipient ~** 反对的初期迹象 **3** (against authority, parents) 叛逆

rebellious /rɪ'belɪəs/ *adj* **1** Mil 叛乱的 ‹*subjects, troops*› **2** (defiant) 叛逆的 ‹*child, behaviour*›；**my class was getting a bit ~** 我的班有点儿管不住了

rebelliously /rɪ'belɪəsli/ *adv* 反抗地

rebelliousness /rɪ'belɪəsnɪs/ *n* [u] 反抗

rebirth /ˌriː'bɜːθ/ *n* [u] **1** Relig 新生；**his spiritual ~** 他精神的重生 **2** (of a movement, an industry) 复兴；**the ~ of a defeated nation** 一个战败国的重新崛起

reboot /ˌriː'buːt/ *vt, vi* 重新启动

rebore
A /'riːbɔː(r)/ *n* 重镗
B /ˌriː'bɔː(r)/ *vt* 镗大…的孔径

reborn /ˌriː'bɔːn/ *adj* **1** Relig 重生的 ‹*person*›；**to be ~ into ...** 获得新生成为… **2** (revived) 复活的 ‹*person*›；复兴的 ‹*movement*›；**to be ~ as sth.** 复活为某物；**a ~ version of social democracy** 社会民主主义的翻版

rebound
A /rɪ'baʊnd/ *vi* **1** (bounce) «*ball, projectile*» 反弹 **2** (affect adversely) «*action, intervention, scheme*» 产生相反效果；**to ~ on sb.** 使某人自食其果 **3** (recover) «*prices, interest rates*» 回升；**the Share Index ~ed to show a twenty-point gain** 股票指数回升了 20 个点
B /'riːbaʊnd/ *n* **1** (of ball, stone) 反弹；**I hit/caught the ball on the ~** 我击中/接住了反弹回来的球；**to be on the ~** «*prices*» 在回升；colloq «*person*» 在失意之时；**I was on the ~ when I met Jack** 我在失意之时遇到了杰克；**I suppose I married her on the ~ from Jane** 我想我是在跟简分手后心灰意冷之时和她结的婚 **2** (ball, shot) 反弹球；**to hit/catch the ~** 打到/接到反弹球 **3** (increase) 回升；**a sharp ~ in prices** 价格的大幅反弹；**I think the paper industry is poised for a ~** 我认为造纸业就要复苏了；**on the ~** 正在复苏

rebrand /ˌriː'brænd/ *vt* 重塑 ‹*image*›；重塑…的形象 ‹*company*›

rebranding /riː'brændɪŋ/ *n* [u] 重塑形象

rebroadcast /ˌriː'brɔːdkɑːst, Amer -kæst/
A *n* **1** [u] (relayed signal) 转播 **2** [c] (repeated) 重播
B *vt* (*pt, pp* **rebroadcast** *or* **~ed**) **1** (relay message, programme) «*channel, station*» 转播 ‹*signal, message*›；**the programmes are ~ from a central transmitter** 这些节目是从一个中心发射台转播的 **2** (repeat) «*channel, station*» 重播 ‹*programme, message*›；**the series will be rebroadcast next year** 这部连续剧明年会重播

rebuff /rɪ'bʌf/
A *n* 断然拒绝；**to meet with a ~** 遭到断然拒绝
B *vt* 断然拒绝；**she politely ~ed his advances** 她礼貌而坚决地回绝了他的求欢

rebuild /ˌriː'bɪld/ *vt* (*pt, pp* **rebuilt** /ˌriː'bɪlt/) **1** (reconstruct, repair) 重建 ‹*factory, house, town, pier*› **2** (reassemble) 重新组装 ‹*engine, machine*› **3** (re-establish) 使…复原 ‹*system, structure, company, society*›；**he called on the people to ~ their country** 他号召人民重建祖国；**I had to ~ my whole life after my divorce** 离婚后我不得不重新安排整个生活；**to ~ one's confidence/health** 恢复信心/健康

rebuilding /ˌriː'bɪldɪŋ/ *n* [u] 重建

rebuke /rɪ'bjuːk/
A *n* 指责；**a mild/sharp/scathing/stern/stinging ~** 温和/尖锐/刻薄/严厉/尖刻的指责；**to administer** *or* **deliver** *or* **give a ~** 进行斥责；**to draw/receive a ~** 引起/受到非难
B *vt* 指责

rebus /'riːbəs/ *n* (*pl* **~es**) [通过图案猜词的] 字画谜

rebut /rɪ'bʌt/ *vt* (*pres p etc.* **-tt-**) 反驳 ‹*accusation, suggestion, criticism*›

rebuttal /rɪ'bʌtl/ *n* **1** [u] (negation) 反驳；**in ~ of ...** 作为对…的驳斥；**by way of ~** 作为反驳 **2** [c] (refutation) 反证；**to offer/make a ~** 提出/举反证

recalcitrance /rɪ'kælsɪtrəns/ *n* [u] formal 拒不服从

recalcitrant /rɪ'kælsɪtrənt/ *adj* formal 桀骜不驯的 ‹*child*›；难驯服的 ‹*animal*›

recalculate /ˌriː'kælkjʊleɪt/ *vt* 重新计算

recall
A /rɪ'kɔːl/ *vt* **1** (summon back) «*government, leader*» 召回 ‹*parliament, MP, ambassador, troops*› **2** (request the return of) «*library, librarian*» 收回 ‹*book, tape*›；«*manufacturer*» 召回 ‹*product*› **3** (order money to be repaid) «*bank*» 回收 ‹*loan, sum*› **4** (remember) 回忆起 ‹*incident, moment, occasion, name*›；**I ~ seeing them before** 我记得以前见过他们；**as I ~** 就我回忆；**you will ~ that ...** 你会回想起…；**'it was in 1972,' he ~ed** “那是在 1972 年，”他回忆道；**I ~ her as a lovely young girl** 我记得她是个可爱的小姑娘 **5** (bring to mind) «*music, incident, encounter*» 使人想起 ‹*occasion, episode*›；**a tune that ~ed the past for me** 一首让我想起过往的曲子 **6** (bring back) «*doctor*» 使…恢复 ‹*person, animal*›；**to ~ sb. to sth.** 使某人恢复到某状态；**to ~ sb. to life/consciousness** 使某人復活/苏醒
B /'riːkɔːl/ *n* **1** [c] (of parliament, ambassador) 召回；**the government ordered the ~ of its troops from the island** 政府命令其部队撤出该岛 **2** [c] (of books) 收回；(of product) 召回；**the library's termly ~ of books** 图书馆对图书的定期收回 **3** [c] (order for money to be returned) 还款令；**the bank is contemplating the ~ of its loan/funds** 银行正在考虑收回贷款/资金 **4** [u] (memory) 回忆；**powers of ~** 记忆力；**to have total ~ of sth.** 完全记得某事 **5** [c] (summons to troops) 归队号声；**to sound the ~** 吹响归队号 **6** [u] (undoing) 取消；**the past was gone and beyond ~** 过去的事情一去不复返了

recant /rɪ'kænt/
A *vt* 宣布放弃 ‹*belief, heresy*›
B *vi* 公开放弃

recantation /ˌriːkæn'teɪʃn/ *n* **1** [u] (repudiation) 公开放弃主张；**the philosopher was eventually driven to ~** 这位哲学家最终被迫放弃主张 **2** [c] (statement) 放弃信仰声明

recap /'riːkæp/ colloq
A *vi* (*pres p etc.* **-pp-**) 总结；**to ~ on what I have been saying ...** 概括一下我之前所说的…
B *vt* (*pres p etc.* **-pp-**) 总结
C *n* 概述

recapitalization /ˌriːkæpɪtəlaɪ'zeɪʃən/ *n* [u and c] 资产重组

recapitalize /ˌriː'kæpɪtəlaɪz/ *vt* 对…进行资产重组

recapitulate /ˌriːkə'pɪtʃʊleɪt/ formal
A *vt* 总结；**in his talk he ~d what the others had said** 他在讲话中概括了别人的发言
B *vi* 总结；**to ~ on sth.** 对某事进行总结

recapitulation /ˌriːkəpɪtʃʊ'leɪʃn/ *n* formal 概述；**she gave a brief ~ of the day's events** 她对当天发生的事情作了简要总结

recapture /ˌriː'kæptʃə(r)/
A *vt* **1** (catch) 再俘虏 ‹*prisoner*›；再捕获 ‹*animal*› **2** (recover) «*army*» 收复 ‹*town, position*›；«*candidate, party*» 重新获得 ‹*seat*› **3** fig (recreate) 使…再现 ‹*mood, period*›；**the book successfully ~s the atmosphere of this dramatic period** 这本书成功地再现了这个激动人心时期的气氛
B *n* [u] **1** (of prisoner) 再俘虏；(of animal) 再捕获 **2** (of town, position) 收复

recast /ˌriː'kɑːst, Amer -'kæst/ *vt* (*pt, pp* **recast**) **1** (reshape) 重新浇铸 ‹*metal, object*› **2** (rewrite) 改写 ‹*sentence, chapter*›；**he ~ the lecture as a radio talk** 他把讲座改写成广播讲话 **3** (change cast of) 重新安排…的演员阵容 ‹*film, series, part*› **4** (change role of) 改变…的角色；**to ~ sb. as sb.** 让…改演某角色 ‹*actor, actress*›

recce /'reki/ *n* Brit colloq 侦察；**to be on a ~** 在侦察

recd *abbr* **= received**

recede /rɪ'siːd/ *vi* **1** (retreat, go back) «*tide, footsteps*» 后退；**the flood waters ~d** 洪水退去了 **2** (disappear from view) «*lights, person, coast*» 渐渐远去；**to ~ into the distance** 消失在远处 **3** (slope backwards) 向后倾斜；**a receding chin/forehead** 向后缩的下巴/发际线移的前额 **4** fig (fade) «*memory, features*» 变得模糊；«*hopes*» 变得渺茫；«*threat, danger*» 逐渐減弱；**prospects of a reconciliation are receding** 和解的前景越来越渺茫 **5** «*hair, hairline*» 变秃

receipt /rɪ'siːt/
A *n* **1** [c] (proof of purchase) 收据；**a ~ for sth.** 某物的收据；**to sign a ~** 在收条上签字；**to give** *or* **make out** *or* **write out a ~** 开收据 **2** [u] (receiving) 收到；**within 30 days of ~** 收到后 30 天内；**to acknowledge ~ of sth.** 确认收到某物；**on ~ of sth.** 一俟收到某物；**to be in ~ of** 业已收到 ‹*income, benefits*›
B **receipts** *npl* (income) 进款；**net/gross ~s** 净/总收入
C *vt* «*shop, person*» 在…上注明收讫 ‹*bill*›

receipt book *n* 发票簿

receivable /rɪ'siːvəbl/
A **receivables** *npl* 应收款项
B *adj* 应收款的；**accounts/bills ~** 应收账款/账单

receive /rɪ'siːv/
A *vt* **1** (get) 收到 ‹*gift, letter, payment, reply*›；接到 ‹*phone call*›；得到 ‹*information, support*›；接受 ‹*prize, advice, help*›；**he ~d 50 enquiries after advertising the job** 登出招聘广告后，有 50 人次向他咨询；**he ~d an award for bravery from the police service** 他因其勇敢行为受到警方嘉奖；**'~d with thanks'** (on receipt) “收悉，多谢”；**'all contributions gratefully ~d'** (on notice, letter) “捐助均已收到，我等不胜感激” **2** (sustain, undergo) 受 ‹*injury*›；遭受 ‹*blow, setback*›；接受 ‹*training, education*›；**he ~d a 30-year sentence** 他被判 30 年徒刑；**the event ~d wide press coverage** 该事件被新闻界广泛报道；**the film ~d its premiere in London** 该电影在伦敦首映；**the Bill will ~ its first reading today** 今天将对该法案进行第一次宣读 **3** (meet with) «*person, book, film, performance*» 受到 ‹*ovation, welcome*›；«*person*» 接受 ‹*congratulations, thanks*›；**I ~d a lot of criticism for that** 因为那件事我遭到许多批评；**the rulings have ~d widespread acceptance** 裁决受到广泛赞同；**she ~d hearty congratulations from the head teacher**

r

她受到了校长的衷心祝贺 **4** formal (welcome) 欢迎; **to be warmly ~d** 受到热烈欢迎; **the King ~d the French delegation/ambassador at his palace** 国王在宫中接见了法国代表团一行/大使; **I was ~d with open arms** 我受到了热情的欢迎 **5** (react to) 对…作出反应 ‹*performance, reform, suggestion, article*›; **how was the play ~d?** 这部戏反响如何？; **the play was well ~d by the critics** 这部戏得到了评论家的好评; **to be warmly ~d** 受到热心关注; **the package of reforms was positively ~d** 人们对整套改革方案反应积极; **to ~ sth. with sth.** 以某种态度对待某事物; **the statistics were ~d with concern** 人们对统计数据表示担忧 **6** (accept as member) 接纳…加入 ‹*person*›; **to be ~d into sth.** 获准加入 ‹*church, order*› **7** Radio, TV (pick up) 接收 ‹*programme, channel, signal*› **8** Radio, Telecom (hear) 收听到; **are you receiving me?** 你听到我的声音了吗？; **I'm receiving you loud and clear** 我能听到你的声音，又响亮又清晰 **9** esp Brit (buy illegally) 非法收购 ‹*jewellery, paintings*›; **to ~ stolen goods** 收购赃物 **10** Amer (in baseball) 接 ‹*ball*›

B *vi* **1** esp Brit (buy stolen goods) 收赃 **2** (in baseball) 接球

received /rɪˈsiːvd/ *adj* 公认的

Received: ~ Pronunciation *n* [u] Brit 标准发音 [以英格兰南部受过教育者的发音为基础]; **~ Standard** *n* Amer = **~ Pronunciation**; **r~ wisdom** *n* 普遍看法

receiver /rɪˈsiːvə(r)/ *n* **1** (of consignment, mail) 收件人; **who was the ~ of the parcel?** 包裹的收件人是谁？ **2** (telephone) 听筒; **to pick up/put down the ~** 拿起/放下听筒 **3** (equipment) 接收机; **a satellite ~** 卫星接收器 **4** Brit (legal official) **the (official) R~** 官方接管人 **5** Brit (of stolen goods) 收赃人

receiver dish *n* 碟型卫星天线

receivership /rɪˈsiːvəʃɪp/ *n* [u] Brit 破产接管; **to go into ~** 被破产接管

receiving /rɪˈsiːvɪŋ/

A *adj attrib* 收货的 ‹*department, office*›; **to be on the ~ end (of sth.)** colloq 成为（某事物的）承受者; **she got in a rage and I was on the ~ end** 她大发雷霆，我成了出气筒; **he was on the ~ end of a punch on the nose** 他鼻子上挨了一拳

B *n* [u] Brit 收赃

receiving: ~ blanket *n* Amer 婴儿浴巾; **~ clerk** ▸**p. 409** *n* 收货员; **~ line** *n* Amer 迎宾队列

recent /ˈriːsnt/ *adj* **1** (occurring recently) 不久前的 ‹*visit, event, invention*›; **on a ~ trip to France** 在前一阵去法国旅行时; **she's quite a ~ acquaintance/arrival** 她是不久前认识的/她初来乍到 **2** (latest, new) 最新的 ‹*development*›; 最近的 ‹*weeks, months*›; **in ~ times/years** 近来/近年; **to be a ~ graduate** 刚毕业

recently /riːˈsntli/ *adv* 不久前; **I saw them only ~** 我才见过他们; **a ~ discovered phenomenon** 最近发现的现象; **as ~ as Monday/yesterday/last week** 刚刚在周一/昨天/上周; **until (quite) ~** 直到最近; **it was quite** *or* **only ~ that we last met** 我们最近一次见面也就是不久前的事; **I've not heard from them ~** 我最近没有收到他们的来信

receptacle /rɪˈseptəkl/ *n* 容器

reception /rɪˈsepʃn/ *n* **1** [u] (formal welcoming) 欢迎 **2** [u] (admission) 接纳; **her ~ into the Church** 她的加入基督教 **3** [c] (response) 接待; **to get** *or* **be given a favourable/hostile ~** 受到友好的/怀有敌意的接待; **the film got a favourable ~** 影片收到良好的反响; **they gave us a great ~** 他们热情地接待了我们 **4** [c] (area in hotel, office) 接待处 **5** [c] (gathering, social occasion) 招待会; **an official/a wedding ~** 正式招待会/婚宴; **to attend a ~** 出席招待会; **to give/hold/host a ~** 举行/举办/主持招待会; **a ~ for sb.** 为某人举办的招待会 **6** [u] (of signal) 接收; **good/strong/poor/weak ~** 接收信号好/强/差/弱

reception: ~ area *n* 接待大厅; **~ camp** *n* 难民收容营; **~ centre** *n* Brit [苦难者的] 救助站; **~ class** *n* Brit [幼儿的] 预备班; **~ committee** *n* 接待委员会; **~ desk** *n* Brit 接待处

receptionist /rɪˈsepʃənɪst/ ▸**p. 409** *n* 接待员; **the ~ fixed a dental appointment for me** 前台服务员为我做好了牙科预约

reception room *n* **1** (in house) 会客室 **2** (in hotel) 活动室

receptive /rɪˈseptɪv/ *adj* 接受力强的 ‹*person, mind*›; 乐于接受的 ‹*attitude*›; **when he's in a more ~ mood** 在他更能听得进去时; **to be ~ to sth.** 能迅速接受某事物

receptiveness /rɪˈseptɪvnɪs/, **receptivity** /ˌriːsepˈtɪvəti/ *ns* [u] 乐于接受; **I wish she would show a bit more ~** 但愿她能更包容一些; **~ to sth.** 对某事物的接纳

receptor /rɪˈseptə(r)/ *n* 感受器

recess /rɪˈses, Amer ˈriːses/

A *n* **1** Jur, Pol 暂停; **the summer ~** 暑假; **to be in ~** «*parliament*» 正在休会; «*court*» 正在休庭 **2** Amer (class break) 课间休息 **3** (alcove) 凹处; **a ~ in the wall** 壁龛 **4** (hollow space) 洞

B **recesses** *npl* (remote places) 隐秘处; **in the ~es of her mind/memory** fig 在她内心/记忆深处

C *vt* **1** (set into wall or surface) 把…放进凹处; **~ed shelves/windows/ceiling lights** 嵌入墙壁的架子/窗户/天花板吊灯 **2** Amer (interrupt) 使…暂停 ‹*meeting, hearing*›

D *vi* Amer 暂停

recess appointment *n* Amer [总统在参议院休会期间作出的] 休会任命

recession /rɪˈseʃn/ *n* 衰退; **a world ~** 世界经济衰退; **to go into/be in ~** 陷入/处于衰退; **a deep ~** 严重衰退

recessional /rɪˈseʃənl/

A *n* 退场赞美诗

B *adj* formal 退场的 ‹*hymn*›

recessionary /rɪˈseʃənri, Amer -neri/ *adj* 经济衰退的 ‹*period, conditions*›; 引起衰退的 ‹*pressure, effect*›

recessive /rɪˈsesɪv/ *adj* 隐性的; **~ gene** 隐性基因

recharge /ˌriːˈtʃɑːdʒ/ *vt* 给…充电; **to ~ one's mobile/camera battery** 给手机/相机电池充电; **to ~ one's batteries** fig 养精蓄锐

rechargeable /ˌriːˈtʃɑːdʒəbl/ *adj* 可充电的; **~ batteries** 充电电池

recidivism /rɪˈsɪdɪvɪzəm/ *n* [u] formal 累犯

recidivist /rɪˈsɪdɪvɪst/ *n* formal 累犯; **~ rate** 屡犯率

recipe /ˈresəpi/ *n* **1** (list of ingredients) 食谱; **a ~ for sth.** 某食品的做法 **2** (means of achieving) 诀窍; **a ~ for business success** *or* **for succeeding in business** 做生意成功的秘诀; **a ~ for disaster** 灾祸之因

recipe book *n* 烹饪书

recipient /rɪˈsɪpɪənt/ *n* 接受者; **welfare ~** 接受福利救济的人; **a worthy ~ of this generous prize** 这个丰厚奖品当之无愧的得主

reciprocal /rɪˈsɪprəkl/

A *adj* **1** (mutual) 互惠的 ‹*help, relations, trade, agreement*›; **a strong ~ affection** 彼此间强烈的爱慕之情; **~ obligations and duties** 对等的责任和义务 **2** Ling 相互的; **~ pronouns** 相互代词

B *n* 倒数

reciprocally /rɪˈsɪprəkli/ *adv* **1** (mutually) 对等地 ‹*help, apply*›; **~ agreed trading regulations** 双方同意遵守的贸易规则; **a ~ damaging relationship** 互相损害的关系 **2** Math (inversely) 互逆地

reciprocate /rɪˈsɪprəkeɪt/

A *vt* 回报 ‹*feeling, help, smile, wish*›; 互给 ‹*love*›; **her compliments/invitations were not ~d** 她的问候/邀请没有得到回应; **she did not ~ his affection** 她对他的爱慕无动于衷

B *vi* **1** (respond in kind) 回报; **after all their invitations I think we should ~** 在他们邀请我们这么多次后，我想我们应该回请他们 **2** Mech «*engine, valve*» 往复运动; **a reciprocating blade** 往复式叶片

reciprocating engine *n* 往复式发动机

reciprocation /rɪˌsɪprəˈkeɪʃn/ *n* [u] 回报

reciprocity /ˌresɪˈprɒsəti/ *n* [u] 互惠; **there is no ~ of trade agreements between the two nations** 两国之间没有互惠贸易协议

recital /rɪˈsaɪtl/ *n* **1** [c] (performance) [个人或小组举行的] 表演会; **to give a piano ~** 举办钢琴独奏会; **in ~** 在表演会上; **a song/dance/poetry ~** 独唱会/独舞会/诗歌朗诵会 **2** [u] (action of reciting) 吟诵 **3** [c] (account) 叙述; **a long ~ of complaints** 连篇累牍的抱怨

recitation /ˌresɪˈteɪʃn/ *n* **1** [u] (in theatre) 朗诵; (in school) 背诵 **2** [c] (passage, verse) 背诵的诗文

recitative /ˌresɪtəˈtiːv/ *n* **1** [u] (declamation) 宣叙调 **2** [c] (passage, part) 叙唱部

recite /rɪˈsaɪt/

A *vt* **1** (read aloud from memory) 背诵 ‹*poem, passage*›; **the poet ~d his latest work before an invited audience** 诗人为特邀观众朗诵了他的新作 **2** (list) 列举 ‹*facts, list*›; 历数 ‹*litany, grievances*›; **he ~d the names of the European capitals** 他一一说出了欧洲国家首都的名称

B *vi* 背诵

reckless /ˈreklɪs/ *adj* 鲁莽的 ‹*gambler, behaviour, move, assault*›; 胡乱的 ‹*spender, extravagance*›; **~ driving** 莽撞驾驶; **it was very ~ of her to go out alone at night** 她夜里独自外出太鲁莽了; **to be ~ of the dangers/consequences** 不顾及危险/后果

recklessly /ˈreklɪsli/ *adv* 鲁莽地 ‹*gamble, behave, rush, drive, impetuous*›; 胡乱地 ‹*spend*›; **she was ~ determined to win** 她不顾一切地下决心要赢

recklessness /ˈreklɪsnɪs/ *n* [u] 鲁莽; **the ~ of his schemes/spending** 他计划的草率/花钱的大手大脚

reckon /ˈrekən/

A *vt* **1** (consider) 认为; **to ~ (that) ...** 认为…; **to be ~ed (to be) sth.** 被认为是某事物; **the region is ~ed to be uninhabitable** 该地区被认为不适宜居住; **to be ~ed among sb./sth.** 被认为属于某类人/事物; **he is ~ed among our best salesmen** 他被看作是我们最好的推销员之一 **2** esp Brit colloq (think) 觉得; **to ~ (that) ...** 觉得…; **he'll be famous one day; what do you ~?** 他有朝一日会出名的，你觉得呢？ **3** (estimate) 估计; **what do you ~ our chances of survival are?** 依你看我们活下来的可能性有多大？; **I ~ he's about 50** 我估计他在 50 岁上下; **to be ~ed to do sth.** 据估计要做某事; **the journey was ~ed to take about two hours** 路上估计要花大约两小时 **4** (calculate accurately) 计算; **to be ~ed at sth.** 经计算为某数字; **the number of part-time workers is ~ed at two million** 兼职工作者人数共计 200 万; **to ~ (that) ...** 计算出…; **they ~ that their profits are down by 20%** 他们算下来利润下降了 20% **5** Brit colloq (expect) 希望; **to ~ to do sth.** 希望做某事; **I ~ to leave here tomorrow** 我希望明天可以离开这里 **6** Brit colloq (rate highly) 看好 ‹*person, odds*›; **I don't ~ your chances of success** 我认为你不太可能成功

B *vi* **1** (calculate) 计算; **~ing from tomorrow** 从明天算起 **2** (estimate) 估计; **there were about forty, I ~** 大约有 40 个，我估计 **3** esp Brit colloq (think) 认为; **it's worth a lot of**

money, I ～ 我想，这东西很值钱；**they'll never find out — you ～?** 他们永远也不会发现——是吗？

Phrasal verbs

- **reckon on** *vt* 1 [**～ on sth.**] (expect, take into account) 期待；**they had ～ed on a day or two more of privacy** 他们希望多一两天的清静；**he's ～ing on a big reward** 他指望能得到一大笔酬金；**they hadn't ～ed on a visit from her** 他们没料到她来访；**to ～ on doing sth.** 希望做某事；**I wasn't ～ing on having to stay** 我不想留下；**he hadn't ～ed on anyone coming to check up on him** 他没指望会有人来找他核实情况 2 [**～ on sb./sth.**] (rely on) 依赖；**to ～ on sb. to do sth.** 指望某人做某事；**to ～ on sb.** *or* **sb.'s doing sth.** 指望某人做某事
- **reckon up** esp Brit
  A *vi* 结算
  B *vt* [**～ sth. up. ～ up sth.**] 结算；**to ～ up the bill** 结账
- **reckon with** *vt* [**～ with sb./sth.**] 1 (consider as important) 重视；**she's a person to be ～ed with** 她这个人不可小觑；**to be a force to be ～ed with** 是一股不可小看的力量 2 (take into account) 考虑；**you've still got John to ～ with** 你还有约翰可以考虑；**to ～ with doing sth.** 考虑做某事；**I didn't ～ with bumping into him** 我没料到会撞见他
- **reckon without** *vt* [**～ without sb./sth.**] esp Brit 没有考虑；**she had ～ed without the fact that ...** 她没考虑到…的事实

reckoner /ˈrekənə(r)/ *n* = **ready reckoner**

reckoning /ˈrekənɪŋ/ *n* 1 [c and u] (estimation, opinion) 估计；**by my ～** 据我估计；**in your ～** 照你推测 2 [u] (calculation) 计算；**the ～ of debts/accounts** 债务/账目的核算 3 [c and u] (retribution) 报应；**the day of ～** 遭报应的日子；**there's bound to be a day of ～ for him/them** 他/他们总有一天会遭报应的；**to bring sb./to come into the ～** 使某人遭报应/受到惩罚

reclaim /rɪˈkleɪm/ *vt* 1 (for cultivation, building) 开垦 ‹*marshland, desert, waste ground*›；**to ～ an area from the sea/jungle** 从大海/丛林里开辟出一块地 2 (recycle) 回收利用 ‹*plastic, glass*› 3 (recover) 拿回 ‹*possessions, luggage*›；**some customers tried to ～ their money** 一些顾客试图要回他们的钱

reclaimable /rɪˈkleɪməbl/ *adj* 1 (for cultivation, building) 可开垦的 ‹*marshland, desert, waste ground*› 2 (recyclable) 可回收的 ‹*glass, metal*› 3 (recuperable) 可收回的 ‹*tax, expenses, money*›

reclamation /ˌrekləˈmeɪʃn/ *n* [u] 1 (for cultivation, building) 开垦 2 (recycling) 回收

recline /rɪˈklaɪn/
A *vt* 1 (tilt backwards) 使…后倾 ‹*seat*› 2 (rest, lean) 使…斜靠 ‹*back*›；**she ～d her head on his shoulder** 她把头靠在他的肩上
B *vi* 1 (tilt backwards) 后倾；**I couldn't get the seat to ～** 我无法让座椅向后倾斜 2 (lie back) 倚靠；**to ～ on a pillow/sofa** 斜靠在枕头/沙发上

reclining /rɪˈklaɪnɪŋ/ *adj* 1 (able to tilt) 可后仰的；**she fell asleep in a ～ chair/seat** 她在躺椅/靠椅中睡着了 2 (lying back) 斜躺着的；**a ～ figure/nude** 侧卧人像/裸体像

recluse /rɪˈkluːs/ *n* 隐居者；**he's something of a ～** 他有点像个隐士

reclusive /rɪˈkluːsɪv/ *adj* 隐居的；**she's becoming increasingly ～** 她越来越离群索居

recoat
A *vt* /ˌriːˈkəʊt/ 重新涂刷
B *n* /ˈriːkəʊt/ 重刷的涂料层

recognition /ˌrekəɡˈnɪʃn/ *n* [u] 1 (identification) 认出；**beyond** *or* **out of all ～** 无法辨认；**they've changed the town beyond ～** 他们把城市弄得面目全非 2 (realization) 认识；**there is a growing ～ that ...** 越来越多的人认识到… 3 (acknowledgement) 承认；**to gain international ～** 获得国际承认；**to receive** *or* **win ～ for sth.** 在…上获得承认 ‹*work, achievement, contribution*›；**in ～ of ...** 作为对…的承认 4 (by a computer) 识别；**voice ～** 语音识别 5 (appreciation) 赞誉；**to give** *or* **grant sb. ～** 给予某人表彰；**general/universal/growing/official/public ～** 普遍的/一致的/日益增加的/官方的/公众的赞誉；**～ for sth.** 对某事的赞赏；**in ～ of sth.** 作为对某事的表彰

recognizable /ˈrekəɡnaɪzəbl, ˌrekəɡˈnaɪzəbl/ *adj* 可认出的 ‹*person, face, statue*›；可辨认的 ‹*picture, symptoms*›；**～ signs of anxiety** 明显的焦虑迹象

recognizably /ˌrekəɡˈnaɪzəbli, ˈrekəɡnaɪzəbli/ *adv* 可辨别地；**the writing is ～ contemporary** 这篇文章显然是当代的

recognize /ˈrekəɡnaɪz/ *vt* 1 (identify) 认出 ‹*voice, friend, tune, quotation*›；**did you ～ each other?** 你们认出对方了吗？；**the shopkeeper ～d him as a local vagrant** 店主认出他是当地的一个流浪汉 2 (identify from knowledge) 辨别 ‹*symptom, sign*› 3 (officially acknowledge) 承认 ‹*person, government, claim, right*›；**to ～ that ...** 承认…；**to be ～d as ...** 被认定是 ‹*heir, owner*›；**to be ～d by law** 受到法律承认；**to ～ sb.'s claim to ownership** 承认某人的物权要求 4 (show appreciation of) «*person, government, firm*» 赞赏 ‹*talent, person*›；**her services to the nation have now been ～d** 她为国家做的贡献现在得到了嘉奖 5 (acknowledge) 认识到 ‹*problem, phenomenon*›；**we ～d it as a genuine need** 我们意识到这是个真实的需求；**they refuse to ～ that they have done wrong** 他们拒不承认他们做错了；**nobody had ～d his artistic gift** 没人赏识他的艺术天分

recognized /ˈrekəɡnaɪzd/ *adj* 1 (acknowledged) 公认的 ‹*leader, expert, technique*›；**a widely/universally/generally ～ authority** 广泛/一致/普遍公认的权威；**she's a ～ expert in the field** 她是这个领域内公认的专家 2 (granted status) 认可的 ‹*representative, supplier, dealer*›

recoil
A /rɪˈkɔɪl/ *vi* 1 (jump back) «*person*» 后退；**to ～ from** *or* **at sth.** 躲开某物；**to ～ in horror/disgust** 恐惧/厌恶地往后缩 2 (feel revulsion at) 畏缩；**to ～ at** *or* **from sth.** 对某事畏缩不前 3 (jerk backwards) «*gun, rifle*» 反冲 4 (rebound) «*spring*» 反弹；**the muscle has the ability to ～** 肌肉有弹力 5 (affect adversely) **to ～ on sb.** 报应到某人头上
B /ˈriːkɔɪl/ *n* 1 (of gun) 后坐；(of spring) 弹回 2 (revulsion) 畏缩；**～ from sth.** 对某物的畏惧

recollect /ˌrekəˈlekt/
A *vt* 回忆起 ‹*number, date, childhood*›；**I can ～ meeting the Governor** 我能回忆起见州长的情形；**I ～ that she was veiled** 我记得她戴着面纱
B *vi* 回忆；**as far as I ～** 据我回忆

recollection /ˌrekəˈlekʃn/ *n* formal 1 [u] (ability to remember) 记忆力；**she has no ～ of it** 她不记得这件事了；**to the best of my ～** 如果我没记错的话；**within my ～** 在我的记忆中 2 [c] (memory) 往事

recommence /ˌriːkəˈmens/ *vt, vi* 重新开始

recommend /ˌrekəˈmend/ *vt* 1 (commend, suggest) 推荐 ‹*doctor, film, book*›；**to ～ sb. for a job** 推荐某人做一份工作；**she comes highly ～ed** 她深受好评；**a policy that is to be ～ed** 受推崇的政策 2 (advise) 建议 ‹*closure, reduction, measure*›；**the scheme is ～ed for approval** 这个计划被提请审批 3 (favour) 使…受欢迎 ‹*idea, place*›；**the strategy has much to ～ it** 这个策略有很多可取之处；**the hotel has little to ～ it** 这个旅馆毫无可取之处；**her reputation for laziness did not ～ her to potential employers** 她懒惰的名声使她找不到雇主 4 archaic (entrust) «*priest, father*» 托付 ‹*oneself, one's soul*›；**he ～ed the child to her care** 他把孩子托付给她照料

recommendable /ˌrekəˈmendəbl/ *adj* 可推荐的

recommendation /ˌrekəmenˈdeɪʃn/ *n* 1 [u] (commendation, suggestion) 推荐；**on the ～ of ...** 经…的推荐；**to speak in ～ of sb./sth.** 口头推荐某人/某事物 2 [c] (official suggestion) 建议；**to make a ～** 提出建议；**he was sentenced to life imprisonment with a ～ that he serve at least 30 years** 他被判无期徒刑，并建议至少服刑 30 年 3 [c] (letter, statement) 推荐信；**to write sb. a ～** 给某人写推荐信 4 [c] (good quality, advantage) 可取之处

recommended: ～ daily amount *n* 建议每日摄取量；**～ reading** *n* [u] 推荐阅读书目；**～ retail price** *n* 建议零售价

recommit /ˌriːkəˈmɪt/ *vt* (*pres p etc.* **-tt-**) 1 (commit again) «*offender*» 重犯 ‹*offence, crime*› 2 (promise again) 再次承诺 ‹*funds*›；**to ～ oneself to sth./to doing sth.** 再次承诺致力于某事/做某事

recompense /ˈrekəmpens/
A *n* [u] 1 formal (reward) 报酬；**as (a) ～ for ...** 作为对…的酬劳；**in ～ for sth.** 为酬谢某事 2 (compensation) 赔偿；**～ for ...** 对…的补偿
B *vt* 1 formal (reward) 酬报；**to ～ sb. for his/her work/trouble/efforts** 酬谢某人的工作/费心/努力 2 (compensate) 赔偿 ‹*damage, loss*› 3 (make amends to) 补偿；**he was ～d for the wasted time** 他浪费的时间得到了补偿

reconcilable /ˈrekənsaɪləbl/ *adj pred* 1 (able to be reunited) 可和好的 ‹*couple*› 2 (able to be resolved) 可调解的 ‹*differences, disagreements*› 3 (compatible) 可调和的 ‹*ideas*›；**those two views/opinions are quite ～** 那两种见解/意见很容易协调；**to be ～ with sth.** 与某事物可达成一致

reconcile /ˈrekənsaɪl/ *vt* 1 (reunite) 使和好；**to be** *or* **become ～d with sb.** 与某人和解；**to ～ sb. with sb.** 使某人与某人和好 2 (make compatible) 使…一致 ‹*views, approaches*›；**I'm trying to ～ her testimony with the others'** 我正试图使她的证词与其他人的证词相符 3 (persuade to accept) «*salary, compensation*» 使…将就 ‹*person, oneself*›；**to ～ sb. to sth./to doing sth.** 使某人无奈接受某事物/做某事；**to become ～d to sth./to doing sth.** 甘于接受某事物/做某事 4 (resolve) «*institution, department*» 调停 ‹*disagreement*›；«*people*» 调解 ‹*quarrel*›；**we have ～d our differences** 我们已消除分歧 5 Fin 核对 ‹*accounts*›

reconciliation /ˌrekənˌsɪlɪˈeɪʃn/ *n* 1 [c and u] (of people) 和好；**～ with sb.** 与某人的和解；**～ between ... and ...** …和…之间的和解 2 [u] (of ideas, attitudes, beliefs) 协调；**the ～ of conflicting ideas/approaches** 冲突的观念/方法之间的调和 3 Fin (of accounts) 对账

recondite /ˈrekəndaɪt/ *adj* formal 深奥的 ‹*subject, area*›；写艰深题材的 ‹*writer*›；晦涩难懂的 ‹*book, discussion*›

recondition /ˌriːkənˈdɪʃn/ *vt* 修复；**a ～ed engine** 经过翻新的发动机；**a ～ed refrigerator/washing machine** 修好的冰箱/洗衣机；**～ed toner cartridges** 再生硒鼓

reconnaissance /rɪˈkɒnɪsns/ *n* [c and u] 侦察；**aerial ～** 空中侦察；**to carry out** *or* **conduct ～** 进行侦察；**to be on ～** 在侦察；**～ of ...** 对…的侦察

reconnoitre Brit, **reconnoiter** Amer /ˌrekəˈnɔɪtə(r)/ *vt, vi* 侦察；**to send sb. out to ～** 派某人出去侦察

reconquer /ˌriːˈkɒŋkə(r)/ *vt* 再征服

reconquest /ˌriːˈkɒŋkwest/ *n* 再征服

reconsider /ˌriːkənˈsɪdə(r)/ *vt, vi* 重新考虑

reconsideration /ˌriːkənsɪdəˈreɪʃn/ *n* [u] 重新考虑

reconstitute /ˌriːˈkɒnstɪtjuːt, Amer -tuːt/ *vt* **1** (reorganize) 改组 ‹*committee, cabinet*› **2** (restore) 使…复原 ‹*dried milk, powdered soup, dried yeast*›; **~d food** 复水食品

reconstruct /ˌriːkənˈstrʌkt/ *vt* **1** (rebuild) «*builder, company*» 重建 ‹*building, shop, block*›; **the ~ed palace buildings** 修复的宫殿 **2** (reorganize) 改革 ‹*system, policy*› **3** (recreate) «*historian, writer*» 再现 ‹*event, atmosphere*›; **the police plan to ~ the crime** 警方打算重现犯罪情形

reconstruction /ˌriːkənˈstrʌkʃn/ *n* **1** [u] (rebuilding) 重建 **2** [c] (re-enactment) 再现; **police staged a ~ of the crime** 警方放映了重现犯罪情形的短片 **3** [c] (model) 重构物; **a ~ of the skeleton of a brontosaurus** 雷龙的骨骼复原模型 **4** [u] (reorganization) 重组; **a system badly in need of ~** 亟待改革的制度

reconstructive /ˌriːkənˈstrʌktɪv/ *adj attrib* 整形的; **he had ~ surgery on his damaged right knee** 他损坏的右膝盖做了整形手术; **a ~ surgeon** 整形外科医生

reconvene /ˌriːkənˈviːn/ *vt, vi* 再次召开; **let's ~ (the meeting) after lunch** 我们午餐后继续开会吧

r

record

A /ˈrekɔːd, Amer ˈrekərd/ *n* **1** (of facts, proceedings) 记录; (of events) 记载; **to have a ~ of sth.** 有某事物的记录; **to make a ~ of sth.** 记下某事物; **to keep a ~ of sth.** 记下 ‹*orders, calls, expenses*›; **since ~s began** 自从有文字记载以来; **official/parish ~s** 官方/教区记录; **public ~s** 公共档案; **medical/dental ~s** 病历/牙科病历; **for the ~** (in order that sth. be noted) 供记录; (emphasizing a statement) 必须指出; **just for the ~, did you really do it?** 仅供记录，你真的那么干了吗？; **for the ~, the statement is wrong** 必须指出的是，该说法是错的; **off the ~** 非正式的; **to say sth. off the ~** 私下说某事; **off the ~, I think ...** 随便说说，我觉得…; **an off-the-~ briefing** 简报会; **on ~** 在历史记录中; **the hottest summer on ~** 有历史记载以来最热的夏天; **to be on (the) ~** 被记录在案; **to put** *or* **place sth. on (the) ~** 将某事物记录在案; **I would like to place on ~ my sincere thanks** 我要郑重致谢; **to be/go on (the) ~ (as saying sth.)** 公开表态（说某事物）; **he is on ~ as saying that the tax is unfair on the poor** 他公开表示这项税收对穷人不公平; **to put** *or* **set the ~ straight** 澄清事实; **a matter of ~** 有案可查的事 **2** (of student, employee) 履历; (of group, organization) 历史; **she had a good ~ at school** 她学业成绩很好; **sb.'s past ~** 某人的过去; **sb.'s ~ as sth.** 某人从事某工作的履历; **she has a distinguished ~ as a diplomat** 作为外交官，她有着出色的履历; **an academic ~** 学业成绩; **a service/war/safety ~** 服役记录/战绩/安全记录; **a ~ for** *or* **of sth.** 某事物的记录; **the airline has a poor ~ for safety** 这家航空公司飞行安全记录很差; **a child with a poor ~ of school attendance** 经常缺课的孩子; **he has an impressive ~ of achievement** 他取得了令人瞩目的成就; **sb.'s/sth.'s ~ on sth.** 某人/某事物在某方面的记录; **to have a good ~ on sth.** 在…方面有良好记录 ‹*human rights, recycling, safety*› **3** (disc) 唱片; **a pop/jazz ~** 流行乐/爵士乐唱片; **to make** *or* **cut** *or* **record a ~** 灌唱片; **to put on** *or* **play a ~** 放唱片; **change the ~!** colloq 换个话题吧！ **4** (in sport) 最好成绩; (of temperature, speed, output) 最高纪录; **an all-time ~** 历史最佳纪录; **the long-jump/100-metres ~** 跳远/100米跑的纪录; **a speed ~** 最高速度纪录; **the ~ for sth.** 某事的最佳纪录; **what's the ~ for the 100 metres?** 100米跑的最好成绩是多少？; **to break/beat a ~** 打破/超越纪录; **to set/hold a ~** 创造/保持纪录; **~ score/profits** 创纪录的得分/收益; **to reach/be at a ~ high/low** 达到/处于最高/最低纪录; **to do sth. in ~ time** 在最短时间内做某事 **5** (of criminal) 前科; **to have a ~** 有前科; **to have no ~** *or* **a clean ~** 没有前科; **to have a ~ as long as sb.'s arm** colloq 有一长串前科记录 **6** Comput 记录

B /rɪˈkɔːd/ *vt* **1** (keep account of) 记录; **to ~ the minutes (of a meeting)** 做会议记录; **to ~ that ...** 记下…; **his job is to ~ how politicians vote on major issues** 他的工作是记录政要们是如何就重大问题进行投票的; **to ~ the way in which ...** 记录…的方式 **2** (on tape, video, CD) 录下 ‹*speech*›; 为…录制 ‹*artist*›; 录制 ‹*music, programme, film, interview, game, race, CD, DVD*›; **to ~ sb./sth. on sth.** 在某物上录下某人/某事物; **the incident was ~ed on video/on a mobile phone** 这事件已用录像/移动电话摄录下来; **to ~ sth. from sth.** 从某处录下某事物; **to ~ sb./sth. doing sth.** 录下某人/某物做某事; **I ~ed her playing the piano** 我录下了她的钢琴演奏 **3** (register) 显示 ‹*temperature, speed, time, pressure*› **4** (reveal) «*voice, face, expression*» 流露出 ‹*emotion*› **5** (state officially) «*coroner*» 宣布 ‹*verdict*›

C /rɪˈkɔːd/ *vi* **1** (copy) «*person, tape*» 录音; «*person, video*» 录像 **2** (be copied) «*song, programme*» 被录制; **her voice ~s very well** 她的声音录下来很好听 **3** (tape, video) 录制节目; **to ~ live** 现场录制节目

record /ˈrekɔːd, Amer ˈrekərd/**: ~ book** *n* 记录簿; **to go down in the ~ books as ...** 作为…载入史册; **~-breaker** *n* (person) 打破纪录者; (thing) 创纪录的事物; **~-breaking** *adj* 打破纪录的 ‹*effort, pace, event, attempt*›; **~ button** /rɪˈkɔːd ˌbʌtn/ *n* (on tape recorder) 录音键; (on video recorder) 录像键; **~ card** *n* 记录卡; **~-changer** *n* 自动换片装置; **~ deck** *n* 唱机转盘装置

recorded /rɪˈkɔːdɪd/ *adj* **1** (on tape, CD, DVD) 录制的 ‹*speech, concert, image, interview*› **2** (documented) 记录在案的 ‹*history, proceedings, details*›; **it is a matter of ~ fact that ...** 有案可查的事实是…; **the largest earthquake in ~ history** 有历史记载以来最大的一次地震

recorded delivery *n* [u] Brit 挂号邮寄; **to send sth. (by) ~** 挂号邮寄某物

recorder /rɪˈkɔːdə(r)/ *n* **1** (apparatus for recording) (sound) 录音机; (picture) 录像机; **a voice ~** 录音装置 **2** ▸ **p. 395** Mus (instrument) 竖笛; **to play the ~** 吹竖笛; **a tenor/bass ~** 次中音/低音竖笛 **3** Brit (part-time judge) 刑事法院法官 **4** (person who keeps records) 记录员; **the official ~ of local history** 地方史记录官

record: ~ head /rɪˈkɔːd/ *n* 记录磁头; **~-holder** /ˈrekɔːd/ *n* 记录保持者

recording /rɪˈkɔːdɪŋ/ *n* **1** [u] (action) 录制; **sound-/video-~** 录音/录像; **a ~ engineer/artist/studio** 录音工程师/唱片艺人/录音室; **the ~ of sth.** 某物的录制 **2** [c] (recorded image, sound) 录制的音像; **a tape-~** 一段磁带录音; **a video-~** 一段录像; **a ~ of sth.** 某物的录制品; **I'm going to make a ~ of the next tune** 我准备把下一支曲子录下来; **a ~ on sth.** 录在某物上的东西; **a ~ of the concert on CD/DVD** 录制在CD/DVD上的音乐会; **to play a ~** 播放录制品

recording head *n* 记录磁头

record /ˈrekɔːd/**: ~ label** *n* 唱片品牌; **~ library** *n* 唱片租借馆; **~-player** *n* 唱机; **~ sleeve** *n* 唱片套; **~s office** *n* 档案室; **~ token** *n* 唱片礼券

recount /rɪˈkaʊnt/ *vt* 详细叙述 ‹*story, adventures*›

re-count

A /ˈriːkaʊnt/ *n* 重新计算

B /ˌriːˈkaʊnt/ *vt* 重新计算 ‹*votes, money*›

recoup /rɪˈkuːp/ *vt* **1** (regain) 收回 ‹*loss, cost*›; 恢复 ‹*strength*› **2** (reimburse) 补偿 ‹*person, company*›; **I needed to do sth. to ~ myself for these losses** 我需要做些事情来弥补自己这些损失

recourse /rɪˈkɔːs/ *n* **1** [u] (resort) 求助; **to have ~ to sth.** 诉诸某物; **without ~ to ...** 无须求助于… **2** [c] (option) 手段; **surgery may be the only ~** 手术也许是唯一的办法

recover /rɪˈkʌvə(r)/

A *vt* **1** (get back) 追回 ‹*document, jewellery, vehicle, debt*›; 收复 ‹*territory*›; **they ~ed the car from the river** 他们从河里把汽车捞上来了 **2** (regain) 恢复 ‹*faculties, health, sight*›; **to ~ one's confidence/strength/breath** 恢复信心/体力/正常呼吸; **to ~ consciousness** 苏醒过来 **3** (recoup) 挽回 ‹*expenses, loss, time*›; **the right to ~ damages** 获得损害赔偿的权利 **4** (reclaim for use) 利用 ‹*acres, area*›; **to ~ land from the sea** 填海造地 **5** (regain control of) 重新获得 ‹*balance, peace of mind*›; **to ~ one's composure, to ~ oneself** 使自己平静下来 **6** (retrieve) 回收 ‹*space capsule*›; 找回 ‹*body*›

B *vi* **1** (recuperate) «*person*» 康复; **to ~ from ...** 从…中康复; **he fell into a coma and did not ~** 他昏迷后再也没醒过来 **2** (regain equilibrium) «*person, family, community*» 恢复正常; **to ~ from ...** 从…中恢复正常 **3** (regain financial strength) «*economy, stock market*» 复苏; «*currency, shares*» 回升

re-cover /ˌriːˈkʌvə(r)/ *vt* 给…换新面子

recoverable /rɪˈkʌvərəbl/ *adj* **1** (of compensation, money) 能收回的 ‹*deposits, assets, debts*›; **which are the ~ losses?** 哪些是可挽回的损失？ **2** (of mineral reserves) 可开采的 ‹*reserves, gas*›

recovered /rɪˈkʌvəd/ *adj* 康复的; **she isn't fully** *or* **completely ~** 她尚未完全康复

recovery /rɪˈkʌvəri/ *n* **1** [c and u] (recuperation) 康复; **~ from sth.** 从某疾病中的康复; **to make a ~** 复元; **she's well on the way** *or* **road to ~** 她正在顺利康复; **best wishes for a speedy ~** 祝早日康复; **to be past** *or* **beyond ~** 病入膏肓 **2** [u] (retrieval) 找回; **the ~ of the stolen property** 赃物的追回 **3** [c] (of a vehicle, aircraft) 回收 **4** [u] (regaining) 恢复; **the slow ~ of her hearing/eyesight** 她听力/视力的缓慢恢复 **5** [u] (recouping) 收回; **~ of expenses is a priority** 收回费用是当务之急 **6** [c and u] (regaining of financial strength) 复苏; **the Stock Exchange staged a dramatic ~** 股票市场出现大幅反弹 **7** [u] (of reusable substance) 再生回收

recovery: ~ position *n* 复原卧式 [防止病人窒息的姿势，面朝地面，略侧身，身体弯曲]; **~ room** *n* Amer 术后监护室; **~ ship** *n* 航天器回收船; **~ team** *n* 搜救小组; **~ vehicle** *n* 故障抢修车; **~ vessel** *n* 航天器回收船

recreate /ˌriːkrɪˈeɪt/ *vt* **1** (remake) 再创造 **2** (simulate) 再现 ‹*life, the past*›; **scientists ~d the explosion on computer** 科学家用计算机再现了爆炸场景

recreation[1] /ˌrekrɪˈeɪʃn/ *n* [c and u] (leisure) 娱乐; **what do you do for ~?** 你做什么来消遣？; **swimming is my favourite ~** 游泳是我最喜欢的娱乐活动

recreation[2] /ˌriːkrɪˈeɪʃn/ *n* **1** [u] (remaking) 再创造 **2** [c] (simulation) 再现

recreational /ˌrekrɪˈeɪʃənl/ *adj* 娱乐的; **~ facilities/activities** 娱乐设施/活动

recreational: ~ drug *n* 消遣性毒品; **~ user** *n* **1** (of drugs) 消遣性毒品使用者; **2** (of countryside, land) 娱乐消遣者; **~ vehicle** *n* Amer [露营等用的] 休闲车

recreation: ~ ground *n* Brit 公共娱乐场; **~ room** *n* 娱乐室

recrimination /rɪˌkrɪmɪˈneɪʃn/ *n* [c and u] 反责

rec room /ˈrek ruːm, rʊm/ *n* Amer 娱乐活动室

recruit /rɪˈkruːt/
A *n* **1** (in armed forces) 新兵；(in police force) 新警员 **2** (in company, department) 新成员；**a ~ to sth.** 某处的新成员；**a ~ from sth.** 从某处招来的新成员
B *vt* **1** (in armed forces, police) 征募 ‹*soldier, mercenaries*› **2** (enrol) «*club, party*» 招收 ‹*member*›；«*society, movement, sect*» 吸纳 ‹*person, member*› **3** (hire) «*company, organization*» 招聘 ‹*staff, employee*›；**to be ~ed to do ...** 被招收来做…；**to ~ sb. from sth.** 从某处招来某人 **4** (muster) 召集 ‹*force, team, squad, corps*›
C *vi* «*army*» 征兵；«*police*» 招募新警员；«*party, movement*» 招收新成员

recruiting office *n* 征兵处

recruitment /rɪˈkruːtmənt/ *n* [u] **1** (to armed forces) 征兵；(to police) 招募警员 **2** (to company, department) 招聘新员工；(to club, party) 招收新成员；(to society, sect) 吸纳新人

recruitment agency *n* 招聘中介

recta /ˈrektə/ *pl* ▸**rectum**

rectal /ˈrektəl/ *adj* 直肠的

rectangle /ˈrektæŋɡl/ *n* **1** (figure) 长方形；**in the shape of a ~** 呈长方形 **2** (object) 长方形物；**a ~ of cloth, a cloth ~** 一块长方形布

rectangular /rekˈtæŋɡjʊlə(r)/ *adj* 长方形的 ‹*table, sheet of paper, garden*›；**a ~ pattern of intersecting streets** 成直角交叉的街道

rectifiable /ˈrektɪfaɪəbl, ˌrektɪˈfaɪəbl/ *adj* 可纠正的 ‹*error, omission*›；可矫正的 ‹*deficiency*›

rectification /ˌrektɪfɪˈkeɪʃn/ *n* [u] 纠正

rectifier /ˈrektɪfaɪə(r)/ *n* 整流器

rectify /ˈrektɪfaɪ/ *vt* **1** (correct) 改正 ‹*error*›；修复 ‹*damage*›；**to ~ an omission/the situation** 纠正疏忽/扭转形势 **2** Elec 把…变成直流电 ‹*alternating current*›

rectilinear /ˌrektɪˈlɪnɪə(r)/ *adj* **1** (in a straight line) 沿直线的 ‹*motion*›；**the ~ propagation of light** 光的直线传播 **2** (having straight lines) 直线构成的 ‹*figure, design, form*›

rectitude /ˈrektɪtjuːd, Amer -tuːd/ *n* [u] formal 正直；**financial ~** 清廉

rector /ˈrektə(r)/ *n* **1** Brit (in Church of England) 教区牧师长 **2** (in Catholic Church) 教区首席神父 **3** Scot (student representative) [大学行政机构中的] 学生代表

rectory /ˈrektəri/ *n* 教区牧师长住所

rectum /ˈrektəm/ *n* (*pl* **~s** *or* **recta**) 直肠

recumbent /rɪˈkʌmbənt/ *adj* formal 躺着的 ‹*posture, statue*›；**a ~ figure** 卧姿人像

recuperate /rɪˈkuːpəreɪt/
A *vt* 挽回 ‹*costs, losses*›；追回 ‹*object*›；**he won his appeal and ~d the money** 他上诉获胜，要回了钱
B *vi* 恢复；**to ~ from sth.** …后康复 ‹*operation, illness*›

recuperation /rɪˌkuːpəˈreɪʃn/ *n* [u] **1** (of lost objects) 收回；**the ~ of forgotten and neglected texts** 被遗忘和疏忽文本的挽回 **2** (of one's health) 恢复；**a fortnight by the sea might aid ~** 在海边住两周可能有助于康复

recuperative /rɪˈkuːpərətɪv/ *adj* formal 有助于康复的；**~ powers** 恢复力

recur /rɪˈkɜː(r)/ *vi* (*pres p etc.* **-rr-**) **1** (happen again) «*error, circumstances, theme, phrase*» 再现；«*illness, symptom*» 复发 **2** (return to one's mind) «*idea, memory*» 重新忆起 **3** (repeat infinitely) «*digit, number*» 循环

recurrence /rɪˈkʌrəns/ *n* [c and u] (of error, incident) 再现；(of illness, symptom) 复发

recurrent /rɪˈkʌrənt/ *adj* 一再发生的 ‹*attack, problem*›；反复出现的 ‹*phrase, feeling*›；周期性的 ‹*headaches, fits*›；**this is a ~ theme in her work, this theme is ~ in her work** 这是她作品中惯有的主题

recurring /rɪˈkɜːrɪŋ/ *adj* **1** (frequent) 反复出现的 ‹*problem, complaint*›；复发的 ‹*illness*›；**I have this ~ dream/nightmare** 我经常做这个梦/恶梦 **2** (repeating infinitely) 循环的 ‹*digit*›；**a ~ decimal** 循环小数

recyclable /ˌriːˈsaɪkləbl/ *adj* 可回收利用的

recycle /ˌriːˈsaɪkl/ *vt* **1** (make reusable) 回收利用 ‹*glass, product, waste*›；**~d paper** 再生纸；**rice straw can be ~d into a very good insulation material** 稻草可以回收制成很好的隔热材料 **2** (reuse) 重新使用 ‹*ideas*›

recycle bin *n* **1** (recycling bin) 废品回收箱 **2** Comput 回收站

recycling /ˌriːˈsaɪklɪŋ/ *n* [u] 回收利用；**the ~ of plastics/glass/paper** 塑料/玻璃/纸张回收利用；**a ~ facility/plant** 废品回收场/加工厂

recycling bin *n* 废品回收箱

red /red/ ▸**p. 134**
A *adj* **1** (of colour) 红色的；**to go** *or* **turn ~** 变红；**to colour sth. ~** 将某物涂成红色；**dark** *or* **deep ~** 深红的；**light** *or* **pale ~** 浅红的 **2** (bloodshot) 充血的；**he had ~ eyes from lack of sleep** 他因缺乏睡眠双眼布满血丝；**her eyes were ~ with weeping** 她两眼哭得红红的 **3** (irritated) 红肿的 ‹*skin, hands*›；充血的 ‹*eyes*›；**he had come out in dark ~ blotches** 他身上起了深红色的疹块 **4** (flushed) 涨红的 ‹*face, cheeks*›；脸涨得通红的 ‹*person*›；**to go ~** «*face, cheeks*» 涨得通红；«*person*» 脸涨得通红；**to grow ~** «*face, cheeks*» 涨得通红；**to be/go ~ in the face** 脸红/脸涨红；**was my face ~!** 我真是赧颜啊！；**there were ~ faces at the Embassy** 使馆人员感到很尴尬；**to be ~ with sth.** 因某事脸红；**she was ~ with anger** 她气得满脸通红 **5** (ginger) 红褐色的 ‹*hair, curls*›；有红褐色皮肤的 ‹*person*› **6** **Red** Pol colloq pej (communist) 赤色的；(left-wing) 左翼的；**he's pretty ~** 他很左
B *n* **1** [u and c] (colour) 红色；**a rich/dark ~** 鲜红/深红；**in ~** 红色的；**I've marked the corrections in ~** 我已经用红笔改正过了；**the traffic lights were on ~** 红灯亮了；**to see ~** colloq 火冒三丈 **2** [u] (clothing) 红衣服；**to wear ~** 穿红衣服；**dressed in ~** 穿着红衣服的 **3** [u] (material) 红色材料；**do you have the sofa in ~?** 这种沙发有红色的吗？ **4** [u and c] (wine) 红葡萄酒 **5** [u] (deficit) **the ~** 赤字；**to be in/get out of the ~** 负债/偿清债务；**to be £500 in the ~** 亏欠 500 英镑；**to go/plunge into the ~** 开始/陷入亏损；**the company has plunged $37 million into the ~** 该公司一下子负债 3,700 万美元 **6** [c] **Red** Pol colloq pej 赤色分子；**Reds under the bed** 无处不在的赤色分子 **7** [c] (snooker ball) 红球 **8** [u] (in roulette) 红方

red: ~ admiral *n* 赤蛱蝶；**~ alert** *n* **1** (for military) 紧急戒备状态；**the country's armed forces were on ~ alert** 该国的武装部队处于紧急戒备状态；**2** (for hospitals and other organizations) 紧急警报；**to be on** *or* **to be put on ~ alert** 处于紧急状态；**to issue** *or* **put out** *or* **send out a ~ alert** 发布紧急警报；**~ blood cell** *n* 红细胞；**~-blooded** *adj* 血气方刚的；**~ box** *n* Brit [英国大臣用的] 公文匣；**~brick university** *n* Brit 红砖大学 [19世纪末到20世纪初建立的地方大学，区别于剑桥和牛津等古老大学]；**~ cabbage** *n* 紫甘蓝；**~cap** *n* **1** Brit colloq (military policeman) 宪兵；**2** Amer (railway porter) 铁路搬运工；**~ card** *n* 红牌；**to be shown** *or* **given the ~ card** 被红牌罚下场；**~ carpet** *n* [迎接贵宾用的] 红地毯；**to roll out the ~ carpet for sb.** 隆重欢迎某人；**to give sb./get the ~ carpet treatment** 给予某人/受到隆重接待；**~ cent** *n* colloq **1** Amer (one cent) 1分钱硬币；**not to have a ~ cent** 身无分文；**2** (small amount of money) 很少的钱；**he never gave a ~ cent to the poor** 他一个子儿都不给穷人；**~coat** *n* **1** Brit (at holiday camp) 度假营地招待员；**2** (soldier) [尤指18世纪和19世纪初期的] 英国士兵；**Red Crescent** *n* **the Red Crescent** 红新月会；**Red Cross** *n* **the Red Cross** 红十字会；**~currant** *n* **1** (berry) 红醋栗；**2** (shrub) 红醋栗树；**~ deer** *n* 马鹿

redden /ˈredn/
A *vt* «*blood*» 染红 ‹*water, river*›
B *vi* **1** (blush) 脸红；**his face ~ed with shame** 他的脸羞红了 **2** (become red) «*leaves, skin*» 变红

red diesel *n* [u] Brit 红色柴油

reddish /ˈredɪʃ/ *adj* 微红的；**~ hair** 浅红色头发

red duster *n* Brit colloq = **red ensign**

redecorate /ˌriːˈdekəreɪt/ *vt, vi* 重新装饰

redecoration /ˌriːdekəˈreɪʃn/ *n* [u] 重新装饰

redeem /rɪˈdiːm/
A *vt* **1** (buy back) 赎回 ‹*watch, jewellery*› **2** (exchange for cash, goods) 兑现 ‹*bond, share, banknote*›；兑换 ‹*coupon, voucher*› **3** (pay off) 清偿 ‹*mortgage, debt*› **4** formal (salvage, compensate for) 弥补 ‹*plot, poor quality, situation*›；**a mediocre play ~ed by X's performance** 因X的表演而增色的平庸戏剧 **5** (satisfy) 履行 ‹*obligation*›；**the Government's pledge to the strikers has yet to be ~ed** 政府对罢工者的保证还有待兑现 **6** (save from sin) 救赎 ‹*person, sinner*›
B *v refl* formal **to ~ oneself** 补救；**to ~ oneself by doing sth.** 通过做某事弥补过失

redeemable /rɪˈdiːməbl/ *adj* **1** (able to be bought back) 可赎回的 ‹*watch*› **2** (convertible into cash) 可兑现的 ‹*bond, share, token*›；**these vouchers are ~ for goods or cash** 这些票券可兑换成物品或现金 **3** (repayable) 可偿还的 ‹*debt, mortgage*›

Redeemer /rɪˈdiːmə(r)/ *n* **the ~** 耶稣基督

redeeming /rɪˈdiːmɪŋ/ *adj* 起补偿作用的 ‹*feature*›

redefine /ˌriːdɪˈfaɪn/ *vt* 重新定义；**they've ~d the terms of the agreement** 他们重新解释了协议的条款

redemption /rɪˈdempʃn/ *n* [u] **1** (repossession from pawn) 赎回 **2** (conversion) (into cash) 兑现；(into goods) 兑换 **3** (payment of debt, loan) 偿还；**the time came for the ~ of the mortgage** 支付账单的时间到了 **4** (saving from sin) 救赎；**beyond** *or* **past ~** «*situation*» 无法挽回；«*person*» 不可救药

red ensign /ˌred ˈensən/ *n* 英国商船旗

redeploy /ˌriːdɪˈplɔɪ/ *vt* «*government, company*» 调配 ‹*staff, funds*›；«*government, army*» 重新部署 ‹*troops, police, tanks*›

redeployment /ˌriːdɪˈplɔɪmənt/ *n* (of staff, resources) 调配；(of troops, police) 重新部署

redesign /ˌriːdɪˈzaɪn/ *vt* 重新设计

redevelop /ˌriːdɪˈveləp/ *vt* 再开发；**to ~ the city centre** 改造市中心

redevelopment /ˌriːdɪˈveləpmənt/ *n* (of site, town) 再开发；(of run-down area) 改建；**urban ~** 城市改造

red: ~-eye *n* **1** [u] Phot 红眼；**2** [c] colloq (flight) **to take the ~-eye** 乘坐红眼航班 [指乘客无法获得充足睡眠的夜间航班]；**~-eyed** *adj* 眼睛发红的；**~-faced** *adj* **1** (embarrassed) 面红耳赤的；**2** (from exercise, heat) 红脸的；**he emerged ~-faced from the gym** 他脸色红扑扑地从健身房出来；**~ flag** *n* **1** Pol 红旗；**2** (as warning) 示警红旗；**~ fox** *n* 赤狐；**~ giant** *n* 红巨星；**Red Guard** *n* **1** (organization) (in Russia) [尤指俄国十月革命时期的] 赤卫队；(in China) [中国"十年文革"期间的] 红卫兵；**2** (member) (in Russia) 赤卫队员；(in China) 红卫兵；**~-haired** *adj* 红头发的；**~-handed** *adj* **to catch sb. ~-handed** 当场抓住某人；**~head** *n* 红发人；**~headed** *adj* 红头发的；**~ heat** *n* [u] 炽热；**~ herring** *n* **1** (fish) 熏干鲱鱼；**2** (misleading information) 转移注意力的东西；

r

~-hot *adj* 1 (glowing, very hot) 炽热的 ‹*iron, metal*›; 2 (passionate) 强烈的 ‹*enthusiasm*›; **her ~-hot anger** 她的狂怒; 3 (good, exciting) 激动人心的 ‹*campaign, performance*›; 4 (new) 最新的 ‹*news, issue*›; 5 (expected to win) **~-hot favourite** 热门人选

redial
A *vt* /ˌriːˈdaɪəl/ 重拨
B *vi* /ˌriːˈdaɪəl/ 重拨
C *n* /ˈriːdaɪəl/ (last number) ~ 重拨键

redial /ˈriːdaɪəl/: **~ button** *n* 重拨键; **~ facility** *n* 重拨功能

redid /ˌriːˈdɪd/ *pt* ▸ **redo**

Red Indian *n* dated or offensive 印第安人

redirect /ˌriːdaɪˈrekt, -dɪ-/ *vt* 1 (use differently) 重新调配 ‹*industries, resources*›; **to ~ one's energies to sth.** 把精力用在某些地方 2 (divert) «*police*» 使…改道 ‹*vehicles*›; **traffic was being ~ed away from the motorway** 车辆正在被引导离开高速公路 3 (send to different address) «*post office, new occupant*» 改寄 ‹*letters*›

redirection /ˌriːdaɪˈrekʃn, -dɪ-/ *n* [u] (of resources) 重新定向; (of mail) 信件改投

rediscover /ˌriːdɪˈskʌvə(r)/ *vt* 1 (find again) 重新找到 ‹*map, letter, document*› 2 (regain) 重新获得 ‹*magic, skill, enthusiasm*›; **to ~ one's form** 再次恢复状态

rediscovery /ˌriːdɪˈskʌvəri/ *n* [c and u] 重新发现

redistribute /ˌriːdɪˈstrɪbjuːt/ *vt* 重新分配

redistribution /ˌriːdɪstrɪˈbjuːʃn/ *n* 重新分配; **the ~ of land/wealth/profits** 土地/财富/利润的再分配

redistrict /ˌriːdɪsˈtrɪkt/ Amer
A *vt* 把…重新划区
B *vi* 重新划区

red: **~ lead** /led/ *n* [u] 红丹; **~-letter day** *n* 重要纪念日

red light *n* 红灯; **to go through a ~** 闯红灯

red light area, red light district *ns* 红灯区

redline /ˈredlaɪn/ Amer colloq
A *vt* 1 (drive) 使…超速运转 ‹*engine*› 2 (refuse insurance) 拒绝对…承保 ‹*person, area*›; (refuse loan) 拒绝给…贷款 ‹*person, district*›
B *n* [汽车引擎的] 红线转速

red: **~lining** *n* [u] Amer colloq 画红线拒贷 [指银行等拒绝发放贫民窟住房抵押贷款]; **~ meat** *n* [u] 红肉 [指牛肉或羊肉]; **~neck** *n* Amer colloq pej 红脖子 [指美国南部政治保守的白人农民]; **a ~neck farmer/trucker/thug** 红脖子农民/货车司机/暴徒

redness /ˈrednɪs/ *n* [u] 红色

redo /ˌriːˈduː/ *vt* (*pt* **redid**, *pp* **redone**) 1 (do again) 重做 ‹*job, assignment*› 2 colloq (redecorate) 重新装饰 ‹*room*›

redolent /ˈredələnt/ *adj* 1 (smelling of) **to be ~ of sth.** 有某物的强烈气味 2 (reminiscent of) **to be ~ of sth.** 使人联想起某事物

redone /ˌriːˈdʌn/ *pp* ▸ **redo**

redouble /ˌriːˈdʌbl/
A *vt* 加强; **to ~ one's efforts** 加倍努力
B *vi* 倍增

redoubt /rɪˈdaʊt/ *n* 棱堡

redoubtable /rɪˈdaʊtəbl/ *adj* 令人敬畏的 ‹*fighter, opponent*›

redound /rɪˈdaʊnd/ *vi* formal 有助益; **to ~ to sb.'s honour** Brit *or* **honor** Amer 增进某人的荣誉

red: **~-pencil** *vt* 用红笔审核 ‹*request*›; 用红笔修改 ‹*work, word*›; **~ pepper** *n* 1 [c] (fruit) 辣椒; 2 [u] (spice) 辣椒粉

redraft /ˌriːˈdrɑːft, Amer -ˈdræft/ *vt* 重新起草

redress /rɪˈdres/ formal
A *n* 补偿; **~ for sth.** 对某事的补偿; **to seek/obtain (legal) ~ for ...** 因…提起赔偿诉讼/获得对…的（法律）赔偿
B *vt* 1 (make even) 使均衡; **to ~ the balance** 恢复平衡 2 formal (rectify) 纠正 ‹*error, abuse*›; (compensate for) 赔偿 ‹*damage*›; **he strove to ~ her grievances** 他力争为她申冤; **her efforts to ~ the situation** 她挽救局面的努力

red: **~ ribbon** *n* Amer [授予亚军的] 红绶带; **Red River** ▸ **p. 663** *pr n* **the Red River** 红河; **~ route** *n* 红色干线; **Red Sea** *n* **the Red Sea** 红海; **~skin** *n* dated or offensive 印第安人; **~ squirrel** *n* 红松鼠; **~ tape** *n* [u] 繁文缛节

reduce /rɪˈdjuːs, Amer -ˈduːs/
A *vt* 1 (make less) 减少 ‹*quantity, pressure, cost*›; 降低 ‹*level, rate*›; 减轻 ‹*swelling, weight*›; 削弱 ‹*strength, effect*›; 缩短 ‹*length*›; **to ~ speed** 减速; **'~ speed now'** Aut "减速行驶" 2 Comm 降低 ‹*price*›; 降低…的价格 ‹*item, goods*›; **to ~ the price by 10%** 打九折; **the carpet was ~d in a sale** 大减价时这条地毯降了价; **the jackets have been ~d by 50%** 夹克衫五折销售; **to ~ sth. (from sth.) to sth.** 将某事物（从某水平）减少到某水平 3 (make smaller) 缩小 ‹*map, drawing*› 4 (shorten in length) 减少…的篇幅 ‹*essay, report*›; **to ~ an article by 200 words** 把文章删减 200 字 5 (shorten in duration) 缩短; **the law ~d the term of conscription from three years to two** 该法令将服兵役年限从 3 年缩短至 2 年; **the ban on her competing was ~d by two years** 她的禁赛期限缩短了 2 年; **the judge ~d his sentence by six months** 法官将他的刑期减少了 6 个月 6 (bring forcibly) 迫使; **to ~ sb. to sth.** 迫使某人进入某状态; **to ~ sb. to tears** 使某人流泪; **to be ~d to silence/prostitution** 被迫缄口/卖淫; **to ~ sb. to doing sth.** 迫使某人做某事; **to be ~d to begging/apologizing** 被迫乞讨/道歉 7 (change physical state) 改变…的状态; **to ~ sth. to sth.** 把某物变成某物; **to ~ sth. to shreds/ashes** 把某物撕碎/使某物化为灰烬; **to ~ sth. to dust/(a) powder** 使某物成为尘土/粉末 8 Mil **to ~ sb. to sth.** 把某人降至某级别; **to be ~d to the ranks** 被降为普通士兵 9 (simplify) 简化 ‹*argument, issue*›; **to ~ sth. to sth.** 将某事物简化为某事物; **we can ~ the problem to two main issues** 我们可以把这个问题概括为两个要点 10 Culin 使…变浓 ‹*liquid, sauce*›; **to ~ the stock to about a third/by half** 使汤浓缩至原来的三分之一/一半 11 Math 约简 ‹*equation, expression*›; **to ~ sth. (from sth.) to sth.** 将某物（从某物）约简为某物
B *vi* 1 (become less) «*quantity, pressure, cost*» 减少; «*level, rate*» 降低; «*swelling, weight*» 减轻; «*length*» 缩短; «*strength, effect*» 削弱; **inflation has ~d since ...** 通货膨胀自…后已减缓; **shareholders' funds have ~d by £3 million** 股东资金减少了 300 万英镑; **by 1995 this figure had ~d (from 5%) to under 4%** 截至 1995 年这个数字已（从 5%）降至 4% 以下 2 Culin «*liquid, sauce*» 变浓; **let the stock ~ to half its volume** 让汤浓缩至原来的一半 3 esp Amer colloq (lose weight) 减肥; **she's reducing again** 她又在减肥了

reduced /rɪˈdjuːst, Amer -ˈduːst/ *adj* 1 (lowered in price) 降低的 ‹*price, rate*›; 减价的 ‹*item*›; **to sell sth. at a ~ price** 削价出售某物 2 (made smaller) 缩小的 ‹*number, capacity, demand*›; **a map on a ~ scale** 缩尺地图 3 formal (straitened) 沦落的; **in ~ circumstances** 落泊的

reducible /rɪˈdjuːsəbl, Amer -ˈduːsəbl/ *adj* 1 (able to be made smaller) 可减少的 ‹*volume, pressure, expenditure*›; 可降低的 ‹*height, speed*›; **the weight of the machine is not ~ any further** 机器的重量不能再减轻了 2 formal (able to be altered) 可转变的; **to be ~ to ...** «*chaos, idea*» 可转变为… 3 formal (able to be simplified) 可简化的; **to be ~ to ...** «*argument, problem*» 可简化成…

reductio ad absurdum /rɪˌdʌktɪəʊ æd əbˈsɜːdəm/ *n* 归谬法

reduction /rɪˈdʌkʃn/ *n* 1 [c and u] (lessening) 缩减; **~ in** *or* **of sth.** 某物的削减; **~ of taxes, tax ~s** 减税 2 [c] (amount decreased) 减少量; (discount) 折扣; **a 33 per cent ~** 33% 的下降; **to sell sth. at a huge ~** 大减价出售某物; **to make a ~ on an article** 给一件物品打折; **a ~ for cash** 付现金可打折 3 [u] (simplification) 简化; **the ~ of the problem to two main issues** 将问题归结为两个要点

reductionist /rɪˈdʌkʃənɪst/ formal pej
A *n* 简化论者
B *adj* 简化论的; **it is ~ to say that ...** 说…太简单化了

redundancy /rɪˈdʌndənsi/ *n* 1 [c] Brit (dismissal) 解雇; **400 redundancies** 400 个被裁减人员 2 [u] (unemployment) 失业; **compulsory ~** 强制失业; **to take/face ~** 接受/面临失业 3 [u] (of machinery) 多余 4 [u] (in language) 冗长 5 [u] Civ Eng, Tech 冗余

redundancy: **~ notice** *n* 1 [c] (letter) 解雇函; 2 [u] (period of notice) 离职期限; **~ payment** *n* 遣散费

redundant /rɪˈdʌndənt/ *adj* 1 Brit (laid-off) 被裁减的 ‹*staff, miner*›; **to be made/to become ~** 被裁减员/成为冗员 2 (superfluous) 多余的 ‹*skills, word, detail*› 3 Civ Eng, Tech 冗余的 ‹*circuit, system*›

reduplicate /rɪˈdjuːplɪkeɪt, Amer -ˈduː-/ *vt* «*efforts, work*» 重复; «*word, sound*» 使重叠; **these cells are able to ~ themselves** 这些细胞能自我复制

reduplication /rɪˌdjuːplɪˈkeɪʃn, Amer -ˈduː-/ *n* [u] (of efforts, work) 重复; (of words, sounds) 重叠

red: **~ wine** *n* [u and c] 红葡萄酒; **~wood** *n* 红杉

re-echo /ˌriːˈekəʊ/ (*pt, pp* **~ed**)
A *vt* 1 (resound again) «*walls, caves*» 使…反复回响 ‹*shouts, cries*›; **the hills ~ed the sounds of battle** 山谷里回荡着战斗的呼喊 2 (repeat again) «*person*» 一再重复 ‹*sentiments, words, ideas*›
B *vi* 1 (resound again) «*cries, sounds*» 反复回响; «*valleys, hills*» 有声音反复回响; **their cries ~ed around the valley** 他们的叫喊声在山谷中回响不已; **the valley ~ed with the sound** 山谷中声音回响不绝 2 (be repeated again) «*words*» 一再重复

reed /riːd/ *n* 1 [c] (plant) 芦苇 2 [u] (clump, patch) 芦苇丛 3 [c] (stalk) 芦苇秆; **a ~ basket/hut** 用芦苇编的篮子/茅草屋 4 [c] (in musical instrument) 簧片; **the ~s** 簧乐器

reed instrument *n* 簧乐器

re-educate /ˌriːˈedʒʊkeɪt/ *vt* 再教育

re-education /ˌriːedʒʊˈkeɪʃn/ *n* [u] 再教育; **he was sentenced to six months ~ through labour** 他被判处 6 个月的劳教; **a ~ camp** 再教育训练营

reedy /ˈriːdi/ *adj* 1 (full of reeds) 芦苇丛生的 ‹*banks, area, waters*› 2 (high-pitched) 尖厉的 ‹*tone, sound, voice*›; **a thin, ~ tenor** 尖细的男高音

reef[1] /riːf/ *n* (in sea) 礁; **they ran aground on a ~** 他们在礁石上搁浅了

reef[2]
A *n* (on a sail) 缩帆部
B *vt* (reduce area of) 收 ‹*sail*›

reefer /ˈriːfə(r)/ *n* 1 **~ (jacket)** 双排扣厚毛上衣 2 colloq (cannabis cigarette) 大麻香烟

reef knot *n* 平结

reek /riːk/
A *n* 恶臭; **the ~ of corruption** fig 腐败之风
B *vi* 1 (stink) 发臭; **to ~ of sth.** «*breath, room, air*» 散发着某种臭气 2 (be suggestive of) 强烈地意味着; **to ~ of sth.** «*letter, book, speech*» 明显带有某物; **her denials ~ed of hypocrisy** 她那样否认显然很虚伪

r

reel /riːl/

A *n* **1** (on fishing rod) 绕线轮 **2** (spool) 卷轴; **the projectionist is changing ~s** 放映员在换片; **off the ~** Amer colloq 接连地; **he won four races off the ~** 他一连在4项赛跑中获胜 **3** (quantity) (of thread, cotton) 一轴; (of wire, cable) 一卷; (of tape) 一盘 **4** Cin (part of film) 部分; **in the final ~** 在电影的结尾; **a three-~ film** 一部有3盘胶片的电影 **5** (dance) 里尔舞 [苏格兰、爱尔兰和美国等地的一种轻快的民间舞蹈] **6** (music) 里尔舞曲

B *vt* 将…卷起 ‹*thread, line, cable*›

C *vi* **1** (sway) 蹒跚; **to send sb. ~ing** 使某人踉踉跄跄; **the blow sent me ~ing** 那一拳打了我一个趔趄; **the two ~ed out of the bar** 这俩人跌跌撞撞地走出酒吧 **2** (feel shocked) 感到震惊; **to send sb. ~ing** 使某人震惊; **to ~ at sth.** 对某事物感到不知所措; **his mind was ~ing at the thought of losing her** 一想到要失去她，他就心烦意乱; **to ~ from** *or* **with sth.** 因某事物感到不知所措; **I was ~ing from** *or* **with the shock** 这个打击把我弄得心烦意乱 **3** (spin) 旋转; **the street ~ed before my eyes** 街道在我眼前打旋

Phrasal verbs

- **reel back** *vi* 跌跌撞撞地后退; **she ~ed back against the wall** 她跌跌撞撞地退到墙边
- **reel in** *vt* [**~ sth. in, ~ in sth.**] 收钓丝钓起 ‹*fish*›; 收绕 ‹*thread, line, cable*›
- **reel off** *vt* [**~ sth. off, ~ off sth.**] **1** (say) 一口气报出 ‹*list, names*›; 一口气说出 ‹*answers*› **2** (unwind) 放出 ‹*thread, line, cable*›
- **reel out** *vt* [**~ sth. out, ~ out sth.**] 从卷轴上放出 ‹*thread, line, cable*›

re-elect /ˌriːɪˈlekt/ *vt* 再次选举; **she was ~ed with a big majority** 她以压倒多数再次当选

re-election /ˌriːɪˈlekʃn/ *n* [u] 再次选举; **to stand** Brit *or* **run for ~** 竞选连任

reel-to-reel *adj* 盘式的 ‹*tape recorder*›

re-embark /ˌriːɪmˈbɑːk/

A *vt* 使重新上船

B *vi* 再次登船

re-emerge /ˌriːɪˈmɜːdʒ/ *vi* **1** (come up again) «*person, moon*» 再次出现; **the sun ~d from behind the clouds** 太阳再次从云中露出 **2** (return to prominence) «*person*» 再度崛起; **he ~d into prominence after a few years** 他几年后东山再起 **3** (return) «*problem, tension*» 重新发生; **the cancer may ~ years later** 癌症可能在多年后复发

re-employ /ˌriːɪmˈplɔɪ/ *vt* 重新雇用

re-enact /ˌriːɪˈnækt/ *vt* **1** (act out) 上演 ‹*play, scene*›; 再现 ‹*crime, attack*›; **a ritual that was ~ed year after year** 年复一年举行的仪式 **2** (enact again) «*Parliament*» 重新制订 ‹*law*›

re-enactment /ˌriːɪˈnæktmənt/ *n* **1** [c and u] (of scene) 上演; (of crime) 再现; **a ~ of the victim's last hours** 受害者最后几个小时情形的再现 **2** [u] (of a law) 重新制定

re-engage /ˌriːɪnˈgeɪdʒ/ *vt* **1** (re-employ) 重新雇用 ‹*staff*› **2** Aut «*switch, person*» 使…重新啮合 ‹*gears, clutch*›

re-engagement /ˌriːɪnˈgeɪdʒmənt/ *n* [u] **1** formal (of staff) 重新雇用 **2** (of gears, clutch) 重新啮合

re-enlist /ˌriːɪnˈlɪst/

A *vt* 再征…入伍

B *vi* 再从军

re-enter /ˌriːˈentə(r)/

A *vi* **1** (come back in) «*person, vehicle*» 重返 **2** (enrol again) «*person*» 重新报名; **to ~ for an exam** 重新报名参加考试

B *vt* «*person, vehicle, army*» 重新进入 ‹*room, area, town, country*›; «*spacecraft, capsule*» 重返 ‹*atmosphere*›; **at the age of fifty she ~ed the art scene** 她在50岁时重返艺术舞台

re-entry /ˌriːˈentri/ *n* [u] **1** (to a room, town) 重新进入; **a proviso allowing the landlord a right of ~** 认可房东有权收回房屋的附加条款 **2** (of spacecraft) 重返大气层; **~ capsule** 返回舱 **3** fig (return) 重返; **~ to the political scene** 向政治舞台的回归; **the ~ of offenders into society** 犯人的重返社会

re-entry visa *n* 再入境签证

re-equip /ˌriːɪˈkwɪp/ *vt* 重新装备

re-erect /ˌriːɪˈrekt/ *vt* 重新建造 ‹*building, bridge*›; 重新架设 ‹*scaffolding*›

re-establish /ˌriːɪˈstæblɪʃ/

A *vt* **1** (set up again) 重新建立 ‹*business*› **2** (restore) 恢复 ‹*order, relationship, contact*› **3** (reaffirm) 重新确立 ‹*reputation*›; **this book ~ed her fame as a writer** 这本书重新确立了她的作家声誉

B *v refl* **to ~ oneself** 使自己重新立足; **she ~ed herself as a doctor in another town** 她在另一个镇又当起了医生

re-establishment /ˌriːɪˈstæblɪʃmənt/ *n* [u] **1** (of business) 重新建立; (of dynasty) 复辟 **2** (of order, relationship) 恢复; (of contact) 重新订立 **3** (of status, reputation) 重新确立

re-evaluate /ˌriːɪˈvæljʊeɪt/ *vt* 重新评价 ‹*oneself, approach, costs*›; 对…进行复诊 ‹*patient*›; **to ~ one's own family relations** 重新审视自己的家庭关系

re-evaluation /ˌriːɪˌvæljʊˈeɪʃn/ *n* [c and u] 重新评价

re-examination /ˌriːɪgˌzæmɪˈneɪʃn/ *n* [c and u] 重新检查; **a ~ of strategy** 对战略的重新审视; **the question requires ~** 这个问题需要重新考虑

re-examine /ˌriːɪgˈzæmɪn/ *vt* **1** (scrutinize again) 重新检查 ‹*problem, assumptions*›; **I will have the body ~d** 我要复查一下身体 **2** Jur «*lawyer*» 再次盘问 ‹*witness, accused*›

ref.¹ /ref/ *abbr* = **reference** (in/at top of letter) 文件编号

ref² *n* colloq = **referee A1**

refectory /rɪˈfektri/ *n* 食堂

refer /rɪˈfɜː(r)/ (*pres p etc.* **-rr-**) *vt* 退回; **the cheque has been ~red** 支票遭拒付

Phrasal verbs

- **refer back** *vt* **1** **to ~ back to sb./sth.** (mention) 提起某人/某事物 **2** **to ~ sth. back to sb./sth.** (send back) 将…发回至某人/某处 ‹*matter, decision, question*›
- **refer to**

A [**~ to sb./sth.**] *vt*

1 (allude to, talk about) 提及; **I wasn't ~ring to you** 我指的不是你; **we shall not ~ to it again** 我们不会再提它了; **what can she have been ~ring to?** 她指的会是什么?; **to ~ to sb. by name** 提到某人的姓名; **~ring to your letter of 10 June** formal 参阅您6月10日的来函 **2** (call) 称呼; **to ~ to sb./sth. as sb./sth.** 称呼某人/某事物为某人/某事物; **this is what I ~/what is ~red to as 'art'** 这就是我所说的/所谓的"艺术"; **he's always ~red to as 'the secretary'** 大家总是叫他"秘书"; **don't ~ to him as an idiot** 别叫他白痴 **3** (apply to) «*remark, comment*» 适用于 **4** (signify) «*term, name, number, date*» 指的是 **5** (consult) 参考 ‹*notes, article*›; 查阅 ‹*dictionary, original*›; 请教 ‹*person*›; **'please ~ to page 1'** "请参见第一页"; **she ~red to the director** 她请示了主管; **'~ to drawer'** Brit "请与出票人接洽" [支票背面戳记] **6** (pass on) **to ~ sth. to sb./sth.** 将…提交某人/某处 ‹*problem, enquiry*›; **to ~ a dispute to arbitration** 将纠纷提交仲裁; **we ~red the matter to the committee for a decision** 我们将问题提交给委员会裁定

B [**~ sb. to sth.**] *vt* formal (direct attention of) 让…参考; **the reader is ~red to chapter four** 读者请参阅第4章; **may I ~ you to my letter of 14 May?** 请你看一下我5月14日的信好吗?

C [**~ sb. to sb./sth.**] *vt*

1 Admin 让…向…求助 ‹*person, department*›; **she was ~red to the enquiry office** 有人指点她去问讯处询问 **2** Med 让…转诊到…处 ‹*specialist, psychiatrist, hospital*›; **she was ~red to a clinical psychologist for counselling** 她被转诊到临床心理学家处做心理咨询

referee /ˌrefəˈriː/

A *n* **1** Sport 裁判 **2** Brit (for job application) 推荐人; **to act as a ~ for sb.** 做某人的推荐人

B *vt* Sport 为…担任裁判 ‹*match, contest, fight*›

C *vi* Sport 担任裁判

reference /ˈrefərəns/

A *n* **1** [c] (mention) 提及; **the work is full of biblical ~s** 这部作品通篇多处引用《圣经》; **a ~ to sb./sth.** 对某人/某事物的提及; **there are three ~s to his son in the article** 这篇文章有三处提到了他儿子; **to make a ~ to sth.** 提及某事物; **a pointed ~ (to sth.)** (对某事物的)一针见血的谈及 **2** [u] (allusion) 引用; **to make ~ to sb./sth.** 引用某人的话/某作品 **3** [u] (consideration) 考虑; **to do sth. with/without ~ to sb./sth.** 考虑/不考虑某人/某事物就做某事 **4** [u] (consultation) 参考; **for easy ~, we recommend the pocket edition** 为方便查阅，我们推荐袖珍本; **for future ~** 以备日后参考; **for future ~, dogs are not allowed** 今后请注意，禁止狗入内; **a work of ~** 参考书; **'for ~ only'** (on library book) "仅供查阅"; **to do sth. without ~ to sb./sth.** 不征求…就做某事 ‹*opinion*›; 不请示…就做某事 ‹*superior*›; **the publishers reprinted and sold the work without ~ to the author** 出版商未征求作者意见就重印并销售这部作品 **5** [u] (connection) 关系; **~ to sb./sth.** 与某人/某事物的关系; **this has no ~ to the matter in hand** 这与手头的问题没关系 **6** [c] (note) 引文出处; **a ~ to sb./sth.** 关于某人/某事的引文 **7** [c] (source of information) 参考文献; **what are your ~s for this?** 你的这份东西的参考文献是哪些?; **a list of ~s** 参考书目; **to cite a ~** 引用文献 **8** [c] Comm (on letter, memo) 编号 **9** [c] (testimonial) 推荐信; **to give** *or* **write sb. a ~** 给某人写推荐信 **10** [c] (referee) 推荐人; **to be/act as a ~ for sb.** 是/做某人的推荐人 **11** [c] Geog (on map) 标示; **the map ~ is Y4** 地图编号是Y4 **12** [u] Ling 所指

B *prep phr* formal **with** *or* **in ~ to ...** 关于…; **with ~ to your letter of June 15, ...** 关于您6月15日的来信…; **with particular** *or* **specific ~ to sb./sth.** 针对某人/某事物

C *vt* formal **1** (provide with source of information) 为…附参考资料 ‹*article*›; **the book is not well ~d** 这本书的参考书目不全; **the quotation isn't ~d** 这段引文未注明出处 **2** (cite as source of information) 引用…作参考 ‹*book, article*›

reference: ~ book *n* 参考书; **~ library** *n* [不供外借的] 参考图书馆; **~ mark** *n* 参照符号; **~ number** *n* 编号; **~ point** *n* 参照标准

referendum /ˌrefəˈrendəm/ *n* (*pl* **referenda** /ˌrefəˈrendə/ *or* **~s**) 公民公决; **to hold a ~** 举行公投

referral /rɪˈfɜːrəl/ *n* **1** [c and u] Med (person) 转诊病人; (appointment) 转诊介绍 **2** [u] (of matter, problem) 提交处理; **~ to the committee** 向委员会的提交

refill

A /ˌriːˈfɪl/ *vt* 重新注满 ‹*bottle, pen, lighter*›; **our host ~ed our glasses** 主人又为我们把酒杯斟满

B /ˈriːfɪl/ *n* **1** (for fountain pen) 替换墨水管; (for ball-point, pencil) 替换笔芯; (for lighter, perfume) 补充装; (for album, notebook, etc.) 活页芯 **2** colloq (drink) 又一份饮料

refinancing /ˌriːfaɪˈnænsɪŋ, ˌriːˈfaɪnænsɪŋ/ *n* [u] 再筹措资金; **a ~ package/agreement/deal** 再融资一揽子计划/协议/交易

r

refine /rɪˈfaɪn/
A *vt* **1** (purify) 提炼 ‹*sugar*›; **the process of refining oil** 炼油工序 **2** (improve) 改进 ‹*system, design, essay*› **3** (make cultured) 使…优雅 ‹*manners, language*›
B *vi* 改进; **to ~ upon sth.** «*person, thinker, writer*» 对某物进行润色

refined /rɪˈfaɪnd/ *adj* **1** (purified) 精炼的 ‹*oil, ore*›; **highly ~ sugar** 高精制糖 **2** (cultured, elegant) 优雅的 ‹*person, manners, style*›; **a person of ~ tastes** 趣味高雅的人 **3** (improved) 改进的 ‹*theory, system*›

refinement /rɪˈfaɪnmənt/ *n* **1** [u] (purification) 精炼; **techniques for the ~ of sugar** 炼糖技术 **2** [u] (elegance, sophistication) 优雅; **a person entirely lacking in ~** 毫无教养的人 **3** [c] (small improvements) 细微改进; **an oven with automatic timer and other ~s** 带有自动计时器并作了另外一些精细改进的烤炉 **4** [c and u] (of theory, method) 微调; (of plan, joke) 雕琢 **5** [c] (subtlety) 细微差别

refiner /rɪˈfaɪnə(r)/ *n* (person, firm) 精炼加工者; (machine) 炼制设备; **he works for a sugar ~** 他在炼糖厂工作

refinery /rɪˈfaɪnəri/ *n* 精炼厂

refining /rɪˈfaɪnɪŋ/ *n* 提炼

refit
A /ˌriːˈfɪt/ *vt* (*pres p etc.* **-tt-**) **1** (re-equip, refurbish) «*company, yard*» 整修 ‹*factory, ship*›; **the liner was ~ted as a warship** 邮轮被改装成一艘战舰 **2** (reinstall) 重新安装 ‹*bolt, spark, plugs*›
B /ˈriːfɪt/ *n* (of shop, factory, ship) 整修

reflate /ˌriːˈfleɪt/ *vt* 以通货再膨胀刺激 ‹*economy*›

reflation /ˌriːˈfleɪʃn/ *n* [u] 通货再膨胀

reflationary /ˌriːˈfleɪʃnri, Amer -neri/ *adj* 通货再膨胀的

reflect /rɪˈflekt/
A *vt* **1** (show image of) «*window, water, mirror*» 映出 **2** (throw back) «*surface, sand*» 反射 ‹*light, heat, sound*›; **to bask in ~ed glory** *fig* 沾别人的光 **3** (embody, represent) 显示 ‹*tastes, growth, problems*›; **a cultural development that ~s a change in values** 反映价值观变化的文化发展; **his music ~s his feelings** 他的音乐表达了他的感情 **4** (think) 认真思考; **to ~ that …** 琢磨着…
B *vi* (think) 深思; **to ~ on** *or* **upon sth.** 思考某事

Phrasal verb
- **reflect on, reflect upon** *vt* «*behaviour, courage, betrayal*» 导致; «*scandal, accusation, incident*» 给…带来影响; **a success that ~s great credit on all concerned** 给所有相关人员带来荣誉的成功; **how is this going to ~ on the school?** 这对学校的声誉会有什么影响?; **to ~ badly/well on sb./sth.** 给某人/某事物造成坏的/好的影响

reflecting telescope *n* 反射望远镜

reflection /rɪˈflekʃn/ *n* **1** [u] (act of reflecting) 反射; **the laws of the ~ of light** 光的反射定律 **2** [c] (image) 映像; **to see one's ~ in a window** 在窗户上看到自己的影子 **3** [c] (representation) 反映; **the time taken is a ~ of the degree of difficulty involved** 花多少时间要看有多大的难度 **4** [u] (thought) 深思; **on ~** 经深思熟虑; **lost in ~** 陷入沉思 **5** [c] (idea) 想法; (remark) 意见; **~ on sth.** 对某事物的看法; **the ~ that …** …的想法 **6** [c] (criticism) 非议; **to be a ~ on sb./sth.** 是对某人/某事物的指责; **no ~ on you, but …** 不是想批评你，但是…

reflective /rɪˈflektɪv/ *adj* **1** (throwing back light, heat) 反射的; **a ~ surface** 反射面; **~ clothing/strip/number plate/material** 反光衣/带/车牌/材料 **2** *pred* (representative) 典型的; **to be ~ of …** 代表… ‹*public interest*› **3** (thoughtful) 沉思的 ‹*person, mood*›; **~ powers/faculty** 思辨能力

reflectively /rɪˈflektɪvli/ *adv* 仔细地 ‹*ponder*›; 若有所思地 ‹*say*›

reflector /rɪˈflektə(r)/ *n* **1** (on vehicle, bicycle) 反光片 **2** (of light, sound, radio waves) 反射器 **3** = **reflecting telescope**

reflex /ˈriːfleks/
A *n* **1** (movement of body part) 反射动作; **abnormal/diminished/hyperactive/normal ~es** 异常/减弱/过度/正常的反射动作 **2** (reaction) 反应能力 **3** (automatic response) 本能反应
B *adj* **1** (automatic) 本能的 ‹*action, movement, decision*› **2** Math **~ angle** 优角 [大于180度，小于360度]

reflex camera *n* 反射式照相机

reflexive /rɪˈfleksɪv/
A *n* **1** **~ (verb)** 反身动词 **2** **~ (form)** 反身形式; **in the ~** 以反身形式
B *adj* 反身的; **~ pronoun/construction** 反身代词/结构

reflexively /rɪˈfleksɪvli/ *adv* 以反身形式; **the verb is used ~ here** 这个动词在这里是反身用法

reflexive verb *n* 反身动词

reflexology /ˌriːflekˈsɒlədʒi/ *n* [u] **1** (massage) [通过按摩手足等松弛神经的] 反射疗法 **2** Psych 反射学

refloat /ˌriːˈfləʊt/
A *vt* 使再浮起
B *vi* 再浮起

reforestation /ˌriːfɒrɪˈsteɪʃn/ *n* [u] 重新造林

reform /rɪˈfɔːm/
A *vt* 改良 ‹*ways, habits*›; 改造 ‹*person*›; 改革 ‹*law, institution*›
B *vi* «*person*» 改过自新
C *n* **1** [u] (improvement) 改革; **the ~ of criminal justice/the penal system** 刑事司法/刑罚制度的改革 **2** [c] (change) 变革; **far-reaching/radical/sweeping ~s** 意义深远/根本性/大刀阔斧的变革

re-form /ˌriːˈfɔːm/
A *vt* 使…重新编队 ‹*ranks, troops*›; 重新组成 ‹*group, committee*›
B *vi* «*soldiers, ranks*» 重新编队; «*band*» 重新组成; «*ice*» 重新形成

reformable /rɪˈfɔːməbəl/ *adj* 可改革的

reformat /ˌriːˈfɔːmæt/ *vt* **1** Comput, Tech 重新格式化 ‹*hard drive, computer, mobile phone*›; 重新设定…的格式 ‹*text*› **2** (redesign) 重新编排 ‹*movie, show*›

reformation /ˌrefəˈmeɪʃn/
A *n* **1** [u] (of person, character) 改造; (of society, system, procedure) 改革 **2** [c] (change) 革新
B **Reformation** *pr n* **the R~** 宗教改革 [16世纪欧洲改革天主教会的运动]

reformed /rɪˈfɔːmd/ *adj* **1** (improved) 改过的; **she's a ~ alcoholic** 她已戒掉了酒瘾; **~ measures/proposals** 改进的措施/提议 **2** (amended) 修正的; **the introduction of a ~ orthography** 经过修订的正字法的推行

reformer /rɪˈfɔːmə(r)/ *n* 改革者

reformist /rɪˈfɔːmɪst/
A *adj* 改良主义的; **~ parties/movement** 改良派/运动
B *n* 改良主义者

refract /rɪˈfrækt/ *vt* 使折射

refracting telescope *n* 折射望远镜

refraction /rɪˈfrækʃn/ *n* [u] 折射

refractive /rɪˈfræktɪv/ *adj* 折射的; **~ index/power/lens** 折射率/力/透镜; **a ~ material/medium** 折射材料/介质

refractor /rɪˈfræktə(r)/ *n* **1** (substance) 折射物; (object) 折射器 **2** = **refracting telescope**

refractory /rɪˈfræktəri/ *adj* **1** (obstinate) 难管教的 ‹*pupil, child*›; 难驾驭的 ‹*horse*› **2** (resistant to heat) 耐高温的 ‹*substance*›; 难熔的 ‹*metal*›; **a ~ brick** 耐火砖

refrain[1] /rɪˈfreɪn/ *n* **1** (in song) 副歌; (in poem) 叠句 **2** (comment) 一再重复的话; **'Poor Tom' had become the constant ~ of his friends** "可怜的汤姆"成了朋友们的口头禅

refrain[2] *vi* «*person*» 忍住; «*committee, company, government*» 节制; **to ~ from sth./doing sth.** 克制某事/做某事; **please ~ from smoking** 请勿吸烟

refresh /rɪˈfreʃ/
A *vt* **1** (invigorate) «*rest, drink, holiday, bath*» 使…恢复活力 ‹*person, body*›; **to feel ~ed** 感到又有精神了; **I felt so ~ed after the rest** 休息后我感觉精力充沛 **2** (renew) 更新 ‹*design, experience*›; **the company needs to ~ its image** 公司需要重塑其形象 **3** (stimulate) 激发; **to ~ one's/sb.'s memory about sth.** 唤起自己/某人对某事物的回忆 **4** Comput 刷新
B *v refl* **to ~ oneself** 恢复精力; **I need some sleep to ~ myself** 我需要睡一觉提提神
C *vi* 刷新

refresher /rɪˈfreʃə(r)/
A *n* Brit [因案子审议超过一天付给律师的] 额外诉讼费
B *modif* 复习进修的; **~ leave** 进修假期

refresher course *n* 进修课程; **to be sent on a ~** 被送去读进修课程

refreshing /rɪˈfreʃɪŋ/ *adj* **1** (invigorating) 提神的 ‹*drink, break, shower*›; 凉爽的 ‹*breeze*› **2** (novel, interesting) 给人新鲜感的 ‹*personality, approach, news, sight*›; **it is ~ to see/to hear …** 看见/听见…令人耳目一新; **it makes a ~ change** 这带来了别开生面的变化

refreshment /rɪˈfreʃmənt/
A *n* [u] 恢复活力
B **refreshments** *npl* 茶点; **light ~s** 小食品; **~s will be served** 将会有茶点供应

refreshment: ~ stall, ~ stand *ns* 小吃部; **~s tent** *n* 活动小吃摊

refresh rate *n* 刷新率

refrigerant /rɪˈfrɪdʒərənt/
A *n* 制冷剂
B *adj* 致冷的 ‹*qualities, gas*›; 清凉的 ‹*effect*›; **the ~ system in a car's air-conditioner** 汽车空调的制冷系统

refrigerate /rɪˈfrɪdʒəreɪt/ *vt* 使…冷却 ‹*meat, food*›; **'keep ~d'** "冷藏保存"

refrigerated /rɪˈfrɪdʒəreɪtɪd/ *adj* 冷藏的; **sales of ~ food** 冷藏食品的销售量

refrigeration /rɪˌfrɪdʒəˈreɪʃn/ *n* [u] 冷藏; **to keep food under ~** 冷藏保存食品; **~ facilities** 冷藏设备

refrigerator /rɪˈfrɪdʒəreɪtə(r)/ *n* (appliance) 冰箱; (room) 冷库; **the food was kept in the ~** 食品保存在冰箱里; **a ~ truck** *or* **van** *or* **wagon** 冷藏货车

refuel /ˌriːˈfjʊəl/ (*pres p etc.* **-ll-** Brit, **-l-** Amer)
A *vt* **1** (fill with fuel) 给…加燃料 ‹*aircraft, ship*› **2** *fig* (intensify) 加剧 ‹*fears, speculation*›
B *vi* «*aircraft, ship, car, driver*» 加燃料; **we need to stop to ~** 我们需要停下来加油

refuelling Brit, **refueling** Amer /ˌriːˈfjʊəlɪŋ/ *n* [u] 加燃料; **~ stop** 加油停留

refuge /ˈrefjuːdʒ/ *n* **1** [u] (safety) 庇护; **a place of ~** 避难所 **2** [u] (consolation, escape) 慰藉; **to seek** *or* **take ~ in sth.** 在某物中寻求慰藉; **I sought ~ in drink** 我借酒浇愁 **3** [c] (safe place, situation) 避难所; (hostel) 收容所; **a ~ for battered wives/a women's ~** 受虐待妇女庇护所/妇女收容所 **4** [c] Brit (traffic island) [街道中央的] 安全岛

refugee /ˌrefjuˈdʒiː, Amer ˈrefjuːdʒiː/ *n* 难民; **a ~ camp** 难民营

refund
A /ˌriːˈfʌnd/ *vt* **1** (pay back) 退还 ‹*expenses, postage*›; **I took the sweater back and the shop ~ed the money** 我把毛衣拿了回

去，商店把购物款退给了我 2 (reimburse) 退款给 ‹customer›
B /ˈriːfʌnd/ n 1 (sum) 退款金额; **to get a ~** 得到一笔退款 2 (reimbursement) 退还

refundable /ˌriːˈfʌndəbl/ adj 可退还的; **tickets are not ~** 不可退票

refurbish /ˌriːˈfɜːbɪʃ/ vt 整修

refurbishment /ˌriːˈfɜːbɪʃmənt/ n [u and c] 整修

refurnish /ˌriːˈfɜːnɪʃ/ vt 给…添置新家具

refusal /rɪˈfjuːzl/ n 1 [c and u] (in response to order) 拒绝; **his ~ to move/cooperate/hand over the keys** 他拒绝搬家/合作/交出钥匙 2 [u and c] (in response to request) 不答应; **the doctor's ~ to see me** 医生拒绝给我看病 3 [u and c] (in response to offer) 回绝; **our offer was met with a firm ~** 我们的建议被断然回绝了 4 [u] (opportunity to acquire) 优先取舍权; **to give sb. first ~ on sth.** 给予某人对某物的优先取舍权 5 [c] Equit 拒跳障碍物

refuse¹ /rɪˈfjuːz/
A vt 1 (decline) 拒绝; **he ~d to leave** 他拒绝离开; **the car ~d to start** 汽车发动不起来 2 (withhold, deny) 拒绝给予; **the bank ~d them the loan** 银行拒绝给他们贷款 3 (turn down) 回绝 ‹gift, offer›; **she ~d him** 她拒绝了他的求婚 4 Equit 拒绝跳跃
B vi 1 (in response to order) 拒绝; **I asked her to leave, but she ~d** 我让她离开，但她拒绝了 2 (in response to request) 不答应; **we asked her for a day off, but she ~d** 我们向她请一天假，但她没有答应 3 (in response to offer) 回绝; **he offered to drive but I ~d** 他提出让他来开车，我没同意 4 Equit 拒跳障碍物

refuse² /ˈrefjuːs/ n [u] (rubbish) 垃圾; (material thrown away) 废弃物; **household ~** 生活垃圾

refuse /ˈrefjuːs/: **~ bin** n 垃圾桶; **~ chute** n 垃圾槽; **~ collection** n [u and c] 垃圾收集; **~ collector** ▸p. 409 n 垃圾工

refuse disposal /ˈrefjuːs dɪˌspəʊzl/ n [u] 垃圾处理

refuse /ˈrefjuːs/: **~ disposal service** n 垃圾处理部门; **~ disposal unit** n 垃圾粉碎机

refuse: ~ dump n 垃圾场; **~ lorry** n Brit 收垃圾车

refusenik /rɪˈfjuːznɪk/ n 1 Hist 被拒移民者 [指被禁止移民到以色列的苏联犹太人] 2 (protester) [尤指为表示抗议] 拒不服从法规者

refuse skip /ˈrefjuːs skɪp/ n Brit 大垃圾箱

refutable /rɪˈfjuːtəbl, ˈrefjʊtəbl/ adj 可驳倒的

refutation /ˌrefjuːˈteɪʃn/ n 1 [u] (act of disproving) 驳斥; **claims that require ~** 必须驳斥的断言 2 [c] (argument disproving sth.) 反驳论据

refute /rɪˈfjuːt/ vt 驳斥

regain /rɪˈgeɪn/ vt 1 (recover) 收回 ‹possession›; 收复 ‹territory›; 恢复 ‹strength, composure, consciousness›; **he fought hard to ~ the lost time** 他拼命想要找回失去的时间; **to ~ one's balance/footing** 恢复平衡/重新站稳 2 (return to) 返回; **the company has ~ed its leading position** 这家公司再次占据了领先地位

regal /ˈriːgl/ adj 1 (royal) 帝王的; **~ power** 王权 2 (magnificent, stately) 庄严的 ‹air, bearing›; 王者般的 ‹authority›; **a ~ feast was laid before him** 一席华筵摆在他面前; **the ~ splendour of the ceremony** 庆典的富丽堂皇

regale /rɪˈgeɪl/ vt 1 (entertain) 使高兴; **to ~ sb. with sth.** 用某物逗某人开心; **he ~d his guests with hilarious stories** 他令人喷饭的故事使客人们乐不可支 2 (lavishly supply) 款待; **to ~ sb. with sth.** 用某物款待某人; **she ~d her guests with champagne** 她用香槟款待客人

regalia /rɪˈgeɪlɪə/ npl (of royalty) [加冕时用的] 王位标志; (of an order) 勋位标志; (of rank or office) 官位标志; **she was in full ~** hum 她从上到下身着盛装

regally /ˈriːgəli/ adv 庄严地

regard /rɪˈgɑːd/
A n 1 [u] formal (consideration) 考虑; **~ for sb./sth.** 对某人/某事物的考虑; **to do sth. without ~ for sb./sth.** 不考虑某人/某事物做某事; **he was driving without ~ to the speed limits** 他开着车，根本不顾限速是多少; **he had acted without ~ for the rules** 他没有按规定行事; **to do sth. with scant** or **little/no ~ for sb./sth.** 根本不考虑某人/某事做某事; **to have** or **pay (proper** or **due) ~ to sb./sth.** （适当）考虑某人/某事物; **to show ~ for sb./sth.** 顾及某人/某事物; **out of ~ for sb./sth.** 出于对某人/某事物的考虑 2 [u and c] formal (esteem) 尊敬; **sb.'s ~ for sb./sth.** 某人对某人/某事物的尊敬; **to have little ~ for money** 对钱不屑一顾; **to hold sb./sth. in high/low ~** 对某人/某事物评价高/低; **to have (a) great** or **a high ~ for sb./sth.** 对某人极其敬佩/对某事物评价很高 3 [u and c] formal (respect, consideration) 方面; **in this/that ~** 在这/那方面; **she is very careful in this ~** 她在这一点上非常谨慎; **with** or **in ~ to sb./sth.** 关于某人/某事物; **he made enquiries with ~ to her** 他询问了有关她的情况; **with ~ to the question of pay, I would like to say that ...** 关于工资问题，我要说的是…; **having ~ to sb./sth.** 关于某人/某事物 4 [c] liter (gaze) 注视; **beneath their clear/piercing ~** 在他们清澈/锐利目光的注视下
B **regards** npl 问候; **kindest** or **warmest ~s** 最衷心的问候; **with kind ~s** 谨致问候; **to give sb. one's ~s** 向某人问好; **give them my ~s** 代我向他们问好; **to send one's ~s** 传达问候
C **as regards** prep phr formal 关于; **as ~s the question of pay, I would like to point out that ...** 关于报酬问题，我要指出的是…; **as ~s content, the programme will ...** 至于内容，本节目将…
D vt 1 (consider) 看待; **her work is very highly ~ed** 人们对她的工作评价很高; **they ~ him very highly** 他们很器重他; **to ~ sb./sth. with sth.** 以…的态度看待某人/某事物 ‹contempt, suspicion›; **he ~s me with favour** 他很赏识我; **to ~ sb./sth. as sth.** 将某人/某事物当作某情况; **I ~ her achievement as unique** 我认为她的成就独一无二 2 formal (look at) 注视; **to ~ sb./sth. closely** 紧盯着某人/某物 3 formal (pay attention to) 考虑 ‹advice›; **without ~ing our wishes** 未考虑我们的愿望 4 formal (concern) 《point》涉及 ‹topic›; **the next item on the agenda ~s our current situation** 议事日程上的下一项与我们的现状有关

regardful /rɪˈgɑːdfl/ adj pred formal 关注的; **he's not very ~ of people's feelings** 他不太尊重他人的感情; **you should be more ~ of your interests** 你应该更关心自己的利益

regarding /rɪˈgɑːdɪŋ/ prep 关于; **~ your work, I don't have much to say** 关于你的工作，我没有太多要说的

regardless /rɪˈgɑːdlɪs/
A adj pred 不理会的; **~ of cost** or **expense** 不计开支; **~ of rank** or **status** 不管地位如何
B adv 不顾一切地; **he protested, but they carried on ~** 他提出了抗议，但他们毫不理会，照常进行

regatta /rɪˈgætə/ n 划船比赛

regency /ˈriːdʒənsi/
A n (office) 摄政; (period) 摄政期; **the R~** Brit 摄政时期 [指1811至1820年威尔士亲王乔治代摄政王的时期]
B **Regency** modif 摄政时期的; **~ architecture/furniture** 摄政时期风格的建筑/家具

regenerate /rɪˈdʒenəreɪt/
A vt 1 (revive) 振兴 ‹city, industry› 2 (regrow) 重新长出; **the lizard ~s its tail** 蜥蜴的尾巴可再生
B vi 1 (reform) 《party, movement》革新; 《city, area》复兴 2 (regrow) 再生; **once destroyed, brain cells do not ~** 一旦遭到破坏，脑细胞就不能再生了

regeneration /rɪˌdʒenəˈreɪʃn/ n [u] 1 (renewal) 革新; **he showed no desire for ~** 他没有改过自新的愿望 2 (regrowth) 再生; **the ~ of cells in the body** 体内细胞的再生

regenerative /rɪˈdʒenərətɪv/ adj 1 (reinvigorating) 革新的 2 Biol 再生的; **the ~ powers of nature** 大自然的再生力

regent /ˈriːdʒənt/ n 1 Pol 摄政王 2 Amer Univ 校务委员

reggae /ˈregeɪ/ n [u] 雷盖 [一种节奏强劲的西印度流行音乐]; **a ~ band** 雷盖乐队

regicide /ˈredʒɪsaɪd/ n 1 [u] (crime) 弑君罪; **to commit ~** 犯弑君罪 2 [c] (person) 弑君者

regime, régime /ˈreʒiːm, reɪˈʒiːm/ n 1 pej (government) 政权; **a puppet/totalitarian ~** 傀儡/极权主义政权; **to establish/overthrow a ~** 建立/推翻一个政权 2 (management) 管理体制 3 Med (programme) 养生法; **a low-fat, low-calorie ~** 低脂肪低热量的饮食养生法

regime change n [c and u] 政权更迭

regimen /ˈredʒɪmen/ n 养生之道

regiment /ˈredʒɪmənt/
A n 1 Mil (unit) 团; **a crack infantry ~** 精锐步兵团 2 fig (large number) 一大群; **a whole ~ of helpers** 众多帮手
B vt pej 严格管制

regimental /ˌredʒɪˈmentl/ adj 团的; **a ~ commander** 团长; **~ colours** 团旗

regimental sergeant major n 准尉

regimentation /ˌredʒɪmenˈteɪʃn/ n [u] pej 严格控制

regimented /ˈredʒɪmentɪd/ adj pej 刻板的

Regina /rəˈdʒaɪnə/ pr n Brit 女王 [用于名字后或诉讼案名称中]; **Elizabeth ~** 伊丽莎白女王; **~ v. Jones** 女王诉琼斯案

region /ˈriːdʒən/
A n 1 (area) 地带; **a border/mountain/remote/polar/desert ~** 边境/高山/偏远/极地/沙漠地带 2 (administrative district) 行政区 3 Physiol 身体部位; **pains in the lower-back ~** 腰背部的疼痛 4 fig (sphere) 领域; **a ~ of moral uncertainty** 存有道德不确定性的领域 5 (approximately) **in the ~ of** 大约
B **the regions** npl Brit [首都以外的] 全部地区; **the rate of unemployment in the ~s** 地方失业率

regional /ˈriːdʒənl/ adj 1 (district) 地区的 ‹administration› 2 (local) 地方的 ‹flavour, wine›; **the study of ~ accents** 地方口音研究

regional: ~ council n Scot 地方议会; **~ development** n [u] 区域发展

regionalism /ˈriːdʒənəlɪzəm/ n [u] 地方主义

regionalist /ˈriːdʒənəlɪst/
A adj 地方主义的; **~ feeling is running high** 地方主义情绪高涨
B n 地方主义者

register /ˈredʒɪstə(r)/
A n 1 [c] (of people, items, shareholders, land) 登记簿; (of names) 名册; (of trademarks, companies) 注册簿; **a hotel ~** 旅馆登记簿; **a ~ of births, marriages and deaths** 出生、结婚和死亡登记簿; **to be on the ~ of voters** 《name》在选民名册上; **a missing persons' ~** 失踪人员名册; **to make an entry in a ~** 在登记簿上增加一条记录; **to enter sth. in a ~** 将某事物记入登记簿; **to keep a ~** 作记录; **the company must keep a ~ of shareholders** 公司必须对股东进行登记 2 [c] Brit Sch 点名册; **to call** or **take the ~** 点名 3 [c] esp Amer (cash till) 现金出纳机; **to ring sth. up on the ~** 将…记入收银机 ‹amount› 4 [u and c] Mus (range) 音区; **the lower/middle/upper ~** 低音/中音/高音区; **boy trebles singing in a high ~** 童声男高音 5 [u and c] Ling 语域; **the**

r

informal ~ 非正式语体; a specialist ~ 专业语域 6 [c] Comput 寄存器 7 [c] esp Amer (adjustable plate) [冷暖气设备的] 节气门 8 [u] Print (of printed matter) 正反页对版; in ~ 正反页对版的 9 [u] Phot, Print (of coloured components) 套准; in ~ 套准的

B vt 1 (enter or get entered on register) 登记 ‹*name, birth, marriage, vehicle*›; 注册 ‹*trademark, company*›; if you have a firearm, you must ~ it 枪支持有者必须办理登记; to ~ sb./sth. with sb./sth. 在某人处/某处为某人/某事物登记; you are advised to ~ your family with a doctor as soon as possible 建议你尽快找医生登记你家人的资料; to ~ sb./sth. for sth. 为某人/某事物登记某事物; they've ~ed their children for the course 他们已经为孩子们注册修读这门课; students will be ~ed for new courses at the beginning of term 学生们将在开学时注册修读新课程; the ship was ~ed in Panama 这艘船是在巴拿马注册的 2 formal (present) 提出 ‹*protest, objection*›; to ~ sth. with sb. 向某人提出某事; he ~ed a complaint with the appropriate authorities 他向有关部门投诉了 3 (show, indicate) 显示…的读数 ‹*temperature, pressure, speed, quantity*›; the instrument that ~s the airspeed 显示飞行速度的仪器; the gale ~ed 8 on the Beaufort scale 这场大风的风力为蒲福风级 8 级; the earthquake ~ed 6 on the Richter scale 地震震级为里氏 6 级 4 formal (show) 流露出 ‹*emotion*›; his expression ~ed utter dismay 他的表情显得非常惊愕; he ~ed his disapproval by walking out of the meeting 他离开了会场以示反对 5 (take in) 记住 ‹*fact*›; 注意到 ‹*presence*›; he barely ~ed our arrival 他几乎没注意到我们到来; I ~ed the fact that he was late 我记得他迟到了; she suddenly ~ed that ... 她突然注意到… 6 (sink in) 被意识到; it just hadn't ~ed that I would never see him again 我当时只是没有意识到我再也见不到他了; it suddenly ~ed with her that ... 她突然意识到… 7 (achieve) 取得 ‹*success, victory, gain*›; 遭受 ‹*loss*›; the British team has ~ed its first win in the competition 英国队在比赛中首次获胜; they ~ed their third consecutive draw 他们连续第三次打成平局; the retail price index is expected to ~ a rise/fall of 0.6% this month 预计零售价格指数本月将上升/下降 0.6% 8 Post 挂号邮寄 ‹*letter, parcel*› 9 Print 使套准 10 Tech 使…对正 ‹*parts*›; to ~ sth. with sth. 将某物与某物对正

C vi 1 (record name) 登记; to ~ at ... 在…登记 ‹*hotel, reception*›; to ~ with sb. 在…处挂号 ‹*doctor, dentist*›; you need to ~ with the police as soon as you arrive 你一到就得到警察局登记; to ~ for/to do sth. 登记某事物/做某事; to ~ for a course 注册修读课程; have you ~ed to vote yet? 你办好选民登记了吗?; to ~ as a new student 作为新生登记注册 2 (be shown) «*temperature, pressure, speed, quantity*» 被显示 3 (be taken in) 被注意; I told her my name, but it obviously didn't ~ 我把名字告诉了她, 但她显然没在意; the enormity of the accident just didn't ~ 事故的严重性并未引起注意; to ~ with sb. 引起某人注意 4 Tech «*parts*» 对正; to ~ with sth. 与某物对正

registered /ˈredʒɪstəd/ adj 1 (on list) 已登记的 ‹*voter, vehicle, share, firearm*›; 登记在册的 ‹*student, company, patent*›; he is a ~ drug addict 他是个在警署挂了号的瘾君子; she has a German-~ car 她有一辆在德国注册的汽车; to be ~ with sb./sth. 在某人处/某处登记; is your gun ~ with the police? 你的枪在警局登记过吗?; to be ~ as sth. 以某身份登记; she is ~ as blind 她登记为盲人 2 Post 挂号邮寄的 ‹*letter, parcel*›; ~ mail 挂号邮件

registered: ~ **general nurse** n Brit 注册护士; ~ **nurse** n Amer 注册护士; ~ **partnership** n 注册的同性伴侣关系; ~ **post** n [u] Brit 挂号邮寄; to send sth. by ~ post 挂号邮寄某物; ~ **shareholder** n 注册股东; ~ **trademark** n 注册商标

register office n Brit = registry office

registrar /ˌredʒɪsˈtrɑː(r), ˈredʒ-/ ▸p. 409 n Brit 1 Admin 户籍管理员 2 Univ 教务长 3 Med 专科住院医生; Junior/Senior R~ 初级/高级专科住院医生 4 Jur 高等法院注册官

Registrar of Companies n 公司注册官

registration /ˌredʒɪˈstreɪʃn/ n 1 [u] (of person, birth, marriage, firearm) 登记; (of student, trademark, patent, company) 注册; gun/voter ~ 枪支/选民登记; land ~ 土地注册; ~ for …的登记 ‹*work, tax, shares*›; the ~ of students for a course 学生的选课登记 2 [c] (entry) 登记项目; a ~ for …的登记项目 ‹*work, tax, shares*›; we have had a lot of ~s for the French class 我们这儿有很多人注册法语班 3 [c] Brit Aut (number) 车牌号码 4 [c] Amer Aut (document) 行车执照

registration: ~ **form** n 登记表; ~ **number** n 车牌号码; ~ **plate** Brit, ~ **tag** Amer ns 车牌

registry /ˈredʒɪstri/ n 1 [c] Brit (in church) 登记处; (in university) 注册处; a parish ~ 教区登记处; the land ~ 土地注册处 2 [u] Naut 船籍登记; a ship of Panamanian ~ 一艘巴拿马籍轮船; a vessel's port/certificate of ~ 一艘船的船籍港/船籍证明

registry office n 户籍登记处

regress /rɪˈgres/ vi 1 Psych 回归 2 (relapse) «*economy, civilization*» 倒退

regression /rɪˈgreʃn/ n [c and u] 1 Psych 回归; ~ therapy 回归疗法; a past-life ~ 前世回溯 2 (relapse) 倒退; economic ~ 经济倒退 3 Med (deterioration) 恶化

regressive /rɪˈgresɪv/ adj 1 Psych 回归的 ‹*behaviour*› 2 pej (retrogressive) 倒退的 ‹*policies*› 3 Econ 递减的; a ~ tax 递减税

regret /rɪˈgret/ ▸p. 29

A vt (pres p etc. -tt-) 1 (be sorry for) 为…懊悔 ‹*words, mistake*›; I ~ my decision 我后悔作了这个决定; you won't ~ it! 你绝不会后悔的!; to ~ doing sth. 后悔做某事; I ~ted having left so early 我后悔这么早就离开了; to live to ~ sth. 为某事抱憾终生 2 (feel sad about) 为…惋惜 ‹*death, absence*›; we ~ to hear that you have been ill 听说你病了, 我们感到很难过 3 (express apology for) 对…表示遗憾 ‹*fact, situation*›; your court case is not going at all well, I ~ to say 说来很遗憾, 你的案子进展得很不顺利

B n 1 [u] (remorse) 懊悔; to feel/express ~ for one's actions/words 对某人的行为/言辞感到/表示懊悔; with ~ 懊悔地 2 [u] (sadness) 惋惜; our ~ at his death/the sad news/your loss 我们对他的死/这不幸消息/痛失所爱的惋惜; with ~ 惋惜地 3 [c and u] (disappointment) 遗憾; ~s about sth. 对某事物的遗憾 4 [c and u] (apology) 道歉; please give your grandmother my ~s 请向你祖母转达我的歉意

regretful /rɪˈgretfl/ adj 1 (sorry) 后悔的 ‹*look, attitude*›; to be ~ about sth. 对某事感到懊悔 2 (sad) 惋惜的; to feel ~ 感到惋惜

regretfully /rɪˈgretfəli/ adv 1 (regrettably) 遗憾的是 2 (with sadness) 惋惜地 ‹*smile, depart*›

regrettable /rɪˈgretəbl/ adj 令人遗憾的

regrettably /rɪˈgretəbli/ adv 1 (unfortunately) 遗憾的是 2 (very) 令人扼腕地 ‹*high, weak*›

regroup /ˌriːˈgruːp/

A vt 1 Mil 重新部署 ‹*forces*› 2 (rearrange) 重新组合 ‹*people, numbers*›

B vi 1 Mil 重新整编 2 (form into new groups) 重新组合

regrouping /ˌriːˈgruːpɪŋ/ n [u] 1 Mil 重新部署 2 (reorganization) 重新组合

Regt abbr = regiment A

regular /ˈregjʊlə(r)/

A adj 1 (evenly spaced in time) 定期的 ‹*activity, payment, service*›; 均匀的 ‹*footsteps*›; the ~ ticking of the clock 钟有规律的滴答声; her ~ walk before breakfast 她早餐前固定要有的散步; at ~ intervals 每隔一定时间; on a ~ basis 定期地; ~ weekly deliveries 每周固定的送货; as ~ as clockwork 极有规律地 ‹*appear, wake*› 2 (evenly arranged in space) 间隔均匀的 ‹*milestones, lampposts, trees*›; 整齐的 ‹*footprints, lines, pattern*›; at ~ intervals or points 间隙均匀地 ‹*plant, place*›; in ~ formation 按整齐编队 ‹*march, fly*›; the trees made ~ patches of shade along the road 一路上片片树荫均匀有致; the curtains have ~ vertical stripes in red and black 窗帘上均匀分布着红色和黑色的竖条 3 Med 有规律的 ‹*heartbeat, breathing, bowel movements, periods*› 4 (frequent) 频繁的; a fairly ~ occurrence 出现频率相当高的事情; to take ~ exercise 经常锻炼; I make ~ payments into a savings account 我常常往储蓄账户里存钱 5 (habitual) 惯常的; ~ customers/listeners/viewers/travellers 老顾客/老听众/老观众/经常出行者; he was a ~ visitor to her house 他是她家的常客; a ~ offender 惯犯; to be ~ in one's habits 有固定习惯 6 attrib (usual) 通常的 ‹*time, activity, walk*›; 平常的 ‹*price*›; my ~ bedtime 我通常就寝的时间; my ~ doctor/hairdresser 平常给我看病的医生/为我理发的理发师; a ~ sexual partner 固定的性伙伴; one of his ~ haunts 他经常光顾的地方之一; sb.'s ~ duties 某人的日常工作; to keep (very) ~ hours 作息(非常)有规律 7 (conventional) 传统的 ‹*method*›; 通常的 ‹*channels*›; to follow ~ procedures 按正常程序办事 8 (permanent) 稳定的 ‹*job, income*›; to be in ~ use 被持久使用; to be in ~ employment 有固定工作 9 (even) 端正的 ‹*features*›; 匀称的 ‹*pattern, design*›; 整齐的 ‹*teeth*›; 规则的 ‹*shape, pattern*› 10 esp Amer (standard) 标准的 ‹*size*›; 标准装的 ‹*fries, milkshake*› 11 attrib esp Amer (ordinary) 普通的 ‹*cola, pasta*›; ~ gasoline 普通汽油 12 attrib esp Amer colloq (unpretentious) 诚实可靠的; he's a ~ guy 他是个好人 13 attrib Admin, Mil 正规的 ‹*soldier, police force*›; 正规军的 ‹*staff, officer*›; a ~ civil servant 正编公务员; the ~ army 正规军 14 Ling 规则的 ‹*plural, form, ending*›; ~ verbs 规则动词 15 attrib dated colloq (complete) 十足的 ‹*fool, idiot, villain*›; 真正的 ‹*hero, genius*›; 彻底的 ‹*mess, muddle*›; their dog is a ~ nuisance! 他们的狗真讨厌!; the whole thing was a ~ disaster 整件事完全是场灾难 16 Math 正的; a ~ geometrical figure/polygon 正几何形/多边形

B n 1 [c] (visitor, guest) 常客; (customer) 老顾客; (traveller) 老乘客; (listener) 老听众; (viewer) 老观众; pub ~s 酒吧的常客 2 [c] Mil (soldier) 正规军人 3 [c] Sport (player) 正式队员 4 [c] Radio, TV 老主持人; Theat (performer) 正式演员 5 [u] Amer (petrol) 普通汽油 6 [c] Amer Pol (party stalwart) 忠诚党员; Democratic ~s 民主党的忠诚党员

regularity /ˌregjʊˈlærəti/ n [u] 规律性; with increasing ~ 越来越频繁地; with unfailing ~ 一成不变地

regularize /ˈregjʊləraɪz/ vt formal 使合法化; immigrants applying to ~ their status as residents 申请成为合法居民的移民

regularly /ˈregjʊləli/ adv 1 (at fixed intervals or times) 有规律地; we meet ~ to discuss the progress of the project 我们定期会面商讨项目的进展情况 2 (often) 经常 3 (evenly) 均匀地

regulate /ˈregjʊleɪt/ vt 1 (control) 控制 ‹*behaviour, actions, speed, temperature*›; traffic lights ~ the flow of traffic 红绿灯控制交通流量; government-~d 政府管制的; this valve ~s the flow of water back to the boiler 这个阀门可以控制返回锅炉的水流

2 (adapt, change in response) 调节; **to ~ one's lifestyle to fit in with sth.** 调节生活方式以适应某事物 **3** (adjust) 调整 ‹*mechanism, appliance*›; 校准 ‹*clock*›

regulation /ˌregjʊˈleɪʃn/
A *n* **1** [c] (rule) 规定; **a set of ~s** 一套规定; **under the new ~s** 按新规定; **~s for sth./for doing sth.** 某事/做某事的章程; **~s for environmental protection** 环境保护规定; **~s for granting passports to foreign nationals** 向外国人签发护照的规定; **strict ~s are laid down governing the use of firearms** 已颁布了严格的枪支使用管理法规; **to comply with the ~s** «*person, organization*» 遵守规定; «*product*» 符合规定; **to follow** *or* **abide by (the) ~s** 遵守规定; **to meet the ~s** «*person, company, equipment*» 符合规定; **against the** *or* **contrary to ~s** 违反规定的; **rules and ~s** 规章制度; **building/planning ~s** 建筑/规划条例; **traffic ~s** 交通规则; **college/school ~** 大学校规/校规; **EU/police/government ~s** 欧盟/警方/政府规定 **2** [u] (control) 管理; **government ~** 政府控制; **strict ~ of sth.** 对某事物的严格管制; **~ of financial markets** 金融市场的管理; **the voluntary ~ of the press** 新闻界的自律 **3** [u] (adjustment) 调整
B *modif* **1** (standard) 标准化的; **~ army footwear** 正规的军用鞋; **in ~ uniform** 身穿规定制服的; **of the ~ length/width** 规定长度/宽度的 **2** colloq (predictable) 老套的; **a ~ parody** 毫无新意的滑稽模仿作品

regulator /ˈregjʊleɪtə(r)/ *n* **1** (person) 监管者; (body) 监管机构 **2** (device) 调节阀

regulatory /ˈregjʊlətri, Amer -tɔːri/ *adj* 监管的; **~ breaches** 违背监管条例; **a market without a ~ framework** 缺乏管理框架的市场; **~ enzymes/genes** 调节酶/基因

regulatory: ~ authority *n* 监管部门; **~ body** *n* 管理部门

regulo® /ˈregjʊləʊ/ *n* Brit 煤气灶火力控制器

regurgitate /rɪˈgɜːdʒɪteɪt/ *vt* **1** (bring up) «*person, animal*» 使…返回口中 ‹*food*› **2** (disgorge) «*drain*» 使…返流 ‹*liquid*›; «*machine*» 使…来回翻转 ‹*coins, paper*› **3** fig pej (repeat blindly) 机械重复 ‹*facts, opinions*›

regurgitation /rɪˌgɜːdʒɪˈteɪʃn/ *n* [u] **1** (of food) 返回口中 **2** fig pej (blind repetition) 机械重复

rehab /ˈriːhæb/
A *n* **1** [u] (rehabilitation) 康复 **2** [c] (clinic) 康复诊所; (programme) 康复疗程 **3** [c] Amer Constr (refurbishment) 修复的建筑
B *vt* Amer **1** (after imprisonment, addiction) 使改过自新; (after illness) 使康复 **2** (reinstate) 恢复…的名誉 ‹*dissident, politician*› **3** Constr 修复 ‹*building*›

rehabilitate /ˌriːəˈbɪlɪteɪt/ *vt* **1** (to health) 使…康复 ‹*patient*›; (to normal life) 使…恢复正常生活 ‹*drug user, ex-offender*› **2** (reinstate) 恢复…的名誉 ‹*dissident, politician*› **3** (to former condition) 修复 ‹*building*›

rehabilitation /ˌriːəbɪlɪˈteɪʃn/ *n* **1** [u] (to health) 康复; (after prison, addiction) 改过自新 **2** [u] Pol (reinstatement) 恢复名誉 **3** [c and u] Constr (of building) 修复; (of area) 恢复

rehabilitation centre *n* 康复中心

rehash colloq pej
A /ˌriːˈhæʃ/ *vt* 把…炒冷饭; **he endlessly ~es songs from his American years** 他没完没了地改编自己在美国那些年唱过的歌曲
B /ˈriːhæʃ/ *n* 炒冷饭; **his first book was just a ~ of his doctoral thesis** 他的第一本书只是他博士论文的翻版

rehear /ˌriːˈhɪə(r)/ *vt* (*pt, pp* **reheard** /ˌriːˈhɜːd/) **1** (listen to again) 重听 ‹*story, music*› **2** Jur 再审 ‹*case, plaintiff*›

rehearsal /rɪˈhɜːsl/ *n* **1** [c and u] (practice) 排练; **to have** *or* **hold** *or* **conduct a ~** 进行排练; **to attend/call a ~** 参加/召集排练; **to go into ~** 进入排练 **2** [c] (recounting) 复述

rehearse /rɪˈhɜːs/
A *vt* **1** (practise) 排练 ‹*play, sonata, speech*› **2** (supervise) 监督…排练 ‹*actors, animals*› **3** (mentally prepare) 默记 ‹*apology, explanation*› **4** (recount) 反复讲 ‹*grievances, arguments*›; 历数 ‹*evidence*›
B *vi* «*performer*» 排练; **to ~ for sth.** 为某事排练

reheat /ˌriːˈhiːt/ *vt* 重新加热

reheel /ˌriːˈhiːl/ *vt* 给…装新鞋跟

rehouse /ˌriːˈhaʊz/ *vt* 给…安排新住处

reign /reɪn/
A *vi* **1** (rule) «*monarch*» 为王; **to ~ over a country** 做一国君主 **2** (be the best) 独占鳌头; **among pianists, she still ~s supreme** 在众多钢琴演奏家当中，她仍然是最杰出的 **3** (prevail) «*justice*» 占上风; «*violence*» 盛行; **peace ~s in the house** 房子里一片宁静; **chaos and confusion ~ed** 充斥着混乱与迷茫
B *n* **1** (period as monarch) 君主统治时期; **in the ~ of Queen Elizabeth the Second** 在女王伊丽莎白二世统治时期 **2** (period of power, influence) 当政期; **the dictator's ~ is nearly over** 独裁者的时代即将结束; **during the ~ of violence** fig 在暴力泛滥的时期; **a ~ of terror** fig 恐怖统治时期; **during his ~ as champion** 在他保有冠军称号期间

reigning /ˈreɪnɪŋ/ *adj attrib* **1** (ruling) 在位的 ‹*monarch*› **2** (current) 本届的; **the ~ world champion** 本届世界冠军 **3** (prevailing) 盛行的 ‹*attitude, custom*›

reimburse /ˌriːɪmˈbɜːs/ *vt* **1** (refund) 报销 ‹*expenses*›; 赔偿 ‹*losses*›; 退还…的款项 ‹*unused ticket*› **2** (repay) 赔偿 ‹*customer*›; **to ~ sb. for time spent** 补偿某人所花的时间

reimbursement /ˌriːɪmˈbɜːsmənt/ *n* [u] **1** (of expenses) 报销; (of losses) 赔偿; (of unused ticket) 退款 **2** (of customer) 赔偿

reimpose /ˌriːɪmˈpəʊz/ *vt* 重新实施 ‹*curfew, ban*›; 重新征收 ‹*tax*›

rein /reɪn/
A *n* **1** Equit 缰绳; **to pull at the ~s** 收缰; **to give a horse full ~** 给马松开缰绳 **2** fig (control) 控制; **to give sb. (a) free ~ to do sth.** 任由某人做某事; **primary education should give free ~ to a child's imagination** 初等教育应该让孩子自由发挥想象力; **to take up the ~s** 掌权; **to seize the ~s** 抓住权力; **to keep a tight ~ on public expenditure** 严格控制公共支出; **to keep sb. on a ~ rein** 牢牢控制某人; **she keeps her husband on a ~ rein** 她把丈夫管得很紧
B **reins** *npl* Brit (for child) [系在儿童身上防止其走失的] 保护带

Phrasal verb

• **rein back, rein in** *vt* [**~ back sth.**] **1** Equit 勒 ‹*horse*› **2** fig (curb, restrain) 控制 ‹*expenditure, expansion, inflation*›

reincarnate
A /ˌriːɪmˈkɑːneɪt/ *vt* 使投胎; **when he dies he hopes he'll be ~d as a bird** 他希望死后会转世投胎为一只鸟
B /ˌriːɪmˈkɑːnət/ *adj postpos* 转世的; **he thinks he's Hitler/Christ ~** 他认为自己是希特勒/基督转世

reincarnation /ˌriːɪnkɑːˈneɪʃn/ *n* **1** [c] (person, animal) 转世化身 **2** [u] (rebirth) 转世说

reindeer /ˈreɪndɪə(r)/ *n* (*pl* **~** *or* **~s**) 驯鹿; **a herd of ~** 一群驯鹿

reindeer moss *n* [u] 驯鹿苔

reinforce /ˌriːɪnˈfɔːs/ *vt* **1** (in number) 增加 ‹*labour force, staff*›; Mil 增援 ‹*troops, fleet*› **2** (strengthen) 加固 ‹*foundation, seam*› **3** (promote) 强化 ‹*demand, trend, hopes*› **4** (confirm) 证实 ‹*view, idea, conviction*›; (emphasize) 加深 ‹*prejudices, contention*›

reinforced concrete *n* [u] 钢筋混凝土

reinforcement /ˌriːɪnˈfɔːsmənt/
A *n* **1** [u] (of labour force) 增加; Mil (of troops, fleet) 增援 **2** [u] (of foundation, seam, structure) 加固 **3** [c] (beam, bar, pillar) 加固结构; (material) 加固物 **4** [u] (of demand, trend) 强化 **5** [u] (of view, conviction) 证实; (of prejudice) 加深 **6** [u] Psych 强化; **psychological ~** 心理强化; **conditioned ~ in dog training** 驯狗过程中的条件强化; **negative ~** 负强化
B **reinforcements** *npl* (troops, ships) 增援部队

reinsert /ˌriːɪnˈsɜːt/ *vt* 重新插入

reinstate /ˌriːɪnˈsteɪt/ *vt* **1** (to position) 使…恢复原职 ‹*employee*›; (bring back) 恢复 ‹*service, tax*› **2** (recover) 使复原; **to ~ deleted text or files** 恢复已删除的文本或文件

reinstatement /ˌriːɪnˈsteɪtmənt/ *n* [u] (of employee) 恢复原职; (of legislation, service) 恢复

reinstitute /ˌriːˈɪnstɪtjuːt, Amer -tuːt/ *vt* 重新设立; **a bill to ~ the death penalty** 重设死刑的议案

reinsurance /ˌriːɪnˈʃɔːrəns, Amer -ˈʃʊər-/ *n* [u] 分保保险

reinsure /ˌriːɪnˈʃɔː(r), Amer -ˈʃʊə(r)/ *vt* 分保

reintegrate /ˌriːˈɪntɪgreɪt/ *vt* **1** (restore) 使重新成为一体; **to ~ the country into the world economy** 把国家重新纳入世界经济体系 **2** (rehabilitate) 使重新融入; **it can be difficult for an offender to be ~d into the community** 违法者要重新融入社会会很困难

reintegration /ˌriːɪntrˈgreɪʃn/ *n* [u] 再融合; **the ~ of Germany into Europe** 德国的重入欧洲; **prisoner rehabilitation and ~** 犯人的改造和重新融入社会

reinvest /ˌriːɪnˈvest/ *vt* 把…再投资

reinvestment /ˌriːɪnˈvestmənt/ *n* [u and c] 再投资

reinvigorate /ˌriːɪnˈvɪgəreɪt/ *vt* 给…注入新的活力 ‹*economy, area*›; 使…精神焕发 ‹*person*›

reissue /ˌriːˈɪʃuː/
A *vt* 重新发行 ‹*ticket, stamp, film*›; 重新发给 ‹*catalogue*›; **to ~ sb. with sth.** 再发给某人某物
B *n* **1** [c] (new release) 新版 **2** [u] (act) 再版

REIT *abbr* Amer = **real estate investment trust**

reiterate /ˌriːˈɪtəreɪt/ *vt* 重申

reiteration /riːˌɪtəˈreɪʃn/ *n* [c and u] 重申

reject
A /rɪˈdʒekt/ *vt* **1** (turn down) 驳回 ‹*plea, bid, amendment*›; 拒收 ‹*gift, damaged goods*›; 拒绝 ‹*offer, applicant, suggestion*› **2** (spurn) 嫌弃 ‹*child*›; **~ed by his friends, he fell into despair** 由于遭到朋友们的嫌弃，他陷入了绝望 **3** Med 排斥 ‹*transplant*› **4** (not accept) «*machine, computer*» 不接受 ‹*coin, data*›
B /ˈriːdʒekt/ *n* **1** (person) 被拒者; **he sees himself as a social ~** 他把自己看成是社会的弃儿 **2** Comm (product) 次品; **~ goods/china** 次品/有瑕疵的瓷器

rejection /rɪˈdʒekʃn/ *n* **1** [c] (of plea, bid) 驳回; (of applicant, offer) 拒绝 **2** [u] (by family, friend, loved one) 嫌弃; **to meet with** *or* **encounter ~** 遭到嫌弃 **3** [u] Med 排斥; **the risk of ~ of a newly transplanted organ** 新移植器官排异反应的风险

rejection: ~ letter *n* 回绝信; **I got a ~ letter from the editor** 我从编辑那里收到了退稿信; **~ slip** *n* 退稿附条

reject shop /ˈriːdʒekt ʃɒp/ *n* 次品店

rejig /ˌriːˈdʒɪg/ Brit, **rejigger** /ˌriːˈdʒɪgə(r)/ Amer *vt* **1** dated (refit) 重新装配 ‹*lathe*›; (re-equip) 重新装备 ‹*factory*› **2** (rearrange) 重新布置 ‹*room*›; 重新摆放 ‹*furniture*›; 更改 ‹*schedule*›

rejoice /rɪˈdʒɔɪs/ *vi* 欣喜; **to ~ at** *or* **over sth.** 为某事物欢欣鼓舞; **the prisoner ~d in his new found freedom** 这名囚犯为重获自由

r

感到欣喜; **he seems to positively ~ in the misfortunes of others** 他好像对别人的不幸无比开心; **she ~s in the name of Ermintrude** Brit hum 她有个滑稽的名字叫厄敏特鲁德

rejoicing /rɪˈdʒɔɪsɪŋ/ *n* [u] 喜庆; **an occasion for ~** 欢庆的时刻

rejoin /ˌriːˈdʒɔɪn/ *vt* **1** (return to) 重新加入 ‹*club*›; 返回 ‹*train, main road*›; **the sailor had to ~ his ship by midnight** 水手必须不迟于午夜回到船上 **2** (join together again) 重新接上 ‹*broken pieces, thread*›

rejoinder /rɪˈdʒɔɪndə(r)/ *n* 反驳

rejuvenate /rɪˈdʒuːvɪneɪt/ *vt* 使…年轻 ‹*person*›; 使…更有活力 ‹*institution, economy*›

rejuvenation /rɪˌdʒuːvɪˈneɪʃn/ *n* [u] (of person) 变得年轻; (of institution, economy) 焕发生机

rekey /ˌriːˈkiː/ *vt* 重新键入 ‹*data*›

rekindle /ˌriːˈkɪndl/ *vt* **1** (relight) 重新点燃 **2** fig (reawaken) 重新激起 ‹*love, hope*›

relabel /ˌriːˈleɪbl/ *vt* (*pres p etc.* **-ll-** Brit, **-l-** Amer) **1** (label again) 给…重贴标签 ‹*goods*› **2** (rename) 给…重新命名

relaid /ˌriːˈleɪd/ *pt, pp* ▸ **relay²**

relapse

A /rɪˈlæps/ *vi* **1** Med 旧病复发 **2** (revert) 退回原状; **the conversation ~d into silence** 谈话复又陷入了沉默; **prisoners who cannot find work tend to ~ into crime** 找不到工作的犯人往往会再次犯罪

B *also* /ˈriːlæps/ *n* **1** Med 旧病复发 **2** (into bad habit) 故态复萌

relate /rɪˈleɪt/

A *vt* **1** (connect) 把…联系起来 ‹*person, object, idea*›; **a supercomputer could ~ all those factors** 超级计算机能将所有那些因素联系起来; **to ~ sb./sth. and** *or* **to sb./sth.** 将某人/某事物与某人/某事物联系起来; **logic is chiefly concerned with relating cause and effect** 逻辑主要是建立因果之间的联系 **2** formal (recount) 讲 ‹*tale, story*›; 讲述 ‹*adventures, happenings*›; **to ~ sth. to sb.** 把某事讲给某人听; **she ~d how he had run away from home** 她讲述了他是如何离家出走的; **in his memoirs he ~s that they first met in Shanghai** 在回忆录中他讲述说他们在上海初次相遇

B *vi* 有关联; **the two things ~** 这两件事是有联系的

Phrasal verb

• **relate to**

A [**~ to sb./sth.**] *vt*

1 (concern) 涉及; **the figures ~ to last year** 这些数字是去年的; **everything relating to him** *or* **that ~s to him** 所有牵涉到他的东西 **2** (identify with) 理解某人/某事物; **I can't ~ to the painting** 我看不懂这幅画; **I can ~ to that!** 那个我懂！; **an image that people can ~ to** 人们能理解的形象; **to ~ to avant garde music** 了解前卫音乐

B [**~ to sb.**] *vt* (communicate with) 与…沟通; **the way children ~ to their teachers** 孩子与老师交流的方式

related /rɪˈleɪtɪd/

A *adj* **1** (of the same family) 有亲属关系的; (of the same group, type) 同一类型的 ‹*animals, plants*›; **to be ~ to sb.** 和某人是亲戚; **to be ~ by marriage** 有姻亲关系; **our two families are distantly/closely ~** 我们两家是远亲/近亲; **sleeping sickness and ~ diseases** 昏睡病及同类疾病 **2** (connected) 相关的 ‹*subjects, information*›; **these facts are ~** 这些事实之间有关联; **his death was ~ to drug abuse** 他的死和滥用药物有关 **3** Mus 有密切关系的 ‹*passage*›; **a ~ key** 关系调

B **-related** *combining form* 与…有关的; **stress~** 与压力相关的; **alcohol~ violence** 酗酒引起的暴力

relating /rɪˈleɪtɪŋ/ *adj* **~ to ...** 与…有关的; **the law ~ to marriage** 婚姻法

relation /rɪˈleɪʃn/

A *n* **1** [c and u] (connection) 关系; **~ between sth. and sth.** 某事物与某事物之间的关系; **his story bears absolutely no ~ to the truth** 他的说法与事实毫无关联; **the meagre result bears little ~ to the effort involved** 微不足道的结果和付出的努力完全不相称 **2** [c] (relative) 亲戚; **distant/close ~** 远亲/近亲; **friends and ~s** 亲戚朋友 **3** [u] (narration) 叙述 **4** [u] **in ~ to sb./sth.** (in comparison to) 与某人/某事物相比; (in the context of) 关于某人/某事物; **with ~ to sb./sth.** 涉及某人/某事物

B **relations** *npl* **1** (mutual dealings) 往来; **to improve/promote/cement ~s** 改善/促进/巩固关系; **to break off** *or* **sever ~s** 断绝关系; **East-West ~s** 东西方关系 **2** euph (sex) 肉体关系

relational database /rɪˌleɪʃənl ˈdeɪtəbeɪs/ *n* 关系数据库

relationship /rɪˈleɪʃnʃɪp/ *n* **1** (connection) 联系 **2** (family bond) 亲属关系; **family ~s** 家庭关系; **a father-son ~** 父子关系 **3** [c] (human connection) 人际关系; **a business/working ~** 业务/工作关系 **4** (romance, affair) 情爱关系; **to have a ~ with sb.** 与某人有亲密关系; **a sexual ~** 性关系 **5** Math 逻辑关系

relationship marketing *n* [u] [旨在建立长久关系的] 关系营销

relative /ˈrelətɪv/

A *adj* **1** (comparative) 相对而言的 ‹*peace, happiness*›; **he was a ~ stranger** 他相对来说是个陌生人 **2** Sci (not absolute) 相对的 ‹*standard*›; **~ value** 相对值 **3** (respective) 各自的 ‹*values, merits, importance*› **4** (corresponding) 相应的; **to be ~ to sth.** 与某事物相对应; **petrol consumption is ~ to speed** 耗油量与速度是成比例的 **5** formal (relevant) 相关的 ‹*fact, document*› **6** Ling 关系的; **a ~ pronoun** 关系代词; **a ~ clause** 关系从句

B *n* (relation) 亲戚

relative: ~ density *n* 相对密度; **~ humidity** *n* 相对湿度

relatively /ˈrelətɪvli/ *adv* **1** (quite) 相当 ‹*difficult, cheap*› **2** (comparatively) 相对 ‹*young, successful*›; **~ speaking, the winter's been quite mild** 比较而言，这个冬天不太冷

relativism /ˈrelətɪvɪzəm/ *n* [u] 相对主义

relativist /ˈrelətɪvɪst/

A *adj* 相对主义者的

B *n* 相对主义者

relativistic /ˌrelətɪˈvɪstɪk/ *adj* **1** Art, Philos 相对主义的 ‹*argument*›; **the postmodern, ~ view** 后现代的相对主义观点 **2** Phys 相对论性的 ‹*physics, cosmology*›; **~ theory** 相对论; **a ~ electron** 相对论性电子

relativity /ˌreləˈtɪvəti/ *n* [u] **1** (fact of being relative) 相对性; **the ~ of truth** 真理的相对性 **2** Phys 相对论; **Einstein's theory of ~** 爱因斯坦的相对论

relativize /ˈrelətɪvaɪz/ *vt* 使相对化

relax /rɪˈlæks/

A *vt* **1** (slacken) 使…松弛 ‹*muscle, limb*›; 松开 ‹*grip*›; 使…松懈 ‹*vigilance, concentration, attention*› **2** (moderate) 放宽 ‹*tariffs, sanctions*›; **the government has ~ed its immigration procedures** 政府已经简化了移民手续

B *vi* **1** (unwind) 放松; **everyone needs to ~ sometimes** 每个人都不时需要放松一下 **2** (loosen up) «*person, manner*» 变得随和; **her face ~ed into a smile** 她转而轻松一笑

relaxant /rɪˈlæksnt/ *n* 弛缓药

relaxation /ˌriːlækˈseɪʃn/ *n* **1** [c and u] (recreation) 消遣; **his only ~ is gardening** 他唯一的消遣就是园艺; **it's a form of ~** 这是一种娱乐方式 **2** [u] (of body, mind) 放松; **~ of mind and body** 身心的放松 **3** [u and c] (of rules, restrictions) 放宽; **a ~ of import controls** 进口限制的放宽; **there should be no ~ of educational standards** 教育的标准不应该降低

relaxed /rɪˈlækst/ *adj* **1** (free from tension) 轻松的 ‹*atmosphere, discussion, meeting*›; **to feel ~** 感觉轻松自在; **he's always totally ~ when he comes here** 他来这里时总是无拘无束 **2** (loosened up) 放松的; **after a massage the body is ~** 按摩后身体就放松了

relaxing /rɪˈlæksɪŋ/ *adj* 使人放松的; **she spent a ~ weekend at home** 她在家里过了一个轻松的周末

relay¹

A /ˈriːleɪ/ *n* **1** (team, shift) 轮换者; **the rescuers worked in ~s throughout the night** 救援人员整个晚上轮班工作; **teams of horses worked in ~s** 几组马轮流干活儿 **2** (race) 接力赛 **3** Elec 继电器 **4** Telecom (device) 中继设备 **5** Radio, TV 转播节目; **a live/recorded ~** 直播节目/录制节目转播

B /rɪˈleɪ/ *vt* (retransmit) 转播 ‹*signal, programme*›; 转达 ‹*message, orders*›

relay² /riːˈleɪ/ *vt* (lay again) 重新铺设 ‹*track, cable*›

release /rɪˈliːs/

A *vt* **1** (set free) 释放 ‹*person, animal*›; **to ~ sb./sth. from sth.** 将某人从…中释放出来 ‹*prison, custody*›; 将某人/某物从…中解救出来 ‹*trap, rubble, wreckage*›; **to be ~d from captivity** 被释放; **the swan will be ~d into the wild** 天鹅会被放归野外; **the accused was ~d on bail of £5,000** 被告在缴纳了5,000英镑保释金后获释 **2** fig (from debt) 免除…的债务; (from responsibility) 免除…的责任; **to ~ sb. from sth.** 免除某人的 ‹*obligation, undertaking*›; **she ~d him from his promise** 她使他不必履行承诺; **to ~ a monk from his vows** 免除修道士履行誓言的义务; **to ~ sb. from a debt/tax** 免除某人的债务/纳税义务; **to ~ sb. to attend a course** 使某人免修课程 **3** Tech 开启 ‹*mechanism*›; 打开 ‹*lock, shutter*›; 拉动 ‹*clutch, handle*›; 松开 ‹*catch, lever, spring*› **4** (let go of) 放开 ‹*person, arm, object*›; 松开 ‹*hand, grasp*›; **to ~ one's hold (of sth.)** 松开（拿着的某物）; **to ~ one's grip (on** *or* **of sth.)** 松开（抓紧的某物）; **he wouldn't ~ his grip on the rope** 他紧紧抓住绳子不放 **5** (set off) 发射 ‹*missile*›; 投放 ‹*bomb*›; 射出 ‹*arrow, bullet*›; 放飞 ‹*bird, balloon*›; **to ~ sth. from sth.** 从某处射出某物 **6** (make known) 发布 ‹*news, information, bulletin*›; 发表 ‹*report, statement*›; 公开 ‹*details, photo, picture*›; **to ~ sth. to sb./sth.** 向某人/某处公布某事 **7** (make available to the public) 发行 ‹*CD, video, film, software*›; **new products ~d on to the market** 投放市场的新产品; **to ~ sth. to sb./sth.** 对…发行某物 ‹*market, customer*› **8** (end restrictions on) 放开对…的控制 ‹*funds, forces*› **9** (let out) 释放 ‹*pressure, steam*›; 排放 ‹*gas, liquid, chemicals*›; **to ~ sth. into/from sth.** 将某物排入某处/从某处排出; **growth hormone is ~d into the blood during sleep** 生长激素在睡眠时被释放到血液中; **the water ~d from the dam** 从大坝中排出的水 **10** (express) 发泄 ‹*emotions, anger, frustration*› **11** (relieve) 缓解 ‹*tension*› **12** Jur (surrender) 放弃 ‹*right, property*›

B *n* **1** [u and c] (liberation) 释放; **to pay a ransom for sb's ~** 支付赎金使某人获释; **~ from sth.** 从…中的解救 ‹*trap, rubble, wreckage*›; **~ from captivity/custody** 监禁/拘留释放; **~ from prison** 释放出狱 **2** [u and c] (of CD, DVD, video, software) 公开发行; (of film) 公映; **to be due for ~** 预定公开发行; **to be/go on general ~** «*film*» 公开发行/开始公开发行 **3** [c] (product) 新发行的产品 [如CD、影片、软件等] **4** [u and c] (relief) 解脱; **a feeling** *or* **a sense of (intense) ~** （强烈的）解脱感; **to come as** *or* **be a (welcome) ~ (from sth.)** «*death*» 是一种（可喜的）（从…中的）解脱 ‹*pain, suffering*› **5** [u and c] (of pressure, steam, hormones) 释放; (of gas, liquid, chemicals) 排放; **the ~ of**

sth. into the atmosphere 某物向大气中的排放; **the ~ of water from a dam** 水坝的放水 **6** [u and c] (of missile) 发射; **the aircraft turned away after the ~ of its bombs** 飞机投放炸弹后便掉头飞走了 **7** [u and c] Tech (of mechanism) 移动; (of handle, lever, catch) 松开; **~ of the catch starts the mechanism** 松开锁扣就能启动这个机械装置; **the ~ button** 锁键 **8** [c] Tech (mechanism) 擒纵装置; (handle) 操作手柄; (lever) 操控杆; (catch) 固定装置 **9** [u and c] (of news, information, bulletin) 发布; (of report, statement) 发表; (of details, photo, picture) 公开 **10** [c] (announcement) 声明; **to put out a ~** 发表声明; **to issue a news ~** 发表新闻稿 **11** [u and c] Transp 许可; **~ for shipment** 启运许可; **the ~ of goods against payment** 付款发货 **12** [c] Admin (waiver) 弃权文书; **~ forms/documents** 转渡表/文件

relegate /ˈrelɪɡeɪt/ *vt* **1** (downgrade) 降低…的地位; **to ~ sth. to the scrap heap** fig 把某物当作废物处理掉 **2** Brit Sport 降级; **to be ~d** 被降级

relegation /ˌrelɪˈɡeɪʃn/ *n* [u] **1** (downgrading) 降低地位 **2** Brit Sport 降级; **our team is facing ~** 我们队面临降级

relent /rɪˈlent/ *vi* **1** (soften) «*person, authority*» 变宽容; **his parents ~ed and let him go on holiday with his friends** 他的父母心软了, 允许他和朋友一起去度假 **2** (ease) «*wind*» 减缓; «*heat*» 消退; **the rain shows no signs of ~ing** 雨势没有减弱的迹象

relentless /rɪˈlentlɪs/ *adj* **1** (never-ending) 没完没了的 ‹*noise, storm*›; 持续的 ‹*pressure, thirst, heat*›; 不懈的 ‹*pursuit, ambition*› **2** (implacable) 无情的 ‹*enemy, cruelty, advance*›; (inflexible) 固执的 ‹*hostility*›

relentlessly /rɪˈlentlɪsli/ *adv* **1** (unceasingly) 持续地 ‹*rain, argue*›; **the traffic thundered ~ across the bridge** 车辆接连不断轰隆隆地开过大桥 **2** (implacably) 无情地 ‹*advance, fight, attack*›; **~ cold** 酷寒

relet /ˌriːˈlet/ *vt* (*pres p* **-tt-**; *pt, pp* **relet**) Brit 再出租

relevance /ˈreləvəns/ *n* [u] 相关; **to have ~ to sth.** 和某事物有关系

relevant /ˈreləvənt/ *adj* 有关的; **all the facts ~ to the case** 和这个案子相关的所有事实; **I found much of my course was not really ~** 我发现我所学的课程没多大意思; **is religion really ~ today?** 如今宗教还有什么意义吗?

reliability /rɪˌlaɪəˈbɪləti/ *n* [u] **1** (trustworthiness, dependability) 可靠性 **2** (accuracy) 准确性

reliable /rɪˈlaɪəbl/ *adj* **1** (trustworthy, dependable) 可靠的 ‹*service, product, memory*› **2** (accurate) 准确的 ‹*statistics, account*›

reliably /rɪˈlaɪəbli/ *adv* 可靠地; **I am ~ informed that there are no snakes on the island** 我被确切告知这个岛上没有蛇; **who can ~ predict the future?** 谁能准确预言未来?

reliance /rɪˈlaɪəns/ *n* [u] 依赖; **we should avoid ~ on a single country for our energy supplies** 我们应该避免只依赖单一国家提供能源

reliant /rɪˈlaɪənt/ *adj* 依赖的; **to be ~ on sb./sth.** 依赖某人/某事物; **they are ~ on unemployment benefit** 他们靠失业救济生活; **she is far too ~ on her husband** 她过分依赖丈夫

relic /ˈrelɪk/ *n* **1** (artefact) 文物; (building) 遗迹; (custom) 遗俗 **2** Relig 圣人遗物 **3** fig hum (old person, thing) 老古董; **where did you get that old ~ of a car?** 你从哪儿弄来了那部老爷车?

relict /ˈrelɪkt/ *n* formal **1** (object) 残遗物; **the area includes ~ medieval features** 这个地区还残存着一些中世纪的遗迹 **2** (animal, plant) 孑遗种

relief /rɪˈliːf/

A *n* **1** [u] (from pain, distress, anxiety) 解脱; **to breathe** *or* **heave a sigh of ~** 松一口气; **she tried all sorts of remedies, but nothing brought any lasting ~** 她试了各种疗法, 但没有一种有持久的疗效; **to my immense ~, they didn't recognize me** 让我感到万分庆幸的是, 他们没有认出我 **2** [u] (help) 救助; **famine ~** 饥荒救济; **fresh troops came to the ~ of the beleaguered forces** 援军赶来解救被困部队 **3** [u] (from poverty) 减轻; **~ from tax** 税收减免 **4** [u and c] (diversion) 调剂; **Shakespeare uses the device of comic ~ in most of his plays** 莎士比亚在他的大部分剧作中都融入了轻松幽默的元素 **5** [u] Mil 解围; **it was spring before any troops came to the ~ of Leningrad** 直到春天才有部队来为列宁格勒解围 **6** [c] (replacement on duty) 换班者 **7** [c] Brit (vehicle) 临时增开的车辆 **8** [u] Art (technique) 浮雕法; **in ~** 用浮雕法; **in high/low ~** 用高/低浮雕 **9** [c] Art (carving, moulding) 浮雕作品 **10** [u] (sharpness, clarity) 凸显; **to bring** *or* **throw sb./sth. into ~** 使某人/某物变得鲜明 **11** [u] Geog 起伏; **in ~** 起伏不平; **the sharp ~ of the mountains** 山脉的高低起伏

B *modif* 救援的 ‹*brigade*›; 轮班的 ‹*staff*›; 临时增加的 ‹*bus*›; **the ~ column is expected to arrive tomorrow** 救援小分队可望明日到达

relief: **~ agency** *n* 救济机构; **~ convoy** *n* 救济物资护送队伍; **~ effort** *n* 救济工作; **~ fund** *n* 救济基金; **~ map** *n* 地形图; **~ organization** *n* 救济组织; **~ road** *n* Brit [减缓交通拥挤的] 疏导路; **~ shift** *n* (covering for absent staff) 顶替班; (taking over from existing staff) 轮班; **~ supplies** *npl* 灾难救济; **~ troops** *npl* 换防部队; **~ valve** *n* 安全阀; **~ work** *n* [u] 救灾工作; **~ worker** *n* 救灾工作人员

relieve /rɪˈliːv/

A *vt* **1** (alleviate) 减轻 ‹*pain, disease*›; 消除 ‹*anxiety, symptoms*›; 缓解 ‹*poverty, shortage*› **2** (aid, assist) 救济 ‹*population, country*› **3** (on duty) 给…换班 ‹*worker, sentry*›; **I've come to ~ you for lunch** 我来换你的班, 你去吃中饭 **4** (of burden) 卸除; **he ~d her of her suitcase when she got off the train** 她下了火车后, 他帮她拎行李箱 **5** Mil 解…之围 ‹*fortress, blockade*›; **the general sent assault troops to ~ the garrison** 将军派突击部队去要塞解围 **6** (provide contrast to) 调剂 ‹*drabness, seriousness*›; **not a single tree ~d the barren landscape** 没有一棵树来点缀这片荒芜之地

B *v refl* euph 方便; **some men think nothing of relieving themselves in public** 有些男人对当众解手不以为然

relieved /rɪˈliːvd/ *adj* 感到宽慰的; **I'm so ~ to see you** 看到你我大大松了一口气; **how ~ were you that he returned safely?** 他平安回来让你心情有多放松?

religion /rɪˈlɪdʒən/ *n* **1** [u] (faith, belief) 宗教信仰; **a house of ~** 宗教场所; **to get ~** colloq 信教 **2** [c] (system of faith) 宗教; **the world's great ~s** 世界几大宗教; **freedom to practise one's ~ is a basic human right** 宗教信仰自由是一项基本人权; **the wars of ~** 宗教战争 **3** [c] fig (pursuit) 虔诚追求; **to make a ~ (out) of sth./doing sth.** 把某事/做某事当成一种孜孜追求的目标

religiosity /rɪˌlɪdʒɪˈɒsəti/ *n* [u] pej 笃信宗教

religious /rɪˈlɪdʒəs/ *adj* **1** (believing in a god or gods) 信教的 ‹*person, tribe, way of life*›; 虔诚的 ‹*temperament*›; **are you ~?** 你信教吗? **2** (relating to worship) 宗教的 ‹*doctrine, rites*›; **~ belief/freedom** 宗教信仰/自由 **3** (relating to an order or a group) 教派的 ‹*vows*›; **a very wide range of ~ orders** 形形色色的宗教派别; **all ~ communities** 所有宗教团体 **4** fig (treated with devotion) 十分认真的 ‹*attention, care, observance*›; 肃穆的 ‹*silence*›

religious: **~ affairs** *npl* 宗教事务; **~ education, ~ instruction** *ns* [u] 宗教教育; **~ leader** *n* 宗教领袖

religiously /rɪˈlɪdʒəsli/ *adv* **1** (piously) 虔诚地 ‹*kneel, pray*›; **the Arab countries are all ~ bound to Islam** 阿拉伯国家都笃信伊斯兰教 **2** (scrupulously) 十分认真地 ‹*clean, visit*›; (conscientiously) 郑重地 ‹*promise*›

religiousness /rɪˈlɪdʒəsnɪs/ *n* [u] 虔诚

Religious Society of Friends *n* **the ~** 教友会

reline /ˌriːˈlaɪn/ *vt* 给…换衬里 ‹*coat, curtains*›; 换…的闸衬片 ‹*brakes*›

relinquish /rɪˈlɪŋkwɪʃ/ *vt* 放弃 ‹*property, hope, responsibility*›; 松开 ‹*hold, control*›; **to ~ a habit** 改掉习惯; **the minister was forced to ~ his seat after the scandal** 丑闻披露后部长被迫辞职; **the goods will not be ~ed until they are paid for** 付款后才能发货

relinquishment /rɪˈlɪŋkwɪʃmənt/ *n* [u] 放弃; **political union will require some ~ of sovereignty on both sides** 政治联盟需要双方在主权上作出一些让步

reliquary /ˈrelɪkwəri, Amer -kweri/ *n* [尤指盛放圣人遗骨的] 圣物盒

relish /ˈrelɪʃ/

A *n* **1** [u] (enjoyment) 享受; **to eat/drink with ~** 吃/喝得津津有味 **2** [u] (pleasurable anticipation) 兴趣; **he's a peaceable boy and has no ~ for fighting** 他是个温和的孩子, 不喜欢打架 **3** [u] (pleasing taste) 美味; **spices can add a little ~ to the most ordinary dish** 即便是最普通的菜肴, 香料也能增加一点滋味 **4** [u and c] Culin (condiment) 作料

B *vt* **1** (enjoy) 享受 ‹*food, joke*› **2** (look forward to) 盼望 ‹*fight, prospect, idea*›; **she didn't ~ going home alone on the underground** 她可不想独自一人乘地铁回家

relive /ˌriːˈlɪv/ *vt* 再体验 [尤指追忆令人不快的经历]

reload /ˌriːˈləʊd/ *vt* 重装 ‹*software*›; **to ~ a gun** 重新给枪装子弹; **they ~ed the lorry and drove off** 他们把卡车又装上货, 然后开走了

relocate /ˌriːləʊˈkeɪt, Amer ˌriːˈləʊkeɪt/

A *vt* 搬迁 ‹*family, department, sign*›; 调动 ‹*personnel*›

B *vi* 迁移; **our company is relocating to the centre of town** 我们公司即将搬到市中心

relocation /ˌriːləʊˈkeɪʃn/ *n* 迁移; **~ costs** *or* **expenses** 搬迁费用

relocation: **~ allowance** *n* 调职津贴; **~ package** *n* 调职一揽子补偿

reluctance /rɪˈlʌktəns/ *n* [u] 不情愿; **~ to do sth.** 不愿意做某事; **with great ~** 非常勉强地

reluctant /rɪˈlʌktənt/ *adj* 不情愿的; **to be ~ to do sth.** 不愿意做某事; **I prised the letter from his ~ fingers** 他不愿撒手, 但我硬把信夺了下来

reluctantly /rɪˈlʌktəntli/ *adv* 不情愿地

rely /rɪˈlaɪ/ *vi* **1** (be dependent) 依靠; **to ~ on** *or* **upon sb./sth.** 依靠某人/某事物; **she relied entirely on her writing for her income** 她完全靠写作挣钱 **2** (trust) 信赖; **to ~ on** *or* **upon sb./sth.** 信任某人/某事物; **government statistics are not to be relied on** 政府的统计不可信; **one can never ~ on the weather in Britain** 英国的天气根本靠不住

remade /ˌriːˈmeɪd/ *pt, pp* ▸**remake**

remailer /ˌriːˈmeɪlə(r)/ *n* 回邮器 [一种匿名转发邮件的互联网服务]

remain /rɪˈmeɪn/ *vi* **1** (stay in same place) 逗留; **to ~ behind** 留下 **2** (stay in same condition) 保持不变; **your season ticket will ~ valid until the end of the year** 你的季票有效期一直到年底; **her question ~s unanswered** 她的问题仍未得到解答; **the location of the**

r

treasure ~s a secret to this day 那批财宝的存放地点直到今天仍是个秘密 3 (be left over) 剩下; **if any bread ~s, give it to the birds** 如果有剩余面包的话，喂给鸟吃吧; **a lot of work ~s to be done** 还有许多活儿要干; **it ~s to be seen whether her leg is broken or not** 她的腿是否骨折有待检查 4 (continue to exist) 遗留; **not much ~ed of the aircraft after it crashed** 飞机坠毁以后残骸所剩无几

remainder /rɪˈmeɪndə(r)/
A *n* 1 (leftover) 剩余物; **my dog will always eat up the ~** 我的狗总会把剩饭吃掉; **on release from prison he spent the ~ of his life in Jamaica** 他出狱后在牙买加度过了余生 2 Math 余数 3 (unsold item, esp book) 滞销品; **we're selling off ~s at half price** 我们把那些滞销书以半价出售
B *vt* 削价处理; **to be ~ed** 《*book*》 削价出售

remaining /rɪˈmeɪnɪŋ/ *adj attrib* 剩余的 ‹*scraps, time, stock*›

remains /rɪˈmeɪnz/ *npl* 1 (parts left over) 剩余物; **she used the ~ of the dress material to make a scarf** 她用做连衣裙的剩料做了一块头巾; **the rain has washed away the last ~ of the snow** 雨冲走了最后一丝残雪 2 (of building, city, civilization) 遗迹; **~ of the Inca civilization** 印加文明的遗迹 3 (of body) 遗骸; **his mortal ~** 他的尸骨

remake
A /ˌriːˈmeɪk/ *vt* (*pt, pp* **remade**) 重做 ‹*model*›; 重拍 ‹*film*›; 重建 ‹*society*›; 重铺 ‹*bed*›
B /ˈriːmeɪk/ *n* (film) 新版电影; (piece of music) 新版音乐

remand /rɪˈmɑːnd, Amer rɪˈmænd/ Jur
A *vt* 将…还押候审; **to ~ sb. in custody** 让某人还押候审; **to ~ sb. on bail** 准予某人取保候审
B *n* 押候; **on ~** 还押候审

remand: ~ centre *n* Brit 候审拘留所; **~ home** *n* Brit Hist 少年拘留所; **~ prisoner** *n* Brit 在押未决犯; **~ wing** *n* Brit 候审犯隔离区

remanufacture /ˌriːmænjʊˈfæktʃə(r)/
A *vt* 改制 ‹*component, cartridge*›
B *n* [u] 改制; **the ~ of car parts** 汽车部件的改制; **engine ~** 发动机改造

remark /rɪˈmɑːk/
A *n* 1 [c] (comment) 言论; **to make some ~s** 说几句话; **opening/closing ~s** 开场白/结束语; **concluding ~s** 结语; **a personal ~** 人身攻击; **his throwaway ~ caused a political furore** 他随口说的一句话却引起了一场政治骚乱 2 [u] (notice) 注意; **worthy of ~** 值得关注的
B *vt* 1 (comment) 评论道; (mention) 说道 2 (notice) 注意到
C *vi* 议论; **to ~ on** *or* **upon sth.** 议论某事物; **everyone ~ed on her beauty and charm** 人人都对她的美艳品头论足

remarkable /rɪˈmɑːkəbl/ *adj* 出色的 ‹*performer, performance, work of art*›; 非凡的 ‹*achievement, courage, skill, efficiency*›; 引人注目的 ‹*event, sight*›; **the fire brigade arrived with ~ speed** 消防队火速赶到; **it is ~ that she is still unmarried** 令人惊讶的是，她还未结婚

remarkably /rɪˈmɑːkəbli/ *adv* 非同寻常地; **the boys play tennis ~ well** 这些男孩网球打得非常棒; **I'm afraid I found the entire play ~ boring** 我觉得整出戏非常没劲; **~, he escaped without a scratch** 他居然毫发无伤地躲了过去，真是万幸

remarry /ˌriːˈmæri/ *vi* 再婚; **she is now remarried to her former husband** 现在她和前夫复婚了

remaster /ˌriːˈmɑːstə(r)/ *vt* 重新录制

rematch /ˈriːmætʃ/ *n* 复赛

remediable /rɪˈmiːdɪəbl/ *adj* formal 可纠正的 ‹*mistake, injustice*›; 可弥补的 ‹*loss, deficiency*›

remedial /rɪˈmiːdɪəl/ *adj attrib* 1 Med 治疗的; **~ treatment** *or* **therapy** 治疗 2 (measures to redress) 补救的; **to take ~ action** 采取补救措施 3 Sch 补习的 ‹*teaching, pupil*›

remedy /ˈremədi/
A *n* 1 [c] Med 治疗药物; **a ~ for the common cold** 感冒药; **sometimes the ~ is worse than the disease** 治不得法，不如不治 2 [c] fig (means of counteracting) 改进措施; **the best ~ for boredom is hard work** 克服烦闷无聊的最佳办法是努力工作; **to be past** *or* **beyond ~** 无可救药; **desperate diseases require desperate remedies** 重病需下猛药 3 [c and u] Jur 补偿; **to seek (a) ~** 寻求赔偿; **to pursue a legal ~** 寻求通过法律手段补救
B *vt* 纠正 ‹*wrongs, mistake*›; 弥补 ‹*loss*›; **fresh fruit can ~ a vitamin deficiency in diet** 新鲜水果可以弥补饮食中维生素的不足

remember /rɪˈmembə(r)/
A *vt* 1 (recollect) 记得 ‹*person, event, place*›; **a night to ~** 难忘的夜晚; **I ~ a time when ...** 我记得曾几何时…; **to ~ sb./sth. as sth.** 记得某人/某事物是某情形; **I ~ him as a very dynamic man** 在我的记忆中，他非常有活力; **he is best ~ed as the man who brought jazz to England** 他因为将爵士乐传入英格兰而为人所熟知; **to ~ sb./sth. for/by sth.** 因/通过某事物记得某人/某事物; **I wish I had something to ~ him by** 我希望能有什么让我记起他来; **to ~ (sb.) doing sth.** 记得（某人）做过某事; **I vaguely ~ hearing him come in** 我依稀记得听见他进来; **I can still vividly ~ my grandfather teaching me to play cards** 祖父教我打牌的情景我仍然记忆犹新; **to ~ when ...** 记得那时…; **to ~ (that) ...** 记得…; **to ~ sth. about sb./sth.** 记得关于某人/某事物的某事; **I don't ~ anything about it** 我不记得任何关于它的事; **what do you ~ best about your trip to India?** 印度之行给你印象最深的是什么？; **do you ~ anything of your early schooldays?** 你记得学生时代初期的事吗？ 2 (recall to mind) 记起; **I can't ~ her name right now** 我现在一时想不起她的名字; **to be worth ~ing** 《*advice*》 值得铭记; **to ~ that/what ...** 记起…; **~ you're only young once!** 别忘了青春只有一次！; **I wish I could ~ what she said** 但愿我能想起她的话; **to ~ where/how ...** 记起在哪里/如何…; **I can never ~ where I've put my keys** 我怎么也想不起把钥匙放在哪儿了 3 (bear in mind) 记着; **to ~ (that) ...** 想着…; **~ that he was only 20 at the time** 别忘了那时他才 20 岁; **it must/should be ~ed that ...** 必须/应该记住…; **~ where you are!** 别忘了这是什么地方！ 4 (not forget to bring or do sth.) 记得做; **to ~ one's umbrella/coat/sweater** 记得带伞/外衣/毛衫; **to ~ one's milk/bread** 记得拿牛奶/面包; **did you ~ your homework?** 你记得做功课了吗？; **to ~ to do sth.** 记得要做某事; **~ to call me when you arrive!** 你到了之后别忘了给我打电话！ 5 (mark with present) 送礼祝贺 ‹*birthday, anniversary*›; (mark with card) 送贺卡祝贺 ‹*birthday, anniversary*› 6 (give money to) 给…送钱 ‹*person, organization*›; 给…小费 ‹*waiter, guide*›; (give present to) 给…送礼 ‹*person, organization*›; **to ~ sb. in one's will** 在遗嘱中给某人留下遗赠 7 (commemorate) 纪念 ‹*victims, war dead, disaster, war*› 8 **to ~ sb. to sb.** esp Brit (pass on good wishes to) 代某人问候某人; **she asks to be ~ed to you** 她让我代她问候您 9 (mention) 求神保佑; **to ~ sb. in one's prayers** 祈祷神保佑某人
B *vi* 1 (recollect) 记得; **as you may ~, the day was hot and sunny** 你也许还记得，那天很热，阳光灿烂; **if I ~ correctly** *or* **rightly** 如果我没记错的话; **as far as I (can) ~, this is ...** 我记得这是…; **not as far as I (can)** *or* **not that I ~** 我不记得了; **that's longer ago than I care to ~** 那事久远得我都记不得了 2 (recall to mind) 记起来; **you must ~! it's very important** 你必须想起来！那很重要; **you were going to help me with this: ~?** 你要帮我这个忙的，还记得吗？; **if only I could ~** 但愿我想得起来
C *v refl* **to ~ oneself** 自我控制; **he swore, but then quickly ~ed himself** 他咒骂了一句，不过很快就收敛了; **she was about to reply and then ~ed herself** 她正要回答，不过还是控制住了自己

remembrance /rɪˈmembrəns/ *n* 1 [u] (act of remembering) 纪念; **in ~ of sb./sth.** 为纪念某人/某事物; **day of ~** 纪念日; **a service** *or* **ceremony of ~** 纪念仪式 2 [c and u] formal (recollection) 回忆; **~ of sb./sth.** 对某人/某事物的回忆; **within the ~ of sb.** 在某人的记忆中; **I have no ~ whatever of the occasion** 我一点也不记得那个活动了; **to the best of my ~** 就我记忆所及

remembrance: ~ ceremony *n* 纪念仪式; **R~ Day, R~ Sunday** *ns* Brit 荣军纪念日 [最接近11月11日的星期天]

remind /rɪˈmaɪnd/ *vt* 1 (cause to remember) 提醒; **to ~ sb. to do sth.** 提醒某人做某事; **she hated to be ~ed of her age** 她讨厌别人提醒她的年龄 2 (look like, call to mind) 使想起; **to ~ sb. of sb./sth.** 使某人想起某人/某事物; **the hills ~ed him of home** 那些山丘使他想起了老家

reminder /rɪˈmaɪndə(r)/ *n* 1 (sth. that jogs one's memory) 提醒人的事物; (prompt) 提示; **to receive a ~** 收到通知单; **to send/write a ~** 送/写通知单; **the child tied a knot in her handkerchief as a ~ that she had a music lesson after school** 那个孩子在手帕上打了个结，提醒自己放学后要上音乐课; **we needed no ~s that time was running out** 我们不需要提醒就知道时间不多了 2 (memory) 记忆; **the barbed wire barricades were grim ~s of the war** 带刺的铁丝网让人回忆起战争的残酷

reminisce /ˌremɪˈnɪs/ *vi* 缅怀往事; **we often ~ about our college days** 我们经常缅怀我们的大学时光

reminiscence /ˌremɪˈnɪsns/ *n* 1 [u] (recalling) 回忆 2 [c] (story) 旧事; **you should write up your wartime ~s** 你应该把你的战时回忆写下来

reminiscent /ˌremɪˈnɪsnt/ *adj* 1 (absorbed in memories) 怀旧的 ‹*mood, smile*› 2 *pred* (suggestive) 引人联想的; **to be ~ of sth./sb.** 让人联想到某事物/某人; **his style is vaguely ~ of Matisse** 他的风格隐约使人联想起马蒂斯

remiss /rɪˈmɪs/ *adj pred* 懈怠的; **it was really very ~ of me not to come and see you on your birthday** 在你生日那天没有过来看你确实是我的疏忽大意

remission /rɪˈmɪʃn/ *n* 1 [c and u] formal (of debt, charge) 免除; **winning a scholarship entitles pupils to ~ of school fees** 获得奖学金可以使学生免交学费 2 [u] Brit Jur 减刑 3 [u] Med 缓解; **~ of pain** 疼痛的减轻; **the cancer appears to be in ~** 癌症看来处在缓解期

remit
A /rɪˈmɪt/ *vt* (*pres p etc.* **-tt-**) 1 Jur 把…发回重审; **his case was ~ted to the Crown Court** 他的案件被发回到刑事法院重审 2 formal (reduce) 减免 ‹*sentence, tax, debt*› 3 formal (send) 汇寄 ‹*money, payment*›
B /ˈriːmɪt/ *n* 职权范围; **to be within/outside sb.'s ~** 在某人的职权范围内/外; **to exceed one's ~** 超出职权范围; **the council has a ~ to ensure that educational opportunities are available to all** 地方议会有权保证人人享有教育机会

remittance /rɪˈmɪtns/ *n* 1 [c] (payment) 汇款额 2 [u] (sending money) 汇款

remittance advice *n* [尤指邮购货物的] 付款通知单

remix
A /ˌriːˈmɪks/ *vt* **1** (mix again) 再搅和; **to ~ the paint thoroughly before use** 使用前把漆彻底搅一下 **2** Mus 对…进行混音处理 ‹*track, recording*›
B /ˈriːmɪks/ *n* Mus 混音版

remnant /ˈremnənt/ *n* **1** (part left over) 剩余部分; **the ~s of the army** 残余部队 **2** (trace) 残迹; **a ~ of the past** 遗迹 **3** (of fabric) 布头

remodel /ˌriːˈmɒdl/ *vt* (*pres p etc.* Brit, **-ll-**, Amer **-l-**) 改造 ‹*building*›; 修改 ‹*constitution*›; 改制 ‹*dress*›; 整修 ‹*nose*›

remonstrance /rɪˈmɒnstrəns/ *n* **1** [c] (protest) 抗议的呼声 **2** [u] (protesting) 抗议

remonstrate /ˈremənstreɪt/ *vi* 抗议; **to ~ with sb.** 向某人提出抗议; **to ~ about** *or* **against sth.** 抗议某事

remorse /rɪˈmɔːs/ *n* [u] 懊悔; **to show ~ for sth.** 对某事表示懊悔; **to be filled with ~** 充满自责

remorseful /rɪˈmɔːsfl/ *adj* 懊悔的

remorsefully /rɪˈmɔːsfəli/ *adv* 懊悔地

remorseless /rɪˈmɔːslɪs/ *adj* **1** (pitiless) 残酷的 ‹*bullying, person*› **2** (relentless) 无休止的; **the ~ sun** 酷热的太阳; **the ~ gale** 肆虐的大风; **the ~ march of time** 时间永无休止的流失; **the ~ progress of science** 科学永无止境的发展

remorselessly /rɪˈmɔːslɪsli/ *adv* **1** (pitilessly) 无情地 ‹*beat*› **2** (relentlessly) 无休止地 ‹*pursue, argue*›

remote /rɪˈməʊt/
A *adj* **1** (distant in space, time) 遥远的 ‹*place, planet*›; **in the ~ future/past** 在遥远的将来/过去; **in the ~ distance** 在很远的远处; **stories of ~ antiquity** 远古时期的传说 **2** (isolated) 偏远的 ‹*farmhouse, village*› **3** (distantly connected) 关系远的; **~ relatives/ancestors** 远房亲戚/远古先人; **a ~ cause** 远因; **a ~ effect** 间接后果 **4** (slight) 细微的 ‹*resemblance, possibility, link*›; **I haven't the ~st idea what you mean!** 我根本不知道你是什么意思！; **I don't see the ~st connection between the two incidents** 我看不出两个事件之间有一丝一毫的联系 **5** (aloof) 冷傲的 ‹*person, manner*›
B *n* 遥控器

remote: ~ access *n* [u] 远程访问; **~ central locking** *n* [u] 遥控中央门锁; **~ control** *n* **1** [u] (operation) 遥控; **2** [c] (device) 遥控器; **~-controlled** *adj* 遥控的; **a ~-controlled car/plane** 遥控汽车/飞机; **~ learning** *n* [u] 远程学习

remotely /rɪˈməʊtli/ *adv* **1** (in space, time) 遥远地 ‹*located*›; 远程地 ‹*read*›; **they live in a ~ situated farm house** 他们住在一个偏远的农舍; **electronic sensors that can be operated ~** 可遥控的电子传感器 **2** (to small degree) 细微地 ‹*relevant, connected*›; **he doesn't ~ resemble his father** 他一点儿都不像他父亲; **it's ~ possible that he'll pass the exam** 他通过考试的可能性微乎其微

remoteness /rɪˈməʊtnɪs/ *n* [u] **1** (isolation) 偏僻; **she loved the tranquillity and ~ of the island** 她喜欢这个岛屿的安宁与僻静 **2** (in time) 远古 **3** (aloofness) 孤傲

remote: ~ printer *n* 远程打印机; **~ sensing** *n* [u] 遥感; **satellite ~ sensing** 卫星遥感; **~-sensing technology** 遥感技术; **~ surveillance** *n* [u] 远程监视; **~ terminal** *n* 远程终端

remould Brit, **remold** Amer
A /ˌriːˈməʊld/ *vt* **1** (reshape) 改铸 ‹*pot, clay*›; 改造 ‹*character, society*› **2** Brit Aut 翻新 ‹*tyre*›
B /ˈriːməʊld/ *n* Brit 翻新的轮胎

remount /ˌriːˈmaʊnt/
A *vt* **1** (get back on) 重新跨上 ‹*horse, bicycle*› **2** Art 重新镶嵌 ‹*jewel*›; 重裱 ‹*painting*› **3** (restage) 重新上演 ‹*play*›; 重新举办 ‹*exhibition*›
B *vi* «*cyclist*» 重新骑上车; «*jockey*» 重新上马

removable /rɪˈmuːvəbl/ *adj* 可拆装的 ‹*part, battery*›; 可移动的 ‹*cassette, disk*›; 可免职的 ‹*employee*›

removal /rɪˈmuːvl/ *n* **1** [c] Brit (when moving house) 搬迁; **~s** 搬家; **furniture ~ costs a fortune!** 搬运家具要花一大笔钱呢！; **~ from/to somewhere** 从/到某处的搬家; **a ~ company** *or* **firm** 搬家公司 **2** [u] (abolition) 消除; **the ~ of the subsidy** 补贴的取消; **the total ~ of inequality in the world** 世上不平等的完全消除 **3** [u] (from office) 免职; **~ from sth.** 从某职位的解职; **after the ~ of the populist leader** 这位民粹主义领袖被解职后 **4** [u] (of demonstrators, troublemakers) 驱散 **5** [u] (collecting) 收走; **the ~ of rubbish** 垃圾收运 **6** [u] (transfer of patient, prisoner) 转移 **7** [u] (cleaning) 清除; **for the ~ of grease stains** 用于清除油渍 **8** [u] (of troops) 撤退 **9** [u] Med (excision) 切除; **the ~ of sb.'s tonsils/the tumour** 扁桃体/肿瘤切除 **10** [u] colloq euph (killing) 干掉

removal: ~ expenses *npl* 搬迁费; **~ man** *n* 搬家工人; **~ van** *n* 搬家卡车

remove /rɪˈmuːv/
A *vt* **1** (take away) 拿走 ‹*object*›; 带走 ‹*person*›; **the waiter came and ~d their plates** 侍者过来收走了他们的盘子; **~ the prisoner!** 把这个犯人带下去！; **to ~ sb./sth. from sth.** 将某人从某处带走/将某物从某处移走; **we've decided to ~ our children from the school** 我们已决定让孩子们转学了; **three children were ~d from the school for persistent bad behaviour** 3个孩子因一贯表现恶劣被学校开除了; **over 30 bodies were ~d from the rubble** 从瓦砾堆中清理出30多具尸体; **she ~d her hand from his shoulder** 她把手从他肩上挪开; **the product was ~d from the market** 该产品已从市场撤回; **to be ~d to hospital** Brit 被送往医院 **2** (free) 取消; **to ~ sb./sth. from sth.** (from control) 解除某事物对某人/某事物的控制; (from protection) 撤除某事物对某人/某事物的保护; **to ~ the industry from state control** 取消对该产业的政府监管; **they have ~d thousands of needy youngsters from the benefit system** 他们将数千名贫困儿童排除在了福利体制之外 **3** (take off) 脱下 ‹*clothing, shoes*›; 摘下 ‹*hat, glasses*›; 拆下 ‹*bandage*›; **I went to the hospital to have my plaster ~d** 我去医院拆了石膏 **4** (take out) 取下 ‹*dentures, glass eye*› **5** (get rid of) 去除 ‹*dirt, nail polish, unwanted hair*›; **to ~ one's make-up** 卸妆; **to ~ sth. from sth.** 从某处去除某物 **6** Med (extract, excise) 拔下 ‹*tooth*›; 切除 ‹*appendix, tonsils, tumour, organ*› **7** (oust) 把…免职 ‹*official*›; 辞退 ‹*employee*›; **to ~ sb. from sth.** 免除某人的 ‹*position*›; **to be ~d from office/power** 被撤职/被罢免 **8** (dispel) 消除 ‹*threat, boredom*›; 打消 ‹*doubt, fears*›; 排除 ‹*obstacle*›; 解决 ‹*problem*› **9** (cause to disappear) 去除 ‹*stain, dirt*› **10** (delete) 删去 ‹*passage, word, scene*›; **to ~ sth. from sth.** 将某物从某处删掉 **11** Comput 删除 ‹*software, program, file*›; **to ~ sth. from sth.** 将某物从…上删除 ‹*computer, disk*› **12** (abolish) 取消 ‹*tax, subsidy, barrier*› **13** euph (kill) 干掉 ‹*opponent, enemy*› **14** (in kinship) 隔代的; **cousin once/twice ~d** (male on father's side) 堂侄/堂侄孙; (female on father's side) 堂侄女/堂侄孙女; (male on mother's side) 表侄/表侄孙; (female on mother's side) 表侄女/表侄孙女
B *vi* dated «*person, family*» 搬家; «*company*» 搬迁; **to ~ to a country/city** 搬到某国/某城市
C *v refl* formal **to ~ oneself** 走开; **to ~ oneself to a country/city** 去某国/某城市
D *n* formal 间距; **to be (at) one ~ from sb./sth.** 与某人/某事物隔开一段距离; **to live at one ~ from reality** 生活在现实之外; **to be several/many ~s from sb./sth.** 与某人/某事物相差颇远/很远; **life in some villages is only a few ~s from a feudal society** 某些村庄的生活与封建社会相差无几; **it is a far ~ from sth. (to sth.)** 从某事物（到某事物）差距很大; **at this ~** 如此看来

remover /rɪˈmuːvə(r)/ *n* **1** (for stains) 去污剂; (for make-up) 卸妆用品; (for nail varnish) 指甲油清除剂 **2** (person) 搬家工人; (firm) 搬家公司

REM sleep *n* [u] 快速眼动睡眠

remunerate /rɪˈmjuːnəreɪt/ *vt* formal 付酬给

remuneration /rɪˌmjuːnəˈreɪʃn/ *n* [u] **1** (salary, fee) 酬金 **2** (act of paying) 付酬金

remunerative /rɪˈmjuːnərətɪv, Amer -nəreɪtɪv/ *adj* formal 报酬丰厚的 ‹*employment, deal*›

Renaissance /rɪˈneɪsns, Amer ˈrenəsɑːns/
A *pr n* Hist **the ~** 文艺复兴; **~ art** 文艺复兴时期的艺术
B **renaissance** *n* (revival) 复兴

Renaissance man *n* 博学多才的人

renal /ˈriːnl/ *adj* 肾脏的; **he has acute ~ failure** 他得了急性肾功能衰竭

renal dialysis *n* [u] 肾透析

rename /ˌriːˈneɪm/ *vt* 重新命名; **Stalingrad was ~d Volgograd** 斯大林格勒被重新命名为伏尔加格勒

renascence /rɪˈnæsns/ *n* formal 复兴

renascent /rɪˈnæsnt/ *adj* formal 复兴的

rend /rend/ *vt* (*pt, pp* **rent**) **1** lit (tear, rip) 撕扯 ‹*hair, clothes, curtain*›; «*explosion*» 炸碎 ‹*wall*›; **to ~ to pieces** 撕成碎片; **to ~ in two** 撕成两半 **2** fig (tear apart) 使…分崩离析 ‹*family, community*›; «*sound*» 划破 ‹*air*›; 打破 ‹*silence*›; «*experience*» 撕裂 ‹*heart*›

render /ˈrendə(r)/
A *n* [u] 底灰
B *vt* **1** formal (cause to be) 使成为; **to ~ sb. unconscious/homeless/speechless** 使某人失去知觉/无家可归/说不出话; **to ~ sth. impossible** *or* **unlikely** 使某事不可能实现; **the explosives experts came and ~ed the bomb harmless** 爆破专家赶来拆除了炸弹; **I'd like to come, but the continued bad weather ~s that less likely** 我很想来，但是持续的恶劣天气让我难以成行; **to ~ sb. liable for sth.** 使某人对某事物负责; **to ~ sth. null and void** Jur 宣布…无效 ‹*contract*› **2** formal (provide) 提供 ‹*service, assistance, aid*›; **to ~ sth. to sb., to ~ sb. sth.** 向某人提供某物; **you've ~ed me a great service** 你帮了我一个大忙 **3** formal (submit) 提交 ‹*account, statement, report*›; **'for account ~ed'** Comm "发票已开"; **'payment for services ~ed'** (on invoice) "服务酬金" **4** Art formal (depict) 描绘 ‹*landscape*›; 描写 ‹*mood*›; 对…作艺术处理 ‹*effect, portrait*› **5** Mus formal (perform) 演奏 ‹*piece*›; 演唱 ‹*song*› **6** (translate) 翻译; **the Italian phrase can be ~ed as 'I did my best'** 这个意大利短语可以翻译成"我尽力了"; **to ~ sth. into sth.** 将某物译成某物; **it's a concept that is difficult to ~ into English** 这是个很难译成英语的概念 **7** formal (give) 给予; **to ~ sth. to sb./sth.** 给予某人/某团体 ‹*tribute*›; **to ~ sth. to sb./sth.** 向某人/某团体表示 ‹*homage, obedience*› **8** Jur 宣布 ‹*verdict*›; 给出 ‹*opinion*› **9** Constr 给…抹灰 ‹*wall, brickwork*› **10** (melt down) 熔化; **the fat was ~ed for lard** 肥肉已熬成了猪油 **11** (process) 加工 ‹*meat, carcass*›

Phrasal verbs

- **render down** *vt* [**~ sth. down, ~ down sth.**]
1 (melt down) 熔化 ‹*fat*› **2** (process) 加工 ‹*meat, carcass*›
- **render up** *vt* liter [**~ up sth., ~ sth. up**]
1 (surrender) 交出 ‹*arms, prisoners, treasure, town*›; **to ~ sth. up to sb.** 把某物交给某人 **2** Relig 献出 ‹*soul, spirit*›

rendering /ˈrendərɪŋ/ *n* [1] [u] Constr (material) 灰泥层; (application) 抹灰泥 [2] [c] (translation) 翻译; **a literal ~ of an idiom** 一个成语的直译 [3] [c] (performance) 表演

rendezvous /ˈrɒndɪvuː, -deɪ-/

A *n* (*pl* **rendezvous** /ˈrɒndɪvuːz, -deɪ-/) [1] (meeting) 约会; **to have a ~ with sb.** 和某人有约会 [2] (place) 约会地点

B *vi* 会面; **to ~ with sb.** 与某人会面

rendition /renˈdɪʃn/ *n* (performance) 表演; (interpretation) 演绎

renegade /ˈrenɪɡeɪd/

A *n* [1] (deserter, traitor) 叛徒 [2] (outlaw) 叛逆者

B *adj attrib* 叛教的 ‹*priest*›; 变节的 ‹*spy, party member*›; 反叛的 ‹*soldier, supporter*›

renege /rɪˈniːɡ, -ˈneɪɡ/ *vi* **to ~ on sth.** 违背某事; **he's not a man to ~ on his responsibilities** 他不是那种推卸责任的人

renegotiate /ˌriːnɪˈɡəʊʃɪeɪt/ *vt* 重新协商 ‹*deal, contract, terms*›; 重新谈判 ‹*ceasefire, settlement*›; **the parties will ~ the price** 各方将重议价格

renegotiation /ˌriːnɪˌɡəʊʃɪˈeɪʃn/ *n* [c and u] 重新协商

renegue /rɪˈniːɡ, -ˈneɪɡ/ *vi* = **renege**

renew /rɪˈnjuː, Amer -ˈnuː/ *vt* [1] (resume) 重新开始 ‹*relationship, negotiations, efforts*› [2] (repeat) 重申 ‹*protest, promise*›; 重新提出 ‹*offer, bid*› [3] (extend validity of) 续签 ‹*contract*›; 延长…的期限 ‹*licence, visa, loan*›; **to ~ a library book/a subscription** 续借图书馆的书/续订 [4] (replace) 更换 ‹*light bulb, tyres, battery*›; (replenish) 补充 ‹*goods, stocks*› [5] (restore) 恢复 ‹*strength, courage*›

renewable /rɪˈnjuːəbl, Amer -ˈnuːəbl/

A *adj* [1] (with extendable validity) 可延期的 ‹*membership, permit, passport, contract*› [2] (reusable) 可再生的 ‹*resources, energy*›; **~ technology** 可再生能源技术

B **renewables** *npl* 可再生能源

renewal /rɪˈnjuːəl, Amer -ˈnuːəl/ *n* [1] (extension of validity) 续延; **my passport is due for ~** 我的护照该延期了 [2] (regeneration) 复兴; **urban ~** 城市重建

renewed /rɪˈnjuːd, Amer -ˈnuːd/ *adj* 重新开始的 ‹*effort, attack*›; 重新燃起的 ‹*enthusiasm, faith*›; 恢复的 ‹*life, vigour*›

renminbi /renˈmɪnbi/ ▸ **p. 174** *n* 人民币

rennet /ˈrenɪt/ *n* [u] 凝乳酶

renounce /rɪˈnaʊns/ *vt* [1] (abandon) 宣布放弃 ‹*title, privilege, ownership*› [2] (give up) 抛弃 ‹*principles, religious belief, family*›; 退出 ‹*treaty*›; **to ~ the world** 脱离红尘 [3] (reject) 摒弃 ‹*smoking, gambling, alcohol*› [4] (stop) 宣布停止 ‹*violence, force, war*›

renovate /ˈrenəveɪt/ *vt* 翻新 ‹*house*›; 修复 ‹*painting, machine, furniture*›; 修补 ‹*clothes, curtains*›

renovation /ˌrenəˈveɪʃn/

A *n* [u] (process) 翻新; **under ~** 在翻修中; **clumsy ~ has ruined many a good painting** 拙劣的修复工作毁坏了很多优秀的画作; **a ~ scheme/project** 翻新计划/项目

B **renovations** *npl* (works) 翻新工作; **to undertake** *or* **carry out ~s** 进行修复

renovation grant *n* Brit 房屋翻修补助金

renown /rɪˈnaʊn/ *n* [u] 声望; **authors of great ~** 极有名望的作家; **a sculptor of wide ~** 远近闻名的雕塑家

renowned /rɪˈnaʊnd/ *adj* 著名的; **to be ~ for sth.** 因某事物而出名

rent[1] /rent/

A *n* [1] (for property, land) 租金; **the ~ for a two bedroom flat** 一套两居室的房租; **for ~** 招租; **to be behind with one's** *or* **the ~** 拖欠租金; **to collect the ~** 收租金 [2] (for equipment) 租用费

B *vt* [1] (let out) «*owner*» 出租 ‹*house, equipment*› [2] (hire) «*tenant, client*» 租用 ‹*house, equipment*›; **to ~ sth. from sb.** 向某人租用某物; **our TV is only ~ed** 我们的电视只是租来的; **he ~s a room for £180 a month** 他租了一个房间，每月租金为 180 英镑

Phrasal verb

• **rent out** *vt* [**~ sth. out, ~ out sth.**] 出租

rent[2]

A *n* (tear) 裂口

B *pt, pp* ▸ **rend**

rent: ~-a-crowd *n* = **~-a-mob**; **~ agreement** *n* 租赁合同

rental /ˈrentl/ *n* [u] [1] (payment) 租金; **annual/quarterly/monthly/weekly/daily ~** 年度/季度/月/周/日租费 [2] (renting) 租赁; **car/office ~** 汽车/办公室租赁; **a ~ firm** 租赁公司; **an exorbitant ~ rate** 离谱的租费

rental: ~ agreement *n* 租赁合同; **~ building** *n* Amer 出租大楼; **~ car** *n* = **hire car**; **~ company** *n* 租赁公司; **~ income** *n* [c and u] 租金收入

rent: ~-a-mob *n* colloq pej 雇来的乌合之众; **~ arrears** *npl* 拖欠租金; **~ book** *n* 租金册; **~ boy** *n* 年轻男妓; **~ collector** *n* 收租人; **~-controlled** *adj* 租金受管制的 ‹*apartment, tenancy*›

renter /ˈrentə(r)/ *n* [1] (person) 租户 [2] Amer colloq (car) 租来的车; (video cassette) 租来的录像带

rent-free

A *adj* 免租金的

B *adv* 免租金

rent tribunal *n* Brit 租务仲裁处

renumber /ˌriːˈnʌmbə(r)/ *vt* 把…重新编号

renunciation /rɪˌnʌnsɪˈeɪʃn/ *n* [u] 宣布放弃; **~ of faith** 放弃信仰的声明

reoccupy /ˌriːˈɒkjʊpaɪ/ *vt* 再占领

reoffend /ˌriːəˈfend/ *vi* 再次犯罪

reoffender /ˌriːəˈfendə(r)/ *n* 累犯

reopen /ˌriːˈəʊpən/

A *vt* [1] (open again) 重新打开 ‹*door, box*›; 重新开张 ‹*shop*›; 重新开放 ‹*frontier, route*›; **I slept soundly, and when I ~ed my eyes it was already light** 我呼呼大睡，等我再睁开眼时已经天亮了; **to ~ old wounds** fig 揭旧伤疤 [2] Jur 再次开始 ‹*trial, inquiry*› [3] (make operational again) 重新启用 ‹*account*›; 恢复 ‹*enquiry*›

B *vi* [1] (open again) «*hospital, shop*» 重新开业; «*flower*» 重新绽放; «*wound*» 再次裂开 [2] Jur «*trial*» 再次开庭 [3] (resume) «*play, opera*» 重新上演

reopening /ˌriːˈəʊpənɪŋ/ *n* (of building) 重新开放; (of trial) 再次开庭; (of play) 重新上演; **the ~ of the inquiry** 调查的重新开始

reorder /ˌriːˈɔːdə(r)/

A *vt* [1] (request again) 再订购 ‹*goods*› [2] (rearrange) 重新整理 ‹*books*›; 重新安排 ‹*life*›

B *n* 再订购; **to put in a ~** 追加订货; **to receive a ~** 收到再订购单

reorganization /ˌriːɔːɡənaɪˈzeɪʃn/ *n* [c and u] 整顿; **to undergo ~** 受到整顿

reorganize /ˌriːˈɔːɡənaɪz/

A *vt* 重新整理 ‹*room, library, database*›; 重新安排 ‹*life, timetable*›; 整顿 ‹*hospital, service*›

B *vi* 整顿

rep[1] /rep/

A *n* colloq [1] (representative) 代表; **she's the local union ~** 她是本地工会代表 [2] (sales representative) 推销员; **the area ~** 地区推销员

B *vi* colloq 做推销员

rep[2] *n* [1] [u] (repertory) 保留剧目轮演 [2] [c] (company) 保留剧目轮演剧团; (theatre) 保留剧目轮演剧院

repackage /ˌriːˈpækɪdʒ/ *vt* [1] Comm 重新包装 ‹*product, goods*› [2] fig (present differently) 为…重塑形象 ‹*proposal, politician*›

repaginate /ˌriːˈpædʒɪneɪt/ *vt* 给…重标页码

repaid /ˌriːˈpeɪd/ *pt, pp* ▸ **repay**

repaint /ˌriːˈpeɪnt/ *vt* 重新油漆

repair /rɪˈpeə(r)/

A *n* [1] [u and c] (of furniture, window, pipe, machine, roof) 修理; (of wall, road, building) 整修; (of clothes, carpet, sheet) 缝补; **'heel ~s while you wait'** "修理鞋后跟，立等可取"; **a ~ to sth.** 对某物的修理; **to do** *or* **carry out ~s (to** *or* **on sth.)** 修理（某物）; **to undergo ~s** 接受修理; **my car had to undergo extensive ~s after the accident** 车祸后我的车只好进行大修; **to take sth. in for ~** 将某物送去修理; **to be (badly) in need of ~** （非常）需要维修; **to be under ~** 正在修理; **to be (damaged) beyond ~** （损坏得）无法修理; **extensive ~ work** 大修工作; **a TV ~ shop** 电视机修理铺 [2] [u] formal (condition) 状况; **to be in a good/bad state of ~, to be in good/bad ~** 状况良好/不佳; **that jacket of yours looks in a pretty poor state of ~!** 你的那件夹克衫看起来真破！; **he was generally in a pretty poor state of ~** hum 他总是一副邋遢样儿; **to keep sth. in good ~** 使某物保持状况良好

B *vt* [1] (mend) 修理 ‹*furniture, window, pipe, machine, roof*›; 整修 ‹*wall, road, building*›; 缝补 ‹*clothes, carpet, sheet*›; **to have sth. ~ed** 让人修理某物; **it isn't worth having it ~ed** 这东西不值得送去修理了 [2] (make good) 修复 ‹*damage*›; **builders have been working seven days a week to ~ the storm damage** 建筑工人一周工作 7 天来修复暴风雨造成的破坏 [3] fig (put right) 弥补 ‹*wrong*›; 补偿 ‹*damage*›; 补救 ‹*relations*›; **it was too late to ~ their relationship** 要挽回他们的关系已经太迟了

C *vi* formal (go) 去; **we ~ed to the tranquillity of a quiet cafe** 我们去享受咖啡馆的恬静

repairable /rɪˈpeərəbl/ *adj* 可修理的; **this watch is not ~** 这块表没法修了

repair: ~ kit *n* 维修工具; **~man** /-mæn/ ▸ **p. 409** *n* 修理工

repaper /ˌriːˈpeɪpə(r)/ *vt* 给…重新贴墙纸

reparable /ˈreprəbl/ *adj* 可补偿的 ‹*damage, loss*›; 可治愈的 ‹*injury*›

reparation /ˌrepəˈreɪʃn/ *n* [1] [u] (compensation) 赔偿; **no ~ is possible for the terrible wrong they have suffered** 他们所受的可怕冤屈无法补偿; **to make financial ~ to the victim** 对受害者进行经济赔偿 [2] **reparations** *pl* (for war damage) 战争赔款; **to pay/demand ~s** 支付/要求战争赔款

repartee /ˌrepɑːˈtiː/ *n* [u] 连篇妙语

repast /rɪˈpɑːst, Amer rɪˈpæst/ *n* formal 餐; **a sumptuous ~** 华宴

repatriate /ˌriːˈpætrɪeɪt, Amer -ˈpeɪt-/ *vt* [1] (send home) 遣返 ‹*person*› [2] (transfer) 把…调回本国 ‹*money*›

repatriation /ˌriːpætrɪˈeɪʃn, Amer -peɪt-/ *n* [u] [1] (of people) 遣返; **forced/voluntary ~** 强行/自愿遣返 [2] (of money) 调回本国; **the ~ of profit or capital** 利润或资本向本国的回流

repay /rɪˈpeɪ/ *vt* (*pt, pp* **repaid**) [1] (reimburse) 偿还 ‹*money, debt*›; **to ~ sb.** 还某人钱; **I've agreed to ~ the loan in instalments** 我已经同意分期还款 [2] fig 报答 ‹*favour, kindness*›; **she repaid his devotion with indifference** 对他的忠诚，她报之以冷漠 [3] (reward) 使…值得 ‹*work, time*›; **this article ~s careful reading** 这篇文章值得细读

repayable /rɪˈpeɪəbl/ *adj* (must be repaid) 必须偿还的; (may be repaid) 可以偿还的; **~ on demand** 即时偿还的

repayment /rɪˈpeɪmənt/ *n* [1] [c] (amount) 偿还额; **you may spread ~s over five years** 你可以分 5 年还款 [2] [u] (action) 偿还

repayment: ~ mortgage *n* 固定偿还期按揭; **~ schedule** *n* 还款计划

repeal /rɪˈpiːl/

A *vt* 废除 ‹*law*›

r

B 废除; **the ~ of the Corn Laws** Hist 谷物法的废除

repeat /rɪ'piːt/

A *vt* **1** (say again) 重复说; (write again) 重复写; **could you ~ that once more?** 请再说一遍好吗? ; **the opposition have been ~ing their calls for ...** 反对派在反复要求…; **to ~ the same old thing** 老调重弹; **the claims are, I ~, totally unfounded** 这些要求，我再说一遍，是毫无道理的; **I am not, ~ not, travelling in the same car as him!** 我不，再说一遍，不和他乘同一辆车!; **to ~ (that) ...** 重复说…; **to be ~ed** «*event, attack*» 再次发生 **2** (pass on) 转述 ‹*gossip, secret*›; **I'm only ~ing what I've heard!** 我只是把我听到的话告诉你!; **the rumour has been widely ~ed in the press** 报界普遍转载了这一传闻; **to ~ sth. to sb.** 将某事告诉某人; **I don't want you to ~ a word of this to anyone** 这件事我希望你一个字也不要告诉别人 **3** (say verbatim) 复述; **to ~ sth. word for word** 一字不差地复述某事; **to ~ sth. after sb.** 跟着某人读 ‹*sentence, word*› **4** (redo, rerun) 重复 ‹*mistake, experiment, pattern*›; **they are hoping to ~ last year's victory** 他们希望像去年一样再次获胜; **the Americans plan to ~ their attempt to launch a spacecraft** 美国人计划再次尝试发射一部航天器; **a bargain offer that cannot be ~ed** 机不可失的减价优惠 **5** Radio, TV 重播 ‹*programme, series*› **6** Sch 重读 ‹*class, grade*›; 重修 ‹*course, subject*› **7** Mus 重奏 ‹*passage, motif*›

B *vi* **1** (do again) 重复; **lift and lower the right leg 20 times; ~ with the left leg** 右腿提放 20 次，左腿重复该动作 **2** esp Brit (be tasted again) 返味; **cucumber has a tendency to ~** 吃了黄瓜口中会有一股味儿; **to ~ on sb.** 在某人口中留有余味

C *v refl* **1** (say the same thing) **to ~ oneself** 重复说过的话 **2** (recur) **to ~ itself** 重复发生; **history is ~ing itself** 历史正在重演

D *n* **1** Radio, TV 重播节目; **is it a new series? — no, a ~** 这是新的连续剧吗? —— 不，是重播的 **2** (of event, performance) 重演; (of action, statement) 重复; **a ~ of the 1906 earthquake could kill up to 11,000 people** 如果再发生 1906 年的地震，死亡人数可能会达到 11,000 人; **~ orders/attacks** 续订的订单/后续攻击 **3** Mus (passage) 反复段; (mark) 反复符

repeatable /rɪ'piːtəbl/ *adj* 再次说得出口的; **that anecdote wouldn't be ~ at many dinner tables!** 那个趣闻在许多饭桌上不便复述!

repeated /rɪ'piːtɪd/ *adj* 不停的 ‹*warnings, efforts*›; 一再的 ‹*delays, failures*›; **we have received ~ assurances** 我们得到再三的保证

repeatedly /rɪ'piːtɪdli/ *adv* 不停地 ‹*ask, complain*›; 一再 ‹*tell, inform*›; **drivers are ~ warned to reduce speed** 司机们被多次警告要减速

repeater /rɪ'piːtə(r)/ *n* **1** (gun) 连发枪 **2** Radio, TV 转发器 **3** Amer Sch colloq 留级生

repeat fee *n* 重播费

repeating /rɪ'piːtɪŋ/ *adj* **1** (recurring) 重复的 ‹*design, motif, rhythm*› **2** (multiple shot) 连发的 ‹*gun, pistol, firearm*›

repeat: ~ offender *n* 累犯; **~ prescription** *n* Brit 连续处方

repel /rɪ'pel/ *vt* (*pres p etc.* **-ll-**) **1** (drive back) 击退 ‹*attacker, invader*› **2** (disgust) 使厌恶; **he was ~led by the sight of blood** 他一看见血就恶心 **3** Phys 排斥; **like poles ~ one another** 同极相斥 **4** (resist mixing with) 与…不融合; **oil ~s water** 油不溶于水; **this new material ~s moisture** 这种新材料能防潮

repellent /rɪ'pelənt/

A *adj* **1** (arousing disgust) 令人讨厌的 ‹*sight, person*›; 令人反感的 ‹*ideas, views*› **2** (impervious) 隔绝的; **water-~ fabrics** 防水面料

B *n* 驱除剂; **a flea ~** 驱跳蚤剂

repent /rɪ'pent/

A *vt* **1** (feel remorse for) 忏悔 ‹*crime, sins*›; 为…自责 ‹*words, deed, hurt*› **2** (regret) 对…后悔 ‹*action, omission*›; **I hope I don't live to ~ my decision** 我希望我永远不会对自己的决定后悔

B *vi* **1** (feel remorse) 自责; **to ~ of sth.** 为某事物自责 **2** (regret) 后悔

repentance /rɪ'pentəns/ *n* [u] 悔悟

repentant /rɪ'pentənt/ *adj* 悔过的

repercussion /ˌriːpə'kʌʃn/ *n* 间接后果; **to have ~s on sth.** 对某事物造成不良影响; **to bring about ~s** 产生影响

repertoire /'repətwɑː(r)/ *n* **1** (of plays, dances, music) 可表演节目; **in sb.'s ~** 在某人的节目单上 **2** (regularly performed items) 常规节目; **the mainstream concert ~** 主流音乐会的常规曲目 **3** (stock of skills) 全部本领; **she has a whole ~ of hostile looks** hum 她能做出各种各样表示敌意的表情

repertory /'repətri, Amer -tɔːri/ *n* **1** [u] (performance) 保留剧目轮演; **to be in ~** 参加保留剧目轮演; **a ~ actor/theatre** 参加保留剧目轮演的演员/轮演剧目剧院 **2** [u] (theatres) 保留剧目轮演剧场 **3** [c] (company) 保留剧目轮演剧团 **4** = **repertoire**

repertory company *n* 保留剧目轮演剧团

repetition /ˌrepɪ'tɪʃn/ *n* **1** [u] (repeating) 重复; **all musicians learn by ~** 音乐家都是通过重复来学习的 **2** [c] (repeated action) 重做的事; (repeated words) 重复的话 **3** [c] (recurrence) 重现

repetitious /ˌrepɪ'tɪʃəs/ *adj* 重复的; **he has a dull ~ style** 他的风格枯燥而烦琐

repetitive /rɪ'petɪtɪv/ *adj* 重复的; **the work is dull and ~** 这项工作单调重复

repetitively /rɪ'petɪtɪvli/ *adv* 反复地

repetitiveness /rɪ'petɪtɪvnɪs/ *n* [u] 重复

repetitive strain injury *n* [u and c] 重复性劳损

rephrase /ˌriː'freɪz/ *vt* 改变…的措词

replace /rɪ'pleɪs/ *vt* **1** (put back) 放回; **please ~ all books on the shelf after use** 用完后请把所有的书放回到书架上 **2** (take the place of) 取代; **Mr Smith ~s Mr Brown as area manager** 史密斯先生接替布朗先生做地区经理; **craft workers are being ~d by electronic machines** 手艺工正在被电子仪器所取代; **he could find nobody to ~ her in his affections** 他对她的感情无人能代替 **3** (supply replacement for) 更换 ‹*goods, property*›

replaceable /rɪ'pleɪsəbl/ *adj* 可更换的 ‹*blade, tyres*›; 可替代的 ‹*employee, person*›

replacement /rɪ'pleɪsmənt/ *n* **1** [u] (replacing) 更换; **~ cost** 更替费用; **~ staff** 更替的人员 **2** [c] (person) 接替者; (part) 替代品

replant /ˌriː'plɑːnt/ *vt* **1** (of new plants) 新栽种 ‹*plants, trees*›; 在…再植 ‹*area*›; **the old orchard was ~ed this year** 老果园今年种上了新果树 **2** (of existing plants) 移栽 ‹*trees, roses*›; 移栽到 ‹*area*›

replay

A /ˌriː'pleɪ/ *vt* **1** (listen to or watch again) 重放 ‹*CD, DVD*› **2** Sport 重新举行 ‹*game*› **3** fig (repeat) 重温; **she ~ed in her mind every detail of the night before** 她在脑海里重温了前一个晚上的所有细节

B /'riːpleɪ/ *n* **1** (of tape, recording) 重放 **2** Sport 重赛 **3** fig (of event, incident) 重演; **a ~ of the Vietnam War** 越战的重演

replenish /rɪ'plenɪʃ/ *vt* **1** (refill) 再装满 ‹*glass*›; **the recent rain has ~ed our reservoirs** 最近的降雨又使我们的水库蓄满了水 **2** (restore) 补充 ‹*stocks, energy*›

replenishment /rɪ'plenɪʃmənt/ *n* [u] 补充

replete /rɪ'pliːt/ *adj* **1** (with food) 饱食的 ‹*person*› **2** (fully supplied) 装满的 ‹*house*›; **the textbook is ~ with facts, figures and charts** 课本里有丰富的资料、数据和图表

replica /'replɪkə/ *n* **1** (exact copy) [尤指缩小比例的] 复制品 **2** (of work of art) 艺术复制品

replicate /'replɪkeɪt/

A *vt* **1** (reproduce) 复制; **to ~ a document** 复制文件; **is it practical to ~ eastern culture in the west?** 在西方复制东方文化行得通吗? **2** (repeat) 重复获得 ‹*result, data*› **3** Biol 使自我复制; **to ~ itself** 自我复制

B *vi* Biol 自我复制

replication /ˌreplɪ'keɪʃn/ *n* [u] **1** (of experiment, procedure) 重复; **we obtained ~ of the results** 我们得到了同样的结果 **2** Biol 自我复制

reply /rɪ'plaɪ/

A *n* **1** (answer) 答复; **to make no ~** 不回答; **in ~ to your letter of 26th January ...** 1 月 26 日来函收悉，现答复… **2** (response) 回应; **a shrug of the shoulders was his only ~** 耸肩就是他的唯一反应

B *vi* **1** (answer) 答复; **none of my letters have been replied to as yet** 迄今为止我所有的信都未得到答复; **to ~ to an email/text message** 回复电子邮件/短信 **2** (respond) 回应; **she replied with a smile** 她以微笑作答

C *vt* 回答道

reply coupon *n* [用于国际信函的] 预付回信邮资券

repoint /ˌriː'pɔɪnt/ *vt* 重新勾嵌 ‹*wall, house*›

repointing /ˌriː'pɔɪntɪŋ/ *n* [u] 重新勾嵌接缝

repo man /'riːpəʊ mæn/ *n* Amer colloq 货品收回人

report /rɪ'pɔːt/

A *n* **1** (written or spoken assessment of situation) 报告; **a police/medical ~** 警方/医疗报告; **a ~ on sb./sth.** 关于某人/某事物的报告; **I want a full ~ of your date tomorrow morning** hum 你明天上午给我详细汇报约会的事 **2** (notification) 通报; **a ~ of sth.** 关于…的通报 ‹*illness, crime, accident*› **3** (official document) 调查报告; **an air accident ~** 航空意外事故调查报告; **a ~ on sth.** 关于某事物的调查报告; **to deliver/prepare/publish a ~ (on sth.)** 发布/准备/发表（关于某事物的）调查报告; **to present a ~ to sb./sth.** 向某人/某机构呈交调查报告; **an annual ~** 年度报告; **the chairman's/committee's ~** 董事长/委员会的报告 **4** Journ, Radio, TV 报道; **to carry a ~ (of sth.)** 登载（关于某事物的）报道; **a ~ on sb./sth.** 关于某人/某事物的报道; **a newspaper/press/TV ~** 报纸/报刊/电视报道; **a news ~** 新闻报道; **a ~ from sb./sth.** 来自某人/某处的报道 **5** (rumour) 传闻; **according to ~s, ...** 据传…; **to get ~s of sth.** 获悉关于某事物的传闻; **conflicting ~s of** *or* **as to sth.** 关于某事物的自相矛盾的传闻; **I've heard ~s that ...** 我听说…; **~s are circulating that ...** 人们纷纷传说… **6** Brit Sch (on student's work) 成绩报告单; **to get a good/bad ~** 成绩出色/糟糕; **he received a glowing ~** 他成绩优异; **to give sb. a good/bad ~** 给某人一张出色/糟糕的成绩报告单 **7** Amer Sch (review) 读书报告; **to write a ~ (on sth.)** 写（关于某书的）读书报告 **8** (of gun) 枪声; (of shell, explosion, firework) 爆炸声; **the tyre exploded with a loud ~** 随着一声巨响，轮胎爆了

B *vt* **1** (relay) 汇报 ‹*fact, findings, progress*›; **I have nothing to ~** 我没什么要汇报的; **to ~ sth. to sb./sth.** 向某人/某处汇报 ‹*result, decision*›; **to ~ (that) ...** 汇报说…; **to ~ sb./sth. (as) sth.** 宣布某人/某事物处于某状态; **the doctor ~ed the patient fully recovered** 医生说这名病人已完全康复; **to ~ sb./sth. as doing sth.** 宣布某人/某物做某事; **the house was ~ed as being in excellent condition** 据说这幢房子状况极佳; **to ~ doing sth.** 陈述做过某事; **the**

r

neighbours ~ed seeing him leave the building around noon 邻居们反映中午时分看见他离开了大楼; to be ~ed to do sth. 据说做某事; she was ~ed by the hospital spokesman to be making excellent progress 医院发言人说她恢复得相当快 [2] Journ, Radio, TV 报道; the papers ~ed their presence in Paris 各家报纸报道他们在巴黎现身; it was ~ed that ... 据报道…; to ~ sb./sth. to be sth. 报道某人/某事物处于某状态; the newspaper ~ed him to be dead 报纸报道他死了 [3] (allege) 传闻; it is ~ed that ... 据传…; to be ~ed to do/as doing sth. 据传做某事; she is ~ed to have changed her mind 据说她改主意了; the President is ~ed as saying that ... 据传总统说… [4] (give notification of) 报告; I want to ~ the loss of a package 我丢了一个包裹，要报案; ~ed cases of AIDS 已报告的艾滋病病例; no casualties have been ~ed 尚未有人员伤亡的报告; to ~ sth. to sb. 向某人报告某事; to ~ sb. (as) dead/missing 报告某人死亡/失踪; to ~ (as) absent without leave 报告擅自缺席 [5] (complain about) 举报; to ~ sb./sth. to sb. 向某人举报某人/某事; you will be ~ed to the boss 我要向老板告发你; to ~ sb. for sth./doing sth. 因某事物/做某事而举报某人; I'm ~ing you for insolence/being late 我要投诉你的傲慢无礼/举报你迟到

C vi [1] (give account) to ~ on sth. 报告 ‹*situation, progress*›; he will ~ to Parliament on the negotiations 他会向议会汇报谈判事宜 [2] (present findings) 公布调查结果; to ~ on sth. 公布关于某事物的调查结果; the committee will ~ on its research next month 委员会将于下月公布研究结果 [3] Journ 报道; she's been ~ing for over ten years now 她已经当了十多年记者了; to ~ on sth. 报道 ‹*event*›; he ~s on royal stories for the BBC 他为英国广播公司报道王室新闻; to ~ for sb./sth. 为某人/某处提供新闻报道; to ~ from sth. 从某处进行报道 [4] (present oneself) 报到; to ~ to sb./sth. 向某人/到某处报到; please ~ to reception on arrival 到达后请到接待处报到; to ~ to one's unit Mil 到所在部队报到; to ~ sick 告病; to ~ for duty 报到上班

(Phrasal verbs)

• **report back**

A vi [1] (after absence) 报告返回; to take an hour for lunch and ~ back at 2 花 1 小时吃午饭，2 点钟返回; to ~ back from sth. 做完某事后报告返回; he ~s back from leave on Wednesday 他将在星期三休假结束后回来上班 [2] (present findings) 发回报告; to ~ back to sb./sth. 向某人/某处发回报告; to ~ back about *or* on sb./sth. 发回关于某人/某事物的报告

B vt (relay) 汇报; to ~ back that ... 汇报说…

• **report to** vt [~ to sb.] 从属于 ‹*manager, superior*›; she ~s directly to the Head of Department 她直接向部门主管汇报工作

reportage /ˌrepɔːˈtɑːʒ/ *n* [u] [1] (reporting) 新闻报道 [2] (factual presentation) 报告文学

report card *n* esp Amer 成绩报告单

reportedly /rɪˈpɔːtɪdli/ *adv* 据说; the star is ~ gravely ill 那位明星据说病得很厉害

reported speech *n* [u] 间接引语

reporter /rɪˈpɔːtə(r)/ ▸p. 409 *n* 记者; our on-the-spot ~ in Moscow 我们在莫斯科的现场记者; the ~s' gallery 记者席

reporting /rɪˈpɔːtɪŋ/ *n* [u] 报道; accurate/balanced/objective ~ 准确/公正/客观的报道

reporting restrictions *npl* 报道限制; to impose/lift ~ 实施/取消报道限制

report stage *n* 审议阶段 [英国、加拿大议会立法程序之一]

repose /rɪˈpəʊz/ formal or liter

A *n* [u] [1] (rest) 小憩 [2] (state of peace) 安息; the ~ of souls 灵魂的安息 [3] (composure) 镇静; studied ~ 故意装出的从容姿态; nothing seemed to shake her inner ~ 似乎什么都不能打破她内心的镇定平和

B *vt* (place) 寄托 ‹*confidence, trust*›

C *vi* [1] (rest) «*person*» 休息; «*arm, head*» 靠着; he liked to lie with his head reposing in her lap 他喜欢头靠在她大腿上躺着 [2] (be stored) 存放; the painting now ~s in the Louvre 这幅画现在存放在卢浮宫

repository /rɪˈpɒzɪtri, Amer -tɔːri/ *n* [1] (for storage) 存放处; the museum is a ~ of art treasures from all over the world 该博物馆收藏有来自世界各地的艺术珍品 [2] (for knowledge) 智囊; (for information) 信息库

repossess /ˌriːpəˈzes/ *vt* 收回 ‹*house, furniture*›

repossession /ˌriːpəˈzeʃn/ *n* [u] 收回; the bank is seeking ~ of the flat 银行正设法收回拖欠贷款的公寓

repossession: ~ man *n* Amer 货品收回人 [向拖欠货款者追回货品的人]; **~ order** *n* [法院发出的] 物品收回令

repost /ˌriːˈpəʊst/ *vt* [在互联网上] 重新发布 ‹*information, article*›

reprehend /ˌreprɪˈhend/ *vt* formal 指责

reprehensible /ˌreprɪˈhensɪbl/ *adj* 应受指责的

reprehensibly /ˌreprɪˈhensɪbli/ *adv* 应受指责地; the evidence clearly indicated that the accused acted ~ 证据清楚地表明被告的行为该受到谴责

represent /ˌreprɪˈzent/ *vt* [1] (correspond to) 相当于; for the artist those five pictures ~ed a year's work 对那位画家而言，那 5 幅画相当于一年的工作; the new engine ~s a major breakthrough in car design 这款新发动机代表了汽车设计的重大突破 [2] (act on behalf of) 代表; Prince Charles ~ed the Queen at the ceremony 查尔斯王子代表女王参加庆典; he ~ed Great Britain at the Olympics 他代表英国参加这届奥运会; the disaster victims could not afford a lawyer to ~ them 灾难的受害者请不起律师为他们打官司 [3] (form part of) 占据; women writers are strongly ~ed in the list of new fiction published today 在当今新出版小说书单中，女性作家的作品占了很大比例 [4] (depict, portray) 描绘; the painting ~s a battle at sea 这幅画表现的是一场海战 [5] (typify) 体现 ‹*political climate, values, ideals*› [6] (symbolize) 象征; on this map a cross ~s a church 在这张地图上，十字代表教堂; open frontiers ~ political freedom 开放的边界象征着政治自由 [7] (convey in words) 表达; words cannot adequately ~ our anger 言语不足以表达我们的愤怒 [8] (portray on stage, film) 演绎 ‹*character, situation*› [9] (present) 声称; he ~ed himself as a technical expert 他声称自己是技术专家; his supporters ~ him to be a great statesman 他的支持者把他说成是一个伟大的政治家

re-present /ˌriːprɪˈzent/ *vt* 再提交 ‹*cheque, bill*›

representation /ˌreprɪzenˈteɪʃn/ *n* [1] [u] (participation, embodiment) 代表; they are calling for worker ~ on the board 他们要求工人在董事会里要有代表; our firm has exclusive ~ in the Japanese market 我们公司在日本市场有独家代理权 [2] [c] (depiction, portrayal) 描述; an objective ~ of the facts 对事实的客观描述 [3] representations *pl* (formal statement) 交涉; to make ~(s) to sb. about sth. 就某事物向某人提出抗议

representational /ˌreprɪzenˈteɪʃənl/ *adj* [1] Art 具象派的 ‹*art, painter*› [2] Pol 代表性的; ~ democracy/politics 代议民主制/代议政治

representative /ˌreprɪˈzentətɪv/

A *adj* [1] (typical) 典型的 ‹*sample, survey*›; the museum has a good ~ collection of local flora and fauna 这个博物馆收藏了本地区动植物群的典型样本 [2] Pol 代表制的 ‹*government, council*›; a ~ election 代表选举; a ~ assembly 代表大会

B ▸p. 409 *n* [1] (spokesperson) 代表; union ~s 工会代表 [2] Comm (agent) 销售代理; area *or* local *or* regional ~ 地区销售代理; sole ~ 独家代理商 [3] Pol 议员

repress /rɪˈpres/ *vt* [1] (suppress) 忍住 ‹*tears, anger, smile*› [2] (subjugate) 镇压 ‹*revolt, protest, opposition*› [3] Psych 压抑 ‹*instincts, thoughts*›; to ~ subconscious desires 压抑潜意识中的欲望

repressed /rɪˈprest/ *adj* 受压抑的 ‹*person, desire, sexuality, childhood*›; ~ indigenous groups 受压迫的原住民群体; he was a bundle of ~ energy 他浑身精力无处发泄

repression /rɪˈpreʃn/ *n* [u] [1] (of revolt, opposition) 压制; the minister advocated the ~ of dissent 这位部长主张压制持不同政见者 [2] Psych 压抑

repressive /rɪˈpresɪv/ *adj* 专制的 ‹*regime, government*›; 严厉的 ‹*law*›; 强硬的 ‹*measure, action*›

reprieve /rɪˈpriːv/

A *n* [1] (from punishment) 缓刑 [2] (from closure, destruction) 暂时解救; a government grant has given the scheme a last-minute ~ 一笔政府补助款使这个项目在危急关头获得了一线生机

B *vt* [1] (from punishment) 暂缓对…的刑罚 [2] (from closure, destruction) 暂时解救

reprimand /ˈreprɪmɑːnd, Amer -mænd/

A *n* 训斥; to be let off with a ~ 被训斥一通了事

B *vt* 训斥; to ~ sb. for sth. 因某事物训斥某人; to be ~ed for doing sth. 因为做某事遭到训斥

reprint

A /ˌriːˈprɪnt/ *vt* 重新印刷 ‹*book*›; 重新打印 ‹*leaflet, label*›

B /ˌriːˈprɪnt/ *vi* «*book*» 重印

C /ˈriːprɪnt/ *n* [1] (of book) 复印本; (of other printed matter) 复印件 [2] (offprint) 重印本

reprisal /rɪˈpraɪzl/ *n* [c and u] 报复; to carry out ~s 进行报复; in ~ (for sth.) 为了报复（某事）; if we put a tariff on their goods, then they may do the same by way of ~ 如果我们对他们的商品征收关税，那么他们也会同样做进行报复

reprise /rɪˈpriːz/

A *n* 重复; a ~ of the role 角色的重复

B *vt* 重演 ‹*role*›

repro /ˈriːprəʊ/ *n* (*pl* ~s) colloq 仿制品 [尤指家具]

reproach /rɪˈprəʊtʃ/

A *n* [1] [c] (rebuke) 责备的言辞; to heap ~es on sb. 对某人横加指责 [2] [u] (disapproval, criticism) 责备; with a note of ~ 带着责备的口吻; above *or* beyond ~ 无可指摘 [3] [c and u] (disgrace) 耻辱; to be a ~ to sb. 对某人而言是个耻辱; she feels that her runaway daughter is a living ~ to her 她觉得出走的女儿活活让她丢人现眼; to bring ~ on *or* upon sb. 给某人带来耻辱

B *vt* 责备; to ~ sb. with *or* for sth. 为某事物责备某人; don't ~ yourself for it 别为此自责

reproachful /rɪˈprəʊtʃfl/ *adj* 表示责备的; a ~ tone 责备的语气; ~ eyes 责备的目光

reproachfully /rɪˈprəʊtʃfəli/ *adv* 责备地

reprobate /ˈreprəbeɪt/

A *n* 混球 [常表示幽默或亲昵]; my uncle's an old ~ 我叔叔是个老混球

B *adj* 混账的

reprocess /ˌriːˈprəʊses, Amer -ˈprɒses/ *vt* 对…进行再加工

reprocessing /ˌriːˈprəʊsesɪŋ, Amer -ˈprɒs-/ *n* [u] 再加工

reprocessing plant *n* 后处理工厂

reproduce /ˌriːprəˈdjuːs, Amer -ˈduːs/
A *vt* **1** (copy) 复制 ‹*artefact, document, music*›; 模仿 ‹*accent, sound*› **2** (repeat) 使…重现 ‹*process, result*›; 再现 ‹*effect*› **3** Biol 繁殖; **to ~ itself** 自我繁殖
B *vi* **1** (copy) 被复制; **certain colours ~ better than others** 有些颜色比其他颜色复制效果更好 **2** Biol 繁殖

reproducible /ˌriːprəˈdjuːsəbl, Amer -ˈduːsəbl/ *adj* **1** (able to be copied) 可复制的 ‹*format, image*› **2** (able to be repeated) 可再现的 ‹*effect, result, conditions*›

reproduction /ˌriːprəˈdʌkʃn/ *n* **1** [u] Biol 繁殖 **2** [c] (painting, artefact) 复制品 **3** [u] (process) 复制 **4** [u] Audio (sound quality) 声音效果

reproduction furniture *n* [u] 仿古家具

reproductive /ˌriːprəˈdʌktɪv/ *adj* 繁殖的; **~ capacity** 繁殖能力; **~ organs** 生殖器官

reprogram, reprogramme /ˌriːˈprəʊgræm/ *vt* lit 为…重新设计程序 ‹*system, machine*›; fig 重新整合 ‹*brain*›; **to manipulate and ~ DNA** 操控和改变 DNA 编码

reprographic /ˌriːprəˈgræfɪk/ *adj* 复印的; **~ equipment** 复印设备

reproof /rɪˈpruːf/ *n* [c and u] 责备

re-proof /ˌriːˈpruːf/ *vt* **1** (make impervious) 为…重做防水处理 ‹*garment, tent*› **2** Publg (make new proof of) 重新给…打样 ‹*text, page*›

reprove /rɪˈpruːv/ *vt* 责备; **to ~ sb. for sth.** 因某事物责备某人

reproving /rɪˈpruːvɪŋ/ *adj* 责备的

reprovingly /rɪˈpruːvɪŋli/ *adv* 责备地

reptile /ˈreptaɪl, Amer -tl/ *n* **1** Zool 爬行动物 **2** fig pej 卑鄙小人

reptile house *n* 爬行动物馆

reptilian /repˈtɪliən/ *adj* **1** Zool 爬行动物的 **2** fig pej 卑劣的 ‹*smile, eyes*›

republic /rɪˈpʌblɪk/ *n* 共和国; **the People's R~ of China** 中华人民共和国

republican /rɪˈpʌblɪkən/
A *adj* **1** (of or relating to a republic) 共和国的 ‹*system, government*› **2** (in favour of republican system) 拥护共和政体的 ‹*tendency, movement*› **3** **Republican** Amer 共和党的 ‹*voter, policy*› **4** (in Irish politics) 北爱尔兰共和主义的 ‹*movement, party, politician*›
B *n* **1** (supporter of republican system) 共和政体拥护者 **2** **Republican** Amer (supporter) 共和党支持者; (member) 共和党党员 **3** (in Irish politics) 北爱尔兰共和主义者

republicanism /rɪˈpʌblɪkənɪzəm/ *n* [u] **1** (support of republican system) 共和主义 **2** **Republicanism** Amer (support of Republican Party) 对共和党的支持 **3** (in Irish politics) 北爱尔兰共和主义

> **the Republican Party**
>
> 共和党，美国两大政党之一。1854 年由主张废除奴隶制度的人士创立，第一任共和党总统为亚伯拉罕·林肯（Abraham Lincoln）。和民主党（▸**the Democratic Party**）相比，共和党较为保守，主张降低赋税、减少政府干预。简称 GOP，一般认为是 Grand Old Party（大老党）的缩写。官方标志是"大象"，源自 19 世纪 70 年代的一幅政治漫画。和民主党（非官方标志为"驴"）的竞争常被称为"驴象之争"。

Republic of Ireland *pr n* **the ~** 爱尔兰共和国

republish /ˌriːˈpʌblɪʃ/ *vt* 再出版 ‹*book*›; 再刊行 ‹*article, leaflet*›

repudiate /rɪˈpjuːdieɪt/ *vt* **1** (reject) 否认 ‹*accusation*›; 拒绝承认 ‹*violence, validity*›; **he strongly ~d any suggestion that he had acted illegally** 他强烈驳斥了任何指责他行为非法的暗示 **2** Jur 拒绝履行 ‹*contract, treaty*›; 拒付 ‹*debt*› **3** (disown) 与…断绝关系 ‹*child, family*›

repudiation /rɪˌpjuːdɪˈeɪʃn/ *n* **1** (rejection) 否认; **the ~ of a charge** 对指控的否认 **2** Jur (of contract, treaty) 拒绝履行; (of debt) 拒付 **3** (of child, family) 断绝关系

repugnance /rɪˈpʌgnəns/ *n* [u] 憎恶; **~ for** *or* **to sth.** 对某事物的憎恶; **she tried to hide the ~ she felt at his disfigurement** 她试图掩饰看到他容貌被毁时内心的厌恶

repugnant /rɪˈpʌgnənt/ *adj* 令人憎恶的; **she found him totally ~** 她觉得他极其讨厌

repulse /rɪˈpʌls/ *vt* **1** (drive back) 击退 ‹*attack, army*› **2** (rebuff) 断然拒绝 ‹*offer, advances*›

repulsion /rɪˈpʌlʃn/ *n* [u] **1** (feeling of disgust) 嫌恶感 **2** Phys 排斥力

repulsive /rɪˈpʌlsɪv/ *adj* **1** (disgusting) 令人厌恶的 ‹*behaviour, thought*›; **to find sth. ~** 觉得某物很恶心; **~ table manners** 讨厌的吃相 **2** Phys 排斥的

repulsively /rɪˈpʌlsɪvli/ *adv* 令人厌恶地

repulsiveness /rɪˈpʌlsɪvnɪs/ *n* [u] 可憎

repurchase /ˌriːˈpɜːtʃɪs/
A *n* [u] 回购
B *vt* 购回

repurchase agreement *n* 回购协议

reputable /ˈrepjʊtəbl/ *adj* 声誉好的

reputation /ˌrepjʊˈteɪʃn/ *n* 名声; **to live up to one's ~** 名副其实; **to acquire/establish/earn a ~** 获得/确立/赢得名声; **to ruin/lose/tarnish one's ~** 毁掉/失去/玷污名声; **he has a ~ for laziness** 他以懒惰出名; **he has quite a ~ with the girls!** 他玩弄女性是出了名的!

repute /rɪˈpjuːt/
A *n* [u] **1** (reputation) 名声; **of good/bad ~** 名声好的/坏的; **to bring into bad ~** 坏掉名声; **a house of ill ~** euph 妓院 **2** (fame) 知名度
B *vt usu passive* **to be ~d to be/do sth.** 据说是某事物/做某事; **that old house is ~d to be haunted** 那间老屋据说闹鬼

reputed /rɪˈpjuːtɪd/ *adj attrib* 普遍认为的 ‹*intelligence, skill*›; 号称的 ‹*ancestor*›; **her three daughters are ~ beauties** 她的 3 个女儿是出了名的美人

reputedly /rɪˈpjuːtɪdli/ *adv* 据说

request /rɪˈkwest/
A *n* **1** (act of asking) 要求; **to make a ~** 提出要求; **to grant/refuse a ~** 批准/拒绝要求; **at sb.'s ~** 应某人要求; **by** *or* **on ~** 经要求 **2** Radio 点播节目; **to play a ~ for sb.** 为某人播放点播节目
B *vt* 要求 ‹*action, assistance*›; 请求给予 ‹*bill, facts*›; **to ~ sb. (not) to do sth.** 要求某人（不）做某事; **as ~ed** 按照要求; **to ~ the company of sb.** 敬请某人的光临; **to ~ a favour of sb.** 请求某人帮忙

request stop *n* Brit [公共汽车的] 招呼站

requiem /ˈrekwɪem/ *n* **1** Relig 安魂弥撒 **2** Mus 安魂曲

requiem mass *n* 安魂弥撒

require /rɪˈkwaɪə(r)/ *vt* **1** (need) 需要; **my car ~s servicing at least once a year** 我的车每年最起码需要检修一次 **2** (specify) 要求具备 ‹*skill*›; 规定 ‹*action*›; **what qualifications are ~d for the job?** 这份工作要求具备什么样的资格? **3** (oblige, demand) 要求; **those instruments ~ very careful handling** 那些仪器需要小心轻放; **I'm not ~d to tell you where I've been!** 我没义务告诉你我去过哪里!

required /rɪˈkwaɪəd/ *adj* 规定的; **a ~ course** 必修课

requirement /rɪˈkwaɪəmənt/ *n* **1** (need) 需要; **to meet sb.'s ~s** 满足某人的需要; **surplus to ~s** 供过于求; **a pressing ~** 急迫的需求 **2** (condition) 必备条件; **to fulfil** *or* **meet** *or* **satisfy the ~s** 符合要求; **what are the ~s of the job?** 这份工作有什么要求? **3** (obligation) 规定; **a legal ~** 法律规定; **it is a ~ that guns be registered** 按规定枪支必须登记

requisite /ˈrekwɪzɪt/
A *n* 必需物; **to be a ~ for sth.** 是某事物的必要条件; **a good figure is a prime ~ for a fashion model** 好身材是时装模特的首要条件; **toilet ~s** 卫生间必需品
B *adj attrib* 必要的 ‹*qualifications, resources*›

requisition /ˌrekwɪˈzɪʃn/
A *n* **1** [u] Mil 征用; **under ~** 被征用 **2** [c] (formal request) 正式要求; **a ~ order** *or* **form** 需求单; **I've sent in** *or* **submitted a ~ for stationery** 我递交了一份购买文具的申请单; **to be on ~** 已订购
B *vt* **1** (commandeer) 征用 **2** (formally request) 正式要求

requital /rɪˈkwaɪtl/ *n* [u] formal **1** (of good action) 报答; (of bad action) 报复 **2** (of love) 回报

requite /rɪˈkwaɪt/ *vt* formal **1** (return) 报答 ‹*service, favour*›; **to ~ sb. for sth.** 因某事物报答某人 **2** (avenge) 为…报复 ‹*injury, action*›; **to ~ sb. for sth.** 因某事物而报复某人 **3** (reciprocate) 回报 ‹*love, feelings*›

reran /ˌriːˈræn/ *pt* ▸**rerun A**

reread /ˌriːˈriːd/ *vt* (*pt, pp* **reread** /ˌriːˈred/) 重读

reroof /ˌriːˈruːf/
A *vt* 为…换屋顶
B *vi* 换屋顶

reroute /ˌriːˈruːt/ *vt* 使…改道 ‹*goods, traffic*›

rerun
A /ˌriːˈrʌn/ *vt* (*pt* **reran,** *pp* **rerun**) **1** Sport 重新参加 ‹*race*› **2** (show again) 重映 ‹*film*›
B /ˈriːrʌn/ *n* **1** (of race) 重赛; **to stage a ~** 重赛一场 **2** (of film) 重映; **to show a ~** 重新播放

resale /ˈriːseɪl, ˌriːˈseɪl/ *n* [u and c] 转卖

resat /ˌriːˈsæt/ *pt, pp* ▸**resit A, B**

reschedule /ˌriːˈʃedjuːl, Amer -ˈskedʒʊl/ *vt* **1** (change time of) 将…改期 ‹*flight, itinerary*›; 重新编排 ‹*timetable*›; 修改…的时间表 ‹*plans, course*› **2** Fin 修改…的偿还计划 ‹*loan, debt*›

rescind /rɪˈsɪnd/ *vt* 取消; **the government eventually ~ed the directive** 政府最终取消了该指令

rescue /ˈreskjuː/
A *vt* **1** (save from danger) 解救; **he was ~d in the nick of time before the ship blew up** 他在船就要爆炸的节骨眼上被救了出来; **thank you for rescuing me from those boring people!** hum 谢谢你帮助我摆脱了那些无聊的人! **2** (release) 营救 ‹*prisoner, hostage*› **3** (salvage, preserve) 挽救; **the ancient site has been ~d from the threat of redevelopment** 那处古迹已不再受重新开发的威胁
B *n* 救援; **a ~ attempt** 救援行动

rescue: ~ bid *n* **1** (attempt at saving) 拯救行动; **2** Fin 援救倡议; **~ cover** *n* [u] 车辆损坏保险; **~ package** *n* 一揽子援救计划; **~ party** *n + v sing or pl* 救援队

rescuer /ˈreskjuːə(r)/ *n* 救援人员

rescue worker *n* 救援人员

research /rɪˈsɜːtʃ, ˈriːsɜːtʃ/
A *n* [u] 研究; **to do/be engaged in ~** 做/从事研究; **to carry out ~** 进行研究; **a piece of ~** 一项研究
B *vi* 做研究; **to ~ into sth.** 研究某事物
C *vt* «*academic*» 研究 ‹*subject*›; «*journalist*» 调查 ‹*background, market*›

research: ~ and development *n* [u] 研究与开发; **our ~ and development budget was cut by 50%** 我们的研发预算资金被砍掉了一半; **~ assistant** ▸p. 409 *n* 研究助理; **~ degree** *n* 研究学位

r

researcher /rɪ'sɜːtʃə(r), 'riːsɜːtʃə(r)/ ▸**p. 409** *n* 研究人员

research: ~ **establishment** *n* Brit 研究机构; ~ **fellow** *n* Brit 全职研究员; ~ **fellowship** *n* Brit 全职研究员职位; ~ **grant** *n* 研究经费; ~ **laboratory** *n* 研究实验室; ~ **worker** ▸**p. 409** *n* 研究人员

reseat /ˌriː'siːt/ *vt* **1** (show to new seat) 给…找新座位; **to ~ oneself** (sit down again) 使再坐下; **the audience ~ed themselves after the interval** 观众在幕间休息过后又重新就座 **2** (repair) 为…装设新座 ‹*chair*›; 给…换臀部 ‹*trousers*› **3** (realign) 调整…的底座 ‹*valve, bearing*›

resect /ˌriː'sekt/ *vt* 切除 ‹*bowel, tumour*›

resection /ˌriː'sekʃn/ *n* 切除; **a lung ~** 肺切除

reselect /ˌriːsɪ'lekt/ *vt* 重新选举 ‹*candidate, Member of Parliament*›

reselection /ˌriːsɪ'lekʃn/ *n* [u] 重选; **the party endorses Ms Smith's ~ to stand as their candidate** 该党支持史密斯女士再次作为他们的候选人参选

resell /ˌriː'sel/ *vt* (*pt, pp* **resold**) 转卖; **products can be resold on the black market for huge profits** 产品可以在黑市上转卖, 获取巨额利润

r

resemblance /rɪ'zembləns/ *n* **1** [u] (being alike) 相似; **to bear no/some ~ to sb./sth.** 与某人/某事物没有/有一些相似之处; **degree of ~** 相似程度 **2** [c] (likeness) 相像; **a ~ between X and Y** X和Y的相像; **a family ~** 家族相似性

resemble /rɪ'zembl/ *vt* (look like) 像 ‹*person, object*›; (share features with) 类似于 ‹*situation*›; **she ~s her grandmother** 她像她祖母; **he had never had anything resembling a steady job** 他从来没有谋到一份称得上稳定的工作; **he ~d nothing so much as a tramp** 他跟流浪汉也差不了多少

resent /rɪ'zent/ *vt* 对…感到愤恨 ‹*person, comment, treatment*›; **to ~ having to do sth.** 讨厌必须做某事; **she ~ed being treated like a servant** 她讨厌别人把她当仆人对待; **the women ~ the fact that male staff get paid more for the same work** 那些妇女感到气愤的是, 男性员工干同样的活儿拿的工资却多

resentful /rɪ'zentfl/ *adj* 气愤的; **it's pointless to be ~ about such a trivial matter** 对这种琐事愤愤不平毫无意义; **the boy was ~ at being excluded from the school team** 那个男孩对校队不收自己感到气愤

resentfully /rɪ'zentfəli/ *adv* 气愤地; **he brooded ~ on his misfortune** 他对自己的不幸耿耿于怀

resentment /rɪ'zentmənt/ *n* [u and c] 气愤; **to stir up** *or* **arouse ~** 引起愤慨; **to show** *or* **express ~ at sth.** 对某事表示愤慨; **to harbour ~ against sb.** 对某人心怀怨恨

reservation /ˌrezə'veɪʃn/ *n* **1** [c] (booking) 预订; **I should like to make a ~ for a double room** 我想预订一个双人间; **to confirm/cancel a ~** 确认/取消预订 **2** [u] (setting aside) 预留; **the ~ of positions for non-Americans** 为非美人士预留的职位 **3** [c and u] (doubt, qualification) 保留意见; **with ~s** 有所保留; **without ~** 毫无保留; **I support the plan without ~** 我毫无保留地支持这个计划; **legal ~s** 法律上的质疑 **4** [c] (area of land) 居留地; **a wildlife ~** 野生动物保护区

reservation desk *n* 预订处

reserve /rɪ'zɜːv/

A *n* **1** [u and c] (of oil, food, parts, ammunition, currency) 储备; (of strength, patience) 积聚; **to fall back on one's ~s** 依靠自己的储备; **oil/capital ~s** 石油/资金储备; **to have ~s of sth.** 有…储备 ‹*energy*›; 保留 ‹*strength*›; 保持 ‹*patience*›; **in ~** 备用的; **to keep** *or* **hold sb./sth. in ~** 让某人预备待命/储备某物; **the money was being kept in ~ for their retirement** 这笔钱是存给他们退休后用的; **200 police officers were held in ~** 有200名警察随时待命; **~ supplies/funds** 储备补给/储备金; **~ police** 预备役警察 **2** [c] (area of land) 自然保护区; **he works on a ~** 他在自然保护区工作 **3** [u] (reticence) 拘谨; **her natural ~** 她天生的矜持; **to break through sb.'s ~** 消除某人的拘谨; **to lose one's ~** 变得开朗 **4** [u] formal (doubt) 保留; **with ~** 谨慎地; **I trust him without ~** 我完全信任他 **5** [c] Sport 替补队员; **a ~ player/goalkeeper** 替补队员/守门员 **6** [c] Mil **the ~(s)** 后备部队; **the army ~** 预备役部队; **to call up the ~s** 动用后备军; **~ forces** 后备军 **7** [c] Brit Comm 底价; **to put a ~ on sth.** 给某物设定底价

B **reserves** *npl* (team) 预备队; **he plays in the ~s** 他是替补队员

C *vt* **1** (book) 预订 ‹*seat, place, table, ticket*›; **to ~ sth. for sb./sth.** 为某人/某事物预订某物 **2** (set aside) 预留 ‹*seat, place, table, ticket*›; **to ~ sth. for sb./sth.** *or* **to ~ sb./sth. sth.** 为某人/某事预留某物 **3** (save for later) 留下; **roll out half the dough and ~ the other half** 把一半面团擀平, 留下另一半 **4** (save for special situation) 储备; **to ~ sth. for sb./sth.** 为某人/某事物储备某物; **the runner ~d his strength for the final mile of the marathon** 这名马拉松参赛选手为最后1英里赛程保存了体力; **she ~s her fiercest criticism for him** 她准备对他进行最严厉的批评; **to ~ a warm welcome for sb.** 准备热烈欢迎某人 **5** (retain as right) 保留 ‹*power*›; **all rights ~d** 版权所有; **the publisher ~s the film rights on the novel** 出版商保留这部小说的电影版权; **to ~ the right to do sth.** 保留做某事的权利 **6** (not make) 暂不作 ‹*decision, verdict*›; 保留 ‹*opinion*›; **to ~ (one's) judgement** 暂不评判

reserve: ~ **bank** *n* **1** Amer (regional bank) 储备银行; **2** Austral, NZ (central bank) 中央储备银行; ~ **currency** *n* 储备货币

reserved /rɪ'zɜːvd/ *adj* 矜持的; **the English are noted for being ~** 英格兰人的矜持是众所周知的

reservedly /rɪ'zɜːvɪdli/ *adv* (reticently) 矜持地; (reluctantly) 有保留地

reserved word *n* 保留字

reserve: ~ **list** *n* **1** Mil 预备役军官名单; **2** Sport 替补队员名单; ~ **petrol tank** *n* 备用油箱; ~ **price** *n* [拍卖品的] 底价

reservist /rɪ'zɜːvɪst/ *n* 预备役军人

reservoir /'rezəvwɑː(r)/ *n* **1** (lake) 水库; (tank) 储水罐; **a natural ~** 天然蓄水池; **an artificial ~** 人造水库; **an underground ~** 地下水库 **2** fig (large supply) 储备; **a ~ of funds** 资金储备; **a ~ of cheap labour** 廉价劳动力储备; **a ~ of musical talent** 音乐人才库

reset /ˌriː'set/ *vt* (*pres p* **-tt-**; *pt, pp* **reset**) **1** (adjust) 调整 ‹*dial, machine*›; **I must ~ my alarm clock** 我一定要重新调一下闹钟 **2** Med 重接 ‹*broken bone*› **3** (of jewellery) 重镶 ‹*gemstone, ring*› **4** Print 重排 ‹*text*› **5** Comput 重设 ‹*password*›; 重启 ‹*system*›

reset button *n* 复原按钮

resettle /ˌriː'setl/

A *vt* 重新安置 ‹*population, refugees*›; 移居到 ‹*area*›

B *vi* «*refugees*» 重新定居

resettlement /ˌriː'setlmənt/ *n* [u] (settling) 重新定居; (being settled) 重新安置

reshape /ˌriː'ʃeɪp/ *vt* 重塑 ‹*clay, dough, society*›; 重排 ‹*text*›; 调整 ‹*policy*›

reshuffle

A /ˌriː'ʃʌfl/ *vt* **1** (change order of) 打乱…的顺序 ‹*papers, raffle tickets*›; **to ~ the cards** 重新洗牌 **2** (reorganize) 改组 ‹*cabinet, board of directors*›; 重新安排 ‹*staff, jobs*›

B /'riːʃʌfl/ *n* **1** (of cards) 重新洗牌; (of papers) 打乱顺序 **2** (of positions, people) 改组; **to carry out a ~** 进行改组

reside /rɪ'zaɪd/ *vi* **1** (live permanently) 居住; **to ~ with sb.** 和某人住在一起; **she ~s in London, but spends a lot of time in France** 她在伦敦定居, 但有大段时间在法国度过 **2** (be present) 属于; **supreme political power ~s in the President** 最高政治权力属于总统; **justice ~s in the hearts of men** 公道自在人心

residence /'rezɪdəns/ *n* **1** [c] (house, home) 住所; **a permanent ~** 永久住所; **an official ~** 官邸 **2** [u] (fact of living) 居住; **place of ~** 居住地; **you need three years' ~ in the country before you can apply for citizenship** 申请公民资格前你需要在本国居住满3年; **in ~** 常驻的; **a writer/composer/artist in ~** 常驻作家/作曲家/艺术家

residence permit *n* 居留许可证

residency /'rezɪdənsi/ *n* **1** [u] (residing) 定居; **they took up ~ in Yorkshire** 他们在约克郡定居下来 **2** [c] (post) 访问讲学职位; **she is taking up a three months' ~ with an arts foundation in New York** 她正在纽约的一个艺术基金会进行为期3个月的访问讲学 **3** [c] Amer Med 高级专科住院医生实习期

resident /'rezɪdənt/

A *n* **1** (of country, town, house) 居民; **he's one of the ~s in the old people's home** 他是老人之家的一员; **parking in this street is for ~s only** 这条街道只允许住户停车 **2** (in hotel) 住客; **this bar is reserved for hotel ~s** 这个酒吧是专为入住本酒店的客人服务的

B *adj* **1** (in country, town, house) 常住的; **the ~ population** 常住人口 **2** (live-in) 住在任所的 ‹*artist, landlord*›; **~ maid** 住家保姆; **~ physician/nurse** 住院医师/护士

residential /ˌrezɪ'denʃl/ *adj* **1** (allocated to housing) 住宅的; (suitable for housing) 适合居住的; **~ areas** *or* **districts** 住宅区; **~ development on the outskirts of the city** 市郊的住宅开发 **2** (involving residence) 需要居住的 ‹*course, post*›; **a ~ school** 寄宿学校; **~ students** 住校生; **~ care** 提供食宿的护理

residential qualification *n* 居留资格

resident: ~**s' association** *n* 居民委员会; ~ **student** *n* Amer (in home state) 本州学生; (living on campus) 住校生

residual /rɪ'zɪdjʊəl, Amer -dʒʊ-/ *adj* 剩余的 ‹*income, material, magnetism*›; 残余的 ‹*unrest, resistance*›; 残留的 ‹*error*›

residual current *n* [u] 剩余电流

residual current device *n* 漏电断路器

residue /'rezɪdjuː, Amer -duː/ *n* **1** (remainder) 残留物; **a ~ of pesticides** 杀虫剂残留; **I've spent the bulk of my winnings, and I intend to invest the ~** 我把赢来的钱大部分都花掉了, 剩下的我打算投资 **2** Chem, Ind 残渣

residue-free *adj* **1** (free from residues) 无残渣的 ‹*surface, finish*›; (not leaving a residue) 不留残渣的 ‹*incineration, breakdown*› **2** (free from pesticides) 无农药残留的 ‹*product, diet*›

resign /rɪ'zaɪn/

A *vi* 辞职

B *vt* 辞去; **she has ~ed her seat in Parliament** 她辞去了议会席位

C *v refl* 听任; **to ~ oneself to sth.** 对某事听之任之; **the party will never ~ itself to defeat** 该党决不会安于失败的; **she had to ~ herself to the fact that the relationship was over** 她不得不接受这段恋爱关系已经结束的事实

resignation /ˌrezɪg'neɪʃn/ *n* **1** [c] (from post) 辞职; **to accept sb.'s ~** 接受某人的辞职 **2** [u] (document) 辞呈; **to tender** *or* **hand in** *or* **send in one's ~** 递交辞呈; **a letter of ~** 辞职信 **3** [u] (acceptance) 听任; **he had no**

choice but to bow to his fate with ～ 他别无选择，只能低头认命

resigned /rɪˈzaɪnd/ *adj* 顺从的 ‹*person, manner*›; 无奈的 ‹*smile, gesture, voice*›; **to be ～ to sth.** 对某事听之任之; **she seems ～ to not having a holiday this year** 她似乎对今年没有假期这件事认了

resignedly /rɪˈzaɪnɪdli/ *adv* 无可奈何地

resilience /rɪˈzɪliəns/ *n* [u] **1** (of substance, structure) 还原能力 **2** (of person, character) 适应能力

resilient /rɪˈzɪliənt/ *adj* **1** 有弹性的 ‹*material, structure*› **2** 适应能力强的 ‹*person, character*›; **to be ～ to sth.** 对某事物有适应能力; **these fish are ～ to most infections** 这些鱼能抵抗大多数病毒感染

resin /ˈrezɪn, Amer ˈrezn/ *n* [u and c] **1** (natural) 树脂 **2** (synthetic) 合成树脂

resinous /ˈrezɪnəs, Amer ˈrezənəs/ *adj* (of resin) 树脂的; (like resin) 似树脂的; **a ～ deposit** 树脂沉积物

resist /rɪˈzɪst/

A *vt* **1** (fight) 抵抗 ‹*enemy, attack*›; 阻止 ‹*coup*›; **to ～ arrest** 拒捕 **2** (oppose) 抵制 ‹*plan, attempt, takeover*› **3** (be unaffected by) 抗 ‹*heat, cold, rust*›; **the body's ability to ～ disease and infection** 身体的抗病和抗感染能力 **4** (refrain from) 拒受…的诱惑 ‹*food, money*›; **to ～ doing sth.** 忍住不做某事; **I couldn't ～ having another chocolate** 我忍不住又吃了一块巧克力

B *vi* **1** (fight) 反抗 **2** (put up opposition) 抵制

resistance /rɪˈzɪstəns/ *n* [u] **1** (to enemy) 抵抗; **～ to sb./sth.** 对某人/某事物的抗拒; **to put up** *or* **offer ～** 进行抵抗; **armed ～** 武装抵抗; **a pocket of ～** 一小股抵抗力量; **a policy of passive ～** 消极抵抗政策 **2** (to change, innovation) 抵制; **to meet with ～** 遇到抵制; **to take the line** *or* **path of least ～** 采取阻力最小的办法 **3** (to damage, injury, infection) 抵抗力; **to build up a ～ to sth.** 增强对某物的抵抗力 **4** Phys 电阻 **5** **the R～** Hist 抵抗运动［二战期间法国反对德国占领军和维希政府的地下运动］

resistance: ～ fighter *n* 抵抗组织战士; **～ movement** *n* 抵抗运动

resistant /rɪˈzɪstənt/

A *adj* 抵抗…的 ‹*disease, material*›; **a ～ strain of the virus** 耐药病毒株; **the infection is ～ to penicillin** 这种感染是抗青霉素的; **he is very ～ to innovation** 他非常反对革新

B **-resistant** *combining form* 抗…的; **heat/rust～** 耐热的/防锈的; **water～** 防水的

resistor /rɪˈzɪstə(r)/ *n* 电阻器

resit

A /ˌriːˈsɪt/ *vt* (*pt, pp* **resat**) 重新参加 ‹*exam*›

B /ˌriːˈsɪt/ *vi* (*pt, pp* **resat**) 重考; **I failed Maths and will have to ～** 我数学不及格，必须补考

C /ˈriːsɪt/ *n* 重考

resize /ˌriːˈsaɪz/ *vt* 改变…的大小 ‹*window, text*›

reskill /ˌriːˈskɪl/ *vt* 教…新技能 ‹*employee*›

reskilling /ˌriːˈskɪlɪŋ/ *n* [u] 传授新技能; **the ～ of existing staff** 现有员工的再培训

resold /ˌriːˈsəʊld/ *pt, pp* ▸**resell**

resole /ˌriːˈsəʊl/ *vt* 给…换鞋底

resolute /ˈrezəluːt/ *adj* 有决心的 ‹*person, champion*›; 坚决的 ‹*refusal, attitude*›; 坚定不移的 ‹*approach, faith*›; **to be ～ in sth.** 在某事上很坚决

resolutely /ˈrezəluːtli/ *adv* 坚决地

resoluteness /ˈrezəluːtnɪs/ *n* [u] 坚定

resolution /ˌrezəˈluːʃn/ *n* **1** [u] (determination) 坚定; **to show/lack ～** 表现出/缺乏决断 **2** [c] (decision) 决心; **to make a ～** 下决心; **he made a firm ～ to lead a healthier life** 他下定决心要过更健康的生活; **to keep/break a ～** 坚持/放弃决心; **a New Year's ～** 新年立志 **3** [c] (by committee, meeting) 决议; **to table/pass/adopt/reject a ～** 提出/通过/采纳/否决一项决议 **4** [u and c] (of problem, argument) 解决; **a problem that defies ～** 无法解决的问题 **5** [u] Phys (separation) 分解; **the ～ of light into the colours of the spectrum** 光分解为光谱颜色

resolvable /rɪˈzɒlvəbl/ *adj* 可解决的 ‹*problem, difficulty*›; 可化解的 ‹*crisis, doubts*›

resolve /rɪˈzɒlv/

A *vt* **1** (decide firmly) 决定; **to ～ that ...** 下决心…; **to ～ to do sth.** 决定做某事 **2** (decide by vote) 表决 **3** (solve) 解决 ‹*problem, difficulty*›; 化解 ‹*crisis*› **4** Phys (separate) 分解 ‹*light, gas*› **5** (divide) 解析 ‹*argument, theory*›

B *vi* **1** (decide) 下决心; **they ～d on** *or* **upon an early start next morning** 他们决定第二天一早出发 **2** (separate) «*light*» 分解 **3** (divide) «*argument, theory*» 被解析

C *n* **1** [c] (decision) 决定; **to make a ～ to do sth.** 决定做某事 **2** [u] (determination) 决心; **to show ～** 表现出决断; **to strengthen sb.'s ～** 坚定某人的决心; **to be strong/weak in one's ～** 决心很坚定/不坚定

resolved /rɪˈzɒlvd/ *adj pred* 坚决的; **to be ～ to do sth.** 决意做某事; **she is ～ to lose weight** 她决心减肥

resonance /ˈrezənəns/ *n* [c and u] 回响; **the ～ of his deep voice** 他低沉嗓音的回响; **the rich ～ of African-American culture in her work** fig 她作品中散发出浓郁的美国黑人文化的气息

resonant /ˈrezənənt/ *adj* **1** (echoing) 回响的 ‹*sound*›; **the deep, ～ voice of the baritone** 那位男中音歌手低沉、浑厚的嗓音 **2** (of rooms, instruments) 产生共鸣的 ‹*hall, instrument*›; **an ancient site ～ with history** fig 充满历史沧桑的古迹

resonate /ˈrezəneɪt/ *vi* **1** (with sound) «*sound, footsteps, hall, cave*» 发出回响 **2** fig (with memories, images) 产生共鸣; **to ～ with sb.** 引起某人的共鸣; **what you say does not ～ with me** 你说的话不能引起我的共鸣

resonator /ˈrezəneɪtə(r)/ *n* 共鸣器

resort /rɪˈzɔːt/

A *n* **1** [u] (action, strategy) 招数; **without ～ to sth.** 不借助某事物; **to have ～ to sth.** 诉诸于某事物; **if the state cannot provide, our only ～ is charity** 如果国家不抚养，我们只能求助于慈善机构; **as a last ～** 作为最后一招; **in the last ～** 最后 **2** (holiday destination) 度假胜地

B *vi* 诉诸; **to ～ to violence and intimidation** 诉诸武力与恐吓

resound /rɪˈzaʊnd/ *vi* **1** (fill with echoing sound) «*sound, music*» 发出回响 **2** (be filled with echoing sound) «*church, cave*» 回荡着 **3** fig liter «*deed, name*» 被传颂

resounding /rɪˈzaʊndɪŋ/ *adj* **1** (loud and echoing) 响亮的 ‹*cheers, footsteps*› **2** *attrib* (notable) 轰动的 ‹*victory, success*›; 惊人的 ‹*failure*›; **our team had suffered a ～ defeat** 我们队遭到了惨败

resoundingly /rɪˈzaʊndɪŋli/ *adv* **1** (with reverberation) 响亮地 ‹*echo, ring*› **2** (emphatically) 轰动地 ‹*successful*›; **to be defeated ～** 遭到惨败

resource /rɪˈsɔːs, -ˈzɔːs, Amer ˈriːsɔːrs/

A *n* **1** (raw material) 资源; **natural/untapped/unlimited ～s** 自然/尚未开发的/无限的资源 **2** [u] (resourcefulness) 智谋; **he is a man of great ～** 他是一个足智多谋的人

B **1** **resources** *pl* (money) 财力; (staff) 人力; **to pool one's ～s** 集中人力物力 **2** (attributes, capabilities) 才智; **to draw on one's ～s** 依靠自己的才智; **as an only child, he is often left to his own ～s** 作为独生子，他常常要独力解决问题

resource: ～ allocation *n* **1** [u] Comput 资源分配; **2** [c and u] Admin 资源配置; **～ centre** *n* 资源中心

resourceful /rɪˈsɔːsfl, -ˈzɔːs-, Amer ˈriːsɔːrsfl/ *adj* 足智多谋的

resourcefully /rɪˈsɔːsfəli, -ˈzɔːs-, Amer ˈriːsɔːrsfəli/ *adv* 随机应变地

resourcefulness /rɪˈsɔːsflnɪs, -ˈzɔːs-, Amer ˈriːsɔːrsflnɪs/ *n* [u] 足智多谋

resource: ～ management *n* [u] **1** Admin 资源配置; (in conservation) 资源管理; **human ～ management** 人力资源管理; **natural ～ management** 自然资源管理; **2** Comput 资源管理; **～ sharing** *n* [u] 资源共享

respect /rɪˈspekt/

A *n* **1** [u and c] (admiration, politeness) 尊敬; **mutual love and ～** 互敬互爱; **～ for sb./sth.** 对某人/某事物的尊敬; **to have (the greatest** *or* **highest) ～ for sb./sth.** （极其）敬重某人/某事物; **to win** *or* **earn/enjoy the ～ of sb.** 赢得/受到某人的尊敬; **to command ～** 值得尊敬; **to do sth. as a mark** *or* **token of ～** 做某事以示尊敬; **in Japan you are taught great ～ for your elders** 在日本，人们会教你尊重长辈; **you've got no ～!** 你不尊重人！; **to show no ～ for sb., to show sb. no ～** 不敬重某人; **to treat sb. with ～** 尊重某人; **everyone has a right to be treated with ～** 每个人都有权得到尊重; **out of ～** 出于尊重; **with (all due** *or* **the utmost) ～** formal 恕我直言 **2** [u] (consideration) 考虑; **to have no ～ (for sth.)** 不考虑（某事物）; **he has no ～ for her feelings** 他根本不在乎她的感受; **to show no ～ for sth., to show sth. no ～** 不考虑某事物; **I have a lot of ～ for people like him** 我很重视像他这样的人; **～ for all living creatures** 对所有生命的重视 **3** [u] (for human rights, privacy, the law) 认可; **～ for sth.** 对某事物的认可; **a regime with little ～ for human rights** 无视人权的政体; **to show a lack of ～ for authority** 表现出对权威的漠视 **4** [u] (caution) 谨慎态度; **(a healthy) ～ for sb./sth.** （正常的）对待某人/某事物的谨慎态度; **to treat sb./sth. with ～** 谨慎对待 ‹*person*›; 谨慎使用 ‹*machine, appliance*› **5** [c and u] (aspect) 方面; **in this/that ～** 在这/那方面; **in some/all/many/several/other ～s** 在某些/所有/许多/几个/其他方面; **in what ～?** 在哪方面？; **in ～ of sth.** formal (concerning) 关于某事物; (in payment for) 作为某事的报酬; **a writ was served on the firm in ～ of their unpaid bill** 该公司因未付账单而接到法院令状; **money received in ～ of overtime** 加班所得报酬; **with ～ to sth.** formal 就某方面而言; **to be similar with ～ to income and status** 在收入和地位方面相似

B **respects** *npl* 问候; **they called at his house and offered him their ～s** 他们去他家问候他; **please pass on my ～s to your mother** 请代我问候你的母亲; **to pay one's ～s (to sb.)** （向某人）表示问候; **to pay one's last ～s (to sb.)** (at funeral) （向某人遗体）告别

C *vt* **1** (admire) 尊敬 ‹*person*›; 钦佩 ‹*ideal, work, purpose*›; **a man I greatly** *or* **deeply ～ed** 我以前非常敬重的人; **she was ～ed by everyone** 她受到所有人的尊敬; **to ～ sb./sth. for sth.** 因某事物尊敬某人/钦佩某事物; **I ～ him for his integrity** 我敬佩他的正直; **to ～ sb./sth. as sth.** 尊敬有某身份的某人/钦佩作为…的某事物; **I ～ him as a doctor** 我很钦佩他的医术 **2** (have regard for) 尊重 ‹*person, feelings, views, rights*›; **to ～ sb.'s wishes/privacy** 尊重某人的愿望/隐私 **3** (not harm) 爱护 ‹*property, environment*› **4** (abide by) 遵守 ‹*treaty, contract*›; 保持 ‹*neutrality*›; 服从 ‹*authority*›; **to ～ the law** 守法 **5** formal (concern) 关于; **as ～s sth.** 关于某事物; **as ～s your rights in the affair ...** 关于在这件事中你享有的权利…

D *v refl* **to ～ oneself** 自重

respectability /rɪˌspektəˈbɪləti/ *n* [u] 体面

r

respectable /rɪ'spektəbl/ *adj* **1** (proper, correct) 体面的 ‹*family, background*›; **highly** *or* **eminently ~** 非常体面的; **~ society** 上流社会; **a ~ married couple** 一对正派夫妻 **2** (adequate) 不错的 ‹*standard, mark*›; 可观的 ‹*amount*›; **a ~ wage** 一份可观的工资; **he plays a ~ game of tennis** 他网球打得相当不错; **there was a ~ crowd at the match** 有不少人到场观看这场比赛

respectably /rɪ'spektəbli/ *adv* **1** (properly) 体面地 ‹*dressed*›; **a ~ behaved child** 一个举止得体的小孩 **2** (adequately) 相当不错地; **he is paid quite ~** 他的收入相当可观; **a ~ high salary** 一份不错的薪水

respectful /rɪ'spektfl/ *adj* 尊敬的; **to be ~ to** *or* **towards sb.** 对某人很尊敬; **she is always ~ of other people's feelings** 她总是尊重别人的感情; **a ~ silence** 出于尊敬的沉默

respectfully /rɪ'spektfəli/ *adv* 尊敬地

respectfulness /rɪ'spektflnɪs/ *n* [u] 尊敬

respecting /rɪ'spektɪŋ/ *prep* formal 关于; **laws ~ property** 关于财产的法律

respective /rɪ'spektɪv/ *adj attrib* 各自的; **they parted and went their ~ ways** 他们分手后各奔前程; **both men excel in their ~ fields** 两个人在各自的领域都出类拔萃

respectively /rɪ'spektɪvli/ *adv* 各自; **German and Italian courses are held in Munich and Rome ~** 德语和意大利语课程分别在慕尼黑和罗马开设

respiration /ˌrespɪ'reɪʃn/ *n* [u] **1** (breathing) 呼吸; **~ rate** 呼吸速率 **2** Bot 呼吸作用

respirator /'respɪreɪtə(r)/ *n* **1** (machine) 人工呼吸器 **2** (protective mask) 防毒面具

respiratory /rɪ'spɪrətri, Amer -tɔːri/ *adj* 呼吸的; **the ~ tract/system** 呼吸道/系统; **~ disease** 呼吸道疾病

respite /'respaɪt, 'respɪt/ *n* **1** [u] (relief) 喘息; **they longed for a moment of ~** 他们渴望稍作休息; **without ~** 不停歇地 **2** [c] (delay) 暂缓; **to be granted a short ~** 获准暂缓; **to grant a ~ for payment** 准予暂缓付款; **a ~ of a day/week/month** 一天/一周/一个月的暂缓期

resplendent /rɪ'splendənt/ *adj* 华丽的; **she looks ~ (in her new dress)** 她（穿上新连衣裙）看上去光彩照人

respond /rɪ'spɒnd/ *vi* **1** (give answer) 答复; **to ~ to sb./sth.** 答复某人/某事; **she did not ~ to my letter** 她没有给我回信; **to ~ to a toast** 答谢敬酒 **2** (react) 回应; **I smiled at her and she ~ed** 我向她微笑，她也作出了回应; **he ~ed with an uppercut** 他用一记上勾拳反击; **to ~ in kind** 以同样的方式回敬; **the car ~s well** 这辆车开起来很顺手

respondent /rɪ'spɒndənt/ *n* [尤指离婚或上诉案中的] 被告

response /rɪ'spɒns/ *n* **1** (answer) 答复; **a ~ to sb./sth.** 对某人/某事的答复; **to bring a ~** 得到答复; **in ~ to your enquiry ...** 作为对你询问的答复… **2** (reaction) 反应; **a ~ to sb./sth.** 对某人/某事作出的反应; **to get a favourable/unfavourable ~** 得到良好的/不良的反响

response time *n* 反应时间; **the ~ of the police was too slow** 警方反应太慢了

responsibility /rɪˌspɒnsə'bɪləti/ *n* **1** [u] (for action, crime, task) 负责; **to take** *or* **accept full ~ for sb./sth.** 为某人/某事承担全部责任; **to claim/disclaim ~ for sth.** 声称/否认对某事物负责; **a sense of ~** 责任感; **without ~ on our part** 我方概不负责 [商业用语] **2** [c] (commitment) 义务; (duty) 职责; **a joint** *or* **shared ~** 连带责任; **owners have a ~ to control their dogs** 主人有义务管好自己的狗; **the minister assumes his responsibilities at the end of the month** 部长在月底就职; **to be weighed down by one's responsibilities** 被自己的职责压垮

responsible /rɪ'spɒnsəbl/ *adj* **1** *pred* (for action, crime, task) 负有责任的; **to be ~ for sb./sth.** 对某人/某事物负责; **the police are ~ for maintaining order** 警察负有维持治安的责任; **the individual is ~ for his own actions** 每个人都要为自己的行为负责 **2** *pred* (accountable) [对主管部门或上级] 承担责任的; **the foreign minister is ~ to the president** 外交部长向总统负责 **3** (trustworthy) 可靠的 ‹*person, nature*›; **a ~ citizen** 有责任感的公民 **4** (involving important duties) 责任重大的 ‹*position*›; **is he really up to such a ~ job?** 他真的能胜任这样责任重大的工作吗? **5** *pred* (for illness, accident) 成为起因的; **smoking is ~ for many cases of lung cancer** 许多肺癌病例是由吸烟引起的

responsibly /rɪ'spɒnsəbli/ *adv* 负责任地

responsive /rɪ'spɒnsɪv/ *adj* **1** (enthusiastic) 热情的 ‹*person, service*›; 反应热烈的 ‹*audience, class*› **2** (quick to react) 反应灵敏的 ‹*brakes, dog*›; **a virus that is not ~ to treatment** 治疗无效的病毒

responsively /rɪ'spɒnsɪvli/ *adj* 热情地 ‹*smile, nod, gesture*›

responsiveness /rɪ'spɒnsɪvnɪs/ *n* [u] **1** (of person, audience) 反应热烈 **2** (of brakes, equipment) 反应灵敏

respray

A /ˌriː'spreɪ/ *vt* 重新喷涂

B /'riːspreɪ/ *n* 再喷涂

rest¹ /rest/

A *n* **1** [u] (repose, inactivity) 休息; **a day of ~** 休息日; **to be at ~** formal (unworried) 不担心; euph (dead) 安息; **my mind is at ~ now** 我现在不担心了; **to set** *or* **put sb.'s mind at ~** 使某人放心; **you can set your mind at ~ on that score** 在那一点上你可放心; **to lie at ~ (in a grave/cemetery)** formal euph 被安葬（在墓地/公墓）; **to lay sb. to ~** formal euph 安葬某人; **he was laid to ~ beside his parents** 他被葬在父母身边; **to lay sth. to ~** 终结 ‹*doubts, dispute*›; **~ day/period** 休息日/休养期 **2** [c] (break) 休息时间; **we stopped for a well-earned ~** 我们停下来好好歇了一会儿; **a ~ from sb./sth.** 安置好某人/料理好某事后的休息; **a ~ from doing sth.** 做某事的间歇; **at least it's a ~ from continually having to watch what I eat** 至少这能让我歇口气，用不着一直注意饮食了; **to need a ~ (from sth.)** 需要（停下某事）休息; **to have** *or* **take a ~ (from sth.)** （停下某事）休息一段时间; **we took ~s every hour or so during the climb** 我们在登山过程中每一小时左右休息一次; **to give sb. a ~ (from sth.)** 让某人（不做某事）休息一下; **I took the day off just to give myself a ~ from the office** 我请了一天假，只是为了放下工作休息一下; **to give sth. a ~** colloq 暂停某事; **to give jogging/the television a ~** 暂停慢跑锻炼/关掉电视片刻; **give it a ~!** Brit colloq 别说了!; **a change is as good as a ~** Prov 改变就相当于休息 **3** [c] (support) 撑架; **she put the receiver back on its ~** 她把听筒放回机座上; **a ~ for a snooker cue** 斯诺克球杆支架 **4** [u] (immobility) 静止; **at ~** 静止的; **at ~ the insect looks like ...** 这种昆虫不动时看起来像…; **starting from ~ the projectile accelerates at an extremely rapid rate** 抛射物进入运动状态后增速极快; **to come to ~** 停下; **the lift came to ~ at the first floor** 电梯停在了二楼; **his eyes came to ~ on her face** 他的目光停在了她脸上 **5** [u and c] Mus (silence) 休止; **a crotchet/minim ~** Brit 四分音/二分音休止; **a quarter-note/half-note ~** Amer 四分音/二分音休止; **30 bars' ~** 30 小节的休止 **6** [c] Mus (sign) 休止符

B *vt* **1** (allow to relax, recover) 使休息; **~ your eyes every half an hour** 每隔半小时让眼睛休息一次; **God ~ his/her soul** 愿上帝保佑他/愿她的灵魂得到安息 **2** (lean) 使依靠; **to ~ sth. on** *or* **against sth.** 将某物靠在某物上; **~ your head on my shoulder** 把你的头靠在我的肩上; **I ~ed my back against the table leg** 我背靠着桌腿; **to ~ sth. in sth.** 将某物搁在某物里; **he ~ed his chin in his hands** 他两手托着下巴 **3** Jur (conclude) 中止; **to ~ one's case** 结案; **my standards are not impossibly high! — name somebody who's met them — um ... — I ~ my case** hum 我的标准并没有高得离谱! ——那么说说有谁达到了呢——嗯…我不多说了 **4** Sport ‹*manager, coach*› 让…停赛 ‹*player*› **5** Agric 让…休耕 ‹*land, field*›

C *vi* **1** (relax) 休息; **to ~ from sth./doing sth.** 停下某事/做某事休息; **he was ~ing from his labours** 他放下活儿正在休息; **you should ~ from studying for at least an hour** 你应该停止学习，休息至少一个小时; **he/we/they won't ~ until ...** (stop) 他/我们/他们直到…才会停下; (be satisfied) 他/我们/他们直到…才会满意; **I won't ~ until I know** 我要了解到情况才罢休; **to ~ easy** 放心; **I can ~ easy knowing that she's safely home** 我知道她已平安到家就放心了 **2** (be supported) 被支撑; **to ~ on** *or* **against sth.** 靠在…上 ‹*shoulder, table, wall, fence*›; **his hands ~ed lightly on the arms of the chair** 他双手轻轻搭在椅子扶手上; **the whole weight of the bridge is ~ing on those two girders** 整个桥的重量都落在那两根座梁上; **he stood there ~ing on his spade** 他拄着铲子站在那儿 **3** (stand, remain) «*question, matter*» 被搁置; **to let sth. ~, to allow sth. to ~** 搁下某事; **to let things ~** 把事情搁置起来; **you can't just let it ~ there!** 你不能就这么不管了!; **so that is where things ~ for the present** 那么这就是目前的状况 **4** Amer Jur «*defence, prosecution*» 中止 **5** euph (be unemployed) 赋闲; **to be ~ing** «*actor*» 无戏可演 **6** euph (be buried) 安息; **to ~ in peace** 安息

Phrasal verbs

- **rest in** *vt* **1** [**~ sth. in sb./sth.**] (place in) 将…寄托在…上 ‹*hopes*› **2** [**~ in sth.**] (lie in) «*key, strength*» 在于 ‹*change*›; **to ~ in doing sth.** 在于做某事; **they argued that the solution ~ed in resurrecting the country's independence** 他们主张解决办法在于恢复国家独立
- **rest on** *vt* **1** [**~ on sb./sth.**] (be directed towards) «*eyes, gaze*» 凝视 **2** [**~ on sb./sth.**] (depend on) 依靠; **all our hopes now ~ on you** 我们现在就指望你了; **so much ~s on the outcome of this trial** 很多事都取决于这次审判的结果 **3** [**~ on sth.**] (be based on) «*argument, case*» 基于 ‹*assumption, premise, reasoning*›
- **rest up** *vi* 好好休息
- **rest with** *vt* [**~ with sb./sth.**] «*decision, choice*» 取决于; **the final say ~s with the regional assemblies** 最终还是地区议会说了算; **it ~s with sb. to do sth.** 某事要由某人来做

rest² *n* **1** + *v sing* (remaining part) **the ~** 剩余部分; **you can keep/leave the ~** 剩下的你留着/放着吧; **the ~ of sth.** 某物的剩余部分; **the ~ of the time** 剩下的时间; **the ~ of one's life** 余生; **I'm not doing this job for the ~ of my life** 我这辈子再也不做这样的工作了; **and the ~** colloq 不止这些; **you mean it took three hours? — and the ~!** 你是说那花了3个小时——还要多呢!; **and (all) the ~ (of it)** colloq 诸如此类; **he wants a big house and an expensive car and all the ~ of it** 他想要一所大房子、一辆昂贵的汽车，如此等等; **for the ~** Brit formal (other part) 至于其他部分; (other matters) 至于其他事情; **for the ~, the usual rules apply** 至于其他情况，遵从一般规定 **2** + *v pl* (remaining people) **the ~** 其余的人; **the ~ of us/them** 我们/他们中的其他人; **all the ~ of the members** 所有其他成员 **3** + *v pl* (remaining things) **the ～** 其余的东西; **the ～ of the tables were all empty** 其余几桌都空了

rest area *n esp* Amer [高速公路旁的] 服务区

restart

A /ˌriːˈstɑːt/ *vt* **1** (cause to operate again) 重新启动 ‹*engine*›; 重启 ‹*computer*› **2** (resume) 继续 ‹*talks, match, work*›

B *vi* **1** (start functioning again) «*engine*» 重新发动 **2** (resume) «*activity*» 继续; **school ～s a week from today** 从今天起再有一个星期学校就又要开学了

C /ˈriːstɑːt/ *n* **1** (of talks, work) 新的开始 **2** Sport 重新开赛

restate /ˌriːˈsteɪt/ *vt* 重述 ‹*case, problem*›; 重申 ‹*position*›

restatement /ˌriːˈsteɪtmənt/ *n* (of case, problem) 重述; (of position) 重申

restaurant /ˈrestrɒnt, Amer -tərɑnt/ *n* 餐馆

restaurant: ～ car *n* Brit 餐车; **～ guide** *n* 餐馆指南; **～ owner** *n* 餐馆老板

restaurateur /ˌrestərəˈtɜː(r)/ ▸**p. 409** *n* (manager) 餐厅经理; (owner) 餐馆老板

rest cure *n* 休养疗法

rested /ˈrestɪd/ *adj* 休息后精力恢复的; **I awoke feeling ～ and refreshed** 我睡醒后感觉精力充沛，神清气爽

restful /ˈrestfl/ *adj* 有益休息的 ‹*sleep, break*›; 闲适宁静的 ‹*weekend, place, colour*›

restfulness /ˈrestfəlnɪs/ *n* 宁静; **the ～ of country scenery** 静谧的乡村景色

rest home *n* (for the aged) 养老院; (for the frail) 疗养院

resting place *n* 休息处; **sb.'s last ～** 某人的长眠之地

restitution /ˌrestɪˈtjuːʃn, Amer -ˈtuː-/ *n* [u] **1** formal (restoration) 归还; **the ～ of land and personal property** 土地和个人财产的物归原主 **2** Jur 赔偿; **to make ～ for sth.** 为某事作出赔偿; **he was ordered to pay ～ to the injured party** 他被命令向受损的一方支付赔偿; **to pay £5,000 in full and final ～** 全额最终赔付 5,000 英镑

restitution order *n* 赔偿令

restive /ˈrestɪv/ *adj* 躁动不安的 ‹*person, audience*›; 难驾驭的 ‹*population, region*›; **to grow** *or* **become ～** 变得躁动不安

restively /ˈrestɪvli/ *adv* 躁动不安地

restiveness /ˈrestɪvnɪs/ *n* [u] 躁动不安

restless /ˈrestlɪs/ *adj* **1** (agitated) 躁动的; **I had a ～ night** 我辗转反侧了一夜; **the ～ motion of the sea** fig 大海波涛的汹涌不息 **2** (fidgety, unsettled) 焦躁的; **to get** *or* **grow ～** 变得烦躁不安; **she's too ～ to stay in one place for very long** 她静不下心来，无法在一个地方待长

restlessly /ˈrestlɪsli/ *adv* 焦躁不安地

restlessness /ˈrestlɪsnɪs/ *n* [u] 焦躁不安

restock /ˌriːˈstɒk/ *vt* 再装满 ‹*freezer*›; 为…补货 ‹*shelves, shop*›; **the river was ～ed with trout** 这条河里重新放养了鳟鱼

Restoration /ˌrestəˈreɪʃn/ *n* Brit **the ～** [1660 年英国的] 王政复辟

restoration /ˌrestəˈreɪʃn/ *n* **1** [u] (of building, painting) 修复 **2** [u] (to former state) 恢复; **the ～ of order/the death penalty** 秩序/死刑的恢复; **we are celebrating his ～ to complete health** 我们在庆祝他的完全康复; **the ～ of the monarchy** 王政的复辟 **3** [u] (return) 归还; **the ～ of stolen property** 被窃财物的归还 **4** [c] (building) 修复的建筑物; **the castle is very largely a ～** 这座城堡的很大一部分是重建的 **5** [c] (model) 重建模型; **a ～ of Tyrannosaurus Rex** 暴龙复原模型

Restoration drama *n* [u] Hist 王政复辟时期戏剧

restorative /rɪˈstɒrətɪv/ *adj* 促进康复的; **the ～ powers of rest and a good diet** 休息与合理膳食的康复功效

restore /rɪˈstɔː(r)/ *vt* **1** (rebuild, repair) 修复 ‹*building, vehicle, painting*›; **craftsmen are restoring the furniture to its original state** 工匠们正在将家具修复到原样 **2** (bring back) 使…复职 ‹*person*›; 把…放回 ‹*object*›; **management agreed to ～ the strikers to their former jobs** 资方同意罢工者恢复原先的工作 **3** (return) 使…复元 ‹*faculty*›; **to ～ sb.'s sight** 恢复某人的视力; **to be ～d to health** 恢复健康; **success has ～d his confidence** 成功让他重拾信心 **4** (reintroduce) 恢复 ‹*tax*›; **to ～ law and order** 恢复治安 **5** (give back to owner) 归还 ‹*property*›

restorer /rɪˈstɔːrə(r)/ *n* 修复者; **a furniture/picture ～** 家具/图画修复师

restrain /rɪˈstreɪn/ *vt* **1** (hold back) 阻止 ‹*person, crowd*›; **to ～ sb. from doing sth.** 阻止某人做某事 **2** (physically control) 制止 ‹*patient*›; **policemen had to ～ the accused** 警察不得不强行控制住被告; **the dog was ～ed with a stout lead** 那只狗被一条很结实的皮带拴着 **3** (curb) 抑制 ‹*feelings, laughter*›; 控制 ‹*prices, inflation*›; **to ～ oneself** 克制自己

restrained /rɪˈstreɪnd/ *adj* **1** (kept in check) 克制的 ‹*language, protest, silence*›; **a man with self-control and a ～ manner** 一个有自我克制、举止拘谨的男子 **2** (sober) 素淡的 ‹*colours, clothes, decoration*›; 含蓄的 ‹*style*›

restraining order *n* 限制令

restraint /rɪˈstreɪnt/ *n* **1** [u] (control) 控制; **to put** *or* **place sb./sth. under ～** 将某人/某物控制起来 **2** [c] (restriction) 限制; **to impose ～s on sth.** 对某事物实施限制; **subject to ～s** 受到限制的; **a ～ on the freedom of expression** 对言论自由的限制 **3** [u] (moderation) 克制; **to show** *or* **exercise ～** 表现出克制; **lack of ～** 无所顾忌 **4** [c] (rope, strap) [用于限制精神病人、囚犯等活动自由的] 束缚索带

restrict /rɪˈstrɪkt/

A *vt* 限制 ‹*speed, freedom, rights*›; **a law ～ing access to the area** 限制进入该地区的法令

B *v refl* **to ～ oneself** 约束自己; **they ～ themselves to one foreign holiday a year** 他们限自己每年只能到国外度一次假

restricted /rɪˈstrɪktɪd/ *adj* 有限的 ‹*circulation, choice, visibility*›; 受控制的 ‹*development, quantity*›; **a ～ market** 限制性市场; **a ～ document** 保密文件

restricted: ～ access *n* [u] (to place) 限制进入; (to file, books, Internet) 限制使用; **～ area** *n* **1** (with restricted access) 禁区; **2** Brit (with parking restrictions) 限停区; (with speed restrictions) 限速区; **～ parking** *n* [u] 有限制停车

restriction /rɪˈstrɪkʃn/ *n* **1** [u] (limitation) 限制; **the ～ of local government power** 对地方政府权力的限制; **～ of the money supply** 对货币供应量的限制 **2** [c] (limit) 限制规定; **speed ～s** 限速规定; **to enforce a ～** 实行限制; **to be subject to ～s** 受到限制; **to raise/abolish/lift a ～** 撤销/废除/取消限制规定; **～s on arms sales** 针对武器销售的限制条款

restrictive /rɪˈstrɪktɪv/ *adj* **1** (imposing limitations) 限制性的 ‹*measure, routine*›; **～ rules/clauses** 限制性规定/条款; **if you want to swim, do not wear ～ clothing** 如果你想去游泳，就不要穿束缚手脚的衣服 **2** Ling 限定性的; **～ and non-～ clauses** 限定性和非限定性从句

restrictive practice *n* **1** (by companies) 限制竞争协议 **2** Brit (by employees) 限制竞争的行为

re-string (*pt, pp* **re-strung**) *vt* **1** (attach to new string) 重串 ‹*pearls*› **2** (affix new strings on) 给…重新装弦 ‹*violin, racket*›

restroom /ˈrestruːm, -rʊm/ *n* **1** Amer (lavatory) 洗手间 **2** Brit (rest area) 休息室

re-strung /ˌriːˈstrʌŋ/ *pt, pp* ▸**re-string**

restyle

A /ˌriːˈstaɪl/ *vt* 改变…的款式 ‹*coat, car*›; **the hairdresser ～d her hair** 理发师给她做了个新发型

B /ˈriːstaɪl/ *n* 新样式

result /rɪˈzʌlt/

A *n* **1** (effect, outcome) 结果; **as a ～** 因此; **as a ～ of sth.** 因为某事物; **without ～** 毫无结果; **his limp is the ～ of an accident** 他的跛足是事故造成的; **all our efforts produced little or no ～** 我们所有的努力几乎都是徒劳 **2** (of exam) 成绩; (of event) 竞赛结果; **football ～s** 足球比赛比分; **the ～ of the election** 选举结果 **3** Sport colloq [尤指足球赛中的] 获胜 **4** Math 计算结果

B **results** *npl* 成果; **to get** *or* **yield ～s** 取得成效; **to produce/show ～s** 产生/显示成效; **trading ～s** 营业效益; **payment by ～s** 绩效付酬

C *vi* 发生; **to ～ in sth.** 导致某事; **all his hard work ～ed in failure** 他所有的努力都失败了; **injuries ～ing from a fall** 摔伤

resultant /rɪˈzʌltənt/ *adj attrib* 因而产生的

resume /rɪˈzjuːm, Amer -ˈzuːm/

A *vt* **1** (continue) 继续 ‹*voyage, work*›; **to ～ doing sth.** 接着做某事; **to ～ negotiations** 重启谈判; **normal service will be ～d as soon as possible** 正常的服务会尽快恢复 **2** (use again) 重新得到 ‹*title, seat*›

B *vi* «*discussion, lecture*» 继续; «*service, hostilities*» 恢复

resumé /ˈrezjuːmeɪ, Amer ˌrezʊˈmeɪ/ *n* **1** (summary) 摘要 **2** Amer (curriculum vitae) 简历

resumption /rɪˈzʌmpʃn/ *n* 恢复; **the ～ of power supplies** 恢复供电; **a ～ of negotiations** 重启谈判

resurface /ˌriːˈsɜːfɪs/

A *vt* 重铺 ‹*road*›; 重铺…的地面 ‹*tennis court, car park*›

B *vi* **1** (come to surface) «*submarine, diver*» 重新露出水面 **2** fig (become apparent) 重新浮现; **old prejudices began to ～** 旧时的偏见重新开始抬头 **3** fig (from hiding) 重新露面; (from obscurity) 重新活跃

resurgence /rɪˈsɜːdʒəns/ *n* 复兴; **a ～ of interest** 兴趣的重新激发; **the ～ of the flagging economy** 疲软经济的复苏

resurgent /rɪˈsɜːdʒənt/ *adj* 复苏的 ‹*economy, hope*›; 复兴的 ‹*nationalism, militarism*›; 重新产生的 ‹*threat, force*›

resurrect /ˌrezəˈrekt/ *vt* **1** (restore to life) 使复活 **2** fig (revive) 恢复 ‹*tradition, memory*›; **she ～ed an old dress from the sixties** 她又穿起了 60 年代的一件旧连衣裙

resurrection /ˌrezəˈrekʃn/ *n* **1** **the Resurrection** Relig 耶稣复活 **2** (revival) 复兴; **the ～ of old country customs** 古老乡村习俗的恢复; **the ～ of hope** 希望的复苏

resuscitate /rɪˈsʌsɪteɪt/ *vt* **1** Med 使苏醒 **2** fig (make active, vigorous) 使复苏; **to ～ the flagging economy** 重振萧条的经济

resuscitation /rɪˌsʌsɪˈteɪʃn/ *n* [u] Med 抢救; **he died in spite of their attempts at ～** 尽管他们努力抢救，他还是死掉了; **～ equipment** 急救设备

resuscitator /rɪˈsʌsɪteɪtə(r)/ *n* 急救器

ret. *abbr* = **retired**

retail /ˈriːteɪl/

A *n* [u] 零售; **by ～** 通过零售

B *vt* **1** (sell) 零售 **2** (recount) 反复讲述 ‹*scandal, details*›; **to ～ gossip to all and sundry** 向每个人散布小道消息

C *vi* (be sold) 零售; **these shoes ～ for £60** 这种鞋子零售价是 60 英镑

D *adv* 以零售方式 ‹*sell, buy*›

retailer /ˈriːteɪlə(r)/ *n* 零售商

retailing /ˈriːteɪlɪŋ/ *n* [u] 零售业; **a ～ giant** 零售业巨头

retail park *n* [城郊的] 零售商业区

r

retail price *n* 零售价

retail price: ~ **index** *n* Brit 零售价格指数; ~ **maintenance** *n* [u] 零售价格维持

retail: ~ **sales** *npl* 零售额; ~ **space** *n* [u] 零售区; ~ **therapy** *n* [u] hum 购物疗法; ~ **trade** *n* [u] 1 (sales) 零售; 2 (companies) 零售业

retain /rɪˈteɪn/ *vt* 1 (continue to have) 保留 ‹*property, salary, right*›; 保持 ‹*control, dignity, independence*›; **to ~ one's composure** 保持镇静 2 (in memory) 记住 ‹*fact, memory*›; **I have ~ed a vivid image of the accident** 我对那次事故记忆犹新 3 (hold, contain) 挡住 ‹*water, floods*›; 留住 ‹*moisture*›; **in winter the sea ~s heat longer than the land can** 在冬天海洋比陆地保留热量的时间要长 4 Jur 付定金聘定 ‹*barrister*›

retained earnings *npl* 留存盈余

retainer /rɪˈteɪnə(r)/ *n* 1 (fee) [尤指付给律师的] 预付金 2 (servant) 家仆; **an old family/a faithful ~** 老家仆/忠实的仆从

retaining: ~ **fee** *n* = **retainer 1**; ~ **wall** *n* 护墙

retake

A /ˌriːˈteɪk/ *vt* (*pt* **retook**; *pp* **retaken**) 1 (recapture) 夺回 ‹*town, ship, fortress*› 2 Phot, Cin 重拍 ‹*scene, shot*› 3 Mus 重录 ‹*song*› 4 (resit) 重新参加 ‹*exam*›

B /ˈriːteɪk/ *n* 1 (of scene) 重拍; (of music) 重录 2 (exam) 重考

retaliate /rɪˈtælieɪt/ *vi* 报复; **to ~ against sb./sth.** 报复某人/某事; **to ~ by doing sth.** 通过做某事进行报复

retaliation /rɪˌtæliˈeɪʃn/ *n* [u] 报复

retaliatory /rɪˈtæljətri, Amer -tɔːri/ *adj* 报复性的; **to take ~ action/measures** 采取报复行动/措施

retard

A /rɪˈtɑːd/ *vt* 1 (make slower) 减慢 ‹*ignition, mechanism*› 2 (hinder) 阻碍 ‹*growth, progress*›

B /ˈriːtɑːd/ *n* colloq pej 弱智

retarded /rɪˈtɑːdɪd/ *adj* (mentally) 弱智的; (in development) 迟钝的

retch /retʃ/ *vi* 1 (heave) 干呕 2 (vomit) 呕吐

retd *abbr* = **retired**

retell /ˌriːˈtel/ *vt* (*pt, pp* **retold**) 复述

retelling /ˌriːˈtelɪŋ/ *n* [c and u] 复述

retention /rɪˈtenʃn/ *n* [u] 1 (continued possession, control) 保留; **the ~ of skilled staff** 熟练员工的留用 2 (in memory) 记忆力; **powers of ~** 记忆力 3 Med 阻滞; **fluid ~** 体液潴留

retentive /rɪˈtentɪv/ *adj* 记忆力好的; **to have a ~ memory** 有很强的记忆力

rethink

A /ˌriːˈθɪŋk/ *vt* (*pt, pp* **rethought** /ˌriːˈθɔːt/) 重新考虑 ‹*plan, situation*›

B *vi* (*pt, pp* **rethought**) 重新考虑

C /ˈriːθɪŋk/ *n* 反思; **to have a ~ about sth.** 反思某事物

reticence /ˈretɪsns/ *n* [u] 缄默; **~ about sth.** 对某事的缄默; **~ on matters concerning one's private life** 在有关私生活的事情上讳莫如深

reticent /ˈretɪsnt/ *adj* 缄默的; **he was very ~ about his real intentions** 他绝口不提他的真实意图

reticently /ˈretɪsntli/ *adv* 有保留地 ‹*speak, write*›; 矜持地 ‹*behave*›

reticle /ˈretɪkl/ *n* [光学仪器上的] 分划板

retile /ˌriːˈtaɪl/ *vt* 给…重贴瓷砖

retina /ˈretɪnə, Amer ˈretənə/ *n* 视网膜; **a detached ~** 脱落的视网膜

retinue /ˈretɪnjuː, Amer ˈretənuː/ *n* 随从人员

retire /rɪˈtaɪə(r)/

A *vi* 1 (from work) «*person, employee*» 退休; **to ~ early** *or* **prematurely** 提前退休; **retiring age** 退休年龄; **the retiring manager** 即将退休的经理 2 formal (retreat) 退下; **the jury ~d from the courtroom** 陪审团退庭; **to ~ from public life** 从公众视野中消失; **to ~ into oneself** 冥思苦想 3 formal or hum (go to bed) 就寝 4 Sport 退出比赛; **to ~ injured** 受伤退出比赛

B *vt* 使…退休 ‹*employee*›; **to be ~d on grounds of ill health** 病退; **to be compulsorily ~d** 被强制退休

retired /rɪˈtaɪəd/ *adj* 退休的

retirement /rɪˈtaɪəmənt/ *n* 1 [u] (action) 退休; **to take early ~** 提前退休; **over** *or* **above/under** *or* **below the age of ~** 超过/未到退休年龄; **compulsory ~** 强制退休 2 [c] (instance) 退休个例; **we have had several ~s at the office this year** 今年我们办公室有好几个人退休了 3 (state) 退休生活; **to live in ~** 过退休生活; **a peaceful ~** 平静的退休生活; **he decided to spend his ~ painting** 他决定退休后以绘画打发时间

retirement: ~ **age** *n* 退休年龄; **to reach ~ age** 达到退休年龄; ~ **bonus** *n* 退休红包; ~ **home** *n* 1 (house) 退休之家; 2 (care home) 养老院; ~ **pension** *n* Brit 退休金

retiring /rɪˈtaɪərɪŋ/ *adj* 孤僻的 ‹*nature, disposition, person*›

retool /ˌriːˈtuːl/

A *vt* 为…更新设备

B *vi* 更新设备

retort /rɪˈtɔːt/

A *vt* 反驳; **'Nonsense!' she ~ed** "胡说!" 她反驳道

B *n* 反驳; **to make a witty ~** 机智地回一句嘴

retouch /ˌriːˈtʌtʃ/ *vt* 修整 ‹*photograph, painting*›

retrace /ˌriːˈtreɪs/ *vt* 1 (go back over) 沿…返回; **to ~ one's steps** 沿原路返回; **to ~ one's path** *or* **route** 重走原路 2 (recall) 追溯 ‹*movements, events*›

retract /rɪˈtrækt/

A *vt* 1 (withdraw) 撤回 ‹*charge, allegation*›; 收回 ‹*statement, remark*›; **the defendant ~ed his confession** 被告翻了供 2 (go back on) 违背 ‹*promise, agreement*›; 撤销 ‹*offer, undertaking*› 3 (pull back or in) 缩回 ‹*claws, tentacles*›; 收起 ‹*undercarriage*›

B *vi* «*claws, tentacle*» 缩回; «*undercarriage*» 收起

retractable /rɪˈtræktəbl/ *adj* 可缩回的 ‹*claws*›; 可收起的 ‹*awning, top*›

retraction /rɪˈtrækʃn/ *n* 1 [u and c] (withdrawal) 撤回; **the newspaper has published a ~ of the allegation** 报纸刊登了一份撤回指控的声明 2 [u and c] (of promise) 违背; (of undertaking) 撤销 3 [u] (of claws) 缩回

retrain /ˌriːˈtreɪn/

A *vt* 再培训

B *vi* 再培训; **to ~ as a midwife** 接受助产士再培训

retraining /ˌriːˈtreɪnɪŋ/ *n* [u] 再培训

retransmit /ˌriːtrænzˈmɪt/ *vt* 再发送

retread[1]

A /ˌriːˈtred/ *vt* (*pt, pp* **~ed**) 翻新 ‹*tyre*›

B /ˈriːtred/ *n* 翻新的轮胎

retread[2] *vt* (*pt* **retrod,** *pp* **retrodden**) 再踏上 ‹*steps, path*›

retreat /rɪˈtriːt/

A *n* 1 [c] (withdrawal) 撤退; **an orderly ~** 有序的撤退; **an undignified ~** 不光彩的撤退; **to beat a hasty ~** 仓皇撤退 2 [u] Mil **the ~** 撤退信号; **to sound the ~** 发出撤退信号; **to beat the ~** 击鼓撤退 3 [c] (secluded place) 隐居处; **a mountain ~** 深山隐居所; **a country ~** 乡间幽静的住所 4 [c and u] Relig 静修期; **to go into** *or* **on a ~** 去静修; **to be in ~** 在静修

B *vi* 1 Mil «*army, soldiers, enemy*» 撤退; **to ~ to a safe distance** 撤退到安全的距离 2 fig (withdraw) 隐退; **to ~ into oneself** 躲进自己的世界里 3 (recede) «*glacier, flood*» 后退

retrench /rɪˈtrentʃ/ *vi* 紧缩开支

retrenchment /rɪˈtrentʃmənt/ *n* [c and u] 紧缩开支

retrial /ˌriːˈtraɪəl/ *n* 复审; **to order a ~** 下令再审

retribution /ˌretrɪˈbjuːʃn/ *n* [u] formal 惩罚; **he was jailed in ~ for his crimes** 他被关入监狱以惩罚他的罪行; **to make ~ for one's crimes** 惩罚所犯罪行

retrievable /rɪˈtriːvəbl/ *adj* 1 (recoverable) 可取回的 ‹*equipment, cash*›; 可挽回的 ‹*loss, situation*›; **the situation is still ~** 局面还能挽回; 可纠正的 ‹*error*› 2 Comput 可检索的 ‹*data, file*›

retrieval /rɪˈtriːvl/ *n* [u] 1 (getting sth. back) 失而复得; **beyond** *or* **past (all hope of) ~** 无可挽回 2 Comput 检索; **information ~** 信息检索

retrieve /rɪˈtriːv/ *vt* 1 (get back) 取回 ‹*object, possessions*›; **she ~d her ball from the neighbour's garden** 她从邻居的花园里把球拿了回来 2 Comput 检索 ‹*data, file*› 3 (save) 挽回 ‹*loss, situation*›; 纠正 ‹*error*› 4 (restore) 挽救 ‹*fortunes*›; 恢复 ‹*honour, position*›

retriever /rɪˈtriːvə(r)/ *n* 寻回犬

retro /ˈretrəʊ/

A *adj* 再度流行的 ‹*fashion, music*›

B *n* [u] 再度流行的事物

retroactive /ˌretrəʊˈæktɪv/ *adj* 有追溯效力的 ‹*law*›; 追加的 ‹*award*›; **a ~ payment** 回溯支付

retroactively /ˌretrəʊˈæktɪvli/ *adv* formal 有追溯效力地; **the ruling should be applied ~** 这个裁决执行时应追溯过往

retro-engineer *vt* 逆向研发 ‹*technology, design, product*›

retrofit /ˈretrəʊfɪt/ *vt* (*pres p etc.* **-tt-**) 加装 ‹*component, accessory*›; 为…加装新设施 ‹*building, car*›

retroflex /ˈretrəfleks/ *adj* 卷舌的

retrograde /ˈretrəgreɪd/ *adj* 1 Tech (backwards) 逆行的; **Jupiter's ~ motion is more pronounced than that of Saturn** 木星的逆行运动比土星明显得多 2 (retrogressive) 退步的; **a thoroughly ~ policy** 彻底倒退的政策

retrogress /ˌretrəˈgres/ *vi* 1 (go backwards) 后退 2 (deteriorate) 恶化; **civilization has ~ed to a primitive state** 文明倒退到了原始状态

retrorocket /ˈretrəʊrɒkɪt/ *n* 制动火箭

retrospect /ˈretrəʊspekt/ *n* **in ~** 事后看来

retrospection /ˌretrəˈspekʃn/ *n* [u] 回顾; **he was much given to ~** 他沉湎于回忆

retrospective /ˌretrəˈspektɪv/

A *adj* 1 (looking back) 回顾的 ‹*survey, review*› 2 Art 回顾性的; **a ~ exhibition** 回顾展 3 (retroactive) 有追溯效力的 ‹*law*›; 追加的 ‹*pay award*›

B *n* 回顾展

retrospectively /ˌretrəˈspektɪvli/ *adv* (looking back) 回顾地; (retroactively) 有追溯效力地

retroviral /ˈretrəʊˌvaɪərəl/ *adj* 逆转录病毒的

retrovirus /ˈretrəʊvaɪərəs/ *n* 逆转录病毒

retry /ˌriːˈtraɪ/ *vt* 1 Jur 复审 2 Comput 重试; **the '~' icon/button** "重试"图标/按钮

retsina /retˈsiːnə, Amer ˈretsɪnə/ *n* [u] 松香味希腊葡萄酒

retune /ˌriːˈtjuːn, Amer -ˈtuːn/

A *vt* 1 Radio, TV 转换…的频道; **she ~d the radio to a different station** 她把收音机调到了另外一个台 2 Mus 为…重新调音; **the piano needs to be ~d** 这架钢琴需要重新调音了

B *vi* 转换频道

return /rɪˈtɜːn/

A *n* 1 [c] (coming or going back) (to place) 返回; (to home) 回家; (to home country) 回国; **on sb.'s ~**

某人返回时; **on my ~ home** 我回到家时; **sb.'s/sth.'s ~ to sth.** 某人/某物的回到某处; **I saw the play on its ~ to Broadway** 这部戏再度在百老汇上演时我看了; **sb.'s ~ from sth.** 某人从某处的返回; **her ~ from sick leave** 她病假后回到工作岗位; **they celebrated his safe ~ from the war** 他们庆祝他从战场平安归来; **I'm delaying my ~ to Rome by three more days** 我打算推迟3天再回罗马; **a ~ visit to sth.** 重游某地; **a ~ match** 回访赛 **2** [u and c] (giving or sending back) (of borrowed, stolen object) 归还; (of unwanted object) 退回; (of person, hostage, child) 送回; **I am hoping for its ~** 我希望它能被还回来; **on ~ of the vehicle/documents** 归还车辆/送回文件时; **the ~ of sb./sth. to sb./sth.** 将某人/某物交还某人/某处; **by ~ (of post)** Brit 由下一班邮递; **please reply by ~ of post** 请尽快回复 **3** [c] (recurrence) 重现; **a ~ of sth.** …的重现 ‹feeling, symptoms, doubts›; …的恢复 ‹law, practice›; **the ~ of spring** 春回大地; **we're hoping for a ~ of the fine weather** 我们盼望天气好转; **many happy ~s (of the day)** formal (as birthday wish) 祝你长命百岁 **4** [c] (resumption) 恢复; **a ~ to sth.** 某事的恢复; **on your ~ to work** 在你重返工作岗位之际; **they appealed for a ~ to work** 他们要求复工; **her ~ to politics/power** 她的重返政界/重新掌权; **a ~ to normal/the status quo** 恢复正常/现状; **a ~ to one's old habits** 恢复旧有习惯 **5** [u and c] (reward) 回报; **a (small) ~ for sth.** 对某事的（小小）回报; **this is a poor ~ for all your kindness** 这辜负了你的一片好意; **a ~ for doing sth.** 对做某事的回报; **in ~** (in exchange) 作为回报; (in response) 作为回应; **in ~ I'd like to ...** 作为回报，我想…; **in ~ for sth./doing sth.** (in exchange for) 作为对某事/做某事的回报; **to do sth. in ~ for sth./doing sth.** 做某事以回报某事/做某事 **6** [u and c] Fin (from land, investment) 收益; (from business, shares) 利润; **a ~ from sth./doing sth.** 某事/做某事的收益; **a ~ on an investment** 一项投资的收益; **a high rate of ~ on capital** 资本的高收益率; **the law of diminishing ~s** 报酬递减律 **7** [c] Brit (ticket for travel) 往返票; **a day/mid-week ~** 当天/周中往返票; **a ~ to Cardiff** 去加的夫的往返票 **8** [c] (ticket for performance, event) 退票; **do you get any money back on ~s?** 票退钱了吗？; **'~s only'** "只有退票" **9** [c] Comm (purchase) 退货 **10** [c] Publg (book) 退书 **11** [u] Comput (key) 回车键; **to press ~** 按回车键 **12** [c] Sport (of ball, shuttlecock) 回击; **to hit a winning back-hand ~** 打出一记制胜的反手球 **13** [c] Tax 报税表 **14** [c] Admin (official statement) 报告; **census ~s** 人口普查报告 **15** [c] Pol (vote) 选票; **~s from sth.** 来自某处的投票结果; **election ~s** 选票统计结果 **16** [u] Pol (election) 选举

B vt **1** (give back) 送还; **when does the video have to be ~ed by?** 这盘录像带应该什么时候还？; **to ~ sth. to sb./sth.** 将某物归还某人/某处 **2** (take back) 退回 ‹purchase›; 归还 ‹library book›; **~ed goods** 退货; **to ~ sth. to sb./sth.** 将某物退还某人/某处 **3** (put back) 将…放回原处; **to ~ sb./sth. to sth.** 将…送回某处 ‹baby, book›; **to ~ sth. to its place** 将某物放回原处 **4** (send back) 送回 ‹person, refugee›; 将…退回 ‹letter, parcel›; **to ~ sb./sth. to sb./sth.** 将某人送回/某物退回给某人/到某处; **'~ to sender'** (on envelope etc.) "退回发件人" **5** (in response) 回敬 ‹salute›; 回应 ‹wave, greeting›; **she ~ed his kiss** 她回吻了他; **it's time we ~ed their invitation** 我们该回请他们了; **to ~ the compliment (by doing sth.)** （通过做某事）回敬; **to ~ the favour** 报答好意; **I'll be glad to ~ the favour** 我会很乐意报答你的帮助; **to ~ sb.'s call** 给某人回电话; **to ~ (sb.'s) fire** «troops, police» 还击（某人） **6** (reciprocate) 以…回报 ‹feelings›; **he loved her, but his love was not ~ed** 他爱她，但他只是一厢情愿 **7** Sport 回击 ‹ball, shuttlecock›; **I was finding it impossible to ~ his serve** 我发现没法打回他发的球 **8** (reply) 应答; **'is that all?' she ~ed somewhat incredulously** "就这些吗？" 她有些怀疑地回应说 **9** Jur 宣告 ‹verdict, decision› **10** Fin (yield) 产生 ‹profit›; **to ~ approximately 7% after tax** 有约7%的税后收益; **to ~ a loss of £157 million** 损失1.57亿英镑 **11** Brit Pol (elect) 选出 ‹person, candidate›; **she was ~ed with an increased majority** 她以更大的优势当选; **to ~ sb. to sth.** 选举某人进入 ‹parliament, House of Commons›; **to ~ sb. as MP for ...** 选举某人为…议员 **12** Tax 申报; **to ~ details of one's income** 详细申报收入

C vi **1** (to place) 返回; (to home) 回家; (to home country) 回国; **the plane ~ed empty** 飞机空载返回; **to ~ from sb./sth.** 从某人处/某处返回; **to ~ from work/the trip** 下班/旅行回来; **to ~ to do sth.** 回来做某事; **we ~ed by the same route** 我们原路返回; **to ~ to sb./sth.** 回到某人处/某处 **2** (recur) 重现; **my doubts about the relationship have ~ed** 我对这层关系又起了疑心; **those days, alas, will never ~** 唉，那些日子一去不复返了

Phrasal verb

- **return to** vt [~ to sth.]
  1 (resume activity) 继续; **to ~ to work/school** 返岗/返校; **to ~ to one's work/book** 继续干活/看书; **she's ~ed to her old habits** 她又恢复了老习惯 **2** (start discussing again) 重提 ‹topic›; **to ~ to the point I made earlier, ...** 再谈谈我刚才提到的那一点，… **3** (revert to former state) 恢复; **to ~ to normal/power** 恢复正常/重新掌权

returnable /rɪ'tɜːnəbl/ *adj* 可回收的 ‹bottle, packaging›; 可退回的 ‹goods, purchase›

return: ~ address *n* 回寄地址; **~ envelope** *n* Amer 回寄信封

returner /rɪ'tɜːnə(r)/ *n* 重返工作岗位者

return: ~ fare *n* 来回票价; **~ flight** *n* 往返航班

returning officer *n* Brit 地方选举监察官

return: ~ journey Brit, **~ trip** Amer *ns* 返程; **~ ticket** *n* Brit 往返票; **~ visit** *n* 回访

reunification /ˌriːjuːnɪfɪ'keɪʃn/ *n* [u] 重新统一

reunify /ˌriː'juːnɪfaɪ/ *vt* 重新统一

reunion /ˌriː'juːnɪən/ *n* **1** [u] (with friend, child, sister) 团聚; **the children's desire for ~ with their parents** 孩子们想与父母团圆的愿望 **2** [c] (gathering, event) 重聚联欢会; **to hold** *or* **have a ~** 举办重聚联欢会; **the annual ~ of war veterans** 年度老兵联欢会

reunite /ˌriːjuː'naɪt/
A *vt* 使…再联合 ‹group, factions›; 使…重聚 ‹people›; 使…再统一 ‹countries›; **to be ~d with sb.** 与…团聚 ‹child, family›
B *vi* «group, factions» 再联合; «countries» 再统一; «people» 重聚

reusable /ˌriː'juːzəbl/ *adj* 能重复使用的; **~ battery** 充电电池

reuse
A /ˌriː'juːz/ *vt* 重复使用; **there are lots of ways to ~ scrap metal** 重新利用废金属的方法有很多
B /ˌriː'juːs/ *n* [u] 再使用; **the ~ and recycling of paper and cardboard** 纸张和纸板的回收利用

Rev *abbr* = **reverend A**

rev /rev/ colloq
A *n* (revolution) 每分钟转速; **maximum ~s** 最大转速; **an engine speed of 1,750 ~s** 每分钟1,750转的发动机转速
B *vt* (*pres p etc.* **-vv-**) 使加快转速; **don't ~ the engine so much** 别让发动机转得这么快
C *vi* (*pres p etc.* **-vv-**) «engine, car» 加快转速; **the roar of aircraft engines ~ving** 飞机发动机加速时的轰鸣声

Phrasal verb

- **rev up**
  A *vt* [~ **up sth.** *or* ~ **sth. up**] 加快…的转速 ‹engine, car›
  B *vi* «engine, car» 加快转速

revaluation /riːˌvæljuˈeɪʃn/ *n* **1** (of asset) 重新估价; **the ~ of a property** 对财产的重新估价 **2** (of currency) 升值; **the ~ of the euro** 欧元的升值

revalue /ˌriː'væljuː/
A *vt* **1** (reassess value of) 对…重新估价 ‹property, jewellery› **2** Fin 使…升值 ‹currency›
B *vi* 升值

revamp
A /ˌriː'væmp/ *vt* 翻新 ‹model, machine, room›; 改组 ‹company›; 修改 ‹play, script›
B /'riːvæmp/ *n* **1** (result) 改造过的东西; **a ~ of an old comedy** 一部老喜剧的改编本 **2** (action) 翻新; **a ~ of the living room** 翻新起居室

rev counter *n* 转速表

Revd *abbr* = **reverend A**

reveal /rɪ'viːl/ *vt* **1** (make known) 披露 ‹facts, details›; **accidents which ~ed faults in the design** 暴露了设计缺陷的事故; **the report ~ed long suppressed secrets** 报道披露了被长期隐瞒的秘密; **to ~ sb.'s whereabouts** 透露某人的行踪; **to ~ a talent for sth.** 展示某方面的天才; **to ~ oneself** 现身 **2** (make visible) 展现 ‹scene, view, object›; **he drew back the curtain to ~ the plaque on the wall** 他把幕布拉开，墙上的一块匾展现在眼前

r

revealing /rɪ'viːlɪŋ/ *adj* **1** (causing to be known) 揭露真相的 ‹report, document›; 发人深省的 ‹experience, action›; 暴露细节的 ‹examination›; **a ~ slip of the tongue** 暴露真实想法的口误 **2** (causing to be visible) 暴露身体的 ‹dress, costume, sight›; **a rather ~ low-cut dress** 领口很低、十分暴露的连衣裙

reveille /rɪ'væli, Amer 'revəli/ *n* 起床号; **to sound (the) ~** 吹起床号; **~ was at 5.30 a.m.** 起床时间是清晨5点30分

revel /'revl/
A *vi* (*pres p etc.* **-ll-**, Amer **-l-**) **1** (take pleasure) 狂欢; **to ~ in sth./in doing sth.** 陶醉于某事/做某事; **he ~led in his sudden and unexpected success** 他对自己不期而至的成功陶醉不已 **2** (party) 痛饮; **we ~led all night long** 我们彻夜狂欢
B **revels** *npl* 喧闹的欢庆

revelation /ˌrevə'leɪʃn/ *n* **1** [u] (making known) 披露; **the ~ of the truth** 对真相的揭露; **divine ~** 上帝的启示 **2** [c] (fact) 被暴露的真相; (secret) 被曝光的秘密; **to be a ~ (to sb.)** 出乎（某人的）意料; **her cooking skills were a ~ to me** 她的烹饪技巧让我大开眼界; **the progress he was making at school was a ~** 他在学校取得的进步出人意料

revelatory /ˌrevə'leɪtrɪ, Amer -tɔːri/ *adj* 启发性的

reveller /'revələ(r)/, **reveler** Amer *n* 狂欢者

revelry /'revəlri/ *n* [u] **revelries** /-riz/, *n pl* 狂欢作乐

revenge /rɪ'vendʒ/
A *n* [u] **1** (punishment) 报复; **an act of ~** 报复行为; **to exact ~** 进行报复; **he pledged ~ on his persecutors** 他发誓要向那些迫害他的人报复; **~ is sweet** 复仇是甜蜜的 **2** (desire to punish) 报复心; **in a spirit of ~** 出于报复心理
B *vt* **1** (inflict punishment for) 报…之仇 ‹insult, crime, injustice›; **he ~d the murder of his elder brother** 他报了杀兄之仇 **2** (take vengeance for) 替…报仇 ‹victim› **to be ~d on sb.** 报复某人
C *v refl* 复仇; **to ~ oneself (on sb.)** （向某人）报仇

revengeful /rɪ'vendʒfl/ *adj* 想报复的

revenue /'revənju:, Amer -nu:/ *n* **1** [u] (income) 岁入; **a source of ~** 收入来源; **public/private ~** 公共/私人收入; **a ~ tax** 岁入税; **advertising ~** 广告收入 **2** **revenues** *pl* (money received) 总收入; **oil ~s** 石油总收入; **tax ~** 税收收入

revenue-sharing *n* [u] Amer 岁入分享

reverberate /rɪ'vɜ:bəreɪt/ *vi* **1** (resound repeatedly) «*sound, thunder*» 回响; **his words ~d in my ears** 他的话在我耳边回响 **2** «*hills, tunnel*» 震颤; **the room ~d with the noise of gunshots** 隆隆的枪炮声在房间里回荡; **my ears ~d with the sound of the bells** 我的耳畔回荡着钟声 **3** (fig) (have repercussions) «*shock, rumour*» 产生严重后果; **the bank's collapse ~d throughout the financial sector** 该银行的倒闭给整个金融行业造成了严重影响

reverberation /rɪ,vɜ:bə'reɪʃn/ *n* **1** [u] (of sound) 回响 **2** [c] (echo) 回声 **3** [c] fig (repercussion) 后果; **psychological ~s** 心理后遗症

revere /rɪ'vɪə(r)/ *vt* 尊敬 ‹*person*›; 推崇 ‹*teaching, work, life*›; **to ~ sb.'s memory** 向某死者致敬; **a ~d figure** 受人尊敬的人

reverence /'revərəns/ *n* **1** [u] (respect) 尊敬; **~ for sb./sth.** 对某人/某物的尊敬; **in ~** 出于尊敬; **with ~** 怀着敬意 **2** [c] **Reverence** (in title) 尊敬的阁下 [对神职人员的尊称]; **Your/His R~** 尊敬的神父

reverend /'revərənd/

A *adj* 尊敬的大人 [对神职人员的尊称]; **the R~ Jones** 尊敬的琼斯神父; **R~ Mother** 院长嬷嬷

B *n* colloq 教士

reverent /'revərənt/ *adj* 恭敬的

reverential /,revə'renʃl/ *adj* 恭敬的

reverently /'revərəntli/ *adv* 恭敬地

reverie /'revəri/ *n* [c and u] 遐想; **to be deep** *or* **lost** *or* **sunk in ~** 沉浸在遐想中; **to fall** *or* **lapse into a ~** 陷入遐思

reversal /rɪ'vɜ:sl/ *n* **1** [u and c] (of order, sequence) 颠倒; (of policy, method) 背离; (of trend, tendency) 逆转; **a ~ of fortune(s)** 运势的逆转 **2** [u and c] (exchange) 转换; **a complete ~ of roles/positions** 彻底的角色转换/位置对调 **3** [c] Jur 撤销; **~ of sth.** 对…的撤销 ‹*ruling, verdict*› **4** [c] (defeat) 失败 **5** [c] (setback) 挫折

reverse /rɪ'vɜ:s/

A *n* **1** [u] (opposite) 相反情况; **the ~ (of sth.)** (某事的) 相反情况; **your behaviour was the ~ of polite** 你的举止很不礼貌; **the ~ is in fact the case** 实际情况正相反; **quite the ~** 正相反; **quite the ~ seems to be true** 似乎实际情况正好相反; **to be rather/exactly the ~** 恰恰/截然相反 **2** [u] (back) **the ~** (of medal, coin, banknote, paper) 背面; (of cloth, fabric, garment) 反面; **sign the cheque on the ~** 请在支票背面签字 **3** [u] Aut 倒挡; **in ~** 使用倒挡的; **you're/the car's in ~** 你/汽车挂的是倒挡; **to go into ~** 挂倒挡; **to put the car into ~** 给车挂倒挡 **4** [u] (opposite direction, order, way) **in ~** (in opposite direction) 向相反方向; (in opposite order) 按逆序; (in opposite way) 相反地; **we'll have to go through the whole process in ~** 我们得把整个过程倒推一遍; **the image appears in ~ in the mirror** 镜像是反的; **to go into ~** 发生逆转; **the upward trend went into ~, and recession loomed** 上升势头发生了逆转，经济衰退迫在眉睫; **to put sth. into ~** 使某事逆转; **to put a plan/policy into ~** 与计划/政策背道而驰 **5** [c] (defeat) 失败; **a heavy ~** 惨败 **6** [c] (setback) 挫折

B *adj* **1** (opposite) 相反的 ‹*process, effect*›; **to travel in the ~ direction** 朝相反方向行进; **in ~ order** 按逆序 **2** (other) 反面的; **the ~ side** (of medal, coin, banknote, paper) 背面; (of cloth, fabric, garment) 反面 **3** (backwards) 向后的 ‹*somersault*› **4** Aut 倒挡的; **to do a ~ turn** 倒挡转弯

C *vt* **1** (change to opposite) 彻底转变 ‹*direction*›; 逆转 ‹*process, trend*›; **to ~ the economic decline** 扭转经济滑坡局面 **2** Jur 撤销 ‹*decision, verdict*› **3** (turn opposite way around) 反转 ‹*image*›; 反穿 ‹*garment*›; **writing is ~d in a mirror** 字迹在镜子里的映像是反的 **4** (switch order of) 颠倒; **you should ~ the order of these pages** 你应该把这些页的顺序颠倒一下 **5** (swap) 对调 ‹*roles, positions*›; **if we ~ these two wires, ...** 如果我们把这两条电线调换一下，… **6** Brit (change to success) 扭转 ‹*defeat, result*› **7** esp Brit Aut 使…倒行 ‹*vehicle*›; **he ~d the car out of the garage/around the corner** 他将车倒出车库/倒过街角 **8** Tech 使…倒转 ‹*machine, projector*› **9** Brit Telecom **to ~ the charges** 让受话方支付话费

D *vi* esp Brit «*driver, vehicle*» 倒车; **caution! this vehicle is reversing** 注意！车辆倒车; **to ~ into sth.** 倒车进入 ‹*parking space*›; 倒车撞上 ‹*tree*›; **to ~ across a road** 倒车穿过公路

reverse: ~-charge *adj* Brit 由受话方付费的; **will you accept a ~-charge call?** 你愿意接一个由你付费的电话吗？; **~ discrimination** *n* [u] = **positive discrimination**; **~ engineer** *vt* 逆向制造; **~ engineering** *n* [u] 逆向制造 [指拆解别人产品后进行仿制的做法]; **~ gear** *n* 倒挡装置; **~ thrust** *n* [u] 逆推力

reversible /rɪ'vɜ:səbl/ *adj* **1** (able to be turned) 可翻转的 ‹*image, positions*›; 两面可用的 ‹*cloth, garment*› **2** (revocable) 可撤销的 ‹*decision*›; 可逆转的 ‹*trend, decline*›

reversing light /rɪ'vɜ:sɪŋ laɪt/ *n* Brit 倒车灯

reversion /rɪ'vɜ:ʃn, Amer -ʒn/ *n* **1** [u and c] (going back) 回复; **~ to his former habits** 他以往习惯的恢复 **2** Biol 返祖现象 **3** Jur (on death) 继承权; (at end of lease) 归复权

revert /rɪ'vɜ:t/ *vi* **1** (return) 回复; **to ~ to sth.** 回复到某状态; **fields that have ~ed to moorland** 恢复为高沼地的田野; **the company has ~ed to outdated methods of distribution** 公司又恢复了过时的分销方式 **2** Biol «*animal, plant*» 返祖; **to ~ to type** 返祖 **3** (return to topic) «*speaker*» 重提; **to ~ to sth.** 又提到某事物; **he ~ed to the original matter under discussion** 他又回到原来讨论的问题上 **4** Jur «*title, estate*» 归属; **if he dies without an heir, his property ~s to his brother** 如果他死亡时没有继承人，他的财产归属他兄弟

review /rɪ'vju:/

A *n* **1** [u and c] (of situation, developments) 检查; (of event, tax) 审查; (of facts) 审核; **a policy ~** 政策审查; **a pay** *or* **salary ~** 工资评审; **to be/come under ~** «*pay, salaries*» 在评审中/接受评审; «*policy, contract*» 在审查中/接受审查; **to keep sth. under ~** 持续审查某事物; **salaries are kept under constant ~** 对薪金情况会进行经常性审查; **to be** *or* **come up for ~** 准备接受审查 **2** [u and c] (of prices) 评估; (of research) 评价; (of events) 评述; **an annual/monthly** *etc.* **~ (of sth.)** (某事物的) 年度/月度等述评; **the director-general's end-of-year ~** 署长的年终报告; **the week in ~** Journ, Radio, TV 本周要闻回顾 **3** [u and c] Jur 复审; **to come up for ~** «*case*» 准备复审 **4** [u and c] (by critic) 评论; **a book/play/film/exhibition/music ~** 书评/剧评/影评/展评/乐评; **a restaurant ~** 餐馆点评; **a rave ~** colloq 高度赞誉的评论; **to get a good/bad** *etc.* **~** 获得好评/差评等; **to write a ~ (of sth.)** 撰写 (某事物的) 评论; **to send/submit a book for ~** 寄出/提交一本书供评论 **5** [c] (magazine) 评论杂志; **the Saturday R~** 《星期六评论》 **6** [c] Mil (of troops, regiment) 阅兵式; (of ships, aircraft) 检阅仪式; **to hold a ~** (of troops, regiment) 举行阅兵式; (of ships, aircraft) 举行检阅仪式 **7** [c] Amer Sch, Univ 复习课; **a ~ of sth.** 某科目的复习课

B *vt* **1** (assess) 检查 ‹*situation, progress*›; 审核 ‹*facts, salaries, pension*›; 审查 ‹*contract, policy*› **2** (study, consider) 回顾 ‹*subject, research, events*› **3** Jur 复审 ‹*judgement, sentence, case*› **4** (write critique of) 评论 ‹*book, play, film, exhibition*›; 品评 ‹*restaurant, food*›; **to ~ sth. for sth.** 为某机构评论某作品; **she ~s films for The Guardian** 她为《卫报》写影评; **to be well** *or* **favourably/badly ~ed** 得到好评/劣评 **5** Mil (inspect) 检阅 ‹*troops, regiment, ships, aircraft*› **6** Amer Sch, Univ 复习 ‹*subject, lesson, notes*›

C *vi* **1** (act as critic) 写评论; **to ~ for/in sth.** 为…写/在…上发表评论 ‹*magazine, newspaper*› **2** Amer Sch, Univ 复习功课; **to ~ for sth.** 为准备…而复习功课 ‹*exam*›

review: ~ article *n* 评论文章; **~ board, ~ body** *ns* 审查机构; **~ copy** *n* [供人写评论用的] 评阅本; **~ date** *n* 审查日; **~ document** *n* 评审意见书

reviewer /rɪ'vju:ə(r)/ *n* 评论者; **a film/play/book ~** 影评/剧评/书评家; **a restaurant ~** 美食评论家

review process *n* 评审程序

revile /rɪ'vaɪl/ *vt* 谩骂; **to ~ sb. for sth.** 因某事物辱骂某人

revisable /rɪ'vaɪzəbl/ *adj* 可修改的; **the rent is ~ every five years** 租金每 5 年可以变动一次

revise /rɪ'vaɪz/

A *vt* **1** (re-examine) 修改 ‹*proposal, estimate, figures*›; **to ~ one's opinion of sb./sth.** 改变对某人/某事物的看法; **a ~d offer** 修改后的报价 **2** Brit (for exam) 复习 ‹*notes, subject*› **3** (review, alter) 修订 ‹*book, dictionary*›; 校正 ‹*article*›; **a ~d edition** 修订本

B *vi* Brit 复习功课

reviser /rɪ'vaɪzə(r)/ ▸ **p. 409** *n* 修订者

revision /rɪ'vɪʒn/ *n* **1** [u and c] (amendment) 修改; **our budget needs drastic ~** 我们的预算需要大幅修正 **2** [u] Brit (for exam) 复习; **I've got to do some ~ for my 'A' levels** 我得复习准备高级证书考试 **3** [c] (corrected form) 修订本

revisionism /rɪ'vɪʒənɪzəm/ *n* [u] pej 修正主义

revisionist /rɪ'vɪʒənɪst/ pej

A *adj* 修正主义的

B *n* 修正主义者

revisit /,ri:'vɪzɪt/ *vt* **1** (visit again) 重访; **he went back to ~ his old school** 他回去重访了母校 **2** fig (go back over) 重提; **~ing painful memories isn't advisable** 重提痛苦的回忆是不可取的; **we will need to ~ this issue at a later meeting** 我们需要在以后的会议上重新探讨这个问题

revitalization /,ri:vaɪtəlaɪ'zeɪʃn, Amer -lɪ'z-/ *n* [u] 重振; **~ of the economy/the old town** 经济的振兴/旧城的复兴

revitalize /ri:'vaɪtəlaɪz/ *vt* 使恢复元气; **investment in technology will ~ the economy** 对技术的投资将重振经济

revival /rɪ'vaɪvl/ *n* **1** [c] (to health, strength) 复元; (to consciousness) 苏醒; **the patient's speedy ~** 病人的迅速康复 **2** [u] (of activity, fashion, language) 复兴; **the Gothic ~** 哥特式风格的复兴 **3** [c] (of economy, religion, artistic form) 复苏; **an economic ~** 经济复苏; **a ~ in traditional jazz** 传统爵士乐的复苏; **a ~ of hope** 希望的重燃 **4** [c] Theat 重演; **a ~ of a Restoration comedy** 王政复辟时期喜剧的重新上演

revive /rɪ'vaɪv/

A *vt* **1** (to health, strength) 使复元; (to consciousness) 使苏醒; **the fresh air will ~ you** 新鲜空气会让你振作起来的; **the flowers were ~d by fresh water** 这些花浇了淡水以后就活过来了 **2** (improve condition of) 振兴; **to ~ the economy** 振兴经济; **to ~ sb.'s hopes** 重振某人的希望 **3** (restore to popularity) 恢复 ‹*practice, trend*› **4** Theat 重新上演

B *vi* **1** (return to health) «*person*» 康复; «*flowers*»

恢复生机；(regain consciousness) 苏醒 **2** (improve) «*economy, industry*» 复苏；«*hope, spirits*» 重振 **3** (regain popularity) «*practice, trend*» 恢复

revocation /ˌrevəˈkeɪʃn/ *n* [c and u] (of law) 废除；(of licence) 吊销；(of membership) 取消

revoke /rɪˈvəʊk/
A *vt* 废除 ‹*law, edict*›；吊销 ‹*licence*›；取消 ‹*orders, membership*›
B *vi* (in card game) 藏牌

revolt /rɪˈvəʊlt/
A *vi* **1** (rebel) «*people, army*» 反抗；**to ~ against sb./sth.** 反抗某人/某事；**after years of oppression the population are ~ing** 受压迫多年以后人民开始反抗 **2** (protest) «*person, group*» 违抗；**teenagers often ~ against parental discipline** 青少年常常反叛父母的管教 **3** (feel horror) 感到惊骇；(feel disgust) 感到厌恶；**to ~ at sth.** 对某事物反感
B *vt* (horrify) «*injustice*» 使惊骇；(disgust) «*bad habits*» 使厌恶；**such unnecessary cruelty ~s me** 这种残酷虐待令我震惊
C *n* [c and u] 反抗；**open/armed ~** 公开/武装反抗；**the people rose in ~** 人民起来反抗；**to put down** *or* **suppress a ~** 镇压反抗；**a ~ against a cruel tyrant** 对残酷暴君的反抗

revolting /rɪˈvəʊltɪŋ/ *adj* **1** (causing horror) 令人惊骇的 ‹*cruelty, atrocity*›；(causing disgust) 令人厌恶的 ‹*habit, act*› **2** colloq (nasty) 令人作呕的 ‹*smell, taste*›；难看的 ‹*dress, colour*›；**he was a ~ sight in his dirty clothes** 他穿着那些脏衣服的样子难看死了

revoltingly /rɪˈvəʊltɪŋli/ *adv* 令人惊骇地 ‹*cruel, violent*›；令人反感地 ‹*behave, act*›；令人作呕地 ‹*smell, smelly*›；**~ wet weather** colloq 令人无法忍受的多雨天气；**he's quite ~ healthy!** colloq hum 他的身体棒极了！

revolution /ˌrevəˈluːʃn/ *n* **1** [c and u] (against government) 革命；**to stir up** *or* **foment** *or* **incite ~** 煽动革命；**the French R~** 法国大革命 **2** [c] fig (dramatic change) 革命性巨变；**to bring about a ~** 带来巨变；**the Industrial R~** 工业革命；**the green ~** 绿色革命 **3** [c] (circular motion) 天体运行；**a ~ round sth.** 围绕某物的旋转；**the ~ of the moon round the earth** 月亮绕着地球的运行；**200 ~s per minute** 每分钟 200 转；**each ~ of the wheel takes ten seconds** 车轮每转一周需要 10 秒

revolutionary /ˌrevəˈluːʃənəri, Amer -neri/
A *adj* **1** Pol 革命的 ‹*movement, leader*› **2** (radical, dramatic) 革命性的 ‹*change, invention*›
B *n* 革命者

revolutionize /ˌrevəˈluːʃənaɪz/ *vt* 使发生革命性剧变；**computers have ~d banking/publishing** 计算机使银行业/出版业产生了革命性的改变

revolve /rɪˈvɒlv/
A *vi* **1** lit (rotate) «*wheel, fan*» 旋转；**the earth ~s on its axis/around the sun** 地球绕地轴自转/绕太阳公转 **2** fig **to ~ around sb./sth.** (focus on) 以某人/某事物为中心；**his life ~s around his work** 他的生活以工作为中心
B *vt* 反复掂量；**she ~d the possibilities in her mind** 她在心中反复思考了各种可能性

revolver /rɪˈvɒlvə(r)/ *n* 左轮手枪；**he fired his ~ at the enemy** 他用左轮手枪向敌人射击

revolving /rɪˈvɒlvɪŋ/ *adj attrib* 旋转的；**a ~ stage** 旋转舞台

revolving: ~ credit *n* [u] 循环信贷；**~ door** *n* 旋转门

revue /rɪˈvjuː/ *n* 时事讽刺剧；**a ~ artist(e)** 时事讽刺剧演员

revulsion /rɪˈvʌlʃn/ *n* [u] (disgust) 厌恶；(loathing) 憎恶；(horror) 惊恐；**to feel ~ at sth.** 对某事物感到厌恶；**to feel ~ at having to do sth.** 很讨厌不得不做某事；**when she saw the snake, she jumped back in ~** 当看到那条蛇时，她惊恐地向后跳去

reward /rɪˈwɔːd/
A *n* **1** [c and u] (recompense) 报偿；**as a ~ for sth./for doing sth.** 作为某事/做某事的奖励；**virtue is its own ~** 善行本身就是回报；**she was given a medal in ~ for saving the little girl's life** 为奖励她挽救了小姑娘的生命，她获颁一枚奖章 **2** [c] (money) 酬金；**to offer a ~ for sth.** 为某物提供赏金 **3** fig (compensation, return) 回报；**to get** *or* **receive one's just ~** 获得应得的回报；**one ~ of my job is foreign travel** 我工作的一个回报是可以去国外旅行
B *vt* **1** (recompense) 酬谢；**to ~ sb. for sth.** 因某事物酬谢某人；**the finder will be ~ed** 寻得者有赏；**if you persist, your efforts will be ~ed** fig 如果你坚持不懈，你的努力是不会白费的 **2** fig (merit) 值得；**it's a subject that ~s further investigation** 这是一个值得进一步研究的课题

rewarding /rɪˈwɔːdɪŋ/ *adj* **1** (profitable) 有利的；**teaching is not very ~ financially** 教书并不是一个报酬很高的工作 **2** (satisfying) 有益的 ‹*activity, trip*›；**a ~ novel** 值得一读的小说

rewind /ˌriːˈwaɪnd/ *vt* (*pt, pp* **rewound**) 倒回

rewind button *n* 倒退键

rewire /ˌriːˈwaɪə(r)/ *vt* 为…换新电线

reword /ˌriːˈwɜːd/ *vt* 改写 ‹*sentence, speech*›；修改…的措词 ‹*idea, law*›

rework /ˌriːˈwɜːk/ *vt* 改编 ‹*theme, play*›；修订 ‹*plan*›；修改 ‹*figures, garment*›

reworking /ˌriːˈwɜːkɪŋ/ *n* [c and u] (of song, book, play) 改编；(of plan) 修订；(of figures, garment) 修改

rewound /ˌriːˈwaʊnd/ *pt, pp* ▸**rewind**

rewritable /ˌriːˈraɪtəbl/ *adj* 可擦写的 ‹*CD, DVD*›

rewrite
A /ˌriːˈraɪt/ *vt* (*pt* **rewrote**; *pp* **rewritten**) 重写 ‹*essay, sentence*›；修改 ‹*law, rule*›；**to ~ a poem as a piece of prose** 把诗改写成散文
B /ˈriːraɪt/ *n* **1** (action) 改写 **2** (book, song) 改写的作品

rewritten /ˌriːˈrɪtn/ *pp* ▸**rewrite A**

rewrote /ˌriːˈrəʊt/ *pt* ▸**rewrite A**

Rex /reks/ *pr n* Brit 国王；**George ~** 乔治国王；(in lawsuits) **~ v. Jones** 国王诉琼斯案

Reykjavik /ˈreɪkjəvɪk/ *pr n* 雷克雅未克

RFC *abbr* = **rugby football club** 橄榄球俱乐部

RGN *abbr* Brit = **registered general nurse**

rhapsodic /ræpˈsɒdɪk/ *adj* **1** Mus 狂想曲的 **2** fig (enthusiastic) 热情的；(ecstatic) 狂热的

rhapsodize /ˈræpsədaɪz/ *vi* (talk) 热情洋溢地谈论；(write) 热情洋溢地写；**to ~ about** *or* **over sb./sth.** 热情称赞某人/某事物

rhapsody /ˈræpsədi/ *n* **1** Mus 狂想曲；**Liszt's Hungarian Rhapsodies** 李斯特的《匈牙利狂想曲》 **2** (effusive expression) 热情的表达；**to go into rhapsodies over sb./sth.** 热情赞美某人/某事物

rhenium /ˈriːnɪəm/ *n* [u] 铼

rheostat /ˈriːəstæt/ *n* 变阻器

rhesus /ˈriːsəs/: **~ baby** *n* 溶血性疾患儿；**~ factor** *n* 猕因子；**~ monkey** *n* 恒河猴；**~ negative** *adj* Rh 阴性的；**~ positive** *adj* Rh 阳性的

rhetoric /ˈretərɪk/ *n* [u] **1** (persuasive language) 雄辩 **2** pej (meaningless language) 虚夸的言辞；**the empty ~ of politicians** 政客的大话空话

rhetorical /rɪˈtɒrɪkl, Amer -ˈtɔːr-/ *adj* **1** Literat 修辞的；**~ figures** 修辞手法 **2** (persuasive) 雄辩的；**her ~ skills** 她的辩才 **3** pej (meaningless) 虚夸的；**~ speeches containing nothing of any substance** 词藻华丽、没有任何实质性内容的演讲

rhetorical question *n* 反问句

rheumatic /ruːˈmætɪk/
A *adj* (affected by rheumatism) 患风湿病的 ‹*joint, fingers*›；(of or causing rheumatism) 风湿病的；**a ~ condition** 风湿病；**~ pain** 风湿痛
B *n* 风湿病患者

rheumatic fever ▸**p. 377** *n* [u] 风湿热

rheumatism /ˈruːmətɪzəm/ ▸**p. 377** *n* [u] 风湿病；**to suffer from ~** 患风湿病

rheumatoid arthritis ▸**p. 377** *n* [u] 类风湿性关节炎

rheumatologist /ˌruːməˈtɒlədʒɪst/ ▸**p. 409** *n* 风湿病学专家

rheumatology /ˌruːməˈtɒlədʒi/ *n* [u] 风湿病学

Rhine /raɪn/ ▸**p. 663** *pr n* **the ~** 莱茵河

rhinestone /ˈraɪnstəʊn/ *n* 莱茵石［用铅玻璃制成的钻石仿制品］

rhino /ˈraɪnəʊ/ *n* (*pl* **~** *or* **~s**) colloq 犀牛

rhinoceros /raɪˈnɒsərəs/ *n* (*pl* **~** *or* **~es**) 犀牛；**to have a hide** *or* **skin like a ~** 脸皮和犀牛皮一样厚

rhinoceros horn *n* [c and u] 犀牛角

rhizome /ˈraɪzəʊm/ *n* 根茎

Rhode Island /ˌrəʊd ˈaɪlənd/ *pr n* 罗得岛州

rhodium /ˈrəʊdɪəm/ *n* [u] 铑

rhododendron /ˌrəʊdəˈdendrən/ *n* 杜鹃花

rhombus /ˈrɒmbəs/ *n* (*pl* **~es** *or* **rhombi** /ˈrɒmbaɪ/) 菱形

rhubarb /ˈruːbɑːb/ *n* [u] **1** Bot 大黄 **2** Culin 大黄茎 **3** colloq (nonsense) 废话；**that's complete ~!** 那是一派胡言！

rhumba /ˈrʌmbə/ *n* = **rumba**

rhyme /raɪm/
A *n* **1** [u] (between words) 押韵；**a sense of ~** 韵律感 **2** [c] (rhyming word) 押韵词；(rhyming sound) 韵脚；**can you think of a ~ for 'orange'?** 你能想出一个和orange押韵的词吗？ **3** [c] (poem, verse) 押韵诗 **4** [u] (verse form) 韵文 **5** **~ or reason** (sense) 道理；(logic) 条理；**there is no ~ or reason to the way they work** 他们的工作方式毫无条理
B *vt* 使押韵；**~d verse** 押韵诗；**to ~ sth. with sth.** 使…和…押韵
C *vi* 押韵；**that doesn't ~** 那不押韵；**it ~s with my name** 这与我的名字押韵

rhyming /ˈraɪmɪŋ/: **~ couplet** *n* 押韵对句；**~ slang** *n* [u] 同韵俚语

> **rhyming slang**
>
> 同韵俚语。指用和某个单词押韵的短语来代替这个单词，常含喜剧效果，伦敦东区的人即以使用同韵俚语著称（▸**cockney**）。如用 brown bread（棕色面包）指代和 bread 同韵的 dead（死翘翘），trouble and strife（麻烦之源）指代 wife（婆娘）。有时候短语中押韵的单词会省略，如 china plate（瓷盘子）是 mate（哥们儿）的同韵俚语，但有时会省略 plate，只用 china 表示 mate。少数同韵俚语已进入日常词汇。如 apples and pears（苹果和梨）用于指代 stairs（楼梯）。

rhythm /ˈrɪðəm/ *n* **1** [u] (pattern of movement, sound) 节奏；**a sense of ~** 节奏感；**the ~ of the drums** 鼓点的节奏；**the ~ of his breathing** 他的呼吸节奏 **2** [c] (individual pattern) 韵律；**the song has an infectious ~** 这首歌有一种感染人的韵律 **3** [c] fig (recurring sequence) 循环往复；**the ~ of the tides** 潮起潮落；**the ~ of the seasons** 四季更替；**biological ~s** 生物节律

rhythm: ~ and blues *n + v sing* 节奏布鲁斯；**~ guitar** *n* [u] 节奏吉他

rhythmic, rhythmical /ˈrɪðmɪk, ˈrɪðmɪkl/ *adj* 有节奏的 ‹*movement, beat*›

rhythmically /ˈrɪðmɪkli/ *adv* 有节奏地

rhythmic gymnastics *npl + v sing* 韵律体操

r

rhythm: ~ method *n* 安全期避孕法; **~ section** *n + v sing or pl* 节奏乐器组

RI *abbr* 1 **= religious instruction** 2 Amer **= Rhode Island**

rial /rɪ'jɑːl/ ▸**p. 174** *n* 里亚尔 [伊朗、阿曼等国的货币]

rib /rɪb/

A *n* 1 肋骨; **a broken/fractured ~** 折断的肋骨; **a floating ~** 浮肋; **to dig** *or* **nudge sb. in the ~s, to give sb. a dig** *or* **nudge in the ~s** 轻轻捅一下某人的肋部 2 Culin 排骨; **a ~ of beef** 一块牛肋排

B *vt* (*pres p etc.* **-bb-**) colloq 打趣; **to ~ sb. about sth.** 因某事物取笑某人

ribald /rɪbld/ *adj* 下流粗俗的

ribbed /rɪbd/ *adj* 有棱纹的 ‹*stockings, jumper*›; 用肋状物支撑的 ‹*ceiling, shell*›

ribbing /'rɪbɪŋ/ *n* [c and u] 1 (structure, pattern) 罗纹; **a line of ~ round the neck** 领沿的一圈罗纹针 2 colloq (teasing) 打趣; **to give sb. a ~** 取笑某人

ribbon /'rɪbən/ *n* 1 [c and u] (strip of fabric) 丝带; **to tie sth. with a ~** 用丝带扎某物; **a length of ~** 一条丝带; **in ~s** 丝丝缕缕的; **to tear sth. to ~s** 将某物扯成碎片 2 [c] (in machines) 色带; **a typewriter ~** 打字机色带; **to change the ~** 更换色带

ribbon development *n* [u] Brit 带状房屋开发 [指沿主干道进行的住房建设]

ribcage /'rɪbkeɪdʒ/ *n* 胸廓

ribonucleic acid /ˌraɪbəʊnjuːˌkliːɪk 'æsɪd, Amer -nuː-/ *n* [u] 核糖核酸

rib: ~-tickler *n* colloq (joke) 笑话; (story) 逗人的故事; **~-tickling** *adj* colloq 逗人的

rice /raɪs/ *n* [u] 1 Bot 水稻; **a ~ field** *or* **paddy** 稻田 2 Culin 大米; **boiled/fried ~** 米饭/炒饭

rice: ~ bowl *n* 1 (container) 饭碗; 2 (rice-producing area) 稻米之乡; **~paper** *n* [u] [用作小蛋糕底托等的] 米纸; **~ pudding** *n* [c and u] 大米布丁

ricer /'raɪsə(r)/ *n* Amer 压粒器

rice wine *n* [u and c] 米酒

rich /rɪtʃ/

A *adj* 1 (wealthy) 富有的; **to grow** *or* **get ~** 发财; **to make sb. ~** 让某人富起来; **to strike it ~** 发横财; **(as) ~ as Croesus** 富可敌国 2 (expensive) 昂贵的 ‹*gift, clothes*›; (luxurious) 奢华的 ‹*banquet, furnishings*› 3 (having abundance) 丰富的; **to be ~ in sth.** 含有大量某物; **oranges are ~ in vitamin C** 橙子富含维生素C; **South Africa is ~ in diamonds** 南非盛产钻石; **the whole area is ~ with historical interest** 整个地区遍布历史遗迹 4 (abundant, fertile) 肥沃的 ‹*soil*›; 富饶的 ‹*land*›; 丰厚的 ‹*profit*›; **a ~ harvest** 丰收; **a ~ display of talent** 才华横溢; **a ~ supply of ideas** 层出不穷的想法; **a ~ vein of minerals** 矿藏丰富的矿脉 5 Culin 油腻的 ‹*food, cake, sauce*›; 醇厚的 ‹*port*› 6 (full-bodied) 浓艳的 ‹*colour*›; 浓郁的 ‹*smell*›; 圆润的 ‹*sound*› 7 (interesting) 丰富多彩的 ‹*life, history*› 8 colloq (causing indignant amusement) 荒唐的; **that's ~!** 这太可笑了!

B *npl* **the ~** 富人; **the idle ~** 富贵闲人; **to take from the ~ to give to the poor** 劫富济贫

C riches *npl* (wealth) 财富; (abundant resources) 丰富的资源; **natural ~es** 大自然的财富

richly /'rɪtʃli/ *adv* 华丽地 ‹*decorated, dressed*›; 丰厚地 ‹*reward*›; 浓艳地 ‹*coloured*›; 浓郁地 ‹*flavoured*›; **a ~ talented writer** 一位才华横溢的作家

richness /'rɪtʃnɪs/ *n* [u] 1 (of person, country) 富有 2 (of soil) 肥沃 3 (of deposit, vein) 丰富 4 (of colour) 浓艳; (of voice) 圆润 5 (of ornament, quality) 富丽堂皇 6 (of food) 油腻; (of drink) 醇厚

Richter scale /'rɪktə skeɪl/ *n* 里氏震级; **an earthquake measuring 5 on the ~** 里氏5级的地震

rich text format *n* [u] RTF格式

ricin /'raɪsɪn/ *n* [u] 蓖麻毒素

rick[1] /rɪk/ *n* Agric 草垛

rick[2]

A *n* (sprain) 扭伤; **to have a ~ in sth.** 扭伤某处

B *vt* (sprain) 扭伤 ‹*ankle, joint*›

rickets /'rɪkɪts/ ▸**p. 377** *npl + v sing* 佝偻病

rickety /'rɪkəti/ *adj* 摇晃的 ‹*bridge, stairs*›; **a ~ old car** 一台摇摇晃晃的老爷车

rickshaw /'rɪkʃɔː/ *n* 1 (two-wheeled) 黄包车 2 (three-wheeled) 三轮车

ricochet /'rɪkəʃeɪ, Amer ˌrɪkə'ʃeɪ/

A *vi* (*pt, pp* **~ed, ~ted**) 弹开; **the bullet ~ed off the wall** 子弹从墙上弹飞了

B *n* (rebound) 弹开; (hit) 跳弹; **an unfortunate soldier who was killed by a ~** 一个被跳弹击中身亡的倒霉士兵

rictus /'rɪktəs/ *n* 龇牙咧嘴

rid /rɪd/

A *vt* (*pres p* **-dd-**; *pt, pp* **rid**) 使摆脱; **to ~ sb./sth. of sb./sth.** 使…摆脱…; **plans to ~ the world of famine** 使世界摆脱饥荒的计划; **to ~ the house of mice** 消灭房子里的老鼠; **to be** *or* **get ~ of sb./sth.** 摆脱某人/某物; **they could not get ~ of the old house** 他们无法卖掉老房子; **you're well ~ of him; he's caused nothing but trouble** 你把他打发走了是件好事, 他只会添麻烦

B *v refl* **to ~ oneself of sb./sth.** 摆脱某人/某物; **we tried hard to ~ ourselves of debt** 我们尽力还清债务; **he's trying to ~ himself of his irritating girlfriend** 他正在极力摆脱他那个烦人的女友

riddance /'rɪdns/ *n* [u] **good ~** 总算摆脱了; **good ~ to bad rubbish!** 谢天谢地总算解脱了!

ridden /'rɪdn/

A *pp* ▸**ride A, B**

B *adj pred* **to be ~ with sth.** 充满某物; **he was ~ with guilt** 他充满了负罪感

C -ridden *combining form* 充满…的; **a flea~ bed** 满是跳蚤的床; **a guilt~ person** 负罪感深重的人; **a debt~ family** 负债累累的家庭

riddle[1] /'rɪdl/ *n* 1 (puzzle) 谜语; **to ask sb. a ~** 让某人猜谜; **to solve a ~** 解谜; **to talk in ~s** 说话拐弯抹角 2 (mystery) 谜; **he's a ~** 他是个谜一样的人; **the ~ of the origin of the universe** 宇宙起源之谜; **the ~ of the Sphinx** 斯芬克斯之谜

riddle[2]

A *n* (sieve) 粗筛

B *vt* 1 (sieve) 用粗筛筛 ‹*soil, sand*› 2 (make holes in) 使布满窟窿; **the body was ~d with bullets** 那具尸体布满了子弹孔; **his clothes were ~d with holes** 他的衣服上到处都是窟窿 3 (permeate) «*disease, cancer*» 充斥; **an administration that was ~d with graft and corruption** 一个贪污腐败成风的政府

ride /raɪd/

A *vt* (*pt* **rode,** *pp* **ridden**) 1 (sit on animal) «*rider*» 骑 ‹*horse*› 2 (in race) «*jockey*» 骑…参赛 ‹*horse*› 3 (compete in) «*rider, cyclist*» 乘骑参加; **to ~ a good race** 在乘骑比赛中表现出色 4 (sit on vehicle) «*cyclist, child*» 骑 ‹*bicycle, motorbike*› 5 Amer (travel in vehicle) 搭乘 ‹*bus, train, subway*› 6 Amer (travel in or on) 乘坐 ‹*elevator, escalator*› 7 (travel through) «*rider, cowboy*» [骑马、自行车等] 穿越 ‹*prairie, range*› 8 (float on) «*surfer, boat*» 乘 ‹*wave*›; «*bird*» 翱翔在…之上 ‹*thermal, air current*› 9 (absorb) «*person, boxer*» 躲闪 ‹*punch, blow*›; **he rode the first punch easily** 他轻松躲过了第一拳 10 colloq esp Amer (criticize) «*person*» 数落 ‹*person, employee*›; **you're riding them too hard** 你把他们批得太狠了; **to ~ sb. about sth.** 因某事物数落某人

B *vi* (*pt* **rode,** *pp* **ridden**) 1 (be able to ride a horse) 骑马; **to ~ astride/side-saddle** 跨骑/侧坐马背骑 2 (go horse riding) 去骑马; **we ~ most weekends** 我们大多数周末都去骑马; **to ~ to hounds** 骑马纵犬猎狐; «*horse*» 适于乘骑; **this mare ~s well** 这匹母马很好骑 3 (race) (on horse) 骑马参赛; (on bicycle) 骑车参赛; **to ~ in sth.** «*rider, jockey*» 骑马参加某比赛; «*cyclist*» 骑车参加某比赛; **have you ever ridden in the Tour de France?** 你参加过环法自行车赛吗? 4 (travel on animal) «*rider*» 乘骑旅行; **they had been riding for hours** 他们骑马好几个小时了; **to ~ on sth.** «*rider*» 骑 ‹*horse, animal*›; «*person*» 骑牲畜行走在…上 ‹*path, road*›; **she was riding on a camel** 她当时正骑着一头骆驼; **to ~ across sth.** 骑马穿过某处; **to ~ at sth.** 骑马冲向某物; **to ~ behind sb.** (on same horse) 坐在某人身后共骑一匹马; (on different horse) 骑马跟在某人后面; **to ~ over** 骑马过去; **to ~ over/through sth.** 骑马穿越/穿过某处; **to ~ along sth.** 骑马沿某处前行; **to be riding for a fall** colloq 做事莽撞 5 (travel on vehicle) «*cyclist, motorcyclist*» 骑乘; **to ~ on** «*cyclist, motorcyclist*» 骑在…上 ‹*bicycle, motorbike*›; «*cyclist*» 骑车在…上行进 ‹*road, pavement*›; **she rode all the way to London on her bike** 她一路骑自行车到了伦敦; **to ~ along** 骑车前行; **to ~ along sth.** 沿某处骑车; **to ~ along the lane and back** 沿着这条小路骑, 然后返回; **to ~ over** 骑车过去; **to ~ over/through sth.** 骑车轧过某物/穿过某处; **to ~ behind** (on same vehicle) 坐在后座上; (on different vehicle) 骑车跟在后面; **to ~ behind sb.** (on same vehicle) 坐在某人后座上; (on different vehicle) 骑车跟着某人 6 (travel in vehicle) «*passenger*» 搭车; **to ~ in** *or* **on sth.** 搭乘某交通工具; **he's never ridden on a bus** 他从来没坐过公共汽车; **to ~ along** 搭车前行 7 Amer (travel in elevator, on escalator) 乘坐; **to ~ up and down the escalators** 乘自动扶梯上下 8 (on shoulders) 骑在肩上; (on back) 骑在背上; **to ~ on sth.** «*baby, child*» 骑在…上 ‹*shoulders, back*› 9 (float) «*boat*» 漂浮; «*surfer*» 踏浪; «*bird*» 飞翔; **to ~ on sth.** 乘 ‹*wave, wind, air current*›; **to be riding on a wave of popularity** 十分流行; **to be riding high** fig «*person, team*» 获得成功; **to let sth. ~** 听任某事发展

C *n* 1 (journey) 短途旅程; **a train/taxi ~** 乘火车/出租车的旅程; **a bike/horse ~** 骑自行车/骑马的出行; **it's a five-minute ~ in a taxi** 乘出租车要花5分钟; **it's a £3 bus ~** 这段路程坐公共汽车要花3英镑; **it's a short/long ~** 乘车去很近/很远; **to go for a ~** 去乘车兜风; **a ~ on sth.** 骑某物的旅程; **to have a ~ on a horse** 骑马; **a ~ in sth.** 乘某物的旅程; **to have a ~ in a steam train** 乘蒸汽火车; **to take sb. for a ~** lit 开车带某人去兜风; fig colloq (cheat) 忽悠某人; **to go along for the ~** colloq lit 一起开车出行; fig 凑热闹; **to be in for a rough/bumpy/difficult ~** 即将举步维艰/坎坷不平/困难重重; **an easy ~ to the Presidency** 一帆风顺赢得总统选举 2 (carriage on sb.'s shoulders, back) 骑; **to give sb. a ~** 让…骑 ‹*person, baby*›; **give the child a ~ on your shoulders** 让孩子骑在你肩膀上 3 esp Amer (person giving lift) 让人搭车者; **their ~ into town dropped them off near the bridge** 带他们进城的人让他们在桥附近下车了 4 esp Amer (lift) 搭便车; **to give sb. a ~** 让某人搭便车; **to get** *or* **hitch a ~** 搭便车 5 Amer Transp colloq (degree of smoothness) 旅途平稳性; **a comfortable/bumpy ~** 舒适/颠簸的旅途 6 (at fair or amusement park) 乘坐; **to have a ~ on a merry-go-round/roller coaster** 骑旋转木马/乘坐过山车 7 Horse racing 赛马; **he's got three ~s today** 他今天参加了三场赛马

Phrasal verbs

• **ride around, ride about** *vi* 1 (on animal) 骑牲畜到处走 2 (in vehicle) «*passenger*» 乘车兜风; (on vehicle) «*rider, cyclist*» 骑车兜风;

I thought I'd ～ around a bit and try out my new motorbike 我想我应该骑车转一圈，试试我的新摩托车

- **ride back** *vi* [1] (on animal) 骑牲畜返回 [2] (in vehicle) «*passenger*» 乘车返回；(on vehicle) «*rider, cyclist*» 骑车返回；**he rode back to the airport in a taxi** 他乘出租车返回机场
- **ride down** *vt* [～ **sb. down,** ～ **down sb.**] [1] (hit) 骑马撞倒 [2] (catch up with) «*rider, cyclist, motorcyclist*» 骑马赶上
- **ride off** *vi* [1] (on animal) 骑牲畜离开；**to ～ off to …** 骑牲畜去… [2] (in vehicle) «*passenger*» 乘车而去；(on vehicle) «*rider, cyclist, motorcyclist*» 骑车而去
- **ride on** *vt* [～ **on sth.**] (depend) «*money, future*» 取决于；**he has a lot riding on this project** 这个项目对他影响很大
- **ride out**

A *vt* [～ **sth. out,** ～ **out sth.**] [1] (come safely through) «*ship*» 安然渡过 ‹*gale*›；**to ～ out the storm** 安然渡过暴风雨 [2] (person, company) 经受住 ‹*crisis, recession*›

B *vi* [1] (on animal) «*rider*» 骑牲畜出行 [2] [～ **out to sth.**] (in vehicle) «*passenger*» 乘车出行；(on vehicle) «*rider, cyclist, motorcyclist*» 骑车出行

- **ride up** *vi* [1] **to ～ up to sb./sth.** (approach on animal) «*person, rider*» 骑牲畜向某人/某处走去 [2] **to ～ up to sb./sth.** (approach in vehicle) «*passenger*» 乘车向某人/某处行进；(approach on vehicle) «*rider, cyclist, motorcyclist*» 骑车向某人/某处行进 [3] **to ～ up over sth.** (move up) «*dress*» 向上方某处收；**her skirt rode up over her knees** 她的裙摆拱到了膝盖上面

ride-on *adj* 乘骑式的 ‹*lawn mower*›

rider /ˈraɪdə(r)/ *n* [1] (person) 骑手；**an experienced/inexperienced ～** 熟练的/经验不足的骑手；**the leading ～ at this stage of the Tour de France** 环法自行车赛本段的领先车手 [2] Amer (passenger) 乘客；**a taxi ～** 出租车乘客 [3] (condition) 附文；**the committee added a ～ to the minutes** 委员会在会议记录上又补充了一条

ridge /rɪdʒ/

A *n* [1] (on roof) 屋脊 [2] (on mountain, hillside) 山脊 [3] Meteorol 高压脊；～ **of high pressure** 高压脊 [4] (raised band) 隆起

B *vt* 使隆起；**a ～d surface** 隆起的表面

ridge: ～ **pole** *n* [帐篷的] 横梁；～ **tent** *n* 尖顶帐篷；～ **tile** *n* 脊瓦

ridicule /ˈrɪdɪkjuːl/

A *n* [u] 嘲弄；**an object of ～** 被嘲笑的对象；**to hold sb./sth. up to ～** 公然取笑某人/嘲笑某事物；**to be met with ～** 被嘲笑；**to lay oneself open to ～** 使自己成为笑柄

B *vt* 嘲笑；**the opposition ～d the government's proposals** 反对党嘲笑政府的提议

ridiculous /rɪˈdɪkjʊləs/ *adj* 可笑的 ‹*person, dress*›；荒唐的 ‹*price, behaviour, excuse*›；荒谬的 ‹*idea*›；**to look ～** 看起来滑稽可笑；**to make oneself (look) ～** 使自己出丑；**stop being** *or* **don't be ～!** 别犯蠢了！

ridiculously /rɪˈdɪkjʊləsli/ *adv* 可笑地 ‹*behave, dressed*›；不可思议地 ‹*expensive, cheap*›

ridiculousness /rɪˈdɪkjʊləsnɪs/ *n* [u] 荒谬；**the height of ～** 荒谬透顶

riding /ˈraɪdɪŋ/ ▸**p. 307** *n* [u] 骑马；**to go ～** 去骑马；～ **gear** 骑具；**a ～ jacket** 骑马装

riding: ～ **boots** *npl* 马靴；～ **breeches** *npl* 马裤；～ **crop** *n* 马鞭；～ **habit** *n* 女式骑马装；～ **lesson** *n* 骑术课；～ **school** *n* 骑术学校

rife /raɪf/ *adj pred* [1] (widespread) **to be ～** «*crime, corruption*» 猖獗的；«*unemployment*» 普遍的；«*rumour*» 盛传的 [2] (full) **to be ～ with** 充斥着… ‹*crime, rumour*›

riff /rɪf/ *n* [流行乐或爵士乐的] 重复段

riffle /ˈrɪfl/

A *vt* (shuffle) 洗；**to ～ (through) the cards/pack** 洗牌

B *vi* (leaf through) 飞快翻动；**to ～ through sth.** 随意浏览某物

C *n* [1] (shuffle) 洗牌 [2] (leafing through) 飞快翻阅 [3] esp Amer (shallows in river) 浅滩

riff-raff /ˈrɪfræf/ *n + v sing or pl* 不三不四的人

rifle¹ /ˈraɪfl/ *n* 步枪；**to point** *or* **aim a ～ at sb./sth.** 用步枪瞄准某人/某物；**to fire a ～** 击发步枪

rifle² *vt* 快速翻查 ‹*drawers, safe*›；**thieves had broken in and ～d the house** 窃贼破门而入，把屋子翻了一遍

Phrasal verb

- **rifle through** *vt* [～ **through sth.**] 快速翻查 ‹*drawers, safe*›；迅速翻阅 ‹*papers, contents*›

rifle: ～ **butt** *n* 步枪枪托；～**man** /-mən/ *n* 步兵；～ **range** *n* [1] (for practice) 步枪靶场；[2] (at fair) 打靶游戏场；[2] [u] (range) 步枪射程；**to be within/out of ～ shot** 在步枪射程内/外

rift /rɪft/ *n* [1] (crack, split) 裂缝；**a landscape full of ～s and crevasses** 沟壑丛生的景色；**a ～ in the clouds** 云罅 [2] (disagreement) 分歧；**a ～ between sb. and sb.** 某人与某人之间的分歧；**to cause a ～** 引起分歧；**a growing** *or* **widening** *or* **deepening ～** 不断加深的分歧

rift valley *n* 裂谷

rig¹ /rɪg/

A *n* [1] Naut 帆装 [2] (piece of equipment) 设备；**a test ～** 试验台；**a lighting ～** 照明设备 [3] (for drilling oil) 钻井设备；**an oil ～** 石油钻塔；**a drilling ～** 钻井架；**a floating ～** 浮动钻井平台 [4] colloq (clothes) 装束 [5] Amer (lorry) 铰接式卡车

B *vt* (*pres p etc.* **-gg-**) 给…装帆具 ‹*ship*›

Phrasal verbs

- **rig out** *vt* [～ **sb./sth. out,** ～ **out sb./sth.**] [1] (with clothes, equipment) 给…提供装备；**the recruits had been ～ged out with uniforms and equipment** 新兵都已配好制服和装备 [2] colloq (in outfit) 为…提供装束；**he was ～ged out as a fireman** 他被装扮成一个消防员
- **rig up** *vt* [～ **sth. up,** ～ **up sth.**] 草草搭建

rig² *vt* (*pres p etc.* **-gg-**) (change fraudulently) 暗箱操纵 ‹*election, result*›

Riga /ˈriːgə/ *pr n* 里加

rigger /ˈrɪgə(r)/ ▸**p. 409** *n* [1] (oil-rig worker) 钻井工人 [2] (on lighting rigs, cranes) 装配吊运工

rigging¹ /ˈrɪgɪŋ/ *n* [u] [1] Naut 索具 [2] (lifting gear) 升降装置

rigging² *n* [u] (of election, result) 暗箱操作

right /raɪt/

A *n* ▸**p. 905** [1] [u] (moral correctness) 正当；**he doesn't know ～ from wrong** 他分不清是非；**they both had some ～ on their side** 他们双方都有点道理；**to be in the ～** 有理 [2] [u and c] (just claim) 权利；**consumer ～s** 消费者权益；**everyone has a ～ to a fair trial** 每个人都有权获得公正的审判；**to have a** *or* **the ～ to do sth.** 有权做某事；**you have every ～ to be angry** 你完全有权发脾气；**to be within one's ～s (to do sth.)** (做某事) 在某人的权利范围内；**you would be quite within your ～s to refuse** 你完全有权拒绝；**in one's own ～** 凭本人的资格；**her husband is a celebrity in his own ～** 她丈夫本身就是一位名人；**she was already established as a poet in her own ～** 她自身就是位无可争议的诗人；**as of/by ～** 作为合法权利；**the property belongs to him as of/by ～** 这份财产依法归他所有；**British by ～ of birth** 生来就是英国人；**by ～s** 按理；**by ～s half the money should be mine** 按理说有一半的钱应该是我的 [3] [u] (side, direction) 右；**to look from left to ～** 左顾右盼；**keep to the ～** Aut 靠右行驶；**on the ～ of sth.** 在某物的右边；**on** *or* **to the** *or* **sb.'s ～** 在右边；**the third turning on the** *or* **your ～** 右边的第三个路口；**on** *or* **to your ～ is the town hall** 在你的右边是市政厅 [4] [c] (road) 右侧道路；**the first/second ～** 右侧第一/第二条路 [5] [c] (turn) 右转弯；**to take** *or* **make a ～** 向右转弯；**to hang a ～** Amer colloq 向右拐弯 [6] **Right** [u] Pol (grouping, wing of party) 右派；**the R～ got in at the election** 右派在选举中获胜；**he's on the R～ of the Labour Party** 他是工党中的右翼成员 [7] [c] (in boxing) (fist, punch) 右手拳；**you need to use your ～ more** 你应该多用右手拳；**he hit him with a ～ to the jaw** 他一记右手拳打在他的下巴上

B **rights** *npl* [1] Comm, Jur 权利；**he sold the ～s for £2 million** 他以 200 万英镑出售了版权；**mining** *or* **mineral ～s** 采矿权；**human ～s** 人权；**film/translation/paperback ～s** 电影/翻译/平装本版权；**all ～s reserved** 版权所有 [2] (moral aspects) 正确性；**the ～s and wrongs of a matter** 一件事情的是非曲直；**to put** *or* **set sth. to ～s** 纠正某事

C *adj* [1] (true, correct, accurate) 准确的；**to get sth. ～** 把某事弄准确；**to get one's facts ～** 澄清事实真相；**that's the ～ answer** 这就是正确答案；**he was ～ about that restaurant: the food was awful** 他对那家饭店的看法是对的，那里的菜很差劲；**let me get this ～: you want us to pay extra?** 让我把这一点弄清楚，你想要我们额外付费吗？；**that's ～, call me a liar!** iron 你说对了，我就是谎话精！；**is that clock ～?** 那只钟准吗？；**to put** *or* **set sb. ～** 纠正某人的看法；**to put or set a clock/one's watch ～** 调准时钟/手表 [2] (morally correct) 正当的；(legally correct) 合法的；**to be ～ to do sth.** 做某事是正当的；**to think it ～ to do sth.** 认为做某事是对的；**to be ～ in doing sth.** 做某事是对的；**to do the ～ thing** 做正当的事情；**to do the ～ thing by sb.** 做某人开创的正义事业；**it's not ～ to steal** 盗窃是不对的；**it is only ～ that …** 就应该…；**it is ～ and proper that …** …是正当合理的；**it wouldn't look ～ if we didn't attend** 我们不参加似乎不妥 [3] (appropriate) 合适的 ‹*choice, conditions*›；对头的 ‹*decision, direction, road*›；**to choose the ～ candidate** 选择合适的候选人；**is this the ～ train for Dublin?** 这是去都柏林的火车吗？；**to be in the ～ place at the ～ time** 在适当的时间出现在适当的地点；**the ～ moment to ask/get sb. to do sth.** 询问/让某人做某事的恰当时间；**to be ～ for sb./sth.** 对某人/某事物是合适的；**she was never ～ for you** 她根本不适合你；**the ～ side of a piece of material** 一块布料的正面 [4] *attrib* (socially important) 关键的；**to know the ～ people** 认识头面人物；**to go to the ～ schools** 上知名学校；**to be seen in the ～ places** 在重要场合出现 [5] *pred* (functioning properly) 正常的；**sb./sth. is not quite ～** 某人/某事物不太正常；**I don't feel quite ～ today** 我今天感觉不太舒服；**to put** *or* **set sth. ～** 使…恢复正常 ‹*situation, machine, vehicle*›；纠正 ‹*mistake, injustice*›；**to put** *or* **set sb. ～** 使某人恢复正常；**this medicine should put** *or* **set you ～** 这种药会使你康复；**to see sb. ～** Brit colloq 确保满足某人的需求；**you needn't worry about money: I'll see you ～** 你不必担心钱，我会给你的；**in one's ～ mind** 头脑正常；**no one in their ～ mind would wear that!** 没有哪个精神正常的人会穿那种衣服！ [6] *attrib* (not left) 右边的；**my ～ foot** 我的右脚；**the ～ bank** 右岸；**take a ～ turn at the intersection** 在十字路口右拐；**on my ～ hand** (position) 在我的右边 [7] *attrib* Brit colloq (complete) 完全的；**I felt a ～ idiot!** 我感觉像个十足的傻瓜！；**it's a ～ mess** 真是一团糟 [8] *pred* Brit colloq (ready) 准备好的；**are you ～?** 你准备好了吗？ [9] *attrib* Math 直的；**a ～ pyramid** 直立棱锥

D *adv* [1] (exactly) 正好；～ **in the middle of the room** 恰好在房间的中央；**the bullet hit him ～ in the forehead** 子弹正好击中了他的前额；～ **now** (immediately) 立即；(at this point in time) 此刻；**do it ～ now!** 立即去做！；**he's not in**

r

the office ~ now 他此刻不在办公室 **2▸** (directly) 直接地; **he was standing ~ behind her** 他就站在她身后; **go ~ home** 直接回家 **3▸** (completely) 完全地; **a wall goes ~ around the garden** 一面墙整个围住了花园; **go ~ to the end of the street** 一直走到街道的尽头; **we're ~ behind you!** 我们完全支持你! **4▸** (immediately) 立即; **I'll be ~ back** 我马上回来 **5▸** (correctly) 正确地; **I guessed ~** 我猜对了; **if I remember ~** 如果我没记错的话; **you did ~ not to speak to her** 你不跟她说话是对的; **~ enough** colloq 毫无疑问; **you heard me ~ enough** 你肯定听到我说的话了 **6▸** (on the right) 在右边; (to the right) 向右; **to go** *or* **turn ~** 向右转; **keep ~** Aut 靠右行; **eyes ~!** Mil 向右看齐!; **stage ~** Theat 舞台右侧 **7▸** (very) 非常; **it's ~ spooky in there!** Brit colloq 这里太诡异了!; **he knew ~ well what was happening** archaic 他很清楚正在发生的事

E *excl* **1▸** (expressing agreement) 是的; **you may find it hurts a little at first — ~** 一开始你会觉得有点疼——是啊; **I'll have a whisky and soda — ~ you are, sir** 我要一杯威士忌加苏打水——好的, 先生; **too ~** Brit colloq 一点不错; **you're going, then? — too ~ I am!** 那么你要走了吗? ——对啦, 我要走了! **2▸** (for getting attention) 嗨; **~, let's get going** 喂, 我们开始吧; **~, let's have a look** 好吧, 让我们看看 **3▸** colloq (seeking confirmation) 对吗; **it was Monday you went to see her, ~?** 你是在星期一去看她的, 对吗?; **so that's twenty of each sort, ~?** 那么每一类是 20 个, 对不对? **4▸** colloq (checking attention, understanding) 明白吗; **and I didn't think any more of it, ~, but Mum says I should see a doctor** 我本来也不再想这件事了, 知道吗? 但妈妈说我应该去看医生 **5▸** iron (expressing disbelief, disagreement) 是吗; **I won't be late tonight — yeah, ~!** 我今晚不会迟到——是啊, 真的吗!

F *vt* **1▸** (restore to upright position) 把…扶正 ‹*vehicle, ship*›; 使…站起来 ‹*person*›; **to ~ a capsized canoe** 让倾覆的独木舟正过来; **he ~ed the chair that had fallen over** 他把倒下的椅子扶了起来 **2▸** (correct) 使…恢复常态 ‹*circumstances, system*›; **to ~ a situation** 使局势恢复正常 **3▸** (rectify) 纠正 ‹*injustice*›; **she was determined to ~ the wrongs done to her father** 她决心为她父亲平反昭雪

G *v refl* **1▸** (regain upright position) 恢复直立; **she quickly ~ed herself and continued along the path** 她迅速站直, 继续沿着小路前行; **to ~ itself** «*vehicle, ship, plane*» 恢复平稳 **2▸** (return to normal) 恢复正常; **to ~ itself** «*situation*» 恢复正常; «*problem*» 得到纠正

right: ~ angle *n* 直角; **at ~ angles to sth.** 与某物成直角; **~-angled triangle** *n* 直角三角形; **~ away** *adv* 立即; **~ back** *n* 右后卫

right-click
A *vi* 点击鼠标右键
B *vt* 点击…的右键 ‹*mouse*›; 用鼠标右键点击 ‹*icon*›; **~ the folder** 用鼠标右键点击文件夹
C *n* 右键点击

righteous /ˈraɪtʃəs/
A *adj* 正直的; **a ~, God-fearing man** 一位正直虔诚的人
B *npl* **the ~** 正直的人

righteously /ˈraɪtʃəsli/ *adv* 正当地; **she was ~ indignant when her car was broken into** 她的车被撬后, 她理所当然地大为光火

righteousness /ˈraɪtʃəsnɪs/ *n* [u] 正直

rightful /ˈraɪtfl/ *adj* 合法的 ‹*owner, inheritance*›; 恰当的 ‹*place, position*›; **the feminist movement enabled women to take their ~ place in society** 女权运动帮助妇女得到应有的社会地位

rightfully /ˈraɪtfəlɪ/ *adv* 合法地 ‹*claim, own*›; 理所应当地 ‹*give, belong*›

right hand
A *n* **1▸** (on body) 右手; **I'd give my ~ to know the answer** fig 为了得到答案我愿意付出任何代价 **2▸** (person, assistant) 左膀右臂 **3▸** (side, direction) 右方; **she sat on his ~** 她坐在他的右边
B **right-hand** *adj attrib* 右边的; **the top right-hand corner** 右上角

right-hand drive
A *n* **1▸** [u] (steering system) 右侧驾驶 **2▸** [c] (vehicle) 右侧驾驶的车辆
B *adj* 右侧驾驶的 ‹*car, vehicle*›

right-handed /ˌraɪtˈhændɪd/
A *adj* 惯用右手的 ‹*person*›; 适合右手使用的 ‹*golf clubs, scissors, tools*›; **she is ~** 她是右撇子
B *adv* 用右手 ‹*play, write*›

right: ~-handedness /-ˈhændɪdnɪs/ *n* 惯用右手; **~-hander** /raɪtˈhændə(r)/ *n* **1▸** (person) 惯用右手的人; **2▸** colloq (blow) 右手的一击

right-hand man *n* 左膀右臂

Right Honourable *adj attrib* Brit **1▸** (as title of nobility) **the ~ ...** …阁下 **2▸** Pol **the** *or* **my ~ ...** 尊敬的…议员阁下; **my ~ friend** 尊敬的议员同僚

rightism /ˈraɪtɪzəm/ *n* [u] 右翼主义

rightist /ˈraɪtɪst/
A *adj* 右翼的
B *n* 右翼分子

rightly /ˈraɪtli/ *adv* **1▸** (accurately) 正确地 ‹*describe, assign, give*›; **as you ~ said/commented** 正如你所说的/所评论的; **you acted ~ in calling the police** 你叫来警察做得对 **2▸** (justifiably) 理所当然地 ‹*furious, upset, believe*›; **and ~ so** 这是理所当然的; **~ or wrongly** 且不管正确与否 **3▸** (with certainty) 确切地; **I can't ~ say** 我说不准; **I don't ~ know** 我知道得不确切

right-minded *adj attrib* 思想正常的

righto /ˈraɪtəʊ/, **right-oh** *excls* = **righty-ho**

right: ~-of-centre *adj* 中间偏右的; **~ off** *adv* colloq 立刻; **~ of way** *n* **1▸** [u] (right to cross land) 通行权; **2▸** [c] (path) 公用通道; **3▸** [u] (of pedestrian, driver) 优先通行权; **pedestrians have ~ of way here** 行人在这里有优先通行权; **~-on** *adj* colloq esp pej 新潮的 ‹*person, views*›; **my parents are a pair of ~-on ageing hippies** 我父母是一对入时的老嬉皮士; **R~ Reverend** *adj attrib* **the R~ Reverend ...** 尊敬的…; **~s issue** *n* 配股; **~-thinking** *adj attrib* 思想正常的; **~-to-die** *adj attrib* 有权选择死亡的; **~-to-life** *adj attrib* 反对堕胎的; **~ triangle** *n* Amer 直角三角形

right wing
A *n* **1▸** Pol **the ~** 右翼 **2▸** Sport 右翼; **to play on the ~** 打右翼位置
B **right-wing** *adj* Pol 右翼的

right-winger /ˌraɪt ˈwɪŋə(r)/ *n* **1▸** Pol 右翼人士 **2▸** Sport 右边锋

righty-ho /ˈraɪtɪhəʊ/ *excl* Brit colloq 对啊; **I've come to pick up the kids — ~** 我来接孩子们——是啊

rigid /ˈrɪdʒɪd/ *adj* **1▸** (stiff, firm) 坚硬的 ‹*structure, support, material*›; **he was ~ with fear when he saw the snake** 当看到那条蛇时, 他吓呆了; **to shake sb. ~** fig colloq 把某人吓惨; **to bore sb. ~** fig 使某人感到无聊透顶 **2▸** (inflexible) 死板的 ‹*person, attitude*› **3▸** (unchangeable) 苛严的 ‹*system, discipline, control*›; **a man of ~ and unbending principles** 一个坚持原则不让步的人; **~ and inflexible laws** 苛严僵化的法令

rigidity /rɪˈdʒɪdəti/ *n* [u] **1▸** (stiffness, firmness) 坚固 **2▸** (inflexibility) 死板 **3▸** (unchangeability) 苛严

rigidly /ˈrɪdʒɪdli/ *adv* **1▸** (firmly) 坚固地 ‹*fix, construct*›; **to stand ~ to attention** 笔直立正 **2▸** (inflexibly) 严格地 ‹*control, enforce*›; 刻板地 ‹*behave*›; **to be ~ opposed to sb./sth.** 坚决反对某人/某事

rigmarole /ˈrɪgmərəʊl/ *n* **1▸** (procedure) 冗长烦琐的手续 **2▸** (story) 冗长的叙述

rigor /ˈrɪgə(r)/ *n* Amer = **rigour**

rigor mortis /ˌrɪgə ˈmɔːtɪs/ *n* [u] 尸僵

rigorous /ˈrɪgərəs/ *adj* **1▸** (strict) 严格的 ‹*discipline, law*›; 严苛的 ‹*regime*› **2▸** (careful) 缜密的 ‹*check, analysis, assessment*› **3▸** (harsh) 严酷的 ‹*climate*›

rigorously /ˈrɪgərəsli/ *adv* 严格地

rigour /ˈrɪgə(r)/ Brit
A *n* [u and c] **1▸** (of discipline, law) 严格; (of regime) 严苛 **2▸** (of check, analysis) 缜密; **intellectual ~** 学术的严谨
B **rigours** *npl* 严酷; **the ~s of the Arctic winter** 北极冬天的严寒; **the ~s of prison life** 监狱生活的严酷

rig-out *n* Brit colloq 一套衣服

rile /raɪl/ *vt* colloq 惹恼; **to be ~d at** *or* **about sth.** 对某事感到恼火; **his whole attitude really ~d me** 他的那副德性真让我火冒三丈

rim /rɪm/
A *n* **1▸** (of container) 边沿; **the ~ of the cup** 杯子的边沿; **a pair of spectacles with gold ~s** 一副金边眼镜; **a cup with a chipped ~** 有缺口的杯子 **2▸** (of wheel) 轮辋 **3▸** (of dirt, grease) 圆圈; **a thick ~ of soap suds** 一圈厚厚的肥皂泡
B *vt* (pres p etc. **-mm-**) «*border*» 给…镶边 ‹*cup, plate*›; «*mountain*» 环绕 ‹*valley*›
C **-rimmed** *combining form* 有…边的; **she wears gold~ spectacles** 她戴着金边眼镜; **her eyes were red~ with fatigue** 她的双眼通红, 满是疲惫

rime /raɪm/ *n* [u] 雾凇

rimless /ˈrɪmlɪs/ *adj* 无框的 ‹*glasses*›

rind /raɪnd/ *n* [u and c] **1▸** (on cheese, bacon) 外皮; **bacon ~** 熏猪肉皮; **cheese ~** 奶酪皮 **2▸** (on fruit) [尤指柑橘类水果的] 皮; **the thick ~ on an orange** 厚厚的橙皮; **to peel the ~ off a lemon** 剥柠檬皮

ring¹ /rɪŋ/
A *n* **1▸** (on finger) 戒指; (on toe) 趾环; (in nose) 鼻环; **a diamond/gold ~** 钻戒/金戒指; **a wedding/engagement ~** 结婚/订婚戒指; **to wear a ~** 戴戒指 **2▸** Brit (on bird) [鸟腿上的] 铝环 **3▸** (on bull, pig, etc.) 鼻圈 **4▸** (for attaching things) 环状物; (for mooring) 系船环; (for curtains) 窗帘环; (for keys) 钥匙环 **5▸** (for juggling) 杂耍圈 **6▸** (for swimming) 救生圈 **7▸** Med (for sitting on) 环形坐垫 **8▸** (mark on page) 圈; **a ~ around sth.** 围绕某物的圈; **to put a ~ around** «*person*» 圈出 ‹*name, ad*› **9▸** (around eyes) 晕圈; **to have ~s under one's eyes** 眼睛下部有黑眼圈 **10▸** Bot (in tree trunk) 年轮 **11▸** esp Brit (on electric cooker) 灶盘; (on gas cooker) 灶口; **a three-~ hob** 三炉盘炉灶 **12▸** Astron [围绕行星的] 光环; **Saturn's ~s** 土星环 **13▸** (circular arrangement) (of people) 围成一圈的人; (of things) 围成一圈的物; **to form a ~** 围成一圈; **to stand in a ~ (around sb./sth.)** (围着某人/某物) 站成一圈 **14▸** (circular movement) 环形路线; **to run ~s round** *or* **around sb.** colloq 远远超过某人 **15▸** (for boxing) 拳击场; (for wrestling) 摔跤场; **he knocked his opponent out of the ~** 他将对手摔出场外 **16▸** (boxing profession) **the ~** 拳击运动; **he retired from the ~ at the age of 35** 他 35 岁时退出拳坛 **17▸** (at circus) 马戏场; (for bullfighting) 斗牛场; (for showjumping) 马术障碍赛场; (at dog show) 犬展场 **18▸** (at livestock fair) 牲畜卖场 **19▸** (at racecourse) 下注区 **20▸** (illegal group) 团伙; **a spy/drugs ~** 间谍网/贩毒集团
B **rings** *npl* **the ~s** (in gymnastics) 吊环
C *vt* (*pt, pp* **~ed**) **1▸** (surround) «*trees, buildings*» 环绕 ‹*area*›; «*police, troops, protesters*» 包围 ‹*area, building*›; **a small valley ~ed by steep cliffs** 被悬崖峭壁环抱的小山谷; **to ~ sth. with sb./sth.** 用某人/某物围住某物

2 esp Brit (circle) 《*person*》圈出〈*name, ad*〉; **to ~ sth. in pencil/ink** 用铅笔/墨水将某物圈出; **her name was ~ed in black** 她的名字用黑笔圈了出来 3 Brit (tag) 给…戴上铝环〈*bird, leg*〉 4 Agric 环割…的皮〈*tree*〉

ring²

A *vi* (*pt* **rang,** *pp* **rung**) 1 Brit (telephone) 《*person, caller*》打电话; **to ~ for sb./sth.** 打电话找〈*person*〉; 打电话要〈*taxi, ambulance*〉; **to ~ from home** 从家里打来电话; **to ~ about sth.** 就某事打电话; **to ~ to do sth.** 打电话要做某事 2 (indicate incoming call) 《*telephone*》响起铃声; **it's** *or* **the number's ~ing** 这个号码拨通了; **to ~ off the hook** esp Amer 铃声大作 3 (produce bell sound) 《*church bell, handbell, bicycle bell, alarm clock*》响起; **the doorbell rang** 门铃响了 4 (cause bell to sound) 按铃; 《*bell ringer*》敲钟; **you rang, sir/madam?** 先生/夫人，是您按铃了吗？; **to ~ at the door** 按门铃; **to ~ for sb.** 按铃叫某人; **to ~ for** 按铃引起〈*attention*〉; **'please ~ for service'** "需要服务请按铃" 5 (be filled with sound) 《*place*》回响; **to ~ with sth.** 回响着某声音; **the house rang with laughter** 屋子里回荡着笑声 6 (fill place with sound) 《*footsteps, laughter*》响彻; **his words were still ~ing in my ears** 他的话还在我耳畔回响; **their steps rang down the corridor** 他们的脚步声在走廊里回荡 7 liter (possess quality) 充满; **to ~ with sth.** 《*voice, words*》充满〈*emotion, pride, contempt, sincerity*〉; **to ~ true/false/hollow** 给人以真实/虚假/空洞的印象 8 (be filled with buzzing sound) 《*head*》嗡嗡作响; **that noise makes my ears ~** 那噪音震得我的耳朵嗡嗡响

B *vt* (*pt* **rang,** *pp* **rung**) 1 Brit (telephone) 给…打电话〈*person, office*〉; 拨〈*number*〉; **to ~ Directory Enquiries** 打电话到电话号码查询台 2 (cause to sound) 敲响〈*church bell*〉; 摇响〈*handbell*〉; 按响〈*bicycle bell*〉; **to ~ the doorbell** *or* **bell** 按门铃; **to ~ the hours** 敲钟报时

C *n* 1 (sound of bell) 铃声 2 (act of ringing bell) 鸣铃; **there was a ~ at the door** 有人按门铃 3 (sound of phone) 电话铃声; **hang up after three ~s** 电话铃响三次后挂机 4 Brit colloq (phone call) 打电话; **to give sb. a ~** 给某人打电话 5 (of crystal, hooves, hammer) 清脆而响亮的声音 6 (set of bells) [尤指教堂钟楼的] 一套钟 7 (particular quality) 特质; **her name has an exotic ~ to it** 她的名字有点外国味儿; **that story has a familiar ~ to it** 这个故事听起来耳熟; **to have a nice ~ (to it)** (它) 很好听; **to have a ~ of truth** 听起来真实可信; **to have a hollow ~** 听起来不真诚

Phrasal verbs

• **ring around** Brit

A *vi* 挨个给人打电话

B *vt* = **ring round B**

• **ring back**

A *vi* 1 (phone again) 再打电话 2 (return call) 回电话

B *vt* [**~ sb. back**]

1 (phone again) 再给…打电话〈*person, place*〉; 再拨〈*number*〉 2 (return call to) 给…回电话〈*person, place*〉; 回拨〈*number*〉

• **ring down** *vt* [**~ down sth., ~ sth. down**] Theat 降下〈*curtain*〉; **to ~ down the curtain on one's career** 结束职业生涯

• **ring in**

A *vi* Brit 1 (to work) 给工作单位打电话; **to ~ in sick** 给单位打电话请病假 2 **to ~ in to sth.** (to radio show) 给某广播节目打电话; (to TV show) 给某电视节目打电话; **he rang in to express his view on the subject** 他打进电话表达对这个问题的看法

B *vt* **to ~ in the New Year** 鸣钟欢庆新年

• **ring off** *vi* Brit 挂断电话

• **ring out**

A *vi* 《*voice, cry*》大声响起; 《*shot, bell*》发出清脆的响声

B *vt* [**~ out sth., ~ sth. out**]

1 (celebrate) **~ out the old, ~ in the new** 辞旧迎新 2 (announce) 《*bells*》鸣钟宣布〈*news, message*〉

• **ring round** Brit

A *vi* **to ~ round to sb./sth.** (to organize sth.) 逐一打电话通知某人/某处; (for information) 逐一打电话询问某人/某处

B *vt* [**~ round sb./sth.**]

1 (to organize sth.) 逐一打电话通知〈*group, people, members*〉 2 (for information) 逐一打电话咨询〈*shops*〉

• **ring through** *vi* **to ~ through to sb./sth.** Brit 打电话给某人/某处 [尤指给同一栋楼内的人]; **to ~ through to do sth.** 给同一楼的人打电话做某事

• **ring up**

A *vi* Brit 打电话

B [**~ sb./sth. up, ~ up sb./sth.**] *vt* Brit (telephone) 《*person*》给…打电话〈*person, office*〉; 拨〈*number*〉

C [**~ sth. up, ~ up sth.**] *vt* (on cash register) 《*cashier*》把…输入收银机〈*figure, total*〉

D [**~ sth. up, ~ up sth.**] *vt*

1 (amass) 拢总〈*sales, profits, losses*〉 2 Theat 响铃开启〈*curtain*〉; **to ~ up the curtain on sth.** fig 开始某事

ring: ~-a-ring o' roses *n* [u] 编玫瑰花环 [一种游戏，儿童手拉手围成一圈跳舞，歌曲结束时一起蹲在地上]; **~ binder** *n* 活页夹

ringer /ˈrɪŋə(r)/ *n* 1 colloq (substitute) 冒名顶替者; (replacement horse) 冒名顶替的马 2 (double) 酷似的人; **to be a (dead) ~ for sb.** 酷似某人; **you're a dead ~ for Marilyn Monroe** 你和玛丽莲·梦露简直是一个模子里刻出来的

ring: ~ fence *n* 1 (enclosing barrier) 围栏; 2 (guarantee) [确保资金不被挪用的] 隔离屏障; **~-fence** *vt* 1 (enclose) 用围栏围; 2 Brit (guarantee) 确保…不被挪用〈*funds, grant*〉; **~ finger** *n* 无名指

ringing /ˈrɪŋɪŋ/

A *adj* 1 (resonating) 清脆响亮的〈*voice, sound*〉 2 fig (forceful) 强有力的; **a ~ denunciation of racial hatred** 对种族仇恨的有力谴责

B *n* [u] 鸣响声; **the ~ of the alarm clock** 闹钟的蜂鸣声; **there's a ~ noise in my ears** 我耳朵里有嗡嗡声

ringing tone *n* 振铃音

ringleader /ˈrɪŋliːdə(r)/ *n* 元凶

ringlet /ˈrɪŋlɪt/ *n* 垂下的长卷发

ring: ~ main *n* [房子里的] 环形主线; **~master** *n* 马戏表演领班; **~-pull** *n* 易拉环; **a ~-pull can** 易拉罐; **~ road** *n* Brit 环路

ringside /ˈrɪŋsaɪd/ *n* [拳击场或马戏表演场等的] 台边区

ring: ~side seat *n* 1 (at boxing ring) 台边前排座位; 2 fig (prime position) 最佳目击位置; **~ spanner** *n* Brit 梅花扳手; **~tone** *n* 手机铃声; **~ vaccination** *n* [u] 环状疫苗接种 [指对传染病爆发点周围所有人进行的接种]

rink /rɪŋk/ *n* 1 (surface) (for ice skating) 溜冰场; (for roller skating) 旱冰场 2 (building) (for ice skating) 溜冰馆; (for roller skating) 旱冰馆

rinky-dink /ˌrɪŋkɪˈdɪŋk/ *adj* Amer colloq 1 (old-fashioned) 老旧的 2 (amateurish, shoddy) 拙劣的

rinse /rɪns/

A *n* 1 [c] (wash) 冲洗; **give your hair a thorough ~ after shampooing it** 用过洗发液以后把头发彻底冲洗一下; **just give your mouth a ~ out** 漱一下你的口 2 [c and u] (in hairdressing) 染发剂; **a hair ~** 染发剂 3 [c and u] (mouth freshener) 漱口液

B *vt* 1 (wash quickly) 冲洗〈*hands, clothes, stain*〉; 漱〈*mouth*〉 2 (remove soap, dirt from) 漂洗〈*hair, clothes*〉

Phrasal verb

• **rinse out** *vt* [**~ out sth., ~ sth. out**]

1 (wash) 清洗〈*clothes, container*〉; 漱〈*mouth*〉 2 (remove) 冲洗掉〈*stain, dirt, dye*〉

rinse: ~ aid *n* 碗碟光亮剂; **~ cycle** *n* [洗衣机或洗碗机的] 漂洗过程

rinsing agent /ˈrɪnsɪŋ ˌeɪdʒənt/ *n* 漂洗剂

riot /ˈraɪət/

A *n* 1 (disturbance) 骚乱; **a prison ~** 监狱暴乱; **to run ~** (behave wildly) 撒野; (grow wildly) 疯长; **inflation is running ~, and prices are out of control** 通胀在肆虐，物价已失控 2 (profusion) 丰富多彩; **a ~ of emotion** 一阵情感的爆发; **a ~ of colour** 五彩缤纷; **a ~ of flowers** 花的海洋 3 colloq **to be a ~** 《*person, film, show*》非常滑稽有趣; **this new comedy is a ~** 这部新拍的喜剧非常搞笑

B *vi* 发生骚乱

riot: R~ Act *n* **to read the R~ Act (to sb.)** 严重警告（某人）; **~ control** *n* [u] 防暴

rioter /ˈraɪətə(r)/ *n* 聚众闹事者

riot: ~ gear *n* [u] 防暴服; **~ gun** *n* 防暴枪

rioting /ˈraɪətɪŋ/ *n* [u] 骚乱

riotous /ˈraɪətəs/ *adj* 1 (disorderly) 骚乱的〈*assembly, crowd*〉; **~ behaviour** 暴乱行为 2 (boisterous, unrestrained) 狂欢的〈*dancing, party*〉; 热烈的〈*welcome*〉; 放纵的〈*lifestyle, laughter*〉; **a ~ success** 轰轰烈烈的成功; **to have a ~ time** 玩得非常痛快 3 (vivid) 缤纷的〈*colour, display*〉

riotously /ˈraɪətəsli/ *adv* 极端; **~ funny** 滑稽至极

riot: ~ police *n* [u] + *v pl* 防暴警察; **~ shield** *n* 防暴盾牌; **~ squad** *n* 防暴警察队

RIP *abbr* = **rest in peace** 安息 [书于墓碑上]

rip¹ /rɪp/

A *vt* (*pres p etc.* **-pp-**) 1 (tear) 撕破; **to ~ sth. with one's teeth/a knife** 用牙撕开/用刀割开某物; **to ~ sb./sth. in two** 将某人/某物撕成两半; **to ~ sb./sth. to pieces** *or* **shreds** lit 《*person, animal*》将某人/某物撕成碎片; 《*bomb*》将某人/某物炸成碎片; fig 《*person*》将…批得体无完肤〈*person, argument*〉 2 (create) 《*bomb, wind, lightning*》撕出; **to ~ a hole in sth.** 在某物上撕出一个洞 3 (tear off) 猛力扯掉; **storms ~ped tiles from the roof** 暴风雨掀掉了屋顶上的瓦片 4 colloq (copy) 刻录〈*CD, DVD, track*〉

B *vi* (*pres p etc.* **-pp-**) 《*material, fabric*》被撕破; **to let ~** colloq (behave without restraint) 为所欲为; (happen in uncontrolled way) 不受控制地发展; (speak vehemently) 激动地说; **let it** *or* **her ~!** colloq 让车全速前进吧!; **to let sth. ~, to let ~ sth.** colloq (utter) 激动地说某事; (allow to happen in uncontrolled way) 听任某事发生; **he let ~ a stream of abuse** 他大骂了一通; **to let ~ at sb./sth.** 破口大骂某人/某事物

C *n* 裂口; **a ~ in sth.** 某物上的裂口

Phrasal verbs

• **rip apart** *vt* [**~ sb./sth. apart, ~ apart sb./sth.**]

1 (tear into pieces) 将…撕成碎片 2 (destroy physically) 《*blast, bomb*》将…炸成碎片〈*person, object*〉 3 (have harmful effect on) 《*person, disagreement*》损害〈*family, country, reputation*〉 4 (overwhelm) 击溃〈*defences*〉; 击垮〈*person, team*〉 5 (prove wrong) 将…驳得体无完肤〈*person, argument, thesis*〉

• **rip at** *vt* [**~ at sb./sth.**] 猛烈撕扯〈*animal, flesh, clothes*〉

• **rip down** *vt* [**~ down sth., ~ sth. down**] 撕下〈*picture, notice*〉; 扯下〈*curtains*〉

• **rip into** *vt* [**~ into sb./sth.**]

1 (enter forcefully) 《*knife*》猛力扎入〈*flesh*〉; 《*bullet, missile*》穿透〈*building, flesh*〉 2 colloq (criticize) 《*person, article*》斥责

• **rip off**

A [**~ off sth., ~ sth. off**] *vt*

1 (remove forcefully) 迅速脱掉〈*dress*〉; 迅速解下〈*tie*〉; **to ~ sth. off sb./sth.** 把某物从某人身上/某处扯掉; **he ~ped the cloth off the table** 他一把扯掉了桌子上的布; **she ~ped his trousers off him** 她拽下了他的裤子 2 (blow off) 《*wind, blast*》掀掉〈*roof*〉 3 colloq (steal) 偷窃〈*goods*〉; 剽窃〈*idea*〉

r

B [~ **off sb.**, ~ **sb. off**] *vt* colloq (cheat) 敲诈 ‹*customer, tourist*›; **to get ~ped off** 被敲竹杠
• **rip open** *vt* [~ **open sth.**, ~ **sth. open**] 撕开 ‹*envelope, parcel*›; 割开 ‹*bag*›
• **rip out** *vt* [~ **out sth.**, ~ **sth. out**] 拆掉 ‹*fireplace, kitchen units*›; 撕下 ‹*page*›
• **rip through** *vt* [~ **through sb./sth.**] «*bullet*» 穿透 ‹*person, flesh*›; «*fire*» 猛力窜入 ‹*building, area*›; «*blast*» 猛力穿过 ‹*building, area*›
• **rip up** *vt* [~ **up sth.**, ~ **sth. up**] [1] (tear up) «*person*» 将…撕成碎片 ‹*paper, cloth*›; 撕毁 ‹*evidence, document*› [2] (take up) 挖开 ‹*pavement, street*›; 掀起 ‹*floorboards, carpet*›

rip² *n* (in sea) 裂流

ripcord /ˈrɪpkɔːd/ *n* [降落伞的] 开伞索

ripe /raɪp/ *adj* [1] (ready to be eaten) 成熟的 ‹*fruit, crop, grain*› [2] (fully matured) 酿好的 ‹*port, wine*›; **a ~ cheese** 熟干酪 [3] *attrib* (advanced) 年高的; **to live to a ~ old age** 活到高龄; **at the ~ old age of 21 I find myself on the shelf** hum 活到 21 岁高龄之时，我发现自己成了剩女 [4] *pred* (ready for sth.) **to be ~ for sth.** 做某事的时机已成熟; **apples ~ for (the) picking** 成熟待摘的苹果; **land ~ for development** 适合开发的土地 [5] *pred* (full of sth.) **to be ~ with sth.** 充满某事物; **a job ~ with opportunities for promotion** 有充分升职机会的工作 [6] colloq (coarse) 粗俗的; **we thought his humour was a bit ~** 我们觉得他的幽默有点粗俗

ripen /ˈraɪpən/
A *vt* 使…成熟 ‹*fruit, crop*›; 促熟 ‹*cheese*›; **peaches ~ed by the sun** 被太阳晒熟了的桃子
B *vi* «*fruit, crop*» 成熟; «*cheese*» 变熟

ripeness /ˈraɪpnɪs/ *n* [u] [1] (of fruit, crop) 成熟; (of cheese) 酿熟 [2] colloq (of language, humour) 粗俗

rip-off *n* colloq [尤指价格离谱的] 骗人的东西; **£1 for a glass of water? what a ~!** 一杯水要 1 英镑？简直是敲竹杠！

rip-off artist, rip-off merchant *ns* colloq 骗子老手

riposte /rɪˈpɒst/
A *n* [1] (retort) 即刻反驳 [2] (in fencing) 还击
B *vi* (retort) 机敏地反驳

ripper /ˈrɪpə(r)/ *n* [1] (murderer) 杀人碎尸者 [2] colloq dated (good thing) 极品; **a ~ of a motorbike/party** 摩托车极品/妙不可言的聚会

ripping /ˈrɪpɪŋ/ *adj* Brit colloq dated 绝妙的; **a ~ yarn** 妙不可言的故事; **a ~ time at the beach** 沙滩上的绝妙好时光

ripple /ˈrɪpl/
A *n* [1] (in water) 细浪 [2] (in corn, hair) 波纹状物; **the breeze made ~s in the cornfield** 微风中麦浪起伏 [3] (of laughter, voices, stream) 起伏声; **the ~ of a woodland stream** 林地里溪水的潺潺声 [4] (of feeling, effect) 波动; **this measure will send ~s through the economy** 这项措施将会引发经济波动
B *vi* «*water, waves*» 起涟漪; «*corn, hair*» 如波浪般起伏; «*laughter, murmur*» 轻轻荡漾; «*applause*» 此起彼伏; «*anger*» 涌动
C *vt* 使…起涟漪 ‹*water*›; 使…飘起来 ‹*hair*›; 使…条条凸起 ‹*muscles*›

ripple effect *n* 连锁反应; **to have a ~ on sth.** 在…中引起连锁反应

rip: ~-roaring /ˈrɪprɔːrɪŋ/ *adj attrib* colloq 喧闹的 ‹*party, show*›; **to have a ~-roaring time (doing sth.)** （做某事）欢闹地乐一场; **~saw** *n* 粗齿锯; **~tide** *n* 裂流

rise /raɪz/
A *vi* (*pt* **rose**, *pp* **risen**) [1] (move upwards) 上升; **the aircraft rose from the ground** 飞机从地面起飞 [2] (appear over horizon) «*sun, moon, star*» 升起; **to ~ over** *or* **above sth.** 上升至某物上方 [3] (increase in level) «*lake, sea*» 上涨; **the river level rose so high that the work had to be abandoned** 河水上涨得太高，只好停工 [4] (slope upwards) «*surface, road*» 隆起 [5] (tower) «*tower, wall, peak*» 矗立; **the cliff rose above us** 峭壁耸立在我们上方; **to ~ to a height of 2 metres** 高达 2 米 [6] (be built) 被建起; **an office block rose on the site of the old temple** 老寺院旧址上建起了一座办公大楼 [7] formal (stand up) 站起来; **'all ~'** “全体起立”; **to ~ from** 从…上站起来 ‹*chair, floor*›; 从…旁站起来 ‹*desk, table*›; **to ~ on tiptoe/to one's feet** 踮着脚/站起身来; **I rose to take my leave** 我起身告辞 [8] formal (get out of bed) 起床; **~ and shine!** hum 赶快起床！ [9] formal (come to life again) 复活; **to ~ from the dead** 起死回生 [10] esp Brit formal (adjourn) «*committee, parliament*» 闭会; «*court*» 退庭 [11] (increase) «*amount, value, volume, rate, cost of living, pressure*» 增加; «*price*» 上涨; «*level, standard, temperature*» 提高; «*inflation*» 加剧; **to ~ in** 增加 ‹*amount, value, volume, pressure*›; 提高 ‹*level, standard, temperature, rate, price*›; **to ~ to/above sth.** 增加到/超出某数量 [12] (become louder) «*sound*» 变响; (become higher in pitch) «*sound*» 提高; **his voice rose to a shout** 他提高嗓门喊起来; **his voice rose in anger** 他气得嗓门大了起来 [13] (blow stronger) 刮得更猛; **the wind continued to ~** 风力继续增强 [14] (intensify) «*hopes, anger, frustration*» 变得强烈; «*tension*» 加剧; «*pressure*» 增大 [15] (progress) «*person*» 更加成功; **to ~ in the world** 事业发达; **to ~ (from sth.) to sth.** （从某职位）升至 ‹*director*›; **to ~ to fame** 成名; **he rose from apprentice to manager** 他从学徒步步晋升为经理; **she rose from nothing to become a major Hollywood star** 她从一个无名小卒成了好莱坞大明星 [16] Culin «*dough, bread*» 发酵 [17] (stand on end) «*hair, fur*» 竖起 [18] (appear on skin) «*bump, weal*» 出现; **blisters rose on his burned hand** 他烧伤的手上起了水疱 [19] formal (with embarrassment) «*colour*» 涨红; **she could feel her colour rising** 她觉得自己脸红了 [20] (give higher reading) «*barometer, glass, mercury*» 读数升高 [21] Geog (have source) 发源; **to ~ in** «*river, stream*» 发源于 ‹*mountains, area*› [22] (be produced) «*cry, cheer*» 发出; **a great shout rose from the crowd** 人群中一声大喊 [23] formal (rebel) 起义; **to ~ against sb./sth.** 奋起反抗某人/某事物 [24] **rising** colloq (approaching) 接近; **she was thirty-nine, rising forty** 她 39 岁，快到 40 了
B *n* [1] (increase) (in amount, number, rate, value, volume, cost of living) 增加; (in level, standard) 提高; (in price) 上涨; (in temperature, pressure) 升高; (in inflation) 加剧; **a ~ in sth.** 某物的增加; **a ~ from sth. to sth.** 从某水平到某水平的增长; **to be on the ~** «*crime, number*» 在增加; «*inflation*» 在加剧; «*prices*» 在上涨 [2] (increase in importance) (of person) 出头; (of country, company, empire) 兴起; (of doctrine, ideology) 发展; **the ~ and fall of the Roman Empire** 罗马帝国的兴衰; **her ~ to fame** 她的成名; **his ~ through the ranks** 他地位的上升 [3] Brit (increase in pay) 加薪; **a ~ in salary, a salary ~** 加薪 [4] (upward movement) 上升; (of water, liquid, sea) 上涨; **the ~ and fall of his chest** 他胸膛的起伏; **a ~ into/to sth.** 进入/到某处的上升; **we watched the balloon's slow ~ into the air** 我们看着气球缓缓升到了空中; **the submarine's ~ to the surface** 潜艇浮出水面 [5] (hill) 小山 [6] (slope) 坡; **there's a slight ~ in the road here** 路这处有一个缓坡 [7] (source) 源头; **the river has its ~ in …** 这条河的源头在…; **to give ~ to** 招致 ‹*rumour*›; 引起 ‹*problem, emotion*›

Phrasal verbs
• **rise above** *vt* [~ **above sth.**] [1] (not be hindered by) 不受…的影响 ‹*misfortune, problems, background*› [2] (be morally superior to) 摆脱 ‹*bitterness, jealousy, disagreements*› [3] (be better than) 超出 ‹*standard, level*›
• **rise to** *vt* [~ **to sth.**] [1] (meet successfully) 能够应付 ‹*occasion, task*›; **he was determined to ~ to the challenge** 他决心克服困难，迎接挑战 [2] (react to) 对…作出反应 ‹*insult, provocation*›; **he didn't ~ to my teasing** 我戏弄他，他并未被激怒
• **rise up** *vi* [1] (move upwards) «*aircraft, bird, ball, balloon*» 上升; «*steam, smoke*» 升腾 [2] (tower, wall) 矗立; **the mountains ~ up on all sides** 四周山峰高耸 [3] (be produced) «*shout, cry*» 发出; **a tremendous cheer rose up from the audience** 观众当中欢呼声雷动 [4] (rebel) «*people, region*» 奋起反抗; **to ~ up in revolt** *or* **rebellion** 起来造反

risen /ˈrɪzn/
A *pp* ▸ **rise A**
B *adj* 复活的

riser /ˈraɪzə(r)/ *n* [1] (person) **an early/a late ~** 早起/晚起的人 [2] (on staircase) 楼梯踏步竖板

risible /ˈrɪzəbl/ *adj* 可笑的 ‹*idea, proposal*›

rising /ˈraɪzɪŋ/
A *adj* [1] (moving upwards) 上升的 ‹*sun, trend*›; 向上倾斜的 ‹*ground*› [2] (increasing) 上涨的 ‹*prices*›; 增长的 ‹*unemployment, costs*›; 加剧的 ‹*inflation, tension*› [3] (becoming successful) 崭露头角的 ‹*actor, politician*›
B *n* 叛乱; **an armed ~** 武装叛乱

rising: ~ damp *n* [u] Brit [从地下渗入墙壁的] 上升潮气; **~ fives** *npl* Brit 快五岁的儿童 [尤指可上学的适龄儿童]

risk /rɪsk/
A *n* [1] [u] (chance, peril) 风险; **a ~ of sth.** …的风险; **a ~ of sb./sth. doing sth.** 某人/某物做某事的风险; **a ~ (that) …** …的风险; **there's a ~ of her failing** *or* **that she'll fail** 她有遭遇失败的危险; **is there any ~ of him catching the illness?** 他有染病的危险吗？; **there is no ~ to consumers** 对消费者没有风险; **to be at ~** 有危险; **my job is at ~** 我有失业的危险; **to be at ~ from starvation** 面临饥饿的威胁; **children at ~** 处于危险中的孩子们; **to put sth. at ~** 使某事物受到威胁; **to put oneself/one's life/one's health at ~** 使自己/生命/健康受到威胁; **at one's own ~** 自己负责; **'at owner's ~'** “由所有人自行负责”; **he saved the child at considerable ~ to himself** 他冒着相当大的危险救了那个孩子 [2] [c] (possible bad situation) 危险; **it's not worth the ~** 不值得冒这个险; **without ~s to health** 不危害健康地; **they run a higher ~ of cancer** 他们患癌症的风险比较大; **to run the ~ of a strike/being arrested** 冒着罢工/被捕的危险; **to take ~s** 冒险; **at the ~ of sounding ungrateful/showing one's ignorance** 冒着显得忘恩负义/无知的危险 [3] [c] (potentially bad person) 危险人物; (thing) 具有危害性的事物 [4] [c] Insur (person) 被保险人; (company) 保险对象; **to be a good/bad (insurance) ~** 风险小/大等的保险对象 [5] [c] Insur (thing that is insured against) 险别; **an all-~s policy** 全险保单 [6] [u and c] Fin 风险; **to spread a ~** 分散风险
B *vt* [1] (endanger) «*person*» 使面临危险; **to ~ one's life** 冒生命危险; **to ~ one's health** 使健康遭受威胁; **to ~ one's all** 押上一切; **to ~ one's neck (doing sth.)** 冒死（做某事） [2] (dare to experience) «*person*» 冒…的风险 ‹*injury, loss, failure*›; **to ~ death** 冒死; **to ~ doing sth.** 冒险做某事 [3] (take chance on) 大胆做; **we decided to ~ it** 我们决定豁出去了; **let's ~ it anyway** 不管怎么说，我们冒险试一试吧

risk: ~ capital *n* [u] = **venture capital**; **~ factor** *n* 风险因素

riskiness /ˈrɪskɪnɪs/ *n* [u] 风险性

risk: ~ management *n* [u] 风险管理; **~ manager** ▸ **p. 409** *n* 风险管理经理; **~-taker** *n* 冒险者; **~-taking** *n* [u] 冒险

risky /ˈrɪski/ *adj* 危险的 ‹*course of action, journey*›; 有风险的 ‹*investment, business*›

risotto /rɪˈzɒtəʊ/ *n* [c and u] (*pl* **~s**) 意大利烩饭

risqué /ˈriːskeɪ, Amer rɪˈskeɪ/ *adj* 有伤风化的 ‹*clothing, story, joke*›

rissole /ˈrɪsəʊl/ *n* 炸肉饼

rite /raɪt/ *n* 1 Relig 仪式; **to perform a ~** 举行仪式; **marriage/funeral ~s** 婚礼/葬礼; **to administer the last ~s** 举行临终仪式 2 (custom, convention) 礼节; **fertility ~s** 生殖庆典; **initiation ~s** 入会仪式; **a ~ of passage** [标志人生重要阶段的] 通过仪式

ritual /ˈrɪtʃʊəl/
A *n* 1 [u] Relig 仪式; **the ~ of the Catholic Church** 天主教仪式; **the ~ of the law** 法律程序 2 [c] (ceremony) 程式; **a solemn ~** 庄严的庆典; **pagan/satanic ~s** 异教徒/魔鬼的仪式; **the courtship ~ of some animals and birds** 某些动物和鸟类的求偶仪式 3 [c] (regular behaviour) 惯例; **to make a ~ of sth.** 使某事成为习惯; **he went through his ~ of filling and lighting his pipe** 他例行公事地把烟丝塞进烟斗, 然后点燃
B *adj* 仪式的; **a ~ dance/murder** 仪式上的舞蹈/活人祭仪; **~ phrases of greeting** 惯常的招呼语; **a ~ visit** 礼节性的访问; **~ sexual abuse** 仪式性虐待

ritual abuse *n* [u] 宗教仪式性侵害

ritualism /ˈrɪtʃʊəlɪzəm/ *n* [u] 仪式主义

ritualistic /ˌrɪtʃʊəˈlɪstɪk/ *adj* 仪式的 ‹*words, abuse*›; 老一套的 ‹*activity, ceremony*›; **~ sacrifice/slaughter** 仪式祭祀/宰杀

ritually /ˈrɪtʃʊəli/ *adv* 仪式性地 ‹*wash, bless, kill*›; 惯常地 ‹*eat, serve*›

ritzy /ˈrɪtzi/ *adj* colloq 豪华的 ‹*decor, hotel*›; 时尚的 ‹*clothing*›

rival /ˈraɪvl/
A *n* 竞争对手; **a ~ for** *or* **in sth.** 某方面的竞争对手; **~s in love** 情敌; **without ~** 无与伦比
B *adj* 相互竞争的 ‹*firm, group, suitor*›; 对抗的 ‹*competitor, team*›
C *vt* (*pres p etc.* **-ll-** Brit, **-l-** Amer) 与…不相上下 ‹*person, thing*›; **to ~ sb. (for** *or* **in sth.)** (在某方面) 比得上某人; **his stupidity is ~led only by his meanness** 他有多卑鄙, 就有多愚蠢

rivalry /ˈraɪvlri/ *n* 1 [u] (adversarial state) 竞争; **~ with sb./sth.** 与某人/某物的竞争; **~ between sb./sth.** 某人/某物之间的竞争; **fierce** *or* **intense** *or* **keen ~** 激烈的竞争 2 [c] (competition) 竞争行为; **political rivalries** 政治对抗

riven /ˈrɪvn/ *adj* liter 撕裂的; **a family ~ by ancient feuds** 因世仇而四分五裂的家族; **a tree ~ by lightning** 被闪电劈开的树

river /ˈrɪvə(r)/ *n* 1 (gen) 河流; **the R~ Thames/Seine/Amazon** 泰晤士河/塞纳河/亚马孙河; **down/up the ~** 向下游/上游; **to sell sb. down the ~** colloq 出卖某人 2 (of lava, mud, oil) 涌流; **~s of lava flowed down the mountainside** 大量的熔岩顺着山坡流下来; **~s of blood flowed during the war** 战争期间血流成河

river: ~bank *n* 河岸; **along the ~bank** 沿着河岸; **~ basin** *n* 流域; **the Congo ~ basin** 刚果河流域; **~bed** *n* 河床; **a dried-up ~bed** 干涸的河床; **~boat** *n* 内河船; **~ bus** *n* 水上巴士; **~front** *n* 滨河地区; **~ mouth** *n* 河口; **~ police** *n* [u] + *v pl* 水警

riverside /ˈrɪvəsaɪd/ *n* 河畔; **to go for a walk along the ~** 沿着河边散步; **a ~ inn** 河边小旅馆; **a ~ car park** 河边停车场

river traffic *n* [u] 内河航运船只

rivet /ˈrɪvɪt/
A *n* 铆钉
B *vt* 1 (fasten, secure) 铆接; **to ~ together** 铆接在一起; **to ~ down** *or* **in place** 用铆钉固定住 2 (fix) 使…固定 ‹*person, eyes, gaze*›; **we stood ~ed to the spot with fear** 我们吓得呆若木鸡 3 (hold attention of) 吸引住 ‹*audience*›; **we were absolutely ~ed by the story** 我们完全被那个故事吸引住了

riveter /ˈrɪvɪtə(r)/ ▸**p. 409** *n* 铆工

riveting /ˈrɪvɪtɪŋ/ *adj* 引人入胜的; **a ~ thought** 极吸引人的想法

riviera /ˌrɪvɪˈeərə/ *n* 1 (coastal region) 海滨度假胜地 2 **the R~** (region in France, Italy) 里维埃拉地区 [法国、摩纳哥及意大利的地中海沿岸地区]

rivulet /ˈrɪvjʊlɪt/ *n* 小溪; **~s of sweat** fig 津津汗水

Riyadh /riːˈæd/ *pr n* 利雅得

riyal /rɪˈjɑːl/ ▸**p. 174** *n* = **rial**

RM *abbr* Brit = **Royal Marines**

RMB *abbr* = **renminbi**

RN *abbr* 1 Brit = **Royal Navy** 2 Amer = **registered nurse**

RNA *abbr* = **ribonucleic acid**

RNIB *abbr* Brit = **Royal National Institute for the Blind** 皇家国立盲人学院

RNLI *abbr* Brit = **Royal National Lifeboat Institution** 皇家全国救生艇协会

roach¹ /rəʊtʃ/ *n* (fish) (*pl* **roach**) 拟鲤

roach² *n* Amer colloq (insect) (*pl* **~es**) 蟑螂

road /rəʊd/ *n* ▸**p. 905** 1 [u and c] (between towns) 道路; **the ~ to Leeds, the Leeds ~** 通往利兹的公路; **the ~ from Edinburgh to Glasgow** 从爱丁堡到格拉斯哥的公路; **the ~ back to sth.** 回某处的路; **are we on the right ~ for Oxford?** 我们走的这条路是去牛津的吗?; **the ~ north/inland** 通往北方/内地的路; **the ~ home** 回家的路; **to follow the ~ ahead** 沿着前面的路走; **a country ~** 乡间小路; **~ safety/condition** 道路安全/路况; **by ~** 由公路; **transported by ~** 由公路运输的; **off the ~** 不能行驶; **on the ~** (on tour) 在途中; (drivable) 可行驶; (homeless) 在流浪; **I've been on the ~ all night** 我整晚都在旅行; **after three hours on the ~** 旅行 3 小时后; **to go on the ~ with the show** 去巡回演出; **to be/get back on the ~** ‹*car*› 重新上路; **let's get the show on the ~!** colloq (start an activity) 我们开始吧!; (start a journey) 我们上路吧!; **to hit the ~** colloq 出发; **to take to the ~** 出发; **one for the ~** colloq 临行前的最后一杯酒; **the ~ to hell is paved with good intentions** Prov 光想不练是不够的 2 [c] (in towns) 街道; **across the ~** 在街对面; **at the top** *or* **end of the ~** 在街的尽头; **along** *or* **down the ~** 沿着街; **it's just down the ~** 它就在这条街前面不远处; **my friend from down the ~** 住在这条街那边的我的朋友; **35 York Road** *or* **Rd** 约克路 35 号 3 [c] fig (way) 途径; **a difficult ~ to follow** 艰难的途径; **to be on the ~ to success/disaster** 走向成功/灾难; **we think we're on the right ~** 我们认为我们的路子是对的; **we don't want to go down that ~** 我们不想采用那种方法; **(further) down** *or* **along the ~** 在将来; **further down** *or* **along the ~ (to sth.)** 在 (成就某事的) 道路上迈进一步; **today the country is much further along the ~ to democracy** 如今该国在民主的道路上取得了很大进展 4 [c] Brit colloq (way) 路线; **to be in the** *or* **sb.'s ~** 挡某人的道; **to get out of the** *or* **sb.'s ~** 给某人让路; **just keep out of the ~ and you won't get into trouble** 你只要不碍事就不会有麻烦 5 [c] Hist (trade route) 贸易路线; **the Silk R~** 丝绸之路 6 [c] *usu pl* Naut 近岸锚地; **the deeper waters of Boston R~s** 波士顿近岸锚地中较深的水域

road: ~ accident *n* 道路交通事故; **~bed** *n* 1 (of road) 路床; 2 Rail 路基; **~block** *n* 路障; **a police/army ~block** 警方/军方路障; **~ bridge** *n* 公路桥; **~ fund licence** *n* Brit 路税付讫证; **~ haulage** *n* [u] 公路运输; **~ haulier** ▸**p. 409** *n* (company) 公路运输公司; (person) 公路运输承运人; **~ hog** *n* colloq 猪头司机 [指莽撞而不顾及他人的司机]; **~holding** *n* [u] [车辆的] 抓地性; **~house** *n* 路边旅馆; **~ hump** *n* [道路上的] 减速垄

roadie /ˈrəʊdi/ *n* colloq 巡回乐队设备管理员

road: ~ junction *n* 交叉路口; **~ kill** *n* 1 [c] (killing of an animal) 路杀 [路上撞死动物]; 2 [u] (animals killed) 路杀动物 [指路上被撞死的动物]; **~ manager** ▸**p. 409** *n* 巡回乐队演出经纪人; **~ map** *n* 1 lit (for motorists) 公路交通图; 2 fig (plan of action) 路线图; **~ movie** *n* 公路电影; **~ noise** *n* [u] 路面噪声; **~ pricing** *n* [u] [繁忙路段的] 道路收费; **~ rage** *n* [u] 公路泄愤 [因交通不畅引发的情绪激愤行为]; **a ~ rage incident** 公路泄愤事件; **~roller** *n* 压路机; **~ sense** *n* [u] Brit 路感; **~show** *n* 1 Radio, TV [远赴外地拍摄的] 现场节目; 2 (political campaign) 巡回宣传; (promotional campaign) 巡回推销; **~side** *n* 路边;

r

Rivers

■ The word 河 (river) always follows the name of the river in Chinese, and no article is used before the name of a river:

the Thames
= 泰晤士河

the River Danube
= 多瑙河

the Mississippi River
= 密西西比河

■ 'River' may be translated as 河, 江, or 水:

the Huai River
= 淮河

the Yellow River
= 黄河

the Chang Jiang
or *the Yangtze River*
= 长江

the Pearl River
= 珠江

the Han River
or *the Hanshui River*
or *the Han Shui*
= 汉水

the Xiu River
or *the Xiushui River*
or *the Xiu Shui*
= 秀水

Combinations

River Rhine cruises
= 莱茵河观光船游览

a Chang Jiang lighthouse
= 长江上的灯塔

a tributary of the Amazon River
= 亚马孙河的一条支流

the source of the Jin River
= 锦江水源

the mouth of the Red River
= 红河河口

the Nile estuary
= 尼罗河河口

the upper/middle/lower reaches of the Yellow River
= 黄河上游 / 中游 / 下游

at *or* by the ~side 在路边; along *or* by the ~side 沿着路边; a ~side café 路边咖啡馆; ~ sign *n* 路标

road movie

公路电影。一种电影类型，20 世纪 60 年代出现于美国。剧情一般为主人公结伴开车逃避警察的追捕，多含暴力镜头。逃亡的旅程是主人公发现自我的过程，同时也是对社会现实的批判。知名的影片包括《逍遥骑士》（*Easy Rider*, 1969）、《末路狂花》（*Thelma and Louise*, 1991）等。

roadster /ˈrəʊdstə(r)/ *n* 敞篷双座汽车

road: ~sweeper ▸p. 409 *n* (person) 街道清扫工; (machine) 街道清扫机; ~ **tax** *n* [u] Brit 公路税; ~ **tax disc** 公路税付讫证

road test

A *n* **1** (of vehicle, engine) 道路试验 **2** fig (of equipment) 实地测试 **3** = **driving test**

B **road-test** *vt* **1** (test out) 对…进行道路试验 ‹*vehicle, engine*› **2** fig 对…进行实地测试 ‹*equipment*›

road: ~ transport *n* [u] 公路运输; ~ **trip** *n* **1** (journey) 公路旅行; **2** Amer (away game) 客场比赛; ~ **user** *n* 道路使用者; **~way** *n* **1** (road) 道路; **2** (part for vehicle use) 车道; **3** (of bridge, railway) 车行道; **~works** *npl* 道路施工; **~worthy** *adj* 适合行驶的

r

roam /rəʊm/

A *vi* «*person, group*» 漫步; «*animal*» 游荡; «*gaze*» 扫视; «*thoughts*» 徜徉; **to ~ about the streets/the countryside** 在街上/在乡间溜达; **all the while his eyes were ~ing round the room** 他的目光一直在房间里四下扫视

B *vt* 在…漫步 ‹*streets, country, hills*›; 漫游 ‹*world*›

C *n* 漫步; **to go for** *or* **have a ~** 去溜达

Phrasal verb

- **roam around** *vi* «*person*» 四处走动; «*animal*» 游荡; «*gaze, eyes*» 扫视; «*thoughts*» 徜徉

roamer /ˈrəʊmə(r)/ *n* (person) 漫游者; (animal) 流浪的动物

roaming /ˈrəʊmɪŋ/ *n* [u] **1** (wandering) 闲逛 **2** Telecom 漫游

roan /rəʊn/ *n* 毛色斑杂的动物 [尤指马或牛]

roar /rɔː(r)/

A *n* **1** (of large animal) 咆哮; **to give a ~** 嗥叫 **2** (of person) 叫喊; **he gave a ~ of rage** 他怒吼了一声 **3** (of amusement) 大笑声; **a ~ of laughter** 一阵哈哈大笑 **4** (of applause) 鼓掌声; **the audience gave a ~ of applause** 观众报以雷鸣般的掌声 **5** (of machine, traffic) 轰鸣声 **6** (of water, wind) 呼啸声; **the wind howled above the ~ of the sea** 风在咆哮的大海上呼号; **the ~ of the waterfall deafened them** 瀑布的轰鸣声让他们什么也听不见 **7** (of flames) 呼呼声; **the ~ of the forest fire was terrifying** 熊熊燃烧的林火令人恐惧

B *vt* **1** (shout) 大喊; **to ~ one's approval** 大声叫好; **'quiet!' he ~ed** "安静！"他吼道 **2** (rev up) 使…快速运转 ‹*engine*›

C *vi* **1** (howl) «*lion, bull*» 吼叫; **to ~ with fury** 怒吼 **2** (bellow) «*person*» 大喊; **to ~ at sb.** 冲某人喊叫 **3** (shout together) «*crowd*» 喧哗; **to ~ with pain/rage** 痛苦/愤怒地大喊大叫 **4** (laugh) 放声大笑; **to ~ in amusement** 开心地大笑; **to ~ with laughter** 哈哈大笑 **5** (rumble) «*machine, traffic*» 轰鸣; **the car ~ed into life** 汽车轰鸣着发动起来 **6** (move noisily) 呼啸而行; **to ~ past sb./sth.** 从某人/某物旁呼啸而过; **to ~ along** 轰鸣着前行; **the car ~ed away** 汽车呼啸而去; **to ~ down/up the street** 轰鸣着沿街开去/开来 **7** (make long, loud, deep sound) «*wind, sea*» 呼啸; «*waterfall*» 轰鸣; «*fire, flames*» 熊熊燃烧

Phrasal verb

- **roar out** *vt* [~ **sth. out,** ~ **out sth.**] 大声喊出 ‹*command*›; **the fans ~ed out their approval** 粉丝们大声叫好

roaring /ˈrɔːrɪŋ/

A *adj attrib* **1** (expressing pain, anger, approval) 吼叫的 ‹*lion, crowd*›; ~ **drunk** 烂醉的; ~ **mad** 暴怒的 **2** (making deep sound) 隆隆的 ‹*thunder*›; 咆哮的 ‹*sea*›; 呼啸的 ‹*wind*›; **a ~ fire** 熊熊大火; **the ~ forties** 咆哮西风带 **3** (highly popular or successful) 成功的; **to do a ~ trade** 生意火爆; **the ~ twenties** 繁荣的 20 年代; **a ~ success** 巨大的成功

B *n* [u] **1** (of lion, person) 吼叫声 **2** (of thunder, waterfall, machinery) 轰鸣声

roast /rəʊst/

A *vt* **1** (cook) 烤 ‹*meat, potatoes*› **2** (process) 烘焙 ‹*coffee beans, peanuts*›; 焙烧 ‹*metal, ore*› **3** (in heat of fire) 烤; (in heat of sun) 晒; **to ~ one's toes in front of the fire** 在炉火前烤脚趾; **I'm being ~ed alive in this heat!** 太热了，我要被烤焦了！ **4** colloq (criticize severely) 猛烈抨击 ‹*play, film, book*›

B *vi* **1** (cook) «*meat, potatoes*» 烤 **2** (process) «*coffee beans*» 烘焙 **3** (in heat of fire) 烤火; (in heat of sun) 晒太阳

C *adj* 烤过的; ~ **beef/potatoes/vegetables/chestnuts** 烤牛肉/土豆/青菜/板栗

D *n* **1** (meat) 烤肉 **2** (dish, meal) 烤制的饭菜 **3** (outdoor party) 户外烧烤; **a pig ~** 乳猪烧烤野餐

roaster /ˈrəʊstə(r)/ *n* **1** (container) 烘烤器 **2** (food) 适合烧烤的食物 [尤指鸡肉]

roasting /ˈrəʊstɪŋ/

A *adj* **1** (being cooked) 在烘烤的; ~ **coffee beans** 正在烘焙的咖啡豆 **2** colloq (hot, dry) 炙热的 ‹*weather*›; **to be ~** «*person, room*» 非常燥热; ~ **heat** 酷热

B *n* colloq 猛烈抨击; **to give sb. a ~** 猛烈抨击某人

roasting tin *n* 烤盘

rob /rɒb/ *vt* (*pres p etc.* **-bb-**) **1** (take property from illegally) 抢劫; **to ~ sb./sth. (of sth.)** 抢劫某人/某物（的某物）; **I was ~bed of my life savings** 我被抢走了一生的积蓄; **to ~ Peter to pay Paul** 借新债还旧账 **2** (deprive) 剥夺; **to ~ sb. of their sleep/rights** 使某人不能入睡/剥夺某人的权利 **3** Sport colloq 抢…的球 ‹*opposing player*›

robber /ˈrɒbə(r)/ *n* 强盗; **a bank/train ~** 银行/列车抢劫犯

robber baron *n* 强盗富豪

robbery /ˈrɒbəri/ *n* [u] **1** (activity) 抢劫; **armed/daylight/highway ~** 持械/光天化日下的/拦路抢劫; **it's sheer ~!** fig 这完全是敲竹杠！ **2** [c] (incident) 抢劫案; **three robberies in one week** 一周内发生的三起抢劫案

robe /rəʊb/

A *n* **1** (outer garment) 长袍; **a beach ~** 沙滩袍 **2** (ceremonial garment) [标志级别、职位等的] 礼服; **to wear one's ~ of office** 穿上制服; **coronation/christening ~** 加冕礼袍/洗礼袍 **3** Amer (bathrobe) 浴袍

B *vt* 给…穿上长袍; **~d in silk/in white** 身穿丝质/白色长袍; **black-~d academics** 身穿黑色礼袍的大学教师

robin /ˈrɒbɪn/ *n* **1** (European) ~ **(redbreast)** 欧亚鸲 **2** (North American) 旅鸫

robot /ˈrəʊbɒt/ *n* **1** (in industry, science fiction) 机器人 **2** fig (person) 机械呆板的人 **3** S Afr (traffic lights) 交通信号灯

robotic /rəʊˈbɒtɪk/ *adj* **1** (relating to robots) 机器人的 ‹*movement, operation*›; 自动控制的 ‹*equipment, system*› **2** (like a robot) 机械呆板的 ‹*movement, gesture*›

robotics /rəʊˈbɒtɪks/ *npl* + *v sing* 机器人学

robust /rəʊˈbʌst/ *adj* **1** (healthy, strong) 强壮的 ‹*person*›; 结实的 ‹*furniture*›; 强劲的 ‹*economy*›; 旺盛的 ‹*appetite*›; 茁壮的 ‹*plant*› **2** (uncompromising) 坚定的 ‹*defence, tactics*›; 斩钉截铁的 ‹*reply*› **3** (strong) 醇厚的 ‹*wine*›; 浓郁的 ‹*aroma*›; 浓烈的 ‹*smell*›

robustly /rəʊˈbʌstli/ *adv* **1** (strongly) 结实地 ‹*built, made*› **2** (vigorously) 斩钉截铁地 ‹*answer*›; 坚定地 ‹*defend*›

robustness /rəʊˈbʌstnɪs/ *n* [u] **1** (of object) 结实; (of economy) 强劲 **2** (of reply) 斩钉截铁

rock[1] /rɒk/

A *n* **1** [u] (substance) 岩石; **solid/molten ~** 坚固的岩石/熔岩 **2** [c] (rising from ground) 石山; **(as) firm** *or* **solid as a ~** (sturdy) 坚如磐石的; (determined) 坚定的; (reliable) 十分可靠的; **to be solid as a ~ in defence** 防守固若金汤; **(as) steady as a ~** (not moving) 岿然不动的; (steady and calm) 沉着冷静的; (reliable) 十分可靠的; **(as) hard as a ~** (solid and rigid) 坚硬的; (unemotional) 冷漠的; **between a ~ and a hard place** fig colloq 进退两难的; **to be caught** *or* **stuck between a ~ and a hard place** 进退两难; **he was a real ~ in my life** fig 他是我生命中真正的依傍 **3** [c] (rising from seabed) 礁石; **the ship hit the ~s** fig 船触礁了; **to be on the ~s** Naut 触礁; fig (in predicament) 陷于困境; fig «*business*» 濒临破产; fig (with ice) 加冰块的; **their marriage was on the ~s** 他们的婚姻濒临破裂; **Scotch on the ~s** 加冰块的苏格兰威士忌酒 **4** [c] (boulder) 巨岩块; **'danger: falling ~s'** "危险：前方有滚石" **5** [c] Amer (stone) 石块 **6** [u] Brit (sweet) 棒棒糖 **7** [c] colloq (jewel) 宝石; (diamond) 钻石 **8** [u and c] colloq (crack cocaine) 强效可卡因

B **rocks** *npl* sl (testicles) 睾丸; **to get one's ~s off** (enjoy oneself) 做开心的事; (have orgasm) 达到性高潮

rock[2]

A *vt* **1** (move gently) «*child, wind, waves*» 轻轻摇晃 ‹*person, cradle, boat*›; **I ~ed the baby to sleep** 我轻轻摇着婴儿入睡; ▸**cradle A1** **2** (shake) «*earthquake, bomb, wave*» 使…剧烈晃动 ‹*town, vessel*› **3** (shock) «*scandal, revelation, news*» 使…震惊 ‹*government, country, society*›

B *vi* **1** (sway) «*person, ship, cradle*» 轻轻摇晃; **he sat ~ing in his chair** 他坐在椅子上轻轻摇晃着; **to ~ back and forth** *or* **backwards and forwards** 前摇后晃; **to ~ from side to side** 左右摇晃; **to ~ with laughter** 笑得前仰后合 **2** (shake) «*building, ground*» 剧烈摇晃 **3** colloq (be excellent) «*person, film, book*» 很棒; **her new movie ~s!** 她的新电影棒极了！ **4** colloq (be lively) «*club*» 挤满欢快起舞的人; **by midnight, the place is ~ing** 到午夜时分，全场的人都跳起舞来 **5** dated colloq (dance) «*person*» 跳摇滚舞; **they seemed ready to ~ all night long** 他们似乎准备跳一晚上摇滚舞 **6** dated colloq (play music) «*person, band*» 演奏摇滚乐; **they've been ~ing (away) for more than twenty years now** 他们演奏摇滚乐已有 20 多年

C *v refl* **to ~ oneself** 轻轻摇晃; **he sat ~ing himself in his chair** 他坐在摇椅里轻轻地摇晃着

D *n* [u] 摇滚乐; **a ~ band/concert/musician** 摇滚乐队/音乐会/乐师

rockabilly /ˈrɒkəbɪli/ *n* [u] [起源于美国东南部的] 乡村摇滚乐

rock: ~ and roll *n* [u] 摇滚乐; **the ~ and roll era** 摇滚乐时代; ~ **band** *n* 摇滚乐队; ~ **bottom** *n* [u] 最低点; **to reach** *or* **hit** *or* **touch ~ bottom** 降到最低点; **to be at ~ bottom** 处于最低水平; **~-bottom prices/rates** 最低价格/费用; ~ **cake,** ~ **bun** *ns* Brit 岩皮糕饼; ~ **candy** *n* [u] Amer 冰晶硬糖; ~ **carving** *n* 石刻; ~ **climber** *n* 攀岩者; ~ **climbing** ▸p. 307 *n* [u] 攀岩; **to go ~ climbing** 去攀岩

rocker /ˈrɒkə(r)/ *n* **1** (on cradle, chair) 弧形摇杆; **to be/go off one's ~** colloq 疯了/发疯 **2** Amer (chair) 摇椅 **3** (switch) 簧压摇杆开关 **4** Brit Hist 摇滚小子 [指身穿皮夹克骑摩托车的青少年]

rocker: ~ **arm** *n* 摇臂; ~ **switch** *n* 摇杆开关

rockery /'rɒkəri/ *n* 假山花园

rocket /'rɒkɪt/

A *n* **1** (spacecraft) 火箭; (missile) 火箭弹; (firework) 焰火; **a space/carrier** ~ 太空/运载火箭; **like a** ~ 迅速地 **2** Brit colloq (severe reprimand) 斥责; **to give sb. a** ~ 痛骂某人; **to get a** ~ 受到斥责

B *vi* **1** (increase rapidly) 飙升; **to** ~ **(up)** «*price, profits, amount*» 急速上升 **2** (move quickly) «*person*» 飞奔; «*vehicle*» 疾驰; **to** ~ *or* **go** ~**ing along/away/past** 飞速行进/离开/经过; **to** ~ **to fame** *or* **stardom** 一举成名; **to** ~ **to the top** 蹿升到高层

rocket² *n* [u] Culin 芝麻菜

rocket: ~ **attack** *n* 火箭弹袭击; ~ **engine** *n* 火箭发动机; ~ **fuel** *n* 火箭燃料; ~ **launcher** *n* 火箭筒; ~ **plane** *n* 火箭推进式飞机; ~**-propelled** *adj* 火箭推进的; ~ **propulsion** *n* [u] 火箭推进

rocketry /'rɒkɪtri/ *n* [u] **1** (subject) 火箭学 **2** (use of rockets) 火箭应用

rocket: ~ **science** *n* [u] **1** (designing rockets) 火箭科学; **2** colloq hum (difficult subject) 高深的事; **it isn't** *or* **it's hardly** ~ **science** 这并非难事; ~ **scientist** *n* **1** (specialist in rockets) 火箭科学家; **2** colloq hum (intelligent person) 绝顶聪明的人; ~ **ship** *n* 火箭航天器

rock: ~ **face** *n* 垂直岩石表面; ~**fall** *n* **1** (event) 岩崩; **2** (rocks) 落石; ~ **festival** *n* 摇滚音乐节; ~ **formation** *n* 岩石构造; ~ **garden** *n* 假山庭园; ~ **group** *n* 摇滚乐队; ~**-hard** *adj* 坚如岩石的 ‹*earth, bread, bed*›

Rockies /'rɒki:z/ *pr npl* **the** ~ = **Rocky Mountains**

rocking /'rɒkɪŋ/ *n* [u] 摇摆

rocking: ~ **chair** *n* 摇椅; ~ **horse** *n* [儿童游戏用的] 木马

rock: ~**'n'roll** /,rɒkən'rəʊl/ *n* [u] = ~ **and roll**; ~ **plant** *n* 岩生植物; ~ **pool** *n* 岩石区潮水潭; ~ **salt** *n* [u] 岩盐; ~**slide** *n* (avalanche) 岩滑; (rocks) 岩滑堆; ~ **solid** *adj* 坚固的 ‹*post, building*›; fig 坚如磐石的 ‹*relationship, building, defence, basis*›; ~ **star** *n* 摇滚乐明星; ~**-steady** *adj* 稳固的 ‹*chair, relationship*›; 稳定的 ‹*prices*›; ~ **wool** *n* [u] 矿毛绝缘纤维

rocky /'rɒki/ *adj* **1** (formed of rock) 岩石的 ‹*outcrop, crag*›; **a** ~ **mountain** 石头山 **2** (covered in rocks) 布满岩石的 ‹*ground, shore, hill*›; **a** ~ **road** lit, fig 崎岖的道路 **3** (unsteady) 摇摇晃晃的 ‹*furniture, person*›; **to be** ~ **on one's feet** 站不稳 **4** colloq (unstable) 不牢靠的 ‹*person*›; 不稳定的 ‹*marriage, relationship*›

Rocky Mountains *pr npl* **the** ~ 落基山脉

rococo /rə'kəʊkəʊ/

A *adj* 洛可可式的 ‹*style, architecture, furniture*›

B *n* [u] **the R**~ 洛可可式 [18世纪盛行于欧洲的精巧的装饰风格]

rod /rɒd/ *n* **1** (thin bar) 杆; **a wood/metal** ~ 木杆/铁棒; **a nuclear fuel** ~ 核燃料棒 **2** (for punishment) 棍棒; **spare the** ~ **and spoil the child** Prov 孩子不打不成器; **a** ~ **to beat sb. with** 攻击某人的把柄; **to make a** ~ **for one's own back** 自讨苦吃; **to rule with a** ~ **of iron** 实行铁腕统治 **3** (for fishing) 钓竿; **to fish with** ~ **and line** 用鱼竿钓鱼 **4** Anat 视网膜杆 **5** Amer colloq (pistol) 手枪

rode /rəʊd/ *pt* ▸ **ride A, B**

rodent /'rəʊdnt/ *n* 啮齿动物

rodeo /'rəʊdiəʊ/ *n* (*pl* ~**s**) 牛仔竞技会

roe /rəʊ/ *n* **1** (of female fish) 鱼卵; (when used as food) 鱼子 **2** (of male fish) 雄鱼生殖腺; (when used as food) 鱼白 **3** (edible shrimp) 虾子; (edible crab) 蟹膏

roebuck /'rəʊbʌk/ *n* (*pl* **roebuck**) 雄狍

roe deer *n* 狍

roentgen /'rɜ:ntjən/ *n* 伦琴 [射线剂量单位]

rogation /rə'geɪʃn/ *n* [基督教祈祷日的] 祈祷

roger /'rɒdʒə(r)/

A *excl* **1** Telecom 收到; ~**(, over and out)** 明白，完毕 **2** colloq (OK) 行

B *vt* Brit taboo sl 与…性交 ‹*woman*›

rogue /rəʊg/

A *n* **1** (dishonest man) 无赖; ~**s' gallery** (of criminals) 罪犯照片档案; (of people) 一群讨厌的人 **2** hum (disreputable but charming man) 调皮鬼; **a lovable/handsome** ~ 可爱/英俊的捣蛋鬼

B *modif* **1** Zool 离群的 ‹*beast, elephant*› **2** fig 异常的; **a** ~ **machine/example/politician** 捣蛋机器/坏榜样/胡作非为的政客

roguery /'rəʊgəri/ *n* [u] **1** (dishonesty) 无赖行为 **2** (mischief) 调皮捣蛋

rogue state *n* 无赖国家 [指无视国际法的国家]

roguish /'rəʊgɪʃ/ *adj* 调皮的 ‹*look, wink*›

roguishly /'rəʊgɪʃli/ *adv* 调皮地 ‹*grin, wink*›

roister /'rɔɪstə(r)/ *vi* dated 喧闹作乐

role /rəʊl/ *n* **1** (part in play, film) 角色; **to play** *or* **take the** ~ **of sb./sth.** 扮演某人/某物; **the leading/supporting** ~ 主角/配角; **to be cast in the** ~ **of sb./sth.** (in play, film) 被分派扮演某人/某物; fig 老是被看作某人/某物 **2** (function, importance) 作用; **to fulfil one's** ~ **as wife and mother** 履行作为妻子和母亲的职责; **a vital/key/leading** ~ **(in sth.)** (在某事中) 至关重要/关键/主要的作用

role model *n* 行为榜样; **to use sb. as a** ~ 拿某人当楷模

role play

A *n* **1** [u] (technique) 角色扮演 **2** [c] (instance) 角色扮演活动

B **role-play** *vt* 演习对付 ‹*situation, scene*›

role reversal *n* 角色倒转

roll /rəʊl/

A *vt* **1** (move on wheels, rollers, etc.) 使滚动; **to** ~ **a ball along/across the ground** 沿着球场往前带球/将球传到球场的另一边; **to** ~ **barrels up the ramp** 把桶滚上斜坡; **to** ~ **sth. across sth.** 将…推到某处的另一边 ‹*vehicle, trolley, piano*›; **to** ~ **sth. forward** 往前推某物; **to** ~ **the car back a few metres** 把汽车往回推几米 **2** (make into tube, ball) 将…卷起 ‹*cigarette, paper*›; **to** ~ **into a ball** 将…揉成团 ‹*paper, dough, clay*›; 将…绕成团 ‹*wool*›; **(all)** ~**ed into one** (全部) 融为一体; **to** ~ **one's own** 自己卷烟 **3** (flatten) 擀 ‹*dough, pastry*›; 推平 ‹*lawn*›; 碾平 ‹*road*›; 轧平 ‹*metal*›; **to** ~ **sth. into sth.** 将…轧成某物 ‹*sheets, bars*› **4** (rotate in place) 转动; **to** ~ **sth. between one's fingers** 在手指间转动某物 **5** (turn to different position) 使翻转; **to** ~ **the patient on to his back** 给病人翻身成仰卧姿势 **6** (turn upwards) **to** ~ **one's eyes** 翻白眼 **7** colloq (overturn) «*person, driver*» 弄翻 ‹*vehicle*›; **she** ~**ed her car** 她开翻了车 **8** (fold up) 卷起 ‹*sleeves, trousers*› **9** (start operating) 启动 ‹*movie camera, presses*›; ~ **'em!** colloq 开拍! **10** (throw) 掷 ‹*dice*› **11** colloq (rob) [尤指趁人醉酒或熟睡时] 抢劫 **12** Ling 用颤音发出; **to** ~ **one's r's** 发r的舌尖颤音

B *vi* **1** (move on wheels, rollers, etc.) 滚动; **to** ~ **into sth.** 驶进某处; **to** ~ **down sth.** 滚下 ‹*hill, slope*›; **to** ~ **forwards/backwards** 向前/向后滚动; **to** ~ **to a halt** 滚动后停下 **2** (move by turning over) 翻滚; **to** ~ **behind sb./sth.** 滚到某人/某物后面; **to** ~ **on to sb./sth.** 滚到某人身上/某物上面; **to** ~ **under sb./sth.** 滚到某人身下/某物下面; **the ball** ~**ed over the line** 球滚过了线; **to** ~ **down/off sth.** 滚下/滚离某处; **he** ~**ed out of bed** 他从床上滚了下来; **to** ~ **clear (of sth.)** 避开 (某物); **heads will** ~ **(for sth.)** (因某事物) 有些人要掉脑袋; **to** ~ **with the punches** (in boxing) 躲闪对手的猛击; fig (adapt) 适应艰苦环境 **3** (move smoothly) 平稳移动; **to** ~ **on to** *or* **up sth.** 挪动到某物上; **to** ~ **away** 缓缓离开 **4** (curl up) «*person, hedgehog*» 蜷曲 **5** (rotate in place) 原地打滚; **to** ~ **in sth.** «*person, animal*» 在…里打滚 ‹*grass, mud, dust*›; **to be** ~**ing (in it** *or* **money)** colloq 财源滚滚; **to be** ~**ing in the aisles** 笑声不断; ~**ing drunk** 醉得摇摇晃晃 **6** (turn in different direction) «*person*» 翻身; **to** ~ **on to sth.** 翻身呈某姿势; **to** ~ **on to one's back/front/side** 翻身仰卧/俯卧/侧卧 **7** (rotate lengthwise) «*aircraft, vehicle*» 翻滚 **8** (turn upwards) 向上翻; **her eyes** ~**ed** 她翻了翻白眼 **9** (sway) «*person, ship, aircraft*» 摇晃; **to** ~ **to and fro/from side to side** 前后/左右摇晃 **10** (rumble) «*thunder*» 隆隆响 **11** Mus «*drum*» 咚咚响 **12** (start operating machine) 开动; **cameras,** ~! 开拍! ; **let's** ~ esp Amer colloq 咱们开始吧; **to get (sth.)** ~**ing** colloq (使某事) 顺利开始; **to keep sth.** ~**ing** colloq 使某事顺利进行下去; **let the good times** ~! colloq 尽情享乐吧!

C *n* **1** [c] (cylinder) 一卷; **a** ~ **of film/paper/cloth/tobacco** 一卷胶卷/纸/布/烟 **2** [c] Amer, Austral (wad) 一沓; **a** ~ **of banknotes** 一沓钞票 **3** [c] Amer (packet) 一管; **a** ~ **of candy/mints** 一管糖/薄荷糖果 **4** [c] (of flesh, fat) 一堆; (of skin) 一圈 **5** [c] (piece of bread) 小圆面包 **6** [u and c] (pressed meat) 肉卷 **7** [c] (in gymnastics) 翻跟头; **a forward/backward** ~ 前/后滚翻 **8** [c] Aviat (rotation in flight) 翻滚 **9** [u and c] (swaying) 摇晃; **the car corners well with a minimum of** ~ 这辆车拐弯性能良好，晃动轻微; **to walk with a** ~ **of the hips** 走起路来臀部一扭一扭的 **10** [c] (throw of dice) 掷骰子; **to be on a** ~ colloq 连连获胜 **11** [c] (of thunder) 隆隆声 **12** [c] (of drums) 咚咚声 **13** [c] (register) 花名册; **we have about ninety members on our** *or* **the** ~**(s)** 我们的名单上大约有 90 名会员; **to call** *or* **take the** ~ 点名; **a class** ~ 班级学生名册; **an electoral** ~ 选民名册; **to be struck off the** ~ 被除名 **14** [c] (number on list) 名单总人数; **falling school** ~**s** 下降的在校学生人数

Phrasal verbs

- **roll about** *vi* Brit = **roll around**
- **roll along** *vi* «*vehicle*» 平稳向前行驶
- **roll around** *vi* «*person, animal*» 原地打滚; «*marble, tin*» 原地滚动; **to** ~ **around on the grass** 在草地上打滚
- **roll back**

A *vi* «*person, computer*» 回退

B *vt* [~ **sth. back,** ~ **back sth.**]
1 (roll up) 卷起 ‹*carpet, sleeve*› **2** (reverse progress of) «*person, event, film*» 使…倒流 ‹*years*› **3** (move farther away) 使…后退 ‹*frontier, desert*› **4** Mil «*troops*» 击退 ‹*enemy*› **5** (reduce power of) 削弱…的影响 ‹*state, ideology*› **6** Fin 使…回落 ‹*prices, inflation*›

- **roll down** *vt* [~ **sth. down,** ~ **down sth.**] 放下 ‹*sleeve, trouser leg, blind*›
- **roll in**

A *vi* **1** colloq (arrive in large numbers) «*letters, offers, money, tourists*» 纷至沓来 **2** colloq (arrive late) «*person*» 姗姗来迟; **he didn't** ~ **in until 3 am** 他直到午 3 点才慢吞吞地来了 **3** (move, flow) «*waves, smoke, cloud, fog*» 滚滚而来 **4** (arrive) «*truck, tank*» 驶来

B *vt* **1** (coat in) **to** ~ **sth. in sth.** 把某物裹在某物里; **to** ~ **the meat in the breadcrumbs** 将肉裹上面包屑 **2** (wrap in) **to** ~ **sb. in sth.** 把某人裹在某物里

- **roll off** *vt* [~ **off sth.**] «*vehicles*» 从…生产出 ‹*production line*›; «*newspapers*» 从…印出 ‹*presses*›
- **roll on**

A *vi* «*time, hours*» 流逝; ~ **on Christmas/next week!** Brit 圣诞节/下一周快点来吧!

B *vt* [~ **sth. on,** ~ **on sth.**]
1 (by unravelling) «*person*» 滚卷着穿 ‹*stockings*›
2 (apply) **to** ~ **on deodorant** 滚抹除臭剂

- **roll out** *vt* [~ **sth. out,** ~ **out sth.**]
1 (flatten) 碾平 ‹*bumps*›; 擀平 ‹*pastry, dough, lumps*›; 轧平 ‹*metal*› **2** (unroll) 将…铺开

r

‹*carpet, map*› **3** (launch) 推出 ‹*product, model*›; 开展 ‹*campaign*›

• **roll over**

A *vi* **1** (turn over) «*vehicle, ship*» 侧翻; **to ~ over on one's back/stomach** 翻身仰卧/俯卧 **2** colloq (be easily defeated) «*player, team*» 不堪一击

B [**~ sb. over**] *vt*
1 (turn over) 使…翻身 ‹*patient, invalid*›; **to ~ sb. over on to sth.** 将某人翻转成某姿势 ‹*back, front, stomach, side*›; **they ~ed him over on to his back** 他们给他翻身使他仰卧 **2** colloq (defeat easily) 轻易击败 ‹*player, team*›

C [**~ sth. over**] *vt* Fin 准许…延期偿还 ‹*loan, debt*›

• **roll up**

A *vi* **1** colloq (arrive) «*guests, visitors*» [尤指迟到或不合时宜、衣着不整等情况下] 到来; **~ up!** (at fairground) 快来看哪! **2** (form ball, tube) «*person, animal*» 蜷缩; «*carpet, paper, map, garment*» 卷起

B [**~ sth. up, ~ up sth.**] *vt*
1 (shorten) 挽起 ‹*sleeve, trouser leg*› **2** (make into ball, tube) 卷起 ‹*carpet, map, paper*›

C [**~ sb./sth. up, ~ up sb./sth.**] *vt* (wrap) 将…裹起来; **to ~ sb./sth. up in a blanket** 用毛毯将某人/某物裹起来

rollaway /ˈrəʊləweɪ/ *n* Amer 滚轮床

rollback /ˈrəʊlbæk/
A *n* **1** Amer (of wages, taxes) 削减; (of prices) 回落 **2** Comput 还原
B *vt* 使…还原 ‹*database*›

roll: ~bar *n* 翻车保护杠; **~ cage** *n* 翻滚护架; **~-call** *n* **1** (in army, school) 点名; **2** (of notable people) 要人名单; (of notable things) 重要事项清单

rolled /rəʊld/: **~ gold** *n* [u] 轧制金箔; **a ~ gold watch/bracelet** 包金手表/手镯; **~ oats** *npl* 燕麦片; **~-up** *adj* 卷起的 ‹*newspaper, blanket*›; 收拢的 ‹*umbrella*›

roller /ˈrəʊlə(r)/ *n* **1** Ind (rotating cylinder) 滚筒; **road ~** 压路机 **2** (for painting) 涂料辊; (for inking) 墨辊 **3** (for blind) 滚轴 **4** (for hair) 卷发筒; **to have** *or* **put one's hair in ~s** 用卷发筒卷头发 **5** (wave) 巻浪

roller: ~ball *n* **1** (pen) 水笔; **2** Comput 鼠标; **~ bandage** *n* 绷带卷

Rollerblade® /ˈrəʊləbleɪd/ *n* 直排轮滑鞋

rollerblade /ˈrəʊləbleɪd/ *vi* 轮滑

rollerblader /ˈrəʊləbleɪdə(r)/ *n* 轮滑者

rollerblading /ˈrəʊləbleɪdɪŋ/ *n* [u] 轮滑

roller: ~ blind *n* 卷轴窗帘; **~ coaster** *n* **1** (fairground ride) 过山车; **2** fig (film, novel) 情节跌宕起伏的作品; (situation) 急剧变化的局势; **the holiday was a bit of a ~ coaster** 这个假期过得有点跌宕起伏; **~ disco** *n* **1** [c] (event) 旱冰迪斯科舞厅; **2** [u] (dancing) 旱冰迪斯科; **~ rink** *n* 旱冰场; **~ skate** *n* 旱冰鞋; **~ skater** *n* 溜旱冰者; **~ skating** ▸**p. 307** *n* [u] 溜旱冰; **to go ~ skating** 去溜旱冰; **~ towel** *n* [挂在滚筒上的] 环状擦手巾

roll film *n* 胶卷

rollick /ˈrɒlɪk/ *vi* colloq 欢闹; **to ~ about** *or* **around** 四处嬉耍

rollicking /ˈrɒlɪkɪŋ/
A *adj* 欢闹的 ‹*play, party*›; **to have a ~ good time** 过得非常快活
B *n* Brit colloq 斥责; **to give sb. a ~** 训斥某人; **to get a ~ from sb.** 挨某人的骂

rolling /ˈrəʊlɪŋ/ *adj attrib* **1** (undulating) 起伏的 ‹*hills, countryside*›; 汹涌的 ‹*waves, sea*› **2** (swaying) 摇摆的 ‹*walk, gait*› **3** (ongoing) 周而复始的 ‹*programme, reforms*›

rolling: ~ mill *n* (factory) 轧钢厂; (machine) 轧钢机; **~ news** *n* [u] 滚动播放的新闻; **~ pin** *n* 擀面杖; **~ stock** *n* [u] [铁路上运行的] 全部车辆; **~ stone** *n* colloq 居无定所的人; **~ strike** *n* [分小组连续进行的] 滚动罢工

roll: ~-neck *n* **1** (collar) 高翻领; **a black ~-neck sweater** 黑色高翻领毛线衣; **2** (garment) 高翻领衣服; **~ of honour** *n* **1** Sch, Sport 光荣榜; **2** Mil 阵亡将士名册

rollocking /ˈrɒləkɪŋ/ *n* = **rollicking B**

roll-on
A *n* (deodorant) 走珠除臭剂; (container, mechanism) 走珠瓶
B *adj attrib* 走珠式的 ‹*deodorant, cologne*›

roll-on roll-off *adj* 滚装滚卸的; **a ~ ferry/system** 滚装渡轮/滚装滚卸系统

rollout /ˈrəʊlaʊt/ *n* [u] **1** (of product, service) 首次发布 **2** (of aircraft, spacecraft) 首次公开展出

rollover /ˈrəʊləʊvə(r)/ *n* [c and u] **1** Fin (extension) 展期; (transfer) 转让 **2** and Brit (of lottery) 滚动增加 **3** (of vehicle) 翻车

rollover: ~ credit *n* 浮动利率信贷; **~ jackpot** *n* 滚动增加的累积奖金

roll-top desk *n* 卷盖式书桌

roly-poly /ˌrəʊliˈpəʊli/
A *adj* colloq 矮胖的 ‹*person, body*›; 胖乎乎的 ‹*baby*›
B *n* **1** colloq (plump person) 矮胖子 **2** Brit Culin 卷布丁; **~ pudding** 卷布丁; **jam ~** 果酱卷布丁

ROM /rɒm/ *n* = **read-only memory**

Roman /ˈrəʊmən/
A *adj* **1** (of city) 罗马的 ‹*citizens, architecture, fashion*› **2** (of empire, culture) 古罗马帝国的 ‹*civilization, history, ruins*›; 罗马式的 ‹*amphitheatre, architecture*› **3** **roman** Print 罗马体的; **~ type/characters** 罗马体/罗马体字
B *n* **1** [c] (ancient) 古罗马人 **2** [c] (medieval or modern) 罗马人 **3** [u] **roman** Print 罗马体

Roman: ~ baths *npl* 罗马浴场; **~ Britain** *n* [公元43-410年间的] 罗马帝国统治下的不列颠; **~ candle** *n* [可连续喷发彩色火球和火花的] 罗马焰火筒

Roman Catholic
A *adj* 天主教的 ‹*service, tradition*›; **a ~ cathedral** 天主教大教堂
B *n* 天主教教徒

Roman Catholic Church *n* [u] **the ~** 天主教会

Roman Catholicism *n* [u] 天主教

Romance /rəʊˈmæns/ *adj* 罗曼语的; **a ~ word/dialect** 罗曼语词/罗曼语方言; **the ~ languages** 罗曼诸语言

romance /rəʊˈmæns/
A *n* **1** [u] (romantic quality) 浪漫氛围; (romantic feeling) 浪漫情调; **an air of ~ (about sb./sth.)** (某人/某物的) 浪漫气息 **2** [c] (love affair) 风流韵事; **to have a ~** 经历一段浪漫的爱情; **a holiday** Brit *or* **vacation** Amer **~** 假日里的风流韵事; **a whirlwind ~** 旋风式恋爱 **3** [u] (genre of fiction) 传奇文学; **medieval/historical ~** 中世纪的传奇文学/历史传奇 **4** [c] (story) 传奇故事; **I'm fond of historical ~s** 我喜欢历史传奇故事 **5** [c] (love story) 爱情故事 **6** [u] (exaggeration) 夸张的描述 **7** [c] Mus 浪漫曲
B *vt* 与…谈情说爱
C *vi* 渲染; **to ~ about sth.** 添枝加叶地谈论某事物

Romanesque /ˌrəʊməˈnesk/
A *adj* 罗马式的 ‹*architecture, features*›; 罗马风格的 ‹*painting, sculpture, style*›
B *n* 罗马式建筑

Romania /rəʊˈmeɪnɪə/ *pr n* 罗马尼亚

Romanian /rəʊˈmeɪnɪən/ ▸**p. 503, p. 426**
A *adj* (of Romania) 罗马尼亚的; (of the people) 罗马尼亚人的; (of the language) 罗马尼亚语的
B *n* **1** [c] (person) 罗马尼亚人 **2** [u] (language) 罗马尼亚语

romanize /ˈrəʊmənaɪz/ *vt* 用拉丁字母拼写 ‹*words*›; 用罗马体书写 ‹*language*›

Roman: ~ law *n* [u] 罗马法; **~ nose** *n* 高鼻梁; **~ numerals** *npl* 罗马数字; **~ road** *n* 罗马式大道

romantic /rəʊˈmæntɪk/
A *adj* **1** (appealing to emotions) 浪漫的 ‹*landscape, adventure, tale*›; 夸张的 ‹*nonsense*›; **to have ~ notions about doing sth.** 对做某事抱有浪漫的想法; **the ~ lead** 爱情剧中的主角; **to give a ~ account of sth.** 添油加醋地叙述某事 **2** (relating to love) 情爱的 ‹*complications*›; **to form a ~ attachment with sb.** 对某人产生绵绵情意; **to have a ~ assignation/involvement with sb.** 与某人有一个情意绵绵的幽会/与某人谈情说爱 **3** (inclined to romance) 多情的 ‹*person, character, nature*› **4** **Romantic** (relating to romanticism) 浪漫主义的 ‹*poetry, artist, period*›
B *n* **1** (person) 浪漫的人; **to be a hopeless ~** 是一个无可救药的浪漫的人 **2** **Romantic** (artist, writer, musician) 浪漫主义艺术家

romantically /rəʊˈmæntɪkli/ *adv* 浪漫地 ‹*behave, write, play*›; 情意绵绵地 ‹*attached, linked*›; **to be ~ involved with sb.** 与某人坠入情网

romantic: ~ comedy *n* **1** [u] (genre) 浪漫喜剧; **2** [c] (film) 浪漫喜剧片; **~ fiction** *n* [u] 言情小说

romanticism /rəʊˈmæntɪsɪzəm/ *n* [u] **1** (feelings) 浪漫情感; (attitudes) 浪漫态度; (behaviour) 浪漫行为 **2** **Romanticism** (in art, music, literature) 浪漫主义

romanticize /rəʊˈmæntɪsaɪz/
A *vi* «*story, film*» 浪漫地刻画; «*person, report*» 夸张地描述; **to ~ about the past** 把过去理想化
B *vt* 使…浪漫化 ‹*past, facts*›; 使…理想化 ‹*reality, person*›

Romany /ˈrɒməni/ ▸**p. 426**
A *n* **1** [c] (gypsy) 吉卜赛人 **2** [u] Ling 吉卜赛语
B *adj* 吉卜赛人的

> **Romany**
>
> 吉卜赛人。这种说法源自 rom，吉卜赛语指"男子，丈夫"。现多认为吉卜赛人初现于印度，旧时则被认为初现于埃及，故称埃及人（Egyptian），经音变成为 gypsy。吉卜赛人散居于世界很多地方，16 世纪前后进入英国。历史上多乘大篷车（caravan），过流浪生活。一般认为女性多从事算命和巫术，男性则为马贩子、修补匠（tinker，英语中亦用作对吉卜赛人的贬称）等。一般不与外族通婚。吉卜赛人因生活方式难以被当地人理解，历史上备受歧视。Romany 亦指吉卜赛语。

Rome /rəʊm/ *pr n* 罗马; **~ wasn't built in a day** Prov 伟业非一日之功; **all roads lead to ~** Prov 条条大路通罗马; **when in ~, do as the Romans do** Prov 入乡随俗

Romeo /ˈrəʊmɪəʊ/ *pr n* 风流男子

Romish /ˈrəʊmɪʃ/ *adj* pej 天主教的 ‹*beliefs*›

romp /rɒmp/
A *vi* **1** (play, run, jump) 嬉闹; **to ~ about** *or* **around** 到处嬉耍 **2** (succeed easily) 轻易取胜; **to ~ home** *or* **in** 轻易获胜; **to ~ through sth.** 轻松完成 ‹*work, exams*›
B *n* **1** (frolic) 嬉闹; **a ~ in the snow** 雪中的嬉戏 **2** (film) 节奏轻快的电影 **3** (easy victory) 轻而易举的胜利; **to come in at a ~** 轻松取得名次 **4** colloq (sexual activity) 做爱 [尤指淫乱]; **three-in-bed (sex) ~s** 一床三人的淫乱

rompers /ˈrɒmpəz/ *npl*, **romper suit** *n* [幼儿穿的] 连衫裤

rondo /ˈrɒndəʊ/ *n* (*pl* **~s**) 回旋曲

roo /ruː/ *n* Austral colloq 袋鼠

roo bar *n* Austral colloq 防撞架

rood screen /ˈruːd skriːn/ *n* [教堂中的] 祭台屏风

roof /ruːf/
A *n* **1** (of building) 屋顶; (of vehicle) 车顶; **a tiled/thatched/flat/sloping ~** 瓦屋顶/茅草屋顶/平屋顶/斜屋顶; **under one** *or* **the same ~**

同在一个屋檐下; **under sb.'s ~** 在某人家里; **to have a ~ over one's head** 有栖身之地; **the ~ of the world** 世界屋脊 [指喜马拉雅山脉]; **to hit** *or* **go through the ~** 《*person*》暴跳如雷; 《*prices*》飞涨; 《*costs, figure*》急剧增加 **2** (of cave) 洞顶; (of mine) 巷道顶 **3** (of mouth) 腭

B *vt* 给…盖顶 ‹*house, building*›; **to ~ sth. with sth.** 用某物给某物盖顶

Phrasal verbs

• **roof in** *vt* [**~ in sth., ~ sth. in**] 给…盖顶 ‹*area, space*›

• **roof over** *vt* [**~ over sth., ~ sth. over**] 给…盖顶 ‹*area, space*›

roofer /'ru:fə(r)/ ▸**p. 409** *n* 屋顶工

roof garden *n* 屋顶花园

roofing /'ru:fɪŋ/ *n* [u] **1** (material) 盖屋顶用的材料; **~ tiles/slates** 屋顶瓦片/石板瓦 **2** (process) 盖屋顶

roofing: ~ contractor *n* (person) 屋顶承建工; (company) 屋顶承建商; **~ felt** *n* [u] 屋顶油毡

roof: ~ light *n* **1** (on building) 天窗; **2** (in vehicle) 顶灯; **3** (on emergency vehicle) 警灯; **~ rack** *n* 车顶架

rooftop /'ru:ftɒp/ *n* 屋顶; **a ~ garden/bar/swimming pool** 屋顶花园/酒吧/游泳池; **to shout** *or* **proclaim sth. from the ~s** fig 公开宣布某事

rook /rʊk/

A *n* **1** (bird) 秃鼻乌鸦 **2** (in chess) 车

B *vt* colloq dated 骗取…的钱财 ‹*person, organization*›; **they ~ed him out of £100** 他们骗了他 100 英镑

rookery /'rʊkəri/ *n* **1** (colony) 秃鼻乌鸦群 **2** (trees) 秃鼻乌鸦群结巢处

rookie /'rʊki/ *n* Amer colloq 新手; **a ~ cop/half-back** 新警察/新中卫

room /ru:m, rʊm/

A *n* **1** [c] (in house, hotel, office) 房间; **in the next ~** 在隔壁房间; **a three-~ flat** 三室的套房; **~ 159** 159 号房间; **~ and board** 食宿; **'~s to let: apply within'** "房间出租: 有意请进"; **a meeting ~** 会议室 **2** [c] (people) 房间里所有的人; **the ~ fell silent** 屋里的人突然鸦雀无声 **3** [u] (space) 空间; **to take up ~** 占地方; **to be short of ~** 缺少空间; **~ for sb./sth.** 某人/某物的位置; **to make ~ (for sb./sth.)** (给某人/某物) 腾出地方; **~ to do sth.** 做某事的空间; **there is always ~ at the top** 总有向上发展的空间 **4** [u] (scope) 机会; **~ for improvement/manoeuvre** 改进/回旋的余地; **no ~ for doubt** 不容置疑; **~ to do sth.** 做某事的机会

B rooms *npl* Brit dated (lodgings) [尤指租住的] 寓所

C *vi* Amer 租房; **to ~ with sb.** 与某人合住; **to ~ together** 租住在一起

D -roomed *combining form* 有…房间的; **a four~ cottage** 有 4 个房间的村舍

room: ~ clerk ▸**p. 409** *n* Amer 客房调配员; **~ divider** *n* 房间隔板

roomer /'ru:mə(r)/ *n* Amer 房客

roomette /ru:'met, rʊ'met/ *n* Amer [火车卧铺车厢的] 小包间

roomful /'ru:mfʊl/ *n* 满房间; **a ~ of children/antiques** 一屋子的孩子/古董

roominess /'ru:mɪnɪs/ *n* [u] 宽敞

rooming house /'ru:mɪŋ haʊs/ *n* [带家具的] 出租公寓住房

room: ~mate *n* **1** (in same room) 室友; **2** Amer (flatmate) 合住公寓套间者; **~ service** *n* [u] 客房送餐服务; **~ temperature** *n* 室温; **to be kept at ~ temperature** 在室温下保存

roomy /'ru:mi/ *adj* 宽敞的 ‹*flat, car*›; 宽松的 ‹*clothes*›; 宽大的 ‹*cupboard, bag*›

roost /ru:st/

A *n* 栖息处; **to rule the ~** 主宰一切

B *vi* 栖息; **the chickens have come home to ~** fig 自作自受

rooster /'ru:stə(r)/ *n* 公鸡

root /ru:t/

A *n* **1** (of plant) 根; **to take ~** 《*plant*》生根; 《*idea, feeling*》深入人心; **to pull sth. up** *or* **out by the ~s** 将某物连根拔起 **2** (of hair, tooth) 根 (部); **electrolysis kills off the hair at the ~** 电解脱毛可以杀死毛体根部 **3** fig (of problem, matter) 起因; (of unhappiness, evil) 根源; **to get at** *or* **to the ~(s) of the problem** 找到问题的根源; **the ~ of all evil** 万恶之源 **4** Ling 词根 **5** Math 根; **square/cube ~** 平方根/立方根

B roots *npl* (origins) [家族、种族、文化等的] 根; **to get back to one's ~s** 回到故乡; **to have ~s** 有根基; **to put down new ~s** 在新地方扎根

C *vt* **1** Bot 使…生根 ‹*cuttings, plants*› **2** **to be/stand ~ed to the spot** *or* **ground** fig (unmoving) 在/站在原地一动不动 **3** (establish deeply) 使…根深蒂固 ‹*feelings, emotions*›; **to be ~ed in sth.** 深深扎根于某事物; **a story firmly ~ed in reality** 牢固建立在现实基础上的故事; **to have a deeply ~ed dislike of sth.** 对某事物怀有根深蒂固的厌恶

D *vi* **1** Bot 生根 **2** (search) 翻找; **he opened a drawer and ~ed through it** 他打开抽屉翻了个遍 **3** (turn up the ground) 《*animal*》用嘴拱土觅食; **to ~ for sth.** 用嘴拱土寻找某物

Phrasal verbs

• **root around, root about** *vi* 搜寻; **to ~ around** *or* **about for sth.** 四处搜寻某物

• **root for** *vt* [**~ for sb./sth.**] colloq (cheer) 为…加油; **good luck in the exams; we're all ~ing for you!** 祝你考试有好运, 我们都为你加油鼓劲!

• **root out** *vt* [**~ out sth., ~sth. out**] 根除 ‹*corruption, dissent, dissenter*›

• **root up** *vt* [**~ up sth., ~ sth. up**] 连根拔起 ‹*plant, bush*›

root and branch /,ru:t ənd 'bra:ntʃ/

A *adj attrib* 彻底的 ‹*purge, reform*›

B *adv* 彻底地 ‹*purge, reform*›

root: ~ beer *n* Amer 根汁饮料; **~ cause** *n* 根本原因; **~ canal** *n* (牙) 根管; **~ canal treatment** *or* **work** (牙) 根管填充术; **~ crop** *n* 根用作物; **~ directory** *n* 根目录; **~ ginger** *n* [u] 姜根

rootless /'ru:tlɪs/ *adj* **1** lit 无根的 ‹*plant*› **2** fig 无根基的 ‹*person*›; 漂泊不定的 ‹*vagabond, life*›; 不稳固的 ‹*society*›

root: ~stock *n* **1** (rhizome) 根茎; **2** (for graft) 根砧木; **~ vegetable** *n* 根菜

rope /rəʊp/

A *n* **1** [u and c] (thick string) 绳索; **a piece of ~** 一根绳子; **to give sb. plenty of** *or* **enough ~** fig 放任某人为所欲为; **give him enough ~ and he'll hang himself** 让他由着性子来, 他就会自取灭亡; **to be at the end of one's ~** Amer colloq 计穷力尽 **2** [c] (set) 一串; **a ~ of pearls/onions** 一串珍珠/洋葱 **3** [u] (hanging) **the ~** 绞刑; **to bring back the ~** 恢复绞刑

B ropes *npl* **1** Sport **the ~s** [拳击或摔跤场四周的] 围绳; **on the ~s** (in boxing) 被逼到围绳上; fig colloq (in trouble) 濒于失败; **behind its apparent success the bank was actually on the ~s** 这家银行表面看起来很成功, 实际上濒临破产 **2** colloq (established procedures) **the ~s** 既定程序; **to know the ~s** 知道办事规矩; **to show sb. the ~s** 向某人演示操作程序

C *vt* **1** (attach) 用绳子将…捆起 ‹*person, animal*›; **a ~d party of climbers** 用绳索串系起来的登山队 **2** (make secure) 用绳子系牢 ‹*trunk*› **3** esp Amer (lasso) 用套索套 ‹*cattle, horse*›

Phrasal verbs

• **rope in** *vt* [**~ sb. in, ~ in sb.**] colloq 说服…加入; **~ sb. in to do sth., ~ in sb. to do sth.** 劝说某人做某事; **~ sb. into doing sth.** 说服某人做某事; **to get ~d in** 被说动

• **rope off** *vt* [**~ off sth., ~ sth. off**] 用绳子围起 ‹*area, scene, street*›

rope: ~ ladder *n* 绳梯; **~ trick** *n* (Indian) **~ trick** 爬绳魔术 [爬上似悬空的绳子]

ropy, ropey /'rəʊpi/ *adj* Brit colloq 差劲的 ‹*book, food, entertainment*›; 体弱的 ‹*person*›; **to feel a bit ~** 觉得有点不舒服

RORO, ro-ro /'rəʊrəʊ/ *abbr* = **roll-on roll-off**

rosary /'rəʊzəri/ *n* **1** (prayer) 玫瑰经; **to say the ~** 念玫瑰经 **2** (beads) 念珠

rose¹ /rəʊz/ *pt* ▸**rise A**

rose² *n* **1** [c] (shrub) 玫瑰; **a climbing/rambling ~** 攀缘的/蔓生的蔷薇; **everything's coming up ~s** 一切都很顺利 **2** [c] (flower) 玫瑰花; **a bunch of red ~s** 一束红玫瑰花; **life is not a bed of ~s** 生活并非总是称心如意; **to come up smelling of ~s** 保持名誉无损; **~ petals** 蔷薇花瓣 **3** [u] (colour) 玫瑰红 **4** [c] (on shower, watering can) 莲蓬式喷嘴

rosé /'rəʊzeɪ, Amer rəʊ'zeɪ/

A *n* [u and c] 玫瑰红葡萄酒

B *adj* 玫瑰红的

roseate /'rəʊziət/ *adj* liter 玫瑰色的 ‹*glow, sky*›

rose: ~ bowl *n* 玫瑰花钵; **~bud** *n* 玫瑰花蕾; **~-coloured** ▸**p. 134** *adj* **1** (pink) 玫瑰色的; **2** (optimistic) 乐观的; **to look at** *or* **see sth. through ~-coloured glasses** *or* **spectacles** fig 乐观地看待某事物

rosehip /'rəʊzhɪp/ *n* 玫瑰果

rosehip syrup *n* [u] 玫瑰果糖浆

rosemary /'rəʊzməri, Amer -meri/ *n* [u] **1** (shrub) 迷迭香 **2** (herb) 迷迭香叶

rose pink ▸**p. 134**

A *adj* 浅玫瑰红的

B *n* [u] 浅玫瑰红色

rose-tinted /'rəʊztɪntɪd/ ▸**p. 134** *adj* = **rose-coloured**

rosette /rəʊ'zet/ *n* **1** (decoration) 光荣花 [政党或运动队支持者或竞赛获胜者佩戴的玫瑰形饰物] **2** (design) 玫瑰花形图案

rose: ~ water *n* [u] 玫瑰水; **~ window** *n* 圆花窗

rosewood /'rəʊzwʊd/ *n* **1** [u] (timber) 黄檀木; **~ furniture** 黄檀木家具 **2** [c] (tree) 黄檀

rosin /'rɒzɪn, Amer 'rɒzn/

A *n* 松香

B *vt* 用松香擦

RoSPA /'rɒspə/ *abbr* Brit = **Royal Society for the Prevention of Accidents** 皇家事故预防协会

roster /'rɒstə(r)/

A *n* 值勤名单; **to draw up** *or* **compile a ~** 编制一份花名册

B *vt* 将…列入名单 ‹*person, worker*›

rostrum /'rɒstrəm/ *n* (*pl* **rostra** /'rɒstrə/ *or* **~s**) (for making speech) 讲坛; (at award ceremony) 领奖台; (for conducting orchestra) 指挥台

rosy /'rəʊzi/ *adj* **1** (pink) 玫瑰色的 ‹*hue, tinge, colour*›; 红润的 ‹*cheeks, complexion*› **2** (favourable) 美好的 ‹*future, picture, prospects*›; 乐观的 ‹*view*›; **to paint a ~ picture of sth.** 把某事物描绘得非常美好; **to feel a ~ glow** 感到得意洋洋

rot /rɒt/

A *vi* (*pres p etc.* **-tt-**) **1** lit (decompose) 《*substance, food*》腐烂; **to ~ away** 烂掉 **2** fig (deteriorate) 《*person, garden*》渐衰; 《*car, house*》日渐破损; **to ~ in prison** 在监狱内日渐萎靡

B *vt* (*pres p etc.* **-tt-**) **1** lit (cause to decay) 使…腐烂 ‹*body, plant, matter*›; 腐蚀 ‹*rubber, metal*› **2** fig (damage) 使…迟钝 ‹*mind*›; **too much sugar will ~ your teeth** 吃糖太多会发生蛀牙; **too much television ~s your brain** 看电视太多脑子会迟钝

C *n* [u] **1** lit (decay) 腐烂; fig 腐败; **the ~ in the system** 体制中的腐败 **2** Brit fig (deterioration)

r

恶化; **the ~ has set in** 情况开始恶化 **3** Brit colloq dated (rubbish) 废话; **what ~!** 胡说! **4** Bot (disease) 枯病

rota /'rəʊtə/ *n* Brit 勤务轮值表; **to do one's duty on a ~ basis** 轮值

Rotarian /rəʊ'teərɪən/ *n* "扶轮国际"成员

rotary /'rəʊtəri/
A *adj* **1** (revolving) 旋转的 ‹*action*›; **~ motion/movement** 转动/旋转运动 **2** (operating by rotation) 旋转式的 ‹*drier, lawn mower, flight*›; **a ~ switch/drill** 旋转开关/旋转钻机
B *n* Amer 交通环岛

rotary: ~ clothes line *n* 旋转式晾衣架; **R~ club** *n* **the R~ club** "扶轮国际"分社; **~ engine** *n* 旋转式发动机; **~ press, ~ printing press** *ns* 轮转印刷机; **~ wing** *n* 旋翼; *modif* **a ~-wing aircraft** 旋翼机

rotate /rəʊ'teɪt, Amer 'rəʊteɪt/
A *vi* **1** (move) «*blades, wings*» 旋转 **2** (take turns) «*position, worker*» 轮换; **the post of chairman ~s among members of the committee** 主席一职由委员会委员轮流担任
B *vt* **1** (cause to move) 使…旋转 ‹*blades, handle*› **2** (cause to take turns) 轮换 ‹*roles, jobs*›; 轮种 ‹*crops*›

rotation /rəʊ'teɪʃn/ *n* **1** [u] (movement) 旋转; **the ~ of the Earth** 地球的旋转 **2** [c] (circle) [旋转的] 一周; **five ~s per hour** 每小时旋转五圈 **3** [u] (taking turns) 轮换; **to work in ~** 轮流工作; **crop ~** 轮作

rotavate /'rəʊtəveɪt/
A *vt* 用旋耕机耕 ‹*soil*›
B *vi* 用旋耕机耕地

rotavator /'rəʊtəveɪtə(r)/ *n* Brit (for garden) 旋转碎土器; (on farm) 旋耕机

rote /rəʊt/ *n* [u] **by ~** 死记硬背; **to do/say/learn … by ~** 生搬硬套地做/生搬硬套地说/死记硬背地学…

rote learning *n* [u] 死记硬背的学习

rotgut /'rɒtgʌt/ *n* [u] colloq pej 劣质酒

rotisserie /rəʊ'tiːsəri/ *n* **1** (device) 旋转烤肉架 **2** (restaurant) 烤肉馆

rotor /'rəʊtə(r)/ *n* 转子

rotor: ~ arm *n* 分火头; **~ blade** *n* 旋翼叶片

rototiller /'rəʊtətɪlə(r)/ *n* Amer 旋转碎土器

rotovator /'rəʊtəveɪtə(r)/ *n* **= rotavator**

rotproof /'rɒtpruːf/ *adj* 防腐的 ‹*material*›

rotten /'rɒtn/
A *adj* **1** (decayed) 腐烂的 ‹*food, ironwork, smell*›; **a mouthful of ~ teeth** 满口蛀牙 **2** (corrupt) 腐败的 ‹*government, regime*›; 堕落的 ‹*person*›; **to be ~ to the core** 腐败透顶 **3** colloq (bad) 糟透的; **what ~ luck!** 真倒霉!; **to feel ~** 感到不舒服; **to feel ~ about doing sth.** 做某事感到很讨厌
B *adv* colloq 很大程度上; **to spoil sb. ~** 宠坏某人; **to tease sb. something ~** 极尽能事戏弄某人

rotten apple *n* fig 害群之马

rottenness /'rɒtnnɪs/ *n* [u] **1** (state of decay) 腐烂 **2** fig (corruptness) 腐败

rotter /'rɒtə(r)/ *n* Brit colloq dated 无赖

Rottweiler /'rɒtvaɪlə(r)/ *n* 罗威纳犬

rotund /rəʊ'tʌnd/ *adj* 圆胖的 ‹*person, figure*›; 肥圆的 ‹*stomach*›

rotunda /rəʊ'tʌndə/ *n* (building) 圆形建筑; (room) 圆形大厅

rouble /'ruːbl/ ▸**p. 174** *n* 卢布

roué /'ruːeɪ/ *n* liter [尤指上了年纪的] 酒色之徒

rouge /ruːʒ/
A *n* [u] (for cheeks) 胭脂; (for lips) 口红
B *vt* 在…上搽胭脂 ‹*cheeks*›; 在…上涂口红 ‹*lips*›

rough /rʌf/
A *adj* **1** (not smooth) 粗糙的 ‹*skin, hands, material*›; 凹凸不平的 ‹*rock, surface*›; 参差不齐的 ‹*edge*›; 高低不平的 ‹*grass, country*›; 崎岖的 ‹*road, track*›; **~ edges** (of character) 瑕疵 **2** ▸**p. 32** (approximate) 粗略的 ‹*sketch, description*›; 不精确的 ‹*translation, calculation*›; 大概的 ‹*figure, estimate*›; **can you give me a ~ idea of the cost?** 请告诉我费用大致是多少好吗? **3** (violent) 粗暴的 ‹*person, behaviour*›; 粗野的 ‹*game, sport*›; **to be ~ with sb./sth.** 粗暴对待某人/某物; **to get ~ (with sb.)** (对某人) 动粗 **4** (containing violent people) 充斥暴力的 ‹*area, bar*› **5** (stormy) 恶劣的 ‹*weather, conditions*› **6** (with large waves) 波涛汹涌的 ‹*sea, lake*› **7** (uncomfortable) 颠簸的 ‹*landing, ride*›; 有风浪的 ‹*crossing*› **8** (plain, basic) 简陋的 ‹*furniture, house*› **9** (makeshift) 临时拼凑的 ‹*dwelling, shelter*› **10** (unsophisticated) 质朴的 ‹*person, manners, appearance*› **11** (harsh-sounding) 刺耳的 ‹*voice, sound*› **12** (unpleasant-tasting) 味道差的 ‹*wine*›; 涩的 ‹*taste*› **13** (difficult) 艰难的 ‹*life, period*›; **to give sb. a ~ ride** 使某人吃苦头; **he's had a ~ deal** colloq 他受到了不公平的待遇; **to be ~ on sb.** (difficult) 对某人来说很困难; (unfair) 对某人来说不公平; **that was ~ luck** 真倒霉 **14** (severe, strict) 粗暴严厉的; **to be ~ on sb.** 粗暴严厉地对待某人 **15** *pred* colloq (unwell) 不适的; **to feel/look ~** 感到/好像不舒服
B *n* **1** [u and c] (draft) 草稿; **a ~ for sth.** (design) 某物的草稿; (drawing) 某物的草图; **to write sth. out in ~** 给某物打草稿 **2** [u] (in golf) 深草区 **3** **to take the ~ with the smooth** 既能享乐也能吃苦
C *adv* **1** Brit (outdoors) 在街头; **to live** *or* **sleep ~** 露宿街头 **2** colloq (violently) 粗暴地 ‹*fight, treat*›; 粗野地 ‹*play*›; **to cut up ~** Brit colloq 大发脾气
D *vt* colloq **to ~ it** 暂时过艰苦生活

Phrasal verbs

- **rough in** *vt* [**~ in sth., ~ sth. in**] **1** (sketch) 勾画出…的轮廓 ‹*scene, object, figures*› **2** (estimate) 估计 ‹*details, figures*›
- **rough out** *vt* [**~ sth. out, ~ out sth.**] 草拟 ‹*report, plan*›; 粗略勾画 ‹*drawing*›; 简略写出 ‹*idea*›
- **rough up** *vt* [**~ sb. up, ~ up sb.**] colloq 殴打

roughage /'rʌfɪdʒ/ *n* [u] [食物中的] 粗纤维

rough: ~-and-ready *adj* **1** (unsophisticated) 粗犷的 ‹*person, manners*›; **2** (improvised) 粗糙但实用的 ‹*method, equipment*›; **~-and-tumble** *n* 吵闹捣蛋的行为; fig 混战; **to have a ~-and-tumble** 打闹; **the ~-and-tumble of party politics/the free market** 党派政治/自由市场的混乱; **in the ~-and-tumble world of politics** 在混乱的政界

roughcast /'rʌfkɑːst, Amer -kæst/
A *n* 粗灰泥
B *adj* 涂粗灰泥的 ‹*wall*›; 墙面拉毛的 ‹*house*›
C *vt* (*pt, pp* **roughcast**) 用粗灰泥涂 ‹*building, wall*›

rough diamond *n* **1** (uncut stone) 未经琢磨的钻石 **2** Brit fig (person) 外粗内秀的人

roughen /'rʌfn/
A *vt* 使…变粗糙 ‹*surface, skin, hands*›
B *vi* «*skin, hands*» 变粗糙; «*voice*» 变粗哑

rough-hewn /'rʌfhjuːn/ *adj* 胡乱砍成的 ‹*wood*›; fig 粗犷的 ‹*facial features*›

rough house esp Amer colloq
A *n* 打闹
B *vt* 粗暴地对待

rough justice *n* [u] 不太公平的惩罚

roughly /'rʌfli/ *adv* **1** (without detail) 粗略地 ‹*calculate, describe, sketch*›; **~ speaking** 粗略地说 **2** ▸**p. 32** (more or less) 大致 ‹*equal, equivalent*›; 近似 ‹*triangular, circular*›; **~ 10%/100 people** 约 10% / 100 人; **~ the same age/size** 年龄相仿/尺寸差不多 **3** (with force) 粗暴地 ‹*handle*› **4** (severely, strictly) 严厉地 ‹*speak*› **5** (without care) 漫不经心地; **I painted it very ~ because I was in a hurry** 我因为有急事漆得非常马虎; **to chop/grate the vegetables ~** 粗粗地切一下蔬菜/把蔬菜磨碎; **a ~ built brick fireplace** 胡乱砌成的砖壁炉 **6** (not smooth) 粗糙地; **a ~ plastered wall** 灰泥抹的凹凸不平的墙壁

roughneck /'rʌfnek/ ▸**p. 409** *n* **1** colloq (violent person) 粗汉 **2** (oil-rig worker) 石油钻井工人

roughness /'rʌfnɪs/ *n* [u] **1** (of skin, surface, material, edge) 粗糙; (of road, terrain) 高低不平 **2** (of person, treatment, behaviour) 粗暴; (of game, sport) 粗野 **3** (of sound) 粗哑刺耳 **4** (of wine, alcohol) 口感差 **5** (of weather) 风雨交加 **6** (of sea) 波涛汹涌; **it all depends on the ~ of the sea** 这全得看海上的风浪有多大 **7** (of crossing, landing, ride) 颠簸 **8** (of furniture, house) 简陋 **9** (lack of sophistication) 质朴; **his accent contributed to a general impression of ~** 他的口音更使他给人一种质朴的总体印象; **he made no apology for the ~ of his appearance** 他没有为自己不修边幅的样子道歉

rough: ~shod /'rʌfʃɒd/ *adj* **to ride ~shod over sb./sth.** 对某人/某物为所欲为; **~-spoken** *adj* 谈吐粗俗的; **~ stuff** *n* [u] colloq 暴力行为; **~ trade** *n* [u] colloq [尤指伴有暴力或虐待行为的] 男性同性卖淫; **~ work** *n* [u] 粗制品

roulade /ruː'lɑːd/ *n* (meat roll) 包馅肉卷; (fish roll) 鱼肉卷; (sweet roll) 蛋糕卷

roulette /ruː'let/ *n* [u] 轮盘赌; **to play ~** 玩轮盘赌

roulette: ~ table *n* 轮盘赌台; **~ wheel** *n* 轮盘赌轮

Roumania *pr n* **= Romania**

Roumanian *adj, n* **= Romanian**

round /raʊnd/
A *adj* **1** (circular) 圆形的; **these glasses suit people with ~ faces** 这种眼镜适合圆脸的人; **a ~-necked T-shirt** 一件圆领T恤衫 **2** (spherical) 球形的; **the earth is ~** 地球是圆的 **3** (hemispherical) 半球形的; **the ~ green hills** 圆圆的绿山岗 **4** (curved) 弧形的; (containing curves) 圆体的 ‹*handwriting*›; **the cloisters have ~ arches** 修道院有圆弧形的拱门; **he writes a neat ~ hand** 他写得一手工整的圆体字 **5** (bent forwards) 前曲的; **~ shoulders** 驼背 **6** (plump) 丰满的; **she had ~ pink cheeks** 她的面颊粉嘟嘟的 **7** *attrib* (in convenient units) 整数的; **a ~ figure** *or* **number** 整数; **in ~ figures** 以整数 **8** *attrib* (complete) 十足的; **a ~ dozen** 整整一打; **the batsman made a ~ 100** 击球手整整得了 100 分 **9** *attrib* (considerable) 可观的; **a nice ~ sum** 一笔相当大的金额
B *prep* esp Brit **1** (on all sides of, surrounding, in circumference) 围绕; **they were all sitting ~ the table** 他们都围坐在桌边; **the fence ~ the garden** 环绕着花园的栅栏; **she looked ~ her** 她环顾四周; **to put one's arm ~ sb.** 拥抱某人; **what do you measure ~ the waist?** 你的腰围是多少? **2** (past obstacle or point) 绕过; **the baker's is just ~ the corner** 面包店就在那个拐角处; **there's one way ~ this difficulty** 有一种避开这个难题的办法; **they've found a way to get ~ the new law** 他们找到了一个规避新法律的方法 **3** (taking in whole area) 在…各处; **to go ~ the shops** 逛商店; **she looked all ~ the room** 她看遍了房间里的每一个角落; **we've been travelling ~ France** 我们一直在周游法国; **to lie ~ sth.** «*clothes, papers, toys*» 散落在… ‹*room*› **4** (to fit in with) 适应; **he has to organize his life ~ the kids** 他不得不以孩子为中心来安排他的生活
C *adv* **1** (in circular movement) 旋转地; **to go ~** «*wheel*» 转动; **what speed does the Earth go ~ at?** 地球以什么样的速度旋转?; **the tune was going ~ and ~ in my head** 那支曲子一直萦绕在我的头脑里; **a plane circled ~ overhead** 一架飞机在头顶上盘旋 **2** (in circumference) 以周长计; **a tree three**

metres ～ 周长3米的一棵树 3 (forming edge) 围绕着; **to go all the way** ～ ‹*fence, wall, moat*› 环绕四周; **a garden with a wall all** ～ 有围墙的花园 4 (on all sides) 在周围; **to crowd/gather** ～ 围拢/聚集在周围 5 (here and there) 到处; **to stand** ～ 站在四处; **to show sb.** ～ 领某人到处看看; **we could have a look** ～ **if you've got time** 如果你有时间的话，我们可以到处看看; **a large valley with a number of small farms scattered** ～ 有许多小农场散落其间的大山谷; ～ **here** 在附近 6 (in opposite direction) 反方向地; **to look** ～ 回头看; **to turn sth.** ～ 把某物掉转过来; **turn your chair the other way** ～ 把你的椅子转过去; **it's the wrong way** ～ 方向弄反了 7 (changing direction) 向另一侧; **it was the last house before the road curved** ～ 过了这座房子，这条路就要拐弯了; **we walked** ～ **to the back of the house** 我们兜到房子后面; **we had to drive the long way** ～ 我们不得不开车兜远路 8 (relative or different position) [表示相对位置或位置的变动]; **which way** ～ **does it go?** 它通往哪一个方向？; **is this the right way** ～**?** 这是正确的路线吗？; **they've moved all the furniture** ～ 他们移动了所有家具的位置 9 (to various people) 逐个; **there were smiles all** ～ 每个人的脸上都露出了微笑; **to pass/hand sth.** ～ 把某物传给大家; **to go** ～ 流传; **there's a rumour going** ～ **that ...** 有传言说… 10 (to office, work, home) 到某处; (at office, work, home) 在某处; **she's coming** ～ **today** 她今天要过来; **to be** ～ 在这里; **I'll be** ～ **in an hour** 我一小时后到; **to be** ～ **at a place** 在某处; **I'll be** ～ **at Joe's later** 过一会儿我会在乔那儿; **to go** ～ 顺便拜访; **to go** ～ **to a place** 去某处 11 (as part of cycle) 循环地; **as summer comes** ～ 当夏天到来时; **this time** ～ 又到了这个时候; **all year** ～ 一年到头

D **round about** *adv phr* esp Brit 1 ▸**p. 32** (approximately) 大约; ～ **about 50 people** 大约50人; **it happened** ～ **about here** 这件事大约发生在这儿 2 (nearby) 在附近

E *n* 1 (of events, in contest) 轮次; **a** ～ **of sth.** 一轮 ‹*meetings, discussions, negotiations*›; **the next** ～ **of talks** 下一轮会谈; **the qualifying** ～ 资格赛; **the final** ～ **of voting** 最后一轮投票; **the first** ～ **of the World Cup** 世界杯的首轮比赛; **he was knocked out in the third** ～ 他在第三回合被淘汰 2 (in golf) 整场比赛; **to play a** ～ **of golf** 打一场高尔夫球赛 3 Equit 整套跳跃; **a clear** ～ 没有失误的整套跳跃动作 4 (series of activities) 一连串; **the daily** ～ **of activities** 日常活动; **her life is one long** ～ **of parties and fun** 她的生活就是没完没了的聚会和玩乐 5 (of postman, milkman, paper boy or girl) 巡回; (of watchman, security guard) 巡视; **we saw the postman pass by on his** ～ 我们看到邮差在送信的路上从这儿经过 6 (of drinks) 一巡; **to pay for a** ～ 支付一巡酒钱 7 (burst) 一阵; **a** ～ **of applause/cheering** 一阵掌声/欢呼 8 Mil (unit of ammunition) 一发弹药; **a** ～ **of ammunition** 一发弹药; **we only have three** ～**s left** 我们只剩下三发子弹了 9 Mil (shot) 一次射击; **to fire** ～ **after** ～ 一次又一次射击; ～**s of machine-gun fire** 机枪的连续射击 10 (circular shape) 圆团; **cut the pastry into** ～**s** 把油酥面团切成圆块 11 Mus (canon) 轮唱 12 Dance 圆圈舞 13 Theat **in the** ～ 舞台在观众中央的; **theatre in the** ～ 环形剧场 14 Art **in the** ～ ‹*sculpture*› 立体的; **Canova's work in the** ～ 卡诺瓦的立体雕塑作品 15 Culin (of cheese) 圆形奶酪; (of meat) 牛股肉; **a** ～ **of beef** 一大块牛腿肉 16 Brit Culin (of sandwiches) 整片三明治; **a** ～ **of ham sandwiches** 一份火腿三明治 17 Brit Culin (slice of bread) 一整片面包; **a** ～ **of toast** 一整片吐司面包

F **rounds** *npl* 巡行; **to do one's** ～**s** ‹*security guard*› 巡视; ‹*postman, milkman*› 挨户递送; ‹*refuse collector*› 挨户收取; **the doctor was on her daily ward** ～**s** 大夫在例行查房; **to do** *or* **go** Brit *or* **make** Amer **the** ～**s** ‹*rumour, story, joke, flu*› 传播; ‹*document*› 传递; **to do** *or* **make the** ～**s of sb./sth.** 逐一巡访某人/某处; **she did the** ～**s of the employment agencies, but couldn't find anything suitable** 她去了一家又一家职业介绍所，但是没找到合适的工作

G *vt* 1 (go around) 绕过; **the car** ～**ed the corner** 汽车绕过了拐角 2 (make round) 使成圆形; **a lathe that** ～**ed chair legs** 旋椅子腿的车床; **he** ～**ed his lips to whistle** 他嘟起嘴唇吹口哨 3 Phon 以圆唇发 ‹*vowel*›

H *vi* (become round) 成圆形; **her eyes** ～**ed with delight/horror** 她高兴得眼睛睁得大大的/恐惧得两眼圆睁

Phrasal verbs

- **round down** *vt* [～ **sth. down,** ～ **down sth.**] 把…下舍入 ‹*figure, number*›
- **round off** [～ **sth. off,** ～ **off sth.**] *vt* 1 (finish off) 圆满结束; **she** ～**ed off the tour with a concert at Carnegie Hall** 她在卡内基音乐厅举行的音乐会圆满结束了这次巡回演出; **a dance to** ～ **off the evening** 圆满结束晚会的舞蹈节目 2 (make smooth) ‹*plane, tool*› 使…平整光滑 ‹*corner*›; **to** ～ **sth. off with sth.** 用某物使某物变得平滑; **you can** ～ **off the corners with sandpaper** 你可以用砂纸将角磨光; **use a plane to** ～ **off the sharp edges** 用刨子刨平尖利的边沿 3 (change) 把…舍入 ‹*figure, number*›; **use** ～**ed off figures to simplify the calculations** 用经过凑整的数字简化计算
- **round on** *vt* [～ **on sb.**] 突然对…发难; **she** ～**ed on me angrily** 她突然对我大发雷霆
- **round out** *vt* [～ **sth. out,** ～ **out sth.**] 使…更完整 ‹*list, numbers, range, education*›
- **round up** *vt* 1 [～ **sb./sth. up,** ～ **up sb./sth.**] (assemble) 聚集; **I** ～**ed up a few friends for a party** 我召集了几个朋友搞了个聚会 2 [～ **sb. up,** ～ **up sb.**] (arrest) 拘捕; **thousands of students were** ～**ed up when the military took power** 军队夺取了政权以后，成千上万的学生遭到拘捕 3 [～ **sth. up,** ～ **up sth.**] (increase) 把…上舍入 ‹*figure, number*›; **we'll** ～ **the weight up to the nearest kilo** 我们会把重量上舍入最接近的公斤数
- **round upon** *vt* = **round on**

roundabout /ˈraʊndəbaʊt/

A *n* Brit 1 (in fairground) 旋转木马 2 (in playground) 旋转平台; **it's swings and** ～**s, what you gain on the swings you lose on the** ～**s** fig 这是有得有失的事，失之东隅，收之桑榆 3 Transp 环岛

B *adj* 1 (circuitous) 迂回的; **to come by a** ～ **way** *or* **route** 绕道而来; **by** ～ **means** 以迂回的方式 2 (not straightforward) 绕圈子的; **to ask in a** ～ **way** 拐弯抹角地问

round: ～ **brackets** *npl* 圆括号; ～ **dance** *n* 轮舞 [围成一个大圈跳的民间舞]

rounded /ˈraʊndɪd/ *adj* 1 (curved) 圆形的; ～ **hills/cheeks/edges** 圆顶小山/圆圆的脸颊/圆边 2 Ling 圆唇的 ‹*vowel*› 3 (balanced) 发展全面的 ‹*character, personality*›; 完整的 ‹*period, sentence*›

roundel /ˈraʊndl/ *n* 1 Aviat [军用飞机上的] 圆形识别标志 2 (pattern, picture) 圆形图案

rounder /ˈraʊndə/ *n* [圆场棒球中的] 得分

rounders /ˈraʊndəz/ *npl* + *v sing* Brit 圆场棒球

round: ～**-eyed** *adj* 双目圆睁的; ～**-faced** *adj* 圆脸的; **R**～**head** *n* Brit Hist 圆颅党人 [英国内战期间的议会派成员或其支持者]

roundly /ˈraʊndli/ *adv* 1 (frankly) 坦率地 ‹*inform, assert*›; (vehemently) 严厉地 ‹*condemn, criticize*› 2 (convincingly) 彻底地 ‹*beat, defeat*›

round-neck sweater, round-necked sweater *n* 圆领套衫

roundness /ˈraʊndnɪs/ *n* [u] 饱满; **the** ～ **of her face/cheek/curves** 她那圆圆的脸/饱满的脸颊/浑圆的曲线

round: ～ **robin** *n* 1 (petition) 联名请愿书; 2 Sport 循环赛; *modif* **a** ～ **robin tournament/competition** 循环联赛/比赛; ～**-shouldered** *adj* 双肩前曲的 ‹*person*›; **to be** ～**-shouldered** 拱背曲肩的

roundsman /ˈraʊndzmən/ *n* (*pl* **roundsmen**) 1 (for deliveries) 送货员; **a milk** ～ 送奶工 2 Amer (police officer) 巡警

round table

A *n* 圆桌会议

B **round-table** *modif* **round-table talks/sessions** 圆桌会谈/圆桌会议

round-the-clock

A *adj* 日夜不停的 ‹*surveillance, service, care*›; ～ **shifts** 24小时轮班

B **round the clock** *adv phr* 日夜不停地 ‹*work*›

round-the-world *adj* 环球的; ～ **ticket/cruise** 环球机票/航行

round: ～ **trip** *n* 1 (journey) 环程旅行; 2 Amer (ticket, fare) 往返旅行; **a** ～**-trip ticket** Amer 往返票; ～**up** *n* 1 (of animals) 赶拢; (of people) 聚拢; 2 (summary) 摘要; **a** ～**up of the day's sport** 一天体育综述

rouse /raʊz/

A *vt* 1 (wake) 唤醒; **to** ～ **sb. from a deep sleep** 将某人从沉睡中唤醒 2 (stir) 激起; **to** ～ **public opinion** 激起公众舆论; **to** ～ **sb. to anger/action** 激怒某人/激励某人行动起来; **to** ～ **sb.'s anger/interest/curiosity** 激起某人的愤怒/兴趣/好奇心

B *vi* 醒来

rousing /ˈraʊzɪŋ/ *adj* 激动人心的 ‹*chorus, music, speech, words*›; 热烈的 ‹*cheers, applause*›

roustabout /ˈraʊstəbaʊt/ *n* 1 (labourer) 非技术工 2 (on oil rig) 油井杂工 3 Amer (docker) 码头工人

rout[1] /raʊt/

A *n* 1 [u] (defeat) 彻底失败; **to put sb. to** ～ 彻底打垮某人 2 [c] (disorderly retreat) 溃退

B *vt* 彻底击败 ‹*enemy, political party*›

Phrasal verb

- **rout out** *vt* [～ **sth./sb. out,** ～ **out sth./sb.**] 1 (find) 搜寻到 ‹*object, person, animal*› 2 (force out) 拖出 ‹*person, animal*›; **to** ～ **sb. out of their bed** 把某人从床上拖起来

rout[2] *vt* 在…上刨槽 ‹*wood, metal*›

route /ruːt, Amer raʊt/

A *n* 1 (path) 路途; **to plan a** ～ 安排路线; **on the** ～ **to Oxford** 在去牛津的路上; **by a different** ～ 走不同路线的; **the main/shortest** ～ **(to sth.)** (去某处的) 主要/最短路线 2 Transp (for bus, train, goods) 常规路线; (for bicycles) 自行车道; (for ship, aircraft) 航线; **a bus/rail** ～ 公交线/铁路线; **a traffic** ～ 交通路线 3 Amer (main road) 公路; **R**～ **86** 86号公路 4 (official itinerary) 规定路线; **they lined the** ～ 他们站在行进路线的两旁 5 fig (means of achieving sth.) 途径; **a** ～ **to sth.** 获得…的途径 ‹*power, promotion*›; 导致…的做法 ‹*disaster*›; **the** ～ **to success/health** 成功/健康之路 6 Amer (round) 递送路线; **a newspaper** ～ 送报纸的路线 7 Med [药剂等进入人体的] 途径; **a** ～ **of infection** 传染途径

B *vt* 按路线发送 ‹*person, goods, bus, train*›; **this flight is** ～**d to Chicago via New York** 这个航班途经纽约飞往芝加哥

route: ～ **map** *n* 线路图; ～ **march** *n* 1 Mil 拉练; 2 fig (long walk) 长途步行; ～ **planner** *n* 线路查询程序

router[1] /ˈraʊtə(r)/ *n* (power tool) 刨槽机

router[2] /ˈruːtə(r), Amer ˈraʊtə(r)/ *n* Comput 路由器

routine /ruːˈtiːn/

A *n* 1 (regular procedure) 常规; **the daily** ～ 日常的例行公事; **to establish a** ～ (at work) 确

r

立常规; (for spare time) 形成习惯; **as a matter of ~** 按常规 **2** (in dance, performance) 一套动作; **a dance/skating/comic ~** 一套舞蹈/溜冰/滑稽动作 **3** Comput 例行程序

B *adj* **1** (normal) 例行的 ‹*procedure*›; 常规的 ‹*maintenance, medical*› **2** (uninspiring) 平淡乏味的 ‹*tasks, chores, work, job, performance*›

routinely /ruːˈtiːnli/ *adv* 例行地 ‹*examine, question*›; **firefighters ~ put themselves at risk to save others** 消防队员一向都是冒着危险抢救他人

routing code *n* **1** Telecom, Comput 路径选择码 **2** (on cheque) 转账代码

rove /rəʊv/

A *vt* 在…漫游 ‹*countryside, hills*›; 在…闲荡 ‹*streets*›

B *vi* **to ~ (around** *or* **about)** «*person, animal, group*» 游荡; «*eyes, gaze*» 左顾右盼

rover /ˈrəʊvə(r)/ *n* 漫游者

roving /ˈrəʊvɪŋ/ *adj* **1** (roaming) 游牧的 ‹*peoples*›; 流窜的 ‹*criminals*›; **to have a ~ eye** fig 时刻找机会寻花问柳 **2** Journ, Pol **a ~ reporter/ambassador** 流动新闻记者/巡回大使

roving commission *n* Brit [给予调查者的] 自由旅行权; **to have a ~** 得到自由旅行权

row¹ /rəʊ/ ▸**p. 307** *n* **1** (line) 一排; **a ~ of cars** 一排汽车; **in the front ~** 在前排; **seated in a ~/in ~s** 坐成一排/成排坐着 **2** (succession) 连续; **six times in a ~** 连续6次; **~ upon** *or* **after ~ of sth.** 接二连三的某物; **~s (and ~s) of sth.** 一连串某物

row² /rəʊ/

A *vi* **1** (using oars) 划船; **to ~ across the lake/up the river** 划船到湖对岸/沿河而上 **2** Sport 参加划船赛; **he ~s for Oxford** 他代表牛津大学参加划船比赛

B *vt* **1** (propel) 划; **to ~ a boat across/up the river** 划船过河/划船沿流而上 **2** (convey) 划运 ‹*person, thing*›; **to ~ sb. across the lake/river** 划船送某人过湖/河

C *n* 划船小游; **to take sb. for a ~** 带某人去划船; **to go for a ~** 去划船

row³ /raʊ/

A *n* **1** (dispute, argument) 争吵; **a ~ about** *or* **over sth.** 因某事物发生的争吵; **to have** *or* **get into a ~ with sb. (about** *or* **over sth.)** (因某事物) 与某人争吵 **2** Brit colloq (uproar) 喧闹声; **to make a ~** 发出吵闹声; **to start** *or* **have** *or* **kick up a ~** 吵闹起来

B *vi* 争吵; **to ~ (with sb.) about** *or* **over sth.** (与某人) 因某事物发生争吵

rowan /ˈrəʊən, ˈraʊ-/ *n* 花楸

rowboat /ˈrəʊbəʊt/ *n* Amer 划艇

rowdiness /ˈraʊdɪnɪs/ *n* [u] 闹哄哄

rowdy /ˈraʊdi/

A *adj* (noisy) 闹哄哄的 ‹*crowd, party*›; (disorderly) 捣乱的 ‹*behaviour, gang*›

B *n* 吵嚷者; **football rowdies** 足球流氓

rowdyism /ˈraʊdɪɪzəm/ *n* = **rowdiness**

rower /ˈrəʊə(r)/ *n* 桨手

rowhouse /ˈrəʊhaʊs/ *n* Amer 一栋排屋

rowing /ˈrəʊɪŋ/ ▸**p. 307** *n* [u] 划船; **to go (out) ~** 去划船; **a ~ club** 划船俱乐部

rowing: ~ boat *n* Brit 划艇; **~ machine** *n* 划船练习架

rowlock /ˈrəʊlɒk, ˈrɒlək/ *n* Brit [船侧的] 桨架

royal /ˈrɔɪəl/

A *adj* **1** (of king or queen) 王室的 ‹*arms, power, visit, prerogative*›; **R~ prince/princess/household** *or* **family** 王子/公主/王室 **2** (in service of king or queen) 皇家的; **R~ Commission/Society** 皇家委员会/皇家学会 **3** (fit for king or queen) 适于君王的 ‹*style*›; 盛大的 ‹*welcome*›; **a ~ fortune** 巨额财富

B *n* colloq 王室成员

royal: R~ Air Force, the R~ Air Force *n* Brit 皇家空军; **R~ assent** *n* [u] Brit 御准 [君主对议会通过的议案的批准]

royal blue ▸**p. 134**

A *n* [u] 品蓝

B *adj* 品蓝的

royal: ~ family *n* 王室; **R~ Highness** *n* 殿下; **His/Her/Your R~ Highness/Their R~ Highnesses** 殿下; **~ icing** *n* [u] Brit [蛋糕等的] 蛋白糖霜硬皮

> **the Royal Family**
>
> 王室。目前英国的王室为温莎 (Windsor) 王室, 成员包括伊丽莎白女王和她的丈夫、子女及其配偶以及孩子。广义的王室成员亦可包括以前君主的子女、儿媳及孙子、孙媳等。英国的君主 (monarch 或 sovereign) 名义上是国家元首、武装部队总司令, 也是英联邦 (Commonwealth) 元首。君主的儿子及孙子享有王子 (prince) 称号; 女儿及孙女享有公主 (princess) 称号。长子传统上受封为威尔士亲王 (Prince of Wales), 同时被封为康沃尔公爵 (Duke of Cornwall), 为王位继承人; 其妻子常受封为威尔士王妃 (Princess of Wales)。次子一般被封为约克公爵 (Duke of York)。当面称呼君主要用 Your Majesty, 第三人称则用 His/Her Majesty。对王室其他成员当面一般称 Your Royal Highness, 第三人称则用 His/Her Royal Highness (HRH)。

royalist /ˈrɔɪəlɪst/

A *n* **1** (supporter) 君主主义者 **2** Brit Hist (in English Civil War) 保皇党人 **3** Amer Hist (in War of Independence) 亲英分子

B *adj* 君主主义者的 ‹*tendencies, principles*›

royally /ˈrɔɪəli/ *adv* fig 以盛情 ‹*entertain, receive*›

Royal: ~ Mail *n* Brit **the ~ Mail** 英国邮政; **~ Marines** *npl* Brit **the ~ Marires** 皇家海军陆战队; **~ Navy** *n* Brit **the ~ Navy** 皇家海军

royalty /ˈrɔɪəlti/ *n* + *v sing or pl* **1** [u] (king, queen, etc.) 王室成员; **to treat sb. like ~** 给某人以君王般的礼遇 **2** [u] (status) 王权 **3** [c] (for copyright) 版税 **4** [c] (for patent) 专利权费 **5** [c] (for mineral rights) 矿区土地使用费

royal: R~ Ulster Constabulary *n* Brit Hist **the R~ Ulster Constabulary** 北爱尔兰皇家警察; **~ warrant** *n* 英廷供货许可证

RP *abbr* Brit = **Received Pronunciation**

RPI *abbr* = **retail price index**

rpm *abbr* = **revolutions per minute** 每分钟转数

RRP *abbr* Brit = **recommended retail price**

RRSP *abbr* = **Registered Retirement Savings Plan** 注册退休储蓄计划

RSA *abbr* **1** = **Republic of South Africa** 南非共和国 **2** Brit = **Royal Society of Arts** 皇家艺术学会

RSI *abbr* = **repetitive strain injury**

RSM *abbr* = **regimental sergeant major**

RSPB *abbr* Brit = **Royal Society for the Protection of Birds** 皇家鸟类保护协会

RSPCA *abbr* Brit = **Royal Society for the Prevention of Cruelty to Animals** 皇家防止虐待动物协会

RSVP *abbr* = **répondez s'il vous plaît** 敬请赐复

RTF *abbr* = **rich text format**

Rt Hon *abbr* Brit = **Right Honourable**

RU *abbr* = **rugby union**

rub /rʌb/

A *vt* (*pres p etc.* **-bb-**) **1** (massage) 按摩 ‹*shoulders*›; **she ~bed my back** 她给我按摩后背 **2** (press on) 揉搓 ‹*chin, eyes, nose*›; **to ~ sb. up the wrong way, to ~ sb. the wrong way** Amer fig colloq 无意中惹恼某人; **to ~ sb.'s nose in it** fig colloq 老揭某人的伤疤 **3** (move back and forth) 抚摩 ‹*hand, finger, leg, cloth*› **4** (press together) 摩擦 ‹*hands*›; **to ~ noses** (in greeting) 行碰鼻礼; **to ~ one's hands with** *or* **in glee** 高兴得直搓手; **to ~ shoulders** *or* **elbows** Amer **with sb.** 与某名人交往 **5** (polish) 擦拭; **to ~ sth. with sth.** 用某物擦拭 ‹*surface, object*›; **to ~ the glass with a cloth** 用布擦玻璃杯 **6** (produce by friction) 磨出 ‹*bald patch*›; **to ~ a hole in sth.** 在某物上磨出洞 **7** (to dry) 擦干; (to clean) 擦净; (to smooth) 磨平; **to ~ sth. dry** 将…擦干 ‹*surface, hair*›; **to ~ sth. clean** 将…擦干净 ‹*surface, table, blackboard*›; **to ~ sth. smooth** 把…磨光 ‹*surface*›; **to ~ sth. away** 擦去 ‹*stain, tears*› **8** (apply ointment, polish, etc.) 涂抹; **to ~ sth. on to the skin** 将某物搽在皮肤上; **~ the cream into your skin** 把润肤霜揉进皮肤里; **to ~ salt into the wound** fig 往伤口上抹盐 **9** (chafe) «*shoe*» 磨 ‹*heel*›; «*wheel*» 蹭 ‹*mudguard*›; **to ~ sth. raw** 擦破…的皮 ‹*skin, neck*›

B *vi* (*pres p etc.* **-bb-**) **1** (press) 揉搓; **to ~ at sth.** «*person*» 揉搓 ‹*chin, eyes, nose*›; **to ~ against sth.** 揉搓某物 **2** (polish) 擦拭; **to ~ at sth.** «*person*» 擦拭 ‹*surface, table, silverware*› **3** (be pressed together) «*surfaces, objects*» 互相摩擦 **4** (to dry) 擦干; (to clean) 擦净; (to smooth) 磨平; **to ~ at sth.** 擦掉 ‹*stain, mark*› **5** (chafe) «*wheel*» 磨擦; «*shirt, collar*» 磨损; **these shoes ~** 这双鞋子磨脚; **to ~ on** *or* **against sth.** 蹭擦某物

C *v refl* **1** (press oneself) **to ~ oneself on** *or* **against sth.** 蹭某物 **2** (dry oneself) **to ~ oneself with** 用…擦干身体 ‹*towel*›; **to ~ oneself dry** 把自己擦干

D *n* **1** (with hand) 按摩; **to give sth. a ~** 按摩 ‹*back, knee, elbow, horse*› **2** (with cloth) 抹; **to give sth. a ~** 抹 ‹*spoon, table, stain*› **3** (ointment) 药膏 **4** liter or hum (difficulty) 难题; **there's the ~** 这就是症结所在

Phrasal verbs

- **rub along** *vi* Brit colloq **1** (manage) «*person, couple, family*» 勉强过活; **they ~ along because their overheads are so low** 他们勉强能生活, 因为他们的日常开支很低 **2** **to ~ along with sb.** (get on) 与某人相处融洽
- **rub down** *vt* [**~ sb./sth. down, ~ down sb./sth.**] **1** (smooth) 将…打磨光滑 ‹*wood, paint, surface, wall, plaster*› **2** (make dry and clean) 彻底擦干 ‹*person, horse*›; **to ~ oneself down** 把自己彻底擦干
- **rub in** *vt* [**~ sth. in, ~ in sth.**] 把…揉进表层 ‹*ointment, shampoo*›; **to ~ it in** colloq 不断触及痛处; **there's no need to ~ it in!** 没必要老是哪壶不开提哪壶!; **he's always ~bing it in how rich he is** 他总是爱说自己如何富有
- **rub off**

A *vt* [**~ sth. off, ~ off sth.**] 擦掉 ‹*stain, pattern*›

B *vi* **1** (come off) 掉落; **to ~ off on sb./sth.** «*dye, ink*» 掉色沾到某人身上/某处; **the ink ~bed off on my hands** 油墨掉色沾到我手上了 **2** (wipe off) «*mark, stain*» 被擦掉; **the chalk/the pencil ~s off easily** 粉笔/铅笔痕迹容易擦掉 **3** fig (be transferred) 传给; **I hope your enthusiasm ~s off on him** 我希望你的热情能感染他

- **rub out**

A *vt* [**~ sth. out, rub out sth.**] Brit (erase) 擦掉 ‹*word, drawing*›

B *vt* [**~ sb. out, ~ out sb.**] Amer colloq (kill) 干掉

C *vi* Brit «*mark, stain*» 被擦掉

rubber /ˈrʌbə(r)/

A *n* **1** [u] (substance) 橡胶; **a ~ ball/hose** 皮球/橡胶软管 **2** [c] Brit (for erasing mistakes) 橡皮擦 **3** [c] (for blackboard, whiteboard) 板擦 **4** [c] Amer colloq (condom) 避孕套 **5** [c] (contest) [板球、网球等的] 胜局比赛; **Sweden won the ~ five-nil** 瑞典队以5比0获胜 **6** (in bridge) 一盘胜局; **to play a ~** 获得一盘胜局

B **rubbers** *npl* Amer (boots) 橡胶套鞋

rubber: ~ band *n* 橡皮筋; **~ bullet** *n* 橡皮子弹; **~ cheque** *n* colloq 空头支票; **~ dinghy** *n* 橡皮艇; **~ glove** *n* 橡胶手套

rubberneck /'rʌbənek/ colloq pej
A *n* 东张西望的人
B *vi* 东张西望

rubbernecker /'rʌbənekə(r)/ *n* colloq pej 东张西望的人

rubber: ~ plant *n* 橡胶植物; **~ plantation** *n* 橡胶种植园; **~ sheet** *n* 橡胶床单; **~-soled** *adj* 有橡胶鞋底的; **~ solution** *n* [u] 橡胶胶水

rubber stamp
A *n* **1** lit (stamp) 橡皮图章 **2** fig pej (body) 橡皮图章 [指履行审批手续而没有实权的人或机构]
B **rubber-stamp** *vt* **1** lit 在…上盖橡皮图章 ‹*document, form*› **2** fig (approve) 例行公事般地批准 ‹*decision, policy*›

rubber: ~ tapper /'rʌbə ˌtæpə(r)/ ▸**p. 409** *n* 割胶工; **~ tapping** *n* [u] 割胶; **~ tree** *n* 橡胶树; **~-tyred** *adj* 装有橡胶轮胎的 ‹*vehicle*›

rubbery /'rʌbəri/ *adj* **1** (resembling rubber) 橡胶似的 ‹*substance, smell*›; 有弹性的 ‹*lips, texture*›; 软绵绵的 ‹*legs*› **2** (tough) 嚼不动的 ‹*meat, steak, bread*›

rubbing /'rʌbɪŋ/ *n* [u] **1** (action) 摩擦 **2** (impression) 拓印; **to make a ~** 制作拓本

rubbish /'rʌbɪʃ/
A *n* **1** Brit (waste) 垃圾 **2** (inferior goods) 差劲的东西 **3** (nonsense) 胡说; **(what a load of) ~!** 一派胡言！; **to talk ~** 胡说八道
B *vt* Brit colloq 狠批 ‹*idea, film, author*›
C *adj* Brit colloq 糟透的

rubbish: ~ bin *n* Brit 垃圾箱; **~ chute** *n* Brit 垃圾道; **~ collection** *n* Brit 垃圾收集; **~ dump, ~ tip** *ns* Brit 垃圾场

rubbishy /'rʌbɪʃi/ *adj* colloq 蹩脚的 ‹*goods, newspaper, entertainment*›; **they like ~ food like chips and burgers** 他们喜欢吃薯片和汉堡包这样的垃圾食品

rubble /'rʌbl/ *n* [u] 碎石; **the house was reduced to a pile of ~** 这幢房子被毁成了一堆瓦砾

rub-down *n* **1** (drying) 擦干; (smoothing) 打磨; **to give sb./sth. a ~** 给某人擦身/将某物磨光 **2** (massage) 按摩

rube /ru:b/ *n* Amer colloq 乡巴佬

rubella /ru:'belə/ ▸**p. 377** *n* [u] 风疹; **to be suffering from ~** 患风疹

Rubicon /'ru:bɪkən, Amer -kɒn/ *pr n* **the ~** 鲁比肯河; **to cross the ~** 破釜沉舟

rubidium /ru:'bɪdɪəm/ *n* [u] 铷

Rubik's cube /'ru:bɪks kju:b/ *n* 魔方

ruble /'ru:bl/ *n* = **rouble**

rubric /'ru:brɪk/ *n* formal **1** (instruction) (on exam paper) 说明; (in liturgical book) 礼拜规则 **2** (category) 类目; (heading) 标题; **courses taught under the ~ of human sciences** 人文科学类目下的讲授课程

ruby /'ru:bi/
A *n* **1** [c] (gem) 红宝石 **2** ▸**p. 134** [u] (colour) 红宝石色
B *modif* 镶红宝石的 ‹*necklace, bracelet*›
C *adj* 红宝石色的 ‹*liquid, lips, glow*›

ruby-coloured ▸**p. 134** *adj* 红宝石色的

ruby red ▸**p. 134**
A *n* [u] 宝石红
B *adj* 宝石红的

ruby wedding *n* 红宝石婚 [结婚40周年纪念]

RUC *abbr* = **Royal Ulster Constabulary**

ruck /rʌk/
A *n* **1** (in rugby) 密集争球 **2** (crowd, group) 密集的人群 **3** **the ~** (mass) 普通人; **to escape from the ~** 出人头地 **4** (crease) 褶皱
B *vi* «*bedclothes, clothes*» 起皱
C *vt* 弄皱 ‹*bedclothes, clothes*›

Phrasal verb
• **ruck up** *vt* 将…弄皱 ‹*skirt, bedclothes, cloth*›

ruckle *vi, vt* = **ruck B, C**

Phrasal verb
• **ruckle up** *vt* = **ruck up**

rucksack /'rʌksæk/ *n* Brit 帆布背包

ruckus /'rʌkəs/ *n* colloq 喧闹

ructions /'rʌkʃnz/ *npl* Brit colloq 争吵; **the police heard of some ~ outside the town hall** 警察听到市政厅外面有人在抗议; **we don't want any ~ in the family over this** 我们不希望家人因此起争执

rudder /'rʌdə(r)/ *n* **1** (on boat) 舵 **2** (on plane) 方向舵

rudderless /'rʌdəlɪs/ *adj* **1** lit (having no rudder) 无舵的 ‹*boat*›; 无方向舵的 ‹*plane*› **2** fig (purposeless) 无领导的 ‹*government, management*›

ruddy /'rʌdi/
A *adj* **1** (in complexion) 红润的 ‹*face, cheeks, complexion*› **2** (in colour) 红彤彤的 ‹*colour, sky, autumn leaves*›; **the ~ glow of the setting sun** 落日的红色霞辉 **3** Brit colloq dated (bloody) 该死的 ‹*person, animal, car*›; **~ hell!** 该死的！
B *adv* Brit colloq dated [用于加强语气，表示愤怒]; **don't be so ~ stupid!** 别那么傻了！

rude /ru:d/ *adj* **1** (impolite) 粗鲁的 ‹*person, remark, behaviour*›; **to be ~ to sb.** 粗鲁地对待某人; **to be ~ of sb. to do sth.** 某人做某事很无礼 **2** (offensive) 猥亵的 ‹*gesture, behaviour*›; 下流的 ‹*joke, remark*› **3** (abrupt) 突然的 ‹*shock, dismissal*›; 猛然的 ‹*awakening*› **4** liter (simple) 简陋的 ‹*dwellings, implements*› **5** *attrib* Brit (vigorous) **to be in ~ health** 身强体壮

rudely /'ru:dli/ *adv* **1** (impolitely) 粗鲁地 ‹*behave, remark*› **2** (offensively) 下流地 ‹*gesture*› **3** (abruptly) 猛然 ‹*awakened*›; 突然 ‹*shattered*› **4** liter (simply) 简陋地 ‹*constructed, made*›

rudeness /'ru:dnɪs/ *n* [u] **1** (of behaviour, remark) 粗鲁; **~ to sb.** 对某人的粗鲁态度; **she was brusque to the point of ~** 她唐突到了粗鲁无礼的地步 **2** (of gesture) 下流 **3** (abruptness) 猛然 **4** liter (simplicity) 粗陋

rudimentary /ˌru:dɪ'mentri/ *adj* **1** (undeveloped) 早期的 ‹*system*›; 原始的 ‹*tools, techniques*› **2** (basic) 基本的 ‹*knowledge, facts, skills*›; **a ~ course** 基础课程; **~ mathematics** 基础数学; **I have only a ~ grasp of physics** 我只是粗通物理罢了 **3** Biol 未完全发育的 ‹*brain, stage*›

rudiments /'ru:dɪmənts/ *npl* **1** (basic facts, elements) 基本原理; **the ~ of economics/life/tennis** 经济学基础/生活常识/网球入门 **2** (elementary form) 雏形; **the ~ of a central heating system** 中央供暖系统的雏形 **3** Biol 未完全发育的器官

rue /ru:/ *vt* (*pres p* **ruing** *or* **~ing**) 对…感到懊悔 ‹*action, decision*›; **you'll ~ the day you joined up** 你一入伍就会后悔的

rueful /'ru:fl/ *adj* 懊悔的 ‹*sigh, thoughts, mood*›; **to feel ~ about sth./doing sth.** 对某事/做某事感到懊悔

ruefully /'ru:fəli/ *adv* 懊悔地 ‹*sigh, say, smile*›

ruff[1] /rʌf/ *n* **1** (of lace) [16和17世纪服装上的] 轮状皱领 **2** (of a bird or animal) 翎颌

ruff[2] (in cards)
A *vt* 以将牌吃进 ‹*card, opponent*›
B *vi* 出将牌
C *n* (*pl* **~** *or* **~s**) (bird) 毛领鸽

ruffian /'rʌfiən/ *n* 恶棍; **he was set upon by a gang of ~s** 他遭到一群暴徒的袭击

ruffle /'rʌfl/
A *vt* **1** (stroke) 弄乱 ‹*hair, fur*› **2** (turn quickly) 快速翻动 ‹*pages, papers*› **3** (of bird) 竖起 ‹*feathers*› **4** (disturb) 使…起伏不平 ‹*sea, grass, surface*›; 扰乱 ‹*peace, tranquillity, event*› **5** (disconcert) 使生气; **to ~ sb.'s feathers** fig 惹恼某人
B *n* 褶裥饰边

ruffled /'rʌfld/ *adj* 弄乱的 ‹*hair*›; 弄皱的 ‹*bedclothes*›; 起伏的 ‹*waters, surface*›

rug /rʌg/ *n* **1** (small carpet) 小地毯; **to be as snug as a bug in a ~** colloq 感到温暖舒适; **to pull the ~ out from under sb.'s feet** fig 突然停止支持某人 **2** Brit (blanket) (for person) [用于盖肩或膝的] 盖毯; (for horse) [护马用的] 披毯

rugby /'rʌgbi/ ▸**p. 307** *n* **~ (football)** 橄榄球运动; **a ~ player/tournament/coach/fan** 橄榄球队员/比赛/教练/迷; **~ boots** 橄榄球钉鞋

rugby: ~ league *n* [每队13人参赛的] 联盟橄榄球; **~ tackle** *n* [橄榄球运动中的] 擒抱; **~ union** *n* [每队15人参赛的] 联合会橄榄球

rugged /'rʌgɪd/ *adj* **1** (rough) 崎岖的 ‹*terrain, path*›; 起伏的 ‹*coastline, mountains*›; **~ rocks/cliff** 凹凸不平的石块/岩石突兀的悬崖 **2** (manly) 粗犷的 ‹*face, features*› **3** (tough) 坚毅的 ‹*explorer, character*›; 坚定的 ‹*determination*›; 坚决的 ‹*resistance*› **4** (durable) 坚固的 ‹*construction, defences*›; 耐用的 ‹*equipment*›

ruggedness /'rʌgɪdnɪs/ *n* **1** (of terrain) 崎岖不平; (of coastline) 起伏 **2** (of appearance) 粗犷; **there was a certain ~ about his features** 他的相貌有些粗犷 **3** (of character, nature) 坚毅 **4** (of construction) 坚固; (of vehicle) 耐用

rugger /'rʌgə(r)/ ▸**p. 307** *n* Brit colloq dated 橄榄球运动; **to play ~** 打橄榄球

ruin /'ru:ɪn/
A *vt* **1** (destroy) 毁坏 ‹*furniture, relationship, economy, reputation*›; **smoking can ~ your health** 吸烟有损健康; **to ~ sb.'s prospects/career** 葬送某人的前程/事业; **to ~ sb.'s chances of doing sth.** 断送某人做某事的机会 **2** (spoil) 破坏 ‹*holiday, atmosphere, view*›; 宠坏 ‹*child, pet*› **3** (reduce to poverty) 使…破产 ‹*person, company*›
B *n* **1** [u] (state of collapse) (physical) 毁坏; (financial) 破产; (moral) 堕落; **in a state of ~** «*town, building*» 破败不堪; **to fall** *or* **go into ~** 毁灭; **to be on the brink of financial ~** 处于破产的边缘; **a man brought to ~ by debt/drugs** 因债务/吸食毒品而一贫如洗的人; **to be reduced to (a state of) ~** 落到破产的地步; **to go to rack and ~** «*building, object*» 变得破败不堪; «*person*» 彻底毁掉 **2** [c] (building) 破败的建筑; **the abbey/castle is now a ~** 这座修道院/城堡现在已破败不堪 **3** [u] (downfall) 毁灭的原因; **that woman will be the ~ of him!** 那个女人会毁了他！
C **ruins** *npl* (remains) 废墟; **the ~s of Pompeii/an old castle** 庞贝城/古城堡遗迹; **an earthquake left the whole town in ~s** 地震使整座城市成为废墟; **our marriage/her reputation/the economy is in ~s** 我们的婚姻已经破裂/她已经身败名裂/经济已经崩溃; **their plan/her career now lay in ~s** 他们的计划泡汤了/她的事业被葬送了

ruination /ˌru:ɪ'neɪʃn/ *n* [u] formal **1** (financial downfall) 破产; (moral downfall) 堕落 **2** (of a plan, process) 毁坏

ruined /'ru:ɪnd/ *adj* **1** (spoilt) 毁掉的 ‹*furniture, career, marriage*› **2** (financially) 破产的 ‹*businessman, company*› **3** (derelict) 破败不堪的 ‹*castle, abbey, town*›

ruinous /'ru:ɪnəs/ *adj* **1** (expensive) 无法承担的 ‹*damages, expense, cost*›; **the prices in that restaurant are absolutely ~** 那家餐馆的价格绝对高得离谱 **2** (disastrous) 灾难性的 ‹*event*›; 毁灭性的 ‹*war*›

ruinously /'ru:ɪnəsli/ *adv* 无法承受地; **~ expensive** 贵得离谱

rule /ru:l/
A *n* **1** [c] (regulation) (of game, sport, system) 规则; (of religion) 教规; (of school, company, organization) 规章; **~s and regulations** 规章制度; **school/EU ~s** 校规/欧盟法规; **to break the ~s** 违规;

to obey/follow/observe the ~s 服从/遵循/遵守规则; to be against the ~s (to do sth.) 违反规定（做某事）; under this ~ 按照这条规定; it is a ~ that ... …是规定; the ~s of the game lit 游戏规则; fig 行为准则; to play by the ~s lit 按规则玩游戏; fig 处事公正诚实; to play by one's own/sb.'s ~s 按自己的原则/某人的规矩行事; to bend or stretch the ~s 通融 [2] [c] (piece of advice) 建议; hard and fast ~s 一定之规; there are two vital ~s to remember 有两条极其重要的原则要记住 [3] [c] (usual occurrence) 常规; I make it a ~ always/never to do ... 我的习惯是一向/从不做…; hot summers are the ~ here 这里的夏天通常很炎热; as a ~ 通常; as a general ~ 一般说来 [4] [u] (authority) 统治; colonial/civilian/military ~ 殖民/文官/军人统治; majority/minority ~ 多数派政党/少数派政党执政; under the ~ of a tyrant 在暴君的统治下 [5] [c] (for measuring) 直尺; a metre ~ 米尺

[B] vt [1] (govern) «monarch, dictator» 统治 ‹country›; to ~ with a rod of iron or with an iron hand 实行铁腕统治 [2] (dominate) 主宰; eighty million years ago, dinosaurs ~d the earth 8,000 万年前，地球是恐龙的天下 [3] (influence) «money, appetite» 支配 ‹person, life, character›; «person, consideration» 控制 ‹behaviour›; «factor» 决定 ‹strategy›; to be ~d by 受…支配 ‹emotion, greed, need›; to let one's heart ~ one's head 感情用事 [4] (decide) 裁定; to ~ sb./sth. (to be) sth. «judge, court» 裁定某人/某事为某情况; to ~ sth. unlawful or illegal 判定某事非法; to ~ that ... 裁定… [5] (draw) 用直尺画 ‹line, margin›

[C] vi [1] (govern) «monarch, dictator» 统治; to ~ over sb./sth. 统治某人/某处 [2] (dominate) «order» 起支配作用; «chaos, fashion» 成风; anarchy ~s 无政府主义猖獗 [3] Jur «judge, court» 作出裁定; to ~ in favour of sb./sth. 判定某人/某机构胜诉; to ~ against sb./sth. 判定某人/某机构败诉; to ~ on sth. 对某事作出裁决 [4] colloq (be excellent) 很棒; Leeds United ~ OK! 利兹联队必胜!

Phrasal verbs

- **rule off**
  [A] vi 画分隔线
  [B] vt [~ sth. off, ~ off sth.] 画线隔开 ‹section, column›
- **rule out** vt [~ sb./sth. out, ~ out sb./sth.] [1] (exclude) «person, police» 排除 ‹person, suspect, possibility›; to ~ sb./sth. out as sth. 因某情况而排除某人/某事物; to ~ sb./sth. out of sth. 从某事中排除某人/某事物 [2] (prevent) «person, weather, situation» 阻止 ‹activity, person›; rain ~d out play for the day 白天的比赛因雨取消; to ~ out doing sth. 阻止做某事; the chairman has ~d out spending any more money on the project 董事长已决定不再给这个项目投资了; his age effectively ~d him out as a possible candidate 他的年龄使他根本不可能成为候选人; to ~ sb./sth. out of sth. 阻止某人/某物参加某事; he has been ~d out of the match with a knee injury 他因膝盖受伤而无缘这场比赛

rule book n 规则手册; to throw away the ~ fig 不按规则办事; to throw the ~ at sb. fig 严惩某人

ruled /ruːld/ adj 有横格的

rule: ~ of law n [u] 法治; **~ of the road** n 行路规则; **~ of thumb** n [根据经验得出的] 粗略估算方法; as a ~ of thumb, you'll need two cups of water for every cup of rice 根据经验粗算一下，每杯大米需要加两杯水

ruler /ˈruːlə(r)/ n [1] (leader) 统治者 [2] (measure) 直尺

rules of engagement npl 交战规则

ruling /ˈruːlɪŋ/
[A] adj attrib [1] (in power) 统治的 ‹faction, class›; the ~ party 执政党 [2] (dominant) 占支配地位的 ‹passion, principle›; ~ prices on the international market 国际市场上的主导价格
[B] n 裁决; to give a ~ on sth. 对某事作出裁决

rum¹ /rʌm/ n [1] [u and c] (drink) 朗姆酒 [2] [c] (serving) 一杯朗姆酒

rum² adj Brit colloq dated 古怪的 ‹chap, idea›; 离奇的 ‹situation, tale›; a ~ do 离奇的事

Rumania /ruːˈmeɪnɪə/ pr n = Romania

Rumanian /ruːˈmeɪnɪən/ adj, n = Romanian

rumba /ˈrʌmbə/ n [1] (dance) 伦巴舞 [2] (music) 伦巴舞曲

rumble /ˈrʌmbl/
[A] n [1] (of thunder, artillery, vehicles, machine) 隆隆声; (of stomach, in pipes) 咕噜声; a or the ~ of sth. 某物的隆隆声 [2] (of voices) 咕哝声; a ~ of discontent went through the hall 大厅里发出了一阵不满的咕哝声 [3] Amer colloq (fight) 街头群架
[B] vt Brit colloq 识破 ‹identity, fraud›; 看穿 ‹intentions, person›
[C] vi [1] (make noise) «thunder, artillery» 发出隆隆声 [2] (trundle) «old vehicle, heavy object» 隆隆地行进; to ~ along/into/past ... 隆隆地沿着…行进/进入…/经过… [3] (with hunger) «stomach» 发出咕噜声 [4] Amer colloq (brawl) 打群架

Phrasal verb

- **rumble on** vi «debate, controversy» 没完没了地进行

rumble strip n [路面的] 齿纹震动带

rumbling /ˈrʌmblɪŋ/
[A] n (of thunder, artillery, vehicles, machines) 隆隆声; (of stomach, in pipes) 咕噜声; the ~ of thunder 隆隆的雷声
[B] **rumblings** npl 不满声; ~s of discontent 怨声载道

rumbustious /rʌmˈbʌstɪəs/ adj Brit colloq 欢闹的 ‹atmosphere, comedy›; 喧闹的 ‹party›

ruminant /ˈruːmɪnənt/ n 反刍动物

ruminate /ˈruːmɪneɪt/ vi [1] (deliberate) 沉思; to ~ on or about sth. 反复思考某事 [2] Zool «cow, sheep» 反刍

rumination /ˌruːmɪˈneɪʃn/ n [1] [c] (deliberation) 沉思 [2] [u] Zool 反刍

rummage /ˈrʌmɪdʒ/
[A] n [1] [c] (search) 翻找; I had a ~ in the attic 我在阁楼里翻找了一下 [2] [u] Amer (old things) 供义卖的捐献物
[B] vi 翻找; to ~ in or among or through sth. 在某物中搜寻; to ~ for sth. 翻找某物

Phrasal verb

- **rummage about, rummage around** vi 东翻西找; to ~ about in sth. 在某物中东翻西找

rummage sale n Amer 旧杂物义卖

rummy /ˈrʌmi/ ▸p. 307 n [u] 拉米纸牌游戏

rumor /ˈruːmə(r)/ n Amer = rumour

rumored /ˈruːməd/ adj Amer = rumoured

rumormonger /ˈruːməmʌŋɡə(r)/ n Amer = rumourmonger

rumour /ˈruːmə(r)/ n [c and u] (story) 谣言; (information considered unreliable) 传闻; to start or spread a ~ 散布谣言; to deny/quash a ~ 否认谣传/平息流言; ~s of or about ... 关于…的传言; there is no truth in or to the ~ that ... …谣传毫无真实性可言; I heard a ~ (to the effect) that ... 我听到谣言（大意是）说…; according to ~ ... 据传…; ~ has it that ... 有传闻说…

rumoured /ˈruːməd/ adj 谣传的 ‹disagreement, plot, pregnancy›; it is ~ that ... 据谣传…; to be ~ to be sth./to have done sth. 据传是某物/做了某事; she is ~ to be a millionaire 有传言说她是百万富翁

rumour: ~ mill n colloq 谣传; according to the ~ mill ..., the ~ mill has it that ... 据谣传…; **~monger** /-mʌŋɡə(r)/ Brit n 散布谣言者

rump /rʌmp/ n [1] (of animal) 臀部; (of bird) 尾部 [2] hum (of person) 屁股蛋子 [3] pej (of party, group) 残留部分

rumple /ˈrʌmpl/ vt 弄皱 ‹clothes, bedclothes›; 弄乱 ‹papers, hair›

rumpled /ˈrʌmpld/ adj 弄皱的 ‹clothes, bedclothes›; 凌乱的 ‹hair, papers›

rump steak n 臀肉牛排

rumpus /ˈrʌmpəs/ n (pl ~es) colloq (disturbance) 喧闹; (protest) 吵闹; a ~ about or over sth. 关于某事物的争执; to have a ~ (with sb.)（与某人）发生口角; to make or create or cause or raise or kick up a ~ 引起骚动

rumpus room n Amer [常设于地下室的] 娱乐室

run /rʌn/
[A] vi (pres p -nn-, pt ran, pp run) [1] (move quickly) 跑; to ~ to meet sb. 跑着去见某人; to ~ to catch the bus/to help sb. 跑着去赶公交车/去帮助某人; ~ and catch him! 赶紧去追他！; to ~ across/along/down/up 跑步穿过/一路跑/跑下/跑上; will you ~ over to the shop and get some milk? 你去趟商店买牛奶好吗？; to ~ for the bus/the train 跑着去赶公交车/火车; to come ~ning lit 跑过来; fig 赶紧做某人喜欢的事; the customers will come ~ning 顾客会踊跃购买的 [2] (as sport or for exercise) 跑步 [3] (compete in race) «athlete, dog, horse» 参加赛跑; to ~ in the 100 metres/in the 3:30 (race) 参加100 米/3:30 开始的赛跑; to ~ for one's country 代表祖国参加赛跑 [4] (flee) 逃跑; I dropped everything and ran 我扔掉所有的东西跑掉了; to ~ for the exit 朝出口处跑去; there's nowhere to ~ (to) 无处可逃; ~ for your life! 快逃命吧！; ~ for it! 快跑！; I had to ~ for it 我只好撒腿跑 [5] colloq (leave) 赶紧离开; sorry, must ~! 对不起，得赶紧走了！ [6] (function) «machine» 运转; to leave the engine ~ning 让引擎运转; to ~ off sth. 靠…运转 ‹mains, battery›; to ~ on sth. 用…作燃料 ‹diesel, unleaded›; to ~ fast/slow «clock, watch» 走快/走慢; to be up and ~ning 全面准确地运行 [7] (proceed) «event, organization» 进行; to ~ smoothly 进展顺利 [8] (provide service) the buses don't ~ on Sundays 公交车周日不开; a taxi service/ferry ~s between A and B A和B之间有出租车/渡轮 [9] (with reference to timetable) 发生; to ~ ahead of/behind schedule 比预定时间提前/推后开始; the train is ~ning late 火车晚点了 [10] (move) 快速行进; a pain ran up my leg 我的腿突然疼了起来; the rope ran through my hands 绳子从我的双手滑过; a wave of excitement ran through the crowd 一阵兴奋迅速在人群中蔓延; his eyes ran over the page 他把那一页浏览了一遍; the news ran from house to house 消息迅速传得家喻户晓 [11] (extend in space) «line, boundary, road, river» 延伸; the stripes ~ vertically 这些条纹是纵向的; to ~ parallel to sth. 与某物平行; to ~ (from) east to west 从东向西延伸; the road ~s north for about ten kilometres 这条路向北延伸约 10 公里; a scar ~s down his cheek 他脸颊上竖着一道伤疤; a bird with a green stripe ~ning down its back 背部有一道绿色斑纹的鸟 [12] (extend in time) 持续; the course ~s for 6 months 这门课程持续 6 个月; the school year ~s from September to July 学年从 9 月份直到 7 月份 [13] (be valid) «contract, permit» 有效; to have another month to ~ 还有一个月的有效期 [14] (be performed) «play, performance» 上演; «TV show» 被播放; «film» 被放映; this show will ~ and ~! 这台节目将会连演!; to ~ for about 3 months 上演约 3 个

月; **the film will ~ for another week** 这部影片将再放映一周 [15] (be worded) «*message, speech*» 被表达; «*argument*» 被陈述; **the telex ~s ...** 电传的内容是…; **so the argument ~s** 论点就是这样 [16] (flow) 流淌; **tears ran down his face** 泪水顺着他的面颊淌下来; **there was water ~ning down the walls** 水顺着墙壁往下流; **the river ran red with blood** liter 河水被鲜血染红了; **the meat juices ran pink/clear** 渗出的肉汁呈粉红色/很清 [17] (release water) «*tap, hose*» 放水 [18] (fill with water) 被注入水; **is the bath still ~ning?** 还在往浴缸里放水吗? [19] (excrete liquid) «*eyes*» 排出体液; **my nose is ~ning** 我在流鼻涕 [20] (be covered with) 流满; **my body was ~ning with sweat** 我浑身是汗; **the streets will ~ with blood** fig 街上会血流成河 [21] (spread) «*dye, colour*» 渗化; «*garment*» 渗色; **this fabric is likely to ~** 这种布料会渗色 [22] (melt) «*butter, wax*» 融化 [23] (become) 变得; **to ~ dry** «*well, river*» 干涸; «*pen*» 没墨水; **to ~ low** «*supplies, stocks, reserves*» 变少; **to ~ short (of sth.)** 缺少(某物); **we've ~ short of milk** 我们没有牛奶了; **to ~ scared** «*person*» 害怕 [24] Pol (stand as candidate) 参加竞选; **to ~ for sth.** 竞选 ‹*mayor, governor, President, office*›; **to ~ against sb.** 与某人竞选 [25] (ladder) «*stockings, pantyhose, material*» 抽丝

B *vt* (*pres p* **-nn-**, *pt* **ran**, *pp* **run**) [1] (sprint) 跑 ‹*distance*›; **I ran the rest of the way** 我跑完了剩下的路 [2] (take part in) 参加; **she ran a brilliant race/a very fast time** 她在赛跑中表现出色/跑得非常快 [3] (take place) 开始; **the race will be ~ at 10:30** 赛跑将于10:30开始 [4] (enter in race) «*person, owner*» 给…报名参赛 ‹*horse, dog*› [5] (enter in election) «*party*» 提名 ‹*person, candidate*› [6] (drive) 驾驶 ‹*vehicle*›; **to ~ the car over to the garage** 把车开到修车厂去; **to ~ the car into a tree** 开车撞到树上 [7] (take in vehicle) «*person, driver*» 用车载送 ‹*person, passenger, object*›; **to ~ sb. home/to the station/to hospital** 开车送某人回家/去车站/去医院; **to ~ sth. over to sb.'s house** 开车将某物送到某人家 [8] (pass, move) 使快速移动; **to ~ one's hand over sth.** 用手抚过某物; **to ~ one's finger down the list** 用手指比着从上到下快速看一遍名单; **to ~ one's eye(s) over sth.** 快速看一遍某物; **to ~ a duster/the vacuum cleaner over sth.** 用掸子/吸尘器清理某物; **to ~ one's pen/pencil through sth.** 用钢笔/铅笔画掉某物; **to ~ a comb through one's hair** 梳头 [9] (wind) 绕; **to ~ a tape/film back/forward** 将磁带/胶片往回倒/往前进 [10] (manage) 经营; **a well-/badly-~ organization** 管理良好/不善的机构; **who is ~ning things around here?** 这儿谁负责?; **I'm ~ning this show!** colloq 这一摊儿现在归我管!; **stop trying to ~ my life!** 别总想操纵我的生活! [11] (organize, offer) 举办 ‹*competition, raffle*›; 提供 ‹*train service*›; 开设 ‹*lessons, course*› [12] (put in service) 使…按路线行驶 ‹*train, bus, ferry*› [13] (conduct) 进行; **to ~ tests on sth.** 对某事物进行测试; **to ~ a check on sb.** «*police*» 对某人进行调查 [14] (own, use) «*person*» 拥有 ‹*car, machine*›; **the car is cheap to ~** 养这辆车花销不大 [15] (operate) 运行 ‹*engine, program*›; **to ~ sth. off the mains/off batteries** 用交流电源/电池使某物运作; **to ~ a machine on gas** 用燃气驱动机器; **to be ~ by sth.** 靠…运转 ‹*solar power, compressed air*› [16] (extend) 使…延伸 ‹*wire, rope, pipe*›; **to ~ a cable from the house to the garage** 从屋子里拉一根电线到车库; **to ~ sth. around/between/under** 把某物绕在…上/设在…之间/铺在…下面; **to ~ a rope through a ring** 将绳子穿过环 [17] (smuggle) 走私 ‹*drugs, guns, contraband*› [18] (cause to flow) 使流动; **to ~ water into sth.** 将水注入 ‹*container*›; **to ~ water over sth.** 将水浇在某物上 [19] (release water from) 拧开 ‹*tap*› [20] (fill with water) 往…中放水 ‹*bath*›; **to ~ sb./oneself a bath** 给某人/自己放洗澡水 [21] (carry) «*newspaper*» 刊登 ‹*story, article*› [22] (navigate) 在…上漂流 ‹*rapids, waterfall*› [23] esp Amer (not stop at) «*person, driver*» 闯 ‹*red light*› [24] (get past) «*person, ship*» 偷越 ‹*blockade*›

C *n* [1] (act of running) 跑; (period of running) 跑步的时间; **a two-mile ~** 两英里的跑步; **to go for a ~** 去跑步; **to take the dog for a ~ in the park** 到公园里溜狗; **on the ~** (escaping) «*prisoner*» 在逃; (retreating) «*army, soldier*» 在溃退; (facing defeat) «*team, competitor, opponent*» 显现颓势; (very busy) «*person*» 在忙碌; (hurrying) «*person*» 在奔波; **to be on the ~ from sb./sth.** 正在躲避某人/某机构的追捕; **to have sb. on the ~** 把…击退 ‹*soldier, army*›; 把…打得无招架之力 ‹*opponent, competitor, team*›; **to go on the ~** «*prisoner*» 开始逃亡; **to make a ~ for the door** 向门口跑去; **to make a ~ for it** 逃跑 [2] (run-up) 助跑; (distance of run-up) 助跑距离; **to take a ~ at sth.** «*person, athlete, rider, horse*» 助跑冲向 ‹*fence, hedge, stream*› [3] (running pace) 跑步; **to do sth. at a ~** 跑着去做某事; **to break into a ~** 突然跑起来 [4] (car trip) 乘车短途旅行; **to go for a ~ (in the car)** 乘车兜风; **it's only a short ~ into town** 开车进城只需一小会儿; **the ~ up to London** 上伦敦去的旅程; **to take sb. for a ~** 让某人搭车 [5] (regular route) (of driver, delivery vehicle) 旅程; (of pilot, aircraft, ship) 航程; **he does the Leeds ~ twice a week** 他每周去两趟利兹 [6] (by bomber) [投弹前或投弹中的] 平直匀速飞行 [7] (opportunity) 机会; **to give sb. a clear ~** 把机会拱手让给某人 [8] (spell) 一段时间; **a ~ of fine weather** 一段时间的好天气; **we had a long ~ without any illness** 我们很久没得病了; **the product has had a good ~ but ...** 该产品问世很久了, 但是…; **to have a ~ of good/bad luck** 好运连连/厄运不断; **in the long ~** 从长远来看; **in the short ~** 从短期看来 [9] (series of performances) 连续上演; **the play is beginning its Broadway ~** 这部戏在百老汇开始连续演出; **to have a long ~** 长时间连续演出; **to have a six-month ~** 连演6个月 [10] (in printing) 一次印数; (in industry) [一段时间内的] 额定产量; **a paperback ~ of 10,000 copies** 印数1万册的平装本; **a production ~ of only 150 cars** 只有150辆车的额定产量 [11] (widespread demand) 抢购; **a ~ on sth.** 对某物的抢购 [12] Fin (widespread trading) [因货币贬值而] 抛售; **a ~ on sterling/the dollar** 英镑/美元的抛售 [13] Fin (repayment demand) 挤兑; **a ~ on the bank** 到银行挤兑 [14] (trend) 趋势; **against the ~ of play** 出人意料; **the ~ of the cards/dice was against her** 她打牌/掷骰子的手气很差; **in the normal ~ of things** 在正常情况下 [15] (type) 普通类型; **the general** *or* **ordinary** *or* **usual ~ of things** 普通的事物 [16] (track for skiing, bobsleighing, tobogganing) 滑道 [17] (enclosure for rabbits, chickens) 饲养场 [18] (unrestricted use) 自由使用; (unrestricted access) 自由出入; **to give sb. the ~ of** 允许某人自由出入 ‹*place, house*›; **to have the ~ of** 能随意去 ‹*place, house*› [19] Sport (point in cricket, baseball) 得分; **to score** *or* **make a ~** 得1分 [20] Mus (rapid passage of notes) 急奏 [21] (in cards) 同花顺; **a ~ of three** 3张同花顺 [22] (in stocking, pantyhose) 抽丝 [23] Amer (in election) 竞选; **a ~ for** 为…的竞选 ‹*nomination, office*›

D runs *npl* **the ~s** colloq (diarrhoea) 腹泻; **to have the ~s** 拉肚子

Phrasal verbs

- **run about** *vi* Brit = **run around A**
- **run about with** *vt* Brit colloq = **run around with**
- **run across** *vt* [1] [**~ across sb.**] (meet) 偶然遇见 ‹*person, acquaintance*› [2] [**~ across sth.**] (find) 偶然发现 ‹*object, reference, quotation*›
- **run after** *vt* [1] [**~ after sb./sth.**] (try to catch) 追赶 ‹*person, thief, vehicle, animal, ball*› [2] [**~ after sb.**] colloq (seek relationship with) 追求
- **run along** *vi* dated colloq [尤指命令儿童] 走开; **~ along (now)!** (马上) 走开!
- **run around**

A *vi* 到处跑; **I've been ~ning around all over the place looking for you** 我在到处找你

B *vt* [**~ around sth.**] 在…处跑来跑去; **the children were ~ning around the house** 孩子们在屋子里跑来跑去

- **run around with** *vt* [**~ around with sb.**] colloq 与…鬼混
- **run at** *vt* [1] [**~ at sb./sth.**] (charge towards) 冲向 [2] [**~ at sth.**] (be at) «*inflation, unemployment*» 达到 ‹*percentage, level, rate, figure*›; **with inflation ~ning at 2.2%** 通胀率达到2.2%
- **run away** [1] (flee) 逃跑 [2] colloq (go away) 离开; **don't ~ away; the play has only just started** 别走, 戏才刚刚开始 [3] **to ~ away from sb./sth.** (leave) 逃离某人/某处; (try to avoid) 回避某人/某事物; **to ~ away from home/one's husband** 离家出走/离开丈夫; **to ~ away from one's responsibilities/a problem** 逃避责任/问题 [4] (elope) 私奔; **to ~ away together** 一起私奔 [5] (flow away) «*water, liquid*» 流掉
- **run away with**

A [**~ away with sth.**] *vt*

[1] (abscond with) 偷走 ‹*profits, takings, money*› [2] (mistakenly believe) 错误地相信 ‹*impression*›; **I don't want him ~ning away with that idea** 我不想让他有那种错误想法; **to ~ away with the idea** *or* **notion that ...** 误以为… [3] (win easily) «*person, team, company*» 轻松赢得 ‹*prize, title, match*› [4] Brit (use up) «*activity, project*» 耗费 ‹*money, resources*›

B [**~ away with sb.**] *vt*

[1] (overwhelm) «*emotions*» 脱离…的控制; **to let one's emotions/enthusiasm/imagination ~ away with one** 按捺不住情感/被热情冲昏了头/想入非非 [2] (elope with) 和…私奔 ‹*boyfriend, lover*›

- **run by** *vt* **to ~ sth. by sb.** colloq [为了解反应] 把…告诉某人 ‹*idea, proposal*›; **can you ~ that plan by me again?** 把那个计划再说给我听听好吗?
- **run down**

A *vi* [1] (lose power) «*battery*» 耗尽; «*watch, machine*» 停止运转 [2] (decline) «*industry, operation*» 萎缩 [3] (decrease) «*reserves, stocks*» 减少

B [**~ sb./sth. down, ~ down sb./sth.**] *vt*

[1] (knock down) «*driver, vehicle*» 撞倒 ‹*person, animal*›; **to be** *or* **get run down by sb./sth.** 被某人/某物撞倒 [2] (criticize) 诋毁 ‹*person, institution*› [3] (catch) 抓到 ‹*person, animal*› [4] (find after a search) 找到 ‹*person, object*›

C [**~ sth. down, ~ down sth.**] *vt*

[1] (make lose power) 耗尽 ‹*battery*›; 使…停止运转 ‹*watch, machine*› [2] (reduce) 减少 ‹*production, reserves*›; 使…萎缩 ‹*industry*›

- **run in** *vt* [1] [**~ sth. in, ~ in sth.**] Brit Aut 磨合 ‹*car, engine*›; **'~ning in — please pass'** "磨合驾驶——请先行" [2] [**~ sb. in**] colloq (arrest) «*person, police*» 拘留
- **run into**

A [**~ into sb./sth.**] *vt* (collide with) «*person, vehicle*» 撞上 ‹*person, vehicle, tree, wall*›

B [**~ into sth.**] *vt*

[1] (experience) 遇到 ‹*difficulties*›; **to ~ into debt** 负债 [2] (enter area of) 遭遇 ‹*bad weather*› [3] (amount to) «*debt, sales*» 达到 ‹*hundreds, millions*›; **an income ~ning into six figures** 高达6位数的收入

C [**~ into sb.**] *vt* (meet) 偶然遇见

- **run off**

A *vi* [1] (flee) «*person, animal*» 跑掉 [2] (abscond) 逃走 [3] colloq (go away) 离开; **don't let him ~ off without saying goodbye** 别让他不辞而别 [4] (flow off) «*water, liquid*» 流掉

B *vt* [**~ sth. off, ~ off sth.**]

[1] (print) «*person, machine*» 复印 ‹*copy*›; **to ~**

sth. off on sth. 用某物复印某物 2 (contest) «organizers» 使…进行 ‹heats› 3 (drain off) 使…流出 ‹liquid›; ~ off the water that has been standing in the pipes 把管子里积存的水排干

- **run off with** vt 1 [~ off with sth.] (abscond with) 偷走 ‹takings, money› 2 [~ off with sb.] (elope with) 和…私奔
- **run on**

A vi «meeting, seminar, programme, person» 拖延
B vt 1 [~ sth. on, ~ on sth.] Print 接排 2 [~ on sb./sth.] (be concerned with) «thoughts, discussion, conversation» 围绕 ‹person, subject, event›; «mind» 总想着 ‹person, subject, event›

- **run out** vi 1 (be used up) 被耗尽; my money ran out 我的钱花完了; time is ~ning out 剩下的时间不多了; my patience is ~ning out 我越来越没耐心了; their luck ran out 他们的好运到头了 2 (become empty) «pen» 用干墨水; «vending machine» 售光 3 (exhaust supply) 用完; sorry, I've ~ out 对不起, 我用完了; the car ran out of petrol 车没油了 4 (expire) «passport, licence, agreement» 过期; «contract» 失效
- **run out on** vt [~ out on sb.] colloq 抛弃 ‹wife, husband, partner›
- **run over**

A [~ sb./sth. over, ~ over sb./sth.] vt (knock down) 撞倒
B [~ over sth.] vt
1 (drive over) 从…上压过 ‹body, log, bump, stone› 2 (explain) 快速解释 ‹schedule, main points, figures› 3 (read through) 浏览 ‹notes, text›
C vi 1 (overrun) «meeting, programme» 超时; to ~ over by 10 minutes 超时 10 分钟 2 (overflow) «container, water» 溢出

- **run past** vt colloq = run by
- **run round** vi, vt Brit = run around
- **run round with** vt Brit colloq = run around with
- **run through**

A [~ through sb./sth.] vt «murmur, excitement, thrill» 迅速传遍 ‹crowd, audience›; «thought, tune» 在…里闪过 ‹head, mind›
B [~ through sth.] vt
1 (pervade) «theme, prejudice» 遍布 ‹work, society› 2 (present, explain) 快速说明 ‹schedule, main points, figures› 3 (read through) 浏览 ‹notes, text› 4 (use up) 挥霍掉 ‹money, inheritance› 5 (rehearse) 排练 ‹speech, scene, act›
C [~ sth. through sth.] vt
1 (process) «person» 用…处理…; to ~ sth. through the computer 用计算机处理 ‹data, figures› 2 (subject to) 使…经受…; to ~ sth. through a series of tests 对…进行一系列检测 ‹machine, device, sample›
D [~ sb./sth. through] vt liter (stab) 刺穿; to ~ sb./sth. through with a sword/spear 用剑/矛刺穿某人/某物

- **run to**

A [~ to sb./sth.] vt (have recourse to) 向…求助 ‹person, authority›; to go ~ning to one's parents 去找父母帮忙; to go ~ning to the police 去找警察求助; don't come ~ning to me for a handout 别来求我施舍
B [~ to sth.] vt
1 (extend to) 达到; to ~ to 300 pages 长达 300 页; her tastes don't ~ to modern jazz 她还欣赏不了现代爵士乐 2 (be enough for) «income, savings» 足够…之用 ‹object, activity›; his salary doesn't ~ to Caribbean cruises 他的薪水不足以去加勒比海乘船游览 3 (afford) 买得起; I don't think I can ~ to that 我想我买不起那个

- **run up** vt [~ sth. up, ~ up sth.] 1 (accumulate) 积欠 ‹bill, debt› 2 (make) 赶制 ‹dress, curtains› 3 (raise) 升起 ‹flag›
- **run up against** vt [~ up against sth.] «person, proposal, scheme» 遭遇 ‹difficulty, obstacle, opposition›
- **run with** vt Amer colloq = run around with

run: ~**about** n Brit colloq (small car) 小型汽车; (light aircraft) 小型飞机; ~**around** n colloq to give sb. the ~around 对某人敷衍了事; to get or be given the ~around 被草草打发

runaway /ˈrʌnəweɪ/
A n (adult) 逃跑者; (child) 离家出走的孩子
B adj attrib 1 (escaped) 离家出走的 ‹teenager, child›; 逃跑的 ‹offender› 2 (out of control) 失控的 ‹horse, car, train› 3 fig (rapidly increasing) 发展迅猛的; ~ inflation 失控的通货膨胀; a ~ success 巨大的成功

run: ~**down** n 1 (report) 概述; to give sb. a quick ~down on sth. 向某人扼要介绍某事物; 2 (of industry, factory) 缩减; ~**-down** adj 1 (exhausted) 疲惫不堪的 ‹person›; 2 (dilapidated) 破败的 ‹area, building, hotel›

rune /ruːn/ n 1 Ling [古日耳曼语中的] 如尼字母 2 (stone) [用于占卜等的] 如尼文石块; to cast the ~s (tell fortune) 算命; (cast a spell) 施魔法; to read the ~s lit 算命; fig 解读

rung¹ /rʌŋ/ n 1 (of ladder) [梯子的] 横档 2 (in society, organization) 等级; the lowest/bottom ~ of a hierarchy 等级制度中的最低一级/底层

rung² pp ▸ring² A, B

runic /ˈruːnɪk/ adj 如尼文的 ‹symbol, inscription›

run-in n colloq 争吵; to have a ~ with sb. over sth. 因某事物与某人争吵

runnel /ˈrʌnl/ n 细流

runner /ˈrʌnə(r)/ n 1 (person) 奔跑的人; (animal) 奔跑的动物; to do a ~ colloq 溜走 2 Sport 赛跑运动员; a 100-metre/marathon/long-distance ~ 100 米跑/马拉松/长跑选手 3 Equit 赛马 4 (on door, furniture) 滑槽 5 Bot 长匍茎 6 (on sledge) 滑板 7 (on skate) 冰刀 8 (covering table) 桌旗 9 (carpet) 长条地毯

runner: ~ **bean** n Brit 红花菜豆; ~**-up** n (pl **runners-up**) 亚军; the 50 ~s-up 50 名二等奖获得者; to be ~-up to sb. 是仅次于某人的亚军

running /ˈrʌnɪŋ/
A n [u] 1 (sport, exercise) 跑步; to take up ~ 开始跑步; to be in the ~ (for sth.) (某事) 有成功的机会; to be out of the ~ (for sth.) (某事) 没有成功的机会; to make the ~ Brit colloq (in race) 领跑; (in activity) 带头 2 (management) 管理; the ~ of sth. …的经营 ‹business›; …的管理 ‹organization›; …的统治 ‹country›
B modif 赛跑用的 ‹shorts, gear›; ~ shoes 跑鞋
C adj 1 postpos (in succession) 连续的; five days ~ 连续5天 2 attrib (flowing) 流动的 ‹water› 3 attrib (supplied by tap) ~ water 自来水 4 attrib (releasing water) 淌水的 ‹tap› 5 attrib (exuding liquid) 流鼻涕的 ‹nose›; a ~ sore lit 流脓的疮; fig 不断的烦扰 6 attrib (ongoing) 连续不断的 ‹argument, joke› 7 attrib (done while running) 边跑边进行的 ‹kick›; to (go and) take a ~ jump dated colloq 滚开

running: ~ **battle** n Mil 游击战; (disagreement) 长期对抗; ~ **board** n 踏板; ~ **commentary** n 实况报道; ~ **costs** npl (of factory, scheme) 经营费用; (of machine, car) 运行成本; ~ **head** n 页首标题; ~ **mate** n Amer 竞选伙伴; ~ **order** n (of programme) 播放顺序; (of items in programme) 节目顺序; (of acts in show) 演出顺序; ~ **race** n 赛跑; ~ **repairs** npl [使用过程中进行的] 小修小补; to make ~ repairs to sth. 对某物进行临时检修; ~ **time** n 1 (of film) 放映时间; (of play) 上演时间; 2 (of train, bus) 运行时间; ~ **total** n 流水式总计; ~ **track** n 跑道

runny /ˈrʌni/ adj 1 (liquid) 水分过多的 ‹jam, sauce, butter› 2 (exuding liquid) 流鼻涕的 ‹nose›; 流泪的 ‹eyes›

runoff /ˈrʌnɒf/ n 1 Sport 附加赛 2 (of water, liquid) 地表径流

run: ~**-of-the-mill** adj 平凡的; ~**-on** adj [诗行] 意义连贯的; a ~-on sentence 连写句 [尤指用连词连接从句构成的冗长句子]; ~**proof** adj 1 (resistant to laddering) 防抽丝的 ‹stockings, pantyhose, fabric›; 2 (waterproof) 防水的 ‹make-up, mascara›

runt /rʌnt/ n 1 (baby animal) [一胎中] 最弱小的幼崽 2 pej (person) 小不点儿

run: ~**-through** n 1 (rehearsal) 排练; 2 (reading) 浏览; (discussion) 概述; ~**-up** n 1 Sport 助跑距离; to begin one's ~-up 开始助跑; to take a ~-up of about 20 feet 需要约 20 英尺的助跑; 2 Brit (preparatory period) 准备期; a ~-up to sth. 某事的准备阶段; ~**way** n 飞机跑道; ~way lighting 跑道照明

rupee /ruːˈpiː/ ▸p. 174 n 卢比

rupture /ˈrʌptʃə(r)/
A n 1 (in relations) 断绝; a ~ with sb. 与某人的绝交; a ~ between A and B A 和 B 的关系的破裂 2 (of vessel, membrane) 破裂 3 Med 疝气
B vt 1 Med 使…破裂 ‹blood vessel, membrane, ligament›; a ~d appendix/spleen 阑尾穿孔/脾破裂 2 (end) 断绝 ‹relationship, connection›; 破坏 ‹unity›
C vi «membrane, seed pod, appendix, spleen» 破裂
D v refl to ~ oneself 发疝气; to ~ oneself doing sth. 因做某事而发疝气

rural /ˈrʊərəl/ adj 1 (in countryside) 农村的 ‹population, traditions›; ~ France 法国农村 2 (typical of the countryside) 乡村的 ‹beauty, smells›; 田园的 ‹scene›

ruse /ruːz/ n 诡计; a ~ for doing sth. 做某事的计谋

rush¹ /rʌʃ/
A vi 1 (move with urgency) «person, vehicle» 急促移动; to ~ at sb./sth. 向某人/某物冲去; to ~ down/up the stairs 冲下/冲上楼梯; to ~ round the house 在屋子里四下忙活; to ~ along the street 沿街冲去; to ~ out of the room/up to sb. 冲出房间/冲向某人; he ~ed off before I could tell him 我还没来得及告诉他, 他就急着走了 2 (flow strongly) «water, river» 奔腾; «wind» 猛烈地刮; «air» 急速流动; the sound of ~ing water 湍急的水声; a ~ing stream 湍急的小溪; the stream ~ed down the mountainside 小溪从山坡上急流而下; the blood ~ed to his face 血一下子涌到了他的脸上 3 (act quickly) 匆忙行事; don't ~ 别急; to ~ at sth. 匆忙做某事; to ~ to do sth. 匆忙做某事; to ~ to explain 急忙解释
B vt 1 (send urgently) 紧急运送; to ~ sb./sth. to sb./sth. 将…紧急运送至… ‹supplies, troops›; to be ~ed to hospital Brit or the hospital Amer 被紧急送到医院; police reinforcements were ~ed to the scene 增援的警力被火速派往现场 2 (send quickly) 迅速发送; to ~ sb. sth. 将…迅速发送给某人 ‹copy, book›; please ~ me my copy 请把我的那本赶紧送来 3 (do hastily) 仓促做; don't try to ~ things 不要草率行事 4 (pressurize, hurry) 催促 ‹person›; I don't want to ~ you, but ... 我不想催你, 但是…; to be ~ed off one's feet 忙得不可开交 5 (charge at) 冲向 ‹building, platform, position› 6 Amer Univ «fraternity, sorority» 特别关注 ‹student, freshman›
C n 1 [c] sing (fast movement) 快速的移动; a ~ of photographers/volunteers 一拥而上的摄影师/志愿者; a ~ for sth. 朝…冲去 ‹exit, train, toilet›; a ~ for the door/towards the buffet 朝门口/自助餐台涌去; a ~ to do sth. 冲去做某事; to make a ~ at or for sb./sth. 朝某人/某处冲去 2 [c] sing (fast flow of water, blood, air) 涌动; to have a ~ of blood to one's cheeks 血涌上了双颊; a ~ of blood to the head 头脑一热 3 [u and c] (hurry) 匆忙; to be in a ~ (to do sth.) 匆忙 (做某事); to do sth. in a ~ 急匆匆地做某事; it all happened in such a ~ 一切都发生得如此

匆忙; **we had a ~ to make the deadline** 我们匆匆赶在最后期限前完成任务; **is there any ~?** 着急吗?; **there's no ~** 不必着急; **what's the ~?** 干吗这么急匆匆的?; **why (all) the ~?** 急什么? **4** [c] (busy time) 繁忙; **the morning/evening ~** (交通的)早上/晚上高峰; **the Christmas/summer ~** 圣诞节购物热潮/夏季旅游热潮; **beat the ~!** 避开交通高峰! **5** [c] (sudden demand) 抢购; **a ~ on** *or* **for sth.** 抢购某物 **6** [c] (of emotion) 冲动; (of energy) 涌动; **to experience a sudden ~ of adrenalin** 突然热血沸腾 **7** [c] colloq (thrill) [吸毒后的] 快感; **it gives you a ~** 它会让你感到亢奋 **8** [c] Amer Univ 学生联谊会纳新活动; **~ party/week** 学生联谊会纳新晚会/周

D rushes *npl* Cin 样片

Phrasal verbs

- **rush into** *vt* **1** [**~ into sth.**] (undertake hastily) «*person*» 仓促进行 ‹*purchase, sale*›; **to ~ into marriage/a decision/a commitment** 仓促结婚/作出决定/作出承诺 **2** (make do hastily) 使仓促进行; **to ~ sb. into sth./doing sth.** 催促某人做某事; **don't be ~ed into it** 不要因为有人催就草率行事
- **rush out** *vt* [**~ sth. out, ~ out sth.**] 匆匆印制 ‹*edition, pamphlet*›; 匆匆作出 ‹*announcement, statement*›
- **rush through** *vt* [**~ through sth., ~ sth. through**] 快速通过 ‹*bill, amendment*›; 迅速处理 ‹*order, application*›; **to ~ a bill through parliament** 使议案在议会匆匆通过

rush² *n* Bot 灯心草; **a ~ mat** 灯心草席

rushed /rʌʃt/ *adj* **1** (hurried) 仓促的 ‹*decision*›; 草率的 ‹*job*› **2** (in a hurry) 匆忙的 ‹*person, staff*›

rush: ~ hour *n* 交通高峰时间; **in** *or* **during the ~ hour** 在交通高峰期; **~ hour congestion/problems** 交通高峰期的拥堵/问题; **to get caught in the ~ hour traffic** 被堵在交通高峰期的车流中; **~ job** *n* colloq 紧急任务; **to have a ~ job on** 有紧急任务要完成; **~ order** *n* 加急订货

rusk /rʌsk/ *n* [尤指给婴儿食用的] 脆饼干

russet /ˈrʌsɪt/ ▸**p. 134**

A *adj* 赤褐色的 ‹*leaves, hair*›; **to go** *or* **turn ~** 变成赤褐色

B *n* **1** (colour) 赤褐色 **2** (apple) 冬季粗皮苹果

Russia /ˈrʌʃə/ *pr n* 俄罗斯

Russian /ˈrʌʃn/ ▸**p. 503, p. 426**

A *adj* (of Russia) 俄罗斯的; (of the people) 俄罗斯人的; (of the language) 俄语的

B *n* **1** [c] (person) 俄罗斯人 **2** [u] (language) 俄语

Russian Federation *n* **the ~** 俄罗斯联邦

Russianist /ˈrʌʃnɪst/ *n* 俄罗斯语言文学研究者

Russian: ~ Orthodox *adj* 俄罗斯东正教的 ‹*cathedral, tradition*›; **the ~ Orthodox Church** 俄罗斯东正教会; **~ Revolution** *n* **the ~ Revolution** 俄国十月革命; **~ roulette** *n* **1** (with revolver) 俄罗斯轮盘赌; **2** fig (risky action) 玩命的行为

Russophile /ˈrʌsəʊfaɪl/ *n* 亲俄者

rust /rʌst/

A *n* [u] 锈

B *vi* **1** lit «*metal, nails*» 生锈 **2** fig (deteriorate) «*talents, faculties*» 荒废

C *vt* **1** (corrode) 使…生锈 ‹*metal, tools, pipes*› **2** fig (cause to deteriorate) 使…荒废 ‹*talents, faculties*›; 使…变迟钝 ‹*reflexes*›

Phrasal verbs

- **rust away** *vi* «*lock, blade, hinge*» 因生锈而烂掉
- **rust in** *vi* «*screw, nail*» 锈住
- **rust up** *vi* «*lock, mechanism, moving parts*» 锈住

rust belt *n* Amer colloq 衰落地带 [尤指美国中西部和东北部衰败、萧条的工业区]; **a rust-belt town** *or* **city/state** 衰落地带的城市/州

rusted /ˈrʌstɪd/ *adj* 生锈的

rustic /ˈrʌstɪk/ *adj* **1** (unsophisticated) 乡村的 ‹*scene, cottage, life*›; **~ fare/food** 农家菜 **2** (unrefined) 质朴的 ‹*manners, accent*› **3** (made of rough timber) 用粗木材做成的 ‹*furniture, bridge, fence*›

rustle /ˈrʌsl/

A *vi* **1** (crinkle) «*leaves, papers*» 发出沙沙声 **2** (move) «*birds, material*» 窸窸窣窣地移动; **to ~ about** 窸窸窣窣地四处活动

B *vt* **1** (crinkle) «*wind, person, movement*» 使…发出沙沙声 ‹*leaves, skirt, newspaper*› **2** (steal) 偷盗 ‹*cattle, horses*›

C *n* (of paper, leaves, fabric) 沙沙声

Phrasal verb

- **rustle up** *vt* [**~ up sth., ~ sth. up**] colloq **1** (prepare quickly) 草草弄好 ‹*meal, snack, sandwich*›; **to ~ up sth. for sb.** 为某人匆匆弄 ‹*meal, cup of coffee*› **2** (find at short notice) 匆忙凑集 ‹*money, volunteers, costumes*›

rustler /ˈrʌslə(r)/ *n* Amer (cattle thief) 偷牛贼; (horse thief) 盗马贼

rustling /ˈrʌslɪŋ/ *n* **1** [u and c] (of paper, fabric, leaves) 沙沙声; **a ~ sound** 窸窸窣窣的声音 **2** [u] Amer (of cattle) 偷牛; (of horses) 盗马

rustproof /ˈrʌstpruːf/

A *adj* 抗锈的 ‹*metal, alloy, chassis, fittings, lock*›; **~ paint** 防锈漆; **a ~ coating** 防锈涂层

B *vt* 使…不生锈 ‹*metal, fittings*›

rustproofing /ˈrʌstpruːfɪŋ/ *n* [u] 防锈处理

rust-resistant *adj* 抗锈的 ‹*metal*›; 防锈的 ‹*paint*›

rusty /ˈrʌsti/ *adj* **1** (corroded) 生锈的 ‹*car, machinery, nail*›; **to grow** *or* **become ~** 变得锈迹斑斑 **2** (out of practice) 衰退的 ‹*memory*›; 荒废的 ‹*knowledge*›

rut¹ /rʌt/

A *n* **1** (in ground) 车辙 **2** (routine) 常规; **to be (stuck) in a ~** 墨守陈规; **to get into/out of a ~** 陷入老一套/摆脱陈规

B *vt* (*pres p etc.* **-tt-**) «*vehicle, wheels*» 在…上留下车辙 ‹*road, lane, surface*›

rut² zod

A *vi* (*pres p etc.* **-tt-**) «*stag, goat, ram*» 发情

B *n* 发情期

rutabaga /ˌruːtəˈbeɪɡə/ *n* Amer **= swede**

ruthenium /ruːˈθiːnɪəm/ *n* [u] 钌

ruthless /ˈruːθlɪs/ *adj* **1** (harsh) 无情的 ‹*adversary, punishment*›; 残忍的 ‹*tyrant*›; **to be ~ towards** *or* **with sb.** 无情地对待某人; **to be ~ in sth./doing sth.** 在某事/做某事上很无情 **2** (determined) 意志坚定的 ‹*businessman, boss*›; 义无反顾的 ‹*determination*›; 彻底的 ‹*investigation*›; **to be ~ in sth./doing sth.** 在某事/做某事上下定决心 **3** (unremitting) 不松懈的 ‹*pace, schedule*›; 不罢休的 ‹*demands*›

ruthlessly /ˈruːθlɪsli/ *adv* **1** (harshly) 无情地 ‹*punish, destroy*›; 残忍地 ‹*torture*› **2** (determinedly) 坚决地 ‹*pursue, enforce*›; 义无反顾地 ‹*determined*›; 彻底地 ‹*investigate*›; 极其 ‹*efficient*›

ruthlessness /ˈruːθlɪsnɪs/ *n* [u] **1** (harshness) 无情 **2** (determination) 坚决; (thoroughness) 彻底

Rutland /ˈrʌtlənd/ *pr n* 拉特兰郡

rutted /ˈrʌtɪd/ *adj* 有车辙的

rutting /ˈrʌtɪŋ/ *n* [u] 发情; **the ~ season/behaviour** 发情期/行为

RV *abbr* Amer **= recreational vehicle**

Rwanda /rʊˈændə/ *pr n* 卢旺达

Rwandan /rʊˈændən/ ▸**p. 503**

A *adj* (of Rwanda) 卢旺达的; (of the people) 卢旺达人的

B *n* 卢旺达人

rye /raɪ/ *n* **1** [u] Agric, Culin 黑麦; **~ bread/flour/field** 黑麦粉/黑麦田 **2** [u and c] Amer **= rye whiskey**

rye: ~ grass *n* [u] 黑麦草; **~ whiskey** *n* [u] 黑麦威士忌酒

r

Ss

S, s /es/

A *n* (*pl* **Ss** *or* **S's**) [英语字母表的第19个字母]

B *abbr* **1** **S** Geog **= south, southern; ~ America** 南美洲 **2** **s** Brit Hist (shilling) 先令; **3s 4d** 3 先令 4 便士 **3** **S = small** 小号 [服装的尺码]

SA *abbr* **1** **= South Africa** **2** **= South America** **3** **= South Australia**

sabbath, Sabbath /'sæbəθ/ *n* 安息日; **to observe/break the ~** 守/不守安息日

sabbatical /sə'bætɪkl/

A *n* 学术假; **to be on ~** 在休假; **to go on** *or* **take a ~** 去度学术假

B *adj attrib* 学术假的; **~ leave/year** 学术假/休假学年

saber /'seɪbə(r)/ *n* Amer **= sabre**

sable /'seɪbl/

A *n* **1** [u] (fur) 貂皮; **to wear** *or* **be dressed in ~** 穿着貂皮衣服 **2** [c] (animal) 紫貂

B *adj* liter 黑色的 ‹*hair*›; 深褐色的 ‹*eyes*›

sabotage /'sæbətɑːʒ/

A *n* [u] 蓄意破坏; **to commit ~** 蓄意破坏; **an act of ~** 人为破坏

B *vt* 蓄意破坏; **the terrorists must not ~ the peace efforts** 不能让恐怖分子破坏和平努力

saboteur /ˌsæbə'tɜː(r)/ *n* 蓄意破坏者

sabre /'seɪbə(r)/ *n* Brit **1** Mil 马刀 **2** Sport 佩剑

sabre: ~ rattling *n* [u] fig 武力恫吓; **~tooth, ~-toothed tiger** *ns* 剑齿虎

sac /sæk/ *n* 囊; **hernial/scrotal ~** 疝囊/阴囊; **the honey ~ of a bee** 蜜蜂的蜜囊

saccharin /'sækərɪn/ *n* [u] 糖精

saccharine /'sækəriːn/

A *adj* pej 故作多情的 ‹*verse, music*›; 过分甜蜜的 ‹*smile*›

B *n* 糖精

sachet /'sæʃeɪ, Amer sæ'ʃeɪ/ *n* **1** Brit (bag) 密封小袋 **2** Brit (contents) 一小袋; **a ~ of sugar/shampoo/ketchup** 一小袋糖/洗发剂/番茄酱 **3** (scented) [盛熏衣草等的] 小香袋

sack /sæk/

A *n* **1** [c] (bag) [结实耐用的] 大口袋; **a coal/mail ~** 煤袋/邮袋 **2** [c] (contents) 一大袋; **a ~ of flour/coal/mail** 一大袋面粉/煤/邮件; **a ~ of potatoes** pej 粗陋难看 **3** [u] colloq (dismissal) **the ~** 开除; **to get the ~** 被炒鱿鱼; **to give sb. the ~** 开除某人; **to be threatened with the ~** 受到解雇的威胁 **4** [u] colloq (bed) **the ~** 床; **to hit the ~** 上床睡觉; **to be great in the ~** 床上功夫了得 **5** [u] liter (pillage) 劫掠

B *vt* **1** colloq (dismiss) 解雇 ‹*worker, employee*›; **to ~ sb. for sth./doing sth.** 因某事/做某事而解雇某人; **to be/get ~ed** 被炒鱿鱼; **to be ~ed from one's job** 被解雇 **2** liter (pillage) 洗劫

Phrasal verb

• **sack out** *vi* Amer colloq 上床睡觉

sackable /'sækəbl/ *adj attrib* 可作为解雇理由的; **a ~ offence/matter** 可据以解雇的过失/事情

sack: ~cloth *n* [u] 粗麻布; **to be in** *or* **wear ~cloth and ashes** fig 忏悔; **~ dress** *n* 布袋裙

sackful /'sækfʊl/ *n* 一大袋; **a ~ of toys** 一大袋玩具; **cash/letters by the ~** 整袋的现金/信件

sacking /'sækɪŋ/ *n* **1** [c and u] colloq (dismissal) 解雇; **there are rumours of more ~s to come** 据传会有更多的人被裁员 **2** [u] Tex 粗麻布 **3** [u] (pillaging) 劫掠

sack: ~load *n* **= sackful**; **~ race** *n* 套袋赛跑 [将双腿套在袋中跳跃前进的赛跑]

sacrament /'sækrəmənt/ *n* **1** (of ritual) 圣事 **2** (for communion) 圣餐; **to receive the ~(s)** 领圣餐; **the Blessed** *or* **Holy ~** 圣餐

sacred /'seɪkrɪd/ *adj* **1** (holy) 神圣的 ‹*place, image, rite*›; **to be ~ to sb.** 对某人来说是神圣的 **2** (religious) 宗教的 ‹*art, text*›; **~ music/building** 圣乐/圣堂 **3** (revered) 受尊崇的 ‹*tradition, life*›; **~ to the memory of ...** 谨纪念…; **to hold sth. ~, to regard sth. as ~** 把某物奉为圣物; **is nothing ~?** hum 难道什么都可以冒犯吗? **4** (binding) 庄严的 ‹*duty, mission, vow*›; 郑重的 ‹*promise*›; **the law is ~** 法律是神圣的

sacred cow *n* fig 神圣不可冒犯的事物

sacrifice /'sækrɪfaɪs/

A *n* **1** [c and u] (act) 献祭; **to make a ~ for sb./sth.** 为某人/某物献祭; **the ~ of sth./sb. (to sb.)** 供奉（给某人）的某物/某人; **getting rich isn't worth the ~ of your principles** 为致富牺牲原则是不值得的 **2** [c] Relig (offering) 祭品; **a human ~** 用作祭品的人

B *vt* **1** Relig 以…为祭品 ‹*animal, person*›; **to ~ sth. to sb.** 把某物献祭给某人 **2** fig (give up) 牺牲 ‹*time, career, principle*›; 舍弃 ‹*opportunity, freedom, comfort*›

C *v refl* **to ~ oneself** 牺牲自己

sacrificial /ˌsækrɪ'fɪʃl/ *adj* 用于献祭的 ‹*animal, virgin*›; 献祭的 ‹*ritual*›

sacrificial lamb *n* (animal) 祭献的羔羊; fig (person) 牺牲品

sacrilege /'sækrɪlɪdʒ/ *n* [u] **1** Relig 亵渎; **to commit ~** 犯亵渎罪; **it is ~ to do ...** 做…是亵渎行为 **2** fig (outrageous behaviour) 不敬的行为

sacrilegious /ˌsækrɪ'lɪdʒəs/ *adj* **1** Relig 亵渎神圣的 **2** fig (disrespectful) 不敬的 ‹*act, criticism*›

sacristan /'sækrɪstən/ *n* 圣器守司

sacristy /'sækrɪsti/ *n* 圣器室

sacrosanct /'sækrəʊsæŋkt/ *adj* 神圣不可改变的 ‹*tradition, idea*›; 不可违背的 ‹*principle, routine*›

SAD /sæd/ *abbr* **= seasonal affective disorder**

sad /sæd/ *adj* **1** (sorrowful) 悲伤的 ‹*person, feeling, expression, voice*›; **I was ~ to leave home** 离开家我很难过; **a ~ smile** 苦笑; **autumn always makes me feel ~** 秋天总是让我伤感; **to grow** *or* **become ~** 变得哀伤; **to look ~** 看上去很伤心; **I am ~ to inform you that ...** 我很遗憾地通知你…; **~der but wiser** 吃了苦头但长了心眼 **2** (causing upset) 令人伤心的 ‹*news, death, ending*›; **a very ~ film** 一部悲剧电影; **it is my ~ duty to inform you that ...** 我很遗憾，但有责任通知你… **3** (unfortunate, deplorable) 糟透的 ‹*affair, mistake*›; **it is ~ that ...** 真可惜…; **it's a ~ fact** *or* **truth that ..., the ~ fact** *or* **truth is that ...** 糟糕的是…; **it's a ~ day for democracy/football** 对民主/足球而言，那是一个可悲的日子; **~ to say, she failed** 可惜她失败了 **4** (inspiring pity) 悲惨的 ‹*sight, plight*›; **this once beautiful ship is in a ~ condition now** 这艘曾经很漂亮的船现在破烂不堪; **a ~ case of cruelty/neglect** 惨不忍睹的残忍/令人痛心疾首的疏忽 **5** colloq pej or hum (inadequate) 很不像样的; (unfashionable) 老气的; (uninteresting) 乏味的; **you haven't been out for a month?! you're ~!** 你都一个月没出门了？！你真没劲！; **a really ~ shirt** 土不拉叽的衬衫

sadden /'sædn/ *vt* 使悲伤; **it ~s me that/to think that ...** …让我感到伤心/想起…我感到伤心

saddening /'sædnɪŋ/ *adj* 令人悲伤的; **it is ~ to hear/think that ...** 听说/想起…令人伤心

saddle /'sædl/

A *n* **1** (on horse) 马鞍; **to climb into the ~** 上马; **she would spend hours in the ~** 她骑马常常一骑就是几个小时; **the party leader is very firmly in the ~** fig 该党领导人的地位非常稳固 **2** (of bicycle) 车座 **3** Brit Culin 脊肉 **4** (ridge) 山鞍

B *vt* **1** Equit **~ (up)** 给…备鞍 ‹*horse*› **2** (impose) 使肩负重担; **to ~ sb./oneself with sth./sb.** 使某人/自己承担某重任/担负某人的重任; **he was ~d with the running of the club** 他负起了管理俱乐部的重任

saddle: ~bag *n* **1** Equit 鞍囊; **2** (on bicycle) [自行车车座后的] 挂包; **~cloth** *n* [垫在鞍下防摩擦的] 鞍褥; **~ horse** *n* esp Amer 骑用马

saddler /'sædlə(r)/ ▸p. 409 *n* (maker) 马具匠; (seller) 马具商

saddlery /'sædləri/ *n* **1** [u] (equipment) 马具 **2** [c] (premises) 马具店

saddle: ~ shoes *npl* Amer 鞍脊鞋 [部分鞋帮与其他部分色彩和皮革截然不同的鞋]; **~-sore** *adj* 坐鞍疼的 ‹*rider, bottom*›; **I was really ~-sore after that long ride** 骑了那么长时间的马，我屁股疼得要命

saddo /'sædəʊ/ *n* Brit colloq pej 土傻冒

sad: ~-eyed *adj* **1** (looking upset) 眼神哀伤的 ‹*person*›; **2** Amer (causing sadness) 伤感的 ‹*lyric*›; **~-faced** *adj* 面容哀伤的

sadism /'seɪdɪzəm/ *n* [u] 施虐狂 [尤指性施虐狂]

sadist /'seɪdɪst/ *n* 施虐狂者 [尤指性施虐狂者]

sadistic /sə'dɪstɪk/ *adj* 施虐狂的

sadistically /sə'dɪstɪkli/ *adv* 施虐狂般地 ‹*treat, punish*›; 施虐狂地 ‹*evil, inclined*›

sadly /'sædli/ *adv* **1** (with sadness) 悲伤地 ‹*look, sigh*› **2** (unfortunately) 不幸地; **~, he did not survive** 很不幸，他没有活下来 **3** (regrettably) 令人遗憾地 ‹*ignorant, neglected*›; **he is ~ lacking in sense** 很遗憾，他缺乏理智

sadness /ˈsædnɪs/ *n* **1** [u] (sorrow) 悲伤; **to feel a great deal of ~ at sth.** 对某事深感悲伤; **to feel no ~ at sth.** 对某事一点也不悲伤; **the recollection filled me with ~** 想起那段往事我满怀悲伤 **2** [u] (poignancy) 辛酸 **3** [c] (misfortune) 令人悲伤的事

sadomasochism /ˌseɪdəʊˈmæsəkɪzəm/ *n* [u] 施虐受虐狂

sadomasochist /ˌseɪdəʊˈmæsəkɪst/ *n* 施虐受虐狂者

sadomasochistic /ˌseɪdəʊˌmæsəˈkɪstɪk/ *adj* 施虐受虐狂的〈*tendency*〉; 施虐受虐狂者的〈*practice*〉

sad sack *n* Amer colloq 不中用的人

sae *abbr* Brit = **stamped addressed envelope**

safari /səˈfɑːri/ *n* [在热带非洲进行的] 游猎; **to go on ~** 去游猎

safari: ~ hat *n* [圆顶、前后檐略宽的] 瑟法里帽; **~ jacket** *n* 狩猎夹克 [一种有腰带和4个口袋的上衣]; **~ park** *n* 野生动物园; **~ suit** *n* 猎装

safe /seɪf/

A *adj* **1** (unharmed) 平安的; **~ and sound** 安然无恙的; **to hope for sb.'s ~ return/arrival** 希望某人平安归来/到达; **have a ~ journey!** 一路平安! **2** *pred* (unlikely to be harmed) 安全的; **is the bike ~ here?** 自行车放在这里没事吧? ; **your reputation is ~, at least** 至少你的名誉不会受损; **to be ~ from sth.** 免受某事物的危害; **if we go up the tree, will we be ~ from attack?** 我们爬到树上是否就能不受攻击? ; **to keep the documents ~** 放好文件; **your secret is ~ with me** 我不会泄露你的秘密; **the money is ~ with him** 钱放在他那里尽可以放心; **as ~ as houses** 十分安全的 **3** (not harmful) 无害的; **the water is ~ for drinking** 这水可以喝; **the drug is ~ for pregnant women** 这种药对孕妇无害; **to make a stadium ~ for the public** 让体育馆成为公众放心的去处 **4** (prudent) 稳妥的〈*choice, estimate, topic*〉; **a ~ investment** 无风险投资; **that would be the ~st thing to do under the circumstances** 在这种情况下那是最稳妥的做法; **it would be ~r not to mention that** 最好别提那件事 **5** (probably correct) 有把握的; **it's ~ to say that ...** 可以肯定地说… **6** (reliable) 可靠的; **a ~ driver** 谨慎的司机; **to be in ~ hands** 由可靠的人照管; **to have a ~ pair of hands** 手法稳健; **better ~ than sorry** 谨慎总比后悔好; **to be on the ~ side** 谨慎起见; **to play (it) ~** 稳扎稳打

B *n* **1** (for valuables) 保险箱 **2** (for meat) 冷藏柜

safe: ~ bet *n* 把握很大的事; **it's a ~ bet that ...** …是十拿九稳的事; **he's a ~ bet** 他是肯定没问题的; **~-blower** *n* 炸开保险箱行窃的盗贼; **~-breaker** *n* 撬窃保险箱的罪犯; **~ conduct** *n* **1** [u] (guarantee) 安全通行权; **2** [c] (document) 通行许可证; **~-cracker** *n* colloq = **~-breaker**; **~-deposit box** *n* [银行或宾馆等处的] 保管箱

safeguard /ˈseɪfgɑːd/

A *vt* 保护; **to ~ the health and safety of employees** 保护员工的健康和安全

B *n* 保护措施; **the union is your ~ against exploitation** 工会是防止遭受剥削的保障

safe: ~ haven *n* **1** (place of safety) 避难所; **a ~ haven for the Muslim minority** 穆斯林少数派的避难所; **2** Fin 避险工具; **~ house** *n* [恐怖分子或谍报人员使用的] 安全房; **~keeping** *n* [u] 妥善保管; **in sb.'s ~keeping** 由某人妥善保管; **to entrust sth. to sb.'s ~keeping, to give sth. to sb. for ~keeping** 将某物交给某人妥善保管

safely /ˈseɪfli/ *adv* **1** (unharmed) 平安地〈*return, arrive*〉 **2** (without risk) 安全地; **your keys can ~ be left with me** 你的钥匙可以放心地交给我保管; **we can ~ assume/conclude/say that ...** 我们有把握认为/下结论/说… **3** (causing no concern) 安稳地〈*hidden, stored*〉; **the children are ~ tucked up in bed** 孩子们好好地盖着被子睡觉了; **he's ~ behind bars** 他已被关入监狱, 不会造成危害了; **she is ~ through to the next round** 她顺利进入下一轮 **4** (carefully) 小心地; **to drive ~** 安全驾驶

safeness /ˈseɪfnɪs/ *n* [u] **1** (of method, treatment, product) 安全性; (of structure) 稳定性 **2** (of investment) 稳妥性 **3** (of assumption) 有把握

safe: ~ passage *n* [c and u] 安全通行权; **to grant sb. (a) ~ passage** 给予某人安全通行权; **~ period** *n* 安全期 [女性月经周期中不易受孕的日子]; **~ seat** *n* 保险席位 [选举中稳操胜券的议会席位]; **~ sex** *n* [u] [采取了性病预防措施的] 安全性交

safety /ˈseɪfti/

A *n* [u] **1** (being out of danger) 安全; **in ~** 安全地; **she helped the survivors to ~** 她帮助幸存者转移到安全的地方; **to reach ~** 到达安全地点; **to seek ~ in flight** 逃跑; **~ first** 安全第一; **there's ~ in numbers** 人多保险 **2** (accident prevention) 保险; **road ~** 道路安全 **3** (of method, treatment, product) 安全性; (of structure) 稳定性 **4** (of investment) 稳妥性

B *modif* 保障安全的; **a ~ strap/bolt** 安全带/闩; **~ inspections/measures** 安全检查/措施

safety: ~ belt *n* 安全带; **~ catch** *n* 保险栓; **to put on/release the ~ catch** 上/松开保险栓; **~ chain** *n* (on door) 防盗门链; (on jewellery) 珠宝链; **~ curtain** *n* 防火幕; **~-deposit box** *n* = **safe-deposit box**; **~ glass** *n* [u] 安全玻璃; **~ helmet** *n* 安全帽; **~ lamp** *n* 安全灯; **~ match** *n* 安全火柴; **~ net** *n* **1** lit [杂技表演时使用的] 安全网; **2** fig (safeguard) 安全措施; **~ pin** *n* 安全别针; **~ razor** *n* 安全剃刀; **~ valve** *n* **1** lit 安全阀; **2** fig (outlet) 疏导方法

saffron /ˈsæfrən/ ▸**p. 134**

A *n* [u] **1** Culin 藏红花柱头 [用于调味或食物着色] **2** (colour) 橘黄色

B *adj* **1** *attrib* Culin 藏红花的〈*flavour, powder*〉; 用藏红花调味的〈*rice*〉 **2** (colour) 橘黄色的〈*flag, cloth*〉

saffron crocus *n* 藏红花

sag /sæg/

A *vi* (*pres p etc.* **-gg-**) **1** «*mattress, ceiling*» 凹陷; «*canvas, rope*» 下垂; «*beam*» 下弯 **2** (hang loosely) «*cheeks, breasts, jacket*» 松垂 **3** (weaken) «*spirits*» 委靡不振; «*courage*» 衰落; «*economy*» 衰退 **4** (fall) «*price, sales*» 下降; «*exports, profits*» 减少; «*shares*» 下跌

B *n* **1** (in ceiling, mattress) 下陷 **2** (in price, value) 下跌; **a ~ in price** 价格的下降

saga /ˈsɑːgə/ *n* **1** (medieval epic) 萨迦 [尤指中世纪斯堪的纳维亚地区的英雄传奇故事] **2** (popular novel) 长篇小说 **3** colloq (lengthy story) 长篇叙述; **he told me the whole ~ of their divorce** 他对我讲述了他们离婚的漫长过程

sagacious /səˈgeɪʃəs/ *adj* formal 睿智的〈*person, remark, advice, decision, attitude*〉

sagaciously /səˈgeɪʃəsli/ *adv* formal 睿智地

sagacity /səˈgæsəti/, **sagaciousness** /səˈgeɪʃəsnɪs/ *ns* [u] formal 睿智

sage¹ /seɪdʒ/

A *n* (wise person) [尤指年长的] 智者

B *adj* 贤明的〈*philosopher*〉; 睿智的〈*advice, opinion, guidance*〉

sage² *n* [u] Bot 鼠尾草; **~ plant/seed/stuffing** 鼠尾草植物/籽/填料

sage: ~-and-onion stuffing *n* [u] 鼠尾草加洋葱填料 [烹调家禽用]; **~brush** *n* 灌木蒿

sage green ▸**p. 134**

A *adj* 灰绿色的

B *n* [u] 灰绿色

sagely /ˈseɪdʒli/ *adv* 睿智地

sagging /ˈsægɪŋ/ *adj* **1** (curving down) 凹陷的〈*bed, roof*〉; 下弯的〈*beam*〉; 下垂的〈*hem*〉 **2** (drooping) 松垂的〈*flesh, cheeks, breasts*〉 **3** (weakening) 衰退的〈*economy, market*〉; 低落的〈*spirits*〉; 减弱的〈*demand*〉 **4** (falling) 下降的〈*prices, sales*〉; 减少的〈*profits*〉

Sagittarian /ˌsædʒɪˈteərɪən/

A *n* 属人马座的人

B *adj* 属人马座的

Sagittarius /ˌsædʒɪˈteərɪəs/ *n* **1** [u] Astron 人马(星)座 **2** [u] Astrol (sign) 人马宫 [黄道第九宫] **3** [c] *sing* Astrol (person) 属人马(星)座的人

sago /ˈseɪgəʊ/ *n* [u] 西米

sago pudding *n* [u and c] 西米布丁

Sahara /səˈhɑːrə/ *pr n* **the ~ (Desert)** 撒哈拉沙漠

Saharan /səˈhɑːrən/ *adj* 撒哈拉沙漠的

sahib /ˈsɑːhɪb/ *n* 先生 [印度人对男子的尊称]

said /sed/

A *pt, pp* ▸**say A, B**

B *adj attrib* formal or hum 上述的; **the ~ Mr X** 这位前面提及的某先生

sail /seɪl/

A *n* **1** [c and u] (for boat) 帆; **to hoist/lower the ~s** 扬帆/降帆; **to put on more ~** 增帆; **to take in ~** 收帆; **to have the wind in one's ~s** 志在必得; **to take the wind out of sb.'s ~s** fig 使某人突然泄气 **2** [u] (navigation) 帆船航行; **under ~** 张着帆; **to cross the ocean under ~** 扬帆渡海; **to set ~ from .../for ...** 从…起航/起航前往…; **in full ~** 张着满帆 **3** [c and u] (voyage in sailing vessel) 乘船航行; **to go for a ~** 乘船出游; **how many days' ~ is it from Hull to Oslo?** 从赫尔到奥斯陆要航行几天? **4** [u] dated (ships) 帆船 **5** [c] (of windmill) [风车的] 翼板

B *vi* **1** (move across water) «*boat, ship*» 航行; **the ship ~ed into Brest** 船驶入布雷斯特港 **2** (travel by boat) 乘船旅行; **to ~ north** 乘船北上; **to ~ around the world** 乘船环游世界; **to ~ close** *or* **near to the wind** 顶风冒险; fig 冒大风险 **3** (start a voyage) «*ship, person*» 起航; **what time do we/does the boat ~?** 我们/船何时起航? ; **to ~ from/for somewhere** 从某处起航/起航前往某处 **4** (sail yacht for leisure) 乘游艇游玩; **to go ~ing** 乘船去游玩 **5** (move in air) 掠过; **the ball ~ed over the fence** 球飞过了栅栏; **clouds were ~ing across the sky** 云在天上飘 **6** (move in stately manner) «*person*» 昂首而行; «*vehicle*» 徐徐驶过; «*swan*» 款款游过; **to ~ into the room** 优雅地走进那房间; **to ~ into work** 悠然自得地上班工作

C *vt* **1** (pilot) 驾驶〈*yacht, catamaran*〉; **she ~ed the boat around the cape/into the harbour** 她驾船绕过了海角/进入港口; **little boys were ~ing model boats on the pond** 小男孩们正在操控池塘上的模型船 **2** (travel across) 在…上航行〈*sea, ocean*〉

Phrasal verbs

- **sail in** *vi* colloq «*person*» 昂首进入
- **sail through** *vt* [**~ through sth.**] 顺利通过〈*exam, interview*〉; **she ~ed through college** 她轻松读完了大学

sail: ~board *n* 帆板; **~boarding** *n* [u] 帆板运动; **to go/enjoy ~boarding** 去玩帆板/享受帆板运动; **~boat** *n* Amer 帆船; **~cloth** *n* [u] 厚篷帆布

sailing /ˈseɪlɪŋ/ ▸**p. 307** *n* **1** [u] (sport) 帆船运动; (hobby) 帆船航行; **a ~ vessel/club** 帆船/帆船俱乐部 **2** [c] (departure) 水运航班; **a ~ schedule** 水运航班时刻表

sailing: ~ boat *n* Brit 帆船; **~ dinghy** *n* 帆艇; **~ ship** *n* 大型帆船

sailmaker /ˈseɪlmeɪkə(r)/ ▸**p. 409** *n* 制帆工

sailor /ˈseɪlə(r)/ *n* **1** (seaman) 海员; **a ~ in the Royal Navy** 皇家海军水兵 **2** (sea traveller) 乘船者; **a good/bad ~** 不晕船/晕船的人

sailor: ～ **hat** *n* 水手帽; ～ **suit** *n* [儿童穿的] 水手装

sailplane /ˈseɪlpleɪn/ *n* 轻型滑翔机

saint /seɪnt, *before names* snt/ *n* **1** Relig 圣徒; **S～ Mark** 圣马可 **2** fig colloq (virtuous person) 圣人般的人; **he's no** ～ 他可不是什么圣人

sainted /ˈseɪntɪd/ *adj* **1** Relig lit 被册封为圣徒的 ‹*pope, martyr*› **2** fig dated (virtuous) 圣人般的; **my** ～ **aunt!** 天哪! [表示吃惊]

sainthood /ˈseɪnthʊd/ *n* [u] 圣徒的地位

Saint Lawrence River /sənt ˈlɒrəns ˌrɪvə(r)/ ▸**p. 663** *pr n* **the** ～ 圣劳伦斯河

saintliness /ˈseɪntlɪnɪs/ *n* [u] 圣洁

saintly /ˈseɪntli/ *adj* 圣洁的 ‹*person, quality*›; 圣人般的 ‹*forbearance, status*›; 神圣的 ‹*devotion, virtues*›

saint's day *n* 圣徒节

sake[1] /seɪk/ *n* **1** (purpose) 目的; **for the** ～ **of clarity, for clarity's** ～ 为了清楚起见; **to do sth. for its own** ～ *or* **for the** ～ **of it** *or* **for sth.'s** ～ 为某事本身的缘故而做某事; **to kill for the** ～ **of killing** 为了杀戮而杀戮; **for old times'** ～ 念及旧日的情分; **art for art's** ～ 为了艺术而艺术 **2** (benefit) 利益; **for my/her** ～ 看在我/她的份上; **for God's** *or* **pity's** *or* **heaven's** *or* **goodness'** ～**!** 看在上帝的份上! [表示生气、不耐烦或加强语气]

sake[2] /ˈsɑːki, ˈsækeɪ/ *n* [u and c] (drink) 日本清酒

salable /ˈseɪləbl/ *adj* Amer = **saleable**

salacious /səˈleɪʃəs/ *adj* 淫秽的 ‹*book, picture*›; 下流的 ‹*gossip, remark, joke*›

salaciousness /səˈleɪʃəsnɪs/ *n* [u] 淫秽

salad /ˈsæləd/ *n* [u and c] 色拉; **to prepare/mix a** ～ 做/拌色拉

salad: ～ **bar** *n* 色拉自助台; ～ **bowl** *n* 色拉碗; ～ **cream** *n* [u] Brit 色拉酱; ～ **days** *npl* liter 少不更事的年岁; ～ **dressing** *n* [u and c] 色拉调味料; ～ **oil** *n* [u] 色拉油; ～ **servers** *npl* 色拉餐具; ～ **shaker** *n* [去除色拉水分的] 色拉摇杯; ～ **spinner** *n* esp Amer 色拉脱水器

salamander /ˈsæləmændə(r)/ *n* **1** Zool 蝾螈 **2** Mythol 火蜥蜴

salami /səˈlɑːmi/ *n* [u and c] 萨拉米香肠

salaried /ˈsælərɪd/ *adj* 领薪水的

salary /ˈsæləri/ *n* 薪水; **a high/low** ～ 高/低薪; **a** ～ **cheque/increase** 薪金支票/加薪

salary: ～ **scale** *n* 薪金级别; ～ **structure** *n* 薪金结构

sale /seɪl/ *n* **1** [u] (selling) 出售; **for** ～ 供出售; **up for** ～ 待售 [主要用于房屋或私有财产]; **to put sth. up** *or* **offer sth. for** ～ 出售某物; **on** ～ Brit (available) 出售; Amer (at reduced price) 减价出售; **(on)** ～ **or return** 剩货包退 **2** [c] (instance) 一笔买卖; **to make a** ～ 做成一笔买卖; **she gets ten pounds commission on each** ～ 她从每笔买卖中抽取 10 英镑佣金; **no** ～ 无交易 [收银机钱箱开启后显示] **3** [c] (cut price period) 廉价出售; **to buy sth. in a** ～ *or* **the** ～**s** 在大减价时买某物; **to put sth. in the** ～ Brit *or* **on** ～ Amer 降价销售某物; **the summer** ～**s are on** 夏季大甩卖正在进行 **4** [c] (public auction) 拍卖会; (for charity) 义卖; **to have** *or* **hold a** ～ 举行拍卖; **a** ～ **in aid of a charity** 为援助慈善团体进行的义卖

saleable /ˈseɪləbl/ *adj* (fit to be sold) 适销的 ‹*product*›; (able to be sold) 可供出售的 ‹*commodity*›

sale: ～ **bin** *n* 特价商品柜; ～**-bin purchases** 购买的特价商品; ～ **item** *n* (at reduced price) 降价物品; (available) 供出售的物品; ～ **of work** *n* Brit 自制物品义卖; ～ **price** *n* (reduced cost) 特价; (cost of item) 售价; ～**room** *n* 拍卖场

sales /seɪlz/ *npl* **1** (amount sold) 销售量; ～ **are up/down** 销售量上升/下降了; ～ **growth** 销量增长; **car** ～ **rose/fell** 汽车销量上升/下降了 **2** + *v sing or pl* (activity) 销售工作; **in charge of** ～ 负责销售 **3** + *v sing or pl* (department) 销售部门; ～ **department/revenue** 销售部门/收入; **director of** ～ **and marketing** 市场销售主管

sales: ～ **assistant** ▸**p. 409** *n* Brit 售货员; ～ **chart** *n* 销量图; ～ **clerk** ▸**p. 409** *n* Amer 售货员; ～ **conference** *n* 展销会; ～ **director** ▸**p. 409** *n* 销售主管; ～ **drive** *n* 促销活动; ～ **executive** ▸**p. 409** *n* 销售代理; ～ **figures** *npl* 销售额; ～ **force** *n* + *v sing or pl* 销售人员; ～ **forecast** *n* 销量预测; ～**girl** ▸**p. 409** *n* 女售货员; ～**lady** ▸**p. 409** *n* Amer 女售货员; ～**man** /-mən/ ▸**p. 409** *n* (representative) 推销员; (in shop) 男售货员; ～ **manager** ▸**p. 409** *n* 销售经理

salesmanship /ˈseɪlzmənʃɪp/ *n* [u] 推销术

sales: ～ **office** *n* 销售办事处; ～**person** ▸**p. 409** *n* (representative) 推销员; (in shop, salesroom) 售货员; ～ **pitch** *n* [u] 推销游说; ～ **point** *n* **1** (outlet) 零售点; **2** (feature) 卖点; ～ **promotion** *n* [u and c] (activity, technique) 促销术; (offer, campaign) 促销; ～ **representative**, colloq ～ **rep** ▸**p. 409** *ns* 销售代表; ～ **resistance** *n* [u] 抵制推销; ～ **slip** *n* 销货单; ～ **staff** *n* + *v sing or pl* 销售人员; ～ **talk** *n* [u] 推销游说; ～ **target** *n* 销售目标; ～ **tax** *n* [u and c] esp Amer 销售税; ～**woman** ▸**p. 409** *n* (representative) 女推销员; (in shop) 女售货员

salient /ˈseɪlɪənt/

A *adj* (striking) 显著的 ‹*feature*›; (principal) 主要的 ‹*fact*›; **to summarize the** ～ **points of ...** 总结…的要点

B *n* Mil 突出部

saline /ˈseɪlaɪn/ *adj* 含盐的; **concentrated** ～ **solution** 浓缩盐溶液

salinity /səˈlɪnəti/ *n* [u] 盐度

saliva /səˈlaɪvə/ *n* [u] 唾液

salivary gland /səˈlaɪvəri glænd/ *n* 唾液腺

salivate /ˈsælɪveɪt/ *vi* 流口水

salivation /ˌsælɪˈveɪʃn/ *n* [u] 唾液分泌

sallow /ˈsæləʊ/

A *adj* 灰黄的 ‹*cheeks, complexion, skin*›; **his face was thin and** ～ 他的脸瘦削蜡黄

B *n* 黄华柳

sally /ˈsæli/ *n* **1** (incursion, sortie) 出击; (quick journey) 短途旅行; **to make a** ～ 进行突袭; **a brief** ～ **to the shops** 匆匆去一趟商店 **2** (witty remark) 妙语; **to make a** ～ 说句俏皮话

Phrasal verb

- **sally forth** *vi* formal or hum 出发

Sally Army *n* Brit colloq = **Salvation Army**

salmon /ˈsæmən/ *n* (*pl* **salmon**) **1** [c] (fish) 鲑 **2** [u] (flesh) 鲑鱼肉, 三文鱼肉

salmonella /ˌsælməˈnelə/ *n* (*pl* **salmonellae** /ˌsælməˈneliː/) **1** [c] Biol 沙门菌 **2** [u] Med 沙门菌感染

salmonella poisoning ▸**p. 377** *n* [u] 沙门菌中毒

salmon farm *n* 鲑鱼养殖场

salmon pink ▸**p. 134**

A *adj* 橙红色的

B *n* [u] 橙红色

salon /ˈsælɒn, Amer səˈlɒn/ *n* **1** (hairdressing parlour) 美发厅; (beauty parlour) 美容厅; (clothes shop) 高级服装店 **2** (reception room) [大宅中的] 客厅 **3** Hist (social gathering) 沙龙; **a literary** ～ 文学沙龙

saloon /səˈluːn/ *n* **1** Brit ～ **(car)** 小轿车 **2** Amer dated or hum (bar) 酒馆 **3** Brit (lounge bar) ～ **(bar)** 雅座酒吧 **4** (on ship) 交谊厅 **5** (public room) 活动室; **a dancing/billiard** ～ 舞厅/弹子房

saloon car racing ▸**p. 307** *n* [u] Brit 家庭轿车比赛 [参赛车辆为加大马力的普通轿车, 赛道通常是越野车道]

salsa /ˈsælsə/ *n* [u] **1** (dance) [源于拉丁美洲的] 萨尔萨舞曲 **2** (sauce) 辛香番茄酱

salsify /ˈsælsɪfi/ *n* [u] 蒜叶婆罗门参

salt /sɔːlt/

A *n* **1** [u] Culin 食盐; **a pinch of** ～ 一小撮盐; **a grain of** ～ 一粒盐; **the** ～ **of the earth** fig (person) 诚实可信的人; (group) 社会中坚; **to take sth. with a pinch** *or* **grain of** ～ fig 对某事将信将疑; **worth one's** ～ fig 称职的; **to be above/below the** ～ fig 属于上层/下层社会的 **2** [c] Chem 盐; **the** ～**s of sulphuric acid** 硫酸盐 **3** [c] colloq (sailor) [有经验的] 水手; **an old** ～ 老水手

B *modif* **1** (of sodium chloride) 盐的 ‹*molecule, crystal*›; **a** ～ **solution** 盐溶液; **a** ～ **factory** 盐厂; **the** ～ **industry** 制盐业 **2** Culin 腌制的 ‹*beef, pork*›; 咸的 ‹*taste*› **3** (brackish) 咸水的 ‹*springs*›; 海水的 ‹*spray*›; **a** ～ **lake** 盐湖

C *vt* **1** (season) 在…中放盐 ‹*food*›; fig 点缀; **his work is** ～**ed with slogans and phrases in capital letters** 他的作品中穿插了大写的口号和短语 **2** (preserve) 用盐腌制 ‹*meat, fish*› **3** (spread salt on) 在…上撒盐 ‹*road, path*›

Phrasal verb

- **salt away** *vt* [～ **away sth.,** ～ **sth. away**] colloq 私下积攒 ‹*amount, money*›

salt: ～**box** *n* Amer 坡顶盐盒式双层楼房; ～ **cellar** *n* Brit [盖上有小孔的餐桌用] 盐瓶

salted /ˈsɔːltɪd/ *adj* 加盐的 ‹*butter*›; ～ **peanuts/beef** 咸花生/腌牛肉

salt: ～ **flat** *n* 盐滩; ～**-free** *adj* 不含盐的

saltine /sɔːlˈtiːn/ *n* Amer 咸饼干

saltiness /ˈsɔːltɪnɪs/ *n* [u] **1** (taste) 咸 **2** (salt content) 含盐度

saltings /ˈsɔːltɪŋz/ *npl* Brit 盐滩岸

salt: ～ **lick** *n* **1** (place) [动物前往舔食的] 盐碱地; **2** (block of salt) [供家畜等舔食的] 盐砖; ～ **marsh** *n* 盐碱滩; ～ **mine** *n* 盐矿; **it's back to the** ～ **mines for me** fig colloq 我又要辛苦一番了; ～ **pan** *n* [海边自然形成的] 盐池

saltpetre Brit, **saltpeter** Amer /ˌsɔːltˈpiːtə(r)/ *n* [u] 硝酸钾

salt: ～ **shaker** *n* esp Amer 盐瓶; ～ **spoon** *n* 盐匙; ～ **tablet** *n* 盐片 [用于补充盐分]; ～**water** *adj* **1** (living in sea) 海产的; **a** ～**water fish/plant** 海鱼/海洋植物; **2** (containing seawater) 含海水的; **a** ～**water lake/aquarium** 咸水湖/海洋水族馆; ～ **water** *n* [u] 盐水; ～**works** *npl* + *v sing or pl* 盐厂

salty /ˈsɔːlti/ *adj* **1** (in taste) 咸的 ‹*water, food, flavour*›; **to taste** ～ 有咸味 **2** Miner 含盐的 ‹*substance, texture*› **3** fig (coarse) 粗俗的 ‹*language, humour*›

salubrious /səˈluːbrɪəs/ *adj* **1** (health-giving) 有益健康的 ‹*climate, atmosphere*› **2** (pleasant) 环境宜人的 ‹*place*›; **one of the less** ～ **parts of town** 城市中环境较为逊色的地区之一

salubrity /səˈluːbrəti/ *n* [u] formal (healthiness) 有益健康; (pleasantness) 环境宜人

salutary /ˈsæljʊtri, Amer -teri/ *adj* 有益的; **it is** ～ **to do sth.** 做某事是有益的; **a** ～ **lesson** 有益的教训

salutation /ˌsæljuˈteɪʃn/ *n* **1** [c and u] formal (greeting) 招呼; **to raise one's hat in** ～ 举帽致意; ～**s!** 向你问候! [带有玩笑意味] **2** [c] (in letter) 称呼语

salutatorian /səˌljuːtəˈtɔːrɪən/ *n* Amer 致开幕词的学生 [在毕业典礼上致词, 一般为毕业班名列第二者]

salute /səˈluːt/

A *n* **1** (greeting) 敬礼; **to give (sb.) a** ～ (向某人) 行礼; **to return sb.'s** ～ 向某人回礼; **in** ～ **to sb.** 以表示对某人的敬意; **to take the** ～ [国家元首等在阅兵时] 接受敬礼 **2** (firing of guns) 鸣礼炮; **a 21-gun** ～ 21 响礼炮 **3** (tribute) 敬意; **a** ～ **to sb./sth.** 对某人/某物的致敬

B *vt* **1** (greet) 向…行军礼 ‹*soldier*›; 向…致敬

S

‹*royalty, visitor*›; **to ~ the flag** 向旗帜敬礼 **2** fig (honour) 赞扬 ‹*person, achievement, efforts*›; **to ~ sb. for sth.** 因某事物而赞扬某人; **to ~ sb./sth. as sth.** 将某人/某事物赞美作某事物

C *vi* «*soldier*» 行军礼

Salvadorean, Salvadorian /ˌsælvəˈdɔːrɪən/ ▸**p. 503**

A *adj* 萨尔瓦多的

B *n* 萨尔瓦多人

salvage /ˈsælvɪdʒ/

A *vt* **1** Naut 打捞 ‹*wreck, cargo, treasure*›; (from building) 抢救 ‹*painting, furniture*›; **a ~ company/vessel** 打捞公司/打捞船; **the ship was ~d and towed into port** 船得救被拖回港内 **2** fig (save) 挽回 ‹*reputation, self-respect*›; 挽救 ‹*situation, marriage*›; 留存 ‹*memories*› **3** (for recycling) 回收利用 ‹*newspapers, cardboard*›

B *n* [u] **1** (recovery) 抢救; **the ~ of treasures from a bombed church** 对被炸教堂中贵重物品的抢救 **2** (goods recovered) 抢救出的财物 **3** (reward) 救助酬金 **4** (recycling) 废物回收; **to collect sth. for ~** 为了回收利用而收集某物

salvation /sælˈveɪʃn/ *n* [u] **1** esp Relig 得救 **2** fig 拯救; **I get so depressed about life; work is my only ~** 生活令我如此沮丧，工作是我唯一的解脱

Salvation Army *n* **the ~** 救世军

salve /sælv, Amer sæv/

A *n* [u and c] **1** (balm) 药膏 **2** fig (comfort) 慰藉; **as a ~ to sb.'s conscience** 作为对某人良心的宽慰

B *vt* **1** (apply balm to) 在…上敷药膏 ‹*wound*› **2** (soothe) 安慰; **to ~ one's conscience** 使良心得到宽慰

salver /ˈsælvə(r)/ *n* [用于正式场合的] 银质托盘

salvo /ˈsælvəʊ/ *n* (*pl* **~s** *or* **~es**) **1** Mil 齐射; **a ~ of gunfire** 炮火的齐发 **2** fig (burst) 一阵; **a ~ of laughter/applause/questions** 一阵笑声/一阵掌声/一连串的问题

sal volatile /ˌsælvəˈlætəli/ *n* [u] 挥发盐

SAM *abbr* = **surface-to-air missile** 地对空导弹

Samaritan /səˈmærɪtən/ *n* **1** Hist 撒马利亚人; **a good ~** fig 善人 **2** **the ~s** (organization) 撒马利亚会 [提供谈心服务的慈善团体]

samarium /səˈmeərɪəm/ *n* [u] 钐

samba /ˈsæmbə/ *n* [c and u] (dance) 桑巴舞; (music) 桑巴舞曲

sambo /ˈsæmbəʊ/ *n* (*pl* **~s** *or* **~es**) dated colloq offensive 黑仔

Sam Browne /ˌsæm ˈbraʊn/, **Sam Browne belt** /ˌsæm braʊn ˈbelt/ *ns* [军官或警官使用的] 武装带

same /seɪm/

A *adj* **1** (just referred to) 同一的; (identical with) 相同的; **we both went to the ~ school** 我们俩曾在同一所学校念书; **later that ~ day/year** 当天/当年稍晚一些时候; **that was the very ~ day that my father died** 那正好是我父亲去世的那天; **(in) the ~ way** 同样地; **the two hats are the ~ colour** 这两顶帽子颜色相同; **one and the ~** 同一个; **they are one and the ~ person** 他们就是同一个人; **at the ~ time** (simultaneously) 同时; (nevertheless) 然而; **she was laughing and crying at the ~ time** 她又笑又哭的; **at the ~ time, you can't help liking him** 不过，你没法不喜欢他; **to go the ~ way (as sb./sth.)** (与某人/某物) 走同一条路; fig (与某人/某物) 有相同经历; **~ difference!** colloq 一码事! **2** (unchanged) 无变化的; **it's still the ~ town** 镇上还是老样子; **she's not the ~ woman** 她已经不是原来那个女人了; **the ~ old excuse** 老一套借口; **the ~ old story** colloq 还是老样子

B *adv* 同样地; **life goes on just the ~** 生活一如既往; **to feel the ~ as sb.** 和某人有同感; **we treat boys exactly the ~ as girls** 我们对男孩和女孩一视同仁; **the ~ as usual** 同往常一样

C *pron* **1** (identical people) 同样的人; (identical things) 同样的事; **I'll have the ~** 同样的给我来一份; **don't do the ~ as I did and get married too young** 别走我的老路，年纪轻轻就成家了; **more of the ~** 老一套; **(the) ~ again, please** (food, drink) 请再来一份同样的; **(the) ~ for me, please** 请给我也来一份; **(the) ~ here** colloq (expressing agreement) 我也是; (ordering food, drink) 我也要一样的; **I don't know much about cars — ~ here, I'm afraid** 我不太懂汽车——恐怕我也差不多; **(the) ~ to you** (as greeting or insult) 你也一样; **you're a complete moron! — ~ to you!** 你是一个十足的笨蛋! ——你也一样! ; **all** *or* **just the ~** 尽管如此; **all the ~, there's some truth in what she says** 尽管如此，她的话还是有些道理; **thanks all the ~** 还是要谢谢你; **it's all the ~ to me** 我无所谓 **2** **to remain** *or* **stay the ~** (unchanged) 保持不变; **she's much the ~** 她几乎还是老样子; **the village is still the ~** 村庄仍然是老样子; **my views are the ~ as always** 我的观点一贯如此 **3** Brit formal (aforementioned person) 该人; (aforementioned thing) 上述事物; **a dwelling together with all the movable property contained within the ~** 一套住宅以及其中的所有动产; **was that George on the phone? — the ~!** 打电话的是乔治吗? ——正是他! **4** *without 'the'* Comm formal (aforementioned thing) 上述情况; **to installing ~** 安装事宜同前; **re your order for four wooden doors plus furniture for ~** 事涉你方订购的 4 扇木门及其配件

same-day *adj attrib* 当日完成的; **the hotel offers a ~ laundry service** 宾馆提供当日可取的洗衣服务

sameness /ˈseɪmnɪs/ *n* [u] pej 千篇一律

same-sex *adj* **1** (of the same sex) 同性别的; **the child's ~ parent** 孩子的同性家长 **2** (involving people of the same sex) 涉及同性别的; **a ~ relationship/marriage** 同性恋关系/同性婚姻

samey /ˈseɪmi/ *adj* Brit colloq 千篇一律的

Samoa /səˈməʊə/ *pr n* 萨摩亚群岛

Samoan /səˈməʊən/ ▸**p. 503, p. 426**

A *adj* (of Samoa) 萨摩亚的; **the ~ Islands** 萨摩亚群岛; (of the people) 萨摩亚人的; (of the language) 萨摩亚语的

B *n* **1** [c] (person) 萨摩亚人 **2** [u] (language) 萨摩亚语

samosa /səˈməʊsə/ *n* 萨莫萨三角煎饺

sampan /ˈsæmpæn/ *n* 舢板

sample /ˈsɑːmpl, Amer ˈsæmpl/

A *n* **1** (of product) 样品; (for test) 抽样; **to take a ~ (of sth.)** (对某物) 进行取样; **free ~s** 免费试用品; **~ questions** 样题 **2** Med 试样; **a blood/urine ~** 血样/尿样 **3** (of population, voters, etc.) 样本; **a representative/limited ~** 代表性/有限样本; **a random ~** 随机样本

B *vt* **1** (try) 品尝 ‹*food, wine*›; **to ~ the pleasure of being waited on** 体验被人服侍的快乐 **2** (get a representative judgement of) 抽样调查 ‹*product, opinion, market*›

sampler /ˈsɑːmplə(r), Amer ˈsæmplər/ *n* **1** (embroidery) 刺绣样品 **2** (collection) 集锦 **3** (person taking samples) 采样者; (device taking samples) 采样机 **4** Mus 取样器

sample survey *n* 抽样调查

sampling /ˈsɑːmplɪŋ, Amer ˈsæm-/ *n* **1** [u] (taking of specimens) 抽样; **random ~** 随机采样; **a ~ technique** *or* **method** 抽样方法 **2** [u and c] (of population group) 抽样调查 **3** [u and c] (tasting) 品尝 **4** [u] Mus 取样

samurai /ˈsæmʊraɪ/ *n* (*pl* **samurai**) Hist [旧时日本的] 武士; **~ warriors** 武士; **a ~ sword** 武士刀

San Andreas fault /ˌsæn ˌændreɪəsˈfɔːlt/ *pr n* **the ~** 圣安德列亚斯断层 [美国加利福尼亚州的地壳断层]

sanatorium /ˌsænəˈtɔːrɪəm/ *n* (*pl* **~s** *or* **sanatoria** /ˌsænəˈtɔːrɪə/) **1** (clinic) 疗养院 **2** Brit (in boarding school) 医务室

sanctify /ˈsæŋktɪfaɪ/ *vt* 使…神圣化 ‹*marriage, life*›; 使…合法化 ‹*practice, usage*›

sanctimonious /ˌsæŋktɪˈməʊnɪəs/ *adj* pej 伪善的 ‹*smile, remark*›; 假装圣洁的 ‹*person, manner*›

sanctimoniously /ˌsæŋktɪˈməʊnɪəsli/ *adv* 伪善地

sanctimoniousness /ˌsæŋktɪˈməʊnɪəsns/ *n* [u] 伪善

sanction /ˈsæŋkʃn/

A *n* **1** [u] (authorization) 准许; (approval) 批准; **with the ~ of ...** 经…的批准 **2** [c] (deterrent) 处罚; **legal/criminal ~** 法律制裁/刑事处罚; **the ultimate ~** 最严厉的处罚

B **sanctions** *npl* Pol 国际制裁; **economic/trade ~s** 经济/贸易制裁; **to impose ~s on ...** 对…实施制裁; **to lift** *or* **raise ~s** 取消制裁

C *vt* (give permission for) 准许; (give approval to) 批准

sanctions busting /ˈsæŋkʃnz ˌbʌstɪŋ/ *n* [u] 违反国际制裁

sanctity /ˈsæŋktəti/ *n* [u] **1** (holiness) 神圣 **2** (of life) 圣洁; (of law) 至高无上

sanctuary /ˈsæŋktʃʊəri, Amer -tʃʊeri/ *n* **1** [c] (holy place) 圣所 **2** [u and c] (refuge) 庇护; **a place of ~** 避难所; **to take ~** 避难; **to claim/seek ~** 要求/寻求庇护; **to offer sb. ~** 为某人提供庇护; **to be a ~ for sb. from sth.** 是某人躲避某事物的避难所 **3** [c] (for wildlife) 保护区; (for mistreated animals) 收容所

sanctum /ˈsæŋktəm/ *n* (*pl* **~s**) **1** (holy place) 圣地; (in Jewish temple) 圣所 **2** (private place) 私室

sand /sænd/

A *n* [u] **1** (fine grit) 沙; **fine/coarse ~** 细沙/粗沙; **a grain of ~** 一粒沙子; **to bury one's head in the ~** 不愿正视现实 **2** Amer colloq (courage) 胆量; **to have the ~ to do sth.** 有勇气做某事

B **sands** *npl* **1** (beach) 沙滩; **on the ~s** 在沙滩上 **2** (desert) 沙漠; **the shifting ~s of international politics** fig 国际政治的风云变幻 **3** (moment) 时刻; **the ~s (of time) are running out** (time is getting short) 时间不多了

C *vt* **1** (smooth) **~ (down)** (with sandpaper, sander) 打磨 ‹*woodwork, floor*› **2** (apply sand to) 在…上撒沙 ‹*road, runway*›

sandal /ˈsændl/ *n* 凉鞋

sandalwood /ˈsændlwʊd/

A *n* **1** [c] (tree) 檀香 **2** [u] (wood) 檀香木

B *modif* 檀香木制的 ‹*box*›; 含檀香油的 ‹*talc*›; **~ perfume/soap** 檀香木香水/檀香皂

sandbag /ˈsændbæg/

A *n* 沙袋

B *vt* (*pres p etc.* **-gg-**) **1** (protect) 用沙袋封堵 ‹*doorway, parapet*›; 用沙袋加固 ‹*dam, gun-emplacement*› **2** (hit with sandbag) 用沙袋击打 ‹*person*› **3** fig colloq (bully) 胁迫; **to ~ sb. into doing sth.** 胁迫某人做某事

C *vi* (*pres p etc.* **-gg-**) colloq 隐藏实力

sand: ~bank *n* 沙洲; **~bar** *n* [河口的] 沙洲; **~blast** *vt* 对…喷沙; **a ~blasted jean jacket** 砂洗牛仔夹克; **~blaster** *n* 喷沙器; **~blasting** *n* [u] 喷沙; **~ box** *n* Amer = **~pit**; **~boy** *n* **as happy as a ~boy** 快乐无比; **~castle** *n* 沙堡; **~ dollar** *n* 饼海胆; **~ dune** *n* 沙丘

sander /ˈsændə(r)/ *n* 打磨机

sand: ~fly *n* 白蛉; **~glass** *n* 沙漏

sanding disc *n* 研磨盘

sandlot /ˈsændlɒt/ Amer

A *n* [供儿童玩耍的] 沙地

B *modif* 业余的 ‹*baseball, team*›

S

S & M /ˌes ənd ˈem/ *abbr* = **sadism and masochism** 施虐受虐狂
sand: ~**man** /-mæn/ *n* **the** ~**man** [童话中在孩子眼皮上撒沙使其熟睡的] 睡魔; ~ **martin** *n* 崖沙燕
sandpaper /ˈsændpeɪpə(r)/
A *n* [u] 砂纸
B *vt* 用砂纸打磨
sand: ~ **piper** *n* 鹬; ~**pit** *n* esp Brit 沙坑; ~**shoe** *n* esp Scot, Austral 胶底帆布鞋; ~**stone** *n* [u] 砂岩; ~**stone cliff/walls** *n* 砂岩峭壁/墙; ~**storm** *n* 沙尘暴; ~ **trap** *n* Amer (in golf) 沙坑
sandwich /ˈsænwɪdʒ, Amer -wɪtʃ/
A *n* **1** (bread snack) 三明治 **2** Brit (cake) 夹心蛋糕
B *vt* 将…插在中间; **to be** ~**ed between sth. and sth.** 被夹在某物与某物之间

sandwich

三明治。用两片或多片面包夹蔬菜、肉、黄油、奶酪或果酱等做成。Sandwich本为英国肯特郡（Kent）一城镇。第四代 Sandwich 伯爵（Earl of Sandwich）约翰·蒙塔古（John Montagu）生性好赌，常用面包裹上肉片，边赌边吃，以节省时间。三明治以此得名。如果只有一片面包，则称 open sandwich，美国英语称 open-faced sandwich。

sandwich: ~ **bar** *n* 三明治快餐店; ~ **board** *n* [挂在身体前后的] 夹板广告牌; ~ **box** *n* 午餐盒; ~ **course** *n* Brit 工读交替制课程; ~ **loaf** *n* 三明治面包
sandy /ˈsændi/ *adj* **1** (of sand) 含沙的 ‹*soil, deposit*›; 覆盖着沙的 ‹*path, seabed*›; ~ **beach/terrain** 沙滩/沙质地形 **2** (yellowish) 沙褐色的 ‹*hair, colour*›
sand: ~ **yacht** *n* 沙地帆车; ~ **yachting** *n* [u] 沙地帆车运动
sane /seɪn/ *adj* **1** (not mad) 神志正常的 ‹*person, behaviour*›; **it's the only thing that keeps me** ~ 这是唯一不让我发疯的事 **2** (reasonable) 明智的 ‹*policy, judgement*›; ~ **response/thinking** 合乎情理的反应/想法
sanely /ˈseɪnli/ *adv* **1** (not madly) 神志正常地 ‹*behave, talk*› **2** (wisely) 明智地 ‹*judge, reason*›
San Francisco /ˌsæn frənˈsɪskəʊ/ *pr n* 旧金山
sang /sæŋ/ *pt* ▸ **sing A, B**
sangfroid /sɒŋˈfrwɑː/ *n* [u] 镇定; **to show** *or* **evince** ~ 表现出沉着冷静
sangria /sæŋˈgriːə/ *n* [u and c] 桑格里亚酒 [用红葡萄酒、果汁和苏打水制成的西班牙饮料]
sanguine /ˈsæŋgwɪn/ *adj* **1** (optimistic) 乐观的 ‹*person, temperament*›; **to be** ~ **about sth.** 对某事很乐观; **to take a** ~ **view** 抱乐观的态度 **2** formal or dated (ruddy) 红润的 ‹*complexion*›
sanguinely /ˈsæŋgwɪnli/ *adv* 乐观地
sanitarium /ˌsænɪˈteərɪəm/ *n* (*pl* ~**s** *or* **sanitaria** /ˌsænɪˈteərɪə/) Amer = **sanatorium**
sanitary /ˈsænɪtri, Amer -teri/ *adj* **1** (of public health) 公共卫生的 ‹*facilities, inspector*› **2** (hygienic) 卫生的 ‹*state*›; ~ **condition/measure** 卫生条件/措施
sanitary: ~ **engineer** ▸ **p. 409** *n* 卫生工程师; ~ **napkin,** ~ **pad** *ns* Amer = ~ **towel**; ~ **protection** *n* [u] 月经用品; ~ **towel** *n* Brit 卫生巾; ~**ware** *n* [u] 卫生洁具
sanitation /ˌsænɪˈteɪʃn/ *n* [u] 公共卫生
sanitation department *n* Amer 环境卫生部门
sanitize /ˈsænɪtaɪz/ *vt* **1** (make hygienic) 使卫生 **2** pej (make palatable) 净化 ‹*politics*›; 美化 ‹*war*›; 删除…中令人不快的内容 ‹*record*›; **a film that tries to** ~ **violence** 试图淡化暴力的电影
sanitized /ˈsænɪtaɪzd/ *adj* pej 净化了的 ‹*art, politics, document, version*›
sanity /ˈsænəti/ *n* [u] **1** (mental health) 精神正常; **to keep** *or* **preserve** *or* **retain one's** ~ 保持精神正常; **to question** *or* **doubt sb.'s** ~ 怀疑某人是否神志正常; **to lose one's** ~ 精神失常 **2** (good sense) 通情达理; **to restore** ~ **(to sth.)** （使某事物）恢复常理; ~ **prevailed** 常理占了上风
San José /ˌsæn həʊˈzeɪ/ *pr n* 圣何塞
sank /sæŋk/ *pt* ▸ **sink A, B**
San Marino /ˌsæn məˈriːnəʊ/ *pr n* 圣马力诺
San Salvador /ˌsæn ˈsælvədɔː(r)/ *pr n* 圣萨尔瓦多
Sanskrit /ˈsænskrɪt/ ▸ **p. 426** *n* [u] 梵语
Santa Claus /ˈsæntə klɔːz/, **Santa** *pr ns* 圣诞老人

Santa Claus

圣诞老人，简称 Santa。英国英语中常作 Father Christmas。其形象为胖胖的、和蔼可亲的白胡子老头，身穿白色毛皮镶边的红色衣裤，头戴红帽，脚蹬黑色皮靴。每年圣诞节前，孩子们会给圣诞老人写信，告诉他自己希望得到的礼物。圣诞节前夜（Christmas Eve），圣诞老人驾着驯鹿（reindeer）拉的雪橇（sled或sleigh）从北极出发，顺着烟囱进入每个孩子的家里，将礼物放在他们睡觉前挂在床边的长筒袜（stocking）内。孩子们则可能会留下一盘圣诞饼干（美国称为 Christmas Cookie，英国称为 mince pie，即百果馅饼），供圣诞老人享用。

Santiago /ˌsæntɪˈɑːgəʊ/ *pr n* 圣地亚哥
Santo Domingo /ˌsæntəʊ dəˈmɪŋgəʊ/ *pr n* 圣多明各
São Tomé and Príncipe /saʊ ˌtəʊmeɪ ənd ˈprɪnsɪpeɪ/ *pr n* 圣多美和普林西比
sap /sæp/
A *n* **1** [u] (in plants) 液; **in early spring the** ~ **starts to rise and buds appear** 初春时分，树液开始增加，于是树芽冒出; **the hot heady days of youth when the** ~ **was rising** fig 朝气蓬勃的青春岁月 **2** [u] (vigour) 活力 **3** [c] esp Amer colloq (gullible person) 傻瓜
B *vt* (*pres p etc.* **-pp-**) 使…虚弱 ‹*person*›; 消耗 ‹*strength, vigour*›; 削弱 ‹*confidence, pride*›; **to** ~ **sb. of sth.** 使某人逐渐失去某物
saphead /ˈsæphed/ *n* Amer colloq 笨蛋
sapling /ˈsæplɪŋ/ *n* 幼树
sapper /ˈsæpə(r)/ *n* Brit Mil (engineer) 工程兵; (laying, disarming mines) 地雷工兵
sapphic /ˈsæfɪk/ *adj* formal or hum 女同性恋的 ‹*inclination, pleasure*›; ~ **love** 女同性恋
sapphire /ˈsæfaɪə(r)/ ▸ **p. 134**
A *n* **1** [c] (stone) 蓝宝石; ~ **earrings** 蓝宝石耳环 **2** [u] (colour) 天蓝色
B *adj* 天蓝色的 ‹*waters, lake*›
sappy /ˈsæpi/ *adj* **1** Amer colloq (soppy) 多愁善感的 ‹*character, story*› **2** Bot 汁液多的 ‹*plant, branch*›
SAR *abbr* = **Special Administrative Region**
Saracen /ˈsærəsn/ *n* Hist **1** (at time of Roman Empire) 撒拉森人 [骚扰罗马帝国的阿拉伯部落] **2** (at time of Crusades) 穆斯林
Sarajevo /ˌsærəˈjeɪvəʊ/ *pr n* 萨拉热窝
Saran® /səˈræn/ *n* [u] Amer ~ **(Wrap)** 赛纶保鲜膜
sarcasm /ˈsɑːkæzəm/ *n* [u] 讽刺; **a note of** ~ **in sb.'s voice** 某人声音中挖苦的语气
sarcastic /sɑːˈkæstɪk/ *adj* 讽刺的 ‹*smile, remark*›; 爱挖苦人的 ‹*person*›; **a** ~ **tone** *or* **voice** 挖苦的语气
sarcastically /sɑːˈkæstɪkli/ *adv* 讽刺地 ‹*say, write, comment*›
sarcoma /sɑːˈkəʊmə/ *n* (*pl* ~**s** *or* **sarcomata** /sɑːˈkəʊmətə/) 肉瘤
sarcophagus /sɑːˈkɒfəgəs/ *n* (*pl* **sarcophagi** /sɑːˈkɒfəgaɪ/) [尤指带雕饰或铭文的] 石棺
sardine /sɑːˈdiːn/ *n* 沙丁鱼; **to be packed** *or* **squashed (in) like** ~**s** 拥挤不堪
Sardinia /sɑːˈdɪnɪə/ *pr n* 撒丁岛
Sardinian /sɑːˈdɪnɪən/ ▸ **p. 503, p. 426**
A *adj* (of Sardinia) 撒丁岛的; (of the people) 撒丁人的; (of the language) 撒丁语的
B *n* **1** [c] (person) 撒丁人 **2** [u] (language) 撒丁语
sardonic /sɑːˈdɒnɪk/ *adj* 讥讽的 ‹*tone, comment, laugh*›; 轻蔑的 ‹*look, expression*›; **a** ~ **smile** 讪笑; ~ **humour** 讥刺的幽默
sardonically /sɑːˈdɒnɪkli/ *adv* 讥讽地
Sargasso Sea /sɑːˌgæsəʊ ˈsiː/ *pr n* **the** ~ 马尾藻海
sarge /sɑːdʒ/ *n* colloq = **sergeant**
sari /ˈsɑriː/ *n* 莎丽 [南亚妇女的传统服饰]
sarin /ˈsɑːrɪn/ *n* [u] 沙林 [一种神经毒气]
sarky /ˈsɑːki/ *adj* Brit colloq = **sarcastic**
sarnie /ˈsɑːni/ *n* Brit colloq = **sandwich A1**
sarong /səˈrɒŋ/ *n* 莎笼 [马来群岛和太平洋岛屿的传统裙装]
SARS /sɑːz/ ▸ **p. 377** *abbr* = **severe acute respiratory syndrome** 严重急性呼吸道综合征 [通称非典型肺炎或非典]
sarsaparilla /ˌsɑːsəpəˈrɪlə/ *n* [u and c] Amer **1** (drink) 菝葜汽水 **2** (plant) 菝葜
sartorial /sɑːˈtɔːrɪəl/ *adj* formal (of tailoring) 缝纫的 ‹*style*›; (of men's clothes) 男装的; **Savile Row in London was long considered a centre of** ~ **excellence** 伦敦的萨维尔街长期被视为高级男装中心
SAS *abbr* Brit = **Special Air Service**
sash /sæʃ/ *n* **1** (round waist) 腰带 **2** (ceremonial) [制服上的] 饰带 **3** (window frame) 窗框; ~ **weight** 吊窗平衡锤
sashay /ˈsæʃeɪ/ *vi* esp Amer colloq (with a swagger) 大摇大摆地走; (seductively) 装腔作势地走
sash: ~ **cord** *n* 吊窗绳; ~**lock** *n* 窗锁; ~ **window** *n* 垂直推拉窗
Saskatchewan /səˈskætʃəwən/ *pr n* 萨斯喀彻温省
sass /sæs/ Amer colloq
A *n* [u] 粗鲁无礼
B *vt* 对…出言不逊
sassafras /ˈsæsəfræs/ *n* 檫树; ~ **oil/tea** 檫树油/茶
Sassenach /ˈsæsənæk/ *n* Scot pej or hum 英格兰人
sassy /ˈsæsi/ *adj* esp Amer colloq **1** (lively) 调皮的 ‹*person, character*›; (impertinent) 莽撞的 ‹*tone, manner*› **2** (smart) 别致的 ‹*hat, appearance*›
SAT /sæt/ *abbr* Sch **1** Brit = **Standard Assessment Task** **2** Amer = **Scholastic Aptitude Test**
sat /sæt/ *pt, pp* ▸ **sit**
Sat. ▸ **p. 182** *abbr* = **Saturday**
Satan /ˈseɪtn/ *pr n* 魔鬼
satanic /səˈtænɪk/ *adj* **1** lit (devilish) 撒旦的 ‹*symbol*›; 崇拜撒旦的 ‹*cult*›; ~ **rites/worship** 撒旦崇拜仪式/撒旦崇拜 **2** fig (evil) 极其邪恶的 ‹*smile*›; ~ **slums** 地狱般的贫民窟
satanic abuse *n* [u] 仪式性侵害 [撒旦崇拜仪式的一部分，通常是对儿童的性侵害或残杀]
satanically /səˈtænɪkli/ *adv* 恶魔般地
satanism /ˈseɪtənɪzəm/ *n* [u] 撒旦崇拜
satanist /ˈseɪtənɪst/
A *n* 撒旦崇拜者
B *adj* 崇拜撒旦的
satay /ˈsæteɪ/ *n* [c and u] 沙嗲烤肉 [印尼和马来西亚食品]
satchel /ˈsætʃəl/ *n* 肩背书包
Satcom /ˈsætkɒm/ *n* [u] = **Satellite Communications System** 卫星通信系统

sate /seɪt/ *vt formal* 充分满足 〈*appetite, curiosity*〉

sated /ˈseɪtɪd/ *adj formal* 餍足了的; **to be ~ with sth.** 对某物感到满足

sateen /sæˈtiːn/ *n* [u] 棉缎

satellite /ˈsætəlaɪt/ *n* **1** (celestial) 卫星 **2** (man-made) 人造卫星; **meteorological** *or* **weather ~** 气象卫星; **to transmit by** *or* **via ~** 通过人造卫星传输; **~ broadcasting/transmission** 卫星广播/播送 **3** (dependent country) 卫星国; **a ~ state** 卫星国 **4** (community) 卫星城; **a ~ town** 卫星城

satellite: ~ channel *n* 卫星频道; **~ dish** *n* 卫星碟形天线; **~ link** *n* 卫星链路; **~ navigation** *n* [u] 卫星导航; **~ operator** *n* 卫星电视运营商; **~ photograph** *n* 卫星照片; **~ receiver** *n* **= ~ dish**; **~ technology** *n* [u] 卫星通信技术; **~ telephone** *n* 卫星电话; **~ television, ~ TV** *ns* [u] 卫星电视

satiate /ˈseɪʃɪeɪt/ *vt* 充分满足

satiated /ˈseɪʃɪeɪtɪd/ *adj* 腻足了的

satiation /ˌseɪʃɪˈeɪʃn/ *n* [u] 餍足

satiety /səˈtaɪəti/ *n* [u] *formal* 餍足

satin /ˈsætɪn, *Amer* ˈsætn/ *n* [u] 缎子; **a ~ dress** 缎子连衣裙; **a ~ finish** 缎子般的光泽度

satinwood /ˈsætɪnwʊd, *Amer* ˈsætnwʊd/ *n* **1** [c] (tree) 椴木树 **2** [u] (wood) 椴木; **with ~ inlays** 有椴木镶嵌的

satiny /ˈsætɪni, *Amer* ˈsætni/ *adj* (in texture) 缎子般的; (in appearance) 光滑的

satire /ˈsætaɪə(r)/ *n* **1** [u] (ridicule) 讽刺; **to be the object of ~** 是讽刺的对象 **2** [c] (novel, play etc.) 讽刺作品; **a stinging ~ on American politics** 尖刻讽刺美国政治的作品

satirical /səˈtɪrɪkl/, **satiric** /səˈtɪrɪk/ *adj* 讽刺的 〈*novel, play, comment, tone*〉

satirically /səˈtɪrɪkli/ *adv* 讽刺地

satirist /ˈsætərɪst/ *n* (writer) 讽刺作家; (artist) 讽刺艺术家

satirize /ˈsætəraɪz/ *vt* 讽刺

satisfaction /ˌsætɪsˈfækʃn/ *n* **1** [u and c] (pleasure) 满足感; **to get** *or* **derive ~ out of** *or* **from sth.** 从某事物中获得满足感; **I assure you I derive no ~ whatever from your defeat** 我向你保证，我对你的失败没有半点幸灾乐祸; **to express one's ~ (at sth.)** 表示（对某事物）满意; **with ~** 心满意足地 **2** [u] (fulfilment) 满足; (gratification) 满意; **the ~ of your every wish is our desire** 我们的目标是满足您每一个心愿; **the ~ of consumer demand** 消费者需求的满足; **the matter was settled to everyone's ~** 这件事以令大家都满意的方式得到了解决 **3** [u] (reparation) 补偿; **to seek/demand ~** 寻求/要求补偿 **4** [u] Jur (payment of debt) 清偿; (fulfilment of obligation or claim) 履行; **in full and final ~** 一次性清偿; **he received no ~ from the company** 他没有获得公司的赔偿 **5** [u] (self-satisfaction) 自满; **a look** *or* **an expression of ~** 自鸣得意的表情

satisfactorily /ˌsætɪsˈfæktərəli/ *adv* 令人满意地

satisfactory /ˌsætɪsˈfæktəri/ *adj* **1** (good enough) 令人满意的; **to be ~ to sb.** 令某人满意; **the solution is less than ~** 这个解决方案不尽如人意; **to bring a matter to a ~ conclusion** 使事情有圆满的结局; **this product should reach you in a ~ condition** 本产品交货时应完好无损 **2** (acceptable) 尚可的 〈*achievement, arrangement, state of health, performance, product*〉; **her condition was said to be ~** Med 据说她的健康状况还可以; **his school report says his work is ~ but not good** 成绩报告单上说他的功课尚好，但并不出色

satisfied /ˈsætɪsfaɪd/ *adj* **1** (pleased) 满意的 〈*customer, smile*〉; **I am more than ~ with the result** 我对结果太满意了; **now are you ~?** 这下你满意了吧? **2** (convinced) 确信的; **to be ~ that ...** 确信…; **I'm not entirely ~ by** *or* **with your explanation** 我并不完全相信你的解释

satisfy /ˈsætɪsfaɪ/

A *vt* **1** (fulfil) 满足 〈*need, curiosity, desire*〉; 使满意; **I need someone who can ~ me both physically and intellectually** 我需要一个身体和精神上都能使我满意的人 **2** (comply with, meet) 符合 〈*terms, condition*〉; 达到 〈*requirement*〉; 偿还 〈*debt*〉; **our firm is unable to ~ the demand for our goods** 本公司无法满足对我们商品的需求 **3** (persuade, convince) 使…确信 〈*public*〉; 向…证实 〈*jury, court*〉; **the employer wanted to ~ himself as to the applicant's honesty** 雇主想弄清楚求职者是否诚实

B *vi* 《*food, book*》 令人满意; **to fail to ~** 未令人满意

satisfying /ˈsætɪsfaɪɪŋ/ *adj* **1** (filling) 丰足的 〈*meal, diet*〉 **2** (rewarding) 让人满意的 〈*feeling, experience, conclusion*〉 **3** (pleasing) 令人高兴的; **it is ~ to see/know that ...** 看到/知道…很让人高兴

satisfyingly /ˈsætɪsfaɪɪŋli/ *adv* 令人满意地

satnav /ˈsætnæv/ *n* [u] 卫星导航

satphone /ˈsætfəʊn/ *n* 卫星电话

satsuma /sætˈsuːmə/ *n* 蜜橘

saturate /ˈsætʃəreɪt/ *vt* **1** (soak) 将…浸透 〈*carpet, soil, bandage*〉; 使…湿透 〈*clothes, body, hair*〉; **sweat had ~d his shirt** 汗水湿透了他的衬衫 **2** (fill to capacity) 使…充满 〈*area, media*〉; 使…饱和 〈*market*〉; **to ~ the market with sth.** 以某物充斥市场 **3** Chem 使…饱和 〈*vapour, solution*〉 **4** Mil (bomb, shell) 对…进行饱和轰炸; **we ~d the area with artillery fire** 我们对该地区进行了饱和炮击

saturated /ˈsætʃəreɪtɪd/ *adj* **1** (soaked) 浸透的 〈*bandage, soil, carpet*〉; 湿透的 〈*clothes, hair*〉 **2** (filled to capacity) 充满的; **the air was ~ with the scent of sth.** 空气里弥漫着某物的气味; **the market is already ~** 市场已经饱和 **3** Chem 饱和的; **~ fat/solution** 饱和脂肪/溶液 **4** Art 深浓的 〈*colour*〉

saturation /ˌsætʃəˈreɪʃn/ *n* [u] **1** (act) 饱和; (state) 饱和状态 **2** Art 色饱和度

saturation: ~ bombing *n* [u] 饱和轰炸; **~ point** *n* [u] 饱和点; **to reach ~ point** fig 达到饱和状态

Saturday /ˈsætədeɪ, -di/ ▸p. 182 *n* 星期六; **on ~** 在星期六; **on ~s/every ~** 每周星期六; **~ morning/afternoon/night** 星期六早晨/下午/晚上; **this/last/next ~** 本周六/上周六/下周六

Saturday night special *n Amer colloq* 小口径手枪

Saturn /ˈsætən/ *pr n* 土星; **the rings of ~** 土星环

saturnine /ˈsætənaɪn/ *adj liter* 阴沉的 〈*expression, face*〉; 阴郁的 〈*character*〉

satyr /ˈsætə(r)/ *n* 萨堤尔 [希腊神话中好酒色、半人半羊的森林之神]

sauce /sɔːs/

A *n* **1** [u and c] Culin 调味汁; **orange/pepper ~** 桔子酱/胡椒酱; **what's ~ for the goose is ~ for the gander** 适于此者也适于彼; **hunger is the best ~** 饥饿是最好的调味料 **2** [u] Amer (stewed fruit) 炖水果 **3** [u] colloq (cheeky behaviour) 无礼的举动; (cheeky attitude) 无礼的态度; (cheeky language) 无礼的话 **4** [u] colloq esp Amer (alcohol) 烈酒; **to be on** *or* **hit the ~** 酗酒

B *vt colloq* 对…无礼

sauce: ~ boat *n* 船形调味碟; **~pan** *n* 深煮锅

saucer /ˈsɔːsə(r)/ *n* 茶托; **cups and ~s** 茶杯和茶碟; **with eyes like** *or* **as big as ~s** 惊讶得眼睛瞪得溜圆

saucily /ˈsɔːsɪli/ *adv colloq* 风骚地 〈*wink, grin, dress*〉; 轻佻地 〈*look, speak*〉

sauciness /ˈsɔːsɪnɪs/ *n* [u] colloq **1** (sexual suggestiveness) 风骚 **2** (cheek) 鲁莽

saucy /ˈsɔːsi/ *adj colloq* **1** (sexually suggestive) 风骚的 〈*smile, wink, dress*〉; 轻佻的 〈*look, lyric*〉; **~ comedy/picture** 情色喜剧/图画 **2** (impudent) 鲁莽的 〈*person, reply*〉

Saudi /ˈsaʊdi/ ▸p. 503

A *adj* (of Saudi Arabia) 沙特阿拉伯的 〈*monarchy, economy*〉; (of the people) 沙特阿拉伯人的

B *n* 沙特阿拉伯人

Saudi Arabia *pr n* 沙特阿拉伯

Saudi Arabian ▸p. 503

A *adj* (of Saudi Arabia) 沙特阿拉伯的; (of the people) 沙特阿拉伯人的

B *n* 沙特阿拉伯人

sauerkraut /ˈsaʊəkraʊt/ *n* [u] 泡菜

sauna /ˈsɔːnə, ˈsaʊnə/ *n* **1** (bath) 桑拿浴; **to have** *or* **take a ~** 洗桑拿浴 **2** (room) 桑拿浴室; **it's like a ~ in here!** 这里热得像桑拿浴室!

saunter /ˈsɔːntə(r)/

A *vi* **~ (along)** 闲逛; **to ~ off** 悠闲地走开

B *n* 闲逛; **to go for a ~** 去漫步

sausage /ˈsɒsɪdʒ, *Amer* ˈsɔːs-/ *n* **1** [c] (for cooking) 香肠; **not a ~** 一点都没有 **2** [u] (eaten cold) 干熏香肠

sausage: ~ dog *n Brit colloq* 腊肠犬; **~ meat** *n* [u] 香肠肉馅; **~ roll** *n Brit* 香肠卷

sauté /ˈsəʊteɪ, *Amer* səʊˈteɪ/

A *vt* (*pres p* **~ing**; *pt, pp* **~d** *or* **~ed**) 嫩煎 〈*potatoes, vegetables*〉

B *adj* (*also* **sautéd** *or* **sautéed**) 嫩煎的 〈*potatoes, vegetables*〉

savage /ˈsævɪdʒ/

A *adj* **1** lit (violent) 残暴的 〈*person, reprisals, temper*〉 **2** fig (hostile) 猛烈的 〈*attack*〉; 凶狠的 〈*treatment*〉; 恶毒的 〈*satire, criticism*〉 **3** (severe) 极度的; **~ cuts** 大幅度削减; **~ cold/heat/wind** 严寒/酷热/狂风 **4** (uncivilized) 未开化的 〈*people, tribe*〉; 未驯服的 〈*animal*〉; 野蛮的 〈*customs*〉

B *n* **1** liter or dated (primitive) 未开化的人; **the children roamed wild like young ~s** 孩子们四处撒野 **2** (brutal person) 凶残的人

C *vt* **1** (attack) 凶猛地攻击 〈*person, animal*〉 **2** fig 猛烈抨击 〈*politician, policy, play*〉

savagely /ˈsævɪdʒli/ *adv* **1** lit 残暴地 〈*kill*〉; 猛烈地 〈*attack*〉; 凶狠地 〈*bite, beat*〉 **2** fig 充满恶意地 〈*criticize, satirical*〉

savagery /ˈsævɪdʒri/, **savageness** /ˈsævɪdʒnɪs/ *ns* [u] (of war, people) 残暴; (of attack) 凶狠; (verbal) 恶毒攻击; **an act of ~ of the worst kind** 最残暴的行为

savannah, savanna /səˈvænə/ *n* [u and c] [亚热带的] 稀树草原

savant /ˈsævənt, *Amer* sæˈvɑːnt/ *n* 智者

save¹ /seɪv/

A *vt* **1** (rescue) 挽救 〈*person, life*〉; **he was ~d by an overhanging branch** 一根伸出的树枝救了他一命; **to ~ the whale/rain forests** 拯救鲸鱼/雨林; **to ~ the set/match** 挽回这一局/这场比赛; **to ~ oneself** 自救; **to ~ sb./sth. from sth./sb.** 使某人/某物免遭某状况/免于落入某人之手; **that loan ~d us from bankruptcy** 那笔贷款使我们免遭破产; **she ~d him from making an awful fool of himself** 她使他避免了大出洋相; **they managed to ~ a few things from the fire** 他们从火里抢救出了几样东西; **to ~ sb. from himself/herself** 使某人免于自我毁灭; **to ~ sb.'s life** lit 救某人的命; fig 帮某人的大忙; **she can't use a computer to ~ her life** colloq 她死活不会用电脑; **to ~ the day** *or* **situation** 挽回败局; **Emily ~d the day by whipping up a meal from some leftovers** 艾米莉匆匆用剩菜做了一顿饭使大家免于挨饿 **2** (keep for future) 积攒 〈*money*〉; 留存 〈*food*〉; **~ me a piece of cake, will you?** 给我留一块蛋糕，好吗?; **to ~ sth. for sb./**

S

sth. 为某人/某事物保留某物; **to ~ a building/an art treasure for posterity/the nation** 把建筑物/艺术珍宝留给后人/民族; **you can ~ your explanations for the police** 你等着向警察解释吧; **she asked us to ~ her a seat** 她要我们给她留一个座位; **I was saving this dance for you** 我在等着和你跳这支舞; **he's saving himself for the big match** 他在为准备参加大赛保存体力; **she's saving herself for Mr Right** 她守身如玉，等待如意郎君的出现; **~ your strength, you'll never break that rope** 省省力气吧，你拉不断那根绳子; **~ it!** colloq 住口! **3▸** (spare) 节省; **why not phone and ~ yourself a journey** 为什么不打个电话省得跑一趟呢; **going via Gloucester will ~ you twenty miles/minutes** 取道格洛斯特可以少走 20 英里/少用 20 分钟; **to ~ one's breath** 少费口舌 **4▸** (avoid need for) 免去; **thanks, you've ~d me an awful lot of trouble** 谢谢，你为我省去了一大堆麻烦; **to ~ sb./sth. (from) doing** *or* **having to do sth.** 使某人/某物不必做某事; **take the stuff now, it'll ~ you having to come back tomorrow** 现在就把东西拿走吧，这样你明天就不用再回来了; **to ~ doing sth.** 免得做某事; **I'll take a key to ~ disturbing you when I come in** 我带一把钥匙免得进来时打扰你 **5▸** Comput 保存 ‹*data, file*› **6▸** Sport 救 ‹*goal, shot*› **7▸** (collect) 收集 ‹*beer mats, matchboxes, collectible items*› **8▸** (keep in health) 护佑; **God ~ the Queen/King** 上帝佑女王/国王 **9▸** Relig 救赎 ‹*soul, sinner, mankind*›

B *vi* **1▸** (keep back money) 攒钱; **to ~ for** *or* **towards sth.** 为某事物攒钱; **I'm saving for a holiday abroad** 我在攒钱准备去国外度假 **2▸** (economize) 节约; **to ~ on sth.** 节省某物; **to ~ on labour costs** 降低劳动力成本; **to ~ on petrol** 节约汽油 **3▸** Relig 救赎; **Jesus ~s** 耶稣救赎世人

C *n* 救球; **to make a ~** 救球

Phrasal verb

- **save up**

A *vi* 攒钱; **to ~ up for** *or* **towards sth.** 为某事物攒钱; **we're saving up for a skiing trip** 我们正在攒钱准备去滑雪旅行

B *vt* [**~ sth. up, ~ up sth.**] 积攒; **they ~d up enough money to pay off the debt** 他们攒够钱把债务还清了

save² *prep* formal or liter 除…之外; **the house was deserted, ~ for one old housekeeper** 除了一个老管家之外，房子里空无一人; **~ that ...** 除了…; **nothing moved, ~ that here and there a slight breeze stirred the treetops** 除了微风时不时吹动树梢以外，一切都是静止的

save as you earn *n* [u] Brit 工资定额扣存储蓄

saveloy /ˈsævəlɔɪ/ *n* [u and c] Brit 萨维罗猪肉熏肠

saver /ˈseɪvə(r)/

A *n* 储户

B **-saver** *combining form* 有助于节省的事物; **a time/money~** 省时/省钱的事物

Savile Row /ˌsævɪlˈrəʊ/ *pr n* 萨维尔街 [伦敦的高档裁缝街]; **a ~ suit** 伦敦裁缝街定制的西服

saving /ˈseɪvɪŋ/

A *n* **1▸** [c] (reduction) 节省; **a ~ in time and money** 省时省钱; **a ~ in fuel** 燃料的节约 **2▸** [u] (activity) 储蓄

B **savings** *npl* 存款; **to live off one's ~s** 靠存款生活; **to lose one's life ~s** 损失毕生的积蓄

C *prep* formal 除…之外; **~ your presence** dated 恕我冒昧

saving: ~ clause *n* 保留条款; **~ grace** *n* 弥补缺点的特点; **that's his one ~ grace** 那是他的唯一可取之处; **~s account** *n* Brit 储蓄账户; **~s and loan association** *n* Amer 储蓄借贷协会 [即建房互助协会]; **~s bank** *n* 储蓄银行; **~s bond** *n* **1▸** Amer (government bond) 储蓄公债; **2▸ = Premium Bond**; **~s book** *n* 存折; **~s certificate** *n* Brit 储蓄存单 [英国政府发行的5年期固定利率存单]; **~s plan** *n* 储蓄计划; **~s stamp** *n* Brit 储蓄印花 [表示存储了一定数量的金额]

saviour Brit, **savior** Amer /ˈseɪvɪə(r)/ *n* **1▸** (gen) 救助者 **2▸** Relig 救世主 [指耶稣]

savoir-faire /ˌsævwɑːˈfeə(r)/ *n* [u] **1▸** (social graces) 处世能力 **2▸** (know-how) 专业技能

savor /ˈseɪvə(r)/ *n, vt, vi* Amer **= savour**

savory /ˈseɪvəri/

A *n* **1▸** [u] (herb) 香薄荷 **2▸** Amer **= savoury B**

B *adj* Amer **= savoury A**

savour /ˈseɪvə(r)/ Brit

A *n* **1▸** lit (flavour) 滋味; (smell) 气味; **to lose/keep its ~** 失去/保持其味道 **2▸** fig (enjoyable quality) 趣味; **life has lost its ~ for her** 对她来说生活已没有了乐趣 **3▸** (trace, hint) 微量; **to have a ~ of ...** 略有…的味道

B *vt* **1▸** (taste and enjoy) 品尝 ‹*food, drink*› **2▸** fig (revel in) 享受 ‹*freedom, peace*›; 欣赏 ‹*idea*›; 品味 ‹*words*›; **I want to ~ every moment** 我想细细品味每一刻; **he didn't ~ the prospect of telling the family** 他可不愿意告诉家人

C *vi* **to ~ of sth.** formal «*remarks, attitude, situation*» 意味着某事物

savoury /ˈseɪvəri/

A *adj* Brit **1▸** (appetizing) 美味的 ‹*dish, food*›; (tasty) 可口的 ‹*taste*› **2▸** (not sweet) 咸味的 ‹*fishcake, eggs*›; 不甜的 ‹*dish*› **3▸** fig (morally wholesome) **not a very ~ individual/area/club** 名声不太好的人/地区/俱乐部; **the less ~ aspects of the matter** 这件事不太光彩的方面

B *n* esp Brit 咸味小吃

savoy cabbage /səˌvɔɪ ˈkæbɪdʒ/ *n* [u and c] Brit 皱叶甘蓝

savvy /ˈsævi/ esp Amer colloq

A *n* [u] **1▸** (common sense) 常识; **you can find your way back by yourself — just use your ~!** 你能自己找到回家的路——运用常识就行! **2▸** (know-how) 技能; **marketing ~** 营销技能

B *adj* (shrewd) 精明的; (well-informed) 有见识的; **to be ~ about sth.** 在某事上精明

saw¹ /sɔː/ *pt* ▸**see¹**

saw²

A *n* (tool) 锯

B *vt* (*pt* **~ed**; *pp* **sawn** esp Brit, **~ed** esp Amer) 锯 ‹*logs, plank, metal*›; **to ~ through sth.** 锯穿某物; **to ~ sth. down** 锯倒某物; **to ~ sth. in half** 将某物锯成两半

Phrasal verbs

- **saw away** *vi* 拉锯似地来回移动; fig 努力重复做; **to ~ away at the bread/violin** 拉锯似地切面包/不停地拉小提琴; **I was ~ing away for hours, cutting all the struts to the right length** 我努力锯了很久，把支杆切成合适的长度
- **saw off** *vt* [**~ sth. off, ~ off sth.**] 锯掉 ‹*branch, table leg, end*›
- **saw up** *vt* [**~ sth. up, ~ up sth.**] 将…锯成小块 ‹*timber, logs, planks*›

saw³ *n* dated (saying) 谚语

saw: ~bones *n* hum (doctor) 医生; (surgeon) 外科医生; **~dust** *n* [u] 锯末

sawed /sɔːd/ *pp* Amer ▸**saw² B**

sawed-off *adj* Amer **= sawn-off**

saw: ~fish *n* (*pl* **~fish** *or* **~fishes**) 锯鳐; **~horse** *n* 锯木架; **~mill** *n* 锯木厂

sawn /sɔːn/

A *pp* Brit ▸**saw² B**

B *adj* 锯好的 ‹*logs*›; **~ timber** 锯材

sawn-off *adj* Brit 锯短的 ‹*barrel, stump*›; **a ~ shotgun** 枪管锯短的猎枪

sawyer /ˈsɔːjə(r)/ ▸**p. 409** *n* 锯木工

sax /sæks/ ▸**p. 395** *n* colloq 萨克斯管

saxhorn /ˈsækshɔːn/ ▸**p. 395** *n* 萨克斯号

saxifrage /ˈsæksɪfreɪdʒ/ *n* [u and c] 虎耳草

Saxon /ˈsæksn/

A *adj* **1▸** (of the people) 撒克逊人的 **2▸** (of the language) 撒克逊语的

B *n* **1▸** [c] (person) 撒克逊人 **2▸** [u] (language) 撒克逊语

saxophone /ˈsæksəfəʊn/ ▸**p. 395** *n* 萨克斯管; **a ~ player/solo** 萨克斯管演奏者/独奏曲

saxophonist /sækˈsɒfənɪst/ ▸**p. 395, p. 409** *n* 萨克斯管演奏者

say /seɪ/

A *vt* (*pt, pp* **said**) **1▸** (utter) 说; **to ~ hello/goodbye** 问好/道别; **she ~s he's ill** 她说他病了; **it's just a way of ~ing thank you** 这只是一种道谢的方式; **to ~ a prayer** 祈祷; **'hello,' he said** "嗨，"他说道; **I've got nothing to ~** (to police, media, etc.) 我无可奉告; **to have a lot to ~** 有很多话要说; **the boss will have something to ~ about that** 关于那件事老板有话要讲; **to ~ sth. to oneself** 心里想某事; **I wouldn't ~ no to a lift to the station** 我不反对搭车去车站; **to ~ one's piece** 说出心里话; **to have a lot to ~ for oneself** 有一肚子话要说; **what have you got to ~ for yourself?** 你还有什么可辩解的吗? ; **I should ~ so** *or* **it is!** 的确如此! ; **you said it!** colloq 说得对! ; **you can ~ that again!** colloq 你说得一点不错! ; **and so ~ all of us** 我们都这么想; **~ no more** colloq 不用再说了; **enough said** colloq 不必多说; **the manager said he'd ~ no more about it if we returned the money immediately** 经理说如果我们马上把钱还回去，他就不再追究; **when all is said and done** 说到底; **it goes without ~ing (that ...)** 不用说 (…) ; **so to ~** 可以说; **as you/they ~** 正如你/人们所说; **so they/you ~** 大家都这么说/那是你说的 **2▸** (claim, assert) 宣称; **the weather forecast said it would be fine today** 天气预报说今天是晴天; **the rules/statutes/regulations ~ associate members have full voting rights** 规定/条例/规章里说明准会员有完全的投票权; **it is said that ...** 据说…; **he's said to be worth millions** 据说他身家数百万; **don't ~ I didn't warn you** 别说我没有警告过你; **don't ~ you forgot!** 别说你忘了! ; **to ~ sth. for sb./sth.** 替某人/某事物说某话; **it ~s a lot for him (that ...)** (…) 说明他很好; **it doesn't ~ much for them (that ...)** (…) 说明他们不怎么样; **it doesn't ~ much for their marriage/her commitment** 这说明他们的婚姻/她的承诺有问题; **there's a lot to be said for sth./doing sth.** 某物/做某事有很多优点; **that isn't ~ing much** 那说明不了什么; **to ~ nothing of ...** 更不用说…; **it will cost millions, to ~ nothing of the amount of disruption it will cause** 这将花去数百万，更何况还会造成极大的混乱 **3▸** (state, indicate) «*writer, gesture, sign*» 表达; «*dial*» 显示; **the letter said nothing about any additional payments** 信中没有提到额外付款; **what do you think the poet is trying to ~?** 你认为诗人想表达什么? ; **the music ~s something to me** 这音乐向我传达了某种意思; **~ it with flowers** 以花传情 [花商广告语]; **a card/gift can ~ so much** 一张贺卡/一份礼物可以传达无限情谊; **the sign ~s 'keep off the grass'** 牌子上写着"勿踏草地"; **the clock ~s half past three** 钟上的时间是 3 点半; **what does your watch ~?** 你的手表几点了? ; **that ~s it all** 那说明了一切; **that is to ~ that ...** 也就是说…; **this is the method we recommend, but that's not to ~ it's the only method** 我们推荐这个方法，但并不是说这是唯一的方法 **4▸** (guess) 估计; (conjecture) 认为; **there's no ~ing** 很难说; **it's a good bargain, I'd ~** 我觉得这个交易蛮划算的 **5▸** (be of the opinion of) 主张; **he ~s I should**

accept 他认为我应该接受; **what do you ~ to that?** 你对那件事有何想法? **6** (assume) **~ (that) ...** 假如…; **~ you have an accident, who would look after you?** 假如你出了事故，谁来照顾你呢? **7** (admit) 承认; **it seems very expensive, I must ~** 我得说这似乎很贵 **8** (instruct, order) 告诉; **she said that we were to wait here** 她要我们在这里等; **to ~ to do sth.** 要求他人做某事; **the man said to pay at the cash desk** 那个人让我们到收银台付款; **do as** *or* **what I ~** 照我说的做 **9** (decide) 决定; **the boss will ~ whether you're to go or not** 老板会决定你的去留; **that's not for me to ~** 这事不由我决定 **10** colloq (in suggestions, offers) [用于提建议]; **what ~ we go for a stroll before lunch?** 我们午饭前去散个步怎么样? ; **~ I drove you to the station; would that help?** 我开车送你去车站吧，这样有帮助吗?

B *vi* (*pt, pp* **said**) **1** colloq (speak) 说; **~s who?** (sceptical) 谁说的? ; **~s you!** (taunting) 你在瞎说! ; **you don't ~!** 不会吧! ; **the boss is in a bad mood again — you don't ~!** iron 老板又不高兴了——不至于吧! **2** Brit dated (hey) 喂 [用来引出一句话]; **I ~, that is a shame!** 哎呀，太遗憾了! ; **I ~, waiter!** 喂，服务员! **3** (for example) 比方说; **you're expecting, ~, 500 guests** 你们需要接待，比方说，500 位客人

C *n* **1** (power to influence) 发言权; **to have a ~ in sth./doing sth.** 在某事物/做某事上有发言权; **to have a/no ~ in the matter** 在此事上有/没有发言权 **2** (chance to speak) 发言机会; **to have one's ~** 发表意见; **no, let him have his ~** 不，让他把话说出来

D *excl* Amer colloq 嘿 [表示惊讶或提请注意]; **~, that's a great idea!** 嘿，这个主意好极了!

SAYE *n* Brit **= save as you earn**

saying /ˈseɪŋ/

A *n* (proverb) 谚语; (epigram) 警句; (maxim) 格言; **as the ~ goes** 常言道

B sayings *npl* (of leader, politician) 格言集

say-so *n* colloq **1** (permission) 许可; **without sb.'s ~** 未经某人的准许 **2** (assertion) 无根据的断言; **on sb.'s ~** 仅凭某人的空口白话

S-bend *n* S 形弯

SC *abbr* Amer **= South Carolina**

scab /skæb/

A *n* **1** Med 痂 **2** colloq pej (strike-breaker) 破坏罢工者; **~! ~!** 工贼! 工贼!

B *vi* (*pres p etc.* **-bb-**) «*wound, cut*» 结痂; **to ~ over** 结痂

scabbard /ˈskæbəd/ *n* (for sword) 剑鞘; (for dagger) 刀鞘

scabby /ˈskæbi/ *adj* **1** (covered in scabs) 结痂的 ‹*leg, skin*› **2** (diseased) 患疥癣的 ‹*animal*›; 有疮痂斑点的 ‹*fruit, bark of tree*›

scabies /ˈskeɪbiːz/ **▸p. 377** *n* [u] 疥疮

scab labour *n* [u] colloq pej 破坏罢工者

scabrous /ˈskeɪbrəs, Amer ˈskæb-/ *adj* 下流的 ‹*jokes, novel, remarks*›

scads /skædz/ *npl* Amer colloq 大量; **he's got ~ of money** 他的钱超多

scaffold /ˈskæfəʊld/ *n* **1** Constr 脚手架 **2** (gallows) 绞刑架

scaffolder /ˈskæfəʊldə(r)/ **▸p. 409** *n* 脚手架搭建工

scaffolding /ˈskæfəldɪŋ/ *n* [u] **1** (structure) 脚手架; **to build** *or* **erect** *or* **put up ~** 搭脚手架; **to take down ~** 拆除脚手架 **2** (materials) 搭脚手架的材料; **a piece of ~** 一块脚手架; **a ~ pole/plank** 脚手架支柱/脚手架板

scalable /ˈskeɪləbl/ *adj* **1** (climbable) 可攀登的 ‹*mountain*› **2** (resizable) 大小可改变的 **3** Comput 可扩展的 ‹*program, system*›

scalar /ˈskeɪlə(r)/

A *adj* 纯量的; **a ~ property/quantity** 无向性/无向量

B *n* 纯量

scalawag /ˈskæləwæg/ *n* Amer colloq **= scallywag**

scald /skɔːld/

A *vt* **1** (burn) 烫伤 ‹*hand, tongue, person*›; **to ~ one's arm with boiling water** 被开水烫伤手臂; **like a ~ed cat** fig 飞快地 **2** Culin (nearly boil) 将…加热到接近沸腾 ‹*liquid, milk*› **3** Culin (blanch) 焯 ‹*tomatoes, meat*›

B *v refl* 烫伤; **to ~ oneself with/on sth.** 被某物烫伤

C *n* 烫伤

scalding /ˈskɔːldɪŋ/

A *adj* **1** (very hot) 滚烫的 ‹*drink, coffee, kettle*› **2** fig (painful) 尖刻的 ‹*criticism*›; 伤人的 ‹*humiliation*›; **the ~ tears ran down her cheeks** 滚烫的泪水从她脸上流下

B *adv* **~ hot** 滚烫的

scale¹ /skeɪl/

A *n* **1** [c] (grading system) 等级; **we assess performance on a ~ of 0 to 10** 我们按 0 到 10 级来评估成绩; **to move up the (social) ~** (社会) 等级上升; **a ~ of values** 价值观体系; **at the other end of the ~** 在等级的另一端; **a ~ of charges** 收费等级; **a pay** *or* **wage ~** 工资级别; **a graduated ~** 级差制; **an incremental ~** 递进级别制 **2** [c] (measuring mark) 刻度 **3** [c] (ratio) 比例; **the ~ (of the plans) is one to a hundred** (设计图的) 比例为 1 : 100; **to ~** 按比例; **out of ~** 不成比例; **the ~ of the map is too small to see anything clearly** 地图比例太小，什么都看不清; **a ~ model/drawing** 按比例缩放的模型/图画 **4** [u] (size) 规模; (degree) 程度; (scope) 范围; **the ~ of the disaster** 受灾程度; **the ~ of change** 变化的程度; **the ~ of production/operations** 生产/运营规模; **on a large** *or* **grand ~** 大规模地; **she loves entertaining on a grand ~** 她喜欢大宴宾客; **on a monumental ~** 规模宏大地; **on a small/an inadequate ~** 小/不够规模地; **on a national ~** 在全国范围内; **she had never seen destruction on such a ~** 她从未见过这么大规模的破坏 **5** [c] Mus 音阶; **to play/sing/practise a ~** 演奏/唱出/练习音阶; **the ~ of C major** C 大调音阶

B *vt* 爬上 ‹*wall, ladder*›; 攀上 ‹*mountain, tower*›

Phrasal verbs

- **scale down,** esp Amer **scale back** *vt* [**~ sth. down, ~ down sth.**] 缩小 ‹*drawing, plan*›; 削减 ‹*production, imports, expenditure, investment*›; 降低 ‹*price, earnings*›; **a ~d down version (of sth.)** (某物的) 缩小版; **the army is scaling down its operations** 军队现正把军事行动降级
- **scale up** *vt* [**~ sth. up, ~ up sth.**] 放大 ‹*drawing, plan*›; 增加 ‹*production, imports, expenditure, investment*›; 提高 ‹*price, earnings*›; **a ~d up version (of sth.)** (某物的) 扩大版; **the army is scaling up its operations** 军队现正把军事行动升级

scale² *n* **~(s** *pl***)** (weighing device) (in kitchen, bathroom) 秤; (for luggage) 磅秤; (for letters) 天平; **a pair** *or* **set of ~s** 一台天平; **to put sth. on the ~(s)** 将某物过秤; **to tip** *or* **turn the ~(s) at 10 kilos** 称得重量为 10 公斤; **to tip** *or* **turn the ~(s)** fig 打破均衡; **her experience in marketing tipped the ~ in her favour** 她的市场营销经验使她处于有利位置

scale³ *n* **1** [c] (on fish, reptile) 鳞; (on insects' wings) 翅瓣; **the ~s fell from my eyes** fig 我恍然大悟 **2** [u] (in pipe, kettle, tank) 水垢; (on teeth) 牙垢 **3** [c] (of skin) 鳞屑; (of rust) 氧化皮; (of paint, plaster) 鳞皮

scaled-down *adj* **1** (in amount, extent) 缩减的 ‹*version, proposal*›; 简化的 ‹*plan*› **2** (reduced according to scale) 按比例缩减的 ‹*model, plane*›

scale: ~ drawing *n* 比例图样; **~ model** *n* 比例模型; **~ pan** *n* 天平盘

scallion /ˈskæliən/ *n* esp Amer (spring onion) 大葱; (shallot) 青葱

scallop /ˈskɒləp, ˈskæləp/

A *n* **1** Zool 扇贝 **2** Culin 扇贝肉 **3** Sewing 扇形饰边

B *vt* **1** Culin [加牛奶或酱汁] 烤制 ‹*mushroom, egg*›; **~ed potatoes/fish** 烤土豆/烤鱼 **2** Sewing 给…缝上扇形饰边 ‹*edge, dress, blouse*›; 把…做成扇贝形 ‹*hem, tablecloth*›

scallywag /ˈskælɪwæg/ *n* colloq 淘气鬼

scalp /skælp/

A *n* **1** Anat 头皮 **2** Hist (war trophy) [旧时北美原住民杀死敌人后割下作为战利品的] 带发头皮; fig 战利品; colloq (sporting or business conquest) 击败; **to be out for** *or* **after sb.'s ~** 决心击败某人

B *vt* **1** (remove scalp of) 剥下…的带发头皮 **2** colloq (punish) 严惩 **3** Amer colloq (resell at a profit) 炒卖 ‹*securities, shares*›; 倒卖 ‹*tickets*›

scalpel /ˈskælpl/ *n* 解剖刀

scalper /ˈskælpə(r)/ *n* Amer colloq **1** (speculator) 炒卖股票者 **2** (ticket tout) 票贩子

scaly /ˈskeɪli/ *adj* **1** (covered in scales) 有鳞的 ‹*fish, reptile*›; 鳞片覆盖的 ‹*legs*› **2** (flaking) 一片片剥落的 ‹*paint, plaster, bark of tree*›; 有鳞屑的 ‹*skin*›

scam /skæm/

A *n* colloq (swindle, fraud) 诈骗; (dishonest scheme) 骗局

B *vt* (*pres p etc.* **-mm-**) 欺诈; **to ~ sb. out of sth.** 从某人处骗得某物

scamp /skæmp/ *n* colloq 淘气鬼

scamper /ˈskæmpə(r)/

A *vi* **to ~ (about** *or* **around)** «*mouse, dog, child*» 蹦蹦跳跳; **to ~ in and out** 蹦进跳出; **to ~ away** *or* **off** 跑开; **to ~ along/across ...** 沿着…奔跑/奔跑着穿过…

B *n* 奔跑

scampi /ˈskæmpi/ *n + v sing or pl* (fresh) 大虾; (breaded) 炸大虾

scan /skæn/

A *vt* (*pres p etc.* **-nn-**) **1** (examine) 仔细观察 ‹*horizon, sea, crowd*›; **to ~ sth. for sth.** 仔细观察某物以寻找某物; **to ~ sb.'s face intently** 细细端详某人的脸 **2** (traverse) 横扫; **the searchlight beam ~ned the sky/every corner** 探照灯的光束扫过天空/每个角落 **3** Literat 标出…的格律 ‹*poem, verse, line*› **4** Med «*doctor, machine*» 扫描检查 ‹*patient, knee, brain*› **5** Comput (convert to digital form) 扫描 ‹*image, data*›; **to ~ a photo on to a computer** 把一张照片扫描到计算机里 **6** Comput (check) 扫描…查病毒 ‹*e-mail, file*› **7** (pass across) «*radar, sonar*» 扫描 ‹*region, space*›

B *vi* (*pres p etc.* **-nn-**) «*poem, line, verse*» 符合格律; **the poem ~s well** 这首诗格律工整

C *n* **1** Med (examination) 扫描检查; (image) 扫描图; **to do** *or* **perform a ~** 进行扫描检查; **to have** *or* **undergo a ~** 接受扫描检查 **2** Comput (check) 扫描查找 **3** Phys 扫描图像

Phrasal verb

- **scan in** *vt* [**~ sth. in, ~ in sth.**] 扫描输入

scandal /ˈskændl/ *n* **1** [c] (incident) 丑事; (action, behaviour) 丑行; **to be involved in a ~** 卷入一桩丑事; **it's a ~ that ...** …太不像话了 **2** [c] (outrage) 愤慨; **to cause** *or* **create a ~** 引起公愤; **the Watergate/arms/drugs ~** 水门事件/军火丑闻/毒品丑闻 **3** [u] (gossip) 流言蜚语; **~ about sb./sth.** 关于某人/某事物的流言蜚语; **a hint** *or* **breath of ~** 一丝流言

scandalize /ˈskændəlaɪz/ *vt* (shock) 使震惊; (horrify) 使愤慨

scandalized /ˈskændəlaɪzd/ *adj* (shocked) 震惊的; (horrified) 愤慨的; **to be ~ by** *or* **at sth.** 对某事感到震惊

scandalmonger /ˈskændlmʌŋgə(r)/ *n* 散布丑闻者

scandalmongering /ˈskændlmʌŋgərɪŋ/ *n* [u] 散布丑闻

scandalous /ˈskændələs/ *adj* 1 (causing outrage) 令人愤慨的 ‹*behaviour, situation, publication*› 2 (disgraceful) 骇人听闻的 ‹*extravagance, waste, neglect*›; **the price of the drug is ~** 这种药的价格太不像话 3 (defamatory) 诽谤性的 ‹*story, rumour*›

scandalously /ˈskændələsli/ *adv* 1 (outrageously) 令人愤慨地 ‹*behave*›; **to get ~ drunk** 醉得丢人现眼 2 (disgracefully) 骇人听闻地 ‹*corrupt, abuse, extravagant, overcharge*›; **~ expensive clothes** 贵得不像话的衣服

scandal sheet *n* pej (newspaper) 丑闻报; (magazine) 丑闻杂志

Scandinavia /ˌskændɪˈneɪvɪə/ *pr n* 1 (Norway and Sweden) 斯堪的纳维亚［包括挪威和瑞典的地理区域］2 (cultural region) 斯堪的纳维亚地区 ［指挪威、瑞典和丹麦，通常还包括冰岛、法罗群岛和芬兰］

Scandinavian /ˌskændɪˈneɪvɪən/
A *adj* (of Scandinavia) 斯堪的纳维亚的; (of the people) 斯堪的纳维亚人的; (of the languages) 斯堪的纳维亚诸语言的
B *n* 1 [c] (person) 斯堪的纳维亚人 2 [u] (languages) 斯堪的纳维亚诸语言

scandium /ˈskændɪəm/ *n* [u] 钪

scanner /ˈskænə(r)/ *n* 1 Med 扫描器 2 (for receiving radar signals) 扫掠天线 3 Comput (for electronic data) 扫描仪; **a bar-code ~** 条形码扫描仪 4 Comput (for viruses) 病毒扫描程序; **an e-mail ~** 邮件病毒扫描程序

scanning /ˈskænɪŋ/ *n* [u] 1 Med 扫描检查 2 (with sonar, radar) 电子光束扫描 3 Comput (of bar codes, ID card) 扫码 4 Comput (checking) 扫描; **virus ~** 病毒扫描; **anti-virus ~ software** 防病毒扫描软件

scansion /ˈskænʃn/ *n* [u] 1 (analysis) ［诗的］韵律分析 2 (rhythm) ［诗行的］韵律

scant /skænt/ *adj* 一丁点的; **a ~ five metres** 5米不到; **he has been given ~ credit for his work** 他的工作几乎没有得到赞许; **to show ~ regard for sth., to pay ~ attention to sth.** 很少关注某事物

scantily /ˈskæntɪli/ *adv* 1 (meagrely) 不足地 ‹*informed*›; **the room was ~ furnished** 房间里几乎没什么家具 2 (skimpily) 暴露地 ‹*dressed, clothed*›

scantiness /ˈskæntɪnɪs/ *n* [u] 1 (of meal, income) 少量; (of information) 不足; (of knowledge) 缺乏; (of crowd) 稀稀拉拉 2 (of dress) 衣着暴露

scanty /ˈskænti/ *adj* 1 (meagre) 量少的 ‹*meal, income, harvest*›; 不足的 ‹*supply, information*›; 缺乏的 ‹*knowledge, choice*›; 稀稀拉拉的 ‹*crowd, audience*› 2 (skimpy) 暴露的 ‹*garment*›

scapegoat /ˈskeɪpɡəʊt/ *n* 替罪羊; **to make a ~ of sb.** 使某人成为替罪羊; **to look for a ~** 寻找替罪羊

scapula /ˈskæpjʊlə/ *n* (*pl* **scapulae** /ˈskæpjʊliː/) 肩胛

scar /skɑː(r)/
A *n* 1 (mark on skin) 疤; **acne ~s** 痤疮疤痕; **to have a ~ on one's knee** 膝盖上有一道疤; **to leave a ~** 留下疤痕; **to bear the ~s of sth.** 带有某事物留下的伤疤; **~s of battle** 搏斗的伤痕 2 fig (psychological damage) 心理创伤; **to leave ~s on sb.** 给某人留下心灵创伤; **psychological/mental ~s** 心灵/精神创伤 3 fig (blemish) 瑕疵; (ugly mark) 污点; **racism has been a ~ on the game** 种族主义为比赛抹了黑; **the town still bore the ~s of war** 城里依旧可见战争的疮痍
B *vt* (*pres p etc.* **-rr-**) 1 (mark) «*accident, disease*» 给…留下疤痕 ‹*person, face, arm*›; **to ~ sb. for life** 给某人留下终生伤疤 2 fig (traumatize) «*experience, event*» 给…造成精神创伤 ‹*person, psyche*›; **to be ~red for life** 留下终生的心理创伤 3 fig (spoil) «*action, damage, crime*» 给…留下瑕疵 ‹*surface, structure*›; **the stone walls were ~red with graffiti** 涂鸦破坏了这些石墙的外观; **a society ~red by crime** 被犯罪活动玷污的社会

Phrasal verb

• **scar over** *vi* «*wound, cut*» 结疤

scarce /skeəs/ *adj* 1 (rare) 稀有的 ‹*edition, plant, animal*› 2 (insufficient) 不足的 ‹*oil, food, houses*›; **water became ~ during the drought** 旱灾期间水很缺乏; **to make oneself ~** colloq 溜走

scarcely /ˈskeəsli/ *adv* 1 (barely) 几乎不 ‹*know, changed, recognize, remember*›; **~ (big) enough** 勉强够（大）; **it ~ matters** 那没什么要紧; **she could ~ believe her eyes** 她几乎不敢相信自己的眼睛; **he was ~ more than a child** 他还是个孩子; **~ at all** 几乎从不 2 (only just) 刚一…就; **~ had she finished when the door opened** 她刚做完，门就开了 3 iron (not really) 根本不; **you can ~ expect me to ...** 你压根儿别指望我…; **that's ~ the point** 那根本不是重点 4 (rarely) 很少; **I ~ ever see him these days** 我现在难得见到他

scarceness /ˈskeəsnɪs/ *n* [u] **= scarcity 2**

scarcity /ˈskeəsəti/ *n* 1 [c and u] (shortage) 匮乏; (inadequate supply) 供不应求; **a time of ~** 物资短缺时期; **~ value** 稀缺价值 2 [u] (rarity) 稀有

scare /skeə(r)/
A *vt* 使害怕; **to ~ sb. into/out of doing sth.** 吓得某人做/不敢做某事; **to ~ sb. stiff** *or* **rigid** *or* **stupid** colloq 把某人吓呆; **to ~ the life** *or* **living daylights out of sb., to ~ sb. out of their wits** colloq 把某人吓得魂不附体; **to ~ sb. to death** colloq 把某人吓得要死
B *vi* 感到害怕; **to ~ easily** 很容易害怕
C *n* 1 (fright) 惊吓; **to give sb. a ~** 使某人受到惊吓; **to get a ~** 受到惊吓 2 (alarm) 恐慌; **a bomb/rabies ~** 炸弹/狂犬病恐慌

Phrasal verbs

• **scare away, scare off** *vt* [**~ away sth./sb., ~ sth./sb. away**] 1 (drive away) 把…吓跑 ‹*person, attacker, animal*› 2 (put off) 使…生畏 ‹*burglars, investors*›; **he often ~s the customers away** 他常常使顾客退避三舍

• **scare up** *vt* [**~ up sth., ~ sth. up**] Amer colloq 勉强凑集 ‹*money, people*›; 费力地张罗 ‹*food, meal*›

scare campaign *n* 恐吓活动［指试图利用人们的惧怕心理来操控公众反应］

scarecrow /ˈskeəkrəʊ/ *n* 1 Agric 稻草人 2 fig colloq (badly dressed person) 衣衫褴褛的人; (odd-looking person) 容貌古怪的人; (thin person) 骨瘦如柴的人

scared /skeəd/ *adj* 惊恐的 ‹*person, animal, look*›; **to be** *or* **feel ~ of sb./sth./doing sth.** 害怕某人/某事物/做某事; **to be ~ about sth.** 对某事物感到害怕; **to be ~ that .../to ...** 害怕…/害怕做…; **to be ~ stiff** *or* **stupid** colloq 吓呆; **to be ~ to death** 怕得要死

scaredy cat /ˈskeədɪkæt/ *n* colloq 胆小鬼

scaremonger /ˈskeəmʌŋɡə(r)/ *n* 散播恐怖谣言的人

scaremongering /ˈskeəmʌŋɡərɪŋ/ *n* [u] 散播恐怖谣言

scare: ~ story *n* 耸人听闻的报道; **~ tactics** *npl* 恐吓战术

scarf¹ /skɑːf/ *n* (*pl* **scarves**) (for head) 头巾; (for neck) 围巾; (for shoulders) 披肩

scarf² *vt* Amer colloq 狼吞虎咽地吃 ‹*food, meal*›; 狼吞虎咽地喝 ‹*drink*›

Phrasal verbs

• **scarf down** *vt* Amer colloq [**~ down sth., ~ sth. down**] 狼吞虎咽地吃下

• **scarf up** *vt* Amer colloq [**~ up sth., ~ sth. up**] 狼吞虎咽地吃完

scarify /ˈskeərɪfaɪ/ *vt* 1 Med 划破 ‹*skin*› 2 Agric 翻松 ‹*soil*›

scarifying /ˈskeərɪfaɪɪŋ/ *adj* colloq 令人恐惧的

scarlatina /ˌskɑːləˈtiːnə/ ▸**p. 377** *n* [u] **= scarlet fever**

scarlet /ˈskɑːlət/ ▸**p. 134**
A *adj* 猩红的; **to blush** *or* **go ~** 变得满脸通红
B *n* [u] 1 (colour) 猩红色; **dressed in ~** 穿着鲜红色衣服的 2 (clothes) 猩红色的衣服 3 (cloth) 猩红色的布料

scarlet: ~ fever ▸**p. 377** *n* [u] 猩红热; **to have ~ fever** 患猩红热; **~ pimpernel** *n* 海绿; **~ runner** *n* 红花菜豆

scarp /skɑːp/ *n* (escarpment) 悬崖; (steep slope) 陡坡

scarper /ˈskɑːpə(r)/ *vi* Brit colloq 溜走

Scart connector /ˈskɑːt kəˌnektə(r)/ *n* 21 针音视频信号连接器

scar tissue *n* [u] 疤痕组织

scarves /skɑːvz/ *pl* ▸**scarf¹**

scary /ˈskeəri/ *adj* 1 colloq (frightening) 可怕的 ‹*moment, situation, experience, person*›; **a ~ story/film** 恐怖故事/电影 2 (uncanny) 怪异的 ‹*fact, circumstance, event*›

scat¹ /skæt/ *vi* (*pres p etc.* **-tt-**) colloq 走开

scat² *n* [u] Mus ［爵士乐中模仿乐器声音的］拟声唱法

scathing /ˈskeɪðɪŋ/ *adj* 尖刻的 ‹*criticism, comment, review*›; **a ~ glance/reply** 严厉的一瞥/回答; **to be ~ about sb./sth.** 苛刻地对待某人/某事物

scathingly /ˈskeɪðɪŋli/ *adv* 严厉地 ‹*look, glance, reply*›; 尖刻地 ‹*criticize, comment*›

scatological /ˌskætəˈlɒdʒɪkl/ *adj* 与粪便有关的 ‹*comedy, humour*›

scatology /skæˈtɒlədʒi/ *n* [u] 1 (interest in excrement) 排泄物迷恋 2 (literature) ［与排泄物有关的］污秽文学

scatter /ˈskætə(r)/
A *vt* 1 (throw around) **to ~ (about** *or* **around)** 撒 ‹*sand, salt, ashes, seeds*› 2 (place haphazardly) **to ~ (about** *or* **around)** 随处放置 ‹*papers, toys*›; **clothes were ~ed on every chair** 每把椅子上都有随手乱放的衣服 3 (cause to disperse) 驱散 ‹*crowd, birds, clouds*› 4 Phys 散射 ‹*electrons, photons*›
B *vi* 散开
C *n* 散落; **a ~ of houses/rain drops** 稀稀落落的房屋/雨滴

scatter: ~brain *n* 思想不集中的人; **~-brained** *adj* 思想不集中的 ‹*person*›; 轻率的 ‹*plan, suggestion*›; **~ cushion** *n* 散放的装饰垫; **~ diagram, ~ graph** *ns* 散布图

scattered /ˈskætəd/ *adj* 分散的 ‹*villages, population*›; 稀疏的 ‹*houses, audience*›; **~ showers** 短时阵雨

scattering /ˈskætərɪŋ/ *n* 零散的东西; **a ~ of sth.** 零零落落的某物

scatter: ~ rug *n* 小装饰毯; **~shot** *adj* esp Amer 随意的; **a ~shot collection of stories** 随意拼凑的故事集

scattiness /ˈskætɪnɪs/ *n* [u] Brit colloq 思想不集中

scatty /ˈskæti/ *adj* Brit colloq 思想不集中的; **to go ~** 思想不集中

scavenge /ˈskævɪndʒ/
A *vt* 1 (search through) 在…中搜寻 ‹*dustbin, scrapyard*›; **to ~ sth. for sth.** 在某物中搜寻某物 2 (search for) 捡拾 ‹*junk, food*›; **they ~d metal from the scrapyard** 他们在废品场捡废金属 3 (eat) «*animal*» 吃 ‹*carrion*› 4 (beg, borrow) 乞求 ‹*funds, subsidies*›; **he had to ~ a part from another machine** 他只好从另一台机器上拆借一个零件
B *vi* «*person, animal*» 搜寻; **to ~ in** *or* **through the dustbins for sth.** 在垃圾箱里搜寻某物

scavenger /ˈskævɪndʒə(r)/ *n* 1 Zool 食腐动物 2 (person) 拾荒者

scenario /sɪˈnɑːrɪəʊ, Amer -ˈnær-/ *n* (*pl* **~s**) **1** (for film, television) 剧本; (for play) 剧情梗概 **2** (sequence of events) 设想的情况; **a nightmare** *or* **worst-case ~** 最糟的情况; **a possible ~ for war** 可能爆发战争的局面

scenarist /sɪˈnɑːrɪst, Amer -ˈnær-/ ▸p. 409 *n* 电影剧本作家

scene /siːn/ *n* **1** (in play, film, novel) 场景; **the opening** *or* **first ~** 第一场; **the final** *or* **last ~** 最后一场; **to steal a ~** «*actor*» 抢戏; **my big ~** 我的重头戏; **to set the ~** Theat (position scenery) 放置布景; (describe setting) 叙述背景; **the ~ is set in Chicago** 这一幕发生在芝加哥; **to set the ~ for sth.** fig 为某事物创造条件 **2** Cin, TV (sequence of action) 镜头; **a ~ from a film** 一个电影镜头; **a comic/frightening/breathtaking ~** 滑稽/恐怖/惊险的镜头 **3** Theat (stage setting) 布景; **to change the ~** 更换布景; **behind the ~s** lit 在后台; fig 秘密地; **can't we do a deal behind the ~s?** 难道我们不能私下达成交易吗? **4** (place where action occurs) 现场; **at the ~ of the crime/accident** 在犯罪/事故现场; **to arrive** *or* **appear on the ~** 露面; **the police arrived on the ~ shortly afterwards** 警方不久就赶到了现场; **when the headmaster appeared on the ~, the children fell silent** 校长一到, 孩子们便安静了下来; **what was Britain like before Mrs Thatcher came on the ~?** 撒切尔夫人上台前英国的情况怎样? **5** Mil **the ~ of operations** lit 战场; fig 着重点 **6** (incident) 事件; (situation) 场面; **~s of utter confusion** 极端混乱的场面; **the peaceful demonstration degenerated into ~s of violence** 和平示威演变成了暴力事件; **horrific/hilarious ~s** 恐怖/欢闹的场面 **7** (image, sight) 景象; (landscape) 景色; **a delightful rural ~** 赏心悦目的乡村风光; **a depressing ~** 令人压抑的景象; **~s of Victorian life** 维多利亚时代生活的景象 **8** (emotional incident) 当场发作; **to make a ~** 大闹一场; **to have a ~ with sb.** (have a row) 和某人当场翻脸; Amer colloq (have sex) 和某人交欢 **9** (sphere, field) 圈子; **the political ~** 政界; **the pop/fashion ~** 流行音乐界/时装界; **London has a lively gay ~** 伦敦的同性恋圈子很活跃; **a change of ~** 环境的改变; **it's not his ~** colloq 这不合他的胃口

scene: ~ change *n* 布景变换; **~ designer** *n* ▸p. 409 布景设计师; **~-of-crime** *adj attrib* Brit 犯罪现场的; **a ~-of-crime unit/expert** 刑事技术大队/专家; **police ~-of-crime officers** 在作案现场取证的警察; **~-of-crime evidence/pictures** 作案现场的证据/照片

scenery /ˈsiːnəri/ *n* [u] **1** (landscape) 风景; **a change of ~** fig 环境改换 **2** Theat 舞台布景; **a piece of ~** 一块布景

scene shifter ▸p. 409 *n* 布景人员

scenic /ˈsiːnɪk/ *adj* 风景秀丽的 ‹*village, route*›; **to be well-known for its ~ beauty** 以风景优美著称

scenic railway *n* [游乐场等处的] 观景小铁路

scent /sent/
A *n* **1** [c] (pleasant smell) 香味; (distinctive odour) 气味; **the ~ of sth.** 某物的气味 **2** [c] Hunt (trail of animal) 臭迹; fig (trail of crime, scandal) 线索; **to pick up the ~** 闻出臭迹; fig 发现线索; **to throw** *or* **put sb./sth. off the ~** 使某人/某物迷失追踪方向; fig 使某人/某物失去线索; **to be on the ~ of sth./sb.** 已掌握某物/某人的蛛丝马迹 **3** [u] (perfume) 香水; **to wear/put on ~** 搽着/涂抹香水
B *vt* **1** lit (smell) 嗅到 ‹*prey, explosive, drugs*› **2** fig (sense) 察觉出 ‹*danger, ambush*›; 预感到 ‹*trouble, trap*› **3** (sniff) «*hound, fox*» 嗅 ‹*air, wind*› **4** (perfume) «*person, incense, flowers*» 使…带有香味 ‹*air, hair, handkerchief*›

Phrasal verb
• **scent out** *vt* [**~ sth. out, ~ out sth.**] 嗅出 ‹*prey, explosive, drugs*›

scented /ˈsentɪd/ *adj* 散发香味的 ‹*air*›; 芳香的 ‹*shampoo, hairspray*›; **~ flowers/sachets** 香花/香囊

scented candle *n* 芳香蜡烛

scentless /ˈsentlɪs/ *adj* 无气味的 ‹*gas, chemical*›; 无香味的 ‹*cosmetic, flower*›

scepter /ˈseptər/ *n* Amer **= sceptre**

sceptic /ˈskeptɪk/ *n* Brit 怀疑论者

sceptical /ˈskeptɪkl/ *adj* Brit 怀疑的; **to be ~ about sth.** 对某事物持怀疑态度

sceptically /ˈskeptɪkli/ *adv* Brit 怀疑地

scepticism /ˈskeptɪsɪzəm/ *n* [u] Brit 怀疑态度; **~ about sth.** 对某事物的怀疑态度; **to treat** *or* **greet sth. with ~** 对某事物持怀疑态度

sceptre /ˈseptə(r)/ *n* Brit [象征君主权位的] 节杖

schedule /ˈʃedjuːl, Amer ˈskedʒʊl/
A *n* **1** (timetable for bus, train, etc.) 时刻表; **railway** *or* **train ~s** 火车时刻表; **to arrive on/ahead of/behind ~** 准点/提前/晚点到达 **2** (projected plan) 计划; **to draw up** *or* **make out a ~** 起草计划; **to adhere** *or* **stick** *or* **keep to a ~** 按计划行事; **to** *or* **on** *or* **according to ~** 按计划; **everything went off smoothly, according to ~** 一切照计划进展顺利; **behind/ahead of ~** 落后于/早于计划进度; **a tight ~** 紧张的日程安排 **3** (day-to-day plans, timetable) 日程安排; **a full/busy/crowded ~** 满满/忙碌/紧张的日程安排; **the agency has arranged an absolutely exhausting ~ for the trip** 旅行社安排的旅行日程令人疲惫不堪 **4** Jur (of items) 清单; (of legal documents) 附件; (of prices, charges, contents) 一览表; **the ~ of postal charges** 邮资明细表; **as per the attached ~** (to a contract) 参见附件 **5** Brit Tax 报税表
B *vt* 安排; **the publication of the novel is ~d for September** 小说定于九月出版; **the plane/flight is ~d to arrive at midday** 飞机/航班定于正午到达; **as ~d** 按计划; **the power station was ~d for completion in 2005** 发电站计划于 2005 年完工

scheduled /ˈʃedjuːld, Amer ˈskedjʊld/ *adj* **1** (planned) 预先安排的 ‹*time, date, meeting*›; esp Aviat 定期的 ‹*service, airline*› **2** Brit (listed for preservation) 列入文物保护的 ‹*structure, monument*› **3** (included on list) 列名的

scheduled: ~ building *n* Brit 列入文物保护的建筑; **~ flight** *n* 定期航班; **~ territories** *npl* Brit 英镑区

scheduling /ˈʃedjuːlɪŋ, Amer ˈskedʒʊl-/ *n* [u] **1** (of project, work, event) 时间安排; (of TV programme) 节目安排 **2** Brit (of monument, building) 文物列名保护

schema /ˈskiːmə/ *n* (*pl* **schemata** /skiːˈmɑːtə/ *or* **~s**) 纲要

schematic /skɪˈmætɪk/ *adj* **1** (illustrative) 示意的 ‹*diagram*›; 概略的 ‹*plan*›; **a ~ layout of the wiring system** 线路系统的布局图 **2** (simplistic) 粗线条的 ‹*thought, idea*›

schematically /skɪˈmætɪkli/ *adv* 用图表 ‹*represent, illustrate*›

scheme /skiːm/
A *n* **1** (plan) 计划; **a ~ for sth./doing sth.** 某事/做某事的计划 **2** pej (impractical idea) 不切实际的念头; **a ~ for sth./doing sth.** 某事/做某事的念头; **to think up** *or* **dream up a ~** 冒出一个念头 **3** (plot) 阴谋 **4** Brit (system) 体系; **a road/an insurance ~** 道路系统/保险制度; **~ of work** 工作流程; **in the (big) ~ of things** 在(大的)格局中 **5** (arrangement) 结构; **the ~ of the novel/symphony** 小说/交响乐的结构; **a rhyme ~** 韵律 **6** (design, plan for house, garden, etc.) 方案; **a decorating ~** 装修方案
B *vi* pej 密谋; **to ~ to do sth.** 密谋做某事; **to ~ against sb./sth.** 算计某人/某事物; **to ~ for sb./sth.** 为某人/某事物策划

schemer /ˈskiːmə(r)/ *n* pej 搞阴谋的人

scheming /ˈskiːmɪŋ/ pej
A *adj* 诡计多端的 ‹*traitor*›; 狡诈的 ‹*person, lies*›
B *n* [u] 阴谋诡计; **all his ~ got him nowhere** 他的种种诡计均未能得逞

schism /ˈsɪzəm/ *n* [宗派或政党间的] 分裂; **a ~ in the church/party** 教会分立/党内分裂; **a ~ between the reformers and the traditionalists** 革新派与守旧派之间的分裂

schismatic /sɪzˈmætɪk/ *adj* 分裂的 ‹*tendency*›; 引起分裂的 ‹*sect, pope*›

schist /ʃɪst/ *n* [u and c] 片岩

schizo /ˈskɪtsəʊ/ colloq pej
A *adj* 精神分裂症的 ‹*behaviour*›
B *n* 精神分裂症患者

schizoid /ˈskɪtsɔɪd/
A *adj* **1** Psych 性格孤僻的 ‹*person*›; 孤僻的 ‹*personality, tendency*› **2** colloq (crazy) 类精神分裂症的 ‹*person*›; 颠三倒四的 ‹*idea*›
B *n* **1** Psych 性格孤僻的人 **2** colloq (crazy person) 精神分裂症患者

schizophrenia /ˌskɪtsəˈfriːnɪə/ *n* [u] **1** ▸p. 377 Psych 精神分裂症 **2** colloq (contradictory behaviour) 矛盾行为

schizophrenic /ˌskɪtsəˈfrenɪk/
A *adj* **1** Psych 精神分裂症的 ‹*symptoms, behaviour*›; 患精神分裂症的 ‹*patient*› **2** colloq (contradictory) 自相矛盾的 ‹*feelings, behaviour*›; **to be/feel ~ about sth.** 对某事物有矛盾心理/感到矛盾
B *n* 精神分裂症患者

schlemiel, schlemihl /ʃləˈmiːl/ *n* Amer sl 笨蛋

schlep, schlepp /ʃlep/ esp Amer sl
A *vi* (*pres p etc.* **-pp-**) **to ~ (around)** 缓慢费力地行进
B *vt* (*pres p etc.* **-pp-**) (drag) 费力地拖拽; (carry) 费力地搬
C *n* (journey) 艰难乏味的旅行

schlock /ʃlɒk/ *n* [u] Amer sl (goods or produce) 低档货; (art, films) 垃圾作品

schmaltz, schmalz /ʃmɔːlts/ *n* [u] colloq 过分伤感

schmaltzy, schmalzy /ˈʃmɔːltsi/ *adj* colloq 过分伤感的 ‹*music, literature, film*›

schmooze /ʃmuːz/ *vi, n* esp Amer colloq 亲密交谈

schmuck /ʃmʌk/ *n* Amer colloq pej 笨蛋

schnapps, schnaps /ʃnæps/ *n* [u] [谷物酿制的] 烈酒

schnitzel /ˈʃnɪtzl/ *n* [u and c] 炸小牛肉片

schnook /ʃnʊk/ *n* Amer colloq pej 笨蛋

schnozz /ʃnɒz/, **schnozzle** /ˈʃnɒzl/ *ns* Amer colloq 鼻子

scholar /ˈskɒlə(r)/ *n* **1** (academic) 学者; **a Shakespeare ~** 研究莎士比亚的学者; **he's not much of a ~** 他算不上学者 **2** (student with scholarship) 奖学金获得者

scholarly /ˈskɒləli/ *adj* **1** (erudite) 有学问的 ‹*person*›; **~ approach** 高深的方法; **to lead a ~ life** 过学者的生活 **2** (academic) 学术的 ‹*publication, thesis, achievements*›; **to move in ~ circles** 进入学术圈

scholarship /ˈskɒləʃɪp/ *n* **1** [u] (learning) 学问; (academic study) 学术研究; (academic achievement) 学术成就; **the book is a fine piece of ~** 这是一本学术杰作 **2** [c] (award) 奖学金; **to win a ~ to …** 赢得…的奖学金; **to award a ~ to sb.** 给予某人奖学金; **he went up to Cambridge on a ~** 他靠奖学金去剑桥大学求学; **a ~ student** 获奖学金的学生

scholastic /skəˈlæstɪk/ *adj* 学校的 ‹*work*›; 学业的 ‹*achievement, aptitude, levels*›; **the ~ profession** 教职

Scholastic Aptitude Test *n* Amer 学业能力倾向测试 [美国大学的入学考试]

S

school /skuːl/
A *n* 1 [c and u] (institution, building) [未成年人上的] 学校; **to go to ~** 去上学; **at ~** 在上学; **she started ~ at the age of six** 她6岁入学; **to drop out of ~** 辍学; **he's not old enough for ~ yet** 他还没到上学年龄; **a comprehensive ~** 综合中学; **a ~ for the blind/deaf** 盲人/聋人学校; **a ballet/dancing/music/drama ~** 芭蕾/舞蹈/音乐/戏剧学校; **an art ~** 美术学校; **to grow up/learn sth. in a hard ~** fig 在逆境中成长/学习某技能; **to go to the ~ of hard knocks** fig 经受艰苦的磨炼 2 [u] (pupils and staff) **the ~** 全校师生 3 [u] (day's work at school) 上课; **before/after ~** 上课前/放学后; **during ~** 上学期间; **~ begins/ends** 上课了/放学了; **no ~** 不上学; **~ restarts on January 7** 学校1月7日开学 4 [c] Univ (institution) 学院; (department) 系; **graduate/medical/business/law ~** 研究生院/医学院/商学院/法学院 5 [c] (group of people) 流派; **the Venetian ~ of painting** 威尼斯画派; **the Frankfurt ~ of critical theory** 批评理论中的法兰克福学派 6 [c] (of gamblers, drinkers, etc.) 狐朋狗友; **a card ~** 一帮牌友 7 [c] (of fish, whales) 群
B *vt* 1 (educate) 教育; (train or discipline) 训练; **to ~ sb. (in sth.)** 教某人(某事); **military service had ~ed him in the art of self-preservation** 军旅生涯教会了他自我保护的技巧; **to be well-~ed** 受过良好训练 2 (train) 驯 ‹*horse*›
C *v refl* **to ~ oneself (in sth.)** 学会(某事物); **to ~ oneself in the art of taking exams** 学会应试技巧; **she ~ed herself not to be impatient** 她学会了忍耐

school: ~ age *n* 学龄; **~ age children** 学龄儿童; **~bag** *n* 书包; **~ board** *n* Amer 地方教育董事会; **~book** *n* 教科书; **~boy** *n* 男生; **~boy humour/crush** 男生的幽默感/热恋; **~ bus** *n* 校车; **~ captain** *n* Brit 学生代表; **~child** *n* 学童; **~ council** *n* 学校董事会; **~ crossing patrol** *n* 学童过街护送员; **~days** *npl* 学生时代; **~ dinner** *n* 学校午餐; **~ district** *n* Amer 学区; **~ fees** *npl* 学费; **~fellow** *n* dated 同学; **~friend** *n* 学友; **~girl** *n* 女生; **~ holidays** *npl* 学校假期; **~ hours** *npl* 上课时间; **~house** *n* 1 (school building) 校舍; 2 (for teacher) 教师宿舍

schooling /ˈskuːlɪŋ/ *n* [u] 学校教育; **formal ~** 正规的学校教育

school: ~ inspector ▸**p. 409** *n* 督学; **~kid** *n* colloq 学童; **~-leaver** /ˈskuːlˌliːvə(r)/ *n* Brit 中学毕业生; **~-leaving age** *n* 中学生可离校年龄; **~ lunch** *n* (provided by school) 学校午餐; (provided by child's family) 自备的学校午餐; **~master** ▸**p. 409** *n* esp Brit 男教师; **~mate** *n* 学友; **~ meal** *n* = **~ lunch**; **~mistress** ▸**p. 409** *n* 女教师; **~ of thought** *n* 学派; **~ playground** *n* 校园操场; **~ prefect** *n* Brit 级长 [指维持纪律的高年级学生]; **~ record** *n* 学生档案; **to be in** *or* **on sb.'s ~ record** 在某人的学生档案中; **~ report** Brit, **~ report card** Amer *ns* 成绩报告单; **~room** *n* 教室; **~ run** *n* Brit 接送孩子上下学的行程; **~teacher** ▸**p. 409** *n* 教师; **~teaching** *n* [u] 教职; **~ time** *n* [u] 上课时间; **~ trip** *n* 学校旅行; **~ uniform** *n* 校服; **~ visit** *n* (from school) 学生参观; (to school) 学校参观; **~work** *n* [u] 1 (pupils' work) 功课; **to do well in one's ~work** 功课很好; 2 (correcting work) 作业批改; **~yard** *n* esp Amer 校园操场

schoolmarm, schoolma'am /ˈskuːlmɑːm/ *n* pej [常指拘谨的] 女教师

schoolmarmish /ˈskuːlmɑːmɪʃ/ *adj* 女教师式的 ‹*tone of voice*›; 古板的 ‹*person*›

school year *n* 学年

schooner /ˈskuːnə(r)/ *n* 1 (boat) [至少有二桅的] 纵帆船; **~-rigged** 纵帆船式装置的 2 Amer, Austral (beer glass) 大啤酒杯 3 Brit (sherry glass) 雪利酒杯

schwa /ʃwɑː/ *n* 非重读央元音 [如ago中的第一个元音]

sciatic /saɪˈætɪk/ *adj* 1 (relating to hip) 髋部的 ‹*artery, muscle*› 2 (relating to nerve) 坐骨神经的 ‹*damage*›; **~ nerve/pain** 坐骨神经/坐骨神经痛; **~ complaint** *or* **condition** 坐骨神经疾病

sciatica /saɪˈætɪkə/ ▸**p. 377** *n* [u] 坐骨神经痛

science /ˈsaɪəns/ *n* 1 [u] (study of physical universe) 科学; **the Faculty of S~** 理学院; **to blind sb. with ~** fig 用专业知识使某人摸不着头脑; **~ correspondent** 科技记者 2 [c] (branch of knowledge) 学科; **the physical/natural/social ~s** 物理/自然/社会科学; **an applied ~** 应用科学

science: ~ fiction *n* [u] 科幻小说; **~ fiction book/film/writer** 科幻小说/影片/小说作家; **~ park** *n* 科技园区

scientific /ˌsaɪənˈtɪfɪk/ *adj* 1 (relating to natural science) 科学(上)的 ‹*experiment, discovery, journal*›; **~ expert/instrument/research** 科学专家/仪器/研究 2 (systematic) 科学的 ‹*approach, proof*›; 有条理的 ‹*person*›; 细致严谨的 ‹*study*›; **to be ~ about** *or* **in sth.** 对某事抱严谨的态度; **to prove/test sth. using the ~ method** 用科学的方法证明/检验某物

scientifically /ˌsaɪənˈtɪfɪkli/ *adv* 1 (relating to natural science) 科学上 ‹*advanced, trained, proven, flawed*› 2 (systematically) 科学地 ‹*devise, plan*›; 细致严谨地 ‹*investigate*›

scientific method *n* 科学方法

scientist /ˈsaɪəntɪst/ ▸**p. 409** *n* 科学家

Scientologist /ˌsaɪənˈtɒlədʒɪst/ *n* 山达基信徒

Scientology® /ˌsaɪənˈtɒlədʒi/ *n* [u] 山达基 [倡导自我认识和精神完善的信仰]

sci-fi /ˈsaɪfaɪ/ *n* [u] colloq 科幻小说; **~ film/book/writer** 科幻电影/作品/作家

Scillies /ˈsɪlɪz/, **Scilly Isles** /ˈsɪli aɪlz/ *pr ns* **the ~** 锡利群岛 [由英格兰西南面140个小岛组成]

scimitar /ˈsɪmɪtə(r)/ *n* [东方人用的] 短弯刀

scintilla /sɪnˈtɪlə/ *n* 一星半点

scintillate /ˈsɪntɪleɪt, Amer -təleɪt/ *vi* 1 (sparkle) «*stars, jewels, eyes*» 闪烁 2 fig «*person*» 焕发才智

scintillating /ˈsɪntɪleɪtɪŋ, Amer -təleɪtɪŋ/ *adj* 1 (sparkling) 闪耀的 ‹*star, jewel*› 2 fig (brilliant, dazzling) 才华横溢的 ‹*humour, personality*›; **~ conversation/performance** 妙趣横生的谈话/精彩的演出

scion /ˈsaɪən/ *n* 1 formal (descendant) [尤指名门的] 后裔 2 Bot 接穗

scissor /ˈsɪzə(r)/ *vt* [用剪刀] 剪; **to ~ sth. out of sth.** 从某物上剪下某物

scissor: ~ hold *n* 剪夹 [用双腿钳夹对手的摔跤动作]; **to put** *or* **get sb. in a ~ hold** 剪夹住某人; **~ jump** *n* (in gymnastics) 剪式跳; (in high jump) 剪式跳高; **~ kick** *n* (in swimming) 剪步打腿; (in football) 倒钩

scissors /ˈsɪzəz/ *npl* 剪刀; **a pair of ~** 一把剪刀; **a ~-and-paste job** fig pej 剪刀加浆糊的拼凑之作

scissors: ~ hold *n* = **scissor hold**; **~ jump** *n* = **scissor jump**; **~ kick** *n* = **scissor kick**

sclerosis /skləˈrəʊsɪs/ ▸**p. 377** *n* [u] 1 Med 硬化 2 fig (rigidity) 僵化; **institutional/economic ~** 机构/经济僵化

scoff[1] /skɒf, Amer skɔːf/ *vi* (mock) 嘲弄; **to ~ at sb./sth.** 嘲笑某人/某事物

scoff[2] Brit colloq
A *vt* (eat) «*person, animal*» 狼吞虎咽地吃 ‹*food*›
B *n* [u] 食物

scoffer /ˈskɒfə(r), Amer ˈskɔːf-/ *n* 嘲弄者

scoffing /ˈskɒfɪŋ, Amer ˈskɔːf-/
A *adj* 嘲弄的 ‹*remark, laugh*›
B *n* [u] 嘲弄

scofflaw /ˈskɒflɔː, Amer ˈskɔːf-/ *n* Amer colloq 无视法律者

scold /skəʊld/
A *vt* 责骂; **to ~ sb. for sth./doing sth.** 因某事/做某事而训斥某人
B *vi* 责骂; **to ~ about sth.** 责怪某事

scolding /ˈskəʊldɪŋ/ *n* [u and c] 责骂; **to give sb. a ~** 数落某人; **to receive** *or* **get a ~** 遭到训斥; **do shut up with your ~!** 你不要再责骂了!

scone /skɒn, skəʊn, Amer skəʊn/ *n* [用面粉、脂肪、牛奶等制成的] 烤饼

scoop /skuːp/
A *n* 1 (utensil) 勺; (for ladling) 长柄勺; (for measuring) 量勺; (for ice cream) 挖球勺 2 (on excavator) 铲斗 3 (of sugar, ice cream) 一勺; (of earth, stones) 一铲 4 Journ colloq 抢先报道; **to get a ~** 挖到一条独家新闻
B *vt* 1 (in cooking) 用勺舀 ‹*food*›; (in shovel) 用铲挖 ‹*earth*›; (in pail) 提 ‹*water*›; **to ~ nuts out of/into a bowl** 用勺把坚果从碗里舀出来/舀入碗里; **to ~ sand out of/into a hole** 把沙子从洞里铲出来/铲入洞内 2 (win) 赢得 ‹*prize, amount*› 3 Journ colloq 抢在…之前报道 ‹*reporter, newspaper*›

Phrasal verbs
- **scoop out** *vt* [**~ out sth., ~ sth. out**] 1 (remove) 舀出 ‹*liquid, ice cream, grapefruit*›; 挖出 ‹*sand, earth*› 2 (create) 挖成 ‹*burrow*›; **to ~ out a hole** 挖出一个洞
- **scoop up** *vt* [**~ sth. up, ~ up sth.**] 迅速挖起 ‹*earth*›; 迅速舀起 ‹*water, rice*›; 迅速捡起 ‹*coins, change*›; 一把抱起 ‹*child, puppy*›

scoopful /ˈskuːpfʊl/ *n* 一勺

scoot /skuːt/ *vi* colloq «*person*» 疾走; «*vehicle*» 疾驰; **I must ~ or I'll miss my bus** 我必须快点走, 否则就赶不上公共汽车了; **to ~ in and out of the traffic** «*motorbike*» 在车流中穿进穿出

scooter /ˈskuːtə(r)/ *n* 1 (with engine) **(motor) ~** 踏板车 2 (foot-powered) 滑板车

scope /skəʊp/ *n* [u] 1 (of plan, report, power, book) 范围; (of study, knowledge) 领域; **to define/extend/restrict the ~ of sth.** 规定/扩展/限制某事物的范围; **within/beyond/outside the ~ of sth.** 在某事物的范围之内/超越某事物的范围/在某事物的范围之外 2 (opportunity) 机会; **~ for sth.** 实现某事物的机会; **~ for improvement** 提高的余地; **~ for sb. to do sth.** 某人做某事的机会; **to have ~ to do sth.** 有机会做某事; **to give sb. ~ to do sth.** 给某人做某事的空间

Phrasal verb
- **scope out** *vt* [**~ sth. out, ~ out sth.**] 考量 ‹*market, competition, project*›

scope creep *n* [u] 范围蔓延 [指产品等在开发过程中超出计划目标的倾向]

scoping meeting /ˈskəʊpɪŋ ˌmiːtɪŋ/ *n* 审议会议

scorch /skɔːtʃ/
A *vt* «*person, chemical, iron, heat*» 把…烧焦 ‹*shirt, material*›; «*sun*» 把…烤焦 ‹*grass, trees*›; **~ed earth policy** Mil fig 焦土政策
B *vi* 1 (get burnt) «*fabric*» 烧焦; «*grass, countryside*» 烤焦 2 (move fast) «*driver, cyclist, car*» 疾驰
C *n* **~ (mark)** 焦痕

scorcher /ˈskɔːtʃə(r)/ *n* colloq 大热天; **today is going to be a ~** 今天会是个大热天

scorching /ˈskɔːtʃɪŋ/ *adj* 1 **~ (hot)** 灼热的 ‹*sun, sand*›; 酷热的 ‹*weather, day*› 2 fig (severe) 严厉的 ‹*criticism*› 3 colloq (fast) 飞快的 ‹*pace*›

score /skɔː(r)/
A *n* 1 Sport 得分; **a high/low ~** 高分/低分; **what's the ~ now?** 比分现在是多少?; **the**

S

final ～ was two-one 最终比分是二比一; **there was no ～ in the first half of the match** 比赛上半场双方均未得分; **to keep the ～** 记分; **to make a good/poor ～** (in cards) 得高分/低分 **2** esp Amer (in exam, test) 分数; **she made a record ～ of 173 in the IQ test** 她在智商测试中得到了创纪录的 173 分; **a good/poor ～** 高分/低分 **3** (twenty) 二十; (about twenty) 约 20 个; **four ～** 八十; **three ～ years and ten** 古稀之年 [《圣经》用语, 指70岁]; **the farm has a ～ of milking cows** 这家农场有 20 头奶牛; **I've received ～s of letters of protest** 我收到了一大堆抗议信; **by the ～** 大量地 **4** Mus (written music) 总谱; (for film, play etc.) 配乐; **the ～ for Swan Lake** 《天鹅湖》总曲谱; **a full/short ～** 全谱/缩编谱 **5** (account) 根据; **on this/that ～** 就这个/那个而言; **on what ～ does he think he's got the right to interfere?** 他凭什么认为自己有权干涉? **6** (grievance) 夙怨; **to settle a** *or* **the ～** 清算旧账; **I have an old ～ to settle with you** 我要跟你算笔旧账 **7** (facts) 实情; **to know the ～** colloq 知道是怎么回事 **8** dated (running account) 欠账; **can you put my drinks on the ～?** 你能把我喝的酒记账吗? ; **to settle** *or* **pay a** *or* **the ～** 结清欠账; **what's the ～ for this consignment of goods?** 这批货的运费是多少? **9** (cut, groove) 刻痕

B *vt* **1** Sport (gain) 赢得 ‹*points, runs*›; fig 取得 ‹*marks, success*›; **he ～d a fantastic goal in the first minute of the match** 比赛第一分钟他就进了精彩的一球; **she ～d 51% in the reading test** 她在总分 100 分的阅读测验中得了 51 分; **to ～ a hit** (in fencing, shooting) 击中得一分; fig (make a favourable impression) 留下好印象; (be very successful) 大获成功; **the play ～d a great success** 该剧取得了巨大成功 **2** (award points to) 给…打分; **they ～d her performance very highly** 他们给她的表演打了高分 **3** (cut, mark) 在…上刻痕 ‹*cardboard*›; Culin 划开 ‹*meat*›; **the old man's face was heavily ～d by the years** 老人的脸上深深地刻着岁月的痕迹; **the water had ～d deep channels into the rock** 水在岩石上冲刷出很深的沟槽; **the brambles ～d her legs** 黑莓灌木划伤了她的腿 **4** Mus 改编 ‹*composition, tune*› **5** sl (obtain) 把…弄到手 ‹*drugs*›

C *vi* **1** Sport (gain points) 得分; **he ～d twice in the second half** 他在下半场两次得分 **2** Sport (record the score) 记分; **who's going to ～?** 谁来记分? **3** colloq (succeed, impress) «*action, company*» 成功; «*idea, proposal*» 胜出; **when it comes to speaking foreign languages, that's where she ～s** 谈到说外语, 那可是她的强项; **the new product ～d with the public** 新产品受到了公众的欢迎; **to ～ over sb.** 胜过某人

Phrasal verbs

- **score out, score through** *vt* [～ **sth. out,** ～ **out sth.**] 删去
- **score up** *vt* [～ **sth. up,** ～ **up sth.**] 记下; **to ～ up points** 记分

score: ～board *n* 记分牌; **～card** *n* 记分卡; **～ draw** *n* [足球比赛的] 平局; **～line** *n* [比赛的] 最终得分

scorer /ˈskɔːrə(r)/ *n* **1** (scorekeeper) 记分员 **2** (person getting point, goal) 得分者

scoresheet /ˈskɔːʃiːt/ *n* (card) 记分卡; (sheet) 记分单; **to add one's name to the ～** 有一球记入名下

scoring /ˈskɔːrɪŋ/ *n* [u] **1** (score keeping) 记分 **2** (getting point, goal) 得分 **3** Mus 总谱写作 **4** (cuts) 刻痕; (on rocks) 磨痕; (on gun) 擦痕 **5** Culin 拉刀剞

scorn /skɔːn/

A *n* [u] 轻蔑; **to treat sb. with ～** 轻蔑地对待某人; **to be the ～ of sb.** 受某人的奚落; **to be held up to ～ by sb.** 受到某人的鄙视; **to pour** *or* **heap ～ on ...** 对…嗤之以鼻; **to draw down ～ upon one's head** 招来嘲笑; **to point the finger of ～ at sb./sth.** 嘲笑某人/某物

B *vt* **1** (deride) 鄙视; **hell hath no fury like a woman ～ed** 地狱烈焰不及受拒女人的怒火 **2** (reject) 不屑接受 ‹*offer, advice*›

C *vi* **to ～ to do sth.** 不屑于做某事

scornful /ˈskɔːnfl/ *adj* 轻蔑的 ‹*person, glance, remark*›; **to be ～ about** *or* **of sth.** 鄙视某物

scornfully /ˈskɔːnfəli/ *adv* 轻蔑地 ‹*say, glance, laugh*›

Scorpio /ˈskɔːpɪəʊ/ *n* **1** [u] Astron 天蝎(星)座 **2** [u] Astrol (sign) 天蝎宫 [黄道第八宫] **3** [c] (*pl* **～s**) Astrol (person) 属天蝎(星)座的人

scorpion /ˈskɔːpɪən/ *n* 蝎子

Scot /skɒt/ ▸**p. 503** *n* 苏格兰人

Scotch /skɒtʃ/

A *adj* dated **= Scottish**

B *npl* dated **the ～** 苏格兰人

C *n* [u and c] 苏格兰威士忌; **a glass of ～** 一杯苏格兰威士忌

scotch /skɒtʃ/ *vt* «*person, government, event*» 阻止 ‹*person, plan*›; 平息 ‹*rumour, revolt*›; 挫败 ‹*plot*›; **devaluation ～ed our hopes of buying a property in Italy** 货币贬值使我们在意大利购买房产的希望破灭了

Scotch: ～ broth® *n* [u] [用羊肉、大麦和蔬菜做成的] 苏格兰浓汤; **～ egg** *n* Brit [用香肠肉包裹后沾上面包屑炸制成的] 苏格兰香肠蛋; **～ mist** *n* [u] 苏格兰霭 [常见于苏格兰高地的有雨浓雾]; **～ pancake** *n* Brit 平锅烙饼; **～ pine** *n* **= Scots pine**; **～ tape®** *n* [u] esp Amer 透明胶带; **～ terrier** *n* **= Scottish terrier**; **～ whisky** *n* [u and c] 苏格兰威士忌

scot-free /ˌskɒtˈfriː/ *adv* **to get off** *or* **go ～** (unpunished) 未受惩处; (unharmed) 安然逃脱

Scotland /ˈskɒtlənd/ *pr n* 苏格兰

Scotland Yard *pr n* Brit (place) 苏格兰场 [即伦敦警察厅总部]; (CID) 伦敦警察厅刑侦处

Scots /skɒts/ ▸**p. 426**

A *adj* 苏格兰的 ‹*accent*›; 苏格兰英语的 ‹*word, pronunciation*›

B *n* [u] 苏格兰英语

Scots: ～ Guards *npl* 苏格兰近卫步兵; **～man** /-mən/ *n* 苏格兰男子; **～ pine** *n* 欧洲赤松; **～woman** *n* 苏格兰女子

Scotticism /ˈskɒtɪsɪzəm/ *n* 苏格兰特色英语

Scottie /ˈskɒti/ *n* colloq 苏格兰㹴

Scottish /ˈskɒtɪʃ/ ▸**p. 503** *adj* (of Scotland) 苏格兰的; (of the people) 苏格兰人的

Scottish: ～ country dancing *n* [u] 苏格兰乡村舞蹈; **～ Highlands** *npl* **the ～ Highlands** 苏格兰高地; **～ Islands** *npl* **the ～ Islands** 苏格兰群岛; **～ Nationalism** *n* [u] 苏格兰民族党纲领; **～ Nationalist** *n* (politician) 苏格兰民族党党员; (supporter) 苏格兰民族党的支持者; **～ National Party** *n* **the ～ National Party** 苏格兰民族党; **～ Parliament** *n* Brit 苏格兰议会; **～ Secretary** *n* Brit 苏格兰事务大臣; **～ terrier** *n* 苏格兰㹴

scoundrel /ˈskaʊndrəl/ *n* pej 无赖

scour[1] /ˈskaʊə(r)/

A *vt* **1** (scrub) 擦净 ‹*surface*› **2** (remove) 擦去 ‹*dirt*›

B *n* 擦净; **to give sth. a good ～** 把某物好好擦一擦

Phrasal verb

- **scour out** *vt* [～ **out sth.,** ～ **sth. out**] **1** (scrub) 擦净 ‹*pan, sink*› **2** (form by erosion) «*water*» 冲刷出 ‹*pool, hole*›

scour[2] *vt* (search) 四处搜寻 ‹*place, text*›; **to ～ sth. for sb./sth.** 在某处彻底搜寻某人/某物

scourer /ˈskaʊərə(r)/ *n* **1** [c] (nylon pad) 塑料丝球; (wire pad) 金属丝球 **2** [u and c] (powder) 洗涤粉

scourge /skɜːdʒ/

A *n* **1** (whip) [用于惩罚或施刑的] 鞭子 **2** fig (affliction) 祸害; **the ～ of war/famine** 战争/饥荒之苦; **to be the ～ of developing countries** 为害发展中国家

B *vt* **1** (whip) 鞭打 **2** fig (afflict) 使…受苦难 ‹*person, country*›

C *v refl* **to ～ oneself** 折磨自己

scouring: ～ pad *n* 百洁布; **～ powder** *n* [u and c] 洗涤粉

Scouse /skaʊs/ Brit colloq

A *n* **1** [u] (dialect) 利物浦方言; (accent) 利物浦口音 **2** [c] (person) **= Scouser**

B *adj* 利物浦的 ‹*person, group*›; 利物浦人的 ‹*accent*›

Scouser /ˈskaʊsə(r)/ *n* Brit colloq 利物浦人

scout /skaʊt/

A *n* **1** Mil (person) 侦察员; (unit) 侦察部队; (aircraft) 侦察机; (ship) 侦察舰 **2** Mil (reconnaissance) 侦察; **to have a ～ around** 展开侦察 **3** (search) 搜寻; **to have a ～ around (for sth.)** 四处寻找(某物) **4** Theat, Sport **= talent scout** **5** **Scout** (member of association) 童子军成员; **the S～s** 童子军; **S～ uniform/camp/movement** 童子军制服/营地/运动

B *vi* **1** Mil 侦察 **2** (search) 搜寻; **to ～ for sb./sth.** 四处寻找某人/某物; **to ～ around the area/shops** 在此地/店铺周围搜寻 **3** (look for talent) 物色人才

Phrasal verb

- **scout around, scout about** *vi* 到处寻找; **to ～ around for sth.** 四处搜寻某物

Scout: ～ Association *n* **the ～ Association** 童子军协会; **～ hut** *n* 童子军协会活动中心

scouting /ˈskaʊtɪŋ/ *n* [u] **1** Mil (reconnaissance) 侦察 **2** **Scouting** (activities) 童子军活动; (movement) 童子军运动 **3** (talent-spotting) 物色人才

Scoutmaster /ˈskaʊtmɑːstə(r), Amer -mæst-/ *n* colloq 男童子军团长

scowl /skaʊl/

A *n* 怒容

B *vi* 怒视; **to ～ at sb.** 怒视某人

scowling /ˈskaʊlɪŋ/ *adj* 怒气冲冲的 ‹*face, expression*›

scrabble /ˈskræbl/

A *vi* **1** (grope) 摸寻; **to ～ around** *or* **about** 四处摸索; **to ～ for a foothold** 摸索找个蹬脚的地方 **2** (claw) «*person*» 乱抓; «*animal, bird*» 用爪子抓 **3** (scramble) «*person, animal*» 飞快地爬

B **Scrabble®** *n* [u] 拼字游戏; **s ～board** 拼字游戏板

scrag /skræg/ *n* [u] Brit **～ (end)** 羊颈背肉

scragginess /ˈskrægɪnɪs/ *n* [u] pej 瘦骨嶙峋

scraggly /ˈskrægli/ *adj* esp Amer **= scraggy 2**

scraggy /ˈskrægi/ *adj* pej **1** (thin) 瘦骨嶙峋的 ‹*person, animal, neck*› **2** (unkempt) 参差不齐的 ‹*weeds, beard*›

scram /skræm/ *vi* (*pres p etc.* **-mm-**) colloq 走开; **～!** 滚开!

scramble /ˈskræmbl/

A *vi* **1** (clamber) 爬; **to ～ up/down the slope** 爬上坡/爬下坡; **to ～ over the rocks** 爬过岩石; **to ～ through the gap in the hedge** 从篱笆的豁口爬过去; **to ～ up on to the chair** 爬上椅子 **2** (rush) 仓促行动; **the little dog ～d out of the car and ran off into the fields** 小狗从车里连滚带爬地跑出来走到田里; **she ～d into her clothes** 她匆匆穿上衣服; **to ～ to one's feet** 匆忙站起身; **to ～ to do sth.** 赶紧做某事; **when the rain started, we all ～d for shelter** 天开始下雨了, 我们赶紧找地方躲雨 **3** (compete) 争抢; **to ～ for sth.** 争抢 ‹*ball, contract, prize*›; **to ～ to do sth.** 抢着做某事

B *vt* **1** (jumble) 胡乱收起 ‹*papers, clothes*›; **the cat has ～d my wool into a hopeless tangle** 猫把我的毛线弄得一团糟 **2** Culin 炒;

S

to ~ eggs 炒蛋 3 Mil 命令…紧急起飞 ‹*aircraft, air crew*› 4 (make unintelligible) 通过倒频扰乱 ‹*transmission, message*›

C *n* 1 (climb) 爬 2 (rush) 争先恐后; **there was a wild ~ to sell shares** 人们争相抛售股票 3 Brit (motorcycle race) 摩托车越野赛 4 Mil 紧急起飞

scrambled egg *n* [u and c] **we had ~(s) for breakfast** 我们早餐吃的是炒蛋

scramble net *n* 1 Naut [紧急情况下离船用的] 攀网 2 (for children) 攀爬网

scrambler /ˈskræmblə(r)/ *n* 1 Radio, Telecom 保密器 2 Brit (motorcycle) 越野摩托车; (rider) 越野摩托车选手

scrambling /ˈskræmblɪŋ/ ▸**p. 307** *n* [u] 1 Radio, Telecom 扰频 2 Brit (motocross) 摩托车越野赛

scrap /skræp/

A *n* 1 [c] (of paper, cloth) 碎片; (of verse, conversation) 片段; (of news, information) 点滴; **a ~ of paper** 一小片纸; **~s of material** 碎布料; **the occasional ~ of the conversation** 谈话的片言只语; **~s of news/information** 零星消息/信息 2 [c] (of meat) 下脚料; (of bread) 面包屑; (of cake) 蛋糕渣; (of leftover food) 残羹剩饭; **the ~s are fed to the pigs** 剩饭拿去喂猪 3 [c] (small amount) 少量; **not a ~** 丝毫没有; **he never does a ~ of work!** 他一点儿活儿都不干!; **it doesn't make a ~ of difference!** 这毫无差别!; **there isn't a ~ of truth in what he says** 他说的话没有丝毫事实根据 4 [u] (waste articles or materials for reprocessing) (metal) 废金属; (other materials) 废料; **there's a thriving trade in ~** 废金属生意很兴旺; **to sell sth. for ~** 把某物当废金属出售; **the ~ value** 废金属价值 5 [c] colloq (fight) 打架; fig (quarrel) 争吵; **to get into a ~ with sb.** 和某人打架; **a fierce ~** 激烈争吵

B *vt* (*pres p etc.* **-pp-**) 1 (dispose of) 报废 ‹*car, equipment, missile*› 2 colloq (do away with) 取消 ‹*project, plan*›; 废除 ‹*system, policy, tax*›; **the two governments ~ped the peace talks** 两国政府停止了和谈

C *vi* (*pres p etc.* **-pp-**) colloq (fight) 打架; fig (quarrel) 争吵

scrap: ~book *n* 剪贴簿; **~ dealer** ▸**p. 409** *ns* 废金属回收商

scrape /skreɪp/

A *vt* 1 (clean) 刮; **to ~ sth. clean** 擦干净 ‹*carrot, wood, boots*›; **to ~ one's plate (clean)** 把盘里的食物吃得一干二净; **to ~ the (bottom of the) barrel** colloq 不得已将就 2 (remove) 刮掉; **to ~ sth. off sth.** 将…从某物上刮掉 ‹*mud, layer*›; ▸**scrape off** 3 (hollow out) 挖出 4 (damage) 刮花 ‹*car, door*›; (injure) 擦伤 ‹*hand, leg*› 5 (rub against) 碰擦 6 (make noise with) 吱嘎地拖拽 ‹*chair*›; 吱嘎地用…刮擦 ‹*knife*› 7 fig (barely manage) 勉强获得 ‹*amount, level*›; **to ~ a living** 勉强度日

B *vi* 1 (grate) «*door, boots*» 吱嘎地移动; **to ~ against/on/over sth.** 贴着某物/在某物上/在某物上方吱嘎地移动 2 (narrowly pass) 勉强通过; **to ~ past/through sth.** 勉强通过/穿过某物; **to ~ between sth.** 勉强从某物间穿过 3 fig (economize) 节衣缩食

C *n* 1 (act of scraping) 刮; **to give sth. a ~** 把某物擦一擦 2 (sound) 刮擦声 3 (mark) (on object) 擦痕; (on body) 擦伤; **to give the car/one's knee a ~** 划伤汽车/擦破膝盖 4 fig (difficult situation) 窘境; **to get (sb.) into a ~** (使某人)陷入窘境; **to get (sb.) out of a ~** (使某人)摆脱困境 5 Brit (small amount) **a ~ of jam/butter** 一丁点果酱/黄油

Phrasal verbs

- **scrape along** *vi* 勉强度日
- **scrape away** *vt* [~ **away sth.**, ~ **sth. away**] 刮去 ‹*layer, substance*›
- **scrape by** *vi* 1 (manage to live) 勉强度日 2 (barely succeed) 勉强通过
- **scrape home** *vi* 勉强成功
- **scrape in** *vi* 勉强进入
- **scrape into** *vt* [~ **into sth.**] 勉强进入 ‹*university, college*›
- **scrape off** *vt* [~ **off sth.**, ~ **sth. off**] 刮去; **to ~ the skin off one's knee** 擦破膝盖上的皮
- **scrape out** *vt* [~ **out sth.**, ~ **sth. out**] 1 (empty) 擦干净 ‹*container*› 2 (remove) 将…掏空 ‹*contents*›
- **scrape through** *vi* lit, fig 勉强通过
- **scrape together** *vt* [~ **sth. together**, ~ **together sth.**] 艰难地积攒 ‹*money*›; 艰难地凑集 ‹*people, evidence*›
- **scrape up** *vt* 1 lit 刮拢 2 fig = **scrape together**

scraper /ˈskreɪpə(r)/ *n* (for wallpaper, paint, ice) 刮刀; (for boots) 刮泥器

scrap heap *n* 废物堆; **cars on a ~** 报废的汽车; **to be thrown on** *or* **consigned to the ~** fig 被丢弃; **the ~ of history** fig 历史的垃圾堆

scrapie /ˈskreɪpi/ *n* [u] [羊的] 痒病

scraping /ˈskreɪpɪŋ/

A *n* 1 [u] (action) 刮擦; **a ~ sound** *or* **noise** 刮擦声 2 [u] (noise) (of feet, chairs) 吱嘎声; (of cutlery) 碰擦声 3 [c] Brit (small amount) **a ~ of jam/butter** 一丁点果酱/黄油

B **scrapings** *npl* Brit 刮屑

scrap: ~ iron *n* [u] 废铁; **~ merchant** ▸**p. 409** *n* 废品回收商; **~ metal** *n* [u] 废金属; **a ~ metal dealer** 废金属回收商; **~ paper** *n* [u] 便条纸

scrappage /ˈskræpɪdʒ/ *n* [u] 汽车补贴报废; **a ~ scheme** 汽车补贴报废方案

scrappy[1] /ˈskræpi/ *adj* (disorganized) 匆忙拼凑的 ‹*essay, collection, meal*›; 杂乱无章的 ‹*game, playing*›

scrappy[2] *adj* Amer pej (pugnacious) 好斗的; (full of fighting spirit) 敢作敢为的

scrapyard *n* 废品场

scratch /skrætʃ/

A *vt* 1 (mark with a scratch) 划破 ‹*face, car, glass*›; **the cat ~ed me on the arm** *or* **~ed my arm** 猫抓伤了我的胳膊; **to (only** *or* **merely** *or* **just) ~ the surface of sth.** 对某事物(仅仅)作肤浅的探讨 2 (rub with fingernails) 挠 ‹*itch, spot, bite, part of body*›; **to ~ one's head** fig 冥思苦想; **you ~ my back and I'll ~ yours** fig 你给我好处, 我也给你好处 3 (make by scratching) 抠出 ‹*hole*›; 戳刻 ‹*line, name*› 4 Sport 使…退出比赛 ‹*horse, competitor*›; Amer Pol 画掉…的名字 ‹*candidate*› 5 (cancel, abandon) 取消 ‹*project*›; **to ~ the charges** 取消收费

B *vi* 1 (make marks) 抓; (wound) 抓伤; **be careful of the cat, she ~es** 小心那只猫, 它会抓人; **a few hens were ~ing in the dust of the yard** 几只母鸡在院子里刨土; **bramble bushes have thorns, and they ~** 黑莓灌木上有刺, 能伤人 2 (relieve itch) 挠痒 3 (make grating noise) «*pen*» 发出刮擦声; **I ~ed very lightly on the window pane** 我轻轻地刮窗玻璃 4 (withdraw) «*competitor, horse, candidate*» 退出比赛

C *n* 1 [c] (wound) 划伤; (graze) 擦伤; **he got a nasty ~ on his cheek** 他脸上有严重的抓伤; **he came out without a ~** 他毫发未伤地逃了出来 2 [c] (mark) 划痕; **how are we going to remove these ~es from the table?** 我们怎么才能除去桌子上的这些划痕? 3 [c] (act of scratching) 挠; **the cat was lying in the sun having a ~** 猫躺在阳光下挠痒痒; **one ~ with the tip of this arrow and you are dead** 只要被这个箭头蹭到就会丧命 4 [c] (rasping noise) 刮擦声; **there was a ~ at the door** 门上传来了抓挠的声音; **the ~ of quill pens on paper** 鹅毛笔在纸上发出的沙沙声 5 [u] (zero) **from ~** 从零开始; **to start from ~** 从零开始; **she built up this company from ~** 她白手起家创办了这家公司; **he lost the manuscript and had to write the whole thing again from ~** 他把手稿弄丢了, 只好再从头写起 6 [u] (standard) **up to ~** 达标的; **to be** *or* **come up to ~** 达标; **to keep sb./sth. up to ~** 使某人/某事物符合标准; **to bring sb./sth. up to ~** 使某人/某事物达标 7 [u] (in golf) 零让杆; **he plays off ~** 他参加无让杆比赛

D *adj attrib* 1 (hastily assembled) 仓促拼凑的 ‹*team, crew, meal*› 2 (in golf) 无让杆的 ‹*golfer*›

Phrasal verbs

- **scratch around, scratch about** *vi* 四处扒拉; **the hen was ~ing around in the dirt** 那只母鸡在到处刨土; **I spend hours ~ing around for ideas** fig 我花了很长时间苦思冥想新创意
- **scratch out** *vt* [~ **sth. out**, ~ **out sth.**] 1 (erase) 勾去 ‹*word, line*› 2 (in attack) **to ~ sb.'s eyes out** 抠出某人的眼珠 [一般为威胁用语]
- **scratch together** *vt* [~ **sth. together**, ~ **together sth.**] 凑集 ‹*money, people*›

scratch: ~card *n* 刮奖卡; **~ mark** *n* = **scratch C1, C2**; **~ pad** *n* 1 esp Amer (notepad) 便笺簿; 2 Comput 高速暂存存储器; **~ test** *n* 划痕试验

scratchy /ˈskrætʃi/ *adj* 1 (rough) 扎人的 ‹*texture*› 2 (scratched) 有沙沙杂音的 ‹*recording*› 3 (grating) 吱嘎作响的 ‹*pen*›; 粗哑的 ‹*voice*› 4 (careless) 潦草的 ‹*writing, sketch*› 5 colloq (irritable) 易怒的

scrawl /skrɔːl/

A *n* 1 [u] (writing) 潦草的笔迹; **can you read his ~?** 你看得懂他的鬼画符吗? 2 [c] (note) 潦草的便条; (mark) 胡乱的符号

B *vt* (write) 潦草地写; (draw) 潦草地画

C *vi* (write) 潦草地写; (mark) 乱涂

scrawny /ˈskrɔːni/ *adj* 瘦巴巴的

scream /skriːm/

A *n* 1 (of person, animal) 尖叫; (of brakes, engine) 尖利刺耳的声音; **he let out a ~ of terror** 他发出一声惊叫; **~s of laughter were coming from the dining room** 餐厅里传来了刺耳的笑声 2 colloq (funny person) 可笑的人; (funny thing) 可笑的事物; **the last act is an absolute ~** 最后一幕滑稽可笑至极

B *vi* 1 (utter a cry) «*person, animal*» 尖叫; «*baby*» 大哭; **to ~ at sb.** 对某人大喊; **to ~ for help** 高声求救; **they're ~ing for John out there** 他们在外头大喊约翰的名字; **to ~ with pain/fright/rage/delight** 痛苦/惊恐/愤怒/快乐地尖叫; **the whole audience was ~ing with laughter** 全场观众哄然大笑起来 2 (make piercing noise) «*wind*» 呼啸; «*engine, brakes*» 发出刺耳声; **the vehicle ~ed to a halt** 车嘎吱一声刹住了

C *vt* 高喊 ‹*order, abuse*›; **'let go of me', he ~ed** "放开我," 他大声喊道; **'MP IN DRUGS SCANDAL' ~ed the headlines** 报纸用惊人的大字标题写着"国会议员卷入毒品丑闻"

Phrasal verb

- **scream out**

A *vt* [~ **out sth.**, ~ **sth. out**] 高喊 ‹*warning, order*›

B *vi* **to ~ out for sth.** lit 呼唤某物; fig 亟需某物; **people ~ing out for help** 高声求救的人们

screamer /ˈskriːmə(r)/ *n* 1 Sport colloq (hard shot) 快球; **to hit a ~** 击快球 2 Amer Journ colloq 耸人听闻的大标题

screaming /ˈskriːmɪŋ/

A *n* [u] 1 (with emotion, pain) 尖叫 2 (of brakes, tyres) 尖厉的嘎吱声

B *adj* 1 (with emotion, pain) 尖叫的 ‹*baby, fans*›; (squealing) 发出尖厉声音的 ‹*brakes, siren*› 2 fig (striking) 惹人注目的 ‹*headline, colour*›

screamingly /ˈskriːmɪŋli/ *adv* 极其 ‹*funny, obvious, dull*›

scree /skriː/ *n* 1 [u] (stones) 岩屑堆 2 [c] (slope) 碎石坡

screech /skriːtʃ/
A vi **1** (scream) «*animal, child*» 尖叫 **2** (squeal) «*brakes, door*» 嘎吱作响; «*vehicle*» 发出尖利的嘎吱声; **to ~ to a halt** 嘎的一声停住
B vt 尖声喊出 ‹*orders, abuse*›
C n **1** (of animal, child) 尖叫 **2** (of brakes, tyres) 尖利的嘎吱声

screech-owl n 仓鸮

screed /skriːd/ n **1** [c] (writing) 冗长的文章 **2** [u and c] Constr 砂浆层

screen /skriːn/
A n **1** (panel, partition) (movable) 屏风; (fixed) 围屏; **there were ~s over the windows to keep out mosquitoes** 窗户上装了防蚊的纱窗; **a bullet-proof glass ~** 防弹玻璃屏; **a ~ of trees/bushes** 树木/灌木丛屏障; **the main column advanced behind a ~ of cavalry** *or* **a cavalry ~** 主力纵队在骑兵的掩护下向前推进 **2** Cin, Phot 银幕; **the (big) ~** 电影; **a ~ role/actor/debut** 电影角色/演员/首映 **3** TV, Comput 屏幕; **a television/radar ~** 电视/雷达屏幕; **a 20-inch ~** 20 英寸屏幕 **4** (sieve) 粗筛
B vt **1** (conceal) 遮蔽 ‹*window, door*›; (protect) 保护 ‹*person*›; **to ~ sth. from sth.** 使某物遮挡住某物; **we're pretty well ~ed from the wind by the railway embankment** 铁路路基为我们挡了很多风; **to ~ sb./sth. from sight** *or* **view** 把某人/某物隐藏起来; **his friend had often ~ed him from punishment** 他的朋友经常庇护他免受惩罚 **2** Cin, TV 播放 ‹*programme*›; 放映 ‹*film*› **3** (sieve) 筛 ‹*gravel, compost*› **4** (subject to a test) 筛选 ‹*candidates, applicants, staff*›; Med 筛查 ‹*patients*›; **to ~ women for cervical cancer** 为妇女做宫颈癌筛查

Phrasal verbs
- **screen off** vt [**~ sb./sth. off, ~ off sb./sth.**] 隔开; **I'm planting some bushes to ~ that part of the garden off** 我在种一点灌木，想把花园的那一部分隔出去
- **screen out** vt [**~ sb./sth. out, ~ out sb./sth.**] 把…排除在外 ‹*troublemakers, undesirables*›; 遮挡 ‹*light, noise*›; 筛除 ‹*unwanted data, nuisance calls*›; **a set of electronic filters ~s out any interference** 一套电子过滤器可以筛除所有干扰

screen: ~ capture n [u and c] (process) 屏幕图像捕获; (image) 屏幕截图; **~ door** n 纱门; **~ dump** n **1** (process) 屏幕打印; **2** (printout) 屏幕打印件; **~ editing** n [u] 屏幕编辑; **~ editing software** 屏幕编辑软件; **~ editor** n 屏幕编辑程序

screening /ˈskriːnɪŋ/ n **1** [c] Cin, TV 放映 **2** [u] (sieving) 筛分 **3** [u] (testing) (of candidates) 筛选; (of patients, animals) 筛查; **cancer ~** 癌症筛查

screening: ~ room n 放映室; **~ service** n 健康筛查服务

screen: ~play n 电影剧本; **~ printing** n [u] 丝网印刷法; **~ rights** npl 电影改编权; **~ saver** n 屏幕保护程序; **~shot** n 屏幕快照; **~ test** n 试镜头; **~wash** n [u] 挡风玻璃清洗剂; **~writer** ▸p. 409 n 电影剧本作家

screw /skruː/
A n **1** Tech 螺丝; **to have a ~ loose** colloq 有些古怪; **to put the ~s on sb.** colloq 胁迫某人 **2** Naut (propeller) 螺旋桨 **3** colloq (prison guard) 监狱看守 **4** taboo sl (sex) 交媾; **to have a ~** 性交 **5** taboo sl (sexual partner) 性伴侣; **to be a good ~** 床上功夫很好 **6** Brit dated (twist of paper) 小纸卷; **a ~ of sweets/salt/tobacco** 一小包糖果/盐/烟草 **7** Brit dated colloq (wage) 工资; **to be on a good ~** 赚高薪
B vt **1** Tech 用螺丝固定 ‹*piece of wood, metal plate*›; **to ~ sth. on to sth.** 把某物用螺丝固定在某物上 **2** (twist) 拧紧 ‹*screw, threaded part*›; **to ~ sth. into sth.** 把某物拧入某物 **3** (distort) 扭曲 ‹*face*› **4** colloq (extort, extract) 勒索; **to ~ sth. out of sb.** 向某人勒索某物; **it took the threat of strike action to ~ concessions out of the management** 以罢工相威胁才迫使资方作出了让步 **5** colloq (swindle) 诈骗 **6** colloq (thwart) 搅乱 ‹*system*› **7** taboo sl (have sex with) 与…性交 **8** taboo sl (damn) (in insults) 让…见鬼去; **~ you!** 去你妈的!; **~ the government!** 让政府见鬼去吧!
C vi **1** Tech 拧上; **to ~ into** *or* **on to sth.** 拧到某物上 **2** taboo sl (have sex) 交媾

Phrasal verbs
- **screw around** vi **1** taboo sl (sleep around) 乱交 **2** Amer colloq (joke) 胡闹; **quit ~ing around! I'm being serious!** 别闹了! 我是认真的!
- **screw in**
A vt [**~ sth. in, ~ in sth.**] 把…拧上 ‹*screw, bolt*›
B vi 拧上
- **screw off**
A vt [**~ sth. off, ~ off sth.**] 拧掉 ‹*cap, lid*›
B vi «*cap, lid*» 旋开
- **screw on**
A vt [**~ sth. on, ~ on sth.**] 拧上 ‹*cap, lid, handle*›; **to have one's head ~ed on (the right way)** colloq 头脑清醒
B vi «*cap, lid, handle*» 拧上
- **screw round** vt [**~ sth. round**] 把…转过来; **to ~ oneself/one's head round** 转身/扭过头来
- **screw together**
A vt [**~ sth. together, ~ together sth.**] 把…拧在一起 ‹*parts*›
B vi «*parts*» 拧在一起
- **screw up**
A vt [**~ sth. up, ~ up sth.**]
1 (tighten) 拧紧 ‹*screw, nut*› **2** (crumple) 把…揉成团 ‹*paper, handkerchief*›; **she ~ed up her eyes because of the glare of the lights** 亮光刺得她眯起了眼睛; **don't ~ your face up like that, try to look natural** 别那样绷着脸，自然一点吧 **3** colloq (mess up) 搞砸 ‹*plan, project*› **4** colloq (make unhappy) 使心烦意乱 **5** (summon) 振作; **to ~ up one's courage (to do sth.)** 鼓起勇气（做某事）
B vi **1** (become tighter) «*nut*» 拧紧 **2** esp Amer colloq (mess up) 搞砸

screw: ~ball n esp Amer colloq 怪人; *modif* 古怪的 ‹*aunt, uncle*›; 描写怪人的 ‹*comedy*›; **~ bolt** n 螺栓; **~ cap** n 螺旋盖; **a ~-cap bottle** 带螺旋盖的瓶子; **~driver** n **1** (tool) 螺丝刀; **2** (drink) 伏特加橙汁鸡尾酒

screwed /skruːd/ adj pred colloq 处境糟糕的 ‹*person*›; **either way we're ~** 无论怎样我们都死定了

screw: ~-in adj 螺旋式安装的 ‹*attachment*›; **a ~-in bulb** 螺口灯泡; **~-off** adj 螺旋式取下的 ‹*lid*›; **~ thread** n 螺纹; **~ top** n = **~ cap**; **~-up** n esp Amer colloq (mess) 搞糟; (bungler) 弄砸的人

screwy /ˈskruːi/ adj esp Amer colloq (crazy) 疯狂的; (strange) 古怪的

scribble /ˈskrɪbl/
A vi **1** (write) (messily) 潦草地写; (hastily) 匆忙地写 **2** (draw) 乱画 **3** pej or hum (write) 要笔杆子
B vt (messily) 潦草地写; (hastily) 匆忙地写
C n **1** [u] (handwriting) 潦草的字迹; **can you read my ~?** 你能看懂我涂写的东西吗? **2** [c] (mark) 乱写的东西; (picture) 乱涂的画

scribbler /ˈskrɪblə(r)/ n **1** esp Amer (notebook) [尤指供学童使用的] 练习本 **2** pej or hum (author) 要笔杆子的人

scribbling /ˈskrɪblɪŋ/ n [u and c] lit 潦草写成的东西; fig 胡写乱画

scribbling: ~ pad n 便笺簿; **~ paper** n [u] 便笺纸

scribe /skraɪb/ n **1** Hist 抄写员 **2** **Scribe** Relig (record-keeper) [古代犹太人的] 记录官; (theologian) 神学家; (jurist) 法理学家 **3** colloq hum (writer) 作家; (journalist) 记者

scrimmage /ˈskrɪmɪdʒ/ n **1** [c and u] Amer Sport 争球 **2** [c] (struggle) 胡乱争抢

scrimp /skrɪmp/ vi 节俭; **to ~ and save** 省吃俭用; **to ~ on sth.** 在某物上很节省; **we never ~ed on food** 在吃的方面我们从来不俭省

scrimshaw /ˈskrɪmʃɔː/
A n [u] (ivory) 牙雕; (shells) 贝雕
B vt 在…上雕刻 ‹*ivory, shell*›; **a ~ed tusk/handle** 牙雕品/雕刻的手柄

scrip /skrɪp/ n **1** [c] (certificate) [一张] 代价券 **2** [u] (certificates) 代价券 **3** [c] = **scrip issue**

scrip issue n 红利股发行

script /skrɪpt/ n **1** [c] Cin, TV, Theat 剧本; Journ, Radio 广播稿 **2** [u] (handwriting) 笔迹; (font) 书写体 **3** [c] Brit Sch, Univ 笔试答卷 **4** [c] Comput 脚本

scripted /ˈskrɪptɪd/ adj 照本宣科的 ‹*dialogue, interview*›

scriptural /ˈskrɪptʃərəl/ adj 圣经的 ‹*study, tradition, basis*›; 圣经中的 ‹*passage, account*›

scripture /ˈskrɪptʃə(r)/ n [u] (*also* **scriptures** *pl*) **1** (Christian) 圣经; **(the) holy ~** *or* **Holy S~** 《圣经》; **in (holy) ~** 在《圣经》里; **~ lesson** 《圣经》选读 **2** (of other religions) 圣典

scriptwriter /ˈskrɪptraɪtə(r)/ ▸p. 409 n 编剧

scroll /skrəʊl/
A n **1** (paper) [书写用的] 卷纸; (parchment) 羊皮卷纸 **2** (document) 古卷; **the Dead Sea S~s** 《死海古卷》 **3** (on column) 涡卷形装饰; (on violin) 涡卷形琴头
B vi 滚屏; **to ~ up/down** 向上/下滚屏
C vt **to ~ sth. up/down** 使…向上/下滚动 ‹*text*›

scrollable /ˈskrəʊləbl/ adj 可滚动的 ‹*text, page, window*›

scroll: ~ arrow n 滚动箭头; **~ bar** n 滚动条; **~ box** n 滚动框

scrolling /ˈskrəʊlɪŋ/ n [u] 上下滚动

scroll: ~ key n 滚动键; **~work** n [u] 涡卷形装饰

Scrooge /skruːdʒ/ n colloq 守财奴; **don't be such a ~** 别这么一毛不拔

scrotum /ˈskrəʊtəm/ n (*pl* **scrota** /ˈskrəʊtə/ *or* **~s**) 阴囊

scrounge /skraʊndʒ/ colloq pej
A vt **1** (borrow) 白要 ‹*cigarette, money*›; **to ~ sth. off sb.** 从某人处白拿某物; **to ~ a free meal** 蹭一顿饭 **2** (forage) 搜寻; **to ~ around for sth.** 四处寻找某物
B vi 白要; **to ~ off sb.** 从某人处白拿
C n **1** (person) = **scrounger** **2** (act of scrounging) 白要; **to be on the ~** Brit 讨要

scrounger /ˈskraʊndʒə(r)/ n colloq pej (habitual borrower) 白吃白拿的人; (sponger) 寄生虫

scrub¹ /skrʌb/
A n **1** (clean) 擦洗; **to give sth. a good ~** 彻底擦洗某物 **2** Cosmet 磨砂膏
B vt **1** (clean) 擦洗 ‹*hands, floor, saucepan*›; **will you ~ my back for me?** 你给我擦擦背好吗? **2** colloq (scrap) 取消 ‹*party, plan*›; **~ that** 删去刚才那一句
C vi 擦洗

Phrasal verbs
- **scrub down** vt [**~ sth./sb. down, ~ down sth./sb.**] 彻底擦洗 ‹*wall, table*›
- **scrub in** vi «*surgeon*» [手术前] 彻底清洗并穿上手术服
- **scrub off** vt [**~ sth. off, ~ off sth.**] 擦去 ‹*mark, dirt*›
- **scrub out** vt [**~ sth. out, ~ out sth.**]
1 (rub out) 擦掉 ‹*mark, writing*› **2** (clean inside) 洗刷 ‹*pan, oven*›
- **scrub up** vi «*surgeon*» [手术前] 彻底清洗手臂

scrub² n [u] Bot 灌木丛

S

scrubber /ˈskrʌbə(r)/ *n* **1** (brush) 刷子; (scourer) 清洁球 **2** Brit, Austral colloq pej (loose woman) 婊子

scrub brush, scrubbing brush *ns* 硬毛刷

scrubby /ˈskrʌbi/ *adj* **1** (small) 低矮的 ‹*tree, bush*› **2** (covered in scrub) 灌木丛生的 ‹*land*› **3** Brit pej (shabby) 破旧的

scruff[1] /skrʌf/ *n* (nape) 后颈; **by the ～ of the neck** 揪着脖子

scruff[2] *n* Brit colloq (untidy person) 邋遢的人

scruffily /ˈskrʌfɪli/ *adv* 邋遢地; **～ dressed** 衣着邋遢的

scruffiness /ˈskrʌfmɪs/ *n* [u] (of person) 邋遢; (of clothes) 不整洁; (of building, area) 破旧

scruffy /ˈskrʌfi/ *adj* 邋遢的 ‹*person*›; 不整洁的 ‹*appearance, clothes, hair*›; 破旧的 ‹*flat, town*›

scrum /skrʌm/ *n* **1** (in rugby) 并列争球 **2** Brit colloq (crowd) 推搡的人群; **a ～ of reporters** 一群乱哄哄的记者

Phrasal verb

• **scrum down** (*pres p etc.* **-mm-**) *vi* (in rugby) 排成并列争球队形

scrum half *n* (position) 争球前卫的位置; (player) 争球前卫

scrummage /ˈskrʌmɪdʒ/

A *n* **1** (in rugby) 并列争球 **2** Brit colloq (crowd) 推搡的人群

B *vi* **1** Sport (form scrum) 排成并列争球队形; (take part in scrum) 并列争球 **2** Brit colloq (jostle) 推搡

scrump /skrʌmp/ *vt* Brit colloq [从果园或花园]偷窃 ‹*fruit*›

scrumptious /ˈskrʌmpʃəs/ *adj* colloq 美味的

scrumpy /ˈskrʌmpi/ *n* [u] Brit [尤指英格兰西部产的] 烈性苹果酒

scrunch /skrʌntʃ/

A *n* 嘎吱声

B *vt* 嘎吱嘎吱地压 ‹*paper, packet*›; 嘎吱嘎吱地嚼 ‹*food*›

C *vi* 发出嘎吱声

Phrasal verb

• **scrunch up** *vt* [**～ sth. up, ～ up sth.**] 揉皱 ‹*paper, box*›; 皱起 ‹*face*›

scrunchie /ˈskrʌntʃi/ *n* 布发圈

scruple /ˈskruːpl/

A *n* [u and c] 顾虑; **he has no ～s** 他无所顾忌; **without ～** 毫无顾忌地; **to have ～s about sth./doing sth.** 对某事/做某事有所顾忌; **to have no ～s about sth./doing sth.** 对某事/做某事无所顾忌

B *vi* 顾虑; **not to ～ to do sth.** 无所顾忌地做某事

scrupulous /ˈskruːpjʊləs/ *adj* **1** (upright) 审慎正直的 ‹*person*› **2** (meticulous) 一丝不苟的; **to be ～ about sth.** 对某事一丝不苟; **～ honesty** 严谨诚实

scrupulously /ˈskruːpjʊləsli/ *adv* 审慎正直地 ‹*act*›; **～ honest/fair** 严谨诚实的/严谨公平的; **～ clean/exact** 一尘不染的/分毫不差的

scrutineer /ˌskruːtɪˈnɪə(r), Amer -tnˈɪər/ *n* esp Brit Pol 监票人; (in competition) 监督人

scrutinize /ˈskruːtɪnaɪz, Amer -tənaɪz/ *vt* 仔细观察 ‹*face*›; 仔细检查 ‹*object*›

scrutiny /ˈskruːtɪni, Amer ˈskruːtni/ *n* [u] (observation) 仔细观察; (investigation) 仔细检查; **to be under ～** (observation) 受到密切注意; (investigation) 受到检查

scuba /ˈskuːbə/ *n* **1** [c] (aqualung) 水肺 **2** [u] (diving) 戴水肺潜水

scuba: ～-diver *n* 戴水肺的潜水员; **～ diving** ▸**p. 307** *n* [u] 戴水肺潜水

scud /skʌd/ *vi* (*pres p etc.* **-dd-**) «*ship*» 疾行; **the clouds ～ded across the sky** 云彩掠过天空

scuff /skʌf/

A *n* (on leather, floor, furniture) 磨损处

B *vt* **1** (scrape) 磨坏 ‹*shoe, bag*›; **to ～ the heel of one shoe** 磨坏一只鞋跟 **2** (mark) 在…上留下磨痕 ‹*shoe, floor*› **3** (drag) **to ～ one's feet** 拖着脚走路

C *vi* 磨损

Phrasal verb

• **scuff up** *vt* [**～ sth. up, ～ up sth.**] **1** (mark) 磨坏 ‹*shoe, leather*› **2** (raise) 扬起 ‹*dust*›

scuffle /ˈskʌfl/

A *n* 扭打; **to get into a ～** 扭打起来

B *vi* «*person, group*» 扭打; **to ～ with sb.** 与某人扭打

scull /skʌl/

A *n* **1** (boat) 双桨赛艇 **2** (single oar) 单桨 **3** (one of a pair of oars) 短桨 **4** **sculls** + *v sing or pl* (race) 双桨赛艇比赛; **single/double ～s** 单人/双人双桨赛艇比赛

B *vi* **1** (with one oar) 用单桨划船 **2** (with two oars) 用双桨划船; **to go ～ing** 去划船

C *vt* **1** (with one oar) 用单桨划 **2** (with two oars) 用双桨划

scullery /ˈskʌləri/ *n* Brit 洗涤室

sculpt /skʌlpt/

A *vt* **1** (shape, mould) 使…成形 ‹*clay*›; 塑成 ‹*shape*›; (carve) 雕刻 ‹*wood, ivory*›; 雕成 ‹*shape*›; **to ～ sth. out of stone/wood** 用石头/木头雕刻某物 **2** (represent, create) 塑造 ‹*bust, figure*›; **～ed heads** 雕塑头像 **3** fig (shape) «*wind, rain*» 使…具有某种形状 ‹*rock, coastline*›; 形成 ‹*hole, form*›

B *vi* (shape) 雕塑; (carve) 雕刻

sculptor /ˈskʌlptə(r)/ ▸**p. 409** *n* (in clay) 雕塑家; (in marble, wood) 雕刻家

sculptress /ˈskʌlptrɪs/ ▸**p. 409** *n* (in clay) 女雕塑家; (in marble, wood) 女雕刻家

sculptural /ˈskʌlptʃərəl/ *adj* **1** (of moulding) 雕塑的 ‹*technique*›; (of carving) 雕刻品的; **～ works/decoration** 雕塑作品/雕饰 **2** (like sculpture) 雕塑般的 ‹*quality*›

sculpture /ˈskʌlptʃə(r)/

A *n* **1** [u] (moulding) 雕塑; (carving) 雕刻; **～ class** 雕塑班 **2** [u and c] (moulded piece) 雕塑作品; (carved piece) 雕刻作品; **～ gallery** 雕塑馆

B *vt* **1** **= sculpt A1** **2** fig (shape) **= sculpt A3**

scum /skʌm/ *n* [u] **1** (film) (on pond) 浮渣; (on liquid) 浮沫; (in bath) 浮垢 **2** colloq pej (worthless person, people) 人渣

scumbag /ˈskʌmbæg/ *n* colloq pej 卑鄙的家伙

scummy /ˈskʌmi/ *adj* **1** (like scum) 似浮渣的 ‹*deposit, froth*› **2** (covered in scum) 盖满浮渣的 ‹*pond*›; 盖满浮沫的 ‹*liquid*›; 满是浮垢的 ‹*container*› **3** colloq pej (rotten) 卑鄙的 ‹*person, behaviour*›

scupper /ˈskʌpə(r)/ Brit

A *n* 甲板排水孔

B *vt* **1** Naut 故意使…沉没 ‹*ship*› **2** fig (ruin) «*person, event*» 使…泡汤 ‹*plans, chances*›; **we're ～ed!** colloq 我们完蛋了!

scurf /skɜːf/ *n* [u] colloq 头皮屑

scurrility /skəˈrɪləti/ *n* [u] **1** (abuse) 辱骂 **2** (vulgar humour) 粗鄙的笑话; (vulgar language) 污言秽语

scurrilous /ˈskʌrɪləs/ *adj* **1** (abusive) 恶意诽谤的 ‹*person, rumour*› **2** (vulgar) 粗俗下流的 ‹*person, joke*›

scurrilously /ˈskʌrɪləsli/ *adv* **1** (abusively) 恶意诽谤地 **2** (vulgarly) 粗俗下流地

scurry /ˈskʌri/

A *n* 疾走; **the ～ of feet** *or* **footsteps** 急促的脚步

B *vi* 碎步疾行; **to ～ to and fro** 来回奔忙; **to ～ away** *or* **off** 匆忙离开

scurvy /ˈskɜːvi/ *n* [u] 坏血病

scuttle[1] /ˈskʌtl/ *vi* (scamper) 小步疾走; **to ～ across sth.** 急速穿过某处; **to ～ after sb./sth.** 急速追赶某人/某物; **to ～ away** *or* **off** 迅速跑开

scuttle[2]

A *n* **= coal scuttle**

B *vt* **1** Naut [以打开通海阀或凿洞等方式] 使…沉没 ‹*ship*› **2** fig (ruin) 使…成泡影 ‹*plan*›

scuttlebutt /ˈskʌtlbʌt/ *n* [u] Amer colloq 谣言; **the ～ had it that ...** 有传言说…

scuzz /skʌz/ *n* esp Amer colloq **1** [u] (muck) 脏东西 **2** [u] (disgusting book, film) 讨厌的东西 **3** [c] (person) 讨厌鬼

scuzzball /ˈskʌzbɔːl/, **scuzzbag** /ˈskʌzbæg/ *ns* esp Amer colloq 讨厌鬼

scuzzy /ˈskʌzi/ *adj* esp Amer colloq **1** (dirty) 肮脏的 ‹*clothes, water*›; 邋遢的 ‹*person*› **2** (sleazy) 讨厌的 ‹*person*›; 乌烟瘴气的 ‹*bar, hotel*›

Scylla /ˈsɪlə/ *pr n* 斯库拉 [希腊神话中从过往船只上掳走水手的多头怪兽]; **～ and Charybdis** 两难的境地; **to be between ～ and Charybdis** fig 进退两难

scythe /saɪð/

A *n* 长柄大镰刀

B *vt* **1** lit 用长柄大镰刀割 ‹*grass*› **2** fig 劈出; **to ～ the air with one's hand** 用手在空中比划; **to ～ a path through sth.** 穿过某处开出一条路

C *vi* «*blade*» 切割; «*hand*» 挥动; **a motorway scything through a city** 穿城而过的高速公路

SD *abbr* Amer **= South Dakota**

SDI *abbr* Amer **= Strategic Defense Initiative** 战略防御计划

SDLP *abbr* **= Social Democratic and Labour Party** 社会民主工党

SE ▸**p. 142** *abbr* **1** **= south-east** **2** **= south-eastern**

sea /siː/

A *n* **1** (ocean) 海; **at ～** 在海上航行; **burial at ～** 海葬; **to be (all) at ～** fig colloq 茫然无绪; **a village beside** *or* **by the ～** 海边的村庄; **by ～** 经由海路; **I'd prefer to go by ～ if I can get a passage** 如果能够买到船票, 我更想走海路; **her husband is home from ～ again** 她丈夫又出海归来了; **I went swimming in the ～** 我去海里游泳了; **out at** *or* **to ～** 在海上; **the ship was heading out to ～** 船正在出海; **a greeting from over the ～s** 来自海外的问候; **to go to ～** (sail) 出海; (become a sailor) 当海员; **to put (out) to ～** 起航; **worse things happen at ～!** 比这糟糕的事情多着呢! ; **the Dead/Caspian Sea** 死海/里海; **an inland ～** 内海; **the Sea of Storms/Serenity** 风暴海/平静海 [指月球表面大片的阴暗区] **2** (oceanic conditions) 海面状况; **a rough** *or* **heavy ～** 波涛汹涌的海面; **a calm ～** 风平浪静的海面 **3** fig (broad expanse) 大片; **a ～ of troubles** 无穷的麻烦; **a ～ of corn** 一大片玉米地; **the stand where the Irish fans were sitting was a ～ of green and white** 爱尔兰球迷就座的看台是一片绿白交织的海洋

B *modif* **1** Zool 海生的 ‹*creature, animal*›; **a ～ bird/fish** 海鸟/海鱼 **2** (used on board ship) 水手用的 ‹*boot, chest*› **3** (naval) 海军的 ‹*power*›; **a ～ battle** 海战

sea: ～ anemone *n* 海葵; **～ bass** *n* 海鲈; **～bed** *n* 海床; **～board** *n* (coast) 海岸; (coastal region) 沿海地区; **～borne** *adj* 海运的 ‹*force, trade*›; **the greatest ～borne invasion in history** 历史上规模最大的海上入侵; **～ bream** *n* 海鲷; **～ captain** ▸**p. 409** *n* [通常指商船的] 船长; **～ change** *n* 巨变; **～ cow** *n* 海牛; **～ defences** *npl* 海岸防护设施; **～ dog** *n* 老水手; **～ dumping** *n* [u] 海洋倾废; **～ eagle** *n* 海雕; **～farer** *n* 水手

seafaring /ˈsiːfeərɪŋ/

A *adj* 当水手的 ‹*man, days*›; 水手的 ‹*life*›; ～

S

nation/prowess 航海民族/技能
B *n* [u] 航海; **a life of ～** 航海生涯
seafood /ˈsiːfuːd/ *n* [u] 海味; **a ～ cocktail** 海味冷盘; **the ～ industry** 海产品工业; **a fancy ～ restaurant** 高档海鲜馆
sea: ～front *n* [城镇的] 滨海区; **a hotel on the ～front** 滨海旅馆; **to stroll along the ～front** 沿着海边漫步; **～going** *adj* 航海的 ‹*experience*›; **a ～going ship/officer** 海船/高级远洋船员
sea green ▸**p. 134**
A *n* [u] 淡蓝绿色
B *adj* 淡蓝绿色的
sea: ～gull *n* 海鸥; **～ horse** *n* 海马; **～ lane** *n* 海上航路
seal[1] /siːl/ Zool
A *n* 海豹; **a performing ～** 会表演的海豹
B *vi* 猎取海豹; **to go ～ing** 猎海豹
seal[2]
A *n* **1** (closure) 密封口; (made of wax) 封蜡; (made of lead) 封铅; **the customs officer checked the ～s on the container** 海关关员检查了集装箱上的封条; **given under my hand and ～** Jur 经我本人签名密封 **2** (authenticating stamp) 印章; **the royal ～** 玺印 **3** fig (confirmation, guarantee) 保证; **the ～ of approval** 正式批准; **under the ～ of confession** Relig 在告解保密的情况下 [天主教牧师对告解者的忏悔内容予以保密]; **under the ～ of secrecy** 在承诺保密的情况下 **4** (symbol of office) 官方的标志; **the ～s of office** 官方特权的标志; **to set one's ～ on sth.** 在某物上盖上自己的图章; fig 在某物上留下自己的风格; **to set** *or* **put the ～ on sth.** 使某事完美收场 **5** (tight closure) 密封; (device to form closure) 密封物; **the rubber ring acts as a ～ around the neck of the jar** 广口瓶瓶颈处的橡胶圈起密封作用 **6** (ornamental stamp) 装饰性贴签 [用于信件、包裹或慈善目的]
B *vt* **1** (authenticate) 在…上盖章了; **the document has been signed and ～ed** 文件已经签字盖章了 **2** (close) 把…封口 ‹*envelope, parcel*›; 封好 ‹*container, consignment, lorry*›; **～ed orders** 封缄命令; **my lips are ～ed** 我守口如瓶 **3** (make airtight, watertight) 把…封死 ‹*joint, wall, cement*›; 把…密封 ‹*container*›; 把…过油 ‹*steak, meat*› **4** (confirm) 达成 ‹*bargain*›; 缔结 ‹*alliance, friendship*›; **to ～ a contract** 签下合同; **to ～ sth. with a kiss/an embrace** 亲吻/拥抱以达成某事; **to ～ sb.'s fate/the fate of sth.** 某人/某物在劫难逃

Phrasal verbs
• **seal in** *vt* [**～ sth. in, ～ in sth.**] 密封住 ‹*smell, flavour*›
• **seal off** *vt* [**～ sth. off, ～ off sth.**] **1** (make separate from) 隔开 ‹*section of building*› **2** (prevent access to) 封锁 ‹*building, street, area*›
• **seal up** *vt* [**～ sth. up, ～ up sth.**] 封死 ‹*door, window*›

sealant /ˈsiːlənt/ *n* [u and c] 密封材料
sea-launched missile *n* 海射
seal cull *n* 选择性的猎杀海豹
sea legs *npl* **to find** *or* **get one's ～** 习惯船上生活
sealer /ˈsiːlə(r)/ *n* **1** [c and u] (substance) 密封材料 **2** [c] (device) 密封机
sea-level *n* 海平面; **500 ft above/below ～** 海拔/海平面以下 500 英尺
sealing /ˈsiːlɪŋ/ *n* [u] 猎杀海豹
sealing wax *n* [u] 封蜡
sea: ～ lion *n* 海狮; **～ loch** *n* [苏格兰的] 狭长海湾
sealskin /ˈsiːlskɪn/ *n* [u and c] 海豹皮
seam /siːm/
A *n* **1** Tex 线缝; **to be bursting at the ～s** lit (coming apart) 线缝破裂; fig (full) 人满为患; **to come apart at the ～** lit (come unstitched) 线缝破裂; fig (fail) 接近崩溃 **2** (line of joint) 接缝; (on boat) 缝隙; (in metal, welding) 焊缝 **3** Geol 矿层; **a rich ～ of iron ore** 富铁矿层 **4** fig (supply, source) 宝藏; **a rich ～ of information** 丰富的信息宝库
B *vt* 缝合
seaman /ˈsiːmən/ *n* (*pl* **seamen**) **1** Naut 水兵 **2** (amateur sailor) 擅长航海者
seamanlike /ˈsiːmənlaɪk/ *adj* 熟练水手般的; **in a ～ manner** 以娴熟的航海技能
seamanship /ˈsiːmənʃɪp/ *n* [u] 航海技能
seamed /siːmd/ *adj* 有缝的; **a face ～ with wrinkles** fig 布满皱纹的脸
sea mist *n* [u and c] 海上的薄雾
seamless /ˈsiːmlɪs/ *adj* **1** (without seams) 无线缝的 ‹*garment, carpet*›; 无接缝的 ‹*wallpaper, panel*› **2** fig (unbroken) 连续的 ‹*process*›; 不间断的 ‹*transition*›; **a ～ narrative** 连贯的叙述
seamstress /ˈsemstrɪs/ ▸**p. 409** *n* 女裁缝
seamy /ˈsiːmi/ *adj* 龌龊的 ‹*scandal, newspaper story*›; 卑鄙的 ‹*intrigue*›; **the ～ side of sth.** 某事物的阴暗面
seance /ˈseɪɑːns/ *n* 降神会
sea: ～ otter *n* 海獭; **～plane** *n* 水上飞机; **～ pollution** *n* [u] 海洋污染; **～port** *n* 海港城市
sear /sɪə(r)/ *vt* **1** (burn, scorch) 烧灼 **2** Culin 轻煎 ‹*meat*› **3** lit (cause to feel pain) 使感到剧痛; fig (brand) 使铭记; **to ～ sth. into sth.** 将某物铭刻在某物上; **the image was ～ed into his brain** 这个形象已深深烙在了他的脑海里 **4** (make insensitive) 使变得冷酷
search /sɜːtʃ/
A *vi* **1** (look, seek) 搜寻; **to ～ for sth./sb.** 搜寻某物/某人; **to ～ through sth.** 找遍某处; **she spends hours ～ing through her wardrobe for** *or* **to find something to wear** 她用了好几个小时在衣橱里翻找可穿的衣服; **I don't like the idea of somebody ～ing through my belongings** 我不喜欢别人翻我的东西 **2** Comput 搜索; **to ～ for data/a file** 搜索数据/文件
B *vt* **1** (examine) 搜查; **he was stopped and ～ed by an army patrol** 他被巡逻兵拦住搜身; **to ～ a catalogue/list** 查目录/清单; **to ～ one's memory** 努力回忆; **～ me!** colloq 我怎么知道! **2** (scan) 仔细察看 ‹*map*› **3** Comput 搜索 ‹*file, document*›
C *n* **1** (hunt) 寻找; **in ～ of ...** 寻找…; **he went into the kitchen in ～ of sth. to drink** 他到厨房去找一点儿喝的 **2** (of area, house, person) 搜查; (into drawer, cupboard, handbag) 翻找; **a body ～** 搜身; **a customs ～** 海关检查; **right of ～** Jur, Naut 搜查权 **3** Comput 搜索; **to do a ～** 进行搜索

Phrasal verbs
• **search about, search around** *vi* **to ～ about for sth./sb.** 四处寻找某物/某人
• **search out** *vt* [**～ sb./sth. out, ～ out sb./sth.**] 找出; **she ～ed out her old school photographs to show me** 她找出上学时的老照片给我看

searchable /ˈsɜːtʃəbl/ *adj* 可检索的
search-and-replace *n* [u] 查找并替换
search engine *n* 搜索引擎
searcher /ˈsɜːtʃə(r)/ *n* 搜索者
searching /ˈsɜːtʃɪŋ/ *adj* 探究的 ‹*look*›; 寻根究底的 ‹*enquiry, investigation*›
searchingly /ˈsɜːtʃɪŋli/ *adv* 探究地; **to look at sb. ～** 用犀利的目光看某人
search: ～light *n* 探照灯; **～ party** *n* 搜索队; **～ warrant** *n* 搜查证
searing /ˈsɪərɪŋ/ *adj* **1** (extremely hot) 灼热的; **～ heat** 灼热 **2** (intense) 剧烈的; **～ abdominal pain** 火辣辣的腹痛 **3** (scathing) 严苛的; **a ～ indictment of the present regime** 对现政权的严厉控诉
sea: ～ route *n* 海上航道; **～ salt** *n* [u] 海盐; **～scape** *n* **1** (view) 海景; **2** (picture) 海景画; **Sea Scout** *n* 海上童子军; **～ shanty** *n* 水手号子; **～shell** *n* 海贝壳; **～shore** *n* **1** (part of coast) 海岸; **2** (beach) 海滩; **～sick** *adj* 晕船的; **to be** *or* **feel ～sick** 晕船; **～sickness** *n* [u] 晕船; **to suffer from ～sickness** 晕船
seaside /ˈsiːsaɪd/ *n* 海滨; **to go to the ～** 去海边; **a ～ holiday** 海滨假日
seaside resort *n* 海滨胜地
season /ˈsiːzn/
A *n* **1** ▸**p. 692** (time of year) 季节; **the four ～s** 四季; **the dry/rainy ～** 旱季/雨季 **2** (for particular activity) 时节; **the growing/planting ～** 生长/种植季节; **the mating/breeding ～** 交配/繁殖季节; **to be in/out of ～** 当令/不当令; **vegetables in ～** 时令蔬菜; **nowadays you can get apples in and out of ～** 现在一年四季都能买到苹果; **the tourist ～** 旅游旺季; **the football/cricket/rugby ～** 足球/板球/橄榄球赛季; **the hunting/fishing ～** 狩猎期/渔汛期 **3** (holiday period) 节期; **the Christmas ～** 圣诞节期; **S～'s greetings!** (on Christmas card) 圣诞快乐!; **the ～ of Advent/Lent** 降临节/大斋节期; **the ～ of good will** 圣诞节 **4** Radio, TV, Theat 上演期; **a Shaw/Beethoven ～** 萧伯纳/贝多芬作品演出季 **5** dated (period of social activity) **the ～** 社交季节 [传统上英国上层社会进行时尚社交活动的时期] **6** (suitable moment) 时机; **to every thing there is a ～** liter 万物皆有时 **7** (period of sexual receptivity) [雌性哺乳动物的] 发情期; **to come into ～** 发情 **8** colloq (season ticket) 季票
B *vt* **1** (prepare by drying) 风干处理 ‹*timber*›; (prepare by steeping) 浸泡处理 ‹*cask*›; (prepare for use) 用油润 ‹*pan*› **2** Culin 给…加作料; **a well-～ed dish** 味道调得极好的一道菜 **3** fig liter (enliven) 为…增添趣味; **a speech ～ed with wit** 妙趣横生的演讲
seasonable /ˈsiːznəbl/ *adj* 应时的; **～ dishes** 当令菜肴
seasonal /ˈsiːzənl/ *adj* **1** (of the season) 节令性的 ‹*food, activity*› **2** (befitting festive period) 适合节日的; **he's full of ～ cheer** 他内心充满了节日的喜悦 **3** (fluctuating with seasons) 随季节变化的; **to vary on a ～ basis** 随季节变化
seasonal affective disorder *n* [u] 季节性情感紊乱
seasonally /ˈsiːzənəli/ *adv* 季节性地; **～ adjusted unemployment figures** 经季节因素调整的失业统计数字
seasoned /ˈsiːznd/ *adj* **1** (experienced) 经验丰富的 ‹*traveller*› **2** Constr 风干的 ‹*timber*› **3** Culin 调好味的 ‹*dish*›; **highly ～** 加了很多作料的
seasoning /ˈsiːznɪŋ/ *n* [c and u] 调味品
season ticket *n* 长期票; **a monthly/quarterly/yearly ～** 月票/季票/年票
season ticket holder *n* 长期票持有者
seat /siːt/
A *n* **1** (chair) (in room, at table) 椅子; (in car) 座椅; (in bus, train, hall, cinema, theatre) 座位; **an adjustable/a reclining ～** 可调节式座椅/靠椅; **a bicycle ～** 自行车车座; **to keep** *or* **save a ～ for sb.** 给某人留座位; **remain in your ～s, please** 请坐在原位; **take** *or* **have a ～!** 坐下! **2** (of chair) 座部; (of trousers) 后裆; (of lavatory) 座圈; **(to fly) by the ～ of one's pants** colloq 凭感觉(行事) **3** euph (buttocks) 臀部 **4** Brit (in parliament) 席位; (on committee etc.) 职位; **to win/lose a ～** 赢得/失去一席; **to take one's ～ in the Commons/Lords** Brit 就任下议院/上议院议员; **a ～ on the board/committee** 董事会/委员会职位 **5** (centre, base) 所在地; **the ～ of commerce** 商业重镇; **a ～ of learning** 学府; **the ～ of consciousness** 意识所在 **6** (residence) 宅邸
B *vt* **1** formal (assign place to) 为…安排座位 ‹*person*› **2** (have seats for) «*hall, coach*» 可供…就座; **the table ～s 12 at a pinch** 这张桌子挤得下 12 个人
C *v refl* **to ～ oneself at sth./next to sb.** 坐在某物/某人旁边

S

seatbelt /'si:tbelt/ *n* 安全带; **to put on one's ~** 系上安全带

seatbelt tensioner /'si:tbelt ˌtenʃənə(r)/ *n* 安全带张力器

seated /'si:tɪd/ *adj* 就座的; **please wait until everybody is ~** 请等到所有人都坐下

-seater /'si:tə(r)/ *combining form* (vehicle, sofa) 有…座位的; **a two~** (plane) 双座飞机; (car) 双座汽车; (sofa) 双人沙发

seating /'si:tɪŋ/ *n* [u] 1 (places) 座位 2 (arrangement) 座位安排

seating: ~ accommodation *n* [u] 座位; **~ arrangements** *npl* 座位安排; **~ capacity** *n* [u] 座位数量; **~ plan** *n* 座位表

sea: ~ urchin *n* 海胆; **~ view** *n* 海景; **~ wall** *n* 防波堤

seaward /'si:wəd/
A *adj* 朝海的
B *adv* (*also* **seawards**) 朝海

sea: ~water *n* [u] 海水; **~way** *n* 1 (sea route) 海上航道; 2 (inland channel) 海道 [可供海船通行的内陆水道]; **~weed** *n* [u] 海藻; **~worthiness** *n* [u] (of a ship) 适航性; **~worthy** *adj* 适于航海的

sebaceous /sɪ'beɪʃəs/ *adj* 1 (resembling sebum) 皮脂状的 2 (secreting sebum) 分泌皮脂的; **~ duct** *or* **gland/cyst** 皮脂腺/囊肿

seborrhoea, Amer **seborrhea** /ˌsebə'rɪə/ ▸**p. 377** *n* [u] 脂溢性皮炎

sebum /'si:bəm/ *n* [u] 皮脂

S

SEC *abbr* Amer = **Securities and Exchange Commission**

sec¹ /sek/ *n* colloq (second) 秒; (short instant) 片刻; **hang on a ~!** 稍等一会儿!

sec² *abbr* = **secant**

Sec. *abbr* = **secretary**

secant /'si:kənt/ *n* 割线

secateurs /ˌsekə'tɜ:z, 'sekətɜ:z/ *npl* Brit 整枝剪

secede /sɪ'si:d/ *vi* [从政党等中] 退出; **to ~ from sth.** 退出某组织

secession /sɪ'seʃn/ *n* [u] [从政党等中的] 退出

secessionist /sɪ'seʃənɪst/
A *adj* 支持脱离的
B *n* 分离主义者

seclude /sɪ'klu:d/ *vt* 隔离; **to ~ oneself from the world** 与世隔绝

secluded /sɪ'klu:dɪd/ *adj* 僻静的 ‹*spot, corner*›

seclusion /sɪ'klu:ʒn/ *n* [u] 1 (privacy) 僻静; **~ from sth.** 离开某物的清静; **to live in ~** 隐居; **in the ~ of one's own home** 在僻静的家中 2 (isolation from others) 隔绝; **certain religions demand the ~ of women** 某些宗教要求妇女与社会隔离

second¹ /'sekənd/ ▸**p. 521**
A *adj* 1 (next after first) 第二的; **the ~ row** 第二排; **a ~ marriage** 二婚; **(in) the ~ person** Ling （以）第二人称; **the ~ person singular** Ling 第二人称单数; **the ~ house** Cin, Theat 第二场; **to be ~ nature (to sb.)** 成为（某人的）第二天性; **one's ~ teeth** 恒齿 2 (in sequence) 第二的; **it's her ~ birthday** 这是她 2 岁生日; **on the ~ floor** 在 3 楼 3 (in name, title) 二世; **Henry the S~ of England** 英王亨利二世 4 (as fraction) 二分之一的 5 (additional) 另外的; **(to ask for) a ~ opinion** （征求）他人的意见; **to have a ~ look** 再仔细看一下; **a ~ helping** 添菜; **I want a ~ go on the ride** 我想再骑一次; **to get one's ~ wind** 恢复精力; **he didn't give it a ~ thought** 他想都没想; **to do sth. without (giving it) a ~ thought** 不假思索做某事; **to have ~ thoughts about sth./doing sth.** 对某事物/做某事有别的想法; **on ~ thoughts** 经重新考虑 6 (less important) 居第二位的 ‹*team*›; **the ~ violin** 第二小提琴手; **a ~ car/house** 第二辆车/第二套房子; **to be ~ only to sb./sth.** 仅次于某人/某事物 7 (alternate) 隔一的; **every ~ day** 每隔一天 8 (similar to predecessor) 类似的; **a ~ Watergate** 水门事件第二; **he thinks he's a ~ Churchill** 他把自己当作丘吉尔第二
B *n* 1 (in sequence) **the ~** 第二; **a good** *or* **close ~** 和第一名差距很小的第二名; **a poor ~** 和第一名差距很大的第二名; **~ in line (to the throne)** 排在第二位的（王位）继承者 2 (additional one) 第二个 3 Brit Univ 二级优等学位; **to get** *or* **be awarded a ~** 获得二级优等学位 4 Aut 二挡; **to put the car into ~** 给汽车挂二挡; **to change from first to ~** 从一挡换到二挡 5 (in date) 2 日; **the ~ of September** 九月二日 6 *usu pl* (defective goods) 次等品 7 **seconds** colloq (second helping) 加菜; **he had ~s of the meat and potatoes** 他吃了土豆烧肉添菜 8 (in boxing, wrestling) 助手; **~s out (of the ring)** 助手请退出（拳击台） 9 (speech of support) 附和 10 Mus (interval) 二度音; (notes constituting interval) 二度音程
C *adv* 1 (in sequence, competition) 第二位地; **I agreed to speak ~** 我答应第二个发言; **to come** *or* **be placed ~** 获得第二名; **to be ~ to none** 无与伦比; **to row ~** Sport 担任尾桨手 2 (in importance) 其次 3 (also, in addition) 另外
D *vt* 1 (assist) 做…的助手 ‹*boxer, duellist*› 2 (formally support) 支持 ‹*motion, resolution, vote*›; **to be ~ed by sb.** 得到某人的支持; **I'll ~ that!** colloq 我完全赞成!

second² /'sekənd/ *n* 1 ▸**p. 831** (unit of time) 秒; **one ~ past 4 o'clock** 4 点零 1 秒 2 colloq (instant, moment) 片刻; **in ~s** 片刻之间; **within ~s he was asleep** 不一会儿他就睡着了; **wait just a ~** 稍等片刻; **in a ~** (immediately) 马上; (very quickly) 很快; **we'll be taking off in a ~** 我们很快就要起飞了; **this** *or* **it won't take a ~** 这马上就好; **just a ~! I was in the queue before you** 等一下!

Seasons

■ There are various names for each season in Chinese:

spring	春天	春季	春
summer	夏天	夏季	夏
autumn/fall	秋天	秋季	秋
winter	冬天	冬季	冬

The four seasons of the year are spring, summer, autumn and winter
= 一年有四季，春、夏、秋、冬

■ Parts of each season:

early spring	初春	早春	
the middle of spring	仲春		
late spring	晚春	残春	暮春
early summer	初夏		
midsummer	仲夏		
late summer	晚夏	夏末	残暑
early autumn	初秋		
the middle of autumn	仲秋		
late autumn	晚秋	暮秋	残秋
early winter	初冬		
midwinter	仲冬		
late winter	晚冬	残冬	

Note that 残春, 暮春, 残暑, 暮秋, 残秋 and 残冬 are fairly literary.

With / without prepositions

■ In Chinese, the only preposition used with a season is 在. Otherwise the preposition is omitted entirely:

I like to travel in the summer
= 我喜欢夏天旅游

We often go to Edinburgh in the summer, when the Festival is on
= 我们常在夏天举办艺术节的时候去爱丁堡

She will stay with her grandparents during the summer
= 她夏季将和祖父母待在一起

I need to prepare myself for the driving test throughout the summer
= 我整个夏天都要准备驾驶考试

He was born in the summer of 1995
= 他 1995 年夏天出生

My brother will graduate in early summer
= 我弟弟将在初夏毕业

I met her on a summer evening
= 在一个夏天的晚上我遇见了她

■ In the following phrases, Chinese and English both omit the preposition:

every summer
= 每年夏天

this summer
= 今年夏天

that summer
= 那年夏天

next summer
= 明年夏天

last summer
= 去年夏天

every other summer
= 每隔一个夏天

one day in summer
= 夏季的一天

Combinations

spring colours
= 春色

spring flowers
= 春花

summer school
= 夏季学校

midsummer nights
= 仲夏之夜

autumn leaves
= 秋叶

an autumn day
= 秋季的一天

the winter sales
= 冬季大减价

winter sports
= 冬季运动

我刚才排在你前面; **within ~s he was asleep** 他一下子就睡着了 3 (of angle, longitude, latitude) 秒; **20 degrees and 15 ~s west** 向西 20 度 15 秒

second³ /sɪ'kɒnd/ *vt* Brit 调遣; **to ~ sb. overseas** *or* **abroad** 把某人调往海外服役; **I was ~ed to a public relations unit** 我被调到公关部

secondarily /'sekəndrəli, Amer ˌsekən'derəli/ *adv* 次要地; **it was agreed, ~, that ...** 其次，大家同意…

secondary /'sekəndri, Amer -deri/

A *adj* 1 (less important) 次要的; (subsidiary) 从属的; **to be ~ to sth.** 次于某事物; **two ~ subjects** 两门副科; **~ stress** *or* **accent** Ling 次重音 2 (derived from primary source) 间接的; **~ industry** 二次产业 3 Sch 中等的 ‹*education*›; 中学的 ‹*student*›

B *n* 继发性癌症

secondary: ~ colour *n* 间色; **green is a ~ colour** 绿色是一种合成色; **~ evidence** *n* [u] 间接证据; **~ forest** *n* [u and c] 次生林; **~ glazing** *n* [u] [窗框的] 第二层玻璃; **~ health care** *n* [u] 二级医疗保健; **~ infection** *n* [c and u] 继发性感染; **~ modern, ~ modern school** *ns* Brit Hist 现代中等学校; **~ picket** *n* Brit [阻止未参加罢工的工人向公司供货的] 二级纠察员; **~ picketing** *n* [u] Brit 二级纠察封锁; **~ road** *n* 支路; **~ school** *n* [c and u] 中等学校; **a ~-school teacher** 中学教师; **~ tumour** *n* 继发瘤

second: ~ ballot *n* 二次投票; **~ base** *n* (position) 二垒; (player) 二垒手; **to be on/reach ~ base** 在第二垒/跑上二垒

second best

A *n* 次优者; **to settle for** *or* **take ~** 退而求其次

B **second-best** *adj* 1 次优的; **to come off second-best (in sth.)** （在某事上）居第二位; **he came off** Brit *or* **out** Amer **second-best** 他被击败了 2 (inferior) 退而求其次的

second chamber *n* 上议院

second class

A *n* 1 [c] (in rank) 二级; **to rank sb./sth. in the ~ (of sth.)** 将某人/某事物列为（某事物的）二流 2 [u] Brit Post 第二类邮件 3 [u] Transp 二等舱 4 [c] Brit Univ 二级优等

B **second-class** *adj* 1 pej (second rate) 二流的; (inferior) 次等的; **a second-class citizen** 二等公民 2 Brit Post 第二类的 ‹*letter, postage*› 3 (standard-class) 二等的 ‹*hotel, carriage, seat*› 4 Brit Univ 二级优等的 ‹*degree*›

C *adv* 1 Post 按第二类邮件 ‹*send, post*› 2 Transp 乘二等舱 ‹*travel, fly*›

second: S~ Coming *n* [最后审判时的] 基督复临; **~ cousin** *n* (male, on the paternal side) 远房堂兄弟; (female, on the paternal side) 远房堂姐妹; (male, on the maternal side) 远房表兄弟; (female, on the maternal side) 远房表姐妹; ▸remove B14; **~-degree burns** *npl* 二度烧伤; **~-degree murder** *n* Amer 二级谋杀罪

seconder /'sekəndə(r)/ *n* 附议者

second: ~-generation *adj* 1 (denoting origin) 第二代的; **she was a ~-generation American** 她是第二代美国人; 2 (advanced) 改进型的 ‹*model, device*›; **~-generation computers** 第二代电脑; **~-guess** *vt* colloq 1 (predict) 预测 ‹*decision, consequence*›; 2 (outguess) 比…猜得更准; 3 esp Amer 放马后炮; **~ hand** *n* 秒针

second-hand

A *adj* 1 (pre-owned) 二手的; **~ books** 旧书 2 (selling used goods) 出售旧货的; **a ~ bookshop** 旧书店 3 (indirect) 间接的 ‹*report, account*›

B *adv* 1 (from previous owner) 作为旧货 ‹*buy, obtain*› 2 (indirectly) 间接地 ‹*hear, learn*›

second: ~ in command *n* 副指挥官; **the managing director and his ~ in command** 董事总经理和他的副手; **~ language** *n* 第二语言; **~ lieutenant** *n* (in army) 陆军少尉; (in US air force) 空军少尉

secondly /'sekəndli/ *adv* 其次

second mate *n* = **second officer**

secondment /sɪ'kɒndmənt/ *n* Brit 临时调任; **to be on ~ (from sth.) (to sth.)** （从某职位）临时调任（到某职位）

second: ~ mortgage *n* 二次抵押; **~ name** *n* 1 (surname) 姓; 2 (second forename) 中间名; **~ officer** *n* (position) 二副职位; (person) 二副; **~ person** *n* [u] 第二人称; **in the ~ person** 为第二人称形式; **~ person singular/plural** 第二人称单数/复数; **~-rate** *adj* 二流的 ‹*actor, performance, novel*›; 次等的 ‹*goods, product*›; **~-rater** *n* colloq 平庸的人; **~ sight** *n* [u] 预见力; **to have the gift of ~ sight** 有天生的预见力; **~ strike** *n* 第二次打击 [指核战争中的还击]; **~ string** *n* (player) 替补队员; (event) 替补; **a ~-string goalkeeper** 替补守门员

secrecy /'siːkrəsi/ *n* [u] (condition) 秘密; (act) 保密; **in ~** 秘密地; **why all the ~?** 为什么要遮遮掩掩？; **to swear sb. to ~** 要某人发誓保密

secret /'siːkrɪt/

A *n* 1 [c] (undisclosed fact) 秘密; **to keep a ~** 保守秘密; **to let sb. in on a ~** 把秘密透露给某人; **to make no ~ of sth.** 不隐瞒某事; **to have no ~s from sb.** 对某人毫无隐瞒 2 [c] (key factor) 诀窍; **the ~ of success** 成功的秘诀 3 [u] (secrecy) **in ~** 秘密地; **there's no ~ about ...** 关于…没有任何秘密可言

B *adj* 1 (kept private) 秘密的 ‹*plan, negotiations, admirer*›; **to keep sth. ~ from sb.** 对某人隐瞒某事; **to be a ~ drinker** 偷偷摸摸喝酒 2 (concealed, hidden) 隐蔽的 ‹*door, passage, drawer*› 3 (secretive) 遮遮掩掩的; **to be ~ about sth.** 对某事守口如瓶

secret agent *n* 特工人员

secretarial /ˌsekrə'teəriəl/ *adj* 秘书的 ‹*work, skills*›; **the ~ staff** 秘书人员; **a ~ course/college** 文秘课程/学院

secretariat /ˌsekrə'teəriət/ *n* 秘书处

secretary /'sekrətri, Amer -teri/ ▸**p. 409** *n* 1 Admin 秘书 2 (official of club etc.) 干事 3 **Secretary** Brit Pol 大臣; Amer 部长

Secretary: ~ General *n* 秘书长; **~ of State** *n* 1 (in UK) 大臣; 2 (in US) 国务卿

secret ballot *n* [c and u] 无记名投票

secrete¹ /sɪ'kriːt/ *vt* Biol 分泌 ‹*fluid, hormone*›

secrete² *vt* (hide) 藏匿

secretion /sɪ'kriːʃn/ *n* 1 [c] (substance) 分泌物 2 [u] (process) 分泌

secretive /'siːkrətɪv/ *adj* 遮遮掩掩的; **to be ~ about sth.** 对某事守口如瓶

secretively /'siːkrətɪvli/ *adv* (mysteriously) 神秘地; (furtively) 遮遮掩掩地

secretiveness /'siːkrətɪvnɪs/ *n* [u] 遮遮掩掩

secretly /'siːkrɪtli/ *adv* 秘密地 ‹*plot, work*›; 暗暗地 ‹*hope, believe, admire*›

secret: ~ police *n* + *v sing or pl* **the ~ police** 秘密警察; **~ service** *n* Brit [政府的] 特务机关; **S~ Service** *n* (in US) **the S~ Service** [财政部的] 特工处; **~ society** *n* 秘密社团; **~ weapon** *n* lit, fig 秘密武器

sect /sekt/ *n* 教派

sectarian /sek'teəriən/

A *adj* 教派的 ‹*beliefs, views*›; 教派间的 ‹*conflict, violence*›

B *n* 教派成员

sectarianism /sek'teəriənɪzəm/ *n* [u] 宗派主义

section /'sekʃn/

A *n* 1 (part) 部分; (of book, text) 节; **to divide the cake/fruit into ~s** 把蛋糕/水果分成几份; **~ 1, paragraph 3** 第 1 节第 3 段; **the front/rear ~ of the train** 火车的前部/后部; **this ~ of the wood is planted with beech** 树林的这一片种的是山毛榉; **you'll find that book in the reference ~** 你可以在工具书部找到那本书 2 (of population, group) 阶层; (in organization, party, etc.) 部门; (in orchestra, band) 乐器组; **the finance ~ of the company** 公司的财务部; **the brass ~** 铜管乐器组 3 Mil 小分队 4 Rail (part of network) 路段 5 Math 截面; **a horizontal/longitudinal ~** 横截面/竖截面 6 Biol, Geol 切片 7 Med 切开; **delivered by Caesarean ~** 剖腹生产的 8 Amer (district) 地段; **the business/residential ~** 商业区/住宅区 9 Amer (in land surveying) 平方英里

B *vt* 1 (divide up) 把…分成部分 ‹*text, library*› 2 Med 切开 3 Brit (confine to psychiatric hospital) 把…送入精神病院

Phrasal verb

- **section off** *vt* [**~ sth. off, ~ off sth.**] 隔出 ‹*area*›

sectional /'sekʃənl/ *adj* 1 (made in parts) 组合式的 2 (factional) 阶层的

sectionalism /'sekʃənəlɪzəm/ *n* [u] pej (to own group) 本位主义; (to local concerns) 地方主义

sector /'sektə(r)/ *n* 1 Comm 行业; **the manufacturing/service/banking ~** 制造业/服务业/银行业 2 (part) 部分; **a broad ~ of the viewing public** 广大电视观众 3 Mil (zone) 防区 4 Math (of circle) 扇形 5 Math (instrument) 函数尺 6 Comput 扇区

sectorial /sek'tɔːrɪəl/ *adj* formal 部门的

secular /'sekjʊlə(r)/ *adj* 1 (non-religious) 世俗的 ‹*education, music, outlook*› 2 Relig 在俗的 ‹*priest*›

secularism /'sekjʊlərɪzəm/ *n* [u] (doctrine) 世俗主义; (political system) 世俗制度

secularization /ˌsekjʊləraɪ'zeɪʃn, Amer -rɪ'z-/ *n* [u] 世俗化

secularize /'sekjʊləraɪz/ *vt* 使世俗化 ‹*society, education*›

secure /sɪ'kjʊə(r)/

A *adj* 1 (firmly fixed) 牢固的 ‹*structure, ladder*›; **to make sth. ~** 把某物弄牢固; **she made the rope ~ around the trunk of a tree** 她把绳子牢牢地系在树干上 2 (protected) 安全的 ‹*place, hideout*›; 稳定的 ‹*job, income*›; **to be ~ against** *or* **from sth.** 不受某事物的威胁; **make sure the house is ~ before you leave it** 出门前确保把门窗关好; **is your pension ~ against inflation?** 你的养老金不会受通货膨胀的影响吗？ 3 (untroubled) 安宁的 ‹*feeling, family background*›; **he didn't feel ~ on his own** 他自己一个人感觉不太踏实; **to be ~ in the knowledge that ...** 知道…而感到踏实

B *vt* 1 (fix or fasten firmly) 系牢 ‹*rope*›; 关紧 ‹*door, window*› 2 (make safe) 保护 ‹*house, premises*›; 使…稳固 ‹*position*› 3 Fin 为…担保 ‹*debt*›; **the loan is ~d on your house** 这笔贷款是拿你的住房作抵押的 4 (acquire) 获得 ‹*position, funds, consent*›

secured: ~ bond *n* 1 Fin 担保债券; 2 Amer Jur (bail) 保释金; **~ loan** *n* 担保贷款

securely /sɪ'kjʊəli/ *adv* 1 (firmly) 牢固地 ‹*fasten, wrap*› 2 (safely) 安全地 ‹*locked up*›

secure unit *n* (for young offenders) [关押14至20岁罪犯的] 青少年监狱; (in psychiatric hospital) 安全隔离区

securities /sɪ'kjʊərətɪz/ *npl* 证券; **~ market/company** 证券市场/公司

Securities and Exchange Commission *n* Amer 证券交易委员会

securitization /sɪˌkjʊərɪtaɪ'zeɪʃn/ *n* [u] 证券化; **the ~ market** 证券化市场

securitize /sɪ'kjʊərɪtaɪz/ *vt* 使证券化

security /sɪ'kjʊərəti/ *n* 1 [u] (of person, state, investment) 安全; **~ from** *or* **against sth.** 免遭

S

某物; ~ **of employment** 就业安全 **2** [u] (procedures, measures) 安全措施; ~ **is very strict at the site** 这个工地的安保措施非常严格; **a ~ barrier/camera** 安全屏障/监控摄像头 **3** [u] + *v sing or pl* (department) 保安部门; **call ~!** 去叫保安! **4** [u and c] (guarantee) 担保; **to take/leave sth. as ~** 接受某物/把某物作为抵押; **to stand ~ for sb.** 为某人担保 **5** [c and u] (safeguard) 保障; ~ **against sth.** 免受某物之苦的保障 **6** [c] *usu pl* Fin 证券; ~ **company/market/trading** 证券公司/市场/交易

security: ~ **alarm** *n* 安全报警器; ~ **blanket** *n* **1** (for child) 安乐毯; fig 安慰物; **2** fig (protection) 安全保障; **3** Brit (on information) 保密措施; ~ **clearance** *n* [u and c] 忠诚度审核批准; **S~ Council** *n* **the S~ Council** (联合国) 安全理事会; ~ **forces** *npl* 保安部队; ~ **guard** ▸p. 409 *n* 保安; ~ **leak** *n* 泄密; ~ **measures** *npl* 安全措施; ~ **officer** ▸p. 409 *n* 安全官员; ~ **police** *n* [u] + *v sing or pl* 治安警察; ~ **precaution** *n* 安全预防措施; ~ **risk** *n* (thing) 威胁因素; (person) 危险分子; ~ **van** *n* Brit 押钞车

sedan /sɪ'dæn/ *n* **1** Hist ~ **(chair)** 轿子 **2** Amer Aut 小轿车

sedate¹ /sɪ'deɪt/ *adj* **1** (unhurried) 不慌不忙的 **2** (quiet) 平淡的

sedate² *vt* 给…服用镇静剂

sedately /sɪ'deɪtli/ *adv* 镇定地

S

sedateness /sɪ'deɪtnɪs/ *n* [u] (of manner, pace) 从容不迫; (of person) 镇定; (of town, lifestyle) 平淡

sedation /sɪ'deɪʃn/ *n* [u] 药物镇静; **to be under ~** 处于用药后的镇静状态

sedative /'sedətɪv/
A *n* 镇静剂
B *adj attrib* 镇静的 ‹*effect*›; ~ **drug/action** 镇静剂/作用

sedentary /'sedntri, Amer -teri/ *adj* 需要久坐的 ‹*occupation*›; 惯于久坐的 ‹*person*›; ~ **lifestyle/habits** 坐着不动的生活方式/久坐的习惯

sedge /sedʒ/ *n* [u and c] 莎草

sediment /'sedɪmənt/ *n* [u and c] **1** (dregs) 沉淀物 **2** Geol 沉积物

sedimentary /ˌsedɪ'mentri, Amer -təri/ *adj* 沉积形成的; ~ **rock** 沉积岩

sedimentation /ˌsedɪmen'teɪʃn/ *n* [u] Geol 沉积; Chem 沉淀

sedition /sɪ'dɪʃn/ *n* [u] formal (action) 煽动叛乱; (speech) 煽动性言论

seditious /sɪ'dɪʃəs/ *adj* formal 煽动叛乱的 ‹*act, faction*›; 煽动性的 ‹*pamphlet, speech*›

seduce /sɪ'djuːs, Amer -'duːs/ *vt* **1** fig (attract, charm) 引诱; **to ~ sb. into doing sth.** 诱使某人做某事; **to ~ sb. away from sth.** 诱使某人离开某事物; **he was ~d by the prospect of easy money** 他受到轻松赚钱前景的诱惑 **2** (sexually) 诱奸

seducer /sɪ'djuːsə(r), Amer -'duːs-/ *n* 引诱者

seduction /sɪ'dʌkʃn/ *n* [c and u] **1** (sexual enticement) 诱奸 **2** (attractive quality) 魅力; **the ~s of city life** 城市生活的诱惑

seductive /sɪ'dʌktɪv/ *adj* **1** (sexually alluring) 性感撩人的 **2** (attractive) 吸引人的 ‹*offer, argument*›

seductively /sɪ'dʌktɪvli/ *adv* **1** (alluringly) 勾人地; **she winked at him ~** 她对他使了个撩人的眼神 **2** (temptingly) 吸引人地

seductiveness /sɪ'dʌktɪvnɪs/ *n* [u] **1** (sexual charm) 撩人 **2** (attractiveness) (of offer) 诱惑; (of argument) 吸引

seductress /sɪ'dʌktrɪs/ *n* 勾引男人的女子

sedulous /'sedjʊləs, Amer 'sedʒʊləs/ *adj* formal 孜孜不倦的 ‹*person*›; 小心周到的 ‹*attention*›; 不懈的 ‹*devotion*›

sedulously /'sedjʊləsli, Amer 'sedʒʊləsli/ *adv* formal 孜孜不倦地 ‹*pursue, strive*›; 小心周到地 ‹*guard*›

see¹ /siː/ (*pt* **saw**, *pp* **seen**)
A *vt* **1** (perceive) 看见; **to ~ (that) ...** 看见…; **to ~ what/where/how/if ...** 看到什么/哪里/如何/是否…; **I couldn't ~ if anyone was at the door** 我看不到门口是否有人; **to ~ sb./sth. do sth.** 看见某人/某物做某事; **to ~ sb./sth. doing sth.** 看到某人/某物正在做某事; **I saw him break the window/climbing into the house** 我看见他打破窗户/爬进房子里了; **it was too dark to ~ anything** 天太黑了, 什么都看不见; **to ~ with one's own eyes** 亲眼看见; **for all (the world) to ~** 显而易见; **not to be seen dead (doing sth.)** colloq 死也不(做某事); **I wouldn't be seen dead in that dress/jogging!** 我坚决不穿那件连衣裙/参加慢跑!; **to ~ sb. damned** *or* **hanged (first)** colloq (先) 让某人见鬼去吧; **to ~ the back** *or* **last of sb./sth.** colloq 终于摆脱某人/某事物; **to ~ sth. coming** 看到某物过来; fig 预料到会出某问题; **to ~ one's way (clear) to doing sth.** colloq (be able) 认为有可能做某事; (find convenient) 方便做某事; **could you ~ your way clear to lending me £500?** 你能借给我 500 英镑吗?; **not to be able to ~ the wood for the trees** colloq 只见树木不见森林; **to ~ stars** colloq 眼冒金星; **to ~ the light (of day)** (be born) 出生; fig (be produced) 问世; **he didn't think the footage should ever ~ the light of day** 他认为那段片子根本就不该播出 **2** (watch) 看 ‹*film, TV programme*›; 观看 ‹*match, game*› **3** (inspect) 查看 **4** (meet by chance) 遇见; **you'll never guess who I saw at the party!** 你绝对猜不出我在聚会上看到谁了!; **to happen to ~ sb.** 碰巧遇见某人; **I'm off now! ~ you (around)!** colloq 我得走了! 再见!; **I'll be ~ing you** colloq 再见 **5** (visit a person) 拜访; (visit a place) 参观; **do come and ~ us again** 一定要再来看我们; **I've always wanted to ~ India** 我一直希望去印度游玩; **to ~ the sights** 观光; **to ~ the world** 游历世界 **6** (have a meeting with) 会晤; (receive a visit from) 接见; **to ~ sb. about sth.** 为某事物会见某人; **what is it you want to ~ me about?** 你找我有什么事?; **to ~ a** *or* **one's doctor** 去看医生; **you should ~ a lawyer** 你应该见一下律师; **he's far too ill to ~ anyone** 他身体很不好, 不能见任何人 **7** (spend time with) 与…在一起; colloq (have relationship with) 与…交往; **to ~ a lot of sb.** 与某人常待在一起; **she's ~ing a married man** 她和一个已婚男子有染; **are you ~ing anyone?** 你在跟谁交往吗? **8** (understand, grasp) 领会 ‹*meaning*›; 看清 ‹*problem*›; **to ~ a joke** 听懂笑话; **can't you ~ (that) she loves you!** 你看不出来她爱你吗!; **to ~ how/where/what ...** 明白如何/哪里/什么…; **do you ~ what I mean?** 你明白我的意思吗?; **I just can't ~ what you're driving at** 我就是不明白你到底想说什么 **9** (interpret) 看待; **to ~ sth. from sb.'s point of view** 从某人的角度看待某事物; **the way** *or* **as I see it ...** 在我看来…; **to ~ eye to eye (with sb./on sth.)** (和某人/在某事上) 意见一致 **10** (envisage) 设想; **I don't ~ her changing her mind** 我无法想象她会改变主意; **I just don't ~ him in that role** 我无法想象他扮演这个角色 **11** (understand, find out) 得知; **I ~ (that) the minister has resigned** 我获悉部长已经辞职; **~ who's (knocking) at the door** 看看谁在敲门; **I think I ~ where the problem lies** 我想我知道问题出在哪儿了; **I'll ~ what I can do to help** 我看看能帮什么忙; **to ~ into the future** 预见未来; **it remains to be seen (if** *or* **whether ...)** (是否…) 有待揭晓 **12** (make sure) 确保; **~ that all the doors are locked** 确保所有的门都已锁好; **to ~ sb. right** colloq 保证不亏待某人 **13** (experience, witness) 经历; **my coat has seen a lot of hard wear** 我的外套已经穿得很旧了; **to have seen better days** 曾经有过一段好日子; **we'll never ~ his like** *or* **the like of him again** 我们再也不会遇到他这样的人了; **to have seen it all** *or* **everything** 什么都见识过; **to ~ service** 服役; **a period which saw the birth of computer science** 见证了计算机科学诞生的时代 **14** (be the scene of) 是…的发生地; **the theatre saw many fine productions in its heyday** 该剧院在鼎盛时期上演过许多精品 **15** (escort) 送; **to ~ sb. across** *or* **over sth.** 护送某人走过某处; **to ~ sb. across the road** 护送某人过马路; **to ~ sb. home** 送某人回家; **to ~ sb. off the premises** 送某人离场 **16** (find in particular condition) 发觉; **he hated to ~ her so unhappy** 他不愿意看她这么不高兴; **it was unpleasant ~ing the house so neglected** 看到房子这样疏于照管, 真让人难过 **17** (find quality in) 看中; **to ~ sth. in sb./sth.** 看中某人/某物的某种品质; **what on earth does she ~ in him?** 她到底看上他什么了? **18** (imagine) 好似看到; **to ~ things** 幻视; **in the darkness I saw a monster lurking behind every tree** 在黑暗中我仿佛看到每棵树后都潜伏着怪物 **19** (demonstrate) 表明; **it has already been seen that ...** 我们已经看到… **20** (refer to) 参看; ~ **page 120** 见第 120 页
B *vi* **1** (have the power of sight) 有视力; (use sight) 看得见; **as you can ~** 正如你所看到的; **to ~ for miles** 看到很远的地方; **it's too dark! I can't ~ to read** 天太黑了! 我看不成书了; **so I ~** fig 我知道了; **to ~ double** 看成重影; **to ~ red** fig colloq 火冒三丈 **2** (understand) 明白; **the whole thing is out of the question, ~?** 整件事情已经不可能了, 明白吗?; **~ here (now)!** 听好了!; **as far as I can ~** 在我看来; **you ~** colloq 要知道 [插入语] **3** (find out, check) 查看; **has the post come yet? — I don't know, I'll go and ~** 邮件到了吗? ——我不知道, 我去看看; **wait and ~!** 等着瞧吧!; **suck it and ~** colloq 自己试试看 **4** (think, consider) 想一想; **let me/let's ~** 让我/让我们考虑一下
C *v refl* **he saw himself already elected** 他设想自己已经当选; **I can't ~ myself as** *or* **being ...** 我无法想象自己成为…; **I can't ~ myself as a writer** 我无法想象自己是个作家

Phrasal verbs

- **see about** *vt* [~ **about sth.**] 处理; **I must ~ about lunch soon** 我马上得去做午饭; **he needs to ~ about getting the car serviced** 他需要找人修车; **we'll (soon) ~ about that!** colloq 我们(很快)就会见分晓!
- **see in** *vt* [~ **sth. in,** ~ **in sth.**] 迎接…的到来; **we're going to ~ in the New Year** 我们就要过新年了
- **see off** *vt* [~ **sb. off,** ~ **off sb.**] **1** (say farewell to) 送别; **we all went to the airport to ~ her off** 我们都去机场为她送行了 **2** (chase after) 驱赶
- **see out**
  A [~ **sb. out**] *vt* **1** (escort from premises) 送…出去 **2** (be present at sb.'s death) 看着…死去; (live or last till sb.'s death) 寿命比…长
  B [~ **sth. out**] *vt* (remain till end of) 持续到…结束; **we've got enough fuel to ~ the winter out** 我们有足够的燃料过冬
- **see over** *vt* [~ **over sth.**] 察看
- **see through** *vt* **1** [~ **through sb./sth.**] (not be deceived by) 看穿; **to ~ through sb.'s little game** colloq 看穿某人的小伎俩 **2** [~ **sth. through**] (not abandon) 把…做到底 ‹*undertaking*›; **to ~ sth. through to the bitter end** 把某事坚持到底 **3** [~ **sb. through**] (support) 帮助…度过; (satisfy) 使维持下来; **to ~ sb. through sth.** 帮助某人度过某事; **I've got just enough money to ~ me through until pay day!** 我的钱只能撑到发工资的那天!
- **see to** *vt* [~ **to sth.**] 处理; **the sink is**

blocked; I'll have to ~ to it 洗涤槽堵了，我得疏通一下；**all the sweets have gone; the children saw to that!** hum 所有的糖果全没了；这都是那帮孩子干的好事！；**to ~ to it that ...** 确保…；**will you ~ to it that all the windows are shut?** 麻烦你把所有的窗户关上好吗？

see² *n* Relig 主教教区；**the Holy See** 宗座

seed /siːd/

A *n* **1** [u and c] Bot, Hort (fruit pip) 籽；(for sowing) 种子；**the pod bursts, and the ~s are scattered** 豆荚爆裂，豆粒散落一地；**grape/pomegranate ~s** 葡萄籽/石榴籽；**a packet of ~(s)** 一包种子；**to sow the ~s in a shallow trench** 在浅沟里播种；**to go** *or* **run to ~** «*plant*» 花谢结籽；fig «*person*» 衰败 **2** [c] fig (beginning) 萌芽；**the ~s of doubt were already sown in her mind** 她的头脑中已经埋下了怀疑的种子 **3** [c] Sport 种子选手；**the top** *or* **first ~** 头号种子选手 **4** [u] archaic (descendants) 后裔

B *vt* **1** (sow) 在…播种 ‹*bed, lawn*›；**to ~ a field with rye** 在地里播下黑麦种子 **2** (remove seeds from) 去掉…的籽 ‹*grape, raisin*› **3** Meteorol 催…化雨 ‹*clouds*› **4** Sport 确定…为种子选手 ‹*player*›；**a ~ed player** 种子选手

C *vi* **1** (produce seeds) 结籽；**mulch encourages plants to ~ freely** 护根能促进植物顺利结实 **2** (sow seeds) 播种；**I have ~ed along the edge of the lawn** 我沿着草坪的边缘撒了种子

D *v refl* **to ~ itself** 靠自身种子繁殖

seed: ~bed *n* **1** (for plants) 苗床；**2** fig (breeding ground) 温床；**~ box** *n* 播种箱；**~ corn** *n* **1** (corn kept for sowing) 粮种；**2** fig (assets) 种子资产

seedily /ˈsiːdɪlɪ/ *adv* 不体面地 ‹*live*›；脏兮兮地 ‹*dress*›

seediness /ˈsiːdɪnɪs/ *n* [u] **1** (sordidness) 肮脏 **2** (shabbiness) 破旧 **3** dated (sickness) 身体不适

seeding /ˈsiːdɪŋ/ *n* **1** [u] Agric 播种 **2** [u] Meteorol (of clouds) 撒干冰 **3** [u and c] Sport 种子选手排名

seed leaf *n* 子叶

seedless /ˈsiːdlɪs/ *adj* 无核的 ‹*grape, raisin*›

seedling /ˈsiːdlɪŋ/ *n* 幼苗

seed: ~ merchant ▸**p. 409** *n* 种子商；**a ~ merchant's** 种子店；**~ money** *n* [u] 本钱；**~ pod** *n* 种荚；**~ potato** *n* 种用马铃薯；**~ tray** *n* 播种盘

seedy /ˈsiːdi/ *adj* **1** (sordid) 脏兮兮的 ‹*person*›；乌七八糟的 ‹*area*› **2** (shabby) 破旧的 ‹*hotel*› **3** dated colloq (unwell) 不舒服的；**to feel ~** 感到不适

seeing /ˈsiːɪŋ/

A *conj* **~ as** *or* **that ...** 因为…；**~ as he's ill, he's not very likely to come** 他生病了，所以不太可能会来；**~ as how ...** colloq 既然…

B *n* [u] 看见；**~ is believing** Prov 眼见为实

seek /siːk/ (*pt, pp* **sought**)

A *vt* **1** (try to obtain) 寻找 ‹*explanation, solution*›；追求 ‹*agreement, fame, person*›；**to ~ revenge** 伺机报复；**to ~ sb.'s approval** 征求某人的同意；**to ~ a second term of office** 争取连任；**to ~ one's fortune** 寻找发财机会 **2** (ask for) 请求 ‹*advice, permission*›；**she sought help from the police** 她向警察求助

B *vi* 寻找；**to ~ for** *or* **after sth.** 追求某物；**to ~ to do sth.** 试图做某事；**I was merely ~ing to clear up some of the confusion** 我只是想澄清一些混淆的地方

Phrasal verb

- **seek out** *vt* [**~ out sb./sth., ~ sb./sth. out**] 找出；**to ~ out and destroy** Mil 找到并消灭

seeker /ˈsiːkə(r)/ *n* 探求者；**a ~ after truth** 追求真理的人

-seeking /ˈsiːkɪŋ/ *combining form* 寻找的；**sun~/fun~ holidaymakers** 想晒日光浴/找乐子的度假者

seem /siːm/ *vi* **1** (look, feel) 好像；**how does she ~ today?** 她今天气色如何？；**taste a bit — it ~s all right to me** 你尝尝——我觉得还行；**they ~ like nice people** 他们看上去是好人；**we had to wait for what ~ed like ages** 我们不得不度日如年般地等待；**to ~ to do sth.** 好像做某事；**she ~s to have gone out** 她似乎已经出门了；**what ~s to be going on?** 出了什么事？；**to ~ as if** *or* **as though ...** 看起来好像… **2** (give impression) 让人觉得似乎；**it ~s ages since we got here** 我们来这里似乎已经很久了；**it ~s (that)** *or* **as if** *or* **as though ...** 看来…；**does it ~ as if the rain's stopping?** 雨有停下来的迹象吗？；**there ~ to me to be two possibilities** 我觉得有两种可能

seeming /ˈsiːmɪŋ/ *adj attrib* 表面上的 ‹*inability, indifference*›

seemingly /ˈsiːmɪŋli/ *adv* **1** (apparently) 表面上 ‹*innocent, interminable*› **2** (as far as one knows) 据我所知；**they've split up? — ~!** 他们分手了？——据说是的！

seemliness /ˈsiːmlɪnɪs/ *n* [u] (of behaviour, dress) 得体

seemly /ˈsiːmli/ *adj* 得体的 ‹*behaviour, dress*›；**it would be more ~ to ...** …会更恰当

seen /siːn/ *pp* ▸**see¹**

seep /siːp/ *vi* «*liquid, gas*» 渗出；«*light*» 透出；**to ~ out of sth.** 从某物中渗出；**to ~ into/under sth.** 渗入某物/渗到某物下面；**to ~ away** 渗漏掉；**to ~ through sth.** 渗透过某物

seepage /ˈsiːpɪdʒ/ *n* **1** [u] (escape of liquid, gas) 渗漏 **2** [c and u] (amount) 渗漏量

seer /ˈsiːə(r), sɪə(r)/ *n* **1** (prophet) 预言家 **2** (forecaster) [政治或经济前景的] 预测者

seersucker /ˈsɪəsʌkə(r)/ *n* [u and c] 泡泡纱

seesaw /ˈsiːsɔː/

A *n* **1** (for children) 跷跷板；**let's go on the ~!** 我们去玩跷跷板吧！ **2** (fluctuating situation) 交替局面；**the emotional ~ of a first love affair** 初恋的情感起伏

B *vi* **1** (move up and down) «*children*» 玩跷跷板；«*branch*» 上下摆动 **2** fig (vacillate) «*price*» 涨落；«*exchange rates, market*» 起伏；**the fight/debate ~ed** 战斗/辩论处于拉锯状态

seethe /siːð/ *vi* **1** (boil) «*water, sea*» 翻腾 **2** (be angry) 发怒；**to ~ with rage/impatience** 怒火中烧/因不耐烦而发怒 **3** (teem) 充满；**to ~ with sth.** 充满某物；**a country seething with unrest** 动荡不安的国家

see-through *adj* 透明的

segment

A /ˈsegmənt/ *n* **1** (of economy, market) 部门；(of population, vote) 部分 **2** Math (of circle) 圆缺；(of line) 线段 **3** Zool (of arthropod) 体节；(of worm, skull, limb) 节 **4** (of orange, grapefruit) 瓣

B /segˈment/ *vt* 分割；**insects with ~ed bodies** 节肢昆虫

C *vi* 分割；**to ~ into sth.** 切分成某物

segmental /segˈmentl/ *adj* **1** (divided into parts) 分节的 ‹*body*›；零碎的 ‹*arrangement*›；弓形的 ‹*arch, window*› **2** (of segments) 部分的 ‹*duplication*›；分割开的 ‹*boundary*› **3** Zool 体节的 **4** Phon 切分的

segmentation /ˌsegmenˈteɪʃn/ *n* [u] 分割；**market ~** 市场划分

segregate /ˈsegrɪgeɪt/ *vt* **1** (separate) 使…分开 ‹*sexes, fans*›；隔离 ‹*races*›；**to ~ sth./sb. from sth./sb.** 将某物/某人从某物/某人中分离出来 **2** (isolate) 使孤立；**to ~ sb. from society** 使某人脱离社会

segregated /ˈsegrəgeɪtɪd/ *adj* 按种族分开的 ‹*audience, facilities*›；种族隔离的 ‹*society, education*›

segregation /ˌsegrɪˈgeɪʃn/ *n* [u] **1** (of races) 种族隔离；(of rivals) 分离；(of prisoners) 隔离 **2** (separation) 分开；**~ from sth.** 从某物中的分离

segregationist /ˌsegrɪˈgeɪʃənɪst/

A *adj* 隔离主义的

B *n* 隔离主义者

Seine /seɪn/ ▸**p. 663** *pr n* **the (River) ~** 塞纳河

seine /seɪn/ *n* **~ (net)** 围网

seismic /ˈsaɪzmɪk/ *adj* **1** (connected with earthquakes) 地震的；(caused by earthquakes) 地震引起的；**~ area** *or* **region** 地震区 **2** fig (huge) 巨大的；(important) 重大的

seismograph /ˈsaɪzməgrɑːf, Amer -græf/ *n* 地震仪

seismographic /ˌsaɪzməˈgrɑːfɪk, Amer -ˈgræfɪk/ *adj* 地震仪的 ‹*data, network*›；测震学的 ‹*study*›

seismography /saɪzˈmɒgrəfi/ *n* [u] 测震学

seismologist /saɪzˈmɒlədʒɪst/ ▸**p. 409** *n* 地震学家

seismology /saɪzˈmɒlədʒi/ *n* [u] 地震学

seismometer /saɪzˈmɒmɪtə(r)/ *n* = **seismograph**

seize /siːz/

A *vt* **1** lit (take hold of) 抓住；**to ~ hold of sb./sth.** 抓住某人/某物；**to ~ sb. around the waist** 搅住某人的腰；**to ~ sb. by the arm/hair** 揪住某人的胳膊/头发 **2** fig (make use of, grasp) 利用；**to ~ an opportunity to ...** 抓住机会来…；**to ~ the initiative** 把握主动 **3** fig (affect) 攫住；**to be ~d by fear/pain** 感到一阵恐惧/疼痛；**~d by** *or* **with a sudden impulse** 一时冲动；**I was ~d by a sudden desire to tell her everything** 我突然想把一切都告诉她 **4** Mil (capture) 夺取；**rebel troops ~d the television station** 叛军占领了电视台 **5** (kidnap, abduct) 绑架 **6** (confiscate) 没收；(apprehend, arrest) 拘押

B *vi* = **seize up**

Phrasal verbs

- **seize on** *vt* = **seize upon**
- **seize up** *vi* **1** (cease to operate) «*engine, mechanism*» 停止运转；«*piston*» 卡住 **2** (stop moving) 活动困难；**my back has ~d up** 我的背发僵
- **seize upon** *vt* [**~ upon sth.**] 抓住…以利用；**he immediately ~d upon the weakness in the argument** 他一下子抓住了论点中的漏洞

seizure /ˈsiːʒə(r)/ *n* **1** [u] (of territory, building) 占领；(of power, control) 夺取 **2** [u] (of hostage) 绑架 **3** [u and c] (of contraband, drugs) 扣押；(of goods) 没收；(of property) 查封 **4** [u] (arrest) 拘押 **5** [c] Med 发作；**to have a ~** 突发心脏病；**dad will have a ~ if he sees you wearing that** fig colloq 如果爸爸看到你穿成那样，他会受不了犯病的

seldom /ˈseldəm/ *adv* 很少地；**~ if ever** 几乎从不

select /sɪˈlekt/

A *vt* 挑选；**to ~ sb. to do sth.** 选择某人做某事；**to be ~ed for the team** 被选入队中

B *vi* 挑选；**to ~ from (among) sth.** 从某物中挑选

C *adj* **1** (carefully chosen) 精选的 ‹*group, audience*›；**only a ~ few can afford such luxuries** 只有极少数人买得起这种奢侈品 **2** (exclusive) 上层人士的 ‹*neighbourhood*›；**a ~ club** 名流俱乐部

select committee *n* Brit 特别委员会

selected /sɪˈlektɪd/ *adj* 精选的 ‹*poems, ingredients*›；挑选出来的 ‹*candidate, question, country*›

selectee /ˌsɪlekˈtiː/ *n* **1** (person selected) 人选 **2** Amer Mil (conscript) 应征入伍者

selection /sɪˈlekʃn/ *n* **1** [u] (act of choosing) 挑选；**~ panel** 选拔小组 **2** [c] (choice) 被选

中者; **to make a ~** 作出选择; **~s from Mozart** 莫扎特作品选 **3** [c] (range, assortment) 供挑选的范围; **to have a wide ~** 有多种选择

selection: ~ committee *n* 选拔委员会; **~ procedure, ~ process** *ns* 选拔程序

selective /sɪˈlektɪv/ *adj* **1** (based on selection) 有选择的 ‹*admission, recruitment*›; **a ~ school** 择优录取学生的学校 **2** *pred* (discriminating) 精挑细选的; **to be ~ about** *or* **in sth.** 对某事物很讲究; **to be ~ about what one reads** 对所读的东西很挑剔; **she should be more ~ in the friends she makes** 她挑选朋友时应该更小心些 **3** Hort 选择性的 ‹*pesticide*›

selective breeding *n* [u] 选择性繁殖

selectively /sɪˈlektɪvli/ *adv* 有选择地; **watching television is fine, as long as you watch ~** 看电视没错，只要看的时候有选择就行

selectivity /ˌsɪlekˈtɪvəti/ *n* [u] 选择性

selectman /sɪˈlektmæn, -mən/ ▸**p. 409** *n* (*pl* **selectmen**) Amer [新英格兰的] 市镇管理委员会成员

selector /sɪˈlektə(r)/ *n* **1** Brit (person) 选拔人 **2** (device) 选择器

selenium /sɪˈliːnɪəm/ *n* [u] 硒

self /self/

A *n* (*pl* **selves**) **1** [u] (person's essence) 自我; **the ~ in relation to others** 个性 **2** [c] (usual character) 本性; **he's back to his old ~ again** 他又恢复了本来面目; **one's former ~** 以前的样子 **3** [u] formal (self-interest) 私利; **without thought of ~** 没有私心地

B *pron* **1** (oneself) 自己; **your good ~** 您本人; **tickets for ~ and secretary** (on memo) 给自己和秘书的票 **2** (on cheque) 本人; **pay ~** 认票不认人

self: ~-abasement *n* [u] 自贬; **~-absorbed** *adj* 只顾自己的; **~-absorption** *n* [u] 只顾自己; **~-abuse** *n* [u] **1** (self-harm) 自虐; **2** (masturbation) 手淫; **~-accusation** *n* [u] 自责; **~-addressed envelope** *n* 写明回邮地址的信封; **~-adhesive** *adj* 自粘的; **~-adjusting** *adj* 自动调节的; **~-advertisement** *n* [u] 自我宣传; **~-aggrandizement** *n* [u] pej 自我扩张; **~-analysis** *n* [u] 自我分析; **~-apparent** *adj* 显而易见的; **~-appointed** *adj* 自封的; **~-appraisal** *n* [c and u] 自我评价

self-assembly

A *adj* [家具等] 自己组装的

B *n* [u] 自己组装

self: ~-assertion *n* [u] 自作主张; **~-assertive** *adj* 自作主张的; **~-assessment** *n* **1** [c and u] (self-appraisal) 自我评价; **2** [u] Brit Fin 自行估税; **a ~-assessment tax return** 自行估税申报单; **~-assurance** *n* [u] 自信; **~-assured** *adj* 自信的; **~-aware** *adj* 自知的; **~-awareness** *n* [u] 自知; **~-belief** *n* [u] 自信; **~-betterment** *n* [u] 自我完善; **~-build** *n* [u] Brit 自建房屋

self-catering Brit

A *n* 自理饮食

B *adj* 自理饮食的 ‹*holiday, accommodation*›

self: ~-censorship *n* [u] 自我约束; **~-centred** *adj* pej 自我中心的; **~-centredness** *n* [u] pej 自我中心; **~-certification** *n* [u] Brit **1** (of information) 自我证明; **2** (of illness) [员工自己写的] 病假证明; **~-cleaning** *adj* 自洁式的; **~-closing** *adj* 自动关闭的; **~-coloured** *adj* 单色的 ‹*fabric, carpet*›; **~-conceit** *n* [u] 自大; **~-conceited** *adj* 自大的 ‹*person, attitude*›; **a ~-conceited smile** 自负的微笑; **~-confessed** *adj attrib* 自己承认的 ‹*liar, womanizer*›; **~-confidence** *n* [u] 自信; **~-confident** *adj* 自信的; **~-congratulation** *n* 沾沾自喜; **~-congratulatory** *adj* 沾沾自喜的; **~-conscious** *adj* **1** (shy) 害羞的; (awkward) 尴尬的; (ill at ease) 不安的; **to be ~-conscious about sth./about doing sth.** 因某事物而害羞/对做某事感到难为情; **2** (deliberate) 刻意的; **3** Psych 有自我意识的; **~-consciously** *adv* **1** (shyly) 害羞地; (awkwardly) 尴尬地; **2** (deliberately) 刻意地; **3** Psych 有自我意识地; **~-consciousness** *n* [u] **1** (shyness) 害羞; (embarrassment) 尴尬; **2** (deliberateness) 刻意; **3** Psych 自我意识; **~-contained** *adj* **1** (complete) 自给自足的 ‹*unit, module*›; **2** Brit (of accommodation) 独门独户的 ‹*flat*›; **3** (independent) 独立的 ‹*person*›; (reserved) 持重的; **~-contempt** *n* [u] 自卑; **~-contradiction** *n* [u and c] 自相矛盾; **~-contradictory** *adj* 自相矛盾的; **~-control** *n* [u] 自制; **to lose/regain one's ~-control** 失去/恢复自制力; **~-controlled** *adj* 有自制力的; **~-correcting** *adj* 自动校正的; **~-critical** *adj* 自我批评的; **~-criticism** *n* [u and c] 自我批评; **~-deception** *n* [u] 自我欺骗; **~-defeating** *adj* 事与愿违的; **that would be ~-defeating** 那会弄巧成拙; **~-defence** *n* [u] **1** (skill) 防身术; **~-defence course** 防身术课程; **2** Jur 自卫; **to shoot sb. in ~-defence** 出于自卫向某人开枪; **~-delusion** *n* [u] 自我; **~-denial** *n* [u] 克己; **~-denying** *adj* 克己的; **~-deprecating** *adj* 自我贬低的; **~-deprecation** *n* [u] 自我贬低

self-destruct

A *vi* 自毁

B *adj attrib* 自毁的 ‹*button, sequence*›

self: ~-destruction *n* [u] 自毁; **~-destructive** *adj* 自毁的; **~-determination** *n* [u] 自决权; **~-determining** *adj* 有自决权的; **~-diagnosis** *n* [u] 自我诊断; **~-discipline** *n* [u] 自律; **~-disciplined** *adj* 有自我约束力的; **~-discovery** *n* [u] 自我发现; **~-disgust** *n* [u] 自我厌恶; **~-doubt** *n* [u] 自我怀疑; **~-doubting** *adj* 自我怀疑的; **~-drive** *adj* **1** Brit (driven by oneself) 租车人自驾的 ‹*vehicle*›; **2** (using own car) 自己驾车的 ‹*tourist*›; **a ~-drive tour** 自驾游; **~-educated** *adj* 自学的; **~-effacement** *n* [u] 自谦; **~-effacing** *adj* 自谦的; **~-elected** *adj* lit 自选的 ‹*committee, leader*›; fig 自命的; **he's a ~-elected expert on ...** 他自命是…方面的行家

self-employed

A *adj* 单干的 ‹*worker, writer*›; 自由职业者的 ‹*work*›; **to be ~** 从事自由职业

B *npl* **the ~** 自由职业者

self: ~-employment *n* [u] 从事自由职业; **~-esteem** *n* [u] 自尊; **~-evident** *adj* 显而易见的; **~-evidently** *adv* 显而易见地; **~-examination** *n* [u] (of conscience, motives) 自省; (of body) 自我检查; **~-explanatory** *adj* 不需解释的; **~-expression** *n* [u] 自我表达; **~-fertilization** *n* [u] (of plants) 自花授粉; (of animals) 自体受精; **~-fertilizing** *adj* 自花授粉的 ‹*plants*›; 自体受精的 ‹*animals*›; **~-financing** *adj* 自筹资金的; **~-fulfilling prophecy** *n* 自我应验的预测; **~-fulfilment** *n* [u] 自我实现; **~-funded** *adj* 自筹资金的 ‹*project, retirement, retiree*›; 自费的 ‹*trip, student*›; **~-glorification** *n* [u] pej 自命不凡; **~-governing** *adj* **1** Pol 自治的; **2** Brit Admin [医院或学校] 不受地方政府控制的; **~-government** *n* [u] **1** Pol 自治; **2** Brit Admin 不受地方控制; **~-gratification** *n* [u] 自我满足

self-harm

A *n* [u] 自残

B *vi* 自残

self-hate, self-hatred *ns* [u] 自我憎恨

self-help *n* [u] 自助; **to learn ~** 学会自立

self-help group *n* 自助小组

selfhood /ˈselfhʊd/ *n* [u] formal 自我

self: ~-hypnosis *n* [u] 自我催眠; **~-ignite** *vi* 自燃; **~-ignition** *n* [u] 自燃; **~-image** *n* [u] 自我形象; **~-importance** *n* [u] pej 妄自尊大; **~-important** *adj* pej 妄自尊大的; **~-imposed** *adj* 自愿承担的; **~-improvement** *n* [u] 自我改进; **~-incrimination** *n* [u] 自证其罪; **~-induced** *adj* 自己造成的; **~-indulgence** *n* [u] 自我放纵; **~-indulgent** *adj* 放纵自己的; **~-injury** *n* [u] 自伤; **~-inflicted** *adj* 加于自身的; **~-interest** *n* [u] 私利; **~-interested** *adj* 自私的 ‹*person, behaviour*›; **~-involved** *adj* 专注的

selfish /ˈselfɪʃ/ *adj* 自私的

selfishly /ˈselfɪʃli/ *adv* 自私地

selfishness /ˈselfɪʃnɪs/ *n* [u] 自私

self: ~-justification *n* [u] 自我辩解; **~-justifying** *adj* 自我辩解的; **~-knowledge** *n* [u] 自知之明

selfless /ˈselflɪs/ *adj* 无私的; **an act of ~ devotion** 无私奉献的行为

selflessly /ˈselflɪsli/ *adv* 无私地; **to be ~ devoted to sth.** 无私地为某事奉献

selflessness /ˈselflɪsnɪs/ *n* [u] 无私

self: ~-loader *n* 自动装填式武器; **~-loading** *adj* 自动装填的; **~-loathing** *n* [u] 自我厌恶; **~-locking** *adj* 自动上锁的 ‹*door, gate*›; 自动锁定的 ‹*catch, screw*›; **~-love** *n* [u] 自爱; **~-lubricating** *adj* 自动润滑的; **~-made** *adj* 靠自己奋斗成功的; **a ~-made millionaire** 白手起家的百万富翁; **~-management** *n* [u] **1** (of life, behaviour) 自我管理; (of illness) 自我处理; **2** Comm 自主经营; **~-medicate** *vi* 自我药疗; **~-mockery** *n* [u] 自嘲; **~-mocking** *adj* 自嘲的; **~-mockingly** *adv* 自嘲地 ‹*laugh, remark*›; **~-motivated** *adj* 自我激励的; **~-motivation** *n* [u] 自我激励; **~-mutilate** *vi* 自残; **~-mutilation** *n* [u] 自残; **~-neglect** *n* [u] 自我忽略; **~-obsessed** *adj* pej 自恋的; **~-opinionated** *adj* pej 刚愎自用的 ‹*person*›; **~-ordained** *adj* lit 自任的 ‹*priest*›; fig 自封的 ‹*expert*›; **~-parody** *n* [u] 自我嘲弄; **~-perpetuating** *adj* 自我持续的; **~-pity** *n* [u] 自怜; **~-pitying** *adj* 自怜的; **~-portrait** *n* 自画像; **~-possessed** *adj* (composed) 沉着的; (assured) 泰然自若的; **~-possession** *n* [u] (composure) 沉着; (assured manner) 泰然自若; **~-praise** *n* [u] 自夸; **~-presentation** *n* [u] 自我表现; **~-preservation** *n* [u] 自我保护; **the instinct for ~-preservation** 自卫的本能; **~-proclaimed** *adj* 自称的 ‹*heir*›; 自封的 ‹*ruler, expert*›; **~-professed** *adj attrib* 自己宣称的; **~-promoting** *adj* 自我推销的; **~-promotion** *n* [u] 自我推销; **~-propelled** *adj* 自力推进的; **~-protection** *n* [u] 自我保护; **in ~-protection** 出于自卫; **~-protective** *adj* 自我保护的; **~-publicist** *n* pej 自我炒作者; **~-punishment** *n* [u] 自罚; **~-raising flour** *n* [u] Brit 自发面粉; **~-realization** *n* [u] (discovery) 自我发现; (fulfilment) 自我实现; **~-referential** *adj* 自指的; **~-regard** *n* [u] **1** pej (vanity) 自负; **2** (self-respect) 自尊; **~-regarding** *adj* pej 关注自己的; **~-regulating, ~-regulatory** *adjs* 自我调节的 ‹*system, economy*›; 自动调节的 ‹*mechanism*›; **~-regulation** *n* [u] (of system, economy) 自我调节; (of mechanism) 自动调节; **~-reliance** *n* [u] 自力更生; **~-reliant** *adj* 自力更生的; **~-renewal** *n* [u] 自我更新; **~-renewing** *adj* 自我更新的 ‹*organization, tissue, stem cell*›; **~-replicating** *adj* 自我复制的; **~-representation** *n* [u] (gen) 自我表现; Jur 自我辩护; **~-reproach** *n* [u] 自我谴责; **~-respect** *n* [u] 自尊; **~-respecting**

adj 有自尊心的; **no ~-respecting journalist would ever work for that newspaper** 任何有自尊心的记者都不会为那家报社工作; **~-restraint** *n* [u] 自我克制; **~-revelation** *n* [u] 自我揭示; **~-ridicule** *n* [u] 自嘲; **~-righteous** *adj* pej 自以为正直的; **~-righteous indignation** 自以为是的义愤; **~-righteously** *adv* pej 自以为正直地; **~-righteousness** *n* [u] pej 自以为正直; **~-righting** *adj* 能自动扶正的 ‹*boat*›; **~-rising flour** *n* [u] Amer = **~-raising flour**; **~-rule** *n* [u] 自治; **~-ruling** *adj* 自治的; **~-sacrifice** *n* [u] 自我牺牲; **~-sacrificing** *adj* 自我牺牲的; **~same** *adj* 同一的; **~-satisfaction** *n* [u] pej 沾沾自喜; **~-satisfied** *adj* pej 沾沾自喜的; **~-sealing** *adj* 1 (self-adhesive) 自行封口的 ‹*envelope, bag*›; 2 (in case of leak) 自动密封的 ‹*tyre, container*›

self-seeking pej
A *adj* 追逐私利的
B *n* [u] 追逐私利

self-service
A *n* [u] 自助
B *adj* 自助的

self: **~-serving** *adj* pej 谋私利的; **~-starter** *n* 做事主动的人; **~-study** *n* [u] 自学; **a ~-study book/aid** 自学课本/辅助材料; **~-styled** *adj attrib* 自封的; **~-sufficiency** *n* [u] 1 (in resources) 自给自足; 2 (in emotions) 自立; **~-sufficient** *adj* 1 (in resources) 自给自足的; **to be ~-sufficient in sth.** 在某事上能自给自足; 2 (in emotions) 自立的; **~-supporting** *adj* 1 (self-sufficient) 自给的 ‹*person, business*›; 2 Constr 自撑式的 ‹*structure*›; **~-sustaining** *adj* 自我维持的; **~-sustaining populations** 自我延续种群; **~-sustaining growth** 自续增长; **~-tanner** *n* [u] 仿古铜色霜; **~-tanning** *adj* 仿古铜色的 ‹*lotion*›; **~-tapping screw** *n* 自攻螺丝; **~-taught** *adj* 自学成才的

self-test
A *vi* Comput, Tech 进行自我测试
B **self test** *n* 1 Comput, Tech 自检 2 Educ 自我测试; **~ questions/exercises** 自测题/练习

self: **~-titled** *adj* [尤指发行的唱片、CD等] 以创作者名字命名的; **~-torture** *n* [u] 自我折磨; **~-treatment** *n* [u] 自我治疗; **~-will** *n* [u] (determination) 执著; pej (stubbornness) 固执; **~-willed** *adj* pej 固执的; **~-winding** *adj* 自动上发条的 ‹*watch*›; 自动卷紧的 ‹*hose*›; **~-worth** *n* [u] 自尊

sell /sel/
A *vt* (*pt, pp* **sold**) 1 (exchange for money) 卖; **to ~ sth. to sb.** 把某物卖给某人; **to ~ sth. at a loss/profit** 亏本/赢利出售某物; **I sold the car for £2,000** 我把车卖了 2,000 英镑; **to ~ sth. at** *or* **by auction** 拍卖某物; **to ~ sth. cheaply** 贱卖某物; **to ~ sb. a pup** colloq 卖给某人伪劣品; **to ~ sth. retail/wholesale** 零售/批发某物; **sold/to be sold** (on notice) 已售出/待售; **to ~ sth. for cash/on credit** 以现金结算方式/赊账方式销售某物; **to ~ sb. into slavery** 把某人卖作奴隶 2 (stock for sale) «*retailer*» 经营; **stamps/newspapers sold here** 此处经销邮票/报纸 3 (promote sale of) «*salesperson*» 推销 ‹*insurance, equipment, property*›; «*publicity, quality, craftsmanship*» 促进…的销路 ‹*product*›; **sex and scandal: that's what ~s the tabloids!** 性与丑闻: 这是小报的卖点! 4 colloq (persuade of the merits of) «*person, campaign*» 推荐 ‹*ideas, party*›; **to ~ sb. sth.** 说服某人采纳某事; **to ~ oneself** 自我推销; **to be sold on sth.** colloq 热衷于某事 5 colloq (make believe) 使…被相信 ‹*excuse, explanation*›; **to ~ sth. to sb., to ~ sb. sth.** 使某人相信某事; **you can't ~ that old excuse to me!** 你那套老借口对我已经不灵了!; **to ~ sb. a** *or* **some line about sth.** 蒙骗某人相信某事 6 (surrender, betray) 出卖; **a traitor who sold his country** 卖国贼; **to ~ one's honour/principles for sth.** 为某事物出卖名誉/原则; **to ~ oneself** 出卖自己; **to ~ oneself to sb.** 被某人收买; **to ~ one's soul (to the devil)** (向魔鬼)出卖灵魂; **to ~ oneself** *or* **one's body** 卖淫; **to ~ sb. down the river** colloq 出卖某人
B *vi* (*pt, pp* **sold**) 1 (exchange sth. for money) 出售; **we are ~ing at a loss** 我们在亏本销售; **he knew I was ~ing short** 他知道我在做卖空交易 2 (be bought) 有销路; **to ~ well/badly** 畅销/滞销; **the car sold to a Russian millionaire** 这辆车卖给了一个俄国百万富翁; **it is ~ing at a discount/for £50** 该商品在打折销售/以 50 英镑的价格出售; **to ~ like hot cakes** 热销
C *n* Brit colloq 失望; **Hawaii's a bit of a ~ — not a patch on Corfu** 夏威夷相当令人失望——远远比不上科孚岛

Phrasal verbs
• **sell off** *vt* [**~ sth. off, ~ off sth.**] 廉价出售
• **sell on** *vt* 1 [**~ sth. on, ~ on sth.**] Comm 转售 ‹*goods*› 2 [**~ sb. on sth.**] 使相信…有价值; colloq **he's completely sold on the idea of a new sports centre** 他完全接受了修建新体育中心的想法
• **sell out**
A *vi* 1 Comm 售完; **the concert has** *or* **is completely sold out** 音乐会的门票已经售完; **we've sold out, I'm afraid** 恐怕已经售完了; **to ~ out of sth.** 卖完某物; **to ~ out (to sb.)** 被(某人)收买 2 (abandon one's principles) 背弃原则; **to ~ out to sb.** 屈服于某人
B *vt* [**~ out sth.**] 售出; **he decided to ~ out his interest in the company** 他决定出售自己在公司拥有的股份
• **sell up**
A *vi* 变卖
B *vt* [**~ up sth.**] 变卖; **they sold up their property** 他们变卖了自己的财产

sell-by date *n* Brit 最晚销售日期
seller /'selə(r)/ *n* 1 (person) 售卖者; **~ of sth.** 某物的销售者; **a street ~** 街头小贩; **a newspaper ~** 报贩 2 (product, book etc.) 商品; **a best-~** 畅销商品
seller's market *n* 卖方市场
selling /'selɪŋ/ *n* [u] 销售; **direct ~** 直销; **telephone ~** 电话销售
selling: **~-off** *n* [u] (of company, assets) 贱卖; (of stock) 低价抛售; **~ point** *n* 卖点; **~ price** *n* 售价; **~ rate** *n* 卖出汇率
sell-off *n* 1 (of goods, assets) 贱卖 2 esp Amer Fin (causing fall in price) 抛售
Sellotape® /'seləʊteɪp/ Brit
A *n* [u] 透明胶带
B **sellotape** *vt* 用透明胶带粘贴
sell-out *n* 1 (event) 满场; **the show was a ~** 这次演出全场爆满; **they played to a ~ crowd of 12,000** 他们演出时现场座无虚席, 观众人数达 12,000 人; **the play was a ~ success** 这场戏观众爆满, 大获成功 2 (betrayal) 出卖; **this is not a compromise, it's a ~** 这不是妥协, 而是背叛
sell-through *n* [u] 1 (goods sold) [与进货量相对的] 销售量; **an 11 per cent ~ rate** 11% 的销售率 2 (sale) [尤指录像带的] 销售
selvage, selvedge /'selvɪdʒ/ *ns* 织边
selves /selvz/ *pl* ▸**self A**
semantic /sɪ'mæntɪk/ *adj* 语义的 ‹*analysis, difference*›; 语义学的 ‹*evaluation*›
semantically /sɪ'mæntɪkli/ *adv* 在语义上
semanticist /sɪ'mæntɪsɪst/ *n* 语义学家
semantics /sɪ'mæntɪks/ *npl* 1 + *v sing* (subject) 语义学; **~ lecture** 语义学讲座 2 + *v pl* (meaning) 含义; **let's not argue over ~** 我们别咬文嚼字了
semaphore /'seməfɔː(r)/
A *n* [u] (using arms) 臂板信号; (using flags) 旗语
B *vt* (using arms) 用臂板信号发出; (using flags) 用旗语发出
semblance /'sembləns/ *n* [u and c] 外貌; **a** *or* **some ~ of ...** 一副…的样子; **to show/put on a ~ of sth.** 表现出/摆出某种样子; **to maintain a ~ of composure** 保持表面镇静
semen /'siːmən/ *n* [u] 精液
semester /sɪ'mestə(r)/ *n* esp Amer 学期
semi /'semi/ *n* colloq 1 Brit (semi-detached house) 半独立式住宅 2 Amer (semi-trailer) 半挂车 3 (semi-final) 半决赛
semi- /'semi/ *combining form* 1 (half) 半; **a ~serious suggestion** 半带严肃的建议 2 (almost) 不完全的
semi: **~-annual** *adj* 半年一次的; **~aquatic** *adj* Zool 半水栖的; Bot 半水生的; **~-arid** *adj* 半干旱的
semi-automatic
A *adj* 半自动的 ‹*gearbox, machine, firearm*›
B *n* 半自动武器
semi: **~-autonomous** *adj* 1 (partially independent) 半自主的 ‹*department, unit*›; 2 (partially self-governing) 半自治的 ‹*region, province*›; **~-basement** *n* Brit 半地下室; **~bold** *n* [u] 半黑体; **~breve** *n* Brit 全音符; **~circle** *n* 半圆; **~circular** *adj* 半圆形的; **~colon** *n* 分号; **~commercial** *adj* 半商业性的 ‹*property, business*›; **~conducting** *adj* 半导体的; **~conductor** *n* 半导体; **~-conscious** *adj* 半清醒的; **~-consciousness** *n* [u] 半清醒; **~-darkness** *n* [u] 半明半暗; **~-desert** *n* [u] 半沙漠; **~-detached** *adj* Brit 半独立式的; **a ~-detached house** 半独立式住宅; **~-final** *n* 半决赛; **~-finalist** *n* (person) 半决赛选手; (team) 进入半决赛的运动队
semi-fluid
A *adj* 半流体的
B *n* 半流体
semi: **~-liquid** *adj, n* = **semi-fluid**; **~-literate** *adj* 半文盲的 ‹*person*›; 蹩脚的 ‹*composition*›
semi-monthly esp Amer
A *adj* 每月两次的 ‹*publication, event*›
B *n* 半月刊
seminal /'semɪnl/ *adj* 1 (important, influential) 开创性的 ‹*work, thinker, idea*›; 重大的 ‹*influence*› 2 Physiol 精液的; **examination of ~ fluid** 精液检查
seminar /'semɪnɑː(r)/ *n* 1 (conference) 研讨会; **to hold a ~ (on sth.)** 举行(关于某事物的)研讨会 2 (class) 研讨班; **a graduate ~** 研究生研讨班
seminarian /ˌsemɪ'neərɪən/, **seminarist** /'semɪnərɪst/ *ns* 神学院学生
seminar: **~ leader** *n* 研讨会主持人; **~ room** *n* (for conference) 研讨会会议室; (for class) 研讨班教室
seminary /'semɪnəri, Amer -neri/ *n* 神学院
semi-official *adj* 半官方的
semiology /ˌsemɪ'ɒlədʒi/ *n* [u] 符号学
semi-opaque *adj* 半透明的
semiotic /ˌsemɪ'ɒtɪk/ *adj* 符号学的
semiotics /ˌsemɪ'ɒtɪks/ *npl* + *v sing* 符号学
semi: **~-permanent** *adj* 半固定的; **~permeable** *adj* 半渗透性的; **~-precious** *adj* 次贵重的 ‹*metal, stone*›; **~-precious gems** 半宝石
semi-professional
A *adj* 半职业的 ‹*player, musician, baseball*›
B *n* 半职业人员
semi: **~quaver** *n* Brit 十六分音符; **~-retired** *adj* 半退休的; **~-rigid** *adj* 1 (solid but flexible) 半刚性的 ‹*material, hose*›; 2 Aerosp, Naut 半硬式的; **~-skilled** *adj* 半熟练的 ‹*worker*›; **~-skilled work** *or* **job** 半技术工作; **~-skimmed** *adj* Brit 半脱脂的

S

‹*milk*›; **~-solid** *adj* 半固态的; **~-submersible** *adj* 半潜式的 ‹*platform, barge*›

Semite /'si:maɪt, 'se-/ *n* 闪米特人

Semitic /sɪ'mɪtɪk/ *adj* 闪语族的 ‹*language, people, culture*›

semi: ~tone *n* Brit 半音; **~-trailer** *n* esp Amer (truck) 铰接式卡车; (trailer) 半挂车; **~-tropical** *adj* = **subtropical**; **~vowel** *n* 半元音

semi-weekly
A *adj* 一周两次的 ‹*column, event*›
B *n* 半周刊

semi-yearly *adj* Amer = **semi-annual**

semolina /ˌsemə'li:nə/ *n* [u] **1** (grain) 粗麦粉 **2** (pudding) 粗麦粉布丁

sempstress /'sempstrɪs/ *n* = **seamstress**

SEN *abbr* Brit = **State Enrolled Nurse**

Sen 1 Amer = **senator 2** Amer = **senate 1 3** = **senior A3**

senate /'senɪt/ *n* **1** **Senate** Pol 参议院 **2** Univ 理事会 **3** Hist (council) [古罗马的] 元老院; (building) 元老院大楼; **the Roman ~** 罗马元老院

> **the Senate**
>
> 参议院，美国国会（▸**Congress**）上院。共有 100 名参议员（Senator），每州两名，任期六年，每两年改选三分之一，可连任。参议院和众议院（House of Representatives）负责起草并通过法律提案，经总统批准后生效。美国政府和其他国家签署的条约须经参议院批准。总统任命某些官员时也需要征求参议院的意见，并获得其批准（advice and consent）。参议院议长由副总统兼任。

S

senator /'senətə(r)/ *n* 参议员

senatorial /ˌsenə'tɔ:rɪəl/ *adj* 参议院的 ‹*debate*›; 参议员的 ‹*campaign, election*›

send /send/ (*pt, pp* **sent**)
A *vt* **1** (dispatch) 发送; **to ~ a telegram** 发电报; **to ~ a letter/parcel** 寄信/寄包裹; **to ~ reinforcements** 派出增援部队; **to ~ sth. to sb., to ~ sb. sth.** 给某人送去某物; **to ~ sb. for sth.** 派某人取某物; **to ~ sb. to do sth.** 派某人做某事; **~ him in as soon as he arrives** 他一到就让他进来; **two children were sent out of class** 两个孩子被赶出了课堂; **management have closed the factory and sent the workers home** 资方关闭了工厂，遣散了工人; **to ~ sb. to bed** 让某人上床睡觉; **to ~ sb. on an errand/a mission** 派某人去办事/履行使命; **he was sent to hospital for treatment** 他被送进医院治疗; **he was sent to prison for five years** 他被监禁 5 年; **to ~ help** 派人援助; **to ~ one's children away to school** 送孩子上寄宿学校; **I'll ~ a car for you** *or* **to fetch you** 我派车去接你; **to ~ one's best wishes/kindest regards** 送上良好祝愿/亲切问候; **to ~ sb. one's love** 向某人问好; **these things are sent to try us!** 这些都是上天安排来考验我们的! **2** Radio 发射 ‹*signal, transmission*›; 发出 ‹*appeal, SOS*›; **the satellite sent pictures back** 卫星发回了一些照片 **3** (cause to move) 使移动; **a sudden cold snap sent the temperature down** 突然而至的寒潮造成气温下降; **favourable economic news sent shares up** 经济方面的利好消息抬升了股价; **to ~ sb./sth. flying** 把某人/某物撞飞; **the sudden gust of wind sent the pieces of paper flying** 一阵疾风把纸张吹得四处乱飞 **4** (drive into certain condition) 使进入某状态; **the pain was ~ing him mad** 他快疼得发疯了; **falling prices sent the market into a panic** 价格下跌造成了市场恐慌; **to ~ sb. to sleep** 使某人入睡 **5** (dismiss) 驱赶; **to ~ sb. packing** *or* **about his business** colloq 叫某人卷铺盖走人; **to ~ sb. off** *or* **away with a flea in his ear** 喝退某人 **6** dated colloq (make ecstatic) 使陶醉; **she really ~s him!** 她使他神魂颠倒!
B *vi* formal 捎信; **he sent to ask if he could do anything to help** (by letter) 他写信问他能不能帮上什么忙

Phrasal verbs

• **send away**
A *vt* **1** [**~ sb. away**] (order to leave) 把…打发走 **2** [**~ sth. away**] (for repair or processing) 发送出去 [以便修理或处理]
B *vi* 写信索取; **to ~ away to sb./sth. (for sth.)** 写信向某人/某处索要（某物）; **he sent away to the warehouse for additional supplies** 他向货栈发函要求追加供货

• **send down** *vt* [**~ sb. down, ~ down sb.**]
1 Brit Univ (expel) 开除 **2** Jur colloq (send to prison) 判…入狱

• **send for** *vt* [**~ for sb./sth.**] 叫…过来; **to ~ for a taxi/an ambulance** 叫出租车/救护车; **to ~ for a doctor** 请医生来

• **send forth** *vt* [**~ forth sb./sth.**] liter «*king*» 派出 ‹*army*›; «*tree*» 长出 ‹*leaves*›; «*star*» 发出 ‹*light*›

• **send in** *vt* **1** [**~ sb. in, ~ in sb.**] (order to a place) 派…去; **troops have been sent in to quell the riots** 部队已被调去镇压骚乱 **2** [**~ sth. in**] (submit) 提交; **to ~ in a job application** 提交求职申请

• **send off** *vt* **1** = **send away A 2** [**~ sb. off, ~ off sb.**] Brit Sport 把…罚下场

• **send on**
A [**~ sth. on**] *vt*
1 (send in advance) 先期发送 **2** (forward) 转送; **to ~ sth. on to sb.** 把某物转运给某人
B [**~ on sb., ~ sb. on**] *vt* Sport 派…上场比赛

• **send out**
A [**~ out sth.**] *vt*
1 (emit) 发出 ‹*light, heat, smoke*› **2** (produce) «*tree, plant*» 长出 ‹*leaves, roots*› **3** (dispatch) 分发 ‹*leaflets, information, invitations*›
B [**~ sb. out**] *vt* 派…出去; **she sent him out to buy some flour** 她遣他出去买些面粉

• **send up** *vt* [**~ sb./sth. up, ~ up sb./sth.**]
1 Brit colloq (imitate) 滑稽模仿 **2** Amer (sentence) 判…入狱

sender /'sendə(r)/ *n* 发送人; **if undelivered, please return to ~** 如无法投递，请退给寄信人

send: ~-off *n* 送别; **a warm/big ~-off** 温馨的送别/大型送别会; **~-up** *n* Brit colloq 滑稽模仿; **a ~-up of sth.** 对某事物的滑稽模仿

Senegal /ˌsenɪ'gɔ:l/ *pr n* 塞内加尔

Senegalese /ˌsenɪgə'li:z/ ▸**p. 503**
A *adj* (of Senegal) 塞内加尔的; (of the people) 塞内加尔人的
B *n* 塞内加尔人

senile /'si:naɪl/ *adj* **1** (infirm through old age) 老迈的 ‹*person, eyes*›; 老态龙钟的 ‹*behaviour*› **2** (relating to old age) 年老所致的 ‹*problem, decay*›

senile dementia *n* [u] 老年性痴呆

senility /sɪ'nɪləti/ *n* [u] 衰老

senior /'si:nɪə(r)/
A *adj* **1** (older) 年长的; **to be ~ to sb. (by ... years)** 比某人年长（…岁） **2** (superior) 较高的 ‹*rank*›; (in rank) 级别较高的 ‹*appointment*›; (in status) 地位较高的; **to be ~ to sb.** 是某人的上级 **3** (*also* **Senior**) esp Amer (in name) [表示同名者中较年长者，两者多为父子] 老，大; **Bob Mortimer ~** 老鲍勃·莫蒂默 **4** Brit Sch 高年级的 [尤指11岁以上] **5** Amer Sch, Univ 毕业年级的 **6** Sport 成人的; **the ~ men's 400 metres** 男子甲组 400 米赛跑
B *n* **1** (older person) 年长者; **to be sb.'s ~ by ten years** 比某人年长 10 岁 **2** (superior) (in rank) 级别较高者; (in status) 地位较高者; **colleagues and ~s** 同事与上司 **3** Brit Sch 高年级学生 **4** Amer Sch, Univ 毕业年级学生

senior: ~ aircraftman *n* Brit (in RAF) (rank) 一等兵军衔; (person) 一等兵; **~ aircraftwoman** *n* Brit (in RAF) (rank) 女一等兵军衔; (person) 女一等兵; **~ airman** *n* Amer (in US Air Force) (rank) 下士军衔; (person) 下士; **~ citizen** *n* [尤指领取养老金的] 长者; **~ editor** ▸**p. 409** *n* 高级编辑; **~ executive** *n* (body) 高级管理部门; (person) 高级主管; **~ high school** *n* Amer 高中

seniority /ˌsi:nɪ'ɒrəti, Amer -'ɔ:r-/ *n* [u] **1** (in age) 年长; **in order of ~** 以年龄大小为序 **2** (in rank) 级别高; **in order of ~** 按职位高低排序 **3** (in years of service) 资历; **in order of ~** 按资历深浅排序

senior: ~ lecturer *n* Brit Univ 高级讲师; **~ management** *n* [u] **1** (highest level) 高级管理层; **2** + *v sing or pl* (senior managers) 高级经理; **~ manager** *n* 高级经理; **~ master sergeant** *n* Amer (in US Air Force) (rank) 二级军士长军衔; (person) 二级军士长; **~ moment** *n* colloq hum 老糊涂时刻 [指因年老记忆力下降导致的健忘]; **~ officer** *n* (in police) 高级警官; (in army) 高级军官; (high-level official) 高级官员; **inform your ~ officer** 通报你的上级; **~ official** *n* 高级官员; **~ partner** *n* (head) 资深合伙人; (joint head) 主要合伙人; **~ registrar** *n* Brit 高级专科住院医师; **~ school** *n* Brit **1** (secondary school) 中学; **2** + *v sing or pl* (older pupils) 高年级学生; **S~ Service** *n* Brit **the S~ Service** (Royal Navy) 皇家海军; **~ staff** *n* [u] **1** Admin 高级职员; **2** Brit Univ 高级导师; **~ year** *n* **1** Brit Sch (final year) 最后学年; (final year pupils) + *v sing or pl* 毕业年级学生; **2** Amer Sch, Univ 毕业年级

senna /'senə/ *n* [u] 番泻叶

sensation /sen'seɪʃn/ *n* **1** [c] (physical feeling) 感觉; (perception) 知觉; **a ~ of falling** 坠落感 **2** [u] (ability to feel) 感觉能力; **loss of ~ in the left arm** 左臂失去知觉 **3** [c] (awareness) 觉察; (impression) 直觉; **the ~ that ...** …的直觉; **he had the eerie ~ of being watched** 他有一种遭人监视的怪异直觉 **4** [c] (stir) 轰动; **to cause** *or* **create a ~** 引起轰动 **5** [c] colloq (person) 引起轰动的人; (object) 引起轰动的东西; (event) 引起轰动的事件; **when she first performed, she was a ~** 她的首次演出引起了轰动; **the new model was the ~ of the motor show** 这款新车在车展上引起了轰动

sensational /sen'seɪʃənl/ *adj* **1** (thrilling, dramatic) 引起轰动的 **2** pej (sensationalist) 耸人听闻的 **3** colloq (very good) 极好的; **you look ~ in that dress!** 你穿这件连衣裙漂亮极了!

sensationalism /sen'seɪʃənəlɪzəm/ *n* [u] **1** pej (of tabloid newspapers etc.) 耸人听闻 **2** Philos 感觉主义

sensationalist /sen'seɪʃənəlɪst/
A *n* **1** pej (person) 追求轰动效应者 **2** Philos 感觉论者
B *adj* **1** Journ pej 耸人听闻的 ‹*story, newspaper*› **2** Philos 感觉论的

sensationalize /sen'seɪʃənəlaɪz/ *vt* pej 大肆渲染

sensationally /sen'seɪʃənəli/ *adv* **1** pej (overdramatically) 耸人听闻地 ‹*write, describe*›; 夸张地 ‹*dress, act*› **2** colloq (extremely) 极度地; **~ good-looking/beautiful/bad** 帅呆了/美若天仙/糟糕得无以复加 **3** colloq (extremely well) 一级棒; **how did she do? — ~!** 她做得怎么样? ——棒极了!

sense /sens/
A *n* **1** [c] (faculty) 感官; **the five ~s** 五种感官; **a sixth ~** 第六感; **to bring sb. to his** *or* **her ~s** 使某人恢复知觉; **to come to one's ~s** 恢复知觉 **2** [u] (ability to appreciate) 理解力; **a ~ of right and wrong/justice/duty** 是非感/正义感/责任感; **a ~ of humour** *or* **fun** 幽默感 **3** [u] (feeling) 感觉; **a ~ of guilt/shame** 负罪感/羞耻感; **a strong ~ of foreboding**

强烈的不祥预感; **a ~ of belonging/security** 归属感/安全感 **4** [u] (practical quality) 判断力; **a man quite devoid of ~** 一个缺少见识的男人; **a grain of ~** 一点见识; **good ~** 明智; **there's some/a lot of ~ in what he suggests** 他的建议有些/很有道理; **to beat** *or* **knock** *or* **drive (some) ~ into sb.** colloq 强使某人开（点）窍 **5** **senses** *pl* (sanity) 理智; **to lose/regain one's ~s** 丧失/恢复理智; **to bring sb. to his** *or* **her ~s** 使某人清醒过来; **to come to one's ~s** 恢复理智; **to be out of one's ~s** 失去理智; **to take leave of one's ~s** 发疯 **6** [u] (reason) 合理性; **there's little ~ in what he plans/says** 他的计划/话几乎没什么道理; **to make ~** (be understandable) 有意义; (be sensible) 合乎情理; **to make ~ of sth.** 理解某事物; **can you make ~ of this sentence?** 你明白这个句子的意思吗？; **to talk ~** 说话有道理; **to see ~** 开始明白事理 **7** [c] (meaning) 意义; **a word with several ~s** 多义词; **it should not be understood in its literal ~** 这不能从字面意义理解; **to get** *or* **grasp the ~ (of sth.)** 领会（某事物的）意义; **in a ~** 从某种意义上讲 **8** [u] (general opinion) 意向; **the ~ of sth.** formal 对某事物的一般看法

B *vt* **1** (feel, detect) 感觉到; **I could ~ somebody out there in the darkness** 我感觉到黑暗中有人出现; **I could ~ what was upsetting her** 我能感到是什么事情在使她烦心 **2** (detect) «*sensor, system*» 检测出 ‹*movement, heat*› **3** Comput (locate) 探出 ‹*position*›; (read) 读取 ‹*data*›

senseless /ˈsenslɪs/ *adj* **1** (pointless) 无意义的 ‹*waste, idea, chatter*›; **it is ~ to do** *or* **doing anything now** 现在做什么都是无意义的; **~ violence** 无谓的暴力 **2** (foolish) 愚蠢的 ‹*act, behaviour*›; **it was an utterly ~ thing to do** 这么做愚蠢透顶 **3** (unconscious) 失去知觉的; **to knock sb. ~** 把某人打昏

senselessly /ˈsenslɪsli/ *adv* **1** (pointlessly) 无意义地 **2** (foolishly) 愚蠢地

senselessness /ˈsenslɪsnɪs/ *n* [u] **1** (pointlessness) 无意义 **2** (foolishness) 愚蠢 **3** (unconsciousness) 失去知觉

sense organ *n* 感觉器官

sensibility /ˌsensəˈbɪləti/

A *n* [u] **1** formal (sensitivity) 鉴赏力 **2** colloq (sensibleness) 明智

B **sensibilities** *npl* 感情; **to offend sb.'s sensibilities** 伤害某人的感情

sensible /ˈsensəbl/ *adj* **1** (showing common sense) 明智的 ‹*person, idea, choice*›; **it is (for sb.) to do ...** （某人）做…是妥当的 **2** (practical) 实用的 ‹*clothing, footwear*› **3** *pred* formal or liter (aware) 意识到的; **to be ~ of** *or* **to sth.** 知道某事

sensibleness /ˈsensəblnɪs/ *n* [u] 明智

sensibly /ˈsensəbli/ *adv* **1** (prudently) 明智地; **are you eating ~?** 你的饮食合理吗？ **2** (practically) 实用地; **~ priced** 合理定价的

sensitive /ˈsensətɪv/ *adj* **1** (easily affected) 敏感的 ‹*instrument, skin, nerve*›; **to be ~ to light/heat/pain** 对光/热/疼痛敏感 **2** fig (easily hurt) 易恼怒的; **he is very ~ to criticism** 他一听到批评就急 **3** (sympathetic, aware) 善解人意的; **he is ~ to the needs of others** 他善于体察别人的需要 **4** (discriminating, appreciative) 细腻的 ‹*interpretation, performance*› **5** (delicate) 微妙的 ‹*situation, problem, matter*›; **negotiations are at a very ~ stage** 谈判处在一个非常敏感的阶段 **6** (confidential) 机密的 ‹*information, material*›

sensitive data *n* [u] (confidential information) 机密资料; (under data protection act) 敏感数据

sensitively /ˈsensətɪvli/ *adv* **1** (sympathetically) 善解人意地 ‹*chosen*›; 细腻地 ‹*portrayed*› **2** (delicately) 谨慎周到地 ‹*act, respond*›

sensitiveness /ˈsensɪtɪvnɪs/ *n* [u] = **sensitivity A**

sensitivity /ˌsensəˈtɪvɪti/

A *n* [u] **1** (responsiveness) 敏感（性）; **~ to sth.** 对某事物的敏感; **the ~ of the instrument** 仪器的灵敏度 **2** (touchiness) 容易生气; **~ on the subject** 对这个话题的敏感 **3** (consideration) 善解人意; **~ to the needs of children** 对孩子所需的体察 **4** (of interpretation, performance) 悟性 **5** (of situation, problem) 谨慎周到; **to handle sth. with ~** 谨慎处理某事 **6** (confidentiality) 机密性

B **sensitivities** *npl* (feelings) 微妙的情感; **you must respect local sensitivities** 你必须尊重当地人的感情

sensitize /ˈsensɪtaɪz/ *vt* **1** (make sensitive) 使敏感; **skin ~d to sunlight** 对阳光过敏的皮肤 **2** fig (make aware) 使意识到; **to ~ sb. to a problem/need** 使某人意识到问题/需要

sensor /ˈsensə(r)/ *n* 传感器

sensory /ˈsensəri/ *adj* 感觉的 ‹*impression, input*›; **~ nerve/organ** 感觉神经/器官

sensory deprivation *n* [u] 感觉丧失

sensual /ˈsenʃʊəl/ *adj* **1** (physical) 感官的 ‹*pleasure*› **2** (sexual) 性感的 ‹*movement, person, nature, lips*›

sensualism /ˈsenʃʊəlɪzəm/ *n* [u] (sensuality) 感官享受; (sensual indulgence) 耽于酒色

sensualist /ˈsenʃʊəlɪst/ *n* 耽于酒色者

sensuality /ˌsenʃʊˈæləti/ *n* [u and c] **1** (physical gratification) 感官满足; **the ~ of sleeping in silk sheets** 盖着丝绸被单睡觉的舒适感受 **2** (enjoyment of physical or sexual pleasure) 感官享受

sensually /ˈsenʃʊəli/ *adv* **1** (in way that is pleasing to the senses) 愉悦感官地 **2** (in voluptuous manner) 性感地 ‹*dance, speak, arousing*›

sensuous /ˈsenʃʊəs/ *adj* **1** (pleasing to the senses) 愉悦感官的 **2** (sexually attractive) 性感的 ‹*person*›; 令人着迷的 ‹*nature, character*›; **her voice was rather deep but very ~** 她的嗓音相当低沉，但非常性感

sensuously /ˈsenʃʊəsli/ *adv* **1** (in a way that is pleasing to the senses) 愉悦感官地 **2** (in a voluptuous manner) 性感地

sensuousness /ˈsenʃʊəsnɪs/ *n* [u] **1** (quality of being pleasing to senses) 感官愉悦 **2** (seductiveness, voluptuousness) 性感

sent /sent/ *pt, pp* ▸**send**

sentence /ˈsentəns/

A *n* **1** Ling 句子; **he never finishes his ~s** 他从来不把句子说完整 **2** (punishment) 判决; **a jail** *or* **prison ~** 判处监禁; **a life ~** 无期徒刑; **to be under ~ of death** 被判死刑; **to serve/commute a ~** 服刑/减刑; **to pass ~ on sb.** 对某人作出判决

B *vt* 判决; **to ~ sb. to sth. (for sth.)** （因某事）判处某人某刑罚; **to ~ sb. to jail** 判决某人入狱; **he was ~d to pay a £500 fine** 他被判支付 500 英镑罚款

sentence adverb *n* 句副词

sententious /senˈtenʃəs/ *adj* formal pej 爱说教的 ‹*person*›; 说教式的 ‹*remark, opinion*›

sententiously /senˈtenʃəsli/ *adv* formal pej 说教式地

sentient /ˈsenʃnt/ *adj* 有感觉能力的 ‹*creature, being*›

sentiment /ˈsentɪmənt/ *n* **1** [u] (general opinion) 情绪; **racist ~** 种族主义态度 **2** [c] (feeling, emotion) 感情; **a ~ of unease** 不自在的感觉 **3** [c] (opinion) 观点; **what are your ~s about this?** 你对这件事的看法是什么？ **4** [u] pej (sentimentality) 伤感; **the sickly ~ of the letter** 信里令人作呕的多愁善感

sentimental /ˌsentɪˈmentl/ *adj* **1** (nostalgic) 深情的; **to be ~ about sth.** 对某物一往情深; **of (purely) ~ value** （纯粹）情感价值的; **the ring was of great ~ value** 这枚戒指有极大的情感价值; **we can't afford to be ~** 我们不能感情用事; **it's too ~** colloq 这太滥情了 **2** pej (mawkish) 多愁善感的 ‹*person*›; 令人伤感的 ‹*story, comedy*›

sentimentalism /ˌsentɪˈmentəlɪzəm/ *n* [u] pej 多愁善感

sentimentalist /ˌsentɪˈmentəlɪst/ *n* 多愁善感的人

sentimentality /ˌsentɪmenˈtæləti/ *n* **1** [u] pej (mawkishness) 多愁善感; **the ~ of the poem** 这首诗的伤感的情调 **2** [c] (idea) 多愁善感的想法; (act) 多愁善感的行为

sentimentalize /ˌsentɪˈmentəlaɪz/

A *vt* (treat sentimentally) 深情地描述; (turn into object of sentiment) 伤感地对待; (be sentimental about) 对…伤感

B *vi* 感伤; **to ~ over** *or* **about sth.** 因某事物而感伤

sentimentally /ˌsentɪˈmentəli/ *adv* 多愁善感地

sentinel /ˈsentɪnl/

A *n* **1** esp Mil (guard) 哨兵; **to stand ~** 站岗; **a tall round tower standing ~ over the river** fig 一座镇守在河边的圆形高塔 **2** Comput 标记

B *vt* (*pres p etc.* **-ll-** Brit, **-l-** Amer) esp Mil 在…设岗哨 ‹*place, area*›

sentry /ˈsentri/ *n* 哨兵

sentry: ~ box *n* 岗亭; **~ duty** *n* [u] 放哨; **to be on ~ duty** 站岗; **~ post** *n* 哨位

Seoul /səʊl/ *pr n* 首尔

Sep *abbr* = **September**

sepal /ˈsepl/ *n* 萼片

separable /ˈsepərəbl/ *adj* **1** (detachable) 可分离的; **to be ~ from sth.** 可从某事物上分离 **2** Ling 可分开的 ‹*phrasal verb*›

separate

A /ˈsepərət/ *adj* **1** (unconnected) 分开的 ‹*piece, area*›; 单独的 ‹*room, sheet, issue*›; **a ~ department for after-sales service** 专门负责售后服务的部门; **I want a ~ opinion** Amer Jur 我想听听独立意见; **~ bathroom and WC** 独立的浴室和洗手间; **to keep the rams ~ from the ewes** 把公羊和母羊分开 **2** (individual) 独有的; **they sleep in ~ rooms** 他们分房睡; **can we have ~ bills, please?** 请给我们分别开账单好吗？; **a ~ entrance to each flat** 每套公寓的单独入口 **3** (independent) 独立的; **the young animals are now capable of ~ existence** 幼兽现在能独立生存了; **a ~ school** Can 教会独立学校

B **separates** /ˈsepərəts/ *npl* [通常指女性的] 单件衣服

C /ˈsepəreɪt/ *vt* **1** (divide) 隔开; **a community ~d by intolerance** 一个因为互不宽容而分裂的社区; **the railway ~s the residential areas from the industrial estate** 铁路把住宅区和工业区隔开 **2** (force apart) 分开; **to ~ the yolks from the whites** 把蛋黄和蛋清分开 **3** (sort) 区分 ‹*people, strands, wires*›; **will you ~ the children according to age** 请你按年龄把孩子们分组; **I have ~d the different threads in the story** 我把故事中不同的线索理清楚了

D /ˈsepəreɪt/ *vi* **1** (part) «*couple, lovers*» 分居 **2** (come away from) 分离; **the oil ~s from the water** 油不溶于水

Phrasal verb

• **separate out** *vt* 分离; **to ~ out elements/ingredients/factors** 把元素/成分/因子分解出来

separately /ˈsepərətli/ *adv* **1** (apart) 分别地 ‹*discuss, treat*›; 分开地 ‹*live, educate, rear*›; **~ from sth.** 与某事物分开 **2** (individually) 单独地 ‹*sell*›; **she spoke to each of us ~** 她与我们逐一谈了话

separation /ˌsepəˈreɪʃn/ *n* **1** [c and u] (break-up of couple) 分居; (time apart) 离别; **they decided on a trial ~** 他们决定尝试分居 **2** [u] (parting) 分开; **the child suffered as a result of ~ from his mother** 孩子因和母亲分开而受苦 **3** [u and c] (distinction) 分离;

a clear ~ between church and state 教会和政府的明确分离 **4** [u] Chem 离析

separatism /'sepərətɪzəm/ *n* [u] 分离主义

separatist /'sepərətɪst/
A *n* 分离主义者
B *adj* (of separatism) 分离主义的; (of separatists) 分离主义者的

separator /'sepəreɪtə(r)/ *n* **1** (machine) 分离器 **2** (person) 分离者

sepia /'siːpɪə/ ▸**p. 134** *n* **1** [u] (substance) 乌贼墨颜料; **~ ink** 乌贼墨墨水 **2** [u] (colour) 棕褐色; **in ~** 以棕褐色; **a ~ photograph/print** 棕褐色照片/印刷品 **3** [c] (drawing) 棕褐色绘画

sepsis /'sepsɪs/ *n* [u] 脓毒症

Sept *abbr* **= September**

septa /'septə/ *pl* ▸**septum**

September /sep'tembə(r)/ ▸**p. 490** *n* 九月; **last/this/next ~** 上个/本年/下个九月份; **in early/late ~** 九月上旬/下旬; **~ weather/morning** 九月的天气/早晨

septet /sep'tet/ *n* **1** (singers) 七重唱组合; (players) 七重奏组合 **2** (composition) 七重奏曲

septic /'septɪk/ *adj* 脓毒性的 ‹*infection*›; 化脓的 ‹*cut, wound*›; **to go** *or* **turn ~** 化脓; **~ poisoning** 败血症

septicaemia Brit, **septicemia** Amer /ˌseptɪ'siːmɪə/ ▸**p. 377** *n* [u] 败血症

septic tank *n* 化粪池

septuagenarian /ˌseptjʊədʒɪ'neərɪən, Amer -tʃʊdʒə-/
A *n* 70多岁的人
B *adj* 70多岁的

septum /'septəm/ *n* (*pl* **septa**) 隔膜; **the nasal ~** 鼻中隔

septuplet /'septjʊplɪt, sep'tjuːplɪt/ *n* **1** (offspring) 七胞胎之一 **2** Mus 七连音符

sepulchral /sɪ'pʌlkrəl/ *adj* **1** (relating to burial) 埋葬的 ‹*rites*›; **~ tomb/monument/statue** 坟墓/墓碑/死者的雕像 **2** formal (gloomy) 阴森森的 ‹*darkness, voice, tone*›

sepulchre Brit, **sepulcher** Amer /'seplkə(r)/ *n* 坟墓

sequel /'siːkwəl/ *n* **1** (consequence) 结果; **~ to sth.** 某事的结局 **2** (to book) 续篇; (to film) 续集; **~ to sth.** …的续篇 ‹*book*›; …的续集 ‹*film*›

sequence /'siːkwəns/ *n* **1** [c] (succession) 一系列; **a ~ of unlucky events** 一连串不幸事件 **2** [c and u] (order) 顺序; **in ascending/chronological ~** 按升序/按年代顺序; **in ~ of sth.** 按某种次序 **3** [c] (of film) 一组镜头

sequence: ~ dancing *n* [u] 序列舞; **~ of tenses** *n* 时态的呼应

sequencer /'siːkwənsə(r)/ *n* **1** Mus 音序器 **2** Biochem 序列测定仪

sequential /sɪ'kwenʃl/ *adj* **1** (forming sequence) 序列的 ‹*numbers*› **2** (consequent, resultant) 作为结果产生的 ‹*event, link, deduction*›; **to be ~ to** *or* **on** *or* **upon sth.** 因某事物而产生 **3** (completed one after the other) 顺序的 ‹*data processing, computer search*›

sequester /sɪ'kwestə(r)/ *vt* **1** formal (lock away) 藏匿 ‹*valuables, treasure*›; 使…隔绝 ‹*person*› **2** Jur 扣押 ‹*assets, property*›

sequestered /sɪ'kwestəd/ *adj* liter 僻静的 ‹*place*›; 隐退的 ‹*life*›

sequestrate /'siːkwestreɪt/ *vt* 扣押 ‹*assets, property*›

sequestration /ˌsiːkwɪ'streɪʃn/ *n* [u] 扣押

sequin /'siːkwɪn/ *n* [装饰衣服的] 亮片

sequinned, sequined /'siːkwɪnd/ *adj* 用亮片装饰的

sequoia /sɪ'kwɔɪə/ *n* **1** [c] (tree) 红杉 **2** [u] (wood) 红杉木

sera /'sɪərə/ *pl* ▸**serum**

seraglio /se'rɑːlɪəʊ/ *n* (*pl* **~s**) [伊斯兰宫殿中女眷居住的] 后宫

seraph /'serəf/ *n* (*pl* **seraphim** *or* **~s**) 六翼天使 [基督教中级别最高的天使，又称撒拉弗]

seraphic /sə'ræfɪk/ *adj* liter 天使般的

seraphim /'serəfɪm/ *pl* ▸**seraph**

Serb /sɜːb/ ▸**p. 426, p. 503**
A *adj* (of Serbia) 塞尔维亚的; (of the people) 塞尔维亚人的; (of the language) 塞尔维亚语的
B *n* **1** [c] (person) 塞尔维亚人 **2** [u] (language) 塞尔维亚语

Serbia /'sɜːbɪə/ *pr n* 塞尔维亚

Serbia and Montenegro *pr n* 塞尔维亚和黑山共和国

Serbian ▸**p. 426, p. 503**
A *adj* (of Serbia) 塞尔维亚的; (of the people) 塞尔维亚人的; (of the language) 塞尔维亚语的
B *n* **1** [c] (person) 塞尔维亚人 **2** [u] (language) 塞尔维亚语

Serbo-Croat /ˌsɜːbəʊ'krəʊæt/, **Serbo-Croatian** /ˌsɜːbəʊkrəʊ'eɪʃn/ ▸**p. 426**
A *adj* (of the language) 塞尔维亚－克罗地亚语的
B *n* **1** [c] (person) 讲塞尔维亚－克罗地亚语的人 **2** [u] (language) 塞尔维亚－克罗地亚语

serenade /ˌserə'neɪd/
A *n* 小夜曲; **a ~ to sb.** 献给某人的小夜曲
B *vt* (play to) 对…奏小夜曲; (sing to) 对…唱小夜曲

serendipitous /ˌserən'dɪpɪtəs/ *adj* formal (chance) 机缘凑巧的 ‹*meeting, event*›; (unexpected) 意外的 ‹*find, discovery*›

serendipity /ˌserən'dɪpəti/ *n* formal **1** [u] (luck) 机缘凑巧 **2** [c] (unplanned event) 巧事

serene /sɪ'riːn/ *adj* 安详的 ‹*person, temperament, expression*›; 宁静的 ‹*landscape, sea*›; 晴朗无云的 ‹*sky*›

serenely /sɪ'riːnli/ *adv* 安详地 ‹*smile, move, beautiful*›; 平静地 ‹*move, preside, survey*›; **~ indifferent** 淡然的

serenity /sɪ'renəti/ *n* [u] (of person, temperament, expression) 安详; (of landscape, sea) 宁静

serf /sɜːf/ *n* 农奴

serfdom /'sɜːfdəm/ *n* [u] (state) 农奴身份; (system) 农奴制

serge /sɜːdʒ/ *n* [u and c] 哔叽布料

sergeant /'sɑːdʒənt/ *n* **1** Mil 中士 **2** (in British police) 巡佐; (in American police) 警佐

sergeant: ~ at arms *n* **= serjeant-at-arms**; **~ first class** *n* Amer 陆军上士; **~ major** *n* **1** Brit 准尉副官; **2** Amer 军士长

serial /'sɪərɪəl/
A *n* (on TV, radio) 连续剧; (in magazine) 连载小说
B *adj attrib* **1** (repeated) 一连串的 ‹*killing, murder, rape*›; **a ~ murderer/rapist** 连环杀人犯/强奸犯 **2** (divided into episodes) 连播的 ‹*drama, documentary*›; 连载的 ‹*story*› **3** Mus 序列的 ‹*tone, note*›

serial comma *n* 序列逗号 [用于倒数第二个列举项之后，在and或or之前]

serialization /ˌsɪərɪəlaɪ'zeɪʃn, Amer -lɪ'z-/ *n* [u] (of TV or radio programmes) 连播; (of novels) 连载

serialize /'sɪərɪəlaɪz/ *vt* (in magazine, newspaper) 连载; (on radio, TV) 连播

serial killer *n* 连环杀手

serially /'sɪərɪəli/ *adv* **1** (in numbered sequence) 按顺序 ‹*number, arrange, present*› **2** (in episodes) 连续地 ‹*publish, broadcast*›

serial: ~ monogamy *n* [u] 连续性一夫一妻制; **~ number** *n* (on product) 序列号; (on cheque) 编号; **~ port** *n* 串行端口; **~ rights** *npl* (of novel) 连载版权; (of TV or radio programme) 连播版权

sericulture /'serɪkʌltʃə(r)/ *n* [u] 养蚕业

series /'sɪəriːz/ *n* (*pl* **series**) **1** [c] (sequence) 一系列; **a ~ of attacks/measures** 一连串的袭击/一系列的措施 **2** [c] (set) 一套; **a ~ of stamps/coins/books** 一套邮票/钱币/丛书 **3** [c] (on TV, radio) 系列节目; (in magazine, newspaper) 系列作品; **a drama/comedy ~** 系列剧/喜剧; **paperback ~** 平装丛书 **4** [u] Elec, Electron 串联; **in ~** 串联的; **~ circuit** 串联电路

serio-comic /ˌsɪərɪəʊ'kɒmɪk/ *adj* 亦庄亦谐的

serious /'sɪərɪəs/ *adj* **1** (not frivolous) 严肃的; **a ~ child** 不苟言笑的孩子; **a ~ look on his face** 他脸上的严肃表情; **to have ~ intentions towards sb.** dated hum 对某人是真心的; **deadly ~** colloq 非常严肃的; **you can't be ~** 你在开玩笑吧; **to be ~ (about sb./sth.)** (对某人/某事物) 是认真的; **a ~ business** 正经事 **2** *attrib* (careful) 需认真思考的 ‹*reading, study*›; (important, weighty) 重要的 ‹*matter*›; **a ~ book/film** 严肃的书/影片 **3** (grave) 严重的 ‹*problem, flaw*›; 严正的 ‹*allegation, charge*›; **the patient's condition is ~** 这个病人的病情很严重

Serious Fraud Office *pr n* Brit **the ~** 重大欺诈案调查局

seriously /'sɪərɪəsli/ *adv* **1** (in earnest) 严肃地 ‹*speak*›; 认真地 ‹*listen, write*›; **to ~ consider doing sth.** 认真考虑做某事; **but ~, ...** colloq 不过，说正经的…; **to take sb./sth. ~** 认真对待某人/某事物; **he takes himself too ~** 他太把自己当回事了 **2** (gravely) 严重地 ‹*wounded, offended*›; 非常 ‹*concerned, worried*›

seriousness /'sɪərɪəsnɪs/ *n* [u] **1** (of style, expression, occasion) 严肃; **in all ~** 说实在的 **2** (of illness, injury, damage) 严重; (of situation) 严峻; (of threat, allegation) 重大

serjeant-at-arms /ˌsɑːdʒəntət'ɑːmz/ *n* (*pl* **serjeants-at-arms**) 警卫官

sermon /'sɜːmən/ *n* **1** (religious address) 布道; **to give** *or* **preach a ~** 布道 **2** (tedious lecture) 说教

sermonize /'sɜːmənaɪz/
A *vi* 说教; **to ~ about** *or* **on sth.** 就某事物进行说教
B *vt* 对…说教; **to ~ sb. about sth.** 就某事物对某人进行说教

sermonizing /'sɜːmənaɪzɪŋ/ *n* [u] 说教

seropositive /ˌsɪərəʊ'pɒzɪtɪv/ *adj* 血清反应阳性的

serotonin /ˌserə'təʊnɪn/ *n* [u] 血清素

serous /'sɪərəs/ *adj* 浆液的 ‹*discharge*›; **~ fluid/membrane/tissue** 浆液/浆膜/浆液组织

serpent /'sɜːpənt/ *n* **1** liter (snake) 巨蛇 **2** fig (treacherous person) 阴险狡诈的人 **3** (musical instrument) 蛇形管

serpentine /'sɜːpəntaɪn, Amer -tiːn/
A *n* [u] 蛇纹石
B *adj* **1** (winding) 弯弯曲曲的 ‹*river, road, coils*› **2** (complicated) 阴险的

SERPS /sɜːps/ *abbr* Brit **= state earnings-related pension scheme** 国家收入关联养老金计划

serrated /sɪ'reɪtɪd, Amer 'sereɪtɪd/ *adj* 锯齿状的 ‹*edge, leaf, tooth*›; 带锯齿的 ‹*knife, blade*›

serration /sɪ'reɪʃn/ *n* 锯齿

serried /'serɪd/ *adj* 密集排列的

serum /'sɪərəm/ *n* (*pl* **sera** /'sɪərə/ *or* **~s**) **1** [u] (in blood) 血清 **2** [c and u] (antidote) 免疫血清; **tetanus ~** 抗破伤风血清

servant /'sɜːvənt/ *n* **1** ▸**p. 409** (household employee) 用人; **to treat sb. like a ~** 像对待用人一样对待某人 **2** (government employee) 职员; **a public/government ~** 公务员/政府雇员; **parliament should be the ~ of the people** 议会应该是人民的公仆 **3** (supporter) 奉献者; (follower) 追随者

servant: ~ girl *n* 女仆; **~s' hall** *n* 用人房间

serve /sɜːv/
A *vt* **1** (work for) 伺候 ‹*master, mistress*›; 为…效力 ‹*company*›; 侍奉 ‹*God*›; **to ~ the cause of freedom** 为自由的事业而奋斗; **to ~**

one's country/the public 为国家/公众服务; **to ~ Queen and Country** 为女王和国家从军; **to ~ two masters** 侍奉二主 **2** (wait on) 招待 ‹*customer*›; **have you ~d the people at table 11?** 你为 11 号桌的客人服务了吗? ; **I can't ~ you; you're under age** 我不能卖酒给你; 你还不到法定年龄 **3** (give) 端上 ‹*food, wine*›; (give food and drink to) 给…端上饭菜 ‹*guest*›; **let me ~ you some more beef** 我再给你添点儿牛肉 **4** (provide) 供应 ‹*meal*›; **we don't ~ hot meals after nine o'clock** 9 点以后我们不卖热餐; **dinner is ~d!** 请来用餐! ; **to ~ sb. sth.** 供应某人某食物; **to ~ sth. with sth.** 以某物配某物一起上; **~s 4** (in recipe) 4 人份 **5** (provide assistance, facility to) 为…提供服务; **the library exists to ~ the community/university** 图书馆是为社区/大学服务的; **towns not ~d by the railway** 未通火车的城镇; **we're very well ~d with shops in this district** 我们这个地区购物很便利 **6** (be useful for) 对…有用; **this old fountain pen has ~d me well over the years** 这支旧钢笔我多年来用着都很好; **her sense of direction ~d her well** 她的方向感帮了她的大忙; **to ~ a purpose** 派上用场; **to ~ the/sb.'s purpose** 满足需求/某人的需求; **(it) ~s you right** fig colloq 你活该 **7** (spend) 度过; **to ~ a** *or* **one's term** 任职一届; **Eisenhower ~d two terms as President** 艾森豪威尔担任了两届总统; **to ~ one's time** (as apprentice) 当学徒; (in prison) 服刑; (in the armed forces) 服役; **to ~ time** *or* **a sentence** 服刑 **8** Jur 送达 ‹*summons, court order*›; **to ~ notice on sb.** 向某人发出警告 **9** Sport (in tennis) 发 ‹*ace, let*› **10** «*bull, stag*» 与…配种 ‹*cow, mare, deer*›

B *vi* **1** (provide food and drink) 招待; **to ~ at table** 侍候进餐; **I usually ~ in the cocktail lounge** 我通常在鸡尾酒吧间做招待 **2** (work) 供职; **to ~ on a committee/jury** 担任委员/陪审员; **to ~ as sth.** 担任某职务 **3** Mil 服役; **to ~ in the army/navy** 在陆军/海军服役; **to ~ as sth.** 担任某军职 **4** formal (meet a need) 有用; **any old excuse will ~ when they're late** 他们如果迟到了, 随便说个老掉牙的理由就管用; **this room ~s as a spare bedroom** 这个房间用作备用卧室; **to ~ to do sth.** 用来做某事 **5** Sport (in tennis) 发球; **to ~ for the set/match** 局点/赛点发球 **6** Relig 担任辅祭

C *n* (in tennis) 发球; **he has a very big ~** 他擅长大力发球

Phrasal verbs

• **serve out** *vt* [**~ sth. out, ~ out sth.**] **1** (distribute) 分发 ‹*provisions*› **2** (complete) 完成; **to ~ out a** *or* **one's sentence** 服满刑期

• **serve up**

A *vi* 上饭菜

B *vt* [**~ sth. up, ~ up sth.**] **1** (put on to plates) 端上 ‹*food, meal*› **2** pej (offer, present) 提供; **they ~ up the same old programmes week after week** 他们一周又一周地重复播放老掉牙的节目

server /ˈsɜːvə(r)/ *n* **1** Amer (waiter, waitress) 侍者 **2** Sport 发球者 **3** Comput 服务器 **4** (food utensil) 上菜器具

servery /ˈsɜːvəri/ *n* Brit (room) 备餐室; (counter) 备餐台

service /ˈsɜːvɪs/

A *n* **1** [u] (by employee, supplier) 效劳; (in army) 服役; **years of ~** 工作年限; **a life of (public) ~** (为公众) 服务的一生; **ten years' ~ in the army** 在部队服役 10 年; **at sb.'s ~** 听候某人吩咐; **he gave his life in the ~ of his country** 他为国捐躯; **can I be of ~?** 我能帮忙吗? ; **on Her Majesty's ~** 为女王陛下效劳 **2** [u] (attention, assistance) 接待; **we add on 10% for ~** 我们加收 10% 的服务费; **~ to the customer/client** 为顾客/客户提供的服务 **3** [u] (use) 使用; **this coat should be good for a lifetime's ~** 这件外套能穿一辈子; **the van has given me excellent ~, I've had excellent ~ from the van** 那辆运货车帮了我大忙; **to be in ~** 在使用中; **to come into** *or* **enter ~** 开始被采用; **to go out of ~** 被停用 **4** [c] (favour) 帮助; **to do sb. a ~** 帮某人个忙 **5** [c] Comm 服务; **a dry-cleaning/money-changing ~** 干洗/货币兑换服务; **it's all part of the ~** 这是份内事; **we badly need the ~s of a good accountant** 我们急需一名优秀的会计; **for ~s rendered** 服务费 **6** [c] (government department) 行政部门; **the customs/diplomatic/health ~** 海关/外交/卫生部门; **the emergency ~s** 应急部门 **7** [c] Mil 军种; **high-ranking officers from (each of) the three ~s** 来自陆海空三军的高级军官; **the ~s** 军队; **he joined the ~ at the age of 18** 他18岁参军 **8** [c] Transp 交通服务; **a bus/train/ferry ~** 公共汽车/火车/轮渡运输服务; **it's a 10 minute ~ on this route** 这条线路每隔 10 分钟发一班车 **9** [u and c] Aut (maintenance) 检修 **10** [c] Relig 宗教仪式; **morning/evening ~** 晨祷/晚祷; **a wedding/funeral ~** 婚礼/葬礼 **11** [c] (dinner set) 成套餐具; **a silver tea ~** 一套银质茶具 **12** [c] (in tennis) 发球; **return of ~** 接发球 **13** [c] Jur (of summons, warrant, writ) 正式送达 **14** **services** *pl* Brit (on motorway) [高速公路旁的] 服务区

B *modif* **1** Mil 军队的 ‹*personnel, life*›; **a ~ rifle** 军用步枪; **~ pay** 军饷 **2** (for employees or servants) 供员工或下人使用的 ‹*entrance, stairs*›

C *vt* **1** (do maintenance on) 检修 ‹*machine, car*› **2** Fin 支付…的利息 ‹*debt, loan*›

serviceable /ˈsɜːvɪsəbl/ *adj* **1** (usable) 可用的 ‹*part, condition*› **2** (practical) 实用的 ‹*clothing, shoes*›

service: ~ area *n* **1** (for motorists) [高速公路旁的] 路边服务区; **2** (of TV, radio station) 信号覆盖区域; **~ break** *n* [尤指网球或羽毛球的] 破发局; **~ call** *n* 上门服务; **~ centre** *n* Brit 维修中心; **~ charge** *n* **1** (in restaurant, at bank) 服务费; **2** (for property maintenance) 维护费; **~ company** *n* 维修服务公司; **~ contract** *n* **1** (employment agreement) 劳务合同; **2** (agreement covering equipment) 服务合同; **~ department** *n* (office) 维修部; (workshop) 维修车间; **~ economy** *n* 服务型经济; **~ elevator** *n* Amer **= ~ lift**; **~ engineer** ▸**p. 409** *n* 维修工程师; **~ entrance** *n* [宾馆用于送货、清运垃圾等的] 服务通道; **~ family** *n* 军人家庭; **~ flat** *n* Brit 酒店式公寓; **~ hatch** *n* 上菜窗口; **~ industry** *n* 服务业; **~ lift** *n* Brit 运货电梯; **~ line** *n* [网球、羽毛球等场地的] 发球线; **~man** /-mən/ *n* 军人; **~ module** *n* [航天器的] 服务舱; **~ operation** *n* 服务运营; **~ provider** *n* 服务提供商; **~ road** *n* Brit [由主干道通往商铺或住宅等的] 支路; **~ sector** *n* **the ~ sector** 服务业; **~ station** *n* 加油站; **~ till** *n* Brit 收银机; **~woman** *n* 女军人

servicing /ˈsɜːvɪsɪŋ/ *n* [u] 维修保养

serviette /ˌsɜːvɪˈet/ *n* Brit 餐巾

servile /ˈsɜːvaɪl, Amer -vl/ *adj* 奴颜婢膝的

servility /sɜːˈvɪləti/ *n* [u] 奴性

serving /ˈsɜːvɪŋ/

A *n* (helping) [食物的] 一份; **a ~ of vegetables** 一份蔬菜; **enough for four ~s** 足够四人吃的

B *adj* (currently in office) 在任的 ‹*chairman, official*›; 现役的 ‹*officer*›

serving: ~ dish *n* 上菜盘子; **~ hatch** *n* 上菜窗口; **~ spoon** *n* 菜勺

servitude /ˈsɜːvɪtjuːd, Amer -tuːd/ *n* [u] (slavery) 奴隶身份; (subjugation) 屈从地位

servo /ˈsɜːvəʊ/ *n* **= servomechanism**

servo: ~ brake, ~ assisted brake *ns* 伺服刹车; **~ control** *n* [c and u] 伺服控制; **~mechanism** *n* 伺服机构; **~motor** *n* 伺服电动机

sesame /ˈsesəmi/ *n* [u] 芝麻; **~ oil/seed** (芝) 麻油/芝麻籽

session /ˈseʃn/ *n* **1** (meeting) 集会; (of law court) 开庭; (of committee, parliament) 会议; **to go into closed** *or* **private ~** 召开秘密会议; **the court is in ~** 法庭正在开庭 **2** (period for specific activity) [进行某活动的] 一段时间; **a bull ~** 闲聊; **a ~ with my analyst** 与我的分析师的讨论 **3** Brit (school year) 学年; Amer (school term) 学期; (period of lessons) 上课时间 **4** (in recording studio) 录音时段 **5** colloq (drinking bout) 畅饮

session: ~ man ▸**p. 409** *n* 录音乐师; **~ musician** ▸**p. 409** *n* 录音乐师

set /set/

A *vt* (*pt, pp* **set**) **1** (place, position) 放置 ‹*object*›; 安置 ‹*person*›; **his hat was ~ at a rakish angle** 他歪戴着帽子; **the castle is ~ on the bank of a river** 城堡位于河岸上; **to ~ guards around the building** 在大楼周围布置警卫; **I would ~ the university just below Oxford and Cambridge in terms of prestige** 从声望上讲, 我觉得这所大学仅次于牛津和剑桥 **2** (arrange, establish) 确定 ‹*time, venue, target, standard*›; 树立 ‹*fashion*›; **to ~ a reserve price for sth.** 为某物定底价 **3** (adjust) 设定; **to ~ the alarm** (on building) 设定警报器; (on clock) 设闹钟; **to ~ the switch in the on/off position** 把开关调到开/关的位置 **4** (put in motion) 使开始; **I'll soon ~ them on the right track** 我很快会拨正他们的思路; **she ~ the motor going** 她开动了马达; **to ~ sb. thinking** 引发某人的思考; **to ~ sb. to do sth.** *or* **doing sth.** 让某人做某事; **to ~ oneself to do sth.** 给自己安排做某事 **5** (assign, arrange) 布置 ‹*task, job*›; 出…的题目 ‹*test*›; **who is ~ting the biology exam?** 谁出生物试题? ; **to ~ sb. a question** *or* **problem** 给某人出题; **the committee has been ~ the task of drafting a new constitution** 委员会受命起草新宪法 **6** (in work of fiction) 以…为背景; **the next scene is ~ in an antechamber** 下一个场景设在接待室 **7** (fix in decorative setting) 镶嵌 ‹*gemstone*›; **to ~ sth. in sth.** 把某物镶嵌入某物; **a gold necklace ~ with rubies and emeralds** 一条镶有红宝石和翡翠的金项链 **8** (write musical accompaniment) 为…谱曲 ‹*words, libretto*›; **to ~ a poem to music** 为一首诗谱曲 **9** Print 排 ‹*type*›; 为…排版 ‹*book*› **10** Med 使…复位 ‹*bone, limb*›; **to ~ a leg/arm in plaster** 用石膏固定腿/胳膊 **11** (cause to harden) 使…凝固 ‹*jam, concrete, dye*› **12** (style) 使定型; **to have one's hair ~** 做发型

B *vi* (*pt, pp* **set**) **1** (go down) «*sun, moon*» 落下 **2** (solidify) «*jam, concrete, dye*» 凝固; **the glue/cement is very quick to ~** 这种胶水/水泥凝固得很快 **3** Med «*bone*» 复位 **4** (begin) 着手; **to ~ to doing sth.** 开始做某事; **to ~ to work** 着手工作 **5** (assume a fixed expression) 呈现; **her features ~ into a grimace** 她的面部扭曲了

C *n* **1** (of tools, spanners, knives etc.) 一套; (of keys) 一串; (of weights) 一组; **a ~ of cutlery** 一套餐具; **a complete ~ of Beethoven's symphonies** 贝多芬交响乐全集; **a ~ of false teeth** 一副假牙; **sold in ~s** 整套出售的; **to make up** *or* **complete a ~** 凑成一套 **2** (group with a shared interest) 一类人; **the smart** *or* **fashionable ~** 时尚一族; **a member of the literary ~** 文学圈中的一员; **he's not part of our ~** 他和我们不是一类人 **3** Radio 收音机; TV 电视机; **please do not adjust your ~** 请不要调台 **4** (of head, shoulders) 姿态; (of sails, tide) 方向; **the ~ of his jaw** 他下巴的姿态; **the particular ~ of his mind** 他特有的思想倾向 **5** Cin, Theat (scenery, setting) 布景; (filming area) 摄影场; (stage) 舞台; **to build/erect a ~** 搭建/竖起布景; **the director gave orders to clear the ~** 导演命令清场; **on (the) ~** 在拍摄现场 **6** Sport (in tennis) 盘; **a 5-~ match** 5 盘制比赛 **7** Math 集 **8** Brit Sch [按学生能力划分的] 教学组; **to be in the top/bottom ~ for maths** 数学成

S

绩名列前茅/垫底 9 (of hair) 发型 10 Culin 凝结 11 Hunt (of hound) [猎犬发现猎物时所摆出的]指示姿势; **(dead) ～** (固定) 指示姿势; **to make a dead ～ at sb.** (attack) 猛烈攻击某人; fig (try to win the affections of) 竭力讨好某人 12 liter (setting) 下落; **at ～ of sun** 日落时分

D *adj* 1 (established) 固定的; **events usually follow a ～ pattern** 事态通常按固有的模式发展; **a ～ procedure** 固定程序; **a ～ phrase/expression** 固定词组/表达方式 2 (rigid, unchanging) 呆板的 ‹*expression*›; 不变的 ‹*idea, attitude, position*›; **to be ～ in one's ways** 固执己见; **to be ～ fair** «*weather*» 持续晴好 3 Sch (assigned for study) 指定的 ‹*book, subject, topic*› 4 (ready) 作好准备的; **ready, (get) ～, go!** 各就位, 预备, 跑! ; **to be all ～** 一切准备就绪 5 (determined) 下定决心的; **to be ～ on sth./doing sth.** 对某事物下了决心/决心做某事; **they seem ～ on ruining our chances** 他们似乎一心想毁掉我们的机会; **to be ～ against sth./doing sth.** 坚决反对某事物/做某事 6 (likely) 很有可能的; **to be ～ to do sth.** 很可能做某事 7 **～ meal** *or* **menu** (in restaurant) 套餐

Phrasal verbs

- **set about** *vt* 1 [**～ about sth.**] (begin purposefully) 着手干 ‹*job*›; **to ～ about doing sth.** 着手做某事 2 [**～ about sb.**] Brit colloq (attack) 袭击; **to ～ about sb. with a stick/hammer** 用棍子/锤子打某人
- **set against** *vt* 1 (cause to be in conflict with) **to ～ sb. against sb./sth.** 使某人反对某人/某事物; **the dispute ～ father against son, brother against brother** 这一争端使得父子成仇, 兄弟反目 2 (offset against) **to ～ sth. against sth.** 把某事物与某事物相比; **the benefits seem very small ～ against the magnitude of the risk** 与巨大的风险相比, 收益似乎太微不足道了
- **set apart** *vt* [**～ sb./sth. apart, ～ apart sb./sth.**] 使与众不同; **what ～s her apart is the elegance of her prose style** 她的散文风格典雅, 使她的写作独具特色
- **set aside** *vt* [**～ sth. aside, ～ aside sth.**] 1 (put to one side) 把…放到一边; **he ～ aside his newspaper** 他把报纸搁到一边 2 (disregard, ignore) 抛开 ‹*differences, prejudices, pride, jealousy*› 3 (dedicate) 省出 ‹*money*›; 留出 ‹*time*› 4 Jur (cancel) 撤销 ‹*decision*›; 驳回 ‹*sentence*›
- **set back** *vt* 1 [**～ sth. back, ～ back sth.**] (position to the rear) 把…往后放; **the house is ～ back from the road** 房子离公路有一段距离 2 [**～ sb./sth. back, ～ back sb./sth.**] (cause delay to) 耽搁 ‹*project, work*›; **a technical problem ～ us back three days** 一个技术问题让我们耽搁了 3 天 3 [**～ sb. back**] colloq (be an expense to) **that must have ～ you back a bit!** 那一定花了你不少钱! ; **it only ～ me back $5** 这只花了我 5 美元
- **set by** *vt* [**～ sth. by, ～ by sth.**] 留出 ‹*money*›
- **set down**

A [**～ sth. down, ～ down sth.**] *vt* 1 (put down) 放下 2 (record) 写下; **to ～ sth. down in writing** *or* **on paper** 把某事物记录在案 3 (fix, arrange) 确定; **they've ～ down Friday as the day for the hearing** 他们确定于星期五召开听证会 4 (land) 使…降落 ‹*plane*›

B [**～ sb. down, ～ down sb.**] *vt* (allow to alight) 让…下车 ‹*passengers*›

- **set forth**

A *vi* liter 出发; **to ～ forth on a journey** 动身旅行

B *vt* [**～ sth. forth, ～ forth sth.**] formal 陈述 ‹*conditions, proposal*›

- **set in** *vi* «*winter, bad weather*» 来临; «*disease, complications*» 发作; **the frosts have ～ in early this year** 今年霜来得早; **the rain has ～ in for the night** 晚上下起了雨
- **set off**

A *vi* «*traveller, expedition*» 动身; **she ～ off down the hill/for the station** 她向山下/车站走去; **to ～ off on a journey** 动身上路; **to ～ off to do sth.** 出发去做某事; **she ～ off on a long explanation** fig 她开始进行冗长的解释

B [**～ off sth., ～ sth. off**] *vt* 1 (trigger) 触发 ‹*alarm*›; 引爆 ‹*firework, bomb*› 2 (initiate) 引发; **to ～ off a chain of events** 引发一连串事件 3 (enhance) 衬托 ‹*colour, jewel, decoration*› 4 (counterbalance) 弥补 ‹*loss, withdrawal*›; **to ～ sth. off against sth.** 用某事物抵消某事物

C [**～ sb. off**] *vt* colloq (cause to begin) 使开始; **you've ～ the baby off again!** 你又把孩子弄哭了! ; **to ～ sb. off doing sth.** 使某人开始做某事; **the tickle in his throat ～ him off coughing** 他嗓子发痒, 引起了一阵咳嗽

- **set on** *vt* 1 [**～ on sb.**] (attack) 袭击; **they were ～ on by a gang of bigger boys** 他们遭到了一伙年纪稍大的男孩的攻击 2 (cause to pursue) **to ～ sth./sb. on sb.** 让某物/某人追击某人; **they ～ the police on me** 他们叫警察来抓我
- **set out**

A *vi* 1 (leave) 出发; **to ～ out on sth.** 动身开始某事; **to ～ out on a long journey** 动身踏上长途旅行 2 (begin with intention) **to ～ out to do sth.** 有意做某事; **to ～ out to earn a lot of money** 打算挣大钱

B *vt* [**～ sth. out, ～ out sth.**] 1 (display, lay out) 摆放 ‹*goods, chess pieces*› 2 (present) 陈述 ‹*ideas, proposals, reasons*›

- **set to** *vi* dated 1 (begin energetically) 起劲地干起来; **they ～ to and soon finished the job** 他们大干起来, 很快就完成了工作 2 (begin to fight) 开始扭打; **they ～ to with fists and feet (flying)** 他们开始拳打脚踢起来
- **set up**

A [**～ sth. up, ～ up sth.**] *vt* 1 (erect) 搭起 ‹*stall, stand*›; 建起 ‹*monument, memorial*›; **the photographer took some time to ～ up all her equipment** 这位摄影师花了点时间把全部摄影器材布放到位 2 (establish) 开办 ‹*company*›; 设立 ‹*tribunal, fund*› 3 (produce, start) 引发; **to ～ up a commotion/turbulence/noise** 引起喧闹/骚乱/吵闹; **the monkeys ～ up a great racket when the tiger approached** 老虎走近时, 猴子们大叫起来 4 (arrange) 安排 ‹*meeting, discussion*› 5 Print 排 ‹*type*›; 为…排版 ‹*page*›; **to ～ up a column in type** 为一个专栏排版

B [**～ sb. up, ～ up sb.**] *vt* 1 (establish) 扶持; **to ～ sb. up in business** 扶助某人创业 2 (equip) 配备; **to ～ sb. up with sth.** 用某物装备某人; **I'm pretty well ～ up with the sort of tools I need** 我已经把我需要的工具准备齐全; **to be ～ up for life** 一生衣食无忧 3 Brit colloq (frame) 诬陷; **I was well and truly ～ up** 我被他们彻底陷害了 4 **to ～ sb. up as** *or* **to be sth.** (claim) 声称某人是某物; (pretend) 假称某人是某物; **the critics are trying to ～ her up as the great white hope of British cinema** 评论家们试图把她捧为英国电影界的巨大希望

C *vi* **to ～ up in business** 创业; **to ～ up as sth.** 从事某事; **I hear you're ～ting up as a caterer** 我听说你要做餐饮

D *v refl* 1 (establish oneself) **to ～ oneself up as sth.** 从事某事; **she ～ herself up as a hairdresser** 她做起了美发师 2 (claim to be) **to ～ oneself up as sth.** 自夸为某物; **I don't ～ myself up as** *or* **to be an expert** 我不敢自诩为专家

- **set upon = set on**

set: ～-aside *n* 1 [u] (agricultural policy) 退耕; 2 [u] (agricultural land) 退耕地; 3 [c] Amer (government contract) [少数族裔公司无须竞争直接获得的] 政府合同; 4 [u] Amer (funds) 预留资金; **～back** *n* (problem) 挫折; (reversal) 倒退; **to suffer a ～back** 遭遇挫折; **to be a ～back to** *or* **for sth.** 对某事物来说是个挫折; **～ designer** ▸p. 409 *n* 布景设计师

set piece

A *n* 1 Sport 固定打法 2 Mus, Cin 固定套路

B **setpiece** *modif* 固定套路的 ‹*play, move, finale*›

set: ～ play *n* 固定打法; **～ point** *n* 盘点; **～ scrum** *n* 判罚对阵争球; **～ square** *n* Brit 三角板

sett /set/ *n* 1 (burrow) 獾穴 2 (paving stone) 铺路石

settee /se'tiː/ *n* 长沙发

setter /'setə(r)/ *n* 赛特犬

set theory *n* [u] 集 (合) 论

setting /'setɪŋ/ *n* 1 (surroundings, location) 环境; (background) 背景; **a riverside/mountain ～** 傍水/依山的环境; **this street was the ～ for a murder** 这条街是一起谋杀案的案发地 2 (of play, novel, film) 情节背景; **short stories with a contemporary ～** 以当代生活为背景的短篇小说 3 (jewellery mount) 镶座; **a sapphire in a gold/silver ～** 镶嵌在金/银底座上的蓝宝石 4 (of machine, dial) 挡; **the oven's highest ～** 烤箱的最高挡 5 (piece of music) 配曲; **an orchestral ～** 一首管弦乐曲 6 (of jam, cement) 凝固 7 (descent of sun, moon) 降落; **before/at the ～ of the sun/moon** 在日落/月落之前/时分 8 (plates and cutlery) [摆在桌上供一人使用的] 一套餐具

setting lotion *n* [c and u] 头发定型水

setting-up *n* [u] (of committee) 成立; (of business, factory) 建立; (of programme, scheme) 设立; (of inquiry) 开展

settle¹ /'setl/

A *vi* 1 (come to rest) «*bird, insect*» 飞落; «*dust*» 落下; **it's snowing quite hard, but it's not settling** 雪下得很大, 但并未在地面上堆积起来; **to ～ on sth.** 落在某物上; **dust soon began to ～ on the furniture** 家具很快就蒙上了灰尘; **silence ～d over the room** 屋子里陷入了寂静 2 (subside, drop) «*building, grounds, dregs*» 沉降; **the contents of the packet may have ～d in transit** 包裹里的东西可能在运输途中摇晃密实了; **the ship ～d in the water** 轮船沉到了水底 3 (become calm) «*baby*» 平静下来; **let your lunch ～ before swimming** 午饭后消化一下再游泳 4 (take up residence) «*family, emigrant, colonist*» 定居 5 (pay bill, debt) 付清欠款; **to ～ out of court** 在庭外和解; **to ～ with sb.** 和某人算账

B *vt* 1 (position) 安放 ‹*object*›; 安顿 ‹*person*›; **to ～ an invalid** *or* **get an invalid ～d for the night** 让病人安然过夜; **Percy ～d himself in an armchair** 珀西舒舒服服地坐在扶手椅里 2 (keep down) 使…沉降 ‹*sediment, dregs*› 3 (calm) 放松 ‹*nerves*›; 消除 ‹*doubts*› 4 (resolve) 解决 ‹*dispute, conflict, question*›; 达成 ‹*terms, details*›; **the game was ～d in the first half** 比赛结果在上半场就见分晓了; **to ～ one's affairs** 料理事务; **that ～s it!** 就这么定了! ; **to ～ sth. with sb.** 和某人协商解决某事; **～ it amongst yourselves** 你们自行解决 5 (pay) 付清 ‹*bill, account, debt*› 6 (colonize) 定居于 ‹*area, country*› 7 (give land or housing to) 安置 ‹*people, immigrants*› 8 colloq (stop from causing trouble) 使…就范 ‹*youngster, mischief-maker*›

Phrasal verbs

- **settle back** *vi* (relax) 处于舒适位置; **I ～d back in my chair** 我舒舒服服地在椅子上坐下
- **settle down**

A *vi* 1 (make oneself comfortable) 歇息; **to ～ down to do sth.** 坐下来做某事; **everybody ～d down to listen to the music** 大家都坐下来听音乐; **it's time to ～ down for the night** 到了晚上睡觉的时间了 2 **to ～ down to sth.** (apply oneself to) 开始认真对待某事物

3 (calm down) «*person, situation, country*» 平静下来 **4** (marry) 成家 **5** (become more stable) 过安定的生活

B *vt* **1** [∼ **sb. down**] (into sitting position) 使舒服地坐下; (into recumbent position) 使舒服地躺下 **2** [∼ **sth. down**] (make calm) 使平静下来

• **settle for** *vt* [∼ **for sth.**] 勉强接受 ‹*second best, second-rate job*›

• **settle in** *vi* 安顿下来

• **settle into** *vt* [∼ **into sth.**] 适应 ‹*routine, role*›

• **settle on** *vt* **1** [∼ **on sth./sb.**] (choose) 选定 **2** **to** ∼ **sth. on sb.** (bequeath) 把某物遗赠给某人

• **settle up** *vi* **1** (pay up) 付清账目; **to** ∼ **up with sb.** 与某人结清账款 **2** (do calculations) 理清欠账

settle² *n* (wooden bench) [座板下通常带柜的] 高背长椅

settled /'setld/ *adj* 持续不变的 ‹*weather, way of life*›; 固定的 ‹*habits, routine*›; **to feel** ∼ 感到舒适自在

settlement /'setlmənt/ *n* **1** [c] (village) 定居点; **stone-age** ∼**s** 石器时代的村落 **2** [u] (colonization, occupation) 殖民 **3** [c] (agreement) 协议; **to reach a** ∼ **(with sb.)** (和某人) 达成协议 **4** [u] (resolution) 解决; **pending** ∼ **of the financial details** 财务细节问题的悬而未决 **5** [c] (arrangement between the parties to a lawsuit) 和解 [尤指庭外和解] **6** [u] (payment) 支付; **a cheque in** ∼ **of your account** *or* **invoice** 用于结账的支票 **7** [c] (conveyance of property) 财产转让; ∼ **on sb.** 对某人的财产让与 **8** [u] (subsidence) 沉降

settlement day *n* Brit 交割日

settler /'setlə(r)/ *n* 移民

set-to *n* (*pl* ∼**s**) colloq (quarrel) 争吵; (fight) 打斗; **to have a** ∼ **with sb.** (quarrel) 与某人争吵; (fight) 与某人打架

set-top box *n* 机顶盒

set-up *n* colloq **1** (of system) 建制; (of equipment) 配置; (of company, organization) 设置 **2** (organization, company) 机构 **3** Sport 得分套路 **4** (trick) 陷害

seven /'sevn/ ▸**p. 15, p. 521, p. 831**

A *n* **1** (number, quantity) 七; ∼ **plus two equals nine** 7 加 2 等于 9; **in December nineteen hundred and** ∼ 在 1907 年 12 月; **we live at (number)** ∼**, Victoria Road** 我们住在维多利亚路 7 号; **her phone number is two six double** ∼ 她的电话号码是 2677; **there are** ∼ **of them** 他们有 7 个人 **2** (in time) 7 点钟; **at** ∼ **(o'clock)** 在 7 点 **3** (on playing card) 7 点; **the** ∼ **of diamonds** 方块 7 **4** (age) 7 岁

B *adj* **1** (as quantity) 七的; ∼ **cats** 7 只猫; ∼ **books** 7 本书; ∼ **weeks** 7 周; **the** ∼ **wonders of the world** 世界七大奇观; ∼**-league boots** [童话中] 一步可跨七里格的靴子 **2** (in age) 7 岁的; **he's nearly** ∼ 他快 7 岁了; **our house is only** ∼ **years old** 我们的房子才造了 7 年 **3** (in series) 第七的; **number** ∼ 7 号; **page** ∼ 第 7 页

C **sevens** *npl* (rugby) 七人制橄榄球; **a** ∼**s tournament** 七人制橄榄球巡回赛

seven-a-side *n* [u] 七人制橄榄球; ∼ **rugby/football** 七人制橄榄球/足球

sevenfold /'sevnfəʊld/ *adj, adv* 七倍的 (地)

seventeen /,sevn'tiːn/ ▸**p. 15, p. 521**

A *n* **1** (number, quantity) 十七 **2** (in age) 17 岁

B *adj* **1** (in number) 十七的; ∼ **metres** 17 米; ∼ **paintings** 17 张画 **2** (in age) 17 岁的; **to be** ∼ **(years old)** 17 岁大; **to be over/under** ∼ 超过/不到 17 岁 **3** (in series) 第十七的; **size/number** ∼ 17 码/号

seventeenth /,sevn'tiːnθ/ ▸**p. 521, p. 181**

A *n* **1** (in sequence) 第十七个 **2** (in date) 17 日 **3** (fraction) 十七分之一

B *adj* **1** (in sequence) 第十七的 **2** (in name, title) 十七; **Louis the S**∼ 路易十七 **3** (as fraction) 十七分之一的

C *adv* 第十七

seventh /'sevnθ/ ▸**p. 181, p. 521**

A *n* **1** (in sequence) 第七 **2** (in date) 7日 **3** (fraction) 七分之一

B *adj* **1** (in sequence) 第七的; **it's her** ∼ **birthday** 这是她 7 岁生日; **on the** ∼ **floor** 在 8 楼; **to be in (one's)** ∼ **heaven** 乐到天上 **2** (in name, title) 七世; **Henry the S**∼ **of England** 英王亨利七世 **3** (as fraction) 七分之一的

C *adv* 第七

seventies /'sevntɪz/ ▸**p. 15, p. 181** *npl* **1** (period) **the** ∼ 70 年代 **2** (age) 七十几岁; **to be in one's** ∼ 70 多岁了 **3** (temperature) 七十多度; **temperatures climbed into the** ∼ 温度升到了 70 多度

seventieth /'sevntɪəθ/ ▸**p. 521**

A *n* **1** (in sequence) 第七十个 **2** (fraction) 七十分之一

B *adj* **1** (in sequence) 第七十的 **2** (as fraction) 七十分之一的

C *adv* 第七十

seventy /'sevnti/ ▸**p. 15, p. 521**

A *n* **1** (number, quantity) 七十; **there are** ∼ **of us** 我们有 70 个人 **2** (in age) 70 岁

B *adj* **1** (in number) 七十的; ∼ **boys** 70 个男孩 **2** (in age) 70 岁的; **I'm nearly** ∼ 我快 70 岁了 **3** (in series) 第七十的

seventy-eight, 78 *n* 七十八转粗纹唱片; **a** ∼ **(record** *or* **disc)** 一张七十八转粗纹唱片

seven-year itch *n* colloq hum 七年之痒 [指夫妇在结婚七年后常会出现厌倦对方的倾向]

seven-year-old

A *n* (child) 7 岁的孩子; (animal) 7 岁的动物

B *modif* 7 岁的

sever /'sevə(r)/

A *vt* **1** (cut) 割断 ‹*branch, rope, wire*›; 切下 ‹*head, limb, finger*›; **to** ∼ **sth. from sth.** 将某物从某物上割下 **2** (break off) 断绝 ‹*ties, communication, relationship*›

B *vi* **1** (be cut) «*rope, cord*» 被割断 **2** (be broken off) «*link, communications*» 中断

severable /'sevrəbl/ *adj* 可分开的 ‹*clause*›

several /'sevrəl/ ▸**p. 32**

A *pron* (more than two) 几个; ∼ **of you/us** 你们/我们中的几个人

B *adj* **1** (a few) 几个的; ∼ **books** 几本书 **2** formal (respective) 各自的; **their** ∼ **briefcases** 他们各自的公文包 **3** formal (separate) 分别的; **they went their** ∼ **ways** 他们各走各的路了 **4** Jur 单独的; ∼ **tenancy** 单独租赁

severally /'sevrəli/ *adv* **1** (separately) 分别地 **2** Jur 单独地

severance /'sevərəns/ *n* **1** (of rope) 割断; (of limb) 切断 **2** (redundancy) 解雇 **3** fig (of relations, connection) 断绝 **4** = **severance pay**

severance pay *n* [u] 解雇金

severe /sɪ'vɪə(r)/ *adj* **1** (very bad, serious) 严重的 ‹*injury, illness*›; 剧烈的 ‹*pain*›; 沉重的 ‹*blow*› **2** (harsh) 严厉的 ‹*person, discipline, treatment*›; 苛刻的 ‹*criticism, judgement*› **3** (austere) 简朴的 ‹*style, clothes*› **4** (enormous) 巨大的 ‹*risk, damage*› **5** (extreme) 严酷的 ‹*weather*›; ∼ **cold/winter** 严寒/严冬 **6** (stern) 严肃的 ‹*person, expression*›; **to be** ∼ **to** *or* **towards** *or* **with sb.** 严肃对待某人

severely /sɪ'vɪəli/ *adv* **1** (seriously) 严重地 ‹*injured, damaged*› **2** (harshly) 严厉地 ‹*treat, punish*›; 苛刻地 ‹*judge, criticize, act*› **3** (austerely) 简朴地 ‹*dress, decorate*› **4** (sternly) 严肃地 ‹*look, speak*› **5** (extremely) 极度 ‹*embarrassed, impeded*›

severity /sɪ'verəti/ *n* [u] **1** (of problem, injury, damage) 严重; (of pain) 剧烈 **2** (of punishment, sentence, treatment) 严厉 **3** (of hair, dress, style) 简朴 **4** (of person, expression) 严肃 **5** (of weather) 严酷

Severn /'sevən/ ▸**p. 663** *pr n* **the (River)** ∼ 塞汶河

Seville orange /,sevɪl 'ɒrɪndʒ, sə'vɪl/ *n* [制果酱的] 酸橙

sew /səʊ/ (*pt* ∼**ed**; *pp* **sewn** *or* ∼**ed**)

A *vt* **1** (stitch) «*person, machine*» 缝 ‹*seam, hem, skirt, patch*›; «*surgeon*» 缝合 ‹*cut, wound*›; **to** ∼ **sth. on to sth.** 把某物缝到某物上; **to** ∼ **sth. into sth.** 把某物缝入某物内 **2** (make) 缝制 ‹*clothes, table linen*›

B *vi* «*person, machine*» 缝

Phrasal verb

• **sew up** *vt* [∼ **sth. up,** ∼ **up sth.**] **1** (close by stitching) 缝合 ‹*hole, gash*› **2** colloq (secure) 使…万无一失 ‹*deal, match*›

sewage /'suːɪdʒ, 'sjuː-/ *n* [u] 污水

sewage: ∼ **disposal** *n* [u] 污水排放; ∼ **farm** *n* 污水处理场; ∼ **outfall,** ∼ **outlet** *ns* 污水排放口; ∼ **sludge** *n* [u] 污水淤泥; ∼ **system** *n* 污水排放系统; ∼ **treatment** *n* [u] 污水处理; ∼ **works** *npl* + *v sing or pl* 污水处理厂

sewer /'suːə(r), 'sjuː-/ *n* 下水道

sewerage /'suːərɪdʒ, 'sjuː-/ *n* [u] **1** (drains) 排水系统 **2** = **sewage**

sewer: ∼ **gas** *n* [u] 阴沟气; ∼ **rat** *n* 褐家鼠

sewing /'səʊɪŋ/ *n* [u] **1** (activity) 缝纫; (skill) 缝纫法; **a** ∼ **table/class** 缝纫桌/班 **2** (piece of work) 针线活

sewing: ∼ **basket** *n* 针线篮; ∼ **bee,** ∼ **circle** *ns* 缝纫小组; ∼ **cotton** *n* [c and u] 缝纫棉线; ∼ **machine** *n* 缝纫机; ∼ **silk** *n* [c and u] 缝纫丝线; ∼ **thread** *n* [c and u] 缝纫线

sewn /səʊn/ *pp* ▸**sew**

sex /seks/

A *n* **1** [c] (gender) 性别; **people of both** ∼**es** 男人和女人; **the fair** ∼ dated or hum 女人; **the stronger/weaker** ∼ dated 男人/女人 **2** [u] (intercourse) 性交; **to have** ∼ **with sb.** 与某人性交; **premarital/extramarital** ∼ 婚前/婚外性行为; **he thinks about nothing but** ∼ 他满脑子都是性

B *modif* **1** Biol 性的; ∼ **chromosome/hormone/organ** 性染色体/激素/器官 **2** (referring to sexual activity) 性行为的; **the** ∼ **trade** 性交易; **a** ∼ **attacker** 性侵犯者

C *vt* (determine sex of) 确定…的性别 ‹*chick, kitten, puppy*›

Phrasal verb

• **sex up** *vt* [∼ **up sth.,** ∼ **sth. up**] colloq 使…更吸引人 ‹*information, report, image*›

sex: ∼ **abuse** *n* [u] 性侵犯; ∼ **act** *n* 性行为; **to perform the** ∼ **act (with sb.)** (与某人) 性交

sexagenarian /,seksədʒɪ'neərɪən/ *n* 60 多岁的人

sex: ∼ **aid** *n* 性辅助器具; ∼ **appeal** *n* [u] 性魅力; ∼ **attack** *n* 性侵害; ∼ **change** *n* 变性; **to have a** ∼ **change** 接受变性手术; ∼**-crazed** *adj* 性狂乱的; ∼ **crime** *n* [c and u] 性犯罪; ∼ **discrimination** *n* [u] 性别歧视; ∼ **drive** *n* 性冲动

sexed /sekst/ *adj* ▸**highly-sexed**

sex: ∼ **education** *n* [u] 性教育; ∼ **game** *n* 性游戏; ∼ **god** *n* colloq 性感的男子; ∼ **goddess** *n* colloq 性感的女人; ∼ **industry** *n* [u] **the** ∼ **industry** 性产业

sexism /'seksɪzəm/ *n* [u] (discrimination) [尤指对女性的] 性别歧视

sexist /'seksɪst/

A *adj* 性别歧视的 ‹*comment, behaviour*›

B *n* 性别歧视者

sex kitten *n* colloq 性感女郎

sexless /'sekslɪs/ *adj* 1 (genderless) 无性别的 ‹*insect, organism*› 2 (without sexual desire) 没有性欲的 ‹*person, life, existence*›

sex: ~ **life** *n* 性生活; ~**-linked** *adj* 伴性的; ~ **machine** *n* fig colloq 性交机器 [尤指性事频繁的男子]; ~**-mad** *adj* colloq 沉溺于性的; ~ **maniac** *n* colloq 色情狂; ~ **object** *n* 性玩物; ~ **offence** *n* Brit 性犯罪; ~ **offender** *n* 性犯罪者

sexologist /sek'sɒlədʒɪst/ ▸**p. 409** *n* 性学家

sexology /sek'sɒlədʒɪ/ *n* [u] 性学

sexploitation /ˌseksplɔɪ'teɪʃn/ *n* [u] 色情利用

sex: ~**pot** *n* colloq 性感的人; ~ **scandal** *n* 性丑闻; ~ **scene** *n* 性场面; ~ **shop** *n* 性用品商店; ~ **show** *n* 色情表演; ~**-starved** *adj* colloq 性饥渴的; ~ **symbol** *n* 性感偶像

sextant /'sekstənt/ *n* 六分仪

sextet /sek'stet/ *n* 1 (group of singers) 六重唱组合; (of players) 六重奏乐队 2 (composition for six voices) 六重唱曲; (for six instruments) 六重奏曲 3 (group of six people) 六人一组; (of six things) 六件套

sex: ~ **therapist** ▸**p. 409** *n* 性功能治疗师; ~ **therapy** *n* [u] 性功能治疗

sexton /'sekstən/ *n* 教堂司事

sex: ~ **tourism** *n* [u] 性旅游 [指到色情业管制宽松的地方旅游度假]; ~ **tourist** *n* 性旅游者

S

sextuple /seks'tju:pl/

A *adj* 1 (of six parts) 六个部分组成的 2 (sixfold) 六倍的

B *n* (sixfold number) 六倍的数; (sixfold amount) 六倍的量

C *vt* 使…变成六倍 ‹*number, figure*›

D *vi* 成为六倍

sextuplet /'sekstjʊplɪt, seks'tju:plɪt/ *n* 六胞胎之一; **a set of ~s** 六胞胎; **to give birth to ~s** 生六胞胎

sexual /'sekʃʊəl/ *adj* 1 (erotic) 性的; ~ **liberation/behaviour/habit/innuendo** 性解放/性行为/性习惯/性暗示; ~ **desire/pleasure/attraction/repression** 性欲/性快感/性吸引/性压抑 2 (relating to gender) 性别的; ~ **discrimination/difference** 性别歧视/差异 3 (reproductive) 生殖的; ~ **organ/characteristic** 性器官/性特征; ~ **reproduction** 有性繁殖

sexual: ~ **abuse** *n* [u] [对儿童的] 性虐待; ~ **assault** *n* [c and u] 性侵犯; ~ **discrimination** *n* [u] [尤指针对女性的] 性别歧视; ~ **harassment** *n* [u] 性骚扰; ~ **intercourse** *n* [u] 性交

sexuality /ˌsekʃʊ'ælətɪ/ *n* [u] 1 (sexual orientation) 性倾向 2 (sexual instincts) 性能力

sexualization /ˌsekʃjʊəlaɪ'zeɪʃn/ *n* [u] (of person) 性感化; (of culture) 赋予性别角色

sexualize /'sekʃjʊəlaɪz/ *vt* (make sexual) 使性感化; (attribute sex or a sex role to) 使有性别角色; **a highly ~d society** 性别特征很明显的社会

sexually /'sekʃʊəlɪ/ *adv* 1 (in sexual manner) 在性方面 ‹*attract, attractive, mature*›; ~ **abused** 受到性虐待的 2 (according to gender) 在性别上 ‹*discriminate, segregate*› 3 (through sexual intercourse) 通过性行为 ‹*transmit, infect*›

sexually transmitted disease *n* 性病

sexual: ~ **organs** *npl* 性器官; ~ **partner** *n* 性伴侣

sex: ~ **urge** *n* 性欲; ~ **worker** ▸**p. 409** *n* 性工作者

sexy /'seksɪ/ *adj* colloq 1 (erotic) 色情的 ‹*book, play, film*›; 性感的 ‹*person, underwear, nightdress*› 2 (appealing) 迷人的 ‹*advertisement, image, product*›

Seychelles /seɪ'ʃelz/ *pr npl* **the** ~ 塞舌尔群岛

SEZ *abbr* = **Special Economic Zone**

sez /sez/ colloq = **says** = **say A, B**

SF *abbr* = **science fiction**

SFO *n* Brit = **Serious Fraud Office**

SGML *abbr* = **Standard Generalized Mark-up Language** 标准通用标记语言

Sgt. *n* = **sergeant**

Shaanxi /ˌʃɑ:n'ʃi:/ ▸**p. 604** *pr n* ~ **(Province)** 陕西（省）

shabbily /'ʃæbɪlɪ/ *adv* 1 (scruffily) 破破烂烂地 ‹*dress, furnish*› 2 (shoddily) 不公正地 ‹*treat*›; 卑鄙地 ‹*behave*›

shabbiness /'ʃæbɪnɪs/ *n* [u] 1 (of clothes) 破破烂烂; (of place) 破败 2 (of treatment) 不公正; (of behaviour) 卑鄙

shabby /'ʃæbɪ/ *adj* 1 (scruffy) 破破烂烂的 ‹*appearance, clothing, furnishings*›; 破败的 ‹*house, neighbourhood*›; **a ~ old man** 衣衫褴褛的老头 2 (shoddy) 不公正的 ‹*treatment*›; 卑鄙的 ‹*behaviour*›

shabby: ~**-genteel** *adj* 穷摆阔的 ‹*person, apartment*›; ~**-looking** *adj* 外表破旧的 ‹*house, car*›; 衣衫褴褛的 ‹*person*›

shack /ʃæk/ *n* 棚屋

Phrasal verb

- **shack up** *vi* colloq **to ~ up with sb.** 和某人同居

shackle /'ʃækl/

A *n* 1 (on wrist) 手铐; (on leg) 脚镣; **prisoners in ~s** 戴着镣铐的囚犯 2 (coupling link) [挂锁的] 钩链 3 fig (constraint) 桎梏; **to throw off the ~s of sth.** 摆脱某事物的束缚; **to cast off one's ~s** 摆脱枷锁

B *vt* 1 (chain) 给…上镣铐 ‹*person, animal*›; 用…锁住 ‹*ring, chain*›; **to ~ sb. to sth.** 将某人锁在某物上 2 fig (restrain, limit) 束缚

shade /ʃeɪd/

A *n* 1 [u] (shadow) 阴影; **light and ~** 光与影; **to put sb./sth. in the ~** fig 使某人/某事物相形见绌 2 [c] (gradation) (of colour) 色度; (of meaning, opinion) 差别; **there are several ~s of meaning in this line** 这句话有好几层意思; **all ~s of opinion** 各种意见 3 [c] (small amount, degree) 些许; **this one is a ~ better** 这个略好一点; **turn the music down a ~** 把音乐声量调小一点 4 [c] (lampshade) 灯罩 5 [c] Amer (window shade) 窗帘; **to pull down/raise the ~** 拉下/拉起窗帘 6 [c] (eye visor) 遮阳帽舌 7 [c] liter (ghost) 鬼魂

B **shades** *npl* 1 colloq (sunglasses) 太阳镜 2 (undertones) 痕迹; **there are ~s of the fifties in that outfit you're wearing** 你的装束有 50 年代的余韵

C *vt* 1 (protect from glare) 为…遮阴 ‹*room*›; (prevent glare from) 遮挡 ‹*light*›; **I ~d my eyes against the sun** 我罩住眼睛以遮挡阳光; **a blind ~d the window** 百叶窗遮挡了窗外的光线 2 (add shadow to) «*paint, colour*» 给…加阴影 ‹*picture, contours, shadows*› 3 (blend) 揉合 ‹*colour, tone*›; **I'll ~ the orange into the brown** 我要把橙色调成褐色

D *vi* «*colour, tone*» 渐变; **to ~ to** *or* **into ...** 渐变为…; **right ~s into wrong** 正确与错误之间没有明显的界限

shadiness /'ʃeɪdɪnɪs/ *n* [u] 1 (of room, garden) 背阴 2 colloq (dishonesty) 不诚实

shading /'ʃeɪdɪŋ/ *n* 1 [u] (in painting) 明暗法; (in drawing) 影线法 2 [c] (of opinions) 细微差别

shadow /'ʃædəʊ/

A *n* 1 [c] (shade) 阴影; **the tree cast a ~ on** *or* **against the wall** 树在墙上投下影子; **his mother's ill health cast a ~ over his childhood** 他母亲的多病给他的童年蒙上了阴影; **to be/live in sb.'s ~** 处于/生活在某人的阴影里; **in the ~s** 在阴影里; **to have ~s under one's eyes** 有黑眼圈; **five o'clock ~** 新长出的胡子茬; **to be afraid of one's own ~** 胆小如鼠 2 [u] (slightest trace) 少许; **without a ~ of doubt** 毫无疑问; **is there any ~ of truth in this story?** 这个说法有什么真实性吗? 3 [c] (inferior version) 较差状况; **his illness has worn him to a ~** 疾病把他折磨得不成人形; **he was (but) a ~ of his former self** 他与以前相比憔悴得不成样子 4 [c] (companion) 形影不离的人; **he is his big sister's ~** 他是他姐姐的跟班 5 [c] (person following and observing sb.) 暗中跟踪者; **to put a ~ on sb.** 派人盯某人的梢

B *vt* 1 (shade) 在…上投下阴影; **the playground is ~ed by a big block of flats** 操场笼罩在一座公寓大楼的阴影中 2 (tail) 跟踪 3 (in order to gain experience) 跟随…学习技能 ‹*worker, colleague*›

C *modif* Brit 影子内阁的; **the ~ minister for homeland security** 负责国土安全事务的影子内阁大臣; **the S~ Home Secretary** 影子内阁的内政大臣

shadow: ~**-box** *vi* 进行空拳训练; ~ **boxing** *n* [u] 空拳训练; ~ **cabinet** *n* Brit 影子内阁; ~ **economy** *n* 影子经济 [指非法经济活动]; ~ **minister** *n* Brit [反对党提名的] 影子内阁大臣; ~ **play** *n* 皮影戏; ~ **puppet** *n* 皮影戏木偶

shadowy /'ʃædəʊɪ/ *adj* 1 (full of shadows) 多阴影的 ‹*wood, area*›; 幽暗的 ‹*room, path, street*› 2 (indistinct) 模糊的 ‹*recollection, image, outline*› 3 (mysterious) 神秘莫测的 ‹*group, person*›

shady /'ʃeɪdɪ/ *adj* 1 (shaded) 阴凉的 ‹*spot, garden, veranda*› 2 (providing shade) 成荫的 ‹*tree, wood, grove*› 3 colloq (dubious) 靠不住的 ‹*businessman, deal*›

shaft /ʃɑ:ft, Amer ʃæft/

A *n* 1 (of mine) 矿井; **to bore** *or* **drive** *or* **sink a ~** 打矿井 2 (for lift) 升降机井 3 (for ventilation) 通风井 4 (of tool, sword, etc.) 柄; (of arrow, golf club, etc.) 杆 5 (rotating rod) 轴; **a drive ~** 驱动轴 6 (on cart, carriage) 辕 7 (of feather) 羽干; (of bone) 骨干 8 (ray, bolt) 一道; **a ~ of light** 一束光; **a ~ of lightning** 一道闪电

B *vt* Amer sl (cheat) 欺骗; (treat unfairly) 亏待; **I was completely ~ed by the company** 我被公司骗惨了

shag[1] /ʃæg/ *n* [u and c] (tobacco) 粗切烟丝

shag[2] *n* (bird) 鸬鹚

shag[3] Brit taboo sl

A *vt* (*pres p etc.* **-gg-**) (have sex with) 与…性交

B *vi* (*pres p etc.* **-gg-**) (have sex) 性交

C *n* (sexual intercourse) 性交; **to have a ~ (with sb.)** （与某人）性交

shagged /ʃægd/ *adj* Brit colloq ~ **(out)** 疲惫不堪的

shaggy /'ʃægɪ/ *adj* 皮毛乱蓬蓬的 ‹*dog, horse*›; 蓬乱的 ‹*mane, hair*›; 粗硬的 ‹*rug, fabric*›

shaggy dog story *n* 冗长乏味的笑话

Shah /ʃɑ:/ *n* 沙 [旧时伊朗国王的称号]

shake /ʃeɪk/

A *vt* 1 (*pt* **shook,** *pp* **shaken**) (move vigorously) 抖动 ‹*mat, bag*›; 甩动 ‹*prey*›; 摇动 ‹*branch*›; ~ **the bottle** 摇瓶子; **it was a rough road, and we were shaken around quite a bit inside the car** 道路崎岖不平, 我们在车里颠得很厉害; **to ~ sth. at sb./sth.** 对某人/某物挥动某物; **she shook the snow off** *or* **from her coat** 她抖落了外衣上的雪; **to ~ hands** 握手; **to ~ hands with sb., to ~ sb.'s hand, to ~ sb. by the hand** 和某人握手; **to ~ one's head** 摇头; **there'll be a few heads shaken over this scheme when it's made public** 这一计划公布后会有人反对的; **to ~ a leg** colloq 快点儿; **more than you can ~ a stick at** Brit colloq 多得不得了 2 (shock) 使震惊; **his death/the news had clearly shaken them** 他的死讯/这一消息使他们大为震惊 3 (weaken, impair) 动摇 ‹*faith, confidence, theory*›; **to ~ sth. to its foundations** 彻底动摇 ‹*belief, system*› 4 colloq = **shake off 2**

B *vi* (*pt* **shook,** *pp* **shaken**) 1 (vibrate, tremble) «*hand, person, voice*» 颤抖; «*ground, building*» 颤动; «*grass, leaves*» 摇动; **to ~ with laughter/fear/fright/cold** 笑得/吓得/害怕得/冻得浑身发抖 **2** colloq (shake hands) 握手; **to ~ on sth.** 为某事握手祝贺; **can we ~ on it?** 我们可以握手祝贺达成协议了吗?

C *v refl* (*pt* **shook**, *pp* **shaken**) **to ~ oneself** 抖动身体; **he shook himself to try and get the spiders off him** 他试图抖落身上的蜘蛛

D *n* **1** (act of shaking) 摇动; **with a ~ of the** *or* **one's head** 摇了摇头; **give the bottle a ~ before you pour** 倒东西之前先摇一摇瓶子; **to have a ~ in one's voice** 声音有些颤抖; **to have the ~s** colloq 发抖; **in a ~** colloq 马上; **in two ~s (of a lamb's tail)** colloq 马上; **no great ~s** colloq 不出色; **to be no great ~s (at sth.)** (在某方面) 很一般; **to get/give sb. a fair ~** Amer colloq 得到公平对待/公平对待某人 **2** Amer (milkshake) 奶昔 **3** Amer (earthquake) 地震 **4** (amount sprinkled) [从容器里] 摇出的东西; **add a few ~s of sea salt and black pepper** 撒点儿海盐和黑胡椒

Phrasal verbs

• **shake down**

A *vi* **1** colloq (settle) «*machine*» 运转正常; «*person*» 适应新环境 **2** (in container) «*contents, powder, granules*» 变得密实

B [**~ sb./sth. down, ~ down sb./sth.**] *vt* **1** (cause to fall) 摇落 ‹*fruit, object*›; (cause to settle) 摇密实 ‹*contents, powder*› **2** Amer colloq (search) 彻底搜查 ‹*person, building, club*›; **the store detective shook him down** 那名商场保安搜了他的身

C [**~ sb. down, ~ down sb.**] *vt* Amer colloq (extort money from) 敲诈

• **shake off** *vt* [**~ sb./sth. off, ~ off sb./sth.**] **1** (let go by shaking) 抖落; **the boy was clinging to Peter's neck, and Peter was trying to ~ him off** 男孩抱住彼得的脖子不放, 彼得正想法把他甩下来 **2** (get rid of, escape from) 摆脱 ‹*bad mood, habit, tiresome person*›; **they shook off the car that was tailing them** 他们甩掉了尾随他们的汽车; **I can't seem to ~ off this flu** 我这次感冒好像怎么也好不了

• **shake out** *vt* [**~ sth. out, ~ out sth.**] (empty by shaking) 摇出 ‹*coins, contents*›; **to ~ the bag out over the table** 把袋子里的东西抖在桌子上

• **shake up**

A [**~ sth. up, ~ up sth.**] *vt* **1** (mix) 摇松 ‹*cushion, pillow*›; 摇匀 ‹*medicine, mixture*› **2** (reorganize) 重组 ‹*company, organization*›

B [**~ sb. up, ~ up sb.**] *vt* **1** (make uncomfortable by jolting) 使…受颠簸 ‹*passengers*› **2** colloq (distress, shock) 震动 **3** colloq (rouse to activity) 使振作; **they need shaking up!** 得让他们振作起来!

shakedown /ˈʃeɪkdaʊn/ *n* Amer colloq **1** (improvised bed) 临时床铺 **2** (swindle) 勒索 **3** (search) 彻底搜查 **4** (final test) 试运行; **a ~ voyage/flight/run** 试航/试飞/试车

shaken /ˈʃeɪkən/
A *pp* ▸**shake**
B *adj* (shocked) 受惊的; (upset) 心烦意乱的

shake-out *n* **1** Fin (crisis) 震仓; (fall in prices) 暴跌 **2** (reorganization) 重组

shaker /ˈʃeɪkə(r)/ *n* **1** (for mixing) 混合器; (for shaking) 摇动器; (for cocktails) 摇酒壶; (for dice) 摇骰子器; (for salad) 摇匀器 **2** (for salt, pepper) [盖上有小孔的] 佐料瓶

Shakespearean, Shakespearian /ʃeɪkˈspɪərɪən/ *adj* 莎士比亚的 ‹*play, sonnet*›; 莎士比亚作品的 ‹*research, style*›; **a ~ scholar/expert** 研究莎士比亚的学者/专家

shake-up *n* colloq 大改组

shakily /ˈʃeɪkɪlɪ/ *adv* **1** (unsteadily) 颤抖着 ‹*say, answer*›; 颤巍巍地 ‹*stand, walk*› **2** (uncertainly) 不稳定地 ‹*begin*›

shakiness /ˈʃeɪkɪnɪs/ *n* [u] **1** (of person, hand, voice) 颤抖 **2** (of bridge, house) 摇晃 **3** (of arguments, evidence) 不可靠 **4** (of marriage, business) 成问题

shaky /ˈʃeɪki/ *adj* **1** (trembling) 颤抖的 ‹*voice, hands, person*› **2** (unstable) 摇晃的 ‹*wall, structure*› **3** (unreliable) 靠不住的 ‹*argument, evidence, position, knowledge*› **4** (uncertain) 成问题的 ‹*marriage, relationship, business, performance*›; **my French is a bit ~** 我的法语不太流利; **to be based on ~ grounds** 基于靠不住的理由

shale /ʃeɪl/ *n* [u and c] 页岩

shale oil *n* [u] 页岩油

shall /ʃæl/ *modal aux* (*short form* colloq **'ll**; *negative* **shall not** *or* colloq **shan't**) **1** (expressing future) 将; **I ~ see you tomorrow** 我明天见你; **we ~ not have a reply before Friday** 我们在星期五之前不会得到答复; **I ~ have retired by then** 到那时我已经退休了 **2** (in offers or suggestions, asking for advice) [在疑问句中表示提议或征求意见]; **~ I pick you up from the station?** 要我去车站接你吗?; **~ we go to the cinema tonight?** 我们今晚去看电影好吗?; **I'll drive, ~ I?** 我来开车, 好吗?; **let's buy some peaches, ~ we?** 咱们买点桃子, 好不好?; **what ~ we do this weekend?** 我们这个周末干什么呢?; **the meat was, how ~ I put it?, a little overdone** 这肉嘛, 怎么说呢, 做得稍微老了点儿 **3** formal (in commands) 应该; **you ~ do as I say** 你应该照我说的做; **candidates ~ remain in their seats until all the papers have been collected** 考生应等所有试卷收毕方可离座 **4** formal (expressing determination) 一定; **you ~ not frighten me out of this** 这事你吓不倒我; **he is determined that you ~ succeed** 他决心使你成功 **5** Jur formal 必须; **the sum ~ be paid on signature of the contract** 合同一经签署即须支付此款项

shallot /ʃəˈlɒt/ *n* Brit 青葱

shallow /ˈʃæləʊ/ ▸**p. 436**

A *adj* **1** (not deep) 浅的 ‹*water, river, earth, hole, container*›; **~ dip** 低洼地带 **2** (taking in little air) 微弱的 ‹*breathing*› **3** (superficial) 浅薄的 ‹*mind, artist*›; 肤浅的 ‹*idea, analysis, remark*›

B **shallows** *npl* 浅滩

shallow-minded *adj* 头脑简单的

shallowness /ˈʃæləʊnɪs/ *n* [u] **1** (of water, river, hole, topsoil) 浅 **2** (of person) 浅薄; (of conversation) 肤浅 **3** (of breathing) 微弱

sham /ʃæm/

A *n* **1** [c] (falsehood) 虚假事物; **let's put an end to this ~** 让我们揭穿这一骗局; **to be a ~** «*person, doctor, expert*» 是假冒的; «*situation, business*» 是虚假的; «*tears, sympathy*» 是虚伪的 **2** [u] (pretence) 假装

B *adj attrib* 假冒的 ‹*doctor, expert*›; 虚假的 ‹*thing, situation*›; 虚伪的 ‹*tears, piety*›

C *vt* (*pres p etc.* **-mm-**) «*person*» 假装 ‹*sympathy, anxiety*›; **to ~ death/sleep** 装死/装睡

D *vi* (*pres p etc.* **-mm-**) «*person, animal*» 装假

shaman /ˈʃeɪmən/ *n* 萨满 [据信有通灵能力的人]

shamanism /ˈʃeɪmənɪzəm/ *n* [u] 萨满教

shamanist /ˈʃeɪmənɪst/
A *n* 萨满教徒
B *adj* 萨满教的

shamateur /ˈʃæmətɜː(r)/ *n* Brit 冒牌业余运动员

shamble /ˈʃæmbl/ *vi* 蹒跚

shambles /ˈʃæmblz/ *npl* + *v sing* colloq (of organization, meeting) 混乱; (of room, house) 凌乱; **to be a ~** 一团糟; **to be in a ~** 处于混乱状态; **the house is in a complete ~** 屋子里一片狼藉

shambolic /ˌʃæmˈbɒlɪk/ *adj* Brit colloq 混乱的

shame /ʃeɪm/

A *n* [u] **1** (painful emotion) 羞愧感; **to feel ~** 感到羞愧; **a sense of ~** 羞愧感; **to nearly die of ~** 羞愧难当; **to put sb./sth. to ~** (cause to feel ashamed or disgraced) 使某人蒙羞; (totally surpass) 使某人/某事物相形见绌; **to bring ~ upon** *or* **on sb.** *or* **sb.'s head** 使某人蒙羞 **2** (disgrace, humiliation) 耻辱; **there's no ~ in being poor** 贫穷并不丢人; **the ~ of it!** 真丢脸!; **~ on you!** 你真不害臊!; **to sb.'s ~** 令某人惭愧地 **3** (pity) 令人遗憾的事物; **what a ~!** 真遗憾!; **it's a great** *or* **dreadful** *or* **terrible ~** 这事非常令人遗憾; **it's a damned** *or* **crying ~** 这事令人后悔莫及

B *vt* **1** (embarrass) 使羞愧; **don't ~ him in front of his children** 不要在孩子们面前让他丢面子; **to ~ sb. into sth.** *or* **doing sth.** 使某人羞愧而不得不做某事; **to ~ sb. out of sth.** 使某人羞愧而放弃某事物 **2** (disgrace) 使…蒙羞 ‹*family, regiment, school*›

shamefaced /ˌʃeɪmˈfeɪst/ *adj* 羞愧的

shamefacedly /ˌʃeɪmˈfeɪsɪdli/ *adv* 羞愧地

shameful /ˈʃeɪmfl/ *adj* 可耻的 ‹*conduct, lies*›; 丢脸的 ‹*ignorance, neglect*›; 不像话的 ‹*treatment*›; **it was ~ of her to do ...** 她做…是可耻的; **it is ~ that ...** …是很丢脸的

shamefully /ˈʃeɪmfəli/ *adv* 令人丢脸地 ‹*behave*›; **we're ~ late** 不好意思我们迟到了

shameless /ˈʃeɪmlɪs/ *adj* 无耻的; **a ~ display of wealth/extravagance** 不以为耻的财富炫示/铺张浪费; **to be quite ~ about sth.** 在某方面很无耻

shamelessly /ˈʃeɪmlɪslɪ/ *adv* 无耻地

shamelessness /ˈʃeɪmlɪsnɪs/ *n* [u] 无耻

shaming /ˈʃeɪmɪŋ/ *adj* 令人羞愧的; **it is ~ that ...** …是令人羞愧的

shammy /ˈʃæmi/ *n* **~ (leather)** Brit colloq **= chamois A2**

shampoo /ʃæmˈpuː/

A *n* **1** [c and u] (for hair) 洗发剂; (for carpet) 洗涤剂 **2** [c] (act of washing hair) 用洗发剂洗; (act of cleaning carpet) 用洗涤剂洗; **to have a ~** 洗头; **to give sb. a ~** 给某人洗头

B *vt* (*pres* **~s**; *pt, pp* **~ed**) 用洗发剂为…洗发 ‹*animal, customer, hair*›; 用洗涤剂洗 ‹*carpet*›

shampooer /ʃæmˈpuːə(r)/ *n* **1** (person) 洗发师 **2** (carpet cleaner) [使用洗涤剂的] 地毯清洗机

shamrock /ˈʃæmrɒk/ *n* [c and u] 三叶草

Shandong /ˌʃænˈdɒŋ/ ▸**p. 604** *pr n* **~ (Province)** 山东 (省)

shandy /ˈʃændi/ Brit, **shandygaff** /ˈʃændɪgæf/ Amer *ns* **1** [u] (mixture) 香蒂啤酒 [掺姜啤或柠檬汁的啤酒] **2** [c] (glass) 一份香蒂啤酒

Shanghai /ʃæŋˈhaɪ/ ▸**p. 604** *pr n* 上海; **~ Municipality** 上海市

shanghai /ʃæŋˈhaɪ/ *vt* **1** (kidnap) «*navy, captain*» 绑架…当水手 ‹*person*› **2** colloq (trick) 诱骗; (coerce) 强迫; **to ~ sb. into doing sth.** 诓骗某人做某事

Shanghainese /ˌʃæŋhaɪˈniːz/ *n* **1** [c] (person) 上海人 **2** [u] (dialect) 上海话

Shangri-La /ˌʃæŋgrɪˈlɑː/ *pr n* 香格里拉 [指世外桃源]

shank /ʃæŋk/ *n* **1** (of person) 小腿; (of animal) [前肢的] 小腿; **Shanks's pony** Brit *or* **mare** Amer colloq 自己的双腿 **2** (joint of meat) [猪、羊等的] 腿肉 **3** (of knife, drill-bit, screw) 柄 **4** (loop) 扣环; (of button) [纽扣背面的] 扣眼

shan't /ʃɑːnt/ colloq **= shall not**

shantung /ˌʃænˈtʌŋ/ *n* [u and c] [柞蚕丝制的] 山东绸

shanty[1] /ˈʃænti/ *n* (hut) 棚屋

shanty[2] *n* (song) 水手号子

shantytown /ˈʃæntɪtaʊn/ *n* [城郊的] 棚户区

Shanxi /ʃænˈʃiː/ ▸**p. 604** *pr n* **~ (Province)** 山西 (省)

SHAPE /ʃeɪp/ *abbr* **= Supreme Headquarters Allied Powers Europe** 欧洲盟军最高司令部

S

shape /ʃeɪp/
A *n* **1** (outer form, outline) 形状; **a square/rectangular/triangular ~** 正方形/矩形/三角形; **the children were cutting out ~s from paper** 孩子们在剪纸; **animal ~s** 动物图形零食; **a streamlined ~** 流线型; **I'm the wrong ~ for this jacket** 我的身材不适合穿这件夹克衫; **to carve/cut/mould sth. into ~** 把某物雕刻/切割/塑造成形; **the bush is losing its ~; it needs a good trim** 灌木丛杂乱一片，需要好好修剪一下; **to take ~** 成形; **(in/of) all ~s and sizes** 各式各样的; **in any ~ or form** 以任何形式 **2** (indistinguishable form) 模糊的影像; **I could only just make out the ~ of the building in the morning smog** 晨雾中的大楼只能看出个轮廓 **3** (guise) 外表; **a fiend** *or* **monster in human ~** 幻化为人形的妖魔; **help arrived in the ~ of a burly policeman** 前来帮忙的是一位魁梧的警察 **4** (optimum condition) 状态; **to be in/out of ~** 状态良好/不佳; **I've got a bit out of ~ during the holidays** 我在度假期间身体有些不适; **to knock** *or* **lick sb./sth. into ~** 使某人/某事物进入良好状态 **5** (character) 特征; (structure) 结构; **the basic ~ of the essay** 文章的基本框架; **technological developments which have changed the ~ of our lives** 改变了我们生活方式的科技发展; **the ~ of things to come** 未来的状况 **6** (mould for jelly, pastry) 模子 **7** (moulded food) 成型食品
B *vt* **1** (fashion, mould) 使…成形 ‹*wood, hair, figure*›; **use both hands to ~ the clay** 用双手把黏土捏成形; **rocks that have been ~d by the tide** 潮水冲刷成形的岩石; **to ~ sth. into sth.** 把某物做成某种形状; **to ~ sth. out of** *or* **from sth.** 用某物做出某物 **2** (influence, determine) 影响 ‹*character, events*›; 决定 ‹*development*› **3** (tailor) 使合身; **this jacket is ~d at the waist** 这件夹克的腰部剪裁很合身
C *vi* colloq (progress, develop) «*plan, project*» 进展; **the way things are shaping, we should be able to come** 看目前的情况我们应该能来

Phrasal verb
- **shape up** *vi* colloq **1** (develop) «*plan, project, team*» 进展; **the new intake seem to be shaping up quite well** 新招的员工看上去适应得不错; **to ~ up to be sth.** 发展成某事物 **2** (meet expectations) «*person*» 称职; **~ up or ship out** 表现不好就走人 **3** (improve one's figure) 改善身材

shaped /ʃeɪpt/
A *adj* 有特定形状的; **a ~ jacket/waist** 合身的夹克/背心; **~ hair** 做成发型的头发; **a rock ~ like a lion's head** 一块狮子头形状的石头
B -shaped *combining form* 有…形状的; **star/V~** 星形/V字形的; **a delicately~ nose** 形状精巧的鼻子; **well~** 身材好的

shapeless /ˈʃeɪplɪs/ *adj* **1** (amorphous) 无定形的 ‹*lump, mass*›; (baggy, unshapely) 样子难看的 ‹*dress, sweater*› **2** (disorganized) 杂乱无章的 ‹*composition, lecture*›

shapelessness /ˈʃeɪplɪsnɪs/ *n* [u] **1** (of lump, mass) 不定形; (of dress, sweater) 样子难看 **2** (of essay) 杂乱无章

shapeliness /ˈʃeɪplɪnɪs/ *n* [u] (of vase, column) 形状优美; (of woman, leg) 线条匀称

shapely /ˈʃeɪpli/ *adj* 形状优美的 ‹*vase, column*›; 线条优美的 ‹*woman, figure, leg*›

shard /ʃɑːd/ *n* [陶器、金属等带锋利边缘的] 碎片

share¹ /ʃeə(r)/
A *n* **1** (part owned or allotted) 一份; **here's your ~!** 这是你那一份! ; **to bear a ~ in** *or* **of sth.** 承担某事的一部分; **he's already spent his ~ of the family inheritance** 他已经把自己继承的那份家族遗产挥霍光了; **to go ~s (on sth.)** colloq 分摊 (某物) **2** (part contributed) 付出的部分; **to do one's ~** 尽一份力 **3** (of company stock) 股份; **to issue ~s** 发行股份; **to buy/sell ~s** 购买/售出股票; **to have** *or* **hold ~s** 持有股份
B *vt* **1** (use or enjoy together) 共用 ‹*room, taxi, bed*›; **to ~ sth. with sb.** 和某人共用某物 **2** (contribute towards) 分担 ‹*cost, chores, responsibility*›; 分享 ‹*credit, praise*› **3** (experience in common) 共同感受; **we ~d each other's sorrows and joys** 我们同悲同喜; **they ~d an interest in history/cooking/motorbikes** 他们都对历史/烹调/摩托车感兴趣; **I don't ~ your optimism about the future of Europe** 我不认同你对欧洲前途的乐观看法 **4** (confide) 透露 ‹*news, thoughts, secret*›; **to ~ sth. with sb.** 把某事告诉某人
C *vi* (give part) 分担; (take part) 参与; **to ~ in the expenses** 分担费用; **to ~ in the work of reconstruction** 参与重建工作; **thank you for letting me ~ in your triumph** 谢谢你让我分享你的胜利; **~ and ~ alike** 平均分担

Phrasal verb
- **share out** *vt* [**~ sth. out, ~ out sth.**] 平均分配 ‹*profits, food, rations, spoils*›

share² *n* (of plough) 犁铧

share: ~ capital *n* [u] 股本; **~ certificate** *n* 股票; **~cropper** *n* Amer 佃农; **~cropping** *n* [u] Amer 佃农耕作制

shared /ʃeəd/ *adj* **1** (used jointly) 共用的 ‹*accommodation, bathroom*›; 共享的 ‹*glory*›; **a trouble ~ is a trouble halved** 苦恼让人知，烦恼少一半 **2** (in common) 共同的 ‹*belief, experience*›; **a ~ interest** 共同的兴趣

shared: ~ care *n* [u] Brit [福利机构与病人家属达成的] 共同护理计划; **~ ownership** *n* [u] Brit 房产共有制 [指住户购买房屋的部分产权并以租金支付余款的制度]

shareholder /ˈʃeəhəʊldə(r)/ *n* 股东

shareholder: ~s' equity *n* [u] 股东权益; **~s' meeting** *n* 股东大会

share: ~holding *n* **1** [u] (possession) 持股; **2** [c] (stake) 股权; **a majority ~** 多数股权; **~ index** *n* 股票指数; **~ option** *n* 股票期权; **~-out** *n* 分配; **~ premium** *n* 资本盈余; **~ware** *n* [u] 共享软件

Sharia /ʃəˈriːə/ *n* [u] **~ (law)** 伊斯兰教教法

shark /ʃɑːk/ *n* (*pl* **~** *or* **~s**) **1** (animal) 鲨鱼 **2** (swindler) 诈骗者; **loan ~** 放高利贷者 **3** Amer (expert) 行家

shark: ~-infested *adj* 鲨鱼出没的 ‹*waters, sea*›; **~'s fin soup** *n* [u] 鱼翅汤; **~skin** *n* [u] **1** (skin) 鲨鱼皮; **2** (synthetic fabric) 雪克斯金细呢

sharp /ʃɑːp/
A *adj* **1** (pointed) 尖的 ‹*fangs, rock, nose*›; **a ~ angle** 尖角; **a ~ corner** *or* **turn** 急转弯; **she had ~ features** 她的面部棱角分明; **to be at the ~ end (of sth.)** 处于 (某事的) 风口浪尖 **2** (abrupt, intense) 骤然的 ‹*drop, incline*›; 刺耳的 ‹*sound, cry*›; 剧烈的 ‹*pain*›; **to make a ~ movement** 猛地一动; **a ~ fall/rise in price** 价格的陡降/陡升 **3** (clearly defined) 清晰的 ‹*image, picture, shape*›; 鲜明的 ‹*contrast, difference*›; **a ~ distinction** 明显的区别 **4** (keen, astute) 聪颖的 ‹*person, child*›; 敏锐的 ‹*mind, eyesight*›; 灵敏的 ‹*ears*›; **to keep a ~ lookout (for sth.)** 密切注意 (某事物); **she has a ~ eye for a bargain!** 她很会淘便宜货! **5** (in business) 精明的 ‹*person, businessman*›; **he is a ~ operator** 他是个老狐狸; **that's ~ work!** 这事干得真绝! **6** (acrid, bitter) 苦涩的 ‹*taste, fruit*›; 刺鼻的 ‹*smell*› **7** (biting) 刺骨的 ‹*wind*›; 剧烈的 ‹*pain*› **8** (harsh) 尖刻的 ‹*rebuke, tone*›; **the school teacher had a ~ tongue** 那个老师说话尖酸刻薄 **9** (smart, stylish) 时髦的 ‹*suit, style, cut*›; **he/she is a ~ dresser** 他/她衣着入时 **10** Mus (raised a semitone) 升半音的; (too high in pitch) 偏高音的 ‹*note*›
B *adv* **1** (higher in pitch) 以偏高音 ‹*play, be tuned*›; **sopranos tend to sing ~ on the high notes** 女高音在唱高音时往往偏高 **2** (abruptly) 骤然 ‹*stop, pull up*›; **you need to turn ~ left/right** 你得马上左转/右转 **3** (punctually) 准时地; **at 9 o'clock ~** 在 9 点整; **the party had to stop ~ on midnight** 聚会不得不在午夜 12 点整结束; **look ~!** 赶快! ; **you'll have to look ~ or you'll miss the train!** 你得快点儿，否则就赶不上火车了!
C *n* Mus 升半音

sharpen /ˈʃɑːpən/
A *vt* **1** (make sharper) 磨快 ‹*blade, razor, scissors*›; **to ~ sth. to a point** 把某物磨尖; **to ~ a pencil/knife** 削铅笔/磨刀; **to ~ its claws** 将它的爪子磨尖 **2** (make clearer) 使…更清晰 ‹*image, outline*›; **we need to ~ the focus of the discussion** 我们要使讨论的重点更明确 **3** (make stronger) 增强 ‹*desire, feeling, longing*›; 加剧 ‹*anger, pain*›; 使…敏锐 ‹*intelligence, reactions*›; **to ~ sb.'s wits** 使某人头脑灵敏 **4** (raise pitch) 使…升高 ‹*note, pitch*›
B *vi* **1** (become piercing) «*voice, tone*» 变尖 **2** (intensify) «*pain, tension*» 加剧

Phrasal verb
- **sharpen up**
A *vt* [**~ up sth., ~ sth. up**] 使…更灵敏 ‹*reflexes*›; 提高 ‹*skills*›; **to ~ oneself up for ...** 为了…而磨砺自己; **to ~ up one's image** 改善形象
B *vi* «*person, team, company*» 改善

sharpener /ˈʃɑːpənə(r)/ *n* (device, machine) 磨具; (for pencil) 卷笔刀; (for knife) 磨刀石

sharper /ˈʃɑːpə(r)/ *n* colloq [尤指扑克牌赌博中的] 骗子

sharp: ~-eyed *adj* **1** (with good eyesight) 视力好的 ‹*person, animal, bird*›; **2** (observant) 目光敏锐的 ‹*person, child*›; **a ~-eyed reader** 眼尖的读者; **~-featured** *adj* 面部棱角分明的 ‹*person*›; 棱角分明的 ‹*face*›

sharpie /ˈʃɑrpi/ *n* Amer colloq **= sharper**

sharpish /ˈʃɑːpɪʃ/ *adv* Brit colloq 立刻; **I'd leave ~ if I were you** 如果我是你，我会拔腿就走

sharply /ˈʃɑːpli/ *adv* **1** (abruptly) 突然 ‹*turn, stop, rise, fall*›; (by large degree) 突然大幅度地 ‹*rise, fall, fluctuating*› **2** (harshly) 尖刻地 ‹*speak, retort*› **3** (distinctly) 鲜明地 ‹*stand out, contrast, differing*›; **to bring sth. ~ into focus** lit 使某事物变清晰; fig 使某事物成为焦点 **4** (perceptively) 机敏地 ‹*say, look at, aware*›; **to be ~ intelligent** 绝顶聪明 **5** (quickly and suddenly) 猛地 ‹*move, look up, knock*›

sharpness /ˈʃɑːpnɪs/ *n* [u] **1** (of blade, scissors) 锋利 **2** (of pencil, needle, nail) 尖利; (of peak, rock) 尖突 **3** (of rise, fall) 突然 **4** (of angle) 夹角大小; (of turn, bend) 急转程度 **5** (of image, outline, sound) 清晰 **6** (of voice, tone) 刺耳; (of words, criticism) 尖刻 **7** (of pain) 剧烈; (of guilt) 强烈 **8** (of taste, smell) 刺激性 **9** (of wind) 凛冽

sharp: ~ practice *n* [u] 不诚实的交易; **~ sand** *n* [u] 尖角沙砾; **~shooter** *n* 神枪手; **~-sighted** *adj* 目光敏锐的; **~-spoken** *adj* 讲话严厉刺耳的 ‹*person*›; 严厉刺耳的 ‹*words*›; **~-tempered** *adj* 脾气暴躁的; **~-tongued** *adj* 说话尖刻的; **~-witted** *adj* 机智的

shat /ʃæt/ *pt, pp* ▸**shit B, C, D**

shatter /ˈʃætə(r)/
A *vt* **1** (break into pieces) «*person, object, action*» 打碎 ‹*window, vase, mirror*› **2** (destroy) 破坏 ‹*peace, silence, life*›; 损害 ‹*career, faith, health*›; 使…破灭 ‹*hopes*›; 损伤 ‹*eardrums, nerves*› **3** (shock, upset) «*event, news*» 使…震惊 ‹*person*› **4** Brit colloq (exhaust) «*work, exertion*» 使精疲力竭
B *vi* «*vase, glass*» 碎裂; **to ~ into pieces** *or* **smithereens** 破成碎片

S

shattered /ˈʃætəd/ *adj* 1 Brit colloq (exhausted) 精疲力竭的 2 (devastated) 被击垮的; **to be ~ by sth.** 被某事物击垮

shattering /ˈʃætərɪŋ/ *adj* 1 (destructive) 毁灭性的 ‹*blow, explosion*› 2 (devastating) 令人惊骇的 ‹*experience, disappointment, news*›

shatter-proof *adj* 防碎的 ‹*glass, lenses*›

shave /ʃeɪv/

A *vt* 1 (remove hair from) 剃…上的毛发 ‹*person, face*›; (remove with razor) 刮 ‹*beard*›; 剃 ‹*hair*›; **to ~ one's legs/head** 剃腿上的汗毛/剃头 2 (graze) «*plane, ball*» 擦过 ‹*arm, goalpost, treetop*› 3 (trim) 刨掉 ‹*surface*›; **to ~ sth. off ...** 从…上刨去 ‹*wood, fraction*› 4 (reduce) «*person, company*» 削减 ‹*profits, prices*›

B *vi* 刮脸

C *n* 刮脸; **to have a ~** 刮脸; **to give sb. a ~** 给某人刮脸; **a narrow** *or* **close ~** 侥幸脱险

Phrasal verb

- **shave off** *vt* [**~ sth. off, ~ off sth.**] 1 (remove with razor) 剃掉 ‹*beard, moustache, hair*› 2 (trim) 刨掉 ‹*wood*› 3 (take off) 减少 ‹*amount, time, distance*›

shaven /ˈʃeɪvən/ *adj* 剃光的

shaver /ˈʃeɪvə(r)/ *n* 1 (electric) 电动剃须刀 2 colloq (boy) 小伙子

shaver point Brit, **shaver outlet** Amer *ns* 电动剃须刀插座

shaving /ˈʃeɪvɪŋ/ *n* 1 [u] (process) 刮脸 2 [c] (of wood) 刨花; (of metal) 切屑

shaving: ~ brush *n* 修面刷; **~ cream** *n* [u and c] 剃须膏; **~ foam** *n* [u and c] 刮胡泡; **~ gel** *n* [u and c] 剃须啫喱; **~ kit** *n* 剃须用具; **~ mirror** *n* 剃须镜; **~ soap** *n* [u and c] 剃须皂; **~ stick** *n* 剃须皂条

shawl /ʃɔːl/ *n* 披巾

she /ʃiː, ʃɪ/

A *pron* (referring to woman, girl) 她; (referring to female animal) 它; (referring to ship, vehicle, country) 她

B *n* 1 (woman) 女人; (girl) 女孩; **is the baby a he or a ~?** 这个婴儿是男孩还是女孩? 2 (female animal) 雌性动物; **what a sweet little dog! is it a he or a ~?** 多么可爱的小狗! 是公的还是母的?

sheaf /ʃiːf/ *n* (*pl* **sheaves**) (of corn) 一捆; (of flowers) 一束; (of papers) 一沓

shear /ʃɪə(r)/ *vt* 1 (*pp* **~ed** *or* **shorn**) (remove fleece, hair from) 剪…的毛 ‹*animal, sheep*› 2 (*pp* **~ed** *or* **shorn**) (cut) 剪去 ‹*hair, wool, grass*› 3 (*pp* **shorn**) (strip, divest) **to be shorn of** 被剥夺 ‹*influence, power, money*›

Phrasal verbs

- **shear off** *vi* (break off) «*metal, handle, key*» 折断
- **shear through** *vt* [**~ through sth.**] 切割 ‹*wood, metal, bolt*›; «*vessel, ship, shark*» 劈开…前进 ‹*water*›

shearer /ˈʃɪərə(r)/ ▸**p. 409** *n* 1 (farm worker) 剪羊毛的人 2 (machine) 剪切机 3 (metalworker) 剪切工

shearing /ˈʃɪərɪŋ/

A *n* [u] 剪羊毛

B **shearings** *npl* 剪下的羊毛

shearing shed *n* 剪羊毛工棚

shears /ʃɪəz/ *npl* 大剪刀

sheath /ʃiːθ/ *n* 1 (for weapon) 鞘; **sword/knife ~** 剑鞘/刀鞘 2 (for cable) 护套 3 Zool (wing case) [鞘翅目昆虫的] 翅鞘 4 (condom) 避孕套

sheath dress *n* 女式紧身衣

sheathe /ʃiːð/ *vt* 1 (place in sheath) 把…插入鞘中 ‹*sword, dagger*› 2 (encase, protect) «*person*» 将…包入护套 ‹*limb, cable*›; «*cat, insect*» 缩回 ‹*claws, wings, sting*›; **to ~ sth. in sth.** 将某物包裹在某物中; **to ~ sth. with sth.** 用某物将某物裹起来

sheath knife *n* 带鞘短刀

sheaves /ʃiːvz/ *pl* ▸**sheaf**

shebang /ʃɪˈbæŋ/ *n* Amer colloq (matter, operation) 事务; (set of circumstances) 状况; **the whole ~** colloq 整个事态

shebeen /ʃɪˈbiːn/ *n* Ir 无执照酒馆

shed[1] /ʃed/ *n* 1 (for storage) 储物棚; (for animals) 牲口棚 2 (at factory site, port) 工棚; (for maintaining vehicles) 修车棚; (for maintaining other machinery) 机修棚

shed[2] *vt* (*pt, pp* **shed**) 1 (spill) «*person*» 流 ‹*tears*›; **to ~ blood** 流血牺牲 2 (let fall) «*tree, plant*» 使…脱落 ‹*leaves, petals, blossom*› 3 (discard, get rid of) «*person, company*» 摆脱 ‹*inhibitions, responsibility*›; «*employer, company*» 削减 ‹*staff, employees*›; **what do I need to do to ~ 6 kilos?** 我怎样才能减掉 6 公斤体重? 4 (take off) «*person*» 脱去 ‹*clothes*› 5 (repel) «*garment, feathers*» 不透 ‹*water*› 6 Brit (accidentally spill) «*lorry*» 意外掉落 ‹*load*› 7 (moult) «*animal*» 脱 ‹*hairs, fur*› 8 (cast off) «*insect, snake*» 蜕 ‹*skin, shell*› 9 (radiate) «*person*» 流露出 ‹*happiness*›; «*lamp*» 散发出 ‹*warmth*›; **to ~ light on** *or* **upon sth.** fig «*person, investigation*» 使某事物为人所知

she'd /ʃiːd/ colloq 1 = **she had** ▸**have** 2 = **she would** ▸**would**

she-devil *n* 恶毒女人

sheen /ʃiːn/ *n* 1 (of hair, silk) 光泽 2 (of a victory, an experience) 光彩; **to take the ~ off sth.** 使某事物黯然失色

sheep /ʃiːp/ *n* (*pl* **sheep**) 1 (animal) 羊; **a flock of ~** 一群羊; **may as well be hung for a ~ as for a lamb** 反正都是死, 不如干大事; **to make ~'s eyes at sb.** 含情脉脉地看某人; **to separate** *or* **divide** *or* **sort out the ~ from the goats** 分清能手与常人; **to count ~** [为了入睡] 数羊 2 (person) 懦弱的人

sheep dip *n* 1 [u and c] (liquid) 浴羊药液 2 [c] (bath) 浴羊槽

sheep dog *n* 牧羊犬

sheep dog trials *npl* 牧羊犬竞技赛

sheep: ~ farm *n* 养羊农场; **~ farmer** ▸**p. 409** *n* 养羊农民; **~ farming** *n* [u] 养羊; **~fold** *n* 羊圈

sheepish /ˈʃiːpɪʃ/ *adj* 难为情的

sheepishly /ˈʃiːpɪʃli/ *adv* 难为情地

sheepishness /ˈʃiːpɪʃnɪs/ *n* [u] 难为情

sheep: ~shank *n* [为缩短绳子而打的] 缩结; **~shearer** ▸**p. 409** *n* 剪羊毛的人; **~shearing** *n* [u] 剪羊毛

sheepskin /ˈʃiːpskɪn/ *n* [c and u] 带毛绵羊皮; **a ~ coat/rug** 羊皮大衣/地毯

sheep: ~'s milk *n* [u] [尤指供人饮用的] 羊奶; **~'s milk cheese** *n* [u and c] 羊奶酪; **~ station** *n* [尤指澳大利亚的] 大牧羊场; **~ stealing** *n* [u] 窃羊; **~ track** *n* 羊径

sheer /ʃɪə(r)/

A *adj* 1 (pure) 十足的 ‹*ignorance, folly*›; 完全的 ‹*desperation, impossibility, necessity*›; **it was ~ coincidence/luck** 那纯属巧合/全凭运气; **out of ~ malice/stupidity** 完全出于恶意/因为愚蠢; **by ~ accident** 纯属意外; **to charge £25 for one ticket is ~ robbery!** 一张票要 25 英镑绝对是抢钱! 2 (steep) 陡峭的 ‹*cliff, rock face*›; 垂直的 ‹*drop, fall, descent*› 3 (fine) 轻薄的 ‹*material, stockings, tights, net curtains*›

B *adv* 陡直地 ‹*drop, rise*›; **the cliff falls away ~ to** *or* **into the bay** 悬崖笔直地插入海湾

Phrasal verb

- **sheer away, sheer off** *vi* «*person, horse, vehicle*» 躲闪; **to ~ away to the right/left** 向右/向左闪躲

sheet /ʃiːt/

A *n* 1 (for bed) 床单; **single/double ~s** 单人/双人床单; **linen/cotton ~s** 亚麻/棉布床单; **to be as white as a ~** 面无血色 2 (of paper, metal) 薄片; **a ~ of plastic** 一块塑料布; **a blank ~ of paper** 一张白纸; **a ~ of stamps** 一版邮票 3 (of water, ice) 大片; **the fields were covered in a solid ~ of water** 田野被一大片水淹没了; **the oil tank exploded in a ~ of flames** 油罐在一片火海中爆炸了; **the rain came down in ~s** 大雨倾盆而下 4 (sail) 帆; **two** *or* **three ~s to the wind** colloq 醉得东倒西歪

B *vi* **to ~ (down)** «*rain*» 倾盆而下; **to ~ against sth.** 对着某物倾泻; **the water was ~ing down off the steep roof** 水从尖屋顶上倾泻而下

sheet: ~ anchor *n* 1 Naut 备用大锚; 2 fig 靠山; **~ feeder** *n* 进纸器

sheeting /ˈʃiːtɪŋ/ *n* [u] 薄片材料; **plastic/vinyl ~** 塑料/乙烯薄膜; **five metres of cotton ~** 5 米棉质床单布

sheet: ~ iron *n* [u] 薄铁板; **~ lightning** *n* [u] 片状闪电; **~ metal** *n* [u] 金属薄板; **~ music** *n* [u] 1 (music published on single sheets) 活页乐谱; 2 (printed music) 乐谱上的曲子

sheikh, sheik /ʃeɪk, Amer ʃiːk/ *n* 1 (Arab leader) 谢赫 [指阿拉伯国家的政治或宗教领袖] 2 (Muslim leader) [伊斯兰教] 教长

sheikhdom, sheikdom /ˈʃeɪkdəm, Amer ʃiːk-/ *n* 酋长国

sheila /ˈʃiːlə/ *n* Austral, NZ colloq (girl) 小妞; (woman) 女郎

shekel /ˈʃekl/

A *n* ▸**p. 174** (currency) 谢克尔 [以色列货币单位]

B **shekels** *npl* colloq (money) 钱; (wealth) 财富; **to be raking in the ~s** 在挣大钱; **to count the ~s** 算着花钱

shelduck /ˈʃeldʌk/ *n* (*pl* **~** *or* **~s**) 翘鼻麻鸭

shelf /ʃelf/ *n* (*pl* **shelves**) 1 (on wall, in cupboard) 架子; (in fridge) 搁板; (in shop) 货架; (in library) 书架; **top/bottom ~** 最上层/最底下的架子; **a whole ~ of books** 整整一书架的书; **on the ~** 大龄未婚的; **to be left on the ~** (unmarried) 嫁不出去; (unwanted) 没人要; (unused) 闲置 2 (shelfful) (of books, china) 一架子 3 (of rock) 陆架; (of ice) 冰架

shelfful /ˈʃelffʊl/ *n* 一架子

shelf-life *n* 1 (of product) 保存期 2 fig colloq (of technology) 有效期; (of pop music) 流行期; (of politician, star) 受欢迎期

shelf mark *n* [图书馆标在书上的] 排架号

shell /ʃel/

A *n* 1 [c] (of egg) 蛋壳 2 [c] (of nut) 果壳 3 [u and c] (of snail, crab, shrimp, etc.) 壳; **lobster in the ~** 带壳龙虾; **one's ~** 羞怯; **to come out of one's ~** 不再羞怯; **to withdraw** *or* **retreat into one's ~** 变得羞怯; **to develop a hard ~** 自我封闭 4 [c] (bomb) 炮弹 5 [c] Amer (cartridge) 弹夹 6 [c] (of building, machine, ship) 骨架; **the ~ of the new theatre** 新剧院的框架 7 [c] (of car) 车架 8 [c] (pastry case) [馅饼或糕点的] 皮

B *vt* 1 (bombard) 炮击 ‹*town, troops, civilians*› 2 (take off husk) 给…去壳 ‹*peas, nuts*›; **to be as easy as ~ing peas** 轻而易举

Phrasal verb

- **shell out** colloq

A *vt* [**~ out sth.**] 大笔支付 ‹*money, taxes, donations*›

B *vi* 大笔付款; **to ~ out on sth.** 支付某物的费用

she'll /ʃiːl/ colloq 1 = **she shall** ▸**shall** 2 = **she will** ▸**will**[1]

shellac /ʃəˈlæk, ˈʃelæk/ Amer

A *n* [u] 虫胶清漆; **to apply ~ (to sth.)** (在某物上) 涂虫胶清漆; **to coat sth. with ~** 给某物表面涂虫胶清漆

B *vt* (*pres p* **shellacking**; *pt, pp* **shellacked**) 1 (varnish) «*person*» 用虫胶清漆涂刷 ‹*article*› 2 Amer colloq (beat) «*person, party*» 彻底击败 ‹*opponent*›

shellacking /ʃəˈlækɪŋ, ˈʃelækɪŋ/ *n* Amer colloq 彻底击败; **to give sb. a ~** 彻底击败某人; **to get a ~** 遭到惨败

S

shell: ~ company *n* 空壳公司; **~fire** *n* [u] 炮火; **~fish** *n* 1 [c] Zool (crustacean) 水生有壳动物; 2 [u] + *v sing or pl* Culin 贝类水产; **~hole** *n* 弹坑

shelling /ˈʃelɪŋ/ *n* [u] 炮击

shell pink ▸**p. 134**
A *adj* 淡粉色的
B *n* [u] 淡粉色

shell: ~-proof *adj* 防炮击的; **~ shock** *n* [u] 炮弹休克 [指长期作战引起的精神紊乱]; **~-shocked** *adj* 1 (suffering shell shock) 患炮弹休克的; 2 fig (shaken) 极为震惊的; **~ suit** *n* 休闲装

shelter /ˈʃeltə(r)/
A *n* 1 [c] (building) 庇护所; **a night ~ for the homeless** 无家可归者夜间收容所; **an animal ~** 动物收容处; **this monastery was a ~ for several Jewish families in the war** 这所修道院在战争期间是一些犹太人家庭的避难之地 2 [c] (structure) (against cold, rain, hurricane) 遮蔽物; **a flimsy ~ made out of branches** 用树枝搭起的简易窝棚; **we crowded under the ~ waiting for the bus** 我们挤在候车亭里等公共汽车; **the air-raid siren sent us running to the ~s** 听到空袭警报，我们都奔向防空洞 3 [u] (protection) (from wind, rain, hurricane) 遮蔽; (from bombing) 躲避; (from attack) 庇护; **the cave offered** *or* **provided ~ from the rain** 这个洞穴可以避雨; **we took** *or* **sought ~ in an old barn** 我们在一处旧谷仓里躲了起来; **to refuse/give sb. ~** 拒绝保护某人/为某人提供庇护; **in the ~ of the cliff/wall** 躲在悬崖/墙壁处
B Shelter *pr n* Brit (charity) 无家可归者之家
C *vt* 1 (protect against weather) «*building, tree, harbour wall*» 遮蔽 ‹*person, place, vessel*› 2 (protect from competition, reality, truth) 保护 ‹*person*› 3 (give refuge, succour to) «*place*» 为…提供庇护 ‹*fugitive*›; 为…提供救助 ‹*orphan*›; **to ~ sb. from sb./sth.** 使某人免受某人/某物所害
D *vi* «*person, animal*» 躲避; **to ~ from the storm** 躲避暴风雨; **to ~ under a tree** 躲在树下

shelter belt *n* 防护林带

sheltered /ˈʃeltəd/ *adj* 1 (from bad weather) 有遮蔽物的 ‹*place, garden, harbour*›; **a ~ spot** 遮风挡雨的地方 2 (from outside influences) 受庇护的 ‹*childhood, environment*›; **to lead a ~ life** 过受庇护的生活

sheltered accommodation, sheltered housing *ns* [u] Brit 福利院的住宿

shelve /ʃelv/
A *vt* 1 (place on shelf) 将…放在架子上 ‹*books, goods*› 2 (provide with shelves) 给…装搁架 ‹*room, wall, cupboard*› 3 (postpone) 搁置 ‹*plans, project, idea*›
B *vi* «*beach, hillside, sea bed*» 倾斜; **to ~ away** *or* **down** 向外/向下倾斜

shelves /ʃelvz/ *pl* ▸**shelf**

shelving /ˈʃelvɪŋ/ *n* [u] 1 (materials) 做架子的材料 2 (shelves) 搁板; (in library) 书架; (in shop) 货架

shemozzle /ʃɪˈmɒzl/ *n* colloq (row) 喧闹; (state of chaos) 混乱; **to make** *or* **create a ~** 制造混乱

shenanigans /ʃɪˈnænɪgənz/ *npl* 1 colloq (mischief) 恶作剧; **please stop the ~** 别胡闹了 2 (dishonesty) 鬼把戏

shepherd /ˈʃepəd/ ▸**p. 409**
A *n* 牧羊人
B *vt* 1 (herd) 放牧 ‹*sheep*›; **to ~ animals into a pen** 将动物赶入圈中 2 (guide, direct) 引领 ‹*guests, children, tourists, passengers*›; **to ~ sb. into/out of ...** 引领某人进入/离开…

shepherd boy *n* 小羊倌

shepherdess /ˌʃepəˈdes, Amer ˈʃepərdɪs/ ▸**p. 409** *n* (girl) 牧羊姑娘; (woman) 牧羊女

shepherd: ~'s crook *n* [一端带金属钩的] 牧羊杖; **~'s pie** *n* [c and u] 肉馅土豆泥饼

sherbet /ˈʃɜːbət/ *n* 1 [u] Brit (sweet) 果汁牛奶冻 2 [u and c] Amer (water ice) 冰糕

sheriff /ˈʃerɪf/ ▸**p. 409** *n* 1 (in England and Wales) (representative of monarch) 郡行政司法长官 2 (in Scotland) (judge) 郡法院法官 3 Amer (law enforcement officer) 县治安官

sheriff court *n* 郡法院

Sherpa /ˈʃɜːpə/ *n* (*pl* **~** *or* **~s**) 夏尔巴人 [尼泊尔一部族]

sherry /ˈʃeri/ *n* 1 [u and c] (wine) 雪利酒 2 [c] (glass of sherry) 一杯雪利酒

she's /ʃiːz/ colloq 1 = **she is** = **be** 2 = **she has** ▸**have**

Shetland /ˈʃetlənd/
A *pr n* 设得兰群岛
B *modif* 1 (of Shetland) 设得兰群岛的 ‹*coast, weather*› 2 (made from Shetland wool) 设得兰羊毛制成的 ‹*scarf, sweater, gloves*›

Shetlander /ˈʃetləndə(r)/ *n* 设得兰群岛人

Shetland: ~ Islands *pr n* **the ~ Islands** 设得兰群岛; **~ pony** *n* 设得兰矮种马; **~ sheep** *n* 设得兰羊; **~ wool** *n* [u] 设得兰羊毛

shhh /ʃ/ *excl* 嘘 [示意需要安静]

Shia, Shiah /ˈʃiːə/ *n* 1 [u] (religion) 什叶派 [伊斯兰教一教派]; **a ~ Muslim/leader/mosque** 什叶派穆斯林/领袖/清真寺 2 [c] (*pl* **~** *or* **~s**) (person) 什叶派教徒

shibboleth /ˈʃɪbəleθ/ *n* (custom) 过时习俗; (belief) 过时信仰

shied /ʃaɪd/ *pt, pp* ▸**shy**[1] **B, shy**[2] **A**

shield /ʃiːld/
A *n* 1 (of soldier, policeman) 盾牌; **to act as a ~** 起保护作用; **the hedge acts as a ~ against the wind** 树篱可以抵挡大风侵袭 2 (coat of arms) 盾形纹徽 3 (trophy) 盾形奖牌 4 (protective plate) 防护板; (protective screen) 防护屏; (on machine) 防护装置; (around gun) 护钣; (in tunnel) 掩护支架
B *vt* 1 (protect) «*person, armour, barrier, law*» 保护 ‹*person, object, place*›; **to ~ one's eyes from the sun** 保护眼睛不受阳光照射; **to ~ sb. with one's body** 用身体护住某人 2 (conceal) 庇护 ‹*person*›; 掩藏 ‹*face*› 3 (enclose) «*barrier, screen*» 给…加防护罩 ‹*machine, equipment, blade*›

shift /ʃɪft/
A *vt* 1 (move) 挪动; **will somebody help me ~ this piano?** 谁来帮我挪一下这架钢琴?; **I can't ~ the lid from this jar** 我揭不开这个坛子的盖子; **~ yourself over/up!** 你们过来/上去!; **the detergent wouldn't ~ the stain** 这种洗涤剂洗不掉这块污渍; **to ~ a cold** colloq 感冒痊愈; **~ your arse** *or* Amer **ass!** taboo sl 滚蛋!; **to ~ one's position** lit 挪地方; fig 改变立场; **to ~ one's ground** 改变立场 2 (transfer) «*lorry, company*» 转移 ‹*weight, production*›; fig «*report, person*» 转嫁 ‹*blame*›; 改变 ‹*attention*›; **he ~ed the load from his left shoulder to his right** 他把扛的东西从左肩换到右肩; **he's trying to ~ the responsibility onto us** 他在试图把责任推卸到我们头上 3 Amer Aut **to ~ gear** 换挡 4 colloq (eat, drink) 大吃 ‹*food*›; 大喝 ‹*beer*› 5 colloq (sell) 卖出 ‹*clothes, stock, goods*›
B *vi* 1 (move around) «*animal, person, object*» 挪动; «*vowel, consonant*» 演变; **the audience ~ed uneasily in their seats** 观众在座位上不安地动来动去; **to ~ from ... to ...** 从…转向…; **the wind ~ed from north to north west** 风向由北转成了西北; **he refused point blank to ~ from his position** lit 他坚决不挪地方; fig 他断然拒绝改变立场; **the ship's cargo ~ed in the rough seas** 船上的货物在波涛汹涌的大海上颠簸; **he's made his mind up, and I can't make him ~** 他已经下定了决心，我无法动摇他 2 Amer (change gear) 换挡; **to ~ into second** 换到二挡; **to ~ up/down (a gear)** (把挡位) 换到高挡/低挡 3 Brit colloq (move quickly) 快速移动; **get ~ing! we're late!** 快走! 我们迟到了!; **look at that car! it's really ~ing!** 瞧那辆车! 跑得真快啊! 4 **to ~ for oneself** 独自谋生
C *n* 1 (change) 变换; **a ~ in the government's policy** 政府政策的转变; **a ~ in the wind from north to north west** 风由北向西北的转变; **to bring about** *or* **produce a ~** 导致转变; **a ~ of emphasis** 重点的转移; **the gradual ~ of people from the country to the town** 人口从乡村到城镇的逐步迁移 2 (group of workers) 轮班员工; (time worked) 轮班工作时间; **the day/night ~** 白班/夜班; **an 8-hour ~** 8小时轮班; **to work ~s** *or* **in ~s** 轮班工作; **to be on the day/morning/evening ~** 上白班/早班/晚班; **to be paid ~ rates** 按轮班标准领工资 3 **to make ~** (manage) 将就着用 4 (woman's dress) 直筒连衣裙 5 (on keyboard) 转换键 6 (of rock) 断层 7 Amer = **gear shift**

shiftily /ˈʃɪftɪli/ *adv* (of behaviour, manner) 鬼鬼祟祟地; (of person, look) 贼眉鼠眼地

shiftiness /ˈʃɪftɪnɪs/ *n* [u] (of behaviour, manner) 鬼祟; (of person, look) 贼眉鼠眼

shifting /ˈʃɪftɪŋ/ *adj* 变化的 ‹*opinion*›; 变换的 ‹*scene*›

shifting: ~ agriculture, ~ cultivation *ns* [u] 轮垦; **~ sands** *npl* 1 lit 流沙; 2 fig (situation) 变化无常

shift key *n* 切换键

shiftless /ˈʃɪftlɪs/ *adj* 1 (lazy) 懒惰的 2 (lacking initiative) 无进取心的

shiftlessness /ˈʃɪftlɪsnɪs/ *n* [u] 不思进取

shift: ~ lock *n* 切换锁定键; **~ system** *n* 轮班工作制; **~ work** *n* [u] 轮班作业; **to be on ~ work** 倒班工作; **~ worker** *n* 倒班工作的员工

shifty /ˈʃɪfti/ *adj* 鬼鬼祟祟的 ‹*behaviour, manner*›; 贼眉鼠眼的 ‹*person, look*›

shiitake /ʃɪˈtɑːki/ *n* **~ (mushroom)** 香菇

Shiite /ˈʃiːaɪt/
A *n* [伊斯兰教的] 什叶派教徒
B *adj* 什叶派的

shilling /ˈʃɪlɪŋ/ ▸**p. 174** *n* Brit 先令 [旧时英国货币单位，等于12便士]; **to take the King's** *or* **Queen's ~** fig 当兵; **not the full ~** fig colloq 脑子不灵光的; **to be down to one's last ~** fig colloq 几乎身无分文

shillyshally /ˈʃɪlɪʃæli/ colloq
A *vi* 犹犹豫豫
B *n* [u] 犹犹豫豫

shillyshallying /ˈʃɪlɪʃælɪŋ/ *n* [u] colloq 犹豫不决

shimmer /ˈʃɪmə(r)/
A *vi* «*stars, light*» 闪烁; «*water, jewels, fabric, metal*» 闪光; «*heat*» 蒸腾
B *n* [u] (of stars, light) 闪烁; (of jewels, water, fabric, metal) 闪光; (of heat) 蒸腾

shimmering /ˈʃɪmərɪŋ/ *adj* 闪烁的 ‹*stars, light*›; 闪光的 ‹*water, jewels, fabric, metal*›; 飘动的 ‹*haze*›

shimmy /ˈʃɪmi/
A *n* **the ~** 希米舞 [舞动时摇摆或抖动全身]
B *vi* 1 (dance) 跳希米舞 2 (glide) 优雅地移动

shin /ʃɪn/
A *n* 1 [c] Anat 胫; **to kick sb. in the ~(s)** 踢某人的胫部 2 [u] (cut of beef) 牛小腿肉
B *vi* (*pres p etc.* **-nn-**) 攀爬; **to ~ up/down sth.** 爬上/爬下某物

shinbone /ˈʃɪnbəʊn/ *n* 胫骨

shindig /ˈʃɪndɪg/ *n* colloq 狂欢聚会

shindy /ˈʃɪndi/ *n* colloq 1 (disturbance) 喧闹; (quarrel) 吵闹 2 = **shindig**

shine /ʃaɪn/
A *vi* (*pt, pp* **shone**) 1 (emit light) «*stars, light, lamp*» 发光; «*sun, moon*» 照耀; **to ~ through sth.** 透过…照射过来 ‹*mist, gloom*›; **the light is shining in my eyes** 亮光照到了我的眼睛; **to ~ in/out** 照进/射出; **to ~ up to sb.** Amer colloq «*person*» 试图讨好某人 2 (glow) «*metal,*

shoes, hair, eyes》闪光 **3** fig (be radiant)《excitement, goodness, courage》显露;《eyes》发亮; **to ~ out of sth.** 从某物中透出; **her courage shone forth** liter 她的勇气表露无遗; **to ~ with sth.** 因某事物而放光; **his face shone with exertion** 他的脸因为用力而发红 **4** (excel)《person》表现出色; **he never shone at school** 他的学业成绩从来都不出色; **to get** or **have a chance to ~** 得到出人头地的机会

B vt **1** (pt, pp **shone**) (direct) 将…照向〈searchlight, headlamps, spotlight〉; **~ your torch over here please** 把你的手电往这边照 **2** (pt, pp **~d**) (polish) 将…擦亮〈buttons, silver, furniture〉; **I ~ my shoes every morning** 我每天早晨都擦鞋

C n [u] **1** (brightness) 光亮; **the ~ of sunlight/moonlight on water** 水面上太阳/月亮的闪光 **2** (polish) 光泽; **to give sth. a ~** 给…上光〈floor, shoes〉; **to take the ~ off sth.** fig 使某物黯然失色; **to take a ~ to sb.** fig colloq 喜欢上某人

shiner /ˈʃaɪnə(r)/ n colloq 青肿眼眶

shingle /ˈʃɪŋɡl/ n **1** [u] (pebbles) 鹅卵石; **a ~ beach** 卵石滩 **2** [c] (wooden tile) 木瓦 **3** [c] Amer colloq (sign) 招牌; **to put up one's ~** fig 挂牌开业

shingled /ˈʃɪŋɡld/ adj 盖木瓦的〈roof, house〉

shingles /ˈʃɪŋɡlz/ ▸**p. 377** npl + v sing 带状疱疹; **to have ~** 患带状疱疹

shingly /ˈʃɪŋɡli/ adj 遍布鹅卵石的〈beach〉

shin guard n 护胫

shininess /ˈʃaɪnɪnɪs/ n [u] 闪亮

shining /ˈʃaɪnɪŋ/ adj **1** (shiny) 有光泽的〈hair〉; 亮闪闪的〈room, vehicle, tools〉; **there stood the car in all its ~ splendour** 那辆汽车停在那里，车身闪亮，尽显华丽 **2** (radiant) 发光的〈face〉; **with ~ eyes she tore the ribbon off the present** 她两眼放光，解开了礼物上的绸带 **3** fig (excellent) 杰出的; **to be a ~ example of sth.** 是某方面的杰出榜样

shining light n fig 杰出者

shinny[1] /ˈʃɪni/ vi Amer = **shin B**

shinny[2] n [u] Amer [尤指儿童玩的] 简化冰球

shin pad n 护胫

Shinto /ˈʃɪntəʊ/, **Shintoism** /ˈʃɪntəʊɪzəm/ ns [u] [日本的] 神道教

Shintoist /ˈʃɪntəʊɪst/ n 神道教教徒

shinty /ˈʃɪnti/ n [u] 苏格兰式曲棍球

shiny /ˈʃaɪni/ adj 闪闪发亮的〈metal, eyes, surface〉; 锃亮的〈jacket, shoes〉; **~ hair/nose/pate** 有光泽的头发/油光光的鼻子/光亮的秃头顶

ship /ʃɪp/

A n 轮船; **to board a ~** 登船; **to disembark from a ~** 下船; **to load/unload a ~** 给船装货/卸货; **to travel by ~** 乘船旅行; **to take ~ for somewhere** dated 乘船去某处; **a ~ of the line** Hist 战列舰; **to keep** or **run a tight ~** fig colloq 严格管理; **the ~ of state** fig 政府; **at the helm of the ~ of state** fig 执掌国家大权; **when someone's ~ comes in** or **home** fig colloq 发了大财时; **a ~ of the desert** liter 沙漠之舟 [指骆驼]; **to jump ~**《crew member》擅自弃职离船; **we are like ~s that pass in the night** 我们只是萍水相逢; **like a ~ without a rudder** 像无舵之船一样漫无目标

B vt (pres p etc. **-pp-**) **1** (transport by sea) 用船运〈commodities〉 **2** (transport by air or land) 运输 **3** (take on board)《crew》把…装船〈cargo, supplies〉; **to ~ oars** 收桨入船; **to ~ water** 从舷侧进水

Phrasal verbs

- **ship off** vt [**~ off sb./sth., ~ sb./sth. off**] **1** (send by ship or air)《firm》运送〈goods, order〉;《government》派遣〈troops〉 **2** hum (dispatch) 送走〈patients, children〉; **we ~ped the kids off to summer camp** 我们送孩子们去了夏令营
- **ship out** vt [**~ out sth., ~ sth. out**] 运送〈goods, order〉

ship: ~board adj attrib 船上发生的〈ceremony, romance〉; 船上的〈duties, life〉; **~broker** ▸**p. 409** n (person) 船舶经纪人; (firm) 船舶经纪公司; **~builder** ▸**p. 409** n (person) 造船工人; (firm) 造船公司; **a firm of ~builders** 造船公司; **~building** n [u] 造船; **~ canal** n [可通大船的] 运河; **~load** n 船舶运载量; **~mate** n 同船船员

shipment /ˈʃɪpmənt/ n **1** [u] (act of shipping) 运输; **on** or **at the time of ~** 在装运时 **2** [c] (consignment) 运输的货物; **a ~ of sth.** 运送的一批某物

ship owner n (person) 船主; (company) 轮船公司

shipper /ˈʃɪpə(r)/ n (person) 托运人; (company) 托运公司

shipping /ˈʃɪpɪŋ/

A n [u] **1** (ships) 船舶; **a danger to ~** 航船面临的危险; **open/closed to ~** 可通航的/不通航的; **attention all ~!** 所有船只注意! **2** (transport) 货运; **the ~ of sth.** 某物的运输; **he's in ~** 他从事运输业

B modif **1** (transportation) 运输的; **~ costs/instructions** 运费/装货指示 **2** (by sea) 船运的; **~ exchange** 航运交易所; **~ magnate** 货运巨头

shipping: ~ agent ▸**p. 409** n (person) 船运代理; (firm) 船运代理公司; **~ charges** npl 运费; **~ clerk** ▸**p. 409** n 货运办事员; **~ company** n (by sea) 海运公司; (by air, road) 运输公司; **~ forecast** n 海上天气预报; **~ lane** n 海上航道; **~ line** n 海运公司; **~ master** ▸**p. 409** n Brit 海员契约监护官; **~ office** n 船运代理行

ship: ~'s biscuit n [u and c] [旧时供船员食用的] 硬饼干; **~'s boat** n 船载救生艇; **~'s chandler** ▸**p. 409** n 船具商; **~'s company** n + v pl 全体船员; **~'s doctor** ▸**p. 409** n 随船医生

shipshape /ˈʃɪpʃeɪp/ adj Brit colloq 整洁的〈room, camp, condition〉; **~ and Bristol fashion** 井井有条

ship: ~'s mate ▸**p. 409** n 大副; **~-to-shore radio** n 船岸通信无线电台

shipwreck /ˈʃɪprek/

A n **1** (accident) 海难; **the entire crew perished in the ~** 在这次海难中全部船员遇难 **2** (ship) 失事船只

B vt 使遭遇海难; **to be ~ed**《person, ship》遭遇海难

ship: ~wright /ˈʃɪpraɪt/ ▸**p. 409** n (person) 造船者; (firm) 造船公司; **~yard** n (for building ships) 造船厂; (for repairing ships) 修船厂

shire /ˈʃaɪə(r)/

A n **1** Brit (county) 郡 **2** Austral (district) 有自选议会的农村行政区

B **Shires** npl Brit **the S~s** 英国中部诸郡 [被视为传统乡村文化的大本营]

shire horse n 夏尔马 [体型大、旧时用于干农活]

shirk /ʃɜːk/ vt 逃避〈work, task, duty, obligation〉; 回避〈problem〉; **to ~ doing sth.** 逃避做某事; **don't ~ the issue!** 不要回避问题!

shirker /ˈʃɜːkə(r)/ n 逃避责任者

shirr /ʃɜː(r)/ vt **1** Sewing 将…抽出褶子〈fabric, garment, cuff〉 **2** Amer Culin 焙〈egg〉

shirring /ˈʃɜːrɪŋ/ n [u] Sewing (action) 抽褶; (result) 抽出的褶

shirt /ʃɜːt/ n 衬衫; **to wear a ~** 穿衬衫; **to put on/take off one's ~** 穿上/脱下衬衫; **to button up one's ~** 扣上衬衫的扣子; **a football/rugby/tennis/sports ~** 足球衫/橄榄球衫/网球衫/运动衫; **to lose one's ~** fig colloq 血本无归; **to put one's ~ on sth.** fig colloq 把全部家当押在某事物上; **keep your ~ on!** fig colloq 保持镇静! ; **to sell the ~ off sb.'s back** fig colloq 为了筹钱卖光某人的全部家当

shirt: ~ dress n 衬衫式连衣裙; **~ front** n 衬衫前襟

shirting /ˈʃɜːtɪŋ/ n [u and c] 衬衫料子

shirt: ~sleeve n 衬衫袖子; **in one's ~sleeves** 只穿着衬衫的; **to roll up one's ~sleeves** lit 卷起衬衫袖子; fig 准备大干一番; **~ tail** n 衬衫下摆; **~waist** n **1** Amer (blouse) 仿男式女衬衫; **2** **~waist (dress)** = **~waister**; **~waister** /ʃɜːtˈweɪstə(r)/ n [上身像衬衫的] 衬衫式连衣裙

shirty /ˈʃɜːti/ adj Brit colloq 脾气坏的; **I'm sorry I was so ~ on the phone** 对不起，我在电话里脾气很不好; **to get ~** 发脾气; **don't get ~ with me!** 别冲我发脾气!

shish kebab /ˈʃɪʃkəbæb/ n [肉片和蔬菜串在一起的] 烤肉串

shit /ʃɪt/ taboo sl

A n **1** [u] (excrement) 粪便; **dog ~** 狗屎; **a load of horse ~** 一担马粪; **to scare the ~ out of sb.** 把某人吓个半死; **to beat** or **kick** or **knock the ~ out of sb.** 把某人打得屁滚尿流; **to be in the ~/to land sb. in the ~** 处于困境/陷某人于困境; **to not give a ~ for** or **about sb./sth.** 毫不在乎某人/某事物; **when the ~ hits the fan** (when trouble starts) 等麻烦开始时; (when things become chaotic) 当事情变得不可收拾时; **no ~?** (as response) 这还用说? **2** [c] (nasty person) 卑鄙的人 **3** [c] (act of defecating) 拉屎; **to need a ~** 要拉屎; **to have a ~** 拉屎 **4** **shits** pl (diarrhoea) **to have** or **get the ~s** 拉肚子 **5** [u] (rubbish, nonsense) 废话; **a piece of ~** 废话; **don't give me that ~!** 少跟我废话! ; **a load of ~** 胡说八道; **you're talking ~** 你胡扯; **to be up ~ creek (without a paddle)** 陷入困境 (而无望逃脱) ; **if the car breaks down we're really up ~ creek** 如果车抛锚，我们就惨了 **6** [u] (stuff) 东西; **have you got all your ~ ready for the holiday?** 你把度假用的东西都准备好了吗? ; **to get (one's) ~ together** (put one's affairs in order) 处理好自己的事情; (put one's possessions in order) 收拾好自己的东西 **7** [u] (intoxicating drug) 毒品 [尤指大麻]

B vi (pres p etc. **-tt-**; pt, pp **-tt-** or **shit** or **shat**) 拉屎; **to ~ on sb.** fig 骑在某人头上拉屎 [指恶意对待或不尊重某人]

C v refl (pres p etc. **-tt-**; pt, pp **-tt-** or **shit** or **shat**) **to ~ oneself** 把屎拉在裤子里; fig (be very afraid) 吓得屁滚尿流; (be very excited) 激动万分

D vt (pres p etc. **-tt-**; pt, pp **-tt-** or **shit** or **shat**) **to be ~ting bricks** fig 把屎拉在裤子里

E excl 妈的; **(oh) ~! I've missed the turning** 妈的! 我开过了转弯处

shitake /ʃɪˈtɑːki/ n = **shiitake**

shitbag /ˈʃɪtbæɡ/ n taboo sl 蠢货 pej

shite /ʃaɪt/ Brit taboo sl

A n = **shit A1, A2, A3, A5**

B excl ▸**shit E**

shit: ~face n taboo sl 讨厌鬼 offensive; **~-faced** adj pred taboo sl (drunk) 喝得脸色煞白的; (on drugs) [因吸毒] 飘飘然的; **~head** n taboo sl = **shitbag**; **~hole** n taboo sl 肮脏不堪的地方; **this place is a ~hole!** 这地方简直是个猪圈! ; **~-hot** adj taboo sl 极出色的〈person, place, activity〉; **the film is ~-hot** 这部电影棒极了; **~house** n taboo sl **1** (toilet) 茅房; **2** fig (unpleasant place) 极脏乱的地方

shitless /ˈʃɪtlɪs/ adj taboo sl **to scare sb. ~** 把某人吓得屁滚尿流; **to be scared/bored ~** 被吓得屁滚尿流/感到无聊透顶

shit: ~-scared adj taboo sl 吓得屁滚尿流的; **~-stirrer** n taboo sl 爱惹是生非的人

shitter /ˈʃɪtə(r)/ n Amer taboo sl 抽水马桶; **he was on the ~** 他在蹲厕所

shitty /ˈʃɪti/ adj taboo sl **1** fig (unpleasant) 肮脏的〈place, person〉 **2** lit (covered with excrement) 沾满粪便的 **3** fig (contemptible) 卑鄙的〈action, trick, person〉

S

shiv /ʃɪv/ *n* Amer colloq (knife) [用作武器的] 小刀; (razor) [用作武器的] 剃刀

shiver[1] /ˈʃɪvə(r)/

A *vi* (with cold, fever or emotion) 颤抖; **to ~ with cold/fever** 冷得发抖/因发烧打寒战; **to ~ with fear/excitement/disgust** 吓得/激动得/厌恶得发抖; **to ~ at the thought of sth.** 一想到某事物就发抖

B *n* 颤抖; **to send a ~ down sb.'s spine** 使某人不寒而栗; **to give a ~** 哆嗦一下

C **the shivers** *npl* 寒战; **an attack of the ~s** 一阵寒战; **to give sb. the ~s** 使某人打寒战; fig 吓得某人发抖

shiver[2]

A *n* (fragment) 碎片; **I cut myself on a small ~ of glass** 我被一片碎玻璃划伤了

B *vi* «*window, wine glass, light bulb*» 碎裂

C *vt* «*explosion, bullet*» 打碎 ‹*window, wine glass, light bulb*›; **~ my timbers!** 真是活见鬼!

shivery /ˈʃɪvəri/ *adj* 颤抖的

shoal[1] /ʃəʊl/ *n* **1** (of fish) 鱼群 **2** Brit (of people) 一大群人

shoal[2] *n* **1** (shallows) 浅水处 **2** (sandbank) 沙洲 **3** fig (hidden danger) 陷阱

shock[1] /ʃɒk/

A *n* **1** [u] (distress) 震惊; **numb with ~** 惊呆的; **speechless from ~** 吃惊得说不出话的 **2** [c] (thing causing distress) 令人震惊的事物; **her sudden death was a terrible ~** 她的突然死亡让人震惊; **to give sb. a ~** 让某人吃一惊; **to come as a ~ (to sb.)** (对某人而言) 是个打击; **~s and upheavals** 动荡不安 **3** [u] (of collision, jolt) 撞击; (of earthquake, blast, explosion) 震动; **the ~ of the collision demolished the front of both cars** 两辆车的车头都撞毁了; **to withstand a ~** 承受冲击; **to absorb ~s** 抵消冲击 **4** [c] (electric current) 电击; **to receive *or* get a ~** 触电; **to give sb. a ~** 让某人遭电击 **5** [u] Med 休克; **to be in a state of ~** 处于休克状态; **severe/mild ~** 严重/轻度休克 **6** [c] colloq (shock absorber) 消震器

B *vt* (surprise, distress) «*speech, action, behaviour*» 使震惊; (offend, disgust) 使厌恶; **you can't ~ me! I've seen everything!** 你吓不着我! 我什么没见过! ; **to be ~ed at sth.** 对某事物感到震惊; **I was ~ed to hear about your accident** 听说你出了事故我很震惊; **to be ~ed by sth.** 因某事物感到震惊

shock[2] *n* (sheaves of corn) [竖在田野里晾晒的] 庄稼捆

shock[3] *n* (of hair) 浓密的一堆头发

shock absorber /ˈʃɒk əbˌzɔːbə(r)/ *n* 减震器

shocked /ʃɒkt/ *adj attrib* 震惊的 ‹*response, person*›; **the terrible news was greeted in ~ silence** 听到这可怕的消息大家非常震惊, 一言不发

shocker /ˈʃɒkə(r)/ *n* colloq **1** (thing, event) 令人震惊的事物 **2** (person) 令人震惊的人

shock: ~-headed *adj* 头发蓬乱浓密的 ‹*person*›; **~-horror** *adj attrib* Brit colloq 激起公愤的 ‹*event, behaviour, statement*›

shocking /ˈʃɒkɪŋ/ *adj* **1** (causing offence, disgust) 令人厌恶的 ‹*speech, words*›; **a ~ book** 惊世骇俗的书; **~ behaviour/insults** 令人发指的行为/侮辱 **2** (causing distress, surprise) 令人震惊的 ‹*news, event, sight*› **3** Brit colloq (very bad) 糟糕的 ‹*spelling, result, luck, weather*›; 严重的 ‹*cold, headache*›

shockingly /ˈʃɒkɪŋli/ *adv* (disgustingly) 令人厌恶地; (surprisingly, distressingly) 令人震惊地; **to behave *or* act ~** 行为可憎; **~ expensive/difficult** 贵得惊人的/极其困难的; **a ~ bad play** 一出糟糕透顶的戏

shocking pink ▸ p. 134

A *adj* 艳粉色的

B *n* [u] 艳粉色

shock: ~ jock *n* colloq 惊悚主播 [指脱口秀节目中故意发表冒犯、煽动性言论的主持人]; **~proof, ~-resistant** *adjs* 防震的 ‹*watch, instrument, case*›; **~ tactics** *npl* 突击战术; **~ therapy, ~ treatment** *ns* [u] **1** Med 休克疗法; **2** fig 断然措施; **~ troops** *npl* 突击部队; **~ value** *n* [u] 震撼性; **it's just for ~ value** 那只是为了产生震撼性效果; **~ wave** *n* **1** lit 冲击波; **2** fig 震惊; **the news has sent ~ waves through the stock market** 消息震动了整个股市

shod /ʃɒd/ *pt, pp* ▸ **shoe B**

shoddily /ˈʃɒdɪli/ *adv* **1** (in quality) 粗劣地; **to be ~ made/built** 做工粗糙/粗制滥造 **2** fig (in behaviour) 卑鄙地 ‹*act, treat*›; **he behaved very ~ towards his parents** 他对待父母非常刻薄

shoddiness /ˈʃɒdɪnɪs/ *n* [u] **1** (of quality) 劣质; **that firm's name has become a byword for ~** 那家公司的名字成了粗制滥造的代名词 **2** fig (of behaviour) 卑鄙

shoddy /ˈʃɒdi/

A *adj* **1** (poor in quality) 劣质的 **2** (unkind) 卑劣的 ‹*act, behaviour, treatment*›; **a ~ trick** 卑鄙的伎俩

B *n* [u] (yarn) 软再生毛; (fabric) 软再生毛织物

shoe /ʃuː/

A *n* **1** (footwear) 鞋; **ballet/beach ~s** 芭蕾舞鞋/沙滩鞋; **a pair of ~s** 一双鞋; **the left/right ~** 左脚/右脚的鞋; **a ~ box/factory/brush/cupboard** 鞋盒/鞋厂/鞋刷/鞋柜; **to take one's ~s off, to take off one's ~s** 脱鞋; **to put on one's ~s** 穿鞋; **to do up *or* tie *or* fasten one's ~s** 系鞋带; **to undo *or* untie *or* unfasten one's ~s** 解开鞋带; **to shake *or* shiver in one's ~s** fig 非常害怕; **to be in sb. else's ~s** fig 处于其他某人的境地; **another pair of ~s** fig 另外一回事; **to step into *or* fill sb.'s ~s** fig 接替某人的位置; **dead men's ~s** fig (property) 别人死后才能得到的遗产; (position) [因死亡或退休而] 空出的职位; **to wait for dead men's ~s** fig 等着别人空出职位 **2** (of horse) 马蹄铁 **3** Tech (brake shoe) 闸瓦; (cable shoe) 套管; (guiding shoe) 导块; (track shoe) 跑鞋

B *vt* (*pres p* **~ing**; *pt, pp* **shod**) 给…穿鞋 ‹*person*›; 给…钉蹄铁 ‹*horse*›; **well/poorly/suitably shod** 鞋穿得很好的/很差的/很合适的

shoehorn /ˈʃuːhɔːn/

A *n* 鞋拔

B *vt* fig 使…硬挤入 ‹*person*›; 把…硬塞入 ‹*thing*›; **to ~ sb. into a room/vehicle** 使某人硬挤入房间/车里; **to ~ sth. into sth.** 将某物硬塞入某物中; **to ~ oneself into a seat/pair of jeans** 勉强挤坐到座位上/硬套上一条牛仔裤

shoe: ~lace *n* 鞋带; **to do up *or* tie (up) one's ~laces** 系鞋带; **~maker** ▸ p. 409 *n* (person) 鞋匠; (firm) 制鞋公司; **~ polish** *n* [u and c] 鞋油; **~ rack** *n* 鞋架; **~ repairer** ▸ p. 409 *n* 修鞋匠; **~ repairs** *npl* 修鞋; **~ repair shop** *n* 修鞋店; **~shine** ▸ p. 409 *n* Amer **~shine (boy)** 擦鞋男童; **~shop** *n* 鞋店; **~ size** *n* 鞋码; **what's your ~ size?** 你的鞋码是多少?

shoestring /ˈʃuːstrɪŋ/ *n* **1** colloq (small budget) 小额预算; (inadequate budget) 不充足的预算; **on a ~** (budget) 以极少的资金; **the film/play was produced on a ~ budget** 这部影片/戏是小成本制作 **2** Amer = **shoelace**

shoe tree *n* 鞋楦

shogun /ˈʃəʊgʊn/ *n* **1** Hist [日本旧时的] 幕府将军 **2** fig [企业界等的] 大亨

shone /ʃɒn/ *pt, pp* ▸ **shine A, B1**

shoo /ʃuː/

A *excl* 嘘 [表示驱赶]

B *vt* [用嘘声] 赶走; **to ~ sb./sth. away** 赶走某人/某物; **to ~ sb./sth. out of the way** 将某人/某物轰走不再挡路; **to ~ sb./sth. out of somewhere** 将某人/某物赶出某处

shoo-in *n* Amer colloq (person) 稳操胜券者; (thing) 十拿九稳的事; **Bates is a ~ to win the election** 贝茨赢得选举十拿九稳

shook /ʃʊk/ *pt* ▸ **shake**

shoot /ʃuːt/

A *vt* (*pt, pp* **shot**) **1** (fire) 射击; **to ~ a gun/an arrow** 打枪/射箭; **the aircraft shot its missiles at the enemy positions** 飞机向敌人阵地发射了导弹; **to ~ it out (with sb.)** colloq (和某人) 火拼; **to ~ oneself in the foot** fig colloq 无意中坏自己的事; **to ~ the breeze** colloq 闲聊 **2** (kill, wound) 射杀; **to go ~ing pheasants** 去打野鸡; **to ~ sb./sth. in the arm/leg/head** *etc.* 射中某人/某动物的胳膊/腿/头等; **he had been shot in the back** 他后背中弹; **he was shot as a spy** 他被作为间谍枪决了; **to be shot for desertion/cowardice** 因开小差/胆小受到严厉惩处 **3** (create by shooting) 开枪打出; **to ~ one's way into/out of sth.** 开枪冲入/冲出某处; **the gunman had shot a large hole in the door** 枪手在门上射出了一个大洞 **4** (throw or push out) 抛出; **the impact had shot the driver out of the car** 撞击把司机抛出车外; **the snake shot its tongue out** 那条蛇唰的一下伸出了舌头; **the volcano shot lava high into the air** 火山把熔岩喷向高空 **5** (direct) 急速发出 ‹*accusation, remark*›; **journalists were ~ing questions at the minister** 记者们连珠炮般向部长提问; **she shot a smile/glance at him** 她向他投去一笑/瞥了他一眼; **'what do you mean by that?' she shot back** "你这话什么意思?" 她冷不丁地反问; **to ~ a line** Brit colloq 吹牛皮; **to ~ one's mouth off** sl (talk indiscreetly) 胡说; (boast, exaggerate) 吹牛皮 **6** (photograph) 拍摄 ‹*film, object, scene*›; **to ~ sb. doing sth.** 拍摄某人做某事的画面; **to ~ sth. in black and white/colour** 用黑白/彩色胶片拍摄某事物; **to ~ sth. on location** 在外景场地拍摄某事物 **7** (pass swiftly over or through) 飞速通过; **to ~ the rapids** 飞速穿过急流; **to ~ the lights** 闯红灯 **8** (push) 闩 ‹*door bolt*›; **to ~ the bolt home** 上好门闩 **9** Sport (in golf) 击出…杆; (in football) 将…射门; (in basketball) 将…投篮; **he shot a 73** 他打出了 73 杆; **to ~ a hole in one** 一击入洞; **he shot the ball at the keeper** 他把球踢向守门员 **10** Amer colloq (play) 玩; **to ~ craps/pool/dice** 玩双骰赌博/打落袋台球/掷骰子 **11** sl (inject) 注射 ‹*heroin, cocaine*›

B *vi* (*pt, pp* **shot**) **1** (fire a gun) «*soldier, marksman, huntsman*» 开枪; «*aircraft, ship*» 射击; **to ~ at sb./sth.** 向某人/某物射击; **to ~ to kill/wound** 开枪射杀/射伤; **to ~ from the hip** fig colloq 鲁莽行事 **2** (use a gun) «*marksman, huntsman*» 射击; **he enjoys riding, fishing and ~ing** 他喜欢骑马、钓鱼和射击; **to ~ straight/accurately** *etc.* 打得直/准等 **3** (fire bullets or arrows) 发射 **4** (move suddenly) 快速移动; **the car shot past** 那辆车飞驰而过; **a meteor shot across the sky** 一颗流星划过天空; **the pain shot down *or* along his arm** 他突然感到胳膊一阵疼痛; **to be *or* get shot of sb./sth.** colloq 摆脱某人/某事物 **5** (sprout) «*plant, bush, shrub*» 发芽 **6** (attempt to score) «*player, forward*» 射门; **to ~ at sth./sb.** 把球射向某处/某人 **7** colloq (speak out) 说出来; **if you've got something to tell me, ~!** 如果你有话对我讲, 那就说吧! ; **you ~ first** 你先说

C *n* **1** (of plant) 幼芽 **2** Brit (shooting expedition) 狩猎活动; **a grouse/tiger ~** 打松鸡/打老虎; **to go on a ~** 去狩猎; **the whole (bang) ~** fig colloq 悉数 **3** Brit (area of land) 狩猎场

Phrasal verbs

- **shoot away** *vt* [**~ sth. away, ~ away sth.**] 射落; **most of the ship's rigging had been shot away in the battle** 战斗中船上的索具大多都被枪炮打掉了
- **shoot down** *vt* [**~ sb./sth. down, ~ down sb./sth.**] 击倒; fig 痛斥; **to ~ sb. down in cold blood** 残忍地枪杀某人
- **shoot off**

A *vt* [**~ sth. off, ~ off sth.**]

S

1 (sever) 开枪打掉; **his arm/foot had been shot off in the war** 他的胳膊/脚在战争中被打断了 **2** (fire) 鸣〈*gun*〉; 发射〈*missile*〉

B *vi* colloq 马上离开; **I must ~ off now** 我必须走了

• **shoot up**

A *vi* **1** (rise up) 向上喷射; **the flames shot up into the sky** 火焰腾空而起 **2** (grow rapidly) 《*plant*》疯长; 《*child*》迅速长高 **3** colloq (inject drug) 注射毒品

B *vt* [**~ sth. up, ~ up sth.**] colloq 朝…扫射〈*car, room*〉; **the gangsters ran into the bar and started to ~ it up** 匪徒们冲进酒吧里就是一阵乱射

shoot-'em-up /ˈʃuːtəmʌp/ *n* colloq **1** (film) 枪战片 **2** (computer game) 射击游戏

shooter /ˈʃuːtə(r)/ *n* **1** (gun user) 射手 **2** colloq (gun) 枪 **3** Sport 得分手

shooting /ˈʃuːtɪŋ/ *n* **1** [u and c] (action) 枪击; (sound) 枪声; **there have been three ~s in the last week** 上个星期发生了3起枪击案; **a drive-by ~** 飞车枪击 **2** ▸**p. 307** [u] Sport 射击运动 **3** [u] Hunt 狩猎; **to go ~** 去打猎 **4** [u] (making films) [电影的] 拍摄; (taking photographs) 摄影

shooting: ~ gallery *n* 打靶场; **~ incident** *n* 枪击事件; **~ iron** *n* Amer colloq 枪支; **~ party** *n* 狩猎队; **~ range** *n* **1** (place) 打靶场; **2** (distance) 有效射程; **within/out of ~ range** 在有效射程内/外; **~ spree** *n* 连环枪击事件; **~ star** *n* 流星; **~ stick** *n* 折叠座手杖

shoot-out *n* colloq 枪战

shoot-to-kill policy *n* 一枪毙命的策略

shop /ʃɒp/

A *n* **1** esp Brit (selling goods or services) 商店; **a corner/duty-free/clothes ~** 街角小店/免税店/服装商店; **to mind the ~** 看管商店; fig 临时照看; **to set up ~** 开业; **to shut up ~** lit 打烊; fig 停业; **to live over the ~** lit 住在店铺的楼上; fig 住在工作地点附近; **to talk ~** 说行话; **like a bull in a china ~** 笨手笨脚地碰东碰西; **all over the ~** colloq (in disarray) 杂乱无章; (in every direction) 到处; **I've been all over the ~ to find a present for her** 我四下为她寻找礼物 **2** (workshop) 车间; **an engineering/machine/assembly ~** 机械加工/机器制造/组装车间; **a repair/print/paint ~** 维修/印刷/喷漆车间 **3** (shopping trip) 购物; **she's gone into town to do her weekly ~** 她进了城购物，每周一次

B *vi* (*pres p etc.* **-pp-**) 购物; **to ~ for (sth.)** 购买（某物）; **to go ~ping** 去购物; **to go Christmas ~ping** 去购买圣诞节用品

C *vt* (*pres p etc.* **-pp-**) Brit colloq (betray) 告发

Phrasal verb

• **shop around** *vi* 货比三家; **we ~ped around for a long time before deciding on this school** fig 我们考察比较了很长时间才选定这所学校

shopaholic /ˌʃɒpəˈhɒlɪk/ *n* colloq 购物狂

shop: ~ assistant ▸**p. 409** *n* Brit 店员; **~ fitter** ▸**p. 409** *n* Brit 商店货架安装工; **~ fitting** *n* [u] Brit 商店货架安装

shopfloor /ʃɒpˈflɔː(r)/

A *n* Brit [工厂的] 生产区; **problems/conditions on the ~** 生产区的问题/工作条件

B *modif* 从事生产的〈*worker*〉; 工人的〈*experience, militancy*〉

shop: ~ front *n* Brit 店面; **~ girl** *n* dated 女店员; **~keeper** esp Brit ▸**p. 409** *n* 店主; **~lift** *vi* 在商店行窃; **~lifter** *n* 商店扒手; **~lifting** *n* [u] 商店行窃

shopper /ˈʃɒpə(r)/ *n* **1** (person) 购物者 **2** Brit (bag) 购物袋; (trolley) 购物推车

shopping /ˈʃɒpɪŋ/ *n* [u] **1** (activity) 购物; **to do some or the ~** 买东西; **we are open for lunch-time ~** 午餐时间我们是开门营业的; **a ~ area/street** 购物区/街 **2** (purchases) 购买的东西; **don't forget your ~** 别忘了带走您买的东西

shopping: ~ bag *n* 购物袋; **~ basket** *n* 购物篮; **~ cart** *n* Amer = **~ trolley**; **~ centre** *n* 购物中心; **~ complex** *n* 大型购物中心; **~ list** *n* 购物单; **~ mall** *n* 购物商场; **~ precinct** *n* 步行购物区; **~ trip** *n* 购物之旅; **to go on a ~ trip** 去作一次购物旅行; **~ trolley** *n* Brit 购物车; **~ village** *n* 购物村 [指位于市郊的高档购物中心]

shop: ~-soiled *adj* Brit 在商店陈列旧了的〈*article, goods, garment*〉; **to be ~-soiled** 因陈列而变旧; **~ steward** *n* esp Brit 工会谈判代表; **~talk** *n* [u] 关于工作的谈话; **~ window** *n* 商店橱窗; **agricultural shows are the ~ window for many rural businesses** 农业展览会是很多农村企业的展示窗口; **~worn** *adj* Amer = **~-soiled**; **~ worker** ▸**p. 409** *n* Brit 店员

shore[1] /ʃɔː(r)/

A *n* **1** [c] (of sea) 海滨; (of lake) 湖滨; **on the ~** 在岸上; **off the ~ of ...** 离开…岸 **2** [u] (land) 陆地; **on ~** 在陆上; **from ship to ~** 从船上到陆上 **3** [c] (tidal area) 潮水涨落之间的地带

B **shores** *npl* (country) 沿海国家; (area) 沿海地区

shore[2] *n* (prop) 支柱; **to use a chair as a ~** 用椅子作支撑

Phrasal verb

• **shore up** *vt* [**~ up sth., ~ sth. up**] **1** (prop up) 《*person, prop*》支撑〈*building, wall, beam*〉 **2** fig (support) 支持〈*organization, economy, argument*〉

shore: ~-based *adj* 以陆上为基地的〈*staff, facilities, event*〉; **~-based guns** 岸基炮; **a ~-based vacation** 海滨度假; **~ leave** *n* [u] [水手的] 登岸假; **to be on ~ leave** 在岸上度假; **~line** *n* [大片水体的] 岸线; **~ patrol** *n* Amer 岸上宪兵队

shorewards /ˈʃɔːwədz/ *adv* 向岸地; **to sail/look/turn ~** 向岸航行/向岸上看/朝岸上的方向掉头

shorn /ʃɔːn/ *pp* ▸**shear**

short /ʃɔːt/

A ▸**p. 436** *adj* **1** (not long in length) 短的; **a ~ dress** 短裙; **to cut sth. ~** 把某物剪短; **a ~ distance away or off** 不远的距离 **2** (below average height) 矮的; **he's rather ~ in stature** 他个头很矮; **~ and stocky** 矮壮的 **3** (not lasting long) 短暂的; **we met in the street and had a ~ conversation** 我们在街上碰面后聊了几句; **he gave a ~ speech of welcome** 他发表了简短的欢迎讲话; **he gave a ~ cry of delight** 他惊喜地叫了一声; **she gave a ~ gasp of pain** 她疼得倒吸了一口气; **to have a ~ memory** 健忘; **a ~ time or while ago** 刚才; **a ~ course** 短期课程; **in ~ order** 迅速地; **to make ~ work of sb./sth.** 干净利落地打败某人/解决某事; **~ and sweet** 简明扼要的; **in two ~ months the political climate had changed completely** 短短两个月后政治气候完全变了 **4** (inadequate) 不足的; **it was mid-summer, and water was very ~** 时值仲夏，水源紧缺; **time is getting ~** 时间越来越少; **the shopkeeper gave us ~ change** 店主少找了我们钱; **the results are far ~ of what we expected** 结果远远达不到我们的预期 **5** (lacking) **to be ~ of sth.** 缺乏某物; **I'm very ~ of ready cash** 我手头很缺现金; **the car is ~ of petrol** 汽车的油不够用了; **to be five ~** 少5个; **we're ~ by two players for the match** 我们比赛还差两个队员; **to be (a bit) ~** 手头（有点儿）拮据; **he is ~ on experience** colloq 他经验不足 **6** (in abbreviation) 简略的; **to be ~ for sth.** 是某事物的简写; **UN is ~ for United Nations** UN是United Nations的缩写; **call me Frank for ~** 为简单起见叫我弗兰克好了 **7** (abrupt) 生硬无礼的; **to be ~ with sb.** 对某人简慢 **8** (expressed in few words) 简短的〈*comment, question, explanation*〉; **~ and to the point** 言简意赅的; **in ~** 简而言之; **to cut a long story ~** 长话短说 **9** Ling 发音时间短的; **a ~ vowel/syllable** 短元音/短音节 **10** Fin 空头交易的; **a ~ contract/bill of exchange/position** 空头交易合同/空头交易票据/空头; **a ~ seller** 卖空者 **11** (crumbly) 松脆的〈*cake, pastry, crust*〉

B *adv* **1** (suddenly) 突然; **to bring or pull sb. up ~** 使某人突然停下 **2** (before the expected place or time) **~ of sth.** 达不到某物; **the plane landed ~ of the runway** 飞机在跑道外迫降着陆; **his second drive landed ~ of the green** 他第二杆击出的球就落在球穴区边上; **to be caught or taken ~** colloq 内急; **a brilliant career tragically cut ~ by illness** 不幸因病半途而废的美好前程; **to stop ~ of sth./doing sth.** 不尝试某事物/做某事; **I'm sure he'd stop ~ of anything/doing anything illegal** 我肯定他不会做违法的事 **3** (less than) **~ of** 不到; **there were just ~ of two thousand people in the hall** 礼堂里有将近两千人; **~ of the truth** 与事实有出入; **we collected not far ~ of £500** 我们募集了差不多500镑; **to fall ~ of sth.** 未达到某状况; **his achievements have fallen ~ of all he hoped to do** 他所取得的成就全部未达到自己的期望; **to go ~ (of sth.)** 缺少（某物）; **to run ~ (of sth.)** 快用完（某物）; **to sell sb./sth. ~** 低估某人/某事物 **4** **~ of ...** (except for) 除…之外; **~ of resigning, there isn't much I can do** 除了辞职，我没多少能做的; **it's little or nothing ~ of scandalous** 简直就是丑闻 **5** (in cricket) **to bowl ~** 投球不够远 **6** Fin 空头交易地; **to sell ~** 卖空

C *n* **1** colloq = **short circuit A** **2** (film) [在正片之前放映的] 电影短片 **3** (alcoholic drink) 少量烈酒

D *vi* colloq = **short circuit B**

E *vt* colloq = **short circuit C1**

shortage /ˈʃɔːtɪdʒ/ *n* 缺乏; **a ~ of sth.** 某物的缺乏; **~s of fuel and food** 燃料和食物的短缺; **at a time of ~** 在匮乏时期; **a housing ~** 住房短缺; **there is no ~ of applicants/opportunity** 申请人/机会很多

short: ~-arse *n* sl pej 矮子; **~ back and sides** *n* Brit [男子脑后和头部两侧都剪得很短的] 盖式发型; **~bread** *n* [u and c] 黄油甜酥饼; **~cake** *n* [u and c] **1** = **~bread**; **2** Amer (dessert) 水果酥饼; **~ change** *vt* **1** lit 少给…找头; **2** fig (treat unfairly) 亏待

short circuit

A *n* 短路

B **short-circuit** *vi* 发生短路

C **short-circuit** *vt* **1** lit 使短路 **2** fig (circumvent) 绕过〈*procedure*〉; **we must ~ the formalities and get a quick decision** 我们必须绕过那些繁文缛节，尽快作出决定

short: ~coming *n* 缺点; **~crust** *n* [u] Brit **~ crust (pastry)** 脆皮油酥; **~cut** *n* **1** (route) 近路; **to take a ~cut through the park** 穿过公园走近路; **2** (method) 捷径; **to take ~cuts** colloq 走捷径; **there are no ~cuts to becoming a musician** 想要成为音乐家是无捷径可走的; **3** Comput 快捷键; **a keyboard ~cut** 快捷键; **a ~cut key** 键盘快捷键; **~ division** *n* [u] 短除法

shorten /ˈʃɔːtn/

A *vt* **1** (reduce) 截短〈*garment, rope, chain*〉; 缩短〈*journey, talk, text*〉; **to ~ a skirt by a few inches** 把一条裙子改短几英寸; **to ~ the journey time to two hours** 把旅程缩短到两小时; **to ~ the odds** 减少几率 **2** Naut 《*sailor*》收起〈*sail*〉; **~ the sails!** 收帆! **3** Culin 在…中加起酥油〈*pastry*〉

B *vi* 《*days, nights*》变短; **the odds have ~ed considerably** 几率大大减少了

shortening /ˈʃɔːtnɪŋ/ *n* [u] **1** (reduction) 缩短; **the ~ of sth.** 某物的缩短; **~ has much improved the book** 经过删减后这本书大有改观 **2** Culin 起酥油

S

short: **~fall** *n* (in budget, accounts) 不足; (in earnings, exports) 差额; **a ~fall in of sth.** 某物的缺额; **there is a ~fall of £10,000 in our budget** 我们有10,000英镑的预算缺口; **to meet** *or* **make up the ~fall between cost and subsidy** 补足支出与补贴间的差额; **~-haired** *adj* 短发的 ‹*person*›; 短毛的 ‹*animal*›; **~hand** *n* [u] **1** (rapid writing) 速记(法); **to take sth. down in ~hand** 采用速记法记下某事; **a ~hand letter/note** 速记信/笔记; **2** fig (verbal shortcut) 简略表达方式; **~ for sth.** 某事物的简略表达; **a ~hand term** *or* **expression** 简略措词; **~-handed** *adj* 人手不足的; **we are ~-handed at the office** 我们部门人手不足

shorthand: **~ typing** *n* [u] esp Brit 速记打字; **~ typist** ▸**p. 409** *n* esp Brit 速记打字员

short haul
A *n* (of goods) 短途货运; (of passengers) 短途客运
B **short-haul** *modif* 短途运输的 ‹*route, market, business*›; **a ~-haul flight** 短途航班

short head *n* Brit Horse racing 不到一个马头的距离; **to lose by a ~** 以不到一个马头的差距输掉

shorthorn /ˈʃɔːthɔːn/ *n* 短角牛

shortie /ˈʃɔːti/ *n* colloq **= shorty**

shortish /ˈʃɔːtɪʃ/ *adj* 相当短的

shortlist /ˈʃɔːtlɪst/
A *n* 入围名单
B *vt* 把…列入入围名单 ‹*applicant, candidate*›; **to ~ sb. for sth.** 把某人列入某事的候选名单

short-lived /ˌʃɔːtˈlɪvd/ *adj* **1** (living for a short time) 短命的 ‹*person*›; 存活期短的 ‹*plant, animal*› **2** (lasting for a short time) 短暂的 ‹*relationship, interest, success, triumph*›

shortly /ˈʃɔːtli/ *adv* **1** (a short time) 不久; **~ beforehand/afterwards** 之前/之后不久; **~ before/after lunch** 午饭前/后不久 **2** (soon) 马上; **she'll be back ~** 她马上就回来; **volume four will be published ~** 第四卷很快就会出版 **3** (succinctly) 简短地; **a letter ~ outlining the proposals** 一封简要说明提案内容的信 **4** (curtly) 没好气地 ‹*speak, reply*›

shortness /ˈʃɔːtnɪs/ *n* [u] **1** (in duration, height, length) 短; **~ of breath** 呼吸的短促; **the ~ of the letter/document/book** 信件/文件/书内容的简短 **2** (abruptness) 没好气

short: **~ odds** *npl* [赌博中] 输赢几乎相等的机会; **~ order** *n* Amer 快餐; **a ~-order cook/chef** 快餐厨师/大厨; **~ pants** *npl* Amer **= ~ trousers**; **~-range** *adj attrib* **1** (of time) 近期的 ‹*plan, forecast*›; **2** (of distance) 短程的 ‹*missile, aircraft, transmission*›

shorts /ʃɔːts/ *npl* **1** (short trousers) 短裤 **2** Amer (underpants) 男式内裤

short: **~-selling** *n* [u] 卖空; **~ sharp shock** *n* Brit 立竿见影的惩罚; **~ shrift** *n* [u] 淡漠处置; **to give sb./sth. ~ shrift** 不理会某人/某事物; **to get ~ shrift from sb.** 受到某人冷遇; **~ sight** *n* [u] esp Brit 近视; **~-sighted** *adj* **1** esp Brit lit 近视的 ‹*person, eye*›; **2** fig (lacking foresight) 目光短浅的 ‹*person, plan, measure*›; **it would be very ~-sighted to ...** …是很缺乏远见的; **to have a ~-sighted attitude** 持目光短浅的态度; **to be ~-sighted about sb./sth.** 对某人/某事物缺乏远见; **~-sightedness** *n* [u] **1** esp Brit lit 近视; **2** fig (lack of foresight) 目光短浅; **~-sightedness about sb./sth.** 对某人/某事物的缺乏远见; **~-sleeved** *adj* 短袖的 ‹*dress, shirt, blouse*›; **~-staffed** *adj* 缺人手的 ‹*company, shop, office, service*›; **to be ~** 人手不足; **~-stay** *adj* 供暂住的 ‹*hostel, housing*›; 临时的 ‹*car park, parking*›; **~ story** *n* 短篇小说; **a ~-story writer/competition** 短篇小说作家/竞赛; **~-tailed** *adj* 短尾的; **~ temper** *n* 暴躁脾气; **to have a ~ temper** 脾气暴躁; **~-tempered** *adj* 脾气暴躁的

short-term
A *adj* 短期的 ‹*plan, arrangement, loan*›; 短时间的 ‹*appointment, car park, parking*›; **~ memory** 短时记忆
B *n* 短期; **in the ~** (looking to future) 在近期内; (looking to past) 眼下

short: **~-time** *n* [u] 短工时; **to be on ~ time** 开工不足; **~-time working** 短工时工作; **~ ton** ▸**p. 909** *n* 短吨; **~ trousers** *npl* 穿短裤的学童

short wave
A *n* [u] (signal) 短波; **I listened on ~** 我收听短波频道
B **short-wave** *modif* 短波的; **a short-wave broadcast/signal** 短波广播/信号

short: **~ weight** *n* [u] 重量不足; **to give ~ weight** 短斤缺两; **~-winded** *adj* 呼吸急促的; **to be ~-winded** 气喘吁吁

shorty /ˈʃɔːti/ *n* colloq **1** (person) 矮子 **2** (garment) 短小衣服; **a ~ mackintosh/nightie** 短雨衣/睡衣

shot /ʃɒt/
A *n* **1** (act of shooting) 射击; (sound of shooting) 枪声; **to take** *or* **fire a ~ at sb./sth.** 对某人/某物射击; **he fired a ~ at the burglar** 他对着盗贼开了一枪; **to have a ~ (at sb./sth.)** (对某人/某物)开一枪; **to fire the first ~** 打响第一枪; **like a ~** colloq (at once) 马上; (very fast) 飞快地 **2** colloq (attempt at shooting) 射击尝试; fig (attempt) 尝试; **he asked me if I would like to have a ~ at a pheasant** 他问我是否愿意去打野鸡; **a ~ at sth./doing sth.** 尝试某事/做某事; **to have a ~** 尝试一下 **3** (in cricket, tennis, billiards, golf, etc.) 击球; (in football, hockey) 踢球; **that was a fine ~!** 那个球打得真漂亮! ; **a backhand/forehand ~** 反手/正手击球; **to have** *or* **take a ~ at goal** 射门; **good ~!** 好球! ; **two ~s behind sb.** 落后某人两个球 **4** (in athletics) 铅球; **to put the ~** 推铅球 **5** [u] (lead pellets) 铅弹; (coarse metal powder) 金属粒屑; **lead ~** 铅弹; **bird ~** 打鸟用的铅弹 **6** (person who shoots) 射击手; **a good/poor ~** 好的/差的射击手; **a crack ~** 神枪手 **7** (photograph) 照片; **a long/close-up ~** 远景/特写照片 **8** (continuous film sequence) 一段影片; **a slow-motion ~** 慢镜头 **9** (launch of space vehicle) 发射; **a moon/Mars ~** 登月/火星探测航天器发射 **10** colloq (injection) 注射; **to give sb. a ~** 给某人注射; **the doctor gave her a ~ to kill the pain** 医生给她打了止痛针; **a ~ in the arm** fig 激励; **the improved trade figures are a much-needed ~ in the arm for the economy** 贸易数字的改善为经济打了一剂急需的强心针
B *adj* **1** (streaked) 闪色的 ‹*satin*›; **a dress of ~ silk** 用闪色绸做成的连衣裙; **brown hair ~ with grey** 花白的褐色头发; **(to be) ~ through with sth.** 充斥某事物; **humour ~ through with sadness** 饱含哀伤的幽默 **2** colloq (worn out) 累坏的; (used up) 用完的; (wrecked) 毁坏的; **his nerves were completely ~** 他的神经脆弱到了极点 **3** Brit colloq (rid) **to be/get ~ of sb./sth.** 摆脱某人/某事物; **I just can't get ~ of this cold!** 我的感冒就是好不了!
C *pp, pt* ▸**shoot A, B**

shot-blasting /ˈʃɒtblɑːstɪŋ, Amer -blæstɪŋ/ *n* [u] 喷砂

shotgun /ˈʃɒtɡʌn/ *n* 猎枪; **to ride ~** esp Amer (on a vehicle) 押车; fig 充当保护人

shotgun marriage, shotgun wedding *ns* colloq [尤指因女方怀孕而仓促举行的]闪电式结婚

shot: **~ hole** *n* **1** (made by shot) 弹孔; **2** (in blasting) 爆破孔; **~-put, ~-putting** /ˈʃɒtpʊtɪŋ/ *ns* [u] 推铅球; **~-putter** /ˈʃɒtpʊtə(r)/ *n* 铅球运动员

should /ʃʊd, ʃəd/ ▸**p. 147** *modal aux* (*negative* **should not** *or* colloq **shouldn't**) **1** (expressing obligation) 应该; **you shouldn't drink and drive** 不应该酒后驾车; **he ~ have been more careful** 他本应该再小心一点儿的; **everything is as it ~ be** 一切正常; **a present for me? you shouldn't have!** 给我的礼物吗? 你太客气了! **2** (giving or asking for advice) 该; **I ~ resign if I were you** 如果我是你的话, 我就辞职不干了; **she recommended that I ~ take some time off** 她建议我休息一段时间; **she doesn't think she'll get a job — she ~ worry, with all her qualifications** iron 她认为自己找不到工作——她那么好的条件, 可真该担心的; **~ I call him and apologize?** 我是不是该打电话向他道歉? **3** (expressing probability) 应该会; **the parcel ~ arrive today** 包裹应该今天到; **I ~ have finished the book by Friday** 到星期五我应该能读完那本书 **4** (indicating that sth. has not happened) 本应; **it ~ be snowing now, according to the weather forecast** 按天气预报的说法, 现在本该下雪才是; **the bus ~ have arrived ten minutes ago** 公共汽车10分钟前就该到了 **5** Brit formal (indicating consequence, purpose) 会; **if they didn't invite me, I ~ be offended** 要是他们没邀请我的话, 我会生气的; **we ~ never have succeeded without you** 要是没有你, 我们绝不会成功; **in order that training ~ be effective** 为了让训练有效; **in order that they ~ not be worried** 为了不让他们担心 **6** formal (indicating possibility) 假如; **if you ~ (ever) change your mind, do let me know** 你(一旦)改变主意的话, 一定要告诉我; **~ anyone call, please tell them I'm busy** 如果有人打电话来, 请告诉他我正忙着; **supposing he ~ die?** 万一他死了呢? **7** (expressing future in reported speech) [用于引语中表示将来动作] **I said that I ~ be pleased to help** 我说过我乐意帮忙 **8** (in expressions of feelings) 竟然; **it's sad that he ~ object** 令人遗憾的是, 他竟然会反对; **I find it astonishing that he ~ be so rude to you** 我很吃惊, 他居然对你这样无礼 **9** Brit formal (in polite requests) [用于表示礼貌请求, 仅与I或we连用] **I ~ like to call my lawyer** 我希望给我的律师打个电话; **I ~ like a drink** 我想喝一杯; **I ~ like to ask whether ...** 我想问一问是否… **10** (expressing uncertain opinion) [表示不确定, 仅与I或we连用]; **I ~ imagine it will take about three hours** 我想得用差不多3个小时吧; **I ~ think so** 我想是吧; **will it matter? — I shouldn't think so** 这有关系吗? ——不会吧 **11** (expressing strong agreement) [用于表示强烈赞同] **nobody will oppose it — I ~ think not!** 谁也不会反对——的确不会! ; **I'll pay you for it — I ~ hope so!** 我会付钱给你的——但愿如此! **12** (expressing annoyance, refusal, surprise) [表示气恼、拒绝或惊讶] **why ~ I help him?** 我干吗要帮他呢? ; **how ~ I know where you've left your bag?** 我怎么知道你把包丢到哪里去了? ; **who ~ walk in but John!** 没想到走进来的居然是约翰! **13** (emphasizing sth. remarkable) [用于强调某事不同凡响] 真该; **you ~ hear her play the cello!** 你真该听听她拉大提琴!

shoulder /ˈʃəʊldə(r)/
A *n* **1** ▸**p. 71** [c] Anat 肩; **to have round/broad/narrow ~s** 长着溜肩/宽肩/窄肩; **to carry sb. on one's ~s** 背某人; **to carry sb. ~ high** 把某人举到肩上; **to look (back) over one's ~** 回过头去看; **to stand ~ to ~ (with sb.)** (和某人)肩并肩站立; **to work ~ to ~** fig 齐心协力; **a ~ to cry on** fig 倾诉对象; **to fall on sb.'s ~s** fig «*responsibility*» 落到某人肩上; **to put one's ~ to the wheel** fig 全力以赴; **straight from the ~** fig 直截了当地 **2** *usu pl* [c] (part of garment) 肩部; **padded ~s** 有衬垫的肩部 **3** [u] Culin 肩肘肉; **a ~ of lamb** 羊前腿连肩肉 **4** [c] (of mountain, hill) 山肩 **5** [c] (of road) 路肩

B vt **1** (take on one's shoulder) 扛起 **2** fig (take on) 承担 ‹*blame, responsibility*› **3** (push with shoulder) 用肩推搡; **to ~ sb. aside/out of the way** 肩部一顶把某人挤到一边儿去/挤开

shoulder: ~ bag n 挎包; **~ belt** n 肩带; **~ blade** n 肩胛骨

shoulder charge
A n 用肩冲撞
B **shoulder-charge** vt 用肩冲撞 ‹*person, door*›

shoulder-high
A adj 齐肩高的
B adv 齐肩高地; **to carry sb. ~** 把某人抬上肩头

shoulder: ~ holster n 腋下手枪套; **~ joint** n 肩关节; **~-length** adj 齐肩的 ‹*hair*›; **~ pad** n **1** (for bulk and shape) 垫肩; **2** (for protection) 护肩; **~ patch** n 臂章; **~ strap** n (of garment) 肩带; (of bag) 背带

shouldn't /ˈʃʊdnt/ colloq = **should not** ▸**should**

should've /ˈʃʊdəv/ colloq = **should have** ▸**should**

shout /ʃaʊt/
A vi **1** (speak at full volume) 大喊; **to ~ at** or **to** or **for sb. to do sth.** 喊某人做某事; **that's nothing much to ~ about!** 用不着这么嚷嚷! ; **to ~ for help** 高声呼救; **to ~ for joy/with excitement** 高兴/兴奋得大喊大叫 **2** (talk angrily) 愤怒地大声嚷嚷; (scold) 呵斥; **to ~ at sb.** 呵斥某人
B vt 高声说出 ‹*answer, question*›; 大声喊 ‹*order, slogan*›; **people were ~ing abuse** 人们在破口大骂; **to ~ one's head off** 拼命喊叫
C n **1** (loud cry) 喊叫; **a ~ of protest** 抗议的呼声; **~ of excitement** 兴奋的叫声; **to give a ~ of laughter/pain** 发出笑声/痛苦的叫声; **to give sb. a ~** colloq 告诉某人; **give me a ~ when you're ready** 你准备好了就喊我一声 **2** colloq (turn to pay for drinks) 轮到买酒水请客; **it's my ~** 该我请客

Phrasal verbs
- **shout down** vt [**~ sb. down, ~ down sb.**] 压倒…的声音 ‹*speaker*›; **he tried to finish, but was ~ed down by the audience** 他想讲完，但观众的呼喊声让他闭了嘴
- **shout out** vt [**~ out sth. ~ sth. out.**] 大声说出 ‹*answer, question*›; 大声喊 ‹*order, slogan*›

shouting /ˈʃaʊtɪŋ/ n 叫喊声; **it's all over bar the ~** fig colloq 胜负已定

shouting match n 大声争吵

shove /ʃʌv/
A vt **1** (push) 猛推 ‹*person, box, trolley, furniture*›; **to ~ sth. through** 将某物用力塞进 ‹*letter-box*›; **to ~ sth. about** or **around** 把某物到处胡乱摆放; **to ~ sb./sth. back** 将某人/某物推回去; **to ~ sb./sth. aside** or **out of the way** 将某人/某物推到一边; **they ~d him down the stairs/out of the window** 他们把他推下了楼梯/从窗户推了出去; **to be ~d into ...** colloq 被迫进入 ‹*room, institution*›; **to ~ sth. in sb.'s face** 把…推到某人面前 ‹*camera, microphone*›; **to ~ sth. down sb.'s throat** fig 强行向某人灌输某事物 **2** (place carelessly) 乱放 ‹*book, money, furniture*›; 胡乱添加 ‹*paragraph, comment*›; **to ~ sth. into** 把某物塞入 ‹*container, pocket, room, gap*›; **to ~ one's finger into the jelly** 把手指插入果酱; **she ~d the clothes back in the drawer** 她将衣服塞回了抽屉里
B vi 猛推; **to ~ past sb.** 从某人身边挤过去; **stop shoving!** 别挤啦! ; **people were pushing and shoving** 人群推推搡搡
C n 猛推; **to give sb./sth. a ~** 推某人/某物一把; **she gave me a ~ in the back** 她在我后背上推了一把; **the door needs a good ~** 这扇门得用力推

Phrasal verbs
- **shove off** vi **1** colloq (go away) 离开; **(why don't you) ~ off!** (你干嘛不) 滚开! **2** Naut 把船撑离河岸
- **shove over** colloq
A vt [**~ sth. over, ~ over sth.**] 把…推过来 ‹*object*›; **~ it over here!** 把它推过来!
B vi 挪开; **~ over so that I can sit down** 挪过去点儿让我坐下
- **shove up** vi colloq 挪开; **~ up a bit, you're taking up too much room!** 挪过去点儿吧，你占的地方太多了!

shove-halfpenny ▸p. 307 n [u] Brit 推硬币游戏 [用手掌将硬币推过带格木盘进入指定区域]

shovel /ˈʃʌvl/
A n **1** (spade) 铁铲 **2** (machine) 挖掘机; (part of machine) 铲形部分; **the ~ of a digger** 挖掘机的铲斗 **3** = **shovelful**
B vt **1** (pres p etc. **-ll** Brit, **-l-** Amer) 铲起 ‹*earth, gravel, coal, snow*›; **to ~ sth. into sth.** 将某物铲入某物中 **2** colloq (put, push) 胡乱塞入; **to ~ sth. into sth.** ‹*person*› 把…胡乱塞入某物中 ‹*substance*›; **to ~ food into one's mouth** 一个劲往嘴里塞吃的

shoveler /ˈʃʌvlə(r)/ n 琵嘴鸭

shovelful /ˈʃʌvlfʊl/ n 一铲子; **three ~s of sand** 3 铲沙子

show /ʃəʊ/
A vt (pt **~ed**, pp **shown** or **~ed**) **1** (allow or cause to be seen) 出示 ‹*ticket, passport*›; 上映 ‹*film*›; 展出 ‹*book, goods*›; **the photograph ~s the position of the house very clearly** 这张照片非常清楚地显示了房子的位置; **to ~ sb. sth., to ~ sth. to sb.** 把某物拿给某人看; **the film ~s her completely naked** 这部电影里有她的全裸镜头 **2** (reveal, disclose) 显露; **a light colour that ~s every mark on the dress** 把裙子上的每个污点都暴露无遗的浅颜色; **to ~ how/what/when** etc. 显示如何/什么/何时等; **worn hands that ~ how hard the work is** 表明工作辛苦的那双粗糙了的手; **~ us what you've been doing** 让我们看看你一直在做什么; **to ~ signs of sth.** 表现出某事物的迹象; **the leading runners are ~ing signs of fatigue** 领跑的运动员们看上去疲乏了; **to ~ the symptoms of sth.** 呈现某疾病的症状; **to ~ contempt** 表现出蔑视; **to ~ one's face** Brit 露面 **3** (point out, indicate) 指示; **to ~ sb. sth.** 把某物指给某人看; **can you ~ me the picture you painted?** 指给我看看你画的画好吗? ; **a cross ~s where the treasure is buried** 十字标出了埋藏宝藏的地方; **to ~ a loss/profit** 显示亏损/赢利; **to ~ red/green** etc. 亮红灯/亮绿灯等 **4** (be visible) 显现; **his anger ~ed on his face** 他面露怒容 **5** (be present) **to ~ oneself** 露面; **a timid creature that very rarely ~s itself** 一种很少出来的胆小动物; **to ~ oneself in public** 公开露面; **she doesn't like ~ing herself in public** 她不喜欢抛头露面; **the sun hasn't shown itself all day** 太阳一整天都没有露脸 **6** (give, grant) 给予 ‹*respect*›; 表现出 ‹*cruelty, contempt*›; **~ a little consideration for the rest of us!** 想着点儿我们大家! ; **you have shown me great kindness** 你待我太好了 **7** (prove) 表明; **to ~ one's gratitude** 表示谢意; **he has shown himself (to be) a liar** 他的所作所为证明他是个骗子; **to ~ one's age** 显老; **she ~s no sign of remorse** 她没有丝毫悔过的表现 **8** (demonstrate) 证明; **overwhelming evidence that clearly ~ed his guilt/innocence** 清楚表明他有罪/无罪的铁证; **to ~ that ...** 说明…; **to ~ what/where/how** etc. 说明什么/何处/如何等; **to ~ sb. that ...** 向某人说明…; **to ~ sb. what/where/how** etc. 向某人说明什么/何处/如何等; **~ me what to do and where to go!** 告诉我做什么、去哪里! ; **to ~ sb. what's what** colloq (explain sth.) 把基本原理告诉某人; (show the truth about sth.) 让某人知道是怎么回事儿; **to ~ sth. to sb., to ~ sb. sth.** 向某人展示某物; **~ me your proof** or **evidence!** 把你的证据拿给我看! ; **to ~ sb. to be sth.** 证明某人是某情况; **to ~ sth. to be true/false/right/wrong** 证明某事是真的/假的/正确的/错误的; **as shown on** or **in** or **by** etc. 如…所示; **as shown in the illustration/on the graph** 如插图/图表所示; **to go to ~** 证明; **it (just) goes to ~! you can't trust anyone these days!** 这下你明白了吧! 这个世道谁也不能相信! ; **they don't think I've got a chance, but I'll ~ them!** colloq 他们认为我没有机会，我倒要让他们看看! **9** (lead to specified place) 为…引路; **to ~ sb. out of the building/off the premises** 引领某人离开大楼/离场; **to ~ the children over the road** 带孩子们过马路; **to ~ sb. round the museum/over the castle** 带某人参观博物馆/城堡; **allow me to ~ you out** 我来送您; **to ~ (sb.) the way** (guide sb. to a place) (给某人) 指路; (be an example to sb.) (为某人) 树立榜样; **would you ~ me the way to the station?** 请告诉我去车站怎么走好吗?
B vi (pt **~ed**, pp **shown** or **~ed**) **1** (be visible) ‹*scar, fear, stain*› 显出; **stark terror ~ed in his eyes/on his face** 他眼中/脸上露出了极其惊恐的表情; **to ~ through** 透出来; **his shirt was so thin that his vest ~ed through** 他的衬衫太薄，都可以看见里面的背心 **2** (exhibit) 展出; **an artist who is ~ing at the Tate Gallery** 正在泰特美术馆办画展的画家; **to ~ to advantage** or **to good effect** 鲜明地展示; **what's ~ing at the Regal?** 皇家影院在上映什么片子? **3** colloq (appear) 露面 **4** Amer Horse racing 获得好名次
C n **1** (act of making visible) 表现; **a ~ of generosity** 慷慨表示; **without any ~ of anger/emotion/grief** 没有表现出任何愤怒/感情/悲伤; **a ~ of hands** 举手表决 **2** (public entertainment) 演出; **a quiz ~** 智力竞赛节目; **a variety ~** 杂耍表演; **to stage** or **put on a ~** 演出; **to go to** or **do a ~** 去看演出 **3** (exhibition) 展出; **an art ~** 艺术展览会; **to hold a ~** 举办展览 **4** (outward appearance) 装出的样子; **a ~ of defiance/friendship/affection** 反抗/友好/爱恋的假象; **nothing but** or **all ~** 纯属装样子; **to make (a) great ~ of sth./doing sth.** 极力装出某样子/做某事的样子; **to be for ~** 是装点门面的 **5** (display) 景象; **to make (a) great ~ of sth./doing sth.** 大力展示某事物/高调做某事; **the roses are a splendid ~ this year** 今年的玫瑰花展真是绚烂多彩 **6** Brit colloq (effort) 表现; **a bad** or **poor/good ~** 很差/很好的表现; **to put up a good ~ (in sth.)** (在某方面) 表现好; **good ~!** 真棒! **7** colloq (activity, business) 事情; **you'll have to ask her, she runs the whole ~** 你要问她才行，事情都归她管; **let's get the ~ on the road!** colloq (start an activity) 我们开始吧! ; (start a journey) 我们上路吧!

Phrasal verbs
- **show off**
A vi 炫耀
B vt 使显眼; **the dress ~s off her figure rather well** 这件连衣裙衬托出她优美的身材; **the dark background ~s off the vase to good effect** 暗色的背景把花瓶衬托得很漂亮; **he wanted to ~ off his new car to us** 他想向我们炫耀他的新车
- **show up**
A vi **1** (become visible) 显现; **the dust on the shelves ~s up in the sunlight** 搁板上的灰尘在阳光照射下看得一清二楚 **2** colloq (arrive) 如约赶到; **I wonder when he's going to ~ up** 我不知道他什么时候能来
B [**~ up sth.**] vt (make visible) 使显露; **close examination ~s up all the faults in the woodwork** 仔细观察就可以看出这件木制品的诸多缺陷
C [**to ~ sb. up**] vt
1 colloq (make feel embarrassed) 使难堪; **he got**

S

drunk at the party and ~ed me up 他在聚会上喝醉了，真让我难堪; **to ~ sb. up in front of sb.** 让某人在某人面前难堪; **he ~ed me up in front of all my friends** 他在我所有朋友面前让我难堪 **2** **to ~ sb. up as** *or* **for sth./to be sth.** (show to be) 表明某人是…; **research has shown him up as** *or* **for a fraud** 调查表明他是个骗子; **his autobiography ~s him up to be immensely ambitious** 他的自传表明他雄心勃勃

show: ~biz *n* [u] colloq = ~ **business**; **~boat** *n* Amer 演艺船; ~ **business** *n* [u] 演艺界

showcase /ˈʃəʊkeɪs/
A *n* **1** (display case) 玻璃陈列柜 **2** (advantageous setting) 展示场合; **a ~ for sth.** 某事物的展示场所; **the programme is a ~ for young talent** 这个节目可以让年轻人展示才华; *modif* **a ~ village/prison/hospital** 示范村/监狱/医院
B *vt* 展示 ‹*actor, musician, brand, talent*›

showdown /ˈʃəʊdaʊn/ *n* (final test, fight) 对决; **a ~ with sb./between two people** 和某人的摊牌/两人之间的决战

shower /ˈʃaʊə(r)/
A *n* **1** Meteorol 阵雨; **a heavy/light ~** 一阵大雨/小雨; **to get caught in a ~** 遇上阵雨; **a snow ~** 雨夹雪 **2** (of leaves, confetti, insults) 一阵; (of gifts) 一大批; **we were suddenly covered in a ~ of petals** 突然花瓣雨点般落在我们身上; **a ~ of sparks flew out from the fire** 炉火中迸发出一串火星 **3** (apparatus) 淋浴器; (unit) 淋浴间; **I won't be long, I'm in the ~** 我用不了多久，我在淋浴; **an electric ~** 电淋浴器 **4** (wash) 淋浴; **to have** *or* **take a ~** 冲淋浴 **5** Brit colloq pej (group) 乌合之众; **they're just a ~ of druggies** 他们只是一伙瘾君子; **what a ~!** 真是一帮废物! **6** Amer (party) [为即将结婚或分娩的妇女举办的] 送礼聚会; **to give a ~ for sb.** 为某人举办送礼会; **a baby ~** 新生儿送礼会
B *vt* **1** (spray) 使纷纷降落; **to ~ sth. on** *or* **over sb.** 把某物抛撒在某人身上; **the tree was ~ing petals everywhere** 这棵树掉落了一地的花瓣; **the fire ~ed us with sparks** 火星四溅，落到我们身上 **2** fig (lavish) 大量给予; **to ~ sb. with sth.** 慷慨给予某人 ‹*gifts, praise, affection*›; **to ~ sth. on sb.** 送给某人许多某物
C *vi* **1** (have a shower) 洗淋浴 **2** (fall in a shower) «*leaves, sparks, stones*» 纷纷落下; **to ~ on** *or* **down on ...** 雨点般地落到…上

shower: ~ attachment *n* 喷淋头; **~ cap** *n* 浴帽; **~ curtain** *n* 浴帘; **~ head** *n* 喷淋头; **~proof** *adj* 防雨的 ‹*clothing, fabric*›; **~ rail** *n* 浴帘杆; **~ room** *n* (in house) 淋浴间; (in gym, school) 公共淋浴室; **~ spray** *n* 淋浴花洒; **~ tray** *n* 淋浴底盆; **~ unit** *n* 淋浴房

showery /ˈʃaʊəri/ *adj* 有阵雨的 ‹*day, afternoon*›; 多阵雨的 ‹*month, weather*›; **it will be ~ tomorrow** 明天有阵雨

show: ~girl *n* 歌舞女演员; **~ground** *n* 展览场地; **~ house, ~ home** *ns* Brit 样板房

showily /ˈʃəʊɪli/ *adv* (ostentatiously) 俗艳地 ‹*dressed*›; **a ~ decorated room** 装修华丽的房间

showing /ˈʃəʊɪŋ/ *n* **1** [u] (action) 展示 **2** [c] (of film) 放映; (of programme) 播出; **there are two ~s daily** 每天上演两场 **3** (performance) 表现; **to make a good/poor ~ in sth.** 在某方面表现出色/糟糕; **if his last ~ is anything to go by ...** 如果他上次的表现可以作为参考的话… **4** [c] (evidence) 迹象; **on sb.'s own ~** 就某人自己的表现来看

showing-off *n* [u] colloq 炫耀

show: ~jumper *n* **1** (person) 障碍赛马骑手; **2** (horse) 参加障碍赛的赛马; **~jumping** ▸**p. 307** *n* [u] 障碍赛马; **a ~jumping arena/event/competition** 障碍赛马场地/赛事/比赛; **~man** /-mən/ *n* **1** (performer) 演出经纪人; (presenter) 演出主持人; **2** (show-off) 爱炫耀的人

showmanship /ˈʃəʊmənʃɪp/ *n* [u] **1** (organizing) 组织演出的才能; (performing) 主持演出的才能 **2** (showing off) 炫耀

shown /ʃəʊn/ *pp* ▸**show A, B**

show: ~-off *n* colloq 爱炫耀的人; **~ of hands** *n* 举手表决; **~piece** *n* **1** (outstanding example) 展示品; **that picture is a real ~piece** 那幅画极具代表性; **this hospital is a ~piece** 这是一家模范医院; **2** (opportunity) 展示机会; **the serenade was a ~piece for the orchestra's wind section** 这首小夜曲是乐队的管乐部展示技艺的好机会; **~place** *n* 游览胜地; **~room** *n* 陈列室; **to look at cars/kitchens in a ~room** 观看展销厅里的汽车/厨房; **in ~room condition** «*furniture, car*» 在展出陈列; **~-stopper** *n* colloq 受到鼓掌喝彩的节目; **~ trial** *n* 摆样子的公审

showy /ˈʃəʊi/ *adj* 俗艳的 ‹*dress, jewellery, hairstyle, colour*›; **a book written in a somewhat ~ style** 文笔有些花哨的一本书

shrank /ʃræŋk/ *pt* ▸**shrink A, B**

shrapnel /ˈʃræpnl/ *n* [u] [飞溅的] 弹片; **a piece of ~** 一块弹片

shred /ʃred/
A *n* **1** (of paper, fabric) 细条; **~s of paper** 碎纸片; **to hang in ~s** 一条条挂着; **to tear** *or* **rip sth. into** *or* **to ~s** 将某物撕成碎片; **his theory was quickly torn to ~s by the discovery** fig 他的理论很快被这一发现击得粉碎 **2** fig (small amount) 些许; **~ of sth.** 一点点某物; **there isn't a ~ of evidence against her** 没有丝毫不利于她的证据
B *vt* (*pres p etc.* **-dd-**) 撕碎 ‹*documents, fabric, evidence*›; 切碎 ‹*vegetables*›; **~ding attachment** Culin 粉碎装置

shredder /ˈʃredə(r)/ *n* (for paper) 碎纸机; (for other things) 切碎机; **to put sth. through a ~** 将某物放入碎纸机

shrew /ʃruː/ *n* **1** Zool 鼩鼱 **2** pej (woman) 泼妇

shrewd /ʃruːd/ *adj* 精明的 ‹*person, investment, suggestion*›; **a ~ move** 高招; **to have a ~ idea that ...** 有…的机敏想法; **to make a ~ guess/decision** 作出明智的猜测/决定

shrewdly /ˈʃruːdli/ *adv* 精明地 ‹*judge, invest, handle*›; **to ~ decide/suggest that ...** 机敏地决定/建议…

shrewdness /ˈʃruːdnɪs/ *n* [u] 精明; **to have the ~ to do sth.** 机敏地做某事

shrewish /ˈʃruːɪʃ/ *adj* pej 泼妇似的 ‹*woman*›

shriek /ʃriːk/
A *vi* 尖叫; **to ~ at sb. to do sth.** 尖叫着让某人做某事; **to ~ in** *or* **with ...** 因…而尖叫; **to ~ with laughter** 尖声大笑; **to ~ in terror** 吓得尖叫起来
B *vt* 尖声喊出 ‹*insult, warning*›; **'no!' he ~ed** "不!"他尖叫道; **to ~ abuse at sb.** 对某人尖声叫骂
C *n* 尖叫; **to give a ~ of pain** 疼得尖叫起来; **~s of laughter** 尖声大笑

shrike /ʃraɪk/ *n* 伯劳鸟

shrill /ʃrɪl/
A *adj* **1** (piercing) 刺耳的 ‹*scream, cry, whistle, ring*› **2** pej (forceful) 不依不饶的 ‹*protests, demands*›; **to be ~ in one's criticism/protests** 批评尖刻/抗议强烈
B *vi* «*bird*» 尖叫; «*whistle, telephone*» 发出刺耳的声音
C *vt* «*person, voice*» 尖声喊出 ‹*words, objection*›

shrillness /ˈʃrɪlnɪs/ *n* [u] **1** (of scream, cry, whistle, ring) 尖锐刺耳 **2** pej (of protests, demands) 不依不饶

shrilly /ˈʃrɪli/ *adv* **1** (piercingly) 尖锐刺耳地 ‹*scream, cry, whistle, ring*› **2** pej (forcefully) 不依不饶地 ‹*protest, demand*›

shrimp /ʃrɪmp/ *n* (*pl* ~ *or* **~s**) **1** Zool, Culin 虾 **2** colloq pej (person) 矮小的人

shrimping /ˈʃrɪmpɪŋ/ *n* [u] 捕虾; **to go ~** 去捕虾; **~ nets** 捕虾网

shrine /ʃraɪn/ *n* **1** (place of worship) 圣殿 **2** (casket) 圣物箱 **3** (tomb) 圣陵 **4** (niche, wayside building) 圣祠 **5** fig (special place) 圣地; **Wimbledon is a ~ for all lovers of tennis** 温布尔登是所有网球爱好者心中的圣地; **a ~ to sb./sth.** 纪念某人/某物的圣地

shrink /ʃrɪŋk/
A *vi* (*pt* **shrank**; *pp* **shrunk** *or* **shrunken**) **1** (become smaller) «*garment, fabric, forest, area*» 缩小; «*resources, revenue*» 减少; «*economy, trade*» 萎缩; **to have shrunk to nothing** «*team, household*» 已经解体 **2** (recoil) 退缩; **to ~ from sth.** 从某物处缩回 **3** fig (avoid) 回避; **to ~ from sth.** 回避某物; **to ~ from doing ...** 逃避做…; **he didn't ~ from the task** 他没有逃避任务
B *vt* (*pt* **shrank,** *pp* **shrunk**) 使…缩小 ‹*jeans, jumper*›
C *n* colloq 精神病医生

Phrasal verb

• **shrink back** *vi* 退缩; **to ~ back from sth.** 从某物处缩回; **to ~ back in horror** 因恐惧而退缩

shrinkage /ˈʃrɪŋkɪdʒ/ *n* [u] **1** (of garment, fabric, forest, area) 缩小; (of resources, revenue) 减少; (of economy, trade) 萎缩; **to allow for ~** 以备缩水 **2** (in takings) 短耗

shrinking /ˈʃrɪŋkɪŋ/ *adj* 正在缩小的 ‹*forest, area*›; 正在减少的 ‹*resources, revenue*›; 正在萎缩的 ‹*market*›

shrinking violet *n* colloq 羞怯的人; **she's no ~!** 她可不是胆小怕羞的人!

shrink-resistant *adj* 防缩的 ‹*fabric, garment*›

shrink-wrap
A *vt* (*pres p etc.* **-pp-**) 用收缩薄膜包装 ‹*product, goods*›
B *n* [u] [包装用的] 收缩薄膜

shrink: ~-wrapped *adj* 用收缩薄膜包装的 ‹*product, goods*›; **~-wrapping** *n* [u] **1** (process) 用收缩薄膜包装; **2** (material) 收缩薄膜包装材料

shrivel /ˈʃrɪvl/ (*pres p etc.* **-ll-** Brit, **-l-** Amer)
A *vi* «*plant, leaves*» 枯萎; «*skin, meat*» 皱缩; «*fruit, mushrooms*» 变得干瘪; **the young seedlings had ~led and died** 幼苗蔫死了; **to ~ up** 皱缩
B *vt* 使…枯萎 ‹*plant, leaves*›; 使…变得干瘪 ‹*fruit, mushrooms*›; 使…皱缩 ‹*skin, meat*›; **the heatwave ~led the grapes in every vineyard** 热浪使所有葡萄园的葡萄都蔫了

shrivelled /ˈʃrɪvld/ *adj* 枯萎的 ‹*plant, leaves*›; 干瘪的 ‹*fruit*›; 皱缩的 ‹*skin, meat*›

Shropshire /ˈʃrɒpʃə(r)/ *pr n* 什罗普郡

shroud /ʃraʊd/
A *n* **1** (burial cloth) 裹尸布 **2** fig (covering) 覆盖物; (aura) 笼罩物; **a ~ of sth.** 一层某物; **the whole town was enveloped in a ~ of fog** 整座城市被一层雾气笼罩着; **a ~ of secrecy** 隐秘的气氛 **3** (on parachute) **~ (line)** 吊伞索
B *vt* **1** (wrap) 用裹尸布裹 ‹*body*› **2** fig (cover) 掩盖 ‹*events, negotiations, death*›; (envelop) «*fog, clouds, night*» 笼罩 ‹*cliffs, buildings, town*›; **to be ~ed in mist/cloud** 被笼罩在雾霭/云层中; **the project was ~ed in secrecy/mystery** 这个计划蒙上了隐秘/神秘的色彩
C **shrouds** *npl* Naut 侧支索

Shrove Tuesday /ˌʃrəʊv ˈtjuːzdeɪ, -di, Amer ˈtuːz-/ *n* 忏悔日 [基督教大斋期的前一天]

shrub /ʃrʌb/ *n* 灌木

shrubbery /ˈʃrʌbəri/ *n* 灌木丛

shrub rose *n* 灌木蔷薇

shrug /ʃrʌg/
A *vt* (*pres p etc.* **-gg-**) 耸 ‹*shoulders*›

S

B *vi* (*pres p etc.* **-gg-**) 耸肩
C *n* 耸肩; **with a ～ (of one's** *or* **the shoulders)** 耸一下肩; **to give a ～** 耸肩

Phrasal verb

- **shrug off** *vt* [**～ off sth., ～ sth. off**] 对…满不在乎 ‹*criticism, remark, failure*›; 对…不加理会 ‹*cold, injury*›

shrunk /ʃrʌŋk/ *pp* ▸ **shrink A, B**

shrunken /ˈʃrʌŋkən/
A *pp* ▸ **shrink A, B**
B *adj* 皱缩的 ‹*fruit, vegetable*›; 满是皱纹的 ‹*face*›; 干瘪的 ‹*person, body*›

shtick /ʃtɪk/ *n* [u and c] colloq 固定节目

shuck /ʃʌk/ Amer
A *n* (of nut, clam, oyster) 壳; (of bean, pea) 荚; (of grain) 外皮
B *vt* 剥…的壳 ‹*nuts, clam, oyster*›; 剥…的荚 ‹*beans, peas*›; 去…的外皮 ‹*grain*›

Phrasal verb

- **shuck off** *vt* [**～ sth. off, ～ off sth.**] colloq 脱掉 ‹*clothes*›

shucks /ʃʌks/ *excl* Amer colloq **1** (in surprise, regret, irritation) 糟糕; **oh** *or* **aw ～! I forgot all about it** 哎呀糟糕! 我全给忘了 **2** (in self-deprecation) 真是的; **oh ～, it was nothing!** 哎, 不必客气, 这没什么!

shudder /ˈʃʌdə(r)/
A *vi* **1** (tremble) 颤抖; **to ～ in** *or* **with sth.** 因某事而发抖; **to ～ at the sight/thought of sth.** 一看到某物/想到某事就发抖; **I ～ to think!** 我想想就发怵! **2** (shake) «*vehicle, engine, building*» 强烈震动; **to ～ to a halt** 剧烈晃动着停下来
B *n* **1** (trembling) 颤抖; **the news sent a ～ of terror through them** 他们听到这个消息吓得不寒而栗; **to give a ～** 打战; **to give sb. the ～s** 让某人害怕 **2** (of vehicle, engine, building) 强烈震动

shuddering /ˈʃʌdərɪŋ/ *adj* 颤抖的 ‹*breathing*›

shuffle /ˈʃʌfl/
A *vi* **1** (drag feet) 拖着脚走; **to ～ along/in** 拖着脚向前走/走进来; **to ～ about** 拖着脚走来走去 **2** Games «*person, dealer*» 洗牌
B *vt* **1** (change position of) 把…移来移去; **to ～ one's feet (in embarrassment)** (尴尬地) 来回倒换双脚 **2** Games «*person, dealer*» 洗 ‹*cards, pack*› **3** **to ～ (about** *or* **around)** (move around) 挪动 ‹*objects*›; (change order of) 弄乱 ‹*papers, numbers, data*›; (change position of) 重组 ‹*personnel*›; **to ～ things/people about** *or* **around** 将东西移来移去/把人调来调去
C *n* **1** (movement) 拖着脚走 **2** (sound) 拖拉的脚步声 **3** Games 洗牌; **to give the cards a ～** 洗牌 **4** Dance 曳步舞 **5** Pol 改组; **a Cabinet ～** 内阁改组

Phrasal verb

- **shuffle off**

A *vi* 拖着脚走开
B *vt* [**～ sth. off, ～ off sth.**] 摆脱 ‹*duty*›; 逃避 ‹*responsibility, blame*›; **he tried to ～ the job off on to me!** 他试图把活儿推给我!

shufti /ˈʃʊfti/ *n* (*pl* **～s**) Brit colloq 一瞥; **to take** *or* **have a ～ (at sth.)** 看一眼 (某物)

shun /ʃʌn/ *vt* (*pres p etc.* **-nn-**) **1** (avoid) 避开 ‹*person, society, luxuries*›; 避免 ‹*publicity*› **2** (reject) 拒绝 ‹*help, job*›

shunt /ʃʌnt/
A *vt* **1** Rail (from one track to another) 使…转轨 ‹*engine, train, carriage*›; (from one location to another) 使转换地点; **to ～ sth. into/along/out of sth.** 使某物转轨到某物上/沿着某物行进/离开某物 **2** colloq (push around) 把…推来推去 ‹*person*›; 把…移来移去 ‹*furniture, object*›; **to be ～ed from place to place** 被从一个地方移动到另一个地方; **to ～ sb. back and forth** 来回推某人; **we were ～ed from one official to the next** 我们被从一个官员那里推到另一个官员那里 **3** colloq (move around) 将…移至别处 ‹*furniture, books, papers*›; **to ～ sb. into another department** 将某人调到另一个部门; **to ～ sb. into a siding** fig 将某人打入冷宫
B *n* Med 分流管; **～ surgery** 分流手术

shunter /ˈʃʌntə(r)/ *n* **1** (engine) 调车机车 **2** (person) 扳道工

shunting /ˈʃʌntɪŋ/ *n* [u] 调轨

shunting: **～ engine** *n* 调车机车; **～ yard** *n* 调车场

shush /ʃʊʃ/
A *excl* 嘘; **～! he'll hear you!** 嘘! 他会听见你说话的!
B *vt* 发嘘声让…安静

shut /ʃʌt/
A (*pres p* **-tt-**; *pt, pp* **shut**) *vt* **1** (close) 关上 ‹*window, drawer*›; 合上 ‹*book*›; 闭上 ‹*eyes*›; 关闭 ‹*road, rail line*›; **come in and ～ the door** 进来把门关上; **I can't ～ this suitcase!** 我合不上这个手提箱! ; **shut your mouth** *or* **gob** *or* **trap** *or* **face!** colloq 闭嘴! **2** (trap) 夹住 ‹*curtain, dress*›; **to ～ sth. in a door/window/drawer** *etc.* 将某物夹在门/窗/抽屉等里 **3** (stop activity of) 使停止营业; **we ～ the shop at 5:30** 我们店 5 点 30 分关门
B *vi* (*pres p* **-tt-**; *pt, pp* **shut**) **1** 停止营业; **the pub ～s at 11:00** 这家酒馆 11 点打烊 **2** 关闭; **this window won't ～** 这扇窗户关不上; **it ～ with a bang** *or* **crash** 砰的一声关上了
C *adj* **1** (closed) 关上的 ‹*box, lid*›; 合上的 ‹*book, purse*›; 闭上的 ‹*eyes*›; **you have to slam the door ～** 你要用力才能把门关上; **she sat with her mouth tightly ～** 她紧闭着嘴坐着 **2** *pred* (not serving or working) **to be ～** «*shop, pub*» 已打烊的; «*business*» 暂停营业的; «*factory*» 已下班的

Phrasal verbs

- **shut away** *vt* [**～ sb./sth. away**] 把…放好 ‹*papers, jewellery*›; 隔离 ‹*person*›
- **shut down**

A *vt* [**～ sth. down, ～ down sth.**]
1 (close temporarily) 使暂停营业; (permanently) 使停业; **the company has had to ～ down many of its retail outlets** 该公司不得不关闭很多零售点 **2** (cease operation of) 使…停止运转 ‹*machinery, plant*›; **how long does it take to ～ down a nuclear reactor?** 让核反应堆停止运行要用多长时间?
B *vi* «*machinery, factory*» 停止运转; «*business*» 停止营业

- **shut in** *vt* [**～ sb. in**] 把…关起来; **to ～ oneself in** 把自己关在屋里; **she's ～ herself in and won't come out!** 她把自己关在房间里不肯出来!
- **shut off** *vt* **1** [**～ off sth., ～ sth. off**] (cut supply of) 切断…的供应 ‹*water, gas, electricity*›; (to individual appliance) 关掉 ‹*water, gas, electricity*› **2** (isolate) **to ～ sth./sb. off (from ...)** 将某物/某人 (与…) 隔离; **to ～ oneself off (from ...)** 把自己封闭起来 (不接触…)
- **shut out** *vt* [**～ sth./sb. out, ～ out sth./sb.**]

1 (keep out) «*person*» 把…关在外面; «*double glazing, barrier*» 挡住 ‹*noise, water*› **2** fig (exclude) 摆脱 ‹*memory*›; 克制 ‹*sadness, misery*›; **to ～ sb. out** 把某人排除在外; **she wants to ～ him out of her life completely** 她想彻底地把他赶出自己的生活 **3** (block out) «*trees, curtains, wall*» 挡住 ‹*sun, light, view*›

- **shut up**

A *vi* colloq **～ up!** 闭嘴! ; **when he was shown the evidence, he soon ～ up** 当证据摆在他面前时, 他很快便不吭声了
B [**～ sb. up**] *vt*
1 (silence) 使…住口 ‹*person*›; 使…停止发表意见 ‹*critics, journalists*› **2** (imprison) 把…关进监狱
C [**～ up sth., ～ sth. up**] *vt* 关闭 ‹*house, shop*›

shut: **～down** *n* **1** [c] (of factory, shop, company) [尤指临时的] 停工; (of system, machine, reactor) 关闭; **2** [c and u] Comput 关机; **～-eye** *n* [u] colloq 小睡; **to get some ～-eye** 打个盹儿

shut-in *adj* 被关起来的 ‹*person, animal*›; fig (claustrophobic) 压抑的 ‹*feeling*›; 闭塞的 ‹*village*›

shut-off
A *n* [u] (of flow) 切断; (of supply) 停止
B *modif* 关闭用的 ‹*switch, device*›

shut-off valve *n* 关闭阀

shutout /ˈʃʌtaʊt/ *n* Amer 完胜 [输家一分未得的比赛]

shutter /ˈʃʌtə(r)/ *n* **1** (on window) 百叶窗 **2** (on shop) 卷帘门; **to put up the ～s** lit 拉上卷帘门; fig 停止营业 **3** (on camera) 快门

shuttered /ˈʃʌtəd/ *adj* 关着百叶窗的 ‹*building, room*›; **the house was ～ (up)** 这房子的百叶窗是关着的

shutter: **～ release** *n* 快门按钮; **～ speed** *n* 快门速度

shuttle /ˈʃʌtl/
A *n* **1** Transp (plane, bus, train) 往返两地间的运输工具; (service) 往返两地间的运输服务 **2** Aerosp **(space) ～** 航天飞机 **3** (on loom) 梭 **4** (on sewing machine) 摆梭 **5** (in badminton) **= shuttlecock**
B *vi* «*vehicle*» 往返运行; «*person*» 往返旅行; «*goods*» 往返流动; **to ～ between A and B** 往返于 A 和 B 之间; **to ～ to and fro** *or* **back and forth** 往返穿梭
C *vt* 往返运送; **to ～ sb./sth. backwards and forwards** *or* **to and fro between A and B** 在 A 和 B 之间往返运送某人/某物; **to ～ sb./sth. from one place to another** 将某人/某物从一地运往另一地

shuttle: **～ bus** *n* 班车; **～cock** *n* 羽毛球; **～ diplomacy** *n* [u] 穿梭外交; **～ mission** *n* 航天飞行任务; **～ programme** Brit, **～ program** Amer *n* 航天飞行计划; **～ service** *n* 短程往返运输服务; **～ train** *n* 短途往返火车

shy[1] /ʃaɪ/
A *adj* **1** (timid) 害羞的 ‹*person, look, smile*›; 易受惊吓的 ‹*animal*›; **to be ～ with** *or* **of sb.** 在某人面前腼腆 **2** *pred* (wary) 心怀顾忌的; **to be ～ of sth./doing sth.** 忌讳某事物/做某事; **to make sb. feel ～** 让某人感到有所顾忌; **to fight ～ of sth./sb./doing sth.** fig 逃避某事物/某人/做某事; **to be camera/work ～** 不爱照相/不愿工作 **3** (of wild mammal, bird) 怕人的; **deer are very ～ of humans** 鹿非常怕人 **4** *pred* colloq (short) 不足的; **I'm 10 cents ～ of a dollar** 我还差 10 美分就够 1 美元; **he's two years ～ of 40** 他还差两年就 40 了
B *vi* «*horse, pony*» 被惊走; **to ～ at sb./sth.** 见到某人/某物惊走

Phrasal verb

- **shy away** *vi* 躲避; **to ～ away from sb./sth./doing sth.** 回避某人/某事物/做某事

shy[2] dated
A *vt* (throw) 投 ‹*ball, stone, object*›; **to ～ sth. at/into/over sth.** 将某物投向某物/扔进某物中/从某物上方扔过
B *n* 投掷; **to have** *or* **take a ～ at sb./sth.** 向某人/某物投掷

shyly /ˈʃaɪli/ *adv* 害羞地 ‹*look, smile, say*›

shyness /ˈʃaɪnɪs/ *n* [u] 害羞

shyster /ˈʃaɪstə(r)/ *n* colloq 不择手段的人 [尤指律师]

SI *abbr* **= Système International** 国际单位制

si /siː/ *n* Mus **= te**

Siam /saɪˈæm/ *pr n* Hist 暹罗 [泰国的旧称]

Siamese /ˌsaɪəˈmiːz/ ▸ **p. 503, p. 426**
A *adj* dated or Hist (of Siam) 暹罗的; (of the people) 暹罗人的; (of the language) 暹罗语的
B *n* (*pl* **Siamese**) **1** [c] dated or Hist (person) 暹罗人 **2** [u] dated or Hist (language) **= Thai B2** **3** [c] **= Siamese cat**

Siamese: **～ cat** *n* 暹罗猫; **～ twins** *npl* 联体双胎

Siberia /saɪˈbɪərɪə/ *pr n* 西伯利亚

Siberian /saɪˈbɪərɪən/ **▸p. 503**

A *adj* (of Siberia) 西伯利亚的; (of the people) 西伯利亚人的

B *n* 西伯利亚人

sibilant /ˈsɪbɪlənt/

A *adj* **1** (hissing) 咝咝的; **a ～ sound/noise/whispering** 咝咝声/咝咝的噪声/窃窃私语 **2** Phon 发咝音的 ‹*consonant*›; **a ～ sound** 咝音

B *n* 咝音

sibling /ˈsɪblɪŋ/ *n* **1** (elder brother) 兄; (younger brother) 弟 **2** (elder sister) 姐; (younger sister) 妹

sibling rivalry *n* [u] 手足竞争

sic /sɪk/ *adv* 原文如此

Sichuan /sʌˈtʃwæn/ **▸p. 604** *pr n* **～ (Province)** 四川（省）

Sicilian /sɪˈsɪlɪən/ **▸p. 503, p. 426**

A *adj* (of Sicily) 西西里的; (of the people) 西西里人的; (of the language) 西西里方言的

B *n* **1** [c] (person) 西西里人 **2** [u] (language) 西西里方言

Sicily /ˈsɪsɪli/ *pr n* 西西里岛

sick /sɪk/

A *adj* **1** (ill) 有病的 ‹*person, animal*›; fig 衰落的 ‹*organization*›; 病态的 ‹*society*›; **a ～ passenger** 身体不适的乘客; **that rose is looking a bit ～!** 那朵玫瑰花看上去有点蔫！; **to feel ～** 感觉不舒服; **at that time Turkey was the ～ man of Europe** fig 那时候土耳其是"欧洲病夫"; **to fall** *or* **get** Amer *or* **take** dated **～ (with sth.)** 患（某）病; **she fell ～ with some sort of flu** 她患上了某种流感; **to be off ～** 因病休息; **to go ～** 请病假［不上班］ **2** *pred* esp Brit (nauseous) 恶心的; **to feel ～** 感到恶心; **to make sb. ～** 使某人呕吐; **to make oneself ～** 呕吐; **to be (violently) ～** Brit （剧烈）呕吐; **to get ～** Amer 恶心; **to be ～ to one's stomach** 感到很厌恶; **to be ～ at heart** liter 十分不快; **to be worried ～ (about sth.)** （对某事）极度担忧; **(as) ～ as a dog** colloq 吐得一塌糊涂; **(as) ～ as a parrot** Brit colloq hum 大失所望 **3** *pred* colloq (disgusted) 厌恶的; **to be** *or* **feel ～ at** *or* **about sth.** 厌恶某事; **to look ～** 面露不快; **to make sb. ～** 使某人感到厌烦; **you make me ～!** 你真烦人！ **4** *pred* colloq (fed up) 厌倦的; **to be/get ～ of sth./sb./doing sth.** 厌恶某事物/某人/做某事; **to be/get ～ and tired of sth./sb./doing sth.** 厌倦某事物/某人/做某事; **to be/get ～ to death of sth./sb./doing sth.** 极其讨厌某事物/某人/做某事; **to be ～ of the sight of sth./sb.** 一看到某物/某人就腻味 **5** colloq (tasteless) 乏味的 ‹*joke, prank, sense of humour*› **6** (disturbed) 变态的 ‹*imagination, behaviour, person*› **7** *attrib* (causing nausea) 令人极度厌恶的 ‹*emotion*›; **he had a ～ fear of returning** 他对回来既厌恶又恐惧

B *n* [u] Brit colloq (vomit) 呕吐物

C *npl* (ill people) **the ～** 病人; **ambulances carrying the ～ and the wounded** 运送伤病员的救护车

Phrasal verb

- **sick up** *vt* [**～ sth. up, ～ up sth.**] Brit colloq 吐出

sick: ～ bag *n* [供晕机、晕船者使用的] 卫生袋; **～ bay** *n* [学校、军营或船上的] 医务室; **～bed** *n* 病床; **to rise from** *or* **leave one's ～bed** 离开病榻; **～ building syndrome** *n* [u] 病楼综合征

sicken /ˈsɪkən/

A *vt* 使…感到厌恶 ‹*person*›; **to be ～ed (by sth.)** （对某事物）感到厌恶

B *vi* **1** liter (become sick) 生病 **2** Brit (show symptoms) **to be ～ing for sth.** 显露出某病症; **you look as if you might be ～ing for sth.** 你看起来好像是哪儿不舒服

sickening /ˈsɪkənɪŋ/ *adj* **1** (nauseating) 令人作呕的; (disgusting) 令人厌恶的 **2** colloq (annoying) 让人烦恼的

sickeningly /ˈsɪkənɪŋli/ *adv* **1** (nauseatingly) 令人作呕地; (disgustingly) 令人厌恶地; **～ sweet** 甜得发腻的 **2** (annoyingly) 令人烦恼地; **he is ～ smug** 他自鸣得意得令人厌烦

sickie /ˈsɪki/ *n* colloq **1** Brit 假病假; **to take** *or* **throw a ～** 称病缺勤 **2** Amer **= sicko**

sickle /ˈsɪkl/ *n* 镰刀

sick leave *n* [u] 病假; **to be on ～** 在休病假; **to give** *or* **grant sb. ～** 准许某人休病假

sickle-cell anaemia ▸p. 377 *n* [u] 镰状细胞性贫血

sickliness /ˈsɪklɪnɪs/ *n* **1** (frequent illness) 多病 **2** (looking unhealthy) 病态 **3** (nauseousness) 令人作呕; **the ～ of the smell** 这种气味的难闻 **4** (sentimentality) 多愁善感; **I found the film's ～ hard to take** 我觉得这电影过于伤感

sick list *n* 病人名单; **to be on the ～** 在生病

sickly /ˈsɪkli/ *adj* **1** (frequently ill) 多病的 ‹*person, animal*›; 长势差的 ‹*plant*› **2** (unhealthy-looking) 不健康的 ‹*complexion, expression*› **3** (nauseating) 令人作呕的 ‹*smell, taste, colour*›; **～ sweet** 甜得发腻的 **4** (sentimental) 过于伤感的 ‹*story, film, account*›; **to be ～ sentimental** 故作多愁善感; **she gave a ～ smile** 她苦笑了一下

sick-making *adj* colloq **1** (nauseating) 令人作呕的 ‹*smell, taste*› **2** (sentimental) 过分伤感的 ‹*story, film, account*›

sickness /ˈsɪknɪs/ *n* **1** [u] (illness) 疾病; **to be absent because of ～** 因病缺席; **there has been a lot of ～ in the school lately** 近来学校里有很多人生病; **the ～ of the economy** 经济的弊病; **in ～ and in health** (in marriage vow) 无论病弱与健康 **2** [c] (specific illness or disease) 病症 **3** [u] (nausea) 恶心; **to suffer bouts of ～** 觉得一阵阵恶心

sickness benefit *n* [u] Brit 疾病补助金

sick note *n* 病假条

sicko /ˈsɪkəʊ/ *n* (*pl* **～s**) colloq [尤指施虐型的] 变态狂

sick: ～ pay *n* [u] Brit 病假工资; **～room** *n* 病房

side /saɪd/

A *n* **1** [c] (surface of container, cube, paper) 面; **the six ～s of a cube** 立方体的六个面; **right ～ up** 正面朝上; **this ～ up** 此面朝上; **fry the steaks for two minutes on each ～** 牛排两面各煎两分钟; **the right/wrong ～** 正面/反面; **you've got it wrong ～ out** 你把衣服穿反了; **the right(-hand)/left(-hand) ～ of a page** 书页的右面/左面; **the A-～/B-～** [唱片的] A 面/B 面 **2** [c] (surface other than top or bottom) 侧面; **to put** *or* **place** *or* **set sth. down on its ～** 把某物侧放; **on/from all ～s** *or* **every ～** 在/从四面八方 **3** [c] (surface other than front, back, top, bottom) 一侧; **a house with a garage built on to the ～** 挨着山墙建有车库的房子; **to be** *or* **lie on its ～** 侧翻; **the ～ of the car was badly dented in the accident** 汽车一侧在车祸中严重凹陷; **the houses were built ～ by ～** 这些房子成排相连 **4** [c] (surface of upright thing) 壁; **paintings on the ～ of the cave wall** 洞壁上的绘画; **a deep slash in the ～ of the tyre** 轮胎壁上一道深深的划口; **the party had to bivouac on the ～ of the mountain** 这一行人只好在山坡上宿营 **5** [c] (edge) 边缘; **at the ～ of the bed** 在床边; **by the ～ of the road** 在路边; **over the ～ of the ship** 到船舷外; **from ～ to ～** 从一边到另一边; **the campus stretches for four miles from ～ to ～** 校园横跨4英里 **6** [c] Math (boundary of figure) 边 **7** [c] (part of body of person, animal) 肋部; **she was lying on her ～** 她侧卧着 **8** [c] (area next to person) 旁边; **at** *or* **by sb.'s ～** 在某人旁边; **she stayed by his ～ through thick and thin** 她和他相濡以沫，同甘共苦; **on sb.'s left(-hand)/right(-hand) ～** 在某人左边/右边; **～ by ～** (close together) 肩并肩; fig (supporting each other) 休戚与共; fig (at the same time, alongside each other) 同时; **we have been using both systems, ～ by ～, for two years** 两年来我们一直同时使用这两套系统; **to get on the right/wrong ～ of sb.** 讨得某人欢心/惹恼某人; **he tilted his head to one ～** 他把头歪向一边; **to put** *or* **leave sth. on** *or* **to one ～** (put aside) 把某物放在一边; (leave to be dealt with later) 暂时搁置某事 **9** [c] (cut of meat) 半边肋肉; **a ～ of beef** 一扇牛肉 **10** [c] (half, part) 一边; **the sunny ～ of the street** 街道朝阳的一边; **the driver's/passenger's ～ of a car** 车上司机/乘客的一边; **to drive on the left/right ～ of the road** 靠道路左边/右边开车; **the left/right ～ of the brain** 大脑的左/右半球; **the far/near ～** 较远/较近的一边; **he was on the far ～ of the room** 他在房间的另一边; **the debit/credit ～** Fin 借方/贷方; **the north/south ～ of the town** 城镇的南区/北区; **the right/wrong ～** 社会上层/底层; **the arts/science ～** fig 艺术/科学领域; **on the ～** colloq (as a sideline) 作为兼职; (in addition, illegally) 秘密地; esp Amer (serving of food) 作为配菜; **a club sandwich with French fries on the ～** 配有炸薯条的总会三明治; **to have a bit on the ～** colloq 有情人; **people on both ～s of the Atlantic** 大西洋两岸的人们; **from ～ to ～** 从一边到另一边; **the rope swung from ～ to ～** 绳子荡来荡去; **to take sb. on** *or* **to one ～** 把某人拉到一边; **to be on the safe ～** 稳妥起见; **to be (a bit) on the big/small/high/low ～** colloq （有点）偏大/偏小/偏高/偏低; **to be on the right/wrong ～ of forty** colloq hum 不到/超过 40 岁; **this ～ of sth.** (in position) 某物这边; (in time) 某时间以前; **the bank is this ～ of the station** 银行在车站这边; **this ～ of midnight** 午夜前; **the best coffee this ～ of Brazil** colloq 可与巴西咖啡媲美的最好咖啡 **11** [c] (direction) 方向; **we were being attacked on** *or* **from all ～s** 我们四面受敌; **devastation on every ～** 全面的破坏 **12** [c] (group, individual) [对抗双方中的] 一方; **the government/opposition ～** 执政方/反对方; **faults on both ～s** 双方的过错; **to change ～s, to go over to the other ～** 改变立场; **the two ～s agreed to resume border talks** 两国同意重开边界谈判; **the right/wrong ～** 正确/错误的一方; **to be on sb.'s ～, to be on the ～ of sb.** 站在某人一边; **to have right on one's ～** 有理; **to have time on one's ～** 还有时间; **time is on sb.'s ～** 某人还有时间; **to take ～s with sb., to take sb.'s ～** 站在某人一边; **he tried not to take ～s in the dispute** 他在这一争端中尽量不偏不倚 **13** [c] (position, point of view) 一方的立场; **I'd like to hear your ～ of the story** 我想听一听你的说法; **try to see it from my ～** 试着从我的立场看问题 **14** [c] Brit Sport 运动队; **the England/Brazil** *or* **English/Brazilian ～** 英格兰队/巴西队; **seven-a-～ rugby** 七人制橄榄球; **the home/away ～** 主队/客队; **the winning/losing ～** 胜队/负队; **the defending/attacking ～** 防守方/进攻方 **15** [c] (aspect) 方面; **all ～s of the problem** 问题的各个方面; **the seamy ～ of life** 生活的阴暗面 **16** [c] (line of descent) 血统; **on sb.'s ～** 在某人血统一方; **she's a cousin on my father's ～** 她是我堂姐; **she gets her good looks from her mother's ～** 她的美貌是从母亲那里遗传来的 **17** [u] Brit colloq (arrogance) 傲慢; **there was absolutely no ～ to him** 他一点架子也没有 **18** [u] esp Brit (in billiards, snooker, etc.) 侧旋

B *modif* **1** (situated on flank) 侧面的 ‹*door, window, entrance*› **2** (secondary) 附带的 ‹*benefit*›

C *vt* «*hill, structure*» 形成…的侧翼 ‹*valley, street*›

D **-sided** *combining form* 有…面的; **a six～d**

body 六面体; **a glass~d container** 玻璃面容器

Phrasal verbs

- **side against** *vt* [~ **against sb.**] 反对; **as usual the government has ~d against the workers** 政府和往常一样站在了工人的对立面; **to ~ with sb. against sb.** 和某人一道与某人作对
- **side with** *vt* [~ **with sb.**] 支持

side: ~ arms *npl* 随身武器; **~board** *n* 1 (piece of furniture) 餐具柜; 2 Brit = **~burn**; **~burn** *n usu pl* 鬓角; **~car** *n* 1 Aut [摩托车的] 跨斗; 2 (cocktail) 赛德卡鸡尾酒 [用白兰地、橘子酒和柠檬汁调制]; **~ dish** *n* 配菜; **~ drum** ▸**p. 395** *n* 小鼓; **~ effect** *n* 1 Med 副作用; 2 fig (consequence) 意外后果; **~-foot** *vt* 用脚内侧踢 ‹*ball*›

side impact *n* 侧面碰撞

side-impact bars *npl* 侧撞保险杠

side: ~ issue *n* 次要问题; **~kick** *n* colloq 帮手

sidelight /ˈsaɪdlaɪt/

A *n* 1 Brit Aut 侧灯 2 (window) 侧窗 3 fig (piece of information) 侧面情况; **a ~ on sb./sth.** 关于某人/某事物的间接消息

B sidelights *npl* Naut (to port) 左舷灯; (to starboard) 右舷灯

sideline /ˈsaɪdlaɪn/

A *n* 1 (secondary job) 兼职 2 (secondary products) 兼售的货品; **he sells clothes as a ~** 他兼售服装 3 Sport 边线

B sidelines *npl* **the ~s** 场外区域; **on the ~s** fig 从旁观者的角度; **as a reporter, I was on the ~s during the attack** 作为一名记者, 我见证了这次袭击

C *vt* 1 Sport 使…退出比赛 ‹*player*›; **to be ~d** 被停赛 2 (remove from centre of activity) 把…排除在外 ‹*person*›

sidelong /ˈsaɪdlɒŋ/

A *adj* 向旁边的; **a ~ glance/look** 斜眼一瞥/一看

B *adv* 向旁边地; **to look/glance ~** 斜扫一眼/斜眼看一看

side: ~-on *adv* 从侧面 ‹*hit, collide, approach*›; 在侧面 ‹*stand*›; **~-on to sth.** 侧对着某物; **~ order** *n* 另点的配菜; **~ plate** *n* 小吃盘

sidereal /saɪˈdɪərɪəl/ *adj* 恒星的; **~ time/day/month/year/period** 恒星时间/日/月/年/期

side road *n* 旁路

side-saddle

A *n* [尤指供穿裙女子用的] 侧座鞍

B *adv* 在侧座鞍上; **to ride** *or* **sit ~** 坐在侧座鞍上

side: ~ salad *n* 配菜色拉; **~ shoot** *n* 侧枝; **~ show** *n* 1 (at fair) 杂耍; 2 fig (minor incident, issue) 次要事件; **~slip** *n* (of vehicle) 侧滑; (of skier, surfer) 横滑; **~splitting** *adj* colloq 令人捧腹的 ‹*performance, speech, anecdote*›

sidestep /ˈsaɪdstep/

A *vt* 1 (*pres p etc.* **-pp-**) (avoid) 侧跨步躲开 ‹*blow, tackle, person*› 2 (evade) 回避 ‹*question, problem*›

B *n* [躲闪的] 侧跨步

side: ~ street *n* 小街; **~stroke** *n* 侧泳

sideswipe /ˈsaɪdswaɪp/

A *n* 1 (critical remark) 顺带批评 2 esp Amer (glancing blow) 擦撞

B *vt* «*vehicle*» 擦撞 ‹*vehicle, lamp post, bollard*›

side table *n* 茶几

sidetrack /ˈsaɪdtræk/

A *vt* 1 (divert) 使…转移话题 ‹*person, speaker*›; **to get ~ed** 转变话题 2 esp Amer Rail 将…转到侧线 ‹*train*›

B *n* 1 (path, track) 小路 2 esp Amer Rail 侧线

side: ~ view *n* 侧视图; **~walk** *n* Amer = **pavement**

sideways /ˈsaɪdweɪz/

A *adj* (to the side) 向旁边的; (from the side) 从旁边的; **a ~ look/glance** 斜眼的一看/一瞥; **a ~ move in his career** 他的一次平级工作变动

B *adv* 1 (to the side) 向旁边; (from the side) 从旁边; **he looked at me ~** 他斜眼看我; **to be turned ~** «*person*» 被迫侧过身; **~ on** 从侧面; **to knock sb. ~** 出其不意地打击某人 2 (side-facing) 侧身; **turn it round and push it in ~** 把它侧过来推进去; **~ on to sth.** 侧对着某物

side: ~-whiskers *npl* 络腮胡子; **~winder** *n* 1 Zool 角响尾蛇; 2 Amer (in boxing) 侧击

siding /ˈsaɪdɪŋ/ *n* 1 [c] Rail 侧线 2 [u] Amer Constr 墙板

sidle /ˈsaɪdl/ *vi* (furtively) 悄悄地走; (timidly) 战战兢兢地走; **to ~ into/out of/along ...** 溜进…/溜出…/悄悄地沿…走; **to ~ up to sb./sth.** 悄悄地朝某人/某物走去

SIDS /sɪdz/ *abbr* = **sudden infant death syndrome**

siege /siːdʒ/ *n* 1 Mil 围困; **to lay ~ to sth.** lit 包围某处; fig 对某处进行围攻; **to come under ~** 被围困 2 (by police) 包围

siege warfare *n* [u] 围困战

sienna /sɪˈenə/ *n* [u] 1 (pigment) 褐土 2 (colour) 赭色

sierra /sɪˈerə/ *n* 齿状山脉

Sierra Leone /sɪˌerə lɪˈəʊn/ *pr n* 塞拉利昂

Sierra Leonean /sɪˌerə lɪˈəʊnɪən/ ▸**p. 503**

A *adj* (of Sierra Leone) 塞拉利昂的; (of the people) 塞拉利昂人的

B *n* 塞拉利昂人

siesta /sɪˈestə/ *n* [尤指最炎热时段的] 午睡; **to have** *or* **take a ~** 睡午觉

sieve /sɪv/

A *n* 筛子; **to put sth. through a ~** 用筛子筛某物; **to have a head** *or* **memory like a ~** 记性差

B *vt* 筛 ‹*flour, sugar*›; **to ~ sth. into sth.** 将某物筛入某物

Phrasal verb

- **sieve through** *vt* [~ **through sth.**] 仔细检查 ‹*evidence, data, information, correspondence*›

sievert /ˈsiːvərt/ *n* 西韦特 [射线剂量单位]

sift /sɪft/ *vt* 1 (sieve) 筛 ‹*flour, coal, wheat*›; **to ~ sth. into sth.** 将某物筛入某物; **to ~ sth. from** *or* **out of sth.** 将某物从某物中筛出 2 fig (examine thoroughly) 仔细检查 ‹*evidence, data, information, correspondence*›

Phrasal verb

- **sift through** *vt* [~ **through sth.**] 仔细检查 ‹*evidence, data, information, correspondence*›

sifter /ˈsɪftə(r)/ *n* 筛子

sigh /saɪ/

A *vi* 1 (emit breath) 叹气; **to ~ with relief** 舒一口气 2 (make sound) «*wind*» 呜咽; **the sound of the trees ~ing in the wind** 树在风中的悲泣声 3 (yearn) 渴望; **to ~ for sth.** 渴望得到某物

B *n* 叹气; **to breathe** *or* **give** *or* **heave a ~** 发出叹息; **a deep/long/heavy ~** 深深的叹息/长叹/沉重的叹息

C *vt* 叹息着说 ‹*words*›; **'how beautiful!' she ~ed** "多美啊!" 她感叹道

sight /saɪt/

A *n* 1 [u] (faculty of seeing) 视力; **he's always had good/poor ~** 他的视力一向很好/很差; **birds of prey have very keen ~** 猛禽视力敏锐; **to lose one's ~** 失明; **to regain one's ~** 恢复视力; **long/short ~** 远视/近视; **a ~ test** 视力测试 2 [u] (act of seeing) 看见; **love at first ~** 一见钟情; **our first ~ of the Himalayas** 我们第一次看到喜马拉雅山; **at the ~ of sth.** 在看到…时 ‹*place, luxury, injustice*›; **he faints at the ~ of blood** 他晕血; **to catch ~ of sb./sth.** 看到某人/某物; **to lose ~ of sb.** 某人从视线中消失; **to lose ~ of sth.** (stop seeing) 看不见某物; fig (overlook) 忽略某事物; **to know sb. by ~** 和某人面熟; **at** *or* **on ~** 一看到; **to shoot sb. on ~** 一发现某人就射杀; **I took a dislike to him on ~** 我第一眼看见他就讨厌他; **in the ~ of sb., in sb.'s ~** formal 在某人看来; **do what is right in your own ~** 做你认为对的事 3 [u and c] (visible, range of vision) 视野; **to be in** *or* **within (sb.'s) ~** lit «*thing, place*» 在 (某人) 视野之内; fig «*victory, freedom*» 即将到来; **the end of the project is at last in ~** 这个项目终于快要完成了; **the war goes on with no end in ~** 战争没完没了地持续着; **our goal is in ~** 我们的目标就要实现了; **all men are equal in the ~ of God** 在上帝眼里人人平等; **in the ~ of the law** 从法律角度看; **to be in** *or* **within ~ of sth.** 在看得到某物的地方; **to come into ~** 进入视野; **the ship came into ~ out of the fog** 轮船穿过雾霭进入视野; **at last we came in ~ of a few houses** 我们终于看到了几座房子; **to keep ~ of sb., to keep sb. in ~** 监视某人; **to keep ~ of sth., to keep sth. in ~** 一直看着某物; fig (remain aware of sth.) 一直留意某事物; **to be out of (sb.'s) ~** 从 (某人的) 视野中消失; **the house was out of ~ behind a high wall** 房子消失在一堵高墙的后面; **leave any valuables in your car out of ~** 车里的贵重物品不要放在明处; **to be out of ~ of sth.** 看不到某物; **to do sth. out of ~ of sb.** 背着某人做某事; **to keep** *or* **stay out of ~** 躲起来; **to keep sb./sth. out of ~** 将某人/某物藏起来; **get out of my ~!** 滚开! ; **not to let sb./sth. out of one's ~** 盯紧某人/某物; **out of ~, out of mind** Prov 眼不见, 心不烦; **out of ~** colloq dated (excellent) 非常出色; **man, it was out of ~!** 哇, 这东西棒极了! ; **from ~** 从视野中; **line of ~** 视线 4 [c] (glimpse) 一瞥; **to get a ~ of** *or* **to catch ~ of sb./sth.** 瞥见某人/某物 5 [c] (thing seen) 景观; **a familiar ~** 常见的景象; ▸**sore A1** 6 [c] colloq (repulsive, ridiculous person) 不顺眼的人; (object) 不顺眼的东西; **she looked a frightful ~** 她看上去真怪

B sights *npl* 1 (places of interest) 名胜; **she offered to show me the ~s** 她主动提出带我游览名胜 2 (on rifle, telescope) 瞄准具; **he had me in his ~s** 他瞄准了我; fig 他的目光落在我身上

C *vt* 看见; **let me know when you ~ Tower Bridge** 你看见塔桥时就告诉我

sighted /ˈsaɪtɪd/ *adj* 有视力的 ‹*person*›; **the ~** *pl* 有视力的人

sighting /ˈsaɪtɪŋ/ *n* 看见; **there have been a number of reported ~s of the animal/the escaped prisoner** 有很多人声称见过该动物/这名逃犯

sightly /ˈsaɪtli/ *adj* 漂亮的 ‹*person*›; 悦目的 ‹*object, place, view*›

sight-read

A *vt* (sing) 视唱 ‹*score, music*›; (perform) 视奏 ‹*score, music*›

B *vi* (sing) 视唱; (perform) 视奏

sight: ~-reading *n* [u] (singing) 视唱; (performing) 视奏; **~seeing** *n* [u] 观光; **to go ~seeing** 去观光; **~seer** /ˈsaɪtsiːə(r)/ *n* 观光客; **~ unseen** *adv* 事先未看现货地 ‹*buy*›; 事先未看实物地 ‹*order, accept*›

sign /saɪn/

A *n* 1 (symbolic mark) 符号 2 (notice) (giving information) 公告; (giving direction) 路标; (giving instruction, warning) 提示牌; (advertising sth.) 招牌; **follow the ~s for the city centre** 按照路标的指引去市中心; **'open'/'closed' ~** 营业/关门告示牌; **a pub/inn ~** 酒馆/旅店招牌 3 (gesture) 手势; **to give sb. a ~** 向某人打手势; **she nodded as a ~ for us to sit down** 她点头示意我们坐下; **the ~ of the cross** Relig [基督徒祈祷时的] 画十字 4 (visible evidence) 迹象; **~s of suffering on his face** 他脸上痛苦的表情; **there's no ~ of life in the house** 屋子里没有一点住人的迹象;

S

there's not the slightest ～ of him anywhere 哪里都见不到他的踪影 5 (indication, pointer) 征兆; **call the police at the first ～ of trouble** 一旦发现危险苗头就报警; **flowers are often given as a ～ of affection** 人们经常通过送花表达爱意; **a ～ of the times** 时代特征 [含贬义]; **a good/bad ～** 好/坏兆头; **an ominous ～** 不祥的征兆; **there are ～s that the crisis is ending** 有迹象显示危机即将过去 6 Astrol **～ (of the zodiac)** 星座; **what ～ are you?, what's your ～?** 你是什么星座?

B *vt* 1 (write) 签 ‹*one's name*›; **read the statement and ～ your name at the bottom/where indicated** 阅读本声明后在页尾/指定位置签名 2 (put one's signature on) 在…上签名 ‹*cheque, document, painting*›; 签订 ‹*treaty, warrant*›; **a ～ed copy of her latest novel** 她最新小说的签名本; **to ～ a contract** 签合同; **the two countries ～ed a non-aggression treaty** 两国签署了互不侵犯条约; **a ～ed confession** 有签名的供词; **～ed, sealed, and delivered** 成定局的; **to ～ one's own death warrant** *fig* 自寻死路 3 (place under contract) 和…签约 ‹*performer*›; **to ～ sb. for sth.** 为某事和某人签约 4 (perform in sign language) 用手语表演 ‹*programme, play*›; 用手语传达 ‹*message*› 5 (indicate with notice) 以路牌指示; **the footpath is ～ed next to the gate** 门边路牌指示了小道的方向 6 (signal) 示意; **to ～ to sb. that ...** 向某人示意…; **he ～ed to me that I should leave the room** 他示意我应该离开房间; **to ～ to sb. where/when/who/what ...** 向某人示意哪里/何时/谁/什么…; **to ～ (to) sb. to do sth.** 示意某人做某事

C *v refl* **to ～ oneself ...** 在署名中把自己叫做; **he ～s himself Jimmy** 他署名吉米

D *vi* 1 (write one's signature) 签名; **to ～ for sth.** «*recipient*» 签收某物 2 (sign contract) «*performer, player*» 签约; **to ～ for** *or* **with sb./sth.** 和某人/某机构签约 3 (use sign language) 打手语

Phrasal verbs

• **sign away** *vt* [**～ sth. away, ～ away sth.**] 签字放弃 ‹*property, inheritance, rights*›

• **sign in**

A *vi* «*guest*» 登记入住

B *vt* [**～ sb. in, ～ in sb.**] 替…签到 ‹*guest*›

• **sign off**

A *vi* 1 (at work) «*employee*» 辞职 2 colloq (end letter) 结束写信; (end telephone call) 挂电话; **it's getting late, so I must ～ off now** 时间很晚了，我先写到这里吧; **to ～ off on sth.** 批准某事 3 Radio, TV «*broadcaster*» 结束广播; **this is X ～ing off and wishing you goodnight** 我是X，今天的节目到此结束，祝您晚安

B *vt* [**～ sb. off, ～ off sb.**] «*doctor*» 给…签病假条 ‹*patient*›

• **sign on**

A *vi* 1 (enrol) «*applicant*» 报名; **to ～ on for sth.** 报名参加某活动; **I've ～ed on for the French course** 我报名上法语课了; **to ～ on with sth.** 报名加入某组织 2 Brit (register as unemployed) 登记失业

B *vt* [**～ sb. on, ～ on sb.**] «*employer, club*» 签约聘用

• **sign out**

A *vi* (record one's departure) 登记离开; **you must ～ out when you leave the hotel** 离开酒店时必须登记; **to ～ out of** 登记离开 ‹*hotel*›

B *vt* [**～ sb./sth. out, ～ out sb./sth.**] 1 (record departure of) 登记…外出; **all students staying away overnight must be ～ed out by a member of staff** 所有在外过夜的学生都必须经过工作人员登记 2 (record borrowing of) 登记借 ‹*library book*›

• **sign over** *vt* [**～ sth. over, ～ over sth.**] 签字转让 ‹*property, estate*›; **to ～ sth. over to sb.** 签字把某物转让给某人

• **sign up**

A *vi* 1 Mil «*recruit*» 报名从军 2 (conclude deal) «*person, company*» 签约; **to ～ up with sb./sth.** 和某人/某机构签约

B *vt* [**～ sb. up, ～ up sb.**] 与…签约 ‹*performer, worker*›; **the club has ～ed up a new goalkeeper** 该俱乐部签下了一名新守门员; **to ～ sb. up for sth.** 为…签约某人 ‹*club, show, job*›

signal /ˈsɪgnl/

A *n* 1 (gesture, sound) 信号; **to give** *or* **send a ～** 发出信号; **a ～ to do sth.** 做某事的信号; **the policeman raised his hand as a ～ to stop** 警察举手示意停车; **the ～ for violent protest** 强烈抗议的信号 2 (indication) 标志; **the rise in inflation is a clear ～ that government policies are not working** 通货膨胀率的上升清楚地表明政府的决策不起作用; **a ～ of** *or* **about sth.** 某事物的标志; **is this white paper a ～ of a change in government thinking?** 这份白皮书是否标志着政府思路的转变?; **chest pains can be a warning ～ of heart disease** 胸部疼痛可能是心脏病的警示信号 3 Rail 信号灯 4 Radio, TV, Electron 讯号; **to send/transmit a ～** 发出/传输讯号; **to receive** *or* **pick up a ～** 收到讯号

B *vt* (*pres p etc.* **-ll-** Brit, **-l-** Amer) 1 (show by signal) «*person, ship*» 传达 ‹*intention, message*›; Sport «*referee*» 示意 ‹*free kick, penalty*›; **the yellow light ～s 'proceed with caution'** 黄灯表示"小心前行"; **the referee ～led a foul** 裁判示意犯规; **to ～ sth. to sb.** 向某人示意某事; **to ～ to do sth.** 示意做某事; **to ～ which/what/where ...** 示意哪一个/什么/哪里…; **you must ～ which way you are going to turn** 转向前一定要打信号; **to ～ right/left** 打左转/右转信号 2 fig (indicate) «*situation, decision, attitude*» 表明 ‹*shift, determination, intention*› 3 fig (mark) «*event, statement*» 标志 ‹*beginning, stage*›

C *vi* (*pres p etc.* **-ll-** Brit, **-l-** Amer) 发信号; **he was ～ling frantically** 他发疯似地比划着; **you didn't ～!** Aut 你没打转向灯!; **I ～led for him to bring the bill** 我示意他把账单拿来

D *adj attrib* 极大的 ‹*triumph, failure, disaster*›

signal: ～ box *n* Brit 信号房; **～ generator** *n* 信号发生器

signalize /ˈsɪgnlaɪz/ *vt* 表明 ‹*event, change*›

signally /ˈsɪgnəli/ *adv* 显而易见地 ‹*fail, incompetent, important*›

signal: ～man /-mən/ ▸ **p. 409** *n* 1 Rail 信号员; 2 Naut 信号收发员; Mil 信号兵; **～ strength** *n* [u] 信号强度; **～ tower** *n* Amer **= ～ box**

signatory /ˈsɪgnətri, Amer -tɔːri/ *n* 签署方; **a ～ to sth.** 某文件的签署方; **a ～ power** 缔约大国

signature /ˈsɪgnətʃə(r)/ *n* 1 [c] (person's name) 签名; **to put** *or* **set one's ～ to sth.** 在…上签字 ‹*letter, document*› 2 [u] (action of signing) 签字; **please return the document to us for ～** 请将文件交还我们签署

signature: ～ file *n* 签名文件; **～ tune** *n* Brit [广播或电视的] 信号曲

signboard /ˈsaɪnbɔːd/ *n* (of business) 招牌; (of product) 广告牌

signer /ˈsaɪnə(r)/ *n* 手语译员

signet /ˈsɪgnət/ *n* 戒指图章

signet ring *n* 图章戒指

significance /sɪgˈnɪfɪkəns/ *n* [u] 1 (importance) 重要性; (noteworthiness) 可关注性; **not of any ～, of no ～** 无关紧要的 2 (meaning) 意义; **to have** *or* **carry no ～ (for sb./sth.)** (对某人/某事物) 毫无意义

significant /sɪgˈnɪfɪkənt/ *adj* 1 (important) 重要的; (noteworthy) 值得关注的 2 (explicitly meaningful) 有意义的; **it is ～ that ...** …很能说明问题 3 (implicitly meaningful) 意味深长的

significantly /sɪgˈnɪfɪkəntli/ *adv* 1 (notably) 显著地; **～ higher/lower** 明显更高/更低的; **～ different** 大不相同的; **not ～ bigger/faster** 并不大的/没快多少的 2 (meaningfully) 带有含义地 ‹*name, label*›; 耐人寻味地 ‹*glare, look, smile*›

significant other *n* 重要的另一位 [指情人或配偶]

signification /ˌsɪgnɪfɪˈkeɪʃn/ *n* 1 [u] (representation of meaning) 表意 2 [c and u] (exact meaning) 含义

signify /ˈsɪgnɪfaɪ/

A *vt* 1 (indicate) «*person, fact, gesture*» 表示 ‹*approval, displeasure, willingness*› 2 (denote) «*sign, dress*» 表明 ‹*position, loss*›; «*cloud*» 预示 ‹*rain, weather*›; **the symbol signifies a registered trademark** 这个符号是注册商标的标志

B *vi* «*fact*» 要紧; **it doesn't ～** 那无关紧要

signing /ˈsaɪnɪŋ/ *n* 1 [u] (of treaty, official document) 签署 2 [u] (recruitment) 签约雇用; **the ～ of overseas players** 海外队员的签约聘用 3 [c] Brit (newly recruited person) 签约受雇者; **Liverpool's latest ～** 利物浦队最新签约的队员 4 [c] (by author) 签名售书活动 5 [u] (using sign language) 手语的使用

sign language *n* [u] 手语; **to talk in ～** 用手语交谈

signpost /ˈsaɪnpəʊst/

A *n* 路标

B *vt* 1 (mark with signpost) 给…设置路标 ‹*road*› 2 esp Brit (indicate) 用路标标示 ‹*place, attraction, venue*›; **to be ～ed** 有路标

sign writer ▸ **p. 409** *n* 画招牌者

Sikh /siːk/

A *n* 锡克教教徒

B *adj* 锡克教的 ‹*custom, temple, religion*›; 信奉锡克教的 ‹*community, province*›; 锡克教教徒的 ‹*identity*›

Sikhism /ˈsiːkɪzəm/ *n* [u] 锡克教

silage /ˈsaɪlɪdʒ/ *n* [u] 青贮饲料

silence /ˈsaɪləns/

A *n* 1 [u] (absence of sound) 寂静; **～ fell** 安静下来; **～ reigns** 一片寂静; **the sound of a dog barking broke the ～** 犬吠声打破了寂静 2 [c and u] (absence of speaking) 沉默; **～ please!** 请安静!; **to call for ～** 要求保持安静; **to reduce sb. to ～** 使某人安静下来; **in ～** 一言不发地; **a one/two minute ～** 一分钟/两分钟的沉默 3 [c] (absence of communication) 缄默; **to break one's ～** 打破沉默 4 [u and c] (discretion) 不声张; **to buy sb.'s ～** 花钱让某人保密

B *vt* 1 (quieten) 使不出声; **to ～ the enemy's guns** 把敌人的枪炮打哑 2 (gag) 压制 ‹*critics, opposition, criticism*›; **the government has passed new laws to ～ the radical press** 政府已通过了新法令来压制激进的新闻媒体

silencer /ˈsaɪlənsə(r)/ *n* Brit 消音器

silent /ˈsaɪlənt/ *adj* 1 (soundless) 无声的 ‹*footstep, piano keys*›; 寂静的 ‹*atmosphere, forest*›; **she sat alone in the ～ house** 她独自坐在静静的屋子里; **as ～ as the grave** 悄无声息的 2 (wordless) 安静的 ‹*person, audience, room*›; **to be ～** 不出声; **to keep** *or* **remain** *or* **stay ～** 保持沉默; **to fall ～** 安静下来 3 (unexpressed) 未说出来的 ‹*emotion, prayer, curse*› 4 Ling 不发音的 5 Cin 无声的; **the ～ screen** *or* **movies** 无声电影 6 (uncommunicative) 不提供情况的; **to remain ～ about** *or* **on the matter of ...** 对…问题避而不谈; **the law is ～ on this point** 法律没有涉及这一点 7 (taciturn) 沉默寡言的 ‹*person, child*›

silently /ˈsaɪləntli/ *adv* 1 (soundlessly) 无声地 ‹*play, walk, appear*› 2 (without words) 沉默地 ‹*sit, walk, hope, nervous*›

silent: ～ majority *n* 沉默的大多数; **～ partner** *n* Amer **= sleeping partner**

silhouette /ˌsɪluːˈet/

A *n* [浅色背景映衬出的] 轮廓; **in ～** 以轮廓形式; **the ～ of a tree against the sky** 天空映衬下的一棵树的轮廓

B *vt* 使呈现轮廓; **to be ~d against sth.** 在某物的映衬下显出轮廓

silica /ˈsɪlɪkə/ *n* [u] 二氧化硅

silica gel *n* [u] 硅胶

silicate /ˈsɪlɪkeɪt/ *n* **1** [c and u] Chem 硅酸盐 **2** [u] Miner 硅酸盐矿物

silicon /ˈsɪlɪkən/ *n* [u] 硅

silicon chip *n* 硅片

silicone /ˈsɪlɪkəʊn/ *n* [u and c] 硅酮; **a ~ (breast) implant** 硅酮（乳房）假体

silicone rubber *n* [u] 硅（氧）橡胶

Silicon Valley *pr n* 硅谷 [指信息技术产业聚集地]

silicosis /ˌsɪlɪˈkəʊsɪs/ ▸p. 377 *n* [u] 硅肺病

silk /sɪlk/ *n* **1** [u] (fibre) 丝 **2** [u] (fabric) 丝绸; **a ~ shirt/tie/flower** 真丝衬衫/真丝领带/绢花; **~ production/industry** 丝织品生产/丝织业; **as smooth as ~** 如丝绸般光滑的 **3** [u] (thread) 丝线 **4** [c] (clothing) 丝绸服装 **5** [u] (of spider) 蛛丝 **6** [u] (of sweetcorn) 须 **7** [u] Brit Jur colloq 王室律师; **to take ~** 担任王室律师

silken /ˈsɪlkən/ *adj* **1** (made of silk) 丝制的; **a ~ ribbon/gown/underwear** 丝带/丝绸睡衣/丝绸内衣 **2** (like silk) 柔软光滑的 ‹*hair, fabric, skin, sheen*› **3** fig (suave) 柔和的 ‹*voice*›; 温和的 ‹*manner*›

silk: ~ factory *n* 丝织厂; **~ farming** *n* [u] 养蚕业; **~ finish** *n* 缎光; **a paint with a ~ finish** 缎光油漆

silkiness /ˈsɪlkɪnɪs/ *n* [u] **1** (of hair, fabric, skin) 柔软光滑 **2** (of voice) 柔和; (of manner) 温和

silk: ~ moth *n* 蚕蛾; **S~ Road, S~ Route** *pr ns* **the S~ Road** *or* **Route** 丝绸之路; **~-screen printing** *n* [u] 丝网印刷术; **~ square** *n* 丝绸方巾

silk stocking
A *n* **1** lit 长筒丝袜 **2** Amer fig (rich person) 有钱人; (member of the upper class) 上流社会成员
B **silk-stocking** *modif* **1** Amer fig (rich) 富有的 **2** (of the upper class) 上流社会的

silkworm /ˈsɪlkwɜːm/ *n* 蚕

silky /ˈsɪlki/ *adj* **1** (silk-like) 柔软光洁的 ‹*hair, fabric, skin*› **2** fig (suave) 柔和的 ‹*voice, tone*›; 温和的 ‹*manner*›

silky smooth *adj* 柔软光滑的 ‹*hair, skin*›

sill /sɪl/ *n* **1** (of door) 门槛; (of window) 窗台 **2** (of vehicle) 底框梁

silliness /ˈsɪlɪnɪs/ *n* [u] 愚蠢

silly /ˈsɪli/
A *adj* 愚蠢的 ‹*person, question, story, behaviour*›; **he made me feel really ~!** 他让我觉得自己很蠢！; **you ~ fool!** 你这个蠢货！; **what a ~ thing to do!** 这么做太愚蠢了！; **don't be ~** 别犯傻了; **to do something ~** 做傻事; **to make sb. look ~** 让某人看起来很蠢; **to drink oneself ~** 喝醉
B *n* colloq 傻瓜

silly: ~ billy *n* esp Brit colloq 傻瓜; **~ season** *n* esp Brit 无聊季节 [指无重大新闻而只得报道无聊内容的盛夏]

silo /ˈsaɪləʊ/ *n* (*pl* **~s**) **1** (for grain) 筒仓 **2** (for silage) 青贮窖 **3** (for missiles) 发射井

silt /sɪlt/ *n* [u and c] [水渠或港口等处的] 泥沙

Phrasal verb

• **silt up**
A *vi* «*canal, harbour, river*» 被淤塞
B *vt* [**~ sth. up, ~ up sth.**] «*mud, clay*» 使…淤塞 ‹*canal, harbour, river*›

Silurian /saɪˈlʊərɪən/
A *adj* (of the period) 志留纪的; (of the rock system) 志留系的
B *n* **the ~** (period) 志留纪; (rock system) 志留系

silvan /ˈsɪlvən/ *adj* = **sylvan**

silver /ˈsɪlvə(r)/ ▸p. 134
A *n* **1** [u] (metal) 银 **2** [u] (colour) 银色 **3** [u] (dishes) 银器; (cutlery) 银餐具; ▸**cloud A1** **4** [u] (coins) 银币; **in ~** 用银币; **£10 in ~** 10 英镑银币 **5** [c] (medal) 银牌
B *adj* **1** (made of silver) 银质的 ‹*bracelet, watch, cutlery*› **2** (colour) 银色的 ‹*paint, glitter, hair*›
C *vt* 给…镀银 ‹*metal, fork, mirror, glass*›

silver birch *n* 银桦

silvered /ˈsɪlvəd/ *adj* 银灰色的 ‹*hair, landscape, tree, metal*›

silver: ~ fir *n* 银冷杉; **~fish** *n* 蠹鱼; **~ foil** *n* [u] Brit 铝箔; **~ fox** *n* **1** [c] Zool 银狐; **2** [u] (fur) 银狐毛皮; **a coat with a ~ fox collar** 带银狐皮领子的外套; **~ gilt** *n* [u] (silver covered with gold) 镀金银器; (imitation) 仿镀金银器; **a ~-gilt bowl/goblet** 镀金的银碗/银高脚杯; **~-haired** *adj* 银发的 ‹*person*›; 银色毛的 ‹*animal*›; **~ jubilee** *n* [重大事件的] 25 周年纪念; **~ lining** *n* 一线光明; **~ medal** *n* 银牌; **~ mine** *n* 银矿; **~ paper** *n* [u] (made of aluminium) 锡纸; (made of other silvery material) 银色纸; **~ plate** *n* [u] 镀银器皿; **~-plated** *adj* 镀银的 ‹*cutlery, teapot*›; **~ polish** *n* [u] 银器擦亮剂; **~ screen** *n* (films) 银幕; (film industry) 电影业; **a star of the ~ screen** 电影明星; **~ service** *n* 银器服务 [正式宴会上侍者用银匙和银叉向用餐者盘中上菜]; **a ~ service dinner/waiter/waitress** 提供银器服务的宴会/男服务员/女服务员; **~side** *n* [u] 牛臀肉; **~smith** ▸p. 409 *n* 银匠; **~ surfer** *n* colloq 银发网民; **~ tongue** *n* 口才; **~ware** *n* [u] (solid) 银器; (plated) 镀银器; **~ wedding** *n* 银婚 [结婚25周年纪念]

silvery /ˈsɪlvəri/ *adj* **1** (in colour) 银色的 ‹*hair, moon, light*›; **a ~ grey colour** 银灰色 **2** (in sound) 银铃般的 ‹*voice, tinkle*›; 悦耳的 ‹*bells*›

silviculture /ˈsɪlvɪkʌltʃə(r)/ *n* [u] 造林学

SIM card /ˈsɪm kɑːd/ *n* [手机的] SIM 卡

simian /ˈsɪmɪən/
A *adj* **1** Zool 类人猿的 ‹*creature, behaviour, virus*› **2** pej (ape-like) 像猴的 ‹*face, features*›
B *n* 类人猿

similar /ˈsɪmɪlə(r)/ *adj* 相似的; **something ~** 类似的某物; **ten ~ offences** 10 项相似的罪行; **to be ~ to sb./sth.** 与某人/某物相像; **it's ~ to riding a bike** 那就像是骑自行车; **~ in size/price** 尺寸/价格相仿的; **~ in colour** 颜色相似的; **~ in appearance to ...** 外观与…相似的

similarity /ˌsɪmɪˈlærəti/ *n* **1** (fact of resembling) 相似; **a (striking) ~ between sth. and sth.** 某物和某物之间的（明显）相似; **~ with** *or* **to sth.** 与某事物的相似; **~ in sth.** 在某方面的相似 **2** (aspect of resemblance) 相似之处

similarly /ˈsɪmɪləli/ *adv* **1** (in similar way) 相似地 **2** (likewise) 同样; **and ~, ...** 而同样，…

simile /ˈsɪmɪli/ *n* **1** [c] (figure of speech) 明喻 **2** [u] (usage) 明喻运用

similitude /sɪˈmɪlɪtjuːd, Amer -tuːd/ *n* [u] formal 相似

simmer /ˈsɪmə(r)/
A *vt* 煨炖 ‹*fruit, beans, soup, stew*›
B *vi* **1** Culin «*fruit, beans, soup, stew*» 煨炖; «*water*» 慢慢沸腾 **2** fig (seethe) «*person*» 充满怒火; «*unrest, row*» 即将爆发; **to ~ with rage** 怒火中烧; **unrest and dissatisfaction are ~ing** 动荡和不满一触即发
C *n* [u] 即将沸腾状态; **to bring sth. to a ~** 改用文火炖某物; **to keep sth. at a ~** 煨炖某物

Phrasal verb

• **simmer down** *vi* colloq «*row*» 平息下来; «*person*» 平静下来; **after I had had a chance to ~ down, I saw things differently** 有机会冷静下来后，我对事情有了不同的看法

simmering /ˈsɪmərɪŋ/ *adj* fig 一触即发的 ‹*conflict, tension, revolt, anger*›

simnel cake /ˈsɪmnl ˌkeɪk/ *n* [u and c] Brit [复活节和大斋节期间吃的] 水果蛋糕

simper /ˈsɪmpə(r)/
A *vi* (ingratiatingly) 谄媚地笑; (coquettishly) 媚笑; (foolishly) 傻笑
B *n* (ingratiating smile) 谄媚的笑; (coquettish smile) 媚笑; (foolish smile) 傻笑

simpering /ˈsɪmpərɪŋ/
A *adj* (ingratiating) 谄媚的; (coquettish) 卖弄风情的; (foolish) 犯傻的
B *n* [u] (ingratiating behaviour) 谄媚; (coquettish behaviour) 卖弄风情; (foolish behaviour) 犯傻

simple /ˈsɪmpl/ *adj* **1** (uncomplicated) 简单的 ‹*task, method, instructions, solution*›; **it's quite ~** 这很简单; **it's a ~ matter to change a wheel** 换轮子是件简单的事; **for the ~ reason that ...** 只是因为…; **computing made ~** 《数据处理简易通》; **in ~ terms** *or* **language** 简单地说; **as ~ as ABC** 非常简单; **it's a ~ matter of choice** 这只不过是个选择的问题; **for the ~ reason that he hasn't got any money** 就是因为他没有钱 **2** (not elaborate) 朴素的 ‹*clothes, furniture, design*›; 简朴的 ‹*food, lifestyle*› **3** (basic) 原始的 ‹*tool, life form, structure*› **4** (unsophisticated) 普通的 ‹*labourer, soldier*›; **her parents were ~ shopkeepers** 她的父母是普普通通的小商店店主; **I'm a ~ soul** iron 我是个单纯的人 **5** (unintelligent) 智力低的 ‹*person*› **6** (plain) 显而易见的 ‹*truth, fact, difference*›

simple: ~ equation *n* 一次方程; **~ fraction** *n* 简分数; **~ fracture** *n* 单纯骨折; **~ interest** *n* [u] 单利; **~-minded** *adj* **1** (unintelligent) 头脑简单的; **2** (unsophisticated) 纯真的; **~ time** *n* [u] 单拍子

simpleton /ˈsɪmpltən/ *n* 傻瓜

simplicity /sɪmˈplɪsəti/ *n* [u] **1** (of task, instructions, solution) 简单; **it's ~ itself** 这非常简单 **2** (of dress, furniture) 朴素 **3** (of food, taste) 简朴

simplification /ˌsɪmplɪfɪˈkeɪʃn/ *n* **1** [c] (simplified form) 简化的事物; **the final design is a ~ of our original plan** 最终的设计方案是我们最初计划的简化形式 **2** [u] (process) 简化; **the system will need some ~** 该系统需要进行简化

simplify /ˈsɪmplɪfaɪ/ *vt* 简化 ‹*job, task, process*›; 精简 ‹*system*›; 使…简明 ‹*instructions, explanation*›; **this should ~ matters** 这会使情况变得简单

simplistic /sɪmˈplɪstɪk/ *adj* 过分简单化的 ‹*view, attitude, approach*›

simply /ˈsɪmpli/ *adv* **1** (straightforwardly) 简单地; **to put it ~** 简而言之 **2** (not elaborately) 朴素地 ‹*dress, decorated*›; 简朴地 ‹*eat, live*› **3** (merely) 仅仅; **it's ~ a question of concentrating** 这只不过是一个集中精力的问题 **4** (absolutely) 的确; **the concert was ~ wonderful** 音乐会真是精彩极了; **I ~ must dash!** 我真得赶紧走了!

simulate /ˈsɪmjʊleɪt/ *vt* **1** (feign) 假装 ‹*pleasure, anger*›; **she tried hard to ~ interest in what he was saying** 她竭力装作对他所说的很感兴趣 **2** (imitate) 模拟 ‹*conditions, appearance, colour*› **3** (reproduce) 模仿 ‹*sound, background*›; **on TV they use tomato ketchup to ~ blood** 在电视上他们用番茄汁充当人血

simulated /ˈsɪmjʊleɪtɪd/ *adj* **1** (feigned) 假装的 ‹*pleasure, anger*› **2** (imitation) 仿造的; **~ fur/pearls/leather** 仿裘皮/人造珍珠/人造革

simulation /ˌsɪmjʊˈleɪʃn/ *n* **1** (act) 模仿 **2** (model) 模式

simulator /ˈsɪmjʊleɪtə(r)/ *n* 模拟装置

simulator program *n* 模拟程序

simulcast /ˈsɪməlkɑːst, Amer -kæst/
A *n* 联播
B *vt* 联播 ‹*programme, event*›

simultaneous /ˌsɪmlˈteɪmɪəs, Amer ˌsaɪm-/ *adj* 同时发生的 ‹*events, failure, occurrence*›; 同时进行的 ‹*experiments, translation*›; **to be ~ (with ...)** «*events*»（与…）同时发生; «*experiments*»（与…）同时进行

simultaneous equations *npl* 联立方程

simultaneously /ˌsɪmlˈteɪmɪəsli, Amer ˌsaɪm-/ *adv* 同时地; **~ with ...** 与…同步地

sin¹ /sɪn/
A *n* 1 [u] (breaking of divine law) 罪过 [指对宗教戒律的违犯]; **original ~** 原罪 2 [c] (transgression) [宗教意义上的] 罪行; **the ~ of pride** 傲慢之罪; **to commit a ~** 犯罪; **to forgive sb.'s ~s** 宽恕某人的罪孽; **to confess one's ~s** 悔罪; **a ~ against sb./sth.** 冒犯某人/亵渎某事物的罪过 3 [c] (fault, offence, omission) 过错; **it's a ~ to do sth.** 做某事不应该; **a ~ of omission** 渎职; **for one's ~s** Brit 自作自受地
B *vi* (*pres p etc.* **-nn-**) 犯过失; **to ~ against sb./sth.** 亵渎某人/某物; **to be more ~ned against than ~ning** fig 过错无多而报应太重

sin² *abbr* Math = **sine**

sin bin *n* colloq 受罚席

since /sɪns/
A *prep* 自…以来; **~ then** 自那以后; **we've lived here ~ 2004** 从 2004 年起我们一直住在这里; **it's been three years ~ his death** 他去世已经 3 年了; **the worst disaster ~ Chernobyl** 切尔诺贝利核事故以来最严重的灾难; **he's been working in a bank ~ leaving school** 他中学毕业后一直在一家银行工作; **~ when?** (from what time) 从什么时候起?; (expressing anger) 何曾?; **they've split up — ~ when?** 他们分手了——什么时候的事?; **~ when did he ever listen to me?** 他何曾听过我的话?
B *conj* 1 (from the time when) 从…以后; **I've known him ~ I was 12** 我从 12 岁起就认识他了; **she had been worrying ever ~ the letter arrived** 自从那封信来了后, 她就一直焦虑不安; **how long is it ~ we last went to the theatre?** 我们多久没去看戏了? 2 (given that) 由于; **~ it was raining, I stayed at home** 因为在下雨, 我就待在家里; **~ you're so clever, why don't you do it yourself?** 既然你如此聪明, 为什么不自己做呢?
C *adv* 1 (from that time) 自那以后; **he left home two weeks ago, and we haven't heard from him ~** 他两周前离开了家, 我们至今还没有他的音信; **ever ~** 自那后一直 2 (at some time in past) 后来; **the play has ~ been filmed** 这个剧本后来被拍成了电影 3 (ago) 之前; **long ~** 很久以前; **I posted the letter long ~** 我早就把信寄出去了; **not long ~** 不久前

sincere /sɪn'sɪə(r)/ *adj* 真诚的 ‹*good wishes*›; 真挚的 ‹*friendship*›; 诚实的 ‹*person*›; 忠实的 ‹*believer*›; **~ thanks** 诚挚的谢意; **it is my ~ belief that ...** 我真心实意地相信…

sincerely /sɪn'sɪəli/ *adv* 真诚地 ‹*say, apologize, offer, believe*›; 发自内心地 ‹*delighted*›; **Yours ~** 你的真诚的 [正式信函末尾署名前的套语]

sincerity /sɪn'serəti/ *n* [u] 真诚; **in all ~** 十分坦诚地

sine /saɪn/ *n* 正弦

sinecure /'saɪnɪkjʊə(r), 'sɪn-/ *n* 闲职

sine qua non /ˌsɪneɪ kwɑː 'nəʊn/ *n* 必要条件; **the ~ of sth.** 某事物的先决条件

sinew /'sɪnjuː/ *n* 1 [u and c] (tendon, ligament) 肌腱 2 **sinews** *pl* (source of strength) 力量的源泉

sine wave *n* 正弦波

sinewy /'sɪnjuːi/ *adj* 肌肉发达的

sinfonietta /ˌsɪnfən'jetə/ *n* 1 (symphony) 小交响曲 2 (orchestra) 小交响乐队

sinful /'sɪnfl/ *adj* 1 (wicked, immoral) 罪恶的 ‹*person, desires, thought*› 2 (reprehensible) 应受谴责的 ‹*indulgence, waste*› 3 hum (indulgent) 味浓且热量高的 ‹*dessert*›

sinfully /'sɪnfəli/ *adv* 1 (wickedly) 罪恶地 ‹*behave, act, live*› 2 (reprehensibly) 应受谴责地 ‹*waste, polluted*› 3 hum (indulgently) 油腻诱人地 ‹*sweet*›

sinfulness /'sɪnflnɪs/ *n* [u] (of person) 有罪; (of action, behaviour) 罪恶

sing /sɪŋ/
A *vt* (*pt* **sang,** *pp* **sung**) 1 Mus (vocalize) 唱; **to ~ a song** 唱歌; **can you ~ the soprano part?** 你能唱女高音声部吗?; **to ~ sth. to** *or* **for sb.** 为某人唱某歌曲; **to ~ one's troubles/blues away** 借唱歌忘掉烦恼/忧伤; **to ~ a different** *or* **another tune** *or* **song** fig 改弦易辙; **a nightingale was ~ing its song in the twilight** 一只夜莺在暮色中歌唱 2 liter (celebrate in words) 《*poet, poetry*》颂扬
B *vi* (*pt* **sang,** *pp* **sung**) 1 Mus (vocalize) 唱歌; **to ~ in/out of tune** 唱歌合调/走调; **to ~ like a lark** 歌声优美; **to ~ from the same hymn** *or* **song sheet** Brit fig colloq 对外口径一致; **the birds ~ every day at daybreak** 鸟儿每天在破晓时分啼鸣 2 (make high-pitched sound) 《*insect, kettle*》尖叫; **to make sb.'s ears ~** 使某人耳朵嗡嗡作响; **the wind sang in the treetops** 风在树梢间呼啸; **a bullet sang past my ear** 一颗子弹从我耳边嗖的一声飞过 3 colloq (act as informer) 《*criminal*》当线人; **to ~ like a canary** 向警方和盘托出 4 liter (celebrate in words) 《*poet, poetry*》**to ~ of sb./sth.** 歌颂某人/某事物
C *n* colloq 1 (act of singing) 歌唱; **to have a ~** 唱支歌 2 Amer (sing-along) 合唱聚会

(Phrasal verbs)

- **sing along** *vi* 跟着唱; **he played the piano and we all sang along** 他弹钢琴, 我们都跟着唱; **to ~ along with sb.** 随着某人唱
- **sing out**
A *vi* 1 《*singer, choir*》放声高歌 2 colloq (call out) 《*person*》叫喊; 《*voice*》高声发出; **~ out if you need some more** 还需要就喊一声
B *vt* [**~ out sth.,** **~ sth. out**] colloq 高声说出; **he sang out a greeting** 他高声问候
- **sing up** *vi* esp Brit 更大声地唱; **~ up!** 放开嗓门唱!

sing. *abbr* = **singular A, B1**

sing-along *n* 1 Amer (occasion) 众人自娱歌唱会 2 (song) 跟唱歌; (tune) 跟唱曲

Singapore /ˌsɪŋə'pɔː(r)/ *pr n* 新加坡

Singaporean /ˌsɪŋə'pɔːrɪən/ ▸**p. 503**
A *adj* 新加坡的
B *n* 新加坡人

singe /sɪndʒ/
A *vt* (*pres p* **~ing**) 把…轻微烧焦
B *vi* (*pres p* **~ing**) 轻微地烧焦
C *n* **~ (mark)** 轻微的焦痕

singer /'sɪŋə(r)/ *n* 歌手; **he's a ~ in a band** 他是一名乐队歌手

Singhalese *n, adj* = **Sinhalese**

singing /'sɪŋɪŋ/ *n* [u] 1 (act) 唱歌; (sound) 歌声; **opera ~** 歌剧演唱; **to have** *or* **take ~ lessons** 上声乐课 2 (of kettle) 鸣响声; (in ears) 耳鸣声; (of wind) 呜呜声; (of whistling) 啸声

singing voice *n* 歌喉

single /'sɪŋgl/
A *adj* 1 attrib (just one) 仅有一个的; **he won by a ~ vote** 他以仅一票的优势获胜; **we walked thirty miles in a ~ day** 我们一天内走了 30 英里 2 attrib (not double) 单一的; **(in) ~ figures** (以) 一位数; **a ~ cassette player** 单卡放音机; **a ~-barrelled gun** 单管枪; **a ~-masted vessel** 单桅船; **a ~ whisky** 单份威士忌 3 attrib (for one) 单人的; **the hotel only has two ~ rooms** 这家旅馆只有两间单人房 4 attrib Brit Transp 单程的 ‹*fare, journey*›; **a ~ ticket** 单程票 5 (unmarried) 单身的; **a ~ man/woman** 单身汉/单身女人; **are you married or ~?** 你已婚还是单身? 6 Bot 单瓣的 ‹*flower, tulip, rose*› 7 attrib (used emphatically) **every ~ thing/person/time** 每件事/每个人/每一次; **there isn't a ~ word of truth in it!** 那里面没有一句真话!; **heart disease is the ~ biggest killer in Britain** 心脏病在英国是名列榜首的致死因素; **even if there is a ~ vote against, the motion fails** 即便只有一票反对, 这个动议也不能通过
B *n* 1 Brit Transp (one-way ticket) 单程票 2 Tourism (room for one) 单人房间 3 Mus 单曲唱片 4 Sport (in cricket, baseball) 一垒打; **to score** *or* **hit a ~** 打出一垒得分 5 Amer colloq (dollar note) 一元纸币 6 (individual seat) 散座 7 (measure of spirits) 单份; **a ~ or double, sir?** 先生是要单份还是双份?
C **singles** *npl* 1 (unmarried people) 单身人士 2 Sport 单打 (比赛); **the first round of the men's/women's ~s** 男子/女子单打第一轮
D **singles** *modif* 1 (for unmarried people) 单身人士的; **a ~s club/vacation** 单身俱乐部/假期 2 Mus 单曲的 ‹*sales*› 3 Sport 单打的; **a ~s final/champion** 单打决赛/冠军

(Phrasal verb)

- **single out** *vt* [**~ sb./sth. out,** **~ out sb./sth.**] 单独挑出; **to ~ sb./sth. out for attention** 挑出某人/某事物加以留意; **the teacher ~d out her poem for special praise** 老师挑出她的诗给予了特别表扬; **to ~ out sb./sth. as sb./sth.** 选出某人/某事物作为某人/某事物; **she seems to have been ~d out as the ringleader** 她好像被单挑出来认定为元凶

single: ~-action *adj* (of a gun) 单发的; **~-breasted** *adj* 单排扣的; **~ carriageway** *n* 单车道公路; **~-cell, ~-celled** *adj attrib* 单细胞的; **~ combat** *n* [u] 一对一的打斗; **~ cream** *n* [u] Brit 低脂稀奶油; **~ currency** *n* 单一货币; **~-decker** *n* 单层公共汽车; **~-entry** *modif* 单式记账的; **a ~-entry account/book-keeping** 单式记账账目/单式记账法; **~ European currency** *n* 单一欧洲货币 [指欧元]; **~ malt, ~ malt whisky** *ns* [u and c] 纯麦威士忌

single file
A *n* [u] 一路纵队; **in ~** 成一路纵队
B *adv* 成一路纵队

single-handed /ˌsɪŋgl'hændɪd/
A *adj* 1 (solo) 独自一人的 ‹*voyage, crossing*› 2 (for one hand) 单手使用的 ‹*axe, fishing rod, keyboard*›
B *adv* (alone) 独自一人地 ‹*move, sail*›; (independently) 独立地 ‹*manage, achieve*›

single-handedly /ˌsɪŋgl'hændɪdli/ *adv* 单独地

single: ~-lens reflex *adj* 单镜头反射式的; **~ market** *n* 单一市场; **~-minded** *adj* 一心一意的; **to be ~-minded about doing ...** 一心做…; **to be ~-minded in sth.** 专注于某事物; **~-mindedness** *n* [u] 专注; **~ mother** *n* 单身母亲

singleness /'sɪŋglnɪs/ *n* [u] 专一

single parent *n* 单亲

singles /'sɪŋglz/
A *npl* ▸**single C**
B *modif* ▸**single D**

singles: ~ bar *n* 单身酒吧; **~ charts** *npl* 一周流行单曲榜

single: ~ seater *n* (vehicle) 单座车; (aircraft) 单座飞机; **a ~-seater aircraft/racing car** 单座飞机/赛车; **~-sex** *adj* 单性别的; **a ~-sex school** (for boys) 男校; (for girls) 女校; **~-sex education** 男女分校教育; **~ spacing** *n* [u] 单倍行距; **~-storey** *adj* 单楼层的

singlet /'sɪŋglɪt/ *n* Brit 无袖汗衫

singleton /'sɪŋgltən/ *n* 1 (single item) 单个物件 2 colloq (unmarried person) 单身人士 3 (card) 单张花色牌

single: ~-track *adj* 1 lit 单线的; **a ~-track railway/road** 单线铁路/单车道公路; 2 fig 单一的 ‹*mind*›; **~ transferable vote** *n* 单一可转移投票制; **~ yellow line** *n* Brit [路边限制停车的] 单黄线

Singlish /ˈsɪŋglɪʃ/ *n* [u] (English spoken in Singapore) 新加坡式英语; (English spoken in Sri Lanka) 斯里兰卡式英语

singly /ˈsɪŋgli/ *adv* 单个地

sing-song Brit
A *n* 众人自娱歌唱会; **to have a ~** 举行自娱歌唱会
B *adj* 音调起伏的 ‹*voice, intonation*›

singular /ˈsɪŋgjʊlə(r)/
A *n* 单数形式
B *adj* **1** (referring to one person or thing) 单数的; **a ~ noun/form/ending** 单数名词/形式/词尾 **2** (outstanding) 非凡的 ‹*beauty, success, achievement*› **3** (strange) 异常的 ‹*event, behaviour*›

singularity /ˌsɪŋgjʊˈlærəti/ *n* **1** [u] (of beauty, success) 突出 **2** [c] (peculiarity) 特点 **3** [c] Phys 奇点

singularly /ˈsɪŋgjʊləli/ *adv* 突出地

Sinhalese /ˌsɪŋhəˈliːz/ ▸**p. 426, p. 503**
A *adj* (of the people) 僧迦罗人的 ‹*community, tradition, architecture*›; (of the language) 僧迦罗语的
B *n* (*pl* **Sinhalese**) **1** [c] (person) 僧迦罗人 **2** [u] (language) 僧迦罗语

sinister /ˈsɪnɪstə(r)/ *adj* **1** (suggestive of evil) 邪恶的 ‹*person, character, place*›; 恶意的 ‹*behaviour, action, event*›; 阴险的 ‹*plot*› **2** Herald 左侧的

sink /sɪŋk/
A *vi* (*pt* **sank**, *pp* **sunk**) **1** (go below surface) «*object, submarine, material*» 下沉; **to ~ to the bottom/below the surface** 沉底/沉到水下; **the wheels started to ~ in the mud** 车轮开始陷入泥里; **the rain sank into the dry ground** 雨水渗进了干燥的地面; **my warning hasn't sunk into your thick skull yet, has it?** fig colloq 你的笨脑瓜还没明白我的警告, 是不是?; **~ or swim** fig 不自救, 必沉沦; **to ~ without trace** «*ship*» 消失得无影无踪; fig «*idea, book*» 销声匿迹 **2** (become lower) 倒下; **to ~ to the ground/floor** 倒在地上/地板上; **to ~ down/back** 倒下/仰面倒下; **a shot rang out, and he slowly sank to his knees** 一声枪响之后他慢慢跪到了地上; **to ~ under the weight of sth.** lit «*container*» 在某物的重压下塌陷; fig «*company, person*» 被某事物拖垮 **3** (go below horizon) «*sun, moon*» 下落; **Venus was ~ing below the horizon** 金星正缓缓落下地平线 **4** fig (in strength) «*person*» 衰弱; (in volume) «*voice*» 变低; (in value) «*currency*» 贬值; **to ~ fast** 行将就木; **to ~ in value** 贬值; **to ~ in sb.'s estimation** 在某人心目中的地位下降; **my spirits sank** 我情绪低落; **to ~ into oblivion** 逐渐被大家遗忘; **to ~ so low (as to do sth.)** 沉沦至如此地步 (以至于做出某事)
B *vt* (*pt* **sank**, *pp* **sunk**) **1** (in the sea) 使…沉没 ‹*ship, vessel*› **2** fig (destroy) 毁掉 ‹*hope, chance, project*›; **to be sunk** colloq 完蛋; **we'll be absolutely sunk if the train is late** 如果火车晚点我们就彻底完了 **3** (lower) 放下 ‹*cable, pipe*›; fig 放低 ‹*voice*› **4** (embed) 埋下 ‹*stake, pillar*›; **to ~ one's differences** 抛开分歧; **to be sunk in despair/thought** 陷入绝望/沉思中; **the dog sank its teeth into my arm** 狗咬了我胳膊一口; **his hands were sunk deep into the pockets of his coat** 他的双手深深插在外衣兜中 **5** (bore, excavate) 挖掘 ‹*shaft, tunnel*›; **we shall have to ~ a well to obtain water** 我们只好打井取水了; **to ~ a gold mine** 开掘金矿; **we shall ~ the swimming pool into the ground** 我们要在地上挖游泳池 **6** Sport «*snooker player*» 把…击入洞中 ‹*ball*›; «*golfer*» 以…击球入洞 ‹*shot, putt*›; **to ~ the ball into the middle pocket** 击球入中区/入袋 **7** Brit colloq (drink) 猛喝 ‹*beer, pint*› **8** Fin 投入; **he sank all his savings into the family business** 他把自己的积蓄都投到了家族企业
C *n* **1** (basin) 洗碗槽; **a double ~** 双水槽 **2** (cesspit) 污水坑; **a ~ of iniquity** fig 罪恶的巢穴 **3** Tech 汇; **a heat ~** 热汇; **a carbon ~** 碳库
D *modif* Brit 污秽贫困地区的 ‹*estate*›; **a ~ school** 渣滓学校

Phrasal verb
• **sink in** *vi* **1** (penetrate) «*water, lotion*» 渗入; **rub the cream into your skin and let it ~ in** 把面霜揉进皮肤让皮肤充分吸收 **2** fig (be understood) «*news, facts*» 被领会; **he read the letter twice before the meaning sank in** 他把信读了两遍才搞明白意思

sinker /ˈsɪŋkə(r)/ *n* **1** (weight) [钓线的] 坠子 **2** Amer (doughnut) 炸面圈

sinkhole *n* 落水洞

sinking /ˈsɪŋkɪŋ/
A *adj* (because of anxiety) 颓丧的 ‹*heart, feeling*›; (because of hunger) 虚脱的 ‹*feeling*›
B *n* **1** (of ship) (accidental, by flooding) 沉没; (by torpedo) 炸沉 **2** (of well, foundations, shaft) 挖掘

sinking fund *n* 偿债基金

sink: ~ tidy *n* 洗涤槽垃圾网罩; **~ unit** *n* 洗涤槽组合台

sinless /ˈsɪnlɪs/ *adj* 圣洁的

sinner /ˈsɪnə(r)/ *n* 罪人

Sinn Féin /ˌʃɪn ˈfeɪn/ *n* [爱尔兰的] 新芬党

Sino- /ˈsaɪnəʊ/ *combining form* 中国的; **~-Soviet relations** 中苏关系

sinologist /saɪˈnɒlədʒɪst/ ▸**p. 409** *n* 汉学家

sinology /saɪˈnɒlədʒi/ *n* [u] 汉学

sinuous /ˈsɪnjʊəs/ *adj* 婀娜多姿的 ‹*dance, movements*›; 起伏有致的 ‹*ripples*›; 盘曲的 ‹*snake*›; 蜿蜒的 ‹*trail, river*›

sinuously /ˈsɪnjʊəsli/ *adv* 蜿蜒地

sinus /ˈsaɪnəs/ *n* (*pl* **~es**) (body cavity) 窦; (of nostrils) 鼻窦

sinusitis /ˌsaɪnəˈsaɪtɪs/ ▸**p. 377** *n* [u] 鼻窦炎

Sioux /suː/
A *adj* (of the Sioux people) 苏人的 ‹*warrior, tradition, dance*›; (of the language) 苏语的
B *n* (*pl* **Sioux**) **1** [c] (person) 苏人 **2** [u] (language) 苏语

sip /sɪp/
A *vt* (*pres p etc.* **-pp-**) 小口喝 ‹*drink, water, juice*›
B *vi* (*pres p etc.* **-pp-**) 小口喝; **to ~ at sth.** 小口喝 ‹*drink, water, juice*›
C *n* 一小口; **to have** *or* **take a ~ (of sth.)** 抿一小口 (某物)

siphon /ˈsaɪfn/
A *n* 虹吸管
B *vt* **1** (suck up) «*person, equipment*» 用虹吸管抽 ‹*water, petrol*›; **to ~ sth. out of** *or* **from/into sth.** 从某物中吸出某物/把某物吸到某物中 **2** (divert) 抽走 ‹*money, resources*›; **to ~ sth. from** *or* **out of/into sth.** 从某物中抽走某物/把某物转移至某物中

Phrasal verb
• **siphon off** *vt* [**~ sth. off, ~ off sth.**] **1** (suck out) 用虹吸管抽 ‹*water, petrol*› **2** (divert) 抽走 ‹*money, resources*›

SIPP /sɪp/ *abbr* Brit = **self-invested personal pension** 自我投资型退休金计划

sir /sɜː(r)/ *n* **1** (form of address, in correspondence) 先生; **Dear S~** (in letter) 亲爱的先生 **2** Brit (title) 爵士; **S~ James** 詹姆斯爵士

sire /ˈsaɪə(r)/
A *n* **1** (of horse, pig) 雄性种兽 **2** archaic (term of address) 陛下
B *vt* «*man*» 成为父亲; «*stallion, boar*» 繁殖

siree, sirree /sɜːˈriː/ *n* Amer colloq [用于加强语气]; **yes/no ~!** 当然是/不是!

siren /ˈsaɪərən/ *n* **1** (alarm) 警报器; **an air raid/police/ambulance/fire engine ~** 空袭/警车/救护车/消防警报器 **2** (in mythology) 塞壬 [希腊神话中以歌声诱惑水手使船触礁的女海妖] **3** (woman) 妖魅的女子

siren song, siren call *ns* 危险的诱惑

sirloin /ˈsɜːlɔɪn/ *n* 牛里脊肉

sirocco, scirocco /sɪˈrɒkəʊ/ *n* (*pl* **~s**) 西罗科风 [从北非穿过地中海吹向南欧的湿热风]

sirup /ˈsɪrəp/ *n* Amer = **syrup**

sirupy /ˈsɪrəpi/ *adj* Amer = **syrupy**

sis /sɪs/ *n* colloq (older) 姐姐; (younger) 妹妹

sisal /ˈsaɪsl/ *n* [u] **1** (plant) 剑麻; **a ~ carpet/bag** 剑麻地毯/口袋 **2** (fibre) 剑麻纤维

siskin /ˈsɪskɪn/ *n* 黄雀

sissy /ˈsɪsi/ colloq
A *n* (coward) 胆小鬼; (effeminate man) 女里女气的男人
B *adj* (cowardly) 怯懦的 ‹*behaviour*›; (effeminate) 女孩子气的 ‹*clothes*›

sister /ˈsɪstə(r)/
A *n* **1** ▸**p. 419** (older sibling) 姐姐; (younger sibling) 妹妹; **big/little ~** 大姐/小妹 **2** **Sister** Brit (nurse) 护士长 **3** **Sister** (nun) 修女 **4** (fellow woman) 姐妹 **5** Amer colloq (form of address) (to older woman) 大姐; (to younger woman) 小妹
B *modif* 同类型的; **~ country** *or* **state** 姊妹国家; **~ nation** 姊妹民族

sisterhood /ˈsɪstəhʊd/ *n* **1** [u] (feeling of kinship) 姐妹情谊 **2** [c] + *v sing or pl* (foundation) 妇女会 **3** [u] (being sisters) 姐妹关系

sister-in-law ▸**p. 419** *n* (*pl* **sisters-in-law**) (sister of one's wife) 姨子; (sister of one's husband) 姑子; (wife of one's older brother) 嫂子; (wife of one's younger brother) 弟媳; (wife of one's husband's brother) 妯娌

sisterly /ˈsɪstəli/ *adj* **1** (like a sister) 姐妹般的 ‹*feeling, behaviour, attitude*› **2** (of a sister) 姐妹的; **~ rivalry** 姐妹相争

sister ship *n* 姊妹船

sit /sɪt/ (*pres p* **-tt-**; *pt, pp* **sat**)
A *vi* **1** (be seated) 坐; **to ~ at a desk** *or* **table** 坐在桌旁; **to ~ still** 坐着一动不动; **to ~ at home (all day)** (整日) 闲坐在家; **~ting and waiting** 坐等; **don't just ~ there! do something!** 别老坐着! 做点儿事啊!; **to ~ at sb.'s feet** fig 是某人的弟子; **to ~ on one's hands** fig 袖手旁观; **to ~ on one's arse** fig sl 屁都不干; **to ~ tight** (remain in place) 守在原地; fig (refrain from taking action) 静观事态发展; **to be ~ting pretty** 处于极为有利的地位 **2** (pose) [为画像等] 摆好坐姿; **to ~ for sb.** 摆好姿势让某人画 **3** (meet) «*committee, parliament, board of directors*» 开会 **4** (hold office) 任职; **he ~s in the House of Commons/in Congress** 他在下议院/国会担任议员; **to ~ for ...** «*MP*» 担任…的议员 ‹*constituency*›; **to ~ as ...** 担任…职务 ‹*judge, magistrate*› **5** (on hindquarters) «*dog, animal*» 蹲坐 **6** (perch) 栖息; **to ~ on ...** «*bird*» 栖息在…上 ‹*tree, fence*› **7** (on nest) «*bird*» 孵蛋 **8** (fit) «*clothes, suit*» 合身; fig «*fame, prosperity*» 影响; **to ~ well/badly/loosely** 合身/不合身/很宽松; **those trousers ~ very nicely on you** 你穿这条裤子很合身; **greatness ~s lightly on him** 他对名声地位看得很淡 **9** (lie, be) «*building*» 位于; «*object*» 搁置; **the little farmhouse ~s in a fold between two hills** 小农舍位于两座小山之间的山坳处; **the letter was ~ting unopened on his desk** 那封信就放在他的写字台上没有拆开; **to ~ on sb.'s tail** fig 紧随某人的车尾; **to ~ (heavy** *or* **heavily) on the** *or* **one's stomach** «*food*» 难消化; **his crime sat heavy on his conscience** 他的罪行成了压在他良心上的沉重负担 **10** **to ~ with sth.** (be harmonious with) 为…所接受; **his shyness does not ~ easily with Hollywood tradition** 他的羞怯不太符合好莱坞的传统 **11** Brit Sch, Univ 参加考试; **to ~ for sth.** 参加 ‹*exam*›; **to ~ for the Bar** Jur 参加律师考试
B *vt* **1** (put) 使坐下; **I sat the baby on my lap** 我把宝宝放在腿上坐着; **she sat him by the fire** 她让他坐在炉火边 **2** (be candidate for) 参加 ‹*exam, test*› **3** (accommodate) «*table, bench*» 可坐下; «*auditorium, building*» 能容纳; **how many does the sofa ~?** 这个沙发能坐几个人?

S

C *v refl* **to ～ oneself** 坐下; **he sat himself at the table/desk** 他在桌边/写字台边坐下了

Phrasal verbs

• **sit around, sit about** *vi* 无所事事地闲坐; **to ～ around waiting** 坐着干等

• **sit back** *vi* 1 (lean back) 仰靠着坐; **to ～ back on one's heels** 蜷腿仰靠坐着 2 (relax) 休息; **it's time to ～ back and listen to some soothing music** 现在应该放松下来听一些舒缓的音乐

• **sit by** *vi* 坐视不管

• **sit down**

A *vi* 坐下; **wait till they're all ～ting down** 等到他们都坐好; **please ～ down** 请坐下; **to ～ down to a meal** 坐下来吃饭; **to ～ down and do sth.** 坐下来做某事; **we must ～ down together and settle our differences** 我们必须一起坐下来解决我们之间的分歧

B *vt* [**～ sb. down**] 让…坐下; **they sat him down and gave him a drink** 他们让他坐下，然后递给他一杯饮料

C *v refl* **to ～ oneself down** 坐下; **get a chair/come in and ～ yourself down** 拿把椅子/进来坐下吧

• **sit in** *vi* 1 (as protest) «*students, workers*» 静坐抗议 2 **to ～ in on sth.** (as observer) 旁听 ‹*class*›; 列席 ‹*meeting*› 3 **to ～ in for sb.** (be substitute for) 临时代替某人

• **sit on** *vt* [**～ on sth.**]

1 (be member of) 是…的成员 ‹*jury, board, committee*›; **he has been invited to ～ on the committee** 他受邀担任委员会委员 2 colloq (not deal with) 搁置 ‹*piece of work, document*› 3 colloq (suppress) 不发布 ‹*report, news*›; **I want this story sat on** 我要求把这件事压下来

• **sit out**

A *vi* 坐在外面; **to ～ out in the garden** 坐在花园里

B *vt* [**～ sth. out, ～ out sth.**]

1 (stay to end of) 坚持看完 ‹*performance, play*› 2 (not take part in) 坐在一旁不参加 ‹*game, dance*›; **I think I'll ～ out the tango** 我不想跳探戈舞 3 (wait for end of) 熬到…结束 ‹*storm, air raid*›; fig 对…坐视不管 ‹*crisis, war*›

• **sit through** *vt* [**～ through sth.**] 耐着性子看完 ‹*performance, ceremony*›; 耐着性子听完 ‹*lecture*›

• **sit up**

A *vi* 1 (raise oneself upright) 坐直; **take your elbows off the table and ～ up!** 把胳膊肘从桌子上放下来，坐直！; **the invalid was ～ting up reading** 那位病人坐起来看书了; **to ～ up straight** 坐直; **to make sb. ～ up (and take notice)** fig colloq 使某人警觉起来（开始关注） 2 (stay up late) 熬夜; **to ～ up doing sth.** 熬夜做某事; **to ～ up with sb.** 熬夜照顾某人

B *vt* [**～ sb./sth. up, ～ up sb./sth.**] 使坐起来; **the little girl sat her doll up in the pram** 小姑娘让她的洋娃娃坐在婴儿车里

sitar /ˈsɪtɑː(r), sɪˈtɑː(r)/ ▸**p. 395** *n* 锡塔尔琴 [一种形似吉他的印度弦乐器]

sitcom /ˈsɪtkɒm/ *n* colloq = **situation comedy 1**

sit-down

A *n* 1 Brit colloq (rest) 坐下休息 2 (protest) 静坐抗议

B *adj* 1 (at table) 坐着吃的 ‹*lunch*› 2 (in protest) 静坐的; **a ～ demonstration/protest** 静坐示威/抗议

sit-down strike *n* 静坐罢工

site /saɪt/

A *n* 1 (**building** *or* **construction**) ～ (before building) 地点; (during building) 工地; **on ～** 在工地; **to choose a ～ for sth.** 为某物选址 2 (for camping) 营地 3 (of event, accident) 现场

B *vt* (decide location of) 给…选址 ‹*building, factory*›; **to be ～d in ...** 坐落于…

site: ～ map *n* 网站地图; **～ office** *n* 工地办公室

sit-in *n* 静坐示威; **to stage** *or* **hold a ～** 举行静坐示威

siting /ˈsaɪtɪŋ/ *n* [u] (of building) 选址; (of weaponry) 部署

sits vac /ˌsɪts ˈvæk/ *npl* Brit colloq [报纸等的] 招聘广告

sitter /ˈsɪtə(r)/ *n* 1 (model) [供画像或拍照的] 模特 2 (for children) 保姆; (for the sick) 护工; (for animals) 照看动物的人 3 colloq (easy shot, catch) 机会球; **to miss a ～** 错过机会球 4 (hen) 抱窝母鸡

sitting /ˈsɪtɪŋ/

A *n* 1 (meeting) 开会期 2 Brit (of law court) 开庭期; **in ～** 在开庭 3 (serving period) 一批人就餐时间; **we ate in two ～s** 我们分两批就餐 4 (period of being seated) 坐着的一段时间; **to read a book at one ～** 坐着一口气把书读完 5 (period modelling for artist) 一次当模特儿的时间

B *adj* 1 (seated) 坐着的 ‹*person*›; **to be in a ～ position** 采用坐姿 2 (current) 现任的; **a ～ judge** 任期内的法官

sitting: ～ duck *n* colloq 容易击中的目标; **～ room** *n* Brit 起居室; **～ target** *n* 易受攻击者; **～ tenant** *n* 现有房客

situate /ˈsɪtjʊeɪt, Amer ˈsɪtʃʊeɪt/ *vt* 1 (place, locate) 使…位于 ‹*building, town*› 2 (put into context) 将…置于 ‹*idea, fact, attitude*›; **the book ～s the danger in its real context** 这本书将危险置于真实的情景

situated /ˈsɪtjʊeɪtɪd, Amer ˈsɪtʃʊeɪtɪd/ *adj* 1 (in location) 位于…的; **to be ～ next to/in sth.** 紧挨着某处/位于某处内; **it is ～ in a valley** 它位于山谷中; **conveniently/well/badly ～** 位置便利的/好的/不好的 2 (of circumstances) 处于…状况的; **how are you ～ financially?** 你的经济状况如何？; **to be well/badly ～ (to do sth.)** 处于有利/不利（于做某事）的境况; **how are you ～ for money at the moment?** 你目前钱的问题怎么样了？

situation /ˌsɪtjʊˈeɪʃn, Amer ˌsɪtʃʊ-/ *n* 1 (circumstances) 情况; **in the present economic ～** 在目前的经济形势下; **to get oneself into/out of a ～** 陷入/摆脱某情形 2 (of house, town, school) 位置; **to be in a beautiful ～** 位于风景秀丽的地方 3 formal (job) 职位; **to offer sb. a ～** 给某人提供一个职位; **to look for a ～** 求职

situation comedy *n* 1 [c] (programme) 情景喜剧节目 2 [u] (genre) 情景喜剧

sit-up *n* 仰卧起坐; **to do ～s** 做仰卧起坐

SI unit *n* 国际标准单位

six /sɪks/ ▸**p. 15, p. 521, p. 831**

A *n* 1 (number, quantity) 六; **～ plus two equals eight** 6 加 2 等于 8; **in December nineteen hundred and ～** 在 1906 年 12 月; **we live at (number) ～, Victoria Road** 我们住在维多利亚路 6 号; **her phone number is two ～ double ～** 她的电话号码是 2666; **there are ～ of them** 他们有 6 个人; **to be (all) at ～es and sevens** colloq 乱七八糟; **it's ～ of one and half a dozen of the other** colloq 两者本是一回事; **to be ～ foot** *or* **feet under** colloq 入土了 2 (in time) 6 点钟; **at ～ (o'clock)** 在 6 点 3 (on playing card) 6 点; **the ～ of diamonds** 方块 6 4 (age) 6 岁 5 (in cricket) 六分打; **to hit a ～** 击出六分打; **to hit** *or* **knock sb. for ～** fig colloq 彻底击垮某人

B *adj* 1 (as quantity) 六的; **～ cats** 6 只猫; **～ books** 6 本书; **～ weeks** 6 周 2 (in age) 6 岁的; **he's nearly ～** 他快 6 岁了; **our house is only ～ years old** 我们的房子才造了 6 年 3 (in series) 第六的; **number ～** 6 号; **page ～** 第 6 页

six: Six Counties *pr npl* **the Six Counties** 爱尔兰北部六郡; **～-eight time** *n* 八六拍; **～-footer** colloq *n* 六英尺高的人; **they were both ～-footers** 他俩都有六英尺高; **～-gun** *n* colloq 六发左轮手枪; **～-pack** *n* 1 (of bottles) 六瓶装; (of cans) 六罐装; 2 colloq (muscles) 发达的腹肌; **～pence** *n* 1 Brit (coin) 六便士硬币; 2 (sum of money) [1971年币制改革前的] 六便士; **～penny** *adj attrib* Brit [1971年币制改革前] 值六便士的; **～-shooter** *n* 六发左轮手枪

sixteen /sɪkˈstiːn/ ▸**p. 15, p. 521**

A *n* 1 (number, quantity) 十六 2 (in age) 16 岁

B *adj* 1 (in number) 十六的; **～ metres** 16 米; **～ paintings** 16 张画 2 (in age) 16 岁的; **to be ～ (years old)** 16 岁大; **to be over/under ～** 超过/不到 16 岁 3 (in series) 第十六的; **size/number ～** 16 码/号

sixteenth /sɪkˈstiːnθ/ ▸**p. 181, p. 521**

A *n* 1 (in sequence) 第十六个 2 (in date) 16 日 3 (fraction) 十六分之一

B *adj* 1 (in sequence) 第十六的 2 (in name, title) 十六; **Louis the S～** 路易十六 3 (as fraction) 十六分之一的

C *adv* 1 (sixteenthly) 第十六 2 (in sixteenth position) 居第十六位

sixteenth note *n* Amer = **semiquaver**

sixth /sɪksθ/ ▸**p. 181, p. 521**

A *n* 1 (in sequence) 第六 2 (in date) 6 日 3 (fraction) 六分之一

B *adj* 1 (in sequence) 第六的; **on the ～ floor** 在 7 楼; **it's her ～ birthday** 这是她 6 岁生日 2 (in name, title) 六世; **Henry the S～ of England** 英王亨利六世 3 (as fraction) 六分之一的

C *adv* 1 (sixthly) 第六 2 (in sixth position) 居第六位

sixth form *n* Brit 第六年级

sixth-form college *n* Brit 第六年级学院

sixth former *n* Brit 第六年级学生

sixthly /ˈsɪksθli/ *adv* 第六; **～, they had to adopt a life of poverty** 第六，他们不得不过贫困的生活

sixth sense *n* 第六感觉

sixties /ˈsɪkstɪz/ ▸**p. 15, p. 181** *npl*

1 (decade) **in the ～** 在 60 年代; **the swinging ～** 活跃的 60 年代 2 (age) 六十多岁; **to be in one's ～** 六十多岁了 3 (temperature) 60 度; **temperatures climbed into the ～** 温度攀升至 60 度

sixtieth /ˈsɪkstɪəθ/ ▸**p. 521**

A *n* 1 (in sequence) 第六十个 2 (fraction) 六十分之一

B *adj* 1 (in sequence) 第六十的 2 (as fraction) 六十分之一的

C *adv* 1 (sixtiethly) 第六十 2 (in sixtieth position) 居第六十位

sixty /ˈsɪksti/ ▸**p. 15, p. 521**

A *n* 1 (number, quantity) 六十; **there are ～ of us** 我们有 60 个人 2 (in age) 60 岁

B *adj* 1 (in number) 六十的; **～ boys** 60 个男孩 2 (in age) 60 岁的; **I'm nearly ～** 我快 60 岁了 3 (in series) 第六十的

sixty: ～-four thousand dollar question *n* colloq 关键问题; **～ nine** *n* [u] colloq 相互口交 [两人身体姿势如69]

six: ～ yard area, ～ yard box *ns* 六码区; **～ yard line** *n* 六码线

sizable /ˈsaɪzəbl/ *adj* = **sizeable**

sizably /ˈsaɪzəbli/ *adv* = **sizeably**

size¹ /saɪz/

A *n* 1 [u and c] (dimensions) 大小; **the same ～** 一样大; **a building of vast ～** 巨大的建筑物; **of some ～** 很大的; **chairs of all ～s** 各种大小的椅子; **a good ～** 不算小; **what's the ～ of the house?** 这房子有多大？; **they were shocked by the ～ of his debts** 他的巨额债务让他们感到震惊; **forests the ～ of Wales** 面积和威尔士一样大的森林; **to increase** *or* **grow in ～** «*plant, tree*» 长高; «*town, area*» 变大; **to be of a ～** «*boxes, containers, people*» 同样大; **the two girls are of a ～** 两个女孩身高相当; **that's (about) the ～ of it** colloq 情况大概就是这样; **to ～** 尺寸合适; **to cut sb. down to ～** 使某人有自知之明 2 [u and c] (number) 数量; **what's the ～**

of the population of China? 中国的人口数量是多少?; **schools/firms of all ~s** 各种规模的学校/公司; **to increase** *or* **grow in ~** «*town, company*» 规模得到扩大; **the school has grown in ~ and now has 900 pupils** 学校规模扩大了，现在有 900 名学生 **3** [c] Clothg (standard measurement) 尺码; **what ~ do you take?** 你穿多大号?; **a small/large/medium ~** 小号/大号/中号; **~ 36 shoes** 36 号鞋; **one ~ fits all** 均码; **to try sth. (on) for ~** 试试某物看尺码是否合适; fig 试试某事物看是否合适; **what ~ are you?** 你穿多大尺码?

B **-size** *combining form* = **-sized**

C *vt* **1** (grade) «*person, machine*» 标定…的大小 ‹*items*› **2** (change size of) «*jeweller*» 改变…的大小 ‹*ring*›; Comput 调节…的大小 ‹*window, font*›

Phrasal verb

- **size up** *vt* [~ **sb./sth. up**, ~ **up sb./sth.**] colloq 估量 ‹*problem, surroundings*›; 评价 ‹*person*›; **to ~ up the situation** 判断形势; **to ~ up who/what/where ...** 琢磨谁/什么/哪里…; **to ~ up what is going on** 判断发生了什么事

size²

A *n* [u] (sealer, filler) 浆料

B *vt* 给…上浆 ‹*textile, paper*›; 给…上涂料 ‹*wall*›

sizeable /ˈsaɪzəbl/ *adj* 相当大的 ‹*house, portion*›; 相当多的 ‹*inheritance*›; 大块头的 ‹*person*›; **the Democrats have a ~ majority in the House** 民主党在众议院占明显多数

sizeably /ˈsaɪzəbli/ *adv* 相当大地

-sized /saɪzd/ *combining form* …大小的; **a small/medium~ dress** 小号/中号连衣裙; **Jumbo/man~** 特大的/如人一般大的; **marble~ hailstones** 石块大小的冰雹

sizeism /ˈsaɪzɪzəm/ *n* [u] 体形歧视

sizzle /ˈsɪzl/

A *n* 嗞嗞声

B *vi* 发出嗞嗞声; **to ~ away** 嗞嗞响着变小

sizzler /ˈsɪzlə(r)/ *n* colloq 大热天

sizzling /ˈsɪzlɪŋ/ *adj* **1** (hissing) 嗞嗞作响的 ‹*fat, bacon, sausages*›; **a ~ sound** 嗞嗞声 **2** colloq (hot) 灼热的 **3** colloq (erotic) 激情热辣的 ‹*magazine, film*›

ska /skɑː/ *n* [u] 斯卡 [一种源于牙买加、盛行于20世纪60年代的流行乐]

skag /skæg/ *n* [u] colloq = **heroin**

skanky /ˈskæŋki/ *adj* Amer colloq 倒胃口的

skate¹ /skeɪt/

A *n* **1** (for ice) 冰鞋; **to get** *or* **put one's ~s on** 穿上冰鞋; fig (hurry up) 赶紧 **2** (roller skate) 轮滑旱冰鞋; (in-line skate) 直排轮滑旱冰鞋

B *vt* 滑出 ‹*figure*›; **to ~ one's way to sth.** fig 靠滑冰获得某物

C *vi* 滑冰; **to ~ across** *or* **over ...** 在…上滑冰; **to go skating** 去溜冰; **to be skating on thin ice** fig 冒风险

Phrasal verbs

- **skate around** *vt* [~ **around sth.**] 回避 ‹*problem, requirement*›
- **skate over** *vt* [~ **over sth.**] 对…一带而过 ‹*issue, fact*›
- **skate round** *vt* Brit = **skate around**

skate² *n* (*pl* ~ *or* ~**s**) **1** [c] (fish) 鳐 **2** [u] (flesh) 鳐肉

skateboard /ˈskeɪtbɔːd/

A *n* 滑板

B *vi* 踩滑板

skate: ~boarder *n* 滑板运动员; **~boarding** ▸**p. 307** *n* [u] 滑板运动; **to go ~boarding** 去踩滑板; **~park** *n* 滑板运动场

skater /ˈskeɪtə(r)/ *n* (on ice skates) 滑冰的人; (on roller skates or in-line skates) 滑轮滑旱冰的人; (on skateboard) 踩滑板的人

skating /ˈskeɪtɪŋ/ ▸**p. 307**

A *n* [u] (on ice) 滑冰; (on roller skates or in-line skates) 滑轮滑旱冰; **to go ice/roller ~** 去滑冰/去溜旱冰

B *modif* (on ice) 滑冰的; (on roller skates or in-line skates) 滑旱冰的

skating: ~ boots *npl* Brit 冰鞋; **~ rink** *n* (ice) 滑冰场; (for roller-skating) 旱冰场

skedaddle /skɪˈdædl/ *vi* colloq 匆匆离开

skein /skeɪn/ *n* **1** (of wool) [羊毛或线的] 一束 **2** (of geese, swans) [野禽的] 一群

skeletal /ˈskelɪtl/ *adj* **1** (relating to skeleton) 骨骼的; **~ muscles** 骨骼肌; **the ~ structure** 骨架; **~ remains** 骨骼残骸 **2** (emaciated) 骨瘦如柴的 ‹*person, body*› **3** (outline) 梗概性的; **a ~ plot for a novel** 小说的情节梗概

skeleton /ˈskelɪtn/

A *n* **1** (bone framework) 骨架; **a living** *or* **walking ~** 骨瘦如柴的人; **to be reduced to a ~** 瘦得皮包骨; **to have a ~ in the cupboard** fig 有不可外扬的家丑 **2** (study aid) 骨骼标本 **3** (framework) 构架; **the ~ of a building** 建筑物的构架 **4** (outline) 纲要; **we have the ~ of a plan/the novel** 我们有计划/小说的框架

B *modif* 概要的; **a ~ plan/project/scheme** 概要的计划/方案/安排; **a ~ staff** 骨干人员

skeletonize /ˈskelɪtnaɪz/ *vt* 使…成骨架 ‹*remains*›; 使…减到最小 ‹*organism*›; **larvae ~ leaves in early season** 幼虫在初春时把叶子蛀得只剩叶脉

skeleton key *n* 万能钥匙

skeptic /ˈskeptɪk/ *n* Amer = **sceptic**

skeptical /ˈskeptɪkl/ *adj* Amer = **sceptical**

skeptically /ˈskeptɪkli/ *adv* Amer = **sceptically**

skepticism /ˈskeptɪsɪzəm/ *n* Amer = **scepticism**

sketch /sketʃ/

A *n* **1** Art (drawing, painting) 素描; **a ~ of sth./sb.** 某物/某人的素描; **to draw** *or* **make a ~ of sb./sth.** 为某人/某物画素描; **a quick ~** 速写; **a rough ~** 草图 **2** (brief account) 概述; **a biographical ~ of Ernest Hemingway** 欧内斯特·海明威的生平简介 **3** (on stage, TV, radio) 幽默短剧; (in newspaper) 小品文

B *vi* 画素描

C *vt* **1** Art 为…画素描 ‹*person, scene*›; **to ~ sb.'s likeness** 为某人画素描; **to ~ the outline of sth.** 画出某物的轮廓 **2** (describe briefly) 简要说明; **a briefly ~ed history of the town** 该镇的简史

Phrasal verbs

- **sketch in** *vt* [~ **sth. in**, ~ **in sth.**] **1** Art 草草把…画入 **2** (add brief details to) 简要补充 ‹*details, background*›
- **sketch out** *vt* [~ **sth. out**, ~ **out sth.**] **1** Art 画出…的草图 ‹*composition, outline*› **2** (outline) 简述 ‹*plot, policy, agenda*›

sketchbook /ˈsketʃbʊk/ *n* 素描本

sketchily /ˈsketʃɪli/ *adv* 粗略地

sketch: ~ map *n* 草图; **~pad** *n* 速写簿

sketchy /ˈsketʃi/ *adj* (lacking thoroughness) 粗略的 ‹*information, account, details*›; (rough) 草草完成的 ‹*essay, work*›

skew /skjuː/

A *vt* **1** (distort) 歪曲 ‹*result, data, view*›; (bias) 使…有倾向性 ‹*distribution, priority*›; **to ~ sth. towards** *or* **in favour of sth.** 使某事倾向于某事 **2** (angle) 使…歪斜 ‹*structure, object*› **3** (change heading of) 使…偏斜 ‹*vehicle, aircraft, ball*›

B *vi* «*vehicle, aircraft, ball*» ~ **(round)** 偏斜

C *n* (angle) 斜角; (slant) 倾斜度; **on the ~** 倾斜的

D *adj* 斜的; **a ~ angle/picture/edge** 斜角/倾斜的画/斜边

skewbald /ˈskjuːbɔːld/

A *n* 白花斑马

B *adj* 白花斑的

skewer /ˈskjuːə(r)/

A *n* 串肉扦

B *vt* 用串肉扦串

skew-whiff /ˌskjuːˈwɪf/ *adv* Brit colloq 歪斜地; **he had his hat on ~** 他歪戴着帽子

ski /skiː/

A *n* **1** (for snow) 滑雪板; **cross-country ~s** 越野滑雪板; **a ~ suit** 滑雪服 **2** (for water) 滑水橇 **3** (on aircraft) 滑橇

B *vi* (*pt, pp* **ski'd** *or* **~ed**) 滑雪

ski: ~ binding *n* 雪靴固定装置; **~ boot** *n* 滑雪靴; **~ club** *n* 滑雪俱乐部

skid /skɪd/

A *vi* (*pres p etc.* **-dd-**) «*person, car, lorry, driver*» 打滑; **to ~ into a wall/off the road** 打滑撞到墙上/滑出路面; **to ~ to a halt** 滑行一段后停下来

B *n* **1** (slide) 打滑; **to go** *or* **get into a ~** 打滑; **to be on/hit the ~s** 每况愈下/开始衰落 **2** (runner) 滑橇; **to put the ~s under sb./sth.** 加速某人的失败/某事的衰败

skid: ~ mark *n* [车辆的] 打滑痕迹; **~pan** *n* Brit [供驾车者练习防滑技术的] 转向试验场

Skidoo® /skɪˈduː/, **skidoo** *n* 摩托雪橇

skid: ~ road *n* Amer **1** (log track) 木材滑道; **2** = **~ row**; **~ row** *n* Amer colloq **1** (area) [流浪汉和酒鬼聚集的] 贫民区; **2** (bad situation) 绝境; **to be/end up on ~ row** 处于/陷入绝境

skier /ˈskiːə(r)/ *n* 滑雪者

skies /skaɪz/ *pl* ▸**sky**

skiff /skɪf/ *n* (working boat) [通常为单人的] 小划艇; (for racing) 小赛艇

skiffle /ˈskɪfl/ *n* [u] [流行于20世纪50年代的] 噪音爵士乐

ski hat *n* 滑雪帽

skiing /ˈskiːɪŋ/ ▸**p. 307** *n* [u] (activity) 滑雪; (sport) 滑雪运动

skiing: ~ holiday *n* 滑雪假期; **~ instructor** ▸**p. 409** *n* 滑雪教练; **~ resort** *n* 滑雪旅游胜地

ski: ~ instructor ▸**p. 409** *n* = **skiing instructor**; **~ jump** *n* **1** (jump) 跳台滑雪; **2** (ramp) 跳台滑雪助滑道; **3** (event) 跳台滑雪比赛; **~ jumper** *n* 跳台滑雪运动员; **~ jumping** *n* [u] ▸**p. 307** (sport) 跳台滑雪运动; (activity) 跳台滑雪

skilful /ˈskɪlfl/ *adj* Brit **1** (proficient) 娴熟的 ‹*driver, doctor, gardener*›; **~ at sth.** 在某方面很熟练的; **~ at doing ...** 做…很熟练的; **~ with one's hands/feet** 手巧的/脚灵活的 **2** (requiring proficiency) 需要高超技术的 ‹*operation*›

skilfully /ˈskɪlfəli/ *adv* Brit 娴熟地 ‹*play, work, perform*›; 精妙地 ‹*constructed, carved*›; 巧妙地 ‹*worded*›

skilfulness /ˈskɪlflnɪs/ *n* Brit [u] (mental) 老练; (physical) 娴熟; **her ~ at negotiating** 她的谈判技巧老练; **my ~ as a negotiator/writer** 我熟练的谈判/写作技巧

ski lift *n* [运送滑雪者的] 上山吊椅

skill /skɪl/ *n* **1** [u] (ability) 能力; **~ in** *or* **at doing ...** 做…的能力; **to have ~** 有能力; **with ~** 熟练地; **a writer of great ~** 颇为老练的作家 **2** [c] (for a particular activity) 专长; **to acquire/learn a ~** 获得/学习一门技术; **language ~s** 语言技能; **her ~s as a linguist/mechanic** 她的语言学专长/机械师的技能; **the necessary ~s for the job** 做这份工作必需的技能; **to have no social ~s** 没有社交能力

skilled /skɪld/ *adj* **1** (proficient) 熟练的 ‹*teacher, musician, doctor*›; 老练的 ‹*negotiator, diplomat*›; **to be ~ in** *or* **at sth.** 在某方面很熟练; **to be ~ in the use of ...** 在使用…上很娴熟; **to be ~ at translation** 擅长翻译; **a ~ worker/labour force** 熟练工/熟练劳动力 **2** *attrib* (requiring skill) 技术性的 ‹*job,* *occupation*›; ~ **and semi-~ work** 技术性和半技术性工作

skillet /ˈskɪlɪt/ *n* **1** Amer (for frying) 长柄平底煎锅 **2** Brit dated (for general cooking) 长柄小烧锅

skillful /ˈskɪlfl/ *adj* Amer = **skilful**

skillfully /ˈskɪlfəli/ *adv* Amer = **skilfully**

skillfulness /ˈskɪlflnɪs/ *n* Amer = **skilfulness**

skill: ~ **level** *n* 技术水平; ~ **sharing** *n* [u] 技术分享; **~s shortage** *n* 技术短缺

skim /skɪm/

A *vt* (*pres p etc.* **-mm-**) **1** (remove) 撇去 ‹*cream, fat, scum*›; **to ~ sth. from** *or* **off sth.** 把某物从某物上撇掉 **2** (remove surface of) 撇去…上的浮沫 ‹*stock, jam*› **3** colloq (embezzle) 盗用 ‹*money, amount*› **4** Amer colloq (not declare) 瞒报 ‹*part of income*› **5** (copy fraudulently) 仿制 ‹*credit card, debt card*› **6** (pass lightly over) «*flying insect, speedboat*» 掠过 ‹*treetops, sea*›; **swallows ~ming the surface of the lake** 掠过湖面的燕子; **the article only ~s the surface of the problem** fig 这篇文章只谈了问题的皮毛 **7** (bounce across water) 拿…打水漂 ‹*pebble*› **8** (read quickly) 浏览 ‹*newspaper, report*›; **I always ~ the financial section of the newspaper** 我总要浏览一下报纸的财经版

B *vi* (*pres p etc.* **-mm-**) **1** (pass lightly) «*bird, speedboat*» 掠过; **to ~ over sth.** 从某物上掠过 **2** (read quickly) «*reader, eye*» 浏览; **to ~ through an article/a magazine** 浏览文章/杂志 **3** (give little attention to) **to ~ over sth.** 忽略某事物; **his speech ~med over the unpalatable facts** 他在讲话中没有提那些令人不快的事实 **4** Amer Tax colloq (not declare full income) 瞒报收入

C *n* **1** (thin layer of plaster, cement) 薄层 **2** (quick read) 浏览; **a quick ~ through the pamphlet** 对小册子的快速浏览

Phrasal verb

- **skim off** *vt* [~ **sth. off,** ~ **off sth.**] 撇去 ‹*grease, scum*›; **to ~ off sth. from sth.** 从某物上撇掉某物; **to ~ off the cream from the top of the milk** 撇掉牛奶表层的奶油

ski mask *n* [露出眼、鼻和嘴的] 滑雪头罩

skimmed milk /ˌskɪmd ˈmɪlk/ Brit *n* [u] 脱脂奶

skimmer /ˈskɪmə(r)/ *n* Culin 撇油漏勺

skim milk *n* Amer = **skimmed milk**

skimp /skɪmp/ *vi* 节省; **to ~ on ...** 节省 ‹*paint, food*›; 在…方面吝啬 ‹*insurance*›

skimpily /ˈskɪmpɪli/ *adv* 敷衍了事地 ‹*made*›; 不足地 ‹*feed, provide*›; 短而暴露地 ‹*clothed, dress*›

skimpiness /ˈskɪmpɪnɪs/ *n* [u] (of portion, income) 不足; (of clothing) 短而暴露

skimpy /ˈskɪmpi/ *adj* 短而暴露的 ‹*dress, clothing*›; 不足的 ‹*portion, income*›; 敷衍了事的 ‹*piece of work*›

skin /skɪn/

A *n* **1** [u and c] (of person, live animal) 皮肤; **to have dry/greasy/sensitive ~** 皮肤为干性/油性/过敏性; **to be no ~ off one's nose** *or* **back** fig colloq 不关自己的事; **by the ~ of one's teeth** fig colloq 勉强; **to get under sb.'s ~** fig colloq (irritate) 惹恼某人; (attract) 吸引某人; **to have sb. under one's ~** fig colloq 迷恋某人; **to jump out of one's ~** fig colloq 吓一大跳; **to be nothing but** *or* **to be all ~ and bone(s)** fig colloq 瘦得皮包骨头; **to have a thin/thick ~** fig colloq 脸皮薄/厚; **a ~ like a rhinoceros** 皮糙肉厚 [指对批评或攻击不敏感]; **to save one's (own) ~** 保全自己; **to be/get soaked** *or* **wet to the ~** 浑身湿透/弄得浑身湿透 **2** [u and c] (of dead animal) 兽皮 **3** [c] (of fruit, vegetable) 表皮 **4** [c] (of sausage) 肠衣 **5** (on hot milk) 奶皮; (on hot cocoa) 薄层 **6** (outer layer of ship, plane) 外壳 **7** colloq = **skinhead**

B *vt* (*pres p etc.* **-nn-**) **1** (remove skin from) 剥去…的皮 ‹*animal*›; 去…的表皮 ‹*fruit, vegetable*›; **to keep one's eyes ~ned (for sb./sth.)** 密切注意（某人/某事物） **2** (graze) 擦破 ‹*knees, elbow*› **3** Amer colloq 欺骗

skin: ~ **cancer** ▸p. 377 *n* [u and c] 皮肤癌; ~ **care** *n* [u] 皮肤护理; ~ **cream** *n* [c and u] 护肤霜; **~-deep** *adj* 表面的 ‹*commitment*›; ~ **disease** *n* 皮肤病; ~ **diver** *n* 自由潜水者; ~ **diving** ▸p. 307 *n* [u] 自由潜水; ~ **flick** *n* Brit colloq 色情电影; **~flint** *n* colloq 吝啬鬼

skinful /ˈskɪnfʊl/ *n* Brit colloq 足以喝醉的量; **he's had a ~** 他喝得烂醉; **a ~ of sth.** 足以让人喝醉的某物

skin: ~ **graft** *n* **1** (operation) 植皮; **2** (grafted area) 皮移植片; **~head** *n* 光头仔 [崇尚暴力的青年种族主义者]; ~ **lotion** *n* [u and c] 润肤液

-skinned /skɪnd/ *combining form* 有…皮肤的; **dark/fair~** 皮肤黑/白皙的; **thin/thick~** 脸皮薄/厚的

skinner /ˈskɪnə(r)/ *n* **1** (person who prepares skins) 兽皮加工者 **2** (dealer in skins) 皮革商

skinny /ˈskɪni/ *adj* colloq **1** (thin) 瘦得皮包骨的 ‹*person, arms, legs*› **2** (tight-fitting) 紧身的 ‹*garment, top, jeans*›

skinny: **~-dip** *vi* colloq 裸泳; **~-dipping** *n* [u] colloq 裸泳; **~-rib, ~-rib sweater** *ns* 紧身毛衫

skint /skɪnt/ *adj* Brit colloq 身无分文的

skin: ~ **test** *n* 皮试; **~tight** *adj* 紧身的 ‹*jeans, top*›

skip /skɪp/

A *vi* (*pres p etc.* **-pp-**) **1** (jump) «*child, animal*» 蹦蹦跳跳地走; **he came along the road, ~ping and jumping** 他一路连蹦带跳地走来; **to ~ with joy** 高兴得跳起来; **to ~ about** 四处蹦跳; fig «*writer*» 不停地转换话题; **a speaker ~ping about from subject to subject** 一再转换话题的演讲者 **2** Brit (with rope) 跳绳 **3** colloq (from one place to another) 赶去; (from one thing to another) 跳到; **to ~ from A to B** 从A处赶去B处; **I suggest we ~ to the next item on the agenda** 我建议我们跳到下一项日程; **to ~ over sth.** «*reader*» 跳过某段落

B *vt* (*pres p etc.* **-pp-**) **1** (not attend) 不参加 ‹*appointment, event*›; **he's in trouble for ~ping classes** 他因为逃课有麻烦了; **to ~ school/the exams** 逃学/逃避考试 **2** (leave out, miss) 省略; **try not to ~ breakfast** 尽量不要不吃早饭; **you can ~ the formalities** 不必多礼; **my heart ~ped a beat** 我的心里咯噔一下; **~ it!** colloq 不提这个! **3** (not read or view) «*reader*» 跳过 ‹*chapter, section*›; **I read the whole report very carefully, without ~ping a single page** 我一页不漏地仔细读了整篇报告 **4** colloq (flee) «*criminal, fugitive*» 逃离 ‹*country, town*› **5** (jump over) 跳过 ‹*puddle, low obstacle*›; **to ~ rope** Amer 跳绳 **6** (skim) 拿…打水漂 ‹*pebble*›

C *n* **1** (jump) 蹦跳 **2** Brit (for rubbish) 废料桶

Phrasal verb

- **skip off** *vi* colloq 溜走; **I'm not giving them a chance to ~ off again** 我不会再让他们有机会开溜的

ski: ~ **pants** *npl* **1** (women's trousers) 踏脚健美裤; **2** (skiing trousers) 滑雪裤; **~-plane** *n* 雪上飞机; ~ **pole** *n* 滑雪杖

skipper /ˈskɪpə(r)/

A *n* **1** (of ship) 船长 **2** (of team) 队长 **3** (of aircraft) 机长

B *vt* 当…的船长 ‹*boat*›; 当…的队长 ‹*team*›; 当…的机长 ‹*aircraft*›

skipping /ˈskɪpɪŋ/ *n* [u] 跳绳

skipping: ~ **rhyme** *n* 跳绳童谣; ~ **rope** *n* Brit 跳绳

skip rope *n* Amer **1** [c] = **skipping rope** **2** [u] (game) 双摇跳绳游戏

ski: ~ **racer** *n* (cross-country) 越野滑雪赛选手; (downhill) 滑降赛选手; ~ **racing** ▸p. 307 *n* [u] (cross-country) 越野滑雪赛; (downhill) 滑降赛; ~ **resort** *n* 滑雪胜地

skirl /skɜːl/ *n* [风笛等发出的] 尖厉高音

skirmish /ˈskɜːmɪʃ/

A *n* **1** Mil (minor battle) 小规模战斗 **2** (between gangs, protesters) 打斗; **a ~ between sb. and sb.** 某人与某人间的小打小闹; **a ~ with sb.** 与某人发生的小打小闹 **3** (argument) 争执

B *vi* «*soldiers, ship, patrol*» 进行小规模战斗; **to ~ with sb.** 与某人发生冲突; **the leader of the opposition ~ed with ministers in the debate** 辩论中反对派领导人与部长们发生了交锋

skirt /skɜːt/

A *n* **1** [c] (garment) 裙子; **to cling to one's mother's ~s** 依赖母亲 **2** [c] (part of dress) 裙摆; (part of coat) 下摆 **3** [c] (of vehicle, machine) 挡板 **4** [u] colloq (women) 骚妞 **5** [u] Brit (cut of beef) 牛腩

B *vt* **1** (move along edge of) 沿…的边缘走 ‹*field, town, lake*› **2** (avoid) 回避 ‹*issue, problem*›

Phrasal verb

- **skirt around,** esp Brit **skirt round** *vt* [~ **round sth.**] **1** (move along edge of) 绕…的边缘前行 ‹*field, town, lake*› **2** (avoid) 回避 ‹*issue, problem*›

skirting /ˈskɜːtɪŋ/ *n* [u] **1** Brit (in room) 踢脚板 **2** (fabric) 裙料

skirting board *n* Brit 踢脚板

skirt length *n* **1** (piece of fabric) 一块裙料 **2** (measurement) 裙长

ski: ~ **run** *n* 滑雪道; ~ **slope** *n* 滑雪坡; ~ **suit** *n* 滑雪服

skit /skɪt/ *n* (parody) 滑稽短剧; (sketch) 幽默小品文; **a ~ on sth.** 讽刺某事的小品文

ski: ~ **touring** ▸p. 307 *n* [u] 滑雪旅行; ~ **tow** *n* [运送滑雪者的] 上山缆车

skitter /ˈskɪtə(r)/

A *vi* (skim) «*bird, insect*» 飞掠; «*stone*» 掠过

B *vt* (in fishing) 沿水面拉动 ‹*bait*›

skittish /ˈskɪtɪʃ/ *adj* **1** (nervous) 受惊难以驾驭的 ‹*horse, behaviour*› **2** (playful) 易变而顽皮的 ‹*person, behaviour*›

skittishly /ˈskɪtɪʃli/ *adv* **1** (unpredictably) 易变地 ‹*act, behave*› **2** (playfully) 顽皮地 ‹*act, behave*›

skittle /ˈskɪtl/

A *n* [撞柱游戏的] 木柱

B **skittles** ▸p. 307 *npl* + *v sing* 撞柱游戏

skittle alley *n* 撞柱游戏球道

skive /skaɪv/ Brit colloq

A *vi* 逃避工作

B *n* **1** (easy job) 轻松的活儿 **2** (absence) 逃避工作; **to be on the ~** 溜掉

Phrasal verb

- **skive off** Brit colloq

A *vi* 溜走

B *vt* [~ **off sth.**] 逃避 ‹*work, duty*›; **to ~ off school** 逃学

skiver /ˈskaɪvə(r)/ *n* Brit colloq 开溜的人

skivvy[1] /ˈskɪvi/ Brit colloq

A *n* **1** (servant) 下等女佣 **2** (menial worker) 干粗活儿的人; **to treat sb. like a ~** 如使唤丫头般对待某人

B *vi* 做下等女佣的活儿; **to ~ for sb.** 为某人干粗活儿

skivvy[2] Amer colloq

A *n* (T-shirt, vest) 男式汗衫

B **skivvies®** *npl* (underwear) 男式内衣

Skopje /ˈskɒpjeɪ/ *pr n* 斯科普里

skua /ˈskjuːə/ *n* 贼鸥

skulduggery /skʌlˈdʌgəri/ *n* [u] colloq 阴谋

skulk /skʌlk/ *vi* 鬼鬼祟祟地活动; **to ~ in/out** 溜进/溜出; **to ~ about** 鬼鬼祟祟地走动; **to ~ off** 溜走

skull /skʌl/ *n* 1 (bone structure) 颅骨; **he has a fractured ~** 他颅骨破裂 2 fig colloq (brain, head) 脑筋; **to have a thick ~** 笨头笨脑

skull: ~ and crossbones *n* (emblem) 骷髅图; (flag) 骷髅旗; **~ cap** *n* 1 (Catholic, Jewish) 无檐便帽; 2 (helmet) 防护帽

skunk /skʌŋk/ *n* 1 [c] (animal) 臭鼬 2 [u] (fur) 臭鼬皮 3 [c] colloq pej (person) 讨厌的人

sky /skaɪ/

A *n* [u and c] 天空; **a clear/cloudy ~** 晴朗/多云的天空; **a blue/sunny ~** 蓝天/晴空; **a patch of blue ~** 一小块蓝天; **a starry ~** 星空; **the night ~** 夜空; **in the ~** 在天上; **the sun climbed up into the ~** 太阳升起来了; **to see nothing but sea and ~** 只见海天茫茫; **to sleep under the open ~** 露天睡觉; **the ~'s the limit** colloq 无穷尽; **to reach for the ~** colloq 志向远大; **out of a** *or* **the (clear) blue ~** colloq 晴天霹雳; **red ~ at night, shepherd's** *or* **sailor's delight; red ~ in the morning, shepherd's** *or* **sailor's warning** Prov 晚霞旅人笑盈盈，朝霞旅人慎出行

B **skies** *npl* 天气; **clear/blue skies** 晴朗的天气; **a day of cloudy skies** 多云的一天; **starry skies** 繁星点点的天空; **to take to the skies** 起飞; **to praise** *or* **laud sb./sth. to the skies** fig 把某人/某事物捧上天; **there are blue skies ahead** fig 前景看好

C *vt* Sport 把…击向高空; **to ~ a ball** *or* **shot** 打高球; **to ~ a ball out of the ground/bunker** 把球高高地击离地面/沙坑

sky blue ▸**p. 134**

A *n* [u] 天蓝色

B *adj* 天蓝色的

sky-blue pink *n* [u] hum 天蓝粉红色 [指不存在的颜色]; **Bill could swear that black was white, or green was ~** 比尔会信誓旦旦地把黑说成白，或把绿色说成天蓝粉红色

sky: ~box *n* Amer 贵宾包厢; **~cap** *n* Amer 机场行李工; **~dive** *vi* 进行特技跳伞; **~diver** *n* 特技跳伞者; **~diving** ▸**p. 307** *n* [u] 特技跳伞

sky-high

A *adj* 1 (very high) 高耸的 ‹*structure*›; 很高的 ‹*ceiling*› 2 (at very high level) 极高的 ‹*prices, rate, premiums*›; (very great) 极大的 ‹*ambition, expectation, confidence*›

B *adv* 1 (high up) 在高空; **to rise ~** 升到高空; **to blow sth. ~** 彻底摧毁某物 2 (at or to high level) 极高地

skyjack /ˈskaɪdʒæk/

A *n* 劫机

B *vt* 空中劫持

sky: ~jacker *n* 劫机者; **~jacking** *n* 劫机

skylark /ˈskaɪlɑːk/

A *n* 云雀

B *vi* 嬉闹

skylarking /ˈskaɪlɑːkɪŋ/ *n* [u] 嬉闹

skylight /ˈskaɪlaɪt/ *n* 天窗

skylight filter *n* 天光滤光片

sky: ~line *n* (in countryside) 地平线; (in city) [建筑物、高山等在天空映衬下的] 空中轮廓线; **~ marshal** *n* Amer 空中警察

skyrocket /ˈskaɪrɒkɪt/

A *n* [作为信号或焰火的] 冲天火箭

B *vi* 飞涨

sky: ~scape *n* (view) 天空景色; (picture) 天空景色画; **~scraper** *n* 摩天大楼; **~ train** *n* 空中列车; **~walk** *n* [大楼间的] 人行天桥

skyward /ˈskaɪwəd/, **skywards** /ˈskaɪwədz/

A *adj* 朝向天空的

B *adv* 朝天空

sky: ~way *n* 1 (aircraft route) 航线; 2 (walkway) [大楼间的] 人行天桥; 3 (motorway) 高架公路; **~writing** *n* [u] [飞机释放烟雾形成的] 空中文字

slab /slæb/ *n* 1 (of stone, wood) 厚板; **a ~ of marble** 一块大理石板 2 (of meat, cheese, cake, chocolate) 大块 3 (in rock climbing) 石板 4 colloq (operating table) 手术台; (mortuary table) 停尸台

slack /slæk/

A *adj* 1 (loose, limp) 松垂的 ‹*rope*›; 松弛的 ‹*muscles, skin*›; **to go ~** 松开; **his mouth went ~** 他的嘴巴微张开来; **to have a ~ grip on sth.** 对某物抓得不紧 2 pej (negligent) 懒散的 ‹*worker, student*›; **to get** *or* **grow ~** 变得懒散; **to be ~ (in) doing sth./at** *or* **about sth.** 做某事/在某事物上马虎 3 pej (lax) 松懈的 ‹*organization, discipline*›; **to get** *or* **grow ~** 变得松懈 4 (not busy) 萧条的 ‹*market, conditions*›; 疲软的 ‹*sales*›; 生意清淡的 ‹*week*›; **business/trading is ~** 生意/贸易不景气; **the ~ period/season (of the year)** 萧条期/（一年中的）淡季 5 (sluggish) 缓慢的 ‹*current, pace*›; 柔和的 ‹*winds*›; 缓慢流动的 ‹*area of water*›

B *n* [u] 1 (sag, looseness) 松弛; **there's too much ~ (in the rope)** （绳子）太松了; **there's very little ~ in the budget** 预算很紧; **to take** *or* **pick up the ~** 收紧松弛处; fig 提高使用效率; **take up the ~!** (in sail) 把帆收紧！; **to cut (sb.) some ~** Amer sl （对某人）宽容一些 2 fig (lull, reduced activity) 松懈; **there is no ~ in my day** 我在工作日里根本没有空闲; **to have little ~ in the day** 整日不得空闲; **economic ~, ~ in the economy** 经济萧条; **to pick up the ~** Econ 提振不景气的状况 3 (coal) 煤屑

C **slacks** *npl* 便裤; **a pair of ~s** 一条便裤

D *vi* Brit colloq **to be ~ing** (be idle) 懒散; (work slowly) 工作懈怠; **stop ~ing!** 别松松垮垮的!

E *vt* 1 (loosen) 松开 ‹*rope*› 2 (reduce) 放缓 ‹*pace*›; 减少 ‹*activity*›

Phrasal verbs

- **slack off** *vi* = **slacken off B1**
- **slack up** *vi* = **slacken up**

slacken /ˈslækən/

A *vi* 1 (loosen) «*rope, reins, nut*» 变松弛 2 (diminish) «*pace, speed*» 慢下来; «*pressure, enthusiasm, sales*» 降低; «*gale, rain, wind*» 减弱; «*trade*» 萎缩; **to ~ in one's efforts** 放松努力

B *vt* 1 (loosen) 松开 ‹*reins, rope, cable*›; 减少 ‹*pressure*›; **to ~ one's grip** *or* **hold (on sth.)** 放松（对某物的）抓握 2 (make slower) 减缓; **to ~ one's pace** 放慢脚步

Phrasal verbs

- **slacken off**

A *vt* [**~ sth. off, ~ off sth.**] 松开 ‹*cable, nut, bolt*›

B *vi* 1 (subside) «*gale, wind*» 减弱; «*business*» 不景气; «*demand*» 萎缩 2 (slow down) «*person, driver*» 减速

- **slacken up** *vi* 减少活动量

slackening /ˈslækənɪŋ/ *n* [u] (of grip, rope, reins) 变松; (of discipline) 松懈; (of skin) 松弛; (of pace, speed) 减慢; (of business, trade, economy) 不景气; (of demand) 萎缩; (of tension) 缓和; **a ~ of sth.** 某物的减少; **a ~ in sth.** 某方面的减少

slacker /ˈslækə(r)/ *n* colloq 懒鬼

slackly /ˈslækli/ *adv* 松弛地

slackness /ˈslæknɪs/ *n* [u] (of worker, student) 懒散; (in trade, business, economy) 不景气; (in discipline, security) 松懈

slack water *n* [u] 憩流

slag /slæg/ *n* 1 [u] (from coal mining) 煤渣 2 [u] Brit (from metal smelting) 熔渣 3 [c] Brit colloq pej (promiscuous woman) 荡妇

Phrasal verb

- **slag off** *vt* [**~ off sb./sth., ~ sb./sth. off**] Brit colloq 贬损

slag heap *n* 矿渣堆

slain /sleɪn/

A *pp* ▸**slay 1**

B *npl* (people killed) 被杀害者; (from armed forces) 阵亡士兵

slake /sleɪk/ *vt* 1 (quench) 满足; **to ~ one's thirst** 解渴; **to ~ one's thirst/desire for sth.** fig 满足对某事物的渴望/愿望 2 Chem, Ind 使…熟化 ‹*lime*›

slaked lime /ˌsleɪkt ˈlaɪm/ *n* [u] 熟石灰

slalom /ˈslɑːləm/ ▸**p. 307**

A *n* 1 (ski race) 滑雪回转赛 2 (canoe race) 独木舟障碍赛

B *vi* (on skis) 参加滑雪回转赛; (in canoe) 参加独木舟障碍赛; **she ~ed through the crowd** 她在人群里迂回前进

slam /slæm/

A *vt* (*pres p etc.* **-mm-**) 1 (shut loudly) 砰的一声关上; **to ~ sth. shut** 砰的一声关上 ‹*door, window*›; 啪的一声合上 ‹*book*›; 砰的一声盖上 ‹*lid*›; **to ~ the door in sb.'s face** 砰的一声把某人关在门外; fig 拒绝某人 2 (thrust, strike) 使劲扔; **to ~ sth. on (to) sth.** 把某物摔到某物上; **he ~med his fist on the table** 他一拳砸在桌子上; **to ~ sth. through sth.** 用某物打穿某物; **to ~ sb. against a wall/door** 把某人往墙上/门上撞; **to ~ the ball into the net** 把球射入网中 3 colloq (criticize) 猛烈抨击; **to ~ sb./sth. for sth./doing sth.** 因某事物/做某事而激烈抨击某人/某事物; **to ~ a speech for going on too long** 因发言冗长而对之猛批; **to ~ sb./sth. as incompetent/useless** 劈头盖脸地骂某人无能/疾言厉色地指斥某事物无用; **to be ~med as a dictator** 被骂是独裁者; **to be ~med by the media/one's rivals** 受到媒体/对手的猛烈抨击 4 colloq (defeat) 轻松击败 ‹*opponent*›

B *vi* (*pres p etc.* **-mm-**) 1 (shut loudly) **to ~ (shut)** 砰的一声关上; **to ~ against sth.** 砰地合到某物上 2 (rush violently) 猛冲; **to ~ out of the room** 冲出房间 3 colloq (crash) **to ~ into sb./sth.** «*vehicle*» 猛撞某人/某物; «*boxer*» 猛击某人/某物 4 colloq (criticize) **to ~ into sb./sth.** 猛烈抨击某人/某事物; **his father ~med into him** 他父亲狠狠训斥了他

C *n* 1 (bang) 砰的一声 2 Amer colloq (jail) 监狱 3 (at bridge, whist) 满贯; **a grand/little** *or* **small ~** 大/小满贯; **to bid/make a ~** 叫/得满贯

Phrasal verbs

- **slam down**

A *vt* [**~ sth. down, ~ down sth.**] 猛摔 ‹*glass, coins*›; 猛地盖上 ‹*lid, car bonnet*›; 猛地合上 ‹*book*›; **to ~ sth. down on (to) sth.** 把某物猛摔在某物上

B *vi* «*lid*» 猛地落下; **to ~ down on (to) sth.** 砸在某物上

- **slam on** *vt* colloq **to ~ on the** *or* **one's brakes** 猛踩刹车

slam-bang

A *adj* Amer colloq 1 (exciting) 令人兴奋的 ‹*film, performance*› 2 (forceful) 有力的

B *adv* 猛地; **to walk/go ~ into sth.** 猛地撞上某物; **to walk ~ into sb.** 和某人撞个满怀

slam dunk

A *n* 1 (in basketball) 扣篮 2 Amer colloq (certain result) 稳操胜券的事; **a ~ victory** 十拿九稳的胜利

B **slam-dunk** *vt* «*player*» 灌 ‹*ball*›

slammer /ˈslæmə(r)/ *n* 1 (cocktail) **tequila ~** 龙舌兰鸡尾酒 2 colloq (prison) **the ~** 监狱

slander /ˈslɑːndə(r), Amer ˈslæn-/

A *n* [c and u] (defamation) 诽谤; **a ~ on sb./sth.** 对某人/某事物的诽谤; **to sue sb. for ~** 控告某人诽谤

B *vt* 诽谤

slanderer /ˈslɑːndərə(r), Amer ˈslæn-/ *n* 诽谤者

slanderous /ˈslɑːndərəs, Amer ˈslæn-/ *adj* 诽谤性的

slanderously /ˈslɑːndərəsli, Amer ˈslæn-/ *adv* 诽谤性地

S

slang /slæŋ/
A *n* [u] 俚语; **a ～ term** *or* **word for sth.** 某物的俚语词
B *vt* colloq 谩骂; **to ～ sb. for sth./doing sth.** 因某事物/做某事谩骂某人

slanginess /ˈslæŋınıs/ *n* [u] 使用俚语的特点

slanging match /ˈslæŋıŋ mætʃ/ *n* Brit 互相谩骂; **a ～ between A and B** A与B之间的相互谩骂; **a ～ about** *or* **over sth.** 因某事物的相互谩骂

slangy /ˈslæŋi/ *adj* 俚语的 ‹*expression*›; 使用俚语的 ‹*style, letter, book*›

slant /slɑːnt, Amer slænt/
A *n* 1 *sing* (slope) 倾斜; **the floor had a ～** 地板不平; **to hang at a ～** «*picture, fan*» 歪斜地挂着; **to cut sth. on a ～** 斜切 ‹*stem*› 2 pej (bias) 偏见; **with a right-/left-wing ～** 有右派/左派偏见的; **a ～ on sth.** 对某事物的偏见; **to have a ～ on sth.** 对某事物有偏见 3 (perspective) 看法; **to give (sb.) a (new) ～ on sth.** （向某人）提出有关某事物的（新）看法; **to get a (different) ～ on sth.** 对某事物形成（不同的）看法 4 (point of view) 角度; **a humorous/ironic/liberal/conservative ～ on sth.** 对某事物的幽默/讥讽/开明/保守态度 5 Print 斜线
B *vt* 1 (lean) 使倾斜; **to be ～ed (from sth.) to the left/right** （从某处）向左/向右倾斜; **to ～ sth. (up) against sth.** 把某物斜靠在某物上; **to ～ one's letters** 用斜体写字母 2 (twist) «*network, journalist*» 有倾向地报道 ‹*news*›; **to ～ the facts** 歪曲事实; **to be ～ed in favour of sb./sth.** «*report, finding*» 偏向某人/某事物
C *vi* «*ground, roof*» 倾斜; «*handwriting*» 歪斜; «*eyes*» 斜眼看; **to ～ to the left/right** 向左/向右倾斜; **to ～ from left to right** 从左向右倾斜; **to ～ up/down** 向上/向下倾斜; **to ～ across the mountains** «*sun*» 斜照群山

slanted /ˈslɑːntıd, Amer ˈslæn-/ *adj* 有倾向性的

slant-eyed /ˌslɑːntˈaıd, Amer ˌslænt-/ *adj* colloq 斜眼角的

slanting /ˈslæntıŋ/ *adj* 斜的

slap /slæp/
A *vt* (*pres p etc.* **-pp-**) 1 (hit) 拍打; **to ～ sb. across the face, to ～ sb.'s face** 打某人耳光; **to ～ sb. for sth./doing sth.** 因某事物/做某事打某人耳光; **to ～ a child's bottom** 打孩子屁股; **to ～ one's thighs** 拍大腿; **to ～ sb. on the arm/leg** 拍某人的胳膊/腿; **to ～ sb. on the back** (in praise) 赞扬某人; (in congratulation) 拍打某人后背以示祝贺; **to ～ sb. in the face** 侮辱某人; **to ～ sb. with sth.** fig colloq 对某人加以 ‹*penalty*›; 对某人处以 ‹*fine*› 2 (put) **to ～ sth. on (to) sth.** 把…啪的一声摔在某物上 ‹*paper, money*›; 把…涂抹在某处 ‹*paint, make-up*›; **to ～ sth. on the table** 啪的一声把某物摔在桌子上
B *vi* (*pres p etc.* **-pp-**) **to ～ against sth.** «*water*» 拍打 ‹*wall, boat*›; **to ～ into sth.** «*water*» 涌入 ‹*doorway, pipe*›
C *n* 1 (blow) 拍打; **to give sb./sth. a ～** 拍某人/拍某物; **to give sb. a ～ for sth./doing sth.** 因某事/做某事而拍某人; **a ～ on sth.** 拍打某物; **to deserve a ～ (on the bottom)** 该挨巴掌; **a ～ across** *or* **in the face** 一记耳光; **a ～ in the face** (rebuff) 拒绝; (snub) 怠慢; **(to give sb.) a ～ on the back (for sth./doing sth.)** fig (in praise) （因某事物/做某事）表扬（某人）; (in congratulation) （因某事物/做某事）（向某人）祝贺; **a ～ on the wrist** 警告; **to get a ～ on the wrist for sth./doing sth.** 因某事物/做某事而受训诫 2 (sound) 拍打声; **the ～ of the waves against the rocks/hull** fig 浪打在礁石/船体上的声音
D *adv* **= slap bang**

Phrasal verbs

• **slap down** *vt* 1 [**～ sth. down, ～ down sth.**] (put down) 把…啪地一放 ‹*money, paper*›; **to ～ sth. down on (to) sth.** 把某物啪地扔在某物上 2 [**～ sb. down**] colloq (silence) 粗暴地打断; (reprimand) 训斥

• **slap on** *vt* [**～ sth. on, ～ on sth.**] colloq 1 (put on) 随意涂抹 ‹*paint, make-up*›; **just ～ the paint on** 随便刷点漆就行了 2 fig (apply) 加以 ‹*penalty*›; **to ～ on (an extra) 50p** (add) （又）加价50便士; **to ～ an embargo on imports/a ban on using email on the staff** 对进口货物实行禁运/禁止员工使用电邮; **to ～ a fine on sb.** 对某人处以罚款

slap: ～ and tickle *n* [u] Brit hum colloq 打情骂俏; **～ bang** *adv* colloq 1 (directly) 径直地; **to run ～ bang into sb./sth.** (bump into) 猛地撞上某人/某物; (meet) 猛然撞见某人/某物; **to run ～ bang into the wall** 猛地撞到墙上; 2 (exactly) 正好; **to be ～ bang in the middle (of a place/event)** 正在某个地点的中心地带/正经历某事件; ‹*place*› 在（…的）正当中 ‹*event*›; **to hit sb. ～ bang on the nose** 打中某人的鼻子; **～dash** *adj* 草率的; **～-happy** *adj* colloq 1 (careless) 大大咧咧的 ‹*person*›; (poorly thought out) 考虑不周的 ‹*procedure, method*›; 2 (carefree) 无忧无虑的 ‹*attitude*›; **～head** *n* Brit colloq pej 秃子

slapper /ˈslæpə(r)/ *n* colloq pej (promiscuous woman) 荡妇; (vulgar woman) 泼妇

slapstick /ˈslæpstık/ *n* [u] 打闹剧

slap-up *adj* Brit colloq 丰盛的 ‹*dinner, lunch*›; **～ celebration** 奢华的庆典

slash /slæʃ/
A *n* 1 (wound) 砍伤; **the ～ on his cheek** 他脸颊上的刀伤 2 (cut in fabric, wood, etc.) 切口; **a ～ in the jacket** 夹克衫上的豁口; **to make a ～ (in sth.)** （在某物上）划出口子 3 (knife stroke) 砍; **a ～ with a sword/knife** 用剑/刀劈; **to take a ～ at sb./sth. (with sth.)** （用某物）砍向某人/某物 4 Fashn (slit) 开衩; **a ～-neck top** 开领上衣 5 (streak of colour, light) 条纹; **a ～ of red/red lipstick** 一道红色/口红 6 Print, Comput 斜杠; **bbc dot co dot uk ～ radio** bbc点co点uk斜杠radio [即bbc.co.uk/radio] 7 colloq (reduction in rate, output, etc.) 大幅度削减; **a 20% ～ in prices** 20%的大减价 8 Brit colloq (pee) 撒尿; **to go for/have a ～** 去撒尿/撒尿
B *vt* 1 (wound with knife) 砍伤; (cut) 割; **to ～ sb./sth. (with sth.)** （用某物）砍伤 ‹*person, animal*›; **to ～ sb./sth. to the bone** 砍到某人/某物的骨头; **to ～ sb. across the face** 划破某人的脸; **to ～ one's wrists** 割腕; **to ～ sth. (with sth.)** （用某物）划破 ‹*tyre, painting*›; （用某物）割断 ‹*rope*›; （用某物）砍 ‹*wood*›; **to ～ one's way through** *or* **past sth.** 披荆斩棘地穿过 ‹*jungle, undergrowth*›; **to ～ sth. open with a knife** 用刀将某物划开 2 colloq (reduce) 大幅度削减 ‹*cost, output*›; 大幅度减小 ‹*size*›; **20%/£100 has been ～ed from the cost** 成本砍掉了20%/100英镑; **expenditure has been ～ed drastically** 开支大幅降低; **the workforce was ～ed by 2,000/half** 员工被裁减了2,000人/一半; **'prices ～ed'** "大减价" 3 Fashn (slit open) 给…做开衩; **a suit with ～ed sleeves** 袖子开衩的套装
C *vi* 1 (hit at with knife) 砍; **to ～ at sb.** 向某人砍去; **to ～ at sb. with a knife/broken bottle** 持刀砍向/用破酒瓶砸向某人 2 (slice through) 割; **to ～ at sth.** 割 ‹*undergrowth*›; **to ～ at a ball** 击球; **the rain was ～ing at the window** fig 雨水猛烈地击打在窗户上; **to ～ through sth.** 割断 ‹*cord*›; 裁开 ‹*fabric*›

slash-and-burn *adj attrib* 刀耕火种的

slasher film /ˈslæʃə fılm/, esp Amer **slasher movie** *ns* colloq 血腥恐怖片

slashing /ˈslæʃıŋ/ *adj* 猛烈的

slash pocket *n* 斜插兜

slat /slæt/
A *n* 1 (in shutter, blind) 板条 2 (on aircraft) 前缘缝翼
B *vt* (*pres p etc.* **-tt-**) 给…装板条; **a ～ted blind** *or* **shutter** 板条百叶窗

slate /sleıt/
A *n* 1 [u] (rock) 页岩; **～ quarry/mine/mining** 页岩采石场/矿/采矿 2 [c] (piece) 小石板; (on roof) 石板瓦; **a ～ tile/roof/floor** 石板瓦/屋顶/地面 3 [c] (for writing) 石板; **to put sth. on the ～** 把某物挂在账上; **to wipe the ～ clean** fig 既往不咎 4 [u] (colour) 暗蓝灰色 5 [c] Amer (candidate list) 候选人名单; **to have a full ～** 每个选区都有候选人
B *vt* 1 (cover with slate) 用石板铺 ‹*roof*› 2 colloq (criticize) «*person, critic, newspaper*» 抨击 ‹*person, play, book*›; **to ～ sb./sth. for sth.** 因某事物抨击某人/某事物 3 Amer (propose for office) 推举 ‹*person, candidate*›; **to ～ sb. for sth.** 推选某人担任某职务 4 Amer (plan) 安排 ‹*event, meeting*›; **the conference is ～d for June** 会议定于6月份举行; **to be ～d to go far** «*person*» 注定会前程远大

slate blue ▸**p. 134**
A *n* [u] 暗蓝灰色
B *adj* 暗蓝灰色的

slate-coloured /ˈsleıtkʌləd/ ▸**p. 134** *adj* 暗蓝灰色的

slate grey ▸**p. 134**
A *n* [u] 青灰色
B *adj* 青灰色的

slater /ˈsleıtə(r)/ ▸**p. 409** *n* 石板瓦工

slating /ˈsleıtıŋ/ *n* 1 [u] (laying slates) 铺石板 2 [u] (material) 石板瓦 3 [c] Brit colloq (criticism) 抨击; **to give sb. a ～** 批评某人; **to get a ～ from sb.** 受到某人的批评

slatted /ˈslætıd/ *adj* 用板条做的 ‹*shelving, table*›; **a ～ blind** *or* **shutter** 百叶窗

slattern /ˈslætən/ *n* dated pej 邋遢女人

slatternly /ˈslætənli/ *adj* dated pej 邋遢的

slaty /ˈsleıti/ *adj* 1 (containing slate) 含板岩的 ‹*coal*› 2 (of or like slate) 深蓝灰的 ‹*colour*›

slaughter /ˈslɔːtə(r)/
A *n* 1 [u] (of animals) 屠宰; **to send sth. for ～** 将某物送去屠宰; **to go to ～** 被送去屠宰 2 [u] (of people) 屠杀 3 [c] colloq (defeat) 惨败
B *vt* 1 (butcher) 屠宰 ‹*animal*› 2 (massacre) 屠杀 ‹*animals, civilians, victims*›; **to be ～ed in (their) thousands** 成千上万地被屠杀 3 colloq (defeat) 彻底击败 ‹*person, team*›; **to ～ sb. at sth.** 在某方面彻底击败某人

slaughter: ～house *n* 屠宰场; **～man** /-mən/ *n* 屠夫

Slav /slɑːv, Amer slæv/ ▸**p. 426, p. 503**
A *adj* **= Slavic A**
B *n* (person) 斯拉夫人

slave /sleıv/
A *n* 1 (servant) 奴隶; **to treat sb. like a ～** 像对待奴隶般对待某人; **to work like a ～** 像奴隶般劳作 2 (victim of habit, interest) 完全受控制的人; **to be a ～ to sth.** 完全依赖某事物; **a ～ to convention** 循规蹈矩的人; **she became a ～ to drugs** 她变得离不开毒品
B *vi* 苦干; **to ～ (away) at sth./at doing sth.** 拼命干某事; **to ～ over ...** 辛苦地忙于…

slave: S～ Coast *pr n* Hist **the S～ Coast** 奴隶海岸 [位于西非，16至19世纪为主要的非洲奴隶来源地]; **～ driver** *n* 1 lit (overseer) 奴隶监工; 2 fig colloq (taskmaster) 残酷的监工; **～ labour** *n* [u] (activity) 繁重且报酬低的工作; (manpower) 苦役

slaver[1] /ˈsleıvə(r)/ *n* 1 (dealer) 奴隶贩子 2 (ship) 奴隶贩运船

slaver[2] /ˈslævə(r)/
A *n* 口水
B *vi* 1 (drool) 流口水; **to ～ over sth.** 对某物垂涎; **to ～ at the mouth** 嘴边淌口水 2 (show eagerness, desire) 渴望; **to ～ over sb./sth.** 渴望得到某人/某物; **to ～ over the prospect of doing sth.** 迫切希望做某事

slavery /ˈsleıvəri/ *n* [u] 1 (state) 奴隶身份; (condition) 受奴役的状态; **to be sold into ～** 被卖作奴隶 2 (owning slaves) 奴隶制; **the**

abolition of ~ 奴隶制的废止; white ~ 逼良为娼 [3] (hard work) 苦役 [4] (devotion) 沉迷; ~ to 受…支配 ‹*fashion, convention*›

slave: S~ State *n* Amer [美国废除奴隶制之前的] 蓄奴州; **~ trade** *n* [尤指16至19世纪对非洲黑人的] 奴隶贸易; **~-trader** *n* 奴隶贩子; **~-trading** *n* [u] 奴隶买卖

Slavic /ˈslɑːvɪk, Amer ˈslæv-/ ▸**p. 426, p. 503**
A *adj* (of the people) 斯拉夫人的 ‹*custom, dance*›; (of the language) 斯拉夫语的
B *n* [u] (language) 斯拉夫语

slavish /ˈsleɪvɪʃ/ *adj* [1] (servile) 奴隶般的 ‹*devotion, obedience, condition*› [2] (imitative) 无独创性的 ‹*copy, remake, reworking*›

slavishly /ˈsleɪvɪʃli/ *adv* [1] (like a slave) 奴隶般地 ‹*work, obey, adhere*› [2] (imitatively) 无独创性地 ‹*copy, remake, rework*›

Slavonic /sləˈvɒnɪk/ ▸**p. 426** *adj, n* = **Slavic**

Slavophile /ˈslɑːvəfaɪl, Amer ˈslæv-/
A *n* 亲斯拉夫者
B *adj* 亲斯拉夫的

slaw /slɔː/ *n* [u] Amer = **coleslaw**

slay /sleɪ/ *vt* [1] (*pt* **slew,** *pp* **slain**) (kill) 杀死 ‹*person, animal*›; **to be slain in battle** 在战斗中被杀 [2] (*pt, pp* **slayed**) colloq (impress) «*act, performance*» 深深打动; (amuse) «*act, performance*» 逗乐

slayer /ˈsleɪə(r)/ *n* 杀戮者

sleaze /sliːz/ *n* [u] Brit [1] (corruption) [尤指政治或商业中的] 龌龊行为 [2] (of behaviour) 卑鄙; (of newspaper) 不正派; (of place) 肮脏

sleazebag /ˈsliːzbæg/, **sleazeball** /ˈsliːzbɔːl/ *ns* Amer colloq [1] (corrupt person) 不正派的人 [2] (sordid person) 卑鄙小人

sleazy /ˈsliːzi/ *adj* colloq [1] (corrupt) 龌龊的 [2] (sordid) 卑鄙的 ‹*behaviour*›; 不正派的 ‹*newspaper*›; 肮脏的 ‹*place*›

sled /sled/ *n, vi, vt* Amer = **sledge**[1]

sled dog *n* Amer 拉雪橇的狗

sledge[1] /sledʒ/ Brit
A *n* 雪橇; **a dog ~** 狗拉雪橇
B *vi* 滑雪橇; **to go sledging** 去滑雪橇
C *vt* «*person*» 用雪橇运送 ‹*load, passengers*›

sledge[2] *n* colloq = **sledgehammer A**

sledgehammer /ˈsledʒhæmə(r)/
A *n* 长柄大锤
B *modif* [1] (powerful) 有力的 ‹*punch, blow*› [2] (ruthless) 毫不留情的 ‹*approach, tactic*›
C *vt* [1] (hit, strike) 用大锤砸 ‹*rock, post, pipe*› [2] fig (destroy) 沉重打击 ‹*community*›; 无情压制 ‹*freedom, activity*›

sleek /sliːk/
A *adj* [1] (smooth, glossy) 油亮的 ‹*hair, coat*› [2] (prosperous-looking) 阔气的 ‹*person, appearance, manner*›; (stylish) 时髦的 ‹*person, appearance, manner*› [3] (streamlined) 造型优美的 ‹*plane, boat, lines*›
B *vt* «*person, animal, bird*» 使…变得油亮 ‹*hair, coat, feathers*›

Phrasal verb

- **sleek down** *vt* [~ **down sth.,** ~ **sth. down**] 使…平整光亮 ‹*hair, fur*›

sleekly /ˈsleekli/ *adj* 衣冠楚楚地

sleekness /ˈskiːknɪs/ *n* [u] [1] (of hair, coat) 油亮 [2] (of person, appearance) 衣冠楚楚 [3] (of plane, lines) 造型优美

sleep /sliːp/
A *vi* (*pt, pp* **slept**) [1] (be asleep) 睡着; **to ~ well/badly** 睡得好/没睡好; **to ~ deeply** *or* **soundly** 熟睡; **to ~ lightly/fitfully** 睡得很浅/时睡时醒; **to ~ (for) eight hours/round the clock** 睡 8 个小时/ 12 小时; **~ tight!** 睡个好觉!; **to ~ like a log** *or* **top** *or* **baby** colloq 睡得很香; **a city that never ~s** fig 不夜城 [2] (stay overnight) 过夜; **where did you ~ last night?** 昨晚你在哪里过的夜?; **to ~ in sth.** 在…上过夜 ‹*bed, hammock*›; 在…里过夜 ‹*car*›; **his bed has not been slept in** 他的床没人睡过; **to ~ on sth.** 在…上过夜 ‹*sofa, train*›; **to ~ at sb.'s house/the station** 在某人家里/车站过夜; **to ~ together** colloq euph 睡在一起 euph; **to ~ with sb.** colloq euph 和某人睡觉 euph [3] euph (be at peace in death) 安息; **he/she ~s in Holywell Cemetery** 他/她安息在霍利韦尔墓地
B *vt* (*pt, pp* **slept**) 可供…住宿 ‹*number of people*›; **how many people can you ~?** 你这里可住多少人?; **to (comfortably) ~ six** 能 (舒舒服服地) 睡下 6 个人; **'accommodation, ~s 6'** "提供住宿, 有 6 张床位"
C *n* [1] [u and c] (state) 睡眠; (period) 睡眠时间; **to go (back)** *or* **get (back) to ~** (又) 睡着; **to go to ~** fig «*arm, leg*» 发麻; **to get** *or* **have enough/a good night's ~** 睡足/一夜安睡; **to have a ~** Brit *or* **get some ~** 睡一会儿; **to not get any** *or* **a wink of ~ all night** 一夜没合眼; **not enough ~, (a) lack of ~** 睡眠不足; **deep** *or* **heavy** *or* **sound/peaceful** *or* **restful ~** 熟睡/安睡; **light/fitful ~** 浅睡/时睡时醒; **a long/short ~** 久睡/小睡; **to send** *or* **put sb. to ~** «*heat, tablet*» 使某人入睡; fig «*speech*» 让人感到无聊透顶; **to sing/rock sb. to ~** 唱歌/摇晃着哄某人入睡; **to read oneself to ~** 看书看得睡着; **to talk/walk in one's ~** 说梦话/梦游; **to cry oneself to ~** 哭到睡着; **not to lose ~ over sth., to lose no ~ over sth.** fig 不大为某事物操心; **to be able to do sth. in one's ~** colloq 闭着眼睛都能做某事 [2] [u] euph (death) 安息; **the big ~** 长眠; **to put an animal to ~** [通过注射药物] 无痛苦地杀死动物 [3] [u] (in eyes) 眼屎

Phrasal verbs

- **sleep around** *vi* colloq 乱搞男女关系
- **sleep in** *vi* (lie in) 睡懒觉; (oversleep) 睡过头
- **sleep off** *vt* [~ **sth. off,** ~ **off sth.**] 靠睡觉消除 ‹*headache, jet lag, hangover*›; **to ~ it off** colloq 睡一觉恢复过来
- **sleep on** *vt* [~ **on sth.**] colloq 把…留到第二天解决 ‹*problem*›; 把…留到第二天再作 ‹*decision*›; **maybe you should ~ on it first** 也许你应该把它留到明天再说
- **sleep over** *vi* 在别人家过夜; **to ~ over at sb.'s house** *or* **with sb.** 在某人家过夜; **he's ~ing over at my house tonight** 今晚他住我家
- **sleep through**
A *vt* [~ **through sth.**] **to ~ (right) through the noise/storm** 没有被噪声/暴风雨吵醒; **to ~ through a film/speech** 电影放映时/演讲时从头睡到尾; **she ~s through anything!** 什么声都吵不醒她!
B *vi* **to ~ through until noon/the middle of the afternoon** 一直睡到中午/半下午

sleeper /ˈsliːpə(r)/ *n* [1] (person) 睡眠者; **to be a sound ~** 睡眠好; **a heavy/light ~** 睡觉沉/轻的人 [2] (train) 卧铺列车 [3] (sleeping car) 卧铺车厢 [4] (train berth) 卧铺 [5] Brit (railway track beam) 枕木 [6] Brit (earring) 耳钉 [7] Amer colloq (successful book, film, play) 爆冷门的作品; **a ~ hit** *or* **success** 爆冷门成功的事物 [8] (secret agent) 潜伏特工

sleepily /ˈsliːpɪli/ *adv* 昏昏欲睡地

sleep-in *n* 在工作地就寝

sleepiness /ˈsliːpɪnɪs/ *n* [u] (of person) 困倦; (of village, town) 宁静

sleeping /ˈsliːpɪŋ/ *adj* [1] (asleep) 睡着的 ‹*person, animal*›; **the S~ Beauty** 睡美人; **to let ~ dogs lie** 不招惹麻烦 [2] *attrib* (for the night) 供住宿的 ‹*accommodation*›

sleeping: ~ bag *n* 睡袋; **~ car** *n* 卧铺车厢; **~ draught** *n* 安眠药水; **~ partner** *n* Brit 隐名合伙人; **~ pill** *n* 安眠药; **~ policeman** *n* Brit colloq 减速带; **~ quarters** *npl* (place) 睡觉的地方; (rooms) 卧室; **~ sickness** ▸**p. 377** *n* [u] 昏睡病; **~ tablet** *n* 安眠药

sleep: ~ laboratory *n* 睡眠障碍实验室; **~ learning** *n* [u] 睡眠学习法 [睡眠中听录音学习]

sleepless /ˈsliːplɪs/ *adj* [1] (without sleep) 不睡觉的 ‹*vigil, hours*›; 失眠的 ‹*night*› [2] (moving) 不停息的 ‹*wind*›; 摇摆不停的 ‹*trees*›

sleeplessly /ˈsliːplɪsli/ *adv* 不睡觉地 ‹*watch, work, pace*›; 失眠地 ‹*toss, lie*›

sleeplessness /ˈsliːplɪsnɪs/ *n* [u] 失眠

sleep: ~ mode *n* 休眠模式; **~out** *n* [1] (sleeping outdoors) 露宿; (as protest) [为无家可归者举行的] 户外睡觉抗议; [2] Austral, NZ (outbuilding) 卧廊; **~over** *n* 在外过夜; **~ research** *n* [u] 睡眠研究; **~walk** *vi* 梦游; **to ~walk into sth.** 稀里糊涂地做某事; **~walker** *n* 梦游者; **~walking** *n* [u] 梦游; **~wear** *n* [u] 睡衣

sleepy /ˈsliːpi/ *adj* [1] (needing sleep) 困倦的 ‹*person, animal, voice*›; 惺忪的 ‹*eyes*›; **to feel/be ~** 感到困倦/昏昏欲睡; **to make sb. ~** 使某人犯困 [2] (not busy) 宁静的 ‹*town*›

sleepyhead /ˈsliːpɪhed/ *n* colloq 瞌睡虫

sleet /sliːt/
A *n* [u] (snow with rain) 雨夹雪; (hail with rain) 雨夹雹; **to turn to ~** 转成冻雨
B *v impers* **it's ~ing** (snow with rain) 正在下雨夹雪; (hail with rain) 正在下雨夹冰雹

sleety /ˈsliːti/ *adj* (with snow) 夹雪的; (with hail) 夹雹的; **~ rain/shower** (with snow) 雨/阵雨夹雪; (with hail) 雨/阵雨夹冰雹

sleeve /sliːv/
A *n* [1] (of garment) 袖子; **short/long ~s** 短袖/长袖; **to pull** *or* **tug at sb.'s ~** 拉某人的袖子; **to roll up one's ~s** 挽起袖子; fig 准备大干一场; **(to have) sth. up one's ~** (有) 锦囊妙计; **to have another idea up one's ~** 另有主张; **what's she got up her ~?** 她葫芦里到底卖的什么药?; **(to have) a trick (or two) up one's ~** (还有) 留着的一 (两) 招; **to keep sth. up one's ~** 对某事保密; **to laugh up one's ~** 暗暗发笑; **to wear one's heart on one's ~** 流露感情 [2] (for record, CD) 唱片套; **an album ~** 专辑唱片套 [3] Tech (inner liner) 套筒; (axle casing) 轴套; (casing pipe) 套管
B **-sleeved** *adj* 有…袖的; **long/short~d** 长袖/短袖的; **a cap~d shirt** 小包肩衬衫

sleeve design *n* [c and u] 唱片套设计

sleeveless /ˈsliːvlɪs/ *adj* 无袖的 ‹*shirt, top*›

sleeve: ~ note *n* Brit 唱片套说明; **~ valve** *n* 套筒式气门

sleigh /sleɪ/
A *n* 雪橇
B *vi* 乘雪橇

sleigh: ~ bell *n* 雪橇铃; **~ ride** *n* 乘雪橇

sleight of hand /ˌslaɪt əv ˈhænd/ *n* [c and u] [1] (manual dexterity) [变魔术时的] 敏捷手法 [2] (trick, deception) 花招

slender /ˈslendə(r)/ *adj* [1] (thin) 苗条的 ‹*person, build*›; 纤细的 ‹*waist, hand, neck*›; 细长的 ‹*stem, column*› [2] (slight) 微小的; **~ chance/hope/majority** 很小的机会/渺茫的希望/微弱的多数; **to win by a ~ margin** 以微弱优势获胜 [3] (meagre) 微薄的 ‹*income*›; 贫乏的 ‹*resources, means*›

slenderize /ˈslendəraɪz/ esp Amer
A *vt* «*garment, style*» 使…显苗条 ‹*person*›; 使…显得纤细 ‹*waist, thighs*›
B *vi* «*person*» 变苗条

slenderness /ˈslendənɪs/ *n* [u] [1] (of person) 苗条; (of waist, neck) 纤细; (of stem, column) 细长 [2] (of funds) 不足; (of chance) 渺茫; (of majority, margin) 微小

slept /slept/ *pt, pp* ▸**sleep A, B**

sleuth /sluːθ/
A *n* 侦探
B *vi* 当侦探; **to ~ around** *or* **about** 四处侦查

S

S-level
A *n* Brit = **Special Level** 特别级考试 [与高级考试同时进行但水准更高]
B *modif* 特别级的 ‹*study, standard, physics, French*›

slew¹ /sluː/ *pt* ▸**slay 1**

slew²
A *vi* «*vehicle, lorry, person*» 猛地转向; **to ~ to the left/right** 向左/向右急转
B *vt* (turn) «*person, impact, collision*» 使…急转 ‹*vehicle, car, lorry*›; **to ~ sth. to the left/right** 将某物向左/向右急转

slew³ *n* Amer colloq (pile) 大量; **a ~ of sth.** 大量某物

slewed /sluːd/ *adj* colloq 喝醉了的

slice /slaɪs/
A *n* **1** Culin (piece) 薄片; **a ~ of cake/cheese/lemon** 一片蛋糕/乳酪/柠檬; **a ~ of bread and butter** 涂黄油的面包片; **a generous** *or* **large/small/thin ~** 大片/小片/薄片; **to cut a ~ (of ...)** 切一片 (…); **to cut sth. into ~s** 把某物切成片 **2** fig (proportion, share) 部分; **a (large/small) ~ of sth.** (很大/很小的)一份 ‹*profits, market*›; **a large ~ of the territory/population** 大片领土/大批民众; **a ~ of the credit** 一部分荣誉; **(to have) a ~ of luck** (有)一些运气; **a ~ of the cake** fig 应得的利益 **3** Culin (utensil) 铲; **a cake/cheese ~** 蛋糕铲/干酪铲 **4** Sport (in golf) 右旋削球; (in tennis) **a (forehand/backhand) ~** (正手/反手)削球; **a ~ to the baseline** 打到底线的削球
B *vt* **1** (cut into slices) 把…切片 ‹*bread*›; **to ~ sth. thin** *or* **thinly/thick** *or* **thickly** 把某物切成薄片/厚片; **to ~ sth. in two** *or* **half** 把某物切成两半; **thinly** *or* **thin-~d/thickly** *or* **thick-~d** 切成薄片/厚片的; **~d meat/cucumber** 肉片/黄瓜片 **2** (cut from whole) 切下; **to ~ sth. off** *or* **from sth.** 把某物从某物上切下来; **to ~ two seconds off the record** 把纪录缩短两秒钟; **to ~ £300 off the budget** 把预算减少 300 英镑 **3** (cut through) «*knife*» 划破 ‹*flesh, cloth*›; «*fin, wing*» 划过 ‹*water, air*›; **to ~ a leg/an arm to the bone** 把腿/胳膊划破深及骨头; **to ~ the water** «*ship, bow*» 破浪前进 **4** Sport 削 ‹*ball*›; **to ~ a ball** *or* **shot into/to sth.** (in tennis) 把球斜切打进/打到某处; **to ~ a catch to the wicketkeeper** (in cricket) 把球斜切击出给捕手接住; **to ~ a corner into the net** (in football) 使角球斜切进网
C *vi* **1** (cut) «*knife*» 切; **a knife that ~s well** 很好切的刀; **to ~ through sth.** «*knife*» 切开 ‹*object*›; «*fin, boat, bow, wing*» 划过 ‹*water, air*›; **to ~ through sb.'s defence** fig 突破某人的防守; **to ~ through the confusion** fig 澄清混淆; **to ~ into sth.** «*knife*» 划破 ‹*arm, leg*›; «*spade*» 铲入 ‹*earth*› **2** (be cut) 被切; **this bread ~s easily/does not ~ very well/will not ~** 这块面包容易切片/不容易切片/切不了片

(Phrasal verbs)
- **slice off** *vt* [**~ sth. off, ~ off sth.**] 切下 ‹*piece of meat*›; 割掉 ‹*head, arm*›
- **slice up** *vt* [**~ sth. up, ~ up sth.**] 把…切片 ‹*bread*›; **to ~ up the land into lots** 把土地分成多块

sliced /slaɪst/: **~ bread** *n* [u] 切片面包; **the best** *or* **greatest thing since ~ bread** colloq hum 极好的东西 [对新发明或发现等的赞美语]; **~ loaf** *n* 切片面包条

slice of life
A *n* [文艺作品中] 生活片段的如实再现
B **slice-of-life** *modif* 反映现实生活的 ‹*story, film*›

slicer /ˈslaɪsər/ *n* 切片机

slick /slɪk/
A *adj* **1** (adept) 精明的 ‹*deal, takeover*›; 娴熟的 ‹*operation, manoeuvre*› **2** pej (adept but superficial) 华而不实的 ‹*presentation, broadcast, style*› **3** pej (suave, insincere) 圆滑的 ‹*person, excuse, explanation*›; **a ~ operator** colloq 圆滑的骗子 **4** (glossy) 光滑润泽的 ‹*hair, coat, skin*› **5** Amer (slippery) 滑溜溜的 ‹*surface*›
B *n* **(oil) ~** [油罐泄漏等造成的] 浮油

(Phrasal verbs)
- **slick back** *vt* [**~ sth. back, ~ back sth.**] 将…朝后梳光滑 ‹*hair*›
- **slick down** *vt* [**~ sth. down, ~ down sth.**] 将…向下梳光滑 ‹*hair*›

slicker /ˈslɪkə(r)/ *n* Amer **1** colloq (rogue) 油嘴滑舌的骗子 **2** (raincoat) 油布雨衣 **3** = **city slicker**

slickly /ˈslɪkli/ *adv* **1** (adeptly) 娴熟地 ‹*perform, do, presented*›; (cleverly) 巧妙地 ‹*achieve, presented, produced*› **2** (smoothly) 顺利地 ‹*do, achieve, operate*›; (efficiently) 高效地 ‹*do, achieve, operate*› **3** (stylishly) 时髦地 ‹*dress, dressed, combed*›; (elegantly) 雅致地 ‹*dress, dressed, combed*›

slickness /ˈslɪknɪs/ *n* [u] **1** (cleverness) (of film, production, style) 巧妙; (of answer, person) 圆滑 **2** (of magician, of operation) 娴熟

slide /slaɪd/
A *vi* (*pt, pp* **slid** /slɪd/) **1** (glide, move smoothly) 滑行; **to ~ down sth.** 顺着…滑下 ‹*banisters, rope*›; **to ~ down the bank into the water** 从岸上滑入水中; **to ~ along sth.** 沿着…滑动 ‹*rail, ice*›; **to ~ around** *or* Brit **about (on sth.)** (在某物上)四处滑动; **to ~ by** *or* **past** «*toboggan*» 滑过; fig «*time*» 流逝; **to ~ open/shut/open and shut** 徐徐打开/关闭/开合; **to ~ up/down/up and down** 滑上/滑下/滑上滑下; **to ~ in/out/in and out** 滑进/滑出/滑进滑出 **2** (slip accidentally) 打滑; **to ~ off** 滑落; **to ~ off sth.** 从…上滑下来 ‹*shelf, roof*›; **to ~ off the road** «*car*» 滑出路面; **to ~ into sth.** 打滑撞上 ‹*wall, bank*›; **to ~ on the floor/ice** 在地板上/冰上打滑 **3** (slip quietly) 溜; **to ~ away/out** 悄悄溜走/溜出去; **to ~ out of/into the room** 悄悄溜出/溜进房间; **to ~ into the driver's seat** 悄悄溜到驾驶座上; **to ~ towards sth.** 悄悄靠近某物; **to ~ over an issue** 回避问题 **4** fig (decline) 降低; **to ~ (downwards)** «*price, value*» 下跌; «*shares, currency*» 贬值; **to ~ to a new low** 降到新低; **to ~ into/towards sth.** 陷入/逐渐衰落到 ‹*bankruptcy, recession, anarchy*›; **to ~ into bad habits** 渐渐染上坏习惯; **to let sth. ~** colloq 放任某事物衰退; **to let things ~** colloq 得过且过
B *vt* (*pt, pp* **slid** /slɪd/) **1** (move smoothly) 使滑行; **to ~ sth. out of/into/across/over sth.** 把某物从某物中抽出来/滑入某物中/滑过某物/滑到某物上方; **to ~ a sword out of its scabbard** 拔剑出鞘; **to ~ a boat into the water** 把小船滑到水中; **to ~ sth. on/off** 把…滑动着盖上/打开 ‹*lid*›; **to ~ the cover over the hatch** 把舱盖推合到舱口; **to ~ sth. shut/open** 把…徐徐推上/推开 ‹*door, window*›; **to ~ sth. back/forward** 把…往后推 ‹*seat, hatch, sunroof*›; **to ~ back the bolt** 上保险栓 **2** (slip quietly) 悄悄移动; **to ~ sth. into/under sth.** 把某物悄悄放进某物/塞到某物下
C *n* **1** (in playground) 滑梯; (for swimmers) 滑道; (on ice, in mud) 滑行面; **an escape ~** 逃生滑梯; **to go down a ~ (into sth.)** 顺着滑道滑(入某物); **the frozen brook is a good ~** 冻结的小河很适合溜冰 **2** *sing* (act of sliding) 滑行; **to have a ~ on sth.** 在某物上滑行; **to go into a ~** «*vehicle*» 打起滑来; **to have a ~ on the ice** «*child*» 在冰面上溜冰 **3** Phot 幻灯片; **colour ~s** 彩色幻灯片; **to be on ~(s)** 映现在幻灯片里 **4** (microscope plate) 载玻片 **5** fig (decline) 下降; **a ~ in sth.** …的下跌 ‹*price, value*›; **a ~ into sth.** 陷入…状况 ‹*poverty, war*›; **to be on the ~** «*price, value*» 逐步下跌; «*economy*» 日益衰退 **6** Brit = **hair-slide** **7** Mus (slur) 滑音 **8** Mus (on instrument) 滑管 **9** Mech 滑块

slide: **~-action** *adj* 滑动式的 ‹*shotgun*›; **~ fastener** *n* Amer 拉链; **~ guitar** ▸**p. 395** *n* [u] 吉他滑奏; **~ projector** *n* 幻灯机; **~ rule** Brit, **~ ruler** Amer *ns* 滑尺; **~ show** *n* 幻灯片放映; **~ trombone** ▸**p. 395** *n* 滑管长号; **~ valve** *n* 滑阀

sliding /ˈslaɪdɪŋ/
A *n* [u] 滑动
B *adj attrib* 滑动的; **a ~ lid/roof** 滑盖/滑动式活顶

sliding: **~ door** *n* 滑门; **~ scale** *n* 浮动计算法; **~ seat** *n* 滑座

slight /slaɪt/
A *adj* **1** (small in degree) 小的; (inconsiderable) 微不足道的; (not big or strong) 细微的; **a ~ error/risk/problem** 小错误/风险/问题; **a ~ hope/possibility** 极小的希望/可能性; **a ~ hesitation/improvement/decrease/accent** 略微的犹豫/改进/减少/口音; **a ~ noise/sound/movement** 细微的噪声/声音/动作; **not to have the ~est difficulty/idea** 毫无困难/丝毫不知; **at the ~est provocation** 动不动就; **not in the ~est** 丝毫不 **2** (slender) 瘦小的 ‹*person, figure*›; (frail) 纤弱的 ‹*person, figure*› **3** (insubstantial) 肤浅的 ‹*novel, film, book*›
B *n* 冒犯; **to suffer a ~** 受到冒犯; **a ~ on sb./sth.** 对某人/某事物的简慢; **a ~ from sb.** 来自某人的轻慢
C *vt* Amer 轻视; **to feel ~ed** 感觉受到冷落

slighting /ˈslaɪtɪŋ/ *adj* 侮慢的

slightingly /ˈslaɪtɪŋli/ *adv* 侮慢地

slightly /ˈslaɪtli/ *adv* **1** (a little) 略微地 ‹*worse, thinner, sweet, dry*›; **the patient is ~ better today** 病人的病情今天稍有好转 **2** (slimly) 纤细地; **~ built** 身材瘦小的

slightness /ˈslaɪtnɪs/ *n* [u] **1** (slenderness of build) 纤细 **2** (of film, book) 肤浅 **3** (of risk, improvement) 微小

slim /slɪm/
A *adj* **1** (slender) 苗条的 ‹*person, figure*›; 纤细的 ‹*ankle, wrist, leg*›; 薄的 ‹*book*›; **a ~ volume of poems** 薄薄的诗集 **2** (slight) 些许的 ‹*prospects, expectations*›; **a ~ hope of sth./of doing sth.** 某事物/做某事的一线希望; **the ~mest of evidence** 极薄弱的证据
B *vi* (*pres p etc.* **-mm-**) Brit 减肥

(Phrasal verb)
- **slim down**
A *vi* «*person*» 减肥
B *vt* [**~ down sth., ~ sth. down**] 压缩 ‹*budget*›; 精简 ‹*business*›; 减少 ‹*portfolio*›

slime /slaɪm/ *n* [u] **1** (slippery substance) 黏质物; (on riverbed) 黏泥 **2** (of slug, snail) 黏液

sliminess /ˈslaɪmɪnɪs/ *n* [u] **1** (of substance, mud) 黏糊; (of snail, slug) 黏滑 **2** Brit colloq (obsequiousness) 谄媚

slimline /ˈslɪmlaɪn/ *adj* **1** (slim) 瘦长的 ‹*garment, dress, trousers*›; 小巧的 ‹*mobile phone, appliance, model*› **2** (low-calorie) 低热量的 ‹*drink, food*›

slimmer /ˈslɪmə(r)/ *n* Brit 减肥者

slimming /ˈslɪmɪŋ/ *n* [u] Brit 减肥

slimming pill *n* 减肥药

slimness /ˈslɪmnɪs/ *n* [u] **1** (of person, figure) 苗条; (of waist) 纤细; (of book) 薄 **2** (of chance) 些许; (of margin) 微小

slimy /ˈslaɪmi/ *adj* **1** (slime-like) 黏糊糊的 ‹*substance, liquid, mud*›; (slippery) 黏滑的 ‹*creature, floor, wall*›; (covered in slime) 沾满黏液的 ‹*trail*› **2** Brit colloq (obsequious) 谄媚的

sling /slɪŋ/
A *n* **1** (catapult) 投石器; (slingshot) 弹弓; **~s and arrows** 命运的矢石 [指厄运] **2** Med 吊腕带; **to have one's arm in a ~** 用悬带吊着胳膊 **3** (support for load) 吊索 **4** (for baby) 吊兜; **to carry a baby in a ~** 用吊兜背婴儿 **5** (for climbing) 钩悬带
B *vt* (*pt, pp* **slung**) **1** esp Brit colloq (throw) 扔; **to ~ sth. at sb./sth.** 把某物投向某人/某物; **to ~ sth. into/on (to)/out of/over sth.** 把某物扔到某物中/上面/外/上方; **to ~ sth. over**

the chair/one's shoulder 把…搭在椅子上/挎在肩上 ‹*coat, bag*›; **to ~ sth. round** *or* **around one's neck** 把…搭在脖子上 ‹*shawl, sweater*›; **to ~ a few things into a bag** 往包里丢几样东西; **to ~ mud** *or* **insults (at sb.)** 玷污（某人的）名声 **2** (hang, carry) 吊挂 ‹*load, hammock*›; **to ~ sth. from sth.** 把某物挂在…上 ‹*hook, beam*›; **to ~ sth. between two trees/poles** 把某物挂在两棵树/两个杆子之间; **to ~ sth. over sth.** 把某物搭在…上 ‹*chair, handlebars*›; **to ~ sth. around one's shoulders** 把某物搭在肩上; **to ~ sth. across** *or* **over one's shoulder** 把某物挎在肩上; **to ~ sth. on one's back** 背起某物

Phrasal verbs

- **sling away** *vt* [**~ sth. away, ~ away sth.**] Brit colloq 扔掉
- **sling on** *vt* [**~ sth. on, ~ on sth.**] Brit colloq 匆匆穿上 ‹*clothes*›
- **sling out** *vt* Brit colloq **1** [**~ sth. out, ~ out sth.**] (throw away) 扔掉 **2** [**~ sth. out, ~ out sth.**] (reject) 拒绝接受; **the proposal/amendment/plan was slung out** 方案/修订/计划被否决了 **3** [**~ sb. out, ~ out sb.**] (eject) 赶走; **to ~ sb. out of a bar/club** 把某人轰出酒吧/俱乐部
- **sling over** *vt* [**~ sth. over, ~ over sth.**] Brit colloq 把…扔过来

sling: ~back *n* 露跟女鞋 [后帮为窄带]; **~shot** *n* **1** (catapult) 弹弓; **2** (shot) 弹弓射出的弹丸

slink /slɪŋk/ *vi* (*pt, pp* **slunk**) **1** (move stealthily) 偷偷摸摸地走; **to ~ out (of sth.)** 溜出（某处） **2** colloq (move seductively) 风情万种地走

slinkily /ˈslɪŋkɪli/ *adv* colloq 调情地 ‹*walk, move, dance, sway*›

slinkiness /ˈslɪŋkinɛs/ *n* [u] colloq 柔媚

slinky /ˈslɪŋki/ *adj* colloq 线条优美的 ‹*clothing, fabric*›; 撩人的 ‹*walk*›

slip /slɪp/

A (*pres p etc.* **-pp-**) *vi* **1** (lose footing) «*person, animal*» 滑倒; «*foot, vehicle*» 打滑; **to ~ in/on sth.** 在某物中/上滑倒; **to ~ on a banana skin** 踩到香蕉皮滑倒; fig (difficulty) 遭遇挫败; (embarrassment) 遭遇尴尬; **to ~ down sth.** 滑下 ‹*slope, stairs*› **2** (slide accidentally) 滑动; **the knife ~ped and cut my cheek** 剃刀一滑割伤了我的面颊 **3** (fail to grip) «*clutch, brake*» 没挂上; «*rope, knot, catch*» 松脱; **to ~ on sth.** 在…上滑行 ‹*rail, surface*›; **to ~ off the hook** «*rope*» 从钩子上掉下来; **to let one's control ~** 失控 **4** (slide easily) 轻快地滑动; **to ~ down sth.** 轻快地滑下 ‹*rope, ladder*›; **to ~ past/across sth.** 轻快地从某物边/上滑过; **to ~ along the bench** 顺着长凳滑溜; **to ~ through the water** «*boat*» 掠过水面; **to ~ into place** *or* **position** «*piece*» 滑到位; **to ~ into sleep/a coma/debt** 睡着/陷入昏迷/开始负债; **to ~ into bad habits** 染上恶习; **to ~ behind schedule** 落后于进度安排 **5** (move quietly) 悄悄移动; **to ~ (unnoticed)** （趁人不注意）偷偷溜走; **to ~ over** *or* **across** 悄悄越过 ‹*border*›; 悄悄渡过 ‹*mountains*›; 悄悄渡过 ‹*river*›; **to ~ through sth.** 悄悄穿过 ‹*lines, checkpoint*›; **to ~ into/out of sth.** 溜进/溜出某处; **to ~ into bed** 悄悄上床; **to ~ into port** «*ship*» 悄然进港; **several errors have ~ped into the text** 文中不经意出现了几处错误 **6** (fall, escape) «*person, animal*» 逃脱; «*object*» 滑落; **to ~ from** *or* **out of sth.** 从…中滑落 ‹*hand*›; 从…中逃脱 ‹*grasp*›; **to ~ through sth.** 从…间滑落 ‹*fingers*›; **to let happiness ~ through one's fingers** 让幸福从指缝间溜掉; **to ~ free** 挣脱; **to let sth. ~** (miss) 错过 ‹*chance*›; (reveal) 走漏 ‹*information*›; **he let (it) ~ that ...** 他不小心说出… **7** **to ~ into/out of sth.** (put on/take off) 穿上/脱下 ‹*clothes, shoes*›; **to ~ into something more comfortable** 套上件更舒服的衣服 **8** fig (drop) «*standard, popularity*» 降低; «*person, team*» 降级; Fin «*shares*» 下跌; **to ~ to third place/37p** 降到第三名/跌到 37 便士; **to be ~ping** colloq 退步

B *vt* (*pres p etc.* **-pp-**) **1** (put unobtrusively) 悄悄放 ‹*object, hand*›; fig 插入 ‹*joke, question*›; **to ~ sth. into sth.** 把某物放入某物中; **I ~ped the money into his pocket** 我把钱悄悄塞进他口袋里; **to ~ a car into gear** 给车挂挡; **to ~ sth. into place** 把某物放到位; **an additional clause had been ~ped into the contract** 合同里增添了附加条款; **to ~ sth. through sth.** 通过…塞入某物 ‹*opening, gap*›; **she ~ped her arm through mine** 她挽住了我的胳膊 **2** (give unobtrusively) 悄悄给; **to ~ sb. sth., to ~ sth. to sb.** 把某物塞给某人; **I'll get you to the front of the queue if you want to ~ me a fiver** 你给我 5 英镑，我就让你加塞儿到队伍前面 **3** (put on or take off) **to ~ sth. on/off** 穿上/脱下 ‹*garment, shoe*›; 戴上/摘下 ‹*ring, gloves, handcuffs*›; **to ~ sth. on (to) one's finger/wrist** 把某物套在手指/手腕上; **to ~ sandals on one's feet** 匆匆穿上便鞋; **to ~ sth. over one's head** 把某物套在头上; **to ~ sth. round one's shoulders/neck** 把某物披在肩上/围在脖子上 **4** (release) 解开 ‹*knot*›; **to ~ a (dog's) leash** 解开（拴狗的）皮带; **to ~ a dog off its leash** 解开皮带放开狗 **5** (escape from) «*animal*» 挣脱 ‹*collar*›; «*ship*» 使…松脱 ‹*moorings*›; «*balloon*» 从…上松脱 ‹*rope*›; fig «*matter*» 没有引起 ‹*attention*›; **to ~ anchor** 弃锚起航; **to ~ one's mind** *or* **memory** 被遗忘; **it quite ~ped my mind that ...** 我都忘了… **6** (in knitting) **to ~ a stitch** 跳针; **knit one, ~ one** 织一针，跳一针 **7** Med **to ~ a disc** 椎间盘突出 **8** Aut **to ~ the clutch** 滑挡

C *n* **1** [c] *usu sing* (act of sliding) 滑倒; **a ~ on sth.** 在…上的滑倒 ‹*ice*›; **to give sb. the ~** (avoid) 避开某人; (escape) 甩掉某人 **2** [c] (error) 差错; **a ~ in sth.** …中的差错 ‹*calculation*›; **to make a ~** 出错; **a ~ of the pen/tongue** 笔误/口误; **one ~ and you're out** 你只要犯一次错就走人; **there's many a ~ 'twixt cup and lip** Prov 杯子到口，还会失手 **3** [c] (reduction) (in level, standard) 下降 **4** [c] Fashn (undergarment) 衬裙; Sch (gymslip) 体操衫 **5** [c] (pillow over) 枕套 **6** [c] (piece of paper) 纸片; (notice) 通知单; **a ~ of paper** 一片纸; **a credit card ~** 信用卡交易签账单; **an advice ~** (for salary) 薪金收据; (for payment made) 付款收据; **a salary** *or* **pay ~** 工资单 **7** [u] (clay) 泥釉 **8** [c] (in cricket) (position) 防守位置; (fielder) 守场员; **to be** *or* **field (at) (first/second)** ~ 打（第一/第二）防守位置 **9** [c] (landslide) 滑坡 **10** [u] Geol (movement) 滑移; (deformation) [金属晶体的] 滑动变形; **a ~ fault** 滑断层 **11** [c] colloq dated **a ~ of a boy/girl** 瘦削的男孩/苗条的女孩

D **slips** *npl* (in cricket) **the ~s** 防守位置; **to field/be caught in the ~s** 在防守位置接球/被截住

Phrasal verbs

- **slip away** *vi* **1** (leave quietly) 溜走; (leave briefly) 离开一会儿; **to ~ away to Paris for the weekend** 去巴黎度周末 **2** euph (die) «*person*» 去世; **his life is ~ping away** 他行将就木
- **slip back** *vi* **1** (return quietly) 溜回去; (return briefly) 回去一会儿; **to ~ back (to the house) and do sth.** (quietly) 溜回（家）去做某事; (briefly) 回（家）去一会儿做某事; **to ~ back into port** 悄然回港 **2** Fin «*shares*» 贬值; «*prices*» 降低
- **slip by** *vi* «*time, life*» 流逝; «*opportunity*» 溜掉
- **slip down** *vi* **1** (fall) «*person*» 滑倒; «*socks, hat*» 往下滑 **2** (go down) 喝下; **this wine ~s down well** 这葡萄酒真好喝
- **slip in**

A *vi* 溜进; **a few errors ~ped in** 不经意出了几个错

B *vt* [**~ sth. in, ~ in sth.**] 放入 ‹*object*›; 把…伸进去 ‹*hand*›; fig 插入 ‹*remark, question*›; **to ~ in the clutch** 挂挡

- **slip off**

A *vi* **1** (come off) «*lid, object*» 滑落 **2** (leave quietly) 溜走; (leave briefly) 离开一会儿

B *vt* [**~ sth. off, ~ off sth.**] 脱下 ‹*clothes, shoes*›; 摘下 ‹*ring, gloves*›

- **slip on** *vt* [**~ sth. on, ~ on sth.**] 穿上 ‹*clothes, shoes*›; 戴上 ‹*ring, gloves*›
- **slip out**

A *vi* **1** (leave quietly) 溜出去; (leave briefly) 出去一会儿; **to ~ out for a moment/for a newspaper** 出去一会儿/买份报纸 **2** (escape) «*animal*» 挣脱; «*object*» 滑脱; fig «*words*» 无意中说出; **the words ~ped out before he ...** 他还未…，话就出口了; **it (just) ~ped out** （就那么）说漏了

B *vt* **to ~ out the clutch** 松开离合器

- **slip over** *vi* 滑倒
- **slip past** *vi* = **slip by**
- **slip through** *vi* «*error*» 被忽略
- **slip up** *vi* colloq 弄错; **to ~ up on sth.** 弄错某事

slip: ~ case *n* 封套; **~ cover** *n* **1** (for furniture) 家具套; **2** (for book) 书套; **~ knot** *n* **1** (running knot) 滑结; **2** (knot that is easily undone) 活结

slip-on

A *n* (garment) 套头装; (shoe) 无带便鞋

B *adj* 无带的 ‹*shoe*›; 开合简易的 ‹*connection*›

slipover /ˈslɪpəʊvə(r)/

A *adj* 套头的

B *n* 套头衫

slippage /ˈslɪpɪdʒ/ *n* **1** [u] (subsidence) 沉陷 **2** [u] (of wheel, clutch) 动力传递损耗 **3** [c and u] (decline in standard, popularity) 下降; (delay) 延误

slipped disc /ˌslɪpt ˈdɪsk/ *n* 椎间盘突出

slipper /ˈslɪpə(r)/ *n* **1** (indoor shoe) 拖鞋 **2** (dance, evening shoe) 轻便舞鞋

slippery /ˈslɪpəri/ *adj* **1** (slippy) 滑的 ‹*path, steps*›; 滑溜溜的 ‹*fish, reptile*›; **to be ~ underfoot** 脚下滑 **2** (difficult to deal with) 棘手的 ‹*subject, topic, situation*›; **to be on ~ ground** 处境困难; **to be on the ~ slope** 处境堪忧 **3** colloq (untrustworthy, unreliable) 靠不住的; (evasive) 油滑的

slippy /ˈslɪpi/ *adj* colloq **1** (slippery) 滑的 ‹*path, surface*›; **he skidded on a ~ road** 他在滑溜溜的路面上滑了一下 **2** Brit dated (quick) 快的; **look ~ about it!** 快点！

slip: ~ road *n* Brit [进出高速公路的] 匝道; **~shod** /ˈslɪpʃɒd/ *adj* 马虎的 ‹*person*›; 敷衍了事的 ‹*worker, style*›; **a ~shod piece of work** 一件粗糙的作品; **to be ~shod in** *or* **about sth.** 在某事上敷衍了事

slip stitch

A *n* 挑针

B *vt* 用挑针缝 ‹*hem*›

slipstream /ˈslɪpstriːm/

A *n* **1** (from propeller) 滑流; (from jet engine) 气流 **2** (behind car, motorbike) 低压气穴

B *vt* [为减少空气阻力] 紧跟 ‹*person, vehicle*›

slip: ~-up *n* colloq 差错; **a ~-up in** *or* **with sth.** 对某事的疏忽; **~ware** *n* [u] 施釉陶器; **~way** *n* [造船或修船的] 滑台

slit /slɪt/

A *n* 窄缝; **to make a ~ in sth.** 在某物上切开一条缝; **his eyes narrowed to ~s** 他的双眼眯成了一条缝; **a narrow ~ in the fence** 栅栏上的一条窄缝

B *vt* **1** (*pres p* **-tt-**, *pt, pp* **slit**) (by cutting) 割开 ‹*material*›; (by slitting) 拆开 ‹*envelope*›; **to ~ a letter open with a paper-knife** 用裁纸刀划开信; **to ~ sb.'s throat** 割破某人的喉咙; **to ~ one's (own) throat** 割喉; **to ~ one's wrists** 割腕 **2** (*pres p* **-tt-**, *pp* **slit**) (cut into strips) 把…切成条; **the material had been ~ into narrow strips** 布料被裁成了窄条 **3** (*pres p etc.* **-tt-**) colloq (narrow) **to ~ one's eyes at sb.** 眯缝眼睛看某人

S

slit-eyed /ˈslɪtaɪd/ *adj* 眯缝眼的 ‹*person*›; 眯眼的 ‹*expression, look*›

slither /ˈslɪðə(r)/ *vi* 1 (move smoothly) «*person*» 滑行; «*snake*» 爬行; **to ~ about on ...** 在…上滑行 ‹*ice, surface*›; **to ~ down the bank** 滑下堤岸; **to ~ into one's seat** 滑到座位上; **the snake ~ed across the path** 蛇爬过小径 2 (move unsteadily) «*person*» 踉踉跄跄地走; «*car*» 打滑着开; **he ~ed and fell on the ice** 他在冰上滑倒了; **when we got to the embankment we ~ed down (it)** 到达堤岸后，我们摇摇晃晃地滑了下去

slit: ~ pocket *n* 侧开缝衣袋; **~ trench** *n* 狭长掩壕

sliver /ˈslɪvə(r)/
A *n* 长薄片; **cake? — just a ~!** colloq 要蛋糕吗？——一小片就好！; **the glass broke into ~s when it hit the ground** 玻璃杯掉到地上摔成了碎片
B *vi* «*glass, wood*» 裂成碎片
C *vt* 使裂成碎片; **the impact ~ed the windscreen** 挡风玻璃被撞碎了

Sloane /sləʊn/ *n* Brit pej colloq **~ (Ranger)** [尤指住在伦敦的] 富家女

slob /slɒb/ *n* colloq (lazy person) 懒汉; (slovenly person) 邋遢的人; (ill-mannered person) 粗鲁的人; **get up, you lazy ~!** 起床，你这懒猪！

slobber /ˈslɒbə(r)/ colloq
A *vi* 淌口水; **to ~ at the mouth** 嘴角流口水; **to ~ at the smell/sight of sth.** 一闻到/看到某物就流口水; **to ~ over sb./sth.** 对某人/某物垂涎三尺; **the visitors ~ed over the new baby** 客人们毫不掩饰对新生婴儿的喜爱
B *n* [u] 口水

slobbery /ˈslɒbəri/ *adj* pej colloq 淌口水的; **a ~ kiss** 湿吻

slobbish /ˈslɒbɪʃ/ *adj* Brit colloq (lazy) 懒惰的; (slovenly) 邋遢的; (ill-mannered) 粗鲁的

sloe /sləʊ/ *n* 1 (fruit) 黑刺李果 2 (bush) = **blackthorn**

sloe: ~-eyed *adj* (with dark eyes) 黑眼睛的; (with slanted eyes) 细长眼的; (with almond-shaped eyes) 杏眼的; **~ gin** *n* [u] 黑刺李杜松子酒

slog /slɒg/ colloq
A *n* 1 [c] (hard stroke) 猛击; **to have** *or* **take a ~ (at sth.)** (朝某物) 猛击; **it was just a ~!** (without skill) 那纯属乱打一气！ 2 [u and c] **a (hard) ~** (work) 苦差事; (walk) 跋涉; **a long, hard ~** 艰苦的长途跋涉; **getting this done is going to be a long hard ~** 做这件事可谓任重道远啊
B *vt* (*pres p etc.* **-gg-**) 1 (hit hard) 猛击; **to ~ sb. on the chin** 猛击某人的下巴; **to ~ sth. to/over sth.** 把某物猛击到/过某处; **to ~ the ball for six** (in cricket) 大力击球得六分; **to ~ it out (for sth.)** Brit (为某事物) 一决胜负 2 (progress with effort) **to ~ one's way** 艰难前进; **to ~ one's way through/to** *or* **towards/across somewhere** 坚持不懈地穿过/走向/穿越某处 3 (work hard) 埋头苦干; **to ~ one's guts out** 苦干
C *vi* (*pres p etc.* **-gg-**) 1 (hit hard) 猛击; **to ~ at sb./sth.** 对着某人/某物猛击 2 (progress with effort) 迎难而进; **to ~ up/down the slope** 艰难地上坡/下坡; **to ~ through sth.** 艰难地穿过 ‹*snow*›; **to ~ through one's work/a task** 辛苦地工作/完成任务 3 (work hard) 苦干; **to ~ from morning to night** 从早忙到晚

Phrasal verb
- **slog away** *vi* colloq 苦干; **to ~ away at sth.** 努力做某事; **to ~ away to meet a deadline** 为赶工期而苦干

slogan /ˈsləʊgən/ *n* 1 (short phrase) 广告口号 2 (motto) 口号; **a political ~** 政治口号

sloganeer /ˌsləʊgəˈnɪə(r)/ pej
A *vi* 拟订口号
B *n* 口号拟订者

sloganeering /ˌsləʊgəˈnɪərɪŋ/ *n* [u] pej 拟订口号; **political/shallow ~** 政治口号的拟订/拼凑拟订

slogger /ˈslɒgə(r)/ *n* colloq 1 Sport (hard-hitter) [板球或拳击运动中的] 猛击者 2 (hard worker) 埋头苦干的人; **he may not be very bright, but he's a real ~** 他可能不太聪明，但干活很卖力

slo-mo /ˈsləʊməʊ/ *n* [u] colloq = **slow motion**

sloop /sluːp/ *n* 单桅帆船

slop /slɒp/
A *vi* (*pres p etc.* **-pp-**) «*liquid*» 溅出; **to ~ out (of sth.)** (从某物中) 溅出; **to ~ over sth.** 溅到某物上
B *vt* (*pres p etc.* **-pp-**) 使…溅出 ‹*liquid*›; **to ~ sth. on to sth.** 把某物溅到某物上; **to ~ sth. into sth.** 把某物倒入某物; **to ~ sth. over sth.** 把某物泼在某物上
C *n* [u] colloq pej 味淡的流体食物; **they fed us on insipid ~ in hospital** 在医院他们让我们吃淡而无味的流食
D **slops** *npl* 1 (dirty water) 脏水 2 (human waste) 粪便 3 (kitchen waste) 泔脚

Phrasal verbs
- **slop about, slop around** *vi* 1 (slap noisily) «*liquid*» [在容器中] 晃荡; **I could hear the soup ~ping about** 我听到汤在晃荡 2 esp Brit (referring to dress) 不修边幅; (referring to behaviour) 举止懒散; **she never does anything; she just ~s about at home all day long** 她什么都不干，终日在家里晃来晃去
- **slop out** *vi* «*prisoner*» 倒便桶

slop: ~ basin Brit, **~ bowl** Amer *ns* 茶渣盆; **~ bucket, ~ pail** *ns* (in prison) 便桶; (in kitchen) 泔脚桶

slope /sləʊp/
A *n* 1 (incline) 倾斜; **to be on a ~** 呈倾斜状; **the ~ on the road is considerable** 公路的坡度很大; **a 40° ~, a ~ of 40°** 40 度的斜面; **a steep/gentle ~** 陡坡/缓坡; **a ~ of 1 in 10** 1 比 10 的斜率; **at the ~** Mil 在肩上; **we carried our rifles at the ~** 我们扛着步枪 2 (on hill, mountain) 山坡; (road) 坡; **halfway up** *or* **down the ~** 在半山坡上; **the northern/southern ~s** 北坡/南坡
B *vi* «*ground, roof, handwriting*» 倾斜; **to ~ down** *or* **away (to ...)** (向…) 倾斜; **to ~ to the left/right** 向左/向右倾斜
C *vt* Mil 扛 ‹*firearm*›; **the sergeant gave the command: ~ arms!** 中士命令道：枪上肩！

Phrasal verb
- **slope off** *vi* colloq 溜走; **I called for volunteers, but everyone had ~d off!** 我招呼志愿帮忙的人，但大伙都开溜了！

sloping /ˈsləʊpɪŋ/ *adj* 倾斜的 ‹*ground, floor, handwriting*›; **a house with a ~ roof** 带坡顶的房子

sloppily /ˈslɒpɪli/ *adv* 1 (carelessly) 马虎地 ‹*write, made, presented*›; 邋遢地 ‹*dress*›; **he was dismissed for working ~** 他因干活马虎被解雇; **a ~ run organization** 管理松散的机构; **a ~-built house** 草草建造的房屋 2 (sentimentally) 伤感地 ‹*behave, talk*›; **he smiled ~ at her** 他伤感地朝她笑着

sloppiness /ˈslɒpɪnɪs/ *n* [u] 1 (of thinking, discipline) 无条理; (of work) 马虎; (of dress) 邋遢 2 (sentimentality) 伤感 3 (wateriness) 稀薄

slopping out *n* [u] Brit 倒便桶

sloppy /ˈslɒpi/ *adj* 1 (untidy) 邋遢的 ‹*dress*›; (careless) 马虎的 ‹*work*›; 松散的 ‹*procedure, management*›; **a ~ dresser** 穿着邋遢的人; **a ~ worker** 工作马虎的人; **a ~ eater** 吃东西弄得到处都是的人; **a ~ writer** 写作不严谨的人; **his work is ~ in the extreme** 他的工作极其草率; **~ English** 错误百出的英语 2 colloq (sentimental) 感情脆弱的 ‹*girl*›; 庸俗伤感的 ‹*film, letter, words*›; **he gave her a ~ grin** 他伤感地朝她咧嘴一笑 3 (watery) 太稀的; **a bowl of ~ porridge** 一碗稀粥

sloppy joe /ˌslɒpi ˈdʒəʊ/ *n* colloq 1 Brit (sweater) 宽大套衫 2 Amer (hamburger) 辣番茄肉馅汉堡

slosh /slɒʃ/
A *vi* **~ (about)** «*liquid*» [在容器中] 咣当作响
B *vt* 1 (make splash) 搅动 ‹*liquid*›; (apply) 胡乱涂抹 ‹*paint, glue, oil*›; **to ~ sth. on** *or* **on to sth.** 把某物胡乱涂在某物上; **to ~ sth. over sth.** 把某物泼在某物上; **to ~ sth. in** *or* **into sth.** 把某物匆忙倒入某物 2 Brit colloq (hit) 揍 ‹*person*›; **he ~ed him on the nose** 他一拳打在他的鼻子上

sloshed /slɒʃt/ *adj* colloq 喝醉的; **to be ~ out of one's head** *or* **mind** 酩酊大醉

slot /slɒt/
A *n* 1 (slit) 狭缝; (for coin) 投币口; (for ticket) 投票口; (for letters) 投信口; **a ~ for sth./doing sth.** 塞入某物/做某事的窄缝; **to push sth. through a ~** 把某物塞入狭缝 2 (groove) 槽沟; **a ~ for/in sth.** 装某物的/某物里的槽沟; **to make** *or* **cut a ~** 挖出槽沟 3 (scheduled time) 时段; **landing ~s** Aviat 着陆时间; **a prime-time/comedy ~** 黄金/喜剧时段; **a (five-minute) ~ for sth.** (五分钟的) …时间 ‹*announcement, take-off*›; **the band has a regular ~ in the bar** 乐队定时在酒吧演出; **to find a ~ (for sb./sth.)** (为某人/某事物) 留出时间; **to fit sb./sth. into a ~** 为某人/某事物安排时间 4 (job) 职位; **a ~ in the personnel department** 人事部的职位; **to create a ~ for sb.** 为某人设一个职位
B **slots** *npl* colloq **the ~s** 吃角子老虎机; **to play the ~s** 玩老虎机
C *vt* (*pres p etc.* **-tt-**) 1 (make slot in) 在…上挖出沟槽 ‹*wood, metal*›; **a ~ted tube** 开缝管 2 (fit in slot) **to ~ sth. into sth.** 把…塞入某物 ‹*piece, pipe*›; **to ~ a rail into the groove** 把铁轨铺到轨槽里 3 (schedule, assign) 为…安排时段 ‹*program, event*›; **to ~ an appointment into the schedule/for one o'clock** 将约见排进日程/安排在1点钟; **to ~ sb. into a position** 给某人安排职位
D *vi* (*pres p etc.* **-tt-**) 插入; **to ~ into sth.** 插入 ‹*hole, machine*›; **to ~ into place** *or* **position** «*piece*» 安装到位; **the two parts ~ into each other** 这两个部件互相插接; **to ~ into one's new position very well** fig 对新职位很适应

Phrasal verbs
- **slot in**
A *vi* «*shelf, rod*» 可放入; «*part*» 可安装
B *vt* [**~ sth./sb. in, ~ in sth./sb.**]
1 (fit into opening) 铺入 ‹*rail*›; 塞进 ‹*shelf, rod*›; 安装进 ‹*part*› 2 (schedule) 为…安排时段 ‹*meeting, event*› 3 Brit Sport colloq 踢进 ‹*goal, shot*›
- **slot together**
A *vi* «*components, parts*» 插接起来
B *vt* [**~ sth. together, ~ together sth.**] 把…插接起来 ‹*components, parts*›

slot car *n* Amer 槽轨电动玩具赛车

sloth /sləʊθ/ *n* 1 [c] Zool 树懒 2 [u] (laziness) 懒散

slothful /ˈsləʊθfl/ *adj* 懒散的

slothfully /ˈsləʊθfəli/ *adv* 懒散地

slothfulness /ˈsləʊθfəlnɪs/ *n* [u] 懒散

slot machine *n* 1 (for gambling) 吃角子老虎机 2 Brit (for vending) 投币式自动售货机

slouch /slaʊtʃ/
A *n* 1 (posture) 无精打采的姿势; **to walk with a ~** 无精打采地走路; **she's got a terrible ~** 她垂头丧气 2 colloq (lazy person) 懒散的人; (slow person) 迟钝的人; (incompetent person) 无能的人; **he's no ~** 他绝非等闲之辈; **he's no ~ at tennis** 他网球打得很好
B *vi* (sit badly) 低头垂肩地坐着; (stand badly) 无精打采地站着; **tall people often ~ in an attempt to disguise their height** 高个子的人总爱佝偻着腰，试图掩饰他们的身高

slough[1] /slaʊ, Amer *also* sluː/ *n* **1** (bog) 沼泽; **to be stuck in a ～** 陷入泥沼 **2** fig (of despair) 绝境; (static situation) 困境

slough[2] /slʌf/ *vt* **1** (shed) 蜕 ‹*scab*›; 使…脱落 ‹*dead tissue*›; **a snake regularly ～s its skin** 蛇定期蜕皮 **2** fig (get rid off) 摆脱 ‹*responsibility, worry*›; **he has ～ed off all his bad habits** 他已经改掉了所有的恶习

Slovak /ˈsləʊvæk/ ▸**p. 426, p. 503**

A *adj* (of Slovakia) 斯洛伐克的; (of the people) 斯洛伐克人的; (of the language) 斯洛伐克语的

B *n* **1** [c] (person) 斯洛伐克人 **2** [u] (language) 斯洛伐克语

Slovakia /sləˈvækɪə/ *pr n* 斯洛伐克

Slovakian /sləˈvækɪən/ *adj, n* = **Slovak**

Slovene /ˈsləʊviːn/ ▸**p. 426, p. 503**

A *adj* (of Slovenia) 斯洛文尼亚的; (of the people) 斯洛文尼亚人的; (of the language) 斯洛文尼亚语的

B *n* **1** [c] (person) 斯洛文尼亚人 **2** [u] (language) 斯洛文尼亚语

Slovenia /sləˈviːnɪə/ *pr n* 斯洛文尼亚

Slovenian /sləˈviːnɪən/ *adj, n* = **Slovene**

slovenliness /ˈslʌvnlɪnɪs/ *n* [u] **1** (of person, appearance) 邋遢 **2** (carelessness) 马虎; (laziness) 懒散; **there is no room for ～ in this business** 这事容不得半点马虎; **the ～ of his language was quite disgraceful** 他用词低俗随便，很丢人

slovenly /ˈslʌvnli/ *adj* **1** (untidy) 邋遢的 ‹*appearance, dress, person*›; 懒散的 ‹*habits*›; **even at his wedding he looked ～** 即使在婚礼上他看上去也是邋里邋遢的; **the ～ state of the room** 房间的凌乱状况 **2** (careless) 马虎的 ‹*performance*›; 无条理的 ‹*speech*›; 不地道的 ‹*language*›; **I've never seen such ～ work!** 我从未见过干得这么马虎的工作!

slow /sləʊ/

A *adj* **1** (taking long time) 耗时的; (low in speed) 缓慢的; **to make ～ progress/a ～ recovery** 进展/恢复缓慢; **at a ～ speed/tempo** 以缓慢的速度/节拍; **to be a ～ grower** «*plant*» 生长缓慢; **to be a ～ reader/driver** 阅读/开车速度慢; **a ～ pace of life** 慢悠悠的生活节奏; **to fall into a ～ decline** 开始缓慢衰退; **it's ～ work (doing sth.)** （做某事）快不得; **a ～ poison** 慢性毒药; **the ～ movement** Mus 慢板乐章; **to have a ～ eye** 有只眼睛不灵敏 **2** (mentally dull) 迟钝的; **he's a bit ～** 他有点笨; **a ～ learner** 学东西慢的人; **to be ～ at** *or* **in sth.** 在…上迟钝 ‹*maths*›; **to be ～ at** *or* **in doing sth.** 做某事迟钝 **3** *pred* (not hasty) 慢吞吞的; **to be ～ to do sth., to be ～ in** *or* **about doing sth.** 做某事很慢; **to be ～ to anger/chide** 不轻易生气/责备; **to be ～ of speech** 说话慢吞吞; **she's not ～ to give her opinion** 她会及时给出自己的意见 **4** (uneventful) 乏味的 ‹*film, plot*›; 沉闷的 ‹*town, life*› **5** (sluggish) 缓慢的 ‹*pulse*›; 不景气的 ‹*economy, business*› **6** *pred* (behind correct time) 走时慢的; **to be ten minutes ～** «*clock, watch*» 慢十分钟 **7** (impeding speed) 难走的 ‹*road, route*›; Sport 妨碍速度的 ‹*court, surface*›; **rain made the pitch ～** 下雨导致投球速度不快 **8** Phot 曝光慢的 ‹*film, lens*› **9** (not hot) 烧得不旺的 ‹*oven*›; 缓慢的 ‹*combustion*›; **cook over a ～ heat** 用文火煮

B *adv* 缓慢地; **to go/drive ～** 慢慢走/开车; **please speak a little ～er** 请说得慢一点; **you're walking too ～** colloq 你走得太慢了; **～-cooked food** 慢煮的食物; **a ～-acting fertilizer** 慢效肥料; **～ astern/ahead!** Naut 慢速后退/前进!; **a '～' sign** Aut 减速标志牌

C *vi* «*vehicle, runner*» 减速; «*breathing, pulse*» 变慢; «*output, demand*» 减少; «*progress, growth*» 放缓; **to ～ to a walking pace/a stop** 减慢到步行速度/减速停下来; **to ～ to 30 mph** 减速到每小时 30 英里; **to ～ to a crawl** «*traffic, driver*» 慢如爬行

D *vt* 使…减速 ‹*vehicle, runner*›; 使…变慢 ‹*breathing, pulse*›; 使…放缓 ‹*progress, growth*›; 减少 ‹*output, demand*›; **to ～ sb./sth. to a walking pace/30 mph** 使某人/某物减慢到步行速度/减速到每小时 30 英里; **age had ～ed his reactions** 他上了年纪，反应慢了

Phrasal verbs

- **slow down**

A *vi* **1** (reduce speed) «*vehicle, runner*» 减速; «*breathing, pulse*» 变慢; «*demand, output*» 减少; «*progress, growth*» 放缓; **～ down a bit!** 慢一点! **2** colloq (reduce pace of life) 放松; **he'll never ～ down** 他总是闲不住; **you should ～ down a bit** 你应该放松点

B *vt* [**～ sth./sb. down, ～ down sth./sb.**] 使…减速 ‹*vehicle, runner*›; 使…变慢 ‹*breathing, pulse*›; 减少 ‹*demand, output*›; 使…放缓 ‹*progress, growth*›

- **slow up** *vi, vt* = **slow down**

slow: ～ bowler *n* (in cricket) （旋转）慢球投手; **～ burner** *n* fig 慢热的事物 [指没有立即受到瞩目的事物]; **～-burning** *adj* **1** lit 燃烧缓慢的 ‹*fuel*›; 不易熔断的 ‹*fuse*› **2** fig (slowly developing) 逐渐到来的 ‹*success*›; 逐渐产生的 ‹*effect*›; 逐渐发作的 ‹*anger*›; **a ～-burning film** 一部渐入佳境的电影; **～coach** *n* Brit colloq 慢条斯理的人; **get a move on, you old ～coach!** 快一点，你这个磨磨蹭蹭的老家伙!; **～ cooker** *n* 焖炖锅; **～down** *n* **1** (decline) 衰退; **a ～down in demand** 需求量的减少; **a ～down in the housing market** 房地产市场的衰退; **2** (reduction in speed) 减速; **～ food** *n* [u] 慢餐 [与快餐相对，提倡有机食物、本土生产与消费等]; **～ handclap** *n* [表示不满或不耐烦的] 缓慢鼓掌; **～ lane** *n* Brit 慢车道

slowly /ˈsləʊli/ *adv* **1** (not quickly) 慢悠悠地 ‹*go, drive, speak*›; **to walk/react ～** 慢慢走/反应慢; **life moves ～ in the countryside** 乡间生活节奏缓慢; **～, she opened the door** 慢慢地，她打开了门 **2** (over period of time) 渐渐地 ‹*change, realize*›; 缓慢地 ‹*improve, develop*›; **～ but surely** 缓慢但有把握地; **～ but surely, he began to get better** 虽然不是很明显，但他确实开始好转了

slow: ～ march *n* 慢步走; **'～ ..., march!'** "慢步…走!"; **～ motion** *n* [u] 慢动作; **the scene was shot in ～ motion** 这一场是用慢镜头拍摄的; **～-moving** *adj* 行进缓慢的 ‹*traffic*›; 情节发展缓慢的 ‹*film, book*›; **a ～-moving farm vehicle** 一辆慢腾腾的农用车; **～-moving ocean currents** 流速缓慢的洋流

slowness /ˈsləʊnɪs/ *n* [u] **1** (of motion, vehicle, pace, response, voice) 缓慢 **2** (of intellect, ability) 迟钝 **3** (of business, market) 不景气 **4** (of plot, film, novel) 进展迟缓 **5** (of route, road) 难走 **6** Sport (of surface, court, track) 妨碍速度 **7** Phot (of film) 曝光慢

slow: ～poke *n* Amer colloq = **～coach**; **～ puncture** *n* 慢撒气扎孔; **to get a ～ puncture** 车胎被扎了个孔，缓慢漏气; **～ reactor** *n* 慢中子反应堆; **～ train** *n* 慢车; **～-witted** *adj* 迟钝的; **～-worm** *n* 慢缺肢蜥

SLR *abbr* = **single-lens reflex**

sludge /slʌdʒ/ *n* [u] **1** (muddy substance) 烂泥状物质; (in drain) 淤泥; **you can't swim in that lake, it's full of ～** 你不能在那湖里游泳，里面全是烂泥 **2** (oily sediment) 油泥

sludgy /ˈslʌdʒi/ *adj* 淤泥般的; **the bottom of the lake is all ～!** 湖底全是烂泥!

slug /slʌg/

A *n* **1** Zool 蛞蝓 **2** esp Amer (bullet) 子弹; (of lead) 铅弹 **3** (gulp) 一口; (shot) 一杯; **a few ～s of gin made her feel more relaxed** 几口杜松子酒下肚后她放松了一些

B *vt* (*pres p etc.* **-gg-**) esp Amer colloq (hit) 重击; **to ～ sb. one** 打某人一拳; **to ～ it out** 一决高下; **I want to discuss our differences but he just wants to ～ it out** 我希望探讨我们之间的分歧，但是他只想比出个高下

slug: ～ bait *n* [u] 蛞蝓饵; **～fest** *n* Amer colloq (struggle) 激烈的争斗; (contest) 激烈的比赛 [尤指拳击比赛或棒球赛]

sluggard /ˈslʌgəd/ *n* 懒人; **he's a ～ who never gets up before noon** 他是个从不在中午前起床的懒汉

slugger /ˈslʌgə(r)/ *n* colloq (in baseball) 强击手; (in boxing) 重拳手

sluggish /ˈslʌgɪʃ/ *adj* 行动缓慢的 ‹*person, animal*›; 缓慢的 ‹*river, flow, pulse, reaction*›; 没有活力的 ‹*heartbeat*›; 疲软的 ‹*sales, economy*›; 性能差的 ‹*engine, car*›; **the heat made us ～** 高温使我们萎靡不振; **after a ～ start** 在经历起步阶段的不景气之后

sluggishly /ˈslʌgɪʃli/ *adv* 缓慢地 ‹*move, flow, react, respond*›; 疲软地 ‹*sell*›; **to move ～ in the intense heat** 在酷热中萎靡不振地行进; **his liver was functioning very ～** 他的肝脏功能很差

sluggishness /ˈslʌgɪʃnɪs/ *n* [u] (of person, animal) 行动缓慢; (of river, flow, reaction) 缓慢; (of heartbeat) 没有活力; (of sales, economy) 疲软; (of engine, car) 性能差; **～ of blood circulation** 血液循环的不畅

slug pellet *n* 杀蛞蝓药丸

sluice /sluːs/

A *n* **1** **～ (gate)** 水闸 **2** (channel) 泄水道; **the water is diverted along the ～** 水被引到闸沟中 **3** (act of rinsing) 冲洗

B *vt* (rinse) 洗 ‹*face*›; 冲洗 ‹*floor*›

C *vi* «*liquid*» 泄出

Phrasal verbs

- **sluice down** *vt* [**～ sth. down, ～ down sth.**] 冲洗 ‹*floor, deck*›
- **sluice out** *vt* [**～ out sth, ～ sth. out**] 冲洗 ‹*stables, garage*›

sluiceway /ˈsluːsweɪ/ *n* = **sluice A2**

slum /slʌm/

A *n* **1** (poor area) 贫民窟; **～ area/property/conditions/clearance** 贫民区/贫民区房产/贫民窟状况/贫民窟的清除; **the ～s (of ...)** （…的）贫民区 **2** colloq (house) 破旧房屋; (building) 破旧建筑

B *vi* (*pres p etc.* **-mm-**) colloq **to ～ it** 过穷日子; **they spend their leisure time ～ming and visiting lowlife bars** 他们闲暇时体验贫民生活并出入低档酒吧

slumber /ˈslʌmbə(r)/

A *n* [u] 睡眠; **to fall into a heavy** *or* **deep/peaceful ～** 陷入沉睡/安睡

B **slumbers** *npl* 睡眠; **the blast woke them from their ～s** 爆炸声将他们从熟睡中惊醒

C *vi* **1** lit (sleep) 睡觉 **2** fig (lie dormant) 蛰伏; **a ～ing volcano** 休眠火山; **the revolutionary spirit which has ～ed for so long** 长期蛰伏的革命精神

slumber party *n* Amer [尤指十几岁女孩子的] 留宿聚会

slum: ～ dwelling *n* 贫民窟住所; **～lord** *n* Amer colloq pej [尤指牟取暴利的] 贫民窟房东

slummy /ˈslʌmi/ *adj* colloq 肮脏的 ‹*area, house, appearance*›; **what a ～ kitchen!** 多脏的厨房啊!

slump /slʌmp/

A *n* **1** (fall in value, profit etc.) 骤降; **a ～ in the property market** 房地产市场的急剧衰退; **to experience a ～** «*economy, market*» 经历滑坡; **last year's dramatic shares ～** 去年的股票大跌; **the worldwide ～ in oil demand** 全世界石油需求量的锐减 **2** (period of low economic activity) 萧条期; **the company is slowly recovering from a prolonged ～** 该公司正从漫长的低迷中慢慢恢复过来 **3** (period of decline) 低潮期; **the team/party is experiencing a ～** 该球队/政党正处于低潮

B *vi* **1** (fall, reduce) «*demand, trade, sales, profits*» 猛跌; «*business, economy*» 滑坡; «*popularity, support*» 锐减; **the newspaper's circulation has ～ed** 该报纸的发行量大幅度下降 **2** (sit heavily) 重重地坐下; (fall heavily) 重重地倒下; **to**

S

~ **into an armchair/to the ground** 一屁股坐在扶手椅里/扑通一声摔倒在地 **3** (fail) 惨败; (decline) 衰败 ; **the team ~ed to another one-nil defeat** 这个队又以一比零落败

slung /slʌŋ/ *pt, pp* ▸ **sling B**

slunk /slʌŋk/ *pt, pp* ▸ **slink**

slur /slɜː(r)/
A *vt* (*pres p etc.* **-rr-**) **1** (say indistinctly) 含糊不清地说; **'goodnight,' he ~red** "晚安," 他咕哝着地说; **to ~ one's speech** *or* **words** 说话不利索 **2** Mus 《*singer*》 连唱 〈*notes*〉; 《*player*》 连奏 〈*notes*〉
B *vi* (*pres p etc.* **-rr-**) 含糊不清地说话
C *n* **1** (allegation, insinuation) 诋毁; (aspersion) 诽谤; **to cast a ~ on sb./sth.** 诋毁某人/某事物; **to be a ~ on sb./sth.** 是对某人/某事物的诽谤; **an outrageous ~** 无耻的中伤; **a racial ~** 种族侮辱语 **2** Mus 连奏线 **3** (indistinct speech) 含糊不清的讲话

slurp /slɜːp/
A *vi* 发出啧啧声; **she ~ed loudly as she drank her coffee** 她啧啧地喝咖啡
B *vt* (when eating) 啧啧地吃; (when drinking) 啧啧地喝; **the baby ~ed his orange juice** 婴儿吸溜着橙汁
C *n* 啧啧声; **she drank her tea with a ~** 她咂着嘴喝茶

slurred /slɜːd/ *adj* **1** (indistinct) 含混不清的 〈*speech, remark, utterance*〉 **2** Mus 连奏的 〈*notes*〉

slurry /ˈslʌri/ *n* [u and c] 稀泥浆; **the rain turned the ground into ~** 雨水把地面变成了一片泥浆

slush /slʌʃ/ *n* [u] **1** (melted snow) 融雪; (melted ice) 融冰; **she walked through the wet, slippery ~** 她从潮湿、溜滑的雪泥中走过 **2** colloq pej (excessive sentimentality) 矫揉造作; (romance) 庸俗的言情; **a romantic novel full of ~** 充斥着缠绵感伤情节的爱情小说

slush fund *n* [尤指用于政治贿赂的] 非法基金

slushy /ˈslʌʃi/ *n* **1** (melting) 半融化的 **2** (covered in melted snow) 雪泥覆盖的 〈*pavement, ground*〉; **the streets were ~ and slippery** 街道上满是雪泥, 滑溜溜的 **3** colloq (excessively sentimental) 矫揉造作的 〈*film, story*〉; **a book full of false, ~ sentiment** 一本充斥着虚情假意的书

slut /slʌt/ *n* colloq pej **1** (promiscuous woman) 荡妇; (prostitute) 妓女 **2** (slovenly woman) 邋遢女人

sluttish /ˈslʌtɪʃ/ *adj* colloq pej **1** (promiscuous) 淫荡的 **2** (dirty) 邋遢的; **she looked ~ and unkempt** 她看上去邋里邋遢、不修边幅

slutty /ˈslʌti/ *adj* colloq pej 淫荡的

sly /slaɪ/ *adj* **1** (cunning) 狡猾的 〈*person*〉; **a ~ (old) dog** colloq (老) 滑头; **I don't trust him, he seems really ~** 我不信任他, 他看起来很油滑; **that was a ~ trick they played on us** 那是他们对我们耍的诡计 **2** (surreptitious) 偷偷的; **on the ~** 偷偷地 **3** (knowing) 诡秘的 〈*smile, wink, remark*〉

slyboots /ˈslaɪbuːts/ *n* colloq 滑头; **you never told me you had a girlfriend, you old ~!** 你从没告诉过我你有女朋友, 你这个老滑头!

slyly /ˈslaɪli/ *adv* **1** (with cunning) 狡猾地 〈*behave, speak*〉; **~, he slipped the letter into his pocket** 他把信偷偷地塞进口袋 **2** (knowingly) 诡秘地 〈*smile, look, wink, remark*〉

slyness /ˈslaɪnɪs/ *n* [u] **1** (cunning of person, act) 狡猾; **I can't believe he's capable of such ~!** 我无法相信他能如此狡诈! **2** (knowingness of smile, look, remark) 诡秘

smack¹ /smæk/
A *n* **1** [c] (sharp slap) 猛拍; (sharp blow) 猛击; (slap on face) 打耳光; **if you don't behave, you'll get a ~** 如果你不规矩些, 你就要挨揍 **2** [c] (sharp sound) (of object) 撞击声; (of waves) 拍击声; (of hand) 掌掴声; **the books fell to the floor with a ~** 那些书啪的一声掉到了地板上; **the ~ of waves against the harbour wall** 海浪拍打港口护堤的啪啪声 **3** [c] (loud kiss) 响吻; **the boy's aunt gave him a big ~ on the cheek** 男孩的姨妈在他脸上亲了一个响吻 **4** [c] (flavour, taste) 味道 **5** [c] (hint) 暗示; (trace) 痕迹 **6** [u] colloq (heroin) 海洛因
B *vt* **1** (strike) 猛拍 〈*person, hand, leg*〉; 掴 〈*face*〉; 猛击 〈*ball*〉; **she is always ~ing her children** 她老是打孩子; **she ~ed him in the face** 她扇了他一耳光 **2** (open and close noisily) 咂 〈*lips*〉 **3** (smash) 啪地一放; (drive) 冲撞; **he ~ed his hand down flat on the table** 他用手拍了一下桌子; **he ~ed his car into a lamp post** 他开车猛地撞在了灯柱上
C *vi* 暗示; **to ~ of sth.** 有某事物的味道; **this drink ~s of gin** 这种饮料有杜松子酒味; **their remarks ~ed of bigotry** 他们的话有点偏执
D *adv* colloq **1** (unexpectedly) 猛然; (sharply) 猛烈地; **he ran ~ into his boss** 他和上司撞了个满怀; **the car went ~ into the lamp post** 汽车猛地撞在了灯柱上; **he hit him ~ on the jaw** 他猛击他的下巴 **2** (directly, precisely) 恰好; **~ in front of ...** 在…的正前方; **he lives ~ in the middle of town** 他住在市中心

smack² *n* [c] Naut (boat) 单桅小帆船

smack bang *adv* colloq = **smack¹ D**

smacker /ˈsmækə(r)/ *n* colloq **1** (kiss) 响吻; **give her a great big ~!** 使劲亲她一个响吻! **2** Brit (one pound) 一英镑 **3** Amer (one dollar) 一美元

smacking /ˈsmækɪŋ/ *n* **1** [u] (action, practice) [尤指对孩子的] 掴打 **2** [c] (act, instance) 一顿掴打; **to get a ~** 挨一顿揍

small /smɔːl/
A *adj* **1** (not big) 小的 〈*object*〉; 矮小的 〈*person, animal*〉; **a ~ hill/room/car** 小山/小屋/小汽车; **~ size/proportion** 小尺寸/小部分; **to be (a bit/too) ~** 《*clothes, shoes*》 穿着 (有点/太) 小; 《*hat, gloves*》 戴着 (有点/太) 小; **to count in its** *or* **their own ~ way** 《*aid, contribution*》 有其意义; **it's a ~ world!** colloq 世界真小啊! ; **the ~est room** colloq euph 厕所; **all creatures great and ~** 万物生灵; **~ is beautiful** 小的就是好的 **2** (few in number) 成员少的 〈*family*〉; 小型的 〈*wedding, celebration*〉; **a ~ crowd/quantity** 一小群/少量; **a ~ party/theatre company** 小党派/小剧团 **3** (minor) 次要的 〈*problem*〉; 不大的 〈*effect, difference*〉; 简单的 〈*task*〉; **a ~ mistake/change** 小错误/小改动; **the ~est details** 微不足道的细节 **4** (young) 年幼的; **when I was ~** 我小时候; **I was only ~** 那时候我还小 **5** *usu attrib* (lower-case) 小写的 〈*letter*〉; **it's de Broglie with a ~ d** 是de Broglie, d 小写 **6** *usu attrib* pej (petty) 卑鄙狭隘的; **that was a ~ thing to do** 做这事真卑鄙; **to have a ~ mind** 为人卑鄙 **7** *attrib* (not much) 极少的 〈*reason, comfort*〉; **to have ~ cause to worry** 几乎没有什么可担心的; **~ wonder ...** 怪不得…; **to be of no ~ consequence** *or* **importance** 极其重要 **8** (quiet) 微弱的 〈*noise*〉; **in a ~ voice** 小声地 **9** (humiliated) 丢脸的; (embarrassed) 尴尬的; **to make sb. look/feel ~** (humiliated) 使某人显得/感觉很丢脸; (embarrassed) 使某人显得/感觉很尴尬
B *adv* **1** (into small pieces) 小块地; **to cut/chop/fold sth. up ~** 把某物切/砍/折成小块 **2** (in small size) 小规模地; **to start ~** 从小本经营开始; **to think/live ~** 思想/生活谦卑; **write it ~er** 把它写得再小点
C *n* **(in) the ~ of the** *or* **one's back** (在) 后腰
D **smalls** *npl* Brit colloq dated euph 小件衣服

small ad *n* Brit 分类小广告; **the ~s section** 分类广告栏

small arms *npl* 轻武器

small arms fire *n* [u] 轻武器火力

small: ~ beer *n* [u] Brit colloq (thing) 微不足道的东西; (person) 小人物; **to be ~ beer (beside sth.)** colloq (和某物比起来) 微不足道; **~ business** *n* 小企业; **~ businessman** ▸ **p. 409** *n* 小商人; **~ change** *n* [u] 零钱; **£10,000 is ~ change to someone as rich as him** fig 1万英镑对像他这样的富人来说是小钱; **~ claims court** *n* Brit 小额索赔地方法院; **~ fortune** *n* colloq 一大笔钱; **to cost a ~ fortune** 花费一大笔钱; **~ fry** *npl* **1** (young fish) 小鱼; (young animals) 幼畜; (young children) 幼儿; **2** (insignificant people) 小人物; (insignificant things) 微不足道的东西; **~holder** ▸ **p. 409** *n* Brit 小农场主; **~holding** *n* Brit **1** [c] (agricultural holding) 小块农田; **2** [u] (practice) 小块农田的耕作; **~ hours** *npl* **the ~ hours** 凌晨时分 [从1时至3时]; **in the (wee) ~ hours** 在凌晨; **~ intestine** *n* 小肠

smallish /ˈsmɔːlɪʃ/ *adj* 相当小的; **a ~ company with thirty employees** 有 30 名雇员的的小公司

small: ~ letter *n* 小写字母; **~-minded** *adj* (with rigid opinions) 固执己见的; (with narrow outlook) 狭隘的; **~-mindedness** *n* [u] 狭隘

smallness /ˈsmɔːlnɪs/ *n* [u] (of object, person, group) 小; (of sum) 少量; **they chose the car for its ~** 他们选择那款车是因为它车型小

small potatoes *npl* esp Amer colloq = **small beer**

smallpox /ˈsmɔːlpɒks/ ▸ **p. 377** *n* [u] 天花

small: ~ print *n* [u] **1** lit 小号字体印刷品; **2** fig (details, conditions) [小号字体印刷的] 附加细则; **to read the ~ print of a contract** 阅读合同的附加细则; **~-scale** *adj* 小规模的; **~ screen** *n* **the ~ screen** 电视 [与电影银幕相比较而言]; **~ shopkeeper** ▸ **p. 409** *n* 小商店店主; **~ talk** *n* [u] 闲聊; **to make ~ talk** 闲谈; **~-time** *adj* colloq (unimportant) 无关紧要的; (minor) 三流的; **a ~-time crook** 小骗子; **~-town** *adj* (provincial) 小镇的 〈*life, gossip*〉; (unadventurous, narrow-minded) 保守狭隘的 〈*mentality, life*〉; (bigoted) 顽固的 〈*mentality*〉

smarm /smɑːm/ esp Brit colloq
A *vi* 谄媚; **to ~ over sb.** 拍某人的马屁; **it's disgusting the way they ~ all over him** 他们巴结他的方式令人厌恶
B *vt* **1** (ingratiate) 讨好; **he ~ed his way into high society** 他靠阿谀奉承进入上流社会 **2** (smooth) 使平滑; **he had ~ed his hair down before the interview** 在采访前他把头发梳得溜光
C *n* [u] 谄媚

smarmy /ˈsmɑːmi/ *adj* esp Brit colloq 讨好的; **to be ~** 阿谀奉承; **a ~ waiter** 点头哈腰的侍者; **a ~ remark** 谄媚的话; **he's a ~ git** sl 他是个只会拍马屁的饭桶

smart /smɑːt/
A *adj* **1** (stylish, neat) 漂亮的 〈*appearance, clothes, car, office*〉; **a ~ young officer** 衣冠楚楚的年轻军官; **you're looking very ~** 你看上去很漂亮啊 **2** (fashionable) 时尚的 〈*hotel, street*〉; 时髦的 〈*person, group*〉; **the ~ set** 时髦一族 **3** (clever) 聪明的; (shrewd) 精明的; **to be ~ at doing sth.** 做某事精明; **he thinks he's so ~** 他自作聪明; **that wasn't very ~ of you** 你那件事办得不太漂亮; **that was a really ~ thing to do!** iron 这事干得真够高明的! ; **she's a ~ kid** 她是个聪明的孩子 **4** esp Amer colloq (cheeky) 厚脸皮的; **to be** *or* **get ~** 放肆; **don't get ~ with me!** 别跟我油嘴滑舌的! **5** Tech (controlled by computer programme) 智能的 〈*washing machine*〉 **6** (stinging) 引起剧痛的 〈*slap*〉; 尖刻的 〈*retort*〉; **to deal sb. a ~ blow** 狠狠打某人一下 **7** (brisk, sharp) 轻快的 〈*pace*〉; 清脆的 〈*crack*〉; **that was ~ work!** 干得真利落! ; **look ~ (about it)!** Brit 赶快 (处理这件事) !
B *vi* **1** (sting) 引起剧痛; **the cut on my finger is ~ing** 我手指的伤口疼死了; **his eyes ~ed from the smoke** 他双眼被烟熏得两眼生疼 **2** fig (mentally) 感到痛楚; **to ~ from sth.** 因…而痛心 〈*attack, failure*〉; **he is ~ing**

S

over his defeat/the insult 他因失败/受辱而难过

C *n* [u] (pain) 剧痛; fig (mental) 痛楚

D smarts *npl* Amer sl (intelligence) 聪明; (shrewdness) 能干

smart: ~ alec, ~ aleck /'smɑːt ˌælɪk/ *n* colloq 自作聪明的人; **she's a proper little ~ alec!** 她完全是个自以为是的小女人! ; **there's always some ~ alec who knows the answer** 总有一些自以为无所不知的万事通; **~-arse** Brit, **~-ass** Amer *ns* colloq 自作聪明的人; **don't be such a ~-arse** 不要这么自以为是; **~ bomb** *n* 智能炸弹; **~ card** *n* 智能卡; **~ drink** *n* 益智饮料; **~ drug** *n* 智能药 [据说可提高认知能力]

smarten /'smɑːtn/

Phrasal verb

• **smarten up**

A *vt* [**~ sth./sb. up, ~ up sth./sb.**] 使…漂亮 ‹*person*›; 使…整洁 ‹*house, room*›; **go and ~ yourself up** 你去打扮一下吧; **we'll have to ~ you up** 我们得把你打扮打扮; **can't you ~ this place up a bit?** 你不能把这个地方收拾一下吗?

B *vi* **1** (improve in appearance) «*person*» 变得漂亮; «*town*» 变得整洁; **I'll just ~ up, then we can go to dinner** 我打扮一下, 我们就可以去吃晚饭了; **this area is really ~ing up** 这个地区真是焕然一新 **2** (behave more wisely) 变得更聪明; **if you don't ~ up, you 'll end up just like her** 如果你不聪明点, 就跟她一样的下场

smartly /'smɑːtli/ *adv* **1** (neatly) 整洁地; (elegantly) 优雅地; **a ~ dressed young man** 衣着讲究的男青年 **2** (quickly) 迅猛地 ‹*strike*›; (sharply) 猛烈地 ‹*rebuke*›; **she slapped him ~ on the cheek** 她狠狠地给了他一记耳光 **3** (briskly) 轻快地 ‹*move*› **4** (cleverly) 机敏地 ‹*act, respond*›; **he answered all the examiner's questions ~** 他巧妙地回答了主考官的所有问题

smart money *n* [u] colloq (bet) 明智的赌注; (investment) 明智的投资; **the ~ was on Desert Orchid** 内行把赌注押在了"沙漠兰花"身上

smartness /'smɑːtnɪs/ *n* [u] **1** (of clothes, appearance) (attractiveness) 漂亮; (tidiness) 整洁; **the interviewers were impressed by his ~** 那些主持面试的人被他的帅气打动了; **I was surprised by the ~ of his dress** 我对他衣着的考究感到惊讶 **2** (cleverness) 机智; **they were amazed at the ~ of the child's answer** 孩子机敏的回答让他们感到惊讶 **3** (promptness) 敏捷; (sharpness) 有力

smart: ~ phone *n* 智能手机; **~ quotes** *npl* (电脑) 智能引号; **~ weapon** *n* 智能武器

smarty /'smɑːti/, **smarty-pants,** Brit **smarty-boots** *ns* colloq **= smart alec**

smash /smæʃ/

A *vt* **1** (shatter) 击碎 ‹*object, skull*›; 打断 ‹*leg*›; **to ~ sth. to bits** *or* **into pieces** 把某物击碎; **to ~ sth. open** 砸开 ‹*door, safe*›; **to ~ the atom** colloq 使原子分裂 **2** (crash) «*person*» 驾驶…碰撞 ‹*vehicle*›; «*waves*» 把…打碎 ‹*boat*›; **to ~ sth. into** *or* **against sth.** 使某物撞上某物; **he ~ed his fist into my face** 他一拳捶在我脸上; **to ~ a hammer down on to sth.** 用榔头砸某物 **3** (break open) 砸出 ‹*hole*›; **to ~ one's way (into ...)** 闯进 (…) **4** fig (destroy) 摧毁 ‹*political system, terrorism, crime ring*›; 镇压 ‹*protest*›; 打垮 ‹*enemy, opponent*› **5** (surpass) 打破 ‹*record*› **6** Sport (hit) 扣 ‹*ball*›

B *vi* **1** (shatter) «*object*» 哗啦一声碎掉 **2** (crash) 猛撞; **to ~ into sth.** «*vehicle, person*» 猛地撞上 ‹*wall*›; «*fist*» 猛地砸中 ‹*face*›; **to ~ through sth.** «*ball*» 猛地撞破 ‹*window*›; «*waves*» 冲破 ‹*dyke*›

C *n* **1** *sing* (crash) (of glass, china) [破碎时的] 哗啦声; (of vehicles) [撞击时的] 轰响; **to collide/break with a ~** 轰的一声相撞/哗啦一声打碎; **there was a ~ of breaking plates** 盘子打碎的哗啦声传了过来 **2** colloq (accident) 撞车; **a rail ~** 火车相撞事故 **3** (blow) 猛击; **a forearm ~** 挥舞前臂的重击 **4** *usu sing* colloq (success) **~ (hit)** 巨大成功; **a box-office ~** 票房的巨大成功; **to be a ~** 获得巨大成功 **5** Sport (hit) 扣球

D *adv* **to fall** *or* **go ~ on to sth.** «*object*» 哗啦一声掉到某物上摔碎; **to run** *or* **go ~ into sth.** «*vehicle*» 轰的一声撞到某物上; **then ~ it was all gone** 然后轰的一声, 就都没了

Phrasal verbs

• **smash down** *vt* [**~ sth. down, ~ down sth.**] 撞破 ‹*door, barrier*›

• **smash in** *vt* [**~ sth. in, ~ in sth.**] 砸破 ‹*door, window*›; **to ~ sb.'s face/head in** colloq 打瘪某人的脸/脑袋

• **smash up** *vt* [**~ sth. up, ~ up sth.**] 捣毁 ‹*place*›; 毁坏 ‹*vehicle, furniture*›

smash-and-grab Brit colloq

A *adj* 砸橱窗抢劫的; **a ~ raid at a jeweller's** 砸橱窗抢劫珠宝店事件; **a ~ robbery/theft/thief** 砸橱窗抢劫/偷窃/窃贼

B *n* 砸橱窗抢劫

smashed /smæʃt/ *adj* **1** (broken) 严重损坏的 ‹*vehicle*›; (shattered) 粉碎的 ‹*bone*› **2** *pred* colloq (intoxicated) (on alcohol) 大醉的; (on drugs) 迷醉的; **to get ~** 酩酊大醉; **he's ~ out of his head** 他醉得不省人事

smasher /'smæʃə(r)/ *n* Brit colloq (attractive woman) 极漂亮的女人; (attractive man) 极帅的男人; (attractive thing) 极漂亮的东西; **she's a real ~** 她真是貌若天仙! ; **her car is a real ~!** 她的车真是漂亮极了!

smashing /'smæʃɪŋ/ *adj* Brit colloq 极好的; **she's a really ~ person** 她真是个出色的人; **we had a ~ time on holiday** 我们假期玩得十分痛快; **you get a ~ view out of this window** 这扇窗外景色绝妙

smash-up *n* colloq **= smash C2**

smattering /'smætərɪŋ/ *n* **1** (slight knowledge) 略知; **to have a ~ of Russian** 略懂俄语; **to have a ~ of culture** 有一点点文化 **2** (small amount) 少量; **there was a ~ of snow on the pavement** 人行道上有一点残雪

smear /smɪə(r)/

A *vt* **1** (spread) 涂抹 ‹*lotion, oil, mud*›; **she ~ed eyeshadow on her eyelids** 她在眼睑上涂了眼影; **he ~ed butter on to a slice of bread** 他在面包片上抹了黄油; **the baby ~ed his food over his face** 婴儿把食物抹到了脸上 **2** (blur, smudge) 使…变模糊 ‹*paint, lipstick, charcoal*›; **try not to ~ the ink with your hand** 尽量不要用手蹭油墨 **3** (coat, mark) 弄脏 ‹*window, glass, lens*›; **her face was ~ed with jam** 她的脸被果酱弄脏了; **to ~ the walls with paint** 用漆在墙上乱涂 **4** fig (slander) 诽谤 ‹*person*›; 玷污 ‹*reputation, name*›

B *vi* «*ink, lipstick, make-up*» 变模糊; **let the paint dry completely or it will ~** 让漆干透, 否则会走漆

C *n* **1** (mark, streak) 污斑; **a ~ of grease/paint/blood** 一片油渍/漆斑/血迹; **there is a ~ on this fork** 这把叉子上有污渍 **2** fig (false accusation) 诽谤; **a ~ on sb.'s character** 对某人人格的诋毁; **he dismissed the rumour as a ~** 他把谣言当作毁谤而置之不理 **3** Med (sample) 涂片 **4** Med **= smear test**

smear: ~ campaign *n* 造谣中伤活动; **~ tactics** *npl* 造谣中伤策略; **~ test** *n* 子宫颈涂片检查

smeary /'smɪəri/ *adj* colloq 弄脏的 ‹*glass, window, face*›; 模糊的 ‹*paint*›; **the page was impossible to read because of the ~ ink** 因为墨迹模糊不清, 这一页无法阅读

smell /smel/

A *n* **1** [u and c] (odour) 气味; **a sweet/musty ~** 香气/霉味 **2** [u and c] (stink) 臭味; **there's a ~ in here!** 这里有臭味! ; **what a ~!** 真臭! ; **to get rid of ~s** 除臭 **3** [u] (sense) 嗅觉; **(a good/bad) sense of ~** (灵敏/迟钝的) 嗅觉 **4** [c] *usu sing* (sniff) 嗅; **to have a ~ of** *or* **at sth.** 嗅一下某物; **give it a ~** 闻闻这东西; **one ~ of the meat and ...** 一闻到肉味就… **5** [c] *usu sing* fig (hint) 迹象; **the ~ of suspicion/dishonesty** 怀疑/欺诈的迹象

B *vi* (*pt, pp* **~ed** *or* esp Brit **smelt**) **1** (have odour) 有气味; **to ~ nice/awful** 好闻/难闻; **dinner ~s good** 饭真香; **the wine/meat ~s off** 葡萄酒香气四溢/肉香扑鼻; **to ~ of sth.** 有…的气味 ‹*socks, garlic*›; **to ~ like sth.** 闻上去像 ‹*curry, roses*›; **what does it ~ like?** 它是什么味儿? ; **▸rose² 2** **2** (stink) 发臭; **your feet ~!** 你的脚真臭! ; **his breath ~s** 他有口臭; **to start to ~** 开始发臭; **it/your idea ~s** fig colloq 这事真糟糕/你这主意真馊 **3** (have sense of smell) 有嗅觉; **can fish ~?** 鱼有嗅觉吗? ; **he can't ~ anything because of his cold** 他感冒了, 闻不出气味 **4** fig colloq (be dubious) «*affair, situation*» 不正常; **the whole thing ~s** 整件事不对劲儿; **to ~ fishy** *or* **dodgy** 可疑; **to ~ of racism/corruption** 有种族歧视/腐朽堕落的意味; **it ~s like a hoax** 那像是一场恶作剧

C *vt* (*pt, pp* **~ed** *or* esp Brit **smelt**) **1** (notice, detect) 闻到…的气味; **I can ~ lemons/alcohol on his breath** 我闻得到他呼出的柠檬味儿/酒气; **to ~ (sth.) burning** 闻到 (某物) 烧焦 **2** (sniff) 嗅; **to ~ a rose** 闻一闻玫瑰 **3** fig (identify) 察觉到 ‹*danger, problem, change*›; 发现 ‹*news scoop*›; 识破 ‹*liar*›; **to ~ blood** 察觉到对方的弱点

Phrasal verb

• **smell out** *vt* [**~ sth. out, ~ out sth.**] **1** (sniff out) 嗅出 ‹*drugs, explosives*› **2** fig (identify) 查出 ‹*plot, corruption, spy*› **3** (fill with smell) 把…弄臭 ‹*room, place*›

smelliness /'smelɪnɪs/ *n* [u] 臭; **the ~ of the room was indescribable** 房间里臭不可闻

smelling salts /'smelɪŋ sɔːlts/ *npl* esp Hist 嗅盐

smelly /'smeli/ *adj* (having strong smell) 有强烈气味的; (having unpleasant smell) 发臭的; **this cheese is a bit ~** 这种干酪有点难闻

smelt¹ /smelt/ *pt, pp* **▸smell B, C**

smelt² *vt* **1** (melt) 熔炼 ‹*ore*› **2** (extract) 提炼 ‹*metal*›; **they ~ copper in that factory** 那个工厂炼铜

smelter /'smeltə(r)/ *n* (installation) 熔炉; (factory) 冶炼厂

smelting /'smeltɪŋ/ *n* [u] **1** (melting) 熔炼; **a ~ furnace** 熔炉 **2** (extracting) 提炼; **a copper-~ works** 炼铜厂

smidgen, smidgin /'smɪdʒən/ *n* colloq **a ~ of sth.** 一点点 ‹*food, emotion*›; **just a ~** 就一点儿; **do I detect a little ~ of jealousy?** 我好像觉得有人有点儿嫉妒啊!

smile /smaɪl/

A *n* 微笑; **a big/broad/winning ~** 灿烂/满面/迷人的微笑; **a ~ of welcome/approval** 欢迎/赞成的微笑; **a stupid ~** 傻笑; **to have a ~ on one's face** 面带笑容; **to break into a ~** 露出笑容; **to give (sb.) a ~** (对某人) 笑一笑; **with a ~** 微笑着; **take that ~ off your face!** 不许笑; **to wipe the ~ off sb.'s face** 让某人笑不出来; **to be all ~s** colloq 笑容满面; **to crack a ~** Amer colloq 强作笑颜

B *vi* 微笑; **to ~ with pleasure/delight** 高兴/开心地微笑; **to ~ at sb.** 对某人微笑; **to ~ back** 回以微笑; **to ~ to oneself** 心中暗喜; **to ~ at sth.** 觉得某事物好笑; **to ~ to think of sth./how ...** 想到某事物/如何…就觉得好笑; **to come up smiling** colloq 摆脱困境, 笑迎未来

C *vt* **1** (say with smile) 微笑着表示 ‹*greeting, one's thanks, agreement*›; **'yes,' he ~d** "是的," 他微笑着说 **2** (produce) 露出 ‹*smile*›; **to ~ a bitter ~/a ~ of welcome** 苦笑一下/以微笑表示欢迎

Phrasal verb

• **smile on** *vt* [**~ on sb./sth.**] liter «*fortune*»

S

垂青 ‹*person, event*›; «*authority*» 赞成 ‹*project*›; **the weather has ∼d on us today** 我们今天有幸赶上了好天气

smiley /ˈsmaɪlɪ/
A *adj* colloq (smiling) 微笑的; (cheerful) 兴高采烈的; **the child had a ∼ face** 那孩子有一张笑脸
B *n* **1** (happy symbol) 笑脸标志 **2** (emoticon) 微笑符 [即:-)]

smiling /ˈsmaɪlɪŋ/ *adj* 微笑的; **a happy ∼ face** 一张幸福的笑脸

smilingly /ˈsmaɪlɪŋlɪ/ *adv* (with a smile) 面带微笑地; (cheerfully) 兴高采烈地; **'I'm only teasing', she said ∼** "我只是开个玩笑," 她微笑着说

smirch /smɜːtʃ/
A *vt* **1** (soil, stain) 弄脏 ‹*skin, garment*› **2** fig (discredit) 败坏…的名声 ‹*person, family*›; 败坏 ‹*reputation, name*›
B *n* **1** (dirty mark) 污渍; **a ∼ on sth.** 某物上的污斑 **2** fig (blot, flaw) 污点; **a ∼ on the family's name** 家族声誉的一个污点

smirk /smɜːk/
A *vi* (smile in self-satisfied way) 得意地笑; (smile knowingly) 诡秘地笑; **to ∼ at sth.** 嘲笑某事物
B *n* (self-satisfied smile) 得意的笑; (knowing smile) 诡秘的笑

smite /smaɪt/ *vt* archaic or liter (*pt* **smote,** *pp* **smitten**) 重击 ‹*person, door*›; **he smote the man a mighty blow with his stick** 他用手杖狠狠地打了那个男子一下; ▸**smitten**

smith /smɪθ/ ▸**p. 409** *n* **1** (blacksmith) 铁匠 **2** (metal worker) 锻工

smithereens /ˌsmɪðəˈriːnz/ *npl* colloq 碎片; **in ∼** 成为碎片; **to smash sth. to ∼** 将某物打碎

smithy /ˈsmɪðɪ/ *n* (workshop) 铁匠铺; (forge) 锻工车间

smitten /ˈsmɪtn/
A archaic or liter *pp* ▸**smite**
B *adj pred* **1** (affected, afflicted) **to be ∼ with** *or* **by** 受…折磨 ‹*remorse, guilt, terror*›; 患 ‹*illness*›; **he was ∼ with grief** 他深感悲痛; **she's been ∼ with flu** 她得了流感 **2** (enamoured) **to be ∼ with sb./sth.** (in love) 爱上某人; (infatuated) 迷上某人/某事物; **she's completely ∼ with him** 她完全被他迷住了

smock /smɒk/
A *n* 罩衣; **an artist's ∼** 艺术家的工作服
B *vt* 给…缝褶裥

smocking /ˈsmɒkɪŋ/ *n* [u] 褶裥

smog /smɒg/ *n* [u and c] 烟雾

smog mask *n* 防废气面罩

smoke /sməʊk/
A *n* **1** [u] (fumes) 烟; **a cloud/wisp/puff of ∼** 一团/一缕/一股烟; **cigarette ∼** 香烟的烟气; **to go up in ∼** colloq «*building, town*» 被烧毁; fig «*plan, hopes*» 化为乌有; **∼ and mirrors** (magic trick) 障眼法; fig 欺诈; **there's no ∼ without fire,** Amer **where there's ∼ there's fire** Prov 无风不起浪 **2** [c] *usu sing* (act of smoking) 吸烟; **to go out for a (quick) ∼** colloq 出去抽 (一小会儿) 烟; **to have a ∼** 抽支烟
B *vi* **1** (give off smoke) 冒烟 **2** (inhale tobacco) 吸烟; **to stop smoking** 戒烟; **he ∼s too much** 他烟抽得很凶; **to ∼ like a chimney** colloq (a lot) 抽烟很凶; (constantly) 是个老烟枪 **3** (be smoky) «*wood, fireplace, lamp*» 多烟; **to ∼ badly** 冒烟很厉害
C *vt* **1** (inhale) 吸 ‹*cigarette, marijuana*›; **to ∼ a pipe/20 a day** 抽烟斗/一天抽 20 支烟 **2** Culin 熏制 ‹*meat, fish*›; **∼d mackerel** 熏鲭鱼 **3** (darken) 把…熏黑; **the ∼d glass of a lens** 烟色玻璃镜片

Phrasal verb

- **smoke out** *vt* [**∼ sb./sth. out, ∼ out sb./sth.**]
1 (drive out with smoke) 用烟把…熏出来 **2** fig (expose) 揭露 ‹*traitor*›; 查出 ‹*culprit, fugitive*›

smoke: ∼ alarm *n* 烟雾报警器; **∼ bomb** *n* 烟幕弹; **∼ detector** *n* 烟雾探测器; **∼-dried** *adj* 熏制的; **∼-dry** *vt* 熏制; **delicious ∼-dried herring** 美味的熏鲱鱼; **∼-filled** *adj* 烟雾弥漫的; **a ∼-filled room** 密室; **∼-free** *adj* 禁止吸烟的 ‹*office, zone*›

smokeless /ˈsməʊklɪs/ *adj* 无烟的; **coke is a ∼ fuel** 焦炭是无烟燃料

smokeless zone *n* Brit 无烟区 [禁止使用有烟燃料的地区]

smoker /ˈsməʊkə(r)/ *n* **1** (person) 吸烟者; **a heavy/light ∼** 烟瘾大/小的人; **a ∼'s cough** 吸烟引起的咳嗽 **2** (carriage on train) 吸烟车厢

smoke: ∼screen *n* **1** Mil 烟幕; **2** fig (ruse) 障眼法; **to create** *or* **throw up a ∼screen** 制造烟幕; **∼ signal** *n* **1** (column of smoke) 烟雾信号; **2** fig (indication) 迹象; **∼stack** *n* (chimney) 大烟囱; (funnel) [船舶或机车的] 烟囱

smokey /ˈsməʊki/ = **smoky**

smoking /ˈsməʊkɪŋ/
A *n* [u] 吸烟; **to give up ∼** 戒烟; **to cut down on one's ∼** 减少抽烟; **a ban on ∼** 禁烟令; **'no ∼'** "禁止吸烟"; **they want to reduce ∼ among pupils** 他们希望减少小学生吸烟的情况
B *adj attrib* 冒烟的 ‹*volcano, chimney*›

smoking: ∼ ban *n* 禁烟令; **∼ compartment** *n* 吸烟车厢; **∼ jacket** *n* [旧时男子在家吸烟穿的] 宽松便服; **∼-related** *adj* 与吸烟有关的 ‹*disease, death*›; **∼ room** *n* 吸烟室

smoky /ˈsməʊki/ *adj* **1** (full of smoke) 烟雾弥漫的 ‹*room, atmosphere*›; **it's a bit ∼ here** 这儿有点烟雾腾腾 **2** (producing smoke) 冒大量烟的 ‹*flame, lamp, fuel*› **3** (smoky-tasting) 有烟熏味的 ‹*drink, taste*› **4** (looking like smoke) 烟青色的 ‹*eyes, light, glass*›

smolder /ˈsmɔːldə(r)/ *vi* Amer = **smoulder**

smoldering /ˈsmɔːldərɪŋ/ *adj* Amer = **smouldering**

smooch /smuːtʃ/ colloq
A *vi* «*couple*» 搂抱亲吻; **they were ∼ing in the car** 他们在汽车里拥吻
B *n* 搂抱亲吻; **to have a ∼** 拥吻

smoochy /ˈsmuːtʃi/ *adj* colloq 搂抱慢舞的 ‹*song, music*›

smooth /smuːð/
A *adj* **1** (even, flat) 光滑的 ‹*skin, fabric, stone*›; 平坦的 ‹*road*›; 风平浪静的 ‹*sea, lake*›; **to wear** *or* **be worn ∼** «*tyre, tread, surface*» 磨光; ▸**baby A1** **2** (well blended) 混合均匀的 ‹*mixture, sauce*› **3** (steady, without jolts) 平稳的 ‹*motion*›; **to bring the car to a ∼ stop** 把车停稳; **to have a ∼ ride/landing** 平稳乘坐/降落; **to write in one ∼ movement** 一挥而就; **the ∼ running of sth.** 某物的顺畅运转; fig (of organization) 某组织的平稳运作 **4** (flowing) 圆润的 ‹*music, voice*›; 流畅的 ‹*verse, style, rhythm*› **5** (mellow) 醇和的 ‹*taste, drink*› **6** fig (problem-free) 顺利的 ‹*event, delivery*›; **to have a ∼ journey** 一路顺风; **to have a ∼ passage** «*bill*» 顺利通过 **7** usu pej (suave) 圆滑的; **a ∼ talker** 油腔滑调的人
B *vt* **1** (even, flatten out) 抚平 ‹*cloth, hair*›; 磨平 ‹*wood, surface*›; **to ∼ the letter flat on the table/the wallpaper into place** 把信平摊在桌上/把壁纸抚平贴好; ▸**feather A** **2** (remove) 消除 ‹*creases*› **3** fig (make easier) 使…顺利 ‹*process, transition*›; **to ∼ the way (for** *or* **towards sth./for sb.)** (为某事物/某人) 铺平道路; **to ∼ the path towards peace** 铺平通往和平的道路; **to ∼ sb.'s way** *or* **path (into business)** 为某人铺平 (从商的) 道路

Phrasal verbs

- **smooth away** *vt* [**∼ sth. away, ∼ away sth.**] (remove) 消除 ‹*wrinkles*›; fig (solve) 解决 ‹*problems*›; (clear away) 扫清 ‹*obstacles*›
- **smooth back** *vt* [**∼ sth. back, ∼ back sth.**] 向后理顺 ‹*hair, covering*›
- **smooth down** *vt* [**∼ sth. down, ∼ down sth.**] 抚平 ‹*clothing, hair*›; 磨平 ‹*wood, surface*›
- **smooth out** *vt* [**∼ sth. out, ∼ out sth.**]
1 (flatten) 把…铺平 ‹*covering, cloth*› **2** (remove) 消除 ‹*creases*›; **to ∼ the wrinkles out of a piece of paper** 抚平纸上的褶皱 **3** fig (lessen) 解决 ‹*difficulties, problems*›; **to ∼ out the impact of sth.** 消除某事物的影响 **4** Stat 修正 ‹*curve, fluctuations*›
- **smooth over** *vt* [**∼ sth. over, ∼ over sth.**] 缓和 ‹*problems, bad feelings*›; 减少 ‹*difficulties, differences*›; **to ∼ things over** 平息事端

smoothe /smuːð/ *vt* = **smooth B**

smooth-faced /ˌsmuːðˈfeɪst/, **smooth-cheeked** /ˌsmuːðˈtʃiːkt/ *adjs* 脸部光滑的

smoothie, smoothy /ˈsmuːði/ *n* **1** colloq pej (person) 圆滑讨好的男人; **don't trust him, he's a real ∼** 别信任他, 他滑头得很 **2** (drink) 水果奶昔

smoothly /ˈsmuːðli/ *adv* **1** (evenly) 平稳地 ‹*run, glide, brake*› **2** (easily) 顺利地 ‹*go, start, begin*›; **the key turned ∼ in the lock** 钥匙在锁眼里很容易就转动了; **to run ∼** «*engine, machinery*» 运转顺利; **things are going very ∼ for me** 对我来说事情进展得一帆风顺 **3** (suavely) 圆滑地 ‹*speak, persuade*›; **he talked us into it very ∼** 他花言巧语地说服我们做了这件事

smoothness /ˈsmuːðnɪs/ *n* [u] **1** (of surface, skin, hair) 光滑 **2** (of whisky, sauce) 均匀 **3** (of motion) 平稳 **4** usu pej (suaveness) 圆滑; **don't be fooled by his ∼ — he's as dishonest as they come** 别让他的油嘴滑舌给骗了——他很不老实

smooth: ∼-running *adj* 平稳运转的 ‹*machine*›; 进展顺利的 ‹*operation*›; **∼ talk** *n* [u] 花言巧语; **∼-talk** *vt* 对…花言巧语; **don't try to ∼-talk me into it!** 别想用花言巧语说服我!; **∼-talking** *adj* 油嘴滑舌的; **don't trust ∼-talking young men** 不要信任油嘴滑舌的年轻男子; **∼ tongue** *n* 巧舌如簧; **to have a ∼ tongue** 巧舌如簧; **∼-tongued** *adj* = **∼-talking**

smorgasbord /ˈsmɔːgəsbɔːd/ *n* 自助餐

smote /sməʊt/ *pt* ▸**smite**

smother /ˈsmʌðə(r)/ *vt* **1** (kill) 使窒息而死; **he ∼ed the baby with a pillow** 他用枕头把婴儿闷死了; **I hate sleeping with a lot of covers, I feel as if I'm being ∼ed** 我讨厌盖很多被子睡觉, 感觉要憋死了 **2** (cover) 厚厚地覆盖; **to ∼ sb. with kisses** 吻得某人透不过气来; **a cake ∼ed in cream** 裹了厚厚一层奶油的蛋糕; **her face was ∼ed in powder** 她脸上涂了厚厚的粉; **to be ∼ed in blankets/furs** 盖着厚厚的毯子/披着厚厚的毛皮 **3** (overwhelm) 使觉得压抑; **you can ∼ children with too much attention** 过多的关注会让孩子觉得不自在 **4** (suppress) 抑制; **to ∼ a yawn/sob** 强忍住哈欠/呜咽 **5** (extinguish) 把…闷熄 ‹*fire*›

smoulder /ˈsməʊldə(r)/ *vi* **1** (burn slowly) «*fire, cigarette, ruins*» 闷燃; **the embers ∼ed in the grate** 余烬在壁炉里闷燃; **the rubble ∼ed for many days after the fire** 火灾之后瓦砾阴燃了许多天 **2** fig (continue to feel, be felt) «*hatred, jealousy, anger*» 郁积; **to ∼ with ...** 按捺不住 ‹*resentment, jealousy, anger*›; **they were ∼ing with desire** 他们欲火中烧

smouldering /ˈsməʊldərɪŋ/ *adj* **1** (burning slowly) 闷燃的 ‹*fire, cigarette, ashes*›; **nothing was left but ∼ ruins** 除了阴燃的废墟外什么也没有剩下 **2** fig (persistently felt) 郁积的 ‹*hatred, jealousy, desire, anger*›

SMS *abbr* = **Short Message (***or* **Messaging) Service** (service) 短信服务; (message) 短信; **∼ message/messaging** 短信/短信通信

smudge /smʌdʒ/
A *vt* 把…弄模糊 ‹*ink, print, paint*›; 把…弄脏 ‹*paper, cloth*›; **his signature was ∼d** 他的

签名被弄得模糊不清; **careful, you'll ~ my lipstick** 小心点，不要把我的口红弄糊了
B *vi* «*ink, print, paint*» 变模糊; **mind your lipstick doesn't ~** 当心不要把口红抹糊了
C *n* 污迹; **a ~ of dirt/ink** 泥点/墨渍

smudgy /ˈsmʌdʒi/ *adj* 有污迹的 ‹*paper*›; 模糊不清的 ‹*painting, writing, photograph*›; **his face was ~ with tears** 他满脸泪痕

smug /smʌg/ *adj* 沾沾自喜的 ‹*person, smile, remark, attitude*›; **don't be so ~!** 不要这么自鸣得意！; **I can't afford to be ~** 我可不敢得意洋洋; **a look of ~ satisfaction** 洋洋自得的神态

smuggle /ˈsmʌgl/ *vt* **1** (take illegally) 走私; **to ~ sth. through** *or* **past customs** 走私某物过海关 **2** (take secretly) 偷带 ‹*person*›; 偷运 ‹*object*›; **to ~ sth./sb. in** 把某物/某人偷运进来; **to ~ sb. into Britain/the club** 带某人偷渡进入英国/把某人偷偷带进俱乐部

smuggler /ˈsmʌglə(r)/ *n* 走私者; **a drug ~** 毒品走私者

smuggling /ˈsmʌglɪŋ/ *n* [u] 走私; **a large drug-~ cartel** 一个大型毒品走私集团

smuggling ring *n* 走私集团; **a drugs ~** 毒品走私集团

smugly /ˈsmʌgli/ *adv* 沾沾自喜地; **he spoke ~ about his victory** 他自鸣得意地谈论自己的胜利

smugness /ˈsmʌgnɪs/ *n* [u] 沾沾自喜; **his ~ and arrogance haven't won him many friends** 他因自满和傲慢而朋友甚少

smut /smʌt/ *n* **1** [u] (vulgarity) (words) 污言秽语; (stories) 淫秽故事; (pictures) 淫秽图片; **the novel's just ~, not worthy to be called literature** 这部小说只是淫秽故事而已，不配称为文学作品 **2** [c] (particle of dirt) 污迹; (soot) 煤灰

smuttiness /ˈsmʌtɪnɪs/ *n* [u] 淫秽

smutty /ˈsmʌti/ *adj* **1** (vulgar) 淫秽的 ‹*humour, remark, film, book*› **2** (dirty) 煤灰色的 ‹*spots*›; 脏污的 ‹*face, cloth*›; **~ marks on the tablecloth** 台布上的黑色污点

snack /snæk/
A *n* **1** (small meal) 快餐; **to have** *or* **eat a ~** 吃快餐; **a midnight ~** 宵夜 **2** (item of food) 小食品; **party ~s** 宴会小点心
B *vi* (have a small meal) 吃快餐; (eat an item of food) 吃点心; **to ~ on sth.** 吃某物当快餐

snack bar *n* (cafe) 快餐店; (counter) 快餐柜台; **they stopped at a ~ for a sandwich** 他们在快餐店停下来买三明治

snaffle /ˈsnæfl/
A *n* Equit **~ (bit)** 嚼子; **to use a ~** 带嚼子
B *vt* Brit colloq 偷窃 ‹*object, food*›

snafu /snæˈfuː/ Amer colloq
A *n* 混乱局面
B *adj pred* **to be ~** 混乱的 ‹*situation*›; 运转不灵的 ‹*machine*›; **the brakes are ~** 刹车失灵了
C *vt* (*pres* **~es**; *pt, pp* **~ed**) 扰乱 ‹*situation, deal*›; **you ignored the warning signs and ~ed everything** 你没有注意警示标志，把一切都搞砸了

snag /snæg/
A *n* **1** colloq (obstacle, drawback) 障碍; **there's just one ~** 只有一个问题; **that's the ~** 那正是症结; **the ~ is that ...** 麻烦的是…; **to hit** *or* **run into a ~** 遇到麻烦 **2** (tear) 钩破处; **there's a ~ in my tights** 我的连裤袜有一处抽丝; **a ~ in the curtain** 窗帘上的挂破处 **3** (sharp projection) 突出物
B *vt* (*pres p etc.* **-gg-**) 钩破 ‹*tights, sleeve*›; 擦破 ‹*hand, fingernail*›; **mind you don't ~ your trousers on that barbed wire** 当心不要被那些带刺铁丝网挂破裤子
C *vi* (*pres p etc.* **-gg-**) **to ~ on sth.** 钩在某物上; **the fishing net has ~ged on the propeller** 渔网缠住了螺旋桨

snail /sneɪl/ *n* 蜗牛; **at a ~'s pace** 极慢地

snail: ~-like *adj* **1** lit (like a snail) 蜗牛状的 ‹*organism, structure, shell*›; **2** fig (very slow) 非常缓慢的 ‹*pace, speed, progress, traffic*›; **~ mail** *n* [u] colloq 蜗牛式邮寄 [指比电子邮件慢得多的传统邮政系统]; **to send sth. by ~ mail** 平邮某物; **~ shell** *n* 蜗牛壳

snake /sneɪk/
A *n* **1** Zool 蛇 **2** pej (person) 阴险的人; **a ~ in the grass** 背后捣鬼的人
B *vi* «*river, path, rope*» 蜿蜒延伸; «*queue, column, fugitive*» 曲折前进; **the river ~d across the plain** 这条河弯弯曲曲地穿过平原; **the column of marchers ~d in an untidy line round the park** 游行队伍散乱地地绕着公园曲折前行

snake: ~bite *n* **1** [c] (wound) 蛇咬伤; **2** [u] Brit (drink) 苹果鸡尾酒 [苹果酒和淡啤酒各半]; **~ charmer** *n* 耍蛇人; **~head** *n* [组织偷渡的] 蛇头; **~-like** *adj* 蛇一般的 ‹*curve, expression, eyes*›; **a sinuous ~-like movement** 弯弯曲曲、蛇一样的动作; **~ oil** *n* [u] Amer colloq [据称能治百病的] 蛇油; **a charlatan selling ~ oil** 卖万灵油的骗子; **~pit** *n* **1** (hole for snakes) 蛇洞; **2** fig (ruthless scene) 冷酷无情的地方; **the literary ~pits of New York** 纽约文学界的冷酷竞争环境; **~s and ladders** ▸**p. 307** *n + v sing* Brit 蛇梯棋 [遇梯子图案前进，遇蛇图案后退]

snakeskin /ˈsneɪkskɪn/
A *n* [u and c] 蛇皮
B *modif* 蛇皮制的; **~ shoes/belt** 蛇皮鞋/皮带

snap /snæp/
A *n* **1** [c] *usu sing* (sound) 啪的一声; (action) 发出啪的一声; **with a ~** 啪的一声 ‹*close, break*›; **the ~ of a twig** 小树枝的喀嚓声; **to call a waiter with a ~ of one's fingers** 打响指叫服务员来; **(to be ready) in a ~** esp Amer colloq 马上（准备好） **2** [c] *usu sing* (bite) 猛咬; **to make a ~ at sth.** 对准某物猛咬; **with a sudden ~ (of one's jaws)** 猛地一口 ‹*bite*› **3** [c] Phot colloq 快照; **a ~ of sb./sth.** 某人/某物的快照; **to take a ~** 拍快照 **4** [c] (biscuit) 薄脆小饼 **5** [u] Brit Games 对儿牌; **to have** *or* **play a game of ~** 玩一局对儿牌 **6** [c] *sing* Amer colloq (cinch) 容易的事; **it is a ~ doing sth.** *or* **to do sth.** 做某事很容易; **this job's a ~!** 这活儿不过是小菜一碟! **7** [u] colloq (vigour) 劲头; **to have plenty of ~** 劲头十足; **put a bit of ~ in it!** 拿出点劲头来! **8** [c] Amer **= press stud**
B *vi* (*pres p etc.* **-pp-**) **1** (break) 啪的一声断裂; **to ~ (off sth.)** «*twig, section*» （从某物上）啪地折断; **to ~ in two** 啪的一声断为两截 **2** fig (lose control) 情绪失控; (have breakdown) 崩溃; **my temper/patience ~ped** 我忍不住发火了/失去了耐性; **something just ~ped in me** 我内心一下子翻腾起来 **3** (click) (with noise) 啪地一动; (move quickly) 迅速移动; **to ~ open/shut** «*lid, purse*» 啪的一声打开/关上; **his eyes ~ped open** 他猛地睁开了眼睛; **to ~ together** «*jaws*» 啪的一声合上; **to ~ into place** «*piece*» 啪的一声放到位 **4** (speak sharply) 厉声说话 **5** (act quickly) 迅速行动; **~ to it!** 加把劲！; **~ out of it!** 振作起来！; **to ~ to attention** Mil 啪地立正
C *vt* (*pres p etc.* **-pp-**) **1** (break) 使啪的一声断裂; **to ~ sth. off sth.** 使某物从…上喀嚓一声折断 ‹*mast, branch*›; **to ~ sth. in two** 啪的一声把某物折成两截 **2** (click) (with noise) 使啪地一动; (move quickly) 使迅速移动; **to ~ sth. open/shut** (move quickly) 迅速打开/关上某物; (with noise) 啪的一声打开/关上某物; **to ~ sth. on sth./into place** 把…咔嗒一声与某物连接/放到位 ‹*piece, lid*›; **to ~ one's fingers** 打响指 **3** (say sharply) 厉声说 ‹*words*›; **to ~ a reply** 厉声作答; **'no!' she ~ped (at him)** "不!"她厉声（对他）说; **she ~ped that ...** 她气冲冲地说… **4** Phot 给…拍快照; **to ~ the incident** 拍下这一事件
D *adj attrib* 仓促的 ‹*judgement*›; 紧急的 ‹*vote, election*›
E *adv* **to go ~** «*branch*» 啪的一声折断
F *excl* Brit **1** Games **~!** [在对儿牌游戏中喊的] 对儿! **2** colloq (finding similarity) 真巧; **~! you've got the same shoes as me!** 巧了! 你和我穿的鞋是一样的!

Phrasal verbs

- **snap at** *vt* [**~ at sb./sth.**]
  1 (speak sharply to) 对…厉声说话 **2** (bite) «*animal*» 对准…咬; fig 欣然接受 ‹*idea, chance*›
- **snap away** *vi* **to ~ away (at sb./sth.)** 对着某人/某物不停拍照
- **snap back**
  A *vi* **1** (click back) 啪的一声归位; **the lid/his jaw ~ped back** 盖子/下巴吧嗒一声合上了; **to ~ back into place** «*component*» 啪的一声放到原位 **2** (reply sharply) 厉声回嘴; **to ~ back at sb.** 顶撞某人
  B *vt* [**~ sth. back, ~ back sth.**]
  1 啪的一声把…归位; **to ~ the bolt back** 啪的一声闩上门 **2** (reply sharply) 生气地说 ‹*words*›; **'no!' she ~ped back (at him)** "不!"她气冲冲地（对他）说道
- **snap off**
  A *vi* «*branch*» 啪的一声折断
  B *vt* [**~ sth. off, ~ off sth.**] 啪的一声折断
- **snap out** *vt* [**~ sth. out, ~ out sth.**] 厉声喊出 ‹*words*›; 厉声发出 ‹*order*›
- **snap up** *vt* [**~ sth. up, ~ up sth.**] colloq 抢购; **the tickets were ~ped up** 票被一抢而空

snap: ~ decision *n* 仓促的决定; **~dragon** *n* 金鱼草; **~ fastener** *n* **= press stud**; **~-on** *adj* 带揿扣的

snapper /ˈsnæpə(r)/ *n* 红鲷鱼

snappily /ˈsnæpɪli/ *adv* **1** (sharply, irritably) 厉声地; **'go away,' she said ~** "走开，"她厉声说道 **2** (elegantly) 优雅地; **he always dresses very ~** 他总是穿着讲究

snappish /ˈsnæpɪʃ/ *adj* **1** (likely to bite) 爱咬人的 ‹*dog*› **2** (irritable) 急躁的; **a ~ old man** 脾气暴躁的老头

snappy /ˈsnæpi/ *adj* colloq **1** (likely to bite) 爱咬人的 ‹*dog*› **2** (irritable) 厉声的; **he can be very ~ if he's in one of his moods** 如果他心情不好，说话就会恶声恶气的 **3** (lively, punchy) 轻快的 ‹*pace*›; 简洁的 ‹*routine, reply*›; **to be ~ on one's feet** 步子敏捷; **make it ~!** 赶快! **4** (smart, elegant) 漂亮优雅的 ‹*person, clothes*›; **he's a ~ dresser** 他是个穿着讲究的人 **5** (clever) 短小精悍的; **she's always ready with a ~ comment** 她总能作出言简意赅的评论

snapshot /ˈsnæpʃɒt/ *n* **1** (photograph) 快照 **2** (summary) 简况 **3** Comput 数据快照

snare /sneə(r)/
A *n* **1** lit (trap) 罗网 **2** fig (pitfall, temptation) 陷阱
B *vt* **1** lit (trap) [用罗网等] 捕捉 **2** fig (tempt) 引诱…入圈套

snare drum ▸**p. 395** *n* 小鼓

snarl¹ /snɑːl/
A *vi* (growl) 吼叫; (grimace) 龇牙咧嘴; **to ~ at sb./sth.** «*animal*» 对某人/某物嚎叫; **to ~ at sb.** «*person*» 对着某人怒吼
B *vt* (growl) «*person*» 吼叫出 ‹*words, command*›; **to ~ abuse/a threat at sb.** 叫骂着/咆哮着威胁某人; **he ~ed that ...** 他吼叫着说…; **'no!' he ~ed** "不行!"他吼道
C *n* **1** (growl of animal) 吼叫; **a low ~/a ~ of rage** 低声吼叫/怒吼; **the ~ of a race car engine** 赛车引擎的轰鸣 **2** (growl of person) 叫嚷; **to give a ~ of pain** 痛苦地叫起来; **'no!' he said with a ~** "不行!"他怒吼道; **his expression was a ~ of hate** 他愤恨不已，表情扭曲

snarl²
A *vt* (tangle) 把…缠作一团 ‹*rope, hair, wool*›
B *vi* «*rope, hair, wool*» 缠作一团
C *n* **1** **a ~ (of ...)** 乱蓬蓬的一团 ‹*wire, wool*›; **the ~s in my hair** 我头发的缠结; **to get the ~s out of a rope** 把缠结的绳子理顺 **2** colloq **= snarl-up 1**

S

Phrasal verb

- **snarl up**

A *vi* **1** (get tangled) «*rope, hair, wool*» 缠作一团 **2** (get jammed) «*traffic, network*» 拥堵不堪

B *vt* [～ **sth. up,** ～ **up sth.**]
1 (tangle) 把…缠作一团 ‹*rope, hair, wool*›; **to be** *or* **get ～ed up in sth.** 被缠在某物中 **2** (jam) 使…瘫痪 ‹*traffic, system*›; fig 使…陷入僵局 ‹*trade, plans, talks*›; **to be ～ed up (in sth.)** (be jammed) 受到（某事物）阻碍; fig 受到（某事物）妨碍; **to be** *or* **get ～ed up in a traffic jam** 遭遇交通堵塞

snarl-up *n* colloq **1** (in traffic) 交通拥堵 **2** (in distribution network) 混乱

snatch /snætʃ/

A *vt* **1** (grab) 抢走 ‹*object*›; fig 抓住 ‹*opportunity, moment*› **2** (rescue) 救回 ‹*person*›; (win) 夺得 ‹*opportunity, victory*›; **to ～ sb. from the jaws of death** 把某人从鬼门关救回来 **3** (take hurriedly) 抓紧时间做; **to ～ a week's holiday/a few hours' sleep** 抓紧时间度一周假/睡几小时; **to ～ a meal/a bite to eat** 匆匆吃一顿饭/吃一口东西; **to ～ a kiss** 飞快地吻一下 **4** colloq (steal) 抢夺; (kidnap) 绑架

B *vi* 争抢; **children, don't ～!** 孩子们，不要抢！; **to ～ at sth.** 抓取 ‹*object*›; fig 争取 ‹*opportunity*›

C *n* **1** (grab) 抓; **to make a ～ at sth.** 伸手去抓某物; **a quick ～ of breath** 快速吸气 **2** colloq (theft) 抢夺; (kidnapping) 绑架; **a wages ～** 抢工资 **3** (fragment) 片段; **a brief ～ of sleep** 片刻小睡; **a ～ of their conversation** 他们谈话的只言片语; **I remember odd ～es of the song** 我只记得歌曲的零星片段 **4** (in weightlifting) 抓举 **5** taboo sl (female genitals) 阴户

Phrasal verb

- **snatch away** *vt* [～ **sth. away,** ～ **away sth.**] 一把拿走

snatch squad *n* Brit [抓捕闹事者的] 搜捕队

snazzily /ˈsnæzɪli/ *adv* 时髦地 ‹*dress*›

snazzy /ˈsnæzi/ *adj* colloq 时髦的 ‹*clothes, car, design*›

sneak /sniːk/

A *vi* (*pt, pp* **～ed,** esp Amer colloq **snuck**) **1** (move furtively) 溜; **to ～ in/away** 溜进去/溜走; **to ～ past (sb./sth.)** 从（某人/某物）旁边溜过去; **to ～ up** 溜近; **to ～ up on/behind sb.** 悄悄/从背后悄悄接近某人 **2** Brit colloq (tell tales) **to ～ (on sb.)** [尤指学童间] 打（某人的）小报告; **to ～ to sb. (about sth.)** 向某人告发（某事）

B *vt* (*pt, pp* **～ed,** esp Amer colloq **snuck**) (take secretly) 偷偷拿; (bring secretly) 偷偷带; (put secretly) 偷偷放; **can I ～ another glass of wine?** 我能再偷偷拿一杯葡萄酒吗？; **to ～ a glance/look (at sth.)** 偷偷瞥/看一眼（某物）; **I managed to ～ a note to him** 我设法把纸条偷偷递给了他; **someone ～ed a camera inside** 有人偷偷把相机带了进去

C *n* colloq pej **1** Brit (telltale) 打小报告者 [尤指学童] **2** (devious person) 鬼鬼祟祟的人 [尤指告密者]

D *adj attrib* 偷偷的; **a ～ attack** 偷袭; **a ～ visit** 暗访; **to take a ～ look at sth.** 偷看一眼某物

Phrasal verb

- **sneak out**

A *vi* 溜出

B *vt* [～ **sb./sth. out,** ～ **out sb./sth.**] 悄悄放走 ‹*person*›; 偷偷拿出 ‹*object*›

sneaker /ˈsniːkə(r)/ *n* esp Amer 运动鞋

sneaking /ˈsniːkɪŋ/ *adj attrib* **1** colloq (furtive) 鬼鬼祟祟的 ‹*traitor, informer*›; 暗中的 ‹*advantage*› **2** (persistent) 潜在萦绕的; **to have a ～ suspicion that ...** 一直暗自怀疑…; **to have a ～ admiration/respect for ...** 私底下钦佩/尊敬…

sneak: ～ preview *n* (of film) 预映; (of exhibition) 预展; **to give sb. a ～ preview of sth.** 让某人预先观摩某事物; **～ thief** *n* [溜进屋内行窃的] 小偷

sneaky /ˈsniːki/ *adj* colloq **1** (furtive) 鬼鬼祟祟的; **～, underhand tactics** 偷偷摸摸的狡诈战术 **2** (secret) 暗中的 ‹*affection, desire, feeling*›

sneer /snɪə(r)/

A *n* **1** (facial expression) 冷笑 **2** (remark) 讥笑

B *vi* **1** (smile contemptuously) 冷笑 **2** (speak contemptuously) 讥笑; **to ～ at sb.** 嘲笑某人

sneering /ˈsnɪərɪŋ/

A *n* [u] (smiling contemptuously) 冷笑; (speaking contemptuously) 讥笑

B *adj* 讥笑的; **in a ～ tone** 带着嘲笑的口吻

sneeringly /ˈsnɪərɪŋli/ *adv* 讥笑地

sneeze /sniːz/

A *vi* 打喷嚏; **it is not to be ～d at** 这不可小视

B *n* (act) 喷嚏; (sound) 喷嚏声

snick /snɪk/ colloq

A *n* **1** (small cut) 小切口; (small notch) 细刻痕; **to cut a ～ in sth.** 在某物上切一道小口子 **2** (in cricket) 削打; **to give the ball a ～** 削球

B *vt* **1** (cut) 割破 ‹*skin, toe*›; 在…上刻细痕 ‹*fabric, wood*› **2** (in cricket) 削打 ‹*ball*›

snicker /ˈsnɪkə(r)/ *n, vi* Amer = **snigger**

snide /snaɪd/ *adj* 挖苦的

sniff /snɪf/

A *n* **1** (audible breath) [用鼻子的] 吸气; **'stupid,' she said, with a disdainful ～** "真笨，" 她轻蔑地哼了一声; **he gave a ～ of disapproval** 他哼了一声，表示不同意 **2** (inhalation) (in order to perceive smell) 嗅; (in order to inhale drug) 吸入; **to take** *or* **have a ～ (at** *or* **of sth.)** 嗅一嗅（某物）; **to give sb. a ～ of sth.** 让某人闻一闻某物; **a single ～ of the substance can be fatal** 吸一口这种物质就会致命 **3** (scent) 气味; **a ～ of gas/alcohol** 煤气味/酒精味; **a ～ of sea air will do you the world of good!** 呼吸海边的空气对你大有好处！ **4** colloq (hint, trace) 迹象; **a ～ of trouble/scandal** 问题/丑闻的苗头; **not to get a ～ of money/the ball/a medal** 根本得不到钱/碰不到球/拿不到奖牌

B *vi* 抽鼻子

C *vt* **1** (smell at) 嗅; (inhale as drug) 吸; **he stopped and ～ed the air** 他停下来嗅了嗅空气 **2** (say with audible breath) 抽着鼻子说; **he ～ed his disapproval** 他轻轻地表示不同意

Phrasal verbs

- **sniff around** *vi* colloq 打探; **to ～ around for sth.** 四处打探某事
- **sniff at** *vt* [～ **at sth.**]
1 (smell at) 嗅 **2** fig (be disdainful of) 对…嗤之以鼻; (reject) 摈弃; **what are you ～ing at?** 你有什么看不惯的？; **not to be ～ed at** 不容轻视
- **sniff out** *vt* [～ **sb./sth. out,** ～ **out sb./sth.**]
1 (detect by smell) 闻出 **2** fig (expose) 查出 ‹*crime, criminal*›; 发现 ‹*news story, bargain*›

sniffer dog /ˈsnɪfə dɒg/ *n* 嗅探犬

sniffle /ˈsnɪfl/ colloq

A *n* 抽鼻子; **to have the ～s** 患轻感冒

B *vi* 抽鼻子

sniffy /ˈsnɪfi/ *adj* colloq 轻蔑的; **to be ～ about sth.** 对某事物嗤之以鼻

snifter /ˈsnɪftə(r)/ *n* colloq **1** Brit dated (small drink) 少量烈酒 **2** Amer (glass) 白兰地酒杯

snigger /ˈsnɪgə(r)/

A *n* 窃笑; **the boy replied with a ～** 男孩以窃笑作答

B *vi* 窃笑; **to ～ at sb./sth.** 窃笑某人/某事物

sniggering /ˈsnɪgərɪŋ/

A *n* [u] 窃笑

B *adj attrib* 窃笑的

snip /snɪp/

A *n* **1** (cutting) 剪 **2** (piece of fabric) 剪下的小片 **3** Brit colloq (bargain) 便宜货; **the dress was a ～ at only £12!** 这件连衣裙只卖 12 英镑，真便宜！

B *vt* (*pres p etc.* **-pp-**) 剪

Phrasal verb

- **snip off** *vt* [～ **sth. off,** ～ **off sth.**] 剪下

snipe /snaɪp/

A *n* 沙锥鸟

B *vi* **1** (shoot) 狙击; **to ～ at sb./sth.** 对某人/某物打冷枪 **2** (criticize) 抨击; **to ～ at sb.** 指摘某人

sniper /ˈsnaɪpə(r)/ *n* 狙击手

sniper fire *n* [u] 冷枪

sniping /ˈsnaɪpɪŋ/ *n* [u] 抨击

snippet /ˈsnɪpɪt/ *n* 片断

snitch /snɪtʃ/ colloq

A *vi* 告密; **to ～ on sb.** 告发某人

B *vt* 偷

C *n* **1** (nose) 鼻子 **2** (informer) 告密者

snivel /ˈsnɪvl/ *vi* pej 哭哭啼啼

sniveller Brit, **sniveler** Amer /ˈsnɪvlə(r)/ *n* pej 哭哭啼啼者

snivelling Brit, **sniveling** Amer /ˈsnɪvlɪŋ/ pej

A *n* [u] 哭哭啼啼

B *adj attrib* 哭哭啼啼的

snob /snɒb/

A *n* **1** (in social life) 势利的人 **2** (in specific sphere) 自以为懂行者; **a coffee ～** 自诩精于品鉴咖啡的人

B *modif* 势利者的 ‹*following*›; **to have ～ appeal** 对爱慕虚荣的顾客有吸引力; **there's a certain ～ value in shopping at Harrods** 在哈罗兹百货公司购物能满足某种庸俗的虚荣心

snobbery /ˈsnɒbəri/ *n* [u] 势利

snobbish /ˈsnɒbɪʃ/ *adj* 势利的

snobbishness /ˈsnɒbɪʃnɪs/ *n* [u] 势利

snobby /ˈsnɒbi/ *adj* colloq 势利的

snog /snɒg/ Brit colloq

A *vt, vi* (*pres p etc.* **-gg-**) 拥吻

B *n* 拥吻

snogging /ˈsnɒgɪŋ/ *n* [u] Brit colloq 拥吻

snook /snuːk/ *n* Brit **to cock a ～ at sb.** lit, fig 对某人做拇指抵鼻的轻蔑手势; fig 蔑视某人

snooker /ˈsnuːkə(r)/ ▸**p. 307**

A *n* **1** [u] (game) 斯诺克; **a ～ player/champion** 斯诺克选手/冠军 **2** [c] (shot) [斯诺克中的] 障碍球; **to play a ～** 做斯诺克

B *vt* **1** (leave opponent in unfavourable position) 为…设障碍球 ‹*opponent*› **2** (thwart) 阻挠; **I'm ～ed** 我一筹莫展了 **3** Amer (deceive) 欺骗; **to ～ sb. into sth.** *or* **into doing sth.** 欺骗某人做某事

snoop /snuːp/ colloq

A *vi* 窥探; **to ～ into sth.** 探听某事; **to ～ on sb.** 跟踪某人

B *n* 窥探; **to have a ～ around** 四处打探

Phrasal verb

- **snoop around, snoop about** *vi* colloq 四下窥探

snooper /ˈsnuːpə(r)/ *n* colloq 窥探者

snooping /ˈsnuːpɪŋ/ colloq

A *n* [u] 窥探; **～ on sb.** 对某人的跟踪

B *adj attrib* 窥探的

snoot /snuːt/ *n* colloq **1** (nose) 鼻子 **2** (person) 势利眼

snooty /ˈsnuːti/ *adj* colloq (snobbish) 势利的; (aloof) 傲慢的

snooze /snuːz/ colloq

A *n* [尤指白天的] 小睡; **to have a ～** 打个盹儿

B *vi* 打盹儿

snooze button *n* [闹钟上的] 小睡按钮

snore /snɔː(r)/

A *vi* 打鼾

B *n* (act) 打鼾; (sound) 打鼾声

snorer /ˈsnɔːrə(r)/ *n* 打鼾者

snoring /ˈsnɔːrɪŋ/ *n* [u] 打鼾

snorkel /ˈsnɔːkl/

A *n* 呼吸管

B *vi* (*pres p etc.* **-ll-** Brit, **-l-** Amer) 带呼吸管潜水

S

snorkelling /ˈsnɔːklɪŋ/ ▸**p. 307** *n* [u] 带呼吸管潜水; **we went ~** 我们去徒手潜水

snort /snɔːt/
A *n* **1** (noise) (of horse, bull) 喷鼻息; (of person, pig) 哼声; **to give a ~ of indignation** 气愤地哼一声 **2** colloq (drug-taking) (act) 用鼻子吸毒; (quantity) 吸入的毒品 **3** colloq (drink) 一口烈酒
B *vt* **1** (say contemptuously) 哼着鼻子说 ‹*remark*› **2** (inhale) 用鼻子吸 ‹*drug*›
C *vi* **1** (make noise) «*person, pig*» 发哼声; «*horse, bull*» 喷鼻息; **to ~ with laughter** 噗嗤一声笑出来 **2** colloq (take drug) 用鼻子吸毒

snot /snɒt/ *n* colloq **1** [u] (mucus) 鼻涕 **2** [c] pej (person) 卑鄙下贱的人

snotty /ˈsnɒti/ *adj* colloq **1** (full of mucus) 满是鼻涕的 **2** (snobbish) 自以为是的

snotty-nosed /ˈsnɒtɪnəʊzd/ *adj* colloq **1** (with runny nose) 满是鼻涕的 **2** (snobbish) 自以为是的

snout /snaʊt/ *n* **1** (of animal) 口鼻部 **2** pej (of person) 鼻子 **3** Brit colloq (informer) 警方线人

snow /snəʊ/
A *n* [u] **1** (ice crystals) 雪; **a fall of ~** 下雪 **2** TV [电视或雷达屏幕上的] "雪花" **3** colloq (cocaine) 白面儿
B **snows** *npl* 降雪; **the eternal ~s of the Frozen North** 严寒北方的永久积雪
C *v impers* 下雪; **it's ~ing** 下雪了
D *vt* Amer colloq 用花言巧语蒙骗; **to ~ sb. into doing sth.** 用花言巧语哄某人做某事

Phrasal verbs
- **snow in** *vt usu passive* **to be ~ed in** «*person, family*» 被雪困住; «*house, farm*» 被雪封住
- **snow under** *vt usu passive* **to be ~ed under** (covered with snow) «*fields, village*» 被雪覆盖; fig (inundated with work, letters, etc.) 应接不暇; **I'm ~ed under with work at the moment** 眼下我正忙得不可开交
- **snow up** *vt* = **snow in**

snowball /ˈsnəʊbɔːl/
A *n* **1** (ball of snow) 雪球; **they haven't got a ~'s chance in hell (of doing that)** 他们毫无机会(做那件事) **2** (drink) [用柠檬水和白兰地蛋酒调制成的] 雪球鸡尾酒 **3** (dessert) 冰霜卷 **4** (rapidly growing thing) 滚雪球般发展的情形; **to have a ~ effect on ...** 使…产生滚雪球效应
B *vt* 向…扔雪球
C *vi* 滚雪球般增长

snowball fight *n* 打雪仗

snow: ~bank *n* Amer [被风吹成的] 雪堆; **~belt** *n* Amer 霜冻地带 [尤指美国五大湖区以南地带]; **~-blind** *adj* 雪盲的; **~ blindness** *n* [u] 雪盲症

snowboard /ˈsnəʊbɔːd/
A *n* 滑雪板
B *vi* 用滑雪板滑雪

snow: ~boarder *n* 用滑雪板滑雪的人; **~boarding** ▸**p. 307** *n* [u] 滑雪板运动; **~boot** *n* 雪地靴; **~bound** *adj* 被雪困住的 ‹*person, vehicle*›; 被雪封住的 ‹*house, region*›; **~ cannon** *n* 造雪机; **~-capped** *adj* 有雪冠的; **~ chains** *npl* 雪地防滑链

Snowdon /ˈsnəʊdən/ *pr n* 斯诺登山

Snowdonia /snəʊˈdəʊnɪə/ *pr n* 斯诺登尼亚

snow: ~drift *n* [被风吹成的] 雪堆; **~drop** *n* 雪花莲; **~fall** *n* **1** [c] (event) 降雪; **2** [u] (amount) 降雪量; **~field** *n* 雪原; **~flake** *n* 雪花; **~ goose** *n* (*pl* **~ geese**) 雪雁; **~ job** *n* Amer colloq 花言巧语诱骗; **~ leopard** *n* 雪豹; **~ line** *n* 雪线; **~man** /-mæn/ *n* 雪人

snowmobile /ˈsnəʊməbiːl/
A *n* 机动雪橇
B *vi* 乘机动雪橇

snowplough Brit, **snowplow** Amer /ˈsnəʊplaʊ/
A *n* **1** (vehicle for clearing snow) 扫雪机 **2** (turn of skis inward) 犁式制动
B *vi* 作犁式滑降

snow: ~ report *n* 雪况预报; **~ shoe** *n* 雪鞋; **~slide** *n* Amer 雪崩; **~storm** *n* **1** (event) 雪暴; **2** (toy) 雪暴玩具 [内装液体及白色颗粒, 摇晃时若雪花飘舞]; (ornament) 雪暴装饰物; **~ suit** *n* Amer 风雪服; **~ tyre** Brit *n* 雪地防滑轮胎; **S~ White** *pr n* 白雪公主

snowy /ˈsnəʊi/ *adj* **1** (covered with snow) 白雪覆盖的 **2** (characterized by snow) 多雪的 ‹*weather, climate, journey*›; **it was very ~ yesterday** 昨天雪很大 **3** ▸**p. 134** (white as snow) 雪白的

snowy owl *n* 雪鸮

SNP *abbr* Brit = **Scottish National Party**

Snr *abbr* = **senior A3**

snub /snʌb/
A *vt* (*pres p etc.* **-bb-**) 冷落; **to be ~bed (by ...)** 受到(…的)怠慢
B *n* 冷落

snub: ~ nose *n* 短翘鼻; **~-nosed** *adj* 塌鼻子的 ‹*child, animal*›; 枪管短的 ‹*pistol*›; 顶端扁平的 ‹*bonnet of car*›

snuck /snʌk/ *pt, pp* Amer colloq ▸**sneak A, B**

snuff[1] /snʌf/ *n* [u] 鼻烟

snuff[2] *vt* 熄灭; **to ~ it** Brit colloq 断气

Phrasal verb
- **snuff out** *vt* [**~ sth. out, ~ out sth.**] **1** (extinguish) 熄灭 ‹*candle, lamp*› **2** (suppress) 扼杀 ‹*rebellion, enthusiasm*› **3** colloq (kill) 杀死 ‹*person*›

snuffbox /ˈsnʌfbɒks/ *n* 鼻烟盒

snuffle /ˈsnʌfl/
A *vi* **1** (breathe noisily) 抽鼻子 **2** (smell) «*animal*» 哧哧地嗅
B *n* (sniff) 抽鼻子; (sound) 抽鼻子声
C **snuffles** *npl* colloq (cold) 感冒; (other infection) 鼻塞; **to have the ~s** 患感冒

snuffling /ˈsnʌflɪŋ/ *n* [u] 呼哧声

snuff movie *n* colloq 凶杀纪实片

snug /snʌg/
A *adj* **1** (warm, cosy) 温暖舒适的 ▸**rug 1** **2** (tight) 紧身的 ‹*garment*›; 严实的 ‹*door, cabin*›; **the ~ fit of a jacket** 夹克衫的紧贴合身; **a ~ little boat** 一条紧凑小巧的船
B *n* Brit [酒馆或客栈中的] 雅间

snuggery /ˈsnʌgəri/ *n* 温暖舒适的地方

snuggle /ˈsnʌgl/ *vi* 偎依; **to ~ together** 偎依在一起; **to ~ against sb./sth.** 倚靠着某人/某物

Phrasal verbs
- **snuggle down** *vi* 舒舒服服地躺下; **to ~ down in (one's) bed** 舒舒服服地躺上床
- **snuggle up** *vi* 偎依; **to ~ up to sth./sb.** 偎依着某物/某人

snugly /ˈsnʌgli/ *adv* **1** (cosily) 温暖舒适地 ‹*lie*› **2** (tightly) 紧贴地 ‹*fit, buttoned up*›; 严实地 ‹*close, wrap*›

so[1] /səʊ/
A *adv* **1** (to such a degree, extent) 如此; **don't talk ~ fast!** 别说得那么快!; **there's no need to worry ~** 没必要这么着急; **not ~ ... as ...** 不像…那样…; **it's not ~ easy as you'd think** 这并非你想象的那么容易; **he's not ~ stern a father as yours** 作为父亲他不像你父亲那样严厉; **she spoke ~ quietly I could hardly hear her** 她说话轻得我几乎听不见; **the current is ~ strong as to be dangerous for swimmers** 水流湍急, 对游泳者很危险 **2** (very) 非常; **I'm ~ glad you're here** 你来这儿我非常高兴; **he sat there ever ~ quietly** Brit 他静悄悄地坐在那儿; **she loved him ~** 她非常爱他 **3** (demonstrating size, technique) 这么; **she's about ~ tall** 她差不多有这么高; **stand with your arms out, ~** 两臂伸开站着, 这样; **it fastens (like) ~** 是这样系的 **4** (that is the case, the truth) 是这样; **he said ~** 他这样说过的; **if ~** 要是那样; **I'm afraid ~** 恐怕是这样; **I hope ~** 希望如此; **is that ~?** 是吗?; **~ I see!** 这下我明白了!; **I told you ~!** 我早就对你说过!; **he thinks I dislike him, but that just isn't ~** 他以为我讨厌他, 其实不是那么回事 **5** (this) 如此 [指以前提到的事物]; **~ saying ...** 如此说…; **they asked me to call them, and I did ~** 他们要我给他们打电话, 于是我就打了; **it is a secret, and will remain ~** 这是秘密, 将来也仍然如此; **he opened the drawer, and while he was ~ occupied ...** 他打开抽屉, 而正当他忙于开抽屉时…; **yes, if you ~ wish** formal 是的, 如果你希望如此; **he looked exactly as I expected him to, only more ~** 他的长相和我想象的完全一样, 甚至是更像; **he's conscientious, perhaps too much ~** 他勤勉认真, 也许过头了 **6** (also) 也; **he's French, and ~ is she** 他是法国人, 她也是; **if they accept, ~ do I** 如果他们答应, 我也答应 **7** (expressing agreement) 的确如此; **there's another one — ~ there is** 还有一个——可不是嘛; **I thought you liked it? — ~ I do** 我以为你是喜欢它的?——当然喽 **8** (in such a way) 像这样; **~ it was that he finally returned home** 就这样, 他终于回到了家; **the contract is ~ worded that ownership is unclear** 合同这样措词使得所有权不明确; **~ to speak** 可以说; **they were all very similar: all cut from the same cloth, ~ to speak** 他们都十分相像: 可以说如出一辙; **~ be it** formal 就这样吧; **if he doesn't want to be involved, then ~ be it** 如果他不想参与, 那就随他的便; **and ~ forth, and ~ on** 等等 **9** (for that reason) 所以; **he's young, and ~ impulsive** 他年轻, 所以容易冲动; **she was tired and ~ went to bed** 她累了, 于是上床睡觉去了 **10** ▸**p. 32** (thereabouts) 大约; **or ~** 左右; **there were twenty or ~ people there** 那儿有 20 人左右; **a year or ~ ago** 大约1年前 **11** colloq (definitely) 的确; **that's ~ not fair** 那确实不公平; **you are ~ going to regret this** 你肯定会为此后悔的 **12** colloq (contradicting a statement) 偏就是; **he didn't hit you — he did ~!** 他没有打你——他就是打了的!
B *conj* **1** (in order that) 为了; **but I gave you a map ~ you wouldn't get lost!** 但我怕你迷路, 给过你一张地图! **2** (introducing next part of narrative) 就这样; **~ after shouting and screaming for an hour, she walked out in tears** 就这样, 大喊大叫了 1 个小时后, 她泪流满面走了出来 **3** (and therefore, with the result that) 因此; **it's Sunday, ~ the shops are shut** 今天是星期天, 所以商店都不开门; **~ there!** colloq 就是这样!; **well, you can't have it, ~ there!** 好啦, 就是不给你, 没什么好说的! **4** colloq (defending self, dismissing sth.) 那又怎样; **~ I had a couple of drinks on the way home: what's wrong with that?** 不错, 我在回家的路上是喝了两杯: 这有什么不对吗?; **you've been smoking again — ~?** 你又抽烟了——那又怎样?; **I'm leaving — ~?** 我要走了——那又怎样?; **he's fifteen years younger than you! — ~ what?** 他比你小 15 岁呢! ——那又怎么啦? **5** (introductory or ensuing or concluding remark) 那么; **~, what have you been doing today?** 那你今天都干什么了?; **~ you're going, are you?** 这么说, 你要走了, 是吗?; **~, that's it for today** 好, 今天就到这里 **6** (in the same way) 同样; **(just) as ... ~ ...** (正) 像…一样, …也; **as prices go up, ~ sales decline** 物价在上涨, 销售额则在下降; **just as you need him, ~ he needs you** 正如你需要他一样, 他也需要你 **7** (next) 然后; **and ~ to the final** 然后进入决赛
C **so that** *conj phr* 以便; **she wrote the**

S

instructions ~ that they'd be easily understood 她写了用法说明以使其易于理解; she fixed the party for 8 ~ that he could come 她把聚会时间定在8点为的是他能来

D so as *conj phr* 为了; he tiptoed out, ~ as not to disturb people 为了不惊动别人, 他踮着脚走了出去

E so many *adv and pron phr* **1** (a certain number, such a large number) 这么多; the hostel can only take ~ many 这家招待所只能接待这么多人; there are only ~ many hours in a day 一天就只有这么多个小时; I've warned him about it ~ many times 这事我已经提醒他好多次了; he's wasted ~ many of the opportunities he's had 他得到的好多机会都浪费掉了 **2** (in comparisons) [表示对应或等同] they were behaving like ~ many schoolgirls 他们的表现跟那些学校的小女生没什么两样

F so much *adv and pron phr* **1** (amount of sth.) 这么多; I can only pay ~ much 我只能付这么多; his family's got ~ much money 他家这么有钱; the article was just ~ much nonsense 这篇文章纯属无稽之谈; ~ much of sth. 相当多的某事物; ~ much of the information was useless 这些信息很多都是无用的 **2** (in comparisons, contrasts) [表示对应或等同] they were tossed like ~ much flotsam 它们就像废物一般被扔掉了; not ~ much X as Y 与其说是甲, 不如说是乙; it doesn't annoy me ~ much as surprise me 与其说令我气愤, 还不如说令我吃惊 **3** (to such an extent) 到这种程度; you've made things ~ much worse 你把事情弄得更糟了; she hates him ~ much she can't even stand to be in the same room as him 她对他恨之入骨, 以至于无法忍受和他待在同一间屋子里; I haven't enjoyed myself ~ much for a long time 我好久没这么开心过了; thank you ~ much/ever ~ much 太感谢你了; ~ much ~ (that) ... 以至到…的程度; we are very busy, ~ much ~ that we won't be able to take time off this year 我们很忙, 忙得今年都没时间休假了; ~ much the better/worse 那就更好/更糟了; if it arrives by then, ~ much the better 如果那时候到了就更好

G so much as *adv phr* 甚至; he never ~ much as apologized 他甚至没有道个歉; she left without ~ much as a goodbye *or* without ~ much as saying goodbye 她都没道个别就离开了; ▸much B2

H so much for *prep phr* **1** (having finished with) 关于…到此为止; ~ much for the situation in Germany; now we turn our attention to France 德国的形势就讲到这里, 现在我们来看看法国 **2** colloq (used disparagingly) 作罢好了; ~ much for that idea! 别提那个主意了!; ~ much for saying you'd help! 得了, 别再说你愿意帮忙了!

I so long as *conj phr* ▸long¹ C2

so² *n* Mus = soh

soak /səʊk/

A *vt* **1** (wet) «*rain, dew*» 打湿; «*person*» 弄湿; to ~ sb. to the skin 使某人浑身湿透; to be/get ~ed 湿透; to get one's feet/head ~ed 把脚/头弄湿 **2** (immerse) 浸泡; to ~ sth. in sth. 把某物浸泡在…里 ‹*water, detergent, dye*›; to be ~ed in sex/sentiment fig 纵欲/过度感伤 **3** colloq (take excess money from) 向…敲竹杠; to ~ the rich 敲富人的竹杠

B *vi* **1** (penetrate) to ~ into sth. 渗入 ‹*earth, leather*›; to ~ through sth. 渗透 ‹*clothes, bandages*› **2** (be immersed) «*clothes, foodstuffs*» 浸泡; to leave a garment to ~ 把衣服放在一边泡着; she spent some time ~ing in a hot bath 她泡了一会儿热水澡 **3** dated (drink heavily) 狂饮

C *v refl* **1** (get wet) 湿透; to ~ oneself from head to foot 浑身湿透 **2** (become immersed) to ~ oneself in sth. 浸泡在…中 ‹*bath*›; fig 沉浸在…中 ‹*atmosphere, music*›

D *n* **1** [c and u] (immersing) 浸泡; to give sth. a ~ 把某物泡一泡; to have a ~ 泡个澡; to be in ~ «*washing*» 浸泡着 **2** [c] colloq (drunk) 酒鬼

E -soaked *combining form* 被…浸透的; blood~ed 浸透血的 ‹*bandages*›; 血流成河的 ‹*battlefield*›; rain/dew~ed 被雨/露水打湿的; wine~ed 醉醺醺的 ‹*brain*›; sun~ed 阳光普照的

Phrasal verbs

- **soak away** *vi* 渗完
- **soak in** *vi* «*liquid*» 渗入; fig «*words, ideas*» 被理解
- **soak off**

A *vt* [~ sth. off, ~ off sth.] 把…泡掉 ‹*label, dressing*›

B *vi* «*label, dressing*» 被泡掉

- **soak out**

A *vt* [~ sth. out, ~ out sth.] 把…泡掉 ‹*stain, dirt*›

B *vi* «*stain, dirt*» 被泡掉

- **soak through**

A *vi* «*liquid*» 渗透; to ~ right through (to sth.) 完全渗透 (到某物中)

B *vt* [~ through sth./sb., ~ sth./sb. through] 使湿透; my raincoat is ~ed through! 我的雨衣湿透了!; to ~ sb. right through to the skin 使某人浑身湿透

- **soak up** *vt* [~ sth. up, ~ up sth.] 吸掉 ‹*liquid*›; fig 吸取 ‹*information*›; 感受 ‹*atmosphere*›; use your handkerchief to ~ up the blood 用你的手帕把血吸干; to ~ up the sun 晒太阳

soakaway /ˈsəʊkəweɪ/ *n* Brit 渗水坑

soaked /səʊkt/ *adj* 湿透的

soaking /ˈsəʊkɪŋ/

A *n* 湿透; to get a ~ 全身湿透; to give sb./sth. a ~ 使某人浑身湿透/把某物浸湿

B *adj* 湿透的; ~ wet 湿淋淋的

so-and-so *n* (*pl* ~s) **1** (unspecified person) 某某人; (unspecified thing) 某某事; Mr ~ 某某先生 **2** colloq (disliked person) 讨厌鬼; he's an old ~ 他是个讨厌的老家伙

soap /səʊp/

A *n* **1** [c and u] (for washing) 肥皂 **2** [c] colloq = soap opera

B *vt* 用肥皂洗

soapbox /ˈsəʊpbɒks/ *n* **1** (box, crate) 临时演讲台; to get on one's ~ 大发议论 **2** fig (opportunity) 大发议论的机会

soapbox: ~ **orator** *n* (from soapbox) 街头演说者; (expressing strong opinions) 大发议论的人; ~ **oratory** *n* [u] (from soapbox) 街头演说; (expression of strong opinions) 大发议论

soap: ~**dish** *n* 肥皂盘; ~ **dispenser** *n* 皂液器; ~**flakes** *npl* 肥皂片; ~ **opera** *n* 肥皂剧; ~ **powder** *n* [u and c] 肥皂粉; ~ **star** *n* 肥皂剧明星; ~**stone** *n* [u] 皂石; ~**suds** *npl* 肥皂沫

soap opera

肥皂剧, 亦称 soap。一种电视连续剧 (serial), 通常每周播放3到5次, 每集约30分钟, 讲述普通人的日常生活故事。源于20世纪30年代美国的广播节目。因当时听众多为家庭主妇, 赞助商为肥皂等洗涤用品公司, 故名。情节进展缓慢, 以对话为主。在英国一般于晚间播出, 较受欢迎的有独立电视台 (▸ITV) 的《加冕街》(*Coronation Street*) 和 BBC 的《东区人》(*EastEnders*)。美国的肥皂剧多数在下午播出, 故亦称日间剧 (daytime drama)。其中哥伦比亚广播公司 (▸CBS) 播出的《指路明灯》(*Guiding Light*) 始于1937年, 是迄今为止历史最悠久的肥皂剧。

soapy /ˈsəʊpi/ *adj* **1** (containing soap) 含肥皂的; (covered in soap) 涂满肥皂的; (covered in lather) 盖满肥皂泡的 **2** (of soap) 肥皂的; (like soap) 像肥皂的 **3** (obsequious) 讨好的; a ~ remark 恭维话

soar /sɔː(r)/ *vi* **1** (fly up or rise high in the air) «*bird, kite*» 高飞; «*aircraft, flames*» 升空; «*tower, mountain*» 高耸; the eagle/glider ~ed high above us 老鹰/滑翔机在我们头顶的高空翱翔 **2** (rise in pitch) «*voice, pitch*» 升高; «*instrument*» 音调增高 **3** (in spirits) «*hopes, expectations, morale*» 高涨 **4** (increase rapidly) 猛增; to ~ beyond *or* above *or* through ... 猛升至…以上; to ~ to 激增到 ‹*amount, figure*›; to ~ from X to Y 从X骤升到Y

Phrasal verb

- **soar up** *vi* 飞上天空

soaring /ˈsɔːrɪŋ/ *adj* **1** (in height) 高耸的 ‹*skyscraper, tower, mountain*›; 腾空的 ‹*rocket, flames*› **2** (in pitch) 高昂的 ‹*voice, pitch, volume*› **3** (in level, rate) 高涨的 ‹*hopes, spirits*›; 骤升的 ‹*popularity, price, temperature*›

sob /sɒb/

A *vi* (*pres p etc.* -bb-) 啜泣

B *vt* (*pres p etc.* -bb-) 抽噎着说

C *n* (act) 啜泣; (sound) 啜泣声

Phrasal verb

- **sob out** *vt* [~ out sth., ~ sth. out] 哭诉 ‹*tale, story*›; she ~bed out her trouble to him 她向他哭诉自己的烦恼; to ~ one's heart out 哭得死去活来

sobbing /ˈsɒbɪŋ/

A *n* [u] (action) 啜泣; (sound) 啜泣声

B *adj* 啜泣的

sober /ˈsəʊbə(r)/ *adj* **1** (not drunk) 未醉的; to be ~ 没有喝醉 **2** (serious) 严肃的 ‹*person, mood, truth*›; 冷静的 ‹*judgement, estimate*› **3** (sombre) 素净的 ‹*colour, pattern, garment*›

Phrasal verb

- **sober up**

A *vi* **1** (become less drunk) 醒酒 **2** (become sensible) 变得冷静; (become serious) 变得严肃

B *vt* [~ sb. up] **1** (make less drunk) 使醒酒 **2** (make sensible) 使理智; (make serious) 使严肃

sobering /ˈsəʊbərɪŋ/ *adj* 令人清醒的 ‹*thought, phone call*›

soberly /ˈsəʊbəli/ *adv* 严肃地 ‹*act, say*›; 素净地 ‹*dress, furnished, decorated*›

soberness /ˈsəʊbənɪs/ *n* [u] **1** (of demeanour, person) 持重 **2** (of dress, decor) 素净

sobriety /səˈbraɪəti/ *n* [u] **1** (moderation) 饮酒适度 **2** (seriousness) 严肃; (calm) 冷静; (sensibleness) 理智 **3** (simplicity of dress, decor) 素净

sobriquet /ˈsəʊbrɪkeɪ/ *n* formal 绰号

sob: ~ **sister** *n* colloq **1** (female journalist) 写伤感文章的女记者; **2** (actress) 演伤感角色的女演员; ~ **story** *n* colloq 伤感故事; ~ **stuff** *n* [u] colloq pej 伤感的故事

so-called *adj* **1** (popularly) 号称…的 **2** (falsely) 所谓的

soccer /ˈsɒkə(r)/ ▸p. 307 *n* [u] 足球运动; ~ boots 足球鞋

soccer: ~ **mom** *n* Amer colloq 足球妈妈 [指生活在郊区的中产阶级家庭妇女, 子女常踢足球而不是参加美国传统体育项目]; ~ **player** *n* 足球运动员; ~ **season** *n* 足球赛季

sociability /ˌsəʊʃəˈbɪləti/ *n* [u] 好交际

sociable /ˈsəʊʃəbl/ *adj* 好交际的 ‹*person, mood*›; 群居的 ‹*animal*›; 社交的 ‹*occasion, place, activity*›; 友好的 ‹*community*›

sociably /ˈsəʊʃəbli/ *adv* 友好地

social /ˈsəʊʃl/

A *adj* **1** (relating to society) 社会性的; man is a ~ animal 人是社会性的动物 **2** (relating to position in society) 社会地位的 ‹*mobility, order*›; ~ position *or* status 社会地位 **3** (recreational) 社交的 ‹*activity, occasion*›; a ~ drinker/smoker 应酬时才喝酒/吸烟的人 **4** (gregarious) 爱交际的 ‹*person*›; 群居的 ‹*animal*›

B *n* 联谊会

S

social: ～ **anthropology** *n* [u] 社会人类学; ～ **charter** *n* [尤指规范劳工权利与福利的] 社会宪章; ～ **climber** *n* pej 一心向上爬的人; ～ **climbing** *n* [u] pej 一心向上爬; ～ **club** *n* 联谊会; ～ **column** *n* [报道上流社会活动等的] 社会新闻栏; ～ **conscience** *n* 社会良知; ～ **contact** *n* **1** [u] (association, communication) 交往; **2** [c] (friend) 朋友; (acquaintance) 熟人; ～ **democracy** *n* [u] 社会民主主义; ～ **democrat** *n* (member) 社会民主党人; (advocate) 社会民主主义者; ～ **democratic** *adj* 社会民主主义的; ～ **disease** *n* **1** (societal ill) 社会弊病 [如贫穷、饥饿等]; **2** colloq (venereal disease) 性病; ～ **duty** *n* 社会责任; ～ **engagement** *n* **1** [u] (involvement in society, community) 社会参与; **2** [c] (meeting) 社交聚会; (arrangement) 社交安排; **3** [u] (socializing) 参加社交活动; ～ **engineering** *n* [u] 社会工程; ～ **evening** *n* 社交晚会; ～ **event** *n* 社交活动; ～ **exclusion** *n* [u] 社会排斥; ～ **fund** *n* Brit [向困难者提供资助的] 社会基金; ～ **gathering** *n* 社交聚会; ～ **geography** *n* [u] 社会地理学; ～ **historian** ▸**p. 409** *n* 社会历史学家; ～ **history** *n* [u] 社会史; ～ **housing** *n* [u] Brit 社会福利住房; ～ **inclusion** *n* [u] 社会包容; ～ **insurance** *n* [u] Amer 社会保险

socialism /'səʊʃəlɪzəm/ *n* [u] 社会主义

socialist /'səʊʃəlɪst/
A *adj* 社会主义的
B *n* 社会主义者

socialite /'səʊʃəlaɪt/ *n* 社交名流

socialization /ˌsəʊʃəlaɪ'zeɪʃn, Amer -lɪ'z-/ *n* [u] **1** (acquiring of social behaviour) 社会化 **2** (placing under government control) 社会主义化

socialize /'səʊʃəlaɪz/
A *vi* 交际; **to ～ with sb.** 同某人交往
B *vt* **1** (cause to adapt to society) 使适应社会 **2** (organize according to socialism) 使社会主义化

socializing /'səʊʃəlaɪzɪŋ/ *n* [u] 社交

social life *n* 社交生活

socially /'səʊʃəli/ *adv* 在社交方面 ‹*acceptable, mix*›; 社交性地 ‹*meet, visit*›; 在社会地位上 ‹*inferior, superior*›; 在社会意义上 ‹*valid*›; ～ **inept** 不擅交际的; **I knew her ～, but I wouldn't say we were friends** 我是在社交场合认识她的，但不能说我们是朋友

socially excluded *adj* 被社会排斥的; **the ～ + *v pl*** 被社会排斥的人

social: ～ **marketing** *n* [u] 社会营销; ～ **misfit** *n* 与社会格格不入的人; ～ **mobility** *n* [u] 社会流动

social networking *n* [u] 网络社交; ～ **services** 网络社交服务

social networking site *n* 社交网站

social: ～ **outcast** *n* 社会弃儿; ～ **partner** *n* 社会伙伴 [指参加互惠合作的个人或组织]; ～ **rank** *n* 社会等级; ～ **register** *n* Amer 社会名人录; ～ **scene** *n* 社交界; ～ **science** *n* **1** [u] (study) 社会科学; **2** [c] (subject) 社会科学学科; ～ **scientist** ▸**p. 409** *n* 社会科学家; ～ **secretary** *n* 社交秘书

social security *n* [u] 社会保障金; **to live off ～** 靠社会保障金生活; **to be on ～** 领取社会保障金

Social Security Administration *n* Amer 社会保障局

social: ～ **services** *npl* Brit 社会福利事业; ～ **studies** *npl + v sing* 社会学科; ～ **welfare** *n* [u] 社会福利; ～ **work** *n* [u] 社会福利工作; ～ **worker** ▸**p. 409** *n* 社会福利工作者

societal /sə'saɪətl/ *adj* 社会的

society /sə'saɪəti/ *n* **1** [u] (community) 社会; **in Western/American/British ～** 在西方/美国/英国社会中 **2** [c] (individual social system) 社会制度; **a civilized/closed/multicultural ～** 文明/封闭/多元文化社会 **3** [c] (organized group) 社团; **a learned ～** 学术团体; **a debating ～** 辩论社; **to set up a ～** 建立协会 **4** [u] (fashionable, wealthy, and influential group) 上层社会; **fashionable ～** 上流社会; ～ **gossip** 上流社会的琐闻

society: ～ **column** *n* 社会新闻栏; **S～ of Friends** *pr n* 公谊会 [即贵格会，17世纪40年代产生于英格兰的宗教组织]

sociobiology /ˌsəʊsɪəʊbaɪ'ɒlədʒi/ *n* [u] 社会生物学

sociocultural /ˌsəʊsɪəʊ'kʌltʃərəl/ *adj* 社会与文化的

socio-economic /ˌsəʊsɪəʊiːkə'nɒmɪk/ *adj* 社会与经济的 ‹*context, factor, influence*›; **the lower ～ groups** 社会和经济地位较低的群体

sociolinguistic /ˌsəʊsɪəʊlɪŋ'gwɪstɪk/ *adj* 社会语言学的

sociolinguistics /ˌsəʊsɪəʊlɪŋ'gwɪstɪks/ *npl + v sing* 社会语言学

sociological /ˌsəʊsɪə'lɒdʒɪkl/ *adj* 社会学的

sociologically /ˌsəʊsɪə'lɒdʒɪkli/ *adv* 在社会学方面; ～ **speaking, ...** 从社会学角度来说，…

sociologist /ˌsəʊsɪ'ɒlədʒɪst/ ▸**p. 409** *n* 社会学家

sociology /ˌsəʊsɪ'ɒlədʒi/ *n* [u] **1** (study of society) 社会学 **2** (social aspects) 社会学研究; **the ～ of sth.** 对某事物的社会学研究

sociopath /'səʊsɪəpæθ/ *n* 反社会者

sociopolitical /ˌsəʊsɪəʊpə'lɪtɪkl/ *adj* 社会与政治的

sock /sɒk/
A *n* **1** (garment) 短袜; **to pull one's ～s up** colloq 加油干; **to put a ～ in it** Brit colloq 闭嘴 **2** (insole) 鞋垫 **3** colloq (blow) 猛击; **to give sb. a ～** 朝某人猛击一拳
B *vt* colloq 猛击; **～ him one!** 揍他一顿！; **to ～ it to sb.** (attack) 猛击某人; (make impression on) 给某人留下深刻印象

socket /'sɒkɪt/ *n* **1** (for plug) 插座; (for bulb) 灯泡插口; (for aerial) 插孔 **2** (hollow) 孔穴; (eye socket) 眼窝

socket set *n* 套筒扳手组

socko /'sɒkəʊ/ *adj* Amer colloq 大获成功的

Socratic /sə'krætɪk/ *adj* 苏格拉底的 ‹*dialogue, philosophy, irony*›; 苏格拉底哲学的 ‹*method, question, tradition*›

sod¹ /sɒd/ Brit
A *n* sl (person) 讨厌鬼; (task) 难办的事; **you stupid ～** 你这个讨厌的蠢货; **poor little ～s** 可怜的小家伙
B *excl* taboo sl **～ it!** 该死！; **～ him!** 去他妈的！

Phrasal verb
- **sod off** *vi* Brit taboo sl 滚开 offensive

sod² *n* **1** [c] (turf) 草皮 **2** [u] (ground) 长草的土层; **under the ～** 入土的

soda /'səʊdə/ *n* **1** [u] (sodium carbonate) 碳酸钠 **2** [c and u] (carbonated water) **～ (water)** 苏打水 **3** [c and u] Amer (soft drink) 汽水

soda: ～ **ash** *n* [u] 苏打灰 [即纯碱]; ～ **biscuit** *n* Brit 苏打饼干; ～ **bread** *n* [c and u] 苏打面包; ～ **cracker** *n* Amer **= ～ biscuit**; ～ **fountain** *n* Amer **1** (device) 汽水机; **2** (shop) 汽水店; (counter) 汽水柜台; ～ **pop** *n* Amer **= soda 3**; ～ **siphon** *n* 汽水机

sod all *n* [u] Brit taboo sl 屁都没有; **he knows ～ about it** 他屁都不知道; **to do ～** 屁事不做

sodden /'sɒdn/ *adj* 湿透的

sodding /'sɒdɪŋ/ *adj* Brit taboo sl 该死的; **that ～ manager** 那个混蛋经理

sodium /'səʊdɪəm/ *n* [u] 钠

sodium: ～ **bicarbonate** *n* [u] 碳酸氢钠; ～ **carbonate** *n* [u] 碳酸钠; ～ **chloride** *n* [u] 氯化钠; ～ **hydroxide** *n* [u] 氢氧化钠; **～-vapour lamp, ～ lamp** *ns* [常用于街道照明的] 钠蒸气灯

sodomite /'sɒdəmaɪt/ *n* 鸡奸者

sodomize /'sɒdəmaɪz/ *vt* 鸡奸

sodomy /'sɒdəmi/ *n* [u] 鸡奸

sod's law *n* [u] Brit hum 造物弄人法则; **It's ～ that he got injured just before the most important game** 真是天不遂人愿，他在最重要的比赛即将开始前受伤了

sofa /'səʊfə/ *n* 长沙发

sofa bed *n* 沙发床

Sofia /'səʊfɪə/ *pr n* 索非亚

soft /sɒft, Amer sɔːft/
A *adj* **1** (yielding) 软的; **to grow *or* get ～** 变软; **to make sth. ～** 使某物变软; ～ **stone/pencil** 软石/软铅笔; **as ～ as butter** 非常软的; **a book in ～ covers** 平装书; ～ **brakes** 偏软的刹车 **2** (smooth and delicate) 柔滑的; **～ to (the) touch** 手感柔滑的; **as ～ as silk *or* velvet** 非常柔滑的 **3** (muted) 柔和的 ‹*colour, tone, lighting*› **4** (not sharp) 线条柔和的 ‹*outline, shape*› **5** (mild, gentle) 和煦的 ‹*climate, weather, breeze*›; **～ rain/wind** 细雨/和风 **6** (quiet, subdued) 轻柔的 ‹*music, tone, steps*›; 轻声的 ‹*whisper, laugh*›; **to say in a ～ voice** 轻声细语 **7** (gentle, conciliatory) 温和的 ‹*reply, expression*›; **～ and gentle words** 温柔的话语 **8** (not forceful) 轻轻的 ‹*impact, tap, touch*› **9** (lenient) 宽厚的; **to be ～ on *or* with sb.** 仁慈地对待某人; **to be ～ on sth.** 对某事宽大处理; **the ～ left** Pol 温和的左派; **to take a ～ line on sth./with sb.** 对某事物/某人采取温和态度 **10** colloq (weak, cowardly) 软弱的 **11** **～ (in the head)** colloq (stupid) 傻的 **12** colloq (easy, agreeable) 轻松的 ‹*job, life*›; **to have a ～ time of it** 过舒适的生活 **13** Ling 发软音的; **'c' is ～ in 'city'** c在city中发软音; **a ～ consonant** 软辅音 **14** (not alcoholic) 不含酒精的 ‹*drink*›; **would you prefer something ～?** 你想喝点软饮料吗？ **15** Chem 软性的 ‹*water*› **16** Econ (unstable) 疲软的 ‹*price, market, currency*›; (favourable) 优惠的 ‹*terms*›
B *adv* colloq **1** (quietly) 轻柔地 ‹*speak, sing, play*› **2** (foolishly) 傻乎乎地; **don't talk ～!** 别说傻话了！

soft: **～back** *n* 平装本; **～ball** *n* **1** [u] Amer (game) 垒球运动; **to play ～ball** 打垒球; **2** [c] (ball) 垒球; **～-boiled** *adj* 煮得嫩的; **～-boiled egg** 溏心鸡蛋; **～-centred** *adj* 软夹心的; ～ **cheese** *n* [c and u] 软干酪; ～ **coal** *n* [u] 烟煤; ～ **copy** *n* 软拷贝; **～-core** *adj* 软色情的; **～cover** *n* **= paperback**; ～ **currency** *n* 软通货; ～ **drink** *n* 软饮料; ～ **drug** *n* 软毒品 [指危害较小不易成瘾的毒品]

soften /'sɒfn, Amer 'sɔːfn/
A *vi* **1** (become less hard) «*ground, material*» 变软; «*light, outline, voice, consonant*» 变柔和; «*colour*» 变淡 **2** (become less harsh) «*person, character, attitude, expression*» 变温和
B *vt* **1** (make less firm or rough) 使…变软 ‹*ground, material*›; 使…变柔和 ‹*light, voice, music, outline*›; 使…变淡 ‹*colour*›; 使…变缓和 ‹*resistance*› **2** Chem 软化 ‹*water*› **3** (cause to become kinder) 使变温和; **to ～ sb.'s attitude** 软化某人的态度 **4** (make less painful, harsh) 使…减轻 ‹*effect, blow, shock*›; 使…变委婉 ‹*refusal*›

Phrasal verb
- **soften up** *vt* [**～ sb. up, ～ up sb.**] 打动 ‹*person, client, customer*›; 削弱 ‹*enemy*›

softener /'sɒfnə(r), Amer 'sɔːf-/ *n* [c and u] **1** **(fabric) ～** 织物柔顺剂 **2** (substance) **(water) ～** 硬水软化剂; (device) 硬水软化器

soft focus *n* [u] 焦点柔和; **in ～** 用柔焦

soft-focus lens *n* 柔焦镜头

soft: ～ **fruit** *n* [u and c] Brit 无核小果; ～ **furnishings** *npl* Brit 软装饰; ～ **goods** *npl* Brit 纺织品; **～-headed** *adj* colloq 愚蠢的; **～-hearted** *adj* 心肠软的

softie /'sɒfti, Amer 'sɔːfti/ *n* **= softy**

softish /'sɒftɪʃ, Amer 'sɔːft-/ *adj* colloq 有点软的

S

soft: ~ landing *n* 软着陆; **~ loan** *n* 软贷款 [常指发放给发展中国家的优惠贷款]

softly /'sɒftli, Amer 'sɔ:ft-/ *adv* 1 (quietly) 轻声地 ‹*speak, tread, play, close*›; 温柔地 ‹*smile*›; **~, ~ catchee monkey** 耐心点，不着急，你会心想事成的 2 (gently) 轻柔地 ‹*touch, fall*›; 柔和地 ‹*shine*›

softly-softly *adj* Brit 谨慎耐心的; **to take a ~ approach** 采用耐心细致的方法

softness /'sɒftnɪs, Amer 'sɔ:ft-/ *n* [u] (of texture, skin, surface, material) 柔软; (of colour, light, outline, sound) 柔和; (of impact, touch) 轻柔; (of character, attitude, view) 温和; (in economy) 缓和; **to have a ~ for sb.** 对某人温柔

soft: ~ option *n* 轻松的选择; **to take the ~ option** 选择轻松的方案; **~ palate** *n* 软腭

soft pedal
A *n* 弱音踏板
B **soft-pedal** *vt* 低调处理 ‹*issue, problem, significance*›

soft porn *n* [u] colloq 软色情作品

soft sell
A *n* 软推销
B **soft-sell** *vt* 软推销

soft: ~-shoe *n* 软鞋踢踏舞; **~ shoulder** *n* Amer [公路边不适合车辆行驶的] 软质路肩; **~ skills** *npl* 软技能 [指沟通、灵活性、团队合作等技能]

soft soap
A *n* 1 [c and u] (soap) 软皂 2 [u] colloq (flattery) 奉承劝诱的话
B **soft-soap** *vt* colloq 给…灌迷魂汤

soft: ~-spoken *adj* 声音柔和的; **~ spot** *n* fig colloq **to have a ~ spot for sb./sth.**; 喜爱某人/某事物; **she always had a ~ spot for rural Ireland** 她过去一直很喜欢爱尔兰的乡村; **~ target** *n* 易受攻击的目标; **~ tissue** *n* [c and u] 软组织; **~-top** *n* 1 (car) 软顶篷汽车; 2 (roof) 软车篷; **~ touch** *n* colloq (person who does sth. if asked) 易被说动的人; (easily manipulated person) 易受摆布的人; **~ toy** *n* 软体玩具; **~ verge** *n* 路边草带; **~-voiced** *adj* 声音柔和的

software /'sɒftweə(r), Amer 'sɔ:ft-/ *n* [u] 软件

software: ~ developer ▸**p. 409** *n* (person) 软件开发者; (company) 软件开发公司; **~ engineer** ▸**p. 409** *n* 软件工程师; **~ engineering** *n* [u] 软件工程; **~ house** *n* 软件公司; **~ package** *n* 软件包

softwood /'sɒftwʊd, Amer 'sɔ:ft-/ *n* [c and u] 软质木材; **~ furniture** 软木家具

softy /'sɒfti, Amer 'sɔ:fti/ *n* colloq 心肠软的人

soggy /'sɒgi/ *adj* 湿软的; **I can't stand ~ cornflakes** 我最讨厌吃受潮的玉米片; **her clothes were ~ from** *or* **after falling into the river** 她的衣服掉到河里变湿了

soh /səʊ/ *n* 1 (in tonic sol-fa) [大调音阶的第5音] 2 (in fixed-doh system) [固定唱法的G音]

soil /sɔɪl/
A *n* 1 [c and u] (upper layer of earth) 土壤 2 [u] (land) 土地; (farmland) 农田; **to make one's living from the ~** 务农为生 3 [u] (territory) 国土; **on British/foreign ~** 在英国/外国国土上; **native ~** 故土 4 [u] (waste matter) 废物 [尤指含有粪便的污水]
B *vt* 1 (make dirty) 弄脏 2 (defecate in) 在…上大便 3 (tarnish) 玷污 ‹*good name, reputation*›

soiled /sɔɪld/ *adj* 1 (dirtied) 弄脏的; (with excrement) 沾上粪便的 2 (discredited, corrupted) 受到玷污的

soilless culture *n* [u] 无土栽培

soil: ~ pipe *n* (sewage) 下水道; (waste water pipe) 污水管; **~ sample** *n* 土样; **~ science** *n* [u] 土壤学

soirée /'swɑ:reɪ, Amer swɑ:'reɪ/ *n* (evening party) 社交晚会; (evening gathering) 社交聚会

sojourn /'sɒdʒən, Amer səʊ'dʒ3:rn/ formal *n, vi* 逗留

sol /sɒl/ *n* = **soh**

solace /'sɒləs/
A *n* formal 1 [u] (feeling of comfort) 安慰; **to seek** *or* **find ~ in sth.** 在某事物中寻求慰藉; **to draw ~ from sth.** 从某事物中得到安慰 2 [c] (source of comfort) (person) 安慰者; (thing) 安慰物; **to be a ~ to sb.** 是对某人的安慰
B *vt* liter 安慰; **to ~ sb. with sth.** 用某事物抚慰某人; **to ~ sb. for sth.** 因某事物安慰某人

solar /'səʊlə(r)/ *adj* 太阳的 ‹*cycle*›; **~ radiation/energy/year** 太阳辐射/太阳能/太阳年

solar: ~ battery, ~ cell *ns* 太阳能电池; **~ calculator** *n* 太阳能计算器; **~ constant** *n* 太阳常数; **~ eclipse** *n* 日食; **a total/partial ~ eclipse** 日全食/日偏食; **~ farm** *n* 太阳能发电站; **~ flare** *n* 太阳耀斑; **~-heated** *adj* 太阳能加热的; **~ heating** *n* [u] 太阳能采暖

solarium /sə'leərɪəm/ *n* 1 (with glass walls) 日光室 2 (with sunbeds) 日光浴室

solar panel *n* 太阳能电池板

solar plexus /,səʊlə 'pleksəs/ *n* 腹腔神经丛

solar: ~ power *n* [u] 太阳能; **~-powered** *adj* 使用太阳能的; **~ system** *n* 太阳系; **~ wind** *n* 太阳风

sold /səʊld/ *pt, pp* ▸**sell A, B**

solder /'səʊldə(r), 'sɒld-, Amer 'sɒd-/
A *vt* 焊; **to ~ sth. to** *or* **on to sth.** 把某物焊接在某物上; **to ~ sth. up** 焊补某物
B *n* [u] 焊锡

soldering iron /'səʊldə(r), 'sɒld-, Amer 'sɒd-/ *n* 烙铁

soldier /'səʊldʒə(r)/ ▸**p. 409**
A *n* 士兵; **to play at ~s** «*children*» 玩打仗游戏; «*adults*» 气势汹汹; **~s and civilians** 军民
B *vi* 从军

Phrasal verb
- **soldier on** *vi* Brit 硬挺着; **to ~ on with sth./doing sth.** 坚持某事/做某事

soldier ant *n* 兵蚁

soldiering /'səʊldʒərɪŋ/ *n* [u] 从军

soldierly /'səʊldʒəli/ *adj* 有军人气质的 ‹*person*›; **a ~ manner** 军人风度

soldier of fortune *n* 雇佣兵

sole[1] /səʊl/
A *n* 1 (of foot) 脚掌 2 (of shoe) 鞋底; (of sock) 袜底; (of iron) 底板
B *vt* 给…换底

sole[2] *adj* 1 (single, unique) 仅有的; (one and only) 唯一的; **for the ~ purpose of ...** 只是为了…; **the ~ survivor** 唯一的幸存者 2 (exclusive) 独家的 ‹*dealer, stockist*›; 独占的 ‹*right*›; **for the ~ use of ...** 由…专用; **to have the ~ agency for ...** 拥有…的独家代理权; **to be in ~ charge of sth.** 全权掌管某事物

sole[3] *n* (*pl* **sole**) (fish) 鳎

sole beneficiary *n* 唯一受益人

solecism /'sɒlɪsɪzəm/ *n* 1 (mistake in grammar or usage) 语病 2 (gaffe) 失礼

solely /'səʊlli/ *adv* (wholly) 完全地; (only) 单独地; **it was ~ for her benefit** 这完全是为了她好; **to be ~ responsible for ...** 单独负责…

solemn /'sɒləm/ *adj* 1 (serious) 严肃的 ‹*person, face, voice*›; 庄重的 ‹*clothes*› 2 (formal, dignified) 庄严的 ‹*occasion, procession, music*› 3 (sincere) 郑重的 ‹*promise, warning, plea, word*›; 庄严的 ‹*duty, truth*›

solemnity /sə'lemnəti/
A *n* [u] 庄严; **with all due ~** 庄严肃穆地; **the ~ of the occasion** 场面的隆重
B **solemnities** *npl* 庄重的仪式

solemnize /'sɒləmnaɪz/ *vt* 为…举行仪式

solemnly /'sɒləmli/ *adv* 1 (seriously) 严肃地 2 (sincerely) 郑重地

solenoid /'səʊlənɔɪd/ *n* 螺线管

sol-fa /,sɒl'fɑ:, Amer ,səʊl-/ *n* 首调唱名法

solicit /sə'lɪsɪt/
A *vt* 1 (request) 索求 ‹*money*›; 请求 ‹*attention, help*›; 征求 ‹*opinion, view, information*›; **to ~ sth. from sb.** 向某人索要某物 2 (offer sexual services in exchange for money) 招徕 ‹*custom*›; **the women were ~ing clients in the red-light district** 那些女人在红灯区拉客
B *vi* 1 (request) **to ~ for sth.** «*beggar*» 索要某物; «*tradesperson*» 招揽某物; **to ~ for custom** 招揽顾客 2 (offer sexual services in exchange for money) 拉客

solicitation /sə,lɪsɪ'teɪʃn/ *n* formal 1 [c and u] (request) 请求; **~(s) for sth.** 对某物的索求 2 [u] (offer of sexual services in exchange for money) 拉客

soliciting /sə'lɪsɪtɪŋ/ *n* [u] 拉客

solicitor /sə'lɪsɪtə(r)/ ▸**p. 409** *n* 1 Brit (lawyer) 事务律师 2 Amer (chief law officer) 法务官 3 Amer (canvasser) (for votes) 游说者; (for custom) 推销员; (for contributions) 募捐者

solicitor: S~ General *n* 1 Brit (Crown law officer) 副检察长; 2 Amer (in Department of Justice) 司法部副部长; **~'s fees** *npl* Brit 律师费

solicitous /sə'lɪsɪtəs/ *adj* formal 关切的; **to be ~ about sth.** 关心某事物; **to be ~ for** *or* **of sth.** 为某事物操心

solicitude /sə'lɪsɪtju:d, Amer -tu:d/ *n* [u] formal 关切; **to show ~ for sb./sth.** 关心某人/某事物

solid /'sɒlɪd/
A *adj* 1 (not liquid or gaseous) 固体的 ‹*food, substance*›; **a ~ body** 固体; **on ~ ground** *or* **land** 在陆地上; **to go** *or* **become ~** 成为固体; **to freeze ~** 冻结 2 (dense, compact) 密实的 ‹*substance, texture, crowd*›; **a ~ bank of cloud** 厚厚的一片云; **~ to the core** 非常坚实的; **to press/pack sth. ~** 按/塞得严严实实; **to have a heart of ~ stone** *or* **ice** 有铁石心肠 3 Math (three-dimensional) 立体的; **a ~ figure with six plane faces** 六面体 4 (not hollow) 实心的 5 *attrib* (of one substance) 纯的; **~ meat/chocolate** 纯精肉/纯巧克力; **(of) ~ gold/steel** 纯金/纯钢（的） 6 *attrib* (of one colour) 纯色的; **~ white/blue** 纯白/纯蓝 7 (unbroken) 连绵的 ‹*blue sky, block*›; 不间断的 ‹*line*›; **a ~ mass of colour** 一大团色块 8 (full) 挤满的; **to be ~ with sth.** 挤满某物; **to be packed ~ (with sth.)** 挤满（某物）; **the town was ~ with shoppers** 城里到处都是购物的人; **to be booked ~** 被预订一空 9 (uninterrupted) 连续的; **five days ~, five ~ days, a ~ five days** 整整5天; **fifteen minutes' ~ conversation** 15分钟不间断的谈话; **a ~ day's work** 一整天的工作; **~ rain for three weeks** 连续3周的降雨 10 (well-established) 稳固的 ‹*control, base*›; **the strike remains ~** 罢工仍然势头不减 11 (large, secure) 一致的 ‹*vote, support*›; **to win a ~ majority** 赢得绝对多数票; **to hold ~** 持稳 12 *attrib* (of one main type) 单一的 ‹*party, class*›; **this area is ~ Tory, this is a ~ Tory area** 这个地区是保守党的地盘 13 *pred* (staunch) **to be ~ for/against sth.** 坚决支持/反对某事物; **to be ~ behind sb.** 坚定地支持某人; **to be ~ on sth.** 在某事上立场坚定 14 (unshakeably close) 密切的 ‹*relationship*›; 牢固的 ‹*marriage*›; **to be (in) ~ with sb.** Amer colloq (intimate) 和某人关系很铁; (staunch) 得到某人的坚定支持 15 (physically strong or dense) 结实的 ‹*structure, foundation, muscles*›; **the Scottish defence remained ~** 苏格兰队的防守一直很严密; **to be of ~ build** 体格健硕 16 (firm) 有力的 ‹*grip, blow, push*›; **a ~ driving rhythm section** 活力四射的节奏乐器组 17 *attrib* (reliable) 可信赖的; (respectable) 值得尊敬的; **a banker of ~ character** 信誉可嘉的银行家 18 (satisfactory) 牢靠的 ‹*work, employee*› 19 Fin (secure, dependable) 稳健的 ‹*investment, company*› 20 (substantial) 切实的 ‹*comfort*›; **a ~ meal** 份量充足的一餐

21 *attrib* (well-founded) 可靠的 ‹*common sense, experience*›; 扎实的 ‹*basis*› **22** *attrib* (factual) 确凿的 ‹*evidence, facts*›; 有力的 ‹*argument, reason*›; **to rest** *or* **be on ~ ground(s)** 基于充分的理由 **23** *attrib* (thorough) 全面的 ‹*investigation, understanding*›

B *n* **1** Math 立体图形 **2** Chem 固体

C solids *npl* **1** (foodstuffs) 固体食物; **to start on/take ~s** 开始吃/吃固体食物 **2** (particles) [液体中的] 固形物; **blood/non-fat ~s** 血液中的/非脂乳固形物

solidarity /ˌsɒlɪˈdærəti/ *n* [u] **1** (unity of feeling, action) 团结; **to feel ~ with sb.** 感到与某人团结一心; **to do sth. out of ~ with sb.** 同某人团结一致做某事; **to show ~ with** *or* **towards sb.** 表示支持某人 **2 Solidarity** (Polish independent trade union movement) 团结工会

solidarity fund *n* 团结基金

solid: ~ compound *n* 连写复合词; **~ fuel** *n* [c and u] 固体燃料

solidi /ˈsɒlɪdiː/ *pl* ▸**solidus**

solidification /səˌlɪdɪfɪˈkeɪʃn/ *n* [u] 固化

solidify /səˈlɪdɪfaɪ/

A *vt* 巩固 ‹*opinion, law, resolve*›

B *vi* **1** (harden) «*lava, paint*» 凝固 **2** (reinforce) «*opinion, measure, support*» 巩固; **to ~ into sth.** 变为某物

solidity /səˈlɪdəti/ *n* [u] **1** (of object, substance) 坚硬 **2** (of friendship, support) 稳固; (of currency) 坚挺 **3** (of construction) 坚固 **4** (of person, organization) 可靠 **5** (of research, argument, theory) (soundness) 严密; (thoroughness) 完整

solidly /ˈsɒlɪdli/ *adv* **1** (firmly, densely) 密实地; **cars were parked ~ on both sides of the street** 街道两旁汽车停得密密麻麻 **2** (continuously) 不间断地 **3** (staunchly) 坚定地; (predominantly) 占主导地位地; (unanimously) 一致地; **to be ~ against sb./sth.** 一致反对某人/某事物 **4** (strongly) 结实地 **5** (properly) 扎实地; (respectably) 稳妥地 **6** (convincingly) 严谨地

solid-state *adj* 固态的

solidus /ˈsɒlɪdəs/ *n* (*pl* **solidi**) Brit 斜线分隔符

solid word *n* 连写词

soliloquize /səˈlɪləkwaɪz/ *vi* liter «*person*» 自言自语; «*character*» 独白

soliloquy /səˈlɪləkwi/ *n* **1** [c] (part of play) 独白 **2** [u] liter (speaking of thoughts out loud) 自言自语

solipsism /ˈsɒlɪpsɪzəm/ *n* [u] 唯我论

solitaire /ˌsɒlɪˈteə(r), Amer ˈsɒlɪteər/ ▸**p. 307** *n* **1** [c] (gemstone) 独粒宝石; (ring) 独粒宝石戒指 **2** [u] (card game) 单人纸牌戏; **to play ~** 玩单人纸牌戏 **3** [u] (board game) 单人跳棋

solitary /ˈsɒlɪtri, Amer -teri/

A *adj* **1** (unaccompanied) 独自的 **2** (lonely) 孤单的 **3** (fond of being alone) 喜欢独处的 **4** (isolated) 孤零零的 ‹*tree, figure*›; 荒凉的 ‹*farm, village*› **5** (empty, deserted) 空旷的 **6** *attrib* (single) 唯一的; **with the ~ exception of ...** 唯独除了…之外

B *n* **1** [c] (loner) 独居者; (recluse) 隐士 **2** [u] colloq **= solitary confinement**

solitary confinement *n* [u] 单独监禁; **to put** *or* **place sb. in ~** 把某人单独囚禁; **to be in ~** 被单独监禁

solitude /ˈsɒlɪtjuːd, Amer -tuːd/ *n* [u] 独处

solo /ˈsəʊləʊ/

A *n* **1** [c] Mus (for voice) 独唱; (for instrument) 独奏; (for dancer) 单人舞; **to play a ~** 弹奏独奏曲 **2** [u] (card game) **~ (whist)** 惠斯特纸牌戏 [一人对多人的纸牌戏] **3** [c] (flight by one person) 单飞

B *adv* 单独地; **to go ~** 独自做

C *adj* **1** Mus 单独表演的; **for ~ piano** 钢琴独奏的; **a passage for ~ voice** 一段独唱曲; **for ~ violin** (with orchestra) 小提琴独奏的; **a ~ piece** (for voice) 独唱曲; (for instrument) 独奏曲 **2** (single-handed) 独自的

soloist /ˈsəʊləʊɪst/ *n* (singer) 独唱演员; (instrumentalist) 独奏演员

Solomon /ˈsɒləmən/

A *pr n* 所罗门

B Solomons *pr npl* **the ~s = Solomon Islands**

Solomon Islands *pr npl* (country) **the ~** 所罗门（群岛）; (archipelago) 所罗门群岛

solstice /ˈsɒlstɪs/ *n* 至; **the summer/winter ~** 夏至/冬至

solubility /ˌsɒljʊˈbɪləti/ *n* [u] **1** (of substance) 可溶性 **2** (of problem) 可解决性

soluble /ˈsɒljʊbl/ *adj* **1** (dissolvable) 可溶的; **to be ~ in sth.** 可溶于某物 **2** (having an answer) 可解开的 ‹*puzzle*›; (solvable) 可解决的 ‹*problem*›

solution /səˈluːʃn/ *n* **1** [c] (answer to problem, difficulty) 解决办法; **a ~ to sth.** 解决某事的办法 **2** [c and u] (mixture) 溶液; **in ~** 处于溶解状态 **3** [c] (answer to puzzle) 答案

solvable /ˈsɒlvəbl/ *adj* 可解决的 ‹*problem*›; 可解开的 ‹*puzzle*›

solve /sɒlv/ *vt* **1** (resolve) 解开 ‹*problem, puzzle*›; 解 ‹*equation*› **2** (find explanation for or solution to) 破解; **to ~ a murder** 侦破谋杀案 **3** (provide way of dealing with) 解决 ‹*problem, difficulty*›

solvency /ˈsɒlvənsi/ *n* [u] 偿付能力

solvent /ˈsɒlvənt/

A *adj* **1** (able to meet financial obligations) 有偿付能力的 **2** *attrib* (able to dissolve other substances) 有溶解力的

B *n* **1** (liquid) 溶剂; **water is a ~ for** *or* **of salt** 水能溶解盐 **2** (cleaning agent) 清洁溶剂

solvent abuse *n* [u] 溶媒滥用 [例如吸胶毒]

solver /ˈsɒlvə(r)/ *n* 解答者

Somali /səˈmɑːli/ ▸**p. 503, p. 426**

A *adj* (of Somalia) 索马里的; (of the people) 索马里人的; (of the language) 索马里语的

B *n* **1** [c] (person) 索马里人 **2** [u] (language) 索马里语

Somalia /səˈmɑːlɪə/ *pr n* 索马里

somatic /səˈmætɪk/ *adj* (of the body) 躯体的; (as distinct from the mind) 肉体的; **~ cells** 体细胞

sombre Brit, **somber** Amer /ˈsɒmbə(r)/ *adj* **1** (dark in colour, tone) 灰暗的 ‹*colour, clothing*›; 昏暗的 ‹*room, day*› **2** (gloomy, sad and serious) 沮丧的 ‹*face, tone, character*›; 严峻的 ‹*thought, remark, prospect*›; 沉重的 ‹*music*›

sombrely Brit, **somberly** Amer /ˈsɒmbəli/ *adv* **1** (darkly) 灰暗地; **we dressed ~ for the funeral** 我们穿着暗色调衣服去参加葬礼 **2** (gloomily) 沮丧地

sombreness Brit, **somberness** Amer /ˈsɒmbənɪs/ *n* [u] **1** (of clothes) 灰暗; (of room) 昏暗 **2** (gloominess) 沮丧

sombrero /sɒmˈbreərəʊ/ *n* (*pl* **~s**) 墨西哥阔边帽

some /sʌm/ ▸**p. 162**

A *det* **1** (an unspecified amount or number) 一些; **~ cheese/apples** 一些奶酪/苹果; **would you like ~ breakfast?** 你想吃点早饭吗? **2** (certain members of a group or type) 有的; **~ tulips are black** 有的郁金香是黑色的; **in ~ parts of Europe** 在欧洲的某些地方; **~ people find this more difficult than others** 这件事有人觉得难，有人觉得不难; **I like ~ modern music** 有些现代音乐我喜欢; **~ people!** 总有这样的人! **3** (a considerable amount or number) 相当多的; **we stayed there for ~ time** 我们在那里待了相当长时间; **he hadn't seen her for ~ years** 他好多年没见到她了; **his suggestion was greeted with ~ hostility** 他的建议受到相当大的敌视; **she'll take ~ persuading** 需要费点口舌才能说服她 **4** (a small amount or number) 少量的; **to have ~ knowledge of computers** 有点计算机知识; **there are ~ tickets left** 还剩几张票; **to ~ extent** 在某种程度上; **in ~ way or (an)other** 以某种方式 **5** (an unidentified or unknown) 某个; **she married ~ poet** 她嫁了一个诗人; **there must be ~ mistake** 一定是出了什么差错; **a car of ~ sort** 某种汽车; **~ day** 总有一天; **I'll see you again ~ time, I'm sure** 我敢肯定，什么时候我还会见到你的; **she won a competition in ~ newspaper or other** 她在某报举办的竞赛中得了奖 **6** colloq (a remarkable) 了不起的; **that's ~ woman!** 那真是个了不起的女人!; **that was ~ film!** 那部影片真棒!; **that was ~ goal!** 好一记漂亮的射门! **7** colloq iron (not much) 真可谓; **~ dictionary that is!** 那也算词典!; **I'd like the work to be finished by Monday — ~ hope!** 我想星期一之前完成工作——好有希望啊!

B *pron* **1** (unspecified amount or number of things) 一些东西; (unspecified amount or number of people) 一些人; **I've made coffee: would you like ~?** 我煮了咖啡: 想喝点儿吗?; **~ say that ...** 有些人说…; **and then ~** colloq 还不止这些; **we got our money's worth and then ~** 我们的钱花得值，而且还不止这个 **2** (certain members of a group or set) 部分; **here are ~ of our suggestions** 这是我们的一部分建议; **~ of them are French, others Spanish** 他们中有一部分是法国人，其他的是西班牙人

C *adv* **1** (approximately) 大约; **~ 70 people/20 years ago** 大约 70 人/20 年前 **2** (to some degree) 稍微; **from here to town in 5 minutes: that's going ~** 从这里到城里只花了 5 分钟: 相当快啊; **are you finding the work any easier? — ~** colloq 你觉得工作顺手些了? ——是顺手些了

somebody /ˈsʌmbədi/ *pron* **1** (unspecified person) 某人; **there's ~ at the door** 门口有个人; **we need ~ who speaks Japanese** 我们需要一个会讲日语的人; **should we call a doctor or ~?** colloq 我们要不要请个大夫什么的?; **she's ~ famous** 她是个名人; **~ else** 另外某个人; **~ or other** 某某人; **Mr S~(-or-other)** 某某先生; **~ up there likes me** hum 我福星高照; **~ up there doesn't like me** hum 老天不助我 **2** (important person) 重要人物; **he really thinks he's ~** 他真以为自己是个人物呢

somehow /ˈsʌmhaʊ/ *adv* **1** (by some means) 以某种方式; **we'll get there ~** 我们总会想办法到达那儿的; **he ~ broke his leg** 他不知怎么把腿弄断了; **~ or other** 以某种方式; **~ or other I must get a new job** 我必须想方设法找份新工作 **2** (for some reason) 出于某种原因; **~, I don't feel I can trust him** 不知为什么，我觉得信不过他

someone /ˈsʌmwʌn/ *pron* **= somebody**

someplace /ˈsʌmpleɪs/ *adv, pron* Amer colloq **= somewhere**

somersault /ˈsʌməsɒlt/

A *n* **1** (acrobatic movement) (of gymnast, child) 筋斗; (of diver) 翻腾; (accidental) 跟头; **to turn ~s** 翻筋斗; **a front** *or* **forward ~** 前空翻 **2** (turning over of vehicle) 翻滚; **to do** *or* **turn a ~** 做翻滚动作

B *vi* **1** (move body) 翻筋斗 **2** (turn over) «*driver*» 翻车; «*vehicle*» 翻滚

Somerset /ˈsʌməset/ *pr n* 萨默塞特郡

something /ˈsʌmθɪŋ/

A *pron* **1** (unspecified thing) 某事物; **you learn ~ new every day** 你每天都学新东西; **~ happened** 发生了一件事; **go and put ~ on!** 去穿点衣服!; **would you like ~ to eat?** 你想吃点什么吗?; **there's ~ odd about her** 她有点儿怪; **he's ~ in television** 他是做电视的; **~ to do with sb./sth.** 与某人/某事物有关; **his job is ~ to do with oil** 他的工作与石油有关; **to get ~ for nothing** 不劳而获; **~ or other** 某个事物; **they were protesting about ~ or other** 他们正在对一件什么事表示抗议; **she's a professor of ~ or other at Leeds** 她是利兹大学某个学科的教授; **~ else** 另外一件事; **it's ~ else!** (another thing) 这是另一码事!; colloq (exceptional

S

person) 这人出类拔萃！; (exceptional thing) 这事很棒！; **the reaction from the crowd was ~ else** colloq 人群的反应有点异常 2 (thing of importance, value, etc.) 重要的事; **it means ~ to her** 这对她意义重大; **there's ~ in what he says** 他的话不无道理; **you've got ~ there!** 你说得真好！; **do you want to make ~ (out) of it?** 你想找茬吗？; **to make ~ of oneself** *or* **one's life** 有所成就; **to have a certain ~** 具有某种魅力; **that little boy is quite ~!** 那小男孩确实了不起！ 3 (some money) 小费; **did you leave ~ for the waiter?** 你给服务员留小费了吗？; **we gave him ~ for his trouble** 他辛苦了一趟，我们给了他赏钱 4 (forgotten or unknown name etc.) …什么的; (forgotten or unknown amount etc.) 大约; **his name's Andy ~** 他的名字叫安迪什么的; **he's six foot ~** 他大约6英尺高; **in nineteen-sixty-~** 在大约20世纪60年代; **or ~** 诸如此类的事; **do you want to phone or ~?** 你想打电话还是做什么？; **are you stupid or ~?** 你傻了还是怎么的？

B *adv* 1 (a little) 有点; **it tastes ~ like melon** 这吃起来有点像甜瓜; **~ under 20 people** 不太够20人; **they pay six pounds an hour; ~ like that** 他们按每小时6英镑付费; 差不多就是这个数吧; **~ between 50% and 70%** 大概在50%到70%之间 2 colloq (extremely) 非常; **she was swearing ~ terrible** 她骂得难听极了; **he was carrying on ~ awful** 他胡闹得太不像话了

C **something of** *adv phr* 相当; **he is ~ of a writer** 他可以说是个作家; **it was ~ of a surprise** 这有点出人意料; **the evening was ~ of a disaster** 那个晚上可以说是个灾难

sometime /ˈsʌmtaɪm/

A *adv* 在某个时候; **~ soon** 不久的某个时候; **I'll tell you about it ~** 我找个时间告诉你; **all holidays have to end ~** 假期早晚都会结束; **I'll phone you ~ tomorrow** 我明天找时间给你打电话; **~ or other** 任何时间

B *adj attrib* 1 (former) 从前的 ‹*chairman, captain*›; **the ~ editor of the paper** 报纸的前任编辑; **the ~ president** 前总统 2 Amer (occasional) 临时的 ‹*employee*›; **a ~ contributor to this magazine** 一位偶尔给这家杂志投稿的作者

sometimes /ˈsʌmtaɪmz/ *adv* 有时; **~ I go by car** 有时我开车去; **he ~ writes to me** 他偶尔给我写封信; **he was ~ angry, ~ depressed** 他时而愤怒时而沮丧

somewhat /ˈsʌmwɒt/ *adv* 有点; **it was ~ of a disappointment** 这有点儿令人失望; **she was ~ disturbed by his demeanour** 他的行为使她颇感不安; **he answered ~ ironically** 他的回答带有几分挖苦; **it annoyed her more than ~** 这使她感到很不愉快

somewhere /ˈsʌmweə(r)/

A *adv* 1 (in some place) 在某处; **to be ~ about** *or* **around** 在附近某个地方; **~ else** 在别处; **his mind was/his thoughts were ~ else** 他心不在焉; **to have a holiday ~ hot** 在某个炎热地方休假; **I've seen him ~ before** 我以前在哪儿见过他; **~ or other in Asia** 在亚洲的某个地方; **or ~** 或别的什么地方 2 (to some place) 到某处; **are you going ~ this summer?** 你今年夏天要去什么地方吗？; **are you going ~ special?** 你打算去什么特别的地方吗？; **to get ~** fig 取得进展 3 (approximately) 大约; **~ between 50 and 100 people** 50到100人之间; **~ around 10 o'clock** 10点钟左右

B *pron* 某处; **we need to find ~ to live** 我们需要找个住的地方; **I know ~ we can go** 我知道有个地方我们可以去

somnambulist /sɒmˈnæmbjʊlɪst/ *n* formal 梦游者

somnolence /ˈsɒmnələns/ *n* [u] formal 瞌睡

somnolent /ˈsɒmnələnt/ *adj* 1 formal (drowsy) 瞌睡的; **to feel ~** 感到昏昏欲睡 2 (causing drowsiness) 催眠的

son /sʌn/ ▸p. 419 *n* 1 (male child) 儿子; **an only ~** 独生子; **my ~ and heir** 我的嗣子; **he's his father's ~** 他酷似他父亲; **like father, like ~** 有其父必有其子; **every mother's ~** 人人 2 liter (descendant) 子孙; **the ~s of the revolution** 革命的后代; **Scotland's favourite ~** 苏格兰的宠儿 3 **Son (Christ) the S~** 圣子 4 colloq (form of address) 孩子; **come here, ~** 过来，孩子

sonar /ˈsəʊnɑː(r)/ *n* 1 [u] (system) 声呐 2 [c] (apparatus) 声波定位仪 3 [u] Zool (echolocation method) 回声定位

sonata /səˈnɑːtə/ *n* 奏鸣曲

sonata form *n* [u] 奏鸣曲式

sonde /sɒnd/ *n* (probe) (underground) 地下探测仪; (underwater) 水下探测仪; (in atmosphere) 探空仪

son et lumière /ˌsɒneɪˈluːmjeə(r)/ *n* 声光表演

Song /sɒŋ/ *pr n* 宋（朝）

song /sɒŋ/ *n* 1 [c] (vocal piece) 歌曲; **(to go) for a ~** colloq 以极低价格（出售） 2 [u] (singing) 唱歌; **to burst into ~** 突然唱起歌来; **the art of ~** 歌唱艺术; **(to be) on ~** 处于良好状态 3 [u] (sound made by birds) 鸣啭

song: ~ and dance *n* 1 colloq (fuss) 大惊小怪; (commotion) 骚动; **to make a ~ and dance (about sth.)** （对某事物）小题大做; 2 Amer (explanation) 啰嗦的话; **(to give sb.) the same old ~ and dance** （对某人说）絮絮叨叨的老一套; **~bird** *n* 鸣禽; **~book** *n* (of songs) 歌曲集; (of hymns) 赞美诗集; **~ cycle** *n* 声乐套曲; **~smith** *n* colloq 流行曲作家

songster /ˈsɒŋstə(r)/ *n* dated 1 (singer) 歌手 2 (bird) 鸣禽

songstress /ˈsɒŋstrɪs/ *n* dated 女歌手

song: ~ thrush *n* 歌鸫; **~writer** ▸p. 409 *n* 流行歌曲作家; **~writing** *n* [u] 流行歌曲创作

sonic /ˈsɒnɪk/ *adj* 1 (relating to sound waves) 声音的; (using sound waves) 利用声波的; **~ interference** 声波干涉; **a ~ vibration** 声振动 2 (as fast as sound) 音速的

sonic: ~ barrier *n* = **sound barrier**; **~ boom** *n* 音爆

sonics /ˈsɒnɪks/ *npl* 音乐声

son-in-law ▸p. 419 *n* (*pl* **sons-in-law**) 女婿

sonnet /ˈsɒnɪt/ *n* 十四行诗

sonny /ˈsʌni/ *n* colloq (kind address) 老弟; (patronizing address) 小伙子

sonny boy, sonny Jim /ˌsʌni ˈdʒɪm/ *n* colloq 老兄

son of a bitch *n* (*pl* **sons of bitches**) Amer sl 王八蛋 offensive

son of a gun *n* (*pl* **sons of guns**) Amer colloq 哥们儿

sonority /səˈnɒrəti, Amer -ˈnɔːr-/ *n* [u] liter 浑厚

sonorous /ˈsɒnərəs, səˈnɔːrəs/ *adj* 1 (rich in sound) 浑厚的 2 (rhetorical) 语调夸张的 ‹*speech*›; 华丽的 ‹*words, language, style*›

sonorously /ˈsɒnərəsli, səˈnɔːrəsli/ *adv* 浑厚地

soon /suːn/ *adv* 1 (in a short time) 不久; **the book will be published ~** 这本书即将出版; **I'll ~ be ready** 我马上就好; **~ after(wards)** 不久以后; **see you ~!** 一会儿见！; **they left ~ after us** 我们走后不久他们就离开了; **no ~er had I done that than ...** 我刚做这事就…; **no ~er had she said it than she burst into tears** 她话一出口，泪水便夺眶而出 2 (quickly) 迅速地; **as ~ as possible** 尽快; **I ~ realized the mistake** 我很快意识到了错误; **how ~ can you get here?** 你多快能赶到这儿？; **I'll tell him as ~ as I see him** 我一见到他就告诉他; **all too ~ the summer was over** 转眼之间，夏天就结束了; **we arrived not a moment too ~** 我们差点迟到 3 (early) 早; **to speak too ~** 言之过早; **~ enough** 很快; **~er or later** 迟早; **~er rather than later** 赶早不赶晚; **at the ~est** 最早; **no ~er said than done** 说干就干; **least said ~est mended** Prov 少说为妙 4 (rather) 宁可; **I'd just as ~ stay at home as go out tonight** 今晚我还是愿意待在家里不外出; **I would ~er not go** 我宁愿不走; **he would ~er die than lose you** 他宁愿死也不愿失去你; **~er you than me!** 我才不愿做你做的事呢！

soot /sʊt/ *n* [u] 煤烟子; **as black as ~** 乌黑的

soothe /suːð/

A *vt* 1 (calm) 安慰 ‹*person, animal, group*›; 平息 ‹*fear, anxiety, anger*›; **to ~ sb.'s fears/nerves** 消除某人的恐惧/紧张 2 (ease) 减轻…的疼痛 ‹*patient, wound*›; 减轻 ‹*pain*›

B *vi* «*person, speech, presence*» 起抚慰作用; «*drug, ointment*» 起缓解作用

Phrasal verb

- **soothe away** *vt* [**~ away sth., ~ sth. away**] 减轻 ‹*pain*›; 平息 ‹*fear, anxiety, anger*›

soothing /ˈsuːðɪŋ/ *adj* 1 (calming, reassuring) 安慰的 ‹*person, tone, effect*›; 抚慰的 ‹*action, policy*› 2 (easing pain) 镇痛的 ‹*medicine, ointment, drug*›

soothingly /ˈsuːðɪŋli/ *adv* 1 (reassuringly) 安慰地 ‹*speak*›; 抚慰地 ‹*gentle, reassuring*› 2 (in a manner that eases pain) 镇痛地

soothsayer /ˈsuːθseɪə(r)/ *n* (in ancient times) 占卜者; hum pej (in modern times) 预言者

soothsaying /ˈsuːθseɪɪŋ/ *n* (in ancient times) 占卜; hum pej (in modern times) 预言

sooty /ˈsʊti/ *adj* (covered in soot) 满是煤烟子的; (dirty with soot) 被煤烟子熏黑的; (consisting of soot) 煤烟子构成的; (producing soot) 产生煤烟子的; **~ from doing sth.** 做某事而被煤烟子弄脏的

sop /sɒp/ *n* 抚慰品; **to offer sth. as a ~ to sb.** 给某物作为对某人的安抚; **to throw a ~ to sb.** 给某人小恩小惠

Phrasal verb

- **sop up** *vt* [**~ up sth., ~ sth. up**] 吸干

sophism /ˈsɒfɪzəm/ *n* (argument) 诡辩; (reason) 谬论

sophist /ˈsɒfɪst/ *n* 1 Philos 智者派 2 (person using specious arguments) 诡辩者

sophisticate

A /səˈfɪstɪkət/ *n* 老于世故的人

B /səˈfɪstɪkeɪt/ *vt* 使…更精确 ‹*process*›; 使…老于世故 ‹*person*›

sophisticated /səˈfɪstɪkeɪtɪd/ *adj* 1 (worldly) 老于世故的; (cultured) 有修养的 2 (intelligent, aware) 老练的 3 (appealing to the cultured, refined) 高雅的 4 (elaborate) 精密的; (complex) 复杂的

sophistication /səˌfɪstɪˈkeɪʃn/ *n* [u] 1 (experience) 老于世故; (refinement) 修养 2 (intelligence and subtlety) 老练 3 (complexity of argument) 复杂; (modernity of equipment) 先进

sophistry /ˈsɒfɪstri/ *n* 1 [u] (use of specious arguments) 诡辩术 2 [c] (specious argument) 诡辩

sophomore /ˈsɒfəmɔː(r)/ *n* Amer 大二学生; **~ student** 大二学生

sophomoric /ˌsɒfəˈmɔːrɪk/ *adj* Amer 1 (relating to university sophomore) 大二的 2 (juvenile) 幼稚的

soporific /ˌsɒpəˈrɪfɪk/

A *adj* 1 (sleep-inducing) 催眠的 2 (sleepy) 瞌睡的; **to make sb. ~** 使某人昏昏欲睡

B *n* (drug) 催眠药; (substance) 催眠物

soppiness /ˈsɒpɪnəs/ *n* [u] pej (of person) 自作多情; (of book, song) 多愁善感

sopping /ˈsɒpɪŋ/ *adj* **~ (wet)** 湿透的 ‹*person, clothes, floor, walls*›

soppy /ˈsɒpi/ *adj* Brit colloq pej 自作多情的; **to be ~ about sth.** 痴迷于某事物; **~ romantic novels** 多愁善感的言情小说

soprano /sə'prɑːnəʊ, Amer -'præn-/
A *n* (*pl* ~**s**) **1** (singer) (female) 女高音歌手; (male) 童声高音歌手 **2** (voice) 女高音 **3** (part) 女高音声部
B *adj* 高音的

sorbet /'sɔːbeɪ, 'sɔːbət/ *n* [c and u] 冰糕

sorcerer /'sɔːsərə(r)/ *n* 男巫

sorceress /'sɔːsərɪs/ *n* 女巫

sorcery /'sɔːsəri/ *n* [u] **1** (witchcraft) 巫术; **to practise ~** 施巫术 **2** (magic) 魔法

sordid /'sɔːdɪd/ *adj* **1** (ignoble, contemptible) 卑劣的 ‹*affair, motive*›; 丑恶的 ‹*story, life*› **2** (dirty) 肮脏的

sordidness /'sɔːdɪdnɪs/ *n* [u] **1** (immorality) 无耻 **2** (dirtiness) 肮脏

sore /sɔː(r)/
A *adj* **1** (sensitive) 易疼痛的; (painful) 痛的; **to have a ~ throat** 嗓子疼; **a sight for ~ eyes** colloq 使人乐于看的事物; **to be like a bear with a ~ head** colloq 脾气暴躁 **2** *pred* (suffering pain) 感到疼痛的; **to be** *or* **feel ~ (all over)** 感到(浑身)疼痛; **to be ~ from exercise/running** 锻炼/跑得浑身酸痛 **3** colloq (peeved, angry) 气恼的; **to be ~ about** *or* **over sth.** 因某事物生气; **to be ~ at sb.** 生某人的气; **to get ~** 生气 **4** *attrib* liter (urgent) 紧迫的; (severe) 剧烈的; (extreme) 极度的; **to be in ~ need of sth.** 急需某事物
B *n* **1** (on body) 疮; **an open ~** 疮口 **2** (cause of annoyance) 痛处; **there is no point opening old ~s** 没必要揭开旧伤疤

sorehead /'sɔːhed/ *n* Amer colloq 脾气暴躁的人

sorely /'sɔːli/ *adv* 非常地; **~ needed funds** 急需的资金; **you will be ~ missed** 大家会非常想念你的

soreness /'sɔːnɪs/ *n* [u] **1** (pain) 疼痛 **2** Amer colloq (anger) 恼怒

sorghum /'sɔːgəm/ *n* [c and u] 高粱

SORN *abbr* Brit = **Statutory Off Road Notification** 车辆停驶申报

Soroptimist /sə'rɒptɪmɪst/ *n* 国际职业妇女和女企业家联谊会会员

sorority /sə'rɒrəti, Amer -'rɔːr-/ *n* **1** Amer (society of female students) 女生联谊会 **2** (sisterhood) 妇女联谊会

sorrel *n* **1** [c and u] (plant) 酸模 **2** [u] (edible leaves of plant) 酸模叶

sorrow /'sɒrəʊ/
A *n* **1** [u] (grief) 悲伤; **to feel ~** 感到悲哀; **to my ~** 令我伤心的是; **more in ~ than in anger** 出于悲哀而不是愤怒 **2** [c] (misfortune) 伤心事; **the ~s of sth.** 某事物带来的悲伤; **joys and ~s** 悲欢
B *vi* liter (feel grief) 感到悲伤; (express grief) 表达悲伤

sorrowful /'sɒrəʊfl/ *adj* **1** (feeling grief) 悲伤的; (expressing grief) 表示哀痛的; **to be ~ about** *or* **at** *or* **over sth.** 对某事物感到悲伤 **2** (causing grief) 可悲的

sorrowfully /'sɒrəʊfəli/ *adv* 悲伤地

sorry /'sɒri/ ▸**p. 29** *adj* **1** *pred* (apologetic) 抱歉的; **I'm (terribly) ~, I haven't a clue** (非常)抱歉, 我一点都不知道; **he didn't look the slightest bit ~** 他看似毫无歉意; **to be ~ about sth.** 为某事物抱歉; **(I'm really) ~ about the mess** (非常)抱歉, 这里太乱了; **to be ~ for sth./doing sth.** 为某事物/做某事而抱歉; **~ for breaking your vase/the delay** 对不起, 把你的花瓶打碎了/耽搁时间了; **to be ~ to do/be ...** 因为做/是…而感到抱歉; **I'm ~ to be a nuisance but ...** 抱歉打扰你了, 可是…; **to be ~ that ...** 为…抱歉; **~ I'm late** 对不起, 我来晚了; **to say (that one is) ~** 道歉; **(I'm) ~ if I am interrupting/was rude** 抱歉, 我想打断一下/失礼了; **~, but we can't serve children** 抱歉, 我们不接待儿童; **we are ~ to inform you that ...** 我们抱歉地告知您…; **I'm ~ to disappoint you** 抱歉, 让您失望了 **2** *pred* (sympathetic) 难过的; **to be ~ about sth.** 为某事物而难过; **he was ~ about what had happened to her** 他同情她的遭遇; **to be ~ that ...** 为…而难过 **3** *pred* (regretful) 后悔的; **to be ~ that ...** 为…而后悔; **to be ~ to do sth.** 为做某事而后悔; **no one will be ~ to say goodbye** 大家都巴不得说再见; **to be ~ at** *or* **about sth.** 因某事物而后悔; **you'll be ~ about this later** 你以后会为此后悔的; **to feel ~** 感到后悔; ▸**safe A6** **4** *pred* (correcting oneself) 不对 [用于纠正自己的话]; **his name's Johnson, ~, Jason** 他叫约翰逊, 不好意思, 是贾森 **5** *pred* esp Brit (requesting repeat) [用于听不清时请求对方重复]; **you can't go — ~?** 你不能去——你说什么? **6** *pred* (pitying) 可惜的; (feeling pity and disapproval) 遗憾的; **to be** *or* **feel sorry for sb.** (sympathetic) 同情某人; (feeling pity and disapproval) 觉得某人倒霉; **to be** *or* **feel ~ for oneself** (self-pitying) 自怨自怜 **7** *attrib* (pathetic) 悲惨的; (deplorable) 可悲的; **a ~ bunch of failures** 一群可悲的失败者; **a ~ state of affairs** 悲惨的处境; **to be in a ~ state** *or* **plight** 处境悲惨; **to cut a ~ figure** (pathetic) 显得很悲惨; (undignified) 显得很不像样 **8** *attrib* (worthless) 徒劳的 ‹*attempt, excuse*› **9** *attrib* (saddening) 令人伤心的 ‹*story, sight*›

sort /sɔːt/
A *n* **1** (kind, type) 种类; **this/that ~ of X** 这种/那种X; **people of that ~** 那种人; **the same ~ of thing** 同一类事情; **what ~ of dog/man is he?** 它是什么品种的狗/他是什么样的人?; **what ~ of car is it?** 那是什么类型的汽车?; **several/different ~s of cake** 好几种/不同种类的蛋糕; **A, B, that ~ of thing** A、B之类的东西; **all ~s of reasons** 各种原因; **you know the ~ of thing I mean** 你知道我在说什么; **a cheap ~ of cotton** 一种廉价的棉布; **in an embarrassed ~ of way** 有点尴尬地; **that's my ~ of holiday** 这是我喜欢的度假方式; **that's the ~ of person I am** 我就是这样的人; **what ~ of people does he think we are?** 他把我们当成什么人了?; **I'm not that ~ of girl!** 我不是那种随随便便的女孩!; **what ~ of a reply/an excuse is that?** 那算什么回答/理由啊?; **radiation of any ~, any ~ of radiation** 任何种类的辐射; **a liar of the worst ~** 最恶劣的说谎者; **it takes all ~s (to make a world)** Prov 大千世界无奇不有; **I wouldn't want to do that myself, but it takes all ~s** 我自己不想做那件事, 但各人有各人的爱好; **nothing** *or* **not anything of the ~** 一点也不; **I shall do/say nothing of the ~!** 我绝不做这种事/说这种话! **2** (in vague description) 某种; **a ~ of X** 类似X的东西; **a ~ of elephant without a trunk** 某种没有长鼻子的大象; **I had a ~ of (a) feeling that ...** 我依稀觉得…; **in a ~ of way I'm sorry** 我有点抱歉; **he must be some ~ of madman** 他一定是有点疯了; **there must be some ~ of mistake** 一定是出了什么差错; **you must have some ~ of idea** 你肯定多少了解一点的; **(an) X of some ~** 某种X; **we made progress of ~s** 我们勉强取得了一点进步; **X or something of the ~** X或诸如此类的东西; **to be** *or* **feel out of ~s** (ill) 感到不适; (grouchy) 心情烦躁 **3** (type of person) 某一类人; **to be sb.'s ~** 是某人那种人; **they're not our ~** 他们和我们不是一类人; **people of her ~** 她那类人; **we see all ~s here** 我们这里三教九流的人都有 **4** colloq (person) 人; **a good/bad ~** 好人/坏人
B **sort of** *adv* colloq **1** (a bit, somewhat) 有点; **~ of cute/eccentric** 有点可爱/古怪的; **to ~ of understand/sympathize** 有点理解/同情; **I've ~ of heard of her vaguely** 我对她略有耳闻; **it just ~ of happened** 事情就这么发生了; **aren't you pleased? — ~ of** 你难道不满意吗?——还可以吧; **do you see what I mean? — ~ of** 你明白我的意思吗?——差不多吧 **2** (approximately) 大约; **it's ~ of behind her** 那东西就在她身后; **come at ~ of 6 o'clock** 6点左右来吧; **it happened ~ of recently** 事情算是最近发生的
C *vt* **1** (classify, arrange) 把…分类 ‹*items, collection*›; Comput 整理 ‹*data, files*›; Post 分拣 ‹*mail, parcels*›; **he ~ed the clothes into piles/into clean and dirty** 他把衣服分成一堆堆/干净的和脏的; **to ~ sth. by colour** 按颜色给某物分类; **to ~ things into sizes** *or* **according to size** 把东西按大小分类; **to ~ one's cards** *or* **hand** 按花色理牌 **2** (select) 挑出; (separate) 分开; **to ~ sth. from sth.** 把某物和某物分开; **a machine for ~ing potatoes** 挑选土豆的机器 **3** colloq (mend) 修理; **I've ~ed your bike** 我修好了你的自行车

Phrasal verbs

• **sort out**
A [**~ sth. out, ~ out sth.**] *vt*
1 (select) 挑出; (separate) 分开; **to ~ out sth. from sth.** (select) 从某物中挑出某物; (separate) 把某物和某物分开 **2** (organize) 整理; (arrange) 安排; (fix) 处理; **did you ~ it out with him when you were there?** 你在那里时和他安排好了吗? **3** (tidy up) 整理 ‹*objects*›; 打理 ‹*affairs*›; **it was left to me to ~ out the mess** 收拾烂摊子的事留给了我 **4** (distinguish) 识别; (establish) 确定; **I couldn't ~ out what had happened** 我弄不明白出了什么事; **to ~ out who is responsible** 查出负责人 **5** (resolve, put right) 纠正; **we've got it all ~ed out now** 我们目前把一切都搞定了; **to ~ out one's life** 恢复正常生活; **can you ~ this out for me?** (help) 你能帮我弄好这个吗?; (explain) 你能帮我弄清楚这个吗? **6** (mend) 修理 ‹*machine*›; 纠正 ‹*fault*›; **I've ~ed out the television** 我把电视机修好了
B [**~ sb. out**] *vt* colloq **1** (help) 安顿 ‹*person*›; **the doctor will soon ~ her out** 医生很快就会治好她的 **2** (punish) 收拾 ‹*person*›; **I'll ~ him out!** 我会收拾他的!
C *v refl* **1** **to ~ oneself out** (sort out one's life) 恢复正常生活; (get organized) 安顿自己 **2** **to ~ itself out** ‹*situation*› 圆满结束; ‹*problem*› 圆满解决

• **sort through** *vt* [**~ through sth.**] 翻查 ‹*items, cupboard*›

sort code *n* 银行代码

sorted /'sɔːtɪd/ *adj* Brit colloq **1** (arranged, organized) 整理好的; **it's all ~** 全都整理好了; **to get sth. ~** 整理好某物 **2** (well-balanced) 神智健全的

sorter /'sɔːtə(r)/ ▸**p. 409** *n* **1** (person) 分类者; **a mail** *or* **postal ~** 邮件分拣员 **2** (mail-sorting machine) 邮件分拣机

sortie /'sɔːti/ *n* **1** (troop attack) 出击 **2** (operational flight) 出动架次 **3** (short trip) 外出; **to make a ~ to ...** 出门去…

sorting /'sɔːtɪŋ/: **~ machine** *n* 邮件分拣机; **~ office** *n* 邮件分拣室

sort: ~ key *n* 排序关键词; **~-out** *n* Brit colloq (tidying) 清理; (organizing) 整理; **to give sth. a ~-out** 整理某物; **to have a ~-out** 进行清理

SOS *n* (*pl* **~s**) **1** (code signal) 紧急呼救信号 **2** fig (appeal for help) 紧急求救

so-so *adj* colloq 一般的; **his work is only ~** 他的工作不怎么样; **I'm feeling ~ this morning** 今天早上我感觉一般

sot /sɒt/ *n* Brit pej 酒鬼

sottish /'sɒtɪʃ/ *adj* 醉醺醺的

sotto voce /ˌsɒtəʊ 'vəʊtʃeɪ/ *adj, adv* 小声的(地)

sou /suː/ *adj* colloq 一点点钱; **I haven't (got) a ~!** 我一个子儿也没有!

soubriquet /'suːbrɪkeɪ/ *n* formal = **sobriquet**

souchong /ˌsuː'tʃɒŋ/ *n* [u] 小种茶 [一种上等的中国红茶]

soufflé /'suːfleɪ, Amer suː'fleɪ/ *n* 蛋奶酥

S

sought /sɔːt/ *pt, pp* ▸ **seek A, B**

sought-after *adj* 广受欢迎的

soul /səʊl/ *n* 1 [c] (spirit) 灵魂; **to sell one's ~ for ... /to do ...** 为…/为了做…而出卖灵魂 2 [c] (innermost nature) 内心; **to have the ~ of a poet** 有诗人的心灵; **to put one's heart and ~ into sth.** 全心全意专注在某事物上; **with all one's ~** 一心一意地; **to bare one's ~** 袒露心扉 3 [c] (essence) 精髓; **the ~ of the British middle classes** 英国中产阶级的典范; **to be the ~ of kindness** 是善良的化身 4 [u] (emotional appeal) 热情; (emotional depth) 灵性; (emotional warmth) 生气; **to lack ~** 缺乏灵气 5 [c] (character type) 某种人; **a sensitive ~** 敏感的人 6 [c] (individual) 人; **not a ~ is here** 这里一个人也没有; **a village of 200 ~s** 有 200 人的村子; **poor ~!** 可怜的家伙! 7 [u] (central part) 中心人物; **the life and ~ of the party** 聚会的活跃分子 8 [u] **= soul music**

soul: ~-destroying *adj* 极为单调的; **~ food** *n* [u] Amer [美国南方] 黑人的传统食物

soulful /'səʊlfl/ *adj* 深情的

soulfully /'səʊlfəli/ *adv* 深情地

soulless /'səʊllɪs/ *adj* 1 (lacking humanity) 无情的 2 (lacking interest, appeal) 呆板的 3 (lacking character) 没有生气的

soul: ~mate *n* 知己; **to find one's ~mate** 找到知心朋友; **~ music** *n* [u] 灵乐

soul-searching
A *n* [u] 反省
B *adj* 反省式的

sound[1] /saʊnd/
A *n* 1 [u] (audible vibrations) 声响; **the speed of ~** 音速 2 [u] Audio (quality) 音质; (volume) 音量; **to turn up/down the ~** 调高/调低音量; **poor/good ~** 差/好音质; **a ~ mixer** 混音师; **~ quality** 音质 3 [c and u] (noise) 声音; **a high/low ~** 高音/低音; **a vowel ~** 元音; **the ~ of sth.** 某物发出的声音; **the ~ of the wind/voices/steps** 风声/说话声/脚步声; **without a ~** 悄无声息地; **to emit** *or* **produce** *or* **utter a ~** 出声; **(not) to make a ~** (不) 出声; **I left, trying not to make a ~** 我轻手轻脚地离开了; **a soft** *or* **faint ~** 微弱的声音; **a grating** *or* **rasping ~** 刮擦声 4 [u] esp Mus (controlled vibrations) (乐) 音; **musical ~** 乐音; **to the ~ of a drum/trumpet** 伴着鼓声/号声 5 [u and c] Mus (distinctive style) 音乐风格; (distinctive quality) 乐曲特色; **the ~s of the sixties** 60 年代的流行乐; **the Motown ~** 摩城之音; **the ~ of rap** 说唱乐风格 6 [c] fig (idea, impression) 印象; **the latest news has a sinister ~ (to it)** 最新的消息给人不祥之感; **reorganization? I don't like the ~ of that** 重组? 这消息不太好哇; **by the ~ of it, ...** 听起来…; **from the ~ of things** 看样子 7 [u] (hearing distance) 听力范围; **within/out of** *or* **beyond (the) ~ of sth.** 在听得到/听不到某声音的地方 8 [c] Geog 海峡; **Plymouth S~** 普利茅斯海峡
B *vt* 1 (cause to emit noise) 吹响 ‹*trumpet*›; 敲响 ‹*bell, alarm*›; **the driver ~ed his horn** 司机按响了喇叭 2 (ring out) 发出…的信号; **a bell began to ~ midnight** 午夜的钟声敲响了; **to ~ reveille/the retreat/lights out/the charge** Mil 吹起床/撤退/熄灯/冲锋号; **to ~ a warning** 发出警告声 3 (express) 表示; **to ~ a note of caution** 提出告诫; **her words ~ed a sombre note** 她的话里带着忧郁; **to ~ a warning** 发出警告; **the news ~ed the death knell for our chances of winning** 这消息意味着我们已获胜无望 4 (pronounce) 发 ‹*vowel*›; **you don't ~ the 'h' in 'hour'** hour 一词中的 h 不发音; **he doesn't ~ his aitches** 他说话时h都不发音 5 (test by sound) (in health examinations) 对…听诊 ‹*chest*›; (in mechanics) 敲击检查 ‹*object, wheel*› 6 Naut (measure depth of) 测…的深度 ‹*water*›
C *vi* 1 (emit sound) «*bell, alarm, trumpet*» 响起; **a note of terror ~ed in her voice** 她的声音中带着恐惧 2 (give impression) 听起来; **the cat ~ed hurt** 那只猫听上去像是受了伤; **his voice ~s hoarse/wonderful** 他的声音听起来很哑/很棒; **he ~s ill** 他听上去病了; **she likes to ~ grown-up** 她喜欢用大人的口气说话; **his words ~ed threatening** 他的话里透着威胁; **the situation doesn't ~ too promising** *or* **good** 情况听上去不妙; **she ~s Japanese to me** 我觉得她的口音听起来像日本人; **we'll leave at ten — how does that ~ to you?** 我们 10 点出发——你觉得怎么样? ; **to spell a word as it ~s** 根据发音拼写一个单词; **to ~ like sb./sth.** 听起来像是某人/某事物; **that ~s like fun** 那听起来很有趣; **that ~s like a good idea** 那听起来是个好主意; **it ~s as if** *or* **as though** *or* **like ...** 听起来好像…; **she ~s just the person we need** 听起来她正是我们需要的人

Phrasal verbs

- **sound off** *vi* colloq pej **to ~ off about sth.** 高谈阔论某事物; **he's ~ing off about how good he is at bridge** 他在吹嘘自己打桥牌有多厉害; **to ~ off at sb./against sth.** 对某人夸夸其谈/大肆抨击某事物
- **sound out** *vt* 1 [**~ sb. out, ~ out sb.**] (question) 试探; **to ~ sb. out about** *or* **on sth.** 试探某人对某事物的看法; **we'll ~ out parliament first** 我们首先要探听一下议会的意见 2 [**~ sth. out, ~ out sth.**] (ascertain) 打探 ‹*opinion*›

sound[2]
A *adj* 1 (in good condition) 健康的 ‹*limb, heart, teeth*›; 完好的 ‹*structure, foundations*›; **~ in** *or* **of mind and body** 身心健康的; **to be of ~ mind** 心智健全; **safe and ~** 安然无恙的; **~ in wind and limb** dated hum 身体硬朗的 2 (well-founded) 合理的; (solid) 坚实的; **a ~ education** 良好的教育; **to give sb. ~ advice** 对某人提出忠告; **everything he says makes ~ (economic) sense** 他说的一切 (从经济收益角度看) 完全合情合理; **their policies are environmentally ~** 他们的政策对环境没有不利影响 3 Fin, Econ (secure) 稳固的 ‹*currency, financial position, organization, bank*›; 稳妥的 ‹*investment, deal*› 4 (competent) 实实在在的; **this is a ~ piece of writing** 这篇文章写得不错; **he's a very ~ golfer** 他的高尔夫球打得相当不错; **to be ~ on sth.** «*book*» 在某方面相当翔实; «*person*» 在某方面很在行 5 (acceptable, reliable) 可靠的 ‹*person*›; **to be politically ~** 政治上可靠 6 (thorough) 彻底的 ‹*investigation, understanding*›; **he gave his opponent a ~ thrashing** 他痛击了对手; **what he needs is a ~ telling-off** 他需要狠狠训一顿; **a ~ grasp of sth.** 对某事物的全面把握 7 (deep, undisturbed) 酣畅的; **she's a very ~ sleeper** 她睡眠很沉; **a ~ night's sleep** 一夜的酣睡 8 Jur (valid) 合法的 ‹*claim, case*›
B *adv* 酣畅地; **to be/fall ~ asleep** 酣睡/进入酣睡; **sleep ~!** 睡个好觉!

sound: ~ archive *n* 音响档案; **~ barrier** *n* 声障; **to break the ~ barrier** 突破声障; **~ bite** *n* [采访或演讲的] 录音片断; **~board** *n* 共鸣板; **~ box** *n* 共鸣箱; **~ card** *n* 声卡; **~ change** *n* [c and u] 音变; **~ effect** *n* 音响效果; **~ hole** *n* 音孔

sounding /'saʊndɪŋ/ *n* 1 [u] (measuring depth) 水深测量 2 [c] (measurement taken) 水深; **to take ~s** lit 测量水深; fig 征求意见

-sounding /'saʊndɪŋ/ *combining form* 听起来…的; **a grand~/an English~ name** 听起来很气派/像英国人的名字; **unlikely~** 听上去不可能的

sounding: ~ board *n* 1 lit (board, screen) [讲台上的] 增音板; 2 fig (test audience) 决策征询人; **can I use you as a ~ board?** 我能否咨询你的意见? ; 3 fig (channel) 宣传渠道; (means) 宣传手段; 4 **= soundboard**; **~ line** *n* 测深绳

sound insulation *n* [u] 1 (property) 隔音 2 (material) 隔音材料

soundless /'saʊndlɪs/ *adj* 无声的; **a ~ night** 万籁俱寂的夜晚

soundlessly /'saʊndlɪsli/ *adv* 无声地

sound: ~ level *n* 声级; **~ library** *n* 音效样本库

soundly /'saʊndli/ *adv* 1 (deeply) 酣畅地 ‹*sleep*› 2 (utterly) 彻底地 ‹*defeat*› 3 (severely) 严厉地; **to be ~ thrashed** 被痛打一顿 4 (competently) 娴熟地 ‹*play, write*›; (reliably) 可靠地 ‹*advise*› 5 (securely) 安全地; **the money has been invested ~** 这笔投资很稳妥

soundness /'saʊndnɪs/ *n* [u] 1 (good condition) (of constitution, health) 健康; (of structure, foundations) 完好; **~ of mind and body** 身心健康 2 (solidness) 合理; **the ~ of the advice** 这一建议的可靠性; **~ of judgement** 判断的正确性 3 Fin, Econ (of currency, financial position) 稳定; (of investment, business) 低风险; (of bank) 资金充裕

soundproof /'saʊndpruːf/
A *adj* 隔音的
B *vt* 给…隔音; **a poorly ~ed door** 隔音效果差的门

soundproofing /'saʊndpruːfɪŋ/ *n* [u] 1 (action, process) 隔音; **to enhance the ~** 增强隔音效果 2 (material) 隔音材料; **to cover sth. in ~** 用隔音材料覆盖某物

sound: ~ shift *n* 语音演变; **~ stage** *n* 录音平台; **~ system** *n* (for personal use) 高保真音响; (for use on stage, in disco etc.) 音响系统; **~track** *n* 1 (recording of music from film) 配乐录音; **I've bought the ~track of the film** 我买了这部电影的音乐带; 2 (strip on film) 音轨; **~ wave** *n* 声波

soup /suːp/ *n* 1 [u and c] Culin 汤; **the ~ of the day** 时日例汤; **to land sb./be in the ~** fig 使某人陷入/处于困境; **my big mouth has landed me in the ~ again!** 我随便乱说话又给我惹了麻烦! 2 [u] fig (mixture, substance) 汤一般的东西

Phrasal verb

- **soup up** *vt* [**~ up sth., ~ sth. up**] colloq (increase) (in power) 加大…的马力; (in efficiency) 提高…的效率; (in speed) 增加…的速度

soupçon /'suːpsɒn, Amer suː'pˈsɒn/ *n* 少量; **a ~ of sth.** 一点儿某物

souped-up *adj* colloq (having greater power) 加大马力的; (having greater efficiency) 提高效率的

soup: ~ kitchen *n* 施食处; **~ plate** *n* 汤盆; **~ spoon** *n* 汤匙; **~ tureen** *n* [瓷或银质的] 汤碗

soupy /'suːpi/ *adj* 1 (like soup) 羹一般浓稠的 2 (thick, dense) 浓的 ‹*fog*›; 浓厚的 ‹*atmosphere*›

sour /'saʊə(r)/
A *adj* 1 (bitter, sharp) 酸的; **to taste ~** 有酸味 2 (off, bad) 馊的 ‹*milk, wine*›; 酸臭的 ‹*taste, flavour, smell*›; **to go** *or* **turn ~** 变馊 3 fig (bitter) 辛酸的; (resentful) 怨恨的; (bad-tempered) 脾气坏的 ‹*person*›; 坏的 ‹*temper*›; (angry) 阴郁的 ‹*mood*›; **to go** *or* **turn ~** 变得令人不快; **relations between them have turned ~** 他们的关系恶化了; **to have a ~ look on one's face** 阴沉着脸; **to feel ~** 闷闷不乐
B *n* 酸味鸡尾酒; **a rum/vodka/whisky ~** 酸味朗姆/伏特加/威士忌鸡尾酒
C *vt* 1 (make sour) 使…变酸 ‹*milk*› 2 fig (make unpleasant) 使…恶化 ‹*relationship, atmosphere*›; 使…变坏 ‹*personality*›
D *vi* 1 (turn bad) «*milk*» 变酸腐 2 fig (become bitter, acrimonious) «*relationship, friendship*» 恶化

source /sɔːs/
A *n* 1 (of river) 源头; **the ~ of the Nile** 尼罗河发源地 2 (origin) 来源; **at ~** 在源头; **our wages are taxed at ~** 我们的工资下发前已扣税; **a ~ of income** 收入来源 3 (of information) (person) 提供消息者; (place) 消息来源; **to hear sth. from a reliable ~** 从可靠人士

S

那里听说某事; **an original ~ for ...** …的原始出处; **to cite one's ~s** 引用原始资料; **~s close to sb./sth.** 接近某人/某物的消息人士 **4** (of trouble, problem) 根源; **a** *or* **the ~ of ...** …的缘由; **you're a constant ~ of disappointment to your parents** 你总是让父母失望

B *vt* 获得; **the coffee is ~d from overseas** 这咖啡是进口的; **to ~ a supply of sth.** 得到某物的供给

source: ~book *n* 原始资料集; **~ code** *n* [u] 源代码; **~ directory** *n* 源目录; **~ language** *n* [翻译的] 源语言; **~ material** *n* [u] [尤指报告、学术论文等的] 原始资料; **~ program** *n* 源程序

sour cream *n* [u] 酸奶油

sourdough /ˈsaʊədəʊ/ *n* [u] **1** (fermented dough) 酸面团 **2** (bread) 发面面包

sourdough bread *n* [u] 发面面包

sour: ~-faced *adj* 面色阴沉的; **~ grapes** *npl* colloq 酸葡萄; **it's (a touch of) ~ grapes!** 这（有点儿）是吃不着葡萄说葡萄酸!

sourish /ˈsaʊərɪʃ/ *adj* **1** (acidic) 微酸的 ‹*taste, smell*› **2** (peevish, resentful) 略带怒气的

sourly /ˈsaʊəli/ *adv* 怨恨地

sourness /ˈsaʊənɪs/ *n* [u] **1** (acidity) 酸味; **the ~ of these grapes hurts my teeth** 这些葡萄酸倒了我的牙 **2** fig (resentfulness, peevishness) (of person) 阴郁; (of expression) 尖酸; (of remark) 刻薄

sourpuss /ˈsaʊəpʊs/ *n* colloq 脾气乖戾的人; **you can be such a ~ sometimes!** 有时候你真难缠啊!

sousaphone /ˈsuːzəfəʊn/ ▸**p. 395** *n* 苏萨大号

souse /saʊs/ *vt* **1** (soak, drench) 浸透; **to ~ sth. in** *or* **with sth.** 把某物浸在某物中; **he ~d his chips with vinegar** 他用醋泡薯条 **2** Culin **to ~ sth. in sth.** 用某物腌渍某物

soused /saʊst/ *adj* **1** Culin 腌制的 **2** colloq dated (drunk) 喝醉的

south /saʊθ/ ▸**p. 142**

A *n* [u] (direction) 南; (position or location) 南方; (southern part) 南部; **the sun/wind is in the ~** 太阳在南面/吹的是南风

B *adj* **1** (southern) 南边的; **on the ~ side of the island** 在岛屿的南侧; **the ~ bank/coast** 南河岸/南海岸 **2** *attrib* (from the south) 来自南边的; **a ~ wind** 南风

C *adv* **1** (to the south, on the southern side) 在南边; **~ of sth.** 在某物的南边 **2** (towards the south) 向南; **due ~** 向正南; **to go ~ of sth.** 向某物的南面走去; **down ~** 向南部; **due ~** 正南方; **to be heading ~** fig colloq 滑坡

South Africa *pr n* 南非

South African ▸**p. 503**

A *adj* (of South Africa) 南非的; (of the people) 南非人的

B *n* 南非人

South America *pr n* 南美洲

South American

A *adj* (of South America) 南美洲的; (of the people) 南美洲人的

B *n* 南美洲人

South: ~ Asian *adj* 南亚的; **~ Australia** *pr n* 南澳大利亚; **~ Bank** *pr n* **the ~ Bank** 南岸地区 [指泰晤士河以南地区]; **s~bound** *adj* **1** 南行的 ‹*traffic, train, passenger*› **2** 向南的 ‹*road, line, platform*›; **~ Carolina** *pr n* 南卡罗来纳州; **~ China Sea** *pr n* **= China Sea**; **~ Dakota** *pr n* 南达科他州

south-east ▸**p. 142**

A *n* [u] **1** (direction) 东南; (position or location) 东南方; (south-eastern part) 东南部; **the sun/wind is in the ~** 太阳在东南方/吹的是东南风 **2** (compass point) 东南方 **3** (of country, region, town) 东南部

B *adj* **1** (south-eastern) 东南边的; **on the ~ side of the island** 在岛屿的东南侧; **~ London** 伦敦东南部 **2** *attrib* (from the south-east) 来自东南边的; **a ~ wind** 东南风

C *adv* **1** (to the south-east, on the south-eastern side) 在东南边; **~ of sth.** 在某物的东南边 **2** (towards the south-east) 向东南; **due ~** 向正东南; **a village ~ of Oxford** 牛津东南部的一个村子

South-East Asia, South East Asia *pr n* 东南亚

southeaster /ˌsaʊθˈiːstə(r)/ *n* 东南风

south-easterly /ˌsaʊθˈiːstəli/ ▸**p. 142**

A *adj* **1** (in a south-eastward position) 东南的 ‹*point, area*› **2** (in a south-eastward direction) 向东南的 ‹*aspect, course, journey*› **3** (from a south-eastward direction) 从东南方来的; **a ~ wind** 东南风; **a ~ breeze** 东南微风

B *adv* (from south-east) 从东南方; (towards south-east) 向东南方

C *n* 东南风

south-eastern ▸**p. 142** *adj attrib* **1** (of or in the south-east) 东南方的; **~ France** 法国东南部 **2** (facing south-east) 向东南的; (going towards south-east) 东南行的

south-eastward

A *adj* 向东南的

B *adv* (*also* **south-eastwards**) 向东南

southerly /ˈsʌðəli/ ▸**p. 142**

A *adj* **1** (in a southward position) 南方的 ‹*point, area*› **2** (in a southward direction) 向南的 ‹*aspect, course, journey*› **3** (from a southward direction) 从南方吹来的; **a ~ wind** 南风; **a ~ breeze** 南微风

B *n* 南风

southern /ˈsʌðən/ ▸**p. 142** *adj attrib* **1** (of or in the south) 南方的; **~ France** 法国南部; **the ~ wall of the city** 南城墙 **2** (facing south) 向南的 ‹*window, wall*›; (going towards south) 南行的 ‹*journey, route*› **3** (*also* **Southern**) Pol, Geog 南方的

Southern: ~ Comfort® *n* [u and c] 南方安逸酒 [美国原产的加香料威士忌烈酒]; **~ Cross** *n* **the ~ Cross** 南十字星座

southerner, Southerner /ˈsʌðənə(r)/ *n* (native) [尤指美国或英格兰的] 南方人; (inhabitant) [尤指美国或英格兰的] 南方居民

southern: ~-fried chicken *n* [u] Amer 南方炸鸡; **~ hemisphere** *n* 南半球; **S~ Lights** *npl* **the S~ Lights = aurora australis**

southernmost /ˈsʌðənməʊst/ *adj* 最南的

Southern Ocean *pr n* **the ~** 南大洋

south-facing *adj* 面朝南的

South Georgia *pr n* 南乔治亚岛

South Island *pr n* [新西兰的] 南岛

South Korea *pr n* 韩国

South Korean ▸**p. 503**

A *adj* (of South Korea) 韩国的; (of the people) 韩国人的

B *n* 韩国人

south: ~paw *n* **1** (in boxing) 左势拳击手; **2** esp Amer colloq (left-handed person) 左撇子; **S~ Pole** *n* **1** (of Earth) **the ~** 南极; **2** Astron 南天极; **3** **south pole** (of magnet) [磁体的] 南极

south-south-east

A *n* [u] 南东南

B *adj* **1** (in direction) 南东南的 ‹*position*› **2** (from direction) 从南东南吹来的 ‹*wind*›

C *adv* (to direction) 向南东南; (in direction) 在南东南

south-south-west

A *n* [u] 南西南

B *adj* **1** (in direction) 南西南的 ‹*position*› **2** (from direction) 从南西南吹来的 ‹*wind*›

C *adv* (to direction) 向南西南; (in direction) 在南西南

southward /ˈsaʊθwəd/ ▸**p. 142**

A *adj* 向南的

B *adv* (*also* **southwards**) 向南

south-west ▸**p. 142**

A *n* [u] **1** (direction) 西南; (position or location) 西南方; (south-western part) 西南部; **the sun/wind is in the ~** 太阳在西南方/吹的是西南风 **2** (compass point) 西南方 **3** (of country, region, town) 西南部

B *adj* **1** (south-western) 西南边的; **on the ~ side of the island** 在岛屿的西南侧; **~ France** 法国西南部 **2** *attrib* (from the south-west) 来自西南边的; **a ~ wind** 西南风

C *adv* **1** (to the south-west, on the south-western side) 在西南边; **~ of sth.** 在某物的西南边 **2** (towards the south-west) 向西南; **due ~** 向正西南

southwester /ˌsaʊθˈwestə(r)/ *n* 西南风

south-westerly /ˌsaʊθˈwestəli/ ▸**p. 142**

A *adj* **1** (in a south-westward position) 西南方的 ‹*point, area*› **2** (in a south-westward direction) 向西南的 ‹*aspect, course, journey*› **3** (from a south-westward direction) 从西南方来的; **a ~ wind** 西南风; **a ~ breeze** 西南微风

B *adv* (from south-west) 从西南方; (towards south-west) 向西南方

C *n* 西南风

south-western /ˌsaʊθˈwestən/ ▸**p. 142** *adj attrib* **1** (of or in the south-west) 西南方的; **~ France** 法国西南部 **2** (facing south-west) 向西南的; (going towards south-west) 西南行的

south-westward

A *adj* 向西南的

B *adv* (*also* **south-westwards**) 向西南

South Yorkshire /ˌsaʊθ ˈjɔːkʃə(r)/ *pr n* 南约克郡

souvenir /ˌsuːvəˈnɪə(r), Amer ˈsuːvənɪər/ *n* 纪念品; **a ~ of sth.** 某事物的纪念

souvenir: ~ hunter *n* 纪念品收藏者; **~ shop** *n* 纪念品商店

sou'wester /ˌsaʊˈwestə(r)/ *n* [水手或渔民用的] 防水帽

sovereign /ˈsɒvrɪn/

A *n* **1** (ruler) 元首; (monarch) 君主 **2** Hist (coin) [面值1英镑的] 金币

B *adj* **1** (highest) 至高无上的 ‹*power, authority, rights*› **2** *attrib* (independent) 有主权的; **a ~ state** 主权国家

sovereignty /ˈsɒvrənti/ *n* [u] **1** (supreme power) 至高无上的权力; (supreme authority) 至高无上的权威; **the ~ of Parliament** 议会的最高权威 **2** (authority) 主权; **national ~** 国家主权; **to claim ~ over ...** 对…宣称主权

sovereign wealth fund *n* 主权财富基金

Soviet /ˈsəʊvɪət, ˈsɒv-/ Hist

A *adj* 苏联的

B *n* **1** **soviet** (elected body) 苏维埃 [苏联的各级代表会议] **2** (person) 苏联人

Soviet Union *pr n* Hist 苏联

sow¹ /saʊ/ *n* 母猪; **you can't make a silk purse out of a ~'s ear** Prov 粗瓷碗雕不出细花

sow² /səʊ/ *vt* (*pt* **~ed**, *pp* **sown** *or* **~ed**) **1** (plant by scattering) 播撒; **to ~ sth. in** *or* **on** *or* **around somewhere** 在某地播种某物; **to ~ one's wild oats** [年轻时] 生活放荡 **2** (plant seed on) 播种于; **to ~ a garden with grass seed** 在花园撒草籽 **3** fig (cause to appear, spread) 散布; **to ~ the seeds of doubt (in sb.)** 使（某人）起疑心; **to ~ the wind and reap the whirlwind** 作恶必遭加倍报应

sower /ˈsəʊə(r)/ *n* **1** (person) 播种者; (machine) 播种机 **2** fig (initiator) 煽动者; **a ~ of sth.** 某事的散布者; **a ~ of discontent and disorder** 挑起不满与骚动的人

sown /səʊn/ *pp* ▸**sow²**

sox /sɒks/ *npl* Amer colloq 短袜

soy /sɔɪ/ *n* [u] **1** **~ (sauce)** 酱油 **2** **= soya**

soya /ˈsɔɪə/ *n* [u] **1** (protein) 大豆蛋白 **2** (plant) 大豆

soya: ~ **bean** *n* [u and c] = **soybean**; ~ **milk** *n* [u and c] 豆浆; ~ **sauce** *n* [u] esp Brit 酱油

soybean /ˈsɔɪbiːn/ *n* [u and c] 大豆

sozzled /ˈsɒzld/ *adj* colloq 烂醉的; **to get completely** ~ 烂醉如泥

spa /spɑː/ *n* 1 (spring) 矿泉; ~ **water** 矿泉水 2 (town) 矿泉城; (resort) 矿泉疗养地 3 (health club) 休闲健身中心

space /speɪs/

A *n* 1 [u] (room) 空间; **to take up a lot of** ~ 占很大地方; **the amount of** ~ **occupied by sth.** 某物所占的空间; ~ **to do sth.** 做某事所需的空间; **to have some** ~ **to exercise in** 有一点可供锻炼的地方; ~ **for sth./sb.** 可供某物占用/某人使用的空间; **there's ample** ~ **for parking** 有足够的地方停车; **to leave some** ~ **for dessert** 留出肚子吃甜点; **living/storage** ~ 生活/储存空间; **to make** ~ **for sb./sth.** 为某人/某物腾出地方; **a feeling** *or* **an impression of** ~ 空旷感; **a player in** ~ Sport 单刀直入的运动员; **he's got no sense of** ~ 他没有空间感; **to invade sb.'s (personal)** ~ 侵占某人的（个人）空间; **(a journey in)** ~ **and time** 时空（旅行）; **to stare into** ~ 茫然直视前方 2 [u] (outer space) 太空 3 [c] (empty place, gap) 空隙; (blank area) 空地; **a small/narrow** ~ 小的/窄的空当; **some empty** ~**s on the bookshelves** 书架上的几处空隙; **there's a** ~ **next to me** 我旁边空着; **a** ~ **to park one's car** 可供停车的地方; **a fear of enclosed** *or* **confined** ~**s** 对封闭空间的恐惧; **leave a** ~ **after your name** 在名字后面留空; **large, empty** ~**s in the crowd** 人群中大片的空隙; **there's a** ~ **on page three for your article** 第三版上有空隙可登你的文章; **in/into a** ~ 在/进入空隙中; **a** ~ **of two metres (between ...)** （…间）两米的间隙; **open** ~**s** 开阔的空地; **a country of wide open** ~**s** 幅员广袤的国家; **watch this** ~! colloq 请关注本版！ 4 [u] (amount of airtime) 时段; (amount of paper) 版面; **the newspaper gives** ~ **to local news/young writers** 这家报纸刊登地方新闻/年轻作者的文章; **a** ~ **for the public to air their views** 供公众发表意见的时段; **to buy/sell** ~ **in a newspaper** (for advertising) 购买/出售报纸版面; **in her book, she devotes a lot of** ~ **to this theory** 她在书中花了大量篇幅阐述这一理论 5 [c] Print 空白; **to type a** ~ 键入一个空格; **to leave a** ~ 空一格; ~**s between the words/lines** 字间距/行间距 6 [c] (interval of time) 期间; **a short** ~ **of time** 一会儿; **after a** ~ **of about fifteen minutes** 约 15 分钟后; **there will be a** ~ **of two weeks between appointments** 每隔两周约见一次; **in** *or* **within the** ~ **of two hours** 两小时内 7 [c] (zone) 区域; **green** ~**s** 绿地; **a women-only** ~ 女性专用区; **sb.'s private** ~ 某人的私人领域 8 [u] (freedom, scope) 余地; **to give each other** ~ 互留余地; ~ **to develop one's talents** 发展才干的余地 9 [c] Mus (on stave) 线间空白

B *vt* 1 (arrange in space) 以一定间隔排列 ‹*objects, lines, words*›; **to** ~ **the chairs evenly/two metres apart/further apart** 把椅子均匀地摆开/以两米间距摆开/摆得更开一点; **the letter was well** ~**d** 信文排得很舒服; **widely-/closely-**~**d eyes** 间距很宽/很近的眼睛 2 (arrange in time) 把…间隔开 ‹*events*›; **to be better** ~**d** 时间间隔被安排得更好; **he** ~**d his visits over a period of three years** 他把访问分散安排在三年内

Phrasal verb

• **space out**

A *vt* [~ **sth. out**, ~ **out sth.**] 1 (separate physically) 使…拉开间距 ‹*objects, lines, words*›; **to** ~ **the trees out** 把树种得稀疏些; **the houses are well** ~**d out** 房子的间距拉得很开; **they** ~**d themselves out around the room** 他们分散在房间各处 2 (separate in time) 把…间隔开 ‹*events, holidays*›; **you can** ~ **out the payments over (a period of) 20 years** 你可以在 20 年内分期付款; **the ten broadcasts were** ~**d out over a period of six months** 十次节目分别在六个月内播出

B *vi* esp Amer colloq [使用致幻毒品后] 精神恍惚

space age

A *n* 太空时代

B **space-age** *modif* (very modern) 非常现代的 ‹*design, music*›; (very hi-tech) 非常先进的 ‹*technology, car*›

space: **S**~ **Agency** *n* 航天局; **the US S**~ **Agency** 美国太空总署; ~ **bar** *n* [打字机或计算机的] 空格键; ~ **blanket** *n* [主要用于户外的] 太空毯; ~ **cadet** *n* 1 (trainee astronaut) 见习宇航员; 2 esp Amer hum (absent-minded person) 外星人 [指注意力不集中、行为怪异的人]; ~ **capsule** *n* 太空舱; ~**craft** *n* (*pl* ~**craft** *or* ~**crafts**) 太空船

spaced out *adj* colloq (on drugs) 飘飘然的; (disorientated) 恍惚的; **I was so tired that I began to feel totally** ~ 我困得开始觉得完全迷糊了

space: ~ **exploration** *n* [u] 太空探索; ~ **flight** *n* 1 [u] (space travel) 航天; 2 [c] (single journey) 宇宙飞行; ~ **heater** *n* 小型取暖器; ~ **heating** *n* [u] 室内取暖; ~ **helmet** *n* 宇航头盔; ~ **industry** *n* 航天工业; **S**~ **Invaders** *npl* + *v sing* 太空侵入者 [一种电脑游戏]; ~ **lab** *n* 太空实验室; ~**man** /-mæn/ *n* 太空人; ~ **opera** *n* esp Amer colloq 1 [u] (genre) 太空探险题材; 2 [c] (story) 太空探险故事; (novel) 太空探险小说; (film) 太空探险电影; ~**plane** *n* 航天飞机; ~ **platform** *n* 宇宙空间站; ~**port** *n* 宇航基地; ~ **probe** *n* 航天探测器; ~ **programme** *n* 太空计划; ~ **race** *n* **the** ~ **race** [尤指美国和苏联之间的] 太空竞赛; ~**-saving** *adj* 节省空间的 ‹*device, design*›; ~ **science** *n* [u] 航天科学; ~ **scientist** ▸p. 409 *n* 航天科学家; ~**ship** *n* 宇宙飞船; ~ **shot** *n* 空间发射; ~ **shuttle** *n* 航天飞机; ~ **sickness** *n* [u] 宇航病; ~ **station** *n* 宇宙空间站; ~**suit** *n* 宇航服; **to put on/wear a** ~**suit** 穿上/穿着航天服; ~ **technology** *n* [u] 航天技术; ~ **telescope** *n* 空间望远镜; ~**-time** *n* [u] 时空; ~ **travel** *n* [u] 航天旅行

space walk

A *n* 航天舱外活动; **to make a** ~ 进行太空行走

B **space-walk** *vi* 进行航天舱外活动

spacewoman /ˈspeɪswʊmən/ *n* 女太空人

spacey /ˈspeɪsi/ *adj* 1 colloq (bewildered or on drugs) 精神恍惚的 2 Mus 飘渺的 ‹*sound*›

spacing /ˈspeɪsɪŋ/ *n* [u] 1 Print (between words) 字距; (between lines) 行距; **in single/double** ~ 以单/双倍行距 2 (between objects, events) ~ **(out)** 间隔; **the** ~ **of the windows** 窗距; **the** ~ **(out) of loan repayments** 还款间隔

spacious /ˈspeɪʃəs/ *adj* 宽敞的 ‹*room, garden, car park*›; 宽松的 ‹*garment*›

spaciousness /ˈspeɪʃəsnɪs/ *n* [u] (of room, garden, car park) 宽敞; (of garment) 宽松

spade[1] /speɪd/ *n* 锹; **a garden** ~ 园艺铲; **to call a** ~ **a** ~ 直言不讳; **he's plump, or, to call a** ~ **a** ~**, just plain fat** 他长得圆滚滚的，或者说白了，就是胖

spade[2] *n* 1 (in cards) 黑桃; **the ace/five/king of** ~**s** 黑桃A/五/老K; **to play a** ~ 出一张黑桃; **in** ~**s** 大量的; **she has leadership qualities in** ~**s** 她很有领导素质 2 sl offensive (black person) 黑鬼 offensive

spadeful /ˈspeɪdfʊl/ *n* 一铲; **three** ~**s of sand** 三锹沙子; **by the** ~ fig 大量地

spadework /ˈspeɪdwɜːk/ *n* [u] 艰苦的准备工作; **to do the** ~ **(for sb.)** （为某人）做艰苦的准备工作

spaghetti /spəˈgeti/ *n* [u] 意大利细面条

spaghetti western *n* colloq 意大利人摄制的美国西部影片

Spain /speɪn/ *pr n* 西班牙

spam /spæm/

A *n* [u] 1 **Spam®** Culin 斯帕姆午餐肉 2 Comput 垃圾邮件

B *vt* (*pres p etc.* **-mm-**) 向…发垃圾邮件; **we were** ~**med over a hundred times today** 今天我们收到了一百多封垃圾邮件

spammer /ˈspæmə(r)/ *n* 垃圾邮件发送者

spamming /ˈspæmɪŋ/ *n* [u] 大量发送垃圾邮件; **software that can help block** ~ 能够帮助屏蔽垃圾邮件的软件

span /spæn/

A *n* 1 (period of time) 持续时间段; **the** ~ **of sb.'s life/career** 某人的一生/事业生涯; **over a** ~ **of several years** 数年间; **concentration** ~ 注意力持续时间 2 (extent, range) 范围; **to have a wide** ~ **of interests** 兴趣广泛; **the whole** ~ **of human history** 整个人类历史 3 (width) 宽度; (across hand) 一拃; (across arms) 臂展; (across wings) 翼展 4 (of bridge) 全长; (of arch) 跨度; (between supports) 墩距; **the bridge crosses the river in a single** ~ 河上的这座桥是独拱桥

B *vt* (*pres p etc.* **-nn-**) 1 (cross, extend over) 跨越; **the Thames is** ~**ned by many bridges** 泰晤士河上架着许多桥 2 (in time) «*reign, state of affairs*» 持续 ‹*period of time, generations*›; **her life** ~**ned most of the nineteenth century** 她活过了 19 世纪的大部分时间 3 fig (in scope) 涵盖; **a group** ~**ning the age range 10 to 14** 包括 10 到 14 岁年龄段的小组 4 (with hand) 用手指拃; **I can** ~ **about 20 centimetres with my right hand** 我右手一拃能达到大约 20 厘米; **he could** ~ **the tree trunk with his hands** 他能用双手卡住树干

spandex® /ˈspændeks/ *n* [u] 斯潘德克斯弹性纤维

spandrel /ˈspændrəl/ *n* 拱肩

spangle /ˈspæŋgl/ *n* (of metal) [装饰服装或头发的] 闪光金属片; (of plastic) 闪光塑料片

spangled /ˈspæŋgld/ *adj* 1 (sparkling) 闪闪发光的 ‹*surface, sky*›; **to be** ~ **with sth.** 因某物而闪闪发光 2 (covered in spangles) 缀满闪光饰片的 ‹*dress, hair*›; **to be** ~ **with sth.** 缀满闪光的某物

Spaniard /ˈspænjəd/ ▸p. 503 *n* 西班牙人

spaniel /ˈspænjəl/ *n* 西班牙猎犬 [一种长毛垂耳狗]

Spanish /ˈspænɪʃ/ ▸p. 503, p. 426

A *adj* (of Spain) 西班牙的; (of the people) 西班牙人的; (of the language) 西班牙语的

B *n* [u] 西班牙语

C *npl* **the** ~ (people) 西班牙人

Spanish America *pr n* 通用西班牙语的拉丁美洲国家

Spanish American

A *adj* (from Spanish America) 西班牙语拉美国家的 ‹*people, culture, tradition*›; 西班牙语拉美人的 ‹*nation, food, word*›; (in US) 母语为西班牙语并拥有美国公民权的 ‹*people*›; 母语为西班牙语的美国人的 ‹*culture, food, word*›

B *n* 1 (from Spanish America) (native) 说西班牙语的拉美人; (inhabitant) 说西班牙语的拉美居民 2 (in US) (native) 母语为西班牙语的美国人; (inhabitant) 母语为西班牙语的美国居民

Spanish: ~ **Armada** *n* **the** ~ **Armada** [1588年西班牙派往英国而被击败的] 无敌舰队; ~ **chestnut** *n* 1 (nut) 欧洲栗子; 2 (tree) 欧洲栗树; ~ **Civil War** *pr n* **the** ~ **Civil War** [1936-1939年的] 西班牙内战; ~ **fly** *n* [u] 欧芫青; ~ **guitar** ▸p. 395 *n* 西班牙吉他; ~ **Inquisition** *n* Hist **the** ~ **Inquisition** 西班牙宗教法庭; ~ **Main** *pr n* archaic **the** ~ **Main** 美洲大陆加勒比海沿岸; ~ **omelette** *n* [尤指包土豆丁的] 西班牙煎蔬菜蛋卷; ~ **onion** *n* 西班牙洋葱; ~ **rice** *n* [u] 西班牙什锦菜饭 [用米饭加剁青椒、洋葱、

S

番茄等蔬菜制成]; ~-**speaking** *adj* 讲西班牙语的 ‹*people, country*›

spank /spæŋk/
A *vt* 打…的屁股; **if you do that again, I'll ~ your bottom!** 如果你再那样做, 我就揍你的屁股!
B *n* 打屁股; **to give sb. a ~** 打某人的屁股一下

spanking /ˈspæŋkɪŋ/
A *n* 打屁股; **to give sb. a ~** 打某人一顿屁股
B *adj attrib* 1 colloq (impressive) 漂亮的; **a ~ new car/kitchen** 崭新的汽车/厨房 2 colloq (very good) 极好的; **to have a ~ (good) time** 玩得很愉快 3 (quick) 轻快的; **at a ~ pace** 以飞快的速度

spanner /ˈspænə(r)/ *n* Brit 扳手; **to throw** *or* **put a ~ in the works** fig 从中捣乱; **the car won't start; that's really thrown a ~ in the works** 汽车发动不起来; 那可真要坏事了

spar[1] /spɑː(r)/
A *vi* (*pres p etc.* **-rr-**) 1 Sport **to ~ with sb.** «*boxer*» 与某人练习拳击 2 (argue) **to ~ with sb.** 与某人争论
B *n* (sparring) 一阵争论

spar[2] *n* 1 Naut [尤指用作桅杆的] 圆材 2 Aviat 翼梁

spare /speə(r)/
A *adj* 1 (not occupied) 闲置的 ‹*room, desk*›; (not used) 不用的; (in reserve) 备用的; **a ~ bed/seat** 空床/空座; **~ cash for the book/winter holiday** 买书/过寒假的闲钱; **will there be any ~ men/women at the party?** colloq 聚会上会有没伴的男人/女人吗?; **do you have a ~ shirt by any chance?** 或许你有不穿的衬衫?; **a ~ ticket for the match** 比赛多余的门票; **to be going ~** Brit colloq 没人要; **this food/desk is going ~** 这些食物没人想吃/这张书桌没人用 2 (free) 空闲的 ‹*time*›; **do you have a ~ minute?** 你现在有空吗?; **not to have a ~ moment** 没有一点空 3 (lean) 瘦削的; **to be ~ of build** *or* **stature** 体形瘦削; **his body was lean and ~** 他骨瘦如柴 4 (elegantly simple) 简朴的 ‹*decoration, style*›; **the precise, ~ movements of the dancers** 舞蹈演员们准确而简洁的动作 5 (meagre) 简单的 ‹*diet, meal*› 6 *pred* Brit colloq (frantic) **to go ~** 气急败坏; **to drive sb. ~ (with worry)** 使某人 (忧虑得) 发狂
B *n* (object) 备用品; (component) 备件; (wheel) 备用轮; (tyre) 备用胎; (ticket) 余票; **a set of ~s** 一套备用品; **have my pen: I've got a ~** 用我的钢笔吧, 我还有一支; **take a ~ (just in case)** 带一件备用 (以防万一) 吧; **~s for sth.** 某物的配件
C *vt* 1 (give, lend) 匀出; (be able to afford to give or spend) 花得起; (make available) 拿得出; **can you ~ a cigarette?** 能给我一支烟吗?; **I've got plenty of pens, so I suppose I can ~ one** 我有很多钢笔, 所以我想我可以让出一支; **if you can ~ a moment, …** 如果你能空出一点时间的话, …; **I can ~ 5 minutes** 我能抽出 5 分钟; **can you ~ me ten pounds?** 你能借给我 10 英镑吗?; **I can't ~ the time to stand about chatting to you!** 我可没闲功夫站在一边跟你聊天!; **I can ~ £250 for Christmas presents** 我可以拿出 250 英镑买圣诞礼物; **to ~ a thought for sb.** 为某人着想; **to have sth. to ~** 有多余的某物; **there's no time to ~!** 不能再耽搁了!; **I had no energy/time to ~ for the housework** 我没力气/时间做家务; **I caught the train with only a couple of minutes to ~** 我赶上火车时就剩几分钟了; **that turkey will feed ten people with some to ~** 那只火鸡十个人也吃不完; **they won the match with something to ~** 他们没费全力就赢了比赛 2 colloq (manage without) 用不着 ‹*person*›; **I just can't ~ him today** 我今天实在缺不了他 3 (treat leniently) 放过; **the plague did not ~ any of the villagers** 村民们无一幸免于瘟疫; **to ~ sb.'s life** 饶某人的命; **please ~ me!** 求求你饶了我吧!; **if I'm ~d** hum 如果我能活下来; **the lumberjack ~d a few trees** 伐木工人留了几棵树没砍; **to be ~d from demolition** «*building*» 未遭毁坏; **the report ~s no one** (criticizes all) 这份报告批评了所有人; (blames all) 这份报告认为所有人都有责任; **to ~ sb.'s feelings** 照顾某人的感受 4 (protect from) 免去; **to ~ sb. sth.** 为某人免除某事; **try to ~ her as much distress as possible** 尽量不要让她难受; **I'll ~ you the suspense, and tell you exactly what happened** 我就不卖关子了, 直接告诉你发生了什么事吧; **I'll ~ you the job of washing up** 我就免了你洗碗吧; **I just wanted to ~ her any trouble** 我就是不想让她受累; **to ~ sb. the details** 不告诉某人细节; **~ me the sarcasm** 没必要对我冷嘲热讽吧; **to ~ sb. the expense of sth./doing sth.** 省去某人购买某物/做某事的花费; **he was ~d his life** 他捡回了一条命; **the surgeon ~d him the knife** hum 外科医生没有给他做手术; **the north will be ~d much of the bad weather** 这种糟糕的天气将基本不会出现在北方 5 (withhold) 吝惜; **to ~ no effort/inconvenience/pains (doing** *or* **to do sth.)** (做某事) 不遗余力/不厌其烦/不辞辛劳; **no trouble was ~d to ensure our comfort** 为了保证我们的舒适, 什么办法都用过了; **~ your pains: I've done it myself!** 不用麻烦了, 我自己已经做好了!; **a willing helper who never ~s any effort** 竭诚助人的人
D *v refl* 1 (not make effort) **not to ~ oneself** 不遗余力 2 (avoid) **to ~ oneself expense/effort** 节省开支/少费劲; **to ~ oneself an unnecessary trip** 省得跑一趟; **to ~ oneself the bother** *or* **trouble (of doing sth.)** 避免 (做某事的) 麻烦

spare part *n* (mechanical) 机器零件; (electrical) 电子备件; **to feel like a ~** 感到多余

spare part surgery *n* [u] 器官移植手术

spare: ~ **rib** *n* 猪排骨; ~ **room** *n* [尤指客人用的] 备用房间; ~ **time** *n* [u] 业余时间; **to do sth. in one's ~ time** 在闲暇时间做某事; ~ **tyre** *n* 1 Aut 备用轮胎; 2 colloq hum (roll of fat) 腰部赘肉; ~ **wheel** *n* 备用车轮

sparing /ˈspeərɪŋ/ *adj* 节俭的 ‹*use, user*›; 谨慎的 ‹*advice, praise*›; **to be used only in ~ amounts** 只需使用少量; **to be ~ with sth.** 节俭使用某物; **to be ~ of sth.** 吝惜某物

sparingly /ˈspeərɪŋli/ *adv* 节俭地 ‹*spend*›; 量少地 ‹*eat*›; 谨慎地 ‹*praise*›; **to use sth. ~** 节约使用某物; **she gives her advice ~** 她不轻易提建议

spark /spɑːk/
A *n* 1 (from fire) 火花; **(the) ~s will fly** (there will be an argument) 会发生激烈争吵; (there will be a fight) 会打架; **to strike ~s off each other** 互相启发 2 Elec 电火花 3 fig (sparkle) 闪现; **there was a ~ of mischief/excitement/interest in her eyes** 她的眼睛闪出一丝调皮/兴奋/兴致 4 fig (small amount) 一点儿; **he hasn't a ~ of generosity/decency in him** 他没有一点起码的宽宏/体面
B *vi* «*fire*» 飞火星; «*firework, electrical appliance*» 冒火花
C *vt* «*event, electrical failure*» 引发; **the explosion ~ed a fire** 爆炸引起了火灾

Phrasal verb
• **spark off** *vt* 1 [**~ off sth., ~ sth. off**] (provide stimulus for) 引起 ‹*conflict, riot, controversy*› 2 [**~ off sb.**] (stimulate mentally) 启发

sparking plug /ˈspɑːkɪŋ plʌg/ *n* Brit = **spark plug**

sparkle /ˈspɑːkl/
A *vi* 1 (flash, shine brightly) «*flame, firework, eyes*» 发光; «*jewellery, tinsel, snow*» 闪耀; **to ~ with …** fig 因…而闪闪发光 ‹*happiness, wit*› 2 (be vivacious) 生动活泼; (be witty) 富于机智 3 (effervesce) 发泡; (fizz) 发嘶嘶声; **the champagne ~d in the glasses** 香槟酒在玻璃杯里泛着气泡
B *n* 1 [u and c] (flash of light) 闪光; **to add ~ to sth.** 使某物发光; **there was a ~ of mischief/excitement in his eyes** 他的眼睛里闪着调皮/激动的光芒 2 [u] (vivacity) 活力; (wit) 才智; **to lose one's ~** 失去活力; **to add some ~ to one's life** 给生活增添一些激情

sparkler /ˈspɑːklə(r)/ *n* 1 (firework) 烟花棒 2 colloq (jewel, gemstone) 宝石 [尤指钻石]

sparkling /ˈspɑːklɪŋ/
A *adj* 1 (with light) 闪闪发光的 ‹*flame, jewellery, eyes*› 2 (vivacious) 活跃的; (witty) 机智的; **~ with wit/humour** 富于才思/幽默的 3 (carbonated) 起泡的 ‹*mineral water*›; **~ wine** 汽酒
B *adv* 闪光地; **~ clean/white** 洁净得/白得耀眼的

spark plug *n* 火花塞

sparky /ˈspɑːki/ *adj* 活泼的 ‹*person, performance*›; 机敏的 ‹*humour*›

sparring /ˈspɑːrɪŋ/: ~ **match** *n* fig 友好的争论; ~ **partner** *n* 1 (in boxing) 陪练; 2 (in argument) 争论的对手

sparrow /ˈspærəʊ/ *n* 麻雀

sparrowhawk /ˈspærəʊhɔːk/ *n* 雀鹰

sparse /spɑːs/ *adj* 稀少的 ‹*population, vegetation, hair*›; 简朴的 ‹*furnishings, room*›; 匮乏的 ‹*resources, amount*›

sparsely /ˈspɑːsli/ *adv* 稀少地 ‹*populated, wooded, grow*›; 简朴地 ‹*furnished*›

sparseness /ˈspɑːsnɪs/ *n* [u] (of population, vegetation) 稀少; (of furnishings, room) 简朴; (of resources) 匮乏

Spartan /ˈspɑːtən/
A *adj* 1 Hist (of Sparta) 斯巴达人的 2 (*also* **spartan**) fig 清苦的 ‹*conditions, life*›; 简朴的 ‹*meal, accommodation*›
B *n* Hist 斯巴达人 [传统上不追求舒适奢华]

spasm /ˈspæzəm/ *n* 1 [c and u] (of muscle) 痉挛; **to go into ~** 开始抽搐; **to have ~s** 抽搐 2 [c] (of energy, activity, pain) 阵发; **a sudden ~ of pain in the chest** 胸部的突然疼痛; **a ~ of rage swept over him** 他突然感到一阵愤怒; **(to do sth.) in ~s** 一阵一阵地 (做某事)

spasmodic /spæzˈmɒdɪk/ *adj* 1 (caused by spasm) 痉挛性的 ‹*cough*› 2 (intermittent) 一阵阵的 ‹*asthma, cramp, cough*›; **~ periods of intense activity** 时断时续的剧烈活动

spasmodically /spæzˈmɒdɪkli/ *adv* 一阵阵地; **he tends to work ~, only when the mood takes him** 他往往凭性情工作, 没有常性

spastic /ˈspæstɪk/
A *adj* 1 dated (relating to cerebral palsy) 患痉挛性麻痹症的 ‹*person, child*›; 痉挛性的 ‹*paralysis*› 2 colloq offensive (clumsy) 笨拙的; (incompetent) 无能的; **she's ~ at gymnastics** 她做体操动作很笨拙
B *n* 1 dated (person with cerebral palsy) 痉挛性麻痹症患者 2 colloq offensive (clumsy person) 笨蛋; (incompetent person) 无能的人; **he's a total ~!** 他是个十足的笨蛋!

spat[1] /spæt/ *pt, pp* ▸**spit**[1] **A, B**

spat[2] *n* esp Hist (on shoe) [男子穿的] 鞋罩; **a pair of ~s** 一副鞋套

spat[3]
A *n* colloq (quarrel) 小争吵; **to have a ~ with sb.** 同某人争执; **a ~ between sb. and sb.** 某人与某人之间的口角
B *vi* (*pres p etc.* **-tt-**) 发生小争吵; **to ~ with sb.** 与某人发生口角

spatchcock /ˈspætʃkɒk/
A *n* (chicken) 烤炙的开膛鸡; (game bird) 烤炙的开膛猎禽
B *vt* 1 Culin 把…开膛烤炙 ‹*bird*› 2 Brit colloq (incorporate inappropriately) 生硬地插入; **a new**

clause was ~ed into the bill 法案中生生地增加了新的条款

spate /speɪt/ *n* 突然迸发; **a ~ of sth.** 突然涌出的某物; **in full ~** Brit «*river*» 泛滥的; fig «*person*» 滔滔不绝的; «*work*» 全速进行的

spatial /ˈspeɪʃl/ *adj* 空间的

spatial awareness *n* [u] 空间意识

spatiotemporal /ˌspeɪʃəʊˈtempərəl/ *adj* 时空的

spatter /ˈspætə(r)/

A *vt* (scatter, splash) 溅 ‹*mud, oil, blood*›; (deliberately splash, sprinkle) 洒 ‹*mud, oil, blood*›; **to ~ sth. on/over sb./sth., to ~ sb./sth. with sth.** 将某物溅某人一身/洒满某物; **blood-~ed** 血迹斑斑的

B *vi* «*rain*» 滴滴答答地落下; «*mud, blood*» 飞溅; **to ~ down on** *or* **against sb./sth.** 洒落在某人/某物上

C *n* **1** (sprinkling, small shower) 洒落; **a ~ of rain** 一阵雨 **2** (sound) 溅落声; **a ~ of applause** 稀稀落落的掌声

spatula /ˈspætʃʊlə/ *n* **1** (tool) [尤指烹饪和绘画用的] 铲 **2** Brit Med (for pressing the tongue) 压舌板; (for taking cell samples) 切片刀

spawn /spɔːn/

A *n* [u] 卵

B *vi* 产卵

C *vt* **1** Zool 产 ‹*eggs*›; 繁殖 ‹*offspring*› **2** fig often pej (result in) 滋生 ‹*imitators, imitations*›

spawning ground *n* [鱼的] 产卵场

spay /speɪ/ *vt* 切除…的卵巢; **to have** *or* **get one's cat ~ed** 骟猫

SPCA *abbr* Amer = **Society for the Prevention of Cruelty to Animals** 防止虐待动物协会

SPCC *abbr* Amer = **Society for the Prevention of Cruelty to Children** 防止虐待儿童协会

speak /spiːk/

A *vi* (*pt* **spoke**; *pp* **spoken**) **1** (talk) 说话; **please ~ more slowly** 请说得再慢一点; **sorry, did you ~?** 抱歉, 你说话了吗?; **she got up without ~ing** 她一声不吭站了起来; **she ~s so beautifully** 她说话非常动听; **to ~ in a loud/deep/soft voice** 高声/低声/轻声说话; **to ~ in a whisper/monotone** 耳语/声音单调地说话; **she spoke with a broad Irish accent/without a trace of an accent** 她说话爱尔兰口音很重/不带一点口音; **to ~ in Hindi** 说印地语; **permission to ~, sir!** 长官, 请允许我发言!; **~ when you're spoken to!** 别人跟你说话你再开口!; **who's ~ing, please?** (on telephone) 请问是哪位?; **this is Jason ~ing** (on telephone) 我是贾森; **can I ~ to Mr Brown? — ~ing** (on telephone) 我找布朗先生——我就是; **this is your captain ~ing** 我是本次航班的机长; **to ~ in public** 公开讲话; **to ~ to sb.** 对某人说; **~ to me, Albert!** 你倒是说话呀, 艾伯特!; **I am ~ing to you from the People's Square** (radio announcer) 我在人民广场向大家报道; **don't you ~ to me like that/in that tone!** 不许你那样/用那种语气对我说话!; **to ~ about** *or* **of sth./sb.** 谈起某事物/某人; **the person you were ~ing of** 你刚才说到的那个人; **the book ~s of betrayal** 这本书讲述的是背叛的故事; **~ing of lunch/Simon, ...** 说到午餐/西蒙, …; **to ~ well** *or* **highly of sb./sth.** 对某人/某事物评价很高; **she's well spoken of in academic circles** 她在学术界口碑很好; **to ~ about** *or* **of doing sth.** 提及做某事; **he spoke of selling the house** 他说到了卖房子的事情; **~ing as a parent, ...** 作为家长来说, …; **to ~** *or* **~ing personally, I ...** 就我个人而言, …; **she was ~ing personally** 她在表达个人看法; **do you mind if I ~ technically** *or* **scientifically for a moment?** 你介意我说两句行话吗?; **politically/sociologically ~ing** 从政治上/社会学角度讲; **metaphorically ~ing** 打个比方; **generally/roughly/strictly** *or* **properly ~ing** 一般/粗略/严格说来; **no X to ~ of** (very little, if any) 几乎没有 X; (no X worth mentioning) X 不值一提; **had any complaints? — none to ~ of** 有什么不满意的吗? ——那倒说不上; **nothing/nobody to ~ of** 没什么大不了的事物/了不得的人; **there's nothing to ~ of on television tonight** 今晚电视没什么好节目; **not to ~ of ...** 更不用说…; **so to ~** 可以说 **2** (converse) 谈话; **they're not ~ing (to each other)** 他们谁也不和谁说话了; **would you prefer it if we spoke in Russian?** 我们用俄语交谈好吗?; **to ~ about** *or* **of sth./sb.** 谈论某事物/某人; **we spoke of this and that** 我们谈天说地; **to ~ to** *or* esp Amer **with sb. about sth.** 和某人谈某事物; **who was that you were ~ing to?** 你刚才在和谁说话?; **I won't ~ to her again** 我再也不和她说话了; **I need to ~ to him urgently** 我有急事要跟他谈; **I don't know them to ~ to** 我知道他们, 但没说过话; **to ~ through an interpreter/a solicitor** 通过传译员交谈/事务律师来交涉 **3** (make a speech) 发言; **to rise to ~** 起立发言; **are you ~ing at the conference?** 你要在会上发言吗?; **to ~ in the Assembly/House/Senate** 在州议会/众议院/参议院发言; **to ~ (to sb.) about** *or* **on sth.** (对某人) 发言讲述某事; **to ~ on** *or* **about cultural diversity** 作文化多样性方面的演讲; **to ~ against/in favour of sth.** 发言反对/赞成某事物 **4** fig (express sth.) «*scene, gesture*» 有意义; **this poem ~s to me in a very special way** 这首诗向我传达了很特别的意义; **the story spoke to him directly** 这个故事触动了他; **that look spoke louder than any words could have done** 那个表情胜过千言万语

B *vt* (*pt* **spoke**; *pp* **spoken**) **1** (communicate in) 说 ‹*language*›; **can** *or* **do you ~ Chinese?** 你会说汉语吗?; **'French/Italian spoken'** "本处说法语/意大利语"; **English as it is spoken** 英语口语; **we don't ~ the same language** lit 我们语言不通; fig 我们没有共同语言 **2** (utter) 说出 ‹*name*›; 念出 ‹*line, poem*›; **to ~ the truth** 说真话; **to ~ one's mind** 说心里话

C **-speak** *combining form* colloq 行话; **computer/management/lawyer~** 计算机业/管理界/律师的行话

Phrasal verbs

- **speak for** *vt* [**~ for sb./sth.**] **1** (on behalf of) 为…讲话 ‹*person, organization*›; **to ~ for the working classes** 代表劳动阶级; **I think I ~ for everyone here when I say ...** 当我说…时, 我认为是反映了在场所有人的心声; **~ing for myself ...** 就我而言…; **~ for yourself!** 那只是说你自己吧!; **let her ~ for herself** 让她自己说; **he's old enough to ~ for himself** 他不小了, 可以自己表达意见了; **the facts ~ for themselves** 事实不言自明 **2** **to be spoken for** (be reserved) 被预订; (be engaged) 已订婚; **he's spoken for** 他已名草有主
- **speak out** *vi* (say what one thinks) 表明意见; (speak openly) 公开宣布; **he's not afraid to ~ out** 他不怕畅所欲言; **to ~ out about** *or* **on sth.** 表明对某事物的看法; **to ~ out against/in favour of sth.** 公然反对/赞成某事物
- **speak to** *vt* **1** [**~ to sb.**] (reprimand, advise) 责备; **to ~ to sb. about sth.** 就某事数落某人 **2** [**~ to sth.**] (talk about) 谈论; **please ~ to the point** 请不要走题
- **speak up** *vi* **1** (talk louder) 大声说话; **please ~ up!** 请大点声讲! **2** (dare to talk) 大胆讲话; **nobody spoke up** 没人敢说话; **to ~ up for sb./sth.** 为某人/某事物仗义执言

speakeasy /ˈspiːkiːzi/ *n* Amer Hist (club) 非法售酒的夜总会; (shop) 非法经营的酒店

speaker /ˈspiːkə(r)/ *n* **1** (person talking) 发言者; **a ~ from the floor** 台下发言的听众 **2** (at event, lecture) 演讲者; **the previous ~** 前一位发言人; **a guest/an after-dinner ~** 特邀/宴会后演讲人; **to be a good/poor ~** 擅长/不擅长演讲 **3** (of language) 讲某种语言的人; **a Japanese/Russian ~** 讲日语/俄语的人 **4** **Speaker** esp Brit Pol [议院的] 议长; **Mr/Mdm S~** 议长先生/女士 **5** Audio 扬声器; **a pair of ~s** 一对扬声器

speaking /ˈspiːkɪŋ/

A *adj attrib* **1** (involving speech) 讲话的; **a ~ robot** 语音机器人; **a normal ~ voice** 正常的说话声 **2** (lifelike) 逼真的 ‹*likeness*›; 栩栩如生的 ‹*portrait*›

B *n* [u] **1** (conveying information, emotion) 讲话; **~ and writing in a foreign language** 外语的说与写 **2** (in public) (act) 演讲; (skill) 演讲术

C **-speaking** *combining form* **1** (specifying language) 讲…语言的; **English/French~** 讲英语/法语的 **2** (describing vocal quality) 说话有…特点的; **slow/soft~** 说话慢的/轻柔的; **plain ~** 心直口快的

speaking: ~ clock *n* Brit 电话报时服务; **~ engagement** *n* 演讲预约; **~ part, ~ role** *ns* 有台词的角色; **~ terms** *npl* **to be on ~ terms with sb.** 与某人是泛泛之交; **to be on ~ terms with sb. again** 与某人言归于好; **we're not on ~ terms** 我们互不搭腔; **~ tour** *n* 巡回演讲; **to be on a ~ tour** 作巡回演讲

speak-your-weight machine *n* 语音体重机

spear /spɪə(r)/

A *n* **1** (weapon) 矛; **warriors armed with ~s** 持长矛的勇士; **to catch fish with ~s** 用叉捕鱼 **2** (stalk) 嫩枝; (of asparagus, broccoli) 嫩茎

B *vt* **1** (pierce with weapon) 用矛刺; **to ~ fish** 叉鱼; **to ~ sb. to death** 刺死某人 **2** (pierce with cutlery) 用叉子叉起

spear: ~ carrier *n* colloq **1** (actor) 龙套; **to be a ~ carrier** 跑龙套; **2** (unimportant person) 无足轻重的参与者; **~gun** *n* 水下鱼矛枪

spearhead /ˈspɪəhed/

A *n* **1** lit (point) 矛头 **2** fig (leader) 先锋; (group) 先头部队; **to act as (a) ~** 担当前导

B *vt* 做…的先锋 ‹*attack, campaign*›

spearmint /ˈspɪəmɪnt/ *n* [u] 绿薄荷; **~ gum/toffee** 绿薄荷口香糖/太妃糖

spec[1] /spek/ *n* [u] colloq (speculation) **on ~** 碰运气; **to buy shares on ~** 凭运气购买股票

spec[2] *n* colloq = **specification 2**

special /ˈspeʃl/

A *adj* **1** (out of the ordinary) 特别的; **to pay ~ attention to sth.** 特别注意某事物; **to take ~ care of sth.** 特别照管某物; **he regarded such people with ~ hatred/contempt/affection** 他特别痛恨/鄙视/喜欢这类人; **~ concessions for regular customers** 针对常客的特价让利; **a ~ discount** 特价折扣; **~ offers this week** 本周的特价商品; **to be on ~ offer** 正在特价出售; **would you, as a ~ favour, let me choose?** 你能不能特别照顾我一下, 让我来选?; **she did me a ~ kindness by letting me borrow her car** 她对我特别好, 把车借给了我; **~ treatment** 特殊待遇; **a ~ occasion** 特殊场合; **you're a ~ case** 你是特例; **~ powers to deal with the emergency** 处理紧急情况的特权; **he has a ~ place in our affections** *or* **hearts** 我们特别喜欢他; **a ~ feature of sth.** 某事物的特色; **a ~ feature on sth.** Journ 关于某事物的专题文章; **we decided to give ~ prominence to that story** 我们决定重点报道那一事件; **to cook something ~** 做一道特别的菜; **anything ~ on TV tonight?** 今晚电视上有什么特别节目吗?; **there wasn't anything ~ about him** 他没有什么与众不同的; **the wine is nothing ~** 这种葡萄酒没什么特别的; **someone ~** 出众的人 **2** (for specific purpose) 专用的 ‹*tool, notebook*›; 专门的 ‹*meeting*›; **to wear ~ clothing** 穿着特制服装; **a ~ account** Fin 特别账户; **a ~ train/flight** 专列/专机; **if it**

means a ~ journey 如果需要专程前往; UK ~ forces 英国特种部队; a ~ ambassador/representative 特命大使/特别代表 3 (particular) 具体的; the official with ~ responsibility for public health 具体负责公共卫生的官员; in this one ~ instance 就这一次; I made a ~ point of asking her 我特地问了她; there was one ~ job she wanted 有一个职位她特别想得到; to have something ~ to do 有要做的具体事情; to be ~ to sb./sth. 仅限于某人/某物 4 (personal) 独有的 ‹interest›; 专用的 ‹pen, bowl›; sb.'s ~ way of doing sth. 某人做某事的独特方法; sb.'s ~ friend/chair 某人的密友/专座
B n 1 [c] (dish) 特色菜; the chef's ~ 大厨推荐的特色菜 2 [c and u] colloq (special offer) 特价; to be on ~ esp Amer 卖特价; sth. on ~ this week 本周的特价某商品 3 [c] TV, Radio (additional service) 特别节目; Journ 特别报道; Transp 专门的交通工具; an all-night/a late-night ~ 通宵/深夜特别节目; this train is a football ~ 这列火车是足球迷专列; a holiday ~ to Brighton 去布赖顿的度假专线车 4 [c] (speciality) 专长; the ~s of a barman 酒吧服务员的招牌饮料; get Jim to bowl one of his ~s 让吉姆来投他最擅长的球 5 [c] Brit colloq = special constable

special: S~ Administrative Region n [中国的] 特别行政区; ~ **agent** n 特工; **S~ Air Service** n Brit 空军特勤团; **S~ Branch** n Brit 政治保安处; ~ **constable** n Brit 临时警察; ~ **delivery** n [u] 1 Brit 次日达; to send sth. by ~ delivery 用次日达邮寄某物; 2 Amer [比普通邮件收费高的] 特快专递; ~ **drawing rights** npl 特别提款权; **S~ Economic Zone** n 经济特区; ~ **edition** n 特别版; ~ **education** n [u] [残疾儿童的] 特殊教育; ~ **effects** npl 特技效果; ~ **hospital** n Brit 精神病医院; ~ **interest group** n 特殊利益集团; ~ **interest holiday** n [参加某个活动的] 特色假期

specialism /'speʃəlɪzəm/ n 1 [c] (special interest) 专业 2 [u] (specialization) 专业化

specialist /'speʃəlɪst/
A n 1 (expert) 专家; a ~ in sth. 某方面的专家 2 ▸p. 409 Med 专科医生; a cancer ~ 癌症专科医生
B adj 专业的 ‹knowledge, area, magazine›; 专门的 ‹shop›

speciality /ˌspeʃɪ'æləti/ n (special service) 特色服务; (special product) 特产; (special food) 特色菜; (special skill) 专长; (special interest) 专业; a local ~ 土特产; a ~ dish 特色菜; a house ~ 私家菜; pizza is his ~ 比萨饼是他的拿手菜; his ~ is telling bad jokes 他专爱讲下流的笑话

speciality act n (performer) [尤指娱乐性的] 特色演员; (performance) 特色表演

specialization /ˌspeʃəlaɪ'zeɪʃn, Amer -lɪ'z-/ n [u] (act) 专门化; (area) 专业领域; ~ in sth. 某方面的专业化

specialize /'speʃəlaɪz/ vi 从事专门研究; to ~ in sth. 专攻某领域

specialized /'speʃəlaɪzd/ adj 专业的 ‹knowledge, skill, job›

special licence n Brit 结婚特别许可 [允许不在通常规定的时间及地点结婚]

specially /'speʃəli/ adv 1 (specifically) 专门地; I came over ~ to see her 我特意过来看她 2 colloq (particularly) 特别地 ‹interesting, helpful, difficult›; I like animals, ~ dogs 我喜欢动物，尤其是狗

special: ~ measures npl 1 Brit Sch [对不达标学校所采取的] 特殊扶持措施; to place a school on ~ measures 对一个学校进行特殊扶持; to be on ~ measures 受到特殊扶持; 2 Jur [为证人提供的] 特别保护措施; ~ **needs** npl [残疾儿童的] 特殊教育需要; a ~ needs teacher 特殊教育教师; ~ **pleading** n [u] [尤指规避一方缺点的] 诡辩; ~ **relationship** n [二战后英美之间的] 特殊关系; ~ **school** n Brit [为残疾儿童设立的] 特殊学校

specialty /'speʃəlti/ n Amer = speciality

specie /'spi:ʃi:/ n [u] formal 硬币; in ~ 以硬币形式

species /'spi:ʃi:z/ n (pl **species**) 种; the human ~ 人种; an endangered ~ 濒危物种

species barrier n 物种屏障; to cross or jump the ~ 越过物种屏障

specific /spə'sɪfɪk/
A adj 1 (detailed) 详细的; (precise) 明确的; (exact) 具体的; to be ~ on or about sth. 对某事说得很明确 2 (unique) 特定的; to be ~ to sb./sth. 为某人/某事物特有
B **specifics** npl (particular aspects or details) 详情; to get down to ~s 进入细节

specifically /spə'sɪfɪkli/ adv 1 (specially) 特别地; ~, we must focus on the following points 我们尤其要集中探讨以下几点; ~ for children/rough terrain 专门针对儿童/崎岖不平的地形 2 (explicitly) 明确地; more ~ 更明确地说; to state ~ that ... 清楚地说明… 3 (in particular) 具体来说

specification /ˌspesɪfɪ'keɪʃn/ n 1 [u] (making specific) 明确说明 2 [c] (detailed description) 规格; a standard ~ 标准规格; built to sb.'s ~s 按照某人的设计建造的; to comply with ~s 遵照规格; a job ~ 工作规范; technical ~s 技术规格 3 [c] (requirement) 要求; the only ~ is that previous experience is necessary 唯一的要求是必须有过工作经历

specification sheet n (产品) 说明书

specific gravity n = relative density

specify /'spesɪfaɪ/ vt 具体说明; as specified above 如上所述; unless otherwise specified 除非另有规定; not specified elsewhere 未在别处说明的

specimen /'spesɪmən/ n 1 (of animal, plant, mineral, handwriting) 样本; to collect ~s 收集标本; to analyse a ~ 分析样品 2 Med 抽样; a blood/urine ~ 血样/尿样; a tissue ~ 组织样本 3 colloq (person) 某种人; a fine ~ of manhood hum 男子汉的典型; an odd or weird ~ 古怪的家伙

specimen: ~ charge, ~ count ns 主要指控; ~ **jar** n 1 Med (for urine sample) 尿样缸; 2 (for preservation of specimen) 标本缸

specious /'spi:ʃəs/ adj formal 1 (superficially plausible) 似是而非的 ‹argument, reason›; ~ logic 貌似有理的逻辑 2 (deceptively attractive) 华而不实的 ‹appearance, beauty, glamour›

speck /spek/
A n 1 (spot) 斑点; (of dust, soot) 污点; (of metal) 锈斑; a ~ of blood 一滴血迹; a ~ on the horizon 地平线上的一个小点 2 (particle) 微量; just a ~ 就一点点
B vt usu passive 使有斑点; to be ~ed with blood 布满点点血迹; a skirt with a ~ed pattern 有斑点花纹的裙子

speckle /'spekl/
A n (spot) 斑点; (patch of colour) 色斑
B vt 使有斑点; to be ~d with sth. 布满点点的某物

speckled /'spekld/ adj 有斑点的

specs /speks/ npl colloq 眼镜

spec sheet n colloq = specification sheet

spectacle /'spektəkl/
A n 1 (performance) 精彩的表演; (display) 壮观的场面; to stage or put on a ~ 举行盛大的演出 2 (sight) 奇观; a tremendous ~ 宏伟的场景; a daunting/frightening ~ 令人望而却步的/骇人的场面 3 pej (event, scene) 引人注目的景象; to make a ~ of oneself 出洋相
B **spectacles** npl Brit 眼镜; a pair of ~s 一副眼镜

spectacled /'spektəkld/ adj 1 (wearing glasses) 戴眼镜的 2 Zool 有眼镜状斑纹的

spectacular /spek'tækjələ(r)/
A adj 1 (dramatic, eye-catching) 壮观的; the erupting volcano was a ~ sight 这次火山爆发的景象很壮观 2 (impressive) 引人注目的; (extraordinary) 惊人的; a ~ success 辉煌的成功; a ~ increase in the number of holidaymakers 度假者人数的剧增; a ~ rise in house prices 房价的暴涨
B n 壮观场面; a TV ~ 场面宏大的电视节目; a Christmas ~ 壮观的圣诞节表演; a 3-hour ~ 长达 3 小时的盛大演出

spectacularly /spek'tækjʊləli/ adv 引人注目地 ‹win, collapse, rise, fail›; 惊人地 ‹good, bad, stupid›; it was ~ successful/unsuccessful 它取得了辉煌的成功/遭到了惊人的失败

spectate /spek'teɪt/ vi 观看

spectator /spek'teɪtə(r)/ n 观众; I didn't take part in the demonstration, I was just a ~ 我没有参加示威，我只是个旁观者; to be present as a ~ 到现场观看

spectator sport n 吸引大量观众的体育运动

specter /'spektə(r)/ n Amer = spectre

spectra /'spektrə/ pl ▸spectrum

spectral /'spektrəl/ adj 1 (ghostlike) 幽灵似的 2 (of spectrum) 光谱的

spectre /'spektə(r)/ n Brit 1 (ghost) 幽灵 2 fig (mental image) [似幽灵般] 缠绕内心的恐惧; the ~ of war 战争的魔影

spectrogram /'spektrəgræm/ n 光谱图

spectrograph /'spektrəgrɑ:f, Amer -græf/ n 光谱仪

spectrometer /spek'trɒmɪtə(r)/ n 分光计

spectroscope /'spektrəskəʊp/ n 分光镜

spectroscopic /ˌspektrə'skɒpɪk/ adj 分光镜的 ‹image›; 使用分光镜的 ‹technique, examination›; ~ analysis/measurement 光谱分析/分光测定

spectroscopy /spek'trɒskəpi/ n [u] 光谱学

spectrum /'spektrəm/ (pl **spectra**) n 1 (of colours) 光谱 2 (range) 电磁波谱 3 (distribution) 频谱 4 fig (of ideas, emotions, abilities) 范围; at the other end of the ~ 在领域的另一端; a broad ~ of views 广泛的不同意见; people across the political ~ 各个政治派别的人

specula /'spekjʊlə/ pl ▸speculum

speculate /'spekjʊleɪt/
A vi 1 (form theory, opinion) 猜测; to ~ as to why 推测为什么; to ~ about or on sth. 推断某事 2 Fin 投机; to ~ on the Stock Exchange 炒股; to ~ for or on a rise/fall 看涨/看跌投机; to ~ in sth. 做某物的投机买卖; one must ~ to accumulate 想发财就得敢冒险
B vt 猜测; to ~ that ... 推测…; it has been widely ~d that ... 人们普遍猜测…; to ~ what/where/who ... 对是什么/在哪里/是谁…作推测

speculation /ˌspekjʊ'leɪʃn/ n [u and c] 1 (conjecture) 猜测; ~ about or over sth. 关于某事物的推测; ~ that sth. will happen 某事会发生的推断; ~ as to why 有关为什么的猜测; to give rise to/be the subject of ~ 引起猜测 2 Fin 投机; ~ in sth. 某物的投机买卖

speculative /'spekjʊlətɪv, Amer also 'spekjəleɪtɪv/ adj 1 (based on conjecture) 推测的; his conclusions are purely ~ 他的结论纯粹是猜测; to give sb. a ~ glance 向某人投去试探的一瞥 2 Comm, Fin 投机性的 ‹investment›; a ~ venture 投机生意

speculatively /'spekjʊlətɪvli, Amer also 'spekjəleɪtɪvli/ adv 1 (based on conjecture) 推测性地 ‹ask, think, discuss›; 探究地 ‹look at› 2 Comm, Fin 投机性地

S

speculator /ˈspekjʊleɪtə(r)/ *n* 投机者; **a ~ in sth.** 某物的投机商

speculum /ˈspekjʊləm/ *n* (*pl* **specula**) 扩张器; **a nasal/vaginal ~** 鼻镜/阴道窥器

sped /sped/ *pt, pp* ▸**speed B, C**

speech /spiːtʃ/ *n* **1** [u] (faculty) 说话能力; (action) 言语; **the power** *or* **faculty of ~** 言语能力; **in** *or* **by ~** 以口头形式 **2** [u] (language) 口语; **everyday ~** 日常会话; **direct/indirect** *or* **reported ~** 直接/间接引语 **3** [u] (manner of speaking) 说话方式; **clear** *or* **distinct ~** 清楚的口齿 **4** [c] (oration) 演讲; **to give** *or* **make** *or* **deliver a ~** 作演讲; **a ~ on** *or* **about sb./sth.** 关于某人/某事物的讲话; **the S~ from the Throne** Brit 君主致词 **5** [c] Theat 台词

speech: ~ act *n* 言语行为; **~ clinic** *n* 言语障碍矫正所; **~ community** *n* 言语社区; **~ day** *n* Brit [一年一度的] 授奖演讲日; **~ defect** *n* **= ~ impediment**; **~ difficulty** *n* [c and u] 言语障碍; **~ disorder** *n* 言语失常

speechify /ˈspiːtʃɪfaɪ/ *vi* pej 喋喋不休

speechifying /ˈspiːtʃɪfaɪɪŋ/ *n* [u] pej 喋喋不休; **there was much ~ at the opening ceremony** 开幕式上很多人在高谈阔论

speech: ~-impaired *adj* 有言语障碍的; **~ impediment** *n* 言语障碍

speechless /ˈspiːtʃlɪs/ *adj* 说不出话的; **to be ~ with ...** 因…而说不出话来; **I was ~ at the sight/the news** 看到那一幕/听到那消息我一时说不出话来; **I'm ~!** colloq 我无话可说!

speech: ~ maker *n* 演讲人; **~ organ** *n* 言语器官; **~ pattern** *n* 言语模式; **~ recognition** *n* [u] 语音识别; **~ sound** *n* 语音; **~ synthesis** *n* [u] 语音合成; **~ therapist** ▸**p. 409** *n* 言语矫治师; **~ therapy** *n* [u] 言语矫治; **~ training** *n* [u] (for public speakers, actors, etc.) 演讲训练; (to improve speech) 言语训练; **~-writer** ▸**p. 409** *n* 演讲稿撰写人

speed /spiːd/

A *n* **1** [c and u] (rate of movement or action) 速度; (quickness of movement) 快速; **with (great) ~** 快速地; **~ of hand** 变换手法的速度; **with the ~ of light/an arrow** 以光速/离弦之箭般; **to gather** *or* **build up** *or* **pick up ~** 加速; **to reduce** *or* **drop one's ~** 减速; **high** *or* **great ~** 高速; **at ~** 快速地; **to put on a burst of ~** 突然加速; **with lightning ~** 以闪电般的速度; **to have a (good) turn of ~** 能突然加速; **with all ~** 以全速; **to make all ~** 全速前进; **full ~ ahead!** 全速前进! ; **at a ~ of 150 mph** 以150英里的时速; **trains travelling at ~s in excess of 150 mph** 以超过150英里时速行驶的火车; **the ~ of light/sound** 光速/音速; **an aircraft with a maximum** *or* **top ~ of 300 mph** 最高时速为300英里的飞机; **an average/a steady ~ of ...** …的平均速度/匀速; **at breakneck ~** 以危险的速度; **to be up to ~** colloq (fully informed, up to date) 了解最新情况; **to bring sb. up to ~** colloq (fully inform) 告知某人全部情况; (make perform at the required rate or level) 使某人达到应有水准; **the cost of bringing the schools up to ~** 使学校达标需要的费用; **for ~** 为了快速起见; **shorthand ~** 速记速度; **that's about my ~** Amer 这才合我的心愿 **2** [c] Phot (sensitivity) 感光度; (time) 快门速度; **to take photographs at a ~ of ...** 以…的快门速度拍照 **3** [u] colloq (drug) 安非他明 **4** [c] (gear) (of bicycle) 变速器; Amer (of motor vehicle) 排挡; **a car with five forward ~s** 有五个前进挡的汽车; **a ten-~ bicycle** 十速自行车; **a three-~ gear** 三挡变速器

B *vi* **1** (*pt, pp* **sped**) 快速前行; **to ~ along sth.** 沿着某物快速移动; **to ~ past sth.** 从某物旁边疾驰而过; **the car sped along the road** 汽车在路上疾驰; **to ~ on one's way** 疾驰上路; **we got into the car and sped home** 我们上了车，疾驰回家; **to ~ to the rescue** 急驰前往救援; **the hours sped by** fig 时间飞逝 **2** (*pt, pp* **~ed**) (drive too fast) 超速行驶; **to be caught ~ing** 超速驾车被抓

C *vt* (*pt, pp* **~ed** *or* **sped**) **1** (make quicker) 加快…的速度 ‹*work*›; **to ~ sb.'s recovery** 加快某人的康复 **2** (take quickly) 快速运送 ‹*passenger, freight*›; **the taxi sped us into the city centre** 出租车把我们急送到了市中心

Phrasal verb

- **speed up** (*pt, pp* **~ed**)

A *vi* 加速; **work has ~ed up** 工作已经加快了速度

B *vt* [**~ sth. up, ~ up sth.**] 加快…的速度; **to ~ up the introduction of sth.** 加快引入某物; **output must be ~ed up** 必须加快产出; **can you ~ things up a bit?** 你们能不能做事快一点?

speed: ~ball *n* colloq **1** [c] (drug) "急速球" [指掺了安非他明或可卡因的海洛因]; **2** [c] (punchball) 拳击小吊球; **3** [u] Amer (game) 速球运动 [一种类似于足球的运动，但是手可以触球]; **~boat** *n* 快艇; **~ bump** *n* 减速垄; **~ camera** *n* 超速监控摄像机; **~ dating** *n* [u] 快速约会

speed dial

A *n* [u] [电话的] 快速拨号功能

B **speed-dial** *vt* (*pres p etc.* **-ll-** Brit, **-l-** Amer) 快速拨 ‹*number*›; 给…快速拨号 ‹*person*›

speed: ~ freak *n* colloq 安非他明瘾君子; **~ hump** *n* Brit **= ~ bump**

speedily /ˈspiːdɪli/ *adv* 迅速地; **as ~ as possible** 越快越好

speediness /ˈspiːdɪnɪs/ *n* [u] 快速; **thank you for the ~ of your reply** 感谢您立即回复

speeding /ˈspiːdɪŋ/ *n* [u] 超速行驶; **a ~ fine** 超速罚款

speeding offence *n* 超速违法

speed: ~ limit *n* 速度限制; **to drive within the ~ limit** 在限速范围内行驶; **to exceed** *or* **break the ~ limit** 超速; **~ limiter** *n* 限速器; **~ merchant** *n* colloq 飙车者

speedo /ˈspiːdəʊ/ *n* colloq **= speedometer**

speedometer /spɪˈdɒmɪtə(r)/ *n* 速度计

speed: ~-read *vt* 快速阅读; **~ reading** *n* [u] 快速阅读; **~ restriction** *n* 速度限制; **~ skating** ▸**p. 307** *n* [u] 速度滑冰

speedster /ˈspiːdstə(r)/ *n* colloq (fast person) 速度快的人; (fast driver) 快速驾驶者; (fast vehicle) 高速行驶的车辆; **a nippy little second-hand ~** 小巧灵便的二手跑车; **he's a bit of a ~** 他开车相当快

speed: ~ trap *n* 雷达测速器; **~-up** *n* colloq 增速; **a ~-up in production/the work rate** 生产的加速/工作效率的提高

speedway /ˈspiːdweɪ/ *n* **1** [u] Brit (motorcycle racing) 摩托车赛 **2** [c] (track) 摩托车赛道; (stadium) 摩托车赛场

speedway racing ▸**p. 307** *n* [u] Brit 摩托车赛

speedwell /ˈspiːdwel/ *n* [u and c] 婆婆纳 [一种爬行植物]

speedy /ˈspiːdi/ *adj* **1** (occurring quickly) 迅速的; **to wish sb. a ~ recovery** 祝愿某人早日康复; **a ~ settlement of the strike** 罢工的即时解决 **2** (moving quickly) 动作快的 ‹*person*›; 快速的 ‹*animal, vehicle, movement*›

speleologist /ˌspiːlɪˈɒlədʒɪst/ *n* (expert) 洞穴学家; (explorer) 洞穴探险家

speleology /ˌspiːlɪˈɒlədʒi/ ▸**p. 307** *n* [u] (study) 洞穴学; (exploration) 洞穴探险; **to have an interest in ~** 对洞穴探险感兴趣

spell[1] /spel/ *n* **1** (magic words) 咒语; **to recite** *or* **chant a ~** 念咒; **a magic/an evil ~** 魔咒/毒咒; **to be under a ~** 中了魔法; **to cast** *or* **put a ~ on** *or* **over sb./sth.** 对某人/某物施咒; **a ~ had been laid over the land** 这片土地中了魔咒; **to break/remove a ~** 打破/去除魔咒 **2** (attractive power) 魅力; **the mysterious ~ of music** 音乐的神秘魅力; **to be under sb.'s ~** 被某人迷住; **to be under the ~ of sb.'s beauty/stories** 被某人的美貌/故事迷住; **he is waking from her ~** 他正摆脱她的诱惑

spell[2]

A *n* **1** (period) 一段时间; **after a brief** *or* **short ~** 短暂的一段时间以后; **to do a ~ in prison** 坐一阵子牢; **to go through a bad ~** 有一段痛苦经历; **a rainy/sunny ~** 一段多雨/晴好的天气; **a long/short ~ of windy weather** 长/短时间的大风天气; **she suffers from dizzy ~s** 她一阵阵头晕 **2** (turn) 一段工作时间; **can I have a ~ on the computer now?** 现在我能用一会儿计算机吗? ; **he spent a brief ~ on the Washington Post** 他在《华盛顿邮报》短暂工作过; **a ~ of gardening/of duty in the Far East** 做园丁/在远东服役的一阵子; **he did two ~s as director** 他当过两任主任; **to take a ~ at sth./doing sth.** 轮流做某事; **to take ~s at the wheel** *or* **at driving** 轮流驾驶

B *vt* esp Amer 暂时替换; **I'll find someone to ~ him** 我会找人顶他一阵; **to ~ sb. at the wheel/oars** 替换某人开车/划桨

spell[3] (*pt, pp* **~ed,** esp Brit **spelt**)

A *vt* **1** (in writing) 拼写; (aloud) 拼读; **the word is ~ed like this** 这个词是这样拼的; **will you ~ that please?** 请你拼一下那个词好吗? ; **the dictionary ~s it R-H-Y-M-E** 它在词典里拼作R-H-Y-M-E; **to ~ sth. with/without sth.** 某词的拼写中带有/不带某字母; **to ~ sth. correctly** *or* **right/wrong** 拼对/拼错某词 **2** (be spelling of) 拼作; **C-A-T ~s 'cat'** C-A-T拼成cat一词 **3** fig (imply) 意味着 ‹*success, danger, end*›; **to ~ disaster (for sb.)** (对某人来说) 意味着灾难

B *vi* 拼写; **to ~ well/badly** 拼写能力强/差

Phrasal verb

- **spell out** *vt* [**~ sth. out, ~ out sth.**] **1** (write) 拼写; (say) 拼读 **2** (make clear) 讲清楚; (explain in detail) 详细说明; **let me ~ it out to** *or* **for you: you're fired!** 我跟你明说吧，你被解雇了!

spell: ~binding *adj* 迷人的; **a place of ~binding beauty** 美丽迷人的地方; **~bindingly** *adv* 迷人地; **~bound** *adj* 入迷的; **to hold sb. ~bound** 使某人着迷

spellcheck

A *n* **1** (action) 拼写检查; **to do** *or* **run a ~** 进行拼写检查 **2** **= spellchecker**

B *vt* 检查…的拼写

spell: ~checker *n* 拼写检查程序; **~checking** *n* [u] 拼写检查; **a ~checking program/facility** 拼写检查程序/工具

speller /ˈspelə(r)/ *n* **1** (person) 拼写单词者; **a good/bad ~** 拼写能力强/差的人 **2** Amer (book) 单词拼写课本

spelling /ˈspelɪŋ/ *n* **1** [u] (action, process) 拼写; **~ mistake/test** 拼写错误/测验 **2** [c] (way spelled) 拼法 **3** [u] (ability) 拼写能力

spelling: ~ bee *n* 拼单词比赛; **~ checker** *n* **= spellchecker**

spelt /spelt/ *pt, pp* esp Brit ▸**spell**[3]

spelunker /spɪˈlʌŋkə(r)/ *n* Amer 洞穴探险爱好者

spelunking /spɪˈlʌŋkɪŋ/ ▸**p. 307** *n* [u] Amer 洞穴探险

spend /spend/

A *vt* (*pt, pp* **spent**) **1** (pay out, use) 花 ‹*time, energy*›; **to ~ money on clothes/rent** 花钱买衣服/付租金; **he spent too much on that second-hand car** 他买那辆二手车花了太多的钱; **she spent all her money** 她把钱花光了; **to ~ a fortune (doing sth./on sth.)** 花大钱 (做某事/在某事物上); **not to ~ a penny** *or* **halfpenny on sb./sth.** 不为某人/某事物花一分钱; **we have spent far too**

long on the matter 我们在这件事情上花的时间实在太多了; to ～ time/energy (in) doing sth. 花时间/费精力做某事; to ～ one's life doing sth. 花一生的时间做某事 2 (exhaust) 耗尽; (use up) 用完; they had spent all their ammunition 他们打完了全部弹药; to ～ all one's resources on sth./(in) doing sth. 把所有资源耗在某事/做某事上; the storm had spent its fury *or* itself 暴风雨平息了 3 (pass) 度过 ‹*holiday, weekend*›; how do you ～ your spare time? 你业余时间怎么过?; he ～s hours watching TV/whole days fishing 他一连几个小时看电视/一天到晚地钓鱼; he spent a long time in the library 他在图书馆里待了很长时间; to ～ many happy hours 度过许多快乐时光; he spent five years as a teacher/travelling 他教了5年书/游历了5年; he wanted to ～ more time with his family 他想抽出更多的时间和家人在一起; to ～ the night with sb. euph 和某人一起过夜 [指发生性关系]
B *vi* (*pt, pp* **spent**) 花钱; he ～s as if money grew on trees! 他挥金如土!
C *n* colloq 花费; the average ～ at the restaurant 该餐馆的人均消费

spender /'spendə(r)/ *n* 花钱者; to be a big ～ 花钱大手大脚; an extravagant *or* lavish ～ 挥金如土的人; he's the last of the big ～s iron hum 他真是个挥霍者

spending /'spendɪŋ/ *n* [u] 开销; ～ on education/defence 教育/国防开支

spending: ～ **cut** *n* 开销削减; big ～ cuts in education 教育开支的大幅度削减; ～ **limit** *n* 开销限额; ～ **money** *n* [u] 零用钱; ～ **power** *n* [u] 购买力; ～ **spree** *n* 拼命花钱; to go on a ～ spree 去疯狂购物

spendthrift /'spendθrɪft/
A *n* 挥霍者; to be a ～ 是个浪费金钱的人; she's an awful ～! 她挥金如土!
B *adj attrib* 挥霍的

spent /spent/
A *pt, pp* ▸ **spend A, B**
B *adj* 1 (used up) 用过失效的; a ～ match 擦过的火柴; a ～ force fig (with no power) 权力不再的事物; (with no influence) 不再有影响力的事物 2 (exhausted) 精疲力竭的 ‹*person*›; 平息了的 ‹*storm*›; 枯竭的 ‹*emotion*›

sperm /spɜːm/ *n* 1 [c] (cell) 精子 2 [u] (semen) 精液

spermatic /spɜː'mætɪk/ *adj* (of sperm) 精子的; (of semen) 精液的; the ～ cord 精索

spermatozoon /ˌspɜːmətə'zəʊɒn/ *n* (*pl* **spermatozoa** /ˌspɜːmətə'zəʊə/) 精子

sperm: ～ **bank** *n* 精子库; ～ **count** *n* 精子计数; ～ **donation** *n* [u and c] 精子捐献; ～ **donor** *n* 精子捐献者

spermicidal /ˌspɜːmɪ'saɪdl/ *adj* 杀精的 ‹*foam, cream, jelly*›

spermicide /'spɜːmɪsaɪd/ *n* [c and u] 杀精剂

sperm: ～ **oil** *n* [u] 鲸油; ～ **whale** *n* 抹香鲸

spew /spjuː/
A *vt* 1 (expel) ～ **(out)** 喷出; to ～ (out) smoke and soot 冒出烟尘 2 colloq (vomit) ～ **(up)** 呕出; to ～ sth. on *or* over sth. 把某物呕吐在某物上
B *vi* 1 (pour or rush out) ～ **(out)** 喷出; lava ～ed from the volcano 岩浆从火山喷出; water ～ed out of the hole 水从孔眼中涌出 2 colloq (vomit) ～ **(up)** 呕吐; you make me ～ 你让我恶心

SPF *abbr* = **sun protection factor**

sphagnum /'sfægnəm/ *n* [u and c] ～ **(moss)** 泥炭藓

sphere /sfɪə(r)/ *n* 1 (shape) 球形 2 (round object) 球体 3 (area of activity, interest, or expertise) 领域; physics is quite outside *or* beyond my ～ 物理学不在我的研究范围内 4 (section of life or society) 阶层; the highest ～ of society 社会最上层; to move in different ～s 出入不同的社会阶层 5 liter (heavenly body) 星球; the music of the ～s 天籁

sphere of influence *n* 势力范围

spherical /'sferɪkl/ *adj* 1 (round) 球形的; a ～ object 球体 2 Math 球面的

spherical: ～ **aberration** *n* [u] 球面像差; ～ **angle** *n* 球面角; ～ **geometry** *n* [u] 球面几何学

spheroid /'sfɪərɔɪd/ *n* 球状体

spheroidal /'sfɪərɔɪdl/ *adj* 球状的

sphincter /'sfɪŋktə(r)/ *n* 括约肌

sphinx /sfɪŋks/ *n* (*pl* ～**es** *or* **sphinges** /'sfɪndʒiːz/) 1 **Sphinx** Mythol 斯芬克斯 [传说中的狮身人面女怪, 常叫人猜谜] 2 (stone figure) the S～ 狮身人面像 3 fig (enigmatic person) 猜不透的人

sphinxlike /'sfɪŋkslaɪk/ *adj* 谜一样的; she gave a ～ smile 她神秘地笑了笑; ～ riddles 难解之谜

sphygmomanometer /ˌsfɪgməʊmə'nɒmɪtə(r)/ *n* 血压计

spic and span /ˌspɪkən'spæn/ *adj* = **spick and span**

spice /spaɪs/
A *n* 1 [c and u] Culin 香料 2 [u] fig (excitement) 趣味; to add/lack ～ 增加/缺乏情趣; variety is the ～ of life 生活丰富多彩才有乐趣
B *vt* 1 Culin 给…加香料; to ～ sth. with sth. 用某物给某物调味 2 fig (add zest to) ～ **(up)** 给…增添趣味; to ～ up one's sex life 给性生活增添情趣

spiced /spaɪst/ *adj* 加香料的; heavily ～ 加香料过多的

spiciness /'spaɪsɪnɪs/ *n* [u] 1 Culin 香辣; I like the ～ of Indian food 我喜欢印度食品的香辣 2 fig (raciness, excitement) 淫猥

spick and span /ˌspɪkən'spæn/ *adj* 整洁的 ‹*room, house, office*›; to make the house ～ 把房子整理得清清爽爽

spicy /'spaɪsi/ *adj* 1 Culin (flavoured with spice) 加香料的; (fragrant with spice) 香辣的 2 fig (racy, exciting) 淫猥的; ～ stories 荤段子

spider /'spaɪdə(r)/ *n* 1 Zool 蜘蛛; a ～'s web 蜘蛛网 2 Brit (elastic ties) 弹性束带 3 (snooker rest) 架杆 4 Comput 蜘蛛程序

spider: ～ **crab** *n* 蜘蛛蟹; ～**man** /-mæn/ *n* Brit colloq [高空作业的] 蜘蛛人; ～ **monkey** *n* 蜘蛛猴; ～ **plant** *n* 蛛状吊兰; ～**web,** ～**'s web** *n* 1 Zool 蜘蛛网; 2 fig (complex structure, tangle) 蜘蛛网状的东西

spidery /'spaɪdəri/ *adj* 蜘蛛般的 ‹*shape, structure, form*›; 细长的 ‹*scrawl, handwriting*›

spied /spaɪd/ *pt, pp* ▸ **spy B, C**

spiel /ʃpiːl, Amer spiːl/ *n* colloq 油嘴滑舌的讲话; a ～ about sth. 关于某事物的夸夸其谈; to give sb. a ～ about sth. 口若悬河地对某人谈论某事物; to make a ～ 夸夸其谈

spiffing /'spɪfɪŋ/ *adj* Brit colloq dated 极好的; what a ～ idea! 这主意真棒!

spigot /'spɪgət/ *n* 1 (of cask) 栓; to remove the ～ 卸掉塞子 2 (flow control) 阀门; to open/close a ～ 打开/关上阀门 3 Amer (tap) 龙头; to turn a ～ on/off 打开/关上龙头

spike /spaɪk/
A *n* 1 (pointed object) 尖状物 2 Rail 道钉 3 Sport 鞋钉; a set of ～s 一套鞋钉 4 Elec (variation in voltage) 尖峰 5 (of flower) 穗状花序; (of corn) 穗
B **spikes** *npl* 钉鞋
C *vt* 1 (pierce) 用尖物刺穿; to be ～d on sth. 被钉在某物上 2 colloq (add alcohol to) 将烈酒掺入; to ～ sth. with sth. 把某种酒掺入某物; to be ～d with sth. 被掺入某种酒 3 Journ 弃用 4 (thwart) 挫败; to ～ sb.'s guns 打乱某人的计划

spike heel *n* 细高跟

spiky /'spaɪki/ *adj* 1 (sharp, pointed) 细尖的; (having sharp points) 有尖刺的; ～ hair 刺猬头发式 2 colloq (easily offended) 易怒的

spill[1] /spɪl/
A *vi* (*pt, pp* **spilt** *or* ～**ed**) 1 (pour out) 溢出; to ～ from *or* out of sth. 从某物中溢出; to ～ over/on to sth. «*ink, salt*» 洒满某处/洒到某物上; the water spilt all over the floor 水泼了一地; the wind spilt from the sail 风对帆的压力减小了 2 (disgorge) «*contents, load*» 散落; fig «*light*» 散射; the coins spilt on to the floor 硬币散落到了地板上; the crowds ～ed into the street 人群涌到了街上
B *vt* (*pt, pp* **spilt** *or* ～**ed**) 1 (tip out) 使…溢出 ‹*liquid*›; 使…散落 ‹*powder, salt*›; to ～ water/salt from *or* out of sth. 把水/盐从某物中洒出来; he spilt wine down his suit 他把葡萄酒洒在了西装上; to ～ blood (shed blood) 流血; (kill) 杀死; much innocent blood was spilt (blood was shed) 很多无辜的人流血了; (people were killed) 很多无辜的人被杀了; it is no use crying over spilt milk Prov 覆水难收; to ～ the wind from the sail 减小风对帆的压力 2 (overturn) 打翻; to ～ sb.'s drink 弄翻某人的饮料 3 (disgorge) 使…散落 ‹*contents, load*›; the sack burst and spilt grain all over the floor 麻袋破了, 粮食洒了一地 4 colloq (reveal) (deliberately) 透露; (unintentionally) 泄露; who spilt the news? 是谁走漏了风声?; to ～ the beans 泄露消息 [尤指泄密] 5 (unseat) «*horse, bicycle*» 把…摔下来 ‹*rider*›
C *n* 1 (liquid spilt) 溢出物 2 (spilling action) 溢出 3 (fall from horse, bicycle) 摔下; there were many ～s at the gymkhana 那次马术比赛中有很多人摔下来; to have a ～ 摔下来; a nasty ～ 重重的一摔

Phrasal verbs

- **spill out**
A *vi* 1 (pour out) «*liquid, powder*» 洒出 2 (be disgorged) «*contents, load*» 散落; «*crowd*» 涌出; to ～ out on to the pavement/into the street 涌上人行道/涌到街上 3 colloq (be revealed) 被泄露; (become known) 被公开
B *vt* [～ sth. out, ～ out sth.]
1 (disgorge) 使…散落 ‹*contents, load*›
2 (reveal) 泄露; she spilt out the whole story 她把事情原原本本说了出来; to ～ out one's troubles to sb. 向某人倾诉烦恼
- **spill over** *vi* 1 (overflow) 溢出; the milk boiled and ～ed over 牛奶潽出来了; to ～ over on to sth. 溢到某物上; five years of frustration spilt over into violence 五年的挫败感最终演化成了暴力 2 (spread beyond boundary) 涌出; to ～ over on to the pavement/into the neighbouring country 涌上人行道/涌入邻国

spill[2] *n* (lighter) (of wood) 引火木片; (of paper) 纸捻

spillage /'spɪlɪdʒ/ *n* 1 [c] (spill) 溢出液; an oil/chemical ～ 石油/化学品泄漏 2 [u] (spilling) 溢出

spillikins /'spɪlɪkɪnz/ ▸ **p. 307** *npl + v sing* 挑棒游戏; a game of ～ 一局挑棒游戏

spill: ～**over** *n* 1 (overflow) 溢出; (spread) 外流; there has been a ～over of workers into unorganized non-agricultural activities 出现了工人转向从事无组织非农业活动的情况; 2 (consequence) 后果; ～**way** *n* 溢洪道

spilt /spɪlt/ *pt, pp* ▸ **spill**[1] **A, B**

spin /spɪn/
A *vt* (*pres p* **-nn-**; *pt, pp* **spun**) 1 (rotate) 快速转动; a child ～ning a top 抽陀螺的孩子; a cricketer who ～s the ball a lot 投出的球旋转很多的板球手; to ～ the wheel (to the left/right) 快速 (向左/向右) 打方向盘; to ～ the wheels [突然原地加速] 使车轮空转; to ～ one's wheels Amer colloq 徒劳无功; to ～ a coin 投硬币 [决定次序]; they spun a coin for service 他们投硬币决定谁先发球; to ～ a record 播放唱片 2 Tex 纺 ‹*thread, yarn*›; to ～ cotton into thread 把棉花纺成

线; **to ~ wool from goat's hair** 用山羊毛纺毛线; **hair like spun gold** 金丝般的毛发 **3** Zool 结 ‹*web, cocoon*› **4** (wring out) 甩干 ‹*washing*› **5** fig (tell) 编造; **to ~ (sb.) a yarn** *or* **tale (about sb./sth.)** 编造（关于某人/某事物的）故事（给某人听） **6** colloq (give bias to) 有倾向性地发布 ‹*news story*›; **to ~ sth. as sth.** 有倾向性地把某事说成某事

B *vi* (*pres p* **-nn-**; *pt, pp* **spun**) **1** (rotate) 快速旋转; **she spun on her heel and left** 她猛地转身走开了; **to ~ on one's toes** 踮着脚转圈; **to ~ across/through/off sth.** 打着旋穿过/通过/离开某处; **to go ~ning** 旋转起来; **to send sth. ~ning** 使某物旋转起来; **the aircraft was ~ning out of control** 飞机失控，不停地旋转; **the car's wheels were/the compass needle was ~ning** 车轮/罗盘指针转个不停; **my head is ~ning** 我晕头转向; **my head is ~ning with ideas** 我头脑中闪过了很多想法; **I feel the room is ~ning** 我感觉屋子在打转 **2** Tex 纺线 **3** Fishg 用旋式诱饵钓鱼; **to ~ for sth.** 用旋式诱饵钓某种鱼 **4** colloq (move along rapidly) 疾驰; **to ~ along** *or* **down the road on one's bike** 骑车在路上飞驰

C *n* **1** [c and u] (rapid turn on turning motion) 高速旋转; **to do** *or* **perform a ~** 做旋转动作; **he did a ~ on the ice** 他在冰上做了一个旋转动作; **the ~ of the earth as it goes round the sun** 地球绕太阳公转同时的自转; **to give sth. a ~** 转动某物; **to put (a) ~ on a ball** 打转球; **the ~ of the wheel** (in roulette) 轮盘的转动; **to give washing a (long/short) ~**（长/短时间地）甩干衣物; **this load is on its final ~** 这缸衣服正在进行最后的甩干; **to give a record a ~** 播放唱片; **everything was in a ~** colloq 天旋地转; **to be** *or* **get in a (flat) ~** colloq 惊慌失措 **2** [c] Aviat 尾旋; **to go** *or* **get into a ~** «*aircraft*» 进入尾旋; «*pilot*» 使飞机进入尾旋; **to come** *or* **get out of a ~** «*aircraft, pilot*» 改出尾旋 **3** [c] colloq (pleasure trip) (in car, on bicycle) 兜风; (in aircraft) 短途飞行; **to go for** *or* **take a ~** 去兜风 **4** [c and u] colloq (biased presentation) [尤指对己方有利的] 倾向性陈述; **to put a positive ~ on sth.** 正面描述某事物

Phrasal verbs

- **spin along** *vi* colloq «*vehicle*» 疾驰; «*driver*» 开车疾驰
- **spin around** *vi* = **spin round**
- **spin off** *vt* [~ **off sth.**, ~ **sth. off**] **1** (produce as by-product) 衍生出 ‹*product, result*› **2** Fin 使…脱离出来 ‹*company, business*›; **to be spun off into a separate company** 脱离出来组建成一家独立公司
- **spin out** *vt* [~ **sth. out**, ~ **out sth.**] 拉长 ‹*story, explanation, time*›; **to ~ out the food/visit** 尽量使食物能多吃几天/延长访问的时间
- **spin round**

A *vi* **1** (through 360°) 旋转; **we cannot see the earth ~ning round** 我们看不到地球的转动; **to ~ round and round** 不停地打转 **2** (through 180°) 转过来; **he spun round in the chair** 他在椅子上转过身来

B *vt* [~ **sb./sth. round**] 使转过来; **he spun his chair round** 他把椅子转了过来

spina bifida /ˌspaɪnə ˈbɪfɪdə/ ▸**p. 377** *n* [u] 脊柱裂

spinach /ˈspɪnɪdʒ, Amer -ɪtʃ/ *n* [u] 菠菜

spinal /ˈspaɪnl/ *adj* 脊的; **the ~ nerve** 脊神经; **a specialist unit for ~ injuries** 脊柱损伤专家组

spinal: ~ **canal** *n* 椎管; ~ **column** *n* 脊柱; ~ **cord** *n* 脊髓; ~ **fluid** *n* [u] 脊髓液; ~ **tap** *n* Amer 腰椎穿刺

spindle /ˈspɪndl/ *n* **1** (on spinning wheel) 纺锤 **2** (on spinning machine) 绕线轴 **3** (axle) 轴

spindly /ˈspɪndli/ *adj* **1** (long and thin) 细长的 **2** (weak) 纤弱的; ~ **dining chairs** 不结实的餐椅

spin doctor *n* colloq 舆论导向专家

spindrift /ˈspɪndrɪft/ *n* [u] 海浪溅沫

spin: ~**-dry** *vt* 为…旋转脱水; ~ **dryer** *n* 旋转式脱水机

spine /spaɪn/ *n* **1** [c] (spinal column) 脊柱; **it sent shivers up and down my ~** 这使我后背直冒凉气 **2** [c] (of plant) 刺; (of animal) 刺毛 **3** [c] (of book) 书脊 **4** [u] fig (nerve, backbone, endurance) 骨气; **a person who lacks ~** 没有骨气的人

spine: ~**-chiller** *n* 恐怖作品; ~**-chilling** *adj* 令人毛骨悚然的 ‹*story, event, sight*›

spineless /ˈspaɪnlɪs/ *adj* **1** (invertebrate) 无脊柱的; ~ **creatures** 无脊椎动物 **2** fig (weak, cowardly) 没有骨气的

spinelessly /ˈspaɪnlɪsli/ *adv* 没有骨气地

spinelessness /ˈspaɪnlɪsnɪs/ *n* [u] fig 没有骨气

spine-tingling *adj* colloq 令人毛骨悚然的 ‹*scream, sight*›

spinnaker /ˈspɪnəkə(r)/ *n* 大三角帆; **to have a ~ up** 升起大三角帆

spinner /ˈspɪnə(r)/ *n* **1** ▸**p. 409** (worker) 纺纱工 **2** colloq = **spin dryer** **3** (fishing bait) 旋式诱饵; **to fish with a ~** 用旋式诱饵钓鱼

spinneret /ˈspɪnəret/ *n* 吐丝器

spinney /ˈspɪni/ *n* (*pl* ~**s**) Brit 小树林

spinning /ˈspɪnɪŋ/ *n* [u] 纺纱

spinning: ~ **machine** *n* 纺纱机; ~ **mill** *n* 纺纱厂; ~ **top** *n* 陀螺; **to play with a ~ top** 抽陀螺; ~ **wheel** *n* 纺车

spin-off

A *n* **1** (incidental benefit) 意外收获 **2** (by-product) 副产品; **a ~ from** *or* **of sth.** 某物的副产品 **3** TV 衍生节目; Cin 衍生电影; **a TV ~ from the film** 电影衍生的电视作品 **4** (company) 分公司

B *modif* 派生的 ‹*series, effect*›

spin setting *n* [洗衣机的] 转速设定; **a ~ of 1,400 rpm** 每分钟 1,400 转的设定转速

spinster /ˈspɪnstə(r)/ *n* pej 老处女

spinsterhood /ˈspɪnstəhʊd/ *n* [u] 老处女身份

spinsterish /ˈspɪnstərɪʃ/ *adj* pej 老处女般的

spiny /ˈspaɪni/ *adj* 多刺的

spiral /ˈspaɪərəl/

A *adj* 螺旋形的 ‹*staircase, motif, horns, structure, spring*›

B *n* **1** (curve, shape, pattern) 螺旋形; **in a ~** 以螺旋形; **a right-/left-handed ~** 向右/向左旋转的螺旋形 **2** Econ (progressive rise) 不断上升; (progressive fall) 不断下降; **an inflationary ~** 日益恶化的通货膨胀; **a ~ of violence** 暴力升级; **a downward/upward ~** 螺旋式下降/上升

C *vi* (*pres p etc.* **-ll-** Brit, **-l-** Amer) **1** (move upward) 螺旋式上升; (move downward) 螺旋式下降; **to ~ up** *or* **upwards/down** *or* **downwards** 螺旋式上升/下降; **to ~ to sth.** (moving upward) 盘旋上升到某物上; (moving downward) 盘旋下降到某物上; **the leaf ~led to the ground** 叶子旋转着飘落到地上 **2** Econ (increase continuously) 持续上升; (decrease continuously) 持续下降

spiral: ~ **binding** *n* [c and u] 螺旋装订; ~**-bound** *adj* 螺旋装订的 ‹*book, pad*›; ~ **galaxy** *n* 漩涡星系

spirally /ˈspaɪərəli/ *adv* 成螺旋形地

spiral: ~ **notebook** *n* 螺旋装订笔记本; ~ **staircase** *n* 螺旋式楼梯

spire /ˈspaɪə(r)/ *n* 尖顶; **a church ~** 教堂尖塔

spirit /ˈspɪrɪt/

A *n* **1** [u and c] (mind, will) 精神; **the power of the human ~** 人的精神力量; **I'll be with you in ~** 我的心将会和你在一起; **the ~ is willing but the flesh is weak** 心有余而力不足 **2** [u and c] (soul) 灵魂; **body and ~** 形与神; **sb.'s ~ is troubled, sb. is troubled in ~** 某人内心苦恼; **brothers/sisters in ~** 精神上的兄弟/姐妹 **3** ▸**p. 325** [c] (supernatural being) 神灵; **nature ~s** 自然神灵; **the (Holy) S~** 圣灵; **an evil ~** 恶魔 **4** [c] (person) 一类人; **a great/bold ~** 伟人/大胆的人; **a leading ~ in the movement** 运动的领袖 **5** [c] *sing* (essence, character) 实质; **the ~ of the declaration/agreement** 宣言/协议的精神; **in the ~ not the letter of the law** 根据法律的精神实质而不是字面意思; **to be faithful to the ~ of the original** «*translation, film*» 忠实于原作的精神; **the ~ of the age** *or* **times** 时代精神 **6** [u and c] *sing* (mood) 心境; (attitude) 态度; **in a friendly/forgiving ~, in a ~ of friendship/forgiveness** 以友好/宽容的态度; **the party/holiday ~** 聚会/度假的心情; **community/team ~** 集体/团队精神; **a ~ of resistance/optimism** 反抗/乐观情绪; **to take sth. in the wrong ~** 误解 ‹*remark, words*›; **that's the ~!** 那才是好样的！ **7** [u] (will) 意志; (courage) 勇气; (energy) 活力; **fighting ~** 斗志; **to break sb.'s ~** 摧垮某人的意志; **to be full of ~** 充满活力; **to play with great ~** «*team, player*» 表现得极为勇猛 **8** [u] Chem (distilled liquid) 精; (distilled alcohol) 酒精; **aviation ~** 航空汽油; **a ~ lamp/stove** 酒精灯/炉

B **spirits** *npl* **1** (mood) 情绪; **to be in good/poor/high/low ~s** 情绪好/不好/高昂/低落; **to keep one's ~s up** 保持高昂的情绪; **to raise sb.'s ~s** 使某人精神振奋; **my ~s rose/sank** 我的情绪振奋/低落了 **2** esp Brit (alcohol) 烈酒 **3** Pharm (essence) 精; **~s of turpentine** 松节油

C *vt* 偷偷带走; **to ~ sb./sth. away** 把某人/某物偷偷带走

spirited /ˈspɪrɪtɪd/

A *adj* 精神饱满的 ‹*reply, performance*›; 热烈的 ‹*conversation*›; 勇猛的 ‹*attack, defence*›

B **-spirited** *combining form* 有…精神的; **high ~** 兴高采烈的; **a generous~ woman** 宽宏大量的女性

spirit lamp *n* 酒精灯

spiritless /ˈspɪrɪtləs/ *adj* 无精打采的

spirit level *n* 气泡水平仪

spiritual /ˈspɪrɪtʃʊəl/

A *adj* **1** (of the spirit) 精神的 **2** Relig 宗教的; **the country's ~ leader** 这个国家的宗教领袖; **the Lords S~** Brit 上议院的神职议员 **3** (not material) 心灵的

B *n* 灵歌

spiritualism /ˈspɪrɪtʃʊəlɪzəm/ *n* [u] 通灵术

spiritualist /ˈspɪrɪtʃʊəlɪst/

A *n* 灵媒; **to go to a ~** 找巫师作法

B *adj* 招魂术的; ~ **practices** 招魂术

spirituality /ˌspɪrɪtʃʊˈæləti/ *n* [u] 精神性; **monuments to the ~ of medieval thought** 中世纪思想灵性的不朽之作

spiritually /ˈspɪrɪtʃʊəli/ *adv* 在精神上; **to feel ~ uplifted** 感觉精神得到升华

spirituous /ˈspɪrɪtʃʊəs/ *adj* formal 含酒精的; ~ **liquors** 烈酒

spirit world *n* **the ~** 阴间

spirometer /spaɪˈrɒmɪtə(r)/ *n* 肺活量计

spit¹ /spɪt/

A *vt* (*pres p* **-tt-**; *pt, pp* **spat** *or* esp Amer **spit**) **1** (eject from mouth) 吐出 ‹*seeds, pips*›; **to ~ blood** 吐血; **to ~ milk (all) over the table** 把奶吐得满桌子都是 **2** (sputter) 喷出; **a volcano ~ting lava** 喷出熔岩的火山; **to ~ oil/water** «*pan, kettle*» 溅出油/水 **3** (utter) 厉声说出 ‹*insult*›; **to ~ curses at sb.** 怒骂某人

B *vi* (*pres p* **-tt-**; *pt, pp* **spat** *or* esp Amer **spit**) **1** (eject saliva) 吐口水; **to clear one's throat and ~** 清清嗓子吐口痰; **to ~ at each other** «*children*» 互相吐口水 **2** (in contempt) [表示鄙夷地] 啐唾沫; **to ~ on sb./sth.** 朝某人/某物啐唾沫; fig 鄙视某人/某事物; **to ~ at sb./in sb.'s face** 朝某人/某人的脸上啐一口唾沫 **3** (hiss) 发嘶嘶声; **to ~ at sb./sth.** «*cat*» 朝某人/某物发出嘶嘶声; **to ~ with**

rage *or* **anger** 《*person*》 气得直喘粗气 [4] (eject venom) 《*snake*》 喷射毒液 [5] (sputter) 劈啪作响; **logs ~ting in the fire** 火中劈啪作响的木柴; **sausages ~ting in the frying pan** 在煎锅里嘶嘶冒油的香肠

C *v impers* Brit **it's ~ting (with rain)** 天空飘着小雨

D *n* [1] [u] (saliva) 口水; **his mouth was full of ~** 他嘴里满是口水 [2] [c and u] (act of spitting) 吐口水; **to give a ~** 啐口唾沫; **~ and polish** 彻底的擦洗; **to be the (dead) ~ of sb.** colloq 和某人简直一模一样 [3] [c] Brit (of rain) 小雨; **a few ~s of rain** 几滴小雨

Phrasal verbs

- **spit out** *vt* [**~ sth. out, ~ out sth.**] [1] (eject from mouth) 吐出; **to ~ sth. on to one's plate** 把某物吐到盘子里 [2] (sputter) 《*volcano*》 喷出 ‹*lava, fire*› [3] (utter) 快速说出 ‹*insult*›; **~ it out!** colloq 有什么话说吧!
- **spit up** *vt* [**~ sth. up, ~ up sth.**] [1] (eject from mouth) 吐出; **to ~ up blood** 咯血 [2] Amer (regurgitate) 《*baby*》 回呕 ‹*food*›

spit²

A *n* [1] Culin 烤肉扦 [2] Geog (cape) 岬; **a ~ of land shelters the bay** 一个岬角掩蔽了海湾; **a ~ of sand** (shoal) 一道沙嘴 [3] Brit (spade depth) 一锹的深度; **a hole two-~s deep** 两锹深的洞

B *vt* (*pres p etc.* **-tt-**) 把…串到烤肉扦上 ‹*meat*›

spite /spaɪt/

A *n* [u] 恶意; **out of** *or* **from (pure) ~** （纯粹）出于恶意

B **in spite of** *prep phr* 不管; **in ~ of sb./sth.** 不顾某人/某事物; **in ~ of (the fact that) ...** 尽管…; **in ~ of oneself** 不由自主地

C *vt* 故意惹恼 ‹*person*›; **to cut off one's nose to ~ one's face** 害人不成反害己

spiteful /ˈspaɪtfl/ *adj* 心怀叵测的 ‹*person*›; 恶意的 ‹*remark, action, story*›; **~ gossip** 恶意中伤的流言; **to have a ~ tongue** 说话尖酸刻薄

spitefully /ˈspaɪtfəli/ *adv* 充满恶意地 ‹*act, laugh, speak, worded*›

spitefulness /ˈspaɪtflnɪs/ *n* [u] 恶意; **out of ~** 出于恶意

spit-roast *vt* 用烤肉扦烤

spitting /ˈspɪtɪŋ/ *n* [u] 吐痰; **'~ prohibited'** "严禁吐痰"; **within ~ distance (of sth.)** fig 在（离某物）很近的地方

spitting image *n* colloq (of person) 一模一样的人; (of thing) 一模一样的东西; **to be the ~ of sb./sth.** 和某人/某物一模一样

spittle /ˈspɪtl/ *n* [u] 唾沫

spittoon /spɪˈtuːn/ *n* 痰盂

spitz /spɪts/ *n* 狐狸犬

spiv /spɪv/ *n* Brit colloq 衣冠楚楚的奸商

spivvish /ˈspɪvɪʃ/ *adj* Brit colloq 坑蒙拐骗的 ‹*person*›; 像模像样的 ‹*clothes*›

spivvy /ˈspɪvi/ *adj* Brit colloq 坑蒙拐骗的 ‹*person*›; 像模像样的 ‹*clothes*›; **to be/look ~** 是/像个骗子

splash /splæʃ/

A *n* [1] (sound) 溅泼声; (effect) 飞溅; **to go ~** 发出扑通声; **to fall into the water with a ~** 扑通一声落入水中; **to make a (big) ~** 溅起（一大片）水花 [2] fig colloq (sensation) 轰动; **to make a ~** 惹人注目; **to cause** *or* **make quite a ~** 《*news, scandal*》 引起很大的轰动 [3] (paddle, swim) 戏水; **to go for a ~** 去游一会儿泳 [4] (spot) (of water) 溅上的液体; (of mud) 溅上的泥点; **~es of water on the floor** 地板上的一摊摊水渍 [5] (patch of colour) 色块; **a ~ of white** 白斑 [6] colloq (small amount) [掺入的] 少量; **to add a ~ of milk** 稍加点儿牛奶

B *vt* [1] (spatter, spray) 溅起 ‹*water*›; 溅湿 ‹*person*›; **to ~ mud all over sb./sth.** 把泥浆溅得某人浑身都是/溅得某物到处都是; **he got ~ed as the car drove through the puddle** 车子开过水坑时溅了他一身水; **to ~ one's way through a swamp** 哗哗地趟水穿过沼泽 [2] (sprinkle) 泼; **to ~ water on (to) one's face, to ~ one's face with water** 往脸上泼水; **to ~ each other with water** 互相泼水 [3] *usu passive* (decorate) [用颜料等] 泼洒; **a towel ~ed with blue and green** 泼洒有蓝色和绿色的毛巾 [4] Journ 在显著位置刊登; **to be ~ed across the front pages** 刊登在头版的显著位置

C *vi* [1] (spatter) 溅落; **raindrops ~ing against the windscreen** 劈里啪啦打在挡风玻璃上的雨点; **water was ~ing from the tap** 水从龙头里哗哗地流出来 [2] (move with splashing action) **to ~ across the river** 哗哗地趟水过河; **to ~ into the pond** 《*pebble*》 扑通一声落入水塘; **he ~ed into the pond to retrieve the ball** 为了拿回球，他扑通一声跳下池塘 [3] (play in water) 戏水

Phrasal verbs

- **splash around, splash about**

A *vi* 戏水

B *vt* [**~ sth. around**]
[1] (spatter) 到处泼溅 ‹*liquid, mud*› [2] (publicize) 大肆炒作 ‹*news, scandal*›; **the story was ~ed around** 那篇报道被大肆炒作 [3] colloq (spend) 挥霍 ‹*money*›

- **splash down** *vi* 《*spacecraft*》 溅落
- **splash out** Brit colloq

A *vi* **to ~ out on sth.** 花大把的钱买某物

B *vt* [**~ out sth.**] 大把地花; **to ~ out thousands of pounds on sth.** 花几千英镑在某事物上

- **splash up** *vi* 《*water, mud*》 溅起来

splash: ~back *n* Brit [洗涤槽等后面的] 防溅挡板; **~board** *n* 挡泥板; **~down** *n* 溅落

splat /splæt/ colloq

A *n* 啪嗒声; **heavy ~s of rain started to fall** 大雨开始啪嗒啪嗒地落下; **the tomato hit the wall with a ~** 西红柿啪嗒一声打在墙上

B *adv* 啪嗒一声; **he landed ~ on his right elbow** 他啪的一声右胳膊肘着地摔了下去

C *vt* 拍打

D *vi* 啪嗒落下

splatter /ˈsplætə(r)/

A *vt* 使…泼溅 ‹*liquid, water, paint, blood*›; **to ~ sb./sth. with sth.** 把某物泼溅到某人身上/某物上; **to ~ sth. over sb./sth.** 用某物泼溅某人/某物; **the car ~ed mud everywhere** 汽车把泥溅得到处都是

B *vi* 啪嗒作响; **to ~ down** 《*rain, water*》 劈里啪啦地落下; **to ~ on (to) sth.** 啪嗒溅到某物上

C *n* 啪嗒声

splay /spleɪ/

A *vt* 叉开 ‹*legs, feet, fingers*›

B *vi* **~ (out)** 《*legs, fingers*》 张开; 《*window, arrow slit*》 成喇叭口形

splayed /spleɪd/ *adj* 叉开的

splay: ~foot *n* Med 八字脚; Vet 外翻足; **to have ~feet** 长了一双八字脚; **~footed** *adj* 长八字脚的 ‹*person*›; 长外翻足的 ‹*animal*›

spleen /spliːn/ *n* [1] [c] Anat 脾 [2] [u] (bad temper) 怒气; **to vent one's ~ on sb.** 把怒气撒在某人身上; **an outburst of ~** 大发雷霆

splendid /ˈsplendɪd/ *adj* [1] (magnificent) 壮丽的 ‹*sunset, view*›; 华丽的 ‹*dress*› [2] colloq (excellent) 极好的; **we had a ~ time!** 我们玩得非常开心！; **she did a ~ job** 她干得非常漂亮; **~!** 棒极了!

splendidly /ˈsplendɪdli/ *adv* [1] (magnificently) 华丽地 ‹*dress*›; 豪华地 ‹*furnish, equip*›; **a ~ appointed suite of rooms** 富丽堂皇的套房 [2] colloq (excellently) 极好地 ‹*progress*›; **everything is going ~** 一切进展顺利; **he was ~ rude to his critics** 他振振有词地责骂批评他的人

splendiferous /ˌsplenˈdɪfərəs/ *adj* colloq hum 壮丽的

splendour Brit, **splendor** Amer /ˈsplendə(r)/

A *n* [u] 辉煌; **to live/dine in ~** 奢华地生活/用餐; **the ~ of the view** 景色的壮丽; **to restore sth. to its former ~** 使某物恢复昔日的辉煌

B **splendours** *npl* 恢宏气势; **the ~s of the imperial court** 帝王宫廷的富丽堂皇

splenetic /splɪˈnetɪk/ *adj* liter 脾气坏的 ‹*person*›; 恶狠狠的 ‹*speech*›

splice /splaɪs/

A *vt* [1] (join by interweaving the strands) 绞接 ‹*rope(s)*›; **to ~ sth. to sth.** 把某物与某物捻接起来; **to ~ two things together** 绞接两样东西; **to get ~d** Brit colloq 结婚 [2] (join at the ends) 粘接 ‹*pieces of timber, film, tape*›; **to ~ two things together** 把两样东西粘接起来

B *n* (in rope) 绞接点; (in film, tape) 粘接点; (in wood) 交接点; **a ~ in sth.** 某物的拼接点; **to join sth. with a ~** 把某物拼接起来; **a ~ joint** 绞接点

splicer /ˈsplaɪsə(r)/ *n* (person) 粘接者; (device) 绞接器

spliff /splɪf/ *n* colloq 大麻烟卷; **to roll/smoke a ~** 卷/抽大麻烟卷

splint /splɪnt/

A *n* [1] Med 夹板; **to put sb.'s leg/arm in a ~** 给某人的腿/手臂上夹板; **to have sth. in a ~** 用夹板固定某物; **to apply a ~ to sth.** 给某物上夹板; **a ~ for sb.'s arm/leg** 用于固定某人手臂/腿的夹板 [2] (sliver of wood) 薄木条

B *vt* 用夹板固定

splinter /ˈsplɪntə(r)/

A *n* 尖碎片; **shell ~s** 弹片; **to get** *or* **have a ~ in sth.** 某物中扎有尖刺; **to extract** *or* **remove a ~ from sth.** 从某物中拔去尖刺; **to get a ~ out of sth.** 把尖刺从某物中取出; **to break into ~s** 裂成许多尖碎片

B *vi* [1] (break, shatter) 裂成碎片; **to ~ off (from sth.)** （从某物中）碎裂出来; **to ~ into pieces** 碎裂; **to ~ on impact** 撞碎 [2] fig (separate off) 分裂; **to ~ off (from sth.)** （从某物中）分裂出来; **to ~ into factions** 分裂成派系

C *vt* 使裂成碎片; **to ~ sth. to pieces** 把某物打碎; **to ~ a party/group** 使政党/小组分崩离析

splinter: ~ group *n* 分裂出来的小派别; **~-proof** *adj* 防碎的 ‹*material, glass*›

split /splɪt/

A *vt* (*pres p* **-tt-**; *pt, pp* **split**) [1] (cut) 切开; (crack) 劈开; **to ~ logs for kindling** 劈一些圆木做引火柴; **to ~ one's lip** 把嘴唇划破; **to ~ a seam** 开线; **to ~ sth. into pieces/in half** *or* **two** 把某物切成几块/两半; **to ~ sth. into X and Y** Chem 把某物分解成 X 和 Y; **to ~ the atom** 使原子核裂变; **lightning ~ the sky** 闪电划破了天空; **to ~ one's sides** colloq 笑破肚皮 [2] (divide) 把…分开 ‹*text, work*›; **to ~ sth. into two areas/groups/sections** 把某物分成两个区/小组/部分; **to ~ an infinitive** 使用分裂不定式 [3] fig (cause division in) 使…分裂 ‹*group*›; **to ~ an alliance into three camps** 使联盟分裂成三个阵营; **to be ~ on an issue** 《*group*》 在某个问题上存在分歧; **to ~ the Conservative vote** 分散保守党阵营的选票; **to ~ the** *or* **one's ticket** Amer Pol 投票给不同党派的候选人; **to ~ enemy forces** 分散敌人的兵力 [4] (share) 分担; **to ~ sth. three ways** 把…分成三份 ‹*profit, cost*›; **to ~ the rent between four people** 在四个人之间分摊租金; **shall we ~ a bottle of wine (between us)?** 我们（俩）一起喝一瓶葡萄酒好吗？; **to ~ the difference** 折中 [5] Comput 分割 ‹*window*›

B *vi* (*pres p* **-tt-**; *pt, pp* **split**) [1] (crack, tear) 《*wood, seam, sack*》 裂开; **the ship ~ in two** 轮船断成两截; **my head is ~ting** 我头痛欲裂 [2] (divide) 《*cell, atom*》 分裂; 《*road, stream*》 分岔; **to ~ into small groups** 分成小组 [3] (disagree) 《*group, alliance*》 分裂; **to ~ on** *or* **over (the question of) ...** 在…（问题）上存在分歧; **to ~ along party lines** 《*government*》 在政党路线上有分歧 [4] (end relationship) 关系破裂; **to ~ with/from sb.** 和某人分手/断绝关系; **to ~ from the band** 和乐队分道扬镳 **5** Brit colloq (tell tales) **to ~ on sb. (to sb.)** (向某人) 告发某人 **6** colloq (leave) 跑开; **he ~ when he saw the cops** 他一看到警察就开溜了

C *n* **1** (crack, tear) 裂缝; **a ~ in a seam** 绽开的线缝 **2** fig (division) 分裂; **a two-way ~** 分裂成两派 **3** *usu sing* colloq (share) 划分; **a ~ of the profits** 利润的分配; **to do a five-way ~ of sth.** 把某物分成五份 **4** Culin 水果船; **a banana ~** 香蕉船 **5** esp Amer (half-size bottle) 小瓶饮料 [容量为通常的1/2] **6** Sport (time) 分段计时; (point in race) 分段计时点

D splits *npl* **the ~s** 劈叉; **to do the ~s** 劈叉

E *adj* 裂开的; **a ~ log** 劈开的圆木; **~ bamboo** 剖开的竹片; **to give sb. a ~ lip** 把某人的嘴唇打裂

Phrasal verbs

• **split off, split away**

A *vi* **1** (crack off) 断裂; (fall off) 断落; **to ~ off from the trunk** «*branch*» 从树干上断裂 **2** fig (diverge) 分离; **to ~ off from the main group** 脱离大部队; **to ~ off and found one's own political party** 分裂出去成立自己的政党

B *vt* [**~ sth. off, ~ off sth.**] **1** (detach) 使…断裂 ‹*branch*›; **to ~ a piece off (from) sth.** 从某物上切下一块 **2** (separate) 使…分离 ‹*group*›; **to ~ sth. off from the rest of the organization** 把…从机构的其他部门独立出来

• **split open**

A *vi* 裂开; **the bag ~ open, and all my shopping fell out** 袋子破了，我买的东西都掉了出来

B *vt* [**~ sth. open, ~ open sth.**] 使裂开; **to ~ sth. open with an axe** 用斧子把某物劈开; **his cheek was ~ right open** 他的脸颊被划了一道口子

• **split up**

A *vi* **1** (disperse) «*crowd*» 散开; **we stayed together as far as London, where we ~ up to return to our separate homes** 我们一起到了伦敦，然后分手各自回家 **2** (divide) «*company, group, alliance*» 分开; **to ~ up into sth.** 分成某物; **the children ~ up into smaller groups for art** 孩子们学习美术时分成了人数更少的小组 **3** (end relationship) «*couple, friends*» 分手; «*group, band*» 解散; **to ~ up with sb.** 和某人分手

B *vt* [**~ sth. up, ~ up sth.**] 使分开; **you can ~ the work up any way you want to, so long as it gets done** 只要活儿能够做完，你们之间怎么分工都行; **they ~ the household effects up between them** 他们把家产分了; **to ~ sth. up into sth.** 把某物分成某物

split: ~ decision *n* [尤指拳击赛中的] 分歧裁定; **~ end** *n* 分叉的发梢; **~ infinitive** *n* 分裂不定式 [在to和动词之间插入副词的不定式]; **~-level** *adj* **1** Archit 错层式的 ‹*house, building, flat, room*›; **2** (with separate oven and hob) 分层式的 ‹*cooker*›; **~ peas** *npl* 干豌豆瓣; **~ personality** *n* 分裂人格; **to have *or* be a ~ personality** 患有人格分裂; **~ screen** *n* 分画面; **~-screen** *adj* 分画面的; **a stylish TV with ~ facility** 有分屏功能的新潮电视机; **~ second** *n* 一刹那; **in *or* for a ~** 一瞬间; **~-second** *adj* 一瞬间作出的 ‹*decision, reflex*›; 分秒不差的 ‹*timing*›; **~ shift** *n* 间隔班 [指分成间隔时间段的轮班]; **to work ~ shifts** 上间隔班; **~-site school** *n* 多校区学校

splitter /ˈsplɪtə(r)/ *n* **1** (person) 劈开者; (machine) 劈裂机; **a log *or* wood ~** 劈木机 **2** Comput, Telecom 分路器; TV 分配器

split ticket *n* Amer 分裂选票

splitting /ˈsplɪtɪŋ/

A *n* [u] (of wood, stone) 碎裂; (of profits, proceeds) 分享; (of group) 分裂

B *adj attrib* colloq 剧痛的; **to have a ~ headache** 头痛欲裂

splotch /splɒtʃ/, Brit **splodge** /splɒdʒ/ colloq

A *n* (of ink, paint, mud, etc.) 污渍; (of light, colour, etc.) 斑点

B *vt* 涂抹; **to ~ sth. with sth.** 用某物涂抹某物; **to ~ sth. on (to) sth.** 把某物涂抹到某物上

splurge /splɜːdʒ/ colloq

A *n* **1** (spending money) 挥霍; **a ~ on sth.** 为某物的乱花钱; **to have a ~** 挥霍一把 **2** (large, excessive amount) 巨量; **to make a ~ (of sth.)** (把某物) 搞得很铺张

B *vt* 挥霍; **to ~ money on sth.** 在某事物上大把花钱

C *vi* 挥霍; **to ~ on sth.** 在某事物上大把花钱

splutter /ˈsplʌtə(r)/

A *vi* **1** (speak quickly and with spitting sound) 慌张地说话; **to ~ with rage/astonishment** 愤怒/吃惊得说话颠三倒四; **to ~ in confusion/anger** 语无伦次/气愤得语无伦次 **2** (spit) «*person*» 喷吐; (sputter) «*engine, fire, fat*» 发劈啪声; **to ~ out** 劈里啪啦地熄灭; **to cough and ~** 一边咳嗽一边噗噗地吐气; **to ~ to a halt** 劈里啪啦地停下来

B *vt* 语无伦次地说 ‹*words, apology*›; **to ~ sth. out** 语无伦次地说出某事

C *n* 劈啪声; **to give a ~** 发出劈啪声; **a ~ of sth.** 某物的劈啪声

spoil /spɔɪl/

A *vt* (*pt, pp* **~ed,** Brit **spoilt**) **1** (ruin, damage) 毁掉; **to ~ one's chances of getting/doing sth.** 断送自己获得某事物/做某事的机会; **spoilt ballots** 废选票; **to ~ one's appetite** 败坏食欲; **to ~ sb.'s (little) game** colloq 拆穿某人的 (小) 把戏; **too many cooks ~ the broth** Prov 人多添乱 **2** (mar) 败坏 ‹*event, evening*›; **to ~ the fun/sb.'s fun** 扫兴/扫某人的兴; **to ~ the view** 破坏景致; **a holiday spoilt by rain** 让雨搅了的假期; **to ~ sth. for sb.** 破坏某人对某事物的兴致; **the bad news spoilt the day for me** 坏消息把我这一天都给毁了; **to ~ everything** 把整个事情搞砸; **to be spoilt for choice** Brit 因选择太多而拿不定主意 **3** (overindulge) 宠坏 ‹*child*›; **to ~ sb. rotten** colloq 宠坏某人; **to be ~ed by sb.** 被某人惯坏 **4** (pamper) 娇惯; **to ~ sb. with presents** 用礼物善待某人; **I'm very ~ed living by the sea** 住在海边，我很享受

B *v refl* (*pt, pp* **~ed,** Brit **spoilt**) **to ~ oneself** 善待自己; **let's ~ ourselves and eat out** 我们享受享受，出去吃顿饭吧

C *vi* (*pt, pp* **~ed,** Brit **spoilt**) «*food, dinner*» 变质

D *n* [u] (waste) 弃土

E spoils *npl* **1** (booty) 赃物; **to get a share of the ~s** 分得一份赃物; **the ~s of war** 战利品 **2** fig (reward, prize) 奖品; **to carry off the ~s** Sport 夺得奖项

Phrasal verb

• **spoil for** *vt* **to be ~ing for a fight** 一心想打架; fig (for argument) 一心想争吵; **to be ~ing for trouble** 存心想找麻烦

spoilage /ˈspɔɪlɪdʒ/ *n* [u] **1** (decay) 变质 **2** (waste) 废弃物 [尤指印坏的纸张]

spoiled /spɔɪld/

A *pt, pp* ▸**spoil A, B, C**

B *adj* **1** pej (overindulged) 宠坏了的; **to be terribly ~, to be ~ rotten** colloq 被宠得不像样; **a ~ brat** colloq 被惯坏的小顽皮 **2** (made invalid) 作废的 ‹*ballot paper*›

spoiler /ˈspɔɪlə(r)/ *n* **1** Aut 气流偏导器 **2** Aviat 扰流板 **3** Journ 抵消影响的新闻报道 **4** (revelation of plot) [电影、书籍等推出前的] 泄露情节者 **5** Amer Pol 拆台者

spoil: ~ heap *n* 弃土堆; **~sport** *n* colloq 扫兴的人; **~s system** *n* Amer 政党分肥制

spoilt /spɔɪlt/ Brit

A *pt, pp* ▸**spoil A, B, C**

B *adj* **= spoiled B**

spoke¹ /spəʊk/ *n* **1** (in wheel) 辐条; **a bicycle ~** 自行车辐条; **to put a ~ in sb.'s wheel** fig 阻挠某人实施计划 **2** (in umbrella) 伞骨

spoke² *pt* ▸**speak A, B**

spoken /ˈspəʊkən/

A *pp* ▸**speak A, B**

B *adj attrib* 口头的 ‹*word, command*›; **~ English** 英语口语; **the ~ language** 口语

spokeshave /ˈspəʊkʃeɪv/ *n* 辐刨

spokesman /ˈspəʊksmən/ *n* (*pl* **spokesmen**) (for government or office) 发言人; (for company or product) 代言人

spokesperson /ˈspəʊkspɜːsn/ *n* (for government or office) 发言人; (for company or product) 代言人

spokeswoman /ˈspəʊkswʊmən/ *n* (*pl* **spokeswomen**) (for government or office) 女发言人; (for company or product) 女代言人

spoliation /ˌspəʊlɪˈeɪʃn/ *n* [u] formal **1** (ruining) 损坏 **2** (taking of property) 抢劫

spondaic /spɒnˈdeɪɪk/ *adj* 扬扬格的 ‹*verse, rhythm*›

spondee /spɒnˈdiː/ *n* 扬扬格

spondulicks, spondulix /spɒnˈdjuːlɪks/ *n* [u] esp Brit colloq hum 钞票

sponge /spʌndʒ/

A *n* **1** [c] (for cleaning) 海绵块; **a bath ~** 浴用海绵; **to throw in the ~** fig colloq 认输; **to have a mind like a ~** 有海绵一样的头脑 [指吸收知识快]; **a contraceptive ~** 避孕绵 **2** [u] (material) 海绵; **cushions filled with ~** 海绵靠垫 **3** [c] *sing* (wipe) 用海绵揩拭; **to give sth. a ~** 用海绵擦拭某物 **4** [c] Med 消毒纱布; **a surgical ~** 医用纱布 **5** [c] Zool 海绵 **6** [u and c] Brit Culin (cake) 松糕; (pudding) 松软布丁 **7** [c] colloq pej **= sponger**

B *vt* **1** (wipe) 用海绵擦拭 ‹*object, material, face*›; **to ~ sth. with cleaning fluid** 用海绵蘸清洁剂擦洗某物; **to ~ sth. clean** 用海绵把某物擦干净 **2** (remove) **to ~ the dirt off sth.** 用海绵擦拭某物; **to ~ water off the floor** 用海绵擦去地板上的水 **3** colloq pej (scrounge) 白得 ‹*money, food*›; **he ~d £10 from *or* off me** 他白拿了我 10 英镑; **to ~ a lift with sb.** 搭某人的顺风车; **he's always sponging meals** 他老是在蹭饭吃

C *v refl* **to ~ oneself** 用海绵擦洗身体

D *vi* colloq pej 当食客; **to ~ on *or* off one's friends** 揩朋友的油; **to ~ off the state** 依靠国家养活

Phrasal verbs

• **sponge down** *vt* [**~ sth. down, ~ down sth.**] 用海绵擦拭; **to ~ the car down after washing** 洗完车后用海绵把车擦干

• **sponge off** *vt* [**~ sth. off, ~ off sth.**] 用海绵擦去 ‹*dirt, water*›

• **sponge out** *vt* [**~ sth. out, ~ out sth.**] 用海绵擦去 ‹*stain*›

• **sponge up** *vt* [**~ sth. up, ~ up sth.**] 用海绵吸掉 ‹*liquid*›

sponge: ~ bag *n* Brit 盥洗用品袋; **~ bath** *n* [不入水的] 海绵擦身浴; **~ cake** *n* [u and c] 松糕; **~ diver** ▸**p. 409** *n* 潜水采集海绵者; **~ diving** *n* [u] 潜水采集海绵; **~-down** *n* 海绵擦洗; **to have a ~-down** 做海绵擦身洗浴; **to give sth./sb. a ~-down** 用海绵擦洗某物/某人; **~ finger** *n* Brit 松手指饼; **~ mop** *n* 海绵拖把; **~ pudding** *n* [u and c] Brit 松软布丁

sponger /ˈspʌndʒə(r)/ *n* colloq pej 揩油的人

sponge: ~ roll *n* [c and u] Brit [海绵纸包的] 甜馅卷筒蛋糕; **~ rubber** *n* [u] 海绵橡胶

sponginess /ˈspʌndʒɪnɪs/ *n* [u] (of ground, bread) 松软; (of texture, material) 有弹性

spongy /ˈspʌndʒi/ *adj* (like a sponge) 海绵般的 ‹*bread*›; (absorbent) 柔软吸水的 ‹*material*›; (porous) 多孔的 ‹*rotten wood*›; 有弹性的 ‹*flesh*›; **wet ~ ground consisting of decaying vegetation** 由腐败植物形成的湿软地面;

S

the flesh of the aubergine has a ~ texture 茄子瓤绵软多孔

sponson /ˈspɒnsən/ *n* 1 Naut (gun platform) 舰侧凸出炮座 2 Aviat (short wing) 翼梢浮筒

sponsor /ˈspɒnsə(r)/
A *n* 1 (advertiser, backer) 赞助者 2 (for charity) 捐助人 3 Pol (of bill, motion) 倡议者 4 (guarantor) 保人; **to act as ~ for sb.** 为某人担保; **to be sb.'s ~** 做某人的担保人 5 Relig (godfather) 教父; (godmother) 教母
B *vt* 1 (fund) 资助 ‹*programme, event*›; **a ~ed walk/swim** 步行募捐/游泳筹款义赛 2 (support) 支持; **UN-~ed** 联合国支持的 3 Pol (advocate) 倡议 ‹*bill, motion*› 4 (act as guarantor for) 做…的保证人 ‹*apprentice*› 5 (be godfather to) 做…的教父; (be godmother to) 做…的教母

sponsored /ˈspɒnsəd/ *adj* 1 (for charity) 捐助性的 ‹*event*› 2 Advertg 有赞助的

sponsorship /ˈspɒnsəʃɪp/ *n* [u] 1 (backing) (financial) 资助; (moral, political) 支持; **under sb.'s ~** 由某人资助的 2 (corporate funding) 赞助; **to seek ~ for sth.** 为某事寻求赞助 3 Pol (of bill, motion) 倡议 4 (by guarantor) 担保

spontaneity /ˌspɒntəˈneɪəti/ *n* [u] 自发性; **with ~** 自发地

spontaneous /spɒnˈteɪnɪəs/ *adj* 1 (without premeditation or stimulus) 主动的 ‹*offer*›; 自发的 ‹*applause, action*›; 不由自主的 ‹*impulse*› 2 (natural) 自然的 ‹*manner*›; 无雕饰的 ‹*gaiety, friendliness*›; 淳朴的 ‹*person*›

spontaneous combustion *n* [u] 自燃

spontaneously /spɒnˈteɪnɪəsli/ *adv* 1 (without premeditation or stimulus) 不由自主地 ‹*react*›; 自发地 ‹*ignite, decide*› 2 (naturally) 自然地 ‹*react*›

spoof /spuːf/ colloq
A *n* 1 (parody) 滑稽模仿; **a ~ on sth.** 对某事物的滑稽模仿; **a ~ horror film/crime novel** 恶搞的恐怖电影/犯罪小说 2 (hoax, trick) 哄骗
B *vt* 1 (parody) 滑稽地模仿 ‹*book, film*› 2 (trick) 哄骗

spook /spuːk/ colloq
A *n* 1 (ghost) 鬼 2 Amer (spy) 间谍
B *vt* esp Amer 吓唬
C *vi* 受惊

spookiness /ˈspuːkɪnɪs/ *n* [u] colloq 阴森可怕

spooky /ˈspuːki/ *adj* colloq 阴森可怕的 ‹*house, atmosphere*›; 令人毛骨悚然的 ‹*story*›; **to find sb. ~** 觉得某人吓人

spool /spuːl/
A *n* (of thread) 线轴; (of tape, film) 卷盘; (for fishing line) 绕线轮
B *vt* 1 (wind) 把…绕在线轴上 ‹*thread*›; 把…绕在卷盘上 ‹*film, tape*›; 把…缠在绕线轮上 ‹*fishing line*› 2 Comput 假脱机输送 ‹*data, file*›

spoon /spuːn/
A *n* 1 (utensil) 匙; **a measuring ~** 量匙; **to be born with a silver ~ in one's mouth** fig 生在富贵人家; **wooden ~** Culin 木勺; Sport 末名奖 2 (measure) 一匙; **two ~s of sugar** 两匙糖; **a level/heaped ~ (of sth.)** 一平匙/满满一匙（某物）
B *vt* 1 (scoop) 用匙舀 ‹*food, liquid*›; **to ~ sth. up** *or* **out** 用勺舀起某物; **to ~ sth. into sth.** 用勺把某物舀到某物中; **to ~ sth. out of sth.** 用勺把某物从某物中盛出来; **to ~ sth. over sth.** 用勺把某物浇到某物上; **to ~ sth. off, to ~ off sth.** 用勺把某物撇去 2 colloq (in golf, cricket) 轻轻向上击 ‹*ball*›
C *vi* colloq dated 拥吻

spoonbill /ˈspuːnbɪl/ *n* 琵鹭

spoonerism /ˈspuːnərɪzəm/ *n* 首音误置

spoon-feed *vt* 1 (with food) 用匙喂 ‹*baby, invalid*› 2 fig pej (with help, information) 填鸭式灌输; **to ~ the public with sth.** 向公众灌输某事

spoonful /ˈspuːnfʊl/ *n* 1 (measure) 一匙; **a level/heaped ~** 一平匙/满满一匙 2 colloq (small amount) 少量

spoor /spɔː(r), Amer spʊər/ *n* [c and u] (track) 足迹; (scent) 臭迹; **to follow the ~ of sth.** 循迹追踪某物

sporadic /spəˈrædɪk/ *adj* 零星的 ‹*fighting*›; 偶尔的 ‹*outbursts*›; 间或出现的 ‹*patches*›; **~ rain showers** 阵雨

sporadically /spəˈrædɪkli/ *adv* 断断续续地 ‹*rain, work*›; 偶尔 ‹*occur, appear*›; **theatre reviews appeared only ~ in the paper after he left** 他离开后，戏剧评论只是零星地见诸报端

spore /spɔː(r)/ *n* 孢子

sporran /ˈspɒrən/ *n* [垂在苏格兰裙前的] 毛皮袋

sport /spɔːt/ ▸p. 307
A *n* 1 [c and u] (physical activity) 运动; **to be good/bad at ~** 擅长/不擅长运动; **team ~s** 团体运动项目; **amateur/professional ~s** 业余/职业体育运动; **to go in for ~** 参加体育运动; **to win a prize in the school ~s** 参加学校运动会获奖; **~s coverage/programmes** 体育报道/节目 2 [c] colloq (person) **to be a good/bad ~** 为人乐观/患得患失; (in games) 输得起/输不起; **to be a good** *or* **real ~ about doing sth.** 对做某事内心不存芥蒂; **come on, be a ~!** 得啦，要输得起！ 3 [u] Austral colloq (term of address) 老兄; **how's it going, ~?** 还好吗，伙计？ 4 [u] formal (fun) 娱乐; **to have great ~** 非常开心; **to do sth. for ~** 为寻开心而做某事; **to make ~ of sb.** 拿某人开玩笑; **to say sth. in ~** 开玩笑地说某事
B *vt* (have, wear proudly) 得意地戴着 ‹*flower, ring, rosette*›; 故意蓄起 ‹*moustache*›; **to ~ a black eye** 有一只眼睛发青
C *vi* liter (frolic) 嬉戏

sportiness /ˈspɔːtɪnɪs/ *n* [u] (fondness for sport) 爱好运动; (ability at sport) 擅长体育运动

sporting /ˈspɔːtɪŋ/ *adj* 1 *attrib* (relating to sport) 体育运动的 ‹*event, occasion*›; (interested in sport) 爱好体育运动的 ‹*person*› 2 (generous) 大度的; (fair) 公正的; (sportsmanlike) 有良好体育风尚的; **it's very ~ of you to do ...** 你做…非常大度; **a ~ gesture** 大度的姿态; **there is a ~ chance that they'll win** 他们有望取胜; **a ~ offer** 高风格的提议

sportingly /ˈspɔːtɪŋli/ *adv* 慷慨大度地

sportive /ˈspɔːtɪv/ *adj* liter 好玩的 ‹*person, behaviour*›; 轻松愉快的 ‹*mood*›

sports: ~ bar *n* 运动酒吧; **~ bra** *n* 运动文胸; **~ car** *n* 跑车; **~cast** *n* Amer 体育节目; **~caster** ▸p. 409 *n* Amer 体育节目播音员; **~ centre** *n* 体育中心; **~ channel** *n* 体育频道; **~ club** *n* 体育俱乐部; **~ complex** *n* 综合体育馆; **~ day** *n* Brit [小学生] 运动会; **~ desk** *n* [报社、电视台或电台的] 体育组; **~ drink** *n* 运动型饮料; **~ ground** *n* 运动场; **~ hall** *n* 运动大厅; **~ jacket** *n* Brit 男式便服外套

sportsman /ˈspɔːtsmən/ *n* 1 (competing in sport) 运动员; (fond of sport) 体育运动爱好者 2 (behaving sportingly) 有运动员风范的人

sportsmanlike /ˈspɔːtsmənlaɪk/ *adj* 有运动员风范的 ‹*person, behaviour, attitude, gesture*›

sportsmanship /ˈspɔːtsmənʃɪp/ *n* [u] (generous behaviour) 运动员风范; (skill in sports) 体育运动技能

sports: ~ page *n* [报纸的] 体育版; **~person** *n* (*pl* **~people**) 运动员; **~wear** *n* [u] (for sport) 运动服装; (leisurewear) 便装; **~woman** *n* 1 (competing in sport) 女运动员; (fond of sport) 爱好运动的女性; 2 (behaving sportingly) 有运动员风范的女性; **~ writer** ▸p. 409 *n* 体育记者

sporty /ˈspɔːti/ *adj* colloq 1 (fond of sport) 爱好运动的; (good at sport) 擅长体育运动的; **I'm not the ~ type** 我不是爱运动的那类人 2 (dashing) 漂亮帅气的 ‹*person, clothes*› 3 (compact and fast) 运动型的 ‹*car*›

spot /spɒt/
A *n* 1 (dot on fabric, dice, domino) 点; (on animal, insect) 斑点; **a red dress with white ~s** 红底白点的连衣裙; **to change one's ~s** fig 改变本性 2 (stain) 污渍; **a grease/rust/blood ~** 油渍/锈斑/血迹; **~s of mud** 泥点; **to knock ~s off sb./sth.** Brit colloq 远远胜过某人/某事物 3 (pimple) 丘疹; (bump on fruit, leaves) 疤点; **to have a ~ on one's nose** 鼻子上长了个粉刺; **to have ~s** (acne) 长青春痘; **to come** *or* **break out in ~s** (rash) 身上长皮疹 4 (drop) 滴; **a few ~s of rain** 几滴雨 5 Brit (small amount) 一点; **care for a ~ of lunch?** 想吃点午饭吗？; **to have a ~ of bother with sth.** 某事出了点麻烦 6 (place) 地点; (in or on body) 部位; **a good picnic ~** 野餐的好去处; **a bald ~** 秃斑; **sb.'s tender** *or* **vulnerable ~** 某人的痛处; **to rush to/be on the ~** (scene) 火速赶到/在现场; **to do sth. on the ~** 当场做某事; **the (only) bright ~** fig （唯一的）亮点; **to hit the ~** colloq ‹*drink, meal*› 正合所需; **to hit the high ~s** colloq 游览精华景点 7 colloq (difficulty) **to be in tight** *or* **difficult ~** 身处困境; **to be on the ~** 处于困境; **to put sb. on the ~** 使某人为难 8 TV, Radio (slot) 节目档; (for commercial) 广告位; **to have a regular five-minute ~ on the radio** 在广播中有一档5分钟的固定栏目 9 colloq (ranking) 排名位置; **to have** *or* **be in the top** *or* **number-one ~** 排名第一 10 fig (blemish) 污点; **a ~ on sb.'s reputation** 某人名誉上的污点; **his record is without ~ or stain** 他的履历清清白白 11 Theat, Cin = **spotlight A** 12 (in football) **the ~** 罚球点
B *vt* (*pres p etc.* **-tt**) 1 (see) 看见; **she was ~ted at a hotel** 有人看见她在一家旅馆; **to ~ that something is wrong** 发现有问题 2 (identify) 认出; **to ~ sb. by his beard** 通过胡子认出某人; **to ~ the difference between two pictures** 找出两张画的不同之处 3 (dot) 使有斑点; **she ~ted the blue with yellow** 她在蓝底上打上了黄点; **trees ~ted the land** 地里稀稀拉拉地长着几棵树 4 *usu passive* (stain) 使有污渍; **to be ~ted with grease/mud** 满是油渍/泥点 5 Amer colloq (lend) 借给; **I'll ~ you $500** 我会借给你500美元
C *vi* (*pres p etc.* **-tt-**) 1 (become stained) 沾上污渍; **the cloth has ~ted rather badly** 这块布上沾了很多污渍 2 Mil [尤指从空中] 探察敌军位置; **to ~ for the artillery** 为炮兵探明敌军位置
D *v impers* (*pres p etc.* **-tt-**) **it's ~ting (with rain)** 在下着零星小雨

spot: ~ advertising *n* [u] 电视插播广告; **~ cash** *n* [u] 当场交付的现金; **~ check** *n* (random) 抽查; (without warning) 突击检查; **to carry out a ~ check on sth.** 对某物进行抽查; **~-check** *vt* (randomly) 抽查; (without warning) 突击检查; **~ fine** *n* 当场罚款; **~ goods** *npl* 现货; **~ height** *n* [尤指地图上的] 地面点高度

spotless /ˈspɒtlɪs/ *adj* 1 (clean) 非常洁净的 ‹*clothes, room, house, person*› 2 (beyond reproach) 清白的 ‹*record, reputation*›; 没有污点的 ‹*career*›

spotlessly /ˈspɒtlɪsli/ *adv* 极清洁地; **~ clean** 一尘不染的

spotlessness /ˈspɒtlɪsnɪs/ *n* [u] 1 (of clothes, room, house, person) 非常洁净 2 (of reputation) 清白

spotlight /ˈspɒtlaɪt/
A *n* 1 (light) 聚光灯 2 fig (focus of attention) 公众注意中心; **to be in** *or* **under the ~** 受到人们的关注; **the ~ is on sb./sth.** 公众关注着某人/某事物; **to turn** *or* **put the ~ on sb./sth.** 把公众的注意力转移到某人/某事物上
B *vt* (*pt, pp* **~ed** *or* **spotlit** /ˈspɒtlɪt/) 1 Cin, Theat 用聚光灯照 ‹*stage, actor*› 2 fig (highlight) 突出 ‹*situation, plight*›

spot market *n* 现货市场

S

spot on Brit colloq
A *adj pred* 精准的 ‹*hit, guess*›
B *adv* 精准地 ‹*hit, guess*›

spot: ~ **price** *n* 现货价格; ~ **prize** *n* 现场奖; ~ **rate** *n* 即期汇率; ~ **sale** *n* 现货销售

spotted /'spɒtɪd/ *adj* 有斑点的; **mud/blood/grease-~** 沾有泥点/血渍/油渍的

spotted dick *n* [u] Brit 葡萄干布丁

spotter /'spɒtə(r)/ *n* **1** (observer) 观察者; (person looking for sth.) 探子; **a trend-~** 潮流猎人; **celebrity-~s** 狗仔队 **2** Mil (for artillery fire) 弹着观察员; (for aircraft) 航空观察员

spotter plane *n* 侦察机

spot test *n* **1** (random check) 抽查 **2** (chemical test) 点滴试验

spot: ~ **trader** ▸p. 409 *n* 现货交易商; ~ **trading** *n* [u] 现货交易; ~ **transaction** *n* 现货交易

spotty /'spɒti/ *adj* **1** (pimply) 多粉刺的 ‹*face*›; 多丘疹的 ‹*back*› **2** (patterned) 有斑点图案的 ‹*fabric*›; 长斑点的 ‹*animal*› **3** (marked, stained) 有污渍的 ‹*linen, mirror*› **4** esp Amer (uneven) 不稳定的 ‹*performance*›; 断断续续的 ‹*coverage*›

spot: ~ **weld** *n* 点焊; **to do a ~ weld** 进行点焊; **~-weld** *vt* 对…进行点焊; **~-welder** *n* 点焊工

spouse /spaʊs, spaʊz/ *n* 配偶

spout /spaʊt/
A *n* **1** (of kettle, teapot) 嘴; (of tap, hose) 口 **2** (pipe of fountain, gutter) 出水管 **3** (spurt of liquid) 水柱 **4** **to be up the ~** Brit colloq (ruined, lost) 完蛋; **all our plans are up the ~** (wrecked) 我们所有计划都泡汤了
B *vi* **1** (spurt) «*liquid*» 喷出; **to ~ out of sth.** 从某物中喷出来 **2** Brit colloq pej (talk) ~ **(forth)** 滔滔不绝地说; **to ~ (on) about sth.** 唠叨某事; **to ~ at sb.** 喋喋不休地对某人说话 **3** Zool «*whale*» 喷水柱
C *vt* **1** (spurt) 喷出 ‹*liquid*› **2** pej (declaim) 滔滔不绝地聊 ‹*poetry*›; 喋喋不休地谈 ‹*advice, opinions, statistics*›; **to ~ sth. at sb.** 对某人没完没了地说某事; **to ~ sth. out.** 唠叨某事

sprain /spreɪn/
A *n* 扭伤; **a slight/bad ~** 轻微/严重扭伤
B *vt* 扭伤; **to have a ~ed ankle** 踝骨扭伤

sprang /spræŋ/ *pt* ▸**spring B, C**

sprat /spræt/ *n* 西鲱; **to use a ~ to catch a mackerel** Brit 施小惠而得大利

sprawl /sprɔːl/
A *vi* **1** (sit) 伸展四肢坐; (lie) 伸展四肢躺; (fall) 伸展四肢倒下; **to ~ across/in/on sth.** 伸开四肢横躺在某物上/躺在某物里/躺在某物上; **to send sb. ~ing** 把某人摔趴下 **2** (spread out) «*suburb, town*» 蔓延扩展; **to ~ out** 杂乱地扩展开来; **to ~ across/over sth.** «*handwriting*» 无章法地布满某物
B *n* [c and u] 杂乱无序扩展的地区; **a suburban ~** 无计划蔓延的郊区地带

sprawling /'sprɔːlɪŋ/ *adj* 无序蔓延扩展的 ‹*suburb, city*›; 蜘蛛爬似的 ‹*handwriting*›

spray[1] /spreɪ/
A *n* **1** [u and c] (flying droplets) 飞沫; **sea ~** 海面的浪花; **the ~ of a waterfall** 瀑布的水花; **a cloud of fine ~** 一片水雾 **2** [u and c] (fine jet of liquid) 喷剂; **a throat/nasal ~** 润喉/鼻雾喷剂; **to apply sth. in** *or* **as a ~** 把…喷涂上去 ‹*paint, glaze*›; **a ~ deodorant** 除臭喷剂 **3** [c] (atomizer, device) 喷雾器; **a throat ~** 润喉剂喷筒; **a ~-head/nozzle** 喷头/喷嘴 **4** [c] (act) 喷洒; **to give the flowers a quick ~** 给花迅速喷点水 **5** [c] fig (shower) 一阵; **a ~ of bullets/sparks** 一阵弹雨/火花
B *vt* **1** (apply) 喷; **to ~ paint (on to sth.)** (给某物) 喷漆; **to ~ water at/over sth.** 对着某物/往某物上喷水; **to ~ perfume on one's cheeks** 往脸上喷香水 **2** (apply liquid to) 向…喷洒; **to ~ crops** 给庄稼喷水; **to ~ sb./sth. with sth.** 给某人/某物喷某物 **3** fig (emit) «*furnace, explosion*» 溅落 ‹*shards*›; **to be ~ed with sparks** 溅满火星; **to ~ bullets** 扫射 **4** fig (shower) 倾泻; **to ~ sb./sth. with sth.** «*fire, explosion*» 使某人身上/某物上散落 ‹*sparks, debris*›; **to ~ rioters with sth.** 用某物喷射暴徒; **to ~ sth. with bullets** 对着某物扫射
C *vi* **1** lit 喷; **water ~ed all over the floor** 水喷了一地 **2** fig (shower) «*bullets, sparks*» 倾泻; **to ~ all over the room** «*shards*» 溅落至房间各个角落

spray[2] /spreɪ/ *n* **1** (sprig) 小花枝 **2** (bunch of flowers) 一簇花; **a ~ of roses** 一簇玫瑰花

spray: ~ **attachment** *n* 喷头; ~ **can** *n* 喷雾罐; **~deck** *n* [套在单人划子座舱口的] 防水裙

sprayer /'spreɪə(r)/ *n* **1** (equipment) 喷雾器 **2** (person) 喷漆者

spray: ~ **gun** *n* 喷枪; **~-on** *adj* 喷雾式的; ~ **paint** *n* [u and c] 喷漆; **~-paint** *vt* (cover) 为…喷漆 ‹*wall, vehicle*›; (paint) 喷绘 ‹*image*›

spread /spred/
A *vt* (*pt, pp* **spread**) **1** (open out) 展开 ‹*sails*›; (lay out) 铺开 ‹*groundsheet*›; **to ~ one's arms wide** 张开双臂; **to ~ its tail** «*peacock*» 开屏; **to ~ its wings** «*bird*» 展翅; **to ~ sth. on the table/floor** 在桌子/地板上摊开某物; **to ~ sth. over the furniture** (as cover) 把某物盖在家具上; **~ 'em!** colloq (police command) 手脚伸开! **2** (smear) 涂; **to ~ sth. on sth.** 在某物上涂 ‹*butter, paste*›; **to ~ sth. with sth.** 在…上涂某物 ‹*surface, paper*›; **to ~ cream over one's cheeks** 把护肤霜涂抹在脸颊上; **to ~ butter on the bread** 在面包上抹黄油 **3** *usu passive* (lay, cover) 覆盖; **to be ~ with gravel** 铺上了砾石; **to be ~ with sheets** 铺着床单; **the table is ~ with cakes/for lunch** 桌上摆满了蛋糕/已摆好午饭 **4** (distribute, disperse) 使分散; **seeds are ~ by the wind** 种子是随风传播的; **to ~ the compost/sand evenly** 均匀地施堆肥/撒沙子; **to ~ mud everywhere** 把烂泥弄得到处都是; **to ~ the workload fairly** 公平地分摊工作量; **to ~ resources thinly** 分散使用资源; **to be ~ all over the country** 遍布全国 **5** (diffuse) 传播; **to ~ gossip** 散布流言; **to ~ a disease** 传播疾病; **the wind ~ the fire to ...** 火借风势蔓延到…; **to ~ the word** 传播消息; **word had been ~ among the staff that ...** 员工们一直在传言说… **6** (space out) 分布; **to be ~ (out) over several months** «*meetings*» 延续几个月; **five interviews will be ~ over three days** 将分3天进行5个访谈
B *vi* (*pt, pp* **spread**) **1** (proliferate) 扩散; **to ~ from place to place** «*fire, fear*» 四处蔓延; **to ~ to other countries** «*disease, religion*» 传播到其他国家; **water ~ across the floor** 水漫过了地板; **the settlers began to ~ inland** 移民们开始向内地迁移; **a smile ~ across his face** 他脸上露出了笑容; **gossip ~s rapidly** 流言传播得很快; **reports were ~ing that ...** 有传闻说… **2** (cover area) 延伸; (cover time) 延续; **the forest ~s for miles in all directions** 这片森林方圆好几英里; **a desert which ~s over the whole of the north of the country** 覆盖该国整个北部地区的沙漠; **experience ~ing over thirty years** 30多年的经验 **3** (be spreadable) «*butter, cream*» 可以涂抹; **to ~ easily** 容易涂开
C *v refl* (*pt, pp* **spread**) **to ~ oneself over** *or* **across sth.** 伸展四肢躺在…上 ‹*sofa, bed*›; **to ~ oneself too thinly** fig colloq 样样都抓, 哪样都抓不好
D *n* **1** [u] (diffusion) (of information, disease) 传播; (of fire, plague) 蔓延; (of nuclear weapons) 扩散; **the ~ of religion/democracy** 宗教/民主思想的传播; **the ~ of education/ideas** 教育/观念的普及; **the ~ of a population into an area** 人口向一个地区的迁移 **2** [c] *usu sing* (width) 宽度; (range) 范围; **the ~ of a bird's wings** 鸟的翼展; **there is quite a ~ in terms of age** 年龄段分布相当广泛; **the ~ between borrowing and deposit rates** (difference) 存贷款利差 **3** [c] Journ 跨数栏的文章; **a double-/full-page ~** 横贯两版/整版的文章 **4** [u and c] Culin 酱; **cheese ~** 奶酪酱 **5** [c] colloq (assortment of dishes) 丰盛的饭菜; **a magnificent ~** 盛宴 **6** [c] Amer (ranch) 大牧场; (farm) 大农场 **7** [c] Amer = **bedspread**

Phrasal verbs

• **spread around, spread about** *vt* [~ **sth. around**] 散布 ‹*rumour*›; **it's being ~ around that ...** 有传言说…

• **spread out**
A *vi* **1** (move apart) 散开; **the police ~ out to search the hillside** 警察分散开来搜索山坡 **2** (extend) 延伸; **the woods ~ out as far as the eye could see** 树林一望无际
B *vt* **1** [~ **sth. out,** ~ **out sth.**] (open out) 摊开 ‹*map, cloth*›; ~ **one's arms out** 张开双臂; **the plans were ~ out on the table** 设计图摊开放在桌上; **the whole town lay ~ out before them** 整个小镇都展现在他们眼前 **2** [~ **sth./sb. out,** ~ **out sth./sb.**] (distribute over area) 使分散; ~ **your men out** 让你的人散开; **houses were ~ out all over the valley** 房子零散分布在山谷各处

spread betting *n* [u] 差额投注

spreadeagled /ˌspred'iːgld/ *adj* 四肢摊开的; **to be/lie ~ over sth.** 伸开四肢摊在某物上/四肢张开躺在某物上

spreader /'spredə(r)/ *n* **1** (for glue) 涂抹用具 **2** Agric 撒播机

spreadsheet /'spredʃiːt/ *n* 电子表格程序

spree /spriː/ *n* 狂热; **to have a ~** 狂欢一番; **to go on a ~** (drink to excess) 狂喝痛饮; **to go on a shopping ~** 疯狂购物; **to go on a spending ~** 大肆挥霍; **a crime ~** 一通犯罪活动; **to go on a killing ~** 滥杀一番

spree killer *n* 杀人狂

sprig /sprɪg/ *n* [带叶或花的] 小枝; **a ~ of holly/lavender** 一小枝冬青/熏衣草

sprightliness /'spraɪtlɪnɪs/ *n* [u] 精神矍铄

sprightly /'spraɪtli/ *adj* 精神矍铄的 ‹*person*›; 轻快的 ‹*walk*›

spring /sprɪŋ/
A *n* **1** ▸p. 692 [u and c] (season) 春天; **in (the) ~** 在春天; **in the ~ of 2006** 在2006年春季; **~ is in the air** 已经有春天的气息了; **a bright ~ day** 明媚的春日 **2** [c] (leap) 跳跃; **with a ~ he was up on the wall** 他纵身跃上了墙头 **3** [c] (coil) (in chair, vehicle) 弹簧; (in watch, clock) 发条; **to be like a coiled ~** (ready to take off, tense) 像绷紧的弹簧 **4** [u and c] *usu sing* (bounce) 弹性; **to have a ~ in one's step** 脚步轻快 **5** [c] (water source) 泉; ~ **water** 泉水
B *vi* (*pt* **sprang** *or* esp Amer **sprung**; *pp* **sprung**) **1** (leap) 跳跃; **to ~ over** *or* **across sth.** 跳过某物; **to ~ to one's feet/out of bed** 一跃而起/跳下床来; **to ~ lightly up the steps** 轻快地拾级而上; **the dog sprang at me** 狗向我扑来 **2** (move quickly) 飞快行动; **to ~ into action** «*team*» 迅速行动起来; **to ~ to** *or* **into life** «*person*» 突然活跃起来; «*engine, machine*» 一下运转起来; «*place*» 突然热闹起来; **to ~ to attention** 迅速立正; **to ~ to sb.'s defence/rescue** 立即为某人辩护/救助某人; **to ~ to one's lips** «*name*» 脱口而出; **to ~ to mind** 突然在脑海中闪现; **to ~ into focus** 一下子成为焦点; **tears sprang to her eyes** 她的眼泪夺眶而出; **where did you ~ from?** 你是从哪儿冒出来的? **3** (be released quickly) 突然弹开; **the lid sprang open/shut** 盖子啪地打开/关上了 **4** (make known suddenly) **to ~ sth. on sb.** 突然向某人提出 ‹*idea, plan*›; 突然把…交给某人 ‹*task, problem*›; **to ~ bad news on sb.** 突然把坏消息告诉某人; **I hate to ~ this on you, but ...** 我不想让你没有心理准备就知道这件事, 但是…
C *vt* (*pt* **sprang** *or* esp Amer **sprung**; *pp*

sprung) [1] (set off) 触发 ‹*trap, mechanism*›; **to ~ a mine** 使地雷爆炸; **to ~ a surprise (on sb.)** 做出（使某人感到）突然的举动 [2] colloq (liberate) 帮助…越狱 ‹*prisoner*›; **to ~ the hostages** 营救人质 [3] (warp) 使…翘曲 ‹*board*›; (split) 使…开裂 ‹*board*›; **to ~ a leak** «*container, boat*» 出现裂缝 [4] Hunt «*dog, beater*» 使…受惊跳出来 ‹*game*›

Phrasal verbs

- **spring back** *vi* [1] (leap back) «*person*» 向后跳 [2] (return with elastic force) «*branch*» 弹回; **to ~ back into position** «*part*» 弹回原位
- **spring for** *vt* [**~ for sth.**] Amer colloq 付钱买; **I'll ~ for dinner tonight** 今天晚饭我来付钱
- **spring from** *vt* [**~ from sth.**] (originate from) 起源于; **the dispute sprang from a misunderstanding** 这一争端是由误解引起的; **his problems ~ from overconfidence** 他的问题是过度自信造成的
- **spring up** *vi* [1] (get up) 跃起 [2] (appear) 涌现; **new industrial estates are ~ing up everywhere** 到处都在兴建新工业区; **a gale sprang up during the night** 夜里突然刮起了大风; **a group of onlookers sprang up from nowhere** 一群旁观者不知从哪里冒了出来

spring: ~ balance *n* 弹簧秤; **~ binder** *n* 弹簧活页夹; **~board** *n* [1] Sport 跳板; [2] fig (sth. giving impetus) 动力; **a ~board to** *or* **for sth.** 达成某事的跳板; **a ~board to success** 走向成功的跳板

springbok /ˈsprɪŋbɒk/ *n* [1] Zool 跳羚 [2] **Springbok** Sport 跳羚队队员［尤指南非橄榄球联盟球队队员］

spring: ~ chicken *n* [1] [c and u] Culin 雏鸡; [2] [c] fig (young person) 年轻人; **he's no ~ chicken** 他已经不是毛头小伙了; **~ clean** *n* Brit 大扫除; **~-clean** *vt* Brit 彻底打扫; **~ cleaning** *n* [u] 大扫除; **to do the ~ cleaning** 进行大扫除; **~ equinox** *n* 春分; **~ fever** *n* [u] 春躁症; **~ greens** *npl* Brit 嫩卷心菜叶

springiness /ˈsprɪŋɪnɪs/ *n* [u] 弹性

spring: ~-like *adj* 春天般的 ‹*weather, day*›; **~-loaded** *adj* 用弹簧顶住的 ‹*latch, bolt*›; **~ lock** *n* 弹簧锁; **~ mattress** *n* 弹簧床垫; **~ onion** *n* Brit 大葱; **~ roll** *n* 春卷; **~ tide** *n* 朔望大潮［指在新月和满月期间潮差较大的潮汐］; **~time** *n* [u] 春天; **in the ~time** 在春天; **~ vegetable** *n* 春季蔬菜; **~ water** *n* [u] 泉水

springy /ˈsprɪŋi/ *adj* 有弹性的

sprinkle /ˈsprɪŋkl/

[A] *vt* 洒 ‹*water*›; 撒 ‹*sand, salt, powder*›; **to ~ sth. over sb./sth.** 把某物撒到某人身上/某物上; **to ~ sth. with water** 向某物洒水; **to ~ oneself with talc** 往自己身上撒爽身粉; **to ~ a speech with quotations** 在演讲中穿插引用一些话

[B] *vi* «*water, rain*» 轻轻洒落; **to ~ on** *or* **on to sb./sth.** 洒落在某人/某物上

[C] *n* (small amount) 少量; **a ~ of rain** 一阵小雨

sprinkler /ˈsprɪŋklə(r)/ *n* [1] (for lawn, field) 喷水装置; **a garden ~** 花园喷水器 [2] (to extinguish fires) 喷水灭火装置 [3] (for condiments) 撒作料瓶; **a sugar ~** 撒糖瓶

sprinkler: ~ ban *n* 花园洒水器禁用令; **~ system** *n* (for extinguishing fires) 自动喷水灭火系统; (for crops) 自动喷灌系统

sprinkling /ˈsprɪŋklɪŋ/ *n* [1] [c] (small amount) 少量; **a ~ of sth.** 少量的某物; **a ~ of snow/rain/people** 少量降雪/稀稀拉拉的几点雨/几个人; **to put a ~ of sugar on top of the cake** 在蛋糕上撒点儿糖 [2] [c and u] (use of sprinkler) (for lawn, field or fires) 喷洒; (for condiments) 喷撒; **the garden could do with a good ~** 花园需要好好喷灌一下

sprint /sprɪnt/

[A] *n* [1] (race) 短跑比赛; **the final ~** lit, fig 最后冲刺 [2] (in cycling) 短程赛; (in swimming) 短泳比赛 [3] (quick run) 短距离全速奔跑; **to break into a ~** 突然开始飞奔; **to put in a ~** 拼全力冲刺; **a ~ start** 起跑阶段的冲刺; **a ~ finish** 终点前的冲刺

[B] *vi* 冲刺; **to ~ past** *or* **by** 飞奔过去; **he had to ~ to catch the bus** 他只好一路飞奔去赶公交车

[C] *vt* 全速跑完 ‹*distance, lap*›; **to ~ the length of sth.** 全速跑过某长度

sprinter /ˈsprɪntə(r)/ *n* (in athletics) 短跑运动员; (in cycling) 短程赛手; (in swimming) 短距离游泳选手

sprite /spraɪt/ *n* [1] (fairy) 小仙子; (elf) 小妖精; **a water ~** 小水怪 [2] Comput (graphic) 子画面

spritzer /ˈsprɪtsə(r)/ *n* [u and c] 汽酒

sprocket /ˈsprɒkɪt/ *n* [1] **~ (wheel)** (toothed wheel) 链轮 [2] (projection on wheel) 链齿

sprog /sprɒg/ *n* Brit colloq 小孩

sprout /spraʊt/

[A] *n* [1] Bot (shoot) 新芽 [2] **= Brussels sprout**

[B] *vi* [1] (put forth shoots) «*potato, tree*» 发芽; **buds are ~ing on the trees** 树木正在发芽 [2] (grow) «*grass, plant*» 长出; **hair ~ing from one's ears** 耳朵上长出的毛 [3] fig (appear) **= sprout up**

[C] *vt* 长出 ‹*new growth*›; **to ~ shoots** 发芽; **to ~ a horn/beard** 长角/长胡子

Phrasal verb

- **sprout up** *vi* [1] lit 迅速生长; **to ~ up overnight** 一夜之间长出来 [2] fig «*buildings*» 涌现; **office blocks are ~ing up in the city centre** 一幢幢办公大楼在城市中心拔地而起

spruce[1] /spruːs/ *n* [1] [c] (tree) 云杉; **white/black ~** 白/黑云杉 [2] [u] (wood) 云杉木; **a floor made of ~ blocks** 云杉木地板

spruce[2] *adj* 整洁悦目的; **to keep sth. ~ and tidy** 保持某物整洁

Phrasal verb

- **spruce up**

[A] *vt* [**~ sb./sth. up, ~ up sb./sth.**] 将…收拾整洁 ‹*house, clothes, vehicle*›; 打扮 ‹*person*›; **she ~d herself up for the interview** 他为参加面试而把自己打扮了一番

[B] *vi* 收拾打扮; **to ~ up for sth.** 为某事而打扮自己

sprucely /ˈspruːsli/ *adv* 整洁地

spruceness /ˈspruːsnɪs/ *n* [u] 整洁

sprung /sprʌŋ/

[A] *pp and esp Amer pt* ▸ **spring B, C**

[B] *adj* 装弹簧的 ‹*floor, mattress, seat*›

sprung rhythm *n* [u] 跳跃韵

spry /spraɪ/ *adj* 充满活力的; **to be ~ for one's age** 相对自己的年龄而言仍精力充沛

spud /spʌd/ *n* colloq 土豆

spud-bashing *n* [u] Brit colloq［尤指长时间的］削土豆皮

spume /spjuːm/ *n* [u] liter［尤指浪花的］泡沫

spun /spʌn/

[A] *pt, pp* ▸ **spin A, B**

[B] *adj* 纺成的 ‹*yarn*›; **~ gold** 金丝; **~ glass** 玻璃纤维; **~ sugar** 拔丝糖

spunk /spʌŋk/ *n* [u] [1] colloq (courage, spirit) 勇气 [2] Brit taboo sl (semen) 精液

spunky /ˈspʌŋki/ *adj* colloq 勇敢的 ‹*fighter*›; 顽强的 ‹*resistance*›; 十足的 ‹*effort*›

spun: ~ silk *n* [u] 绢丝; **~ sugar** *n* [u] 棉花糖

spur /spɜː(r)/

[A] *n* [1] *usu pl* Equit 踢马刺; **to dig** *or* **drive in one's ~s** 用踢马刺策马; **to win one's ~s** fig 获得声誉 [2] *usu sing* fig (incentive) 激励; **a ~ to greater achievements** 争取更大成就的动力; **on the ~ of the moment** 一时冲动之下; **a ~-of-the-moment decision** 一时冲动的决定 [3] Zool (on bird's wing, cock's leg) 距 [4] **= spur road** [5] **= spur track** [6] Geol 支脉

[B] *vt* (*pres p etc.* **-rr-**) [1] Equit 用踢马刺策…前进 ‹*horse*›; **to ~ one's horse into a trot** 用踢马刺策马小跑 [2] fig (urge) 激励 ‹*person, group*›; 促进 ‹*growth*›; **to cut interest rates to ~ demand** 降低利率以刺激需求; **to ~ sb. into action** 激励某人采取行动; **~red by the response, she ...** 在这种反应的激励下，她…

[C] *vi* (*pres p etc.* **-rr-**) liter 策马飞奔; **to ~ onward** 策马向前飞奔

Phrasal verb

- **spur on** *vt* [**~ sth./sb. on, ~ on sth./sb.**] [1] lit 用踢马刺策…前进 ‹*horse*› [2] fig (urge) 激励; **to ~ sb. on to try again/to greater efforts** 鞭策某人再次尝试/作出更大的努力; **~red on by ambition** 受野心的驱策

spur gear *n* 正齿轮

spurious /ˈspjʊərɪəs/ *adj* 站不住脚的 ‹*claim, accusation*›; 伪造的 ‹*document, evidence*›; 虚假的 ‹*affection, interest, sympathy*›; **a ~ argument** 谬论

spuriously /ˈspjʊərɪəsli/ *adv* 虚假地

spuriousness /ˈspjʊərɪəsnɪs/ *n* [u] 虚假; **the ~ of an argument** 论点的谬误

spurn /spɜːn/ *vt* 轻蔑地拒绝 ‹*help, gift, lover*›; **to be ~ed by sb.** 被某人傲慢回绝

spur road *n* 岔路

spurt /spɜːt/

[A] *n* [1] (gush) (of liquid) 喷射流; (of flame) 喷出的火舌; (of steam) 汽浪; **to come out in ~s** 喷射出来 [2] (burst) (of energy, enthusiasm) 迸发; (of activity) 突发性开展; (of speed) 突然加大; (in growth) 猛增; **to put on a ~** 突然提速; **to do sth. in ~s** 不时地心血来潮做某事

[B] *vi* [1] (gush) «*liquid, flame*» 喷射; **to ~ from** *or* **out of sth.** 从某物中喷出; **to ~ up/out** 喷涌而上/出 [2] (speed up) «*runner, athlete*» 突然加速

[C] *vt* 喷出 ‹*liquid*›; «*gun*» 射出 ‹*bullets*›; **to ~ sth. out** 喷射出某物; **to ~ flames** 喷出火舌

spur track *n* 支线

sputnik /ˈspʊtnɪk/ *n*［苏联的］人造地球卫星

sputter /ˈspʌtə(r)/ *n, vt, vi* **= splutter**

sputum /ˈspjuːtəm/ *n* [u] 痰; **to cough up ~** 咳痰

spy /spaɪ/

[A] *n* [1] (political, industrial) 间谍; **an industrial ~** 工业间谍; **a ~ film** 间谍电影; **a ~ trial** 间谍案审判 [2] (for police) 密探; **a police ~** 警方密探; **to act** *or* **work as a ~ for sb.** 做某人的暗探

[B] *vi* [1] (collect secret information) «*secret agent*» 从事间谍活动; «*person*» 当间谍; **to ~ for sb.** 为某人刺探情报; **to be accused/found guilty of ~ing** 被控从事间谍活动/被判犯间谍罪 [2] **to ~ on sb.** (keep watch) 暗中监视某人; **to ~ on** *or* **into sth.** 刺探某事; **his neighbours were ~ing on him** 他的邻居们在偷偷监视他

[C] *vt* liter 看见; **to ~ sb./sth. doing sth.** 看见某人/某物在做某事; **I ~ with my little eye ...** 我看见…［儿童游戏用语，一人说出某物的首字母，其他人猜此物］

Phrasal verb

- **spy out** *vt* [**~ out sth., ~ sth. out**] 探明 ‹*situation, plan*›; **to ~ out the land** 摸清虚实

spy: ~catcher *n* 反间谍特工; **~glass** *n* 小型望远镜; **~hole** *n* Brit 观察孔

spying /ˈspaɪɪŋ/ *n* [u] 间谍活动; **to be accused of ~** 被控从事间谍活动

spy: ~-in-the-cab *n* (*pl* **spies-in-the-cab**) colloq 计速器; **~-in-the-sky** *n* (*pl* **spies-in-the-sky**) 空中间谍; **~-in-the-sky technology/satellite** 空中间谍技术/间谍卫星; **~master** *n* 间谍组织首脑; **~ ring** *n* 间谍网; **~ satellite** *n* 间谍卫星; **~ story** *n* 间谍小说

spyware /ˈspaɪweə(r)/ *n* [u] 间谍软件

Sq *abbr* = **Square** 广场 [用于街道名称]; **16, Hanover ~** 汉诺威广场 16 号

sq = **square** 平方; **50 ~ km** 50 平方公里

SQL *abbr* = **Structured Query Language** 结构化查询语言

Sqn Ldr *abbr* Brit = **squadron leader**

squabble /ˈskwɒbl/
A *n* 争吵; **to have a ~ with sb. about** *or* **over sth.** 为某事物与某人发生口角; **a family ~** 家庭口角
B *vi* «*people*» 争吵; «*birds, monkeys*» 叽叽喳喳; **to ~ with sb.** 与某人争吵; **to ~ about** *or* **over sth.** 为某事物争吵

squabbler /ˈskwɒblə(r)/ *n* 争吵的人

squabbling /ˈskwɒblɪŋ/ *n* [u] 口角

squad /skwɒd/ *n* [1] Sport 运动队; **the Olympic ~** 奥林匹克运动队; **the England ~** 英格兰队 [2] Mil 班 [3] (small group) 小队; **a ~ of construction workers** 一组建筑工人 [4] Police 警察小组; **the drug(s)/anti-riot ~** 缉毒/防暴小组

squad car *n* 警车

squaddie, squaddy /ˈskwɒdi/ *n* Brit colloq 列兵

squadron /ˈskwɒdrən/ *n* [1] Brit (air force unit) 空军中队; **a fighter ~** 战斗机中队 [2] (in cavalry regiment) 骑兵中队; (in armoured regiment) 装甲兵连 [3] Naut 海军中队 [4] fig colloq (large group) 一大群

squadron leader *n* Brit 空军中队长

squalid /ˈskwɒlɪd/ *adj* [1] (dirty) 极肮脏的; **the prisoners were living in ~ conditions** 囚犯们生活在十分肮脏的环境里 [2] (degraded, immoral) 丑恶的 ‹*affair*›; 卑鄙的 ‹*deal, business, motive*›; 淫秽的 ‹*story*›

squall /skwɔːl/
A *n* [1] Meteorol 飑; **a rain/snow ~** 雨飑/雪飑 [2] (cry) 大声啼哭; (scream) 大叫
B *vi* «*baby*» 大声啼哭

squally /ˈskwɔːli/ *adj* 多飑的 ‹*showers, conditions, day*›

squalor /ˈskwɒlə(r)/ *n* [u] (of living conditions) 极其肮脏; (of life) 邋遢; **to live in ~** 生活在十分肮脏的环境中

squander /ˈskwɒndə(r)/ *vt* 挥霍 ‹*money, time*›; 浪费 ‹*opportunity*›; **to ~ sth. on sb./sth.** 在某人/某事物上糟蹋某物; **to ~ one's talents** 浪费才华; **to ~ one's affections** 浪费感情

squanderer /ˈskwɒndərə(r)/ *n* 挥霍者

square /skweə(r)/
A *n* [1] (shape) 正方形; **the ~s on a chess board** 国际象棋棋盘上的方格; **a silk ~** 方丝巾; **to cut sth. into ~s** 把某物切成方块; **to be** *or* **go back to ~ one** 从头再来; **on the ~** 成直角的; fig (honest) 正直的; (proper) 正当的; **to cut sth. on the ~** 方方正正地切某物; **out of ~** 不成直角的; **the frame is out of ~** 画框不正 [2] (plaza) 广场; Mil 操练场; **the town ~** 市中心广场; **Red S~** 红场 [3] Amer (block) 街区 [4] Math (product) 平方; **9 is the ~ of 3** 9 是 3 的平方 [5] Math, Tech (tool) 直角尺 [6] colloq (conventional person) 老古板
B *adj* [1] (in shape) 正方形的 ‹*object*›; **to cut sth. ~** 把某物切成方形; **a man of ~ build** 壮实的男人; **to have ~ shoulders** 肩膀宽阔结实; **to be a ~ peg (in a round hole)** 格格不入 [2] (right-angled) 成直角的; **a ~ corner** 方角; **to be ~ to** *or* **with sth.** 与某物成直角; **to be ~ to the bottom edge** (vertical) 与底边垂直 [3] *attrib* Meas 平方的; **four ~ metres** (in area) 4 平方米; **a rug two foot** *or* **feet ~** (across) 一块 2 英尺见方的地毯; **the S~ Mile** Brit colloq 伦敦城 [4] *pred* fig (balanced, settled) 扯平的; **to be (all) ~** «*books*» (全部) 结清; **to get the accounts ~** 把账目结清; **I'll give you £5, and we'll be ~** 我给你5英镑，那么我们就两清了; **the teams are (all) ~** 两队打成平局 [5] fig (honest) 诚实的; (fair) 公平的; **to be ~ with sb.** 对某人以诚相待; **to give sb. a ~ deal** 公正地对待某人 [6] *pred* (in order) 整齐的; (aligned) 对齐的; **to be ~ with the frame** «*photo*» 与相框对齐 [7] *usu pred* colloq (conventional) 古板的 [8] Sport 横向的 ‹*kick*›; **a ~ pass** 一记横传
C *adv* [1] (directly) 正对着; **to look sb. ~ in the eye** 直视某人的眼睛; **to hit sb. ~ on the jaw** 对准某人的下颌打 [2] Sport 横向地; **to kick the ball ~** 横向踢球
D *vt* [1] (make square) 使…成正方形 ‹*object*›; **to ~ one's shoulders** fig 挺起胸膛 [2] (make right-angled) 使成直角; **to ~ both edges** 使两条边垂直 [3] (mark off squares on) 把…分成方格; **a sheet of ~d paper** 一张方格纸 [4] (settle) 结清 ‹*account, debt*›; 与…结清账目 ‹*creditor*›; **to ~ one's account(s) with sb.** 和某人结账; fig 跟某人算账 [5] Sport 使打平; **his goal ~d the match 2-2** 他进了一球，使比分打成了2比2平 [6] Math 使…成平方 ‹*number*›; **6 ~d is 36** 6 的平方是 36 [7] **to ~ sth. with sb.** (get agreement for) 征得某人对…的同意 ‹*proposal, decision*›; **please ~ your budget with the finance department** 你的预算请提交财务部门审批 [8] **to ~ sth. with sth.** (reconcile) 使某物与某物一致; **to ~ sth. with one's conscience** 对某事问心无愧 [9] colloq (secure agreement) 说服; (bribe) 收买; **they must have ~d the mayor before they won the contract** 他们一定是买通了市长才赢得了合同
E *v refl* **to ~ oneself (to face sth.)** 挺起胸膛 (面对某事物)

Phrasal verbs

- **square off**
A *vt* [**~ sth. off, ~ off sth.**]
[1] (make square) 把…做成方形; **the posts should be ~d off** 柱子应该加工成方形 [2] (mark into squares) 把…分成方格 ‹*paper*›
B *vi* esp Amer = **square up B**

- **square up**
A *vt* [**~ sth. up, ~ up sth.**]
[1] (make square) 使成方形; **to use a T-square to ~ up the fabric** 用丁字尺把布裁成方形 [2] (align) 把…弄整齐; **to ~ up the papers on one's desk** 把桌上的文件收拾整齐 [3] (settle) 结清 ‹*account, debt*›
B *vi* [1] (prepare to fight) 摆好架势; **to ~ up for sth.** 摆好架势准备进行 ‹*fight, match*›; **to ~ up to sb./sth.** 勇敢面对 ‹*person, reality*› [2] (settle accounts) 结清账目; **to ~ up with sb.** 与某人结清账

- **square with** *vt* [1] **to ~ with sth.** (be consistent with) 和某事物一致; **that doesn't ~ with what you said yesterday** 那和你昨天所讲的不吻合 [2] **to ~ with sb.** (come to agreement) 征得某人的同意

square: ~-bashing *n* [u] Brit Mil colloq 队列训练; **~ brackets** *npl* 方括号; **~ dance** *n* [4对男女跳的] 方块舞; **to do a ~ dance** 跳方块舞; **~ dancing** *n* [u] 跳方块舞

squarely /ˈskweəli/ *adv* [1] (directly) 直接 ‹*confront*›; **to hit sb. ~ on the jaw** 正好打在某人下巴上; **to look ~ at ...** 正视 ‹*problem*›; **to look at sb. ~** 直视某人; **to position oneself ~ behind the desk** 正好坐在桌子后面 [2] (honestly) 公正地 ‹*win, deal*› [3] (fully) 完全; **the blame rests ~ on his shoulders** 责难完全落到他一人肩上; **to fit ~ into the liberal tradition** 完全符合自由传统

square: ~ meal *n* 丰盛的一餐; **~-rigged** *adj* 横帆装置的; **~ root** *n* 平方根; **~-shouldered** *adj* 肩膀宽厚的; **~-toed** *adj* 方头的 ‹*shoes*›

squash¹ /skwɒʃ/
A *n* [1] [c] (crush) 拥挤; **it will be a bit of a ~** 这会有点儿挤 [2] [c] (crowd) 拥挤的人群 [3] [u] Sport ▸**p. 307** 软式壁球; **a ~ court** 软式壁球球场 [4] [u and c] (drink) 果汁饮料; **lemon/orange ~** 柠檬汁/橙汁
B *vt* [1] (crush) 把…压扁 ‹*hat, box, car*›; 把…压烂 ‹*fruit*›; **to be ~ed out of shape** 被压得变形; **to ~ sth. flat** 把某物压扁; **four of us were ~ed in the back of the car** 我们 4 个人挤坐在汽车后座; **to ~ sth. into shape** 把某物挤压成形 [2] (squeeze in) 硬塞; **she ~ed the clothes into the suitcase** 她把衣服塞进了手提箱; **they managed to ~ forty passengers into the bus** 他们设法往公共汽车上塞了 40 个乘客 [3] colloq (silence, subdue) 使无言以对; **to feel ~ed** 一时语塞; **to ~ sb. with a single look** 只看一眼便噎住某人 [4] colloq (reject) 打消 ‹*idea, plan*›; 否定 ‹*proposal*›; 驳回 ‹*argument*› [5] colloq (defeat) 镇压 ‹*rebellion*›; 粉碎 ‹*rumour*›
C *vi* [1] (become crushed out of shape) «*fruit*» 压坏; «*clothes*» 压走形; «*box*» 压扁; **to ~ easily** 容易压坏 [2] (squeeze) 硬挤; **to ~ through sth.** 从某物中挤过; **to ~ together** 挤在一起; **they all ~ed into the back seat of the car** 他们全都挤坐在汽车后排座位上

Phrasal verbs

- **squash in** *vi* 挤进来
- **squash up** *vi* 挤紧; **if I ~ up, you can fit in** 我再挤挤你就可以进来

squash² *n* [c and u] (vegetable) 南瓜小果

squashy /ˈskwɒʃi/ *adj* colloq 易压坏的 ‹*fruit, chair*›; 柔软易压扁的 ‹*cushion*›

squat /skwɒt/
A *adj* 矮胖的 ‹*person, shape*›; 低矮的 ‹*building*›
B *vi* (*pres p etc.* **-tt-**) [1] (crouch) 蹲坐; **to ~ down** 蹲下; **they were ~ting around the fire** 他们蹲在火炉周围 [2] colloq (sit) 坐 [3] colloq (occupy building) 偷住空屋; (occupy land) 擅自占用土地; **to ~ in an empty house** 偷住空房
C *n* [1] (position) 蹲坐 [2] colloq (building) 偷住的空屋

squatter /ˈskwɒtə(r)/ *n* colloq (in building) 偷住空屋的人; (on land) 擅自占地的人

squatter's rights, squatters' rights *npl* (to building) 偷住空房者的权利; (to land) 擅自占用空地者的权利

squat thrust *n* 俯撑下蹲促腿

squatting /ˈskwɒtɪŋ/ *n* [u] [1] (crouching) 蹲坐; **(in) a ~ position** (以) 蹲坐姿势 [2] (in building) 偷住空屋; (on land) 擅自占用土地

squaw /skwɔː/ *n* [1] offensive (North American Indian) (woman) 北美印第安女人; (wife) 北美印第安人的老婆 [2] Amer colloq (woman) 娘们儿; (wife) 老婆

squawk /skwɔːk/
A *vi* [1] (make harsh cry) 嘎嘎叫; **the parrot ~ed loudly and flew away** 鹦鹉尖声叫着飞走了 [2] colloq (complain) 大声抱怨; **to ~ about sth.** 嚷嚷着抱怨某事物
B *n* [1] (of duck, parrot, crow, etc.) 嘎嘎的叫声; (of hen) 咯咯的叫声 [2] fig colloq (complaint) 大声抱怨; (protest) 大声抗议; **he let out a ~ of protest** 他嚷嚷着抗议

squawk box *n* Amer colloq [尤指内部通信系统的] 扬声器

squeak /skwiːk/
A *n* [1] (of door, wheel, chalk, shoes) 嘎吱声; (of mouse) 吱吱声; (of infant) 尖叫声; **to let out** *or* **give a ~ (of surprise)** (惊得) 发出一声尖叫; **without a ~** colloq 毫无异议地; **there wasn't a ~ from her** colloq 她一声不吭; **not a ~!** 不准吱声！; **a ~ of terror/delight** 惊恐/欣喜的尖叫声 [2] colloq (escape) **a narrow** *or* **near ~** 侥幸逃脱
B *vi* [1] (make high-pitched sound) «*person, animal*» 尖叫; «*door, wheel, chalk, shoes*» 嘎吱作响; **to ~ out** 尖叫 [2] colloq (inform) 告密; **to ~ to sb.** 向某人告密
C *vt* 尖声说出 ‹*reply, apology*›

squeaker /ˈskwiːkə(r)/ *n* [尤指玩具熊等内置的] 嘎吱作响的装置

squeaky /'skwi:ki/ *adj* 尖厉的 ‹*voice, sound*›; 吱吱作响的 ‹*door, wheel, shoes*›; **in a ~ voice** 声音尖厉地

squeaky-clean *adj* colloq ① (completely clean) 十分干净的 ‹*room, house*› ② fig (beyond reproach) 无可指责的 ‹*person, reputation*›

squeal /skwi:l/

A *n* (of animal, person) 长而尖的叫声; (of brakes, tyres) 拖长的嘎吱声; **a ~ of pain/excitement** 疼痛/激动的尖叫声; **to give** *or* **let out a ~** 发出尖叫

B *vi* ① «*person, animal*» 发出长而尖的叫声; «*brakes, vehicle*» 发出嘎吱声; **to ~ with delight** 高兴得尖叫起来; **to ~ to a ~ with laughter** 尖声笑起来; **to ~ to a stop** *or* **halt** 嘎的一声停住 ② colloq (inform) 告密; **to ~ on sb.** 告发某人; **to ~ to sb.** 向某人告密; **the gang was arrested after somebody ~ed** 经人举报后，这伙人被逮捕了

squealer /'skwi:lə(r)/ *n* colloq ① (person making squealing) sound 尖叫的人; (animal making squaling sound) 尖叫的动物 ② (informer) 告密者

squeamish /'skwi:mɪʃ/ *adj* ① (easily sickened) 易恶心的; **as the boat left harbour, he began to feel ~** 船离港时，他开始有些反胃 ② (easily shocked) 大惊小怪的; (easily offended) 易生气的; **to be ~ about sth.** 对某事物神经质; **I don't like explicit violence in films, I'm rather ~** 我不喜欢电影中赤裸裸的暴力，我神经很脆弱

squeamishness /'skwi:mɪʃnɪs/ *n* [u] ① (nauseousness) 恶心; **a feeling of ~** 恶心的感觉 ② (sensitivity) 神经质; (prudishness) 易心烦; **~ at sth.** 易对某事物产生反感

squeegee /'skwi:dʒi:/ *n* (for windows) 橡皮刮水刷; (for floor) 胶绵拖把

squeeze /skwi:z/

A *vt* ① (press) 挤 ‹*tube*›; 榨 ‹*orange*›; 拧 ‹*mop*›; **to ~ the trigger** 扣扳机; **to ~ sb./sb.'s hand** 紧抱某人/紧握某人的手; **to ~ sth. dry** 把…拧干 ‹*cloth*›; **to ~ sb. dry** fig 榨干某人; **to ~ sb. for £500/information** 逼某人拿出 500 英镑/说出情报 ② (extract) **to ~ toothpaste out of the tube** 从管子里挤出牙膏; **to ~ information out of sb.** 逼迫某人吐露信息; **to ~ juice** 榨汁; **to ~ water out of sth.** 把水从…里拧出来 ‹*cloth, mop*›; **to ~ three meals out of one chicken** 靠一只鸡对付三顿饭; **to ~ money/the truth out of sb.** 勒索某人钱财/逼某人说出实情 ③ (cram) 塞入; **to ~ sth. into a suitcase** 把某物塞进手提箱; **to ~ more people into the car/more books on to the shelf** 让更多的人挤进汽车/把更多的书塞入书架; **to ~ the car into a parking space** 把车勉强开进停车位; **to ~ one's way through a gap** 从豁口挤过去; **to ~ a lot into a week** 把一周的日程安排得满满的 ④ Econ, Fin 使受到挤压; **companies are being ~d by high interest rates** 高利率使公司举步维艰; **profit margins are being ~d** 利润空间正逐渐减小

B *v refl* **to ~ oneself into sth.** 挤入 ‹*small space*›; 勉强穿上 ‹*garment*›

C *vi* ① (compress) 挤压; **take hold of the tube and ~** 抓住管子挤就行了 ② (cram) 塞入; **to ~ into sth.** «*people*» 挤进 ‹*place, car*›; **to ~ into a dress** 勉强穿上连衣裙; **to ~ through to the finals** 挤入决赛

D *n* ① (application of pressure) 挤压; **to give sth. a ~** 挤一下 ‹*tube, orange*›; **to give sb./sb.'s hand a ~** 紧紧抱一抱某人/紧紧握一握某人的手; **a ~ of the trigger** 扣扳机; **to put the ~ on sb./sth.** colloq 对某人/某事物施加压力 ② (small amount) 挤出的一点儿; **to add a ~ of sth.** 再挤一点儿某物; **a ~ of lemon (juice)** 挤出的一点儿柠檬汁 ③ *sing* colloq (crush) 拥挤; **it will be a (tight) ~** (in car, small space) 会很挤 ④ Econ, Fin 削减; **the current ~ on borrowing** 目前的银根紧缩; **a credit ~** 信贷紧缩; **to feel the ~** 感到手头拮据 ⑤ Amer colloq (sweetheart) **(sb.'s) main ~** (某人的）恋人

Phrasal verbs

• **squeeze in**

A *vt* [**~ sb./sth. in, ~ in sb./sth.**] ① lit 使…挤入 ‹*person*›; 塞入 ‹*object*›; **to ~ a few more people in** 再多挤进几个人 ② fig 为…挤出时间; **I can ~ you in tomorrow** 我明天可以挤出时间来见你; **to ~ in lunch** 挤出吃午饭的时间

B *vi* 挤入; **we can just about ~ in** 我们可以勉强挤进来; **to ~ in between two people** 挤在两个人中间

• **squeeze out** *vt* ① [**~ sth. out, ~ out sth.**] (wring) 把…拧干 ‹*cloth*›; (extract) 挤出 ‹*liquid*› ② Comm **to ~ sb./sth. out (of the market)** 把某人/某物（从市场中）排挤掉; **to ~ out small shops** 挤垮小商店

• **squeeze up**

A *vi* 挤紧; **could you ~ up a bit?** 你们能不能稍微挤一挤？; **to ~ up against sb./sth.** 紧贴着某人/某物

B *vt* [**~ sb./sth. up, ~ up sb./sth.**] 使挤在一起; **to be ~d up in one corner of the room** 挤在房间的一角; **to be ~d (tightly) up against sb./sth.** （紧紧）挤着某人/某物

squeeze: ~ bottle *n* Amer 塑料挤瓶; **~ box** *n* colloq 六角手风琴

squeezer /'skwi:zə(r)/ *n* 榨汁机; **a lemon ~** 柠檬榨汁机

squelch /skweltʃ/

A *vi* 吧嗒作响; **to ~ along** 吧嗒吧嗒地向前走; **water ~ed in my shoes** 水在我的鞋子里吧唧吧唧响

B *vt* colloq (silence) 镇住 ‹*person*›; (repress) 压制 ‹*protest*›

C *n* 吧嗒声; **with a ~** 吧唧一声

squelchy /'skweltʃi/ *adj* ① (soft, muddy) 松软的 ‹*mud*›; 泥泞的 ‹*path, ground*› ② (overripe) 软熟的 ‹*fruit*›

squib /skwɪb/ *n* 小爆竹; **a damp ~** 让人扫兴的事

squid /skwɪd/ *n* [c and u] (*pl* **~** *or* **~s**) 鱿鱼

squidgy /'skwɪdʒi/ *adj* Brit colloq 湿软的

squiffy /'skwɪfi/ *adj* Brit colloq 微醉的; **to feel ~** 感觉有点儿醉

squiggle /'skwɪgl/

A *n* (wavy line) 弯弯曲曲的线条; **her signature looks like nothing more than a ~** 她的签名看上去只不过是一堆曲线

B *vi* esp Amer «*insect, worm*» 蠕动

squint /skwɪnt/

A *vi* ① Med 患斜视 ② (look with narrowed eyes) 眯着眼看; **to ~ at sb./sth.** 眯着眼看某人/某物; **to ~ through sth.** 眯着眼通过…看 ‹*peephole*›

B *n* ① Med 斜视; **to have a ~** 眼睛斜视 ② colloq (look) 看; **to have** *or* **take a ~ (at sth.)** 看一眼（某物）

squint-eyed *adj* colloq ① pej 斜眼的 ② (sidelong) 向旁边的 ‹*glance, look*›

squirarchy /'skwaɪərɑ:ki/ *n* = **squirearchy**

squire /'skwaɪə(r)/

A *n* ① (country gentleman) 乡绅 ② Hist (knight's retainer) 扈从 ③ Brit colloq hum (form of address) 先生

B *vt* dated 殷勤伴护 ‹*lady*›

squirearchy /'skwaɪərɑ:ki/ *n* 地主阶层

squirm /skwɜ:m/ *vi* ① (wriggle) «*reptile, worm*» 蠕动; «*person*» 扭动; **to ~ around** 左右扭动; **to ~ through sth.** 蠕动着从某物中穿过去; **he was ~ing in agony** 他痛苦地扭动着 ② (feel embarrassment) 局促不安; **to make sb. ~** 使某人难堪; **to ~ with embarrassment/shame** 尴尬/羞愧得无地自容

squirrel /'skwɪrəl, Amer 'skwɜ:rəl/ *n* ① [c] Zool 松鼠; **a red/grey ~** 红/灰松鼠 ② [u] (as fur) 松鼠毛皮; **a ~ hat** 松鼠皮帽子 ③ [c] colloq (hoarder) 东掖西藏的人

squirt /skwɜ:t/

A *vt* 喷射 ‹*liquid, powder, foam*›; **to ~ sth. into sth.** 把某物注入某物; **to ~ water/ink at sb., to ~ sb. with water/ink** 向某人喷水/喷墨水

B *vi* «*liquid, powder, foam*» 喷出; **to ~ out of** *or* **from sth.** 从某物中喷出

C *n* ① (jet) 喷流; **a ~ of sth.** 喷出的一股某物 ② (small amount) 喷出的少量东西; **a ~ of perfume** 喷出的一股香水 ③ colloq pej (insignificant person) 无足轻重的人; (presumptuous person) 妄自尊大的人

squirt gun *n* Amer 玩具水枪

Sr *abbr* ① **= senior** 老; **John Smith ~** 老约翰·史密斯 ② Relig **= Sister** 修女; **~ Mary Francis** 玛丽·弗朗西斯修女

Sri Lanka /ˌʃri: 'læŋkə/ *pr n* 斯里兰卡

Sri Lankan /ˌʃri: 'læŋkən/ ▸**p. 503**

A *adj* (of Sri Lanka) 斯里兰卡的; (of the people) 斯里兰卡人的

B *n* 斯里兰卡人

SRN *abbr* Brit **= State Registered Nurse**

SS *abbr* ① Naut **= steamship** ② Relig **= Saints** 圣人

SSE *abbr* **= south-south-east**

SSSI *abbr* Brit **= Site of Special Scientific Interest** 有特殊科学价值的地点

SSW *abbr* **= south-south-west**

St *abbr* ① **= Saint** 圣人; **~ John/Paul** 圣约翰/圣保罗 ② **= Street** 街; **43 Acacia ~** 阿卡西亚街 43 号

st *abbr* Brit **= stone A7**

stab /stæb/

A *vt* (*pres p etc.* **-bb-**) ① (pierce) 刺 ‹*person, animal*›; 扎 ‹*food*›; **to ~ sb. to death** 把某人刺死; **to ~ sb. in the heart** 刺某人的心脏; **to ~ sb. in the back** lit, fig 在某人背后捅刀子 ② (poke hard) 戳; **to ~ the air** 强调自己的观点

B *vi* (*pres p etc.* **-bb-**) ① (aim blow) 刺; **to ~ at sb./sth. with sth.** 用某物刺某人/某物 ② (tap, poke) 戳; **to ~ at sb./sth.** 捅某人/某物; **to ~ at sth. with one's finger** 用手指捅某人

C *n* ① (act) 刺; **a ~ wound in the chest** 胸口上被刺的伤口; **a ~ in the back** lit, fig 背后捅的一刀 ② (wound) 刺破的伤口 ③ (feeling, pain) 突发的一阵; **a ~ of pain/jealousy/fear** 一阵剧痛/嫉妒/害怕 ④ colloq (attempt) 尝试; **to make** *or* **have a ~ at sth./at doing sth.** 尝试某事物/做某事

stabbing /'stæbɪŋ/

A *n* 持刀伤人事件

B *adj attrib* ① (sharp) 剧烈的 ‹*pain*› ② (poking) 戳刺似的 ‹*gesture, action*›

stability /stə'bɪləti/ *n* [u] ① (steadiness) 稳定; (of character) 坚定; **to give** *or* **lend ~ to sth.** 使某事物稳定 ② Chem (of substance) 稳定性

Stability Pact *n* ① EU 稳定与增长公约 ② (in South Eastern Europe) 东南欧稳定公约

stabilization /ˌsteɪbəlaɪ'zeɪʃn, Amer -lɪ'z-/ *n* [u] 稳定

stabilize /'steɪbəlaɪz/

A *vt* 使…稳定 ‹*condition, prices, population, economy*›

B *vi* «*condition, prices, population, country, economy*» 保持稳定

stabilizer /'steɪbəlaɪzə(r)/

A *n* ① Tech (device) 稳定装置; Naut 减摇装置; Aviat 水平安定面 ② (substance) 稳定剂

B **stabilizers** *npl* Brit (on bicycle) 平衡轮 [童车后轮两侧的支撑轮]

stabilizing /'steɪbəlaɪzɪŋ/ *adj attrib* 稳定的 ‹*effect, influence*›

stable¹ /'steɪbl/ *adj* ① (steady) 稳定的 ‹*relationship, job, structure, prices*›; **his condition is said to be ~** 据说他病情稳定 ② (psychologically) 稳重的 ‹*person, temperament*›; **mentally and emotionally ~** 心理和情绪稳定的

S

stable²
A *n* **1** (building) 马厩; **a livery ~** 代养马房; **to clean the Augean ~s** 进行大扫除 **2** Horse racing (establishment) 赛马训练场 **3** fig (organization) 培训机构; **the latest addition to the Ferrari ~** 法拉利车队最新增加的赛车
B **stables** *npl* + *v sing or pl* 养马场; **a riding ~s** 骑用马养马场
C *vt* 把…关进马厩 ‹*horse*›

stable: ~ block *n* 马厩房; **~ boy** ▸p. 409 *n* 马倌; **~ companion** *n* = **~mate**; **~ door** *n* 两截门 [上下两部分可分别开关]; **to shut** *or* **bolt the ~ door after the horse has bolted** Brit fig 亡羊补牢; **~ girl** ▸p. 409 *n* 女马倌; **~ lad** *n* ▸p. 409 马倌; **~man** /-mən, -mæn/ ▸p. 409 *n* esp Amer 马倌; **~mate** *n* **1** (horse) 同一马厩的马 [尤指赛马]; **2** fig (person from same organization) 同事; (person from same background) 背景相同的人; (product) 同一系列的产品; **~ yard** *n* 马厩院子

stabling /ˈsteɪblɪŋ/ *n* [u] 马厩

stab wound *n* 刺伤

staccato /stəˈkɑːtəʊ/
A *adj* **1** Mus 断音的 ‹*note*›; 断奏的 ‹*passage*› **2** fig (short and sharp) 短促刺耳的 ‹*command, gunfire, style*›
B *adv* 以断奏方式 ‹*play*›

stack /stæk/
A *n* **1** (pile) 一叠; **a ~ of plates** 一摞盘子; **to put the chairs together into a ~** 把椅子叠放在一起 **2** Agric 垛; **a ~ of straw** 稻草垛 **3** (chimney) 烟囱; (exhaust pipe) 排气管; **to blow one's ~** colloq 发脾气 **4** (shelves) (**book**) **~** 书架 **5** Aviat 分层盘旋的待降机群; **to hold aircraft in a ~** 让飞机分层盘旋等待着陆 **6** Brit Geol 岩柱 **7** Comput (存贮) 栈 **8** Audio 组合音响 **9** colloq (a lot) 大量; **she's got a ~ of clothes** 她有许多衣服; **there has been a whole ~ of complaints** 有一大堆投诉
B **stacks** *npl* **1** colloq (lots) 大量; **I've got ~s of time/things to do** 我有的是时间/有一大堆事情要做; **to have ~s of money** 有大把大把的钱 **2** (in library) **the ~s** 书库; **open/closed ~s** 开架/闭架书库
C *vt* **1** (pile) 把…叠起来 ‹*books, chairs*›; 把…堆成垛 ‹*hay*›; **to ~ sth. into neat piles** 把…整齐地码放成堆 ‹*bricks, boxes*› **2** (fill) 在…上堆放; **to ~ the shelves** (in shop) 摆货物上架; **a lorry ~ed with boxes of sth.** 码放着一箱箱某物的卡车; **to be (well) ~ed** colloq «*woman*» 胸部丰满 **3** Games colloq 对…作弊; **to ~ the cards** Brit *or* **deck** Amer **(against sb.)** (对某人) 洗牌作弊; **the cards** *or* **odds are ~ed in favour of/against sb.** fig 情况对某人有利/不利 **4** pej colloq (fill with supporters) 在…中安插支持者 ‹*jury*›; **the committee was ~ed** 委员会被人暗中控制了 **5** Aviat 使…分层盘旋待降 ‹*aircraft*› **6** Telecom 使…排队等候 ‹*incoming calls*›
D *vi* **1** (able to be piled) 可叠放; **~ing chairs** 可叠放的椅子; **(not) easily/well ~ed** (不) 容易码放/码放得 (不) 好的 **2** Aviat «*aircraft*» 分层盘旋待降

Phrasal verb

• **stack up**
A *vt* [**~ sth. up, ~ up sth.**]
1 (put in pile) 把…叠放起来 ‹*books, plates*›; **to ~ up the boxes** 把箱子摞起来 **2** (cause to build up) 使积聚成一堆
B *vi* **1** (build up) «*work, bills*» 积聚成一堆 **2** colloq (compare) 相比; **how does this brand ~ up?** 这个品牌怎么样?; **to ~ up well against sb./sth.** 比得上某人/某事物 **3** colloq (make sense) «*account*» 讲得通; **it doesn't ~ up** 这不合情理 **4** Aviat «*aircraft*» 分层盘旋待降

stacker /ˈstækə(r)/ *n* (person) 堆垛工; (device) 堆垛机

stadium /ˈsteɪdɪəm/ *n* (*pl* **~s** *or* **stadia** /ˈsteɪdɪə/) 体育场; **a sports ~** 体育场; **an indoor** *or* **a covered ~** 室内体育场

staff /stɑːf, Amer stæf/
A *n* **1** + *v sing or pl* (employees) 全体职员; **editorial/medical/clerical/managerial ~** 编辑/医疗/办事/管理人员; **kitchen/hotel/senior ~** 厨房/旅馆/高级员工; **a business with a ~ of ten** 一家有 10 名员工的企业; **to join/leave the ~** 入职/离职; **the ~ in this shop are** Brit *or* **is** Amer **very helpful** 这家店的店员非常乐于助人; **a ~ party** 员工聚会; **the ~ canteen** 职工食堂; **~ development** 员工培养 **2** + *v sing or pl* (*pl* **~s**) Sch, Univ (teachers) 全体教职工; **the school has 50 ~** *or* **a ~ of 50** 这所学校有 50 名教职工; **the teaching ~** Brit 教学人员; **Mr Jones is joining the ~ of St Francis (as a French teacher)** 琼斯先生将加入圣弗朗西斯学院 (担任法语教师); **he's on the ~ of the local comprehensive school** 他在本地综合中学任职; **students, faculty, and ~** 学生及教职工; **a ~ party** 教职工聚会 **3** + *v sing or pl* Mil 参谋人员; **the general and his ~** 将军及其参谋人员; **a ~ posting** 参谋职位 **4** (*pl* **staves**) (stick) (for walking) 拐杖; (of shepherd) 曲柄杖; (as weapon) 棍棒; (as emblem of office) 权杖; (of bishop) 牧杖; (for flag) 旗杆; **to lean** *or* **rest on one's ~** 倚靠在拐杖上 **5** (*pl* **staves**) Mus = **stave 4**
B *vt usu passive* 为…配备职员; **a school ~ed by bilingual teachers** 一所由双语教师执教的学校; **the centre is ~ed entirely by volunteers** 在该中心工作的全部是志愿者; **a well-~ed hotel** 员工充足的旅馆

staff: ~ association *n* 职员联合会; **~ college** *n* 参谋学院; **~ discount** *n* [c and u] [购买内部产品的] 员工折扣

staffing /ˈstɑːfɪŋ, Amer ˈstæf-/ *n* [u] (appointment) 人员配备; (total number) 员工总数

staffing levels *npl* 员工数量

staff: ~ meeting *n* 员工大会; **~ nurse** *n* 医院护士; **~ officer** *n* 参谋; **~ of life** *n* liter 主食 [尤指面包]; **~ of office** *n* 权杖

Staffordshire /ˈstæfədʃə(r)/ *pr n* 斯塔福德郡

staff: ~-pupil ratio *n* 师生比; **~room** *n* esp Brit 教师休息室; **~ sergeant** *n* **1** Brit (in army) 陆军上士; **2** Amer (in air force) 空军中士; **~-student ratio** *n* 师生比; **~ training** *n* [u] 职员培训

Staffs. *abbr* Brit = **Staffordshire**

stag /stæg/ *n* **1** Zool 雄鹿 **2** Brit Fin 股民

stag beetle *n* 锹甲 [一种大型甲虫]

stage /steɪdʒ/
A *n* **1** (platform) (for play, show, ceremony) 舞台; (for speaker) 讲台; **to go up on (the) ~** 上台; **to go** *or* **be on ~** (perform) 登台演出; **a star of ~ and screen** 舞台银幕两栖明星; **to hold the ~** «*actor*» 吸引观众; fig 引人注目; **to set the ~ (for sth.)** (使某事物) 成为可能 **2** Theat **the ~** (the theatre as medium) 戏剧界; (profession) 戏剧表演; **a ~ actor** 戏剧演员; **to go on/give up the ~** 当演员/告别舞台; **to retire after 40 years on the ~** 从事戏剧表演 40 年后退休; **to write for the ~** 写舞台剧本; **to adapt a novel for the ~** 把小说改编为戏剧; **her play never reached the ~** 她的剧本从未上演 **3** *sing* fig (setting, place) 活动舞台; **the ~ for meetings of world leaders** 世界领导人召开会议的场所; **the ~ of international politics** 国际政治舞台 **4** (phase in journey, process, project, etc.) 阶段; **~ one/two** 第一/第二阶段; **at an early ~ in** *or* **of our history** 在我们历史发展的早期; **to reach/be at the talking ~** «*child*» 到了/处于开口说话的阶段; **I've reached the ~ where I have to make a decision** 我已经到了必须作决定的时候; **at this ~** (at this point) 此刻; (for the time being) 眼下; **at an earlier/later ~** 早些/晚些时候; **by** *or* **in ~s** 逐步地; **by** *or* **in easy ~s** 从容不迫地; **we did the trip from Rome to Paris in easy ~s** 我们走走歇歇地从罗马旅行到了巴黎; **they learnt German by easy ~s** 他们循序渐进地学会了德语; **it's just a ~!** (as child grows) 这只是一个必经的阶段! **5** Aerosp 级; **a three-~ rocket** 三级火箭 **6** Brit (on bus route) 行程 **7** (on microscope) 镜台 **8** Geol 阶 **9** Hist = **stagecoach**
B *vt* **1** Theat 上演 ‹*play, performance*› **2** (organize) 组织; **to ~ a demonstration/strike/ceremony** 举行示威/罢工/仪式; **to ~ a football match** 举办足球赛; **to ~ a comeback** 复出; **the dollar ~d a recovery** 美元汇率出现了回升 **3** (fake) 刻意安排 ‹*event, scene*›; **the interview was obviously ~d** 这次采访显然是做样子的

stage: ~coach *n* Hist 驿站马车; **~craft** *n* [u] (performing) 舞台表演技艺; (writing) 编剧技巧; **~ designer** ▸p. 409 *n* 舞台设计师; **~ direction** *n* 舞台指示; **~ door** *n* (at back) 剧场后门; (at side) 剧场边门; **~ fright** *n* [u] 怯场; **~hand** ▸p. 409 *n* 舞台工作人员; **~ left** *adv* 从舞台左侧 ‹*enter, exit*›; **~-manage** *vt* 精心安排 ‹*event, election*›; **~ management** *n* [u] **1** Theat 舞台监督工作; **2** fig (organization) 精心安排; **~ manager** ▸p. 409 *n* 舞台监督; **~ name** *n* 艺名; **~ right** *adv* 从舞台右侧 ‹*enter, exit*›; **~ show** *n* 舞台娱乐演出; **~-struck** *adj* 渴望当演员的; **~ whisper** *n* 舞台低语

stagey /ˈsteɪdʒɪ/ *adj* = **stagy**

stagflation /ˌstægˈfleɪʃn/ *n* [u] 滞胀

stagger /ˈstægə(r)/
A *vi* 蹒跚; **to ~ along the road** 沿路蹒跚而行; **to ~ to one's feet** 摇摇晃晃地站起来; **to ~ from one crisis to the next** 在接踵而至的危机中举步维艰
B *vt* **1** *usu passive* (astonish) 使震惊; **I was ~ed by his audacity** 他的放肆让我震惊; **I was ~ed when I heard the news** 我听到这个消息时大吃一惊; **it ~ed me that ...** 我觉得不可思议的是… **2** (spread out in space) 使交错; **to be ~ed along sth.** 沿某物交错分布; **~ed seating** 交错式座位; **a ~ed junction** 错位式交叉口; **a ~ed start** Sport 梯形起跑 **3** (spread out in time) 使…错开 ‹*shifts*›; **equal payments ~ed over six months** 分 6 个月等额支付的款项; **we work ~ed hours** 我们的上班时间是错开的; **a ~ed start** Sport 错时起跑 **4** (totter) 蹒跚前行; **to ~ a few feet** 踉踉跄跄地走几英尺
C *n* **1** (movement) 蹒跚; **to walk with a ~** 摇摇晃晃地走 **2** (arrangement) 交错安排; **to be arranged in a ~** 交错安排 **3** Sport (at start) 梯形起跑

staggering /ˈstægərɪŋ/ *adj* 令人难以相信的 ‹*news, success, loss*›; 巨大的 ‹*amount*›

staggeringly /ˈstægərɪŋlɪ/ *adv* 令人难以置信地 ‹*beautiful, expensive*›

staghorn /ˈstæghɔːn/ *n* [u] 鹿角 [用作雕刻材料]

staging /ˈsteɪdʒɪŋ/ *n* [u] **1** Theat (act) 上演; (method) 表演技巧 **2** Constr (scaffolding) 脚手架; (platform) 临时工作台

staging: ~ area *n* 集结地; **~ post** *n* 中途站

stagnant /ˈstægnənt/ *adj* **1** (still and gone stale) 不流动而污浊的 **2** fig (sluggish) 停滞的 ‹*economy, prices*›; 不景气的 ‹*business*›

stagnate /stægˈneɪt, Amer ˈstægneɪt/ *vi* **1** lit (cease to flow and become stale) 因不流动而变得污浊 **2** fig (become inactive) «*economy, trade*» 停滞; «*person*» 不进步; **I am stagnating in this job; I need more of a challenge!** 我做这份工作没有长进，我需要来点挑战!

stagnation /stægˈneɪʃn/ *n* [u] 停滞

stag night, stag party *ns* Brit 男子婚前聚会 [仅有男性朋友参加]

stagy /ˈsteɪdʒɪ/ *adj* pej 装腔作势的 ‹*manner, voice*›

S

staid /steɪd/ *adj* 古板的 ‹*person, appearance, approach*›

staidness /ˈsteɪdnɪs/ *n* [u] 古板

stain /steɪn/

A *vt* **1** (soil) 弄脏 ‹*clothes, carpet, fingers*› **2** (dye) 给…染色 ‹*wood, fabric*›; **to ~ sth. with sth.** 用某物给某物染色; **to ~ sth. teak/mahogany** 把某物漆成柚木色/红木色 **3** fig (damage) 玷污 ‹*reputation, honour*›; **his good name was ~ed by the accusation** 这一指控玷污了他的好名声

B *vi* **1** (mark) «*wine, ink, blood*» 留下污渍 **2** (be marked) «*clothes, material*» 被弄脏; **this fabric ~s easily** 这种布料容易脏

C *n* **1** (mark) 污迹; **a blood/coffee ~** 血污/咖啡污渍; **to remove a ~ from sth.** 除去某物上的污点; **it will leave a ~** 这会留下污渍 **2** (dye) 染色剂 **3** fig (moral blemish) 污点; **without a ~ on one's character** 品行没有任何污点的; **a ~ on the reputation** *or* **good name of one's family** 对家族声誉的玷污

-stained /steɪnd/ *combining form* 沾有…污渍的; **oil/ink~** 有油污/墨污的; **tear~** 泪痕斑斑的; **teak/mahogany~** 涂成柚木色/红木色的

stained glass *n* [u] 彩色玻璃

stained glass window *n* 彩色玻璃窗

stainless /ˈsteɪnlɪs/ *adj* **1** (unmarked) 无污点的 ‹*garment, surface*› **2** fig (unsullied) 洁白无瑕的 ‹*reputation, past*›

stainless steel *n* [u] 不锈钢; **a ~ sink** 不锈钢洗碗槽

stain: ~ remover *n* [u and c] 去污剂; **~-resistant** *adj* 耐脏的

stair /steə(r)/

A *n* **1** (step) 梯级; **the top/bottom ~** 楼梯最上/最下端 **2** formal (staircase) 楼梯

B **stairs** *npl* 楼梯; **a flight of ~s** 一段楼梯; **to go up** *or* **climb the ~s** 上楼; **to come** *or* **go down the ~s** 下楼; **to run up the ~s** 跑上楼; **to fall down the ~s** 从楼梯上摔下来; **below ~s** 在地下室 [旧时常指仆人住的地方]

stair: ~ carpet *n* 楼梯毯; **~case** *n* 楼梯; **a spiral/moving ~case** 旋转式/活动楼梯; **~gate** *n* 楼梯安全门; **~lift** *n* 座椅电梯; **~ rod** *n* 楼梯毯压条; **~way** *n* = **~case**; **~well** *n* 楼梯井

stake /steɪk/

A *n* **1** (pole) (for support) 桩; (as marker) 标桩; **to drive a ~ through sth.** 把桩子钉入某物; **to pull up ~s** Amer 搬家 **2** Hist (for execution) 火刑柱; **to be burnt at the ~** 被处以火刑; **to go to the ~** 受火刑; **to go to the ~ over sth.** fig 誓死捍卫某事 **3** (amount risked) 赌注; **to put a ~ on …** 对…押注 ‹*horse*›; **high/low ~s** 大笔/小笔赌注; **to play for high ~s** lit, fig 下大赌注; **to raise the ~s** lit 提高赌注; fig 增加危险; **to be at ~** 有风险; **there is a lot at ~** 有很大风险; **to put sth. at ~** lit 对某事物下赌注; fig 使某事物处于危险中 **4** (investment) 股本; **to have a large/small ~ in sth.** 在某事物中占很大/很小的股份

B **stakes** *npl* (prize money) 奖金; (race) 赛马锦标会; fig 比赛; **she always comes first in the fashion ~s** 她参加时装比赛总是拿冠军

C *vt* **1** (support) 用桩支撑 ‹*tree, plant*› **2** (mark) 立桩标出 ‹*area, plot*›; **to ~ a claim (to sth.)** 声明（对某物的）所有权 **3** (gamble) 以…打赌 ‹*money, hopes*›; 拿…冒险 ‹*one's life*›; **to ~ sth. on sth.** 用某物赌某物; **I would ~ my life on it** 我愿拿脑袋打赌; **to ~ one's all on …** 为…赌上全部身家 **4** Amer colloq (back) 资助 ‹*person, business, project*›

Phrasal verb

- **stake out** *vt* [**~ out sth./sb., ~ sth./sb. out**] **1** (mark) 立桩标出 ‹*area, plot*› **2** colloq (keep under surveillance) 监视 ‹*building, person*›

stake boat *n* [赛船时用以标示起点的] 标柱艇

stakeholder /ˈsteɪkhəʊldə(r)/ *n* **1** (in gambling) 赌金保管人 **2** (interested party) 有权益关系者; **a ~ economy/society** 利益相关者经济/团体

stakeholder pension *n* Brit 存托养老金计划

stake-out *n* [c and u] colloq 监视; **to be on (a) ~** 受到监视

stalactite /ˈstæləktaɪt, Amer stəˈlæk-/ *n* 钟乳石

stalagmite /ˈstæləɡmaɪt, Amer stəˈlæɡ-/ *n* 石笋

stale /steɪl/ *adj* **1** (not fresh) 不新鲜的 ‹*food*›; 难闻的 ‹*tobacco, beer, urine*›; 污浊的 ‹*air*›; **to go ~** 走味; **to smell ~** «*room*» 有霉味 **2** (hackneyed) 陈腐的 ‹*joke, idea*›; **~ news** 老掉牙的新闻 **3** (tired) 厌倦的 ‹*person, sportsman, performer*›; **to feel ~** 感觉腻烦; **to get ~ in a job** 厌倦工作; **their marriage had gone ~** 他们的婚姻已不再有激情了

stalemate /ˈsteɪlmeɪt/

A *n* [u and c] **1** (in chess) 僵局 **2** fig (deadlock) 僵持局面; **a military/political ~** 军事/政治僵局; **an industrial ~** 劳资谈判僵局; **to break a/reach (a) ~** 打破/陷入僵局

B *vt* 使…陷入僵局 ‹*progress, negotiations*›

staleness /ˈsteɪlnɪs/ *n* [u] **1** (of food) 走味; (of air) 污浊 **2** fig (of ideas) 陈腐 **3** (of performer, sportsman) 厌倦; **a feeling of ~** 厌倦感

Stalinism /ˈstɑːlɪnɪzəm/ *n* [u] 斯大林主义

Stalinist /ˈstɑːlɪnɪst/

A *n* 斯大林主义者

B *adj* 斯大林主义的

stalk[1] /stɔːk/ *n* **1** Bot (main stem) 茎; **a ~ of grass** 一株草; **he's got legs like ~s** 他的腿细如麻秆; **to have one's eyes (out) on ~s** fig 两眼发直 **2** Bot, Culin (stem) (of leaf, mushroom) 柄; (of flower, grapes) 梗 **3** Zool 肉柄 **4** (slender supporting structure) 柄状物; **drinking glasses with long ~s** 高脚酒杯 **5** Aut [车辆转向柱上控制指示仪、灯光等的] 手柄

stalk[2]

A *vi* **1** (stride) 昂首阔步; **to ~ in/out** 昂首阔步走进来/出去; **to ~ away** *or* **off** 气呼呼地走开; **to ~ out of the room** 怒冲冲地大步走出房间 **2** esp liter (prowl) 潜行; **to ~ through sth.** «*famine, disease*» 蔓延于 ‹*place*›; **fear ~ed through the streets** 街上弥漫着恐惧; **to ~ along the streets/through the area** «*killer*» 在街头/在该地区出没

B *vt* **1** lit, fig 偷偷接近 ‹*prey, victim*›; **to ~ sb.** 悄悄逼近某人 **2** Jur (harass) 骚扰 **3** (prowl through) «*person, animal*» 出没于 ‹*area*›; (haunt) «*famine, disease*» 在…蔓延 ‹*area, land*›; **the tiger ~s the jungle** 老虎出没于丛林地带; **fear was ~ing the camp** 营地里笼罩着恐怖气氛

stalker /ˈstɔːkə(r)/ *n* 跟踪者

stalking horse *n* 掩护性候选人

stall /stɔːl/

A *n* **1** (at market, fair) 货摊; (newspaper stand) 报刊亭; **a cake ~** 蛋糕摊; **to run a ~** 经营摊位; **to buy sth. from a ~** 从摊位上买某物; **to set up/take down a ~** 搭起/拆掉摊位; **to set out one's ~** Brit 表明立场 **2** (in stable) 牲畜棚隔间 **3** Aviat 失速; (of engine) 熄火; (of car) 抛锚; **to go** *or* **get into a ~** 进入失速状态; **to get out of a ~** 脱离失速状态 **4** Archit (in church) 靠背扶手座位; **the choir ~s** 唱诗班座位 **5** (cubicle for shower, toilet) 小隔间 **6** Amer (parking space) 车位

B **stalls** *npl* Brit 正厅前排座位

C *vi* **1** Aviat «*pilot, aircraft*» 失速; Aut «*engine*» 熄火; «*driver, vehicle*» 抛锚; **the car ~ed at a roundabout** 汽车在交通环处熄火了 **2** (play for time) 拖延时间; **to ~ for time** 拖延时间; **quit** *or* **stop ~ing!** 不要拖延了！ **3** (stop, stagnate) «*market, talks*» 停顿

D *vt* **1** Aviat 使…失速 ‹*aircraft*›; Aut 使…熄火 ‹*engine*›; 使…抛锚 ‹*vehicle*› **2** (hold up) 拖延 ‹*negotiations, process, person*›

stall: ~-fed *adj* 圈养的; **~-feed** *vt* 圈养; **~holder** *n* 摊贩

stalling tactic *n* 拖延战术

stallion /ˈstæliən/ *n* 牡马 [尤指种马]

stalwart /ˈstɔːlwət/

A *n* 坚定分子; **a party ~** 一名党内坚定分子

B *adj* 忠实的 ‹*defender, person*›; 坚决的 ‹*resistance, support*›; **to do ~ work** 勤奋可靠地工作

stamen /ˈsteɪmən/ *n* 雄蕊

stamina /ˈstæmɪnə/ *n* [u] 耐力; **to have/lack ~** 有/缺乏耐力; **to have the ~ for sth./to do sth.** 对某事物/做某事有耐性

stammer /ˈstæmə(r)/

A *vi* 结结巴巴地说话; **he tends to ~ when he is nervous** 他常常一紧张就结巴

B *vt* 结结巴巴地说出 ‹*words, reply*›; **to ~ sth. out** 结结巴巴地说出某事物

C *n* 口吃; **to have a ~** 说话结巴; **to speak with a ~** 结结巴巴地说话

stammerer /ˈstæmərə(r)/ *n* 口吃的人

stammering /ˈstæmərɪŋ/

A *n* [u] 口吃

B *adj attrib* 口吃的 ‹*person*›; 结结巴巴的 ‹*words, answer*›

stamp /stæmp/

A *n* **1** Post 邮票; **a 32p ~** 一枚面值 32 便士的邮票; **a first-/second-class ~** 第一类/第二类邮件所贴的邮票; **a book** *or* **booklet/sheet of ~s** 一本/一版邮票; **to put** *or* **stick a ~ on (sth.)** （给某物）贴上邮票; **to collect ~s** 集邮 **2** Comm (coupon) 赠券 **3** (marking tool) (made of rubber) 橡皮图章; (made of metal) 钢印; **a (die) ~** (for coins) 冲模 **4** (mark) 戳记; (seal) 印章; **visa ~s** 签证章; **a document bearing the official ~** 盖有公章的文件; **a ~ of approval** 许可; **to get the parental ~ of approval** 得到父母的同意 **5** (beating with foot) 跺脚; (sound) 跺脚声; **with a ~ of one's foot** 一跺脚; **to give a ~ of anger** 气愤地跺一下脚; **the ~ of horses' hoofs** 马蹄踩踏的声音 **6** (marking) (with rubber stamp) 盖章; (with die) 冲压 **7** fig (hallmark) 特征; **the ~ of truth** 真实性; **to bear the ~ of greatness** «*person*» 具有高贵的气质; **to set/leave one's ~ on sth.** 给某事物打上/留下自己的印记 **8** *sing* (type) 类型; **women of her ~** 她那样的女人

B *vt* **1** (print) (with rubber stamp) 盖上 ‹*mark*›; (with die) 冲压上 ‹*design*›; **the date of entry is ~ed in my passport** 我的护照盖上了入境日期; **the name is ~ed on the box** 名字印在了盒子上; **the crime has revenge ~ed all over it** fig 从各方面看，这一犯罪都是为了复仇 **2** (mark) (with rubber stamp) 在…上盖章 ‹*document, book*›; (with die) 在…上压印图案; **to be ~ed 'paid'** «*invoice*» 盖有“付讫”章 **3** (with foot) 跺; **to ~ one's feet** 跺脚; **to ~ one's foot in anger** 气得直跺脚; **to ~ sth. flat** 把某物踩平; **to ~ sth. into the ground** 把某物踩进土里 **4** *usu passive* Post 在…上贴邮票; **to be insufficiently ~ed** «*letter*» 邮资不足 **5** Tech 冲压; **to ~ metal discs from** *or* **out of a sheet of copper** 用一张铜板压制金属圆盘 **6** fig (imprint) 铭刻; **to ~ one's personality on sth.** 给…注入自己的个性 ‹*project, place*›; **it remains ~ed on my memory** 这件事一直铭刻在我的记忆中 **7** fig (identify) 表明; **his denial ~ed him as a liar** 他加以否认表明他在撒谎; **his clothes ~ him as a foreigner** 他的衣着表明他是个外国人

C *vi* **1** (bring foot down) «*person*» 跺脚; «*horse*» 用蹄子踩地; **to ~ on sth.** 用力踩某物; fig 压制 ‹*rebellion*›; **you ~ed on my foot!** 你踩到我的脚了！; **to ~ on the brakes** 猛踩刹车 **2** (tread heavily) 重步走; **don't ~!** 走路脚步别那么重！

S

Phrasal verbs

• **stamp off**

A *vt* [~ **sth. off,** ~ **off sth.**] 跺掉 ‹*mud, dirt*›; **to ~ sth. off one's shoes** 把某物从鞋子上跺掉

B *vi* 重步走开; **to ~ off in anger** 气冲冲地走开

• **stamp on** *vt* [~ **on sth.**] 坚决压制

• **stamp out**

A *vt* [~ **sth. out,** ~ **out sth.**]

1 (beat out) 踩灭 ‹*fire, embers*› **2** fig (crush) 镇压 ‹*rebellion*›; (wipe out) 消除 ‹*terrorism, crime*›; **to ~ out tax evasion** 打击逃税行为; **to ~ out the disease** 消灭这种疾病 **3** Tech 冲压; **to be ~ed out from a strip of steel** 用钢条冲压而成

B *vi* 重步走出; **to ~ out in a huff** 气冲冲地走出去

stamp: ~ **album** *n* 集邮册; ~ **collecting** *n* [u] 集邮; ~ **collection** *n* 邮票藏品; ~ **collector** *n* 集邮爱好者; ~ **duty** *n* [u and c] 印花税

stamped addressed envelope *n* Brit [邮资已付并写好地址的] 回邮信封

stampede /stæmˈpiːd/

A *n* **1** (rush of animals) 惊跑 **2** (rush of humans) 奔逃; (sudden movement of people) 蜂拥; fig (of people doing the same thing) 热潮; **there was a sudden ~ towards the exit** 人们突然涌向出口; **falling interest rates have led to a ~ to buy property** 利率持续下降引发了一阵购房热; **a ~ for sth.** 做某事的热潮 **3** Amer (rodeo) 牛仔竞技表演

B *vi* (charge) «*animals, crowd*» 惊跑; (move quickly and in large numbers) 蜂拥; **to ~ towards/into ...** 涌向/涌进 ‹*doors*›; **a stampeding elephant** 受惊狂奔的大象

C *vt* **1** (cause to stampede) 使…狂奔 ‹*animals, crowd*› **2** fig (force the hand of) 使…冲动行事 ‹*person*›; **to ~ sb. into doing sth.** 使某人仓促做某事

stamping ground *n* Brit 常去的地方

stamp machine *n* 邮票自动出售机

stance /stɑːns, stæns/ *n* **1** (attitude) 态度; **a ~ on sth.** 对某事物的态度; **to take up** *or* **adopt a ~** 采取一种态度; **to maintain a ~** 保持一种立场 **2** (way of standing) 站立姿势; (in sport) 击球姿势; **to adopt a ~** 摆出一种姿势

stanch /stæntʃ/ *vt* esp Amer = **staunch²**

stanchion /ˈstænʃən, Amer ˈstæntʃən/ *n* 支柱

stand /stænd/

A *vi* (*pt, pp* **stood**) **1** (get to or be on feet) 站立; **she was too weak to ~** 她虚弱得站都站不住; **everyone stood when the prime minister entered the room** 首相进屋时，大家都站了起来; **they were ~ing at the bar** 他们站在吧台旁; **a bird ~ing on one leg** 单腿独立的鸟; **don't just ~ there, do something!** 别光站在那儿! 找点儿事做!; **to ~ still** 停住不动; **to ~ at attention/ease** 立正/稍息; **they were left with nothing but the clothes they stood (up) in** 他们除了身上穿的衣服已一无所有; **to ~ on sb.'s foot** 踩到某人的脚; **to leave sb. ~ing** 把某人远远甩在后面; **as a cook, she leaves me ~ing** 她的厨艺比我高明多了 **2** (be or become upright) 直立; **these walls have stood for centuries** 这些墙已经矗立了好几个世纪; **after the shelling only a few houses were left ~ing** 炮击之后只剩几幢房子没倒; **the earthquake destroyed the village completely; not a stone remained ~ing** 地震完全摧毁了村庄，一切都被夷为平地; **to ~ on one's hands** 双手倒立 **3** (measure in height) 高度为; **he ~s 6 feet in his bare feet** 他赤脚身高为 6 英尺; **the tower ~s 60 metres high** 这座塔高 60 米 **4** (be positioned) 位于; (be) 处于; **a tree once stood there** 那儿曾经有过一棵树; **a little town ~ing by the sea** 坐落在海边的小镇; **the house has stood empty for years** 这栋房子空置了多年; **he stood firm against her attempts to persuade him** 她试图说服他，但他坚决不让步; **I ~ corrected** 我欢迎指正; **as things ~** 就目前情况来看; **when it came to practical jokes Tom stood alone** 说到恶作剧，汤姆无人能比; **how do things ~ between the two of you at the moment?** 你们俩现在关系如何?; **nothing ~s between me and getting the job** 什么也阻止不了我得到那份工作; **I won't ~ between them** 我不会拆散他们; **to ~ in sb.'s way** 挡住某人的路; fig 阻拦某人 **5** (remain stationary) 停住; **our train stood outside the station for half an hour** 我们的列车在站外停了半个小时; **time seemed to ~ still** 时间好像停止了 **6** (remain valid) 保持有效; (remain unchanged) 保持不变; **the agreement ~s** 协议仍然有效; **the world record stood for 43 years** 这项世界纪录保持了 43 年; **we must let the matter ~ and see what happens** 我们对此事一定不要插手，静观其变即可 **7** (be at certain level) 达到特定水平; (be at certain point of a scale) 达到特定数值; **the thermometer ~s at 40°C** 温度计的读数为 40 摄氏度; **the budget stood at £2,000 million per annum** 预算为每年 20 亿英镑; **to ~ at an all-time high/low** 创历史最高/最低纪录 **8** (be liable) 很可能会; **to ~ to do sth.** 很可能会做某事; **he ~s to make a lot of money** 他准能赚大钱 **9** (rest) 静止; **mix the batter and then let it ~ for 20 minutes** 搅好面糊后醒 20 分钟 **10** Brit (be candidate) 参加竞选; **to ~ for parliament/president** 竞选议员/总统; **to ~ as the Labour candidate** 作为工党候选人参选 **11** (act as) 担任; **will you ~ as godfather for him?** 你愿意当他的教父吗?; **he refused to ~ as guarantor for me/the loan** 他拒绝为我/这笔贷款担保 **12** (have opinion) 持某观点; **where do you ~ on abortion?** 你对堕胎持什么观点?

B *vt* (*pt, pp* **stood**) **1** (place) 使…站立 ‹*person*›; 使…直立 ‹*object*›; **he stood the child on a stool** 他让孩子站到凳子上; **he stood the ladder against the wall** 他把梯子立在墙边; **to ~ sth. on (its) end** 把某物倒置; **he stood himself near the door** 他站在门边 **2** (bear, withstand) 忍受; **I can't ~ liars!** 我无法容忍撒谎的人!; **I can't ~ her laughing at me** 我不能容忍她嘲笑我; **she couldn't ~ to wait a moment longer** 她一刻也等不下去了; **modern plastics can ~ very high temperatures** 新型塑料能承受很高的温度; **it won't ~ close scrutiny** 那事经不起仔细审查; **he can't ~ the sight of spiders** 他一看到蜘蛛就难受; **more than flesh and blood can ~** 凡人难以忍受的 **3** (pay for) 为…付账; **I'll ~ you a slap-up dinner!** 我要请你们吃大餐!; **he's ~ing drinks all round** 他做东，请大家喝饮料

C *n* **1** (attitude) 立场; **the party's tough ~ on immigration** 该党在移民问题上的强硬立场; **he has always taken a firm ~ on capital punishment** 他在死刑问题上一直立场坚定 **2** (resistance to attack) 抵抗; **to make** *or* **put up a ~** 进行抵抗; **you must make a ~ for your principles** 你必须捍卫自己的原则; **we have to make a ~ against racism** 我们必须抵制种族主义 **3** (rack, frame) 架; (pedestal) 座; **he hung his coat on the ~ in the hall** 他把外套挂在门厅里的衣帽架上; **a book ~** 书架 **4** (table for selling sth.) 货摊; (kiosk) 售货亭; **a newspaper ~** 报摊; **a hamburger ~** 汉堡包售卖亭; **to set up a ~ in the market** 在市场上摆摊 **5** (promoting area or structure) 展台; **a display/trade ~** 展位/展销台 **6** (place for vehicles to wait) 停车候客处 **7** Sport (seating structure for spectators) 看台 **8** (platform) (for a band, orchestra) 舞台; (for speaker) 讲台 **9** (witness box) 证人席; **to take the ~** 出庭作证 **10** (stop for performance) 停留演出; **to get a ~ in Liverpool for three performances** 在利物浦停留演出三场 **11** (standstill) 停止; **to come to a ~** 停下来; **owing to heavy snowfalls all trains were at a ~ in Scotland** 由于下大雪，苏格兰的所有火车都停运了; **to bring sth. to a ~** 使某事物停下来 **12** (cricket partnership) 双人配对 **13** (growth of plants) 林分; **a fine ~ of wheat/trees** 一片长势很好的小麦/树林

Phrasal verbs

• **stand about, stand around** *vi* 站着; **to ~ about doing sth.** 闲站着做某事; **I can't ~ about waiting for you all day!** 我不能整天闲着等你!

• **stand aside** *vi* **1** (move) 站到一边; **to ~ aside to do sth.** 站到一边做某事 **2** (refuse to act) 不作为; **she just stood aside and let me do everything** 她只是袖手旁观，什么事都让我做 **3** (withdraw) 退居一旁; **he stood aside as leader of the party** 他让出了该党领袖的位子

• **stand back** *vi* **1** (move) 往后站; **the policeman ordered us to ~ back** 警察命令我们退后; **you should ~ back from the painting** 你应该站得离那幅画远一些 **2** (become detached, objective) 置身事外; **to ~ back from sth.** 置身于某事物之外; **it's time to ~ back and look at your career so far** 现在你该从旁观者的角度来看一看自己到目前为止的职业生涯了 **3** **to ~ back from sth.** (be situated) 不是紧挨着某物; **the house ~s back from the road** 房子离公路有一段距离

• **stand by**

A *vi* **1** (be prepared) 做好行动准备; **the army is ~ing by with additional supplies** 军队随时准备提供更多的补给品; **to ~ by for sth.** 为某事物做好准备; **~ by for lift-off!** 准备发射!; **to ~ by to do sth.** 准备好做某事; **we stood by to receive instructions** 我们正在待命 **2** (remain uninvolved) 袖手旁观; **you can't just ~ by and do nothing** 你不能只是袖手旁观，什么都不做

B *vt* **1** [~ **by sb.**] (be loyal to) 支持; **whatever he does, she always ~s by her man** 不管她丈夫做什么，她都支持他 **2** [~ **by sth.**] (not break or retract) 遵守; **he ~s by everything he said** 他从不食言; **to ~ by one's pledges** 信守诺言

• **stand down**

A *vi* **1** (resign) «*candidate*» 退出; **the President has stood down after five years in office** 总统任职 5 年后下台了 **2** (relax after alert) «*army, emergency services*» 解除警戒状态 **3** (leave witness box) «*witness*» 退出证人席

B *vt* [~ **sb./sth. down,** ~ **down sb./sth.**] 命令…解除警戒状态 ‹*army, emergency services*›

• **stand for** *vt* [~ **for sth.**]

1 (denote) 表示; **OUP ~s for Oxford University Press** OUP 代表牛津大学出版社 **2** (represent) 主张; **I condemn fascism and all it ~s for** 我谴责法西斯主义以及它的一切主张 **3** (support) 支持; **a party that ~s for racial equality** 一个支持种族平等的政党 **4** colloq (tolerate) 忍受; **I will not ~ for such outrageous behaviour** 我不能容忍如此无礼的行为; **to ~ for sb. doing sth.** 容忍某人做某事; **I will not ~ for him behaving like that** 我不能容忍他那样行事

• **stand in** *vi* 代替; **to ~ in for sb.** 代替某人

• **stand off**

A *vi* **1** (move or keep away) 走开; **the women stood off at a slight distance** 妇女们站得稍远 **2** (reach deadlock) «*adversaries, opponents*» 陷入僵局

B *vt* [~ **sb. off,** ~ **off sb.**] Brit (lay off) 解雇

• **stand out** *vi* **1** **to ~ out from** *or* **against sth.** (be noticeable) 在某物的衬托下显眼; **the yellow letters ~ out well against the black background** 黄色字母在黑色背景的衬托下很醒目; **to ~ out like a sore thumb** colloq 扎眼 **2** **~ out from sb./sth.** (be better) 比某人/某事物出色; (be more important)

S

比某人/某事物重要; **she ~s out a mile from other candidates** 和其他候选人相比，她非常出众 **3** (protrude) 凸出; **veins stood out on his forehead** 他额头上青筋凸起; **to ~ out in (sharp) relief** （清晰地）凸显 **4** (resist) 坚持抵抗; **the workers stood out against attempts to close the company down** 工人们坚决抵制关闭公司的企图

• **stand to**

A *vi* «*sailors, soldiers*» 进入戒备状态

B *vt* [**~ sb. to, ~ to sb.**] 使…进入戒备状态 ‹*sailors, soldiers*›

• **stand up**

A *vi* **1** (get to or be on feet) 站立; **we stood up when the teacher came into the room** 老师走进教室时，我们都站了起来; **to ~ up straight** 站直; **to be ~ing up** 站着 **2** (stay upright) 直立; **the tripod wouldn't ~ up properly** 这副三脚架立不起来 **3** **to ~ up for sth.** (defend, support) 维护某事物; **~ up for what you believe in** 你要捍卫你的信仰; **she stood up for him when he was accused of dishonesty** 他被人指责不诚实时，她站出来为他辩护; **to ~ up for oneself** 自我保护 **4** (withstand investigation) 经得起检验; **the evidence will never ~ up in a court of law** 这一证据在法庭上根本站不住脚; **his case didn't ~ up to close scrutiny** 他的论据经不起仔细推敲 **5** **to ~ up to sb.** (resist) 抵抗某人; **to ~ up to a bully** 反抗恶霸逞凶 **6** **to ~ up to sth.** (withstand) 经受得住某事物; **the car is designed to ~ up to our harsh winter climate** 这种车的设计使其能够在我们这里冬季的严寒气候里正常行驶; **to ~ up to a lot of wear and tear** 十分耐用

B *vt* **1** [**~ sb./sth. up, ~ up sb./sth.**] (set upright) 使…站立 ‹*person*›; 使…直立 ‹*object*›; **to ~ a ladder up against a wall** 把梯子靠墙立着; **after the little boy had fallen over, she stood him up** 小男孩摔倒后，她把他扶了起来 **2** [**~ sb. up, ~ up sb.**] colloq (fail to meet) 让…白等; **she said she'd meet me at 7 o'clock, but she stood me up** 她说7点钟和我见面，但她失约了; **I was stood up** 我空等了一场

stand-alone *adj* 独立的 ‹*hardware, software, company*›

standard /ˈstændəd/

A *n* **1** (official specification) 度量衡标准; **to comply with EU ~s** 符合欧盟标准; **an industry/international ~** 行业/国际标准; **to adhere** *or* **conform to a ~** 遵照执行一项标准; **to apply** *or* **enforce/abandon a ~** 实施/放弃一项标准 **2** (level of quality) 水平; (requirement, yardstick) 标准; **a ~ of culture in a society** 社会文化水平; **academic** *or* **scholastic ~s** 学术水准; **by European ~s, pollution in parts of this country is appalling** 按欧洲标准衡量，这个国家部分地区的污染令人震惊; **has he reached the required ~?** 他达到规定水平了吗？; **to be below ~** 未达标; **to be up** *or* **come up to ~** 达标 **3** (banner, emblem) 旗帜; **the royal ~** 王旗; **to raise one's** *or* **the ~ (against sb.)** (take up arms) 拿起武器（反抗某人）; fig (oppose) 起来反抗（某人） **4** (song) 经典歌曲; **the old ~s** 经典老歌 **5** (tree or shrub) 茎干挺直的植物

B **standards** *npl* 行为规范; **moral ~s** 道德规范; **to maintain** *or* **keep up one's ~s** 坚持自己的行为准则

C *adj* **1** (officially specified) 标准的; **~ weights and measures** 标准度量衡; **the ~ rate of tax** 标准税率 **2** (normal) 普通的; **a ~ letter** 平信; **it is ~ practice to act in this way** 采取这样的行动是例行做法; **these vehicles now come with a CD player as ~** 这些车辆现在都标配CD播放机 **3** (authoritative) 权威性的; **a ~ author** 权威作家 **4** Ling 标准的; **~ English** 规范英语 **5** (growing on stem) 茎干挺直的

standard: **~ amenities** *npl* 房屋标准卫生设施; **S~ Assessment Task** *n* Brit 标准会考; **~-bearer** *n* **1** Mil 旗手; **2** fig 领袖; **~ cost** *n* 标准成本; **~ deviation** *n* 均方差; **~ gauge** *n* [u] 标准轨距; **a ~-gauge railway** 标准轨距铁路; **~-issue** *adj* **1** Mil 标准配发的 ‹*uniform, firearm*›; **2** colloq (unexceptional) 典型的 ‹*clothes, person, haircut*›

standardization /ˌstændədaɪˈzeɪʃn, Amer -drˈz-/ *n* [u] 标准化; **to aim for** *or* **seek ~** 追求标准化; **to bring about** *or* **achieve ~** 实现标准化

standardize /ˈstændədaɪz/ *vt* 使标准化

standard: **~ lamp** *n* Brit 落地灯; **~ of living** *n* 生活水平; **to raise the ~ of living** 提高生活水平; **~ time** *n* [u] 标准时

standby /ˈstændbaɪ/

A *n* (*pl* **~s**) **1** [u and c] (backup) 备用品; (person) 后备人员; **to be on ~** «*army*» 待命; **to be put on ~** «*army*» 进入待命状态 **2** [u and c] (in travel) (state of waiting for ticket) 等待退票; (person waiting for ticket) 等退票的旅客; **to be on ~** 候补待位; **to be put on ~** 被列入候补待位名单 **3** [u] Elec 待机状态; **to save energy, don't leave appliances on ~** 为省电起见，不要让电器处于待机状态

B *adj* **1** (emergency) 备用的 ‹*vehicle, supply, lighting*›; 待命的 ‹*mode*› **2** (in travel) 等待退票的 ‹*passenger*›; 作为退票处理的 ‹*ticket*›

standee /stænˈdiː/ *n* esp Amer (person standing) (passenger) 站立乘客; (spectator) 站票观众

stand-in

A *n* **1** (replacement) 代替人 **2** Cin, Theat 替身演员

B *adj attrib* 替补的 ‹*goalkeeper*›; 代课的 ‹*teacher*›; 替身的 ‹*actor*›; 临时的 ‹*leader*›

standing /ˈstændɪŋ/

A *n* [u] **1** (reputation) 名声; (position) 地位; **of high** *or* **considerable ~** 声望高的; **one's ~ among ...** 在…中的地位; **social/academic/professional/financial ~** 社会/学术/专业/金融地位 **2** (length of time) **of long/ten years ~** 长期的/持续10年的

B *adj attrib* **1** (permanent) 常设的 ‹*committee*›; 常备的 ‹*army*›; (continuing) 长期有效的 ‹*rule, charge, invitation*› **2** Sport (from standing position) 站立的 ‹*position*›; **a ~ jump/start** 立定跳远/站立式起跑 **3** Agric 生长的 ‹*crop*› **4** Transp 站着的 ‹*passenger*›

standing: **~ charge** *n* 固定费用; **~ joke** *n* 活笑柄; **it's a ~ joke that he always forgets his key** 大家总是笑他老忘记带钥匙; **~ order** *n* **1** Fin 按期付款委托书; **2** Brit Comm 长期订单; **a ~ order for sth.** 某物的长期订单; **~ ovation** *n* 起立鼓掌; **to give sb. a ~ ovation** 为某人起立鼓掌; **~ room** *n* [u] [剧场、体育馆等处的] 站立空间; **~ stone** *n* 巨石柱

stand-off *n* 僵局; **his surrender ended a dramatic ~ with the police** 他投降了，从而结束了与警方的紧张对峙

stand-offish /ˌstændˈɒfɪʃ/ *adj* colloq 冷漠的 ‹*person, manner*›

stand-offishness /ˌstændˈɒfɪʃnɪs/ *n* [u] colloq 冷漠

stand: **~pipe** *n* 竖管; **~point** *n* 立场; **from sb.'s ~point** *or* **the ~point of sb.** 从某人的立场

standstill /ˈstændstɪl/ *n* (stop) (of traffic, production) 停止; (of economy, growth) 停滞; **to be at a ~** «*traffic*» 处于堵塞状态; **to come to a ~** 停下来; **to bring sth. to a ~** 使…陷入停顿状态 ‹*service*›

standstill agreement *n* 维持现状协议

stand-up

A *adj attrib* **1** (eaten standing) 站着吃的 ‹*meal*› **2** Theat, TV 表演独角喜剧的 ‹*comedian, comedy*› **3** (aggressive) 激烈的 ‹*row, fight*›

B *n* **1** [u] **~ (comedy)** 独角喜剧 **2** [c] **~ (comedian)** 独角喜剧演员

stank /stæŋk/ *pt* ▸**stink A**

Stanley knife® /ˈstænli naɪf/ *n* Brit 斯坦利工艺刀

stannic /ˈstænɪk/ *adj* 锡的

stannous /ˈstænəs/ *adj* 亚锡的

stanza /ˈstænzə/ *n* 诗节

staphylococcus /ˌstæfɪləˈkɒkəs/ *n* (*pl* **staphylococci** /ˌstæfɪləˈkɒkaɪ/) 葡萄球菌

staple[1] /ˈsteɪpl/

A *adj attrib* 主要的 ‹*product, crop*›; **~ foods/industries** 主食/基本工业; **violence is the ~ diet of the video generation** 暴力是影像时代的人的主要精神食粮

B *n* **1** (basic food) 主食 **2** (crop) 主要作物; (product) 主要产品; (industry) 基本工业 **3** fig (main element) 主要内容

staple[2]

A *n* **1** (for paper) 订书钉 **2** Constr (U-shaped) U形钉

B *vt* **1** (fasten) 用订书机订 ‹*papers, cloth*›; **to ~ sth. to sth.** 用订书机把某物订到某物上; **to ~ two sheets of paper together** 把两张纸装订到一起 **2** Med 为…做间隔手术 ‹*stomach*›

staple gun *n* 订书钉射枪

stapler /ˈsteɪplə(r)/ *n* 订书机

staple remover *n* 起钉器

star /stɑː(r)/

A *n* **1** Astron 星; **under the ~s** 在星空下; **to camp out under the ~s** 露天宿营; **to reach for the ~s** 有远大志向; **to see ~s** colloq 眼冒金星; **to have ~s in one's eyes** 渴望成名 **2** (shape) 星形; **the walls were painted with moons and ~s** 墙上画着月亮和星星 **3** (celebrity) 明星; **a pop/Hollywood ~** 流行音乐歌星/好莱坞影星; **a tennis ~** 网球明星; **the film made him a ~ overnight** 这部影片使他一夜成名 **4** (main performer) 主角 **5** (best of group) 最优秀者; **she is the ~ of the class** 她是班上最优秀的学生 **6** (rating mark for hotel or restaurant) 星级; **this hotel has three ~s** 这家旅馆是三星级的; **a four-~ restaurant** 四星级餐馆 **7** (asterisk) 星号 **8** (badge of law enforcement officer) 星徽 **9** (mark of rank on military uniform) 星章; **how many ~s does the general have?** 这位将军有几颗星？; **a five-~ general** 五星上将 **10** Sch (award sticker) [作为表扬的] 星形贴; **I got a gold ~ for my work** 我的作业得了一颗金星 **11** (white patch on an animal's forehead) 白斑 **12** colloq (helpful person) 给予帮助的人; **thanks! you're a ~!** 谢谢！你真是个大好人！ **13** (planet or constellation influencing person's fate) 星宿; **it's written in the ~s** 这是命中注定的; **to be born under a lucky/an unlucky ~** 生来命好/命不好; ▸**lucky 2**

B **stars** *npl* Brit colloq (horoscope) 星象; **do you read your ~s?** 你读星象方面的内容吗？; **what do my ~s say?** 我的星象怎么样？

C *modif* **1** (of a celebrity) 明星的; **~ treatment** 明星级的待遇 **2** (main) 主角的; **to have a ~ role in a play** 在一部剧中担任主角 **3** (outstanding, best) 最优秀的; **the ~ performer** 表现最佳者; **the ~ prize** 特等奖

D *vt* (*pres p etc.* **-rr-**) **1** (feature) «*film, play*» 由…担任主角; «*director, studio*» 使主演; **a movie ~ring Leonardo DiCaprio** 一部由莱昂纳多·迪卡普里奥主演的电影; **Hitchcock ~red her in many of his films** 希区柯克让她主演了他执导的多部电影 **2** (mark with asterisk) 用星号标出; **~red dishes on the menu are suitable for vegetarians** 菜单上标有星号的菜品适合素食者 **3** (decorate) 用星形物装饰; **sea urchins ~red the pale rocks** 海胆像星星一样点缀着灰白的礁石; **a meadow ~red with wild flowers** 野花星星点点点缀其间的草地

E *vi* (*pres p etc.* **-rr-**) 主演; **he ~s as Henry V** 他扮演主角亨利五世; **she ~red with** *or*

opposite Keanu Reeves in The Matrix 她和基努·里维斯搭档，在《黑客帝国》中饰演男女主角; **she has a ~ring role in the new play** 她在新剧中担任主角

star anise *n* [u] 八角茴香

starboard /ˈstɑːbəd/ *n* [u] Naut, Aviat 右舷; **to ~** 向右舷方向; **hard a-~!** 向右舷打满舵！; **to alter course** *or* **turn to ~** 将航线转向右侧; **to bank to ~** 向右倾斜转弯; **a ~ tack** 右舷抢风行驶

starch /stɑːtʃ/

A *n* **1** [u and c] (carbohydrate) 淀粉; (food) 含淀粉食物; **potato/wheat ~** 马铃薯/小麦淀粉 **2** [u] (for clothes) 淀粉浆; **to put ~ on sth.** 给某物上浆; **spray ~** 喷雾淀粉浆

B *vt* 给…打浆 ‹*clothes, sheet*›; **a shirt with ~ed cuffs and collar** 袖口和领子浆过的衬衣

star chart *n* 星图

starchy /ˈstɑːtʃi/ *adj* **1** (containing starch) 含淀粉的 ‹*food, diet*›; (resembling starch) 淀粉似的 ‹*substance*› **2** colloq pej (formal, stiff) 刻板的 ‹*person, manner*›

star: ~ connection *n* 星形三相绕组; **~-crossed** *adj* liter 命运不好的

stardom /ˈstɑːdəm/ *n* [u] 明星地位; **to rise to ~** 成为明星; **he is being groomed for ~** 他正在接受明星培训

stardust /ˈstɑːdʌst/ *n* [u] fig 魔力

stare /stɛər/

A *vi* **1** (gaze) 注视; **I screamed, and everyone ~d** 我尖叫起来，大家都盯着我看; **to ~ back at sb.** 与某人对视; **to ~ up/down at sb./sth.** 抬头/低头盯着某人/某物; **to ~ into space/the distance** 茫然直视/凝视远方 **2** (be wide open) «*eyes*» 睁大注视; **her angry eyes ~d back at him** 她生气地瞪大眼睛与他对视

B *vt* 注视; **the teacher ~d the child into silence** 老师把那个孩子盯得不再说话; **to be staring sb. in the face** (be obvious) 对某人来说显而易见; (be unavoidable) 对某人来说不可避免; **defeat was staring them in the face** 他们必败无疑; **to be staring sth. in the face** 某事物不可避免; **they were staring defeat in the face** 他们必败

C *n* 注视; **we received curious ~s from the passers-by** 过路人向我们投来好奇的目光; **he fixed her with an angry ~** 他愤怒地瞪着她; **she gave him a blank ~** 她面无表情地看了他一眼; **to return/hold sb.'s ~** 与某人对视/目光相接

Phrasal verbs

- **stare down** *vt* [**~ sb. down, ~ down sb.**] 盯得…转移目光; **he easily ~d her down** 他轻易就把她盯得低下了头
- **stare out** *vt* [**~ sb. out, ~ out sb.**] 盯得…转移目光; **the children were trying to ~ each other out** 两个孩子对视着，看谁能把对方瞪得受不了

star: ~fish *n* (*pl* **~fish** *or* **~fishes**) 海星; **~fruit** *n* **1** [c and u] (fruit) 杨桃; **2** [c] (plant) 七瓣莲; **~gazer** /ˈstɑːɡeɪzə(r)/ *n* colloq **1** (astronomer) 天文学家; **2** (astrologer) 占星术家; **~gazing** /ˈstɑːɡeɪzɪŋ/ *n* [u] **1** (astronomy) 观星; **2** (astrology) 占星学

staring /ˈsteərɪŋ/ *adj attrib* 凝视的 ‹*crowd*›; **to look at sb. with ~ eyes** 目不转睛地看某人

stark /stɑːk/

A *adj* **1** (bare) 荒凉的 ‹*landscape, scene*›; 单调的 ‹*lighting, decor*›; 无生气的 ‹*appearance*›; 无修饰的 ‹*beauty*› **2** fig (unadorned) 赤裸裸的 ‹*fact, truth*›; 严酷的 ‹*reality, realism*›; 鲜明的 ‹*contrast*›; 无情的 ‹*reminder, warning*›; **to face a ~ choice** 面临残酷的选择 **3** *attrib* (sheer) 极度的 ‹*terror*›

B *adv* 完全地 ‹*naked, crazy*›; **to be ~ staring** *or* **raving mad** colloq 完全疯了

starkers /ˈstɑːkəz/ *adj pred* Brit colloq 一丝不挂的

starkly /ˈstɑːkli/ *adv* **1** (austerely) 粗陋地 ‹*outlined, lit, simple*› **2** (bluntly) 明显地 ‹*contrast, highlight, contradict*›; 非常 ‹*evident, honest, realistic*›; 极其 ‹*violent*›

starkness /ˈstɑːknɪs/ *n* [u] **1** (bareness) (of landscape, appearance) 荒凉; (of decor, room) 简朴 **2** fig (directness) 率直

starless /ˈstɑːlɪs/ *adj* 无星星的 ‹*night, sky*›

starlet /ˈstɑːlɪt/ *n* 尚未成名的年轻女演员

starlight /ˈstɑːlaɪt/ *n* [u] 星光

starling /ˈstɑːlɪŋ/ *n* 椋鸟

starlit *adj* 星光照耀的

Star of David *n* 大卫之星 [犹太教的标志]

starry /ˈstɑːri/ *adj* **1** (full of stars) 繁星闪烁的 ‹*night, sky*› **2** (shining) 明亮的 ‹*eye*› **3** colloq (all-star) 明星云集的 ‹*cast*›

starry-eyed *adj* 天真的 ‹*admiration*›; 空想的 ‹*person, notion*›; **to be ~ about sb./sth.** 对某人/某事物过分乐观

star: S~s and Bars *n + v sing* Hist **the S~s and Bars** [美国南北战争中的] 南部邦联旗; **S~s and Stripes** *n + v sing* **the S~s and Stripes** 星条旗 [美国国旗]; **~shell** *n* 照明弹; **~ sign** *n* 星座

> **the Stars and Stripes**
>
> 星条旗。美国国旗，亦称古老的荣耀（Old Glory）或星光闪耀的旗帜（Star-Spangled Banner）。为长方形，左上角为蓝色方框，内有 50 颗白色五角星，象征美国的 50 个州——最早为 13 颗，后每新增一个州，就增加一颗星。方框外为红白相间的 13 道条纹（stripe），7 红 6 白，代表最早的 13 个州。1777 年 6 月 14 日经第二届大陆会议（Second Continental Congress）确定为国旗，后来把 6 月 14 日定为国旗日（flag day）。举办大型活动时，人们常需向国旗宣誓效忠（Pledge of Allegiance）。

star-spangled *adj* **1** liter (covered with stars) 布满星星的 ‹*sky, cloth*› **2** fig (impressively successful) 非常成功的 ‹*career, cast*›

Star-spangled Banner *n* **1** (flag) **the ~** 星条旗 **2** (anthem) **the ~** 《星条旗永不落》[美国国歌]

star: ~-struck *adj* colloq 追星族的; **~-studded** *adj* **1** (filled with stars) 繁星点点的 ‹*sky*›; **2** colloq 明星荟萃的 ‹*cast, film*›

start /stɑːt/

A *vi* **1** (begin to happen) 开始; **when does the class ~?** 什么时候上课？; **have you any idea where the rumour ~ed?** 你知不知道谣言是从哪儿传出来的？; **the custom ~ed in the Middle Ages** 这一习俗始于中世纪 **2** (begin doing sth.) 开始做; (begin saying sth.) 开始说; **can you ~ on Monday?** 你能星期一开始上班吗？; **it's a long story; where shall I ~?** 说来话长，我该从哪儿说起呢？; **the best professional musicians ~ young** 顶尖的音乐家都从小就接触音乐; **we'll ~ at the top of page 20** 我们从第 20 页的上端开始读; **to ~ on one's journey** 起程; **as soon as they'd finished the first bottle, they ~ed on the next** 他们刚喝完第一瓶就打开了第二瓶; **it's time we got ~ed** 我们该动手了; **I must get ~ed on my revision in good time** 我必须及早开始复习 **3** (do as a first stage) 首先做; **let's ~ by reviewing what we did last week** 我们先来复习一下上周学的内容; **let's ~ with the case you mentioned** 我们先来说说你提到的情况; **she ~ed as a secretary but ended up running the department** 她起初是一位秘书，但最后掌管了整个部门; **I ~ed in marketing** 我是从销售干起的; **to ~ as one means to go on** 始终如一 **4** (have as a first stage) 开头是; (have as a starting point) 起始; **the day ~ed badly: I overslept!** 那天一开始就不顺利，我睡过了头！; **her name ~s with (an) M** 她名字的首字母是M; **this is where the desert ~s** 沙漠从这里延伸开去; **prices ~ at 50 dollars** 价格从 50 美元起 **5** (leave) 出发; (begin to move) 开始走; **we must ~ at 6 o'clock** 我们必须 6 点钟动身; **to ~ for/from sth.** 起程去某处/从某处出发; **I ~ed after her to tell her the news** 我起身朝她追去，要把消息告诉她; **he ~ed for the door, but I blocked his way** 他向门口走去，但我拦住了他 **6** (begin to operate) 启动; **the car won't ~** 这辆车发动不起来 **7** (jump) 突然一惊; **the sudden noise made her ~** 突如其来的声音吓了她一跳 **8** colloq (begin to complain) 开始抱怨; **don't ~! I told you I'd be late** 别抱怨啦！我跟你说过我会迟到的

B *vt* **1** (begin to do) 开始做; (begin to engage in) 开始从事 ‹*occupation*›; (begin to experience) 开始经历; (begin to attend) 开始上; (begin to use) 开始用; **he's just ~ed a new job** 他刚刚开始干上一个新工作; **the ship ~ed its voyage at Auckland** 船从奥克兰起航; **I only ~ed this book yesterday** 我昨天才开始看这本书; **he ~ed laughing** 他大笑起来; **it ~ed to rain** 下起雨来了; **he ~ed life as a teacher before turning to journalism** 他一开始当过教师，后来改行从事新闻工作; **do you ~ the day with a good breakfast?** 你早晨起来先要好好吃一顿早饭吗？; **she ~s school today** 她今天开学; **we need to ~ a new jar of coffee** 我们得新开一罐咖啡了 **2** (cause to begin activity) 使动手; **to ~ sb. in business** 帮助某人创业; **the news ~ed me thinking** 那条消息让我思考起来; **I must just get the kids ~ed on their homework** 我必须让孩子们动手做作业了 **3** (give signal in race) 给…发起跑信号 ‹*runners*› **4** (cause to begin) 使开始; (cause to happen) 使发生; **to ~ a fire/an argument** 生火/挑起争论; **to ~ a family** 开始生儿育女; **to ~ something** colloq 惹事; **stop fighting, you two! — he ~ed it!** 你们俩不要打了！——是他先动的手！ **5** (cause to begin operating) 启动; **I can't get the car ~ed** 这辆车我发动不起来

C *n* **1** (beginning) 开端; **tomorrow's the ~ of a new school year** 明天是新学年的第一天; **the ~ of his speech was rather boring** 他演讲的开头部分很乏味; **the ~ of something big** colloq 大事的苗头; **that's a good ~** 那是个不错的开端; **the meeting got off to a good ~** 会议有了一个良好的开端; **a perfect ~ to the holidays** 假期的完美开端; **at the ~, I thought I could trust him** 开始时我以为可以信赖他; **at the ~ of the year** 在年初; **(right) from the ~ (of sth.)** 从（某事物）一开始; **from ~ to finish** 自始至终; **for a ~** 首先 **2** (act of beginning sth.) 开始; **I think you should make a ~ on your homework now** 我想你现在该动手做作业了; **to make an early ~** (on journey) 早早动身; (on work) 早早开始; **to make a fresh** *or* **new ~** 开始新的生活 **3** (opportunity for beginning sth.) 起始优势; **to give one's children a good ~ in life** 为孩子们奠定一个良好的人生基础; **the job gave him his ~ in journalism** 那份工作使他走上了从事新闻业的道路 **4** (useful initial contribution) 良好开端; **I've written one page of my essay; it's not much, but it's a ~** 我的文章写了一页，虽然不多，却是个良好的开端 **5** (beginning of race) 起跑; **the runners lined up at the ~** 赛跑运动员在起跑线上一字排开; **the pistol went for the ~ of the 100 metres** 百米赛跑起跑的发令枪响了 **6** (distance or time advantage) 起跑提前量; **they gave me a 10-metre ~ in the race** 他们在赛跑中让了我 10 米; **he had an hour's ~ on me** 他比我先出发 1 小时 **7** (race, competition) 参加的比赛; **she has been beaten only once in six ~s** 她参加了 6 次比赛，只输了一次 **8** (sudden movement) 突然一动; **she woke from the dream with a ~** 她从梦中惊醒; **you gave me quite a ~!** 你吓了我一大跳！

D **to start with** *adv phr* **1** (firstly) 首先; **to ~ with, we haven't enough money** 首先我们

S

的钱不够 2 (at first) 起初; **she wasn't very keen on the idea to ~ with** 她一开始并不太喜欢这个主意 3 (at all) 丝毫; **I should never have told her to ~ with** 我根本就不该告诉她

Phrasal verbs

- **start back** *vi* 1 (begin to return) 动身返回; **isn't it time we ~ed back?** 我们是不是该回去了? 2 (step back) 突然后退
- **start in on** *vt* [**~ in on sb.**] colloq (criticize) 开始批评; (scold) 开始斥责; (shout at) 开始冲…叫嚷; **she ~ed in on me for being late** 她因为我迟到了而数落我
- **start off**

A *vi* 1 (set off) 出发; **the horse ~ed off at a steady trot** 这匹马稳步小跑起来; **he ~ed off down the path to the village** 他沿着小路向村庄走去; **to ~ off on one's journey** 踏上旅途 2 (do as a first stage) 首先做; **let's ~ off with some gentle exercises/by introducing ourselves** 我们先来做点强度小的运动/进行自我介绍; **I ~ed off working quite hard, but it didn't last** 我一开始干得很卖力, 但没有坚持多久; **she ~ed off as a secretary and ended up a director** 她起初是一名秘书, 但最后成了主管 3 (have as a first stage) 一开始是; **the leaves ~ off green but turn red later** 树叶一开始是绿色, 但后来会变红

B [**~ sb. off**] *vt*

1 (cause to begin) 使开始做; **the company ~ed him off as a shipping clerk** 公司一开始让他做的是运务员; **don't ~ her off crying** 别把她惹哭了; **my mother ~ed me off on the piano when I was three** 我三岁时母亲就开始让我学钢琴了; **what ~ed her off on that crazy idea?** 她怎么会有那么古怪的念头呢? 2 colloq (make angry) 使生气; (cause to laugh) 使发笑; (cause to cry) 弄哭 3 (in race) 给…发起跑信号 ‹*runners*›

C [**~ sth. off, ~ off sth.**] *vt* (do first stage of) 首先进行; **we ~ed off our tour with a visit to the palace** 游览一开始, 我们就先去参观了宫殿; **they ~ed off the season by losing their first four matches** 赛季刚开始, 他们就输了前 4 场比赛

- **start on** *vt* [**~ on sb.**] colloq (criticize) 批评; (complain about) 抱怨; **don't ~ on me** 别数落我
- **start on about** *vt* [**~ on about sb./sth.**] colloq 开始抱怨; **don't ~ on about him not having a job** 不要埋怨他没有工作
- **start on at** *vt* [**~ on at sb.**] colloq 开始责备; **she ~ed on at me again about getting some new clothes** 她因为我买了几件新衣服又开始数落我了
- **start out** *vi* 1 (begin to do sth.) 开始起步; **he was just ~ing out in life when the accident happened** 他的人生才开始, 就出了那起事故; **she ~ed out on her legal career in 1997** 她在 1997 年开始从事司法工作 2 (do sth. initially) 最初做; **he ~ed out as a salesman** 他一开始做的是推销员; **he ~ed out in TV, but always hoped to move into films** 他起初做电视业, 但一直希望进入电影业发展 3 (be initially) 一开始是; **the morning ~ed out so beautifully** 早晨刚开始的时候天气很好; **what ~ed out as a sideline soon became a major earner for the company** 最初的副业很快成了公司利润的主要来源 4 (intend initially) 起先打算; **I ~ed out to write a short story, but it soon developed into a novel** 我本来打算写一部短篇小说, 但很快就写成了一部长篇小说 5 (set off) 出发; **they ~ed out on their 20-mile hike** 他们开始了 20 英里的远足; **to ~ out for the airport** 动身去机场
- **start over** *vi* 重新开始; **she wasn't happy with our work and made us ~ over** 她对我们干的活儿不满意, 让我们返工
- **start up**

A *vi* 1 (be set up) «*business, organization*» 成立 2 (set up business) 创业; **to ~ up in business** 开始经商; **he's ~ed up as a consultant** 他开始是做顾问 3 (begin working) 启动; **I heard his car ~ up** 我听见他的车发动了 4 (begin to be heard) «*noise, music*» 响起

B *vt* [**~ sth. up, ~ up sth.**]

1 (found) 创办 ‹*business, organization*› 2 (cause to begin working) 启动; **can you ~ the car up please?** 请你把车发动起来好吗?

starter /ˈstɑːtə(r)/ *n* 1 Sport (participant) (person) 参赛人; (horse) 参赛马 2 Sport (official) 发令员; **to be under ~'s orders** 等待发令起跑 3 (person) 起步…的人; **to be a fast ~** Sport 起跑快; **I'm just a slow/fast ~** 我只是做事起步慢/快; **a late ~ on guitar/in art** 弹吉他/学美术起步晚 4 Aut, Tech 启动装置; **a ~ button/motor** 启动按钮/引擎 5 esp Brit Culin 第一道菜; **a seafood ~** 海鲜头道菜 6 (in quiz) 第一个问题; (in discussion, study) 引子; **for ~s** colloq 首先

starter: ~ home *n* [针对首次买房年轻人的] 过渡房; **~ kit, ~ pack** *ns* 启动工具包

starting: ~ block *n* 起跑器; **~ gate** *n* [赛马等的] 起跑门; **~ grid** *n* 发车排位; **~ handle** *n* 启动曲柄; **~ line** *n* 起跑线; **to be quick off the ~ line** 起跑快; **~ pistol** *n* 发令枪; **~ point** *n* (of journey, race, project) 起点; (of discussion) 出发点; **~ post** *n* 起跑点; **~ price** *n* [赛马等的] 临赛赔率; **~ salary** *n* 起薪

startle /ˈstɑːtl/ *vt* «*person, sight, news*» 使吃惊; «*sound*» 使…受惊 ‹*animal, person*›; **to ~ sb. out of their wits** 把某人吓得失魂落魄

startled /ˈstɑːtld/ *adj* 吃惊的 ‹*person, look, voice, cry*›; 受惊的 ‹*animal*›; **to be ~ at sth.** 对某事物感到吃惊; **to be ~ to see/learn/hear sth.** 看到/了解到/听到某事物大吃一惊

startling /ˈstɑːtlɪŋ/ *adj* 惊人的 ‹*likeness, news, results*›; **~ blue eyes** 蓝盈盈的眼睛

startlingly /ˈstɑːtlɪŋli/ *adv* 惊人地 ‹*beautiful, different, vivid*›; **to be ~ similar** 惊人地相似

start-up *n* 1 [u] (setting up) 启动; **~ money/expenses/time** 启动资金/费用/时间; **a ~ business** 新创办的公司 2 [c] (new business) 新公司; **an Internet ~** 刚成立的互联网公司

start-up costs *npl* 启动经费

star turn *n* (act) 主要环节; (person) 主要演员

starvation /stɑːˈveɪʃn/ *n* [u] (hunger) 饥饿; (resulting in death) 饿死; **to face ~** 面临挨饿; **to die of ~** 死于饥饿; **~ wages** 不够填饱肚子的工资

starvation diet *n* 节食减肥型饮食; **to be/go on a ~** 正在/进行节食减肥

starve /stɑːv/

A *vi* 挨饿; **to ~ (to death)** 饿死

B *vt* 1 (withhold food from) 使挨饿; (causing death) 使饿死; **to ~ oneself/sb. to death** 绝食而死/把某人饿死; **to ~ a city into submission** 断绝一城人的食物来源迫使其投降 2 fig (deprive) 使匮乏; **to ~ sb./sth. of sth.** 使某人/某物缺乏某物; **children who have been ~d of affection** 缺乏关爱的儿童; **to be ~d for choice** 急需进行选择

Phrasal verb

- **starve out** *vt* [**~ sb. out, ~ out sb.**] 以断绝食物来源迫使…出来

starving /ˈstɑːvɪŋ/ *adj* 1 (hunger-stricken) 挨饿的 2 colloq (hungry) 饥肠辘辘的; **to be ~** 非常饿; **I'm ~!** 我快饿死了!

Star Wars *n* colloq 星球大战 [美国的一项战略防御计划]

stash /stæʃ/ colloq

A *vt* 藏匿 ‹*heirlooms, stolen goods*›; **to ~ money under the floorboards** 把钱藏在地板下面

B *n* 藏匿物; **they found a ~ of heroin in the car** 他们发现了藏在车里的一批海洛因

Phrasal verb

- **stash away** *vt* [**~ sth. away, ~ away sth.**] 藏匿

stasis /ˈsteɪsɪs, ˈstæsɪs/ *n* [u] (inactivity) 停滞; (equilibrium) 静止

state /steɪt/

A *n* 1 [c] (condition) 状况; **sb.'s financial ~** 某人的经济状况; **he is in a confused ~ of mind** 他思维混乱; **she's in a poor ~ of health** 她健康状况不佳; **the building is in a bad ~ of repair** 这幢建筑年久失修; **in a ~ of undress** 赤身裸体的; **he's not in a fit ~ to drive** 他现在的状态不宜开车 2 [c] colloq (agitated condition) 焦虑不安; **to be in a ~** 焦虑不安; **to get (oneself) in** *or* **into a ~** 变得焦虑不安 3 [c] Brit colloq (mess) 脏乱; **what a ~ this place is in!** 这地方真够乱的!; **look at the ~ of you!** 看看你这副邋遢样子! 4 [c] (molecular condition) 态; **a gaseous/solid ~** 气态/固态; **water in a liquid ~** 液态水 5 **State** [c] (country) 国家; **a sovereign S~** 主权国家; **EU member S~** 欧盟成员国; **the S~ of Israel** 以色列国; **a S~ within a S~** 国中之国 6 **State** [c] (part of country) 州; **the southern S~s of the US** 美国南部各州 7 [c and u] (government) 政府; **matters** *or* **affairs of ~** 国家大事; **the separation of church and ~** 政教分离 8 [u] (formal ceremony) 国事礼仪; **robes of ~** 御礼袍; **the President was driven in ~ to the White House** 总统隆重地乘车前往白宫; **she will lie in ~ in Westminster Abbey** 她的遗体下葬前将安放在威斯敏斯特大教堂接受吊唁

B **States** *npl* **the S~s** colloq = **the United States of America** 美国

C *modif* 1 (of government) 国家的; **a ~ school/company** 公立学校/国有企业; **~ benefits** 政府救济金; **~ secrets** 国家机密 2 (of part of country) 州的; **the ~ taxes** 州税; **the ~ legislature** 州立法机关 3 (ceremonial) 国事礼仪的; **a ~ banquet/coach** 国宴/皇家马车; **to go on a ~ visit to Tokyo** 对东京进行国事访问; **the ~ apartments** 国事活动厅

D *vt* 1 (say, write) 陈述; **to ~ one's position** 阐明立场; **to ~ one's intention to run for election** 表示打算参加竞选; **he ~d categorically that he knew nothing about the deal** 他明确表示对此交易一无所知; **it was ~d that standards at the hospital were dropping** 据称这家医院的医疗水准在下降; **to ~ the obvious** 陈述人尽皆知的情况; **as ~d above/below** 如上/下所述 2 (provide as information) 说明; **to ~ one's name and address** 报出姓名和住址; **~ clearly how many tickets you require** 说清楚你需要多少张票 3 (specify) 规定; **this is not one of their ~d aims** 在他们的既定目标里没有这一条; **do not exceed the ~d dose** 不要超过规定的剂量; **you must arrive at the ~d time** *or* **at the time ~d** 你必须在规定时间到达 4 Jur 陈述; **to ~ one's case** 陈述案情

state: ~ bank *n* Amer 州立银行; **~ capital** *n* Amer 州府; **~ capitalism** *n* [u] 国家资本主义; **S~ Capitol** *n* Amer 州议会大厦; **~ control** *n* [u] 国家控制; **to bring sth. under ~ control** 将某事物纳入国家管理体系; **~-controlled** *adj* 国家控制的; **~craft** *n* [u] 治国才能; **S~ Department** *n* Amer **the S~ Department** 国务院; **S~ Enrolled Nurse** ▸p. 409 *n* Brit 国家登记护士; **~-funded** *adj* 政府出资的

the State Department

美国国务院, 亦作 the Department of State。位于华盛顿特区 (▸**Washington, DC**)。主管外交及部分内政事务, 地位居于政府各部门之首。前身为外交部 (Department of Foreign Affairs), 1789 年改组成为国务院。负责人称国务卿 (Secretary of State), 经参议院批准, 由总统任命。

statehood /ˈsteɪthʊd/ *n* [u] 独立国家地位; **to achieve ~** 取得独立国家地位

S

state house *n* Amer 州议会大厦

stateless /ˈsteɪtlɪs/ *adj* 无国籍的 ‹*person, refugee*›

statelessness /ˈsteɪtlɪsnɪs/ *n* [u] 无国籍

state line *n* Amer 州界

stateliness /ˈsteɪtlɪnɪs/ *n* [u] (of building, surroundings) 壮观; (of person) 优雅从容; (of movement, procession) 缓慢庄严

stately /ˈsteɪtli/ *adj* (grand, dignified) 壮观的 ‹*building, procession*›; 优雅高贵的 ‹*person, manner, grace*›; 庄重的 ‹*furnishings, surroundings*›; (slow, unhurried) 缓慢庄重的 ‹*pace, progress*›

stately home *n* Brit [尤指供人参观的] 豪华古宅

statement /ˈsteɪtmənt/ *n* **1** (expression of view) 声明; **a ~ on** *or* **about sth.** 关于某事物的声明; **to make** *or* **issue** *or* **release a ~** 发表声明; **a ~ of belief** 信仰声明; **a ~ of intent/principle** 意图/原则说明; **a ~ of fact** 情况说明 **2** Jur 口供; **to make a false ~** 做假口供; **to take a ~** 录口供 **3** Fin **(bank) ~** 结算单; **a ~ of account** 账户结算单

statement of claim *n* Brit 起诉书

state: ~ of affairs *n* 事态; **the present ~ of affairs** 当前的局势; **this ~ of affairs can no longer be ignored** 再不能无视这种情况了; **~ of emergency** *n* 紧急状态; **to declare a ~ of emergency** 宣布进入紧急状态; **~ of grace** *n* 天恩眷顾; **she died in a ~ of grace** 她受天恩眷顾，寿终正寝; **~ of play** *n* **1** (current situation) 进展情况; **2** (current score) 当前比分; **~ of the art** *n* [u] 当前发展水平; **a ~-of-the-art computer program** 最先进的计算机程序; **S~ of the Union address** *n* Amer 国情咨文 [美国总统向国会提交宣读的年度报告]; **~ of war** *n* 战争状态; **to declare a ~ of war** 宣布进入战争状态; **S~ Opening of Parliament** *n* Brit 议会开幕典礼; **~-owned** *adj* 国有的 ‹*company, enterprise*›; **~ police** *n* Amer 州警; **S~ Registered Nurse** ▸**p. 409** *n* Brit 国家注册护士; **~room** *n* **1** (ceremonial hall) 国事活动厅; **2** Naut (captain's room) 船长室; (private cabin) 特等客舱; **~-run** *adj* 国营的 ‹*company*›; 官方的 ‹*newspaper*›; **~'s attorney** *n* Amer 州检查官; **~ school** *n* Brit 公立学校; **~ senator** *n* Amer 州参议员; **~'s evidence** *n* [u] Amer 同案犯证据; **to turn ~'s evidence** 供出对同案犯不利的证据

stateside /ˈsteɪtsaɪd/ esp Amer colloq

A *adj* 在美国的

B *adv* (in the US) 在美国; (to or towards the US) 向美国

statesman /ˈsteɪtsmən/ *n* (*pl* **statesmen**) 政治家

statesmanlike /ˈsteɪtsmənlaɪk/ *adj* 有政治家才干的 ‹*person*›; 有政治家风范的 ‹*ability, quality, approach, act, speech*›

statesmanship /ˈsteɪtsmənʃɪp/ *n* [u] 政治才能; **to show ~** 表现出政治才能

statesmen /ˈsteɪtsmən/ *npl* ▸**statesman**

state: ~ socialism *n* [u] 国家社会主义; **~-sponsored terrorism** *n* [u] 国家支持的恐怖主义

stateswoman /ˈsteɪtsˌwʊmən/ *n* (*pl* **stateswomen**) 女政治家

state: ~ trooper *n* Amer 州警察; **~ university** *n* Amer 州立大学

statewide

A *adj* Amer 全州范围的 ‹*campaign, election, poll, strike*›

B *adv* 在全州范围内

static /ˈstætɪk/

A *adj* **1** (stationary) 静止的 ‹*person, image, scenes*›; 停滞的 ‹*water, traffic*› **2** (unchanging) 一成不变的 ‹*way of life, values, quality, role*› **3** (stable) 稳定的 ‹*population, price, interest rate*› **4** Phys 静力的 ‹*pressure*›; 静电的 ‹*discharge*› **5** Comput 静态的 ‹*memory, data*›

B *n* [u] **1** Radio, Telecom (interference) 静电干扰 **2** = **static electricity**

static electricity *n* [u] (electric charge) 静电; (sparks) 静电火花

statics /ˈstætɪks/ *npl* + *v sing* 静力学

statin /ˈstætɪn/ *n* 他丁类降脂药

station /ˈsteɪʃən/

A *n* **1** (train stop) 火车站; (for underground train) 地铁站; **I get off at the next ~** 我在下一站下车; **the ~ platform** 站台 **2** **the ~** (police office) 警察局 **3** TV (company, building) 电视台; (programming) 电视节目; (frequency) 电视频道; Radio (company, building) 电台; (programming) 电台节目; (frequency) 电台频道; **to tune to** *or* **into another ~** 换一个台 **4** Mil (base) 军事基地; (people at base) 驻军; **on a ~** 在基地里 **5** Austral, NZ (farm) 大牧场 **6** (place for particular activity) 站; **an agricultural research ~** 农业研究所; **a pollution monitoring ~** 污染监测站 **7** dated formal (social rank) 社会地位; **one's ~ in life** 所处的阶层; **to get ideas above one's ~** 抱有超出自己身份的想法 **8** (work post) 岗位 **9** **S~ of the Cross** (religious picture or carving) 苦路十四处之图 [描写耶稣受难的画像]; **the S~s of the Cross** 耶稣苦路十四处之图; **to do the S~s of the Cross** 做苦路祈祷

B *vt* 派驻; **troops ~ed abroad** 驻外部队; **they're ~ed in Germany** 他们驻扎在德国; **they ~ed two police officers in the grounds of the house** 他们在那幢房子周围派了两名警官巡视

C *v refl* **to ~ oneself** 待在某处; **she ~ed herself at the window to await his return** 她守在窗前等他回来; **he ~ed himself behind the door** 他藏在门后

stationary /ˈsteɪʃənri, Amer -neri/ *adj* 停着的 ‹*vehicle*›; 停滞的 ‹*traffic, queue*›; 固定的 ‹*target, position*›

station break *n* Amer [播报台名的] 播出间歇

stationer /ˈsteɪʃnə(r)/ ▸**p. 409** *n* **1** (person) 文具商 **2** (shop) 文具店; **a ~'s (shop)** 一家文具店

stationery /ˈsteɪʃnəri, Amer -neri/ *n* [u] **1** (writing materials) 文具; **a ~ order** 文具用品订单 **2** (letter paper) 信笺

stationery shop Brit, **stationery store** Amer ▸**p. 409** *ns* 文具店

station: ~master ▸**p. 409** *n* Brit 站长; **~ wagon** *n* esp Amer 客货两用小轿车

statistic /stəˈtɪstɪk/ *n* 统计数字; **official/government ~s** 官方/政府统计数字; **unemployment ~s** 失业统计数据; **the ~s on ...** 关于…的统计资料 ‹*prices*›; **~s show that ...** 统计数字表明…; **to collect** *or* **gather ~s** 收集统计数据

statistical /stəˈtɪstɪkl/ *adj* 统计的 ‹*evidence, analysis, error, work*›

statistically /stəˈtɪstɪkli/ *adv* 从统计角度 ‹*analyse, prove*›

statistician /ˌstætɪˈstɪʃn/ ▸**p. 409** *n* 统计学家

statistics /stəˈtɪstɪks/ *npl* **1** + *v sing* (practice) 统计; (science) 统计学 **2** + *v pl* (figures) 统计数据

stative /ˈsteɪtɪv/ *adj* 表示状态的 ‹*verb, relation*›

stats /stæts/ *npl* colloq = **statistics**

statuary /ˈstætʃʊəri, Amer -eri/ *n* [u] 雕塑; **Roman ~** 古罗马雕塑

statue /ˈstætʃuː/ *n* (carved figure) 雕像; (cast figure) 塑像

statuesque /ˌstætʃʊˈesk/ *adj* 高挑优美的 ‹*woman, figure*›

statuette /ˌstætʃʊˈet/ *n* 小雕塑

the Statue of Liberty

自由女神像。正式名称为“自由照亮世界之神”（Statue of Liberty Enlightening the World）。美国的象征。位于纽约港自由岛（Liberty Island）上。1884 年由法国赠送给美国。女神头戴冠冕，身穿飘逸的长袍。右手高举象征自由和光明的火炬，左手铜板上用罗马数字刻着《独立宣言》的发表日期——1776 年 7 月 4 日。脚底是挣断的铁链。铜像连同底座高 93 米。1984 年被列为世界遗产。

stature /ˈstætʃə(r)/ *n* [u] **1** (height) 身高; **small/tall of** *or* **in ~** 身材矮小/高大的 **2** (status) 名望; **one's ~ as sth.** 作为某事的声望; **to give sb. ~** 使某人获得声望; **intellectual ~** 在知识界的名望; **to be of some/considerable/international ~** 具有一定/相当/国际声望

status /ˈsteɪtəs/ *n* (*pl* **~es**) **1** [u and c] (social position) 地位; **her ~ as manager** 她的经理身份 **2** [u] (prestige) 社会上层地位; **to have ~** 有显赫地位 **3** [u and c] (legal position) 法律地位; **sb.'s employment/refugee ~** 某人的职业/难民身份; **marital ~** 婚姻状况; **to have most favoured/non-aligned nation ~** 拥有最惠国待遇/不结盟国家地位 **4** [u and c] (level of importance) 重要程度; **top priority ~** 最高的重视程度

status: ~ bar *n* [电脑屏幕或程序窗口显示文件编辑或程序运行信息的] 状态条; **~ meeting** *n* 工作情况报告会; **~ quo** /ˌsteɪtəs ˈkwəʊ/ *n* 现状; **to restore the ~ quo** 恢复原状; **~ symbol** *n* 地位象征

statute /ˈstætʃuːt/ *n* **1** [u and c] (written law) 成文法; **by ~** 按照法令 **2** [c] (formal rule) 章程; **the University ~s** 大学规章制度

statute: ~ book *n* **the ~ book** 法令全书; **to be on the ~ book** 成为正式法规; **to reach the ~ book** 成为法律; **~ law** *n* [u] 成文法; **~ of limitations** *n* 诉讼时效法规

statutory /ˈstatʃʊtəri, Amer -tɔːri/ *adj* **1** Jur 法定的 ‹*rights, duty, control, holidays*›; **a ~ offence** Brit 法定罪行 **2** fig (customary) 惯常的

statutory: ~ instrument *n* 有效立法; **~ rape** *n* [u and c] Amer 法定强奸罪

staunch¹ /stɔːntʃ/ *adj* (loyal, committed) 坚定的 ‹*supporter, defender*›; 忠实的 ‹*ally, believer*›

staunch² *vt* **1** lit (stop, control the flow of) 止住 ‹*blood, flow*›; 给…止血 ‹*wound*› **2** fig (curb) 制止; **to ~ the loss of customers** 阻遏顾客流失

staunchly /ˈstɔːntʃli/ *adv* 坚定地 ‹*support, defend*›; **~ Republican/Catholic** 坚定支持共和党的/虔诚信仰天主教的

stave /steɪv/ *n* **1** (vertical support) 木柱 **2** (stick) 棍; (weapon) 棒 **3** (of barrel) 桶板 **4** Mus 五线谱 **5** (stanza) 诗节

Phrasal verbs

- **stave in** *vt* (*pt, pp* **staved** *or* **stove**) [**~ sth. in, ~ in sth.**] 打穿 ‹*door, boat*›; 打破 ‹*skull, crate*›
- **stave off** *vt* (*pt, pp* **staved**) [**~ sth. off, ~ off sth.**] 暂时消除 ‹*fatigue, threat*›; 挡住 ‹*attack*›; 推迟 ‹*defeat, ruin, bankruptcy, illness*›; **to ~ off hunger/thirst** 暂时解饿/解渴

staves /steɪvz/ *pl* **1** ▸**staff A4, A5** **2** ▸**stave**

stay /steɪ/

A *vi* **1** (remain in place) 停留; **I can't ~** 我得走了; **~!** (to dog) 别动！; **to ~ in bed/(at) home** 待在床上/家里; **~ on this road until you come to a fork** 沿着这条路一直走到岔路口; **to ~ to dinner** 留下来吃晚餐; **to ~ for lunch/a cup of coffee** 留下来吃午饭/喝杯咖啡; **it will have to ~ there (for) a few weeks** 它还得在那儿放几周; **I'll ~ and help you** 我会留下来帮你; **to ~ put** colloq 留在原地; **I taped the latch so that it would**

~ **put** 我用胶带粘住了门闩，这样它就掉不下来了; **to be here to ~, to have come to ~** colloq 为多数人所接受; **it looks like televised trials are here to ~** 看来电视直播审判已经成了一种风气 2 (remain in particular state) 保持; **he never ~s angry for long** 他生气的时间向来不会长; **we promised to ~ friends for ever** 我们保证永远做朋友; **inflation ~ed below 4% last month** 上个月的通货膨胀率保持在 4% 以下; **to ~ in teaching** 继续教书 3 (be guest or visitor) 暂住; **do you like having people to ~?** 你喜欢留客人住在家里吗? ; **he's coming to ~ (for) a few days** 他要来住几天; **to ~ in a hotel** 住在宾馆里; **he's ~ing with friends this weekend** 这个周末他要和朋友们一起过 4 (spend the night) 留宿; **to ~ the night** 过夜 5 Scot, S Afr (live permanently) 居住; **where do you ~?** 你家住在哪儿?

B *vt* 1 (suspend, postpone) 延缓 ‹*proceedings*› 2 (stop) 阻止; (delay) 推迟; (check) 抑制; **to ~ the progress of a disease** 防止病情恶化; **to ~ sb.'s hand** (take hold of sb.'s hand) 抓住某人的手; (stop sb. from doing sth.) 阻止某人做某事; **to ~ one's hand** 住手; fig 作罢 3 (run all of) **to ~ the distance/course** 跑完全程/坚持到底

C *n* 1 (period) 停留; **I'm planning a ~ of ten days** *or* **a ten day ~ in London** 我计划在伦敦逗留 10 天; **to have an overnight ~ in Singapore** 在新加坡住一晚; **he found out about her ~s in mental hospitals** 他发现她住过几次精神病院 2 Jur 延缓; **a ~ of execution** (court order) 缓期执行; (postponement) 暂缓执行; **to grant (sb.) a ~ of execution** 准予（某人）缓期执行 3 (rope, wire) 支索

D **stays** *npl* Hist (corset) 胸衣

Phrasal verbs

• **stay around** *vi* 待着不走; **I'll ~ around in case you need me** 我就待在这儿，万一你用得着我
• **stay behind** *vi* 留下
• **stay down** *vi* 1 (remain in stomach) «*food, drink*» 留在胃里; **I was so ill that not even water would ~ down** 我病得很重，连喝水都吐 2 (remain lowered) 保持在低处; **the switch wouldn't ~ down** 这个开关按不下去 3 (remain lying) 躺倒; **when he knocks you down, you ~ down** 如果他把你击倒，你就爬不起来了 4 Brit (at school) 留级
• **stay in** *vi* 1 (not go out) 待在家里 2 (remain inserted) 固定住; **the nail wouldn't ~ in as the wood was rotten** 木头烂了，钉子钉不住
• **stay on** *vi* 1 (not fall off) 留在上面; **my hat wouldn't ~ on** 我的帽子老是掉下来; **the lid won't ~ on properly** 这个盖子盖不严实 2 Brit (continue education) 留下继续学习; **to ~ on in full-time education** 继续接受全日制教育; **he hopes to ~ on at university and do research** 他希望留在大学里继续学习并做研究工作 3 (remain behind) 留下; **to ~ on in Britain** 留在英国 4 (continue in work post) 继续在岗; **I would like him to ~ on after his present contract expires** 他现在的合同到期后，我想让他继续干下去; **to ~ on as a board member** 继续担任董事
• **stay out** *vi* 1 (not return home) 待在外面; **to ~ out all night** 彻夜不归 2 (continue on strike) 继续罢工; **the miners ~ed out (on strike) for a year** 矿工们连续罢工一年
• **stay out of** *vt* [~ **out of sth.**] 1 (not enter) 待在…外面; **~ out of my room** 不要进我的房间 2 (not interfere in) 不介入; **just ~ out of my business!** 别插手我的事! 3 (avoid) 避开; **to ~ out of trouble/the sun** 远离是非/避免日晒 4 (not come within) 在…之外; **tell him to ~ out of my way!** 叫他不要挡我的路! ; **to ~ out of sight** 不让人看见
• **stay over** *vi* 过夜
• **stay together** *vi* 待在一起
• **stay up** *vi* 1 (not fall down) 保持不掉落; **the trousers were so big they just wouldn't ~ up!** 裤子太大了，老是掉下来! ; **one wonders how these jerry-built houses ~ up!** 这些豆腐渣房子居然没倒掉，真是太奇怪了! 2 (go to bed late) 深夜不睡; **to ~ up late** 熬夜; **I ~ed up until 2 in the morning** 我一直熬到凌晨两点 3 (not be relegated) «*team, club*» 成功保级
• **stay with**

A *vt* [~ **with sb.**] 1 (be remembered by) 留在…的记忆中; **his words ~ed with her all evening** 整个晚上她的耳边都回响着他的话 2 (keep up with) 跟上

B [~ **with sth.**] *vt* (persevere with) 坚持做; **it's a difficult book to get into, but ~ with it and you'll enjoy it** 这本书很难读进去，但只要你坚持读，就会喜欢上它

stay-at-home *n* colloq 恋家的人; **working and ~ mums** 上班族妈妈和全职妈妈

stayer /ˈsteɪə(r)/ *n* Brit (person) 有耐力的人; (horse) 有耐力的马

staying power *n* [u] 持久力

St Bernard /ˌsnt ˈbɜːnəd, Amer ˌseɪnt bərˈnɑːrd/ *n* 圣伯纳救护犬

STD *abbr* 1 = **sexually transmitted disease** 2 Brit = **subscriber trunk dialling**

St David's Day /ˌsnt ˈdeɪvɪdz deɪ/ *n* 圣大卫节 [3月1日，纪念威尔士主保圣人的节日]

stead /sted/ *n* [职位等的] 代替; **in sb.'s/sth.'s ~** 代替某人/某事物的; **to do sth. in sb.'s ~** 替某人做某事; **she went in my ~** 她代我去了; **to stand sb. in good ~** 对某人有用

steadfast /ˈstedfɑːst, Amer -fæst/ *adj* 坚定的 ‹*supporter, determination*›; 坚决的 ‹*refusal*›; 目不转睛的 ‹*look, gaze*›; **a ~ friend** 坚贞不渝的朋友; **to be ~ in adversity** 在逆境中不动摇; **to be ~ to one's beliefs/principles** 坚持信念/原则

steadfastly /ˈstedfɑːstli, Amer -fæstli/ *adv* 坚定地 ‹*believe, follow*›; 坚决地 ‹*refuse*›; 目不转睛地 ‹*look, gaze*›

steadfastness /ˈstedfɑːstnɪs, Amer -fæst-/ *n* [u] (of supporter, determination) 坚定; (of refusal) 坚决

steadily /ˈstedɪli/ *adv* 1 (gradually) 逐步地 ‹*rise, fall, improve*›; 越来越 ‹*louder*› 2 (regularly) 均匀地 ‹*breathe*›; 有规律地 ‹*bang, pump*› 3 (without interruption) 持续地 ‹*work, rain, progress*› 4 (without wavering) 平静地 ‹*say*›; 平稳地 ‹*drive*›; **to look ~ at sb.** 凝视某人

steadiness /ˈstedɪnɪs/ *n* [u] 1 (of table, chair, etc.) 平稳; (of hand) 稳当 2 (of voice, gaze) 镇定 3 (of temperament) 稳重可靠

steady /ˈstedi/

A *adj* 1 (unchanging, lasting) 稳定的; (regular) 均匀的; **a ~ job** 固定工作; **a ~ stream of visitors** 稳定的游客流量; **a ~ outflow of oil from the tank** 从油箱里源源不断流出的油; **they set off at a ~ pace** 他们以不急不慢的速度出发了; **to drive at a ~ 80 km/h** 以每小时 80 公里的匀速行驶; **the ~ beat of the drums** 均匀的鼓点; **his breathing was ~** 他呼吸平稳; **to keep one's weight ~** 保持体重; **to hold ~** «*share prices, interest rates*» 保持稳定 2 (not wobbly) 稳的; **to make a table ~** 使桌子不摇晃; **a good eye and a ~ hand** 眼尖手稳; **to hold a ladder/needle ~** 把梯子扶稳/把针拿稳; **to be not very ~ on one's feet** 走路不稳当 3 (not wavering) 镇定的; **a ~, even voice** 沉稳平和的嗓音; **a ~ gaze** 凝视的目光; **my nerves aren't very ~ today** 我今天有点儿心神不定 4 (gradual) 稳步的; **a ~ decline in numbers** 数量的持续下降; **five years of ~ economic growth** 持续 5 年的经济平稳增长 5 (long-term) 关系稳定的 ‹*boyfriend, girlfriend*›; **I'm in a ~ relationship** 我有确定的恋爱对象; **to go ~ (with sb.)** dated colloq （与某人）保持稳定的男女朋友关系 6 (resolute) 坚定的 ‹*purpose*›; **her faith remained ~ throughout this crisis** 在这场危机中，她的信念始终没有动摇过 7 (level-headed) 沉着的 ‹*young man, worker*›

B *excl* (keep calm) 小心; **~! don't fall off** 当心! 别摔下来; **~ on!** Brit colloq (be more careful!) 小心点儿! ; (calm down!) 冷静!

C *vt* 1 (prevent from wobbling) 使平稳; **to ~ one's hand** 稳住手; **to ~ a ladder** 放稳梯子 2 (calm) 使镇定; **I took a deep breath to ~ my nerves** 我深吸一口气，让自己平静下来

D *vi* 1 (stop wobbling) «*boat, hand*» 变稳; **the lift rocked slightly, steadied, and the doors opened** 电梯微微一晃，稳定下来，然后门开了 2 (become calm) «*tone, nerves*» 镇定下来; **his voice steadied as his confidence returned** 他恢复了信心，声音变得镇定自若 3 (stop changing) «*prices, interest rates*» 稳定下来; **the pound steadied against the dollar** 英镑对美元的汇率稳定下来了 4 (become regular) «*heartbeat, pulse*» 恢复平稳; **her breathing slowly steadied** 她的呼吸慢慢平稳下来

E *v refl* 1 (physically) **to ~ oneself** 站稳; **she steadied herself against the wall** 她靠墙站稳 2 (mentally) **to ~ oneself** 镇定下来

steady state theory *n* [u] **the ~** 稳恒态学说

steak /steɪk/ *n* [u and c] (of beef) 牛排; (of other meat) 肉块; (of fish) 鱼块

steak: ~ and kidney pie, ~ and kidney pudding *ns* [u and c] 牛肉腰子馅饼; **~house** *n* 牛排餐馆; **~ knife** *n* 牛排餐刀; **~ sandwich** *n* 牛排三明治

steal /stiːl/

A *vt* (*pt* **stole**, *pp* **stolen**) 1 (take illegally) 偷 ‹*money, property*›; **to ~ sth. from sb./sth.** 偷某人/某处的某物; **to ~ sb.'s heart** fig 博得某人的欢心; **to ~ the show** fig 抢风头 2 fig (take surreptitiously) 偷偷夺取; **to ~ an idea** 剽窃观点; **to ~ a few minutes' sleep/peace** 偷闲睡几分钟/享受几分钟的安静; **to ~ the credit for sth.** 把某事的功劳据为己有; **to ~ a glance at sth.** 偷看某物一眼; **to ~ a kiss** 偷吻; **to ~ a scene from sb.** 抢某人的镜头; **to ~ a march on sb.** 抢先某人一步

B *vi* (*pt* **stole**, *pp* **stolen**) 1 (take illegally) 偷盗; **to ~ from sb.** 偷某人的东西; **to ~ from a car/house** 从汽车/房子里偷东西 2 (creep) 偷偷移动; **to ~ up on sb.** 蹑手蹑脚靠近某人; **to ~ away** 溜走; **a sad expression stole across her face** 她脸上流露出一丝伤感

C *n* 1 colloq (bargain) 便宜货; **the watch was a ~!** 那块手表等于白送! 2 esp Amer (act of theft) 偷盗

stealing /ˈstiːlɪŋ/ *n* [u] 盗窃

stealth /stelθ/ *n* [u] 偷偷摸摸; **by ~** 偷偷地

stealth bomber *n* 隐形轰炸机

stealthily /ˈstelθɪlɪ/ *adv* 偷偷地 ‹*move, follow, introduce*›; 不知不觉地 ‹*erode, take effect*›

stealth: ~ tax *n* 隐性税; **~ technology** *n* [u] [飞机的] 隐形技术

stealthy /ˈstelθi/ *adj* 偷偷摸摸的

steam /stiːm/

A *n* [u] 1 (vapour) 水蒸气; (as source of power) 蒸汽动力; **engines powered by ~** 蒸汽机; **to let off** *or* **blow off ~** colloq (release energy) 消耗精力; (release strong emotions) 宣泄情绪; (release anger) 发泄怒气; **under one's own ~** colloq 靠自己的力量; **she says she'll get there under her own ~** colloq 她说她会自个儿去那里; **to get** *or* **pick up ~** (increase speed) «*vehicle*» 逐渐加速; (get more powerful) «*campaign*» 逐渐形成声势; **to raise ~** 提高蒸汽压力; **to run out of ~** colloq «*person*» 筋疲力尽; «*campaign, economy*» 失去活力; **to go full ~ ahead** «*production*» 全力进行 2 (locomotives, railways) 蒸汽机车; **the age of ~** 蒸汽时代 3 (air moisture, condensation) 水汽; **my breath turned to ~ in the cold** 我呼出的气在寒冷的天气中化成了汽雾

S

B *vi* **1** (cook over boiling water) «*food*» 蒸煮; **add the mussels and leave them to ~** 加上贻贝，然后蒸一蒸 **2** (give off hot gas) 散发蒸汽; **a kettle was ~ing on the stove** 水壶在炉子上冒着蒸汽; **a mug of ~ing hot coffee** 一大杯热气腾腾的咖啡 **3** (produce moisture in air) 形成水汽; **the roofs were ~ing in the early-morning sunlight** 在清晨的阳光下，屋顶上冒出了汽雾 **4** (move under steam power) 靠蒸汽动力行驶; **the boat ~ed across the lake** 汽船驶过湖面 **5** colloq (move fast) 快速行进; **to ~ down the motorway at 100 mph** 以 100 英里的时速沿着高速公路疾驰; **she ~ed out of his office when she heard this** 她听到这话后冲出了他的办公室

C *vt* 蒸; **~ed fish** 清蒸鱼

Phrasal verbs

- **steam ahead** *vi* 进展迅速; **the company is ~ing ahead with its new investment programme** 公司正抓紧实施新的投资方案
- **steam off**
  A *vi* 靠蒸汽动力离开; **the train ~ed off towards London** 蒸汽列车驶向伦敦
  B *vt* [**~ sth. off, ~ off sth.**] 用蒸汽使脱离; **to ~ the stamp off the envelope** 用蒸汽把邮票从信封上揭下来
- **steam open** *vt* [**~ sth. open, ~ open sth.**] 用蒸汽把…拆开; **to ~ an envelope open** 用蒸汽开启信封
- **steam up**
  A *vi* 蒙上水汽; **my glasses have ~ed up!** 我的眼镜上起了一层雾!
  B *vt* [**~ sth. up, ~ up sth.**] 使蒙上水汽

steam: ~ age *n* 蒸汽时代; **~ bath** *n* **1** (room) 蒸汽浴室; **2** (session) 蒸汽浴; **~boat** *n* 汽船; **~ cleaner** *n* 蒸汽清洗机; **~ cooking** *n* [u] 蒸煮

steamed /stiːmd/ *adj* **1** (cooked by steaming) 蒸煮的 **2** *pred* esp Amer colloq (angry) 非常气愤的 ‹*person*›; **to be/get ~ about sth.** 对某事气愤/感到愤怒 **3** *pred* Brit colloq (drunk) 烂醉的; **to get ~** 酩酊大醉

steamed pudding *n* [c and u] Brit 蒸布丁

steamed up *adj pred* Brit colloq 非常气愤的 ‹*person*›; **to be/get (all) ~ about** *or* **over sth.** 为某事物（很）气愤/感到（非常）愤怒

steam engine *n* **1** (engine) 蒸汽机 **2** (locomotive) 蒸汽机车

steamer /ˈstiːmə(r)/ *n* **1** (boat) 汽船 **2** (pan) 蒸锅

steaming /ˈstiːmɪŋ/ *adj* **1** (very hot) 热气腾腾的 ‹*cup of tea, bath*›; **~ hot** 非常热的 **2** Brit colloq (furious) 愤怒的 ‹*person*› **3** Brit colloq (drunk) 烂醉的

steam: ~ iron *n* 蒸汽熨斗; **~ locomotive** *n* 蒸汽机车; **~ museum** *n* 蒸汽机车博物馆; **~ power** *n* [u] 蒸汽动力

steamroller /ˈstiːmrəʊlə(r)/
A *n* 蒸汽压路机
B *vt* pej 以强势手段压服 ‹*person, opposition*›; **to ~ a bill/a plan through** 强行通过一项法案/计划

steam: ~ room *n* 蒸汽浴室; **~ship** *n* 汽船; **a ~ship company** 轮船公司; **~ stripper** *n* 蒸汽式剥墙纸机; **~ train** *n* 蒸汽火车

steamy /ˈstiːmi/ *adj* **1** (full of steam) 蒸汽弥漫的 ‹*kitchen, bathroom*›; 蒙着水汽的 ‹*window, windscreen, glasses*› **2** (humid) 潮湿闷热的 ‹*atmosphere, climate, jungle*› **3** colloq (erotic) 色情的 ‹*book, film, scene, description*›

steed /stiːd/ *n* archaic or liter 骏马

steel /stiːl/
A *n* **1** [u] (metal) 钢; **~ knives** 钢刀; **~ production** 钢铁生产 **2** [c] (knife sharpener) 磨刀钢棒 **3** [u] fig (in character) 坚韧; **nerves of ~** 钢铁般的气魄
B *vt* 坚定 ‹*resolve*›; 鼓足 ‹*courage, nerve*›
C *v refl* **to ~ oneself to do sth.** 下决心做某事

steel band *n* 钢鼓乐队

steel blue ▸ **p. 134**
A *adj* 铁青色的
B *n* [u] 铁青色

steel: ~ engraving *n* **1** [u] (process) 钢版雕刻; **2** [c] (print) 钢凹版印刷品; **~ erector** *n* 钢架工

steel grey ▸ **p. 134**
A *adj* 青灰色的
B *n* [u] 青灰色

steel: ~ guitar ▸ **p. 395** *n* **1** [u] (technique) 钢棒吉他弹奏法; **to play ~ guitar** 弹奏钢棒吉他; **2** [c] (instrument) 钢棒吉他; **~ industry** *n* 钢铁工业; **~ mill** *n* 炼钢厂; **~-stringed guitar** ▸ **p. 395** *n* 钢弦吉他; **~ wool** *n* [u] 钢丝球; **~worker** ▸ **p. 409** *n* 炼钢工人; **~works** *n + v sing or pl* 炼钢厂

steely /ˈstiːli/ *adj* **1** (in colour) 灰蓝色的 ‹*sky, eyes*› **2** fig (in character) 冷冰冰的 ‹*look, eyes, voice, person*›; 坚定的 ‹*determination, resolve*›

steelyard *n* 杆秤

steep[1] /stiːp/ *adj* **1** (rising or falling at a sharp angle) 陡峭的 ‹*hill*›; 陡的 ‹*slope, street, stairs, roof*›; **a ~ climb/descent/drop** 陡直的攀升/下降/下落 **2** (sharp) 急剧的 ‹*rise, increase, fall, decline*› **3** colloq (unreasonable) 过高的 ‹*price, cost, fee*›; **that's a bit ~** 那有点儿离谱

steep[2]
A *vt* (soak) 浸泡 ‹*onions, fruit, wool, fabric*›; **to ~ sth. in sth.** 把某物浸泡在某物中
B *vi* 浸泡; **to ~ in sth.** 在某物中浸泡
C *v refl* **to ~ oneself in sth.** 沉浸在某事中; **to ~ oneself in the history of a place** 潜心研究一个地方的历史

steeped /stiːpt/ *adj pred* «*place, building, society, person*» 饱含…的; **to be ~ in sth.** 深深浸淫某物; **a history ~ in violence** 充斥暴力的历史

steeple /ˈstiːpl/ *n* [教堂的] 尖塔

steeple: ~chase *n* **1** Horse racing 障碍赛马; **2** (in athletics) 障碍赛跑; **~jack** *n* [高塔、烟囱等的] 高空作业工人

steeply /ˈstiːpli/ *adv* **1** (at a sharp angle) 陡直地 ‹*climb, descend, drop, rise, fall away*› **2** (sharply) 急剧地 ‹*rise, increase, fall, decline*›

steepness /ˈstiːpnɪs/ *n* [u] **1** (quality) 陡峭 **2** (degree) 陡度

steer[1] /stɪə(r)/
A *vt* **1** (control direction of) 驾驶; **to ~ a bicycle** 骑自行车; **to ~ the car through the entrance** 把车开进大门; **he ~ed the boat into the harbour** 他将船开进港口 **2** (escort) 带领; **she took my arm and ~ed me towards the door** 她抓住我的胳膊，把我带往门口; **he was ~ed to a chair in the corner** 他被领到角落里的一把椅子前 **3** (follow forward) 沿着…前进; **to ~ a direct course for the port** 沿着一条笔直的航线驶往港口; **he ~ed his way towards the buffet table** 他朝自助餐桌走去 **4** (bring to desired state) 引导; **he tried to ~ the conversation away from his divorce** 他试图把谈话从他离婚一事上转移开; **to ~ a bill through parliament** 使法案在国会通过; **she ~ed the team to victory** 她率领全队取得了胜利 **5** (adopt, follow) 遵循; **the skill is in ~ing a middle course between the two extremes** 技巧在于避开两个极端，走中间路线; **to ~ one's way towards a solution/to success** 寻求解决的办法/走上成功的道路
B *vi* **1** (control direction of movement) 驾驶; **you row and I'll ~** 你划桨，我来掌舵; **they ~ed due south** 他们朝着正南方行驶; **he ~ed into the parking area** 他把车开进了停车位; **to ~ by the stars** 根据星星的位置导航; **to ~ clear of sb./sth.** 避开某人/某事物; **you'd best ~ clear of him** 你最好离他远点儿 **2** (move in particular direction) 行驶; **the ship ~ed into port** 船驶进了港口 **3** (be able to be guided in particular way) «*vehicle, ship, plane*» 可驾驶; **how does the car ~ now?** 现在这辆车开起来怎么样?; **the boat didn't ~ very well because the rudder was bent** 这条船驾驶起来不太灵活，因为舵弯了
C *n* colloq (tip) 指点; **to ask for a ~** 征求建议; **to give sb. a bum ~** Amer 误导某人

steer[2] *n* (male cow) [阉过的] 小公牛

steerage /ˈstɪərɪdʒ/ *n* [u] Hist 统舱; **to travel ~** 坐统舱旅行

steering /ˈstɪərɪŋ/ *n* [u] **1** (action) 操舵 **2** (mechanism) 转向装置

steering: ~ column *n* [连接方向盘与转向装置的] 转向柱; **~ committee** *n + v sing or pl* 指导委员会; **~ lock** *n* 方向盘锁; **~ wheel** *n* 方向盘

steersman /ˈstɪəzmən/ *n* 舵手

stellar /ˈstelə(r)/ *adj* **1** *attrib* Astron 恒星的 ‹*light, system, movement*› **2** fig (outstanding) 杰出的 ‹*career*›; 精彩的 ‹*performance, cast*›; 极高的 ‹*rating*›

stem[1] /stem/
A *n* **1** (of fruit, flower, leaf) 梗 **2** (of feather) 羽干 **3** (of glass, vase) 柄脚 **4** (of pipe) 烟斗柄 **5** (of letter) 干线 **6** (of musical note) 符干 **7** (of word) 词干 **8** (of ship) 船头; **from ~ to stern** 从船头到船尾
B *vi* (*pres p etc.* **-mm-**) 起源; **to ~ from sth.** «*problem, anger*» 起因于某事物

stem[2] *vt* (*pres p etc.* **-mm-**) (prevent, restrain) 阻止 ‹*flow, spread*›; 止住 ‹*blood*›; 遏制 ‹*loss*›; 控制 ‹*tide, flood*›

stem cell *n* 干细胞

stem cell research *n* [u] 干细胞研究

-stemmed /stemd/ *combining form* 有…梗的; **long/short~** 长/短梗的

stench /stentʃ/ *n* 臭气

stencil /ˈstensɪl/
A *n* **1** (template) [印刷图案或文字用的] 模板 **2** (design) [用模板印的] 图案
B *vt* (*pres p etc.* **-ll-** Brit, **-l-** Amer) 用模板印 ‹*design, pattern, letters*›; 用模板在…上印图案 ‹*fabric, walls, cupboard*›; **to ~ sth. with sth.** 用模板把某物印在某物上

stencilling Brit, **stenciling** Amer /ˈstensɪlɪŋ/ *n* [u] 模板印刷

steno /ˈstenəʊ/ *n* Amer **1** colloq [c] = **stenographer** **2** [u] = **stenography**

stenographer /steˈnɒgrəfə(r)/ ▸ **p. 409** *n* Amer 速记员

stenography /steˈnɒgrəfi/ *n* [u] Amer 速记

stentorian /stenˈtɔːrɪən/ *adj* liter 洪亮的 ‹*voice, tone, roar*›

step /stɛp/
A *n* **1** [c] (act of lifting foot) 迈步; **to walk with slow ~s** 缓步行走; **the water got deeper and deeper at** *or* **with every ~** 每走一步水就更深一些; **she took a ~ towards the window** 她向窗户迈了一步; **to retrace one's ~s** 按原路返回; **to change/break ~** 换步/走乱步伐; **to fall into ~ (with** *or* **beside sb.)** （和某人）齐步行进; **in/out of ~ (with sb./sth.)** (when walking, marching, dancing) （与某人/某物）步伐一致/不一致; (in conformity with/at odds with) （与某人/某物）想法一致/不一致; **one ~ out of line, and you're finished!** 只要越轨一步，你就完蛋了!; **to march in ~ with the music** 踏着音乐的节拍齐步走; **to be out of ~ with the times** 跟不上时代; **to watch** *or* **mind one's ~** (walk carefully) 走路小心; (behave properly) 言行谨慎; **a** *or* **one ~ at a time** 一步一个脚印地 **2** [c] (distance covered by pace) 一步; **she moved a ~ closer to me** 她向我走近了一步; **it's only a few ~s further** 再走几步就到了 **3** [c] (distance to or from somewhere) 步行距离; **it's only a**

S

~ **to the station** 到车站只有几步路; **it was a good ~ from our house to the shops** 从我们家到商店很远 **4** [c] (sound of footsteps) 脚步声; **we heard ~s outside** 我们听到外面有脚步声 **5** [c] (footprint) 脚印; **a line of ~s in the snow** 雪地上的一行脚印 **6** [c] (way of walking) 步态; **to walk with a quick/light ~** 快步走/以轻松的步子行走; **to know/recognize sb.'s ~** 知道/认出某人走路的样子 **7** [c] (of dance) 舞步; **tango ~s** 探戈舞的舞步 **8** [c] (stair) 梯级; **we walked down some stone ~s to the beach** 我们走下几级石阶, 来到海滩上; **a flight of ~s** (inside building) 一段楼梯; (outside building) 一段台阶; **she was sitting on the top/bottom ~ of the staircase** 她坐在最上面/最下面一级楼梯上 **9** [c] (doorstep) 门阶 **10** [c] (ladder rung) [梯子的] 横档 **11** [c] (move) 步骤; **the first/next ~** 第一步/下一步; **it's a ~ in the right direction** 这是朝正确方向迈出的一步; **a major ~ forward in the treatment of the disease** 治疗这一疾病的重大进展; **to be a** *or* **one ~ ahead of sb./sth.** 领先某人/某事物一步; **he was now one ~ closer to winning the title** 他现在离赢得冠军又近了一步; **they were one ~ away from victory** 他们距离胜利仅一步之遥; **one ~ forward, two ~s back** 进一步, 退两步; **to do sth. one ~ at a time** 按部就班 **12** [c] (measure) 措施; **to take ~s to reduce pollution** 采取措施减少污染 **13** [c] (stage) 阶段; **to go a** *or* **one further** 再进一步; **to take an idea a** *or* **one ~ further** 进一步深化想法; **I'm with you every ~ of the way** 整个过程的每一步, 我都和你在一起 **14** [c] (position in hierarchy) 级别; **the first ~ on the managerial ladder** 初级管理层; **it represents an important ~ up in his career** 这是他在事业上的一次重要晋升 **15** [u] (aerobic exercise) 踏板操; **a ~ class** 踏板操训练班 **16** [c] Amer (musical interval) 音级

B **steps** *npl* **1** (small ladder) 折梯 **2** (stairs) (to upper floor) 楼梯; (in front of building) 台阶

C *vi* (*pres p etc.* **-pp-**) **1** (walk) 迈步; **to ~ across a stream/in a puddle** 趟过小溪/踏进水坑; **to ~ into a boat/on to a train** 登上小船/火车; **she ~ped into/out of the dress** 她穿上/脱下了连衣裙; **to ~ on sb.'s foot** 踩到某人的脚; **to ~ on it** *or* **the gas** colloq 加快; **to ~ out of line** (break military ranks) 出列; (behave badly) 出格 **2** formal (come) 行走; **please ~ this way** 请走这边; **to ~ into sb.'s office** 走进某人的办公室

D *vt* (*pres p etc.* **-pp-**) **1** (construct in series of levels) 使成阶梯状; **the garden was ~ped** 花园建成了阶梯状 **2** (organize in stages) 分段安排; **the tax should be ~ped** 税收应该划分等级

Phrasal verbs

- **step aside** *vi* **1** (move to one side) 让开; **she ~ped aside to let them pass** 她站到一边让他们过去 **2** (leave post) 让位; **to ~ aside for** *or* **in favour of sb.** 让位于某人
- **step back** *vi* **1** (move backwards) 后退; **she ~ped back from the table** 她从桌子旁向后退; **going into the hotel is like ~ping back in time** 走进这家宾馆就像是回到了过去 **2** (mentally detach oneself from) 退后一步思考; **we are learning to ~ back from ourselves** 我们正努力学着走出自我的樊篱来看问题
- **step down** *vi* **1** (come down) 走下来; **to ~ down from the train** 走下火车 **2** (resign) 让位; **he ~ped down from the chairmanship of the party** 他从党主席的位置上退了下来; **to ~ down in favour of sb.** 让位于某人; **he ~ped down as Scotland's coach** 他辞去了苏格兰队教练的职务
- **step forward** *vi* **1** (move forward) 向前迈步 **2** (offer help or information) 主动站出来; **we are appealing for volunteers to ~ forward** 我们呼吁志愿者自告奋勇
- **step in** *vi* **1** (intervene) 介入; **a local businessman ~ped in with a large donation for the school** 当地一位商人出面捐了一大笔钱给学校; **the coach was forced to ~ in to stop the two athletes from coming to blows** 教练被迫出面干预, 阻止这两名运动员斗殴 **2** (act as substitute) 代替; **thanks for ~ping in when David became ill** 谢谢你在戴维生病期间接替他
- **step out** *vi* **1** (go out) 出去; **she's just ~ped out for a few minutes** 她刚出去了几分钟 **2** Amer colloq dated (have relationship) 约会; **to ~ out with sb.** 与某人约会 **3** (stride) 大步走
- **step out on** *vt* [**~ out on sb.**] Amer colloq 对…不忠
- **step outside** *vi* **1** (go out) 出去; **I opened the door and ~ped outside** 我开门走了出去 **2** (go out for fight) 出去较量
- **step up**

A *vi* **1** (move forward) 向前走; **she ~ped up to receive her prize** 她走上前去领奖 **2** esp Amer (agree to help) 同意帮忙; **it's time you ~ped up** 该你站出来帮忙了

B *vt* [**~ sth. up, ~ up sth.**] (increase) 增加; **to ~ up one's efforts to do sth.** 更加努力地做某事; **he has ~ped up his training to prepare for the race** 他加强了训练, 为那场赛跑做准备

step: ~ aerobics ▸p. 307 *npl + v sing* 有氧踏板操; **~brother** *n* (elder brother by same father) 同父异母哥哥; (elder brother by same mother) 同母异父哥哥; (younger brother by same father) 同父异母弟弟; (younger brother by same mother) 同母异父弟弟

step-by-step

A *adj attrib* 逐步的 ‹*description, reduction*›; 分步的 ‹*guide, instructions*›; 循序渐进的 ‹*policy, programme*›

B **step by step** *adv* 逐步地 ‹*analyse, explain*›; **to take sb. through sth. step by step** 引导某人一步步完成某事; **to take things step by step** 按部就班地做事

step: ~ change *n* (sudden change) 突变; (major change) 巨变; **~child** *n* (son) 继子; (daughter) 继女; **~daughter** *n* 继女; **~father** *n* 继父; **~ladder** *n* 折梯; **~mother** *n* 继母; **~-parent** *n* (stepfather) 继父; (stepmother) 继母; **his ~-parents** 他的继父母

steppe /step/ *n* **steppe(s** *pl***)** 干草原

stepping stone *n* **1** lit 踏脚石 **2** fig 进身之阶; **a ~ to sth.** 某事的敲门砖; **a ~ to the Presidency** 通向总统宝座的阶梯

step: ~sister *n* (elder sister by same father) 同父异母姐姐; (elder sister by same mother) 同母异父姐姐; (younger sister by same father) 同父异母妹妹; (younger sister by same mother) 同母异父妹妹; **~son** *n* 继子

stepwise /ˈstepwaɪz/

A *adj* 逐步的

B *adv* 逐步地

stereo /ˈsterɪəʊ/ *n* **1** [u] (sound) 立体声; **to broadcast in ~** 用立体声广播 **2** [c] (*pl* **~s**) (system) 立体声音响

stereochemistry /ˈsterɪəʊˌkemɪstri/ *n* [u] 立体化学

stereogram /ˈsterɪəgræm/ *n* **1** (image) 立体图像 **2** dated (stereo radiogram) 立体声收音唱机

stereomicroscope /ˈsterɪəʊˌmaɪkrəskəʊp/ *n* 立体显微镜

stereophonic /ˌsterɪəˈfɒnɪk/ *adj* 立体声的 ‹*recording, equipment, system*›; 立体效果的 ‹*sound*›

stereoscope /ˈsterɪəskəʊp/ *n* 体视镜

stereoscopic /ˌsterɪəˈskɒpɪk/ *adj* 立体的 ‹*vision, image, photograph*›

stereoscopy /ˌsterɪˈɒskəpi/ *n* [u] 体视术

stereo system *n* 立体声音响

stereotype /ˈsterɪətaɪp/

A *n* **1** (idea) 模式化观念; (person) 模式化的人; **to perpetuate** *or* **conform to a ~** 墨守陈规; **sexual/racial ~s** 有关性/种族的旧框框 **2** Print 铅版

B *vt* 对…形成模式化看法; **to ~ sb. as sth.** 把某人模式化地归入某类

stereotyping /ˈsterɪətaɪpɪŋ/ *n* [u] 模式化

sterile /ˈsteraɪl, Amer ˈsterəl/ *adj* **1** (germ-free) 无菌的 **2** (infertile) 不育的 ‹*man, woman, animal*›; 只具雄蕊的 ‹*plant*›; 贫瘠的 ‹*land*› **3** fig (unfruitful) 无结果的 ‹*debate, discussion, relationship*›

sterility /stəˈrɪləti/ *n* [u] **1** (cleanliness) 无菌 **2** (infertility) 不育; (barrenness) 贫瘠 **3** fig (unfruitfulness) 无结果

sterilization /ˌsterəlaɪˈzeɪʃn, Amer -lɪˈz-/ *n* **1** [u] (removal of germs) 消毒 **2** [u and c] (making infertile) 绝育

sterilize /ˈsterəlaɪz/ *vt* **1** (remove germs from) 给…消毒 ‹*bottle, instrument, dressing*›; **~d milk** 杀菌牛奶 **2** (make infertile) 使…绝育 ‹*person, animal, plant*›

sterling /ˈstɜːlɪŋ/

A ▸p. 174 *n* [u] 英镑; **~ rose/fell** 英镑升值/贬值了; **to quote ~ prices** 按英镑报价

B *adj attrib* 出色的 ‹*work*›; 优秀的 ‹*qualities*›; 高尚的 ‹*character*›

sterling: ~ area *n* **the ~ area** 英镑区; **~ silver** *n* [u] 标准纯银 [纯度不低于92.5%]; **a ~-silver necklace** 纯银项链

stern¹ /stɜːn/ *adj* (severe) 严厉的 ‹*person, warning, expression, face*›; 苛刻的 ‹*treatment*›; **to be ~ with sb.** 对某人严厉; **to be made of ~er stuff** 性格坚毅

stern² *n* Naut 船尾

sternly /ˈstɜːnli/ *adv* 严厉地 ‹*look, say*›; 苛刻地 ‹*treat, deal with*›

sternness /ˈstɜːnnɪs/ *n* [u] 严厉

sternum /ˈstɜːnəm/ *n* (*pl* **~s** *or* **sterna** /ˈstɜːnə/) 胸骨

steroid /ˈstɪərɔɪd, ˈste-/ *n* 类固醇; **to be on ~s** 在服用类固醇

stertorous /ˈstɜːtərəs/ *adj* liter 有鼾声的 ‹*breathing*›; 打鼾的 ‹*sleeper*›

stet /stet/

A *vi* 保留不删 [批注用语]

B *vt* (*pres p etc.* **-tt-**) 给…加注 "保留不删" ‹*section, word*›

stethoscope /ˈsteθəskəʊp/ *n* 听诊器

Stetson /ˈstetsn/ *n* 斯泰森宽边帽

stevedore /ˈstiːvədɔː(r)/ ▸p. 409 *n* 码头工人

stew /stjuː, Amer stuː/

A *n* [u and c] 炖菜; **to be/get in a ~ over** *or* **about sth.** fig colloq 为某事物坐立不安/变得坐立不安

B *vt* 煨炖 ‹*fruit, vegetables, meat*›; **~ed lamb** 炖羊肉

C *vi* **1** Culin «*fruit, meat, vegetables*» 炖; «*tea*» 长时间泡 **2** fig colloq (be uncomfortably hot) 感觉闷热 **3** fig colloq (worry) 担忧; **to ~ over about sth.** 为某事物坐卧不宁; **to ~ in one's own juice** 自作自受

steward /ˈstjʊəd, Amer ˈstuːərd/ ▸p. 409 *n* **1** (on ship, aircraft, train) 乘务员; **the chief ~** 乘务长 **2** (of college or club) 管理员 **3** (at race, match) 组织者 **4** (of estate) 管家

stewardess /ˈstjʊədes, Amer ˈstuːərdəs/ ▸p. 409 *n* 女乘务员

stewardship /ˈstjʊədʃɪp, Amer ˈstuːərdʃɪp/ *n* [u] **1** (management, leadership) 管理; **under sb.'s ~** 在某人的管理下 **2** (position) 管理职位

stg *abbr* = **sterling A**

St George's /ˌsnt ˈdʒɔːdʒɪz/ *pr n* 圣乔治

stick¹ /stɪk/

A *n* **1** [c] (piece of wood from tree) 枝条; **a dry ~**

S

枯枝; **her arms were like ∼s** 她的双臂骨瘦如柴; **to get (hold of)/have the wrong end of the ∼** Brit colloq 出错/误解; **to up ∼s** Brit colloq 突然搬家 **2** [c] esp Brit (walking aid) 拐棍; **the old lady leant on her ∼ as she talked** 老太太说话时拄着拐棍 **3** [c] (as weapon) 棍子 **4** [c] (in hockey, polo, lacrosse) 球棍 **5** [c] (for food item) 小棍; **pieces of pineapple on ∼s** 一串串插在小棍上的菠萝块 **6** [c] (stalk) 茎; **a ∼ of celery/rhubarb** 一株芹菜/大黄 **7** [c] (cylindrical container) 棍状物; **a ∼ of dynamite/glue** 一根炸药棒/胶棒 **8** [c] (strip, length) 条状物; **carrot ∼s** 胡萝卜条; **a ∼ of butter** Amer 一条黄油; **a ∼ of gum** 一支口香糖 **9** [c] (group of bombs) 集束炸弹 **10** [c] *usu pl* colloq (piece of furniture) **a few ∼s (of furniture)** 几件家具; **there wasn't a ∼ of furniture left** 一件家具也没剩下 **11** [u] Brit colloq (criticism) 批评; **to get** *or* **take (some** *or* **a lot of) ∼ (from sb.)** 受到（某人的）严厉批评; **to give sb. (some** *or* **a lot of) ∼** 严厉批评某人 **12** [c] Brit dated colloq (person) **he's a funny/dull old ∼** 他是个老活宝/无趣的老家伙 **13** [c] esp Amer colloq (joystick) 操纵杆 **14** [c] Amer colloq (gear lever) 变速杆

B **sticks** *npl* colloq **the ∼s** 边远乡村地区; **we live out in the ∼s** 我们住在偏远的乡下

stick² (*pt, pp* **stuck**)

A *vt* **1** (fix with adhesive substance) 粘贴; **she stuck a stamp on the letter** 她把一张邮票贴在信封上; **you'll have to ∼ the broken plate with some superglue** 你得用强力胶把破了的盘子粘起来 **2** (push) 把…插入; **the nurse stuck the needle into my arm** 护士把针扎进我的胳膊; **don't ∼ your fingers through the bars of the cage** 不要把手指伸进笼子 **3** (impale) 插牢; **to ∼ the balls of wool on knitting needles** 把毛线团插在编结针上 **4** (penetrate, stab) 刺; **a board stuck with pins** 扎着大头针的木板 **5** colloq (place carelessly or quickly) 放置; **to ∼ one's head out the window** 把头探出窗户; **he stuck his hands in his pockets/the pencil behind his ear** 他把手揣在口袋里/把铅笔夹在耳后; **just ∼ that sandwich on my desk** 把那个三明治搁我桌上就行 **6** colloq (post, announce) 列出; **why don't you ∼ an advert in the paper?** 你干吗不在报上登个广告呢？; **to ∼ the drinks on sb.'s bill** 把酒水记到某人的账上 **7** colloq (cause to go) 使前往; **I gave her some money and stuck her on a train back home** 我给了她一些钱，把她弄上了回家的火车 **8** colloq (expressing rejection of offer) [表示愤怒的拒绝]; **∼ the job! I don't want it anyway!** 让那份工作见鬼去吧！反正我也不想干！ **9** Brit colloq (tolerate) 容忍; **he can't ∼ living with his parents** 他不能忍受和父母住在一起; **I can't ∼ it any longer** 我再也受不了了

B *vi* **1** (become fixed) 被粘住; **this stamp won't ∼!** 这张邮票粘不住！; **her wet clothes were ∼ing to her body** 湿衣服贴在她身上 **2** (be pushed) 被插入; **the needle stuck in my finger** 针扎进了我的手指; **there was a post ∼ing into the ground beside her** 她身边的地上竖着一根立柱 **3** (have adhesive properties) 有黏性; **this glue ∼s very well** 这种胶水黏性很强 **4** (jam) 卡住; **he drove into a bog, where his wheels stuck fast** 他把车开进了泥地里，车轮陷得死死的; **the key had stuck in the lock** 钥匙卡在了锁里 **5** (remain the same) «*person, prices*» 保持不变; **he had lost a lot of weight, but had stuck at 15 stone** 他减去了很多体重，但减到15英石时就减不下去了 **6** (be remembered) «*event, remark, sight*» 经久难忘; **to ∼ in sb.'s mind** *or* **memory** 铭记在某人心中 **7** colloq (remain valid) 继续有效; **the police didn't have enough evidence and couldn't make the charges ∼** 警察没有足够的证据，无法证明那些指控成立 **8** colloq (continue to be used) 仍在使用; **they called him 'Snoopy' at school, and the name stuck** 有人在学校叫他“史努比”，后来这名字就叫开了 **9** colloq (become established) «*practice*» 长久保留; **he started smoking when he was fifteen, and the habit stuck** 他15岁时开始抽烟，这一习惯已经无法戒掉了 **10** (in cards) 不再要牌

Phrasal verbs

- **stick around** *vi* colloq 待在原地; **∼ around; we'll need you to help us later** 别走开，过一会儿我们还要你帮忙呢
- **stick at** *vt* [**∼ at sth.**] 坚持不懈地做; **if you want to play an instrument well, you've got to ∼ at it** 要想练好一种乐器，必须持之以恒; **to ∼ at nothing** 不择手段
- **stick by** *vt* **1** [**∼ by sb.**] (support) 忠于; **she stuck by her husband through thick and thin** 在任何情况下，她都对丈夫忠贞不渝 **2** [**∼ by sth.**] (adhere to) 坚持; **they stuck by their decision** 他们决心已下，不会动摇; **he usually stuck by his word** 他通常说话算话
- **stick down** *vt* [**∼ sth. down, ∼ down sth.**]
  1 (fasten) 粘住 **2** colloq (put down) 放下; **to ∼ it down on the table** 把它放在桌子上 **3** colloq (write down) 写下; **∼ your name down on the list** 把你的名字写在名单上
- **stick on** *vt* [**∼ sth. on, ∼ on sth.**] 粘上
- **stick out**

A *vi* **1** (protrude) 突出; **his ears ∼ out** 他长着一对招风耳; **there was a large nail ∼ing out of the back tyre** 后轮胎扎上了一根大钉子 **2** (be noticeable) 引人注目 **3** (be memorable) «*person, event*» 令人难忘

B *vt* [**∼ sth. out, ∼ out sth.**]
1 (cause to protrude) 使突出; **to ∼ one's tongue out (at sb.)** （朝某人）吐舌头; **don't ∼ your arm out of the car window** 别把胳膊伸出车窗; **he proudly stuck out his chest** 他骄傲地挺起了胸膛 **2** colloq (keep at) 把…坚持到底 ‹*activity, job*›; **she didn't like the course, but she stuck it out** 她不喜欢这门课，但还是耐着性子学完了

- **stick out for** *vt* [**∼ out for sth.**] colloq 坚持要求; **they are ∼ing out for a higher pay rise** 他们坚持要求更大幅度的加薪
- **stick to**

A [**∼ to sth.**] *vt*
1 (keep up) 坚持做; **to ∼ to a diet** 坚持节食 **2** (continue using) 继续使用; **I'll ∼ to my old washing powder** 我会继续用我以前用的那种洗衣粉 **3** (keep to) 局限于; **∼ to what you know** 只讲你知道的; **would you like some wine? — no, I'll ∼ to beer** 喝点儿葡萄酒吗？——不了，我还是喝啤酒吧 **4** (not digress from) 紧扣 ‹*subject, point*›; **to ∼ to the facts** 就事论事 **5** (adhere to) 坚持; **to ∼ to one's word** 守信; **shall we meet on Friday this week? — no, let's ∼ to Saturdays** 这周我们星期五见面好吗？——不，还是照旧在星期六吧 **6** (continue along) 继续沿着…行进 ‹*road*›

B [**∼ to sb.**] *vt* (stay close to) 紧跟; **to ∼ close to sb.** 紧跟某人

- **stick together**

A *vi* **1** (become fixed together) «*pages, sweets*» 粘在一起 **2** colloq (remain united) «*group, people*» 团结在一起 **3** colloq (remain in relationship) «*couple*» 维持关系

B *vt* [**∼ sth. together, ∼ together sth.**] 把…粘在一起 ‹*objects, pieces*›

- **stick up**

A *vi* 竖立; **the branch was ∼ing up out of the water** 树枝从水下伸了出来; **his hair was ∼ing up** 他的头发翘起来了

B [**∼ sth. up, ∼ up sth.**] *vt*
1 (fix on surface) 张贴; **he stuck up a notice on the noticeboard** 他在布告栏里贴了一张通知 **2** colloq (raise) 举起 ‹*hand, arm, head*›; **∼ 'em up!** colloq (in robbery) 举起手来！

C [**∼ sb./sth. up, ∼ up sb./sth.**] *vt* esp Amer colloq (rob) 持枪抢劫 ‹*person, bank*›

- **stick up for** *vt* [**∼ up for sb./sth.**] (support) 支持; (defend) 捍卫; **to ∼ up for one's rights** 维护自己的权利; **to ∼ up for oneself** 保护自己
- **stick with** colloq

A [**∼ with sb.**] *vt*
1 (stay close to) 紧跟 **2** (be remembered by) «*event, remark*» 被…记住; **this story has stuck with me** 我一直记得这个故事

B [**∼ with sth.**] *vt*
1 (continue using) 继续使用; **I'm ∼ing with that old car for now** 我暂时还在用那辆旧车 **2** (continue doing) 继续做; **I'm going to ∼ with my original plan** 我将继续执行我原来的计划; **be patient and ∼ with it** 耐心点儿，坚持下去

stickball /ˈstɪkbɔːl/ *n* [u] Amer 棍球

sticker /ˈstɪkə(r)/ *n* 贴纸

sticker price *n* Amer 标价

stickiness /ˈstɪkɪnɪs/ *n* [u] **1** (adhesiveness) 黏附性 **2** (of food, substance) 黏性 **3** (of weather, climate) 闷湿 **4** (of person, skin) 汗湿 **5** colloq (of problem, situation) 棘手 **6** Comput colloq (of website) 吸引力

sticking: **∼ plaster** *n* [c and u] Brit 创可贴; **∼ point** *n* 症结; **to be a ∼ point for sb.** 是某人的难题

stick: **∼ insect** *n* **1** Zool 竹节虫; **2** fig (person) 骨瘦如柴的人; **∼-in-the-mud** *n* colloq 墨守成规的人; **a ∼-in-the-mud approach** 守旧的方式

stickleback /ˈstɪklbæk/ *n* 刺鱼

stickler /ˈstɪklə(r)/ *n* 坚持…的人; **to be a ∼ for sth.** 拘泥于某事; **a ∼ for accuracy/spelling/punctuation/protocol** 斤斤计较准确性/拼写/标点/礼仪的人

stick: **∼-on** *adj* 可粘贴的 ‹*beard, tattoo*›; **∼-on labels** 背胶标签; **∼pin** *n* Amer **1** (tiepin) 领带夹; **2** (brooch) 胸针; **∼ shift** *n* Amer **1** (gear lever) 换挡杆; **2** (manual transmission) 手动换挡; **3** (vehicle) 手动变速车; **∼-up** *n* esp Amer colloq 持枪抢劫

sticky /ˈstɪki/ *n* **1** (tending to adhere) 黏乎乎的 ‹*fingers, floor, dough, cake*›; 有背胶的 ‹*label, plaster*›; 粘牙的 ‹*toffee, syrup*›; **to be ∼ to the touch** 摸上去黏糊糊的; **to have ∼ fingers** 有顺手牵羊的毛病 **2** (hot and humid) 闷热的 ‹*weather, climate*›; (damp with sweat) 汗津津的 ‹*person, skin*› **3** colloq (difficult) 棘手的 ‹*problem, situation*›; **to be ∼ about sth./doing sth.** 对于某事/做某事很不爽快; **to come to a ∼ end** 落得可悲的下场 **4** Comput colloq 富有吸引力的 ‹*website, page*›

sticky: **∼ bun** *n* Brit 糖衣圆面包; **∼ tape** *n* [u and c] Brit 透明胶带

stiff /stɪf/

A *adj* **1** (rigid) 硬的; **∼ cardboard** 硬纸板; **a pair of ∼ shoes** 一双坚硬的鞋子; **a ∼ upper lip** [面对痛苦或困境时的] 泰然自若; **to keep a ∼ upper lip** 不动声色 **2** (hard to move) 不易移动的; **the windows were ∼, and she couldn't get them open** 窗户很紧，她打不开 **3** (unable to move easily) 僵硬的; **to have ∼ legs** 两腿僵直; **she was really ∼ after sleeping on the floor** 在地板上睡了一觉之后，她觉得浑身酸痛 **4** (thick) 稠的; **to beat the egg whites until ∼** 把蛋清打到变稠为止 **5** (difficult) 艰难的; **a pretty ∼ exam/climb** 相当难的考试/相当费劲儿的攀爬; **∼ competition/opposition** 激烈的竞争/强烈的反对 **6** (severe) 严厉的 ‹*penalty, warning*› **7** (greater than normal) 过高的; **∼ fines** 高额罚款; **£2,000? that's a bit ∼, isn't it!** 2,000英镑？那太贵了点儿吧！ **8** (blowing strongly) 强劲的 ‹*wind*› **9** (high in alcohol) 烈性的 ‹*drink*› **10** (formal, not relaxed) 生硬的; **a ∼ smile** 牵强的微笑

B *adv* colloq 极其; **that man bores me ∼!** 那人让我厌烦透了！; **to be scared ∼** 怕得要死

C *n* colloq **1** (corpse) 死尸 **2** Amer (stuffy person) 古板的人

D *vt* Amer colloq **1** (fail to pay) 不付钱给; **she ~ed an appliance store on a refrigerator** 她没给一家电器商店付冰箱钱 **2** (fail to tip) 不给…小费

stiffen /'stɪfn/
A *vt* **1** (make rigid) 使…变硬 ‹*fabric, paper, dough, mixture*› **2** fig (make stronger) 使…更加坚定 ‹*resolve, resistance*›; 使…更加激烈 ‹*competition*›; 使…更加严厉 ‹*penalty*›
B *vi* **1** (become rigid) «*limbs, joints, shoulder, neck*» 变得僵硬 **2** fig (become stronger) «*resolve*» 变得坚定; «*resistance*» 变得顽强; «*competition*» 变得激烈 **3** Culin «*dough*» 变硬; «*mixture, paste, egg whites*» 变稠

stiffener /'stɪfnə(r)/ *n* (in collar) 立领料; (in packaging) 加固材料

stiffly /'stɪfli/ *adv* **1** (in rigid way) 僵硬地 ‹*walk, bend, stand*› **2** (formally) 牵强地 ‹*smile*›; 生硬地 ‹*say, greet*›

stiff-necked /'stɪfnekt/ *adj* 固执的 ‹*person, official*›

stiffness /'stɪfnɪs/ *n* [u] **1** (of fabric, substance) 硬 **2** (physical) 僵硬 **3** (of manner) 生硬 **4** Culin 黏稠

stifle /'staɪfl/ *vt* **1** (suppress) 扼杀 ‹*creativity, initiative*›; 阻止 ‹*progress, debate*›; 镇压 ‹*rebellion*›; 克制 ‹*impulse, anger, desire*› **2** (suffocate) 使…窒息 ‹*person*›

stifling /'staɪflɪŋ/ *adj* **1** (hot) 闷热的 ‹*atmosphere, heat, room*›; **it's ~!** 闷死了! **2** fig (repressive) 令人窒息的 ‹*atmosphere, climate, effect*›

stigma /'stɪgmə/
A *n* **1** (*pl* **~s**) (disgrace) 耻辱 **2** (*pl* **~s** *or* **stigmata** /stɪg'mɑːtə/) Bot 柱头
B **stigmata** *npl* 圣伤痕 [据称出现在某些人身上, 与耶稣基督受刑时留下的伤痕相似]

stigmatize /'stɪgmətaɪz/ *vt* 使感到羞耻; **to be ~d as sth.** 被诬蔑为某状况

stile /staɪl/ *n* **1** (in wall, hedge) 梯蹬 **2** (of window) 窗梃; (of door) 门梃

stiletto /stɪ'letəʊ/ *n* (*pl* **~s**) **1** esp Brit (shoe) 细高跟女鞋 **2** esp Brit (heel) 细高跟 **3** (dagger) 匕首

still¹ /stɪl/ *adv* **1** (referring to situation now or to come) 仍然; **he ~ can't read** 他仍然不识字; **eat them while they're ~ hot** 趁热把这些东西吃了吧; **prices are ~ expected to rise** 预计价格还可能上涨; **I have four exams ~ to go** 我还要参加4次考试; **~ to come, a report on …** Radio, TV 接下来的报道是… **2** (nevertheless) 然而; **the weather was cold and wet; ~, we had a great time** 天气又冷又潮, 不过我们还是玩得很开心; **it was very dear; ~, it was worth it** 这很贵, 但物有所值 **3** (even) 甚至更; **faster/better/worse ~, ~ faster/better/worse** 甚至更快/更好/更糟; **if you can manage to get two tickets that's better ~** 要是你能设法弄到两张票, 那就更好了; **~ less** 更不用说; **no explanation was offered, ~ less an apology** 没有任何解释, 更不用说道歉了 **4** (yet) 还有; **many died; ~ others emigrated** 许多人死了, 还有的人移居国外了; **~ more money was spent** 花掉了更多的钱; **she made ~ another excuse** 她又找了一个借口

still²
A *adj* **1** (motionless) 静止的 ‹*body, hand, person, animal, image*›; 平静的 ‹*water*›; 无风的 ‹*air*›; **~ waters run deep** Prov 静水流深; **the ~ small voice (of conscience)** 良心的呼唤; **do stand ~!** 站好别动! **2** (peaceful) 寂静的 ‹*countryside, streets, house*› **3** esp Brit (not fizzy) 不起泡的 ‹*drink, mineral water*›
B *n* **1** [c] Phot 定格画面; **a ~ from a film** 电影剧照; **a ~ camera** 剧照照相机 **2** [u] liter (calmness) 寂静; **(in) the ~ of the night/forest** (在) 夜深人静 (时) / (在) 寂静的森林 (中)
C *vt* 消除 ‹*doubts, fears*›; 平息 ‹*voices*›
D *vi* liter «*noise, voices, music*» 平静下来

still³ *n* (apparatus) [制酒的] 蒸馏器; (distillery) 蒸馏酿酒厂

still: ~birth *n* [c and u] 死产; **~born** *adj* **1** lit 死产的 ‹*baby, calf*›; **2** fig (unrealized) 夭折的 ‹*idea, plan, attempt*›; **~ life** *n* **1** [c] (*pl* **~ lifes**) (work) 静物画; **a ~ life painting** *or* **drawing** 一幅静物画; **2** [u] (genre) 静物画艺术

stillness /'stɪlnɪs/ *n* [u] **1** (lack of motion) (of water) 平静; (of air) 无风 **2** (calmness) 宁静

still photographer ▸p. 409 *n* 剧照摄影师

stilt /stɪlt/ *n* **1** (pole) 高跷; **on ~s** 踩着高跷; **a pair of ~s** 一副高跷 **2** Constr 支柱; **a house on ~s** 用支柱撑着的房屋

stilted /'stɪltɪd/ *adj* 生硬的 ‹*language, conversation, style*›

Stilton /'stɪltən/ *n* [u and c] 斯提耳顿干酪

stimulant /'stɪmjʊlənt/ *n* **1** (substance) 兴奋剂; **to act as a ~** 有兴奋剂的作用 **2** fig (stimulus) 刺激物; **to act as a ~ to sth.** 对某事物有刺激作用

stimulate /'stɪmjʊleɪt/ *vt* **1** (encourage) 刺激 ‹*development, appetite*›; 激励 ‹*person*›; 激发 ‹*interest, creativity*›; **to ~ sb. to do sth.** 激励某人做某事 **2** Physiol «*hormone, process*» 促进…的功能 ‹*ovulation, gland, cell, nerve*›

stimulating /'stɪmjʊleɪtɪŋ/ *adj* **1** (interesting, exciting) 激动人心的 ‹*discussion, person, environment*› **2** Physiol 增加活力的 ‹*property, effect*›

stimulation /ˌstɪmjʊ'leɪʃn/ *n* [u and c] 刺激; **to need intellectual ~** 需要智力刺激

stimulus /'stɪmjʊləs/ *n* (*pl* **stimuli** /'stɪmjʊliː/) 刺激; **the ~ of competition** 竞争刺激; **the ~ given to the economy** 对经济的刺激措施; **auditory stimuli** 听觉刺激

sting /stɪŋ/
A *vt* (*pt, pp* **stung**) **1** (wound) «*bee*» 蜇; «*insect*» 叮 **2** (cause pain to) «*smoke, whip, wind, nettle*» 刺疼 ‹*person, skin, eyes*› **3** fig (hurt) «*remark, insult, criticism*» 刺痛; **to ~ sb. into action** 刺激某人采取行动 **4** colloq (swindle) 敲诈; **to ~ sb. for sth.** 宰某人某数额; **to ~ sb. for £10** 敲某人 10 英镑的竹杠
B *vi* (*pt, pp* **stung**) **1** (hurt, be site of pain) «*cut, hand, eyes*» 感觉刺痛; **it ~s!** 真蜇人!; **to ~ from** *or* **with sth.** 因某物而感到刺痛 **2** (cause pain) «*nettle, insect*» 引起刺痛感; **bitter remarks that really stung** 十分伤人的刻薄话
C *n* **1** (wound) (of bee, wasp, scorpion) 蜇伤; (of mosquito) 叮伤; (of plant) 刺伤 **2** (organ) (of insect, scorpion) 蜇针; (of plant) 刺 **3** (pain) 刺痛 **4** fig (hurtful effect) 痛苦; **to take the ~ out of sth.** 减轻某事物引起的痛苦; **a ~ in the tail** 煞风景的结局 **5** esp Amer colloq (in con game, law enforcement) 圈套; **a ~ operation** 诱捕的圈套

stinger /'stɪŋə(r)/ *n* **1** (stinging insect or animal) 蜇人的动物 **2** (stinging part) (of insect) 蜇针; (of plant) 刺 **3** **Stinger®** Amer 斯丁格刺钉路障

stingily /'stɪndʒɪli/ *adv* colloq 吝啬地 ‹*allocate, behave, treat*›

stinginess /'stɪndʒɪnɪs/ *n* [u] colloq 吝啬

stinging /'stɪŋɪŋ/ *adj* **1** (causing physical pain) 刺痛的 ‹*blow, sensation, feeling*› **2** fig (unkind) 尖刻的 ‹*remark, criticism*›; 沉重的 ‹*blow*›

stinging nettle *n* 大荨麻

stingray /'stɪŋreɪ/ *n* 魟

stingy /'stɪndʒi/ *adj* colloq 吝啬的 ‹*person, government, decision*›; 微小的 ‹*amount, grant*›; **to be ~ with …** 对…吝啬 ‹*money*›

stink /stɪŋk/
A *vi* (*pt* **stank** *or* **stunk,** *pp* **stunk**) **1** (smell) 有臭味; **to ~ of sth.** 有某种臭味; **to ~ of petrol/garlic** 有汽油/大蒜味; **the room is filthy, it ~s** 房间很脏, 熏死人 **2** colloq (be unpleasant) «*organization, place*» 令人厌恶; «*situation, state of affairs*» 糟糕透顶; **to ~ of sth.** 有做某事的嫌疑; **to ~ of corruption/injustice** 有腐败/不公正的嫌疑; **the contract ~s!** 这份合同糟糕透了!
B *n* [u] **1** (smell) 恶臭 **2** colloq (row) 吵闹; **there'll be a (hell of a) ~ over this!** 此事会引起轩然大波!; **to kick up** *or* **cause a ~ about sth.** 为某事物大闹一场; **like ~** 十分卖力地

Phrasal verb

• **stink out** *vt* [**~ sth. out, ~ out sth.**] «*person*» 使…充满臭气 ‹*house, place*›; «*smell*» 熏臭 ‹*house, place*›

stink bomb *n* 臭弹

stinker /'stɪŋkə(r)/ *n* colloq **1** (person) 讨厌的人; (child) 讨厌的孩子; (thing) 讨厌的事物; **he's been a real little ~ today** 他今天可真是够烦人的 **2** (difficult task) 棘手的事

stinkhorn /'stɪŋkhɔːn/ *n* 鬼笔 [一种真菌, 会产生恶臭黏液]

stinking /'stɪŋkɪŋ/
A *adj* **1** (foul-smelling) 发恶臭的 ‹*mess, corpse, cesspool*› **2** *attrib* colloq (wretched) 破烂的 ‹*place, house*›; 讨厌的 ‹*money*›; **a ~ cold** 重感冒
B *adv* colloq 非常 ‹*rich*›; **~ drunk** 烂醉如泥

stint /stɪnt/
A *n* **1** [c] (period of work) 规定工作时间; **to do one's ~ at the wheel** 驾驶规定时数; **during my three-day ~ as a secretary** 在我做秘书的 3 天时间里; **I've done my ~ for today** 今天的活儿我已经干完了 **2** [u] (limitation) 限量; **without ~** 不受限制地
B *vt* 对…吝啬 ‹*person, oneself*›; **to ~ sb. (of sth.)** 小气地供应某人 (某物)
C *vi* «*person, organization*» 节省; **to ~ on** 对…吝惜 ‹*presents, food, fabric*›

stipend /'staɪpend/ *n* [尤指神职人员、教师和公务员的] 薪金

stipendiary /staɪ'pendɪəri, Amer -dieri/
A *adj attrib* 有薪俸的 ‹*priest, service, office*›
B *n* 受薪俸者

stipendiary magistrate *n* Brit 领薪治安官

stipple /'stɪpl/ *vt* 点刻 ‹*design, pattern*›; 用…点画 ‹*paint, powder*›; 把…弄毛糙 ‹*surface, plaster*›; **a ~d effect** 点画效果

stipulate /'stɪpjʊleɪt/ *vt* 规定 ‹*price, condition, quantity*›

stipulation /ˌstɪpjʊ'leɪʃn/ *n* **1** [c] (stated condition) 条款 **2** [u] (directive) 规定

stir /stɜː(r)/
A *vt* (*pres p etc.* **-rr-**) **1** (mix) 搅动; **she ~red her tea with a silver spoon** 她用银汤匙搅了搅茶; **the vegetables are ~red into the rice while it is hot** 趁米饭热时把蔬菜拌进去 **2** (move slightly) 使微动; **a gentle breeze ~red the branches** 微风吹动了树枝 **3** (cause to take action) 使行动; **their complaints have finally ~red him into action** 他们的抱怨最终促使他采取了行动; **a noise ~red me from sleep** 响声把我从睡梦中惊醒 **4** (affect emotionally) 使…激动 ‹*person*›; 激发 ‹*emotions, imagination, curiosity*›; **the film ~red many memories of my childhood** 这部电影唤起了我童年的许多记忆; **the sight of the hungry children ~red her to pity** 孩子们饥饿的样子使她动了恻隐之心; **to ~ the blood** 令人激动 **5** Brit colloq **to ~ it** (cause trouble) 挑拨是非
B *vi* (*pres p etc.* **-rr-**) **1** (mix) 搅动; **~ well before use** 使用前先充分搅拌 **2** (move slightly) 微动; **she ~red in her sleep** 她在睡梦中微微动了一下 **3** (wake up) 醒来; **it was 11 o'clock, and still no one was ~ring** 已经 11 点了, 还没有人起床 **4** (budge) 离开; **you haven't ~red from the sofa all evening!** 你坐在沙发上一晚上没动了!; **he seldom ~red out of his house** 他很少出门 **5** (begin to be felt) 萌生; **old memories began**

S

to ~ as we talked 我们交谈时，对往事的回忆渐渐涌上心头; **a feeling of guilt began to ~ in her** *or* **in her heart** 她心里渐渐生出了内疚感 6 Brit colloq (cause trouble) 挑拨是非

C *v refl* (*pres p etc.* **-rr-**) **to ~ oneself** 行动起来; **come on, ~ yourself! you're late!** 快，快走吧！你要迟到了！

D *n* 1 [c] (act of mixing) 搅动; **to give sth. a ~** 把某物搅一搅 2 [c] (commotion) 骚动; **to cause** *or* **create** *or* **make a ~** 引起骚动; **her resignation caused quite a ~** 她的辞职引起很大震动 3 [u] colloq (prison) 监牢; **to be in ~** 坐牢

Phrasal verbs

- **stir in** *vt* [**to ~ sth. in, to ~ in sth.**] 把…搅进去 ‹*liquid, substance*›
- **stir up**

A [**~ sth. up, ~ up sth.**] *vt*
1 (elicit) 激起 ‹*emotions*›; **the photographs ~red up old memories** 这些照片唤起了对往事的记忆; **a campaign to ~ up support for the plan** 为该计划寻求支持的活动 2 (cause) 挑起 ‹*trouble, debate*›; **to ~ things up** 挑起事端 3 (move around) 搅起; **the swirling wind ~red up dust and sand** 旋风扬起了沙尘

B [**~ sb. up, to ~ up sb.**] *vt* (excite) 鼓动; **they were ~red up to rebellion** 他们被煽动起来参加叛乱

stir crazy *adj* esp Amer colloq [因囚禁而] 精神失常的; **to go ~** 发疯

stir-fry
A *vt* (*pt, pp* **stir-fried**) 煸炒
B *n* 炒菜; **a beef/vegetable ~** 一盘炒牛肉/青菜; **~ vegetables** 炒蔬菜

stirrer /ˈstɜːrə(r)/ *n* 1 (implement for stirring) 搅拌器; **plastic coffee ~s** 塑料咖啡搅拌条 2 Brit colloq pej (troublemaker) 煽动者; **a political ~** 政治事端制造者

stirring /ˈstɜːrɪŋ/
A *adj* 激动人心的 ‹*speech, performance, story, music*›
B *n* 1 (of emotion) [感情等的] 萌动; **to feel a ~ of hope** 感觉到一丝希望 2 (sign) 迹象; **the first ~s of revolt/nationalism** 造反/民族主义的苗头

stirrup /ˈstɪrəp/ *n* 1 Equit 马镫; **to lose one's ~s** 踩空马镫; **to stand up in the ~s** 脚踩马镫而立 2 Med [妇科检查用的] U 形支架

stirrup: ~ cup *n* [给骑马者的] 饯行酒; **~ iron** *n* 马镫踏板; **~ leather** *n* 马镫皮带; **~ pump** *n* 手摇灭火泵

stitch /stɪtʃ/
A *n* 1 [c] (in sewing, embroidery, knitting, crochet) 一针; **to drop a ~** 漏一针; **very small, neat ~es** 很细密整齐的针脚; **a ~ in time saves nine** Prov 小洞不补，大洞吃苦; **she didn't have ~ on** *or* **wasn't wearing a ~** 她一丝不挂 2 [u and c] (style) (of crochet) 针法; (of knitting) 编结法; **embroidery/knitting ~** 刺绣/编织法 3 [c] Med 缝线; **to have ~es** 缝针; **she had 10 ~es** 她被缝了 10 针; **to have one's ~es out** 拆线 4 [c] (sharp pain) [胁部的] 突然剧痛; **to have a ~** 出现岔气; **to be in ~es** 岔气; **to have sb. in ~es** 逗得某人笑岔气
B *vt* 1 (in sewing) 缝 ‹*seam, buttonhole*›; (in embroidery) 绣 ‹*fabric*›; (in knitting, crochet) 编织; **hand-~ed** 手工缝制的; **machine-~ed** 机器缝制的; **to ~ sth. on to/into sth.** 把某物缝到某物上/里面 2 Med 缝合 ‹*wound, cut, body part*›

Phrasal verbs

- **stitch down** *vt* [**~ sth. down, ~ down sth.**] 缝住 ‹*facing, flap, lining*›
- **stitch on** *vt* [**~ sth. on, ~ on sth.**] 把…缝上 ‹*button, braid*›
- **stitch together** *vt* [**~ sth. together**] 1 lit 缝合 ‹*wound*›; 缝补 ‹*pieces of cloth*› 2 fig (arrange, secure) 促成 ‹*package, deal, compromise*›
- **stitch up** *vt* 1 [**~ up sth., ~ sth. up**] lit 缝 ‹*hem*›; 缝合 ‹*wound*› 2 [**~ up sb., ~ sb. up**] Brit colloq (make appear guilty) 诬陷

stitching /ˈstɪtʃɪŋ/ *n* [u] 针脚

St John Ambulance /snt ˌdʒɒn ˈæmbjʊləns/ *pr n* Brit 圣约翰救护组织

St John's /ˌsnt ˈdʒɒnz/ *pr n* 圣约翰斯

St Kitts and Nevis /snt ˌkɪts ənd ˈniːvɪs/ *pr n* 圣基茨和尼维斯

St Lucia /ˌsnt ˈluːʃə/ *pr n* 圣卢西亚

stoat /stəʊt/ *n* 短尾鼬

stochastic /stəˈkæstɪk/ *adj* 随机的 ‹*geometry, analysis, process*›

stock /stɒk/
A *n* 1 [u and c] (available goods) 存货; **we don't carry a large ~ of pine furniture** 松木家具我们备货不多; **to be in/out of ~** 有货/没货; **to take ~ (of sth.)** (make list) 清点（某物的）存货; (carry out review) （对某事物）作出评估 2 [u and c] (supply, store, accumulation) 储备; **to build up a good ~ of teaching materials** 积累大量的教学资料; **food ~s are running low** 食物储备越来越少了; **the housing ~** 住房存量; **his vast ~ of knowledge** 他丰富的知识储备 3 [u] Fin (capital) 股本 4 *usu pl* Fin (portion of capital) 股份; **~s closed higher on Wall Street last night** 昨晚华尔街股市收高 5 [u and c] Brit Fin (government securities) 公债券 6 [u] (farm animals) 家畜; **dairy ~** 奶畜 7 [u] (descent) 世系; **she was of French ~** 她是法国人的后裔; **to come from farming ~** 出身农民世家 8 [u and c] Culin (liquid) 高汤; **fish/vegetable ~** 鱼汤/菜汤 9 [u] formal (personal standing or reputation) 名声; **her ~ is high/low** 她的声望很高/很低; **his ~ is rising/falling** 他声誉日隆/日衰 10 [c] (part of firearm, instrument, tool etc.) (handle) 柄; (base) 基座; (support) 支座; **a gun ~** 枪托 11 [u and c] (garden plant) 紫罗兰 12 [u and c] (plant receiving graft) 砧木 13 [c] Games (pile of cards) 发剩下的牌
B **stocks** *npl* 1 Hist, Jur 刑枷; **to be put in the ~s** 被戴上刑枷 2 Naut 船台; **to be on the ~s** (be under construction) ‹*ship*› 在建造中; fig (be in preparation) 在准备中; **our new model is already on the ~s and will be available in the spring** 我们已着手生产新的款式，春天就可以上市
C *modif* 1 (usually kept for sale) 常备的 ‹*item, size*› 2 (relating to goods kept) 存货的 ‹*level, valuation*›; **~ turnover** 存货周转率 3 pej (hackneyed) 陈腐的; **a ~ answer/phrase** 老一套的回答/说法 4 (typical) 常见的 ‹*character, theme, scene*› 5 Cin, TV 现成的 ‹*footage, shot*› 6 Fin 股票的; **~ prices/dividends** 股价/股息 7 Agric 家畜的; **~ farming** 畜牧业
D *vt* 1 (sell) 库存 ‹*goods*›; **do they ~ green tea?** 他们有绿茶卖吗？; **they ~ all sizes** 他们的库存尺码齐全 2 (fill) 在…中贮存; **the pond was well ~ed with fish** 池塘里有很多鱼; **a well-~ed library** 馆藏丰富的图书馆

Phrasal verb

- **stock up**

A *vi* 贮备; **to ~ up on** *or* **with sth.** 备足某物; **we ought to ~ up with film before our trip** 我们应该在旅行前备足胶卷; **to ~ up for Christmas** 为过圣诞节大采购
B *vt* [**~ sth. up, ~ up sth.**] 把…装满 ‹*freezer, cupboard*›

stockade /stɒˈkeɪd/
A *n* 1 (fence) 一排栅栏; (enclosure) 围场 2 Amer Mil (prison) 军人监狱; (detention centre) 战俘拘留营
B *vt* 用栅栏围起 ‹*area, settlement*›

stock: ~breeder ▸p. 409 *n* 牲畜饲养者; **~breeding** *n* [u] 畜牧

stockbroker /ˈstɒkbrəʊkə(r)/ ▸p. 409 *n* 股票经纪人

stockbroker belt *n* Brit [大城市外围的] 富人住宅带

stockbroking /ˈstɒkbrəʊkɪŋ/ *n* [u] 股票经纪业务; **a ~ firm** 股票经纪公司

stock car *n* 1 Aut [普通汽车加固而成的] 改装赛车 2 Amer Rail 牲口车皮

stock-car racing ▸p. 307 *n* [u] Brit 改装车车赛

stock: ~ clearance *n* 清仓甩卖; **~ company** *n* Amer 保留剧目剧团; **~ control** *n* [u] 库存管理; **~ cube** *n* 固体汤料

stock exchange *n* 股票交易所; **to work on the ~** 在股票交易所工作; **to be listed on the ~** 在股票交易市场挂牌

stock exchange listing *n* 股票上市

stockholder /ˈstɒkhəʊldə(r)/ *n* esp Amer 股东

stock: ~holders' equity *n* [u] esp Amer 股东权益; **~holders' report** *n* esp Amer 股东年度报表

Stockholm /ˈstɒkhəʊm/ *pr n* 斯德哥尔摩

stockily built /ˌstɒkɪli ˈbɪlt/ *adj* 矮壮的

stockiness /ˈstɒkɪnɪs/ *n* [u] 矮壮

stockinet, stockinette /ˌstɒkɪˈnet/ *n* [u] 松紧织物

stocking /ˈstɒkɪŋ/ *n* 1 (for woman) 长筒女袜; **a pair of ~s** 一双长筒女袜; **in (one's) ~(ed) feet** 只穿袜不穿鞋的 2 (for presents) 圣诞袜

stocking: ~ filler *n* Brit 圣诞袜小礼物; **~ mask** *n* 蒙面袜; **terrorists wearing ~ masks** 戴着蒙面袜的恐怖分子; **~ stitch** *n* [u] 隔行正反针编结法; **~ stuffer** *n* Amer **= ~ filler**

stock-in-trade *n* 1 (goods, subject) [某一行业的] 用具设备 2 fig (repertoire) 常用手法

stock issue *n* 1 (authorization) 股票发行 2 (shares) 股票

stockist /ˈstɒkɪst/ *n* 零售商; **a sole ~** 专营商

stock: ~jobber /-dʒɒbə(r)/ ▸p. 409 *n* Brit 股票经纪人; **~ list** *n* Brit 货物价格清单; **~man** /-mən/ ▸p. 409 *n* 饲养员; **~ market** *n* 1 (stock exchange) 股市; **to be quoted** *or* **listed on the ~ market** 在股市挂牌; **~-market price** *or* **value** 股市价格; 2 **the ~ market** (trading activity) 股票交易; **~ option** *n* 优先认股权

stockpile /ˈstɒkpaɪl/
A *n* 储备物资
B *vt* 储备 ‹*supplies, weapons*›

stock: ~piling /-paɪlɪŋ/ *n* [u] 储备; **~pot** *n* 1 (container) 汤锅; 2 (contents) 一汤锅; **~ rearing** *n* [u] 畜牧业; **~ room** *n* 仓库; **~ sheet** *n* 存货清单; **~ shortage** *n* 缺货; **~ split** *n* Amer 股份分割; **~-still** *adv* 静止地; **to stand ~-still** 一动不动地站着; **~take** *n* 一次盘存; **to do a ~take** 盘点存货; **~taking** *n* [u] 1 Comm 盘存; **to do (the) ~taking** 清点存货; 2 fig (review) 反思; **~ warrant** *n* 认股权证; **~whip** *n* 短柄长鞭

stocky /ˈstɒki/ *adj* 矮壮的 ‹*man, animal*›; **of ~ build** 体格敦实的

stockyard /ˈstɒkjɑːd/ *n* 牲畜栏

stodge /stɒdʒ/ *n* [u] Brit colloq 1 (food) 易饱的食物 2 fig (writing, speech) 枯燥乏味的东西

stodginess /ˈstɒdʒɪnɪs/ *n* [u] Brit colloq 1 (heaviness of food) 易饱 2 (dullness of writing, speech, style) 枯燥乏味

stodgy /ˈstɒdʒi/ *adj* Brit colloq 1 (heavy) 容易吃饱的 ‹*food, meal*› 2 fig (dull) 枯燥乏味的 ‹*writing, speech, style, person*›

stogy, stogie /ˈstəʊgi/ *n* Amer 廉价细雪茄

stoic /ˈstəʊɪk/
A *n* 1 (uncomplaining person) 坚忍的人 2 **Stoic** Philos 斯多葛派学者
B *adj* 1 **= stoical** 2 **Stoic** Philos 斯多葛派的

stoical /ˈstəʊɪkl/ *adj* 坚忍的 ‹*person*›; 泰然的 ‹*attitude, acceptance, resignation*›

stoically /ˈstəʊɪkli/ *adv* 坚忍地 ‹*loyal, behave*›; 泰然地 ‹*accept*›

stoicism /ˈstəʊɪsɪzəm/ *n* [u] 坚忍

stoke /stəʊk/ *vt* ~ **(up)** 1 (add fuel to) 给…添加燃料 ‹*fire, furnace, boiler*›; 给…加油 ‹*engine*› 2 fig (stir up) 激起 ‹*emotion, resentment, prejudice*›; 煽起 ‹*unrest, anger*›

stoke: **~hold** *n* 锅炉舱; **~hole** *n* 1 (area) 炉前; 2 (opening) 炉膛口

stoker /ˈstəʊkə(r)/ ▸**p. 409** *n* 锅炉工

STOL *abbr* Aviat = **short take-off and landing** 短距起降; **a ~ plane** *or* **aircraft** 短距起降飞机; **a ~ operation** 短距起降操作

stole¹ /stəʊl/ *pt* ▸**steal A, B**

stole² *n* Fashn 女用披肩

stolen /ˈstəʊlən/ *pp* ▸**steal A, B**

stolid /ˈstɒlɪd/ *adj* 不动感情的 ‹*person, speech, character*›

stolidly /ˈstɒlɪdli/ *adv* 冷淡地

stoma /ˈstəʊmə/ *n* 气孔

stomach /ˈstʌmək/

A *n* 1 ▸**p. 71** [c] (internal organ) 胃; **he says he's got a pain in his ~** 他说他胃疼; **my ~ started rumbling with hunger** 我的肚子饿得开始咕咕叫了; **a ~ upset** Brit 胃部不适; **you shouldn't exercise on a full/an empty ~** 你不应该吃饱了就运动/空腹去运动; **the pit of one's ~** 心窝; **he had a sudden sinking feeling in the pit of his ~** 他内心深处突然涌起一阵不祥之感; **to have a strong ~** (have good digestion) 胃口好; (not be squeamish) 能忍受恶心事物; **to turn sb.'s ~** 使某人恶心; **to be sick to one's ~** (be upset) 感到心烦意乱; (be afraid) 感到非常害怕; esp Amer (want to vomit) 感觉想吐; **to be sick to one's ~ of sb./sth.** (be fed up) 对某人/某事物感到厌烦; **sb.'s eyes are bigger than their ~** 某人眼大肚子小 2 ▸**p. 71** [c] (front part of body) 腹部; **she kicked him in the ~** 她踢在他的肚子上; **a dog lying on its ~** 一条趴着的狗; **an army marches on its ~** Prov 兵马未动，粮草先行; **~ muscles** 腹肌 3 [u and c] (appetite) 胃口; **she had no ~ for the leftover stew/to eat anything** 她不想吃剩下的炖菜/什么也不想吃 4 [u and c] (desire) 欲望; **he had no ~ for a fight** 他不想打架

B *vt* 1 (endure, tolerate) 欣然接受 ‹*thing*›; 喜欢和…相处 ‹*person*›; **I can't ~ violent films** 我不喜欢暴力影片; **I find him very hard to ~** 我发现很难和他相处 2 (physically tolerate) 吃得下; **she couldn't ~ any breakfast** 她早饭一点都吃不下

stomach: **~ ache** *n* [u and c] 胃痛; **to have/get ~ ache** 胃痛/患胃痛; **~ powder** *n* [u] 胃舒粉; **~ pump** *n* 胃唧筒; **~ stapling** *n* [u] 胃间隔手术; **~ ulcer** *n* 胃溃疡; **~ wall** *n* 胃壁

stomp /stɒmp/

A *vi* 1 (walk heavily) 重踏; **to ~ in/out** 踩着重步走进去/出去 2 esp Amer (dance) 跳顿足爵士舞

B *vt* esp Amer = **stamp B3**

C *n* esp Amer colloq 1 (dance) 顿足爵士舞 2 (tune) 顿足爵士舞曲; (song) 顿足爵士舞歌

stomping ground *n* Amer = **stamping ground**

stone /stəʊn/

A *n* 1 [c] (small rock) 石块; **a pile of ~s** 一堆石块; **to leave no ~ unturned** fig 想尽一切办法; **to sink like a ~** 急速下沉; **a ~'s throw** fig 很近的距离; **we live just a ~'s throw from here** 我们就住在附近; **to cast** *or* **throw the first ~ (at sb.)** fig 率先责难（某人） 2 [u] (hard substance) 石头; **a slab of ~** 一块石板; **to work ~** 加工石料; **~ walls/jars** 石墙/石坛; **to be made of ~** lit 是用石头造的; fig (unfeeling) 冷酷无情; **to have a heart of ~** 铁石心肠; **to be as hard as ~** lit 和石头一样坚硬; fig (unfeeling) 冷酷无情; **to be set** *or* **written in (tablets of) ~** fig 板上钉钉; **to set sth. in ~** fig 使某事不可更改 3 [c] (for particular purpose) [有特定用途的] 石块; **a commemorative ~** 纪念碑; **a ~ for grinding knives** 磨刀石 4 [c] (gem) 宝石; **to set a ~ in sth.** 在某物上镶宝石 5 [c] esp Brit (of fruit) 果核; **a peach/cherry ~** 桃核/樱桃核 6 [c] Med 结石 7 [c] (*pl* **stone**) ▸**p. 909** Brit Meas 英石 [合14磅或6.35千克]; **he's trying to lose a ~** 他试图减去 1 英石的体重

B *vt* 1 (throw rocks at) 向…扔石块; **to ~ sb. to death** 用石头砸死某人; **~ me** *or* **the crows!** Brit colloq dated 天哪！; **well, ~ the crows! he's done it all by himself!** 哎呀！全是他自己做的！ 2 (remove stone from) 去掉…的核 ‹*peach, cherry*›

Stone Age *n* **the ~** 石器时代; **~ tools** 石器时代的工具; **~ man** 石器时代的人; **~ equipment/computers** fig 老掉牙的设备/电脑

stone circle *n* [西欧的] 史前环状巨石阵

stone cold

A *adj* 冰凉的

B **stone-cold** *adv* 完全地; **stone-cold sober** 完全清醒的

stoned /stəʊnd/ *adj* colloq 1 (with cannabis) 神志恍惚的 2 (with alcohol) 醉醺醺的

stone: **~ dead** *adj pred* 完全死了的; **~ deaf** *adj* 完全聋的; **~ fruit** *n* [u and c] 核果; **~ground** *adj* 用石磨磨碎的; **~ground flour** 石磨研磨的面粉; **~ mason** ▸**p. 409** *n* 石匠

stonewall /ˈstəʊnwɔːl/

A *vt* 阻碍 ‹*person, investigation, question*›

B *vi* 1 (be obstructive) 阻碍 2 Sport (in cricket) «*batsman*» 防守挡击

stoneware /ˈstəʊnweə(r)/ *n* [u] 粗陶器; **attractive ~ pottery** 漂亮的粗陶器

stone: **~washed** *adj* 砂洗的 ‹*denim, jeans, jacket*›; **~work** *n* [u] [建筑物的] 石造部分

stonily /ˈstəʊnɪli/ *adv* 冷漠地 ‹*stare, say*›; 无情地 ‹*indifferent*›

stonking /ˈstɒŋkɪŋ/ *adj* Brit colloq 极大的; **the book is a ~ good read** 这真是本好书

stony /ˈstəʊni/ *adj* 1 (rocky) 多石的 ‹*riverbed, beach, field*›; **a ~ path** 石头路; **~ soil** 多石的土壤; **to fall on ~ ground** fig (be badly received) 受到冷遇; (be ignored) 被忽视 2 (resembling stone) 坚硬如石的 ‹*substance, material*› 3 fig (cold) 冷漠的 ‹*look, silence*›

stony: **~ broke** *adj* Brit colloq 身无分文的; **~-faced** *adj* 冷漠的 ‹*person, look, silence*›

stood /stʊd/ *pt, pp* ▸**stand A, B**

stooge /stuːdʒ/ *n* 1 pej (subordinate, assistant) 奴才 2 Theat 丑角

stook /stuːk, stʊk/ Brit

A *n* 禾束堆

B *vt* 把…堆成堆 ‹*sheaves*›

stool /stuːl/ *n* 1 (seat) 凳子; **high ~** 高脚凳; **to fall between two ~s** esp Brit fig 两头落空 2 (faeces) 粪便

stool pigeon *n* colloq 1 (decoy) 用作诱饵的人 2 (informer) 线人

stoop¹ /stuːp/

A *vi* 1 (lean forward) 俯身; **to ~ down** 弯下腰; **to ~ over sth.** 俯身到某物上 2 (be bent over) 弓背; **to ~ with age** 因上了年纪而驼背 3 (debase oneself) 降低身份; (condescend) 屈尊; **to ~ to do sth.** 降低身份做某事; **to ~ so low as to do sth.** 卑鄙到做某事的程度

B *vt* 使…弯曲 ‹*head, shoulders*›

C *n* 弓背; **to have a ~** 驼背; **to walk with a ~** 驼着背走路

stoop² *n* Amer (of house) 门廊

stooping /ˈstuːpɪŋ/ *adj attrib* 弯下的; **~ shoulders** 曲背

stop /stɒp/

A *vi* (*pres p etc.* **-pp-**) 1 (cease moving) 停住; **~ or I'll shoot!** 站住，否则我要开枪了！; **the car ~ped at the traffic lights** 汽车在交通信号灯前停下来 2 (not continue, end) 停止; **we'll work until seven and then ~ for the day** 我们将工作到 7 点，然后今天就不干了; **the bus service ~s at midnight** 公交车午夜收车; **the rain seems to be ~ping** 雨好像要停了; **the bleeding's ~ped** 血止住了; **without ~ping** 毫不停歇地; **not to know when to ~** 不知道适可而止; **to ~ at nothing (to do sth.)** 不择手段（做某事） 3 (pause for short time) 暂停; **I'm hungry, let's ~ for lunch** 我饿了，我们停下来吃午饭吧; **people just don't ~ to think about the consequences of their actions** 人们做事情就是不肯停下来想想他们行为的后果; **he ~ped and bought some flowers** 他停下来买了一些花 4 Brit colloq (stay) 停留; **we ~ped two days in Paris on the way back** 我们回来时在巴黎停留了两天; **will they be ~ping for dinner?** 他们会留下来吃晚饭吗？; **I'd love to ~ and chat, but I'm late already** 我很愿意留下来聊聊，可是我已经迟到了 5 Transp (make scheduled halt) 靠站; **main-line trains ~ at platform 5** 干线火车停靠第 5 站台 6 (cease operating) 停止运转; **my watch has ~ped** 我的表停了; **I felt as if my heart had ~ped** 我觉得好像我的心都不跳了

B *vt* (*pres p etc.* **-pp-**) 1 (halt action of, put an end to) 使停止; **we were ~ped by the police for speeding** 我们因为超速被警察截住了; **to ~ an engine** 使发动机停转; **to ~ the clock** 停止计时; **~ me if I'm boring you** 你要觉得我烦就打断我; **the pistol will ~ a man at 30 metres** 这把手枪能把距离 30 米远的人撂倒; **rain ~ped play** 因雨停赛; **I can't ~ the bleeding** 我止不住血; **strikes have ~ped production in several factories** 罢工已经造成好几家工厂停产 2 (quit) 停止; **to ~ smoking** 戒烟; **he never ~s talking** 他总是说个没完; **please ~ crying and tell me what's wrong** 快别哭了，告诉我出了什么事; **~ it! you're hurting me** 住手！你把我弄疼了; **I'm ~ping my subscription as from next month** 我将从下月起停止订阅 3 (prevent) 阻止; **to ~ pollution** 防止污染; **I'm leaving and you can't ~ me!** 我要走，你拦不住我！; **how can I ~ this bowl (from) leaking?** 我怎样才能让这个碗不漏呢？ 4 (refuse to provide) 停止提供; **to ~ sb.'s salary** 停发某人的薪水 5 Brit (deduct) 扣除; **they've ~ped the money out of my wages** 他们从我的工资里扣除了那笔钱 6 Brit (withhold payment on) 止付 ‹*cheque*› 7 colloq (be hit by) 被…击中 ‹*bullet*›; **he ~ped one just as he was climbing out of the trench** 他爬出战壕时被一颗子弹击中 8 (plug) 堵塞; **to ~ a bottle** 把瓶子塞住; **to ~ one's ears** 捂住耳朵 9 Mus (press down or cover with finger) 按住 ‹*string, hole*›

C *n* 1 (halt) 停止; **they worked six hours without a ~** 他们连续工作了 6 个小时; **in ~s and starts** 时断时续地; **she brought the car to a ~** 她停下了车; **work on the project is at** *or* **has come to a full ~** 这个项目的工作完全停了下来; **to put a ~ to sth.** 结束某事 2 (short break in journey) 停留; **we had** *or* **made a short ~ for coffee** 我们曾短暂停下来喝咖啡; **we made an overnight ~ in Hong Kong** 我们在香港停留过夜 3 Transp (stopping place) 车站; **I'm getting off at the next ~** 我在下一站下车; **it's about two ~s farther on** 还要过去大约两站路 4 Brit dated (punctuation mark) 标点符号 [尤指句号] 5 (in telegrams) [句号的代字]; **meet you at the airport ~** 在机场接你，句号 6 (object preventing movement) 止动器; **the door was pushed back on to the ~** 门被推开固定在门吸上 7 Mus (knob on organ) 音栓; **to pull out all the ~s (to do sth.)** colloq (try one's utmost) 竭尽全力（做某事）; (go to a lot of trouble) 煞费苦心（做某事） 8 Mus (set of organ pipes) 音管 9 Phot (aperture) 光圈

S

D *v refl* (*pres p etc.* **-pp-**) **1** to ~ oneself (prevent oneself) 阻止自己; **I nearly fell, but I ~ped myself** 我差点跌倒，不过我稳住了我自己; **to ~ oneself doing** *or* Brit **from doing sth.** 阻止自己做某事; **he couldn't ~ himself from thinking about it** 他忍不住去想这件事; **she had to grab on to a crate to ~ herself overbalancing** 她只得抓住一个板条箱，以使自己保持平衡 **2** **to ~ oneself** (restrain oneself) 克制自己; **I couldn't ~ myself** 我忍不住; **to ~ oneself doing** *or* Brit **from doing sth.** 克制自己不做某事; **he tried to ~ himself from telling her** 他努力忍住不告诉她; **I had to ~ myself laughing out loud** 我只好忍住不大声笑出来; **I tried to ~ myself (from) crying** 我努力忍住不哭; **I only just ~ped myself giving the game away** 我勉强没有泄露秘密

Phrasal verbs

- **stop away** *vi* Brit colloq **1** (not go) 不去; **if you ~ away from lectures, you may fail the exams** 如果你不去上课，就可能会考试不及格 **2** (not come) 不来; **to ~ away from sth.** 不来某处
- **stop behind** *vi* Brit colloq 留下; **I had to ~ behind after school** 我不得不在放学之后留下; **to ~ behind to do sth.** 留下来做某事
- **stop by**

A *vi* 顺路造访; **I'll ~ by this evening for a chat/at his place** 今晚我想过去聊聊/顺路去他家坐坐

B *vt* [**~ by sth.**] 顺路造访; **could you ~ by the shop on the way home for some bread?** 你回家时顺路到那家店买些面包好吗？; **we ~ped by her house to give her the tickets** 我们顺便到她家去把票给她

- **stop down** *vt* [**~ sth. down, ~ down sth.**] 缩小…的光圈 ‹*lens*›; 缩小 ‹*aperture*›
- **stop in** *vi* Brit colloq **1** (stay in) 待在家里 **2** (call in) 顺路造访; **he ~ped in to buy some bread on his way home** 回家路上他顺便去买了一些面包
- **stop off** *vi* 中途停留; **we ~ped off at a hotel for the night** 我们中途停下来在一家旅馆过夜
- **stop out** *vi* Brit colloq 夜里很晚不回家; **to ~ out all night** 整夜不回家
- **stop over** *vi* **1** (break journey) 中途停留; **I wanted to ~ over in India on the way to Australia** 去澳大利亚的途中我想在印度稍作停留 **2** Brit colloq (stay over) 过夜
- **stop up**

A *vt* [**~ sth. up, ~ up sth.**] 堵塞 ‹*hole, opening*›; **the drainpipe was ~ped up with leaves** 排水管被树叶堵住了

B *vi* Brit colloq 熬夜; **to ~ up to see the New Year in** 熬夜等待新年的到来

stop-and-start *adj* = **stop-start**

stop: ~ bath *n* 停显液; **~cock** *n* 旋塞

stopgap /ˈstɒpgæp/

A *n* 权宜之计

B *adj attrib* 临时的 ‹*measure, arrangement, job*›

stop: ~-go *adj* **1** lit 走走停停的; **2** Econ 交替刺激与紧缩的; **~ lamp** *n* Amer 刹车灯; **~ light** *n* **1** Brit (red traffic light) 红灯; **2** Amer (set of traffic lights) 交通信号灯; **3** (on vehicle) 刹车灯; **~-loss** *adj* 止损的 ‹*order, policy, protection*›; **the ~ strategy** 止损策略; **~-off** *n* [短暂的] 中途停留; **~over** *n* [较长的] 中途停留

stoppage /ˈstɒpɪdʒ/ *n* **1** (strike) 停工; **a 24-hour ~** 24 小时罢工 **2** Sport 中断比赛 **3** Brit (deduction from wages) 扣除款

stoppage time *n* [u] 伤停补时

stop payment *n* 止付; **~ order** 止付通知书

stopper /ˈstɒpə(r)/

A *n* 塞子; **to put the ~ in a bottle** 盖上瓶塞; **to take the ~ out of a bottle** 取下瓶塞

B *vt* 给…塞上塞子 ‹*bottle*›; **a ~ed jar** 用塞子塞住的罐子

stopping /ˈstɒpɪŋ/ *n* [u] 停止; **'no ~'** "不准停车"

stopping: ~ distance *n* 制动距离; **~ place** *n* 停留处; **~ train** *n* Brit [几乎每站都停的] 慢车

stop: ~ press *n* [u] Brit [报纸临付印前或开始付印后插入的] 最新消息; **~ press news** 最新消息; **~ sign** *n* 停车标志; **~ signal** *n* 停车信号灯; **~watch** *n* 秒表; **~-start** *adj* colloq 断断续续的 ‹*journey, game, career*›; **~word** *n* 停用词 [指电脑检索中的非检索用字]

storage /ˈstɔːrɪdʒ/ *n* **1** (of food, fuel, goods) 贮藏; (of furniture, document, file) 存放; (of heat, energy, electricity) 存储; **~ costs** 存储费用; **to be in ~** 在贮存中; **to put sth. in(to) ~** 把某物储藏起来 **2** (space) 贮存空间 **3** Comput 存储; **~ on disk** 磁盘存储; **~ space/problems/disc** 存储空间/问题/盘

storage: ~ area *n* 存储区; **~ battery** *n* 蓄电池; **~ capacity** *n* [u] 存储容量; **~ device** *n* 存储设备; **~ heater** *n* Brit 蓄热电暖器; **~ jar** *n* **1** (glass) 储物瓶; **2** (ceramic) 储物罐; **~ tank** *n* 储存柜; **~ unit** *n* **1** (cupboard) 橱柜; **2** (room) 储藏室; **3** Comput 存储单位

store /stɔː(r)/

A *n* **1** [c] (large shop) 大型百货商店 **2** [c] esp Amer (shop of any size) 商店; **the ~ owner** 店主 **3** [c] (supply, stock, accumulation) 贮存物; **to lay in** *or* **keep a ~ of food** 储存食物; **a vast ~ of knowledge** 丰富的知识储备 **4** [c] (storage place) 仓库; **a grain/munition ~** 粮仓/军火库 **5** [u] (storage) 储存; **to put sth. in(to) ~** 把某物储存起来; **in ~** 储存着; fig (waiting to happen) 即将发生; **goods in ~** 存货; **it looks like there's trouble in ~** 看起来好像会有麻烦; **they think it'll be easy, but they have a surprise in ~** 他们认为这很容易，但是他们会大吃一惊的; **what does the future have** *or* **hold in ~ for us?** 我们的未来会是怎样呢？ **6** [u] (importance) 重要性; (value) 价值; **to set** *or* **lay** *or* **put ~ by** *or* **on sth.** 看重某事物; **he sets great ~ by your advice** 他非常重视你的建议

B **stores** *npl* **1** (supplies) 补给品; **medical/military ~s** 医疗用品/军需品 **2** (storage area) 补给品仓库

C *modif* Amer (not home-made) 商店售卖的 ‹*cake, cookies*›

D *vt* **1** (put away, accumulate) 储存; **to ~ lemons in a cool dry place** 把柠檬存放在凉爽干燥处; **the squirrels ~ nuts for the winter** 松鼠会为过冬储存坚果 **2** (put into storage) 收存 ‹*furniture, personal belongings*› **3** (hold) 容纳; **the cupboard can ~ all the books** 这个橱柜放得下所有的书 **4** Comput 存储; **the data is ~d on disk** 数据存在磁盘上 **5** (retain mentally) 记住; **I can't ~ these dates in my memory** 我记不住这些日期

E *vi* ‹*food*› 可保存; **these truffles will ~ for up to two weeks in the fridge** 这些松露在冰箱里可以存放两个星期

Phrasal verbs

- **store away** *vt* [**~ sth. away, ~ away sth.**]
  1 (put away) 储存; **those old clothes are ~d away in the attic** 那些旧衣服存放在阁楼上 **2** (retain mentally) 记住; **she wondered what secrets were ~d away in his brain** 她想知道他的头脑中都藏了些什么秘密
- **store up** *vt* [**~ sth. up, ~ up sth.**]
  1 (accumulate) 储备; **animals were storing up food for the winter** 动物们在储备过冬的食物 **2** (bottle up) 把…郁积在心 ‹*strong feelings*›; **she had ~d up all her anger and eventually snapped** 她把所有的愤怒都憋在心里，最后终于爆发了 **3** (not deal with) 使…积累 ‹*problems*›; **by ignoring your feelings, you are only storing up trouble for yourself** 你回避自己的感情问题，将来必有麻烦

store: ~ card *n* [商店或连锁店的] 赊账卡; **~ cupboard** *n* 储物柜

stored /stɔːd/ *adj* **1** *usu attrib* (put away) 储存的; **~ information/food** 储存的信息/食物; **~ data** 存储数据 **2** *attrib* (bottled up) 郁积的 ‹*feelings*›; **sb.'s ~ resentment** 某人的积怨 **3** *attrib* (not dealt with) 积累的 ‹*troubles, problems*› **4** *pred* (stocked) 储存…的; **a mind well ~ with esoteric knowledge** 充满深奥知识的头脑

store: ~ detective ▸p. 409 *n* [受雇在商店里专抓行窃者的] 商店侦探; **~front** *n* Amer **1** = **shop front**; **2** (premises) 店面; **a ~front eatery** 开在铺面房里的饭馆; **3** Comput **(electronic) ~front** 电子店面; **~house** *n* **1** (building) 仓库; **2** fig (repository) 宝库; **~keeper** ▸p. 409 *n* Amer = **shopkeeper**; **~man** /-mən/ ▸p. 409 *n* Brit 仓库保管员; **~ manager** ▸p. 409 *n* 零售商店经理; **~room** *n* 储藏室

storey /ˈstɔːri/ *n* (*pl* **~s**) 楼层; **on the top ~** 在顶楼; **a single-~ building** 单层建筑; **a three-~ed building** 一座三层楼

stork /stɔːk/ *n* 鹳

storm /stɔːm/

A *n* **1** (very bad weather) (with rain) 暴风雨; (with snow) 暴风雪; (with thunder and lightning) 雷暴; **we were** *or* **got caught in the ~ and got drenched to the skin** 我们遭遇了暴风雨，浑身都湿透了; **a ~ is brewing** *or* **gathering** 暴风雨要来了; **the ~ broke, and the rain began to pour down** 暴风雨降临了，大雨开始倾盆而下 **2** Meteorol (force 10 wind) 狂风 **3** (controversy) 风暴; **to cause** *or* **create** *or* **raise a political ~** 引发一场政治风暴; **a ~ is brewing over ...** 一场风暴正在酝酿; **to bring a ~ (down) about sb.'s ears** 导致某人遭受激烈的批评 **4** (outburst) 爆发; **a ~ of applause** 暴风雨般的掌声; **a ~ of protest** 抗议的浪潮 **5** (large number) 纷飞; **a ~ of bullets** 枪林弹雨 **6** (direct assault) 猛攻; **to take a city/fortress by ~** 突袭城市/要塞; **to take sb./sth. by ~** fig 使某人为之倾倒/在某地大获成功; **the play took London by ~** 这部剧风靡伦敦

B **storms** *npl* Amer (protective windows) 外重窗; (protective doors) 外重门

C *vt* **1** (attack) 突袭 ‹*building, place*› **2** (shout) 怒吼; **'don't you know who I am?' she ~ed** "你不知道我是谁吗？" 她怒喝道

D *vi* **1** (move angrily) 气呼呼地走; (move at a pace) 向前闯; **to ~ into** 怒气冲冲地闯入 ‹*room, house*›; 闯进 ‹*semi-finals, lead position*›; **to ~ off** 气呼呼地跑开 **2** (launch attack) 突袭; **troops ~ed into the city at dawn** 部队在拂晓时分攻入城内 **3** (be angry) 大发雷霆; **to ~ at sb.** 对某人大发雷霆 **4** Meteorol (with rain) 有暴风雨; (with snow) 有暴风雪; (with thunder and lightning) 有雷暴; **it ~ed last night** 昨夜雷雨大作

stormbound /ˈstɔːmbaʊnd/ *adj* 为暴风雨所阻的 ‹*ships, travellers*›; 因暴风雨而与外界隔绝的 ‹*island, lighthouse*›

storm: ~ cellar *n* 防风地窖; **~ centre** *n* **1** lit 风暴中心; **2** fig 麻烦的中心; **~cloud** *n* **1** lit 暴风云; **2** fig 凶兆; **~ cone** *n* Brit 风暴信标; **~ damage** *n* [u] 暴风雨造成的破坏; **~ door** *n* esp Amer [防雨雪及风等的] 风门; **~ drain** *n* 雨水管; **~ flap** *n* **1** (on tent) 防雨盖; **2** (on coat) 门襟; **~ force wind** *n* 暴风

storminess /ˈstɔːmɪnɪs/ *n* [u] **1** (of weather) 风暴度 **2** (of relationship, meeting, debate) 冲突激烈程度

storming /ˈstɔːmɪŋ/

A *n* [u] 突袭

B *adj attrib* Brit colloq 精彩的 ‹*debut, appearance, race, finish*›

storm: ~ lantern *n* esp Brit 防风灯; **~-lashed** *adj* 暴风雨吹打的; **~ petrel** *n* （预示风暴的）海燕; **~ sewer** *n* Amer

= ~ **drain**; ~**-tossed** *adj* 在风暴中颠簸的; ~ **trooper** *n* 突击队员; ~ **troops** *npl* = **shock troops**; ~ **warning** *n* 风暴警报; ~ **water** *n* [u] 暴雨积水; **a ~ water drain/channel** 暴雨积水排水道/渠; ~ **window** *n* esp Amer 防风窗

stormy /'stɔːmi/ *adj* 1 (having heavy rain) 有暴风雨的 ‹*weather, sky, day*›; 多暴风雨的 ‹*period, season*›; (having heavy snow) 有暴风雪的 ‹*weather, sky, day*›; 多暴风雪的 ‹*period, season*›; 波涛汹涌的 ‹*sea*› 2 fig (turbulent) 冲突不断的 ‹*relationship*›; 争论激烈的 ‹*meeting*›; 激烈的 ‹*debate*›

story /'stɔːri/ *n* 1 (tale) 故事; **to tell/read (sb.) a ~** （给某人）讲/读故事; **stories of ancient Greece** 古希腊故事; **the ~ of Robin Hood** 罗宾汉的传说; **the ~ goes that ...** 据说…; **she never saw him again, or so the ~ goes** 她再也没有见到他，或者据说如此 2 (account) 对往事的叙述; **the true ~ is that ...** 事情的真相是…; **he told us the ~ of his life** 他给我们讲述了他的生平经历; **the ~ of the Beatles** 披头士乐队的来龙去脉; **there are two sides to every ~** fig 每个故事都可以从两个方面看; **to have similar stories** 有相似的经历; **to tell the same ~** 有相同的经历; **it's a long ~** colloq 说来话长; **to cut** Brit *or* **make** Amer **a long ~ short** colloq 长话短说; **a likely ~!** colloq iron 听上去像是那么回事！; **that's the ~ of my life** colloq 我就是这个命 3 (version) 陈述; **we must stick to our ~ about the accident** 对事故的说法我们必须一口咬定 4 *sing* (situation) 情况; **the whole** *or* **full ~** 全部情况; **only part** *or* **half of the ~** 只是部分情况; **it's the same old ~, it's always the same ~** 还是老一套; **many years later I returned to Africa, but that's another ~** 多年后我又重返非洲，不过这是后话了; **in public the couple were all smiles; in private it was a different ~** 这对夫妻在公开场合满面笑容，私下里则完全两样 5 Journ 新闻报道; **an exclusive ~ on** *or* **about sth.** 有关某事物的独家报道; **the incident will make a good ~** 这一事件将成为新闻报道的好题材; **to carry** *or* **run a ~** 刊登一篇报道 6 (plot, events) 情节; **a film with a good ~ to it** 情节精彩的电影; **the ~ was taken from a Russian novel** 故事情节取材自一部俄罗斯小说; **the ~ is set in Normandy** 故事发生的背景是诺曼底 7 colloq (lie) 谎言; **to tell stories** 撒谎; **to make up** *or* **invent a ~ (about sb./sth.)** 编造（关于某人/某事物的）谎言 8 (rumour) 谣传; **all sorts of stories about him are going round the office** 办公室里流传着关于他的种种流言 9 Amer (floor) = **storey**

story: ~**board** *n* 剧情梗概系列图片; ~**book** *n* 故事书; **an affair with a ~book ending** 结局如传奇故事的风流韵事; ~**teller** *n* 1 (writer) 讲故事的人; 2 (liar) 说谎者

storyline /'stɔːrɪlaɪn/ *n* 故事情节

story-telling *n* [u] 讲故事

stout /staʊt/

A *adj* 1 (fat) 肥胖的 ‹*person, pet animal*›; **to grow ~** 发胖 2 (strong) 厚实耐穿的 ‹*footwear*›; 粗壮的 ‹*leg, arm*›; 粗大的 ‹*stick, branch*›; 坚固的 ‹*ship, walls*› 3 (valiant) 勇敢的 ‹*heart*›; 顽强的 ‹*supporter, support, opposition, defence, resistance*›

B *n* [u and c] 烈性黑啤酒

stout-hearted /ˌstaʊt'hɑːtɪd/ *adj* 勇敢坚毅的 ‹*person*›; 顽强的 ‹*supporter, support, opposition, defence, resistance*›

stoutly /'staʊtli/ *adv* 1 (strongly) 坚固地 ‹*build, construct*›; ~ **made** 做得结实的 2 (valiantly) 坚决地 ‹*maintain, deny, believe*›; 顽强地 ‹*support, oppose, defend, resist, fight*›; ~ **held beliefs** 坚定的信念

stoutness /'staʊtnɪs/ *n* 1 (of person, animal) 肥胖 2 (of footwear) 结实; (of stick, branch) 粗壮 3 (of heart) 勇敢; (of support, opposition, defence, resistance) 顽强

stove /stəʊv/ *n* 1 (cooker, heater) 炉; **an electric/a gas ~** 电炉/煤气炉 2 (kiln) 窑

stove: ~ **enamel** *n* [u] Brit 耐热搪瓷制品; ~**pipe** *n* 火炉管

stove in *pt, pp* = **stave in**

stow /stəʊ/ *vt* 1 (pack) 装填; **to ~ sth. in(to) sth.** 把某物装进某物中; **to ~ cargo in the hold** 把货物装进货舱 2 Brit colloq (shut) 闭上 ‹*mouth*›; ~ **it!** 住嘴！

Phrasal verb

• **stow away**

A *vi* 无票偷乘 [指乘船、乘飞机等]; **to ~ away in** *or* **on sth.** 无票偷乘某交通工具

B *vt* [~ **sth. away,** ~ **away sth.**] 收好 ‹*luggage, cargo, sail*›

stowage /'stəʊɪdʒ/ *n* [u] 1 (action) 装载 2 (space) 载货容积 3 (cost) 装货费

stowaway /'stəʊəweɪ/ *n* [乘船、乘飞机等的] 逃票乘客

St Patrick's Day /ˌsnt 'pætrɪks deɪ/ *n* 圣帕特里克节 [3月17日，爱尔兰节日]

straddle /'strædl/

A *vt* 1 (sit or stand across) 跨 ‹*fence, ditch*›; 跨坐 ‹*chair*›; 骑 ‹*cycle, horse*› 2 (extend across) «*bridge*» 横跨 ‹*border, river*› 3 Amer fig (be equivocal about) 对…含糊其辞; **to ~ (both sides of) an issue** pej 对一个问题持骑墙态度 4 (fire at) 夹叉射击; (bomb) 夹叉轰炸

B *n* 1 (action, position) 叉腿 2 ~ **(jump)** Sport 俯卧式跳高

strafe /strɑːf, Amer streɪf/ *vt* 低空轰炸

strafing /'strɑːfɪŋ, Amer 'streɪf-/ *n* [u] 低空轰炸

straggle /'strægl/ *vi* 1 (spread untidily) «*plant, vine, weed*» 蔓生; «*village, houses*» 散乱地分布; «*hair, beard*» 散乱; **to ~ along sth.** 沿某物蔓延; **to ~ along ...** 沿…散乱分布 ‹*road*› 2 (move slowly) 掉队; **the injured soldiers ~d behind** 受伤士兵落到了后面

Phrasal verb

• **straggle in** *vi* 拖拖拉拉到达

straggler /'stræglə(r)/ *n* 掉队者

straggling /'stræglɪŋ/ *adj* 蔓生的 ‹*plant, vine, weed*›; 零散的 ‹*village, houses*›; 蓬乱的 ‹*hair, beard*›

straggly /'strægli/ *adj* 蔓生的 ‹*plant, vine, weed*›; 蓬乱的 ‹*hair, beard*›

straight /streɪt/

A *adj* 1 (not bent, curved, curly, wavy) 直的; **a ~ line/road** 直线/直路; **she has long, ~ hair** 她的头发又长又直 2 (not flared or close-fitting) 直筒式的; **a ~ skirt** 直筒裙 3 (going direct to target) 正中目标的; **a ~ punch to the face** 不偏不倚打在脸上的一拳 4 (properly positioned) 平正的; **your tie isn't ~** 你的领带不正; **the walls aren't ~** 墙不平; **to keep** *or* **have a ~ face** 板着脸 5 *usu pred* (neat and tidy) 整洁的; **it took hours to get** *or* **put the house ~** 用了好半天才把房子收拾好 6 *usu pred* (in order) 有条理的; **to get** *or* **put sth. ~** 把某物整理好 7 *pred* (clear) 清楚明了的; **to get sth. ~** 把某事弄清楚; **to put** *or* **set things** *or* **matters ~** 将事情弄清楚; **to put** *or* **set the record ~** 澄清事实; **to put** *or* **set sb. ~ (about sth.)** 纠正某人（对某事物）的错误认识 8 (honest, direct) 坦率的; **it's time for some ~ talking** 现在该开诚布公地谈一谈了; **I don't think you're being ~ with me** 我觉得你没有跟我坦诚相见 9 (involving only two) 仅涉及两者的; **it was a ~ choice between taking the job and staying out of work** 要么接受这份工作，要么继续失业，此外别无选择; **the election was a ~ fight between the two main parties** 那次选举是两大政党的直接交锋 10 (outright) 完全的; **he issued a ~ denial of all charges** 他发表声明，断然否认了所有的指控; **that's ~ dishonesty** 那是纯粹的欺诈 11 *attrib* (serious) 严肃的 ‹*actor, role, play*› 12 *attrib* (consecutive) 连续的; **the team has had five ~ wins** 该队已经连赢了5场比赛 13 *attrib* (involving every subject) 每门科目的; **to get** *or* **earn ~ As** 成绩全优; **a ~ A student** 全优生 14 (undiluted) 纯的 ‹*whisky, brandy*› 15 colloq (heterosexual) 异性恋的 16 colloq (not criminal) 规规矩矩的 ‹*person*› 17 colloq pej (conventional) 正统的 ‹*person*› 18 colloq (not on drugs) 不吸毒的 19 *pred* colloq (quits, even) 扯平的; **if I give you $10, we'll be ~** 如果我给你 10 美元，我们就两清了; **to get oneself ~ (with sb.)** 还清欠（某人）的钱

B *adv* 1 ▸ p. 905 (in direct line) 笔直地; **she held her arm out ~** 她把胳膊伸直; **to go ~ ahead** 一直往前走; **to look sb. ~ in the eye** 直视某人; **she drove ~ into a tree** 她开车一头撞在了树上; **this wind is terrible; it goes ~ through you** 这场风太大，把人都吹透了 2 (without delay) 立即; **to go ~ home** 直接回家; **I was so tired, I went ~ to bed** 我太累，径直上床睡了; **to come ~ to the point** 开门见山; **you shouldn't go swimming ~ after a meal** 你不应该一吃完饭就去游泳; ~ **off** (colloq) (immediately) 立即; (without hesitation) 毫不犹豫地; **he drank it ~ off** 他一口把它喝了 3 (in proper position) 端正地; **stand up ~!** 站直了！; **she pulled her hat ~** 她把帽子拉正 4 (clearly) 清楚地; **I can't see/think ~** 我看/想不清楚 5 (honestly and directly) 坦率地; **to give it to sb. ~** colloq 对某人实话实说; ~ **out** colloq 直截了当地; ~ **up** Brit colloq 真的 [用以询问或强调所说内容的真实性]; **to play ~ with sb.** colloq 跟某人坦诚相见; **to play it ~** 诚实无欺; **you'd better be playing it ~** 你最好别要花招; **to go ~** «*criminal*» 改邪归正 6 (continuously) 连续地; **they had been working for 16 hours ~** 他们一连工作了 16 个小时 7 (seriously) (in drama, film, etc.) 严肃地 ‹*play, act*› 8 (neat) 不掺杂地; **to drink one's whisky ~** 喝纯威士忌酒

C *n* 1 colloq (heterosexual) 异性恋者 2 colloq pej (conventional person) 正统的人 3 *sing* esp Brit (of road, racetrack) 直道; **the ~ and narrow** 诚实正当的生活; **to keep sb. on the ~ and narrow** 让某人走正路; **to keep to/get back on the ~ and narrow** 走正路/改邪归正 4 Games (in poker) 顺子

straight arrow *n* Amer colloq 诚实正直的人

straightaway /ˌstreɪtə'weɪ/

A *adv* 立刻

B *n* Amer (of road) 直道; (of racetrack) 直道部分

straight: ~ **chair** *n* 直背椅; ~ **edge** *n* 直尺

straighten /'streɪtn/

A *vt* 1 (stop being bent, curved, curly, wavy) 使变直; **to ~ one's arm/back/shoulders** 伸直胳膊/挺直后背/挺起肩膀; **to ~ one's hair** 把头发弄直 2 (make upright or level) 使端正; **I ~ed my tie and walked in** 我把领带正了正，走了进去 3 (tidy) 使整洁; **to ~ the room** 整理房间

B *vi* 1 (stop being bent or curved) «*road*» 变直 2 (become upright) «*person*» 挺直身体; «*back, shoulders*» 挺直

Phrasal verbs

• **straighten out**

A *vi* «*road, stem*» 变直

B [~ **sth. out,** ~ **out sth.**] *vt*

1 (stop being bent or curved) 使变直; **she sat down, ~ing out one leg** 她伸着一条腿坐了下来; **he untwisted the wire and ~ed it out** 他解开缠绕的电线后又把它拉直 2 (sort out) 清理; **I need time to ~ out the mess** 我需要时间来收拾这个烂摊子; **to ~ out a misunderstanding** 澄清误会

C [~ **sb. out,** ~ **out sb.**] *vt*

1 colloq (help to behave better) 帮…改进; **I used**

S

to eat loads of junk food, but my husband ~ed me out 我过去经常吃大量垃圾食品，但我的丈夫帮我改掉了这个习惯; to ~ oneself out 改过自新 2 (help to understand the real situation) 为…解除困惑; she ~ed me out about a lot of things 她帮我弄清楚了很多事情

• **straighten up**

A vi 1 (become upright) 挺直身体; to ~ up and fly right Amer 改邪归正 2 (tidy up) 整理

B vt [~ up sb./sth., ~ sb./sth. up]

1 (make upright or level) 把…收拾整齐; to ~ up one's tie 把领带拉正 2 (stop being bent or curved) 挺直 ‹back› 3 (tidy) 使整洁; to ~ up the room 整理房间; go and ~ yourself up: you look a bit of a mess 去把自己弄干净: 你看上去有点邋遢

straight: **~-faced** *adj* 绷着脸的; **~ flush** *n* 同花顺子; **~forward** *adj* 1 (simple) 简单的 ‹*case, matter, question, answer*›; 2 (honest) 坦率的 ‹*person*›; **~forwardly** *adv* 1 (honestly) 坦率地 ‹*answer, speak, deal*›; 2 (simply) 简单地 ‹*set out, describe, explain*›; **~forwardness** *n* [u] 1 (honesty) 坦率; 2 (simplicity) 简单; **~-laced** *adj* = strait-laced; **~ left** *n* 左直拳; **~-line depreciation** *n* [u] [资产的] 直线折旧法; **~ man** *n* 搭档; to be *or* play the ~ man (to sb.) (为某人) 做配角

straightness /'streɪtnɪs/ *n* [u] 1 (honesty) 直率 2 (of hair, shoulders) 直挺; (of line, alignment) 直 3 (heterosexuality) 异性恋的性取向

straight: **~-out** *adj* 直截了当的 ‹*answer, refusal*›; **~ right** *n* 右直拳; **~ sex** *n* [u] 异性性行为; **~ ticket** *n* Amer 投给同一政党所有候选人的选票; to vote a ~ ticket 投清一色选票

strain /streɪn/

A *n* 1 [u and c] (pressure on person or relationship) 压力; I found it a ~ having to concentrate for so long 我觉得这么长时间全神贯注挺累的; these repayments are putting a ~ on our finances 偿还这些债款使我们背负上了财务压力; their marriage is under great ~ at the moment 眼下他们的婚姻关系非常紧张; relax, and let us take the ~ 你歇一歇，让我们来顶一会儿 2 [u] (tense state) 紧张; mental/nervous ~ 精神/神经紧张 3 [u and c] (force) 作用力; the rope broke under the ~ 绳子拉断了; don't place too much ~ on muscles and joints 不要让肌肉和关节太吃力 4 [u and c] (injury) 劳损; a muscle/thigh ~ 肌肉劳损/大腿拉伤 5 [c] (type) 种类; a new ~ of rice 水稻新品种; this is only one of the many ~s of the disease 这种病有许多类型，这只是其中一种 6 [c] (quality) 特性; there is a ~ of musical talent in the family 这一家人有音乐天赋; a ~ of melancholy runs through his poems 他的诗歌当中贯穿着一种忧伤的格调 7 [c] formal (style) 风格; to continue to speak in the same ~ 用同样的语气往下说

B **strains** *npl* liter 旋律; they left the church to the ~s of Mendelssohn's Wedding March 他们在门德尔松的《婚礼进行曲》的音乐声中离开了教堂

C vt 1 (injure) 使劳损; to ~ a muscle 拉伤肌肉; to ~ one's eyes reading by candlelight 因就着烛光看书弄坏眼睛; exercise gently and avoid ~ing yourself 运动的时候动作要轻柔，以免弄伤自己 2 (exert) 尽力使用; to ~ one's ears (to hear sth.) 竖起耳朵 (听某声响); to ~ one's neck (to do sth.) 伸长脖子 (做某事); to ~ oneself to do sth. 竭尽全力做某事 3 (make excessive demands on) 使不堪承受; to ~ relations between two countries 使两国关系紧张起来; to ~ sth. to the limit 使某事物达到极限 4 (stretch) 拉紧; the rope was ~ed to breaking point 绳子快要拉断了 5 (remove liquid from) 过滤; to use a colander to ~ the vegetables 把蔬菜放在滤篓里控水; to ~ the water from the vegetables 把蔬菜里的水滤掉

D vi 1 (exert oneself) 尽力; if you ~ too hard, you'll injure yourself 如果太用力，你会弄伤自己的; I had to ~ to hear what they were saying 我得竖起耳朵去听他们在说些什么; he burst to the surface, ~ing for air 他猛地冒出水面，拼命吸气 2 (pull on) 用力拉; (push against) 用力推; she ~ed against the ropes that held her 她使劲想挣脱拴住她的绳子; the bear ~ed at the chain around its neck 熊使劲拽脖子上的链子

Phrasal verb

• **strain off** vt [~ sth. off, ~ off sth.] 滤掉 ‹*liquid*›; she ~ed the water off (from) the vegetables 她把蔬菜滤干

strained /streɪnd/ *adj* 1 (worried) 焦虑的 ‹*person, face, expression*› 2 (tense) 不自然的 ‹*smile, voice, style, gesture*›; 紧张的 ‹*atmosphere*› 3 (injured) 扭伤的 ‹*muscle, wrist, ankle*› 4 (sieved) 滤过的 ‹*food, liquid, sauce*›

strainer /'streɪnə(r)/ *n* 滤器; a sink/drain/dishwasher ~ 洗涤池/下水管/洗碟机滤网

strait /streɪt/

A *n* ~(s *pl*) Geog 海峡

B **straits** *npl* to be in difficult ~s 身处困境; to be in dire ~s 境况岌岌可危

straitened /'streɪtnd/ *adj* 穷困的; in ~ circumstances 处于贫困境地

straitjacket /'streɪtdʒækɪt/

A *n* 1 lit 约束衣 [尤用于束缚精神病患者]; to put sb. in(to) a ~ 给某人穿上约束衣 2 fig (restriction) 约束

B vt 1 lit 用约束衣束缚 2 fig (restrict) 严加束缚 ‹*person, government, activity*›

strait-laced /ˌstreɪt'leɪst/ *adj* pej 古板的 ‹*person, attitude*›

Strait of Magellan /ˌstreɪt əv mə'gelən/ *n* the ~ 麦哲伦海峡

strand[1] /strænd/

A vt 1 (leave or drive ashore) 使…搁浅 ‹*person, fish, whale, dolphin*›; a ship ~ed on a beach 搁浅在海滩上的轮船 2 fig 使…受困 ‹*person*›; to be ~ed 受困; to leave sb./sth. ~ed 使某人/某物滞留

B *n* liter (of sea) 海滨; (of lake) 湖岸; (of river) 河滩

strand[2] *n* 1 (of fibre, web, wire) 股 2 (of hair) 缕 3 (of beads) 串 4 fig (of story, argument, thought) 部分

stranded /'strændɪd/ *adj* 滞留的 ‹*traveller, climber, motorist*›

strange /streɪndʒ/ *adj* 1 (odd) 奇怪的 ‹*dream, noise*›; 奇特的 ‹*clothes*›; 异常的 ‹*phenomenon*›; it's ~ to be back in my old job again 我又重操旧业，真是不可思议; it is ~ (that) ... 奇怪的是…; there's something ~ about her/this place 她/这个地方有些古怪; in a ~ way 古怪地; ~ to say *or* relate, ... 奇怪的是; ~ as that might seem 那也许看起来有点儿怪; ~ but true 奇怪但真实的; truth is ~r than fiction 真实情况离奇得超乎想象 2 (unwell) 不舒服; to look/feel ~ 看上去/感觉不自在 3 (unfamiliar) 陌生的 ‹*person, object, situation*›; don't talk to ~ men 别和陌生人讲话; I never sleep well in a ~ bed 我一到生地方就睡不好觉 4 pred (new) 不习惯的; to be ~ to city life/a task 不习惯城市生活/某项工作

strangely /'streɪndʒli/ *adj* 怪异地 ‹*silent, calm, act*›; ~ shaped 奇形怪状的; she looks ~ familiar 很奇怪，她看起来面熟; ~ enough, ... 奇怪的是…

strangeness /'streɪndʒnɪs/ *n* [u] 1 (oddness) 奇怪 2 (unfamiliarity) 陌生

stranger /'streɪndʒə(r)/ *n* 1 (unknown person) 陌生人; a complete *or* total ~ 素未谋面的人; to be a ~ to sb. 对某人来说是陌生人; hello, ~! 你好，久违了！; a little ~ hum 新生儿 2 (newcomer) 新来者; she's a ~ to the town 她刚到这个镇子; to be no ~ to sth. 习惯某事物; he's no ~ to misfortune/controversy/tragedy/hardship 他对不幸之事/争论/惨事/困难见得多了

stranger crime *n* [c and u] 陌生人犯罪

strangle /'stræŋgl/ vt 1 (throttle) 扼死; to ~ sb. to death 把某人掐死; to ~ sb. with sth. 用某物勒死某人; this collar is strangling me 这领子快勒死我了; I could cheerfully have ~d him hum 我真想掐死他; to ~ an idea at birth 把想法扼杀在萌芽状态 2 (curb, repress) 阻碍 ‹*project, development, economy*›; 压制 ‹*protest, free speech*›; a ~d cry/sob 压抑的哭声/啜泣

stranglehold /'stræŋglhəʊld/ *n* 1 (in combat) 勒颈; to have sb. in a ~ 卡住某人的脖子 2 fig (control) 压制; to have a ~ on sth. 束缚某事物; to put a ~ on sth. 压制某事物

strangler /'stræŋglə(r)/ *n* 扼死人者

strangling /'stræŋglɪŋ/ *n* [u and c] (with hands) 掐死; (with rope etc.) 勒死

strangulate /'stræŋgjʊleɪt/ vt 1 colloq (strangle) 扼死; the poor woman was ~d 那个可怜的女人被勒死了; a ~d tone of voice fig 哽塞的语调 2 Med 绞窄; a ~d hernia 绞窄性疝

strangulation /ˌstræŋgjʊ'leɪʃn/ *n* [u] 1 (strangling) 扼杀 2 Med 绞窄

strap /stræp/

A *n* 1 (gen) 带子; (for holding on to on bus, train) 拉手吊环; a watch with a leather ~ 有皮表带的手表; to fasten/undo a ~ 系好/解开带子 2 (bandage) 绷带 3 Hist (for punishing) 皮鞭; to give sb. the ~ 鞭打某人

B vt (*pres p etc.* **-pp-**) 1 (secure) 用带子固定; the load needs to be ~ped more tightly 货物需要捆得再紧些; he ~ped the knife to his leg 他把刀绑到腿上; don't forget to ~ the child into the pushchair 别忘了把推车上的安全带给孩子系上 2 (bandage) 用绷带包扎

Phrasal verbs

• **strap down** vt [~ sb./sth. down, ~ down sb./sth.] 用带子把…固定住; everything had to be ~ped down to stop it from sliding around 所有东西都必须绑定，免得来回滑动

• **strap in** vt [~ sb. in, ~ in sb.] 给…系上安全带; are you ~ped in? 你系好安全带了吗?

• **strap on** vt [~ sth. on, ~ on sth.] 用带子把…固定; to ~ a watch on 戴上手表; to ~ on skis 穿上滑雪板

• **strap up** vt [~ sth. up, ~ up sth.] 用绷带包扎; the nurse ~ped the wound up 护士把伤口包扎起来

strap: **~ fastening** *n* 带扣; **~hang** *vi* colloq [在公交车上] 拉吊环站立; **~hanger** *n* colloq 拉吊环站立的乘客

strapless /'stræplɪs/ *adj* 无吊带的 ‹*garment, top, bra*›

strapline /'stræplaɪn/ *n* 1 Journ 眉题 2 (slogan) 广告口号

strapped /stræpt/ *adj* colloq 短缺的; to be ~ for cash 缺现金

strapping /'stræpɪŋ/

A *adj attrib* 魁梧的

B *n* [u and c] 1 Med 橡皮膏 2 (fastening, strengthening) 胶带

strata /'strɑːtə, Amer 'streɪtə/ *pl* ▸ **stratum**

stratagem /'strætədʒəm/ *n* 计策; to use *or* employ a ~ 用计

strategic /strə'tiːdʒɪk/ *adj* 1 (long-term) 战略的 ‹*decision, objective, interests, investor*›; ~ materials/bombing/missiles 战略物资/轰炸/导弹 2 (key) 关键的 ‹*location, move, alliance, asset*›

Strategic Air Command *n* Amer 战略空军司令部

strategical /strəˈtiːdʒɪkl/ *adj* = **strategic 1**

strategically /strəˈtiːdʒɪkli/ *adv* 在战略上 ‹*important, relevant*›; 战略性地 ‹*placed, plan, develop*›

Strategic Defence Initiative *pr n* Amer 战略防御计划

strategics /strəˈtiːdʒɪks/ *npl + v sing* 战略学

strategist /ˈstrætədʒɪst/ *n* 战略家; **an armchair ~** 对战略一知半解的空想战略家

strategy /ˈstrætədʒi/ *n* 1 [u] (art, skill) 战略 2 [c] (plan) 策略; **a reading ~** 阅读策略; **a wrong/correct** *or* **right ~** 错误/正确的策略

stratification /ˌstrætɪfɪˈkeɪʃn/ *n* [u] (of rocks) 成层; (of social classes) 阶层化

stratify /ˈstrætɪfaɪ/

A *vt usu passive* **a stratified society** 分化成不同阶层的社会; **stratified rock** 成层岩

B *vi* «*rock*» 成层; «*society*» 形成阶层; **to ~ into sth.** 分化成某些阶层

stratocumulus /ˌstrætəʊˈkjuːmjʊləs/ *n* [u] 层积云; **~ clouds** 层积云

stratosphere /ˈstrætəsfɪə(r)/ *n* [u] 1 (atmospheric layer) 平流层 2 fig colloq (very high level) 极高水平; **the fashion ~** 时装的最高档次

stratospheric /ˌstrætəˈsferɪk/ *adj* 1 lit 平流层的 ‹*ozone, height, conditions*› 2 fig (very high) 极高的

stratum /ˈstrɑːtəm, Amer ˈstreɪtəm/ *n* (*pl* **strata**) 1 Geol 地层 2 (social class) 阶层

straw /strɔː/ *n* 1 [u] (substance) 禾秆; **a piece of ~** 一根稻草; **a bale of ~** 一包稻草; **a man of ~** 傀儡; **a ~ hat** 草帽 2 [c] (single stalk) 一根禾秆; **to draw ~s** 抽签; **to draw** *or* **get the short ~** 倒霉; **the last** *or* **final ~** 最后一根稻草; **to clutch** *or* **grasp at ~s** 抓救命稻草; **to not care** *or* **give a ~** dated 毫不在乎; **a ~ in the wind** esp Brit 征兆 3 [c] (for drinking) 吸管; **to drink sth. with** *or* **through a ~** 用吸管喝某物

strawberry /ˈstrɔːbəri, Amer -beri/ *n* 草莓; **~ flowers/tart** 草莓花/馅饼

strawberry blonde, strawberry blond ▸p. 134

A *adj* 草莓红色的 ‹*hair*›

B *n* 头发呈浅红黄色的人 [尤指女子]

strawberry mark *n* 草莓斑

straw: ~-blonde, ~-blond *adjs* 浅黄色的 ‹*hair*›; **~board** *n* [u] 黄纸板; **~board panelling** 硬纸板镶板; **~-coloured** *adj* 浅黄色的 ‹*hair, beer, lawn, stalk*›; **~ man** *n* esp Amer 1 (person with no real power) 傀儡; 2 (easy target) (person) 易受攻击的人; (idea) 易受攻击的观点; **~ mat** *n* 稻草垫; **~ poll,** Amer **~ vote** *ns* 非正式民意测验

stray /streɪ/

A *vi* 1 (wander) 走失; **the military arrested anyone who ~ed into the exclusion zone** 军方逮捕了所有误入禁区的人; **to ~ from the path** 偏离道路 2 (move casually) 漫不经心地移动; **her eyes kept ~ing over to the clock on the wall** 她的目光不时瞟向墙上的钟 3 (be distracted) 偏离正题; **to let one's thoughts ~** 分心; **to ~ from sth./back to sth.** 偏离某事物/失神回想某事 4 euph (be unfaithful) «*husband, wife, partner*» 有外遇 5 formal dated Relig 误入歧途; **to ~ from the path of righteousness** 偏离正道

B *adj attrib* 1 (lost) 流浪的; **a ~ dog/child** 流浪狗/流浪儿 2 (isolated, random) 零星的; **a ~ bullet** 流弹; **there were a few ~ passers-by in the empty streets** 空荡荡的街上只有寥寥几个行人; **a few ~ hairs** 几根散乱的头发

C *n* 1 (domestic animal) 走失的宠物; (farm animal) 走失的家畜; **a home for ~s** 流浪动物收容所 2 (lost person) 走散者

streak /striːk/

A *n* 1 (of paint, substance, water) 条痕; (of light) 光带; **a ~ of lightning** 一道闪电 2 (in character) 性格特征; **to have a ~ of sth. in one's character** 性格中有某种特点; **a cruel/mean ~, a ~ of cruelty/meanness** 残忍/吝啬的本性; **he's got a real mean ~ in him** 他真是卑鄙无耻; **a yellow ~** colloq 懦弱的性格 3 (run) 一阵子; **to be on a winning/losing ~** 一切顺风顺水/在走背运; **a lucky/unlucky ~** 走运/不走运的时期 4 colloq (naked run) 裸奔; **to do a ~** 进行裸奔

B *vt* 1 (cover or mark with lines) «*person, colour, light*» 在…上留下条纹 ‹*face, clothes, sky*›; «*tears, colour, mud*» 在…上留下痕迹 ‹*face, clothes, window*›; **to ~ sth. with sth.** 在某物上留下一道道某物; **to be ~ed with sth.** 布满一道道的某物 2 Cosmet 把…条染; **to ~ sb.'s hair** 把某人的头发染成一绺一绺的; **~ed hair** 染得一绺一绺的头发

C *vi* 1 (move fast) «*person*» 飞跑; «*train*» 疾驰; «*aircraft, rocket*» 高速飞行; **to ~ across** *or* **through sth.** 飞驰过某物; **to ~ off** 飞奔而去 2 colloq (run naked) 裸奔

streaker /ˈstriːkə(r)/ *n* colloq 裸奔的人

streak lightning *n* [u] 枝状闪电; **like ~** 闪电般地

streaky /ˈstriːki/ *adj* 有条纹的 ‹*pattern, finish, paintwork*›; 条染的 ‹*hair*›

streaky bacon *n* [u] Brit 五花咸肉

stream /striːm/

A *n* 1 (small river) 溪流; **a mountain/an underground ~** 山涧/地下溪流; **a trout ~** 有鳟鱼的小河 2 (flow, moving mass) 涌流; **a ~ of blood** 一股鲜血; **a ~ of smoke/light** 一缕烟/一道光; **to flow in a steady ~** 源源不断地流出; **I've had a steady ~ of visitors** 我这里不断有客人来; **cars filed past in an endless ~** 过往汽车一辆接着一辆，川流不息 3 (series) 一连串; **a constant ~ of enquiries** 接连不断的询问; **a steady ~ of work** 接二连三的工作; **to hurl a ~ of abuse (at sb.)** 不停地辱骂（某人） 4 (current) 水流; **the river is high, and the ~ is strong** 河流水位很高，水流很急; **against/with the ~** 逆流/顺流的; fig 逆潮流/顺应潮流的; **to swim with the ~** 顺流游泳; fig 顺应潮流; **on ~** (in operation) 在运转中; (in existence) 存在的; **the new computer system comes on ~ next month** 新的电脑系统下月投入使用; **more jobs are coming on ~** 更多的工作不断涌现 5 esp Brit Sch 学生小组 [由相同年龄和能力的学生组成]; **the fast ~** 快班 6 Comput 数据流

B *vi* 1 (flow) 流动; **tears ~ed down her cheeks** 泪水顺着她的面颊流下; **black smoke ~ed from the exhaust** 排气管里冒出黑烟; **sunlight ~ed through the windows** 阳光洒入窗户 2 (move) 涌动; **people ~ed across the bridge** 桥上行人川流不息; **the audience ~ed out of the concert hall** 观众涌出了音乐厅 3 (be wet) 流淌; **his face was ~ing with sweat** 他脸上汗水直流; **her head was ~ing with blood** 她头上在流血; **the walls were ~ing with condensation** 墙壁上有冷凝的水流下来; **the cold wind made his eyes ~** 寒风吹得他的眼睛流泪; **pollen makes his nose ~** 花粉使他的鼻子流涕 4 (float, wave) (in wind) 飘扬; (in water) 漂动; **the banner ~ed out behind them** 旗帜在他们身后飘扬

C *vt* 1 (produce flow of) 流出; **the wound was ~ing blood** 伤口在流血; **the exhaust ~ed black smoke** 排气管里冒出了黑烟 2 esp Brit Sch 把…按年龄和能力分组 ‹*students*› 3 Comput 流播; **if you visit their website, you can ~ the whole album** 如果你浏览他们的网站，你可以通过流播在线收听整张唱片

streamer /ˈstriːmə(r)/ *n* 横幅

streaming /ˈstriːmɪŋ/

A *adj attrib* 1 Comput 流播的 ‹*video, media, technology*› 2 (runny) 流鼻涕的 ‹*cold, nose*›; 流眼泪的 ‹*eyes*›

B *n* [u] 1 Comput 流播 2 Brit Sch 能力分组

streamline /ˈstriːmlaɪn/ *vt* 1 lit 使…成流线型 ‹*car, aircraft, body*› 2 fig (make more efficient) 提高…的效率 ‹*method, procedure, production, organization*›

streamlined /ˈstriːmlaɪnd/ *adj* 1 (in shape) 流线型的 ‹*car, aircraft, body*› 2 fig (efficient) 效率高的 ‹*method, procedure, production*›; 精简的 ‹*organization*›

stream of consciousness *n* 意识流; **a ~ novel** 意识流小说

street /striːt/ *n* ▸p. 905 街道; **in** *or* **on the ~** 在街上; **across** *or* **over the ~** 在街对面; **to keep people/trouble off the ~s** 不让人们上街/保持街道平安; **a dead-end ~** 死路; **the man in the ~** 普通人; **to take to the ~s** «*crowd*» 上街示威; **the two sides are ~s apart** 双方意见相去甚远; **to be ~s ahead of** *or* **better than sb./sth.** Brit 比某人/某事物强得多; **not in the same ~ (as sb./sth.)** Brit （与某人/某物）不在一个档次; **to put** *or* **turn sb. out in the ~** 把某人赶出家门; **to be on** *or* **walk the ~s** (be homeless) 无家可归; **a woman of the ~s** 妓女; **to work** *or* **go on the ~s** 做站街女; **to be right up sb.'s ~** 正符合某人口味; **~ kids** 流浪儿童; **a ~ map** 街道地图; **~ crime/culture** 街头犯罪/文化

street: ~car *n* Amer 有轨电车; **~ cleaner** ▸p. 409 *n* 1 (person) 街道清洁工; 2 (machine) 街道清扫车; **~ cleaning, ~ cleansing** *ns* [u] Brit 街道清洁; **~ clothes** *npl* Amer 日常便装; **~ cred, ~ credibility** *ns* [u] colloq 街头声望 [城市时髦青年认同的着装风格等]; **it gives him ~ cred** 这会使他看上去很时尚; **~ cry** *n usu pl* 街头叫卖声; **~ directory** *n* 街道地图; **~ door** *n* 街门; **~ entertainer** ▸p. 409 *n* 街头艺人; **~ entertainment** *n* [u] 街头表演; **~ fighting** *n* [u] (of armies) 巷战; (of groups) 街头斗殴; **~ furniture** *n* [u] 街道设施 [指邮筒、路标等公共设施]; **~ guide** *n* 街道指南; **~ lamp** *n* = **~ light**; **~-legal** *adj* 符合道路法规的 ‹*vehicle*›; **~ level** *n* [u] 街面; **at ~ level** 在街面上; **a ~-level shop** 街面商店; **~ light** *n* 路灯; **~ lighting** *n* [u] 街道照明; **~ market** *n* 街头市场; **~ newspaper** *n* [供无家可归者阅读的] 街头小报; **~ performer** ▸p. 409 *n* 街头艺人; **~ plan** *n* 1 (layout) 街道布局; 2 = **~ guide**; **~ sweeper** ▸p. 409 *n* = **~ cleaner**; **~ theatre** *n* [u] 街头戏剧; **~ trader** ▸p. 409 *n* 街头小贩; **~ value** *n* 黑市价; **~walker** *n* 街头拉客妓女; **~wise** *adj* colloq 熟悉都市世态的 ‹*teenager, style*›; **~worker** ▸p. 409 *n* Amer 街道工作者 [指帮助弱势青少年的社会工作者]

strength /streŋθ/ *n* 1 [u and c] (physical power) 体力; **a man of great ~** 强壮的男子; **she didn't have the ~ to walk any further** 她再也走不动了; **he has great ~ in his arms** 他的手臂力气很大; **to build up one's ~** (by exercise) 增强体力; (after illness) 恢复体力; **to summon (up) all one's ~** 使出全身力气; **to recover** *or* **regain one's ~** 恢复体力; **with all one's ~** 用全力; **give me ~!** colloq 真受不了! 2 [u] (of natural force) (potency, intensity) 力度; (speed) 速度; **the wind had markedly increased in ~** 风力明显增强了; **the ~ and direction of the tide** 潮水的流速与方向 3 [u] (ability to perform function) (of lens) 光焦度; (of electric current) 强度; (of bulb) 功率 4 [u] (robustness) 结实; **the ~ of a retaining wall** 挡土墙的坚固程度; **the hook has the ~ to withstand the pull** 这个钩子经得住拉拽 5 [u and c] (concentration, potency) (of flavouring, drink, solution) 浓度; (of drug) 效力; **add more curry powder depending on the ~ required** 按所要求的口味轻重再加点咖喱粉; **a range of beers with different ~s** 各种度数不同

S

的啤酒 6 [u] (influence) 实力; **economic/military ~** 经济/军事实力; **to be in a position of ~** 处于有利地位; **to go from ~ to ~** 不断取得成功; **since her appointment the department has gone from ~ to ~** 自她上任以来，这个部门越来越兴旺了 7 [u] (of currency) 强弱（程度）; **to gain ~** 变得坚挺 8 [u and c] (resolution) 坚强; **to draw ~ from one's faith** 从信仰中汲取力量; **to show great ~ of character** 表现出很大的毅力; **she has (a) remarkable inner ~** 她具有非凡的意志力 9 [u] (intensity of emotion, opinion, etc.) 强烈程度; **this view has gathered ~** 这种观点已为更多人接受了; **don't underestimate the ~ of feeling about this!** 不要低估对这件事的强烈情绪! 10 [u] (effectiveness of protest, influence, performance) 效力 11 [u] (noticeability) (of sound, voice, accent) 清晰度; (of light) 亮度 12 [u] (ability to endure) 持久性; **the ~ of their attachment to each other was obvious to all** 他们相互之间深深依恋是大家有目共睹的 13 [u] (persuasiveness) 说服力; **to give** *or* **lend ~ to sth.** 使…具有说服力 ‹*argument, theory*›; **on the ~ of sth.** 凭借某事物; **I got the job on the ~ of his recommendation** 由于他的推荐，我得到了那份工作 14 [c] (positive aspect) 优点; **the ability to keep calm is one of her many ~s** 能够保持冷静是她的诸多长处之一; **the ~s and weaknesses of an argument** 论点的有力之处与薄弱之处 15 [u and c] (force of number) 人数多寡; **the ~ of the enemy army** 敌军的兵力; **he is on the ~ of the teaching staff** 他是在编教师; **in ~** 大量地; **the enemy attacked in ~** 敌人投入大批兵力发动进攻 16 [u] (total number) 人手; **to be up to ~** «*army, staff, team*» 达到所需人数; **to bring sth. up to ~** 使…达到所需人数 ‹*army, staff, team*›; **to be at full ~** (have full complement) 人手充足; (use best members) 使用最佳人选; **the team will be back at full ~ for the next match** 下一场比赛，球队将恢复主力阵容; **to be below** *or* **under ~** (lack full complement) 人手不足; (not use best members) 未使用最佳人选; **these cuts have left the local police force under ~** 这几次人员裁减造成地方警力不足

strengthen /'streŋθn/

A *vt* 1 (reinforce) 加固 ‹*object, building, structure, equipment*›; **fluoride ~s the teeth** 氟化物能固齿 2 (increase the power of) 强化 ‹*organization, claim, case, position*›; **to ~ sb.'s hand** 加强某人的实力 3 (increase) 增强 ‹*determination, conviction*›; **to ~ one's lead** 扩大领先优势; **the experience ~ed their faith** 这个经历坚定了他们的信念 4 (build up) 使…强壮 ‹*person, muscle, limb*›; 增强…的功能 ‹*heart, lungs*› 5 fig (shore up) 使…坚挺 ‹*currency*›; 巩固 ‹*economy, relationship*› 6 (increase concentration or potency of) 增加…的浓度 ‹*flavouring, drink, solution*›; 加强…的效力 ‹*drug*›

B *vi* «*wind, current, conviction, feeling, economy*» 变强; «*currency*» 变得坚挺

strengthening /'streŋθnɪŋ/

A *n* [u] (of building, equipment etc.) 加强; (of economy, currency) 坚挺; (of solution) 变浓

B *adj* 1 (becoming stronger) 增强的 ‹*wind, current, conviction*›; 变坚挺的 ‹*currency*›; 变强劲的 ‹*economy*› 2 (that increases strength) 增强体魄的 ‹*exercise, work*›

strenuous /'strenjʊəs/ *adj* 1 (demanding) 繁重的 ‹*work*›; 剧烈的 ‹*activity, exercise*›; 紧张的 ‹*schedule*›; **avoid doing anything too ~** 要避免做过分劳累的事 2 (determined) 奋力的 ‹*attempt*›; 顽强的 ‹*protest, opposition*›

strenuously /'strenjʊəsli/ *adv* 费力地 ‹*work, pull*›; 努力地 ‹*encourage*›; 顽强地 ‹*resist, oppose*›; **she ~ denied the accusation** 她竭力否认指控

strenuousness /'strenjʊəsnɪs/ *n* [u] 1 (of work, activity) 繁重 2 (of protest) 强烈; (of resistance, opposition) 顽强

streptococcal /ˌstreptə'kɒkl/ *adj* 链球菌的 ‹*infection*›

streptococcus /ˌstreptə'kɒkəs/ *n* (*pl* **streptococci** /ˌstreptə'kɒki:/) 链球菌

stress /stres/

A *n* 1 [u] (anxious state) 精神压力; **to be under/suffer from ~** 在压力下/有精神压力; **emotional/mental/nervous ~** 感情负担/思想负担/精神压力 2 [c] (factor causing anxiety) 紧张; **we needed time to rest and relax after the ~es of the journey** 经历了旅途的紧张劳累，我们需要时间休息和放松; **the ~es and strains of modern life** 现代生活的紧张和压力 3 [u and c] (physical pressure) 压力; **to put** *or* **impose ~ on sth.** 给某物加压; **to be under ~** 受到应力; **a ~ of 500 kg** 500千克的压力 4 [u] (emphasis) 强调; **she lays** *or* **puts** *or* **places ~ on punctuality** 她非常注重守时; **a great deal of ~ has been laid on this fact** 这个事实已经得到了极大重视 5 [u and c] Ling 重音; **to put** *or* **place the ~ on sth.** 把重音放在某音节上; **in 'strategic' the ~ falls on the second syllable** “strategic”一词的重音在第二个音节上

B *vt* 1 (emphasize) 强调; **to ~ the importance of sth.** 强调某事物的重要性; **it must be ~ed that this disease is very rare** 必须着重指出，这种病很罕见; **'I want it done very neatly,' she ~ed** 她强调说，“我希望这件事做得非常干净利落” 2 Ling 重读; **the final syllable is ~ed** 最后一个音节要重读 3 (put physical pressure on) 施压于; **this type of workout ~es the knee joints** 这种锻炼增加膝关节的压力 4 colloq (make anxious) 使焦虑不安; **driving in cities really ~es me** 在市内开车让我非常紧张

C *vi* colloq 担心; **stop ~ing about your exams** 别再担心考试了

Phrasal verb

• **stress out** colloq

A *vt* [~ **sb. out**] 使非常焦虑; **travelling always ~ed him out** 旅行总是让他非常紧张

B *vi* 感到非常焦虑; **he's ~ing out about being unemployed** 他十分担心失业

stressed /strest/ *adj* 1 (emotionally) 焦虑不安的; **to feel ~** 感到很紧张 2 Mech 受应力作用的 ‹*component, structure*› 3 Ling 重读的 ‹*syllable, vowel*›

stressed out *adj* colloq = **stressed 1**

stress: ~ factor *n* 紧张因素; **~ fracture** *n* 应力性骨折; **~-free** *adj* 轻松自在的

stressful /'stresfl/ *adj* 压力大的 ‹*situation, job*›

stress: ~ limit *n* 应力极限; **~ management** *n* [u] 压力管理; **~ mark** *n* 重音符号; **~-related** *adj* 压力引起的 ‹*illness*›; **~ relief** *n* [u] 压力消除

stretch /stretʃ/

A *vt* 1 (make bigger) 撑大 ‹*shoe, garment*›; 拉长 ‹*spring, rubber, dough*›; **don't hang your woollens out on the line or you'll ~ them** 不要把羊毛衫挂在绳子上，否则会把它撑大的 2 (pull tight) 拉紧 ‹*rope, cord, bowstring, elastic*›; 绷紧 ‹*canvas, tarpaulin*›; 铺开 ‹*net, fabric*›; **to ~ sth. across sth.** 将某物在某物上铺开; **to ~ sth. on** *or* **over sth.** 把某物绷紧到某物上; **to ~ sth. tight** 拉紧某物 3 (straighten) «*person, animal*» 舒展 ‹*limb, neck*›; **to ~ one's legs** colloq (go for walk) 散散步; **the bird ~ed its wings** 这只鸟张开了翅膀; **to ~ one's wings** fig 进行新的尝试 4 (push bounds of) 耗尽 ‹*budget, resources*›; 超越…的界限 ‹*tolerance*›; **the ending really ~es the audience's credulity** 这个结局实在让观众难以相信; **you're ~ing my patience!** 你让我忍无可忍! ; **to be fully ~ed** «*person*» 竭尽全力; «*company*» 倾尽所能; **to ~ sth. to the limit** 把某物消耗殆尽 5 (cause to do one's best) 使…竭尽全力 ‹*person*›; 尽力发挥 ‹*abilities*›; **she isn't ~ed at school** 她在学校里并未被发掘出所有潜力 6 (exaggerate) 夸大 ‹*meaning*›; **to ~ the truth** 言过其实; **to be ~ing it a bit** *or* **a little** colloq 有点夸张 7 (make exception to) 变通 ‹*rules*›; **to ~ a point** (make exception) 破例; (exaggerate) 夸大 8 (cause to go further) 节约使用 ‹*budget, income, supplies*›; 节约地吃 ‹*meal*› 9 (increase) 扩充 ‹*record, total*›; **they ~ed their lead to 5-0** 他们把领先优势扩大到了5比0

B *vi* 1 (become bigger) «*spring, elastic, rubber*» 被拉长; **this fabric ~es** 这种布料富有弹性 2 (become too big) «*garment, fabric*» 被撑大 3 (straighten body when exercising) 舒展肢体; **he ~ed and yawned** 他伸了个懒腰，打了个哈欠 4 (reach out arm) 伸长胳膊; (reach out leg) 伸出腿; **to ~ across** *or* **over sth.** 把手伸过某物; **he ~ed across and could just touch the other wall with his fingertips** 他伸出手去，指尖刚刚能碰到另一面墙; **to ~ for sth.** 伸手去够某物; **to ~ over** 伸手过来; **to ~ up** 向上伸胳膊 5 (continue in space) 延伸; **how far does the traffic jam ~?** 交通拥堵到多远? ; **to ~ to** *or* **as far as sth.** «*flex, traffic jam, queue*» 延伸到某物; **to ~ from sth. to sth.** 从某物延伸到某物; **his grin ~ed from ear to ear** 他笑得合不拢嘴; **to ~ down to sth.** 一直延伸到某物; **to ~ into sth.** 延伸入某物; **mountains ~ed away into the distance** 山峦绵延伸向远方; **to ~ for miles** 延伸数英里; **to ~ over sth.** 在某物之上延伸; **at that time the empire ~ed over most of Europe** 那时候，该帝国的领土覆盖了欧洲的大部分区域; **to ~ around sth.** 环绕某物延伸 6 (continue in time) 延续; **the weeks ~ed into months** 几周的时间延续成了几个月; **to ~ over** «*festivities, course, talks, work*» 延续 ‹*week, fortnight, month*› 7 (be enough) «*food, supplies, budget*» 够用; **the budget won't ~ to a new computer** 这个数目的预算不够买一台新电脑

C *v refl* **to ~ oneself** 1 (straighten body) 舒展身体 2 (try one's best) 全力以赴

D *n* 1 [c] (narrow area of land, water) 一段; **an unspoilt ~ of coastline** 一段未遭破坏的海岸线; **a dangerous ~ of road** 危险的路段 2 [c] (expanse of land, water) 一片; **a ~ of open country** 一片开阔地区 3 [c] (period) 一段时间; **a short ~** 一小段时间; **a long ~** 很长一段时间; **they worked in four-hour ~es** 他们工作每4小时一班; **to work for a ~** 工作一段时间; **at a ~** 一口气地 4 [c] colloq (prison sentence) 刑期; **a five-year ~** 5年的刑期; **to do a ~ (for sth.)** （因为某事）服刑 5 [u and c] (act of tightening muscles) 伸展; **to do a ~** *or* **some ~es** 做伸展运动; **to have a (good) ~** （好好）舒展身体; **to give sth. a ~** 伸展一下 ‹*arm, leg, neck, back*›; **at full ~** 尽量伸展四肢; fig 竭尽全力地; **I was at full ~, but the lever was still just out of reach** 我尽力伸展手臂，但还是够不着操作杆; **we're at full ~ already and cannot possibly cope with more orders** 我们已经尽了全力，不可能再处理更多的订单了; **at a ~** (with difficulty) 勉强地; (in extreme circumstances) 在极端情况下; **not by any** *or* **by no ~ of the imagination** 任凭如何想象也不 6 [u and c] (pull) 拉紧; **to give sth. a ~** 拉一下 ‹*rope*›; 撑一下 ‹*shoe*›; **to be at full ~** «*rope*» 拉紧; «*cord, bowstring*» 绷紧 7 [u] (elasticity) 弹性; **~ material** 弹性材料; **a pair of ~ jeans** 一条弹力牛仔裤 8 [c] *usu sing* esp Amer (straight) 终点直道; **the home** *or* **finishing** *or* **final ~** 终点直道; fig 最后阶段; **the campaign has entered its final ~** 竞选进入了最后冲刺阶段; **to be on the home** *or* **finishing** *or* **final ~** 接近终点; fig 将要完成

Phrasal verbs

• **stretch back** *vi* 1 (in time) 回溯; **this tradition ~es back (for) centuries** 这个传

S

统可以回溯到几个世纪前; **to ~ back to sb./sth.** 回溯到某人/某事物 **2** (in space) 往后延伸; **to ~ back to sth.** 向后延伸至某物; **the traffic jam ~es back to the motorway** 交通拥堵的车流到了高速公路

• **stretch out**

A *vi* **1** (lie down) 躺下; **to ~ out on sth./in front of sth.** 躺在某物上/在某物的前面 **2** (continue in space) 延伸; **fields and hills ~ed out as far as the eye could see** 田野和山峦向远方延伸至视野所及之处; **the woods seem to ~ out to the horizon** 森林似乎一直延伸到了地平线的尽头 **3** (continue in time) «*life, future, days*» 延续; **the moment seemed to ~ out endlessly** 那一刻似乎无休无止

B *vt* [~ **sth. out,** ~ **out sth.**]

1 (reach out) 伸出 ‹*leg, foot*›; **to ~ out one's hand/arm towards sb./sth.** 朝某人/某物伸出手/手臂; **he ~ed out his hand to the telephone** 他伸手去拿电话; **I ~ed out my hand to grasp hers** 我伸手去握她的手 **2** **to be ~ed out** (be lying down) 躺下; **to be ~ed out on the bed/floor** 躺在床上/地板上; **to be ~ed out in front of the TV/the fire** 躺在电视机/火堆前; **to lie ~ed out** 四肢伸展地躺着 **3** (pull tight) 拉紧 ‹*rope, cord, bowstring*›; 绷紧 ‹*canvas, tarpaulin*›; 铺开 ‹*net, sheet, fabric*›; **they ~ out the hides and leave them in the sun to dry** 他们把兽皮铺开，放在太阳底下晒干 **4** (prolong) 延长 ‹*plot, meeting, work*›; **he tried to ~ out the script with two extra scenes** 他试图多加两幕剧来拖长这剧本; **I ~ed my speech out to an hour** 我把演说延长至一小时

C *v refl* **to ~ oneself out** 躺下; **to ~ oneself out on sth.** 躺在某物上

stretch cover *n* 弹性座套

stretcher /ˈstretʃə(r)/ *n* **1** Med 担架 **2** (for hat) 帽撑; (for shoes) 扩鞋器; (for canvas) 画布框 **3** (strut) (in chair, table) 横档; (in umbrella) 伞骨; (in rowing boat) 踏脚板 **4** Constr (brick) 横砌石

Phrasal verb

• **stretcher off** *vt* [~ **sb. off,** ~ **off sb.**] 用担架抬走

stretcher: ~**-bearer** ▸p. 409 *n* 抬担架者; ~ **case** *n* 重伤员; ~ **party** *n* 担架队

stretch: ~ **limousine,** colloq ~ **limo** *n* 超长豪华轿车; ~ **mark** *n* 妊娠纹

stretchy /ˈstretʃi/ *adj* 有弹性的 ‹*material*›

strew /struː/ *vt* (*pp* **strewn** /struːn/ *or* ~**ed**) 撒 ‹*sand, litter*›; **to ~ sth. on** *or* **over sth.** 把某物撒在某物上; **to ~ the floor with clothes** 把衣服乱扔到地板上; **to be strewn with sth.** 撒满某物; **rock-strewn** 布满岩石的; **the desk was strewn with books** 办公桌上乱放着书

strewth /struːθ/ *excl* colloq 天哪

striate /ˌstraɪˈeɪt, Amer ˈstraɪeɪt/ *vt* 在…上划条纹; **the glacier had ~d the rocks** 冰川在岩石上留下了条痕

striation /ˌstraɪˈeɪʃn/ *n* **1** [u] (striating) 划条纹 **2** [c] (line, groove) 条纹

stricken /ˈstrɪkən/ *adj* (afflicted) 受折磨的 ‹*person*›; 受打击的 ‹*area, industry*›; 苦恼的 ‹*expression, voice*›; **to be ~ with** *or* **by sth.** 受到…的折磨 ‹*fear, illness, poverty*›

strict /strɪkt/ *adj* **1** (not lenient) 严厉的 ‹*person, upbringing, rule, ban*›; **to be ~ with sb.** 对某人严格; **to be ~ about sth.** 在某事上严格; **a ~ Muslim** 恪守教规的穆斯林 **2** (clearly defined) 明确的 ‹*instruction, etiquette*›; (precise) 精确的 ‹*sense, interpretation*›; (stringent) 严格的 ‹*observance, limit*›; 周密的 ‹*schedule*›; **in the ~ sense of the word** 严格说来; **they have to work to ~ deadlines** 他们不得不严格按期完成工作 **3** (absolute) 绝对的 ‹*silence, understanding*›; **in ~ confidence** 绝对保密地

strict: ~ **construction** *n* [u] [法院对法令或文书的] 严格解释; ~ **liability** *n* [u] [并无疏忽行为或犯罪意图情况下仍要承担的] 严格责任

strictly /ˈstrɪktli/ *adv* **1** (not leniently) 严格地 ‹*treat*›; ~ **orthodox Jewish homes** 恪守正统的犹太家庭 **2** (absolutely) 绝对地 ‹*prohibited, confidential, true*›; **what he said is not ~ accurate** 他所说的并不完全准确; ~ **speaking** 严格说来; ~ **between ourselves ...** 就你我私下说说…

strictness /ˈstrɪktnɪs/ *n* [u] (of person, upbringing, law) 严格; (of views, principles) 周密

stricture /ˈstrɪktʃə(r)/ *n* **1** (censure) 指摘; **to pass ~s on sb./sth.** 指责某人/某事物 **2** (restriction) 限制 **3** Med 狭窄

stridden /ˈstrɪdn/ *pp* ▸**stride B, C**

stride /straɪd/

A *n* **1** [c] (long step) 大步; **to cross a room in two ~s** 两大步跨过房间; **to take sth. in one's ~** 从容应对某事; **to make great ~s in sth.** 在某事上取得巨大进步 **2** [u] (gait) 步态; **he has a long ~** 他步幅很大; **to lengthen one's ~** 加大步伐; **to get into one's ~** lit 跟上步调; fig 进入状态; **after a nervous start, the speaker was now getting into his ~** 演讲者开始有点儿紧张，现在比较从容了

B *vi* (*pt* **strode,** *pp* **stridden**) **1** (walk) 阔步行走 **2** (straddle) 跨越; **to ~ over** *or* **across sth.** 跨过某物

C *vt* (*pt* **strode,** *pp* **stridden**) 大步走过 ‹*distance*›

stridency /ˈstraɪdnsi/ *n* [u] **1** (of sound, voice) 刺耳 **2** (of claim, protest) 强硬

strident /ˈstraɪdnt/ *adj* **1** (harsh) 刺耳的 ‹*sound, voice*› **2** (vociferous) 强硬的 ‹*claim, protest*›

stridently /ˈstraɪdntli/ *adv* **1** (harshly) 刺耳地 ‹*shout, yell*› **2** (vociferously) 强硬地 ‹*claim, protest*›

stridulate /ˈstrɪdjʊleɪt, Amer ˈstrɪdʒʊleɪt/ *vi* «*grasshopper*» 尖声鸣叫

strife /straɪf/ *n* [u] (conflict) 冲突; (dissent) 纠纷; **ethnic ~** 种族冲突; **domestic/industrial ~** 家庭/劳资纠纷; **in a state of ~** 处于冲突中; **trouble and ~** 纠纷

strife-torn /ˈstraɪftɔːn/ *adj* 饱经冲突的

strike /straɪk/

A *vt* (*pt, pp* **struck**) **1** (hit with hand, weapon, implement) 击打; **to ~ sb. in the face** 打某人的脸; **to ~ sb. on the head** 砸某人的头; **to ~ sth. with sth.** 用某物捶打某物 **2** (collide with, fall on) 碰撞; **the ship struck a rock** 船触礁了; **the town hall had been struck by a bomb/missile** 市政厅遭到了炸弹/导弹袭击 **3** (knock) 撞击; **the stone struck her on the forehead** 石头击中了她的额头; **he struck his head on the table** 他的头撞到了桌子上 **4** Sport (hit) 击 ‹*tennis ball*›; (kick) 踢 ‹*football*›; **he struck the ball into the back of the net** 他把球踢入网窝 **5** (inflict) 给予 ‹*blow*›; **fate then struck another cruel blow** 接着命运又给了一次残酷的打击; **she struck him a heavy blow on the head** 她重重地打了一下他的头; **who struck the first blow?** 谁先动的手?; **to ~ a blow for sth.** 维护 ‹*cause, belief, principle*›; **to ~ a blow against** *or* **at sth.** 损害 ‹*cause, belief, principle*› **6** (afflict) 侵袭; **disaster struck the family once again** 灾难再次降临这个家庭; **the area was struck by an outbreak of cholera** 这一地区爆发了霍乱 **7** (create) 引起; **to ~ fear** *or* **terror into sb.** *or* **into sb.'s heart** 使某人感到恐惧 **8** (occur to) 使突然想到; **an awful thought struck me** 我突然有了一个可怕的念头; **to (suddenly) ~ sb. that ...** 某人（突然）想起… **9** (seem to) 给…以某种印象; **how does the idea ~ you?** 你觉得这个主意怎么样?; **she ~s me as very efficient** *or* **as a very efficient person** 在我眼里，她是个很干练的人; **it ~s me that nobody is really in favour of the reform** 我觉得没有人真正赞成这项改革 **10** (be taken with) 打动; **I was struck with him** 我被他打动了; **I was struck by her youth and enthusiasm** 她年轻热情，把我迷住了; **to be struck on sb./sth.** Brit colloq 迷恋某人/某事物; **we're not very struck on that new restaurant** Brit colloq 我们不太喜欢那家新餐馆 **11** (fall on) «*light*» 照在…上; «*lightning*» 击中 **12** (be perceived by) 被…感受到; **a terrible sight struck my eyes** 我忽然看到一处可怕的景象 **13** (cause to become) 使处于某状态; **to ~ sb. dead** 劈死某人; **to be struck dumb (with amazement)** （吃惊得）张口结舌; **to be struck blind** 突然失明 **14** (ignite) 划燃; **to ~ a match** 划火柴 **15** (produce by friction) 摩擦出; **he had a flint for striking fire** 他有一块打火的燧石; **the sword struck sparks off the stone floor** 剑砍在石地板上，火星飞溅 **16** (chime) «*clock*» 敲响报出 ‹*time*› **17** Mus 弹奏; **to ~ a chord on the piano** 在钢琴上弹出和弦 **18** (discover) (by drilling) 钻探到; (by mining) 开采出; **miners prospecting in the valley struck a seam of silver** 在山谷里勘探的矿工们发现了一个银矿层; **to ~ a vein of sth.** fig 发现某种特性; **exploring women's everyday lives, she struck a rich vein of humour** 她在对女性的日常生活进行研究时发现其中包含大量的幽默元素 **19** (achieve) 达成; **to ~ a deal** 成交; **to ~ a balance** *or* **happy medium (between sth. and sth.)** （在某事物和某事物之间）找到折中办法; **to ~ a balance between order and freedom** 兼顾秩序和自由 **20** (assume) 摆出; **to ~ a pose** 装腔作势 **21** (delete) 删去; **I will ~ his name from the list** 我要把他的名字从名单里画掉 **22** (produce by stamping metal) 铸造 ‹*coin, medal*› **23** (take down, dismantle) 拆卸 ‹*tent*›; 拆除 ‹*stage set, scenery, scaffolding*›; **to ~ camp** 撤营 **24** (lower) 降下 ‹*sail, flag*›; **to ~ one's colours** Mil 降旗 **25** Hort (develop) **to ~ root** «*plant*» 生根 **26** Fishg (hook) 急拉钓线把…钩住 ‹*fish*›; (bite) «*fish*» 咬 ‹*bait, fly*›

B *vi* (*pt, pp* **struck**) **1** (hit) 撞击; **12 people were killed when the missile struck** 导弹袭击造成 12 人死亡; **my head struck against a beam** 我的头撞在横梁上 **2** formal (with hand, weapon, implement) 击打; **hold the nail, take the hammer, and ~ sharply** 捏住钉子，拿起锤子，使劲敲; ▸**iron A3** **3** (attack) 袭击; **the generals will decide when the time is right to ~** 将军们会决定何时可以发起进攻 **4** (occur) 突然发生; **tragedy struck when her husband was killed in a car crash** 悲剧发生了，她的丈夫在一次车祸中丧生 **5** (take industrial action) 罢工; **to ~ for a pay increase** 罢工要求加薪; **to ~ over job losses** 因失业问题进行罢工 **6** (chime) 报时; **did you hear the clock ~?** 你听到钟响了吗?; **six o'clock was striking as I left** 我离开时，钟正敲6点 **7** (ignite) «*match*» 被划燃; **damp matches won't ~** 湿火柴划不着 **8** (proceed) 行进; **to ~ north** 向北走; **they struck across an open field** 他们穿过了空旷的田野 **9** Fishg (secure hook) «*angler*» 急拉钓线把鱼钩住; (bite) «*fish*» 上钩

C *n* **1** (withdrawal of labour) 罢工; **a one-day/an official ~** 为期一天/得到批准的罢工; **to be (out) on ~** 正在罢工; **to come out** *or* **go on ~** 举行罢工; **to call/break a ~** 号召举行罢工/破坏罢工; **to take ~ action** 采取罢工行动 **2** (attack) 袭击; **the threat of nuclear ~s** 核袭击的威胁; **an air/pre-emptive ~** 空袭/先发制人的打击; **to launch a ~ (against** *or* **on sth.)** （对某处）发动袭击 **3** *usu sing* (hit) 击打 **4** (kick) 踢; **his spectacular ~ in the second half made the score 2-0** 他在下半场的一脚精彩射门把比分改写为 2 比 0 **5** (in baseball) 击球不中; **'~ three'** "三击不中" **6** (in tenpin bowling) 全中 **7** (discovery) 发现; **an oil ~** 石油的发

S

现; **to make a ～** 有发现; **a lucky ～** (lucky chance) 好运; (lucky discovery) 幸运的发现 **8** esp Amer (bad thing or action) 不利因素; **the amount of fuel that this car uses is a big ～ against it** 耗油量大是这辆车的一大缺点; **three ～s, and you're out** 三振出局法 [指三次犯罪即判入狱的法律] **9** (clock mechanism) 报时装置 **10** Fishg 急拉钓线

Phrasal verbs

• **strike at** *vt* [**～ at sb./sth.**]
1 (try to hit with hand, weapon, implement) 朝…打去; **he struck at me repeatedly with a stick** 他拿着棍子连续朝我打过来 **2** (make attack on) 袭击; **to ～ at the enemy's communications network** 攻击敌人的通讯网络 **3** (try to damage) 企图损害; **this ～s at the heart of the democratic system** 这会损害民主体制的根本; **to ～ at the roots of a social malaise** 根绝一种社会弊端

• **strike back** *vi* **1** (use force in return) 反击; **to ～ back at** *or* **against sb./sth.** 对某人/某事物予以反击 **2** (criticize in return) 反驳; **to ～ back at** *or* **against sb./sth.** 对某人/某事物予以回击 **3** Sport 反击; **to ～ back at** *or* **against sb./sth.** 对某人/某队予以反击; **they struck back with two goals in seven minutes** 他们予以反击，7分钟之内进了两个球

• **strike down**
A [**～ sb. down, ～ down sb.**] *vt*
1 (kill) 使丧命; **to be struck down by a bullet/by cancer** 中弹身亡/死于癌症 **2** (incapacitate) ‹*disease*› 使病倒; **he was struck down by a mystery virus** 他感染了一种神秘的病毒，病倒了 **3** (knock down) 击倒
B [**～ sth. down, ～ down sth.**] *vt* Amer (abolish) 废除 ‹*law, regulation*›

• **strike off**
A *vt* [**～ sb./sth. off, to ～ off sb./sth.**]
1 (delete) 删去; **to ～ sb.'s name off (a list)** 把某人的名字（从名单上）画掉 **2** (remove as member) 把…除名; **to be struck off** 被取消资格; **to be struck off the medical register** 被取消医师资格
B *vi* 行进; **we left the road and struck off across the fields** 我们下了公路，穿过田野

• **strike on** *vt* [**～ on sb./sth.**] 突然发现; **I suddenly struck on a good idea** 我突然想到了一个好主意; **we were lucky to ～ on just the right person to do the job** 我们运气好，碰巧找到了合适的人来做这份工作

• **strike out**
A *vi* **1** (start out on new course) 开始新的道路; (start out on independent course) 开始独立; **to ～ out in a new direction** 闯出一条新路; **to ～ out on one's own** (become independent) 开始独立谋生; (start own business) 开创自己的事业; **he's struck out as a private eye** 他开始当私家侦探 **2** (aim blow) 猛击; **he lost his temper and struck out wildly** 他怒不可遏，大打出手; **to ～ out at sb./sth.** 朝某人/某物猛击 **3** (express criticism) 抨击; **to ～ out at sb./sth.** 抨击某人/某事物; **she struck out at her critics, claiming their comments were biased** 她驳斥那些批评她的人，声称他们的评论抱有偏见 **4** (proceed) 行进; **we struck out across the field** 我们穿过了田野; **he struck out strongly for the shore** 他奋力向岸边游去 **5** esp Amer colloq (fail) 失败; **the movie struck out and didn't win a single Oscar** 那部影片拍砸了，奥斯卡奖项一项都没拿到
B *vt* [**～ sth. out, ～ out sth.**] (delete) 删去; (put line through) 在…上画线; **she struck out the whole paragraph** (deleted) 她把一整段都删掉了; (put line through) 她把一整段都画掉了

• **strike through** *vt* [**～ sth. through, ～ through sth.**] (delete) 删去; (put line through) 在…上画线

• **strike up**
A *vt* [**～ up sth., ～ sth. up**]
1 (start to play) 开始演奏; (start to sing) 开始演唱 **2** (begin relationship, conversation) 开始; **to ～ up a friendship** 建立友谊; **to ～ up a conversation with a stranger** 和陌生人攀谈
B *vi* (start to play) 开始演奏; (start to sing) 开始演唱; **the band struck up with a waltz** 乐队开始演奏一支华尔兹舞曲

strike: ～ action *n* [u] 罢工行动; **to take ～ action** 罢工; **～ ballot** *n* [决定罢工与否的] 罢工投票; **～bound** *adj* 因罢工而瘫痪的 ‹*company, area*›; **～-breaker** *n* 破坏罢工者; **～-breaking** *n* [u] 破坏罢工; **～ force** *n* 突击部队; **～ fund** *n* 罢工基金; **～ pay** *n* [u] 罢工津贴

striker /ˈstraɪkə(r)/ *n* **1** (person on strike) 罢工者 **2** Sport (in football) 前锋 **3** Mech (in gun) 撞针; (in clock) 打锤

strike vote *n* = **strike ballot**

striking /ˈstraɪkɪŋ/ *adj* **1** (conspicuous) 明显的 ‹*difference, similarity*›; (impressive) 出众的 ‹*woman, good looks, design*› **2** *attrib* Mech 报时的 ‹*clock, mechanism*› **3** *attrib* (on strike) 罢工的 ‹*worker*›

striking distance *n* [u] 攻击距离; **to be within ～ (of sth.)** 在（某物的）攻击距离内; **we are within ～ of victory** 我们胜利在望

strikingly /ˈstraɪkɪŋli/ *adv* 出众地 ‹*handsome*›; 明显地 ‹*different, similar*›

Strimmer® /ˈstrɪmə(r)/ *n* Brit 草坪修剪器

string /strɪŋ/
A *n* **1** [u and c] (twine) 细绳; **a ball/piece/length of ～** 一团/一根/一段细绳; **to tie sth. (up) with a ～** 用细绳捆扎某物; **the key is hanging on a ～ by the door** 钥匙挂在门边的绳子上; **to untie** *or* **undo a ～** 解开细绳; **how long is a piece of ～?** Brit colloq 谁能说得准呢? **2** [c] (on musical instrument, racket, bow) 弦; **to tune the ～s (on sth.)** （给某乐器）调弦 **3** [c] (on puppet) 牵线; **a puppet on ～s** 牵线木偶; **to pull ～s (for sb.)** colloq （为某人）走后门; **to pull the ～s** 提拉牵线; fig colloq 幕后操纵 **4** [c] (fastening on clothing or headgear, cord around neck) 带子; **the ～s of a bonnet** 女帽的帽带; **a medallion on a ～** 挂在带子上的大奖章 **5** [c] (set of things joined together) 一串; **a ～ of pearls** 一串珍珠; **the molecules join together to form long ～s** 分子连接在一起形成长串 **6** [c] (succession) 一连串; **a ～ of obscenities/hits** 一连串的脏话/接二连三的成功 **7** [c] (group) 一批; **he owns a ～ of racing stables** 他有好多个赛马训练场; **a ～ of racehorses** [在同一训练场里训练的] 一群赛马 **8** [c] (line) 一排; **a ～ of islands in the Pacific** 太平洋中的岛链 **9** [c] Comput (of characters) 字符串; (of other data) 信息串; **a character/numeric ～** 字符串/数字串 **10** *usu pl* [c] (condition) 附加条件; **without** *or* **(with) no ～s (attached)** 没有附加条件 **11** [c] Ling 语符列
B **strings** *npl* Mus **the ～s** (instruments) 弦乐器; (players) 弦乐器演奏者; **the ～s section** 弦乐器组
C *vt* (*pt, pp* **strung**) **1** (hang) 悬挂; **fairy lights were strung on trees** 树上挂着彩色小灯; **the route was strung with flags** 沿途悬挂着旗子 **2** (fit with stretched wire, nylon, etc.) 给…装弦 ‹*musical instrument, bow*›; 给…绷线 ‹*racket*› **3** (thread) 把…串起来; **the jeweller was ～ing pearls on a nylon cord** 珠宝匠正在往一根尼龙绳上串珍珠
D *vi* (*pt, pp* **strung**) colloq 充当报料人; **to ～ for a newspaper** 为报纸充当报料人

Phrasal verbs

• **string along** colloq
A *vi* Brit 跟随; **is it OK if we ～ along?** 我们跟着来可以吗?; **to ～ along with sb.** 伴随某人
B *vt* [**～ sb. along, ～ along sb.**] 耍弄; **he had no plans to marry her: he was just ～ing her along** 他根本没打算娶她：不过是跟她玩玩

• **string out**
A *vt* **1** [**～ sth. out, ～ out sth.**] (prolong) 延长; **they seem determined to ～ the talks out for an indefinite period** 他们似乎一心要把谈判无限期地拖下去 **2** (set at intervals) 间隔排列; **warning notices were strung out along the motorway** 高速公路上每隔一段距离就有一个警示牌
B [**～ sb./sth. out, ～ out sb./sth.**] *vt* (spread out) 使间隔排开; **forty soldiers were strung out in a line** 40名士兵拉开排成一排
C *vi* 分成一列; **don't bunch up: ～ out at intervals of 30 metres** 不要挤在一起：按30米的间隔排开

• **string together** *vt* [**～ sth. together, ～ together sth.**]
1 (combine articulately) 将…联结成句; **I can just manage to ～ a few words together in French** 我的法语只能把几个单词拼凑成句 **2** (add one after another) 把…连在一起; **they strung together seven or eight passes** 他们一连传了七八次球 **3** (form by combining articulately) 联成; **to ～ a sentence together** 造句 **4** (form by adding) 串联成; **the band strung together a great set** 乐队连续演奏了一组动听的乐曲

• **string up** *vt* **1** [**～ sth. up, ～ up sth.**] (hang up) 悬挂; **lanterns were strung up in the trees** 树上挂着灯笼 **2** [**～ sb. up, ～ up sb.**] colloq (kill by hanging) 吊死

string: ～ bag *n* 网兜; **～ bass** ▸ p. 395 *n* 低音提琴; **～ bean** *n* 刀豆

stringed /strɪŋd/ *adj* 有弦的; **a ～ puppet** *or* **marionette** 提线木偶; **a six-～ instrument** 六弦乐器

stringency /ˈstrɪndʒənsi/ *n* [u] (of law, control, requirement) 严格; (of criticism, measure) 严厉; (of reason) 严谨

stringent /ˈstrɪndʒənt/ *adj* 严格的 ‹*law, requirement, control*›; 严厉的 ‹*measure, criticism*›; **a ～ economic climate** 紧缩的经济气候; **a ～ money market** 银根紧缩的金融市场

stringently /ˈstrɪndʒəntli/ *adv* 严格地

stringer /ˈstrɪŋə(r)/ ▸ p. 409 *n* **1** Journ colloq 特约记者 **2** Archit (beam) 纵梁 **3** Naut, Aviat 纵向加强条

string: ～ instrument, ～ed instrument ▸ p. 395 *ns* 弦乐器; **～ orchestra** *n* 弦乐队; **～ player** *n* 弦乐器演奏者; **～-pulling** *n* [u] colloq 幕后操纵; **～ puppet** *n* 牵线木偶; **～ quartet** *n* (ensemble) 弦乐四重奏; (music) 弦乐四重奏曲; **～ vest** *n* 网眼背心

stringy /ˈstrɪŋi/ *adj* **1** (resembling string) 细长的 ‹*hair*› **2** (thin, wiry) 精瘦的 ‹*person, build*› **3** Culin 多纤维的 ‹*beans, celery*›; 多筋的 ‹*meat*› **4** (viscous) 可拉成丝的 ‹*cheese*›

strip /strɪp/
A *vt* (*pres p etc.* **-pp-**) **1** (remove clothing from) 脱掉…的衣服; **he was ～ped naked/to his boxer shorts** 他被扒得一丝不挂/只剩下了短裤; **to be ～ped to the waist** 脱光上衣; **to be ～ped of one's clothes** 衣服被脱光 **2** (remove surface or parts of) 除去; **deer had ～ped the tree (of its bark)** 鹿啃掉了树皮; **the wind had ～ped all the leaves from the trees** 风把树上的叶子都吹落了; **to ～ the paint from the door** 把门上的油漆刮掉; **I ～ped the sheets from the bed** 我把床单撤了下来; **they ～ped all the beds** 他们把床单全都撤了下来; ▸ **bare A2** **3** (remove everything from) 使空无一物; **the thieves ～ped the house bare** 窃贼将房子洗劫一空; **the room had been ～ped of furniture** 房间里的家具都搬走了 **4** (dismantle) 拆卸 ‹*machine*› **5** (deprive) 剥夺; **he was disgraced and ～ped of his title** 他名誉扫地，所获头衔被取消了 **6** (damage) 损坏…的螺纹 ‹*nut, screw*›; 损坏…的齿 ‹*gearwheel*›

B *vi* (*pres p etc.* **-pp-**) **1** (undress) 脱掉衣服; **to ~ naked/to one's underwear** 脱得一丝不挂/只剩内衣; **he ~ped to the waist** 他脱光了上衣 **2** (perform striptease) 跳脱衣舞

C *n* **1** (piece) 条; **a metal/paper ~, a ~ of metal/paper** 金属条/纸条; **to cut sth. into ~s** 把某物切成条; **to tear sb. off a ~, to tear a ~ off sb.** Brit colloq 把某人骂得狗血喷头 **2** (area) (of land) 狭长地带; (of water) 带状水域; **a small ~ of garden** 一个狭长的小花园; **the islands are separated by a narrow ~ of water** 岛屿之间一衣带水 **3** Brit Sport (clothes) 队服; **the England ~** 英格兰队队服 **4** *usu sing* (removal of clothes) 脱衣舞; **to do a ~** 跳脱衣舞 **5** (cartoon) 连环漫画 **6** Amer (street) 商业街; **Sunset S~** 日落大道商业街

Phrasal verbs

- **strip away** *vt* [**~ sth. away, ~ away sth.**]
  1 (remove from surface) 除去 **2** (eliminate) 揭除; **the movie aims to ~ away the lies surrounding the president's life** 电影旨在揭穿有关这位总统生平的种种谎言
- **strip down**
  A *vt* [**~ sth. down, ~ down sth.**]
  1 (dismantle) 拆卸 ‹*machine*›; **the soldier ~ped down his rifle** 那名士兵拆开了他的步枪 **2** (remove applied layer or coverings from) 除去…的覆盖物; **to ~ a door down** 刮掉门上的油漆; **~ the bed down and remake it** 把床单撤下来, 重新铺床
  B *vi* 脱掉衣服; **to ~ down to one's underpants** 脱得只剩内裤
- **strip off**
  A *vt* [**~ sth. off, ~ off sth.**]
  1 (remove from body) 脱掉 ‹*clothes*› **2** (remove from surface) 除去; **squirrels had ~ped the bark off the tree** 松鼠把树皮啃掉了; **to ~ off the old wallpaper** 把旧墙纸刮掉; **I ~ped all the sheets off the beds** 我把床单全都撤了下来
  B *vi* 脱掉衣服
- **strip out** *vt* [**~ sth. out, ~ out sth.**]
  1 (remove all of) 全部去除; **we had to ~ out all the old wiring and start again** 我们只好把原有的线路全部拆除, 从头再来 **2** (remove everything from) 使空无一物; **they ~ped out the interior of the buildings and redesigned them** 他们将房屋内部清空, 重新进行了设计 **3** Fin (disregard) 对…忽略不计 ‹*cost, asset*›

strip: ~ cartoon *n* Brit 连环漫画; **~ club** *n* 脱衣舞夜总会; **~ cropping** *n* [u] Amer 等高条植 [为减少坡地土壤侵蚀而间作密根与松根两类作物]

stripe /straɪp/ *n* **1** (narrow band) 条纹; **with blue and white ~s** 带有蓝白条纹 **2** Mil (chevron) 臂章; **to win/lose one's ~s** 获得军衔晋升/失去军衔 **3** esp Amer (type) 类型; **people of all ~s** 形形色色的人

striped /straɪpd/ *adj* 有条纹的 ‹*material, suit*›; **blue ~** 蓝色条纹的

strip: ~ joint *n* colloq **= ~ club**; **~ light** *n* 长条灯; **~ lighting** *n* [u] 长条灯照明

stripling /ˈstrɪplɪŋ/ *n* archaic or hum 小伙子

strip: ~ mall *n* Amer 商店街; **~ mill** *n* 带钢轧机; **~ mining** *n* [u] 露天开采

stripped-down /ˌstrɪptˈdaʊn/ *adj* 简约的 ‹*decor, version*›

stripper /ˈstrɪpə(r)/ ▸**p. 409** *n* **1** [c] (person) 脱衣舞演员 **2** [c] (device) 除漆器 **3** [u and c] (solvent) 脱漆剂

strip poker ▸**p. 307** *n* [u] 剥猪猡扑克牌戏 [输者被罚脱衣服]

strip-search
A *vt* 对…作光身搜查
B *n* 光身搜查

strip show *n* 脱衣舞表演

striptease /ˈstrɪptiːz/ *n* [u and c] 脱衣舞; **to do a ~** 跳脱衣舞

striptease artist ▸**p. 409** *n* 脱衣舞演员

strip-wash
A *n* 光身洗
B *vt* 给…光身洗

stripy /ˈstraɪpi/ *adj* Brit colloq 有条纹的 ‹*material, dress, suit*›

strive /straɪv/ *vi* (*pt* **strove** *or* **~d**, *pp* **striven** /ˈstrɪvn/ *or* **~d**) **1** (try) 力争; **to ~ to do sth.** 力争做某事; **to ~ for** *or* **after sth.** 争取某事物; **to ~ for independence/perfection** 争取独立/完善; **to ~ hard** *or* **with all one's might** 尽全力争取 **2** liter (struggle) 斗争; **to ~ with sb.** (oppose) 反抗某人; (support) 与某人一起斗争

strobe /strəʊb/ *n* **~ (light)** 频闪闪光灯

strobe lighting *n* [u] **1** (lighting) 频闪光 **2** (equipment) 频闪光设备

stroboscope /ˈstrəʊbəskəʊp/ *n* 频闪仪

strode /strəʊd/ *pt* ▸**stride B, C**

stroke /strəʊk/

A *n* **1** (blow) 一击; **he cut the rope with a ~ of his sword** 他一剑劈断了绳子; **he was given 20 ~s of the cane** 他挨了 20 下笞杖 **2** Sport (hit) 击球; **a forehand/backhand ~** 正手/反手击球 **3** (scoring unit in golf) 杆数; **to have a 3-~ lead** 领先 3 杆; **to win by 2 ~s** 以少于对手 2 杆的成绩获胜 **4** (swimming movement) 划水动作; (swimming style) 游泳姿势; **she took a few more ~s to reach the bank** 她又划了几下, 游到了岸边; **butterfly ~** 蝶泳 **5** (rowing movement) 划桨动作; **a few more ~s and they would be across the finishing line** 再划几桨, 他们就可以越过终点线了; **to put sb. off their ~** (upset timing of) 打乱某人的节奏; Brit (disconcert) 使某人乱了方寸 **6** (rower) 尾桨手 **7** *usu sing* esp Brit (caress) 抚摸; **to give sb./sth. a ~** 抚摸一下某人/某物 **8** (move, accomplishment) 举动; **a bold ~** 大胆的举措; **at one** *or* **a (single) ~** 一下子; **they threatened to cancel the whole project at a ~** 他们威胁要一举砍掉整个项目; **she never does a ~ (of work)** 她一向什么(活儿)都不干 **9** (occurrence) 一次; **a ~ of bad/good luck** 背运/好运; **by a ~ of fortune** 幸运地 **10** (idea) 主意; **your idea was a ~ of genius** 你的主意很高明 **11** (mark, movement leaving mark) 一笔; **the paint had been applied in careful ~s** 油漆已经仔细地刷好了; **he finished the portrait with no more than a few ~s** 他寥寥几笔就画好了肖像; **at the ~ of a pen** 大笔一挥 **12** Brit (slash) 斜线; **the reference number is five three seven ~ six** 编号是 537/6; **his secretary ~ PA** 他的秘书兼私人助理 **13** (time signal) [报时的] 钟声; **on the ~ of five** 在5点整; **at the ~ of midnight** 午夜的钟声敲响时 **14** Med 中风; **to have** *or* **suffer a ~** 患中风; **a ~ patient** 中风病人 **15** Tech (of engine, pump) 冲程; **a 2-~ engine** 二冲程发动机

B *vt* **1** esp Brit (pet, caress) 抚摸; **he's a beautiful dog; can I ~ him?** 这条狗真漂亮, 我可以摸一摸吗?; **he ~d his beard, wondering what to do next** 他捋着胡须, 想着接下来该做什么 **2** (kick ball smoothly) 踢; (hit ball smoothly) 击 **3** (move gently) 轻拂; **she ~d away his tears** 她轻轻拭去他的泪水 **4** esp Amer colloq (flatter) 奉承; **I knew how to ~ his ego** 我知道该如何满足他的虚荣心

stroke of lightning *n* Amer 一道闪电

stroll /strəʊl/

A *n* **1** (walk) 溜达; **to go for** *or* **take a ~** 去散步; **to take sb. for a ~** 带某人溜达一下 **2** fig (easy victory) 轻易取得的胜利; (easy objective) 容易实现的目标

B *vi* (walk) 溜达; **to ~ along the beach** 在海滩上漫步; **to ~ in/out** 溜达进去/出来

stroller /ˈstrəʊlə(r)/ *n* **1** (walker) 散步者 **2** Amer (pushchair) 婴儿车

strolling minstrel, strolling player *ns* Hist 流浪艺人

strong /strɒŋ, Amer strɔːŋ/ *adj* **1** (physically powerful) 强壮的; (powerful in performing activity) 强劲的; **I wasn't ~ enough to lift the box** 我力气不够大, 提不动这个箱子; **to be as ~ as an ox** *or* **horse** 强壮如牛; **she wasn't a ~ swimmer** 她游泳不大行 **2** (performed with physical force) 强有力的 ‹*push, grip*›; **the vacuum cleaner has quite ~ suction** 这台吸尘器吸力很强 **3** (exerting natural force) 强的; **a ~ current/wind** 强流/强风; **now the sun is ~est** 现在阳光最强烈 **4** (very effective) 效力强的; **a ~ painkiller** 强效止痛药; **a ~ microscope** 高倍显微镜 **5** (affecting sb. greatly) 极大的; **~ pressure** 巨大的压力; **to make a ~ impression on sb.** 给某人留下深刻印象 **6** (formidable) 强势的; **a ~ team/leader** 强队/强有力的领导人; **in a ~ bargaining position** 处于强势谈判地位 **7** (likely to succeed) 有望成功的; (likely to happen) 可能性大的; **a ~ candidate for the job** 这份工作的热门人选; **there's a ~ possibility that it's true** 那很可能是真的 **8** (compelling) 有力的; **~ evidence** 有力的证据; **you have a ~ case for getting your job back** 你有充分理由要求恢复你的工作 **9** *attrib* (committed) 坚定的 ‹*believer*›; **a ~ supporter of the government** 坚定拥护政府的人 **10** (felt to high degree) 强烈的; (done to high degree) 激烈的; **people have ~ feelings about this issue** 人们对这个问题反应强烈; **a man of ~ principles** 原则性很强的人; **~ support for the government** 对政府的坚决拥护; **to put up ~ resistance** 进行有力的抵抗 **11** (robust) 牢固的; **nylon rope is light but very ~** 尼龙绳很轻, 但非常结实 **12** (resolute) 坚强的; (not easily influenced) 有主见的; **you need ~ nerves to ride a bike in London** 在伦敦骑自行车, 你得有胆量 **13** (firm, decisive) 坚决的; **to take ~ measures** 采取坚决的措施 **14** (proficient) 擅长的; **the play has a very ~ cast** 这部戏演员阵容强大; **she's ~ in mathematics** 她擅长数学; **to be ~ on sth.** (be good at) 擅长某事; (have a lot of) 有很多某物; **I'm not very ~ on dates** 我不大记得住日期; **the report was ~ on criticism, but short on practical suggestions** 这份报告批评的话说得多, 但可行的建议提得少 **15** *attrib* (best) 最拿手的 ‹*subject*›; **to be sb.'s ~ point** *or* **suit** 是某人的强项 **16** (great in number) 大量的; **there was a ~ police presence at the demonstration** 示威现场出现了大批警察 **17** *postpos* (of number of people in a group) 多达…的; **an army 10,000 ~** 一支 1 万人的军队; **the crowd was about 5,000 ~** 聚集的人群有 5,000 人左右 **18** (healthy) 健康的; **are you feeling ~er now after your rest?** 休息过后你感觉好些了吗?; **to be still going ~** colloq (continue to be healthy) 保持健康; (continue to be successful) 状况良好; **my grandmother is 90 and still going ~** 我奶奶 90 岁了, 身体仍然硬朗; **the firm was founded in 1872 and is still going ~** 这家公司创建于 1872 年, 现在仍然运营良好 **19** (functioning well) 强健的 ‹*heart, lungs*›; 敏锐的 ‹*eyesight*›; 洪亮的 ‹*voice*›; **the patient has a ~ pulse** 病人的脉搏很有力 **20** (solid, lasting) 牢固的 ‹*link, relationship, marriage*› **21** Fin (high in value) 坚挺的 ‹*currency, market*› **22** (successful) 状况良好的; **their catering business remained ~ despite the recession** 尽管经济出现衰退, 他们的餐饮生意依然兴隆 **23** (highly discernible) 明显感觉得到的; (easy to understand) 明显的 ‹*hint*›; **a ~ flavour/smell** 浓烈的味道/气味; **a ~ indication/rhythm** 明显的迹象/强劲的节奏; **she bears a ~ likeness to her father** 她长得同她父亲极其相像; **a face with ~ features** 轮廓分明的脸; **he speaks English with a ~ French accent** 他说英语带有浓重的法国口音 **24** (concentrated) 浓的; (vivid) 浓重的 ‹*colour*›; **~ tea/coffee** 浓茶/咖啡 **25** (highly alcoholic) 酒精度高的; **a ~ drink** 烈酒 **26** (powerfully flavoured) 味重的 ‹*cheese, cigarette*› **27** (outspoken) 激烈的 ‹*words*›; 言辞激烈的 ‹*letter*›; **to be a bit ~** Brit colloq 有点言重了; **to come on ~ (to sb.)** colloq (be overbearing) (对某人) 言行过分; (make sexual advances) (对某人) 露骨地调情 **28** (offensive) 冒犯的; **~ language** 脏话 **29** Ling 重读的 ‹*syllable*›; **the ~ form of 'and'** "and" 的强读形式

strong-arm
A *adj attrib* 强制性的 ‹*measure, methods*›; **~ tactics** 强制手段
B *vt* 强制; **to ~ sb. into doing sth.** 强制某人做某事

strong box *n* 保险箱

stronghold /ˈstrɒŋhəʊld, Amer ˈstrɔːŋ-/ *n* **1** (fortress) 堡垒 **2** Pol fig 势力强大的地方; **a nationalist/socialist ~** 民族主义/社会主义的坚强阵地

strongly /ˈstrɒŋli, Amer ˈstrɔːŋli/ *adv* **1** (with force) 使劲地; **the wind was blowing quite ~** 风刮得很大 **2** (solidly) 坚固地; **he's a ~ built man** 他体格强壮 **3** (in large numbers) 强有力地 **4** (powerfully) 强烈地 ‹*attract*›; 深刻地 ‹*influence*›; 浓重地 ‹*taste*›; **to smell ~** 气味很浓 **5** (emphatically) 坚决地 ‹*believe, support, protest, encourage*›; 强烈地 ‹*advise, suggest*›; 激烈地 ‹*argue, criticize*›; **to feel ~ about sth.** 对某事物态度明确; **to be ~ in favour of/against sth.** 坚决拥护/反对某事

strongly-worded *adj* 措词强硬的 ‹*statement, attack*›

strong: ~man /-mæn/ *n* **1** ▸**p. 409** (in circus) 大力士; **2** fig (leader) 铁腕人物; **~-minded** *adj* 有主见的; **~-mindedness** *n* [u] 意志坚定; **~room** *n* 保险库; **~-willed** *adj* 意志坚强的

strontium /ˈstrɒntɪəm/ *n* [u] 锶

strop /strɒp/
A *n* **1** (strap) 磨剃刀皮带 **2** Brit colloq (temper) 恼怒; **to get** *or* **be in a ~** 发脾气
B *vt* (*pres p etc.* **-pp-**) 在皮带上磨 ‹*razor*›

strophe /ˈstrəʊfi/ *n* (first section of Greek ode) 第一诗节; (group of lines) 诗节

strophic /ˈstrəʊfɪk/ *adj* 分节的 ‹*verse, song*›

stroppy /ˈstrɒpi/ *adj* Brit colloq (hard to deal with) 易怒难处的; (bad tempered) 脾气坏的; **to be** *or* **get ~ with sb.** 对某人发火

strove /strəʊv/ *pt* ▸**strive**

struck /strʌk/ *pt, pp* ▸**strike A, B**

structural /ˈstrʌktʃərəl/ *adj* **1** Constr 结构上的 ‹*damage, stability*›; **to make ~ alterations to a house** 改变房屋的结构 **2** (fundamental) 结构性的 ‹*problem, reform*› **3** Sci, Ling 结构的 ‹*relationship, complexity*›

structural: ~ analysis *n* [u] 结构分析; **~ engineer** ▸**p. 409** *n* 结构工程师; **~ engineering** *n* [u] 结构工程学; **~ formula** *n* 结构式

structuralism /ˈstrʌktʃərəlɪzəm/ *n* [u] **1** Ling, Literat 结构主义 **2** Psych 构造主义

structuralist /ˈstrʌktʃərəlɪst/
A *adj* **1** Ling, Literat 结构主义的 **2** Psych 构造主义的
B *n* **1** Ling, Literat 结构主义者 **2** Psych 构造主义者

structural linguistics *npl + v sing* 结构语言学

structurally /ˈstrʌktʃərəli/ *adv* 结构上

structural: ~ steel *n* [u] 结构钢; **~ survey** *n* Brit 结构勘测; **~ unemployment** *n* [u] 结构性失业

structure /ˈstrʌktʃə(r)/
A *n* **1** [c and u] (overall shape, organization) 结构; **a political/social ~** 政治/社会结构; **a price/wage/career ~** 价格/工资/职业体系 **2** [u] (quality of being well-organized) 条理性; **the essay needs more ~** 这篇文章缺乏条理 **3** [c] (building) 建筑物; (object comprised of connected parts) 结构体; **the human back is a complex ~** 人的背骨结构复杂
B *vt* 安排 ‹*day, life, schedule*›; 组织 ‹*essay, activity, argument*›; 使…形成体系 ‹*society*›

structured /ˈstrʌktʃəd/ *adj* 有组织的 ‹*activity, play, situation*›; 结构严密的 ‹*hierarchy*›; 条理清楚的 ‹*essay*›; **~ programming** 结构化编程

structuring /ˈstrʌktʃərɪŋ/ *n* [u] **1** (arrangement) 结构 **2** (organizing) 安排

struggle /ˈstrʌgl/
A *n* **1** [c and u] (combat) 斗争; **a power ~** 权力斗争; **a ~ against drug dealers/for independence** 打击毒贩/争取独立的斗争; **to give up** *or* **surrender without a ~** 不战而降; **to be engaged in a bitter ~ with sb.** 同某人进行激烈斗争 **2** [c] (scuffle) 打斗; **to be injured in** *or* **during a ~** 在扭打中受伤; **there were no signs of a ~ at the murder scene** 凶杀现场没有搏斗的痕迹 **3** [c and u] (determined effort) 奋斗; **they won't succeed without a ~** 他们不努力就不会成功 **4** [c] (difficult task) 难事; **it was a real ~ to be ready on time** 要按时做好准备确非易事; **I had a ~ to convince them** 说服他们我费了很大力气
B *vi* **1** (try hard) 奋斗; **she ~d for breath** 她费力地喘着气; **a country struggling for independence** 争取独立的国家; **they ~d to make ends meet** 他们努力维持生计 **2** (compete for power or control) 争夺; **to ~ for power** 争夺权力 **3** (try to overcome) 抗争; **he ~d against cancer for two years** 他同癌症抗争了两年; **she ~d with her conscience before talking to the police** 她经过一番良心上的斗争，终于对警方说了 **4** (engage in scuffle) 打斗; (try to get free) 挣扎; **to ~ with sb.** 与某人搏斗; **I ~d and screamed for help** 我挣扎着，高声呼救; **how did she manage to ~ free?** 她是如何挣脱的? **5** (move with difficulty) 艰难地行进; (do with difficulty) 艰难地做; **we ~d to the top of the hill** 我们吃力地爬上山顶; **we eventually managed to ~ back to the camp** 我们终于挣扎着回到了营地; **to ~ to one's feet** 艰难地站起来; **to ~ to keep one's temper** 竭力克制不发脾气 **6** (be in difficulty) 处于困境; **new authors are struggling in the present climate** 新作家在当前的环境中处境艰难

Phrasal verbs

- **struggle along** *vi* **1** (keep going) 勉力向前 **2** (keep doing) 奋力坚持; **the family is struggling along on her pitiful salary** 全家靠她那点可怜的薪水艰难度日
- **struggle on** **1** (keep going) 勉力向前; **we're stopping here, but she's going to ~ on** 我们打算在这里停下来，但她坚持要往前走 **2** (keep doing) 奋力坚持; **despite the injury, he ~d on till half-time** 尽管受了伤，他还是坚持到了中场休息
- **struggle through** *vt* [**~ through sth.**] **1** (move through) 艰难地穿越; **to ~ through the crowds** 从人群中挤过去 **2** (toil through) 艰难地完成 **3** (battle through) 挺过; **Britain had to ~ through this recession** 英国必须挺过这次经济衰退

struggling /ˈstrʌglɪŋ/ *adj attrib* 艰难谋生的 ‹*artist, writer, actor*›

strum /strʌm/
A *vt* (*pres p etc.* **-mm-**) 弹奏 ‹*guitar*›; 弹出 ‹*tune, chords*›
B *vi* (*pres p etc.* **-mm-**) 随意弹拨; **to ~ on sth.** 随意弹奏某乐器
C *n* 弹奏

strumpet /ˈstrʌmpɪt/ *n* archaic or hum (female prostitute) 妓女; (promiscuous woman) 荡妇

strung /strʌŋ/ *pt, pp* ▸**string C, D**

strung out *adj* colloq **1** (stressed) 紧张的; (physically worn) 疲惫不堪的; **to be ~ out by sth.** (stressed) 因某事物而焦虑; (physically worn) 被某事物弄得疲惫不堪 **2** Amer (addicted) (to drugs, alcohol) 神志恍惚的; (to activity, behaviour) 沉迷的

strung up *adj* Brit colloq 紧张不安的; **to be/get (all) ~ about sth.** 因某事物感到焦虑不安

strut[1] /strʌt/
A *vi* (*pres p etc.* **-tt-**) (walk in proud manner) «*person, peacock*» 趾高气扬地走; **to ~ along** 昂首阔步向前走; **the models ~ted along the catwalk** 模特儿昂首走在 T 形台上; **to ~ about** *or* **around** 趾高气扬地走来走去
B *vt* (*pres p etc.* **-tt-**) colloq 在…上高视阔步 ‹*stage, catwalk*›; **to ~ one's stuff** 卖弄自己那一套

strut[2] *n* (support) 支柱

strychnine /ˈstrɪkniːn/ *n* [u] 士的宁 [一种白色结晶状的剧毒生物碱]

stub /stʌb/
A *n* **1** (stump) (of cigarette) 烟蒂; (of tail, stick, lipstick) 残端 **2** (counterfoil) (of cheque) 存根; (of ticket) 票根
B *vt* (*pres p etc.* **-bb-**) 不小心使…碰踢 ‹*foot, toe*›

Phrasal verb

- **stub out** *vt* [**~ sth. out, ~ out sth.**] 掐灭 ‹*cigarette, cigar*›

stubble /ˈstʌbl/ *n* [u] **1** (straw) 根茬 **2** (beard) 胡子茬

stubble-burning /ˈstʌblbɜːnɪŋ/ *n* [u] 焚烧秸秆

stubbly /ˈstʌbli/ *adj* 胡子拉碴的 ‹*chin, face*›; 粗短的 ‹*hair*›

stubborn /ˈstʌbən/ *adj* **1** (difficult to influence) 执拗的 ‹*person*›; 倔强的 ‹*animal*›; 固执的 ‹*government, attitude, behaviour*›; **~ resistance/refusal** 顽强的抵抗/顽固的拒绝; **to be ~ about** *or* **over sth./doing sth.** 在某事/做某事上固执 **2** (difficult to remove) 难开的 ‹*door, lock*›; 难去除的 ‹*stain*›; **a ~ cough/fever** 久治不愈的咳嗽/发烧

stubbornly /ˈstʌbənli/ *adv* 顽固地 ‹*persist, deny*›; **the door ~ refused to move** 门就是转不动

stubbornness /ˈstʌbənnɪs/ *n* [u] 顽固; **I find his ~ infuriating** 我觉得他的执拗令人恼火

stubby /ˈstʌbi/
A *adj* 粗短的 ‹*finger, tail, pencil*›; 矮壮的 ‹*person*›
B *n* Austral, NZ colloq 矮啤酒瓶 [容量通常为0.375升]

stucco /ˈstʌkəʊ/
A *n* [u] (plaster) 粉饰灰泥; (decorative work) 拉毛粉饰; **a house with ~ walls** 墙壁做了拉毛粉饰的房子
B *vt* 用灰泥粉刷 ‹*house, wall*›

stuck /stʌk/ *pt, pp* ▸**stick**[2]

stuck-up *adj* colloq 自命不凡的 ‹*person*›; **he's too ~ to talk to me** 他自以为了不起，不屑和我说话

stud[1] /stʌd/ *n* **1** (fastener) 搭扣; **a collar ~** 领扣; **a press-~** Brit 揿钮 **2** (for decoration) 饰钉 **3** (in ear) 耳钉; (in nose) 鼻钉; (in tongue) 舌钉 **4** (on boot) 鞋钉 **5** (in road) 反光路钉 **6** (in tyre) 防滑钉 **7** (in wall) 板墙筋

stud[2] *n* **1** (animal for breeding) 种畜; **to be** *or* **stand at ~** 可配种; **to put a horse out to ~** 用一匹马当种马 **2** (farm) 种马场 **3** colloq (man) 风流男子 **4** **= stud poker**

stud book *n* 良种登记册

studded /ˈstʌdɪd/ *adj* **1** (set with studs) 用饰钉装饰的 ‹*door, belt, jacket*›; 有防滑钉的 ‹*boot, tyre*› **2** fig (sprinkled) **to be ~ with sth.** 布满某物; **the sky was clear and ~ with stars** 天空晴朗，繁星点点

student /ˈstjuːdnt, Amer ˈstuː-/
A *n* **1** Univ, Sch 大学生; **a part-time/full-time ~** 非全日制/全日制学生; **a medical/an art ~** 医科/艺术专业学生; **a high-school ~** 中学生 **2** (person interested in a subject) 研究者;

a keen ~ of human nature 热衷于探究人性的人
B *modif* 1 Univ 大学生的 ‹*life, club, newspaper*›; ~ **unrest** 学潮 2 (trainee) 实习的

student: ~ **driver** *n* Amer 学车者; ~ **grant** *n* 助学金; ~ **ID card** *n* 学生证; ~ **loan** *n* 学生贷款; ~ **nurse** *n* 见习护士

studentship /ˈstju:dntʃɪp, Amer ˈstu:-/ *n* Brit 奖学金

student: ~ **teacher** *n* 实习教师; ~ **union** *n* 1 (organization) 学生会; 2 ~ **union (building)** 学生活动中心

stud: ~ **farm** *n* 种马场; ~ **fee** *n* 配种费; ~ **horse** *n* 种马

studied /ˈstʌdɪd/ *adj* 刻意的 ‹*casualness, indifference, simplicity*›; 做作的 ‹*look, elegance, pose*›; **his writing style is too ~ and artificial** 他的写作风格太矫揉造作

studio /ˈstju:dɪəʊ, Amer ˈstu:-/ *n* (*pl* ~**s**) 1 (of painter) 画室; (of photographer) 摄影室; (of filmmaker) 摄影棚; (of recording company, broadcaster, musician) 录音室 2 (of production company) [电影、广播节目、唱片等的] 制作公司; **a Hollywood ~** 好莱坞电影制片厂 3 = **studio flat**

studio: ~ **apartment** *n* Amer = ~ **flat**; ~ **audience** *n* 节目现场观众; ~ **couch** *n* esp Amer 沙发床; ~ **flat** *n* Brit 单间公寓; ~ **portrait** *n* 影楼人像照片; ~ **recording** *n* 录音棚录音; ~ **set** *n* Cin 电影拍摄场地; TV 电视演播室; ~ **theatre** *n* 实验剧院

studious /ˈstju:dɪəs, Amer ˈstu:-/ *adj* 1 (hard-working) 勤奋的 2 (deliberate) 刻意的 ‹*avoidance, silence, calm, effort*› 3 (careful) 周密的 ‹*inspection, approach*›

studiously /ˈstju:dɪəsli, Amer ˈstu:-/ *adv* 1 (deliberately) 刻意地 ‹*ignore, avoid*›; ~ **calm/indifferent** 故作镇静/冷漠的 2 (carefully) 周密地 ‹*examine, inspect*›; 勤奋地 ‹*work, study*›

studiousness /ˈstju:dɪəsnɪs, Amer ˈstu:-/ *n* [u] 勤奋

stud poker ▸ p. 307 *n* [u] 明扑克 [一种扑克牌戏，第一张发暗牌，其他四张为明牌]

study /ˈstʌdi/
A *n* 1 [u] (gaining of knowledge) 学习; **I don't have a lot of time for ~** 我可以用来学习的时间不多; **a ~ period** 自习时间; **a ~ room** 学习室 2 [c] (book) 专著; (article) 论文; **a ~ of Jane Austen's novels** 简·奥斯丁小说的研究专著 3 [c and u] (piece of research) 研究; **to make a ~ of sth.** 研究某事物; **studies on animal behaviour** 对动物行为的研究; **the matter is under ~** 此事正在研究中 4 [c] (room) 书房 5 [c] Art 习作 6 [c] Mus 练习曲 7 [c] (embodiment) 化身; (good example) 典型; **she was a ~ in calm** 她一副镇定自若的神情; **the whole affair is a ~ in managerial incompetence** 整个事件充分证明了管理层的无能
B **studies** *npl* 1 + *v pl* (academic activity) 学业 2 + *v sing* (subject) 课程; **Celtic studies** 凯尔特语研究
C *vt* 1 (learn about) 学习 ‹*subject*›; (take course in) 攻读 ‹*subject, language, engineering*›; **I've never studied local history** 我从来没学过地方史 2 (investigate, consider) 研究; **she's ~ing how animals communicate** 她正在研究动物如何交流; **it's a question that hasn't been studied** 这个问题还未研究 3 (examine) 细看 ‹*map, menu, photograph, features*›
D *vi* 1 (learn) 学习; (revise) 复习; **I didn't ~ much over the vacation** 假期里我花在学习上的时间不多; **to ~ for an exam** 复习备考 2 (take course) 攻读; **to ~ for sth.** 攻读某科目; **to ~ under sb.** 在某人指导下学习; **to ~ to be an engineer** 读工程学

study: ~ **aid** *n* 学习辅助物; ~ **bedroom** *n* Brit 书房兼卧室; ~ **group** *n* 专题调查组; ~ **hall** *n* Amer Sch 1 [u and c] (period) 自习课; 2 [c] (room) 自习室; ~ **leave** *n* [u] 脱产学习假

stuff /stʌf/
A *n* [u] 1 colloq (unnamed substance or objects) 东西; **the chairs were covered in some sort of plastic ~** 椅子都包了某种塑料膜; **they sell stationery and ~ (like that)** 他们销售文具之类的东西; **this wine is good ~** 这葡萄酒不错; **a bit of ~** Brit sl 风骚娘们儿; **to do one's ~** 施展本领; **go on! do your ~!** 快点！露一手吧！; **the medicine has clearly done its ~** 这药显然起作用了; **to know one's ~** 精通业务; **that's the ~!** Brit 这就对啦！; **I don't give a ~!** Brit 我一点也不在乎！ 2 colloq (personal items) 私人物品; **where's all my ~?** 我的东西都哪儿去了? 3 colloq (unnamed activities) 事儿; **I've got loads of ~ to do today** 我今天有很多活儿要干; **I like reading and ~ (like that)** 我喜欢看书什么的 4 colloq (information, content, subject matter) 玩意儿; **I don't believe in all that ~ about ghosts** 我不信什么鬼呀魂呀的; **I'm bored by history: dates and battles and all that ~** 我对历史很厌烦：都是日期、战役之类的东西; **what's all this 'Mrs Smith' ~? — call me Anna** 哪来的什么"史密斯夫人"那一套？叫我安娜好了; ~ **and nonsense** dated 胡说八道 5 colloq (work produced) 作品; **this poem is good ~** 这首诗很不错; **the band did some great ~ on their first album** 这支乐队的首张专辑做得很棒 6 formal or liter (main constituent) 要素; **let's see what ~ you're made of** 我们来看看你是怎样一个人; **parades and marches were the very ~ of politics in the region** 游行示威是该地区政治生活的基本内容; **the trip was magical: the ~ that dreams are made of** 那次旅行非常奇妙：宛如梦境 7 colloq (drugs) 毒品 8 colloq (stolen goods) 赃物
B *vt* 1 (pack) 装满; **the fridge is ~ed to bursting** 冰箱满得都快撑破了; **the cupboard was ~ed with old clothes** 衣橱里塞满了旧衣服 2 (fill) 填入; **the sofa was ~ed with horsehair** 沙发里填充了马毛; **she had 500 envelopes to ~ with leaflets** 她得在500个信封里装上传单 3 (cause to be filled with) 使充满; **her head is ~ed with romantic notions** 她满脑子都是不切实际的想法 4 (block up) 堵塞; **to ~ a crack with newspaper** 用报纸塞住缝隙 5 (shove) 把…塞进; **to ~ one's hands in one's pockets** 把手插在口袋里; **to ~ cotton wool in one's ears** 用药棉堵住耳朵 6 Culin 给…装馅; **to ~ a chicken with mushrooms** 在鸡里面放蘑菇 7 colloq (cause to eat a lot) 使吃撑; **don't ~ the kids with** *or* **full of chocolate before dinner** 饭前不要让孩子一个劲地吃巧克力; **to ~ one's face** 大吃特吃 8 (in taxidermy) 把…制成标本 ‹*animal*› 9 Amer Pol 把假选票投入 ‹*ballot box*› 10 Brit sl (expressing indifference or rejection) [表示不感兴趣或拒绝]; **I told them they could ~ their job** 我告诉他们让他们的工作见鬼去吧; **get ~ed!** 去你的！; **she lost her temper and told him to get ~ed** 她大发脾气，叫他滚蛋; ~ **it!** 去它的！ 11 Brit colloq (defeat in sport) 彻底击败; **we ~ed them in the second half** 下半场我们把他们打得落花流水
C *v refl* colloq **to ~ oneself** 大吃特吃; **they sat there ~ing themselves with ice cream** 他们坐在那儿狼吞虎咽地大吃冰激凌

Phrasal verb
• **stuff up** *vt* [~ **sth. up**, ~ **up sth.**] colloq 堵塞 ‹*hole, crack*›; **the drain was ~ed up with leaves** 排水沟被树叶堵住了

stuffed /stʌft/ *adj* 1 Culin 有馅的 ‹*cabbage, olive*› 2 (in taxidermy) 填充制成标本的 ‹*animal*› 3 (filled with padding) 有填充物的 ‹*toy*› 4 *pred* colloq (replete) 饱的; **I feel completely ~!** 我感觉吃撑了！

stuffed: ~ **animal** *n* 1 (toy) 填充式动物玩具; 2 (in taxidermy) 动物标本; ~ **shirt** *n* colloq pej 妄自尊大的人; ~ **up** *adj* colloq 塞住的 ‹*nose*›; **I'm all ~ up** 我的鼻子塞住了

stuffily /ˈstʌfɪli/ *adv* pej 古板地 ‹*say, refuse, formal*›

stuffiness /ˈstʌfɪnɪs/ *n* [u] 1 (airlessness) 通风不畅 2 (staidness) 古板 3 colloq (congestion) 鼻塞

stuffing /ˈstʌfɪŋ/ *n* [u] 1 Culin 填料; **chestnut ~** 栗子馅 2 (of upholstery, pillow etc.) 填充物; **to knock the ~ out of sb.** colloq 使某人丧失信心

stuff sack *n* [放睡袋、衣物等的] 整理袋

stuffy /ˈstʌfi/ *adj* 1 (airless) 不透气的; **it's very ~ in here** 这里很闷 2 (staid) 古板的; **the ~ face of royalty** 王室成员的古板面孔 3 colloq (congested) 塞住的 ‹*nose*›

stultify /ˈstʌltɪfaɪ/ *vt* 使呆滞

stultifying /ˈstʌltɪfaɪɪŋ/ *adj* 使人呆滞的 ‹*effect, work, atmosphere*›

stumble /ˈstʌmbl/
A *vi* 1 (trip) 绊脚; (fall) 绊倒; **to ~ against sth.** 绊在某物上; **to ~ on** *or* **over sth.** 在某物上绊了一跤 2 (stagger) 跌跌撞撞地走; **to ~ in/out/off** 跌跌撞撞地走进/走出/走开 3 (in speech) 结结巴巴地说话; **to ~ over a word/phrase** 磕磕巴巴地念单词/短语; **he ~d through his farewell speech** 他磕磕巴巴地念完了他的告别讲话
B *n* 1 (fall) 绊倒 2 (mistake in speech) 结结巴巴; **he got through the whole speech without a ~** 他的发言从头到尾一点儿都没打奔儿

Phrasal verb
• **stumble across, stumble on, stumble upon** *vt* **to ~ across sth.** 意外发现某事物

stumbling block /ˈstʌmblɪŋ blɒk/ *n* 障碍物; **to be** *or* **prove a ~ to sth.** 是某事物的障碍

stump /stʌmp/
A *n* 1 (of tree) 树墩; **up a ~** Amer colloq 处于困境; **he was up a ~ and he knew it** 他走投无路了，连他自己也知道 2 (remaining piece) 残余部分; **a pencil ~** 铅笔头; **the ~ of a cigar** 雪茄烟头; **the ~ of a tooth** 残牙 3 (of limb) 残肢 4 (in cricket) [三柱门的] 柱 5 esp Amer Pol (campaign) **the ~** 巡回演说; **to be on the ~** 作巡回演说; **the senator gave his standard ~ speech** 那位参议员作了一次常规的巡回演说 6 Brit dated colloq (leg) **to stir one's ~s** 赶快动身
B *vt* 1 colloq (baffle) 难住; **I'm ~ed as to how they got here before us** 我搞不懂他们怎么会比我们先到; **she was ~ed for words** 她张口结舌 2 (in cricket) 使…出局 ‹*batsman*› 3 Amer Pol 在…作巡回演说 ‹*country*›
C *vi* 1 (stomp) 脚步重重地走; **to ~ off** 脚步重重地走开 2 Amer Pol 作巡回演说; **to ~ for votes** 为拉选票进行巡回演说

Phrasal verb
• **stump up** Brit colloq
A *vi* 掏腰包; **we were asked to ~ up for the repairs** 人家要我们出修理费
B *vt* [~ **up sth.**, ~ **sth. up**] 掏腰包付 ‹*money*›

stumpy /ˈstʌmpi/ *adj* 矮胖的 ‹*person, shape*›; 粗短的 ‹*legs*›

stun /stʌn/ *vt* (*pres p etc.* **-nn-**) 1 (render unconscious) 打昏; **all animals should be ~ned prior to slaughter** 所有动物在屠宰前都必须击昏 2 fig (shock) 使震惊; **the community was ~ned by the tragedy** 社区公众对悲剧感到震惊 3 fig (impress) 使惊叹

stung /stʌŋ/ *pt, pp* ▸ sting A, B

stun: ~ **grenade** *n* 眩晕手榴弹; ~ **gun** *n* 眩晕枪

stunk /stʌŋk/ *pt, pp* ▸ stink A

stunned /stʌnd/ *adj* 1 (dazed) 眩晕的; **I lay ~ for a while** 我晕晕乎乎地躺了一会儿 2 (amazed, shocked) 震惊的; **we sat in ~ silence** 我们惊呆了，坐着那里一语不发

S

stunner /ˈstʌnə(r)/ *n* colloq 1 (person) 魅力十足的人; (female) 尤物; **your sister's quite a ~** 你妹妹是个绝色佳人 2 (object) 极品

stunning /ˈstʌnɪŋ/ *adj* 1 (stupefying) 使人眩晕的 ‹*blow, impact*› 2 (shocking) 令人震惊的 ‹*defeat, revelation*› 3 (amazing) 绝色的 ‹*beauty*›; 绝妙的 ‹*view, display*›; **she looked ~ as always** 她看上去一如既往地美艳照人

stunningly /ˈstʌnɪŋli/ *adv* 绝妙地 ‹*dress, perform*›; 极其 ‹*powerful, beautiful*›

stunt[1] /stʌnt/

A *n* 1 (act to gain attention) 噱头 2 (risky act) 特技表演; **to do a ~** 表演特技; **a ~ riding/flying** 特技驾车/飞行

B *vi* 表演特技

stunt[2] *vt* (prevent or impede development of) 遏制 ‹*growth, development*›; 阻碍…的发育 ‹*child*›

stunted /ˈstʌntɪd/ *adj* 1 (undersized) 发育不良的 ‹*person*›; **~ growth** 生长不良 2 fig (blighted) 未能充分发展的 ‹*imagination, intelligence*›

stunt: ~man /-mæn/ ▸**p. 409** *n* 特技替身演员; **~ pilot** ▸**p. 409** *n* 特技飞行员; **~ rider** ▸**p. 409** *n* 特技摩托车手; **~woman** ▸**p. 409** *n* 女特技替身演员

stupefaction /ˌstjuːpɪˈfækʃn/ *n* [u] 1 (astonishment) 惊愕; **to sb.'s ~ ...** 使某人惊愕的是… 2 (befuddlement) 麻木状态

stupefy /ˈstjuːpɪfaɪ, Amer ˈstuː-/ *vt* 1 (astonish) 使惊愕; **I was completely stupefied by the news** 听到这个消息，我完全惊呆了 2 (befuddle) 使…麻木 ‹*person, mind, senses*›; **to be stupefied with sth.** 被某物弄得昏昏沉沉; **the blow left him momentarily stupefied** 那一拳把他打得一时头晕目眩

stupefying /ˈstjuːpɪfaɪɪŋ, Amer ˈstuː-/ *adj* 1 (astonishing) 令人震惊的 2 (befuddling) 使人昏昏沉沉的

stupefyingly /ˈstjuːpɪfaɪɪŋli, Amer ˈstuː-/ *adv* 令人昏昏沉沉地 ‹*boring, tedious*›; **the party was ~ dull** 聚会无聊得令人昏昏欲睡

stupendous /stjuːˈpendəs, Amer stuː-/ *adj* 惊人的; **the hotel is in a ~ location** 那家旅馆的地段好得超乎想象

stupendously /stjuːˈpendəsli, Amer stuː-/ *adv* 超乎想象地 ‹*rich, successful, difficult*›

stupid /ˈstjuːpɪd, Amer ˈstuː-/

A *adj* 1 (unintelligent) 笨的; **she is not ~, just lazy** 她并不笨，只是懒; **I pretended I understood because I didn't want to look ~** 我假装听懂了，因为我不想看上去像个傻瓜 2 (foolish) 愚蠢的; **I've done something ~** 我做了件蠢事; **don't be ~!** 不要犯傻了!; **you ~ idiot!** 你这个蠢货!; **I felt so ~ when I realized I'd been duped** 当我意识到被骗时感觉傻透了 3 (befuddled) 迷糊的 ‹*person*›; **to be ~ with cold/shock/fatigue** 冻得失去知觉/惊得神志不清/累得迷迷糊糊; **to drink oneself ~** (喝酒) 喝得晕头转向; **to be knocked ~ by sth.** 被某物撞得头晕眼花 4 *attrib* colloq (damn) 恼人的; **get your ~ feet off the chair!** 把你的臭脚从椅子上拿开!

B *n* colloq (as term of address) 笨蛋 [一般用作称呼]

stupidity /stjuːˈpɪdəti, Amer stuː-/ *n* 1 [u] (lack of intelligence) 笨; **to feign ~** 装傻 2 [u and c] (foolishness) 愚蠢; **remarks of incredible ~** 愚蠢至极的话

stupidly /ˈstjuːpɪdli, Amer stuː-/ *adv* 1 (unintelligently) 傻乎乎地 2 (foolishly) 愚蠢地; **~, I forgot to bring it** 真笨，我忘带了

stupidness /ˈstjuːpɪdnɪs, Amer ˈstuː-/ *n* [u] 1 (lack of intelligence) 笨 2 (foolishness) 愚蠢

stupor /ˈstjuːpə(r), Amer ˈstuː-/ *n* [c and u] 恍惚; **to be in a ~** 神志不清; **in a drunken ~** 酩酊大醉

sturdily /ˈstɜːdɪli/ *adv* 结实地; **he's pretty ~ built** 他体格很健壮

sturdiness /ˈstɜːdɪnɪs/ *n* [u] (of person, build) 健壮; (of structure, vehicle) 结实

sturdy /ˈstɜːdi/ *adj* 1 (hardy) 结实的; **the bike is ~ enough to cope with bumpy tracks** 这辆自行车很结实，在颠簸的小道上骑没问题; **a ~ pair of boots** 一双耐磨的靴子 2 (strong and healthy) 健壮的; **a ~ breed of cattle** 一种健壮的牛 3 (resolute) 顽强的 ‹*independence, defence*›

sturgeon /ˈstɜːdʒən/ *n* [c and u] (*pl* **~** *or* **~s**) 鲟

stutter /ˈstʌtə(r)/

A *vi* 1 (stammer) «*person*» 结结巴巴地说; «*voice*» 磕磕巴巴 2 (make series of sounds) «*gun, engine*» 突突地响 3 (move with difficulty) «*vehicle*» 突突地费力行驶; (start with difficulty) 突突地费力启动; **to ~ along** 突突地费力驶向前 4 (progress irregularly) 时断时续地发展

B *vt* 结结巴巴地说出 ‹*word, apology*›

C *n* 1 (stammer) 口吃; **to have a ~** 说话结巴 2 (of gun, engine) 突突声

Phrasal verb

• **stutter out** *vt* [**~ sth. out, ~ out sth.**] 结结巴巴地说出 ‹*word, apology*›

stutterer /ˈstʌtərə(r)/ *n* 结巴

stuttering /ˈstʌtərɪŋ/

A *n* [u] 口吃

B *adj attrib* 1 (stammering) 结巴的 ‹*person, voice*› 2 (progressing irregularly) 断断续续发展的 ‹*economy*›; 不顺畅的 ‹*rhythm, beat*›; 磕磕绊绊的 ‹*start*›

St Valentine's Day /snt ˈvæləntaɪnz deɪ/ *n* 情人节 [2月14日]

St Vincent and the Grenadines /snt ˌvɪnsənt ənd ðə ˈɡrenədiːnz/ *pr n* 圣文森特和格林纳丁斯

sty[1] /staɪ/ *n* (*pl* **sties**) 1 (pigsty) 猪圈 2 fig (dirty place) 肮脏的地方

sty[2], **stye** *n* (*pl* **sties** *or* **styes**) (swelling of the eye) 睑腺炎

Stygian /ˈstɪdʒɪən/ *adj* 1 Mythol 冥河的 ‹*waters, boatman*› 2 liter (dark) 阴森森的 ‹*gloom, depths*›

style /staɪl/

A *n* 1 [c and u] (manner) 方式; **a ~ of living** 生活方式; **different teaching ~s** 不同的教学方式; **a ~ of swimming, a swimming ~** 泳姿; **that's the ~!** 就该那样做! 2 [c] (design of object) 样式; (clothing design) 款式; **various ~s of carpet** 各种式样的地毯; **our fireplaces come in several ~s** 我们有多种款式的壁炉; **shoes in the latest ~** 最新款式的鞋 3 [c] (hairstyle) 发型 4 [u] (fashionableness) 时尚; **short skirts are back in ~** 短裙又流行起来了 5 [u] (elegance) 风度; **to do everything with ~ and grace** 事事做得优雅得体; **in ~** 有气派地; **she always celebrates her birthday in ~** 她的生日总是过得很排场; **he won the championship in great *or* fine ~** 他很风光地赢得了冠军 6 [c and u] (characteristic approach) 风格; **a building in Gothic ~** 哥特式建筑; **a parody written in the ~ of Molière** 一部模仿莫里哀风格的滑稽喜剧 7 [c and u] (way of writing or speaking) 文体; **she writes in a journalistic ~** 她用新闻体写作; **a conversational ~** 会话体; **it's not considered good ~ to start a sentence with 'but'** 人们认为，一个句子用 but 开头不是好的文法 8 [u] (usual way of behaving) 作风; **caution was not her ~** 谨小慎微不是她的风格; **I'm surprised he rides a motorbike: I'd have thought cars were more his ~** 他骑摩托让我很惊讶：我倒认为开车更适合他 9 [c] Bot 花柱

B *vt* 1 (design) 把…设计成某种式样; **an elegantly ~d jacket** 式样高雅的夹克; **he's ~d the hair of some Hollywood stars** 他给几位好莱坞明星设计过发型 2 formal (give title) 任命; (give name) 称呼; **he is ~d principal of the university** 他被任命为这所大学的校长; **should he be ~d 'Mr' or 'Dr'?** 应该称他"先生"还是"博士"?; **he ~d himself Major Carter** 他自称卡特少校

C **-style** *combining form* …式样的; **1950s~ chairs** 20 世纪 50 年代款式的椅子

style: ~ guru *n* 时尚大师; **~ sheet** *n* 样式表

styli /ˈstaɪlaɪ/ *pl* ▸**stylus**

styling /ˈstaɪlɪŋ/ *n* [u] 1 (design) 款式 2 (contours, appearance) 式样 3 (hairstyling) 造型; **~ gel/mousse** 定型发胶/摩丝

styling: ~ brush *n* 电热梳; **~ tongs** *npl* 卷发器

stylish /ˈstaɪlɪʃ/ *adj* 1 (smart) 时尚的 ‹*person, outfit*›; (elegant) 高雅的 ‹*district, restaurant, furniture*› 2 (accomplished) 有才艺的 ‹*player, writer*›; 高水平的 ‹*performance*›

stylishly /ˈstaɪlɪʃli/ *adv* 1 (fashionably, elegantly) 时尚地 ‹*dress, design*› 2 (in an accomplished way) 高水平地 ‹*perform, write*›

stylishness /ˈstaɪlɪʃnɪs/ *n* [u] 1 (elegance) (of person, outfit) 时尚; (of district, restaurant, furniture) 高雅 2 (accomplished nature) 高水平

stylist /ˈstaɪlɪst/ ▸**p. 409** *n* 1 (hairdresser) 发型师 2 (image creator) 造型师 3 (clothes designer) 时装设计师 4 (writer) 文体家 5 (film-maker) 有格调的电影导演 6 Sport 动作优美的运动员 7 Mus (player) 有格调的演奏者; (singer) 有风度的歌手; (composer) 有格调的作曲家

stylistic /staɪˈlɪstɪk/ *adj* (in literature) 文体上的 ‹*analysis, similarity, feature*›; (in art, music) 风格的 ‹*variety, innovation*›

stylistically /staɪˈlɪstɪkli/ *adv* 风格上地; **~ (speaking), ...** 风格上（而言），…

stylistic: ~ device *n* 文体手段; **~ marker** *n* 文体标记

stylistics /staɪˈlɪstɪks/ *npl* + *v sing* 文体学

stylized /ˈstaɪlaɪzd/ *adj* 非写实的 ‹*picture, form*›; 程式化的 ‹*gesture, performance*›

stylus /ˈstaɪləs/ *n* (*pl* **~es** *or* **styli**) 1 (on record player) 唱针 2 (for writing, computer) 光笔 3 (tool used in ancient times) [刻写蜡板用的] 尖笔

stymie /ˈstaɪmi/ *vt* colloq 阻碍

stymied /ˈstaɪmɪd/ *adj* colloq 受阻的

styptic /ˈstɪptɪk/

A *adj* 止血的

B *n* [c and u] 止血剂

styptic pencil *n* 止血笔

Styrofoam® /ˈstaɪrəfəʊm/ *n* [u] esp Amer 舒泰龙泡沫塑料; **a ~ cup** 泡沫杯

Styx /stɪks/ *n* **the (River) ~** 冥河

suasion /ˈsweɪʒn/ *n* [u] formal 说服

suasive /ˈsweɪsɪv/ *adj* 1 formal (persuasive) 说服的 ‹*power*›; 有说服力的 ‹*language*› 2 Ling 劝导性的 ‹*verb*›

suave /swɑːv/ *adj* 圆滑的

suavely /ˈswɑːvli/ *adv* 圆滑地

suaveness /ˈswɑːvnɪs/, **suavity** /ˈswɑːvɪti/ *ns* [u] 圆滑

sub /sʌb/

A *n* colloq 1 Sport = **substitute A2** 2 Naut = **submarine A1** 3 Brit (subscription) 会员费; **to pay one's ~s** 交纳会员费 4 Amer (sandwich) = **submarine A2** 5 Brit (subeditor) 审校人 6 Brit (advance) 预支; (loan) 借支

B *vi* (*pres p etc.* **-bb-**) colloq 1 Sport (appear as substitute) 做替补; **to ~ for sb.** 替换某人 2 (be replacement at work) 暂代; **to ~ as sth.** 代任某职; **to ~ for sb.** 顶替某人

C *vt* (*pres p etc.* **-bb-**) colloq 1 Sport 替换 2 (use as replacement) 换用; **to ~ sth. for sth.** 用某物代替某物 3 Brit (lend) 预支给; **to ~ sb. sth.** 给某人预支某物 4 Brit (subedit) 审校

subagent /ˈsʌbeɪdʒənt/ *n* (commercial) 分销商; (political) 副代理人

subalpine /ˌsʌbˈælpaɪn/ *adj* 亚高山带的

subaltern /ˈsʌbltən, Amer səˈbɔːltərn/
A *n* **1** Brit Mil 陆军中尉 **2** formal (subordinate) 下属
B *adj* **1** Brit Mil 陆军中尉的 ‹*rank*›; **one of the ~ officers** 陆军中尉军官之一 **2** formal (subordinate) 下级的

sub-aqua /ˌsʌbˈækwə/
A *adj attrib* 水下的; **~ equipment** *or* **gear** 潜水设备
B *n* [u] (swimming) 潜泳; (exploration) 水下探险

subarctic /ˌsʌbˈɑːktɪk/ *adj* **1** Geog 亚北极的 ‹*zone, habitat, species*› **2** colloq (cold) 北极般冰冷的 ‹*conditions, temperatures*›

sub-assembly *n* 分组合件

subatomic /ˌsʌbəˈtɒmɪk/ *adj* 亚原子的 ‹*theory, physics*›; 小于原子的 ‹*scale, level*›

subatomic particle *n* 亚原子粒子

sub-basement *n* 下层地下室

subclass /ˈsʌbklɑːs, Amer -klæs/ *n* **1** (subordinate group) 基类 **2** Biol 亚纲

subcommittee /ˈsʌbkəmɪti/ *n* + *v sing or pl* 小组委员会

subconscious /ˌsʌbˈkɒnʃəs/
A *n* [u] **the** *or* **one's ~** 潜意识
B *adj* 潜意识的

subconsciously /ˌsʌbˈkɒnʃəsli/ *adv* 潜意识地; **~, she was looking for the father she had never known** 她在下意识地寻找自己从未见过的父亲

subcontinent /ˌsʌbˈkɒntɪnənt/ *n* **1** (part of South Asia) **the (Indian) ~** 印度次大陆 **2** (land mass) 次大陆

subcontract
A /ˌsʌbkənˈtrækt/ *vt* **1** (get done) 转包 ‹*work, construction*›; **to ~ sth. out, to ~ out sth.** 转包某事; **to ~ sth. to sb./sth.** 把某事转包给某人/某公司 **2** (employ) 转包给 ‹*person, company*›; **to ~ sb./sth. to do sth.** 转包给某人/某公司做某事
B /ˈsʌbkɒntrækt/ *n* 分包合同

subcontracting /ˌsʌbkənˈtræktɪŋ/ *n* [u] 转包

subcontractor /ˌsʌbkənˈtræktə(r)/ *n* (person) 分包人; (company) 分包公司

subculture /ˈsʌbkʌltʃə(r)/ *n* **1** [c and u] (behaviour) 亚文化; **youth ~** 青少年群体特有的亚文化 **2** [c] (group) 亚文化人群 **3** [c] Biol 次培养

subcutaneous /ˌsʌbkjuːˈteɪnɪəs/ *adj* 皮下的

subdirectory /ˈsʌbdaɪrektəri, -dɪ-/ *n* 子目录

subdivide /ˌsʌbdɪˈvaɪd/
A *vt* 再分割; **to ~ sth. into sth.** 把某物再分割成某物; **the building has been ~d into flats** 整幢楼被进一步分成若干公寓套房
B *vi* 被再分; **to ~ into sth.** 被再分成某物

subdivision /ˌsʌbdɪˈvɪʒn/ *n* **1** [u] (process) 再分割 **2** [c] (part) 再分成的部分; **a police ~** 警察管辖分区 **3** [c] Amer (housing development) 住宅小区

subduction /səbˈdʌkʃn/ *n* [u] 潜没 [指一个地壳板块下降到另一板块之下的过程]

subdue /səbˈdjuː, Amer -ˈduː/ *vt* **1** (conquer, defeat) 制服 ‹*forces, opponent, prisoner*›; 征服 ‹*country*›; 镇压 ‹*rebellion, rebels*› **2** (hold in check) 克制 ‹*fear, anger, delight*›

subdued /səbˈdjuːd, Amer -ˈduːd/ *adj* **1** (downcast, muted) 闷闷不乐的 **2** (kept in check) 压抑的 ‹*enthusiasm, reaction*› **3** (hushed) 压低的 ‹*voice*›; 小声的 ‹*conversation*› **4** (not bright) 柔和的 ‹*lighting, colour*› **5** (not busy) 低迷的 ‹*trading, market*›

subedit /ˌsʌbˈedɪt/ *vt* Brit 审校

subeditor /ˌsʌbˈedɪtə(r)/ ▸**p. 409** *n* Brit 审校人

subentry /ˈsʌbentri/ *n* **1** (in accounts) 小项 **2** Comput 子项

subfamily /ˈsʌbfæməli/ *n* **1** Biol 亚科 **2** Ling 亚语系

subfield /ˈsʌbfiːld/ *n* 子域

subgroup /ˈsʌbgruːp/ *n* **1** (subdivision) 小小组 **2** Math 子群

subheading /ˈsʌbhedɪŋ/, **subhead** /ˈsʌbhed/ *ns* 小标题

subhuman /ˌsʌbˈhjuːmən/ *adj* pej **1** (unworthy of human being) 不齿于人类的 ‹*person, behaviour*›; 非人的 ‹*treatment*› **2** (unfit for humans) 不适合人类的 ‹*conditions, existence*›

subject
A /ˈsʌbdʒɪkt/ *n* **1** (topic) 主题; **to change the ~** 换个话题; **an article on the ~ of space travel** 一篇谈论太空旅行的文章; **let's just drop the ~** 我们别再谈这事儿了; **how did we get on to the ~ of marriage?** 我们怎么谈到婚姻问题上了?; **we're getting off the ~** 我们跑题了 **2** (branch of knowledge) 科目; **French is her best/favourite ~** 法语是她成绩最好/最喜欢的科目 **3** Art, Phot 表现对象; **to focus the camera on the ~** 将相机聚焦到拍摄对象上; **landscapes were a popular ~ with many 18th century painters** 风景是 18 世纪很多画家喜欢的表现题材 **4** (in experiment) 实验对象; **male ~s between the ages of 18 and 25** 18 至 25 岁之间的男性实验对象 **5** (focus) 缘由; **a ~ of dispute** 争端的起因; **he's become a ~ for ridicule** 他成了别人讥笑讽刺的对象 **6** Ling 主语 **7** (citizen) 臣民; **a British ~** 英国国民
B /ˈsʌbdʒɪkt/ *adj* **1** *pred* (liable) **to be ~ to sth.** 可能遭受…; **prices are ~ to alteration** 价格有可能变动 **2** *pred* (dependent) **to be ~ to sth.** 取决于某事物; **the proposal is ~ to approval by the shareholders** 提案需经股东批准 **3** *pred* (obliged to obey) **to be ~ to sth.** 受某事物支配; **the island is not ~ to British law** 该岛不受英国法律制约 **4** *attrib* formal (subservient) 臣服的; **the Greeks were the first ~ people to break free from Ottoman rule** 希腊人是第一个挣脱奥斯曼帝国统治的民族
C /ˈsʌbdʒɪkt/: **subject to** *prep phr* 取决于; **~ to the EU's agreement, ...** 根据欧盟协议, …; **you will be granted membership, ~ to producing certain documents** 只要提供一些文件, 你就可以成为会员
D /səbˈdʒekt/ *vt* formal 使臣服; **to be ~ed to bombing/ridicule** 遭到轰炸/受到嘲笑

subject: ~ heading *n* 分类类目; **~ index** *n* 分类索引

subjection /səbˈdʒekʃn/ *n* [u] **1** (action of subjugating) 征服; **the ~ of a race/country** 对种族/国家的征服; **the ~ of over three million people to foreign rule** 征服300多万人使其接受外族统治 **2** (state of subjugation) 屈从; **to keep sb. in a state of ~** 使某人处于屈从地位; **~ to foreign rulers** 对外国统治者的服从 **3** (action of forcing to experience) 遭受; **he confessed, after ~ to torture** 他受刑后招供了

subjective /səbˈdʒektɪv/
A *adj* **1** (personal or biased) 主观的 ‹*idea, opinion, perception, judgement*› **2** (existing only in the mind) 臆测的 **3** Ling 主格的 ‹*pronoun*›; **the ~ case** 主格
B *n* Ling 主格

subjectively /səbˈdʒektɪvli/ *adv* **1** (in biased way) 主观臆断地 ‹*talk, judge*› **2** (mentally) 主观地 ‹*exist, perceive*›

subjectiveness /sʌbˈdʒektɪvnɪs/ *n* [u] **= subjectivity**

subjectivism /səbˈdʒektɪvɪzəm/ *n* [u] 主观主义

subjectivity /ˌsʌbdʒekˈtɪvəti/ *n* [u] **1** (biased nature) 主观臆断 **2** (mental nature) 主观性

subject matter *n* 主题

sub judice /ˌsʌb ˈdʒuːdɪsi, ˌsʊb ˈjuːdɪkeɪ/ *adj* formal 在审理中的

subjugate /ˈsʌbdʒʊgeɪt/ *vt* **1** (defeat) 征服 ‹*country, people*› **2** (suppress) 克制 ‹*desire, will*› **3** (make subordinate) **to ~ sb./sth. to sth.** 使某人/某事物受制于某事物

subjugation /ˌsʌbdʒʊˈgeɪʃn/ *n* [u] **1** (of people, country) 征服 **2** (of desire, will) 克制 **3** (subordination) 从属

subjunctive /səbˈdʒʌŋktɪv/
A *n* **1** [u] (mood) 虚拟语气; **in the ~** 用虚拟语气 **2** [c] (form) [动词的] 虚拟式
B *adj* 虚拟的; **~ form/mood/verb** 虚拟式/虚拟语气/虚拟动词

subkingdom /ˌsʌbˈkɪŋdəm/ *n* 亚界

sublease /ˈsʌbliːs/ *vt, vi, n* **= sublet**

sublet
A *vt* /ˌsʌbˈlet/ (*pres p* **-tt-**; *pt, pp* **sublet**) **1** (allow use of) 转租 ‹*flat, land*›; **to ~ sth. to sb./sth.** 把某物转租给某人/某机构 **2** (pay to use) 转租使用 ‹*flat, office*›; **to ~ sth. from sb./sth.** 从某人/某机构转租某物
B *vi* /ˌsʌbˈlet/ (*pres p* **-tt-**; *pt, pp* **sublet**) **1** (allow use of property) 转租; **to ~ to sb./sth.** 转租给某人/某机构 **2** (pay to use property) 转租使用; **to ~ from sb./sth.** 从某人/某机构转租
C *n* /ˈsʌblet/ **1** (lease) 转租 **2** colloq (property) 转租的房产

sublibrarian /ˌsʌblaɪˈbreərɪən/ ▸**p. 409** *n* 图书馆管理员助理

sub-lieutenant /ˌsʌblefˈtenənt, Amer -luːˈtenənt/ *n* (rank) 海军中尉军衔; (person) 海军中尉

sublimate /ˈsʌblɪmeɪt/
A *vt* **1** Psych 使…高尚化 ‹*drive, desire*› **2** Chem 使…升华 ‹*solid, ice*›
B *vi* ‹*solid, ice*› 升华; **to ~ (from sth.) into sth.** (从某物) 升华为某物
C *n* [c and u] 升华物

sublimation /ˌsʌblɪˈmeɪʃn/ *n* **1** [c and u] Psych 高尚化 **2** [u] Chem 升华

sublime /səˈblaɪm/
A *adj* **1** (perfect) 令人赞叹的 ‹*beauty*›; 卓越的 ‹*genius*›; 崇高的 ‹*art*› **2** colloq (excellent) 很棒的 ‹*food, clothes*› **3** *attrib* (utter) 极端的 ‹*indifference, contempt*›
B *n* **the ~** 崇高的事物; **from the ~ to the ridiculous** 由高超到荒谬

sublimely /səˈblaɪmli/ *adv* **1** (perfectly) 令人赞叹地; **~ beautiful** 美艳动人; **~ heroic** 英勇无畏 **2** colloq (excellently) 非常棒地 ‹*play, write*› **3** (utterly) 极端地 ‹*contemptuous*›; **she was ~ indifferent to their presence** 她压根儿不关心他们的存在

subliminal /səbˈlɪmɪnl/ *adj* 潜意识的; **~ advertising** 隐性广告

subliminally /səbˈlɪmɪnəli/ *adv* 下意识地

sublimity /səˈblɪməti/ *n* [u] formal 崇高

sub-machine gun /ˌsʌbməˈʃiːn gʌn/ *n* 冲锋枪

submarine /ˌsʌbməˈriːn, Amer ˈsʌb-/
A *n* **1** Naut 潜艇; **~ warfare** 潜艇战; **a ~ captain** 潜艇艇长 **2** Amer **~ (sandwich)** 潜艇三明治 [长条面包纵向切开, 内夹各种食物]
B *adj attrib* 海底的; **~ life/cables** 海底生物/电缆

submariner /ˌsʌbˈmærɪnə(r), Amer ˈsʌb-/ *n* 潜艇水兵

submenu /ˈsʌbmenjuː/ *n* 子菜单

submerge /səbˈmɜːdʒ/
A *vt* **1** (put under water) 淹没 ‹*field, rock*› **2** (hide) 掩盖 ‹*feeling, opinion*›
B *vi* 潜入水中
C *v refl* **to ~ oneself** **1** (go underwater) 浸入水中 **2** (immerse oneself) 潜心; **to ~ oneself in work/study** 潜心于工作/研究

submerged /səbˈmɜːdʒd/ *adj* 淹没的; **the submarine remained ~ for weeks** 潜艇好几个星期一直待在水下

submergence /səbˈmɜːdʒəns/ *n* [u] **1** (in water) 淹没 **2** fig 沉沦

S

submersible /səbˈmɜːsəbl/
A *n* 潜水器
B *adj* 水下用的

submersion /səbˈmɜːʃn, Amer -ˈmɜːrʒn/ *n* **1** [c and u] (action) 沉没 **2** [u] (state) 淹没

submission /səbˈmɪʃn/ *n* **1** [u] (subjection) 屈服; (obedience) 恭顺; (surrender) 投降; **to beat/frighten/starve sb. into ~** 把某人打得/吓唬得/饿得屈服 **2** [c and u] (in wrestling) 制服 **3** [u] (tendering) 提交; **when is the final date for the ~ of proposals?** 提交提案的最后日期是什么时候? **4** [c] (proposal, report) 提交的文件; **our ~s have to be in by tomorrow** 我们的报告最迟明天必须提交 **5** [c] Jur (proposition or argument) [向法官或陪审团提出的] 意见; **to make a ~ that ...** 提出…的意见 **6** [c] formal (opinion) 看法; **in my ~** 依我之见

submissive /səbˈmɪsɪv/ *adj* 顺从的; **to be ~ to authority** 服从权威

submissively /səbˈmɪsɪvli/ *adv* 顺从地

submissiveness /səbˈmɪsɪvnɪs/ *n* [u] 顺从

submit /səbˈmɪt/
A *vi* (*pres p etc.* **-tt-**) **1** (accept defeat) «*general, opponent*» 认输; «*army, town, tribe*» 投降; **to ~ to sb./sth.** 向…认输 ‹*opponent*›; 向…投降 ‹*army, invader*›; 屈从于 ‹*rule, will, demand*›; **she refused to ~ to threats** 她拒不向恐吓低头 **2** (defer to) 遵从; **to ~ to** 遵从 ‹*arbitration, decision*› **3** (agree to) 听任; **to ~ to** 接受 ‹*examination, treatment*›; 甘受 ‹*humiliation, injustice*›; 遵从 ‹*discipline*›
B *vt* (*pres p etc.* **-tt-**) **1** (present) 提交 ‹*bill, report, budget, appeal, resignation*›; **the findings have been ~ted to the government** 调查结果已经呈送给政府 **2** formal (propose, suggest) 主张; **I would ~ that ...** 我认为… **3** (subject to) 使经受; **to ~ sb./sth. to sth.** 让某人/某物经受某事; **to ~ oneself to** 接受 ‹*examination, treatment*›; 甘受 ‹*humiliation*›; 遵从 ‹*jurisdiction, decision*›

subnetwork /ˈsʌbnetwɜːk/, **subnet** /ˈsʌbnet/ *ns* 子网络

subnormal /sʌbˈnɔːml/ *adj* **1** (unusually low) 低于正常的 ‹*level, intelligence*›; **a week of ~ temperatures** 一个星期的偏低气温 **2** offensive (mentally defective) 弱智的

suborder /ˈsʌbɔːdə(r)/ *n* 亚目

subordinate
A /səˈbɔːdɪnət/ *adj* **1** (lower) 级别低的 ‹*rank, officer*›; **to be ~ to sb.** 从属于某人 **2** (less important) 次要的 ‹*issue, question*›; **to be ~ to sth.** 没有某事物重要
B /səˈbɔːdɪnət, Amer -dənət/ *n* 下属
C /səˈbɔːdɪneɪt/ *vt* 使…服从 ‹*person, need*›; **to ~ sb./sth. to sb./sth.** 使…服从于…; **environmental considerations were ~d to commercial interests** 环境因素让位给了商业利益; **a subordinating conjunction** 从属连词

subordinate clause /səˈbɔːdɪnət klɔːz/ *n* 从句

subordination /səˌbɔːdɪˈneɪʃn/ *n* [u] 从属; **~ of sb./sth.** 某人/某事物的从属地位; **~ to sth.** 对某事的顺从

suborn /səˈbɔːn/ *vt* formal 买通 ‹*witness*›; 唆使 ‹*perjury*›

subparagraph /ˈsʌbpærəgrɑːf/ *n* [尤指法律文件中的] 小段

subplot /ˈsʌbplɒt/ *n* 次要情节

subpoena /səˈpiːnə/
A *n* [c and u] 传票; **to serve a ~ on sb.** 向某人送达传票
B *vt* **1** (order to testify) 用传票传唤 ‹*witness*› **2** (order to be submitted) 发传票命令交出 ‹*evidence, record*›

sub-post office *n* Brit 小邮局

sub-prime *adj* 次级的; **~ loan** 次级贷款; **the ~ mortgage market** 次级抵押贷款

subregion /ˈsʌbriːdʒən/ *n* 分区

subroutine /ˈsʌbruːtiːn/ *n* 子程序

subscribe /səbˈskraɪb/
A *vi* **1** (pay to receive or view sth.) 订购; **to ~ to** 订阅 ‹*magazine*›; 预付费收看 ‹*TV, channel*› **2** (support) 定期捐助; **to ~ to** 定期向…捐助 ‹*fund, charity*› **3** Fin (apply) 认购; **to ~ to** *or* **for sth.** 认购 ‹*issue, shares*› **4** (agree with) **to ~ to an idea/theory** 赞同一个观点/认同一个理论
B *vt* **1** (contribute) 定期捐助 ‹*sum*› **2** *usu passive* (apply for) 报名参加 ‹*course, tour*›; 认购 ‹*issue, shares*›; **the class was fully ~d** 这个班名额已满

subscriber /səbˈskraɪbə(r)/ *n* **1** (customer) 订户; **a ~ to a magazine/TV channel** 杂志的订户/付费频道用户 **2** Telecom 用户 **3** (support) 定期捐助者; **a ~ to** …的定期捐助者 ‹*fund, charity*› **4** Fin (applicant) 认购者; **a ~ to** *or* **for** …的认购者 ‹*issue, shares*› **5** formal (believer) 赞同者; **a ~ to** 赞同…的人 ‹*idea, values, theory*›

subscriber trunk dialling *n* [u] Brit 用户长途直拨

subscript /ˈsʌbskrɪpt/
A *adj* 下标的
B *n* 下标

subscription /səbˈskrɪpʃn/ *n* **1** [c and u] (agreement by customer) 订购; **a ~ to sth.** 订购某物; **on** *or* **by ~** 通过订购; **to take out a ~ to a magazine** 订阅杂志 **2** [c] (payment by customer) 预订费 **3** [c and u] Brit (agreement by contributor) 认捐; **a ~ to sth.** 为某事所作的认捐 **4** [c] Brit (monetary contribution) 捐款; **a ~ to sth.** 对某事的捐款 **5** [c and u] (act of financing) 捐资; **public ~** 公众捐资 **6** [c and u] Fin (application) 认购; **a ~ to** *or* **for** 对…的认购 ‹*issue, shares*›

subscription: **~ concert** *n* Brit 联票音乐会; **~ fee, ~ rate** *ns* 预订费; **~ magazine** *n* [不零售的] 预订版杂志; **~ service** *n* 预订服务

subsection /ˈsʌbsekʃn/ *n* [尤指法律文件的] 分项

subsequent /ˈsʌbsɪkwənt/ *adj* 随后的; **~ to sth.** 继某事之后的; **~ generations** 后代; **~ events proved her wrong** 后来发生的事证明她是错的

subsequently /ˈsʌbsɪkwəntli/ *adv* 随后

subservience /səbˈsɜːvɪəns/ *n* [u] **1** pej (submissiveness) 恭顺; **~ to sb./sth.** 对某人/某物俯首帖耳 **2** (subordination) 从属; **a nation which has been kept in ~ for generations** 连续几代受制于人的民族

subservient /səbˈsɜːvɪənt/ *adj* **1** pej (submissive) 恭顺的 **2** (subordinate) 次要的; **to be ~ to an interest/a need** 服从于利益/需要

subset /ˈsʌbset/ *n* **1** (smaller group) 分组 **2** Math 子集

subside /səbˈsaɪd/ *vi* **1** (diminish) «*storm, flames, threat*» 减弱; «*noise, laughter*» 变轻; «*pain, fever, excitement*» 消退 **2** (become lower) «*waters, river*» 回落 **3** (sink) «*house, foundation*» 坍陷; (cave in) «*land, road*» 下沉 **4** (disappear) «*swelling*» 消失 **5** (drop) (into sitting position) 坐下; (into kneeling position) 跪下; (into recumbent position) 躺下; **to ~ into a chair** 坐到椅子上; **to ~ on to a bed/the ground** 躺到床上/地上

subsidence /səbˈsaɪdns, ˈsʌbsɪdns/ *n* [u] 下陷

subsidiarity /səbˌsɪdɪˈærəti/ *n* [u] 辅助原则

subsidiary /səbˈsɪdɪəri, Amer -dɪeri/
A *n* 子公司
B *adj* **1** (less important) 次要的 ‹*matter, role*› **2** *attrib* Comm 附属的 ‹*company*›

subsidize /ˈsʌbsɪdaɪz/ *vt* **1** (help pay for) 补贴 ‹*education, housing, school meals*› **2** (give money to) 资助 ‹*industry, farming*›

subsidy /ˈsʌbsɪdi/ *n* [c and u] 补贴; **EU farming subsidies** 欧盟农业补贴

subsist /səbˈsɪst/ *vi* **1** (live) 维持生活; **to ~ on sth.** 靠…维持生活 ‹*income*›; 靠…活下去 ‹*fruit*› **2** formal (remain in force) «*contract, visa*» 有效; «*right, marriage*» 存续

subsistence /səbˈsɪstəns/ *n* **1** [u and c] (living) 维持生计; **~ on sth.** 靠…维持生活 ‹*income*›; 靠…活下去 ‹*diet*› **2** [u] formal (continuation in force) (of contract, visa) 有效; (of right, marriage) 存续

subsistence: **~ allowance** *n* esp Brit 生活补助; **~ economy** *n* 自给经济; **~ farmer** *n* 自给自足农户; **~ farming** *n* [u] 生存农业 [指收成仅够自身口粮]; **~ level** *n* [u] 勉强糊口的生活水平; **~ wage** *n* 勉强糊口的工资

subsoil /ˈsʌbsɔɪl/ *n* [c and u] 底土

subsonic /ˌsʌbˈsɒnɪk/ *adj* 亚音速的

subspecies /ˈsʌbspiːʃiːz/ *n* (*pl* **subspecies**) 亚种

substance /ˈsʌbstəns/ *n* **1** [c] (type of matter) 东西; **a chemical ~** 化学物质; **a sticky/dangerous/poisonous ~** 黏性/危险/有毒物质; **this ~ should not come into contact with food** 这种东西不可以和食物接触 **2** [c] (drug) [尤指违法的] 药物; **illegal ~s** 毒品; **a ~ abuser** 滥用药物者 **3** [u] (basis in reality) 事实基础; **to have/lack ~** 具有/缺乏事实根据; **there is no/some ~ to sth.** 某事没有/有一定的依据; **to lend ~ to sth.** 使某事有根有据 **4** [u] (essence) 实质; **in ~** formal 本质上 **5** [u] (importance) 重要性; **talks/matters of ~** 重要的会谈/事务; **the meeting yielded little of ~** 会议几乎没有产生实质性成果 **6** [u] (physical matter) 物质; **proteins compose much of the actual ~ of the body** 蛋白质构成了人体物质的大部分

substance abuse *n* [u] (of drugs) 滥用毒品; (of alcohol) 酗酒

substandard /ˌsʌbˈstændəd/ *adj* **1** (inferior) 不合格的 ‹*quality, housing, education*› **2** Ling (non-standard) 不规范的 ‹*language, usage*›

substantial /səbˈstænʃl/ *adj* **1** (considerable in amount, degree) 可观的 ‹*sum, amount*›; 显著的 ‹*difference, increase, fall*›; 重要的 ‹*role, evidence*›; **~ damages** Jur 巨额赔偿金; **a ~ majority** 绝大多数 **2** (solid, bulky) 结实的 **3** (generous) 丰盛的 ‹*meal*› **4** (fundamental) 基本上的; **to be in ~ agreement (over sth.)** 大体同意（某事物） **5** formal (tangible) 真实的 ‹*thing, being*›

substantially /səbˈstænʃəlɪ/ *adv* **1** (considerably) 可观地 ‹*improve, reduce*›; 相当 ‹*lower, higher, more, less*› **2** (solidly) 结实地 ‹*built*› **3** (fundamentally) 大体上 ‹*correct, unchanged*›

substantiate /səbˈstænʃɪeɪt/ *vt* formal 证实; **this claim is hard to ~** 这个断言很难证明

substantiation /səbˌstænʃɪˈeɪʃn/ *n* [u] formal 证实

substantive
A /ˈsʌbstəntɪv, səbˈstæntɪv/ *adj* 重大的
B /ˈsʌbstəntɪv/ *n* dated 名词

substantive law *n* [u] 实体法

substation /ˈsʌbsteɪʃn/ *n* 变电所

substitute /ˈsʌbstɪtjuːt, Amer -tuːt/
A *n* **1** [c and u] (alternative) 代替者; **a milk ~** 代乳品; **a ~ fuel** 代乳燃料; **the local bus service was a poor ~ for their car** 他们坐当地的公交车，这比坐自己的汽车差远了 **2** [c] Sport 替补队员; **to come on** *or* **be brought on as (a) ~** 作为替补队员上场; **a ~ goalkeeper** 替补守门员 **3** [c] Psych 替身; **when her parents died, we became her ~ family** 她的双亲去世后，我们成了她家人的替身
B *vt* **1** (use as replacement) 用…代替; **an understudy was ~d when the star broke a leg** 那位明星腿断了，由替角代替演出 **2** (replace) 替代; **butter can be ~d with margarine in this recipe** 做这道菜可以用人造黄油代替黄油 **3** Sport 替换 ‹*player*›; **he**

was ~d in the second half because of a knee injury 下半场他因膝盖受伤被换下场
C *vi* **1** (act as replacement) 代替; **to ~ for sth.** 代替某事物; **nothing can ~ for the advice your doctor is able to give you** 医生给你的忠告是无可替代的 **2** Sport 担任替补队员; **to ~ for sb.** 替换某人; **he ~d for Robinson in the second half** 下半场他替下了鲁宾逊

substitute: ~'s bench *n* 替补席; **~ teacher** *n* 代课教师

substitution /ˌsʌbstɪ'tju:ʃn, Amer -'tu:-/ *n* **1** [u and c] (use as replacement) 代替; **the ~ of A for B** 用 A 代替 B **2** [u and c] (replacement) 替代; **the ~ of B with** *or* **by A** 用 A 替换 B **3** Sport 替换; **the manager made two ~s** 主教练换了两次人 **4** [u] Math 代换

substratum /'sʌbstrɑ:təm, Amer 'sʌbstreɪtəm/ *n* (*pl* **substrata** /'sʌbstrɑ:tə, Amer 'sʌbstreɪtə/) **1** (lower level) 底层; (subsoil) 底土; (bedrock) 底层岩 **2** fig (basis) 基础; **a ~ of fact** 事实基础

substructure /'sʌbstrʌktʃə(r)/ *n* 基础

subsume /səb'sju:m, Amer -'su:m/ *vt* formal 把…归入; **to ~ sth. under sth.** 把某事物归入某范畴

subsystem /'sʌbsɪstəm/ *n* 子系统

subteen /'sʌbti:n/ *n* Amer 十一二岁的少年

subtenancy /'sʌbtenənsi/ *n* (position of subtenant) 转租承租人身份; (agreement with subtenant) 转租承租合约

subtenant /'sʌbtenənt/ *n* 转租承租人

subtend /səb'tend/ *vt* 对向 ‹*angle*›

subterfuge /'sʌbtəfju:dʒ/ *n* **1** [c] (trick) 诡计; (excuse) 托词; **she got in by a clever ~** 她找了个巧妙的借口进去了 **2** [u] (trickery) 耍花招

subterranean /ˌsʌbtə'reɪmɪən/ *adj* **1** (underground) 地下的 **2** fig (secret) 秘密的 ‹*force, world*›

subtext /'sʌbtekst/ *n* 潜台词

subtitle /'sʌbtaɪtl/
A *n* Publg 副标题
B **subtitles** *npl* Cin, TV 字幕
C *vt* **1** Publg 给…加副标题 ‹*book*› **2** Cin, TV 给…打字幕 ‹*film, documentary*›

subtitling /'sʌbtaɪtlɪŋ/ *n* [u] (action) 打字幕; (words) 字幕

subtle /'sʌtl/ *adj* **1** (barely perceptible) 细微的 ‹*distinction, shift*›; 微妙的 ‹*allusion, meaning, style, irony*› **2** (sophisticated, finely tuned) 精妙的 ‹*design*›; 精湛的 ‹*performance*›; 巧妙的 ‹*idea, analysis, plot, strategy*› **3** (perceptive) 敏锐的; **it wasn't very ~ of you to mention the war** 你提起战争的事考虑欠妥 **4** (delicate) 隐约的 ‹*lighting, blend, colour, shade*›; 淡雅的 ‹*charm*›; 依稀的 ‹*flavour, fragrance*›

subtleness /'sʌtlnɪs/ *n* [u] = **subtlety 1, 2, 3, 4**

subtlety /'sʌtlti/ *n* **1** [u] (slightness) 细微 **2** [u] (sophistication) 精巧; **the ~ of her arguments** 她的论证巧妙缜密 **3** [u] (perceptiveness) 敏锐 **4** [u] (delicacy) 微妙 **5** [c] (fine point) 微妙之处

subtly /'sʌtli/ *adv* **1** (imperceptibly) 不易察觉地 ‹*change, influence*›; 细微地 ‹*different*› **2** (sophisticatedly) 巧妙地 ‹*argue, analyse, evoke, mock*› **3** (delicately) 淡淡地 ‹*flavoured, coloured*›; 微妙地 ‹*humorous*›

subtopic /'sʌbtɒpɪk/ *n* 副题

subtotal /'sʌbtəʊtl/ *n* 部分和

subtract /səb'trækt/
A *vt* **1** Math 减去 ‹*amount*›; **to ~ A from B** 从 B 中减去 A **2** (remove) 去除 ‹*item, amount*›
B *vi* Math 做减法

subtraction /səb'trækʃn/ *n* **1** [u and c] Math (procedure) 减法 **2** [u] (removal) 去除

subtropical /ˌsʌb'trɒpɪkl/ *adj* 亚热带的 ‹*climate, plant*›

subtropics /ˌsʌb'trɒpɪks/ *npl* **the ~** 亚热带

suburb /'sʌbɜ:b/
A *n* 郊区; **an inner ~** 近郊; **an expensive ~** 地价高的市郊; **a leafy ~** 树木茂密的郊区
B **suburbs** *npl* **the ~s** 郊区; **the outer ~s** 远郊

suburban /sə'bɜ:bən/ *adj* **1** (relating to the suburbs) 郊区的 ‹*development, train*›; **a ~ sprawl** 郊区的无序扩张 **2** pej (dull) 平淡乏味的 ‹*lifestyle*›; 古板的 ‹*values, attitude*›

suburbanite /sə'bɜ:bənaɪt/ *n* 郊区居民

suburbanize /sə'bɜ:bənaɪz/ *vt* 使变成郊区

suburbia /sə'bɜ:bɪə/ *n* [u] 郊区

subvention /səb'venʃn/ *n* formal 资助金

subversion /səb'vɜ:ʃn, Amer -'vɜ:rʒn/ *n* [u] 颠覆

subversive /səb'vɜ:sɪv/
A *adj* 颠覆性的; **his books are highly ~** 他的书具有很大的煽动性
B *n* 颠覆分子

subvert /səb'vɜ:t/ *vt* 颠覆 ‹*state, religion, democracy, authority*›

subway /'sʌbweɪ/ *n* **1** Brit (pedestrian tunnel) 地下人行道 **2** Amer (underground railway) 地铁

sub-zero /ˌsʌb'zɪərəʊ/ *adj* 零下的 ‹*temperature*›

succeed /sək'si:d/
A *vi* **1** (achieve success) 成功; **to ~ in business** 做生意获成功; **to ~ in one's exams** 通过考试; **I only ~ed in making things worse** 我结果却把事情弄得更糟; **nothing ~s like success** Prov 一事成, 百事顺; **if at first you don't ~, try, try again** Prov 如果一开始不成功, 那就努力努力再努力 **2** (accede) **to ~ to** 继承 ‹*throne, title, property*›
B *vt* **1** (take place of) 接替 ‹*person*›; **she ~ed her father as chairman** 她接替父亲任董事长 **2** (follow) 接续; **her embarrassment was ~ed by fear** 她尴尬之后感到害怕

succeeding /sək'si:dɪŋ/ *adj attrib* 后续的; **~ generations** 后代; **each ~ year** 随后的每一年

success /sək'ses/ *n* **1** [u] (achievement) 成功; **to meet with ~** 获得成功; **wishing you every ~** 祝你马到成功; **he never had much ~ with women** 他从来未受女性青睐; **to enjoy the sweet smell of ~** 品尝成功的喜悦 **2** [c] (thing that succeeds) 成功的事; (person that succeeds) 成功的人; **to make a ~ of sth.** 把某事做成功; **to be a ~ with the critics/children** 获得评论家/孩子的青睐; **to be a ~ as a teacher/politician** 教书/从政很成功; **to be a ~ in** 在…方面很成功 ‹*life, career, business*›

successful /sək'sesfl/ *adj* **1** (achieving aim) 成功的; **to be ~ in** *or* **at doing sth.** 做成某事; **she was not ~ in her efforts to raise the money** 她没有筹到钱 **2** (having high status) 有成就的 ‹*politician, actor*› **3** (popular, well regarded) 受好评的; (doing well) 畅销的; (profitable) 卖座的; **this film was less ~** 这部电影的票房差一些 **4** (winning, getting through) 获胜的 ‹*team, candidate*›; 通过的 ‹*application*›; **to be ~ in an exam** 通过考试 **5** (happy) 一帆风顺的 ‹*relationship, partnership*›

successfully /sək'sesfəli/ *adv* 成功地

succession /sək'seʃn/ *n* **1** [c] (consecutive number) 一连串; **the party has had a ~ of poor leaders** 该党连续几任领导人都很无能 **2** [u] (sequence) 连续; **in ~** 连续地; **for five years in ~** 连续 5 年; **in close** *or* **quick** *or* **swift ~** 接连不断地; **the days followed each other in quick ~** 日子一天接一天很快过去 **3** [u] (act of inheriting) 继承; (right of inheriting) 继承权; (line of descent) 继承顺序; **to be fifth in ~ to the throne** 是王位的第 5 顺位继承人

successive /sək'sesɪv/ *adj* 连续的

successively /sək'sesɪvli/ *adv* 连续地

successor /sək'sesə(r)/ *n* **1** (person) 继任者; **to be sb.'s ~ as** 接替某人做 ‹*monarch, minister*›; **a worthy ~ to sb.** 某人优秀的接替者 **2** (invention, concept) 替代物; **it is a possible ~ to silicon** 这可能会成为硅的替代品

success: ~ rate *n* 成功率; **~ story** *n* 获得巨大成功的例子

succinct /sək'sɪŋkt/ *adj* 简明的; **could you be a little more ~?** 你能不能再简明扼要一点?

succinctly /sək'sɪŋktli/ *adv* 简要地

succinctness /sək'sɪŋktnɪs/ *n* [u] 简洁

succor /'sʌkə(r)/ *n, vt* Amer = **succour**

succotash /'sʌkətæʃ/ *n* [u] Amer 煮玉米菜豆

succour /'sʌkə(r)/ formal
A *n* [u] 救援; **to give ~ to sb.** 救助某人
B *vt* 救助

succulence /'sʌkjʊləns/ *n* [u] 鲜美多汁

succulent /'sʌkjʊlənt/
A *adj* **1** (juicy) 鲜美多汁的 **2** Bot 肉质的; **a ~ plant/stem** 肉质植物/肉质茎
B *n* 肉质植物

succumb /sə'kʌm/ *vi* **1** (give in) 屈服; **to ~ to persuasion/desire** 屈从于劝说/欲望 **2** (die) 被压垮; **to ~ to a disease** 死于某种疾病; **he eventually ~ed to his injuries** 他受了伤, 最终没能挺过去

such /sʌtʃ/
A *det* **1** (of that type) 那样的; (of this type) 这样的; **in ~ a situation** 在这种情况下; **there was some ~ case last year** 去年有过这类案件; **in ~ a way that ...** 以…的方式; **there's no ~ person/thing** 没有这样的人/事; **until ~ time as ...** 直到…时候 **2** (so great) 如此程度的; **why are you in ~ a hurry?** 你干吗这么急匆匆的? ; **~ good quality as this is rare** 这么好的质量很罕见; **we've had ~ a lot of problems with the new washing machine** 我们这台新洗衣机问题太多了; **ever ~ a lot of people/money** colloq 特多的人/钱; **thanks ever ~ a lot** colloq 太感谢了 **3** (any) 任何的; **you're welcome to ~ money as I have** 我手头的这点钱你尽管用好了; **~ advice as he was given has proved almost worthless** 他所得到的建议证明几乎毫无价值 **4** **~ as it is/they are** (expressing small worth or quantity) 不怎么样的; **the food, ~ as it was, was served at nine o'clock** 这种不怎么样的饭菜还到 9 点钟才端上来; **you can borrow my boots, ~ as they are** 你可以借用我的靴子, 虽然不怎么好
B *pron* **1** (that) 那; (this) 这; **~ is life** 这就是生活; **the damage was ~ that it would cost thousands to repair** 损坏很严重, 要修好得花几千块钱; **~ as** (for example) 例如; (like) 诸如…之类; **there are loads of things to do — ~ as?** 该做的事有一大堆——比如呢? ; **wild flowers ~ as primroses are becoming rare** 报春花之类的野花越来越稀少了; **inflation ~ as occurred last year** 像去年那样的通货膨胀; **as ~** (as being that) 如所指的那样; (exactly) 严格意义上; **we were second-class citizens and they treated us as ~** 我们是二等公民, 他们就是这样对待我们的; **there is no guest house as ~** 没有严格意义上的旅店 **2** (so great) 如此程度; **~ was his anger that he was unable to speak** 他气得话都说不出来了; **he sends her flowers every morning, ~ is his admiration for her** 他对她十分倾慕, 每天早上都给她送花 **3** (suchlike) 诸如此类; **and ~** (things) 诸如此类的事物; (people) 诸如此类的人; **the centre offers activities like canoeing, sailing and ~** 中心有划艇、帆船之类的活动

such-and-such *det* 某; **at ~ a time** 在某个时候; **Mr S~** 某某先生

S

suchlike /'sʌtʃlaɪk/
A *det* 诸如此类的; **caviar, smoked salmon, and ~ delicacies** 鱼子酱、熏三文鱼诸如此类的美味佳肴
B *pron* 诸如此类的东西; **and** *or* **or ~** 等等之类的东西; **lions, tigers, and ~** 狮子、老虎之类的动物

suck /sʌk/
A *vt* **1** (take into mouth) 吸食; **to ~ milk through a straw** 用吸管喝奶; **to ~ the juice from an orange** 吸橙子的汁; **she ~ed the smoke into her lungs** 她把烟吸进肺里; ▸**grandmother** **2** (keep in mouth) 吮; **she ~ed a mint** 她嘴里咂着一颗薄荷糖; **stop ~ing your thumb!** 别吃大拇指!; **to ~ one's teeth** Brit (when feeling doubtful) 疑惑地吸气 **3** (swallow liquid from) 吸食…的汁液; **the baby is ~ing its mother's breast** 婴儿在吃母亲的奶; **he ~ed the orange dry** 他把橙子吸干了 **4** (draw in) 抽吸; **plants ~ moisture from the soil** 植物从土壤中吸取水分; **I was getting ~ed into the affair** 我正被卷入这一事件 **5** taboo sl (fellate) 对…行口交 ‹*person*›; 舔吸 ‹*penis*›
B *vi* **1** (take liquid into mouth) 吸食; **the baby was finding it difficult to ~** 这个婴儿吸奶有困难 **2** (keep object in mouth) 吮吸; **the old man was ~ing at his pipe** 老人在吸烟斗 **3** (draw in liquid) 抽吸; **to ~ on a tube to draw the liquid up** 用管子把液体吸上来 **4** esp Amer colloq (be bad) 令人讨厌; **the weather here really ~s!** 这里的天气真讨厌!; **it ~ed that we had to leave so soon** 糟糕的是, 我们不得不这么快就离开
C *n* 吮吸; **~s to you!** Brit colloq 瞧你这副熊样!

Phrasal verbs

- **suck in** *vt* [~ sb./sth. in, ~ in sb./sth.]
1 (take into mouth) 把…吸进嘴里 ‹*liquid, air*›; **he ~ed in a mouthful of cigar smoke** 他吸了一大口雪茄烟 **2** (draw in) 吸入 ‹*liquid, air*› **3** (pull inwards) 收缩 ‹*cheeks, stomach*› **4** (pull inside) 把…吸进去; **the marsh ~ed him in remorselessly** 沼泽无情地把他吞没了 **5** (involve) 把…卷入; **don't get ~ed in: you know it's dangerous** 别卷入其中, 你知道这很危险
- **suck off** *vt* [~ sb. off, to ~ off sb.] taboo sl 对…行口交 ‹*man*›
- **suck out** *vt* [~ sth. out, ~ out sth.]
1 (take into mouth) 吸食; **to ~ the juice out of an orange** 吸橙子的汁; **the vampire had ~ed all the blood out of her** 吸血鬼把她的血吸干了 **2** (draw out) 把…吸出来; **the pump ~s air out through the valve** 抽气机通过阀门把空气抽出去
- **suck up**
A *vt* [~ sth. up, ~ up sth.]
1 (take into mouth) 吸食; **she was ~ing up milk through a straw** 她正在用吸管喝牛奶 **2** (draw upwards) 把…吸上来; **to ~ up the petrol through the siphon** 用虹吸管把汽油吸上来
B *vi* colloq pej 奉承; **to ~ up to sb.** 奉承某人; **she's only ~ing up to him** 她只是在拍他的马屁

sucker /'sʌkə(r)/
A *n* **1** colloq (dupe) 易上当的人; **he made a real ~ out of you** 他把你当傻瓜耍了; **to be a ~ for sth.** 不由得对某事物入迷; **he's a ~ for compliments** 他特别喜欢受人恭维 **2** Zool (animal's pad) 吸盘 **3** Bot (shoot) 吸根 **4** (suction pad) 橡皮吸盘
B *vt* colloq (dupe) 欺骗; **to ~ sb. out of sth.** 从某人处骗得某物; **to ~ sb. into sth.** 哄骗某人做某事
C *vi* Bot, Hort 长出吸根

sucking /'sʌkɪŋ/ *adj attrib* 吸溜的 ‹*noise, sound*›

sucking pig *n* = **suckling pig**

suckle /'sʌkl/
A *vt* 给…哺乳 ‹*baby, calf*›
B *vi* «*baby, calf*» 吃奶

suckling /'sʌklɪŋ/
A *n* **1** [u] (act) 哺乳 **2** [c] (offspring) (human) 乳儿; (animal) 乳兽; **out of the mouths of babes and ~s** Prov 童言有道
B *adj* 未断奶的 ‹*baby, calf*›

suckling pig *n* [c and u] 乳猪

sucrose /'su:krəʊz, -rəʊs/ *n* [u] 蔗糖

suction /'sʌkʃn/ *n* [u] **1** (forcing fluid into space) 抽吸 **2** (causing adhesion) 吸力

suction: ~ **pad** *n* 吸盘; ~ **pump** *n* 抽吸泵; ~ **valve** *n* 吸入阀

Sudan /su:'dɑ:n/ *pr n* **(the)** ~ 苏丹

Sudanese /ˌsu:də'ni:z/ ▸**p. 503**
A *adj* (of Sudan) 苏丹的; (of the people) 苏丹人的
B *n* 苏丹人

sudden /'sʌdn/ *adj* 突然的; **all of a ~** 突然; **a ~ increase in applications** 申请的骤然增加; **a ~ inspiration** 刹那间的灵感

sudden: ~ **death** *n* [u] Sport 突然死亡法 [平局后加时赛中先得分一方获胜的规则]; **a ~-death play-off** 采用突然死亡法的加时赛; ~ **infant death syndrome** *n* [u] 婴儿猝亡综合征

suddenly /'sʌdnli/ *adv* 突然地

suddenness /'sʌdnnɪs/ *n* [u] 突然; **the ~ of her death shocked everyone** 她的突然去世震惊了每一个人

sudoku /su:'dəʊku:/ *n* [u] 数独游戏 [一种在格子中填数的游戏]

suds /sʌdz/ *npl* **1** (foam) 肥皂泡沫; (soapy water) 肥皂水 **2** Amer colloq dated (beer) 啤酒

sudsy /'sʌdzi/ *adj* 多肥皂泡沫的

sue /su:, sju:/
A *vt* 控告; **to ~ sb. for libel/negligence** 控告某人诽谤/玩忽职守; **she's suing him for divorce/damages** 她正在起诉他要求离婚/要求赔偿
B *vi* **1** Jur 起诉 **2** formal (appeal) **to ~ for pardon** 请求宽恕

suede /sweɪd/ *n* [u] 绒面革; **imitation ~** 仿麂皮; **a pair of ~ gloves** 一副绒面革手套

suet /'su:ɪt, 'sju:ɪt/ *n* [u] [牛、羊等腰部的] 板油; ~ **pudding** Brit 板油布丁

Suez /'sʊɪz/ *pr n* **1** Geog 苏伊士; **the ~ Canal** 苏伊士运河 **2** Brit Hist **~, the ~ crisis** 苏伊士运河危机 [1956年埃及总统纳赛尔宣布苏伊士运河国有化后发生的短暂危机]

suffer /'sʌfə(r)/
A *vt* **1** (undergo) 遭受; **he ~ed a severe heart attack** 他心脏病严重发作; **the region has ~ed severe job losses** 该地区失业问题严重; **to ~ hunger** 挨饿 **2** formal (tolerate) 忍受; **I won't ~ it a moment more** 我一刻也受不了了; **to not ~ fools gladly** 不能容忍愚蠢的人
B *vi* **1** (feel pain) 受苦; **martyrs who ~ed for their faith** 为信仰而受难的殉道者; **she ~s terribly with her feet** colloq 她的脚痛得不得了; **to be the first to ~** 第一个吃苦头; **to ~ in silence** 默默忍受痛苦 **2** (with illness) 患病; **to ~ from depression/high blood pressure** 患抑郁症/高血压; **she was still ~ing from shock** 她仍然惊魂未定 **3** (be in bad situation) 受到妨碍; **business ~ed badly in the recession** 生意在经济衰退期受到重创; **the project ~s from a lack of funds** 这个项目受困于资金短缺 **4** (become worse) 变差; **she keeps late hours, and her work is beginning to ~** 她睡得很晚, 工作质量开始受影响; **his health will ~** 他的健康将会受到损害

sufferance /'sʌfərəns/ *n* [u] **on ~** 勉强地

sufferer /'sʌfərə(r)/ *n* (afflicted by illness) 患者; (afflicted by painful condition) 受难者; **cancer ~s** 癌症患者

suffering /'sʌfərɪŋ/
A *n* [u] (physical) 疼痛; (mental) 痛苦
B **sufferings** *npl* 苦难

suffice /sə'faɪs/
A *vi* «*warning*» 足以; «*sum*» 足够; **~ (it) to say that ...** 只需说…就够了
B *vt* 满足…的需要; **£500 will ~ us** 500 英镑够我们用了

sufficiency /sə'fɪʃnsi/ *n* 足量; **a ~ of fuel for the winter** 足够冬天用的燃料

sufficient /sə'fɪʃnt/ *adj* 充足的 ‹*food, money, time*›; 足够的 ‹*amount, people, books*›; **to be ~ for sb. to do sth.** 足够供某人做某事; **to be more than ~** 绰绰有余; **to have ~ to drink/to live on** 有足够的喝的东西/足以维持生活

sufficiently /sə'fɪʃntli/ *adv* 足够地 ‹*well, large, knowledgeable*›; 充分地 ‹*develop*›

suffix
A /'sʌfɪks/ *n* 后缀
B /sə'fɪks/ *vt* 在末尾附加

suffocate /'sʌfəkeɪt/
A *vi* **1** (die from asphyxiation) 被闷死 **2** (have difficulty breathing) 呼吸困难
B *vt* **1** (asphyxiate) 闷死; **the smoke almost ~d me** 我几乎被烟闷死 **2** (cause difficulty in breathing) 使呼吸困难 **3** fig (oppress) 扼制; **I felt ~d by London** 我感觉伦敦令我窒息

suffocating /'sʌfəkeɪtɪŋ/ *adj* **1** (causing difficulty in breathing) 令人透不过气的 ‹*fumes, atmosphere*› **2** fig (oppressive) 压抑的 ‹*restrictions, family*›

suffocation /ˌsʌfə'keɪʃn/ *n* [u] 窒息; **he died from ~** 他窒息而死

Suffolk /'sʌfək/ *pr n* 萨福克郡

suffrage /'sʌfrɪdʒ/ *n* [u] **1** (right) 选举权; **universal ~** 普选权 **2** (system) 投票选举; **by ~** 通过投票选举

suffragette /ˌsʌfrə'dʒet/ *n* [20世纪初期的] 妇女争取选举权团体的成员; **the ~ movement** 妇女争取选举权运动

suffuse /sə'fju:z/ *vt* liter 布满; **a blush ~d her cheeks** 她满脸通红; **his eyes were ~d with tears** 他泪水盈眶

sugar /'ʃʊgə(r)/
A *n* **1** [u] (unrefined) [植物所含的] 糖; **to refine ~** 炼糖 **2** [u and c] (refined) 食糖; **brown/white ~** 红糖/白糖; **how many ~s do you take?** 你要加多少糖?; **a ~ spoon** 糖勺 **3** esp Amer colloq (term of endearment) 亲爱的; **bye, ~!** 再见, 宝贝儿!
B *excl* euph colloq 完了 [表示恼怒]; **~! I've forgotten my wallet!** 糟了! 我忘带钱包了!
C *vt* 在…中加糖; **~ed almonds** 糖衣杏仁

sugar: ~ **beet** *n* [u] 甜菜; ~ **bowl** *n* 糖罐; ~ **cane** *n* [u] 甘蔗; **~-coated** *adj* **1** lit (sugar-covered) 裹糖衣的 ‹*cereal, biscuit*›; **2** fig (superficially attractive) 巧加粉饰的 ‹*promise, lie*›; ~ **content** *n* [u] 含糖量; ~ **cube** *n* 方糖; ~ **daddy** *n* colloq 甜爹 [以贵重礼物诱惑年轻女子的阔佬]; ~ **diabetes** ▸**p. 377** *n* [u] 糖尿病; **~-free** *adj* 不含糖的

sugariness /'ʃʊgərɪnɪs/ *n* [u] 甜腻

sugarless /'ʃʊgəlɪs/ *adj* 无糖的

sugar: ~ **loaf** *n* 塔糖; ~ **lump** *n* Brit 方糖; ~ **maple** *n* [u and c] 糖槭; ~ **mouse** *n* 鼠形糖; ~ **plantation** *n* 甘蔗种植园; **~plum** *n* 小圆糖果; ~ **soap** *n* [u] Brit 糖皂; ~ **sprinkler** *n* 撒糖器; ~ **tongs** *npl* 方糖夹钳

sugary /'ʃʊgəri/ *adj* **1** (sweet) 甜的 **2** (sugar-like) 糖一样的 **3** fig pej (sentimental) 甜腻腻的 ‹*voice, tone, person, melody*›

suggest /sə'dʒest, Amer səg'dʒ-/
A *vt* **1** (propose) 建议; **I ~ a little walk** 我建议去散会儿步; **the company ~ed that I resign** *or* **should resign** Brit 公司建议我辞职; **I ~ed going in my car** 我提议坐我的车去 **2** (recommend) 推荐; **may I ~ a white wine with this dish?** 我可以推荐一种白葡萄酒来配这道菜吗?; **who do you ~ for the job?** 你推荐谁来做这份工作? **3** (state as

S

possibility) 认为; **the truth, I ~, is different** 依我看，事实并非如此; **can you ~ how he managed to do it?** 你能不能说说他是如何做到的? **4** (indicate) 表明; **the symptoms ~ a minor heart attack** 症状显示这是轻微的心脏病发作; **what do these results ~ to you?** 你觉得这些结果说明什么呢?; **the evidence ~s that spending should be cut** 证据表明应该削减开支 **5** (evoke) 使人想到; **what did the sound ~ to you?** 那声音让你想到了什么? **6** (insinuate) 暗示; **I would never ~ such a thing** 我决不会有这样的意思; **are you ~ing I'm lazy?** 你言下之意是说我懒吗?

B *v refl* **to ~ itself** 出现; **an idea ~ed itself to me** 我想到了一个主意

suggestible /sə'dʒestəbl, Amer səg'dʒ-/ *adj* 易受他人影响的

suggestion /sə'dʒestʃn, Amer səg'dʒ-/ *n* **1** [c] (proposal) 建议; **to put forward** *or* **offer** *or* **make a ~ (about sth.)** (针对某事物)提出建议; **there is no ~ of any illegality** 没人提出违法指控 **2** [u] (recommendation) 提议; **at** *or* **on sb.'s ~** 在某人的提议之下 **3** [c] (hint) 迹象; **the merest ~ of a smile crossed her face** 她脸上露出一丝不易察觉的微笑 **4** [u] Psych 心理暗示; **the power of ~** 暗示的力量

suggestions box *n* 建议箱

suggestive /sə'dʒestɪv, Amer səg'dʒ-/ *adj* **1** (evocative) 引起联想的 ‹*writing, aroma, effect*›; **to be ~ of sth.** 让人想起某事物 **2** (sexually) 性暗示的 ‹*glance, remark*›

suggestively /sə'dʒestɪvli, Amer səg'dʒ-/ *adv* 性暗示地

suggestiveness /sə'dʒestɪvnɪs, Amer səg-'dʒ-/ *n* [u] 性暗示

suicidal /ˌsuːɪ'saɪdl, ˌsjuː-/ *adj* **1** (tending to suicide) 有自杀倾向的; **I felt completely ~** 我真想自杀 **2** (potentially disastrous) 自杀性的 ‹*policy, attempt, folly*›

suicidally /ˌsuːɪ'saɪdəli, ˌsjuːɪ-/ *adv* **1** (to the extent of suicide) 有自杀倾向地; **~ depressed** 沮丧消沉得想自杀 **2** (potentially disastrously) 自杀性地 ‹*leap, drive*›

suicide /'suːɪsaɪd, 'sjuː-/ *n* **1** [u and c] (action, instance) 自杀; **to attempt/commit ~** 企图自杀/自杀 **2** [c] (person) 自杀者 **3** [u] fig (disastrous course) 自毁; **it would be political ~ to do that** 那么做会断送政治前程

suicide: ~ attack *n* 自杀式袭击; **~ bomber** *n* 人体炸弹; **~ mission** *n* 自杀式任务; **~ note** *n* 绝命书; **~ pact** *n* [集体] 自杀协议; **~ rate** *n* 自杀率

suit /suːt, sjuːt/

A *n* **1** (jacket and trousers) 套装; **he is wearing a grey ~** 他穿着一套灰西装; **a ~ of clothes** 一套衣服 **2** (jacket and skirt) 套裙 **3** (clothes for particular activity) [特种用途的] 成套服装; **a flying/protective ~** 飞行服/防护服 **4** (in cards) 所有同花色的牌; **four cards of the same ~** 4张同花色的牌; **to follow ~** (in card games) 跟牌; fig (do the same) 照着做 **5** Jur (lawsuit) 诉讼; **to lose/win a ~** 败诉/胜诉; **a civil/divorce ~** 民事/离婚诉讼; **they have brought** *or* **filed a ~ for damages against the company** 他们已经起诉该公司要求损害赔偿 **6** colloq pej (person) 要员

B *vt* **1** (be convenient for) 对…方便; (be acceptable to) 中…的意; **it doesn't ~ us to come that day** 我们那天不方便过来; **if you want to go by bus, that ~s me fine** 要是你想坐公交车去，那正合我意; **to ~ sb. down to the ground** Brit colloq 完全合某人的心意; **to ~ sb.'s book** Brit colloq (be convenient for) 对某人方便; (be acceptable to) 中某人的意 **2** (be appropriate for) 适合; **the job doesn't ~ her** 这工作不适合她; **the house ~s our requirements** 这房子符合我们的要求 **3** (look good on) 与…相配; **that dress really ~s you** 那条连衣裙你穿很好看; **red doesn't ~ you** 你不适合穿红色 **4** esp Brit (be beneficial for) 适宜; **this hot weather doesn't ~ me** 天这么热，我真受不了 **5** (match) **to ~ sth. to sb./sth.** 使某事物适合某人/某事物; **to ~ the punishment to the crime** 按罚量刑; **to ~ the action to the word** liter 言行一致

C *vi* 合适; **will ten o'clock ~?** 10点钟方便吗?

D *v refl* **1** (please oneself) **to ~ oneself** 照自己的意愿; **I choose my assignments to ~ myself** 我根据自己的喜好挑选任务 **2** (expressing annoyance) **to ~ oneself** 自便; **I think I'll stay in this evening — ~ yourself!** 我今晚就不出去了——随你的便!

suitability /ˌsuːtə'bɪləti, ˌsjuːt-/ *n* [u] 适合; **~ for sth.** 对某物的适合; **~ for** *or* **to sb.** 适合某人; **she questioned the ~ of the film for young children** 她质疑那部电影是否适合儿童观看

suitable /'suːtəbl, 'sjuː-/ *adj* 合适的 ‹*tool, clothes, colour*›; 恰当的 ‹*moment, choice, example*›; 适宜的 ‹*climate, place*›; **~ for sth./doing sth.** 适合某事/做某事的; **would this be a ~ present for your mother?** 这个作为礼物送给你母亲合适吗?

suitableness /ˌsuːtə'blnɪs, ˌsjuːt-/ *n* [u] **= suitability**

suitably /'suːtəbli, 'sjuː-/ *adv* **1** (appropriately) 合适地 ‹*dressed, equipped, behave*›; **~ qualified** 符合条件的 **2** often hum (to the appropriate degree) 恰如其分地 ‹*amazed, contrite*›; **she looked ~ grateful for this information** 对这个消息她恰如其分地表现出了感激

suitcase /'suːtkeɪs, 'sjuː-/ *n* [旅行用的] 手提箱; **to pack/unpack one's ~** 把东西装进手提箱/从手提箱里取出东西; **to live out of a ~** fig 过居无定所的生活

suite /swiːt/ *n* **1** (of furniture) 一套家具; **a bathroom ~** 一套卫浴设备 **2** (of rooms) 套房 **3** Mus 组曲 **4** Comput 套装软件; **a ~ of programs** 一套程序

suited /'suːtɪd, 'sjuː-/

A *adj* 合适的; **to be ~ to** *or* **for sth.** 适合某事物; **they are ideally ~ to each other** 他俩是天造地设的一对

B -suited *combining form* 着…套装的; **a dark~ man** 身穿深色套装的男子

suiting /'suːtɪŋ, 'sjuː-/ *n* [u and c] 西服料

suitor /'suːtə(r), 'sjuː-/ *n* **1** dated (admirer) 求婚者 **2** Fin (prospective buyer) 有意收购者

sulfate /'sʌlfeɪt/ *n* Amer **= sulphate**

sulfide /'sʌlfaɪd/ *n* Amer **= sulphide**

sulfonamide /sʌl'fɒnəmaɪd/ *n* Amer **= sulphonamide**

sulfur /'sʌlfə(r)/ *n* Amer **= sulphur**

sulfuric /sʌl'fjʊərɪk/ *adj* Amer **sulphuric**

sulfurous /'sʌlfərəs/ *adj* Amer **= sulphurous**

sulk /sʌlk/

A *n* 愠怒; **to be in a ~** 生闷气; **to go into a ~** 闹脾气; **to have (a fit of) the ~s** colloq 生(一阵)闷气

B *vi* 生闷气; **to ~ about** *or* **over sth.** 为某事物生闷气

sulkily /'sʌlkɪli/ *adv* 闷闷不乐地

sulkiness /'sʌlkɪnɪs/ *n* [u] (characteristic) 爱生闷气; (behaviour) 闷闷不乐

sulky /'sʌlki/ *adj* 闷闷不乐的

sullen /'sʌlən/ *adj* **1** (bad-tempered) 郁郁寡欢的 ‹*person, expression*›; **he sat in ~ silence** 他闷闷不乐地坐着，一言不发 **2** liter (dark) 阴沉的 ‹*sky, day*›

sullenly /'sʌlənli/ *adv* 闷闷不乐地

sullenness /'sʌlənnɪs/ *n* [u] 郁郁寡欢

sully /'sʌli/ *vt* liter **1** (dirty) 弄脏 ‹*water, surface*›; 玷污 ‹*purity*›; **to ~ one's hands** 弄脏双手 **2** (damage) 损害 ‹*reputation, honour, name*›

sulphate /'sʌlfeɪt/ *n* Brit 硫酸盐

sulphide /'sʌlfaɪd/ *n* Brit 硫化物

sulphonamide /sʌl'fɒnəmaɪd/ *n* Brit 磺胺

sulphur /'sʌlfə(r)/ *n* [u] Brit 硫磺

sulphur dioxide *n* [u] Brit 二氧化硫

sulphuric /sʌl'fjʊərɪk/ *adj* Brit (containing sulphur) 含硫磺的; (containing sulphuric acid) 含硫酸的; **~ acid** 硫酸

sulphurous /'sʌlfərəs/ *adj* Brit **1** (of sulphur) 硫磺的 ‹*vapour, fumes, smell*› **2** (pale yellow) 淡黄的 ‹*yellow*›

sulphur spring *n* 含硫泉

sultan /'sʌltən/ *n* 苏丹 [某些伊斯兰国家统治者的称号]

sultana /sʌl'tɑːnə, Amer -'tænə/ *n* **1** (raisin) 无核小葡萄干 **2** (wife of sultan) 苏丹后妃

sultanate /'sʌltəneɪt/ *n* **1** (office) 苏丹王位; (rule) 苏丹的统治 **2** (territory) 苏丹统治的领土

sultriness /'sʌltrɪnɪs/ *n* [u] 闷热

sultry /'sʌltri/ *adj* **1** (hot and humid) 闷热的 **2** (sensual) 撩人的 ‹*beauty, look, voice*›

sum /sʌm/ *n* **1** (amount of money) 款项; **a six-figure ~** 一笔6位数的款项; **a large ~ of money** 一大笔钱; **to be fined the ~ of £200** 被罚款200英镑 **2** (total from addition) 总和; **the ~ of 7 and 12 is 19** 7加12的和是19 **3** (totality) 全部; **is that the ~ of their achievements?** 那就是他们的全部成就吗?; **to be greater** *or* **more than the ~ of its parts** 个体相加不如集体的力量大; **the ~ and substance of sth.** 某事物的要点; **in ~** formal 总之 **4** Brit colloq (calculation) 算术; **to be good at ~s** 擅长算术; **to do a ~ in one's head** 做心算; **to do one's ~s** 做算术题; fig 估算一下; **to get one's ~s right** 做对算术题; fig 估算正确

Phrasal verb

• **sum up**

A *vi* (*pres p etc.* **-mm-**) **1** (summarize) 总结; **to ~ up, there are three main ways of tackling the problem** 总而言之，这一问题主要有三种解决办法 **2** Jur «*judge*» 概述要点

B *vt* (*pres p etc.* **-mm-**); **[~ sth. up, ~ up sth.]** **1** (summarize) 总结; **in the last chapter I will briefly ~ up my conclusions** 在最后一章，我会简要总结一下我得出的若干结论 **2** Jur «*judge*» 对…作概述 ‹*evidence, case*› **3** (describe concisely) 概括; **the city's problem can be ~med up in a few words: too many people** 这座城市的问题可以用几个字来概括：人太多 **4** (size up) 估量; **to ~ up a situation/person** 估计形势/对某个人作出评判

sumac, sumach /'ʃuːmæk, 'suː-, 'sjuː-/ *n* [u and c] 漆树

Sumatra /sʊ'mɑːtrə/ *pr n* 苏门答腊岛

summa cum laude /ˌsʊmə kʊm 'laʊdeɪ/ Amer

A *adv* 以最优等级; **he graduated ~** 他以最优异的成绩毕业

B *adj* 最优等级的

summarily /'sʌmərəli, Amer sə'merəli/ *adj* 即刻 ‹*dismissed, executed, evicted*›

summarize /'sʌməraɪz/ *vt* 总结

summary /'sʌməri/

A *n* 总结; **in ~** 总的来说; **here is a ~ of the news** 现在播放新闻概要

B *adj attrib* **1** esp Jur (without usual procedure) 即决的 ‹*fine, arrest*›; **~ execution** 草草处决 **2** (summarizing) 概要的 ‹*account, statement*›

summation /sə'meɪʃn/ *n* **1** [u and c] formal (addition, accumulation) 累加; **the exhibition is a ~ of her life's work** 这次展览是她一生作品的汇总 **2** [u and c] (précis) 总结 **3** [c] Math (total) 总和

summer /'sʌmə(r)/

A ▸**p. 692** *n* 夏天; **in ~** 在夏季; **last/next ~** 去年/明年夏季; **a lovely ~'s day** 美好的夏日; **a ~ tourist** *or* **visitor** 夏季游客; **~ clothes** 夏装; **the golden ~ of her life** fig 她生命中的黄金岁月

B **summers** *npl* liter 年岁; **a youth of sixteen ～s** 一个16岁的花季少年
C *vi* 度夏; **we used to ～ in Provence** 我们过去常在普罗旺斯消夏

summer: ～ camp *n* esp Amer 夏令营; **～ holiday** **1** (vacation) 夏天假期; **2** Univ, Sch 暑假; **the ～ holidays** 暑假; **～ house** *n* 凉亭; **～ lightning** *n* [u] 热闪电; **S～ Palace** *n* **the S～ Palace** 颐和园; **～ pudding** *n* [u and c] Brit [把水果和葡萄干放入面包做成的] 夏令布丁; **～ resort** *n* 避暑胜地; **～ sausage** *n* [u] Amer 夏令香肠 [一种干而硬的烟熏香肠]; **～ school** *n* [c and u] (part of academic course) 暑期班; (independent course) 暑期课程; **～ solstice** *n* [u] 夏至; **～ squash** *n* [c and u] 西葫芦; **～ term** *n* [一学年的] 下半学期; **～ time** *n* [u] Brit 夏令时; **～ vacation** *n* Amer **= ～ holiday**

summery /ˈsʌməri/ *adj* 夏季的 ‹*weather*›; 夏季特有的 ‹*look*›; 适合夏季的 ‹*dress*›; **it's quite ～ today** 今天热得像夏天

summing-up /ˌsʌmɪŋˈʌp/ *n* [c and u] (*pl* **summings-up**) **1** Jur 证据概述 **2** (recapitulation) 总结

summit /ˈsʌmɪt/ *n* **1** (mountain peak) 山顶 **2** fig (high point) 巅峰; **the ～ of his career** 职业生涯的巅峰 **3** Pol (meeting) 首脑会议; **an economic/a peace ～** 经济/和平峰会; *modif* 政府首脑间的 ‹*talks*›; **the annual ～ conference** 年度峰会

summitry /ˈsʌmɪtri/ *n* [u] 峰会外交

summon /ˈsʌmən/ *vt* **1** (call for) 召唤; **to ～ sb. to do sth.** 召唤某人做某事; **to ～ sb. in** 召唤某人进来; **to ～ reinforcements** 调来援军; **to ～ a taxi** 叫出租车 **2** Jur 传唤 ‹*defendant, witness*› **3** (convene) 召集 ‹*parliament, conference*› **4** **= summon up**

Phrasal verb

- **summon up** *vt* [**～ sth. up, ～ up sth.**] **1** (muster) 鼓起 ‹*courage*›; **to ～ up strength/interest** 使出力气/提起兴趣; **she finally ～ed up a smile** 她终于挤出一丝笑容 **2** (acquire, gather) 取得 ‹*support, help, resources*› **3** (call to mind) 唤起; **the photo ～ed up memories of years gone by** 这张照片勾起了对逝去岁月的回忆

summons /ˈsʌmənz/
A *n* **1** Jur 传票; **a ～ for sth.** 因某事收到的传票; **to serve a ～ on sb.** 发出传票 **2** (order) 召见令; **a ～ to do** *or* **for sth.** 做某事的命令
B *vt* 传…出庭; **he was ～ed to attend court** 他被传唤出庭

sumo /ˈsuːməʊ/ ▸**p. 307** *n* **1** [u] **～ (wrestling)** 相扑 **2** [c] **～ (wrestler)** 相扑手

sump /sʌmp/ *n* **1** Aut [发动机下面的] 集油槽 **2** (hollow) 集水坑

sumptuous /ˈsʌmptʃʊəs/ *adj* 奢华的; **a ～ feast** 盛宴

sumptuously /ˈsʌmptʃʊəsli/ *adv* 丰盛地 ‹*feast*›; 奢华地 ‹*decorate*›

sumptuousness /ˈsʌmptʃʊəsnɪs/ *n* [u] 奢华

sum total *n* (of money) 总额; fig (of achievements) 全部

sun /sʌn/
A *n* **1** [c] (in solar system) 太阳; **the ～ is rising/setting** 太阳正在升起/落下; **the ～ is shining** 阳光照耀; **an eclipse of the ～** 日食; **to be up before the ～** 日出之前起床; **with the ～** (at sunrise) 日出时; (at sunset) 日落时; **I get up with the ～** 我日出即起; **under the ～** (on earth) 世上的; (in existence) 存在的; **we talked about everything under the ～** 天南地北, 我们无所不谈; **there's no reason under the ～ why he should be here** 他根本没有任何理由待在这儿 **2** [u] (sunlight) 阳光; **the warmth of the afternoon ～** 午后阳光的温暖; **this room gets (the) ～ in the mornings** 这个房间上午可以晒到太阳; **in the ～** (in sunny position) 在阳光下; (in sunny country) 在阳光充足的地方; **a place in the ～** (sunny position) 阳光充足之处; (home in sunny country) 阳光灿烂的家园; (good situation) 优越的处境; **out of the ～** 不在阳光下; **to keep out of the ～** 避开阳光的照射 **3** [c] Astron (any star) 恒星
B *v refl* (*pres p etc.* **-nn-**) **to ～ oneself** 晒太阳

Sun. ▸**p. 182** *abbr* **= Sunday**

sun: ～-baked *adj* 晒得干硬的; **～bath** *n* 日光浴

sunbathe /ˈsʌnbeɪð/
A *vi* 晒日光浴
B *n* Brit 日光浴

sun: ～bather *n* 晒日光浴的人; **～bathing** *n* [u] 日光浴; **～beam** *n* 阳光光束; **～bed** *n* (lounger) 日光浴椅; (with sunlamp) 太阳灯日光浴床; **～belt** *n* Amer **the ～belt** 阳光地带 [尤指美国南部从佛罗里达州至加利福尼亚州之间的地区]; **the ～belt states** 阳光地带诸州; **～blind** *n* Brit 百叶窗; **～block** *n* [c and u] 防晒霜; **～burn** *n* [u] 晒伤; **～burned, ～burnt** *adj* **1** (burnt) 晒伤的; **2** (tanned) 晒黑的; **～cream** *n* [c and u] 防晒霜

sundae /ˈsʌndeɪ, Amer -diː/ *n* [c and u] 圣代冰激凌 [一种加水果、果仁等的冰激凌]

Sunday /ˈsʌndeɪ, -di/ ▸**p. 182**
A *n* 星期日; **on ～** 在星期日; **on ～s/every ～** 每周星期日; **～ morning/afternoon/night** 星期日早晨/下午/晚上; **this/last/next ～** 本周日/上周日/下周日; **not in a month of ～s** 遥遥无期
B **Sundays** *npl* Brit colloq **the ～s** 星期日报

Sunday: ～ best *n* [去教堂时穿的] 最好的衣服; **～ driver, ～ motorist** *ns* pej [因不熟练等仅偶尔开车的] 星期日司机; **～ observance** *n* [u] 守星期天安息日; **～ opening** *n* [u] 周日营业; **～ paper** *n* 星期日报

Sunday school *n* [c and u] 主日学校

Sunday school teacher *n* 主日学校教师

Sunday trading *n* [u] 周日营业; **～ hours/laws/restrictions** 周日营业时间/法规/限制规定

sun deck *n* **1** (on ship) 日光甲板 **2** esp Amer, Austral (attached to house) 晒台

sunder /ˈsʌndə(r)/ *vt* liter 分开 ‹*family, partners*›; 使分离 ‹*whole*›

sundial /ˈsʌndaɪəl/ *n* 日晷

sundown /ˈsʌndaʊn/ *n* esp Amer **= sunset 1**

sun: ～-drenched *adj* 阳光充足的; **～dress** *n* 太阳裙; **～-dried** *adj* 晒干的 ‹*tomatoes, bricks*›

sundry /ˈsʌndri/
A *adj attrib* 杂七杂八的 ‹*objects, items*›; **all and ～** 所有人; **to all and ～** 对各色人等
B **sundries** *npl* 杂项

sun-filled /ˈsʌnfɪld/ *adj* 充满阳光的

sunflower /ˈsʌnflaʊə(r)/ *n* 向日葵; **～ oil/seed** 葵花籽油/葵花籽

sung /sʌŋ/ *pp* ▸**sing A, B**

sun: ～glasses *npl* 墨镜; **to wear ～glasses** 戴墨镜; **～ god** *n* 太阳神; **～ goddess** *n* 太阳女神; **～ hat** *n* 阔边遮阳帽

sunk /sʌŋk/ *pp* ▸**sink A, B**

sunken /ˈsʌŋkən/ *adj* **1** (submerged) 沉入海底的 ‹*ship, treasure*› **2** (recessed) 凹陷的 ‹*cheeks, eyes*›; 干瘪的 ‹*person*› **3** (low) 低洼的 ‹*terrace, living area*›; **a ～ bath** 嵌入地面的浴缸

sun: ～-kissed *adj* (warmed) 晒暖的; (made brown) 晒黑的; **～lamp** *n* 太阳灯 [能发出紫外线, 用于治疗等]

sunless /ˈsʌnlɪs/ *adj* 没有阳光的

sun: ～light *n* [u] 阳光; **a shaft of ～light** 一道阳光; **～lit** *adj* 阳光照耀的; **～ lotion** *n* **= ～cream**; **～ lounge** *n* Brit 阳光房; **～lounger** *n* Brit 日光浴椅

Sunni /ˈsʌni/ *n* **1** [u] (branch of Islam) 逊尼派 [伊斯兰教两大派别之一] **2** [c] (adherent) **～ (Muslim)** 逊尼派教徒

sunny /ˈsʌni/ *adj* **1** (bright) 阳光充足的; **～ intervals** *or* **periods** 间晴; **a lovely ～ morning** 阳光灿烂的美好早晨 **2** (sunlit, facing the sun) 向阳的 ‹*flat, garden*›; **～ side up** Amer [鸡蛋] 单面煎的 **3** (cheerful) 快乐的 ‹*temperament, person*›; **she usually looks on the ～ side** 她遇事通常都往好处看; **to be on the ～ side of 50** colloq 不到 50 岁

sun: ～ oil *n* 防晒油; **～ protection factor** *n* 防晒系数

sunrise /ˈsʌnraɪz/ *n* **1** [u] (time) 日出时分; **at ～** 日出时 **2** [c] (event) 日出; **it was a beautiful ～** 那是个美丽的日出

sunrise industry *n* [尤指与电子或通信产业相关的] 朝阳产业

sun: ～roof *n* [汽车的] 天窗; **～ room** *n* esp Amer **= ～ lounge**; **～screen** *n* [u and c] 防晒霜; **～seeker** *n* 追求阳光者 [指寻找阳光充裕之地度假或居住的人]

sunset /ˈsʌnset/ *n* **1** [u] (time) 日落时分; **at ～** 日落时 **2** [c] (event) 日落 **3** [u] fig (later years) 晚年

sunset industry *n* 夕阳产业 [指每况愈下的传统产业]

sunshade /ˈsʌnʃeɪd/ *n* (parasol) 遮阳伞; (awning in car) 遮阳板

sunshine /ˈsʌnʃaɪn/
A *n* [u] **1** (sunlight) 阳光; **bright/dazzling/warm ～** 明媚的/耀眼的/和煦的阳光; **their music can bring a ray of ～** fig 他们的音乐可以带来一丝欢乐 **2** (sunny weather) 晴天; **life's not all ～ and roses** 生活并不总是充满阳光与鲜花 **3** Brit colloq (as address) 老兄; **hi, ～!** 嗨, 哥们儿!
B *adj* Amer 阳光的 [指要求政府部门的某些程序透明]; **～ laws/bill** 阳光法律/法案

sunshine: ～ roof *n* **= sunroof**; **S～ State** *n* Amer **the S～ State** 阳光州 [美国的佛罗里达、新墨西哥、加利福尼亚或南达科他州的别称]

sun: ～spot *n* 太阳黑子; **～stroke** *n* [u] 中暑; **～suit** *n* [儿童穿的] 太阳装

suntan /ˈsʌntæn/
A *n* 晒黑; **to get a ～** 被晒黑
B *modif* 防晒的; **～ oil/lotion/cream** 防晒油/乳液/霜

sun: ～tanned *adj* 晒黑的; **～trap** *n* Brit 避风向阳处; **～ umbrella** *n* 阳伞; **～up** *n* esp Amer **= sunrise 1**; **～ visor** *n* [汽车挡风玻璃上方的] 遮阳板; **～ worshipper** *n* **1** Relig 崇拜太阳者; **2** colloq (sunbather) 迷恋日光浴的人

super /ˈsuːpə(r), ˈsjuː-/
A *adj* colloq 顶呱呱的; **how ～ to see you!** 见到你真是好极了!
B *n* **1** [u and c] Amer (petrol) 高级汽油 [指高辛烷值汽油] **2** colloq **= superintendent 2** **3** Amer colloq **= superintendent 3**
C *excl* colloq 好极了

superable /ˈsuːpərəbl, ˈsjuː-/ *adj* formal 能够克服的

superabundance /ˌsuːpərəˈbʌndəns, ˌsjuː-/ *n* [c and u] formal or liter 过剩; **we have food in ～** 我们的食物过多

superabundant /ˌsuːpərəˈbʌndənt, ˌsjuː-/ *adj* formal or liter 过剩的; **a ～ harvest** 大丰收

superannuate /ˌsuːpərˈænjʊeɪt, ˌsjuː-/ *vt* 使领养老金退休

superannuated /ˌsuːpərˈænjʊeɪtɪd, ˌsjuː-/ *adj* **1** (belonging to superannuation scheme) 领养老金退休的 ‹*person, employee*› **2** colloq (outdated) 年老不能工作的 ‹*person*›; 过时的 ‹*vehicle, idea, equipment*›

superannuation /ˌsuːpərˌænjʊˈeɪʃn, ˌsjuː-/ *n* Admin **1** [c] (pension) 养老金; **a ～ fund/scheme** 退休金基金/计划 **2** [c] (amount) [从

S

工资里定期扣除的] 养老基金 3 [u] (process) 领养老金退休

superb /suː'pɜːb, sjuː-/ *adj* 1 (excellent) 极好的 ‹*view, meal*›; 一流的 ‹*facilities, player, skill*› 2 (magnificent) 豪华的 ‹*mansion*›; 极度的 ‹*aplomb*›

superbly /suː'pɜːbli, sjuː-/ *adv* 1 (very well) 出色地 ‹*behave, perform, play*› 2 (extremely) 非常 ‹*fit, skilled*› 3 (magnificently) 极度地 ‹*majestic*›

Super Bowl *n* **the ~** (美国) 超级碗橄榄球赛

> **the Super Bowl**
>
> 超级碗橄榄球赛，美国橄榄球联盟（National Football League，简称 NFL）冠军赛。始于 1967 年。NFL 分为两大联合会：全国橄榄球联合会（National Football Conference）和美国橄榄球联合会（American Football Conference，简称 AFC），各有 16 支球队。两个联合会又各分为东、西、南、北四个赛区，每个赛区 4 支球队。经过常规赛和季后赛的角逐，双方的冠军队最终进行超级碗的争夺。一般在每年 2 月初举行，为美国最受欢迎的体育赛事。

superbug /'suːpəbʌg, 'sjuː-/ *n* [耐抗菌素的] 超级病菌

supercargo /'suːpəkɑːgəʊ, 'sjuː-/ *n* (*pl* **~es** *or* **~s**) [商船上的] 货物管理员

supercharged /'suːpətʃɑːdʒd, 'sjuː-/ *adj* 1 Aut 增压的 ‹*engine, racer*› 2 fig (highly emotional) 极度激动的 ‹*reunion*›; 语气强烈的 ‹*word*›

supercharger /'suːpətʃɑːdʒə(r), 'sjuː-/ *n* 增压器

supercilious /ˌsuːpə'sɪlɪəs, ˌsjuː-/ *adj* pej 傲慢的

superciliously /ˌsuːpə'sɪlɪəsli, ˌsjuː-/ *adv* pej 傲慢地

superciliousness /ˌsuːpə'sɪlɪəsnɪs, ˌsjuː-/ *n* [u] pej 傲慢

superclass /'suːpəklɑːs, 'sjuː-, Amer -klæs/ *n* 总纲

supercomputer /'suːpəkəmˌpjuːtə(r), 'sjuː-/ *n* 超级计算机

supercomputing /'suːpəkəmˌpjuːtɪŋ, 'sjuː-/ *n* [u] 超级运算

superconducting /ˌsuːpəkən'dʌktɪŋ, ˌsjuː-/, **superconductive** /ˌsuːpəkən'dʌktɪv, ˌsjuː-/ *adjs* 超导的 ‹*device, material*›

superconduction /ˌsuːpəkən'dʌkʃn, ˌsjuː-/, **superconductivity** /ˌsuːpəˌkɒndʌk'tɪvəti, ˌsjuː-/ *ns* [u] 超导（电）性

superconductivity /ˌsuːpəˌkɒndʌk'tɪvəti, ˌsjuː-/ *n* [u] 超导（电）性

super-duper /ˌsuːpə'duːpə(r), ˌsjuː-/ colloq hum

A *adj* 特好的

B *excl* 太棒了

superego /'suːpəregəʊ, 'sjuː-, -iːgəʊ/ *n* 超我

superette /ˌsuːpə'ret/ *n* Amer 小型超市

superficial /ˌsuːpə'fɪʃl, ˌsjuː-/ *adj* 1 (surface) 外表的; **only a ~ wound** 只是皮外伤 2 (cursory) 粗略的 ‹*glance*› 3 (apparent) 表面上的 ‹*resemblance*› 4 pej (sketchy) 肤浅的 ‹*book*›; 皮毛的 ‹*knowledge, education*› 5 pej (shallow) 浅薄的 ‹*person*›

superficiality /ˌsuːpəˌfɪʃɪ'æləti, ˌsjuː-/ *n* [u] 1 (surface nature) 表层 2 (mere appearance) 外表 3 pej (sketchiness) 肤浅 4 pej (shallowness) 浅薄

superficially /ˌsuːpə'fɪʃəli, ˌsjuː-/ *adv* 1 (on surface) 外表上 ‹*damage, wound*› 2 (apparently) 表面上 ‹*similar, attractive*› 3 (sketchily) 肤浅地 ‹*know*›

superfine /'suːpəfaɪn, 'sjuː-/ *adj* 1 Comm 特级的; **~ sugar** 精制糖 2 (very subtle) 细微的 ‹*distinction*›

superfluity /ˌsuːpə'fluːəti, ˌsjuː-/ *n* 1 [c and u] (excess) 过剩 2 [c] (unnecessary thing) 多余物 3 [u] = **superfluousness**

superfluous /suː'pɜːfluəs, sjuː-/ *adj* 多余的; **~ hair** 过多的毛发; **I felt rather ~** 我感到自己是多余的

superfluously /suː'pɜːfluəsli, sjuː-/ *adv* 多余地

superfluousness /suː'pɜːfluəsnɪs, sjuː-/ *n* [u] 多余

supergiant /'suːpədʒaɪənt, 'sjuː-/ *n* 超巨星

superglue /'suːpəgluː, 'sjuː-/

A *n* [u and c] 强力胶

B *vt* 用强力胶粘住

supergrass /'suːpəgrɑːs, 'sjuː-, Amer -græs/ *n* Brit colloq [向警方供出大量涉案人员的] 超级告密者

supergroup /'suːpəgruːp, 'sjuː-/ *n* 超级摇滚乐队

superhero /'suːpəˌhɪərəʊ, 'sjuː-/ *n* [小说、电影等中拥有非凡力量的] 超级英雄

superhighway /'suːpəhaɪweɪ, 'sjuː-/ *n* Amer 高速公路

superhuman /ˌsuːpə'hjuːmən, ˌsjuː-/ *adj* 超人的

superimpose /ˌsuːpərɪm'pəʊz, ˌsjuː-/ *vt* 使叠映; **to ~ sth. on sth.** 把…叠放在某物上 ‹*picture*›; 把…套录在某物上 ‹*soundtrack*›; **~d images** 叠映的图像

superintend /ˌsuːpərɪn'tend, ˌsjuː-/ *vt* formal 主管

superintendent /ˌsuːpərɪn'tendənt, ˌsjuː-/ *n* 1 (supervisor) 主管人; **park ~** 公园负责人 2 (police officer) **(police) ~** Brit 警官; Amer 警长 3 Amer (caretaker of large building) [大楼的] 管理员

superior /suː'pɪərɪə(r), sjuː-, sʊ-/

A *adj* 1 (better than average) 上等的 ‹*product*›; 超常的 ‹*intelligence*›; 优秀的 ‹*team, candidate*› 2 (better than another) 更好的 ‹*method, player*›; 占优势的 ‹*forces, numbers*›; **to be ~ in sth.** 在某事上占优; **to be ~ to sth./sb.** 优于某事物/某人 3 (higher in rank) 级别更高的 ‹*officer*›; **to be ~ to sb.** 比某人地位高 4 pej (condescending) 高傲的 5 Print 上标的 ‹*character, number*›

B *n* 1 (in hierarchy) 上司 2 (in quality, achievement) (person) 更优秀的人; (thing) 更好的事物 3 Relig 修道院院长

superior court *n* (in England) 高等法院; (in US) [美国某些州的] 上级法院

superiority /suːˌpɪəri'ɒrəti, sjuː-, Amer -'ɔːr-/ *n* [u] 1 (in quality, achievement) 优越（性）; **~ over sb./sth.** 对某人/某物的优势; **~ in sth.** 在某方面的优势 2 (in hierarchy) 上级 3 pej (condescension) 优越感

superiority complex *n* [为掩饰自卑和挫折感而表现出的] 自大情结

superlative /suː'pɜːlətɪv, sjuː-/

A *adj* 1 (consummate) 最好的; **in ~ condition** 处于最佳状态; **a demonstration of ~ skill** 纯熟技巧的展示 2 Ling 最高级的 ‹*form, adjective, adverb*›

B *n* 最高级; **a review full of ~s** 言过其实的评论

superlatively /suː'pɜːlətɪvli, sjuː-/ *adv* 极度地; **~ well** 绝佳

superman /'suːpəmæn, 'sjuː-/ *n* (*pl* **supermen** /'suːpəmen, 'sjuː-/) 超人

supermarket /'suːpəmɑːkɪt, 'sjuː-/ *n* 超市; **a ~ chain** 连锁超市

supermodel /'suːpəmɒdl, 'sjuː-/ *n* 超级名模

supernatural /ˌsuːpə'nætʃrəl, ˌsjuː-/

A *adj* 超自然的 ‹*being, power*›; 神奇的 ‹*phenomenon, event*›

B *n* **the ~** 超自然现象

supernaturally /ˌsuːpə'nætʃrəli, ˌsjuː-/ *adv* 不可思议地

supernormal /ˌsuːpə'nɔːml, ˌsjuː-/ *adj* 超常的 ‹*power, phenomenon*›; 非同一般的 ‹*human*›; **a ~ rate of growth** 超常的增长率

supernova /ˌsuːpə'nəʊvə, ˌsjuː-/ *n* (*pl* **supernovae** /ˌsuːpə'nəʊvi, ˌsjuː-/) 超新星

supernumerary /ˌsuːpə'njuːmərəri, ˌsjuː-, Amer -'nuːmreri/

A *adj* 1 Admin 编外的 ‹*staff*› 2 (redundant) 多余的 ‹*person, object*› 3 Cin, Theat 跑龙套的 ‹*actor*›

B *n* 1 Admin 编外人员 2 Cin, Theat 龙套

superorder /'suːpərɔːdə(r), 'sjuː-/ *n* 总目

superordinate /ˌsuːpər'ɔːdɪnət, ˌsjuː-/

A *adj* 地位更高的; **to be ~ to sb./sth.** 比某人/某事物级别更高

B *n* 1 (higher in status) (person) 级别更高的人; (thing) 级别更高的事物 2 Ling 上义词

superphosphate /ˌsuːpə'fɒsfeɪt, ˌsjuː-/ *n* [u] 过磷酸钙

superpose /ˌsuːpə'pəʊz, ˌsjuː-/ *vt* formal 叠放; **to ~ sth. on sth.** 把某物叠放在某物上

superpower /'suːpəpaʊə(r), 'sjuː-/ *n* 超级大国; **a ~ summit** 超级大国峰会

super-rich /ˌsuːpə'rɪtʃ, ˌsjuː-/

A *n* **the ~** 超级富豪

B *adj* 超级富有的

supersaturated /ˌsuːpə'sætʃəreɪtɪd, ˌsjuː-/ *adj* 过饱和的

superscript /'suːpəskrɪpt, 'sjuː-/

A *adj* 标在上面的

B *n* 上标字符

supersede /ˌsuːpə'siːd, ˌsjuː-/ *vt* 取代

supersensitive /ˌsuːpə'sensətɪv, ˌsjuː-/ *adj* 超灵敏的 ‹*device, sensor*›; 超敏锐的 ‹*hearing, eyes*›; 非常敏感的 ‹*skin, area*›; **to be ~ to sth.** 对某物极其敏感

supersize /'suːpəsaɪz, 'sjuː-/

A *adj* 超大的

B *vt* 大幅度增大; **~d suitcases on wheels** 超大滚轮行李箱

supersonic /ˌsuːpə'sɒnɪk, ˌsjuː-/ *adj* 超音速的

supersonically /ˌsuːpə'sɒnɪkli, ˌsjuː-/ *adv* 以超音速

superstar /'suːpəstɑː(r), 'sjuː-/ *n* 超级明星; **to achieve ~ status** 获得超级明星的地位

superstate /'suːpəsteɪt, 'sjuː-/ *n* [由数个国家组成的] 超国家

superstition /ˌsuːpə'stɪʃn, ˌsjuː-/ *n* 1 [u] (believing irrationally) 迷信 2 [c] (belief) 迷信观念; (practice) 迷信行为

superstitious /ˌsuːpə'stɪʃəs, ˌsjuː-/ *adj* 迷信的; **to be ~ about sth./doing sth.** 对某事物/做某事心存迷信; **to be ~ about walking under ladders** 迷信在梯子底下走过会不吉利

superstitiously /ˌsuːpə'stɪʃəsli, ˌsjuː-/ *adv* 迷信地

superstore /'suːpəstɔː(r), 'sjuː-/ *n* 1 (large supermarket) 大型超市 2 (specialist shop) 大型专卖场

super-strength *adj* 高度数的 ‹*beer, cider*›

superstructure /'suːpəstrʌktʃə(r), 'sjuː-/ *n* [建筑物或船舶的] 上部结构

supertanker /'suːpətæŋkə(r), 'sjuː-/ *n* 超级油轮

supertax /'suːpətæks, 'sjuː-/ *n* [c and u] 附加税; **the ~ bracket** 附加税税档

supervene /ˌsuːpə'viːn, ˌsjuː-/ *vi* formal «*illness, disaster*» 意外发生

supervention /ˌsuːpə'venʃn, ˌsjuː-/ *n* [c and u] formal 不期而至

supervise /'suːpəvaɪz, 'sjuː-/

A *vt* 1 (oversee activity of) 管理 ‹*worker, team, student*›; 照料 ‹*child, patient*› 2 (oversee execution of) 监督 ‹*job, activity, operation*›; 指导 ‹*thesis, research*›; **to ~ an exam** 监考 3 (oversee

activity in) 监管 ‹*building site, department*›; **a ~d playground** 受监管的游乐场
B *vi* «*manager, supervisor*» 监督; «*doctor, parent*» 照料

supervision /ˌsuːpəˈvɪʒn, ˌsjuː-/ *n* [u] (of staff, work) 监督; (of research student, thesis) 指导; (of child, patient) 照料; (of place, prisoner) 监管; **under (the) ~ of sb.** 在某人的指导之下

supervisor /ˈsuːpəvaɪzə(r), ˈsjuː-/ ▸**p. 409** *n* **1** (of staff, work) 管理人; (of building site) 监督人; **a canteen/factory/shop ~** 食堂/工厂/车间主管; **the site ~** 工地监工 **2** Univ 导师 **3** Amer Sch 督导老师

supervisory /ˈsuːpəvaɪzəri, ˈsjuː-, Amer ˌsuːpəˈvaɪzəri/ *adj* 监督的; **she's a ~ officer** 她是个督导官员

superwoman /ˈsuːpəwʊmən, ˈsjuː-/ *n* (*pl* **superwomen** /ˈsuːpəwɪmɪn, ˈsjuː-/) colloq 女超人

supine /ˈsuːpaɪn, ˈsjuː-/ formal
A *adj* **1** (lying face upwards) 仰卧的 ‹*figure, position*› **2** fig pej (weak or indolent) 懒散的 ‹*person, position*›; 苟安的 ‹*government*›; 消极的 ‹*complacency, submission*›
B *adv* 仰面朝天地 ‹*lie*›

supper /ˈsʌpə(r)/ *n* [u and c] **1** (evening meal) 晚饭; **what's for ~?** 晚饭吃什么? ; **to have** *or* **eat ~** 吃晚饭; **to sing for one's ~** fig 未受恩惠先报恩 **2** (late snack) 夜宵

suppertime /ˈsʌpətaɪm/ *n* [u] 晚饭时间

supplant /səˈplɑːnt, Amer səˈplænt/ *vt* 取代

supple /ˈsʌpl/ *adj* **1** (flexible) 敏捷的 ‹*person, limbs, movement*›; fig 灵活的 ‹*mind*›; **the ~ grace of the dancer** 舞蹈者轻盈优雅的体态 **2** (soft) 柔韧的 ‹*material, skin*›

supplement /ˈsʌplɪmənt/
A *n* **1** (addition) 补充; **a valuable ~ to the regular diet** 常规饮食的重要补充 **2** (additional charge) 附加费; **a ~ for sth.** 某物的附加费 **3** (separate part) (of newspaper, magazine) 增刊; (of reference work) 补编
B *vt* 补充 ‹*diet, knowledge*›; 增加 ‹*income*›; **to ~ sth. with sth.** 用某物补充某物; **he's ~ing his income by doing odd jobs** 他通过打零工来增加收入

supplementary /ˌsʌplɪˈmentri, Amer -təri/
A *adj* 补充的 ‹*item, vitamins, supply*›; 额外的 ‹*payment, charge, income*›; 附加的 ‹*papers, document, question*›
B *n* Brit Pol [尤指议会中的] 附加问题

supplementary benefit *n* [u] Brit [旧时政府发给低收入者的] 补助金

supplementation /ˌsʌplɪmenˈteɪʃn/ *n* [c and u] 补充; **salary/income ~** 额外工资/收入

suppleness /ˈsʌplnɪs/ *n* [u] **1** (flexibility) (of person, limbs, movement etc.) 敏捷; fig (of mind) 灵活 **2** (softness) (of material, skin) 柔韧

supplicant /ˈsʌplɪkənt/ *n* formal 哀求者

supplicate /ˈsʌplɪkeɪt/ formal
A *vi* 祈求; **to ~ for sth.** 祈求某物; **to ~ to do sth.** 恳求做某事
B *vt* **to ~ sb. to do sth.** 恳求某人做某事

supplication /ˌsʌplɪˈkeɪʃn/ *n* [u and c] formal 祈求; **to kneel in ~** 跪地祈求

supplier /səˈplaɪə(r)/ *n* 供货商

supply /səˈplaɪ/
A *n* **1** [c and u] (stock) 供应量; **supplies of food are almost exhausted** 储存的食物快吃完了; **an inexhaustible ~ of jokes** 讲不完的笑话; **in short/plentiful ~** 供应不足/充足 **2** [c and u] (provision) 供应; **the ~ of raw materials to the factory** 向工厂供应原材料; **to allow the ~ of emergency aid** 允许提供紧急援助; **the water ~ is unsafe** 供水不安全 **3** [u] Econ 供给; **demand for the new model is outrunning ~** 这一新款产品现在供不应求 **4** [u] Brit Sch 代课教师; **to do ~ work** 做代课教师; **to be** *or* **work on ~** 做代课教师
B **supplies** *npl* **1** (provisions) 补给品; **our supplies were running out** 我们的补给快用完了; **a transport plane carrying food and medical supplies** 一架运送食物和医疗用品的运输机 **2** Comm (goods) 用品; **office/household supplies** 办公/家庭用品; **electrical supplies** 电气设备
C *vt* **1** (provide) 供应; **they were accused of ~ing arms to the rebels** 他们被指控向叛乱者提供武器; **the hens ~ more eggs than we can eat** 母鸡下的蛋多得我们吃不完 **2** (equip) 为…提供; **the bakery has been ~ing these shops for years** 这家面包房多年来一直给这些商店供货; **the boat is supplied with satellite navigation** 这条船配有卫星导航系统 **3** (satisfy) 满足 ‹*need, requirement*›

supply: ~ and demand *n* [u] 供求关系; **~ chain** *n* 供应链; **~ line** *n* **1** Elec 供电线路; **2** (pipe) (carrying gas supply) 供气管; (carrying water supply) 供水管; **3** (route) 补给线; **~-side economics** *npl* + *v sing* [主张减税以刺激经济的] 供应学派经济学; **~ teacher** *n* 代课老师

support /səˈpɔːt/
A *vt* **1** (back, provide assistance to) 支持; **what team do you ~?** 你支持哪个队? ; **an organization that ~s people with AIDS** 一个向艾滋病患者提供援助的组织 **2** (provide financial backing to) 资助; **the project is ~ed by the EU** 该项目受到欧盟的资助 **3** (provide for) 供养; **to ~ oneself/a wife and children** 养活自己/妻小; **she ~ed her son through college** 她供儿子读完了大学; **the atmosphere of Mars could not ~ life** 生命体无法在火星的大气环境中生存 **4** (pay to sustain) 维持; **to ~ one's drug habit** 维持吸毒的恶习 **5** (bear weight of) 支撑; **a platform ~ed by concrete pillars** 混凝土柱子支撑的平台; **~ the baby's head when you hold it** 抱婴儿时要把头托住 **6** (corroborate) 证实; **the witness's story was not ~ed by the evidence** 目击者的说法没有证据的支持 **7** (perform earlier than) 为…进行垫场表演 ‹*band, performer*› **8** Comput 支持 ‹*program, device, language*›
B *n* **1** [u] (backing, approval) 支持; **there is strong public ~ for the change** 公众大力拥护这一变革; **he spoke in ~ of the motion** 他表示支持这一动议; **the theatre closed because of lack of ~** 由于缺乏观众的支持, 这家剧院关门了 **2** [u] (financial assistance) 资助; **financial ~** 财政资助 **3** [u] (money to live on) 生计; **means of ~** 生计来源 **4** [u] Mil 支援; **air/sea ~** 空中/海上支援 **5** [u] (bearing of weight) 支撑; **to give extra ~** 提供额外支撑; **she held on to his arm for ~** 她抓住他的手臂以便能站稳; **the garment gives excellent ~** 这件衣服起到很好的支托作用 **6** [c] (thing bearing weight) 支撑物; **a ~ for the tent** 帐篷的支架; **the ~s under the bridge** 桥下的支柱; **a knee/neck ~** 护膝/颈托 **7** [u] (supporters) 支持者; **Green Party ~** 绿党的支持者 **8** [c] *sing* (help, comfort) 安慰; **he was a great ~ to me when she died** 她去世的时候, 他给了我极大的帮助 **9** [u] (corroboration) 证实; **the statistics offer further ~ for our theory** 统计数字进一步支持了我们的理论; **there is a lot of evidence in ~ of this point of view** 有大量的证据支持这个观点 **10** [u and c] (secondary act at concert) (individual) 垫场演员; (band) 垫场乐队 **11** [u] (technical assistance) 技术支持; **we offer free technical ~** 我们提供免费的技术支持; **if you have a problem, just call ~** 如有疑问, 请致电技术支持部门查询

supportable /səˈpɔːtəbl/ *adj* **1** (able to be held up) 能支承的 ‹*weight*› **2** (able to be justified) 可证实的 ‹*evidence, premise, conclusion*›; **this view is hardly ~** 这个观点很难站得住脚 **3** (able to be helped) 扶养得起的 ‹*person*› **4** (able to be maintained, used) 能维护的 ‹*machinery*›; Comput 能支持的 ‹*program, language*›

support: ~ act *n* (individual) 垫场演员; (band) 垫场乐队; **~ band** *n* 垫场乐队

supported /səˈpɔːtɪd/ *adj* 支持的 ‹*system, hardware, program, language, device*›

supporter /səˈpɔːtə(r)/ *n* **1** (person) 支持者; **a ~ of sb./sth.** 某人/某事的支持者 **2** Herald [纹章中的] 持盾者

support: ~ group *n* [患病者结成的] 互助小组; **~ hose** *npl* = **~ stockings**

supporting /səˈpɔːtɪŋ/ *adj* **1** (holding sth. up) 支承的 ‹*structure*›; **a ~ wall** 承重墙 **2** Theat, Cin 配角的 ‹*part, role*›; **the award for best ~ actor** 最佳男配角奖

supportive /səˈpɔːtɪv/ *adj* 给予帮助的; **she was very ~ when I lost my husband** 我失去丈夫时她给了我很多帮助

supportively /səˈpɔːtɪvli/ *adv* 起支持作用地

supportiveness /səˈpɔːtɪvnɪs/ *n* [u] 支持

support: ~ network *n* **1** (group) 互助小组; **2** (friends, family etc.) 亲友关系网; **~ personnel** *n* = **~ staff**; **~ price** *n* 维持性价格 [低于此价格政府保证补贴农户或购买剩余的农产品]; **~ scheme** *n* 支援计划; **~ services** *npl* [地方政府对贫困儿童及其家庭提供的] 支持服务; **~ staff** *n* **1** (auxiliary staff) 辅助人员; **2** Comput 维护人员; **~ stockings** *npl* 弹力长袜; **~ system** *n* 互助体系; **~ team** *n* (group of people assisting others) 援助小组; (for assisting customers) 售后服务队; **~ troops** *npl* 辅助部队; **~ vessel** *n* 补给船; **a diving ~ vessel** 潜水给养船

suppose /səˈpəʊz/ *vt* **1** (believe) 认为; **getting a visa isn't as simple as you might ~** 办签证不像你想的那么容易; **it was generally ~d that he had died** 大家都以为他已经死了; **when do you ~ (that) he'll arrive?** 你觉得他什么时候会到? ; **prices will go up, I ~** 我觉得物价会上涨 **2** (imagine) 设想; (introducing hypothesis) 假定; **let us ~ that this theory is correct** 让我们假设这个理论是正确的; **the theory ~s the existence of life on other planets** 这个理论假定其他行星上存在生命; **~ he is dead: what then?** 假如他死了, 那怎么办? **3** (expressing reluctant agreement) [表示勉强同意]; **I ~ you're right** 我看你是对的; **can I borrow the car? — I ~ so** 我能借这辆车吗? ——我看行吧; **I could take you in the car, I ~** 好吧, 你就坐我的车吧 **4** (expressing annoyance) [表示生气]; **I ~ you think it's funny, do you?** 我看你是觉得这挺好玩, 是不是? **5** (making polite request) [表示婉转的建议、提问或请求]; **~ we get a later train?** 要不我们坐晚一点的火车? ; **I don't ~ you know where she's gone?** 您知不知道她去哪儿了? ; **I don't ~ I could have a look at your newspaper, could I?** 我能不能看看您的报纸? **6** (introducing interesting detail) 猜想; **who do you ~ I saw yesterday?** 你猜猜我昨天见着谁了?

supposed *adj* **1** /səˈpəʊzd, səˈpəʊzɪd/ *attrib* (alleged) 误以为的; **when did this ~ accident happen?** 这场所谓的事故发生在什么时候? **2** /səˈpəʊzd, səˈpəʊst/ *pred* (expected, required) 应当的; **to be ~ to do sth.** 应当做某事; **you're ~ to buy a ticket, but not many people do** 按说应当买票, 不过买的人不多; **I thought we were ~ to be paid today** 我原以为我们今天会领到薪水呢; **the engine doesn't sound like it's ~ to** 发动机听起来不对劲 **3** /səˈpəʊzd, səˈpəʊst/ *pred* (believed) 普遍认为的; **to be ~ to be sth./to do sth.** 普遍认为是某物/做某事; **it's ~ to be a good hotel** 这家旅馆口碑不错 **4** /səˈpəʊzd, səˈpəʊst/ *pred* (allowed) 允许的; **to be not ~ to do sth.** 不允许做某事; **you're not ~ to walk on the grass** 不准践踏草地

supposedly /səˈpəʊzɪdli/ *adv* 据说

supposition /ˌsʌpəˈzɪʃn/ *n* **1** [u] (guessing) 推测 **2** [c] (assumption) 推测的想法; **that is only**

S

a ~: you don't know for certain 那只是假设：你并不确切知道

suppositional /ˌsʌpəˈzɪʃənl/ *adj* **1** (unproven) 假定的 ‹*claim, theory*› **2** (supposed) 臆想的 ‹*relationship, event*›

suppository /səˈpɒzɪtri, Amer -tɔːri/ *n* 栓剂

suppress /səˈpres/ *vt* **1** (prevent, quell) 镇压 ‹*riot, uprising, activities*› **2** (withhold, ban) 封锁 ‹*information, facts, evidence, scandal*›; 查禁 ‹*report, newspaper*› **3** (consciously inhibit) 忍住 ‹*anger, sneeze, sob*›; 克制 ‹*feeling*› **4** (retard, weaken) 阻止 ‹*growth*›; **the drugs he had to take have ~ed his growth/immune system** 他被迫服用的药物阻碍了他的发育/抑制了他的免疫系统 **5** Radio, Electron 抑制 ‹*interference, frequency*›

suppressant /səˈpresənt/ *n* 遏抑剂; **a cough ~** 止咳药

suppression /səˈpreʃn/ *n* [u] **1** (prevention, quelling) 镇压; **the deliberate ~ of human freedom/the free market** 对人类自由/自由市场的蓄意压制 **2** (withholding, banning) (of information, facts, evidence, scandal) 封锁; (of report, newspaper) 查禁 **3** (conscious inhibition) (of feeling, memory) 克制; (of sneeze) 忍住 **4** (retardation, weakening) 阻碍 **5** Radio, Electron 抑制

suppressive /səˈpresɪv/ *adj* **1** (repressive) 压制的 ‹*action, attitude*›; **a ~ regime** 高压政权 **2** Med 起抑制作用的 ‹*drug, therapy*› **3** Mil 压制性的; **~ fire/weapon** 压制火力/武器

suppressor /səˈpresə(r)/ *n* 抑制器

suppurate /ˈsʌpjʊreɪt/ *vi* 化脓

suppuration /ˌsʌpjʊˈreɪʃn/ *n* [u] **1** (discharging) 化脓 **2** (pus) 脓

supranational /ˌsuːprəˈnæʃənl, ˌsjuː-/ *adj* 超国家的

supremacist /suːˈpreməsɪst, sjuː-/ *n* 种族优越论者

supremacy /suːˈpreməsi, sjuː-/ *n* [u] **1** (power) 至高无上; **the fight for ~** 对霸权的争夺; **to achieve** *or* **gain ~ (over sb.)** 获得（对某人的）控制权 **2** (superiority) 优势; **the company's ~ is undisputed** 公司的优势地位不容置疑

supreme /suːˈpriːm, sjuː-/ *adj* **1** (highest-ranking) 至上的 ‹*ruler, tribunal*›; **to reign ~** 占绝对优势 **2** (outstanding) 卓越的 ‹*art, skill, heroism*›; 最大的 ‹*endeavour*›; 决定性的 ‹*moment*›; pej 极度的 ‹*ignorance, arrogance*›; **to make the ~ sacrifice** 做出最大的牺牲; **an act of ~ folly** 愚蠢至极的行为

Supreme: ~ Being *n* **the ~ Being** 上帝; **~ Commander** *n* 最高统帅; **S~ court** *n* [美国、英格兰和威尔士的] 最高法院

supremely /suːˈpriːmli, sjuː-/ *adv* 极度地

Supreme Soviet *n* Hist **the ~** 最高苏维埃

supremo /suːˈpriːməʊ, sjuː-/ *n* (*pl* **~s**) Brit colloq 总管

Supt *abbr* = **superintendent 2**

surcharge /ˈsɜːtʃɑːdʒ/

A *n* **1** (payment) (for extra service) 附加费; (on tax) 附加税; (as penalty) 附加罚款; **a 10% ~ on the basic cost of the holiday** 基本费用之外的 10% 假日附加费 **2** Post 改值加盖

B *vt* 向…收附加费 ‹*holidaymaker*›; 向…收附加税 ‹*importer*›; **to ~ sb. 10% (on sth.)** 向某人收取（某物）10% 的附加费

surd /sɜːd/ *n* 不尽根

sure /ʃɔː(r), Amer ʃʊər/

A *adj* **1** *pred* (clear in one's mind) 确信的; **Is that John over there? — I'm not ~** 那边那个人是约翰吗？——我说不准; **I'm not absolutely ~ about** *or* **of this** 对此我没有绝对把握; **are you ~ you don't mind?** 你确实不在意吗？; **I'm not ~ whether I should tell you this** 我拿不准该不该把这事告诉你; **to make ~** (ascertain) 弄清; (ensure) 确保; **I think the door's locked, but I'll just go and make ~** 我觉得门已经锁了，不过我还是要去确认一下; **make ~ no one finds out about this** 绝对不要让任何人发觉这件事; **they scored another goal and made ~ of victory** 他们又进了一个球，确保了胜局; **make** *or* **be ~ to give your family my regards** 务必代我向你的家人问好; **to be ~** formal (conceding point) 固然; dated (adding emphasis) 确实; **he is intelligent, to be ~, but he's also very lazy** 他聪明是聪明，但也很懒 **2** *pred* (guaranteed) 一定的; **we are ~ of success** *or* **succeeding** 我们一定会成功; **England must win this game to be ~ of qualifying for the World Cup** 英格兰队必须赢得这场比赛才能确保获得世界杯的参赛资格; **it's ~ to rain** 准会下雨 **3** (undoubted) 不容置疑的; **~ proof** 确凿的证据; **the war will be long, but victory is ~** 战争会很漫长，但胜利终将到来; **for ~** colloq (without doubt) 无疑; Amer colloq (in answers) 当然; **no one knows for ~ what happened** 没有人确切知道发生了什么事; **one thing is (for) ~: it's not going to be easy** 有一点可以肯定：事情不会很容易; **a ~ thing** colloq 确定的事; **~ thing!** esp Amer colloq 当然！ **4** (reliable) 可靠的; **a ~ friend** 可靠的朋友; **a ~ remedy for colds** 治感冒的良药; **it's a ~ sign of economic recovery** 这是经济复苏的可靠征兆 **5** *pred* (confident) 有信心的; **she seems very ~ of herself** 她好像非常自信 **6** (assured) 有把握的; **with a ~ hand** 沉着自信地

B *adv* **1** colloq (yes) 当然; **will you open the wine? — ~, where is it?** 你把葡萄酒打开好吗？——没问题，在哪儿呢？; **did it hurt? — ~ it hurt** 疼吗？——当然疼了 **2** colloq (used for emphasis) 确实; **it ~ is cold** 确实很冷; **amazing view — ~ is** 景色真美——没错; **(as) ~ as I'm standing here** *or* **as hell** *or* **as eggs are eggs** 千真万确; **I'm ~ as hell not inviting him** 我肯定不会邀请他; **that song ~ sounds familiar** 那首歌确实耳熟 **3** colloq (in reply to thanks) 不用客气 **4** **~ enough** (as predicted) 果然; **I said he'd forget, and ~ enough he did** 我说过他会忘记，他果然忘了

sure: ~-fire *adj attrib* 万无一失的 ‹*recipe, plan, success, winner*›; **~-footed** *adj* 脚步稳的; **~-footedness** *n* [u] 步履稳健; **~-handed** *adj* 巧手的 ‹*person*›; 得心应手的 ‹*performance*›

surely /ˈʃɔːli, Amer ˈʃʊərli/ *adv* **1** (expressing certainty) 肯定 **2** (expressing surprise) 当真; **~ not!** 绝对不可能！; **~ to God** *or* **goodness** colloq [表示诧异] 怎么可能 **3** (expressing disagreement) 确定; **that was in 2002-2003, ~?** 那是在 2002 至 2003 年？你确定吗？ **4** esp Amer colloq (yes) 当然 **5** (in sure manner) 稳步地; **slowly but ~** 缓慢但稳健地

sureness /ˈʃɔːnɪs, Amer ˈʃʊərnɪs/ *n* [u] 有把握; **~ of touch** 笔法的苍劲

surety /ˈʃɔːrəti, Amer ˈʃʊərəti/ *n* **1** [u and c] (money) 保证金 **2** [u and c] (guarantor) 保证人; **to go** *or* **stand ~ for sb.** 为某人做担保人 **3** [u] (assurance, certainty) 自信; **to say sth. with ~** 自信地说某事

surf /sɜːf/

A *n* **1** [u] (waves) 拍岸浪花; **how is the ~?** 冲浪浪头怎么样？ **2** [c] Sport 冲浪; **to go for a ~** 去冲浪

B *vi* 冲浪

C *vt* Comput 浏览; **to ~ the Net** *or* **Internet** *or* **Web** 上网浏览

surface /ˈsɜːfɪs/

A *n* **1** (top, outer layer) 表面; **on the ~ (of sth.)** 在（某物的）表面; **under** *or* **beneath** *or* **below the ~** 在地表下; **to work at the ~** ‹*miner*› 在地面工作 **2** (upper limit of water) 水面; **to float to the ~** 浮到水面; **at the ~** 在水面 **3** (worktop) 操作台; **kitchen ~s** 厨房台面 **4** Math (of solid, cube) 面 **5** (visible aspect) 外表; **to touch** *or* **skim** *or* **scratch the ~ of** 触及…的表面 ‹*issue, subject*›; **on the ~** 表面上; **violence is never far below the ~** 暴力事件随时会发生; **her grief is never far below the ~** 她的悲伤总是难以掩饰; **to come** *or* **rise to the ~** «*tensions, emotions*» 显露

B *modif* **1** (outer) 表面的; **~ layer** 表层; **~ measurements** 表面尺寸 **2** (relating to ground) 地表的 ‹*temperature, feature*› **3** (apparent) 表面上的 ‹*similarity, appearance, meaning, problem*› **4** (relating to transportation on surface of water) 水上的 ‹*vessel, fleet*›; (relating to transportation across land or sea) 水陆路的; **to send sth. by ~ mail** 通过水陆路邮寄某物 **5** Mining 地面上的 ‹*work, worker*› **6** (relating to wound, incision) 表皮的 **7** Ling 表层的 ‹*analysis*›; **~ grammar** 表层语法

C *vi* **1** (emerge from water) 露出水面; **he ~d from his dive** 他潜入水中后钻出水面 **2** (become apparent) «*emotion, problem, evidence*» 显露; «*rumour, scandal, anxiety*» 出现 **3** (re-appear after absence) 重新出现 **4** colloq (get out of bed) 起床; **oh, so you've ~d at last!** 哦，你终于起床啦！

D *vt* 给…加表面层; **to ~ the road/ground with sth.** 用某物铺设路面/地面

surface: ~ area *n* 表面积; **~ mail** *n* [u] 水陆路邮件; **~ structure** *n* [u] 表层结构; **~ tension** *n* [u] 表面张力; **~-to-air** *adj* (from ground) 地对空的 ‹*missile*›; (from ship) 舰对空的 ‹*missile*›; **~-to-~** *adj* (from ground) (at target on ground) 地对地的 ‹*missile*›; (at target on ship) 地对舰的 ‹*missile*›; (from ship) (at target on land) 舰对地的 ‹*missile*›; (at target on ship) 舰对舰的 ‹*missile*›

surfactant /sɜːˈfæktənt/ *n* [c and u] 表面活性剂

surf: ~board *n* 冲浪板; **~boarder** *n* 冲浪者; **~boarding** ▸p. 307 *n* [u] 冲浪运动; **~casting** ▸p. 307 *n* [u] 激浪投钓

surfeit /ˈsɜːfɪt/

A *n* 过量; **a ~ of sth.** 过量的某物; **to have a ~ of food and wine** 暴饮暴食

B *vt* 过量提供; **to be ~ed with sth.** 沉溺于某事

surfer /ˈsɜːfə(r)/ *n* **1** Sport 冲浪者 **2** Comput 网上冲浪者

surfing /ˈsɜːfɪŋ/ ▸p. 307 *n* [u] 冲浪运动; **to go ~** 去冲浪

surf: ~ 'n' turf, ~ and turf *n* [u] Amer 海鲜牛排餐; **~riding** *n* [u] = **surfing**

surge /sɜːdʒ/

A *vi* **1** (rush) 使强烈感受到; **to ~ within sb./sth.** 在某人内心/某物内部迸发; **relief ~d through her** 她顿感如释重负; **the blood ~d to his cheeks** 血涌上了他的脸颊; **indignation ~d up within her** 她内心愤慨难平 **2** (increase) «*prices, shares*» 急剧上涨; «*profits, demand, interest rates*» 激增; **to ~ to a record high** 激增到创纪录的高度; **to ~ upwards** 急剧上涨 **3** (move suddenly) «*crowd, waves, floodwater*» 涌动; **to ~ forward/out** 向前涌动/涌出去; **to ~ into/on to/up** *or* **over/through sth.** 涌入/涌到/涌上/涌过某物 **4** Sport (accelerate) 冲刺; **to ~ into the lead** 冲到最前面; **she ~d through to win** 她不断冲刺直到获胜 **5** Elec 浪涌

B *n* **1** *usu sing* (rush) 突发; **a ~ of emotion/anger/pain** 一股强烈的情感/一阵怒火/一阵疼痛 **2** *usu sing* (rise) 激增; **a ~ of** *or* **in** …的急剧上升 ‹*prices, unemployment, demand*› **3** *usu sing* (sudden movement) 涌动 **4** Sport (increase in speed) 冲刺 **5** **(power) ~** Elec 浪涌

surgeon /ˈsɜːdʒən/ ▸p. 409 *n* 外科医生; **a brain/heart ~** 脑/心外科医生

surgeon general *n* (*pl* **surgeons general**) **1** Mil 军医处处长 **2** (head of US public health service) 卫生局局长

surgery /ˈsɜːdʒəri/ *n* **1** [u] (treatment) 外科手术; (study) 外科学; **to have** *or* **undergo ~** 动手术; **brain/cosmetic ~** 脑部手术/整形手术 **2** [c] (building) 门诊大楼; (room) 门诊室 **3** [c and u]

S

Brit (consultation time) 门诊时间; **to take ~** 看门诊; **~ hours** 门诊时间 **4** [c] Brit Pol [国会议员的] 接待时间

surgical /ˈsɜːdʒɪkl/ *adj* **1** (used in surgery) 外科手术的; (involving surgery) 外科的; **~ cotton/instruments/treatment** 医用药棉/外科手术器械/外科治疗 **2** (corrective) 矫正用的; **~ boot/stocking** 矫正靴/袜 **3** Mil (precise) 精确的 ‹*bombing, strike*›

surgical: ~ appliance *n* 矫形器械; **~ clamp** *n* 手术夹钳; **~ dressing** *n* 消毒纱布

surgically /ˈsɜːdʒɪkli/ *adv* 通过手术

surgical: ~ spirit *n* [u] Brit 医用酒精; **~ strike** *n* 外科手术式打击; **~ ward** *n* 外科手术病房

surging /ˈsɜːdʒɪŋ/ *adj attrib* 猛涨的 ‹*rates, prices*›; 猛增的 ‹*demand, costs, exports*›; 飞速增长的 ‹*economy*›

Suriname, Surinam /ˌsʊərɪˈnæm/ *pr n* 苏里南

Surinamese /ˌsʊərɪnəˈmiːz/ ▸**p. 503**
A *adj* 苏里南的
B *n* 苏里南人

surliness /ˈsɜːlɪnɪs/ *n* [u] 乖戾粗暴

surly /ˈsɜːli/ *adj* 乖戾的 ‹*expression*›; 阴沉的 ‹*face*›; 粗暴的 ‹*manner, refusal*›

surmise /səˈmaɪz/ formal
A *vt* 猜测 ‹*answer*›; **to ~ (from sth.) that ...** (根据某事物) 推测出…; **we can only ~ what happened** 我们只能推测发生了什么事
B *n* [c and u] 推测

surmount /səˈmaʊnt/ *vt* **1** (overcome) 克服 ‹*difficulty, obstacle*›; 解决 ‹*problem*›; 成功应对 ‹*challenge*› **2** formal (be on top of) 居于…之上; **a column/tower ~ed by a statue** 顶端立着一座雕像的柱子/高塔

surmountable /səˈmaʊntəbl/ *adj* 能克服的 ‹*difficulty*›; 可超越的 ‹*barrier*›; 可成功应对的 ‹*challenge*›

surname /ˈsɜːneɪm/ *n* 姓; **they have the same ~** 他们同姓

surnamed /ˈsɜːneɪmd/ *adj attrib* 姓…的

surpass /səˈpɑːs, Amer -ˈpæs/
A *vt* **1** (be better than) 胜过; **to ~ sb./sth. in sth.** 在某方面优于某人/某物; **a performance that far ~es all others** 远远优于其他人的表演 **2** (go beyond) 超出 ‹*expectation, level, record*›
B *v refl* **to ~ oneself** 超越自我; **the chef has ~ed himself with this dessert** 这位厨师在这道甜点上发挥超常

surplice /ˈsɜːplɪs/ *n* [教士或唱诗班穿的] 白色罩衣

surplus /ˈsɜːpləs/
A *n* [c and u] (of production, supply) 剩余; (of income, assets) 盈余; **a trade ~** 贸易顺差; **a labour ~** 劳动力过剩; **in times of ~** 在富足的岁月
B *adj* 剩余的 ‹*material, goods, cash*›; 过剩的 ‹*labour, production*›; **to be ~ to requirements** 不需要; **they told me that I was ~ to requirements!** 他们告诉我我被解雇了!

surplus value *n* [u] 剩余价值

surprise /səˈpraɪz/
A *n* **1** [c] (unexpected event) 意想不到的事物; **it was a lovely ~!** 这真是个意外之喜啊!; **there are few ~s in this year's budget** 今年的预算案没什么出人意料的地方; **there are lots of ~s in store for visitors to the gallery** 参观画展的人将会发现许多令他们惊奇的东西; **it comes as** *or* **it is a/no ~ (to sb.) (to hear/learn/see) that ...** (听到/得知/看见) … (对某人来说) 出乎意料/毫不意外; **to be in for a ~** 肯定会大吃一惊; **to get/have a ~** 吃了一惊; **~, ~!** colloq iron (emphasizing predictability) 果然不出所料!; colloq (announcing sth. unexpected) 想不到吧! **2** [u and c] (astonishment) 惊讶; **he had a look of ~ on his face** 他的脸上带着惊讶的神情; **to show/conceal/express (one's) ~ (at sth.)** 流露出/掩饰/表示 (对某事物的) 惊讶; **imagine my ~ when I saw him there!** 想象一下当我看到他在那儿的时候是多么惊讶吧!; **(much) to sb.'s ~** 令某人感到 (非常) 惊讶的是; **much to my ~, I was given the job** 万万没想到, 我竟然获得了那份工作; **in** *or* **with ~** 惊讶地 **3** [u and c] (treat) 惊喜; **she wants it to be a ~** 她想让它成为一个惊喜; **to have a ~ for sb.** 给某人一个惊喜 **4** [u] (as tactic) 出人意料; **a successful campaign should have an element of ~** 成功的宣传活动应有出奇制胜之处; **to take sb. by ~** 出乎某人意料; **their visit took me completely by ~** 他们的来访完全令我措手不及
B *modif* 意外的 ‹*decision, resignation, result*›; **a ~ attack** 突然袭击; **to pay sb. a ~ visit** 意外拜访某人
C *vt* **1** (astonish) 使…惊讶 ‹*person*›; **what ~s me most is ...** 最让我惊讶的是…; **he ~d everyone by winning** 他的获胜让大家都感到惊讶; **it ~d us to learn that she had got married** 得知她已经结婚, 我们感到很意外; **it wouldn't ~ me if they rejected the proposals** 如果他们拒绝这些提案, 我不会感到意外; **you (do) ~ me!** lit 你 (着实) 让我吃了一惊!; iron 你真令我惊讶!; **~ me!** lit 给我个惊喜!; iron 让我吃惊吧! **2** (catch unawares) 使…措手不及 ‹*intruder, garrison*›; 无意中发现 ‹*person, thief*›; **to ~ sb. doing sth.** 无意中发现某人正在做某事

surprised /səˈpraɪzd/ *adj* 惊讶的; **to be ~ at sb./sth.** 对某人/某事物感到吃惊; **I'm ~ at you!** 我没想到你竟会这样!; **she looked ~ to see me** 她见到我时显得很惊讶

surprising /səˈpraɪzɪŋ/ *adj* 令人吃惊的; **it is ~ (that) ...** 真想不到…; **I find it ~ (that) ...** 我吃惊地发现…

surprisingly /səˈpraɪzɪŋli/ *adv* 惊人地; **~ few people know about it** 知道此事的人少得出奇

surreal /səˈrɪəl/ *adj* 离奇的 ‹*experience*›; 荒诞的 ‹*world, moment, atmosphere, imagery, comedy*›

surrealism /səˈrɪəlɪzəm/ *n* [u] 超现实主义

surrealist /səˈrɪəlɪst/
A *n* (artist) 超现实主义画家; (writer) 超现实主义作家
B *adj* 超现实主义的

surrender /səˈrendə(r)/
A *vi* **1** (submit) (to enemy control) «*soldier, army, country*» 投降; (to authorities) «*criminal, fugitive*» 自首; (to influence) «*person, authority*» 屈服; **to ~ to sb.** 屈服于某人; **the government ~ed to the influence of the unions** 面对工会的影响力, 政府让步了; **I ~** fig 我投降 **2** (give in to emotion) 听任; **to ~ to one's craving for drugs/the desire to retain power** 克制不住犯毒瘾/压抑不住保住权势的渴望
B *vt* **1** (cede to enemy, give up) 放弃 ‹*town, liberties, rights*›; **he agreed to ~ all claims to the property** 他同意放弃所有的产权要求; **to ~ power to the opposition** 将权力交给反对党 **2** (hand over or in) 交出 **3** Insur 撤销 ‹*insurance policy*› **4** Jur 放弃 ‹*lease, tenancy*›
C *v refl* **to ~ oneself** **1** (to the enemy) 投降; (to the authorities) «*criminal, fugitive*» 自首; **the hijackers eventually ~ed themselves to the police** 劫持犯最终向警方投降了 **2** (to emotion) 放任自己; **to ~ oneself to the joy/despair of sth.** 因某事物沉浸在快乐之中/陷于绝望之中 **3** liter (to sexual partner) 听任摆布; **she could hardly wait to surrender herself to him** 她迫不及待地要臣服于他
D *n* [u and c] **1** (submission) (of soldier, army, garrison, town, country) 投降; (of criminal, fugitive) 自首; (of person, authorities) 屈服; **to force sb. into ~** 迫使某人投降; **the ~ of the bank robbers to the police** 银行劫匪向警察投降; **the government's ~ to the unions** 政府对工会组织的让步 **2** (giving up) (of territory) 割让; (of liberties, rights, power) 放弃; **they agreed to the ~ of their land to the Canadian state** 他们同意把他们的土地割让给加拿大 **3** (handing over or in) 交出 **4** (giving in to emotion) 听任; **~ to despair** 陷入绝望 **5** Insur (cancellation of policy) 退保 **6** Jur (giving up of lease, tenancy) 弃租

surrender value *n* 退保金额

surreptitious /ˌsʌrəpˈtɪʃəs/ *adj* 偷偷进行的

surreptitiously /ˌsʌrəpˈtɪʃəsli/ *adv* 偷偷地

Surrey /ˈsʌri/ *pr n* 萨里郡

surrogacy /ˈsʌrəgəsi/ *n* [u] 代孕

surrogate /ˈsʌrəgət/
A *n* **1** (substitute) (for person) 替代者; (for thing) 替代品; **to be a ~ for sb./sth.** 替代某人/某事物 **2** Amer Jur 遗嘱认证法官
B *adj* 替代的

surrogate mother *n* **1** (undertaking pregnancy) 代孕母亲 **2** (undertaking role) 代理母亲

surround /səˈraʊnd/
A *vt* **1** (be all round) «*fence, hills*» 环绕; **to be ~ed by** *or* **with sth.** 被某物环绕; **I'm ~ed by books at home** 我家里到处都是书 **2** (move into position round) «*police, troops*» 包围 **3** (be associated with) «*rumour, doubt*» 围绕 ‹*plan, future*›; **to be ~ed by sth.** 充满某物
B *v refl* **to ~ oneself with sth.** 喜欢身边总有某物
C *n* (of fireplace, door, window) 边; (of painting, quilt) 饰边
D **surrounds** *npl* 周围地区

surrounding /səˈraʊndɪŋ/ *adj* 周围的

surroundings /səˈraʊndɪŋz/ *npl* 环境; **animals in their natural ~** 野生环境中的动物

surround sound *n* [u] 环绕立体声; **a ~ system** 环绕立体声系统

surtax /ˈsɜːtæks/ *n* [u and c] 附加税; **a ~ on sth.** 对某物征收的附加税

surveillance /sɜːˈveɪləns/ *n* [u] 监视; **to put** *or* **place** *or* **keep sb. under ~** 对某人实施监视; **a ~ camera/device/radar/system** 监视摄像机/设备/雷达/系统

survey
A /ˈsɜːveɪ/ *n* **1** (poll, investigation) 调查; **to carry out** *or* **conduct** *or* **do a ~** 开展调查; **the results** *or* **findings of a ~** 调查结果; **a ~ of voting intentions** 一项关于投票意向的调查 **2** (mapping) 测绘; (map) 测绘图; **a geological/an aerial ~** 地质/航空测量 **3** Brit (inspection of building) 房屋检测; (report on building) 房屋检测报告; **to get a ~ (done)** 进行一次房屋检测 **4** (overview) 概述; **a comprehensive ~ of modern music/linguistics/literature** 现代音乐/语言学/文学综述 **5** (careful look) 审视
B /səˈveɪ/ *vt* **1** (investigate) 对…进行调查 ‹*trends, prices, products, market*› **2** (interview) 向…调查 ‹*people, households*› **3** (assess) 对…进行评价 ‹*opinion, views, intentions*› **4** (map) 测绘 ‹*site, coastline, region, seabed*› **5** Brit (in house-buying) 检测 ‹*property, house*› **6** (give overview of) 概述 ‹*research, situation*› **7** (carefully look at) 审视 ‹*audience, countryside, scene*›

surveying /səˈveɪɪŋ/ *n* [u] **1** (mapping) 勘测; **~ instruments** 测绘仪器 **2** Brit (of building) 房屋检测

surveyor /səˈveɪə(r)/ ▸**p. 409** *n* **1** (of land) 勘测员 **2** Brit (of building) 验房师

survey ship *n* 测量船

survivable /səˈvaɪvəbl/ *adj* 非致命的

survival /səˈvaɪvl/
A *n* **1** [u] (continued existence) (of person, animal, plant, project, government) 存留; (of custom, belief) 遗存; **the ~ of the fittest** 适者生存; **what are his chances of ~?** 他存活的可能性有多大? **2** [c] (relic) (of custom, practice) 残存物; (of object) 幸存物; (person) 幸存者; **to be a ~ from sth.** 是…的幸存者
B *modif* 救生的 ‹*equipment, training, expert*›

S

survival: ~ rate *n* 存活率; **~ skills** *npl* 生存技能

survive /sə'vaɪv/
A *vi* «*person, animal, plant, project, government*» 存留; «*custom, belief*» 遗存; **to ~ on sth.** 靠某物活下去; **you haven't had any lunch! — don't worry, I'll ~** 你还没吃午饭! ——别担心, 我活得下去
B *vt* **1** (live through) 经历…而幸存 ‹*heart attack, winter, flood, fire, crisis, recession*› **2** (outlive) 比…活得长; **she is ~d by three daughters** 她身后留下 3 个女儿; **to ~ sb. by 10 years** 比某人多活 10 年

surviving /sə'vaɪvɪŋ/ *adj attrib* 幸存的 ‹*patient, victim*›; 在世的 ‹*relative, children*›

survivor /sə'vaɪvə(r)/ *n* **1** (of accident, attack) 幸存者; **there are no reports of any ~s** 没有任何生还者的报告 **2** (resilient person) 挺过困难者

susceptibility /sə,septə'bɪləti/
A *n* [u] **1** (proneness) (to illness) 易受感染; (to injury, damage) 容易遭受; (to advertising, pressure) 易受影响 **2** (impressionability) 易感性
B **susceptibilities** *npl* 感情脆弱处

susceptible /sə'septəbl/ *adj* **1** (prone, vulnerable) **to be ~ to** 容易感染 ‹*disease*›; 容易遭受 ‹*attack, influence*›; 容易受…的影响 ‹*flattery, advertising*›; **officials who are ~ to bribery** 容易受贿的官员 **2** (impressionable) 善感的 ‹*person, nature, age*› **3** formal (capable) **to be ~ of** 容许 ‹*generalization, explanation*›

sushi /'su:ʃi/ *n* [u] 寿司 [日式料理]; **a ~ restaurant** 寿司店

suspect
A /sə'spekt/ *vt* **1** (think likely) 推测 ‹*conspiracy, crime, sabotage*›; **there is reason to ~ that ...** 有理由认为…; **I ~ she didn't want to leave** 我觉得她并不想离开 **2** (doubt) 质疑 ‹*truth, honesty, motive*› **3** (be suspicious of) 怀疑; **she strongly ~ed her husband of infidelity** 她强烈怀疑丈夫不忠
B /'sʌspekt/ *n* 嫌疑犯; **he is the chief ~ at present** 目前他是头号嫌疑犯
C /'sʌspekt/ *adj* 不可信的 ‹*story, claim*›; 靠不住的 ‹*painting, antique*›; 可疑的 ‹*item, smell*›; 可能有危险的 ‹*equipment, vehicle, foodstuff*›; **a ~ package** 可疑包裹

suspend /sə'spend/ *vt* **1** (hang) 悬挂; **to ~ sb./sth. from/between/over sth.** 将某人/某物吊在某物的下面/中间/上方; **her body was found ~ed by a rope** 她的尸体被发现吊在一根绳子上; **to be ~ed in mid-air** 悬挂在半空 **2** (stop temporarily) 暂停; **to ~ a trial/hostilities** 暂停审判/交战; **to ~ play** Sport 暂停比赛; **to ~ shares** Fin 停牌; **to ~ (one's) disbelief** 暂不质疑; **to be ~ed in time** 身处时间停滞的状态 **3** (delay) 推迟; **to ~ judgement** Jur 延期宣判; (delay opinion) 推迟决定 **4** (remove from activities) 使…暂时停职 ‹*person, employee, official*›; 暂时将…除名 ‹*party member*›; 使…暂时停赛 ‹*player, athlete*›; 使…暂时停学 ‹*student*›; **to be ~ed from duty/a game/school** 被暂时停职/停赛/停学 **5** Jur (not enforce) 缓期执行 ‹*sentence*› **6** (float) 使悬浮; **to be ~ed in** 悬浮在…之中 ‹*air, solution, gel*›

suspended: ~ animation *n* [u] 假死; **to go into ~ animation** fig 进入蛰伏状态; **~ sentence** *n* 缓刑; **to give sb. a two-year ~ sentence** 判某人两年缓刑

suspender /sə'spendə(r)/
A *n* Brit (to hold up stocking) 吊袜带; **a pair of ~s** 一副吊袜带
B **suspenders** *npl* Amer (to hold up trousers) 吊裤带

suspender belt *n* Brit 吊袜腰带

suspense /sə'spens/ *n* [u] **1** (tension) 焦虑; **to wait in ~ for sth.** 焦急地等待某事物; **the ~ is killing me!** 急死我了! ; **to break the ~** 打破悬念 **2** (abeyance) 暂时搁置; **to be** *or* **remain in ~** 悬而未决

suspense account *n* 暂记账户

suspension /sə'spenʃn/ *n* **1** [u] (temporary cessation) 暂停 **2** [u and c] (temporary dismissal) (from job) 暂时停职; (from school, university) 暂时停学; (from team, sport) 暂时停赛; **~ from sth.** 某事的暂停; **he had to serve a two-match ~** 他不得不停赛两场 **3** [u] Aut [车辆减震用的] 悬架 **4** [c and u] Chem (mixture) 悬浮液; (mixed state) 悬浮; **in ~** 处于悬浮状态

suspension: ~ bridge *n* 悬索桥; **~ cable** *n* 悬索

suspicion /sə'spɪʃn/ *n* **1** [u] (mistrust) 怀疑; **to arouse** *or* **create ~** 引起怀疑; **to regard sb./sth. with ~** 以怀疑的眼光看待某人/某事物; **to be under ~** 有嫌疑; **to be above** *or* **beyond ~** 无可置疑; **they arrested him on ~ of murder** 他因涉嫌谋杀被捕 **2** [c] (idea) 看法; (feeling) 感觉; **I have a strong ~ that she is lying** 我强烈感到她在撒谎; **to have a sneaking ~ that ...** 暗自怀疑…; **to have ~s about sb./sth.** 对某人/某事物存有疑虑 **3** [c] (hint) 少许; **a ~ of a smile** 一丝笑意

suspicious /sə'spɪʃəs/ *adj* **1** (mistrustful) 怀疑的 ‹*person, look, attitude*›; **to be ~ of** *or* **about sb./sth.** 对某人/某事物感到怀疑 **2** (dubious) 可疑的 ‹*behaviour, remark, character*›; **it is ~ that ...** 可疑的是…; **the police are asking people to report anything ~** 警方要求人们报告任何可疑情况

suspiciously /sə'spɪʃəsli/ *adv* **1** (mistrustfully) 怀疑地 ‹*ask, watch, treat*› **2** (strangely, ominously) 令人怀疑地 ‹*behave, enthusiastic, heavy*›; **it looks ~ like a plot** 这看起来很可疑, 像是一个阴谋

suspiciousness /sə'spɪʃəsnɪs/ *n* [u] 猜疑

suss /sʌs/ *vt* Brit colloq **1** (realize, grasp) 意识到 ‹*fact*› **2** (discover character of) 了解 ‹*person*›; **to have sb. ~ed** 了解某人

Phrasal verb
- **suss out** *vt* [**~ sth./sb. out, ~ out sth./sb.**] Brit colloq **1** (work out) 弄明白 ‹*truth, problem*› **2** (understand) 了解 ‹*person*›

sustain /sə'steɪn/ *vt* **1** (maintain) 维持 ‹*interest, friendship, life, economy*›; 使…持续 ‹*sound, interest, campaign*›; **a ~ed effort** 不断的努力; **a ~ed note** 持续音; **he cannot ~ a normal conversation** 他无法进行正常的谈话 **2** (provide strength) «*hope, belief, food*» 支撑 ‹*person*›; **they were ~ed by the knowledge that eventually truth would prevail** 他们知道真理必胜, 这给了他们以力量 **3** (suffer) 遭受 ‹*injury, defeat, damage*›; **to ~ a blow to the head** 头上挨一拳 **4** (bear) 承受 ‹*weight*› **5** Jur (confirm) 认可 ‹*claim, allegation*›; (affirm, uphold) 确认 ‹*decision, verdict*›; **objection ~ed!** 反对有效!

sustainable /sə'steɪnəbl/ *adj* **1** (able to be maintained) 能维持的 ‹*growth, rate*›; 可持续发展的 ‹*market, economy*› **2** Ecol 可持续性的 ‹*agriculture, farming, forestry, energy, future*›; **~ development** 可持续发展 **3** (tenable) 站得住脚的 ‹*argument*›

sustained-release /sə,steɪnd rɪ'li:s/ *adj* [胶囊制剂] 缓释的

sustaining /səs'teɪnɪŋ/ *adj* 提供营养的 ‹*meal, drink*›

sustain pedal, sustaining pedal *ns* [钢琴的] 延音踏板

sustenance /'sʌstɪnəns/ *n* [u] **1** (food) 食物; (nourishment) 营养; **the slaughter of animals for ~** 食用动物的宰杀 **2** (maintenance) 维持; **the ~ of the family** 养家

suture /'su:tʃə(r)/ *n* **1** [c] (stitch) 缝合处; (thread) 缝线 **2** [u] (action) 缝合 **3** [c] Anat 骨缝

SUV *abbr* **= sport utility vehicle** 运动型多功能车

Suva /'su:və/ *pr n* 苏瓦

suzerain /'su:zərən/ *n* formal **1** Pol (state) 宗主国; (sovereign) 宗主国国君; **a ~ power** 宗主权 **2** Hist (feudal overlord) 封建主; **a ~ lord** 封建领主

suzerainty /'su:zərənti/ *n* [u] formal 宗主权

svelte /svelt/ *adj* 苗条的

SW *abbr* ▸**p. 142** **1 = south-west 2 = south-western 3** Radio **= short wave**

swab /swɒb/
A *n* **1** Med (pad) 药签 **2** Med (specimen) 拭子标本; **to take a ~** 用药签取样 **3** (mop) 拖把
B *vt* (*pres p etc.* **-bb-**) **1** Med 用拭子擦拭 ‹*wound, mucus*› **2** (mop) **~ (down)** 擦洗 ‹*deck*›

swaddle /'swɒdl/ *vt* **1** Hist [用襁褓] 包裹 ‹*baby*› **2** (wrap warmly) [用毯子等] 裹紧 ‹*baby, oneself*›; **to ~ sb. in sth.** 用某物将某人裹紧

swag /swæg/ *n* **1** [u] colloq (stolen property) 赃物 **2** [u] Austral (bundle of personal belongings) 行囊 **3** [c] (festoon) 装饰性布幔

swagger /'swægə(r)/
A *vi* **1** (walk) 大摇大摆地走 **2** colloq (boast) 自吹自擂; **to ~ about sth.** 吹嘘某事物
B *n* 趾高气扬

swaggering /'swægərɪŋ/ *adj* 趾高气扬的 ‹*gait, person*›; 神气活现的 ‹*style*›

swagger stick *n* 轻便手杖

swagman /'swægmən/ *n* Austral (travelling labourer) 背着行囊的流动工; (tramp) 背着行囊的流浪汉

Swahili /swə'hi:li/ ▸**p. 426**
A *adj* (of the people) 斯瓦希里人的; (of the language) 斯瓦希里语的
B *n* **1** [c] (*pl* **~**) (person) 斯瓦希里人 **2** [u] (language) 斯瓦希里语

swain /sweɪn/ *n* liter 情郎

swallow[1] /'swɒləʊ/
A *vt* **1** (take down throat) 吞下 ‹*food, drink, pill*›; **to ~ sth. whole** 囫囵吞下某物 **2** (engulf) 吞没; **to be ~ed by the darkness/shadows/flames** 被黑暗/阴影/火苗吞没 **3** (use up) 耗尽 ‹*money, resources, supply*› **4** (believe) 相信 ‹*story, excuse, explanation*›; **to be hard to ~** 难以相信; **he told her a pack of lies, but she ~ed it whole** 他对她说了一大堆谎话, 可是她全都信以为真 **5** (repress) 不流露 ‹*pride, disappointment*›; 抑制 ‹*anger, doubts*› **6** (put up with) 忍受 ‹*insult, criticism*›; **her sarcasm was a bit hard to ~** 她的讽刺让人有点难受
B *vi* (take sth. down throat) 咽下去; (move throat muscles) 做吞咽动作; **I've got a really sore throat, and it hurts to ~** 我的喉咙非常疼, 一吞咽食物就疼; **she ~ed hard and told him the bad news** 她硬下心把坏消息告诉了他
C *n* (gulping action) 吞咽; (amount gulped down) 一次吞咽量; **in one ~** 一口吞下; **a ~ of beer** 一大口啤酒

Phrasal verbs
- **swallow down** *vt* [**~ sth. down, ~ down sth.**] 吞下 ‹*food, drink, medicine*›; **he ~ed down his dinner as fast as he could** 他狼吞虎咽地吃完了晚饭
- **swallow up** *vt* [**~ sb./sth. up, ~ up sb./sth.**]
1 (engulf) 吞没; **the dark mist ~ed her up** 她消失在了阴沉的薄雾中; **I was so embarrassed, I wanted the ground to open and ~ me up** 我非常尴尬, 恨不得有个地缝让我钻进去 **2** (incorporate) 吞并 ‹*company, organization, country*› **3** (use up) 耗尽 ‹*money, resources, supply*›

swallow[2] *n* (bird) 燕子; **one ~ doesn't make a summer** Prov 孤燕不成夏 [一次走运并不代表次次好运]

swallow: ~ dive *n* Brit [直体向前的] 燕式跳水; **~tail** *n* **~tail (butterfly)** 凤蝶

S

swam /swæm/ *pt* ▸**swim A, B**

swami /ˈswɑːmi/ *n* (Hindu saint) [印度教的] 圣人; (Hindu teacher) [印度教的] 宗教导师

swamp /swɒmp/
A *n* [c and u] 沼泽
B *vt* **1** (flood) 淹没 ‹*floor, ship*› **2** fig (overwhelm) «*phone calls, requests*» 使…应接不暇 ‹*organization*›; «*people*» 使…人满为患 ‹*place*›; **to be ~ed with** *or* **by sth.** 某物多得难以招架

swamp fever ▸**p. 377** *n* [u] **1** Vet 马传染性贫血 **2** Med dated 疟疾

swampy /ˈswɒmpi/ *adj* 多沼泽的 ‹*area*›; 湿软的 ‹*ground*›

swan /swɒn/
A *n* 天鹅
B *vi* (*pres p etc.* **-nn-**) 悠游; **to ~ in/out/off** 悠然逛入/逛出/离去; **she's ~ned off to the cinema** 她悠哉悠哉的晃到电影院去了; **to ~ around** 四处闲逛

swan dive *n* Amer = **swallow dive**

swank /swæŋk/ colloq pej
A *vi* esp Brit (boast) 吹牛; (show off) 炫耀; **to ~ about sth.** 炫耀某物
B *n* esp Brit **1** [u] (boasting) 吹嘘; (showing off) 炫耀 **2** [c] (boaster) 吹牛的人; (show-off) 爱卖弄的人
C *adj* Amer = **swanky**

swanky /ˈswæŋki/ *adj* colloq pej **1** (fancy) 奢华的 ‹*hotel, car*› **2** (trying to impress) 摆阔的

swan: ~-necked /ˌswɒnˈnekt/ *adj* **1** (curved) 天鹅颈状的 ‹*tube, lamp*›; **2** (with long neck) 脖子细长优雅的 ‹*girl, creature*›; **~song** *n* (last performance) 告别演出; (last achievement) 最后作品; **~-upping** /ˌswɒnˈʌpɪŋ/ *n* [u] Brit 天鹅喙上刻标记 [每年在泰晤士河上举办的活动，以示王室或公司拥有天鹅]

S

swap /swɒp/
A *vt* (*pres p etc.* **-pp-**) **1** (exchange) 交换; **to ~ sth. (with sb.) for sth. else** 用某物（和某人）交换另一物; **will you ~ me a chocolate for this piece of cake?** 给我把这块蛋糕换成巧克力，好吗？; **I wouldn't ~ you for anyone else!** 我舍不得把你换成别人！ **2** colloq (make exchange with) 和…交换; **if you like this one better, I'll ~ you** 如果你更喜欢这个，我和你换 **3** (reverse position of) 对调…的位置; **to ~ things over** *or* **around** 把东西对调 **4** (take part in exchange of) 交流 ‹*news, information*›; 对调 ‹*jobs, places*›; **to ~ phone numbers** 交换电话号码
B *vi* (*pres p etc.* **-pp-**) 交换
C *n* **1** (exchange) 交换 **2** colloq (item exchanged) 交换品

SWAPO /ˈswɒpəʊ/ *abbr* = **South-West Africa People's Organization** 西南非洲人民组织

sward /swɔːd/ *n* **1** liter (lawn) 草坪 **2** Agric (turf, grass) 草皮

swarm /swɔːm/
A *n* **1** (large group of insects) 一大群; **a ~ of bees/ants/flies** 一大群蜜蜂/蚂蚁/苍蝇 **2** (large number) 涌动的人群; **a ~** *or* **~s of people** 涌动的人群
B *vi* **1** (move or fly in large group) «*insects*» 成群结队地飞 **2** (move quickly in large group) «*people, animals*» 成群移动 **3** (be full) 挤满; **the air was ~ing with mosquitoes** 成群的蚊子在空中飞来飞去; **the city was ~ing with tourists** 城市里游客熙熙攘攘 **4** (climb) **to ~ up/down sth.** 攀上/攀下某物; **the child ~ed up the pole** 孩子爬上了杆子

swarthiness /ˈswɔːðinɪs/ *n* [u] (of person) 黝黑的肤色; (of complexion, skin) 黝黑

swarthy /ˈswɔːði/ *adj* 皮肤黝黑的 ‹*person*›; 黝黑的 ‹*complexion, skin*›

swashbuckler /ˈswɒʃbʌklə(r)/ *n* **1** (adventurer) 自吹自擂的冒险者 **2** (film, book) 传奇历险作品

swashbuckling /ˈswɒʃbʌklɪŋ/ *adj* 传奇历险的

swastika /ˈswɒstɪkə/ *n* **1** (religious symbol) 万字饰 [即卐字饰] **2** (Nazi symbol) 卐字饰

swat /swɒt/
A *vt* (*pres p etc.* **-tt-**) **1** (try to kill) 拍 ‹*insect*› **2** (hit) 拍打 ‹*curtains, table*›; **to ~ sth./sb. with sth.** 用某物拍打某物/某人
B *vi* (*pres p etc.* **-tt-**) 拍打; **to ~ at an insect** 对着昆虫拍去
C *n* **1** (action) 拍打 **2** (implement) 苍蝇拍

swatch /swɒtʃ/ *n* (sample) [尤指织物的] 样品; (collection of samples) [尤指做成书本状的] 样品集

swatch book *n* 样品簿

swathe¹ /sweɪð/ Amer **swath** /swɔːθ/ *n* **1** (strip of grass, crops etc.) 一刈幅 **2** (expanse of land) 一长条地; **vast ~s of countryside** 广袤的乡野; **to cut a ~ through sth.** 严重破坏某物; **the hurricane cut a ~ of destruction through the country** 飓风给该国造成严重破坏

swathe² /sweɪð/
A *vt* 包; **to ~ sb. in sth.** 用某物把某人包起来; **his head was ~d in bandages** 他的头上裹着绷带
B *n* [尤指悬挂装饰用的] 长布条

sway /sweɪ/
A *vi* 摇晃; **to ~ to the music** 跟着音乐的节奏摇摆; **to ~ from side to side/backwards and forwards/back and forth** 左右/前后/来回摇摆; **fronds of seaweed ~ed to and fro in the water** 海草的叶子在水中来回摆动; **the stagecoach ~ed along the bumpy road** 驿站马车在崎岖的路上颠簸前行
B *vt* **1** (swing) 使摇摆; **~ your body in time to the music** 跟着音乐的节奏摇动你的身体 **2** (influence) 使动摇; **to be ~ed by sb./sth.** 被某人/某事物左右; **to ~ sb. in favour of doing sth.** 说服某人赞同做某事; **to ~ the outcome in sb.'s favour** 使结果有利于某人
C *n* **1** [u and c] (swing) 摇摆 **2** [u] liter (power) 势力; (influence) 影响力; **under the ~ of sb./sth.** 在某人/某事物的影响下; **to hold ~ (over sb./sth.)** (be supremely powerful) （对某人/某事物）具有绝对的支配力; (be supremely influential) （对某人/某事物）具有极大的影响力; **rebel forces hold ~ over much of the island** 叛军控制了该岛的大部分地区

swaying /ˈsweɪɪŋ/ *adj attrib* 摇晃的; **~ dancers/palms** 摇摆着的舞者/摇曳的棕榈树

Swazi /ˈswɑːzi/ ▸**p. 426, p. 503**
A *adj* (of Swaziland) 斯威士的; (of the people) 斯威士人的; (of the language) 斯威士语的
B *n* (*pl* **~** *or* **~s**) **1** [c] (person) 斯威士人 **2** [u] (language) 斯威士语

Swaziland /ˈswɑːzɪlænd/ *pr n* 斯威士兰

swear /sweə(r)/ (*pt* **swore**, *pp* **sworn**)
A *vt* **1** (vow, affirm) 发誓; **to ~ (to sb./sth.) that .../to do ...** （向某人/某物）发誓…/发誓做…; **I ~ not to breathe a word to anyone** 我发誓不会向任何人吐露一个字; **I ~ to God I had nothing to do with it** 我向上帝发誓我与此毫无关系; **I didn't take the book: I ~ it!** 我没有拿那本书：我发誓！; **to ~ revenge on sb.** 发誓报复某人; **to ~ blind (that) ...** colloq 一口咬定… **2** (promise under oath) 宣誓 ‹*loyalty, allegiance, fidelity*›; (declare) 立 ‹*oath*›; **to ~ (an oath of) allegiance to sb./sth.** 立誓效忠某人/某物; **to ~ in a court of law that ...** 在法庭上宣誓…; **I ~ on my honour that I knew nothing about this** 我以我的名誉发誓，我对此一无所知; **I ~ to tell the truth, the whole truth, and nothing but the truth** Jur 我宣誓所述属实，及为事实之全部，并无虚言 **3** (bind by promise) 使…宣誓 ‹*person, jury, witness*›; **to be sworn to secrecy/silence/celibacy/chastity** 发誓保守秘密/保持沉默/独身/守贞; **the new prime minister was sworn into office** 新任首相已宣誓就职 **4** (curse) 咒骂; **'damn!' he swore** "他妈的！" 他骂道
B *vi* **1** (curse) 咒骂; **I've never heard you ~ before!** 我以前从未听到过你说脏话！; **to ~ in front of sb.** 当着某人的面骂人; **to ~ at sb./sth.** 咒骂某人/某事物 **2** (affirm) 发誓; **I'll be there — do you ~?** 我会到那儿——你保证吗？ **3** (promise under oath) «*person, witness, soldier*» 宣誓; **to ~ on the Bible/one's honour (that ...)** 以《圣经》的名义/以名誉起誓（…）

Phrasal verbs
- **swear by** *vt* [**~ by sb./sth.**] 极其信赖 ‹*remedy, organization, brand*›; **she ~s by meditation as a way of relieving stress** 她深信冥想是一种减压的方法
- **swear in** *vt* [**~ sb. in, ~ in sb.**] 使…宣誓就职 ‹*president, MP*›; 使…宣誓履行职责 ‹*jury, witness*›; **he was sworn in as president** 他宣誓就任总统
- **swear to** *vt* [**~ to sth.**] 一口咬定; **I wouldn't ~ to it** 我对此不能肯定; **to ~ to having done sth.** 断言做过某事

swearing /ˈsweərɪŋ/ *n* [u] (swear words) 诅咒语; (offensive language) 骂人话

swearing-in ceremony *n* 宣誓就职典礼

swear word *n* 骂人话

sweat /swet/
A *n* **1** [u] (perspiration) 汗; **to be covered in ~** 浑身是汗; **to be dripping** *or* **pouring with ~** 大汗淋漓; **beads** *or* **drops of ~** 汗珠; **no ~!** colloq 小事一桩！; **thanks for everything — hey, no ~!** 多谢你所做的一切——哎呀，举手之劳！; **will that be all right? — yeah, no ~** 这样可以吗？——行，别费事了 **2** [c] (state of perspiring) 出汗; **in a ~** 一身汗; **to break (out) into a ~** 浑身冒汗; **to work up a ~** 干出了一身汗; **night ~s** 盗汗 **3** [u] colloq (hard work) 繁重的工作; (hard effort) 艰苦的努力; **by the ~ of one's brow** liter 靠自己的辛勤劳动; **to break ~** Brit *or* **a ~** Amer colloq 费很大力气 **4** [c] colloq (anxious state) 焦虑; **to be in/get in(to) a ~ (over sb./sth.)** （为某人/某事物）感到/陷入焦虑 **5** [c] colloq (demanding task) 苦差事
B **sweats** *npl* esp Amer colloq (trousers) 运动裤; (sweatsuit) 运动服
C *vi* **1** (perspire) 出汗; **to ~ heavily** *or* **profusely** 大汗淋漓; **he stood there, ~ing with fear** 他站在那儿，害怕得直流汗; **to ~ like a pig** colloq 大汗淋漓 **2** colloq (worry) 担忧; **to let** *or* **make sb. ~** 让某人担心 **3** colloq (work hard) 卖力干活; **to ~ over** 努力完成 ‹*homework, task, report*› **4** Brit Culin (be cooked) «*vegetables*» 被焖煮; **to let sth. ~** 焖煮某物 **5** (produce moisture) «*cheese, vegetable*» 渗出水珠
D *vt* **1** colloq (produce) 冒出; **to ~ buckets** 大汗淋漓; **to ~ bullets** Amer 焦急万分; **to ~ blood** (work hard) 累死累活地工作; **I've ~ed blood over this essay** 我在这篇论文上费尽了心血; **she's ~ed blood to support her family** 她为养家卖命工作 **2** Brit Culin 焖 ‹*vegetables*› **3** Amer colloq (worry about) 为…担忧; **don't ~ the small stuff** 别为细枝末节担忧

Phrasal verbs
- **sweat off** *vt* [**~ sth. off, ~ off sth.**] 通过排汗消耗 ‹*calories, food*›; 通过排汗减轻 ‹*weight*›
- **sweat out** *vt* [**~ sth. out, ~ out sth.**] 通过发汗治好 ‹*cold, chill, fever*›; **to ~ it out** colloq (endure heat or exertion) 熬过; (wait anxiously) 焦急地等待

sweat: ~band *n* **1** Sport [缠在头部或手腕处的] 汗巾; **2** (on hat) [帽子里的] 吸汗带; **~ bath** *n* (structure) 蒸汽浴设施; (action) 蒸气浴; **~ duct** *n* 汗腺管

sweater /ˈswetə(r)/ *n* 毛衣

sweat: ~ gland *n* 汗腺; **~ pants** *npl* 厚运动裤; **~shirt** *n* 厚运动衫; **~shop** *n* 血汗工厂; **~-soaked** *adj* 被汗水湿透的; **~-stained** *adj* 汗渍斑斑的

sweaty /ˈsweti/ *adj* **1** (emitting sweat) 汗津津的 ‹*palm, feet*›; 被汗水湿透的 ‹*clothes*›; 冒水

珠的 ‹*cheese*› **2** (caused by sweat) 出汗导致的; **the ~ smell in the school changing rooms** 学校更衣室内的汗臭味 **3** (causing sweating) 热得使人出汗的 ‹*room, climate, climb, work*›

Swede /swi:d/ ▸**p. 503** *n* 瑞典人

swede /swi:d/ *n* [c and u] Brit **1** (root) 大头菜 **2** (plant) 芜菁甘蓝

Sweden /'swi:dn/ *pr n* 瑞典

Swedish /'swi:dɪʃ/ ▸**p. 426, p. 503**

A *adj* (of Sweden) 瑞典的; (of the people) 瑞典人的; (of the language) 瑞典语的

B *n* [u] (language) 瑞典语

C *npl* **the ~** (people) 瑞典人

Swedish massage *n* [u and c] 瑞典式按摩

sweep /swi:p/

A *vt* (*pt, pp* **swept**) **1** (clean with broom) 清扫; **to ~ sth. clean** 把某物清扫干净 **2** (clear away with broom, brush, hand) 扫去; **to ~ sth. into/on to sth.** 将某物扫进某物/扫到某物上; **to ~ the crumbs on to the floor/into the wastebasket/into a heap** 把面包屑扫到地板上/扫进垃圾桶/扫成一堆; **to ~ sth. from** *or* **off sth.** 将某物从某物上扫除; **to ~ the snow from** *or* **off the path** 扫除路上的积雪 **3** (move or push with force) 推送; **the current swept the logs down the river** 激流把圆木冲向河的下游; **to ~ sb./sth. from** *or* **off/into/on to** *or* **over sth.** 将某人/某物推离/推进/推上某处; **he swept me into his arms** 他一下把我揽入怀中; **a huge wave swept us off our feet** 一个巨浪将我们打翻; **to ~ sb./sth. downstream/out to sea** 将某人/某物冲向下游/大海 **4** (clear of obstacles) «*ship*» 清除 ‹*area, channel, sea*›; **to ~ sth. clear** *or* **free (of sth.)** 清理干净某处(的某物) **5** (put in particular state) 一举送入; **to be swept to** *or* **into power/office** 以压倒优势获得选举胜利上台掌权; **to ~ sb. off his/her feet** 使某人对自己一见倾心 **6** (in election) «*party*» 在…范围内大获全胜 ‹*country*› **7** (move through) «*hurricane, wave, fire*» 横扫 ‹*area, coast, city*›; (spread through) «*disease, crime, rumour*» 席卷 ‹*country, area, city*›; (be directed over) «*gaze, searchlight, periscope*» 扫过 ‹*sky, room, area*› **8** (skim) «*dress, coat*» 掠过 ‹*ground, floor*› **9** (search) «*troops, police, vessel*» 搜索 ‹*area, sea*›; **to ~ sth. for sb./sth.** 在某处搜寻 ‹*escapee, mines, bugs*› **10** (arrange hair) 掠; **to ~ the hair from one's eyes** 把眼睛上的头发掠开; **her hair was swept back from her face/into a chignon** 她的头发是从前往后梳的/梳成了发髻 **11** Amer Sport 获得…的全部胜利 ‹*contest, event*›; 完胜 ‹*team*›; **to ~ the series** 囊括系列比赛的全部冠军

B *vi* (*pt, pp* **swept**) **1** (clean with broom) 打扫 **2** (move through area) 横扫; (spread in area) 席卷; **to ~ across sth.** «*hurricane*» 横扫 ‹*land, area*›; «*disease, rumour, news*» 席卷 ‹*area, city, country*›; **the wind swept in from the east** 风从东边吹来; **huge waves were ~ing over the deck** 巨浪冲上了甲板; **fire swept through the building** 大火蔓延到整个大楼 **3** (move quickly) 快速移动; **to ~ down** «*plane*» 俯冲下来; **to ~ into sth.** «*enemy*» 一举攻入 ‹*region*›; **to ~ past sth.** «*vehicle, car*» 在某物旁一掠而过 **4** (move majestically) 堂皇地移动; **a mighty eagle swept across the sky** 一只雄鹰在空中巍然掠过; **she swept in dressed in a magnificent gown** 她穿着华贵的礼服，仪态优雅地走了进来; **to ~ down/into/out of sth.** 庄严地走下/走进/走出某处 **5** (enter particular state) 一举进入; **to ~ to** *or* **into power/office** 以压倒优势在选举中获胜/一举上台; **to ~ into the lead** 一举取得领先; **to ~ to victory** 一举获胜 **6** (extend) «*road, coast, mountains, plain*» 延伸; **to ~ around/down sth.** 绕着/沿着某物延伸; **to ~ down/up to sth.** 向下/向上延伸到某物; **to ~ north** *or* **northwards/south** *or* **southwards** 向北/向南延伸

C *n* **1** [c] (with broom) 扫; **to give sth. a ~** 扫一扫某物; **this room needs a good ~** 这个房间需要好好打扫一下 **2** [c] (swing) 挥动; **the slow ~ of the pendulum** 钟摆的缓慢摆动; **with** *or* **in one ~ of his hand he knocked all the plates off the shelf** 他手一挥，把盘子全部从架子上扫了下来 **3** [c] (movement in curve) 掠; **to make a ~** 掠过 **4** [c] (curved stretch of road, river, country, etc.) 绵延弯曲的地带; **the ~ of the cliffs/hills** 蜿蜒的悬崖/山丘 **5** [u] (curved range) 范围; **outside the ~ of the guns/searchlights/telescope** 在炮火的射程/探照灯的扫射范围/望远镜的视野之外 **6** [u] (scope of events) 广度; **her book covers the long ~ of the country's history** 她这本书内容涵盖这个国家的漫长历史 **7** [c] (search on land, at sea, by air) 搜寻; **a ~ of** *or* **over** *or* **through sth.** 对…的搜寻 ‹*area, room, land, sea*›; **a ~ for sb./sth.** 对…的搜寻 ‹*criminals, mines, bugs*›; **a ~ with sth.** 用…进行的搜索 ‹*periscope, telescope, radar*›; **to make a ~** 进行搜寻 **8** [c] (comprehensive survey) 扫荡; **a ~ of** *or* **over** *or* **through** 对…的扫荡 ‹*area, land, sea*›; **the bombers made a series of ~s over enemy territory** 轰炸机在敌占区进行了一系列轰炸 **9** [c] esp Brit **= chimney sweep** **10** [c] Amer (series of wins) 连胜; (comprehensive win) 全胜; **a World Series ~** 在世界棒球联赛中的全胜 **11** [c] colloq **= sweepstake**

D **sweeps** *npl* Amer **the ~s** 收视率调查

Phrasal verbs

- **sweep along** *vt* [**~ sb./sth. along**]
  1 (force to move) «*current, water, crowd*» 迫使…前移; **to be swept along by the crowd/the strong current** 被人群/激流裹挟着向前 **2** (cause to become carried away with emotion) 使醉心; **to be swept along by the force of one's emotions** 受感情力量的驱使
- **sweep aside** *vt* [**~ sb./sth. aside, ~ aside sb./sth.**]
  1 (move to one side) 把…推到一边 **2** (ignore) 对…置之不理 ‹*person, protest, offer, inhibition*›
- **sweep away**
  A [**~ sth. away, ~ away sth.**] *vt*
  1 (clear away with broom, brush, hand) 扫除 ‹*dirt, snow, leaves*› **2** (get rid of) 彻底消除 ‹*restriction, obstacle, difficulty, doubt*›
  B [**~ sb./sth. away, ~ away sb./sth.**] *vt* «*flood, hurricane, storm*» 卷走 ‹*object, bridge, person*›; **a big wave came in and swept him away** 一个大浪涌来把他冲走了
  C [**~ sb. away, ~ away sb.**] *vt* «*enthusiasm, passion, charm*» 使醉心; **to be swept away by sth.** 对某事物着迷
- **sweep out** *vt* [**~ sth. out, ~ out sth.**] 把…打扫干净 ‹*room*›
- **sweep over** *vt* [**~ over sb./sth.**]
  1 (be directed over) «*eyes, gaze*» 扫视 ‹*person, room*›; «*searchlight, periscope*» 扫过 ‹*sky, area*› **2** (come over) «*panic, guilt, elation*» 强烈影响; **fear swept over him** 恐惧感笼罩着他; **the feeling swept over me that ...** 我猛然觉得…
- **sweep up**
  A *vi* 打扫干净; **after you've finished in the kitchen, please remember to ~ up** 你在厨房里干完活后记得打扫干净
  B *vt* **1** [**~ sth. up, ~ up sth.**] (clear away with broom, brush, hand) 打扫; **he swept the leaves up into a pile** 他把落叶扫成了一堆 **2** [**~ sb./sth. up, ~ up sb./sth.**] (lift) 一把抱起 ‹*person*›; 一把拿起 ‹*object*› **3** [**~ sb. up, ~ up sb.**] (cause to become carried away) «*passion, pleasure, enthusiasm, optimism*» 使忘乎所以; **to be swept up in** 沉醉于 ‹*revolution, wave of nationalism*›

sweepback /'swi:pbæk/ *n* [u] [机翼等的] 后掠

sweeper /'swi:pə(r)/ *n* **1** (cleaner) (person) 清洁工; (machine) 清扫器 **2** Sport [足球赛的] 自由中卫

sweeping /'swi:pɪŋ/

A *adj* **1** (far-reaching) 影响广泛的 ‹*cuts, legislation*›; **~ gains/losses** 重大收益/损失; **~ changes/reforms** 彻底的变化/全面的改革 **2** (decisive) 决定性的 ‹*victory*› **3** pej (without exceptions) 一概而论的 ‹*assertion*›; (too general) 过于笼统的 ‹*generalization, statement, accusation*› **4** (expansive) 幅度大的 ‹*movement, gesture*›; 弧度大的 ‹*bow, curve*›; 下摆大的 ‹*skirt*›

B *npl* **sweepings** 扫拢的垃圾

sweep second hand *n* 长秒针

sweepstake /'swi:psteɪk/ *n* **1** (form of gambling) 赌金全赢制 **2** (race) 赌金全赢制赛马

sweet /swi:t/

A *adj* **1** (sugary) 含糖的 ‹*food, drink*›; (not sour) 甜的 ‹*fruit, flavour*›; (not dry) 口感甜的 ‹*wine, cider*›; **to taste ~** 尝起来是甜的; **to have a ~ tooth** 喜欢吃甜食 **2** (fragrant) 芳香的 ‹*fragrance, flower*›; **to smell ~** 闻上去很香; **an unpleasantly ~ smell** 一种不好闻的香味 **3** (melodious, pleasurable) 甜美的 ‹*sound, voice*›; 美妙的 ‹*feeling, love*›; **to be ~ to sb.'s ear(s)** 是某人乐于听到的 **4** (pure, fresh) 清新的 ‹*air, water, smell*›; 新鲜的 ‹*milk*› **5** esp Brit (cute) 可爱的 ‹*baby, animal, face, expression*› **6** (kind) 善良的 ‹*person, nature*›; **to be ~ to sb.** 对某人友善; **to be ~ of sb.** 某人很好心; **it was ~ of her to offer to help** 她主动提供帮助，真是好心人; **~ sixteen** Amer colloq 甜蜜的 16 岁 [指女孩子的16岁生日聚会]; **to keep sb. ~** colloq 讨好某人 **7** iron (for emphasis) [用以加重语气]; **what had happened? — ~ nothing** 发生了什么事？——啥事儿也没有; **~ f. a., ~ Fanny Adams** Brit euph colloq 啥都没有; **what did I get out of it? ~ f.a.!** 我从中得到了什么？啥都没有！; **in one's own ~ time** *or* **way** colloq 随心所欲地; **to go one's own ~ way** 我行我素 **8** dated colloq (infatuated) 着迷的; **to be ~ on sb.** 迷恋某人

B *n* **1** [c] Brit (candy) 糖果; **a bag of ~s** 一包糖果 **2** [u and c] Brit (dessert) 甜食 **3** [u] dated (darling) 亲爱的; **my ~** 宝贝儿

sweet: ~-and-sour *adj* 糖醋的; **~bread** *n* [食用的小牛或羊的] 胰脏; **~ chestnut** *n* 欧洲栗; **~corn** *n* [u] 甜玉米; **~ course** *n* 甜点

sweeten /'swi:tn/

A *vt* **1** (in taste) 使…变甜 ‹*food, drink*›; **to be ~ed with sth.** 加了某物变甜 **2** (in smell, purity) «*air freshener*» 使…清新 ‹*air*› **3** (improve) «*person, action, news*» 使…变轻松 ‹*mood*›; 使…变温和 ‹*temper*›; «*company, government*» 使…更诱人 ‹*offer, deal, package*› **4** colloq **= sweeten up**

B *vi* **1** (in taste) «*fruit, tomato, sauce*» 变甜 **2** (in manner) «*expression, smile*» 变和蔼

Phrasal verb

- **sweeten up** *vt* [**~ sb. up, ~ up sb.**] colloq 哄

sweetener /'swi:tnə(r)/ *n* [c and u] **1** (substance) 甜味剂 **2** colloq (incentive) 甜头; (bribe) 贿赂

sweetheart /'swi:thɑ:t/ *n* **1** (darling) 亲爱的; (lovable person) 招人喜欢的人 **2** (boyfriend, girlfriend) 恋人

sweetie /'swi:ti/ *n* **1** (term of endearment) 亲爱的 **2** (nice person) 招人喜欢的人 **3** Brit colloq (candy) 糖果

sweetish /'swi:tɪʃ/ *adj* 有点甜的

sweetly /'swi:tli/ *adv* **1** (gently, kindly) 和蔼地 ‹*smile, say, behave*› **2** (attractively) 可爱地 ‹*dressed, decorated*› **3** (melodiously) 悦耳地 ‹*play, sing*› **4** Mech (quietly, efficiently) 平稳地 ‹*go, move*›; **the engine's running ~** 发动机运转顺畅 **5** Sport (accurately, squarely) 顺顺当当地 ‹*hit, kick, pass*›

sweet: ~meat *n* (confectionery or sweet food) 甜食; (sweet delicacy) 蜜饯; **~-natured** *adj* **= ~-tempered**

sweetness /ˈswiːtnɪs/ *n* [u] **1** (in taste) 甜味 **2** (in smell, purity) 清新 **3** (in sound) 悦耳 **4** (in manner, character) 和蔼; **to be all ~ and light** colloq 和蔼可亲 **5** (in appearance) 赏心悦目

sweet: ~ nothings *npl* 绵绵情话; **to whisper ~ nothings (into sb.'s ear)** (对某人) 低诉喁喁情话; **~ pea** *n* 香豌豆; **~ potato** *n* [c and u] 红薯; **~ shop** ▸**p. 409** *n* Brit 糖果店; **~-smelling** *adj* 芬芳的

sweet talk

A *n* [u] 甜言蜜语

B **sweet-talk** *vt* 用甜言蜜语劝说; **to ~ sb. into sth./doing sth.** 用花言巧语哄某人做某事

sweet: ~-tempered *adj* 脾气好的; **~ trolley** *n* Brit [餐厅里的] 手推甜点车; **~ william** *n* 美国石竹

swell /swel/

A *vi* (*pt* **swelled,** *pp* **swollen** *or* **swelled**) **1** (distend) «*part of body*» 肿胀 **2** (increase in number or size) 增长; **the crowd had swollen to about 20,000** 聚集的人群增加到了大约2万人 **3** (expand) «*object, wood, balloon, tyre*» 膨胀 **4** (rise) «*river*» 上涨 **5** (curve out) 鼓起; **the sails ~ed in the wind** 船帆在风中鼓起 **6** (well up) «*emotion*» 涌起; **pride ~ed in her heart as she watched her daughter** 她看着女儿，心中涌起一阵骄傲 **7** (be affected by emotion) «*person, heart*» 充满; **to ~ with emotion** 情绪激动; **she felt herself ~ with indignation** 她感到义愤填膺 **8** (grow louder) 增强; **cheers ~ed through the hall** 欢呼声响彻了大厅

B *vt* (*pt* **swelled,** *pp* **swollen** *or* **swelled**) **1** (increase in number or size) 增加; **to ~ the ranks of sth.** 增加某物的数量 **2** (cause to rise) «*rain, flood water*» 使…上涨 ‹*river*› **3** (cause to curve out) 使鼓起; **the wind began to ~ the sails** 风把船帆吹得鼓了起来

C *n* **1** (movement of sea) 涌动; **the gentle/heavy ~ of the sea** 大海舒缓/巨大的浪涌 **2** (bulge) 隆起; **the firm ~ of her breasts** 她挺拔的双乳 **3** (increase) (in amount of support, opposition, patriotism) 增长; (in loudness of sound) 增强; **a massive ~ of strings** 弦乐声部的磅礴响起 **4** (welling up of emotion) 高涨; **a ~ of pride swept over him** 一股自豪之情涌上他的心头 **5** dated colloq (fashionable person) 时髦人物 **6** (mechanism of organ, harmonium) 音量调节器

D *adj* Amer dated colloq 很棒的 ‹*time, party, guy*›

E *adv* Amer dated colloq 极好地

Phrasal verb

- **swell up** *vi* **1** (distend) «*part of body*» 肿胀; (expand) «*bud, wood, balloon, tyre*» 膨胀 **2** (well up) 涌起; **anger ~ed up in her chest** 她心中涌起愤怒 **3** (be affected by emotion) 充满感情; **I felt my heart ~ up** 我感觉心潮起伏; **to ~ up with pride** 满腔自豪

swelling /ˈswelɪŋ/

A *n* **1** [c] (swollen area) 肿胀处 **2** [u] (swollen condition) 肿胀 **3** [u] (increasing) (in intensity, volume) 增强; (in number, amount) 增加

B *adj* **1** (becoming swollen) 肿胀的 ‹*ankle*›; 饱满的 ‹*fruit*›; 鼓起的 ‹*sails*›; fig 自我膨胀的 ‹*heart, pride*› **2** (increasing) 增加的 ‹*population*›; 上涨的 ‹*river*›

swelter /ˈsweltə(r)/ *vi* 酷热难当

sweltering /ˈsweltərɪŋ/ *adj* 酷热难耐的

swept /swept/ *pt, pp* ▸**sweep A, B**

swept: ~-back *adj* **1** (of aircraft wings) 后掠的; **2** (of hair) 往后梳的; **~-wing** *adj* 有后掠翼的

swerve /swɜːv/

A *vi* **1** (change direction) 突然转向 **2** fig (deviate) 背离

B *vt* 使…突然转向 ‹*vehicle, motorcycle*›

C *n* **1** [c] (act of swerving) 突然转向 **2** [u] Sport (put on ball) [足球等的] 弧线运动

swift¹ /swɪft/ *adj* **1** (happening quickly) 迅速的 ‹*reaction, growth, development*›; 立刻的 ‹*departure, return*›; **to be ~ to do sth.** 迅速做某事; **to be ~ in sth./doing sth.** 在某事上/做某事上动作迅速 **2** (fast-moving) 速度飞快的 ‹*horse, runner, movement*›; 湍急的 ‹*river, current*›; **~-footed** 脚快的

swift² *n* (bird) 雨燕

swiftly /ˈswɪftli/ *adv* **1** (promptly) 迅速地 ‹*respond, decide, return, depart*›; 快速地 ‹*grow, develop*› **2** (fast) 飞快地 ‹*run, swim*›; 湍急地 ‹*flow*›

swiftness /ˈswɪftnɪs/ *n* [u] (promptness) 迅捷; (transitoriness) 瞬间

swig /swɪɡ/ colloq

A *vt* (*pres p etc.* **-gg-**) 大口喝

B *n* [喝的] 一大口

swill /swɪl/

A *vt* **1** Brit (wash, rinse) 冲洗 ‹*draining board, deck, bucket*›; **to ~ sth. with sth.** 用某物冲洗某物; **to ~ one's mouth with water** 用水漱口 **2** Brit (swirl) 使…晃荡 ‹*liquid, drink*› **3** colloq pej (drink) 大口喝 ‹*tea, beer*›

B *vi* Brit «*liquid, water*» 晃荡; **to ~ around** *or* **about** 来回晃荡

C *n* **1** [u] (feed for pigs) 泔脚 **2** [c] colloq (mouthful) 一大口 **3** [c] Brit (wash, rinse) 冲洗

Phrasal verbs

- **swill down** *vt* [**~ sth. down, ~ down sth.**] **1** Brit (wash down) 冲洗 ‹*steps, draining board, deck*› **2** colloq (accompany with large quantities of drink) 边大量喝饮料边吃 ‹*food, meal*›
- **swill out** *vt* [**~ sth. out, ~ out sth.**] Brit 涮洗 ‹*bottle, jug, sink*›

swim /swɪm/

A *vi* (*pres p* **-mm-,** *pt* **swam,** *pp* **swum**) **1** (move through water) 游泳; **to ~ underwater/on one's back/on one's front** 潜泳/仰泳/俯游; **to ~ downstream/upstream** 游向下游/上游; **to ~ across sth.** 游过某物; **to ~ for/to the shore** 游向岸边; **to ~ around/away/past** 来回游动/游走/游过去; **to ~ in/up and down sth.** 在某物中游/游来游去; **to leave sb. to sink or ~** fig 让某人自己去拼搏 **2** (be immersed) 浸泡; **to be ~ming in sth.** 浸泡在某物中; **to be ~ming with sth.** 充溢着某物; **the meat was ~ming in fat** 肉油汪汪的; **her eyes were ~ming with tears** 她眼睛里饱含泪水 **3** (appear to whirl, reel) «*scene, room, mirage*» 仿佛在旋转; «*letters, figures, pages*» 似乎在晃动; «*head*» 眩晕; **to ~ before sb.'s eyes** 仿佛在某人的眼前晃动

B *vt* (*pres p* **-mm-,** *pt* **swam,** *pp* **swum**) **1** (perform action, cover distance) 游过 ‹*length, mile*›; **to ~ the Channel** 游过英吉利海峡 **2** (compete in) 参加…游泳; **to ~ a race/event/heat** 参加游泳比赛/项目/预赛; **the race is swum over 10 lengths** 比赛要游5个来回

C *n* 游泳; **to go for a ~** 去游泳; **to have a ~** 游泳; **in the ~ (of things)** colloq 合潮流

swim bladder *n* (鱼) 鳔

swimmer /ˈswɪmə(r)/ *n* 游泳者

swimming /ˈswɪmɪŋ/ ▸**p. 307** *n* [u] 游泳

swimming: ~ baths *npl* Brit (pool) 室内游泳池; (building) 游泳馆; **~ cap** *n* 游泳帽; **~ costume** *n* Brit **= swimsuit**; **~ instructor** ▸**p. 409** *n* 游泳教练

swimmingly /ˈswɪmɪŋli/ *adv* colloq 顺利地; **to go ~** 一切顺利

swimming: ~ pool *n* (pool) 游泳池; (building) 游泳馆; **~ trunks** *npl* [男式] 游泳裤

swimsuit /ˈswɪmsuːt, -sjuːt/ *n* 游泳衣

swindle /ˈswɪndl/

A *vt* **1** (cheat) 诈骗; **to ~ sb. out of sth.** 诈骗某人某物 **2** (obtain fraudulently) 骗取; **to ~ sth. out of sb.** 骗取某人某物

B *n* (scheme or action) (illegal) 诈骗; (legal but unfair) 欺骗

swindler /ˈswɪndlə(r)/ *n* (acting illegally) 诈骗犯; (acting legally but unfairly) 骗子

swine /swaɪn/ *n* **1** (*pl* **swine**) Amer formal (pig) 猪 **2** (*pl* **~s**) colloq pej (person) 猪猡 **3** (*pl* **~s**) colloq pej (difficult thing) 难对付的事物

swine flu ▸**p. 377** *n* [u] 猪流感

swineherd /ˈswaɪnhɜːd/ *n* 猪饲养员

swing /swɪŋ/

A *vt* (*pt, pp* **swung**) **1** (cause to sway) 摆动 ‹*arms, legs*›; 挥动 ‹*object*›; **to ~ sb./sth. to and fro/backwards and forwards/from side to side** 来回/前后/左右摇晃某人/某物 **2** (move in curve) 使…突然转动 ‹*gate, implement*›; 使…突然转向 ‹*person, vehicle*›; **he swung the camera around to face the opposite direction** 他猛地将照相机转过来对着相反方向; **to ~ sb./sth. around and around** 使某人/某物不停地转动; **the driver swung the car around the corner** 司机猛地将车转过拐角; **she swung the sword at my head** 她挥剑朝我的头砍来; **to ~ sb./sth. into/on to sth.** 将某人/某物抛进某物/抛到某物上; **he swung the sword over his head** 他手拿那把剑在头上挥舞; **the captain swung the periscope through 180°** 船长将潜望镜转动了180度; **he swung the gate open/shut** 他一下推开/关上了大门 **3** (aim) 挥 ‹*blow*›; **she swung a punch at him** 她朝他挥了一拳 **4** (cause to change) 使…转变 ‹*person, jury, election, match*›; **to ~ sb./sth. sb.'s way** 使某人/某事物转而按某人的方式行事/发展; **to ~ sb./sth. in sb.'s favour** 使某人/某事物转而变得对某人有利; **to ~ voters away from/towards the party** 使选民们转而反对/支持这个政党 **5** colloq (cause to succeed) 搞定 ‹*interview, deal*›; 搞到 ‹*job*›; **to ~ it for sb. (to do sth.)** 为某人搞定 (某事); **to ~ it** 搞定; **can you ~ it for me?** 你能为我搞定吗?; **it was the large bribe that swung it** 靠大笔贿赂才把事情办成

B *vi* (*pt, pp* **swung**) **1** (sway) 摇摆; **she sat on the branch with her legs ~ing** 她坐在树枝上，双腿摆动着; **a set of keys swung from her belt** 一串钥匙在她的腰带上摆来摆去; **the boy swung by his hands from the branch** 小男孩用手挂在树枝上来回摆荡; **the bucket was ~ing on the end of a rope** 桶在绳子的一端摇晃着; **to ~ to and fro/backwards and forwards/from side to side** 来回/前后/左右摇摆; **to ~ at anchor** Naut 在锚地摇摆; **to ~ both ways** colloq 是双性恋 **2** (move by holding on to sth.) «*person, animal*» 荡; **to ~ across/down/up sth.** 荡过/荡下/荡上某物; **to ~ on to/along sth.** 荡到某物上去/沿着某物荡; **the ape swung from branch to branch** 大猩猩从一根树枝荡到另一根树枝 **3** (move in curve) «*gate, door*» 转动; «*car, river, road*» 转向; **to ~ around/back/into/out of/to** *or* **towards sth.** 转过/折返回/拐进/拐出/转向某物; **to ~ open/shut** 转动着打开/关闭; **to ~ into action** 立即投入行动; **a full-scale evacuation operation swung into action** 全线撤退行动立即开始实施 **4** (move with swaying gait) 摇摆着行进; **to ~ along/past** 摇摆着向前走/走过去; **to ~ along/down/up the road** 摇摇摆摆地沿路走向前/走下去/走过来 **5** (try to hit) 挥击; **to ~ at sb./sth. (with sth.)** (挥动某物) 朝某人/某物打去 **6** (change) «*person, voting, mood, opinion*» 转变; **the game could ~ either way** 这场比赛胜负未知; **to ~ between sth. and sth./from sth. to sth.** 在某事物和某事物之间摇摆/从某事物转变到某事物; **his mood ~s unpredictably from optimism to pessimism** 他的情绪变化无常，时而乐观，时而悲观; **to ~ to** *or* **towards sth.** 朝某事物转变; **the mood of the voters has swung towards the government** 选民们的态度已经变得倾向于政府了;

to ～ in favour of/against sb./sth. 变得有利/不利于某人/某事物 **7** colloq (be lively) 热闹; (be fashionable) 时髦; **the party was ～ing** 这个聚会很热闹 **8** colloq (in terms of sexual preference) 滥交; (by swapping sexual partner) 交换性伴侣 **9** (be played, play rhythmically) «*music, song, tune*» 具有强劲节奏; «*band, musician*» 以强劲节奏演奏; «*person*» 以强劲节奏演唱

C *v refl* (*pt, pp* **swung**) **to ～ oneself across/along sth.** 荡过某物/沿着某物荡; **to ～ oneself down/up** 荡到下面/上面去; **she swung herself from branch to branch** 她从一根树枝荡到另一根树枝; **he swung himself into the driver's seat/out of the car** 他纵身坐到了驾驶座上/跳下汽车

D *n* **1** [c] (wheeling action of arm, object) 挥动; Sport (hitting action of golf club, bat) 挥击; **to take** *or* **aim a ～ at sb./sth. (with sth.)** (挥动某物) 朝某人/某物打去 **2** [c] (swaying movement of pendulum, instrument, body, hips) 摆动; (wide curved movement of ball, door, gate, window) 转动; **to go with a ～** Brit colloq «*party, event*» 气氛热烈; **to get in** *or* **into the ～ (of it** *or* **things)** colloq (become fully involved) 融入 (某事物); **to get back in** *or* **into the ～ (of it** *or* **things)** colloq (get used to again) 重新熟悉 (某种情况); **to be in full ～** «*party, meeting, strike, inquiry*» 正在热烈进行中 **3** [c] (change) (in voting, public opinion, mood) 变动; (in prices, values, economy, business activity) 波动; **market ～s** Fin 市场波动; **he is prone to abrupt ～s in mood** *or* **mood ～s** 他的情绪容易大起大落; **a ～ to the left/right** Pol 向左翼/右翼的摇摆; **a ～ towards/away from sb./sth.** 向着/背离某人/某事物的变化 **4** [c] (suspended seat) 秋千; **can we go on the ～s?** 我们可以去荡秋千吗? ; **to give sb. a ～** 为某人晃秋千 **5** [u] (type of music) 摇摆乐 **6** [u and c] (rhythm or drive of music, dance) 强劲的节奏; **to go with a ～** «*music, tune, piece*» 有强劲的节奏 **7** [c] Amer (swift tour) [尤指竞选中的] 巡回行程

E *modif* Mus 摇摆乐的; **the ～ era** 摇摆乐时代; **～ dance/music/band** 摇摆舞/摇摆乐/摇摆乐团

(Phrasal verb)

• **swing around,** Brit **swing round** *vi* 突然转向; **to ～ around in one's chair** 坐着椅子突然转身; **to ～ around on sb.** 突然转向某人; **to ～ around to do sth.** 突然转身去做某事

swing: ～bin *n* Brit 推盖垃圾桶; **～boat** *n* Brit 船形秋千; **～bridge** *n* 平转桥; **～ door** *n* 双开式弹簧门

swingeing /ˈswɪndʒɪŋ/ *adj* Brit 大幅度的 ‹*cut, increases*›; 巨额的 ‹*charges*›; 猛烈的 ‹*sanctions, attack*›

swinger /ˈswɪŋə(r)/ *n* colloq 时髦活跃的人; **an ageing ～** pej 老来俏

swinging /ˈswɪŋɪŋ/ *adj usu attrib* 节奏感强的 ‹*music, step*›; 活跃时髦的 ‹*party, nightlife*›; **the ～ sixties** 活跃的 60 年代

swinging door *n* Amer = **swing door**

swing: ～ shift *n* Amer [三班制的] 中班; **～ state** *n* Amer 摇摆州 [指美国大选中选民举棋不定的州]; **～-wing** *n* **1** (aircraft wing) 可变后掠翼; **2** **～ (aircraft)** 可变后掠翼飞机

swipe /swaɪp/

A *vi* 挥击; **to ～ at sth.** 击打某物

B *vt* **1** (hit) 挥击 ‹*person, object*› **2** colloq (steal) 偷窃 **3** (pass through reader) 刷 ‹*credit card, identity card*›

C *n* 挥击

swipe card *n* 磁卡

swipe card reader *n* 磁卡读卡器

swirl /swɜːl/

A *vi* «*water, leaves, smoke*» 打旋儿; «*dancer*» 旋转; «*skirt*» 摆动

B *vt* «*wind, water*» 使…打旋儿 ‹*dust, leaves, smoke*›; «*dancer*» 使…旋转 ‹*dance partner*›; «*wind, dancer*» 使…摆动 ‹*skirt*›; **to ～ coffee** 搅咖啡

C *n* **1** (movement) 旋动 **2** (shape) 螺旋形

swish /swɪʃ/

A *vi* «*skirt, curtain*» 窸窣作响; «*tail, whip, club*» 刷刷作响; «*grass, leaves*» 沙沙作响

B *vt* 窸窣地摆动 ‹*skirt, curtain*›; «*animal*» 刷刷地甩动 ‹*tail*›; 嗖嗖地挥动 ‹*cane, scythe*›

C *n* (of skirt, curtain) 窸窣声; (of grass) 沙沙声; (of tail) 刷刷声; (of whip, cane, club etc.) 嗖嗖声; (of water) 哗哗声

D *adj* Brit colloq (luxurious) 豪华的 ‹*hotel, car*›; 华丽的 ‹*outfit*›

Swiss /swɪs/ ▸**p. 503**

A *adj* (of Switzerland) 瑞士的; (of the people) 瑞士人的

B *n pl* **the ～** 瑞士人

Swiss: ～ Alps *n* **the ～ Alps** 瑞士阿尔卑斯山脉; **～ army knife, ～ army penknife** *ns* Brit 瑞士军刀; **～ chard** *n* [u] 叶甜菜; **～ cheese** *n* [u] 瑞士干酪; **～ Guard** *n* **1** + *v sing or pl* (corps) **the ～ Guard** 瑞士侍卫队; **2** + *v sing* (person) 瑞士侍卫兵; **～ roll** *n* [c and u] Brit 卷筒蛋糕

switch /swɪtʃ/

A *n* **1** Elec 开关; **the ～ is on/off** 开关是开着/关着的; **to press/flick/throw a ～** 按下/啪地按下/推动开关 **2** (change) 转变; **a ～ in** *or* **of policy/styles** 政策/风格的转变; **a ～ from sth. (to sth.)** 从某事物 (到某事物) 的转变; **the polls show a ～ to the Conservatives** 民意调查显示人们转向支持保守党 **3** (substitution) 调换; **a ～ of sb./sth. for sb./sth.** …替换为…; **to make a ～** 进行调换 **4** Amer (points on railway) 道岔 **5** (stick) 细枝条 **6** Equit 鞭子; **a riding ～** 马鞭 **7** (hairpiece) 假发

B *vt* **1** (redirect, change) 改变 ‹*attention, bank account, brands, flights*›; **to ～ lanes** 改变行车道; **the aim is to ～ the emphasis to research and development** 目标是把重点转到研发方面; **he ～ed his allegiance back to Labour** 他转而又效忠工党 **2** (swap around) 调换 ‹*objects*›; (exchange) 交换 ‹*roles, jobs*›; **to ～ sth. with sth./sb.** 用某物调换某物/和某人交换某物

C *vi* **1** (change) 改变; **to ～ from sth./doing sth. to sth./doing sth.** 从某事/做某事转到某事/做某事; **to ～ between languages/programmes** 转换语言/转台; **she ～ed from sales back to teaching** 她从销售工作回到了教学工作 **2** TV, Radio 转换频道; **to ～ to** 转换到 ‹*channel, station, programme*› **3** (swap positions) 交换位置; (swap roles) 交换角色; (swap shifts) 交换班次; **to ～ with sb.** 和某人交换 **4** Comput 转换程序; **to ～ to sth.** 转换到某程序

(Phrasal verbs)

• **switch around**

A *vi* (swap positions) 交换位置; (swap roles) 交换角色

B *vt* [**～ sb./sth. around**] 交换…的位置; **to ～ the players around at half-time** 使运动员在半场结束时交换场地

• **switch off**

A *vt* [**～ sth. off, ～ off sth.**]

1 (turn off) 关掉 ‹*appliance, light*›; 停止 ‹*supply, engine*›; **to ～ itself off** «*appliance, light*» 自动关闭 **2** fig colloq (stop using) 停止施展 ‹*charm*›

B *vi* **1** (turn off light) 关灯; (turn off machine) 关机器 **2** (be turned off automatically) «*appliance, light*» 自动关闭 **3** colloq (stop paying attention) 不再注意

• **switch on**

A *vt* [**～ sth. on, ～ on sth.**]

1 (turn on) 打开 ‹*appliance, light, supply*›; 启动 ‹*engine*›; **to ～ itself on** «*appliance, light*» 自动开启 **2** fig colloq (start using) 开始施展 ‹*charm*›

B *vi* **1** (turn on light) 开灯; (turn on machine) 开机器 **2** (be turned on automatically) «*appliance, light*» 自动打开

• **switch over** *vi* **1** (change) «*consumer, voter, company*» 改变; **to ～ over (from sth.) to sth.** (从某事物) 转变至某事物 **2** Brit TV, Radio 转换频道; **to ～ over to sth.** 换到 ‹*channel, station, programme*› **3** (swap roles) 交换角色

• **switch round** Brit = **switch around**

switch: ～back *n* **1** Brit (railway, road, path) 高低起伏的路线; **2** Brit (roller coaster) 过山车; **3** Amer (bend) [尤指上山坡道上的] 180 度急转弯; **～-blade** *n* = **flick knife**

switchboard /ˈswɪtʃbɔːd/ *n* (installation) 电话总机; (staff) 总机接线员

switchboard operator ▸**p. 409** *n* 总机接线员

switched-on /ˌswɪtʃtˈɒn/ *adj* Brit colloq 新潮的

switcheroo /ˈswɪtʃəruː/ *n* Amer colloq 意想不到的变化

switch: ～-hitter *n* Amer **1** (batter in baseball) 能左右开弓的击球员; **2** colloq (bisexual) 双性恋者; **～-over** *n* 转换; **a ～-over from sth.** 脱离某物的转变; **a ～-over to sth.** 向某事物的转变; **～-yard** *n* Amer 编组场

Switzerland /ˈswɪtzələnd/ *pr n* 瑞士

swivel /ˈswɪvl/

A *n* (coupling device) 联轴器; (pivot) 旋轴; *modif* 旋转的 ‹*seat, lamp, mechanism*›

B *vi* (*pres p etc.* **-ll-** Brit, **-l-** Amer) «*chair, telescope*» 旋转; «*head, eyes, person*» 转动

C *vt* (*pres p etc.* **-ll-** Brit, **-l-** Amer) «*person, mechanism*» 转动 ‹*telescope, gun, head*›; **to ～ one's hips** 扭胯部

(Phrasal verb)

• **swivel round**

A *vi* 转过来

B *vt* [**～ sth./sb. round, ～ round sth./sb.**] 旋转 ‹*telescope, periscope*›; 转动 ‹*chair, head, oneself*›

swivel chair *n* 转椅

swizz, swiz /swɪz/ *n* Brit colloq 骗局

swizzle /ˈswɪzl/ *n* Brit colloq = **swizz**

swizzle stick *n* 搅酒棒

swollen /ˈswəʊlən/

A *pp* ▸**swell A, B**

B *adj* 肿胀的 ‹*ankle, gland*›; 上涨的 ‹*river*›; **to have a ～ head** fig 自命不凡

swollen-headed /ˌswəʊlənˈhedɪd/ *adj* 自命不凡的

swoon /swuːn/

A *vi* **1** (faint) 昏倒 **2** (be in ecstasies) 痴迷; **to ～ over** *or* **at sb./sth.** 为某人/某事物神魂颠倒; **to ～ with excitement** 激动得难以自持

B *n* dated or liter 昏厥; **in a ～** 处于昏迷状态

swoop /swuːp/

A *vi* **1** (fly downwards) «*plane, bird*» 俯冲; **to ～ down** 俯冲下来 **2** (attack) «*army, raider, police*» 突然袭击; **to ～ on sb./sth.** 突袭某人/某处

B *n* **1** (downward flight) 俯冲 **2** (attack) 突然袭击

swoosh /swʊʃ/

A *vi* «*skirt, tall grass, tyre, leaves*» 发出嗖嗖声; «*water, surf*» 发出哗哗声; **cars ～ed past** 汽车嗖嗖地疾驶而过

B *n* **1** (sound and movement) (of fabric, foliage, car etc.) 嗖嗖声; (of water, surf) 哗哗声 **2** (stripe) 彩条标识

swop /swɒp/ *vt, vi, n* = **swap**

sword /sɔːd/ *n* 剑; **to put sb. to the ～** 用剑刺死某人; **he who lives by the ～ dies by the ～** 玩火者必自焚; **to beat** *or* **turn one's ～s into ploughshares** fig 铸剑为犁 [指化干戈为玉帛]; **to cross ～s (with sb.)** (与某人) 发生争执; **to be a double-edged** *or* **two-edged ～** fig 是一把双刃剑; **the ～ of justice** 司法权

S

sword: ~ dance *n* [英格兰北部等地的] 剑舞; **~fish** *n* (*pl* **~fish** *or* **~fishes**) 剑鱼; **~ of Damocles** /ˌsɔːd əv ˈdæməkliːz/ *n* 达摩克利斯剑 [指随时可能降临的灾祸]; **~play** *n* [u] (skill) 剑术; (action) 舞剑; fig (repartee) 机智的巧辩

swordsman /ˈsɔːdzmən/ *n* 剑客

swordsmanship /ˈsɔːdzmənʃɪp/ *n* [u] 剑术

sword: ~stick *n* [内藏剑或匕首的] 剑杖; **~-swallower** *n* 表演吞剑的人

swore /swɔː(r)/ *pt* ▸**swear**

sworn /swɔːn/

A *pp* ▸**swear**

B *adj* **1** (made under oath) 宣誓过的 ‹*declaration, testimony*›; **~ statement** 宣誓声明 **2** (avowed) 发过誓的 ‹*friend, ally*›; 不共戴天的 ‹*enemy*›

swot /swɒt/ Brit colloq

A *vi* (*pres p etc.* **-tt-**) [尤指为准备考试] 刻苦学习; **to ~ for** 用功准备 ‹*exam, interview*›

B *n* pej 书呆子

Phrasal verb

• **swot up** Brit colloq

A *vt* [**~ sth. up, ~ up sth.**] 刻苦学习 ‹*subject*›

B *vi* **to ~ up on** 用功温习 ‹*subject*›

swotting /ˈswɒtɪŋ/ *n* [u] Brit colloq 刻苦学习

swum /swʌm/ *pp* ▸**swim A, B**

swung /swʌŋ/ *pt, pp* ▸**swing A, B, C**

swung dash *n* 代字号

S

sycamore /ˈsɪkəmɔː(r)/ *n* **1** [c] (tree) 西卡莫槭 **2** [u] (wood) 西卡莫木材

sycophancy /ˈsɪkəfənsi/ *n* [u] formal 阿谀奉承

sycophant /ˈsɪkəfænt/ *n* formal 阿谀奉承者

sycophantic /ˌsɪkəˈfæntɪk/ *adj* formal 阿谀奉承的

syllabary /ˈsɪləbəri, Amer -beri/ *n* 音节表

syllabic /sɪˈlæbɪk/ *adj* **1** (involving syllables) 音节的 ‹*division, pattern, elision*› **2** (constituting a syllable) 成音节的; **a ~ consonant** 音节辅音

syllabification /sɪˌlæbɪfɪˈkeɪʃn/ *n* [u] 音节划分

syllabify /sɪˈlæbɪfaɪ/ *vt* 划分…的音节

syllable /ˈsɪləbl/ *n* 音节; **(to explain sth.) in words of one ~** 用简单明了的字眼 (解释某事)

syllabub /ˈsɪləbʌb/ *n* [u and c] 乳酒冻 [用奶油、糖、酒等混合制成的甜食]

syllabus /ˈsɪləbəs/ *n* (*pl* **~es**) (course of study) 教学大纲; (range of topics) 提纲

syllogism /ˈsɪlədʒɪzəm/ *n* [逻辑学中的] 三段论

syllogistic /ˌsɪləˈdʒɪstɪk/ *adj* 三段论的

sylph /sɪlf/ *n* **1** (fairytale creature) 气仙 **2** (slender woman) 苗条女子

sylphlike /ˈsɪlflaɪk/ *adj* 苗条的 ‹*creature, figure*›; 柔美的 ‹*movement*›

sylvan /ˈsɪlvən/ *adj* **1** (wooded) 林木覆盖的 ‹*setting*›; (relating to woods) 森林的; **a ~ landscape** 森林景观; **a ~ glade** 林中空地 **2** (rural) 田园的 ‹*imagery, charm, meadow*›

symbiosis /ˌsɪmbaɪˈəʊsɪs, ˌsɪmbɪ-/ *n* [u and c] (*pl* **symbioses** /ˌsɪmbaɪˈəʊsiːz/) 共生

symbiotic /ˌsɪmbaɪˈɒtɪk, ˌsɪmbɪ-/ *adj* 共生的 ‹*relationship*›

symbol /ˈsɪmbl/ *n* **1** (emblem) 象征 **2** (mark, sign) 符号; **phonetic ~s** 音标

symbolic, symbolical /sɪmˈbɒlɪk(l)/ *adj* 象征性的; **to be ~ of sth.** 是某物的象征

symbolically /sɪmˈbɒlɪkli/ *adv* 象征性地

symbolism /ˈsɪmbəlɪzəm/ *n* [u] **1** (use of symbols) 符号使用; (symbolic meaning) 象征意义 **2** **Symbolism** (artistic movement) [19世纪晚期的] 象征主义

Symbolist /ˈsɪmbəlɪst/ *n* (artist) 象征主义艺术家; (writer) 象征主义作家; **a ~ painter/poet** 象征主义画家/诗人

symbolization /ˌsɪmbəlaɪˈzeɪʃn/ *n* [u] 符号化

symbolize /ˈsɪmbəlaɪz/ *vt* **1** (be symbol of) «*image, object*» 象征 ‹*quality*› **2** (represent symbolically) «*person, art work*» 代表 ‹*quality, fact*›; **to ~ sb./sth. with sth.** 用某物做为某人/某物的标志; **to ~ sb./sth. as sth.** 以某物代表某人/某物

symmetric /sɪˈmetrɪk/, **symmetrical** /sɪˈmetrɪkl/ *adj* 对称的; **to be ~ to** *or* **with sth.** 与某物对称

symmetrically /sɪˈmetrɪkli/ *adv* 对称地

symmetry /ˈsɪmətri/ *n* **1** [u] (quality) 对称性 **2** [c] (instance) 对称

sympathetic /ˌsɪmpəˈθetɪk/ *adj* **1** (compassionate) 有同情心的 **2** (expressing sympathy) 表示同情的 ‹*smile, words, gesture*› **3** (likeable) 讨人喜欢的 ‹*person, character*› **4** (supportive) 赞同的 ‹*person, committee, public opinion*›; **to be ~ to sb./sth.** 支持某人/某事 **5** (suitable) 合意的 ‹*structure*› **6** Anat, Physiol 交感性的; **a ~ ganglion** 交感神经节; **the ~ nervous system** 交感神经系统

sympathetically /ˌsɪmpəˈθetɪkli/ *adv* **1** (compassionately) 同情地 ‹*smile, look, say*› **2** (supportively) 赞同地 ‹*respond, consider, inclined*›

sympathize /ˈsɪmpəθaɪz/ *vi* **1** (feel or express compassion) 同情; **to ~ with sb./sth.** 同情某人/某事物 **2** (support) 支持; **to ~ with sth./sb.** 赞同 ‹*cause, aims, views, person*›

sympathizer /ˈsɪmpəθaɪzə(r)/ *n* **1** (person feeling compassion) 同情者 **2** (political supporter) 支持者

sympathy /ˈsɪmpəθi/

A *n* [u] **1** (compassion) 同情; **~ for** *or* **towards sb.** 对某人的同情; **out of ~** 出于同情 **2** (condolence) 慰唁; **a letter of ~** 吊唁信; **~ at** *or* **on sth.** 对某事的慰唁; **my ~ goes out to him** 我对他深表慰问 **3** (solidarity) 支持; **to be in ~ (with sb./sth.)** 支持 (某人/某事); **to be out of ~ (with sb./sth.)** 不赞同 (某人/某事) **4** (affinity, empathy) 意气相投; **~ between sb. and sb.** 某人与某人的志同道合

B **sympathies** *npl* **1** (condolences) 慰问 **2** (supportive feelings) 同情心

sympathy: ~ strike *n* [为声援其他罢工者而举行的] 同情罢工; **~ vote** *n* 同情票; **he's going for the ~ vote** fig 他试图获得同情

symphonic /sɪmˈfɒnɪk/ *adj* 交响乐的 ‹*form*›; 交响乐团的 ‹*repertoire, concert*›; **great ~ compositions/composers** 伟大的交响乐作品/作曲家

symphonic poem *n* 交响诗

symphonist /ˈsɪmfənɪst/ *n* 交响乐作曲家

symphony /ˈsɪmfəni/ *n* **1** (musical composition) 交响乐 **2** (harmonious assemblage) [尤指色彩的] 和谐 **3** = **symphony orchestra**

symphony orchestra *n* 交响乐团

symposium /sɪmˈpəʊzɪəm/ *n* (*pl* **symposia** /sɪmˈpəʊzɪə/) **1** (conference) 专题研讨会 **2** (collection) 专题论文集

symptom /ˈsɪmptəm/ *n* **1** (indicator of illness) 症状; **to show** *or* **manifest ~s** 出现症状 **2** (indication) 征兆

symptomatic /ˌsɪmptəˈmætɪk/ *adj* Med 症状的; (indicative) 作为征兆的; **inflation was ~ of a decline in the economy** 通货膨胀预示着经济衰退

synagogue /ˈsɪnəgɒg/ *n* (building) 犹太教堂; (congregation) 犹太教徒会众

synapse /ˈsaɪnæps/ *n* [神经元的] 突触

sync, synch /sɪŋk/ *n* [u] colloq = **synchronization**

synchromesh /ˈsɪŋkrəʊmeʃ/ *n* [u] [变速箱中的] 同步齿轮系

synchronic /sɪŋˈkrɒnɪk/ *adj* 共时的

synchronicity /ˌsɪŋkrəˈnɪsəti/ *n* [u] 同步性

synchronism /ˈsɪŋkrənɪzəm/ *n* [u] = **synchrony**

synchronization /ˌsɪŋkrənaɪˈzeɪʃn, Amer -nɪˈz-/ *n* [u] 同时发生; **in/out of ~** 同步/不同步的

synchronize /ˈsɪŋkrənaɪz/

A *vt* 使同步; **to ~ sth. with sth.** 使某事物与某事物同步

B *vi* «*movement, sound, action*» 同时发生; **to ~ with sth.** 与某事物同步

synchronized swimming /ˌsɪŋkrənaɪzd ˈswɪmɪŋ/ ▸**p. 307** *n* [u] 花样游泳

synchronous /ˈsɪŋkrənəs/ *adj* formal 同步的

synchronous: ~ motor *n* 同步电动机; **~ orbit** *n* 同步轨道

synchrony /ˈsɪŋkrəni/ *n* [u] 同步性; **to be in ~ (with sth.)** (与某事物) 同步

syncline /ˈsɪŋklaɪn/ *n* 向斜

syncopate /ˈsɪŋkəpeɪt/ *vt* 切分 ‹*rhythm, beats*›

syncopation /ˌsɪŋkəˈpeɪʃn/ *n* [u] 切分

syndicalism /ˈsɪndɪkəlɪzəm/ *n* [u] 工联主义

syndicalist /ˈsɪndɪkəlɪst/ *n* 工联主义者

syndicate

A /ˈsɪndɪkət/ *n* **1** (group of companies) 辛迪加 [指私人或企业联合组织]; **a banking/financial ~** 银行/金融辛迪加 **2** (news agency) [把文章等同时出售给多家报刊的] 报业辛迪加 **3** (organized group) 有组织团体 [尤指犯罪团伙]; **a drugs/gambling ~** 贩毒/赌博集团

B /ˈsɪndɪkeɪt/ *vt* **1** (publish) 通过报业辛迪加发表 ‹*column, photograph, cartoon*› **2** (sell) 把…出售给多家媒体 ‹*show, programme, series, column, photograph, cartoon*› **3** (provide through a syndicate) 通过辛迪加提供 ‹*project, loan, shares*›

syndrome /ˈsɪndrəʊm/ *n* **1** (set of disease symptoms) 综合征 **2** (characteristic combination) 典型特征

synergy /ˈsɪnədʒi/ *n* [u and c] 协同增效作用; **~ between drug combinations** 联合用药的增效作用

synod /ˈsɪnəd/ *n* (event) 教会会议; (participants) 教会会议会众

synonym /ˈsɪnənɪm/ *n* 同义词

synonymous /sɪˈnɒnɪməs/ *adj* 同义的; **wealth is not necessarily ~ with generosity** fig 财富未必等同于慷慨

synonymy /sɪˈnɒnəmi/ *n* [u] 同义

synopsis /sɪˈnɒpsɪs/ *n* (*pl* **synopses** /sɪˈnɒpsiːz/) 梗概

synoptic /sɪˈnɒptɪk/ *adj* 概要的

synovial /saɪˈnəʊvɪəl/ *adj* 滑液的; **~ fluid/membrane** 滑液/滑膜

syntactic /sɪnˈtæktɪk/, **syntactical** /sɪnˈtæktɪkl/ *adj* 句法的

syntactically /sɪnˈtæktɪkli/ *adv* 句法上

syntax /ˈsɪntæks/ *n* [u] **1** Ling 句法 **2** Comput [计算机语言的] 句法

syntax error *n* [计算机指令语言中的] 句法错误

synthesis /ˈsɪnθəsɪs/ *n* (*pl* **syntheses** /ˈsɪnθəsiːz/) **1** [u] (combining of separate parts) 综合 **2** [c] (product, result) 综合体 **3** [u] (combining of sounds, chemical substances) 合成; **speech ~** 语音合成

synthesize /ˈsɪnθəsaɪz/ *vt* **1** (produce) «*process, plant, cell*» 合成 ‹*substance, protein, chemical element*› **2** (combine) 综合 ‹*elements, data, chemicals*› **3** Audio, Mus [用合成器] 合成 ‹*sound, speech, music*›

synthesizer /ˈsɪnθəsaɪzə(r)/ *n* 音响合成器

synthetic /sɪn'θetɪk/
A *adj* **1** (man-made) 合成的 ‹*chemical, rubber, hormone*›; 人造的 ‹*diamond, fertilizer, fibre*› **2** (not genuine or natural) 假的; (insincere) 虚伪的 ‹*smile, compassion, friendliness*›
B *n* 合成物

synthetically /sɪn'θetɪkli/ *adv* 通过合成

syphilis /'sɪfɪlɪs/ ▸**p. 377** *n* [u] 梅毒

syphilitic /ˌsɪfɪ'lɪtɪk/
A *adj* 患梅毒的 ‹*patient*›; 梅毒的 ‹*symptom*›
B *n* 梅毒患者

syphon /'saɪfn/ *n, vt* = **siphon**

Syria /'sɪrɪə/ *pr n* 叙利亚

Syrian /'sɪriən/
A *adj* (of Syria) 叙利亚的; (of the people) 叙利亚人的
B *n* 叙利亚人

syringe /sɪ'rɪndʒ/
A *n* **1** (used in medicine) 注射器 **2** (used in gardening, cooking) 冲洗器
B *vt* 用注射器灌洗 ‹*wound, body cavity*›; 用冲洗器冲洗 ‹*plant, meat*›

syrup /'sɪrəp/ *n* **1** [u] (sweetened water) 糖水 **2** [u and c] (thick liquid) 糖浆 **3** [u and c] Med 药用糖浆; **cough ～** 止咳糖浆

syrup of figs *n* [u] 无花果糖浆 [一种通便剂]

syrupy /'sɪrəpi/ *adj* **1** lit 糖浆状的 ‹*drink, mixture*› **2** fig pej 缠绵的 ‹*story, film*›; 甜腻腻的 ‹*music, song*›

system /'sɪstəm/ *n* **1** [c] (set of ideas, principles) 制度; **an educational/monetary/legal/economic ～** 教育/金融/法律/经济体制; **the feudal ～** 封建制度 **2** [c] (method) 方法; **a ～ for sth./doing sth.** 用于某事/做某事的方法 **3** [c] (network) 系统; **the state railway/road/telephone/traffic/canal ～** 国家铁路/公路/电话/交通/运河系统 **4** [c] (mechanism) 装置; **the security/electrical/air-conditioning ～** 安全/电力/空调系统; **all ～s are go** 一切就绪; **it was all ～s go for our holiday** colloq 我们已做好休假准备 **5** [c] (set of organs) 生理系统; **the cardiovascular/genito-urinary/reproductive/respiratory ～** 心血管/泌尿生殖/生殖/呼吸系统 **6** [c] (body) 身体; **to be bad/good for the ～** 对身体不好/好的; **to get into/pass out of the** *or* **one's ～** 进入/排出人体; **to get sth. out of one's ～** lit 将某物排出体外; **to get sb./sth. out of one's ～** colloq 淡忘某人/某物 **7** [c] Comput 操作系统; **to reboot the ～** 重新启动系统; **to store sth. in the ～** 在系统中存储某物 **8** [c] *sing* **the ～** colloq (prevailing order) 现行体制; **to beat/buck the ～** 胜过/反抗现行体制; **to be up against the ～** 面对的是整个体制; **to work within the ～** 在体制范围内行事 **9** [u] (planning) 秩序; **to lack ～** 缺乏秩序 **10** [c] Astron 系; **the planets in our ～** 我们太阳系里的行星 **11** [c] Meteorol 天气系统; **a high-pressure/low-pressure ～** 高压/低压天气系统; **a frontal ～** 锋面天气系统 **12** [c] Geol [地层等的] 系; **a mountain/river ～** 山系/河系; **the Jurassic ～** 侏罗纪系 **13** [c] (set of rules for measurement, classification) 规制; **the metric/decimal/classification ～** 公制/十进制/分类系统 **14** [c] (in gambling) 下赌注法

systematic /ˌsɪstə'mætɪk/ *adj* **1** (methodical) 有条理的 ‹*person, arrangement, method*›; 系统的 ‹*training, planning*›; **to be ～ in sth./doing sth.** 在某事上/做某事上有条不紊 **2** pej (deliberate) 有计划有步骤的 ‹*undermining, destruction, prevarication*›

systematically /ˌsɪstə'mætɪkli/ *adv* **1** (methodically) 有条理地 ‹*work, arrange, compile*› **2** pej (deliberately) 有计划有步骤地 ‹*undermine, sabotage, bomb*›

systematization /ˌsɪstəmətaɪ'zeɪʃn, Amer -tɪ'z-/ *n* [u] 系统化

systematize /'sɪstəmətaɪz/ *vt* 使系统化

systemic /sɪ'stemɪk/
A *adj* **1** (in-built) 涉及全系统的 ‹*problem, weakness*›; 影响全局的 ‹*delay, abuse*› **2** (of or affecting the whole body) 全身的 ‹*poison, circulation, infection*› **3** (killing plant pests) 内吸的 ‹*pesticide, fungicide*›; (killing plants) 内吸除草的 ‹*weedkiller*›
B *n* (pesticide) 内吸杀虫剂; (weedkiller) 内吸除草剂

systems: ～ analysis *n* [u] 系统分析; **～ analyst** ▸**p. 409** *n* 系统分析员; **～ disk** *n* 系统盘; **～ diskette** *n* 系统软盘; **～ engineer** ▸**p. 409** *n* 系统工程师; **～ engineering** *n* [u] 系统工程; **～ software** *n* [u] 系统软件

systolic /sɪ'stɒlɪk/ *adj* 收缩的; **～ blood pressure/hypertension** 收缩压/收缩性高血压

Tt

T, t /tiː/

A *n* (*pl* **Ts** *or* **T's**) [英语字母表的第20个字母]; **to a ~** colloq 恰好; **it suits me to a ~** 这个对我最合适不过了

B **t** *abbr* = **ton(s), tonne(s)** 吨

TA *n* Brit = **Territorial Army**

ta /tɑː/ *excl* Brit colloq 谢谢

tab¹ /tæb/

A *n* **1** (projecting piece) (on garment) 挂襻; (for decoration) 小垂片; (for fastening) 鞋舌片; (on file) 检索凸舌; **to keep a ~ or ~s on sb./sth.** colloq 监视某人/某物 **2** Amer (ring pull) [易拉罐的] 拉环 **3** esp Amer colloq (bill) 餐馆账单; **to pick up the ~** 买单 **4** (tally) 赊账; **please put it on my ~** 请把它记到我的账上; **to run up a ~** 赊账大量购物 **5** (flap for identification) 标签 **6** Brit Mil 领章 **7** (on aircraft's wing, tail) 补翼

B *vt* (*pres p etc.* **-bb-**) **1** (label) 在…上贴标签 ‹*garment, file, book*› **2** Amer (identify) 认定; **she was ~bed as a candidate** 她被视为候选人 **3** esp Amer (designate) 指定; **to ~ money/resources for sth.** 指定款项/资源用于某事

tab² *n* Comput = **tabulator 2**

tab³ *n* colloq (tablet) 迷幻药

tabard /ˈtæbəd/ *n* (worn by knight over armour) [中世纪骑士穿在盔甲外面的] 短披风; (as modern fashion) 搭肩衫; (as protective clothing) 无袖防护衫

Tabasco® /təˈbæskəʊ/ *n* [u] 塔巴斯科辣椒酱

tabby /ˈtæbi/ *n* **~ (cat)** 斑猫

tabernacle /ˈtæbənækl/ *n* **1** Bible 会幕 [古代犹太人在荒漠旅途中用作圣所] **2** Relig (receptacle) 圣体盒 **3** Relig (place of worship) 礼拜堂

tab key *n* 跳格键

table /ˈteɪbl/

A *n* **1** (piece of furniture) 桌子; **a kitchen/garden ~** 厨房用桌/花园桌; **to get or sit round or around a ~** 围桌坐下; **to lay or set the ~ for dinner** 为晚餐摆好餐具; **to sit down to ~** 坐下用餐; **children must learn to behave at ~** 孩子们必须学会用餐规矩; **to put sth. on the ~** Brit (propose) 将…提交讨论; Amer (postpone) 搁置 ‹*proposal, offer*›; **to turn the ~s (on sb.)** 扭转局面（使之不利于某人）; **under the ~** fig 私底下的; **to wait at ~** Brit, **to wait on ~** Amer 伺候进餐; **to lay or put one's cards on the ~** fig 摊牌 **2** (company at table) 一桌人; **the whole ~ enjoyed the joke** 全桌人都觉得那个笑话很有趣; **a round ~ conference or discussion** 圆桌会议 **3** (list of facts, figures) 表; **to draw up or compile a ~** 编制表格; **to present or give sth. in ~ form** 以表格形式提交某物 **4** Math 乘法表; **to learn one's ~s** 熟记乘法表; **the six/nine times ~** 6/9 的乘法口诀 **5** Sport 名次表; **to be top/bottom of the ~** 位于榜首/排名末位

B *vt* **1** Brit Pol (submit for discussion) 把…提交讨论 ‹*motion, report, amendment, proposal*›; **to be ~d for discussion** 被提交讨论 **2** Amer (postpone) 搁置 ‹*motion, report, amendment, proposal*›

tableau /ˈtæbləʊ/ *n* (*pl* **tableaux** /ˈtæbləʊz/ *or* **~s**) **1** Theat 舞台造型 **2** (scene) 引人入胜的场面

table: ~cloth *n* 桌布; **~ cream** *n* [u] Amer = **single cream**; **~ dancer** *n* 桌边舞女; **~ dancing** *n* [u] 桌边舞; **~ football** ▸**p. 307** *n* [u] 桌式足球; **~ lamp** *n* 台灯; **~land** /-lænd/ *n* 高原; **~ leg** *n* 桌腿; **~ linen** *n* [u] [桌布、餐巾等] 餐桌用布; **~ manners** *npl* 餐桌礼仪; **~ mat** *n* 餐具垫; **~ napkin** *n* 餐巾; **~ salt** *n* [u] [餐桌上用的] 佐餐盐; **~ soccer** *n* = **~ football**; **~spoon** *n* **1** (serving spoon) 大汤匙; **2** (*also* **~spoonful**) (amount) 一汤匙

tablet /ˈtæblɪt/ *n* **1** (plaque) 匾 **2** Archaeol 刻写板; **to decipher ~s** 译读简; **engraved in ~s of stone** 板上钉钉的 **3** esp Brit (pill) 药片; **to take a ~** 服药片 **4** esp Brit (small block) 小块; **a ~ of scented soap** 一块香皂 **5** Amer (writing pad) 便笺簿 **6** Comput 手写板 **7** Scot (fudge) 乳脂软糖

table: ~ talk *n* [u] 餐桌漫谈; **~ tennis** *n* [u] 乒乓球运动; **to play ~ tennis** 打乒乓球; **a ~ tennis bat/ball** 乒乓球拍/乒乓球

tabletop /ˈteɪbltɒp/

A *n* 桌面

B *modif* 台式的 ‹*unit, device*›

table-top sale *n* Brit 台面商品展销

tablet PC *n* 平板电脑

table: ~ware *n* [u] 餐具; **~ wine** *n* [u and c] 佐餐葡萄酒

tabloid /ˈtæblɔɪd/ *n* **~ (newspaper)** 通俗小报; **a ~ journalist** esp pej 小报记者

taboo /təˈbuː/

A *n* **1** Anthrop 禁忌; **to break or violate a ~** 触犯禁忌 **2** fig (prohibition) 禁止; **a ~ on talking politics at dinner** 晚饭时避谈政治的避讳

B *adj* 忌讳的 ‹*subject, problem*›; 禁忌的 ‹*place, activity*›; **~ words** 禁忌词

C *vt* 禁止 ‹*practice, activity*›

tabu /təˈbuː/ *n, adj* = **taboo**

tabular /ˈtæbjʊlə(r)/ *adj* 列成表的 ‹*data*›; 表格式的 ‹*summary*›; **in ~ form/format** 以表格形式/格式

tabulate /ˈtæbjʊleɪt/ *vt* **1** (put in table form) 列表显示 ‹*data, results*› **2** (format for table form) 将…列成表格 ‹*page, columns*›

tabulation /ˌtæbjʊˈleɪʃn/ *n* [u and c] 列表显示

tabulator /ˈtæbjʊleɪtə(r)/ *n* **1** (arranger) (person) 制表员; (device) 制表机 **2** (formatter on typewriter, keyboard) 跳格键

tachograph /ˈtækəgrɑːf, Amer -græf/ *n* 转速计

tachometer /təˈkɒmɪtə(r)/ *n* 转速表

tachymeter /təˈkɪmɪtə(r)/ *n* **1** (theodolite) [快速测定距离、方位等的] 视距计 **2** (facility on watch) 测速仪

tacit /ˈtæsɪt/ *adj* 心照不宣的; **~ consent/approval** 默许/暗中支持

tacitly /ˈtæsɪtli/ *adv* 心照不宣地

taciturn /ˈtæsɪtɜːn/ *adj* 沉默寡言的

taciturnity /ˌtæsɪˈtɜːnəti/ *n* [u] 沉默寡言

taciturnly /ˈtæsɪtɜːnli/ *adv* 不苟言笑地

tack¹ /tæk/

A *n* **1** (small nail) 平头钉; **a carpet ~** 地毯钉 **2** Amer (drawing pin) 图钉 **3** (temporary stitch) 粗线脚缝; **to put a ~ in sth.** 粗缝某物 **4** Naut (oblique course) 抢风调向; fig (approach) 方法; **to be on the starboard/port ~** 在右/左舷抢风行驶; **to change ~** 改弦易辙; **to try another or different ~** fig 变换策略; **to be on the right/wrong ~** (of vessel) 航向正确/错误; fig (of course of action) 路子正确/错误

B *vt* **1** (nail) 用平头钉钉 ‹*carpet, lino, upholstery*›; **to ~ sth. to sth.** 用平头钉将某物钉在某物上; **to ~ sth. down** 用平头钉将某物固定 **2** (temporarily stitch) 用粗线脚缝 ‹*article of clothing, sheet, hem*›; **to ~ sth. on (to sth.)** 用粗缝针脚将某物缝（在某物）上

C *vi* ‹*person*› 作之字形移动; ‹*sailor, yacht*› 抢风航行; **to ~ to port/starboard** 在左/右舷抢风行驶; **to ~ about** 抢风航行; **to ~ into the wind** 抢风航行

Phrasal verb

• **tack on** *vt* [**~ sth. on, ~ on sth.**] colloq 添加; **to ~ sth. on to sth.** 把某物添加到某物上

tack² *n* [u] Equit 马具

tacking /ˈtækɪŋ/ *n* [u] (stitches) 粗缝针脚; (thread) 粗缝针线

tacking: ~ stitch *n* 粗缝针脚; **~ thread** *n* [u] 粗缝线

tackle /ˈtækl/

A *n* **1** [u] Mech (on ship) 索具; (for lifting weights) 辘轳 **2** [u] (equipment) (for sport) 体育器械; (for task) 工具 **3** [c] (challenge) (in soccer, hockey) 阻截; (in rugby, American football) 擒抱; **a ~ on sb.** 对某人的阻截; **a fair/dangerous ~** 正当/危险的阻截

B *vt* **1** (handle) 处理 ‹*task, problem, fire*›; 应对 ‹*challenge, difficulty*›; 整理 ‹*garden, painting*›; 努力吃下 ‹*food, meal*›; **to ~ sth. head-on** 正面应对某事 **2** (confront) 与…交涉; **to ~ sb. about or over sth.** 与某人就某事交涉 **3** Sport (in soccer, hockey) 阻截抢…的球; (in rugby, American football) 擒抱摔倒; **~ him!** 抢断他! **4** (take on) 抓获 ‹*intruder, animal*›

C *vi* (in soccer, hockey) 阻截; (in rugby, American football) 擒抱

tackle block *n* 滑轮组

tackler /ˈtæklə(r)/ *n* 阻截队员

tackling /ˈtæklɪŋ/ *n* [u] (in soccer, hockey) 阻截; (in rugby, American football) 擒抱

tack room *n* 马具房

tacky /ˈtæki/ *adj* **1** (sticky) 发黏的 ‹*glue, varnish*›; **the paint is still ~** 油漆还未干 **2** colloq (in poor taste, shabby) 俗气的 ‹*decoration*›; 劣质的 ‹*object, jewellery*›; 乏味的 ‹*joke, show*›; **the film has a really ~ ending** 这部电影的结尾真差劲

taco /ˈtɑːkəʊ/ *n* (*pl* **~s**) 墨西哥煎玉米卷; **~ shells** 墨西哥煎玉米卷皮

tact /tækt/ *n* [u] 圆通; **she has or shows great/little ~** 她待人处事很得体/不得体

tactful /ˈtæktfl/ *adj* 圆通的 ‹*person, attitude, intervention, approach*›; 得体的 ‹*behaviour, words*›; **it wasn't very ~ of you to mention his first wife** 你提起他的第一个妻子，这不太得体

tactfully /ˈtæktfəli/ *adv* 得体地 ‹*behave, speak*›; 圆通地 ‹*refuse, worded*›

tactfulness /ˈtæktfʊlnɪs/ *n* [u] = **tact**

tactic /ˈtæktɪk/

A *n* 策略; **a delaying ~** 拖延战术

B tactics *npl* **1** Mil 战术 **2** fig (means) 手段; **to employ** *or* **use ~s** 施手段; **to change ~s** 改变策略; **strong-arm/underhand ~s** 强制手段/不光明手段

tactical /ˈtæktɪkl/ *adj* **1** (strategic) 战术上的; **to make a ~ retreat** 进行战术上的撤退 **2** (showing skilful planning) 有谋略的 ‹*move*›; 高明的 ‹*decision*› **3** *attrib* Mil (providing support) 短程的 ‹*bombing*›; 战术的 ‹*missile*›

tactically /ˈtæktɪkli/ *adv* **1** (in strategic way) 有策略地 ‹*vote, proceed*› **2** (in tactical terms) 在战术上 ‹*sound, unwise*›

tactical voting *n* [u] 策略性投票

tactician /tækˈtɪʃn/ *n* (political strategist) 谋略家; (military strategist) 战术家; (in chess, sport) 高手

tactile /ˈtæktaɪl, Amer -tl/ *adj* **1** (relating to touch) 触觉的 ‹*reflex, organ, stimulus, communication*› **2** (tangible) 可感触到的 ‹*movement, emotion*›; **a ~ fabric** 手感好的织物 **3** (for touching) 触摸的 ‹*map, exhibition*›

tactless /ˈtæktlɪs/ *adj* 不圆通的 ‹*person*›; 不得体的 ‹*behaviour, remark*›; **to be ~ of sb. (to do sth.)** 某人（做某事）不妥当

tactlessly /ˈtæktlɪsli/ *adv* 不得体地

tactlessness /ˈtæktlɪsnɪs/ *n* [u] 不得体

tad /tæd/ *n* colloq **1** **a ~** (somewhat) 有些; **a ~ embarrassed** 有点尴尬的 **2** **a ~** (a little) 微量; **she is a ~ short** 她个子偏矮了点; **just a ~ more milk** 再加一点点牛奶

tadpole /ˈtædpəʊl/ *n* 蝌蚪

Tadzhik /ˈtɑːdʒɪk/ ▸**p. 503** *adj, n* = **Tajik**

Tadzhikistan /tɑːˌdʒɪkɪˈstɑːn/ *n* = **Tajikistan**

tae kwon do /ˌtaɪkwɒnˈdəʊ/ *n* [u] 跆拳道

taffeta /ˈtæfɪtə/ *n* [u] 塔夫绸; **a ~ dress** 塔夫绸连衣裙

Taffy /ˈtæfi/ *n* colloq pej 威尔士佬

taffy /ˈtæfi/ *n* Amer **1** [u and c] (sweet) 太妃糖 **2** [u] colloq (flattery) 拍马屁

tag¹ /tæg/

A *n* **1** (label) (on garment, goods, luggage, file) 标签; (on person, animal) 标牌; **a name/price/luggage ~** 姓名标牌/价格标签/行李挂牌; **a dog** Amer *or* **an identification** Brit **~** 身份识别牌 **2** Jur (electronic device) [戴在罪犯身上的] 电子跟踪器 **3** (loose end) [挂下来的] 碎片 **4** (for hanging clothes) 挂襻 **5** Ling [表示强调的] 附加语 **6** (stock phrase) 警句; **Latin ~s** 拉丁语格言 **7** (on shoelace, cord etc.) 包头 **8** Comput 标识符 **9** (epithet) 称号 **10** Amer colloq (licence plate) 汽车牌照

B *vt* (*pres p etc.* **-gg-**) **1** (attach label to) 给…加标签 ‹*garment, file*›; 给…系标牌 ‹*animal*›; 给…戴电子跟踪器 ‹*criminal*›; **to ~ sb./sth. as sth.** 将某人/某物标明为某物 **2** (name, describe) 把…称作; **the film/novel was ~ged (as) 'surreal'** 该电影/小说被称为"超现实主义"作品 **3** Amer Aut colloq 发违章传票给; **he was ~ged for speeding** 他因超速行驶而收到了违章传票 **4** (add at the end) 给…加结束语 ‹*piece of writing*› **5** Comput 用标识符标记 ‹*document*› **6** Brit colloq (follow closely) 跟随; **I ~ged him to an old house on the outskirts of town** 我尾随他来到城郊的一幢老房子

C *vi* (*pres p etc.* **-gg-**) colloq 尾随; **to ~ after sb.** 尾随某人

Phrasal verbs

- **tag along** *vi* 尾随; **to ~ along after** *or* **behind sb.** 尾随某人; **to ~ along with sb.** 跟随某人一起走
- **tag on**

A *vi* 尾随; **to ~ on to sth.** 跟随某物

B *vt* [**~ sth. on, ~ on sth.**] 添加; **to ~ sth. on to sth.** 将…加在某物上 ‹*label, note*›

tag²

A *n* [u] (game) [儿童的] 捉人游戏; **a game of ~** 捉人游戏; **to play ~** 玩捉人游戏

B *vt* (*pres p etc.* **-gg-**) [在捉人游戏中] 抓住

tag: ~board *n* **1** [u] Amer (cardboard) 卡纸板; **2** [c] Comput 留言板; **~ day** *n* Amer = **flag day**; **~ end** *n* **1** esp Amer (last part) 末尾; **the ~ end of the year** 年末; **2** (loose end) (of thread) 线头; (of cloth) 布边

tagging /ˈtægɪŋ/ *n* [u] [对轻罪犯的] 电子监视

tag: ~ line *n* Amer colloq (catchphrase) 时髦用语; (punchline) 妙语; (advertising slogan) 广告口号; **~ question** *n* 附加疑问句; **~ wrestler** *n* 组合摔跤手; **~ wrestling** ▸**p. 307** *n* [u] 组合摔跤

Tahiti /tɑːˈhiːti/ *pr n* 塔希提岛

Tahitian /təˈhiːʃn/ ▸**p. 503**

A *adj* (of Tahiti) 塔希提岛的; (of the people) 塔希提人的; (of the language) 塔希提语的

B *n* **1** [c] (person) 塔希提人 **2** [u] (language) 塔希提语

tai chi /ˌtaɪ ˈtʃi/ *n* [u] 太极拳; **to practise ~** 练太极拳

taikonaut /ˈtaɪkənɔːt/ *n* 中国宇航员

tail /teɪl/

A *n* **1** Zool (of animal, bird, fish, reptile) 尾; **the sting in the ~** fig 煞风景的结尾; **the ~ wagging the dog** fig 尾巴摇狗 [指本末倒置]; **(to be** *or* **keep) on sb.'s ~** 紧跟着某人; **to have sb./sth. on one's ~** 有某人/某物尾随着; **to go off with one's ~ between one's legs** colloq 夹着尾巴走开; **to turn ~** 逃跑 **2** (end piece) (of kite, aircraft, queue, procession) 尾部; (of comet) 彗尾; **the traffic was nose to ~ for mile after mile** 车辆首尾相接延绵数英里 **3** esp Amer colloq (buttocks) 屁股; **a piece of ~** Amer pej (woman) 娘儿们 **4** colloq (person following another) 尾随者; **to put a ~ on sb.** 派人盯某人的梢

B tails *npl* **1** (of shirt, coat) 燕尾服 **2** colloq (man's evening dress) [男子的] 晚礼服 **3** + *v sing* (sides of a coin) [硬币的] 反面; **heads or ~s?** 正面还是反面?

C *vt* colloq 尾随; **to ~ sb. to a place** 跟踪某人到一个地方

Phrasal verbs

- **tail away** *vi* **1** = **tail off 1** **2** (become fainter) 逐渐消失; **his voice ~ed away to a whisper** 他的声音逐渐减弱成了耳语
- **tail back** *vi* Brit «*vehicles*» 排成长队; «*traffic jam*» 绵延; **lines of cars ~ing back from the roundabout** 从交通环岛绵延开去的一排排汽车; **the traffic jam ~ed back to the previous motorway junction** 堵塞的车辆一直延伸到前一个高速路口
- **tail off** *vi* **1** (decrease) «*numbers, attendance, interest*» 逐渐减少 **2** (fade) «*voice, remarks*» 逐渐减弱; **to ~ off into silence** 渐渐沉寂下来

tail: ~ assembly *n* 尾翼; **~back** *n* Brit [车辆受阻而形成的] 长队; **~board** *n* Brit = **tailgate A**; **~coat** *n* = **tail B1**; **~ end** *n* **1** (last piece) (of meat, cloth, queue) 末端; (of event, film, storm, conversation, day) 尾声; **2** colloq (buttocks) 臀部; **~ feather** *n* 尾羽; **~ fin** *n* 尾鳍

-tailed /teɪld/ *combining form* 有…尾的; **long/bushy~** 有长/毛茸茸的尾巴的

tailgate /ˈteɪlgeɪt/

A *n* (of truck, trailer) 后拦板; (of car) 舱盖式后车门

B *vt* colloq 开车紧随

C *vi* esp Amer colloq 紧随前车行驶

tailgate party *n* Amer [从后车门取用食物和饮料的] 车尾野餐会

tail: ~-heavy *adj* 尾部重的 ‹*aircraft*›; **~ light** *n* 尾灯; **~-off** *n* 逐渐减少

tailor /ˈteɪlə(r)/ ▸**p. 409**

A *n* 裁缝; **a bespoke ~** 专做定制衣服的裁缝

B *vt* **1** (make) 量身定做; **a ~ed jacket** 定做的夹克衫; **a well-~ed suit** 一套做工考究的衣服 **2** (adapt) 定制 ‹*appliance, article*›; 制定 ‹*policy, curriculum*›; **to ~ sth. for sb./sth.** 为某人/某事物定制某物; **homes ~ed to the needs of the elderly** 专为满足老年人需求而设的养老院

tailoring /ˈteɪlərɪŋ/ *n* [u] **1** (making of clothes) 裁缝业 **2** (cut, style) 剪裁 **3** (garments) 成衣

tailor-made *adj* **1** (made to measure) 定做的 ‹*garment*› **2** fig (perfectly suited) 非常合适的 ‹*solution, training*›; **to be ~ for sth./sb.** «*system, course*» 对某事/某人正适合; **the part is ~ for her** 这个角色是为她量身打造的

tailor: ~'s chalk *n* [u] 裁缝粉片; **~'s dummy** *n* 裁缝店的人体模型

tail: ~piece *n* **1** (design in book) 章尾装饰图; **2** (extension) (of story) 附加章节; (of pipe) 接续管; **3** Mus 系弦板; **~pipe** *n* Amer 排气管; **~plane** *n* Brit 水平尾翼; **~ rotor** *n* [直升机的] 尾桨; **~ section** *n* 飞机尾部; **~skid** *n* **1** Aviat 尾橇; **2** Aut 后轮打滑; **~spin** *n* **1** Aviat 尾旋; **2** fig (loss of control) 失控; **to be in a ~spin** 处于一片混乱; **~ unit** *n* 尾翼; **~wheel** *n* [尤指飞机的] 尾轮; **~wind** *n* 顺风

taint /teɪnt/

A *n* **1** (trace of something bad or unpleasant) 瑕疵 **2** (contamination) 污染

B *vt* **1** (sully) 玷污 ‹*reputation, family, lineage*›; **ambition had ~ed his motives** 野心使他的动机变得不纯 **2** (contaminate) 污染 ‹*food, air*›; **the water was ~ed with oil** 水被油污染了

tainted /ˈteɪntɪd/ *adj* 腐坏的 ‹*food*›; 受污染的 ‹*water, air*›; 被玷污的 ‹*family, reputation*›; **~ motives** 不良的动机; **~ money** 脏钱

taipan /ˈtaɪpæn/ *n* 大班 [旧时中国的洋行经理]

Taipei /taɪˈpeɪ/ *pr n* 台北

Taiwan /taɪˈwɑːn/ *pr n* 台湾

Taiwanese /ˌtaɪwəˈniːz/ ▸**p. 503**

A *adj* 台湾的

B *n* 台湾人

Tajik /ˈtɑːdʒɪk/ ▸**p. 503, p. 426**

A *adj* (of Tajikistan) 塔吉克斯坦的; (of the people) 塔吉克人的; (of the language) 塔吉克语的

B *n* **1** [c] (person) 塔吉克人 **2** [u] *also* **Tajiki** (language) 塔吉克语

Tajikistan /tɑːˌdʒɪkɪˈstɑːn/ *pr n* 塔吉克斯坦

take /teɪk/

A ▸**p. 82** *vt* (*pt* **took**, *pp* **taken**) **1** (carry from one place to another) 携带; (accompany from one place to another) 带领; **to ~ sb./sth. with one** 带上某人/某物; **to ~ the car to the garage** 把汽车送到修理厂; **to ~ sth. upstairs/downstairs** 把某物拿到楼上/楼下; **to ~ sb. to school/work/the hospital** 送某人去上学/去上班/去医院; **to ~ sb./sth. swimming/riding** 带某人/某物去游泳/骑马; **to ~ sb./sth. home** 带某人/某物回家; **to ~ the dog for a walk** 去遛狗; **he took her a bunch of flowers** 他给她送去一束花; **~ these chairs into the garden** 把这些椅子搬到花园里; **to ~ sb. to have a haircut** 带某人去理发; **to ~ sth. to be mended** 把某物送去修理; **he was taken before the court** 他被带上法庭; **honestly, I can't ~ you anywhere!** colloq hum 老实说，我不能带你走！ **2** (bring into specified state) 使达到; **I'd like to ~ my argument a stage further** 我想进一步阐述我的论点; **we'll ~ the matter forward at our next meeting** 我们下次开会将继续讨论此事; **the invasion took Europe to the brink of war** 这次入侵将欧洲推到了战争的边缘; **I'll ~ it from here** 我来处理接下来的事 **3** (reach and hold) 拿 ‹*object*›; 抱 ‹*person, animal*›; **to ~ sb. by the arm** 挽着某人的胳膊; **to ~ sb. by the throat** 扼住某人的喉咙; **he took her by the hand** 他牵着她的手 **4** (use) 取用; **~ three eggs and break them into a large bowl** 取三个鸡蛋打进大

t

碗里 5 (remove) (from place, person) 取走; (without permission) 擅自拿走; (by mistake) 错拿; **to ~ sth. from sb./sth.** 从某人那里/某处拿走某物; **he took a book from the shelf** 他从书架上拿了一本书; **these documents may not be taken from the building** 这些文件不能擅自带出大楼; **did the burglars ~ anything valuable?** 盗贼偷走了什么贵重物品吗？; **has someone taken my scarf?** 谁错拿了我的围巾？ 6 (get from source) 取得; **the passage is taken from his latest book** 这段文字出自他的新书; **the machine ~s its name from its inventor** 这机器是以发明者的名字命名的 7 (subtract) 减去 ‹*number, quantity*›; **seven ~ five leaves two** colloq 7 减 5 剩 2 8 (capture) 夺取 ‹*fortress, garrison, town*›; 抓获 ‹*prisoner*›; **to ~ sb. alive** 活捉某人 9 Games 赢 ‹*trick*›; 吃掉 ‹*piece, pawn*›; 赢得 ‹*prize, title*›; **he took my bishop with his rook** 他用车吃了我的象 10 (rent) 租; **to ~ lodgings** 租房子住 11 (buy) 要买 ‹*clothing, goods, article*›; Brit (buy regularly) 订阅 ‹*newspaper, magazine*›; **to ~ three pints of milk every day** 每天订 3 品脱的奶; **I'll ~ a kilo of apples, please** 请给我称一公斤苹果 12 (consume) 吃 ‹*food, medicine*›; 接受 ‹*remedy*›; 喝 ‹*drink, milk*›; **not to be taken internally** Med 不可内服; **you should ~ something for your stomach** 你应当吃点胃药; **do you ~ sugar in your tea?** 你喝茶放糖吗？; **to ~ tea/lunch with sb.** Brit formal 和某人一起喝茶/吃午饭 13 (record) 记录; **can I ~ your name and address, please?** 可否请你留下姓名和地址？; **to ~ the minutes (of a meeting)** 做会议记录 14 Phot 拍 ‹*photo, picture*› 15 (measure) 测量 ‹*pulse, temperature*›; **to ~ sb.'s blood pressure** 给某人量血压; **to ~ a reading** (of thermometer, scale) 记录读数; **to ~ sb.'s measurements** (for clothes) 为某人量尺寸 16 (occupy) 占 ‹*chair, place*›; **~ a seat!** 坐吧！ 17 (consider as example) 以…为例; **let us** *or* **if we ~ the situation in France** 我们以法国的情况为例; **~ John (for example)** 比方说约翰 18 (accept sth.) 接受; (accept, admit sb.) 接纳; **to ~ advice** 接受建议; **to ~ a job** 接受工作; **~ it or leave it** (making offer) 要就要，不要就算; (expressing lack of interest in offer) 无所谓; **to ~ it on** *or* **upon oneself to do sth.** 擅自决定做某事; **(you can) ~ it from me (that) ...** colloq 我（向你）保证…; **to ~ sb. as they come** 不苛求某人; **to ~ sb./sth. as it comes** 顺其自然; **~ that!** 看招！; **the doctor does ~ some private patients** 这位医生的确收诊一些自费病人; **the school doesn't ~ boys** 这所学校不收男生; **do you ~ this man to be your lawful wedded husband?** formal 你愿接受这个男人成为你的合法丈夫吗？ 19 (earn) 收入; **the shop ~s £2,500 a week** 这家商店每周的赢利为 2,500 英镑 20 (consider valid) 认可; **I ~ your point** 我认可你的观点 21 (bear, endure, accept) 承受; **can the ropes ~ the strain?** 这些绳子能承受住拉力吗？; **go on, tell me: I can ~ it!** 说下去，告诉我：我扛得住！; **to ~ a joke** 开得起玩笑; **to ~ a blow/beating** 挨一拳/一顿揍; **she can't ~ being criticized** 她受不了被人批评; **I find it difficult to ~ his rudeness** 我难以接受他的粗鲁; **she just sat there and took it!** 她就这么忍气吞声了！ 22 (react to) 对…作出反应; **to ~ sb./sth. seriously/lightly** 认真/轻率地对待某人/某事物; **to ~ sth. well/badly** 从容接受某事/对某事想不开; **to ~ things one** *or* **a step at a time** 循序渐进; **how did she ~ the news of his death?** 她对他的死讯作何反应？ 23 (believe, regard as being so) 认为; (understand as being so) 理解; **how am I supposed to ~ that remark?** 那句话我该怎么理解？; **to ~ sth. in isolation** 孤立地看待某事; **to ~ sth. as sth.** 将某事看作某事; **she took what he said as a compliment** 她将他的话视作褒扬; **what do you ~ this poem to mean?** 你认为这首诗的意义何在？; **what do you ~ me for?** 你把我当成什么人了？; **I took him to be honest** 我原以为他是诚实的; **I ~ it (that) ...** 我认为…; **I don't think she took my meaning** 我想她没理解我的意思 24 (adopt) 持有; **to ~ the view** *or* **attitude that ...** 持有…的看法/态度; **to ~ a tough/soft line on sb./sth.** 对某人/某事采取强硬/柔和的态度 25 (feel) 感到; **to ~ an interest in sth.** 对某事物感兴趣; **don't ~ offence at what I said** 我的话你别见怪 26 (use course of action) 采取 ‹*action, step*›; 采用 ‹*measures, approach*›; (perform action) [与名词连用，表示具体动作]; **to ~ a shower** 冲澡; **to ~ a walk** 散步; **to ~ a decision** 作决定; **to ~ a short break/deep breath** 休息片刻/深呼吸 27 (develop particular form) 呈现; **our next class will ~ the form of a debate** 我们下一堂课将采用辩论形式 28 (need) 需要; **to ~ sb./sth. a long time/three hours to do sth.** 某人/某物做某事需要很长时间/三小时; **it'll ~ time for her to recover from the illness** 她要过很长时间才能康复; **it would ~ a strong person/a genius to do that** 做那事需要身体健壮的人/天才; **it ~s patience/courage to do sth.** 做某事需要耐心/勇气; **it doesn't ~ much to make her angry** 她动不动就生气; **to ~ some** *or* **a bit of doing** colloq 不容易做到; **she'll ~ some persuading** 想说服她可得费一番口舌; **to have (got) what it ~s (to do sth.)** colloq 具备成功（做某事）的才能 29 (operate using) «*car, machine*» 使用 ‹*unleaded petrol, diesel, battery*› 30 (wear) 穿; **she ~s a size 12/a size 10 in shoes** 她穿 12 号衣服/10 号鞋 31 (hold) 容纳; **the bus can ~ 60 passengers** 这辆公共汽车可载 60 名乘客; **the tank ~s 50 litres** 这个桶能装 50 升; **this suitcase will not ~ any more clothes** 这个手提箱装不下更多衣服了 32 (teach subject) 教授; (study subject) 学习; (be examined in subject) 参加 ‹*exam, test*›; **who ~s you for French?** 谁给你上法语课？; **he took lessons in Arabic** 他上过阿拉伯语课 33 Brit (be awarded) 获得 ‹*degree*› 34 (officiate at) «*priest, vicar*» 主持 ‹*service, mass, prayers, wedding*› 35 (use as means of transport) «*passenger*» 乘 ‹*bus, plane, train, ferry*›; (be means of transport for) «*train, car*» 运送 ‹*passenger, traveller*›; **this bus will ~ you to the station** 坐这辆公共汽车可以到车站 36 (use as route) 取道; (be route for) «*path*» 把…引向 ‹*person, vehicle*›; **to ~ the first (on the) left/right** 在第一个路口左转/右转; **to ~ the coast road** 走沿海公路; **this road ~s you to the Town Hall** 这条路通往市政厅 37 (cause to go) 使…去; **his work ~s him to many different countries** 他常去不同的国家出差; **what took you to Paris?** 你怎么会去巴黎的？ 38 (negotiate) 翻越 ‹*fence, hill*›; 绕过 ‹*bend*›; **he ~s the corners with no concern for his own safety** 他急转弯时不顾自己的安危 39 Sport (kick ball) 踢; (throw ball) 掷; **to ~ a penalty/free kick/corner/throw-in** 主罚点球/主罚任意球/开角球/掷界外球 40 (establish opinions using) 进行 ‹*vote, poll, survey*› 41 Ling «*verb, noun, preposition*» 与…连用 ‹*object, case*› 42 liter (have sex with) 与…性交 43 dated (get by marrying) «*man*» 娶 ‹*wife*›; «*woman*» 嫁给 ‹*husband*› 44 Fishg «*fish*» 咬 ‹*bait, fly*›

B *vi* (*pt* **took**, *pp* **taken**) 1 (need specified time) 费时; **how long will it ~?** 它需要多长时间？; **it does not ~ long to do sth.** 做某事不需要很长时间 2 (have desired effect) «*vaccination, drug*» 奏效; **the dye won't ~ in cold water** 这种染料在冷水中染色效果不理想 3 (grow successfully, become established) «*seed, plant*» 成活; **the skin graft failed to ~** 移植的皮肤没能成活 4 Fishg «*fish*» 咬钩

C *n* 1 Mus, Cin (single recording) (一次) 录音; (single shot) (一次) 拍摄; **they shot the scene in one ~** 这个镜头他们一次就拍好了; **'it's a ~!'** "一次过！" 2 colloq (opinion) 看法; (version) 阐释; **a ~ on sth.** 对某事物的看法; **a new ~ on the Romeo and Juliet story** 《罗密欧与朱丽叶》故事新解 3 colloq (takings) 收入额; **to be on the ~** colloq 受贿 4 Fishg, Hunt (of fish) 捕捞量; (of animals, birds) 捕猎量

Phrasal verbs

- **take aback** *vt* [**~ sb. aback**] 使大吃一惊; **to be taken aback by sb./sth.** 被某人/某事物吓一跳
- **take after** *vt* [**~ after sb.**]
  1 (be like) 像 ‹*parent*› 2 Amer colloq (chase) 追赶
- **take along** *vt* [**~ sb./sth. along, ~ along sb./sth.**] 携带 ‹*object*›; 带着 ‹*person*›; **to ~ sb./sth. along with one** 带着某人/某物
- **take apart** *vt* [**~ sb./sth. apart, ~ apart sb./sth.**]
  1 (dismantle) 拆卸 ‹*car, machine*› 2 (criticize) 严厉批评 ‹*essay, film, book*› 3 colloq (defeat) 轻易打败 ‹*opponent, team*›
- **take around** *vt* **= take round 2**
- **take aside** *vt* [**~ sb. aside**] 把…带到一边
- **take away**

A [**~ sth. away, ~ away sth.**] *vt*
1 Brit (buy for eating elsewhere) 买…带走 ‹*food*›; **two burgers to ~ away, please** 请来两份汉堡包，带走 2 (cause to disappear) 消除 ‹*fear, grief*›; **to ~ the pain away** 止痛; **to ~ away sb.'s appetite** 倒某人的胃口 3 (subtract) 减去 ‹*number*›; **ten ~ away four is** *or* **leaves six, ~ four away from ten and it leaves six** 10 减去 4 等于 6

B [**~ sb./sth. away, ~ away sb./sth.**] *vt* (remove) 弄走 ‹*person, object*›; **to ~ sb./sth. away from sb./sth.** 把某人/某物从某人处/某处弄走; **'not to be taken away'** "请勿带走"

- **take away from** *vt* [**~ away from sth.**] 减少 ‹*success, merits*›; **that doesn't ~ anything away from his achievement** 那丝毫不能贬低他的成绩
- **take back**

A [**~ sth. back, ~ back sth.**] *vt*
1 (return to shop) 退回; **to ~ a faulty product back to the shop** 把有缺陷的商品退回商店 2 (accept back) «*shop, person*» 回收 ‹*goods, gift*› 3 (retract) 收回 ‹*statement, words*›; **I ~ it back** 我收回说过的话; **to ~ back a** *or* **one's promise** 反悔

B [**~ sb. back**] *vt*
1 (cause to remember) 勾起…的回忆; **the smell of the sea took him back to his childhood** 大海的气息让他回想起了童年 2 (allow to come back) 重新接纳 ‹*partner, employee*›; **he took his wife back after she had left him** 妻子离开他之后他又同意她回家了

- **take down**

A [**~ sth. down, ~ down sth.**] *vt*
1 (carry to lower level) 将…拿下来 ‹*book, box*›; **to ~ sth. down to sb./sth.** 将某物拿下来给某人/放到某处; **she took the medicine down to the child** 她把药拿下来给孩子; **to ~ sth. down from sth.** 从某处取下某物; **please ~ the clock down from the shelf** 请把钟从架子上拿下来 2 (remove from fixed position) 摘掉 ‹*picture, sign, curtains*›; **to ~ sth. down from sth.** 从某处摘下某物 3 (lower) 褪下 ‹*skirt, trousers*› 4 (dismantle) 拆除 ‹*tent, gate, barricade*› 5 (write down) 记录 ‹*name, details, speech*›

B [**~ sb. down, ~ down sb.**] *vt* (accompany to lower level) 带…下去 ‹*person, animal*›; **to ~ sb. down to sb./sth.** 带某人下去见某人/到某处

- **take hold** *vi* «*disease*» 加重; «*epidemic*» 爆发; «*idea, ideology*» 产生影响
- **take hold of** *vt* [**~ hold of sb./sth.**]
  1 (grasp) 抓住 ‹*person, animal, object*› 2 (overwhelm) «*feeling, idea*» 完全控制 ‹*person, animal*›; **panic took hold of him** 他惊恐万分

• **take in**

A [**~ sb./sth. in, ~ in sb./sth.**] *vt*
1 (carry, accompany inside) 将…搬进去〈*things, plant*〉; 带…进去〈*person, animal*〉 **2** (allow to stay) 收留〈*person*〉; 让…留宿〈*lodger*〉; 收养〈*stray animal*〉

B [**~ sth. in, ~ in sth.**] *vt*
1 (understand) 理解〈*situation*〉; **I can't ~ it in!** 这个我弄不明白！; **I just couldn't ~ his death in** 他的死让我难以置信 **2** (absorb) 吸收〈*nutrients, oxygen*〉 **3** (start to fill with) 《*boat*》 渗进〈*water*〉 **4** esp Amer (go to see) 去观看〈*movie, play, exhibition, match*〉 **5** (observe) 注意到〈*detail, spectacle, situation*〉; (enjoy) 享受〈*atmosphere*〉; **he took in the scene at a glance** 他一眼就看到了那场面 **6** (accept for payment) 揽…回家做〈*washing, ironing, mending*〉

C [**~ sb. in, ~ in sb.**] *vt* (deceive) 欺骗; **he was taken in** 他上当了; **don't be taken in by appearances!** 不要被外表迷惑！

D [**~ in sth.**] *vt* (include) 包括〈*place, subject, development*〉

• **take off**

A *vi* **1** (start to fly) 《*aircraft, flight*》 起飞; 《*bird*》 飞起来; **to ~ off from sth.** 从某处起飞; **to ~ off for sth.** 飞往某处 **2** (jump) 《*athlete, high jumper*》 起跳 **3** colloq (leave) 开溜 **4** (become popular, successful) 《*idea*》 大受欢迎; 《*fashion*》 迅速流行; 《*product*》 畅销

B [**~ sth. off, ~ off sth.**] *vt*
1 (remove) 脱下〈*coat, trousers, shoes*〉; 摘下〈*gloves, hat*〉; **the nurse took his clothes off** 护士给他脱了衣服; **please ~ your hands off me/your feet off the seat** 请把你的手从我身上拿开/请勿踩踏座位; **to ~ sth. off sb.** (remove from possession of) 从某人手中夺走某物 **2** (stop from being performed or broadcast) 停演〈*show, play*〉; 停播〈*programme*〉; **to ~ sth. off the market** 在市场上停售某物 **3** (withdraw from service) 取消〈*bus, train*〉 **4** (cut off) 截去〈*part of body*〉; 剪掉〈*hair*〉; **his leg had to be taken off just below the knee** 他不得不从膝盖以下截肢 **5** (detach) 拿掉〈*lid*〉; 卸下〈*door*〉; 使…剥落〈*paint*〉; **to ~ sth. off sth.** 从某物上弄掉某物 **6** **to ~ sth. off sth.** (deduct) 从某总量扣除某数量; **to ~ £10 off the price (of sth.)** （将某物）降价 10 英镑; **that experience took ten years off my life** 那段经历让我老了十岁; **that hairstyle ~s 15 years off you!** 那个发型让你看上去年轻了 15 岁！ **7** **to ~ sth. off sth.** (stop including) 从某处去除某项; **my name had been taken off the list** 我的名字从名单上画掉了; **fish has been taken off the menu** 菜单上去掉了鱼

C [**~ sth. off**] *vt* (have as holiday) 休…的假〈*week, morning*〉; **to ~ two days off** 休两天假; **to ~ the afternoon/time off work** 下午请假/请假不上班

D [**~ sb. off, ~ off sb.**] *vt*
1 colloq (imitate) 模仿; **he ~s the Prime Minister off to perfection** 他把首相模仿得惟妙惟肖 **2** (end participation of) 换下〈*player, performer*〉; **to ~ sb. off the case/project** 禁止某人继续办案/参与项目 **3** (remove from ship) 使弃船; **to ~ sb. off sth.** 使某人撤离某处; **a helicopter took the six crew members off** 一架直升机营救了六名船员 **4** **to ~ sb. off sth.** (stop from using) 使某人停止使用某物; **she was taken off the ventilator** 她的呼吸器被拿掉了

E [**~ sb. off**] *vt* (cause to leave) 带走〈*person*〉; **to ~ sb. off to prison** 将某人投入监狱

F *v refl* **to ~ oneself off** 离开; **to ~ oneself off to sth.** 动身去某处

• **take on**

A [**~ sb. on, ~ on sb.**] *vt*
1 (employ) 雇用〈*employee, staff*〉; **to ~ sb. on as sth.** 聘用某人担任某职位 **2** (accept as client) 承接 **3** (compete against) 与…比赛〈*person, opponent, team*〉; **I can beat him! I'll ~ him on!** 我能打败他！我要与他一争高下！; **Liverpool are taking on Arsenal in the Cup Final** 利物浦队将在足总杯决赛中迎战阿森纳队; **to ~ sb. on at tennis/badminton** 与某人打一场网球/羽毛球比赛 **4** (fight) 与…作战〈*person, army*〉

B [**~ sth. on, ~ on sth.**] *vt*
1 (assume) 显现; **the chameleon can ~ on the colour of its background** 变色龙可以呈现与背景一致的颜色; **her eyes took on a hurt look** 她的眼中透出受伤的神色; **her voice took on a pleading note** 她的声音带着恳求的语气; **the word has taken on a whole new meaning** 这个词有了一个全新的意义; **the subject has taken on a new significance** 该主题体现了一个新的意义 **2** (undertake) 承担〈*work, task, job, responsibility*〉; **to ~ on more than one has bargained for** 承担比预期多的工作

C [**~ sb./sth. on, ~ on sb./sth.**] *vt* (accept on board) 装载〈*cargo, freight*〉; 接载〈*passenger*〉; **the plane took on more fuel** 飞机接受了燃油补给; **the ship stops at Cape Town to ~ on more passengers** 轮船停靠在开普敦以接载更多的乘客

D *vi* Brit colloq dated 大惊小怪; **don't ~ on so!** 别这么紧张！

• **take out**

A [**~ sth. out, ~ out sth.**] *vt*
1 (remove) (from container) 取出〈*object, letter*〉; (from place) 将…拿出去〈*object*〉; **to ~ sth. out of a drawer/box/bag** 把某物从抽屉/盒子/袋子里拿出来; **to ~ the excitement/worry out of sth.** 使某事物不再让人兴奋/忧虑; **to ~ sb. out of himself/herself** 使某人摆脱烦恼; **to ~ it** *or* **a lot out of sb.** 让某人精疲力竭 **2** Dent, Med 拔掉〈*tooth*〉; 切除〈*appendix*〉 **3** (withdraw from bank account) 提取〈*cash, amount*〉; **to ~ money out of the bank** 从银行取钱 **4** Amer (buy for eating elsewhere) 买…带走〈*food*〉; **two burgers to ~ out, please** 请来两份汉堡包，带走 **5** (deduct) 扣除〈*money, contributions, tax*〉; **to ~ sth. out of sth.** 从某处扣除某款项 **6** (obtain officially) 获得〈*insurance, loan, patent, licence*〉 **7** (cause to disappear) 除掉〈*mark*〉; **to ~ a coffee/wine stain out of a carpet** 除掉地毯上的咖啡/葡萄酒污渍

B [**~ sb./sth. out, ~ out sb./sth.**] *vt*
1 (go out with, accompany) 带…外出〈*person, dog*〉; (go out with socially) 请…外出〈*person*〉; **to ~ the child/dog out for a walk** 带孩子出去散步/去遛狗; **to ~ sb. out to lunch/dinner** 请某人出去吃午饭/晚饭 **2** colloq (kill) 干掉〈*person, enemy*〉; (destroy) 摧毁〈*site, target, installation*〉 **3** colloq (put out of action) 使…不能工作〈*person*〉; 牵制〈*player*〉; 使…瘫痪〈*network*〉

• **take out on** *vt* **to ~ sth. out on sb./sth.** 对某人/某物发泄某情绪; **she tended to ~ her anger/frustrations out on her family** 她一动怒/受挫就爱拿家人出气; **to ~ it out on sb.** 拿某人当出气筒

• **take over**

A *vi* **1** (assume power) 《*rebels, protesters, faction*》 接管; **to ~ over from sb./sth.** 从某人/某组织手中接管 **2** (dominate) 《*person, feeling*》 起支配作用; **he's always trying to ~ over** 他总想发号施令; **don't let negative thoughts ~ over** 别让消极的想法左右你 **3** **to ~ over from sb.** (assume responsibility in place of sb.) 接替某人; (perform activity in place of sb.) 接手某人的工作; **to ~ over as sth.** 继任某职位; **she's taken over as boss** 她继任老板 **4** **to ~ over from sth.** (be replacement for sth.) 替代某物; **the computer has taken over from the typewriter** 计算机取代了打字机

B *vt* [**~ sth. over, ~ over sth.**]
1 Mil, Pol (assume power over, occupy) 接管〈*town, country, party*〉; 占领〈*building*〉; **to ~ over power from sb.** 从某人处接手权力 **2** (assume charge of or responsibility for) 接管〈*company, business, shop*〉; 接手〈*duty, responsibility, cooking*〉; **CBS Records was taken over by Sony** 哥伦比亚唱片公司被索尼公司收购; **shall I ~ over the driving for a while?** 我替你开一会儿车好吗？; **to ~ over sth. from sb./sth.** 接替某人/某物做某事; **who can ~ over the leadership from the Prime Minister?** 谁能够继任首相的领导职务？

• **take place** *vi* 《*event, incident*》 发生; 《*meeting, ceremony*》 举行

• **take round** *vt* **1** [**~ sth. round, ~ round sth.**] (circulate with) 分发 **2** [**~ sb. round**] (show, accompany) 带…看; **to ~ sb. round sth.** 带某人参观某处

• **take through** *vt* **to ~ sb. through sth.** 帮助某人了解某事; **to ~ the actors through the scene** 给演员说戏

• **take to**

A [**~ to sth.**] *vt*
1 (go to) 去〈*forest, hills*〉; 登上〈*lifeboats*〉; **he's ill and has taken to his bed** 他卧病在床; **to ~ to the streets to protest** 走上街头抗议 **2** (develop habit of) 开始养成…的习惯; **she's taken to drink** 她开始酗酒了; **to ~ to doing sth.** 开始习惯于做某事; **she's taken to watching TV before doing her homework** 她养成了先看电视后做作业的习惯 **3** (develop ability for) 培养…的能力; **she took to tennis as if she'd been playing all her life** 她网球学得很快，好像打了一辈子似的 **4** **to ~ sth. to sb./sth.** (use on) 用…对付某人/某物〈*axe, sledgehammer*〉; **I took a hacksaw to the shaft and cut it into three sections** 我用弓锯把杆子锯成了三段

B [**~ to sb./sth.**] *vt* (develop liking for) 喜欢上〈*person, occupation, idea*〉; **I took to him the moment I saw him** 我对他一见钟情

• **take up**

A [**~ sth./sb. up, ~ up sth./sb.**] *vt* (carry to higher level) 拿…上去〈*book, box, tray*〉; (accompany to higher level) 带…上去〈*person, animal*〉; **to ~ sth. up to sb./sth.** 将某物拿上去给某人/拿到上面某处; **can you ~ the phone up to her?** 请你把电话拿上去给她; **to ~ sb. up to sb./sth.** 带某人上去见某人/带到上面某处; **he took the doctor up to her room** 他带医生上去到她房间里

B [**~ sth. up, ~ up sth.**] *vt*
1 (accept) 接受〈*offer, invitation, challenge*〉 **2** (mention, raise) 提出〈*matter, question*〉; **to ~ up sb.'s case** 提交某人的案件; **to ~ up sth. with sb.** 向某人提出某事; **I suggest you ~ this up with the boss** 我建议你向老板提出此事 **3** (shorten) 将…改短〈*skirt, trousers, curtains*〉 **4** (absorb) 吸收〈*liquid, water, ink*〉 **5** (remove) 掀起〈*carpet, railway track*〉; 翻起〈*road, runway*〉 **6** (pick up) 拿起〈*pen, brush, violin*〉 **7** (start to engage in or work in) 开始从事〈*activity, job, career*〉; 开始学〈*tennis, piano*〉; **to ~ up one's duties** *or* **responsibilities** 担负起职责 **8** (add one's voice to) 加入〈*chorus, refrain*〉; **to ~ up a cry** 齐声高呼 **9** (resume, return to) 继续〈*story, work, discussion*〉; 回到〈*item*〉; **I'd like to ~ up the point you raised earlier** 我想回到你刚才提出的那一点

C [**~ up sth.**] *vt*
1 (use up) 占用〈*space*〉; 耗费〈*energy*〉; **it ~s up too much time** 这太费时间; **to be taken up with sth.** 忙于某事 **2** (move into) 《*troops, army*》 占据〈*position*〉 **3** (adopt) 采取〈*attitude, stance*〉; **to ~ up a high moral tone** 大唱道德高调

D *vi* 《*person, episode, book*》 继续; **to ~ up where sb./sth. left off** 从某人/某事中断的地方接下去

• **take up on** *vt* **to ~ sb. up on sth.**
1 (challenge) 就…质问某人〈*point, assertion*〉 **2** (accept) 接受某人的〈*invitation, offer, challenge*〉; **to ~ sb. up on their promise** 让某人信守承诺

• **take up with** *vt* **1** [**~ up with sb.**] dated colloq (start to associate with) 结交; **he's taken up with a divorced woman** 他和一

t

个离了婚的女人勾搭在一起 2 **to be taken up with sb./sth.** (be preoccupied with) 沉迷于某人/专注于某事; **the Prime Minister is rather taken up with domestic issues** 首相正致力于解决国内的问题

takeaway /ˈteɪkəweɪ/ Brit
A *adj* 外卖的 ‹*food*›
B *n* 1 (restaurant) 外卖餐馆 2 (meal) 外卖食品

take-home pay *n* [u] [扣除税款后的] 实得工资

take-in *n* colloq 欺骗

taken /ˈteɪkən/
A *pp* ▸ **take A, B**
B *adj pred* 1 (reserved) 预留的; **excuse me, but is this seat ~?** 对不起，请问这个座位有人吗？ 2 (impressed) 对…着迷的; **to be ~ with** *or* **by sb./sth.** 对某人/某事物着迷

take: ~-off *n* 1 Aviat 起飞; **the local economy is poised for ~-off** 本地经济呈腾飞之势; **~-off speed** 起飞速度; 2 Sport 起跳; 3 colloq (imitation) 滑稽模仿; **he did a really good ~-off of the prime minister** 他对首相的滑稽模仿惟妙惟肖; **~out** *n* Amer = **takeaway**

takeover /ˈteɪkəʊvə(r)/ *n* 1 Fin 收购 2 Pol 接管

takeover bid *n* 收购出价

taker /ˈteɪkə(r)/ *n* (of food) 食用者; (of drink) 饮用者; (of drugs) 吸食者; (of wager, challenge, offer) 接受者; **there's some cake left — any ~s?** 还剩下一些蛋糕——谁要？

take-up *n* [u] (acceptance) (of benefit, rebate) 领受; (of grant, shares) 认购; **~ rate** (of benefit) 领受率; (of shares) 认购率

take-up spool *n* 收片盘

taking /ˈteɪkɪŋ/
A *n* [u] (of challenge, offer, bribe, money, risk) 接受; (of object, article) 拿取; (of food) 食用; (of drink) 饮用; (of drugs) 吸食; Mil (of town, country) 攻占; **for the ~** 可随意取用的
B **takings** *npl* 进账; **the week's ~s** 本周收入

talc /tælk/ *n* 1 [u] Chem 滑石 2 [u and c] Cosmet 爽身粉

talcum /ˈtælkəm/
A *n* [u and c] **~ (powder)** 爽身粉
B *vt* 给…扑爽身粉

tale /teɪl/ *n* 1 (story) 故事; **a folk ~** 民间传说; **to tell a ~** 讲故事; **a cautionary ~** 警示; **to tell the same/another ~** fig 情况相同/矛盾; **thereby hangs a ~** 说来话长; **dead men tell no ~s** Prov 死人不会说话; **to tell its own ~** 不言自明; **recent events tell their own ~** 新近发生的事一目了然; **a likely ~!** colloq 鬼才信呢！ colloq 2 (piece of hearsay or gossip) 流言; **to tell ~s out of school** 背后说长道短

talent /ˈtælənt/ *n* 1 [u and c] (natural ability) 天赋; **a man of many ~s** 多才多艺的男子; **a ~ for sth./doing sth.** 某事上的/做某事的天赋; **he has a ~ for upsetting people** iron 他特会烦人; **to waste one's ~(s)** 浪费才智 2 [u and c] (people) 天才; **young ~** 青年才俊; **fresh** *or* **new ~** 新锐 3 [u] Brit colloq (members of the opposite sex) 富有魅力的异性; **to eye up the local ~** 色迷迷地打量本地的美妞

talent contest *n* 才艺大赛

talented /ˈtæləntɪd/ *adj* 才华横溢的; **to be ~ at sth./doing sth.** 具有某方面/做某事的天分

talentless /ˈtæləntlɪs/ *adj* 缺乏才能的

talent: ~ scout *n* 星探; **~ show** *n* = **talent contest**; **~ spotter** *n* Brit = **~ scout**; **~-spotting** *n* [u] 物色新秀; **a ~-spotting agency** 星探公司

tale: ~teller *n* 说长道短的人; **~-telling** *n* [u] 说长道短

Taliban /ˈtælɪbæn/ *pr n + v sing or pl* **the ~** 塔利班 [伊斯兰激进武装组织]

talisman /ˈtælɪzmən, ˈtælɪs-/ *n* 护身符

talismanic /ˌtælɪzˈmænɪk, ˌtælɪs-/ *adj* 能驱邪的 ‹*person, quality, object*›

talk /tɔːk/
A *vi* 1 (speak, converse) 谈话; **to ~ to** *or* **with sb. (about sth.)** (就某事物) 与某人谈话; **to ~ to oneself** 自言自语; **to ~ about** *or* **of** *or* **on sb./sth.** 谈论某人/某事物; **to know what one is ~ing about** colloq 精于此道; **he hasn't a clue what he's ~ing about** 他不谙此道; **he's ~ing about** *or* **of getting a job** 他说的是找工作的事; **look** *or* **listen who's ~ing!, you can** *or* **can't ~!** colloq 你还有脸说别人！; **to ~ away** 说个不停; **to ~ for the sake of ~ing** 为了说话而说话; **to love to hear oneself ~** 喜欢夸夸其谈; **he kept me ~ing for an hour!** 他没完没了地同我谈了一个小时！; **~ about ...** colloq 这才叫… [用于表示所说之事非常明显]; **~ about mean/trouble/stupid/expensive!** 这才叫吝啬/麻烦/愚蠢/贵呢！; **~ing of films/holidays** 说到电影/假期; **I don't think it's going to be easy — you're ~ing about at least eight hours' work** 我觉得这件事不容易——至少要花 8 个小时; **it's easy** *or* **all right for you/her to ~!** colloq 你/她说得容易！; **now you're ~ing!** colloq 你这话就对了！ 2 (have the power of speech) 能说话; **can your little boy ~ yet?** 你的小儿子会说话了吗？ 3 pej (gossip) 说闲话; **to give people something to ~ about** 给人们留下谈资; **to be** *or* **get oneself ~ed about** 招人议论 4 (give information under coercion) 招供; **to make sb. ~** 使某人招供; **the prisoner refused to ~** 囚犯拒绝交待
B *vt* 1 (discuss) 谈论 ‹*business, politics, sport*› 2 (express in speech) 说; **you're ~ing sense!** 你说的话有道理！; **to ~ rubbish** *or* **nonsense** 说废话; **we're ~ing £2 million/three years** colloq 这将花费 200 万英镑/3 年; **we're ~ing a huge investment/a major project** colloq 这关系到一笔巨大的投资/一个大项目 3 (persuade) **to ~ sb. into/out of doing sth.** 说服某人做/不要做某事 4 (speak in language) 讲 ‹*English, Chinese, French*› 5 (bring into certain condition) 讲得; **he ~ed himself hoarse/to a standstill!** 他讲得声音都嘶哑了/精疲力竭！; **he's hoping to ~ himself out of trouble** 他希望用力陈理由以摆脱麻烦; **to ~ oneself** *or* **one's way into/out of sth./doing sth.** 靠能说会道使自己做/免于做某事; **to ~ one's head off** colloq 说个不停; **to ~ sb.'s head off** colloq 唠叨得使某人感到厌烦
C *n* 1 [c] (conversation) 谈话; **a formal/an informal ~** 正式/非正式谈话; **to have a ~ with sb. (about sb./sth.)** (就某人/某事物) 同某人交谈; **a heart-to-heart ~** 谈心 2 [u] (talking) 说话; **small/sweet/baby ~** 闲聊/甜言蜜语/儿语; **fast** *or* **double ~** 花言巧语; **blunt** *or* **plain** *or* **straight ~** 直截了当的话; **too much ~ and not enough action!** 说得多做得少！; **to be all ~ (and no action)** 光说不做; **nothing but/a whole lot of ~** 尽是/全是空谈 3 [u] (rumours) 谣言; (gossip) 闲话; **idle/loose ~** 闲话/信口乱说; **the ~ of the town** 街谈巷议; **~ about** *or* **of sb./sth.** 有关某人/某事物的传闻 4 [c] (lecture) 讲座; (speech) 演讲; **an academic/informal ~** 学术/非正式演讲; **a ~ on** *or* **about deep-sea fishing/acupuncture** 关于深海捕鱼/针灸的讲座; **to give/have a ~** 作演说/听讲座; **a ~ on radio/TV** 广播/电视演说
D **talks** *npl* (formal discussions) 商谈; **pay/disarmament/peace/arms ~s** 工资/裁军/和平/军备谈判; **to conduct** *or* **hold ~s** 举行会谈; **~s about sth.** 有关某事物的会谈; **~s between sb. and sb.** 某人与某人之间的洽谈

Phrasal verbs

- **talk at** *vt* [**~ at sb.**] 对…大发议论
- **talk back** *vi* 回嘴; **to ~ back to sb.** 对某人顶嘴; **don't you ~ back to me like that!** 不许你这样和我顶嘴！
- **talk down**
A *vt* [**~ sb. down**]
1 (silence) (by talking loudly) 高声讲话盖过; (talking persistently) 说个不停不让…插话 2 Aviat (guide) 引导…着陆 ‹*aircraft*›; **ground control ~ed the pilot down in thick fog** 地面控制人员引导飞行员在浓雾中着陆
B *vi* 高高在上地说话; **to ~ down to sb.** 以高人一等的口气对某人说话
- **talk out** *vt* [**~ sth. out**]
1 (discuss, resolve by discussion) 协商解决 2 Brit Pol (prevent passing of) 通过冗长发言阻止…通过 ‹*bill*›
- **talk over** *vt* 1 [**~ sb. over**] (persuade) 说服; **we ~ed them over to our way of thinking/to doing it our way** 我们说服他们同意我们的看法/按照我们的方式行事 2 (discuss) **to ~ sth. over (with sb.)** (和某人) 讨论某事; **we must ~ the matter over** 我们必须把这件事议一议
- **talk round** esp Brit *vt* 1 [**~ sb. round**] (persuade) 说服; **to ~ sb. round to sth./doing sth.** 说服某人赞同某事物/做某事; **to ~ sb. round to our way of thinking/to doing it our way** 说服某人同意我们的看法/按照我们的方式行事 2 [**~ round sth.**] (skirt around) 不着边际地谈
- **talk through** *vt* [**~ sth. through**] 谈透
- **talk up** *vt* [**~ sb./sth. up**] 吹捧

talkathon /ˈtɔːkəθɒn/ *n* colloq 马拉松式的长篇大论

talkative /ˈtɔːkətɪv/ *adj* 健谈的; **she was in a ~ mood** 她谈兴正浓

talkativeness /ˈtɔːkətɪvnɪs/ *n* [u] 健谈

talk: ~back *n* 1 (two-way communication) 对讲机; **a ~back system** 对讲系统; 2 TV, Radio = **phone-in**; **~board** *n* (bulletin board) 讨论区; (chat room) 聊天室

talked-about, talked-of *adjs* 常被谈论的 ‹*event, relationship, person*›

talker /ˈtɔːkə(r)/ *n* 讲话者; **he's a great ~!** 他是个相当健谈的人！; **a smooth** *or* **glib** *or* **fast ~** 能说会道的人; **he's just a ~** 他只会说空话

talkie /ˈtɔːki/ *n* colloq [早期的] 有声电影

talking /ˈtɔːkɪŋ/
A *n* [u] 讲话
B *adj* 会说话的 ‹*doll*›; 会学人语的 ‹*bird*›; 有声的 ‹*film*›

talking: ~ book *n* 有声读物; **~ head** *n* colloq [人头特写的] 播音员; **~ point** *n* 话题; **~ shop** *n* Brit pej [只说不做的] 清谈馆; **~-to** *n* colloq 责骂; **to give sb. a ~-to** 斥责某人

talk: ~ radio *n* [u] 听众热线节目; **~ show** *n* 脱口秀; **a ~ show host/audience** 脱口秀主持人/听众; **~time** *n* [u] [手机的] 通话时间

tall /tɔːl/ ▸**p. 436** *adj* 1 (higher than average) 高的 ‹*person, building, tree*›; **to get** *or* **grow ~(er)** 长高; **a ~ order** colloq (difficult task) 难办的事; (unreasonable request) 无理要求; **a ~ story** *or* **tale** colloq 荒诞不经的事; **to walk ~** 趾高气扬; **to stand ~** (proud and confident) 趾高气扬; (resolute) 果敢自信 2 (of specified height) …高的; **how ~ is he?** 他个子有多高？; **to feel** *or* **seem (about) ten feet ~** 自高自大

tall: ~boy *n* Brit 高衣柜; **~ drink** *n* 高脚杯饮料

Tallinn /ˈtælɪn/ *pr n* 塔林

tallness /ˈtɔːlnɪs/ *n* [u] 高

tallow /ˈtæləʊ/ *n* [u] 动物油脂

tallow candle *n* 油脂蜡烛

tall ship *n* 高桅横帆船

tally /ˈtæli/
A *n* 1 (record) 账目; **to keep** *or* **make a ~ (of sth.)** (将某事物) 记账; **a running ~** 流水账 2 (total amount) 账目总数; Sport 总分 3 (label) [尤指植物或树木的] 标签

B *vi* «*accounts, amounts, signatures*» 吻合; **to ~ with sth.** 与某事吻合; **their stories don't ~** 他们的说法有出入
C *vt* **~ (up)** **1** (calculate) 计算 ‹*items, votes*› **2** (record) 记录 ‹*result, total, score*›

tally-ho /ˌtælɪˈhəʊ/ *excl* 呔嗬 [猎人呼唤猎狗追逐猎物时的叫喊]

Talmud /ˈtælmʊd, *Amer* ˈtɑːl-/ *pr n* **the ~** 《塔木德经》[犹太古代法典]

talmudic /tælˈmʊdɪk, *Amer* tɑːl-/ *adj* 《塔木德经》的

talon /ˈtælən/ *n* [尤指猛禽的] 爪

tamable /ˈteɪməbl/ *adj* = **tameable**

tamarin /ˈtæmərɪn/ *n* 小绢猴

tamarind /ˈtæmərɪnd/ *n* **1** [c] (tree) 罗望子树 **2** [c] (pod) 罗望子果 **3** [u] (pulp) 罗望子果酱

tambourine /ˌtæmbəˈriːn/ ▸**p. 395** *n* [镶有金属片的] 铃鼓

tame /teɪm/
A *adj* **1** (not wild) 驯化的 ‹*animal, bird*›; **to become** *or* **grow ~** 变得驯顺 **2** (unadventurous) 枯燥乏味的 ‹*party, life, ending*› **3** *attrib hum* (obliging) 温顺的
B *vt* **1** (domesticate) 驯服 ‹*bird, animal*› **2** *fig* (control) 控制 ‹*passion, river, country*›; 梳理 ‹*hair*›; 抑制 ‹*interest rates, inflation*›

tameable /ˈteɪməbl/ *adj* 可驯养的

tamely /ˈteɪmli/ *adv* **1** (unexcitingly) 平淡地 ‹*end, proceed, worded*› **2** (meekly) 温顺地 ‹*surrender, accede*›; *Sport* 不紧不慢地 ‹*shoot, hit*›

tameness /ˈteɪmnɪs/ *n* [u] **1** (of animal, bird) 驯服 **2** (of story, event) 枯燥乏味

tamer /ˈteɪmə(r)/ *n* 驯养员; **a lion-~** 驯狮员

Tamil /ˈtæmɪl/ ▸**p. 503, p. 426**
A *adj* (of the Tamils) 泰米尔人的; (of the language) 泰米尔语的
B *n* **1** [c] (person) 泰米尔人 **2** [u] (language) 泰米尔语

Tamil Tigers *npl* **the ~** 泰米尔猛虎组织

taming /ˈteɪmɪŋ/ *n* [u] **1** (domestication) 驯化; **lion-~** 驯狮 **2** (controlling) 控制

tam-o'-shanter /ˌtæməˈʃæntə(r)/ *n* [帽顶有绒球的] 苏格兰圆帽

tamp /tæmp/ *vt* 夯实 ‹*hole*›

Phrasal verb
• **tamp down** *vt* [**~ down sth., ~ sth. down**] 压实 ‹*tobacco, earth*›

tamper /ˈtæmpə(r)/ *vi* (meddle) 鼓捣; (alter without authority) 篡改; **to ~ with sth.** 鼓捣 ‹*brakes, safe, food*›; 篡改 ‹*records, evidence*›; **to ~ with a jury** 向陪审团行贿

tamper-proof *adj* 防做手脚的 ‹*ballot box*›; 防胡乱摆弄的 ‹*lock, machine*›

tampon /ˈtæmpɒn/ *n* **1** (for menstruation) [月经期用的] 卫生棉条 **2** *Med* 止血栓

tan¹ /tæn/
A *n* **1** [u] (colour) 棕黄色 **2** [c] (suntanning of skin) 棕褐色肤色; **to get a ~** 被晒黑; **she has a lovely, golden ~** 她的皮肤晒成了可爱的金棕色
B *adj* **1** (yellowish-brown) 棕黄色的 ‹*shoes, fabric, paper*› **2** *Amer* (suntanned) 晒黑的 ‹*skin, person*›
C *vt* (*pres p etc.* **-nn-**) **1** (make into leather) 将…制成革 ‹*hide*›; **to ~ sb.'s hide** *colloq* 打得某人皮开肉绽 **2** (make suntanned) 晒黑 ‹*skin, person*› **3** *colloq* (beat) 猛揍 ‹*child*›
D *vi* (*pres p etc.* **-nn-**) «*skin, person*» 晒黑

tan² *abbr* = **tangent A2**

tandem /ˈtændəm/
A *n* **1** (bicycle) 双人自行车 **2** (pair) 联合作业; **in ~** (one behind the other) 一前一后地; (alongside one another) 同心协力地; **in ~ with sb.** 与某人协同工作
B *adv* 一前一后地 ‹*ride*›

tandoori /tænˈdʊəri/
A *adj attrib* 唐杜里烹饪法的; **~ chicken/oven** 唐杜里鸡/炉
B *n* **1** [u and c] (food) 唐杜里食品; (cooking) 唐杜里烹饪 **2** [c] (restaurant) 唐杜里餐馆

Tang /tæŋ/ *pr n* 唐朝; **a ~ vase** 唐代的花瓶; **the ~ dynasty** 唐朝

tang /tæŋ/ *n* **1** (taste, smell) 强烈味道; **the ~ of blood** 血腥味; **his words came out with a distinct local ~** 他说话带有明显的地方口音 **2** (part of blade) 柄舌

tanga /ˈtæŋgə/ *n* **~ (briefs** *pl***)** *Brit* 丁字裤

tangent /ˈtændʒənt/
A *n* **1** (touching line) 切线; **to fly off at a ~** «*ball*» 突然转向; **to go off at** *or* **on a ~** *fig* 突然转换话题 **2** *Math* (trigonometric function) 正切
B *adj attrib* 正切的

tangential /tænˈdʒenʃl/ *adj* **1** *Math* 正切的 ‹*line, plane*› **2** *fig* (peripheral) 离题的 ‹*point, remark*›; 不相干的 ‹*information, relationship*›; **to be ~ to sth.** 与某事不相干

tangerine /ˌtændʒəˈriːn/
A *n* **1** [c] (fruit) 橘子 **2** [u] (colour) 橘红色 **3** [c] (tree) 柑橘树
B *adj* 橘红色的

tangibility /ˌtændʒəˈbɪləti/ *n* [u] **1** (perceptibility to touch) 可触性 **2** (clearness, definiteness) 明确性; **the ~ of the evidence** 证据的确凿

tangible /ˈtændʒəbl/ *adj* **1** (perceptible to touch) 可触摸的 ‹*object, contact*› **2** (clear, definite) 明显的 ‹*improvement, advantage*›; 确凿的 ‹*evidence*›; 有形的 ‹*property*›

tangible assets *npl* 有形资产

tangibly /ˈtændʒəbli/ *adv* **1** (to the touch) 可触知地 ‹*detect, exist, soft*›; **~ real** 真真切切的 **2** (clearly) 明确地 ‹*prove, demonstrate*›; 显著地 ‹*improve, change*›

tangle /ˈtæŋgl/
A *n* **1** (confused mass of hair, string, etc.) 缠结; **to be in a ~** 乱成一团 **2** *fig* (confused state) 混乱; **his business affairs are in a dreadful ~** 他的生意一塌糊涂
B *vt* 把…缠结在一起 ‹*hair, string*›
C *vi* **1** (get in a tangle) «*hair, string*» 缠成一团 **2** *colloq* (quarrel) 争论; **to ~ with sb.** 与某人争执; **I wouldn't ~ with him if I were you** 我如果是你就不会去惹他; **to ~ over sth.** 就某事发生争执

Phrasal verb
• **tangle up**
A *vt* [**~ sth. up, ~ up sth.**] 把…缠结在一起 ‹*hair, string*›
B *vi* «*hair, string*» 缠成一团

tangled /ˈtæŋgld/ *adj* 缠在一起的 ‹*hair, string, weeds*›; **a ~ web of lies** 谎言的罗网

tangly /ˈtæŋgli/ *adj* 乱糟糟的 ‹*hair, brambles*›

tango /ˈtæŋgəʊ/
A *n* **1** *Dance* 探戈舞 **2** *Mus* 探戈舞曲
B *vi* 跳探戈舞; **it takes two to ~** 一个巴掌拍不响

tangy /ˈtæŋi/ *adj* 味道强烈的 ‹*aroma, flavour*›

tank /tæŋk/
A *n* **1** (container) [贮放液体或气体的] 容器; **a ~ of tropical fish** 一缸热带鱼; **a hot-water/fuel ~** 热水箱/燃料箱; **a developing ~** *Phot* 显影槽 **2** (contents) 一箱; **a ~ of petrol** *Brit or* **gas** *Amer* 一箱汽油 **3** *Mil* 坦克; **a ~ offensive** 坦克攻击; **~ tracks in the mud** 泥地里的坦克辙 **4** (reservoir) （人工）蓄水池
B *vi esp Amer colloq* «*company, stock market*» 遭受重创; «*show, film*» 惨败

Phrasal verb
• **tank up**
A *vt* [**~ sth. up, ~up sth.**] **1** (with fuel) 给…加满油 ‹*vehicle*› **2** *Brit colloq* (with alcohol, drugs) **to get ~ed up** 喝高了
B *vi* **1** (with fuel) «*vehicle*» 加满油 **2** *colloq* (with alcohol) 喝醉; (with drugs) 吸食过量

tankard /ˈtæŋkəd/ *n* **1** (mug) 单柄大酒杯 **2** (amount) 一大酒杯

tank: ~ car *n Amer* [运送液体的] 罐车; **~ engine** *n* 水柜蒸汽机车

tanker /ˈtæŋkə(r)/ *n* (ship) 油轮; (aircraft) 空中加油飞机; (lorry, railway truck) 油罐车

tanker: ~ aircraft *n* 空中加油飞机; **~ lorry** *n Brit* 油罐车

tankful /ˈtæŋkfʊl/ *n* = **tank A2**

tankini /tæŋˈkiːni/ *n* 坦基尼 [两件套女式泳装]

tank: ~ killer *n* 坦克克星 [指能有效攻击坦克的飞机、车辆或导弹]; **~ locomotive** *n* = **~ engine**; **~ top** *n* 坎肩; **~ trap** *n* 坦克路障; **~ truck** *n Amer* 槽车; **~ wagon** *n Amer* = **~ car**

tanned /tænd/ *adj* 晒黑的 ‹*skin, person*›

tanner¹ /ˈtænə(r)/ *n* **1** (person) 鞣皮匠 **2** (lotion) 棕褐色肤色助晒膏

tanner² *n Brit Hist colloq* (sixpence) 6便士; (coin) 6便士硬币

tannery /ˈtænəri/ *n* 皮革厂

tannic /ˈtænɪk/ *adj* 单宁酸的 ‹*dye, wood*›; 似单宁酸的 ‹*taste, wine*›; **~ acid** 单宁酸

tannin /ˈtænɪn/ *n* [u] 单宁酸

tanning /ˈtænɪŋ/ *n* **1** [u] (suntanning) 晒黑; **~ lotion** 防晒油; **a ~ salon** 日光浴沙龙 **2** [u] *Ind* 鞣制皮革 **3** [c] *colloq* (thrashing) 揍; **to give sb. a (good) ~** （狠狠）揍某人一顿

Tannoy® /ˈtænɔɪ/ *n Brit* 天朗扩音设备

tantalize /ˈtæntəlaɪz/ *vt* **1** (tease, torment) 引逗; **he was ~d by the delicious smells coming from the restaurant** 饭店里传出的香味使他垂涎欲滴 **2** (fascinate) 使着迷

tantalizing /ˈtæntəlaɪzɪŋ/ *adj* 逗引的 ‹*hint, offer, smile*›; 诱人的 ‹*smell, sight*›

tantalizingly /ˈtæntəlaɪzɪŋli/ *adv* 逗引地 ‹*say, linger*›; **to be ~ close to victory** 离成功只差一步之遥; **the whole process was ~ slow** 整个过程缓慢得让人干着急

tantalum /ˈtæntələm/ *n* [u] 钽

tantamount /ˈtæntəmaʊnt/ *adj pred* 无异于…的; **to be ~ to sth.** 无异于某事物; **the result was ~ to disaster** 后果近乎灾难; **to be ~ to doing sth.** 无异于做某事; **it's ~ to saying that I'm incompetent** 这等于说我无能

tantrum /ˈtæntrəm/ *n* [尤指儿童的] 耍脾气; **to throw** *or* **have a ~** 使性子

Tanzania /ˌtænzəˈnɪə/ *pr n* 坦桑尼亚

Tanzanian /ˌtænzəˈnɪən/ ▸**p. 503**
A *adj* 坦桑尼亚的
B *n* 坦桑尼亚人

Tao /taʊ, ˈtɑːəʊ/ *n* [u] [道家学说的] 道

Taoiseach /ˈtiːʃəx/ *n* [爱尔兰共和国的] 总理

Taoism /ˈtaʊɪzəm, ˈtɑːəʊ-/ *n* [u] 道教

Taoist /ˈtaʊɪst, ˈtɑːəʊɪst/
A *adj* 道教的
B *n* 道家

tap¹ /tæp/
A *n* **1** *esp Brit* (faucet) 龙头; **to turn the ~ on/off** 打开/关上水龙头; **to leave the ~ running** 让水龙头开着白白流水; **a water/gas ~** 水龙头/煤气阀门; **on ~** (in barrel) «*beer*» 散装的; (available) 随时可用的; **there are plenty of willing hands on ~** *colloq* 有许多随时待命的志愿者 **2** (listening device) 窃听器; **a (telephone) ~** （电话）窃听器; **to put a ~ on a telephone** 在电话上装窃听器 **3** *Med* 抽液; **a spinal ~** 腰椎穿刺 **4** *Tech* **(screw) ~** 螺丝攻
B *vt* (*pres p etc.* **-pp-**) **1** (draw liquid from) 从…中汲取液体 ‹*cask, barrel*›; (draw off) 旋开桶塞放出 ‹*cider*›; **he ~ped off a pint of beer** 他旋开塞子放出了一品脱啤酒; **he ~ped some beer from the barrel** 他从桶里放出了一些啤酒 **2** (cut bark for sap) 在…上切口导出树液 ‹*rubber tree, pine*›; (collect) 开孔导出 ‹*rubber, sap, resin, latex*›; **to ~ a tree for sth.** 在树上开孔导出某物; **workers ~ping off rubber** 采集橡胶的工人 **3** (make use of) 利用 ‹*resources, skills, reserves*›; (extract) 提取; **to ~ the energy of the sun** 利用太阳能; **to ~ an**

informer for information 利用线人获取情报; **to ~ sb. for a loan/money** colloq 向某人借钱/要钱 **4** (fit a listening device to) 在…上装窃听器 ‹*telephone, telephone line*› **5** Ind 从熔炉中放出; **to ~ a furnace** *or* **iron** 出铁 **6** Tech (cut thread of) 在…上攻螺纹 ‹*screw*›

tap²

A *vt* (*pres p etc.* **-pp-**) 轻拍; **to ~ the table with a pencil** 用铅笔轻敲桌子; **to ~ sb. on the shoulder/arm** 轻拍某人的肩膀/胳膊; **to ~ one's feet (to the rhythm/music)** 用脚（随着节奏/音乐）打拍子; **to ~ a rhythm (with sth./on sth.)** （用某物/在某物上）敲节拍; **he ~ped his pipe against the wall/on the table** 他在墙上/桌子上轻轻叩了叩烟斗; **to ~ data into the computer** 用键盘将数据敲入计算机

B *vi* (*pres p etc.* **-pp-**) 轻拍; **to ~ (away) at a typewriter** 轻轻敲着打字机打字; **to ~ on** *or* **against the window** 轻叩窗户

C *n* (light blow, rap) 轻拍; **a ~ on the shoulder/at the window** 在肩膀/窗户上的轻轻一拍; **to give sth. a ~** 轻敲某物

D **taps** *npl + v sing or pl* **1** Mil (bugle call) (for lights out) Amer 熄灯号; (at funeral) 葬礼号 **2** Brit (closing song) [童子军在营火旁或会议结束时所唱的] 结束曲

Phrasal verb

- **tap out** *vt* [~ **out sth.**, ~ **sth. out**] **1** (produce) 轻打出; **to ~ out a rhythm on sth.** 用某物打拍子 **2** (write or enter) 打出 ‹*message*›

tap: ~ **dance** *n* [c and u] 踢踏舞; **~-dance** *vi* 跳踢踏舞; ~ **dancer** *n* 踢踏舞者; **~-dancing** *n* [u] 跳踢踏舞

tape /teɪp/

A *n* **1** [u and c] (strip of material) 带子; **decorative/medical ~** 装饰带/医用胶带; **a name ~** 姓名标签; **to tie sth. with ~** 用带子捆绑某物; **to hold sth. in place with ~s** 用带子固定某物 **2** [u] (adhesive strip) 胶带; **adhesive** *or* Brit **sticky ~** 胶带; **a roll/strip of ~** 一卷/一条胶带; **to stick sth. with ~** 用胶带粘贴某物 **3** [c] (ribbon) (marking end of race) 终点线; (at opening ceremony) 彩带; (indicating road closure) 警示带; **the prime minister cut the ~ to open the new road** 首相为新公路的开通剪彩; **the winner reached the ~** 获胜者冲线了 **4** [c] Telecom (for teleprinter) 纸带 **5** [c and u] (for recording) (audio) 录音带; (video) 录像带; (computer, cassette, reel) 磁带; **to have sth. on ~** 在磁带上录有某物; **to put sth. on ~** 把某物录到磁带上; **to play a ~ (back)** (cassette) （回）放磁带; (video) （回）放录像带; **to erase** *or* colloq **wipe a ~** 抹去磁带 **6** [c] (recording) 录制物; **to make a ~ (of sth.)** (cassette) （给某物）制作录音带; (video) （给某物）制作录像带

B *vt* **1** (fasten with tape) 用带子捆 ‹*object, parcel*›; 用胶带封 ‹*envelope*›; **to ~ sth. up** *or* **together** (with strip of material) 用带子把某物捆起来; (with adhesive strip) 用胶带把某物粘合在一起; **to ~ sth. up with sth.** (with strip of material) 用某物将某物捆起来; (with adhesive strip) 用某物把某物粘牢; **to have** *or* **get sth. ~d** colloq 彻底了解某事物 **2** (record on tape) 把…录到磁带上; **a ~d interview** 采访录音; **he ~d the concert from** *or* **off the radio broadcast** 他从广播中录下了音乐会

Phrasal verb

- **tape up** *vt* [~ **sth. up**, ~ **up sth.**] 用带子捆紧; **to ~ sth. up with sth.** 用某物捆住某物

tape: ~ **cassette** *n* 盒式磁带; ~ **deck** *n* 卡座; ~ **drive** *n* 磁带驱动装置; ~ **head** *n* 磁头; ~ **machine** *n* = ~ **recorder**; ~ **measure** *n* 卷尺

taper /'teɪpə(r)/

A *n* **1** [c] (spill) 点火媒 **2** [c] (candle) 细蜡烛 **3** [c] (narrow part) (of trouser leg, sleeve) 窄细部分; (of blade, column) 尖细部分 **4** [u] (narrowing) 逐渐变细

B *vi* «*trousers, sleeve*» 逐渐变窄; «*blade, aircraft wing, spire*» 逐渐变尖细

C *vt* 使…逐渐变窄 ‹*trousers, sleeve*›; 使…逐渐变尖细 ‹*column, spire*›

Phrasal verb

- **taper off**

A *vi* «*production, sales, demand*» 逐渐减少

B *vt* [~ **sth. off**, ~ **off sth.**] 逐渐减少 ‹*output, production, investment*›

tape: **~-record** *vt* 用磁带录制; ~ **recorder** *n* 磁带录音机; ~ **recording** *n* **1** [u] (process) 磁带录制; **2** [c] (result) 磁带录制内容

tapestry /'tæpəstri/ *n* **1** [u and c] (cloth) 壁毯; **the Bayeux T~** [描绘诺曼人入侵英国的] 贝叶挂毯; **it's part of life's rich ~** 这是复杂人生的一部分 **2** [u] (making) 壁毯编织

tapeworm /'teɪpwɜːm/ *n* 绦虫

tap hole *n* (hole) (for molten metal) 出熔融金属口; (for slag) 出渣口

tapioca /ˌtæpɪ'əʊkə/ *n* **1** [u] (foodstuff) 木薯淀粉 **2** [u and c] ~ **(pudding)** (dessert) 木薯布丁

tapir /'teɪpə(r), -pɪə(r)/ *n* 貘 [生活在美洲和马来西亚热带地区的猪形小动物]

tappet /'tæpɪt/ *n* 挺杆

tap: **~root** *n* 主根; ~ **water** *n* [u] 自来水

tar /tɑː(r)/

A *n* **1** [u] (from wood or coal) 焦油沥青; **a ~ road** 柏油路; **to spoil the ship for a ha'porth of ~** 因小失大 **2** [u] (from cigarettes) 烟碱; **low-/middle-/high-~ cigarettes** 焦油含量低/中/高的卷烟 **3** [c] dated colloq (sailor) 水手

B *vt* (*pres p etc.* **-rr-**) 用焦油沥青覆盖 ‹*road, roof*›; **to ~ and feather sb.** 惩罚某人; **to be ~red with the same brush (as sb.)** 被看成（与某人）是一路货色

tarantula /tə'ræntjʊlə, Amer -tʃələ/ *n* 狼蛛

tardily /'tɑːdɪli/ *adv* **1** (late) 拖拉地; **to arrive ~** 姗姗来迟 **2** (slowly) 缓慢地

tardiness /'tɑːdɪnɪs/ *n* [u] **1** (lateness) 拖拉; **~ in sth./doing sth.** 在某事上/在做某事上的拖拉; **please excuse my ~ in replying to your letter** 迟复为歉 **2** (slowness) 缓慢

tardy /'tɑːdi/ *adj* **1** (late) 拖延的; **to be ~** Amer «*pupil*» 迟到; «*train*» 晚点; **to be ~ for** *or* **to school** Amer 上学迟到 **2** (slow) 缓慢的

tare /teə(r)/

A *n* [u] **1** (weight without contents) 皮重; **allowance for ~** 皮重扣除 **2** (allowance) 皮重的扣除; **a ~ weight of 150 kg** 150 千克的皮重扣除

B *vt* 称…的皮重 ‹*balance, pan*›

target /'tɑːgɪt/

A *n* **1** (in archery, shooting practice) 靶; **to aim/shoot at a ~** 瞄准靶子/向靶子射击; **to hit/miss the ~** 中靶/脱靶; **(dead** *or* **right** *or* **spot) on ~** 正中靶子的; fig 击中要害的 **2** (objective) 目标; **a ~ of sth.** …的目标; **a ~ for sb./sth.** 某人/某物的目标; **to set (oneself) a ~** （为自己）确立目标; **a production/export ~** 生产/出口指标; **to meet** *or* **reach a ~** 达到指标; **on/off ~** 正中/偏离目标的; **output is on ~ so far this year** 目前为止今年的产量指标能实现; **we are (way) off ~ and cannot hope to fulfil our quotas** 我们（远远）无法达标，不能指望完成定额; **a civilian/military/moving/stationary ~** Mil 民用/军事/移动/静止目标 **3** (butt) 批评对象; **to be the ~ of abuse/ridicule** 是谩骂/嘲讽的对象; **to become the ~ for sb.'s anger** 成为某人宣泄愤怒的对象; **to be an easy** *or* **soft ~** 是容易遭受攻击的对象

B *vt* **1** Mil (aim) 把…对准 ‹*weapon, missile, installation*›; 把…作为攻击目标 ‹*town, building, aircraft*›; **to ~ sth. at** *or* **on sb./sth.** 将某物瞄准某人/某物 **2** fig (select for special treatment in marketing) 把…作为对象 ‹*place, group, campaign*›; **to be ~ed at teenagers** 以青少年为对象; **to ~ an advertisement at sb.** 将某人作为广告对象; **he has been ~ed for early promotion** 他被确定为提前晋升的人选; **to ~ sb./sth. as sth.** 把某人/某物确定为某物

targetable /'tɑːgɪtəbl/ *adj* **1** (able to be aimed) 可制导的 ‹*missile, warhead*› **2** (able to be made a target) 可作为目标的 ‹*enemy, place, person, group*›

target: ~ **date** *n* 预定日期; ~ **group** *n* [产品销售、服务等的] 目标群体

targeting /'tɑːgɪtɪŋ/ *n* [u] **1** (for marketing a product) 确定销售对象; (for marketing a service) 确定服务对象 **2** Mil 确定攻击目标

target: ~ **language** *n* **1** (in translation) 译入语; **2** (in learning) 目标语; ~ **practice** *n* [u] 射击练习; ~ **price** *n* **1** (sale price) 目标价; **2** Fin (forecast price) 预测价; (lowest profitable price) 最低赢利价格

tariff /'tærɪf/ *n* **1** (price list) 价目表 **2** (customs duty) 关税; **to impose** *or* **levy a ~ (on sth.)** （对某物）征收关税; **a ~ barrier** 关税壁垒 **3** Jur 量刑标准

tarmac /'tɑːmæk/

A *n* [u] **1** (*also* **Tarmac®** Brit) (black material) [铺路面的] 柏油碎石; **to lay ~** 铺柏油碎石; **a ~ road** 柏油碎石路 **2** Aviat (runway) 柏油碎石跑道; (apron) 柏油碎石停机坪

B *vt* (*pres p etc.* **-ck-**) 用柏油碎石铺 ‹*road*›

tarmacadam /ˌtɑːmə'kædəm/ *n* = **tarmac A1**

tarn /tɑːn/ *n* 山中小湖

tarnish /'tɑːnɪʃ/

A *vi* «*brass, silver*» 失去光泽; «*mirror*» 变得模糊不清

B *vt* **1** (make dull) 使…失去光泽 ‹*metal*›; **badly ~ed mirrors** 变得异常模糊的镜子 **2** fig (damage) 玷污 ‹*reputation, image, record*›; **revelations that have ~ed his good name** 令他好名声受损的爆料

C *n* **1** [u] (dullness) (on metal) 色泽暗淡; (on mirror) 模糊不清 **2** [c] fig (blemish) 瑕疵

taro /'tɑːrəʊ/ *n* **1** [c] Bot 芋; ~ **root** 芋头 **2** [u and c] Culin 芋头

tar oil *n* [u] 焦油

tarot /'tærəʊ/ *n* **1** [u] **the T~** (pack of cards) 一副塔罗纸牌 [用于占卜] **2** [c] ~ **(card)** 塔罗纸牌; **to read (sb.'s) ~s** 用塔罗牌（为某人）算卦 **3** ▸**p. 307** [u] (card game) 塔罗纸牌游戏

tarp /tɑːp/ *n esp Amer colloq* 柏油帆布

tar paper *n* [u] 沥青油纸

tarpaulin /tɑː'pɔːlɪn/ *n* **1** [u] (material) 柏油帆布 **2** [c] (sheet) 油布

tarragon /'tærəgən/ *n* [u] **1** Bot 龙蒿 **2** Culin 龙蒿叶

tarry¹ /'tɑːri/ *adj* **1** (tar-like) 像柏油的 ‹*substance*› **2** (covered with tar) 涂满柏油的 ‹*rope*›

tarry² /'tæri/ *vi* archaic or liter (delay) 耽搁; (stay longer) 逗留

tart¹ /tɑːt/ *adj* **1** (sharp-tasting) 酸的; **this fruit tastes ~** 这种水果味道很酸 **2** fig (sharp in manner) 尖酸刻薄的 ‹*remark, tone*›

tart² *n* **1** (pie) 馅饼 **2** colloq (prostitute) 妓女 **3** colloq pej (promiscuous woman) 荡妇 pej

Phrasal verb

- **tart up** colloq

A *vt* [~ **sth. up**, ~ **up sth.**] colloq 把…搞得花里胡哨 ‹*room, brochure*›; **to be ~ed up** 打扮得花里胡哨

B *v refl* **to ~ oneself up** (dress up) 穿得花里胡哨; (apply make-up) 浓妆艳抹

tartan /'tɑːtn/

A *n* [u and c] **1** (pattern) [尤指作为苏格兰家族标志的] 花格图案 **2** (fabric) 花格呢料; **to wear the ~** 身着花格呢料装

B *modif* **1** (of tartan) 花格呢料的 ‹*rug, kilt*›; **a ~ skirt** 花格呢料裙 **2** (Scottish) 苏格兰人的 ‹*characteristic*›; 苏格兰的 ‹*tax*›; **the ~ army** (football fans) 苏格兰足球迷; (any group) 苏格兰团伙

t

tartan

花格呢料。苏格兰传统呢料，由各种颜色和条纹组成不同的格子图案。苏格兰的多数部族（clan）都有自己的独特图案。花格呢料短裙裙（kilt）和长披肩（plaid）构成高地服装，为苏格兰男子的传统服装（▸ **the Highlands**），多在婚礼等正式场合穿着。

Tartar /ˈtɑːtə(r)/ ▸**p. 503, p. 426**
A *n* **1** [c] Hist 鞑靼人 **2** [c] (person) **= Tatar B1** **3** [u] (language) **= Tatar B2** **4** **tartar** [c] colloq (fierce person) 暴君
B *adj* **= Tatar A**

tartar /ˈtɑːtə(r)/ *n* [u] **1** (deposit on teeth) 牙垢 **2** (deposit in wine) [酒发酵器内壁上的] 酒石

tartare /tɑːˈtɑː(r)/ *adj* 生食的; **steak ~** 鞑靼牛排

tartare sauce *n* [u] 鞑靼酱

tartaric /tɑːˈtærɪk/ *adj* （含）酒石的

tartaric acid *n* [u] 酒石酸

tartar sauce *n* [u] **= tartare sauce**

tartly /ˈtɑːtli/ *adv* 尖酸刻薄地 ‹*say*›

tartness /ˈtɑːtnɪs/ *n* [u] **1** (acidity) 酸 **2** (sharpness of manner) 尖酸刻薄

Tarzan /ˈtɑːzæn/ *pr n* colloq 泰山; **he's no ~** fig 他可不是什么人猿泰山

taser® /ˈteizə(r)/ *n* 泰瑟枪

Tashkent /tæʃˈkent/ *pr n* 塔什干

task /tɑːsk, Amer tæsk/
A *n* 任务; **to perform** *or* **carry out a ~** 执行任务; **a thankless ~** 费力不讨好的差事; **a Herculean ~** 艰苦卓绝的任务; **to take** *or* **hold sb. to ~ (about** *or* **for** *or* **over sth.)** （因某事）训斥某人
B *vt* **1** (charge with) 给…分配任务; **he had been ~ed with drawing up a new timetable** 给他安排的任务是制定新时刻表 **2** (tax) 考验 ‹*patience, imagination, ability*›; **a problem that ~ed his brain** 让他大伤脑筋的问题

taskbar /ˈtɑːskbɑː(r), Amer ˈtæsk-/ *n* 任务栏

task: ~-based learning *n* [u] [尤指学习语言时的] 任务式学习; **~ force** *n* **1** Mil 特遣部队; **2** (special group) [为某任务成立的] 特别工作组; **~master** *n* 监工; **to be a hard ~master** 像工头一样严厉

Tasmania /tæzˈmeɪnɪə/ *pr n* **1** (island) 塔斯马尼亚岛 **2** (state) 塔斯马尼亚州

Tasmanian /tæzˈmeɪnɪən/
A *adj* (of Tasmania) 塔斯马尼亚的; (of the people) 塔斯马尼亚人的
B *n* 塔斯马尼亚人

tassel /ˈtæsl/ *n* **1** (tuft of threads) 流苏 **2** Bot 穗; **corn ~s** 谷穗

tasselled /ˈtæsld/ *adj* 饰有流苏的

taste /teɪst/
A *n* **1** [u and c] (flavour) 味道; **a strong ~ of garlic** 浓烈的大蒜味; **a bad/foul ~** 不好/难闻的味道; **a pleasant** *or* **nice ~** 好味道; **a bitter/sour/sweet/mild ~** 苦味/酸味/甜味/淡味; **to leave a ~ in the mouth** 在口中留有余味; **we won, but the manner of our winning left a nasty ~ in the mouth** 我们赢了，但是获胜的方式却让人感到不是滋味 **2** [u] (sense) 味觉; **his cold deprived him of his sense of ~** 他感冒了，嘴里尝不出味道; **to have a keen/have little sense of ~** 味觉敏锐/迟钝; **sour/bitter/sweet to the ~** 尝起来有酸味/苦味/甜味; **add salt to ~** 适量加盐 **3** [c] *usu sing* (sample, small quantity) 少许尝的东西; **just take a ~ of this!** 尝一点儿这个！; **add just a ~ of brandy to the mixture** 在混合饮料中稍加一点白兰地 **4** [c] fig (brief or first experience) 体验; **he got a ~ of life on the wild side** 他感受到了生活中疯狂的一面; **the ~ of things to come** 对未来事物的体验 **5** [c] (liking) 爱好; (preference) 偏爱; **~s differ** 人各有所好; **a ~ for/in sth.** 对某物/在某方面的爱好; **(not) to sb.'s ~** （不）合某人的口味; **each** *or* **everyone to his ~** 人各有所好 **6** [u] (discernment) (with regard to beauty, appropriateness, etc.) 鉴赏力; (with regard to what is acceptable) 品味; **he's got more money than ~** 他有钱但没什么品味; **to have exquisite ~ in clothes** 对服装很讲究; **to dress in the best (possible) ~** 穿着非常雅致; **to have good/no ~** 品味高雅/没品味; **the room had been furnished in** *or* **with execrable ~!** 房间装修得俗不可耐！; **(to be) in good/the best of ~** 得体/非常得体; **(to be) in bad/the worst of ~** 粗俗/粗俗不堪
B *vi* **1** (perceive flavour) 有味觉 **2** (have specified flavour) 有…的味道; **the drink ~s of mint** 饮料有股薄荷味; **the wine ~s sour** 这葡萄酒有酸味; **to ~ off** 变味
C *vt* **1** (perceive flavour) 尝出…的味道 **2** (sample, test flavour) 品尝 **3** (eat or drink) 吃 ‹*food*›; 喝 ‹*drink*› **4** fig (experience) 体验 ‹*power, freedom, failure, hardship*›

taste bud *n* 味蕾

tasteful /ˈteɪstfl/ *adj* 高雅的 ‹*garment, manner*›; 雅致的 ‹*design, room*›

tastefully /ˈteɪstfəli/ *adv* 高雅地 ‹*dress*›; 雅致地 ‹*furnish, decorate*›

tastefulness /ˈteɪstflnɪs/ *n* [u] 品味高雅

tasteless /ˈteɪstlɪs/ *adj* **1** (lacking flavour) 淡而无味的 ‹*food, drink*›; 没有气味的 ‹*powder, gas*› **2** (lacking discernment) 庸俗的 ‹*joke, ornament, dress*›

tastelessly /ˈteɪstlɪsli/ *adv* 俗气地 ‹*decorate, dress*›

tastelessness /ˈteɪstlɪsnɪs/ *n* [u] **1** (lack of flavour) (of food, drink) 寡淡无味; (of powder, gas) 无味 **2** (lack of discernment) 庸俗

taster /ˈteɪstə(r)/ *n* **1** (appraiser) 品味师; **a wine/tea ~** 品酒师/品茶员 **2** (tasting device) (for wine) 品酒杯; (for cheese) 奶酪取样器 **3** Brit (foretaste) 试样

tastiness /ˈteɪstɪnɪs/ *n* [u] 美味可口

tasting /ˈteɪstɪŋ/
A *n* **1** [u] (action) 品尝 **2** [c] (event) 品尝会
B **-tasting** *combining form* 有…味道的; **sweet ~** 甜味的; **fresh~** 味道清新的

tasty /ˈteɪsti/ *adj* **1** (flavoursome) 美味可口的 **2** esp Brit colloq (sexually attractive) 性感的; **she's a ~ little dish!** 她是个风骚小妞！ **3** Brit colloq (very good) 诱人的 ‹*price, discount*›; 相当不错的 ‹*garment*›

tat¹ /tæt/ *n* [u] Brit colloq 劣质廉价品

tat² (*pres p etc.* **-tt-**)
A *vi* 用梭织法编织
B *vt* 梭织 ‹*mat, edging*›

ta-ta /təˈtɑː/ *excl* Brit colloq 再见

Tatar /ˈtɑːtə(r)/ ▸**p. 503, p. 426**
A *adj* (of the people) 鞑靼人的; (of the language) 鞑靼语的
B *n* **1** [c] (person) 鞑靼人 **2** [u] (language) 鞑靼语

tattered /ˈtætəd/ *adj* **1** (ragged or dilapidated) 破破烂烂的 ‹*garment, book*›; **~ and torn** 又破又烂的 **2** (wearing ragged clothes) 衣衫褴褛的 **3** fig (damaged) 破灭的 ‹*hopes, dreams*›; 毁掉的 ‹*reputation, career, life*›; 破裂的 ‹*relationship*›

tatters /ˈtætəz/ *npl* 碎片; **to be in ~** «*garment, book*» 破旧不堪; «*building*» 坍塌; «*dreams*» 破灭; «*relationship*» 破裂; «*economy*» 受损; **her reputation/career was in ~** 她已名声扫地/她的事业毁了

tatting /ˈtætɪŋ/ *n* [u] **1** (lace) 梭织花边 **2** (lacemaking) 梭织花边工艺

tattle /ˈtætl/
A *vi* **1** (gossip) 闲聊 **2** esp Amer (tell tales) 打小报告; **to ~ on sb.** 打某人的小报告
B *n* [u] 闲聊

tattler /ˈtætlə(r)/ *n* 爱打小报告的人

tattletale /ˈtætlteɪl/ *n* Amer **= telltale A**

tattoo¹ /təˈtuː, Amer tæˈtuː/
A *n* 纹身图案
B *vt* **1** (mark) 在…上刺青 ‹*part of body*›; **his forearm was ~ed with a picture of a butterfly** 他的前臂上纹了一只蝴蝶 **2** (mark on the skin) 刺 ‹*picture, words*›

tattoo² *n* **1** (signal on drum, bugle) 归营号; **to beat/sound the ~** 击响归营鼓/吹响归营号 **2** Brit (parade) [伴有军乐与齐步行进的] 军事表演; **the Edinburgh Military T~** 爱丁堡军事表演 **3** (drumming) 鼓点; (tapping) 连续有节奏的敲击声; **the rain beat a ~ on the roof** 雨水滴答滴答地落在屋顶上

tattoo artist ▸**p. 409** *n* 纹身师

tattooist /təˈtuːɪst, Amer tæˈtuːɪst/ ▸**p. 409** *n* 纹身师

tatty /ˈtæti/
A *adj* esp Brit colloq **1** (shabby) 褴褛的 ‹*garment*›; 破烂的 ‹*carpet, furniture, book*›; 不整洁的 ‹*appearance, garden*›; 破败的 ‹*building, area*› **2** (of poor quality) 劣质的 ‹*goods, furniture, jewellery*›; 俗气的 ‹*decorations*›
B *n* Scot 马铃薯

taught /tɔːt/ *pt, pp* ▸**teach**

taunt /tɔːnt/
A *vt* 奚落; **to ~ sb. about** *or* **over** *or* **with sth.** 就某事奚落某人; **to ~ sb. for sth.** 因某事笑话某人
B *n* 奚落; **racist ~s** 种族歧视的奚落

taunting /ˈtɔːntɪŋ/
A *adj* 讥讽的 ‹*words, criticism*›
B *n* [u] 讥讽

tauntingly /ˈtɔːntɪŋli/ *adv* 讥讽地 ‹*speak*›; 嘲笑地 ‹*stare*›

Taurus /ˈtɔːrəs/ *n* **1** [u] Astron 金牛（星）座 **2** [u] Astrol (sign) 金牛宫 [黄道第二宫] **3** [c] *sing* Astrol (person) 属金牛（星）座的人

taut /tɔːt/ *adj* **1** (tight) 拉紧的 ‹*rope, cloth*›; (tense) 紧张的 ‹*muscle, nerves*› **2** (firm) 结实的 ‹*body, thighs*› **3** (concise) 紧凑的 ‹*writing, music*›

tauten /ˈtɔːtn/
A *vt* 拉紧 ‹*rope, cloth*›
B *vi* «*rope, muscle*» 绷紧

tautly /ˈtɔːtli/ *adv* **1** (tightly) 紧紧地 ‹*stretch, contract*›; (tensely) 紧张地 ‹*reply*› **2** (economically) 紧凑地 ‹*organize, written*›

tautness /ˈtɔːtnɪs/ *n* [u] **1** (tightness, tension) (of rope, cloth) 绷紧; (of nerves, voice) 紧张 **2** (economy of construction) 紧凑

tautological /ˌtɔːtəˈlɒdʒɪkl/ *adj* **1** (repetitious) 赘述的 ‹*phrase, repetition*› **2** Philos 重言式的 ‹*definition, reasoning*›

tautology /tɔːˈtɒlədʒi/ *n* [u and c] **1** (repetition) 赘述 **2** Philos 重言式

tavern /ˈtævən/ *n* Amer *or* archaic 客栈

taverna /təˈvɜːnə/ *n* 希腊小餐馆

tawdriness /ˈtɔːdrɪnɪs/ *n* [u] (of jewellery, clothes) 俗丽而价廉; (of decorations) 花里胡哨; fig (of motives, affair) 龌龊; (of sentiments) 猥琐

tawdry /ˈtɔːdri/ *adj* **1** (showy but cheap) 俗丽而价廉的 ‹*jewellery, clothes*›; 花里胡哨的 ‹*decorations*› **2** fig (sordid) 龌龊的 ‹*motives, affair*›; 猥琐的 ‹*sentiments*›

tawny /ˈtɔːni/
A *adj* 黄褐色的 ‹*mane, eyes*›
B *n* [u] 黄褐色

tawny owl *n* 灰林鸮

tax /tæks/
A *n* **1** [c and u] (duty) 税; **he has to pay a third of his income in ~** 他得将工资的三分之一用于纳税; **a ~ on consumer/luxury items** 消费品/奢侈品税; **to pay ~ (on sth.) (to sb.)** （为某物）（向某人）缴税; **to pay £2,500 in (back) ~** 缴纳2,500英镑的（欠）税; **before/after ~** 税前/税后; **to put** *or* **place** *or* **levy** *or* **impose a ~ (on sth.)** （对某物）征税; **to be liable to** *or* **for ~** 应纳税; **to increase** *or* **raise/cut** *or* **lower** *or* **reduce**

t

~(es) 增税/减税 **2** [c] fig (burden, strain) 负担; **a ~ on sth.** 对某物的负担; **her behaviour was a constant ~ on my patience** 她的行为让我不胜其烦

B *vt* **1** (impose tax on) 对…征税 ‹*person, income, profit, goods*›; **to ~ sb./sth. at a higher/lower rate** 以更高/更低的税率向某人/某物征税; **highly** *or* **heavily ~ed** 课以重税的; **~ed out of existence** 不堪重税而破产的 **2** (pay tax on) 缴纳…的牌照税 ‹*vehicle*› **3** fig (burden, strain) 使…受重负 ‹*strength, resources*›; **to ~ sb.'s patience** 使某人忍无可忍; **to ~ one's/sb.'s brain(s)** 使自己/某人大伤脑筋 **4** formal (accuse) 指责; **to ~ sb. with sth./doing sth.** 因某事/做某事而指责某人

taxable /'tæksəbl/ *adj* 应纳税的 ‹*income, perk*›

tax: ~ accountant ▸p. 409 *n* 税收会计师; **~ adjustment** *n* 税收调整; **~ advantage** *n* 税收优惠; **~ allowance** *n* 收入免税额; **~ arrears** *npl* 拖欠税款

taxation /tæk'seɪʃn/ *n* [u] **1** (imposition of taxes) 征税; **immunity from ~** 免税 **2** (revenue from taxes) 税收

tax: ~ authority *n* 税务部门; **~ avoidance** *n* [u] 避税; **~ bracket, ~ band** *ns* 税收等级; **~ break** *n* 赋税减免; **~ burden** *n* 税负 [尤指重税]; **~ code** *n* 纳税代码 [代表应纳税额, 在英国指免税部分的收入]; **~ collection** *n* **1** [u] (process) 收税; **2** [c] (amount) 收取的税款; **~ collector** *n* 税务员; **~ credit** *n* 抵税额; **~ cut** *n* 减税; **~-deductible** *adj* 可减免课税的 ‹*cost, loss, item*›; **~ demand** *n* **1** (amount of tax) 核定课税额; **2** (notice) 应付税额通知; **~ disc** *n* Brit [贴在汽车挡风玻璃上的] 圆形完税证; **~ dodge** *n* 避税; **~ dodger** *n* 避税人; **~ evader** *n* 逃税人; **~ evasion** *n* [u] 逃税; **~-exempt** *adj* **1** = **~-free**; **2** (not paying tax) 免于缴税的 ‹*investor, status*›; **~ exemption** *n* [u and c] 免税; **~ exile** *n* 越国避税者; **~ form** *n* = **~ return**; **~ fraud** *n* [u and c] 逃税; **~-free** *adj* 免税的 ‹*income, asset*›; **~ haven** *n* 避税港 [指低税率国家]

taxi /'tæksi/

A *n* 出租车; **to call** *or* **hail a ~** 叫出租车; **to take a ~ to the station, to go to the station by ~** 打的去车站

B *vi* **1** Aviat 滑行 **2** colloq (go by taxi) 乘出租车

taxicab /'tæksɪkæb/ *n* = **taxi A**

taxidermist /ˌtæksɪ'dɜːmɪst/ ▸p. 409 *n* 动物标本剥制师

taxidermy /'tæksɪˌdɜːmi/ *n* [u] 动物标本剥制术

taxi: ~ driver ▸p. 409 *n* 出租车司机; **~ fare** *n* 出租车车费; **~ man** *n* colloq = **~ driver**; **~meter** *n* 出租车计价器

tax: ~ immunity *n* [u] 免税; **~ incentive** *n* 减税激励

taxing /'tæksɪŋ/ *adj* 吃力的 ‹*work, role*›; 耗神的 ‹*problem*›; **this shouldn't be too ~ for you** 这对你来说应该不太难

tax inspector ▸p. 409 *n* 税务稽查员

taxi: ~ rank *n* Brit 出租车站; **~ ride** *n* 乘出租车出行; **~ stand** *n* Amer = **~ rank**; **~way** *n* [飞机的] 滑行道

tax: ~ law *n* [u and c] 税法; **~ levy** *n* [u and c] **1** (process) 征税; **2** (amount) 税款; **~ liability** *n* [u and c] 纳税义务; **~ loophole** *n* 税收漏洞; **~man** /-mæn/ *n* colloq **1** (person) 税务员; **2** (department) 税务部门; **~ office** *n* 税务局

taxonomist /tæk'sɒnəmɪst/ *n* 分类学家

taxonomy /tæk'sɒnəmi/ *n* **1** [u] (branch of science) 分类学 **2** [u] (classifying) 分类 **3** [c] (classificatory scheme) 分类系统

tax: ~payer *n* 纳税人; **~ point** *n* [增值税的] 起税日期; **~ purposes** *npl* **for ~ purposes** 应税的; **to declare a sum for ~ purposes** 申报应税收入; **~ rate** *n* 税率; **~ rebate** *n* 退税; **~ relief** *n* [u] 税减免; **~ return** *n* 纳税申报表; **to complete** *or* **fill in/file** *or* **submit a** *or* **one's ~ return** 填写/提交纳税申报表; **~ revenue** *n* [u] 税收; **~ shelter** *n* 避税策略; **~ threshold** *n* 税收起征点; **~ year** *n* 税收年度

TB *abbr* = **tuberculosis**

TBA, t.b.a. *abbrs* **1** = **to be arranged** 待定 **2** = **to be announced** 待通知

T-bar *n* **1** (T-shaped bar) (gen) 丁字钢; (for skiers) 丁字形吊椅 **2** Fashn [鞋上的] 丁字扣; **a pair of ~ sandals** 一双丁字扣凉鞋

Tbilisi /ˌtəbɪ'liːsi/ *pr n* 第比利斯

T-bone steak *n* T字骨牛排

tbsp *abbr* = **tablespoon**

TCFL *abbr* = **Teaching Chinese as a Foreign Language** 对外汉语教学

TD *abbr* = **technical drawing**

te /tiː/ *n* [大调音阶的第7音]

tea /tiː/ *n* **1** [u] (drink) 茶; **morning ~** 早茶; **strong/weak ~** 浓/淡茶; **to make (the) ~** 泡茶; **a pot of ~** 一壶茶; **sb.'s cup of ~** colloq 某人的所好; **he's not really my cup of ~** 他其实并不是我喜欢的那种人; **to give sb. ~ and sympathy** colloq 给某人同情与关怀 **2** [c] (serving) 一杯茶; **two ~s please** 请来两杯茶 **3** [u and c] (substance) (as preparation) 茶叶; (as cash crop) 茶树; **not for all the ~ in China** 无论报酬多少都不 **4** [u and c] (other infusion) 冲泡饮料; **mint** *or* **peppermint ~** 薄荷茶 **5** [u and c] esp Brit (meal) (in late afternoon) 茶点; (in evening) 晚点

tea: ~ bag *n* 袋泡茶; **~ ball** *n* 滤茶球; **~ break** *n* Brit 茶歇; **to have** *or* **take a ~ break** 喝茶休息; **~ caddy** *n* 茶叶罐; **~cake** *n* Brit 茶点饼; **~ cart** *n* Amer = **~ trolley**

teach /tiːtʃ/ (*pt, pp* **taught**)

A *vt* **1** (instruct) 教; **to ~ sb. (how/when) to do sth.** 教某人（如何/何时）做某事 **2** (communicate knowledge or skill to or of) 讲授 ‹*subject, language*›; 训练 ‹*swimming, animal*›; **to ~ music/a class** 教音乐/教一个班; **to ~ sb. sth.** 给某人讲授某课程; **to ~ sb. the ropes** 把窍门教给某人; **to ~ school** Amer 当老师; **(you can't) ~ an old dog new tricks** fig （无法）使守旧的人接受新事物; ▸**grandmother** **3** (advocate) 教导 ‹*virtue, doctrine*›; 倡导 ‹*belief, creed*›; **Christ taught forgiveness** 基督倡导宽恕; **his parents taught him to be truthful/not to tell lies** 他的父母教育他要诚实/不要撒谎 **4** colloq (as correction) 教训; **to ~ sb. to do sth.** 告诫某人要做某事; **to ~ sb. a lesson** 给某人一个教训; **to ~ sb. a thing** *or* **trick or two** ‹*life, experience*› 使某人明白事理

B *vi* 教书; **to ~ in** *or* **at a school** 在学校教书

C *v refl* **to ~ oneself** 自学; **he taught himself to swim** 他自己学会了游泳

teachability /ˌtiːtʃə'bɪlɪti/ *n* [u] **1** (of person) 可教 **2** (of subject, topic) 适于教授

teachable /'tiːtʃəbl/ *adj* 可教的 ‹*person*›; 可传授的 ‹*subject*›

teacher /'tiːtʃə(r)/ ▸p. 409 *n* 教师; **a university ~** 大学教师; **a French/music ~** 法语/音乐老师; **a qualified** *or* **certified** Amer **~** 合格的教师; **experience is the best ~** 经历是最好的老师

teacher: ~ certification *n* [u] Amer 教师资格; **~ education** *n* [u] Amer = **teacher training**; **~ evaluation** *n* [u] 教师评估; **~-pupil ratio** *n* 师生比; **~s' centre** *n* 教学资料中心; **~'s pet** *n* colloq 老师的宠儿

teacher training *n* [u] 教师培训

teacher-training: ~ certificate *n* 教师资格证书; **~ college** *n* 师范学院

tea chest *n* Brit 茶叶箱

teach-in *n* colloq 座谈会

teaching /'tiːtʃɪŋ/ *n* **1** [u] (instruction) 教学; **to go into ~** 开始从事教学工作; **20 hours ~ per week** 每周教学20小时; **she does some ~ in the evenings** 她在晚上授一些课; **~ methods/skills** 教学方法/技巧 **2** [u and c] (doctrine) (of philosopher, prophet) 学说; (of religion, church) 教义

teaching: ~ aid *n* 教辅工具; **~ assistant** ▸p. 409 *n* **1** Sch 教学助理; **2** Amer Univ 助教; **~ fellow** *n* **1** Brit (on fixed term position) 合同教师; **2** (graduate student) 研究生助教; **~ fellowship** *n* **1** Brit (fixed term position) 合同教师职位; **2** (for graduate student) 研究生助教奖学金; **~ hospital** *n* 教学医院; **~ machine** *n* 教学机器; **~ practice** *n* [u and c] Brit 教学实习; **~ profession** *n* **1** (career) 教师职业; **2** (body) 教育工作者

teachware /'tiːtʃweə(r)/ *n* [u] 教学软件

tea: ~ cloth *n* **1** esp Brit (for drying) = **~ towel**; **2** Brit (for table, tray) 台布; **~ cosy** Brit, **~ cozy** Amer *n* 茶壶保温套; **~cup** *n* 茶杯; **a storm in a ~cup** 小题大做; **~cupful** *n* 一茶杯的茶; **to pour a ~cupful** 倒一杯茶; **~ dance** *n* 下午茶舞会; **~ garden** *n* **1** (café) 露天茶座; **2** = **~ plantation**; **~ house** *n* 茶馆; **~-infuser** *n* 滤茶器

teak /tiːk/ *n* **1** [c] (tree) 柚木树; **a ~ forest/plantation** 柚木林/种植园 **2** [u] (timber) 柚木; **~ door/furniture** 柚木门/家具

tea kettle *n* 烧水壶

teal /tiːl/ *n* **1** [c] (*pl* **~** *or* **~s**) Zool 水鸭 **2** ▸p. 134 [u] **~ (blue)** 蓝绿色; **a ~ shirt** 蓝绿色衬衫

tea: ~ lady ▸p. 409 *n* Brit [工作地的] 侍茶女工; **~ leaf** *n* [尤指泡过的] 茶叶; **to read the** *or* **sb.'s ~ leaves** 通过某人杯中的茶叶算命

team /tiːm/

A *n + v sing or pl* **1** Sport 队; **a football/cricket/rugby ~** 足球/板球/橄榄球队; **she didn't make the first ~** 她没入选甲队; **the ~ captain/colours** 队长/队旗 **2** (unit) [一起工作的] 组; **a research/management ~** 研究/管理小组; **they make a good ~** 他们一起工作得很出色; **the ~ leader** 小组长 **3** (pack) [同拉一辆车的] 一组牲畜; **a ~ of huskies** 一队爱斯基摩狗

B *vt* **1** (put into group) 让…结成一队; **to ~ sb. with sb.** 把某人与某人编成一队 **2** (coordinate) 使…搭配 ‹*colour, item*›; **to ~ sth. with sth.** 使某物与某物相配 **3** (harness) 把…套在同一辆车上 ‹*horses, dogs*›

Phrasal verb

- **team up** *vi* 合作; **to ~ up with sb.** 与某人合作

team: ~ bonding *n* [u] 团队凝聚力; **~ building** *n* [u] 团队建设; **a ~ building exercise** 团队建设练习; **~ manager** *n* 运动队经理; **~mate** *n* 队友; **~ member** *n* (of sports team) 队员; (of work team) 组员; **~ player** *n* 善于与团队合作的人; **~ spirit** *n* [u] 团队精神

teamster /'tiːmstə(r)/ *n* Amer **1** (truck driver) 卡车司机 **2** (union member) 卡车司机工会会员

team: ~ teaching *n* [u] 小组协同教学; **~work** *n* [u] 协同工作

tea: ~ party *n* 茶话会; **~ plant** *n* 茶树; **~ plantation** *n* 茶园; **~ planter** ▸p. 409 *n* 茶农; **~ plate** *n* 茶碟; **~pot** *n* 茶壶; **a tempest in a ~pot** Amer 小题大做

tear¹ /teə(r)/

A *vt* (*pt* **tore**, *pp* **torn**) **1** (rip) 撕 ‹*cloth, paper*›; 撕破 ‹*garment, sleeve*›; **to ~ sth. in half** *or* **two** 把某物撕成两半; **to ~ sth. in** *or* **into pieces** *or* **bits** 把某物撕成碎片; **to ~ sth. open** 撕开某物; **to ~ sb.'s argument/the**

film to pieces *or* **shreds** 将某人的论点/这部电影批得体无完肤; **to ~ one's hair (out)** fig 扯自己的头发 [表示愤怒或懊恼]; **to ~ a muscle/hamstring** 拉伤肌肉/腘绳肌腱; **a ~ing sound** 撕裂声; **that's torn it!** 这下完了! **2** (remove by force) 拉掉; **to ~ sth. from** *or* **off** *or* **out of sth.** 从某物中扯掉某物; **you nearly tore my arm out of its socket** 你差点把我的胳膊拉脱臼了 **3** (divide) 使分裂; **a country torn by civil war** 被内战弄得四分五裂的国家 **4** (be in state of indecision) **to be torn** 左右为难; **to be torn between two things/people** 在两个事物间/两人间难以选择

B *vi* (*pt* **tore**, *pp* **torn**) **1** (come apart) 撕裂; **this fabric ~s easily** 这种布很容易扯破 **2** (rip, pull) 撕开; **to ~ along the seam/dotted line** 沿接缝/虚线撕开; **to ~ at sth.** 撕扯某物; **to ~ into sb./sth.** 痛打某人/某物; fig 猛烈抨击某人/某事物 **3** (rush, hasten) «*person*» 飞跑; «*vehicle*» 疾驰; **a car came ~ing round the corner** 一辆汽车飞驰转过街角; **she tore off down the road** 她沿路飞奔而去; **I tore through the first few chapters** 我匆匆浏览了开头几章; **to be in a ~ing hurry to do sth.** Brit 急匆匆地去做某事; **she was in a ~ing hurry to get home** 她急匆匆地回家

C *n* 裂缝

Phrasal verbs

• **tear apart** *vt* [**~ sth./sb. apart**]
1 (rip to pieces, destroy) 撕碎 ‹*body*›; 拆毁 ‹*structure*›; 使…难过 ‹*person*›; fig 使…四分五裂 ‹*organization, party*› **2** (separate) 撕开 ‹*things*›; 拆散 ‹*people*› **3** colloq (criticize) 严厉抨击

• **tear away** *vt* **1** [**~ sth. away, ~ away sth.**] (remove) 扯掉 ‹*wrapping, bandage*› **2** [**~ sb. away**] (compel to leave) 使忍痛离去; **to ~ sb. away from sth.** (make sb. leave) 使某人勉强离开某处; (make sb. stop doing sth.) 使某人勉强停止做某事; **to ~ oneself away from sth.** 勉强离开 ‹*place*›; 勉强放下 ‹*object*›; **if you can ~ yourself away from the television set for one moment ...** iron 别舍不得离开电视了

• **tear down** *vt* [**~ sth. down, ~ down sth.**]
1 (remove by pulling) 撕下 ‹*poster*›; 扯下 ‹*flag*›; **to ~ sth. down from a wall/lamppost** 从墙/灯柱上扯下某物 **2** (demolish) 拆毁 ‹*building*›

• **tear off** *vt* [**~ sth. off, ~ off sth.**]
1 (remove) 扯掉 ‹*piece, edging*›; 一下子脱掉 ‹*clothing*› **2** colloq (write hastily) 匆匆地写 ‹*letter, note*›

• **tear open** *vt* [**~ sth. open, ~ open sth.**] 撕开

• **tear out** *vt* [**~ sth. out, ~ out sth.**] 撕下 ‹*page, cheque*›; **to ~ sb.'s eyes out** fig 挖掉某人的眼睛 [常用于威胁]; **to ~ sth. out of** *or* **from sth.** 从某物上撕下某物

• **tear up** *vt* [**~ sth. up, ~ up sth.**]
1 lit (rip into pieces, destroy) 撕碎 ‹*piece of paper, envelope*›; **to ~ sth. up into little pieces** 把某物撕成碎片 **2** fig (repudiate) 撕毁 ‹*contract, agreement, treaty*›

tear² /tɪə(r)/ *n* 眼泪; **to be in ~s** 在流泪; **to be close** *or* **near to ~s** 快要哭出来; **to burst into ~s** 放声大哭; **to move** *or* **reduce sb. to ~s** 使某人感动落泪; **~s of joy/rage/remorse** 喜悦/愤怒/悔恨的泪水; **to shed** *or* **weep bitter ~s (of contrition)** (因痛悔而) 流下伤心的泪水; **to end in ~s** 下场很惨

tearaway /ˈteərəweɪ/ *n* Brit 小混混

teardrop /ˈtɪədrɒp/
A *n* 泪珠
B *modif* 泪珠状的 ‹*pendant, earring*›

tear duct /ˈtɪə dʌkt/ *n* 泪腺

tearful /ˈtɪəfl/ *adj* **1** (weepy) 哭泣的 ‹*child, mourner*›; 带哭腔的 ‹*voice*›; **to feel ~** 想哭 **2** (marked by tears) 挥泪的 ‹*farewell, speech*›

tearfully /ˈtɪəfəli/ *adv* 哭泣地 ‹*say, beg*›; 眼泪汪汪地 ‹*look, smile*›

tear gas /ˈtɪə gæs/ *n* [u] 催泪瓦斯; **a ~ canister** *or* **grenade** 催泪弹

tear jerker /ˈtɪə ˌdʒɜːkə(r)/ *n* colloq (book) 催人泪下的书; (film) 催人泪下的电影; (story) 催人泪下的故事

tear-off /ˈteərɒf/ *adj* 可撕下的 ‹*strip, calendar*›

tea room *n* 茶室

tear-stained /ˈtɪəsteɪnd/ *adj* 布满泪痕的 ‹*face*›; 泪渍斑斑的 ‹*pillow, letter*›

tease /tiːz/
A *vt* **1** (provoke) (playfully) 打趣; (maliciously) 嘲弄; (sexually) 挑逗 **2** (separate out) 理顺 ‹*wool, hair*› **3** esp Amer (backcomb) 往后梳 ‹*hair*›
B *vi* (provoke) (playfully) 打趣; (maliciously) 嘲弄; (sexually) 挑逗
C *n* **1** (joker) 打趣的人 **2** colloq (woman) 卖弄风骚的人 **3** (act of teasing) 取笑

Phrasal verb

• **tease out** *vt* [**~ sth. out, ~ out sth.**]
1 lit (untangle) 理顺 ‹*hair*›; 解开 ‹*knot*› **2** fig (deduce, retrieve) 梳理清楚 ‹*meaning, information*›

teasel /ˈtiːzl/ *n* **1** [u and c] Bot 起绒草 **2** [c] Tex 起绒机

teaser /ˈtiːzə(r)/ *n* **1** (person) (playfully) 逗弄者; (maliciously) 奚落者; (sexually) 挑逗者 **2** colloq (puzzle) 难题 **3** Advertg 悬念式前导广告; **a ~ ad/trailer** 悬念式广告/预告片

tea: ~ service, ~ set *ns* 一套茶具; **~ shop** *n* 茶馆

teasing /ˈtiːzɪŋ/
A *n* [u] **1** (action) (playful) 逗弄; (malicious) 奚落; (sexual) 挑逗 **2** Advertg 悬念式广告手法
B *adj* (provoking) (playfully) 逗弄的; (maliciously) 奚落的; (sexually) 挑逗的

teasingly /ˈtiːzɪŋli/ *adv* (playfully) 逗弄地; (maliciously) 奚落地; (sexually) 挑逗地

Teasmade® /ˈtiːzmeɪd/ *n* 自动煮茶机

tea: ~spoon *n* **1** (spoon) 茶匙; **2** (amount) 一茶匙; **~spoonful** *n* = **~spoon 2**; **~-strainer** *n* 滤茶器

teat /tiːt/ *n* **1** (nipple) (of animal) 乳头; pej (of woman) 奶头 **2** Brit (on baby's bottle) 奶嘴

tea: ~ table *n* 茶桌; **~ things** *npl* Brit colloq 茶具; **~time** *n* [u] esp Brit 下午茶时间; **~ towel** *n* Brit 茶巾; **~ tray** *n* 茶盘; **~ trolley** *n* esp Brit 茶点车; **~ urn** *n* 大茶壶; **~ wagon** *n* Amer = **~ trolley**

tech /tek/ *n* colloq **1** [c] Brit = **technical college** *or* **school** 技校 **2** [u] = **technology**

techie /ˈteki/ *n* colloq (technology expert) 技术专家; (technology enthusiast) 科技迷; (computer expert) 电脑专家; (computer enthusiast) 电脑迷

technical /ˈteknɪkl/ *adj* **1** (technological) 技术的; **the ~ staff** 技术人员; **~ knowledge/skill** 技术知识/技能; **a ~ hitch** 技术故障 **2** (specialist) 专业的 ‹*language, term*›; **~ jargon** 行话 **3** (legal) 严格依据法律的 ‹*defect, breach*›; **a ~ offence** 法律上成立的违法行为 **4** (of technique) 技巧性的 ‹*brilliance, complexity*›

technical: ~ college *n* 技术学院; **~ drawing** *n* **1** [u] (practice) 机械制图; **2** [c] (product) 机械设计图

technicality /ˌteknɪˈkæləti/
A *n* **1** [c] (point of law) 法律细则; **he got off/the case was dismissed on a ~** 根据诉讼程序上的一个细则, 他逃脱了惩罚/此案被撤销 **2** [u] (technical nature) 技术性; (use of technical terms) 术语使用
B **technicalities** *npl* (technical details) 技术细节; (technical terms) 技术用语

technically /ˈteknɪkli/ *adv* **1** (technologically) 在技术上 ‹*advanced, backward, feasible*› **2** (strictly) 严格地; **~ speaking** 严格说来 **3** (in technique) 在技巧上 ‹*bad, brilliant*›

technical: ~ sergeant *n* Amer (person) 空军上士; (rank) 空军上士军衔; **~ support** *n* [u] **1** (service) 技术支持; **2** (department) 技术支持部

technician /tekˈnɪʃn/ ►**p. 409** *n* **1** (worker) 技师; **a laboratory** *or* **lab ~** 实验室技术员 **2** (master of technique) 技术精湛者

Technicolor® /ˈteknɪkʌlə(r)/
A *n* [u] **1** Cin 彩色印片法 **2** **technicolour** Brit, **technicolor** Amer (bright colours) 色彩缤纷
B **technicolour** Brit, **technicolor** Amer *adj* colloq 色彩缤纷的 ‹*world*›; 绚烂夺目的 ‹*extravaganza*›

technique /tekˈniːk/ *n* **1** (method) 方法; (process) 技术; **printing/processing/manufacturing ~s** 印刷/生产/制造技术 **2** (skill) 技巧; **he hasn't got the ~ to cope with the difficult passages** 他没有处理艰深段落的技巧

technobabble /ˈteknəʊbæbl/ *n* [u] colloq 技术呓语

technocracy /tekˈnɒkrəsi/ *n* **1** [u] (system) 技术专家治国制度 **2** [c] (society) 技术专家治理的社会 **3** [c] (elite) 技术精英

technocrat /ˈteknəkræt/ *n* 技术专家官员

technocratic /ˌteknəˈkrætɪk/ *adj* (of technocrats) 技术专家官员的; (of technocracy) 技术专家治国的

technological /ˌteknəˈlɒdʒɪkl/ *adj* 科技的; **~ change** 科技变革

technologically /ˌteknəˈlɒdʒɪkli/ *adv* 在科技上

technologist /tekˈnɒlədʒɪst/ ►**p. 409** *n* 技术专家

technology /tekˈnɒlədʒi/ *n* **1** [u] (applied science) (application) 技术; **science and ~** 科学技术; **advances in ~** 技术上的发展; **modern ~** 现代技术 **2** [c] (method) 工艺 **3** [u] (resources) 技术设备; **we don't yet have the ~ to isolate the virus** 我们还没有隔离这种病毒的技术

technology park *n* = **science park**

technophile /ˈteknəʊfaɪl/ *n* 新科技迷

technophobe /ˈteknəʊfəʊb/ *n* 科技恐惧者

technospeak /ˈteknəʊspiːk/ *n* [u] 科技呓语

techy /ˈteki/ *n* colloq = **techie**

tectonic /tekˈtɒnɪk/ *adj* 地壳构造的; **~ shift/activity** 板块漂移/构造活动

tectonic plate *n* 构造板块

tectonics /tekˈtɒnɪks/ *npl* + *v sing* 构造地质学

teddy /ˈtedi/ *n* **~ (bear)** 泰迪熊

> **teddy bear**
>
> 泰迪熊, 简称 teddy。儿童毛绒玩具熊。相传美国总统西奥多·罗斯福 (Theodore Roosevelt) 在一次打猎时曾拒绝杀死一头幼熊。后来有人将玩具熊以其名字 Theodore 的昵称 Teddy 命名, 称 teddy bear。现也有成人收集泰迪熊, 以为爱好。

teddyboy /ˈtedɪbɔɪ/ *n* Brit 阿飞 [20世纪50年代穿长上衣、紧身裤的反叛青少年]

tedious /ˈtiːdɪəs/ *adj* 单调乏味的

tediously /ˈtiːdɪəsli/ *adv* 单调乏味地 ‹*talk, repetitive*›; 令人厌烦地 ‹*long, dull*›

tediousness /ˈtiːdɪəsnɪs/ *n* [u] 单调乏味

tedium /ˈtiːdɪəm/ *n* [u] 单调乏味

tee /tiː/
A *n* **1** (peg) 球座 **2** (area) 发球区; **a ~ shot** 开球
B *vt* (*pt, pp* **~d**) **~ (up)** 把…置于球座上 ‹*ball*›

Phrasal verb

• **tee off**
A *vi* **1** (play ball) «*golfer*» 开球 **2** (get under way) «*tournament*» 开始
B *vt* [**~ sb. off, ~ off sb.**] Amer colloq 惹烦

t

tee-hee /ˌtiːˈhiː/
A *excl* 嘻嘻 [窃笑声]
B *n* 窃笑声
C *vi* 窃笑

teem /tiːm/ *vi* **1** (be full) 充满; **to ~ with wildlife/ideas** 遍布野生动物/想法极多; **a river ~ing with fish** 盛产鱼的河流 **2** **to ~ (down)** «*rain*» 倾盆而下; **it is ~ing (down) (with rain)** 大雨如注

teeming /ˈtiːmɪŋ/ *adj attrib* **1** (full) 充满生机的 ‹*river, city, continent*› **2** (pouring) 如注的 ‹*rain*› **3** (swarming) 拥挤的 ‹*crowd, mass*›; 成群结队的 ‹*herd*›

teen /tiːn/ *adj attrib* colloq 青少年的 ‹*fashion, magazine*›

teenage /ˈtiːneɪdʒ/ *adj attrib* **1** (between 13 and 19) 十几岁的 ‹*children, gang*› **2** (of teenagers) 青少年的 ‹*behaviour, rebellion*›; **the ~ years** 青少年时期

teenager /ˈtiːneɪdʒə(r)/ *n* 青少年

teens /tiːnz/ *npl* 十几岁; **children in their mid-~** 十五六岁的孩子们

teeny /ˈtiːni/, **teensy** /ˈtiːnzi/, **teensy weensy** /ˌtiːnzi ˈwiːnzi/ *adjs* colloq 极小的 ‹*bikini, object*›; **a ~ person** 小不点儿

teeny: ~-bopper /ˈtiːnɪbɒpə(r)/ *n* colloq 新潮少年; **~ weeny** /ˌtiːni ˈwiːni/ *adj* colloq **= teeny**

teepee /ˈtiːpiː/ *n* [北美印第安人的] 圆锥形帐篷

tee-shirt /ˈtiːʃɜːt/ *n* **= T-shirt**

teeter /ˈtiːtə(r)/ *vi* «*person*» 踉跄; «*structure, pile*» 摇摇欲坠; **the firm is ~ing on the brink of ruin** 这家公司正濒临倒闭

teeter-totter /ˈtiːtəˌtɒtə(r)/ *n* Amer 跷跷板

teeth /tiːθ/ *pl* ▸ **tooth**

teethe /tiːð/ *vi* «*baby*» 长牙

teething /ˈtiːðɪŋ/ *n* [u] (cutting teeth) 长牙; (period) 长牙期

teething: ~ ring *n* 长牙嚼环; **~ troubles, ~ problems** *nspl* fig 起步时的小困难

teetotal /tiːˈtəʊtl, Amer ˈtiːtəʊtl/ *adj* 滴酒不沾的 ‹*person, lifestyle*›; **to go ~** 戒酒

teetotaler *n* Amer **= teetotaller**

teetotalism /tiːˈtəʊtəlɪzəm/ *n* [u] 绝对戒酒主义

teetotaller /tiːˈtəʊtələ(r)/ *n* 滴酒不沾的人

TEFL /ˈtefl/ *abbr* **= Teaching of English as a Foreign Language** 作为外语的英语教学

Teflon® /ˈteflɒn/
A *n* [u] 特富龙 [不沾锅涂料]
B *modif* 特富龙的 ‹*coating*›; fig 声誉不受负面事件损害的 ‹*politician*›; **a ~ frying pan** 特富龙煎锅

Tehran, Teheran /ˌteəˈrɑːn/ *pr n* 德黑兰

tel. /tel/ *abbr* **= telephone A**

Tel Aviv /ˌtel əˈviːv/ *pr n* **~(-Jaffa)** 特拉维夫

telco /ˈtelkəʊ/ *n* colloq 电信公司

tele-ad /ˈtelɪæd/ *n* 电话约定广告

telebanking /ˈtelɪbæŋkɪŋ/ *n* [u] **= telephone banking**

telecamera /ˈtelɪkæmərə/ *n* 电视摄像机

telecast /ˈtelɪkɑːst, Amer -kæst/
A *n* 电视节目; **a live ~** 电视直播
B *vt* (*pt, pp* **telecast**) 用电视播出 ‹*programme, match*›

telecommunications /ˌtelɪkəˌmjuːnɪˈkeɪʃnz/ *npl* **1** + *v sing* (science) 电信学 **2** + *v sing or pl* (means) 电信; **a ~ network/satellite** 远程通信网络/通信卫星

telecommute /ˌtelɪkəˈmjuːt/ *vi* [通过电信设备] 远程工作

telecommuter /ˌtelɪkəˈmjuːtə(r)/ *n* 远程工作者

telecommuting /ˌtelɪkəˈmjuːtɪŋ/ *n* [u] 远程工作

telecomputing /ˌtelɪkəmˈpjuːtɪŋ/ *n* [u] 远程信息处理; **~ services/technology** 远程信息处理服务/技术

telecoms /ˈtelɪkɒmz/ *npl* + *v sing* 电信; **~ company/technology/industry** 电信公司/技术/业

teleconference /ˈtelɪkɒnfərəns/ *n* 电话会议

teleconferencing /ˌtelɪˈkɒnfərənsɪŋ/ *n* [u] 召开电话会议

telecottage /ˈtelɪkɒtɪdʒ/ *n* [公用] 乡间电脑室

telefilm /ˈtelɪfɪlm/ *n* 电视影片

telegenic /ˌtelɪˈdʒenɪk/ *adj* 上镜的

telegram /ˈtelɪɡræm/ *n* 电报

telegraph /ˈtelɪɡrɑːf, Amer -ɡræf/
A *n* **1** [u] (system) 电报; **a ~ wire/machine/operator** 电报线/发报机/电报员 **2** [c] (device) 电报机
B *vt* **1** (inform) 发电报给 **2** (send) 用电报发送 ‹*message*› **3** (convey, reveal) (unintentionally) 流露 ‹*feeling*›; (intentionally) 泄露 ‹*intention, message*›

telegrapher /təˈleɡrəfə(r)/ ▸**p. 409** *n* 报务员

telegraphese /ˌtelɪɡrəˈfiːz/ *n* [u] colloq 电报文体

telegraphic /ˌtelɪˈɡræfɪk/ *adj* 电报的 ‹*transfer, signal*›

telegraphically /ˌtelɪˈɡræfɪkli/ *adv* 通过电报 ‹*transmit, communicate, transfer*›

telegraphist /təˈleɡrəfɪst/ ▸**p. 409** *n* 报务员

telegraphy /təˈleɡrəfi/ *n* [u] 电报通讯

telekinesis /ˌtelɪkaɪˈniːsɪs, -kɪˈniːsɪs/ *n* [u] 心灵遥感

telekinetic /ˌtelɪkaɪˈnetɪk, -kɪˈnetɪk/ *adj* 心灵致动的 ‹*power, force*›

telemarketer /ˌtelɪˈmɑːkɪtə(r)/ ▸**p. 409** *n* 电话推销员

telemarketing /ˈtelɪmɑːkɪtɪŋ/ *n* [u] 电话推销; **~ calls** 推销电话

telematics /ˌtelɪˈmætɪks/ *npl* + *v sing* 远程信息技术; **~ industry** 远程信息技术业

telemessage /ˈtelɪmesɪdʒ/ *n* 电传信息

telemeter /ˈtelɪmiːtə(r), təˈlemɪtə(r)/ *n* 遥测仪

telemetric /ˌtelɪˈmetrɪk/ *adj* 遥测的

telemetry /tɪˈlemətri/ *n* [u] 遥测术

teleological /ˌtelɪəˈlɒdʒɪkl, ˌtiː-/ *adj* 目的论的

teleology /ˌtelɪˈɒlədʒi, ˌtiː-/ *n* **1** [u and c] Philos 目的论 [认为现象是为了目的而发生] **2** [u] Relig 目的信仰 [认为宇宙有其目的或规划]

telepath /ˈtelɪpæθ/ *n* 传心术者

telepathic /ˌtelɪˈpæθɪk/ *adj* **1** (involving telepathy) 传心术的 ‹*power, understanding*› **2** (able to use telepathy) 会传心术的 ‹*person*›

telepathy /təˈlepəθi/ *n* [u] 传心术

telephone /ˈtelɪfəʊn/
A *n* (system) 电话; (instrument) 电话机; **to be on the ~** (have a telephone) 装有电话机; (be talking on the telephone) 正在打电话; **I tried to reach her by ~** *or* **on the ~** 我试图用电话联系她; **to answer the ~** 接电话; **a ~ wire/switchboard** 电话线/交换机
B *vt* **1** (contact) 给…打电话 ‹*person, country*› **2** (communicate) 打电话告知 ‹*message, news*›
C *vi* 打电话

telephone: ~ answering machine *n* 电话答录机; **~ banking** *n* [u] 电话银行业务; **~ bill** *n* 电话账单; **~ book** *n* **= ~ directory**; **~ booth,** Brit **~ box** *ns* 电话亭; **~ call** *n* 打电话; **~ directory** *n* 电话号码簿; **~ exchange** *n* (equipment) 电话交换台; (office) 电话局; **~ kiosk** *n* Brit **= ~ booth**; **~ line** *n* 电话线路; **~ number** *n* 电话号码; **~ operator** ▸**p. 409** *n* esp Amer 电话接线员; **~ pole** *n* 电话线杆; **~ service** *n* 电话业务; **~ sex** *n* [u] (conversation) 色情电话; (commercial provision) 色情电话服务; **~ subscriber** *n* 电话用户; **~ tapping** *n* [u] 电话窃听

telephonic /ˌtelɪˈfɒnɪk/ *adj* 电话的 ‹*interview, survey*›

telephonist /təˈlefənɪst/ ▸**p. 409** *n* Brit 电话接线员

telephony /təˈlefəni/ *n* [u] 电话通信

telephoto lens /ˌtelɪfəʊtəʊ ˈlenz/ *n* 摄远镜头

teleport /ˈtelɪpɔːt/
A *vt, vi* 用意念传送
B *v refl* **to ~ oneself** *or* **itself** «*person, creature*» 用意念移动

teleportation /ˌtelɪpɔːˈteɪʃn/ *n* [c and u] [科幻小说里的] 远距离即时传送

teleprinter /ˈtelɪprɪntə(r)/ *n* Brit 电传打印机

teleprocessing /ˌtelɪˈprəʊsesɪŋ/ *n* [u] 远程数据处理

teleprompter /ˈtelɪprɒmptə(r)/ *n* [电视广播的] 自动提词机

telesales /ˈtelɪseɪlz/ *npl* + *v sing* esp Brit 电话销售

telesales operator, telesales person ▸**p. 409** *ns* 电话推销员

telescope /ˈtelɪskəʊp/
A *n* 望远镜; **to look at sth. through a ~** 通过望远镜观察某物
B *vi* **1** (slide inside itself) «*umbrella, tripod*» 叠缩; «*leg*» 蜷缩 **2** (be crushed together) «*railway carriages*» 相撞嵌进
C *vt* **1** (slide inside itself) 叠缩起 ‹*rod, tripod*› **2** (condense) 缩短 ‹*period of time, process*›

telescopic /ˌtelɪˈskɒpɪk/ *adj* **1** (magnifying) 放大的 ‹*lens*›; **a ~ sight** (on gun) 望远瞄准器; **~ vision** 远视觉; **a ~ eye** 远视眼 **2** (through telescope) 用望远镜看到的 ‹*image, view*› **3** (collapsible) 可伸缩的 ‹*aerial*›; 可折叠的 ‹*umbrella*›

telescopic rifle *n* 望远瞄准镜步枪

teleshopper /ˈtelɪʃɒpə(r)/ *n* (by telephone) 电话购物者; (by computer) 网上购物者

teleshopping /ˈtelɪʃɒpɪŋ/ *n* [u] (using telephone) 电话购物; (using computer) 网上购物; **~ channels** (using telephone) 电话购物渠道; (using computer) 网上购物渠道

Teletex® /ˈtelɪteks/ *n* [u] 泰来泰克斯电子文本传输系统

teletext /ˈtelɪtekst/ *n* [u] 图文电视

telethon /ˈtelɪθɒn/ *n* [通常为慈善目的的筹款的] 马拉松式电视节目

Teletype® /ˈtelɪtaɪp/ *n* [u and c] 电传打字机

teletypewriter /ˌtelɪˈtaɪpraɪtə(r)/ *n* Amer **= teleprinter**

televangelism /ˌtelɪˈvændʒəlɪzəm/ *n* [u] 电视福音布道

televangelist /ˌtelɪˈvændʒəlɪst/ ▸**p. 409** *n* 电视福音布道者

televise /ˈtelɪvaɪz/ *vt* 用电视播放

television /ˈtelɪvɪʒn, ˌtelɪˈvɪʒn/ *n* **1** [u] (medium) 电视; **to watch ~** 看电视; **to be shown live on ~** 在电视上直播; **a ~ interview/personality** 电视访谈节目/电视圈名人 **2** [u] (programmes) 电视节目; **how much ~ do you watch every day?** 你每天看多长时间电视? **3** [c] (set) 电视机; **to turn the ~ on/off** 打开/关上电视 **4** [u] (activity, profession) 电视行业; **she works in ~** 她从事电视行业

television: ~ announcer ▸**p. 409** *n* 电视节目预告员; **~ cabinet** *n* 电视柜; **~ channel** *n* 电视频道; **~ chef** *n* 电视烹调节目主持人; **~ company** *n* 电视公司; **~ dinner** *n* [预先包装好, 在看电视时吃的]

t

盒饭; ~ **licence** *n* 电视收视许可证; ~ **listings** *npl* 电视节目单; ~ **lounge** *n* 电视厅; ~ **network** *n* 电视广播网; ~ **picture** *n* 电视图像; ~ **programme** *n* 电视节目; ~ **room** *n* 电视厅; ~ **satellite** *n* 电视卫星; ~ **schedule** *n* 电视节目表; ~ **screen** *n* 电视屏幕; ~ **set** *n* 电视机; ~ **tube** *n* 电视显像管

televisual /ˌtelɪˈvɪʒuəl/ *adj* 电视的 ‹*entertainment, image*›

teleworker /ˈtelɪwɜːkə(r)/ *n* [在家通过电话、传真和电邮与工作地点联系的] 远程办公者

telex /ˈteleks/

A *n* **1** [u] (system) 电传系统; **a ~ operator** 电传收发员 **2** [c] (machine) 电传机 **3** [c] (message) 电传

B *vt* **1** (send) 用电传发送 ‹*message*› **2** (contact) 通过电传联系 ‹*person, company*›

tell /tel/ (*pt, pp* **told**)

A *vt* **1** (make known) 讲 ‹*story, joke, history*›; 告诉 ‹*fact, news*›; (say, express in words) 说 ‹*truth, lie*›; **to ~ sb. sth., to ~ sth. to sb.** 告诉某人某事; **to ~ the time,** Amer **to ~ time** 看钟表; **she's only six, but she can ~ the time** 她只有6岁，但是她已经会看时间了; **to ~ sb. about sb./sth.** 告诉某人有关某人/某事物的情况; **don't ~ the world about it!** 不要四处张扬这件事! ; **to ~ sb. a thing or two (about sb./sth.)** 告诉某人（关于某人/某事物的）一些事; **I can't ~ you how happy/sad I am** 我无法向你形容我有多高兴/伤心; **to ~ sb. (sth.) in no uncertain terms** 毫不含糊地对某人说（某事）; **to ~ sth. in one's own words** 用自己的话描述某事物; **something ~s me he won't be very pleased** 我觉得他会不高兴的; **she told me of all her hopes and aspirations** 她对我讲了她所有的希望与抱负; **I'm not going to ~ you again (to do it)** 我不会跟你再说一遍（去做这件事）; **to ~ sb. a secret** 告诉某人一个秘密; **I** *or* **I'll ~ you what ...** colloq 我跟你说…; **I told you (so)** colloq 我早就跟你说过; **you're ~ing me!** colloq 你说得一点不错! ; **I ~ you, I can ~ you, let me ~ you** colloq 我可以肯定地说; **to ~ sb. a pack of lies** 对某人说一大堆谎话; **~ me another!** colloq 我才不信呢! ; **more than words can ~** 非言语所能表达; **I love him more than words can ~** 我对他的爱无法用言语形容; **to ~ it like it is** colloq 实话实说 **2** (give information) «*person, book*» 提供 ‹*information*›; «*instructions, map*» 说明 ‹*way*›; «*gauge, thermometer, signpost*» 显示 ‹*amount, rise, fall*›; **to ~ sb. the way (to sth.)** 给某人指（去某处的）路; **his behaviour told me a great deal about his character** 他的行为向我充分显示了他的性格; **to ~ sb. what's what** 使某人了解底细 **3** (ascertain) 确定; (deduce) 推断; **nobody could ~ how he did the trick** 谁也不知道他那个戏法是如何变的; **who can ~?** 谁知道呢? ; **you can never** *or* **you never can ~ (with sb.)** （对于某人）谁也说不清; **you can ~ a lot from the kind of clothes people wear** 从人的衣着可以看出很多东西; **you couldn't ~ much from his expression** 从他的表情看不出什么来 **4** (distinguish) 辨别 ‹*difference, person, object*›; **to ~ sb./sth. from sb./sth.** 将某人/某物与某人/某物区分开来; **to ~ which is which** 辨认出哪个是哪个; **can you ~ the two sisters apart?** 你能分得出这俩姊妹吗? ; **to ~ right from wrong** 分辨对与错 **5** (order to do) 命令; (direct to do) 指示; **~ him yourself!** 你自己去跟他说! ; **they told me not to interfere** 他们让我不要干涉; **~ him not to bother; I'll do it myself** 叫他不要费心，我自己来做这件事; **will you kindly do what you are told!** 你能不能爽快地让干什么就干什么! ; **he won't be told** (to obey orders) 他不会服从命令的; (to take advice) 他不会听人意见的; **to ~ sb. where to put** *or* **what to do with sth.** colloq 让某人收起那一套; **to ~ sb. where to get off** colloq 严厉斥责某人

B *vi* **1** (know for certain) 确定; **it may rain or it may not; it's very hard to ~** 可能下雨，也可能不下，这很难说; **you just can't ~ with people like that** 像那样的人你可说不准; **to ~ from sth.** 通过某事物确定; **as far as I can ~ ...** 就我所知…; **there is no ~ing ...** 无从知道…; **time (alone) will ~** （只有）时间会证明 **2** (reveal secret) 泄密; **promise you won't ~!** 你必须答应不说出去! ; **that would be ~ing** colloq 那会泄密的 **3** (be evidence of) 表明; **the lines on his face told of years of hardship** 他脸上的一道道皱纹道出了多年来的艰辛; **eyes that ~ of great happiness** 流露出极度喜悦之情的双眼; **ruins that ~ of lost civilizations** 讲述着已逝文明的废墟 **4** (produce effect) 产生效果; **good breeding ~s** 良好的教养会有好的效果; **her age is beginning to ~** 她开始显老了; **a life of hard toil is beginning to ~ on him** 艰辛生活的影响开始在他身上显现出来了; **worry and overworking is ~ing on my health** 忧虑与工作过度劳累开始影响我的健康; **youth and inexperience told against her at the interview** 年轻与缺乏经验在面试中对她不利

Phrasal verbs

- **tell off** *vt* [~ **sb. off**] colloq 责备; **you'll get told off if they catch you doing that!** 如果你做那件事让他们抓住，你会被训斥的! ; **she told him off for his cheek** 她骂他脸皮厚
- **tell on** *vt* [~ **on sb.**] colloq 告发; **to ~ on sb. for doing sth.** 告发某人做了某事; **to ~ on sb. to the headmaster** 向校长告发某人

teller /ˈtelə(r)/ ▸**p. 409** *n* **1** esp Amer (cashier) 出纳员 **2** (vote-counter) 计票员 **3** (narrator) 叙述者; **a ~ of lies** 说谎的人 **4** Amer (cash machine) 自动取款机

telling /ˈtelɪŋ/

A *n* [u] 叙述; **the accounts of his brave exploits gained in the ~** 对他英勇事迹的描述越来越言过其实; **there's no ~** 无法了解

B *adj* **1** (effective) 有力的 ‹*point, blow*›; 有效的 ‹*figures, evidence*› **2** (revealing) 透露真相的 ‹*detail, omission*›

tellingly /ˈtelɪŋli/ *adv* **1** (effectively) 有力地 ‹*speak, punch*› **2** (revealingly) 透露真相地 ‹*convey, illustrate*›

telling-off *n* (*pl* **tellings-off**) Brit colloq 数落

telltale /ˈtelteɪl/

A *n* 告密者 [常指小孩]

B *adj attrib* 泄露秘密的 ‹*sign, blush, stain*›

tellurium /teˈljʊərɪəm/ *n* [u] 碲

telly /ˈteli/ *n* Brit colloq **1** (medium of television) 电视; **a ~ programme** 电视节目 **2** (television set) 电视机

telnet /ˈtelnet/

A *n* [u] 远程登录系统; **a ~ server/command** 远程登录服务器/指令

B *vi* 进行远程登录

temerity /tɪˈmerəti/ *n* [u] 鲁莽; **to have the ~ to do sth.** 竟敢做某事

temp /temp/ colloq

A *n* 临时工

B *vi* 打零工

temper /ˈtempə(r)/

A *n* **1** [c] (nature) 脾气; **a hot** *or* **quick ~** 火爆脾气; **to have a bit of a ~** 有点小脾气; **to lose one's ~** 发脾气 **2** [c] (mood) [尤指坏的] 情绪; **to be in a ~** 正在生气; **to get** *or* **fly into a (bad) ~** 勃然大怒 **3** [u] (anger) 怒气; **a fit of ~** 一阵愤怒

B *vt* **1** Ind 使…回火 ‹*metal, blade*›; **~ed steel** 回火钢 **2** (moderate) 缓和 ‹*effect, rigours*›; 使…下降 ‹*expectation, enthusiasm*›

tempera /ˈtempərə/ *n* [u] **1** (technique) 蛋彩画法 [用蛋清调和颜料]; **~ painting** 蛋彩画 **2** (emulsion) 蛋彩颜料

temperament /ˈtemprəmənt/ *n* **1** [u and c] (nature) 性情; **a cool, phlegmatic man by ~** 性情淡定平和的男子; **the artistic ~** 艺术家的气质 **2** [u] (excitability) 喜怒无常

temperamental /ˌtemprəˈmentl/ *adj* **1** (moody) 喜怒无常的 ‹*person*› **2** fig (likely to go wrong) 性能不稳定的 ‹*machine, vehicle*›; (unpredictable) 时好时坏的 ‹*weather*› **3** (natural) 性格上的 ‹*unsuitability, affinity*›

temperamentally /ˌtemprəˈmentəli/ *adv* 性格上; **they were ~ unsuited** 他们性格不和

temperance /ˈtempərəns/ *n* [u] **1** formal (moderation) 节制 **2** (teetotalism) [出于道德和宗教信仰而实行的] 戒酒; **a ~ movement** 戒酒运动

temperate /ˈtempərət/ *adj* **1** Geog 温带的 ‹*forest, climate*› **2** formal (moderate) 有节制的 ‹*person, habit*›; **to be ~ in sth.** 在某事上有节制

temperature /ˈtemprətʃə(r), Amer -tʃʊr/ ▸**p. 814** *n* [u and c] **1** Phys 温度; **at a ~ of 100°C** 在100摄氏度; **what ~ is the water?** 水温是多少? ; **~s are normal for the time of year** 今年眼下的气温正常; **a ~ gauge/change** 温度计/变化 **2** Med 体温; **to be running** *or* **have a ~** 发烧; **to take sb.'s ~** 给某人量体温

temperature-controlled *adj* 恒温的 ‹*room, storage*›

temper tantrum *n* [尤指小孩子的] 大发脾气; **to throw** *or* **have a ~** 耍小孩子脾气

tempest /ˈtempɪst/ *n* liter 暴风雨

tempestuous /temˈpestʃuəs/ *adj* **1** (emotional) 狂暴的 ‹*person*›; 激烈的 ‹*quarrel*›; 跌宕起伏的 ‹*music, affair*› **2** liter (stormy) 狂风暴雨的; **~ seas** 波涛汹涌的大海

tempestuously /temˈpestʃuəsli/ *adv* 狂暴地 ‹*toss, sweep*›; 奔放地 ‹*play*›; **a ~ competitive match** 争夺激烈的比赛

tempi /ˈtempiː/ *pl* ▸**tempo**

temping /ˈtempɪŋ/ *n* [u] colloq 做临时工

temping job *n* colloq 临时工作

template /ˈtempleɪt/ *n* **1** Sewing, Tech 型板 **2** fig (model) 样板 **3** Comput 模板

temple /ˈtempl/ *n* **1** (place of worship) [非基督教的] 神殿; **a Hindu/Buddhist/Sikh ~** 印度教/佛教/锡克教庙宇; **a ~ of learning** 学术殿堂; **the T~ (at Jerusalem)** （耶路撒冷的）犹太古神殿 **2** Anat 太阳穴

templet /ˈtemplɪt/ *n* = **template**

tempo /ˈtempəʊ/ *n* (*pl* **~s** *or* **tempi**) **1** (musical speed) [乐曲的] 速度 **2** (pace) 节奏

tempo marking *n* [乐曲的] 速度标记

temporal /ˈtempərəl/ *adj* **1** (secular) 世俗的 **2** (concerning time) 时间的; **a ~ adverb/conjunction** 时间副词/连词; **a universe which has spatial and ~ dimensions** 有时空维度的宇宙

temporarily /ˈtempərəli, Amer -pərerɪli/ *adv* (for limited time) 暂时地; (provisionally) 临时地

temporary /ˈtemprəri, Amer -pəreri/ *adj* (for limited time) 短期的 ‹*contract, visa, arrangement*›; (provisional) 临时的 ‹*job, accommodation, solution*›

temporize /ˈtempəraɪz/ *vi* formal 拖延时间

tempt /tempt/ *vt* 引诱; **can I ~ you to a whisky?** 能请你喝一杯威士忌吗? ; **to be** *or* **feel ~ed to do sth.** 动心想做某事; **she ~ed me to dive into the water** 她诱使我潜入水下; **to ~ sb. into sth./into doing sth.** 引诱某人做某事; **to ~ sb. into engineering/a life of crime** 吸引某人学习工程学/引诱某人过犯罪的生活; **he ~ed me with my favourite food** 他用我最爱吃的东西引诱我; **to ~ fate** *or* **providence** 冒险

temptation /tempˈteɪʃn/ *n* **1** [u] (being tempted) 诱惑; **to give in to/to resist ~** 经不

t

住/抵挡诱惑 **2** [c] (tempting thing) 诱惑物; **to feel a ~ to do sth.** 动心想做某事

tempter /'temptə(r)/ *n* 引诱者

tempting /'temptɪŋ/ *adj* 诱人的

temptingly /'temptɪŋli/ *adv* 诱人地; **~ cheap** 便宜得令人心动

temptress /'temptrɪs/ *n* 狐狸精

ten /ten/ ▸**p. 15, p. 521, p. 831**

A *n* **1** (number, quantity) 十; **~ plus two equals twelve** 10 加 2 等于 12; **we live at (number) ~, Victoria Road** 我们住在维多利亚路 10 号; **there are ~ of them** 他们有 10 个人; **to be ~ to one** 十有八九 **2** (in time) 10 点钟; **at ~ (o'clock)** 在 10 点; **at about ~ at night** 在大约晚上 10 点钟 **3** (on playing card) 10 点; **the ~ of diamonds** 方块 10 **4** (age) 10 岁 **5** (set of ten) 十个一组; **to count in ~s** 十个一数; **~s of thousands** 好几万 **6** (banknote) **~(-dollar bill)** 10 美元钞票; **~(-pound note)** 10 英镑钞票

B *adj* **1** (as quantity) 十的; **~ cats** 10 只猫; **~ books** 10 本书; **~ weeks** 10 周; **during the last ~ years** 在过去10年间 **2** (in age) 10 岁的; **he's nearly ~** 他快 10 岁了; **our house is only ~ years old** 我们的房子才造了 10 年 **3** (in series) 第十的; **number ~** 10 号; **page ~** 第 10 页

tenable /'tenəbl/ *adj* **1** (valid) 站得住脚的 ‹*hypothesis, proposition, claim*›; **to be ~ for sb. (to do sth.)** 对某人来说 (做某事) 是行得通的 **2** (available) 可保持的; **a scholarship ~ for up to three years** 为期可达三年的奖学金

tenacious /tə'neɪʃəs/ *adj* 顽强的 ‹*defence, resistance*›; 执着的 ‹*belief, pursuer*›; **a ~ grip** 紧握

tenaciously /tə'neɪʃəsli/ *adv* 顽强地

tenacity /tə'næsəti/ *n* [u] 顽强

tenancy /'tenənsi/ *n* **1** [c and u] (fact of being a tenant) 租赁; (right of being a tenant) 租赁权 **2** [c] (period) 租赁期限

tenancy agreement *n* 租赁协议

tenant /'tenənt/

A *n* (person paying rent) (for land) 租户; (for building) 房客

B *vt* 租赁 ‹*property*›

tenant farmer ▸**p. 409** *n* 佃农

ten-cent store *n* Amer [专卖廉价物品的] 10 美分店

tench /tentʃ/ *n* (*pl* **tench**) 丁鲹

tend[1] /tend/ *vi* (incline, move) 趋向; **to ~ to** *or* **towards sth.** 倾向于某事物; **to ~ to do sth.** 趋向于做某事; **prices are ~ing upwards/downwards** 价格趋涨/趋降; **it ~s to rain a lot at this time of year** 每年的这个时候往往雨水很多

tend[2]

A *vi* 照料; **to ~ to sb./sth.** 照料某人/某事物; **to ~ to sb.'s needs** 关注某人的需求

B *vt* 照管; **to ~ bar** Amer 做酒吧招待

tendency /'tendənsi/ *n* **1** (inclination) 倾向; **a ~ to** *or* **towards sth.** …的趋向; **a ~ to do sth.** 做某事的倾向 **2** (movement) 趋势; **an upward/downward ~** 上升/下降趋势 **3** (group) 派别

tendentious /ten'denʃəs/ *adj* 有偏见的

tendentiously /ten'denʃəsli/ *adv* 有偏见地

tendentiousness /ten'denʃəsnɪs/ *n* [u] 偏见

tender[1] /'tendə(r)/ *adj* **1** (gentle, loving) 温柔的 ‹*tone*›; 慈爱的 ‹*smile*›; **the ~ touch of a mother** 母亲的爱抚; **~ loving care** 体贴入微的关怀; **to give sb. a ~ look/kiss/embrace** 情意绵绵地看某人一眼/吻某人/拥抱某人; **to leave sb. to the ~ mercies of sb.** iron 使某人受某人的任意摆布 **2** (soft, delicate) 嫩的 ‹*meat, vegetable, flower*›; **is the steak ~ enough?** 牛排足够嫩吗? ; **~ blossoms** 娇嫩的花朵 **3** (susceptible to pain) 一触即痛的; **the bruise is still ~** 擦伤处仍然一碰就痛; **a ~ spot** 痛处; **a ~ subject** 敏感的话题 **4** liter (young) 年轻的; **at the ~ age of sixteen** 在 16 岁的小小年纪

tender[2]

A *n* 投标; **to put in** *or* **make** *or* **submit a ~** 投标; **to put a job/contract out to ~** 为工作/合同对外招标; **the ~ has to be in by Monday morning** 标书须在周一早上之前送达

B *vi* 投标; **to ~ for sth.** 投标承包某事; **an invitation to ~** 投标邀请

C *vt* formal **1** (present) 提出 ‹*advice, apology, excuse*›; **to ~ one's resignation** 递交辞呈 **2** (offer as payment) 付 ‹*money*›; **please ~ the exact fare** (on public transport) 自备零钱, 恕不找赎

tender[3] *n* **1** Rail [蒸汽机车的] 煤水车 **2** Naut (for passengers) 交通船; (for coal) 运煤船; (for supplies) 供应船 **3** (fire engine) 消防车

tenderer /'tendərə(r)/ *n* 投标人

tenderfoot /'tendəfʊt/ *n* (*pl* **~s** *or* **tenderfeet**) **1** (novice) 新手 **2** (newcomer) 新来者

tenderhearted /ˌtendə'hɑːtɪd/ *adj* 心肠软的

tendering /'tendərɪŋ/ *n* [u] 招标

tenderize /'tendəraɪz/ *vt* 使变嫩

t

Temperature

■ Temperature scales:

degrees Celsius/centigrade (°C) 摄氏度
degrees Fahrenheit (°F) 华氏度

Note that degrees Celsius is generally adopted in the Chinese-speaking world and that 度 is normally used to refer to 摄氏度.

■ In Chinese, 摄氏 and 华氏 are placed either before the number and the degree or between the number and the degree:

	Spoken	Written
100°C	一百摄氏度	100 摄氏度 or 100°C
0°C	零摄氏度	0 摄氏度 or 0°C
–100°C	零下一百摄氏度	零下 100 摄氏度 or –100°C
212°F	二百一十二华氏度	212 华氏度 or 212°F
–200°F	零下二百华氏度	零下 200 华氏度 or –200°F

above 37°C
= 超过 37 摄氏度

over 32°F
= 在 32 华氏度以上

below 50°
= 在 50 度以下

a Celsius thermometer
= 摄氏温度计

a Fahrenheit thermometer
= 华氏温度计

The thermometer says/shows 28°C
= 温度计显示温度为 28 摄氏度

Body temperature

■ 'Body temperature' is 体温:

The normal human body temperature is close to 37°C or 98°F
= 人的正常体温接近 37 摄氏度或 98 华氏度

What is her temperature?
— Her temperature is 39°C
= 她的体温是多少? —— 39 摄氏度

The nurse took my temperature
= 护士给我量了体温

Things

■ The temperature of something inanimate is referred to as 温度:

What temperature does water boil at?
— It boils at 100°C or 212°F
= 水在什么温度下沸腾?
—— 水在 100 摄氏度或 212 华氏度时沸腾

How hot is the soup? — It's about 80°C
= 汤有多热? —— 大约 80 摄氏度

What temperature is the milk? — It's 55°
= 牛奶多少度? —— 55 度

Water freezes at a temperature of 0°C or 32°F
= 水在 0 摄氏度或 32 华氏度结冰

The oven was preheated to a temperature of 180°C
= 烤箱预热到 180 摄氏度

A is the same temperature as B
or ***A and B are the same temperature***
= A 和 B 温度相同

A is hotter than B
= A 比 B 热

Note that it is conventional to use 凉 and not 冷 in the example below (while 冷 is used to describe weather – see below):

B is colder/cooler than A
= B 比 A 凉

Weather

■ 'Air temperature' is 气温:

What's the temperature today?
= 今天的气温是多少?

It is 12 degrees centigrade
= 12 摄氏度

The maximum temperature is 25°C and the lowest is –5°C
= 最高气温是 25 摄氏度, 最低气温是零下 5 摄氏度

There has been a gradual rise in temperature since last week
= 从上周起, 气温逐渐升高

It's roasting today. It's 42°C
= 今天非常热, 气温是 42 摄氏度

It's freezing today. The temperature is –15°
= 今天非常冷, 气温是零下 15 度

London is warmer than Edinburgh
= 伦敦比爱丁堡暖和

Glasgow is colder in winter than Oxford
= 格拉斯哥冬天比牛津冷

It's the same temperature in Hong Kong as in Singapore
= 香港和新加坡的气温相同

tenderizer /ˈtendəraɪzə(r)/ *n* 嫩肉剂

tenderloin /ˈtendəlɔɪn/ *n* **1** [u and c] (cut of meat) 里脊肉 **2** [c] Amer colloq (district of city) [腐败和罪恶充斥的] 污浊城区; **a ～ bar/motel** 乌七八糟的酒吧/汽车旅馆

tenderly /ˈtendəli/ *adv* 温柔地

tenderness /ˈtendənɪs/ *n* [u] **1** (gentleness) 温柔 **2** (softness) 嫩 **3** (soreness) 痛感

tender offer *n* Amer 要约收购

tendon /ˈtendən/ *n* 腱

tendril /ˈtendrɪl/ *n* **1** (clinging shoot) [攀缘植物的] 卷须 **2** (tendril-like thing) 卷须状物

tenement /ˈtenəmənt/ *n* **1** (building) **～ (building** *or* **block)** Brit, **～ (house)** Amer 经济公寓 **2** (flat) 套间

tenement flat *n* Brit 经济套间

tenet /ˈtenɪt/ *n* 信条

tenfold /ˈtenfəʊld/

A *adj* **1** (ten times as great) 十倍的 ‹*increase*› **2** (having ten parts) 有十部分的

B *adv* 十倍地; **to increase** *or* **multiply ～** 增长十倍

ten four

A *n* 收到信息

B *excl* 信息收到

ten-gallon hat *n* [美国牛仔戴的] 高顶宽边帽

tenner /ˈtenə(r)/ *n* colloq **1** Brit (ten-pound note) 十英镑钞票 **2** Amer (ten-dollar bill) 十美元钞票

Tennessee /ˌtenəˈsiː/ *pr n* 田纳西州

tennis /ˈtenɪs/ ▸**p. 307** *n* [u] 网球

tennis: ～ court *n* 网球场; **～ elbow** *n* [u] 网球肘 [打网球等引起的肘部发炎]; **～ shoe** *n* 网球鞋

tenon /ˈtenən/ *n* 榫舌

tenon saw *n* 开榫锯

tenor /ˈtenə(r)/ *n* **1** [c] (singer) 男高音歌手 **2** [c] (voice) 男高音; **a ～ voice/solo** 男高音/男高音独唱 **3** [c and u] (part) 次中音; **a ～ solo/part** 次中音独奏/声部 **4** [c] (general course, basic character) 基调 **5** [c] (tone, gist) 要旨; **the general ～ of the discussion** 讨论的要点

tenpin bowling /ˌtenpɪn ˈbəʊlɪŋ/ Brit, **tenpins** Amer ▸**p. 307** *ns* [u] 十柱保龄球戏

tense[1]

A *adj* **1** (nervous, strained) 紧张的 **2** (taut) 绷紧的 ‹*muscle, rope*› **3** (pronounced with tight vocal muscles) 紧的; **a ～ vowel** 紧元音

B *vt* 绷紧 ‹*muscle*›

C *v refl* **to ～ oneself** 绷紧身体

D *vi* «*person, muscle*» 绷紧

Phrasal verb

• **tense up** *vi* «*person, muscle*» 绷紧

tense[2] /tens/ *n* [c and u] (category of verb or verbal inflection) 时态; **the present/past/future ～** 现在时/过去时/将来时

tensely /ˈtensli/ *adv* 紧张地

tenseness /ˈtensnɪs/ *n* [u] **1** (nervousness) 紧张 **2** (tautness) 绷紧

tensile /ˈtensaɪl, Amer ˈtensl/ *adj* **1** (ductile) 可拉长的 ‹*material, rubber, cable*› **2** (relating to tension) 拉力的; **～ force/stress** 拉力/张应力

tensile strength *n* [u] 抗拉强度

tension /ˈtenʃn/

A *n* **1** [c and u] (nervousness) (from inability to relax) 紧张; (between two parties) 紧张关系; **～ is mounting** *or* **there is mounting ～ along the border** 边境局势日趋紧张 **2** [u] (tautness) (in cable, racket strings) 张力; (in muscle, body) 绷紧 **3** [u] (suspense) 紧张气氛 **4** [c and u] (conflict) 对立 **5** [u] (voltage) 电压

B *vt* 绷紧 ‹*cable, sail, spring*›

tension headache *n* [c and u] 紧张性头疼

tent /tent/ *n* 帐篷; **to put up/take down a ～** 搭/拆帐篷

tentacle /ˈtentəkl/ *n* **1** Zool 触须 **2** *usu pl* (influence) 影响范围

tentative /ˈtentətɪv/ *adj* **1** (provisional) 暂定的 ‹*arrangement, date, explanation*›; **～ plans/proposals** 临时计划/提议 **2** (hesitant) 犹豫不决的; **a ～ suggestion** 试探性的建议; **a ～ smile/voice** 怯生生的微笑/声音

tentatively /ˈtentətɪvli/ *adv* **1** (provisionally) 暂时地 ‹*arrange, agree*›; 临时性地 ‹*propose, conclude*› **2** (hesitantly) 犹豫不决地 ‹*say, approach*›; 怯生生地 ‹*smile*›

tentativeness /ˈtentətɪvnɪs/ *n* [u] **1** (provisional nature) (of offer) 临时性; (of arrangement, agreement) 暂时性 **2** (hesitancy) 犹豫不决

tenterhooks /ˈtentəhʊks/ *npl* **to be on ～** 坐立不安; **to keep sb. on ～** 使某人如坐针毡

tenth /tenθ/ ▸**p. 181, p. 521**

A *n* **1** (in sequence) 第十 **2** (in date) 10 日 **3** (fraction) 十分之一

B *adj* **1** (in sequence) 第十的; **on the ～ floor** 在 11 楼; **my ～ birthday party** 我的十岁生日聚会 **2** (in name, title) 十世 **3** (as fraction) 十分之一的

C *adv* 第十

tenth-rate *adj* colloq 最劣等的

tent: ～ peg *n* 帐篷桩; **～ pole** Brit, **～ stake** Amer *ns* 帐篷柱; **～ trailer** *n* 帐篷拖车

tenuous /ˈtenjʊəs/ *adj* **1** (weak, slight) 纤细的 ‹*thread*›; 稀薄的 ‹*atmosphere*›; **a ～ hope** 一线希望 **2** (unconvincing) 微弱的 ‹*connection, distinction*›; 站不住脚的 ‹*logic, theory, evidence*› **3** (precarious) 脆弱的 ‹*hold, position, situation*›

tenuously /ˈtenjʊəsli/ *adv* **1** (only slightly) 微弱地 ‹*connect, attach*› **2** (unconvincingly) 没有底气地 ‹*argue, suggest, maintain*› **3** (precariously) 摇摇欲坠地 ‹*cling, balance*›

tenuousness /ˈtenjʊəsnɪs/ *n* [u] (of thread) 纤细; (of plot) 空洞; (of position, situation) 脆弱; (of connection) 微弱; (of argument, evidence) 站不住脚

tenure /ˈtenjə(r) *n* [u] **1** (right of occupancy) [房地产等的] 保有权; **security of ～** 租住权保障 **2** (holding of office) 任职; [c] (period of office) 任期 **3** (permanent status) [尤指教师的] 终身职位; **to have** *or* **get ～** 获得终身职位

tenured /ˈtenjəd/ *adj* Amer 有终身职位的

tenure-track position *n* Amer 可获终身聘用的职位

tepee /ˈtiːpiː/ *n* = **teepee**

tepid /ˈtepɪd/ *adj* **1** (lukewarm) 温热的 ‹*water, tea, bath*› **2** (unenthusiastic) 不温不火的 ‹*response, applause*›

tepidly /ˈtepɪdli/ *adv* 不温不火地

tequila /təˈkiːlə/ *n* **1** [u] (alcoholic drink) [产自墨西哥的] 龙舌兰酒 **2** [c] (serving) 一杯龙舌兰酒

terbium /ˈtɜːbɪəm/ *n* [u] 铽

tercentenary /ˌtɜːsenˈtiːnəri, tɜːˈsentəneri/ *n* 三百周年纪念; **～ celebrations** 300 周年庆典

tercet /ˈtɜːsɪt/ *n* 同韵三行诗节

term /tɜːm/

A *n* **1** (period of time) (political) 任期; (financial, judicial) 期限; **the president's first ～ of** *or* **in office** 总统的第一届任期; **to serve a long ～ of imprisonment ～** 长期服刑; **he was elected for a four-year ～** 他当选了，任期四年; **a short-/medium-/long-～ loan** 短期/中期/长期贷款; **in the long/short ～** 在长期/短期内 **2** formal (end of period) 到期; **his life had reached the end of its natural ～** 他已尽其天年; **her pregnancy was approaching its ～** 她临近产期; **she had her first child at (full) ～** 她的第一个孩子是足月分娩的 **3** (in school, college, university) 学期; **end-of-～ examinations/reports** 期末考试/成绩报告; **the Autumn** *or* Amer **Fall/Spring/Summer ～** 秋季/春季/夏季学期; **in** *or* **during ～ (time)** 在学期中; **out of ～ (time)** 学期结束后 **4** (word, phrase) 术语; **a technical/legal/scientific/general/generic ～** 技术/法律/科学/一般/通用术语; **a ～ for sth.** 代表某事物的词; **a ～ of abuse** 詈词 **5** Math 项 **6** (in logic) (subject or predicate of proposition) [命题的] 项; (name or individual variable) 个体变项

B terms *npl* **1** (conditions of agreement, treaty, contract, will) 条款; **to dictate** *or* **stipulate** *or* **lay down ～s** 规定条件; **by** *or* **under the ～s of sth.** 根据某物的条款; **～s and conditions** 条件 **2** Comm (payment) 付款; (conditions of payment) 付款条件; **cash/credit ～s** 现付/信贷条件; **～s of payment/sale** 付款/销售条件; **on easy ～s** 以分期付款方式; **～s for sth./doing sth.** 某物/做某事的费用; **inclusive ～s** 全包价格 **3** (relations) 关系; **to be on good/bad/friendly/intimate ～s (with sb.)** （同某人）关系好/不好/友好/亲密; **to be on the best of ～s (with sb.)** （与某人）关系极好; **to be on speaking ～s (with sb.)** (to know sb. well enough to speak to him) （和某人）说得上话; (to be willing to talk to each other again) （与某人）和好如初; **we're not really on speaking ～s (with each other)** 我们（互相）几乎说不上话; **we are on first-name ～s** 我们关系很好，相互直呼其名; **to come to ～s with sth.** 对某事物妥协; **at last she has come to ～s with her disability** 她终于接受了自己残疾的现实 **4** (mode of expression) 说话方式; **in loose/endearing ～s** 泛泛地/讨人喜欢地说; **in plain** *or* **simple ～s** 以简明的语言; **glowing/flattering ～s** 溢美之词/奉承的话语 **5** **in ～s of** (in relation to) 就…而言; **to express sth. in ～s of cost/colour** 以成本/颜色表示某物; **they are equals in ～s of age and experience** 他们在年龄与阅历方面不相上下; **the book offers nothing in ～s of a satisfactory conclusion** 该书没有提供令人满意的结论; **in ～s of an investment** 从投资的角度 **6** **on one's own ～s** (in accordance with one's wishes) 根据自己的意愿; (in one's own way) 用自己的方式 **7** (point of view) **in his/their ～s** 在他/他们看来

C *vt* formal 把…称作 ‹*object, person*›; **the offer was ～ed derisory** 那个报价被称为少得可怜; **his behaviour was ～ed lamentable** 他的行为被形容为令人惋惜

terminal /ˈtɜːmɪnl/

A *adj* **1** (fatal) 晚期的 ‹*disease, cancer*›; **a ～ patient** 晚期病人; **～ boredom** hum 极度的无聊 **2** (furthest, last) 终点的 ‹*velocity*›; 到期的 ‹*date*›; (at end of stem) 顶生的 ‹*bud, flower, inflorescence, cluster*›; (at end of word) 词尾的 ‹*string, element*›; **the ～ point** 终点 **3** colloq (extreme) 不可救药的; **to be in ～ decline** 一蹶不振; **a ～ crisis** 致命危机 **4** (happening every school term) 学期末的 ‹*examination*›; (happening every judicial term) 开庭期末的 ‹*report*›

B *n* **1** (building) (at bus or train station) 终点站; (at airport) 航空站; (at port) 码头; **an oil/a freight ～** 输油管终端/货运站; **the ～ building** (at airport) 航站楼; (at train or bus station) 车站大楼 **2** (in electrical system) 端子 **3** (device in computer system) 终端

terminally /ˈtɜːmɪnəli/ *adv* **1** (with fatal disease) 处于晚期; **～ ill** 病入膏肓的 **2** colloq (extremely) 极度地 ‹*bored, stupid, sad, shy*›

terminal ward *n* 临终病房

terminate /ˈtɜːmɪneɪt/

A *vt* **1** (put an end to) 终止 ‹*contract, service, relationship, pregnancy*›; 结束 ‹*discussion, meeting*›; 停止 ‹*treatment*› **2** esp Amer (lay off) 解雇 ‹*employee*› **3** esp Amer (kill) 行刺 ‹*enemy*›

B *vi* **1** (end) «*meeting, programme*» 结束; «*contract, employment*» 终止; **to ～ in sth.** 在某处结束 **2** (reach terminus) «*train, bus*» 到达终点站

termination /ˌtɜːmɪˈneɪʃn/ *n* **1** [u and c] (ending) (of contract, service, relationship, pregnancy)

t

终止；(of discussion, meeting) 结束；(of treatment) 停止 **2** [u and c] (abortion) 终止妊娠

termini /ˈtɜːmɪnaɪ/ *pl* ▸**terminus**

terminological /ˌtɜːmɪnəˈlɒdʒɪkl/ *adj* 术语的

terminologist /ˌtɜːmɪˈnɒlədʒɪst/ ▸**p. 409** *n* 术语学家

terminology /ˌtɜːmɪˈnɒlədʒi/ *n* **1** [u] (technical language) 专门用语 **2** [c] (set of terms) 术语

term insurance *n* [u] 定期人寿保险

terminus /ˈtɜːmɪnəs/ *n* (*pl* **termini** *or* **~es**) **1** (final station) 终点站 **2** (oil, gas terminal) 终端

termite /ˈtɜːmaɪt/ *n* 白蚁

termly /ˈtɜːmli/
A *adj* 每学期的 ‹*assessment, fee, inspection*›
B *adv* 每学期 ‹*occur, pay, publish*›

term: ~ paper *n* Amer 学期论文；**~s of reference** *npl* 受权调查范围；**~s of trade** *npl* 进出口比价

tern /tɜːn/ *n* 燕鸥

terrace /ˈterəs/
A *n* **1** (paved area of patio, balcony) 露台；(roof area) 屋顶平台 **2** Brit (row of houses) 排屋；(one house) 一栋排屋 **3** (field) 梯田
B **terraces** *npl* (wide steps for sports spectators) 阶梯看台
C *vt* 把…筑成梯田 ‹*slope, garden*›

terrace cultivation *n* [u] 梯田耕种

terraced /ˈterəst/ *adj* **1** (formed into fields) 梯田形的 ‹*hillside, garden*› **2** Brit (of housing in terraces) 排屋式的 ‹*housing, cottage*›；有排屋的 ‹*street*›

terraced house, terrace house *ns* Brit 排屋

terracotta /ˌterəˈkɒtə/ *n* **1** [u] (earthenware) 赤陶土；**a ~ pot/statue** 赤陶土罐/雕像 **2** [c] (object) 赤土陶器 **3** [u] (colour) 赤褐色；**a ~ paint** 赤褐色油漆

terra firma /ˌterə ˈfɜːmə/ *n* [u] 坚实的大地

terrain /ˈtereɪn/ *n* [u and c] 地带；**fertile/infertile ~** 肥沃/贫瘠的土地

terrapin /ˈterəpɪn/ *n* **1** (Old World turtle) 水龟 **2** (New World turtle) **(diamondback) ~** 菱背泥龟

terrarium /təˈreərɪəm/ *n* (*pl* **~s** *or* **terraria** /təˈreərɪə/) **1** (for animals) [尤指爬行动物的] 养育箱 **2** (for plants) 玻璃栽培箱

terrestrial /təˈrestrɪəl/ *adj* **1** (of the earth) 地球的 ‹*ecosystem*›；地球上的 ‹*life*›；(similar to the earth) 类地球的 ‹*planet*› **2** (with ground equipment) 地面上的 ‹*channel, station, broadcaster*› **3** (belonging to the land) 陆生的 ‹*animal, plant*›；陆地的 ‹*environment*›

terrestrial: ~ globe *n* 地球仪；**~ telescope** *n* 大地望远镜

terrible /ˈterəbl/ *adj* **1** (tragic) 可怕的；(serious) 严重的；(very unpleasant) 非常讨厌的；**a ~ blow** 沉重的打击；**~ poverty** 赤贫；**a ~ fool/liar** 大傻瓜/大骗子；**a ~ shame** 奇耻大辱 **2** (unwell) 有病的；**to feel/look ~** 感觉不适/看上去有病 **3** (guilty) 负疚的；**to feel ~ about sth.** 对某事感到愧疚 **4** (poor, awful) 糟糕的 ‹*meal, performance, player*›；**you look ~ in that hat** 你戴那顶帽子难看死了；**to be ~ at sth./doing sth.** 在某方面/做某事很差劲 **5** (sinister) 骇人的 ‹*look, scream*›

terribly /ˈterəbli/ *adv* **1** (very) 非常；**~ well/badly** 好极了/糟透了；**I'm ~ sorry** 我十分抱歉 **2** (badly) 糟糕地 ‹*play, drive, write*› **3** (seriously, greatly) 很厉害地；**your father misses you ~** 你爸爸十分想你；**the experiment went ~ wrong** 这次实验出了大问题

terrier /ˈterɪə(r)/ *n* 小猎狗

terrific /təˈrɪfɪk/ *adj* **1** (huge) 巨大的 ‹*size, amount*›；极度的 ‹*heat, shock, worry*›；可怕的 ‹*bust-up, accident*›；激烈的 ‹*argument, struggle*› **2** colloq (wonderful) 很棒的；**to feel ~** 感觉很爽；**to look ~** (healthy) 气色很好；(attractive) 看上去非常迷人；**we had a ~ time** 我们玩得十分尽兴

terrifically /təˈrɪfɪkli/ *adv* colloq **1** (extremely) 非常 ‹*generous, talented, difficult*› **2** (very well) 很棒地 ‹*play, sing*›

terrified /ˈterɪfaɪd/ *adj* **1** (feeling fear) 惧怕的；**to be ~ of sth./doing sth.** 害怕某事物/做某事；**to be ~ of heights** 恐高 **2** *attrib* (expressing fear) 惊恐的 ‹*expression, scream*›

terrify /ˈterɪfaɪ/ *vt* 使恐惧；**to ~ the life out of sb.** colloq 把某人吓得魂飞魄散

terrifying /ˈterɪfaɪɪŋ/ *adj* 可怕的

terrifyingly /ˈterɪfaɪɪŋli/ *adv* 惊人地 ‹*fast, close, large*›；令人恐惧地 ‹*plunge, shake, tilt*›

territorial /ˌterəˈtɔːrɪəl/
A *adj* **1** (relating to national territory) 领土的 ‹*boundary, dispute, sovereignty*› **2** (possessive of land) 地盘性的 ‹*animal, bird, instinct, behaviour*›；**to be very ~** 有很强的地盘意识 **3** **Territorial** Brit Mil 本土防卫义勇军的 ‹*soldier, officer*›
B **Territorial** *n* Brit 本土防卫义勇军

territorial: T~ Army *pr n* Brit **the T~ Army** 本土防卫义勇军；**~ waters** *npl* 领海

territory /ˈterətri, Amer ˈterɪtɔːri/ *n* **1** [u and c] (land) (of nation, army) 领土；(of team, person, animal) 地盘 **2** **Territory** [c] (division within country) (in USA) 准州；(in Canada) 地方；(in Australia) 区 **3** [c] (responsibility of salesperson) [某人负责的] 地区；**to go with the ~** 是难免的事 **4** [c] (sphere, area of knowledge) 领域

terror /ˈterə(r)/ *n* **1** [u and c] (fear) 恐惧；**frozen by** *or* **with ~** 吓呆了的；**to be in ~ of sth./doing sth.** 害怕某事/做某事；**to strike ~ into (the heart of) sb.** 使某人心惊胆战 **2** [c] (person who terrorizes) 可怕的人；(thing that terrorizes) 恐怖的事物；(annoying person) 讨厌的人；(annoying thing) 讨厌的事；**a little** *or* **holy ~** 小捣蛋鬼；**he's a ~ for cleanliness** 他有洁癖 **3** [u] (intimidation, terrorism) 恐怖活动；**a ~ attack** 恐怖袭击

terrorism /ˈterərɪzəm/ *n* [u] 恐怖主义

terrorist /ˈterərɪst/ *n* 恐怖分子；**a ~ gang/organization** 恐怖团伙/组织

terrorize /ˈterəraɪz/ *vt* 恐吓；**to ~ sb. into doing sth.** 胁迫某人做某事

terror-stricken *adj* 心惊胆战的

terry /ˈteri/ *n* [u and c] **~ (towelling** Brit *or* **cloth** Amer**)** [尤指做毛巾用的] 毛圈织物

terse /tɜːs/ *adj* 简短的 ‹*reply, dialogue*›；简练的 ‹*style*›

tersely /ˈtɜːsli/ *adv* 简短地

terseness /ˈtɜːsnɪs/ *n* [u] 简短

tertiary /ˈtɜːʃəri, Amer -ʃieri/
A *adj* **1** (third) 第三的 ‹*level, stage*›；(of services) 第三产业的 ‹*sector*› **2** (beyond school) 高等教育的；**~ education** 高等教育；**a ~ college** 职业专科学校 **3** **Tertiary** (of the period) 第三纪的；(of the rock system) 第三系的
B **Tertiary** *n* **the T~** (period) 第三纪；(rock system) 第三系

Terylene® /ˈterəliːn/ *n* 涤纶

TESL /ˈtesl/ *abbr* = **Teaching English as a Second Language** 作为第二语言的英语教学

tessellated /ˈtesəleɪtɪd/ *adj* 镶嵌铺面小块的

test /test/
A *n* **1** (examination, trial) 试验；**to carry out** *or* **conduct** *or* **run** *or* **do a ~** 进行试验；**a nuclear/lie-detector/personality/means ~** 核试验/测谎/人格测验/经济情况调查；**a ~ of strength/their love/the vehicle's reliability** 对力量的测验/对他们爱情的考验/车辆安全性试验；**a field/laboratory ~** 现场/实验室试验；**to subject sb./sth. to a ~** 使某人/某物经受测验；**to put sb./sth. to the test** 使某人/某物接受考验；**to stand the ~ of time** 经得起时间的考验 **2** (evaluation of knowledge, skill) 测验；**an intelligence/IQ/aptitude ~** 智力/智商/能力倾向测验；**a ~ in** *or* **on arithmetic/irregular verbs** 算术/不规则动词测验；**an oral/aural ~** 口语/听力测验；**to take a ~** 参加测验；**to fail/pass a ~** 测试不及格/及格；**to set** *or* **give a ~** 举行测验；**to mark** *or* **correct a ~** 批考卷 **3** (medical examination) (of fluids) 化验；(of organ) 检查；**to send samples to the laboratory for ~s** 把样本送到实验室化验；**a blood/urine/saliva ~** 验血/验尿/唾液检查；**a negative/positive ~** 阴性/阳性检验 **4** (means of examining) 测试方法；(procedure for examining) 测试过程；**to devise a ~** 设计一个测试
B *vt* **1** (check) 检测；**to have one's eyesight ~ed** 检查视力；**to ~ sb./sth. for sth.** 为某事物检测某人/某物；**applicants are ~ed for AIDS** 申请者接受了艾滋病检查；**to ~ sth. on sb./sth.** 在某人/某物上检测某物；**doctors ~ed the vaccine on volunteers** 医生对志愿者进行了疫苗试种；**to ~ sth. for faults** 对某物做故障检测；**to ~ the water** fig 试探反应 **2** (examine) 测验；**she ~ed the whole class on** *or* **in irregular verbs** 她对全班进行了不规则动词的测验 **3** (strain, tax) 考验；**the climb ~ed our strength and endurance** 登山考验了我们的力气和耐力；**your behaviour is ~ing my patience** 你的行为让我难以忍受；**to ~ sth. to the limit** 最大限度地考验某物
C *vi* 检测；**to ~ for air and water pollution** 检测空气和水污染；**to ~ negative/positive** 化验呈阴性/阳性；**sugar content ~ed low** 检测出来的含糖量很低

testament /ˈtestəmənt/ *n* **1** (person's will) 遗嘱 **2** (evidence) 证明；**to be ~ to sth.** 是某事物的证明 **3** **Testament** (copy or part of the bible) 圣约书；**the Old/New T~** 《旧约全书》/《新约全书》

test: ~ ban *n* 禁止核试验；**a ~ ban treaty** 禁止核试验条约；**the T~ Ban Treaty (1963)** (1963年) 部分禁止核试验条约；**~-bed, ~-bench** *ns* 试验台；**~ bore** *n* 探孔；**~ card** *n* [调试电视机收视效果的] 测试卡；**~ case** *n* 判例；**~ drill** *n* 探孔

test drive
A *n* 试驾
B **test-drive** *vt* 试驾

tester /ˈtestə(r)/ *n* **1** (person) 测试者 **2** (device) 测试仪 **3** (sample) 试用品 [尤指化妆品]

test: ~ flight *n* 试飞；**~-fly** *vt* 试飞

testicle /ˈtestɪkl/ *n* 睾丸

testicular /teˈstɪkjʊlə(r)/ *adj* 睾丸的

testify /ˈtestɪfaɪ/
A *vt* **1** (state in court) «*witness*» 作证；**to ~ that ...** 作证说… **2** (affirm) 证实；**to ~ that ...** 证实…
B *vi* **1** (state in court) «*witness*» 作证；**to ~ in court/under oath** 出庭/宣誓作证；**to ~ for/against sb.** 提供对某人有利/不利的证词；**to ~ to sth.** 为某事作证 **2** (provide evidence) «*fact, presence, behaviour*» 证明；**to ~ to sth.** 证明某事

testily /ˈtestɪli/ *adv* 暴躁地

testimonial /ˌtestɪˈməʊnɪəl/ *n* **1** (reference) 证明信 **2** (tribute) 奖品；**to be a ~ to sth.** 是对某事的嘉奖 **3** (sports game or event) 纪念赛

testimony /ˈtestɪməni, Amer -məʊni/ *n* **1** [c and u] (statement in court) 证词；**to give ~** 作证 **2** [c and u] (statement) 说明 **3** [c] (evidence) 证明；**to be ~ to sth.** 是某事物的见证；**to bear ~ to sth.** 说明某事物

testing /ˈtestɪŋ/
A *adj* 棘手的 ‹*situation, work*›；费劲的 ‹*climb*›
B *n* [u] 检测

testing ground *n* 试验场

test market
A *n* 试销市场
B **test-market** *vt* 试销

test: ～ **marketing** *n* [u] 试销; **T**～ **match** *n* [两支板球或橄榄球队之间进行的]国际锦标赛

testosterone /teˈstɒstərəʊn/ *n* [u] 睾丸酮

test: ～ **paper** *n* **1** (written examination) 试卷; **2** (chemical paper) 试纸; ～ **pattern** *n* Amer 电视测试图案; ～ **piece** *n* 参赛演奏曲目; ～ **pilot** *n* 试飞员; ～ **run** *n* 试运行; ～ **strip** *n* 测试条

test tube *n* 试管

test-tube baby *n* 试管婴儿

testy /ˈtesti/ *adj* 暴躁的

tetanus /ˈtetənəs/ ▸**p. 377** *n* [u] 破伤风; **a** ～ **vaccine** 破伤风疫苗

tetchily /ˈtetʃɪli/ *adv* 暴躁地

tetchiness /ˈtetʃɪnɪs/ *n* [u] 暴躁

tetchy /ˈtetʃi/ *adj* 暴躁的

tête-à-tête /ˌteɪtɑːˈteɪt/
A *n* (*pl* ～ *or* ～**s**) 两人密谈; **to have a** ～ 二人促膝谈心
B *adv* 私下
C *adj* 私下的; **a** ～ **dinner** 二人私密晚餐

tether /ˈteðə(r)/
A *n* [系牲口用的] 拴绳; **to be at the end of one's** ～ 忍无可忍
B *vt* 拴; **to** ～ **sth. to sth.** 把某物拴在某物上

tetherball /ˈteðəbɔːl/ *n* [u] Amer 绳球游戏

tetrahedron /ˌtetrəˈhiːdrən, -ˈhedrən/ *n* 四面体

tetrameter /təˈtræmɪtə(r)/ *n* 四音步诗

Teutonic /tjuːˈtɒnɪk, Amer tuː-/ *adj* **1** (of modern Germans) 德国人的 ‹*thoroughness, efficiency, precision*› **2** dated (relating to ancient Germanic peoples) 日耳曼的 ‹*literature, people, invader*›

Texan /ˈteksn/
A *adj* 得克萨斯州的
B *n* 得克萨斯人

Texas /ˈteksəs/ *pr n* 得克萨斯州

Tex-Mex /ˈteksmeks/ *adj* 得墨式的

> **Tex-Mex**
>
> 得墨式。融合了墨西哥和美国西南部地区特色的食品、音乐和建筑等。Tex-Mex 由 Texan-Mexican 缩略而成，Texan 和 Mexican 分别指美国得克萨斯州和墨西哥。多作定语，如 Tex-Mex restaurant（得墨风味的餐厅）。作语言讲时，指墨西哥西班牙语（Mexican Spanish）的得克萨斯变体。

text /tekst/
A *n* **1** [u] (written matter) 文本; (in computer form) 文档 **2** [c] (wording) 原文 **3** [c] (main content) 正文 **4** [c] (book) 书籍; (textbook) 课本; **a set** ～ 指定书目 **5** [c] (passage from the Bible) [宗教仪式上引用的]《圣经》经文; fig (subject or theme for discussion) 论题 **6** [c] (mobile phone message) 短信息
B *vt* 给…发短信 ‹*person*›; 发送 ‹*message, reply*›

textbook /ˈtekstbʊk/
A *n* 课本
B *adj* 规范的 ‹*landing, description*›; **a** ～ **example** 范例

text editor *n* 文本编辑程序

textile /ˈtekstaɪl/
A *n* (fabric) 纺织品; **a** ～ **factory/worker** 纺织厂/纺织工
B **textiles** *npl* (industry) 纺织业

textile bin *n* 纺织品回收箱

text: ～ **message** *n* 短信息; ～ **messaging** /mesɪdʒɪŋ/ *n* [u] 短信息发送; ～**phone** *n* [供聋哑人使用的] 文本电话; ～ **processing** *n* [u] 文本处理; ～ **processor** *n* 文本处理器

textual /ˈtekstʃʊəl/ *adj* 文本的 ‹*analysis, study, content, error*›

textual harassment *n* [u] colloq 短信骚扰

textually /ˈtekstʃʊəli/ *adv* 在文本上

texture /ˈtekstʃə(r)/ *n* [u and c] **1** (feel) 手感 **2** (consistency) (of mixture, batter, meat) 口感; (of paint, soil) 质地 **3** (quality of life, writing, music) 韵味

textured /ˈtekstʃəd/ *adj* 起纹理的 ‹*fabric, wallpaper*›; 质地不平的 ‹*surface*›; **rough-**～ 质地粗糙的

textured vegetable protein *n* [u] 植物组织蛋白[从大豆中提取制成的肉糜状蛋白质]

TGWU *abbr* Brit = **Transport and General Workers' Union** 运输与普通工人工会

Thai /taɪ/ ▸**p. 503**
A *adj* (of Thailand) 泰国的; (of the people) 泰国人的; (of the language) 泰国语的
B *n* **1** [c] (person) 泰国人 **2** [u] (language) 泰国语

Thailand /ˈtaɪlænd/ *pr n* 泰国

thalamus /ˈθæləməs/ *n* (*pl* **thalami** /ˈθæləmaɪ/) 丘脑

thalidomide /θəˈlɪdəmaɪd/ *n* [u] 酞胺哌啶酮 [镇静剂，因有致胎儿畸形的副作用而被禁用]; **a** ～ **baby** 酞胺哌啶酮药物性畸婴

thallium /ˈθælɪəm/ *n* [u] 铊

Thames /temz/ ▸**p. 663** *pr n* **the (River)** ～ 泰晤士河

than /ðæn, ðən/ ▸**p. 140**
A *prep* **1** (in comparisons) 比; **I'm thinner** ～ **him** 我比他瘦; **we got there later** ～ **usual** 我们比平时晚到那里 **2** (expressing quantity, degree, value) …于; **less** ～ **100** 少于100; **more** ～ **half** 超过一半; **temperatures lower** ～ **30 degrees** 30度以下的温度 **3** (except for) 除…之外; **I don't know any French people other** ～ **you** 我只认识你一个法国人 **4** (in preference to) 而不是; **rather** *or* **sooner sb./sth.** ～ **sb./sth.** 宁可是某人/某事物而不是某人/某事物; **I'd rather** *or* **sooner bread** ～ **rice** 我宁愿要面包不要米饭 **5** esp Amer (from) [用以区分两个人或事物]; **to be different** ～ **sb./sth.** 与某人/某事物不同; **she is different** ～ **I'd expected** 她和我预想中的不一样
B *conj* **1** (in comparisons) 比; **she's much older** ～ **I am** 她比我大得多; **it was further away** ～ **I remembered** 它比我记忆中的更远; **there's nothing better/worse** ～ **doing sth.** 没有什么比做某事更好/更糟糕的了 **2** (except for) 除了; **we had no alternative** ～ **to buy it** 我们除了买下它别无选择 **3** (expressing preference) 而不是; **I'd sooner** *or* **rather do X** ～ **do Y, I'd do X sooner** *or* **rather** ～ **do Y** 我宁愿做X而不做Y; **he would die sooner** ～ **give in** 他宁死不屈 **4** (when) 就; **no sooner ...** ～ **..., hardly ...** ～ **..., scarcely ...** ～ **...,** 刚…就…; **no sooner had he left** ～ **the phone rang** 他刚离开电话铃就响了 **5** esp Amer (from the way that) [用以区分两个人或事物]; **they do it differently** ～ **we do** 他们的做法和我们的不同

thank /θæŋk/ ▸**p. 818** *vt* 感谢; **to** ～ **sb. for sth./doing sth.** 因某事感谢某人/感谢某人做某事; **you've only got yourself to** ～ **for that!** colloq 这事只能怪你自己！; **there's the bus,** ～ **goodness** 公共汽车来了，谢天谢地; ▸**lucky 2**

thankful /ˈθæŋkfl/ *adj* **1** (grateful, relieved) 欣慰的; **to be** ～ **for sth./to do sth.** 因某事/做某事而感到欣慰 **2** (expressing gratitude, relief) 感激的 ‹*smile, look, prayer*›

thankfully /ˈθæŋkfəli/ *adv* **1** (luckily) 幸亏; ～ **another train came along after five minutes** 幸好五分钟后又来了一列火车 **2** (with gratitude, relief) 感激地 ‹*say, acknowledge, accept*›

thankfulness /ˈθæŋkflnɪs/ *n* [u] 感谢

thankless /ˈθæŋklɪs/ *adj* **1** (unrewarding) 吃力不讨好的 ‹*task, role*› **2** (ungrateful) 忘恩负义的

thanks /θæŋks/
A *npl* **1** (expression of gratitude) 感谢; **a letter of** ～ 感谢信 **2** (allocating responsibility) 由于; ～ **to sth./sb.** 多亏了某事物/某人
B *excl* 谢谢; ～ **a lot** 多谢; **no** ～ 不用了，谢谢

thanksgiving /ˌθæŋksˈgɪvɪŋ/ *n* [u] **1** [尤指对上帝的] 感恩 **2** **Thanksgiving** Amer **T**～ **(Day)** 感恩节

thank you
A *n* (*pl* **thank yous**) 谢意; **to say one's** ～**s to sb.** 向某人表示感谢; **a** ～ **letter/present** 感谢信/答献礼物
B *excl* 谢谢你; ～ **for the lovely gift/for having me** 谢谢你送的可爱礼物/请我来; ～ **very much** 非常感谢; **no** ～ 不用了，谢谢你

that /ðæt, ðət/ ▸**p. 193**
A *det* (*pl* **those**) **1** (identifying person or thing, referring to the more distant of two, person or thing previously mentioned) 那（个）; ～ **chair/woman over there** 那边的那把椅子/那个女人; **I said** ～ **dress!** (for emphasis) 我说的是那件连衣裙！; **not** ～ **one!** 不是那个！; **I prefer** ～ **colour to this one** 我更喜欢那种颜色而不是这种; ～ **same day** 那同一天; **you can't do it** ～ **way** 你不能那样做; **he went** ～ **way** 他朝那边走了; **at** ～ **moment/time** 在那一刻/时候; ～ **train crash last year** 去年的那次火车撞车事故; ～ **lazy husband of hers** 她那个懒惰的丈夫; **it's** ～ **Mr Jones from down the road** 是路那头的那位琼斯先生 **2** formal (categorizing person or thing) 那种的; **those patients who are able to walk** 那些能行走的病人
B *pron* (*pl* **those**) **1** (identifying person or thing, referring to the more distant of two, person or thing previously mentioned) 那（个）; **what's** ～**?** 那是什么？; **who's** ～**?** 是谁啊？; **is** ～ **John?** 那是约翰吗？; **is** ～ **you, John?** 是你吗，约翰？; **we prefer this to** ～ 我们更喜欢这个而不是那个; **not this,** ～**!** (for emphasis) 不是这个，是那一个！; ～**'s what he said** 他就是这样说的; ～**'s bureaucrats for you!** 那就是你所谓的官僚！; **which boys? — those over there** 哪些男孩？——那边的那些; **those are the books I wanted** 那些书就是我想要的; **who told you** ～**?** 谁告诉你那事的？; **before** ～**, he had always lived in London** 在那之前，他一直住在伦敦; **he never went there again after** ～ 打那以后他再也没去过那儿; **he's not as greedy as (all)** ～**!** 他才没那么贪心呢！; **... and (all)** ～ Brit colloq …等等; **did you bring the contract and (all)** ～**?** 你把合同之类的都带来了吗？; **at** ～ (furthermore) 而且; (in fact) 实际上; (in reaction) 紧接着; **he managed to buy a car after all, and a nice one at** ～ 他终究设法买了一辆车，而且是辆很好的车; **with** ～ 紧接着; **with** ～ **he got up and left** 然后他起身离开了; ～ **is (to say) ...** (giving explanation) 也就是说…; (adding information) 那是说…; **you'll find her very helpful; if she's not too busy,** ～ **is** 你会发现她很乐于助人; 那是说如果她不太忙的话; ～**'s it!** (that's right) 对了！; (that's the end) 到此为止！; (that's enough) 够了！; (that's the reason) 就是那个原因！; ～**'s** ～**!** colloq 就这么定了！ **2** formal (categorizing person or thing) 那种; **those who ...** 那些…的人; **salaries are higher here than those in my country** 这儿的薪水比我们国家的高 **3** esp Brit colloq (indeed) 那样; **he's a fussy man — he is** ～ 他是个挑剔的人——的确如此
C *rel pron* **1** (introducing defining clause) [引导限定性定语从句]; **the house** ～ **they bought** 他们买的房子; **the woman** ～ **won** 获胜的那个女人; **and fool** ～ **I am, I believed him** 我真傻，竟然相信了他; **Mrs Jones, Miss Simpson** ～ **was** dated 琼斯太太，即原来的辛普森小姐 **2** (for which, in which, when) [代替

t

for which, in which, when 引导定语从句]; **the reason ~ I phoned** 我打电话的原因; **the way ~ she works** 她的工作方式; **the night ~ she arrived** 她到达的那晚

D *conj* **1** (expressing statement or hypothesis, reason or cause, result, purpose) [引导表示陈述、假设、原因、结果、目的的从句]; **he said ~ he had finished** 他说他已经完成了; **it's likely ~ they are out** 他们很可能出去了; **it's important ~ they should realize** 重要的是他们应当意识到; **he seemed pleased ~ I wanted to continue** 我想继续下去，为此他似乎很高兴; **it's just ~ I'm a bit scared** 只不过我有点害怕; **it was so cold ~ the pipes froze** 天气冷得连水管都冻住了 **2** (expressing surprise) 竟然; **~ it should come to this!** 事情怎么会这样啊！; **~ she should treat me so badly!** 她怎么能如此恶劣地对待我！ **3** liter (expressing wish) 要是…就好了; **oh ~ I could fly!** 我会飞的话该多好啊！; **oh ~ he would come** 哦，他如果能来该多好

E *adv* **1** (to such a degree, extent) 那么; **you're not ~ stupid** 你没那么蠢; **I can't do ~ much work in one day** 我一天之内做不了那么多工作; **she's ~ much smaller than me** 她个头比我小那么多 **2** (very) 非常; **not (all) ~** 不很; **it isn't (all) ~ cold** 天气不怎么冷 **3** Brit colloq (so very) 如此; **he was ~ ill that he had to go into hospital** 他病得那么厉害，只好去住院

thatch /θætʃ/

A *n* **1** [u] (roof) 茅草屋顶 **2** [u] (material) [盖屋顶用的] 茅草 **3** [c] colloq (of hair) 浓密的头发

B *vt* 用茅草盖 ‹*roof*›; **a house/cottage ~ed with reeds** 用芦苇盖顶的房子/小屋

thatched /θætʃt/ *adj* 茅草覆顶的

thatched roof *n* 茅草屋顶

thatcher /ˈθætʃə(r)/ *n* 盖茅草屋顶者

Thatcherism /ˈθætʃərɪzəm/ *n* [u] 撒切尔主义 [英国前首相撒切尔夫人所持的政治观点和政策]

thaw /θɔː/

A *vi* **1** (unfreeze) «*ice, snow*» 融化; «*ground, lake*» 化冻 **2** (defrost) «*frozen food*» 解冻 **3** (become friendly) «*atmosphere, relations*» 变得缓和; «*person*» 变得随和

B *vt* **1** (cause to unfreeze) «*sun, heat*» 使…融化 ‹*snow, ice*›; 使…化冻 ‹*ground*› **2** (defrost) 使…解冻 ‹*frozen food*›

C *n* **1** (spell of warm weather) 解冻时期 **2** (state of becoming friendly) 缓和

Phrasal verb

• **thaw out**

A *vi* **1** (unfreeze, defrost) «*frozen food, ground*» 解冻; «*person, extremities*» 暖和过来 **2** fig (become more friendly) «*atmosphere, relations*» 变得缓和

B *vt* [**~ sth. out, ~ out sth.**] 使…化冻 ‹*ground*›; 使…解冻 ‹*frozen food*›; 使…变暖 ‹*extremities*›

the /ðiː, ði, ðə/ ▸p. 2 *det* **1** (referring to person or thing mentioned or known, to unique person or thing, or specifying person or thing) [指已提及或已知的人或事物; 指独一无二的人或事物; 指特定的人或事物]; **two chapters of ~ book** 该书的两章; **I met them at ~ supermarket** 我在那家超市遇到他们; **~ Queen** 女王; **~ Nile** 尼罗河; **~ house at the end of the street** 街道尽头的那所房子; **~ fastest train** 最快的列车; **you're ~ third person to ask me that** 你是第三个问我那件事的人 **2** colloq (replacing possessive) [指代物主代词] **I'm meeting ~ boss** 我要见老板; **how's ~ family?** 家里人好吗？ **3** (with family name) [用于姓氏前] **~ Hapsburgs/Buntings** 哈布斯堡/邦廷一家 **4** (used after name) [用于姓名之后] **George ~ Sixth** 乔治六世; **Alexander ~ Great** 亚历山大大帝 **5** (preceding clause or phrase) [用于短语或从句之前] **~ fuss that he made of her** 他对她的宠爱; **~ top of a bus** 公共汽车的顶部 **6** (in generalized references) [用于某事物的泛指或总称] **to play ~ violin** 拉小提琴; **I heard it on ~ radio** 我从广播里听到的; **~ opera/ballet** 歌剧/芭蕾舞剧; **~ future** 未来 **7** (referring to species, class, or groups, or forming abstract noun) [用于单数名词前，指一类物种、一个阶层或一类人，或用于构成抽象名词] **~ dolphin/African elephant** 海豚/非洲象; **~ French** 法国人; **~ wounded/handicapped** 伤员/残疾人; **~ impossible** 不可能的事; **she buys only ~ best** 她只买最好的东西 **8** (with rates) [表示计量单位] **to do 120 miles to ~ gallon** 每加仑油跑 120 英里; **35p in ~ pound** 每磅 35 便士; **you get paid by ~ hour** 你领时薪 **9** (referring to decade) [指年代] **~ fifties** 五十年代 **10** (enough) 足够的; **he hadn't ~ courage to refuse** 他没有勇气拒绝; **we don't have ~ money for a holiday** 我们没有钱去度假 **11** (best, greatest) 最好的; **she's ~ violinist of the century** 她是本世纪最出色的小提琴家; **~ book of the year** 年度最佳书籍 **12** (famous) 有名的; **do you mean ~ William Blake?** 你说的是那个大名鼎鼎的威廉·布莱克吗？ **13** (with comparative adj or adv) [用于比较级前] **all ~ ...** 更加…; **~ news made her all ~ sadder** 这消息让她更加悲伤; **none ~ ...** 毫不…; **he seems none ~ worse for the experience** 这次经历似乎对他没有丝毫影响 **14** (in double comparatives) [两个比较级连用] **~ more ..., ~ more ...** 越…越…; **~ more I learn, ~ less I understand** 我越学越糊涂; **~ sooner, ~ better** 越快越好

theatre Brit, **theater** Amer /ˈθɪətə(r)/

A *n* **1** [c] (place) 剧场; **to go to the ~** 去看戏 **2** [u] (acting) 演戏; (drama) 戏剧; **the ~ of the absurd** 荒诞派戏剧 **3** [u and c] Brit (hospital operating room) 手术室; **to be in ~** «*patient, medical staff*» 正在做手术 **4** [c] (military area of operations) 战区; **a ~ of war** *or* **operations** 战场

B *modif* **1** (of the theatre) 剧场的 ‹*audience, seat*›; 戏剧的 ‹*buff, lover, performance, workshop*›; **a ~ ticket** 戏票 **2** Brit (of the operating room) 手术室的 ‹*staff, equipment*› **3** Amer (of the cinema) 电影院的 ‹*manager, seat*›

theatre: ~goer *n* 经常看戏的人; **~ group** *n* 剧团; **~-in-the-round** *n* [u] 圆形剧场式演出; **~land** /-lænd/ *n* [u] colloq [尤指伦敦的] 剧院区; **~ weapon** *n* 战区武器 [尤指中程导弹]

theatrical /θɪˈætrɪkl/ *adj* **1** (of the theatre) 戏剧的 **2** (exaggerated) 夸张的

theatrically /θɪˈætrɪkli/ *adv* **1** (for or of the theatre) 在戏剧方面 ‹*gifted, exciting, succeed*› **2** (exaggeratedly) 夸张地 ‹*behave, gesture, sob*›

theatricals /θɪˈætrɪklz/ *npl* [尤指业余演员的] 戏剧演出

thee /ðiː/ *pron* archaic or dial 你 [第二人称单数宾格]

theft /θeft/ *n* [c and u] 偷窃

their /ðeə(r)/ ▸p. 487 *det* **1** (of men, boys, people in general) 他们的; (of women, girls) 她们的; (of animals, things) 它们的; **parents keen to**

ℹ 'Thank you' and 'excuse me'

Expressing thanks

■ The most common expressions of thanks are: 谢谢 (thanks), 谢谢你 (thank you) as in the examples below:

Here is your tea. — Thank you
= 这是你的茶。—— 谢谢你

Shall I wait for you at the bus stop? — No, thanks
= 我在公交车站等你好吗？
—— 不用了，谢谢

Can you explain this to me? Thank you in advance
= 你能把这给我解释一下吗？先谢谢了

Thank you very much for your Christmas presents
= 谢谢你的圣诞礼物

Thank you for picking me up
= 谢谢你来接我

■ Other phrases:

That was a lovely meal. Thank you very much
= 那顿饭好极了，非常感谢

I'm sincerely grateful to you for all your help
= 我衷心感谢你所有的帮助

You've done me a big favour. I can't thank you enough
= 你帮了我的大忙。我感激不尽

I'd like to say a big thank you for your support
= 对你的支持，我深表感谢

Words can not express my gratitude to you or ***I can't express how grateful I am to you***
= 我不知如何表达我对你的谢意

Asking a favour

■ If you want to ask someone a favour, the polite way is to use 劳驾 or phrases with 劳. The literal meaning of 劳驾 is to trouble someone (for something).

Sorry to bother you. Can you help me translate the sentence into Chinese?
= 劳驾，您能帮我把这句话翻译成汉语吗？

Can you do me a favour? I'm wondering if you could give me lift
= 有劳了。不知道你能否让我搭个便车？

Can you please recommend me an interesting Chinese novel?
= 能否劳驾你向我推荐一本有趣的汉语小说？

Excusing oneself

■ 劳驾 (excuse me) is used to attract someone's attention. It is also used to ask someone politely to move so that you can pass:

Excuse me, how can I get to the railway station?
= 劳驾，到火车站怎么走？

Excuse me, can I just get past?
= 劳驾，让我过去好吗？

A. ***Excuse me!***	= 劳驾！
B. ***Can I help?***	我能帮你吗？
A. ***What time is it?***	几点了？
B. ***It's 6***	6 点
A. ***Thanks***	谢谢

help ~ children 急切希望帮助孩子的父母; some of the books had lost ~ covers 有些书的封面不见了 **2** (belonging to person or animal of unspecified sex) [指性别不详者]; I asked a friend if I could borrow ~ car 我问过一个朋友能否把车借给我

theirs /ðeəz/ ▸p. 487 *pron* **1** (referring to men, boys, people in general) 他们的; (referring to women, girls) 她们的; (referring to animals, things) 它们的; **the choice was ~** 选择权在他们手中; **my car is red but ~ is blue** 我的车是红色的，但他们的是蓝色的; **which house is ~?** 他们的房子是哪一幢?; **I'm a friend of ~** 我是他们的一个朋友; **~ was not an easy task** 他们的任务不简单 **2** (referring to person or animal of unspecified sex) [指性别不详者]; **I've got my coat, but someone's left ~ over there** 我拿了我的外套，但有人把外套落在那儿了

theism /'θiːɪzəm/ *n* [u] 有神论

theist /'θiːɪst/ *n* 有神论者

theistic /θiː'ɪstɪk/ *adj* 有神论的

them /ðem, ðəm/ *pron* **1** (referring to men, boys, people in general) 他们; (referring to women, girls) 她们; (referring to animals, things) 它们; **I know ~** 我认识他们; **both of ~ work in London** 他们俩都在伦敦工作 **2** (referring to person or animal of unspecified sex) [指性别不详者]; **I phoned a friend and asked ~ to help** 我给一个朋友打了电话求助

thematic /θɪ'mætɪk/ *adj* 主题的

theme /θiːm/

A *n* **1** (topic) 主题; **on the ~ of ...** 关于…主题; **a ~ bar/party** 主题酒吧/聚会 **2** (musical motif) 主旋律

B *vt* 赋予…某种主题; **the amusement park will be ~d as a Caribbean pirate stronghold** 这个游乐园的主题将被定为加勒比海盗要塞

theme: ~ music *n* [u] 主题音乐; **~ park** *n* 主题公园; **~ pub** *n* Brit 主题酒馆; **~ restaurant** *n* 主题餐厅; **~ song** *n* **1** (song) 主题歌; **2** (sth. frequently repeated) 套话; **~ tune** *n* **1** Cin, Theat 主旋律; **2** = signature tune

themselves /ðəm'selvz/ *pron* **1** (reflexive) (referring to men, boys, people in general) 他们自己; (referring to women, girls) 她们自己; (referring to animals, things) 它们自己; **(all) by ~** (alone) 他们独自地; (unaided) 他们独立地; **(all) to ~** 完全归他们享用 **2** (reflexive) (referring to person or animal of unspecified sex) [指性别不详者]; **I hope nobody will burn ~** 我希望谁都别烧伤自己; **anyone who tells ~ that is a fool** 任何对自己那样说的人都是傻子; **everyone looked very pleased with ~** 大家看上去都沾沾自喜 **3** (emphatic) 他们亲自; **both doctors said so ~** 两个医生都亲口这样说了; **they saw it for ~** 他们亲眼看到了它 **4** (in normal state) 正常状态; **they're not ~ today** 他们今天不对劲; **they hadn't felt ~ for a long time now** 他们感觉不舒服有很长时间了 **5** (not influenced by others) 独立自主; **they needed space to be ~** 他们需要独立的空间

then /ðen/

A *adv* **1** (at that time) (in the past) 当时; (in the future) 到那时; **we were living in Dublin ~** 我们那时住在都柏林; **people were idealistic ~** 当时人们耽于空想; **X, ~ leader of the party** 某某，当时的该党领袖; **I thought so ~, and I still think so** 我过去这么想，现在还是这么想; **just ~** 就在那时; **from ~ on** 从那时起; **since ~** 自那以后; **back ~** 当初; **by** *or* **until ~** 到那时; **they will let us know by ~** 届时他们会让我们知道的; **between ~ and ...** 从那时起到…期间; **between now and ~** 从现在起到那时; **~ and there** 立即; **before ~** 在那之前; **even ~ it still won't be completely finished** 即使到那时还是不会全部完成 **2** (in sequences: afterwards, next) 然后; **wash, ~ slice finely** 先清洗，然后切成薄片; **~ came the big news** 接着传来了重大新闻; **she was an editor, ~ a teacher** 她当过编辑，后来做了教师; **we will ~ start the next project** 我们接下来会开始下一个项目; **~, after that ...** 接着，在那之后…; **and ~ what?** 然后又怎么样?; **and ~ some** colloq 而且还不止这些 **3** (in that case, rounding off, focusing on a topic) 那么; **I saw them if not yesterday, ~ the day before** 我不是在昨天就是在前天见到过他们; **if it's a problem for you, ~ say so** 如果这对你是个问题的话，那就直说吧; **if x = 3, ~ 6x = 18** Math 若 x = 3，则 6x = 18; **when we know what the problem is, ~ we can find a solution** 我们弄清问题就能找到解决方法; **~ why did you tell her?** 那你为什么要告诉她呢?; **well, try this ~** 好吧，那就试试这个; **is it all arranged ~?** 那么一切都安排好了?; **till Tuesday ~** 那就周二见吧; **now ~, what's all this?** 那这是怎么一回事?; **all right ~, who'd like some coffee?** 那好吧，谁想喝咖啡? **4** (summarizing statement: therefore) 总之; **these, ~, are the results of the policy** 总之，这些就是这一政策的结果; **overall ~ it would seem that ...** 而总体上看似乎… **5** (in addition, besides) 而且; **and ~ there's the cost to consider** 况且还要考虑成本 **6** (on the other hand) 另外; **she's good, but ~ so is he** 她不错，可他也一样好; **he looks anxious, but ~ (again) he always does** 他看上去很焦急，不过他一贯如此

B *adj attrib* 当时的; **the ~ mayor of New York, Mr X** 当时的纽约市市长某某先生; **they took over the ~ state-owned sugar factory** 他们接管了那家当时属国有的糖厂

thence /ðens/ *adv* formal **1** (from there) 从那里 ‹*go, travel*› **2** (therefore) 因此

theocracy /θɪ'ɒkrəsi/ *n* **1** [u] (system) 神权制 **2** [c] (state) 神权国 **3** [c] (government) 神权政体

theocratic /ˌθɪə'krætɪk/ *adj* 神权的

theodolite /θɪ'ɒdəlaɪt/ *n* 经纬仪

theologian /ˌθɪə'ləʊdʒən/ *n* 神学家

theological /ˌθɪə'lɒdʒɪkl/ *adj* 神学的

theology /θɪ'ɒlədʒi/ *n* [u and c] 神学

theorem /'θɪərəm/ *n* 定理

theoretical /ˌθɪə'retɪkl/, **theoretic** /ˌθɪə'retɪk/ *adjs* **1** (hypothetical) 假设的 ‹*advantage, possibility, limit*› **2** (involving theory) 理论的 ‹*study, framework, basis*›; **~ physics** 理论物理学

theoretically /ˌθɪə'retɪkli/ *adv* 理论上; **~ speaking** 从理论上说

theoretician /ˌθɪərɪ'tɪʃn/, **theorist** /'θɪərɪst/ *ns* 理论家

theorize /'θɪəraɪz/

A *vi* 从理论上说明; **to ~ about sth.** 从理论上说明某事物

B *vt* 从理论上说明; **to ~ that ...** 从理论上说明…

theory /'θɪəri/ *n* **1** [c] (hypothesis) 学说; **the ~ of evolution/relativity** 进化论/相对论; **my ~ would be that ...** 我的看法是… **2** [u and c] (general principle, set of principles) 理论; **a ~ of education** 教育理论; **in ~** 在理论上

theosophical /ˌθiːə'sɒfɪkl/ *adj* 神智学的

theosophist /θɪ'ɒsəfɪst/ *n* 神智学者

theosophy /θiː'ɒsəfi/ *n* [u] 神智学 [宣称依赖直觉领悟神性的学说]

therapeutic /ˌθerə'pjuːtɪk/ *adj* **1** (beneficial) 有益健康的 ‹*exercise, massage, intervention*›; **a ~ shampoo** 保健香波 **2** (relating to healing) 治疗的; **~ facilities/efficacy** 治疗设施/疗效

therapeutics /ˌθerə'pjuːtɪks/ *npl + v sing* [u] 治疗学

therapist /'θerəpɪst/ *n* **1** (specialist in therapy) 治疗专家 **2** (psychotherapist) 心理治疗师

therapy /'θerəpi/ *n* [u and c] **1** (medical treatment) 治疗; **music ~** 音乐疗法; **a course of antibiotic ~** 抗生素疗程 **2** (psychotherapy) 心理治疗

there /ðeə(r)/ ▸p. 193

A *adv* **1** (that place or position) 那里; (at or in that place) 在那里; (to that place) 到那里; **far/two kilometres from ~** 离那里很远/两公里; **I live near ~** 我住在那附近; **up/down to ~** 到那里; **put it in ~** 把它放在那里面; **in ~ please** (ushering sb.) 请进; **put the bags on ~** 把包放在那上面; **we're almost ~** 我们就快到了; **are you still ~?** (on phone) 你还在听吗?; **back ~** 在后面; **the fact is, they're ~ to make money** 事实是，他们就是要赚钱; **to go ~ and back in an hour** 一小时内去那儿一个来回; **to stand/stop ~** 站/停在那儿; **sign ~ please** 请在那儿签名; **my colleague ~ will show you** 我在那儿的同事会给你看; **what does it say ~?** 那上面怎么说的?; **~ it is!** 就在那儿!; **~ you are!** (seeing sb. arrive) 你来了呀!; **~'s a bus coming** 有辆公共汽车开过来了; **that ~ contraption** colloq 那小玩意儿; **~ and then** 立即; **been, ~ done that** colloq 没意思; **to be ~ for sb.** 随时在某人左右; **to have been ~ before** colloq 以前也经历过 **2** (existing or available) 可得的; **the money's ~ if you need it** 如果你需要钱的话就来取; **take the offer while it's ~** 趁报价还没撤销赶快接受吧 **3** (at that point) 在那一点上; (in that respect) 在那方面; **~ we must finish** 我们到此得结束了; **I'd like to interrupt you ~** 我想在这里插一句话; **~ was our chance** 那就是我们的机会; **I think you're wrong ~** 我认为在那一点上你错了; **you've got me ~!** 你把我难倒了!; **~ again** 但反过来; **he may be guilty; ~ again he may not** 他可能有罪，但也可能无罪 **4** (attracting sb.'s attention) [用以引起注意]; **hello ~!** 你好!; **hey, you ~!** 嘿，说你呢! **5** (giving sth.) 拿去吧; **~ you are** *or* **go** 给你; **~'s the book you wanted to borrow** 这就是你想借的书 **6** (on hearing sth.) [用以引起注意]; **~ goes the phone** 电话铃响啦; **listen, ~'s my sister calling** 听，我姐姐在叫呢 **7** (pointing out fact or situation) [用以指出某种情况或形势]; **~'s why!** 就是这个原因!; **so, ~ you have it: that's how it all started** 所以，你看，一切就是那样开始的; **~ it is** colloq 情况就是这样; **~ you are** *or* **go** colloq (explaining or showing sth.) 你看; (expressing resignation) 就这样吧; **~ you are! I told you it was easy!** 怎么样! 我告诉过你很简单!; **~ you go again** colloq 你又来了; **finish your lunch, ~'s a good boy** colloq 把午饭吃完，乖孩子; **~'s devotion for you** colloq 这才叫忠诚; **~'s gratitude for you!** iron 这真称得上感激啊!

B *pron* [表示存在或发生]; **~ is** *or* **are ...** 有…; **~ is some left** 还剩下一些; **~'s only four days left** colloq 只剩四天了; **~'s no denying that ...** 不可否认…; **~ seems** *or* **appears to be ...** 似乎有…; **~ remains the problem of finance** formal 还有财政问题没解决; **once upon a time ~ was ...** liter 从前有…; **suddenly ~ appeared a fairy** liter 突然出现了一位仙女

C *excl* **1** (expressing satisfaction, annoyance) 你瞧; **~! I told you!** 看到了吧! 我告诉过你的!; **~! you've gone and woken the baby!** 瞧! 你竟然一去就把宝宝吵醒了! **2** colloq (comforting) 好了; **~, ~!** 好啦，好啦!

thereabouts /ˌðeərə'baʊts/ Brit, **thereabout** /'ðeərəbaʊt/ Amer ▸p. 32 *adv* **1** (near that place) 在那附近; **the key is on the table or ~** 钥匙在桌上或是附近的地方 **2** (around that time) 大约在那时; **at 3 o'clock or ~** 3 点钟左右 **3** (around that amount) 大约那个数目; **£500 or ~** 大约 500 英镑

thereafter /ˌðeər'ɑːftə(r), Amer -'æftər/ *adv* formal 此后

thereby /ˌðeə'baɪ, 'ðeə-/ *adv* 因此

there'd /ðeəd/ colloq **1** = **there had** ▸**have C1** **2** = **there would** ▸**would**

therefore /'ðeəfɔː(r)/ *adv* 所以；**I think, ～ I am** 我思故我在

therein /ˌðeər'ɪn/ *adv* archaic or formal **1** (in that respect) 在那方面；**～ lies the difficulty/the key to his success** 那就是困难所在/他成功的秘诀 **2** (in that place) 在其中

there'll /ðeəl/ colloq = **there will** ▸**will**[1]

thereof /ðeər'ɒv/ *adv* formal 其；**born in Britain and subject to the laws ～** 生于英国并受其法律约束

thereon /ˌðeər'ɒn/ *adv* formal 由此

there's /ðeəz/ colloq **1** = **there is** ▸**be A** **2** = **there has** ▸**have C1**

thereto /ðeə'tuː/ *adv* archaic or formal 对此；**the third party assents ～** 第三方对此表示同意

thereunder /ˌðeər'ʌndə(r)/ *adv* archaic or formal 据此

thereupon /ˌðeərə'pɒn/ *adv* formal **1** (immediately) 随即；(for that reason) 于是 **2** (on that) 在其上；**the words written ～** 其上所书文字

therewith /ðeə'wɪð/ *adv* archaic or formal **1** (attached) 与此；**the documents enclosed ～** 随附文件 **2** (with it) 随之；**the person charged ～ in the High Court** 随后在高等法院受到指控的那个人

therm /θɜːm/ *n* 撤姆［英国的煤气热量单位，合10万英制热单位］

thermal /'θɜːml/

A *adj* **1** (relating to heat) 热的；**～ energy** 热能；**a ～ power station** 热电站；**～ reactor** 热反应堆；**～ unit** 热量单位 **2** = **geothermal** **3** (retaining heat) 保暖的 ‹*garment, underwear*›

B *n* 上升热气流

C **thermals** *npl* 保暖内衣

thermal: ～ baths *npl* 温泉浴；**～ efficiency** *n* [u] 热效率；**～ imaging** *n* [u] 热成像

thermic /'θɜːmɪk/ *adj* 热的；**～ energy/response** 热能/热反应

thermionic /ˌθɜːmɪ'ɒnɪk/ *adj* 热离子的

thermionics /ˌθɜːmɪ'ɒnɪks/ *npl* + *v sing* 热离子学

thermionic valve Brit, **thermionic tube** Amer *ns* 热离子管

thermobaric /ˌθɜːməʊ'bærɪk/ *adj* 热气压的

thermocouple /'θɜːməʊkʌpl/ *n* 热电偶

thermodynamic /ˌθɜːməʊdaɪ'næmɪk/ *adj* 热力学的；**～ equilibrium** 热动平衡

thermodynamics /ˌθɜːməʊdaɪ'næmɪks/ *npl* + *v sing* 热力学

thermoelectric /ˌθɜːməʊɪ'lektrɪk/ *adj* 温差电的

thermograph /'θɜːməgrɑːf, Amer -græf/ *n* 温度记录器

thermography /θɜː'mɒgrəfi/ *n* [u] 温度记录法

thermoluminescence /ˌθɜːməʊluːmɪ'nesns/ *n* [u] 热发光

thermometer /θə'mɒmɪtə(r)/ *n* (for measuring temperature of air, oven, meat, etc.) 温度计；(for measuring body temperature) 体温表；**a digital/electronic/mercury ～** 数字/电子/水银温度计

thermonuclear /ˌθɜːməʊ'njuːklɪə(r), Amer -'nuː-/ *adj* **1** (related to high temperatures) 热核的；**～ reaction/fusion** 热核反应/聚变 **2** (related to weapons) 热核武器的 ‹*war, test*›；**a ～ bomb/weapon/warhead** 热核弹/武器/弹头

thermopile /'θɜːməʊpaɪl/ *n* 热电堆

thermoplastic /ˌθɜːməʊ'plæstɪk/

A *adj* 可热塑的

B *n* 热塑性塑料

Thermos® /'θɜːməs/, **Thermos flask** Brit, **Thermos bottle** Amer *ns* 瑟姆斯保温瓶

thermostat /'θɜːməstæt/ *n* 温度自动调节器

thermostatic /ˌθɜːmə'stætɪk/ *adj* 温度自动调节器的

thermostatically controlled /ˌθɜːmə'stætɪkli kən̩trəʊld/ *adj* 温度自动调节的

thesaurus /θɪ'sɔːrəs/ *n* (*pl* **thesauri** /θɪ'sɔːraɪ/ *or* **～es**) **1** (of synonyms) 同义词词典 **2** (of keywords) 主题词表 **3** (of particular field) 分类词典

these /ðiːz/ ▸**p. 193** *pl* ▸**this A, B**

thesis /'θiːsɪs/ *n* (*pl* **theses** /'θiːsiːz/) **1** (dissertation) 论文；**a postgraduate/doctoral/master's ～** 硕士/博士/学士学位论文；**a ～ on sth.** 有关某课题的论文 **2** (argument) 论点

thespian /'θespɪən/ formal or hum

A *n* 演员

B *adj* 戏剧的

they /ðeɪ/ *pron* **1** (men, boys, people in general) 他们；(women, girls) 她们；(animals, things) 它们；**～ go on the bottom shelf** 这些东西放在底层架子上；**here/there ～ are!** 他们在这儿/那儿呢！；**～ won't be there** 他们不会在那里；**she bought one, but ～ didn't** 她买了一个，但他们没买；**things ain't what ～ used to be** colloq 时过境迁 **2** (person, animal of unspecified sex) ［指性别不详者］；**anyone can join if ～ are a resident** 任何常住居民都可参加；**ask a friend if ～ can help** 问问有没有朋友能帮忙 **3** (people in general) 人们；**the rest, as ～ say, is history** 后来的事就尽人皆知，不须赘述了 **4** (people in authority, experts) ［指有权势有地位者］；**～ cut my water off** 管事的人把我的水停了；**I asked whether ～ could change my ticket** 我问过票务是否能给我换票；**～ now say that red wine is good for you** 如今专家说红葡萄酒有益健康

they'd /ðeɪd/ colloq **1** = **they had** ▸**have** **2** = **they would** ▸**would**

they'll /ðeɪl/ colloq = **they will** ▸**will**[1]

they're /ðeə(r)/ colloq = **they are** ▸**be**

they've /ðeɪv/ colloq = **they have** ▸**have**

thiamine /'θaɪəmɪn, -miːn/ *n* [u] 硫胺素［即维生素B］

thick /θɪk/

A *adj* **1** (broad, fat) 厚的 ‹*sweater, book, lips*›；粗的 ‹*wool, rope, waist*›；粗体的 ‹*print*›；**a ～ layer of snow** 厚厚的一层雪；**three inches/feet ～** 3 英寸/英尺厚；**made of six-inch ～ steel** 用 6 英寸厚的钢板制成的；**to give sb./get a ～ ear** colloq 打某人耳光/挨耳光；**to have a ～ head** colloq 头晕脑涨；**to have (a) ～ skin** colloq 脸皮厚 **2** (dense) 茂密的 ‹*forest, vegetation, hedge*›；浓密的 ‹*hair, eyebrows, beard*›；浓的 ‹*fog, cloud, smoke*› **3** (abundantly covered) 密布的；**windows ～ with grime and dirt** 落满尘垢的窗户；**a river ～ with waste** 布满垃圾的河流；**the air/room was ～ with smoke** 空气中/房间里烟雾弥漫；**the ground was ～ with ants** 地面上爬满了蚂蚁 **4** (concentrated) 黏稠的 ‹*liquid, paste*›；**～ soup** 浓汤；**to make sth. ～** 使某物变得黏稠 **5** (husky) 沙哑的 ‹*voice*›；**～ with emotion** 因激动而嗓音沙哑的 **6** (pronounced) 浓重的 ‹*accent*› **7** colloq (stupid) 愚蠢的；**to be as ～ as a brick** *or* **as two short planks** 笨得要死 **8** *pred* colloq (close, intimate) 亲密的；**to be ～ with sb.** 与某人过于亲近；▸**thief** **9** (unreasonable) 过分的；**that's a bit ～** colloq 那有点过分

B *adv* 厚厚地 ‹*slice, cut*›；**to lay it on ～** colloq 夸大其词；**the lies/insults were coming ～ and fast** 谎言/辱骂纷至沓来；**her tears fell ～ and fast** 她泪如雨下

C *n* [u] 厚的部分；**the bullet had hit him in the ～ of the leg** 子弹射在他的大腿上；**to be in the ～ of sth.** (in busiest part) 在某事物最繁忙的时候；(in most crowded part) 在某事物最密集处；**to be in the ～ of the battle** 在战斗白热化的时候；**I found myself in the ～ of things** 我发觉自己已深深卷入其中；**through ～ and thin** 不顾艰难险阻；**he remained a true friend through ～ and thin** 无论在顺境还是逆境中，他都是一个真正的朋友

thicken /'θɪkən/

A *vt* 使…变得黏稠 ‹*liquid, paste*›

B *vi* «*snow*» 变厚；«*neck, waist*» 变粗；«*forest, vegetation*» 变得茂密；«*liquid, paste*» 变得黏稠；«*fog, smoke*» 变浓；«*voice*» 变得沙哑；**the mist had ～ed into a dense fog** 薄雾变成了浓雾；**the plot ～s** 情节变得错综复杂

thickener /'θɪkənə(r)/, **thickening** /'θɪkənɪŋ/ *ns* [u and c] 增稠剂

thicket /'θɪkɪt/ *n* 灌木丛

thickhead /'θɪkhed/ *n* colloq 傻瓜

thickheaded /ˌθɪk'hedɪd/ *adj* colloq 愚蠢的

thickie /'θɪki/ *n* colloq 笨蛋

thick: ～-knit *n* [u] 厚羊毛针织物；**～-lipped** *adj* 嘴唇厚的

thickly /'θɪkli/ *adv* 密集地 ‹*fall*›；厚厚地 ‹*spread, cut*›；沙哑地 ‹*speak, reply*›；**a ～-wooded landscape** 树林密布的景色；**～ covered with** *or* **in sth.** 厚厚覆盖着某物

thickness /'θɪknɪs/ *n* **1** [u] (state or quality of being thick) (of wall, material, lips) 厚；(of waist, ankles) 粗；(of features) 粗犷；(of hair) 浓密；(of fog, mist, smoke) 浓；(of forest, hedge, foliage) 茂密；(of voice) 沙哑；(of accent) 浓重；**a piece of wood half an inch in ～** 一块半英寸厚的木板 **2** [c] (width) 厚度；**wood in different ～es** 不同厚度的木头 **3** [c] (layer of specified material) 层 **4** [u] (broad or deep part) 厚的部分；**the beams were set into the ～ of the walls** 横梁架在了墙壁的最厚处 **5** colloq (stupidity) 愚蠢

thicko /'θɪkəʊ/ *n* colloq 傻瓜

thick: ～set *adj* **1** (stocky) 粗壮的；**2** (with closely growing bushes) 稠密的 ‹*hedge*›；**～-skinned** *adj* 厚脸皮的 ‹*person*›；**～-skulled** /ˌθɪk'skʌld/ *adj* 愚钝的

thief /θiːf/ *n* (*pl* **thieves**) 小偷；**stop ～!** 捉贼！；**a thieves' kitchen, a den of thieves** 贼窝；**set a ～ to catch a ～** 以毒攻毒；**like a ～ in the night** 偷偷摸摸地；**to be as thick as thieves** 亲密无间

thieve /θiːv/ *vt* 偷

thievery /'θiːvəri/ *n* [u] 偷窃

thieves /θiːvz/ *pl* ▸**thief**

thieving /'θiːvɪŋ/ colloq

A *adj attrib* 偷窃的；**～ children** 爱小偷小摸的孩子

B *n* [u] 偷窃

thievish /'θiːvɪʃ/ *adj* 好偷窃的

thigh /θaɪ/ *n* **1** [c] (part of leg) 大腿；**a ～ muscle** 大腿肌肉 **2** [c and u] (top of chicken leg) 鸡腿

thigh: ～bone *n* 股骨；**～boot** *n* ［高及大腿的］长统靴

thimble /'θɪmbl/ *n* 顶针

thimbleful /'θɪmblfʊl/ *n* 极少量［尤指酒］；**a ～ of vodka** 一点点伏特加

thin /θɪn/

A *adj* **1** (slim, bony) 瘦的 ‹*person*›；**he's very ～ in the face** 他脸很瘦；**a man with a long ～ nose** 长着瘦削高鼻子的男人；**to be as ～ as a rake** 骨瘦如柴 **2** (not thick) 细的 ‹*stripe, stick, cord*›；薄的 ‹*layer, paper, lips*›；**a ～ trickle** 涓涓细流；**(it's) the ～ end of the wedge** fig （这是）冰山一角 **3** (watery) 稀的 ‹*liquid, gravy, soup, oil*›；**～ blood** 稀薄的血；**a bowl of ～ gruel** 一碗稀粥 **4** (fine) 稀薄的；**to vanish** *or* **disappear into ～ air** 消失得无影无踪 **5** (sparse) 稀疏的 ‹*hair, forest, population*›；**a ～ straggly beard** 稀疏蓬乱的胡须；**to be** *or* **get ～ on top** colloq 开始谢顶；**to be ～ on the ground** 寥寥无几；**to**

get *or* **become** *or* **grow ~ner** 变得更加稀少 **6▸** fig (unconvincing) 空泛的 ‹*storyline*›; 空洞的 ‹*excuse, argument*›; **a ~ alibi/disguise** 空洞的托词/容易识破的伪装; **to have a ~ time of it** (not very fortunate) 不太走运; (not very prosperous) 处境艰难 **7▸** (in tone) (high-pitched) 尖细的; (weak) 微弱的 **8▸** Fin 不景气的 ‹*trading*›

B *adv* colloq 薄薄地; **to spread/cut sth. ~** 薄薄地涂一层某物/把某物切成薄片

C *vt* **1▸** (dilute) 稀释 ‹*paint*›; 使…变淡 ‹*sauce, soup*› **2▸** (make less dense) 使…稀疏 ‹*plants, vegetation*›

D *vi* «*fog, cloud*» 变稀薄; «*crowd*» 变稀少; «*hair*» 变稀疏

Phrasal verbs

- **thin down**

A *vt* [**~ sth. down, ~ down sth.**] 稀释 ‹*paint*›; 使…变淡 ‹*sauce, soup*›

B *vi* «*person*» 消瘦

- **thin out**

A *vt* [**~ sth. out, ~ out sth.**] 使…稀疏 ‹*seedlings, plants, population*›

B *vi* «*fog, crowd*» 散开; «*traffic*» 变稀少

thin-cut *adj* 切成薄片的; **~ slices of ham** 火腿薄片

thine /ðaɪn/ archaic

A *pron* 你的 [第二人称单数物主代词]

B *adj* 你的 [第二人称单数所有格，用在元音前]

thing /θɪŋ/

A *n* **1▸** (object) 东西; **I haven't got a ~ to wear!** 我没衣服穿了! ; **there's not a ~ to eat in the house!** 屋里一点吃的也没有! ; **what's that ~?** colloq 那是什么东西? ; **what's this ~ for?** colloq 这东西是干什么用的? ; **a big box ~** colloq 大箱子一样的东西; **sweet ~s** 甜食; **there was not a living ~ to be seen in the desert** 沙漠里看不到一个活物; **to see/hear ~s** colloq 产生幻觉/出现幻听; **a ~ of beauty is a joy for ever** Prov 美好的事物是永恒的喜悦 **2▸** (task, action, deed, matter, etc.) 事情; (event) 事件; **I've got ~s to do** 我有事要做; **a difficult ~ to do** 难处理的事; **the right/wrong ~ to do** 应该/不应该做的事; **the first/last ~ to do** 首先/最不该做的事; **the best ~ would be to go** 最好还是去; **that was the worst ~ you could have done** 这事你做得糟糕透了; **an awful ~ happened to me!** 我遇到一件可怕的事! ; **that's a nice** *or* **fine ~ to do** iron 那件事做得可真妙啊; **he did the right ~ by her and apologized** 他向她道歉是做对了; **he did the decent ~ and resigned** 他辞职是做了一件体面的事; **sure ~** esp Amer colloq 当然; **a sure ~** 必定成功的事情; **to do great ~s** 获得成功; **to do (odd) ~s to sb./sth.** 对某人/某事物产生（奇怪的）影响; **to be on to a good ~** colloq 过上舒适的日子; **he's on to a good ~: he married the boss's daughter!** 他交上好运，娶了老板的女儿! ; **one ~ leads to another** 有一就有二; **one ~ is obvious/certain** 有一点是显而易见/肯定的; **the first ~ we must consider is …** 我们首先必须考虑…; **financial/artistic/spiritual ~s** 财政/艺术/精神问题; **it's** *or* **it was (just) one of those ~s** 这是没有办法的事; **I didn't mean to break the vase; it was just one of those ~s** 我无意打碎花瓶，但碎了也只能碎了; **it's one (damned) ~ after another!** colloq 真是祸不单行! ; **what with one ~ and another, I …** colloq 因为杂七杂八的事情，我…; **for one ~ …, and for another ~ …** 一方面…，另一方面…; **if there's one ~ I hate, it's …** 要说到招我讨厌的东西的话，那就是…; **not to know the first ~ about sth.** 对某物一无所知; **to know a ~ or two (about sb./sth.)** colloq (have knowledge) （对某人/某事）非常了解; (have experience) （对某人/某事）有丰富经验; **there's a ~ or two I know about Jane that would surprise you!** 我所知道关于简的一些事情会让你吃惊的! ; **we certainly showed them a ~ or two!** 我们当然让他们有所见识了! ; **to tell sb. a ~ or two (about sb./sth.)** 给某人透露（关于某人/某事物的）秘密; **to make a big ~ of** *or* **out of sth.** colloq 对某事小题大做; **~s of the flesh** [与性有关的] 皮肉之事 **3▸** (statement) 话语; **I said no such ~!** 我没有说过这样的话! ; **to say the right/wrong ~** 说对/说错话; **I couldn't think of a ~ to say!** 我想不出来该说什么! ; **we've heard dreadful ~s about them!** 我们听说了有关他们的可怕事情! **4▸ the ~** (appropriate, suitable matter) 合适的事情; (most important matter) 最重要的事情; **the ~ is …** 需要考虑的是…; **the ~ is, what should we do next?** 问题是，我们下一步该怎样做? ; **the ~ about sb./sth.** 某人/某事物的特点; **the main ~ (to do) is to keep fit and healthy** 关键的问题是保持健康; **to become quite the ~** 成为流行时尚; **just the ~, the very ~** 正是所需要的东西; **the in ~** 时髦的事物; **the done ~** 合乎规范的做法; **the latest ~ (in sth.)** （某方面）最时髦的东西; **to be not the ~ to do** 不符合社会习俗 **5▸** (person, animal) 家伙; **she's a funny, little ~** 她是个有趣的小家伙; **old ~** dated 老伙计; **you lucky ~!** 你这家伙真走运! **6▸** (idea) 想法; **to say the first ~ that comes into one's head** 想到什么就说什么; **to have a ~ about sb./sth.** colloq (like) 对某人/某事物有好感; (be obsessed by) 对某人/某事物着迷; (be prejudiced against) 对某人/某事物有偏见 **7▸** colloq (special interest) [特殊的] 兴趣; **his ~ is cooking** 他的兴趣是烹饪; **to do one's (own) ~** (follow one's own interests and inclinations) 做自己爱做的事; (be independent) 自立; **a loner, who likes to do his own ~** 喜欢自行其是的离群之人; **it's a guy/girl ~** 这是男人/女孩子的事情 **8▸** (monstrous entity) 怪物; **a black, slimy ~** 黑乎乎的黏滑怪物

B things *npl* **1▸** (belongings) [个人的] 物品; **bathing** *or* **swimming ~s** 泳装; **family ~s** 家财; **one's ~s** 个人财物 **2▸** (equipment) 用具; **gardening/DIY ~s** 园艺用具/自己动手用的工具; **wash up the breakfast ~s!** 把早餐餐具给洗了! **3▸** (circumstances) 形势; (conditions) 情况; **how are ~s with you?** 你过得怎么样? ; **how are ~s going?** 近来怎么样? ; **~s are going from bad to worse/are on the up-and-up/are pretty normal** 情况越来越糟/越来越好/很正常; **all sorts** *or* **manner of ~s** 各种情况; **all ~s considered …** 总的说来，…; **in all ~s** 在任何情况下; **(to try) to be all ~s to all people** *or* **men** （试图）八面玲珑; **to change/spoil ~s** 改变局势/扫兴; **~s improve** *or* **get better/deteriorate** *or* **get worse** 形势好转/恶化; **~s take a turn for the better/worse** 局势日趋好转/恶化; **these ~s are sent to try us** 这是对我们的考验; **as ~s stand** 目前的情况是; **as ~s are, …** 按现状看来，…; **~s don't look too good** *or* **bright** 情况看来不妙; **~s are looking up** 情况正在好转; **to take ~s as they come** 顺其自然; **~s aren't what they used to be** 今非昔比; **of all ~s** 在所有情况中偏偏; **he gave her a snake of all ~s!** 他竟然给了她一条蛇! ; **and then, of all ~s, she …** 后来，真没想到，她… **4▸** (matters) 事物; **he's fascinated by ~s Chinese** 他对中国的东西着了迷; **~s eternal and ~s temporal** 永恒和暂时的事物; **all ~s bright and beautiful** 一切光明美丽的事物; **he hasn't a clue about ~s feminine** 他对女人的事情一窍不通

thingumabob /ˈθɪŋəməbɒb/, **thingumajig** /ˈθɪŋəmədʒɪɡ/ *ns* colloq = **thingummy**

thingummy /ˈθɪŋəmi/, **thingy** /ˈθɪŋi/ *ns* colloq (person) 某某; (thing) 那东西

think /θɪŋk/

A *vi* (*pt, pp* **thought**) **1▸** (be capable of thought) 有思考能力; **humans are the only animals that ~** 人是唯一有思想的动物 **2▸** (engage in thought) 思索; **~ before you act!** 想好了再行动! ; **let me ~ a moment** 让我考虑一下; **to make sb. ~** 使某人深思; **she's always ~ing about her children** 她总是想着孩子们; **to ~ on one's feet** (react quickly) 反应快; (be mentally agile) 思维敏捷; **to ~ hard/clearly/carefully** 苦苦思索/清晰地思考/仔细考虑; **to ~ as** *or* **like sb.** 像某人一样思考; **to ~ in French** 用法语思维; **to ~ for oneself** (form one's own opinions) 有主见; (make decisions) 自行决定 **3▸** (consider) **to ~ of** *or* **about sb./sth.** 考虑某人/某事物; **he's ~ing of** *or* **about resignation** *or* **resigning** 他正打算辞职; **just ~ of your family!** 想想你的家人吧! ; **to ~ of** *or* **about oneself** 为自己考虑; **to ~ of** *or* **about sb.'s feelings** 顾及某人的感受; **to ~ on it** colloq 思考这件事; **well ~ again** 还是改主意吧 **4▸** (have in mind or have the idea) **to ~ of sth./doing sth.** 想到某事物/做某事; **she's ~ing of a career in nursing** 她有意从事护士职业; **don't even ~ of it!** 想都不要想! ; **I don't ~!** iron 我才不信呢! ; **I couldn't ~ of letting you take the blame** 我没想过让你承受指责; **she'd never ~ of marrying anyone** 她根本不想嫁人 **5▸** (imagine) **to ~ of sth./doing sth.** 设想某事物/做某事; **just ~!** 想一想吧! ; **just ~, if we won the lottery we would never have to work again!** 想想吧，假如我们彩票中了奖，就再也不用工作了! ; **just ~ of what it would cost!** 想想这会花多少钱! ; **to ~ of his not knowing all about it!** 设想一下，他居然对此事一无所知! **6▸** (remember) **to ~ of sb./sth.** 记得某人/某事物; **to ~ about** *or* **of the past** 回想过去; **I thought about** *or* **of her only yesterday** 我昨天才想起她来; **if you ~ of anything else (we need to buy)** 如果你想起（我们需要买的）任何其他东西 **7▸** (suggest, make mental choice) **to ~ of sth./doing sth.** 想出某事/做某事; **who first thought of the idea?** 谁先想出这个主意的? ; **~ of a number, then double it** 想一个数字，然后乘以 2 **8▸** (have opinion) **to ~ of sb./sth.** 看待某人/某事物; **what do you ~ of my idea?** 你觉得我的主意怎么样? ; **to ~ of sb./sth. as …** 把某人/某事物看作…; **he ~s of himself as an expert** 他以专家自居; **to ~ well of sb.** (approve) 认可某人; (respect) 尊敬某人; (favour) 看重某人 **9▸** colloq (direct one's thoughts) [按特定方式] 思考; **to try to ~ constructively** 试着往积极方面想; **to ~ straight** 清晰地思考; **to ~ thin** (about becoming slim) 想着怎么减肥; (about keeping slim) 想着怎么保持身材

B *vt* (*pt, pp* **thought**) **1▸** (believe, consider) 认为; **I ~ (that) …** 我认为…; **I ~ (that) this is their house** 我想这是他们的房子; **I thought (that) I heard a scream** 我好像听到了一声尖叫; **it's going to rain, I ~** 我看天要下雨了; **we'd better be going now, don't you ~?** 我们现在该走了，你觉得呢? ; **who do you ~ you are?** 你以为你是谁? ; **I really don't know what to ~** 我真是没想法了; **to ~ sb./sth. (to be) sb./sth.** 认为某人/某事物是某人/某事物; **many ~ him a genius** 很多人认为他是天才; **people ~ him quite charming** 人们认为他很有魅力; **to be thought (to be) …** 被认为是…; **I (don't) ~ so** 我觉得（不）是这样; **can I go to the pictures? — no, I ~ not** 我能去看电影吗? ——不，我看不行; **to ~ to oneself (that) …** 心想…; **to ~ (that) …** 竟然会…; **to ~ (that) I believed him!** 我居然会相信他! ; **anyone** *or* **you would ~ (that) …** 别人会以为…; **I hardly ~ it likely** 我认为不大可能; **I ~ it (most) unlikely (that) …** 我认为…是（非常）不可能的; **that's what he ~s!** 那就是他的想法! **2▸** (intend, plan) 打算; **to ~ (that) …** (intend) 打算…; (plan) 计划…; **I ~ I'll go to the cinema tonight** 我想今晚去看电影; **to ~ to do sth.** 打算做某事 **3▸** (imagine) 想象; **~ how nice it would be to spend a day on the beach** 想象一下在海滩上度过一天会多美好; **~ what could happen!** 想一想会发生什么! ; **I can't ~**

t

what you mean 我猜不出你的意思; **you can't begin to ～ how relieved I am** 你根本想象不出我是多么如释重负; **who'd have thought it!** 谁会想到这个!; **to ～ to do sth.** 想象到做某事; **I didn't ～ to find you here** 我没有想到会在这里找到你; **I thought as much** 我也料到了 **4** (rate, assess) 评价; **to ～ the world of sb.** (have high regard for) 非常敬重某人; (like very much) 非常喜欢某人; **to ～ a lot/not much of sb./sth.** 对某人/某事物评价很高/不高; **to ～ the best/worst of sb.** 认为某人尽善尽美/十恶不赦; **to ～ better of sth.** 改变对某事的看法; **he was going to leave her, but then he thought better of it** 他打算离开她，但后来改主意了 **5** (remember) **to ～ to do sth.** 记得做某事; **did you ～ to bring a corkscrew?** 你记得带瓶塞钻来了吗?; **(now/when I) come to ～ of it, ...** （现在/当我）想起来了，… **6** esp Amer colloq (direct thoughts to) [按特定方式] 思考; **if you want to make money, ～ money!** 如果你想挣钱，就得琢磨钱!; **to ～ beautiful/evil thoughts** 想美好的东西/动邪念

C *n* colloq 想; **to have a ～ (about sth.)** 想一想（某事）; **to have a fresh** *or* **another ～** 重新考虑; **have a good ～ about it** 好好想想这事; **to have (got) another ～ coming** colloq (be forced to revise opinions, plans etc.) 还得想一想; (be deluded) 被骗; (be mistaken) 想错了; **if you ～ I'm going to lend you money, then you have another ～ coming** 如果你认为我会借给你钱，那你就想错了

Phrasal verbs

- **think ahead** *vi* (cast one's mind forward) 预想; (anticipate) 预先考虑; **to ～ ahead to sth.** 预想某事; **～ ahead to what the situation will be** 预先考虑一下会是怎样的情形
- **think back** *vi* 回想; **～ back and tell us all you can remember** 回忆一下，告诉我们你记得的一切; **to ～ back to sth.** 回忆某事
- **think out** *vt* [**～ sth. out, ～ out sth.**] (consider carefully) 仔细考虑; (produce by thinking) 想出 ‹*idea*›; **～ it all out before you ...** 在你…之前，通盘考虑一下这事; **～ out what you are going to say/how you are going to respond** 仔细考虑一下你要说些什么/如何应答; **well/badly thought out** 考虑周密/草率的
- **think over** *vt* [**～ sth. over, ～ over sth.**] 仔细考虑
- **think through** *vt* [**～ sth. through, ～ through sth.**] 充分考虑 ‹*problem*›; **to ～ it through carefully** 仔细充分地考虑这事
- **think up** *vt* [**～ sth. up, ～ up sth.**] colloq 想出; **you'll have to ～ up a better excuse!** 你得想出一个更好的借口!; **what can we ～ up for the party next week?** 关于下周的聚会，我们看看能有什么想法?

thinkable /ˈθɪŋkəbl/ *adj* 可想象的; **it is hardly** *or* **scarcely/not ～ that ...** …几乎是难以想象的/是无法想象的

thinker /ˈθɪŋkə(r)/ *n* **1** (person who thinks) 思考者; **a clear ～** 思路清晰的人 **2** (intellectual) 思想家

thinking /ˈθɪŋkɪŋ/

A *adj attrib* (rational) 理性的; (intelligent) 有才智的; (capable of using the mind) 能思考的; **all ～ people** 所有有理智的人; **the ～ person's choice** 聪明人的选择

B *n* [u] **1** (use of the mind) 思维; (thoughts) 思想; (reflection, reasoning) 思考; **to do some ～ (about sth.)** （对某事）作一些思考; **this is going to need some ～** 这需要考虑一下; **there's a lot of ～ to do before ...** 在…之前，有很多事要考虑; **to do some hard ～ about sth.** 对某事苦思冥想一番; **to put on one's ～ cap (to do sth.)** colloq 开动脑筋（想某事） **2** (way one thinks) 思路; **clear/positive/muddled ～** 清楚/积极/混乱的思路; **the ～ of a whole generation of young people** 整整一代青年的思维模式; **to my way of ～, ...** 在我看来，…; **wishful ～** 一厢情愿; **to influence sb.'s ～** 影响某人的思路 **3** (opinions) 意见; (conclusions) 推论; **one's ～ on sth.** 对某事的见解; **current ～ is that ...** Brit 流行的看法是…

think tank *n* 智囊团

thin-lipped /ˌθɪnˈlɪpt/ *adj* 嘴唇抿紧的

thinly /ˈθɪnli/ *adv* **1** 薄薄地 ‹*spread, paint, cut*›; **to slice bread ～** 把面包切成薄片 **2** (sparingly) 节省地; **'apply paint ～'** "节约使用油漆" **3** (weakly) 微弱地; **to smile ～** 淡淡地微笑 **4** (sparsely) 稀疏地; **to sow seeds ～** 稀疏地播种; **～ inhabited** *or* **populated/wooded** 人口稀少/树木稀疏的 **5** fig (scarcely) 几乎没有; **～ disguised** *or* **veiled** 几乎不加掩饰的 ‹*insult, accusation, jealousy*›

thinner /ˈθɪnə(r)/ *n* [u and c] 稀释剂; **paint ～(s)** 油漆稀释剂

thinness /ˈθɪnnɪs/ *n* [u] (of person's body) 瘦; (of fabric, textile, slice, layer, plank) 薄; (of branch, stem) 纤细; (of argument, idea, excuse) 空洞

thin-skinned *adj* **1** (with thin rind) 皮薄的 ‹*fruit*› **2** (touchy) 脸皮薄的 ‹*person*›

third /θɜːd/ ▸p. 181, p. 521

A *n* **1** (in sequence) 第三 **2** (in date) 3日 **3** (fraction) 三分之一

B *adj* **1** (in sequence) 第三的; **it's her ～ birthday** 这是她3岁生日; **on the ～ floor** 在4楼; **～ time lucky,** Amer **～ time is the charm** 第三次运气就好了; **～ finger** 无名指; **in ～ gear** 挂三挡的 **2** (in name, title) 三世; **Henry the T～ of England** 英王亨利三世 **3** (as fraction) 三分之一的

C *adv* **1** (thirdly) 第三 **2** (in third position) 居第三位

third class

A *n* **1** [c] Brit Univ [学位或考试成绩] 第三等学位 **2** [u] Amer (postage) 第三类邮件 [邮资便宜的邮件，包括广告及16盎司以下的印刷品]

B **third-class** *adj* 三流的 ‹*power, education, restaurant*›; 三等的 ‹*ticket, carriage*›; **a ～ degree** Brit 三等学位

C *adv* 作为第三类邮件 ‹*send, mail*›

third degree

A *n* 逼供; **to subject sb. to** *or* **to give sb. the ～** ‹*police, captor*› 对某人逼供; ‹*parent, teacher*› 盘问某人

B **third-degree** *adj attrib* **1** (severe) 三度的; **third-degree burns** 三度烧伤 **2** Amer (least serious) 三级的; **third-degree crime/murder/robbery** 第三等级犯罪/谋杀/抢劫 **3** (intensive) 逼供的 ‹*method*›; **third-degree interrogation** *or* **questioning/torture** 逼供/刑讯逼供

third estate *n* + *v sing or pl* 普通民众

third-hand

A *adj* 第三手的 ‹*goods, information, report, evidence*›

B *adv* 第三手地; **I heard the news ～** 消息到我这里已经转了两道弯

thirdly /ˈθɜːdli/ *adv* 第三

third party

A *n* **1** (external person involved in dispute) 第三当事人 **2** Brit (person other than the insured) 第三方

B **third-party** *adj* **1** (other than the main two) 第三方的 ‹*supplier, operator, software*› **2** Brit (covering damage, injury) 第三方责任的 ‹*claim*›; **third-party liability/insurance** 第三者责任/第三者责任险

third: ～ person *n* **1** Jur (third party) 第三方; **2** (in grammar) **in the ～ person** 第三人称; **～ person singular/plural** 第三人称单数/复数; **～-rate** *adj* 三流的; **～ sector** *n* **the ～ sector** 第三部门 [指介于政府和私营企业之间的民间公益组织]; **T～ Way** *n* **the T～ Way** 第三条道路 [即中间路线]; **T～ World** *n* **the T～ World** 第三世界; **a T～ World country** 第三世界国家

> **the third way**
>
> 第三条道路。指有别于传统的左派和右派分野的政治立场。左派一般指社会主义，强调政府干预。右派则指资本主义，强调个人的责任和市场的自由竞争。第三条道路努力将政府干预与市场导向结合，以发挥各自的优势。1997年，英国的工党靠走第三条道路，改革成为"新工党"（New Labour, ▸**the Labour Party**），从而击败保守党上台执政。

thirst /θɜːst/

A *n* [u and c] **1** (need to drink) 口渴; **to quench** *or* **slake one's ～** 解渴; **to die of ～** 渴死 **2** (desire) 渴望; **～ for sth.** 对某物的渴望

B *vi* 渴求; **to ～ for** *or* **after sth.** 渴望得到 ‹*power, knowledge, affection, drink*›

thirstily /ˈθɜːstɪli/ *adv* 口渴地

thirst quencher /ˈθɜːst ˌkwentʃə(r)/ *n* 解渴饮料

thirsty /ˈθɜːsti/ *adj* **1** (needing drink) 口渴的; **to be ～ for sth.** 想喝 ‹*water, drink*›; fig 渴望 ‹*vengeance, power, knowledge, affection*› **2** (dry, parched) 干旱的 ‹*soil*›; 缺水的 ‹*plant*› **3** (requiring topping up) 耗油的 ‹*engine, car*›; 耗水的 ‹*plant, crop*› **4** colloq (causing thirst) 使人口渴的 ‹*work, weather*›

thirteen /ˌθɜːˈtiːn/ ▸p. 15, p. 521

A *n* **1** (number, quantity) 十三 **2** (in age) 13岁

B *adj* **1** (in number) 十三的; **～ metres** 13米; **～ paintings** 13张画 **2** (in age) 13岁的; **to be ～ (years old)** 13岁大; **to be over/under ～** 超过/不到13岁 **3** (in series) 第十三的; **size/number ～** 13码/号

Thirteen Colonies *n* **the ～** [1776年通过《独立宣言》的] 十三个殖民州

thirteenth /ˌθɜːˈtiːnθ/ ▸p. 181, p. 521

A *n* **1** (in sequence) 第十三个 **2** (in date) 13日 **3** (fraction) 十三分之一

B *adj* **1** (in sequence) 第十三的 **2** (in name, title) 十三; **Louis the T～** 路易十三 **3** (as fraction) 十三分之一的

C *adv* **1** (thirteenthly) 第十三 **2** (in thirteenth position) 居第十三位

thirteen-year-old *n* 十三岁的人

thirtieth /ˈθɜːtɪəθ/ ▸p. 181, p. 521

A *n* **1** (in sequence) 第三十个 **2** (fraction) 三十分之一

B *adj* **1** (in sequence) 第三十的 **2** (as fraction) 三十分之一的

C *adv* **1** (thirtiethly) 第三十 **2** (in thirtieth position) 居第三十位

thirty /ˈθɜːti/ ▸p. 15, p. 521, p. 831

A *n* **1** (number, quantity) 三十; **there are ～ of us** 我们有30个人 **2** (in age) 30岁

B *adj* **1** (in number) 三十的; **～ boys** 30个男孩 **2** (in age) 30岁的; **I'm nearly ～** 我快30岁了 **3** (in series) 第三十的

thirtyfold /ˈθɜːtɪfəʊld/

A *adj* 三十倍的

B *adv* 以三十倍

thirty-second note *n* Amer **= demisemiquaver**

thirty something

A *n* (person) 三十多岁的人; (age) 三十多岁

B *adj* 三十多岁的

thirty: ～-year-old *n* 三十岁的人; **T～ Years War** *n* Hist **the T～ Years War** 三十年战争 [1618-1648年发生在神圣罗马帝国和其他国家之间]

this /ðɪs/ (*pl* **these**) ▸p. 193

A *det* **1** (referring to person or thing nearby, to the nearer of two, to person or thing already mentioned) 这（个）; **～ man is dangerous** 这个人很危险; **do it ～ way, not that way** 要这样做，别那样做; **I said ～ dress** (for emphasis) 我说的是这件连衣裙; **～ way and that** 四处; **all these books belong to her** 这些书全是她的 **2** (referring to present, future) 本; **～ week/month/year** 本星期/这个月/今年;

~ **morning** 今天早上; ~ **minute** 现在; **at ~ moment** 在这一刻; **these days** 现在; ~ **Friday** 本周五; ~ **coming week** 下周 **3** (referring to time just passed) 最近的; **we've lived here these (past) five years** 我们最近五年一直住在这里 **4** colloq (expressing attitude) **these new friends of hers are supposed to be very rich** 她的这些新朋友据说很有钱 **5** colloq (when narrating events) 一个; ~ **woman came up to me** 有个女人走到我跟前

B *pron* **1** (referring to person or thing nearby, to the nearer of two, or to person or thing already mentioned) 这（个）; **what's ~?** 这是什么? ; **who's ~?** (on telephone) 是哪一位? ; **whose is ~?** 这是谁的? ; **who did ~?** 这是谁干的? ; **where's ~?** 这是在哪里? ; ~ **is what happens when you press the red button** 按下红色按钮就会发生这种情况; **we'll need more than ~** 我们需要的不止这个; **it happened like ~** 事情是这样的; **hold it like ~** 像这样握住它; ~ **and that, ~, that, and the other** colloq (various things) 各种各样的东西; (various activities) 各种各样的活动; **not those, these!** 不是那些, 是这些! **2** (introducing sb. or sth.) (referring to event or words spoken) 这; ~ **is the book I was talking about** 这就是我说的那本书; **hello, ~ is Anna Diaz** (on telephone) 你好, 我是安娜·迪亚斯; **what did you mean by ~?** 你这是什么意思? ; ~ **was not what she had intended** 这不是她所希望的; **what's all ~ about?** 这是怎么一回事? ; **after ~ we'll have lunch** 等这事完了我们就吃午饭; **before ~ he'd never been out of France** 此前他从没离开过法国; **at ~** 随即; **with ~** 紧接着; **with ~ she turned and walked away** 她随即转身就走了; ~ **is it** (indicating sth. about to happen) 是这样的; (expressing agreement) 说得对; **well, ~ is it! wish me luck!** 好, 就这样! 祝我好运吧! ; **yes, ~ is it, you just can't trust him** 是的, 说得对, 你根本不能相信他

C *adv* 这么; **it's ~ big** 它有这么大; **I can't eat ~ much** 我吃不了这么多; **to get ~ far** lit 走这么远; fig 进行到这一步

thistle /ˈθɪsl/ *n* 蓟

thistledown /ˈθɪsldaʊn/ *n* [u] 蓟种子冠毛

thistly /ˈθɪsli/ *adj* 多蓟的

thither /ˈðɪðə(r)/ *adv* archaic or liter 向那里

tho' /ðəʊ/ *abbr* = **though**

thong /θɒŋ/

A *n* **1** (lash on whip) [鞭子的] 皮条 **2** (fastener on shoe, garment) 皮带子 **3** (G-string) (as swimwear) 丁字泳衣; (as underwear) 丁字内裤

B **thongs** *npl* Amer, Austral 人字拖鞋

thoracic /θɔːˈræsɪk/ *adj* 胸的

thorax /ˈθɔːræks/ *n* (*pl* **thoraces** /ˈθɔːrəsiːz/ *or* ~**es**) 胸

thorium /ˈθɔːrɪəm/ *n* [u] 钍

thorn /θɔːn/ *n* **1** [c] (on stem, flower, leaf) 刺; **to be a ~ in sb.'s flesh** *or* **side** 是某人的肉中刺 **2** [c] (bush, hawthorn, etc.) 荆棘 **3** [u and c] (ancient letter) 刺形符 [古英语和冰岛语的如尼字母, 表示齿擦音]

thornbush /ˈθɔːnbʊʃ/ *n* 多刺高灌丛

thornless /ˈθɔːnlɪs/ *adj* 无刺的

thorny /ˈθɔːni/ *adj* **1** (bearing thorns) 多刺的 ‹*rose, bramble, branch*› **2** (with thorn bushes) 长满荆棘的 ‹*thicket, scrub, hedge*› **3** (difficult) 棘手的 ‹*issue, problem*›

thorough /ˈθʌrə, Amer ˈθʌrəʊ/ *adj* **1** (carefully done) 彻底的 ‹*examination, search, wash, tidying-up*› **2** (detailed) 透彻的 ‹*understanding*›; 全面的 ‹*knowledge*› **3** (meticulous) 缜密的 **4** Brit pej (out-and-out) 彻头彻尾的 ‹*idiot, nuisance*›

thoroughbred /ˈθʌrəbred, Amer ˈθʌrəʊ-/

A *adj* **1** (of pure breed) 纯种的 ‹*racehorse, stallion*› **2** colloq (first-class) 一流的 ‹*car*›; 优秀的 ‹*performer*›

B *n* **1** (horse) 纯种马 **2** colloq (person) 优秀的人; (thing) 一流的事物

thoroughfare /ˈθʌrəfeə(r), Amer ˈθʌrəʊ-/ *n* 大道; **'no ~'** "禁止通行"

thoroughgoing /ˈθʌrəgəʊɪŋ/ *adj* **1** (in-depth) 彻底的 ‹*investigation, analysis, reform*› **2** (out-and-out) 十足的 ‹*villain, addict*›

thoroughly /ˈθʌrəli, Amer ˈθʌrəʊli/ *adv* **1** (meticulously) 彻底地 **2** (completely) 极其 ‹*dangerous, nice, reliable*› **3** (without reservation) 完全 ‹*agree, approve, enjoy*›

thoroughness /ˈθʌrənɪs, Amer ˈθʌrəʊnɪs/ *n* [u] 彻底

those /ðəʊz/ ▸**p. 193** *pl* ▸**that A, B**

thou¹ /ðaʊ/ *pron* archaic or dial 汝 [第二人称单数主格]

thou² /θaʊ/ *n* (*pl* ~ *or* ~**s**) colloq **1** (thousand) 一千 **2** (thousandth) 千分之一英寸

though /ðəʊ/

A *conj* **1** (despite the fact that) 尽管; **we enjoyed the trip (even) ~ it was very hot** 尽管天气很热, 这次旅行我们还是玩得很高兴; ~ **she's clever** *or* **clever ~ she is, she's not what we're looking for** 尽管她很聪明, 她不是我们要找的人; **strange ~ it may sound ...** 虽然听起来有点怪… **2** (modifying information) 可是; **I think she knows, ~ I can't be sure** 我想她是知道的, 不过我不能确定; **the house was small, ~ well-designed** 那房子设计得很好, 但有点小; **a foolish, ~ courageous act** 勇敢然而愚蠢的行为

B *adv* 然而; **fortunately, ~, they survived** 然而幸运的是, 他们幸免于难了; **in all, ~, we had a good time** 但总的来说, 我们过得很愉快; **travelling abroad's expensive — it's worth it, ~** 出国旅游很费钱——不过也值得

thought /θɔːt/

A *pt, pp* ▸**think A, B**

B *n* **1** [u] (process of thinking, reflection) 思考; (consideration) 考虑; **to put (a lot of) ~ into sth.** (深入) 思考某事; **lost** *or* **deep in ~** 陷入沉思的; **after much ~** 经过长时间的思考; ~ **for** *or* **of sth.** 对某事的考虑; **no ~ of one's own safety** 不顾自身安危; **without any ~ of the trouble he causes** 丝毫不考虑他带来的麻烦; **a moment's ~** (reflection) 片刻的考虑; (hesitation) 片刻的犹豫; **to give ~ to sth.** 考虑某事; **don't give it another ~** 别把这事放在心上; **to give a** *or* **some ~ (to sth.)** (对某事) 考虑一下; **little ~ has been given to how/why ...** 几乎没想过如何/为什么… **2** [c] (idea, mind) 想法; **a brilliant ~** 聪明的想法; **that's a ~!** 那倒是个主意! ; **it's only a ~** 这只是一个想法而已; **the mere** *or* **very ~ of it makes me feel ill** 一想到这事我就难受; **my ~s were elsewhere** 我的心思不在这里; **to read sb.'s ~s** 看出某人的心思; **it's the ~ that counts** 有这份心意就好 **3** [c] (intention) 意图; (ambition) 志向; ~**s of doing sth.** 做某事的打算; **I have no ~ of marrying** 我没有结婚的打算; **he has ~s of entering the church** 他有奉神职的打算 **4** [c] (viewpoint) 观点; (opinion) 意见; **to have some further ~s (about sth.)** (对某事) 有更多的看法; **to keep one's ~s to oneself** 不透露自己的意见 **5** [u and c] Philos (thinking) 思想; **scientific/Greek ~** 科学/古希腊思想; **the ~s of Plato** 柏拉图的思想

thought content *n* [u] 思想内容

thoughtful /ˈθɔːtfl/ *adj* **1** (reflective) 沉思的 ‹*expression, mood*›; **to be ~ about sth.** 深思某事 **2** (well thought-out) 经缜密思考的 ‹*analysis, article, research*› **3** (considerate) 体贴的 ‹*person, act*›

thoughtfully /ˈθɔːtfəli/ *adv* **1** (carefully) 经深思熟虑地 ‹*speak, choose, worded*› **2** (pensively) 沉思地 ‹*stare, smile, walk*› **3** (considerately) 体贴地 ‹*behave, treat*›

thoughtfulness /ˈθɔːtflnɪs/ *n* [u] **1** (carefulness) 深思熟虑 **2** (pensiveness) 沉思 **3** (consideration) 体贴

thoughtless /ˈθɔːtlɪs/ *adj* **1** (inconsiderate) 不顾及他人的 ‹*character, remark, behaviour*›; **to be ~ towards sb.** 不为某人着想; **to be ~ of sth.** 轻率对待某事 **2** (unthinking) 欠考虑的 ‹*behaviour, person*›; **to be ~ of sth.** 对某事不加考虑

thoughtlessly /ˈθɔːtlɪsli/ *adv* **1** (inconsiderately) 不顾及他人地 ‹*speak, behave*› **2** (unthinkingly) 欠考虑地 ‹*behave, move*›

thoughtlessness /ˈθɔːtlɪsnɪs/ *n* [u] **1** (lack of consideration) 不体贴 **2** (lack of forethought) 欠考虑

thought: ~**-out** *adj* 考虑周全的; ~ **police** *n + v pl* **the ~ police** 思想警察 [指镇压思想自由的团体]; ~ **process** *n* 思路; ~**-provoking** *adj* 发人深省的; ~**-reader** *n* 读人心思的人; ~**-reading** *n* [u] 读人心思; ~ **transference** *n* [u] 心灵感应

thousand /ˈθaʊznd/ ▸**p. 521**

A *n* 一千; **a** *or* **one ~ and one** 一千零一; **ten ~** 一万; **by the ~** 成千地; **I have nearly a ~** 我有差不多一千

B *adj* **1** (in number) 一千的; **a three-~-mile journey** 三千英里的旅行 **2** colloq (in large quantities) 许许多多的; **a ~ thanks** 多谢; **to die a ~ deaths** 羞愧难当

C **thousands** *npl* **1** (number range) 千位数 **2** colloq (large numbers, amounts) 成千上万

thousandfold /ˈθaʊzndfəʊld/

A *adj* 千倍的 ‹*increase, reduction*›

B *adv* 千倍地 ‹*increase, decrease*›

Thousand Island Dressing *n* 千岛酱 [用蛋黄酱加番茄酱和醋泡小黄瓜等制成]

thousandth /ˈθaʊznθ/ ▸**p. 521**

A *n* **1** (in sequence) 第一千个 **2** (fraction) 千分之一

B *adj* **1** (in sequence) 第一千的; **for the ~ time** 第一千次 **2** (as fraction) 千分之一的

thrall /θrɔːl/ *n* **1** [u] liter (powerless state) 束缚; **to hold sb. in ~** 完全控制某人; **to be in ~ to sth.** 深受某物的影响 **2** [c] archaic (slave) 奴隶

thrash /θræʃ/

A *vt* **1** (beat with stick or whip) 抽打 **2** (hit hard) 用力击打 **3** colloq (defeat soundly) 彻底击败 **4** (move violently) 使劲晃动 ‹*head, limbs*›; 用力拍击 ‹*wings*›

B *vi* «*legs, arms*» 使劲晃动; «*wing, bird*» 乱扑腾

C *n* **1** [u] (musical style) 快节奏重金属摇滚乐 **2** [c] Brit colloq (party) 聚会

Phrasal verbs

• **thrash about, thrash around**

A *vi* «*person*» 激烈扭动; **somebody was ~ing about in the water** 有人在水里乱扑腾

B *vt* [~ **sth. about**] 使劲晃动 ‹*limbs, stick*›; 用力拍击 ‹*wings*›; **to ~ one's arms/legs about** 乱挥胳膊/乱踢腿

• **thrash out** *vt* [~ **out sth.**] **1** (resolve) 通过讨论解决 ‹*problems, differences, quarrel*› **2** (agree on) 通过讨论达成 ‹*solution, compromise*›

thrashing /ˈθræʃɪŋ/ *n* **1** (punishment) 殴打; **to give sb. a good ~** 痛打某人 **2** colloq (sound defeat) 惨败; **to give sb. a good ~** 把某人打得一败涂地

thread /θred/

A *n* **1** [u and c] (string) 线; **a piece** *or* **length of ~** 一根线; **to hang** *or* **be hanging by a ~** 挂在一根线上; fig 岌岌可危 **2** (theme of argument, story) 脉络; **to follow/lose the ~** 跟上思路/失去头绪; **to pull all the ~s together** 把所有的线索联系起来; **to pick up the ~(s) of** 重续 ‹*conversation, story, career, life*›; **to pick up the ~ of a relationship with sb.** 与某人重拾关系 **3** (line) 线状物; **a ~ of light/smoke** 一线光/一缕烟 **4** (ridge of screw) 螺纹 **5** (linked messages on Internet) 跟帖

t

B *npl* **threads** Amer colloq 衣服
C *vt* 1 (put thread in) 给…穿线; **can you ～ this needle/sewing machine?** 你能穿这根针/为这台缝纫机穿线吗? 2 (insert) 把…装入; **to ～ the film on to the spool** 把底片装在卷轴上; **to ～ sth. through sth.** 将某物穿过某物; **to ～ the rope through a pulley** 把绳子穿进滑轮 3 (move) 穿过; **to ～ one's way through** 在…中间穿行 ‹*tables, obstacles, crowd*›
D *vi* «*needle, sewing machine, bead*» 穿上线; «*film, yarn*» 装入; **the machine ～s from behind** 这台机器从后面穿线; **the tape ～s between these magnetic heads** 磁带在这些磁头中间穿过

threadbare /ˈθredbeə(r)/ *adj* 1 (very worn) 破旧的 ‹*garment, blanket, curtains*› 2 (overused) 老一套的 ‹*argument, excuse, joke*›

threaded /ˈθredɪd/ *adj* 1 (cut with thread) 有螺纹的 ‹*screw, bolt, groove, hole*› 2 (with or like thread) 有线状图案装饰的 ‹*embroidery, glass, carpet*› 3 (involving linked Internet messages) 跟帖的 ‹*email, discussion, forum*›; **a ～ message** 跟帖

thread-like *adj* 线状的

threat /θret/ *n* 1 (verbal abuse) 恐吓; **to make ～s against sb.** 对某人发出恐吓; **to give in to ～s** 屈服于恐吓; **an empty** *or* **idle ～** 虚张声势的恐吓; **it was no idle ～** 那可不是吓唬吓唬而已 2 (danger) 威胁; **to pose a ～ to sb./sth.** 对某人/某物构成威胁; **to be under ～ (from ...)** 受到(来自…的)威胁; **under ～ of** 在…的威胁下 ‹*death, injury, punishment*› 3 (risk, possibility) 凶兆; **a security ～** 安全风险

threaten /ˈθretn/
A *vt* 1 (menace) 恐吓; **to be ～ed with death/prison** 受到死亡/坐牢的威胁 2 (warn of) 发出…的威胁 ‹*revenge, violence*›; **to ～ to do sth.** 威胁要做某事; **the clouds ～ed rain** 云层预示着要下雨 3 (endanger) 危及 ‹*peace, stability, wildlife, planet*›; **to be ～ed with starvation/extinction** 有发生饥荒/灭绝的危险 4 (be likely) «*person, illness, danger*» 威胁着要; **to ～ to do sth.** 可能造成某种恶果; **rain ～s to stop play** 大雨可能造成停赛
B *vi* «*war, famine, danger, adverse weather*» 可能来临

threatened /ˈθretnd/ *adj* 1 (endangered) 有灭绝危险的 ‹*species, culture, forest*› 2 (vulnerable) 受到威胁的; **to feel ～** 感觉受到威胁

threatening /ˈθretnɪŋ/ *adj* 1 (conveying a threat) 威胁的; **a ～ phone call** 恐吓电话 2 (presaging adverse weather) 阴沉沉的 ‹*clouds, weather conditions*›

threateningly /ˈθretnɪŋli/ *adv* 威胁地

three /θriː/ ▸p. 15, p. 521, p. 831
A *n* 1 (number, quantity) 三; **～ plus two equals five** 3 加 2 等于 5; **in December nineteen hundred and ～** 在 1903 年 12 月; **we live at (number) ～, Victoria Road** 我们住在维多利亚路 3 号; **her phone number is two six double ～** 她的电话号码是 2633; **there are ～ of them** 他们有 3 个人; **to play the best of ～** 参加三局两胜制的比赛; **(two's company,) ～'s a crowd** (两人相伴,)三人不欢 2 (in time) 3 点钟; **at ～ (o'clock)** 在 3 点 3 (on playing card) 3 点; **the ～ of diamonds** 方块 3 4 (age) 3 岁
B *adj* 1 (as quantity) 三的; **～ cats** 3 只猫; **～ books** 3 本书; **～ weeks** 3 周 2 (in age) 3 岁的; **he's nearly ～** 他快 3 岁了; **our house is only ～ years old** 我们的房子才造了 3 年 3 (in series) 第三的; **number ～** 3 号; **page ～** 第 3 页

three: ～-colour *adj* 三色的; **～-cornered** *adj* 1 (triangular) 三角形的; 2 (involving three) 有三方参加的 ‹*contest, argument, fight*›; **～-D** *n* [u] 三维; **to film sth. in ～-D** 给某物拍摄立体电影; **a ～-D film/video/model** 立体电影/三维录像/三维模型; **～-day event** *n* 马术三日赛; **～-day eventing** *n* [u] 马术三日全能赛事; **～-decker** *n* 1 (boat) 三层甲板船; 2 (sandwich) 三层夹心三明治; **～-dimensional** /ˌθriːdaɪˈmenʃənl, -dɪ-/ *adj* 1 (solid) 三维的; 2 (believable) 逼真的 ‹*character, portrayal, work*›

threefold /ˈθriːfəʊld/ *adj, adv* 三倍的(地)

three-four time *n* 四三拍; **in ～** 用四三拍

three: T～ Gorges Dam *pr n* **the T～ Gorges Dam** 三峡大坝; **～-legged** /ˌθriːˈlegɪd/ *adj* 三条腿的; **～-legged race** 两人绑腿赛跑; **～pence** /ˈθrəpəns, ˈθrʌpəns/ *n* Brit (sum) 三便士; (coin) 三便士硬币

threepenny /ˈθrəpəni, ˈθrʌpəni/ *adj* Brit 三便士的

threepenny bit *n* Brit 三便士硬币

three: ～-phase *adj* 三相的; **～-piece suit** *n* [由上衣、裤子和马甲组成的]三件套男装; **～-piece suite** *n* 三件套沙发

three-ply
A *n* [u] 1 **～ (wool)** (yarn) 三股头毛线 2 (plywood) 三夹板
B *adj* 三股头的 ‹*knitting, wool*›; 用三股头线织成的 ‹*garment, jumper*›; 三层的 ‹*plywood*›

three: ～-point landing *n* 三点着陆; **～-point turn** *n* 三点转向

three-quarter *adj* 1 (in size, length, weight, time) 四分之三的; (in clothing) 中长的; **～ ton/moon/share** 四分之三吨/四分之三个月亮/四分之三的份额; **～ hour** 三刻钟; **～ sleeves** 中长袖; **～ trousers** 七分裤 2 (not full-face) 展示脸部四分之三的 ‹*portrait, profile*›; **～ face** 四分之三面部的肖像

three-quarter-length *adj* 中长的

three-quarters
A *npl* 四分之三; **～ of an hour** 三刻钟; **～ of the voters** 四分之三的投票人
B *adv* 达四分之三

three-ring circus *n* Amer (circus) [有三块圆形场地的]大马戏团; (disorganized scene) 纷乱的场面

three R's *n* **the ～** 初等教育的三要素 [指reading, writing, arithmetic三种基本技能]

threescore /ˌθriːˈskɔː(r)/ archaic
A *n* 六十; **～ and ten** 七十
B *adj* 六十的; **～ years and ten** 七十年

three-sided *adj* 1 (triangular) 三面的 2 (involving three) 有三方参加的 ‹*contest, discussion, argument*›

threesome /ˈθriːsəm/ *n* (gen) 三人一组; (engaging in sex) 三人性交

three: ～-star *adj* (of restaurant, hotel) 三星级的 ‹*meal, accommodation, rating*›; Amer (denoting military rank) 三星的 ‹*rank, status*›; **a ～-star general** 三星中将; **～-way** *adj* 1 (with three elements) 三向的; **a ～-way junction/switch** 三向接头/开关; 2 (involving three) 有三方参加的 ‹*contest, discussion, argument, fight*›

three-wheeler /ˌθriːˈwiːlə(r)/ *n* (car) 三轮汽车; (tricycle) 三轮车; (motorcycle) 三轮摩托车

three-year-old *n* 三岁的孩子

thresh /θreʃ/
A *vt* 给…脱粒
B *vi* 打谷

thresher /ˈθreʃə(r)/ *n* 1 (machine) 脱粒机 2 (person) 打谷者

threshing /ˈθreʃɪŋ/ *n* [u] 打谷

threshing: ～ floor *n* 打谷场; **～ machine** *n* 脱粒机

threshold /ˈθreʃəʊld, -həʊld/ *n* 1 (bottom of doorway) 门槛 2 (lower limit) 下限; **to have a low pain ～** 忍痛力弱; **he has a low boredom ～** 他很容易厌倦 3 (point of transition) 开端; **on the ～ of a discovery/new career/new era** 即将有所发现/从事新职业/进入新时代 4 (taxation level) 起征点

threshold price *n* 门槛价格 [欧盟规定的进口粮食的最低限价]

threw /θruː/ *pt* ▸**throw**

thrice /θraɪs/ *adv* archaic or liter 三次 ‹*speak, attack*›; 以三倍 ‹*multiply*›

thrift /θrɪft/
A *n* 1 [u] (frugality) 节俭; **to practise** *or* **exercise ～** 厉行节约 2 [u and c] (plant) 海石竹
B **thrifts** *npl* Amer 互助储蓄银行

thriftiness /ˈθrɪftɪnɪs/ *n* [u] 节俭

thrift shop *n* Amer [为慈善目的开设的]廉价旧货店

thrifty /ˈθrɪfti/ *adj* 节俭的 ‹*person, lifestyle, meal*›; **to be ～ in sth.** 在某事上节俭

thrill /θrɪl/
A *n* 1 (sensation) 震颤感; **a ～ of pleasure** 一阵快感; **to feel** *or* **experience a ～ (of joy)** 感觉到一阵(愉悦的)刺激; **to get a ～** *or* **one's ～s (from/out of doing sth.)** (从某事/做某事中)得到刺激; **～s and spills** 紧张和刺激 2 (pleasure) 兴奋; **it was a ～ to meet her** 见到她真是太激动了
B *vt* 使…非常兴奋 ‹*person, crowd, audience*›
C *vi* 感到非常兴奋; **to ～ to sth.** 对某事感到非常兴奋

thrilled /θrɪld/ *adj* 非常兴奋的; **to be ～ to do sth.** 做某事非常兴奋; **to be ～ that ...** …是令人兴奋的; **to be ～ with sth.** 因某事兴奋无比; **to be ～ to bits (with sth.)** colloq (因某事)乐不可支

thriller /ˈθrɪlə(r)/ *n* 1 (film) 惊险电影; (book) 惊险小说; (drama) 惊险戏剧 2 (exciting event) 令人兴奋的事件

thrilling /ˈθrɪlɪŋ/ *adj* 令人兴奋的

thrill-seeker *n* 寻求刺激的人

thrive /θraɪv/ *vi* (*pt* **throve** *or* **～d**; *pp* **thriven** /ˈθrɪvn/ *or* **～d**) 1 (be healthy and strong) «*person, child, animal, plant*» 茁壮成长 2 (be wealthy) «*market, community, business, industry*» 繁荣; **to ～ on sth./doing sth.** 靠某物/做某事而兴旺发达; **to ～ on hard work** 以苦干而发达

thriving /ˈθraɪvɪŋ/ *adj* 1 (in good health) 茁壮成长的 ‹*child, animal, plant*›; 康复进展良好的 ‹*patient*› 2 (wealthy) 繁荣的 ‹*business, community, town, economy*›

throat /θrəʊt/ *n* 1 (passageway in neck) 咽喉; **a ～ infection/injury/disease** 咽喉感染/伤害/疾病; **a ～ lozenge/tablet/spray** 止咳糖/咽喉片/咽喉喷剂; **to cut** *or* **slit sb.'s ～** 割断某人的咽喉; **to clear one's ～** 清清嗓子; **to have a lump in one's ～** 哽咽; **to stick in sb.'s ～** 卡在某人嗓子里; **it sticks in my ～** fig 我难以启齿; **to jump down sb.'s ～** colloq 严厉斥责某人; **to ram** *or* **stuff** *or* **thrust sth. down sb.'s ～** colloq 强行向某人灌输某事 2 (part of neck) (excluding passageway) 喉部; (including passageway) 颈前部; **to grab sb./sth. by the ～** 掐住某人/某物的颈部; **to cut one's own ～** 自寻死路; **to be at each other's ～** *or* **at one another's ～s** (fighting fiercely) 激烈打斗; (arguing fiercely) 激烈争吵 3 (constricted opening) 口子; **the ～ of a chimney** 烟囱口; **the ～ of a shoe** 鞋帮口

throaty /ˈθrəʊti/ *adj* 1 (husky) 嘶哑的 ‹*voice, laugh, sound, cough*›; **the ～ roar of the engine** 引擎低沉的轰鸣声 2 colloq (with sore throat) 喉咙痛的

throb /θrɒb/
A *n* 1 (sound) [有节奏的]震响 2 (movement, sensation) (of heart, pulse) [有节奏的]跳动; (of pain) 抽痛
B *vi* (*pres p etc.* **-bb-**) 1 (pound with pain) «*wound, body part*» 阵阵作痛; **my head is ～bing** 我的头阵阵抽痛 2 (pulsate) «*pulse, heart, blood*» 搏动; **to be ～bing with life** 生机勃勃 3 (make sound) «*motor, machine, music, drums*» 有节奏地震响; **the air/forest ～bed with the call of the birds** 空中/森林里回荡着一阵阵鸟鸣

throbbing /ˈθrɒbɪŋ/
A *n* [u] **1** (of heart, pulse, blood) 搏动; (of pain) 抽痛 **2** (of motor, music) 有节奏的震响 **3** (sensation) 悸动
B *adj* **1** (painful) 抽痛的 ‹*wound*›; **a ~ pain** *or* **ache** 抽痛 **2** (audible) 有节奏地震响的 ‹*sound, music*› **3** (pulsating) 悸动的 ‹*sensation, rhythm*›

throes /θrəʊz/ *npl* **1** (violent struggle) (in death) 剧痛; (in birth) 阵痛; (of revolution) 剧烈的动荡; **to be in one's death ~** *or* **the ~ of death** 处于临终痛苦中 **2** (middle of process) 煎熬; **to be in the ~ of sth./doing sth.** 处于某事/做某事的煎熬之中

thrombosis /ˌθrɒmˈbəʊsɪs/ ▸**p. 377** *n* [u and c] (*pl* **thromboses** /ˌθrɒmˈbəʊsiːz/) 血栓形成

throne /θrəʊn/ *n* **1** (chair) 宝座 **2** (power) 王权; **the ~** 王位; **to be on the ~** 在位; **to ascend (to)/abdicate from the ~** 登基/退位

throne room *n* 觐见室

throng /θrɒŋ, Amer θrɔːŋ/
A *n* 一大群
B *vt* «*people*» 在…处群集 ‹*place, street, platform*›; **to be ~ed with sth.** 挤满了某物
C *vi* 群集; **crowds ~ed to** *or* **towards the main square** 人群向主广场蜂拥而去

thronging /ˈθrɒŋɪŋ/ *adj* 群集的 ‹*crowd, spectators*›; **to be ~ with sth.** «*place, street, platform*» 挤满了某物

throttle /ˈθrɒtl/
A *n* **1** [c] **~ (valve)** (device) 节流阀 **2** [u] (accelerator) 油门; **at full ~** 以全速
B *vt* **1** (strangle) 掐死 ‹*person, animal*›; fig 压制 ‹*press, media*› **2** (control with throttle) 节流调节 ‹*engine, vehicle*›

Phrasal verb

• **throttle back, throttle down**
A *vt* [**~ sth. back, ~ back sth.**] 调节油门使…减速 ‹*engine, vehicle*›
B *vi* 调节油门减速

through /θruː/
A *prep* **1** (into and out the other side of, making hole or opening in, passing among) 穿过; **to look ~ sth.** 通过…观看 ‹*hole, window*›; **go straight ~ that door** 直接穿过那道门; **she stuck her finger ~ the slit** 她将手指插入裂缝; **to cut ~ the fields** 穿越田野; **to go ~ the town centre** 穿过市中心; **they travelled ~ Germany to Poland** 他们取道德国前往波兰; **the nail went right ~ the wall** 钉子直接穿透了墙壁; **he jumped ~ the window to escape** 他破窗而逃; **he drilled ~ a cable** 他将电缆钻透了; **to fly ~ dense clouds** 飞过厚厚的云层 **2** (across) 穿行于; **he's travelling ~ Asia at the moment** 他目前正在周游亚洲; **to fly ~ the air** «*acrobat, arrow, bullet*» 从空中飞过 **3** (throughout) 遍及; **villages were scattered ~ the jungle** 丛林中到处散布着村庄 **4** (from other side of) 从…的另一侧; **the sun was streaming in ~ the window** 阳光从窗外射进来; **I saw a figure inside ~ the net curtains** 透过网眼窗帘我看到里面有个人影; **I couldn't hear their conversation ~ the wall** 隔着墙我听不到他们的谈话; **to feel the stones ~ one's shoes** 感觉到鞋底下面的石子 **5** (past) 经过; **he drove ~ a red light** 他开车闯红灯了; **the water poured ~ the roof** 水透过房顶一泻而下; **the approach to the church is ~ the gate** 去教堂要经过那道大门; **we were ~ customs in less than five minutes** 我们不到五分钟就要通关了 **6** (in course of) 在…期间; **the goal came midway ~ the second half** 下半场进行到一半时进球了 **7** (completing successfully) 通过; **to make it ~ an exam/a test/this round** 顺利通过考试/测试/这一轮; **to get the bill ~ the Lords** 使议案在上议院得以通过 **8** (from beginning to end of) 从头到尾; **to work all** *or* **right ~ the day** 整天工作; **he talked all the way ~ the film** 电影放映期间他一直在说话; **to have been ~ a lot** 遭遇了很多不幸; **to put sb. ~ it** esp Brit colloq 迫使某人吃苦; **I've had a look ~ his file** 我查看过他的档案; **rotate it ~ 180°** 将它旋转 180 度 **9** (by means of sth.) 凭借; (as part of a process) 经由; **to seek justice ~ the proper channels** 通过适当渠道寻求公正; **to look ~ binoculars/a telescope** 用双筒望远镜/望远镜观看; **it was ~ him that I got the job** 我是通过他找到的这份工作; **to speak ~ an interpreter** 通过翻译来讲话; **I heard ~ a friend** 我听一个朋友说的; **to send sth. ~ the post** 邮递某物; **to book sth. ~ a travel agent** 通过旅行社预订某物; **it's been ~ several people's hands** 它已经几易其手 **10** (because of) 因为; **~ carelessness/inexperience/illness** 因粗心/缺乏经验/生病 **11** Amer (until and including) 直到; **March 24 ~ May 7** 从 3 月 24 号直到 5 月 7 号; **open April ~ September** 四月至九月开放; **1939 ~ 1945** 从1939 年到 1945 年
B *adj* **1** *pred* colloq (finished) 结束的; (no longer in a relationship) 断绝关系的; **are we ~ now?** 我们现在结束了吗？; **to be ~ with sb./sth.** (finished with) 处理完某人的事/某事; **I'm not ~ with you yet!** 我还没跟你说完呢！; **are you ~ with the paper?** 你的论文完成了吗？; **Claire and I are ~** 克莱尔和我吹了; **to be ~ with sb./sth.** (no longer have relationship with) 与某人/某事断绝关系; **I'm ~ with men!** 我再也不想和男人谈情说爱了! **2** *pred* colloq (no longer successful) 彻底失败的; **you're ~! get out!** 你被炒鱿鱼了！滚出去! **3** *attrib* (passing from one side to other) 贯穿的; **'~ traffic'** "过境交通"; **'no ~ road'** "此路不通"; **a ~ route/train** 直通路线/直达列车; **a ~ ticket** 联运票 **4** *pred* Brit colloq (worn) 磨破的
C *adv* **1** (into and out the other side, making hole or opening, passing among group) 穿过; **to squeeze ~** 挤过去; **to make one's way ~** 穿过去; **I went up to the kitchen window and looked ~** 我走到厨房窗户前向外望去; **the bullet went straight ~** 子弹一下子打穿了 **2** (from other side, past opening or obstacle, completing successfully) 通过; **the sunlight was streaming ~** 阳光直射进来; **to drive straight ~** 径直开过去; **to make it ~ to the next round/the semifinals/the final** 成功进入下一轮/半决赛/决赛 **3** (in course of a process or period) 持续地; **we'll have to struggle ~ till pay day** 我们一定要坚持到发薪日 **4** (from beginning to end, inspecting sth.) 从始至终; **to play sth. right ~** 将某作品完整演奏一遍; **I'm about halfway ~ already** 我差不多已经完成一半了; **from Friday ~ to Sunday** 从星期五一直到星期天; **this train goes straight ~ to York** 这趟列车直达约克; **I gave the article a quick look ~** 我将文章快速浏览了一遍 **5** Telecom (connected) 接通; **to be ~ to sb./sth.** 接通某人/某处的电话 **6** (completely) 完全; **to be soaked** *or* **wet ~** «*person, clothes*» 湿透; **to be cooked right ~** 熟透; **~ and ~** 彻底地; **to know an area/a city ~ and ~** 对某个地区/城市了如指掌; **he's British ~ and ~** 他是地地道道的英国人

through-draught Brit, **through-draft** Amer *n* 穿堂风

throughout /ˌθruːˈaʊt/
A *prep* **1** (in every part of) 遍及; **~ China/Europe/the world** 遍及全中国/欧洲/世界; **books were scattered ~ the house** 屋子里扔得到处是书; **his confidence had spread ~ the team** 他的自信感染了整个团队 **2** (during the whole of) 贯穿; **~ the year** 全年; **~ April** 整个四月份; **~ the interview** 在整个面试过程中; **~ his life/career** 在他的一生/职业生涯中; **~ history** 从古至今
B *adv* **1** (in every part) 到处; **it is printed in italics ~** 它全部用斜体字印刷; **lined/repainted ~** 全部镶边/粉刷一新的; **the offices are carpeted ~** 办公室全部铺了地毯 **2** (during the whole time) 自始至终地; **to stand ~** 一直站着; **to be faithful ~** 坚贞不渝

throughput /ˈθruːpʊt/ *n* [u and c] **1** (amount of processed data) 吞吐量 **2** (amount of work done) 生产量; **the plant has a ~ of 10 tonnes per day** 这家工厂的日产量为 10 吨

through: ~-ticketing *n* [u] 联程通票; **~way** *n* Amer 高速公路

throve /θrəʊv/ *pt* ▸**thrive**

throw /θrəʊ/
A *vt* (*pt* **threw**, *pp* **thrown**) **1** (send through air) 投掷; **to ~ a ball in** *or* **into the air/across the pitch/over the wall** 把球扔向空中/扔过球场/扔过墙; **he threw the javelin 80m** 他把标枪掷出了 80 米; **to ~ cold water on sth.** 给某事泼冷水; **to ~ a bridge over sth.** 在某物上架桥 **2** (direct) 把…指向; **to ~ sb. a glance/look** 瞥/看某人一眼; **to ~ sb. a smile/kiss** 对某人微笑/向某人抛飞吻; **to ~ a question/remark at sb.** 对某人提出问题/说一句话; **to ~ money at sth.** 在某事上投钱; **to ~ suspicion on sb./sth.** 使某人/某事受到猜疑; **to ~ doubt on sb./sth.** 怀疑某人/某事; **to ~ one's voice** 使说话声听起来似乎来自他处 **3** (disconcert) 使困惑; **I was thrown by the news** 那个消息使我心烦意乱 **4** (activate) 扳动 ‹*switch, lever, gear*›; **the operator threw the machine into gear/reverse** 操作员开动了机器/让机器倒转 **5** colloq (indulge in, succumb to) 使发作; **to ~ a fit** *or* **tantrum** 大发脾气 **6** colloq (organize) 举行; **to ~ a party** 举行聚会 **7** (shape on potter's wheel) 把…拉成坯 ‹*jug, vase*›; (turn on lathe) 车 ‹*wood, chair leg*›; **to ~ a pot** 拉出罐坯; **a hand-thrown piece of pottery** 一件手拉坯的陶器 **8** (give birth to) «*animal*» 产下 ‹*young*› **9** (put or move carelessly) 随手放 ‹*garment, sheet, wood*›; **~ some coal on the fire, it's dying down** 丢几块煤到炉子里，火快灭了 **10** (move part of body) 猛动; **she threw her arms around my neck** 她张开双臂搂住我的脖子 **11** (cause to fall) 把…摔倒 ‹*person, opponent, rider*›; (cause to move) 将…投入; **he threw his opponent in the third round** 他在第三个回合把对手摔倒在地; **to ~ sb. into jail** 把某人投入监狱 **12** (roll) 掷 ‹*dice*›; (score) 掷出 ‹*number*›; **to ~ a six** 掷出六点 **13** (cause to be) 使…处于 ‹*person, army, plans*›; **the strike has thrown hundreds of people out of work** 罢工使几百人失业了; **to ~ sb./sth. into confusion** *or* **disarray** 使某人/某物慌张失措/陷入混乱; **the news ~ me off balance** 这消息使我不知所措 **14** (project) «*sun, building*» 投射 ‹*light, shadow, shade*› **15** (aim at opponent) 挥出 ‹*punch, blow, right*›; **he threw a left at his opponent** 他向对手打出一记左拳 **16** colloq (lose) «*person, boxer*» 在…中放水 ‹*fight, contest, game*›
B *v refl* (*pt* **threw**, *pp* **thrown**) **to ~ oneself** (on to floor, bed, chair) 一头倒下; (with force) 猛冲; **to ~ oneself off a building/in front of a train** 跳楼/卧轨; **to ~ oneself at sb.'s feet** 伏倒在某人脚下; **to ~ oneself at sb.** 向某人猛扑过去; fig 拼命讨好某人; **to ~ oneself into ...** 跳入 ‹*river, sea*›; fig 热衷于 ‹*work, project*›
C *vi* (*pt* **threw**, *pp* **thrown**) 投; **how far can you ~?** 你能投多远？
D *n* **1** (act or instance of casting object) 掷; (distance cast) 投掷距离; **a well-aimed/record ~** 很准的一掷/破纪录的一投; **he won with a ~ of six** 他掷出六点赢了; **whose ~ is it?** (in ball game) 该谁掷球？; (with dice) 该谁掷骰子了？; **a stone's ~** 投石之遥; **a ~ of 70 metres** 70 米的投掷距离 **2** (act of throwing opponent in wrestling, judo etc.) 摔倒; **a shoulder ~** 肩摔 **3** colloq (each) 每一个; **CDs £5 a ~!** 激光唱片 5 英镑一张! **4** (furniture cover) 罩 **5** Mech (action) (of slide valve) 摆度; (of crank) 行程

Phrasal verbs

• **throw about, throw around** *vt* [**~ sth. about, ~ about sth.**]

t

1 (between points) 把…扔来扔去; **to ~ a ball about** 把球扔来扔去 **2** (randomly) 乱扔 ‹*litter, confetti, cushions*›; **to ~ money about** 乱花钱; **to ~ one's weight about** colloq 耀武扬威

• **throw aside** vt [**~ sth. aside, ~ aside sth.**]
1 lit (discard) 把…扔在一边 ‹*object, garment, document*› **2** fig (abandon) 抛弃 ‹*moral standard, principle*›

• **throw away** vt [**~ sth. away, ~ away sth.**]
1 (discard) 扔掉 ‹*unwanted object, rubbish*› **2** (waste) 浪费 ‹*opportunity, advantage, life, money*› **3** (utter casually) 随口说出 ‹*words, remark, information*›

• **throw back** vt [**~ sth. back, ~ back sth.**]
1 (return) 把…扔回 ‹*ball, fish*› **2** (move) 将…向后移 ‹*arm, body part*›; **~ your shoulders back** 把你的胸挺起来 **3** (repulse) 击退 ‹*person, opponent, enemy*›; **to ~ sb. back on to the defensive** 击退某人使其采取守势 **4** (make dependent) 迫使…依靠; **we have been thrown back on our own resources** 我们不得不自己想办法

• **throw down** vt [**~ sth. down, ~ down sth.**]
1 (cast to the ground or floor) 扔下 ‹*object, person*›; fig 抛出 ‹*challenge*› **2 it's (absolutely) ~ing it down!** Brit colloq (raining hard) 雨下得真大!

• **throw in** vt [**~ sth. in, ~ in sth.**]
1 (propel) 把…扔进来 ‹*object, ball*›; **to ~ in the towel** *or* **sponge** fig 认输 **2** colloq (give for free) 附赠 ‹*goods, extra item*› **3** colloq (add) 添加 ‹*ingredient*›; **thrown in for good measure** 额外添加的 **4** colloq (contribute) 随口说出 ‹*remark, suggestion*›

• **throw off**
A [**~ sth. off, ~ off sth.**] vt
1 (take off) 迅速脱去 ‹*garment*›; 匆匆扯掉 ‹*bedclothes*› **2** (compose quickly) 随手写出 ‹*poem, letter*› **3** (overcome) 从…中恢复 ‹*illness, depression, handicap*›
B [**~ sb. off, ~ off sb.**] vt 逐出; **the conductor threw him off the bus** 售票员把他赶下公交车
C [**~ off sb./sth.**] vt 摆脱 ‹*person, pursuer, burden, tradition*›

• **throw on** vt [**~ sth. on, ~ on sth.**] 匆匆穿上 ‹*garment*›

• **throw open** vt [**~ sth. open, ~ open sth.**]
1 (open forcefully) 猛力推开 ‹*door, window*› **2** (make public) 使…公开 ‹*debate*›; **to ~ a discussion open** 把讨论公开 **3** (make accessible) 开放 ‹*market, facility, tourist attraction*›

• **throw out**
A [**~ sth. out, ~ out sth.**] vt
1 (discard) 扔掉 ‹*rubbish, produce, clothing*›; ▸**baby A1** **2** (reject) 否决 ‹*plan, case, bill*› **3** (utter peremptorily) 断然地说 ‹*hint, suggestion*›; (utter casually) 随口说出 ‹*idea, suggestion*› **4** (extend) 伸出; **~ your arms out in front of you** 向前伸出你的胳膊; **~ your chest out** 把你的胸挺起来 **5** (radiate) 发出 ‹*heat, light*› **6** (rapidly develop) «*plant*» 迅速长出 ‹*side shoot, bud, leaves*›
B [**~ sb. out, ~ out sb.**] (eject) 逐出; **to be thrown out of work** 被解雇
C [**~ sb./sth. out**] vt 使…不知所措 ‹*person*›; 使…混乱 ‹*calculation, thought process*›; **that's what threw me out** 正是那件事把我搞糊涂了

• **throw over** vt [**~ sb. over, ~ over sb.**] colloq dated 抛弃 ‹*spouse, lover*›

• **throw together** vt [**~ sth. together, ~ together sth.**]
1 (assemble hastily) 匆匆拼凑 ‹*ingredients, elements*› **2** (make hastily) 仓促弄出 ‹*meal, piece of furniture, entertainment*›

• **throw up**
A vi colloq 呕吐
B vt [**~ sth. up, ~ up sth.**]
1 (reveal) 使…显露 ‹*information, fact, problem*› **2** (emit) «*volcano, geyser*» 喷出 ‹*lava, spray, smoke, ash*› **3** (toss into air) 把…抛向空中 ‹*ball, object*›; **to ~ up one's hands in horror** 惊恐地举起双手 **4** (build hastily) 匆匆建造 ‹*shelter, structure*› **5** colloq (vomit) 呕吐出 ‹*food, drink*› **6** colloq (abandon) 放弃 ‹*job, career*›

throwaway /ˈθrəʊəweɪ/
A *adj attrib* **1** (discardable) 一次性使用的; **~ razor/toothbrush/packaging/goods** 一次性剃刀/牙刷/包装/商品 **2** (wasteful) 浪费的 ‹*society, culture*› **3** (casual) 即兴的 ‹*remark, style, entertainment*›
B *n* 一次性物品

throwback /ˈθrəʊbæk/ *n* **1** (animal with primitive characteristics) 返祖者; (reversion to ancestral characteristic) 返祖 **2** fig (person) 有旧时特点的人; (thing) 有旧时特点的事物; **a lot of his work is a ~ to the fifties** 他的许多作品有50年代的风格

thrower /ˈθrəʊə(r)/ *n* (person) 投掷者; (thing) 投掷器; (in sports) 投手; **a stone-~** 扔石头的人

throw-in *n* 掷界外球; **to take a ~** 接界外发球

throwing /ˈθrəʊɪŋ/ *n* [u] **1** (of javelin etc.) 投掷项目; (of stones etc.) 投掷 **2** (discarding) 扔; **the ~ of litter is forbidden** 禁止乱扔垃圾

thrown /θrəʊn/ *pp* ▸**throw**

thru /θruː/ *prep* Amer = **through**

thrum /θrʌm/
A *n* 连续的轻击声; **the steady ~ of rain on the windows** 雨点打在窗户上的滴滴答答声
B *vi* «*rain, fingers*» 连续轻击; «*engine*» 发出突突的声音
C *vt* = **strum A**

thrush[1] /θrʌʃ/ *n* (bird) 鸫

thrush[2] *n* [u] Med ▸**p. 377** (oral) 鹅口疮; (vaginal) 念珠菌阴道炎

thrust /θrʌst/
A *n* **1** [c] (sudden lunge) (with part of body) 猛推; (with pointed weapon) 刺; **with a powerful/violent ~** 用力/猛地一推; **a ~ of the dagger** 匕首的一刺; **to give sth. a ~** 戳某物一下 **2** [c] (drive) 动力; **a new ~ in business development** 商业发展的新动力 **3** [c] *sing* (of argument, essay, narrative) (main aim, purpose) 目的; (gist) 要旨; (chief meaning) 大意; (direction) 方向; **the main ~ of the policy** 政策的主旨 **4** [u] Mech, Tech (propulsive force) 推力; **engine ~** 发动机的推力; **the ~ of a rocket/propeller** 火箭/螺旋桨的推力 **5** [u] Archit (lateral pressure) 侧向压力
B *vt* (*pt, pp* **thrust**) (push with force) 猛推; **she ~ a dagger into his back** 她把匕首刺入他的后背; **he ~ a glass of wine into my hands** 他将一杯葡萄酒递到我手里; **he ~ his hand into the scalding liquid** 他将手猛地伸入滚烫的液体中; **to ~ one's hands into one's pockets** 把双手插入口袋; **to ~ sth. through sth.** 将某物猛地穿过某物; **he ~ his head/fist through the window** 他猛地将头伸出窗外/一拳打碎窗玻璃; **to ~ sth. at sb.** 将某物刺向某人; **to ~ sb./sth. away** *or* **out of the way** 把某人/某物推开; **to ~ one's way in** *or* **into ...** 挤入…; **to ~ one's way past/through ...** 从旁边挤过/挤过…; **they ~ their way through the crowd** 他们挤过了人群; **he ~ his way to the front of the queue** 他挤到了队伍的前面; **to ~ sth. under sb.'s nose** 将某物伸到某人眼皮底下
C *vi* (*pt, pp* **thrust**) (force one's way) 挤; **she ~ past me** 她从我身边挤了过去; **to ~ sth. upon** *or* **on sb.** fig 强迫某人接受某物; **some have greatness ~ upon them** 有些人是被迫成为伟人的
D *v refl* (*pt, pp* **thrust**) **to ~ oneself** (force one's way) 挤; fig (make oneself noticed) 出风头; (impose oneself) 强加自己的意志; **he ~ himself to the front of the crowd** 他挤到了人群的最前面; **she ~s herself forward whenever the boss is present** 只要老板在, 她就喜欢出风头

Phrasal verbs

• **thrust aside** vt [**~ sb./sth. aside, ~ aside sb./sth.**]
1 lit (push to one side) 把…抛在一边 **2** fig (reject) 对…置之不理

• **thrust out** vt [**~ sth. out, ~ out sth.**] 猛推 ‹*object*›; 突然伸出 ‹*part of body*›; **he ~ out his tongue** 他突然吐出舌头; **she opened the door and ~ her head out** 她打开门, 探出头来; **to ~ sth. out of the way** 将某物推开

thrust bearing, thrust block *ns* 推力轴承

thruster /ˈθrʌstə(r)/ *n* 推进器

thrust fault *n* 冲断层

thrusting /ˈθrʌstɪŋ/ *adj* **1** pej (ambitious) 急功近利的 ‹*person, ambition, campaign, drive*› **2** (jutting) 突出的 ‹*part, jaw, canopy*›

thruway /ˈθruːweɪ/ *n* Amer colloq = **throughway**

thud /θʌd/
A *n* 砰的一声
B *vi* (*pres p etc.* **-dd-**) 发出砰声; **she ~ded on the door** 她砰的一声撞在门上; **they ~ded up the stairs** 他们蹬蹬蹬跑上楼梯; **her heart was ~ding** 她的心怦怦直跳

thug /θʌɡ/ *n* 恶棍

thuggery /ˈθʌɡəri/ *n* [u] 暴行

thulium /ˈθuːlɪəm/ *n* [u] 铥

thumb /θʌm/
A *n* **1** (human finger) 拇指; **to be all (fingers and) ~s** 笨手笨脚; **to be under sb.'s ~** 受某人摆布 **2** (animal finger) 第一指 **3** (part of glove) [手套的] 拇指部分
B *vt* **1** (turn pages of) 用拇指翻动 ‹*book, magazine*› **2** (touch) 用拇指按 ‹*button, nose*›; **to ~ one's nose at sb./sth.** 对某人/某事物不屑一顾 **3** colloq (hitch-hike) 竖起拇指要求; **to ~ a lift** *or* **a ride** 竖起拇指要求搭便车
C *vi* 用拇指示意; **to ~ at** *or* **towards sth.** 用拇指示意某物

Phrasal verb

• **thumb through** vt [**~ through sth.**] 迅速翻阅 ‹*book, magazine, pages*›

thumb: ~ index *n* 拇指索引; **~-indexed** *adj* 带拇指索引的

thumbless /ˈθʌmlɪs/ *adj* 没有拇指的

thumbnail /ˈθʌmneɪl/ *n* **1** (nail of the thumb) 拇指甲 **2** (picture) 略图; (description) 短文 **3** (small picture of image) 缩略图; **a ~ image** 缩略图像

thumbnail sketch *n* (drawing) 微型素描; (description) 简短的描写

thumbscrew /ˈθʌmskruː/ *n* **1** (for torture) 拇指夹 [旧时的一种刑具]; **to put the ~s on sb.** fig 对某人施加压力 **2** (screw) 指旋螺钉

thumbs down *n* colloq 反对; **to give sb./sth. the ~** 反对某人/某事; **the candidate/proposal got the ~** 候选人/提案遭到反对

thumb: ~stall *n* 拇指套; **~sucker** *n* **1** (person) 吮拇指的人; **2** Amer colloq pej (article) 新闻背景分析; **~sucking** *n* [u] 吮吸拇指

thumbs up *n* colloq 翘拇指; **to give sb./sth. the ~** 翘拇指赞成某人/某事; **the candidate/proposal got the ~** 候选人/提案获得了赞同

thumbtack /ˈθʌmtæk/ Amer
A *n* = **drawing pin**
B *vt* 用图钉钉住 ‹*notice, paper, poster*›

thump /θʌmp/
A *n* **1** (whack) 重击; **to give sb. a ~** 给某人重重一击 **2** (sound) 重击声 **3** (heartbeat) 怦怦的跳动

B *vt* **1** (whack) 重击; **to ~ sb. in the jaw/stomach** 重击某人的下巴/肚子 **2** colloq (defeat) «*person, team*» 重挫 ‹*opponent, team*›
C *vi* **1** (pound) «*rhythm, music*» 砰砰作响; «*heart*» 怦怦跳; «*person*» 砰砰敲击; **my head is ~ing** 我的头阵阵抽痛; **to ~ on** 砰砰地敲 ‹*door, floor*›; 猛力弹奏 ‹*piano*›; **her heart ~ed with joy** 她高兴得心怦怦直跳 **2** (clump) 噔噔地走; **to ~ upstairs/along the landing** 噔噔地上楼/在楼梯平台上走

Phrasal verbs

- **thump down**

A *vt* [**~ sth. down, ~ down sth.**] 重重地放下 ‹*object, book*›
B *vi* (sit) 重重地坐下; (fall down) 嘭的一声倒下

- **thump out** *vt* [**~ sth. out, ~ out sth.**] 猛力弹奏出 ‹*tune, dance, rhythm*›

thumping /ˈθʌmpɪŋ/
A *n* [u] **1** (pounding or percussion) 重击 **2** colloq (beating) 重挫; **to get a ~** «*person, team*» 遭遇重挫
B *adj* **1** colloq (big) 巨大的; **a ~ salary/error/majority/lie** 极高的薪水/天大的错误/压倒性多数/弥天大谎 **2** (loud) 砰砰作响的 ‹*sound, rhythm*› **3** (severe) 剧烈的 ‹*headache*›
C *adv* Brit colloq 非常; **a ~ great house/lie** 豪宅/弥天大谎

thunder /ˈθʌndə(r)/
A *n attrib* **1** (noise of storm) 雷声; **a clap** *or* **peal of ~** 一声霹雳; **~ and lightning** 雷电; **with a face like ~** *or* **as black as ~** 怒容满面的; **to steal sb.'s ~** 抢某人的风头 **2** (noise of hooves, traffic, cannons, applause) 隆隆声; **the ~ of artillery** 隆隆的炮声
B *vt* **~ (out)** 吼出 ‹*approval, disapproval, applause, command*›
C *vi* **1** (roar) «*person*» 怒吼; **to ~ at** *or* **against sb./sth.** 怒斥某人/某事物 **2** (rush) «*traffic, horses, water, person*» 隆隆地移动; **to ~ along/past …** 轰隆隆地沿着…向前/从…旁边经过; **he came ~ing down the stairs** 他咚咚咚地跑下楼梯; **the river ~ed over the cliffs** 河水轰隆隆地冲过悬崖 **3** (make loud noise) 发出巨大声响
D *v impers* **it's ~ing** 打雷了

thunder: ~bolt *n* 雷电; **~clap** *n* 雷鸣; **~cloud** *n* 雷雨云; **the ~clouds of war** 战争的阴云

thundering /ˈθʌndərɪŋ/ colloq
A *adj* 极大的 ‹*success*›; **he's a ~ bore!** 他这个人烦死了!
B *adv* Brit 极其; **a ~ good book/film** 非常好的书/电影

thunderous /ˈθʌndərəs/ *adj* **1** (loud) 雷鸣般的 ‹*applause, welcome, crash, roar*› **2** (angry) 怒气冲冲的 ‹*expression, face, mood*›; **a ~ attack on the government** 对政府的猛烈抨击 **3** (powerful) 强有力的 ‹*kick, punch*›

thunder: ~storm *n* 雷暴; **~struck** *adj* 惊呆的

thundery /ˈθʌndəri/ *adj* (characterized by thunder) 有雷的 ‹*rain, weather, season*›; (indicating imminent thunder) 可能有雷的 ‹*weather, season, atmosphere, shower*›; **it's ~** 要打雷了

Thurs. /θɜːz/ ▸**p. 182** *abbr* = **Thursday**

Thursday /ˈθɜːzdeɪ, -di/ ▸**p. 182** *n* 星期四; **on ~** 在星期四; **on ~s/every ~** 每周星期四; **~ morning/afternoon/night** 星期四早晨/下午/晚上; **this/last/next ~** 本周四/上周四/下周四

thus /ðʌs/ *adv* formal **1** (in this way) 这样; **children who have been ~ treated** 受到如此对待的孩子们 **2** (consequently) 因此 **3** **~ far** (to this point) 迄今为止

thwack /θwæk/
A *n* **1** (blow with hand) 拍打; **~!** 啪! **2** (sound) 拍打声
B *vt* 重击

thwart /θwɔːt/
A *vt* 阻挠 ‹*person, plan, candidature, nomination*›; **he was ~ed in his ambitions/in love** 他的雄心/恋爱受挫
B *n* 横坐板

thy /ðaɪ/ *adj* archaic = **your**

thyme /taɪm/ *n* [u] **1** (leaves) 百里香叶; **sprig of ~** 百里香枝 **2** (plant) 百里香

thyroid /ˈθaɪrɔɪd/ *n* **1** (gland) 甲状腺 **2** (cartilage) 甲状软骨

thyself /ðaɪˈself/ *pron* archaic = **yourself**

ti /tiː/ *n* Amer = **te**

Tiananmen Square /ˌtjenənmən ˈskweə(r)/ *pr n* 天安门广场

Tianjin /ˌtɪenˈdʒɪn/ *pr n* **~ (Municipality)** 天津（市）

tiara /tɪˈɑːrə/ *n* 冠状头饰

Tibet /tɪˈbet/ *pr n* [u] 西藏; **~ Autonomous Region** 西藏自治区

Tibetan /tɪˈbetn/ ▸**p. 503, p. 426**
A *adj* (of Tibet) 西藏的; (of the people) 藏族人的; (of the language) 藏语的
B *n* **1** [c] (person) 藏族人 **2** [u] (language) 藏语

tibia /ˈtɪbɪə/ ▸**p. 71** *n* (*pl* **tibiae** /ˈtɪbiiː/ *or* **~s**) 胫骨

tic /tɪk/ *n* 肌肉抽搐

tich /tɪtʃ/ *n* Brit colloq = **titch**

tick¹ /tɪk/
A *n* **1** (noise of clock) 滴答声 **2** Brit colloq (moment) 瞬间; **in half a ~** 一瞬间; **I'll be with you in a** *or* **half a ~** 我马上就回来; **shan't be a ~** 马上就好; **just a ~!, in a ~!, in two ~s!** 马上! **3** Brit (mark on paper) 钩号; **to make** *or* **put a ~ against sth.** 在某物上打钩
B *vt* 给…打钩; **please ~ the appropriate box** 请在合适的框内打钩
C *vi* «*clock, watch, bomb*» 滴答响; **I don't know what makes him ~** fig colloq 我不明白他为什么会那么做

Phrasal verbs

- **tick along** *vi* colloq 进行; **work on her book is ~ing along nicely** 她的书写得相当顺利
- **tick away** *vi* «*meter*» [以滴答声] 标示时间流逝; «*time*» 流逝
- **tick by** *vi* «*time*» 流逝
- **tick off**

A *vt* [**~ sth. off, ~ off sth.**] (put mark against) 给…打钩 ‹*item, name*›
B [**~ sb. off, ~ off sb.**] *vt* **1** Brit colloq (reprimand) 斥责 **2** Amer colloq (annoy) 使恼火; **he was a little ~ed off about the news** 他听到那个消息有点生气

- **tick over** *vi* Brit «*engine, machine, vehicle*» 空转; fig 缓慢进行; **they are keeping things ~ing over until the boss returns** 在老板回来以前，他们做事都是慢慢吞吞的

tick² *n* Vet, Zool 壁虱; **sheep ~** 绵羊虱蝇

tick³ *n* [u] Brit colloq (credit) 赊账; **on ~** 以赊账方式

ticker /ˈtɪkə(r)/ *n* **1** Amer (teleprinter) 自动收报机 **2** colloq (heart) 心脏 **3** colloq (watch) 表

ticker tape *n* [u] 自动收报机纸带; **to give sb. a ticker-tape welcome** *or* **reception** 抛彩带热烈欢迎某人

ticker tape parade *n* 抛投纸带的迎宾仪式

ticket /ˈtɪkɪt/
A *n* **1** (proof of entitlement) 票; **a coach/metro** *or* **underground ~** 长途汽车/地铁票; **a theatre/cinema ~** 戏票/电影票; **a library ~** 图书馆借书证; **a left-luggage/cloakroom ~** 行李/衣帽寄存凭证; **a ~ for an exhibition** 展览会入场券; **'~ holders only', 'admission by ~ only'** "凭票入场"; **that's (just) the ~!** colloq (just right) 一切正好!; (the appropriate or desirable thing) 要的就是这个!; **this car could be just the ~ for a small family** 这辆汽车正适合小家庭; **cooperation, that's the ~** 要的就是合作; **for him, football was a ~ to a better life** 对他来说，足球使他过上了更好的生活 **2** (tag, label) 标签; **a ~ bearing the kite mark** 带有风筝标志的标签 **3** (proof of financial transaction) 交易凭证; **goods cannot be exchanged without the ~** 没有收据的商品不能退换; **the till ~** 收银条 **4** colloq (notification of fine) 罚款单; **a parking ~** 违章停车罚款单; **a ~ for speeding, a speeding ~** 超速驾驶罚款单; **to give sb./get a ~** 给某人开/收到罚款单 **5** Aviat, Naut (certificate of competence) 执照; **a pilot's ~** 飞行员执照 **6** *sing* Amer Pol (list of candidates) 候选人名单; **to run on the Republican ~** 作为共和党的候选人参加竞选; **to be elected on an environmentalist ~** 以注重环境保护的政治主张当选
B *vt* **1** (attach ticket to) 加标签于 **2** Amer (provide with ticket) 给…票; **~ed passengers** 持票旅客; **we can now be ~ed electronically** 我们现在可以电子购票 **3** Amer (fine) 对…开罚款单; **to be ~ed** colloq 被贴罚款单

ticket: ~ agency *n* 代理售票处; **~ agent** ▸**p. 409** *n* 代理售票人; **~ barrier** *n* 验票闸门; **~ booth** *n* 售票亭; **~ clerk** ▸**p. 409** *n* Brit 售票员; **~ collector** ▸**p. 409** *n* Brit 收票员; **~ dispenser** *n* Brit 出票机; **~ holder** *n* 持票人; **~ inspector** ▸**p. 409** *n* 查票员; **~ machine** *n* 自动售票机; **~ office** *n* 售票处; **~ punch** *n* 剪票钳; **~ tout** *n* Brit 票贩子; **~ window** *n* 售票窗口

tickety-boo /ˌtɪkətɪˈbuː/ *adj* Brit colloq dated or hum 良好的; **everything is ~** 一切都好

tick fever *n* [c and u] 蜱热

ticking /ˈtɪkɪŋ/
A *n* [u] 滴答声
B *adj* 滴答作响的 ‹*clock, mechanism*›; **a ~ sound** *or* **noise** 滴答声

ticking-off *n* (*pl* **tickings-off** *or* **~s**) Brit colloq 斥责; **to give sb. a ~** 申斥某人

tickle /ˈtɪkl/
A *vt* **1** (stimulate by touch) 使…发痒 ‹*person, animal, body part*›; **to ~ sb. in the ribs/on the tummy** 胳肢某人的肋部/腹部 **2** fig colloq (gratify) «*news, event, person, food*» 使…满足 ‹*person, palate, appetite, sense of humour*›; (amuse) «*news, event, person, food*» 使…高兴 ‹*person*›; **to ~ sb.'s fancy** (amuse) 使某人开心; (appeal to) 使某人觉得好玩; **to be ~d to death, to be ~d pink** 乐不可支
B *vi* **1** (itch) «*person*» 觉得痒; **my arm ~s** 我手臂发痒 **2** (cause itching) «*blanket, garment, feather, wool*» 使人发痒
C *n* 痒; **to give sb. a ~** 胳肢某人; **I've got a ~ in my throat** 我喉咙发痒; **to have a (bit of) slap and ~** Brit colloq 打情骂俏

tickler /ˈtɪklə(r)/ *n* Brit colloq 难题

tickling /ˈtɪklɪŋ/ *adj* 使人发痒的 ‹*fabric, blanket, jumper*›; 使喉咙发痒的 ‹*cough*›; 痒的 ‹*feeling, sensation*›

ticklish /ˈtɪklɪʃ/ *adj* **1** (sensitive to tickling) 易痒的; (unable to bear being tickled) 怕痒的 **2** (persistently irritating) 使喉咙发痒的 ‹*cough*› **3** (tricky) 棘手的 ‹*problem, situation, subject, question*› **4** (touchy) 易被激怒的 ‹*person*›; **he is ~ on that subject** 他对那个话题很敏感

tickly /ˈtɪkli/ *adj* 痒的 ‹*feeling*›; 使人发痒的 ‹*fabric, garment*›; 使喉咙发痒的 ‹*cough*›

tick: ~over *n* [u] Brit 怠速运转; **to leave the engine on ~over** 让发动机怠速运转; **~-tack** *n* [u] Brit = **tic-tac**; **~-tack-toe** *n* [u] Amer = **tic-tac-toe**; **~-tock** *n* **1** (ticking) [钟的] 滴答声; **2** child lang (clock) 钟

ticky-tacky /ˈtɪkɪtækɪ/ Amer colloq pej
A *n* [u] 劣质建筑材料
B *adj* 用劣质建筑材料制造的

tic-tac /ˈtɪktæk/ *n* [u] Brit [赛马时赌注登记经纪人及其助手相互间用手表示的] 秘密信号; **a ~ man** 发秘密信号的人

tic-tac-toe /ˌtɪktækˈtəʊ/ *n* [u] Amer = **noughts and crosses**

t

tidal /ˈtaɪdl/ *adj* (of the tide) 潮汐的; (influenced by the tide) 受潮汐影响的 ‹*inlet*›; ～ **current** *or* **flow** 潮流; **the Thames is** ～ 泰晤士河是感潮河; **a** ～ **river** 感潮河

tidal: ～ **basin** *n* 有潮港池; ～ **energy** *n* [u] 潮汐能; ～ **power station** *n* 潮汐能电站; ～ **waters** *npl* 感潮水域; ～ **wave** *n* 1 (tsunami) 海啸; 2 fig (of emotion, activity, behaviour) [公众情绪、行为等的] 浪潮

tidbit /ˈtɪdbɪt/ *n* Amer = **titbit**

tiddler /ˈtɪdlə(r)/ *n* Brit 1 (stickleback) 刺鱼; (minnow) 米诺鱼; (any small fish) 小鱼 2 colloq hum (person) 小娃娃

tiddly /ˈtɪdli/ *adj* Brit colloq 1 (drunk) 微醉的 2 (tiny) 微小的 ‹*amount, portion*›

tiddlywinks /ˈtɪdlɪwɪŋks/ Amer **tiddledy-winks** /ˈtɪdldɪwɪŋks/ ▸**p. 307** *npl* + *v sing* 挑圆片游戏

tide /taɪd/ *n* 1 (rise or fall of sea) 潮; **the rising/falling** *or* **ebb** ～ 涨潮/退潮; **the** ～ **is in/out** 涨潮/退潮了; **(at) high/low** ～ (处于) 高潮/低潮; **time and** ～ **wait for no man** Prov 时不我待 2 fig (powerful trend, tendency, surge of feelings) 潮流; **the** ～ **of public opinion** 舆论倾向; **the** ～ **of events/war** 事件/战争的动向; **a rising** ～ **of popular interest/public sympathy** 大众兴趣/公众同情的上升态势; **to go** *or* **swim with the** ～ 顺应潮流; **to go** *or* **swim against** *or* Amer **to buck the** ～ 逆潮流; **to turn the** ～ 扭转形势; **the** ～ **has turned in our favour/against us** 局势发生了有利于/不利于我们的转变; **to stem the** ～ 阻止发展趋势; **to stem the** ～ **of anarchy/public criticism** 阻止无政府状态的进一步恶化/扭转舆论批评 3 fig (surging movement) 奔涌; **a** ～ **of letters/refugees** 潮水般的书信/难民

Phrasal verb

- **tide over** *vt* [～ **sb. over**] «*money, food, clothing*» 帮助…挺过去; **to** ～ **sb. over till pay day/for another year** 帮助某人撑到发薪日/再撑一年; **to** ～ **sb. over the crisis** 助某人度过危机

tide: ～ **gate** *n* 潮闸; ～ **gauge** *n* 测潮仪; ～**land** /-lænd/ *n* Amer 潮浸区; ～**line** *n* 潮位线; ～**mark** *n* 1 (on beach) 高潮痕; 2 Brit colloq (in bathtub) 垢痕; ～ **mill** *n* 潮水动力磨; ～ **race** *n* 急潮流; ～ **rip** *n* 潮激; ～ **table** *n* 潮汐表; ～**way** *n* 潮汐水道

tidily /ˈtaɪdɪli/ *adv* 整齐地; **he doesn't dress very** ～ 他穿得不是很整洁; ～ **written notes** 书写工整的笔记

tidiness /ˈtaɪdɪnɪs/ *n* [u] (of house, desk, person, appearance, etc.) 整洁; (of work, behaviour) 井井有条; **the** ～ **of his handwriting** 他笔迹的工整

tidings /ˈtaɪdɪŋz/ *npl* liter 消息; ～ **of (great) joy** (大) 喜讯; **to be the bearer of bad** ～ 带来坏消息

tidy /ˈtaɪdi/

A *adj* (*comp* **tidier**, *superl* **tidiest**) 1 (neat) 整洁的; (well organized) 有条理的; **to get** *or* **make sth.** ～ 把某物收拾整齐; **to make oneself** ～ 梳理打扮; **to have a** ～ **mind** 思维严谨 2 *attrib* colloq (large, generous) 相当大的 ‹*sum, portion*›; **he earns a** ～ **commission on every sale** 每一笔销售他都能赚取可观的佣金; **a** ～ **penny** 一大笔钱; **they set off at a** ～ **pace** 他们快速出发了

B *v refl* **to** ～ **oneself (up)** 梳理打扮

C *n* Brit [盛零碎物品的] 容器; **a desk** ～ 案头文具盒

Phrasal verbs

- **tidy away** *vt* [～ **sth. away,** ～ **away sth.**] 把…收拾起来
- **tidy out** *vt* [～ **sth. out,** ～ **out sth.**] 清理; **to** ～ **out the garage/store room** 清理车库/储藏室
- **tidy up**

A *vt* [～ **sth. up,** ～ **up sth.**] 整理; **please** ～ **your bedroom up** 请把你的卧室收拾干净

B *vi* 整理; **to** ～ **up after sb.** 收拾被某人弄乱的地方

tidy-minded *adj* (disposed to keeping things neat) 爱整洁的; (preferring things to be well organized) 有条理的

tidy-out, tidy-up *ns* Brit 收拾; **they are having a** ～ **of the house** 他们正在整理房子

tie /taɪ/

A *vt* (*pres p* **tying**; *pt, pp* ～**d**) 1 (fasten, bind) 捆; **to** ～ **sb./sth. to sth.** 把某人/某物捆在某物上; **to** ～ **sth. with string** 用绳子将某物捆起来; **to** ～ **sb. hand and foot** 捆住某人的手脚; fig 限制某人的行动自由; **he was** ～**d hand and foot by the demands of his position** 他被职位的要求束缚住了; **to have one's hands** ～**d** fig 无能为力; **to** ～ **sth. down** 捆住某物; **to** ～ **sb./sth. together** 将某人/某物绑起来; **the peasants remain firmly** ～**d to the land** 农民们依然紧紧依附土地 2 (attach with string) 系; (arrange to form a knot, join in knot) 扎 ‹*hair, bow*›; 打 ‹*necktie, cravat*›; **to** ～ **a string/shoelace** 扎绳子/系鞋带; **to** ～ **a knot in the rope** 在绳子上打结; **to** ～ **sth. on** 把某物系上; **to** ～ **sth. on/round sth.** 将某物系在某物上/周围; **he** ～**d his scarf round his neck** 他将围巾系在脖子上; **to** ～ **the knot** fig colloq 结婚; **to** ～ **oneself into** *or* **(up) in knots** 搞糊涂 3 Mus 用连结线连接 4 Sport, Games **to** ～ **the score/match** 比分相当/比赛打成平局; **Britain is** ～**d with Holland for second place** 英国队与荷兰队并列第二

B *vi* (*pres p* **tying**; *pp* ～**d**) 1 (be fastened) «*string*» 系住; **the ribbon** ～**s in front/at the back** 丝带在前面/后面打结 2 (draw) (in sports match) 打成平局; (in race) 成绩相同; (in vote) 得票相等; **the teams were tying two all** 两队 2 比 2 打成平局; **to** ～ **with sb./sth.** 同某人/某队打成平局; **the runners** ～**d for second place** 这几名赛跑运动员并列第二

C *n* 1 (item of clothing) 领带; **to wear/tie a** ～ 系着/打领带 2 (fastener for bags, plants) (cord) 带子; (wire) 线; **plastic** ～**s** 塑料绳 3 Constr (rod, beam) 系梁 4 (equal score) (in sport, game, competition) 平局; (in election) 等票; **in the event of a** ～ (in sport, game, competition) 如果打成平局; (in election) 如果出现等票; **the match ended in a** ～ **(for first/second** *etc.* **place)** (争夺第一名/第二名等的) 比赛以平局结束 5 Brit Sport (arranged match) 比赛; **(the first leg of) a** ～ **between ...** …之间的比赛 (的第一轮) 6 *usu pl* fig (bond) 纽带; **family** ～**s** 家族关系; **to have (close)** ～**s with sb./sth.** 同某人/某事物有 (密切) 关系; **to cement** *or* **strengthen** ～**s between ...** 加强…之间的联系; **to cut** *or* **sever/loosen the** ～**s with sb./sth.** 切断/疏远与某人/某事物的联系; **to cut the** ～**s with one's past** 和过去一刀两断 7 Amer Rail = **sleeper 5** 8 Mus 连结线 9 *usu pl* fig (limit on person's freedom of action) 累赘; (constraint) 束缚; **feudal** ～**s** 封建束缚

Phrasal verbs

- **tie back** *vt* [～ **sth. back,** ～ **back sth.**] 向后系住; **she** ～**d her hair back** 她把头发向后扎起来
- **tie down** *vt* 1 [～ **sth. down,** ～ **down sth.**] (fasten, bind) 拴住 2 [～ **sb. down**] (commit, restrict) 限制; **children do** ～ **you down, don't they?** 孩子们的确把你拖累住了, 是吗? ; **to** ～ **sb./oneself down to sth.** 把某人/自己束缚在某事物上; **he didn't want to** ～ **himself down to a steady job** 他不想把自己局限在一份固定的工作上; **to be** ～**d down by sth.** 受到某事物的束缚
- **tie in with** *vt* [～ **in with sth.**] (tally with) 与…一致; (have link with) 与…有联系; **to** ～ **sth. in with sth.** (combine) 将某事物同某事物相结合; (connect) 将某物同某物相连接; **her husband is able to** ～ **his shifts in with hers** 她丈夫能够使上班时间和她同步; **her ideas don't** ～ **in with mine** 她的想法和我不一致
- **tie on** *vt* [～ **sth. on,** ～ **on sth.**] 将…系上
- **tie together** *vt* [～ **sth. together**] 将…绑在一起; **we** ～**d his hands together** 我们把他的双手绑在一起
- **tie up**

A [～ **sth. up,** ～ **up sth.**] *vt*
1 (secure) 系紧; **to** ～ **up a boat** 系牢小船; **she** ～**d her hair up** 她扎紧了头发 2 (bring to satisfactory conclusion) 完成; **to** ～ **up the loose ends** 处理未了结的零星事务; **to** ～ **up a business deal** 处理一宗商业交易 3 (invest or reserve) 把…搁死 ‹*capital*›; **money** ～**d up in accounts** 搁死在账户内的资金

B [～ **sb. up**] *vt*
1 (bind with rope etc.) 把…捆起来 2 **to be** ～**d up** (be busy) 被缠住; **he's** ～**d up in a meeting/with a client** 他正在开会/正在见客户无法分身; **I'm a bit** ～**d up right now** 我现在有点忙

tie: ～**back** *n* 1 (cord for curtain) 帘扣带; 2 (curtain) 扣帘; ～ **bar** *n* 系杆; ～ **beam** *n* 系梁; ～ **bolt** *n* 系紧螺栓; ～ **break,** ～ **breaker** *ns* (in tennis) 决胜局; (in quiz) 决胜负的问题; ～ **clasp,** ～ **clip** *ns* 领带夹

tied /taɪd/ *adj* Brit 租给雇工的 ‹*house, cottage*›

tied: ～ **agent** *n* [代表一家或多家保险公司的] 独立代理人; ～ **house** *n* Brit 酒厂酒馆

tie-dye

A *n* 扎染织物

B *vt* 扎染

tie: ～**-in** *n* 1 (link) 关联; **a** ～**-in between sth. and sth.** 某物和某物之间的关系; 2 Amer Comm (spin-off product) 关联产品; 3 Comm (sale) 搭售; (advertisement) 搭卖广告; 4 Comm (item) 搭售的商品; ～**-on** *adj* 可系上的; ～ **pin** *n* 领带别针; ～ **plate** *n* 系板

tier /tɪə(r)/

A *n* 1 (row, layer) (in seating) 排; (of cake, sandwich) 层 2 (grade, level of organization, system) 阶层; **a two/three/four-**～ **system** 二/三/四级系统

B *vt* 使…分层 ‹*seating, organization, system*›; **a four-**～**ed cake** 四层的蛋糕

tie: ～ **rack** *n* 领带架; ～ **rod** *n* (in steering gear) 转向横拉杆; (in building) 拉杆; ～ **tack** *n* Amer = ～ **pin**

tie-up *n* 1 (link) 联合; **a** ～ **with sth.** 与某机构的联合 2 Amer (stoppage) (of work) 停顿; (of traffic) 拥堵 3 Amer colloq (mooring) 停泊处

tiff /tɪf/ *n* colloq 拌嘴; **a lovers'** ～ 情人间的吵嘴; **to have a** ～ 发生口角

tig /tɪg/ ▸**p. 307** *n* [u] 儿童捉人游戏

tiger /ˈtaɪgə(r)/ *n* 老虎; **to have a** ～ **by the tail** fig 遇到出乎意料的困难

tiger: ～ **cub** *n* 虎仔; ～ **economy** *n* 小龙经济 [指蓬勃发展的韩国、新加坡等国家经济]

tigerish /ˈtaɪgərɪʃ/ *adj* 像虎的 ‹*creature, behaviour*›; 狂暴的 ‹*person, attack, mood*›; ～ **colouring** 似虎皮的色彩

tiger: ～ **lily** *n* 卷丹; ～**'s eye** *n* 虎睛宝石; ～ **shark** *n* 鼬鲨

tight /taɪt/

A *adj* 1 (firm) 紧的; **the drawer/window is very** ～ 抽屉/窗户很紧; **to have a** ～ **grasp** *or* **hold on sth.** 紧紧抓住某物; fig 对某事物有很好的把握 2 (close-fitting) 紧身的 ‹*clothes*›; **a** ～ **dress/skirt/jacket** 紧身连衣裙/裙子/夹克; **my shoes are** ～ 我的鞋子很紧 3 (with little space) 挤满的; **a** ～ **squeeze** 极度的拥挤; **it's going to be** ～ **in the back seat** 后座会很挤 4 (difficult to negotiate) 难对付的; **a** ～ **bend** *or* **corner** *or* **curve** 急转弯; **to be in/get oneself into a** ～ **corner** *or* **situation** *or* colloq **spot (over sth.)** (在某事上) 处于/使自己陷入困境 5 (pulled taut) 拉紧的 ‹*rope, string, strap*›; 紧密的 ‹*stitch, weaving*›; 憋闷的 ‹*chest, breathing*›; **your knitting is too** ～ 你

织得太密了; **as ～ as a drum** 非常紧的; **you must stretch the fabric as ～ as a drum** 你必须把布绷得紧紧的; **my nerves are as ～ as a drum** 我的神经绷得紧紧的 **6** (restricted, limited) 严格的 ‹*control, restriction*›; 排满的 ‹*timetable*›; **money is a bit ～ these days** 最近钱有些紧; **a ～ budget** 紧张的预算; **a ～ schedule** 密集的日程安排; **time is rather ～** 时间很紧 **7** (impermeable) 密封的 ‹*container, bottle*›; **a ～ seal/joint** 密封条/严丝合缝的接口; **a ～ roof** 不漏雨的屋顶; **to run a ～ ship** fig 管理有方 **8** colloq (drunk) 醉醺醺的; **to be/feel ～** 喝醉/觉得醉了; **to get ～** 喝醉 **9** Sport (evenly contested) 势均力敌的 ‹*match, competition*› **10** colloq (miserly) 小气的; **she is very ～ (with her money)** 她（对钱）很小气; **he's as ～ as they come** 他太抠门儿了 **11** (compact) 密集的; **they sat in a ～ circle around him** 他们紧紧围坐在他周围

B *adv* **1** (firmly) 紧紧地; **to fasten/close sth. ～** 紧紧系住/关上某物 **2** (closely) 紧紧地 ‹*squeeze, knit, stitch*›; **he pulled the collar of his coat ～** 他把大衣领子拉得紧紧的; **the commuters are packed ～ on the trains** 火车上挤满了上下班的人 **3** (fast) 牢固地; **to hold/sit ～** 抓牢/坐着不动; **to sit ～ and wait for the crisis to blow over** 静待危机结束

C **tights** *npl* **1** esp Brit (worn by women) 连裤袜; **a pair of ～s** 一双连裤袜 **2** (worn by acrobats, dancers, etc.) 紧身衣

tight-arsed /ˈtaɪtɑːst/ Brit, **tight-assed** /ˈtaɪtæst/ Amer *adjs* sl **1** (uptight, conventional) 拘谨的 ‹*person, society*› **2** (mean) 小气的

tighten /ˈtaɪtn/

A *vt* **1** (tauten) 使变紧; (in sewing) 缝紧 ‹*waist, fit*›; (in knitting) 收紧 ‹*stitch, tension*›; **to ～ a lid/screw/rope/clip/spring** 盖紧盖子/拧紧螺丝/系紧绳子/夹紧夹子/拉紧弹簧; **they ～ed their grip on the land** 他们加紧了对这片土地的控制; **to ～ the tension** 使局势更为紧张; **to ～ the purse strings** fig 省吃俭用 **2** (make stricter) 使更严格; **to ～ a budget/credit controls** 紧缩预算/信贷; **to ～ control/security** 加紧控制/加强安全措施; **to ～ laws/regulations/policy** 严格执行法律/规章/政策

B *vi* **1** (narrow) «*screw, nut, rope, grip*» 变紧; «*arm, muscle, lips*» 绷紧; **her mouth ～ed** 她的嘴唇紧闭着; **she felt her throat ～** 她觉得喉咙发紧 **2** (become stricter) «*law, security, credit control, policy*» 变得更严格

Phrasal verb

• **tighten up**

A *vt* [**～ sth. up, ～ up sth.**] **1** (tauten) 收紧 ‹*spring*›; 系紧 ‹*rope, belt, strap, tie*› **2** (make stricter) 使更严格; **to ～ up security** 加强安全措施; **to ～ up laws/regulations/restrictions on sth.** 针对某事物更严格地执行法律/规定/限制规定

B *vi* **1** **to ～ up on sth.** (become stricter) 对某事物更严格 **2** (become tense) 变得紧张

tightening /ˈtaɪtnɪŋ/ *n* [u] **1** (becoming tighter) (of screw, lid) 变紧; (of muscle, lips, mouth) 绷紧; (of throat) 发紧 **2** **～ (up)** (making stricter) (of legislation, security, restrictions, policy) 变严格; (of budget, credit) 紧缩

tight: ～-fisted *adj* colloq 小气的; **～-fitting** *adj* 紧身的; **～-knit** *adj* **1** (bound closely together) 紧密团结的 ‹*group, family, community*›; **2** (close-fitting) 紧密编织的 ‹*garment, fabric, sweater*›; **～-lipped** *adj* (with closed lips) 双唇紧闭的; (determinedly silent) 口紧的

tightly /ˈtaɪtli/ *adv* **1** (firmly) 紧紧地; **her hair was drawn back ～ in a bun** 她的头发向后紧紧地梳成一个圆髻; **a ～ stretched rope** 绷紧的绳索 **2** (closely) 紧密地 ‹*wound*›; **the ～ packed crowd** 挤得严严实实的人群 **3** (strictly) 严格地 ‹*controlled, restricted, budgeted, scheduled*›

tightness /ˈtaɪtnɪs/ *n* [u] **1** (tautness) (of belt, rope) 拉紧; (of stitch, fabric) 紧密 **2** (narrowing) (of muscles, jaw, lip, mouth) 紧绷; (of chest, breathing, throat) 憋闷 **3** (restriction, constraint) (of finances) 紧缩; (of time) 紧凑; (of security, control) 严格 **4** (smallness) (of space) 挤; (of clothing, garment, footwear) 紧

tightrope /ˈtaɪtrəʊp/ *n* (wire) 绷紧的钢丝; (rope) 绷紧的绳索; **to walk the ～** lit 走钢丝; fig 身处险境; **I'm walking the ～ between my family and my job** 我小心翼翼地在家庭与工作之间周旋; **to be on a ～** fig 处于困境

tightrope walker *n* 走钢丝表演者

tightwad /ˈtaɪtwɒd/ *n* Amer colloq pej 小气鬼

tigress /ˈtaɪɡrɪs/ *n* **1** lit (female tiger) 雌虎 **2** fig (woman) 母老虎

tilde /ˈtɪldə/ *n* (in Spanish) 腭化符号; (in Portuguese) 鼻音化符号

tile /taɪl/

A *n* (for roof) 瓦片; (for floor, wall) 瓷砖; **to go out on the ～s, to have a night on the ～s** Brit colloq 晚上出去纵情玩乐

B *vt* 贴瓷砖于 ‹*wall, floor, patio, room*›; 铺瓦于 ‹*roof*›

tiled /taɪld/ *adj* 铺了瓷砖的 ‹*bathroom, kitchen, floor, wall*›; 铺了瓦的 ‹*roof*›

tiler /ˈtaɪlə(r)/ ▸ **p. 409** *n* 砖瓦工

tiling /ˈtaɪlɪŋ/ *n* [u] **1** (tiles) (of roof) 瓦片; (of floor, wall) 瓷砖 **2** (laying tiles) (for roof) 铺瓦; (for floor, wall) 贴砖

till[1] /tɪl/ = **until**

till[2] *n* (drawer) 放钱的抽屉; (box) 钱箱; **to be caught with/have one's fingers** *or* **hand in the ～** fig colloq 偷自己单位的钱时被当场抓住/偷自己单位的钱

till[3] *vt* (work land) 耕种

tillage /ˈtɪlɪdʒ/ *n* [u] (process) 耕种; (land) 耕地

tiller /ˈtɪlə(r)/ *n* 舵柄; **at** *or* **on the ～** 掌舵

till: ～ receipt *n* 购货小票; **～ roll** *n* 收银机纸卷

tilt /tɪlt/

A *vt* 使倾斜; **to ～ one's head to one side** 把头歪向一边; **to ～ sth. to the left/right** 把某物向左/向右倾侧; **to ～ sth. back/forward** 使某物向后仰/向前倾; **to ～ one's cap over one's eyes/to the back of one's head** 把帽子压到眼睛上方/推到脑后; **to ～ the balance in favour of/away from sth.** 使局面有利于/不利于某事物

B *vi* **1** (incline) 倾斜; **to ～ to the left/right/to one side** 向左/右/一边倾斜; **the balance of industrial power ～ed towards the workers** 产业力量的天平向劳工倾斜 **2** (attempt) 尝试; **to ～ at winning the European Cup** 向欧洲杯发起冲击 **3** Hist (joust) 骑马持矛冲刺; **to ～ at sb.** 骑马持矛冲向某人; fig 抨击某人

C *n* **1** (incline) 倾斜; **a slight/definite/45° ～** 稍微/明显/45 度的倾斜; **a ～ to the left/north** 向左/向北的倾斜; **it is on the ～** 它斜了 **2** (bias) 倾向; **a ～ toward** *or* **towards sth./sb.** 对某事物/某人的偏向 **3** (speed, force) **(at) full ～** 全速（地） **4** Hist (jousting contest) 马上比枪; (thrust, blow in contest) 骑马持矛冲刺; **to make** *or* **take a ～ at sb.** 骑马持矛冲向某人; **to have** *or* **take a ～ at sb./sth.** fig 抨击某人/某事物

tilt-and-turn window *n* 内开内倒窗

tilted /ˈtɪltɪd/ *adj* 倾斜的; **～ to the right/to one side** 歪向右边/一边的; **his head was ～ back** *or* **backward/forward** 他的头后仰/前倾着

tilting train /ˈtɪltɪŋ treɪn/ *n* 摆式列车

tilt-top table *n* **1** (hinged table) 翻起式桌子 **2** (sloping table) 斜面桌

timber /ˈtɪmbə(r)/

A *n* **1** [u] esp Brit (wood prepared for use in building etc.) 木材 **2** [u] (trees grown for use in building etc.) [可作木材的] 林木; **to fell ～** 伐木; **'T～!'** "倒啦!" [伐木工的呼喊声] **3** [c] (beam) 栋木; **roof ～s** 房檩

B *modif* **1** (relating to timber) 木材的; **～ preservative/treatment/importer/trade** 木材防护剂/处理/进口商/贸易; **a ～ plantation** 林场 **2** (made of timber) 木制的; **～ panelling/roof/floor/building** 木嵌板/木屋顶/木地板/木结构建筑

timber: ～-clad *adj* 木板包覆的; **～ cladding** *n* [u] 木板包覆

timbered /ˈtɪmbəd/ *adj* **1** (wooded) 林木覆盖的 ‹*hill, slopes*› **2** (made with timber) 木结构的 ‹*building*›; (panelled in timber) 镶木的 ‹*wall, room*›

timber-framed *adj* 木构架的

timbering /ˈtɪmbərɪŋ/ *n* [u] **1** (material) 木材 **2** (finished work) 木结构

timber: ～land /-lænd/ *n* [u] Amer 用材林地; **～ line** *n* = **treeline**; **～ merchant** ▸ **p. 409** *n* Brit 木材商; **～ mill** *n* = **sawmill**; **～ yard** *n* 贮木场

timbre /ˈtɪmbə(r), ˈtæmbrə/ *n* **1** Mus 音质 **2** Ling 音色

Timbuktu /ˌtɪmbʌkˈtuː/

A *pr n* (town in west Africa) 廷巴克图

B *n* [u] (remote or distant place) 偏远的地方

time /taɪm/ ▸ **p. 831**

A *n* **1** [u] (continuum, passing of time) 时间; **～ and space** 时间与空间; **for all ～** 永远; **～ passes** *or* **goes on** *or* **goes by** 时间流逝; **only ～ will tell** 只有时间会证明 **2** [u] (specific duration) 一段时间; **to have a good ～** 过得很愉快; **(at) the present ～** （在）当前; **at this point in ～** 目前; **to take ～ (for sb./sth. to do sth.)** （某人/某物做某事）花费时间; **to need/take ～ (to do sth.)** （做某事）需要时间; **the ～ when ...** …的时候; **all in good ～** 不消多久; **for a ～** 一度; **in a week's ～** 一周以后; **in** *or* **with ～, in the course of ～** 一段时间以后; **over ～** 渐渐地; **to have all the ～ in the world** 有的是时间; **to have ～ (for sth./to do sth.)** 有时间（处理某事物/做某事）; **to have a lot of ～ for sb./sth.** 赞赏某人/某物; **to have no ～ for sb./sth.** 不喜欢某人/某事物; **to have no ～ to lose** 耽误不起时间; **to save/waste ～** 节省/浪费时间; **to find ～ (for sth./to do sth.)** 找时间（处理某事/做某事）; **to spend ～ (in) doing sth.** 花时间做某事; **quite some ～** 很长一段时间; **to take one's ～ (over sth./to do sth.** *or* **doing sth.)** (not hurry) （在某事上/做某事）不着急; iron (be unreasonably late or slow) （在某事上/做某事）慢吞吞; **to leave ～ (for sth./to do sth.)** （为某事/做某事）留出时间; **out of ～** 过了规定的时间; **in one's ～** 在一生中的某个时期; **for the ～ being** 暂时; **～ drags** *or* **hangs heavy (on one's hands)** （觉得）时间过得很慢; **to have ～ on one's hands** 有大把空闲时间; **a long/short ～** 很长/很短的时间; **it's a long ～ since I went to the cinema** 我很久没去看电影了; **long ～ no see!** 好久不见!; **she won't be ready for some ～ yet** 她还得过一段时间才能准备好; **all/most of the ～** 一直/大部分时间; **after a** *or* **some ～** 过了一会儿; **some ～ ago** 不久前; **a period of ～** 一段时间; **in one's own (good) ～** colloq 在自己方便时; **he'll tell you in his own ～** 他到时候会告诉你的; **a ～ gap** 时间间隔 **3** [u] (hour of the day, night) 时刻; **what's the ～?** 几点了?; **until such ～ as ...** 直到…的时候; **local ～** 当地时间; **to show the ～** 显示时间; **to keep good ～** «*watch*» 走得准; «*person*» 守时; **do you have the ～ (on you)?** 你知道现在几点了?; **to pass the ～ of day with sb.** 和某人寒暄; **I wouldn't give him the ～ of day** 我才不会搭理他呢; **from this/that ～ on** 从现在/从那时起 **4** [u and c] (period measured in units) 用时; **cooking ～** 烹饪时间; **record ～** 破纪录时间; **within the agreed/a reasonable ～** 在约定/合理的期限内; **flight/journey ～** 飞行/旅行时间

t

5 [u] (period allocated for purpose) 规定时间; **breakfast/lunch/tea/supper** *or* **dinner ~** 早餐/午餐/喝茶/晚餐时间; **to do sth. to ~** 准时做某事; **in ~** (within the allotted time) 及时; (eventually) 迟早; **we arrived just in ~** 我们差点就晚到了; **you'll learn how to do it in ~** 你最终会学会如何做这件事的; **(and) about time (too)** colloq 早该如此; **they're going to get married, and about ~ too!** 他们要结婚了，也早该结了！; **it's about ~ we were leaving** 我们该走了; **it's ~ for lunch** 该吃午餐了; **the right/wrong ~** 适当的/不适当的时间; **there is a ~ and place for everything** 凡事都有其时机; **now is your ~!** 现在你的机会到了！; **his ~ had come** 他的大限到了; **her ~ was near** 她快要分娩了; **~'s up!** 时间到了！; **to choose one's ~** 选择最佳时机; **this is no ~ for sth./(for sb.) to do sth.** 这不是…/（某人）做某事的时候; **this is no ~ for indecision!** 现在必须当机立断！; **to make ~ with sb.** Amer colloq 勾搭上某人 **6** [c] (occasion, instance) 次; **I play tennis three ~s a week** 我每周打三次网球; **this ~ I'll let you off** 这次我就放过你; **at the ~ we were living in London** 当时我们住在伦敦; **(the) next/last ~** 下次/上次; **for the first ~** 第一次; **~ and again, ~ and again** 再三地; **from ~ to ~** 时不时地; **each** *or* **every ~** 每次; **several ~s** 好几次; **at ~s** 有时候; **at other ~s** 在其他时候; **he comes to see us at odd ~s** 他时不时地来看看我们; **one/two** *etc.* **at a ~** 每次一个/两个等; **there are ~s when ...** 有时候…; **many** *or* **very many** *or* **many many ~s** 很多次; **many's the ~ that ...** 多次…; **nine ~s out of ten, ninety-nine ~s out of a hundred** 十有八九; **there's always a first ~** 总会有第一次; **there's a first ~ for everything** 凡事总有第一次; **the previous ~, the ~ before** 上一次; **~ after ~, ~ and ~ again** 一次又一次地 **7** [c] *usu pl* (period associated with events or people) 时期; **prehistoric/ancient/medieval/modern ~(s)** 史前时代/古代/中世纪/现代; **in Victorian ~s** 在维多利亚时代; **our ~s** 我们的时代; **former** *or* **olden ~s** 旧时; **in ~s past** 在过去; **in ~ of war/peace** 在战争/和平年代; **good/bad ~s** 美好/艰难的时期; **opening/closing ~s** 开门/关门时间; **Christmas/harvest/holiday ~** 圣诞节期/收获期/假期; **spring/summer/winter ~** 春季/夏季/冬季; **he left the company before my ~** 在我来这里上班之前，他就离开了公司; **at my ~ of life** 在我这个年龄; **it's an old house, but it will last** *or* **see out my ~** 这是一所老房子，但在我有生之年将保持完好; **bath ~** [尤指儿童的] 洗澡时间 **8** [u] Brit (closing time in bar, pub) 关门时间; **to call ~** 宣布打烊时间已到; **~ please!** 关门了！; **~, gentlemen, please!** 先生们，要打烊了！ **9** [u] (prison sentence) 刑期; **to do** *or* **serve ~** colloq 坐牢 **10** [u] Mus (rhythm) 节拍; **three eight ~** 八分之三拍; **waltz/march ~** 圆舞曲/进行曲节拍 **11** [u] Mus (tempo) 节奏; **quick/slow ~** 快节奏/慢节奏; **to play in ~ (to** *or* **with the music)** 演奏得合（音乐的）节奏; **out of ~** 不合节奏的 **12** **times** Math (multiplication) 倍; **the nine ~s table** 九九乘法表; **three ~s as long (as sth.)** （某物的）3 倍长; **three ~s longer (than sth.)** （比某物）长 3 倍

B *vt* **1** (schedule) 为…安排时间 ‹*event*›; 选择 ‹*moment*›; **you've ~d your visit just right** 你来得正是时候; **to ~ sth. for sth.** 把某事定在某时间; **kick-off is ~d for 2.30 p.m.** 足球比赛定于下午两点半开始; **to ~ sth. to do sth.** 定于某时做某事; **to ~ the bomb to go off at 8 p.m.** 把炸弹定在晚上 8 点爆炸; **a perfectly-/badly-~d remark** 正合时宜/不合时宜的话 **2** (measure speed, duration) 测定…所需的时间 ‹*person, event, process*›; **to ~ an egg** 设定煮鸡蛋的时间; **I ~d how long it took to empty the bottle** 我记录了清空瓶子所需的时间; **we were ~d and given certificates according to our speed** 有人为我们计时，然后根据各自的速度给我们颁发了证书 **3** Sport ‹*player*› 在某一时刻击 ‹*ball*›; **he ~s his shots beautifully** 他击球的时机恰到好处; **a perfectly-~d stroke** 时机完美的一击 **4** **times** ▸p. 288 colloq (multiply) 乘; **five ~s two is** *or* **equals ten** 5 乘 2 得 10

time-and-motion *adj attrib* 工时学的 ‹*consultant, methods*›

time-and-motion: ~ expert ▸p. 409 *n* 时间与动作研究专家; **~ study** *n* 时间与动作研究 [对工作程序效率的评估]

time: ~ bomb *n* **1** lit 定时炸弹; **2** fig (future problem) 隐患; **the demographic/political ~ bomb** 人口/政治隐患; **~ capsule** *n* 时代文物秘藏器 [存有代表当代特征的器物，供后人去发现]; **~ card** *n* 考勤卡; **~ check** *n* **1** (ascertaining the exact time) (in radio, TV) 报时; **2** (time remaining or time it will take to do sth.) 核对时间; **~ clause** *n* 时间状语从句; **~ clock** *n* **1** (clock for employees) 考勤钟; **2** (switch mechanism) 定时器; **~ code** *n* [电影胶片上表示帧数、曝光度等的] 时间码; **~-consuming** *adj* 耗时的; **the process is very ~-consuming** 这过程很费时间; **~ delay** *n* 延时; **a ~ delay bomb** 延时炸弹; **~ deposit** *n* Amer 定期存款; **~ difference** *n* 时差; **~ dilation** *n* [u] 时间膨胀; **~ exposure** *n* 定时曝光; **~-filler** *n* 打发时间的事物; **~-frame** *n* 时间范围; **~ fuse** *n* 定时引信; **~-honoured** *adj* 由来已久的 ‹*tradition*›; **~keeper** *n* **1** (person monitoring time) 计时员; **2** (punctual person) 守时的人; **3** (watch, clock) 钟表; **~keeping** *n* [u] **1** (punctuality) 守时; **2** (monitoring time) 计时; **~ lag** *n* 时间间隔; **~-lapse photography** *n* [u] 延时摄影

timeless /ˈtaɪmlɪs/ *adj* **1** (not affected by time) 无时间性的 **2** (unending, permanent) 永恒的; **the ~ laws of nature** 永恒的自然法则

time: ~ limit *n* **1** (deadline) 期限; **to put a ~ limit on** 规定…的期限 ‹*work, delivery, improvement*›; **to set a ~ limit for sth.** 为…规定期限 ‹*work, completion*›; **2** (maximum duration) 限期; **there's a 20 minute ~ limit on speeches** 演说时间最长为 20 分钟; **~line** *n* **1** (graphical representation) 大事年表; **2** (schedule) 活动时间表

timeliness /ˈtaɪmlɪnɪs/ *n* [u] 及时

time: ~ loan *n* 定期贷款; **~ lock** *n* **1** (lock with timer) 定时锁; **2** (in computer program) 定时锁程序块

timely /ˈtaɪmli/ *adj* (occurring at the right time) 及时的; (opportune) 适时的; **the ~ arrival of the fire brigade** 消防队的及时赶到

time: ~ machine *n* 时间机器; **~ management** *n* [u] 时间管理; **~ off** *n* [u] 休假时间; **to ask for ~ off** 请假; **to take ~ off** 休假; **to take ~ off from work** 歇班; **~out** *n* **1** (sports break) 暂停; **2** Comput 超时; **~piece** *n* formal (watch) 表; (clock) 钟

timer /ˈtaɪmə(r)/ *n* **1** (for cooking or activating device) 定时器; (for measuring time) 计时器; **the bomb was on a ~** 炸弹上装了定时器 **2** (person) 计时员

> **the Times**
>
> 《泰晤士报》。英国历史最悠久的全国性主流日报。英文原意为"时报"，中文则以伦敦的泰晤士河命名。在英国之外有时亦称为 *London Times* （《伦敦时报》），以和世界其他地方名字含 Times 的报纸相区别。1785 年创刊，始称《每日环球纪闻》（*Daily Universal Register*），1788 年改为现名。报纸以新闻、社论（editorial）和纵横字谜游戏（▸**crossword**）知名。政治立场偏保守，读者多为支持保守党的中上阶层人士。有姊妹报《星期日泰晤士报》（*the Sunday Times*）。1981 年被鲁珀特·默多克（Rupert Murdoch）收购。

time: ~ saver *n* 节约时间的事物; **dishwashers are a real ~** 洗碗机确实节省时间; **~-saving** /ˈtaɪmseɪvɪŋ/ *adj* 节约时间的 ‹*device, method*›; **~ scale** *n* 时间段; **within** *or* **over a 6 month ~ scale** 在 6 个月的时段内; **~-served** *adj attrib* Brit 学徒期满的 ‹*tradesman, craftsman*›; **~-server** *n* **1** pej (trimmer) 趋炎附势者; **2** (worker doing minimum) 混日子的人

timeshare /ˈtaɪmʃeə(r)/

A *n* **1** [c] (house, apartment) 分时度假房 **2** [u] (arrangement) 分时使用度假房的方法

B *modif* 分时享用的 ‹*apartment, studio*›

time: ~-sheet *n* 考勤表; **~-signal** *n* 报时信号; **~ signature** *n* 拍号; **~ slot** *n* 播出时段; **~span** *n* 时间跨度; **~-switch** *n* 定时开关

timetable /ˈtaɪmteɪbl/

A *n* **1** (agenda, schedule) 时间表; (for plans, negotiations) 日程表; **to set up a ~ of meetings/negotiations** 制定会议/谈判的日程表; **to work to a strict ~** 按严格的时间表运作 **2** Brit (class schedule) 课程表 **3** (list of departure and arrival times) 时刻表; **a bus/train ~** 汽车/火车时刻表

B *vt* **1** (include in timetable) 把…排入时间表 ‹*meeting, activity, negotiations*›; 把…排入时刻表 ‹*ferry, train*›; **to ~ the meeting for 9 a.m.** 把会议时间定在上午 9 点; **the bus is ~d to leave at 11.30 a.m.** 公共汽车定于上午 11:30 发车 **2** Brit (include in class schedule) 把…列入课程表 ‹*lesson, subject*›

time: ~ travel *n* [u] 时间旅行; **~ trial** *n* **1** (sports race) 计时赛; **2** (exercise to test time needed) 计时测验; **~ warp** *n* 时间错位; **~-waster** *n* (idle person) 浪费时间的人; (activity) 浪费时间的行为; (thing) 浪费时间的事物; **~-wasting** *n* [u] (act) 浪费时间; (sports tactic) 拖延时间战术; **~-wasting tactics/procedure** 拖延时间的战术/浪费时间的步骤; **~-worn** *adj* **1** (damaged) 陈旧的 ‹*carpet, furnishings, garment*›; 苍老的 ‹*person, face*›; **2** (hackneyed) 陈腐的 ‹*phrase, proverb, tradition*›; **~ zone** *n* 时区

timid /ˈtɪmɪd/ *adj* **1** (fearful) 胆怯的 ‹*person, animal*›; (diffident) 怯生生的 ‹*request, answer, look*› **2** (shy) 羞怯的 ‹*person, behaviour, look, smile*›

timidity /tɪˈmɪdəti/ *n* [u] (state of being fearful) 胆怯; (state of being shy) 羞怯

timidly /ˈtɪmɪdli/ *adv* 胆怯地

timidness /ˈtɪmɪdnɪs/ *n* [u] **= timidity**

timing /ˈtaɪmɪŋ/ *n* **1** [u] (scheduling) 时间选择 **2** [u] (skill) 时机掌握; **to get one's ~ right/wrong** 时机把握适当/错误 **3** [c] (in engine) 点火时间控制 **4** [c] (specific time) 特定时间 **5** [c] (length of time) 时长

timorous /ˈtɪmərəs/ *adj* liter 战战兢兢的

timorously /ˈtɪmərəsli/ *adv* liter 战战兢兢地

timpani /ˈtɪmpəni/ ▸p. 395 *npl* **1** + *v pl* (instrument) 定音鼓 **2** + *v pl* (players) 定音鼓手 **3** + *v sing* (sound) 定音鼓声

timpanist /ˈtɪmpənɪst/ ▸p. 395, p. 409 *n* 定音鼓手

tin /tɪn/

A *n* **1** [u] (metal) 锡 **2** [u] **= tin plate A** **3** [c] Brit (can) 罐头; **to eat out of ~s** 吃罐头食品 [意为吃得不好]; **it does what it says on the ~** fig 名副其实 **4** [c] (airtight container) 金属罐; **a biscuit ~** 饼干听; **a paint ~** 油漆罐 **5** [c] (contents) **a ~ of paint/tobacco/soup** 一罐涂料/烟草/汤; **a whole ~ of biscuits** 整整一听饼干 **6** [c] Brit (container for baking, roasting) 烤模 **7** [c] Brit (pot for donations) 募捐箱

B *modif* 马口铁制的 ‹*cup, mug, bath, roof*›; **to have a ~ ear** fig colloq 没有乐感

C *vt* (*pres p etc.* **-nn-**) **1** (coat with tin) 给…镀锡 ‹*surface, container, pan*› **2** Brit (can) 把…装罐 ‹*food, cat food*›

tin can *n* 马口铁罐

t

Time

What time is it?

What time is it?/What's the time?
= 几点了?

Could you tell me the time?
= 你能告诉我几点了吗?

Do you know what time it is?
= 你知道几点了吗?

It is 5 o'clock
= 5 点（了）

It is about 3
= 大约 3 点

It is exactly 6
= 刚好 6 点

Come at 6 sharp
= 6 点整来

It is nearly 8 o'clock
= 将近 8 点
or 快到 8 点了

It's just before 9
= 就要到 9 点了

It's just after 10
= 10 点刚过

■ In written Chinese, as in English, either a colon (:) or a point (.) is used to separate the hours, minutes and seconds.

■ '5 o'clock' can be translated as 五点 or 五点钟. 钟 is only used for exact times on the hour.

■ 分 (minutes) is normally used if the number of minutes is ten or below ten. However, it is not required if the number of minutes is over ten. 分 must be used if hours, minutes and seconds are all included.

■ Times from just after dusk to 12 midnight are usually expressed as 晚上…点. Times from 12 midnight to the break of dawn are usually expressed as 凌晨…点. Times between daybreak to 8 am are usually expressed as 早上 rather than 上午.

■ 3.07 can be read as 三点零七分 or 三点过七分. 3.18 is read as 三点十八（分）. If the time is a few minutes (from one second to less than ten minutes) past the hour, 零 or 过 is added after 点. 零 is more commonly used than 过. However, if it is more than ten minutes past the hour, 零 or 过 are not required.

4.50 is generally read as 四点五十（分）or 五点差十分. 4.45 can be read as 五点差一刻 / 五点差十五, 差一刻五点 or 四点四十五（分）:

	Written	Spoken
3 am	凌晨三时 凌晨 3 时 凌晨 3:00	凌晨三点
7 am	早上七时 早上 7 时 早上 7:00	早上七点
5 o'clock in the afternoon	下午五时 下午 5 时 下午 5:00	下午五点
10 pm	晚上十时 晚上 10 时 晚上 10:00	晚上十点
three minutes past five	五时三分 5 时 3 分 5:03	五点零三分 五点过三分
ten past five	五时十分 5 时 10 分 5:10	五点十分
a quarter past five	五时十五分 5 时 15 分 5:15	五点一刻 五点十五（分）
half past five	五时半 五时三十分 5 时 30 分 5:30	五点半 五点三十（分）

	Written	Spoken
5.40	五时四十分 5 时 40 分 5:40	五点四十（分） 六点差二十
5:45:46	五时四十五分四十六秒 5 时 45 分 46 秒 5:45:46	五点四十五分四十六秒
a quarter to six	六时差十五分 差一刻六时 5:45	六点差一刻 差一刻六点
5.50	五时五十分 5 时 50 分 5:50 六时差十分 6 时差 10 分	五点五十（分） 六点差十分
two minutes to six	六时差两分 6 时差 2 分 5:58	六点差两分
12 midnight	午夜十二时 凌晨 12 时 凌晨 12:00	午夜十二点 凌晨十二点
12 noon	中午十二时 中午 12 时	中午十二点

When?

■ When referring to a specific time, the only preposition used in Chinese is 在, or the preposition is omitted entirely:

What time will the flight land?
= 飞机什么时候着陆?

What time will he arrive at?
= 他什么时候到达?

What time did it happen?
= 事情是什么时候发生的?

It happened at about 9 pm
= 事情大约发生在晚上 9 点钟

The flight will land at half past 10 in the morning
= 飞机将在上午 10 点半着陆

He will arrive at about 3 o'clock
= 他大约 3 点钟到达

I often send emails to my friends in my lunch hour
= 我常在午饭时间给朋友发电子邮件

Buses arrive at ten to the hour and leave at a quarter past the hour
= 公交车在整点差 10 分时到达，在整点过一刻时开走

The ceremony will start in three hours' time
= 仪式将在 3 个小时之后开始

■ Note the following examples:

The nurse sees him every hour on the hour
= 护士每到整点来查看他一次

Supper will be ready by 6 pm
= 晚饭 6 点钟之前会准备好

The boss won't be in the office until 10 am
= 老板到上午 10 点才会到办公室

I will stay here until midnight
= 我会待到午夜

The library is open from 10 am to 8 pm
= 图书馆从上午 10 点开到晚上 8 点

tincture /ˈtɪŋktʃə(r)/ *n* **1** [u and c] Med, Pharm 酊剂; **a ~ of iodine** 碘酒 **2** [c] (tinge) (of feeling, of flavour, smell) 一丝; (of colour) 些许

tinder /ˈtɪndə(r)/ *n* [u] 引火物; **to be the ~ for sth.** fig 是某事的导火索; **as dry as ~** 非常干燥

tinderbox /ˈtɪndəbɒks/ *n* **1** (box for tinder) 引火盒; **the barn was a (real) ~** fig 这个谷仓（极）容易起火 **2** (tense situation) 一触即发的局势; (tense area) 危险地区

tine /taɪn/ *n* **1** (prong of rake, fork) 尖齿 **2** (terminal branch of antler) [鹿角的] 分叉

tin foil *n* [u] 锡箔

ting /tɪŋ/

A *n* 丁零声

B *vt* 使发丁零声; **to ~ a bell** 敲铃

C *vi* «*clock, bell*» 发丁零声

ting-a-ling /ˌtɪŋəˈlɪŋ/ *n* 丁零声

tinge /tɪndʒ/

A *n* (of colour) 些许; (of feeling, quality) 一丝; **it was pink with a bluish ~** 那粉红色中略带点蓝; **a ~ of sadness** 一丝悲伤

B *vt* **1** (tint) «*person, colour, dye*» 给…稍稍着色 ‹*area, object*›; **to ~ sth. with sth.** 用某物给某物略微着色; **hair ~d with silver** 略带银色的头发 **2** (imbue) **to be ~d with melancholy/regret** 略带一丝哀愁/遗憾; **in a voice ~d with admiration** 以略带羡慕的语气

tingle /ˈtɪŋɡl/

A *vi* **1** (physically) «*fingers, feet, body, person*» 感到刺痛 **2** (psychologically) 感到激动; **to ~ with excitement/anticipation** 激动不已/因期待而激动

B *n* **1** (physical sensation) 刺痛 **2** (psychological sensation) 激动

tingling /ˈtɪŋɡlɪŋ/

A *n* [u and c] 刺痛

B *adj attrib* 刺痛的 ‹*feeling, sensation*›

tingly /ˈtɪŋɡli/ *adj* 有刺痛感的 ‹*body part*›; 刺痛的 ‹*feeling, sensation*›; **my fingers/legs have gone all ~** 我的手指/双腿都感到刺痛

tin: ~ god *n* 妄自尊大的人 [尤指小官员]; **~ hat** *n* Brit colloq 钢盔

tinker /ˈtɪŋkə(r)/

A *n* **1** (itinerant repairer) 白铁匠; **I don't give a ~'s cuss** *or* **damn** colloq 我根本不在乎; **it's not worth a ~'s cuss** *or* **damn** colloq 这毫无价值 **2** Brit pej (gypsy) 吉卜赛人 **3** (attempt to mend) 尝试修理; **to have a ~ with sth.** 试图修理某物

B *vi* **1** **to ~ with sth.** (try and repair) 对…修修补补 ‹*machine, car, computer*›; (attempt to improve sth.) 对…修修改改 ‹*design, essay*› **2** **to ~ with** (play with) 摆弄 ‹*keys, watch, pen*›; **I've been ~ing with the idea of joining the navy** 我一直在琢磨参加海军的事 **3** **to ~ with sth.** (tamper with) 捣鼓 ‹*safe*›; 任意更改 ‹*wording, document*›; **the lock on my car has been ~ed with** 我汽车上的锁被人动过了

tinkle /ˈtɪŋkl/

A *n* **1** (sound) (of glass, bell, ice, piano) 叮当声; (of water) 叮咚声; (of telephone) 丁零声; **give us a ~ (on the piano)** 给我们弹首钢琴曲; **to give sb. a ~** Brit colloq 给某人打电话 **2** Brit colloq (act of urinating) 撒尿; **to have/go for a ~** 尿尿/去尿尿

B *vt* 使发出叮当声; **to ~ the bicycle bell/piano** 按响自行车铃/弹奏钢琴; **the wind ~d the chimes** 风吹响了风铃; **to ~ the ivories** 弹钢琴

C *vi* «*bell, chimes, ice*» 叮当响; «*water*» 叮咚响; «*telephone*» 丁零响

tinkling /ˈtɪŋklɪŋ/

A *n* (of glass, bell, ice, piano) 叮当声; (of water) 叮咚声; (of telephone) 丁零声

B *adj attrib* 叮当响的 ‹*bell, chimes, ice, piano*›; 叮咚响的 ‹*water*›; 丁零响的 ‹*telephone*›

tin mine *n* 锡矿

tinned /tɪnd/ *adj* **1** Brit (canned) 罐装的 ‹*vegetables, fish, meat, fruit*›; **~ food** 罐头食品 **2** (coated with tin) 镀锡的 ‹*surface, pan*›; (coated with tin alloy) 镀锡合金的 ‹*surface, pan*›

tinnie /ˈtɪni/ *n* Austral, NZ colloq = **tinny²**

tinnitus /ˈtɪnɪtəs/ ▸p. 377 *n* [u] 耳鸣

tinny¹ /ˈtɪni/ *adj* **1** (metallic-sounding) 尖细的 ‹*sound, tone, music*›; 声音尖细的 ‹*radio, piano*› **2** (badly made) 质量差的 ‹*washing machine, pan*›

tinny² *n* Austral, NZ colloq (can of beer) 一罐啤酒

tin: ~ opener *n* Brit 开罐器; **T~ Pan Alley** *n* [u] dated colloq 流行音乐界 [本为纽约一个地区的别称，因流行音乐作曲家和发行商曾集中于此而得名]

tin plate

A *n* [u] 镀锡铁皮

B *vt* 给…镀锡

tin: ~-plated *adj* 镀锡的; **~pot** *adj* Brit colloq 无能的 ‹*dictator*›

tinsel /ˈtɪnsl/ *n* [u] **1** (decoration) [用于装饰圣诞树等的] 金属箔; **~ decorations/material/costume** 金属箔饰品/材料/服装 **2** fig (sham brilliance) 浮华; **the ~ world/appearance** 浮华的世界/外表

Tinseltown /ˈtɪnsltaʊn/ *n* [u] pej (Hollywood) 好莱坞; (superficially glamorous world) 浮华之地

tin: ~smith ▸p. 409 *n* 锡匠; **~ soldier** *n* 锡制玩具兵

tint /tɪnt/

A *n* **1** (colour) 色彩; (pale colour) 浅色; (shade) 色调; (hint, trace) 些许; **blue with a purple ~** 略带点紫的蓝色; **a ~ of pink/gold** 一抹粉红色/金色; **autumn ~s** 秋色 **2** (hair dye) (substance) 染发剂; (application) 染发; **a blonde/auburn ~** 金色/赤褐色染发剂; **to have a ~** 染头发

B *vt* **1** (colour) 给…略微着色; **the pinks and golds that ~ the morning sky** 点缀早晨天空的粉色和金色; **to ~ sth. blue/pink** 使某物略呈蓝色/粉红色 **2** (dye) 染 ‹*hair*›; **to ~ one's hair brown/blonde** 把头发染成棕色/金色; **to get one's hair ~ed** 染发

tinted /ˈtɪntɪd/ *adj* **1** (coloured faintly) 略微着色的 ‹*paint, colour, window*›; **blue-~ glass, glass ~ with blue** 略呈蓝色的玻璃; **~ lenses** 有色镜片 **2** (dyed) 染色的 ‹*hair*›

tin whistle *n* 六孔小笛

tiny /ˈtaɪni/ *adj* **1** (very small) 极小的 ‹*piece, budget, hole, bird*› **2** (very young) 幼小的 ‹*child, baby*›

tip¹ /tɪp/

A *n* **1** (end) (of stick, umbrella, sword, branch, shoot, leaf, blade) 尖端; (of mountain, rock) 顶; **a pencil ~** 铅笔尖; **the ~ of one's finger/nose/tongue** 指尖/鼻尖/舌尖; **asparagus ~s** 芦笋尖; **to stand on the ~s of one's toes** 脚尖着地站立; **a house on the ~ of the island** 位于岛屿一端的房子; **at the southernmost ~ of Italy** 在意大利的最南端 **2** (covering) (of cane, umbrella, heels, etc.) 顶端附加物; **a walking stick with a metal ~** 带金属头的手杖; **filter ~s** 过滤嘴

B *vt* (*pres p etc.* **-pp-**) 覆盖…的顶端; **to ~ sth. with sth.** 在某物的顶端装某物; **they ~ their arrows with poison** 他们在箭头上抹了毒药; **steel-~ped heels** 钉有铁掌的鞋跟; **~ped cigarettes** 过滤嘴香烟

tip²

A *vt* (*pres p etc.* **-pp-**) **1** (tilt) 使…倾斜 ‹*cup, seat*›; **to ~ sth. forwards/back/to one side** 使某物向前/向后/向一边倾斜; **don't ~ your chair!** 不要翘椅子！; **to ~ sth. on to its side/back** 把某物向侧边/后侧倾斜; **to ~ sb./sth. off/into sth.** 使某人/某物翻离/翻入某物; **she ~ped all the pots off the tray** 她把托盘上所有的壶都打翻了; **they ~ped him off his sun lounger straight into the pool** 他们把他从日光浴椅上直接掀到泳池里; **to ~ the scales at 60 kg** 体重为 60 公斤 **2** fig (push, overbalance) 使失衡; **to ~ the economy into recession** 使经济转入衰退; **to ~ sb. over the edge** 使某人情绪失控; **to ~ the scales** *or* **balance** 起决定性作用; **her excellent grades ~ the scales in her favour** 她的优秀成绩对她非常有利 **3** (pour, empty, throw away) «*person, lorry*» 倾倒 ‹*dirty water, gravel, contents*›; **to ~ sth. away/out/down** 把某物倒掉/倒出去/倒下去; **to ~ the washing-up water down the sink** 把洗碗水倒下水槽; **'no ~ping'** “禁止倒垃圾”

B *vi* (*pres p etc.* **-pp-**) «*cup, seat, person*» 倾斜; **to ~ forwards/backwards/sideways/on to one side** 向前/向后/向一侧/向一边倾斜

C *n* Brit **1** colloq (mess) 凌乱的地方; **to be (in) a ~** 乱成一堆; **this room is a real** *or* **an absolute ~!** 这个房间太乱了！ **2** (rubbish dump) 垃圾场 **3** (mound of waste) 废物堆

Phrasal verbs

- **tip down** *vi* Brit colloq 下大雨; **it's ~ping down (with rain)** 正在下大雨; **the rain was ~ping down** 大雨倾盆而下
- **tip over**

A *vt* [**~ sth. over, ~ over sth.**] (overturn) 使倾覆; (cause to fall down) 使倒下

B *vi* (overturn) 倾覆; (fall down) 倒下

- **tip up** *vt* [**~ sth. up, ~ up sth.**] 使侧斜

tip³

A *n* **1** (gratuity) 小费; **to give** *or* **leave a ~** 给小费 **2** (helpful hint) 指点; (piece of helpful advice) 提示; **I'll give you a ~ — don't mention politics** 我来给你一个忠告——不要提及政治; **a ~ on** *or* **for ...** 有关…的指点; **cookery/sewing/decorating ~s** 烹调/缝纫/装修贴士; **take a ~ from me** 听我的劝告 **3** (in betting) [尤指赛马或赛狗的] 内幕消息; **a hot ~** 热门的小道消息; **he's a hot ~ for the Grand National** 他是越野障碍赛马的夺冠大热门

B *vt* (*pres p etc.* **-pp-**) **1** (give extra amount of money to) 给…小费; **to ~ sb. 50p/£3** 给某人 50 便士/3 英镑小费 **2** (forecast, predict) 预测…会获胜 ‹*person, horse*›; 预测 ‹*winner*›; **she is ~ped to be the next managing director/to win the election** 有人预测她会担任下一任总裁/赢得选举; **to be ~ped as president** 被预测有望成为总统 **3** (touch lightly) 轻触; **he ~ped the hoof with the blade of his knife** 他用刀刃轻轻碰了碰蹄子; **to ~ the ball** (strike) 轻轻击球; (kick) 轻轻踢球; **he ~ped the ball over the net** 他轻轻一击，将球打过了网

Phrasal verb

- **tip off** *vt* [**~ sb. off, ~ off sb.**] 向…透露消息 ‹*police, gang*›; **to ~ sb. off (about sth.)** 暗中（将某事）告知某人; **she ~ped us off as to his hideaway** 她向我们透露了他的藏身之处

tip: ~ cart *n* Amer 翻斗手推车; **~-off** *n* colloq 密告; **to act on a ~-off** 根据密报采取行动; **to receive a ~-off** 得到举报

tipper /ˈtɪpə(r)/ *n* **1** = **tipper lorry** **2** (person leaving gratuity) 给小费者; **to be a generous/mean ~** 给小费很大方/小气 **3** Brit (person who dumps waste) 乱倒废物的人

tipper lorry Brit, **tipper truck** Amer *ns* 翻斗卡车

Tipp-Ex® /ˈtɪpeks/ Brit

A *n* [u] 迪美斯修正液

B *vt* **~ (out** *or* **over)** 用修正液涂改 ‹*word, mistake*›

tipping point /ˈtɪpɪŋ pɔɪnt/ *n* **1** (of person) 忍受极限 **2** (of social phenomenon) 爆发点 **3** Ecol [天气变化的] 触发点

tipple /ˈtɪpl/ colloq

A *n* 酒精饮料; **sb.'s favourite ~** 某人最爱喝的酒; **what's your ~?** (what would you like) 你想喝什么酒？; (what do you usually drink) 你通常喝什么酒？

B *vi* 饮酒

tippler /ˈtɪplə(r)/ *n* colloq 有酒瘾的人

tipsily /ˈtɪpsɪli/ *adv* 微醉地

tipster /ˈtɪpstə(r)/ *n* 1 (in betting, stock market) 情报贩子 2 (in general) 告密者

tipsy /ˈtɪpsi/ *adj* 微醉的

tiptoe /ˈtɪptəʊ/
A *n* 脚尖; **(to walk) on ~(s)** 踮着脚走
B *vi* 踮起脚走; **to ~ in/out** 蹑手蹑脚地进来/出去

tip-top *adj* colloq 一流的; **to be in ~ condition** 处于最佳状态

tip: ~-up seat *n* 自翻椅; **~-up truck** *n* 翻斗卡车

tirade /taɪˈreɪd, Amer ˈtaɪreɪd/ *n* (speech) 长篇激烈演说; (criticism) 长篇激烈批评

Tirana /tɪˈrɑːnə/ *pr n* 地拉那

tire¹ /ˈtaɪə(r)/
A *vt* (weary) 使疲劳
B *vi* 1 (get weary) 感到疲劳 2 (get bored) 厌倦; **to ~ of sth./doing sth.** 厌烦某事物/做某事

Phrasal verb
• **tire out**
A *vt* [~ sb. out] 使疲惫不堪; **to be ~d out** 精疲力竭
B *v refl* **to ~ oneself out (doing sth.)** (做某事)累垮了

tire² *n* Amer = **tyre**

tired /ˈtaɪəd/ *adj* 1 (weary or showing weariness) 疲劳的; **to be ~ out** 疲惫不堪; **~ voice/eyes** 疲倦的嗓音/眼睛; **~ and emotional** hum 喝醉的 2 (bored) **to be ~ of sth./sb./doing sth.** 厌烦某事物/某人/做某事; **~ of protesting, she agreed** 她对抗议已经厌倦, 于是就答应了; **to grow** *or* **get ~ (of sth./of doing sth.)** (对某事物/做某事)感到厌倦 3 (hackneyed) 陈腐的 〈*joke, cliché, image*〉 4 (worn out) 破旧的 〈*car, clothes, furniture, decorations*〉; 运转不良的 〈*organization, institution*〉 5 (wilted) 萎蔫的 〈*vegetable, cabbage, lettuce*〉; (no longer fresh) 不新鲜的 〈*foodstuff, fish*〉

tiredly /ˈtaɪədli/ *adv* 疲劳地

tiredness /ˈtaɪədnɪs/ *n* [u] 疲劳

tireless /ˈtaɪəlɪs/ *adj* 不知疲倦的; **~ efforts** 不懈的努力

tirelessly /ˈtaɪəlɪsli/ *adv* 不知疲倦地; **to campaign ~ for sth.** 为了某事孜孜不倦地奔走; **to search ~ for …** 坚持不懈地搜寻…

tiresome /ˈtaɪəsəm/ *adj* 令人厌倦的

tiresomely /ˈtaɪəsəmli/ *adv* 令人厌倦地; **~ repetitive/familiar/predictable** 重复/熟悉/老套到令人厌倦的

tiring /ˈtaɪərɪŋ/ *adj* 累人的

tiro /ˈtaɪərəʊ/ *n* (*pl* **~s**) = **tyro**

tissue /ˈtɪʃuː/ *n* 1 [c and u] (cells material) 组织 2 [c] (handkerchief) 纸巾; **a box of ~s** 一盒纸巾 3 [u] 薄纸; **toilet ~** 卫生纸 4 [c] (series) 一系列; **a ~ of lies** 一派谎言

tissue: ~ culture *n* 1 [u] (process) 组织培养; 2 [c] (result) 培养的组织; **~ paper** *n* [u] [包装用的] 薄纸; **~ sample** *n* 组织标本; **~ type** *n* 组织型; **~ typing** *n* [u] 组织分型

tit /tɪt/ *n* 1 (songbird) 山雀 2 taboo sl (woman's breast) 奶子 3 Brit sl (fool) 蠢货 4 **~ for tat** (blow for blow) 以牙还牙; **a ~-for-tat response** 针锋相对的回应

titan /ˈtaɪtn/ *n* 巨人; **a ~ of the political world** 政界巨头

titanic /taɪˈtænɪk/ *adj* 激烈的 〈*struggle, battle, clash*〉; 巨大的 〈*force, figure, effort*〉

titanium /tɪˈteɪnɪəm/ *n* [u] 钛

titbit /ˈtɪtbɪt/ *n* 1 (piece of food) 小片食物 2 (piece of gossip) 趣闻

titch /tɪtʃ/ *n* Brit colloq 小矮子

titchy /ˈtɪtʃi/ *adj* Brit colloq 极小的 〈*garden, car, amount, hands*〉; 极矮的 〈*person, child*〉

tithe /taɪð/ *n* 什一税 [旧时向教会缴纳的税种, 占农产品或收入等的十分之一]

tithe barn *n* 什一税农产品仓库

titillate /ˈtɪtɪleɪt/ *vt, vi* 挑逗

titillating /ˈtɪtɪleɪtɪŋ/ *adj* 挑逗性的

titillation /ˌtɪtɪˈleɪʃn/ *n* [u] 挑逗; **sexual/erotic ~** 情欲/情色挑逗

titivate /ˈtɪtɪveɪt/ *vt* colloq 修饰 〈*hair*〉; 装饰 〈*show*〉; **to ~ oneself** 梳妆打扮

title /ˈtaɪtl/
A *n* 1 [c] (identifying heading) (of book, film, play, piece of music, sculpture) 名称; (of poem, article, photograph, painting) 标题 2 [c] (book, publication) [出版物的] 一种 3 [c] (status, rank, qualification awarded, etc.) 称呼; (profession) 职衔; **~: Mr/Mrs/Ms** 称谓: 先生/夫人/女士 [填写表格时的选项] 4 [c] (descriptive name) (describing position, job) 职位; (earned or chosen) 称号 5 [c] (championship) 冠军; **to win/hold the ~** 获得冠军/拥有冠军头衔 6 [c] (rank of nobility) 贵族头衔; **a man with a ~** 有爵位的男子; **to take/be given a ~** 获得/被授予贵族头衔; **the ~ of Duke of Marlborough** 马尔伯勒公爵爵位 7 [u and c] (right to property or rank or throne) 所有权; (basis of this right) 所有权基础; (documentary evidence of this right) 所有权凭证; (claim based on such a right) 所有权主张; **the ~ to sth.** 某物的所有权; **to register a ~** 注册所有权
B **titles** *npl* 片尾字幕
C *modif* 1 (eponymous) 与作品同名的; **the ~ character** (of play, opera) 剧名角色; (of film) 片名角色 2 (involving championship title) 冠军的; **a ~ bout/defence/challenge/race** 决定冠军归属的回合/卫冕赛/挑战赛/赛跑
D *vt* 给…加标题; **they ~d their first album Ocean Drive** 他们把第一张专辑取名为《海洋之旅》

title bar *n* 标题栏

titled /ˈtaɪtld/ *adj* 有头衔的; **the ~ classes** 贵族阶级

title: ~ deed *n* 所有权证书; **~ fight** *n* 冠军赛; **~-holder** *n* 冠军; **~ music** *n* [u] (at beginning of TV programme) 片头曲; (at end of TV programme) 片尾曲; **~ page** *n* 标题页; **~ role** *n* (in film) 片名角色; (in play) 剧名角色; **~ song** *n* 专辑名歌曲; **~ track** *n* (song) 专辑名歌曲; (instrumental) 专辑名乐曲

titrate /taɪˈtreɪt, tɪ-/ *vt* 滴定测量 〈*solution*〉

titter /ˈtɪtə(r)/
A *vi* (snigger mockingly or in amusement) 窃笑; (laugh nervously or in embarrassment) 傻笑
B *vt* 窃笑着说
C *n* (mocking or amused snigger) 窃笑; (embarrassed or nervous laugh) 傻笑

tittle /ˈtɪtl/ *n* 微量; **not one ~** 一点也不; **to change** *or* **alter sth. not one ~** 丝毫未改变某事物

tittle-tattle /ˈtɪtltætl/
A *n* [u] 闲言碎语
B *vi* 说闲话

titular /ˈtɪtjʊlə(r), Amer -tʃʊ-/ *adj* 1 (providing the title) 与作品同名的 〈*character, role, song, place*〉 2 (nominal) 名义上的 〈*head of state, president, professor, power*〉; **the monarch is ~ head of the Church of England** 君主是英国国教的名义领袖

tizzy /ˈtɪzi/ *n* colloq 慌张; **to be in** *or* **get into a ~** 心慌意乱

T-junction *n* 丁字路口

TM *abbr* 1 = **trademark A1** 2 = **Transcendental Meditation**

TN *abbr* Amer = **Tennessee**

TNT *abbr* [u] = **trinitrotoluene** 梯恩梯 [即三硝基甲苯]

to *before consonant* /tə/; *before vowel* /tʊ, tu/; *stressed* /tuː/
A ▸p. 487 *prep* 1 (indicating destination) 去; **to travel from place ~ place** 四处奔波; **~ the country/town** 到乡下/城里; **~ Paris/Spain** 去巴黎/西班牙; **~ your positions!** 各就各位!; **to go ~ a meeting** 去开会; **~ sb.'s (place)** 去某人家; **she came ~ mine** 她来到我家; **I am going ~ the shop/hospital/station** 我要去那商店/医院/车站 2 (in direction of, facing towards) 向; **to fall ~ the ground** 落到地上; **trains ~ and from Oxford** 进出牛津的列车; **children ~ the front, adults ~ the back** 小孩到前面, 大人到后面; **he turned ~ the wall** 他转身面向墙壁; **he was standing with his back ~ them** 他背对他们站着 3 (indicating recipient of sth.) 给; **give the book ~ Sophie** 把书给索菲; **she's given the meat ~ the dog** 她把肉喂狗了; **to explain sth. ~ sb.** 向某人解释某事; **who was the letter addressed ~?** 那封信寄给谁了?; **~ whom did she address the letter?** formal 她把那封信寄给谁了? 4 (as far as, reaching particular state, indicating end of range or period) 到; **the meadows lead down ~ the river** 草坪一直延伸到河边; **her hair fell ~ her waist** 她的头发垂至腰间; **from this post ~ that tree it's 100 metres** 从这根柱子到那棵树有 100 米; **the vegetables were cooked ~ perfection** 蔬菜烧的火候恰到好处; **to change from amazement ~ joy** 由惊奇变为喜悦; **to count ~ 100** 数到 100; **a cheque ~ the value of £100** 一张面值为 100 英镑的支票; **50 ~ 60 people** 50 到 60 人; **in five ~ ten minutes** 5 到 10 分钟之后; **~ the end/this day** 直到结束/今天; **~ this day, I don't know why he left** 时至今日, 我仍不明白为他为何离去; **it's been three years ~ the day since we met** 从我们认识至今已整整 3 年了 5 (indicating location) 位于…方向; **~ the left/right of sth.** 在某物的左侧/右边; **40 miles ~ the south of the site** 该地点以南 40 英里处 6 (against) 紧挨; **holding the letter ~ his chest** 他把信攥在胸口; **back ~ back** 背靠背 7 esp Brit (before, until) 在…之前; **it's five ~ ten** 现在 10 点差 5 分; **how long is it ~ lunch?** 还有多久吃午餐? 8 (indicating connection) 在; **attach this rope ~ the front of the car** 把这根绳子系在汽车前部; **he had a name tag attached ~ his lapel** 他上衣翻领上贴了一张姓名标签 9 (indicating person or thing affected, relationship) 对; **to be devoted ~ one's family** 深爱家庭; **be nice ~ your brother** 对你弟弟好一点; **she's married ~ an Italian** 她嫁给了一个意大利人; **economic adviser ~ the President** 总统的经济顾问; **the key ~ the door** 门钥匙; **there's no sense ~ it** 这毫无道理 10 (concerning) 关于; **what's it ~ you?** colloq 关你什么事?; **a threat ~ world peace** 对世界和平的威胁; **she made a reference ~ her recent book** 她提到了她最近的新书; **there's nothing ~ it** 非常简单; **that's all there is ~ it** (it's easy) 就这么简单; (not for further discussion) 到此为止 11 (in comparisons, ratios) 比; **I prefer walking ~ climbing** 我喜欢散步胜过登山; **we won by three goals ~ two** 我们以 3 比 2 获胜; **X is ~ Y as A is ~ B** X 比 Y 等于 A 比 B 12 (referring to quantities, measurements) (equalling) 等于; (per) 每; **there are 2.54 centimetres ~ an inch** 1 英寸等于 2.54 厘米; **to do 30 miles ~ the gallon** 每加仑汽油跑 30 英里 13 (in honour of) 向…表示敬意; **a monument ~ the soldiers who died in the war** 阵亡士兵纪念碑; **~ Jean** (in dedication) 献给琼; **~ our dear son** (on tombstone) 致我们的爱子 14 (for exclusive use of) 为…专用; **a room ~ myself** 我自己的房间 15 (with intention of giving sth.) 为了给; **people rushed ~ her rescue** 人们冲上前去救她 16 (indicating accompaniment) 伴随; **they danced ~ the music** 他们随音乐起舞; **~ the sound of the drums** 伴着鼓点声 17 (in accordance with) 与…一致; **it isn't ~ my taste** 这不对我的口味; **is the map ~ scale?** 这张地图符合比例吗?; **the train is running ~ time** 列车准点运行 18 (in the opinion of) 按…的看法; **~ my daughter, it's just a minor problem** 对我女儿来说, 这只是个小问题; **it looks ~ me like rain** 我看像是

要下雨了 **19** (showing reaction) 让; ～ **his dismay/surprise** 令他惊愕/惊讶的是
B *infinitive particle* **1** (expressing intention, outcome, cause) [表示目的、结果或原因]; **he did it ～ impress his friends** 他那样做是为了打动朋友们; **she managed ～ escape** 她设法逃脱了; **I'm sorry ～ hear that** 听到那个消息我很抱歉 **2** (expressing desire, wish) [表示愿望]; **oh ～ be able to stay in bed!** hum 哦, 要是能待在床上该多好! ; **oh ～ be in England!** liter 唉, 能去英格兰就好了! ; **I'd love ～ go to France** 我很想去法国 **3** (indicating desired or advisable action) [表示想要或值得做的事] **the leaflet explains how ～ apply for a place** 手册解释了如何申请入学名额 **4** (indicating sth. known or believed) [表示为人相信的事或传闻]; **the house was said ～ be haunted** 据说那房子闹鬼 **5** (linking consecutive acts) [表示紧接着的动作]; **he looked up ～ see ...** 他抬头看见…; **he woke up only ～ find everyone had left** 他醒来时发现所有人都走了 **6** (expressing obligation or necessity) [表示应该或需要做的事] **to be ～ do sth.** 应该做某事; **you are not ～ talk during the exam** 考试时不得交头接耳 **7** (avoiding repetition of verb) [用以避免动词重复]; **did you go? — no, I promised not ～** 你去了吗? ——没有, 我答应过不去的 **8** (following impersonal verb) [用于以it引导的非人称结构中]; **it is interesting/difficult** *etc.* **～ do sth.** 做某事很有趣/很困难等; **it's hard ～ understand why he did it** 很难理解他为什么那样做 **9** (expressing future) [表示将来的动作]; **to be about ～ do sth.** 即将做某事; **he was about ～ sing** 他就要演唱了 **10** (after noun expressing function) [表示功能或用途]; **something ～ eat** 吃的东西 **11** (after ordinal number, superlative) [用于序数词或最高级之后]; **the first person ～ arrive** 第一个到达的人; **the youngest ～ enter the competition** 最年轻的参赛选手
C /tuː/ *adv* 关上; **push the door ～** 推门关上; **when the curtains are ～** 幕帘拉上时

toad /təʊd/ *n* **1** (animal) 蟾蜍 **2** colloq (person) 讨厌的人

toad: **～-in-the-hole** *n* [u] Brit 裹面糊烤香肠; **～stool** *n* 毒蕈

toady /'təʊdi/ pej
A *n* 马屁精
B *vi* 拍马屁; **to ～ to sb.** 奉承某人

toadying /'təʊdɪɪŋ/ *n* [u] pej 拍马屁

to and fro /ˌtuː ən 'frəʊ/
A *adv* 来回地 ‹*move, travel, run*›; **to go ～** 走来走去
B *vi* **1** (move backwards and forwards) 往返 **2** (vacillate) 犹豫不决
C *n* **1** (movement backwards and forwards) 往返; **we watched the ～ of their dancing** 我们看着他们来来回回地跳舞 **2** (debate, vacillation) 犹豫不决

toast /təʊst/
A *n* **1** [u] Culin 烤面包片; **to do** *or* **make (some) ～** 做（一些）烤面包片; **a piece** *or* **slice of ～** 一片烤面包片; **a round of ～** 一整片烤面包片; **to be ～** esp Amer colloq 要完蛋; **to be as warm as ～** «*person, bed, room*» 很温暖 **2** [c] (tribute) 干杯; **to drink a ～ (to sb./sth.)** （为某人/某事物）干杯; **to propose a ～ (to sb.)** 提议（为某人）干杯; **will you raise your glasses and join me in a ～ to the happy couple** 请大家举起酒杯和我一起为这对幸福的伉俪干杯; **to reply** *or* **respond to the ～** 答谢祝酒 **3** [c] *sing* (popular person) **to be the ～ of sb./sth.** 在…中备受推崇; **she was the ～ of the town** 她在城里有口皆碑
B *vt* **1** Culin (make into toast) 烤; **this bread tastes good ～ed** 这面包烤后味道很好; **a ～ed sandwich** 烤三明治 **2** Culin (brown over heat) 把…烤得焦黄 ‹*grains, seeds, nuts, spices*› **3** (warm) 烘暖 ‹*feet, hands*› **4** (propose a toast to) 提议为…干杯 ‹*person, success, health*›; (drink a toast to) 为…干杯 ‹*person, success, health*›; **they were ～ed with champagne** 大家举起香槟酒为他们干杯
C *v refl* **to ～ oneself** 取暖; **she sat ～ing herself in front of the fire** 她坐在炉火前取暖

toaster /'təʊstə(r)/ *n* 烤面包炉; **a pop-up ～** 弹出式烤面包机

toastie /'təʊsti/ *n* Brit colloq (sandwich) 烤三明治; (snack) 烤点心

toast: **～ing fork** *n* 烤叉; **～master** *n* 宴会主持人; **～ rack** *n* 烤面包片架

tobacco /tə'bækəʊ/ *n* [u] **1** (product) 烟草; **a tin of ～** 一听烟丝; **a ～ tin** 烟草罐; **chewing ～** 口嚼烟 **2** (plant) 烟草植株; **a ～ leaf/plant** 烟叶/烟草植株

tobacconist /tə'bækənɪst/ ▸**p. 409** *n* **1** (seller) 烟草商; **～'s (shop)** 烟草店 **2** (outlet) 烟草店

Tobago /tə'beɪgəʊ/ *pr n* 多巴哥岛

to-be *adj postpos* 将来的; **husband/wife ～** 未来的丈夫/妻子; **the new President ～** 即将上任的新总统

toboggan /tə'bɒgən/
A *n* 平底雪橇
B *vi* 滑平底雪橇; **to ～ down a hill** 坐平底雪橇滑下山

tobogganing /tə'bɒgənɪŋ/ ▸**p. 307** *n* [u] 平底雪橇运动; **to go ～** 去滑平底雪橇

toboggan: **～ race** *n* 平底雪橇比赛; **～ run** *n* 平底雪橇滑道

toby jug /'təʊbi dʒʌg/ *n* (jug) 人形水罐; (mug) 人形水杯

toccata /tə'kɑːtə/ *n* 托卡塔曲 [用管风琴等键盘乐器快速演奏的乐曲]

tod /tɒd/ *n* Brit colloq **(all) on one's ～** 独自地; **I suppose I'll have to go on my ～ then** 我想我得全靠自己了

today /tə'deɪ/ ▸**p. 181, p. 182**
A *adv* **1** (on this day) 在今天; **he's arriving ～** 他于今日到达; **what's the day/date ～?** 今天星期几/几号? ; **it's the fifth of April ～** 今天是 4 月 5 号; **a week from ～** Brit 下星期的今天; **a month ago ～** 一个月前的今天; **all day ～** 今天一整天; **earlier/later ～** 在今天的早些/晚些时候; **here ～, gone tomorrow** 变化无常的; **these fashions are here ～, gone tomorrow** 这些时尚经常变换 **2** (nowadays) 当今; **people ～ live far more comfortable lives** 如今人们过着更为舒适的生活
B *n* **1** (this day) 今天; **what's ～'s date?** 今天几号? ; **as of ～, from ～ onward** 从今天起; **～'s papers** 今天的报纸 **2** (present period) 现在; **the computers/teenagers of ～** 如今的计算机/十几岁的青少年; **～'s X** 时下的 X; **in ～'s rapidly changing society** 在当下迅速变化的社会中

toddle /'tɒdl/
A *vi* **1** (walk unsteadily) «*child*» 蹒跚行走; **to ～ to the door** 蹒跚地走到门口; **to ～ off** 蹒跚地走开 **2** colloq (go) «*person*» 闲逛; **to ～ over to Bob's house** 到鲍勃家去串门; **to ～ down to the shop** 溜达到商店; **to ～ off/along** 溜达着走开/向前走
B *n* **1** (child's walk) 蹒跚行走 **2** colloq (walk) 闲逛; **to go for a ～** 出去溜达一会儿

toddler /'tɒdlə(r)/ *n* 学步的儿童

toddy /'tɒdi/ *n* [c and u] 托迪酒 [用热水和烈酒加糖或香料制成]; **hot ～** 热托迪酒

to-do /tə'du/ *n* colloq 喧闹; **what a ～!** 吵死了!

to-do list *n* 任务一览表

toe /təʊ/ ▸**p. 71**
A *n* **1** (on human or animal foot) 脚趾; **the big/little ～** 大/小脚趾; **to stand** *or* **tread** *or* **step on sb.'s ～s** 踩到某人的脚趾; **to tread on sb.'s ～s** fig colloq 得罪某人; **to keep sb. on their ～s** 使某人保持警觉; **from top** *or* **tip** *or* **head to ～** 从头到脚; fig 完全地 **2** (of sock, shoe) 足尖部
B *vt* (kick) 用脚尖踢; (touch) 用脚尖碰; **to ～ the line** 听从命令; **to ～ the party/management line** 服从党/资方的安排

toe: **～cap** *n* [鞋子的] 外包头; **～ clip** *n* [尤指自行车脚踏板上的] 鞋头夹套; **～-curling** *adj* colloq 令人无地自容的

TOEFL /'təʊfl/ *abbr* = **Test of English as a Foreign Language** 托福考试

> **TOEFL**
>
> 托福考试，全称 Test of English as a Foreign Language。母语不是英语的人进入美国大学学习时必须参加的考试，亦为不少美国以外的国家采用。由美国教育考试服务中心（Educational Testing Service，简称 ETS）组织实施。中国目前采用的是网络考试（Internet-based Test，即 iBT）。分听力、阅读、口语和写作四个部分，满分为 120 分。成绩有效期为两年。

toehold /'təʊhəʊld/ *n* **1** (in climbing) 小立脚点 **2** fig 立足点; **to get** *or* **gain a ～ in ...** 在…中得以立足

toe: **～nail** *n* 脚趾甲; **～rag** *n* Brit colloq (offensive, contemptible person) 浑蛋; (worthless person) 废物

toff /tɒf/ *n* Brit colloq 纨绔子弟

toffee /'tɒfi, Amer 'tɔːfi/ *n* **1** [u] (mixture) 太妃糖 [用糖与黄油混合熬煮制成] **2** [c] (sweet) 一块太妃糖; **he can't sing/act for ～** 他根本不会唱歌/演戏

toffee: **～ apple** *n* 涂太妃糖的苹果 [用签子插起]; **～-nosed** *adj* Brit colloq 势利的

tofu /'təʊfuː/ *n* [u] 豆腐

tog[1] /tɒg/
A **togs** *npl* Brit colloq (clothes) 衣服; **swimming ～s** 游泳衣
B *vt* colloq (*pres p etc.* **-gg-**) **to ～ oneself up** *or* **out (in sth.)** 穿上（某种）衣服; **they were (all) ～ged out in tennis gear** 他们（都）穿着网球服

tog[2] *n* Brit **～ (rating)** 托格 [测量棉被、夹克、睡袋等保暖性的热阻单位]

toga /'təʊgə/ *n* [古罗马男性公民穿的] 托加袍

together /tə'geðə(r)/
A *adv* **1** (as a pair or group) 一起; (in relationship) 共同; (collectively) 整个地; **they're always ～** 他们总是在一起; **let's go there ～** 咱们一道去那儿吧; **to be close ～** «*objects, trees, plants*» 紧挨在一起; **his eyes are too close ～** 他的双眼长得太近; **acting ～, they could have prevented the invasion** 如果统一行动, 他们原本可以阻止入侵的; **we're all in this ～** 这件事我们都有份; **they belong ～** «*objects*» 它们应该放在一起; «*two people*» 他们是天生的一对; **they're not married, but they're living ～** 他们没结婚, 但在同居; **James and Emma have got back ～ again** 詹姆斯和埃玛又在一起了; **he has more money than the rest of us (put) ～** 他的钱比我们所有人的加一块儿还多; **taken ～, these factors are highly significant** 综合起来看, 这些因素至关重要; **these two documents, taken ～, provide crucial evidence** 这两份文件放在一起成为关键证据; **his argument doesn't hold ～ very well** 他的论点前后不太一致 **2** (so as to be joined) 连在一起; **he nailed the two planks ～** 他把两块木板钉在了一起; **he rubbed his hands ～ in satisfaction** 他满意地搓着双手 **3** (in agreement) 一致; **after the meeting the two sides in the dispute were no closer ～** 会谈之后争论双方的立场差距依然如故 **4** (at the same time) 同时; **they were all talking ～** 他们全都在说话; **all my troubles seem to come ～** 我的麻烦似乎凑到一块儿全来了; **all ～ now!** (speaking) 一起说! ; (singing) 一齐唱! ; (pulling, pushing, lifting) 一起加油! **5** Mus 以相同节奏; **the soprano and the orchestra weren't quite ～** 女高音歌手和管弦乐队之间配合不太默契 **6** (without interruption)

接连地; **for four days/three weeks** *etc.* ～ 一连 4 天/3 个星期等

B *adj* colloq 稳妥自信的; **he's a very ～ guy** 他是个很稳重的家伙

C **together with** *prep phr* **1** (including) 包括; **～ with the Johnsons, there were 12 of us** 包括约翰逊一家在内, 我们总共有 12 个人 **2** (as well as) 连同; **he put his wallet, ～ with his passport, in his pocket** 他把钱包连同护照一起放进衣兜; **taken ～ with the rest of the evidence, this proves that he is guilty** 加上其他的证据, 这证明他有罪 **3** (in the company of) 同…一起; **I went there ～ with George** 我和乔治一起去了那儿

togetherness /tə'geðənɪs/ *n* [u] (of team, friendship) 团结友爱; (of family or couple) 亲密无间; **family warmth and ～** 家庭的温暖与和睦

toggle /'tɒgl/ *n* **1** (fastening) 棒形纽扣 **2** Comput **～ (key)** 切换键

toggle: ～ bolt *n* 系墙螺栓; **～ switch** *n* **1** (switch) 拨动开关; **2** Comput **= toggle 2**

Togo /'təʊgəʊ/ *pr n* 多哥

toil /tɔɪl/

A *vi* **1** **～ (away)** (work hard) 辛勤工作; **to ～ (away) at** *or* **over sth.** 辛苦从事某事 **2** (struggle) «*person, animal, lorry, train*» 艰难缓慢地移动; **to ～ up the hill** 艰难地爬上山岗; **to ～ on** 费力前行

B *n* [u and c] 辛劳

toilet /'tɔɪlɪt/ *n* **1** (bowl) 抽水马桶; **to sit on the ～** 坐在马桶上; **to flush the ～** 冲马桶; **the ～ is blocked** 马桶堵了 **2** (room) 厕所; **to go to the ～** 去洗手间; **public ～(s)** 公共厕所; **men's/women's ～(s)** 男/女厕所; **～ facilities** 洗手间设备; **the ～ bowl** 马桶 **3** dated (washing and dressing) 梳洗

toilet: ～ bag *n* Brit **= sponge bag**; **～ brush** *n* 马桶刷; **～ paper** *n* [u] 手纸; **a roll of ～ paper** 一卷卫生纸; **～ pan** *n* 便池

toiletries /'tɔɪlɪtrɪz/ *npl* 洗漱用品

toilet: ～ roll *n* **1** [c] (roll of toilet paper) 卫生纸卷; (cardboard tube inside roll) 手纸卷筒; **2** [u] (tissue) 卷筒纸; **～ seat** *n* 马桶座圈; **～ soap** *n* 香皂; **～-train** *vt* «*parent*» 训练…上厕所 ‹*child*›; **he's not yet ～-trained** 他还不会上厕所; **～ training** *n* [u] [对小孩进行的] 上厕所训练

toiletry bag /'tɔɪlətri ˌbæg/ *n* **= sponge bag**

toilet: ～ tissue *n* [u] **= toilet paper**; **～ water** *n* [u] 花露水

toing and froing /ˌtu:ɪŋ ən 'frəʊɪŋ/ *n* [u] **1** (movement) 来来往往; **all this ～** 来回奔波 **2** (vacillation) 犹豫不决; **after much ～** 经过长时间的犹豫

token /'təʊkən/

A *n* **1** (for machine, phone) (of metal) 金属代币; (of plastic) 塑料代币 **2** (voucher) 代金券 **3** (symbol) 象征; **a ～ of ...** …的标志; **as a ～ of esteem/love** 以表示尊敬/爱意; **by the same ～** 同样地

B *adj attrib* pej 象征性的; **～ strike/resistance/attempt/payment** 象征性罢工/抵抗/尝试/付款; **he was the ～ black person on the committee** 他是委员会里装点门面的黑人成员

tokenism /'təʊkənɪzəm/ *n* [u] pej 表面文章; **a policy of ～** 装点门面的政策; **he has been accused of ～** 他被指责只做表面文章

token money *n* [u] 名目货币

Tokyo /'təʊkɪəʊ/ *pr n* 东京

tolbooth /'təʊlbu:θ/ *n* **= tollbooth**

told /təʊld/ *pt, pp* ▸**tell**

tolerable /'tɒlərəbl/ *adj* **1** (bearable) 可忍受的 ‹*pain, heat, difficulties, conditions*› **2** (adequate) 尚好的 ‹*result, knowledge, weather, meal*›

tolerably /'tɒlərəbli/ *adv* 还可以; **the weather is ～ warm** 天气还算暖和

tolerance /'tɒlərəns/ *n* **1** [u] (broad-mindedness) 宽容; **to show ～** 表现出宽容 **2** [u] (ability to tolerate) 忍耐力; **～ to sth.** 对…的耐受性 ‹*alcohol, cold*› **3** [c] (permitted variation) 公差

tolerant /'tɒlərənt/ *adj* **1** (broad-minded) 宽容的 ‹*person, parents, religion*›; **a racially ～ society** 种族宽容的社会; **to be ～ towards sb.** 对某人持宽容态度; **to be ～ of sb./sth.** 容忍某人/某事物 **2** **to be ～ of sth.** (able to tolerate) 能耐… ‹*heat, cold, conditions, treatment*›; **a plastic that is ～ of high temperatures** 耐高温塑料

tolerantly /'tɒlərəntli/ *adv* 宽容地

tolerate /'tɒləreɪt/ *vt* **1** (permit) 容许 ‹*opinions, rudeness, opposition*›; **I will not ～ this sort of behaviour!** 我不会容忍这种行为! ; **society must not ～ racial violence** 社会决不能容许种族暴力 **2** (able to endure) 忍受 ‹*heat, cold, pain, noise, conditions*› **3** (be able to take) 对…有耐受性 ‹*drug, therapy, treatment, radiation*›

toleration /ˌtɒlə'reɪʃn/ *n* [u] 容忍; **religious ～** 宗教上的宽容; **the ～ of certain drugs** 对某些药物的耐受性

toll¹ /təʊl/ *n* **1** (charge) 通行费; **to pay a ～** 缴纳通行费 **2** (number) 伤亡人数; **the death ～** 死亡人数 **3** (cost, damage) 毁坏; **to take its ～ (on sb./sth.)** (对某人/某事物) 产生恶果; **to take a heavy ～ (on sb./sth.)** (对某人/某事物) 造成严重损失; **the environmental/physical ～** 环境/身体损害 **4** Amer Telecom 长途电话费

toll²

A *vi* «*bell*» 缓慢鸣响; **the bell ～ed for the dead** 为死者鸣钟

B *vt* «*person*» 缓慢敲击; **the verger was ～ing the bell for Matins** 教堂司事为晨祷鸣钟

C *n* (sound) [缓慢而有规律的] 钟声; (for funeral) 丧钟

toll: ～booth *n* 道路收费亭; **～ bridge** *n* 收费桥; **～ call** *n* Amer 长途电话; **～ free** *adj* Amer 免费拨打的; **～ gate** *n* 道路收费站; **～house** *n* 道路收费处; **～ motorway** *n* 收费高速公路; **～ plaza** *n* 道路收费区; **～ road** Brit, **～way** Amer *ns* 收费道路

Tom /tɒm/ *pr n* colloq 汤姆 [Thomas的简写形式]; **any** *or* **every ～, Dick and Harry** 任何人; **I don't want every ～, Dick, and Harry peering through the garden fence!** 我不想让随便什么人都透过花园栅栏往里窥探!

tom /tɒm/ *n* 雄性动物 [尤指雄猫]

tomahawk /'tɒməhɔ:k/ *n* 印第安战斧

tomato /tə'mɑ:təʊ, Amer tə'meɪtəʊ/ *n* (*pl* **～es**) **1** [c] (fruit) 番茄; **～ skins/seeds/plant** 番茄皮/籽/秧; **～ salad/sauce/ketchup** 番茄色拉/沙司/调味酱 **2** [u] (colour) [成熟番茄的] 鲜红色

tomb /tu:m/ *n* **1** (vault) 坟墓 **2** (monument) 墓碑

tombola /tɒm'bəʊlə/ *n* Brit "翻筋斗" 赌戏 [参加游戏者从旋转的鼓中抽出奖券]

tomboy /'tɒmbɔɪ/ *n* 假小子; **to be something of a ～** 有点像假小子

tomboyish /'tɒmbɔɪɪʃ/ *adj* 假小子似的

tombstone /'tu:mstəʊn/ *n* 墓碑

tomcat /'tɒmkæt/ *n* 雄猫

tome /təʊm/ *n* liter or hum 巨著; **university libraries full of weighty ～s** 满是厚重的大部头书的大学图书馆

tomfool /tɒm'fu:l/ *adj attrib* dated 愚蠢的 ‹*behaviour, idea*›; **that was a ～ thing to do, wasn't it!** 那件事干得真蠢, 难道不是吗!

tomfoolery /tɒm'fu:ləri/ *n* [u] 愚蠢行为; **enough of this ～ — let's get down to the serious business!** 别傻了——我们干正经事吧!

Tommy /'tɒmi/ *n* Brit colloq dated 英国兵

tommy /'tɒmi/: **～gun** *n* colloq dated 汤普森冲锋枪; **～rot** *n* [u] colloq dated 胡扯; **he's talking a load of old ～rot!** 他又在胡说八道了!

tomography /tə'mɒgrəfi/ *n* [u] X 线体层照相术

tomorrow /tə'mɒrəʊ/ ▸**p. 182**

A *adv* **1** (on the day after today) 在明天; **see you ～!** 明天见! ; **all day ～** 明天一整天; **a week ～, ～ week** 一周后的明天; **a week ago ～** 6 天前; **they got married a month ago ～** 一个月差一天前, 他们结婚了; **first thing ～** 明天要做的第一件事; **as from ～** 从明天起; **～ morning/afternoon/evening/night** 明天上午/下午/晚上/夜间 **2** (in the near future) 不久; **the government has promised to cut taxes ～** 政府保证马上会减税

B *n* **1** (the day after today) 明天; **the day after ～** 后天; **～'s newspaper** 明天的报纸; **what's ～'s date?** 明天几号? **2** (the future) 未来; **～'s world/citizens** 未来的世界/公民; **who knows what ～ may bring?** 谁知道明天会发生什么?

tomtit /'tɒmtɪt/ *n* Brit 大山雀

tom-tom *n* 手鼓

ton /tʌn/ ▸**p. 909** *n* **1** Brit (in weight) 吨; **a three-～ truck** 一辆三吨的卡车; **to weigh a ～** fig 非常重; **to come down on sb. like a ～ of bricks** (criticize) 严厉斥责某人; (punish harshly) 严厉惩处某人 **2** Brit colloq (a hundred) (speed) 100 英里时速; (score) 100 分 [体育比赛得分]; **to do a ～** 以 100 英里的时速驾驶; **he scored a ～ at cricket** 他在板球比赛中得了 100 分 **3** colloq (a lot) 许多; **a ～ of** 大量的; **～s of** 许多; **we've ～s left** 我们还剩下很多; **her new car is ～s better than the other one** 她的新车比另一辆好得多

tonal /'təʊnl/ *adj* **1** (relating to tone) (of music) 音调的; (of colour) 色调的; (of writing) 风格的; **～ quality/variation/colour** (of music) 音质/音调变化/音色; **～ quality/variation** (of colour) 色质/色调的变化; **～ variation** (of writing) 风格的变化 **2** Mus 调性的; **～ music** 调性音乐 **3** Ling 音调的; **a ～ language** 声调语言

tonality /tə'næləti/ *n* [u and c] **1** Mus 调性 **2** (of picture) 色调

tonally /'təʊnəli/ *adv* 在音调方面; **parts that are rhythmically and ～ coherent** 节奏和音调协调的声部

tone /təʊn/

A *n* **1** [c] (quality of sound) 音调; **the harsh ～ of an alarm bell** 警铃鸣响的刺耳声音 **2** [c] (character of voice) 口气; **to use a sarcastic ～** 用讥讽的口气; **in a(n) ... ～, in ... ～s** 以…的口吻; **to speak in hushed/low/clipped/measured ～s** 用压低/低沉/短促/慢条斯理的语调讲话; **～ of voice** 语气 **3** [u and c] (character) (of letter, speech, meeting, conversation) 调子; (of place) 风气; **the overall ～ of the book was gently nostalgic** 这本书的整体格调是温情的怀旧; **differences in style and ～ between the two prime ministers** 两位首相作风与格调的不同; **to set the ～ (for sth.)** (为某事物) 定基调; **to raise/lower the ～ (of sth.)** 提高/降低 (某事物的) 格调 **4** [u and c] (tint) 色调; **two-～** 双色 **5** [c] (sound) (on telephone) 声音信号; (on answering machine) 答录信号; **the engaged ～** 忙音; **a continuous ～** 连续音 **6** [c] *usu sing* (sound of musical instrument) 音色 **7** [c] Mus (interval) 全音 **8** [c] Audio (quality of sound of radio, CD player, etc.) 音质 **9** [c] Ling 声调; **a rising/falling ～** 升调/降调 **10** [u] Physiol 健康; **muscle/skin ～** 肌肉的结实度/皮肤的柔韧性; **in ～** 健康的

B *vi* 调和; **to ～ (in) with sth.** «*colour, curtains, carpet, paintwork*» 与某物协调

C *vt* «*exercise, treatment*» 使…健壮 ‹*muscles, body*›; «*treatment*» 使…紧致 ‹*skin*›; **a beautifully ～d body** 健美的身体

Phrasal verbs

- **tone down** *vt* [~ sth. down, ~ down sth.] 1 (make less harsh or extreme) 使…缓和 ‹*remark, language, article, policy*› 2 (darken) 使…柔和 ‹*colour*›
- **tone up** *vt* [~ sth. up, ~ up sth.] 使…健壮 ‹*body, muscle*›

tone: ~ arm *n* 拾音器臂; **~ control, ~ control button** *ns* 音调控制钮

toned-down /ˌtəʊnd'daʊn/ *adj* 1 lit (softened) 变柔和的 ‹*colour, sound*› 2 fig (moderated) 缓和的 ‹*version, language, film*›

tone: ~-deaf *adj* 不能辨别音调的; **to be ~ deaf** 五音不分; **~ language** *n* 声调语言

toneless /'təʊnlɪs/ *adj* 单调的

tonelessly /'təʊnlɪsli/ *adv* 单调地

tone poem *n* 音诗

toner /'təʊnə(r)/ *n* 1 [c and u] (for photocopier) 墨粉 2 [c and u] Cosmet 紧肤水 3 [c] (toning device) 健身器; (toning exercise) [某个身体部位的] 锻炼; **a tummy ~** 腹部锻炼

Tonga /'tɒŋgə/ *pr n* 汤加; **the ~ Islands** 汤加群岛

Tongan /'tɒŋgən/ ▸**p. 503, p. 426**
A *adj* (of Tonga) 汤加的; (of the people) 汤加人的; (of the language) 汤加语的
B *n* 1 [c] (person) 汤加人 2 [u] (language) 汤加语

tongs /tɒŋz/ *npl* 1 (for coal) 火钳; (in laboratory) 钳子; (for salad, sugar) 夹子; **a pair of coal ~** 一把火钳; **we've been going at this job hammer and ~** 我们一直在倾尽全力做这项工作 2 (for hair) **(curling) ~** 烫发钳

tongue /tʌŋ/
A *n* 1 [c] Anat 舌头; **to stick** *or* **poke** *or* **put out one's ~** 伸出舌头; **sb.'s ~ is hanging out** 某人垂涎三尺; **to click one's ~** 嘴里发出啧啧声 [表示不满]; **hold your ~!** 住口! ; **to bite/lose/watch one's ~** 忍住不说/哑口无言/说话当心; **to find one's ~** [尤指在受惊说不出话后] 能开口说话; **the cat has got his/her ~** colloq 他/她一声不吭; **on the tip of one's ~** 就在嘴边的; **to be able to get one's ~ round sth.** 能够正确读出某单词; **to trip off the ~** 顺口说出; **to loosen sb.'s ~** 使某人敞开说; **alcohol loosened his ~** 酒后他的话匣子便打开了; **(to say sth.) with one's ~ in one's cheek** *or* **(with) ~ in cheek** 半开玩笑地(说某事物); **to get** *or* **feel the rough side** *or* **edge of sb.'s ~** 受到某人的严厉呵斥; **to set ~s wagging** colloq 引起闲言碎语 2 [c] (manner or style of speaking) 说话方式; **to have a caustic ~** 说话尖刻; **she has a spiteful ~ in her head** 她这人嘴巴很损; **to keep a civil ~ in one's head** dated 说话文明 3 [u and c] liter (language) 语言; **one's native** *or* **mother ~** 母语; **to speak in ~s** 讲未知的语言 [在基督教礼拜中用圣灵所赐的口才] 4 [u] Culin 口条 5 [c] (flap on shoe, boot) 鞋舌 6 [c] Geog 岬; **a ~ of land** 岬角 7 [c] (clapper in bell) 铃锤 8 [c] (pin of buckle) [搭扣上的] 别针 9 [c] Mus (reed) [管乐器的] 簧片 10 [c] Tech 榫舌; **~ and groove** 榫槽接合 11 [c] (of flame, fire) 舌状物; **a ~ of flame** 火舌
B *vt* «*player*» 用运舌法吹出 ‹*note, passage*›

tongue-and-groove *adj* 榫槽接合的 ‹*floorboards, joint*›

tongue-in-cheek
A *adj* (ironic) 挖苦的 ‹*humour, reply*›; (insincere) 随便说说的 ‹*comment, reply*›
B *adv* (ironically) 挖苦地; (insincerely) 随口地; **'and we all know what a passionate love life I have!' he said, ~** "并且大家都知道我的爱情生活多么富有激情!"他自嘲地说

tongue: ~-lashing *n* 呵斥; **~ stud** *n* 舌钉; **~-tied** *adj* 张口结舌的; **~-twister** *n* 绕口令; **~-twisting** *adj attrib* 拗口的 ‹*name, sentence*›

tonic /'tɒnɪk/
A *n* 1 [c and u] (drink) 奎宁水; **a gin and ~** 一杯杜松子酒奎宁水 2 [c and u] Med 补药; **hair ~** 生发水; **skin ~** 护肤液 3 [c] fig (boost) 使精神振奋的东西; **he's a real ~** 他真是令人精神振奋; **to be a ~ for sb.** 使某人精神一振; **success is always a good ~** 成功总是令人精神振奋 4 [c] Mus 主音
B *adj* (thing improving well-being) 滋补的; (thing improving vigour) 振奋精神的; **~ wine** 滋补酒; **a ~ effect** 振奋精神的效果

tonic: ~ sol-fa /ˌtɒnɪk 'sɒlfɑ:/ *n* [u] 首调唱名法; **~ water** *n* [u] 奎宁水

tonight /tə'naɪt/
A *n* 今夜; **have you seen ~'s paper?** 你看到今晚的报纸了吗?
B *adv* 在今夜; **you'll sleep well ~!** 你今晚会睡个好觉!

toning /'təʊnɪŋ/ *n* [u] 1 (firming of muscles) 肌肉锻炼 2 Phot 相片调色; **sepia ~** 调成棕褐色

toning-down *n* [u] 1 (softening) 柔和化 2 (moderation) 缓和

tonnage /'tʌnɪdʒ/ *n* 1 [c] (ship's capacity) 吨位 [表示容量] 2 [u] (amount of shipping) 吨位 [表示载重量] 3 [u] (total weight) 总重量; **road convoys carry more ~** 公路车队能载运更多的货物

tonnage dues /'tʌnɪdʒ dju:z, Amer du:z/ *npl* 船舶吨税

tonne /tʌn/ ▸**p. 909** *n* = **metric ton**

tonometer /tə'nɒmɪtə(r)/ *n* 1 Mus 音调计 2 Med 压力计

tonsil /'tɒnsl/ *n* 扁桃体; **to have one's ~s out** 切除扁桃体

tonsillectomy /ˌtɒnsɪ'lektəmi/ *n* 1 [u] (procedure) 扁桃体切除 2 [c] (operation) 扁桃体切除术

tonsillitis /ˌtɒnsɪ'laɪtɪs/ ▸**p. 377** *n* [u] 扁桃体炎; **she's got ~** 她扁桃体发炎了

tonsure /'tɒnʃə(r)/ *n* 头顶剃光部分

too /tu:, tʊ, tə/ *adv* 1 (excessively) 太; **you've gone ~ far** 你太过分了; **it's ~ hot a day for walking** 天气太热了,不适合散步; **~ silly for words** 愚蠢得难以言表; **I was ~ shocked to speak** 我惊讶得说不出话来; **it was ~ little ~ late** 那太少且为时太晚; **the measures were ~ little ~ late** 那些措施力度不够且为时太晚; **I ate ~ much** 我吃得太饱了; **it's ~ much of a strain** 这扭伤很严重; **she's ~ much of a feminist to do that** 她是十足的女权主义者,不会那样做的; **he was in ~ much of a hurry to talk** 他太匆忙,都来不及说话 2 (also, as well) 也; **have you been to India ~?** (like me) 你也去过印度吗? ; (as well as other countries) 你还去过印度吗? ; **she's kind, but she's strict ~** 她人很好,但也很严厉; **the town has changed, so ~ have the inhabitants** 城市变样了,居民也变了 3 (reinforcing an opinion) 而且; **she broke her leg last week, and on her birthday ~!** 她上周摔断了腿,而且是在她生日那天! ; **they sacked him, and quite right ~!** 他们炒了他鱿鱼,做得很对! 4 (expressing indignation, annoyance) [用以表示生气、惊讶或赞同]; **she gave me the money — about time ~!** 她把钱给我了——早该给了! ; **I'm sorry — I should think so ~!** 我很抱歉——我想应该是这样! ; **and in front of your mother ~!** 居然当着你母亲的面! 5 (in negatives) **not ~** 不太; **he's not ~ keen on jazz** 他不太喜欢爵士乐; **it wasn't ~ bad** 不算太糟糕; **he wasn't ~ bad** (in health) 他身体不算太差; (in appearance) 他外表还过得去; (in his reaction) 他还过得去; **I'm not ~ sure about that** 我对那事没有太大把握; **it's not ~ far removed from blackmail** 这简直是敲诈 6 formal (very) 非常; **you're ~ kind/generous!** (expressing gratitude) 你太好了/太慷慨了! ; hum iron 你真是个大好人啊/你可真大方呀! 7 esp Amer colloq (contradicting) 确实如此; **he didn't touch you — he did ~!** 他没碰过你——他确实碰了! ; **but you can't swim — I can ~!** 可你不会游泳——我当然会了!

took /tʊk/ *pt* ▸**take A, B**

tool /tu:l/
A *n* 1 (device, implement) 工具; **a set of ~s** 一套工具; **garden ~s** 园艺用具; **to down ~s** 停工 2 (aid) (in occupation) 用具; (in pursuit of aim) 手段; **an essential ~ in the classroom** 基本教具; **management ~s** 管理工具 3 Comput 工具软件 4 pej (underling) 爪牙; (puppet) 傀儡; **to be a mere ~ in the hands of …** 只是…手里的工具 5 sl (penis) 鸡巴 offensive
B *vt* 给…压印图案 ‹*leather, silver*›; **volumes bound in green leather and ~ed in gold** 烫金绿革封皮的书卷

Phrasal verb

- **tool up**
A *vt* [~ sth. up, ~ up sth.] 给…配置设备 ‹*factory*›; **as soon as the factory's ~ed up, we can start production** 工厂的设备一旦配置齐全,我们就能开始生产
B *vi* 配置设备

tool: ~ bag *n* 工具袋; **~bar** *n* [计算机程序中的] 工具栏; **~box** *n* 工具箱; **~ chest** *n* 大工具木箱

tooled /tu:ld/ *adj* 压花的 ‹*leather, silver*›

tool house *n* Amer = **tool shed**

tooling /'tu:lɪŋ/ *n* [u] 压花

tool: ~ kit *n* 成套工具; **~maker** ▸**p. 409** *n* 工具制造者; **~making** *n* [u] 工具制造; **~ shed** *n* [尤指花园中的] 工具房; **~ tip** *n* 工具提示

toot /tu:t/
A *vt* 使…嘟嘟响 ‹*whistle*›; **~ your horn to warn other drivers of your approach** 鸣喇叭警告其他司机你开过来了
B *vi* «*driver*» 嘟嘟鸣喇叭; **to ~ at sb.** 对某人按喇叭
C *n* 嘟嘟声

tooth /tu:θ/ *n* (*pl* **teeth**) 1 (in mouth) 牙齿; **a set of teeth** 一副牙齿; **baby** *or* **first teeth** 乳牙; **adult** *or* **second** *or* **permanent teeth** 恒牙; **to bare** *or* **show one's teeth** 露出牙齿; fig 显示出坚定的姿态; **to mutter between one's teeth** 喃喃自语; **to flash one's teeth at sb.** 朝某人咧嘴笑; **to cut one's teeth** 长出牙齿; **to cut one's teeth on …** fig 从…中获得初步经验; **to take out** *or* **extract** *or* **remove a ~** 拔牙; **to sink one's teeth into sth.** (eat) 狼吞虎咽地吃某物; (attack) 用力咬某物; **to get one's teeth into sth.** fig 专注于某事物; **armed to the teeth** 武装到牙齿的; **to fight (for sth.) ~ and nail** (为某事物)奋力抗争; **nature, red in ~ and claw** 残酷无情的大自然; **to be fed up** *or* **sick to the (back) teeth (of** *or* **with sb./sth.)** colloq 受够了(某人/某事物); **he lied through his teeth to get that job!** 为了得到那份工作他公然说谎! ; **to do sth. in the teeth of criticism/opposition/danger** 不顾批评/反对/危险做某事; **in the teeth of the storm/wind/gale** 冒着暴风雨/风/大风; **a kick in the teeth** fig 野蛮的对待; **to be long in the ~** 年事已高; **to have a sweet ~** 喜欢吃甜食; **to escape by the skin of one's teeth** 勉强逃脱 2 (of tool, implement) 齿 3 **teeth** *pl* fig (power) 权力; (effectiveness) 效力; **it's no use setting up a regulatory body if it has no teeth** 设立监管机构却不赋予它权力是毫无用处的; **to give sth. teeth** 赋予某物权力

tooth: ~ache *n* [u and c] 牙痛; **to have (a) ~ache** 牙疼; **~brush** *n* 牙刷; **~ decay** *n* [u] 蛀牙; **~ fairy** *n* 牙仙子 [传说中将儿童脱落的乳牙取走并在枕下留一枚硬币的仙人]; **~ glass** *n* 漱口杯

toothless /'tu:θlɪs/ *adj* 没有牙齿的; **a ~ wonder** 无用的人

tooth: ~ **mug** *n* 漱口杯; ~**paste** *n* [u and c] 牙膏; ~**pick** *n* 牙签; ~ **powder** *n* [u] 牙粉

toothsome /ˈtuːθsəm/ *adj* [1] (of food) (tasting good) 可口的; (looking good) 诱人的; **a ~ selection of cakes and pastries** 多种美味糕饼 [2] colloq (of person) 好看的

toothy /ˈtuːθi/ *adj* 露齿的 ‹*smile*›; **to give a ~ grin** 露齿一笑

tootle /ˈtuːtl/ *vi* [1] Brit colloq (go) 闲逛; **I'll just ~ into town/down to the shops** 我正要去城里/商店逛一逛 [2] (on musical instrument) 悠闲地吹奏; **to ~ on sth.** 悠然自得地吹奏某物

tootsie, tootsy /ˈtʊtsi/ *n* colloq [1] (foot) 脚丫子 [2] dated (young woman) 风骚小妞

top /tɒp/

A *n* [1] [u and c] (highest part) (of mountain, head, roof, car) 顶; (of ridge, cliff, tree, ladder, wall, wave, list, etc.) 顶端; (of cupboard, container) 顶部; **the ~ of the hill/building** 山顶/楼顶; **the very ~** 最顶端; **to fill a glass to the very ~** 斟满杯子; **five lines down from the ~ of the page** 从页首数起第5行; **the ~ of the street/garden** esp Brit 街道/花园的尽头; **the ~ of the table** 桌子的上首; **to be (at the) ~ of the** *or* **one's list (to do sth.)** (做某事) 是最重要的; **to be ~ of the class** 名列班级第一; **~ of the pops** 流行音乐排行榜首位; **from ~ to toe** 从头到脚; **from ~ to bottom** 彻底地; **from the ~** colloq 从头开始; **to take sth. from the ~** 从头再做一遍某事; **to go over the ~** Mil 爬出战壕进攻; **to go over the ~ with anger** 怒不可遏; **to be over the ~** esp Brit colloq (be excessive) 过分; (be exaggerated) 夸张; **not to have much up ~** colloq 没有多少脑子; **~ of the morning** Ir 早上好 [2] [u and c] (upper surface) (of box, desk, sideboard, cake) 上面; (of water, sea, lake) 表面; **on the ~ of sth.** 在某物上面; **the ~ of the table** 桌面; **to come** *or* **rise** *or* **float to the ~** 浮到表面; **off the ~ of one's head** colloq 不假思索地; **to talk through a hole in the ~ of one's head** colloq 趾高气扬地胡说; **on ~** 在上面; **she wore a skirt and blouse with a raincoat on ~** 她穿着裙子和衬衫, 外面罩着雨衣; **to be** *or* **stay on ~** (be in superior position) 处于优势; (be in control) 控制局面; **to come out on ~** 名列前茅; **one thing on ~ of another** 接二连三的事情; **on ~ of all this, she was made redundant** 最糟糕的是, 她还被解聘了; **on ~ of doing sth.** 除了做某事之外; **to be** *or* **get on ~ of sth.** 能够处理某事; **to get on ~ of sb.** 使某人吃不消; **to feel on ~ of the world** colloq 欢天喜地 [3] [u] **the ~** (highest, most important rank) 最高级别; **the decision came from the ~** 决定是最上层作出的; **life can be tough at the ~** 身居高位日子也会不好过; **to get to** *or* **make it to** *or* **reach the ~** 出人头地; **his experience will surely take him to the ~** 他的经验肯定能将他送上高位; **the ~ of the tree** 最高地位 [4] [u and c] (upper part) (of piece of furniture, building, facade) 上部; esp Brit (of milk) 奶皮; **a sliding ~** Aut 滑动天窗; **to sit on ~** (of bus, tram) 在车厢上层就座 [5] [c] (lid) 盖; (pen cap) 帽; **to put on/screw on the ~** 盖上/拧上盖子; **to screw off** *or* **unscrew the ~** 拧开盖子; **to blow one's ~** fig colloq 发脾气 [6] [c] Clothg 上装; **a pyjama/tracksuit ~** 睡衣/运动服上衣 [7] [u] Brit Aut 高挡; **to be in ~** 挂着高挡 [8] [c] (toy) 陀螺; **to spin a ~** 转陀螺; **to sleep like a ~** 睡得很熟

B **tops** *npl* [1] Hort (of plant and vegetable) [根茎类植物的] 茎叶; **turnip/carrot/celery ~s** 芜菁/胡萝卜/芹菜茎叶 [2] colloq (person) 最优秀的人; (thing) 最好的东西; **to be (the) ~s** 出类拔萃

C *adj attrib* [1] (highest) 最上面的 ‹*button, shelf, layer*›; 最高的 ‹*price, class, category*›; **on the ~ floor** 在顶楼; **on the ~ step** 在最高一级的台阶上; **the ~ coat of paint** 最上面的一层漆; **she has difficulty reaching the ~ notes** 她很难唱到最高音; **~ gear** 最高挡; **the ~ right-/left-hand corner** 右上角/左上角; **to get/give sb. ~ marks (for sth.)** (在某方面) 得到最高分/给某人最高分; fig (因某事物) 获得/给某人特别偏爱; **the ~ end of the range/market** 该系列/市场的高端 [2] esp Brit (furthest away) 最远的 ‹*end*›; 最远端的 ‹*part, section*›; **the patient in the ~ bed** 最里边床位的病人 [3] (maximum) 最大的; **this is a matter of ~ priority** 这是最重要的一件事; **(at) ~ speed** (以) 最高速; **in** *or* **on ~ form** 处于最佳状态的; **you could earn ~ money in Saudi Arabia** colloq 你在沙特阿拉伯能挣到大钱 [4] (leading) 最高位的 ‹*authority, politician*›; 顶尖的 ‹*surgeon, adviser, team, job*›; **one of the company's ~ executives** 公司最高层管理人员之一; **he's the ~ scorer this season** 他是本赛季的头号得分手; **the ~ ten/twenty** Mus 流行音乐排行榜前10名/前20名; **he's a ~ bloke** Brit colloq 他是个大好人 [5] (best) 最划算的 ‹*buy*›; 最好的 ‹*choice*›; **one of the city's ~ tourist attractions** 这座城市的最佳观光地之一 [6] (upper) 上部的; **the ~ half of the body** 上半身

D **tops** *adv* colloq 至多; **it couldn't have cost more than £50, ~s** 这应该花了最多不超过50英镑

E *vt* (*pres p etc.* **-pp-**) [1] (surmount, finish off) «*trees, roof, icing, sauce*» 盖在…顶上 ‹*hill, building, dish*›; **to be ~ped by** *or* **with sth.** 以某物做顶; **each cake was ~ped with a cherry** 每只蛋糕顶上都放了一颗樱桃 [2] (head) 到达…的顶部 ‹*mountain, ridge*›; «*team, record, politician, political party, name*» 居…之首 ‹*league, division, charts, list, class*›; **Liverpool are ~ping the first division** 利物浦队目前在甲级联赛中占据首位; **to ~ the polls in an election** 在选举中得票最多; **a chart-~ping new single** 排行榜首的新单曲; **to ~ the bill** (as performer) 领衔主演; (as attraction) 成为主要看点 [3] (surpass) 超过; **to ~ one's best work** 超越自己最好的作品; **that ~s the lot!** colloq 那简直盖了帽了!; **and to ~ it all …** 更有甚者…; **to ~ sb.** 比某人高 [4] (cap) 胜过 ‹*story, remark, action*›; **~ that!** 来比试比试! [5] Culin, Hort «*cook, gardener*» 为…剪顶 ‹*plant, fruit, vegetable, tree*› [6] Brit colloq (kill) 干掉

F *v refl* (*pres p etc.* **-pp-**) [1] **to ~ oneself** Brit colloq (commit suicide) 自杀 [2] **to ~ oneself** Amer (surpass oneself) 超越自己

Phrasal verbs

- **top off** *vt* [**~ sth. off, ~ off sth.**] [以特定方式] 结束 ‹*action, entertainment, meal*›; **to ~ sth. off with sth.** 以某物结束某事; **to ~ sth. off by doing sth.** 以做某事结束某事
- **top out**

A *vt* [**~ sth. out, ~ out sth.**] 为…封顶 ‹*building*›

B *vi* «*expenditure, growth*» 达到顶点

- **top up** esp Brit

A [**~ sth. up, ~ up sth.**] *vt* [1] (refill) 加满 ‹*tank, drink, glass*›; **to ~ up the battery every week** 每周给电池充满电; **to ~ sth. up with sth.** 用某物加满某物 [2] (supplement) 补足 ‹*earnings, savings, payment, rate*›

B [**~ sb. up, ~ up sb.**] *vt* colloq (give refill to) 给…斟满杯子 ‹*person*›

C *vi* 加满; **~ up before you start your journey** 在出发以前把油加满; **to ~ up with sth.** 用某物加满

top and tail *vt* Brit 给…掐头去尾 ‹*fruit, vegetables*›

topaz /ˈtəʊpæz/ *n* [u and c] 黄玉; **a ~ ring** 黄玉戒指

top: ~ **banana** *n* Amer colloq (leader) 头头; (boss) 老板; ~ **brass** *n* [u] + *v pl* colloq (military officers) 高级军官; (business leaders) 高级官员; **the ~ brass of the US military** 美国军方的要员; ~**-class** *adj* 一流的 ‹*person, performance*›; ~**coat** *n* [1] (of paint) 外涂层; [2] (garment) 轻便大衣; ~ **copy** *n* 正本; ~ **dog** *n* colloq 头头; ~**-down** *adj* 自上而下的 ‹*management, structure, approach*›; ~**-drawer** *adj* colloq [1] (of best quality) 最优秀的; [2] dated (of high social standing) 最上层的; ~**-dress** *vt* 在…的表面施肥 ‹*soil*›; ~ **dressing** *n* [1] [c] (substance) 顶肥; [2] [u] (process) 表施; ~**-flight** *adj* 第一流的; **~-flight computer scientists/athletes/universities** 一流的计算机科学家/运动员/大学; ~ **fruit** *n* [c and u] Brit 树果; ~ **gear** *n* [u] 最高挡; ~ **hat** *n* 高顶礼帽; ~**-heavy** *adj* 头重脚轻的; **the structure was too ~-heavy** 这种结构上部过重; **the management structure is ~-heavy** 管理架构头重脚轻; ~**-hole** *adj* Brit colloq dated 极好的; **we had a ~-hole dinner!** 我们美餐了一顿!

topiary /ˈtəʊpɪəri, Amer -ɪeri/ *n* [u] [1] (art) 林木造型艺术; (practice) 林木造型 [2] (clipped shrubs or trees) 修剪后的林木

topic /ˈtɒpɪk/ *n* (subject) (of discussion, conference) 话题; (of essay, project) 题目; **there has been much debate on this ~** 就这一主题有过很多争论

topical /ˈtɒpɪkl/ *adj* 有关时事的 ‹*question, play*›; **of ~ interest** 当前关注的

topicality /ˌtɒpɪˈkæləti/ *n* [u] 时事性

topknot /ˈtɒpnɒt/ *n* 顶髻

topless /ˈtɒplɪs/ *adj* [1] (of woman) 上身裸露的; **'~ bathing forbidden'** "禁止裸胸游泳" [2] (of garment) 袒胸的; **~ swimsuit** 袒胸泳装

topless bar *n* 无上装酒吧 [指雇用袒胸女招待的酒吧]

top: ~**-level** *adj* 最高级的; **~-level talks** 最高层会谈; ~**-loader** *n* 波轮式洗衣机; ~ **management** *n* [u] 高级管理层; ~**mast** *n* 中桅; ~**most** *adj attrib* 最高的; **the ~most branches of the tree** 树的顶端枝条; **the ~most floor** 顶楼; ~**-notch** *adj* colloq 一流的 ‹*person, performance*›; **he's a ~-notch lawyer/film director** 他是顶尖律师/一流的电影导演; ~**-of-the-range** *adj* 最高端的 ‹*model, car*›

topographical /ˌtɒpəˈɡræfɪkl/, **topographic** /ˌtɒpəˈɡræfɪk/ *adjs* 地形的; **~ features/survey/map** 地形特征/测量/图

topography /təˈpɒɡrəfi/ *n* [1] [u] (layout) 地形; **the ~ of the island** 岛屿的地形; **a study of the ~ of the area** 对这一地区地貌的研究 [2] [c] (description) 地形描绘

topper /ˈtɒpə(r)/ *n* colloq 高顶礼帽

topping /ˈtɒpɪŋ/

A *n* [食品顶部的] 配料; **with a ~ of bread crumbs** 顶部撒有面包屑的

B *adj* Brit colloq dated 极好的

topple /ˈtɒpl/

A *vt* [1] (cause to fall) 使…倒下 ‹*tower, structure*›; 使…掉落 ‹*ornament*› [2] fig (overthrow) 颠覆; **the miners' strike eventually ~d the government** 矿工的罢工最终使政府倒台

B *vi* ~ **(over)** 倒下; **the plant grew too tall, and eventually it ~d over** 那株植物长得太高, 最终倒了下去; **to ~ over the edge of a cliff** 从悬崖边缘落下

top: ~**-ranking** *adj* (of the highest rank) 级别最高的; (of the highest importance) 最重要的; ~**sail** *n* 中桅帆; ~ **secret** *adj* 绝密的; ~ **security** *adj* 防备最严的 ‹*prison*›; ~**-selling** *adj attrib* 最畅销的; ~**-shelf** *adj* [1] Brit (pornographic) 色情的; **a ~-shelf magazine** 色情杂志; [2] Amer (first-rate) 一流的; ~**side** *n* [u] [1] (joint of beef) 牛外股肉; [2] Naut (above waterline) 水线以上部分; (above decks) 甲板以上部分; ~ **slice** *n* 上切税; ~**soil** *n* [u and c] 表土; ~**spin** *n* [u] [球的] 上旋; **he bowls/serves with a lot of ~spin** 他投的球/发的球带有强烈的上旋; ~**stitch** *vt* 用明线缝

t

topsy-turvy /ˌtɒpsɪ'tɜ:vi/ *adj* colloq 乱七八糟的 ‹*room, life, story*›; **it's a ~ world** 这是一个颠三倒四的世界; **our plans have been thrown ~** 我们的计划被弄得乱七八糟

top-up *n* Brit colloq 补充饮料; **to give sb. a ~** 给某人再斟满

top-up: ~ card *n* [手机] 充值卡; **~ fees** *npl* Brit [大学的] 附加学费; **~ loan** *n* 补充贷款

tor /tɔ:(r)/ *n* 突岩

torch /tɔ:tʃ/ *n* **1** Brit (flashlight) 手电筒; **to shine a ~ on sb./sth.** 用手电筒照某人/某物 **2** (burning) 火炬; **to be turned into a human ~** 被烧成火人; **to carry a ~ for sb.** fig 单恋某人

torch: ~-bearer *n* 火炬手; **~light** *n* [u] (electric) 手电筒光; (from burning torches) 火炬亮光; **~ relay** *n* 奥运火炬传递

tore /tɔ:(r)/ *pt* ▸**tear¹ A, B**

toreador /'tɒrɪədɔ:(r), Amer 'tɔ:r-/ *n* [尤指骑马的] 斗牛士

torment

A /'tɔ:ment/ *n* **1** [u and c] (physical or mental suffering) 折磨; **to be in ~** 经受折磨; **to suffer ~s of jealousy/remorse** 受到嫉妒/悔恨的煎熬 **2** [c] (cause of suffering) 痛苦的根源; **his failure was a constant ~ to him** 他对自己的失败总是感到痛苦

B /tɔ:'ment/ *vt* **1** (cause suffering to) 折磨; **to be ~ed by jealousy/remorse** 受到嫉妒/悔恨的煎熬; **it's no use ~ing yourself, you can't do anything about it now!** 折磨自己没有用，这件事你现在无能为力了！ **2** (annoy) 烦扰; (provoke) 逗弄; **stop ~ing that poor cat!** 别戏弄那只可怜的猫了！; **exhausted mothers ~ed by uncontrollable children** 被不听管教的孩子弄得不胜其烦的母亲们

tormentor /tɔ:'mentə(r)/ *n* 折磨者

torn /tɔ:n/ *pp* ▸**tear¹ A, B**

tornado /tɔ:'neɪdəʊ/ *n* (*pl* **~es** *or* **~s**) **1** Meteorol 龙卷风 **2** fig (person) 狂暴的人; (thing) 具有巨大破坏性的事物

Toronto /tə'rɒntəʊ/ *pr n* 多伦多

torpedo /tɔ:'pi:dəʊ/

A *n* 鱼雷; **a ~ attack** 鱼雷攻击

B *vt* **1** (attack) 用鱼雷攻击 ‹*ship*›; (hit) 用鱼雷击中 ‹*ship*› **2** fig (wreck) 彻底破坏 ‹*plans, agreement*›

torpedo: ~ boat *n* 鱼雷快艇; **~ tube** *n* 鱼雷发射管

torpid /'tɔ:pɪd/ *adj* **1** (sluggish) 有气无力的; **in a ~ state** 无精打采地; **in ~ silence** 懒散且不出一声 **2** (dormant) 蛰伏的

torpor /'tɔ:pə(r)/ *n* [u] 懒散; **you'd better shake yourself out of this ~** 你最好摆脱这种死气沉沉的状态

torque /tɔ:k/ *n* [u and c] 扭转力

torque: ~ converter *n* 变矩器; **~ wrench** *n* 转矩扳手

torrent /'tɒrənt, Amer 'tɔ:r-/ *n* **1** (of water) 急流; (of rain) 倾注; **the stream had become a raging ~** 小溪变成了汹涌的急流; **the rain is falling in ~s** 大雨如注 **2** fig (of words) 连发; (of feelings) 迸发; **he was met with a ~ of abuse** 他遭到了一阵痛骂; **a ~ of questions from the reporters** 记者们提出的连珠炮似的问题

torrential /tə'renʃl/ *adj* 如注的; **~ rain** 倾盆大雨

torrid /'tɒrɪd, Amer 'tɔ:r-/ *adj* **1** (very hot, dry) 炽烈的 ‹*heat, sun*›; 酷热的 ‹*climate, area*› **2** (passionate) 火辣辣的 ‹*romance, love scene*› **3** (full of difficulty) 艰难的; **the economy is going through a ~ time** 经济正处于困难时期; **to give sb. a ~ time** 使某人经历重重困难

torrid zone *n* 热带

torsion /'tɔ:ʃn/ *n* [u] 扭转

torsion: ~ balance *n* 扭秤; **~ bar** *n* [车辆减震用的] 扭杆; **~ test** *n* 扭力试验

torso /'tɔ:səʊ/ *n* (*pl* **~s**) **1** (of body) 躯干 **2** (of statue) 躯干雕像

tort /tɔ:t/ *n* 侵权行为

tortilla /tɔ:'ti:jə/ *n* [c and u] **1** (omelette) 西班牙土豆炒鸡蛋 **2** (pancake) 墨西哥玉米薄饼

tortoise /'tɔ:təs/ *n* 陆龟

tortoiseshell /'tɔ:təsʃel/ *n* [u] 龟甲; **a comb made of ~** 玳瑁梳子; **glasses with ~ frames** 玳瑁边眼镜

tortoiseshell: ~ butterfly *n* 蛱蝶 [翅膀带黄褐色斑点]; **~ cat** *n* 花斑家猫

tortuous /'tɔ:tʃʊəs/ *adj* **1** (twisty) 弯弯曲曲的 ‹*path*›; **~ progress** 曲折的进程 **2** fig (complex) 拐弯抹角的 ‹*argument, logic, article*›

tortuously /'tɔ:tʃʊəsli/ *adv* **1** (with twists and turns) 弯弯曲曲地 ‹*wind*›; **the road/path/river runs ~ through the fields** 道路/小径/河流蜿蜒曲折地穿过田野 **2** fig 含混不清地 ‹*difficult, complex*›; **a ~ reasoned argument** 一个论证烦琐的观点

torture /'tɔ:tʃə(r)/

A *n* [u and c] **1** (infliction of pain) 酷刑; **under ~** 在严刑拷打之下; **instruments of ~** 刑具 **2** (physical, mental suffering) 折磨; **the ~ of unrequited love** 单相思的苦恼; **these shoes are ~ to wear!** 这双鞋穿着真受罪！ **3** fig (unpleasant experience) 痛苦经历; **the long wait was absolute ~!** 长时间的等候真是煎熬！

B *vt* **1** (inflict pain on) 拷问; **some of the prisoners were ~d** 有些囚犯受到了拷打 **2** fig 折磨; **to be ~d by sth.** 受…的煎熬 ‹*guilt, jealousy*›; **to ~ oneself about** *or* **with sth.** 因某事物折磨自己

torture chamber *n* 刑讯室

torturer /'tɔ:tʃərə(r)/ *n* 拷打者; fig 虐待者

Tory /'tɔ:ri/ Brit

A *n* (*pl* **Tories**) (member) 英国保守党党员; (supporter) 英国保守党支持者; **to vote ~** 投保守党的票

B *adj* 英国保守党的; **a ~ policy/government** 保守党政策/政府

Toryism /'tɔ:rɪɪzəm/ *n* [u] Brit 保守主义 [即英国保守党的主张等]

tosh /tɒʃ/ *n* [u] Brit colloq 废话; **what ~!** 一派胡言！; **don't talk such ~!** 不要讲这样的废话！

toss /tɒs/

A *vt* **1** (throw) 扔; **to ~ sth. to sb., to ~ sb. sth.** 把某物扔给某人; **to ~ one's bag on to the sofa** 把包扔到沙发上; **can you ~ me a box of matches?** 扔一包火柴给我好吗？ **2** Culin 把…抛起翻面 ‹*pancake*› **3** Culin (stir) 拌; **a ~ed green salad** 拌好的生菜色拉; **vegetables ~ed in olive oil** 用橄榄油拌的蔬菜 **4** (throw back) 甩 ‹*hair*›; **she ~ed her head and turned her back on him** 她把头一甩，不再搭理他了; **to ~ one's fringe out of one's eyes** 甩开遮眼的刘海 **5** (flip) 抛 ‹*coin*›; (flip coin with) 与…抛硬币决定 ‹*person*›; **to ~ sb. for sth.** 与某人抛硬币决定某事; **I'll ~ you for the last piece of cake!** 我要和你抛硬币决定谁吃最后那块蛋糕！ **6** (throw up) 抛起; **he was chased by a bull and ~ed over a hedge** 他被公牛追上，然后被抛过了篱笆 **7** (unseat) «*horse*» 把…甩下 ‹*rider*›; **his horse ~ed him into a ditch** 马把他甩到了沟里 **8** (move violently) «*waves*» 使…颠簸 ‹*boat*›; «*wind*» 使…摇摆 ‹*trees, flowers*›; **a storm-~ed sea** 风暴肆虐的大海; **the branch was ~ed to and fro by the wind** 树枝被风吹得摇来摇去

B *vi* **1** (move restlessly) «*person*» 辗转反侧; «*trees*» 摇摆; «*boat*» 颠簸; **to ~ from side to side/back and forth** 摇来摇去/前摇后晃; **to ~ and turn** (in bed) 辗转反侧 **2** (flip coin) 抛硬币; **to ~ to decide sth.** 抛硬币决定某事; **to ~ for sth.** 为某事抛硬币; **we ~ed for the most comfortable bed** 我们抛硬币来决定谁睡最舒服的床

C *n* **1** (throw) 抛; **to give sth. a ~** 扔某物 **2** (flipping of coin) 抛硬币; **it all hung on the ~ of a coin** 一切都取决于抛硬币的结果; **the ~** Sport [为决定场地、发球顺序等的] 抛硬币; **to win/lose the ~** 猜对/猜错所掷硬币朝上的那面; **to argue the ~** esp Brit colloq 作无谓的争执 **3** (jerk) 甩头; **with a disdainful ~ of her head, she marched out of the room** 她轻蔑地把头一甩，大步走出了房间; **not to give a ~ (about sth.)** Brit colloq (对某事物) 毫不在乎

Phrasal verbs

- **toss about, toss around**

A *vt* [**~ sth. about, ~ about sth.**] **1** (move violently) «*waves*» 使…颠簸 ‹*boat*›; «*motion*» 使…摇摆 ‹*person*›; **we got ~ed about in the back of the van** 我们坐在送货车的后部被颠来晃去 **2** (throw) 扔 ‹*ball*›; **several ideas were ~ed about at the meeting** 会议上泛泛讨论了好几个想法

B *vi* «*boat*» 颠簸

- **toss away** *vt* [**~ sth. away, ~ away sth.**] 扔掉 ‹*rubbish*›; fig 丢失 ‹*opportunity*›
- **toss back** *vt* [**~ sth. back, ~ back sth.**] **1** (return) 把…扔回 ‹*object*› **2** (jerk back) 向后甩 ‹*head, hair*›
- **toss off**

A [**~ sth. off, ~ off sth.**] *vt* **1** (dash off) (without effort) 轻松写好; (without care) 草草写好 **2** (drink) 把…一饮而尽

B [**~ sb. off, ~ off sb.**] *vt* Brit taboo sl (masturbate) 给…行手淫

C *v refl* **to ~ oneself off** Brit taboo sl 手淫

- **toss out** *vt* **1** [**~ sth. out, ~ out sth.**] (discard) 把…扔出去 **2** [**~ sb. out, ~ out sb.**] (eject) 赶走; (exclude) 排斥
- **toss up** *vi* 抛硬币决定; **let's ~ up** 我们抛硬币决定吧; **to ~ up to decide sth.** 用抛硬币的方法决定某事; **to ~ up between A and B** 在 A 与 B 之间抛硬币作出取舍

tosser /'tɒsə(r)/ *n* **1** (person who tosses sth.) 抛掷者; (thing that tosses sth.) 抛掷用具; **a ~ of coins** 掷硬币的人 **2** Brit sl (contemptible person) 浑蛋 offensive

toss-up *n* **1** (flip of a coin) 抛硬币; **let's have a ~ to decide** 让我们抛硬币来决定 **2** (two-way choice) 两可的事; **it's a ~ between a pizza and a sandwich** 吃比萨饼还是吃三明治都可以 **3** (even chance) 相等机会; **it was a ~ as to who would be chosen** 很难说谁会被选中

tot /tɒt/ *n* **1** colloq (young child) 幼儿; **tiny ~s** 小娃娃们 **2** Brit (of whisky, rum) 少量烈酒

Phrasal verb

- **tot up** Brit

A *vt* [**~ up sth., ~ sth. up**] 把…加起来 ‹*figures, bill*›

B *vi* 总计

total /'təʊtl/

A *n* 总数; **in ~** 总共; **£200 in ~** 总共 200 英镑; **to come to a ~ of £200** 总计为 200 英镑

B *adj attrib* **1** (added together) 总的; **~ number/amount/quantity/losses/cost/sales** 总数/总额/总量/总亏损/总成本/总销售额 **2** (complete) 完全的 ‹*ignorance, stranger*›; **~ loss/attention** 全部损失/注意力; **~ war** 全面战争; **the ~ effect** 总体效果; **the ~ picture** 整体情况; **~ failure** 彻底的失败; **~ silence** 一片寂静; **a ~ waste of time** 纯粹的浪费时间

C *vt* (*pres p etc.* **-ll-** Brit, **-l-** Amer) **1** (add up) 把…加起来 ‹*numbers*›; **the votes have now been ~led** 选票总数已经计算出来了 **2** (amount to) 总数达到 ‹*sum, number, percentage*›; **their votes ~led two million** 他们的得票共计 200 万张 **3** Amer colloq (destroy) 彻底毁坏 ‹*vehicle, equipment*›; **he ~led his**

father's car 他把他爸爸的汽车撞得面目全非

total: ~ **allergy syndrome** *n* [u] [化学品引起的] 过敏症; ~ **eclipse** *n* 全食; **a ~ eclipse of the sun** 日全食

totalitarian /ˌtəʊtælɪˈteərɪən/
A *adj* 极权主义的 ‹*state, regime, system*›
B *n* 极权主义者

totalitarianism /ˌtəʊtælɪˈteərɪənɪzəm/ *n* [u] 极权主义

totality /təʊˈtæləti/ *n* [u] 全体; **let's consider the universe in its ~** 让我们把宇宙看作一个整体

totalizator /ˈtəʊtəlaɪzeɪtə(r), Amer -lɪz-/, **totalizer** /ˈtəʊtəlaɪzə(r)/ *ns* 赌金数额显示器

totally /ˈtəʊtəli/ *adv* 完全 ‹*forget, change, different, deaf*›; **this is ~ ridiculous!** 这太可笑了!

total: ~ **quality management** *n* [u] 全面质量管理; ~ **recall** *n* [u] [能记住每个细节的] 完全记忆力

tote[1] /təʊt/ *n* colloq (in horse betting) **the ~ = totalizator**

tote[2] *vt* esp Amer (carry) 携带; (wield) 挥动; (convey) 搬运; **gun-toting hooligans** 带枪的流氓; **we ~d a pile of books home from the library** 我们把一摞书从图书馆搬回家

tote bag *n* Amer 大手提袋

totem /ˈtəʊtəm/ *n* 图腾

totemic /təʊˈtemɪk/ *adj* 图腾的; **to have a ~ significance** 具有象征意义

totem pole *n* 图腾柱

totter /ˈtɒtə(r)/ *vi* **1** (walk unsteadily) 蹒跚; **to ~ in/out** 跌跌撞撞地走进来/出去; **the baby ~ed over to her mother** 婴儿摇摇晃晃地向母亲走去; **she ~ed unsteadily towards the bar** 她踉踉跄跄地走向吧台 **2** (wobble) (be about to collapse) «*pile, chimney, regime*» 摇摇欲坠; «*industry*» 濒临崩溃; **a country ~ing on the brink of civil war** 一个处于内战边缘、濒临瓦解的国家

tottering /ˈtɒtərɪŋ/ *adj* **1** (wobbling) 摇摇晃晃的; **the baby took his first ~ steps** 婴儿踉踉跄跄地走出了第一步 **2** fig (failing) 摇摇欲坠的 ‹*government*›; 濒临崩溃的 ‹*industry*›

totty /ˈtɒti/ *n* [u] Brit colloq 骚货

toucan /ˈtuːkæn, -kən, Amer *also* tʊˈkɑːn/ *n* 巨嘴鸟

touch /tʌtʃ/
A *vt* **1** (make physical contact with) 触碰 ‹*person, object*›; **don't let the wires ~ each other!** 不要让两根电线相碰!; **'not to be ~ed'** "不可触摸"; **can you ~ the ceiling?** 你碰得到天花板吗?; **to ~ one's toes** 弯腰用手指触脚趾; **I ~ed him on the arm to attract his attention** 我碰了碰他的胳膊以引起他的注意; **I never (even) ~ed him** 我(甚至连)碰都没有碰过他; **please don't ~ my things!** 请不要动我的东西!; **to ~ bottom** 触底; **he had really ~ed (rock) bottom** 他真是落泊到底了; **the housing market has ~ed bottom** 房市跌到了最低点; **a smile ~ed the corners of his mouth** 他的嘴角掠过一丝微笑; **to ~ one's hat** *or* **cap (to sb.)** 触帽(向某人)致敬; **she wouldn't let him ~ her** 她不会让他碰的; **to ~ sb. for money** colloq (ask for loan) 向某人借钱; (beg) 求某人给钱 **2** (eat) 吃; (drink) 喝; (use) 动用 ‹*money, supplies, inheritance*›; **you've hardly ~ed your food** 你几乎没吃东西啊; **I never ~ cigarettes/drugs** 我从不抽烟/碰毒品 **3** (move emotionally) 打动; **to ~ sb./sth. with sth.** 用某事物打动某人/某物; **his death ~ed our hearts** 他的死令我们感到悲痛; **to ~ sb. deeply** *or* **profoundly** 深深感动某人 **4** (hurt, offend) «*person, words, action*» 伤害 ‹*person, feelings*›; **you've ~ed me on a tender spot** 你触到了我的痛处; ▸nerve A1 **5** (have dealings with) 从事; **to ~ sth. illegal** 染指非法勾当; **everything she ~es turns to disaster** 什么事她一插手就会搞砸; **I haven't ~ed my thesis all week** 我整个星期都没碰论文 **6** (make a difference to, have effect on) 对…起作用; **the police can't ~ me** 警方拿我没办法; **water wouldn't ~ the grass stains** 水洗不掉草渍; **my steak was so tough, the knife wouldn't ~ it** 我的牛排太老，刀子割不动 **7** (equal in excellence) 与…媲美; (rival in excellence) 比得上; **there's nothing to ~ mountain air for giving you an appetite** 没有什么能像山上的空气那样让你胃口大开; **nobody can ~ him as an opening batsman** 作为首发击球手，无人能与他相比 **8** (reach) 达到 ‹*level, speed, temperature*›
B *vi* **1** (make contact) 触碰; **keep your hands to yourself and don't ~!** 管好你的手，不要乱碰!; **'do not ~'** "请勿触摸" **2** (come together) «*people, objects*» 接触; «*areas*» 接壤; **their hands ~ed** 他们的手碰在了一起
C *n* **1** [u and c] (physical contact) 触摸; **a light/delicate/gentle ~** 轻轻/小心/轻柔的触摸; **I felt a ~ on my shoulder** 我感觉有人碰了一下我的肩膀; **the slightest** *or* **merest ~** 轻轻的一碰; **at the ~ of a switch** 一触开关; **soft/hard/rough to the ~** 摸上去柔软/坚硬/粗糙的; **his ankle was painful to the ~** 他的脚踝一碰就痛; **he managed to get a ~ on the ball** 他尽力触到了球 **2** [u] (sense) 触觉; **a highly developed sense of ~** 高度发达的触觉; **to read Braille by ~** 通过触摸读布莱叶盲文 **3** [u] fig (contact) 联系; **to maintain close ~** 保持密切联系; **to be in ~ with sb.** (contact) 与某人有接触; (communication) 与某人有联系; **to be in ~ with current trends/one's feelings** 了解当前的趋势/自己的感情; **to get/stay in ~ (with sb.)** (与某人) 取得/保持联系; **to put sb. in ~ with sb.** 帮某人联系上某人; **to be out of ~ with sb.** (contact) 与某人没有接触; (communication) 与某人没有联系; **to be out of ~ with sth.** 不了解某事物; **I've been away for some time, and I'm rather out of ~** 我离开了一段日子，因此有点孤陋寡闻; **to keep in/lose ~ with sb.** (contact) 与某人保持/不再接触; (communication) 与某人保持/失去联系; **to keep in ~ with all the latest developments** 了解所有最新的进展; **to lose ~ with sth.** 不再了解某事物; **to be out of ~ with reality** 与现实脱节 **4** [c] *sing* (impression) 感觉; **the surface has a smooth, slippery ~** 表面摸上去平顺滑溜; **I felt the soft ~ of her dress as she passed** 当她走过时，我感觉到她的连衣裙很柔软 **5** [c] (detail) (with pen, words) 润色; (with brush) 修饰; **the portrait still needs a few ~es to finish it off** 肖像画还需要修几笔才可以完成; **a humorous/clever ~** 幽默的笔触/灵巧的一笔; **to put** *or* **add the finishing** *or* **final ~(es) (to sth.)** (为某物) 润色; **I must put the finishing ~es to my report** 我必须润色一下我的报告 **6** [c] (trace, element) 些许; **a ~ of sarcasm/colour/garlic** 一丝讽刺/一抹颜色/一点大蒜; **to have a ~ of flu/the sun** 染上轻度流感/轻微中暑; **there's a ~ of class about everything he does** 他做的每件事情都有点派头; **it's a ~ colder today** 今天稍微冷一点; **it's a ~ too hot** 有点太烫了; **add a ~ less/more salt next time** 下次少加/多加一点盐 **7** [c] *sing* (manner, method) 风格; **a feminine ~** 女性气息; **the ~ of a master, the master's ~** 大师风范; **he lacks a human ~** 他缺少人情味 **8** [c] *sing* (skill) 才能; **the ~ of genius** 天赋的才能; **to lose/find one's ~** 失去/找回平日的技能; **I must be losing my ~** 我的技艺肯定在走下坡路; **to have the right ~ with sb./sth.** 对某人/某物有一套; **that inimitable Spielberg ~** 那种无法仿效的斯皮尔伯格风格 **9** [u] Sport [橄榄球和足球的] 边线外区域; **to kick the ball into ~** 把球踢出边线; **the idea was kicked firmly into ~ by the authorities** 这个意见被当局束之高阁 **10** [c] **to be a soft** *or* **an easy ~** colloq (willing to give) 乐意送礼; (willing to lend) 对借钱的请求有求必应

Phrasal verbs

• **touch down**
A *vi* **1** Aviat 着陆 **2** (in rugby) [持球过底线] 触地得分; **the winger ~ed down for a try/five points** 边锋队员持球触地得分/得5分
B *vt* [**~ sth. down, ~ down sth.**] «*rugby player*» 持…触地得分 ‹*ball*›

• **touch off** *vt* [**~ sth. off, ~ off sth.**]
1 lit (ignite) 点燃 ‹*fuse, firework*›; 点 ‹*fire*›; 引起 ‹*explosion*› **2** fig (start) 引发 ‹*riot, crisis, argument*›

• **touch on** *vt* [**~ on sth.**] 提起 ‹*subject, topic*›

• **touch up** *vt* **1** [**~ sth. up, ~ up sth.**] (improve) 修改; **to ~ up sb.'s hair/essay/photograph** 修剪某人的头发/润色某人的文章/修饰某人的照片; **I'm going to ~ up those scratches with a bit of paint** 我打算用点油漆来修补这些擦痕 **2** [**~ sb. up, ~ up sb.**] Brit colloq (touch sexually) 对…动手动脚

• **touch upon** *vt* = **touch on**

touch: **~-and-go** *adj* 不确定的; **it was ~-and-go whether we would get to the airport in time** 我们能否及时到达机场还说不准; **~down** *n* **1** Aviat, Aerosp 着陆; **2** (in rugby) 持球触地; (in American football) 达阵 [带球或传球攻入对方端区得6分]

touché /tuːˈʃeɪ, ˈtuːʃeɪ/ *excl* **1** (in fencing) 有了 [用以表示承认被对方击中] **2** fig (in argument) 击中要害; **'oh, ~,' he said, pretending to look wounded** "噢，一针见血，" 他装出一副受到伤害的样子说道

touched /tʌtʃt/ *adj* **1** (moved) 受感动的; **to be ~ by sth.** 因…而感动 ‹*kindness*›; **to be ~ to hear/receive ...** 因听到/收到…而感动; **I was most ~ when you rang to see how I was** 你打电话来问候我，令我感动不已 **2** colloq (slightly mad) 疯疯癫癫的; **to be (a bit) ~ in the head** 有些神经兮兮

touchily /ˈtʌtʃɪli/ *adv* 暴躁地 ‹*reply, behave*›

touchiness /ˈtʌtʃɪnɪs/ *n* [u] **1** (of person) 暴躁 **2** (of subject, issue, situation) 棘手

touching /ˈtʌtʃɪŋ/ *adj* 感人的 ‹*sight, story, scene*›; **he shows a ~ faith in his own ability** 他对自己能力的自信令人动容

touchingly /ˈtʌtʃɪŋli/ *adv* 感人地 ‹*speak, write*›; **a ~ worded letter of condolence** 措词感人的吊唁信

touch: ~ **judge** *n* (in rugby) 边线裁判员; **~line** *n* [足球或橄榄球场的] 边线; ~ **pad** *n* 触摸板; ~ **panel** *n* 触控式面板; **~paper** *n* 火硝纸; ~ **screen** *n* 触摸屏; **~-sensitive** *adj* 触控式的 ‹*screen, key*›; **~stone** *n* **1** (stone) 试金石; **2** fig (standard) 检验标准; **~-tone** *adj* **1** (of telephone) 按键式拨号的; **2** (of service) 拨号音控制的; **T~-Tone®** *n* 塔奇通按键式电话机; **~-type** *vi* 盲打; **~-typing** *n* [u] 盲打; **~-typist** ▸p. 409 *n* 盲打者; **a fast ~-typist** 盲打速度很快的人

touchy /ˈtʌtʃi/ *adj* **1** (easily offended) 易怒的; **don't be so ~! it was only a joke!** 不要这么不开心! 这不过是开玩笑!; **to be ~ about sth.** 容易为某事物生气 **2** (potentially controversial) 棘手的 ‹*subject, issue, situation*›; **the ~ business of divorce** 难办的离婚事务

touchy-feely /ˌtʌtʃɪˈfiːli/ *adj* colloq usu pej 感情外露的; **he is not exactly known as the ~ type** 他不完全是那种露骨地表达情感的人

tough /tʌf/
A *adj* **1** (strong and durable) 坚固的 ‹*material*› **2** (hard to chew) 咬不动的; **the meat is as ~ as old boots** 这块肉像牛皮一样嚼不动 **3** (hardy) (physically) 强壮的; (mentally) 刚强的; **you have to be ~ to do that** 做那事你必

t

须吃得起苦; **as ~ as old boots** 非常坚强; **to hang ~** Amer 坚定不移; **hang ~!** Amer 顶住! [4] (hardened, determined) 强硬的; (hard-hearted, ruthless) 无情的; **you have to be ~ to be in politics these days** 如今想要从政，就要心肠狠一点儿; **he's a ~ character!** 他是个狠角色!; **a ~ customer** 难对付的人; **a ~ guy** 硬汉; **to talk/act ~** 说话口气/举止强硬 [5] (severe) 严厉的 ‹*policy, law, penalty*›; (firm) 坚决的 ‹*opposition, stance*›; **to be ~ with sb./on sth.** 对某人/某事物很严厉; **'~ on crime'** (government slogan) "严打犯罪"; **to get ~** *or* **to take a ~ line with sb./on sth.** 对某人/某事物采取严厉措施 [6] (hard, difficult) 艰难的; **a ~ problem to solve** 要解决的难题; **to have a ~ time (of it) (with ...)** (因…) 日子很难熬; **to have a ~ time doing sth.** 做某事很艰难 [7] (rough) (of area characterized by crime) 犯罪活动猖獗的; (of area characterized by vandalism) 野蛮的 [8] (unfortunate) 不幸的; **to have a ~ break** 倒霉; **~ luck!** (not showing sympathy) 真倒霉!; (showing sympathy) 真不幸!; **it's** *or* **that's (just) ~ (luck)** 真倒霉; **it's** *or* **that's (just) his ~ luck** *or* **~ luck on him** 他活该倒霉; **~ shit!** taboo sl 倒霉透了!; **poor kid, it's been ~ on her** 可怜的孩子，她太不幸了

B *excl* 多倒霉啊; **I've no money — ~!** 我没带钱——倒霉!

C *n* colloq 粗暴的人

Phrasal verb

• **tough out** *vt* [**~ sth. out, ~ out sth.**] colloq 捱过 ‹*crisis*›; **to ~ it out** 撑到底

toughen /'tʌfn/

A *vt* [1] (make stronger) 使…坚固 ‹*material*›; 使…坚韧 ‹*plastic, cloth, leather, skin*›; **a process that ~s the glass to make it safer** 提高玻璃的强度使其变得更安全的工序 [2] **~ (up)** (make better able to cope) 使…坚强 ‹*person*›; **travelling alone has certainly ~ed him up** 独自旅行确实使他变得坚强了 [3] **~ (up)** (make more stringent) 使…更为苛刻 ‹*penalties*›; **the government should ~ (up) the law on drink-driving** 政府应该强化处罚酒后驾车行为的法律

B *vi* [1] (become less pliable) «*glass, material*» 变坚固; «*plastic, leather, cloth, skin*» 变坚韧 [2] **~ (up)** (become more able to cope) «*person*» 变坚强

toughie /'tʌfi/ *n* colloq [1] (person) 强硬的人 [2] (question, problem) 棘手的问题; (contest) 激烈的竞赛

tough love *n* [u] 严厉的爱 [为促进有毒瘾者、罪犯等改过自新或促使儿童健康成长而采取严厉的限制措施]; **to practise ~** 出于爱护而采取严厉措施

toughly-worded /ˌtʌflɪ'wɜːdɪd/ *adj* 措词强硬的 ‹*speech, ultimatum*›

tough-minded /ˌtʌf'maɪndɪd/ *adj* (strong-willed) 意志坚强的; (realistic) 讲求实际的; **he has a reputation for being ~** 他有讲求实际的名声

toughness /'tʌfnɪs/ *n* [u] [1] (strength, durability) 坚固 [2] (of meat) 咬不动 [3] (hardiness) (physical) 强壮; (mental) 坚强 [4] (determination) 强硬 [5] (severity) 严厉 [6] (difficulty) 艰难 [7] (of area) 犯罪活动猖獗

toupee /'tuːpeɪ, Amer tuː'peɪ/ *n* [男用] 遮秃假发

tour /tʊə(r), tɔː(r)/

A *n* [1] [u and c] (organized trip) 旅行; **a coach/cycling ~** 乘坐长途客车/骑车的旅行; **to go on a ~ to France** 去法国旅游; **to go on a walking ~ of the city** 徒步游览城市; **to go on** *or* **make a ~ of historic sites** 去游览古迹; **to organize/run a ~** 组织/举办一次旅行; **to go on an organized/a sightseeing ~** 参加组团/观光旅行; **'on ~'** (sign on bus) "旅游车" [2] [c] (visit of single place) 参观; **a ~ of the White House** 参观白宫; **to go on** *or* **do a ~ (of somewhere)** 去参观 (某地); **(to go on) a ~ of inspection** (去) 巡视 [3] [u and c] (round of engagements, performances) 巡回演出; Sport 巡回比赛; **a lecture ~** 巡回演讲; **a cricket/concert ~** 板球巡回赛/音乐会巡演; **an eight-match ~ of New Zealand** 在新西兰的 8 场巡回赛; **to do a ~ (of somewhere)** (在某地) 作巡回演出; **to be/go on ~** 在/去巡回演出; **to take a play on ~** 巡回演出一出戏 [4] [c] (period of duty) 任期; **to do a ~ as a lecturer overseas for three years** 在海外任教 3 年; **a ~ of duty** Mil 服役期; **to do a ~ of duty in Germany** 在德国服役

B *vt* [1] (travel in) 在…旅行; **to ~ Wales in a caravan** 乘坐旅行拖车在威尔士旅游 [2] (visit) 参观 [3] (do round of engagements, matches in) «*performer, band, company, play*» 在…巡回演出; «*sports, team*» 在…巡回比赛; «*speaker*» 在…巡回演讲

C *vi* [1] (travel) 旅游; **to be/go ~ing (in France)** 在/去 (法国) 旅游 [2] (do round of engagements, matches) **to ~ (somewhere)** «*performer, band, company, play*» (在某地) 巡回演出; «*sports team*» (在某地) 巡回比赛; «*speaker*» (在某地) 巡回演讲; **to be ~ing in Japan** «*theatre, company*» 在日本巡回演出

tour de force /ˌtʊə də 'fɔːs/ *n* (*pl* **tours de force** /ˌtʊə də 'fɔːs/) 杰作; **her performance was a real ~** 她的表演精彩至极

tourer /'tʊərə(r), tɔːrə(r)/ *n* (sports car) 跑车; (caravan) 旅行拖车; (bicycle) 旅行自行车

Tourette's syndrome /tʊə'rets ˌsɪndrəʊm/, colloq **Tourette's** *ns* [u] 图雷特氏综合征 [一种精神疾病，其症状表现为无意识的身体抽搐和口出污言秽语]

tour guide *n* 导游

touring /'tʊərɪŋ, 'tɔːr-/

A *n* [u] 旅行; **to like ~** 喜欢旅游

B *adj attrib* 巡回的; **a ~ rugby team** 进行巡回比赛的橄榄球队; **a ~ theatre company** 巡回演出的剧团

touring car *n* [1] (for passengers and luggage) 旅行车 [2] (for motor racing) 旅行赛车

tourism /'tʊərɪzəm, 'tɔːr-/ *n* [u] (organization) 旅游业; (operation) 旅游; **~ is growing rapidly in the area** 旅游业在那个地区迅速发展; **increased ~ has resulted in parking problems in the town** 那个城市因旅游业的发展产生了停车问题

tourist /'tʊərɪst, 'tɔːr-/ *n* [1] (on holiday) 旅游者; **the ~ trade** *or* **industry** 旅游业; **the ~ season/attractions** 旅游季节/胜地 [2] Sport (member of touring team) 巡回比赛队员

tourist bus *n* 旅游客车

tourist class

A *n* [u] (in ship, aircraft) 二等舱; (in hotel) 标准间

B *adv* (in ship, aircraft) 乘坐二等舱地; (in hotel) 住标准间地; **she always travels ~** 她出行总是乘坐二等舱

tourist: ~ information *n* [u] 旅游信息; **~ information (office** *or* **bureau)** 旅游局; **~ trap** *n* (place) 敲旅客竹杠的地方; (attraction) 敲旅客竹杠的景点

touristy /'tʊərɪsti, 'tɔːr-/ *adj* colloq pej (heavily touristed) 挤满游客的 ‹*area*›; (overdeveloped for tourism) 旅游开发过度的; **the town is getting more and more ~** 城里游客越来越多; **I don't like going to these ~ resorts** 我不喜欢去这些游客人满为患的景点

tournament /'tɔːnəmənt, Amer 'tɜːrn-/ *n* [1] (in sport, game) 锦标赛; **to hold** *or* **stage a ~** 举行联赛; **the local schools are holding a chess ~** 当地学校正举办国际象棋联赛 [2] Hist (jousting contest) [中世纪的] 骑士比武 [3] (military display) 军事表演; **the Royal T~** 皇家军事表演

tourniquet /'tʊənɪkeɪ, Amer 'tɜːrnɪkət/ *n* 止血带

tour operator *n* (travel agent) 旅游代理商; (company) 旅行社

tousle /'taʊzl/ *vt* 弄乱 ‹*hair, bedclothes*›

tousled /'taʊzld/ *adj* 弄乱的; **~ hair** 蓬乱的头发

tout /taʊt/

A *vt* [1] (attempt to sell) 兜售 ‹*wares, goods*› [2] Brit (sell illegally above face value) 高价倒卖 ‹*tickets*›

B *vi* [1] (solicit) 招揽; **to ~ for business/custom** 招揽生意/顾客; **to ~ for votes** 拉选票 [2] Amer (offer racing tips) 出售赛马情报

C *n* [1] Brit **(ticket) ~** 票贩子 [2] Amer (offering racing tips) 赛马情报贩子

tow /təʊ/

A *vt* 拖 ‹*vehicle, trailer, boat*›; **to ~ a bus up a hill** 牵引公共汽车上坡

B *n* [1] [c and u] (of vehicle) 拖; **to be on ~** 被拖着走; **to give sb. a ~** 给某人拖车; **to need a ~** 需要把车拖走; **to take a vehicle in ~** 拖走一辆车 [2] [u] **in ~** fig (following) 紧随; (accompanying) 陪伴着; **to have sb. in ~** 后面紧跟着某人; **a father with two children in ~** 后面跟着两个孩子的父亲; **he's got a new girlfriend in ~** 他身边有了新女友; **she always seems to have a couple of attractive men in ~** 她好像总有几个帅哥追随左右 [3] [c] (rope) 拖索; **don't let the ~ slacken too much** 不要让拖缆太松弛

Phrasal verb

• **tow away** *vt* [**~ away sth., ~ sth. away**] 拖走

towards /tə'wɔːdz, tɔːdz/, esp Amer **toward** /tə'wɔːd, tɔːd/ *prep* [1] (in the direction of, facing) 向; **the ship was sailing ~ the east** 轮船在向东航行; **she ran ~ him** 她朝他跑去; **he was standing with his back ~ me** 他背对我站着 [2] (closer in space or time, closer to state or condition) 接近; **seats ~ the rear of the plane** 靠近机舱尾部的座位; **~ midnight** 午夜时分; **~ the end of the day/month/one's life** 接近黄昏/月底/生命结束; **to progress ~ democracy/independence** 走向民主/独立; **a first step ~ sth.** 迈向…的第一步 ‹*solution, system*›; **he is moving ~ the idea that ...** 他正盘算着…; **to do what one can ~ improving conditions** 尽自己所能改善条件; **to go some way ~ meeting sb.'s demands** 在满足某人的要求方面作出一些努力 [3] (in relation to) 对于; **our attitude ~ death** 我们对死亡的态度; **their policy ~ Europe** 他们对欧洲的政策; **to be friendly/hostile ~ sb.** 友好对待/敌视某人 [4] (as contribution to) 用于; **to put money ~ one's education** 把钱用在教育上; **to save ~ a holiday** 攒钱去度假

tow bar *n* 牵引杆

towel /'taʊəl/

A *n* (cloth) 毛巾; (paper) 纸巾; **a set of ~s** 一套毛巾; **to throw** *or* colloq **chuck in the ~** 认输; **a ~ rack** 毛巾架; **a ~ dispenser** 纸巾筒

B *vt* (*pres p etc.* **-ll-**, Amer **-l-**) 用毛巾擦干 ‹*person, horse*›; **to ~ sb./oneself down** 用毛巾把某人/自己擦干; **to ~ one's hair** 擦干头发

towelette /ˌtaʊə'let/ *n* Amer (of paper) 湿纸巾; (of cloth) 小湿毛巾

towelling /'taʊəlɪŋ/ *n* [u] 毛巾料; **a ~ robe/dressing gown** 毛巾浴衣/晨衣

towel: ~ rail *n* 毛巾架; **~ ring** *n* 毛巾环

tower /'taʊə(r)/

A *n* 塔; **a church ~** 教堂钟楼; **the Eiffel T~** 埃菲尔铁塔

B *vi* **to ~ above** *or* **over sb./sth.** 高耸于某人/某物上方; **he's growing so fast he ~s above his mother already!** 他长得飞快，都比他母亲高出一大截了!; **the magnificent snow-capped peaks ~ing over the village** 屹立在村庄之上、山顶覆盖着白雪的雄伟山峰

tower block *n* Brit 高层建筑

towering /'taʊərɪŋ/ *adj attrib* [1] (extremely tall) 高大的 ‹*building, figure*›; **a ~ giant redwood** 高大的红杉; **~ cliffs** 高耸的悬崖 [2] (exceptionally important) 极重要的 ‹*decision, work*›; **a ~**

performance (by musician) 出色的演奏; (by actor) 杰出的表演 [3] (extreme) 强烈的; **a ～ rage** *or* **fury** 勃然大怒

Tower of Babel /ˌtaʊə(r) əv ˈbeɪbl/ *pr n* 巴别塔 [世人拟建的通天塔，上帝使他们无法理解彼此的语言，从而阻止其建成]

towing: ～ path *n* = **towpath**; **～ rope** *n* = **tow rope**

towline /ˈtəʊlaɪn/ *n* = **tow rope**

town /taʊn/ *n* [1] (urban area) 城镇; **a small country ～** 小乡镇; **she's out of ～ at the moment** 她眼下不在城里; **he comes from out of ～** Amer 他来自乡下; **to leave ～** 出城; **guess who's back in ～!** colloq 猜猜谁回城里来了！; **look me up next time you're in ～** 你下次进城的时候要来看我; **she's in ～ to publicize her film** 她在城里推销她的电影 [2] (inhabitants) 市民; (officials) 城镇官员; **the whole ～ knows about it** 全镇的人都知道这件事; **～ and gown** Brit 大学城的居民和师生; **to be the talk of the ～** (centre of attraction) 引人注目; (thing talked about most) 是最热门的话题 [3] (central area of town) 商业中心; **to go into ～** Brit, **to go down ～** Amer 到市中心去; **on the ～** 在城里作乐; **to have a night (out) on the ～** 在城里痛快地玩一个晚上; **to go to ～ on sth.** colloq (spare no expense on) 在某物上大量花钱; (put a lot of effort into) 在某事上大干一番; **they've really gone to ～ on the decoration and furnishings** 他们在装修和家居陈设上的确花了大钱

town: ～-and-country planning *n* [u] 城乡规划; **～ centre** *n* 市中心; **～ clerk** *n* [1] Brit Hist [1974年前的] 城镇秘书兼法律顾问; [2] Amer [主管档案的] 城镇文书; **～ council** *n* Brit 市政会; **～ councillor** *n* Brit 市政会委员; **～ crier** /ˌtaʊn ˈkraɪə(r)/ *n* Hist [旧时高声传报消息等的] 街头公告员

townee /ˈtaʊni/ *n* colloq = **townie**

town: ～ hall *n* 市政厅; **～ house** *n* [1] (in town) 城镇住房; [2] (urban terraced house) [市区内三层或三层以上的] 排房

townie /ˈtaʊni/ *n* colloq 城里人

town: ～ meeting *n* Amer 镇民大会; **～ planner** ▸**p. 409** *n* Brit 城镇规划人员; **～ planning** *n* [u] Brit 城镇规划

townscape /ˈtaʊnskeɪp/ *n* [1] (appearance) 城市风景 [2] (picture) 城市风景画

townsfolk /ˈtaʊnzfəʊk/ *npl* dated = **townspeople**

township /ˈtaʊnʃɪp/ *n* [1] (small town) 小镇 [2] (in South Africa) 黑人居住区 [3] Amer (county division) 镇区 [县以下的行政区]

townspeople /ˈtaʊnzpiːpl/ *npl* 城镇居民

tow: ～path *n* [旧时河道旁供拖船马匹行走的] 纤路; **～ rope** *n* 纤绳; **～ truck** *n* Amer 拖车

toxaemia Brit, **toxemia** Amer /tɒkˈsiːmɪə/ ▸**p. 377** *n* [u] 毒血症

toxic /ˈtɒksɪk/ *adj* [1] (poisonous) 有毒的; **this substance is ～ to humans** 这种物质能使人中毒 [2] Fin 不良的 ‹*loan, asset*›; **～ debt** 坏账

toxicity /tɒkˈsɪsəti/ *n* [u] 毒性; **ways of measuring the ～ of the substance/waste** 测量这种物质/废物毒性的方法

toxicological /ˌtɒksɪkəˈlɒdʒɪkl/ *adj* 毒物学的; **～ research/expert/effects** 毒物学研究/毒物学专家/毒理效应

toxicologist /ˌtɒksɪˈkɒlədʒɪst/ ▸**p. 409** *n* 毒物学家

toxicology /ˌtɒksɪˈkɒlədʒi/ *n* [u] 毒物学

toxic: ～ shock syndrome *n* [u] 中毒性休克综合征; **～ waste** *n* [u] 有毒废物

toxin /ˈtɒksɪn/ *n* 毒素

toy /tɔɪ/ *n* 玩具; **a ～ car** 玩具汽车; **a ～ library** [出借玩具的] 玩具馆

Phrasal verb

- **toy with** *vt* [1] [**～ with sth.**] (play with) 摆弄; **he ～ed with the keys** 他摆弄钥匙; **to ～ with one's food** 拨弄饭菜 [2] (consider) 考虑 ‹*thought, possibility*›; **to ～ with the idea of doing sth.** 有做某事的想法 [3] [**～ with sb./sth.**] (treat without seriousness) 把…当儿戏; **he was just ～ing with her affections/with her** 他只是在玩弄她的感情/玩弄她

toy: ～box *n* 玩具盒; **～ boy** *n* Brit colloq [比女友年轻得多的] 小情夫; **～ dog** *n* [供玩赏的] 小种狗; **～ poodle** *n* 小卷毛狗; **～shop** *n* 玩具店; **～ soldier** *n* 玩具士兵; **～ spaniel** *n* 小猎; **～town** *adj* [1] (miniature) 微型的; **a ～town village** 微型村庄; **a ～town replica** 缩微复制品; [2] pej (worthless) 毫无价值的 ‹*politics*›; 无用的 ‹*politician, intellectual*›; **～ train** *n* 玩具火车

TQM *abbr* = **total quality management**

trace¹ /treɪs/

A *n* [1] [u and c] (evidence) 痕迹; **to remove all ～(s) of sb.'s presence** 消除某人在场的所有痕迹; **～s of a struggle/of poison** 搏斗的痕迹/毒药的残留; **～s of a Roman villa** 古罗马别墅的遗迹; **～s of tears/the old way of life** 泪痕/旧生活方式的遗痕; **no ～ remains** *or* **there is no ～ of sth.** 某物没留下一丝痕迹 [2] [u and c] (hint) 微量; **a ～ of sth.** 一丝 ‹*humour, accent*›; **to speak without a ～ of emotion** 丝毫不带感情地讲话; **without a ～ of make-up/a smile** 没化一点妆/没有丝毫笑容; **just a ～ of garlic/chemical** 些许大蒜/一丁点化学品; **a ～ of dampness in the air** 空气中的一丝潮气 [3] [u and c] (aiding retrieval) 踪迹; **a ～ of sb./sth.** 某人/某物的踪迹; **to lose (all) ～ of sb.** 失去某人的（全部）行踪; **to leave no ～ of one's whereabouts** 没留下任何行踪; **to disappear/sink without ～** 消失得/沉没得无影无踪 [4] [c] (on recording instrument) (line) 描记线; (pattern) 描记图 [5] [c] esp Amer (path) 小路; **to follow a ～** 沿小道走

B *vt* [1] (locate) 查出; **I can't ～ any reference to it** 我查不到它的出处; **to ～ sth./sb. to sth.** 追查某物/某人到 ‹*place, number*›; **to ～ sb. to an address in Chicago** 追查到某人在芝加哥的一处地址; **the call was ～d to a London number** 电话被查出是伦敦的一个号码; **the problem was ～d to ...** 问题被归结到… [2] (follow, chart) 追溯 ‹*history, ancestry, life, story, friendship*›; 追踪 ‹*progress, events*›; **to ～ one's origins to ...** 将身世追溯到… [3] (copy) 描摹 ‹*map, drawing*›; **to ～ sth. on to sth.** 把某物描摹到某物上 [4] (draw, form) 勾画出 ‹*letters, figure*›; **a tear ～d a path down her cheek** 一滴眼泪顺着她的面颊流了下来

Phrasal verbs

- **trace back** *vt* [**～ sth. back, ～ back sth.**] 追溯 ‹*history*›; 追踪 ‹*tracks*›; **to ～ footprints/a trail back to sth.** 追踪脚印/踪迹到某处; **the root of the problem was ～d back to ...** 最后查出问题的根源是…; **how far back can you ～ your ancestors?** 你可以追溯自己的祖先到多远?
- **trace out** *vt* [**～ sth. out, ～ out sth.**] [1] (copy) 描摹 ‹*map, drawing, design*› [2] (draw, form) 勾画出 ‹*figure, letters, pattern*›; **to ～ out the route on a map** 在地图上描出路线; **to ～ out sth. in the sand/on the wall** 在沙子里/墙上画写某物

trace² *n* [1] *usu pl* (of harness) 缰绳; **to snap the ～s** «*horse*» 脱缰; **to kick over the ～s** Brit dated 不受管束 [2] (in angling) 引线

traceability /ˌtreɪsəˈbɪləti/ *n* [u] 可追溯性; **Welsh branded beef with full ～** 原产地完全可查的威尔士品牌牛肉

traceable /ˈtreɪsəbl/ *adj* 可追溯的 ‹*origin*›; 可追踪的 ‹*person*›; **easily ～** 可轻易查出的; **to be ～ to sth.** 归因于 ‹*malfunction*›; **such faults are usually ～ to the battery connection** 故障通常源于电池连接环扣

trace element *n* [1] (in sample) 痕量元素 [2] (required for growth) 微量元素

tracer /ˈtreɪsə(r)/ *n* [1] (bullet) 曳光弹; **～ bullet/shell/ammunition** 曳光子弹/炮弹/弹药 [2] (radioactive substance) 示踪剂 [3] (of pattern) (person) 追踪者; (instrument) 追踪装置

tracery /ˈtreɪsəri/ *n* [1] [u] Archit (of window) 窗花格 [2] [c] (pattern) 花饰图案

trachea /trəˈkiːə, Amer ˈtreɪkɪə/ *n* (*pl* **～s** *or* **tracheae** /trəˈkiːiː, Amer ˈtreɪkɪiː/) 气管

tracheotomy /ˌtrækrˈɒtəmi/ *n* 气管切开术

trachoma /trəˈkəʊmə/ ▸**p. 377** *n* [u] 沙眼

tracing /ˈtreɪsɪŋ/ *n* [1] [c] (copy) 描摹; **to make a ～ of sth.** 描画某物 [2] [u] (procedure) 追踪

tracing paper *n* [u] 描图纸

track /træk/

A *n* [1] [c] (print) (of person, animal) 足迹; (of vehicle) 车辙; **tyre ～s** 轮胎辙印; **to follow sb.'s ～ to the river** 顺着某人的脚印来到河边; **to cover one's ～s** 掩盖行踪; **to stop dead in one's ～s** colloq 突然止步; **to make ～s for home** colloq 往家走; **I'd better be making ～s** 我该动身了 [2] [u and c] (trajectory, route) 路径; (whereabouts) 行踪; **to be on sb.'s ～/on the ～ of sth.** 追踪某人/某物; fig 寻觅某人/某物; **to be on the fast ～ to promotion** 即将获得提升; **to be on the right ～** (in terms of thinking) 思路正确; (in terms of action) 做法对路; **to put sb. on the right ～** (in terms of thinking) 使某人思路正确; (in terms of action) 使某人做法对路; **to be on the wrong ～, to be off (the) ～** (in terms of thinking) 思路错误; (in terms of action) 做法不对路; **to get** *or* **set sb. on the wrong ～** (in terms of thinking) 使某人思路出错; (in terms of action) 使某人做法不对路; **to keep ～ of sb./sth.** 跟踪某人/某物; **it's hard to keep ～ of old colleagues** 和旧同事保持联系是很难的; **to keep ～ of the conversation** 跟得上谈话的内容; **to lose ～ of sth./sb.** (fail to follow) 失去…的行踪 ‹*aircraft, fugitive, friend, parcel, document*›; fig 不了解…的进展 ‹*situation*›; **to lose ～ of what sb. is talking about** 不清楚某人在说什么; **to keep/lose ～ of time** 记得/不记得时间 [3] [c] (path, rough road) 小道; **a mountain/cattle ～** 山间小道/牛道; **a side ～** 岔道; **three years down the ～** colloq 3 年以后 [4] [u and c] Rail 铁轨; **a stretch of ～** 一段铁轨; **a double-～ line** 双轨线; **to come off** *or* **leave the ～(s)** «*train*» 脱轨; **～ 3** Amer (platform) 3 号站台; **(to live on/come from) the wrong side of the ～s** esp Amer colloq （住在/来自）贫民区 [5] [c] Sport (circuit) (for runners, horses) 跑道; (for vehicles, bicycles) 车道; **a speedway/motor-racing ～** 快车道/赛车道; **a dog-racing ～** 赛狗道; **four laps of the ～** 4 圈赛道 [6] [u] Sport (running) 径赛; **～ and field** 田径; **a ～ athlete/meet** 径赛运动员/运动会 [7] [c] Audio, Mus 曲目; **the title ～** 标题歌曲; **a two-/four-～ tape** 双声道/四声道磁带 [8] [c] (on tank, tractor) 履带 [9] [u and c] (rail for curtain, door, light) 滑轨 [10] [c] Amer Sch [按学生能力编成的] 班组; **the top/middle/bottom ～** 尖子班/中等班/差班; **to place students in ～s** 把学生分班

B *vt* [1] (follow path of) 跟踪 ‹*person, progress*›; (plot course of) 追踪 ‹*satellite, storm*›; **to ～ sb. to their hideout** 追踪某人至其藏身处 [2] Amer (bring in) «*person, shoes*» 带入 ‹*dirt*›; **to ～ mud into the house/over the carpet** 把泥踩进家里/踩到地毯上

C *vi* [1] Cin «*cameraman, director*» 跟踪拍摄; **the camera ～ed away** 摄像机镜头推远了; **to ～ in/out** 拉回/推出镜头 [2] (travel) 行进; **to ～ across the ground** «*storm*» 横过地面 [3] Audio «*stylus*» [在唱片纹道上] 移动; **to ～ well/badly** 运转流畅/不畅

Phrasal verb

• **track down** *vt* [**~ sb./sth. down, ~ down sb./sth.**] 1 (hunt down) 追踪到 ‹*criminal, animal*› 2 (find) 搜寻到 ‹*old friend, object, reference*›

track: ~ and field events *npl* 田径比赛; **~ athlete** *n* 径赛运动员; **~ball** *n* 轨迹球

tracked /trækt/ *adj* 有履带的 ‹*vehicle*›

tracker /ˈtrækə(r)/ *n* 1 (person) 追踪者; (animal) 循迹追踪的动物 2 Fin (mortgage) 追踪抵押贷款; (loan) 追踪贷款; (fund) 指数追踪基金

tracker: ~ ball *n* **= trackball**; **~ dog** *n* 搜救犬; **~ fund** *n* 指数追踪基金; **~ loan** *n* 追踪贷款; **~ mortgage** *n* 追踪抵押贷款

track events *npl* 径赛项目

tracking /ˈtrækɪŋ/ *n* [u] 1 (monitoring) 跟踪 2 Aut (alignment of wheels) 轮距 3 Amer Sch (streaming) [根据学生能力层次进行的] 分班

tracking: ~ device *n* 跟踪器; **~ shot** *n* 移动镜头; **~ station** *n* [对卫星、火箭等进行跟踪定位的] 跟踪站

track: ~layer *n* 1 (vehicle) 履带车; 2 Amer **= ~man**; **~laying vehicle** *n* 履带式车辆

trackless /ˈtræklɪs/ *adj* 1 (without paths) 无路的 ‹*land*›; (without tracks) 无人迹的 ‹*desert, ocean*›; **~ wastelands** 人迹罕至的荒原 2 (not running on a track) 无轨的; **a ~ train/tram** 无轨列车/电车

track: ~ lighting *n* [u] 轨道式投照灯; **~ maintenance** *n* [u] 路轨维护; **~man** /-mæn/ ▸**p. 409** *n* Amer 铺轨工人; **~pad** *n* 触控盘; **~ record** *n* 1 (of achievements, performance) 业绩记录; **to have a good/poor ~ record** 业绩良好/不佳; **this firm has a poor ~ record on pollution control** 这家公司在控制污染方面做得不好; **a candidate with a proven ~ record in sales** 有良好销售业绩的人选; 2 (in athletics) 径赛纪录; **~ shoe** *n* 跑鞋; **~suit** *n* 运动服; **~suited** *adj* 穿运动服的; **~way** *n* 踏出来的路; **~work** *n* [u] 1 (tracks) 铁路设施; 2 (laying, maintenance) 铁路铺设维护

tract[1] /trækt/ *n* 1 (large area) 大片; **~s of natural forest** 大片大片的天然森林 2 Anat (passage) 道; **the digestive/respiratory ~** 消化/呼吸道

tract[2] *n* (pamphlet) 小册子; **a Catholic/Methodist ~** 天主教/循道宗教会的小册子

tractable /ˈtræktəbl/ *adj* 顺从的 ‹*person, child*›; 驯服的 ‹*pet*›; 易处理的 ‹*material, problem*›

traction /ˈtrækʃn/ *n* [u] 1 (pulling action) 拖拉 2 (of wheel on surface) 附着摩擦力; **to have good ~ on icy roads** 在结冰路面上有很好的附着力 3 Med 牵引; **in ~** 接受牵引治疗的; **to apply ~ to sth.** 对某部位进行牵引

traction: ~ control system *n* 磨擦控制系统; **~ engine** *n* 牵引机车

tractive /ˈtræktɪv/ *adj* 牵引的; **~ force** or **power** 牵引力

tractor /ˈtræktə(r)/ *n* 拖拉机

tractor: ~ feed *n* 送纸器; **~ mower** *n* 机引式割草机; **~-trailer** *n* Amer 牵引式挂车

trad /træd/ Brit colloq

A *n* [u] 传统爵士乐

B *adj* [尤指爵士乐] 传统的

tradable /ˈtreɪdəbl/ *adj* 可买卖的; **a portfolio of ~ assets** 可交易的资产包

trade /treɪd/

A *n* 1 [u] Econ 贸易; **foreign ~** 外贸; **~ is declining/expanding** 贸易量在减少/增长; **restraint of ~** 贸易限制; **~ negotiations/agreement** 贸易谈判/协定 2 [u] Comm (business) 生意; **to do ~ with sb.** 与某人做买卖; **~ is quite brisk/bad** 生意兴旺/惨淡; **to do a good/roaring ~** 生意做得好/红火; **those in ~** 生意人; **~ in sth.** 某物的买卖; **~ terms/price** 交易条款/批发价格 3 [u and c] + *v sing or pl* Comm (sector) 行业; **the X ~** X 行当; **to be in the furniture ~** 从事家具业; **the car/book ~** 汽车业/图书业; **(to be in) the ~** (是) 同行; **to attract the tourist ~** 吸引游客; **'suppliers to the ~'** Brit "酒类批发商"; **known in the ~ as X** 在业界被叫做 X 的; **a ~ journal/paper** 行业期刊/报纸 4 [u and c] + *v sing or pl* (craft) 行当; **to learn/practise a ~** 学习/从事一个行当; **to put sb. to a ~** dated 让某人学一门技术; **I am a designer by ~** 我是搞设计的; **~ courses** 职业培训课程 5 [c] (swap) 交换; **to do** or Amer **make a ~ with sb.** 和某人作交换 6 **trades** *pl* Meteorol 信风

B *vi* 1 Comm 做买卖; **to ~ (directly) with sb.** (直接) 与某人做买卖; **to ~ in sth. (with sb.)** (与某人) 交易某物; **to ~ at a profit/loss** 买卖获利/亏损; **to ~ as sth.** 以某名号做买卖; **to ~ at sth.** Amer 在某处买东西 2 *usu pres p* Fin «*shares, currency*» 交易; **oil is trading at $80 a barrel** 目前石油的交易价为每桶 80 美元 3 Amer (swap) 交换

C *vt* 1 Comm 买卖 ‹*goods, commodity*›; **our products are ~d worldwide** 我们的产品行销全世界 2 esp Amer (swap) 交换 ‹*objects*›; **the two sides ~d hostages** 双方互换了人质; **to ~ sth. with sb.** 和某人交换某物; **to ~ places/blows (with sb.)** (与某人) 调换位置/互殴; **to ~ (sb.) sth. for sth.** 用某物 (和某人) 换某物; **to ~ insults** 互相谩骂

Phrasal verbs

• **trade down** *vi* 1 (sell sth. in order to buy sth. cheaper) 卖好买次; **to ~ down and settle for a more basic model** 卖掉好车买一个较基本的型号凑合着开 2 (spend less money) «*shopper*» 降低消费

• **trade in** *vt* [**~ sth. in, ~ in sth.**] 折价贴换; **to ~ sth. in for sth.** 以某物折价换购某物

• **trade off** *vt* [**~ sth. off, ~ off sth.**] 1 (balance) 平衡 ‹*advantage, gain*›; **to ~ sth. off against sth.** 用某物平衡某物; **you have to ~ the pleasure off against the risk** 你必须在享乐和风险之间权衡 2 (swap) 换取 ‹*advantage, gain*›; **to ~ sth. off for sth.** 以某物换取某物

• **trade on** *vt* [**~ on sth.**] 利用

• **trade up** *vi* (give sth. in part-exchange for sth. more expensive) 折价换购; (sell sth. in order to buy sth. more expensive) 卖次买好; **to ~ up and get sth.** 折价换购某物; **to ~ up to a larger house** 卖掉小房买大房

trade: T~ and Industry Secretary *n* Brit 贸易及工业部大臣; **~ association** *n* 同业公会; **~ balance** *n* **= balance of trade**; **~ barrier** *n* 贸易壁垒; **~ credit** *n* [c and u] 贸易信用; **~ cycle** *n* **= business cycle**; **~ deficit** *n* 贸易赤字; **~ description** *n* 商品描述; **T~ Descriptions Act** *n* Brit 商品描述法; **~ discount** *n* [c and u] (between traders) 商业折扣; (to retailer) 批发折扣; **~ dispute** *n* (between employers and workers) 劳资争议; (between countries) 贸易争端; **~ embargo** *n* 贸易禁运; **~ fair** *n* 商品交易会; **~ figures** *npl* 贸易数据; **~ gap** *n* **= ~ deficit**

trade-in

A *n* 1 (article) 折价旧物 2 (transaction) 折旧贴换交易; **if I buy a new Mini Cooper, will you do a ~ on my old Volvo?** 我的旧沃尔沃能否折价买一辆新的迷你库珀? 3 (money deduction) 折旧价

B *modif* 折旧贴换的; **~ allowance/terms/value** 折旧贴换额/折价条款/抵换价值

trade-in price *n* 贴换价

trademark /ˈtreɪdmɑːk/

A *n* 1 商标; **registered ~** 注册商标 2 fig (distinctive characteristic) 特征; **the professionalism which is his ~** 他所具备的独特专业素质

B *modif* 特别的 ‹*garment, behaviour*›; **he was wearing his ~ flat cap** 他戴着标志性的软水手帽

C *vt* 1 (label) 给…贴商标 ‹*product*› 2 (register) 将…注册为商标 ‹*word, symbol, name*›

trade: ~ minister *n* 贸易部部长; **~ mission** *n* 贸易代表团; **~ name** *n* 品牌名称; **~-off** *n* 1 (balance) 权衡; (compromise) 折中; **a ~-off between sth. and sth.** 某物与某物之间的权衡; **the ~-off between the risk and the potential return** 风险与潜在利润之间的权衡; 2 (exchange) 交易; **to do a ~-off** 做交易; **a ~-off of sth. for sth.** 用某物换某物的交易; **a ~-off of sth. against sth.** 用某物取代某物的交易; **a ~-off of aid against arms contracts** 用援助取代军火合同的交易; **~ pattern** *n* 贸易模式

trader /ˈtreɪdə(r)/ *n* 1 (person) 商人 2 (merchant ship) 商船

trade: ~ restrictions *npl* 贸易限制; **~ sanctions** *npl* 贸易制裁; **~ school** *n* Amer 中等职业学校; **~ secret** *n* 1 Comm 商业秘密; **the recipe for their drink is a closely guarded ~ secret** 他们的饮料配方是严格保守的行业秘密; 2 fig hum 秘诀; **her keep-fit regime is her own ~ secret** 她的养生之道靠的是她自己总结的秘诀; **T~ Secretary** *n* Brit **= Trade and Industry Secretary**; **~ show** *n* 贸易展会

tradesman /ˈtreɪdzmən/ *n* dated 1 esp Brit (retail trader) 上门推销员 2 esp Amer (artisan) 手艺人

tradesman's entrance *n* esp Brit dated 服务人员专用通道

trades union *n* Brit **= trade union**

Trades Union Congress *n* Brit 英国工会联盟

trade: ~ surplus *n* 贸易顺差; **~ union** *n* Brit 工会; **she belongs to a ~ union** 她是工会会员; **~ union movement/meeting/headquarters** 工会运动/集会/总部; **a ~ union member/leader** 工会会员/领导人; **~ unionist** *n* Brit (member) 工会会员; (advocate) 工会主义者; **~ war** *n* 贸易战; **~ wind** *n* 信风

trading /ˈtreɪdɪŋ/ *n* [u] 贸易; **our firm has a long history of ~ with Japan** 我们公司的对日贸易历史很长

trading: ~ card *n* 集换卡 [儿童收集和交换的卡片]; **~ company** *n* 贸易公司; **~ day** *n* 交易日; **~ estate** *n* Brit 工商业区; **~ floor** *n* 交易大厅; **~ nation** *n* 贸易国; **~ post** *n* [边远地区的] 贸易站; **~ stamp** *n* [商店的] 赠券; **T~ Standards Department** *n* Brit 贸易标准部; **T~ Standards Officer** *n* Brit 贸易标准部官员

tradition /trəˈdɪʃn/ *n* 1 [u] (handing down of customs, beliefs) 传说; **by ~** 据传说; **~ has it that ...** 据传…; **in the ~ of ...** 在…的传说中 2 [c] (custom, belief) 传统; **to keep up/break with a ~** 保持/打破传统; **there's a long ~ of public service in our family** 我们家族从事公益事业历史悠久 3 [c] (method) [艺术或文学的] 传统方法; (style) 传统风格; **in the ~ of William Blake** 以威廉·布莱克的风格

traditional /trəˈdɪʃənl/ *adj* 传统的 ‹*design, practice*›; **it is ~ to do sth.** 做某事是传统; **a ~ English breakfast** 传统的英国早餐

traditionalism /trəˈdɪʃənəlɪzəm/ *n* [u] 传统主义

traditionalist /trəˈdɪʃənəlɪst/ *n* 传统主义者; **she's a bit of a ~** 她有点儿守旧

traditionally /trəˈdɪʃənəli/ *adv* 传统上; **～ the English and French are enemies** 英国人和法国人历来就是敌人

traduce /trəˈdjuːs, Amer -ˈduːs/ *vt* formal 诋毁; **to ～ one's rival** 中伤对手

traffic /ˈtræfɪk/

A *n* **1** [u] (movement of road vehicles) 交通; (vehicles) [来往的] 车辆; **the flow of ～** 车流; **light/heavy/rush-hour ～** 车流稀少的/繁忙的/高峰期的交通; **slow-moving ～** 缓缓移动的车流; **to be stuck in ～** 遭遇塞车; **oncoming/through ～** 迎面驶来的/过往的车辆; **～ into/out of London** 进/出伦敦的车辆; **～ conditions/accidents** 交通状况/事故 **2** [u] (movement of trains, planes, ships, people) 运输; (flow, volume) 交通量; **sea/cross-Channel ～** 海上/跨英吉利海峡的运输; **(rail) passenger ～** (铁路) 客运; **the ～ of goods** 货运; **～ through Shanghai has doubled** 途经上海的车流量翻了一番 **3** [u] Comput, Telecom 通信; **data ～** 数据传输 **4** [u and c] (dealings) (in drugs, arms, goods) [尤指非法的] 买卖; fig (in ideas) 交换; **(illegal or illicit) ～ in sth.** 某物的 (非法) 交易; **a two-way ～ in scientific know-how** 科学知识的双向交流

B *vi* (*pres p etc.* **-ck-**) pej **to ～ in sth.** [尤指非法地] 买卖 ‹*drugs, contraband*›

traffic: ～ accident *n* 交通事故; **～ calming** *n* [u] 道路缓行措施; **～ circle** *n* Amer 交通环岛; **～ cone** *n* 锥形警告路标; **～ controller** *n* (person) [尤指空中交通的] 交通管制员; (device) 交通管制设施; **～ cop** ▸**p. 409** *n* Amer colloq 交通警察; **～ court** *n* Amer 交通法庭; **～ duty** *n* [u] 交通执勤; **to be on ～ duty** 在指挥交通; **～ engineer** ▸**p. 409** *n* 交通工程师; **～ flow** *n* [u] (volume of traffic) 交通流量; (movement of traffic) 交通状况; **～-free** *adj* (without traffic) 没有车辆的 ‹*road*›; (from which traffic is banned) 禁止通行的 ‹*area, street*›; **～ island** *n* [道路中间供行人避让车辆的] 安全岛; **～ jam** *n* 交通阻塞; **we got stuck in a ～ jam** 我们遇上了交通阻塞; **a 5-mile ～ jam** 5 英里长的塞车

trafficker /ˈtræfɪkə(r)/ *n* 做非法买卖的人; **to be a ～ in sth.** 非法经营某物; **a drugs ～** 毒品贩子

traffic: ～ lane *n* **1** (carriageway) 车道; **2** (air route) 航线; (sea route) 航道; **～ light** *n* **1** **～ (lights)** *pl* (set of lights) 红绿灯; **2** (individual light) 交通信号灯; **the green ～ light** 绿灯; **～ manager** ▸**p. 409** *n* **1** (for transport of goods) 运输主管; **2** (for road traffic) 交通管理员; **～ offence** *n* 交通违法行为; **～ pattern** *n* esp Amer Aviat 机场区域空中交通图; **～ police** *n* + *v pl* **1** (organization) [警察局的] 交通处; **2** (people) 交通警察; **～ policeman** *n* 交通警察; **～ report** *n* 路况报告; **～ sign** *n* 交通标志; **～ system** *n* 交通系统; **～ warden** ▸**p. 409** *n* Brit 交通管理员

tragedian /trəˈdʒiːdɪən/ *n* **1** (author) 悲剧作家; **the Greek ～s** 希腊悲剧作家 **2** (actor) 悲剧演员

tragedienne /trəˌdʒiːdɪˈen/ *n* 悲剧女演员

tragedy /ˈtrædʒədi/ *n* **1** [c and u] (dreadful occurrence) 灾难; **it's a ～ that ...** …是一场灾难; **the ～ of it is that ...** 不幸的是…; **the ～ of war is that ...** 战争带来的灾难是…; **his death at 25 was a ～** 他在 25 岁时去世是一大不幸 **2** [u and c] (genre, play) 悲剧; **King Lear is probably the greatest of Shakespeare's tragedies** 《李尔王》也许是莎士比亚最伟大的悲剧作品

tragic /ˈtrædʒɪk/ *adj* **1** (characterized by tragedy) 悲惨的 ‹*effect, accident, death*›; **it is ～ that ...** …很可悲 **2** (very sad) 悲伤的 ‹*face, look*›; 令人悲痛的 ‹*story, sight*› **3** Theat, Literat 悲剧性的; **a ～ hero/scene/ending/irony/flaw** 悲剧性的主人公/场景/结局/讽刺/缺点; **～ actor/actress** 男/女悲剧演员

tragically /ˈtrædʒɪkli/ *adv* 悲惨地 ‹*die, end*›; **his ～ short life** 他悲惨而短暂的一生; **her ～ early death** 她的英年早逝

tragicomedy /ˌtrædʒɪˈkɒmədi/ *n* [u and c] 悲喜剧

tragicomic /ˌtrædʒɪˈkɒmɪk/ *adj* 悲喜剧的 ‹*situation, scene*›

trail /treɪl/

A *n* **1** (path) [乡间的] 小径; **to blaze** or Amer **break a ～** 辟出小径; **to set off** or **out on the ～** 上路; **to hit the ～** colloq 出发 **2** (trace, mark) [长串的] 痕迹; **a ～ of blood** 一长串血迹; **to leave a ～ of sth.** 留下一道某物; fig 留下一连串 ‹*clues*›; **to leave a ～ of devastation** «*storm*» 留下满目疮痍; **to leave a ～ of broken hearts** 留下一颗颗破碎的心; **in the ～ of sb./sth.** 随着某人/某物; **he arrived with a crowd of journalists in his ～** 他到了, 身后跟着一大群记者 **3** esp Hunt (track, evidence) 踪迹; **to pick up/lose sb.'s ～** 发现/失去某人的行踪; **to be on the ～ of sb./sth.** 在跟踪某人/某物; **to follow the ～ (of sb./sth.) to somewhere** 追踪 (某人/某物) 到某地; **to be hot on sb.'s ～** colloq 紧追某人; **the ～ was still warm/had gone cold** 踪迹还很明显/消失了 **4** (circuit) 路径; **to be well off the tourist ～** 远离旅游线路

B *vi* **1** (hang, extend) «*hair, vine*» 垂下; (drag) 拖曳; **to ～ on** or **along the ground** 拖在地上; **the bride's dress ～ed behind her** 新娘的礼服拖在身后; **to ～ in the mud** 拖在泥里; **smoke ～ed from the exhaust pipe** 排气管里冒出来一长串烟 **2** (traipse, lag) 无精打采地走; **to ～ home/back** 拖着步子回家/回去; **to ～ along behind sb.** 无精打采地跟在某人后面; **to ～ (a)round after sb.** 跟着某人转; **to have fans ～ing around in one's wake** 身后跟着一群粉丝 **3** (fall behind) 落后; **to ～ (far) behind (sb.)** (远远) 落后 (于某人); **to ～ badly/by 6 points** 落后很多/6 分; **to be ～ing (by) 3 goals to 1/at the bottom of the league** 1 比 3 落后/在联赛中垫底; **to be ～ing in the polls** 在民意调查中落后

C *vt* **1** (follow) 追踪; **to be ～ed by the police** 被警察追踪; **to ～ sb. to his/her front door** 追踪某人直到他/她家大门 **2** *usu pres p* (fall behind) 落后于; **to be ～ing (one's) competitors in sth.** 在某事上落后于竞争者 **3** (let hang) 垂下; (drag) 拖; **to ～ sth. on** or **along the ground** 把某物拖在地上; **to ～ one's hand in the water** 用手划水; **to ～ mud all over the house** 把屋里踩得满地泥巴; **a jeep ～ing a cloud of dust** 扬起一团尘土的吉普车 **4** (publicize) 预告 ‹*film, broadcast*›

Phrasal verbs

- **trail away** *vi* «*voice, sound*» 逐渐消失; «*writing, signature*» 渐渐淡去; **the smoke ～ed away in the wind** 烟在风中渐渐散去
- **trail off** *vi* «*voice, sound, discussion*» 渐渐停止

trail: ～ bike *n* 越野摩托车; **～blazer** *n* **1** (explorer) 拓荒者; **2** (innovator) (person) 创始人; (company, group) 先驱; **～blazing** *adj* 创新的 ‹*discovery, scientist, firm*›; **～breaker** *n* Amer = **～blazer**

trailer /ˈtreɪlə(r)/ *n* **1** (vehicle) 拖车 **2** Amer (caravan) 活动房车 **3** Cin 预告片 **4** Phot 空白胶片头

trailer: ～ park *n* Amer 活动房车停车场; **～-park** *adj* Amer colloq pej (lacking refinement) 粗俗的; (lacking taste) 没有品位的; (lacking quality) 蹩脚的; **her ～-park bleached perm** 她俗气的染成浅色的头发; **a ～-park audience** 趣味低俗的观众; **～ tent** *n* Brit 拖车帐篷; **～ trash** *n* [u] Amer offensive colloq 住活动房车的废物 [指地位低下的贫困白人]; **～ truck** *n* Amer 铰接式卡车

trailing /ˈtreɪlɪŋ/ *adj attrib* 蔓生的 ‹*ivy, branches*›; 下垂的 ‹*hair, skirts*›; 袅袅飘动的 ‹*smoke*›

train /treɪn/

A *n* **1** [c] (overground railway) 火车; (subway) 地铁; **a passenger/goods** Brit or **freight** Amer **～** 客运/货运列车; **a slow/fast/express ～** 慢车/快车/特快列车; **the London ～** 伦敦开来的火车; **the morning/9 o'clock ～** 上午/9 点的列车; **the (six o-clock) ～ to London** (6 点钟) 开往伦敦的火车; **the up/down ～** Brit 上行/下行列车; **to catch/miss a ～** 赶上/错过火车; **when does your ～ go** or **leave?** 你坐的那趟车何时出发? ; **to go** or **travel (to Paris) by ～** 乘火车旅行 (去巴黎); **it's two hours to Paris by ～** 坐火车到巴黎要两个小时; **to change ～s** 倒车; **to transport goods by ～** 用火车运货; **an hourly/a two-hourly ～ service** 每小时/两小时一班的列车运行服务; **a ～ station/robbery/crash** 火车站/火车劫案/列车撞车事故 **2** [c] (procession of animals, vehicles, people) 队列; **a baggage ～** 辎重队 **3** [c] *usu sing* (series of events, ideas) 系列; **to set off a ～ of ideas/events** 引发一连串想法/一系列事件; **(to interrupt sb.'s) ～ of thought** (打断某人的) 思绪 **4** [u] (motion) **to be in ～** 正在进行; **to set** or **put sth. in ～** 促使某事发生 **5** [c] dated (retinue) 侍从; **to bring sth. in its ～** fig 带来某种后果; **famine that followed in the ～ of civil war** 随内战而来的饥荒 **6** [c] Fashn 裙裾 **7** [c] Tech 系; **a ～ of gears** 齿轮系

B *vt* **1** (instruct) 培训 ‹*staff, engineer*›; 训练 ‹*athlete, soldier, animal*›; **to ～ sb. as sth.** 把某人培养成 ‹*scientist*›; **to be ～ed on the job/as a pilot/in the use of sth.** 接受在岗培训/飞行员训练/使用某物的培训; **to ～ sb. for a senior position/the Olympics** 培训某人出任高级职位/为参加奥运会训练某人; **to ～ sb. in sth.** 训练某人某方面的技能; **to ～ sb. to do sth.** 训练某人做某事; **to be ～ed to kill** 受训做杀手; **to ～ a dog to sit** 训练一只狗坐下; **exercises for ～ing the memory** 锻炼记忆力的练习 **2** Hort 使…朝某处生长 ‹*plant*›; **to ～ a branch along a wall/over an archway** 修整枝条使其沿墙/在拱门上方生长 **3** (aim, focus) 把…瞄准 ‹*gun*›; 把…对准 ‹*telescope, camera*›; **to ～ sth. on sth./sb.** 用某物对准某物/某人; **all eyes are ～ed on Geneva** 所有人都在关注日内瓦; **to have one's sights ～ed on stardom** 一心要做明星

C *vi* **1** (for profession) 接受培训; **she ～ed at X University** 她在 X 大学接受培训; **to train as** or **to be a teacher/a mechanic** 接受师资培训/做机修工的培训; **to ～ for sth.** 接受培训做某事; **to ～ for the ministry** 接受培训做牧师; **to ～ for the stage** 接受戏剧训练 **2** Sport 训练; **to ～ with sb.** 与某人一起训练; **to ～ for sth.** 为某事进行训练; **she's ～ing to run the 400 metres** 她在为 400 米跑训练

D *v refl* **to ～ oneself** 自我训练; **to ～ oneself to do sth.** 训练自己做某事

Phrasal verb

- **train up** *vt* [**～ sb. up, ～ up sb.**] 把…培训好 ‹*staff*›; 充分训练 ‹*athlete*›; **to ～ up a successor** 培养好接班人; **to ～ up raw recruits into disciplined fighting men** 把新兵训练成纪律严明的战士

train: ～-bearer *n* [婚礼上新娘身后的] 挽裙裾者; **～ crash** *n* 火车撞车事故; **～ driver** ▸**p. 409** *n* 火车司机

trained /treɪnd/ *adj* 受过培训的 ‹*staff, professional*›; 受过训练的 ‹*athlete, animal*›; **to be fully ～** 得到全面培训; **well-～** 训练有素的 ‹*soldier*›; **to have one's husband well ～** iron or hum 把丈夫管教得很好; **to the ～ ear/eye** 在训练有素的耳朵听来/眼睛看来; **a singer with a ～ voice** 声音受过训练的歌手; **a Harvard-～ lawyer** 哈佛培养出来的律师; **an Irish-～ horse** 在爱尔兰驯过的马

trainee /treɪ'niː/ *n* 受培训者; **a management ~** 管理实习生; **a ~ manager/pilot/salesman** 见习经理人/飞行员/推销员

traineeship /treɪ'niːʃɪp/ *n* (position) 见习职位; (period) 见习期; **she got a ~ in an engineering company** 她获得了一家工程公司的见习职位; **during his ~** 在他实习期间

trainer /'treɪnə(r)/ *n* **1** (of athlete) 教练员; (of horse) 驯马师; (of circus animal, dog) 驯兽师 **2** Brit (sports shoe) 运动鞋; **a pair of ~s** 一双运动鞋 **3** (flight simulator) 飞行练习器; (aircraft) 教练机

trainer pants *npl* 坐便训练裤

train ferry *n* 列车轮渡

training /'treɪnɪŋ/ *n* [u] **1** (for profession) 培训; **on-the-job/staff ~** 在职/员工培训; **~ as** *or* **for sth.** 为做…进行的培训 ‹*teacher*›; **it's good ~ for adult life/a management position** 这是一种为成年生活/担任管理职位作准备的有益训练; **~ in sth.** …方面的培训 ‹*publishing*›; **a ~ programme/course** 培训计划/课程 **2** (for athlete, soldier, animal) 训练; **to break (one's) ~** 中断训练; **to be in ~** 在训练; fig 处于良好状态; **to be in ~ for sth.** 在为某事训练; **in ~ for the World Cup** 备战世界杯; **fitness ~** 健身; **basic ~** Mil 基本训练; **~ method/facilities** 训练方法/设施; **~ exercises** Mil 操练

training: ~ centre *n* 训练中心; **~ college** *n* Brit [尤指培养教师的] 培训学院; **~ ground** *n* **1** Sport, Mil (area) 训练场; **2** (establishment) 培训基地; **~ manual** *n* 培训手册; **~ ship** *n* 教练船; **~ shoe** *n* **= trainer 2**

train: ~load *n* (of commodity) 列车装载量; (of people) 列车载客量; **~ set** *n* Brit 玩具火车; **~spotter** *n* Brit 收集机车号码的人; **~spotting** *n* [u] Brit 收集机车号码; **~ station** *n* 火车站; **~ surfing** *n* [u] 火车顶冲浪 [为寻求刺激而爬上行驶列车的车厢顶部]

traipse /treɪps/
A *vi* (wearily) 疲惫地走; (reluctantly) 磨蹭; **I've been traipsing around town all day** 我一整天都在镇上溜达; **to ~ in and out** 拖沓地进进出出; **to ~ round** 疲惫地四处溜达; **to ~ around after sb.** 围着某人磨蹭
B *n* (tiring journey) 疲惫的步行; (tedious journey) 长途跋涉

trait /treɪ, treɪt/ *n* **1** (distinguishing characteristic) 特点; **personality ~** 性格特征; **a positive/negative ~** 正面的/负面的性格特点 **2** (genetically determined characteristic) 性状

traitor /'treɪtə(r)/ *n* 叛徒; **to turn ~** 叛变; **to be a ~ to oneself** 背叛自己; **he was tried and shot as a ~ during the war** 他在战争期间被指是卖国贼而受审并被枪决

traitorous /'treɪtərəs/ *adj* 叛国的 ‹*act, conduct*›; **a ~ speech** 背叛性的演讲

traitorously /'treɪtərəslɪ/ *adv* 叛逆地 ‹*act, speak*›; **to behave ~** 有背叛表现

trajectory /trə'dʒektərɪ/ *n* Phys 轨迹; Math 轨线; **a low/flat ~** 低/平轨迹; **the ~ of the rocket was flatter than expected** 火箭的运行轨迹要比预想的平

tram /træm/ *n* Brit 有轨电车; **to catch** *or* **take a ~** 乘坐有轨电车

tramcar /'træmkɑː(r)/ *n* Brit 有轨电车

tramline /'træmlaɪn/
A *n* (track) 电车轨道; (route) 有轨电车路线
B tramlines *npl* **1** (on tennis court) 球场两侧的双打加线 **2** fig (rigid principles) 不可改变的原则

trammel /'træml/ formal
A *vt* (*pres p etc.* **-ll-** Brit, **-l-** Amer) 限制 ‹*person*›; **those less ~led by convention than him** 那些受传统束缚比他少的人
B trammels *npl* 束缚; **the ~s of marriage/materialism** 婚姻/实利主义的束缚

tramp /træmp/
A *n* **1** (vagrant) 流浪者 **2** (sound of feet) 沉重的脚步声; **I heard the ~ of feet** 我听到了重重的脚步声 **3** (hike) 远足; **to go for a ~** 去远足 **4** Amer colloq (promiscuous woman) 荡妇 **5** Naut **~ (steamer)** 航线不固定的商船
B *vi* **1** (hike) 长途跋涉; **I've ~ed all round town looking for her birthday present!** 为了给她找生日礼物我走遍了全城! **2** (walk heavily) 脚步沉重地行走; **to ~ up the stairs** 嗵嗵地爬上楼梯
C *vt* 疲惫地走过 ‹*highway, shops*›; **to ~ the streets** 疲惫地走过一条又一条街道; **we ~ed the countryside looking for the lost dog** 我们走遍了乡下寻找那只丢失的狗

trample /'træmpl/
A *vt* 踩 ‹*person, flowers, crops*›; **to ~ sth. underfoot** 把某物踏在脚下; **to be ~d to death** 被踩死
B *vi* **1** lit (tread on) 踩; **to ~ on** *or* **over sth.** 踩踏某物 **2** fig (impose or encroach upon) 侵犯; **she determined she wouldn't be ~d on any longer** 她下决心不再忍受蹂躏; **to ~ on other people's feelings** 伤害他人的感情

trampoline /'træmpəliːn/
A *n* 蹦床
B *vi* 跳蹦床

trampolining /'træmpəliːnɪŋ/ ▸p. 307 *n* [u] 跳蹦床

tramway /'træmweɪ/ *n* **1** Brit (route) 有轨电车轨道 **2** (system) 有轨电车系统

trance /trɑːns, Amer træns/ *n* **1** [c] (hypnotic) 催眠状态; (religious) 入定; **to be in/go into a ~** 处于/陷入昏睡状态; **to put sb. into a ~** 使某人进入昏睡状态; **to come out of a ~** 从昏睡中苏醒过来 **2** [c] fig (state of abstraction) 出神; **to be in a ~** 在发呆; **I listened to the music in a ~** 我迷迷糊糊地听着音乐 **3** [u] **~ (music)** 催眠电子舞曲

trance-like *adj* (hypnotic) 催眠般的; (dreamy) 恍惚的; **to be in a ~ state** 神情恍惚

tranche /trɑːnʃ/ *n* 一部分; **the first ~ of the loan** 第一笔贷款

tranny, trannie /'trænɪ/ *n* colloq **1** Brit dated **= transistor 2** **2** (*usu* **trannie**) **= transvestite**

tranquil /'træŋkwɪl/ *adj* (calm, untroubled) 平静的 ‹*mind, expression, waters*›; (free from disturbance) 恬静的 ‹*scene, setting, life*›

tranquillity Brit, **tranquility** Amer /træŋ'kwɪlətɪ/ *n* [u] (calm) 平静; (peace and quiet) 安宁; **in ~** 宁静地; **the ~ of the scene** 景色的静谧

tranquillize Brit, **tranquilize** Amer /'træŋkwɪlaɪz/ *vt* 使平静; **to have a tranquillizing effect on sb./sth.** 对某人/某物有安定作用

tranquillizer Brit, **tranquilizer** Amer /'træŋkwɪlaɪzə(r)/ *n* 镇静剂; **to be on ~s** 在服用镇静剂; **to take a ~/~s** 服用镇静剂

tranquillizer dart *n* 麻醉射针

tranquilly /'træŋkwɪlɪ/ *adv* (calmly) 平静地 ‹*say, smile*›; (peacefully) 安宁地 ‹*sleep*›; **the stream flowed ~ through the garden** 小溪静静流淌, 穿过花园

transact /træn'zækt/ *vt* 处理 ‹*business, diplomacy*›; 商议 ‹*contract, terms*›; **to ~ a deal** 做交易

transaction /,træn'zækʃn/
A *n* **1** [c] (piece of business) 交易; **a legal ~** 合法交易; **a cash/credit card ~** 现金/信用卡交易 **2** [u] (act) 办理; **the ~ of business** 事务的处理 **3** [c] Comput 数据处理
B transactions *npl* 公报; **the ~s of the Geographical Society are published quarterly** 地理学会的会刊每季度出版一期

transactional /,træn'zækʃənl/ *adj* 交易的

transalpine /,trænz'ælpaɪn/ *adj* 阿尔卑斯山另一侧的 ‹*route, pass*›

transatlantic /,trænzət'læntɪk/ *adj* **1** (across the Atlantic) 大西洋彼岸的 ‹*accent, influence*›; **~ visitors** 来自大西洋彼岸的游客 **2** (crossing the Atlantic) 跨越大西洋的 ‹*flight, telephone call, trade, alliance*›

transceiver /,træn'siːvə(r)/ *n* 无线电收发机

transcend /,træn'send/ *vt* **1** (go beyond) 超越 ‹*limits, expectations, knowledge*›; **it's an issue that ~s petty party differences** 这个问题超越了无足轻重的党派分歧 **2** (surpass, excel in) 胜过 ‹*person, work, performance*›; **his latest novel ~s anything he has ever written before** 他的最近一部小说超越了他从前所写的任何作品; **to ~ sb./sth. in sth.** 在某方面优于某人/某事物 **3** Relig, Philos 超越于…而存在 ‹*material world, human experience*›

transcendence /,træn'sendəns/ *n* [u] 卓越; **to find** *or* **achieve ~** 实现超越

transcendent /,træn'sendənt/ *adj* **1** Relig, Philos (beyond, above) 超然的 ‹*deity*›; 超验的 ‹*idea*›; **the search for a ~ level of knowledge** 对先验知识的探求 **2** (exceptional) 杰出的 ‹*genius*›; 非同寻常的 ‹*piety, significance*›; **to be ~ over sth.** 超越某事物

transcendental /,trænsen'dentl/ *adj* 超凡的 ‹*religion, view*›; 超验论的 ‹*philosophy*›

Transcendental Meditation *n* [u] 超脱禅定法

transcontinental /,trænzkɒntɪ'nentl/ *adj* 横贯大陆的

transcribe /,træn'skraɪb/ *vt* **1** (by writing) 转写; **to ~ sth. into sth.** 把某物转写成某物 **2** Comput 转录 ‹*data*›; **to ~ sth. from ... to ...** 把某物从…转录到… **3** Mus 改编; **she ~d many orchestral pieces for piano** 她把许多管弦乐曲改编成了钢琴曲

transcript /'trænskrɪpt/ *n* **1** (written copy) 抄本; (printed copy) 打印本 **2** Amer (record of student's work) 成绩单

transcription /,træn'skrɪpʃn/ *n* **1** [u] (action) 抄写 **2** [c] (of speech) (written) 抄本; (printed) 打印本 **3** [c] (of music) 改编 **4** [c] (of speech sound) 标注; **phonetic ~s of British English** 英国英语的音标

transcutaneous /,trænzkjuː'teɪnɪəs/ *adj* 经皮肤的

transdermal patch /,trænzdɜːml 'pætʃ/ *n* 透皮贴剂

transduce /,træns'djuːs, Amer -'duːs/ *vt* 转换

transducer /træns'djuːsə(r), Amer -'duː-/ *n* 换能器

transect
A /,træn'sekt/ *vt* 横切
B /'trænsekt/ *n* (through object) 横断面; (across earth's surface) 样条

transept /'trænsept/ *n* [十字形教堂的] 耳堂

transexual /,træn'seksjʊəl/ *n, adj* **= transsexual**

transexualism /træn'seksjʊəlɪzm/ *n* [u] **= transsexualism**

transfer
A /,træns'fɜː(r)/ *vt* (*pres p etc.* **-rr-**) **1** (move) 调动 ‹*employee, soldier*›; 转移 ‹*prisoner, patient, luggage, goods, energy*›; 使…转会 ‹*sportsman, player*›; 转接 ‹*call, caller*›; **to ~ sth./sb. to sth.** 把某物/某人转到某处; **the passengers were ~red to coaches** 乘客被转到了长途客车上; **to be ~red to another hospital** 转到另一家医院; **I'm ~ring you to reception** 我把你的电话转到前台; **to ~ sth./sb. from sth.** 把某物/某人从某处转来; **to ~ credits from junior college** Amer 将大专的学分转过来; **to ~ one's affections to sb.** 把感情转移到某人身上; **to ~ one's support to sb.** 转而支持某人; **to ~ sth. from sb.** 把某物从某人处移走; **to ~ £500 from one's deposit account into one's current account** 从定期账户转 500 英镑到活期账户 **2** esp Jur (hand over) 转让 ‹*right, assets*›;

移交 ‹*power, authority, responsibility*›; **to ~ ownership of sth.** 过户某物; **to ~ sth. to sb./sth.** 把某物让渡给某人/某处; **to ~ sth. from sth.** 从某处转让某物; **the house has been ~red to my name/from his name to mine** 房子过户到了我的名下/从他的名下过户到了我的名下 **3** Comput, Tech (copy) 转存 ‹*drawing, details*›; **to ~ sth. on to sth.** 把某物转存到某物中 **4** (translate) 使转化; **to ~ sth. (on) to sth.** 将某物表现到某物上; **to ~ one's emotions on to canvas** 将情感表现在画布上; **to ~ an idea on to paper** 把概念转化为文字 **5** *usu passive* Ling 转变 ‹*sense*›; **a ~red use of the noun** 这个名词的转义用法 **6** (change) 转换 ‹*objects*›; **to ~ schools** 转学

B /træns'fɜː(r)/ *vi* (*pres p etc.* **-rr-**) **1** (move) «*employee, soldier*» 调动; «*passenger*» 转移; «*sportsman, player*» 转会; **to ~ to/from sth.** 转到某处/从某处转来; **to ~ from the airport to the railway station** 从机场转到火车站; **passengers ~ring at Frankfurt** 在法兰克福转机的旅客; **to ~ to/from another department** 调到另一部门/从另一部门调来; **will my credits ~?** esp Amer 我的学分可以转过来吗? **2** Univ (change institutions) 转学; (change courses) 转专业; **to ~ from one university to another** 从一所大学转到另一所大学 **3** (adapt, translate) 改编; **to ~ (on) to sth.** «*idea, text*» 转换到某媒体; **the novel didn't ~ well to the stage** 这部长篇小说改编成舞台剧的效果不佳

C /'trænsfɜː(r)/ *n* **1** [u and c] (relocation) (of employee, soldier) 调动; (of prisoner, patient, luggage, goods, energy) 转移; (of sportsman, player) 转会; (of call, caller) 转接; **~ to/from sth.** 到某处/从某处的转移; **the ~ from A Hospital to B Hospital** 从A医院到B医院的转院; **the ~ from the airport to the hotel** 从机场到旅馆的转车; **~s between industry and the civil service** 在工业领域与行政部门之间的调动; **to apply** *or* **ask for a ~** Mgmt 申请调动; **to ask for a ~** Sport 要求转会; **heat ~** 热传递 **2** [u and c] (handover) (of funds, ownership, property, rights) 转让; (of power, authority) 移交; **capital ~s** 资本转让; **to make a ~** 转账; **a ~ of funds** 资金转账; **the electronic ~ of cash** 现金的电子转账 **3** [c] (person) 转移者; **she's a ~ from another branch** 她是从另一家分公司调来的; **the club's next ~** 俱乐部下一个转会对象; **~s go to gate 4** 换乘旅客到4号门 **4** [u and c] esp Comput, Tech (copying, copied information) 转存; **file ~** 文件转存; **a ~ of data** 数据传输 **5** [c] Brit (picture, design) 转印图案; **an iron-on ~** 烫印图案 **6** [c] Amer (ticket) **a (bus/train) ~** (公共汽车/火车) 换乘票

transferable /træns'fɜːrəbl/ *adj* **1** (able to be transferred) 可转让的 ‹*right, asset, ticket, pension*›; 可转移的 ‹*debt, vote*› **2** (applicable to different job) 可用于其他工作的 ‹*skill, learning*›

transfer: **~ deed** *n* 产权转让契约; **~ desk** *n* 转机柜台; **~ duty** *n* [u] [由买方支付的] 财产转让税

transference /'trænsfərəns, Amer ˌtræns'fɜːrəns/ *n* [u] **1** (transfer) 转移; **education involves the ~ of knowledge** 教育事关知识的传承 **2** Psych 移情

transfer: **~ fee** *n* Brit 球员转会费; **~ list** *n* Brit 球员转会名单; **~ lounge** *n* 转机休息室; **~ passenger** *n* (air transport) 转机旅客; (road transport) 转车旅客; (water transport) 转船旅客; **~ payment** *n* 转移支付

transferral /træns'fɜːrəl/ *n* [u] 转移; **the ~ of ownership** 所有权的移交

transferred charge call /ˌtrænsfɜːd 'tʃɑːdʒ kɔːl/ *n* 受话方付费电话

transfer: **~ season** *n* 球员转会期; **~ time** *n* [u and c] [尤指从机场到目的地的] 旅客运送时间

transfiguration /ˌtrænsfɪgə'reɪʃn, Amer -gjə'r-/ *n* [u and c] (into more beautiful state) 容光焕发; (into more spiritual state) 更兴奋

transfigure /ˌtræns'fɪgə(r), Amer -gjər/ *vt* 使…容光焕发 ‹*person*›; 使…更兴奋 ‹*expression*›; **her face was ~d with joy at seeing her family once again** 再次见到家人时她喜形于色

transfix /ˌtræns'fɪks/ *vt usu passive* 使怔住; **when she heard the news, she was ~ed with shock** 她听到这个消息时惊呆了; **I was ~ed by an irrational fear** 莫名其妙的恐惧令我感到六神无主

transform /ˌtræns'fɔːm/ *vt* **1** (change) 改变; **to be ~ed into sth.** 被改变成某物; **I intend to ~ the cellar into a dining room** 我打算把地下室改建成餐厅; **losing his job had ~ed him into a radical** 失业使他变得很极端 **2** (convert into different form) 改变…的形态 ‹*matter, energy*›; **cooling ~s the moisture into ice particles** 冷却使湿气变成了冰粒; **to ~ heat into motive power** 将热转化成动力 **3** Math, Elec 变换 ‹*equation, expression, current*›

transformation /ˌtrænsfə'meɪʃn/ *n* **1** [c] (change) 变化; **the change in his appearance was a real ~!** 他看上去真是判若两人! **2** [u] (action) 改变 **3** [u] Phys 形态变化 **4** [c] Math 变换

transformational grammar /ˌtrænsfəmeɪʃnl 'græmə(r)/ *n* [u] 转换语法

transformer /ˌtræns'fɔːmə(r)/ *n* 变压器

transformer station *n* 变电站

transfuse /ˌtræns'fjuːz/ *vt* **1** *usu passive* (permeate) 使弥漫; **to be ~d with sth.** 充满 ‹*joy, excitement*›; **to be ~d with melancholy and anguish** 充满忧郁和苦恼 **2** Med 给…输血 ‹*patient*›; 输 ‹*blood, bone marrow*›

transfusion /træns'fjuːʒn/ *n* [c and u] (of blood) 输血; (of other fluid) 输液; **to give sb. a blood ~** 给某人输血; **to have a blood ~** 接受输血

transgender /ˌtræns'dʒendə(r)/ *adj* 变性的

transgenderism /træns'dʒendərɪzm/ *n* [u] 变性

transgenic /træns'dʒenɪk/ *adj* 转基因的 ‹*plant, material, organism*›

transglobal /ˌtrænz'gləʊbl/ *adj* **1** (extending across the world) 全球的; **a ~ corporation/network/broadcast** 覆盖全球的公司/网络/广播 **2** (moving round the world) 环球的; **~ tourism** 环球旅游; **a ~ journey** 环球旅行

transgress /ˌtrænz'gres/ formal

A *vt* (violate) 违反 ‹*law, convention*›; (overstep) 侵犯 ‹*bounds*›; **to ~ the bounds of decency** 有伤风化

B *vi* **to ~ against sth./sb.** 触犯某物/某人; **to ~ against God's commandments** 违反上帝的戒律; **to ~ against the code of family solidarity** 违反家族团结的准则

transgression /ˌtrænz'greʃn/ *n* [c and u] Jur 过失; Relig 罪过

transgressor /ˌtrænz'gresə(r)/ *n* Jur 违法者; Relig 有罪者

tranship /ˌtræn'ʃɪp/ *vt* = **trans-ship**

transhipment /ˌtræn'ʃɪpmənt/ *n* = **trans-shipment**

transience /'trænzɪəns/, **transiency** /'trænzɪənsi/ *ns* [u] 短暂; **the ~ of youth** 青春的转瞬即逝; **the ~ of romantic relationships** 恋爱关系的多变

transient /'trænzɪənt, Amer 'trænʃnt/

A *adj* 短暂的 ‹*emotion, beauty, phase, friendship*›; 暂住的 ‹*population*›; **that ~ moment of happiness** 那短暂的幸福时刻

B *n* esp Amer 暂住者; **we cater for the needs of tourists and other ~s** 我们能够满足游客以及其他暂住者的需要

transistor /ˌtræn'zɪstə(r), -'sɪstə(r)/ *n* **1** (semiconductor device) 晶体管 **2** **~ (radio)** 晶体管收音机

transistorize /ˌtræn'zɪstəraɪz, -'sɪst-/ *vt* 给…装晶体管 ‹*device, circuit*›

transit /'trænzɪt, -sɪt/ *n* **1** [u] (conveyance) 运输; **in ~** 在运输中; **the rapid ~ of goods** 商品的快速运送 **2** [c] (act of passing through) 通过 **3** [c and u] Astron 凌日

transit camp *n* (for refugees) 临时难民营; (for soldiers) 临时宿营地

transition /ˌtræn'zɪʃn, -'sɪʃn/ *n* [c and u] (process) 过渡; (period) 过渡期; **to make a** *or* **the ~** 进行变革; **in a state of ~** 处于转变状态的; **the ~ from colonial rule to self-government** 从殖民统治到自治的过渡

transitional /ˌtræn'zɪʃənl, -'sɪʃənl/ *adj* 过渡的; **a ~ period/style/government/stage/form** 过渡时期/风格/政府/阶段/形式

transitive /'trænzətɪv/

A *adj* 及物的; **~ use/sense/verb** 及物用法/意义/动词

B *n* 及物动词

transitively /'trænzətɪvli/ *adv* 及物地; **the verb is used ~ in this sentence** 这个动词在本句中是及物用法

transitivity /ˌtrænzə'tɪvəti/ *n* [u] 及物性

transit lounge *n* 中转候机厅

transitoriness /'trænsɪtrɪnɪs, Amer -tɔːrɪnɪs/ *n* [u] 短暂; **the beauty and ~ of the world** 世界的美丽与变幻无常

transitory /'trænsɪtri, Amer -tɔːri/ *adj* 短暂的

transit visa *n* 过境签证

translatable /ˌtrænz'leɪtəbl/ *adj* 可翻译的 ‹*word, concept*›; **her novels are eminently ~** 她的小说非常易于翻译

translate /ˌtrænz'leɪt/

A *vt* **1** (express in a different language) 翻译 ‹*book, text, sentence, poem*›; **how do you ~ this word?** 这个词怎么译? **2** (convert) 转换 ‹*measurement, unit*›; **to ~ sth. into sth.** 将某物转变为某物; **to ~ theory into practice** 将理论转化为实践

B *vi* **1** (express meaning in different language) 翻译; **you speak in your native language, and I'll ~** 你说母语, 我来翻译 **2** (be able to be translated) 可译; **this word does not ~** 这个词没法翻译; **his poetry does not ~ well** 他的诗歌不好翻译

translation /ˌtrænz'leɪʃn/ *n* **1** [c] (of book, text, sentence, poem) 译文; **a free/literal ~** 意译/直译; **to make a ~ (of sth.)** 翻译 (某物); **in ~** 以译本形式; **I never read a book in ~ if I can read it in the original** 如果我能读懂原著就绝不读译本; **the play loses a lot in ~** 这部剧的译本大为失色 **2** [u] (activity) 翻译; **simultaneous ~** 同声传译 **3** [c] (as test) 翻译测试; **I passed the comprehension but failed the ~** 我的阅读理解及格了, 但翻译没通过

translation table *n* 代码转换表

translator /ˌtrænz'leɪtə(r)/ *n* **1** (person) 译者; **he's a professional ~** 他是专业译员 **2** Comput 翻译程序

transliterate /ˌtrænz'lɪtəreɪt/ *vt* 音译 ‹*word, letter*›

transliteration /ˌtrænzlɪtə'reɪʃn/ *n* [c and u] 音译

translucence /ˌtrænz'luːsns/ *n* [u] 半透明

translucent /ˌtrænz'luːsnt/ *adj* 半透明的

transmigrate /ˌtrænzmaɪ'greɪt/ *vi* 转世

transmigration /ˌtrænzmaɪ'greɪʃn/ *n* [u] 转世

transmissible /ˌtrænz'mɪsəbl/ *adj* 可传染的 ‹*disease*›; 可传输的 ‹*energy*›; 可传送的 ‹*information, data*›; 可传达的 ‹*idea*›

transmission /ˌtrænz'mɪʃn/ *n* **1** [u] (broadcast) TV, Radio 播送; Med 传染; Phys 传送; **~ of the virus is only through physical contact** 那种病毒只通过身体接触传播; **the concert has been recorded ready for ~**

t

on Christmas Day 音乐会节目已经录制完毕，将在圣诞节播放 2 [c] (broadcast programme) 广播节目; (broadcast signal) 广播信号; **to broadcast a live ～ of the Prime Minister's speech** 现场直播首相的演讲 3 [c and u] Aut 变速箱; **manual/automatic ～** 手动/自动变速器

transmission: ～ **belt** *n* 传动带; ～ **cable** *n* 输电缆; **high-voltage ～ cables** 高压电缆; ～ **chain** *n* 传染链; ～ **line** *n* 输电线; ～ **shaft** *n* 传动轴

transmit /ˌtrænzˈmɪt/ (*pres p etc.* **-tt-**)
A *vt* 1 (transfer) 传播; **to ～ a report/message** 传送报告/消息; **to ～ sth. to sb.** 把某物传给某人; **to ～ disease** 传播疾病; **to ～ a skill** 传授技能; **to ～ light/an image** 传播光/传送图像 2 (broadcast) 播送 ‹*news, signal*›; **to ～ sth. live** 现场直播某事件; **the programme will be ～ted at a later date** 节目将在日后播放 3 Phys 传 ‹*heat, sound*›; 传递 ‹*vibration*›; 输送 ‹*electricity*›
B *vi* 广播

transmittance /ˌtrænzˈmɪtns/ *n* [u] [光能] 透射比; **high/low ～** 高/低透明度

transmitter /ˌtrænzˈmɪtə(r)/ *n* 1 Radio, TV (device) 发射机; (equipment) 发射设备; **short/long/medium wave ～** 短波/长波/中波发射机; **the radio operator switched on/off his ～** 无线电报务员打开/关闭了他的发报机 2 (person who transmits) 传播者

transmogrify /ˌtrænzˈmɒɡrɪfaɪ/ *vt* hum 使惊人地改变; **his flat was transmogrified into a hippy commune** 他的公寓居然成了嬉皮士的群居地

transmutable /ˌtrænzˈmjuːtəbl/ *adj* 能变化的 ‹*substance, metal*›; **to be ～ into sth.** 可变成某物; **he claimed that lead was ～ into gold** 他宣称铅可以变成金子

transmutation /ˌtrænzmjuːˈteɪʃn/ *n* [c and u] 变化; **the material underwent a series of ～s** 这种材料发生了一系列变化; **the ～ of sadness into joy** 由悲到喜的转变

transmute /ˌtrænzˈmjuːt/ *vt* 1 (transform) 使变化; **life had ～d the lovely girl he remembered into a serene old woman** 生活把他记忆中的那个可爱女孩变成了安详的老妇人 2 (by alchemy) 把…变为贵金属 ‹*element*›; **he claimed to be able to ～ base metal into gold** 他声称能把贱金属变成黄金

transom /ˈtrænsəm/ *n* 1 (in window) 横楣 2 (in boat) 艉横材 3 Amer = **transom window**

transom window *n* 气窗

transparency /ˌtrænsˈpærənsi/ *n* 1 [u] (state, condition) 透明 2 [c] Phot 幻灯片

transparent /ˌtrænsˈpærənt/ *adj* 1 (see-through) 透明的 ‹*fabric, film, coating*› 2 (obvious) 显而易见的 ‹*lie, deception*›; 坦白的 ‹*honesty*›; **a ～ style of writing/meaning** 清晰的写作风格/明确的意思; **a ～ disguise** 容易识破的伪装; **to use ～ language** 使用明白易懂的语言; **he spoke to us with ～ sincerity** 他坦诚地同我们谈话

transparently /ˌtrænsˈpærəntli/ *adv* 显然 ‹*stupid*›; **～ obvious** 显而易见的; **a ～ ridiculous campaign trick** 明显荒谬的竞选伎俩

transpiration /ˌtrænspɪˈreɪʃn/ *n* [u] 蒸腾作用

transpire /ˌtrænˈspaɪə(r)/ *vi* 1 (be revealed) 出现; **it ～d that ...** 结果证实…; **let's wait and see what ～s at the meeting** 咱们等着瞧，看会议上会发生什么事 2 Bot «*plant, leaf*» 蒸腾

transplant /ˌtrænsˈplɑːnt, Amer -ˈplænt/
A *vt* 1 (move) 移栽 ‹*plant, seedling*›; 使…迁移 ‹*population, business*› 2 Med 移植 ‹*organ, tissue, hair*›
B *n* 1 (operation) 移植手术; **to have** *or* **undergo a heart/lung ～** 接受心脏/肺移植手术 2 (organ) 移植器官; (tissue) 移植组织

transplantation /ˌtrænsplɑːnˈteɪʃn, Amer -plæn-/ *n* [u] 移植; **clinical organ ～** 临床器官移植; **the ～ of trees** 树木的移栽

transponder /trænˈspɒndə(r)/ *n* 转发器

transport
A *n* /ˈtrænspɔːt/ 1 [u] (system) 运输; **air/rail ～** 航空/铁路运输; **Ministry** *or* **Department of T～** 交通部; **～ charges/industry** 运输费/运输业/运输工人 2 [u] (conveyance of goods or people) 运送; (means of conveyance) 运输工具; **the ～ of goods by sea** 货物的海运; **his bike is his only means of ～** 自行车是他唯一的代步工具; **～ to and from the airport is included** 往返机场的交通费用包括在内 3 [c] *usu pl* liter (rapture) 狂喜; (fury) 狂怒; **to go into ～s of delight (over sth.)** （对某事）喜不自胜; **his ～s of rage** 他的暴怒 4 [c] Mil (vehicle) 运输车; (ship) 运输船; (aircraft) 运输机
B *vt* /ˌtrænsˈpɔːt/ 1 (convey) 运输 ‹*goods*›; 运送 ‹*people*›; **the van isn't big enough to ～ my furniture** 这辆货车不够大，运不了我的家具 2 (carry) 传送; **blood ～s oxygen round the body** 血液将氧气输送到全身; **the smell ～ed me back to my childhood** 这种气味把我带回童年时代 3 *usu passive* Hist (as punishment) 放逐; **to be ～ed for sheep-stealing** 因为偷羊被流放 4 *usu passive* liter (affect) 使激动万分; **to be ～ed with joy/anger (at seeing sb.)** （见到某人时）高兴极了/气坏了

transportable /ˌtrænsˈpɔːtəbl/ *adj* 可运输的

transportation /ˌtrænspɔːˈteɪʃn/ *n* [u] 1 esp Amer (process) 运输 2 (system) 交通运输系统; (means) 运输工具 3 Brit Hist (as punishment) 流放

transport cafe *n* Brit [供卡车司机进餐的] 路边小餐馆

transporter /ˌtrænsˈpɔːtə(r)/ *n* (vehicle) 运输车; (ship) 运输船; (aircraft) 运输机; **a tank ～** 坦克运输车

Transport Police *n* Brit 铁路警察

transpose /ˌtrænˈspəʊz/ *vt* 1 (cause to change places) 使…调换顺序 ‹*letters, pages, ideas*› 2 Mus 使变调; **to ～ up/down** 调高/调低音调 3 Math 移 ‹*terms*›

transputer /ˌtrænsˈpjuːtə(r), -zˈpjuːtə(r)/ *n* 计算机集成块

transsexual /ˌtrænzˈsekʃʊəl/
A *n* 易性癖者
B *adj* 有易性癖的

transsexualism /ˌtrænzˈsekʃʊəlɪzəm/ *n* [u] 易性癖

trans-ship /ˌtrænsˈʃɪp/ *vt* 转运 ‹*goods, cargo*›

trans-shipment /ˌtrænsˈʃɪpmənt/ *n* [u] 转运

Trans-Siberian Railway /ˌtrænsaɪˈbɪərɪən ˈreɪlweɪ/ *n* **the ～** 西伯利亚大铁路

transverse /ˈtrænzvɜːs/ *adj* 横向的; **a ～ beam/arch/shaft/incision** 横梁/横拱/横柄/横切口; **a ～ engine** 横置发动机; **a ～ wave** 横波

transversely /ˈtrænzvɜːsli/ *adv* 横向地

transvestism /ˌtrænzˈvestɪzəm/ *n* [u] 易装癖

transvestite /ˌtrænzˈvestaɪt/ *n* 易装癖者

trap /træp/
A *n* 1 (snare) 陷阱; (device) 夹子; **to set a ～ for an animal** 布下陷阱诱捕动物; **to lure sb./sth. into a ～** 把某人/某物诱入陷阱; **to fall into a ～** 掉进陷阱; **to spring a ～** 触发夹子 2 fig (stratagem) 圈套; **to fall into the ～ of doing sth.** 陷入做某事的圈套; **to set** *or* **lay a ～** 设圈套 3 dated (carriage) 双轮轻便马车 4 (in waste pipe) 存水弯; **the u-bend ～ was blocked** U形弯管被堵住了 5 (in dog racing) 隔栏 6 sl (mouth) 嘴; **shut your ～!** 闭上你的嘴!
B *vt* (*pres p etc.* **-pp-**) 1 (catch) 设陷阱捕捉 ‹*animal, bird, fish*› 2 (prevent from escaping) 困住 ‹*person*›; **I'm ～ped!** 我被困住了!; **we were ～ped in the lift for four hours** 我们在电梯里困了4小时; **the terrorists ～ped a party of tourists** 恐怖分子劫持了一群游客; **there was air ～ped in the pipe** 管子中有留存的气体; **the child ～ped his fingers in the automatic doors** 孩子被自动门夹住了手指; **the fabric ～s body heat** 这种织物能保暖; **to be/feel ～ped (in a situation/a marriage)** 中圈套/感到中圈套（陷入某情形/一桩婚姻） 3 (trick) 诱骗 ‹*person*›; **to ～ sb. into doing sth.** 诱使某人做某事; **she was ～ped into making an unsuitable marriage** 她被骗进了一桩不相配的婚姻

trapdoor /ˌtræpˈdɔː(r)/ *n* (in floor) 活板门; (in roof) 活动天窗

trapeze /trəˈpiːz, Amer træˈpiːz/ *n* 高空秋千; **to perform on a ～** 在高空秋千上表演

trapeze: ～ **act** *n* 高空秋千表演; ～ **artist** *n* ▸p. 409 高空秋千表演者

trapezium /trəˈpiːzɪəm/ *n* (*pl* **trapezia** /trəˈpiːzɪə/ *or* **～s**) 1 Brit (with two parallel sides) 梯形 2 Amer (with no sides parallel) 不规则四边形

trapezoid /ˈtrəˈpiːzɔɪd/ *n* 1 Brit (with no sides parallel) 不规则四边形 2 Amer (with two parallel sides) 梯形

trapper /ˈtræpə(r)/ *n* 设陷阱捕兽者

trappings /ˈtræpɪŋz/ *npl* 1 (accessories and adornments) 虚饰; **the ～ of ...** …的标志 ‹*wealth, power, success*› 2 (harness) 马饰

Trappist /ˈtræpɪst/
A *adj* 特拉普派的 ‹*monk, monastery*›
B *n* 特拉普派修道士

trap shooting *n* [u] 多向飞靶射击

trash /træʃ/
A *n* [u] 1 Amer (refuse) 垃圾; **to put the ～ out** 把垃圾倒出去 2 colloq (nonsense) 废话; (poor quality art, writing, music) 拙劣作品; **to talk ～** 胡说八道; **the film is (absolute) ～** 这（绝对）是一部垃圾电影; **he thinks her watercolours are just ～** 他认为她的水彩画不过是些平庸之作; **they only sell cheap ～ in that shop** 那家商店只卖廉价的劣质货 3 colloq offensive (person, people) 废物; **don't have anything to do with that family — they're ～** 不要同那家人有任何来往——他们都是下三滥
B *vt* colloq 1 (vandalize, damage) 破坏; **they ～ed his parents' living room** 他们把他父母的起居室弄得乱七八糟 2 (criticize) 严厉批评; **trade associations ～ed the new legislation** 同业公会严厉谴责这项新法规 3 Comput 删除 ‹*file, process*›; 清空 ‹*disk*›

trash can *n* Amer 垃圾箱

trashed /træʃt/ *adj* colloq (on alcohol) 烂醉的; (on drugs) 吸了毒的; **to get ～** (on alcohol) 喝得烂醉; (on drugs) 吸食了毒品

trash: ～ **heap** *n* Amer 垃圾堆; **to throw sb./sth. on the ～ heap, to consign sb./sth. to the ～ heap** fig 抛弃某人/某物; ～ **man** ▸p. 409 *n* Amer 垃圾清理工

trashy /ˈtræʃi/ *adj* colloq pej (cheap) 廉价的 ‹*goods*›; (worthless) 无聊的 ‹*novel, film*›

trauma /ˈtrɔːmə, Amer ˈtraʊ-/ *n* (*pl* **～s** *or* **traumata** /trɔːˈmɑːtə/) 1 [u] (state of shock) 精神创伤; **to suffer from ～** 遭受精神创伤 2 [c] Med (wound) 外伤; **a ～ to the head** 头部损伤; **there are multiple ～s to all parts of the body** 全身上下有多处损伤 3 [c] (distressing experience) 痛苦经历; **what a ～!** 多大的打击啊!

trauma centre *n* 创伤治疗中心

traumatic /trɔːˈmætɪk, Amer traʊ-/ *adj* 1 (emotionally distressing) 令人痛苦的 ‹*event, change*›; **retirement was quite ～ for him** 退休对他来说是一件很痛苦的事; **losing a parent is a ～ experience for a child** 失去父亲或母亲对孩子来说是一种痛苦经历

[2] Med 外伤性的; **he suffered a ~ brain injury** 他遭受了创伤性脑损伤 [3] Psych 精神创伤的

traumatize /'trɔːmətaɪz, Amer 'traʊ-/ *vt* [1] (subject to shock) 使受精神创伤; **innocent civilians are being ~d by repeated air raids** 频繁的空袭使无辜平民在精神上遭受到持续的折磨 [2] Med (cause injury to) 损伤

traumatized /'trɔːmətaɪzd, Amer 'traʊ-/ *adj* 受伤的 ‹*person, mind*›; **emotionally ~** 感情受挫的

travail /'træveɪl, Amer trə'veɪl/ liter *n* **~(s** *pl***)** (work) 艰苦劳动; (effort) 辛勤努力

travel /'trævl/

A *vi* (*pres p etc.* **-ll-**, Amer **-l-**) [1] (journey) 旅行; **to ~ abroad/light/first class** 出国/轻装出行/坐头等舱旅行; **to ~ widely/across Africa/around the world** 广泛游历/穿越非洲/周游世界; **to ~ a long way/all day to reach somewhere** 走很长的路/一整天才到达某地; **to ~ by car/plane** 坐汽车出行/乘飞机旅行; **to ~ to work by train** 坐火车上班; **to ~ on a German passport/a season ticket** 持德国护照/季票旅行; **pilgrims ~ling to Mecca** 去麦加的朝圣者; **are you ~ling to Salzburg?** 你要到萨尔茨堡去吗？; **this is the way to ~!** 这样旅行才像样嘛！ [2] (move) «*object*» 移动; «*sound, light*» 行进; **to ~ at 50 kph/along the motorway** «*vehicle*» 以50公里的时速行驶/在高速公路上行驶; **to be ~ling through a tunnel/down a hill** «*train*» 正在穿越隧道/正在往山下走; **to ~ around the sun** «*planet*» 绕太阳运行; **to ~ at tremendous speed** «*ball*» 以极快的速度移动; **he was really ~ling!** colloq (on feet) 他跑得真快！; (in car) 他开得飞快！; **news ~s fast** 消息传得快; **bad news ~s faster than good** 好事不出门，坏事传千里; **to ~ back/forward in time** 回到过去/进入未来; **her mind ~led back to her youth** 她的思绪回到了青年时代 [3] (withstand journey) **to ~ well** «*foodstuff*» 经得起长途运送; «*person*» 经得起长途旅行; fig «*music, style, humour*» 广为流传; **this wine doesn't ~** 这种葡萄酒经不起长途运输

B *vt* (*pres p etc.* **-ll-**, Amer **-l-**) (traverse) 在…游历 ‹*land*›; (go along) 沿着…走 ‹*road*›; **to ~ the world (with sb.)** （和某人一起）周游世界; **to ~ the highways and byways of Italy** 走遍意大利各地; **to ~ the length and breadth of the country** 走遍全国各地

C *n* [u] [1] (gen) 旅行; **air/sea/space/overland ~** 空中/海上/太空/陆上旅行; **overseas** *or* **foreign ~** 境外旅行; **business/holiday ~** 出差/假日旅行; **~ by car/train/plane** 驾车/乘火车/坐飞机的旅行; **~ to Italy** 到意大利的旅行; **the cost includes ~ to and from the airport** 费用包括往返机场的旅费; **~ broadens the mind** 旅行使人开阔眼界; **~ time/arrangements** 旅行时间/行程安排; **a ~ agency** *or* **service/magazine** 旅行社/旅游杂志; **a ~ bag/case** 旅行包/箱; **~ expenses/grant** 旅行花费/出差补助 [2] Tech 移动; **there's too much ~ on it** 它松动得太厉害了

D **travels** *npl* 旅程; **in the course of my ~s** 在我的旅途中; **on his ~s, he learnt ...** 在旅途中他获悉…; **he's off on his ~s again** 他又外出旅行去了

travel: ~ agency *n* 旅行社; **~ agent** **▸p. 409** *n* 旅行代办人

travelator /'trævəleɪtə(r)/ *n* 自动人行道

travel: ~ bureau *n* **=** **~ agency**; **~ card** *n* Brit 旅游卡; **a weekly/monthly/one-day ~ card** 旅游周卡/月卡/日卡; **~ clock** *n* 旅行闹钟; **~ documents** *npl* 出国旅行证件; **~ flash** *n* 出行简讯; **~ insurance** *n* [u] 旅行保险

-travelled, Amer **-traveled** /'trævld/ *combining form* **a much** *or* **widely~ person** 走南闯北的人; **a well** *or* **much/little~ road** 很多人/很少人走的路

traveller Brit, **traveler** Amer /'trævlə(r)/ *n* [1] (on business, holiday) 旅行者; (regular passenger) 旅客; **~s to Moscow** 到莫斯科的旅客; **a frequent ~ by air** 经常乘飞机出行的人 [2] (salesman) 销售代表; **a ~ in sth.** 某物的销售代表 [3] Brit (gypsy) 吉卜赛人 [4] Brit **= New Age traveller**

traveller: ~'s cheque *n* 旅行支票; **~'s tale** *n* 无稽之谈

travelling Brit, **traveling** Amer /'trævlɪŋ/

A *n* [u] 旅行; **to go ~** 去旅行; **the job involves ~** 这份工作需要出差

B *adj attrib* [1] (mobile) 流动的; **a ~ circus/troupe** 流动马戏团/剧团 [2] (for travellers) 旅行用的; **a ~ companion** 旅伴 [3] (for travel purposes) 旅行的 ‹*allowance*›; **a ~ fellowship** *or* **scholarship** 旅行奖学金

travelling: ~ library *n* 流动图书馆; **~ salesman** **▸p. 409** *n* 销售代表

travel news *n* [u] 交通出行信息

travelogue /'trævəlɒg/ Brit, **travelog** Amer /'-lɔːg/ *n* (film) 旅行纪录片; (book) 游记; (talk) 旅行见闻讲座

travel: ~-sick *adj* (in vehicle) 晕车的; (on boat) 晕船的; (on aircraft) 晕机的; **to be** *or* **get ~-sick** 晕动; **when I fly I tend to get ~-sick** 我常常会晕机; **~-sickness** *n* [u] (in vehicle) 晕车; (on boat) 晕船; (on aircraft) 晕机; **to suffer from ~-sickness** 晕动; **~ writer** *n* 游记作家

traversal /trə'vɜːsəl/ *n* 穿越

traverse /trə'vɜːs/

A *vt* [1] (extend through) «*road, path*» 穿过; **the ancient pilgrims' route ~s the Arabian desert** 古代朝圣者的路线要穿过阿拉伯沙漠 [2] (travel across) 横穿 ‹*desert, mountains*›; 横渡 ‹*ocean*›; «*comet, rocket*» 掠过 ‹*sky*› [3] (move back and forth across) 来回穿行; **searchlights ~d the sky, seeking out enemy aircraft** 探照灯光在夜空里扫来扫去搜寻敌机; **enemy tanks ~d the town during the night** 夜间敌人的坦克在城里开来开去 [4] (in skiing) 作Z字形滑下 ‹*slope*›; (in climbing) 作Z字形攀登 ‹*rock face*›

B *vi* (in climbing) 作Z字形攀登; (in skiing) 作Z字形下滑

C *n* [1] (crossing) 穿越; **his ~ of Persia from north to south** 他从北向南穿越波斯之行 [2] (route, path) 横贯路 [3] (in climbing) Z字形攀登; (in skiing) Z字形下滑

travesty /'trævəsti/ *n* pej 歪曲; **the trial was a ~ of justice** 那次审判是对司法公正的嘲弄; **a ~ of history** 对历史的歪曲

trawl /trɔːl/

A *vt* [1] Fishg 用拖网在…捕鱼 ‹*area, waters*›; 用拖网捕 ‹*fish*› [2] fig (search) 查阅 ‹*reference book*›; 在…搜寻 ‹*crowd*›; **to ~ sth. for sth.** 在某物中寻找某物; **authors often ~ the Bible for a suitable phrase** 作家经常从《圣经》中搜寻合适的短语

B *vi* [1] Fishg **to ~ for sth.** 用拖网捕 ‹*herring*› [2] fig (search) **to ~ (for sth.)** 搜罗（某物）; **to ~ (through a book) for information** （翻遍一本书以）获取信息

C *n* [1] (net) 拖网 [2] Amer (line) **~ (line)** 排钩 [3] fig (search) 搜寻; **to have a ~ through sth.** 找遍某处; **we had a ~ through the old newspaper archives** 我们查遍了旧报档案

trawler /'trɔːlə(r)/ *n* 拖网渔船

trawlerman /'trɔːləmən/ **▸p. 409** *n* 拖网渔民

trawling /'trɔːlɪŋ/ *n* [u] 拖网捕鱼

tray /treɪ/ *n* [1] (for food etc.) 托盘 [2] (salver) [放名片、杯子或作为装饰物的] 浅盘 [3] (for baking) 烤盘; (for roasting) 烤肉盘; (cooling rack) 网眼搁架 [4] (for papers, letters) 文件盘 [5] (for collecting drips) 接油盘

traycloth /'treɪklɒθ, Amer -klɔːθ/ *n* 托盘布

treacherous /'tretʃərəs/ *adj* [1] (traitorous, disloyal) 背叛的; **a ~ person/action** 背叛者/行为; **~ spy/motives/plot** 叛变间谍/动机/阴谋; **a ~ ally** 背信弃义的盟友 [2] (dangerous) 变化莫测的 ‹*conditions, weather, tides*›; 有潜在危险的 ‹*water, ice, slope, cliffs*›

treacherously /'tretʃərəsli/ *adv* [1] (traitorously, disloyally) 背信弃义地 ‹*plot, betray, behave*› [2] (dangerously) 危险地 ‹*slippery, weak*›; (unpredictably) 无法预料地 ‹*uncertain, changeable*›; **~ thin ice** 危险的薄冰层

treacherousness /'tretʃərəsnɪs/ *n* [u] [1] (treachery) 背叛 [2] (dangerousness, unpredictability) 危险

treachery /'tretʃəri/ *n* [u] 背叛; **an act of ~** 变节行为; **~ to sb./sth.** 对某人/某事的背叛

treacle /'triːkl/ *n* [u] esp Brit [1] (molasses) 糖蜜 [2] (golden syrup) 糖浆

treacly /'triːkli/ *adj* [1] esp Brit (treacle-like) 糖蜜似的 ‹*consistency*›; (tasting of treacle) 糖蜜般甜的 ‹*pudding*› [2] fig pej (sickly) 令人腻烦的 ‹*sentiment, sycophancy*›; (sentimental) 过分多情的 ‹*tones, song*›; **a ~ melodrama** 甜腻腻的情节剧

tread /tred/

A *vi* (*pt* **trod**, *pp* **trodden** *or* **trod**) [1] (walk) 行走; **to ~ in/on sth.** 踏进某处/踩到某物; **to ~ all over** 踩上 ‹*flower bed*›; **the horse trod delicately between the puddles** 这匹马在水坑间小心翼翼地行走; **~ softly!** 走路轻一点！; **to ~ carefully (round sth.)** fig 谨慎地谈论（某事物）; **~ carefully when you meet her** fig 你碰到她的时候说话要小心点儿; **to go where others fear to ~** fig 闯入别人不敢涉足的领域; **▸angel 1** [2] esp Brit (squash) 踩踏; **to ~ on sth.** 踩踏某物; **to get trodden on** 被踩了; **to ~ on the brake** 踩刹车; **to ~ on sb.'s heels** 踩某人的脚后跟; fig 紧跟某人

B *vt* (*pt* **trod**, *pp* **trodden** *or* **trod**) [1] (walk) 沿…走 ‹*path, street*›; **to ~ the same path as sb.** fig 走与某人同样的道路; **to ~ a dangerous path** fig 走一条危险的道路; **a well-trodden path** 常有人走的路; fig (to ruin) 重蹈的覆辙; (to success) 成功的老路 [2] (squash) 踩踏; **to ~ ash/mud underfoot** 把灰/泥踩在脚下; **to ~ sth. into the house/carpet** 把某物踩进屋里/踩到地毯上; **to ~ a path across the hillside** 在山坡上踩出一条小径; **the carpet has been trodden bare** 地毯被踩得绒头都秃了; **to ~ grapes** 踩葡萄; **to ~ water** 踩水; fig 裹足不前

C *n* [1] [u] (footstep) 脚步; (sound) 脚步声 [2] [c] (flat surface of stair) 梯面 [3] [u and c] (of wheel, tyre) 胎面; **there's no ~ left on this tyre** 这只轮胎上已经没有花纹了; **~ pattern/mark** 胎面花纹/轮胎印痕 [4] [c] (of shoe) 鞋底

Phrasal verbs

- **tread down** *vt* [**~ sth. down, ~ down sth.**] 踩倒
- **tread out** *vt* [**~ sth. out, ~ out sth.**] 踩灭 ‹*cigarette butt*›

treadle /'tredl/ *n* 踏板

treadmill /'tredmɪl/, **treadwheel** /'tredwiːl/ *ns* [1] esp Hist (driving machinery or for punishment) 踏车 [2] fig (dull routine) 单调乏味的工作; (situation) 令人厌倦的处境; **to be on a ~** 做枯燥的工作 [3] (gym equipment) 跑步机

treas /treʒ/ *abbr* **= treasurer**

treason /'triːzn/ *n* [u] [1] (betrayal of one's country) **(high) ~** 叛国罪; **an act of ~** 叛国行为 [2] 背叛 (disloyalty); **~ against sb./sth.** 对某人/某事物的背叛

treasonable /'triːzənəbl/ *adj* 叛国的 ‹*act, remark, rebellion*›; **to be ~** 是叛国行为

treasure /'treʒə(r)/

A *n* [1] [u] (precious objects) 珍宝; (precious metals) 金银财宝; (gems) 宝石; **buried ~** 埋藏的珍宝 [2] [c] (valuable object) 珍贵之物; (work of art) 珍品; (heirloom) 传家宝; **art/national ~s** 艺术瑰宝/

国宝 3 [c] colloq (much loved person) 心肝宝贝儿; (highly valued person) 珍视的人
B vt 1 (value greatly) 珍爱 ‹*gift, friendship, independence*›; **he ~s his books above everything else** 他爱惜他的书胜过其他任何东西; **I ~ every happy memory of those years** 我珍视那些年的每一个幸福回忆 2 (keep carefully) 珍藏 ‹*souvenir, heirloom*›

treasure: ~ house *n* 1 (building) 宝库; 2 fig (source) 丰富来源; **a ~ house of information** 信息宝库; **~ hunt** *n* 1 (game) 寻宝游戏; 2 (search for treasure) 寻宝; **~ hunter** *n* 1 (in game) 寻宝游戏玩家; 2 (searcher of treasure) 寻宝者

treasurer /ˈtreʒərə(r)/ *n* 1 (of society, club, association) 司库; **to act** *or* **serve as ~** 担任司库 2 Amer (in company) 财务主管

treasure trove *n* 1 [u] Jur (valuables of unknown ownership) 无主财宝 2 [c] fig (store) 宝库; **the entire archaeological site is a ~ of Greek history** 整个考古遗址是一座研究希腊史的宝库; **this book is a ~ of delights** 这本书能给人带来无尽的快乐

treasury /ˈtreʒəri/ *n* 1 (funds) 资金; (revenues) 财政收入; **the treasuries of the Arab States** 阿拉伯国家的财政收入 2 (government department) **the T~** 财政部; **a T~ spokesman** 财政部发言人

Treasury: ~ bill *n* 短期国库券; **~ bond** *n* Amer 国库券; **~ Department** *n* Amer 财政部; **~ Minister** *n* Brit 财政大臣; **~ note** *n* Amer 中期国库券; **~ Secretary** *n* Amer 财政部长

treat /triːt/
A *vt* 1 (behave towards) 对待 ‹*person, animal, object*›; (handle, deal with) 处理 ‹*demand, request, subject, aspect*›; **to ~ sb. well/badly** 对某人好/不好; **to ~ everybody the same** 对大家一视同仁; **to ~ sb. as an enemy/sth. as a joke** 把某人看作敌人/把某事物看作笑话; **I want to be ~ed as an adult** 我想被当作成年人对待; **to ~ sb. like a child/fool** 把某人当成孩子/傻瓜; **to ~ sb. like dirt** 鄙视某人; **stop ~ing this place like a hotel** 不要再把这里当成宾馆了; **to be ~ed with inhuman cruelty/the utmost kindness/respect** 受到残酷虐待/最友善的礼遇/尊敬; **sth. should be ~ed with care/seriousness** 应当小心/严肃对待某事物 2 (pay for) 款待; **go on, have it, I'll ~ you** 来吧, 吃吧, 我请你; **to ~ sb. to sth.** 款待某人某物; **to ~ sb. to lunch at the Savoy/a trip to the circus** 请某人去萨伏伊饭店吃午饭/去看马戏; **to ~ sb. to a long lecture on sth.** 对某人滔滔不绝地谈某事; **we were ~ed to the unusual spectacle of ...** 我们欣赏了…的奇观 3 Med, Vet 治疗 ‹*person, condition*›; **to ~ sb. for sth.** 为某人治疗某疾病; **she's being ~ed for cancer** 她正在接受癌症治疗; **to ~ sb./sth. with sth.** 用某物治疗某人/某病症 4 (subject to a chemical etc. process) 处理; (coat) 涂; **to ~ sth. against damp/fire** 对某物进行防潮/防火处理; **the fabric's been ~ed to make it fire-resistant** 这种织物经过了防火处理; **to ~ sth. with sealant/insecticide** 在某物上喷洒密封剂/杀虫剂; **fence posts ~ed with creosote** 涂过杂酚的围栏桩
B *v refl* **to ~ oneself** 款待自己; **to ~ oneself to sth.** 享用某物; **to ~ oneself to a new hairdo** 换个新发型让自己开心一下
C *n* 1 (pleasure) 乐趣; (event) 款待; (food) 美食; **a birthday ~** 生日款待; **as a special ~, I was allowed to ...** 作为特别优待, 我获准…; **to give sb./oneself a ~** 款待某人/自己; **oysters! what a ~!** 牡蛎! 真是美味佳肴啊! ; **have we got a ~ for you tonight!** 今晚我们为大家准备了一个惊喜! 2 *usu sing* colloq (invitation to meal, outing) 请客; **sb.'s ~** 某人请客; **(this is** *or* **it's) my ~** (是) 我请客; **to stand sb. a ~** 做东请某人; **to stand ~ (for twenty people)** 请 (二十个人的) 客 3 Brit colloq **a ~** (good or well) 棒极了; **to look a ~** 看起来棒极了; **it worked a ~** 这非常有效; **the gift/dessert went down a ~ (with them)** 礼物/甜点大受 (他们的) 欢迎

treatable /ˈtriːtəbl/ *adj* 可治疗的 ‹*disease, condition*›

treatise /ˈtriːtɪs, -ɪz/ *n* 论文; **a ~ on sth.** 关于某研究课题的论文; **a scholarly** *or* **an academic ~** 学术论文

treatment /ˈtriːtmənt/ *n* 1 [u] (handling) 对待; **special/preferential ~** 特殊待遇/优待; **equal ~ for men and women** 男女平等待遇; **it won't stand up to rough ~** 对待此物不可粗手粗脚; **~ of sb./sth.** 对待某人/某事物的态度; **his disdainful ~ of me/my suggestion** 他对我/我的建议的藐视; **to give sb. the (full) ~** colloq 对某人热情备至 2 [u] (discussion) 探讨; (analysis) 论述; **an in-depth ~ of the topic** 对该话题的深入探讨 3 [u and c] Med, Vet 治疗; **preventive/dental ~** 预防性/牙科治疗; **a drug/new ~** 药物/新型疗法; **a course of ~** 疗程; **the patient/infection isn't responding to ~** 治疗对病人/感染不起作用; **~ for sth.** 针对…的疗法 ‹*disease*›; **to receive** *or* **undergo ~ (for sth.)** (为某病症) 接受治疗 4 [u and c] Chem, Ind (process) 处理; (substance) 防护剂; **the ~ of sewage, sewage ~** 污水处理; **various ~s can be applied to protect the wood** 可以涂抹多种防护剂来保护木材; **~ against** *or* **for damp/rust** 防潮/防锈处理; **~ with sth.** 用某材料作的处理

treatment: ~ plant *n* 污水处理厂; **~ room** *n* 治疗室

treaty /ˈtriːti/ *n* 1 Pol 条约; **a peace ~** 和平协定; **the T~ of Rome** 《罗马条约》; **to draw up/sign a ~** 起草/签署条约; **a ~ banning chemical weapons** 禁止使用化学武器的公约; **a ~ with sb.** 同某人签署的条约; **a ~ between ...** …之间签署的条约 2 Jur 合同; **for sale by private ~** 待售, 私下订协议

treble /ˈtrebl/ ▸ **p. 288**
A *adj* 1 (triple) 三重的 ‹*digit*›; 三倍的 ‹*measure*›; **~ nine, five, six** 99956; **to reach ~ figures** 达到三位数; **this blanket is ~ thickness** 这条毯子有三层厚 2 Mus 高音的; **a ~ voice** 男童声高音; **a ~ recorder/aria/line** 高音竖笛/咏叹调/谱线
B *adv* 三倍地; **~ the amount/size** 三倍量/三倍大
C *n* 1 [u] Audio (high-frequency sound) 高音 2 [c] Mus (voice) 高音; (boy singer) 高音男童歌手 3 [c] (in darts) 正中内圈的一投 4 [c] (drink) 三倍分量的酒
D *vt* 使成三倍; **Iran has ~d its oil output** 伊朗的石油产量增加了两倍
E *vi* 成三倍; **to ~ in size** 大小增加两倍

treble: ~ chance *n* Brit 三重彩投注; **~ clef** *n* 高音谱号

trebly /ˈtrebli/
A *adv* 三倍地; **to work ~ hard** 极其努力地工作
B *adj* colloq 尖声的; **~ sound/quality** 尖声/高音音质

tree /triː/
A *n* 树木; **an apple/a cherry ~** 苹果/樱桃树; **the ~ of life/knowledge** 生命/智慧之树; **to be up a ~** esp Amer colloq 骑虎难下; **to not see the wood for the ~s** 见树不见林; **to grow on ~s** colloq (be easily obtained) 容易得到; (plentiful) 多得很; **money doesn't grow on ~s** 钱来之不易; **jobs don't grow on ~s** 工作可不是遍地都有; **to get to/to be at the top of the ~** 达到/处于最高地位; **if you work hard, you'll get to the top of the ~** 如果你努力工作, 就会成为人上人; **to be out of one's ~** colloq (completely stupid) 愚不可及; (mad) 发疯
B *vt* Amer 1 Hunt 把…赶上树 ‹*animal*› 2 fig colloq (force into difficult situation) 把…逼进困境

tree: ~-covered *adj* 林木覆盖的; **~ diagram** *n* 树形图; **~ fern** *n* 桫椤; **~house** *n* 树屋; **~-hugger** *n* colloq pej 抱树人 [指热衷环保的人]

treeless /ˈtriːlɪs/ *adj* 无树木的

tree: ~line *n* 林木线; **~-lined** *adj* 树木成行的 ‹*street, river*›; **~ ring** *n* 年轮; **~ stump** *n* 树桩; **~ surgeon** ▸ **p. 409** *n* 树木修补专家; **~ surgery** *n* [u] 树木修补; **~tops** *n* (branches) 树梢; (silhouette) 树高线; **~ trunk** *n* 树干

trefoil /ˈtrefɔɪl/ *n* 1 Bot 三叶草 2 Archit 三叶形装饰

trek /trek/
A *n* 1 (long journey) 长途旅行; **to make** *or* **do a ~** 作长途旅行; **a mule ~** 骑骡旅行 2 fig (laborious trip) 令人困乏的旅程; **it's a bit of a ~** colloq 这段路有点儿累人
B *vi* (*pres p etc.* **-kk-**) 1 (make a long journey) 长途跋涉; **to ~ across** *or* **through** 长途跋涉穿过 ‹*desert, jungle*› 2 colloq (walk, hike) 长距离步行; **I had to ~ into town** 我不得不步行到市中心

trekking /ˈtrekɪŋ/ ▸ **p. 307** *n* [u] 1 (walking) 远足; **to go ~** 去远足 2 (riding) 骑马旅行

trellis /ˈtrelɪs/ *n* (structure) 格子结构; (pattern) 格子图案; (as screen) 格子屏风; (for climbing plants) 棚架

trelliswork /ˈtrelɪswɜːk/ *n* [u] 格子细工; **a ~ fence** 格子篱笆

tremble /ˈtrembl/
A *vi* 1 (vibrate, quiver) «*leaves, walls*» 颤动 2 (shake involuntarily) «*person, hand, voice*» 颤抖; **to ~ with** *or* **from sth.** 因某事物颤抖; **the poor dog was trembling with cold** 那只可怜的狗冻得直哆嗦; **to ~ all over** 浑身发抖 3 (be apprehensive) 担心; **to ~ at sth.** 为某事物忧虑; **how much does he owe? — I ~ to think!** colloq 他欠了多少钱? ——我一想到这个就不寒而栗!
B *n* 1 (tremor, vibration) 震动; **a ~ ran through the vessel as it changed course** 船在改变航道时猛地晃了一下 2 (quiver from fear, excitement) 颤抖; **to be all of a ~** colloq 浑身哆嗦; **she was all of a ~ at the prospect of meeting the prince** 想到就要见到王子, 她浑身颤抖

trembling /ˈtremblɪŋ/ *n* [u] (of body, voice) 颤抖; (of leaves) 颤动

tremendous /trɪˈmendəs/ *adj* 1 (great) 极大的; (intense) 强烈的; **a ~ amount of sth.** 大量的某物; **it costs a ~ amount** 它花了一大笔钱; **it makes a ~ difference to me** 这对于我来说太重要了 2 (marvellous, excellent) 极好的; **how do you feel after your operation? — ~!** 手术后你感觉怎么样? ——棒极了! ; **a ~ achievement** 了不起的成就

tremendously /trɪˈmendəsli/ *adv* 1 (immensely) 非常; **~ rich/big/pleased/proud** 极富有/特别大/非常高兴/极其自豪的; **to admire/respect/like sb. ~** 非常钦佩/尊敬/喜欢某人; **to be ~ impressed** 印象很深 2 (excellently) 极好地; **the team are playing ~** 队员们表现很棒

tremolo /ˈtreməlәʊ/ *n* 1 (of instrument, voice) 颤音; **to play/sing with a ~** 奏出/唱出颤音 2 (on guitar) **~ (arm)** 震音杆 3 (in organ) 震音音栓

tremor /ˈtremə(r)/ *n* 1 (trembling) (in body, voice) 颤抖; (in sound) 颤动; **a slight ~ in her voice** 她嗓音的轻微颤抖 2 (of delight, fear etc.) 颤栗; **he felt a ~ of fear** 他感到一阵恐惧 3 Geol (slight earthquake) **(earth) ~** 微震

tremulous /ˈtremjʊləs/ *adj* liter 1 (trembling) 颤抖的 ‹*person, voice, hand*› 2 (timid) 胆怯的 ‹*smile, glance*›; (nervous) 紧张的 ‹*entreaty*›; **~ hope** 怯生生的希望

tremulously /ˈtremjʊləsli/ *adv* liter 1 (with trembling voice) 声音颤抖地 ‹*say, plead*› 2 (timidly) 胆怯地 ‹*smile, suggest*›

trench /trentʃ/ *n* 1 (ditch) 沟渠; **to dig/fill in a ～** 挖/填沟 2 Mil 战壕; **in the ～es** 在堑壕中

trenchant /ˈtrentʃənt/ *adj* 尖锐的 ‹*remark, observation, humour*›; 有力的 ‹*debate*›; 有效的 ‹*management*›; **～ wit** 机智

trenchantly /ˈtrentʃəntli/ *adv* 毫不含糊地 ‹*refute, critical, hostile*›; 有力地 ‹*argue, retort*›; **～ held opinions** 明确的意见

trench coat *n* [有宽松腰带、双排纽扣的] 军装式雨衣

trencherman /ˈtrentʃəmən/ *n* (*pl* **trenchermen** /ˈtrentʃəmən/) hum 胃口好的人; **all my family are good trenchermen** 我们全家人胃口都很好

trench: ～ fever ▸ **p. 377** *n* [u] 战壕热 [由虱子传播的传染病]; **～ foot** *n* [u] 壕沟足 [因在冷水或泥水中浸泡时间过长而造成足部变黑、表皮组织坏死]; **～ warfare** *n* [u] 堑壕战

trend /trend/

A *n* 1 (tendency) (in events, prices) 趋势; (in allegiance, public opinion) 倾向; **an upward/downward ～** 上升/下降的趋势; **if the present ～ continues** 如果当前的趋势持续下去; **a ～ in medicine/education** 医学/教育方面的趋势; **a ～ towards doing sth.** 做某事的趋势; **the ～ is towards democracy** 趋势是倾向于民主化; **a ～ away from sth.** 背离某事物的倾向 2 (fashion) 时新款式; **a fashion ～** 流行款式; **to set a new ～** 创新风; **to follow the ～** 赶时髦

B *vi* 趋向; **to ～ higher/lower** 趋向升高/下降; **house prices are ～ing rapidly downwards** 房价呈迅速下行趋势

trendiness /ˈtrendɪnɪs/ *n* [u] colloq 时髦

trend: ～setter *n* 创新风者; **a real fashion ～setter** 真正的新潮倡导者; **～setting** *adj* 创新风的

trendy /ˈtrendi/ colloq

A *adj* 时髦的 ‹*clothes, opinion, art*›; **army haircuts are quite ～ these days** 如今军人发型很时髦

B *n* usu pej 时髦客

trepidation /ˌtrepɪˈdeɪʃn/ *n* [u] (fear) 惊悸; (anxiety) 不安; **it was with some ～ that I confronted my manager** 我有些惶恐不安地来到经理面前; **in ～** 战战兢兢地

trespass /ˈtrespəs/

A *vi* 1 (enter unlawfully) 擅自进入; **to ～ on sth.** 非法侵入某处; **'no ～ing'** "非请莫入" 2 **to ～ on sth.** (take advantage of) 滥用某物; **to ～ on sb.'s time** 占用某人的时间; **to ～ on sb.'s rights** 侵害某人的权利; **to ～ on sb.'s privacy** 侵犯某人的隐私

B *n* 1 [u] (unlawful entry) 擅自进入; **to sue (sb.) for ～** (对某人) 提起非法侵入起诉 2 [c] (unlawful act) 侵害行为; **to be guilty of a ～** 犯侵害罪 3 [c] archaic or liter (sin) 罪过; (offence) 过错

trespasser /ˈtrespəsə(r)/ *n* 擅自进入者; **'～s will be prosecuted'** "非请莫入, 擅闯必究"

tress /tres/ liter

A *n* 一绺长发

B **tresses** *npl* 长发; **her golden ～es** 她的金色长发

trestle /ˈtresl/ *n* 支架; **to rest on ～s** 搁在支架上

trestle table *n* 支架台

triad /ˈtraɪæd/ *n* 1 (group of three) (of people) 三人组合; (of things) 三件套 2 Mus 三和弦 3 (*also* **Triad**) (secret society) 三合会 [源于中国的黑社会组织]; (member) 三合会成员

trial /ˈtraɪəl/

A *n* 1 [u and c] Jur 审判; **to go on** *or* **stand ～ (for sth./doing sth.)** (因某事/做某事) 受审; **to come up for ～ (for sth./doing sth.)** (因某事/做某事) 出庭受审; **to be awaiting ～** 候审; **to bring** *or* **commit sb. to ～, to send sb. for ～** 把某人送交法院审判; **to put sb. on ～** 审判某人; **to hold** *or* **conduct a ～** 进行审判; **at sb.'s ～** 在某人受审时; **(to receive) a fair ～** (接受) 公正的审判; **without ～** 未经审判; **～ by jury/media** 陪审团讯问/媒体审判; **(to be subjected to) ～ by ordeal** Hist (交由) 神明裁决; **～ proceedings/report** 审讯程序/报道 2 [u and c] (test) (of product, drug, process) 试验; (of applicant, recruit) 试用; **medical/clinical ～s** 医学/临床试验; **to carry out** *or* **conduct ～s (on sth.)** (对某物) 进行试验; **to put sth. through ～s** 试用某物; **to use sth. free on ～ for 10 days** 免费试用某物 10 天; **to give sb. a ～ (as sth.)** 试用某人 (担任某职); **(to be) on ～** (在) 试用中; **to take** *or* **employ sb. on ～** 试聘某人; **～ and error** 反复试验; **you learn to teach by ～ and error** 通过反复摸索, 才能学会教书; **a ～ flight/marriage** 试飞/试婚; **for ～ purposes only** 仅供试用; **on a ～ basis** 试验性地; **(for) a ～ period** 试用期 3 [c] (difficulty) 困难; (trying person or thing) 考验; **to be a (sore) ～** 让人伤脑筋; **the ～s of (real) life/old age** (现实) 生活中的磨难/年老的痛苦; **～s and tribulations** 艰难困苦 4 [c] *usu pl* esp Brit (competition) 竞赛 [尤指选拔赛]; **to compete in ～s** 参加选拔赛; **to hold ～s** 举办竞赛; **a ～ of strength** 角力

B *vt* (*pres p etc.* **-ll-**, Amer **-l-**) 试用 ‹*product*›

trial: ～ attorney *n* Amer 出庭辩护律师; **～ balance** *n* 试算表; **～ balloon** *n* Amer (measure) 试探性措施; (statement) 试探性言论; **～ court** *n* esp Amer 初审法院; **～ judge** *n* 承审法官; **～ jury** *n* [6到12人组成的] 小陪审团; **～ run** *n* 1 Aut 试行; **to take a car for a ～ run** 试车; 2 Ind, Tech 试验; **to give sth. a ～ run** 试验某物; **to do a ～ run** 作试运行; 3 Theat 试演; 4 TV 试播; 5 fig (rehearsal, practice) (for exam) 预考; (for competition) 预赛

triangle /ˈtraɪæŋgl/ *n* 1 (figure) 三角形; (shape) 三角形物体 2 Mus 三角铁 3 (group of three people) 三人组; **a love ～** 三角恋爱; **the (eternal) ～** 三角关系 4 Amer (set square) 三角板

triangular /traɪˈæŋgjʊlə(r)/ *adj* 1 (triangle-shaped) 三角形的 ‹*object, formation, pattern*› 2 (involving three people) 三人的; (involving three parties) 三方的; **a ～ contest/relationship** 三方角逐/三角关系

triangulate /traɪˈæŋgjʊleɪt/ *vt* 对…作三角测量 ‹*area, site*›

triangulation /traɪˌæŋgjʊˈleɪʃn/ *n* [u] 三角测量

triangulation: ～ point *n* = **trig point**; **～ station** *n* (on hill) 三角测量站; (on map) 三角测量标点

Triassic /traɪˈæsɪk/

A *adj* (of the period) 三叠纪的; (of the rock system) 三叠系的

B *n* **the ～** (period) 三叠纪; (rock system) 三叠系

triathlete /traɪˈæθliːt/ *n* 三项全能运动员

triathlon /traɪˈæθlɒn/ *n* 三项全能运动

tribal /ˈtraɪbl/ *adj* 1 (of tribes) 部落的 ‹*customs, chiefs, wars*› 2 fig pej (tending to form groups) 有组织集团倾向的; (loyal to a group) 集团意识强的; **～ loyalty/society** 对集团的效忠/宗法社会

tribalism /ˈtraɪbəlɪzəm/ *n* [u] 1 (customs) 部落习俗; (way of life) 部落生活方式 2 fig pej (strong group loyalty) 同族意识

tribe /traɪb/ *n* 1 Anthrop dated 部落; **a primitive/nomadic ～** 原始/游牧部落 2 fig colloq (group) 大群 3 fig pej (close-knit group) 紧密联系的群体

tribesman /ˈtraɪbzmən/ *n* (*pl* **tribesmen**) 部落成员

tribeswoman /ˈtraɪbzwʊmən/ *n* (*pl* **tribeswomen**) 部落妇女

tribulation /ˌtrɪbjʊˈleɪʃn/

A *n* [u] 苦难

B **tribulations** *npl* (mental hardships) 苦恼; (physical hardships) 困苦; **trials and ～s** 艰难困苦

tribunal /traɪˈbjuːnl/ *n* 1 Brit (adjudicating body) 仲裁机构 2 (court) 法庭

tribune /ˈtrɪbjuːn/ *n* 讲坛

tributary /ˈtrɪbjʊtəri, Amer -teri/ ▸ **p. 663**

A *n* 支流

B *modif* 支流的; **a ～ stream** *or* **river** 支流; (secondary) 次要的; (subsidiary) 辅助的

tribute /ˈtrɪbjuːt/ *n* 1 [c and u] (speech) 颂词; (act) 致敬; (gift) 礼物; **a floral ～** 葬礼献花; **to pay ～ to sb./sth.** 赞扬某人/某事物; **as a ～ to my late father** 为了悼念我去世的父亲; **in silent ～ to sb.** 为某人默哀 2 [c] (credit) 体现; **to be a ～ to sb.'s skill/generosity/determination** 显示出某人的技艺/慷慨/决心 3 [u] Hist (payment to ruler) (in cash) 贡金; (in kind) 贡品; **to pay ～ to sb.** 向某人进贡; **to exact ～ from sb.** 向某人索取贡品

tribute band *n* 模仿乐队

trice /traɪs/ *n* **in a ～** 转眼之间

tricentenary /ˌtraɪsenˈtiːnəri/ *n* = **tercentenary**

triceps /ˈtraɪseps/ *n* (*pl* **triceps**) 三头肌

trick /trɪk/

A *n* 1 (cunning or deceitful act) 诡计; (gimmick) 花招; **a mean/clever ～** 卑鄙的伎俩/巧妙的花招; **it's a ～!** 那是一个骗局!; **it's the oldest ～ in the book** 那是众人皆知的老把戏; **to try every ～ in the book** 使尽浑身解数; **a ～ of the light** 光线引起的错觉; **not** *or* **never to miss a ～** 对一切了如指掌 2 (mischievous act) 恶作剧; **he always pulls that ～** 他老是开那种玩笑; **to play a ～ on sb.** 捉弄某人; **my memory plays ～s on me sometimes** 我的记忆有时会发生紊乱; **he's up to his old ～s** 他又要起了老花招; **the computer is up to its ～s again** 电脑又犯老毛病了 3 (stunt) (by conjuror) 魔术; (by juggler or animal) 绝技; **to do (conjuring) ～s** 变魔术; **to perform a ～** 表演绝技; **to have a ～ up one's sleeve** 还有绝招没使出来; **to do the ～** 管用; **the pills seem to have done the ～** 药片好像起效了; **how's ～s?** colloq 最近过得怎么样?; **～ photography/a ～ shot** 特技摄影/镜头; **～ riding** 特技马术表演 4 (knack, technique) 技巧; (secret) 窍门; **there's no special ～ to it** 这没有什么特殊的技巧; **the ～ here is to ...** 这里的窍门在于…; **the ～s of the trade** 门道; **to have a ～ of doing sth.** 掌握做某事的诀窍; **to know a ～ or two** *or* **a few ～s (about sth.)** 精通 (某事) 5 (habit) 习惯; **to have a** *or* **the ～ of doing sth.** 有做某事的习惯 6 (in card games) [桥牌等的] 一圈; **to win/take a ～** 赢/玩一圈 7 sl (prostitute's client) 嫖客; **to turn ～s** «*prostitute*» 接客卖淫

B *vt* 欺骗; **I've been ～ed!** 我上当了!; **to ～ sb. into doing sth.** 欺骗某人做某事; **to ～ sb. into thinking that ...** 骗某人以为…; **to ～ sb. out of sth.** 从某人处骗走某物; **to ～ one's way past the guard/into the club** 骗过保安/蒙混进入夜总会

C *adj attrib* Amer 虚弱的 ‹*shoulder*›; **he has a ～ knee** 他的膝盖不能吃力

Phrasal verb

• **trick out**

A *vt* [**～ sb. out, ～ out sb.**] *usu passive* 精心打扮; **to be all ～ed out (in one's best clothes)** 穿着最好的衣服

B *v refl* **to ～ oneself out** 精心打扮; **he ～ed himself out in tails (for the wedding)** 他特意换上了一套燕尾服 (去参加婚礼)

trick cyclist *n* 1 (rider) 特技自行车手 2 Brit hum (psychiatrist) 精神病医生

trickery /ˈtrɪkəri/ *n* [u] pej 欺骗; **to resort to ～** 要花招; **by ～** 用诡计

trickiness /ˈtrɪkɪnɪs/ *n* [u] (difficulty of manoeuvre, operation) 困难; (complexity of problem, question, situation) 复杂; (awkwardness) 棘手

trickle /ˈtrɪkl/

A *vi* 1 (flow slowly) 小股流淌; **to ～ down sth.** 沿着某物滴下; **to ～ down one's cheeks**

«*tears*» 缓缓流下面颊; **to ~ out of** *or* **from sth.** 从…中淌出; **blood ~d out of the wound** 血从伤口处流出来; **to ~ away into the drain** 缓缓流入下水道; **to ~ into sth.** 滴入某物 **2** fig (move gradually) 缓缓移动; **to ~ down the street** «*people*» 沿着街道缓慢行进; **to ~ away from a place** 从一个地方慢慢离开; **to ~ back to the bus** 陆续返回公共汽车; **to ~ out of/into a building/area** 缓缓走出/进入一座建筑/一地区; **cash is trickling out of the country** 现金正从该国悄然流出; **the news started to ~ out** 消息开始一点一点传出来

B *vt* 使…滴下 ‹*liquid*›; **to ~ sth. into/on (to) sth.** 把某物滴到某物里/上; **he ~d water over the leaves** 他在叶子上洒了几滴水

C *n* **1** lit (of liquid, powder) 细流; **the stream has shrunk to a mere** *or* **bare ~** 小溪水道愈来愈窄，变成了涓涓细流 **2** fig (small amount) (of people, vehicles) 稀稀拉拉; (of information, offers, business, cash) 一点点; **a steady ~ of investment** 源源不断的小额注资; **a slow ~ of orders** 稀稀拉拉的订单; **to be down to a ~** 只剩下一点点; **traffic/the number of refugees dwindled to a ~** 车流/难民数量慢慢变得稀少

Phrasal verbs

- **trickle down** *vi* «*wealth, money*» 下渗; **is any of the fat cats' wealth trickling down to me?** 大款的财富惠及我了吗?
- **trickle in** *vi* «*liquid, money*» 涓涓流入; «*people*» 陆续进入; **orders are trickling in** 订单来得稀稀拉拉
- **trickle out** *vi* (emerge) «*liquid, information*» 泄漏; «*people*» 陆续逃脱

trickle charger *n* 涓流充电器

trickle down

A *n* [u] 滴漏论 [因最富人群的财富增加逐渐惠及最穷人群]

B **trickle-down** *modif* 滴漏的 ‹*theory, effect*›

trick or treat

A *n* [u] **'~!'** "不请吃就捣蛋!" [儿童在万圣节向邻居索要糖果的用语]

B *vi* 敲邻居门要糖果 [万圣节风俗]; **to go trick or treating** 去敲邻居门要糖果

trick: ~ or treater *n* 敲邻居门要糖果的人; **~ question** *n* 使人上当的问题

trickster /ˈtrɪkstə(r)/ *n* pej 骗子

tricky /ˈtrɪki/ *adj* **1** (difficult) 困难的 ‹*operation, decision*›; (complex) 复杂的 ‹*problem*›; (awkward) 棘手的 ‹*situation*›; **it is ~ to find/predict ...** 找到/预测…很难 **2** pej (sly, wily) 狡猾的

tricolour Brit, **tricolor** Amer /ˈtrɪkələ(r), Amer ˈtraɪkʌlə(r)/ *n* 三色旗; **the T~** (French national flag) 三色旗 [即法国国旗]

tricorne /ˈtraɪkɔːn/ *n* **~ (hat)** 三角帽

tricycle /ˈtraɪsɪkl/ *n* **1** (cycle) 三轮脚踏车 **2** (motorized vehicle) 三轮摩托车

trident /ˈtraɪdnt/ *n* **1** (spear) [尤指作为海神标志的] 三叉戟 **2** **Trident** (missile) [美国的] 三叉戟弹道导弹

tried /traɪd/

A *pt, pp* ▸ **try A, B**

B *adj* **~ and tested** 经过考验的

triennial /traɪˈenɪəl/

A *adj* **1** (every three years) 三年一次的 ‹*event*› **2** (lasting three years) 三年期的 ‹*agreement*›

B *n* 三年一次的活动

trier /ˈtraɪə(r)/ *n* colloq 一贯努力的人

trifle /ˈtraɪfl/ *n* **1** [c and u] Brit Culin 屈莱弗甜食 [由松糕、水果和雪利酒上覆蛋奶冻等制成] **2** [c] (triviality) 琐事; (problem) 小问题; (article, gift) 不值钱的东西; **to waste time on ~s** 在鸡毛蒜皮的小事上浪费时间 **3** [c] (small amount) 少量; (of money) 少量的钱; **a ~** (slightly, somewhat) 稍微; **a ~ dull/long** 有点儿单调/长; **a ~ breathlessly** 稍稍气喘地; **to speed up/slow down a ~** 稍微快一点/慢一点

Phrasal verb

- **trifle with** *vt* [**~ with sth.**] **1** (treat lightly) 怠慢; **she's not someone to be ~d with!** 她这个人可怠慢不得! **2** (toy with) 摆弄; **to ~ with sb.'s affections** 玩弄某人的感情

trifling /ˈtraɪflɪŋ/ *adj* 琐碎的 ‹*detail*›; 无足轻重的 ‹*excuse, miscalculation*›; 微不足道的 ‹*sum, cost*›; **a ~ matter/error/misunderstanding** 小事/小错/小误会

trifocal /traɪˈfəʊkl/

A *adj* 三焦距的 ‹*lens, spectacles*›

B **trifocals** *npl* 三焦距眼镜

trigger /ˈtrɪɡə(r)/

A *n* **1** lit (on gun) 扳机; **to pull** *or* **squeeze** *or* **press the ~** 扣扳机; **to be quick on the ~** 反应迅速 **2** (starting mechanism) 触发器 **3** fig (event) 触发因素; **to act as** *or* **be the ~ for sth.** 是某事的导火线

B *vt* = **trigger off**

Phrasal verb

- **trigger off** *vt* [**~ off sth.**] **1** lit (set off) 启动 ‹*mechanism*›; 引发 ‹*explosion*› **2** fig (cause) 引起 ‹*reaction, debate, strike*›

trigger-happy *adj* colloq **1** (quick to shoot) 动辄开枪的; **to be ~** 爱动武 **2** fig (impulsive) 冲动的 ‹*person, temperament*›

trigonometrical /ˌtrɪɡənəˈmetrɪkl/ *adj* 三角学的

trigonometry /ˌtrɪɡəˈnɒmətri/ *n* [u] 三角学

trig point /ˈtrɪɡ pɔɪnt/ *n* [测绘时设的] 三角参照点

trigraph /ˈtraɪɡrɑːf, Amer -ɡræf/ *n* [表示一个音的] 三合字母

trike /traɪk/ *n* colloq 三轮自行车

trilateral /traɪˈlætərəl/ *adj* 三边的 ‹*agreement, trade, treaty*›; 三方的 ‹*negotiations, alliance*›

trilby /ˈtrɪlbi/ *n* esp Brit 软毡帽

trilingual /traɪˈlɪŋɡwəl/ *adj* 三语的

trill /trɪl/

A *n* **1** Mus 颤音 **2** Ling 颤辅音 [尤指 "r"]

B *vt* **1** Mus 用颤音唱 ‹*song*›; 用颤音奏 ‹*notes*›; 用颤音说 ‹*words*› **2** Ling 用颤音发 ‹*consonant*›

C *vi* «*person*» 用颤音唱歌; «*bird*» 啭鸣

trillion /ˈtrɪlɪən/

A *n* 万亿

B **trillions** *npl* colloq 大量; **~s of stars** 无数颗星星

C *adj* **1** (a million million) 万亿的; **a ~ dollars** 一万亿美元 **2** colloq (lots of) 大量的; **a ~ people** 无数人

trilobite /ˈtraɪləbaɪt, ˈtrɪ-/ *n* 三叶虫 [海洋古生物]

trilogy /ˈtrɪlədʒi/ *n* **1** (series of three works) 三部曲; **a ~ of short stories/novels/films** 短篇小说/长篇小说/电影三部曲 **2** (group of three) 三件相关联的事物

trim /trɪm/

A *vt* (pres p etc. **-mm-**) **1** (cut) 修剪 ‹*hair, nails, hedge, lawn*›; 修 ‹*hem*›; **to ~ (the wick of) a lamp** 剪灯花; **to ~ a plank of wood to size** 把一块木料加工成要求的尺寸 **2** (reduce) 削减 ‹*budget, expenditure, workforce*›; 缩短 ‹*text, speech*›; **to ~ sth. to the bone** 把某物减少到最低限度 **3** (remove) 除去 ‹*excess, amount, time*›; **to ~ sth. off** *or* **from sth.** 从某物中去除某物; **to ~ 5% off the budget** 削减 5% 的预算; **to ~ six minutes off a speech** 把讲话缩短 6 分钟 **4** (decorate) 装饰; Culin 修整 ‹*turkey, joint of meat*›; **a coat ~med with fur** 毛皮镶边大衣; **to ~ a shop window** Amer 装点橱窗 **5** Naut 调整…以适应风向 ‹*sail, vessel*› **6** Naut, Aviat (adjust balance of) 使…配平 ‹*ship, aircraft*› **7** (modify) 调整…以适应形势 ‹*opinions, beliefs*›; **to ~ one's words to fit party policy** 使言论与本党的方针政策保持一致

B *vi* (pres p etc. **-mm-**) 见风使舵

C *n* **1** [c] (cut) 修剪; **to give sb./sth. a ~** 为某人剪发/把某物修剪一下; **to need a ~** 需要修剪 **2** [u] (good condition) **to be in ~** 状况良好; **to be out of ~** 乱糟糟; **he's in good ~** 他身体很好; **to get/keep oneself in ~** 使自己/保持身体健康; **to get the garden in ~** 把花园收拾干净 **3** [u and c] (border) (on garment, linen) 饰边; (on woodwork) 贴脸; (on furniture) 镶边; **a red blazer with gold ~** 镶金边的红色夹克; **metal/wood ~** 金属边饰/木包角 **4** [u] Aut 装饰; **interior/exterior ~** 内部/外部装饰; **a car with grey ~** 灰色座椅的汽车 **5** [u] Naut (of ship) 适航状态; **to be in ~** 装备停当; **to be out of ~** 未装备停当 **6** [u] Aviat 配平

D *adj* **1** (neat) 整洁的 ‹*person, appearance, ship*›; 整齐的 ‹*hair*›; 匀整的 ‹*outline*›; **to be neat and ~** 干干净净 **2** (slim) 苗条的 ‹*figure, body*›; 纤细的 ‹*waistline*›

Phrasal verbs

- **trim away** *vt* = **trim off**
- **trim down**

A *vi* 减肥; **to ~ down from 24 stone to 18** 体重从 24 英石减到 18 英石

B *vt* [**~ sth. down, ~ down sth.**] 削减 ‹*budget, workforce, figure*›; 降低 ‹*estimate, ambitions*›

- **trim off** *vt* [**~ off sth., ~ sth. off**] 修剪 ‹*excess, hair, wick*›; **to ~ the fat off the meat** 切掉肉上的肥膘

trimaran /ˈtraɪməræn/ *n* 三体帆船

trimester /traɪˈmestə(r)/ *n* **1** (three months) [尤指妊娠的] 三月期 **2** Amer Sch, Univ [三学期学年的] 学期

trimmer /ˈtrɪmə(r)/ *n* **1** (for hedges, hair, lawn, carpets) 修剪机; (for timber) 截板锯 **2** pej (person) 见风使舵者

trimming /ˈtrɪmɪŋ/

A *n* [u] (on clothing) 镶边; (on curtains, furnishings) 装饰品

B **trimmings** *npl* **1** (decorative additions to a garment) 镶边饰物 **2** (accompaniments to a meal) 配菜; **beef with all the ~s** 备有各种配料的牛排 **3** colloq (extra items) 附件; **the basic car without the ~s** 没有选装件的基本型汽车; **a church wedding with all the ~s** 排场奢华的教堂婚礼 **4** (offcuts) (of pastry) 碎屑; (of fish, meat) 碎肉; (of fabric, paper) 边角料

trimness /ˈtrɪmnɪs/ *n* [u] **1** (neatness of appearance) (of person) 整洁; (of house, garden) 整齐 **2** (slimness of figure) 苗条

trim size *n* [书页切除毛边后的] 切净尺寸

Trinidad /ˈtrɪnɪdæd/ *pr n* 特立尼达岛

Trinidad and Tobago /ˌtrɪnɪdæd ən təˈbeɪɡəʊ/ *pr n* 特立尼达和多巴哥

Trinidadian /ˌtrɪnɪˈdædɪən/ ▸ **p. 503**

A *adj* (of Trinidad) 特立尼达岛的; (of the people) 特立尼达岛人的

B *n* 特立尼达岛人

trinitrotoluene /traɪˌnaɪtrəʊˈtɒljʊiːn/ *n* [u] 三硝基甲苯

trinity /ˈtrɪnəti/ *n* **1** formal (group of three people) 三人小组; (group of three things) 三件套 **2** Relig **the (Holy) T~** [圣父、圣子及圣灵] 三位一体

trinket /ˈtrɪŋkɪt/ *n* (ornament) 小装饰物; (jewellery) 廉价首饰

trio /ˈtriːəʊ/ *n* **1** (group of three musicians) 三重奏组合 **2** (composition) 三重奏曲 **3** (set, group) (of people) 三人小组; (of things) 三件套

triode /ˈtraɪəʊd/ *n* **1** (valve) 三极管 **2** (rectifier) 三接头半导体整流器

trip /trɪp/

A *n* **1** (journey) 旅行; **to go on** *or* **take a ~ (to somewhere)** 去（某地）旅行; **a ~ abroad/round the world** 出国/环球旅行; **a boat ~** 乘船旅行; **the return ~** 返程; **a 12 day/200 km ~** 12 天的/200 公里的旅行; **he's away on a ~ to Europe** 他到欧洲旅行去了; **it's only a short ~ into London** 这只是去伦敦的短程旅游; **I did the ~ in six hours** 我路上花了 6 个小时; **enjoy your ~!** 旅途愉快!; **it's a two-hour ~ from here** 那

儿离这里有两个小时路程; ▸**memory 2** 2 (quick run, visit) 跑一趟; **to make a ～ into town** 进城跑一趟; **to make a ～ to the zoo/dentist/toilet** 去一趟动物园/牙医诊所/厕所; **it took several ～s to bring the equipment over** 往返好几趟才把设备搬过来 3 colloq (hallucinogenic drug experience) [吸毒引起的] 幻觉; **an acid ～** 迷幻药产生的幻觉; **to have a bad/good ～** 吸毒的体验很糟糕/很美妙 4 fig colloq (exciting experience) 令人兴奋的体验; (obsession) 着迷; **sb.'s power ～** 某人对权力的迷恋; **she's on a real guilt ～** 她真正体验到负罪感; **he's on this health food ～** 他迷上了这种保健食品 5 (stumble) 绊; **did she faint or was it a ～?** 她是晕倒了还是绊倒了? 6 Elec, Mech 脱扣装置

B *vi* (*pres p etc.* **-pp-**) 1 (stumble) 绊; **he ～ped and nearly fell** 他绊了一下，差点跌倒; **to ～ on** *or* **over sth.** 被…绊倒 ‹*rock, step*›; **to ～ over one's own feet** 把自己绊倒; **you can't move in here without ～ping over a celebrity** hum 你只要来到此地，必定会碰见名人 2 (step lightly) 轻快地走; fig 《*tune, notes*》 节奏轻快; **to ～ into/out of the room** 轻快地走进/走出房间; **the lies came ～ping off her tongue** 她撒起谎来不假思索 3 colloq (have hallucinogenic drug experience) [服用迷幻药后] 产生幻觉; **he's ～ping** 他产生了腾云驾雾的幻觉

C *vt* (*pres p etc.* **-pp-**) 1 (cause to stumble) 把…绊倒 2 Elec, Mech 触发 ‹*circuit, mechanism*›; **to ～ the alarm** 触响警报器

Phrasal verbs

• **trip out** *vi* colloq [服用迷幻药后] 体验腾云驾雾般的感觉

• **trip over**

A *vi* 被绊倒; **I ～ped over on the carpet** 我在地毯上绊倒了

B *vt* [**～ sb. over**] 绊倒

• **trip up**

A *vi* 1 lit (stumble) 绊倒; **to ～ up over sth.** 被某物绊倒 2 fig (blunder) 犯错; **to ～ up badly on the last question** 在最后一个问题上犯大错

B *vt* [**～ sb./sth. up, ～ up sb./sth.**] 1 (cause to stumble) 绊倒 2 fig (cause to blunder) 使…犯错; **to ～ sb. up with quick-fire questions** 用连珠炮似的问题使某人出错

tripartite /ˌtraɪˈpɑːtaɪt/ *adj* 1 (involving three parties) 三方的 ‹*alliance, agreement, talks*› 2 (having three parts) 有三部分的 ‹*structure, division, composition*›

tripe /traɪp/ *n* [u] 1 Culin [供食用的] 牛肚 2 colloq (nonsense) (written) 拙劣文章; (spoken) 胡说; **a load of ～** 一派胡言

triphthong /ˈtrɪfθɒŋ/ *n* (vowels) 三合元音; (characters) 三元音字母

triplane /ˈtraɪpleɪn/ *n* 三翼飞机

triple /ˈtrɪpl/ ▸**p. 288**

A *adj* 1 (having three parts) 有三部分的 ‹*contest, test, classification*›; 三重的 ‹*role, function, purpose*›; **a ～ murder/alliance** 三重谋杀/三方同盟 2 Mus 三拍的 ‹*beat*›; **in ～ time/rhythm** 以三拍子/三重韵 3 (three times greater) 三倍的 ‹*size, quantity, value*›

B *vi* 《*output, prices, population*》 成为三倍; **to ～ in volume/value** 容量/价值增至三倍; **to ～ in height/width** 高度/宽度增加两倍

C *vt* 使…增至三倍 ‹*output, sales, efficiency*›

D *adv* 三倍地; **to ～ the speed/price/amount** 三倍的速度/价格/数量

triple A *n* Fin 三 A 级的; **a ～ credit rating** 三 A 等级的信用评价

triple: ～-digit *adj* 三位数的 ‹*inflation, growth*›; **～-drug therapy** *n* [u] [尤指治疗肿瘤感染的] 三联药物疗法; **～ jump** ▸**p. 307** *n* [u] **the ～ jump** 三级跳远; **～ jumper** *n* 三级跳远运动员; **～ somersault** *n* 三连空翻

triplet /ˈtrɪplɪt/ *n* 1 (child, animal) 三胞胎之一; **a set of ～s** 三胞胎; **to give birth to ～s** 生三胞胎 2 Literat 三行联句 3 Mus 三连音符

Triplex® /ˈtrɪpleks/ *n* [u] Brit [尤指汽车窗户上的] 三层玻璃; **～ glass** 夹层玻璃

triplicate /ˈtrɪplɪkət/

A *adj* 一式三份的 ‹*copy*›

B *n* **in ～** (in three copies) 一式三份; (three times) 重复三次

triploid /ˈtrɪplɔɪd/ *adj* 三倍体的

trip meter *n* 里程表

tripod /ˈtraɪpɒd/ *n* 三脚架

Tripoli /ˈtrɪpəli/ *pr n* 的黎波里

tripper /ˈtrɪpə(r)/ *n* Brit colloq 短途旅行者; **day ～s** 一日游旅游者

trip switch *n* 转辙器

triptych /ˈtrɪptɪk/ *n* 1 (as altarpiece) 三联画 2 (set of three) (art works) [艺术品的] 三件组; (literary or musical works) 三部曲

trip wire *n* (working a trap) 绊脚线; (setting off an explosion) 触发线; (working an alarm) 拉发线

trireme /ˈtraɪriːm/ *n* [古希腊或罗马的] 三列桨战船

trisect /traɪˈsekt/ *vt* 把…分成三等份

trisyllabic /ˌtraɪsɪˈlæbɪk/ *adj* 有三音节的 ‹*word, foot*›

trisyllable /traɪˈsɪləbl/ *n* (word) 三音节词; (metrical foot) 三音节音步

trite /traɪt/ *adj* pej 老生常谈的 ‹*remark, comment*›; 老一套的 ‹*words, apology*›; 陈腐的 ‹*subject, idea*›

tritely /ˈtraɪtli/ *adv* pej 老一套地 ‹*talk*›; 陈腐地 ‹*write*›; 千篇一律地 ‹*reply, describe*›

triteness /ˈtraɪtnɪs/ *n* [u] pej (of reply, of words) 老一套; (of ideas, thoughts) 陈腐; **the story is commonplace to the point of ～** 这个故事平淡无奇，几近陈腐老套

tritium /ˈtrɪtɪəm/ *n* [u] 氚

triumph /ˈtraɪʌmf/

A *n* 1 [c and u] (victory) 伟大胜利; (success) 巨大成功; (achievement) 重大成就; **a great personal ～** 伟大的个人胜利; **a ～ of** *or* **for sth./sb.** 某事/某人的典范; **it's a ～ over evil/adversity** 这是对抗邪恶势力/逆境的胜利; **to return home in ～** 凯旋而归 2 [u] (joy, satisfaction) 得意扬扬; **a look** *or* **an expression of ～** 欣喜的表情; **～ at doing sth.** 做某事的满足

B *vi* 1 (achieve victory) 获胜; (succeed) 成功; **to ～ over sb./sth.** (defeat) 打败某人/某物; (overcome) 战胜某人/某物; **common sense ～ed in the end** (prevail) 最终是常识占了上风 2 (rejoice) 得意洋洋; **to ～ over sb./sth.** 因某人/某事物而狂喜

triumphal /traɪˈʌmfl/ *adj* 庆祝胜利的 ‹*chorus, parade*›; **a ～ arch** 凯旋门

triumphalism /traɪˈʌmfəlɪzəm/ *n* [u] pej 扬扬得意

triumphalist /traɪˈʌmfəlɪst/ pej

A *adj* 扬扬得意的 ‹*person, manner, celebration*›

B *n* 扬扬得意的人

triumphant /traɪˈʌmfənt/ *adj* 1 (victorious) 大获全胜的 ‹*army, team, soldiers*›; (successful) 获得巨大成功的 ‹*person*›; **a ～ return** 凯旋 2 (exultant) 欢欣鼓舞的 ‹*cheer, behaviour*›; 心满意足的 ‹*look, smile, expression*›

triumphantly /traɪˈʌmfəntli/ *adv* 大获全胜地 ‹*parade, march, return*›; 欢欣鼓舞地 ‹*cheer, behave, smile*›

triumvirate /traɪˈʌmvɪrət/ *n* (people) 三人领导小组; (things) 三方联合领导团体

trivet /ˈtrɪvɪt/ *n* (over fire) 三脚铁架; (on table) 三脚台架; **to be (as) right as a ～** Brit colloq (in good health) 非常健康

trivia /ˈtrɪvɪə/ *npl* 1 (irrelevancies) 琐事; **to worry about ～** 为鸡毛蒜皮的小事担心 2 (unusual or unimportant facts) 无关紧要的信息; **celebrity ～** 无聊的名人传闻

trivial /ˈtrɪvɪəl/ *adj* 1 (unimportant) 不重要的 ‹*matter, discussion*›; 微不足道的 ‹*mistake, offence, comment*›; 琐碎的 ‹*detail, problem*› 2 (banal) 无聊的 ‹*conversation, argument, remark*› 3 pej (frivolous) 狭隘的 ‹*person*›

triviality /ˌtrɪvɪˈæləti/ *n* pej 1 [u] (unimportance) 琐碎; (banality) 乏味无聊 2 [c] (irrelevance) 琐事; **to waste time on trivialities** 把时间浪费在鸡毛蒜皮的小事上

trivialization /ˌtrɪvɪəlaɪˈzeɪʃn, Amer -lɪˈz-/ *n* [u] 平凡化

trivialize /ˈtrɪvɪəlaɪz/ *vt* 使…显得琐碎 ‹*problem, matter*›; 轻视 ‹*subject, role*›

trivially /ˈtrɪvɪəli/ *adv* 琐细地 ‹*deal with, treat*›; 微不足道地 ‹*simple, easy*›

trivia quiz *n* [考查琐细知识的] 知识竞赛

triweekly /traɪˈwiːkli/

A *adj* 1 (three times a week) 每周三次的 2 (every three weeks) 三周一次的

B *adv* 1 (three times a week) 每周三次地 2 (every three weeks) 三周一次地

trochaic /trəʊˈkeɪɪk/

A *adj* 扬抑格的 ‹*rhythm, foot*›

B **trochaics** *npl* 扬抑格

trochee /ˈtrəʊkiː/ *n* 扬抑格

trod /trɒd/ *pt, pp* ▸**tread A, B**

trodden /ˈtrɒdn/ *pp* ▸**tread A, B**

troglodyte /ˈtrɒglədaɪt/ *n* 穴居人

troika /ˈtrɔɪkə/ *n* 1 (sleigh) [俄罗斯的] 三驾马车 2 (triumvirate) 三人领导小组

Trojan /ˈtrəʊdʒən/

A *n* 特洛伊人; **to work like a ～** 埋头苦干

B *adj* 特洛伊的 ‹*war, language, traditions*›

Trojan horse *n* 1 Mythol **the ～** 特洛伊木马 2 fig (person) 颠覆分子; (scheme) 颠覆阴谋; **the policy is a ～ for privatization** 这项政策内含扶持私有化的用意 3 Comput 木马程序

troll[1] /trəʊl/ *n* 1 (giant) [传说中的] 巨怪 2 (dwarf) 侏儒

troll[2]

A *vi* 1 (fish) 曳绳钓鱼; **to ～ for sth.** 曳绳钓某物 2 (search) 搜索; **to ～ for bargains** 淘便宜货 3 esp Brit colloq (stroll) 闲逛; **to ～ into town** 溜达进城 4 Comput colloq (send posting) 发挑衅帖子; (send email) 发挑衅邮件

B *vt* 1 (fish) 在…中曳绳钓鱼 ‹*sea, water*› 2 (search) 搜索 3 (sing) 兴高采烈地唱 ‹*note*›

C *n* 1 (line) 拖钓绳; (bait) 曳绳钓饵 2 Comput colloq (posting) 挑衅帖子; (email) 挑衅邮件

trolley /ˈtrɒli/ *n* 1 Brit (for luggage, shopping) 手推车; (for drinks, desserts) 台车 2 Amer (electric bus) 有轨电车

trolley: ～ bus *n* Brit 无轨电车; **～ car** *n* Amer 有轨电车

trollop /ˈtrɒləp/ *n* pej dated *or* hum 荡妇

trombone /trɒmˈbəʊn/ ▸**p. 395** *n* 1 (instrument) 长号 2 (player) 长号手

trombonist /trɒmˈbəʊnɪst/ ▸**p. 395, p. 409** *n* 长号手

troop /truːp/

A *n* 1 Mil (unit) (of artillery) 坦克连; (of cavalry) 骑兵连 2 (group of people or animals) 群 3 (of Scouts) 童子军中队 [由三个以上小队组成]

B **troops** *npl* (soldiers) 士兵; (armed forces) 部队; **to deploy/dispatch/lead/raise ～s** 部署/派遣/领导/组建部队

C *vi* 1 (come or go in large numbers) 成群结队而行; **to ～ past/over/up/into ...** 成群结队走过…/在…上面走/走上…/走进… 2 (walk) 踱方步

D *vt* **to ～ the colour** Brit 行军旗敬礼分列式

troop carrier *n* (aircraft) 部队运输机; (armoured vehicle) 装甲运兵车

trooper /ˈtruːpə(r)/ *n* 1 (soldier) (in cavalry) 骑兵; (in armoured unit) 装甲兵; **to swear like a ～** colloq 满口粗话 2 Amer (state police officer) 州警察; (mounted police officer) 骑警

troopship /ˈtruːpʃɪp/ *n* 部队运输船

trope /trəʊp/ *n* (word) 比喻用词; (expression) 比喻短语

trophy /ˈtrəʊfi/ *n* **1** Sport (cup) 奖杯; (medal) 奖牌 **2** (souvenir) 战利品; (of hunt) 狩猎纪念品 [尤指动物肢体等]

trophy wife *n* colloq [老年男子炫耀身份的] 花瓶娇妻

tropic /ˈtrɒpɪk/

A *n* 回归线; **the ~ of Cancer/Capricorn** 北/南回归线

B tropics *npl* **the ~s** 热带地区

C *adj* = **tropical**

tropical /ˈtrɒpɪkl/ *adj* **1** Geog 热带的 ‹*region, climate, plants, disease*› **2** (hot, humid) 非常湿热的 ‹*heat, conditions*›

tropical storm *n* 热带风暴

troposphere /ˈtrɒpəsfɪə(r), Amer ˈtrəʊ-/ *n* 对流层

Trot /trɒt/ *n* colloq pej 托洛茨基分子

trot /trɒt/

A *n* **1** *sing* (animal pace) 小跑; **to start off at a brisk/slow ~** 以疾步小跑/慢跑开始; **an extended ~** 伸长快步（赛）; **to break into a ~** «*horse*» 开始小跑; «*rider*» 开始策马小跑 **2** *sing* (human pace) 慢跑; **to break into a ~** 小跑起来; **to be on the ~** colloq (busy) 忙忙碌碌; **to keep sb. on the ~** 让某人忙个不停; **on the ~** 接二连三地; **for several hours on the ~** 一连几个小时

B *npl* **the trots** colloq 腹泻; **to get** *or* **have the ~s** 拉肚子

C *vi* (*pres p etc.* **-tt-**) **1** (move at trot) «*animal, person*» 小跑; «*rider*» 策马小跑 **2** colloq (go) 快步跑; **~ along, I'm busy** 跑开一边去，我忙着呢; **to ~ away to do sth./across to sb.** 快步跑开去做某事/快步跑向某人

D *vt* (*pres p etc.* **-tt-**) **1** (ride at trot) 使小跑; **to ~ one's horse forward** 策马向前小跑 **2** colloq (take briskly) 领…快走 ‹*person*›; **to ~ sb. round town** 带某人在城里兜一圈

Phrasal verb

- **trot out** *vt* [**~ sth. out, ~ out sth.**] colloq pej 动不动就搬出 ‹*phrase, fact*›; **to ~ out the same old excuse** 搬出老一套的借口; **to keep ~ting out one's complaints against sth.** 絮絮叨叨地抱怨某事物

troth /trəʊθ, Amer trɔːθ/ *n* archaic or formal **to plight** *or* **pledge one's ~** [尤指在婚礼上] 发誓信守婚约

Trotskyism /ˈtrɒtskɪɪzəm/ *n* [u] 托洛茨基主义

Trotskyist /ˈtrɒtskɪɪst/

A *n* 托洛茨基主义者

B *adj* 托洛茨基主义的

Trotskyite /ˈtrɒtskɪaɪt/ usu pej

A *n* 托洛茨基分子

B *adj* 托洛茨基主义的

trotter[1] /ˈtrɒtə(r)/ *n* Horse racing 快步马

trotter[2] *n* (of pig) [用作食物的] 猪蹄

trotting /ˈtrɒtɪŋ/ *n* [u] 快步马驾车赛

trotting race *n* 快步马驾车赛

troubadour /ˈtruːbədɔː(r), Amer -dʊər/ *n* **1** Hist (lyric poet) [中世纪的] 抒情诗人; (minstrel) [中世纪的] 行吟诗人 **2** (present-day) (poet) 吟游诗人; (singer) 吟游歌手

trouble /ˈtrʌbl/

A *n* **1** [u and c] (problems) 问题; **what's the ~?** 出什么事了？; **to cause** *or* **give (sb.) ~** （给某人）带来困难; **to make ~ for sb.** 给某人制造麻烦; **to have ~ doing sth.** 做某事有困难; **you may have ~ convincing the police** 你也许很难让警方相信; **to have ~ with sth./sb.** 某事物有麻烦/对付某人有困难; **we're having a bit of ~ with our car** 我们的车出了一点儿毛病; **engine ~** 发动机故障; **to be a ~ (to sb.)** （对某人）是个麻烦; **to be in ~** 处于困境; **she's in ~ with the police** 她犯事落入了警察的手里; **to get** *or* **run into ~** 陷入困境; **he's always getting into ~ at school** 他在学校总惹麻烦; **to get sb. into ~** 让某人有麻烦; **to get a girl in(to) ~** colloq dated 使女孩未婚先孕; **to get out of ~** 脱离困境; **to be asking for ~** colloq 自找麻烦 **2** [u] (discord) 纷争; (fighting) 打斗; (rioting) 动乱; **relationship ~s** 家庭矛盾; **the police had come expecting ~ and were in full riot gear** 警察预料到会有暴乱，所以身穿全套防暴服赶来; **to be looking for ~** colloq 寻衅滋事; **to make ~** 闹事; **they seem bent on making ~** 他们好像执意要闹事; **there's ~ brewing** 骚乱即将发生 **3** [u] (effort, inconvenience) 不便; **it's no ~ (at all)!** （一点儿都）不麻烦!; **it's so much ~ preparing all the ingredients** 准备所有的配料太费事了; **to go to a lot of ~ (to do sth.)** 不辞辛劳（做某事）; **they didn't go to any ~ to disguise what they felt** 他们没有试图掩饰自己的感受; **to go to the ~ of doing sth.** 费力做某事; **to go to** *or* **take a lot of ~ over sth.** 在某事物上花许多工夫; **she went to an awful lot of ~ over the arrangements** 她下了很大工夫进行安排; **to take the ~ to do sth.** 不辞辛苦做某事; **to save sb./oneself the ~ (of doing sth.)** 为某人/自己省却（做某事的）麻烦; **it's not worth the ~** 这不值得费力气 **4** [u] Med 病痛; **heart ~** 心脏病; **back ~** 背痛; **my leg's been giving me ~** 我的腿一直疼

B troubles *npl* **1** (worries, woes) 烦恼; **to tell sb. one's ~s** 向某人诉苦; **to listen to sb.'s ~s** 听某人诉苦; **may all your ~s be little ones!** 但愿你们的烦恼都不是烦恼！ [传统上对新婚夫妇的祝福语]; **his ~s are over** 他死了; **money ~s** 金钱上的困扰 **2 the ~s** Brit Pol 动乱时期 [北爱尔兰民族主义者与反自治主义者、新教徒与天主教徒之间的暴力冲突]

C *vt* **1** (worry) «*problem, anxiety*» 困扰; **I wonder what's troubling her** 我不知道什么事让她愁眉苦脸; **it is going to cost a lot of money, but don't let that ~ you** 这要花很多钱，但你不要担心 **2** (bother) 麻烦; **sorry to ~ you! is this your car?** 对不起，打扰您一下！这是您的车吗？; **may I ~ you for the butter/your signature?** 麻烦递一下黄油/签一下名好吗？ **3** (cause pain, discomfort) «*part of body, illness*» 使疼痛; **my back is troubling me again** 我的背又开始痛了; **to be ~d by** *or* **with sth.** 受某病痛折磨; **he's been ~d by a nasty cough** 他一直在剧烈地咳嗽

D *v refl* **to ~ oneself** 劳神; **don't ~ yourself!** 别费心了！; **they didn't ~ themselves to explain** 他们没有费神去解释

E *vi* **1** (bother) 费心; **don't ~** colloq 别费心了; **don't ~ about me: I'll be OK** 不用担心我，我不会有事的; **don't ~ to meet me, I'll get a taxi** 不必来接我，我打的好了; **don't ~ to knock, will you!** iron 门都懒得敲了，是吧！ **2** (worry) 忧虑; **to ~ about** *or* **over** *or* **with sb./sth.** 为某人/某事物担心; **she was too concerned with her own feelings to ~ about mine** 她一味地想着自己的感受，都不关心我怎么想

troubled /ˈtrʌbld/ *adj* **1** (worried) 烦恼的; **to be ~ about sth.** 因某事物而苦恼; **to be ~ in spirit** 精神上感到苦恼 **2** (interrupted) 不安宁的 ‹*sleep*› **3** (strife-torn) 混乱的 ‹*area*›; **to live in ~ times** 生逢乱世 **4** (having problems) 问题丛生的 ‹*company, economy, industry*›; 麻烦多的 ‹*person, marriage*›

trouble: ~free *adj* (unproblematic) 没有问题的; (free from discord) 没有冲突的; **~maker** *n* 惹是生非者

troubleshoot /ˈtrʌblʃuːt/

A *vi* **1** (for company, organization) 分析解决问题 **2** Tech, Comput 检修故障

B *vt* **1** (for company, organization) 分析解决 ‹*problem*›; 为…解决困难 ‹*company*› **2** Tech, Comput 排除 ‹*problem*›; 检修 ‹*fault*›

troubleshooter /ˈtrʌblʃuːtə(r)/ *n* **1** esp Ind (for company, organization) 分析解决问题者; (mediator, esp in diplomatic affairs) 纠纷调停者 **2** Tech, Comput 检修技工

troubleshooting /ˈtrʌblʃuːtɪŋ/ *n* [u] **1** (for company, organization) 分析解决问题; (in disputes) 调停纠纷 **2** Tech, Comput 检修故障; **hints/tools for ~** 检修指南/工具; **to do some ~** 作一些检修; **~ tips/skills** 检修窍门/技能

troubleshooting guide *n* 故障排除手册

troublesome /ˈtrʌblsəm/ *adj* 令人烦恼的 ‹*problem, issue, cough*›; 讨厌的 ‹*person, child*›

trouble spot *n* 不安定的地区

trough /trɒf, Amer trɔːf/ *n* **1** (for animals to drink out of) 饮水槽; (for animal feed) 饲料槽; **to have one's nose in the ~** fig 拼命捞钱 **2** (for growing plants) 槽形容器 **3** (between waves) 波谷; (between hills) 槽谷 **4** (lowest point) (in economic cycle) 萧条期; (in consumption) 淡季; (in career) 低谷; (on graph) 极小值; **to have peaks and ~s** 有高峰和低谷 **5** Meteorol 低压槽; **a ~ of low pressure** 低压槽

trounce /traʊns/ *vt* 彻底打败 ‹*team, opponent*›

troupe /truːp/ *n* (of actors) [尤指巡回演出的] 剧团; (of dancers) 歌舞团

trouper colloq /ˈtruːpə(r)/ *n* **1** Theat (actor, entertainer) 有经验的演员; **an old ~** 老艺人 **2** (reliable person) 可靠的人; **you've been a real ~** 你真的帮了大忙

trouser: ~ press *n* 夹裤器; **~ suit** *n* Brit 女式衣裤套装

trousers /ˈtraʊzəz/ Brit

A *npl* 裤子; **a pair of ~** 一条裤子; **to wear the ~ (in the house** *or* **family)** fig colloq （在家里）说了算; **to catch sb. with their ~ down** fig colloq 把某人逮个正着

B trouser *modif* 裤子的; **~ belt/leg/pocket** 裤带/裤腿/裤兜

C trouser *vt* Brit colloq (receive) 捞到; (keep for oneself) 私吞; **he trousered a £1,000,000 advance for the book deal** 他从这笔图书生意中捞了 100 万英镑的预付款; **some MPs have been caught trousering considerable sums of money they had claimed was to pay for research staff** 有人发现一些下院议员把他们声称要付给研究人员的巨款私吞了

trousseau /ˈtruːsəʊ/ *n* (*pl* **trousseaux** /ˈtruːsəʊz/ *or* **~s**) 嫁妆

trout /traʊt/ *n* (*pl* **~** *or* **~s**) **1** [u and c] Zool, Culin 鲑鱼; **~ farm/fishing** 鲑鱼养殖场/捕鲑鱼 **2** Brit pej (woman) **an old ~** 讨厌的老太婆

trove /trəʊv/ *n* = **treasure trove**

trowel /ˈtraʊəl/ *n* **1** (for spreading cement, plaster) 瓦刀; **to lay (sth./it) on with a ~** fig colloq 过分夸大（某事/这事） **2** (for digging small holes) 小铲子

troy /trɔɪ/ *n* 金衡 [用于称量贵重金属和宝石]

troy weight *n* [u] 金衡制

truancy /ˈtruːənsi/ *n* [u] 逃学

truant /ˈtruːənt/

A *n* 旷课的学生; **to play ~ (from school)** 逃学

B *adj* 逃学的 ‹*child, pupil*›

truant officer *n* 劝学训导员

truce /truːs/ *n* 停战; **a general ~** 全面休战; **to call a ~** 宣布休战

truck[1] /trʌk/

A *n* **1** (lorry) 卡车; **by ~** 用卡车 **2** Brit (rail wagon) 敞篷车 **3** (trolley) 平板手推车

B *vt* esp Amer 用卡车运送 ‹*goods, livestock*›

C *vi* «*driver*» 驾驶卡车; «*organization*» 用卡车运货

truck[2] *n* [u] **1** (barter) 物物交换; **to have** *or* **want no ~ with sth./sb.** 拒不接受某物/拒不与某人打交道 **2** Amer (produce) 商品蔬菜; **~ produce** 商品蔬菜产品

truckage /ˈtrʌkɪdʒ/ *n* [u] **1** (conveyance) 货车运输 **2** (fee) 货车运费

truck driver ▸p. 409 *n* 卡车司机

trucker /ˈtrʌkə(r)/ ▸p. 409 *n* colloq (长途)货车司机

truck: ~ **farm,** ~ **garden** *ns* Amer 蔬果农场; ~ **farmer,** ~ **gardener** ▸p. 409 *ns* Amer 菜农; ~ **farming,** ~ **gardening** *ns* [u] Amer 商品蔬菜种植

trucking /ˈtrʌkɪŋ/ *n* [u] 1 (transporting) 货车运输 2 (lorry driving) (长途) 货车驾驶 3 (work) 货车司机工作

truckle bed /ˈtrʌkl bed/ *n* esp Brit [可推入大床下的] 滑轮矮床

truck: ~**load** *n* lit 一卡车; fig colloq 许多; **by the** ~**load** lit 整卡车地; fig colloq 大量地; **to eat sth. by the** ~**load** 大吃某物; ~ **stop** *n* Amer 卡车服务站

truculence /ˈtrʌkjʊləns/ *n* [u] (quickness to argue) 爱争吵; (quickness to fight) 好斗

truculent /ˈtrʌkjʊlənt/ *adj* (quick to argue) 爱争吵的; (quick to fight) 好斗的; **to be** ~ **and grumpy** 桀骜不驯, 性情乖戾

trudge /trʌdʒ/

A *vi* (walk heavily) 步履沉重地走; (walk wearily) 疲惫地走; **to** ~ **in/out/up/down/through sth.** 步履艰难地走进/走出/走上/走下/走过某处

B *vt* 步履沉重地走过 ‹*streets, village*›

C *n* 艰难的跋涉; **the five-mile** ~ **home** 令人疲惫不堪的 5 英里返家路程

true /truː/

A *adj* 1 (based on fact, not a lie) 真实的 ‹*fact, version*›; 如实的 ‹*account, report*›; **unfortunately, the rumour turned out to be** ~ 很不幸, 传闻最后证实确有其事; **it can't be** ~**!** 这不可能是真的!; **it is simply not** ~ **that I was there** 我根本不在那里; **it is** ~ **to say that they disliked each other** 的确可以说他们俩相互厌恶; **that is not** ~ **of the people I have met** 我遇到的人可不是这样的; **it is (only) too** ~ **(that ...)** (…) 千真万确; **to be** *or* **hold** ~ **(of sb./sth.)** (对某人/某事物) 同样适用; **what is** ~ **of adults is** ~ **of children** 对大人适用的, 对小孩也一样; **to come** ~ 实现; **may all your wishes/dreams come** ~**!** 愿你所有的愿望都实现/祝你梦想都能成真!; **to be/seem too good to be** ~ 好得/看上去好得令人难以相信; **many a** ~ **word is spoken in jest** Prov 许多真话都是在玩笑中说出的 2 *attrib* (real, genuine) 真正的 ‹*Londoner, professional*›; 纯种的 ‹*mammal*›; **an artist in the** ~ **sense of the word** 名副其实的艺术家; **he reveals his** ~ **character to very few people** 他没有向几个人表露过他的本性; **the** ~ **face of capitalism** 资本主义的真面目 3 (heartfelt, sincere) 真诚的 ‹*feeling, understanding*›; 虔诚的 ‹*faith, believer*›; ~ **love** 真爱 4 (accurate) 逼真的 ‹*copy, bill, likeness*›; 精确的 ‹*judgement, analysis*›; **to be** ~ **to sth.** 忠实于某物; **this new production remains** ~ **to the essence of Shakespeare's play** 新作品保持了莎士比亚戏剧的精髓; **to be** ~ **to life** «*film, book*» 写实; «*painting, sculpture*» 逼真; **to be** *or* **run** ~ **to type** *or* **form** 很典型/一如既往; **his aim was** ~ 他瞄得很准 5 (faithful, loyal) 忠实的 ‹*friend, patriot, servant*›; **to be** ~ **to sb./sth.** 对某人/某事忠诚; **my lover is** ~ **to me** liter 我的爱人对我很忠诚; **to be** ~ **to one's word** *or* **promise** 信守诺言; **to be** ~ **to one's principles/beliefs/ideas** 坚持自己的原则/信念/想法; **to be** ~ **to oneself** 按照自己的信念做事; **good men and** ~ archaic *or* liter 诚实的人 6 Constr (in line) 平的 ‹*surface*›; 直的 ‹*wall, post*›; 处于正确位置的 ‹*frame, wheel, beam*› 7 Geog 根据地极确定的; ~ **north** 真北

B *adv* 1 (straight) 笔直地 ‹*aim, run*›; **the arrow flew** ~**, straight to the mark** 箭不偏不倚地向靶子射去 2 liter (truthfully) 真实地 ‹*say*›; **to speak** ~ 实话实说

C *n* [u] Constr 笔直; **out of** ~ 歪斜的; **this post is half an inch out of** ~ 这根杆子偏斜了半英寸

D *vt* Constr 弄平 ‹*surface*›; 弄直 ‹*wall, post*›; 摆正 ‹*frame, wheel, beam*›

true: ~**-blue** *adj attrib* 1 Brit Pol 忠于保守党的 ‹*voter, Conservative*›; 2 Amer (loyal) 忠贞不渝的 ‹*patriot*›; (typical) 典型的 ‹*American, Californian*›; ~**-born** *adj attrib* 血统纯正的 ‹*national*›; 地道的 ‹*American, Chinese*›; ~**-hearted** *adj* 忠实的 ‹*person, supporter*›; ~**-life** *adj attrib* 忠于现实生活的; **a** ~**-life adventure/story** 真实的冒险活动/故事; ~**love** *n* liter 忠实的爱人 [多指男子]

trueness /ˈtruːnɪs/ *n* [u] 1 (truthfulness) 符合事实; **the** ~ **of sb.'s story/claim** 某人的说法/断言的真实性 2 (accuracy) 准确; **the** ~ **of his aim** 他瞄准的精度; ~ **to life** 逼真 3 (faithfulness) 忠诚; **the** ~ **of their love** 他们的爱的忠贞

truffle /ˈtrʌfl/ *n* 1 (fungus) 块菌 2 (candy) 巧克力软糖

trug /trʌg/ *n* Brit ~ **(basket)** [盛放花、植物等的] 浅筐

truism /ˈtruːɪzəm/ *n* 自明之理; **it's a** ~ **to say ...** 说…是老生常谈

truly /ˈtruːli/ *adv* 1 colloq (really, without doubt) 确实地; **a** ~ **great actor** 真正伟大的演员; **a** ~ **dreadful painting** 糟糕透顶的油画; **really and** ~ 千真万确地; **well and** ~ 彻底地 2 (sincerely) 真诚地 ‹*think, grateful*›; (truthfully) 如实地 ‹*tell, describe*›; (genuinely) 真正地 ‹*believe, sorry*›; **a** ~ **democratic system** 真正的民主政体 3 (accurately) 准确地 ‹*reflect, portray*› 4 **yours** ~ (in letter) 你忠实的; hum (referring to self) 自己

trump /trʌmp/

A *n* 1 *usu pl* (in cards) 王牌; **to call** ~**s** 叫将牌; **clubs/diamonds/hearts/spades are** ~**s** 梅花/方块/红桃/黑桃是主牌; **to play a** *or* **one's** ~ **(card)** 打出王牌; fig 使出绝招 2 ~ **(card)** fig (advantage) 绝招; **to have** *or* **keep a** ~ **up one's sleeve** 有杀手锏; **to hold all the** ~**s** 掌握主动权; **to turn** *or* **come up** ~**s** (come out ahead) 发挥出色; (be helpful) 很有帮助

B *vt* 1 (in cards) 出王牌赢 ‹*card*›; **to** ~ **sb.'s ace** 出王牌赢某人的A 2 fig (surpass) 胜过; (beat) 打败

Phrasal verb

- **trump up** *vt* [~ **up sth.**] pej 捏造 ‹*accusation, excuse*›; **to** ~ **up charges against sb.** 捏造罪名指控某人

trump card *n* 1 (in cards) = **trump A1** 2 fig = **trump A2**

trumped-up /ˌtrʌmptˈʌp/ *adj* pej 捏造的 ‹*charges, evidence*›

trumpet /ˈtrʌmpɪt/ ▸p. 395

A *n* 1 (instrument) 小号; **to blow one's own** ~ esp Brit fig 自我吹嘘; **a** ~ **player/blast/piece** 小号演奏者/吹奏声/演奏曲 2 (player) 小号手 3 (elephant call) 大象的吼声 4 (of flower) 绽开的水仙花

B *vt* 宣扬 ‹*views*›; 吹嘘 ‹*achievements*›; 大肆宣传 ‹*news, victory*›

C *vi* «*elephant*» 吼叫

trumpeter /ˈtrʌmpɪtə(r)/ ▸p. 395, p. 409 *n* (musician) 小号手; (soldier) 号兵

trumpet: ~ **major** *n* [骑兵团的] 号手长; ~ **player** ▸p. 395, p. 409 *n* 小号手

truncate /trʌŋˈkeɪt, Amer ˈtrʌŋ-/ *vt* 1 (cut short) 缩短 ‹*process, journey*›; 删节 ‹*text, article, version*› 2 (cut top or end off) 截去…的梭 ‹*pyramid, cone*›

truncated /trʌŋˈkeɪtɪd, Amer ˈtrʌŋ-/ *adj* 1 (shortened) 缩短了的 ‹*form, process*›; 删节过的 ‹*text, article, version*› 2 (having end or point cut off) 截成平面的 ‹*angle, cone*›

truncation /trʌŋˈkeɪʃn/ *n* [u] (of state, process) 缩短; (of text) 删节

truncheon /ˈtrʌntʃən/ *n* esp Brit 警棍

trundle /ˈtrʌndl/

A *vi* «*vehicle, cart*» 缓慢移动; «*person*» 缓慢地走

B *vt* 缓慢地推动 ‹*cart, luggage*›; **to** ~ **sth. in/out** 缓缓地将某物推入/推出

Phrasal verb

- **trundle out** *vt* [~ **out sth.**] esp Brit pej 重提 ‹*reason, excuse*›

trundle bed *n* esp Amer = **truckle bed**

trunk /trʌŋk/

A *n* 1 (of tree) 树干 2 (of person, animal) 躯干 3 (of elephant) 象鼻 4 (large box) 大箱子 5 Amer (car boot) 行李箱

B **trunks** *npl* 1 (for swimming) 游泳裤 2 (for boxing) 拳击短裤

trunk call *n* esp Brit dated [国内] 长途电话

trunking /ˈtrʌŋkɪŋ/ *n* [u] (for cables) 电缆管道; (for ventilation) 通风管道

trunk: ~ **line** *n* 1 (of railway) 交通干线; 2 Telecom 电话干线; ~ **road** *n* Brit 公路干线

trunnion /ˈtrʌnjən/ *n* (pin, pivot) 枢轴; (for cannon) 炮耳

truss /trʌs/

A *n* 1 Constr 桁架 2 (of flowers) 花束; (of fruit) 果束 3 Med 疝带 4 esp Brit (of hay) 干草捆; (of straw) 秸秆捆

B *vt* 1 = **truss up** 2 Constr 用桁架支撑 ‹*bridge, roof, arch*›

Phrasal verb

- **truss up** *vt* 1 [~ **sb. up,** ~ **up sb.**] (tie up) 把…捆绑起来 ‹*victim, prisoner*› 2 [~ **sth. up,** ~ **up sth.**] Culin [烹调前] 扎紧…的翅膀和腿 ‹*fowl*›

trust /trʌst/

A *vt* 1 (believe in) 相信 ‹*person, advice, memory*›; 依赖 ‹*device, method*›; **I never** ~ **electrical equipment to work** 我从不相信电器能管用; ~ **you to blurt out all the facts!** 你管保会脱口说出所有真相!; **I wouldn't** ~ **him anywhere near my car** 我可不敢让他靠近我的车; **I wouldn't** ~ **her further than I could throw her** 我绝对不会相信她; **not to** ~ **sb. an inch** 丝毫不相信某人 2 (entrust) 托付 ‹*person, object*›; **to** ~ **sb./sth. to sb.** 把某人/某物托付给某人; **I'd** ~ **my life to him** 他是我可以托付一生的人; **to** ~ **sb. to do sth.** 委托某人做某事; **would you** ~ **him to handle your money?** 你放心把钱交给他处理吗?; **to** ~ **sb. with sth.** 把某事物托付给某人; **don't** ~ **little kids with matches** 不要把火柴交给小孩子; **to** ~ **sb. with a secret/one's life's savings** 让某人保守一个秘密/保管一生的积蓄 3 (hope) 希望; **will he tell the newspapers? — I** ~ **not** 他会向报界透露吗? ——我想不会; **I** ~ **you'll pay us soon** 我希望你会很快付我们钱; **I** ~ **that's not the boss's chair you're sitting in!** 我想你坐的椅子不是老板的吧!

B *v refl* **to** ~ **oneself to do sth.** 敢于做某事; **can you** ~ **yourself to keep your temper?** 你能保证不发脾气吗?

C *vi* 相信; **to** ~ **in sb./sth.** 相信某人/某事物; **to** ~ **in God/providence/one's judgement/fate/the future** 相信上帝/天命/自己的判断力/命运/将来; **to** ~ **to luck/memory/instinct** 凭运气/记忆/直觉

D *n* 1 [u] (faith) 信任; **to have** ~ **in sb./sth.** 对某人/某事物有信心; **to put** *or* **place (one's)** ~ **in sb./sth.** 相信某人/某事物; **to take sth. on** ~ 轻信某事; **don't expect me to take what you say on** ~ 别指望我会听信你的话; **a position of** ~ 要职; **a breach** *or* **an abuse of** ~ 背信; **to abuse** *or* **betray sb.'s** ~ 辜负某人的信任; **to earn** *or* **win sb.'s** ~ 赢得某人的信任 2 [c and u] Jur (financial arrangement) 信托; **to set up a** ~ **for sb.** 为某人安排信托财产; **to hold** *or* **leave sth. in** ~ **for sb.** 为某人代管某物; **did he leave any sum in** ~ **for his sisters?** 他有没有为他的姊妹们留下某个数量的托管财产? 3 [c] Jur

t

(organization) 受托基金机构; **a charitable ~** 慈善基金机构 **4** [c] Amer Comm dated 托拉斯

trust: ~ account *n* 信托账户; **~buster** *n* esp Amer colloq (person) 反托拉斯法执行人; (agency) 反托拉斯法执行机构; **~ company** *n* 信托公司; **~ deed** *n* 信托书

trusted /ˈtrʌstɪd/ *adj* 可靠的 ‹*friend, adviser, method*›

trustee /trʌˈstiː/ *n* **1** Jur, Fin 受托人; **a ~ in bankruptcy** 破产财产管理人 **2** (board member of institution) 董事会成员

trusteeship /trʌˈstiːʃɪp/ *n* **1** [u and c] Fin, Jur (office) 受托人职责; (period) 受托人任期 **2** [u and c] (of institution) (office) 董事会成员职责; (period) 董事会成员任期

trustful /ˈtrʌstfl/ *adj* **= trusting**

trustfully /ˈtrʌstfəli/ *adv* **= trustingly**

trust fund *n* 信托基金

trusting /ˈtrʌstɪŋ/ *adj* 轻信的 ‹*person, nature*›

trustingly /ˈtrʌstɪŋli/ *adv* 轻信地; **to do sth. ~** 轻信地做某事

trust: ~ instrument *n* 信托书; **~ territory** *n* [联合国或其委托国家的] 托管领土

trustworthiness /ˈtrʌstwɜːðinɪs/ *n* [u] (of person, company) 值得信任; (of statement, report, evidence, source) 可靠

trustworthy /ˈtrʌstwɜːði/ *adj* 值得信任的 ‹*person, company*›; 可靠的 ‹*statement, report, evidence, source*›

trusty /ˈtrʌsti/

A *adj attrib* dated *or* hum 可信任的 ‹*friend*›; 忠实的 ‹*steed*›; 可靠的 ‹*car, bike, sword*›

B *n* colloq 模范囚犯

truth /truːθ/ *n* **1** [u] (real facts) 实情; **the ~ was beginning to dawn (on them)** 真相开始（在他们面前）渐渐浮出水面; **to tell the ~** 说实话; **to tell you the ~, I don't really know** 说实话，实际上我并不知道; **~ to tell** 说实话; **if ~ be told, she was after his money** 老实说，她图的是他的钱; **to tell the ~, the whole ~, and nothing but the ~** 据实陈述，绝无谎言 [证人在法庭上的誓词]; **to overstep/fall short of the ~** 有虚假成分/不符合事实; **in (all) ~** 事实上; **it wasn't in ~ very difficult** 这其实不太难; **~ is stranger than fiction** Prov 现实比虚构更不可思议; **~ will out** Prov 真相终将大白于天下 **2** [c] (fact) 事实; **I could tell you a few ~s about the family** 我可以告诉你这家人的一些实情 **3** [u] (truthfulness) 真实性; **to confirm/deny the ~ of sth.** 承认/否认某事的真实性; **there's a great deal of ~ in her theory** 她的理论有很多事实依据 **4** [c] (important idea) 真理; **universal ~s** 普遍真理; **scientific ~s** 科学原理

truth drug *n* [c and u] 吐真药

truthful /ˈtruːθfl/ *adj* **1** (honest) 诚实的 ‹*person, character*› **2** (true) 真实的 ‹*statement, account*› **3** (accurate) 逼真的 ‹*portrait, acting*›

truthfully /ˈtruːθfəli/ *adv* **1** (honestly) 诚实地 ‹*speak*›; 如实地 ‹*answer*› **2** colloq (really) 的确; **no, honestly and ~, I know nothing about it** 不，说实在的，我压根不知道这件事

truthfulness /ˈtruːθflnɪs/ *n* [u] **1** (honesty of person) 诚实 **2** (trueness of account) 真实 **3** (accuracy of rendering) 逼真; **~ to life** 栩栩如生

truth value *n* 真假值

try /traɪ/

A *vt* (*pt, pp* **tried**) **1** (attempt) 尝试 ‹*action, trick*›; **I want to ~ something different for a change** 我想尝试别的事情换换口味; **to ~ doing sth.** 试着做某事; **I want to ~ persuading them first** 我想先试试说服他们; **~ telling that to my wife!** 去试试把那话说给我老婆听！; **to ~ to do sth.** 试图做某事; **they were caught ~ing to escape** 他们在试图逃走时被抓了; **are you ~ing to upset me?** 你是不是想烦死我啊？; **to ~ hard to do sth.** 费力做某事; **I've tried very hard to see things from your point of view** 我已经很努力地从你的角度看事情了; **to ~ one's hardest** *or* **best to do sth.** 尽最大努力做某事; **it's ~ing to rain/snow** 看样子要下雨/下雪了; **don't ~ anything!** 别耍花招！; **just you ~ it!** 你试试看！; **to ~ one's hand at sth./doing sth.** 在某事/做某事上初试身手; **I'd like to ~ my hand at driving one of those things** 我想尝试亲手驾驶那种车 **2** (test out) 试用; **plan A doesn't work, so we'd better ~ plan B** 计划 A 行不通，所以我们应该试用计划 B; **~ it; see if it works** 试试这个，看行不行; **let's ~ the table in a different position** 让我们把桌子放到别处看看; **are you any good at this sort of thing? — ~ me** 你擅长这类事情吗？——让我试试看啰; **have you tried sleeping pills?** 你有没有试过服用安眠药？; **to ~ sth. on sb./sth.** 在某人/某物身上试某物; **we tried it on the dog, and even he wouldn't eat it** 我们试着让狗吃它，可狗居然也不吃; **to ~ sth. over** *or* **through** 预先演习某事; **we tried it over a couple of times on the piano** 我们用钢琴演练了好几遍; **to ~ sth. for size/length** 试试…的大小/长短 ‹*shoe, screw*›; **so you need a grammar book, well, ~ this one for size** 这么说你需要一本语法书，那么看看这本合不合适; **to ~ one's luck (at sth.)**（在某事物上）碰运气 **3** (taste, sample) 品尝 ‹*food, wine*›; 尝试 ‹*activity, sport*›; **~ it to see if it needs more salt** 尝尝看是否需要再加点儿盐; **I'd love to ~ skydiving** 我想试试特技跳伞; **I'll ~ anything once** 我什么都想尝一下 **4** (have recourse to) 问询 ‹*person*›; 去…查询 ‹*place*›; 查阅 ‹*book*›; **~ Sylvia, she may know** 问一下西尔维娅，她也许知道; **when I'm stuck, I usually ~ the encyclopedia** 我遇到难题一般会查阅百科全书 **5** (subject to stress) 考验 ‹*nerves, courage, person*›; **these are times that ~ men's souls** 这都是考验人们灵魂的时刻; **his patience has been sorely tried** 他的耐心受到严峻考验; **these things are sent to ~ us** hum 这些东西是上苍送来考验我们的 **6** Jur 审理 ‹*case*›; 审讯 ‹*person, defendant*›; **to ~ sb. for sth.** 因某事物审讯某人; **he was tried for murder/fraud** 他因谋杀/诈骗受审

B *vi* (*pt, pp* **tried**) **1** (make attempt) 尝试; **to ~ again** 再试试; **it's worth ~ing, you might be lucky** 这值得一试，你也许能交好运; **all right, if you're so clever, you ~!** 好吧，如果你那么聪明，就试试看！; **I'd like to see them ~!** 我倒想看看他们会搞什么花样！; **to ~ for sth.** 尝试获取某物; **we thought we'd ~ for a loan** 我们原本想试试贷款; **to ~ and do sth.** colloq 试着做某事; **to ~ and relax** 试着放松; **she did ~ and ring you, but she couldn't get through** 她的确试过给你打电话，但没打通 **2** (enquire) 询问; **I've tried everywhere, but nobody stocks it** 我到处询问，但没人有存货; **you could ~ at the newsagent's** 你可以到报亭问问

C *n* (*pl* **tries**) **1** (attempt) 尝试; **would you like a ~?** 你想试试吗？; **a ~ at sth./doing sth.** 某事/做某事的尝试; **let me have a ~!** 让我试一试！; **you didn't succeed, but you had a good ~** 虽然没有成功，但是你已经很努力了; **to give sth. a ~** (attempt) 尝试某事物; (test out) 试用某物; **it's worth a ~** 这值得一试; **nice ~!** 这招漂亮！ **2** (in rugby) 持球触地得分; **to score a ~** 带球触地得分

Phrasal verbs

• **try on** *vt* **1** [**~ sth. on, ~ on sth.**] (put on in order to test size) 试穿 ‹*garment, shoe*›; 试戴 ‹*hat*›; **why don't you ~ it on for size?** 你为什么不试试大小？ **2** **to ~ it on (with sb.)** Brit colloq (try to provoke) 蒙骗（某人）; **she's just ~ing it on** 她只是在骗人; **don't ~ anything on with me, sonny** 小家伙，不要跟我耍花招

• **try out**

A *vt* [**~ sth. out, ~ out sth.**] 试用 ‹*method, vehicle, drug*›; 试验 ‹*language, recipe*›; **he's itching to ~ out his theories** 他迫不及待地要验证他的理论; **they tried her out in a fairly minor role** 他们让她试演一个小角色; **~ it out on a spare piece of wood** 先在废木块上试一试; **I tried the speech out on my wife** 我在妻子面前预演了一遍演讲

B *vi* Amer 参加选拔; **he tried out, but he didn't make the team** 他参加了选拔，但没能进入那个队; **to ~ out for sth.** 参加…选拔 ‹*team, part*›

trying /ˈtraɪɪŋ/ *adj* 令人厌烦的 ‹*person, experience*›; **a ~ time/task** 难熬的时期/困难的任务

try-on *n* Brit colloq 欺骗; **it's a ~** 这是个骗局

try-out *n* 潜力考核; **to have a ~** 检查衡量潜力; **to give sth./sb. a ~** 考核某物/某人的潜力

tryst /trɪst/ *n* liter 幽会

tsar /zɑː(r)/ *n* **1** (emperor) [1917年之前俄国的] 沙皇 **2** fig (in government) 权威领导人; **energy/drugs ~** 能源大王/禁毒高官

tsarina /zɑːˈriːnə/ *n* (wife of a tsar) 沙皇皇后; (female tsar) 女沙皇

tsarist /ˈzɑːrɪst/

A *n* 沙皇制度追随者

B *adj* (of tsarism) 专制统治的; (of tsar) 沙皇的

tsetse fly /ˈtsetsi flaɪ/ *n* 舌蝇

T: ~-shaped *adj* 丁字形的 ‹*piece, structure*›; **~-shirt** *n* T恤衫

tsp *abbr* **= teaspoonful**

T-square *n* 丁字尺

tsunami /tsuːˈnɑːmi/ *n* (*pl* **~** *or* **~s**) 海啸

TT[1] *abbr* **= teetotal** 滴酒不沾的 ‹*person*›; 绝对禁酒的 ‹*city, movement*›

TT[2] *abbr* **= Tourist Trophy** 旅游杯 [1907年起在马恩岛举行的年度摩托车比赛]

TU *abbr* **= trade union**

tub /tʌb/ *n* **1** (basin) (for water) 盆; (for washing clothes) 洗衣盆 **2** (for plants) 花盆 **3** (container for ice cream, margarine, etc.) 盒; (tubful) 一盒 **4** esp Amer colloq (bath) 浴缸 **5** colloq pej (boat) [短而宽、不易操作的] 老爷船

tuba /ˈtjuːbə, Amer ˈtuː-/ ▸**p. 395** *n* **1** (instrument) 大号 **2** (player) 大号手

tubby /ˈtʌbi/ *adj* colloq 矮胖的

tube /tjuːb, Amer tuːb/ *n* **1** (cylinder) (made of metal) 金属管; (made of plastic) 塑料管; (made of wood) 木管; **to go down the ~** *or* **~s** colloq 完蛋 **2** (of bicycle tyre) 内胎 **3** (of toothpaste, glue) 软管 **4** Anat 管状器官 **5** (in TV set) 阴极射线管; **the ~** Amer colloq 电视机; **to watch the ~** 看电视 **6** **the ~** Brit Transp [伦敦的] 地铁; **to go by ~** 乘地铁去; **a ~ line/ticket** 地铁线/地铁票 **7** Austral colloq (can of beer) 一罐啤酒

tubeless /ˈtjuːblɪs, Amer ˈtuːb-/ *adj* 无内胎的 ‹*tyre*›

tuber /ˈtjuːbə(r), Amer ˈtuːb-/ *n* 块茎

tubercular /tjuːˈbɜːkjʊlə(r), Amer tuːˈb-/ *adj* 结核的 ‹*symptoms, diseases*›; 患结核病的 ‹*patient, lung*›

tuberculin /tjuːˈbɜːkjʊlɪn, Amer tuːˈb-/ *n* [u] 结核菌素

tuberculin-tested *adj* 经过结核菌素试验的 ‹*herd, milk*›

tuberculosis /tjuːˌbɜːkjʊˈləʊsɪs, Amer tuːˌb-/ ▸**p. 377** *n* [u] 结核病 [尤指肺结核]; **a ~ patient/ward** 结核病人/病房

tuberculous /tjuːˈbɜːkjʊləs, Amer tuːˈb-/ *adj* **= tubercular**

tube top *n* Amer **= boob tube 1**

tubing /ˈtjuːbɪŋ, Amer ˈtuː-/ *n* [u] (of metal) 金属管; (of plastic) 塑料管; (of glass) 玻璃管; **a length** *or* **piece of ~** 一节管子

t

tub-thumper /ˈtʌbθʌmpə(r)/ *n* colloq pej 慷慨激昂的鼓吹者

tub-thumping colloq pej
A *adj attrib* 有煽动力的 ‹*orator*›; **a ~ speech** 煽动性的演讲
B *n* [u] 大肆煽动

tubular /ˈtju:bjʊlə(r), Amer ˈtu:-/ *adj* **1** (cylindrical) 管状的 ‹*stem, shape*› **2** (made from tubes) 管子做的 ‹*furniture, scaffolding*›

tubular: ~ bells ▸**p. 395** *npl* 管钟; **~ steel chair** *n* 钢管椅

TUC *abbr* Brit **= Trades Union Congress**

tuck /tʌk/
A *vt* **1** (push or fold into confined or concealed space) 把…塞进 ‹*cloth, garment, paper*›; 挽起 ‹*skirt*›; 掖好 ‹*shirt, sheet*›; 盘起 ‹*hair, legs*›; «*bird*» 收拢 ‹*wings*›; **he ~ed his trousers into his belt/boots** 他把裤腰掖到皮带里/裤腿塞进靴子里; **she carried a shotgun ~ed under her arm** 她腋窝下夹了一把猎枪; **she ~ed the blanket around his legs** 她用毯子裹住他的腿 **2** (make comfortable in bed) 为…掖好被子; **to ~ sb. in(to) bed** 给某人盖好被子; **to ~ a child into bed** 给孩子掖好被窝 **3** (in sewing) 在…上打褶 ‹*dress, cloth*›; **~ it and then press it into shape** 把它打褶熨成型
B *vi* «*garment*» 掖好; **the blouse ~s into the skirt** 衬衫掖在裙子里
C *n* **1** [c] (in sewing) 褶; **to make several ~s in the cloth** 在布上缝几个褶 **2** [c] Sport (in diving) 抱膝; (in gymnastics) 团身; (in downhill skiing) 蹲伏 **3** [c] Med colloq 抽脂术; **a tummy ~** 紧腹手术 **4** [u] Brit colloq dated (school snacks) 零食

Phrasal verbs

- **tuck away** *vt* [**~ sth. away, ~ away sth.**]
1 (hide) (for tidiness) 收起 ‹*document*›; (in reserve) 储存 ‹*money*›; (for safety) 收藏 ‹*valuables*›; **she has £50,000 ~ed away in a personal bank account** 她让人把 50,000 英镑存入个人银行账户 **2** **to be ~ed away** (be secluded) «*village, building*» 被隐藏; **a cottage ~ed away in the depths of a wood** 掩藏在树林深处的小屋
- **tuck in**
A *vt* **1** [**~ sth. in, ~ in sth.**] (fasten in) 掖好 ‹*garment, sheet*›; **~ your shirt in!** 把衬衫掖好! **2** [**~ sb. in, ~ in sb.**] (make comfortable in bed) 为…掖被窝; **I'll read you a story and then ~ you in** 我先给你念一个故事, 然后帮你掖进被窝
B *vi* colloq (eat) 狼吞虎咽
- **tuck into** *vt* [**~ into sth.**] colloq (eat) 大口吃 ‹*food*›
- **tuck up** *vt* **1** [**~ sth. up, ~ up sth.**] (fasten up) 撩起 ‹*garment*›; 盘起 ‹*hair, legs*› **2** [**~ sb. up, ~ up sb.**] (make comfortable in bed) 为…掖被窝

tuck box *n* Brit colloq dated 食盒

tucker /ˈtʌkə(r)/ *n* [u] Austral, NZ colloq 食物

Phrasal verb

- **tucker out** *vt* [**~ sb. out**] Amer colloq 使疲乏; **to be ~ed out** 筋疲力尽

tucker: ~ bag *n* Austral, NZ colloq 食物袋; **~ box** *n* Austral, NZ colloq 食物盒

tuck: ~ jump *n* 团身跳; **~ shop** *n* Brit colloq dated [学校的] 食品饮料店

Tudor /ˈtju:də(r), Amer ˈtu:-/
A *pr n* 都铎王朝时代的人
B *adj* 都铎王朝的 ‹*period*›; 都铎王朝时代的 ‹*theatre, kings*›; 都铎式的 ‹*architecture*›; **the ~ style** 都铎风格

Tue., Tues. ▸**p. 182** *abbr* **= Tuesday**

Tuesday /ˈtju:zdeɪ, -di, Amer ˈtu:-/ ▸**p. 182** *n* 星期二; **on ~** 在星期二; **on ~s/every ~** 每周星期二; **~ morning/afternoon/night** 星期二早晨/下午/晚上; **this/last/next ~** 本周二/上周二/下周二

tufa /ˈtju:fə, Amer ˈtu:-/ *n* [u] 泉华

tuft /tʌft/ *n* (of grass) 一丛; (of feathers, silk) 一簇; (of hair, wool) 一绺

tufted /ˈtʌftɪd/ *adj* 丛生的 ‹*grass*›; 簇生的 ‹*hair*›; 有冠的 ‹*bird*›; 植绒的 ‹*carpet*›

tufted duck *n* 凤头潜鸭

tug /tʌg/
A *vt* (*pres p etc.* **-gg-**) **1** (pull) 拉 ‹*rope*›; 拽 ‹*sleeve*›; 扯 ‹*hair*› **2** (drag) 费力拖 ‹*person*› **3** Naut 用拖船拖 ‹*ship*›
B *vi* (*pres p etc.* **-gg-**) 拉; **to ~ on** *or* **away at sth.** 拉某物; **to ~ at sb.'s sleeve/one's moustache** 拽某人的袖子/扯胡须; **to ~ at sb.'s** *or* **the heartstrings** 令某人心酸
C *n* **1** (pull) (on rope) 拉; (on fishing line) 拽; **to give a rope a ~** 拉一下绳子; **the ~ of old habits/loyalties** 旧习/忠诚的力量 **2** fig (strong feeling) 一股强烈情感 [尤指痛苦]; **a big ~ at parting** 分别时的巨大痛苦; **the ~ of attraction** 强烈的吸引力 **3** **~ (boat)** Naut 拖船

tug of love Brit colloq
A *n* (*pl* **tugs of love**) 孩子监护权的争夺
B *modif* **tug-of-love** 涉及孩子监护权争夺的; **tug-of-love children/case** 监护权有争议的孩子/孩子监护权纠纷案

tug-of-war *n* [u and c] **1** Sport 拔河比赛 **2** fig 激烈争夺

tuition /tju:ˈɪʃn, Amer tu:-/ *n* [u] **1** (tutoring) [对个人或小组的] 讲授; **private ~** 私人教师指导; **to give ~ to sb.** 给某人上课; **~ in** *or* **on sth.** 某方面的课程 **2** Amer (fees) 学费

tuition fees *npl* [大专院校的] 学费

tulip /ˈtju:lɪp, Amer ˈtu:-/ *n* 郁金香

tulip tree *n* 美国鹅掌楸

tulle /tju:l, Amer tu:l/ *n* [u] (for dresses, hats) 薄纱; (for tutus) 绢网

tum /tʌm/ *n* Brit colloq 肚子

tumble /ˈtʌmbl/
A *vi* **1** (fall) «*person*» 跌倒; «*object*» 坠落; «*rocks*» 滚下; «*water*» 泻落; **to ~ down the stairs/slope** 滚下楼梯/斜坡; **to ~ out of bed/the boat** 摔下床/船; **to come tumbling down** «*wall*» 倒塌; **to ~ off sth.** 从…摔下 ‹*cliff, roof, shelf*›; **curls ~d about her shoulders** 卷发垂落在她的肩上 **2** Fin «*prices, shares*» 暴跌 **3** (roll over and over) «*person*» 打滚; «*vehicle*» 侧翻 **4** (do acrobatics) «*clown*» 做空翻动作
B *vt* **1** (toss around) 使…翻滚 ‹*objects, clothes*› **2** (tumble-dry) 甩干 ‹*clothes, washing*› **3** esp Brit (disarrange) 弄乱 ‹*pile, objects, hair*›; **~d sheets** 杂乱的一堆床单
C *n* **1** (fall) 跌倒; **to take a ~** 跌跤; fig 急遽下降 **2** Fin 暴跌; **to take a 50-point ~** «*shares*» 猛跌 50 点 **3** (acrobatic feat) 空翻动作 **4** (jumble) (of clothes) 杂乱; (of objects) 混乱; (of hair) 蓬乱; **a ~ of curls** 蓬乱的卷发

Phrasal verb

- **tumble to** *vt* [**~ to sth.**] Brit colloq 突然意识到 ‹*fact, plan, meaning*›

tumble: ~down *adj attrib* 摇摇欲坠的 ‹*building*›; 破败不堪的 ‹*shack, cottage*›; **~ drier, ~ dryer** *n* Brit 滚筒式烘干机; **~-dry** *vt* 用滚筒式烘干机烘干

tumbler[1] /ˈtʌmblə(r)/ *n* **1** (glass) 玻璃杯 **2** (tumblerful) 一玻璃杯; **a ~ of water/whisky** 一玻璃杯水/威士忌

tumbler[2] *n* (acrobat) [尤指表演翻筋斗的] 杂技演员

tumbler drier *n* **= tumble drier**

tumblerful /ˈtʌmbləfʊl/ *n* 一玻璃杯; **a ~ of sth.** 一玻璃杯某物

tumbleweed /ˈtʌmblwi:d/ *n* [u] 风滚草

tumbling /ˈtʌmblɪŋ/
A *n* ▸**p. 307** [u] 空翻
B *adj attrib* **1** (falling, rushing) 泻落的 ‹*water, hair*›; **a mass of ~ curls** 垂落的一团卷发 **2** (decreasing) 暴跌的 ‹*prices, shares*›

tumescence /tju:ˈmesns, Amer tu:-/ *n* [u] formal 胀大

tumescent /tju:ˈmesnt, Amer tu:-/ *adj* formal [尤指由于性刺激] 胀大的

tummy /ˈtʌmi/ *n* colloq (stomach, abdomen) 肚子; (paunch) 啤酒肚; **~ bug/trouble** 反胃/胃病

tummy: ~ache *n* [c and u] colloq 肚子痛; **~ tuck** *n* colloq 腹部整形术; **to have a ~ tuck** 做腹部整形手术; **~ upset** *n* colloq 反胃

tumour Brit, **tumor** Amer /ˈtju:mə(r), Amer ˈtu:-/ *n* 肿瘤; **brain ~** 脑瘤; **a benign/malignant ~** 良性/恶性肿瘤

tumuli /ˈtju:mjʊlaɪ, Amer ˈtu:-/ *pl* ▸**tumulus**

tumult /ˈtju:mʌlt, Amer ˈtu:-/ *n* [c and u] formal **1** (uproar) 喧哗; (noisy chaos) 吵闹; **to be in ~** 喧嚷吵闹 **2** (confusion, disorder) 混乱; **in the ~ of the fight** 在混战中; **to be in (a) ~** 处于骚动中 **3** (emotional turmoil) 思绪不宁; **to throw sb. into a ~** 使某人心烦意乱; **a ~ of passion/rage/confused feelings** 一阵激动/怒火/迷惑

tumultuous /tju:ˈmʌltjʊəs, Amer tu:ˈm-/ *adj* **1** (noisy) 喧嚣的 ‹*cheers, crowds, meeting*›; 热烈的 ‹*welcome, applause*› **2** (confused, disorderly) 动荡的 ‹*period*›; 狂暴的 ‹*upheaval, protest, parade*› **3** (turbulent) 激动的 ‹*emotions*›; **a ~ life/relationship** 风雨人生/冲突不断的关系

tumultuously /tju:ˈmʌltjʊəsli, Amer tu:ˈm-/ *adv* 热烈地 ‹*welcome, cheer*›; 激动地 ‹*shout*›; 狂暴地 ‹*protest*›

tumulus /ˈtju:mjʊləs, Amer ˈtu:-/ *n* (*pl* **tumuli**) 古坟

tun /tʌn/ *n* **1** (cask) 大酒桶 **2** (as measure) 一大桶; **a ~ of beer** 一大桶啤酒

tuna /ˈtju:nə, Amer ˈtu:-/ *n* (*pl* **~** *or* **~s**) **1** [u and c] Zool 金枪鱼; **~ fishing/canning** 捕金枪鱼/金枪鱼罐头生产; **a ~ rod** 金枪鱼钓竿 **2** [u] **~ (fish)** Culin 金枪鱼肉; **a ~ sandwich/roll/salad** 金枪鱼三明治/卷/色拉

tundra /ˈtʌndrə/ *n* [u] 冻原

tune /tju:n, Amer tu:n/
A *n* **1** [c] (melody) 曲调; **to play/hum/sing/whistle a ~** 弹/哼/唱/用口哨吹曲子; **to compose** *or* **write a ~** 谱曲; **to sing/dance to the ~ of sth.** 随某个曲子唱歌/起舞; **the troops left to the ~ of The British Grenadiers** 部队在《英国掷弹兵进行曲》的乐曲声中离开; **to dance to sb.'s ~** fig 对某人言听计从; **to call the ~** 发号施令; **to change one's ~, to sing another ~** 改口; **she'll change her ~ soon enough when she finds he's left without paying** 等她发现他没有付款就走掉时, 她就会马上换个腔调了; ▸**piper 1** **2** [u] (accurate pitch) 准确的音高; **in/out of ~** 音调准确/不准的; **to be in/out of ~ (with sb./sth.)** (与某人/某事物) 一致/不一致; **few young violinists can play in ~** 没有几个年轻小提琴手能拉琴不走调; **the choir sang the whole piece clearly out of ~** 很明显, 合唱队把整首歌曲唱走调了; **you're out of ~ with current thinking** 你跟不上当今社会的思想潮流; **the government is out of ~ with the electorate** 政府与全体选民唱反调 **3** [c] colloq (amount) **to the ~ of ...** 共计…; **they drank wine and spirits to the ~ of £500** 他们喝葡萄酒和烈性酒花费高达 500 英镑; **the stadium was overfull to the ~ of 2,000 spectators** 体育场爆满观众, 多达 2,000 人
B *vt* **1** Mus 给…调音 ‹*instrument, string*›; **her voice is like a well-~d cello** 她的嗓音宛如音调纯正的大提琴; **to ~ an instrument to concert pitch** 把乐器调到音乐会音高 **2** Mech 调节 ‹*machine, device, part*›; **the car's engine needs tuning** 汽车发动机需要调试 **3** Radio, TV 给…调谐 ‹*radio, TV, signal*›; **to ~ sth. to sth.** 将某物调到 ‹*channel, station, frequency*›; **~ your radio to the**

FM waveband for better reception 要获得更好的收听效果，请把收音机调到调频波段; **stay ~d** 不要换台

(Phrasal verbs)

• **tune in**

A *vt* [**~ sth. in, ~ in sth.**] 把…调好 ‹*radio, television*›; **the television's not ~d in properly** 电视机没有调好; **to ~ one's radio in to the morning programme** 把收音机调到早间节目; **people who are ~d in to what computers can do** 熟谙计算机功能的人们; **it's important to be ~d in to your child's needs** 了解自己孩子的需求很重要

B *vi* (adjust) 调好; (listen) 收听; **when we ~d in, all we heard was martial music** 我们调好后听到的都是军乐; **don't forget to ~ in on Monday!** 别忘了在星期一收听！; **to ~ in to sth.** 收听 ‹*channel, frequency*›; **to ~ in to sb.'s way of thinking** 理解某人的思维方式

• **tune out**

A *vt* **1** [**~ out sth.**] Radio, TV 停止收听 ‹*sound, frequency*› **2** [**~ sth./sb. out, ~ out sth./sb.**] colloq (ignore) 对…充耳不闻 ‹*conversation, person*›

B *vi* colloq 充耳不闻; **when they started arguing, I just ~d out** 当他们开始争吵时，我只当没听见

• **tune up**

A *vt* [**~ sth. up, ~ up sth.**] **1** Mus 为…调音 ‹*instrument*› **2** Aut 调节 ‹*car, engine*›

B *vi* 调音; **I arrived just as the orchestra was tuning up** 我正好在管弦乐队调音时赶到

tuneful /ˈtjuːnfl, Amer ˈtuː-/ *adj* 音调优美的 ‹*music, song, singer*›; 悦耳的 ‹*voice, instrument*›

tunefully /ˈtjuːnfəlɪ, Amer ˈtuː-/ *adv* 音调优美地 ‹*play*›; 悦耳地 ‹*sing*›

tunefulness /ˈtjuːnflnɪs, Amer ˈtuː-/ *n* [u] (of music, instrument) 音调优美; (of singer) 声音悦耳

tuneless /ˈtjuːnlɪs, Amer ˈtuː-/ *adj* 不成调的 ‹*whistling, humming*›; 不好听的 ‹*song*›; 不悦耳的 ‹*music*›

tunelessly /ˈtjuːnlɪsli, Amer ˈtuː-/ *adv* 不悦耳地 ‹*sing, chant*›; 不成调地 ‹*play, whistle*›

tuner /ˈtjuːnə(r), Amer ˈtuː-/ *n* **1** ▸**p. 409** Mus (person) 调音者 **2** Mus (device) 电子调音器 **3** Radio (unit) 调谐器 **4** Radio (knob) 调谐钮

tuner amplifier *n* 调谐放大器

tune-up *n* [对发动机的] 调试

tungsten /ˈtʌŋstən/ *n* [u] 钨; **a ~ lamp/filament/steel** 钨丝灯/钨丝/钨钢

tunic /ˈtjuːnɪk, Amer ˈtuː-/ *n* **1** (loose garment) (**Greek**) **~** 无袖短袍; (for women) 宽松外套; (**gym**) **~** 体操衫 **2** (uniform jacket) 紧身短上衣

tuning /ˈtjuːnɪŋ, Amer ˈtuː-/ *n* **1** [c and u] (of radio, TV) 调谐; (of musical instrument) 调音; (of car, engine) 调节; **~ dial** 调谐刻度盘; **a ~ key/pin** 调音键/弦轴 **2** [c] Mus (key, set of pitches) [尤指弦乐器的] 音调

tuning: ~ fork *n* 音叉; **~ knob** *n* 调谐钮

Tunis /ˈtjuːnɪs, Amer ˈtuː-/ *pr n* 突尼斯（市）

Tunisia /tjuːˈnɪzɪə, Amer tuː-/ *pr n* 突尼斯

Tunisian /tjuːˈnɪzɪən, Amer tuː-/ ▸**p. 503**

A *adj* (of Tunisia) 突尼斯的; (of the people) 突尼斯人的

B *n* 突尼斯人

tunnel /ˈtʌnl/

A *n* **1** (passage) (for vehicles, boats) 隧道; (for pedestrians) 地下通道; **light at the end of the ~** fig 黑暗尽头的光明 **2** (animal burrow) 洞穴通道 **3** (in stadium) 运动员通道

B *vt* (*pres p etc.* **-ll-** Brit, **-l-** Amer) 挖 ‹*passage, hole*›; **to ~ one's way through sth.** 在某物中挖通道; **the river ~led its way through the mountain** 河流在山中冲出一条水道

C *vi* (*pres p etc.* **-ll-** Brit, **-l-** Amer) 挖地道; **to ~ in/under sth.** 在某物中/某物下挖地道; **to ~ through sth.** 开辟通道穿过某物

tunnel: ~ effect *n* 隧道效应; **~ vision** *n* [u] **1** Med 管状视; **2** fig colloq 狭隘的眼光; **to have ~ vision** 见识狭隘

tuppence /ˈtʌpəns/ *n* Brit **1** (twopence) 两便士 **2** colloq (small amount) 很少的量; **it's not worth ~** 这没什么价值; **to not care ~** 毫不在乎

tuppenny /ˈtʌpəni/ *adj attrib* Brit 两便士的 ‹*item, journey*›

tuppenny-ha'penny /ˌtʌpənɪˈheɪpəni/ *adj* Brit **1** (worth two and a half pence) 值两便士半的; **a ~ stamp** 一张两便士半的邮票 **2** colloq (worthless) 无价值的 ‹*item*›; 不重要的 ‹*company, event*›

turban /ˈtɜːbən/ *n* (man's headdress) 包头巾; (lady's hat) 头巾帽

turbaned, turbanned /ˈtɜːbənd/ *adj attrib* 包着头巾的

turbid /ˈtɜːbɪd/ *adj* liter **1** (cloudy, thick) 浑浊的 ‹*waters, stream*› **2** fig (obscure, confused) 朦胧的 ‹*images*›; 混乱的 ‹*thoughts*›

turbine /ˈtɜːbaɪn/ *n* 涡轮机; **a wind/gas/steam ~** 风轮机/燃气涡轮机/汽轮机

turbo /ˈtɜːbəʊ/ *n* **1** (turbocharger) 涡轮增压器; (engine) 涡轮增压发动机 **2** (vehicle) 涡轮增压发动机汽车

turbo: ~charge *vt* 给…安装涡轮增压器 ‹*engine, car*›; **~charged** *adj* 涡轮增压的 ‹*engine*›; 装有涡轮增压发动机的 ‹*car*›; **~charger** *n* 涡轮增压器; **~fan** *n* **1** (engine) 涡轮风扇发动机; **2** (aircraft) 涡轮风扇式飞机; **~generator** *n* 涡轮发电机; **~jet** *n* **1** (engine) **~ (engine)** 涡轮喷气发动机; **2** (aircraft) 涡轮喷气飞机; **~prop** *n* **1** (engine) **~ (engine)** 涡轮螺旋桨发动机; **a ~prop aircraft** 涡轮螺旋桨飞机; **2** (aircraft) 涡轮螺旋桨飞机

turbot /ˈtɜːbət/ *n* (*pl* **~** or **~s**) **1** [c] Zool 大菱鲆 **2** [u] Culin 食用大菱鲆

turbulence /ˈtɜːbjʊləns/ *n* [u] **1** (storminess) (of air) 湍流; (of waves, sea) 紊流 **2** (instability) 动荡; (unrest) 动乱; (emotional) 紊乱

turbulent /ˈtɜːbjʊlənt/ *adj* **1** (rough, stormy) 猛烈的 ‹*air*›; 汹涌的 ‹*sea, waves*› **2** (in turmoil, unstable) 动荡的 ‹*region, times*›; 骚乱的 ‹*mob*›; 混乱的 ‹*thoughts*›; 失控的 ‹*mood, emotions*› **3** Phys 涡旋的 ‹*flow, motion*›

turd /tɜːd/ *n* taboo sl **1** (faeces) 粪块 **2** (objectionable person) 讨厌鬼

tureen /təˈriːn/ *n* [盛汤的] 有盖海碗

turf /tɜːf/

A *n* (*pl* **~s** or **turves**) **1** [u] (lawn) 草地; (peat) 泥炭; **to lay ~** 铺草地 **2** [c] (cut piece of grass and topsoil) 草皮; (piece of peat) 泥炭块 **3** [c and u] (horse racing) **the ~** 赛马 **4** [c] colloq (territory) [自己的] 势力范围; **home ~** 自己的地盘; **to be back on one's own ~** 回到自己的地盘

B *vt* **1** (cover with turf) 用草皮铺 ‹*garden, earth*›; **a newly ~ed lawn/grave** 新铺的草坪/新铺了草皮的坟墓 **2** Brit colloq (eject) **to ~ sb. off (of sth.)** （从某处）把某人撵走; **to be ~ed off the bus** 被赶下公共汽车; **to ~ sb.'s belongings off the chair** 把放在椅子上的某人的物品扔掉

(Phrasal verb)

• **turf out** *vt* Brit colloq **1** [**~ sb. out**] (eject) 赶走; **to be ~ed out of office/the squad** 被逐出办公室/小组 **2** [**~ sth. out, ~ out sth.**] (discard) 扔掉 ‹*objects*›; (reject) 对…不予考虑 ‹*ideas*›

turf: ~ accountant ▸**p. 409** *n* Brit formal [赛马等的] 赌注登记人; **~ war, ~ battle** *ns* colloq 地盘争夺战

turgid /ˈtɜːdʒɪd/ *adj* **1** pej (pompous) 浮夸的 ‹*language, style*›; 华而不实的 ‹*article, speech*› **2** (swollen) 上涨的 ‹*river, waters*›

turgidly /ˈtɜːdʒɪdli/ *adv* **1** pej (pompously) 浮夸地 ‹*speak, worded*›; **a ~ written book** 华而不实的书 **2** (in a swollen manner) 膨胀地 ‹*move*›; **~ flowing water** 上涨的水流

Turk /tɜːk/ ▸**p. 503** *n* 土耳其人

Turkey /ˈtɜːki/ *pr n* 土耳其

turkey /ˈtɜːki/ *n* (*pl* **~s**) **1** [c] Zool 火鸡 **2** [u] Culin 火鸡肉; **to talk ~** Amer colloq 说话直来直去 **3** [c] Amer colloq (flop) [尤指戏剧或电影的] 失败之作 **4** [c] pej (stupid person) 笨蛋

turkey: ~ buzzard *n* Amer = **~ vulture**; **~ cock** *n* **1** Zool 雄火鸡; **2** colloq pej (pompous person) 自负的人; **~ vulture** *n* 红头美洲鹫

Turkish /ˈtɜːkɪʃ/ ▸**p. 503, p. 426**

A *adj* (of Turkey) 土耳其的; (of the people) 土耳其人的; (of the language) 土耳其语的; **the ~ Empire** Hist 奥斯曼帝国

B *n* [u] (language) 土耳其语

C *npl* **the ~** (people) 土耳其人

Turkish: ~ bath *n* 土耳其浴; **~ coffee** *n* [u] 土耳其咖啡; **~ delight** *n* [u and c] 土耳其软糖; **~ towel** *n* 土耳其毛巾

Turkmen /ˈtɜːkmən/ ▸**p. 503, p. 426**

A *adj* (of the people) 土库曼人的; (of the language) 土库曼语的

B *n* (*pl* **~** or **~s**) **1** [c] (person) 土库曼人 **2** [u] (language) 土库曼语

Turkmenistan /ˌtɜːkmenɪˈstɑːn/ *pr n* 土库曼斯坦

turmeric /ˈtɜːmərɪk/ *n* **1** [u] (spice) 姜黄根粉 **2** [c] (plant) 姜黄

turmoil /ˈtɜːmɔɪl/ *n* [u] 混乱; **emotional/political ~** 情绪的纷乱/政治动乱; **to be in (a state of) ~** 处于混乱（状态）之中

turn /tɜːn/

A *vi* **1** (rotate) «*wheel, key, planet*» 转动; **the handle was rusted and wouldn't ~** 把手生锈了，转不动; **to ~ and face sb.** 转过身面对某人; **to ~ on sth.** lit 绕某物转动; fig (have as focus) 以某事物为中心; (depend) 依赖某事物; **our conversation ~ed on matters of mutual interest** 我们的谈话关乎双方共同利益; **everything ~s on who takes over at the top** 一切都取决于谁接替最高领导职位; **to ~ to** or **towards sb./sth.** 转向某人/某物; **my head** or **brain was ~ing** (dizzy) 我感到眩晕; (confused) 我一头雾水 **2** (change direction) «*person, vehicle*» 转向; «*road*» 转弯; fig «*person, mind*» 转变; **to ~ (to the) left** 向左转; **he ~ed into a doorway along the corridor** 他拐进走廊上的一个门廊里; **we ~ed off the main road and travelled along a quiet country lane** 我们离开公路沿着一条寂静的乡村小道前行; **to ~ towards sth.** 转向某处; **her thoughts ~ed to her family at home** 她想到了在家里的家人; **I don't know where** or **which way to ~** 我不知道何去何从; **to ~ to sb./sth.** 求助于某人/某事物; **people ~ed to religion as a refuge from troubled times** 人们转而从宗教中寻求慰藉以逃避乱世; **to ~ to sb./sth. for sth.** 为某事物求助于某人/某事物; **to ~ to page 33** 翻到 33 页 **3** (reverse direction) «*person, vehicle, tide*» 折返; **she ~ed and came back** 她掉头回来了; **'no ~ing'** “禁止转弯”; **your luck may ~** 你会时来运转的; **to ~ on sb.** 突然攻击某人; **the dog ~ed on her and bit her** 那条狗突然扑上去咬了她 **4** (go sour) «*milk, cream*» 变馊 **5** (change) 变化; **to ~ into sth.** 变成某事物; **the situation was rapidly ~ing into a farce** 这一局面正迅速演变成一场闹剧; **his hopes had ~ed to dust and ashes** 他的希望破灭了; **his face ~ed deathly pale** 他的脸变得死灰一般; **she suddenly ~ed all sweet and charming** 她突然变得可爱迷人; **to ~ politician/farmer** 变成政客/农民; **to ~ Catholic/Muslim** 皈依天主教/伊斯兰教 **6** Bot «*tree*» 变枯黄; **as autumn advanced, all the leaves ~ed** 随着秋意渐浓，树叶都变了颜色

B *vt* **1** (rotate) 转动 ‹*screw, wheel*›; **to ~ a knob/**

handle/switch/key to the right 把旋钮/拉手/开关/钥匙向右转; **to ~ sth. through 90°/180°** 把某物转 90 度/180 度; **to ~ the key on sb.** 把某人锁起来 **2** (change direction of) 掉转〈*vehicle, head*〉; **can you ~ your face this way a little?** 你把脸向这边转一点好吗?; **to ~ one's attention/mind to sth.** 把注意力/心思转到某事; **to ~ one's back on sb./sth.** 转身背对某人/某物; **she resolved to ~ her back on her former beliefs** 她决心放弃以前的信仰; **when sb.'s back is ~ed** (no longer present) 当某人离开时; (no longer paying attention) 当某人不注意时; **to ~ one's hand to sth.** 动手做某事; **she can ~ her hand to anything** 她什么活儿都可以干; **to ~ a hose/searchlight on sb./sth.** 把水龙带/探照灯对准某人/某物; **they ~ed their guns on the crowd** 他们把枪口指向人群; **to ~ one's attention/mind to sth.** 把注意力/心思转到某事物上来; **to ~ a corner** 转过街角; **our financial problems have ~ed a corner at last** 我们的财务问题终于出现了转机 **3** (turn over) 翻〈*soil*〉; 翻转〈*mattress, steak*〉; **to be idly ~ing the pages of a magazine** 在悠闲地翻看杂志; **to ~ the pillowcases** 把枕套翻个个儿; **help me ~ him on to his side/back** 帮我把他身子侧过来/翻个身仰卧; **to ~ one's stomach** 反胃; **to ~ one's ankle** 崴脚踝 **4** (transform) 变化; **to ~ sb./sth. ...** 使某人/某物变成…; **to ~ sth. white/black** 把某物变白/变黑; **to ~ one's friends green with envy** 让朋友们嫉妒得要命; **to ~ sb./sth. into sth.** 将某人/某事物变成某状态; **a wicked witch had ~ed him into a frog** 邪恶的女巫把他变成了青蛙; **to ~ a book into a play/film** 将一部书改编成戏剧/电影; **~ your assets into hard cash!** 把你的资产变现! **5** (in time) (reach) 达到; (pass) 超过; **she's just ~ed thirty** 她刚满 30 岁; **it's just ~ed five (o'clock)** 刚过 5 点 **6** (deflect) 推开〈*thrust, person*〉; fig 转移〈*conversation*〉; **the keeper managed to ~ the shot past the post** 守门员将球挡出了门柱; **I tried to ~ the discussion towards a safer topic** 我尽量把讨论引到比较安全的话题上; **she rebuffed all attempts to ~ her from her purpose** 所有试图使她改变主意的尝试都被她一概回绝了; **to ~ sb. from one's door** 把某人拒之门外 **7** (shape on lathe) 车削〈*wood*〉; fig 造〈*phrase*〉; **the spindles were ~ed on a lathe** 这些转轴是在一台车床上车出来的; **he seems incapable of ~ing a reasonably elegant sentence** 他看来写不出像样的文雅句子

C *n* **1** (circular movement) 转动; **to give a screw/handle a couple of ~s** 把螺丝/把手拧几下; **a complicated series of leaps and ~s** 一系列复杂的跳跃和转体; **to go for or take a ~ around the block** 到该街区转一圈; **it was another ~ of the screw** fig 这是雪上加霜; **to be done to a ~** Culin 烹调得恰到火候 **2** (change of direction) (in vehicle) 转向; (on foot) 转身; **a left ~** 左转; **'no right ~'** "禁止右转"; **to make a ~ to port/starboard** 向左舷/右舷转; **a 90°/180° ~** 90 度/180 度转向 **3** (bend, side road) 弯道; **the road is full of twists and ~s** 这条路弯弯曲曲; **a left ~** 左转弯 **4** (change) 转变; (development) 发展; **a ~ in or of sth.** 某事的转变; **a ~ of events** 事态变化; **at the ~ of the century** 在世纪之交; **at every ~** 每次; **she met with disappointment at every ~** 她事事不顺心; **to be on the ~** 《*tide, luck*》即将改变; 《*milk*》即将变质; **to take an unexpected/alarming/encouraging ~** 发生意外的/骇人的/令人鼓舞的转变; **to take a ~ for the better/worse** 《*patient, condition*》好转/恶化; **a ~ of speed** 突然加速 **5** (go) 轮到的机会; **a ~ to do sth.** 轮到的做某事的机会; **it's your ~ to make the coffee** 该你煮咖啡了; **to have a ~ at or on or with sth.** 轮到某事物; **they kindly let me have a ~ at using their new computer** 他们客气地让我用了用他们的新电脑; **by ~s** 轮流地; **I was by ~s elated and utterly miserable** 我时而兴高采烈, 时而痛苦万分; **in ~** 依次; **she said a few words to each of us in ~** 她逐一和我们每个人说了几句话; **out of ~** 未轮到; **she went out of ~ because she has to leave early today** 她不到时间就离开了, 因为她今天得早走; **to miss a or one's ~** 错过一轮; **to speak out of ~** fig 说话冒失; **to take it in ~s to do sth., to take ~s at doing sth.** 轮流做某事; **to do sth. ~ and ~ about** 轮换着做某事; **to wait one's ~** 排队等候 **6** (tendency) 倾向; **to have an enquiring/enterprising ~ of mind** 有好学之心/进取心; **a ~ of phrase** 措词 **7** colloq (attack) 不适感; **a dizzy ~** 一阵眩晕; **it gave me quite a (nasty) ~** 这让我(着实)吓了一跳 **8** (service) 服务; **to do sb. a good/bad ~** 帮某人的忙/坏某人的事; **one good ~ deserves another** Prov 要知恩图报 **9** Theat (performance) 小节目; (performer) 表演者; **a comic/variety ~** 喜剧/杂耍节目

D *v refl* **to ~ oneself into sth.** 将自身变成某状况; **we're going to ~ ourselves into a limited company** 我们要改变成有限公司; **I took evening classes, hoping to ~ myself into a competent painter** 我上了夜校, 希望成为一名出色的画家

Phrasal verbs

• **turn about** *vi* 《*soldier*》向后转; **~ about!** 向后转!

• **turn against** *vt* **1** [**~ against sb./sth.**] 反对; **public opinion is ~ing against the government** 公众舆论开始反对政府了 **2** **to ~ sb./sth. against sb./sth.** 使某人/某派别反对某人/某事; **now she's trying to ~ my own children against me** 她正试图教唆我自己的孩子跟我对着干

• **turn around** *vi, vt* = **turn round**

• **turn aside** *vi* 偏离; **he came towards me, but ~ed aside at the last moment** 他向我走来, 但在最后一刻走开了; **to ~ aside from sth.** 偏离某事; **~ing aside for a moment from the main topic under review, ...** 把主要议题暂且放一下, 说句题外话…

• **turn away**

A *vi* (change direction) 转过脸去; **he ~ed away in disgust/horror** 他厌恶地/恐惧地转过头去; **to ~ away from sth./sb.** 放弃某事物/拒绝某人

B *vt* **1** [**~ sth. away, ~ away sth.**] (face other way) 把…转过去〈*face, object*〉; **he ~ed his head away just as I was taking the photo** 我拍照的时候他把头转过去了 **2** [**~ sb. away, ~ away sb.**] (refuse entry to) 不准…进入; **they got ~ed away from the Ritz because they weren't properly dressed** 他们因为穿着不得体而被丽兹酒店拒之门外

• **turn back**

A *vi* **1** (return) 返回; **we ~ed back when we'd only gone about a mile** 我们只走了一英里就返回了; **there's no ~ing back** 没有回头路 **2** (in book) 翻回; **to ~ back to page 33** 翻回到 33 页

B *vt* [**~ sth. back, ~ back sth.**]

1 (rotate backwards) 使…反转; **~ the knob back as far as it will go** 将旋钮往回拧到底; **don't forget to ~ your clocks back an hour tonight** 别忘了今晚把钟拨慢一小时; **to ~ the control knob back to zero** 把控制钮转回数字 0; **to ~ the clock back to 1900** 让时光倒流至 1900 年; **it's too late now, you can't ~ back the clock** 现在已经太晚了, 你无法让时光倒转 **2** (fold back) 折起〈*sheet, corner of page*〉 **3** (send away) 把…赶回去〈*protester*〉; 遣返〈*refugees*〉; **we were ~ed back by a security guard** 一名保安把我们撵了回去

• **turn down**

A [**~ sth. down, ~ down sth.**] *vt*

1 (fold over) 翻下〈*collar*〉; 叠起〈*sheet*〉; 折起〈*page*〉; **she made the bed, neatly ~ing down the bedclothes** 她铺好床, 把被子整整齐齐地叠好 **2** (reduce) 调低〈*volume, gas*〉; **with the light ~ed down low** 光线调得很暗地 **3** (put face downwards) 使…面朝下〈*card*〉; **look at your card for a moment, then ~ it down on the table** 先看一下你的牌, 然后牌面朝下放在桌上

B [**~ sb./sth. down, ~ down sb./sth.**] *vt* (reject) 拒绝〈*applicant, offer*〉; **they ~ed down all my ideas** 他们否定了我所有的想法

C *vi* 《*line*》向下弯; **the graph ~s down from the end of July** 曲线图从7月底开始呈下降走势

• **turn forward** *vt* [**~ sth. forward, ~ forward sth.**] 把…往前拨; **don't forget to ~ your clocks forward an hour tonight** 别忘了今晚把钟拨快一小时

• **turn in**

A *vi* **1** colloq (go to bed) 上床睡觉; **I think I'll ~ in now** 我想我该睡觉了 **2** (point inwards) 《*foot*》向内弯; **she walks with her toes ~ed in** 她走路内八字; **to ~ in on itself** 向内弯; **to ~ in on oneself** 闭门谢客

B [**~ sth. in, ~ in sth.**] *vt*

1 (hand back) 交还〈*badge*〉; **you must ~ in your pass when you leave the building** 你离开大楼时必须交回通行证 **2** colloq (give up) 放弃〈*activity, membership*〉; **I ~ed in my evening job** 我辞去了晚间的工作; **why don't you ~ it in now and go to bed?** 你为什么不现在把它做完然后上床睡觉呢? **3** (hand in, deliver) 上交〈*homework*〉; 提交〈*resignation*〉; 获得〈*time, figures*〉; **she ~ed in her last assignment two weeks late** 她晚了两个星期才交上次的作业; **he ~ed in a quite magnificent performance** 他表演了一个相当精彩的节目

C [**~ sb. in**] *vt* colloq 告发〈*suspect*〉; **I could ~ you in to the customs** 我可以向海关举报你

D *v refl* **to ~ oneself in** colloq 自首; **he went to the police station and ~ed himself in** 他到警察局自首了

• **turn off**

A *vt* **1** [**~ sth. off, ~ off sth.**] (switch off) 关掉〈*switch, engine*〉; 停止〈*programme*〉; **~ the water off, the bath's full** 不要放水了, 浴缸满了; **to ~ sth. off like a tap** 立刻停下某事 **2** [**~ sb. off, ~ off sb.**] colloq (put off) 使厌烦; **nothing ~s me off more or worse than bad breath** 没有什么比口臭更让我讨厌了; **to ~ sb. off sth.** 使某人对某事物失去兴趣; **it's enough to ~ you off sex/drink for life!** 这足以让你一辈子都厌恶性/酒!

B *vi* **1** (leave road) 换道; **where do we ~ off for Derby?** 我们在什么地方换道去德比? **2** (switch off) 关; **where does this light ~ off?** 这盏灯开关在哪里?; **I couldn't understand the lecture, so I just ~ed off** 我听不懂讲座, 所以干脆不听了

• **turn on**

A *vt* **1** [**~ sth. on, ~ on sth.**] (switch on) 打开〈*tap, radio, television*〉; 启动〈*computer, engine*〉; **I've ~ed the water on for a bath** 我已经开始放洗澡水了; **to ~ on the charm/flattery** 施展魅力/开始奉承; **to ~ on the pressure** 施压; **to ~ sth. on like a tap** 立刻开始某事 **2** [**~ sb. on, ~ on sb.**] colloq (arouse) 引起…的兴趣; **I get ~ed on by short skirts** 我一看到短裙就兴奋; **whatever ~s you on** 随便你怎么想; **to ~ sb. on to sth.** 使某人对某事物着迷

B *vi* 《*light*》打开; 《*machine, appliance*》开启; **I've set the oven to ~ on at half past six** 我已经把烤箱设定在 6 点半启动

• **turn out**

A *vi* **1** (eventually prove to be) 结果是; **it's ~ed out nice again** 后来天气又好了; **to ~ out to be sth.** 结果是某事物; **she's ~ing out to be a first-class manager** 她正在成长为一名一流的经理; **to ~ out to do sth.** 原来是某种情况; **my mother ~s out to have gone to school with him** 我母亲原来同他

一起上过学; **it ~s out that ...** 结果是…; **as it ~ed out, ...** 果不其然, … 2 (come out) «*crowd, people*» 出现; **a large crowd ~ed out in the streets** 街上冒出了一大群人; **to ~ out for sth./to do sth.** 为某事/做某事出来; **only 40% of the electorate ~ed out to vote** 结果只有40%的选民投票 3 (point outwards) «*toe*» 向外撇; **my feet ~ out slightly** 我的脚稍稍有点儿外八字 4 colloq (get up) 起床; **we all ~ed out bright and early** 我们都一大早起床了

B vt [**~ sth./sb. out, ~ out sth./sb.**]
1 (switch off) 关 ‹*light, gas*›; 熄灭 ‹*lamp*›; **~ out the candle before you come to bed** 睡觉前先吹灭蜡烛 2 (empty) 腾空 ‹*attic, cabinet*›; 掏空 ‹*pocket, handbag*›; 把…倒出 ‹*mould, jelly*›; **I'm going to ~ out my desk** 我要清理我的写字台; **I ~ed the blancmange out on a large plate** 我把牛奶冻倒在大盘子上 3 (produce) 生产 ‹*goods*›; 培养 ‹*graduate*›; 写 ‹*script, poem*›; **we've ~ed out some top-rate scientists despite our lack of funds** 尽管我们缺乏资金, 却培养出了一批顶尖科学家 4 (point outwards) 伸出 ‹*feet*›; **the ballet students all ~ed out their toes on cue** 芭蕾舞学生全都按提示伸出脚尖 5 (evict) 赶走 ‹*tenant*›; **the landlord ~ed us out** 房东将我们赶了出来; **go and ~ him out of bed** 去把他从床上弄起来 6 Brit Mil 召集 ‹*troops, police*›; **~ out the guard!** 集合卫兵! 7 (dress, equip) 以…装束出现; **to ~ out a whole cast in Elizabethan costumes** 身穿一整套伊丽莎白女王一世时代的服装

• **turn over**

A vi 1 (roll over) «*person*» 翻身; «*car*» 侧翻; **he ~ed over and went to sleep** 他翻了个身睡着了; **the boat ~ed over, and we were all thrown into the water** 船翻了, 我们都被甩到了水里; **my stomach ~ed over** (from fright, disgust) 我肚子很不舒服 2 (turn page) 翻页; **I ~ed over and read on** 我翻过一页接着读 3 Aut «*engine*» 空转

B vt [**~ sth./sb. over, ~ over sth./sb.**]
1 (reverse) 使…翻过来 ‹*mattress, page*›; **help me ~ the table over** 帮我把桌子翻过来 2 (roll over) 使…翻倒 ‹*vehicle*›; 使…翻身 ‹*patient*›; **a big wave striking the ship side on could ~ it right over** 巨浪打到船舷上, 足以将船掀翻 3 (hand over) 移交 ‹*money, business*›; **customs officials ~ed the man over to the police** 海关官员把那个男子移交给了警方 4 colloq (rob) 抢劫 ‹*shop, person*›; **burglars had ~ed the house over** 盗匪们洗劫了这所住宅 5 (reflect on) 考虑 ‹*idea, offer*›; **I've been ~ing over what you said** 我一直在考虑你的话; **to ~ sth. over in one's mind** 考虑某事 6 Fin 营业额为 ‹*sum*›; **the company ~s over 150 million dollars a year** 这家公司的年营业额为1.5亿美元 7 Comm 销售 ‹*stock, goods*›; **we can't ~ this line over fast enough to make it worth stocking in quantity** 这种产品无法迅速售出, 不值得大量囤货 8 Aut 使…空转 ‹*engine*›

• **turn round** esp Brit

A vi 1 (face different direction) «*person*» 转身; «*vehicle*» 转向; **~ round and face me** 转过来面对我; **to ~ round to do sth.** 转身做某事; **to (just) ~ round and say/do sth.** colloq (只是) 改变主意说某话/做某事 2 (revolve, rotate) «*wheel, planet, dancer*» 旋转; **to ~ round and round** 不断旋转; **to ~ round on its axis** 绕轴转 3 Econ «*business, market*» 向相反方向发展; **we are praying that the sales figures will ~ round before the end of the year** 我们求老天保佑销售量在年底前能有起色 4 Transp (unload and reload) «*aircraft, ship*» 装卸货物

B vt [**~ sth./sb. round, ~ round sth./sb.**]
1 (face other way) 使…转身 ‹*person*›; 使…转向 ‹*vehicle, object*›; **he had ~ed round every single chair in the hall** 他把大厅里的每张椅子都转了过来 2 (reverse) 颠倒 ‹*picture, sentence*› 3 Econ (reverse decline in) 使…好转 ‹*company, economy*›; **it has ~ed my life round** 这使我的生活出现了转机 4 (unload and reload, get ready) 给…装卸货物 ‹*aircraft, ship*›; 装卸 ‹*goods*›; 装卸…的货物 ‹*order*›; **an incoming plane can be ~ed round in under an hour** 一班进港飞机可以在一个小时内装卸完毕

• **turn up**

A vi 1 (arrive) 到来; **she ~ed up in an old shirt and a pair of jeans** 她穿着旧衬衫和牛仔裤来了; **to ~ up for** *or* **to work/for duty** 来上班/值班; **she ~ed up for her appointment two hours late** 她约会迟到了两个小时 2 (be found) 被找到; **I'm sure your watch will ~ up one of these days** 我敢肯定这几天能找到你的手表 3 (present itself) «*opportunity, job*» 出现; **a chance like this doesn't ~ up very often** 这样的机会不常有 4 (point upwards) «*mouth, collar*» 翘起; **his nose ~s up at the end** 他鼻尖上翘

B vt [**~ sth. up, ~ up sth.**]
1 (point upwards) 翻起 ‹*collar*›; **she ~ed up the brim of her hat** 她把帽边翻了起来; **a ~ed-up nose** 朝天鼻 2 (in sewing) 折起 ‹*sleeve, hem*› 3 (discover) 发现 ‹*object, information*›; **I ~ed this up in a little antique shop** 我在一个小古玩店里找到了这个东西 4 (increase, intensify) 调高 ‹*heat, radio, music*›; **can you ~ the sound up a bit, I can't hear** 你能不能把声音弄大点儿, 我听不见 5 Brit colloq (stop) 停止 ‹*activity*›; **~ it up!** 停下来!

turnabout /ˈtɜːnəbaʊt/ *n* 1 (U-turn) 向后转 2 (reversal in policy, opinion, etc.) 转变; **to do a ~ (on sth.)** (在某事上) 彻底改变

turnaround /ˈtɜːnəraʊnd/ *n* 1 (reversal of attitude or trend) 彻底改变 2 (change for the better) 好转 3 Comm, Ind (processing time) 周转期 4 Transp (handling or loading time) 装卸时间 5 Amer (for vehicles) 车辆回转场

turnaround time *n* 1 Comm, Ind (processing time) 周转时间 2 Transp (handling or loading time) 装卸时间

turncoat /ˈtɜːnkəʊt/ *n* 变节者; **a ~ agent** 叛变的特工人员

turndown /ˈtɜːndaʊn/

A *adj attrib* 翻下的 ‹*collar, flap*›

B *n* 1 (downturn) 低落 2 (rejection) 拒绝

turned-out /ˌtɜːndˈaʊt/ *adj* **to be well ~** 打扮得漂漂亮亮; **to be nicely/smartly ~** 穿得漂亮/潇洒

turner /ˈtɜːnə(r)/ *n* 1 (lathe worker) 车工; **a wood-~** 木旋工 2 (implement) 翻动器; **a pancake ~** 翻烙饼的平铲

turning /ˈtɜːnɪŋ/ ▸**p. 905** *n* 1 [c] Brit (turn-off) 转弯处; **to take a wrong ~** 拐错路; **a ~ off the main street** 大街的岔路口 2 [c] (bend) 弯曲处; **at the ~ of the stairs** 在楼梯的拐弯处 3 [u] (using a lathe) (work) 车削工作; (skill, process) 车工工艺

turning: ~ circle *n* 最小回转圆; **~ lathe** *n* 木工车床; **~ point** *n* 转折点; **at a ~ point in one's life/career** 在人生/事业的转折点

turnip /ˈtɜːnɪp/ *n* [c and u] (round root vegetable) 芜菁; (swede) 大头菜; **~ soup** 芜菁汤

turnkey /ˈtɜːnkiː/ *adj attrib* 完整并可立即使用的 ‹*system, operation*›; 总承包的 ‹*contract*›

turnkey project *n* 交钥匙工程

turn-off *n* 1 (in road) 支路; **the Slough ~** 通往斯劳的岔道 2 colloq (repellent factor) 讨厌的事物; (person) 讨厌的人; **to be a (real) ~** «*smell, sight*» (确实) 叫人倒胃口; **to be a ~ to investors** 使投资者望而却步; **he's a total ~** 他一点也不性感

turn-on *n* colloq (stimulating thing) 令人兴奋的事物; (stimulating person) 令人兴奋的人; **to be a total ~** «*scent, style*» 非常刺激; **he's a real ~** 他真性感

turnout /ˈtɜːnaʊt/ *n* 1 [u and c] (attendance) (at meeting) 到会人数; (at event) 到场人数; (at strike, demonstration) 参加人数; **(voter) ~** 投票人数; **a high/low** *or* **poor ~ for the election** 选举的高/低投票率 2 [c] (clean-up) 清理; **to give a room a good ~** 彻底打扫一间屋子 3 [c] *sing* colloq (appearance) (of person) 装束 [尤指制服]; (of thing) 装备 4 [c] Amer (in road) 避车道

turnover /ˈtɜːnəʊvə(r)/ *n* 1 [c and u] (money taken) [一定时期内的] 营业额; **a high/low ~** 高/低营业额; **a ~ of £20,000** 20,000英镑的成交量 2 [c and u] (replacement rate) (of staff) 人员调整率; (of stock) 货物周转率 3 [c] Culin 半圆甜馅饼; **apple ~** 半圆苹果馅饼

turn: ~pike *n* 1 Hist (toll gate) 收税卡; 2 (toll road) 收费公路; 3 Amer (toll expressway) 收费高速公路; **~ signal** *n* Amer 转向灯; **~stile** *n* 旋转栅门

turntable /ˈtɜːnteɪbl/ *n* 1 (of record player) 唱机转盘 2 Rail 转车台

turntable ladder *n* Brit [消防车的] 云梯

turn-up *n* Brit 1 *usu pl* (cuff) 外翻边 2 colloq (surprise) 想不到的事; **a ~ for the books** 出乎意料的事

turpentine /ˈtɜːpəntaɪn/ *n* [u] 松节油

turpitude /ˈtɜːpɪtjuːd, Amer -tuːd/ *n* [u] formal (depravity) 腐化; (wickedness) 邪恶; **moral ~** 道德败坏

turps /tɜːps/ *n* [u] colloq **= turpentine**

turquoise /ˈtɜːkwɔɪz/ ▸**p. 134**

A *n* 1 [u] (colour) 青绿色 2 [u and c] (stone) 绿松石

B *adj* 1 (greenish-blue) 青绿色的 ‹*dress*› 2 (made of turquoise) 绿松石的; **a ~ ring** 绿松石戒指

turret /ˈtʌrɪt/ *n* 1 Archit (on tower) 塔楼; (at corner) 角楼 2 Mil 回转炮塔 3 (of lathe) 转台

turreted /ˈtʌrɪtɪd/ *adj* 1 Archit 有塔楼的 ‹*tower*›; 有角楼的 ‹*castle*› 2 Mil 有回转炮塔的 ‹*tank, cannon*›

turtle /ˈtɜːtl/ *n* 1 [c] Zool (marine) 海龟; (freshwater) 淡水龟; **a fresh-water/mud ~** 淡水龟/泥龟; **a snapping ~** 鳄龟; **to turn ~** «*boat*» 倾覆 2 [u] Culin 海龟肉

turtle: ~ dove *n* 斑鸠; **~ neck** *n* (neckline) 高领; (sweater) 高领套头衫; Amer (polo neck) 高圆翻领; **~-necked** *adj* 高领的

turves /tɜːvz/ *pl* ▸**turf A**

Tuscan /ˈtʌskən/

A *adj* 1 (of Tuscany) 托斯卡纳的; (of the people) 托斯卡纳人的; (of the dialect) 托斯卡纳方言的 2 Archit 托斯卡纳式的

B *n* 1 [c] (person) 托斯卡纳人 2 [u] (dialect) 托斯卡纳方言

Tuscany /ˈtʌskəni/ *pr n* 托斯卡纳区

tusk /tʌsk/ *n* (of elephant, walrus) 长牙; (of wild boar) 獠牙

tusker /ˈtʌskə(r)/ *n* (elephant) 有长牙的大象; (wild boar) 有獠牙的野猪

tussle /ˈtʌsl/

A *n* 1 (struggle) [尤指争夺物品的] 扭打; **to have** *or* **get into a ~ (with sb.)** (与某人) 进行争斗 2 (dispute) 争执; **a ~ about** *or* **over sth.** 关于某事物的争辩; **a verbal/legal ~** 口角/法律争辩

B *vi* 1 (fight) [尤指为争夺物品] 扭打; **to ~ (with sb.) about** *or* **for** *or* **over sth.** (与某人) 争夺某物 2 (dispute) 争执; **to ~ over sth.** 争论某事

tussock /ˈtʌsək/ *n* 草丛

tut /tʌt/ *excl, vi* **= tut-tut**

tutelage /ˈtjuːtɪlɪdʒ, Amer ˈtuː-/ *n* [u] formal 1 (guardianship) (over person) 监护; (over organization) 托管; **(to be) in** *or* **under the ~ of sb.** 受某人监管 2 (tuition) 辅导; (instruction) 指导

tutor /ˈtjuːtə(r), Amer ˈtuː-/ ▸**p. 409**

A *n* 1 (private teacher) **a (private) ~** 家庭教师; **a ~ to sb.** 某人的私人教师; **life is a hard ~** 生活给人以严酷的教训 2 Brit Univ 导师;

an academic/personal ～ 学业/个人指导老师 3 Amer Univ 助教 4 Brit Sch (of class) 班主任; (of year group) 年级组长 5 Brit (book) 课本; **a violin** ～ 小提琴课本

B *vt* 1 (teach privately) 当…的家庭教师; **to ～ sb. in maths/for the exam** 辅导某人的数学/考试 2 Brit Univ 作…的大学导师; **to ～ sb.** 作某人的导师

C *vi* 1 (teach privately) 当家庭教师; **to ～ in French** 做法语私人教师 2 Brit Univ 当大学导师; (as adviser) 做大学辅导老师

tutorial /tjuːˈtɔːrɪəl, Amer tuː-/
A *n* Univ (group) 辅导课; (private) 个别指导; **to give a ～ (in sth.)** (对某课程) 进行辅导
B *adj* (of tutor) 辅导教师的 ‹*duties, capacity*›; (of tuition) 辅导的 ‹*class, session*›

tutorial system 大学辅导制

tutti frutti /ˌtuːti ˈfruːti/ *n* [u] ～ **(ice-cream)** 什锦水果冰激凌

tut-tut /ˌtʌtˈtʌt/
A *excl* 啧啧
B *vi* (*pres p etc.* **-tt-**) 发啧啧声; **to ～ with annoyance** 恼火地咂嘴; **to ～ at sth.** 对某事物咂嘴

tutu /ˈtuːtuː/ *n* 芭蕾舞裙

Tuvalu /ˌtuːvəˈluː/ *pr n* 图瓦卢

tu-whit tu-whoo /təˌwɪt təˈwuː/ *n* 嘟噎嘟呼 [猫头鹰的鸣叫声]

tuxedo /tʌkˈsiːdəʊ/ *n* (*pl* **～s** *or* **～es**) esp Amer 男式无尾礼服

tuyère /twiːˈjeə(r), tuːˈj-/ *n* [冶金炉的] 吹风管嘴

TV *abbr* **= television**

TV dinner *n* [加热即可食用的] 熟食快餐

TVP *abbr* **= textured vegetable protein**

TV: ～ screen *n* 电视屏幕; **～ set** *n* 电视机

twaddle /ˈtwɒdl/ *n* [u] (foolish speech) 蠢话; (foolish writing) 拙劣的文字

twain /tweɪn/ *n* **never** *or* **ne'er the ～ shall meet** 大相径庭

twang /twæŋ/
A *n* 1 (sound of guitar, wire, bow) 拨弦声 2 (accent) 鼻音; **to speak with a bit of a ～** 说话稍带点儿鼻音
B *vt* 弹拨 ‹*guitar, string*›
C *vi* «*bow, guitar*» 发出拨弦声

twangy /ˈtwæŋi/ *adj* 发出拨弦声的 ‹*guitar*›; 带鼻音的 ‹*voice, accent*›

'twas /twɒz, twəz/ archaic or liter **= it was** ▸**be A**

twat /twæt/ *n* 1 sl (unpleasant person) 讨厌鬼 offensive; (stupid person) 蠢材 offensive 2 taboo sl (female genitals) 屄 offensive

tweak /twiːk/
A *vt* 1 (twist, pull) 扭 ‹*cord*›; 拽 ‹*hair*›; 拧 ‹*ear*› 2 colloq (fine-tune) 对…作微调 ‹*engine, machine*›; (improve) 稍稍改进 ‹*system*›; (adjust) 略微改动 ‹*figures, manuscript*›
B *n* 1 (twist) 扭; (pull) 拽; **to give sth. a ～** 拧某物一下 2 colloq (adjustment) [机械装置或系统的] 轻微调整; **to make a few ～s to the script** 对稿子作几处修改

twee /twiː/ *adj* (*comp* **tweer** /ˈtwiːə(r)/, *superl* **tweest** /ˈtwiːɪst/) Brit colloq pej 花里胡哨的 ‹*house, decor*›; 矫揉造作的 ‹*manner*›; 自作多情的 ‹*person*›

tweed /twiːd/
A *n* [u] 粗花呢; **a ～ skirt/rug** 粗花呢裙子/小地毯
B **tweeds** *npl* 粗花呢服装

tweedy /ˈtwiːdi/ *adj* 1 (made from tweed) 粗花呢的 ‹*garment*›; (tweed-like) 似粗花呢的 ‹*material*› 2 colloq (wearing tweeds) 常穿粗花呢衣服的 ‹*farmer*› 3 hum or pej (rural and robust) 乡绅派头的 ‹*person, gathering*›

tweenie, tweeny /ˈtwiːni/ *n* colloq [10至14岁之间的] 小少年

tweet /twiːt/
A *n* 1 (of bird) 啁啾声 2 Comput, Telecom (一条) 微博 [twitter网用户发布的信息]
B *vi* «*bird*» 啁啾

tweeter /ˈtwiːtə(r)/ *n* 高频扬声器

tweeze /twiːz/ *vt* (take hold of) [用镊子等] 钳住 ‹*hair*›; (pluck) 拔 ‹*hair, eyebrows*›

tweezers /ˈtwiːzəz/ *npl* 镊子; **eyebrow ～** 眉钳; **a pair of ～** 一把镊子

twelfth /twelfθ/ ▸**p. 181, p. 521**
A *n* 1 (in sequence) 第十二个 2 (in date) 12 日; **the (Glorious) T～** Brit Hunt 八月十二日 [狩猎松鸡季节的开始日] 3 (fraction) 十二分之一
B *adj* 1 (in sequence) 第十二的 2 (in name, title) 十二; **Louis the T～** 路易十二 3 (as fraction) 十二分之一的
C *adv* 1 (twelfthly) 第十二 2 (in twelfth position) 居第十二位

twelve /twelv/ ▸**p. 15, p. 521, p. 831**
A *n* 1 (number, quantity) 十二 2 (in time) 12 点钟; **at ～ (o'clock)** 在 12 点 3 (age) 12 岁 4 (group) (of people) 十二人一组; (of things) 十二个一组 5 **the Twelve** Bible 十二先知书 6 **(size)** ～ 十二码 7 Brit Cin 适合 12 岁以上观众观看的影片
B *adj* 1 (in number) 十二的; **～ metres** 12 米; **～ paintings** 12 张画; **～ years/miles** 12 年/英里; **～ months/novels** 12 个月/12 本小说 2 (in age) 12 岁的; **to be ～ (years old)** 12 岁大; **to be over/under ～** 超过/不到 12 岁; **she is ～ (years old)** 她 12 岁了 3 (in series) 第十二的; **size/number ～** 12 码/12 号

twelve: ～ mile limit *n* [领海范围的] 十二海里界限; **～ tone** *adj* 十二音的 ‹*piece*›

twentieth /ˈtwentɪəθ/ ▸**p. 181, p. 521**
A *n* 1 (in sequence) 第二十个 2 (in date) **the ～** 20 日 3 (fraction) 二十分之一
B *adj* 1 (in sequence) 第二十的 2 (as fraction) 二十分之一的
C *adv* 居第二十位

twenty /ˈtwenti/ ▸**p. 15, p. 521, p. 831**
A *n* 1 (number, quantity) 二十; **there are ～ of us** 我们有 20 个人 2 (in age) 20 岁 3 (group) (of people) 二十人一组; (of things) 二十个一组 4 **(size)** ～ 二十码
B *adj* 1 (in number) 二十的; **～ boys** 20 个男孩; **～ years/metres** 20 年/米; **～ months/novels** 20 个月/20 本小说 2 (in age) 20 岁的; **I'm nearly ～** 我快 20 岁了 3 (in series) 第二十的; **page/number ～** 20 页/号

twenty-four/seven, twenty-four seven, 24/7, 24-7 *adv* colloq 全天候地 [即每天24小时，每周7天]

twenty: ～-one ▸**p. 307** *n* [u] 二十一点牌戏; **～-～, 20/20** *adj* 正常的 ‹*vision*›; **～-two metre line** *n* [橄榄球运动的] 22 米线

twerp /twɜːp/ *n* colloq pej (fool) 笨蛋; (annoying person) 讨厌鬼

twice /twaɪs/ ▸**p. 288** *adv* 1 (two times) 两次; **to happen ～** 发生两次; **to do/see sth. ～** 两次做某事/看见某物; **～ a day/month** *etc.*, **～ daily/monthly** *etc.* 每天/每月等两次; **～ over** 不止一次，而是两次; **to think ～ about sth./doing sth.** 慎重考虑某事/做某事 2 (double) (in quantity, rate, degree, etc.) 两倍; **～ as long/many** 两倍长/两倍之多; **to be ～ as strong/big as sb.** 比某人强一倍/大一倍; **to be ～ as good (a player) as sb.** (作为运动员) 同某人一样优秀; **to be ～ as careful/likely** 加倍仔细/有两倍的可能性; **to eat/earn ～ as much (as sb.)** (比某人) 食量大一倍/挣钱多一倍; **～ the speed/size** 速度快一倍/尺寸大一倍; **to be ～ sb.'s age** 年龄是某人的两倍; **he is ～ the man that you are** 他比你更有男人味

twiddle /ˈtwɪdl/
A *vt* 旋弄 ‹*knob*›; 捻弄 ‹*hair*›; 摆弄 ‹*ring*›; **to ～ one's thumbs** lit 旋弄两手的大拇指; fig 无所事事
B *vi* 旋弄; **to ～ with one's pen/hair** 摆弄钢笔/捻弄头发
C *n* 1 (twist) 旋弄; **to give sth. a ～** 摆弄 ‹*knob*› 2 (design) 螺旋形图案

twiddly /ˈtwɪdli/ *adj* colloq 烦琐的 ‹*pieces*›; **the ～ bits of the sonata** 繁杂的奏鸣曲片段

twig[1] /twɪg/ *n* (small, thin branch) 细枝

twig[2] *vi, vt* (*pres p etc.* **-gg-**) Brit colloq (understand) 懂得; (realize) 意识到; **to ～ that/what/where/how** *etc.* **...** 弄明白…/什么…/哪里…/如何…等

twilight /ˈtwaɪlaɪt/ *n* [u] 1 (dusk) 黄昏; **at ～** 在黄昏时分; **～ hours** 黄昏时间 2 (half-light) (in evening) 暮色; (in morning) 曙光 3 fig (time of decline) 衰落期; **in the ～ of his career** 在他事业的末期; **his ～ years** 他的暮年

twilight: ～ sleep *n* [u] [无痛分娩时的] 半麻醉; **～ zone** *n* 1 (in city) 衰败城区; 2 fig (undefined area) 模糊区域; **the ～ zone between sth. and sth.** 某领域与某领域之间的过渡区域

twill /twɪl/ *n* [u] 斜纹织物; **cotton/wool ～** 斜纹棉布/羊毛织物; **a ～ rug** 斜纹布地毯

'twill /twɪl/ archaic or liter **= it will** ▸**will**[1]

twin /twɪn/
A *n* 1 (one of two offspring) (human) 双胞胎之一; (animal) 双生崽之一; **to be expecting ～s** 怀着双胞胎; **he has a ～** 他有一个双胞胎兄弟 2 (one of two objects) 一对相像事物中的一个; **the plate was one of a pair, but I broke its ～** 这盘子本来有一对儿，但是我把另一只打碎了 3 (room) [宾馆] 有一对单人床的房间; **I've booked one double and one ～** 我预订了一个双人间和一个标间
B *adj* 1 (born as twins) 孪生的 ‹*girls, boys*›; 双生的 ‹*lambs*›; **she has a ～ sister** 她有一个孪生姐妹 2 (paired) 成对的 ‹*engines*›; **the ～ towers of the World Trade Center** 世贸中心的双子塔; **a ship with ～ propellers** 有双螺旋桨的船 3 (combined) 双重的 ‹*aims, problems, roles*›; **the ～ evils of poverty and violence** 贫穷与暴力双重弊端 4 Bot 并蒂的 ‹*flowers*›; 双生的 ‹*leaves*›
C *vt* (*pres p etc.* **-nn-**) 1 Brit (link for cultural exchange) 使…结成姐妹城市 ‹*town*›; **Oxford is ～ned with Bonn** 牛津与波恩结成了友好城市 2 (combine) 糅合 ‹*ideas, themes*›; **the opera ～s the themes of love and death** 这部歌剧糅合了爱情与死亡的主题

twin: ～-bedded *adj* 有一对单人床的 ‹*room*›; **～ beds** *npl* 一对单人床; **～ bill** *n* Amer 1 Cin **= double feature**; 2 Sport **= double-header**

twine /twaɪn/
A *n* [u] (thread) [两股或多股的] 线; (string) 绳
B *vi* «*plant, vine*» 盘绕; **to ～ round** *or* **around sth.** 缠绕某物; **a twining plant** 缠绕植物
C *vt* 1 (wind) 盘绕 ‹*rope, string*›; **to ～ sth. round** *or* **around sth.** 将某物绕在某物上; **to ～ one's arms around sb.** 双臂搂住某人 2 (interlace) 使交织; **to ～ flowers into a garland** 把花编成花环
D *v refl* **to ～ itself round** *or* **around sth.** «*snake, vine*» 盘绕在某物上

twin-engined /ˌtwɪnˈendʒɪnd/ *adj* 双引擎的 ‹*aircraft, jet*›

twinge /twɪndʒ/ *n* 1 lit (sharp pain) 一阵剧痛; **a ～ of pain** 一阵剧痛 2 fig (pang) 一阵痛苦; **a ～ of conscience/guilt/remorse** 一阵愧疚/负罪感/懊悔

twin jet
A *n* 双喷气发动机飞机
B **twin-jet** *adj attrib* 双喷气式的 ‹*engine*›; 双喷气发动机的 ‹*plane*›

twinkle /ˈtwɪŋkl/
A *vi* «*star, lights, jewel*» 闪烁; **her eyes ～d with mischief** 她双眼闪烁着调皮的神情
B *n* 闪烁; **the distant ～ of lights** 远处灯光的闪耀; **to have a ～ in one's eye** 目光熠熠

t

twinkling /ˈtwɪŋklɪŋ/
A *adj* 闪烁的 ‹*star, light*›; 闪亮的 ‹*eyes*›
B *n* 1 (of stars) 闪烁; (of eyes) 闪亮 2 fig (moment) 瞬间; **in a** *or* **the ~ of an eye** 瞬息之间

twin-lens *adj* 双镜头的 ‹*camera, photography*›

twinning /ˈtwɪnɪŋ/ *n* [u] (linking of towns) 结成姐妹城市

twin: ~set *n* esp Brit 女式两件套毛衣; **~town** *n* Brit 姐妹城市; **~-tub** *n* 双缸洗衣机

twirl /twɜːl/
A *vt* 1 (spin) 旋转 ‹*stick, rope*›; **to ~ sth. round** *or* **around** 旋转某物; **to ~ one's partner round and round** 带着舞伴一圈圈地旋转 2 (curl) 捻弄 ‹*hair, moustache*›; 使…缠绕 ‹*vine, rope*›; **to ~ sth. round** *or* **around sth.** 将某物绕在某物上
B *vi* «*person*» 旋转; **to ~ round and round** 一圈圈地旋转; **a ~ing movement** 转动
C *n* 1 (spin) 旋转; **to give sth. a ~** 转动 ‹*wheel, top*›; **to do a ~** «*person*» 转一圈 2 (spiral) 螺旋形标记

twirler /ˈtwɜːlə(r)/ *n* Amer colloq 军乐队女领队

twirp /twɜːp/ *n* colloq pej = **twerp**

twist /twɪst/
A *vt* 1 (turn) 转动; **to ~ a knob clockwise** 顺时针转动旋钮; **to ~ sb.'s arm** 把某人的胳膊扭到背后; **if I ~ her arm, she'll do it** fig 如果我给她施加一点压力，她会做这事的 2 (wind, twine) 缠绕; **to ~ sth. round** *or* **around sth.** 把某物缠绕在某物上; **she was ~ing a lock of hair round her finger** 她把一缕头发绕在手指上; **to ~ the bed sheets into a rope** 把床单拧成一条绳子 3 (bend, distort) 弯曲 ‹*rod*›; **to ~ sth. out of shape** 把某物扭变形 4 fig (misrepresent) 歪曲 ‹*statement, fact*›; **to ~ logic** 歪曲逻辑 5 (sprain) 扭伤; **to ~ one's neck/wrist/ankle** 扭伤脖子/手腕/脚踝 6 Brit colloq (swindle) 欺骗
B *v refl* 扭转; **he ~ed himself free** 他转身挣脱了; **the snake ~ed itself around its prey** 这条蛇缠住了猎物
C *vi* 1 (curl) «*rope, flex*» 打结; «*person*» 扭动身体; **the cord has (got) ~ed** 线绳打结了; **he ~ed free of their grasp** 他从他们的手中挣脱出来; **to ~ round** *or* **around/up sth.** «*climbing plant, snake*» 缠绕某物 2 (wind) «*road, river, vehicle*» 蜿蜒前行; **to ~ and turn** 蜿蜒曲折; **to ~ in and out of the traffic** 在车流中绕来绕去 3 Dance 跳扭摆舞 4 (in cards) 牌面朝上; **do you want to ~ or stick?** 你要不要牌?
D *n* 1 [c] (action) 旋转; **to give sth. a ~, give a ~ to sth.** 转动一下 ‹*handle, cap*›; 弯一下 ‹*wire*›; **she gave my arm a sharp ~** 她使劲扭了我胳膊一下; **with a sudden ~, she got away from him** 她猛一转身挣脱了他 2 [c] (bend) (in rope, wool) 缠绕; (in pipe, road) 拐弯处; **the path follows the ~s and turns of the stream** 小路沿小河蜿蜒曲折; **to get sth. into a ~** 把某物缠成一团; **he managed to get all his facts into a terrible ~** fig 他居然把所有事实弄得一团糟; **to get oneself into a ~** 把自己搞得焦虑不安; **to be** *or* **go round the ~** Brit colloq 疯了; **to drive sb. round the ~** Brit colloq 逼疯某人 3 [c] fig (in plot, story, series of events) 转折; **a strange ~ of fate** 命运的离奇转折; **to give sth. a new ~** 赋予某事物新意; **(to have) a ~ in the tail** (有) 一个出乎预料的结局 4 [c] (spiral shape) (of yarn) 一匹; (of thread, hair) 一卷; (of smoke) 一缕; **a ~ of paper** 一卷纸; **a ~ of lemon** 一片柠檬 5 [u] (dance) **the ~** 扭摆舞 6 [c] Brit colloq (swindle) 欺诈

Phrasal verbs

- **twist around** *vt, vi* = **twist round**
- **twist off**

A *vt* [~ **sth. off**, ~ **off sth.**] 拧开 ‹*lid*›; 拧掉 ‹*branch*›; **to ~ the cap off** 把盖子拧开
B *vi* «*lid*» 拧开; **the cap ~s off** 盖子拧开了

- **twist round** esp Brit

A *vt* [~ **sth. round**, ~ **round sth.**] 转动; **she ~ed her ring round and round on her finger** 她把手指上的戒指转来转去; **to ~ one's head round** 转过头
B *vi* 转身; **he ~ed round to look at me** 他转过身来看我
C *v refl* **to ~ oneself round** 转身; **he managed to ~ himself round in the restricted space** 他设法在局促的空间里转过身来

- **twist together** *vt* [~ **sth. together**, ~ **together sth.**] 把…缠在一起 ‹*fibres, hairs*›; **she ~ed her hands together nervously** 她紧张地把双手绞在一起
- **twist up** *vt* [~ **sth. up**, ~ **up sth.**] 揉 ‹*paper*›; **she ~ed up the scraps of paper into a ball** 她把纸屑揉成一团; **she ~ed her hair up into a bun** 她把头发盘成髻

twisted /ˈtwɪstɪd/ *adj* 1 (bent) 弯曲的 ‹*wire, limb*›; 变形的 ‹*metal, rod*›; **my belt has got ~** 我的皮带拧了 2 (sprained) 扭伤的 ‹*ankle, wrist*› 3 *attrib* (crooked) 歪斜的; **a ~ grin** *or* **smile** 撇嘴的微笑 4 pej (distorted) 歪曲的 ‹*logic, argument*›; (warped) 偏执的 ‹*personality, person, mind*›

twister /ˈtwɪstə(r)/ *n* colloq 1 Brit (swindler) 骗子 2 Amer (tornado) 龙卷风

twist grip *n* [摩托车的] 扭转把手

twisting /ˈtwɪstɪŋ/ *adj attrib* 弯弯曲曲的 ‹*road, street*›; 蜿蜒曲折的 ‹*path*›

twist-off *adj* 能拧开的 ‹*cap, top*›

twisty /ˈtwɪsti/ *adj* = **twisting**

twit /twɪt/ *n* esp Brit colloq 傻瓜

twitch /twɪtʃ/
A *vi* 1 (quiver) «*mouth, eyelid, nose*» 颤动; «*cheek, muscle*» 痉挛; «*person, animal*» 抽搐 2 (tug) 急拉; **to ~ at sth.** 猛拽某物
B *vt* 急拉; **the dog ~ed its ears** 狗抖了抖它的耳朵
C *n* 1 (spasm, tic) 痉挛; **to have a ~ in the corner of one's eye/mouth** 眼角/嘴角抽动一下; **to give a ~** «*mouth*» 颤动 2 (tug) 急拉; **to give the curtain a ~** 猛地拉一下窗帘

twitcher /ˈtwɪtʃə(r)/ *n* Brit colloq 观鸟痴

twitchiness /ˈtwɪtʃɪnɪs/ *n* [u] 紧张

twitchy /ˈtwɪtʃi/ *adj* Brit (nervous) 神经紧张的; (anxious) 焦虑不安的

twitter /ˈtwɪtə(r)/
A *vi* 1 (chirp) «*bird*» 啁啾 2 (talk) 叽叽喳喳地说话; **to ~ about sth.** 喊喊喳喳地谈论某事物; **to ~ on (about sth.)** pej 叽叽喳喳地絮叨 (某事)
B *vt* (say excitedly) 兴奋地说; (say nervously) 紧张地说
C *n* 1 (of bird) 啁啾; (of voices, laughter) 唧唧喳喳 2 pej (idle talk) 闲聊 3 **to be in** *or* **of** *or* **all of a ~** colloq 紧张而兴奋

two /tuː/ ▸**p. 15, p. 521, p. 831**
A *n* 1 (number, quantity) 二; **~ plus ~ equals four** 2 加 2 等于 4; **in December nineteen hundred and ~** 在1902 年 12 月; **we live at (number) ~, Victoria Road** 我们住在维多利亚路 2 号; **her phone number is ~ six double ~** 她的电话号码是 2622; **there are ~ of them** 他们有两个人; **in a day or ~** 一两天之后; **to break/cut sth. in ~** 把某物掰/切成两半; **to put ~ and ~ together** 根据现有情况推断 2 (in time) 2 点钟; **at ~ (o'clock)** 在 2 点 3 (group) (of people) 两个人; (of things) 两个物; **in ~s** (people) 两人一组地; (things) 两个一组地; **in ~s and threes** 三三两两地; **~ by ~** 成双成对地; **that makes ~ of us** colloq 我也一样; ▸**company 3** 4 (on playing card) 2 点; (domino) 2 点的多米诺骨牌; **the ~ of diamonds** 方块2 5 (age) 2 岁
B *adj* 1 (as quantity) 两的; **~ cats** 两只猫; **~ books** 两本书; **~ weeks** 两周 2 (in age) 两岁的; **he's nearly ~** 他快两岁了; **our house is only ~ years old** 我们的房子才造了两年 3 (in series) 第二的; **number ~** 2 号; **page ~** 第 2 页

two: ~-bit *adj* Amer 1 colloq (costing 25 cents) 两毛五分的 ‹*item*›; 2 pej sl (small-time, inferior) 微不足道的 ‹*thief, town, film*›; (sleazy, cheap) 廉价的 ‹*novel, reproduction*›; **~ bits** *npl* Amer colloq 两毛五分; **~-by-four** *n* 1 截面为 2×4 英寸的木材; 2 *modif* Amer colloq 狭小的 ‹*shack*›; **~-chamber system** *n* [立法机构的] 两院制

twocker /ˈtwɒkə(r)/ *n* Brit colloq 偷车贼

twocking /ˈtwɒkɪŋ/ *n* [u] Brit colloq 偷车

two: ~-cycle *adj* = **two-stroke A**; **~-dimensional** /ˌtuːdaɪˈmenʃnəl, -dɪ-/ *adj* 1 lit 二维的 ‹*drawing, geometry*›; 2 fig 肤浅的 ‹*analysis*›; **a ~-dimensional character** 缺乏深度的人物; **~-edged** *adj* 1 lit 双刃的 ‹*knife, blade*›; 2 fig 双关的 ‹*remark*›; 有利有弊的 ‹*effect*›; **~-faced** *adj* pej 两面派的 ‹*person*›; **he's a very ~-faced person** 他这个人很会搞一套阴一套

twofold /ˈtuːfəʊld/
A *adv* 两倍地; **an investment which increased ~** 翻了一番的投资
B *adj* 1 (double) 两倍的; **a ~ increase in crime** 犯罪案件增加了一倍 2 (of two parts) 有两部分的 ‹*question, answer, argument*›; 双重的 ‹*goal, challenge, effect*›

two: ~-four time *n* 四二节拍; **in ~-four time** 以四二拍; **~-handed** *adj* 1 (using two hands) 用双手的 ‹*stroke, grip, blow*›; 双手握的 ‹*weapon, axe*›; **to have a ~-handed backhand** 双手握拍反手击球; 2 (involving two people) 两人拉的 ‹*saw*›; 两人玩的 ‹*card game*›; 3 (ambidextrous) 左右手都灵活的 ‹*person*›; **~-lane** *adj* 双向两车道的 ‹*road, tunnel*›; **~-party system** *n* 两党制; **~pence** /ˈtʌpəns/ *n* Brit = **tuppence**; **~penny** /ˈtʌpəni/ *adj attrib* Brit 值两便士的 ‹*item*›; **~penny-halfpenny** /ˌtʌpəniˈheɪpəni/ *adj attrib* Brit colloq pej 微不足道的 ‹*dictator, thief*›; 廉价的 ‹*object*›; **~-phase** *adj* 双相的 ‹*circuit, generator*›

two-piece
A *adj attrib* 1 Fashn 两件套的 ‹*outfit, swimsuit*›; **a ~ suit** 两件式西装 2 Mus 有两件乐器的 ‹*band*›; 两人组成的 ‹*group*›
B *n* 1 **~ (suit)** 两件式西装 2 **~ (swimsuit)** 两件式泳衣

two-pin *adj* 双芯的 ‹*plug, socket*›

two-ply
A *adj* (two-layered) 双层的 ‹*wood*›; (two-strand) 双股的 ‹*yarn, rope, wool*›
B *n* [u and c] 1 (yarn) 双股毛线 2 Constr 双层胶合板

two-seater /ˌtuːˈsiːtə(r)/ *n* (car) 双座汽车; (aircraft) 双座飞机; (settee) 双座沙发; (buggy) 双座童车; (canoe) 双座皮划艇; **a ~ car/aircraft/canoe/buggy/settee**双座汽车/飞机/皮划艇/童车/沙发

two-sided /ˌtuːˈsaɪdɪd/ *adj* 1 (having two sides) 双面的 ‹*mat, tape, disc*› 2 (having two aspects) 有争议的; **the ~ nature of the argument** 论点的双重性

twosome /ˈtuːsəm/ *n* 1 (two people) 两人组; (pair) 一对; (lovers) 一对情侣 2 (game) 双人赛; (dance) 双人舞

two-star
A *adj attrib* 1 (of two-star grade) 两星级的 ‹*restaurant, service, petrol*› 2 Amer Mil 两星的 ‹*general, rank*›
B *n* [u] Brit 两星级汽油

two-star hotel *n* 两星级宾馆

two: ~-step *n* 1 (dance) 两步舞; 2 Mus 两步舞曲; **~-storey** *adj* 两层的 ‹*building*›

two-stroke
A *adj* 二冲程的 ‹*engine, vehicle*›
B *n* 二冲程发动机

two-tier *adj* 双重的 ‹*structure, policy, pricing*›; pej 不公平的 ‹*society, health service*›

two-time

A *vt* colloq 对…不忠 ‹*wife, boyfriend*›; **he's been two-timing her for years** 多年来他一直背着她偷情

B *vi* colloq 用情不专; **I'm sure he's two-timing** 我敢肯定他另有所爱

C *adj attrib* 赢过两次的 ‹*winner, champion*›; 有两次前科的 ‹*convict*›

two: ~-timer *n* colloq 用情不专的人; **~-timing** *adj* colloq 用情不专的 ‹*husband, wife, lover*›; **~-tone** *adj usu attrib* **1** (in colour) 两种颜色的 ‹*shoes, jacket, curtains*›; **2** (in sound) 双音的 ‹*bell, horn, whistle*›

two-way *adj usu attrib* **1** (in movement) 双向的 ‹*traffic, trade*›; 双行的 ‹*road, tunnel*› **2** Elec 双路的 ‹*connection, wiring, device*› **3** (in communication) 相互的 ‹*exchange, dialogue*›; 互动的 ‹*process*›; 彼此的 ‹*partnership*›

two-way: ~ mirror *n* 单向透明玻璃镜; **~ radio** *n* 双向无线电通信; **~ street** *n* **1** lit 双行街道; **2** fig (reciprocal process) 互惠关系; **trust/friendship is a ~ street** 信任/友谊是相互的; **~ switch** *n* 双路开关

two: ~-wheeler /ˌtuːˈwiːlə(r)/ *n* colloq (bike) 自行车; (motorcycle) 两轮摩托车; **~-year-old** *n* 两岁的孩子

TX *abbr* Amer = **Texas**

tycoon /taɪˈkuːn/ *n* 巨头; **an oil/a publishing ~** 石油/出版业大亨

tying /ˈtaɪɪŋ/ *pres p* ▸**tie**

tyke /taɪk/ *n* colloq 小淘气

Tyne and Wear /ˌtaɪn ænd ˈwɪə(r)/ *pr n* 泰恩-威尔郡

Tynwald /ˈtɪnwəld/ *n* 马恩岛议会

type /taɪp/

A *n* **1** [c] (variety, kind) 类型; **a ~ of sth.** 某物的一种; **all ~s of jobs, jobs of all ~s** 各种各样的工作; **I'm not the** *or* **that ~** 我不是那种人; **this is definitely my ~ of place** colloq 这毫无疑问是我中意的那种地方; **he's not my ~** colloq 他不是我喜欢的类型 **2** [c] colloq (person) 某种人; **an army ~** 军人一类的人 **3** [u and c] Print (for printing) 活字; (on page) 字体; **metal ~** 金属活字; **bold/italic ~** 黑体/斜体; **to be in ~** 付排 **4** [c] (archetype) 典型; **her characters are ~s rather than individuals** 她塑造的人物是模式化的, 缺乏个性

B **-type** *combining form* …类型的; **a documentary~ film** 纪实类影片

C *vt* **1** (on typewriter, keyboard) 在…上打字 ‹*page*›; 键入 ‹*word*›; **a ~d letter** 打印的信; **to ~ sth. into a computer/on to a screen** 把某内容输入电脑/打到屏幕上; **to ~ over a mistake** 打错字 **2** (classify) 给…分型 ‹*tissue*›; **to ~ blood samples** 给血样分类; **to be ~d as sth.** 被看作某类型

D *vi* 打字

Phrasal verbs

- **type in** *vt* [**~ sth. in, ~ in sth.**] **1** (on computer) 键入 ‹*word, command*›; **to ~ in the file name** 键入文件名 **2** (on typewriter) 打出 ‹*word, letter*›
- **type out** *vt* [**~ sth. out, ~ out sth.**] **1** (put in typed form) 打出 ‹*receipt, letter*›; **I'd prefer it if you ~d out the list** 我希望你把单子打出来 **2** (erase) 打字覆盖 ‹*error, name*›; **if you make a mistake, you can just ~ it out** 打错了就在上面再打字遮住
- **type up** *vt* [**~ sth. up, ~ up sth.**] 把…打出来 ‹*note, draft, report, essay*›

type: ~cast *vt* (*pt, pp* **~cast**) **1** Theat (cast by type) 让…扮演适合类型的角色 ‹*actor*›; (cast in repeat role) 让…扮演同一类型的老角色 ‹*actor*›; **2** fig (stereotype) 模式化地看待 ‹*person*›; **to be ~cast as a killjoy** 被不加区分地看作是杀风景的人; **~casting** *n* [u] **1** Theat (casting by type) 使用适合某类型角色的演员; (casting in repeat role) 分配扮演同一类型角色; **2** fig (stereotyping) 模式化表现; **~face** *n* 字体; **~script** *n* 打印稿; **~set** *vt* (*pt, pp* **~set**) 为…排字 ‹*text*›; 为…排版 ‹*book*›; **~setter** ▸**p. 409** *n* 排字工人; **~setting** *n* [u] 排字; **~ size** *n* 字号; **~writer** *n* 打字机; **a manual/portable ~writer** 手动/便携式打字机; **a ~writer ribbon/keyboard** 打字机色带/键盘; **~writing** *n* [u] 打字; **manual ~writing** 手工打字; **~written** *adj* 打印的 ‹*letter, memo*›

typhoid /ˈtaɪfɔɪd/ ▸**p. 377** *n* [u] **~ (fever)** 伤寒; **a ~ outbreak/epidemic** 伤寒爆发/流行; **~ symptoms/inoculation** 伤寒症状/接种

typhoon /taɪˈfuːn/ *n* 台风

typhus /ˈtaɪfəs/ ▸**p. 377** *n* [u] **~ (fever)** 斑疹伤寒

typical /ˈtɪpɪkl/ *adj* (usual, representative) 典型的 ‹*case, example, symptoms, feature, response*›; (characteristic) 特有的 ‹*behaviour, modesty, rudeness, generosity*›; **to be ~ of the period/area** 是这个时期/地区的特征; **to be ~ of sb.** 是某人的特点; **it's (all too) ~ of him to be late** 他这人就是爱迟到; **(that's) ~!** 一贯如此!

typically /ˈtɪpɪkli/ *adv* 典型地 ‹*behave, respond*›; 一贯地 ‹*rude, generous, inept, modest*›; **~ English behaviour** 英国人特有的行为; **he is ~ English** 他是典型的英国人; **a ~ warm day** 常有的那种暖和日子; **~, it was left to me to do everything** 果然, 一切工作都留给我去做

typify /ˈtɪpɪfaɪ/ *vt* **1** (be typical of) «*feature, quality*» 成为…的特征 ‹*area, period, style*›; **as typified by the EU** 以欧盟为典型; **to be typified by slow growth** 特点是增长缓慢 **2** (embody) «*person, institution*» 体现 ‹*type, system*›; **to ~ all that is best in American society** 体现美国社会所有的最佳方面 **3** (represent) 代表; (symbolize) 象征

typing /ˈtaɪpɪŋ/ *n* [u] **1** (action) 打字; (work) 打字工作; **a ~ class/teacher** 打字班/老师 **2** (text) 打字稿

typing: ~ error *n* 打字错误; **~ paper** *n* [u] 打字纸; **~ pool** *n* 打字小组; **~ skills** *npl* 打字技能; **~ speed** *n* 打字速度

typist /ˈtaɪpɪst/ ▸**p. 409** *n* 打字员

typo /ˈtaɪpəʊ/ *n* (*pl* **~s**) colloq 排印错误

typographer /taɪˈpɒɡrəfə(r)/ ▸**p. 409** *n* 排字工

typographical /ˌtaɪpəˈɡræfɪkl/, **typographic** /ˌtaɪpəˈɡræfɪk/ *adjs* 排印的; **a ~ error/layout** 排印错误/版面设计

typographically /ˌtaɪpəˈɡræfɪkli/ *adv* 在排印上

typography /taɪˈpɒɡrəfi/ *n* [u] **1** (process, work) 排印 **2** (appearance) 版面设计

typology /taɪˈpɒlədʒi/ *n* **1** [c] (classification) 分类法 **2** [u] (study) 类型学

tyrannical /tɪˈrænɪkl/ *adj* **1** (despotic) 专制的 ‹*ruler, regime*› **2** (oppressive) 残暴的 ‹*reign*›

tyrannically /tɪˈrænɪkli/ *adv* 专制地 ‹*rule*›; 残暴地 ‹*oppress*›

tyrannize /ˈtɪrənaɪz/

A *vt* 对…施行暴政 ‹*nation, people*›; 专横地对待 ‹*family, person*›

B *vi* 施行暴政; **to ~ over sb.** 对某人施行暴政

tyrannosaur /tɪˈrænəsɔː(r)/, **tyrannosaurus** /tɪˌrænəˈsɔːrəs/ *ns* 暴龙属; **Tyrannosaurus Rex** 霸王龙

tyrannous /ˈtɪrənəs/ *adj* formal = **tyrannical**

tyranny /ˈtɪrəni/ *n* **1** [u] (despotism) 暴政; (despotic rule) 专制统治; **political/military/Nazi ~** 政治/军事/纳粹专制 **2** [u] (oppression) 暴虐; **the ~ of sb. (over sb.)** 某人(对某人)的暴行; **the ~ of the strong over the weak** 强者对弱者的残暴; **the ~ of domestic routine** 沉重的家务负担 **3** [c] (tyrannical act) 残暴专横的行为 **4** [c] (country, state) 专制国家

tyrant /ˈtaɪərənt/ *n* **1** (despot) 暴君; **to overthrow a ~** 推翻专制君主 **2** fig (bully) 暴虐的人; (dictator) 专横的人; **a ~ of a father** 专横的父亲; **the office ~** 办公室独裁者

tyre /ˈtaɪə(r)/ *n* Brit 轮胎; **to have a flat ~** 轮胎瘪了; **to burst a ~** 爆胎

tyre: ~ centre *n* 汽车轮胎中心; **~ gauge** *n* 轮胎气压计; **~ lever** *n* 外胎撬杆

tyre pressure *n* 轮胎气压

tyre pressure gauge *n* 轮胎气压计

tyre valve *n* 轮胎气门嘴

tyro /ˈtaɪərəʊ/ *n* (*pl* **~s**) 初学者; **to be a ~ at sth.** 是某方面的新手

Tyrone /tɪˈrəʊn/ *pr n* 蒂龙郡

tzar /zɑː(r)/ *n* = **tsar**

tzarina /zɑːˈriːnə/ *n* = **tsarina**

tzarist /ˈzɑːrɪst/ *n, adj* = **tsarist**

t

Uu

U, u /juː/

A *n* (*pl* **Us** *or* **U's**) [英语的第21个字母]

B **U** *abbr* Brit Cin **= universal**; **(a)** ~ **(film)**（一部）U 级电影 [指适合所有观众的电影]

C *adj* Brit colloq hum 上流社会的; **non-**~ 非上流社会的

UAE *abbr* **= United Arab Emirates**

U-bend *n* [尤指污水管的] U形管

ubiquitous /juːˈbɪkwɪtəs/ *adj* 普遍存在的; ~ **presence** 无所不在; **a** ~ **expression** 随处可见的表达方式

ubiquity /juːˈbɪkwəti/ *n* [u] formal 普遍存在; **the** ~ **of rap music** 说唱音乐的无处不在

U-boat *n* [二战时] 德国潜艇

UC *abbr* **= upper case**

UCAS /ˈjuːkæs/ *abbr* Brit **= Universities and Colleges Admissions Service** 高校招生服务处; **a** ~ **form** 高校招生表格

UDA *abbr* **= Ulster Defence Association** 北爱尔兰防务协会

udder /ˈʌdə(r)/ *n* [母牛、母羊等的] 乳房

UDI *abbr* **= unilateral declaration of independence** 单方面宣告独立

UEFA /juːˈeɪfə/ *abbr* **= Union of European Football Associations** 欧洲足球联合会; **the** ~ **cup** 欧洲联盟杯

UFO *abbr* (*pl* ~**s**) **= unidentified flying object** 不明飞行物; **a** ~ **sighting** 飞碟目击

Uganda /juːˈgændə/ *pr n* 乌干达

Ugandan /juːˈgændən/ ▸**p. 503**

A *adj* (of Uganda) 乌干达的; (of the people) 乌干达人的

B *n* 乌干达人

ugh /ʌg/ *excl* 咳 [表示厌恶或恐惧]; ~**, it tastes horrible!** 呸，味道真恶心！

Ugli® /ˈʌgli/ *n* ~ **(fruit)** 丑橘

ugliness /ˈʌglɪnɪs/ *n* [u] (of person, animal, object, place) 丑陋; (of expression) 可怕; **the** ~ **of war/the situation** 战争的丑恶/形势的险恶

ugly /ˈʌgli/ *adj* **1** (hideous) 丑陋的; **an** ~ **sight/building** 难看的景象/建筑; **to be as** ~ **as sin** colloq 非常难看 **2** (vicious) 可怕的 ‹*scene, incident, news, wound*›; **an** ~ **expression/mood** (of person) 骇人的表情/糟糕的情绪; **the mood in the room turned** ~ 屋里的气氛变得很吓人; **to give sb. an** ~ **look** 恶狠狠地看某人一眼; **an** ~ **customer** colloq 难缠的家伙 **3** *usu attrib* (repugnant) 丑恶的; ~ **rumours** 卑劣的谣言; **the** ~ **truth/reality of sth.** 某事的丑恶真相/现实; **the** ~ **face of racism** 种族主义的丑恶面目

ugly duckling *n* fig 丑小鸭 [指起初平庸后来出众的人]; **the** ~**s of the business world** 商界的丑小鸭

UHF *abbr* **= ultra-high frequency**

uh-huh /ʌˈhʌ/ *excl* 嗯 [表示赞同]

UHT *abbr* Brit **= ultra heat treated** 超高温处理的; ~ **milk** 超高温消毒牛奶

UK *abbr* **= United Kingdom**

uke /juːk/ ▸**p. 395** *n* colloq 尤克里里琴

Ukraine /juːˈkreɪn/ *pr n* **(the)** ~ 乌克兰

Ukrainian /juːˈkreɪnɪən/ ▸**p. 503, p. 426**

A *adj* (of Ukraine) 乌克兰的; (of the people) 乌克兰人的; (of the language) 乌克兰语的

B *n* **1** [c] (person) 乌克兰人 **2** [u] (language) 乌克兰语

ukulele /juːkəˈleɪli/ ▸**p. 395** *n* 尤克里里琴

Ulan Bator, Ulaanbaatar /ˌuːlɑːn ˈbɑːtə(r)/ *pr n* 乌兰巴托

ulcer /ˈʌlsə(r)/ ▸**p. 377** *n* 溃疡; **a peptic/bleeding** ~ 消化性/出血性溃疡; **an** ~ **on the body politic** fig 国家身上的溃疡

ulcerate /ˈʌlsəreɪt/ *vi* «*foot, stomach*» 形成溃疡

ulceration /ˌʌlsəˈreɪʃn/ *n* **1** [u] (state, process) 溃疡形成 **2** [c] (ulcer) 溃疡

ulcerous /ˈʌlsərəs/ *adj* 溃疡性的 ‹*sore, inflammation*›; 患溃疡的 ‹*tissue, leg*›

ulna /ˈʌlnə/ *n* (*pl* **ulnae** /ˈʌlniː/ *or* ~**s**) 尺骨

Ulster /ˈʌlstə(r)/ *pr n* **1** (Northern Ireland) 北爱尔兰 **2** Hist **(the province of)** ~ 北爱尔兰省

Ulster: ~**man** /-mən/ *n* 北爱尔兰男人; ~**woman** *n* 北爱尔兰女人

ulterior /ʌlˈtɪərɪə(r)/ *adj* 隐秘的 ‹*purpose, reason*›; **without any** ~ **motive** 没有不可告人的动机

ultimata /ˌʌltɪˈmeɪtə/ *pl* ▸**ultimatum**

ultimate /ˈʌltɪmət/

A *adj attrib* **1** (final) 最终的 ‹*goal, outcome, victory, beneficiary*›; 终极的 ‹*authority, weapon, deterrent*›; **to be carried to the** ~ **extreme** 被推到极致; **the** ~ **responsibility is yours** 责任最终要你来负 **2** (fundamental) 基本的 ‹*principle, truth, source*›; 根本的 ‹*cause, purpose*› **3** (unsurpassed) 极度的 ‹*refinement, luxury*›; 最好的 ‹*accolade, prize*›; 最大的 ‹*insult, test*›; **the** ~ **car** 顶级汽车

B *n* **the** ~ (the best) 最好的事物; (the greatest) 最伟大的事物; **the** ~ **in technology** (the most advanced) 顶级技术; **the** ~ **in comfort/luxury** 极度的舒适/奢侈

ultimately /ˈʌltɪmətli/ *adv* **1** (finally) 最终 ‹*win, succeed, decide*› **2** (fundamentally) 根本上 ‹*derive, consist*›; ~**, it is your fault** 归根结底，这是你的错

ultimatum /ˌʌltɪˈmeɪtəm/ *n* (*pl* ~**s** *or* **ultimata**) 最后通牒; **to issue** *or* **deliver** *or* **give an** ~ **(to sb.)**（向某人）发出最后通牒

ultraconservative /ˌʌltrəkənˈsɜːvətɪv/ *adj* 极端保守的

ultra-high frequency *n* [u] 超高频; ~ **radio** 超高频无线电广播

ultra-left

A *adj* 极左的 ‹*person, policy, newspaper*›

B *n* **the** ~ 极左派

ultramarine /ˌʌltrəməˈriːn/

A *adj* 佛青色的

B *n* [u] 佛青色; **gemstones of a pure** ~ 纯佛青色的宝石

ultramodern /ˌʌltrəˈmɒdən/ *adj* 超现代化的 ‹*factory, hotel*›; 极其时髦的 ‹*building, furniture, design*›

ultrarich /ˌʌltrəˈrɪtʃ/

A *adj* **1** (wealthy) 超富的 ‹*person, country*› **2** Culin 十分油腻的 ‹*dessert*›

B *n* **the** ~ 超富阶层

ultra-right

A *adj* 极右的 ‹*person, policy, newspaper*›

B *n* **the** ~ 极右派

ultrasensitive /ˌʌltrəˈsensɪtɪv/ *n* **1** (touchy) 极为敏感的 ‹*person*›; **to be** ~ **to** 对…极为敏感 ‹*criticism*› **2** (sensitive) 超灵敏的 ‹*instrument, detection*› **3** (confidential) 超级机密的 ‹*information, intelligence*›

ultrasmooth /ˌʌltrəˈsmuːð/ *adj* **1** (smooth) 超光滑的 ‹*surface, material*› **2** (suave) 极其圆滑的 ‹*person*›

ultrasonic /ˌʌltrəˈsɒnɪk/

A *adj* 超声波的 ‹*frequency, technology*›; ~ **waves** 超声波

B **ultrasonics** *npl + v sing* 超声学

ultrasonic testing *n* [u] 超声波探伤

ultrasound /ˈʌltrəsaʊnd/ *n* **1** [u] (waves) 超声波 **2** [c] (procedure) ~ **(scan)** 超声波扫描; **to have** *or* **be given an** ~ 接受超声波扫描

ultrasound scanner *n* 超声波扫描仪

ultrathin /ˌʌltrəˈθɪn/ *adj* 超薄的

ultraviolet /ˌʌltrəˈvaɪələt/

A *adj* 紫外的 ‹*radiation, light*›; 紫外线的 ‹*wavelength*›; ~ **rays** 紫外线; **to have** ~ **treatment** 接受紫外线治疗

B *n* [u] 紫外线

um /əm/ *excl* 呃 [表示犹豫或停顿]; **anyway,** ~**, where was I?** 不管怎么说，呃，我那是在什么地方?

umber /ˈʌmbə(r)/ *n* [u] [用作颜料的] 棕土; ~ **tones** 棕土色调

umbilical /ʌmˈbɪlɪkl, ˌʌmbɪˈlaɪkl/ *adj* 脐带的; ~ **ties** fig 密不可分的关系

umbilical cord *n* **1** Anat 脐带; **to cut/tie the** ~ 剪断/扎上脐带; **to break the** ~ **and leave home** 离开父母开始自立 **2** Aerosp, Naut 空间生命管线

umbrage /ˈʌmbrɪdʒ/ *n* [u] **to take** ~ **at sth.** 因某事不愉快

umbrella /ʌmˈbrelə/

A *n* **1** lit 伞; **to unfurl** *or* **open/furl** *or* **close an** ~ 打开/收起伞 **2** fig 保护伞; **under the** ~ **of sth.** 在…的保护下 ‹*NATO, security forces*›; **an air** ~ 空中掩护

B *modif* 综合的 ‹*committee, project*›; **to be an** ~ **word for sth.** 是某事物的概括词

umbrella: ~ **group** *n* 综合团体; ~ **organization** *n* 综合机构; ~ **stand** *n* 伞架; ~ **term** *n* 总称; ~ **tree** *n* 三瓣木兰

umlaut /ˈʊmlaʊt/ *n* [日耳曼语系中的] 变音符

umpire /ˈʌmpaɪə(r)/

A *n* 裁判员 [不用于足球或橄榄球运动]; **to act as an** ~ **between two parties** 做两党之间的仲裁人

B *vi* 当裁判; **to** ~ **at a match** 当比赛的裁判

C *vt* 当…的裁判 ‹*game, competition*›; fig 对…进行仲裁 ‹*dispute*›

umpteen /ʌmp'tiːn/ colloq
A adj 无数的 ‹*items, people, things to do*›; **I've told him ~ times** 我对他说过无数遍了
B pron 很多; **to have ~ at home** 家里有许许多多

umpteenth /ʌmp'tiːnθ/ adj colloq 第无数个的 ‹*item, person, idea*›; **for the ~ time, I don't know!** 我说过无数次了，我不知道！

UN abbr = **United Nations**

'un /ən/ pron colloq = **one** 一个; **a good ~** (person) 好人; (thing) 好东西; **that's a good ~!** (joke) 多有趣的笑话！; (excuse) 多妙的借口！; (story) 多好听的故事！; **he went fishing and caught a big ~** 他去钓鱼，逮到了一条大家伙

unabashed /ˌʌnə'bæʃt/ adj 不害羞的 ‹*admirer, advocate*›; 不加掩饰的 ‹*enthusiasm*›; **to be ~ by sth.** 对…不感到难为情 ‹*criticism, praise*›

unabated /ˌʌnə'beɪtɪd/ adj usu pred 不减弱的 ‹*enthusiasm, fury*›; **the storm raged ~ for three days** 暴风雨连续肆虐了三天; **to remain ~** «*interest, enthusiasm*» 保持不减

unable /ʌn'eɪbl/ adj **1** (incapable, lacking means) 不能的; **to be ~ to afford the fare** 付不起票钱; **to be ~ to answer the question** 答不出问题 **2** (lacking knowledge, ability) 不会的; **to be ~ to read** 不识字; **to be ~ to move** 动弹不得

unabridged /ˌʌnə'brɪdʒd/ adj 完整未删节的 ‹*version, edition, text, play*›

unaccented /ˌʌnæk'sentɪd/ adj 不带口音的 ‹*English, French*›; 非重读的 ‹*syllable, letter*›; **an ~ beat** Mus 弱拍

unacceptable /ˌʌnək'septəbl/ adj 不能接受的 ‹*terms, solution*›; 不能允许的 ‹*behaviour*›; **it is ~ that ...** …令人难以接受; **to an ~ degree/level** 到达难以容忍的地步/程度; **the ~ face of capitalism** 资本主义令人无法容忍的一面

unacceptably /ˌʌnək'septəbli/ adv 无法容忍地 ‹*poor, slow, expensive*›; **~ low standards** 低得出奇的标准; **costs have risen ~** 成本涨到了无法承受的地步

unaccommodating /ˌʌnə'kɒmədeɪtɪŋ/ adj 不与人方便的 ‹*person, restaurant, reply*›

unaccompanied /ˌʌnə'kʌmpənɪd/ adj **1** (unescorted) 无陪伴的 ‹*person, child*›; 独自的 ‹*tour*›; 非随身携带的 ‹*luggage*› **2** Mus 无伴奏的 ‹*singer, singing, violin*›; **to sing the piece ~** 清唱那首歌

unaccomplished /ˌʌnə'kʌmplɪʃt/ adj **1** (lacking skill, ability) 不熟练的 ‹*performance*›; 无成就的 ‹*person*› **2** (not achieved) 未完成的 ‹*work, task*›; 未实现的 ‹*goal*›

unaccountable /ˌʌnə'kaʊntəbl/ adj **1** (unexplained) 无法解释的 ‹*fact, reason, lack*›; (strange) 莫名其妙的 ‹*behaviour, person*› **2** (not responsible) 不负责任的; **to be** or **remain ~ to sb./sth.** 对某人/某事物不负责任

unaccountably /ˌʌnə'kaʊntəbli/ adv 莫名其妙地 ‹*vanish, appear*›; **to be ~ late/missing/absent** 莫名其妙地迟到/失踪/缺席; **(quite) ~, ...** (非常) 莫名其妙，…

unaccounted /ˌʌnə'kaʊntɪd/ adj pred **to be ~ for** (missing) «*person, object, money*» 下落不明; (unexplained) «*event, disappearance, death*» 未得到解释

unaccustomed /ˌʌnə'kʌstəmd/ adj **1** usu pred (unused) **to be ~ to sth./to doing sth.** 不习惯于某事物/做某事 **2** usu attrib (uncharacteristic) 不寻常的 ‹*generosity, luxury, speed, silence*›

unacknowledged /ˌʌnək'nɒlɪdʒd/ adj **1** (not admitted to) 未被承认的 ‹*problem, reason*›; **her ~ feelings** 她的下意识的感情 **2** (unappreciated) 不被领情的 ‹*help, gift*›; 未受赏识的 ‹*genius, inventor, contribution*›

unacquainted /ˌʌnə'kweɪntɪd/ adj usu pred **to be ~ (with sb.)** (与某人) 不相识; **to be ~ with sth.** 不熟悉某事物; **to be ~ with one another** 互不相识; **two ~ people** 两个从未谋面的人

unadapted /ˌʌnə'dæptɪd/ adj 未经改编的 ‹*text, play*›; **to be ~ to society/conditions** «*person*» 不适应社会/环境

unaddressed /ˌʌnə'drest/ adj **1** (not dealt with) 未处理的 ‹*matter, problem*›; 未考虑的 ‹*question*› **2** (without address) 无地址的 ‹*envelope, parcel*›

unadopted /ˌʌnə'dɒptɪd/ adj **1** (without adoptive parents) 未被领养的 ‹*child*› **2** Brit Admin **an ~ road** or **street** 私有道路 [未被地方当局承担养护的道路]

unadorned /ˌʌnə'dɔːnd/ adj 未装饰的 ‹*wall, building*›; 朴素的 ‹*style, beauty*›; **the ~ human body** 裸体; **the ~ facts/truth** 纯粹的事实/真相

unadulterated /ˌʌnə'dʌltəreɪtɪd/ adj **1** lit (pure) 无杂质的 ‹*food*›; 纯的 ‹*drink*› **2** fig (absolute) 极度的 ‹*joy, hatred*›; 十足的 ‹*nonsense*›; 不折不扣的 ‹*truth*›

unadventurous /ˌʌnəd'ventʃərəs/ adj 无冒险精神的 ‹*person*›; 无新意的 ‹*piece of work, art, food, film*›; 四平八稳的 ‹*career, choice*›

unadventurously /ˌʌnəd'ventʃərəsli/ adv 无新意地 ‹*dress, design*›; 四平八稳地 ‹*perform, select*›

unadvertised /ʌn'ædvətaɪzd/ adj 未作广告的 ‹*product*›; 未公开的 ‹*visit, meeting*›

unaesthetic /ˌʌniːs'θetɪk/ adj 无美感的

unaffected /ˌʌnə'fektɪd/ adj **1** (not contrived) 朴实的 ‹*person, behaviour*›; 真挚的 ‹*pleasure*›; 不做作的 ‹*style*› **2** (not touched) 未改变的 ‹*state, right*›; **to be ~ by** 未受…的影响 ‹*person, event, change*›; 未因…受损 ‹*damp, rust*›

unaffectedly /ˌʌnə'fektɪdli/ adv 朴实地 ‹*behave, dress*›; 真挚地 ‹*pleased*›; **to be ~ simple/natural** 朴实而简单/自然

unaffiliated /ˌʌnə'fɪlieɪtɪd/ adj 非附属的 ‹*club, group*›; 独立的 ‹*college, union*›; **to be ~ to sth.** 独立于某物

unafraid /ˌʌnə'freɪd/ adj pred 不害怕的; **to be ~ of sb./sth./doing sth.** 不害怕某人/某事物/做某事

unaided /ʌn'eɪdɪd/
A adj 独立的; **to do sth. by one's own ~ efforts** 凭自己的努力做某事
B adv 独立地 ‹*walk, work*›; **to do sth. ~** 独立做某事; **she scaled the mountain ~** 她一个人登上了山峰

unaired /ʌn'eəd/ adj **1** (not exposed to air) 不通风的 ‹*room*›; 未晾干的 ‹*damp clothes or sheets*› **2** (undiscussed) 未讨论过的 ‹*issue, problem*› **3** (not broadcast) 未播放过的 ‹*episode, footage*›

unaligned /ˌʌnə'laɪnd/ adj **1** (not in straight line) 未排成直线的 ‹*parts, columns, buttons*› **2** (independent) 无党派的 ‹*voter*›; 不结盟的 ‹*country*›; **to be ~ with sb./sth.** 不与…结盟

unalike /ˌʌnə'laɪk/ adj pred 不相似的; **the two children are very ~** 这两个孩子很不一样; **~ in style and form** 风格和形式不相同的

unalloyed /ˌʌnə'lɔɪd/ adj **1** lit 非合金的 ‹*metal*› **2** fig 纯粹的 ‹*pleasure, joy*›

unalterable /ʌn'ɔːltərəbl/ adj 无法改变的 ‹*fact, truth, reality*›; 不可更改的 ‹*rule, decision*›

unaltered /ʌn'ɔːltəd/ adj 未改变的; **his stance** or **position remains ~** 他的立场保持不变

unambiguous /ˌʌnæm'bɪgjʊəs/ adj 不含糊的; **his attitude on the matter remains ~** 他在这件事情上的态度仍然很明确

unambiguously /ˌʌnæm'bɪgjʊəsli/ adv 不含糊地

unambitious /ˌʌnæm'bɪʃəs/ adj 无抱负的 ‹*person*›; 平凡的 ‹*plan, schedule*›

unambivalent /ˌʌnæm'bɪvələnt/ adj 明确的

un-American /ˌʌnə'merɪkən/ adj **1** (not American) 非美国的 ‹*trait, concept*› **2** (anti-American) 反美的

unamused /ˌʌnə'mjuːzd/ adj pred 不高兴的; **to look/be ~** 看上去不愉快/感到不快

unanimity /ˌjuːnə'nɪməti/ n [U] (unity) 一致; (consensus) 一致同意; **~ among** or **between all members** 所有成员的共识; **to reach** or **arrive at (a state of) ~** 达成一致

unanimous /juː'nænɪməs/ adj **1** usu pred (in agreement) 意见一致的; **to be ~ in sth./doing sth.** «*members, voters*» 一致同意某事/做某事; **to be ~ that ...** 一致认为… **2** (held by all) 一致的 ‹*decision, verdict*›; **to be elected by a ~ vote** 以全票当选

unanimously /juː'nænɪməsli/ adv 一致地 ‹*agree, decide, condemn, vote*›; **to be ~ against/in favour of sth.** 一致反对/赞成某事物; **to be elected ~** 以全票当选

unannounced /ˌʌnə'naʊnst/
A adj 未通知的; **an ~ visit** 突然来访
B adv 未通知地; **to arrive ~** 突然到达

unanswerable /ʌn'ɑːnsərəbl, Amer ˌʌn'æn-/ adj 无可争辩的 ‹*case, argument*›; 无法回答的 ‹*question*›

unanswered /ʌn'ɑːnsəd, Amer ʌn'æn-/ adj 未答复的 ‹*phone call, request, invitation, appeal*›; 未解答的 ‹*problem*›; **an ~ charge/argument** 未经辩驳的指控/论据; **to leave questions/a letter ~** 对问题/信件不予答复; **his cries/prayers went ~** 他的呼喊无人应答/祈祷没有应验

unappealing /ˌʌnə'piːlɪŋ/ adj 无魅力的 ‹*person, character*›; 不吸引人的 ‹*food, place*›

unappetizing /ʌn'æpɪtaɪzɪŋ/ adj 引不起食欲的; **a most ~ individual/sight** 索然无味的人/景象

unappreciated /ˌʌnə'priːʃieɪtɪd/ adj 未受赏识的 ‹*person*›; 不被认可的 ‹*effort, role*›; 不领情的 ‹*offer, help*›

unappreciative /ˌʌnə'priːʃətɪv/ adj (not understanding) 无鉴赏力的 ‹*person, audience*›; (not valuing) 不领情的; **to be ~ of sb.'s help** 不感激某人的帮助

unapproachable /ˌʌnə'prəʊtʃəbl/ adj 难接近的 ‹*person*›

unappropriated /ˌʌnə'prəʊprieɪtɪd/ adj 未被占用的 ‹*land*›; 未被挪用的 ‹*fund, money*›

unarguable /ʌn'ɑːgjʊəbl/ adj 不容置疑的 ‹*fact, right, sovereignty*›; 无可辩驳的 ‹*case*›

unarguably /ʌn'ɑːgjʊəbli/ adv 不容置疑地

unarmed /ʌn'ɑːmd/ adj 不带武器的 ‹*police*›; 非武装的 ‹*civilian*›; 徒手的 ‹*combat*›

unary /'juːnəri/ adj 一元的

unashamed /ˌʌnə'ʃeɪmd/ adj 不害臊的; **to be ~ of one's behaviour** 对自己的行为不感到羞耻; **~ delight** or **pleasure** 坦然的愉快

unashamedly /ˌʌnə'ʃeɪmɪdli/ adv 不害臊地

unasked /ʌn'ɑːskt, Amer ʌn'æskt/ adv **1** (not asked) 没发问的; **so many questions were left ~** 许许多多问题都没有提出来 **2** (uninvited) 未受邀请的 ‹*guest*›; **~ (for) advice/suggestions** 主动提出的劝告/建议

unaspirated /ʌn'æspəreɪtɪd/ adj 不送气的 ‹*consonant, stop*›

unassailable /ˌʌnə'seɪləbl/ adj **1** (very strong) 不容置疑的 ‹*optimism, virtue, reputation*›; 无懈可击的 ‹*argument, case, position*›; **to have an ~ lead** 有无法撼动的领先地位 **2** Mil 攻不破的 ‹*fortress, city, position*›

unassisted /ˌʌnə'sɪstɪd/
A adj 无帮助的; **an ~ goal** 单刀进球; **an ~**

take-off 无助推起飞; **one's own ~ work** 自己独立完成的作品
B *adv* 无帮助地 ‹*stand, walk*›

unassuming /ˌʌnəˈsjuːmɪŋ, Amer ˌʌnəˈsuː-/ *adj* 不爱出风头的; **an ~ young man/manner** 谦逊的年轻人/态度

unassumingly /ˌʌnəˈsjuːmɪŋlɪ, Amer ˌʌnəˈsuː-/ *adv* 谦逊地 ‹*behave, say*›; **to be ~ modest** 谦虚内敛

unattached /ˌʌnəˈtætʃt/ *adj* **1** (not connected) 非附属的 ‹*object, part*›; **she is ~ to any particular organization** 她不属于任何组织 **2** (single) 单身的

unattainable /ˌʌnəˈteɪnəbl/ *adj* 无法实现的 ‹*goal, dream, ambition*›; 达不到的 ‹*standard*›; 得不到的 ‹*prize, woman*›

unattended /ˌʌnəˈtendɪd/ *adj* **1** (unsupervised) 无人看管的 ‹*luggage, child, vehicle, shop*›; (without attendants) 无随员的 ‹*king, judge*›; **to leave sth. ~** 疏于照看某物 **2** (not dealt with) 未处理的 ‹*matter, business*›; **to be ~ to** «*correspondence*» 无人理会

unattractive /ˌʌnəˈtræktɪv/ *adj* **1** (ugly) 难看的 **2** (unappealing) 无吸引力的; **an ~ prospect/career** 缺乏诱惑力的前景/职业; **an ~ quality in a person** 人身上令人反感的品行

unattractiveness /ˌʌnəˈtræktɪvnɪs/ *n* [u] **1** (ugliness) 难看 **2** (lack of appeal) 无吸引力

unauthenticated /ˌʌnɔːˈθentɪkeɪtɪd/ *adj* 未经证实的 ‹*document, evidence, story*›

unauthorized /ʌnˈɔːθəraɪzd/ *adj* 未经授权的 ‹*copy, use*›; 未经允许的 ‹*visit, absence, disclosure*›; **the ~ reproduction/publication of sth.** 某物的越权生产/出版; **an ~ biography** 外传; **no ~ access** 不得擅自进入

unavailable /ˌʌnəˈveɪləbl/ *adj* **1** *usu pred* (unobtainable) 无法得到的; **to be ~ (to sb.)** «*goods, service, care*» 是(某人)得不到的 **2** *pred* (not free) **to be ~** «*person*» 没空; **to be ~ for comment/work** 无暇发表评论/无法工作

unavailing /ˌʌnəˈveɪlɪŋ/ *adj* formal 徒劳的 ‹*effort, attempt, appeal*›

unavailingly /ˌʌnəˈveɪlɪŋli/ *adv* formal 徒劳地 ‹*try, struggle, shout*›

unavoidable /ˌʌnəˈvɔɪdəbl/ *adj* 不可避免的; **it is ~ that ...** 无法避免的是…

unavoidably /ˌʌnəˈvɔɪdəbli/ *adv* 不可避免地 ‹*late, absent*›; **to be ~ delayed** 不可避免地受到耽搁

unaware /ˌʌnəˈweə(r)/ *adj* **1** (having no knowledge) 不知道的; **he was ~ of the fact that she had won the competition** 他不知道她已赢得比赛; **to be politically/environmentally ~** 在政治上/环境问题上无知 **2** (oblivious) 未注意的; **he was ~ of my presence** 他没注意到我在场

unawares /ˌʌnəˈweəz/ *adv* **to catch** *or* **take sb. ~** 使某人措手不及

unbacked /ʌnˈbækt/ *adj* **1** Fin 无经济支持的; **~ credit/debt** 无担保信贷/债务 **2** Sport 无人押注的 ‹*horse, greyhound*›

unbalance /ʌnˈbæləns/ *vt* **1** lit 使…失去平衡 ‹*person, object*› **2** fig (disturb) 使…错乱 ‹*mind*›; 使…失衡 ‹*economy, relationship*›; **to ~ sb.** 使某人心理不平衡

unbalanced /ʌnˈbælənst/ *adj* **1** Psych 精神错乱的 ‹*person*›; 错乱的 ‹*mind*› **2** (biased) 偏颇的 ‹*account, reporting*› **3** (uneven) 不平衡的 ‹*design*›; 不均衡的 ‹*diet*›; **an ~ economy/industrial structure** 失衡的经济/产业结构

unbaptized /ˌʌnbæpˈtaɪzd/ *adj* 未受浸礼的

unbearable /ʌnˈbeərəbl/ *adj* 难以忍受的

unbearably /ʌnˈbeərəbli/ *adv* 难以忍受地 ‹*suffer, hurt*›; **to be ~ cold/painful/rude** 冷得让人吃不消/疼痛难忍/粗鲁难耐

unbeatable /ʌnˈbiːtəbl/ *adj* **1** esp Sport (invincible) 打不垮的 ‹*opponent, team, enemy*›; 无法打破的 ‹*record*›; 无法超越的 ‹*time*›; **to be ~ at** *or* **in sth.** 在某方面是难以战胜的 **2** (unsurpassable) 已达极限的; **an ~ price/offer** 最优惠的价格/报价; **an ~ view/combination** 无与伦比的景色/无敌组合

unbeaten /ʌnˈbiːtn/ *adj* 未败过的 ‹*opponent, team*›; 未曾打破的 ‹*record*›; 未曾超越的 ‹*time*›; **to be ~ at** *or* **in sth.** 在某方面未被击败

unbecoming /ˌʌnbɪˈkʌmɪŋ/ *adj* formal **1** (unflattering) 不合身的 ‹*garment*›; 不相配的 ‹*style, colour, hairstyle*› **2** (unseemly) 不恰当的 ‹*conduct, behaviour*›; **to be ~ (for sb.) to do sth.** (某人)做某事不合适

unbeknown /ˌʌnbɪˈnəʊn/ *adj* **~ to sb., ...** 某人不知道的是…

unbelief /ˌʌnbɪˈliːf/ *n* [u] 无宗教信仰

unbelievable /ˌʌnbɪˈliːvəbl/ *adj* 难以置信的 ‹*news, experience*›; **an ~ speed/amount** 惊人的速度/数量; **~ heat/cold** 极热/极冷; **it was an ~ feeling** 那是一种妙不可言的感觉; **it is ~ that ...** 令人震惊的是…

unbelievably /ˌʌnbɪˈliːvəbli/ *adv* 难以置信地; **~ rich/cold/stupid** 富得/冷得/笨得令人难以置信; **~, he arrived on time** 令人难以相信的是，他准时到达了

unbeliever /ˌʌnbɪˈliːvə(r)/ *n* (in God) 不信上帝者; (in religion) 无宗教信仰者

unbelieving /ˌʌnbɪˈliːvɪŋ/ *adj* 怀疑的 ‹*look, eyes, tone*›

unbelievingly /ˌʌnbɪˈliːvɪŋlɪ/ *adv* 怀疑地 ‹*say, look, stare*›

unbend /ʌnˈbend/ (*pt, pp* **unbent**)
A *vt* 把…弄直; **to ~ one's knees** 伸直膝盖
B *vi* **1** (straighten up) «*hose, stem*» 变直; «*person, animal*» 直起身来 **2** fig (relax) «*person*» 变得随和

unbending /ʌnˈbendɪŋ/ *adj* esp pej 倔强的 ‹*person, attitude*›; 坚定的 ‹*resolve, principle, belief*›

unbent /ʌnˈbent/ *pt, pp* ▸**unbend**

unbiased, unbiassed /ʌnˈbaɪəst/ *adj* 无偏见的; **he is ~ in his views** 他的观点客观公正

unbidden /ʌnˈbɪdn/ *adv* formal **1** (uninvited) 未经邀请地 ‹*come, enter*› **2** (spontaneously) 自发地 ‹*help*›; **to do sth. ~** 主动做某事; **to come ~ into one's mind** «*memory, thought*» 在脑海中闪现

unbind /ʌnˈbaɪnd/ *vt* (*pt, pp* **unbound**) 松开 ‹*person*›; **to ~ sb. from sth.** 把某人从某物解开; **to be unbound** «*prisoner*» 被释放

unbleached /ʌnˈbliːtʃt/ *adj* 未漂白的 ‹*cloth, hair*›

unblemished /ʌnˈblemɪʃt/ *adj* 无瑕疵的 ‹*face*›; 清白的 ‹*reputation*›

unblinking /ʌnˈblɪŋkɪŋ/ *adj* 目不转睛的 ‹*stare, gaze*›; **~ eyes** 一眨不眨的眼睛

unblinkingly /ʌnˈblɪŋkɪŋli/ *adv* 目不转睛地

unblock /ʌnˈblɒk/ *vt* 疏通 ‹*pipe, drain, sink*›

unblocker /ʌnˈblɒkə(r)/ *n* **1** [u] (substance) **(sink/drain) ~** (洗涤池/下水道)疏通剂 **2** [c] (device) 管道疏通器

unblushing /ʌnˈblʌʃɪŋ/ *adj* formal 不害臊的; **an ~ account of sth.** 对某事物厚颜无耻的叙述

unblushingly /ʌnˈblʌʃɪŋli/ *adv* formal 不害臊地 ‹*lie, deny*›

unbolt /ʌnˈbəʊlt/ *vt* 拔去…闩 ‹*door, gate*›

unborn /ʌnˈbɔːn/ *adj* **1** (not yet born) 未出生的 ‹*child*› **2** (of the future) 未来的 ‹*generation*›

unbound /ʌnˈbaʊnd/
A *pt, pp* ▸**unbind**
B *adj* 未装订的 ‹*book, volume, magazine*›

unbounded /ʌnˈbaʊndɪd/ *adj* liter 无限的

unbowed /ʌnˈbaʊd/ *adj pred* 不屈的; **to remain ~ (by sth.)** «*person, nation*» 不为(某物)所屈

unbranded /ʌnˈbrændɪd/ *adj* 没有商标的 ‹*goods*›

unbreakable /ʌnˈbreɪkəbl/ *adj* 不易打碎的 ‹*object, material*›; fig 不可破解的 ‹*code*›; **an ~ bond of friendship** fig 牢不可破的友谊纽带

unbreathable /ʌnˈbriːðəbl/ *adj* 不宜吸入的 ‹*air*›

unbribable /ʌnˈbraɪbəbl/ *adj* 无法贿赂的; **an ~ public official** 无法收买的公职人员

unbridle /ʌnˈbraɪdl/ *vt* 卸除…的辔头 ‹*horse*›

unbridled /ʌnˈbraɪdld/ *adj* **1** *attrib* Equit 无辔头的 ‹*horse*› **2** *usu attrib* fig (unchecked) 不受约束的 ‹*power*›; 无节制的 ‹*rage, jealousy*›; 奔放的 ‹*joy, passion, enthusiasm*›

unbroken /ʌnˈbrəʊkən/ *adj* **1** (uninterrupted) 连续的 ‹*series, sequence*›; **the ~ silence** 持续的沉默; **an ~ view of the hills** 延绵不断的山峦景色; **to get eight hours of ~ sleep** 连续睡8个小时 **2** (intact) 完好的 ‹*pottery, seal, window*›; 完整的 ‹*string, ice*›; **the ~ surface of the lake** 平静的湖面 **3** (unsurpassed) 未打破的 ‹*record*›; 未超过的 ‹*time*› **4** (not subdued) 未驯服的 ‹*horse*›; 不屈服的 ‹*spirit, person*›

unbuckle /ʌnˈbʌkl/ *vt* 解开…的搭扣 ‹*belt, strap*›

unbuilt /ʌnˈbɪlt/ *adj* 尚未修建的 ‹*building, structure*›; 无建筑物的 ‹*land*›

unbundle /ʌnˈbʌndl/ *vt* **1** (charge for separately) 对…分别计价 ‹*product, service*›; **~d software** 非捆绑软件 **2** (split) 分拆 ‹*company, group*›

unburden /ʌnˈbɜːdn/ *v refl* formal **to ~ oneself** 倾诉; **to ~ oneself to sb.** 向某人倾诉; **to ~ oneself of sth.** 诉说某事

unburied /ʌnˈberɪd/ *adj* 未埋葬的

unbusinesslike /ʌnˈbɪznɪslaɪk/ *adj* 无条理的 ‹*person, approach, method*›; 不合规矩的 ‹*attitude, behaviour, transaction*›

unbutton /ʌnˈbʌtn/ *vt* 解开…的扣子 ‹*garment, jacket, coat*›; 解开 ‹*button*›

unbuttoned /ʌnˈbʌtnd/ *adj* **1** (unfastened) 纽扣解开的; **an ~ shirt** 敞开的衬衫 **2** colloq (relaxed) 洒脱的 ‹*attitude*›; (uninhibited) 无拘束的 ‹*behaviour, performance*›

uncalled-for /ʌnˈkɔːldfɔː(r)/ *adj* **1** (undesirable) 不受欢迎的 **2** (unjustified) 不恰当的 **3** (unnecessary) 不必要的

uncannily /ʌnˈkænɪli/ *adv* **1** (eerily) 怪异地 ‹*still, quiet*›; **the old house was ~ silent** 那座老房子安静得有点怪异 **2** (extraordinarily) 非同寻常地 ‹*accurate, familiar, alike*›

uncanny /ʌnˈkæni/ *adj* **1** (eerie) 怪异的 ‹*feeling, occurrence, atmosphere*› **2** (extraordinary) 非同寻常的 ‹*accuracy, ability*›; **to bear an ~ resemblance to sth./sb.** 与某物/某人不可思议地相似

uncap /ʌnˈkæp/ *vt* (*pres p etc.* **-pp-**) 打开…的盖子 ‹*bottle*›

uncared for /ʌnˈkeədfɔː(r)/ *adj* 无人照看的 ‹*child, pet, garden*›; 被忽略的 ‹*appearance*›; **~ old people** 无人照看的老人

uncaring /ʌnˈkeərɪŋ/ *adj* 冷漠的 ‹*person, society, behaviour*›

uncarpeted /ʌnˈkɑːpɪtɪd/ *adj* 未铺地毯的

uncashed /ʌnˈkæʃt/ *adj* 未兑现的 ‹*cheque*›

uncatalogued /ʌnˈkætəlɒgd/ *adj* 未列入目录的

unceasing /ʌnˈsiːsɪŋ/ *adj* 不停的

unceasingly /ʌnˈsiːsɪŋli/ *adv* 不停地

uncensored /ʌnˈsensəd/ *adj* 未经审查的 ‹*book, film*›; **the full, ~ version of the novel** 未经删节的足本小说

unceremonious /ˌʌnserɪˈməʊnɪəs/ *adj* 无礼的

unceremoniously /ˌʌnserɪˈməʊnɪəsli/ *adv* 无礼地

uncertain /ʌn'sɜːtn/ *adj* **1** (unsure) 不确定的; (hesitant) 犹豫不决的; **to be ~ of sth.** 对某事没有把握; **to be ~ about sth./doing sth.** 对某事物/做某事拿不准; **to be ~ (about** *or* **as to) what to do/whether to do sth.** 不能确定该做什么/是否做某事; **in no ~ terms** 直截了当地 **2** (not predictable) 难预料的 ‹*outcome, fate, result*›; (not known) 不确知的 ‹*future, cause*›; **an old man of ~ age** 年龄不详的老头; **a manuscript of ~ origin** 来历不明的手稿 **3** (changeable) 易变的; (erratic) 无常的; **the weather is ~** 天气变幻莫测; **his aim is ~** 他的目标摇摆不定; **a man of ~ moods/temper** 喜怒无常/脾气难以捉摸的男人

uncertainly /ʌn'sɜːtnli/ *adv* 迟疑地

uncertainty /ʌn'sɜːtnti/ *n* **1** [u] (state) 不确定 **2** [c] (thing) 不确定的事物; **the uncertainties of life/of the market** 人生/市场的变幻无常

uncertainty principle *n* 测不准原理

uncertified /ʌn'sɜːtɪfaɪd/ *adj* 未认证的 ‹*accountant, document, software*›; **an ~ cheque** 不保付支票; **an ~ teacher** Amer 无资格证的教师

unchain /ʌn'tʃeɪn/ *vt* **1** (remove chain from) 给…解开锁链; **to ~ sth. from sth.** 把某物的锁链从某物上解开 **2** fig (liberate) 使自由; **the nation has been ~ed** 国家解放了

unchallengeable /ʌn'tʃælɪndʒəbl/ *adj* 不可挑战的 ‹*position, power, leader*›; 无可置疑的 ‹*truth, fact, argument*›

unchallenged /ʌn'tʃælɪndʒd/ *adj* **1** (unquestioned) 不被怀疑的 ‹*person*›; (undisputed) 没有异议的 ‹*statement*›; **to go ~** 未受质疑 **2** (without being asked one's identity) 未受盘查的 **3** (unopposed) 无人反对的 ‹*person, leader*›; 无人挑战的 ‹*power, position*›

unchallenging /ʌn'tʃælɪndʒɪŋ/ *adj* **1** (undemanding) 不具挑战性的 ‹*job, work*›; 不费脑筋的 ‹*film, book*›; **the work is intellectually ~** 这工作不费脑筋 **2** (non-threatening) 没有威胁的 ‹*person, voice*›

unchangeable /ʌn'tʃeɪndʒəbl/ *adj* (not liable to variation) 不变的 ‹*law, system*›; (not able to be altered) 不可改变的 ‹*reality, fact*›

unchanged /ʌn'tʃeɪndʒd/ *adj* 未改变的 ‹*custom, way of life, situation, landscape, rate, price*›

unchanging /ʌn'tʃeɪndʒɪŋ/ *adj* 不变的

uncharacteristic /ˌʌnkærɪktə'rɪstɪk/ *adj* 非典型的; **to be ~ of sb./sth.** 不是某人/某事物特有的

uncharacteristically /ˌʌnkærɪktə'rɪstɪkli/ *adv* 非同寻常地

uncharged /ʌn'tʃɑːdʒd/ *adj* **1** (without electric charge) 不带电的 ‹*particle, battery*› **2** (not charged with offence) 未受指控的 ‹*person*›

uncharitable /ʌn'tʃærɪtəbl/ *adj* 严厉的 ‹*person*›; 刻薄的 ‹*remark, words*›; **to be ~ about sb./sth.** 对某人/某物苛刻

uncharted /ʌn'tʃɑːtɪd/ *adj* **1** (not explored) 未经探测的 ‹*depths*›; 无人涉足的 ‹*territory, area*›; **to sail in ~ waters** lit 在未经探测的水域航行; fig 在未知的领域探索 **2** (not mapped) 地图上未标明的 ‹*island, area*›

unchecked /ʌn'tʃekt/
A *adj* **1** (uncontrolled) 不加约束的; **~ rage/passion** 失控的怒火/激情 **2** (unverified) 未经核对的 ‹*figure, account*›; 未经证实的 ‹*statement*›
B *adv* 不受控制地 ‹*spread, rise, grow*›

unchivalrous /ʌn'ʃɪvəlrəs/ *adj* 不殷勤的

unchristian /ʌn'krɪstʃən/ *adj* **1** (uncharitable) 不慈善的 ‹*person*›; 不宽容的 ‹*behaviour, attitude*› **2** (not Christian) 异端的 ‹*person, place*›

uncircumcised /ʌn'sɜːkəmsaɪzd/ *adj* 未受割礼的 ‹*man, boy*›; 未割包皮的 ‹*penis*›

uncivil /ʌn'sɪvɪl/ *adj* 不礼貌的; **to be ~ to sb.** 对某人粗暴无礼; **to be ~ of sb. to do sth.** 某人做某事有失礼貌

uncivilized /ʌn'sɪvɪlaɪzd/ *adj* **1** (inhumane) 不人道的 ‹*state, conditions*›; 残忍的 ‹*treatment*›; **at an** *or* **some ~ hour** 一大清早 **2** (uncouth, rude) 粗野的 ‹*person, behaviour*› **3** (primitive) 原始的 ‹*people, tribe*› **4** (barbarous) 未开化的 ‹*country, area*›

unclaimed /ʌn'kleɪmd/ *adj* 无人认领的 ‹*prize, property*›; 无人索取的 ‹*reward, benefit*›; **to go** *or* **remain ~** 尚无人领取

unclamp /ʌn'klæmp/ *vt* 松开…的夹钳

unclasp /ʌn'klɑːsp, Amer -'klæsp/ *vt* **1** (release) 松开 ‹*hand, fingers*› **2** (unfasten) 解开…的搭扣 ‹*necklace, bra*›

unclassified /ʌn'klæsɪfaɪd/ *adj* **1** (not categorized) 未分类的 ‹*item, paper, object*›; **an ~ road** 未分级的道路; **to get an ~ grade** Brit 不及格 **2** (not secret) 非机密的 ‹*research, source*›

uncle /'ʌŋkl/ ▶p. 419 *n* (elder brother of father) 伯父; (younger brother of father) 叔父; (brother of mother) 舅父; (husband of father's sister) 姑父; (husband of mother's sister) 姨父; (affectionate term used by children) 叔叔; **Bob's your ~** Brit colloq 易如反掌; **to say** *or* **cry ~** Amer colloq 讨饶

unclean /ʌn'kliːn/ *adj* **1** (dirty) 肮脏的 ‹*area, surface, water*› **2** Relig 邪恶的 ‹*thought, mind*›; 不洁净的 ‹*food*›

unclear /ʌn'klɪə(r)/ *adj* **1** (not evident) 不清楚的 ‹*result, reason, cause*› **2** (not comprehensible) 含糊的 ‹*answer, writing, instruction*› **3** (uncertain) 不肯定的; **to be ~ about sth.** 不明白某事; **to be ~ (as to) how/whether/why** *etc.* …不知道如何/是否/为什么等

uncleared /ʌn'klɪəd/ *adj* 未结关的 ‹*goods*›; 未清扫的 ‹*snow*›; 未清理的 ‹*refuse*›; 未收拾的 ‹*table*›

unclench /ʌn'klentʃ/ *vt* 松开 ‹*teeth, jaw, fist*›

Uncle: ~ Sam *pr n* 山姆大叔 [指美国或美国政府]; **~ Tom** *pr n* Amer colloq pej 汤姆叔叔 [指乐于讨好白人或与白人结交的黑人]

> **Uncle Sam**
>
> 山姆大叔。代表美国及其政府的虚构人物：形象为瘦高个，白胡子，身穿红蓝白三色（美国国旗的颜色）的燕尾服，头戴饰有白色五角星的高礼帽。一般认为这一称呼源自商人塞缪尔·威尔逊（Samuel Wilson）。英美 1812 年战争中，威尔逊为政府提供牛肉。因包装上的 US（United States 的首字母）印记和他的昵称 Uncle Sam 的首字母正好相同，因此 US 被戏称为山姆大叔。1961 年经国会确认，山姆大叔成为美国的象征。

uncloak /ʌn'kləʊk/ *vt* formal 揭开…的覆盖物 ‹*object*›; 揭露 ‹*person, identity*›

unclog /ʌn'klɒg/ *vt* (*pres p etc.* **-gg-**) 疏通 ‹*drain, gutter, pipe*›

unclothed /ʌn'kləʊðd/ *adj* formal 未穿衣服的 ‹*person*›; 赤裸的 ‹*body*›

unclouded /ʌn'klaʊdɪd/ *adj* **1** (clear) 晴朗的 ‹*sky*›; 清澈的 ‹*liquid*›; 明净的 ‹*mirror*› **2** (untroubled) 无忧无虑的 ‹*happiness*›; 光明的 ‹*future*›

uncoded /ʌn'kəʊdɪd/ *adj* 未编码的

uncoil /ʌn'kɔɪl/
A *vt* 展开 ‹*rope, hosepipe, wires*›; **the snake ~ed itself** 蛇展开盘着的身体
B *vi* «*rope, snake, spring*» 展开

uncollected /ˌʌnkə'lektɪd/ *adj* 未收的 ‹*tax, fare*›; 未领取的 ‹*mail, luggage*›; 未收集的 ‹*refuse, litter*›

uncombed /ʌn'kəʊmd/ *adj* 未梳理的

uncomfortable /ʌn'kʌmftəbl, Amer -fərt-/ *adj* **1** (physically) 不舒服的 ‹*shoes, clothes, bed*›; **an ~ journey/temperature** 令人不舒服的旅行/温度; **to sit in an ~ position** 坐的姿势很难受 **2** (emotionally) 不自在的 ‹*feeling*›; 不安的 ‹*thought*›; **to make sb. (feel) ~** 让某人（感到）不自在; **an ~ silence** 令人不安的寂静; **to be ~ about** *or* **with** 对…感到不安 ‹*role, decision, situation, behaviour*›; **to be ~ with sb.** 与某人在一起感到不自在; **I feel ~ talking about it** 谈论这件事我感到不安; **to make life** *or* **things ~ for sb.** 不给某人好日子过

uncomfortably /ʌn'kʌmftəbli, Amer -fərt-/ *adv* **1** (unpleasantly) 不舒服地 ‹*sit, lie*›; **~ hot/cold/tight** 热得/冷得/紧得难受的 **2** (awkwardly) 不自在地 ‹*say, glance, think*›; 令人不安地 ‹*rise, fall*›; **the exam is ~ close** 考试临近，令人不安

uncommercial /ˌʌnkə'mɜːʃl/ *adj* 非商业性的

uncommitted /ˌʌnkə'mɪtɪd/ *adj* **1** (undecided) 未表态的 ‹*person, delegate, voter*›; 不受约束的 ‹*attitude, point of view, position*›; **to be ~ to sb./sth.** 不受某人/某物约束 **2** (not allocated) 未定用途的 ‹*funds, resources*›

uncommon /ʌn'kɒmən/ *adj* **1** (rare, unusual) 不常有的 ‹*sight, occurrence, visitor*›; 罕见的 ‹*plant*›; **it is/is not ~ to ...** 做…很少见/并不少见 **2** formal or liter (exceptional) 异乎寻常的 ‹*likeness, resemblance*›; 特别的 ‹*rapport, liking, intimacy*›

uncommonly /ʌn'kɒmənli/ *adv* formal or liter 异乎寻常地 ‹*kind, generous, intelligent, stupid, talented*›

uncommunicative /ˌʌnkə'mjuːnɪkətɪv/ *adj* 不爱说话的; **to be ~ about sth.** 不愿意谈论某事

uncomplaining /ˌʌnkəm'pleɪnɪŋ/ *adj* 任劳任怨的 ‹*person, service*›; **long years of ~ devotion** 多年的默默奉献

uncomplainingly /ˌʌnkəm'pleɪnɪŋli/ *adv* 无怨言地

uncompleted /ˌʌnkəm'pliːtɪd/ *adj* 未完成的

uncomplicated /ʌn'kɒmplɪkeɪtɪd/ *adj* 简单的

uncomplimentary /ˌʌnkɒmplɪ'mentri, Amer -teri/ *adj* 贬低的

uncomprehending /ˌʌnkɒmprɪ'hendɪŋ/ *adj* 不理解的

uncomprehendingly /ˌʌnkɒmprɪ'hendɪŋli/ *adv* 不理解地

uncompromising /ʌn'kɒmprəmaɪzɪŋ/ *adj* 不妥协的 ‹*person, position, attitude, view*›; 严厉的 ‹*attack*›; 坚定的 ‹*integrity, honesty*›; **to take an ~ stand on sth.** 对某事物不妥协

uncompromisingly /ʌn'kɒmprəmaɪzɪŋli/ *adv* 不妥协地 ‹*reply, respond, say*›; 坚定地 ‹*outspoken, loyal, honest*›

unconcealed /ˌʌnkən'siːld/ *adj* 不掩饰的

unconcern /ˌʌnkən'sɜːn/ *n* [u] **1** (lack of interest) 无兴趣 **2** (lack of care) 不关心 **3** (lack of fear) 不担心

unconcerned /ˌʌnkən'sɜːnd/ *adj* **1** (uninterested) 不感兴趣的 ‹*person, attitude, look*›; **to be ~ with sth./sb.** 对某事/某人不感兴趣 **2** (not caring) 漠不关心的 ‹*person, attitude*›; **to be ~ about** *or* **by sth.** 对某事无所谓 **3** (untroubled) 不担心的 ‹*person, attitude*›

unconditional /ˌʌnkən'dɪʃənl/ *adj* 无条件的 ‹*support, bail, refusal, discharge, surrender*›; 绝对的 ‹*obedience, acceptance, agreement*›; **he has the ~ love of his parents** 他得到父母亲毫无保留的爱

unconditionally /ˌʌnkən'dɪʃənəli/ *adv* 无条件地

unconditioned /ˌʌnkən'dɪʃnd/ *adj* 无条件的; **~ reflexes** 无条件反射

unconfined /ˌʌnkən'faɪnd/ *adj* **1** (not restricted) 自由的 ‹*animal, person*› **2** (unlimited) 无限的 ‹*space, area, joy*›

unconfirmed /ˌʌnkən'fɜːmd/ *adj* 未确认的 ‹*report, information*›; 未经证实的 ‹*rumour*›

unconformity /ˌʌnkən'fɔːməti/ *n* 不整合

U

uncongenial /ˌʌnkənˈdʒiːniəl/ *adj* 意气不相投的〈*person*〉; 不合意的〈*work*〉; 不相宜的〈*place, surroundings*〉; **to be ～ to sb./sth.** 不适合某人/某事物

unconnected /ˌʌnkəˈnektɪd/ *adj* **1** (unrelated) 不相关的〈*events*〉; **the two incidents are quite ～** 这两个事件毫不相干 **2** (not joined) 未连接的〈*appliance, tap, pipe*〉; **an ～ TV set** 未接通电源的电视机

unconquerable /ʌnˈkɒŋkərəbl/ *adj* 不可征服的〈*mountain, adversary, people, army*〉; 坚不可摧的〈*fortress*〉; 不屈服的〈*mind, spirit*〉; 不能控制的〈*feeling*〉

unconquered /ʌnˈkɒŋkəd/ *adj* 未被征服的

unconscionable /ʌnˈkɒnʃənəbl/ *adj* formal **1** (unreasonable) 不合理的〈*action, conduct*〉 **2** (excessive) 过分的〈*demand*〉; **an ～ waste of resources** 资源的极度浪费

unconscious /ʌnˈkɒnʃəs/

A *adj* **1** (senseless) 失去知觉的〈*person, animal*〉; **to knock sb. ～** 打昏某人; **to lie/fall ～** 神志不清地躺着/昏倒; **she remained ～ for several hours** 她几个小时不省人事 **2** (unaware) 未意识到的; **to be ～ of sb./sth.** 未察觉到某人/某事物; **an ～ gesture/assumption** 下意识的手势/设想 **3** (unintentional) 无意的〈*irony, humour, insult*〉 **4** (subconscious) 无意识的〈*impulse, hostility, dislike*〉; **the ～ mind** 无意识

B *n sing* **the ～** 无意识; **in sb.'s ～** 在某人的无意识中

unconsciously /ʌnˈkɒnʃəsli/ *adv* **1** (automatically) 无意地〈*act*〉 **2** (subconsciously) 无意识地〈*feel*〉

unconsciousness /ʌnˈkɒnʃəsnɪs/ *n* [u] **1** (comatose state) 无知觉; **to fall** *or* **lapse into (a state of) ～** 陷入昏迷（状态） **2** (unawareness) 未意识到; **～ of sth.** 未察觉到某事

unconsidered /ˌʌnkənˈsɪdəd/ *adj* 未经考虑的〈*remark, gesture*〉; 被忽视的〈*object, kindness*〉; **an ～ act** 轻率的举动; **～ trifles** 可忽略的琐事

unconstitutional /ˌʌnkɒnstɪˈtjuːʃənl/ *adj* 违反宪法的

unconstitutionally /ˌʌnkɒnstɪˈtjuːʃənəli/ *adv* 违反宪法地

unconstrained /ˌʌnkənˈstreɪnd/ *adv* **1** (unrestricted) 自然的〈*action, growth*〉 **2** (uncontrolled) 不受约束的〈*passion*〉; 自由的〈*person*〉

uncontaminated /ˌʌnkənˈtæmɪneɪtɪd/ *adj* 未被污染的〈*food, drink, area*〉; fig 纯洁的〈*person, mind*〉; **clothing ～ by radioactivity** 未受放射线污染的衣服

uncontested /ˌʌnkənˈtestɪd/ *adj* 无竞争的〈*seat, candidature, election*〉; 无争议的〈*statement, evidence, divorce*〉

uncontrollable /ˌʌnkənˈtrəʊləbl/ *adj* 无法控制的; **an ～ child/fire** 无法管束的孩子/失控的大火

uncontrollably /ˌʌnkənˈtrəʊləbli/ *adv* 不能控制地; **to sob/shake/spin ～** 不由自主地抽泣/颤抖/失控地旋转

uncontrolled /ˌʌnkənˈtrəʊld/ *adj* **1** (not regulated) 不受管束的〈*immigration*〉; **the ～ use of sth.** 某物的滥用 **2** (unrestrained) 失控的〈*emotion, temper, inflation, disease*〉

uncontroversial /ˌʌnkɒntrəˈvɜːʃl/ *adj* 无争议的〈*statement, book, choice*〉; **an ～ figure** 不受争议的人

unconventional /ˌʌnkənˈvenʃənl/ *adj* 不因循守旧的; **an ～ dress/marriage/life** 不落俗套的服装/婚姻/生活

unconventionality /ˌʌnkənˌvenʃəˈnæləti/ *n* [u] (of behaviour) 不按惯例; (of dress) 不落俗套; (of way of life) 不从习俗

unconventionally /ˌʌnkənˈvenʃənəli/ *adv* 不按惯例地〈*live, behave*〉; 不落俗套地〈*dress*〉; 异常地〈*attractive*〉

unconverted /ˌʌnkənˈvɜːtɪd/ *adj* **1** (unaltered in use) 未改变用途的〈*building, vehicle, equipment*〉 **2** (not having adopted different religion) 未改变信仰的〈*person*〉 **3** (in rugby) 未成功射门的〈*try*〉

unconvinced /ˌʌnkənˈvɪnst/ *adj* 未信服的; **to be ～ of sth.** 对某事物不信服; **to be ～ that ...** 不相信…

unconvincing /ˌʌnkənˈvɪnsɪŋ/ *adj* 不令人信服的

unconvincingly /ˌʌnkənˈvɪnsɪŋli/ *adv* 不令人信服地

uncooked /ʌnˈkʊkt/ *adj* 未煮过的; **～ fruit and vegetables** 新鲜蔬果

uncool /ʌnˈkuːl/ *adj* colloq 不时髦的〈*music, appearance*〉; 不酷的〈*person, behaviour*〉

uncooperative /ˌʌnkəʊˈɒpərətɪv/ *adj* 不合作的〈*witness, behaviour, attitude*〉; 不配合的〈*pupil, patient*〉

uncooperatively /ˌʌnkəʊˈɒpərətɪvli/ *adv* 不合作地〈*respond, react, behave*〉

uncoordinated /ˌʌnkəʊˈɔːdɪneɪtɪd/ *adj* **1** (clumsy) 笨拙的〈*person*〉; 不协调的〈*movement, action*〉 **2** (badly organized) 考虑不周的〈*approach, effort, service*〉

uncork /ʌnˈkɔːk/ *vt* 拔去…的塞子〈*bottle*〉

uncorrected /ˌʌnkəˈrektɪd/ *adj* 未改正的〈*error, fault, exercise*〉; 未校正的〈*manuscript, draft*〉; 未矫正的〈*vision*〉

uncorroborated /ˌʌnkəˈrɒbəreɪtɪd/ *adj* 未经证实的〈*statement, evidence*〉

uncorrupted /ˌʌnkəˈrʌptɪd/ *adj* 未堕落的

uncountable /ʌnˈkaʊntəbl/ *adj* **1** (innumerable) 无数的; **an ～ number of people/things** 数不清的人/东西 **2** Ling 不可数的〈*noun*〉

uncounted /ʌnˈkaʊntɪd/ *adj* **1** (not counted) 未数过的〈*item*〉 **2** (innumerable) 无数的〈*objects, number*〉

uncount noun *n* 不可数名词

uncouple /ʌnˈkʌpl/ *vt* 解开…的钩

uncouth /ʌnˈkuːθ/ *adj* 粗鲁的; **～ language** 不雅的话

uncover /ʌnˈkʌvə(r)/ *vt* **1** (expose) 揭露〈*conspiracy, fraud, scandal*〉 **2** (discover) 发现〈*truth, secret*〉 **3** (remove cover from) 揭开…的盖子〈*object*〉; (remove covering from) 移去…的覆盖物〈*part, person*〉

uncovered /ʌnˈkʌvəd/ *adj* 无遮盖物的〈*food*〉; 无盖的〈*receptacle, saucepan*〉; **an ～ grandstand** 露天看台; **an ～ loan** *or* **advance** Fin 无担保贷款

uncritical /ʌnˈkrɪtɪkl/ *adj* **1** (unwilling to criticize) 不加批评的〈*attitude, acceptance*〉; **to be ～ of sb./sth.** 对某人/某事物不加批评 **2** (not using one's critical faculties) 不作评判的〈*person*〉

uncritically /ʌnˈkrɪtɪkli/ *adv* **1** pej (without criticism) 不加批评地〈*accept*〉 **2** (without critical exactness) 不作评判地〈*endorse*〉

uncross /ʌnˈkrɒs, Amer -ˈkrɔːs/ *vt* 使不交叉; **to ～ one's legs** 分开交叉的腿

uncrowded /ʌnˈkraʊdɪd/ *adj* 不拥挤的

uncrowned /ʌnˈkraʊnd/ *adj* 尚未加冕的; **the ～ king** 无冕之王

uncrushable /ʌnˈkrʌʃəbl/ *adj* 揉不皱的〈*fabric, dress*〉; 压不碎的〈*material*〉; **an ～ belief** 压不垮的信念

UNCTAD /ˈʌŋktæd/ *abbr* = **United Nations Conference on Trade and Development** 联合国贸易与发展会议

unction /ˈʌŋkʃn/ *n* [u] **1** (religious rite) 敷油礼 **2** formal pej (effusiveness) 甜言蜜语

unctuous /ˈʌŋktjʊəs/ *adj* formal pej 油滑的〈*person, speech*〉; 虚情假意的〈*tone, smile*〉

unctuously /ˈʌŋktjʊəsli/ *adv* formal pej 油滑地〈*speak, praise*〉; 虚情假意地〈*behave*〉

unctuousness /ˈʌŋktjʊəsnɪs/ *n* [u] formal pej 虚情假意

uncultivated /ʌnˈkʌltɪveɪtɪd/ *adj* **1** (not cultivated) 未耕作的〈*land, field, area*〉 **2** (uneducated) 无教养的〈*person*〉

uncultured /ʌnˈkʌltʃəd/ *adj* 不文雅的〈*person, class, society*〉; 粗俗的〈*taste*〉

uncurl /ʌnˈkɜːl/

A *vt* 伸直〈*oneself, legs*〉; 拉直〈*wire, tendrils*〉; **～ one's fist** 松开拳头

B *vi* «*person, animal*» 伸直; «*leaf, snake*» 展开

uncut /ʌnˈkʌt/ *adj* **1** (not cut) 未割的〈*grass, crops*〉; 未剪的〈*hair*〉; 未修剪的〈*hedge, branch*〉 **2** (unabridged) 未删节的〈*text, book*〉; (uncensored) 未审查的〈*film, version*〉 **3** (not cut open) 未切开的〈*leaves, pages*〉; (not trimmed) 毛边的〈*book*〉 **4** (not shaped) 未雕琢的〈*gemstone*〉

undamaged /ʌnˈdæmɪdʒd/ *adj* 未损坏的〈*goods, building, vehicle*〉; **he left the court with his reputation ～** 他离开了法庭，声誉没有受损

undated /ʌnˈdeɪtɪd/ *adj* 未注日期的

undaunted /ʌnˈdɔːntɪd/ *adj* 不屈不挠的; **he was ～ in his determination to succeed** 他百折不挠，决心取得成功

undeceive /ˌʌndɪˈsiːv/ *vt* liter (free from illusion) 使醒悟; (free from deception) 使不受骗; **to ～ sb. as to sth.** 使某人明白某事的真相

undecided /ˌʌndɪˈsaɪdɪd/ *adj* **1** (not settled) 悬而未决的〈*match, outcome, matter, question*〉 **2** (unsure) 犹豫不决的〈*person*〉; **～ voters** 举棋不定的投票人

undeclared /ˌʌndɪˈkleəd/ *adj* **1** (illegal) 未申报的〈*income, goods*〉 **2** (unannounced) 未宣布的; **an ～ candidate** 未正式表明身份的候选人; **the ～ war** 不宣而战的战争

undefeated /ˌʌndɪˈfiːtɪd/ *adj* 未被击败的

undefended /ˌʌndɪˈfendɪd/ *adj* **1** (unprotected) 未设防的〈*border, outpost, town*〉 **2** (uncontested) 无抗辩的〈*trial, case, divorce*〉

undefined /ˌʌndɪˈfaɪnd/ *adj* 未下定义的〈*term*〉; 不明确的〈*concept, character, emotion, area*〉; **an ～ feeling** 模糊的感觉

undelete /ˌʌndɪˈliːt/ *vt* 恢复〈*text, file*〉

undelivered /ˌʌndɪˈlɪvəd/ *adj* 未投递的

undemanding /ˌʌndɪˈmɑːndɪŋ, Amer -ˈmænd-/ *adj* 要求不高的〈*person*〉; 不费力的〈*task, job*〉; 不紧凑的〈*schedule*〉; **to be ～ of sth.** 不苛求某物

undemocratic /ˌʌndeməˈkrætɪk/ *adj* 不民主的

undemonstrative /ˌʌndɪˈmɒnstrətɪv/ *adj* 感情不外露的; **to be ～ towards** *or* **to sb.** 对某人矜持寡言

undeniable /ˌʌndɪˈnaɪəbl/ *adj* 无可否认的; **it is ～ that ...** …是无可争辩的

undeniably /ˌʌndɪˈnaɪəbli/ *adv* 无可否认地; **what he claims is ～ correct** 他的断言无疑是正确的

undependable /ˌʌndɪˈpendəbl/ *adj* 不可靠的

under /ˈʌndə(r)/

A *prep* **1** (below) 在…下面; (moving below) 到…下面; (passing below) 从…下面; **the box ～ the bed** 床底下的盒子; **the apple rolled ～ the table/sofa** 苹果滚到了床/沙发底下; **to come out from ～ sth.** 从…底下出来〈*table*〉; **to tuck sth. ～ one's arm** 把某物夹在胳膊下面; **to slide sth. ～ the door** 把某物从门下塞进去 **2** (at lower level than) 在…下方; **to shelter ～ the wall** 躲藏在墙根下; **to place a ladder ～ the window** 把梯子支在窗户下面; **to have dark rings ～ one's eyes** 眼睛下面有黑眼圈 **3** (covered by) 由…覆盖着; **fossils buried ～ the earth** 埋在地下的化石; **the cellar was ～ several feet of water** 地下室在水下几英尺; **to sleep ～ a duvet** 盖着羽绒被睡觉 **4** (behind, within) 在…里层;

(moving behind) 到…里面; ～ **the paint there was wallpaper** 涂料下层有墙纸; **she slid the envelope ～ her jacket** 她把信封塞到夹克里面 **5** fig (concealed by) 在…背后; **to have a kind heart ～ a cool exterior** 冷漠的外表下有一颗善良的心 **6** (less than) 不到; **to take (us) ～ an hour** 花（我们）不到一个小时; **temperatures ～ 10°C** 低于 10°C 的气温; **children ～ five** 不满 5 岁的儿童; **an income of ～ £20,000** 不足 2 万英镑的收入 **7** (lower in rank than) 低于; **I was ～ him in the hierarchy** 我比他等级低; **those ～ the rank of sergeant** 军士以下衔级的人 **8** (subordinate to) 从属于; **I have 50 people ～ me** 我手下有 50 个人; **to have 900 men ～ one's command** 指挥着 900 名士兵 **9** (taught by) 以…为师; **to study ～ sb.** 师从于某人 **10** (during) 在…期间; **England ～ the Tudors** 都铎王朝统治时期的英格兰; **plans made ～ the last government** 上一届政府制定的计划 **11** (according to) 根据; ～ **contract** 根据合约; ～ **the law** 依据法律 **12** (in state of) 处于…状况; **land ～ cultivation** 正在耕作的土地; **the situation is ～ control** 局势受到了控制; **to be ～ guarantee** 在保修期内; **to be ～ orders to do sth.** 奉命做某事; ～ **anaesthetic** *or* **anaesthesia** 处于麻醉状态 **13** (using as name) 以…（名字）; **she goes ～ the name of ...** 她名叫…; **to write ～ a pseudonym** 用笔名写作 **14** (in classification) 归入; **books classified ～ Fiction** 小说类书籍; ～ **another heading** 在另一个标题下 **15** Comput 在…环境下; **the program runs ～ DOS** 该程序在 DOS 环境下运行 **16** (planted with) 有…植被; **fields ～ wheat** 麦田; **areas still ～ virgin forest** 仍被原始森林覆盖的区域

B *adv* **1** (below) 在下面; (passing below) 从下面; **to run to the bed and crawl ～** 跑过去钻到床下; **to pull up the covers and crawl ～** 拉起被单钻进去; **to close the door and slide sth. ～** 关上门把某物从下面塞进去 **2** (below surface) 在表面下; **to go ～** ‹*diver*› 下潜; ‹*ship*› 下沉; **he went ～ for the third time** 他第三次潜到水下; **to stay ～** ‹*diver*› 潜在水中; **to sink ～** 沉入水中 **3** (less) 不到; **children of six and ～** 6 岁及以下的儿童; **items at £10 and ～** 10 英镑及以下的物品; **to run five minutes ～** ‹*event*› 持续不足 5 分钟 **4** (unconscious) 处于昏迷; **to put sb. ～** 使某人失去知觉; **to feel oneself going ～** 觉得自己要昏厥; **to be** *or* **stay ～ for three minutes** 昏迷 3 分钟

underachieve /ˌʌndərəˈtʃiːv/ *vi* 未发挥水平

underachiever /ˌʌndərəˈtʃiːvə(r)/ *n* 发挥不佳者

underage /ˌʌndərˈeɪdʒ/ *adj* 未达法定年龄的; ～ **drinking/driving** 未成年饮酒/驾车

underarm /ˈʌndərɑːm/

A *adj* **1** Sport 低手的 ‹*throw, serve, bowling, bowler*› **2** *attrib* (of armpit) 腋下的 ‹*hair, perspiration, deodorant*›

B *adv* 用低手 ‹*throw, bowl, serve*›

C *n* 腋窝

underbelly /ˈʌndəbeli/ *n* **1** (underside of animal's body) 下腹部 **2** (vulnerable part) 薄弱环节; **the soft ～ of the British economy** 英国经济的软肋 **3** pej (underclass) 社会底层; **the dark ～ of the construction industry** 建筑业的阴暗面

underbid /ˌʌndəˈbɪd/ (*pres p* **-dd-**; *pt, pp* **underbid**)

A *vt* **1** (make lower offer than) 投标出价低于 ‹*contractor, rival*› **2** (in card game) 叫牌低于…的实力 ‹*cards, holding*›

B *vi* **1** (make lower offer) ‹*contractor, buyer*› 投标出价过低 **2** (in card game) 叫牌过低

underbody /ˈʌndəbɒdi/ *n* (of animal) 腹部; (of vehicle) 车身底部

underbrush /ˈʌndəbrʌʃ/ *n* [u] Amer = **undergrowth**

undercapitalize /ˌʌndəˈkæpɪtəlaɪz/ *vt* 对…投资不足

undercapitalized /ˌʌndəˈkæpɪtəlaɪzd/ *adj* 投资不足的

undercarriage /ˈʌndəkærɪdʒ/ *n* [飞行器的] 起落架

undercharge /ˌʌndəˈtʃɑːdʒ/

A *vt* 少收…的款 ‹*person, account*›

B *vi* 少收钱

underclass /ˈʌndəklɑːs, Amer -klæs/ *n* 社会底层

underclothes /ˈʌndəkləʊðz/ *npl* 内衣

undercoat /ˈʌndəkəʊt/

A *n* **1** (of paint, varnish) 底漆 **2** Amer (clothing) [穿在外衣内的] 上衣

B *vt* 给…涂底漆 ‹*woodwork, window frame*›

undercook /ˌʌndəˈkʊk/ *vt* 未煮透

undercooked /ˌʌndəˈkʊkt/ *adj* 未煮透的; ～ **meats** 欠火候的肉

undercover /ˌʌndəˈkʌvə(r)/

A *adj* 秘密的; ～ **agent** 密探; ～ **policeman/reporter** 卧底警察/秘密记者

B *adv* 秘密地

undercurrent /ˈʌndəkʌrənt/ *n* **1** lit 潜流 **2** fig 潜在情绪; **an ～ of resentment** 潜在的不满情绪

undercut

A /ˌʌndəˈkʌt/ *vt* (*pres p* **-tt-**; *pt, pp* **undercut**) **1** (set prices lower than) 售价低于; **we have ～ our competitors by 50p per packet** 我们的价格每包比竞争对手低了 50 便士 **2** (cut away) ‹*current*› 冲蚀…的底部 ‹*cliff*›; ‹*machine, erosion*› 切除…的底部 ‹*bank*›; **to ～ spending power/living standards** 削弱购买力/使生活水平下降 **3** (undermine) 削弱 **4** (slice) 下旋削 ‹*ball*›

B /ˈʌndəkʌt/ *n* Brit 牛腰部嫩肉

underdeveloped /ˌʌndədɪˈveləpt/ *adj* **1** (not fully grown) 发育不全的 ‹*person, muscles, physique*› **2** (not yet advanced) 不发达的 ‹*country, area, region*›; 落后的 ‹*economy*› **3** Phot 显影不足的 ‹*film, plate, print*›

underdog /ˈʌndədɒg, Amer -dɔːg/ *n* **1** (in society) 弱者; **in a caring society help is readily available for the ～** 在一个关爱的社会中，弱势群体很容易得到帮助 **2** (in game, contest) (person) 失败者; (team) 失败的一方

underdone /ˌʌndəˈdʌn/ *adj* 未煮熟的; ～ **steak** 嫩牛排

underdressed /ˌʌndəˈdrest/ *adj* 穿着不当的

underemphasize /ˌʌndərˈemfəsaɪz/ *vt* 对…强调不够

underemployed /ˌʌndərɪmˈplɔɪd/ *adj* 大材小用的 ‹*person*›; 未充分就业的 ‹*labour*›; 未充分利用的 ‹*resource, equipment, building*›

underemployment /ˌʌndərɪmˈplɔɪmənt/ *n* [u] (of person) 大材小用; (of labour) 未充分就业; (of resources, equipment, building) 未充分利用

underequipped /ˌʌndərɪˈkwɪpt/ *adj* 设备不全的 ‹*school, hospital, factory*›; 装备不足的 ‹*person*›

underestimate

A /ˌʌndərˈestɪmeɪt/ *vt* 低估

B /ˌʌndərˈestɪmət/ *n* 低估

underestimation /ˌʌndərestɪˈmeɪʃn/ *n* 低估

underexpose /ˌʌndərɪkˈspəʊz/ *vt* 使曝光不足; **an ～d image** 曝光不足的图像

underexposure /ˌʌndərɪkˈspəʊʒə(r)/ *n* **1** [u] (inadequate exposure) 曝光不足 **2** [c] (photograph) 曝光不足的照片; (negative) 曝光不足的底片; (transparency) 曝光不足的幻灯片

underfed /ˌʌndəˈfed/ *adj* 吃不饱的; **to look ～** 看上去营养不良

underfelt /ˈʌndəfelt/ *n* [u and c] Brit 地毯垫毡

underfinanced /ˌʌndəˈfaɪnænst, -fɪˈnænst/ *adj* 资金短缺的

underfloor /ˈʌndəflɔː(r)/ *adj* 地板下的; ～ **heating** 地暖

underfoot /ˌʌndəˈfʊt/ *adv* (under one's feet) 在脚下; (on the ground) 在地上; **to trample sb./sth. ～** 将某人/某物踩在脚下

underframe /ˈʌndəfreɪm/ *n* 底架

underfunded /ˌʌndəˈfʌndɪd/ *adj* 资金不足的; **the library was seriously** *or* **badly ～** 图书馆严重缺乏资金

underfunding /ˌʌndəˈfʌndɪŋ/ *n* [u] 资金不足

undergarment /ˈʌndəgɑːmənt/ *n* 内衣

undergo /ˌʌndəˈgəʊ/ *vt* (*pt* **underwent**, *pp* **undergone**) 接受 ‹*surgery, treatment, training*›; 经历 ‹*change, reform*›; 经受 ‹*test, torture*›

undergraduate /ˌʌndəˈgrædʒʊət/ *n* 本科生; **an ～ grant/student/degree** 本科助学金/本科生/本科学位

underground

A /ˈʌndəgraʊnd/ *adj* **1** (below ground) 地下的; **an ～ railway/car park** 地铁/地下停车场 **2** (secret) 秘密的; **an ～ newspaper/organization/resistance movement** 地下报纸/组织/抵抗运动

B /ˌʌndəˈgraʊnd/ *adv* **1** (below ground) 在地下 **2** (in or into secrecy) 秘密地; **to go/stay ～** 转入地下/隐藏起来; **to drive sb. ～** 迫使某人转入地下

C /ˈʌndəgraʊnd/ *n* [u] **1** Brit (railway) 地铁; **on the ～** 乘坐地铁; **an ～ station** 地铁站 **2** (secret movement) 地下运动; (secret organization) 地下组织; **to work for/join the ～** 为地下组织工作/加入地下组织 **3** (artistic movement) 先锋派运动; ～ **art/music** 先锋派艺术/音乐

underground economy *n* 地下经济

undergrowth /ˈʌndəgrəʊθ/ *n* [u] 下层灌木丛; **to lurk** *or* **skulk in the ～** 潜伏在灌木丛中

underhand /ˌʌndəˈhænd/ *adj* **1** (dishonest) 不光彩的; ～ **trick/dealings** 诡计/非法交易; **I've always regarded his methods as somewhat ～** 我一直认为他的方法有点不那么光明正大 **2** (with palm upward) 手掌向上的; (with palm outwards) 手掌向外的; **to hold the bar with an ～ grip** 反握抓住横杠

underhanded /ˌʌndəˈhændɪd/ *adj* Amer = **underhand 1**

underhandedly /ˌʌndəˈhændɪdli/ *adv* 不光彩地

underinsure /ˌʌndərɪnˈʃɔː(r), Amer -ɪnˈʃʊər/ *vt* 为…投保不足

underinsured /ˌʌndərɪnˈʃɔːd, Amer -ɪnˈʃʊərd/ *adj* 保险额不足的

underinvest /ˌʌndərɪnˈvest/ *vi* 投资不足; **to ～ in sth.** 对某物投资不足

underinvestment /ˌʌndərɪnˈvestmənt/ *n* [u] 投资不足

underlain /ˌʌndəˈleɪn/ *pp* ▸**underlie**

underlay[1] /ˌʌndəˈleɪ/ *pt* ▸**underlie**

underlay[2] /ˈʌndəleɪ/ *n* 地毯衬垫

underlie /ˌʌndəˈlaɪ/ *vt* (*pres p* **underlying**; *pt* **underlay**; *pp* **underlain**) **1** (lie below) 位于…之下 **2** (form basis of) 构成…的基础; **the fundamental issue which ～s the conflict** 引发冲突的根本问题; **a bitter pessimism ～s all his writing** 痛苦的悲观情绪贯穿他的所有作品

underline /ˌʌndəˈlaɪn/ *vt* **1** (draw line under) 在…下面划线 **2** (emphasize) 强调; **ominous words that ～d the danger** 使危险更显突出的不祥语言

underling /ˈʌndəlɪŋ/ *n* pej 走卒; **the underworld boss and his hired ～s** 黑社会头目和他雇用的喽罗

underlining /ˌʌndəˈlaɪnɪŋ/ *n* [u] 下划线

underlit /ˌʌndəˈlɪt/ *adj* 照明不足的

underlying /ˌʌndəˈlaɪɪŋ/

A *pres p* ▸**underlie**

U

B *adj* 隐含的 ‹*guilt, truth*›; 潜在的 ‹*problem, inflation*›; 根本的 ‹*theme, cause*›; **an ~ claim/liability** 优先的权利/责任

undermanager /ˌʌndəˈmænɪdʒə(r)/ ▸**p. 409** *n* 副经理; **the ~ at the local coal pit** 当地煤矿的副矿长

undermanned /ˌʌndəˈmænd/ *adj* 人手不足的

undermanning /ˌʌndəˈmænɪŋ/ *n* [u] 人手不足

undermentioned /ˌʌndəˈmenʃnd/ *adj* Brit formal 下述的; **the ~ items** *or* **articles** 下述物品

undermine /ˌʌndəˈmaɪn/ *vt* 1 (subvert, make weaker) 暗中颠覆 2 (damage) 暗中破坏; **stop undermining me!** 别再挖我的墙角了! 3 (erode) «*sea*» 侵蚀…的基础 ‹*cliff, road*›; «*sea*» 侵蚀 ‹*foundations*› 4 (dig beneath) 在…下挖 ‹*wall*›

underneath /ˌʌndəˈniːθ/

A *prep* 1 (below) 在…下面; (moving below) 到…下面; (passing below) 从…下面; **the box ~ the bed** 床底的盒子; **to have bags ~ one's eyes** 眼睛下方有眼袋; **the apple rolled ~ the sofa/table** 苹果滚到了沙发/桌子底下; **to come out from ~ sth.** 从…底下出来; **to tuck sth. ~ one's arm** 把某物夹在胳膊底下; **to slide sth. ~ the door** 把某物从门下塞进去 2 (below surface of) 在…表面下; **tunnels ~ the earth** 地底下的隧道; **minerals ~ the ground** 地下矿藏; **to dive ~ the water** 潜到水下 3 (behind, within) 在…里层; (moving behind) 到…里层; **the railings were rusty ~ the paint** 漆层底下的栏杆锈迹斑斑; **to wear a swimsuit ~ a dress** 在连衣裙里面穿着游泳衣; **she slid the envelope ~ her jacket** 她把信封塞到夹克里面 4 fig (concealed by) 在…背后; **to have a kind heart ~ a cool exterior** 冷漠的外表下有一颗善良的心

B *adv* 1 (below, lower down) 在下面; (passing below) 从下面; **to look at sth. from ~** 从下面看某物; **the apartment ~** 下面的那套公寓; **to run to the bed and crawl ~** 跑过去钻到床下; **to pull up the covers and crawl ~** 拉起被单钻进去; **to close the door and slide sth. ~** 关上门把某物从下面塞进去 2 (behind layer) 在里层; **to reveal plaster ~** 露出里层的灰泥; **to wear a fur coat with nothing ~** 光身穿裘皮大衣 3 fig (behind appearance) 在外表下; **to be shy ~** 心底里害羞; **to be soft-hearted ~** 有一颗仁心

C *n sing* (lower part) 下面; (underside) 底部; **the ~ of a cup/car/bridge** 杯底/车底/桥底; **the ~ of a drawer** 抽屉底

undernourished /ˌʌndəˈnʌrɪʃt/ *adj* 营养不良的

undernourishment /ˌʌndəˈnʌrɪʃmənt/ *n* [u] 营养不良

underpaid /ˌʌndəˈpeɪd/

A *pt, pp* ▸**underpay**

B *adj* 报酬过低的; **to be ~ for sth.** 做某事所得报酬过低

underpants /ˈʌndəpænts/ *npl* Brit 内裤

underpart /ˈʌndəpɑːt/

A *n* 下部

B underparts *npl* [动物的] 下体

underpass /ˈʌndəpɑːs, Amer -pæs/ *n* 1 (for traffic) 下层通道 2 (for pedestrians) 地下人行道; **to cross the road by the ~** 走地道过马路

underpay /ˌʌndəˈpeɪ/ *vt* (*pt, pp* **underpaid**) 1 (pay badly) 给…报酬过低 2 (pay less than full amount) 少付; **you have underpaid me by £5** 你少付我 5 英镑

underperform /ˌʌndəpəˈfɔːm/ *vi* «*student, player, school, business, stock*» 表现平平

underpin /ˌʌndəˈpɪn/ *vt* (*pres p etc.* **-nn-**) 1 (support) 加固…的基础 ‹*wall, building*› 2 (strengthen) «*fact, statement*» 支持 ‹*argument, case*›; «*morality*» 巩固 ‹*society*›

underplay /ˌʌndəˈpleɪ/ *vt* 淡化…的重要性; **to ~ the negative factors in the matter** 对事情的负面因素轻描淡写

underpopulated /ˌʌndəˈpɒpjʊleɪtɪd/ *adj* 人口不足的; **the ~ areas of the world** 世界上人口稀少的地区

underpowered /ˌʌndəˈpaʊəd/ *adj* 动力不足的 ‹*engine, car, aircraft, ship*›; **to be ~** 动力不足

underprepared /ˌʌndəprɪˈpeəd/ *adj* 准备不充分的

underprice /ˌʌndəˈpraɪs/ *vt* (put too low a price on) 给…定价过低; (sell at too low a price) 以过低的价格销售

underpriced /ˌʌndəˈpraɪst/ *adj* 售价过低的; **this car is ~** 这辆汽车售价过低

underprivileged /ˌʌndəˈprɪvəlɪdʒd/

A *adj* 处于弱势的

B *npl* **the ~** 弱势群体

underproduce /ˌʌndəprəˈdjuːs, Amer -ˈduːs/ *vt* 1 Ind, Com 使生产不足; **goods that have been seriously ~d** 严重减产的商品 2 Mus, Cin 粗糙地制作 ‹*record, song, film*›

underproduced /ˌʌndəprəˈdjuːst, Amer -prəˈduːst/ *adj* 制作粗糙的

underproduction /ˌʌndəprəˈdʌkʃn/ *n* [u] 生产不足; **to lead to ~** 导致减产

underqualified /ˌʌndəˈkwɒlɪfaɪd/ *adj* 资格不够的; **to be ~ for sth.** 不能胜任某事

underrate /ˌʌndəˈreɪt/ *vt* 低估 ‹*number, strength, difficulty*›; 对…评价过低 ‹*person, book, play*›; **to ~ the opposition** 低估对手

underrated /ˌʌndəˈreɪtɪd/ *adj* 被低估的 ‹*opponent, contribution*›; 被评价过低的 ‹*person, book, play*›

underreact /ˌʌndərɪˈækt/ *vi* 反应不够; **to ~ to sb./sth.** 对某人/某事物反应不够

underripe /ˌʌndəˈraɪp/ *adj* 不够成熟的

underscore /ˌʌndəˈskɔː(r)/

A *vt* 1 (underline) 在…下面画线 2 (emphasize) 强调

B *n* 下画线

underscoring /ˌʌndəˈskɔːrɪŋ/ *n* [u] 1 (lines) 下画线; (action) 在下方画线 2 (emphasis) 强调

undersea /ˈʌndəsiː/ *adj attrib* 海面下的

underseal /ˈʌndəsiːl/

A *n* 车身下部防蚀涂料

B *vt* 在…的下部涂防蚀涂料

under-secretary *n* Brit **~ (of state)** 政务次官; **parliamentary ~ to the Treasury** 财政部政务次长

undersell /ˌʌndəˈsel/ (*pt, pp* **undersold**) *vt* 1 (undercut) 以低价出售 ‹*goods, item*›; 以低于…的价格出售 ‹*competitor*›; **our competitors ~ our product/us by £4 per item** 我们的竞争对手比我们的产品/我们每件低 4 英镑 2 (promote insufficiently) 对…推销不够; (undervalue) 过低评价; **to ~ oneself** 过于自谦

underserved /ˌʌndəˈsɜːvd/ *adj* 服务不完备的; **medically ~** 医疗服务不足的

undersexed /ˌʌndəˈsekst/ *adj* 性欲不强的; **to be ~** 性冷淡

undershirt /ˈʌndəʃɜːt/ *n* esp Amer [衬衫内穿的] 背心

undershoot /ˌʌndəˈʃuːt/ (*pt, pp* **undershot**) *vt* 1 (land short of runway) 着陆未达 2 (fall short of) 未达到

undershorts /ˈʌndəʃɔːts/ *npl* [男式] 内裤

undershot /ˌʌndəˈʃɒt/ *pt, pp* ▸**undershoot**

underside /ˈʌndəsaɪd/ *n* 底侧; **the ~ of the car** 汽车的底部; **the sordid ~ of the glamorous 1980s** 迷人的 20 世纪 80 年代的肮脏一面

undersigned /ˌʌndəˈsaɪnd/ formal

A *n* (*pl* **undersigned**) [文件的] 签字人

B *adj* 在文件下面签名的 ‹*person*›; 签在文件下面的 ‹*name*›

undersized /ˌʌndəˈsaɪzd/ *adj* 较矮小的 ‹*person, animal, crops*›; 比一般小的 ‹*portion*›; **~ tomatoes** 个头偏小的西红柿

underskirt /ˈʌndəskɜːt/ *n* 衬裙; **to cling to one's mother's ~s** fig 过分依赖母亲的保护

underslung /ˈʌndəslʌŋ/ *adj* 悬挂的 ‹*cargo, load, section*›; 下悬式的 ‹*chassis, hoist*›

undersoil /ˈʌndəsɔɪl/ *n* [u and c] 底土; **~ heating** 地热

undersold /ˌʌndəˈsəʊld/ *pt, pp* ▸**undersell**

underspend

A /ˌʌndəˈspend/ *vi* (*pt, pp* **underspent**) 花费不足; **to ~ on sth.** 在某事物上花费太少

B /ˌʌndəˈspend/ *vt* (*pt, pp* **underspent**) 花费少于

C /ˈʌndəspend/ *n* 花费不足

underspending /ˌʌndəˈspendɪŋ/ *n* [u] 花费不足

understaffed /ˌʌndəˈstɑːft, Amer -ˈstæft/ *adj* 人员不足的; **to be ~** 人手不足

understaffing /ˌʌndəˈstɑːfɪŋ, Amer -ˈstæfɪŋ/ *n* [u] 人员不足

understand /ˌʌndəˈstænd/ (*pt, pp* **understood**)

A *vt* 1 (grasp meaning of) 懂; (know operation of) 了解; (interpret) 理解; **can you ~ French?** 你懂法语吗?; **I don't ~ what your are saying** 我不明白你在说些什么; **you must be ready on time; is that understood?** 你必须按时做好准备，听明白了吗?; **to make oneself understood** 把自己的意思表达清楚; **doctors still don't ~ much about the disease** 医生对这种疾病还不太了解; **do I ~ you correctly?** 我没有误解你的意思吧?; **her motives, as I ~ them, are purely financial** 据我看，她的动机纯粹是为了钱; **I understood her to imply** *or* **as implying that there was a very remote chance** 我认为她在暗示机会很渺茫 2 (appreciate) 意识到; **they don't ~ the danger they are in** 他们没有意识到自己所处的危险 3 (know reason for) 认识到…的原因; **no one is answering the phone; I can't ~ it** 没人接电话，我不知道是怎么回事; **I could never ~ why she was fired** 我怎么也不明白她为何被解雇; **I just can't ~ his taking the money** formal 我就是不明白他为什么会偷钱 4 (empathize with) 体谅; **I can ~ you feeling angry** *or* **that you feel angry** 你生气我能理解; **we ~ what you're going through** 我们同情你目前的遭遇 5 (believe) 认为; (be told) 得知; **I ~ you wish to see the manager** 听说您想见经理; **am I to ~ that you refuse?** 你是说你拒绝了?; **the Prime Minister is understood to have been extremely angry about the report** 据说首相对该报道大为恼火; **it's generally understood that he will win** 人们普遍认为他会获胜; **I was given to ~ that she had resigned** formal 我获悉她已辞职; **she has let it be understood that she will support the measure** formal 她放出风来说她将支持那项措施; **he's dead — so I ~** 他死了——我听说了 6 (agree) 默认; **it must be understood that ...** …一定不言而喻; **I thought it was understood that my expenses would be paid** 我原以为对方同意支付我的费用 7 Ling (imply) 推断出; **in the sentence 'I can't drive', the object 'a car' is understood** 在 "I can't drive" 一句中，可推测宾语 "a car" 被省略了

B *vi* 1 (comprehend) 懂得; **I'm not sure that I ~: go over it again** 我不敢说我搞懂了，再来一遍吧; **no slip-ups! (do you) ~?** 别出差错! (你) 听明白了吗? 2 (sympathize) 体谅; **I quite ~; it must be very difficult for you** 我很理解，这对你来说一定很艰难

understandable /ˌʌndəˈstændəbl/ *adj* 1 (comprehensible) 易懂的; **such concepts are only ~ to the expert** 这些概念只有专家才懂 2 (natural) 可以理解的; **an ~ error**

情有可原的错误; **it is ~ that they should feel hurt** 他们感到受了伤害是可以理解的

understandably /ˌʌndəˈstændəbli/ *adv* 1 (comprehensibly) 易懂地; **I expressed myself perfectly ~** 我把自己的意思表达得十分清楚 2 (naturally) 可以理解地; **they're ~ disappointed with the result** 他们对结果感到失望是可以理解的

understanding /ˌʌndəˈstændɪŋ/
A *n* 1 [c and u] (comprehension) 理解; **foreign visitors with no ~ of English** 不懂英语的外国游客; **the committee has little ~ of the problem** 委员会对这个问题知之甚少 2 [c] (informal or unspoken agreement) 协议; **to come to** *or* **reach an ~ (with sb.)** (同某人) 达成协议; **we have an ~ that nobody talks about work over lunch** 我们有个默契, 吃午饭时谁也不谈工作; **they agreed to the changes on the ~ that they would be introduced gradually** 他们同意这些变革, 条件是要逐步进行; **on that ~** formal 在此条件下 3 [c and u] (sympathy) 体谅; **we are looking for a better ~ between the two nations** 我们正在寻求两国间的进一步了解; **we must tackle the problem with ~** 我们必须用谅解来处理这个问题 4 [c and u] (interpretation) 解释; **the statement is open to various ~s** 这个声明有多种诠释; **my ~ was that he would find a new supplier** 我的看法是他会找到新的供货商 5 [u] (powers of reason) 理解力; **to be beyond a child's ~** 超出了儿童的理解力
B *adj* 体谅的; **~ parents** 通情达理的父母; **to be ~ about sb.'s position** 体谅某人的处境

understandingly /ˌʌndəˈstændɪŋli/ *adv* 善解人意地

understate /ˌʌndəˈsteɪt/ *vt* 1 (say with reserve) 保守地陈述 ‹*views*›; 有节制地表达 ‹*feeling, reaction*› 2 (play down) 少报 ‹*total, number*›; 对…轻描淡写 ‹*gravity, danger*›

understated /ˌʌndəˈsteɪtɪd/ *adj* 素雅的 ‹*style, fashion*›; 轻描淡写的 ‹*detail*›; **in a natural, ~ way** 以自然低调的方式

understatement /ˈʌndəsteɪtmənt/ *n* 1 [c] (remark) 保守的说法; **that's an ~!** 那是轻描淡写! 2 [u] (style) 低调手法

understood /ˌʌndəˈstʊd/ *pt, pp* ▸**understand**

understudy /ˈʌndəstʌdi/
A *n* 候补演员; **to be (the) ~ to sb.** 是某人的替角; **the Vice President acts as ~ to the President** 副总统做总统的替补
B *vt* 做…的替角 ‹*actor*›; 作为替角排练 ‹*role*›

undertake /ˌʌndəˈteɪk/ *vt* (*pt* **undertook**, *pp* **undertaken**) 1 (carry out) 承担 ‹*mission, task*›; 从事 ‹*job, research*› 2 **to ~ to do sth.** (promise) 答应做某事; (guarantee) 保证做某事

undertaker /ˈʌndəteɪkə(r)/ ▸**p. 409** *n* 殡仪员; **the ~'s** (premises) 殡仪馆; (services) 殡仪服务

undertaking /ˌʌndəˈteɪkɪŋ/ *n* 1 [c] (task) 任务; (job) 工作; (company) 公司 2 [c] (enterprise, venture) 企业; **getting married is a serious ~** 结婚是件严肃的事情 3 [c] (promise) 承诺; (guarantee) 保证; **to give sb. an ~ to do .../that ...** 向某人保证做…/对某人许诺… 4 [u] (funeral business) 殡仪业

undertax /ˌʌndəˈtæks/ *vt* 对…征税不足; **I was ~ed by £500 this year** 今年少收了我 500 英镑的税

under-the-counter
A *adj* 1 (illicit) 非法的 2 (secret) 私下的
B **under the counter** *adv* 1 (illicitly) 非法地 2 (secretly) 私下地

undertone /ˈʌndətəʊn/ *n* 1 (low voice) 低声; **to speak in an ~** 低声说话 2 (undercurrent) 意味; **comic/sinister ~s** 滑稽/险恶的意味; **the music has African/classical ~s** 这音乐有非洲/古典的味道; **sexual ~s** 性暗示 3 (hint) 淡色; **an ~ of green** 浅绿色

undertow /ˈʌndətəʊ/ *n* 1 (undercurrent) 水下逆流; (of wave) 退浪; **a swimmer caught in the ~** 被卷入水下逆流的游泳者 2 (of feeling) 潜在情绪; **an emotional ~** 感情的暗流

underuse /ˌʌndəˈjuːz/ *vt* 未充分利用

underused /ˌʌndəˈjuːzd/ *adj* 未充分利用的 ‹*equipment, resource, technique, land*›; 使用不多的 ‹*expression*›

underutilize /ˌʌndəˈjuːtɪlaɪz/ *vt* = **underuse**

underutilized /ˌʌndəˈjuːtɪlaɪzd/ *adj* = **underused**

undervalue /ˌʌndəˈvæljuː/ *vt* 1 (put low value on) 对…估价太低 ‹*person, building, antique*›; **to ~ sth. by £50** 将某物的价值低估 50 英镑 2 (not appreciate) 轻视; **to ~ sb./sth. as sth.** 将某人/某事物轻视为某事物

undervalued /ˌʌndəˈvæljuːd/ *adj* 1 (underestimated) 估价太低的; **to be ~ by £50** 被低估了 50 英镑 2 (not appreciated) 被看轻的

undervest /ˈʌndəvest/ *n* 汗衫

underwater /ˌʌndəˈwɔːtə(r)/
A *adj attrib* 水下的; **~ camera/floodlighting** 水下照相机/泛光照明; **~ synchronized swimming** 花样游泳
B *adv* 在水下; **to swim ~** 潜泳

underway /ˌʌndəˈweɪ/ *adv* 在航的; **to be ~** 在进行中; **operations were finally ~** 行动终于开始了; **to get ~** 起动; **to get sth. ~** 启动某事物

underwear /ˈʌndəweə(r)/ *n* [u] 衬衣; **thermal ~** 保暖内衣

underweight /ˌʌndəˈweɪt/ *adj* 体重不足的 ‹*person*›; 重量不足的 ‹*goods*›; **this child is four kilos ~** 这个孩子比正常体重轻了四公斤

underwent /ˌʌndəˈwent/ *pt* ▸**undergo**

underwhelm /ˌʌndəˈwelm/ *vt* hum 未给…留下深刻印象; **I was ~ed by the music** 我对那音乐感到腻味

underwired /ˌʌndəˈwaɪəd/ *adj* 钢托式的 ‹*bra*›

underworld /ˈʌndəwɜːld/ *n* 1 (criminal world) **the (criminal) ~** 黑社会 2 (place inhabited by spirits of dead) **the ~** 阴间

underwrite /ˌʌndəˈraɪt/ *vt* (*pt* **underwrote**, *pp* **underwritten**) 1 (issue and sign) 承保 ‹*insurance policy*› 2 (undertake to purchase) 包销 ‹*shares*› 3 (undertake to support) 同意承担…的费用; **to ~ a project** 为项目融资

underwriter /ˈʌndəraɪtə(r)/ *n* 1 (issuer of shares) 包销商; **to act as ~ for sth.** 担当某证券的包销商 2 (assessor of insurance policy) (employee) 保险业者; (agent) 保险代理; (enterprise) 保险商

underwriting /ˈʌndəraɪtɪŋ/ *n* [u] 1 (of share issues) 包销 2 (of policy) 承保 3 (of loan) 贷款审批

underwriting: ~ agent ▸**p. 409** *n* 承保代理人; **~ contract** *n* 证券包销合约; **~ syndicate** *n* 证券包销集团

underwritten /ˌʌndəˈrɪtn/ *pp* ▸**underwrite**

underwrote /ˌʌndəˈrəʊt/ *pt* ▸**underwrite**

undeserved /ˌʌndɪˈzɜːvd/ *adj* 不该受的 ‹*punishment, treatment*›; 不应得的 ‹*reward, reputation*›; **~ praise** 溢美之词

undeservedly /ˌʌndɪˈzɜːvɪdli/ *adv* 不公正地; **an ~ forgotten TV series** 一部不应忘记的电视连续剧; **to be ~ punished** 受冤被罚

undeserving /ˌʌndɪˈzɜːvɪŋ/ *adj* (not worthy of help) 不该得到的; (not worthy of praise or reward) 不配的; **he was an ~ winner** 他不配获胜; **to be ~ of sth.** 不该得到某物

undesirable /ˌʌndɪˈzaɪərəbl/
A *adj* 不受欢迎的 ‹*habit, person, company*›; 令人不快的 ‹*side effect, result, influence*›; **it is ~ for sb. to do ...** 某人做…是令人讨厌的; **it is ~ to do .../that ...** 做…/…是不得人心的; **an ~ alien** 不受欢迎的外国人
B *n* 不受欢迎的人

undesirably /ˌʌndɪˈzaɪərəbli/ *adv* 令人不快地; **~ hot** 热得让人难受

undetected /ˌʌndɪˈtektɪd/ *adj* 未被发现的; **to go** *or* **remain ~** 未被察觉; **to get away/break into the house ~** 不露马脚地逃走/神不知鬼不觉地潜入房子

undetermined /ˌʌndɪˈtɜːmɪnd/ *adj* 1 (unknown) 不明的; **an ~ number of passengers** 不知数量的乘客 2 (not yet settled) 待定的; **an ~ amount of compensation** 未定数额的赔偿

undeterred /ˌʌndɪˈtɜːd/ *adj* 不屈不挠的; **to be ~** 不气馁; **to be ~ by sth./sb.** 未被某物/某人吓住

undeveloped /ˌʌndɪˈveləpt/ *adj* 1 (not fully grown) 未充分发育的 ‹*muscles, organ*›; 未成熟的 ‹*fruit*› 2 (not yet exploited) 未开发的 ‹*land, reserve*›; 未发展的 ‹*idea, theory*›; **politically ~** 政治上落后的 3 Phot 未显影的; **a roll of ~ film** 一卷未冲洗的胶卷

undeviating /ʌnˈdiːvieɪtɪŋ/ *adj* 不偏离的 ‹*course, line*›; 始终如一的 ‹*policy*›; **~ loyalty to ...** 对…始终不渝的忠诚

undiagnosed /ʌnˈdaɪəgnəʊzd/ *adj* 未诊断的; **to be** *or* **go ~** 未得到诊断

undid /ʌnˈdɪd/ *pt* ▸**undo**

undies /ˈʌndɪz/ *npl* colloq [尤指妇女的] 内衣

undigested /ˌʌndaɪˈdʒestɪd/ *adj* 1 (not absorbed by body) 未消化的 2 fig (not assimilated) 未充分理解的

undignified /ʌnˈdɪgnɪfaɪd/ *adj* 无尊严的; **it is ~ to ...** 做…有失体统; **to make an ~ exit** 不体面地退场; **how ~!** 真丢人!

undiluted /ˌʌndaɪˈljuːtɪd/ *adj* 1 (concentrated) 未稀释的; **~ orange concentrate** 未掺水的浓缩橙汁 2 fig (unmixed) 纯真的 ‹*pleasure, emotion*›; 十足的 ‹*nonsense*›

undiminished /ˌʌndɪˈmɪnɪʃt/ *adj* 未减弱的 ‹*strength, vigour, joy*›; **he remains ~ by criticism** 面对批评他不为所动; **with hopes ~** 依旧满怀希望地

undimmed /ʌnˈdɪmd/ *adj* 不减退的 ‹*enthusiasm*›; 不暗淡的 ‹*light*›; 不消退的 ‹*beauty*›; 不模糊的 ‹*memory*›; **~ by age/time** 未因年纪/时间而暗淡失色的

undiplomatic /ˌʌndɪpləˈmætɪk/ *adj* 无外交手腕的 ‹*person*›; 不策略的 ‹*action, answer*›; **it was ~ of you to say that** 你那样说太不婉转

undipped /ʌnˈdɪpt/ *adj* 未把远光调为近光的; **to drive on** *or* **with ~ headlights** 开车时前灯未调为近光

undiscerning /ˌʌndɪˈsɜːnɪŋ/ *adj* 无识别力的; **~ listeners** 不具识别力的听众

undischarged /ˌʌndɪsˈtʃɑːdʒd/ *adj* 未清偿债务的

undisciplined /ʌnˈdɪsɪplɪnd/ *adj* 不遵守纪律的 ‹*person*›; 未受过训练的 ‹*animal*›; **an ~ rabble** 一群散漫的乌合之众

undisclosed /ˌʌndɪsˈkləʊzd/ *adj* 未公开的; **an ~ amount/fact** 未公开的数量/隐匿的事实

undiscovered /ˌʌndɪsˈkʌvəd/ *adj* 未被发现的 ‹*land, crime, secret*›; 未被发掘的 ‹*artist, genius*›; **to lie** *or* **remain ~** 尚不为人所知

undiscriminating /ˌʌndɪˈskrɪmɪneɪtɪŋ/ *adj* 无鉴别力的; **he was an ~ judge of character** 他不会辨别人的个性

undisguised /ˌʌndɪsˈgaɪzd/ *adj* 不掩饰的; **~ hostility/contempt** 公开的敌意/蔑视

undismayed /ˌʌndɪsˈmeɪd/ *adj* (not shocked) 不惊恐的; (not discouraged) 不气馁的; **to be ~ at** *or* **by sth.** 对某事处变不惊; **~, she continued to speak** 她镇定地继续说下去

U

undisputed /ˌʌndɪ'spjuːtɪd/ *adj* 无可争辩的 ‹*champion, fact*›

undistinguished /ˌʌndɪ'stɪŋgwɪʃt/ *adj* 不杰出的; **an ~ speaker/career** 平庸的演讲者/平凡的职业生涯; **he was of ~ appearance, he was ~ in appearance** 他相貌平平

undistributed /ˌʌndɪ'strɪbjuːtɪd/ *adj* 未分配的 ‹*profit, funds*›; 未发行的 ‹*film*›

undisturbed /ˌʌndɪ'stɜːbd/
A *adj* **1** (untouched) 未被碰过的; (not moved) 未被搬动的; (not used) 未被用过的 **2** (uninterrupted) 未受打扰的; **to work/play ~** 不受干扰地工作/玩; **~ peace** 未被打破的宁静
B *adv* 未受打扰地; **to sleep ~** 安稳地睡觉

undivided /ˌʌndɪ'vaɪdɪd/ *adj* 专一的 ‹*loyalty, opposition*›; 未分的 ‹*profit, property*›; **to give sb. one's ~ attention** 全心关注某人

undo /ʌn'duː/ *vt* (*pt* **undid,** *pp* **undone**) **1** (unfasten) 解开 ‹*knot, zip*›; 打开 ‹*lock, parcel*› **2** (cancel out) 消除; **what's done cannot be undone** 覆水难收 **3** formal (be downfall of) 毁灭 **4** Comput 取消; **the '~' button** "撤销"键

undocumented /ʌn'dɒkjʊmentɪd/ *adj* **1** (unrecorded) 无证明文件的 **2** Amer (without papers) 无执照的 ‹*worker, status*›; 无证件的 ‹*immigrant*›

undoing /ʌn'duːɪŋ/ *n* [u] liter (cause) 毁灭的原因; (downfall) 毁灭; **it was her husband's affair that was the ~ of them** 是她丈夫的风流韵事导致了他们婚姻的解体

undomesticated /ˌʌndə'mestɪkeɪtɪd/ *adj* **1** (wild) 未驯化的 ‹*animal*› **2** (unused to housework) 不善做家务的 ‹*person*›

undone /ʌn'dʌn/
A *pp* ▸**undo**
B *adj* **1** (not fastened) 解开的 ‹*buttons, knot, zip*›; 打开的 ‹*lock*›; **to come ~** 松开 **2** (not accomplished) 未完成的; **to leave sth. ~** 留下某事未做完 **3** formal or hum (ruined) 毁了的; **I am ~!** 我完蛋了!

undoubted /ʌn'daʊtɪd/ *adj* 不容置疑的 ‹*skill, ability*›; **to be an ~ success** 无疑是成功的

undoubtedly /ʌn'daʊtɪdli/ *adv* 毫无疑问地

undramatic /ˌʌndrə'mætɪk/ *adj* 缺乏戏剧性的; **an ~ ending** 平淡无奇的结局

undreamed of /ʌn'driːmd ɒv/, **undreamt-of** /ʌn'dremt ɒv/ *adjs* Brit 意想不到的; **~ success/riches** 意想不到的成功/财富; **communication in a way previously ~** 以从未想到的方式交流

undress /ʌn'dres/
A *vt* 脱去…的衣服
B *vi* 脱衣服
C *n* [u] **1** (nakedness) 裸体; (partial nakedness) 半裸; **in a state of ~** 裸体的 **2** Mil (informal clothes) 便装

undressed /ʌn'drest/ *adj* **1** (unclothed) 不穿衣服的; **to get ~** 脱去衣服 **2** (without dressing) 未加调料的 **3** (not processed) 未加工的; **~ stone/metal** 未磨光的石头/金属

undrinkable /ʌn'drɪŋkəbl/ *adj* **1** (unpleasant to taste) 不好喝的 **2** (dangerous to consume) 不可饮用的

undue /ʌn'djuː, Amer -'duː/ *adj* 过度的

undulate /'ʌndjʊleɪt, Amer -dʒʊ-/ *vi* «*wave, surface, terrain*» 起伏; «*body*» 摇摆

undulating /'ʌndjʊleɪtɪŋ, Amer -dʒʊ-/ *adj* 起伏的

undulation /ˌʌndjʊ'leɪʃn, Amer -dʒʊ-/ *n* **1** [c] (curve) 波状弯曲; (slope) 起伏的斜坡 **2** [u] (wavy motion) 波状运动; (wavy appearance) 波浪形

unduly /ʌn'djuːli, Amer -'duːli/ *adv* 过度地; **to surprise sb. ~** 使某人过分吃惊

undying /ʌn'daɪɪŋ/ *adj attrib* 永恒的; **the ~ glory of Greece** 希腊不朽的辉煌; **he pledged his ~ love** liter or hum 他发誓他的爱永恒不变

unearned /ʌn'ɜːnd/ *adj* **1** (not gained through work) 非劳动所得的; **~ income from investments** 投资收入 **2** (undeserved) 不应得的

unearth /ʌn'ɜːθ/ *vt* **1** (dig up) 发掘; **to ~ sth. from sth.** 从某处挖掘某物 **2** (find) 发现

unearthly /ʌn'ɜːθli/ *adj* **1** (supernatural) 超自然的; (mysterious) 神秘的; (frightening) 怪异的; **an ~ silence/scream** 令人毛骨悚然的寂静/尖叫 **2** (unreasonable) 荒唐的; **at an ~ hour** 过分早地

unease /ʌn'iːz/ *n* [u] **1** (worry) 忧虑; **~ at** *or* **about sb./sth.** 对某人/某事物的担心; **a sense** *or* **feeling of ~** 焦虑感 **2** (dissatisfaction) 不满; **social/economic ~** 社会/经济的不安定

uneasily /ʌn'iːzɪli/ *adv* **1** (anxiously) 不安地 **2** (precariously) 不稳定地

uneasiness /ʌn'iːzɪnɪs/ *n* [u] **= unease 1**

uneasy /ʌn'iːzi/ *adj* **1** (worried) 忧虑的; **to grow ~** 变得心神不宁; **to be ~ about** *or* **at sth.** 担心某事物 **2** (worrying) 令人不安的; **an ~ feeling** *or* **sense of danger** 扰人的危险感 **3** (precarious) 不稳定的 ‹*peace, alliance*›; **an ~ truce** 暂时的休战

uneatable /ʌn'iːtəbl/ *adj* 不能吃的

uneaten /ʌn'iːtn/ *adj* 未吃的; **~ food left on the plate** 留在盘子里没吃的食物

uneconomic /ʌnˌiːkə'nɒmɪk, -ˌekə-/ *adj* 不赢利的

uneconomical /ʌnˌiːkə'nɒmɪkl, -ˌekə-/ *adj* 不经济的; **to be ~ to do sth.** 做某事是浪费

unedifying /ʌn'edɪfaɪɪŋ/ *adj* [道德上] 令人厌恶的; **an ~ spectacle** 不光彩的一幕

unedited /ʌn'edɪtɪd/ *adj* 未修改的 ‹*speech, article*›; 未剪辑的 ‹*tape, film*›; 未编辑的 ‹*book, manuscript, version*›

uneducated /ʌn'edʒʊkeɪtɪd/ *adj* **1** (without education) 未受教育的; **the ~ masses** 文盲大众 **2** (vulgar) 缺乏教养的; **common, ~ tastes** 粗俗无知的品味

unemotional /ˌʌnɪ'məʊʃənl/ *adj* **1** (detached) 不露感情的 **2** (rational) 冷静的

unemotionally /ˌʌnɪ'məʊʃənəli/ *adv* **1** (in a detached way) 不露感情地 **2** (rationally) 冷静地

unemployable /ˌʌnɪm'plɔɪəbl/ *adj* 不能被雇用的

unemployed /ˌʌnɪm'plɔɪd/
A *adj* **1** (out of work) 未被雇用的; **~ people** 失业的人 **2** (not in use) 不用的; **~ capital** 闲置资金
B *npl* **the ~** 失业者; **the young ~** 失业的年轻人

unemployment /ˌʌnɪm'plɔɪmənt/ *n* [u] **1** (state) 失业; **to face ~** 面临失业 **2** (amount) 失业人数; (proportion) 失业率

unemployment: ~ benefit Brit, **~ compensation** Amer *ns* [u] 失业救济金; **~ figures** *npl* 失业数据; **~ level, ~ rate** *ns* 失业率

unencumbered /ˌʌnɪn'kʌmbəd/ *adj* 不受妨碍的; **~ by** *or* **with sth.** 没有某物的拖累; **it is best to work ~** 最好是无牵无挂地工作

unending /ʌn'endɪŋ/ *adj* **1** (unceasing) 无尽的 ‹*search, struggle, war, love*›; 不断的 ‹*stream, supply*› **2** (continual) 反复的; **~ complaints** 没完没了的抱怨

unendurable /ˌʌnɪn'djʊərəbl, Amer -'dʊər-/ *adj* 不能忍受的 ‹*pain, conditions, treatment, rudeness*›

unenforceable /ˌʌnɪn'fɔːsəbl/ *adj* 不能实施的

un-English /ʌn'ɪŋglɪʃ/ *adj* (not characteristic of England) 非英国的; (not characteristic of English people) 非英国人的; **with ~ directness** 以非英国式的直率

unenlightened /ˌʌnɪn'laɪtnd/ *adj* (not free from prejudice) 充满偏见的; (not free from ignorance or superstition) 愚昧无知的

unenterprising /ʌn'entəpraɪzɪŋ/ *adj* 无进取心的

unenthusiastic /ˌʌnɪnˌθjuːzɪ'æstɪk, Amer -ˌθuːz-/ *adj* 缺乏热情的; **to be ~ about sb./sth.** 对某人/某事物不热情

unenthusiastically /ˌʌnɪnˌθjuːzɪ'æstɪkli, Amer -ˌθuːz-/ *adv* 缺乏热情地

unenviable /ʌn'envɪəbl/ *adj* 不值得羡慕的

unequal /ʌn'iːkwəl/ *adj* **1** (not equal) 不相等的; (differing) 不同的 **2** (unfair) 不公平的; **the ~ distribution of wealth** 财富的分配不均 **3** (inadequate) 力所不及的; **to be ~ to sth.** 不胜任某事

unequalled Brit, **unequaled** Amer /ʌn'iːkwəld/ *adj* 无可比拟的 ‹*person, animal, object*›; 空前的 ‹*record*›; **a dancer ~ in grace** 优雅无比的舞蹈家

unequally /ʌn'iːkwəli/ *adv* 不相等地 ‹*share*›; 不公平地 ‹*allocate, distribute*›; **~ balanced forces** 悬殊的力量

unequivocal /ˌʌnɪ'kwɪvəkl/ *adj* 毫不含糊的; **to be ~ about sth.** 对某事毫不含糊; **to give sb. an ~ answer** 对某人作出明确的回答

unequivocally /ˌʌnɪ'kwɪvəkəli/ *adv* 毫不含糊地; **to show ~ that ...** 清清楚楚地显示…; **to tell sb. ~ that ...** 明确告诉某人…

unerring /ʌn'ɜːrɪŋ/ *adj* 万无一失的; **an ~ instinct** 准确无误的直觉

unerringly /ʌn'ɜːrɪŋli/ *adv* 万无一失地; **~ accurate** 准确无误的

UNESCO, Unesco /juː'neskəʊ/ *abbr* **= United Nations Educational, Scientific and Cultural Organization** 联合国教科文组织

unescorted /ˌʌnɪ'skɔːtɪd/ *adj* 无人陪同的 ‹*person, dignitary*›; 没有护卫的 ‹*ship, aircraft*›

unessential /ˌʌnə'senʃl/ *adj* 无关紧要的

unesthetic /ˌʌnəs'θetɪk/ *adj* Amer **= unaesthetic**

unethical /ʌn'eθɪkl/ *adj* 不道德的; **it is ~ of sb. to do sth.** 某人做某事是不道德的

unethically /ʌn'eθɪkli/ *adv* 不道德地

uneven /ʌn'iːvn/ *adj* **1** (not level) 不平整的 ‹*surface, ground*›; 不整齐的 ‹*teeth, hem*› **2** (irregular) 不规则的 ‹*pulse, rhythm*›; 不平稳的 ‹*voice*›; 不稳定的 ‹*quality*›; **an ~ heartbeat** 心律不齐 **3** (between unmatched players or teams) 悬殊的 ‹*competition, contest*› **4** Math 奇数的 ‹*number*›

uneven bars *npl* Amer **= asymmetric bars**

unevenly /ʌn'iːvnli/ *adv* 不均等地 ‹*distribute, space*›; 不平整地 ‹*spread*›; 参差不齐地 ‹*arrange, place*›; 不规则地 ‹*beat*›

unevenness /ʌn'iːvənnɪs/ *n* [u] **1** (of surface) 不平整 **2** (of edge, hem, teeth) 不整齐 **3** (of pulse, rhythm) 不规则 **4** (of voice) 不平稳 **5** (of contest) 悬殊

uneventful /ˌʌnɪ'ventfl/ *adj* 平平淡淡的; **an ~ life/career** 平凡的一生/职业生涯; **to have an ~ journey** 旅途平安无事

uneventfully /ˌʌnɪ'ventfəli/ *adv* 平淡地

unexcelled /ˌʌnɪk'seld/ *adj* (unbeaten) 未被击败的; (not bettered) 未被超越的; **to be ~ as sth.** (unbeaten) 作为某物是无敌的; (not bettered) 作为某物是不可超越的

unexceptionable /ˌʌnɪk'sepʃənəbl/ *adj* 无可指摘的 ‹*behaviour, conduct*›; 完美无缺的 ‹*dress*›; **bland, ~ comments** 了无新意的空泛评论

unexceptional /ˌʌnɪk'sepʃənl/ *adj* 普通的; **work of an ~ quality** 质量平平的工作

unexciting /ˌʌnɪk'saɪtɪŋ/ *adj* 枯燥的〈*day, event*〉; 单调的〈*diet, food*〉; **a one-sided, ～ match** 一边倒的无聊比赛

unexpected /ˌʌnɪk'spektɪd/
A *adj* 出乎意料的; **～ guests/question** 不速之客/意外的问题
B *n* [u] **the ～** 意外的事情; **to be prepared for the ～** 防备意外的发生; **all we can expect is the ～!** 我们所能预料到的就是意外!

unexpectedly /ˌʌnɪk'spektɪdli/ *adv* 意外地

unexpired /ˌʌnɪk'spaɪəd/ *adj* 未过期的

unexplained /ˌʌnɪk'spleɪnd/ *adj* 未解释的〈*phenomenon*〉; 莫名其妙的〈*event, occurrence*〉; **the ～ mystery of his disappearance** 他的失踪这一不解之谜

unexploded /ˌʌnɪk'spləʊdɪd/ *adj* 未爆炸的

unexploited /ˌʌnɪk'splɔɪtɪd/ *adj* 未开发的〈*resource, talent*〉; 未利用的〈*wealth*〉

unexplored /ˌʌnɪk'splɔːd/ *adj* 未经勘探的; **the ～ regions of the human soul** 人类心灵中尚未探索的领域

unexposed /ˌʌnɪk'spəʊzd/ *adj* **1** Phot 未曝光的 **2** (covered) 未暴露的; **skin ～ to sunlight** 未遭受日晒的皮肤

unexpressed /ˌʌnɪk'sprest/ *adj* 未表达的〈*feeling*〉; 未说出的〈*word*〉

unexpurgated /ʌn'ekspəgeɪtɪd/ *adj* 未经删节的; **the ～ version of the book** 书的足本

unfading /ʌn'feɪdɪŋ/ *adj* 不灭的〈*hope, memory, light*〉; 不朽的〈*glory*〉

unfailing /ʌn'feɪlɪŋ/ *adj* **1** (constant) 不懈的〈*efforts, support*〉; 永久的〈*devotion, kindness*〉; 一贯的〈*humour*〉; **an ～ supply of fresh water** 源源不断的淡水供应; **an ～ source of inspiration** 无穷无尽的灵感源泉 **2** (reliable) 可靠的; **an ～ memory** 可靠的记忆

unfair /ʌn'feə(r)/ *adj* **1** (unjust) 不公正的〈*person, treatment, verdict*〉; **to be ～ to** *or* **on sb.** 对某人不公平; **to gain/have an ～ advantage (over sb.)** (对某人) 获得/拥有不公正的优势 **2** (not following rules) 不正当的; **～ play** Sport 犯规; **～ trading/competition** 不正当交易/竞争

unfair dismissal *n* [u and c] 不公平解雇

unfairly /ʌn'feəli/ *adv* **1** (unjustly) 不公正地; **rates are ～ high** 费用高得离谱; **to be ～ dismissed** 遭到不公正解雇 **2** (breaking the rules) 不正当地; **to play ～** 犯规

unfairness /ʌn'feənɪs/ *n* [u] 不公正

unfaithful /ʌn'feɪθfl/ *adj* **1** (not loyal) 不忠诚的〈*person*〉; 不如实的〈*representation*〉; **an ～ servant/subject** 不忠的仆人/臣民; **to be ～ to sb./sth.** 不忠实于某人/某事物 **2** (sexually) 不忠的; **her husband had been ～ (to her)** 她丈夫 (对她) 有过不忠行为

unfaithfulness /ʌn'feɪθflnɪs/ *n* [u] (of servant) 不忠诚; (of spouse) 不忠; **～ to sb./sth.** 对某人/某事物的不忠实

unfaltering /ʌn'fɔːltərɪŋ/ *adj* 不摇晃的〈*step*〉; 不动摇的〈*loyalty*〉; **in a clear, ～ voice** 以清楚坚定的嗓音

unfalteringly /ʌn'fɔːltərɪŋli/ *adv* 不摇晃地〈*walk*〉; 坚定地〈*advance, reply*〉

unfamiliar /ˌʌnfə'mɪlɪə(r)/ *adj* **1** (strange) 陌生的; (unusual) 不常见的 **2** *pred* (without working knowledge) 无经验的; **to be ～ with sth.** 不了解某物

unfamiliarity /ˌʌnfəmɪlɪ'ærəti/ *n* [u] **1** (strangeness) 陌生; **～ of sth.** 对某事物的陌生 **2** (lack of knowledge) 无经验; **～ with sth.** 对某事物的不了解

unfashionable /ʌn'fæʃənəbl/ *adj* 不流行的; **an ～ idea** *or* **concept** *or* **notion** 过时的观念; **it's ～ to do sth.** 做某事是不时兴的

unfasten /ʌn'fɑːsn/ *vt* 解开〈*button, clothes*〉; 松开〈*chain, rope*〉; **to ～ sth. from sth.** 从某物上解下某物; **to come ～ed** 松脱

unfathomable /ʌn'fæðəməbl/ *adj* **1** lit (immeasurable) 深不可测的〈*water, depth*〉; 无限的〈*power*〉; 浩瀚的〈*universe*〉 **2** fig (incomprehensible) 不可理解的; (baffling) 难以捉摸的; **for some ～ reason** 莫名其妙地

unfathomed /ʌn'fæðəmd/ *adj* **1** (unexplored) 未测过深度的〈*water*〉; 未测量的〈*depth*〉 **2** fig (mysterious) 捉摸不透的〈*reason, mystery*〉

unfavourable /ʌn'feɪvərəbl/ *adj* **1** (negative) 负面的〈*impression, report, opinion, remark, publicity*〉; **an ～ comparison** 使相形见绌的比较 **2** (adverse) 不适宜的〈*conditions, weather*〉; 不利的〈*effect, outlook, terms*〉; **～ winds** 逆风; **an ～ rate of exchange** 不利的汇率

unfavourably /ʌn'feɪvərəbli/ *adv* **1** (negatively) 负面地〈*comment, review, report*〉; 反对地〈*speak*〉; **to be ～ impressed with ...** 对…印象不佳; **to compare ～ with ...** 比…逊色 **2** (adversely) 不利地〈*end, develop*〉

unfazed /ʌn'feɪzd/ *adj* colloq 处变不惊的; **to be ～ by sth.** 不因某事物慌张

unfeasible /ʌn'fiːzəbl/ *adj* 不可行的; **it is ～ to do sth.** 做某事行不通; **to make sth. ～ for sb.** 使某人做不成某事; **economically/politically ～** 经济上/政治上行不通的

unfeeling /ʌn'fiːlɪŋ/ *adj* 无情的〈*person, remark, attitude*〉; **to be ～ towards sb.** 对某人冷酷无情

unfeelingly /ʌn'fiːlɪŋli/ *adv* 无情地

unfeigned /ʌn'feɪnd/ *adj* 非假装的; **～ joy** 由衷的高兴

unfeminine /ʌn'femɪnɪn/ *adj* 不像女性的; **～ clothes** 没有女人味的衣服; **to be ～ of sb. (to do sth.)** 某人 (做某事) 不符合女性形象

unfettered /ʌn'fetəd/ *adj* formal 不受控制的〈*power, passion*〉; 不受约束的〈*right, expression*〉; 自由的〈*access*〉; **moments of ～ joy** 尽情欢乐的时刻

unfilled /ʌn'fɪld/ *adj* **1** (not made full) 空的 **2** (vacant) 空缺的; **～ school places** 学校的空额

unfinished /ʌn'fɪnɪʃt/ *adj* 未完成的〈*work*〉; 未写完的〈*essay, letter*〉; 未处理完的〈*matter*〉

unfit /ʌn'fɪt/ *adj* **1** (unsuitable) 不合适的; **～ for human habitation** 不适宜人类居住的; **this water is ～ to drink** 这水不宜饮用 **2** (inadequate) 不够好的; (incapable) 无能力的; **an ～ mother** 不称职的母亲; **he is ～ to hold** *or* **for such a senior position** 他不胜任这种高级职务; **he's still ～ for work/to drive** 他还不宜工作/开车 **3** esp Brit (out of condition) 不健康的; **I'm ～** 我身体欠佳 **4** *pred* Jur 不适宜的; **to be ～ to plead/give evidence** 不适宜辩护/作证

unfitness /ʌn'fɪtnɪs/ *n* [u] 不胜任

unfitted /ʌn'fɪtɪd/ *adj pred* formal 不适合的; **to be ～ for sth./to do sth.** 不适合某物/做某事

unfitting /ʌn'fɪtɪŋ/ *adj* formal 不恰当的; **it's ～ that ...** …是不合适的

unfix /ʌn'fɪks/ *vt* 卸下〈*attachment, object, bayonet*〉

unflagging /ʌn'flægɪŋ/ *adj* 不懈的〈*energy, interest, devotion*〉; 不知疲倦的〈*person*〉

unflaggingly /ʌn'flægɪŋli/ *adv* 坚持不懈地〈*pursue, continue, work*〉; 坚定地〈*optimistic, loyal*〉

unflappability /ˌʌnflæpə'bɪlɪti/ *n* [u] 处变不惊

unflappable /ʌn'flæpəbl/ *adj* 处变不惊的

unflattering /ʌn'flætərɪŋ/ *adj* 有损形象的; **to be ～ to sb.** 使某人显得难看; **she was rather ～ about him** 她对他相当不客气

unflatteringly /ʌn'flætərɪŋli/ *adv* 有损形象地; **to portray sb. rather ～** 把某人的肖像画得相当难看

unfledged /ʌn'fledʒd/ *adj* **1** Zool 羽毛未丰的 **2** fig (inexperienced) 年轻而无经验的〈*person*〉; 不成熟的〈*movement*〉

unflinching /ʌn'flɪntʃɪŋ/ *adj* **1** (steadfast) 坚定的 **2** (not showing fear, not shrinking) 不畏缩的; **～ courage** 临危不惧的勇气

unflinchingly /ʌn'flɪntʃɪŋli/ *adv* 不畏缩地; **～ determined** *or* **resolute** 坚定不移的; **～ honest** 直言不讳的

unflyable /ʌn'flaɪəbl/ *adj* 不能飞的

unfold /ʌn'fəʊld/
A *vt* **1** lit (open) 展开; **to ～ the tablecloth** 摊开桌布; **to ～ one's arms** 张开双臂 **2** fig (reveal) 披露; **she listened intently as they ～ed their plans** 她专注地听着他们披露计划
B *vi* **1** (open) «*map, deckchair*» 展开; «*flower*» 开放 **2** fig (be revealed) «*landscape, scene*» 呈现; «*events, inquiry*» 被披露; «*beauty, plot, story*» 展现

unforced /ʌn'fɔːst/ *adj* 自然的〈*style of writing*〉; 非受迫的〈*departure, change*〉

unforced error *n* [尤指网球中的] 非受迫性失误

unforeseeable /ˌʌnfɔː'siːəbl/ *adj* 无法预料的

unforeseen /ˌʌnfɔː'siːn/ *adj* 未预料到的; **the circumstances were totally ～** 情况完全出乎意料

unforested /ʌn'fɒrɪstɪd/ *adj* 无林木覆盖的

unforgettable /ˌʌnfə'getəbl/ *adj* 难忘的〈*experience, scene*〉

unforgettably /ˌʌnfə'getəbli/ *adv* 令人难忘地

unforgivable /ˌʌnfə'gɪvəbl/ *adj* 不可原谅的; **it is ～ of sb. to do sth.** 某人做某事是不可饶恕的; **I find his rudeness ～** 我认为他的粗鲁不可宽恕

unforgivably /ˌʌnfə'gɪvəbli/ *adv* 不可原谅地; **to be ～ rude/biased** 不可饶恕地粗鲁/心存偏见

unforgiven /ˌʌnfə'gɪvn/ *adj* 不被原谅的; **a crime that remains ～ even now** 至今未获宽恕的罪行

unforgiving /ˌʌnfə'gɪvɪŋ/ *adj* **1** (unwilling to forgive) 不原谅人的〈*person, attitude, look*〉 **2** (harsh, hostile) 严酷的〈*terrain, sun*〉

unforgotten /ˌʌnfə'gɒtn/ *adj* 不被遗忘的

unformatted /ʌn'fɔːmætɪd/ *adj* 未按格式编排的〈*text, data*〉; 未格式化的〈*disc, drive*〉

unformed /ʌn'fɔːmd/ *adj* 未定型的〈*character*〉; 不成熟的〈*idea*〉

unforthcoming /ˌʌnfɔːθ'kʌmɪŋ/ *adj* **1** (uncommunicative) 不爱说话的 **2** (unwilling to help) 不乐于助人的; (unwilling to provide information) 不露口风的; **to be ～ about sth.** 不愿谈及某事 **3** (unavailable) 得不到的; **answers, as yet, were ～** 答案尚不得而知

unfortified /ʌn'fɔːtɪfaɪd/ *adj* **1** Mil 未筑防御工事的 **2** Wine 未添加酒精的

unfortunate /ʌn'fɔːtʃənət/
A *adj* **1** (unlucky) 不幸的〈*person, start*〉; 不利的〈*situation*〉; **to be ～ enough to do sth.** 倒霉到做某事; **it was ～ for you that she arrived at that moment** 对你来说, 她来得太不是时候了 **2** *attrib* (pitiable) 可悲的〈*victim, situation*〉 **3** (regrettable) 令人遗憾的〈*incident, remark, coincidence, choice*〉; **it was ～ that ...** …是可惜的
B *n* 不幸的人

unfortunately /ʌn'fɔːtʃənətli/ *adv* 不幸地; **～ I can't come** 可惜我不能来; **an ～ worded letter** 措词不当的信

unfounded /ʌn'faʊndɪd/ *adj* 无根据的; **to prove to be ～** 被证明是空穴来风

unframed /ʌn'freɪmd/ *adj* 无框架的; **an ～ picture** 无框画

U

unfreeze /ʌn'fri:z/ (*pt* **unfroze,** *pp* **unfrozen**)
A *vt* **1** (cause to thaw) 使解冻; **to ~ relations** fig 使关系解冻 **2** Fin (make realizable) 解除对…的冻结; **the company's assets have been unfrozen** 公司的资产被解冻了
B *vi* 解冻

unfreezing /ʌn'fri:zɪŋ/ *n* [u] (of prices) 放开; (of assets, loan) 解冻

unfrequented /ˌʌnfrɪ'kwentɪd/ *adj* 不常有人去的; **remote and ~** 偏僻且人迹罕至的

unfriendliness /ʌn'frendlɪnɪs/ *n* [u] (of person, attitude, reception, act) 不友好; (of place) 不利

unfriendly /ʌn'frendli/ *adj* 不友好的 ‹*person, attitude, reception, act*›; 不利的 ‹*place*›; **to be ~ towards sb.** 对某人不友好; **it was ~ of him to do that** 他做那件事很不友善

unfrock /ʌn'frɒk/ *vt* = **defrock**

unfroze /ʌn'frəʊz/ *pt* ▸ **unfreeze**

unfrozen /ʌn'frəʊzn/ *pp* ▸ **unfreeze**

unfruitful /ʌn'fru:tfl/ *adj* **1** (unproductive) 没有结果的 **2** liter (infertile) 不结果实的 ‹*tree*›; 不毛的 ‹*land*›; 不生育的 ‹*woman*›

unfulfilled /ˌʌnfʊl'fɪld/ *adj* **1** (unrealized) 未实现的 ‹*ambition, condition, promise, prophecy*›; **the country's ~ potential for tourism** 该国未开发的旅游潜力 **2** (dissatisfied) 雄心未了的; **to feel ~** 感到壮志未酬

unfulfilling /ˌʌnfʊl'fɪlɪŋ/ *adj* 不称心的

unfunny /ʌn'fʌni/ *adj* 无趣的

unfurl /ʌn'fɜ:l/
A *vt* 展开; **to ~ an umbrella** 打开伞
B *vi* 展开

unfurnished /ʌn'fɜ:nɪʃt/ *adj* 无家具的; **an ~ apartment** *or* **flat** 不带家具的公寓

unfussy /ʌn'fʌsi/ *adj* 不花哨的

ungainly /ʌn'geɪnli/ *adj* 笨拙的 ‹*movement, walk*›; 不优雅的 ‹*person, manner*›

ungallant /ʌn'gælənt/ *adj* 不殷勤的; **it was ~ of him to do it** 他这样做不太殷勤

ungenerous /ʌn'dʒenərəs/ *adj* **1** (mean) 吝啬的; **the allowance was not ~** 这笔补贴并不少 **2** (unsympathetic) 不宽厚的; **it is ~ of sb. to do sth.** 某人做某事不厚道; **to be ~ towards sb.** 对某人不宽宏大量

ungenerously /ʌn'dʒenərəsli/ *adv* **1** (meanly) 吝啬地 **2** (unkindly) 不宽厚地

ungentlemanly /ʌn'dʒentlmənli/ *adj* 无绅士风度的; **that was a bit ~ of him** 他那样有点没教养

unglazed /ʌn'gleɪzd/ *adj* **1** (lacking glass panes) 没有装玻璃的 **2** (lacking shiny surface) 未上釉的

unglue /ʌn'glu:/ *vt* **1** (unstick) 拆开 ‹*envelope*›; 揭下 ‹*stamp*›; **to ~ one's eyes from the television** fig 把眼睛从电视上挪开 **2** Amer colloq (upset, confuse) 使烦乱

unglued /ʌn'glu:d/ *adj* **1** (unstuck) 分离的; **to come ~** 被拆开 **2** Amer colloq (upset, confused) 烦乱的; **to come ~** 心烦意乱

ungodly /ʌn'gɒdli/ *adj* **1** (irreligious) 不敬神的 **2** colloq (unreasonable) 荒唐的 ‹*speed, amount*›; **at some ~ hour** 在不适当的时候

ungovernable /ʌn'gʌvənəbl/ *adj* **1** (impossible to govern) 难以管治的 ‹*country, people*› **2** liter (uncontrollable) 无法控制的 ‹*rage, desire*›; **to have an ~ temper** 脾气火爆

ungracious /ʌn'greɪʃəs/ *adj* 不礼貌的; **it would be ~ of you to refuse** 你拒绝的话是不礼貌的

ungraciously /ʌn'greɪʃəsli/ *adv* 不礼貌地

ungrammatical /ˌʌngrə'mætɪkl/ *adj* 不合语法的

ungrammatically /ˌʌngrə'mætɪkli/ *adv* 不合语法地

ungrateful /ʌn'greɪtfl/ *adj* 不感激的; **to be ~ to** *or* **towards sb.** 对某人不领情; **it was ~ of you not to say thank you** 你连声谢谢都没说，真是忘恩负义

ungratefully /ʌn'greɪtfəli/ *adv* 不感激地; **to behave ~ towards sb.** 对某人不领情

ungrudging /ʌn'grʌdʒɪŋ/ *adj* 慷慨的 ‹*support, tribute, person*›; 豪爽的 ‹*praise*›

ungrudgingly /ʌn'grʌdʒɪŋli/ *adv* 慷慨地 ‹*respond, give*›; 豪爽地 ‹*praise*›

unguarded /ʌn'gɑ:dɪd/ *adj* **1** (not watched over) 无人看守的 ‹*prisoner, luggage*›; 无保护的 ‹*frontier, depot*› **2** (careless) 不谨慎的 ‹*comment, criticism*›; **in an ~ moment** 一不留神

unguent /'ʌŋgwənt/ *n* formal (as ointment) 药膏; (for lubrication) 油膏

ungulate /'ʌŋgjʊlət/
A *n* 有蹄类动物
B *adj* 有蹄的

unhampered /ʌn'hæmpəd/ *adj* 不受阻碍的; **to be ~ by sth.** 不受某物拖累

unhappily /ʌn'hæpɪli/ *adv* **1** (miserably) 不高兴地; **~ married** 婚姻不幸福的 **2** (regrettably) 遗憾地; (unfortunately) 不幸地; **~, things soon began to go wrong** 不幸的是，事情很快便开始出岔子了

unhappiness /ʌn'hæpɪnɪs/ *n* [u] **1** (misery) 痛苦 **2** (concern, dissatisfaction) 不高兴

unhappy /ʌn'hæpɪ/ *adj* **1** (miserable) 痛苦的; **he looks extremely ~** 他看上去非常难过 **2** (concerned, dissatisfied) 不高兴的; **to be ~ about** *or* **with sth./about doing sth.** 对某事物/做某事不满; **to be ~ at the idea/suggestion that …** 对…的想法/建议感到不高兴 **3** (regrettable) 遗憾的; (unfortunate) 不幸的; **to make an ~ choice** 做出不当的选择; **by an ~ coincidence** 由于不幸的巧合

unharmed /ʌn'hɑ:md/ *adj* 未受伤的 ‹*person*›; 未受损害的 ‹*building, object*›; **to escape** *or* **come out ~** 安然无恙地逃脱

unharness /ʌn'hɑ:nɪs/ *vt* 卸下…的挽具; **she ~ed the horse from the cart** 她把马从马车上解下来

unhealthy /ʌn'helθi/ *adj* **1** (sickly) 不健康的 ‹*person, complexion*›; **the ~ state of the economy** 经济的不良状况; **the engine sounds rather ~** 发动机听上去不太对头 **2** (harmful) 有害健康的 ‹*climate, diet, lifestyle*› **3** (unwholesome) 病态的 ‹*curiosity, interest*›

unheard /ʌn'hɜ:d/ *adj* 未听到的 ‹*voice, music*›; 没人理会的 ‹*case, plea, desire*›; **to enter/leave ~** 悄无声息地进去/离开; **to be condemned ~** 未经审讯即被判刑

unheard of *adj* **1** (previously unknown) 前所未闻的; **to be previously ~** 史无前例; **interest rates are at unheard-of levels** 利率处在前所未有的水平 **2** (shocking) 骇人听闻的

unheated /ʌn'hi:tɪd/ *adj* 无供暖的; **the whole building is ~** 整栋楼都没有供暖

unhedged /ʌn'hedʒd/ *adj* **1** (without a hedge) 未用树篱隔开的 ‹*field, plot*› **2** Fin 未对冲的 ‹*fund, borrowing*›

unheeded /ʌn'hi:dɪd/ *adj* 被忽视的; **our advice/warning went ~** 我们的建议/警告未引起重视

unheeding /ʌn'hi:dɪŋ/ *adj* liter 不注意的; **to be ~ of sth.** 不理会某事

unhelpful /ʌn'helpfl/ *adj* 不肯帮助的 ‹*person*›; 无用的 ‹*advice, intervention*›; **it is ~ of sb. to do sth.** 某人做某事无济于事

unhelpfully /ʌn'helpfəli/ *adv* 不愿帮助地 ‹*refuse*›; 无用地 ‹*suggest*›

unheralded /ʌn'herəldɪd/ *adj* 未事先宣布的; **the arrival of the minister was quite ~** 部长的到来大大出人意料

unhesitating /ʌn'hezɪteɪtɪŋ/ *adj* 不犹豫的; **with ~ generosity** 以毫不犹豫的慷慨

unhesitatingly /ʌn'hezɪteɪtɪŋli/ *adv* 毫不犹豫地

unhide /ʌn'haɪd/ *vt* (*pt* **unhid,** *pp* **unhidden**) 还原 ‹*window, column, taskbar*›

unhindered /ʌn'hɪndəd/
A *adj* 不受阻碍的; **to be ~ by sth.** 不受某事物束缚
B *adv* 不受阻碍地; **to pass ~** 畅通无阻地通过; **to come and go ~** 来去自由

unhinge /ʌn'hɪndʒ/ *vt* (*pres p* **~ing**) **1** (remove from hinges) 把…从铰链上拆下; **to ~ a cupboard door** 把碗橱门从铰链上拆下 **2** fig colloq (unbalance) 使精神失常; **grief totally ~d her** 悲痛使她彻底疯了

unhinged /ʌn'hɪndʒd/ *adj* colloq 精神失常的; **he's completely ~** 他彻底疯了

unhitch /ʌn'hɪtʃ/ *vt* 解下…的套具 ‹*horse*›; 解开 ‹*rope*›

unholy /ʌn'həʊli/ *adj* **1** (profane) 亵渎的; (wicked) 邪恶的; (sinful) 有罪的 **2** (shocking) 危险的 ‹*alliance*›; **an ~ union of prejudice and superstition** 偏见与迷信的危险结合 **3** colloq (dreadful) 可怕的 ‹*muddle, row, din*›; **to be in an ~ mess** 弄得一团糟

unhook /ʌn'hʊk/ *vt* **1** (unfasten) 解开…的钩子 ‹*bra, skirt*›; 解开 ‹*fastener*›; **to come ~ed** 松脱 **2** (remove) 从钩子上取下; **to ~ the picture from the wall** 从墙上取下画

unhoped for /ʌn'həʊpt fɔ:(r)/ *adj* 没有预料到的; **to be ~** 出乎意料

unhopeful /ʌn'həʊpfl/ *adj* (not hopeful) 没有希望的; (not encouraging) 希望渺茫的

unhorse /ʌn'hɔ:s/ *vt* (throw off horse) 把…抛下马; (drag off horse) 把…拖下马

unhurried /ʌn'hʌrɪd/ *adj* 不慌不忙的; **to enjoy an ~ meal** 悠闲地吃一顿饭

unhurriedly /ʌn'hʌrɪdli/ *adv* 不慌不忙地; **calmly and ~** 平静从容地

unhurt /ʌn'hɜ:t/ *adj* 没有受伤的; **to escape ~** 安然无恙地逃脱

unhygienic /ˌʌnhaɪ'dʒi:nɪk/ *adj* 不卫生的

unhyphenated /ʌn'haɪfəneɪtɪd/ *adj* 没有连字符的

uni /'ju:ni/ *n* colloq = **university**

unicameral /ˌju:nɪ'kæmərəl/ *adj* 单院的 ‹*system*›; 一院制的 ‹*structure*›

UNICEF /'ju:nɪsef/ *abbr* = **United Nations Children's Fund** 联合国儿童基金会

unicellular /ˌju:nɪ'seljʊlə(r)/ *adj* 单细胞的

unicorn /'ju:nɪkɔ:n/ *n* **1** Mythol 独角兽 **2** Herald 独角兽标记

unicycle /'ju:nɪsaɪkl/ *n* 独轮车

unidentified /ˌʌnaɪ'dentɪfaɪd/ *adj* **1** (not known) 未知的 ‹*thing, species*›; **an ~ flying object** 不明飞行物 **2** (not recognized) 未认出的 ‹*person, vehicle*› **3** (not named) 无名字的; **quoting from an ~ source, the paper said …** 报纸援引一名未透露姓名的消息人士的话说…

unidirectional /ˌju:nɪdɪ'rekʃənl, ˌju:nɪdaɪ-/ *adj* 单向的

unification /ˌju:nɪfɪ'keɪʃn/ *n* [u and c] 统一; **the ~ of Italy** 意大利的统一; **a process of economic ~** 经济一体化的过程; **the U~ Church** 统一教团 [1954年由文鲜明创立于韩国的宗教组织]

UNIFIL /'ju:nɪfɪl/ *abbr* = **United Nations Interim Force in Lebanon** 联合国驻黎巴嫩临时部队

uniform /'ju:nɪfɔ:m/
A *n* [c and u] 制服; **military/police/school ~** 军装/警服/校服; **out of ~** (gen) 不穿制服的; Mil 穿着便服的; **in full ~** Mil 穿着全套军礼服的
B *adj* (even) 均匀的; (similar) 相同的; (constant) 不变的; **boxes of ~ shape** 形状一致的盒子

uniformed /'ju:nɪfɔ:md/ *adj* 穿制服的 ‹*police*›

uniformity /ˌju:nɪ'fɔ:məti/ *n* [u] (state of being regular) 一致; (state of being homogeneous) 相同; (state of being unvarying) 不变; **rich old cultures reduced to a mediocre ~** 丰富多彩的古

老文化退化成平庸的千篇一律; **the need for ~ in standards** 对统一标准的需要

uniformly /ˈjuːnɪfɔːmli/ *adv* (evenly) 均匀地; (similarly) 相同地; (without varying) 不变地; **the teams have turned in ~ good performances** 各球队一如常态, 表现出色

unify /ˈjuːnɪfaɪ/

A *vt* 统一; **to ~ the country** 统一国家; **a unified system of administration** 统一的管理体制

B *vi* 统一

unifying /ˈjuːnɪfaɪɪŋ/ *adj* 统一的; **a ~ force/theme** 凝聚力/统一的主题

unilateral /ˌjuːnɪˈlætrəl/ *adj* 单边的; **a ~ declaration of independence** 单方面宣布独立; **~ nuclear disarmament** 单方面核裁军

unilateralism /ˌjuːnɪˈlætrəlɪzəm/ *n* [u] **1** (acting or reaching decision unilaterally) 单边主义; **American ~** 美国的单边主义 **2** (unilateral disarmament) 单方面裁军

unilateralist /ˌjuːnɪˈlætrəlɪst/

A *adj* **1** (relating to unilateralism) 单边主义的; **a ~ policy** 单边政策 **2** (relating to unilateral disarmament) 单方面裁军的

B *n* **1** (supporter of unilateralism) 单边主义者 **2** (supporter of unilateral disarmament) 单方面裁军主义者

unilaterally /ˌjuːnɪˈlætrəli/ *adv* 单边地; **to decide ~ to do sth.** 单方面决定做某事

unilingual /ˌjuːnɪˈlɪŋgwəl/ *adj* 单语的; **a ~ country** 单语国家

unimaginable /ˌʌnɪˈmædʒɪnəbl/ *adj* (difficult to imagine) 不能想象的; (difficult to understand) 难以理解的

unimaginably /ˌʌnɪˈmædʒɪnəbli/ *adv* 无法想象地

unimaginative /ˌʌnɪˈmædʒɪnətɪv/ *adj* 缺乏想象力的; **an ~ programme** 无创意的节目

unimaginatively /ˌʌnɪˈmædʒɪnətɪvli/ *adv* 缺乏想象力地 ‹*write*›; 乏味地 ‹*talk*›

unimaginativeness /ˌʌnɪˈmædʒɪnətɪvnɪs/ *n* [u] 缺乏想象力

unimpaired /ˌʌnɪmˈpeəd/ *adj* 未受损的 ‹*health, sight, faculty*›; 未削弱的 ‹*powers*›

unimpeachable /ˌʌnɪmˈpiːtʃəbl/ *adj* 无可指摘的 ‹*honesty, conduct*›; 完美无缺的 ‹*character*›; 无可怀疑的 ‹*source, evidence*›

unimpeded /ˌʌnɪmˈpiːdɪd/ *adj* 无阻挡的; **to be ~ by sth.** 不受某事物的阻碍; **an ~ view across the headland** 一览无余的岬角景色; **the ~ flow of information** 畅通无阻的信息流

unimportant /ˌʌnɪmˈpɔːtnt/ *adj* (not important) 不重要的; (not significant) 无足轻重的; **to be ~ to sb.** 对某人来说微不足道

unimposing /ˌʌnɪmˈpəʊzɪŋ/ *adj* 不壮观的 ‹*building, appearance*›; **an ~ presence/spectacle** 不威严的气质/场面

unimpressed /ˌʌnɪmˈprest/ *adj pred* 无深刻印象的; **to be ~ by sth.** 对某事物印象平平; **she was ~ by his pleas for help** 她不为他的求助所动

unimpressive /ˌʌnɪmˈpresɪv/ *adj* 普通的; **his exam results were rather ~** 他的考试成绩很一般; **an ~ patch of land** 一块不起眼的地

unimproved /ˌʌnɪmˈpruːvd/ *adj* 未改善的 ‹*condition, work, health, patient*›; 未提高的 ‹*position, team*›; **~ land** 未耕作的土地; **to be** *or* **remain ~** «*situation, health*» 没有得到改善

unincorporated /ˌʌnɪnˈkɔːpəreɪtɪd/ *adj* **1** (not united) 未合并的 **2** Jur 未组成法人组织的 ‹*business*›; **his company remains ~** 他的公司仍不具法人资格

uninfluential /ˌʌnɪnfluˈenʃl/ *adj* 没有影响的

uninformative /ˌʌnɪnˈfɔːmətɪv/ *adj* 信息不足的; **to be ~** 信息量很小

uninformed /ˌʌnɪnˈfɔːmd/ *adj* 无知的 ‹*reader*›; 不了解情况的 ‹*public*›; **~ opinion** 没有见识的观点; **to be ~ about sth.** 对某事物一无所知

uninhabitable /ˌʌnɪnˈhæbɪtəbl/ *adj* (unsuitable for habitation) 不宜居住的; (unfit for habitation) 不能居住的

uninhabited /ˌʌnɪnˈhæbɪtɪd/ *adj* 无人居住的; **to be completely ~** 杳无人迹

uninhibited /ˌʌnɪnˈhɪbɪtɪd/ *adj* 无拘无束的 ‹*person, behaviour, attitude*›; 纵情的 ‹*laughter, dance*›; **to be ~ in sth./about doing sth.** 在某方面无拘无束/做某事没有拘束; **she is so ~ in her attitude to sex** 她对于性的态度非常开放

uninhibitedly /ˌʌnɪnˈhɪbɪtɪdli/ *adv* 无拘无束地 ‹*dance, enthusiastic, talk*›; **to express oneself ~** 畅所欲言

uninitiated /ˌʌnɪˈnɪʃɪeɪtɪd/

A *adj* 无专门知识的; **to ~ modern eyes** 对于不谙此道的现代人

B *npl* **the ~** 门外汉

uninjured /ʌnˈɪndʒəd/ *adj* 未受伤的; **to escape ~** 安然无恙地逃脱

uninspired /ˌʌnɪnˈspaɪəd/ *adj* **1** (dull) 无创意的 ‹*person, actor*›; 乏味的 ‹*preacher, artistic, production*› **2** (unimpressed) 无想象力的; (unexcited) 无激情的; **to be ~** «*writer*» 没有灵感; «*team*» 不振奋

uninspiring /ˌʌnɪnˈspaɪərɪŋ/ *adj* (not arousing interest) 引不起兴趣的; (not causing excitement) 令人提不起精神的

uninstall, uninstal /ˌʌnɪnˈstɔːl/ *vt* 卸载

uninsured /ˌʌnɪnˈʃɔːd, Amer ˌʌnɪnˈʃʊərd/ *adj* 未上过保险的; **to be ~** 未投保

unintelligent /ˌʌnɪnˈtelɪdʒənt/ *adj* 不聪明的; **an ~ reading of this remarkable poem** 对这首杰出诗歌的平庸解读

unintelligently /ˌʌnɪnˈtelɪdʒəntli/ *adv* 不聪明地; **to handle the business ~** 愚蠢地处理事情

unintelligible /ˌʌnɪnˈtelɪdʒəbl/ *adj* 不可理解的; **to be ~ to sb.** «*lecture, whisper*» 令某人听不明白

unintelligibly /ˌʌnɪnˈtelɪdʒəbli/ *adv* 不可理解地; **to write/mutter ~** 写得让人看不懂/含糊不清地咕哝

unintended /ˌʌnɪnˈtendɪd/ *adj* 非计划中的; **to be ~** 并非故意; **the ~ consequences of the decision** 这个决定的意外结果

unintentional /ˌʌnɪnˈtenʃənl/ *adj* 非故意的; **an ~ compliment** 非刻意的称赞; **an ~ injury** 无心的伤害

unintentionally /ˌʌnɪnˈtenʃənəli/ *adv* 非故意地; **to be ~ offensive to sb.** 无心地冒犯某人

uninterested /ʌnˈɪntrəstɪd/ *adj* (having no interest) 不感兴趣的; (having no concern) 不关心的

uninteresting /ʌnˈɪntrəstɪŋ/ *adj* 无趣的

uninterrupted /ˌʌnɪntəˈrʌptɪd/ *adj* 不中断的; **~ silence/noise** 持续的沉默/噪音

uninterruptedly /ˌʌnɪntəˈrʌptɪdli/ *adv* 不中断地

uninvited /ˌʌnɪnˈvaɪtɪd/ *adj* **1** (without invitation) 未受邀请的; **an ~ guest** 不速之客; **she turned up completely ~** 她完全是不请自到 **2** (unsolicited) 未经请求的; **his attentions were entirely ~** 他的殷勤完全是自作多情

uninviting /ˌʌnɪnˈvaɪtɪŋ/ *adj* 不吸引人的; **the food looked distinctly ~** 食物看上去一点都不诱人; **the ~ prospect of a war** 令人沮丧的战争前景

union /ˈjuːnɪən/ *n* **1** [u and c] (uniting) 结合; (marriage) 结婚; **political/economic ~** 政治/经济联盟 **2** [c] Ind **(trade) ~** 工会; **to join a ~** 加入工会; **a teachers' ~** 教师工会 **3** **Union** [c] Pol 联邦; Amer [美国内战期间] 支持联邦的北方各州 **4** [c] Brit **(student) ~** (organization) 学生会大楼; (building) 学生会; **the National U~ of Students** 全国学生联合会

union: ~ bashing *n* [u] colloq 对工会的打击; **~ catalogue** *n* [合作图书馆的] 联合图书目录; **~ dues** *npl* 工会会费; **U~ flag** *n* = **Union Jack**

unionism /ˈjuːnɪənɪzəm/ *n* [u] **1** Ind 工会主义 **2** **Unionism** Pol 统一主义

unionist /ˈjuːnɪənɪst/ *n* **1** Ind (member) 工会会员; (supporter) 工会支持者 **2** **Unionist** Pol (person favouring political union) 联合主义者; (in Northern Ireland) 统一派

unionization /ˌjuːnɪənaɪˈzeɪʃn, Amer -nɪˈz-/ *n* [u] 组织工会

unionize /ˈjuːnɪənaɪz/

A *vt* 组织…成立工会 ‹*workers*›; 在…成立工会 ‹*factory*›

B *vi* «*worker*» 加入工会; «*factory*» 成立工会

union: U~ Jack *n* 英国国旗; **~ member** *n* 工会会员; **~ membership** *n* **1** [c] (members) 全体工会会员; **2** [u] (state of being a member) 工会会员身份; **3** [u and c] (number of members) 工会会员总数; **U~ of Soviet Socialist Republics** *pr n* Hist 苏维埃社会主义共和国联盟

the Union Jack

英国国旗, 亦作 Union Flag。Jack 本指船首标志国籍的旗子。英国国旗由 3 个十字旗图案合并而成, 亦称米字旗。1603 年, 苏格兰和英格兰统一, 英格兰的圣乔治红十字旗 (St George's Cross) 和苏格兰的圣安德鲁蓝底白斜十字旗 (St Andrew's Cross) 合并成最早的米字旗。1801 年, 爱尔兰并入大不列颠后, 又加入爱尔兰的圣帕特里克红斜十字旗 (St Patrick's Cross) 图案, 构成今天的米字旗。威尔士被视为英格兰的公国 (principality), 因此在英国国旗上没有体现。20 世纪 50 年代, 卡德瓦拉德红龙 (Red Dragon of Cadwallader) 被确认为威尔士国旗。米字旗多见于公共建筑或体育赛事, 但许多人更加认同英格兰、苏格兰、威尔士和北爱尔兰各自的国旗。

unique /juːˈniːk/ *adj* **1** (sole) 唯一的; (without parallel) 独一无二的; **problems that are not ~ to France** 并非法国独有的问题 **2** (exceptional) 独特的; **the ~ ability of humans to communicate by speech** 人类独具的语言交流能力; **a ~ knowledge of the subject** 关于这个题目的罕见知识; **to be ~ in doing sth.** 做某事是不寻常的

uniquely /juːˈniːkli/ *adv* **1** (exclusively) 独一无二地; (only) 唯一地; **~ Russian** 俄罗斯独有的 **2** (exceptionally) 独特地; **a ~ gifted player** 天赋异禀的选手; **she is ~ suited for the role** 她格外适合这个角色

uniqueness /juːˈniːknɪs/ *n* [u] **1** (singularity) 唯一 **2** (exceptional quality) 独特性

unique selling proposition, unique selling point *ns* 独特卖点

unisex /ˈjuːnɪseks/ *adj* 不分男女的; **~ salon/clothes** 男女皆可光顾的美发店/男女都能穿的衣服

unison /ˈjuːnɪsn, ˈjuːnɪzn/ [u] **1** Mus 同音; **to sing in ~** 齐声歌唱 **2** (in speech, action) 一齐; **to act in ~ with sb.** 同某人一致行动; **'happy birthday!' they cried in ~** "生日快乐!"他们齐声喊道

unit /ˈjuːnɪt/ *n* **1** (part of whole) 单元; **the course book has 15 ~s** 课本有 15 个单元; **the family is the basic ~ of society** 家庭是社会的基本单位 **2** (standard quantity) 单位; **a ~ of length/electricity** 长度/电量单位; **a monetary ~** 货币单位 **3** (group) 小组; (in army, police) 小队; **a bomb-disposal/research ~** 拆弹/研究小组 **4** (building, department) 部门; (in hospital) 科; **a manufacturing ~** 制造部; **the intensive care/maternity ~** 重症监护室/妇产科 **5** (part of machine) 部件; **the lens**

～ in the camera 照相机的透镜组 **6** (piece of furniture) 组合件; **a storage/sink ～** 储藏架/水槽装置; **furniture in ～s** 组装家具 **7** Comm (single item) 一件成品 **8** Math (smallest whole number) 最小整数; (numbers from one to nine) 个位数 **9** Univ (part of course) 教学单元; **students must take three core ～s** 学生必须选修3个核心单元 **10** esp Amer (apartment) 套; **two-bedroomed ～s** 两居室

Unitarian /juːnɪˈteərɪən/
A *n* [基督教的] 神体一位派信徒
B *adj* 神体一位派的

Unitarianism /juːnɪˈteərɪənɪzəm/ *n* [u] [基督教] 神体一位论

unitary /ˈjuːnɪtri, Amer -teri/ *adj* **1** (forming a whole) 单一的 **2** Brit Pol 中央集权制的; **～ authority** [尤指英国的] 单一自治体

unit cost *n* 单位成本

unite /juːˈnaɪt/
A *vt* 使联合; **to ～ the country** 使国家团结; **they are ～d by their love of cars** 对车的喜爱使他们走到一起; **to ～ sth. and** *or* **with sth.** 使某物与某物联合; **an artistic work which ～s freedom and** *or* **with discipline** 将自由创作与规范结合在一起的艺术作品
B *vi* 联合; **to ～ against sb./sth.** 联合起来反对某人/某事; **to ～ behind sb.** 团结支持某人; **to ～ with sb. to do sth.** 联合某人做某事; **to ～ in sth.** 在某事中团结一致; **the two parties ～d in opposing** *or* **to oppose the measure** 两党联合反对该议案; **workers of the world, ～!** 全世界劳动者，联合起来！

united /juːˈnaɪtɪd/ *adj* 联合的 ‹*groups, front, attempt*›; 团结的 ‹*nation, family*›; **to be ～ in sth.** 在做某事中团结一致; **a newly ～ Germany** 新近统一的德国; **～ we stand, divided we fall** 团结就是胜利，分裂必然失败

United: ～ Arab Emirates *pr npl + v sing or pl* **the ～ Arab Emirates** 阿拉伯联合酋长国; **～ Kingdom** *pr n* **the ～ Kingdom (of Great Britain and Northern Ireland)** (大不列颠及北爱尔兰) 联合王国; **～ Nations** *pr npl + v sing* **the ～ Nations (Organization)** 联合国 (组织); **～ States** *pr n + v sing* **the ～ States (of America)** 美利坚合众国

> **the United Kingdom**
>
> 联合王国，即英国，简称 the UK，全称 the United Kingdom of Great Britain and Northern Ireland。由英格兰、威尔士、苏格兰和北爱尔兰组成。1801年，爱尔兰和大不列颠 (▸**Great Britain**) 合并，形成大不列颠及爱尔兰联合王国 (The United Kingdom of Great Britain and Ireland)。1922年，爱尔兰南部宣布成立爱尔兰自由邦 (Irish Free State)，1949年成为完全独立的爱尔兰共和国 (Republic of Ireland)。英国全称由此改为大不列颠及北爱尔兰联合王国。

unit: ～ price *n* 单价; **～ trust** *n* Brit 单位信托投资公司

unity /ˈjuːnəti/ *n* **1** [u and c] (wholeness) 整体性; (oneness) 统一性; **the painting seems to lack ～** 那幅画好像缺乏整体效果; **～ of place, time and action** Theat 三一律 **2** [u] (consensus) 一致; **～ of purpose** 目标的统一; **～ is strength** 团结就是力量 **3** [u] (unification) (of organization) 联合; (of country) 统一; **national ～** 国家统一; **church ～** 教会合一

Univ *abbr* **= university**

univalve /ˈjuːnɪvælv/
A *n* (mollusc) 单壳软体动物; (shell) 单壳
B *adj* 单壳的

universal /juːnɪˈvɜːsl/
A *adj* **1** (general) 普遍的 ‹*fear, grammar, remedy*›; 全体的 ‹*access, acclaim, agreement*›; 通用的 ‹*language*›; **～ health care** 全民医保; **she was a ～ favourite** 她受到所有人的喜爱; **such practices are ～** 这种做法无处不在 **2** (applicable in all cases) 普遍适用的; **a ～ truth** 普遍真理
B *n* **1** Philos 一般概念 **2** Ling (grammatical rule) 通用原则; (linguistic feature) 普遍现象

universal coupling *n* **= universal joint**

universality /juːnɪvɜːˈsæləti/ *n* [u] 普遍性

universalize /juːnɪˈvɜːsəlaɪz/ *vt* 使普遍化; **when education is ～d** 当教育得到普及

universal joint *n* 万向接头

universally /juːnɪˈvɜːsəli/ *adv* 普遍地; **it is ～ acknowledged** *or* **believed** *or* **recognized that ...** …是举世公认的

universal: ～ motor *n* 交直流两用电动机; **～ product code** *n* esp Amer 通用产品码; **U～ Time, U～ Time Coordinated** *ns* [u] **= Greenwich Mean Time**; **～ suffrage** *n* [u] 普选权

universe /ˈjuːnɪvɜːs/ *n* **1** (cosmos) 宇宙 **2** fig (domain) 领域; **the front parlour/her family was the hub of her ～** 前厅是她的主要活动场所/家庭是她生活的中心

university /juːnɪˈvɜːsəti/ *n* 大学; **to have a ～ education** 接受大学教育; **a ～ town/lecturer** 大学城/大学讲师

university entrance *n* [u] 大学入学

unjust /ʌnˈdʒʌst/ *adj* (not fair) 不公平的; (not reasonable) 不合理的; **the manager has been very ～ to her** 经理对她非常不公; **it is ～ of sb. to do sth.** 某人做某事是不公正的

unjustifiable /ʌnˈdʒʌstɪfaɪəbl/ *adj* (unable to be justified) 无正当理由的; (unable to be excused) 不可原谅的; **your rude behaviour is totally ～** 你的粗鲁行为毫无道理

unjustifiably /ʌnˈdʒʌstɪfaɪəbli/ *adv* 没有道理地; **to be ～ anxious/critical** 无端地忧虑/挑剔

unjustified /ʌnˈdʒʌstɪfaɪd/ *adj* (wrong) 无端的; (unnecessary) 不必要的; **completely** *or* **totally ～** 完全没有根据的

unjustly /ʌnˈdʒʌstli/ *adv* (not fairly) 不公平地; (not reasonably) 不合理地; **to be ～ accused/slandered** 被诬告/遭到诽谤

unkempt /ʌnˈkempt/ *adj* 凌乱的 ‹*hair, beard*›; 不整洁的 ‹*person, appearance, garden*›

unkind /ʌnˈkaɪnd/ *adj* 不友善的 ‹*person, act, remark*›; 不宜人的 ‹*climate*›; 残酷的 ‹*fate*›; **it is ～ of sb. to do sth.** 某人做某事很刻薄; **to be ～ to sb.** (in action) 对某人不亲切; (verbally) 对某人刻毒; **to be ～ to animals** 虐待动物

unkindly /ʌnˈkaɪndli/ *adv* 不友善地; **fate/her stepfather had treated her ～** 命运残酷地对待她/继父虐待她; **don't take it too ～ if I say ...** 如果我说…，不要往心里去

unkindness /ʌnˈkaɪndnɪs/ *n* **1** [u] (of person, remark, act) 不友善; (of fate) 残酷; **～ in doing sth.** 做某事表现出的不友好 **2** [c] (act) 不友善的举动

unknot /ʌnˈnɒt/ *vt* (*pres p etc.* **-tt-**) 解开…上的结 ‹*rope, shoelace*›

unknowable /ʌnˈnəʊəbl/ *adj* **1** (not knowable) 不可知的 **2** (beyond human understanding) 超越人类理解力的; (beyond human experience) 超越人类经验的

unknowing /ʌnˈnəʊɪŋ/ *adj* 未察觉的 ‹*person*›; 不是存心的 ‹*cause*›; **she was the ～ victim of a trickster** 她在不知不觉中上了骗子的当

unknowingly /ʌnˈnəʊɪŋli/ *adv* 无心地; **all ～, ...** 在毫不知情的情况下，…

unknown /ʌnˈnəʊn/
A *adj* **1** (not known or identified) 未知的 ‹*result, effect, force*›; 身份不明的 ‹*person, intruder, visitor*›; **it is not ～ for sb. to do sth.** 某人做某事并非不知情; **an ～ quantity** Math 未知数; fig 不知底细的人; **～ to me, the plane had been diverted** 飞机变了航线，我一无所知; **murder by person or persons ～** 身份不明者实施的谋杀 **2** (not publicly recognized) 不出名的 ‹*actress, singer*› **3** (not discovered) 未发现的; (not explored) 未探知的; (not identified) 未确认的; **～ reserves/strengths** 未发现的储备物/长处
B *n* **1** (unidentified thing) 未知事物; (unidentified place) 未知的地方; **fear of the ～** 对未知事物的恐惧; **there are so many ～s in this case** 这个案件中有许许多多未知数 **2** (unheard-of person) 不出名的人; **the director gave the part to a complete ～** 导演把这个角色给了一个寂寂无名的演员 **3** Math 未知数

Unknown Soldier, Unknown Warrior *ns* **the ～** 无名战士

unlace /ʌnˈleɪs/ *vt* 解开…的带子 ‹*shoes, corset*›

unladen /ʌnˈleɪdn/ *adj* 未装货的; **～ weight** 自重 [车辆未装货时的重量]

unladylike /ʌnˈleɪdɪlaɪk/ *adj* 不像淑女的; **it's ～ to swear** 诅咒骂人有失大家闺秀风范; **don't be so ～!** 别这么不文雅！

unlamented /ˌʌnləˈmentɪd/ *adj* 未被悼念的; **his passing went ～** 他的去世无人哀悼

unlatch /ʌnˈlætʃ/
A *vt* 拉开…的插栓; **to leave the door/window ～ed** 没闩大门/窗户
B *vi* 拉开插栓; **how does this door ～?** 这个门怎么开？

unlawful /ʌnˈlɔːfl/ *adj* 不合法的; **～ possession of firearms/drugs** 枪支/毒品的非法拥有

unlawful: ～ arrest *n* [u and c] (without cause) 任意逮捕; (without correct procedure) 非法逮捕; **～ assembly** *n* [u] 非法集会; **～ detention** *n* [u and c] 非法拘禁

unlawfully /ʌnˈlɔːfəli/ *adv* 不合法地

unlawfulness /ʌnˈlɔːflnɪs/ *n* [u] 不合法; **the ～ of such activities/behaviour** 这种活动/行为的违法性

unleaded /ʌnˈledɪd/ *adj* 不含铅的; **～ petrol** 无铅汽油

unlearn /ʌnˈlɜːn/ *vt* (*pt, pp* **～ed** /ʌnˈlɜːnd/ *or* Brit **unlearnt** /ʌnˈlɜːnt/) **1** (discard) 抛弃; **to ～ bad habits** 改掉坏习惯 **2** (try to forget) 故意忘记

unlearned /ʌnˈlɜːnɪd/ *adj* formal 未受教育的

unleash /ʌnˈliːʃ/ *vt* **1** lit (set free) 解除…的束缚; (release) 解皮带放开; **to ～ the guard dogs** 解开看门狗的皮带; **to ～ the dogs of war** fig 发动战争 **2** fig (release, vent) 宣泄 ‹*passion, anger*›; **to ～ one's pent-up rage** 发泄被压抑的愤怒 **3** fig (launch) 发动 ‹*attack, force*›; **to ～ sth. against sth./sb.** 发动某物反对某物/某人

unleavened /ʌnˈlevnd/ *adj* 未发酵的 ‹*bread*›

unless /ənˈles/ *conj* 除非; **I'll have the egg, ～ you want it** 我吃这个蛋吧，除非你想要; **～ something happens, I'll see you tomorrow** 如果没有什么意外，我明天见你; **～ otherwise stated** 除非另有说明; **not ～** 除了; **I won't go, not ～ you say I can** 我不会走的——除非你同意

unlettered /ʌnˈletəd/ *adj* formal or dated (unable to read) 不识字的; (having no education) 未受教育的; **the ～ masses** 文盲大众

unliberated /ʌnˈlɪbəreɪtɪd/ *adj* 未解放的; **to accuse sb. of being old-fashioned and ～** 指责某人守旧和思想不解放

unlicensed /ʌnˈlaɪsnst/ *adj* **1** (having no official licence) 无许可证的; Brit (having no licence to sell alcohol) 无售酒执照的; **to have an ～ gun** 有一把无照枪支 **2** (not authorized) 未经特许的

unlicensed premises *npl* esp Brit 无售酒执照的营业场所

unlike /ʌnˈlaɪk/
A *prep* **1** (in contrast to) 与…相反; **～ me, he ...** 不像我，他… **2** (different from) 和…不同;

they are quite ～ each other 他们彼此迥然不同 **3** (uncharacteristic of) 非…的特点; **how ～ John!** 这可不像约翰！

B *adj pred* 不同的

unlikeable, unlikable /ʌn'laɪkəbl/ *adj* 不可爱的〈*person, place*〉; 招人讨厌的〈*character in book, play*〉

unlikelihood /ʌn'laɪklɪhʊd/ *n* [u] 不大可能

unlikely /ʌn'laɪkli/ *adj* **1** (unexpected) 不大可能的; **highly** *or* **most ～** 极不可能的; **it is/is not ～ that ...** …是不大可能的/…并非不可能; **to be ～ to do sth.** 不大可能做某事; **in the ～ event of his refusing ...** 万一他拒绝… **2** (strange) 想不到的; **a very ～ couple** 很不般配的一对 **3** (probably untrue) 不大可信的; **an ～ story** 不太真实的报道 **4** (not likely to succeed) 不大可能会成功的; **the most ～ men have been successful here** 最不可能成功的人在这里都获得了成功

unlimited /ʌn'lɪmɪtɪd/ *adj* **1** (having no restrictions) 无限制的; **there were ～ drinks at the party** 聚会上饮料无限量供应; **an ～ company** Brit 无限公司 **2** (boundless) 无界限的; **her patience seems ～** 她似乎有无限的耐心; **the ～ expanse of the ocean** 浩瀚的海洋 **3** (absolute) 绝对的; **he has ～ self-confidence** 他绝对自信

unlined /ʌn'laɪnd/ *adj* **1** (without a lining) 无衬里的〈*garment, curtain*〉 **2** (not marked with lines) 无线条的〈*paper*〉; 无皱纹的〈*forehead, complexion*〉

unlisted /ʌn'lɪstɪd/ *adj* **1** (not in a list) 未列表公布的〈*item, hotel*〉 **2** Fin 未上市的〈*company, share*〉 **3** esp Amer Telecom 未列入电话簿的〈*number, person*〉 **4** Brit Constr, Jur 非列入保护名录的〈*building*〉

unlit /ʌn'lɪt/ *adj* **1** (without light) 无灯光的〈*house, street*〉 **2** (without flame) 未点燃的〈*cigarette, fire*〉

unload /ʌn'ləʊd/

A *vt* **1** (remove) 卸下〈*goods, shopping*〉; **to ～ passengers (from a ship)** 让乘客（从船上）下来 **2** (remove load from) 从…上卸货〈*van, ship*〉; 卸下〈*cargo*〉 **3** (remove from gun, camera) 退出〈*charge, film*〉; **to ～ sth. (from sth.)** （从某物中）退出某物 **4** (remove charge from) 从…中退出子弹〈*gun*〉; (remove film from) 从…中退出胶卷〈*camera*〉 **5** Comm (offload large quantity of) 抛售; **to ～ surplus goods** 倾销过剩商品; **to ～ shares** 抛售股票 **6** fig (give vent to) 倾诉〈*anxiety, problem*〉; **he really needed to ～ all his worries** 他真的需要倾吐所有的烦恼 **7** (dispose of, transfer) 摆脱〈*children*〉; 推卸〈*responsibilities*〉; **to ～ one's problems on (to) sb.** 把问题推给某人

B *vi* «*ship, lorry*» 卸货

unloaded /ʌn'ləʊdɪd/ *adj* **1** (without load) 未载货的; **what does the vehicle weigh ～?** 这辆车自重是多少？ **2** (not charged) 未装胶卷的〈*camera*〉; 未装弹药的〈*gun*〉

unloading /ʌn'ləʊdɪŋ/ *n* [u] (of vehicle, ship) 卸货; (of camera, gun) 退出

unlock /ʌn'lɒk/ *vt* **1** lit (with key) 开…的锁; **to leave the door ～ed** 没给门上锁 **2** fig (lay open) 揭开; **to ～ the secrets of one's heart** 倾吐心中的秘密; **this symphony has ～ed the world of classical music to her** 这首交响曲为她打开了古典音乐世界的大门

unlooked for /ʌn'lʊktfɔː(r)/ *adj* 意外的; **this success was quite ～** 这次成功很意外; **they encountered unlooked-for difficulties** 他们遇到了始料不及的困难

unloose /ʌn'luːs/ *vt* **1** (set free) 释放〈*animal, prisoner*〉 **2** (relax) 松开〈*grip, fingers*〉 **3** (unfasten) 解开〈*knot, rope*〉

unlovable /ʌn'lʌvəbl/ *adj* 不可爱的〈*person*〉; 不讨人喜欢的〈*personality, habit*〉

unloved /ʌn'lʌvd/ *adj* 不被喜爱的; **the room/child looked ～** 这房间看上去不受青睐/这孩子看上去不讨人欢喜; **to feel ～** 感到无人疼爱

unlovely /ʌn'lʌvli/ *adj* (without beauty) 不美观的; (without charm) 不吸引人的; **an ～ personality** 令人讨厌的个性

unloving /ʌn'lʌvɪŋ/ *adj* 无爱心的

unluckily /ʌn'lʌkɪli/ *adv* (regrettably) 遗憾地; (unfortunately) 不幸地; **～ for her, the shop was closed** 她很倒霉，商店关门了

unlucky /ʌn'lʌki/ *adj* **1** (having bad fortune) 不幸的; **to be ～ enough to do sth.** 做某事很倒霉; **you were ～ not to get the job** 很遗憾你没有得到那份工作; **he is ～ in love** 他在恋爱方面运气不佳 **2** (causing bad fortune) 不吉利的〈*number, colour*〉; **it is ～ to walk under ladders** 从梯子下走过是不吉利的

unmade /ʌn'meɪd/

A *pt, pp* ▸**unmake**

B *adj* 未做好的〈*thing*〉; 未铺好的〈*bed*〉; **an ～ road** Brit 未铺好的路

unmade-up *adj* 未化妆的〈*person, face*〉

unmake /ʌn'meɪk/ *vt* (*pp, pt* **unmade**) 清理〈*mess*〉; 取消〈*plan*〉; 废除〈*agreement, law*〉

unman /ʌn'mæn/ *vt* (*pres p etc.* **-nn-**) liter 使失去男子气质

unmanageable /ʌn'mænɪdʒəbl/ *adj* 难管理的〈*child*〉; 难控制的〈*animal, system*〉; 难处理的〈*problem, hair, number*〉; 难以清还的〈*debt*〉; 难以负担的〈*burden*〉; **all this data would be ～ without a computer** 没有电脑便难以处理所有这些数据

unmanly /ʌn'mænli/ *adj* 无男子气概的〈*person, behaviour*〉; **crying was considered ～** 哭泣以往被认为是缺乏男子气的表现

unmanned /ʌn'mænd/ *adj* **1** (operated automatically) 无人操纵的〈*flight, lighthouse, crossing*〉; 不载人的〈*probe, spacecraft, rocket*〉; **an ～ train** 无人驾驶火车 **2** (with nobody in attendance) 无人值守的; **they left the telephone ～** 他们没有留人接听电话; **～ positions** Mil 无人守卫的阵地

unmannerly /ʌn'mænəli/ *adj* formal 没有礼貌的

unmapped /ʌn'mæpt/ *adj* 地图上未标明的

unmarked /ʌn'mɑːkt/ *adj* **1** (unblemished) 光洁的〈*face, surface, fruit*〉; 无瑕疵的〈*floor*〉 **2** (without markings) 没有标志的〈*car, suitcase*〉; (unlabelled) 没有标签的〈*linen, merchandise*〉; **～ graves** 无名冢 **3** (not corrected) 未批改的〈*essay, homework*〉 **4** (not noticed) 被忽略的〈*event, anniversary*〉 **5** Ling 无标记的 **6** Sport 无人盯防的〈*player*〉

unmarketable /ʌn'mɑːkɪtəbl/ *adj* **1** (not fit for sale) 不适合销售的 **2** (unable to be sold) 没有销路的

unmarriageable /ʌn'mærɪdʒəbl/ *adj* 不适合结婚的〈*person, age*〉

unmarried /ʌn'mærɪd/ *adj* 未婚的; **to remain ～** 保持独身; **an ～ mother** 未婚母亲

unmask /ʌn'mɑːsk, Amer -'mæsk/

A *vt* **1** lit (remove mask from) 揭下…的面具 **2** fig (expose) 揭露〈*plot, culprit*〉; **the trial ～ed him as a charlatan** 审讯揭露出他是个假内行

B *vi* 摘下面具

unmatched /ʌn'mætʃt/ *adj* 无与伦比的; **to be ～ by sb./sth.** 是某人/某事物无法比拟的; **our products are ～ in quality** 我们的产品质量无与伦比

unmentionable /ʌn'menʃənəbl/

A *adj* **1** (taboo) 难以启齿的〈*word, topic*〉 **2** (unspeakable) 不可提及的

B *npl* **unmentionables** colloq dated or hum 说不出口的东西

unmerciful /ʌn'mɜːsɪfl/ *adj* 不仁慈的; **to be ～ towards sb.** 不怜悯某人

unmercifully /ʌn'mɜːsɪfəli/ *adv* 不仁慈地

unmerited /ʌn'merɪtɪd/ *adj* 不应受的〈*fall, criticism*〉; 不配得到的〈*success*〉

unmet /ʌn'met/ *adj* 未满足的〈*demand, condition*〉

unmethodical /ˌʌnmɪ'θɒdɪkl/ *adj* 没有条理的

unmindful /ʌn'maɪndfl/ *adj* formal **to be ～ of sth.** (not heeding) 不留心某事物; (not caring about) 不在意某事物

unmissable /ʌn'mɪsəbl/ *adj* **1** (not to be missed) 不可错过的〈*film, attraction*〉; 不可失去的〈*experience, opportunity*〉 **2** (impossible to miss) 定能命中的〈*goal*〉; 不可能错过的〈*landmark, relevance*〉

unmistakable /ˌʌnmɪ'steɪkəbl/ *adj* **1** (clearly recognizable) 不会弄错的〈*smell, handwriting*〉; **the ～ sound of her voice** 确定无疑的她本人的嗓音 **2** (unambiguous) 清楚明白的〈*message, honesty*〉; **the ～ evidence of a murder** 谋杀的确凿证据

unmistakably /ˌʌnmɪ'steɪkəbli/ *adv* 毫无疑问地

unmitigated /ʌn'mɪtɪgeɪtɪd/ *adj* 彻底的〈*terror, admiration, disaster*〉; 十足的〈*lie, liar, folly, cruelty*〉

unmixed /ʌn'mɪkst/ *adj* 没有掺杂的〈*seeds*〉; 纯粹的〈*feelings, pleasure*〉; **this gift was not an ～ blessing** 这一天赋并非完全是件幸事

unmoderated /ʌn'mɒdəreɪtɪd/ *adj* **1** (untempered) 不加克制的〈*enthusiasm, harshness*〉 **2** (not monitored) 未加管理的〈*chat room, forum*〉

unmodernized /ʌn'mɒdənaɪzd/ *adj* (not modernized) 未现代化的; (retaining the original features) 保持原有风格的

unmodified /ʌn'mɒdɪfaɪd/ *adj* 未更改的; **the original ～ version of a computer game** 未修改的原版电脑游戏

unmolested /ˌʌnmə'lestɪd/ *adj* 未受干扰的

unmotivated /ʌn'məʊtɪveɪtɪd/ *adj* **1** (lacking drive) 缺乏动力的; **to feel ～ by sth.** 对某事物感到提不起劲来 **2** (lacking motive) 无动机的; **an ～ attack** 无缘无故的攻击

unmounted /ʌn'maʊntɪd/ *adj* **1** (not in a mount) 未装框的〈*photo, stamp, print, painting*〉; 未镶嵌的〈*gem*〉 **2** Equit 不骑马的〈*rider, soldier*〉

unmourned /ʌn'mɔːnd/ *adj* 无人哀悼的〈*person, death*〉

unmoved /ʌn'muːvd/ *adj* **1** (unperturbed) 泰然自若的; (indifferent) 冷淡的; **to be ～ by sth.** (unperturbed by) 未受某事物的烦扰; (indifferent to) 对某事物很冷淡 **2** (not stirred emotionally) 无动于衷的; **she was ～ by his tears** 她不为他的眼泪所动

unmusical /ʌn'mjuːzɪkl/ *adj* **1** (unskilled in music) 不擅长音乐的; (indifferent to music) 对音乐无兴趣的; **to have an ～ ear** 没有乐感 **2** (not harmonious) 不合调的; **the ～ tones of a police siren** 刺耳的警笛声

unnameable /ʌn'neɪməbl/ *adj* 难以形容的〈*horror, monster*〉; 不能命名的〈*disease*〉

unnamed /ʌn'neɪmd/ *adj* **1** (not divulged) 未透露名字的; (not known) 不知其名的; **the source of the rumour went ～** 谣言的来源不得而知 **2** (without a name) 没有名字的〈*thing*〉; 莫名的〈*fear*〉; **as yet ～** 尚未命名的

unnatural /ʌn'nætʃrəl/ *adj* **1** (unusual) 不自然的〈*silence, colour*〉; 反常的〈*event, phenomenon*〉; **it is ～ for sb. to do sth.** 某人做某事很反常 **2** (perverted) 变态的〈*act, desire, interest*〉; **an ～ hatred** 不合常理的仇恨 **3** (wicked) 无人性的〈*crime, murder*〉 **4** (affected) 做作的〈*voice, style*〉; **to smile in an ～ manner** 勉强地微笑

unnaturally /ʌn'nætʃrəli/ *adv* **1** (unusually) 不自然地; **not ～** 自然而然地; **fear made the children ～ silent** 恐惧使孩子们异常安静 **2** (affectedly) 做作地〈*laugh, smile*〉

unnavigable /ʌn'nævɪgəbl/ *adj* 不可通航的〈*river, channel*〉

unnecessarily /ʌnˈnesəsərəli, Amer ʌnˌnesəˈserəli/ *adv* 1 (unjustifiably) 没有理由地; **to be ~ late** 无故迟到 2 (excessively) 不必要地; **~ harsh criticism** 过分严厉的批评

unnecessary /ʌnˈnesəsri, Amer -seri/ *adj* 1 (unjustifiable) 没有理由的; (not required) 不需要的; **it is ~ (for sb.) to do sth.** (某人) 不需要做某事 2 (excessive) 不必要的 ‹*expense, fuss*› 3 (uncalled for) 多此一举的 ‹*reference, jibe*›

unneighbourly Brit, **unneighborly** Amer /ʌnˈneɪbəli/ *adj* 不友善的; **to find sb. a bit ~** 觉得某人不太友善

unnerve /ʌnˈnɜːv/ *vt* (cause to feel uneasy) 使紧张; (cause to lose confidence) 使气馁; (cause to lose courage) 使丧失勇气; **to feel thoroughly ~d (by sth.)** 被 (某事物) 弄得完全不知所措

unnerving /ʌnˈnɜːvɪŋ/ *adj* 令人慌张的; **a thoroughly ~ experience** 令人完全不知所措的经历; **~ accuracy** 极度精准; **I find the way that he stares so ~** 我感到他盯着人的样子令人不安

unnervingly /ʌnˈnɜːvɪŋlɪ/ *adv* 令人慌张地; **~ quiet** 安静得令人不安的

unnoticed /ʌnˈnəʊtɪst/ *adj* 未受到注意的; **to go** *or* **pass ~** 不被察觉; **to slip in ~** 悄悄溜进

unnumbered /ʌnˈnʌmbəd/ *adj* 1 (without a number) 未编号的 ‹*page, seat*› 2 liter (countless) 数不清的 ‹*stars, dead*›

UNO /ˈjuːnəʊ/ *abbr* **= United Nations Organization** 联合国组织

unobjectionable /ˌʌnəbˈdʒekʃənəbl/ *adj* 1 (acceptable) 无异议的 ‹*proposal, idea*› 2 (inoffensive) 不会引起反感的 ‹*person, behaviour, book, language*›

unobservant /ˌʌnəbˈzɜːvənt/ *adj* 观察力不敏锐的; **you're very ~** 你太不留心了

unobserved /ˌʌnəbˈzɜːvd/ *adj* 不被发现的; **to go** *or* **pass ~** 不被察觉; **to slip out ~** 悄悄溜出

unobstructed /ˌʌnəbˈstrʌktɪd/ *adj* 无障碍的 ‹*road, exit, view*›; 未阻塞的 ‹*channel, pipe*›

unobtainable /ˌʌnəbˈteɪnəbl/ *adj* 1 (unable to be procured) 得不到的 ‹*item, parts*› 2 Telecom 无法接通的; **this number is ~** 这个号码无法接通

unobtrusive /ˌʌnəbˈtruːsɪv/ *adj* 不招摇的

unobtrusively /ˌʌnəbˈtruːsɪvli/ *adv* 不招摇地

unobtrusiveness /ˌʌnəbˈtruːsɪvnɪs/ *n* [u] 不招摇

unoccupied /ʌnˈɒkjʊpaɪd/ *adj* 1 (empty) 未被占用的 ‹*room, position*›; **are these seats ~?** 这几个座位是空的吗? 2 (not busy) 空闲的; **in ~ moments** 在空闲时候 3 Mil 未沦陷的 ‹*territory, zone*›

unofficial /ˌʌnəˈfɪʃl/ *adj* 1 (not formally organized or approved) 非官方的; **an ~ strike** 未经批准的罢工 2 (not formally established) 非正式的 ‹*statement, report, result*›

unofficially /ˌʌnəˈfɪʃəli/ *adv* 1 (in informal capacity) 非正式地 ‹*act, open*› 2 (without formal authorization) 未获官方授权地 ‹*speak, report*›; **officially, I'm in favour; ~, I'm very doubtful** 站在官方立场上, 我是赞成的, 但私底下我很怀疑

unopened /ʌnˈəʊpənd/ *adj* 未打开的; **to return a letter ~** 将信原封不动地退回

unopposed /ˌʌnəˈpəʊzd/ *adj* 未遭到抵抗的 ‹*army, invasion*›; 未遭到反对的 ‹*candidate, proposal*›; **to be elected ~** 顺利当选; **the bill was given an ~ second reading** 法案在二读获得一致通过

unorganized /ʌnˈɔːɡənaɪzd/ *adj* 1 (disorganized) 杂乱的 2 (not affiliated to a trade union) 未加入工会的

unoriginal /ˌʌnəˈrɪdʒənl/ *adj* 非原创的; **totally ~** 完全老一套的

unorthodox /ʌnˈɔːθədɒks/ *adj* 1 (unconventional) 非正统的 ‹*approach, technique*›; **it is ~ to do sth.** 做某事是不正规的 2 (independent) 另类的 ‹*person*›; **to be ~ in sth.** 在某方面与众不同

unostentatious /ˌʌnɒstenˈteɪʃəs/ *adj* 不夸耀的; **a fairly ~ way of doing things** 朴实无华的行事方式

unostentatiously /ˌʌnɒstenˈteɪʃəsli/ *adv* 不夸耀地; **an ~ written account** 毫无虚饰的书面报告; **to display one's skills ~** 毫不卖弄地展示自己的技能

unpack /ʌnˈpæk/
A *vt* 1 (empty) 打开…取出东西 ‹*case, luggage*› 2 (remove) [从行李、包裹等中] 取出 ‹*clothes, belongings*›
B *vi* 打开行李; **I haven't ~ed yet** 我还没有打开行李

unpacking /ʌnˈpækɪŋ/ *n* [u] 开包; **to do the ~** 打开行李

unpaid /ʌnˈpeɪd/ *adj* 1 (not yet paid) 未付的 ‹*bill*›; 未偿还的 ‹*debt*› 2 (without salary) 无报酬的 ‹*person, work*›; **~ volunteers** 不领报酬的志愿者; **~ leave** 无薪假

unpainted /ʌnˈpeɪntɪd/ *adj* 未上漆的

unpalatable /ʌnˈpælətəbl/ *adj* 1 (tasting unpleasant) 难吃的 ‹*meal*› 2 fig (hard to accept) 难以接受的 ‹*views, truth, conclusion*›; **to be ~ to sb.** 使某人讨厌

unparalleled /ʌnˈpærəleld/ *adj* 无比的; **a crisis ~ in modern times/history** 现代时期/历史上空前的危机; **her beauty was ~** 她的美貌举世无双

unpardonable /ʌnˈpɑːdənəbl/ *adj* 不可宽恕的; **it was ~ of you to leave her on her own** 你抛下她不管是不可原谅的

unpardonably /ʌnˈpɑːdənəbli/ *adv* 不可宽恕地 ‹*rude, offensive*›; **to behave ~** 行为不可原谅

unparliamentary /ˌʌnpɑːləˈmentri, Amer -teri/ *adj* 违反议会规则的; **~ language** 不适于议会的语言

unpasteurized /ʌnˈpɑːstʃəraɪzd/ *adj* 未进行巴氏消毒的 ‹*milk, cheese*›

unpatched /ʌnˈpætʃt/ *adj* 未打补丁的 ‹*computer, system*›

unpatented /ʌnˈpeɪtəntɪd, ʌnˈpæt-/ *adj* 未获专利权的

unpatriotic /ˌʌnpætrɪˈɒtɪk, Amer ˌʌnpeɪt-/ *adj* 不爱国的

unpatriotically /ˌʌnpætrɪˈɒtɪkli, Amer ˌʌnpeɪt-/ *adv* 不爱国地; **some citizens reacted rather ~** 有些公民的反应显得没有爱国心

unpaved /ʌnˈpeɪvd/ *adj* 未铺砌的

unperturbed /ˌʌnpəˈtɜːbd/ *adj* 不受烦扰的; **to be** *or* **remain ~ (by sth.)** 不受 (某事物的) 干扰

unpick /ʌnˈpɪk/ *vt* 1 (undo) 拆去 ‹*seam, stitches*› 2 (analyse) 对…条分缕析 ‹*facts*›; **you have to try to ~ truth from fantasy** 你必须把事实和幻想仔细区分开来

unpin /ʌnˈpɪn/ *vt* (*pres p etc.* **-nn-**) 1 (remove pins from) 取下…的发卡 ‹*hair*›; 取下…的别针 ‹*sewing, dress*› 2 (unfasten) 取下 ‹*brooch*›; 拔钉使…松开 ‹*paper*›

unplaced /ʌnˈpleɪst/ *adj* 未获名次的 [尤指未获前三名]

unplanned /ʌnˈplænd/ *adj* 未经计划的; **an ~ increase in costs** 计划外的成本增加; **an ~ pregnancy** 意外怀孕

unplayable /ʌnˈpleɪəbl/ *adj* 1 Sport (not returnable) 无法回击的 ‹*serve, ball*›; (unfit for playing on) 不适合比赛的 ‹*pitch*› 2 Mus (impossible to play) 不能演奏的 3 (too damaged to be played) 不能播放的 ‹*CD, video, DVD*›

unpleasant /ʌnˈpleznt/ *adj* 1 (unenjoyable, nasty) 令人不快的; **an ~ smell** 一股难闻的气味; **the ~ truth is that ...** 讨厌的事实是… 2 (disagreeable) 不友善的; **what an ~ character!** 真是个讨厌的人!; **to be ~ to** *or* **with sb.** 对某人不客气

unpleasantly /ʌnˈplezntli/ *adv* 1 (unenjoyably, nastily) 令人不快地 2 (disagreeably) 不友善地; **it was ~ hot in the room** 房间里热得让人难受

unpleasantness /ʌnˈplezntnɪs/ *n* [u] 1 (nastiness) (of smell) 难闻; (of experience) 不愉快; (of remark) 不客气 2 (bad feeling) 不和; (quarrelling) 争执; **in order to avoid ~** 为了避免冲突

unpleasing /ʌnˈpliːzɪŋ/ *adj* 使人不愉快的; **~ to the eye** 不悦目的

unplug /ʌnˈplʌɡ/ *vt* (*pres p etc.* **-gg-**) 1 Elec 拔去…的电源插头 ‹*appliance*› 2 (remove obstruction from) 疏通 ‹*pipe*›; **the drain needs ~ging** 排水管需要疏通

unplugged /ʌnˈplʌɡd/
A *adj* 不插电的 [指不用电子扩音设备]
B *adv* 不插电地

unplumbed /ʌnˈplʌmd/ *adj* 1 lit (not measured) 未用铅垂线测量的; **~ ocean depths** 深不可测的海洋深处 2 fig (not explored) 未探究的; (not understood) 未充分了解的; **to be as yet ~** 尚不为人知

unpoetic, unpoetical /ˌʌnpəʊˈetɪk(l)/ *adj* 无诗意的; **the expression was somewhat ~** 这个词句有点儿平淡无奇

unpolished /ʌnˈpɒlɪʃt/ *adj* 1 lit (not shiny) 没有磨光的 ‹*wood*›; 未擦亮的 ‹*shoe, floor, diamond*› 2 fig (not refined) 粗鲁的 ‹*person, manner*›; 未经润饰的 ‹*style, work*›; **it was rather an ~ performance** 演出稍显粗糙

unpolluted /ˌʌnpəˈluːtɪd/ *adj* 未受污染的 ‹*water, air*›; fig 未被玷污的 ‹*mind*›

unpopular /ʌnˈpɒpjʊlə(r)/ *adj* 不受欢迎的; **a very ~ decision/measure** 非常不得人心的决定/措施; **to make oneself ~** 使自己不受欢迎

unpopularity /ʌnˌpɒpjʊˈlærəti/ *n* [u] 不受欢迎; **~ with sb.** 不受某人的喜欢

unpopulated /ʌnˈpɒpjʊleɪtɪd/ *adj* 无人居住的; **vast ~ plains** 杳无人烟的广阔平原

unpractical /ʌnˈpræktɪkl/ *adj* **= impractical**

unpractised Brit, **unpracticed** /ʌnˈpræktɪst/ Amer *adj* 1 (not skilled) 不熟练的; (without training) 未经训练的; (without experience) 无经验的; **the sound was strange to my ~ ear** 这个声音在我未经训练的耳朵听来有点儿奇怪 2 (neglected) 未运用的 ‹*skill, craft*›

unprecedented /ʌnˈpresɪdentɪd/ *adj* 空前的 ‹*cruelty, situation*›; **~ economic growth** 前所未有的经济增长

unprecedentedly /ʌnˈpresɪdentɪdli/ *adv* 空前地; **~ brave/large** 前所未有地勇敢/规模空前巨大; **the competition was ~ intense** 竞争空前激烈

unpredictability /ˌʌnprɪˌdɪktəˈbɪləti/ *n* [u] 不可预测; **his ~ on the pitch** 他在球场上的善变

unpredictable /ˌʌnprɪˈdɪktəbl/ *adj* 不可预测的 ‹*result, reaction, weather*›; **he's so ~!** 他真是让人捉摸不透!

unpredictably /ˌʌnprɪˈdɪktəbli/ *adv* 不可预测地; **to act ~** 行为反复无常

unprejudiced /ʌnˈpredʒʊdɪst/ *adj* 无偏见的; **~ judgement** 公正的判决

unpremeditated /ˌʌnpriːˈmedɪteɪtɪd/ *adj* (not previously considered) 未事先考虑的; (not previously planned) 未事先策划的; **an ~ crime** 没有预谋的犯罪

unprepared /ˌʌnprɪˈpeəd/ *adj* 1 (not yet ready) 无准备的; **to be ~ to do sth./for sth.** 做某

u

事/对于某事没有准备; **to catch sb. ~** 令某人措手不及 **2** (improvised) 即兴的

unprepossessing /ˌʌnˌpriːpəˈzesɪŋ/ *adj* 不吸引人的; **a somewhat ~ person** 有点儿不讨人喜欢的人; **an ~ house** 不起眼的房子

unpresentable /ˌʌnprɪˈzentəbl/ *adj* 不像样的

unpresuming /ˌʌnprɪˈzjuːmɪŋ, Amer -ˈzuːm-/ *adj* 谦逊的 ‹*person, manner*›; 朴实无华的 ‹*place*›

unpretentious /ˌʌnprɪˈtenʃəs/ *adj* 朴实无华的 ‹*person, manner*›; 简朴的 ‹*car, style, meal*›; **to dress with ~ elegance** 穿着优雅大方

unpretentiously /ˌʌnprɪˈtenʃəsli/ *adv* 朴实无华地

unpretentiousness /ˌʌnprɪˈtenʃəsnɪs/ *n* [u] 朴实无华; **the ~ of his writing/style** 他的文字的平实/风格的朴实

unpriced /ʌnˈpraɪst/ *adj* (without price fixed) 未定价的; (without price marked) 未标价的

unprincipled /ʌnˈprɪnsəpld/ *adj* 不道德的; **he is thoroughly ~** 他无耻之极

unprintable /ʌnˈprɪntəbl/ *adj* [因冒犯或无礼] 不宜刊印的; **her answer was quite ~** 她的回答不太文雅

unprivileged /ʌnˈprɪvɪlɪdʒd/ *adj* 没有特权的; **to be born into the ~ classes** 出身于普通阶层

unproductive /ˌʌnprəˈdʌktɪv/ *adj* 无效益的 ‹*use, work, capital, time*›; 贫瘠的 ‹*land, soil*›; 事半功倍的 ‹*discussion*›; **I spent a very ~ morning in the office** 我上午在办公室一事无成

unproductively /ˌʌnprəˈdʌktɪvli/ *adv* 无益地

unprofessional /ˌʌnprəˈfeʃənl/ *adj* **1** (contrary to standards) 不符合专业要求的; **~ conduct** 违反职业道德的行为 **2** (amateurish) 非专业的

unprofessionally /ˌʌnprəˈfeʃənəli/ *adv* 不符合专业要求地

unprofitable /ʌnˈprɒfɪtəbl/ *adj* **1** Comm 不赢利的; **to have an ~ year** 一年没有赚钱 **2** fig (pointless) 无意义的; (fruitless) 无益的

unprofitably /ʌnˈprɒfɪtəbli/ *adv* **1** Comm 不赢利地; **to trade ~** 做生意不赚钱 **2** fig (pointlessly) 无意义地; (fruitlessly) 无益地

unpromising /ʌnˈprɒmɪsɪŋ/ *adj* 不乐观的; **an ~ task** 难有好结果的任务; **an ~ pupil** 不会有出息的学生

unpromisingly /ʌnˈprɒmɪsɪŋli/ *adv* 不乐观地; **to start ~** 开始时不被看好

unprompted /ʌnˈprɒmptɪd/ *adj* 主动的; **she came to me ~** 她主动向我走来

unpronounceable /ˌʌnprəˈnaʊnsəbl/ *adj* 难发音的; **a completely ~ name** 十分拗口的名字

unprotected /ˌʌnprəˈtektɪd/ *adj* **1** (unsafe) 未受保护的 ‹*family*›; 未设防的 ‹*town*›; **to be ~ against** *or* **from sth./sb.** 对某事物/某人无防范 **2** (not covered) 无预防措施的; **~ against accidental damage** 出现意外损失得不到赔偿的; **(to have) ~ sex** (进行) 无防护性交 [即不采取避孕措施的性交]

unprotesting /ˌʌnprəˈtestɪŋ/ *adj* 不反对的; **to be led away ~** 顺从地被带走

unprovable /ʌnˈpruːvəbl/ *adj* 无法证明的

unprovided for /ˌʌnprəˈvaɪdɪd fɔː(r)/ *adj pred* 无生活来源的; **to leave sb. ~** 让某人生活没有着落

unprovoked /ˌʌnprəˈvəʊkt/
A *adj* 未受挑衅的; **~ aggression** 无端的侵犯
B *adv* 未受挑衅地; **to do sth. ~** 无缘无故做某事

unpublicized /ʌnˈpʌblɪsaɪzd/ *adj* 未加宣扬的

unpublishable /ʌnˈpʌblɪʃəbl/ *adj* **1** (unprintable) 不宜出版的 **2** (outrageous) 骇人的; **her reply was ~!** 她的回答很粗鲁!

unpublished /ʌnˈpʌblɪʃt/ *adj* 未出版的 ‹*manuscript*›; 未公开的 ‹*letter*›

unpunctual /ʌnˈpʌŋktjʊəl/ *adj* 不守时的; **she's inclined to be a bit ~** 她总喜欢晚到一会儿

unpunctuality /ˌʌnpʌŋktjʊˈæləti/ *n* [u] 不守时

unpunished /ʌnˈpʌnɪʃt/ *adj* 未受惩罚的; **to go** *or* **remain ~** 没有得到惩罚

unputdownable /ˌʌnpʊtˈdaʊnəbl/ *adj* colloq 令人不忍释卷的 ‹*book*›

unqualified /ʌnˈkwɒlɪfaɪd/ *adj* **1** (lacking qualifications) 不合格的; **to be ~ (for sth./to do sth.)** (在某方面/做某事) 没资格 **2** (not competent) 没有能力的 **3** (absolute) 绝对的; **he's an ~ idiot/liar** 他是个十足的傻瓜/骗子

unquenchable /ʌnˈkwentʃəbl/ *adj* 不能熄灭的 ‹*fire, inferno*›; 不能遏制的 ‹*fury, zeal*›; 止不住的 ‹*thirst*›

unquestionable /ʌnˈkwestʃənəbl/ *adj* 无疑的; **with ~ sincerity** 绝对真诚地

unquestionably /ʌnˈkwestʃənəbli/ *adv* 毫无疑问地 ‹*real, sincere, miss, feel*›

unquestioned /ʌnˈkwestʃənd/ *adj* **1** (undisputed) 无可争议的; (undoubted) 无疑的 **2** (not subjected to inquiry) 未质询的 ‹*person*›; 未调查的 ‹*fact, report*›

unquestioning /ʌnˈkwestʃənɪŋ/ *adj* 不加质疑的; **he followed her with ~ obedience** 他绝对服从她

unquestioningly /ʌnˈkwestʃənɪŋlɪ/ *adv* 不加质疑地

unquote /ʌnˈkwəʊt/ *adv* 引文结束; ▸ **quote B1**

unquoted /ʌnˈkwəʊtɪd/ *adj* 未上市的 ‹*share, company*›

unranked /ʌnˈræŋkt/ *adj* 未进入排名的 ‹*player, team*›

unravel /ʌnˈrævl/
A *vt* (*pres p etc.* **-ll-** Brit, **-l-** Amer) **1** (undo) 解开; **her knitting became** *or* **got ~led** 她编织的东西脱线了 **2** fig (disentangle) 澄清; **to ~ the mystery** 解开谜团
B *vi* (*pres p etc.* **-ll-** Brit, **-l-** Amer) **1** (become undone) 松散 **2** (become disentangled) 被澄清

unreachable /ʌnˈriːtʃəbl/ *adj* **1** (unable to be reached) 够不到的 ‹*shelf*› **2** (uncontactable) 联系不上的 ‹*person*›; 连不上的 ‹*website, network*› **3** (inaccessible) 不能到达的 ‹*area*› **4** (unattainable) 达不到的 ‹*goal, standard*›

unread /ʌnˈred/ *adj* 未阅读的

unreadable /ʌnˈriːdəbl/ *adj* **1** (not worth reading) 不值一读的 ‹*book*›; **I find her style ~** 我觉得她的文风难以卒读 **2** (illegible) 字迹模糊的 ‹*writing*› **3** fig (unfathomable, inscrutable) 难以捉摸的 ‹*face, expression*›

unreadiness /ʌnˈredɪnɪs/ *n* [u] **1** (lack of preparation) 无准备 **2** (unwillingness) 不愿意

unready /ʌnˈredi/ *adj* **1** (not prepared) 无准备的; **to be ~ for sth.** 没有为某事做好准备 **2** (not willing) 不愿意的; **to be ~ to do sth.** 不情愿做某事; **I'm ~ to go along with that idea** 我不太同意那个想法

unreal /ʌnˈrɪəl/ *adj* **1** (so strange as to appear imaginary) 不真实的; (unrealistic) 不现实的; **there was something ~ about the conversation** 谈话有点儿离谱 **2** esp Amer colloq pej (unbelievable in behaviour) 不可能的 **3** esp Amer colloq (amazingly good) 非常棒的

unrealistic /ˌʌnrɪəˈlɪstɪk/ *adj* 不切实际的; **to be ~ about sth.** 在某事上不实事求是; **it is ~ to suggest that ...** 建议…不现实

unrealistically /ˌʌnrɪəˈlɪstɪkli/ *adv* 不切实际地; **to talk rather ~ about sth.** 空谈某事

unreality /ˌʌnrɪˈælətɪ/ *n* [u] 不真实; **to have a sense of ~** 有一种不真实感

unrealizable /ʌnˈrɪəlaɪzəbl/ *adj* 不能实现的

unrealized /ʌnˈrɪəlaɪzd/ *adj* **1** (not achieved) 未实现的 ‹*ambition, potential*›; **to be** *or* **remain ~** 未能实现 **2** Fin 未变现的 ‹*asset, profit*›

unreasonable /ʌnˈriːznəbl/ *adj* **1** (irrational) 不讲道理的 **2** (excessive) 过分的; **at an ~ hour** 在晚得离谱的时候

unreasonableness /ʌnˈriːznəblnɪs/ *n* [u] **1** (irrationality) 不讲道理; **the ~ of her behaviour** 她行为的不合理 **2** (excessiveness) 过分; **the ~ of the strikers' demands** 罢工者所提的过高要求

unreasonably /ʌnˈriːznəbli/ *adv* **1** (irrationally) 不讲道理地; **not ~** 并非不合理地; **consent shall not be ~ withheld** Jur 同意不得无故撤销 **2** (excessively) 过分地; **~ late at night** 深更半夜的

unreasoning /ʌnˈriːzənɪŋ/ *adj* (not exercising reason) 不理智的 ‹*person, response*›; (not having reason) 无缘无故的 ‹*panic*›

unreceptive /ˌʌnrɪˈseptɪv/ *adj* 不愿接受的; **to be ~ to sth.** 不会接受某事物

unreclaimed /ˌʌnrɪˈkleɪmd/ *adj* 未开垦的

unrecognizable /ʌnˈrekəgnaɪzəbl/ *adj* 难以辨认的; **to be (absolutely** *or* **quite) ~** (完全) 无法识别; **to be ~ as sth.** 辨认不出是某物

unrecognized /ʌnˈrekəgnaɪzd/ *adj* **1** (not realized) 未被意识到的 ‹*danger*›; (not acknowledged) 被忽略的 ‹*significance*›; **to go ~** 被忽视 **2** (not identified) 未被认出的 ‹*person*› **3** (not appreciated) 未得到赏识的 ‹*genius, achievement*›; **to be ~ by sb.** 得不到某人的认可 **4** Pol 未被承认的 ‹*regime*›

unreconstructed /ˌʌnriːkənˈstrʌktɪd/ *adj attrib* (not reconciled) 顽固守旧的; (not converted) 不顺应形势的; **~ Nazi/bigot/believer** 顽固的纳粹分子/偏执者/信徒

unrecorded /ˌʌnrɪˈkɔːdɪd/ *adj* **1** (not written down) 未记录的 **2** (not recorded in sound) 未录音的

unredeemed /ˌʌnrɪˈdiːmd/ *adj* **1** Fin 未赎回的 ‹*pledge, mortgage*›; 未偿还的 ‹*bill, debt*› **2** (not fulfilled) 未履行的 ‹*promise*› **3** Relig 未得救的 ‹*sinner*› **4** (not compensated for) 未弥补的; **to be ~ by sth.** 未得到某事物补救

unreel /ʌnˈrɪəl/
A *vt* 退绕 ‹*line, hose*›; 绕回 ‹*film*›
B *vi* ‹*line, hose*› 退绕; ‹*film*› 绕回

unrefined /ˌʌnrɪˈfaɪnd/ *adj* **1** Ind 未提炼的 ‹*sugar, petroleum*› **2** fig (not polished) 粗俗的 ‹*speech*›; (uncultured) 无教养的 ‹*person, behaviour*›

unreflecting /ˌʌnrɪˈflektɪŋ/ *adj* **1** (not thoughtful) 欠考虑的; **an ~ act** 轻率的举动 **2** (not reflecting light) 不反光的

unreformed /ˌʌnrɪˈfɔːmd/ *adj* 未改革的 ‹*body, society, church*›; 未悔改的 ‹*person, criminal*›

unrefrigerated /ˌʌnrɪˈfrɪdʒəreɪtɪd/ *adj* 未冷藏的

unregarded /ˌʌnrɪˈgɑːdɪd/ *adj* 不重视的; **to pass** *or* **go ~** 被忽视

unregistered /ʌnˈredʒɪstəd/ *adj* 未登记的 ‹*vehicle, birth*›; 未挂号的 ‹*letter*›

unregretted /ˌʌnrɪˈgretɪd/ *adj* 无人惋惜的; **he will die ~** 他死了不会有人觉得可惜的

unrehearsed /ˌʌnrɪˈhɜːst/ *adj* **1** (performed without rehearsal) 未排练的 ‹*play*›; 即兴的 ‹*speech*› **2** (not planned) 无准备的; (without forethought) 未事先考虑的

unrelated /ˌʌnrɪˈleɪtɪd/ *adj* **1** (not logically connected) 不相关的 ‹*event, argument*›; **to be ~ to sth.** 与某事物无关 **2** (not connected by

U

family) 无亲缘关系的 ‹*person*›; 不属于同一科的 ‹*thing*›

unrelenting /ˌʌnrɪˈlentɪŋ/ *adj* [1] (not diminishing) 持续的 ‹*pressure, pursuit, pace*›; 未减弱的 ‹*heat, rain, barrage, zeal*› [2] (unyielding) 不屈服的; **to be ~ in sth.** 在某事上不屈不挠

unreliability /ˌʌnrɪˌlaɪəˈbɪləti/ *n* [u] 不可靠

unreliable /ˌʌnrɪˈlaɪəbl/ *adj* 不可靠的

unrelieved /ˌʌnrɪˈliːvd/ *adj* 未缓和的; **to be ~ by sth.** 未因某事物得到缓和; **a life of ~ misery** 持续不变的悲惨生活

unremarkable /ˌʌnrɪˈmɑːkəbl/ *adj* 平凡的

unremarked /ˌʌnrɪˈmɑːkt/ *adj* 未被注意的; **to go** *or* **pass ~** 未被人注意; **to slip out ~** 偷偷溜出去

unremitting /ˌʌnrɪˈmɪtɪŋ/ *adj* 持续的 ‹*care, demands, boredom, hostility*›; 不懈的 ‹*effort, struggle*›; **to be ~ in sth.** 对某事不松懈

unremittingly /ˌʌnrɪˈmɪtɪŋli/ *adv* 不停地 ‹*continue, attack*›; 持续地 ‹*attentive, dull*›

unremunerative /ˌʌnrɪˈmjuːnərətɪv/ *adj* 不赚钱的

unrepealed /ˌʌnrɪˈpiːld/ *adj* 未被撤销的

unrepeatable /ˌʌnrɪˈpiːtəbl/ *adj* [1] (unique) 不能重复的; **the experiment is ~ in normal conditions** 这个实验在正常条件下是不可重复的 [2] (vulgar) 粗鲁的

unrepentant /ˌʌnrɪˈpentənt/ *adj* 不悔悟的; **to remain ~ (about sth.)** （对某事）不思悔改

unreported /ˌʌnrɪˈpɔːtɪd/ *adj* 未报告的; **the event/incident went ~** 该事件/这件事未被报道

unrepresentative /ˌʌnreprɪˈzentətɪv/ *adj* [1] (not typical) 不典型的 [2] (not representative) 无代表性的; **to be ~ of sth.** 不能代表某事物

unrepresented /ˌʌnreprɪˈzentɪd/ *adj* 无代表的; **the accused appeared before the bench ~** 被告在没有律师辩护的情况下出庭

unrequited /ˌʌnrɪˈkwaɪtɪd/ *adj* 单相思的; **to be tortured by ~ passion** *or* **love** 受单恋的折磨

unreserved /ˌʌnrɪˈzɜːvd/ *adj* [1] (free) 空着的; (not allocated) 未被预订的 [2] *usu attrib* (wholehearted) 毫无保留的; **to have sb.'s ~ admiration** 受到某人的真心仰慕

unreservedly /ˌʌnrɪˈzɜːvɪdli/ ▸**p. 29** *adv* 毫无保留地; **I accept your apology ~** 我真心接受你的道歉

unresisting /ˌʌnrɪˈzɪstɪŋ/ *adj* 不反抗的; **she was led away to prison ~** 她顺从地被带走，关进了监狱

unresolved /ˌʌnrɪˈzɒlvd/ *adj* 未解决的; **an ~ mystery** 未解开的谜团

unresponsive /ˌʌnrɪˈspɒnsɪv/ *adj* 反应迟钝的; **to be ~ to sth.** 对某事毫无反应

unrest /ʌnˈrest/ *n* [u] [1] (rebellious dissatisfaction) 动乱; **to stir up** *or* **foment ~** 激起骚乱; **civil/industrial/political ~** 平民/工业/政治动乱 [2] (agitation, uneasiness) 焦虑不安

unrestrained /ˌʌnrɪˈstreɪnd/ *adj* 无节制的; **~ laughter** 开怀大笑; **to be ~ by sth.** 不受某事物的约束

unrestricted /ˌʌnrɪˈstrɪktɪd/ *adj* 不受限制的; **to have ~ use of sth.** 可以随意使用某物

unrevealed /ˌʌnrɪˈviːld/ *adj* [1] (undetected) 未被发现的; **these problems, ~ until now, ...** 这些至今尚未暴露的问题… [2] (kept secret) 未泄露的; **~ funding for the rebels** 对叛乱者的秘密资助

unrevised /ˌʌnrɪˈvaɪzd/ *adj* 未修订的; **an ~ version** 原版

unrewarded /ˌʌnrɪˈwɔːdɪd/ *adj* 无报偿的; **to go ~** 未得到回报

unrewarding /ˌʌnrɪˈwɔːdɪŋ/ *adj* (unfulfilling) 不令人满意的; (thankless) 无好处的

unrighteous /ʌnˈraɪtʃəs/
[A] *adj* (sinful) 有罪的; (wicked) 邪恶的
[B] *npl* **the ~** 罪人

unripe /ʌnˈraɪp/ *adj* 未成熟的

unrivalled Brit, **unrivaled** Amer /ʌnˈraɪvld/ *adj* 无竞争对手的 ‹*person*›; 无与伦比的 ‹*reputation, collection*›; 至高无上的 ‹*power*›

unroadworthy /ʌnˈrəʊdwɜːði/ *adj* 不适合上路的 ‹*vehicle*›

unroll /ʌnˈrəʊl/ *vt, vi* 展开

unromantic /ˌʌnrəˈmæntɪk/ *adj* 不浪漫的 ‹*person, location*›; 不热烈的 ‹*gesture*›

unruffled /ʌnˈrʌfld/ *adj* [1] (calm) 平静的; **to be ~ (by sth.)** （对某事）处之泰然 [2] (smooth) 平滑的; **calm, ~ waters** 风平浪静的水域

unruled /ʌnˈruːld/ *adj* 未画线的 ‹*paper*›

unruly /ʌnˈruːli/ *adj* [1] (disruptive) 难控制的 ‹*crowd, behaviour*› [2] (wild) 不平整的; **an ~ mop of hair** 乱糟糟的头发

unsaddle /ʌnˈsædl/ *vt* [1] (remove saddle from) 给…卸鞍 ‹*horse*› [2] (unseat) 把…掀下马 ‹*rider*›

unsafe /ʌnˈseɪf/ *adj* [1] (dangerous) 不安全的 ‹*structure, method*› [2] (in danger) 身处险境的 ‹*person*› [3] Jur 证据不可靠的 ‹*verdict, conviction*›

unsaid /ʌnˈsed/
[A] *pt, pp* ▸**unsay**
[B] *adj* 未说出的; **to be** *or* **go ~** 没有讲出口; **to leave sth. ~** 不说出某事

unsalaried /ʌnˈsælərɪd/ *adj* 没有薪金的 ‹*post, staff*›

unsaleable, unsalable /ʌnˈseɪləbl/ *adj* 无销路的

unsalted /ʌnˈsɔːltɪd/ *adj* 不加盐的; **to boil sth. in ~ water** 用白水煮某物

unsatisfactorily /ˌʌnsætɪsˈfæktərəli/ *adv* 不令人满意地

unsatisfactory /ˌʌnsætɪsˈfæktəri/ *adj* 不令人满意的; **the service in the restaurant was very ~** 这家饭店的服务很差

unsatisfied /ʌnˈsætɪsfaɪd/ *adj* 未满足的; **to be ~ (with sth.)** 不满意（某事物）

unsatisfying /ʌnˈsætɪsfaɪɪŋ/ *adj* 不令人满意的

unsaturated /ʌnˈsætʃəreɪtɪd/ *adj* 不饱和的; **~ fat** 不饱和脂肪

unsavoury Brit, **unsavory** Amer /ʌnˈseɪvəri/ *adj* [1] (disagreeable to senses) 难闻的 ‹*smell*›; 难吃的 ‹*food*›; 难看的 ‹*sight*› [2] (objectionable) 讨厌的 ‹*person, reputation, detail*›

unsay /ʌnˈseɪ/ *vt* (*pt, pp* **unsaid**) 收回; **what's said cannot be unsaid** 一言既出，驷马难追

unscathed /ʌnˈskeɪðd/ *adj* 未受伤害的 ‹*person*›; 未受损害的 ‹*reputation*›

unscented /ʌnˈsentɪd/ *adj* 无香味的

unscheduled /ʌnˈʃedjuːld, Amer ʌnˈskedʒʊld/ *adj* 事先未安排的 ‹*halt, appearance*›

unscholarly /ʌnˈskɒləli/ *adj* 非学术性的 ‹*approach*›; 没有学问的 ‹*person*›; 没有学术含量的 ‹*work*›

unschooled /ʌnˈskuːld/ *adj* [1] (without education) 缺乏教育的; **to be ~ in sth.** 在某方面无知 [2] Equit 未驯化的 ‹*horse*›

unscientific /ˌʌnsaɪənˈtɪfɪk/ *adj* [1] (without scientific principles) 不科学的 ‹*approach, argument*› [2] (not skilled at science) 不懂科学的 ‹*person*›

unscramble /ʌnˈskræmbl/ *vt* [1] (decode) 译出 ‹*code, message*› [2] (restore to order) 整理 ‹*thoughts*›

unscratched /ʌnˈskrætʃt/ *adj* 未刮擦的 ‹*vehicle*›; 未损坏的 ‹*paintwork*›; **he emerged from the wreckage ~** 他毫发无损地爬出了废墟

unscrew /ʌnˈskruː/
[A] *vt* [1] (loosen) 拧开 ‹*lid, nut*› [2] (unfasten) 拧下…的螺丝 ‹*sign*›
[B] *vi* «*lid, nut*» 被拧开

unscripted /ʌnˈskrɪptɪd/ *adj* 不用稿子的; **to give an ~ speech** 脱稿演讲

unscrupulous /ʌnˈskruːpjʊləs/ *adj* 不道德的; **to be ~ in sth.** 在某方面不择手段

unscrupulously /ʌnˈskruːpjʊləsli/ *adv* 不道德地; **to treat sb. ~** 不公正地对待某人

unscrupulousness /ʌnˈskruːpjʊləsnɪs/ *n* [u] 不道德

unseal /ʌnˈsiːl/ *vt* [1] (break seal of) 去掉…的封条 ‹*box, container*› [2] (open) 开启 ‹*envelope*›

unsealed /ʌnˈsiːld/ *adj* 未密封的

unseasonable /ʌnˈsiːznəbl/ *adj* [1] (unusual for time of year) = **unseasonal** [2] liter (untimely) 不合时宜的; **at an ~ hour** 在不适当的时候

unseasonably /ʌnˈsiːznəbli/ *adv* 不合时令地; **to be ~ hot/cold** 天气热得反常/冷得反常

unseasonal /ʌnˈsiːzənl/ *adj* (unusual for time of year) 不合节令的; (inappropriate for time of year) 不合时令的

unseasoned /ʌnˈsiːznd/ *adj* [1] Culin 未加调料的 ‹*food*› [2] (not matured) 未经干燥处理的 ‹*timber*› [3] fig (inexperienced) 无经验的 ‹*soldier*›

unseat /ʌnˈsiːt/ *vt* [1] Equit 使…掉下马 ‹*rider*› [2] Pol 使…下台 ‹*MP*›

unseaworthy /ʌnˈsiːwɜːði/ *adj* 不适于航海的 ‹*vessel*›

unsecured /ˌʌnsɪˈkjʊəd/ *adj* [1] Fin 无担保的 ‹*loan*› [2] (not fixed) 未固定的 ‹*ladder*›; 未锁上的 ‹*door*›; 未扎紧的 ‹*hair*›

unseeded /ʌnˈsiːdɪd/ *adj* [1] (without seeds) 无籽的 ‹*grape*› [2] Sport 未列为种子的 ‹*player*› [3] Agric 未播种的 ‹*land*›

unseeing /ʌnˈsiːɪŋ/ *adj* liter 视而不见的; **to gaze at sb. with ~ eyes** 茫然凝视某人

unseemly /ʌnˈsiːmli/ *adj* 不得体的

unseen /ʌnˈsiːn/
[A] *adj* [1] (unperceived) 看不见的; **to slip away ~** 偷偷溜走 [2] Brit Sch 即席的 ‹*translation*›; 无准备的 ‹*exam*›
[B] *n* Brit 即席翻译的文章; **a French ~** 一篇法语即席翻译

unselfconscious /ˌʌnselfˈkɒnʃəs/ *adj* 自然大方的

unselfconsciously /ˌʌnselfˈkɒnʃəsli/ *adv* 自然大方地

unselfish /ʌnˈselfɪʃ/ *adj* 无私的 ‹*person, behaviour, act*›

unselfishly /ʌnˈselfɪʃli/ *adv* 无私地

unselfishness /ʌnˈselfɪʃnɪs/ *n* (state) 无私; (behaviour) 无私行为; **~ in doing sth.** 做某事的慷慨

unsent /ʌnˈsent/ *adj* 未发出的

unsentimental /ˌʌnsentɪˈmentl/ *adj* 不带感情的

unserviceable /ʌnˈsɜːvɪsəbl/ *adj* 不能使用的 ‹*tool, telephone, bicycle*›; 不能运转的 ‹*machine*›

unsettle /ʌnˈsetl/ *vt* 使…担忧 ‹*person*›; 扰乱 ‹*market*›; 使…紊乱 ‹*stomach*›

unsettled /ʌnˈsetld/ *adj* [1] (unstable, upset) 不稳定的 ‹*conditions, market*›; 翻腾的 ‹*stomach*›; **I feel very ~ at work** 我工作时感觉焦躁不安 [2] (uncertain) 多变的 ‹*weather, prospects*› [3] (unresolved) 未解决的 ‹*dispute, issue*› [4] Fin (not paid) 未支付的 ‹*bill*›; 未偿还的 ‹*debt*› [5] Geog (without settlers) 无人居住的 ‹*region*›

unsettling /ʌnˈsetlɪŋ/ *adj* 令人不安的; **psychologically ~** 使人心绪不宁的

unsexy /ʌnˈseksi/ *adj* 不性感的 ‹*person, clothes*›; 无性感镜头的 ‹*film*›

U

unshackle /ʌnˈʃækl/ *vt* 1 (release from chains) 去掉…的镣铐 2 fig (set free) 发挥 ‹*talent*›; 释放 ‹*energy*›; 解放 ‹*worker*›

unshaded /ʌnˈʃeɪdɪd/ *adj* 1 (having no shade) 无灯罩的 ‹*lamp*› 2 (exposed to sunlight) 无荫蔽的 ‹*patch*› 3 Art (not coloured in) 无色调差别的 ‹*part of picture, area*›

unshakeable, unshakable /ʌnˈʃeɪkəbl/ *adj* 不可动摇的; **he's quite ~ in his convictions** 他对自己的信念坚定不移

unshakeably, unshakably /ʌnˈʃeɪkəbli/ *adv* 不可动摇地; **to remain ~ convinced that ...** 依然坚信…

unshaken /ʌnˈʃeɪkən/ *adj* 坚定的; **to be ~ in sth.** 在某方面不动摇

unshapely /ʌnˈʃeɪpli/ *adj* 不匀称的 ‹*figure, legs*›; 不合身的 ‹*clothes*›

unshaven /ʌnˈʃeɪvn/ *adj* 未剃须的

unsheathe /ʌnˈʃiːð/ *vt* 拔…出鞘 ‹*knife*›; 拔出 ‹*weapon*›

unship /ʌnˈʃɪp/ *vt* (*pres p etc.* **-pp-**) 从船上卸下 ‹*cargo*›

unshockable /ʌnˈʃɒkəbl/ *adj* 处变不惊的

unshod /ʌnˈʃɒd/ *adj* 没有穿鞋的 ‹*person*›; 没有钉蹄铁的 ‹*horse*›

unshrinkable /ʌnˈʃrɪŋkəbl/ *adj* 不缩水的

unsighted /ʌnˈsaɪtɪd/ *adj* 1 (blind) 瞎的 2 Sport (without a clear view) 看不清的 ‹*player, referee*›

unsightliness /ʌnˈsaɪtlɪnɪs/ *n* [u] 不悦目

unsightly /ʌnˈsaɪtli/ *adj* 不悦目的

unsigned /ʌnˈsaɪnd/ *adj* 未签名的

unsinkable /ʌnˈsɪŋkəbl/ *adj* 不会下沉的

unskilful Brit, **unskillful** Amer /ʌnˈskɪlfl/ *adj* 无技能的

unskilfully Brit, **unskillfully** Amer /ʌnˈskɪlfəli/ *adv* 不熟练地

unskilled /ʌnˈskɪld/ *adj* 1 (not having training) 未受专门训练的; (not requiring training) 无需专门训练的; **a shortage of ~ labour** 非技术性劳动力的缺乏 2 (not having skill) 无技能的; **to be ~ at sth.** 不擅长某事

unskimmed /ʌnˈskɪmd/ *adj* 全脂的; **~ milk** 全脂乳

unsliced /ʌnˈslaɪst/ *adj* 未切片的 ‹*bread*›

unsmiling /ʌnˈsmaɪlɪŋ/ *adj* (not smiling) 不笑的; (serious) 严肃的; (unfriendly) 不友好的

unsmoked /ʌnˈsməʊkt/ *adj* 未经烟熏的 ‹*bacon, fish*›

unsnarl /ʌnˈsnɑːl/ *vt* 解开…的缠结 ‹*threads*›; 理顺 ‹*traffic jam*›

unsociability /ʌnˌsəʊʃəˈbɪləti/ *n* [u] (not being sociable) 不爱交际; (being withdrawn) 性格内向

unsociable /ʌnˈsəʊʃəbl/ *adj* 1 (not sociable) 不爱交际的; (withdrawn) 性格内向的 2 (socially inconvenient) 不利于交际的; **to work ~ hours** 在非正常工作时间上班

unsocial /ʌnˈsəʊʃl/ *adj* 1 Brit (socially inconvenient) **~ hours** 非正常上班时间 2 (antisocial, disruptive) 反社会的 ‹*person, behaviour*›

unsold /ʌnˈsəʊld/ *adj* 未售出的

unsoldierly /ʌnˈsəʊldʒəli/ *adj* 不像军人的

unsolicited /ˌʌnsəˈlɪsɪtɪd/ *adj* 自动发出的 ‹*mail*›; 主动提出的 ‹*help, advice*›; 未经要求的 ‹*comment, criticism*›

unsolvable /ʌnˈsɒlvəbl/ *adj* 无法解决的 ‹*problem*›; 无法侦破的 ‹*crime*›; 无法解释的 ‹*mystery*›

unsolved /ʌnˈsɒlvd/ *adj* 未解决的 ‹*problem*›; 未侦破的 ‹*crime*›; 未解释的 ‹*mystery*›

unsophisticated /ˌʌnsəˈfɪstɪkeɪtɪd/ *adj* 1 (lacking worldly knowledge) 天真的 ‹*person, reader*›; 单纯的 ‹*taste, mind*›; 质朴的 ‹*style, film*›; **an ~ wine** 味道纯的葡萄酒 2 (basic) 基本的; **an ~ but effective tool/method** 简单而有效的工具/方法

unsought /ʌnˈsɔːt/ *adj* 未经请求的; **to come ~** 不请自来; **to offer one's ~ opinions** 主动提出意见

unsound /ʌnˈsaʊnd/ *adj* 1 (in poor condition) 破旧的 ‹*structure, bridge*›; 腐烂的 ‹*fruit, timber*› 2 (unhealthy) 不健康的 ‹*body, constitution*›; 不佳的 ‹*health*›; **to be of ~ mind** Jur 精神失常 3 (not logically valid) 谬误的 ‹*argument*› 4 (financially unreliable) 资金上不可靠的 ‹*bank, investment*›

unsparing /ʌnˈspeərɪŋ/ *adj* 1 (lavish) 不吝惜的; **~ generosity** 慷慨大方; **to be ~ in one's efforts to do sth.** 不遗余力做某事 2 (merciless) 无情的; **to be ~ in sth.** 在某方面很严厉

unsparingly /ʌnˈspeərɪŋli/ *adv* 1 (lavishly) 不吝惜地 2 (mercilessly) 无情地

unspeakable /ʌnˈspiːkəbl/ *adj* 1 (dreadful) 可怕的 ‹*cruelty, crime, nonsense*› 2 (inexpressible) 难以形容的 ‹*delight*›

unspeakably /ʌnˈspiːkəbli/ *adv* 1 (dreadfully) 可怕地; **a crime that was ~ vile** 极其卑鄙的罪行 2 (inexpressibly) 难以形容地; **~ beautiful/romantic** 美/浪漫得难以形容

unspecified /ʌnˈspesɪfaɪd/ *adj* 未确定的 ‹*date, individual*›

unspectacular /ˌʌnspekˈtækjʊlə(r)/ *adj* 平淡无奇的

unspent /ʌnˈspent/ *adj* 未花费的

unspoilt /ʌnˈspɔɪlt/, **unspoiled** /ʌnˈspɔɪld/ *adj* 1 (not damaged) 未遭破坏的 ‹*flavour, paintwork*›; 未腐坏的 ‹*food, wine*› 2 (unchanged by development) 未遭破坏的; **~ views of the countryside** 未丧失自然美的乡村景色 3 (not ruined in character) 未被宠坏的

unspoken /ʌnˈspəʊkən/ *adj* 1 (secret) 秘密的; (unexpressed) 未表达的; **~ fears** 无以名状的恐惧; **~ longing** 默默的渴望 2 (implicit) 心照不宣的; **~ consent** 默许

unsporting /ʌnˈspɔːtɪŋ/ *adj* (not fair) 不公平的; (not generous) 不大度的; (not sporting) 无体育道德的

unsportsmanlike /ʌnˈspɔːtsmənlaɪk/ *adj* 无运动员风范的; **~ conduct** 有失运动员风度的行为

unstable /ʌnˈsteɪbl/ *adj* 1 (not firm) 不稳固的 ‹*load, structure*› 2 (likely to change) 不稳定的 ‹*situation*› 3 (unbalanced) 反复无常的 ‹*person*›; **to be (mentally/emotionally) ~** (心理/情绪) 易波动

unstained /ʌnˈsteɪnd/ *adj* 1 (not coloured with stain) 未上色的 ‹*wood, surface, glass*› 2 (without blemishes) 未沾污的 3 liter (unsullied) 未被玷污的; **to be ~ (by sth.)** 没有受到 (某事物的) 玷污

unstamped /ʌnˈstæmpt/ *adj* 1 (not marked by stamping) 未盖印的 ‹*form*› 2 (unfranked) 未贴邮票的 ‹*envelope*›

unstated /ʌnˈsteɪtɪd/ *adj* 未陈述的; **~ assumptions** 未说明的假定; **an ~ agreement** 心照不宣的协定

unstatesmanlike /ʌnˈsteɪtsmənlaɪk/ *adj* 不像政治家的; **~ behaviour** 与政治家身份不相称的行为

unsteadily /ʌnˈstedɪli/ *adv* 1 (shakily) 不平稳地; **to sway ~ forwards** 踉踉跄跄地向前走 2 (irregularly) 无规律地; (in non-uniform manner) 不一致地

unsteadiness /ʌnˈstedɪnɪs/ *n* [u] (lack of steadiness) 不平稳; (lack of firmness) 不牢固; **the ~ of the old man's gait** 老人蹒跚的步态

unsteady /ʌnˈstedi/ *adj* 1 (shaky) 站不稳的 ‹*person*›; 不平稳的 ‹*steps*›; 颤抖的 ‹*hand, voice*›; **to be ~ on one's feet** 站不稳 2 (irregular) 无规律的 ‹*pulse, rhythm*›; 不稳定的 ‹*flame*› 3 (fluctuating) 波动的 ‹*market, prices*›

unsterilized /ʌnˈsterəlaɪzd/ *adj* 未消毒的

unstick /ʌnˈstɪk/ *vt* (*pt, pp* **unstuck**) 扯下 ‹*wallpaper, label*›; 撕开 ‹*envelope*›; **the company came badly unstuck over that deal** colloq 公司因那次交易而遭受重大损失

unstinting /ʌnˈstɪntɪŋ/ *adj* 慷慨的; **~ devotion** 无限忠诚; **to be ~ in one's efforts to do sth.** 不遗余力做某事; **to be ~ in one's praise of sb.** 对某人大加赞赏

unstitch /ʌnˈstɪtʃ/ *vt* 拆…的缝线; **to come ~ed** 脱线

unstop /ʌnˈstɒp/ *vt* (*pres p etc.* **-pp-**) 疏通 ‹*pipe, toilet*›; 拔掉…的塞子 ‹*bottle*›

unstoppable /ʌnˈstɒpəbl/ *adj* (unable to be stopped) 不可阻挡的; (unable to be prevented) 不可预防的; **he unleashed an ~ shot high into the net** 他射出的高球势不可挡地钻进球网

unstrap /ʌnˈstræp/ (*pres p etc.* **-pp-**) *vt* 解开…的带子

unstressed /ʌnˈstrest/ *adj* 1 (not under pressure) 心态平和的 ‹*person*›; 无压力的 ‹*work*›; 不受力的 ‹*position*› 2 Ling 非重读的 ‹*syllable, vowel, word*›

unstring /ʌnˈstrɪŋ/ *vt* 1 (*pt, pp* **unstrung**) (remove strings from) 解下…的弦 ‹*racket, violin*› 2 (take from a string) 从线上取下 ‹*beads*›; **to come unstrung** 从线串上脱落 3 (unnerve) 使…紧张不安 ‹*person*›; 使…不稳定 ‹*nerves*›

unstructured /ʌnˈstrʌktʃəd/ *adj* (without structure) 结构凌乱的; (without systematic organization) 无条理的

unstrung /ʌnˈstrʌŋ/
A *pt, pp* ▸**unstring**
B *adj* 1 (without strings) 弦线拆下的; **to come ~** 弦线断了 2 (distressed) 紧张不安的 ‹*person*›; 紧张的 ‹*nerves*›

unstuck /ʌnˈstʌk/ *pt, pp* ▸**unstick**

unstudied /ʌnˈstʌdɪd/ *adj* 不做作的; **the ~ grace of the dancer's movements** 舞蹈演员动作的自然优雅

unstylish /ʌnˈstaɪlɪʃ/ *n* 不漂亮的

unsubdued /ˌʌnsəbˈdjuːd, Amer -ˈduːd/ *adj* 不屈服的

unsubscribe /ˌʌnsəbˈskraɪb/ *vi* 取消订阅

unsubsidized /ʌnˈsʌbsɪdaɪzd/ *adj* 未受资助的

unsubstantial /ˌʌnsəbˈstænʃl/ *adj* 不丰盛的 ‹*meal*›; 不结实的 ‹*structure*›

unsubstantiated /ˌʌnsəbˈstænʃɪeɪtɪd/ *adj* (not proved to be true) 未经证实的; (not backed up by evidence) 无事实根据的

unsuccessful /ˌʌnsəkˈsesfl/ *adj* 不成功的; **to be ~ in** *or* **with sth.** 在某事上失败

unsuccessfully /ˌʌnsəkˈsesfəli/ *adv* 不成功地

unsuitability /ʌnˌsuːtəˈbɪləti/ *n* [u] 不合适; **his ~ for the job** 他不适合这份工作

unsuitable /ʌnˈsuːtəbl/ *adj* 不合适的; **the job is ~ for him** 这份工作不适合他; **she is ~ for you/the position** 她不适合你/这个职位; **to be ~ for young children** «*film*» 儿童不宜

unsuitably /ʌnˈsuːtəbli/ *adv* 不合适地; **to be ~ matched** 不般配; **he is ~ qualified for the job** 他做那份工作不合格

unsuited /ʌnˈsuːtɪd/ *adj* 1 (not appropriate) 不适合的; **to be ~ to** *or* **for sb./sth.** 对某人/某事物来说不适合 2 (not emotionally suited) 志趣不相投的; **to be ~ to sb.** 与某人不般配

unsullied /ʌnˈsʌlɪd/ *adj* liter 1 (clean) 洁净的 2 (free from stigma) 未受玷污的; **to be ~ (by sth.)** 未受 (某事物) 玷污; **an ~ reputation** 清白的名声

unsung /ʌnˈsʌŋ/ *adj* 未被颂扬的 ‹*worker, achievements*›; **the ~ heroes of this forgotten war** 这场被遗忘的战争中的无名英雄

unsupervised /ˌʌnˈsuːpəvaɪzd/ *adj* 无人监督的; **the children were left ～** 孩子们无人照看

unsupported /ˌʌnsəˈpɔːtɪd/ *adj* **1** (without material support) 无资助的 **2** esp Mil (lacking supplies) 无支援的; **to advance ～** 无掩护地前进 **3** (not held up) 无支撑的 ‹*structure*› **4** (unsubstantiated) 未经证实的 ‹*argument, theory, accusation*› **5** Comput 无支持的 ‹*software, hardware*›

unsupportive /ˌʌnsəˈpɔːtɪv/ *adj* (not encouraging) 不鼓励的; (not helpful) 不支持的

unsure /ʌnˈʃɔː(r), Amer -ˈʃʊər/ *adj* **1** (not certain) 不确知的; **to be ～ of sth.** 对某事物没有把握 **2** (lacking in confidence) 缺乏信心的; **to be ～ of oneself** 缺乏自信

unsurpassable /ˌʌnsəˈpɑːsəbl, Amer -ˈpæs-/ *adj* 不可超越的; **～ magnificence/skill** 无与伦比的壮丽/绝技; **a girl of ～ beauty** 美丽绝伦的少女

unsurpassed /ˌʌnsəˈpɑːst, Amer -ˈpæs-/ *adj* 卓越的; **to be ～ (in sth.)** （在某事上）出类拔萃; **to be ～ by sth.** 不被某物胜过

unsurprising /ˌʌnsəˈpraɪzɪŋ/ *adj* 不足为奇的; **it is ～ that ...** …不出预料

unsurprisingly /ˌʌnsəˈpraɪzɪŋli/ *adv* 不足为奇地; **～, she didn't show up** 不出所料，她没有出现

unsuspected /ˌʌnsəˈspektɪd/ *adj* **1** (not known about) 未知的; **～ talent** 潜藏的才能; **～ difficulties** 始料不及的困难 **2** (not under suspicion) 不受怀疑的; **to be** *or* **remain ～** 没有嫌疑

unsuspecting /ˌʌnsəˈspektɪŋ/ *adj* 不怀疑的; **completely ～** 毫无猜疑的; **an ～ victim** 毫无戒心的受害人

unsuspicious /ˌʌnsəˈspɪʃəs/ *adj* (feeling no suspicion) 无疑心的 ‹*person*›; (causing no suspicion) 不令人怀疑的 ‹*behaviour*›

unsustainable /ˌʌnsəˈsteɪnəbl/ *adj* **1** (not maintainable) 无法维持的 ‹*situation, level*› **2** Ecol 破坏生态平衡的 ‹*practice*› **3** (indefensible) 无法辩护的 ‹*claim*›

unswayed /ʌnˈsweɪd/ *adj* 不受影响的; **to be ～ (by sth.)** 不受（某事物）影响

unsweetened /ʌnˈswiːtnd/ *adj* (without added sugar) 未加糖的; (without other sweetener) 未加甜味素的

unswept /ʌnˈswept/ *adj* 未打扫过的

unswerving /ʌnˈswɜːvɪŋ/ *adj* **1** (not turning aside) 直的; **to follow/set an ～ course** fig 走/确定一条笔直的路线 **2** (steady, constant) 不渝的; **to be ～ in one's affections/allegiance** 对感情专一/忠诚程度始终如一

unswervingly /ʌnˈswɜːvɪŋli/ *adv* 坚定不移地; **to be ～ faithful** 忠诚不渝

unsymmetrical /ˌʌnsɪˈmetrɪkl/ *adj* 不对称的

unsympathetic /ˌʌnsɪmpəˈθetɪk/ *adj* **1** (uncaring) 不同情的; **to be ～ to sb.** 对某人冷漠; **don't be so ～!** 不要这么无动于衷！ **2** (unlikeable) 不讨人喜欢的 ‹*person, character*› **3** (not to one's taste) 相违的; **to be ～ to sth.** 与某事物不一致

unsympathetically /ˌʌnsɪmpəˈθetɪkli/ *adv* 不同情地

unsystematic /ˌʌnsɪstəˈmætɪk/ *adj* 杂乱无章的

unsystematically /ˌʌnsɪstəˈmætɪkli/ *adv* 杂乱无章地; **to go about things ～** 做事没有条理

untainted /ʌnˈteɪntɪd/ *adj* 未腐坏的 ‹*food*›; 未被玷污的 ‹*reputation, person*›; **to be ～ by sth.** 未受某物污染

untameable, untamable /ʌnˈteɪməbl/ *adj* 不可驯养的 ‹*animal*›; 无法控制的 ‹*fury, appetite*›

untamed /ʌnˈteɪmd/ *adj* 野性的 ‹*animal, beauty, instinct*›; 未受抑制的 ‹*passion*›

untangle /ʌnˈtæŋgl/ *vt* **1** (bring out of twisted state) 解开; **to ～ sth. from sth.** 把某物从某物上解下来 **2** fig (extricate) 理清; **to ～ oneself (from sth.)** （从某事物中）脱身

untanned /ʌnˈtænd/ *adj* **1** (not suntanned) 未晒黑的 **2** (not converted into leather) 未鞣的

untapped /ʌnˈtæpt/ *adj* (not yet used) 未利用的; (not yet exploited) 未开发的; **～ talents** 潜藏的天赋

untarnished /ʌnˈtɑːnɪʃt/ *adj* **1** lit (still bright) 未失去光泽的 ‹*metal, mirror*› **2** fig (free from blemishes) 清白的; **to be ～ (by sth.)** 未受（某事物）玷污

untasted /ʌnˈteɪstɪd/ *adj* **1** (not sampled) 未尝过的; **she left the meal ～** 她把饭菜搁着一口未动 **2** fig (not experienced) 未体验过的 ‹*pleasure, delight*›

untaught /ʌnˈtɔːt/ *adj* **1** (not instructed) 未受教育的; **an ～ genius** 无师自通的天才 **2** (not acquired by teaching) 天生的 ‹*ability*›

untaxable /ʌnˈtæksəbl/ *adj* 不可征税的

untaxed /ʌnˈtækst/ *adj* 免税的

unteachable /ʌnˈtiːtʃəbl/ *adj* **1** (unresponsive to teaching) 不可教的 ‹*person*› **2** (unable to be taught to sb.) 不适合教的 ‹*subject, course*›; 无法传授的 ‹*skill, language*›

untempered /ʌnˈtempəd/ *adj* **1** Ind 未回火的 ‹*metal*› **2** fig (not moderated) 无节制的 ‹*lust, greed*›; **to be ～ (by sth.)** 不受（某事物）控制

untenable /ʌnˈtenəbl/ *adj* 站不住脚的

untended /ʌnˈtendɪd/ *adj* 无人照看的 ‹*flock, child, garden*›

untested /ʌnˈtestɪd/ *adj* **1** (not yet proved) 未经检验的 ‹*theory, product*›; 未经试验的 ‹*method, drug*› **2** (inexperienced) 未经考验的; **to be ～ in sth.** 未经受某事物的考验

unthinkable /ʌnˈθɪŋkəbl/ *adj* 难以想象的; **it is ～ that ...** 难以置信的是…

unthinking /ʌnˈθɪŋkɪŋ/ *adj* **1** (inconsiderate) 欠考虑的; **to throw out ～ remarks** 随便说话 **2** (careless) 粗心的

unthinkingly /ʌnˈθɪŋkɪŋli/ *adv* 欠考虑地; **she dropped the match ～ on to the floor** 她随手将火柴扔在地板上

unthought of /ʌnˈθɔːt ɒv/ *adj* **1** (not imagined) 没想到的; **hitherto ～** 迄今尚未考虑过的; **an unthought-of piece of luck** 意外的幸运 **2** (unimaginable) 不可想象的

unthread /ʌnˈθred/ *vt* 从…中把线抽出

untidily /ʌnˈtaɪdɪli/ *adv* 凌乱地 ‹*scatter*›; 邋遢地 ‹*dress*›

untidiness /ʌnˈtaɪdɪnɪs/ *n* [u] (state) 凌乱; (trait) 不整洁

untidy /ʌnˈtaɪdi/ *adj* **1** (messy) 凌乱的; **please excuse the ～ writing** 笔迹潦草，万望见谅 **2** (unkempt) 不整洁的; **an ～-looking person** 看上去不修边幅的人

untie /ʌnˈtaɪ/ *vt* **1** (*pres p* **untying**) (undo) 解开 ‹*knot*›; **to come ～d** 松开 **2** (remove fastening from) 打开 ‹*package*› **3** (release from bonds) 给…松绑 ‹*prisoner, hands*›

until /ənˈtɪl/

A *prep* **1** (up to, as far as) 直到; **up ～ 2001/a year ago** 一直到 2001 年/一年前; **～ now** 到目前为止; **to stay ～ Monday** 一直待到星期一; **to wait ～ after Easter** 待到复活节以后; **stay on the bus ～ London** 到伦敦再下车 **2** (used with a negative) **not ... ～** 直到…才…; **they didn't ring ～ the next day** 直到第二天他们才打来电话; **not ～ then did she realize that ...** 直到那时她才意识到…

B *conj* **1** (up to the time when) 直到; **to wait ～ one is alone** 一直等到只剩下自己一个人 **2** (used with a negative) 在…以前; **I can't decide ～ I know the details** 我得了解了详情才能决定; **I won't leave ～ I've seen him** 我要到看见了他以后才离开; **don't look ～ I tell you to** 我让你看你再看

untilled /ʌnˈtɪld/ *adj* 未耕耘的

untimely /ʌnˈtaɪmli/ *adj* **1** (badly timed) 不适时的; **an ～ remark** 不合时宜的话 **2** (uncommonly early) 过早的 ‹*death, disappearance*›; **to come to an ～ end** «*person*» 夭折; «*activity, project*» 过早结束

untiring /ʌnˈtaɪərɪŋ/ *adj* 不知疲倦的 ‹*person*›; 不屈不挠的 ‹*effort*›; 持续不衰的 ‹*energy, enthusiasm*›; **to be ～ in sth.** 在某事上坚持不懈

untiringly /ʌnˈtaɪərɪŋli/ *adv* 孜孜不倦地 ‹*work, continue*›; 持续地 ‹*helpful*›

untold /ʌnˈtəʊld/ *adj* **1** (not quantifiable) 不可计量的; **～ millions/quantities of ...** 数百万/大量的…; **～ damage** 难以估计的破坏 **2** (endless) 无穷的 ‹*suffering, joy*› **3** liter (not told) 未讲过的; **no event is left ～** 事无巨细都讲完了

untouchable /ʌnˈtʌtʃəbl/

A *adj* **1** (unreachable) 管不了的; (invincible) 不可战胜的; **with protection from the police, these criminals are ～** 由于警方的庇护，这些罪犯得以逍遥法外 **2** (unrivalled) 无与伦比的 ‹*feat, beauty*› **3** (unmentionable) 不可提及的 ‹*topic, problem*› **4** (regarded as defiling) [旧时印度] 贱民的

B *n* 贱民 [旧时印度种姓制度下地位最低的阶层]

untouched /ʌnˈtʌtʃt/ *adj* **1** (unchanged) 未改变的; (undisturbed) 未受干扰的 **2** (undamaged) 未受损的 **3** (uneaten) 未吃过的

untoward /ˌʌntəˈwɔːd, Amer ʌnˈtɔːrd/ *adj* **1** (unforeseen) 未预见到的; (unfavourable) 不利的; (unfortunate) 不幸的; **nothing/something ～** 没有/有点儿意外情况 **2** (unseemly) 不适宜的 ‹*behaviour*›

untraceable /ʌnˈtreɪsəbl/ *adj* (not able to be traced) 难以追踪的; (not able to be discovered) 难以发现的

untraced /ʌnˈtreɪst/ *adj* (not traced) 未找到踪迹的; (not discovered) 未被发现的

untrained /ʌnˈtreɪnd/ *adj* **1** (having no education) 未受培训的 **2** (not disciplined) 未受训练的 ‹*eye, ear, mind, voice*› **3** (not taught to obey) 未驯顺的 ‹*animal*›

untrammelled Brit, **untrameled** Amer /ʌnˈtræmld/ *adj* liter (not restricted) 不受限制的; (able to act freely) 自由自在的

untranslatable /ˌʌntrænzˈleɪtəbl/ *adj* 不能翻译的

untravelled Brit, **untraveled** Amer /ʌnˈtrævld/ *adj* **1** (not having travelled) 未旅行过的 ‹*person*› **2** (not travelled over or through) 无人到过的 ‹*area*›; 无人走过的 ‹*route*›; **to be largely ～** 人迹罕至

untreatable /ʌnˈtriːtəbl/ *adj* 不能治疗的; **he has an ～ cancer** 他患了一种无法治愈的癌症

untreated /ʌnˈtriːtɪd/ *adj* 未治疗的

untrendy /ʌnˈtrendi/ *adj* colloq 不时髦的

untried /ʌnˈtraɪd/ *adj* **1** (untested) 未检验的; **raw ～ recruits** 未经考验的新兵; **to leave nothing ～** 用尽一切办法 **2** Jur 未经审讯的 ‹*prisoner*›

untrodden /ʌnˈtrɒdn/ *adj* liter 未被踩踏过的; **an ～ wilderness** 杳无人迹的荒野

untroubled /ʌnˈtrʌbld/ *adj* 未被扰乱的 ‹*calm*›; 平静的 ‹*waters, surface*›; 无忧无虑的 ‹*person, face, appearance*›; **to be ～** (by doubt) 不忧虑; (by news) 不烦恼

untrue /ʌnˈtruː/ *adj* **1** (false) 不真实的 ‹*story, rumour*›; **it is ～ to say that ...** 说…是没有事实根据的 **2** formal (inaccurate) 不精确的 ‹*instrument, tool*› **3** liter (unfaithful) 不忠实的 ‹*lover*›

untrustworthy /ʌn'trʌstwɜːði/ *adj* 不可信赖的

untruth /ʌn'truːθ/ *n* 假话

untruthful /ʌn'truːθfl/ *adj* 爱说谎的 ‹*person*›; 不真实的 ‹*account*›

untruthfully /ʌn'truːθfəli/ *adv* 不真实地

untruthfulness /ʌn'truːθflnɪs/ *n* [u] (of person) 说谎; (of account) 虚假

untuneful /ʌn'tjuːnfl/ *adj* 不悦耳的

untutored /ʌn'tjuːtəd, Amer -'tuː-/ *adj* [1] (untaught) 未受教育的 ‹*person*›; 未受训练的 ‹*taste, ear, eye*› [2] (lacking sophistication) 质朴的 ‹*person*›

untwine /ʌn'twaɪn/ *vt* 解开 ‹*rope, hair*›

untwist /ʌn'twɪst/ *vt* [1] (open) 拧开 ‹*lid*› [2] (untangle) 解开 ‹*wool*›

untying /ʌn'taɪɪŋ/ *pres p* ▸**untie**

untypical /ʌn'tɪpɪkl/ *adj* 非典型的; **to be ~ of sb. (to do sth.)** （做某事）不是某人的特点; **this kind of behaviour is not ~ of her** 这种行为对于她来说很正常

unusable /ʌn'juːzəbl/ *adj* 不能用的 ‹*vehicle*›; **an ~ room/bridge** 不能居住的房间/不能通行的桥梁; **the milk's off; it's ~** 牛奶坏了，不能喝了

unused[1] /ʌn'juːst/ *adj pred* (unaccustomed) **to be ~ to sth./doing sth.** 不习惯某事物/做某事; **they are ~ to hard times** 他们过不惯苦日子

unused[2] /ʌn'juːzd/ *adj* (not used) 未用过的; (not in use) 闲着的; **'computer, ~'** (in advertisement) “出售全新电脑”

unusual /ʌn'juːʒl/ *adj* [1] (uncommon) 不寻常的; **to have an ~ way of doing sth.** 做某事的方式很少见; **it is/is not ~ to find/see ...** 发现/看到…很难得/很平常; **it is ~ (for sb.) to do sth.** （某人）做某事很少见 [2] (exceptional) 与众不同的; **a scene of ~ beauty** 难得一见的美景

unusually /ʌn'juːʒəli/ *adv* [1] (surprisingly, untypically) 出乎意料地 ‹*withdrawn, reluctant*›; **~, she is largely self-taught** 意想不到的是，她主要是靠自学 [2] (exceptionally) 特别地; **it was ~ warm for the time of year** 对于一年中的那个时节来说，天气异常温暖

unutterable /ʌn'ʌtərəbl/ *adj attrib* 难以形容的 ‹*pain, delight*›; **an ~ idiot/bore** 愚蠢/讨厌透顶的人

unutterably /ʌn'ʌtərəbli/ *adv* 难以形容地 ‹*boring, stupid*›

unvaried /ʌn'veərɪd/ *adj* 无变化的; **a writer whose style is ~ from one page to the next** 风格一成不变的作家

unvarnished /ʌn'vɑːnɪʃt/ *adj* [1] (not varnished) 未涂清漆的 ‹*wood*› [2] fig (straightforward) 无掩饰的 ‹*truth*›; 坦率的 ‹*account*›

unvarying /ʌn'veərɪɪŋ/ *adj* 恒久的; **to maintain an ~ temperature** 保持恒温

unvaryingly /ʌn'veərɪɪŋli/ *adv* 恒久地

unveil /ʌn'veɪl/ *vt* [1] (remove covering from) 为…揭幕; **to ~ a statue** 为塑像揭幕 [2] fig (reveal) 推出 ‹*model*›; (announce for the first time) 公布 ‹*plan*›

unveiled /ʌn'veɪld/ *adj* 除去面纱的; **to go ~** 不戴面纱

unveiling /ʌn'veɪlɪŋ/ *n* [1] (of statue) 揭幕; (official ceremony) 揭幕式 [2] fig (revealing) 公布

unventilated /ʌn'ventɪleɪtɪd/ *adj* 不通风的 ‹*room*›

unverifiable /ʌn'verɪfaɪəbl/ *adj* 无法证实的

unverified /ʌn'verɪfaɪd/ *adj* 未证实的

unversed /ʌn'vɜːst/ *adj* 不熟悉的; **to be ~ in sth.** 不熟悉某事物; **to be ~ in correct social etiquette** 不熟悉正确的社交礼节

unvoiced /ʌn'vɔɪst/ *adj* [1] (not expressed) 未用语言表达的; **~ thoughts/doubts** 未说出来的想法/疑惑 [2] Ling 清音的; **an ~ consonant** 清辅音

unwaged /ʌn'weɪdʒd/ Brit
[A] *adj* [1] (out of work) 失业的 [2] (unpaid) 没有工资收入的 ‹*person*›; 无报酬的 ‹*work*›
[B] *npl* **the ~** 失业者

unwanted /ʌn'wɒntɪd/ *adj* 不需要的; **removal of ~ hair** 多余毛发的去除; **an ~ side effect** 有害的副作用; **an ~ pregnancy** 意外怀孕; **~ visitors** 不受欢迎的来访者

unwarlike /ʌn'wɔːlaɪk/ *adj* 不好战的

unwarrantable /ʌn'wɒrəntəbl, Amer -'wɔːr-/ *adj* formal 无法证明为正当的; **it is ~ that ...** …无正当理由

unwarranted /ʌn'wɒrəntɪd, Amer -'wɔːr-/ *adj* (lacking justification) 不合理的; (lacking authorization) 未授权的; **a totally ~ waste of public money** 对公款毫无必要的浪费

unwary /ʌn'weəri/
[A] *adj* (not cautious) 不谨慎的; (not vigilant) 不警觉的; **to be ~ of sb.** 不提防某人
[B] *npl* **the ~** 粗心的人

unwashed /ʌn'wɒʃt/ *adj* 未洗的; **the Great U~** pej hum 下层民众

unwavering /ʌn'weɪvərɪŋ/ *adj* 坚定的; **an ~ gaze** 直视; **to be ~ in one's support** 坚决支持

unwaveringly /ʌn'weɪvərɪŋli/ *adv* 坚定地; **~ loyal** 忠诚不渝的; **~ determined** 坚如磐石的

unweaned /ʌn'wiːnd/ *adj* 未断奶的 ‹*baby, calf*›

unwearable /ʌn'weərəbl/ *adj* (not suitable) 不适合穿戴的; (not comfortable) 穿起来不舒服的

unwearied /ʌn'wɪərɪd/ *adj* [1] (not tired) 不疲倦的 [2] liter (indefatigable) 孜孜不倦的

unwed /ʌn'wed/ *adj* 未婚的 ‹*girl, daughter*›

unwelcome /ʌn'welkəm/ *adj* [1] (not welcome) 不受欢迎的 ‹*visitor*›; **to make sb. feel ~** 使某人觉得不受欢迎 [2] (not received with pleasure) 讨厌的 ‹*news, gift, attentions*›; **it was extremely ~ publicity** 这是极为尴尬的曝光

unwelcoming /ʌn'welkəmɪŋ/ *adj* [1] (uninviting) 不惬意的 ‹*atmosphere, room*› [2] (unfriendly) 冷淡的 ‹*person, expression*›

unwell /ʌn'wel/ *adj pred* 不舒服的; **he looks ~** 他看上去病了

unwholesome /ʌn'həʊlsəm/ *adj* 有损健康的 ‹*diet, climate*›; 不健康的 ‹*interest, literature*›

unwieldy /ʌn'wiːldi/ *adj* [1] (difficult to use) 笨重的 ‹*weapon, tool*›; **an ~ boat** 笨重的大船 [2] fig (difficult to manage) 难操作的 ‹*rules*›; 复杂的 ‹*name*›; **an ~ bureaucracy** 运作不灵的官僚机构

unwilling /ʌn'wɪlɪŋ/ *adj* 勉强的; **to be ~ to do sth.** 不愿意做某事

unwillingly /ʌn'wɪlɪŋli/ *adv* 不情愿地

unwillingness /ʌn'wɪlɪŋnɪs/ *n* [u] 不情愿; **to show an ~ to adapt** 表现得不愿适应变化

unwind /ʌn'waɪnd/ (*pt, pp* **unwound**)
[A] *vt* 解开; **she unwound her legs from the tree trunk** 她松开了盘在树干上的双腿
[B] *vi* [1] (unreel) 解开; **the clock has unwound** 闹钟的发条松了 [2] colloq (relax) 放松; **he ~s by listening to music** 他靠听音乐放松自己

unwise /ʌn'waɪz/ *adj* (foolish) 愚蠢的 ‹*decision, choice*›; (rash) 轻率的 ‹*act*›; **it is ~ (of sb.) to do sth.** （某人）做某事是不明智的

unwisely /ʌn'waɪzli/ *adv* (foolishly) 愚蠢地; (rashly) 轻率地

unwitting /ʌn'wɪtɪŋ/ *adj* (unaware) 不知情的 ‹*accomplice*›; 不了解的 ‹*subject*›; (unintentional) 无意的 ‹*mistake, insult*›

unwittingly /ʌn'wɪtɪŋli/ *adv* 无意地 ‹*harm, offend*›; **he stumbled across the treasure ~** 他意外地发现了这批财宝

unwomanly /ʌn'wʊmənli/ *adj* 不像女人的

unwonted /ʌn'wəʊntɪd/ *adj attrib* formal 异常的; **I was touched by her ~ kindness** 我被她的不寻常的善良打动了

unworkable /ʌn'wɜːkəbl/ *adj* [1] (not practical) 不切实际的 ‹*plan, project*›; **to prove ~** 证明行不通 [2] (not malleable) 不可塑的 ‹*material*› [3] Mining 无法开采的 ‹*mine, seam*›

unworkmanlike /ʌn'wɜːkmənlaɪk/ *adj* (poorly executed) 拙劣的; (unprofessional) 不像能工巧匠的; (slapdash) 草率的

unworldly /ʌn'wɜːldli/ *adj* [1] (naive) 不谙世故的 [2] (not materialistic) 对钱财无兴趣的

unworthiness /ʌn'wɜːðɪnɪs/ *n* [u] 不配; **his ~ for the position he held** 他不适合所担任的职位

unworthy /ʌn'wɜːði/ *adj* (lacking in merit) 缺乏美德的; (undeserving) 不配的; (unsuitable, substandard) 不相称的

unwound /ʌn'waʊnd/ *pt, pp* ▸**unwind**

unwounded /ʌn'wuːndɪd/ *adj* 未受伤的

unwrap /ʌn'ræp/ (*pres p etc.* **-pp-**) *vt* [1] (remove wrapping from) 打开…的包装 ‹*parcel, package*› [2] (remove) 展开 ‹*paper, covering*›; **to ~ sth. from sth.** 从某物上剥去某物; **to come ~ped** 被打开

unwritten /ʌn'rɪtn/ *adj* [1] (not written) 未写下的; **~ songs** 口头流传的歌曲 [2] (tacit) 不成文的; **an ~ agreement between friends** 朋友之间的默契

unyielding /ʌn'jiːldɪŋ/ *adj* [1] (hard) 坚固的 ‹*material*›; (rigid) 不弯曲的 ‹*structure*› [2] (inflexible) 死板的 ‹*law*›; (stubborn) 不屈从的 ‹*person*›

unyoke /ʌn'jəʊk/ *vt* [1] (release from yoke) 给…卸轭 [2] fig (liberate) 解放

unzip /ʌn'zɪp/ (*pres p etc.* **-pp-**)
[A] *vt* [1] (undo) 拉开…的拉链 ‹*skirt, trousers, person*› [2] Comput 将…解压缩 ‹*file*›
[B] *vi* 拉开拉链

up /ʌp/
[A] *adv* [1] (at high position, level) 在上面; **~ here/there** 在这儿/那儿上面; **to be 900 metres ~** 在上面 900 米处; **four floors ~ from here** 从这里再向上 4 层楼; **the notice is ~ on the board** 通知贴在告示板上; **there are clouds ~ in the sky** 天空中有云彩; **the curtains are ~** (installed) 窗帘装上去了 [2] (to high position, level) 向上; **to come/go ~** 上来/上去; **to run ~ to the top of the hill** 跑上山顶; **to put one's hair ~** 把头发束在头顶; **the river is ~** 河水涨了; **the moon is ~** 月亮升起来了 [3] (raised, open) 升起; **to have one's hand ~** 举手; **the tent is ~** 帐篷搭起来了; **to have one's umbrella ~** 撑起雨伞; **the blinds are ~** 窗帘卷起来了; **the hood of the car is ~** 车篷打开了 [4] (greater in intensity) 更大; **the volume is ~ all the way** 音量开到最大; **the wind is ~** 起风了 [5] (higher in amount, price) 更高; **sales are ~ by 10%** 销售量增加了 10%; **carrots are ~ again** 胡萝卜又涨价了 [6] (upstairs) 在楼上; (going upstairs) 向楼上; **I'll be ~ in a minute** 我一会儿就上楼; **can you come ~?** 你能到楼上来吗？ [7] (out of bed) 不在睡觉; **to be ~ early/late** 早起/熬夜; **to be ~ all night** 一夜没睡; **to be ~ and about** (after illness) 起床走动; **to be ~ and about very early** (after sleep) 很早就起床 [8] (upstream) 向上游; **to row ~ to the head of the river** 向河流源头划去 [9] (facing upwards) 朝上; **'this side ~'** (on box) “此面朝上”; **to lay sth. face ~** 将某物面朝上放置; **to lie face ~** 仰面躺着 [10] (in time, scale, rank) 以上; **children from the age of 10 ~** 10 岁以上的孩子; **T-shirts from £5 ~** 售价在 5 英镑以上的T恤衫; **everyone from the cleaning staff ~** 自清洁工以上的每个人; **from the sixteenth**

U

century ~ to the present day 从 16 世纪至今 [11] (rising) 升起; his colour was ~ 他羞红了脸; her temper is ~ 她生气了; his blood was ~ 他血往上涌 [12] (at high status) 居于高位; (to high status) 向高位; to be ~ (there) with *or* among the best 跻身最佳之列; to be ~ (there) with *or* among the leaders 身处领导者之列; to be ~ among the leading contenders for the title 是冠军的主要争夺者之一 [13] (to the far end) 向那头; (at the far end) 在那头; my office is halfway ~ 我的办公室在前面中间的地方 [14] (in north) 在北方; (to north) 向北方; he's ~ in Leeds 他在北方的利兹; to fly ~ to Glasgow 向北飞往格拉斯哥; to move ~ to Edinburgh 北迁到爱丁堡; to move/live ~ north colloq 搬到北方/在北方居住 [15] (in capital, major city) 在大都市; (to capital, major city) 向大都市; ~ in London 在伦敦; to go ~ to London 去伦敦; to be ~ from the country for the weekend 从乡下到城里度周末 [16] Brit (at university) 上大学 [尤指上牛津或剑桥]; he's ~ at Oxford 他在牛津上大学 [17] colloq (wrong) 出错; what's ~? 出什么事啦?; what's ~ with your arm? 你胳膊怎么了?; there's something ~ with the brakes 刹车出问题了 [18] esp Amer colloq (in greeting) hey, what's ~? 嗨，有啥事吗? [19] colloq (informed) to be (well) ~ on sth. （非常）了解某事物 [20] (on trial) to be ~ for murder/fraud 因涉嫌谋杀/诈骗而被审讯; to be ~ before the judge (for sth.) （因某事）而接受法官审理 [21] (in profit) 赢利; to be £100 ~ 获利 100 英镑 [22] Sport (ahead) 领先; to be two points ~ on sb. 领先某人两分; (to get) one ~ (on sb.) fig colloq 超过（某人） [23] colloq (expressing support) ~ with sb./sth.! 支持某人/某事! [24] Brit colloq (ready) 准备好; tea's ~! 茶沏好了!

B *prep* [1] (at higher position) 在…上面; to be ~ a ladder 在梯子上面; to be stuck ~ a tree 被困在树上 [2] (to higher position) 向…上面; to come/go ~ the stairs 上楼; come/go ~ the mountain 上山; the road ~ the mountain 通往山上的路 [3] (along) 沿着; to come/go ~ the street 沿街道过来/过去; to live ~ the road 住在路的那头; to have buttons ~ the front (in vertical row) 前襟有一排扣子 [4] (in) 在…里面; (into) 到…里面; to get water ~ one's nose 让水灌进鼻子; to put sth. ~ one's sleeve 把某物放进袖子里; ~ yours! taboo sl 去你妈的! [5] (upstream) 向…上游; a cruise ~ the Rhine 向莱茵河上游方向的乘船游览 [6] Brit colloq (at) 在…处; (to) 到…处; he's ~ the pub 他在酒吧; she's gone ~ town 她到城里去了

C *adj* [1] *pred* (finished) 完了的; time's ~! 时间到!; his leave is almost ~ 他休假快结束了; the month was finally ~ 一个月的时间终于过去了; to be all ~ (with sb.) colloq （某人）完蛋了 colloq; it's all ~ with this government colloq 这个政府完蛋了 colloq [2] *attrib* (going upward) 向上的 ‹*escalator, stroke*› [3] *pred* colloq (cheerful) 快乐的; he's ~ at the moment 他这会儿很高兴; everyone's mood is ~ 大家情绪高涨 [4] *attrib* Rail 上行的; the ~ train/line/platform 上行列车/线/站台 [5] *pred* Brit (under repair) 在维修的; the road is ~ 道路正在整修; 'road ~' “路面整修” [6] *pred* Comput 运行正常的; is the system ~ today? 今天系统能运行了吗?

D *n* colloq [1] ~s + *v pl* 走运; you can't have ~s all the time 你不可能总是走运; ~s and downs 兴衰; the ~s and downs of being thirty 人到 30 岁的起起落落 [2] on the ~ (increasing) 在增长; (improving) 在改善; confidence is on the ~ (rising) 信心正在提升; on the ~ and ~ (prospering) 日益兴旺; (honest) 诚实; the offer seems to be on the ~ and ~ 出价似乎很有诚意

E **up above** *adv phr, prep phr* [1] (in higher position) 在高处; the clouds ~ above 天上的云; to circle ~ above the lake 在湖面上盘旋 [2] (to higher position) 到高处; to climb ~ above to get a better view 爬到高处以便看得更清楚; she stretched her arms ~ above her head 她双臂举过头顶 [3] Relig 在天堂

F **up against** *prep phr* [1] lit (near) 靠近; (touching) 接触; he left his bike ~ against the wall 他把自行车倚在墙上; to press ~ against sth. ‹*crowd, herd*› 推挤着某物 [2] fig (confronting) 遭遇; to be ~ against strong opposition 遇到强劲对手; to be ~ against it 遇到困难

G **up and down** *adv phr, prep phr* [1] (upwards and downwards) 上上下下; to jump ~ and down with excitement 兴奋得跳上跳下; to bob ~ and down on the water ‹*boat*› 在水面颠簸 [2] (to and fro) 来来回回; to walk/pace ~ and down 来回走/踱步; to walk ~ and down the garden 在花园里走来走去 [3] (throughout) 遍及; to travel ~ and down the country 游遍全国各地 [4] (in and out of bed) 一会儿起来一会儿睡下 [5] (good and bad) ‹*relationship*› 时好时坏; to be (a bit) ~ and down ‹*person*› (depressed) 情绪（有点儿）起伏不定; (ill) 病情（有点儿）反复

H **up and running** *adj phr* ‹*company*› 运行; ‹*project*› 进行; to get the system ~ and running 让系统运行起来

I **up for** *prep phr* [1] (available for) 可供应; to be ~ for sale 可供销售; the subject ~ for discussion/consideration is ... 可讨论/考虑的话题是… [2] (being considered for) 被考虑; to be ~ for election ‹*candidate*› 被提名参加选举; to be ~ for promotion ‹*worker*› 被考虑提拔 [3] (due for) 到期; to be ~ for renewal in June ‹*contract, visa*› 将在 6 月份到期续签 [4] colloq (willing to join) 愿意参加; I'm going out tonight: are you ~ for it? 我今天晚上外出，你想去吗?

J **up to** *prep phr* [1] (as high as, as far as, until) 直到; it has grown all the way ~ to here 它一直长到这里; I was ~ to my knees in water 我站在齐膝深的水里; to read ~ to page 10 读到第 10 页; where are we ~ to? 我们到哪儿了?; ~ to 1994/now 直到 1994 年/现在 [2] (as much, many as) 多达; temperatures of ~ to 35°C 高达 35 摄氏度的气温; to pay ~ to $500 最多支付 500 美元; I can take ~ to four people in my car 我的车最多可以载 4 个人 [3] *with negative* (as good as) 达到; her latest book isn't ~ to her usual standard 她的新书没有达到她一向以来的水准; not to be ~ to much Brit colloq 不怎么样; the play wasn't ~ to much 这部戏很一般 [4] (equal to) 胜任; he's not ~ to the job 他不胜任这项工作; I'm not ~ to writing a book 我没有能力写书; to be ~ for the challenge 准备好迎接挑战 [5] colloq (indicating responsibility) 由…决定; It's ~ to you! 这由你决定!; it's not ~ to you to tell me ... 轮不到你来告诉我… [6] colloq (doing) 正在干; what are they ~ to? 他们在干什么?; to be ~ to something 在干着某种勾当

K *vt* (*pres p etc.* -pp-) 提高 ‹*price, rates*›; to ~ one's offer by £1,000 将出价提高 1,000 英镑; capacity will be ~ped by 70% 产能将提高 70%

L *vi* (*pres p etc.* -pp-) colloq or hum to ~ and do sth. 突然做某事; to ~ and marry someone else 突然和另外一个人结婚; he ~ped and left her 他突然起身离开了她

up-and-coming *adj* 前景好的; an ~ organization 有前途的机构

up-and-down *adj* [1] (to-and-fro) 往复的 ‹*movement*› [2] (variable) 时好时坏的 ‹*career, year*›; 波动的 ‹*economy*›

upbeat /ˈʌpbiːt/
A *adj* colloq (cheerful) 快乐的; (optimistic) 乐观的; to stay *or* remain ~ 保持乐观
B *n* 弱拍

upbraid /ʌpˈbreɪd/ *vt* formal 责骂; to ~ sb. for sth./doing sth. 因某事物/做某事而训斥某人

upbringing /ˈʌpbrɪŋɪŋ/ *n* [c and u] 抚育; a religious ~ 宗教教养

UPC *abbr* esp Amer = universal product code

upchuck /ˈʌptʃʌk/ Amer colloq *vi, vt* 呕吐

upcoming /ʌpˈkʌmɪŋ/ *adj attrib* 即将到来的; next month's ~ movies 下个月即将上映的电影

upcountry /ʌpˈkʌntri/
A *adj attrib* (remote) 偏远的 ‹*region, farm*›; (unsophisticated) 质朴的 ‹*inhabitant, custom*›
B *adv* 往内地 ‹*move*›; 在内地 ‹*live*›; to go back ~ 回内地去

update
A /ʌpˈdeɪt/ *vt* 更新
B /ˈʌpdeɪt/ *n* 最新报道

updraught Brit, **updraft** Amer /ˈʌpdrɑːft, ˈʌpdræft/ *n* 上升气流

upend /ʌpˈend/ *vt* [1] (stand upright) 立起 [2] (turn upside down) 倒放; the boxer ~ed his opponent (knocked down) 那个拳击手把对手打翻在地

upfront /ʌpˈfrʌnt/ *adj* [1] (frank) 坦率的 ‹*person, manner*›; to be ~ about sth. 在某事上很直率 [2] Fin (advance) 预付的 ‹*fee, commission*› [3] esp Amer (prominent) 显要的 ‹*position*›; 重要的 ‹*person, product*›

up front *adv* [1] (towards the front) 在前面 ‹*pass, go*› [2] (in advance) 预先 ‹*pay, put*›; the deal is going nowhere until we've got the money ~ 在我们弄到钱之前这项生意不会有进展

upgrade
A /ʌpˈgreɪd/ *vt* [1] (improve) 改进 ‹*product, machinery*› [2] (raise level of) 提升 ‹*post*›; 提高 ‹*skill*› [3] Comput 给…升级 ‹*program, hardware*›
B /ˈʌpgreɪd/ *n* [1] (act of improving) 改进 [2] (improved version) 改进版 [3] Comput 升级版 [4] Transp [旅客座位、所享受服务标准等的]升级

upheaval /ʌpˈhiːvl/ *n* [c and u] [1] (disturbance) (within society) 动乱; (within organization) 大变动; (within family) 混乱; an emotional ~ 情绪的巨大波动 [2] Geol （地壳的）隆起

uphill /ʌpˈhɪl/
A *adj* [1] (going upwards) 上坡的 ‹*road*› [2] fig (difficult) 费力的 ‹*task, struggle*›
B *adv* 朝上坡方向 ‹*go, push*›; the path led *or* ran ~ 这条小径沿着山坡向上延伸

uphold /ʌpˈhəʊld/ *vt* (*pt, pp* **upheld**) [1] Jur 维持 ‹*verdict, sentence*› [2] (maintain) 保持 ‹*custom*› [3] (support) 支持 ‹*person*›; he fought the duel to ~ his family's honour 他为了维护家族荣誉而决斗

upholder /ʌpˈhəʊldə(r)/ *n* 维护者

upholster /ʌpˈhəʊlstə(r)/ *vt* 为…装软垫 ‹*chair*›; well-~ed hum 虚胖的

upholsterer /ʌpˈhəʊlstərə(r)/ ▸p. 409 *n* 家具装饰商

upholstery /ʌpˈhəʊlstəri/ *n* [u] [1] (covering, padding) 家具装饰 [2] (technique) 家具装饰技能; an ~ business 家具装饰业

upkeep /ˈʌpkiːp/ *n* [u] [1] (care) (of environment) 保护; (of vehicle) 保养; (of animal) 喂养; the ~ of the garden 花园的管理 [2] (cost of care) (of thing) 维护费; (of person) 抚养费

upland /ˈʌplənd/
A *n* [u] 高原; dry ~ soils 干旱的高原土壤
B **uplands** *npl* 高地

uplift
A /ˈʌplɪft/ *n* [1] [c and u] (improving influence) 振奋; he felt his career needed an ~ 他觉得自己的事业需要提高 [2] [u] Geol （地壳的）上升
B /ʌpˈlɪft/ *vt* 振奋 ‹*spirit, heart*›; 抬起 ‹*eyes, arms*›

uplift bra *n* 托高文胸

uplifted /ʌpˈlɪftɪd/ *adj* **1** (raised) 抬起的 ‹*hands, eyes*› **2** (cheerful, enthused) 兴冲冲的

uplifting /ʌpˈlɪftɪŋ/ *adj* 令人振奋的 ‹*experience, speech*›

uplighter /ˈʌplaɪtə(r)/ *n* 上射灯

upload /ˈʌpləʊd/

A *vt* 上传

B *n* **1** (copying of data) 上传 **2** (uploaded data) 上传的文件

upmarket /ʌpˈmɑːkɪt/ esp Brit

A *adj* 高端的

B *adv* 面向高端消费者地; **to go ~** 面向高端市场

upmost /ˈʌpməʊst/ *adj* = **uppermost**

upon /əˈpɒn/ *prep* [on的更为正式的用法，尤用于抽象意义]; ▸**once A2**

upper /ˈʌpə(r)/

A *adj attrib* **1** (higher) 上面的 ‹*shelf, teeth*›; 地势较高的 ‹*village, farm*›; **the ~ deck** 上层甲板; **the ~ jaw/eyelid** 上颌/上眼皮 **2** (superior) [职位或地位] 上层的; **~ management** 高层管理 **3** (higher in scale) 较高一端的 ‹*thirties, register*›; **temperatures are in the ~ twenties** 温度接近 30 度 **4** (inland) 内陆的; (upriver) 上游的; (further North) 北部的; **the ~ reaches of the River Severn** 塞文河上游

B *n* **1** (part of footwear) 鞋帮; **to be (down) on one's ~s** fig 穷困潦倒 **2** sl (drug) 兴奋剂

upper: ~ arm *n* 上臂; **~ atmosphere** *n* [对流层以上的] 高层大气; **~ case** *n* [u] 大写字; **an ~-case letter** 大写字母; **~ circle** *n* 上层环形观众席

upper class

A *n + v sing or pl* 上层社会

B **upper-class** *adj* 上层社会的

upper: ~ crust *n* colloq **the ~ crust** 上流社会; **an ~-crust family** 上流社会家庭; **~cut** *n* 上钩拳; **~ hand** *n* 上风; **to have/get/keep the ~ hand** 占据/得到/保持有利地位; **~ house** *n* 上议院

upper middle class

A *n + v sing or pl* 中上阶层

B **upper middle-class** *adj* 中上层阶级的

uppermost /ˈʌpəməʊst/ *adj* 最高的; **the ~ book in the pile** 书堆最上面的那本; **~ in my mind is ...** 我心里想得最多的是…

upper: ~ school *n* Brit **1** (school) 高中; **2** (part of school) 高中部; **3** + *v sing or pl* (pupils) 高中生; **~ sixth** *n* Brit **1** (year) 高六年级 [英国中学的最高年级]; **2** + *v sing or pl* (pupils) 高六年级生; **to be in the ~ sixth** 是高六年级生

uppish /ˈʌpɪʃ/ *adj* colloq pej (arrogant) 傲慢的; (snobbish) 势利的

uppity /ˈʌpəti/ *adj* colloq pej 自视甚高的 ‹*person, attitude*›

upright /ˈʌpraɪt/

A *adj* **1** (vertical) 垂直的 ‹*tower, wall*›; 挺直的 ‹*posture*›; **'keep ~'** (on box) "请勿倒置" **2** fig (honest) 正直的 ‹*person*›; 规矩的 ‹*dealings*›

B *n* **1** Constr 直柱 **2** Sport 球门柱 **3** = **upright piano**

C *adv* 挺直地 ‹*walk*›; 直立地 ‹*place, hold*›; **to stand ~** 站得笔直

upright: ~ chair *n* 高直背椅; **~ freezer** *n* 立式冰箱

uprightly /ˈʌpraɪtli/ *adv* 公正地 ‹*act, treat*›

uprightness /ˈʌpraɪtnɪs/ *n* [u] **1** (state of being vertical) 垂直 **2** fig (moral correctness) 正直

upright: ~ piano ▸**p. 395** *n* 立式钢琴; **~ vacuum cleaner** *n* 直立式真空吸尘器

uprising /ˈʌpraɪzɪŋ/ *n* 起义; **an ~ against sb./sth.** 反抗某人/某事物的起义

upriver /ʌpˈrɪvə(r)/

A *adj* (direction) 向上游的; (position) 在上游的

B *adv* 向上游; **to go ~** 向上游而去

uproar /ˈʌprɔː(r)/ *n* [c and u] **1** (noise, chaos) 喧嚣 **2** (expressions of indignation, protests) 骚动; **the meeting ended in ~** 会议最后激起了一片义愤

uproarious /ʌpˈrɔːrɪəs/ *adj* **1** (noisy) 喧闹的 ‹*behaviour, occasion*›; **they burst into ~ laughter** 他们哄堂大笑 **2** (funny) 令人捧腹的 ‹*film, joke*›

uproariously /ʌpˈrɔːrɪəsli/ *adv* 喧闹地; **~ funny** 滑稽得令人捧腹的; **to laugh ~** 哄堂大笑

uproot /ʌpˈruːt/ *vt* 连根拔起 ‹*plant*›; **many families were ~ed in the war** 很多家庭在战争中离乡背井

ups-a-daisy /ˈʌpsədeɪzi/ *excl* colloq = **upsy-daisy**

upscale /ˈʌpskeɪl/ Amer

A *adj* 高端的

B *adv* 面向高端消费者地; **to go ~** 面向高端市场

upset

A /ʌpˈset/ *vt* (*pt, pp* **upset**) **1** (distress) 使苦恼; (annoy) 使生气; **it ~ him that nobody had bothered to tell him about it** 谁也没把这件事告诉他，这让他很不高兴; **don't ~ yourself about it: let's just forget it ever happened** 别为这事儿难过，我们就只当它没发生过 **2** (defeat unexpectedly) 意外击败 **3** Med 使…肠胃不适 ‹*person*›; 使…不适 ‹*stomach*›; **too much rich food ~s the digestion** 吃太多的油腻食物会导致消化不良 **4** (throw into disarray) 打乱 ‹*plan, arrangements*›; 搅乱 ‹*situation*›; (destabilize) 打破 ‹*balance, equilibrium*› **5** (knock over) 弄翻; **he ~ the vase** 他把花瓶打翻了

B /ˈʌpset/ *n* **1** [c and u] (upheaval) 混乱; **his health has not been improved by all the ~ at home** 家中的纷乱使他的健康毫无起色 **2** [c] (unexpected defeat) 意外失败; **a big Conservative ~** 保守党的意外惨败 **3** [c] Med 肠胃病; **to have a stomach ~** 拉肚子 **4** [c and u] (distress) 苦恼; **a legal dispute will cause worry and ~** 法律纠纷会使人心烦意乱

C /ˌʌpˈset/ *adj* **1** (distressed) 苦恼的; (annoyed) 生气的; **he was ~ at the news** 那消息让他心烦意乱; **don't get ~ about it** 别为这事难过 **2** Med 肠胃不适的; **an ~ stomach** 肚子痛

upset price *n* [拍卖的] 底价

upsetting /ʌpˈsetɪŋ/ *adj* 令人不快的 ‹*behaviour, news*›

upshift /ˈʌpʃɪft/

A *vi* esp Amer 换高挡

B *vt* 提高

C *n* **1** esp Amer Aut 换高挡 **2** (increase) 提高

upshot /ˈʌpʃɒt/ *n* 结局; **the ~ was that we got the money** 我们最终得到了那笔钱

upside /ˈʌpsaɪd/

A *n* 积极方面; **the recession has its ~s** 经济衰退有它好的方面

B *prep* Amer colloq 在…一边; **I'd like to smack him ~ the head** 我真想掴他的脑袋

upside down

A *adv* **1** (in inverted fashion) 颠倒地 ‹*turn, place*›; **bats hang ~** 蝙蝠倒挂身体 **2** fig (in chaotic manner) 凌乱不堪地; **to turn sb.'s life ~** 把某人的生活搅得一团糟

B *adj* **1** (inverted) 颠倒的 ‹*book*›; 倒立的 ‹*person*›; **the photo is ~** 照片挂反了 **2** fig (in disorder) 杂乱的 ‹*household, organization*›

upsize /ˈʌpsaɪz/

A *vt* 扩大…的规模 ‹*company, industry*›

B *vi* «*company, industry*» 扩张

upsizing /ˈʌpsaɪzɪŋ/ *n* [u] 扩大

upskill /ʌpˈskɪl/

A *vt* 提高…的技能 ‹*staff*›

B *vi* 提高技能

upskilling /ˈʌpskɪlɪŋ/ *n* [u] 雇员技能提高; **the training and ~ of a workforce** 劳动力的培训与技能提高

upstage /ʌpˈsteɪdʒ/

A *adv* (position) 在舞台后部; (direction) 向舞台后部

B *adj* (position) 在舞台后部的; (direction) 向舞台后部的

C *vt* **1** (draw attention from) 抢…的风头 ‹*person*› **2** Theat 抢…的镜头 ‹*actor*›

upstairs /ʌpˈsteəz/

A *adv* **1** (on higher floor) 在楼上; (to higher floor) 往楼上; **to go ~** 走上楼去; **the family ~** 楼上的人家 **2** colloq fig (to more senior post) 往更高职位; **he's been moved ~** 他高升了; **to kick sb. ~** 让某人明升暗降 **3** colloq (in the mind) 在头脑里; **he hasn't got much ~** 他脑子不好使

B *n* 楼上; **there was no social contact between ~ and downstairs** 楼上与楼下之间没有交往

C *adj attrib* 在楼上的; **an ~ room/bedroom** 楼上的房间/卧室

upstanding /ʌpˈstændɪŋ/ *adj* **1** (erect) 直立的; **be ~** 起立 **2** (honest) 诚实的 **3** (strong and healthy) 强健的

upstart /ˈʌpstɑːt/ *n* pej 发迹者

upstate /ˈʌpsteɪt/

A *adv* Amer (location) (in the north) 在州北部; (in the interior part) 在州的边远地区; (direction) (towards the North) 向州北部; (towards the interior part) 向州的边远地区

B *adj attrib* (of the northern part) 州北部的; (of the interior part) 州的边远地区的; **~ New York** 纽约州的边远地区

upstream /ʌpˈstriːm/

A *adv* (in the higher part of a river) 在上游; (towards the higher part of a river) 往上游; (against the flow of the current) 逆流地

B *adj* (of the upper part of a river) 在上游的; (moving against the current) 逆流的

upstroke /ˈʌpstrəʊk/ *n* **1** (in writing) 向上的一笔 **2** (upward movement) (of wing) 向上的拍击; (of machine part) 上冲

upsurge /ˈʌpsɜːdʒ/ *n* 急剧上升; **an ~ of interest** 兴趣倍增; **dramatic ~s of the disease** 这种病的爆发

upswept /ˈʌpswept/ *adj* 向上倾斜的 ‹*line*›; 朝上梳的 ‹*hairstyle*›

upswing /ˈʌpswɪŋ/ *n* **1** (upward movement) 向上摆动 **2** fig (improvement) 改善; **an ~ in profits** 利润的增长

upsy-daisy /ˈʌpsɪdeɪzi/ *excl* colloq (encouraging child to get up) 起来没事啦; (tossing child into air) 上高高喽; **~, you haven't hurt yourself** 起来吧，你没伤着自己

uptake /ˈʌpteɪk/ *n* [u] **1** (use) 使用; **the ~ of free training courses/free school meals** 参加免费培训课程/享用免费学校膳食 **2** Physiol 吸收; **the ~ of oxygen by the body** 身体对氧气的吸收

uptempo /ʌpˈtempəʊ/

A *adj* 快节奏的 ‹*tune, song*›

B *adv* 快节奏地 ‹*play, sing*›

upthrust /ˈʌpθrʌst/ *n* **1** [u] Tech (upward thrust) 上推 **2** [c] Geol (upwards movement of rock) 上冲断层

uptick /ˈʌptɪk/ *n* Amer **1** Fin [股票的] 低买高卖 **2** (small increase) 小幅增加

uptight /ʌpˈtaɪt/ *adj* colloq **1** (tense) 紧张不安的; **to be ~ about sth./sb.** 对某事物/某人紧张 **2** (rigidly conventional) 拘谨的

up to date *adj* **1** (most recent) 最新的 ‹*file, information*›; **to bring/keep sb. ~ (on sth.)** 向某人提供 (某事物的) 最新情况 **2** (modern) 现代的 ‹*course, method*› **3** (fashionable) 时髦的 ‹*attitude, style*›

U

up-to-the-minute *adj* 最新的〈*information, account*〉

uptown /ˈʌptaʊn/ Amer
A *adv* (location) 在住宅区〈*live, work*〉; (direction) **to go ~** 去住宅区
B *adj* 住宅区的; **~ New York** 纽约住宅区; **~ stores** 住宅区的商店
C *n* [u] 住宅区

upturn /ˈʌptɜːn/ *n* (in economy, career) 好转; (in demand, profits) 回升

upturned /ˈʌptɜːnd/ *adj* **1** (upside down) 倒放的〈*container, table*〉 **2** (turned upwards) 仰起的; **an ~ nose** 翘鼻子

upward /ˈʌpwəd/
A *adj attrib* **1** (moving, leading higher) 向上的〈*climb*〉; **to give an ~ glance** 向上瞟一眼; **an ~ stroke with a brush** 画笔的向上一勾 **2** (rising in level) 上升的; **an ~ trend** 上升趋势; **an ~ movement of prices** 价格的上调 **3** (improving) 趋好的; **an ~ spiral** 愈来愈好; **to be on an ~ path** 正在趋向好转
B *adv* = **upwards**

upwardly mobile *adj* 步步高升的〈*person*〉

upward mobility *n* [u] 步步高升

upwards /ˈʌpwədz/
A *adv* **1** (to higher place, facing up) 向上〈*move, look*〉; **the land slopes gently ~** 地面缓缓向上倾斜; **to lie face ~** 仰卧 **2** (to higher level) 向高层次; **the long-term trend is ~** 从长远来看呈上升趋势; **to push prices ~** 把价格抬高 **3** (in scale, degree, rank) 以上; **children of five years (and) ~** 5岁（及）以上的儿童; **prices are from £10 ~** 价格从10英镑起; **everyone from the cleaners ~** 清洁工以上所有人 **4** (to later time) 往后; **from (one's) childhood ~** 自（自己的）童年起
B **upwards of** *prep phr* 多于; **~ of £50** 50多英镑; **to take ~ of an hour** 花一个多小时; **~ of 20% of sales are from one product** 销售额的20%以上来自一种产品

upwind /ʌpˈwɪnd/
A *adv* 逆风地; **to sail ~** 逆风航行; **people living ~ of the fire** 住在火势逆风处的人们
B *adj* 逆风的〈*journey*〉

Ural Mountains /jʊərəl ˈmaʊntɪnz, Amer -tnz/ *pr npl* **the ~** 乌拉尔山脉

Urals /ˈjʊərəlz/ *pr npl* **the ~** = **Ural Mountains**

uranium /jʊˈreɪnɪəm/ *n* [u] 铀; **~ enrichment** 铀浓缩; **the ~ series** 铀系

Uranus /ˈjʊərənəs, jʊˈreɪnəs/ *pr n* 天王星

urban /ˈɜːbən/ *adj* **1** (of the town or city) 城市的; **an ~ dweller** 城市居民 **2** Mus **~ (contemporary)** [源于黑人的] 流行舞蹈音乐的

urban: ~ blight *n* [u] 城市衰败; **~ decay** *n* [u] 城市衰落

urbane /ɜːˈbeɪn/ *adj* 儒雅的〈*person, manner*〉

urbanite /ˈɜːbənaɪt/ *n* colloq 城里人

urbanity /ɜːˈbænəti/ *n* [u] 儒雅

urbanization /ˌɜːbənaɪˈzeɪʃn, Amer -nɪˈz-/ *n* [u] 城市化

urbanize /ˈɜːbənaɪz/ *vt* 使城市化

urban: ~ myth, ~ legend *ns* 都市传奇; **~ planner** ▸**p. 409** *n* 城市规划师; **~ planning** *n* [u] 城市规划; **~ renewal** *n* [u] 城市更新; **~ sprawl** *n* [u] 城市扩张; **~ studies** *npl + v sing or pl* 城市研究

urchin /ˈɜːtʃɪn/ *n* 顽童; **a street ~** 街头小乞丐

Urdu /ˈʊəduː, ˈɜːduː/ ▸**p. 426** *n* [u] 乌尔都语 [巴基斯坦官方语言，亦通行于印度]

urea /jʊˈrɪə, ˈjʊərɪə/ *n* [u] 尿素

ureter /jʊˈriːtə(r)/ *n* 输尿管

urethra /jʊˈriːθrə/ *n* 尿道

urge /ɜːdʒ/
A *n* **1** (desire) 强烈欲望; **I had a sudden ~ to hit him** 我突然很想揍他 **2** (sexual impulse) 性冲动; **sexual ~s** 性冲动
B *vt* **1** (try to persuade) 力劝; **she ~d him to stay** 她竭力劝他留下; **'go and ask him again' she ~d** "再去问他一遍，"她催促道 **2** (advocate) 竭力主张; **he ~d patience on the crowd** 他呼吁那群人保持耐心; **the report ~d that all children (should) be taught to swim** 这份报告呼吁应该教所有的孩子学游泳 **3** formal (encourage to move) 驱赶; **he ~d his horse forward** 他策马向前; **he ~d the sheep through the gate** 他赶着羊群穿过大门

Phrasal verb

- **urge on** *vt* [**~ sb./sth. on, ~ on sb./sth.**] **1** (encourage) 鼓励; **to ~ on the troops** 鼓舞部队的士气 **2** (make go faster) 使加速; **she ~d on her horse** 她策马前进

urgency /ˈɜːdʒənsi/ *n* [u] 紧迫; **a matter of (some) ~** （相当）紧迫的事; **there was a hint of ~ in his voice** 他的声音有点儿急切

urgent /ˈɜːdʒənt/ *adj* **1** (pressing) 紧急的〈*letter, matter*〉; **it is ~ that ...** 需尽快…; **to be in ~ need of sth.** 急需某事物 **2** (earnest and insistent) 迫切的〈*entreaty, tone*〉; **to be ~ about sth.** 在某事上很急切

urgently /ˈɜːdʒəntli/ *adv* 迫切地〈*need, shout*〉; **to be ~ in need of sth.** 急需某事物; **to leave ~** 匆匆离去

urging /ˈɜːdʒɪŋ/ *n* [u] 敦促; **at (sb.'s) ~** 在（某人的）催促下

uric acid /ˌjʊərɪk ˈæsɪd/ *n* [u] 尿酸

urinal /jʊəˈraɪnl, ˈjʊərɪnl/ *n* **1** (public toilet) 男厕所 **2** (fitting) [男用] 小便池

urinary /ˈjʊərɪnəri, Amer --neri/ *adj attrib* (of urine) 尿的; (of the organs) 泌尿器官的; **an infection of the ~ tract** 尿路感染

urinate /ˈjʊərɪneɪt/ *vi* 排尿

urine /ˈjʊərɪn/ *n* [u] 尿

URL *abbr* Comput = **uniform resource locator, universal resource locator** 统一资源定位地址 [即互联网网页地址]

urn /ɜːn/ *n* **1** (vessel) 瓮; **a funeral ~** 骨灰缸 **2** (for tea, coffee) 壶

urogenital /ˌjʊərəˈdʒenɪtl/ *adj* 泌尿生殖系统的

urological /ˌjʊərəˈlɒdʒɪkl/ *adj* 泌尿学的

urologist /jʊəˈrɒlədʒɪst/ ▸**p. 409** *n* 泌尿科专家

urology /jʊəˈrɒlədʒi/ *n* [u] 泌尿学

urticaria /ˌɜːtɪˈkeərɪə/ ▸**p. 377** *n* [u] 荨麻疹

Uruguay /ˈjʊərəgwaɪ/ *pr n* 乌拉圭

Uruguayan /ˌjʊərəˈgwaɪən/ ▸**p. 503**
A *adj* (of Uruguay) 乌拉圭的; (of the people) 乌拉圭人的
B *n* 乌拉圭人

US *abbr* = **United States**

us /ʌs, əs/ *pron* 我们; **he saw ~** 他看见我们了; **both of ~ like jazz** 我们俩都喜欢爵士乐; **none of ~ can drive** 我们谁都不会开车; **give ~ a kiss!** Brit colloq 吻我一下！

USA *abbr* **1** = **United States 2** = **United States Army** 美国陆军; **~ issue** 美国陆军配给

usable /ˈjuːzəbl/ *adj* 可用的

USAF *abbr* = **United States Air Force** 美国空军; **a ~ base** 美国空军基地

usage /ˈjuːsɪdʒ, ˈjuːzɪdʒ/ *n* **1** [c and u] (customary practice) 习俗; **commercial ~** 商业惯例 **2** [c and u] (way of saying sth.) [词语的] 用法; **a ~ borrowed from the Italian** 借自意大利语的惯用法 **3** [u] (use) 使用; **the ~ of equipment** 设备的使用

USB *abbr* = **universal serial bus** 通用串行总线

USB: ~ key *n* **1** (storage device) U盘; **2** (authentication token) 电子钥匙; **~ port** *n* USB接口; **~ stick** *n* U盘

> **USA**
>
> 1\. 美国，全称美利坚合众国（the United States of America），简称 the US、the USA、the States 或 the United States。首都华盛顿（▸**Washington, DC**）。原为英国殖民地，1776年7月4日《独立宣言》发表后，脱离英国独立。最初只有13个州，现在已经扩展为50个州，其中夏威夷州位于太平洋中部，1959年成为美国的第50个州。美国实行立法、行政、司法三权分立的制度。国会为最高立法机构，分为参议院和众议院。总统为国家元首，兼任武装部队总司令。由共和党和民主党两大政党更替执政。国旗为星条旗（▸**the Stars and Stripes** 或 Star-Spangled Banner）。国歌是《星条旗永不落》（*Star-Spangled Banner*）。美国是移民国家，融合了世界各地的不同文化，因此别称大熔炉（melting pot）。
>
> 2\. 美洲，即亚美利加洲。美洲最初并不为人所知，后被航海家克里斯托弗·哥伦布（Christopher Columbus）于1492年发现，但误认为是印度，以致称当地人为印第安人并沿用至今。后以1499年至此的意大利探险家亚美利哥·韦斯普奇（Amerigo Vespucci）的名字命名。

USCG *abbr* = **United States Coast Guard** 美国海岸警卫队

USD *abbr* = **United States dollar** 美元

use
A /juːs/ *n* **1** [c and u] (act of utilizing) 使用; (state of being utilized) 被使用; **the ~ of force** 武力的使用; **a room for ~ as a library** 用作资料室的房间; **textbooks for ~ in universities** 大学用的课本; **the bar is for the ~ of members only** 这个酒吧仅向会员开放; **for external ~ only** Pharm 限外敷; **to make ~ of the most modern technologies** 利用最现代的技术; **we could make better ~ of our resources** 我们可以更有效地利用我们的资源; **to get good** *or* **a lot of ~ out of sth.** 大量使用某物; **to put sth. to good ~** 有效利用某物; **the car gets regular ~** 这辆车经常开; **the chapel was built in the 12th century and is still in ~ today** 这座小教堂建于12世纪，今天仍在使用; **to come into/go out of ~** 开始/停止使用 **2** [c and u] (purpose of utilizing) 用途; (way of utilizing) 用法; **the many ~s of a hairpin** 发夹的多种用途; **have you any ~ for this jug?** 这个罐子你有什么用吗？; **maybe we can find a ~ for him in the kitchen** 也许我们能在厨房给他找点事儿干; **to have no ~ for sb./sth.** (not need) 不需要某人/某事物; (dislike) 不喜欢某人/某事物; **to have one's/its ~s** colloq 有自己的用处/有其用场 **3** [u] (right to avail oneself of sth.) 使用权; **I have the ~ of the car this week** 这辆车本周归我用 **4** [u] (mental or physical ability) 功能; **to lose/regain the ~ of one's arms/legs** 失去/恢复手臂/双腿的功能 **5** [u] (usefulness) 有用; (value) 价值; (advantage) 益处; **to be of ~ (to sb.)** （对某人）有用; **can I be of any ~?** 我能帮什么忙吗？; **to be (of) no ~ (to sb.)** （对某人）没用; **to be no ~ at sth./doing sth.** colloq 不擅长某事/做某事; **what's the ~ of crying?** 哭有什么用？; **it's** *or* **there's no ~ complaining** 抱怨是没用的 **6** [u] (of drug) 吸毒; **widespread drug ~** 普遍的吸毒行为
B /juːz/ *vt* **1** (employ, say or write) 使用〈*word, language*〉; pej (exploit) 利用〈*person*〉; **can I ~ your phone?** 我能用一下你的电话吗？; **how often do you ~ the bus?** 你多长时间坐一次公交车？; **~ your initiative!** 自己想办法！; **he's only using it as an excuse** 他只是拿它当托词; **police ~d tear gas to disperse the crowds** 警察动用了催泪瓦斯驱散人群; **the blue files are ~d for storing old invoices** 蓝色卷宗是用来存放旧发票的; **~ your head** *or* Brit **loaf!** 你动动脑子！; **I have some information you may be able**

to ～ 我有一些可能对你有用的信息; **he's just using you** 他只是在利用你; **I felt ～d** 我感到被利用了 **2** (consume) 消耗; **this type of heater ～s a lot of electricity** 这种取暖器耗电量很大; **he's ～d all the water** 他把水全用完了 **3** (call oneself by) 自称; **she ～s her maiden name** 她用自己的娘家姓 **4** (desire, need) **he could ～ a wash** colloq 他很想洗一洗; **I could ～ a drink!** 我真想喝上一杯! **5** (take habitually) 吸食 ‹*drugs*› **6** archaic (treat) 对待; **to ～ sb. well/ill** 善待/恶劣对待某人

Phrasal verb

• **use up** *vt* [**～ sth. up, ～ up sth.**] 用尽; **the money was soon ～d up** 钱很快就用光了

use-by date *n* esp Brit 保质期

used¹ /ju:st/

A *modal aux* (*negative* **didn't use to**) 曾经; **he ～ to live here** 他曾经住在这里; **there ～ to be a pub here** 这里过去有一家酒吧; **she ～ to go out for walks** 她过去常常外出散步; **he didn't use to smoke** 他过去不抽烟

B *adj pred* 习惯的; **to be** *or* **get ～ to sb./sth.** 习惯某人/某事物; **you'll get ～ to it** 你会习惯的; **to be** *or* **get ～ to doing sth.** 习惯于做某事; **to be** *or* **get ～ to sb. doing sth.** 习惯某人做某事; **he takes a bit of getting ～ to** 要过一段时间才能习惯他

used² /ju:zd/ *adj* **1** (second-hand) 旧的; **～ car(s)** 二手汽车; **£10,000 in ～ notes** 1 万英镑流通纸币 **2** (having served purpose) 用过的 ‹*container, condom*›; **～ syringes** 用过的注射器

useful /'ju:sfl/ *adj* **1** (handy, practical) 有用的 ‹*tool, advice, discussion*›; **to be ～ for doing sth.** 有利于做某事; **to be ～ to sb./sth.** 对某人/某事物有帮助; **the machine is coming to the end of its ～ life** 这台机器的有效使用年限快到了; **to make oneself ～** 帮忙 **2** colloq (competent) 不错的; **to be ～ with one's fists/a paintbrush** 拳打得很好/擅长粉刷

usefully /'ju:sfəli/ *adv* 有用地

usefulness /'ju:sflnɪs/ *n* [u] 有用; **to outlive its** *or* **one's ～** 不再有用

useless /'ju:slɪs/ *adj* **1** (of no use) 无用的 ‹*device, suggestion*›; **his right leg was completely ～ because of the injury** 受伤后他的右腿完全废了 **2** (pointless) 徒劳的 ‹*attempt, waste*›; **it's ～ arguing** *or* **to argue with him** 跟他辩论毫无意义 **3** colloq (incompetent) 无能的 ‹*player, negotiator*›; **to be ～ at sth.** 在某事上差劲

uselessly /'ju:slɪsli/ *adv* 无用地 ‹*stand, lie*›

uselessness /'ju:slɪsnɪs/ *n* [u] 无用

user /'ju:zə(r)/ *n* **1** (person using sth.) 使用者; **a mobile-phone ～** 移动电话用户 **2** (drug) **～** 瘾君子

user: ～ account *n* 用户账号; **～-definable** *adj* 用户可定义的; **～-defined key** *n* 用户自定义键; **～-friendliness** *n* [u] 使用便利性; **～-friendly** *adj* 便于使用的 ‹*program, product*›; **～ group** *n* 用户群; **～ identification** *n* [c and u] 用户识别字符串; **～ interface** *n* 用户界面; **～name** *n* 用户名; **～ software** *n* [u] 用户软件

U-shaped *adj* U形的 ‹*pipe, curve*›

usher /'ʌʃə(r)/ ▸**p. 409**

A *n* (in court) 传达员; (in church) [尤指婚礼仪式上的] 迎宾员; (in cinema, theatre) 引座员

B *vt* 引导; **he ～ed us to our seats** 他把我们领到了座位上

Phrasal verbs

• **usher in** *vt* [**～ sb./sth. in, ～ in sb./sth.**] 迎接; **the railways ～ed in an era of cheap mass travel** 铁路系统开启了廉价的大众旅行时代

• **usher out** *vt* [**～ sb. out, ～ out sb.**] 把…领出去

usherette /,ʌʃə'ret/ ▸**p. 409** *n* 女引座员

USIA *abbr* **= United States Information Agency** 美国新闻署

USMC *abbr* **= United States Marine Corps** 美国海军陆战队

USN *abbr* **= United States Navy** 美国海军

USP *abbr* **= unique selling proposition**

USPS *abbr* **= United States Postal Service** 美国邮政管理局

USS *abbr* **= United States Ship** 美国船

USSR *abbr* Hist **= Union of Soviet Socialist Republics** 苏维埃社会主义共和国联盟

usual /'ju:ʒl/

A *adj* 通常的; **we will meet at the ～ time** 我们还是在老时间见面; **his ～ beer** 他常喝的那种啤酒; **it wasn't our ～ postman today** 今天来的不是我们平时见到的那位邮递员; **they said all the ～ things** 他们说的净是老一套; **he didn't sound like his ～ happy self** 他听起来不像平常那个乐天派了; **it is ～ to start a speech by thanking everybody for coming** 讲话前先感谢大家光临，这是惯例; **he came home later than ～** 他回家比平常晚了些; **as ～** 像平常一样; **Steve, as ～, was the last to arrive** 史蒂夫照例来得最晚; **as ～ at that hour, the place was deserted** 跟平常那个时刻一样，那地方空荡荡的; **it was business as ～ at the school** 学校照常上课; **as is ～ at a wedding, the bride was given away by her father** 按照婚礼的惯例，新娘由她的父亲交给新郎

B *n* colloq **1** (what usually happens) **the ～** 通常的事; **what did he say? — oh, the ～** 他说了什么? ——哦，老一套 **2** **the** *or* **one's ～** (drink) 常喝的饮料; (food) 常吃的食物; **your ～, sir?** 照旧吗，先生?

usually /'ju:ʒəli/ *adv* 通常; **she ～ comes on Thursdays** 她通常星期四来; **we are more than ～ excited about this deal** 我们对这项交易感到特别兴奋

usufruct /'ju:zju:frʌkt/ *n* [u and c] [罗马法的] 使用收益权

usurer /'ju:ʒərə(r)/ *n* pej 放高利贷者

usurp /ju:'zɜ:p/ *vt* pej **1** (seize) 篡夺 ‹*throne, authority, role*›; 侵占 ‹*material*› **2** (supplant) 非法取代 ‹*monarch, rival*›

usurper /ju:'zɜ:pə(r)/ *n* pej 篡位者

usury /'ju:ʒəri/ *n* [u] pej 放高利贷

UT *abbr* Amer **= Utah**

Utah /'ju:tɑ:/ *pr n* 犹他州

ute /ju:t/ *n* Austral, NZ colloq 轻型货车

utensil /ju:'tensl/ *n* 器皿; **kitchen/writing ～s** 厨房用具/文具

uterine /'ju:təraɪn/ *adj* 子宫的; **～ contractions** 子宫收缩

uterus /'ju:tərəs/ *n* (*pl* **uteri** /'ju:təraɪ/ *or* **～es**) 子宫

utilitarian /,ju:tɪlɪ'teərɪən/

A *adj* **1** (functional) 实用的 ‹*furniture, clothing*› **2** Philos 功利主义的 ‹*theory*›

B *n* 功利主义者

utilitarianism /,ju:tɪlɪ'teərɪənɪzəm/ *n* [u] 功利主义

utility /ju:'tɪləti/

A *n* **1** [u] (usefulness) 实用 **2** [c] **(public) ～** (public service) 公用事业 **3** [c] Comput 实用程序

B *modif* **1** (functional) 实用的 ‹*vehicle*› **2** (versatile) 技术全面的 ‹*player*›; 多才多艺的 ‹*actor*›

utility: ～ bill *n* (statement) 公用事业账单; (cost) 公用事业费用; **～ bond** *n* 公用事业债券; **～ company** *n* 公用事业公司; **～ furniture** *n* [u] Brit 实用家具; **～ program** *n* **= utility A3**; **～ room** *n* 杂物间

utilizable /'ju:təlaɪzəbl/ *adj* 可利用的

utilization /,ju:təlar'zeɪʃn/ *n* [u] 利用

utilize /'ju:təlaɪz/ *vt* 利用; **the resources are not fully ～d** 资源没有得到充分利用

utmost /'ʌtməʊst/

A *adj* **1** (greatest) 最大的 ‹*secrecy, honesty*›; **of the ～ importance** 最重要的; **with the ～ speed** 以最快速度 **2** (furthest) 最远的 ‹*point, limit*›; **the ～ ends of the earth** 天涯海角

B *n* 极限; **to the ～** 最大限度地; **at the ～** 至多; **to do one's ～ to do sth.** 竭尽全力做某事

Utopia /ju:'təʊpɪə/ *n* 乌托邦

Utopian /ju:'təʊpɪən/ *adj* **1** (modelled on perfection) 不切实际的 ‹*ideal, dream*› **2** (aiming at perfection) 追求完美的 ‹*person*›

utter¹ /'ʌtə(r)/ *adj attrib* 十足的 ‹*rogue, fool*›; 极度的 ‹*honesty, despair*›; **～ rubbish!** 一派胡言!; **an ～ stranger** 完全陌生的人

utter² *vt* 说出 ‹*prophesy*›; 发出 ‹*warning, cry, curse*›; **I couldn't ～ a word** 我一句话也说不出来

utterance /'ʌtərəns/ *n* **1** [u] (act of speaking) 说出 **2** [c] (statement, remark) 言论; **a prophetic ～** 预言 **3** [c] Ling (speech sequence) 话语 **4** [u] (manner of speaking) 表达方式; **clear/indistinct ～** 清晰/含混的言谈

utterly /'ʌtəli/ *adv* 完全地

uttermost /'ʌtəməʊst/ *adj, n* **= utmost**

U-turn /'ju:tɜ:n/ *n* U形转弯; **'no ～s'** "禁止掉头"; **to do a ～ on sth.** fig 在某事上彻底转变

UV *abbr* **= ultraviolet**

uvula /'ju:vjʊlə/ *n* (*pl* **uvulae** /'ju:vjʊli:/) 小舌

uvular /'ju:vjʊlə(r)/ *adj* 小舌音的; **a ～ fricative/plosive** 小舌摩擦音/爆破音

Uzbek /'ʌzbek, 'ʊz-/ ▸**p. 503, p. 426**

A *adj* (of Uzbekistan) 乌兹别克的; (of the people) 乌兹别克人的; (of the language) 乌孜别克语的

B *n* **1** [c] (person) 乌兹别克人 **2** [u] (language) 乌孜别克语

Uzbekistan /,ʌzbekɪ'stɑ:n, ,ʊz-/ *pr n* 乌兹别克斯坦

V, v /viː/
A *n* (*pl* **Vs** *or* **V's**) [1] (letter) [英语字母表的第22个字母] [2] **V** (number) [罗马数字] 5
B *abbr* [1] **V** Elec = **volt** [2] **v** = **versus 2** [3] **v** = **vide** /ˈviːdeɪ/ 参阅 [4] **v** = **verse 3, 4**

VA *abbr* Amer = **Virginia 1**

vac /væk/ *n* Brit colloq [1] (vacation) 假期 [2] = **vacuum cleaner** [3] *sing* (cleaning) = **vacuum A4**

vacancy /ˈveɪkənsi/ *n* [1] [c] (unoccupied room) (in hotel) 空房; (on campsite) 空位; **'vacancies'/'no vacancies'** "有空房" / "客满" [2] [c] (unfilled job, place) 空职; **a ~ for an accountant** 会计职位空缺; **to advertise a ~** 广告招人填补空职; **to fill/create a ~** 填补/创造职位空缺 [3] [u] (absent-mindedness) 心不在焉 [4] [u] (ignorance) 茫然 [5] [u] (empty space) 空白处

vacancy rate *n* 空房率

vacant /ˈveɪkənt/ *adj* [1] (unoccupied) 空着的 ‹*room, flat, seat, land, office*›; **'~'** (sign on toilet door) "无人" [2] (unfilled) 空缺的 ‹*post, position*›; **to become** *or* **fall ~** 空出来; **'Situations V~'** (section in newspaper) "招聘广告栏" [3] *usu attrib* (absent-minded) 心不在焉的 ‹*gaze, expression*› [4] *usu attrib* (ignorant) 茫然的 ‹*look, reply*›

vacant lot *n* Amer 空地

vacantly /ˈveɪkəntli/ *adv* [1] (absent-mindedly) 心不在焉地 ‹*stare, look*› [2] (ignorantly) 茫然地 ‹*look, answer*›

vacant possession *n* [u] Brit 空置产业合法占有权

vacate /vəˈkeɪt, Amer ˈveɪkeɪt/ *vt* formal [1] (leave empty) 腾出 ‹*house, premises*›; **'guests must ~ their rooms by midday'** "客人必须在中午前退房" [2] (give up) 辞去 ‹*job, post*›

vacation /vəˈkeɪʃn, Amer veɪ-/
A *n* [1] [u and c] Amer (holiday) 假期; **to be/go on ~** 在/去度假; **to take a ~** 休假; **did you have a good ~?** 你假期过得好吗? ; **to spend one's ~ in France** 在法国度假 [2] [c] (recess, break) Sch, Univ 假期; Jur 休庭期; **the long** Brit *or* **summer ~** 暑假; **during** *or* **over** *or* **in the ~** 在假期中 [3] [u] (abandonment of job) 放弃
B *vi* Amer 度假; **to ~ in Miami** 在迈阿密度假

vacationer /vəˈkeɪʃənə(r), Amer veɪ-/ *n* Amer 度假者

vaccinate /ˈvæksɪneɪt/ *vt* 给…接种疫苗; **to ~ sb. against tetanus** 给某人接种破伤风疫苗

vaccination /ˌvæksɪˈneɪʃn/ *n* [u and c] 接种; **a ~ against** *or* **for sth.** 某疫苗的接种; **to have a ~** 接种疫苗; **a ~ programme** 接种计划

vaccine /ˈvæksiːn, Amer vækˈsiːn/ *n* [1] Med, Vet 疫苗; **rabies/tetanus ~** 狂犬病/破伤风疫苗; **a ~ against** *or* **for TB** 预防肺结核的疫苗 [2] Comput 防毒软件

vaccinology /ˌvæksɪˈnɒlədʒi/ *n* [u] 疫苗学

vacillate /ˈvæsəleɪt/ *vi* 犹豫; **to ~ over sth.** 在某事上犹豫不决; **to ~ between teaching and journalism** 拿不定主意是教书还是从事新闻工作

vacillating /ˈvæsɪleɪtɪŋ/
A *adj* 犹豫不决的
B *n* [u] = **vacillation**

vacillation /ˌvæsɪˈleɪʃn/ *n* [u] 犹豫

vacua /ˈvækjʊə/ *pl* ▸ **vacuum A1, A2**

vacuity /vəˈkjuːəti/ *n* formal [1] [c] (empty space) 空白 [2] [u] (blankness) 缺乏思考; (inanity) 愚蠢; **the ~ of her gaze/mind** 她呆滞的目光/心灵上的空虚

vacuous /ˈvækjʊəs/ *adj* formal 茫然的 ‹*expression*›; 空洞的 ‹*remark, article, plot*›; 无意义的 ‹*idea, existence, optimism*›

vacuum /ˈvækjʊəm/
A *n* [1] (*pl* **~s** *or* **vacua**) Phys 真空; **to create a ~** 造成真空 [2] (*pl* **~s** *or* **vacua**) fig (void) 空白; **a cultural/an intellectual ~** 文化/知识空白; **it left a ~ in my life** 这使我的生活变得空虚; **to be in a ~** 与世隔绝 [3] (*pl* **~s**) (appliance) = **vacuum cleaner** [4] (*pl* **~s**) (act of cleaning) 吸尘; **to give sth. a ~** 给…吸尘
B *vt* 用真空吸尘器打扫

vacuum: ~ bottle *n* Amer = **~ flask**; **~-clean** *vt* 用真空吸尘器打扫; **~ cleaner** *n* 真空吸尘器; **~ distillation** *n* [u] 真空蒸馏; **~ flask** *n* esp Brit 保温瓶; **~ gauge** *n* 真空计

vacuum pack
A *n* 真空包装袋
B **vacuum-pack** *vt* 真空包装; **vacuum-packed bacon** 真空包装熏猪肉

vacuum: ~ pump *n* 真空泵; **~ sweeper** *n* Amer = **~ cleaner**; **~ tube** *n* 真空管

vade mecum /ˌvɑːdi ˈmeɪkʊm, ˌveɪdi ˈmiːkəm/ *n* 手册

Vaduz /væˈdʊts/ *pr n* 瓦杜兹

vagabond /ˈvæɡəbɒnd/
A *n* 无业游民
B *adj attrib* [1] (wandering) 流浪的 ‹*person*› [2] (vagrant-like) 流浪汉般的 ‹*lifestyle, habit*›

vagaries /ˈveɪɡəriːz/ *npl* formal 变幻莫测

vagina /vəˈdʒaɪnə/ *n* 阴道

vaginal /vəˈdʒaɪnl/ *adj* 阴道的; **~ intercourse** 阴道性交

vagrancy /ˈveɪɡrənsi/ *n* [u] (gen) 流浪; Jur 流浪罪; **~ laws** 流浪管制法

vagrant /ˈveɪɡrənt/
A *n* 流浪汉
B *adj attrib* 流浪汉的 ‹*lifestyle*›; 流浪的 ‹*beggar*›

vague /veɪɡ/ *adj* [1] (unclearly perceived) 模糊的 ‹*memory, notion*›; **they had only a ~ idea where the place was** 他们只是大概知道那个地方的位置 [2] (not expressed clearly) 含糊的; (evasive) 含糊其辞的; **she gave only a ~ description of her attacker** 她只是粗略地描述了一下那个袭击她的人; **I asked her what she'd like for her birthday, but she was a bit ~** 我问她生日想要什么，但她说得不太清楚; **he was accused of being deliberately** *or* **intentionally ~** 他被指责有意含糊其辞 [3] (unsure) 不确定的; **I am still ~ about what you want** 我还是不清楚你想要什么 [4] (absent-minded) 恍惚的; **his ~ manner concealed a brilliant mind** 他表面上很糊涂，实际上相当聪明 [5] (unclear in shape) 不清晰的; **in the darkness they could see the ~ outline of a church** 他们在黑暗中看到一座教堂模糊的轮廓 [6] (faint, slight) 微弱的 ‹*sound*›; 淡淡的 ‹*smell, taste*›; 轻微的 ‹*feeling*›; **a ~ sense of guilt** 隐隐的内疚感

vaguely /ˈveɪɡli/ *adv* [1] (slightly) 略微地 ‹*familiar, salty, irritated*›; **to be ~ like sth.** 有点像某事物 [2] (faintly) 模糊地 ‹*aware*›; **to feel ~ like a bee sting** 隐约觉得像是被蜜蜂蜇了一下 [3] (distractedly) 心不在焉地 ‹*smile, gaze, say*› [4] (imprecisely) 不确切地 ‹*remember, describe, reply*›

vagueness /ˈveɪɡnɪs/ *n* [u] [1] (imprecision) 不确切 [2] (fuzziness) 模糊 [3] (absent-mindedness) 恍惚

vain /veɪn/ *adj* [1] (conceited) 自负的; **to be ~ about sth.** 为某事自负 [2] *usu attrib* (futile) 徒劳的 ‹*promise, attempt*›; 枉费心机的 ‹*display, boast*›; **to be (all) in ~** (完全) 是白费劲; **in the ~ hope that ...** 徒然希望…; **in a ~ attempt** *or* **effort to do sth.** 徒劳地做某事; **take sb.'s name in ~** 亵渎某人的名字

vainglorious /ˌveɪnˈɡlɔːrɪəs/ *adj* liter 自负的 ‹*person*›; 自吹自擂的 ‹*assessment, ambition*›

vainly /ˈveɪnli/ *adv* [1] (conceitedly) 自负地; **to admire oneself ~ in the mirror** 对着镜子自我欣赏 [2] (futilely) 徒劳地 ‹*struggle, wait*›; **to shout ~** 白费力气大喊大叫

valance /ˈvæləns/ *n* [1] (screen on bed) 床幔 [2] (sheet) 挂布 [3] esp Amer (over curtains) [窗帘上端的] 短幔

vale /veɪl/ *n* liter 山谷; **~ of tears** 尘世

valediction /ˌvælɪˈdɪkʃn/ *n* formal [1] [u] (farewell) 告别 [2] [c] (speech) 告别词; **a funeral** *or* **memorial ~** 悼词

valedictory /ˌvælɪˈdɪktəri/
A *adj usu attrib* 告别的 ‹*speech, wave*›
B *n* Amer [最优毕业生的] 告别演说

valency /ˈveɪlənsi/, **valence** /ˈveɪləns/ *ns* [1] Chem 原子价 [2] Ling 价

valentine /ˈvæləntaɪn/ *n* [1] **~ (card)** 情人节贺卡 [2] (sweetheart) 情人; **will you be my ~** 做我的情人吧

Valentine Day, Valentine's Day *n* 情人节

valet /ˈvælɪt, -leɪ/ ▸ **p. 409**
A *n* [1] (servant) 贴身男仆 [2] (employee in hotel) 客房侍者; Amer (car attendant) 停车管理员 [3] esp Amer (rack) 衣物架
B *vt* [1] (clean) 洗烫 ‹*suit*›; 清洗 ‹*car interior*› [2] (serve) 伺候 ‹*man*›
C *vi* 伺候; **to ~ for sb.** 服侍某人

valeting /ˈvælɪtɪŋ/ *n* [u] 清洗

valeting service *n* 洗车服务

valet: ~ parking *n* [u] 代客停车服务; **~ service** *n* [1] (car cleaning) 洗车服务; [2] (for clothes) 洗衣服务; [3] = **~ parking**

Valhalla /vælˈhælə/ *pr n* 瓦尔哈拉殿堂 [挪威神话中奥丁神接待战死者英灵的殿堂]

valiant /'væliənt/ *adj* 勇敢的 ‹*soldier*›; 英勇的 ‹*attack*›; **to make a ~ attempt to do sth.** 勇敢尝试做某事; **despite their ~ efforts** 尽管他们不懈努力

valiantly /'væliəntli/ *adv* 勇敢地 ‹*fight*›; 大胆地 ‹*strive, try*›

valid /'vælɪd/ *adj* 1 (not expired, acceptable) 有效的 ‹*ticket, licence, passport, offer*›; **to be ~ for sth.** 对某事物有效; **to be no longer ~** 已过期 2 (legally binding) 具有法律效力的 ‹*contract, document*› 3 (well-founded, reasonable) 有根据的 ‹*complaint, criticism, objection*›; 合理的 ‹*argument, reason, excuse, method*›; 符合逻辑的 ‹*theory, comparison, point*› 4 Comput 有效的 ‹*password, address*›

validate /'vælɪdeɪt/ *vt* 1 (make legal, official) 使…生效 ‹*contract, document, passport*›; **to ~ a parking ticket** 确认违章停车罚单有效 2 (substantiate) 证实 ‹*argument, theory, claim*› 3 (approve) 认可 ‹*course, method*›

validation /,vælɪ'deɪʃn/ *n* [u] 认可

validity /və'lɪdəti/ *n* [u] 1 (of ticket, licence, passport, offer) 有效 2 (of argument, reason, excuse, method) 正确; (of complaint, criticism, objection) 正当 3 Comput 有效

valise /və'li:z, Amer və'li:s/ *n* 小旅行包

Valium® /'væliəm/ *n* 瓦利姆镇定药

Valletta /və'letə/ *pr n* 瓦莱塔

valley /'væli/ *n* (*pl* **~s**) 山谷; **the Thames ~** 泰晤士河谷

valor /'vælə(r)/ *n* Amer = **valour**

valorous /'vælərəs/ *adj* liter 英勇的 ‹*conduct, soldier*›

valour /'vælə(r)/ *n* [u] Brit 英勇; **'for ~'** Mil "以彰勇毅"; ▸**discretion**

valuable /'væljuəbl/

A *adj* 1 (precious) 很值钱的 ‹*commodity, asset*›; **a ~ ring/collection** 贵重的戒指/收藏品 2 (useful) 重要的 ‹*member*›; 宝贵的 ‹*information, advice, time*›; **to be ~ in treating ...** 对治疗…很有帮助

B **valuables** *npl* 贵重物品

valuation /,vælju'eɪʃn/ *n* 1 (assessment of monetary worth) 估价; **to have a ~ done on sth.** 请人给某物估价 2 (monetary worth) 估定的价值; **a ~ of £50** 50 英镑的估价; **to put a ~ on sth.** 给某物一个估值 3 fig (assessment of worth) 评价; **to put a high ~ on sth.** 看重某事物; **to take sb. at his own ~** 接受某人的自我评价

value /'vælju:/

A *n* 1 [c and u] (monetary worth) 价值; **a bracelet of great/little ~** 很值钱/不值钱的手镯; **to go up** *or* **rise** *or* **increase in ~** 增值; **to go down** *or* **fall** *or* **decrease in ~** 贬值; **a prize to the ~ of £100** 价值为 100 英镑的奖品; **sports cars tend to hold their ~ well** 跑车往往很保值; **to put** *or* **place a ~ on sth.** lit 给某物估价; fig 重视某事物 2 [u] esp Brit (worth relative to cost) 值得; **the bike is good ~ at $100** 花 100 美元买这辆自行车很值; **to be bad** *or* **poor ~** 不合算; **large sizes give the best ~ for money** 大尺寸的最划算 3 [u] (importance) 重要; (usefulness) 有用; **the ~ of regular exercise** 经常锻炼的好处; **your experience is of ~ to others** 你的经验对其他人有帮助; **the books are of no educational ~** 这些书没有教育意义; **we set great ~ on his friendship** 我们珍视他的友谊; **to be good ~** (important) 很重要; (useful) 很有用; (enjoyable) 很令人愉快 4 [c] Math 值; **let y have the ~ 33** 设 y 的值为 33

B **values** *npl* 价值观; **moral/family ~s** 道德观/家庭价值观

C *vt* 1 (prize) 重视; **I ~ my privacy** 我看重自己的隐私; **I ~ him as a good friend** 我把他视为好朋友 2 (assess worth of) 给…估价; **the property has been ~d at over $200,000** 这处房产估价为 20 多万美元

value-added /,vælju:'ædɪd/ [u] 1 Econ 增值 2 Comm 附加值

value-added tax *n* 增值税

valued /'vælju:d/ *adj* 受敬重的 ‹*friend, employee, customer*›; 宝贵的 ‹*opinion, contribution*›

value: ~ date *n* 起息日; **~ engineering** *n* [u] 价值工程; **~-for-money** *adj* 物有所值的; **~-free** *adj* 客观的 ‹*account, assessment*›; **~ judgement** *n* [根据主观意见的] 价值判断; **~-laden** *adj* 受主观价值影响的 ‹*term, concept*›; **'freedom fighter' is a ~-laden word** "自由战士"是个带有主观性的词汇

valueless /'væljʊləs/ *adj* 无价值的

value: ~-neutral *adj* 客观的 ‹*term, language, fact*›; **~ pack** *n* 超值套装

valuer /'væljʊə(r)/ ▸**p. 409** *n* 估价员

valve /vælv/ *n* 1 (device) (in machine, engine) 阀; (in pipe, duct) 闸阀; (on tyre, football) 气门 2 (in heart, blood vessel) 瓣膜 3 Mus **(air) ~** 阀键 4 (piece of mollusc shell) 贝壳 5 Brit Electron 电子管

vamoose /və'mu:s/ *vi* esp Amer colloq 跑掉; **~!** 开溜吧!

vamp[1] /væmp/ pej

A *n* (seductive woman) 荡妇

B *vt* 勾引 ‹*man*›

vamp[2]

A *n* 1 (front part on shoe upper) 鞋面 2 Mus 即席伴奏

B *vt* 给…换鞋面 ‹*shoe*›

C *vi* 即席伴奏

Phrasal verb

• **vamp up** *vt* [**~ sth. up, ~ up sth.**] colloq 1 (fix up) 润色 ‹*speech, show*›; 修补 ‹*clothing*›; 整修 ‹*house*› 2 (concoct) 编造 ‹*excuse, rumour*›

vampire /'væmpaɪə(r)/ *n* 吸血鬼

vampire bat *n* 吸血蝠

van[1] /væn/ *n* 1 Aut (small) 送货车; (large) 厢式运货车 2 Amer **(camper) ~** 移动房车 3 Brit (caravan) 旅行拖车 4 Brit Rail 行李车厢; **a goods/luggage ~** 行李车厢

van[2] *n* (vanguard) 前卫; **to be in the ~ of** 在…的前头 ‹*procession*›; 处于…的前沿 ‹*movement, field*›

vanadium /və'neɪdiəm/ *n* [u] 钒; **~ steel** 钒钢

vandal /'vændl/ *n* 1 (hooligan) 蓄意破坏者 2 **Vandal** Hist 汪达尔人

vandalism /'vændəlɪzəm/ *n* [u] (action) 破坏行为; (result) 破坏后果

vandalize /'vændəlaɪz/ *vt* lit, fig 蓄意破坏 ‹*property, landscape*›; **to ~ a building/telephone box** 恣意毁坏建筑物/电话亭

van driver ▸**p. 409** *n* 货车司机

vane /veɪn/ *n* 1 (blade of machine, windmill) 叶片 2 = **weathervane** 3 (flat part of feather) 翎 4 (fin or plate) (of torpedo) 舵; (of arrow) 箭翎

vanguard /'vængɑ:d/ *n* Mil 先头部队; fig 先锋; **to be in the ~ (of sth.)** Mil 是（某队伍的）先遣部队; fig 是（…的）先锋 ‹*movement, reform*›

vanilla /və'nɪlə/

A *n* 1 [u] (flavouring) 香草香精 2 [c] **~ (pod)** 香子兰豆 3 [u and c] Bot 香子兰 4 [u and c] (ice cream) 香草冰激凌

B *modif* 1 Culin 香草味的 ‹*sauce, custard*› 2 Bot 香子兰的 ‹*plant, bean*› 3 colloq (ordinary) **(plain) ~** 普通的 ‹*product, version*›

vanilla: ~ essence *n* [u] 香草香精; **~-flavoured** *adj* 香草味的 ‹*cream, drink*›

vanish /'vænɪʃ/ *vi* 1 (disappear) 消失; **to ~ into the distance** 消失在远方; ▸**face A7** 2 fig (leave, be missing) 突然消失; **to ~ without trace** 消失得无影无踪; **to ~ into thin air** 蒸发 3 (cease to exist) «*pain*» 不复存在; «*species, civilization*» 绝迹

vanished /'vænɪʃt/ *adj* 消亡的 ‹*species, civilization*›

vanishing: ~ cream *n* [u and c] 雪花膏; **~ point** *n* [平行线条的] 没影点; **~ trick** *n* 1 (magic trick) 消失术; 2 fig (disappearance) 及时的消失

vanity /'vænəti/ *n* 1 [u] (pride) 虚荣; [c] (feeling of pride) 虚荣心; **to flatter** *or* **tickle sb.'s ~** 满足某人的虚荣心 2 [u] liter (futility) 无用; **all is ~** 一切皆空 3 [c] liter (futile thing) 无价值的事物; **the vanities of the world** 尘世的无谓虚荣 4 [c] Amer **~ (table)** (dressing table) 梳妆台 5 [c] Brit (basin) = **vanity unit**

vanity: ~ bag *n* 梳妆包; **~ case** *n* 梳妆盒; **~ mirror** *n* [汽车副驾驶位前的] 化妆镜; **~ plate** *n* [有车主姓名或姓名首字母的] 个性化汽车牌照; **~ press** *n* 作者自费出书的出版社; **~ unit** *n* Brit 组合式盥洗盆

vanload /'vænləʊd/ *n* 货车载重量

vanquish /'væŋkwɪʃ/ *vt* lit 彻底击败 ‹*foe, rival*›; fig 抑制 ‹*gloom, doubt*›; 克服 ‹*prejudice, fear, despair*›

vantage /'vɑ:ntɪdʒ, Amer 'væn-/ *n* [c] = **vantage point**

vantage: ~ ground *n* 有利地位; **~ point** *n* 1 (high point) 有利地点; **from the ~ point of ...** 从…的有利地位; **from my ~ point I could see ...** 从我这里能清楚地看到…; 2 fig (point of view) 有利视角

Vanuatu /,vɑ:nu:'ɑ:tu:/ *pr n* 瓦努阿图

vapid /'væpɪd/ *adj* pej 乏味的 ‹*remark, conversation*›; 枯燥的 ‹*novel, style*›; 愚蠢的 ‹*smile, expression*›

vapor /'veɪpə(r)/ *n* Amer = **vapour**

vaporization /,veɪpəraɪ'zeɪʃn/ *n* [u] 蒸发

vaporize /'veɪpəraɪz/

A *vt* 1 (convert into vapour) 使…蒸发 ‹*liquid, solid*› 2 (destroy) «*bomb, heat*» 烧化 ‹*person, chemical waste*›

B *vi* «*liquid*» 蒸发

vaporizer /'veɪpəraɪzə(r)/ *n* 1 (device forming vapour) 雾化器 2 (atomizer) 橡皮头喷嘴

vapour /'veɪpə(r)/ *n* [u and c] Brit 蒸汽; **water/exhaust ~** 水蒸气/废气

vapour trail *n* 雾化尾迹

vapourware /'veɪpəweə(r)/ *n* [u] colloq 雾件 [宣布要上市但尚未设计生产的电脑软硬件产品]

variability /,veərɪə'bɪləti/ *n* [u] 可变性

variable /'veərɪəbl/

A *adj* 1 (liable to change) 变化无常的 ‹*mood, temperature, rainfall*›; 方向不定的 ‹*wind*›; 时多时少的 ‹*amount*›; **goods of ~ quality** 质量时好时坏的货物 2 (able to be changed) 可调的 ‹*speed, lighting*›; 调速的 ‹*gear*› 3 Math 变量的; **a ~ quantity** 变量

B *n* 1 (changeable factor) 可变因素 2 Math 变量; **a dependent/free/random ~** 因变量/自变量/随机变数

variable geometry

A *n* [u] 1 Aviat 可变机翼 2 Pol 可变政策地域整合

B **variable-geometry** *adj* 1 Aviat 可变翼的; **a variable-geometry aircraft/wing** 可变翼飞机/可变机翼 2 Pol 可变政策地域整合模型的 ‹*coalition*›

variable rate mortgage *n* 浮动利率抵押贷款

variance /'veərɪəns/ *n* 1 [u] (difference) 不同; (disagreement) 分歧; **to be at ~ with the evidence/facts** 与证据/事实有出入; **my views are at ~ with his** 我和他看法不一致; **~ between A and B** A 与 B 之间的差别; **to be at ~ with sb. (about a subject)** 和某人（在某问题上）看法相悖 2 [c] Math, Stat 方差 3 [c] Amer Jur 规避规定的许可

variant /'veərɪənt/

A *n* 变体; **to be a ~ of sth.** 是…的变体; **a ~ on the theme** 这一主题的另一种说法

B *adj attrib* 不同的 ‹*spelling, tone, species*›; ~

reading *or* text *or* version 不同版本; ～ form Bot 变异体

variation /ˌveərɪ'eɪʃn/ *n* 1 [u and c] (fluctuation) 变化; (difference) 差异; **a wide ～ in prices** 价格的巨大差异; **a slight ～ in** *or* **of colour** 微小的色差; **～ between A and B** A 与 B 之间的差异 2 [c] (different version) 变体; **a ～ of a game/recipe** 游戏/食谱的另一种形式 3 [c] Mus 变奏曲; **～s on a theme** 主题变奏曲; fig 一件事的多种说法

varicoloured Brit, **varicolored** Amer /'veərɪkʌləd/ *adj* 色彩斑斓的

varicose /'værɪkəʊs/ *adj* 曲张的; **a ～ vein, ～ veins** 曲张静脉; **～ ulcer/treatment** 静脉曲张性溃疡/静脉曲张治疗

varied /'veərɪd/ *adj* 各种各样的; **her talents were many and ～** 她多才多艺; **～ sizes** 各种尺码

variegated /'veərɪgeɪtɪd/ *adj* 1 (multicoloured) 色彩斑斓的 ‹*pattern, landscape, flower*›; 斑驳的 ‹*colour, leaf*› 2 Bot 有斑点的 ‹*foliage, plant*›

variegation /ˌveərɪ'geɪʃn/ *n* [u] 1 (multi-coloration) 色彩斑斓 2 Bot 斑驳

variety /və'raɪəti/ *n* 1 [u] (diversity) 多样化; **a lack of ～ in style** 风格变化的缺乏; **to lack ～** «*job, life*» 缺乏变化; **～ is the spice of life** Prov 变化是生活的调味剂 2 [c] (range) 一系列种类; **a wide** *or* **great ～** 很多种类; **a ～ of** 各种 ‹*activities, styles*›; **to come in a ～ of sizes** 有各种尺码; **for a ～ of reasons** 因为种种原因 3 [c] (type) 种类; **lighters of the refillable/disposable ～** 可重注燃气打火机/一次性打火机 4 [c] Biol 品种; **a new plant ～** 新的植物品种 5 [u and c] Theat, TV ～ (show) 综艺节目; **a ～ act** 综艺表演

variety: ～ meats *npl* Amer [食用的] 动物内脏; **～ show** *n* 综艺节目; **～ store** *n* Amer 杂货铺

varifocal /'veərɪfəʊkl/

A *adj* 变焦距的 ‹*lenses*›

B varifocals *npl* 变焦眼镜

various /'veərɪəs/ *adj* 1 *usu attrib* (several) 许多的; **at ～ times** 在很多时候; **in ～ ways** 以多种方式 2 *usu attrib* (different) 各种各样的; **at their ～ addresses** 在他们各自的地址 3 formal (diverse) 多样化的 ‹*landscape, environment*›

variously /'veərɪəsli/ *adv* 以各种方式 ‹*arranged, decorated*›; **it has been ～ suggested that ...** 各方人士建议…

varmint /'vɑːmɪnt/ *n* Amer colloq or dial 1 (animal) 害兽 2 (person) 淘气鬼

varnish /'vɑːnɪʃ/

A *n* [u and c] (for wood, metal) 清漆; Brit (for nails) 指甲油; **an outward ～ of civilization** 文明的外表

B *vt* 给…涂清漆 ‹*wood, furniture*›; Brit 给…涂指甲油 ‹*nails*›; **to ～ the truth** 掩盖真相

varnished /'vɑːnɪʃt/ *adj* 涂了清漆的 ‹*wood, desk*›

varsity /'vɑːsəti/

A *n* Amer 校队

B *modif* 1 Brit 大学的 ‹*match, team*› 2 Amer 校队的; **the ～ team** 校队; **a ～ player** 校队运动员

vary /'veəri/

A *vi* 1 (differ) 相异; **to ～ greatly** 差异极大; **to ～ from sth.** 与…不同 ‹*previous result, response*›; **to ～ from X to Y** 从 X 到 Y 不等; **it varies from one child to another** 孩子和孩子各不相同; **to ～ in size/quality/price** 大小/质量/价格各异; **opinions ～ (on this subject)** 大家（在这个问题上的）意见不尽相同; **results ～ greatly** 结果差异很大 2 (change) ‹*price, colour, mood*› 变化; **to ～ with** *or* **according to sth.** «*weather, height*» 随着…变化 ‹*season, environment*›; **to ～ between X and Y** «*numbers*» 在 X 和 Y 之间变化

B *vt* 使…多样化 ‹*diet, schedule*›; 改变 ‹*temperature, flow, approach, route*›

varying /'veərɪɪŋ/ *adj attrib* 不同的; **～ amounts/opinions** 不同的数量/意见; **with ～ (degrees of) success** 有不同（程度）的成功

vascular /'væskjʊlə(r)/ *adj usu attrib* 1 Anat, Med 血管的 2 Bot 维管的

vase /vɑːz, Amer veɪs, veɪz/ *n* (for flowers) 花瓶; (as ornament) 装饰瓶

vasectomy /və'sektəmi/ *n* 输精管切除术

Vaseline® /'væsɪliːn/

A *n* 凡士林

B vaseline *vt* 给…搽凡士林 ‹*skin*›

vasoconstrictor /ˌveɪzəʊkən'strɪktə(r)/ *n* 血管收缩药

vasodilator /ˌveɪzəʊdaɪ'leɪtə(r)/ *n* 血管舒张药

vasomotor /'veɪzəʊməʊtə(r)/ *adj attrib* 血管舒缩的

vasopressor /ˌveɪzəʊ'presə(r)/ *n* 血管加压药

vassal /'væsl/ *n* 1 Hist 封臣 2 fig (person) 仆从; (country) 附庸国

vassalage /'væsəlɪdʒ/ *n* [u] 1 Hist 封臣地位 2 fig formal (subordination) 附属国; **～ state** 属国

vast /vɑːst, Amer væst/ *adj* 1 (quantitatively) 大量的 ‹*pile, wealth*›; 巨大的 ‹*importance*›; 渊博的 ‹*knowledge*›; **a ～ amount of** 一大笔 ‹*money*›; 大量的 ‹*resources*›; **the ～ majority** 绝大多数 2 (spatially) 宽敞的 ‹*room*›; 辽阔的 ‹*area, ocean, plain*›; **a ～ stretch of desert** 广袤的沙漠

vastly /'vɑːstli, Amer 'væstli/ *adv* 极大地 ‹*overrated*›; 非常 ‹*different, popular, difficult*›; **to be ～ improved** (in ability) 有大幅提高; (in appearance) 有极大改观

vastness /'vɑːstnɪs, Amer 'væstnɪs/ *n* [u] 1 (in quantity) 大量 2 (of space) 辽阔

VAT /ˌviːeɪ'tiː, væt/ *abbr* Brit **= value-added tax**

vat /væt/ *n* 大桶; **a beer/wine ～** 啤酒/葡萄酒桶

Vatican /'vætɪkən/ *pr n* **the ～** (palace) 梵蒂冈宫; (administration) 梵蒂冈 [罗马教廷]

Vatican: ～ City *pr n* 梵蒂冈; **～ Council** *n* 梵蒂冈会议

VAT: ～ man /'væt mæn/ *n* Brit colloq **the ～ man** (officer) 增值税税务员; (department) 税务及海关总署; **～-registered** *adj* Brit 注册增值税的 ‹*company, customer*›

vaudeville /'vɔːdəvɪl/ *n* esp Amer 歌舞杂耍表演厅; **a ～ star** 杂耍明星

vaudevillian /ˌvɔːdə'vɪlɪən/

A *n* esp Amer (performer) 杂耍演员; (writer) 杂耍剧作者

B *adj* 杂耍的 ‹*song, style*›

vault[1] /vɔːlt/ *n* 1 Archit 拱顶; **the ～ of heaven** liter 天穹 2 (underground room) 地窖; (of church, monastery) **(burial) ～** 地下墓室; **wine ～** 酒窖 3 (in bank) 保险库

vault[2]

A *vi* 跳跃; **to ～ over** *or* **across sth.** 跳过某物

B *vt* 跳过 ‹*barrier, ditch*›; **to ～ five metres** 撑杆跳过 5 米高

C *n* 撑跳

vaulted /'vɔːltɪd/ *adj* 拱形的 ‹*ceiling*›; 有拱顶的 ‹*room*›

vaulting[1] /'vɔːltɪŋ/ *n* [u] Archit 拱形结构

vaulting[2] ▸ **p. 307** *n* [u] (in gymnastics) 跳跃

vaulting: ～ horse *n* 鞍马; **～ pole** *n* [撑杆跳运动中的] 撑杆

vaunt /vɔːnt/ *vt* 吹嘘

vaunted /'vɔːntɪd/ *adj* 被吹嘘的; **much ～** 大肆吹嘘的 ‹*success, achievement*›

vblog /'viːblɒg/ *n* 视频博客

VC *abbr* 1 Brit Mil **= Victoria Cross** 2 Brit Univ **= vice chancellor 1**

VCD *abbr* **= video compact disc**

V-chip *n* [装入电视接收器阻断暴力或色情节目的] V 芯片

VCR *abbr* **= video cassette recorder**

VD ▸ **p. 377** *abbr* **= venereal disease** 性病; **a ～ clinic** 性病诊所

VDR *abbr* **= video disc recorder**

VDU *abbr* **= visual display unit**

veal /viːl/ *n* [u] 小牛肉; **～ stew/production** 炖小牛肉/小牛肉生产

veal: ～ calf *n* 肉用小牛; **～ crate** *n* 小牛栏

vector /'vektə(r)/ *n* 1 Math, Phys 矢量, 向量; **～ analysis/field** 向量分析/向量场 2 Biol 传病媒介 3 Aviat 航线

VE day *n* [二次大战的] 欧洲胜利日

veejay /'viːdʒeɪ/ *n* esp Amer colloq 电视音乐节目主持人

veep /viːp/ *n* Amer colloq **= vice-president**

veer /vɪə(r)/ *vi* 1 (change course) «*vehicle, person*» 转向; «*ship, aircraft*» 改变航向; **to ～ to the right** «*car, road*» 向右转弯; **to ～ away from/towards sth.** 转向躲开/冲向某物; **to ～ off the road/across the road** «*vehicle*» 驶出公路/转向横穿马路; **to ～ off course** «*aircraft*» 偏离航线 2 Naut «*wind*» 转向; **to ～ towards the north** 风向转北 3 fig (deviate) 转变; **to ～ (away) from** «*conversation, person*» 转换 ‹*topic, way of thinking*›; **to ～ towards** «*politics, person*» 转向 ‹*idea, stance*›; **to ～ between depression and elation** 一会儿闷闷不乐，一会儿又兴高采烈

veg /vedʒ/ Brit colloq

A *n* (*pl* ～) **= vegetable(s)** 蔬菜; **meat and two ～** 肉和两种蔬菜

B *vi* (*pres p etc.* **-gg-**) **～ (out)** «*person*» 懒散

vegan /'viːgən/

A *n* 严格素食主义者

B *adj* 严格素食的 ‹*diet*›; 严格素食主义的 ‹*chef*›

veganism /'viːgənɪzəm/ *n* [u] 严格素食主义

Vegeburger® /'vedʒɪbɜːgə(r)/ *n* 素汉堡包

Vegemite® /'vedʒɪmaɪt/ *n* [u] 维基米特黑酱

vegetable /'vedʒtəbl/

A *n* 1 (edible plant) 蔬菜 2 fig colloq (brain-damaged person) 植物人; **to become a ～** 变成植物人

B *modif* 1 (of plants) 植物的; **the ～ kingdom** 植物界; **～ matter** 植物性物质 2 (of or for edible plants) 蔬菜的; **～ seeds/plot** 菜籽/菜圃; **～ oil** 植物油; **a ～ knife/dish** 菜刀/一盘蔬菜 3 (containing vegetables) 加蔬菜的 ‹*oil, fat*›; **～ soup/salad/stock** 蔬菜汤/蔬菜色拉/菜味浓汤

vegetable: ～ garden *n* 菜园; **～ marrow** *n* Brit 西葫芦; **～ peeler** *n* 果菜刮皮刀

vegetarian /ˌvedʒɪ'teərɪən/

A *n* 素食者

B *adj* 素食的 ‹*diet, restaurant*›; 素食者的 ‹*society*›; 素食主义的 ‹*ideal*›

vegetarianism /ˌvedʒɪ'teərɪənɪzəm/ *n* [u] 素食主义

vegetate /'vedʒɪteɪt/ *vi* 懒散

vegetation /ˌvedʒɪ'teɪʃn/ *n* [u] 1 (plants) 植被 2 fig (lazing about) 无所事事

vegetative /'vedʒɪtətɪv/ *adj* 1 (asexual) 无性生殖的 ‹*propagation*› 2 Biol (relating to growth) 生长的 ‹*development*›; **a ～ cell** 营养细胞 3 Med 植物人的; **a ～ state/person** 植物人状态/植物人

veggie /'vedʒi/ *n* colloq 1 Brit (vegetarian) 素食者 2 esp Amer (vegetable) 蔬菜

vehemence /'viːəməns/ *n* [u] (of dislike, disapproval, opposition) 强烈; (of speech, action, gesture) 激烈; (of attack, tirade, nod) 猛烈

V

vehement /'viːəmənt/ *adj* 强烈的 ‹*dislike, disapproval, opposition*›; 激烈的 ‹*speech, action, gesture*›; 猛烈的 ‹*attack, tirade, nod*›

vehemently /'viːəməntli/ *adv* 强烈地 ‹*dislike, disapprove, oppose*›; 激烈地 ‹*speak, act*›; 猛烈地 ‹*attack, nod*›; **to ~ oppose** *or* **to be ~ opposed to sth.** 强烈反对某事

vehicle /'vɪəkl, Amer 'viːhɪkl/ *n* 1 Aut 机动车; **'closed to ~s'** "禁止车辆通行"; **~ emissions/registration/tax** 机动车废气排放/车辆登记/车辆税 2 Pharm 赋形药 3 fig (conduit) 手段; **to be a ~ for sth.** «*art, play*» 是表达…的工具 ‹*ideas*›; 是…的手段 ‹*propaganda*› 4 Cin, TV (showcase) **to be a ~ for sb.** 是充分展示某人才艺的作品

vehicular /vɪ'hɪkjʊlə(r), Amer viː-/ *adj* formal 机动车的; **'no ~ access/traffic'** "机动车禁止进入/通行"

veil /veɪl/
A *n* 1 Fashn 面纱; **a bridal ~** 新娘的面纱 2 Relig [修女的] 头巾; **to take the ~** 当修女 3 fig (barrier, disguise) 掩饰物; **a ~ of cloud** 云障; **to draw a ~ over sth.** 避免提及某事物; **to do sth. under a ~ of secrecy** 在秘密掩护下做某事
B *vt* 1 (cover) «*person, scarf, mist*» 遮掩 ‹*face, moon*› 2 fig (disguise) «*expression, smile*» 掩饰 ‹*threat, emotion*›

veiled /veɪld/ *adj* 1 (wearing veil) 戴面纱的 ‹*woman, face*› 2 fig (disguised) 隐含的 ‹*threat, insult*›; **a thinly ~ allusion** 含沙射影

veiling /'veɪlɪŋ/ *n* 1 [u and c] (fabric) 薄纱 2 [u] (wearing of veil) 戴面纱 3 [u] (disguising) 掩饰; **the ~ of the truth** 对事实的掩盖

vein /veɪn/ *n* 1 (blood vessel) 血管 2 (on insect wing) 翅脉 3 (on leaf) 叶脉 4 Geol, Mining 矿脉; **to work a ~** 开矿 5 (in marble, cheese) 纹路 6 *sing* fig (mood, tone) (in text) 主调; (in speech) 语调; **a ~ of nostalgia/seriousness** 怀旧情绪/严肃的语气; **to continue in a similar ~** 用类似的腔调接着说

veined /veɪnd/ *adj* 青筋暴突的 ‹*hand*›; 有翅脉的 ‹*wing*›; 有叶脉的 ‹*leaf*›; 有纹理的 ‹*marble, cheese*›

vela /'viːlə/ *pl* ▸**velum**

velar /'viːlə(r)/ *adj* 软腭音的

Velcro® /'velkrəʊ/ *n* 维可牢搭扣; **a ~ fastener** 维可牢尼龙搭扣

veld, veldt /velt/ *n* [u] [非洲南部的] 无树草原

vellum /'veləm/ *n* [u] 羊皮纸; **in/on ~** 用羊皮纸/在羊皮纸上; **~ paper/binding** 羊皮纸/羊皮纸封皮

velocity /vɪ'lɒsəti/ *n* [u and c] 速度; **to develop** *or* **gain/lose ~** 加速/减速

velodrome /'velədrəʊm/ *n* [自行车或摩托车的] 赛车场

velour, velours /və'lʊə(r)/ *n* [u and c] 丝绒; **~ trousers/curtains** 拉绒裤子/窗帘

velum /'viːləm/ *n* (*pl* **vela**) 软腭

velvet /'velvɪt/
A *n* 1 [u and c] (fabric) 天鹅绒 2 [u] (covering on antler) 鹿茸
B *modif* 1 lit 天鹅绒的; **a ~ robe/cushion** 天鹅绒袍/垫子; **~ curtains** 天鹅绒窗帘 2 fig 柔软的 ‹*skin, paw*›; 柔和的 ‹*voice, eyes*›

velveteen /'velvɪtiːn/ *n* [u and c] 棉绒; **a ~ jacket** 棉绒夹克衫

velvet: ~ glove *n* 1 lit 天鹅绒手套; 2 fig 圆滑的外表; **an iron hand in a ~ glove** 外柔内刚; **~ revolution** *n* 天鹅绒革命 [指非暴力革命]

velvety /'velvɪti/ *adj* 1 lit 光滑柔软的 ‹*skin, leaf, surface*› 2 *attrib* fig 醇和的 ‹*sauce, wine*›; 柔和的 ‹*voice, eyes*›; **the ~ darkness of the night sky** 漆黑的夜空

venal /'viːnl/ *adj* formal 1 (corrupt) 贪赃枉法的 ‹*official, politician*› 2 (resulting from bribery) 贿赂到的 ‹*agreement, acquittal*›

venality /viː'næləti/ *n* [u] formal 贪赃枉法; **political ~** 政治贪腐

vendetta /ven'detə/ *n* 1 (quarrel) 宿怨; **a personal ~** 个人宿仇; **to pursue a ~ against sb.** 长期与某人过不去 2 (blood feud) 家族世仇

vending machine /'vendɪŋ məˌʃiːn/ *n* 自动售货机

vendor /'vendə(r)/ *n* 1 (trader) (in street) 小贩; (in kiosk) 摊贩 2 Jur 卖主 3 esp Amer **= vending machine**

veneer /vɪ'nɪə(r)/ *n* 1 [u and c] (on wood) 镶板 2 [c] *sing* fig (show) 虚饰; **a ~ of kindness** 假装的好心

venerable /'venərəbl/ *adj* 令人敬佩的 ‹*scholar*›; 古老的 ‹*building, tradition*›; **a ~ old man** 德高望重的老人; **a ~ yew tree** 古紫杉

venerate /'venəreɪt/ *vt* 崇敬; **to ~ sb. (for sth.)** (因某事物) 敬重某人

veneration /ˌvenə'reɪʃn/ *n* [u] 敬重; **to have (deep) ~ for sth.** (十分) 尊重; **in ~ of a saint/the dead** 敬奉圣人/敬畏死者

venereal /və'nɪəriəl/ *adj* 性病的 ‹*infection, wart*›

venereal disease *n* [u and c] ▸**p. 377** 性病

venereology /vəˌnɪəri'ɒlədʒi/ *n* [u] 性病学

Venetian /vɪ'niːʃn/
A *adj* (of Venice) 威尼斯的; (of the people) 威尼斯人的
B *n* 威尼斯人

venetian blind *n* 百叶窗帘

Venezuela /ˌvenɪ'zweɪlə/ *pr n* 委内瑞拉

Venezuelan /ˌvenɪ'zweɪlən/ ▸**p. 503**
A *adj* (of Venezuela) 委内瑞拉的; (of the people) 委内瑞拉人的
B *n* 委内瑞拉人

vengeance /'vendʒəns/ *n* [u] 报仇; **to wreak ~** 进行报复; **to take ~ (up)on sb. for sth.** 因某事物对某人进行报复; **with a ~** (to a great degree) 极其; (to a surprising degree) 出乎意料地

vengeful /'vendʒfl/ *adj* 报复的 ‹*act, desire*›; 心存报复的 ‹*person, nature*›

venial /'viːnɪəl/ *adj* esp Relig 轻微可原谅的 ‹*sin, error*›

Venice /'venɪs/ *pr n* 威尼斯

venison /'venɪsn, -zn/ *n* [u] 鹿肉; **~ pie** 鹿肉馅饼

venom /'venəm/ *n* 1 [u and c] Zool 毒液 2 [u] fig (malice) 恶毒

venomous /'venəməs/ *adj* 1 Zool 分泌毒液的 ‹*snake, insect*› 2 Med 有毒的 ‹*wound, bite*› 3 fig (malicious) 恶毒的 ‹*words, look, nature*›

venomously /'venəməsli/ *adv* fig 恶毒地

venous /'viːnəs/ *adj* 静脉的

vent /vent/
A *n* 1 (outlet) 出口; **air/heating ~** 通气口/热风口; **to give ~ to sth.** 发泄 ‹*anger, frustration*› 2 Geol **(volcanic) ~** 火山口 3 Fashn 开衩
B *vt* 1 (release) 排放 ‹*pressure, gas*› 2 fig (express) 发泄 ‹*rage, frustration*›; **to ~ one's anger on** *or* **upon sb./sth.** 对某人/某事物发泄愤怒

ventilate /'ventɪleɪt/ *vt* 1 (provide with air) 使…通风 ‹*room, building*›; **to be well/poorly ~** 通风良好/不畅 2 Med 给…供氧 ‹*patient, lungs*› 3 fig (express) 公开表达 ‹*opinion, anger*›

ventilation /ˌventɪ'leɪʃn/ *n* [u] 1 (provision of air) 通风 2 (equipment) 通风设备 3 Med 供氧

ventilation: ~ shaft *n* 通风井; **~ system** *n* 通风系统

ventilator /'ventɪleɪtə(r)/ *n* 1 Constr (equipment) 通风设备; (opening) 通风口 2 Med 呼吸机; **to turn on/off the ~** 开/关呼吸机; **to be on a ~** «*patient*» 上呼吸机

ventricle /'ventrɪkl/ *n* 心室

ventriloquism /ven'trɪləkwɪzəm/ *n* [u] 腹语术

ventriloquist /ven'trɪləkwɪst/ ▸**p. 409** *n* 口技艺人

ventriloquist's dummy *n* 表演口技用的木偶

ventriloquy /ven'trɪləkwi/ *n* [u] **= ventriloquism**

venture /'ventʃə(r)/
A *n* 1 Comm, Fin 企业; **(business) ~** 企业; **a joint ~** 合资企业; **a publishing/media ~** 出版/传媒企业; **her first ~ into marketing** 她首次涉足市场营销 2 (foray) 探索; **a scientific ~** 科学实验; **his first ~ into fiction** 他第一次写小说的尝试 3 (journey) 冒险旅行
B *vt* 1 (offer) 大胆说出 ‹*remark, guess*›; **may** *or* **might I ~ a suggestion?** 我可以冒昧提个建议吗?; **to ~ to suggest that ...** 斗胆建议…; **to ~ the opinion that ...** 大胆发表…的看法; **'maybe', he ~d** "也许", 他试探着说; **to ~ to do sth.** 鼓起勇气做某事; **nothing ~d nothing gained** 不入虎穴, 焉得虎子 2 (gamble) 拿…冒险 ‹*life, reputation, money*›; **to ~ a bet on sth.** 在某事物上下赌注
C *vi* (go) **to ~ into** 敢于去 ‹*place, street*›; 冒险涉足 ‹*retail market, publishing*›; **to ~ out(doors)** 大胆出门; **to ~ downstairs/further** 敢下楼/继续向前; **to ~ forth** 勇敢地前进

venture: ~ capital *n* [u] 风险资本; **~ capitalism** *n* [u] (practice) 风险投资; (system) 风险投资制度; **~ capitalist** *n* 风险投资人; **V~ Scout** *n* Brit 大龄童子军队员

venturesome /'ventʃəsəm/ *adj* 1 (bold) 大胆的 ‹*person*› 2 (risky) 冒险的 ‹*expedition*›

venue /'venjuː/ *n* 发生地点; **the ~ for a match** 比赛地点; **a change of ~** 地点的变化

Venus /'viːnəs/ *pr n* 1 Astron 金星 2 Mythol 维纳斯 [罗马神话中的爱神]

Venus flytrap /ˌviːnəs 'flaɪtræp/, **Venus's flytrap** /ˌviːnəsɪz 'flaɪtræp/ *n* 捕蝇草

Venusian /vɪ'njuːzɪən/ *adj* 金星的

veracious /və'reɪʃəs/ *adj* formal 真实的 ‹*statement*›; 诚实的 ‹*person*›

veracity /və'ræsəti/ *n* [u] formal (of statement) 真实; (of person) 诚实; **the ~ of the evidence** 证据的真实性

veranda, verandah /və'rændə/ *n* esp Brit 走廊; **on the ~** 在走廊上

verb /vɜːb/ *n* 动词; **a regular/an irregular ~** 规则/不规则动词

verbal /'vɜːbl/ *adj* 1 (spoken) 口头的 ‹*agreement, attack*›; **~ skills/communication** 语言表达技巧/语言交流 2 Ling 动词的

verbal: ~ abuse *n* [u] 言语伤害; **~ diarrhoea** *n* [u] colloq 话痨

verbalize /'vɜːbəlaɪz/
A *vt* 用言语表达
B *vi* 用言辞表达; **to ~ about sth.** 空谈某事物

verbally /'vɜːbəli/ *adv* 口头上; **to communicate ~** 进行语言交流

verbal reasoning *n* [u] 语言推理; **~ skills/test** 语言推理技能/测试

verbatim /vɜː'beɪtɪm/
A *adv* 一字不差地 ‹*repeat, remember*›
B *adj* 一字不差的 ‹*report, quotation*›

verbiage /'vɜːbɪɪdʒ/ *n* [u] pej 连篇累牍

verbless /'vɜːblɪs/ *adj* 无动词的 ‹*sentence, clause*›

verbose /vɜː'bəʊs/ *adj* pej 啰唆的 ‹*person*›; 冗长的 ‹*speech, report, style*›

verbosely /vɜː'bəʊsli/ *adv* pej 啰唆地

verbosity /vɜː'bɒsəti/ *n* pej (of person) 啰唆; (of speech, report, style) 冗长

verb phrase *n* 动词短语

verdant /ˈvɜːdnt/ *adj* liter 碧绿的

verdict /ˈvɜːdɪkt/ *n* 1 Jur [陪审团的] 裁决; **a ~ of guilty/not guilty** 有罪/无罪的裁决; **to arrive at** *or* **reach** *or* **return a ~** 作出裁决; **the ~ was ...** 陪审团的裁决是… 2 *usu sing* fig (opinion) 结论; **to give a** *or* **one's ~ on sth.** 提出对某事的意见; **well, what's the ~?** colloq 那么，有什么意见呢?

verdigris /ˈvɜːdɪgriː, -griːs/ *n* [u] 铜绿

verdure /ˈvɜːdʒə(r)/ *n* [u] liter 青葱的草木

verge /vɜːdʒ/ *n* 1 (brink) **to be on the ~ of sth./doing sth.** 接近于某事/做某事; **to be on the ~ of success/sleep/a discovery** 即将成功/快要睡着/即将发现; **to bring** *or* **drive sb. to the ~ of bankruptcy/despair** 使某人濒于破产/绝望 2 Brit (roadside) 路边; **'soft ~s'** "软路肩"

Phrasal verb

• **verge on** *vt* [~ **on sth.**] 接近; **to be verging on the ridiculous/the illegal** 近乎荒唐/快到了非法的地步

verger /ˈvɜːdʒə(r)/ ▸**p. 409** *n* 教堂司事

verifiable /ˈverɪfaɪəbl/ *adj* 可证实的

verification /ˌverɪfɪˈkeɪʃn/ *n* [u] 1 (confirmation) 证实 2 (checking) 核实

verify /ˈverɪfaɪ/ *vt* 1 (confirm) 证实 ‹*theory, belief*› 2 (check) 核对 ‹*statement, report*›

verisimilitude /ˌverɪsɪˈmɪlɪtjuːd, Amer -tuːd/ *n* [u] formal 貌似真实

veritable /ˈverɪtəbl/ *adj attrib* 真正的 ‹*disaster*›; 名副其实的 ‹*feast, army*›; **a ~ flood of responses/information** 潮水般的回应/信息

vermicelli /ˌvɜːmɪˈseli, -ˈtʃeli/ *n* [u] 1 (pasta) 细面条 2 Brit (chocolate) 巧克力装饰线条

vermiculite /vəˈmɪkjʊlaɪt/ *n* [u] 蛭石

vermifuge /ˈvɜːmɪfjuːdʒ/ *n* 驱肠虫药

vermilion, vermillion /vəˈmɪlɪən/ ▸**p. 134**

A *n* [u] 1 (colour) 朱红色 2 (pigment) 朱红颜料

B *adj* 朱红的

vermin /ˈvɜːmɪn/ *npl* pej 1 (animals) 害兽; (birds) 害鸟 2 (lice) 寄生虫; (insects) 害虫 3 (people) 歹徒

verminous /ˈvɜːmɪnəs/ *adj* (with lice) 生虱子的 ‹*bed, children*›; 有寄生虫的 ‹*animal*›; (with rats) 有鼠患的 ‹*streets*›

Vermont /vɜːˈmɒnt/ *pr n* 佛蒙特州

vermouth /ˈvɜːməθ, Amer vərˈmuːθ/ *n* 1 [u and c] (drink) 味美思酒 2 [c] (glass) 一杯味美思酒

vernacular /vəˈnækjʊlə(r)/

A *n* 1 [c] Ling **the ~** 方言; **in the ~** 用方言 2 [u and c] Archit 民间风格

B *adj* 1 Ling 方言的 ‹*usage*›; **~ language/literature** 方言/方言文学 2 Archit 民间风格的 ‹*architecture, building*›; **the ~ style** 民间风格

vernal equinox *n* 春分

verruca /vəˈruːkə/ *n* (*pl* **verrucae** /vəˈruːkiː/ *or* **~s**) 疣

versatile /ˈvɜːsətaɪl/ *adj* 1 (flexible) 有多种技能的 ‹*person*›; 多才多艺的 ‹*actor, artist*›; 随机应变的 ‹*mind*› 2 (with many uses) 多用途的 ‹*material, vehicle, garment*›; 多功能的 ‹*equipment, tool*›

versatility /ˌvɜːsəˈtɪləti/ *n* [u] 1 (flexibility) (of person) 多才多艺; (of mind) 灵活 2 (usefulness) (of material, vehicle, garment) 多用途; (of equipment, tool) 多功能

verse /vɜːs/ *n* 1 [u] (poetry) 诗; **free ~** 自由诗; **a book of ~** 诗集; **to write ~** 写诗 2 [u] (form) 韵文; **blank ~** 无韵诗; **to write sth. in ~** 用韵文写某物 3 [c] (part) (of poem) 诗节; (of song) 段落 4 [c] Bible 节

versed /vɜːst/ *adj pred* **to be (well) ~ in sth.** 精通某事

versification /ˌvɜːsɪfɪˈkeɪʃn/ *n* [u] 1 (art) 作诗 2 (style, form) 诗律

versifier /ˈvɜːsɪfaɪə(r)/ *n* esp pej 作诗人

versify /ˈvɜːsɪfaɪ/ esp pej

A *vi* 作诗

B *vt* 把…改写成诗 ‹*prose, tale*›

version /ˈvɜːʃn, Amer -ʒn/ *n* 1 (personal account) 说法 2 (form, model) 变体; **an earlier ~ of** …的早期版本 ‹*text, design*› 3 Publg 版本 4 (adaptation) (of book) 改写本; (of song) 改编歌曲; **the jazz ~** 改编成爵士乐的歌曲 5 Comput 更新版本

verso /ˈvɜːsəʊ/ *n* (*pl* **~s**) 1 Print, Publg (back of printed paper) 背面; (left-hand page) 左页 2 (reverse of coin, painting) 反面

versus /ˈvɜːsəs/ *prep* 1 (as opposed to) **sth. ~ sth.** 某事物相对于某事物; **it's integration ~ independence** 这是统一还是独立的问题 2 (against) 对; **sb./sth. ~ sb./sth.** 某人/某物对某人/某物; **Brazil ~ Argentina** Sport 巴西队对阿根廷队; **(the case of) sb. ~ sb.** Jur 某人诉某人（案）

vertebra /ˈvɜːtɪbrə/ *n* (*pl* **vertebrae** /ˈvɜːtɪbreɪ, -briː/) 脊椎

vertebral /ˈvɜːtɪbrəl/ *adj* 脊椎的; **the ~ column** 脊柱

vertebrate /ˈvɜːtɪbrət/

A *n* 脊椎动物

B *adj* 有脊椎的 ‹*animal, species*›; 脊椎动物的 ‹*fossil, evolution*›

vertex /ˈvɜːteks/ *n* (*pl* **vertices** /ˈvɜːtɪsiːz/ *or* **~es**) 1 (top) 最高点 2 Math (angular point) 顶点 3 Math (meeting point) 交点

vertical /ˈvɜːtɪkl/

A *adj* 垂直的 ‹*structure, line, drop*›; **a ~ take-off/landing** Aviat 垂直起飞/垂直降落

B *n* 1 **the ~** (position) 垂直位置; (line) 垂线; (plane) 垂直面; **out of the ~** 不垂直 2 (structure) 垂直结构

vertical: ~ hold *n* 垂直同步; **~ hold control** 帧同步调节; **~ integration** *n* [u] 纵向联合

vertically /ˈvɜːtɪkli/ *adv* 垂直地 ‹*drop, climb*›; 纵向地 ‹*draw, divide, run*›; **to rise ~** 垂直上升

vertices /ˈvɜːtɪsiːz/ *pl* ▸**vertex**

vertiginous /vəˈtɪdʒɪnəs/ *adj* 1 (dizzying) 令人眩晕的 ‹*drop, view*› 2 Med 眩晕的

vertigo /ˈvɜːtɪgəʊ/ *n* [u] 眩晕; **to have/get** *or* **suffer from ~** 感到眩晕

verve /vɜːv/ *n* [u] (enthusiasm) 热情; (vigour) 精力; (liveliness) 活力

very /ˈveri/

A *adv* 1 (extremely) 很; **~ hot/small** 很热/很小; **I'm ~ sorry** 我非常抱歉; **how ~ sad!** 多么令人悲哀啊！; **not ~** (not particularly) 不太; (not at all) 一点也不; **that isn't ~ likely** 那不太可能; **I'm not ~ impressed** 我觉得并不怎么样; **~ good** *or* **well** (extremely good or well) 非常好; dated or formal (expressing agreement) 好吧; **~ good, sir!** 好的，先生！; **I can't ~ well refuse the invitation to her wedding** 我无法拒绝她婚礼的邀请; **she couldn't ~ well do that, knowing it was illegal** 她知道那是非法的，所以没有理由那样 2 (absolutely) 极端地; **the ~ best/worst thing** 最最好/糟糕的事; **at the ~ earliest/latest** 最早/最迟; **at the ~ most/least** 顶多/至少; **the ~ first/last** 第一个/最后一个; **it was the ~ next day** 就是第二天; **I used the ~ same words** 我以前就是这么说的; **her ~ own car** 完全属于她自己的汽车

B *adj attrib* 1 (actual, precise) 正是的; **those were her ~ words** 那就是她的原话; **at that ~ moment** 正在那时 2 (ideal) 最合适的; **the ~ person/thing I need** 我正需要的人/东西 3 (ultimate) 极端的; **from the ~ beginning** 从一开始; **at the ~ beginning/end** 在最初/最后; **to the ~ end** 到最后; **at the ~ front/back** 在最前面/后面; **the ~ top of the hill/profession** 山巅/职业的巅峰 4 (mere) 仅仅的; **the ~ thought of drink made him feel sick** 他一想到酒就感到恶心; **the ~ word conjures up exotic visions** 单是这个字就可让人想到异国情调; **the ~ idea (of it)!** esp Brit hum 想想就不可能!

C **very much** *adv phr, pron phr* 1 (greatly) 非常; **~ much better** 好得多; **I like it ~ much** 我非常喜欢它; **he seemed ~ much the odd one out** 他似乎与别人非常格格不入; **it's ~ much a question of ...** 这完全是…的问题; **~ much a city dweller** 地地道道的城市居民; **~ much so** 确实如此 2 (a large amount) 很多; **there's not ~ much I can do about it** 对此我没有多少可做的; **I didn't eat ~ much** 我吃的不太多

very high frequency *n* 甚高频

Very /ˈveri, ˈvɪəri/: **~ light** *n* 维利式信号弹; **~ pistol** *n* 维利式信号枪

vesicle /ˈvesɪkl/ *n* 囊

vespers /ˈvespəz/ *n* 晚祷

vessel /ˈvesl/ *n* 1 Naut 船 2 (container) 容器 3 Anat, Zool 脉管 4 Bot 导管

vest¹ /vest/ *n* 1 Brit (undergarment) 汗衫 2 (sleeveless garment) 背心; **a bullet-proof ~** 防弹背心 3 Amer (waistcoat) 马甲

vest² *vt usu passive* 授予 ‹*authority, right*›; **to be ~ed with sth.** 被赋予 ‹*responsibility*›; **the powers ~ed in sth./sb.** 属于某物/某人的权力; **to ~ the ownership of sth. in sb.** 使某人拥有某物

vestal virgin /ˌvestl ˈvɜːdʒɪn/ *n usu pl* 维斯太贞女

vested interest /ˌvestɪd ˈɪntrəst/ *n* 既得利益; **to have a ~ in sth.** 在某事中有既得利益

vestibule /ˈvestɪbjuːl/ *n* 1 Archit 门厅 2 Anat 前庭

vestige /ˈvestɪdʒ/ *n* (of system) 残留部分; (of faith, emotion, truth) 丝毫; **there is not a ~ of truth in sth.** 某事毫无真实性; **only a ~ of the city/civilization remains** 这座城市/这一文明仅留下一点残迹; **the last (remaining) ~s of sth.** …的最后残余 ‹*system, society*›

vestment /ˈvestmənt/ *n usu pl* [司祭在礼拜仪式上穿的] 祭衣

vest-pocket *adj attrib* Amer 袖珍的; **a ~ dictionary/calculator** 袖珍词典/计算器

vestry /ˈvestri/ *n* 祭衣室

Vesuvius /vɪˈsuːvɪəs/ *pr n* 维苏威火山

vet¹ /vet/

A *n* (animal doctor) ▸**p. 409 = veterinary surgeon** 兽医; **the ~'s** 兽医诊所

B *vt* (*pres p etc.* **-tt-**) 审查 ‹*person, speech, proposal, material*›; 仔细检查 ‹*place*›; **to be ~ted for the civil service** 为做公务员而受审查

vet² *n* Amer Mil colloq **= veteran 2**

vetch /vetʃ/ *n* [u and c] 野豌豆

veteran /ˈvetərən/ *n* 1 (experienced person) 老手; **a ~ of sth.** 某方面的老手; **a ~ actor/politician/journalist** 资深演员/政治家/记者 2 Mil **(war) ~** 老战士; **a ~ soldier/officer** 老兵/退伍军人

veteran: ~ car *n* Brit [1919年前，尤指1905年前的] 老爷车; **V~s Administration** *n* Amer 退伍军人管理局; **V~s Day** *n* Amer 退伍军人节

veterinarian /ˌvetərɪˈneərɪən/ ▸**p. 409** *n* Amer 兽医

veterinary /ˈvetrɪnri, Amer ˈvetərneri/ ▸**p. 409** *n, adj attrib* 兽医的; **~ medicine/college** 兽医学/学院

veterinary: ~ surgeon ▸**p. 409** *n* Brit formal 兽医; **~ surgery** *n* Brit 兽医院

veto /ˈviːtəʊ/

A *n* (*pl* **~es**) 1 [u and c] (power, rejection) 否决权; **to use** *or* **exercise one's ~** 行使否决权 2 [c] (ban) 禁止; **a ~ on sth.** 对某事的禁止

B *vt* (*pres* **~es**; *pt, pp* **~ed**) 否决 ‹*bill, idea*›

V

vex /veks/ *vt* 使恼火

vexation /vek'seɪʃn/ *n* 1 [u] (annoyance) 恼火 2 [c] (annoying thing) 伤脑筋的事

vexatious /vek'seɪʃəs/ *adj* 1 formal = **vexing** 2 Jur 无理缠讼的 ‹*litigant, claim*›

vexed /vekst/ *adj* 1 *usu pred* (annoyed) 恼火的 2 *usu attrib* (difficult) 棘手的 ‹*question, period, situation*›

vexing /'veksɪŋ/ *adj* 令人烦恼的

VG *abbr* = **very good** 很好

VHF *abbr* = **very high frequency** 甚高频; **a ~ transmitter** 甚高频发射机

via /'vaɪə/ *prep* 1 (by way of) 经由; **to come ~ Paris** 途经巴黎来 2 (by means of) 通过; **(transmitted) ~ satellite** 通过卫星（传送的）; **to get into politics ~ the trade unions** 通过工会进入政界

viability /ˌvaɪə'bɪləti/ *n* [u] 1 (feasibility) (of business, organization, farm) 有望成功; (of plan, project, product) 可行性 2 Biol, Med (of egg, fetus, seed, plant) 可存活

viable /'vaɪəbl/ *adj* 1 (feasible) 有望成功的 ‹*business, organization, farm*›; 切实可行的 ‹*plan, project, product*›; **economically/politically/scientifically ~** 经济上/政治上/科学上可行的 2 Biol, Med 能存活的 ‹*egg, fetus, seed, plant*›

viaduct /'vaɪədʌkt/ *n* 高架桥

Viagra® /vaɪ'ægrə/ *n* 万艾可

vial /'vaɪəl/ *n* 1 (small bottle) 小瓶 2 Pharm 小药瓶

vibe /vaɪb/

A *n* colloq = **B1**

B vibes *npl* 1 colloq (mood of place) 氛围; (feeling of person, situation) 感觉; **to have** *or* **give off good/bad ~s** «*place*» 气氛好/不对头; «*person*» 感觉好/不妙 2 Mus = **vibraphone**

vibrancy /'vaɪbrənsi/ *n* [u] (of person) 精力充沛; (of place) 充满生机; (of light) 明亮; (of colour) 鲜艳; (of sound, tone) 响亮

vibrant /'vaɪbrənt/ *adj* 1 (lively) 活泼的 ‹*person, personality*›; 充满生机的 ‹*place, atmosphere*›; 鲜明的 ‹*image*›; 精彩的 ‹*performance*›; **to be ~ with health** 健康有活力 2 (bright) 明亮的 ‹*light*›; 鲜艳的 ‹*colour*› 3 (resonant) 响亮的

vibrantly /'vaɪbrəntli/ *adv* 鲜艳地

vibraphone /'vaɪbrəfəʊn/ ▸**p. 395** *n* 电颤琴

vibrate /vaɪ'breɪt, Amer 'vaɪbreɪt/

A *vi* «*wings, string*» 颤动; «*building, aircraft, machine, mobile phone*» 震动

B *vt* «*explosion*» 使…震动 ‹*building, bridge*›; «*wind, machine, action*» 使…颤动 ‹*piece of metal, strings*›

vibration /vaɪ'breɪʃn/ *n* [u and c] (of wing, string) 颤动; (of aircraft, machine, mobile phone) 震动

vibrato /vɪ'brɑːtəʊ/ *n* [u and c] (*pl* **~s**) 颤音; **to play/sing ~** 演奏/演唱颤音

vibrator /vaɪ'breɪtə(r)/ *n* 1 (for massage, as sex aid) 颤动按摩器 2 (for concrete) 振捣器

vibratory /vaɪ'breɪtəri/ *adj usu attrib* 震动的 ‹*rate, roller, massage*›

viburnum /vaɪ'bɜːnəm/ *n* [u and c] 荚蒾

vicar /'vɪkə(r)/ *n* 1 (in Church of England) 教区牧师 2 (in Catholic Church, other Anglican churches) 代牧

vicarage /'vɪkərɪdʒ/ *n* 代牧住所

vicarious /vɪ'keərɪəs, Amer vaɪ'k-/ *adj usu attrib* formal 间接感受到的 ‹*pleasure, knowledge*›; **to get a ~ thrill from** *or* **out of sth.** 从某事物间接感受到激动

vicariously /'vɪkeərɪəsli, Amer vaɪ'k-/ *adv* formal 间接地 ‹*enjoy, experience*›; **to live ~ through sb.** 在某人身上实现梦想; **~ liable** Jur 负有替代责任

vice¹ /vaɪs/ *n* 1 [u] (corrupt behaviour) 有伤风化的行为; **~ scandal/law** 有伤风化的丑闻/有伤风化犯罪法 2 [c] (bad habit) 恶习 3 [c] (failing) 缺陷

vice² *n* Brit Tech 台钳

vice- /vaɪs/ *combining form* 副…

vice: V~-Admiral *n* 海军中将; **~-captain** *n* 副队长; **~-chair** *n* 副主席; **~-chairman** *n* 副主席; **~-chairmanship** *n* 副主席职位; **~-chairwoman** *n* 女副主席; **~ chancellor** ▸**p. 409** *n* 1 Brit Univ 副校长; 2 Amer Jur 副大法官; **~-chief** *n* 副职首长; **~-consul** *n* 副领事; **~-like** *adj* Brit 虎钳似的 ‹*grip*›; **~-presidency** *n* (of country) 副总统职位; (of company) 副总裁职位; (of organization) 副主席职位; **~-president** *n* (of country) 副总统; (of company) 副总裁; (of organization) 副主席; **~-presidential** *adj* (of country) 副总统的; (of company) 副总裁的; (of organization) 副主席的; **~-principal** *n* 副校长; **~ ring** *n* 卖淫团伙

viceroy /'vaɪsrɔɪ/ *n* 总督

vice squad *n* [打击性、涉黄和赌博犯罪的]警察缉捕队

vice versa /ˌvaɪsə 'vɜːsə, ˌvaɪs -/ *adv* 反之亦然; **she often helps me with my work and ~** 她经常在工作上帮我，我也经常帮她

vicinity /vɪ'sɪnəti/ *n* 1 lit 邻近地区; **in the ~** 在附近; **in the (immediate) ~ of Oxford/the explosion** 紧邻牛津/爆炸发生地 2 fig **in the ~ of** 大约 ‹*sum, amount*›

vicious /'vɪʃəs/ *adj* 1 (brutal) 凶狠的 ‹*attacker*›; 猛烈的 ‹*attack, kick, attempt*›; 残暴的 ‹*crime, system*› 2 (nasty) 恶毒的 ‹*look, tongue, rumour, criticism*› 3 (dangerous) 凶猛危险的 ‹*animal*› 4 (severe) 剧烈的 ‹*pain*›; 猛烈的 ‹*storm*›; 大幅度的 ‹*price cut*›

vicious circle, vicious cycle *ns* 恶性循环

viciously /'vɪʃəsli/ *adv* 1 (brutally) 猛烈地 ‹*attack, pull, kick*› 2 (nastily) 恶毒地 ‹*say, glare*›; **a ~ worded attack** 恶毒的攻击

viciousness /'vɪʃəsnɪs/ *n* [u] 1 (brutality) (of person) 凶残; (of attack) 猛烈; (of crime, system) 残暴 2 (nastiness) 恶毒

vicissitude /vɪ'sɪsɪtjuːd, Amer -tuːd/ *n usu pl* formal 变迁; **the ~s of life** 人生的沉浮

victim /'vɪktɪm/ *n* lit, fig 受害者; **bomb/earthquake/murder/rape ~** 爆炸伤亡人员/地震灾民/谋杀案受害者/强奸案受害者; **a ~ of one's own success** 为自己的成功所毁的人; **to fall ~ to** 受…的伤害 ‹*disease, developers*›; **a ~ mentality** 受害者心理

victimization /ˌvɪktɪmaɪ'zeɪʃn/ *n* [u] 伤害

victimize /'vɪktɪmaɪz/ *vt* 使受害

victimless /'vɪktɪmlɪs/ *adj* 无受害人的 ‹*crime*›

victim support

A *n* [u] 受害者援助

B Victim Support *pr n* Brit 受害者支援会

victor /'vɪktə(r)/ *n* 胜利者; **to emerge the ~** 胜出

Victoria /vɪk'tɔːrɪə/ *pr n* 维多利亚

Victoria: ~ Cross *n* Brit 维多利亚十字勋章; **~ Day** *n* Can 维多利亚女王纪念日

Victorian /vɪk'tɔːrɪən/

A *adj* 1 (of Queen Victoria's reign) 维多利亚女王的 ‹*times, period*›; 维多利亚女王时代的 ‹*house, dress, novel*› 2 (prudish) 因循守旧的 ‹*attitude, style, parent*›; **~ values** 古板守旧的价值观

B *n* 维多利亚女王时代的人

Victoriana /vɪkˌtɔːrɪ'ɑːnə/ *npl* 维多利亚女王时代的物件

victorious /vɪk'tɔːrɪəs/ *adj* 获胜的; **to be ~ in the election/match** 在选举/比赛中获胜; **to be ~ over sb.** 战胜某人

victoriously /vɪk'tɔːrɪəsli/ *adv* 胜利地 ‹*smile, stride*›; **the army returned ~ to the capital** 军队凯旋回到首都

victory /'vɪktəri/ *n* [u and c] 胜利; **to win** *or* **achieve** *or* **gain** *or* **score a ~ (over sb.)** 战胜（某人）; **to lead sb./sth. to ~** 引领某人/某事物走向胜利; **to snatch ~ from the jaws of defeat** 反败为胜

victory sign *n* [手掌朝外的V字状] 胜利手势; **to give a ~** 做出胜利的手势

victualler Brit, **victualer** Amer /'vɪtlə(r)/ ▸**p. 409** *n* 1 dated (supplier of provisions) 食品供应商 2 Brit (supplier of alcohol) **(licensed) ~** 有许可证的酒商

victuals /'vɪtlz/ *npl* dated (food and drink) 饮食; (provisions) 粮食储备

vid /vɪd/ *n* colloq 录像机

video /'vɪdɪəʊ/

A *n* (*pl* **~s**) 1 [u and c] (medium, film) 录像; **home/commercial ~** 家庭/商业录像; **on ~** 在录像上; **a promotional/training ~** 宣传/培训录像 2 [c] = **video cassette** 3 [c] Brit = **video cassette recorder**

B *modif* 1 Video 录像的 ‹*equipment, collection, interview, film*›; 影像的 ‹*producer, market, age*› 2 Comput 视频的; **~ graphics/link** 可视图像/视频链条

C *vt* 1 (with camera) 给…录像 2 (from TV) 录制

video: ~ art *n* [u] 录像艺术; **~ blog** *n* 视频博客; **~ blogger** *n* 视频博客博主; **~ book** *n* (book in electronic format) 电子书; (electronic device) 电子阅读器; **~ camera** *n* 摄像机; **~ card** *n* 视频卡

video cassette *n* 录像带

video cassette recorder 录像机

video: ~ clip *n* 录像片段; **~ club** *n* 录像带租赁俱乐部; **~ compact disc, ~ compact disk** *n* 激光视盘; **~-conferencing** *n* [u] 视频会议; **~ diary** *n* 录像日记

video disc, video disk *n* 影碟

video disc recorder, video disk recorder *n* 光盘录像机

video: ~ display unit *n* 图像显示器; **~ game** *n* 电子游戏; **~ jock** *n* Amer colloq 电视音乐节目主持人; **~ library** *n* 录像带图书馆; **~ log** *n* = **~ blog**; **~ nasty** *n* Brit (horror film) 恐怖录像片; (pornographic film) 黄色录像片; **~-on-demand** *n* [u] 视频点播; **~phone** *n* 可视电话; **~ piracy** *n* [u] 影像盗版; **~ player** *n* 放像机; **~ recorder** *n* 电视录像机; **~ shop** Brit, **~ store** Amer *ns* 音像商店; **~ surveillance** *n* [u] 录像监控

videotape /'vɪdɪəʊteɪp/

A *n* 1 [u] (medium) 录像带 2 [c] (recording) 录像; **to watch a ~** 看录像 3 [c] = **video cassette**

B *vt* 给…录像 ‹*event*›

videotape recording *n* [c and u] 磁带录像; **digital ~** 数字磁带录像

videotaping /'vɪdɪəʊteɪpɪŋ/ *n* [u] 磁带录像

videotext /'vɪdɪəʊˌtekst/ *n* [u] 视传系统

vie /vaɪ/ *vi* (*pres p* **vying**) 竞争; **to ~ (with sb.) for sth.** （与某人）争夺; **children vying (with each other) for attention** （互相）争着引人注意的孩子们

Vienna /vɪ'enə/ *pr n* 维也纳

Viennese /ˌvɪə'niːz/

A *adj* 维也纳的

B *pr n* 维也纳人; **he's a ~** 他是维也纳人; **the ~** *pl* 维也纳人

Vientiane /ˌvjen'tjɑːn/ *pr n* 万象

Vietcong /ˌvjet'kɒŋ/ *pr n* Hist 越共成员; **the ~** *pl* 越共游击队; **~ attack/forces** 越共游击队的进攻/越共游击队

Vietnam /ˌvjet'næm/ *pr n* 越南

Vietnamese /ˌvɪetnəˈmiːz/ ▸p. 503, p. 426

A *adj* (of Vietnam) 越南的; (of the people) 越南人的; (of the language) 越南语的

B *n* **1** [c] (person) **the ～** *pl* 越南人 **2** [u] (language) 越南语

view /vjuː/

A *n* **1** [c] (opinion) 观点; **to have** *or* **hold strong political ～s** 持强硬的政治观点; **the official ～** 官方态度; **in my ～ it was a waste of time** 依我看，那是浪费时间; **you know my ～s on divorce** 你知道我对离婚的看法 **2** [c] (way of thinking) 思维方式; (way of understanding) 理解方式; **he has an optimistic ～ of life** 他乐观地看待人生; **we take the ～ that ...** 我们认为…; **to take the long ～** 从长远考虑; **in the long ～** 从长远来看 **3** [c and u] (field of vision) 视野; **to block sb.'s ～** 挡住某人的视线; **we had a good ～ of the stage from our seats** 从我们的座位看舞台很清楚; **the bedroom has a side ～ of the lake** 从卧室能看到湖的一侧; **there was nobody in** *or* **within ～** 一个人也看不见; **what do you have in ～?** fig (as aim) 你有什么打算？; (in mind) 你在想什么？; **the lake was within ～ of the house** 从房子能看到湖; **in full ～** 完全看得见的; **he was shot in full ～ of a large crowd** 他在众目睽睽之下被人枪杀了; **to come into/disappear from ～** 进入视野/从视野中消失; **the lake soon came into ～** 那湖很快便映入眼帘; **to be lost to** *or* **from ～** (be no longer seen) 从视野中消失; (become forgotten) 被忘记; **on ～** 在容易看见的地方; **it is advisable not to leave handbags on ～** 明智的做法是不把手提包放在显眼的地方 **4** [c] (vista) 景色; **a room with a ～ (of the lake)** 看得见（那片湖的）风景的房间; **a sea/mountain ～** 海景/山景; **the front ～ of the museum is very imposing** 博物馆的正面看上去非常壮观 **5** [c] (photograph) 风景照; (picture) 风景画; **ten ～s of London** 伦敦十景; **a book with ～s of Paris** 巴黎风光画册 **6** [c and u] (chance to see exhibition, film, TV programme) 观看 **7** [c and u] (inspection before purchase) 察看 **8** [c and u] (presentation of product) 展示; **on ～** 在展出

B **in ～ of** *prep phr* formal 鉴于; **in ～ of the weather, the event will now be held indoors** 由于天气的缘故，这项赛事现在要在室内进行

C **with a ～ to** *prep phr* (with the intention of) 有…的打算; (with the hope of) 有…的指望; **he's painting the house with a ～ to selling it** 他在粉刷房子，想把它卖掉; **they are taking disciplinary action against him, with a ～ to him being dismissed** 他们正要给他纪律处分，目的是要开除他

D *vt* **1** (regard) 看待; **how do you ～ the current situation?** 你如何看待当前的局势？; **she ～ed him as an enemy** 她把他视为敌人; **to ～ the future with optimism** 乐观地看待未来 **2** (see) 看; **this waterfall is best ～ed from the side** 这处瀑布从侧面看效果最佳 **3** formal (watch) 观看 ‹*DVD, film*› **4** (examine) 审查 ‹*exhibition, document, record*›; **people came from all over the world to ～ her work** 人们从世界各地涌来欣赏她的作品 **5** (inspect before buying) 察看 ‹*property, item*›

E *vi* 观看

viewdata /ˈvjuːdeɪtə/ *n* [u] 视传

viewer /ˈvjuːə(r)/ *n* **1** TV 电视观众 **2** (of exhibition, collection) 参观者; (of property) 察看者; (of scene, painting) 观赏者 **3** Phot 观看器

viewership /ˈvjuːəʃɪp/ *n* + *v sing or pl* 电视观众

viewfinder /ˈvjuːfaɪndə(r)/ *n* [照相机的] 取景器

viewing /ˈvjuːɪŋ/ *n* **1** [u] TV 电视的收看; **a programme scheduled for prime-time ～** 安排在收视黄金时段的电视节目; **essential ～ for sb.** 某人必看的电视节目; **that concludes your Saturday night's ～** 周六夜间节目到此结束; **the ～ public** 电视观众; **～ patterns/preferences** 电视收看模式/偏好 **2** [u and c] (of exhibition, collection) 参观; (of property) 察看; (of scene, painting) 观赏; **'early ～ recommended'** "看房请从速"; **'～ by appointment only'** "看房限预约"

viewing gallery *n* 高台观众席

view: ～point *n* **1** (opinion) 观点; **2** (lookout) 观看位置; **～screen** *n* 屏幕

vigil /ˈvɪdʒɪl/ *n* [u and c] (watch) 值夜; (in prayer) 守夜祈祷; **an all-night ～** 彻夜监视; **to keep (a) ～ (over sb.)** 昼夜监护（某人）; **to hold** *or* **stage a ～** (in protest) 举行夜间抗议; **a candlelight** *or* **candlelit ～** 烛光守夜祈祷

vigilance /ˈvɪdʒɪləns/ *n* [u] 警觉

vigilant /ˈvɪdʒɪlənt/ *adj* 警惕的

vigilante /ˌvɪdʒɪˈlænti/ *n* 治安会会员; **a ～ group/attack** 治安小组/治安会突袭

vigilantly /ˈvɪdʒɪləntli/ *adv* 警惕地

vignette /viːˈnjet/ *n* **1** (literary sketch) 花絮; (short scene) 表演片段 **2** (design in book, carving) 小花饰

vigor /ˈvɪɡə(r)/ *n* Amer = **vigour**

vigorous /ˈvɪɡərəs/ *adj* **1** (powerful) 有力的 ‹*push, shake*›; 剧烈的 ‹*exercise*› **2** (healthy) 强健的 ‹*person*›; 茁壮的 ‹*plant, growth*› **3** (vehement) 坚决的 ‹*denial, attempt, defender*›; 声势浩大的 ‹*campaign*›

vigorously /ˈvɪɡərəsli/ *adv* **1** (powerfully) 强有力地 ‹*shake, push, stir*›; 剧烈地 ‹*exercise*›; **to boil ～** 煮得沸腾 **2** (healthily) ‹*plant*› 茁壮地 ‹*grow*› **3** (vehemently) 强烈地 ‹*deny, oppose*›; 坚决地 ‹*defend*›; 积极地 ‹*campaign*›

vigour /ˈvɪɡə(r)/ *n* [u] Brit **1** (energy) (of person) 精力; (of action) 力量 **2** (health) 强壮 **3** (vehemence) (of argument) 激烈; (of effort, words, denial) 强烈; (of campaign) 声势浩大; **with great ～** 十分强烈地

Viking /ˈvaɪkɪŋ/ *n* 维京人 [公元8至11世纪于海上劫掠并贸易的斯堪的纳维亚人]; **～ ship/heritage** 维京人的船/传统

vile /vaɪl/ *adj* **1** (wicked) 邪恶的 ‹*deed*›; 下流的 ‹*language*›; 卑劣的 ‹*person, behaviour*› **2** (awful) 令人恶心的 ‹*taste, smell, medicine*›; 糟糕的 ‹*weather, mood*›; 讨厌的 ‹*place, colour, experience*›

vilely /ˈvaɪli/ *adv* 卑劣地 ‹*murder, torture*›; 无耻地 ‹*swear, abuse*›

vileness /ˈvaɪlnɪs/ *n* [u] **1** (wickedness) 邪恶 **2** (awfulness) 糟糕

vilification /ˌvɪlɪfɪˈkeɪʃn/ *n* [u and c] formal 诋毁

vilify /ˈvɪlɪfaɪ/ *vt* formal 诋毁

villa /ˈvɪlə/ *n* **1** (country house) 乡间庄园 **2** Brit (holiday home abroad) 假日别墅 **3** Brit (detached or semi-detached suburban house) [尤指维多利亚女王或爱德华七世时代风格的] 独立房屋 **4** Hist [古罗马时期的] 乡间宅第

village /ˈvɪlɪdʒ/ *n* **1** (in country) 村庄; **a mountain/farming/fishing ～** 山村/农村/渔村; **～ school/life/fête** 乡村学校/生活/义卖会 **2** (in town, city) 居民村; **the Olympic V～** 奥运村 **3** **the ～** + *v sing or pl* (people) 村民

village: ～ green *n* 村中心绿地; **～ hall** *n* 村政厅; **～ idiot** *n* 村里的傻子

villager /ˈvɪlɪdʒə(r)/ *n* 村民

village shop *n* Brit 乡村商店

villain /ˈvɪlən/ *n* **1** (scoundrel) 坏蛋 **2** (criminal) 罪犯 **3** (in book, film) 反面人物; **the ～ of the piece** esp hum 元凶 **4** fig (agent of harm) 罪魁祸首

villainous /ˈvɪlənəs/ *adj* **1** liter (wicked) 邪恶的 ‹*person, behaviour, plot, deed*› **2** dated colloq (foul) 糟糕的 ‹*weather, smell, taste*›

villainously /ˈvɪlənəsli/ *adv* liter 邪恶地 ‹*behave, smile, look*›

villainy /ˈvɪləni/ *n* [u and c] liter 邪恶行为

Vilnius /ˈvɪlnɪəs/ *pr n* 维尔纽斯

vim /vɪm/ *n* [u] colloq 活力; **full of ～ and vigour** 充满活力的

vinaigrette /ˌvɪnɪˈɡret/ *n* [u and c] **～ (dressing)** 醋油色拉调味汁

vindaloo /ˌvɪndəˈluː/ *n* (*pl* **～s**) **～ (curry)** (meat) 辛辣咖喱肉; (fish) 辛辣咖喱鱼

vindicate /ˈvɪndɪkeɪt/ *vt* **1** (clear of blame) 证明…无辜 ‹*person*›; 证明…清白 ‹*sb.'s honour*› **2** (justify) 证明…有理 ‹*action, claim, judgement*›; **to ～ the doctor's decision** 表明医生的决定是正确的

vindication /ˌvɪndɪˈkeɪʃn/ *n* **1** [u] (clearing of blame) 证明无辜 **2** (justifying) 证明正确; **in ～ of sth.** 作为对…正确性的证明 ‹*action, claim, judgement*› **3** [c] (instance, means) 证明

vindictive /vɪnˈdɪktɪv/ *adj* 有报复心的 ‹*person, attitude*›; 报复性的 ‹*decision, deed, behaviour*›

vindictively /vɪnˈdɪktɪvli/ *adv* 报复地 ‹*say, act*›

vindictiveness /vɪnˈdɪktɪvnɪs/ *n* [u] 报复

vine /vaɪn/ *n* **1** (grapevine) 葡萄藤 **2** (climbing plant) 攀缘植物

vinegar /ˈvɪnɪɡə(r)/ *n* [u] 醋; **cider/malt ～** 苹果醋/麦芽醋; **an oil and ～ dressing** 油醋调味汁

vinegary /ˈvɪnɪɡəri/ *adj* 有酸味的 ‹*sauce, wine*›; 酸的 ‹*taste, smell*›

vine leaf *n* 葡萄叶

vineyard /ˈvɪnjəd/ *n* 葡萄园

viniculture /ˈvɪnɪkʌltʃə(r)/ *n* [u] [为酿酒的] 葡萄栽培

vino /ˈviːnəʊ/ *n* [u and c] (*pl* **～s**) esp Brit colloq [尤指廉价的] 葡萄酒

vintage /ˈvɪntɪdʒ/

A *n* **1** [c] Wine (year, season) 酿造年份; **an excellent ～** 好的酿酒年份; **what's the ～?** 哪年的酒？ **2** [c] Wine (wine) [某年份的] 葡萄酒; (grapes) 葡萄; **the 1986 ～** 1986 年酿造的葡萄酒; **the great ～s** 极好的年份的葡萄 **3** [u] fig (era, date) 优质品生产时期

B *adj* **1** Wine 极佳年份酿造的 ‹*wine, champagne*› **2** *usu attrib* (classic) 经典的 ‹*film, joke*›; **it's ～ Armstrong** 这是阿姆斯特朗的经典佳作 **3** *usu attrib* colloq (ancient) 古老的 ‹*machine, model*› **4** *usu attrib* Aut [制造于1919-1930年间] 老式的 ‹*car*›

vintage: ～ car *n* 老爷车 [制造于1919-1930年间]; **～ year** *n* 葡萄酒的佳酿年份; fig 成功的一年

vintner /ˈvɪntnə(r)/ ▸p. 409 *n* **1** (merchant) 葡萄酒商 **2** Amer (grower) 葡萄酒酿制人

vinyl /ˈvaɪnl/ *n* [u] **1** Tex 乙烯基塑料; **～ wallpaper/paint/chair** 乙烯墙纸/涂料/椅子 **2** (records) 唱片; **on ～** 有唱片版本

viol /ˈvaɪəl/ ▸p. 395 *n* 维奥尔琴

viola[1] /vɪˈəʊlə/ ▸p. 395 *n* **1** (instrument) 中提琴 **2** (player) 中提琴手

viola[2] /ˈvaɪələ/ *n* Bot 堇菜

violate /ˈvaɪəleɪt/ *vt* **1** (contravene) 违犯 ‹*law, agreement, ceasefire, taboo*›; 违反 ‹*rule, regulation, criteria*›; 侵犯 ‹*right, duty, copyright*› **2** (desecrate) 亵渎 ‹*sacred place*› **3** (disturb) 侵扰 ‹*peace, home*›; 侵犯 ‹*privacy*› **4** formal (rape) 强奸

violation /ˌvaɪəˈleɪʃn/ *n* **1** [u and c] (contravention) (of law, agreement, ceasefire, taboo) 违犯; (of rule, regulation, criteria) 违反; (of right, duty, copyright) 侵犯; **in ～ of ...** 违犯… **2** [u and c] (desecration) 亵渎 **3** [u and c] (destruction) (of peace, home) 侵扰; (of privacy) 侵犯 **4** [u and c] formal (rape) 强奸 **5** [c] Jur (minor offence) 违规行为; **parking/traffic ～s** 违章停车/交通违规

violator /ˈvaɪəleɪtə(r)/ *n* **1** [c] (contravener) (of law, agreement, ceasefire, taboo) 违犯者; (of rule, regulation, criteria) 违反者; (of right, duty, copyright) 侵犯者 **2** [u and c] (desecrator) 亵渎者 **3** [u and c]

V

(disturber) (of home, peace) 侵扰者; (of privacy) 侵犯者 **4** [u and c] (rapist) 强奸者

violence /ˈvaɪələns/ *n* [u] **1** (physical aggression) 暴力; **to resort to/use ~** 诉诸/使用暴力; **an outbreak of ~** 暴力的突发; **crimes of ~** 暴力犯罪; **football ~** 足球暴力 **2** (force) 猛力; **he hit the table with such ~ that ...** 他猛地一捶桌子以致… **3** fig (intensity) 猛烈; **the ~ of her feelings/reaction/verbal attack** 她感情的强烈/反应的剧烈/言语攻击的激烈; **the ~ of the storm** 暴风雨的猛烈

violent /ˈvaɪələnt/ *adj* **1** (physically aggressive) 残暴的 ‹*person, criminal*›; 暴力引起的 ‹*death*›; **~ film/clash/attack/protest/behaviour** 暴力电影/冲突/袭击/抗议/行为 **2** (powerful) 猛烈的 ‹*criticism, abuse*›; 剧烈的 ‹*explosion, fit, storm*›; 强烈的 ‹*emotion, dislike, temper*› **3** (sudden) 突然的 ‹*swing, swerve, change*›; 惊人的 ‹*contrast*›; 猛然的 ‹*acceleration, braking*› **4** (harsh, garish) 刺眼的 ‹*colour*›

violently /ˈvaɪələntli/ *adv* **1** (with physical violence) 猛烈地 ‹*attack, hit, push*›; 通过暴力 ‹*demonstrate, struggle*›; 残忍地 ‹*kill*›; **he was ~ kicked** 他被狠狠地踢了一脚; **to die ~** 遭暴力致死 **2** (with great force) 激烈地 ‹*argue, criticize, erupt, rage*›; 强烈地 ‹*disagree, affect, feel*›; 剧烈地 ‹*explode, blow*› **3** (suddenly) 突然 ‹*change, swing, swerve*›; 猛然 ‹*accelerate, brake*› **4** (exceedingly) 极度地; **to be ~ opposed to sth.** 竭力反对某事; **to be ~ ill** *or* **sick** Brit 病得很厉害 **5** (harshly, garishly) 刺眼地 ‹*coloured*›

violet /ˈvaɪələt/ ▸**p. 134**
A *n* **1** [c] Bot 紫罗兰; **African ~** 非洲紫罗兰 **2** [u] (colour) 紫罗兰色
B *adj* 紫罗兰色的

violin /ˌvaɪəˈlɪn/ ▸**p. 395** *n* **1** (instrument) 小提琴; **a ~ concerto/solo** 小提琴协奏曲/独奏曲 **2** (player) 小提琴手; **the first/second ~** 第一/第二小提琴手

violin case *n* 小提琴盒

violinist /ˌvaɪəˈlɪnɪst/ ▸**p. 395, p. 409** *n* 小提琴手

violin player *n* = **violinist**

VIP *abbr* = **very important person** 贵宾; **~ guest/lounge/area/facility** 贵宾/贵宾室/贵宾区/贵宾专用设施; **to give sb. (the) ~ treatment** 给予某人贵宾待遇

viper /ˈvaɪpə(r)/ *n* **1** Zool 蝰蛇 **2** fig liter (malicious person) 毒如蛇蝎的人; **to nurse a ~ in one's bosom** 护恶养奸; **a nest of ~s, a ~'s nest** 一群背信弃义的人

virago /vɪˈrɑːgəʊ/ *n* (*pl* **~es**) **1** pej (violent, ill-tempered woman) 悍妇 **2** (strong, brave woman) 魁梧的女斗士

viral /ˈvaɪərəl/ *adj* 病毒性的 ‹*disease*›; 病毒的 ‹*load*›

viral: ~ infection *n* 病毒性感染; **~ marketing** *n* [u] 病毒式营销 [利用互联网用户自发传播产品信息的营销模式]

Virgin /ˈvɜːdʒɪn/ *pr n* **the ~** 圣母; **the ~ and Child** 圣母子

virgin /ˈvɜːdʒɪn/
A *n* (woman) 处女; (man) 童男
B *adj* **1** (not exploited) 洁白的 ‹*snow*›; 未碰过的 ‹*book, page*›; 初始的 ‹*freshness, purity*› **2** (not processed) 未加工的 ‹*wool*›; 初榨的 ‹*olive oil*›; 未烧过的 ‹*clay*›; 原生的 ‹*metal*› **3** (relating to a virgin) 贞洁的 ‹*person, bride, maid*›; 处女般的 ‹*purity*›

virginal /ˈvɜːdʒɪnl/ *adj* 纯真的 ‹*smile, child, innocence*›; 贞洁的 ‹*woman*›; 纯洁的 ‹*white*›

virgin: V~ Birth *n* **the V~ Birth** 圣母马利亚童贞生子; **~ forest** *n* 原始森林

Virginia /vəˈdʒɪnɪə/ *pr n* **1** Geog 弗吉尼亚州 **2** = **Virginia tobacco**

Virginia creeper *n* [u and c] 五叶地锦

Virginian /vəˈdʒɪnɪən/
A *adj* 弗吉尼亚的
B *n* 弗吉尼亚人

Virginia tobacco *n* [u and c] 弗吉尼亚烟草

Virgin Islands *pr npl* **the ~** [加勒比海的] 维尔京群岛

virginity /vəˈdʒɪnəti/ *n* [u] 处女状态; **to lose one's ~** 失去童贞

Virgin Mary *n* **the ~** 圣母马利亚

Virgo /ˈvɜːgəʊ/ *n* **1** [u] Astron 室女(星)座 **2** [u] Astrol (sign) 室女宫 [黄道第六宫] **3** [c] (*pl* **~s**) Astrol (person) 属室女(星)座的人

virile /ˈvɪraɪl, Amer ˈvɪrəl/ *adj* **1** (manly) 有男子气概的 **2** fig (vigorous) 声势浩大的 ‹*campaign*›; 强势的 ‹*leadership*›

virility /vɪˈrɪləti/ *n* [u] **1** (manliness) 男子气概 **2** fig (vigour) 强壮

virologist /ˌvaɪəˈrɒlədʒɪst/ ▸**p. 409** *n* 病毒学家

virology /ˌvaɪəˈrɒlədʒi/ *n* [u] 病毒学

virtual /ˈvɜːtʃʊəl/ *adj* **1** (almost complete) 实质上的 ‹*bankruptcy, defeat, impossibility*›; **the ~ disappearance of this custom** 这种习俗事实上的消失; **he was a ~ prisoner** 他几乎就是个囚犯; **traffic is at a ~ standstill** 交通几乎陷入停滞 **2** Comput 虚拟的 ‹*memory, storage, hero*› **3** Phys 虚的; **a ~ particle/photon** 虚粒子/虚光子

virtual campus *n* 虚拟校园

virtuality /ˌvɜːtʃʊˈæləti/ *n* [u] **1** (potentiality) 潜在 **2** Comput 虚拟

virtually /ˈvɜːtʃʊəli/ *adv* **1** (almost completely) 实际上; **there is ~ no public transport** 几乎没有公共交通; **it's ~ impossible** 这几乎不可能; **~ every household has one** 差不多每家都有一个; **~ anywhere** 差不多到处 **2** Comput 虚拟地

virtual: ~ memory *n* [u] 虚拟内存; **~ office** *n* 虚拟办公室; **~ pet** *n* 虚拟宠物; **~ private network** *n* 虚拟专用网络; **~ reality** *n* [u] 虚拟现实

virtue /ˈvɜːtʃuː/ *n* **1** [c] (good quality) 美德; **patience is a ~** 耐心是一种美德; **to make a ~ of necessity** 不得已而甘愿为之 **2** [u] (goodness) 高尚品行; **~ is its own reward** Prov 有德便是有报 **3** [c] (advantage) 优点; **to have the ~ of sth.** 有某种优点; **to extol the ~s of sth.** 赞美某事的长处; **by ~ of sth.** 由于某事 **4** [u] archaic (chastity) 贞操; **(a woman) of easy ~** 水性杨花的(女人)

virtuosi /ˌvɜːtʃʊˈəʊsiː/ *pl* ▸**virtuoso A**

virtuosity /ˌvɜːtʃʊˈɒsəti/ *n* [u] esp Mus 精湛演技

virtuoso /ˌvɜːtjʊˈəʊsəʊ, -zəʊ/
A *n* (*pl* **virtuosi** *or* **~s**) esp Mus 技艺超群的人; **a piano/violin/jazz ~** 钢琴/小提琴/爵士乐演奏家
B *adj* 技艺精湛的

virtuous /ˈvɜːtʃʊəs/ *adj* **1** (morally good) 品德高尚的 ‹*person, life, behaviour*› **2** (self-righteous) 自命清高的; **~ indignation** 自以为是的愤怒

virtuous circle *n* 良性循环

virtuously /ˈvɜːtʃʊəsli/ *adv* **1** (morally) 品德高尚地 ‹*live, behave*›; 慷慨地 ‹*act, offer*› **2** (self-righteously) 自命清高地

virulence /ˈvɪrʊləns/ *n* [u] **1** (deadliness) (of pathogen, microorganism) 剧毒; (of disease, poison) 致命性 **2** (fierceness) 恶毒

virulent /ˈvɪrʊlənt/ *adj* **1** Med 剧毒的 ‹*strain, pathogen, microorganism, poison*›; 致命的 ‹*disease*› **2** (fierce) 恶毒的

virulently /ˈvɪrʊləntli/ *adv* **1** Med 恶性地 ‹*spread, infectious*› **2** (fiercely) 恶毒地 ‹*attack, campaign, racist*›; 强烈地 ‹*hate, disagree, hostile*›

virus /ˈvaɪərəs/ ▸**p. 377** *n* (*pl* **~es**) **1** (germ causing disease) 病毒; **the flu/rabies ~** 流感/狂犬病病毒; **a ~ infection/disease** 病毒感染/病毒病 **2** colloq (illness) 病毒病; **to catch** *or* **pick up a ~** 染上病毒性疾病 **3** fig (harmful influence) 毒害; **the ~ of racism** 种族主义的危害 **4** Comput 病毒

virus: ~ checker *n* 查毒程序; **~ protection** *n* [u] 病毒防护软件

visa /ˈviːzə/ *n* 签证; **an entry/exit/transit/tourist ~** 入境/出境/过境/旅游签证

visage /ˈvɪzɪdʒ/ *n* liter **1** (face) 脸 **2** (expression) 表情

vis-à-vis /ˌviːzɑːˈviː/
A *prep* **1** (in relation to) 关于; **China's position ~ climate change** 中国对于气候变化的立场 **2** (as compared with) 同…相比; **the value of the renminbi ~ other currencies** 人民币对其他货币的比值
B *adv* 面对面地 ‹*stand, sit*›
C *n* (*pl* **vis-à-vis**) **1** (counterpart, opposite number) 对等人物 **2** (meeting) 面对面的会面

viscera /ˈvɪsərə/ *npl* 内脏

visceral /ˈvɪsərəl/ *adj* **1** Anat, Med, Zool 内脏的 ‹*nervous system, disease*› **2** (instinctive) 本能的; **a ~ dislike of foreigners/fear of flying** 出于本能的对外国人的厌恶/对乘飞机的恐惧 **3** (raw) 自然的 ‹*power, impact, performance*›

viscose /ˈvɪskəʊz, -kəʊs/ *n* [u] **1** (substance) 黏胶 **2** (fabric) 黏胶织物; (fibre) 黏胶纤维; **a ~ shirt** 黏胶织物衬衫

viscosity /vɪˈskɒsəti/ *n* [u] 黏滞性

viscount /ˈvaɪkaʊnt/ *n* Brit 子爵

viscous /ˈvɪskəs/ *adj* 黏稠的

vise /vaɪs/ *n* Amer = **vice²**

vise-like /ˈvaɪslaɪk/ *adj* Amer = **vice-like**

visibility /ˌvɪzəˈbɪləti/ *n* [u] **1** (clarity of vision) 能见度; **~ is good/poor** 能见度好/差; **~ is below 150 metres** 能见距离不到 150 米; **to have restricted ~** 视野有限 **2** (ability to be seen) 明显性; **light clothes improve your ~** 穿浅色衣服更易引人注目; **to increase a company's ~ in the marketplace** 提升公司在市场上的关注度

visible /ˈvɪzəbl/ *adj* **1** (able to be seen) 看得见的; **to be ~ from space** 从太空可以看得见; **to be ~ for miles around** 周围几英里都可以看得到; **to be ~ to the naked eye** 肉眼可见 **2** (obvious, clear) 明显的 ‹*improvement, sign, change*›; 确实的 ‹*evidence*›; **with no ~ means of support** 生活无着的 **3** (in the public eye) 引人注目的

visible panty line *n* 外露的短裤边

visibly /ˈvɪzəbli/ *adv* **1** (able to be perceived by the eye) 可见地 ‹*shine, move, shrink, pale*› **2** (clearly) 明显地 ‹*relieved, annoyed, moved*›

vision /ˈvɪʒn/
A *n* **1** [u] (ability to see, sight) 视力; **to have poor/good/blurred ~** 视力差/好/模糊; **to come into ~** 进入视野 **2** [u] (imaginative foresight) 眼力; **to have/lack ~** 有/缺乏眼力; **a woman of ~** 有远见的女子 **3** [c] (conception, idea) 想象; **to have ~s of the future** 想象未来; **a romantic ~ of the past** 对于过去的浪漫想象 **4** [c] (mental picture) 幻象; **to have ~s of sth.** 有某事物的幻象; **I had ~s of all sorts of disasters befalling them** 我头脑中是各种各样的灾难降落到他们身上的画面; **to appear to sb. in a ~** 出现在某人的幻象中 **5** [c] esp Relig (dream, hallucination) 幻觉; **the answer came to him in a ~** 他在神示中想到了这个答案 **6** [c] (image) 形象; **a ~ of loveliness/hell** 可爱/可怕的形象 **7** [u] TV 图像; **sound and ~** 音像
B *vt* Amer 想象; **to ~ sth.** 想象某事物

visionary /ˈvɪʒənri, Amer -neri/
A *n* 有远见的人
B *adj* **1** (original, imaginative) 有远见的 ‹*leader*›; 有创见的 ‹*composer, artist, work of art, book*› **2** (relating to visions) 幻觉的 ‹*dream, trance, experience*›; 耽于幻想的 ‹*person*›

vision mixer *n* (person) 图像混调师; (equipment) 视频混合器

visit /ˈvɪzɪt/
A *n* **1** (appointment, call) 访问; **to pay a ~ to sb., to pay sb. a ~** 拜访某人; **to pay a ~ to the dentist/museum** 看牙医/参观博物馆; **a home ~** 上门出诊; **we had a ~ from his parents on Sunday** 星期天他父母来我们家作客了; **he is on an official/a state ~ to Canada** 他正在对加拿大进行正式/国事访问 **2** (stay) 逗留; **this hotel is worth a ~** 这家旅馆值得一住; **it's my first ~ to China** 这是我第一次到中国 **3** Comput 访问; **a ~ to a website/home page** 访问网站/主页 **4** Amer colloq (chat) 聊天; **did you have a nice ~ with him?** 你跟他聊得开心吗?
B *vt* **1** (call on, have appointment with) 访问; (stay with) 在…处做客; (stay in) 在…处逗留; **to ~ a friend/one's parents** 访友/看望父母; **to ~ the dentist/patients** 看牙医/病人; **to ~ the museum** 参观博物馆; **come to** *or* **and ~ us for a few days** 来我们家小住几日吧; **the Prime Minister is ~ing Japan** 首相正在访问日本 **2** (inspect) 视察 ‹*workplace, school*› **3** Comput 访问 ‹*website, home page*› **4** formal (affect) 侵袭; **to be ~ed by nightmares** 做噩梦 **5** *usu passive* liter (inflict) **to ~ sth. upon sb./sth.** 把某事物强加给某人/某事物; **the sins of the fathers are ~ed upon the children** 父辈作的孽报应到子女头上
C *vi* **1** (stay temporarily) 逗留; **to come to** *or* **and ~** 来短暂停留 **2** (call in) 访问 **3** Amer colloq (chat) 聊天

Phrasal verbs

- **visit with** *vt* [~ **with sb.**] Amer colloq **1** (chat with) 跟…聊天 **2** (call on) 在…处做客; **to ~ with a friend** 访友

visitation /ˌvɪzɪˈteɪʃn/ *n* **1** [c] (supernatural sign, visit) (as punishment) 天罚; (as reward) 天赐 **2** [c] (by official person) 视察 **3** [u] Amer Jur [离婚父母对子女的] 探视权

visiting /ˈvɪzɪtɪŋ/ *adj attrib* 访问的; **a ~ scholar** 访问学者

visiting: ~ card *n* 名片; **~ hours** *npl* 探视时间; **~ lecturer** *n* 客座讲师; **~ nurse** ▸**p. 409** *n* Amer 家访护士; **~ professor** *n* 客座教授; **~ room** *n* 探视室; **~ team** *n* 客队; **~ time** *n* 探视时间

visitor /ˈvɪzɪtə(r)/ *n* **1** (to home) (caller, guest) 来客; (intruder) 不速之客; **she didn't often have ~s** 她不常有客人来访; **they were frequent ~s to our house** 他们是我们家的常客 **2** (tourist) 参观者; **I've been a regular ~ to this country/to the museum** 我经常到这个国家/参观博物馆 **3** Sport 客队队员; **the ~s were the first to score** 客队首先得分 **4** (animal, bird) 候鸟; **a summer ~** 夏季来的候鸟

visitor: ~ centre *n* 游客中心; **~s' book** *n* 来宾登记簿

visor /ˈvaɪzə(r)/ *n* **1** (movable part of helmet) 面罩 **2** (piece on cap shielding eyes from the sun) 遮阳帽舌 **3** Aut 遮阳板

vista /ˈvɪstə/ *n* **1** lit (pleasing view) 景色 **2** fig (mental view) (anticipated) 前景; (remembered) 对往事的回忆; **to open up new ~s** 开辟新的前景

visual /ˈvɪʒʊəl/
A *adj* 视觉的
B **visuals** *npl* 视觉资料

visual: ~ aid *n* 直观教具; **~ artist** ▸**p. 409** *n* 视觉艺术家; **~ arts** *npl* 视觉艺术; **~ display unit, ~ display terminal** *ns* 直观显示器; **~ field** *n* 视野

visualize /ˈvɪʒʊəlaɪz/ *vt* **1** (form mental picture of) 使形象化; **she had ~d the house as more modern** 她想象中这所房子要更现代一些; **I met him once, but I can't ~ his face** 我见过他一次, 但现在想不起来他的模样了 **2** (foresee) 预想; **do you ~ yourself staying in the same job for the next few years?** 你能想象自己今后几年要做同样的工作吗?

visually /ˈvɪʒʊəli/ *adv* 在视觉上

visually impaired
A *adj* 视力受损的
B *npl* **the ~** 视力受损的人

vital /ˈvaɪtl/
A *adj* **1** (essential) 必不可少的 ‹*information, supplies*›; 决定性的 ‹*match, factor, point*›; 必要的 ‹*service, help*›; 极其重要的 ‹*treatment, clue*›; **it is ~ that ..., it is of ~ importance that ...** …是极其重要的; **to be ~ to sb./sth.** 对某人/某事极其重要; **it is ~ to do ...** 做…是必要的; **to play a ~ role** *or* **part** 起着至关重要的作用; **to be a ~ force in sth.** 是某事中的重要力量; **news of ~ interest to women** 关乎女性切身利益的消息; **the ~ organs** 重要器官 **2** (lively) 生气勃勃的 ‹*person*›; 充满生机的 ‹*organization, culture*›
B **vitals** *npl* **1** (vital organs) 重要器官 **2** colloq (genitals) 外生殖器

vitality /vaɪˈtæləti/ *n* [u] 活力; **the ~ of youth** 年轻人的朝气蓬勃

vitalize /ˈvaɪtəlaɪz/ *vt* 使…有生命 ‹*person*›; 使…有生机 ‹*scheme, industry*›; 使…有生气 ‹*performance, culture, music*›

vitally /ˈvaɪtəli/ *adv* 极其 ‹*important, urgent*›; 绝对 ‹*necessary, needed*›

vital statistics *npl* **1** Stat 人口动态统计 **2** colloq hum (of woman's body) 女子三围尺寸

vitamin /ˈvɪtəmɪn, Amer ˈvaɪt-/ *n* 维生素; **~ A/B/C** 维生素 A/B/C; **with added ~s, ~ enriched** 添加维生素的; **to have a high/low ~ content** 维生素含量高/低

vitamin deficiency *n* [c and u] 维生素缺乏

vitaminize /ˈvɪtəmɪnaɪz/ *vt usu passive* 在…中加维生素; **a ~d drink** 加维生素的饮料

vitamin: ~ pill, ~ tablet *ns* 维生素片; **~ therapy** *n* [u] 维生素疗法

vitiate /ˈvɪʃɪeɪt/ *vt* formal **1** (spoil) 损坏 ‹*atmosphere, environment*› **2** Jur 使…无效 ‹*decision, claim, contract, judgement*›

viticulture /ˈvɪtɪkʌltʃə(r)/ *n* [u] [酿制葡萄酒的] 葡萄栽培学

vitreous /ˈvɪtrɪəs/ *adj* **1** (glass-like) 玻璃状的 ‹*substance*› **2** (containing glass) 含玻璃的 ‹*rock*›; **a ~ glaze** 玻璃釉; **~ china** 玻璃瓷器

vitrification /ˌvɪtrɪfɪˈkeɪʃn/ *n* [u] (process) 玻璃化; (state) 成玻璃

vitrify /ˈvɪtrɪfaɪ/
A *vt* 使…呈玻璃状 ‹*enamel, glaze*›
B *vi* «*enamel, glaze*» 玻璃化

vitriol /ˈvɪtrɪəl/ *n* [u] 辛辣的批评

vitriolic /ˌvɪtrɪˈɒlɪk/ *adj* 尖刻的 ‹*remark, outburst*›

vitro *n* ▸**in vitro**

vituperation /vɪˌtjuːpəˈreɪʃn, Amer vaɪˌtuː-/ *n* [u] formal 辱骂

vituperative /vɪˈtjuːpərətɪv, Amer vaɪˈtuːpəreɪtɪv/ *adj* formal 谩骂的

viva¹ /ˈviːvə/ *excl* (long live) 万岁; **~ freedom!** 自由万岁!

viva² /ˈvaɪvə/ *n* Brit Univ 口试

vivacious /vɪˈveɪʃəs/ *adj* 活泼的 ‹*person, performance, manner*›; 饱满的 ‹*enthusiasm, high spirits*›

vivaciously /vɪˈveɪʃəsli/ *adv* 活泼地

vivacity /vɪˈvæsəti/ *n* [u] 活泼

vivarium /vaɪˈveərɪəm, vɪ-/ *n* (*pl* **vivaria** /vɪˈveərɪə/) [饲养动物供研究的] 生态缸

viva voce /ˌvaɪvə ˈvəʊtʃi, ˈvəʊsi/ *n* Brit [大学的] 口试; **to have** *or* **take a ~** 参加口试; **~ examination/evidence** 口试/口证

vivid /ˈvɪvɪd/ *adj* **1** (bright) 鲜艳的 ‹*colour, garment, plumage*›; 耀眼的 ‹*light*› **2** (graphic) 清晰的 ‹*memory, picture, dream, impression*›; 生动的 ‹*description, imagination, language, imagery*›

vividly /ˈvɪvɪdli/ *adv* **1** (brightly) 鲜艳地 ‹*colour, paint*›; 耀眼地 ‹*shine, glow*› **2** (graphically) 清晰地 ‹*remember, dream*›; 生动地 ‹*imagine, describe*›

vividness /ˈvɪvɪdnɪs/ *n* [u] **1** (brightness) 鲜艳; **the ~ of the bird's plumage** 鸟儿全身羽毛的光彩夺目 **2** (graphic quality) (of memory, dream, description) 清晰; (of imagination, picture, language) 生动; **the novel contained scenes of incredible ~** 那本小说里有一些逼真得难以置信的场景

vivify /ˈvɪvɪfaɪ/ *vt* 使…生气勃勃 ‹*organization, people, city, process*›; 使…生动 ‹*picture, play, stage set*›

viviparous /vɪˈvɪpərəs, Amer vaɪ-/ *adj* 胎生的

vivisect /ˈvɪvɪsekt/ *vt* pej 对…作活体解剖 ‹*animal*›

vivisection /ˌvɪvɪˈsekʃn/ *n* pej **1** [u] (practice) 活体解剖术 **2** [c] (instance) 活体解剖

vivisectionist /ˌvɪvɪˈsekʃənɪst/ *n* **1** pej (practitioner) 活体解剖者 **2** (supporter) 活体解剖拥护者

vixen /ˈvɪksn/ *n* **1** Zool 雌狐 **2** colloq pej (woman) 泼妇

viz. /vɪz/ *adv* esp Brit formal **= videlicet** 即

VJ *abbr* Amer colloq **= video jock**

vlog /vlɒg/ *n* 视频博客

vlogger /ˈvlɒgə(r)/ *n* 视频博客博主

V-neck *n* (neckline) V字领; (sweater) 鸡心领套衫

V-necked /ˈviːnekt/ *adj* V字领的; **a ~ garment/sweater** 鸡心领服装/毛衣

vocabulary /vəˈkæbjʊləri, Amer -leri/ *n* **1** [c] (of language) 词汇; **to enter** *or* **become part of/drop out of the ~** 成为词汇/成为废弃的词 **2** [c] (of person) 词汇量; **sb.'s active/passive ~** 某人的积极/消极词汇量 **3** [c and u] (of subject) 专业词汇; **the ~ of sociology** 社会学词汇 **4** [c and u] (words being learned) 词汇表

vocal /ˈvəʊkl/
A *adj* **1** (of the voice) 发声的; **~ range/score** 音域/声乐钢琴缩编谱 **2** (vociferous) 直言不讳的; **one of her most ~ critics** 对她最直言的批评者之一
B **vocals** *npl* 演唱; **'with Mick Jagger on ~s'** "由米克·贾格尔演唱"; **who did the ~s?** 谁演唱的?; **to do the backing ~s** 做伴唱

vocal cords *npl* 声带

vocalic /vəˈkælɪk/ *adj* 元音的; **a ~ syllable/sound** 元音音节/元音

vocalist /ˈvəʊkəlɪst/ *n* 歌手

vocalization /ˌvəʊkəlaɪˈzeɪʃn/ *n* [u] **1** (utterance) 发声 **2** (expression) 话语表达; **the ~ of thoughts and emotions** 思想及情感的表达

vocalize /ˈvəʊkəlaɪz/
A *vt* **1** (utter) 发出 ‹*sound*›; 说出 ‹*word*› **2** (express) 用话语表达 ‹*emotion, thought, opposition*› **3** Ling 使…元音化 ‹*sound, consonant*›
B *vi* «*person*» 说话; «*bird*» 唱

vocally /ˈvəʊkəli/ *adv* **1** (using voice) 用嗓音 ‹*express, reproduce*› **2** (vociferously) 大声地 ‹*express, protest, campaign*›

vocal: ~ organs *npl* 发声器官; **~ tract** *n* 声道

vocation /vəʊˈkeɪʃn/ *n* **1** [c and u] (feeling of suitability) 使命感; Relig 神召; **to have a ~ (for sth./for doing sth.** *or* **to do sth.)** 有 (某事/做某事的) 使命感 **2** [c] (ideal job) [特别适合的] 职业; **to find one's ~** 找到理想的工作; **to miss one's ~** 干错行当

vocational /vəʊˈkeɪʃənl/ *adj* 职业的

vocational: ~ course *n* 职业课程; **~ education** *n* [u] 职业教育; **~ guidance** *n* [u] 职业指导; **~ training** *n* [u] 职业培训

vocative /ˈvɒkətɪv/
A *n* (case, form) 呼格; (word) 呼格词
B *adj* 呼格的; **in the ~ case** 以呼格

V

vociferate /vəˈsɪfəreɪt, Amer vəʊ-/ formal
A *vi* 大声疾呼; **to ~ about/against sth.** 大声疾呼某事/反对某事
B *vt* 喧嚷着喊; **to ~ a threat/an opinion** 大声威胁/发表意见

vociferation /vəˌsɪfəˈreɪʃn/ *n* [c and u] formal 大叫大嚷

vociferous /vəˈsɪfərəs, Amer vəʊ-/ *adj* 大叫大嚷的

vociferously /vəˈsɪfərəsli, Amer vəʊ-/ *adv* 大声地

VOD *abbr* = **video-on-demand**

vodka /ˈvɒdkə/ *n* **1** [u and c] (drink) 伏特加酒 **2** (serving) 一杯伏特加酒; **to order two ~s** 要两杯伏特加酒

vogue /vəʊg/ *n* [c and u] 时尚; **to come into/be in ~** 流行起来/成为时尚; **to go out of ~** 不再时髦; **to be out of ~** 不流行; **a ~ word/expression** 时髦词/时尚表达

voice /vɔɪs/
A *n* **1** [c and u] (speaking sound) 说话声; (singing sound) 歌唱声; **to speak in a loud/low ~** 大声/低声说话; **to raise one's ~ (to sb.)** (对某人) 提高嗓门; **to lower one's ~** 压低嗓门; **keep your ~ down!** 小声点!; **don't use that tone of ~ with me!** 别用那种腔调和我说话!; **his ~ is breaking** 他正在变声; **at the top of one's ~** 用最大声音; **to scream at the top of one's ~** 声嘶力竭地尖叫; **to like the sound of one's own ~** 喜欢夸夸其谈; **to give ~ to sth.** 表露某心声; **with one ~** (all together) 异口同声地; (in agreement) 众口一词地; **to have a good ~** 有一副好嗓子; **to be in good ~** 嗓音好 **2** [c] (singer) 声部 **3** [u] (ability to emit sound) 发声能力; **to lose one's ~** (through illness) 倒嗓子; (through emotion) 说不出话; **she is suffering from flu and has lost her ~** 她得了流感, 嗓子哑了; **to find one's ~** 能表达意见 **4** [c] (say) 发言权; **to have a ~ (in sth./doing sth.)** (对某事/做某事) 有发言权; **to give sb. a ~** 给某人发言权 **5** [c] (opinion) 意见; **~s have been raised against the reform** 有些人对改革提出了反对意见; **a dissenting ~** 不同意见; **the ~ of reason/conscience** 理性/良心的声音; **the ~ of the people** 人民的呼声; **to make one's ~ heard** 发表意见 **6** [c] (mouthpiece) 代言人; **the paper was the ~ of middle-class conservatism** 该报纸代表了中产阶级保守主义的声音 **7** [c] (style) 风格; **the poet has her own very distinct ~** 这位诗人有她独具特色的风格 **8** [c and u] (narrator) 叙述者 **9** [c and u] Ling 语态; **the active/passive ~** 主动/被动语态
B *vt* **1** (express) 表达 ‹*opinion, dissatisfaction, doubt*› **2** Phon 使发浊音

voice: ~-activated *adj* 声控的; **a ~-activated phone dialer** 声控电话拨号器; **~ box** *n* 喉; **~ channel** *n* 音频信道

voiced consonant /ˌvɔɪst ˈkɒnsənənt/ *n* 浊辅音

voiceless /ˈvɔɪslɪs/ *adj* **1** Phon 清音的; **a ~ consonant** 清辅音 **2** (silent) 无发言权的 ‹*minority, group*›

voice: ~mail *n* **1** [u] (system) 电话留言系统; **calls were forwarded to ~mail** 来电被转到了语音信箱; **2** [c] (message) 电话留言; **to leave sb. a ~mail** 给某人留一条电话留言; **~ mailbox** *n* 语音信箱; **~ messaging** *n* [u] 电话留言系统; **~-over** *n* [电影或电视节目的] 画外音; **~ print** *n* 声纹; **~ production** *n* [u] [人类语言器官的] 发声; **~ range** *n* 音域; **~ recognition** *n* [u] 声音识别; **~ vote** *n* Amer 口头表决

void /vɔɪd/
A *n* **1** lit (empty space) 空白 **2** fig (emptiness) 空虚; **to fill the ~** 填补空虚感
B *adj* **1** Jur 无效的 ‹*cheque, agreement, contract*›; **to make** *or* **render ~** 使无效 **2** (empty) 空的; **to be ~ of sth.** 没有某物
C *vt* **1** Jur 使…无效 ‹*cheque, contract, statute*› **2** (empty) 排 ‹*water, gas, urine*›

voile /vɔɪl/ *n* [u and c] 薄纱; **~ fabric/garment** 薄纱织物/衣服

vol /vɒl/ *n* (*pl* **~s**) = **volume 1**

volatile /ˈvɒlətaɪl, Amer -tl/ *adj* **1** Chem 易挥发的 ‹*substance, liquid*› **2** fig (changeable) 变化无常的 ‹*person, mood*›; 不稳定的 ‹*situation, market, prices*›

volatility /ˌvɒləˈtɪləti/ *n* [u] **1** Chem 挥发性 **2** fig (of person, mood) 变化无常; (of situation, market, prices) 不稳定

volcanic /vɒlˈkænɪk/ *adj* **1** (of volcanoes) 火山的 **2** fig (extreme, turbulent) 动荡的 ‹*period, era*›; 突然爆发的 ‹*upheaval, passion*›

volcano /vɒlˈkeɪnəʊ/ *n* (*pl* **~es**) **1** Geol, Geog 火山; **an active/extinct ~** 活/死活山; **an inactive** *or* **dormant ~** 休眠火山 **2** fig (explosive situation) 随时可能爆发的状态; **a ~ of resentment** 随时可能发泄的愤恨

volcanologist ▸p. 409 /ˌvɒlkəˈnɒlədʒɪst/ *n* 火山学家

volcanology /ˌvɒlkəˈnɒlədʒi/ *n* [u] 火山学

vole /vəʊl/ *n* 田鼠

volition /vəˈlɪʃn, Amer vəʊ-/ *n* [u] 行使意志; **(to do sth.) of** *or* **by** *or* **on one's own ~** 自愿地 (做某事)

volley /ˈvɒli/
A *n* **1** (of gunfire, missiles, bullets, arrows) 群射; (of stones) 齐投 **2** fig (series) 一连串; **a ~ of insults/questions** 一连串辱骂/问题 **3** (in tennis) 截击空中球; (in football) 凌空踢球; **to miss a ~** (in tennis) 拦截空中球失手; **to hit/kick the ball on the ~** 空中截击球/凌空踢球
B *vt* (in tennis) 空中截击; (in football) 凌空抽射
C *vi* (in tennis) 截击空中球; (in football) 凌空踢球

volleyball /ˈvɒlɪbɔːl/ ▸p. 307 *n* [u] 排球; **a ~ player/ball** 排球运动员/排球

volleyer /ˈvɒlɪə(r)/ *n* 截击空中球的人; **a serve and ~** 发球后上前截击型运动员

volt /vəʊlt/ *n* 伏特; **a nine-~ battery** 9 伏电池

voltage /ˈvəʊltɪdʒ/ *n* 电压; **a high-/low-~ cable** 高压/低压电缆

voltage surge *n* 浪涌电压

voltaic /vɒlˈteɪk/ *adj* 伏打的; **a ~ battery/circuit** 伏打电池/电路

volte-face /ˌvɒltˈfɑːs/ *n* formal 大转弯; **to perform a ~** 彻底转变

voltmeter /ˈvəʊltmiːtə(r)/ *n* 电压表

volubility /ˌvɒljʊˈbɪləti/ *n* [u] 健谈

voluble /ˈvɒljʊbl/ *adj* 健谈的 ‹*person*›; 振振有词的 ‹*protest*›; 流畅的 ‹*discussion, account*›

volubly /ˈvɒljʊbli/ *adv* 振振有词地 ‹*protest, argue*›; 滔滔不绝地 ‹*talk*›

volume /ˈvɒljuːm, Amer -jəm/ *n* **1** [c] (individual book) 册; (part of series) 卷; **a ten-~ set** 十卷套; **in ten ~s** 以十卷套 **2** [c and u] (measurement) 容积; **the ~ of sth.** …的容积 ‹*container, contents*› **3** [u and c] (sound quantity) 音量; **to adjust the ~** 调音量 **4** [c and u] (amount) 量; **the ~ of traffic/production/trade/work** 车流量/产量/贸易量/工作量 **5** (large quantity) 大量; **~s of smoke/steam** 大量的烟/蒸汽; **to speak ~s (about sth.)** 充分表明 (某事); **an expression that speaks ~s** 意味深长的表情

volume: ~ control *n* 音量调控旋钮; **~ discount** *n* 批量折扣

volumetric /ˌvɒljʊˈmetrɪk/ *adj* 测量体积的 ‹*density, data, content*›; **~ efficiency** 容积效率; **~ analysis** 容量分析

voluminous /vəˈluːmɪnəs/ *adj* **1** (extensive) 宽松的 ‹*garment, folds*› **2** (lengthy) 冗长的 ‹*writing, correspondence, notes*›; 长篇的 ‹*works*›

voluntarily /ˈvɒləntrəli/ *adv* **1** (willingly) 自愿地 **2** (for free) 无偿地 ‹*run, organize, help*›

voluntary /ˈvɒləntri, Amer -teri/
A *adj* **1** (not imposed) 自愿的 ‹*participation, donation, recruit, retirement*›; 主动的 ‹*statement, control*›; **on a ~ basis** 基于自愿基础上的 **2** (unpaid) 无偿的 ‹*work, organization*›; **the ~ sector** 非赢利部门 **3** Physiol 随意的; **a ~ movement/muscle** 随意运动/随意肌
B *n* Mus [尤指教堂礼拜仪式上的] 即兴曲

voluntary: ~ euthanasia *n* [u] 自愿安乐死; **~ liquidation** *n* [u] 自愿清算; **to go into ~ liquidation** 进行自愿清算; **~ manslaughter** *n* [u] 故意杀人; **~ redundancy** *n* [c and c] Brit 自愿裁员; **to take ~ redundancy** 自愿接受裁退; **~ repatriation** *n* 自愿遣返; **~ school** *n* Brit 民办学校

volunteer /ˌvɒlənˈtɪə(r)/
A *n* **1** (willing participant) 自告奋勇者 **2** (unpaid worker) 志愿者; **a ~ helper** 自愿提供服务者 **3** Mil 志愿兵; **China's national anthem is the March of the V~s** 中国国歌是《义勇军进行曲》; **a ~ army** 志愿军
B *vt* **1** (offer willingly) 自愿提供 ‹*services, help*›; **to ~ to join/serve** 自愿加入/服务 **2** (divulge willingly) 主动提供 ‹*information, advice, explanation*›; **'it was me,' he ~ed** "是我," 他主动说 **3** (nominate) [尤指擅自地] 举荐 ‹*person*›; **to ~ sb. for sth.** 指派某人担当某事
C *vi* **1** (offer services, with or without payment) 自愿服务; **to ~ for sth.** 自愿为某事服务 **2** Mil 当志愿兵; **to ~ for military service/the army** 志愿服兵役/参军

voluptuous /vəˈlʌptʃʊəs/ *adj* **1** (curvaceous) 丰满性感的 ‹*woman, breasts, curves*› **2** (sensual, sensuous) 感官上的 ‹*sensation, pleasure*›

voluptuously /vəˈlʌptʃʊəsli/ *adv* 性感地 ‹*move, smile, curved*›; 舒适地 ‹*soft, silky*›

voluptuousness /vəˈlʌptjʊəsnɪs/ *n* [u] **1** (curvaceousness) 丰满性感 **2** (sensuality, sensuousness) 感官享受

vomit /ˈvɒmɪt/
A *vi* 呕吐
B *vt* **1** **~ (up)** (throw up) 吐 ‹*food, blood*›; **to ~ sth. up, to ~ up sth.** 呕吐某物 **2** fig (spew forth) 喷出
C *n* [u] 呕吐物

vomiting /ˈvɒmɪtɪŋ/ *n* [u] 呕吐

voodoo /ˈvuːduː/
A *n* [u] [尤指海地等加勒比岛屿的] 伏都教
B *modif* **1** Relig 伏都教的 ‹*priest, doll, ceremony*› **2** fig (not empirical) 伏都巫术般的; **~ economics/science/medicine** 巫术经济/伪科学/巫术医疗

voracious /vəˈreɪʃəs/ *adj* **1** (wanting or eating large amounts of food) 贪吃的 ‹*eater, predator*›; **a ~ appetite for gossip** 对流言蜚语的喜闻乐道 **2** fig (eager) 渴求的 ‹*reader, consumer*›; 贪婪的 ‹*need*›

voraciously /vəˈreɪʃəsli/ *adv* **1** lit (hungrily) 狼吞虎咽地 ‹*eat*›; 大量地 ‹*consume*› **2** fig (eagerly) 贪婪地 ‹*read, consume*›

voracity /vəˈræsəti/ *n* [u] **1** (hunger) 贪食; **the ~ of her appetite** 她的胃口之大 **2** fig (eagerness) 渴求; **a ~ to know/learn** 求知/求学的迫切心情

vortex /ˈvɔːteks/ *n* (*pl* **~es** *or* **vortices** /ˈvɔːtɪsiːz/) **1** (swirling mass) 旋; **a ~ of water** 水流旋涡 **2** fig (whirl) 旋涡; **a swirling ~ of emotions** 感情旋涡

vote /vəʊt/
A *n* **1** [c] (choice) 票; **to cast one's** *or* **a ~** 投票; **to count the ~s** 计票; **the motion was carried by 187 ~s to 93** 这项动议以 187 票对 93 票获得通过; **there were 21 ~s for and 17 against the motion, with 2 abstentions** 这项动议有 21 票赞成, 17 票反对, 2 票弃权; **one man, one ~** 一人一票; **to get sb.'s ~** (in election) 获得某人的投票; fig (be given support) 获得某人的支持 **2** [c] (ballot) 投票; **to**

V

have *or* **take a ~ (on sth.)** （对某事物）进行表决; **the issue was put to the ~** 这一问题被付诸表决; **the Government lost the ~** 政府在投票中失利 **3** [u] (total polled) **the ~** 选票总数; **she obtained 40% of the ~** 她获得了 40% 的选票 **4** [c] (total amount of support) (from particular group) 投票总数; (for particular party) 得票总数; **the female/student ~** 女性/学生的投票总数; **the Labour/Conservative ~** 工党/保守党的得票总数 **5** [u] (franchise) **the ~** 投票权; **in Britain, people get the ~ at 18** 在英国，国民 18 岁开始有选举权 **6** [c] (result of voting) 投票结果; **the ~ was unanimous** 全体表决一致; **the motion was passed by a majority ~** 这项动议以多数票获得通过

B *vt* **1** (give choice to) 投票支持; **to ~ Labour** 投工党的票; **to ~ 'yes'** 投赞成票; **to ~ to strike** 表决举行罢工; **to ~ sb. into office/power** 选举某人任职/当权; **she was ~d on to the board of governors** 她获选进入理事会; **he was ~d the most promising new director** 他当选为最有前途的新导演 **2** (regard as) 认为; **the picnic was ~d a success** 大家认为野餐很成功 **3** (authorize) 投票同意; **to ~ oneself a pay rise** 投票同意给自己涨工资 **4** colloq (propose) 建议; **I ~ we all go** 我建议我们大家都去 **5** colloq (agree) 同意; **we all ~ that you should organize the trip** 我们一致同意应该由你来组织这次旅行

C *vi* 投票; **he's only 17 and not eligible to ~** 他才 17 岁，还没有选举资格; **how are you voting?** 你打算投谁的票？; **to ~ by a show of hands** 举手表决; **to ~ for/against sb./sth.** 投票支持/反对某人/某事物; **60% of members ~d in favour of the motion** 60% 的成员对这项动议投了赞成票; **let's ~ on it** 我们投票表决吧; **to ~ with one's feet** 用脚投票 [用去或不去某处表明态度]; **shoppers ~d with their feet and avoided the store** 购物者对那家商店避而远之

Phrasal verbs

- **vote down** *vt* [~ sb./sth. down, ~ down sb./sth.] 投票击败 ‹*person*›; 投票否决 ‹*proposal, motion*›
- **vote in** *vt* [~ sb. in, ~ in sb.] 投票选…任职; **he was ~d in as treasurer** 他当选为司库
- **vote off** *vt* [~ sb. off sth.] 投票让…离开 ‹*committee, council*›; **he was ~d off the show** 经过投票他被淘汰出了节目
- **vote out** *vt* [~ sb./sth. out, ~ out sb./sth.] 投票免去…的职务 ‹*person*›; 投票否决 ‹*motion, proposal*›; **the ruling party was ~d out of office** 经过投票执政党下台了
- **vote through** *vt* [~ sth. through, ~ through sth.] 投票通过 ‹*bill, budget*›

vote: ~-catching *adj* 吸引选民的 ‹*scheme, policy*›; **~ of censure** *n* 投票谴责; **~ of confidence** *n* 信任票; **to win a ~ of confidence** 赢得信任票; **~ of no confidence** *n* 不信任票; **~ of thanks** *n* 谢辞

voter /ˈvəʊtə(r)/ *n* 投票人

voter registration *n* [u] 选民登记

voter registration card *n* 选民登记卡

voting /ˈvəʊtɪŋ/ *n* [u] 投票; **the second round of ~** 第二轮投票; **~ patterns/habits** 投票模式/习惯

voting: ~ age *n* 选举年龄; **people of ~ age** 达到选举年龄的人们; **~ booth** *n* = **polling booth**; **~ machine** *n* Amer 投票机; **~ paper** *n* 选票; **~ precinct** *n* Amer 选区; **~ record** *n* Amer 投票记录; **~ share** *n* [公司的] 表决权股份

votive /ˈvəʊtɪv/ *adj* [向上帝] 还愿的; **a ~ offering** 还愿奉献物; **a ~ picture/candle** 祈愿用的图画/蜡烛

vouch /vaʊtʃ/ *vt* archaic 保证; **to ~ that ...** 担保…

Phrasal verb

- **vouch for** *vt* [~ for sb./sth.] **1** (confirm character or identity of) (informally) 为…作证 ‹*person, trustworthiness*›; (officially) 为…担保 ‹*person, sb.'s honesty*› **2** (confirm truth or accuracy of) (informally) 证明 ‹*fact*›; (officially) 保证 ‹*authenticity, accuracy*›

voucher /ˈvaʊtʃə(r)/ *n* **1** (for gift, concession) 票券; **a gift/luncheon/discount ~** 礼券/午餐券/打折优惠券 **2** esp Brit (receipt) 收据

vouchsafe /ˌvaʊtʃˈseɪf/ *vt* formal **1** (reveal) 透露 **2** (grant) 惠赐; **to ~ sb. sth.** 给予某人某物 **3** (promise) 允诺; **to ~ to do sth.** 承诺做某事

vow /vaʊ/

A *vt* 对…立誓 ‹*allegiance, revenge, love*›; **he ~ed that he would never return** 他发誓永不回来

B *n* 誓言; **to take** *or* **make a ~** 发誓; **to be under a ~ of silence** 立誓缄口保密; **to keep/break a ~** 遵守/违背誓言

C vows *npl* 誓约; **to take one's ~s** 立誓; **marriage ~s** 婚姻誓约

vowel /ˈvaʊəl/ *n* **1** Ling 元音; **a ~ symbol** 元音符号; **a ~ shift** 元音演变 **2** (letter) 元音字母

voyage /ˈvɔɪɪdʒ/

A *n* 航行; **to go on a ~** 去航行; **a ~ of discovery** *or* **exploration** 探索之旅; **the outward/homeward ~** 出航/归航

B *vi* liter 航行; **to ~ across the ocean** 横渡海洋

voyager /ˈvɔɪɪdʒə(r)/ *n* liter 航行者

voyeur /vɔɪˈɜː(r)/ *n* 窥淫癖者

voyeurism /vɔɪˈɜːrɪzəm/ *n* [u] 窥淫癖

voyeuristic /ˌvɔɪəˈrɪstɪk/ *adj* 有窥淫癖的 ‹*person*›; **to have a ~ interest in other people's lives** 有窥视他人生活隐私的兴趣

VP *n* = **vice-president**

VPN *abbr* = **virtual private network**

vs *prep* = **versus 2**

V-shaped /ˈviːʃeɪpt/ *adj* V字形的

V-sign *n* **1** = **victory sign 2** Brit (offensive gesture) [手背朝外的] V 字形侮辱手势; **to give sb. a ~** 对某人做出侮辱手势

VSO *abbr* Brit = **Voluntary Service Overseas** 海外志愿服务社 [英国慈善机构]; **to do ~** 做海外志愿服务

VT *abbr* Amer = **Vermont**

VTOL *abbr* = **vertical take-off and landing 1** [u] (system) 垂直起落; **~ aircraft/technology** 垂直起落飞机/技术 **2** [c] (aircraft) 垂直起落飞机

vulcanite /ˈvʌlkənaɪt/ *n* [u] 硬质橡胶

vulcanization /ˌvʌlkənaɪˈzeɪʃn, Amer -nɪˈz-/ *n* [u] 硫化

vulcanize /ˈvʌlkənaɪz/ *vt* 硫化处理 ‹*rubber*›

vulcanologist /ˌvʌlkəˈnɒlədʒɪst/ *n* = **volcanologist**

vulcanology /ˌvʌlkəˈnɒlədʒi/ *n* [u] = **volcanology**

vulgar /ˈvʌlgə(r)/ *adj* **1** (tasteless) 庸俗的 **2** (rude) 粗鲁的 ‹*remark, language, joke, gesture*›; 粗野的 ‹*person*›

vulgar fraction *n* 普通分数

vulgarism /ˈvʌlgərɪzəm/ *n* 粗俗词语; **a ~ for sth.** 某物的粗鄙词语

vulgarity /vʌlˈgærəti/ *n* **1** (tastelessness) (of decoration, design) 庸俗; (of person, behaviour) 粗俗; (of furniture, clothes) 俗气 **2** (rudeness) 粗鲁

vulgarization /ˌvʌlgəraɪˈzeɪʃn, Amer -rɪˈz-/ *n* [u] 庸俗化

vulgarize /ˈvʌlgəraɪz/ *vt* **1** (make less refined) 使…通俗化 ‹*place, activity, book, art*› **2** (make rude) 使…庸俗化 ‹*situation, person*›; 使…粗鲁 ‹*remark, behaviour, manners*›

vulgar Latin *n* [u] 俗拉丁语

vulgarly /ˈvʌlgəlɪ/ *adv* **1** (tastelessly) 庸俗地 ‹*furnish, dress, behave*› **2** (rudely) 粗鲁地 ‹*describe, express*›; 下流地 ‹*gesture*›

vulnerability /ˌvʌlnərəˈbɪləti/ *n* [u] (to attack) 易遭攻击; (to injury, harm) 易受伤害; (to criticism) 易遭责难

vulnerable /ˈvʌlnərəbl/ *adj* 脆弱的 ‹*child, young animal, seedling, age*›; 地位不稳固的 ‹*employee, leader*›; 易受影响的 ‹*stock market*›; 易受伤害的 ‹*pedestrian, cyclist*›; 易受攻击的 ‹*country, troops*›; **to be ~ to pressure** 易受压力影响

vulture /ˈvʌltʃə(r)/ *n* **1** lit 兀鹫; **to descend like ~s** 像秃鹫一般扑下来 **2** fig 乘人之危者; **he described lawyers as ~s** 他把律师描绘成趁火打劫的人

vulva /ˈvʌlvə/ *n* (*pl* **vulvae** /ˈvʌlviː/) 外阴

vying /ˈvaɪɪŋ/ *pres p* ▸ **vie**

Ww

W, w /'dʌbljuː/
A *n* (*pl* **Ws** *or* **W's**) [英语字母表的第23个字母]
B **W** *abbr* **1** Elec = **watt** **2** Geog = **west, western**

WA *abbr* Amer = **Washington 2**

wacko /'wækəʊ/ *adj* esp Amer colloq 发疯的 ‹*person*›; 古怪的 ‹*idea*›

wacky /'wæki/ *adj* colloq 古怪的; **a ～ ad campaign/person** 疯狂的广告大战/疯子

wad /wɒd/
A *n* **1** (mass of soft things) 软团; **a ～ of cotton wool** 一团药棉 **2** (portion) 块; **a ～ of tobacco/chewing gum** 一撮烟叶/一块口香糖 **3** (bundle) 叠; **a ～ of bank notes** 一沓钞票 **4** colloq (large amount) 许多; **a ～ of money** 一大把钱
B **wads** *npl* colloq 许许多多
C *vt* (*pres p etc.* **-dd-**) **1** (compress) 将…揉成团 **2** (plug) 填塞 **3** (pad) 用填料填充 ‹*chair, jacket*›

wadding /'wɒdɪŋ/ *n* [u] **1** (padding) 软填料 **2** (in cartridge, gun) 炮塞

waddle /'wɒdl/
A *vi* «*duck, person*» 蹒跚行走
B *n sing* 蹒跚

wade /weɪd/ *vi* **1** (walk through water) 趟水; **to go wading** 去趟水; **to ～ across a river** 趟过河; **to ～ into/through the water** 趟进水里/趟过水 **2** (proceed with difficulty) 艰难进行

Phrasal verbs

- **wade in** *vi* **1** (enter water) 趟进水 **2** colloq (enter into fight) 袭击; (enter into argument) 抨击
- **wade into** *vt* colloq **1** [～ **into sth.**] (physically) 加入 ‹*fight*› **2** [～ **into sb./sth.**] (verbally) 抨击 ‹*critics, opposition, debate*›
- **wade through** *vt* [～ **through sth.**] 费力完成 ‹*task, report, paperwork*›; 费力读完 ‹*book*›

wader /'weɪdə(r)/
A *n* Zool 涉禽
B **waders** *npl* (boots) 高筒防水胶靴

wadi /'wɒdi/ *n* (*pl* **～s** *or* **～es**) [北非和中东地区的] 干河谷

wading /'weɪdɪŋ/**: ～ bird** *n* = **wader A**; **～ pool** *n* Amer = **paddling pool**

wafer /'weɪfə(r)/ *n* **1** Culin 薄酥饼 **2** Relig 圣饼 **3** Electron 晶片

wafer-thin
A *adj* (thin) 很薄的 ‹*slice, metal*›; (too thin) 太薄的 ‹*walls*›; **a ～ majority** 轻微大多数
B *adv* (thinly) 很薄地 ‹*slice, make*›; (too thinly) 太薄地 ‹*build*›

waffle[1] /'wɒfl/ *n* Culin 华夫饼

waffle[2] colloq pej
A *vi* **1** Brit (chatter) **～ (on)** 胡扯; **to ～ on for hours** 絮叨半天 **2** Amer (be indecisive) 犹豫不决
B *n* **1** [u] esp Brit (verbiage) 废话连篇 **2** [c] *sing* Amer (indecision) 犹豫不决

waffle iron *n* 华夫饼烤模

waffler /'wɒflə(r)/ *n* Brit colloq pej 贫嘴子

waffly /'wɒfli/ *adj* Brit colloq pej 含糊其辞的

waft /wɒft, Amer wæft/
A *vi* «*sound, scent, feather*» 飘荡
B *vt* «*breeze*» 使…飘荡 ‹*smell, seeds, clouds*›
C *n* 一阵; **a sudden ～ of air** 突如其来的一阵风; **a ～ of baked bread/perfume** 一股烤面包的香味/香水味

wag[1] /wæg/
A *vt* (*pres p etc.* **-gg-**) «*dog*» 摇摆 ‹*tail*›; «*person, dog*» 摇 ‹*head*›; **to ～ one's finger at sb.** 用手指指某人; fig 责备某人; **it's (a case of) the tail ～ging the dog** 这是本末倒置
B *vi* (*pres p etc.* **-gg-**) «*head, tail*» 摇动; **tongues will ～** fig 人们会说闲话的
C *n* 摇动

wag[2] *n* dated (person who enjoys making jokes) 爱开玩笑的人

wage /weɪdʒ/
A *n* **～(s** *pl*) 工资; **a (legal) minimum ～** (法定) 最低工资; **the ～s of sin is death** Bible 罪恶的代价是死亡; **～ scale/control** 工资级别/额度控制; **a ～ increase/cut** 加薪/减薪
B *vt* 发动 ‹*campaign*›; **to ～ (a) war against sth./sb.** 向某事物/某人开战

wage: ～ bargaining *n* [u] 工资谈判; **～ bill** *n* 工资额; **～ costs** *npl* 工资成本

waged /weɪdʒd/
A *adj* 领工资的 ‹*worker, labour*›
B *npl* **the ～** 工薪阶层

wage: ～ demand *n* 增加工资的要求; **～ earner** *n* **1** (person making wage) 工人; **2** (breadwinner) 养家糊口的人; **～ negotiations** *npl* 工资谈判; **～ packet** *n* Brit **1** (envelope) 工资袋; **2** (pay) 工资

wager /'weɪdʒə(r)/ formal
A *vt* lit, fig 拿…打赌 ‹*amount, one's life*›; **to ～ sth. on sth.** 把某物押在某事物上; **to ～ that ...** 打赌…
B *n* 打赌

wage: ～ restraint *n* [u] [工会作出的] 制止工资增长的决定; **～ round** *n* 年度工资谈判; **～s clerk** ►p. 409 *n* 工资文秘; **～s council** *n* Brit Hist 工资管理委员会; **～ settlement** *n* 工资协议; **～ slip** *n* 工资条; **～ structure** *n* 工资结构; **～ worker** *n* Amer = **～ earner 1**

waggish /'wægɪʃ/ *adj* dated 诙谐的 ‹*person, grin, behaviour*›; **～ remarks** 俏皮话

waggishly /'wægɪʃli/ *adv* dated 诙谐地 ‹*act, say, grin*›

waggle /'wægl/
A *vt* 使…来回动 ‹*screw, ears*›; 使…松动 ‹*tooth*›; **to ～ one's hips/eyebrows** 扭胯/挑动眉头
B *vi* **～ (around** *or* **about)** «*screw, ears*» 来回动; «*tooth*» 松动; **to ～ up and down** 上下动
C *n usu sing* 来回动; **to give sth. a ～** 晃动某物一下

waggon /'wægən/ *n* Brit = **wagon**

waggoner /'wægənə(r)/ *n* Brit = **wagoner**

waggonette /ˌwægə'net/ *n* Brit = **wagonette**

Wagnerian /vɑːg'nɪərɪən/ *adj* 瓦格纳式的 ‹*style, drama, singer*›

wagon /'wægən/ *n* **1** (horse-drawn) 马车; (ox-drawn) 牛车; **to be on/fall off the ～** fig 戒酒/又开始酗酒 **2** Brit Rail 货车车厢 **3** Brit (lorry) 货车 **4** esp Amer (food cart) 手推食品车

wagoner /'wægənə(r)/ ►p. 409 *n* 马车夫

wagonette /ˌwægə'net/ *n* 四轮轻便马车

wagon: ～load *n* [马车、货车等的] 载荷; **～ train** *n* esp Amer 马拉篷车队

wagtail /'wægteɪl/ *n* 鹡鸰

waif /weɪf/ *n* 流浪儿

waif-like *adj* 面黄肌瘦的

wail /weɪl/
A *vi* **1** (cry) 号啕大哭 **2** (make high-pitched noise) «*siren, instrument*» 鸣响; «*wind*» 呼啸
B *vt* (in grief) 哀号着说; (in anger, pain) 叫嚷
C *n* **1** (cry) 号啕大哭 **2** (high-pitched noise) (of siren, instrument) 鸣响; (of wind) 呼啸

wailing /'weɪlɪŋ/
A *n* [u] **1** (crying) 恸哭 **2** (high-pitched noise) (of siren, instrument) 鸣响; (of wind) 呼啸
B *adj attrib* 恸哭的 ‹*sound, voices*›; 鸣响的 ‹*siren, instrument*›; 呼啸的 ‹*wind*›

wainscot /'weɪnskət/ *n* 护墙板

wainscoting, wainscotting /'weɪnskətɪŋ/ *n* [u] (wood for panels) 护墙板材; (panelling) 墙裙

waist /weɪst/ *n* **1** 腰; **to put one's arm around sb.'s ～** 搂某人的腰; **bare to the ～** 光着上身的 **2** Fashn 腰围; **a high/dropped ～** 高腰/低腰 **3** Amer (blouse) 衬衫; (bodice) 连衣裙上身 **4** (of musical instrument) [提琴或吉他类乐器的] 中间细部 **5** (of wasp) [昆虫的] 细腰 **6** (of hourglass) 中窄处

waist: ～band *n* (of skirt) 裙腰; (of trousers) 裤腰; (of underpants) 腰头; **～coat** *n* Brit 马甲

waist-deep
A *adj* 齐腰深的; **to be ～ in ...** 腰部以下埋在…中 ‹*snow, water*›
B *adv* 在齐腰深的水中 ‹*wade, sink*›; **to be standing ～ in ...** 站在齐腰深的…中 ‹*snow, water*›

-waisted /'weɪstɪd/ *combining form* 有某种腰身的; **a narrow** *or* **slim～ girl** 细腰女孩; **a high/low～ dress** 高腰/低腰连衣裙

waist-high
A *adj* 齐腰高的 ‹*grass, railing*›
B *adv* 高至腰部地 ‹*lift*›; **to grow ～** 长得齐腰高

waist: ～line *n* **1** Anat 腰; **2** Fashn 腰围; **～ measurement** *n* 腰围尺寸

wait /weɪt/
A *vi* **1** (stand by) 等候; **I don't mind ～ing** 我不在乎等; **'keys cut, while you ～'** "配钥匙立等可取"; **to ～ for sb./sth.** 等某人/某事物; **～ for me!** 等等我!; **to ～ (for sb.) to do sth.** 等待 (某人) 做某事; **～ until** *or* **till ...** 等到…吧 [用于兴奋地表示或展示某物]; **～ till you see what I've found!** 你等着看我找到了什么吧!; **to keep sb. ～ing** 让某人等着; **～ a minute** *or* **moment** *or* **second!** (asking for delay) 稍等片刻!; (when interrupting) 等一等!; (expressing realization) 慢点!; **I can hardly** *or* **can't ～** 我迫不及待; **～ and see!** 等着看吧!; **what are we/you ～ing for?**

W

我们/你们还在等什么？；**(just) you ~!** (making threat) 你等着瞧！；(making prediction) 你就等着看吧！；**~ for it!** esp Brit (introducing surprise) 听好了！；(ordering delay) 等候通知！；Mil 听命令！；**to be sth. ~ing to happen** 是早晚会发生的事；**everything comes** *or* **all good things come to those who ~** Prov 耐心等候的人交好运 2 (look forward, anticipate) 盼望；**to ~ for sth.** 期待某事；**to ~ (for sb.) to do sth.** 期待（某人）做某事 3 (be ready) 就绪；**there's a letter ~ing for you at home** 家里有你一封信；**the hotel had a taxi ~ing to collect us** 旅馆叫了辆出租车等着接我们 4 (be left until later) 延缓；**he can ~: I'm busy right now** 他得等等，我眼下很忙；**this is important: it can't ~** 这很重要，刻不容缓 5 **to ~ at table** formal (act as waiter) 侍候进餐

B *vt* 1 (watch for) 等待 ‹*chance*›；**he ~ed his opportunity to sneak away** 他等待机会想溜走 2 (stand in line for) 等候；**you'll just have to ~ your turn** 你得等着轮到你 3 esp Amer colloq (delay) 推迟 ‹*meal*›；**don't ~ dinner for me** 吃晚饭不要等我 4 esp Amer (serve at) **to ~ tables** 做餐厅服务员

C *n* 等待；**you'll have a long ~** iron 你就好好等着吧；**to be worth the ~** 值得等待；**to lie in ~ (for sb./sth.)** «*hunter, animal*» 伏击（某人/某物）；**the bandits were lying in ~ just outside the village** 强盗就埋伏在村子外面

Phrasal verbs

- **wait around, wait about** *vi* 空等；**to ~ around for sb. (to do sth.)** 干等着某人（做某事）
- **wait behind** *vi* esp Brit [尤指为了私下交谈] 待他人走后留下来；**to ~ behind after class/a meeting** 在下课/会议之后留下来
- **wait in** *vi* Brit **to ~ in (for sb./sth.)** 在家里等候（某人/某物）
- **wait on** *vt* 1 [**~ on sb./sth.**] (await) 等待；**she is ~ing on the result of a blood test** 她在等验血结果 2 [**~ on sb.**] (serve) 为…服务；(act as attendant to) «*servant*» 服侍；**to ~ on sb. hand and foot** pej 无微不至地服侍某人
- **wait out** *vt* [**~ sth. out, ~ out sth.**] 等待…结束 ‹*storm, crisis*›
- **wait up** *vi* 1 (stay up) **to ~ up (for sb.)** 熬夜等待（某人） 2 esp Amer (stop, pause) 等一等

wait-and-see *adj* 等待观望的 ‹*attitude, policy*›

waiter /ˈweɪtə(r)/ ▸p. 409 *n* [餐馆的] 男服务员

waiter service *n* [u] [餐厅、酒吧等场所的] 男服务员的服务

waiting /ˈweɪtɪŋ/

A *n* [u] 1 (staying, delaying) 等待；**'no ~'** "禁止停车！" 2 (attendance) [尤指宫廷的] 侍奉；**to be in ~ on sb.** 侍奉某人 3 (working as waiter) 当服务员

B *adj attrib* 等待的 ‹*person, crowd, taxi*›；伺机而动的 ‹*ambush, troops*›；**sb.'s ~ arms** 某人张开的臂膀

waiting: ~ game *n usu sing* 伺机而动的策略；**to play a ~ game** 伺机而动；**~ list** *n* 等候者名单；**~ room** *n* (at station) 候车室；(at clinic) 候诊室

wait list Amer

A *n* **= waiting list**

B **wait-list** *vt* 把…列入等候者名单 ‹*person*›；**to be wait-listed for sth.** 被列入某事的等候者名单

waitress /ˈweɪtrɪs/ ▸p. 409 *n* [餐馆的] 女服务员

waitressing /ˈweɪtrɪsɪŋ/ *n* [u] 当女服务员

waitress service *n* [u] [餐厅、酒吧等场所的] 女服务员的服务

waive /weɪv/ *vt* 放弃 ‹*claim, requirement, fee*›；免除 ‹*penalty*›

waiver /ˈweɪvə(r)/ *n* 1 (action) 弃权 2 (statement) 弃权声明 3 (document) 弃权声明书

waiver clause *n* (in employment contract) 弃权条款；(in prospectus) 免责条款

wake /weɪk/

A *vi* (*pt* **woke**, *pp* **woken**) 1 (awake) 醒来；**I always ~ early in the summer** 夏天我总是醒得早；**to ~ from sleep/a dream** 从睡眠/梦中醒来；**I woke to find her gone** 我醒来时发现她已经走了 2 liter or formal (become aware) 醒悟；**to ~ (up) from** 从…中清醒过来 ‹*reverie*›

B *vt* (*pt* **woke**, *pp* **woken**) 1 (awaken) 弄醒 ‹*person*›；**to ~ sb. from sleep/a dream** 将某人从睡眠/梦中弄醒；**to ~ the dead** 能把死人吵醒 2 liter or formal (stir up) 唤起 ‹*memories, feelings*›

C *n* 1 (vigil) [葬礼前的] 守灵 2 (party) [葬礼后的] 守灵 3 (of vessel) [船只行驶留下的] 尾流；**in the ~ of sb./sth.** (in space) 尾随着某人/某物；(in time) 在某人/某事之后；**the storm left a trail of destruction in its ~** 暴风雨过后满目疮痍

Phrasal verb

- **wake up**

A *vi* 1 (awake) 醒来；**what time do you usually ~ up in the morning?** 早上你通常几点醒？；**to ~ up from sleep/a dream** 从睡眠/梦中醒过来；**he woke up to find himself alone in the house** 他醒来时发现独自一人在屋子里；**he woke up in hospital** 他在医院苏醒了过来；**the population woke up to a change of government** 人民一觉醒来发现政府已经易手 2 (become aware) 醒悟；**~ up! can't you see she's only marrying you for your money!** 醒醒吧！难道你看不出来她嫁给你只是为了你的钱！；**to ~ up to the truth/a fact** 意识到真相/事实；**~ up and smell the coffee!** 请清醒地面对现实！

B *vt* [**~ sb. up, ~ up sb.**] 1 (awaken) 弄醒 2 (enliven) 使活跃起来；**a cold shower will soon ~ you up** 冲个冷水澡很快就能让你神清气爽

wakeboard /ˈweɪkbɔːd/ *n* 尾波板

wakeboarding /ˈweɪkbɔːdɪŋ/ *n* [u] 尾流滑水；**to go ~** 去进行尾流滑水运动

wakeful /ˈweɪkfl/ *adj* formal 1 (not sleeping well) 睡得不踏实的 2 (not sleepy) 不困的 3 (sleepless) 失眠的；**a ~ night** 不眠之夜 4 (alert) 警觉的

wakefulness /ˈweɪkflnɪs/ *n* [u] formal 1 (insomnia) 失眠 2 (alertness) 警觉

waken /ˈweɪkən/ *vt, vi* **= wake A, B**

wake-up call *n* 1 lit 叫醒电话 2 fig (warning) 引起警觉的事；**to serve as a ~** «*crisis, news*» 敲响警钟

wakey-wakey /ˈweɪkɪweɪki/ *excl* Brit colloq dated 醒醒；**~, rise and shine!** 醒醒，起床了！

waking /ˈweɪkɪŋ/

A *n* [u] 醒着；**between sleeping and ~** 半睡半醒的

B *adj attrib* 不眠的；**every ~ moment/hour/day** 醒着的每一刻/每小时/每一天；**to spend all one's ~ hours doing sth.** 不睡觉的时候都在做某事；**in** *or* **during one's ~ hours** 在醒着的时候

Waldorf salad /ˌwɔːldɔːf ˈsæləd/ *n* [u and c] 沃尔多夫色拉 [用苹果丁、芹菜丁、果仁和蛋黄酱调制而成]

Wales /weɪlz/ *pr n* 威尔士

walk /wɔːk/

A *vi* 1 (move on foot) 走；(travel on foot) 步行；**to ~ home** 走回家；**it's not very far: let's ~** 那里不太远，我们走着去吧；**don't ~ on the grass** 不要践踏草地；**'~'/'don't ~'** Amer (sign at traffic lights) "通行"/"止步"；**to ~ before one can run** fig 先学会走再学跑；**to run before one can ~** fig 还不会走就想跑；**to ~ in one's sleep** 梦游；**to ~ under a bus** 被公交车撞死 2 (go for stroll) 散步；esp Brit (hike) 远足；**to go out ~ing** 出去散步；**to ~ in the mountains/countryside** 在山里/乡间远足 3 (move at slowest pace) «*horse*» 慢步走 4 colloq hum (disappear) «*possession*» 不翼而飞 5 Amer colloq (be released) (from suspicion) 摆脱嫌疑；(from a charge) 解除指控 6 colloq (leave) «*employee*» 撂挑子 7 liter (appear) «*ghost, phantom*» 出现 8 (in cricket) «*batsman*» 主动离场 9 (in baseball) «*batter*» 自由上垒

B *vt* 1 (go over on foot) 在…上走 ‹*road*›；**to ~ the streets** «*tourist*» 走街串巷；fig «*prostitute*» 在街上拉客；**to ~ it** colloq (go on foot) 走到那儿去；fig (succeed easily) 轻易取胜；**to ~ the ~** colloq 说到做到 2 esp Brit (hike over) 在…远足 ‹*footpath, moors*› 3 (accompany) 陪…走；**to ~ sb. home** 陪某人走回家；**to ~ sb. to their hotel/the station** 陪某人走到酒店/车站；**to ~ sb. around sth.** «*guide*» 带某人徒步游览某处；**to ~ sb. off their feet** colloq 让某人走断腿 4 (cause to go on foot) 使行走；**the guards ~ed him back to his cell** 看守们押着他走回牢房 5 (take out for exercise) 遛 ‹*dog*› 6 (patrol) 在…巡逻 ‹*ramparts, area*›；**to ~ the beat** «*police officer*» 在辖区执勤巡逻 7 liter (appear in) «*ghost*» 出没于 ‹*tower, corridors*› 8 (move from side to side) 挪动 ‹*piece of furniture, ladder*› 9 (wheel) 推着…走 ‹*bicycle*› 10 (ride slowly) 骑着…遛达 ‹*horse*›

C *n* 1 (journey on foot) 步行；**a ~ in the woods/moonlight** 林中/月下漫步；**the ~ home** 步行回家；**to take the dog for a ~** 去遛狗；**to have** *or* **take** *or* **go for a ~** 去散步；**a ten-minute ~** 十分钟的步行；**take a ~!** esp Amer colloq 走开！；**to win in a ~** esp Amer colloq (easily) 轻易获胜 2 (hike) 远足；**to go for a ~** 去远足 3 (route) 散步路线 4 (organized event) 步行出游 5 (gait) 步态；**she has a very strange ~** 她走路的样子很奇怪 6 (pace) (of person) 步伐；(of animal) [尤指马的] 慢步走；**a brisk ~** 轻快的步伐 7 (path) 小径；**shady ~s through the trees** 林荫小路 8 Sport (competitive race) 竞走

Phrasal verbs

- **walk around**

A *vi* 1 (move around) 走来走去；**to ~ around in circles** 兜圈子 2 (wander around) 闲逛 3 (go around perimeter) 绕道走

B *vt* [**~ around sth.**] 1 (go here and there in) 在…闲逛 ‹*city, streets*› 2 (visit all of) 走遍 ‹*museum*› 3 (go around outside of) 绕着…的外面走 ‹*stadium, ruins*›

- **walk away** *vi* 1 (go away) 走开 2 (avoid involvement) 一走了之；**to ~ away from** 甩开 ‹*responsibility, problem*›；**to ~ away from a fight** 逃避斗争；**just ~ away: it's nothing to do with you** 待一边儿去，这跟你没有关系 3 (survive unscathed) **to ~ away from an accident** 从事故中平安脱身
- **walk away with** *vt* [**~ away with sth.**] colloq 1 (win easily) 轻松赢得 ‹*game, election*› 2 (receive) 获得 ‹*prize, medal*› 3 (take unintentionally) 错拿 ‹*coat, book*› 4 (steal) 顺手牵羊拿走 ‹*wallet*›
- **walk in on** *vt* [**~ in on sb./sth.**] 冷不丁进屋撞见 ‹*person, scene*›
- **walk into** *vt* [**~ into sth.**] 1 (enter) 走进 ‹*room, building*› 2 (become entangled in) 陷入 ‹*trap*›；**you ~ed right into that one!** colloq 你撞到枪口上了！ 3 colloq (get easily) 轻易得到 ‹*job*› 4 (collide with) 不小心撞上 ‹*person, wall*›
- **walk off**

A *vi* 愤然离开

B *vt* [**~ sth. off, ~ off sth.**] 散步消除 ‹*headache, hangover*›；散步消化 ‹*meal*›；**to ~ off one's extra weight** 散步减肥

- **walk on** *vi* 1 (continue) 继续走 2 (have acting role) 跑龙套
- **walk out** *vi* 1 (leave) 走出去 2 colloq (abandon relationship) 不辞而别；**to ~ out on** 抛弃 ‹*partner, marriage*›；断绝 ‹*relationship*› 3 colloq (leave job) «*employee*» 撂挑子 4 (leave

early) [为表示不满而] 突然退席; **to ~ out of ...** 突然退出 ‹*negotiations, conference*›; 提前离开 ‹*film, play*› 5 (go on strike) «*workers*» 罢工
- **walk over** *vt* **to ~ (all) over sb.** colloq (take advantage of) 作践 ‹*lover, employee*›; (defeat easily) 轻松打败 ‹*opponent, team*›
- **walk round** *vi, vt* Brit = **walk around**
- **walk up** *vi* 1 (approach) 走上前去; **to ~ up to sb.** (自信地) 走近某人 2 Brit (roll up) 过来看看啊 [常指招徕顾客的喊声]; **~ up, ~ up!** 走过，路过，不要错过!

walkabout /'wɔːkəbaʊt/ *n* 1 Anthrop [澳洲土著人回归传统生活方式的] 短期丛林流浪; fig (roam) «*person*» 闲逛; hum (disappear) «*person*» 跑丢; «*object*» 丢失; **to go ~** «*Aboriginal*» 到丛林去流浪 2 **to go on a** *or* **do a ~** esp Brit (mingle with crowd) «*VIP*» 出巡

walkathon /'wɔːkəθɒn/ *n* colloq [尤指为慈善事业募款的] 步行马拉松

walkaway /'wɔːkəweɪ/ *n* Amer colloq 轻松赢得的比赛; **the race was a ~ for the champion** 对于这位冠军来说这场比赛赢得易如反掌

walker /'wɔːkə(r)/ *n* 1 (person) 步行者; (in race) 竞走者 2 (device) (for invalid) 助行器; (for baby) 学步车

walkie-talkie /ˌwɔːkɪ'tɔːki/ *n* colloq 步话机

walk-in *adj attrib* 1 (able to be entered) 大得能进入的; **a ~ closet/freezer** 步入式衣帽间/冷冻室 2 (not needing appointment) 无需预约的 ‹*clinic, service*› 3 Amer (entered from street) 门挨大街的 ‹*apartment, shop*›

walking /'wɔːkɪŋ/
A *n* [u] (for pleasure, exercise) 步行; (in race) 竞走
B *adj attrib* hum 活的; **she's a ~ dictionary/encyclopedia** 她是本活字典/活的百科全书

walking: ~ boots *npl* 步行靴; **~ distance** *n* [u] 步行距离; **to be within ~ distance** 在步行距离内; **~ frame** *n* 助行架; **~ holiday** *n* 徒步旅行休假; **~ pace** *n sing* 步行速度; **at (a) ~ pace** 以步行速度; **~ papers** *npl* Amer colloq 辞退信; **to get** *or* **be given one's ~ papers** 被炒鱿鱼; **~ race** *n* 竞走; **~ shoes** *npl* 便鞋; **~ stick** *n* 拐杖; **~ tour** *n* 徒步旅行; **~ wounded** *npl* **the ~ wounded** 轻伤员; fig 未伤元气的人

Walkman® /'wɔːkmən/ *n* (*pl* **~s** *or* **Walkmen**) 随身听

walk of life *n* 行业; **people from all (different) walks of life** 各行各业的人

walk-on
A *adj attrib* 跑龙套的 ‹*role, part, actor*›
B *n* 龙套

walk: ~out *n* (in protest) 退场; (strike) 罢工; **to stage a ~out** 举行罢工; **~over** *n* 易如反掌的胜利; **~-up** *n* Amer (building) 无电梯楼房; (apartment) 无电梯公寓套房; **~way** *n* 走道

wall /wɔːl/
A *n* 1 (side of room, building) 墙壁; **an inside/outside ~** 内墙/外墙; **the front/back ~** 前墙/后墙; **these four ~s** 这四堵墙 [尤指私密的处所]; **what I'm telling you should remain within these four ~s** 我现在跟你说的话不得外传; **to drive sb. up the ~** colloq 逼得某人受不了; **to go up the ~** colloq (become exasperated) 非常恼火; (become crazy) 发狂; **to be a fly on the ~** fig 暗中旁观; **to be off the ~** colloq «*person, idea*» 滑稽古怪; **~s have ears** Prov 隔墙有耳; **to push** *or* **drive sb./sth. to the ~** colloq (cause problems for) 使某人/某事物陷入困境; (bankrupt) 使某人/某机构破产; **to have sb. up against the ~** 使某人走投无路; **to go to the ~** colloq «*company*» 破产; **to have one's back to the ~** colloq 被逼得没有退路; **a ~ clock** 挂钟; **~ tiles/lighting** 壁砖/墙照明 2 (barrier) 围墙; **to build a ~** 筑围墙; **the ~s of the city** 城墙 3 (side of hollow structure) 内壁 4 (outer layer) [器官或细胞的] 外壁 5 (of tyre) 轮胎壁 6 (in football) 人墙 7 (large number) (of people) 人墙; (of things) 墙状物; **a ~ of protesters** 抗议者的人墙; **the cliffs form a steep ~** 悬崖像墙一样陡峭; **a ~ of water/flame** 水幕/火墙 8 (non-physical barrier) 隔阂; **a ~ of suspicion/hostility** 怀疑/敌意的隔阂
B *vt* 用墙围住 ‹*area*›

Phrasal verbs
- **wall in** *vt* [**~ sb./sth. in, ~ in sb./sth.**] 围住 ‹*person, area*›; **the lagoon is ~ed in by tall cliffs** 潟湖被高耸的悬崖环绕着
- **wall off** *vt* [**~ sth. off, ~ off sth.**] 1 (block off) 用墙把…封死 ‹*area, room*› 2 (separate) 用墙把…隔开 ‹*area, land*›
- **wall up** *vt* 1 [**~ sth. up, ~ up sth.**] (block up) 用墙把…堵住 ‹*doorway, fireplace*› 2 [**~ sb. up, ~ up sb.**] (imprison) 把…关在高墙后 ‹*prisoner*›

wallaby /'wɒləbi/ *n* 沙袋鼠

wallah /'wɒlə/ *n* colloq dated 从事…的人; **a tea/kitchen ~** 茶商/厨具商

wall: ~bars *npl* Brit 肋木; **~board** *n* [u and c] esp Amer 护墙板; **~ chart** *n* 挂图; **~ covering** *n* [u and c] 覆盖墙壁的装饰; **~ cupboard** *n* 壁柜

walled /wɔːld/ *adj usu attrib* 有围墙的 ‹*garden, town*›

wallet /'wɒlɪt/ *n* 1 (pocket-sized case) 皮夹 2 fig (money) 腰包; **to think about one's ~** 考虑自己掏腰包

wall: ~flower *n* 1 Bot 桂竹香; 2 fig (shy or solitary person) 壁花; **~ hanging** *n* 壁挂; **~ light** *n* 壁灯; **~-mounted** *adj* 壁挂式的 ‹*TV, telephone, unit*›

Wallonia /wɒ'ləʊnɪə/ *pr n* 瓦龙

Walloon /wɒ'luːn/ ▸**p. 503, p. 426**
A *adj* (of Wallonia) 瓦龙的; (of the people) 瓦龙人的; (of the language) 瓦龙语的
B *n* 1 [c] (person) 瓦龙人 2 [u] (language) 瓦龙语

wallop /'wɒləp/ colloq
A *vt* 1 (punch, hit) 痛打 ‹*person, animal*›; 猛击 ‹*ball, punchbag*› 2 (defeat) 大败 ‹*opponent, team*›
B *n usu sing* 1 (punch, hit) 重击; **to give sb./the ball a (good) ~** 给某人一记重拳/猛击一下球; **this vodka packs a ~** fig 这种伏特加酒劲儿大 2 (sound) 重击声; **to hit the door with a ~** «*person*» 大声砸门; «*ball*» 砰地撞在门上
C *adv* 砰的一声; **to run** *or* **go ~ into the wall** 砰的一声撞上墙

walloping /'wɒləpɪŋ/ colloq
A *n* 1 (beating) 痛打; **to give sb. a (good) ~** 痛扁某人 2 (defeat) 惨败; **to get a ~ (from sb.)** 被 (某人) 打得落花流水
B *adj attrib* 很大的 ‹*person, animal, amount*›; **I got a ~ shock** 我惊呆了
C *adv* 极其; **a ~ great** *or* **big fine** 巨额罚款

wallow /'wɒləʊ/
A *vi* 1 (lie, roll) 打滚; **to ~ (about) in sth.** 在…里打滚 ‹*mud, water*›; **to ~ in a hot bath** 泡个热水澡 2 (self-indulge) 沉湎; **to ~ in** 沉湎于 ‹*grief, the past, luxury*› 3 Naut «*ship*» 颠簸
B *n* 1 *usu sing* (action) 打滚 2 (hole for wallowing) 泥沼

wall painting *n* 1 [c] (picture) 壁画 2 [u] (process) 壁画绘制; (technique) 壁画法

wallpaper /'wɔːlpeɪpə(r)/
A *n* 1 [u and c] (for decorating) 墙纸 2 [u] fig colloq (background) 背景; **musical ~** 背景音乐 3 [u and c] Comput 桌面壁纸
B *vt* 给…贴墙纸 ‹*room, wall*›

wallpaper stripper *n* 墙纸剥离机

wall: ~ plug *n* 膨胀螺丝管; **W~ Street** *pr n* Amer 华尔街; **The W~ Street Journal** 《华尔街时报》

> **Wall Street**
>
> 华尔街。美国金融中心。位于美国纽约曼哈顿区。1653年，荷兰殖民者曾在此筑墙 (wall)，防止英军的袭击，街名即源于此。华尔街集中了美国的大公司和大型金融机构，包括著名的纽约证券交易所 (New York Stock Exchange)。现在常用来指代美国金融市场或金融界。

wall-to-wall
A *adj usu attrib* 1 (covering floor) 覆盖整个地板的 ‹*carpet*› 2 (covering wall) 整面墙的 ‹*mirrors, mural*› 3 fig colloq (uninterrupted) 连续的 ‹*news, coverage*›; **to be ~ restaurants** 到处都是饭馆; **~ silence** 无处不在的寂静
B *adv* 整块地板地; **to be carpeted ~** 整个地板都铺上地毯

wally /'wɒli/ *n* Brit colloq 笨蛋

walnut /'wɔːlnʌt/ *n* 1 [c] Bot 核桃; **~ (tree)** 核桃树; **a ~ shell/nut** 核桃壳/仁 2 [c] Culin 核桃仁; **~ oil** 核桃油 3 [u and c] (wood) 核桃木; **~ furniture** 核桃木家具

walrus /'wɔːlrəs/ *n* 海象

walrus moustache *n* 海象胡子

Walter Mitty /ˌwɔːltə 'mɪti/ *pr n* 沃尔特·米蒂 [指幻想出人头地的人]; **a ~ fantasy** 白日梦

waltz /wɔːls, Amer wɔːlts/
A *n* 1 Dance 华尔兹舞 2 Mus 华尔兹舞曲 3 *sing* (skip) 轻快跳跃
B *vi* 1 Dance 跳华尔兹舞 2 (skip) 蹦蹦跳跳 3 colloq (walk jauntily) 神气活现地走; **to ~ in/off** 大摇大摆地走进/走出; **to ~ off with sth.** 顺手牵羊走某物 4 fig colloq (get easily) 轻松完成; **to ~ through an exam** 轻而易举地通过考试; **to ~ off with sth.** 轻松赢得 ‹*prize, medal*›
C *vt* 1 Dance 带…跳华尔兹; **to ~ sb. around the room/across the floor** 带某人绕房间跳华尔兹/跳华尔兹滑过地板 2 (skip with) 带…蹦蹦跳跳; **to ~ sb. around the room/table** 带某人绕房间/桌子雀跃

wampum /'wɒmpəm/ *n* [u] Amer [北美印第安人用作货币的] 贝壳串珠

WAN *abbr* = **wide area network**

wan /wɒn/ *adj* 1 (weak, gaunt) 憔悴的 ‹*person, complexion, expression*› 2 (dispirited) 无精打采的 ‹*look, smile*› 3 (pale) 昏暗的 ‹*light, sky*›

wand /wɒnd/ *n* 1 (for casting spells) **(magic) ~** 魔杖 2 (bar-code reader) 扫描笔 3 (laser pointer) 激光笔 4 Cosmet 睫毛刷 5 (thin rod as symbol of authority) 权杖

wander /'wɒndə(r)/
A *vi* 1 (stroll aimlessly) 游荡; **to ~ around town/in the park** 在城里/公园里闲逛; **they ~ed in and out of the shops** 他们在商店里逛进逛出; **to ~ through** 漫步穿过 ‹*forest, corridor*› 2 (move nonchalantly) 漫不经心地走; **he ~ed into work two hours late** 他磨磨蹭蹭地晚了两个小时来干活 3 (move away) 走散 4 (be distracted) «*thoughts, attention*» 走神 5 (be confused through age, illness) «*person*» 神志恍惚; «*mind*» 混乱; **the old man is ~ing again** 那位老人又在东拉西扯了 6 (digress) «*speaker, speech*» 离题; **to ~ from the topic** 偏离话题 7 (look away) 游离不定; **her gaze ~ed along the row of books** 她的目光扫过那一排书; **his eyes ~ed towards the photograph on the desk** 他的目光慢慢地移向书桌上的照片 8 (touch sb. inappropriately) «*hands*» 乱摸 9 (meander) 蜿蜒; **the road ~s through the hills** 公路蜿蜒穿过丘陵
B *vt* 在…游荡 ‹*streets, hills*›; **to ~ the world** 周游世界
C *n* 闲逛; **to go for** *or* **have** *or* **take a ~** colloq 去逛一圈; **I like going for a ~ around the shops** 我喜欢逛商店

W

Phrasal verbs

• **wander around, wander about**

A *vi* **1** (stroll) 四处游荡 **2** (be lost) [因迷路而]徘徊

B *vt* [~ **around sth.**]

1 (stroll in) 在…游荡 ‹*town, garden*›; **she ~ed aimlessly around the streets** 她在街上瞎逛 **2** [~ **around sb./sth.**] (scan) «*eyes*» 环视 ‹*room, faces*›

• **wander off**

A *vi* **1** (move away, stray) 走散 **2** hum (disappear) «*belongings*» 不翼而飞

B *vt* [~ **off sth.**] 偏离 ‹*topic, subject*›

wanderer /'wɒndərə(r)/ *n* 漂泊者

wandering /'wɒndərɪŋ/ *adj attrib* **1** (travelling) 漂泊的 ‹*person, way of life*›; 流浪的 ‹*animal*› **2** (meandering) 蜿蜒的 ‹*river, road*› **3** (roving) 游离不定的 ‹*eyes, attention*›; 跳跃的 ‹*thoughts, imagination*›; ~ **hands** hum 不老实的手 **4** pej (rambling) 胡言乱语的 ‹*speaker*›; 离题的 ‹*speech*› **5** (confused) 恍惚的 ‹*old person, mind*›

wanderings /'wɒndərɪŋz/ *npl* **1** (of person, animal) 游荡 **2** (of mind, thoughts) 走神

wanderlust /'wɒndəlʌst/ *n* [u] 旅行癖

wane /weɪn/

A *vi* **1** (diminish) «*power, empire*» 衰落; «*influence, popularity*» 减少; «*friendship, enthusiasm*» 冷淡; **the light was beginning to ~** 光线开始变弱了 **2** Astron «*moon*» 亏缺

B *n* **to be on the ~** «*power, empire*» 正在衰落; «*influence, popularity*» 正在减少; «*friendship, enthusiasm*» 正在冷淡; «*moon*» 正在亏缺

wangle /'wæŋgl/ colloq

A *vt* **1** (get, arrange) 设法获得 ‹*favour, object, job*›; **to ~ sth. out of sb.** 从某人那里弄到某物; **to ~ sth. for sb.** 设法为某人弄到某物; **to ~ one's way out of/through** 设法逃脱/挨过 ‹*crisis*›; 设法逃避/进行完 ‹*task*› **2** (persuade) 劝说; **to ~ sb. into sth.** or **doing sth.** 哄某人做某事

B *n* 计谋; **to get sth. by a ~** 耍手段得到某物

wangling /'wæŋglɪŋ/ *n* [u] colloq 用计

waning /'weɪnɪŋ/

A *adj attrib* **1** (diminishing) 衰落的 ‹*power, empire*›; 减少的 ‹*influence, popularity, enthusiasm*›; **the ~ light** 越来越暗的光线 **2** Astron 亏缺的 ‹*moon*›

B *n* **1** (diminution) 减少 **2** Astron 月亏

wank /wæŋk/ Brit taboo sl

A *vi* 手淫 [通常指男性]

B *n* **1** [c] *usu sing* (act of masturbating) [通常指男性的] 手淫; **to have a ~** 手淫 **2** [u] fig pej (rubbish) 垃圾; **a load of ~** 一堆垃圾

Phrasal verb

• **wank off** taboo sl

A *vi* 手淫

B *vt* [~ **sb. off,** ~ **off sb.**] 对…行手淫

wanker /'wæŋkə(r)/ *n* Brit taboo sl **1** (contemptible person) 蠢材 [通常指男性] offensive **2** (person masturbating) 行手淫的家伙 [通常指男性]

wanking /'wæŋkɪŋ/ *n* [u] Brit taboo sl [通常指男性的] 手淫

wanly /'wɒnli/ *adv* **1** (weakly) 虚弱地 ‹*smile, gaze*› **2** (dispiritedly) 无精打采地 ‹*say*› **3** (palely) «*sun, light*» 微弱地 ‹*shine*›

wanna /'wɒnə/ colloq **1** = **want to** 想; **I ~ go** 我想去 **2** = **want a** 想要个; **I ~ cigarette** 我想要根烟

wannabe, wannabee /'wɒnəbiː/ *n* colloq pej 想出名的人; **David Bowie ~s** 大卫·鲍伊的崇拜模仿族; **a ~ model/celebrity** 渴望成为模特/名人的人

wanness /'wɒnnɪs/ *n* [u] (of complexion, state) 憔悴; (of light) 暗淡

want /wɒnt/

A *vt* **1** (desire) 要 ‹*object, money, peace*›; **I ~ a kilo of tomatoes** 我要1公斤西红柿; **where do you ~ this desk?** 你想把桌子摆在哪里?; **what do you ~ for this chair?** 这把椅子你要多少钱?; **to ~ to do sth.** 想做某事; **the party ~s her as leader** 党希望由她做领袖; **what do you ~?** 你想怎样?; ~ **sth. from** or **out of one's life/marriage** 希望从生活/婚姻中得到某物; **what do you ~ from me?** 你想从我这里得到什么?; **you don't ~ much, do you?** colloq iron 你不想要很多，是吗?; **to not ~ to know (about sb./sth.)** colloq 不想知道（某人/某事物） **2** esp Brit (need) 需要; **'gardener ~ed'** "招聘花匠"; **what do they ~ with all that equipment?** 他们要那么多设备干什么?; **to ~ sth. (to be) done** 需要有人做某事; **to ~ doing** «*housework, homework*» 需要做 **3** (require presence of) 需要…到场; **the boss ~s you** 老板想见你; **you're ~ed on the phone** 有你的电话; **I know when I'm not ~ed** 我知道我该何时离开 **4** Brit colloq (deserve) 应挨 ‹*slap, kicking*› **5** (seek) 缉拿 ‹*criminal*›; **to be ~ed by the police** 遭到警方的通缉; **to ~ sb. for murder/fraud** 因谋杀/欺诈而缉拿某人 **6** colloq (should) 应该; **to ~ to do sth.** 应该做某事; **he ~s to get out more often!** 他应该多出去参加社交活动! **7** (desire sexually) 想要 ‹*person*›; **I ~ you so much** 我非常想要你 **8** formal (lack) 缺少 ‹*courage, tact*›

B *vi* formal 缺吃少穿

C *n* **1** [c] (need) 需求 **2** [c and u] formal (lack) 缺乏; **for ~ of sth.** 由于缺乏某物; **for ~ of doing sth.** 因为没做某事; **it's not for ~ of trying** 不是没有努力 **3** [u] formal (deprivation) 贫穷; **to be in ~** 缺衣少食; **the war on ~** 向贫穷开战 [建于1951年的英国组织]

Phrasal verbs

• **want for** *vt* [~ **for sth.**] formal 缺少; **she ~s for nothing** 她什么都不缺

• **want in** *vi* colloq 想要参与; **to ~ in on sth.** 想参与某事; **to ~ in on a deal/project/contract** 想参与一项交易/想加入一个项目/想订立合同

• **want out** *vi* colloq 想要退出; **to ~ out of sth.** 想退出某事; **to ~ out of the marriage/relationship** 想离婚/想脱离关系; **to ~ out of a deal/project/contract** 想取消一项交易/想退出一个项目/想解除合同

want ad *n* Amer colloq 分类广告

wanted /'wɒntɪd/ *adj* **1** (by police) 被通缉的 ‹*criminal, fugitive*›; **a ~ notice** or **poster** 通缉布告 **2** (desired before birth) 被期盼的 ‹*baby*›; (loved after birth) 被喜爱的 ‹*child*›

wanted list *n* 通缉名单

wanting /'wɒntɪŋ/

A *adj pred* **1** (lacking) 缺乏的; **to be ~ in sth.** 缺乏某物; **a performance ~ in fire** 缺乏激情的表演; **to be found ~** 被证明不够好; **to have been tried and found ~** 未经受住考验 **2** colloq (deficient) 低能的; **to be (rather) ~** «*person*» 头脑（相当）愚笨

B *prep* formal 缺; ~ **her sister's natural charm** 缺乏她姐姐的自然妩媚

wanton /'wɒntən, Amer 'wɔːn-/ *adj* **1** *usu attrib* (gratuitous) 恶意的 ‹*cruelty, damage, disregard*› **2** dated (promiscuous) 淫荡的 ‹*woman, behaviour, desire*›

wantonly /'wɒntənli, Amer 'wɔːn-/ *adv* **1** (gratuitously) 恶意地 ‹*destroy, attack*›; **to be ~ cruel/insulting** 肆意施虐/羞辱 **2** dated (provocatively) «*woman*» 淫荡地 ‹*behave, say*›

WAP /wæp/ *abbr* = **wireless application protocol** 无线应用协议

WAP: ~ **phone** *n* 上网手机; ~ **technology** *n* [u] 无线应用协议技术

war /wɔː(r)/

A *n* [c and u] **1** (armed conflict) 战争; **to prepare for ~** 备战; **before/during/after the ~** 战前/战时/战后; **between the ~s** (world wars) 在两次世界大战之间; **to declare/wage ~ (on sb./sth.)** （向某人/某事物）宣战/开战; **to win/lose a ~** 战胜/战败; **to have been in the ~s** (in a fight) 打架受伤; (in an accident) 在事故中受伤; **the ~ zone** 交战地区; **a ~ correspondent** 战地记者; **a ~ medal** 战功勋章 **2** (fierce competition) 激烈竞争; **a circulation/ratings ~** 发行量/收视率大战 **3** (acrimonious situation) 对抗; **to be at ~ (with sb./sth.)** （与某人/某物）处于敌对状态; **a ~ of words** 舌战 **4** (campaign) [为消除有害物而进行的] 长期斗争; **a ~ against** or **on sb./sth.** 对某人/某事物的斗争

B *vi* liter 打仗; **to ~ over sth.** 因某事打仗

war baby *n* 战时出生的孩子 [尤指二战期间]

warble /'wɔːbl/

A *vi* **1** «*bird*» 啭鸣 **2** «*singer*» [用颤音] 高声唱

B *vt* **to ~ sth. out, to ~ out sth.** 高声唱

C *n* 啭鸣

warbler /'wɔːblə(r)/ *n* **1** (bird) 莺 **2** colloq (singer) 颤声高音歌手

warbling /'wɔːblɪŋ/ *n* **1** [u] (of bird) 啭鸣 **2** [u and c] (of person) 颤声高音歌唱

war: ~ **bride** *n* [嫁给军人，尤指长期独自生活的] 战时新娘; ~ **cabinet** *n* 战时内阁; ~ **chest** *n* [尤指用于竞选的] 专用基金; ~ **crime** *n usu pl* 战争罪行; ~ **criminal** *n* 战犯; ~ **cry** *n* **1** Mil [作战时的] 呐喊; **2** fig (slogan) 竞选口号

ward /wɔːd/ *n* **1** [u and c] Med (room) 病房; (department) 住院部; **a maternity/paediatric ~** 产科/儿科病房 **2** [c] Brit Pol, Admin 选区; ~ **councillors/secretaries** 选区政务委员/秘书 **3** [c] Jur 受监护人; **to be made a ~ of the court** 由法院监护

Phrasal verb

• **ward off** *vt* [~ **sth./sb. off,** ~ **off sb./sth.**] 躲避 ‹*attacker, blow, disaster*›; **to ~ off evil spirits** 驱邪; **to ~ off a cold/the flu** 防止感冒/流感

war dance *n* 战舞

warden /'wɔːdn/ ▸p. 409 *n* **1** (supervisor, person policing regulations) 管理员; **a wildlife/park ~** 野生动物保护区巡视员/公园管理员 **2** Brit Sch, Univ 学院院长 **3** Amer (prison governor) 监狱长

warder /'wɔːdə(r)/ *n* **1** esp Brit (prison guard) 监狱看守人 **2** Amer (watchman) 保安

wardrobe /'wɔːdrəʊb/ *n* **1** [c] esp Brit (clothes cupboard) 衣柜 **2** [c] *usu sing* (clothes collection) 全部衣物; Cin, Theat 全部演出服 **3** [u] Cin, Theat (department) 演出服装部

wardrobe: ~ **assistant** ▸p. 409 *n* 演出服助理保管员; ~ **mistress** ▸p. 409 *n* 演出服女保管员; ~ **master** ▸p. 409 *n* 演出服男保管员; ~ **trunk** *n* esp Amer 旅行挂衣箱

ward: ~**room** *n* [战舰上的] 军官餐厅; ~ **round** *n* [医生的] 查房

wardship /'wɔːdʃɪp/ *n* [u] (guardianship) 监护; (period) 监护期; **under the ~ of sb.** 在某人的监护下

ward sister ▸p. 409 *n* Brit 病房女护士长

ware /weə(r)/

A *n* **1** [u and c] (pottery) 陶器 **2** [u] (products) 制品; **crystal/wooden ~** 水晶/木制品; **sanitary/household ~** 卫生/家居用品; **baking ~** 烘烤器皿

B **wares** *npl* 货物; **to peddle one's ~s** 挨门挨户推销货物

war effort *n* 战争投入

warehouse /'weəhaʊs/

A *n* **1** (storage place) 仓库 **2** (store) 批零店

B *vt* 把…存入仓库 ‹*goods*›

warehouse: ~**man** /-mən/ ▸p. 409 *n* (owner) 仓库老板; (employee) 仓库管理员; ~ **party** *n* 仓库聚会 [仓库中举行的非法舞会]

warehousing /'weəhaʊzɪŋ/ *n* [u] 仓储

warfare *n* [u] **1** Mil 战争; **germ/chemical ~** 细菌战/化学战; **open ~** 公开战 **2** fig (conflict) 斗争; **gang/class ~** 帮派/阶级斗争

W

war: ~ game *n usu pl* **1** Games 军事游戏; **2** Mil 军事演习; **~ grave** *n* 阵亡军人墓; **~head** *n* 弹头; **~horse** *n* **1** Mil, Hist 战马; **2** **an old ~horse** colloq (veteran) 久经沙场的老手

warily /ˈweərɪli/ *adv* (cautiously) 谨慎地 ‹*approach, say*›; (mistrustfully) 警惕地 ‹*glance*›

wariness /ˈweərmɪs/ *n* [u] (caution) 谨慎; (mistrust) 警惕; **~ of sth./sb.** 对某人/某事物的警惕; **~ about doing sth.** 做某事的谨慎

war leader *n* 战争领袖

warlike /ˈwɔːlaɪk/ *adj* **1** (eager for war) 好战的 ‹*leader, tribe*›; 进行战争威胁的 ‹*words*›; **to make ~ noises** fig 进行威胁 **2** (for use in war) 用于战争的 ‹*equipment, munitions*›; **~ preparations** 战备

warlock /ˈwɔːlɒk/ *n* 巫师

war: ~lord *n* 军阀; **~ machine** *n* **1** (military resources) 军事资源; **2** (weapon) 战争武器

warm /wɔːm/

A *adj* **1** (moderately hot) 温暖的; **~ weather/climate** 温暖的天气/气候; **a ~ bath** 热水澡; **~ beer** 温啤酒; **the water feels ~** 水摸上去是温的; **we all crowded around the fire to keep ~** 我们都挤在炉火边取暖; **to make things ~ for sb.** colloq dated 刁难某人 **2** (helping body to retain heat) 保暖的 ‹*coat, blanket*›; 暖和的 ‹*room*›; **it's ~ work** 这工作干起来浑身发热 **3** (friendly) 热情的 ‹*person, smile*›; **to give sb. a ~ welcome** 热烈欢迎某人; **~est regards** 最热忱的问候 **4** (enthusiastic) 衷心的 ‹*congratulations, thanks*› **5** (pleasant to look at) 暖色调的; **~ colours** 暖色 **6** (pleasant to hear) 暖人心扉的 ‹*sound*›; **~ tones** 温暖的音色 **7** (recent) 新鲜的; **fortunately, the scent was still ~** 幸运的是气味还很浓; **the police are trying to find new evidence while the trail is still ~** 警方趁线索未断试图找到新的证据 **8** *pred* (as instruction in game) [尤指在儿童游戏中] 快要找到的; (when guessing) 即将猜中的; **you're very ~ now!** 你快要找到了!

B *vt* **1** (heat up) 使…暖和 ‹*person, bed*›; 加热 ‹*food, dish*›; **she was ~ing her hands by the fire** 她正在炉边暖手; **I took a nip of brandy to ~ me** 我呷了一口白兰地来暖暖身子 **2** (gladden) 使…感到温暖 ‹*person, heart*›

C *vi* **1** (heat up) 变暖和; **she put the milk to ~ on the stove for a minute** 她把牛奶放到炉子上热了一分钟 **2** (become happy) «*person, heart*» 变得快活

D *v refl* **to ~ oneself** 取暖

E *n* colloq **1** Brit (place or area) **the ~** 暖和的地方 **2** (action) (of warming sth.) 加热; (of warming oneself) 取暖; **to give sth. a ~** 热一下 ‹*dish*›; 暖一下 ‹*hands*›

Phrasal verbs

- **warm down** *vi* 做放松运动
- **warm over** *vt* Amer [**~ sth. over, ~ over sth.**] 加热 ‹*food*›
- **warm to, warm towards** *vt* [**~ to sb./sth.**] **1** (start to like) 喜欢上 ‹*person, style*› **2** (get more enthusiastic about) 开始热衷于 ‹*idea, cause*›; **the speaker was ~ing to his theme** 演讲者对他的题目越说越来劲
- **warm up**

A *vi* **1** (reach warm temperature) 变暖 **2** (be reheated) «*food*» 重新加热 **3** (prepare for exercise) «*athlete*» 做热身运动 **4** (prepare for performance) «*performer, orchestra*» 做准备 **5** (become ready to operate) «*engine, appliance*» 预热 **6** (become livelier) «*audience, party*» 热烈起来; «*debate, campaign*» 激烈起来

B *vt* [**~ sb./sth. up, ~ up sb./sth.**] **1** (bring to warm temperature) 使…暖和 ‹*person, room, bed*›; 加热 ‹*liquid, dish*› **2** (reheat) 重新加热 ‹*food*› **3** (prepare for exercise) 使…做热身运动 ‹*athlete, team*› **4** (prepare for performance) 使…做准备 ‹*performer, orchestra*›; 准备 ‹*instrument*›; **to ~ up one's voice** 练嗓子 **5** (make ready to operate) 预热 ‹*engine, appliance*› **6** (make livelier) 使…活跃起来 ‹*audience, crowd*›

warm-blooded *adj* **1** Zool 温血的 ‹*animal, bird*› **2** fig (ardent) 感情强烈的 ‹*person*›

war memorial *n* 战争纪念碑

warm: ~ front *n* 暖锋; **~-hearted** *adj* 热心的 ‹*person, character*›; 友好的 ‹*gesture, act*›; 热情的 ‹*welcome*›

warming /ˈwɔːmɪŋ/

A *adj* 暖和的 ‹*sunlight*›; **a ~ drink/bath** 热饮/热水浴

B *n* [u] 变暖; **global ~** 全球变暖

warming: ~ oven *n* 加热箱; **~ pan** *n* [旧时热床用的] 长柄炭炉; **~-up exercises** *npl* **1** Sport 热身运动; **2** Theat, Mus 序曲

warmly /ˈwɔːmli/ *adv* **1** lit «*sun*» 暖和地 ‹*shine*›; **to dress ~** 穿得暖和; **to be ~ lit** 光线温暖 **2** fig 热情地 ‹*embrace, smile, speak, receive*›

warmonger /ˈwɔːmʌŋgər/ *n* pej 战争贩子

warmongering /ˈwɔːmʌŋgərɪŋ/ pej

A *n* [u] 鼓吹战争的行径

B *adj attrib* 鼓吹战争的 ‹*politician, article*›

warmth /wɔːmθ/ *n* [u] **1** (moderate heat) 温暖; **they huddled together for ~** 他们挤在一起取暖 **2** (insulating quality) 保暖 **3** (friendliness, enthusiasm) (of person, feeling, smile) 友善; (of atmosphere, welcome) 热烈; (of thanks, support) 衷心 **4** (fervour) 激动; **he replied with some ~ that ...** 他略显激动地回答…

warm-up *n* **1** Sport 热身活动; Mus 序曲演奏; **a ~ game/lap** 热身赛/绕场热身的一圈 **2** Theat, TV 开场戏; **a ~ act** 序幕

war museum *n* 战争博物馆

warn *vt* /wɔːn/ **1** (alert, advise) 告诫 ‹*person, authorities*›; **to ~ sb. about** *or* **against** *or* **of sth.** 提醒某人提防某事物; **to ~ sb. against complacency** 告诫某人戒骄戒躁; **to ~ sb. (not) to do sth.** 提醒某人（不要）做某事; **you have been ~ed!** 我可警告过你了! **2** (caution officially) «*referee*» 警告 ‹*player*›; **to ~ sb. for sth.** 因某事物而警告某人

Phrasal verbs

- **warn of** *vt* [**~ of sth.**] 预先通知; **police have ~ed of possible delays** 警方通告可能会误点; **traffic signals ~ed of fog** 交通信号提醒有雾
- **warn off** *vt* [**~ sb. off, ~ off sb.**] **1** (tell sb. to keep away) 警告…离开 ‹*trespasser*›; **to ~ sb. off sth.** 警告某人远离某事物 **2** (try to put sb. off) 告诫…不要靠近; **to ~ sb. off alcohol/drugs** 告诫某人不要酗酒/不要吸毒; **we were ~ed off buying the house** 有人劝我们不要买那栋房子

warning /ˈwɔːnɪŋ/

A *n* **1** [c] (alert, official caution) 警告; **a ~ to sb.** 对某人的警告; **a ~ about sth.** 关于某事的警告; **a flood ~** 洪水警报; **to give sb. a ~** 给某人警告; **a verbal/written ~** 口头/书面警告 **2** [u] (cautionary advice) 告诫; **a word of ~** 提醒的话 **3** [u] (advance notice) 预告; **to give sb. ~ (of sth.)** 提前告知某人（某事）; **the bridge collapsed without any ~** 那座桥在没有任何征兆的情况下坍塌了

B *adj attrib* **1** (giving notice of danger) 警告的; **a ~ light/siren/notice** 报警灯/警笛/警告 **2** (deterring) 警告性的 ‹*growl, glance, shout*›

warning: ~ bell *n* **1** lit 警铃; **2** fig 不祥的预感; **~ shot** *n* **1** lit 鸣枪警告; **2** fig 警告; **~ sign** *n* **1** lit 警示标记; **2** fig 危险信号; **~ signal** *n* **1** lit 报警信号; **2** fig 危险信号; **~ triangle** *n* 三角警示架

War of American Independence *n* **the ~** [美国1775-83年间的] 独立战争

warp /wɔːp/

A *vi* «*object, surface, wood*» 变形

B *vt* **1** lit (bend out of shape) 使…变形 ‹*object, surface, wood*› **2** fig (distort) «*experience, upbringing, jealousy*» 扭曲 ‹*mind, personality, judgement, outlook*›

C *n* **1** lit (bend or curve) 变形; **a ~ in the record** 唱片上的一处弯曲 **2** fig (distortion) [人格等的] 扭曲 **3** *sing* Tex **the ~** 经纱

war: ~paint *n* [u] **1** Mil, Anthrop [部落成员涂在脸上和身上的] 出征涂画; **2** colloq (make-up) 浓妆艳抹; **~path** *n* **(to be** *or* **go) on the ~path** colloq hum 怒不可遏

warped /wɔːpt/ *adj* **1** lit 变形的 ‹*object, surface*› **2** fig (distorted) 扭曲的 ‹*mind, personality, judgement, outlook*›

war: ~ pension *n* 战争抚恤金; **~ plane** *n* 战斗机

warp thread *n* 经纱

warrant /ˈwɒrənt, Amer ˈwɔːr-/

A *vt* **1** (justify) «*fact, situation*» 证明…正当 ‹*behaviour, measure*› **2** Comm «*company*» 为…作担保 ‹*product, accuracy*› **3** dated (assure) 打保票; **he'll be back, I'll ~ you** 他会回来的，我向你保证

B *n* **1** [c] Jur 授权令; **an arrest/a search ~** 逮捕/搜查令 **2** [u] (justification) 正当理由; **to be no/sufficient ~ for sth./for doing sth./to do sth.** 某事/做某事没有依据/有足够依据 **3** [c] (voucher) 许可证 **4** [c] Fin 认股权证 **5** [u] formal (legal authority) 授权 **6** [c] Mil 准尉委任状

warrantable /ˈwɒrəntəbl, Amer ˈwɔːr-/ *adj* 正当的 ‹*action, conclusion*›

warrant card *n* 警官证

warranted /ˈwɒrəntɪd, Amer ˈwɔːr-/ *adj* **1** (justified) 正当的 ‹*conclusion, suspicion, action*› **2** *usu pred* Comm **to be ~ (to be) top quality** «*product*» 有优质的保证

warrant officer *n* 准尉

warrantor, warranter /ˈwɒrəntɔː(r), Amer ˈwɔːr-/ *n* 授权人

warranty /ˈwɒrənti, Amer ˈwɔːr-/ *n* **1** [u and c] Comm 保修单; **to be under ~** 在保修期内 **2** [c] Insur 保险单

warren /ˈwɒrən, Amer ˈwɔːrən/ *n* **1** (rabbits' burrows) 野兔洞 **2** (maze) 街道狭窄密集的地方; **a ~ of corridors/streets** 错综的走廊/狭窄密集的街道

warring /ˈwɔːrɪŋ/ *adj attrib* 交战的 ‹*nations, tribes, factions*›; 争吵的 ‹*couple*›; 激烈冲突的 ‹*ideologies*›

warrior /ˈwɒrɪə(r), Amer ˈwɔːr-/ *n* 武士; *modif* 尚武的 ‹*ethos, king*›; 善战的 ‹*nation, race*›

Warsaw /ˈwɔːsɔː/ *pr n* 华沙

Warsaw Pact *n* **the ~** (treaty) [东欧共产党国家和前苏联的] 华沙条约; (signatories) 华沙条约签署者; **a ~ country** 华沙条约签署国

warship /ˈwɔːʃɪp/ *n* 军舰

wart /wɔːt/ *n* **1** Med 疣 **2** *usu pl* fig (defect) 瑕疵; **~s and all** colloq 包括所有缺点在内 **3** Zool [蛤蟆身上的] 瘰

warthog /ˈwɔːthɒg/ *n* 疣猪

war: ~time *n* [u] 战时; **~time Britain/economy** 战时的英国/经济; **~-torn** *adj* 饱受战火蹂躏的 ‹*region, country*›; **~ trial** *n* 战争罪审判

warty /ˈwɔːti/ *adj* **1** (having warts) 长疣的 ‹*face, person*›; 长瘰的 ‹*toad*› **2** *usu attrib* (wart-like) 瘤状的 ‹*growth*›

war: ~ veteran *n* 退伍军人; **~-weary** *adj* 厌战的

Warwickshire /ˈwɒrɪkʃə(r)/ *pr n* 沃里克郡

war: ~ widow *n* [丈夫死于战场的] 战争遗孀; **~-wounded** *npl* **the ~-wounded** 伤兵

W

wary /ˈweəri/ *adj* 警惕的; **to be ~ of sb./sth.** 对某人/某事物警惕; **to be ~ of** *or* **about doing sth.** 谨慎地做某事; **to be ~ of giving offence** 唯恐得罪人; **to keep a ~ eye on sb./sth.** 密切注意某人/某事物

was /wɒz, wəz/ *pt* ▸**be**

wash /wɒʃ/

A *vt* **1** (clean by hand) 给…洗澡 ‹*person, animal*›; 洗 ‹*face, hair, clothes*›; 洗刷 ‹*car, floor*›; **the rain had ~ed the streets clean** 雨把街道冲刷得一干二净; **to ~ one's hands of sb./sth.** 对…甩手不管 ‹*person, matter*› **2** (clean by machine) 机洗 **3** Zool (clean with tongue) 舔 ‹*paws, fur*› **4** (carry) 冲走; **to ~ sth. along** «*tide, river*» 冲走某物; **to ~ sb./sth. into sth.** «*river, current*» 将某人/某物冲入某处; **to be ~ed downstream** 被冲向下游; **to be ~ed out to sea** 被冲到海里; **to be ~ed overboard** «*person, cargo*» 被浪从船上冲入水中 **5** liter (lap against) «*sea, tide*» 拍打 ‹*shore, island*› **6** (dig out) «*river*» 冲蚀出 ‹*channel*›; **the water had ~ed a hole in the bank** 水把堤岸冲出一个洞 **7** (when decorating) 涂; **we ~ed the walls in pink** 我们把墙壁刷成粉色 **8** Art 在…上涂一薄层颜料 ‹*picture*› **9** (sift out) 淘 ‹*gold*›; 洗 ‹*ore*› **10** (purify by separation) 洗涤 ‹*gas, vapour*›

B *vi* **1** esp Brit (clean oneself) 洗澡 **2** (do laundry) 洗衣服 **3** (have effect as detergent) «*detergent*» 有去污力 **4** (withstand cleaning) «*fabric, dye, colour*» 耐洗 **5** (flow) 流动; **the waves ~ed against the side of the boat** 波浪拍打着船舷; **to ~ around** 四处流动 **6** (be carried) **to ~ ashore** «*body, wreckage*» 被冲上岸 **7** colloq (be believed) 可信; **that excuse won't ~ with me** 那个借口我难以相信

C *v refl* esp Brit **to ~ oneself** «*person*» 洗澡; **to ~ itself** «*cat*» 舔自己的身体

D *n* **1** [c] esp Brit (cleaning by hand) 洗; **you need a good ~** 你需要好好洗个澡; **to give sb./sth. a ~** 给某人洗澡/给某物洗一下; **to have a ~** 洗澡 **2** [c] esp Brit (cleaning by machine) 机洗; **a low-temperature ~** 低温洗涤; **my sweater shrank in the ~** 我的毛线衫机洗后缩水了; **it'll (all) come out in the ~** colloq (be revealed) (一切) 终将水落石出; (be resolved) (所有) 问题终会解决 **3** [c] esp Brit (clothes) (to be laundered) 待洗的衣物; (being laundered) 正在洗的衣物; (already laundered) 洗好的衣物 **4** [c] (trail of water) [船驶过引起的] 水流; (sound of trail of water) [船驶过引起的] 波浪拍打声 **5** [c] (movement of waves) 波浪的拍击; (sound of waves) 波浪的拍击声 **6** [c and u] Art (layer, coating) 薄涂层 **7** [u] Art (technique) 淡水彩画技巧 **8** [c] Art (picture) 淡水彩画 **9** [c and u] (skin lotion) 洗液; **a gentle, foaming facial ~** 一种温和的泡沫洁面乳

Phrasal verbs

• **wash away**

A *vt* [**~ sth. away, ~ away sth.**]
1 (carry off) 将…冲垮 ‹*road, bridge*›; 将…冲走 ‹*debris*› **2** (erode) 冲蚀 ‹*cliff, bank*› **3** (remove by cleaning) 洗掉 ‹*dirt*›

B *vi* **1** (be carried off) «*road, bridge*» 被冲垮; «*debris*» 被冲走 **2** (be eroded) «*cliff, bank*» 被冲蚀

• **wash down** *vt* [**~ sth. down, ~ down sth.**]
1 (clean) 冲洗 ‹*wall, deck*› **2** (drink) (as accompaniment) 就着…喝 ‹*food*›; (as aid to swallowing) 用水吞服 ‹*medicine, pill*›; **we ~ed down the hors d'oeuvres with a glass of white wine** 我们吃完开胃小菜后喝了一杯白葡萄酒

• **wash off**

A *vt* [**~ sth. off, ~ off sth.**] 洗掉 ‹*dirt, stain*›; **that red wine is going to be hard to ~ off** 那块红葡萄酒污渍很难洗掉

B *vi* «*dirt, stain*» 被洗掉; **that stain will ~ off easily** 那污渍可以很容易洗掉

• **wash out**

A *vt* [**~ sth. out, ~ out sth.**]
1 (clean inside of) 清洗…的内部 ‹*container*› **2** (remove by cleaning) 洗掉 ‹*stain, dye*› **3** (clean quickly) 洗一洗 ‹*garment, paintbrush*› **4** (rain off) 使…因雨取消 ‹*event, game*› **5** Amer colloq (dismiss) 淘汰 ‹*trainee, student*›

B *vi* **1** (be removed by cleaning) «*stain, dye*» 被洗掉 **2** Amer colloq (be dismissed) «*trainee, student*» 被淘汰

• **wash over**

A [**~ over sth.**] *vt* (flow over) «*water, waves*» 冲过 ‹*deck, bank*›

B [**~ over sb.**] *vt*
1 (affect) «*guilt, pleasure*» 涌上…的心头; **a great feeling of relief ~ed over me** 我突然感到如释重负; **waves of nausea ~ed over him** 一阵阵恶心的感觉涌上他的心头 **2** colloq (not affect) «*criticism, speech*» 对…没有太大影响

• **wash through** *vt* **1** [**~ sth. through, ~ through sth.**] (clean quickly) 洗一洗 ‹*garment, paintbrush*› **2** [**~ through sb.**] (affect) «*anger, relief*» 涌上…的心头

• **wash up**

A *vi* **1** Brit (do dishes) 洗碗 **2** (be carried on to shore) «*debris*» 被冲上岸; **an oil slick ~ed up on the beaches** 浮油被冲上了海滩 **3** Amer (clean one's face and hands) 洗手洗脸

B *vt* [**~ sth. up, ~ up sth.**]
1 Brit (clean) 洗 ‹*dishes, cutlery*› **2** (carry on to shore) 把…冲上岸 ‹*debris*›

washable /ˈwɒʃəbl, Amer ˈwɔːʃ-/ *adj* **1** (able to be washed) 可洗的 ‹*fabric, paint*› **2** (able to be washed out) 可洗掉的 ‹*ink, paint*›

wash: ~-and-wear *adj* 免烫的 ‹*fabric, clothes*›; **~bag** *n* Brit [防水的] 梳妆袋; **~basin** *n* esp Brit 洗脸盆; **~ basket** *n* 洗衣篮

washboard

A *n* **1** (for scrubbing) 搓板 **2** Mus [打击乐器的] 刮板

B *modif* 搓板状的 ‹*stomach, torso*›

wash: ~bowl *n* Amer **= ~basin**; **~cloth** *n* Amer 洗脸巾; **~ cycle** *n* [洗衣机的] 洗涤过程; **~day** *n* [u and c] 洗衣日; **~ drawing** *n* 水彩画

washed-out *adj* **1** (faded) 洗褪的 ‹*colour*›; 洗褪色的 ‹*jeans*› **2** colloq (exhausted) 筋疲力竭的; **to be/look (completely) ~** «*person, face*» 疲惫不堪/显得疲惫不堪

washed-up *adj* **1** colloq (ruined, finished) 完蛋了的 ‹*hero, actress, comedian*›; **his career is all ~** 他的事业全毁了 **2** Amer colloq (tired) 筋疲力竭的; **to look ~** 满面倦容 **3** (left by tide) 被潮水冲上岸的 ‹*jetsam, fish*›

washer /ˈwɒʃə(r), Amer ˈwɔːʃər/ *n* **1** (for nut, bolt, or as seal) 垫圈 **2** **= washing machine**

washer: ~-dryer *n* 洗衣烘干机; **~-up** (*pl* **~s-up**), **~-upper** (*pl* **~-uppers**) *ns* Brit 洗碗工; **~woman** ▸**p. 409** *n* [尤指旧时的] 洗衣女工

wash: ~-hand basin *n* **= ~basin**; **~ house** *n* 洗衣房

washing /ˈwɒʃɪŋ, Amer ˈwɔːʃɪŋ/ *n* [u] **1** (action) (of things) 洗; (of self) 洗漱 **2** (clothes) (to be laundered) 待洗的衣服; (being laundered) 正在洗的衣物; (after laundering) 洗过的衣服; **to do the ~** 洗衣服

washing: ~ day *n* **= washday**; **~ facilities** *npl* 洗涤设施; **~ line** *n* Brit 晾衣绳; **~ machine** *n* 洗衣机; **~ powder** *n* [u and c] Brit 洗衣粉; **~ soda** *n* [u] 洗涤碱

Washington /ˈwɒʃɪŋtən, Amer ˈwɔːʃ-/ *pr n* **1** (city) 华盛顿; **~ DC** 华盛顿哥伦比亚特区; **The ~ Post** 《华盛顿邮报》 **2** (state) 华盛顿州; **~ University** 华盛顿大学

Washingtonian /ˌwɒʃɪŋˈtəʊnɪən, Amer ˌwɔːʃ-/

A *adj* 华盛顿的 ‹*person, custom*›

B *n* 华盛顿人

> **Washington, DC**
>
> 华盛顿，全称华盛顿哥伦比亚特区（Washington, District of Columbia）。美国首都，为美国立法、司法和行政中心。因分别纪念开国总统乔治·华盛顿（George Washington）和美洲发现者克里斯托弗·哥伦布（Christopher Columbus），故名。位于波托马克河（Potomac River）上，马里兰州（Maryland）和弗吉尼亚州（Virginia）之间。1790 年由华盛顿总统选址，1800 年联邦政府机构由费城（Philadelphia）迁入。重要机构有国会大厦（Capitol）、白宫（▸**the White House**）、最高法院（Supreme Court）和国会图书馆（Library of Congress）等。市内的国家草坪广场（National Mall）上有华盛顿纪念碑（Washington Monument）和林肯纪念堂（Lincoln Memorial），总统宣誓就职时普通民众可在草坪上观看。

washing-up *n* [u] Brit **1** (act) 洗餐具; **to do the ~** 洗餐具 **2** (dishes) 待洗的餐具

washing-up: ~ bowl *n* Brit 洗碟盆; **~ cloth** *n* Brit 洗碗布; **~ liquid** *n* [u] Brit 洗涤液; **~ water** *n* [u] Brit 泔水

wash: ~ leather *n* dated 擦洗用麂皮; **~ load** *n* [洗衣机的] 洗衣量; **~out** *n* **1** (cancelled event) 因雨取消的事; **2** colloq (failure) 彻底失败; **~-rag** *n* Amer 洗脸巾; **~room** *n* Amer 盥洗室; **~ sale** *n* Amer 洗售; **~stand** *n* 盥洗台; **~ symbol** *n* [衣物上的] 洗涤说明标签; **~ trough** *n* 洗矿槽; **~tub** *n* (for clothes and linen) 洗衣盆; (for person) 洗澡盆; **~-wipe** *n* 雨刮器

wasn't /ˈwɒznt/ colloq **= was not** ▸**be**

WASP /wɒsp/ *abbr* Amer **= White Anglo-Saxon Protestant** 白种盎格鲁—撒克逊新教教徒; **a ~ candidate/community** 白种盎格鲁—撒克逊新教候选人/社区

wasp /wɒsp/ *n* 黄蜂

waspie /ˈwɒspi/ *n* **1** (corset) 紧身内衣 **2** (belt) 紧身腰带

waspish /ˈwɒspɪʃ/ *adj* 尖刻的 ‹*remark, criticism*›; 暴躁的 ‹*manner, person*›

waspishly /ˈwɒspɪʃli/ *adv* (sharply) 尖刻地; (irritably) 暴躁地

waspishness /ˈwɒspɪʃnɪs/ *n* [u] (of remark) 尖刻; (of manner, person) 暴躁

wastage /ˈweɪstɪdʒ/ *n* [u] **1** (wasting) 浪费; **materials lost through ~** 浪费掉的材料 **2** (amount wasted) (as part of process) 消耗量; (through carelessness) 浪费量; (through pilfering) 损耗量

waste /weɪst/

A *vt* **1** (squander) 浪费 ‹*resources, money*›; **her irony was ~d on him** 她的嘲讽对他没起作用; **she ~d no time in rejecting the offer** 她当即拒绝了那个提议 **2** (not make full use of) 荒废 ‹*opportunity, talents*› **3** (make emaciated) «*illness, hunger*» 使…衰弱 ‹*person*› **4** esp Amer colloq (kill) 干掉 ‹*person*› **5** Amer colloq (defeat) 把…打得落花流水 ‹*player, team*›

B *vi* «*food, material*» 被浪费; **~ not, want not** Prov 勤俭节约，吃穿不缺

C *n* **1** [c and u] (extravagant use) 浪费; **to go to ~** 被浪费掉; **it was a real ~ to spend so much on the shirt** 在那件衬衫上花那么多钱真是浪费 **2** [c] (pointless use) 白费; **a ~ of time/energy** 白费时间/力气; **a ~ of space** colloq 饭桶 **3** [c and u] (unwanted material) 废物; **household ~** 生活垃圾; **radioactive ~** 放射性废物 **4** [u] (product of the body) 排泄物 **5** [c] formal (area of land) 荒野; **icy/snowy ~s** 冰原/雪原

D *adj* **1** (unwanted) 废弃的; **~ water/gases/plastics** 污水/废气/废塑料; **~ materials** *or* **matter** 废物 **2** (derelict) 未开垦的 ‹*ground*›; **to lay sth. ~** *or* **lay ~ (to) sth.** formal 把某处夷为平地

W

Phrasal verb

- **waste away** *vi* 变瘦弱

waste: ~basket *n* = **waste-paper basket**; **~ bin** *n* 垃圾箱

wasted /ˈweɪstɪd/ *adj* 1 (squandered) 白费的 ‹*effort, expense, vote*›; 碌碌无为的一生 2 (emaciated) 瘦弱的 ‹*body, limb*›; 憔悴的 ‹*face*› 3 colloq (high on drink, drugs) 迷醉的

waste depository *n* 垃圾场

waste disposal *n* [u] 废物处理

waste disposal unit *n* Brit [厨房水槽污水管内的] 废物粉碎处理机

waste dump *n* 垃圾场

wasteful /ˈweɪstfl/ *adj* (extravagant) 挥霍的 ‹*person, habit*›; (inefficient) 损耗大的 ‹*machine, method*›; **to be ~ with/of sth.** 浪费某物

wastefully /ˈweɪstfəli/ *adv* (extravagantly) 挥霍地 ‹*use, spend*›; (inefficiently) 损耗大地 ‹*produce, package*›

wastefulness /ˈweɪstflnɪs/ *n* [u] (extravagance) 浪费; (inefficiency) 损耗

waste: ~land /-lænd/ *n* [u and c] 荒地; **~ management** *n* [u] 废物回收处理; **~ material** *n* [c and u] 废弃物; **~ matter** *n* [u] 1 (waste material) 废弃物; (rubbish) 垃圾; 2 (bodily waste) 排泄物

waste paper *n* [u] 废纸

waste-paper basket, waste-paper bin *ns* Brit 废纸篓

waste: ~ pipe *n* 污水管; **~ products** *npl* = **~ matter**

waster /ˈweɪstə(r)/ *n* 1 (squanderer) (extravagantly) 挥霍者; (inefficiently) 造成浪费的物品; **old-fashioned wardrobes are terrible ~s of space** 老式的柜子很占地方 2 colloq pej (worthless person) 废物

waste: ~ recycling *n* [u] 废物回收利用; **~ service** *n* [尤指当地政府提供的] 废物处理服务

wasting /ˈweɪstɪŋ/ *adj attrib* 消耗性的 ‹*disease, disorder*›

wastrel /ˈweɪstrəl/ *n* liter 浪荡子

watch /wɒtʃ/

A *n* 1 [c] (timepiece) (for wrist) 手表; (for pocket) 怀表; **to wear a ~** 戴手表; **to set one's ~** 对表; **my ~ is slow/fast** 我的表慢了/快了; **my ~ keeps perfect time** 我的表走得很准; **to be able to set one's ~ by sb./sth.** 能根据某人/某事物对表 [指某人或某事很有规律]; **a ~ strap/chain** 表带/表链 2 [c and u] (lookout, surveillance) 守望; (attention) 关注; **to keep ~** «*sentry, police, lookout*» 放哨; **to keep (a) ~ on sb./sth.** 监视某人/留意某物; **to keep ~ over sb./sth.** 看守某人/某物; **a hurricane ~** 飓风监视; **to be on the ~ (for sb./sth.)** (try to avoid) 提防（某人/某事物）; (try to get) 等待着（某人/某事物）; **we're always on the ~ for a bargain** 我们随时盯着便宜货 3 [c and u] (period on lookout) 值班时间; **to go on ~** 去值班; **to come off ~** 值完班 4 [c] (guard on lookout) 值班人 5 [c and u] Naut (period on duty) [在船上的] 值班时间; **the ~es of the night** liter 漫漫长夜 6 [c] Naut (crew on duty) 值班船员

B *vt* 1 (look at) 看; **to ~ sb./sth. do** *or* **doing sth.** 看着某人/某物做某事; **~ me play a trick on him** 看我跟他开个玩笑; **now ~ what happens next** 看看接下来会发生什么; **she's a pleasure to ~** 她很养眼; **he never ~es himself on screen** 他从不看自己演出的节目 2 (monitor) 关注 ‹*progress, situation*›; **to ~ sb./sth. do sth.** 观察某人/某物做某事; **she's really somebody to ~** 她绝对是值得关注的人 3 (keep under surveillance) 监视 ‹*suspect, building*›; **I think I'm being ~ed** 我觉得我被盯上了 4 (scrutinize regularly) 留意 ‹*noticeboard, newspaper*›; **to ~ the time** 留意时间; **to ~ the clock** 盯着钟表 [如盼望下班] 5 (look after) 照看 ‹*child, luggage*›; **would you mind ~ing my bag for me?** 你能不能替我看一下包? 6 colloq (beware of) 当心 ‹*person, car*›; **~ the puddle!** 当心水坑!; **~ it!** 当心! 7 colloq (be careful with) 小心 ‹*person, object*›; **to ~ one's back** (in order to avoid injury) 小心弄伤背; **to ~ one's back (with sb./sth.)** (in order to avoid danger) 提防（某人/某事物）; **to ~ sb.'s back** (in order to protect from danger) 在背后保护某人; **to ~ one's language/weight** 注意言辞/体重

C *vi* 1 (look on) 观看 2 (look at TV) 看电视 3 (pay attention to) 注意

D *v refl* **to ~ oneself** 注意; **~ yourself!** 你留点神!; **~ yourself! you're going to fall!** 当心! 你要跌下去了!; **he'd better ~ himself: the boss is gunning for him** 他最好小心一点, 老板正在找他的茬

Phrasal verbs

- **watch for** *vt* [**~ for sb./sth.**] 观察等待 ‹*person, chance*›; **the cat was on the wall, ~ing for birds** 猫在墙上伺机捉鸟
- **watch out** *vi* 1 (beware) 小心; **~ out! you nearly hit me** 小心点! 你差点打到我; **to ~ out for sb./sth.** 当心某人/某事物 2 (keep lookout) 提防; **to ~ out for ...** 密切注意 ‹*person, problem, symptom*› 3 **to ~ out for sb.** (make sure nothing bad happens to) 关照某人
- **watch over** *vt* [**~ over sb./sth.**] 1 (protect) 保护 ‹*person, place*› 2 (safeguard) 维护 ‹*welfare, interests*›

watchable /ˈwɒtʃəbl/ *adj* 不错的 ‹*performer*›; 值得看的 ‹*film, programme*›

watch band *n* Amer = **watch strap**

watchdog /ˈwɒtʃdɒɡ/

A *n* 1 (dog) 看门狗 2 (monitor) (person) 监察人; (organization) 监察机构; **the UN's nuclear ~ body** 联合国核监督机构

B *vt* (*pres p etc.* **-gg-**) 监察 ‹*person, situation*›

watcher /ˈwɒtʃə(r)/ *n* (observer, spectator) 观察者; (viewer) 观看者; **television ~** 电视观众; **China ~** 中国问题观察员

watchfire /ˈwɒtʃfaɪə(r)/ *n* 营火

watchful /ˈwɒtʃfl/ *adj* 警惕的; **to keep a ~ eye on sb./sth.** 密切留意某人/某事; **under the ~ eye of sb.** 在某人的监视下

watching brief *n* Brit 观察委托书; **to have** *or* **keep** *or* **hold a ~ on sth.** fig 监督某事物

watch: ~maker ▸**p. 409** *n* 钟表匠; **~making** *n* [u] 钟表制造修理业; **~man** /-mən/ ▸**p. 409** *n* 1 (guard) [尤指看守空楼的] 守夜人; 2 Hist 巡夜人; **~night, ~night service** *ns* 除夕夜礼拜; **~ strap** *n* 表带; **~tower** *n* 瞭望塔; **~word** *n* (motto) 格言; (slogan) 口号

water /ˈwɔːtə(r)/

A *n* [u] 1 (substance) 水; **a glass/jug of ~** 一杯水/一壶水; **under ~** 被水淹没的; **to make ~** «*ship*» 漏水; **to spend money like ~** colloq 挥金如土; **to not hold ~** «*argument, theory*» 站不住脚 2 (supply) 供水; **to turn on/off the ~** (from tap) 打开/关上水龙头; (at mains) 打开/关闭自来水总管; **running ~** 自来水 3 (area) 一片水; **shallow/deep ~** 浅水区/深水区; **by ~** formal 经由水路; **across** *or* **over the ~** formal 在彼岸 4 (surface) 水面; **can you swim under ~?** 你会潜泳吗?; **to keep one's head above ~** 把头保持在水面上; fig 勉强应付; **to walk on ~** fig 创造奇迹 5 formal (urine) 尿; **to pass** *or* **make ~** 小便

B **waters** *npl* 1 Geog 水体; **the ~s of the Nile** 尼罗河水域; **the stormy ~s of the Atlantic** 大西洋汹涌澎湃的海水 2 Pol 领海; **British ~s** 英国领海 3 (situation) 复杂局面; **to fish in murky ~s** 混水摸鱼; **unknown ~s** 不明朗的局势 4 (in childbirth) 羊水; **her ~s have broken** 她羊水破了 5 dated (of spa) 矿泉水; **to take the ~s** (by drinking) 喝矿泉水; (by bathing) 洗矿泉浴

C *modif* 1 (substance) 水的; **a ~ molecule/vapour/droplet** 水分子/水蒸汽/水滴 2 (containing water) 盛水的 ‹*container*›; **a ~ glass/jug** 水杯/水壶 3 (of supply) 供水的; **~ shortages** 供水短缺; **a ~ tank/pump** 水箱/水泵 4 (aquatic) 水生的 ‹*creature, plant*›

D *vt* 1 Agric, Hort 给…浇水 ‹*crop, lawn, plant*› 2 (provide drink for) 给…水喝 ‹*livestock*›; **the riders stopped to ~ their horses** 骑手们停下来饮马 3 liter (flow through) «*river*» 流经 ‹*region, plain*› 4 (dilute) 在…里掺水 ‹*wine, whisky*›

E *vi* 1 (produce tears) 流泪; **my eyes always ~ when I peel onions** 我剥洋葱时总是流泪 2 (produce saliva) «*mouth*» 流口水

Phrasal verb

- **water down** *vt* [**~ sth. down, ~ down sth.**] 1 (dilute) 在…里掺水 ‹*drink*› 2 fig (tone down) 使…缓和 ‹*criticism, policy*› 3 Fin 虚增 ‹*capital, stock*›

water: ~ bailiff ▸**p. 409** *n* Brit 河道及渔业管理员; **~ bath** *n* 1 Chem 水浴锅; 2 Culin 蒸锅; **~ bed** *n* 水床; **~ beetle** *n* 水生甲虫; **~bird** *n* 水鸟; **~ biscuit** *n* 薄脆水面饼干; **~ boatman** *n* 1 (swimming on surface) 仰泳蝽; 2 (bottom-dwelling) 划蝽; **~ bomber** *n* 森林灭火飞机; **~borne** *adj* 1 Med, Biol 水传播的 ‹*virus, spores*›; 2 Transp 水运的 ‹*goods, trade*›; **~ bottle** *n* 1 (for carrying water) 水壶; 2 = **hot-water bottle**; **~ buffalo** *n* 水牛; **~ butt** *n* [接房檐雨水的] 大水桶; **~ cannon** *n* [驱散闹事者的] 水炮; **~ carrier** *n* 1 (person) 背水者; 2 (container) [汽车上的] 运水桶; 3 Astrol **the W~ Carrier** 宝瓶座; **~ cart** *n* 1 esp Brit (for street cleaning) 洒水车; 2 (for drinking) 卖水车; **~ chestnut** *n* 荸荠; **~ clock** *n* Hist 水钟; **~ closet** *n* dated 1 (flush toilet) 抽水马桶; 2 (room) 厕所; **~colour** *n* 1 [u and c] (paint) 水彩颜料; 2 [c] (painting) 水彩画; **~colourist** Brit, **~colorist** Amer ▸**p. 409** *n* 水彩画家; **~-cooled** *adj* 水冷的 ‹*engine, reactor*›

water cooler

A *n* 饮水冷却器

B **water-cooler** *modif* Amer colloq 职员偷闲时的 ‹*gossip*›; 职员闲聊的 ‹*topic*›

water: ~-cooling *n* [u] 水冷却; **~course** *n* 水道; **~cress** *n* [u] 1 Culin 水田芥叶; 2 Bot 水田芥; **~ diviner** ▸**p. 409** *n* Brit 用占卜杖探水源者; **~ divining** *n* [u] Brit 用占卜杖探水源

watered-down /ˌwɔːtədˈdaʊn/ *adj* 1 (diluted) 掺水的 ‹*beer, paint*› 2 (modified) 轻描淡写的 ‹*language*›; 弱化了的 ‹*legislation*›

watered /ˈwɔːtəd/: **~ silk** *n* [u and c] 波纹绸; **~ stock** *n* [u and c] Amer 掺水股

water: ~fall *n* 瀑布; **~ feature** *n* 水景; **~ filter** *n* 水过滤器; **~fowl** *npl* 水禽; **~-free** *adj* 不含水的 ‹*substance*›; 无水的 ‹*area*›; 免冲水的 ‹*toilet, technology*›; **~front** *n* (street) 滨水路; (area) 滨水区; **a ~front cafe** 滨水咖啡馆; **~ gas** *n* [u] 水煤气; **~ glass** *n* 1 [u] (solution) 硅酸钠; 2 [c] (container) 玻璃水杯; **~ heater** *n* 热水器; **~hole** *n* [沙漠或干旱地区的] 水洼; **~ ice** *n* 冰糕

watering /ˈwɔːtərɪŋ/ *n* [u] (with watering can) 浇水; (with sprinkler) 喷水; (by irrigation) 灌溉

watering: ~ can *n* 洒水壶; **~ hole** *n* 1 colloq hum (pub, bar) 酒吧; 2 = **waterhole**; **~ place** *n* 1 (seaside resort, spa) 海滨胜地; 2 Zool = **waterhole**

water: ~ jacket *n* 水套; **~ jump** *n* Sport 水沟障碍; **~ level** *n* 水位; **~ lily** *n* 睡莲; **~line** *n* 1 Naut (height of water) 吃水线; 2 Naut (structural line) 水线; 3 (mark left by water) 水迹线; **~logged** *adj* 1 (with surface water) 水淹的 ‹*field, soil*›; 2 (saturated with water) 浸透水的 ‹*timber, shoes, carpet*›

W

Waterloo /ˌwɔːtəˈluː/ *pr n* 滑铁卢; **the Battle of ～** 滑铁卢战役; **to meet one's ～** 遭遇最终的失败

water: ～ main *n* 总水管; **～man** /-mən/ *n* 船工; **～mark** *n* [纸张上的] 水印; **～meadow** *n* 浸水草地; **～melon** *n* [c and u] 西瓜; **～ mill** *n* 水磨; **～ nymph** *n* 水中仙女; **～ paint** *n* [u and c] 水粉涂料; **～ pipe** *n* **1** (for sanitation) 水管; **2** (for smoking) 水烟管; **～ pistol** *n* 玩具喷水手枪; **～ polo** ▸**p. 307** *n* [u] 水球; **～ power** *n* [u] 水力; **～ pressure** *n* [u] 水压

waterproof /ˈwɔːtəpruːf/

A *adj* 防水的 ‹*fabric, watch, make-up*›; **～ ink** 防水油墨

B *vt* 使…不透水 ‹*fabric, roof*›

C *n* Brit 雨衣

water: ～proofing *n* [u] 防水处理; **～ purification plant** *n* 水净化工厂; **～ purifying tablet** *n* 净水丸; **～ rail** *n* 普通秧鸡; **～ rat** *n* **1** (large rodent) 水鼠; **2** Brit = **～ vole**; **～ rates** *npl* Brit 水费; **～-repellent** *adj* 抗水的 ‹*fabric, paint*›; **～-resistant** *adj* 抗水的 ‹*coating, ointment, resin*›; **～ retention** *n* [u] 水潴留; **～-saving** *adj* 节水的 ‹*device*›; **～scape** /ˈwɔːtəˌskeɪp/ *n* 水景画; **～shed** *n* **1** Geog 分水岭; **2** (turning point) 转折点; **3** **～shed (hour)** Brit TV [儿童不宜节目的] 播放起始时间; **～ shrew** *n* 水鼩; **～side** *n* 水边; **a ～side path** 水滨小路

waterski /ˈwɔːtəskiː/

A *vi* 水橇滑水

B *n* 滑水橇

water: ～skier *n* 水橇滑水者; **～skiing** ▸**p. 307** *n* [u] 水橇运动; **～ slide** *n* 滑水道; **～ snake** *n* 水蛇; **～ softener** *n* **1** [u and c] (substance) 软水剂; **2** [c] (device) 硬水软化器; **～-soluble** *adj* 水溶性的 ‹*compound, dye*›; **～ sports** ▸**p. 307** *npl* 水上运动; **～spout** *n* 水龙卷; **～ supply** *n* **1** (service) 供水; **2** (ration) [旅行时的] 携带水量; **～ system** *n* **1** Geog 水系; **2** (network of pipes) 供水系统; **～ table** *n* 地下水位; **～tight** *adj* **1** (closely sealed) 不漏水的 ‹*seal, container*›; **2** fig (indisputable) 无懈可击的 ‹*argument, alibi*›; **3** fig (impenetrable) 固若金汤的 ‹*defence, security*›; **～ torture** *n* [u] 水刑; **～ tower** *n* 水塔; **～ treatment** *n* [u] 水处理; **～ trough** *n* 饮水槽; **～ vole** *n* 水田鼠; **～ wagon** *n* Amer (for hauling water) 运水车; (for sprinkling) 洒水车; **～way** *n* 航道; **～weed** *n* [u and c] 水草; **～ wheel** *n* 水轮; **～ wings** *npl* 双翼形浮水袋; **～works** *npl* **1** + *v sing* Tech 自来水厂; **2** **to turn on the ～works** colloq (start to cry) 流眼泪; **3** + *v pl* Brit colloq hum (urinary system) 泌尿系统

watery /ˈwɔːtəri/ *adj* **1** (too dilute) 稀的 ‹*coffee, sauce*›; 太淡的 ‹*colour, paint, ink*› **2** fig (insipid) 惨淡的 ‹*sunshine, sky*›; 淡淡的 ‹*smile*› **3** (water-like) 似水的 ‹*substance*› **4** (involving water) 水的; **a ～ death** or **end** or **fate** 淹死 **5** (full of tears) 泪汪汪的 ‹*eyes*› **6** (secreting liquid) 渗出水的 ‹*wound*› **7** (badly drained) 水浸的 ‹*field, vegetables*›

watt /wɒt/ *n* 瓦特

wattage /ˈwɒtɪdʒ/ *n* [c and u] 瓦特数

wattle¹ /ˈwɒtl/ *n* [u] Constr, esp Hist 编条结构; **a ～ fence/hut** 编条篱笆/小屋

wattle² *n* (skin flap of turkey, lizard) 肉垂

wattle and daub *n* [u] esp Hist 抹灰篱笆墙; **a wattle-and-daub hut** 泥笆墙小屋

wave /weɪv/

A *n* **1** (in water) 波浪; **to ride the ～s** 冲浪; **a huge ～** 巨浪; **to make ～s** lit «*wind, boat*» 掀起波浪; fig colloq (cause a stir) 引起轰动; colloq (cause trouble) 兴风作浪 **2** (hand gesture) 挥手; **to give sb. a ～** 向某人挥手 **3** (gesture with object) 挥动; **with a ～ of his wand** 随着他的魔术棒一挥 **4** (surge of feeling) 一阵; **a ～ of panic/nausea/euphoria** 一阵恐慌/恶心/兴奋; **in ～s** 一阵阵地; **the grief comes in ～s** 悲伤阵阵袭来 **5** (large-scale occurrence) 浪潮; **a ～ of strikes** 罢工浪潮 **6** (large number arriving) (of people) 涌现的人; (of things) 涌现的事物; **we attacked the enemy army in two ～s** 我们分成两个梯队向敌军发起进攻 **7** (radiating surge) 浪; **a ～ of heat** 热浪 **8** Phys 波; **electromagnetic ～s** 电磁波 **9** (curling lock of hair) 卷发 **10** (tendency to curl) 卷曲; **her hair has a slight natural ～ (in it)** 她的头发微微有点自然卷 **11** (undulating shape) 波浪形

B **waves** *npl* **the ～s** liter 大海; **beneath the ～s** 在海底

C *vt* **1** (move as signal) 挥动 ‹*handkerchief, ticket, wand*›; **to be like waving a red flag in front of a bull** 做惹人发怒的事 **2** (brandish threateningly) 挥舞 ‹*gun, stick*›; **he ～d his fist at her angrily** 他愤怒地向她挥拳头 **3** (convey with gesture) 挥臂表示 ‹*greeting, acceptance*›; **I ～d them my thanks** 我向他们挥手致谢; **to ～ goodbye to sb.** 向某人挥手告别; **to ～ goodbye to sth.** (accept loss of) 与某物失之交臂 **4** (direct) 向…挥手示意 ‹*driver, car*›; **to ～ sb./sth. on/through** 挥手示意某人/某物继续前进/通过 **5** (in hairdressing) 把…烫成波浪形; **to have one's hair ～d** 烫发

D *vi* **1** (signal with hand) 挥手示意; **to ～ to sb. to do sth.** 挥手示意某人做某事; **to ～ back** 挥手回应 **2** (move gently) «*branch, grass*» 飘动; **the flag ～d in the breeze** 旗帜在微风中飘扬; **a field of waving corn** 一片起伏的谷浪 **3** (curl slightly) «*hair*» 卷曲

Phrasal verbs

- **wave around, wave about**

A *vi* «*flag*» 飘扬; «*grass, corn*» 波浪般起伏

B *vt* [**～ sth. around, ～ around sth.**] 挥舞 ‹*stick, gun*›

- **wave aside** *vt* [**～ sb./sth. aside, ～ aside sb./sth.**]

1 (dismiss) 对…置之不理 ‹*criticism, suggestion*› **2** (order out of way) 挥手示意…让开 ‹*person*›

- **wave down** *vt* [**～ sb./sth. down, ～ down sb./sth.**] 挥手示意…停下 ‹*car, taxi, driver*›
- **wave off** *vt* [**～ sb./sth. off, ～ off sb./sth.**] 向…挥手告别

wave: ～ action *n* [u] 波浪作用; **～band** *n* 波段; **～ energy** *n* [u] 波浪能; **～ farm** *n* 海浪发电厂; **～form** *n* 波形; **～guide** *n* 波导; **～length** *n* 波长; **to be on the same/a different ～length** fig 想法一致/不一致

wavelet /ˈweɪvlɪt/ *n* 小波浪

wave: ～ machine *n* [游泳池] 造波机; **～ mechanics** *npl* + *v sing* 波动力学; **～ power** *n* [u] 波力

waver /ˈweɪvə(r)/ *vi* **1** (wobble, weaken) «*courage, love*» 消退; «*faith*» 动摇; «*voice*» 发抖; **his determination/concentration seems to be ～ing** 他的决心似乎在动摇/注意力似乎在涣散 **2** (hesitate) 犹豫不决; **to ～ over sth.** 在某事上举棋不定 **3** (flicker) «*light, flame*» 摇曳; «*needle*» 摆动

waverer /ˈweɪvərə(r)/ *n* 犹豫不决的人

wavering /ˈweɪvərɪŋ/

A *n* [u] **1** (hesitation) 犹豫 **2** (unsteadiness) (of flame, image) 摇曳; (of voice) 颤抖

B *adj* **1** (hesitant) 犹豫不决的 ‹*voter, politician*› **2** (unsteady) 动摇的 ‹*courage, confidence*›; 颤抖的 ‹*voice*›; 摇曳的 ‹*light, flame*›; **the baby has taken her first ～ steps** 那个幼儿迈出了摇摇晃晃的第一步

wavy /ˈweɪvi/ *adj* **1** (slightly curling) 稍稍卷曲的; **～ hair** 鬈发 **2** (undulating) 波浪形的 ‹*line, pattern*›

wax¹ /wæks/

A *n* [u and c] **1** (material of honeycomb) 蜂蜡 **2** (processed beeswax) 蜡; **a ～ model/candle** 蜡模/蜡烛 **3** (earwax) 耳屎

B *vt* **1** (treat with wax) 给…上蜡 ‹*furniture, leather, skis*› **2** Cosmet 用蜡除去…的毛 ‹*legs*›

wax² *vi* **1** Astron «*moon*» 渐满 **2** liter (increase) 增加; **to ～ and wane** 兴衰 **3** (express oneself) **to ～ lyrical/eloquent/nostalgic (about** or **over sth.)** 兴高采烈地/滔滔不绝地/伤感地讲（某事物）

waxed /wækst/ *adj* 打过蜡的 ‹*floor, furniture*›; **a ～ jacket** 上过蜡的皮夹克

waxed paper *n* [u] 蜡纸

waxen /ˈwæksn/ *adj* **1** (wax-like) 蜡黄的 ‹*face*› **2** archaic or liter (of wax) 蜡制的 ‹*doll, effigy*›; **a ～ candle** 蜡烛

waxing /ˈwæksɪŋ/ *n* [u and c] **1** (treating with wax) 上蜡 **2** Cosmet 热蜡脱毛

wax: ～ museum *n* = **waxworks**; **～ paper** *n* = **waxed paper**

waxwork /ˈwækswɜːk/ *n* 蜡像; **～ model/figure** 蜡模/蜡像

waxworks /ˈwækswɜːks/ *npl* + *v sing* esp Brit 蜡像馆

waxy /ˈwæksi/ *adj* 似蜡的 ‹*substance, texture*›; 蜡黄的 ‹*skin, complexion*›; **～ potatoes** 蜡质马铃薯

way /weɪ/

A *n* **1** [c] (manner, method) 方式; **in the usual ～** 以通常的做法; **in a friendly ～** 友好地; **there's no ～ of knowing** or **telling** 无从知晓; **that's the ～ (to do it)!** 就是这样（做）！; **to see things my ～** 从我的角度看问题; **～ to go!** Amer colloq 干得好！; **(there's) no ～!** colloq (definitely not) 没门！; (expressing surprise) 不可能！; **to sb.'s ～ of thinking** 在某人看来; **to have a ～ with sb./sth.** 有办法对付某人/某事物; **to have a ～ with one** Brit dated 有不可抗拒的魅力; **in one's** or **its own ～** 以自己特有的方式; **to be born** or **made that ～** 生来如此; **to get into/out of the ～ of sth.** 养成/改掉做某事的习惯; **either ～** (both are the same) 两者都一样; (no matter how/which) 不管怎样; **one ～ and** or **or another** (all things considered) 总的来看; **one ～ or another** or **the other** (by whatever means) 不管怎样; (whichever it is) 无论哪一个; **to have** or **want it both ～s** 想两全其美; **(there are) no two ～s about it** colloq 事实如此 **2** [c] (typical behaviour) 作风; **it was not his ～ to admit that he had made a mistake** 认错可不是他的作风; **to have a ～ of doing sth.** (have habit) «*person*» 惯常做某事; (have tendency) «*situation, event*» 有某种发展倾向; **first love affairs have a ～ of not working out** 初恋通常不会有什么结果; **the ～ of the world** 世道; **that's** or **it's always the ～** colloq 老是这样 **3** [c] (route, path) 路; **a pedestrian ～** 人行道; **to ask the ～** 问路; **the ～ up/down a mountain** 上山/下山的路; **across** or Brit **over the ～ (from sb./sth.)** 在（某人/某物的）路对面; **they live across the ～ from us** 他们住在我们路对面; **can you tell me the ～ to the museum?** 请问到博物馆怎么走？; **the ～ ahead** lit, fig 前面的路; **a ～ around** 绕过…的路 ‹*obstacle*›; fig 避开…的方法 ‹*problem*›; **a ～ back (to sth.)** 回（某处）去的路; **a ～ up/down** 上去/下去的路; **a ～ forward** 向前的路; **a ～ into sth.** (route) 进入某处的路; fig (means of participating) 参与某事的途径; (means of understanding) 理解某事的方法; **the company is looking for a ～ into the European market** 公司正在寻找一条打入欧洲市场的路; **to find one's ～** (reach destination) 找到路; fig (end up) 无意间来到; **a speck of dirt had found its ～ into the mechanism** 一粒脏东西碰巧掉进了机件里; **on the** or **one's ～** (going) 在去的路上; (coming) 在来的路上; (en route) 在路上; colloq (about to be born) 快出生了; **on the ～ to school** 在去学校的路上; **I must be on my ～ now** 我现在必须动身了; **it's not on my ～** 我不顺路; **to be on one's ～ to victory** 即将获得成功; **on the** or **one's ～ to doing sth.** 即将做某事; **to**

go on one's ～ 继续赶路; **to send sb. on their ～** 打发某人离开; **to have sb. on the ～** (be awaiting the arrival of) 马上会见到某人; colloq (be pregnant with) 怀着孩子; **along the ～** (en route) 在路上; (in the course of events) 在进展中; **out of the ～** (remote) 偏远的; (unusual) 不寻常的; **out of sb.'s ～** 不和某人顺道; **to go out of one's ～ (to do sth.)** (make detour) 绕道（去做某事）; (make special effort) 特地（做某事）; **by ～ of sth.** 经由某处; fig (by means of a process) 以某方式; (by means of an intermediate stage) 通过某物; **she rolled her eyes by ～ of an answer and left** 她翻了翻眼睛权作回答，然后就走了; **she came to TV by ～ of drama school** 她通过读戏剧学校进入了电视业; **to go one's own ～** 我行我素; **to go one's separate ～s** lit, fig 分道扬镳; **to go the ～ of sb./sth.** 遭遇和某人/某事物相同的命运; **to see one's ～ (clear) to doing sth.** or **to do sth.** (see as possible) 认为有可能做某事; (see as convenient) 方便做某事; **to make one's ～** (go somewhere) 前往; (make progress) 进步; **to make one's ～ in the world** 闯出一方天地; **to make one's ～ to** or **towards sb./sth.** 向某人/某处走去; **to argue** or **bluff** or **talk one's ～ out of sth.** 蒙混过关; **to cheat/lie one's ～ to sth.** 通过欺骗/说谎获得某物; **to cut** or **hack one's ～ through sth.** 在某物中劈开一条路; **to eat one's ～ through sth.** 把某物吃得精光 **4** [c] (forward route) 通路; **to bar** or **block** or **obstruct the** or **sb.'s/sth.'s ～** 挡住某人/某物的道; **to be** or **get in the** or **sb.'s/sth.'s ～** 妨碍某人/某事物; **to get in the ～ of sth.** 妨碍某事物; **out of the** or **sb.'s/sth.'s ～** lit (not obstructing) 不挡某人/某物的道; fig (not impeding progress) 不妨碍某人/某事物; (over and done with) 处理完某人/某事物; **he pushed me out of the ～ and ran out the door** 他把我推开，跑出门去; **once the wedding is out of the ～, ...** 婚礼一结束，…; **she couldn't get out of the ～ in time** 她没能及时躲开; **out of the** or **my ～!** colloq 滚开！ colloq; **to get sb./sth. out of the** or **sb.'s/sth.'s ～** (remove from place) 让某人/某事物不再挡路; fig (deal with) 对付完某人/处理好某事物; **let me just get lunch out of the ～** 我来搞定午餐吧; **to want sb./sth. out of the** or **sb.'s/sth.'s ～** lit 不想让某人/某事物挡路; fig (want over and done with) 想对付完某人/想处理好某事物; **to keep** or **stay out of the** or **sb.'s/sth.'s ～** 离某人/某事物远远的; **to make ～** 让路; **to make ～ for sb./sth.** (allow to pass) 给某人/某事物让路; (be replaced by) 让位给某人/某事物; **tropical forest is felled to make ～ for grassland** 热带森林被砍伐，以便为草场腾出地方; **spring made ～ for summer** 春去夏来 **5** [c] (direction) 方向; **come** or **step this ～** 到这边来; **look this ～** 朝这个方向看; **the cinema is the other ～** 电影院在相反的方向; **to be going the right/wrong ～** 朝着正确的/错误的方向走; **which ～ for** or **to the dining room?** 去餐厅怎么走？; **'this ～ up'** (on box) “此面朝上”; **to look the other ～** 朝一边看; fig (ignore wrongdoing) 佯作不知; **the other ～ around** or **round** Brit or **about** Brit (reversed) 颠倒过来; (transposed) 调换; (opposite situation) 相反的情况; **I didn't leave you: it was the other ～ around** 我没有离开你，是你离开了我; **the right/wrong ～ around** (not reversed/reversed) 按正确的/相反的方向; (in correct order/transposed) 按正确的/相反的顺序; **you're Ben and you're Tom: have I got that the right ～ around?** 你是本，你是汤姆，我认对了吗？; **to put one's skirt on the wrong ～ around** 把裙子穿反; **you've got the subject and object of the sentence the wrong ～ around** 你把句子的主

ℹ Asking the way

Asking the way

Excuse me, could you tell me the way to the airport?
or ***Excuse me, can you direct me to the airport?***
= 请问怎么去机场？

Excuse me, how can I get to Princes Street?
= 请问到王子大街怎么走？

Excuse me, can you tell me where the theatre is?
= 劳驾，你能告诉我剧院在哪儿吗？

Excuse me, which bus should I take to get to the police station?
= 请问一下，到警察局要坐哪路车？

Excuse me, which line will take me to Oxford Street?
= 打扰一下，到牛津大街坐哪条线？

I'm looking for the train station. Am I anywhere near?
= 我在找火车站，是不是快到了？

Excuse me, is the museum straight ahead?
= 请问博物馆是一直往前吗？

Which way is the bookshop from here?
= 从这儿去书店是哪个方向？

Am I going the right way to the post office?
= 到邮局走这条路对吗？

Can you please tell me if I'm in the right direction for the gallery?
= 你能告诉我去画廊是这个方向吗？

Is there a pharmacy near here?
= 附近有药店吗？

Excuse me, please. Where is the nearest cinema?
= 请问最近的电影院在哪儿？

Sorry to trouble you, but which is the best way to the Holiday Inn?
= 对不起，打扰了。到假日酒店怎么走好？

How far is it from here to the shopping mall?
= 从这儿到购物中心有多远？

How long will it take to get there on foot?
= 步行去那儿需要多长时间？

Giving directions

Take the number 42 bus. Don't get off until the final stop
= 乘 42 路公共汽车，到终点站下车

Take the No. 37 bus from here and get off at Hope Square, then change to the No. 29. This will take you directly to your destination
= 从这儿乘 37 路车，坐到希望广场下车，然后换乘 29 路车，坐那路车可以直接到目的地

Take the Yellow Circle Line to Victoria Station, then change to the Blue Victoria Line and alight at Oxford Circus. From there, follow the exit for Oxford Street
= 先乘黄色的地铁环线到维多利亚站，然后换乘蓝色的维多利亚线，坐到牛津广场站下。下车后，从牛津大街出口出地铁站

The theatre? It's right near here. Just cross the street, and immediately take a left
= 剧院？就离这儿不远。穿过马路，马上往左拐

It's not far from here. Continue on this road (for) about ten minutes. When you see the central library, turn right
= 离这儿不远。沿这条路走大约 10 分钟，看到中心图书馆时往右拐

Go straight ahead. Cut through the shopping mall, and then you exit on to Princes Street
= 一直往前走，穿过购物中心，走出去便是王子大街

I'm sorry. I am new to this city too
= 对不起，我对这座城市也不熟

I live there. If you follow me, I will show you where the post office is
= 我住那儿。跟我走，我指给你看邮局在哪儿

Keep going straight for one mile. The museum is on your left. You can't miss it
= 一直向前走 1 英里，博物馆在你左手边，你不会找不到的

Cross here, and then take the second turning on the right
= 从这儿穿过马路，然后在右手的第二个拐弯处右转

I'm afraid you are going in the wrong direction
= 恐怕你走错方向了

It's the other way. Turn round, and then at the traffic lights turn right
= 是在相反的方向。往回走，看到交通灯时往右拐

There is a pharmacy about half a mile away. I'll walk you there. It's on my way
= 大约半英里远处有家药店。我陪你走到那儿，反正我顺路

The nearest cinema is in Hope Street
= 最近的电影院在希望街

The best way is to take the tube. The nearest tube station is Westminster. Continue on this road, and then take the second turning on the left. You will see the entrance to the station in front of you
= 最好是乘地铁。最近的地铁站是威斯敏斯特站。沿着这条路继续往前走，在左手的第二个拐弯处左转，你就会找到地铁站入口

It's within walking distance
= 走着去就行

It's about two miles away
= 大约两英里远

It's no distance at all
= 一点都不远

It's too far to walk. You'd better take a taxi or bus
= 步行太远了，你最好打出租车或坐公交车

It's about 20 minutes' walk
= 大约要走 20 分钟

You can walk it in 20 minutes
= 20 分钟内就能走到

语和宾语颠倒了; **the other ~ up** 上下颠倒; **the right/wrong ~ up** 上下方向正确/颠倒; **this ~ and that** 前后左右; **to look this ~ and that** 左顾右盼; **to run this ~ and that** 东奔西跑; **to look both ~s** 左右两边都看; **every which ~** colloq (in all directions) 朝四面八方; (by all available means) 用尽一切办法; **her hair tumbled every which ~** 她的头发乱七八糟; **to come sb.'s ~** (approach) 向某人走来; fig (present itself to sb.) 意外落在某人身上; **an opportunity came my ~** 一个机会落在了我的头上; **to go sb.'s ~** 与某人同路; fig (go well for) 对某人有利; **to be going the right ~ to get sth.** colloq 所作所为会招惹某事; **you're going the right ~ to get a smack** 你是想挨一巴掌吧; **to put sth. sb.'s ~** colloq 为某人提供某物; **I might be able to put a bit of business your ~ if I'm elected** 如果我当选也许能为你带来一点生意 **6** **Way** [u] (in street names) 路; **106 Headley Way** 黑德利路 106 号 **7** [c and u] (distance) 距离; (period of time) 时段; **a long** *or* **fair** *or* **good ~** 很长一段距离; **some ~ off** 有一段距离; **Christmas is now just a short ~ off** 圣诞节距现在很近了; **a** *or* **some ~ to go** 还有一段路; **the whole ~** 全程; **all the ~** (for whole distance) 全程; (completely) 完全地; **she cried all the ~ to the church** 她一路哭到了教堂; **he went all the ~ to China with them** 他和他们一路同行去了中国; **there are advertising hoardings all the ~ along this road** 这条街上全是广告牌; **to go all the ~ with sb.** colloq euph 同某人尽情交欢; **to go some/a long ~ towards doing sth.** 对做某事帮助不大/很大 **8** [c] colloq (area) 地区; **down** *or* **around your ~** 在你那儿; **over Bristol ~** 在布里斯托尔一带 **9** [c] (respect, aspect) 方面; **in a ~** (in some respects) 在某些方面; (to a certain extent) 在某种程度上; **in every ~** (in all respects) 在各方面; (from every point of view) 无论从什么观点看; **in more ~s than one** (in more than one respect) 在很多方面; (in more than one sense) 在很多意义上; **in a general ~** 总体而言; **in the ordinary ~** 一般情况下; **there isn't much in the ~ of entertainment in this place** 这个地方没有什么娱乐活动; **what have you got in the ~ of drinks?** 你有没有什么可以喝的? **10** [c] (condition, state) **to be in a bad** *or* **poor ~** 情况危急 **11** [c] (will, desire) 愿望; **to get** *or* **have one's (own) ~** 一意孤行; **have it your (own) ~!** colloq 随你的便吧!; **to have it** *or* **things** *or* **everything one's own ~** 一意孤行; **to have one's (wicked) ~ with sb.** archaic or hum 劝服某人同自己交欢

B **ways** *npl* **1** (behaviour) 习俗; **the old ~s** 旧习俗 **2** (parts) 部分; **to split the money four ~s** 把钱分成四份

C **ways** *n* Amer colloq **1** (distance) 长距离; **they had to walk quite a ~s** 他们不得不走了很长一段路 **2** (time) 长时间

D *adv* colloq **1** (far) 很远; **they live ~ out in the suburbs** 他们住在偏远的郊区; **~ over there** *or* **yonder** 在很远处; **~ up in the air** 在高空中 **2** (a lot) 大大地; **the performance was ~ below their usual standard** 这次表演远远低于他们的正常水平; **they're ~ down in the table at the moment** 眼下他们烂醉如泥; **to be ~ out** (in guess, estimate) 差得太远了; **to be ~ too big** 太大了; **she's ~ bigger than him** 她比他大得多 **3** esp Amer (very) 非常; **the guys behind the bar were ~ cool** 吧台后面的那些小伙子酷毙了

E **by the way** *adv phr* 顺便说一下; **what's the time, by the ~?** 顺便问一下, 几点钟了?; **and she, by the ~, is French** 而她, 顺便说一下, 是个法国人; **all this is by the ~** 所有这些都是次要的

way: ~bill *n* (list) (of passengers) 乘客名单; (of goods) 运货单; **~ in** *n* 入口; **~lay** *vt* (*pt, pp* **~laid**) 拦截; **the travellers were ~laid by bandits** 游客遭到了拦路抢劫

waymark /ˈweɪmɑːk/
A *n* 路标
B *vt* 给…设路标 ‹route›

way: ~marker *n* = **waymark A**; **~ of life** *n* 生活方式; **~ out** *n* **1** (route) 出口; **on the** *or* **one's** *or* **its ~ out** (being eliminated) 遭淘汰的; (stopping operating) 故障的; (dying) 即将灭亡的; (becoming unfashionable) 即将过时的; (when leaving) 离开时; **2** (means of escape) 出路; **~-out** *adj* colloq **1** (unconventional) 前卫的 ‹person, behaviour›; 奇特的 ‹appearance›; 不落俗套的 ‹fashion, idea›; **2** dated (very good) 相当棒的; **~point** *n* **1** (stopping place) 旅途停留处; **2** Aviat, Naut [电脑检测的] 航路点; **~s and means** *npl* 方式方法; **~s and means of doing sth.** *or* **to do sth.** 做某事的方式方法; **~side** *n* 路边; **at** *or* **by the ~side** 在路边; **to fall by the ~side** (stray morally) 误入歧途; (fail, be cancelled) 半途而废; **a ~side inn** 路边小客栈; **~side flowers** 路边的花; **~station** *n* Amer **1** Rail 小站; **2** (staging post) 旅途停留点

wayward /ˈweɪwəd/ *adj* 任性的 ‹person, disposition›; 不忠的 ‹husband, lover›; 难以控制的 ‹horse, missile›; **~ and difficult** 倔强的

waywardness /ˈweɪwədnɪs/ *n* [u] (of person) 任性; (of husband, lover) 不忠实; (of horse, missile) 难控制

wazzock /ˈwæzək/ *n* Brit colloq (stupid person) 蠢货; (annoying person) 讨厌鬼

WC *abbr* Brit = **water closet** 厕所

we /wiː, wɪ/ *pron* **1** (I and my group) 我们; (I and sb. else) 咱们; **~ went yesterday** 我们昨天去的; **~ Scots like the sun** 我们苏格兰人喜欢太阳; **~ four are agreed that ...** 我们四个人一致同意… **2** (people in general) 人们; **~ all make mistakes** 人人都会犯错误; **~ shouldn't lie to our children** 不应该对孩子说谎

WEA *abbr* Brit = **Workers' Educational Association** 工人教育协会

weak /wiːk/
A *adj* **1** (not physically powerful) 软弱无力的 ‹person, arms›; **the ~er sex** dated pej 女性 **2** (debilitated) 虚弱的 ‹patient, heartbeat, voice›; **to be ~ with** *or* **from** 因…而身体发软 ‹hunger, excitement›; 弱的 ‹eyesight, digestion›; **~ at the knees** colloq [因激动、害怕、生病等] 两腿发软的 **3** (functioning poorly) 衰弱的 ‹bladder, immune system›; (with limited effect) 效力不强的 ‹medicine›; **she suffered from a ~ heart** 她心脏不太好; **a very ~ memory** 非常差的记性; **~ spectacles/lenses** 度数浅的眼镜/镜片; **to have a ~ stomach** (have delicate digestion) 胃不太好; fig (be squeamish) 容易心烦意乱 **4** (not performing activity powerfully) 差的; **to be a ~ swimmer** 不善游泳 **5** (not powerful, done to slight degree) 无力的 ‹push, grip, challenge, protest, criticism›; (exerting little natural force) 微弱的 ‹sound, magnet, light›; **~ evidence** 没有说服力的证据; **to give (sb.) a ~ smile** (向某人) 淡淡一笑 **6** (easy to resist or defeat) 软弱的 ‹country, government, president, team›; **a ~ point** *or* **spot** 弱点 **7** (not robust) 不牢固的 ‹structure, joint, beam, foundations› **8** (irresolute, easily influenced) 懦弱的; **a ~ will** 薄弱的意志; **~ nerves** 脆弱的神经; **in a ~ moment** 一时心软 **9** (not firm or decisive) 软弱的 ‹measure, leadership› **10** (not proficient) 不称职的 ‹teacher, parent›; 无把握获胜的 ‹candidate›; (deficient, poor) 不擅长的; **his French is ~** 他的法语说得不好; **to be sb.'s ~ point** «spelling, maths» 是某人的弱项; **to be ~ in** *or* **at** 不擅长 ‹spelling, maths› **11** (of low standard) 水平低的 ‹essay, novel› **12** (not firmly established) 不牢靠的 ‹bond, position› **13** Econ 疲软的 ‹market, currency›; 看跌的 ‹price›; 萧条的 ‹economy, demand›; **the pound is ~ against the dollar** 英镑对美元的走势疲软 **14** (unsuccessful) 疲弱的 ‹industry, economy› **15** (not concentrated, affecting senses slightly) 淡的 ‹taste, smell›; **~ tea/coffee** 淡茶/淡咖啡; **a ~ alkali** 弱碱; **a ~ soup** 稀汤 **16** (not striking) 线条不分明的 ‹features, nose, chin› **17** Ling 弱变化的 ‹verb, form›; 非重读的 ‹form, syllable›
B *npl* **the ~** 弱者

weaken /ˈwiːkən/
A *vi* **1** (lose physical strength) «person, muscle» 变虚弱 **2** (lose power) «resolution, structure, alliance, army, love» 动摇; **the party's grip on power was ~ing** 该党对权力的控制日趋减弱 **3** Econ, Fin «economy» 衰退; «demand» 减少; «price, exchange rate» 降低; «currency» 贬值
B *vt* **1** (physically) 使…虚弱 ‹person, heart›; 减少 ‹stamina, resistance› **2** (in power) 削弱 ‹allegiance, government, will›; **the war ~ed support for the regime** 这场战争削弱了对该政权的支持 **3** Econ 使…衰退 ‹economy›; 使…降低 ‹price, exchange rate›; 使…贬值 ‹currency› **4** (structurally) 动摇 ‹structure, defence›; 使…松动 ‹riverbank› **5** (dilute) 稀释 ‹solution, concentration›

weakening /ˈwiːkənɪŋ/ *n* [u] **1** (physical) 衰弱; **he was alarmed by the progressive ~ of his eyesight** 他对自己逐渐减弱的视力感到紧张 **2** (in power) 削弱 **3** (of economy) 衰退; (of currency) 贬值; (of exchange rate) 降低

weak-kneed /ˌwiːkˈniːd/ *adj* pej 懦弱的 ‹person, subservience›; **~ agreement** *or* **consent** 屈从

weakling /ˈwiːklɪŋ/ *n* **1** (person) (physically) 弱不禁风的人; (morally) 懦弱的人 **2** (animal) 弱小动物

weakly /ˈwiːkli/
A *adv* **1** (without physical force) 软弱无力地 ‹move, hit› **2** (ineffectually) 淡淡地 ‹smile›; 支吾地 ‹say›; 软弱地 ‹protest, defend›
B *adj* 虚弱的 ‹child, animal›

weakness /ˈwiːknɪs/ *n* **1** [u] (of person, health) 虚弱; (of eyesight, digestion) 弱 **2** [u] (of bond, relationship) 不牢靠; (of purpose, resolution, character) 不坚定; (of ability, team) 差; (of legal case) 薄弱环节 **3** [u] (of structure, joint, beam, foundation) 不牢固; (of defence, alliance) 薄弱 **4** [u] Econ (of demand, currency, market) 疲软; (exchange rate) 弱势; (of economy) 衰退 **5** [c] (failing) 缺陷 **6** [c] (liking) 嗜好; **to have a ~ for the bottle/blondes** 嗜酒/迷恋金发女郎

weak-willed /ˌwiːkˈwɪld/ *adj* 意志薄弱的

weal /wiːl/ *n* 红肿

wealth /welθ/ *n* [u] **1** (money) 钱财; (property, valuables) 财产; **to amass ~** 积聚财富; **to flaunt one's ~** 摆阔; **a show of ~** 炫富 **2** (natural resources) 资源; **the oil ~ of the Gulf** 波斯湾的石油资源 **3** Econ 财富; **national ~** 国民财富 **4** (large amount) 大量; **a ~ of ways to do sth.** 许多方式; **a ~ of experience** 丰富的经验

wealth tax *n* 财富税

wealthy /ˈwelθi/
A *adj* 富裕的; **a ~ man** 有钱人
B *npl* **the ~** 有钱人

wean /wiːn/ *vt* **1** (accustom to solid food) 使…断奶 ‹infant› **2** (accustom to go without) **to ~ sb. off** 使某人戒掉 ‹drugs, alcohol›; **to ~ sb. away from sth.** 使某人远离某物 **3** (influence with) 在…的影响下成长; **he was ~ed on Mozart and Beethoven** 他听着莫扎特和贝多芬的音乐长大

weapon /ˈwepən/
A *n* **1** lit (in fight, battle, war) 武器; **to carry** *or* **bear a ~** 携带武器; **conventional ~(s)** 常规武器 **2** fig (in contest, conflict) 手段 **3** Zool 袭击器官
B *modif* (*also* **weapons**) 武器的 ‹deployment, superiority, expert›; **a ~s manufacturer/factory** 军火商/军工厂

weapon of mass destruction *n* 大规模杀伤性武器

W

weaponry /ˈwepənri/ *n* [u] 武器 [总称]

weapons: ～ inspector *n* [联合国] 武器观察员; **～ testing** *n* [u] 武器测试; **a ～ testing programme** 武器测试计划

wear /weə(r)/

A *vt* (*pt* **wore,** *pp* **worn**) **1** (have on) 穿着 ‹*clothing, shoes*›; 戴着 ‹*hat, glasses, watch, ring*›; 涂抹着 ‹*perfume, suncream, make-up*›; **the old lady wore a shawl around her shoulders** 那位老妇人肩上披着一条披巾; **she was ～ing a ribbon in her hair** 她头发上扎着一条丝带; **to ～ black** (as fashion) 穿着黑衣服; (in mourning) 身着丧服 **2** (have in particular style) 留; **to ～ one's hair long/short** 留长发/短发; **to ～ one's hair in plaits** *or* **pigtails** 梳着辫子 **3** (have growth of) 蓄 ‹*beard, moustache*› **4** (display) 流露; **her face wore a shocked expression** 她脸上露出震惊的表情 **5** (damage by use) 穿破 ‹*garment, shoes*›; 磨损 ‹*carpet, tyre*›; 侵蚀 ‹*stone, wood*› **6** (form through use) 磨出 ‹*hole*›; 踩出 ‹*track*›; «*water*» 冲出 ‹*groove, channel*› **7** Brit colloq (accept) 接受 ‹*attitude, excuse*›; **he wouldn't ～ it** 他不会答应的

B *vi* (*pt* **wore,** *pp* **worn**) **1** (become damaged) «*garment, shoes*» 磨破; «*carpet, tyre*» 磨损; «*stone, wood*» 腐蚀; **to ～ smooth/threadbare** 磨滑/磨破; **to ～ thin** (become threadbare) «*fabric, carpet*» 磨薄; fig (be used up) «*patience*» 渐渐耗尽; (become less convincing) «*excuse, joke*» 变得索然无味 **2** **to ～ well** (withstand use) «*garment*» 耐穿; «*carpet, tyre*» 耐磨 **3** **to ～ well** hum (withstand life) 不显老

C *n* [u] **1** (clothing) 服装; **children's ～** 童装; **casual/formal/designer/maternity ～** 休闲装/正装/名牌服装/孕妇装; **summer/winter ～** 夏装/冬装 **2** (ability to last) 耐用性; **I've had three years' ～ out of these boots** 这双靴子我已经穿了三年了; **there's plenty of ～ in the tyres** 这些轮胎还可以用很久 **3** (use) 使用; **the shoes stretched with ～** 鞋穿得撑大了; **to stand up to ～** 经用; **the worse for ～** colloq (damaged) 用坏的; (drunk) 喝醉的 **4** (damage) 磨损; **～ and tear** 磨损

Phrasal verbs

- **wear away**

A *vt* [**～ sth. away, ～ away sth.**] 磨薄 ‹*metal, wood*›; 磨滑 ‹*facade, bank*›; 磨平 ‹*inscription, tread*›; **over a period of years dripping water has worn away the stone** 年复一年的滴水把石头侵蚀了

B *vi* «*cliff, inscription*» 磨蚀

- **wear down**

A *vt* **1** [**～ sth. down, ～ down sth.**] (damage) 磨短 ‹*heel*›; 磨平 ‹*step, stone*›; 磨坏 ‹*brake linings*› **2** [**～ sb./sth. down, ～ down sb./sth.**] (weaken) 削弱…的意志 ‹*enemy*›; 动摇 ‹*will, resolve*›; **he was eventually worn down by the insistent questioning** 他被连番质问弄得垂头丧气

B *vi* 磨损; **the heels on my shoes have worn down** 我的鞋跟磨短了

- **wear off**

A *vi* **1** (lose effect) «*pain, novelty*» 逐渐消失; **the effect of the anaesthetic was beginning to ～ off** 麻醉剂的药效开始逐渐减退 **2** (come off over time) «*colour, varnish, inscription*» 磨掉

B *vt* [**～ sth. off, ～ off sth.**] 磨去 ‹*glaze, paint, inscription*›

- **wear on** *vi* «*time, winter, life*» 慢慢过去; **as the days/evening worn on** 随着日子/傍晚时间缓慢地过去

- **wear out**

A *vt* **1** [**～ sth. out, ～ out sth.**] (damage) 穿破 ‹*clothes, shoes*›; 磨薄 ‹*fabric, carpet*›; 用坏 ‹*equipment*› **2** [**～ sth. out, ～ out sth.**] (use up) 耗尽 ‹*patience*›; **to ～ out one's welcome** 待得太久而不受欢迎 **3** [**～ sb. out, ～ out sb.**] (tire out) «*child, work, journey*» 使精疲力竭; **to ～ oneself out** 筋疲力尽

B *vi* **1** (become unusable through use) «*clothes, shoes*» 穿破; «*fabric, carpet*» 磨薄; «*equipment*» 用坏 **2** (get used up) «*patience*» 耗尽

- **wear through**

A *vi* «*trousers, sole*» 磨破; «*metal*» 磨损; «*glaze*» 磨掉

B *vt* [**～ sth. through, ～ through sth.**] 磨破 ‹*trousers, sole*›; 磨薄 ‹*metal*›; 磨掉 ‹*glaze*›

wearable /ˈweərəbl/ *adj* 适合穿戴的

wearer /ˈweərə(r)/ *n* 穿戴者; **～s of glasses/wigs** 戴眼镜/假发的人

wearied /ˈwɪərɪd/ *adj* 疲倦的; **to be ～ by a long journey** 因长途旅行而疲惫不堪

wearily /ˈwɪərɪli/ *adv* 疲倦地

weariness /ˈwɪərmɪs/ *n* [u] 疲倦

wearing /ˈweərɪŋ/ *adj* 令人倦怠的 ‹*person, behaviour*›; **to be ～ on the nerves** 令人焦虑

wearisome /ˈwɪərɪsəm/ *adj* 令人厌倦的 ‹*complaints, formalities*›

weary /ˈwɪərɪ/

A *adj* **1** (fatigued, showing fatigue) 疲惫的 ‹*traveller, brain, smile*›; **to be ～ in mind and body** 身心疲惫; **to be ～ of life** 厌倦生活 **2** (tiring) 使人疲劳的 ‹*journey, work, day*›

B *vi* 倦怠; **to ～ of sth./of doing sth.** 对某事物/做某事感到倦怠

C *vt* 使疲惫不堪; **to ～ sb. with tedious details** 用繁冗的细节烦扰某人

weasel /ˈwiːzl/

A *n* 鼬

B *vi* (*pres p etc.* **-ll-** Brit, **-l-** Amer) colloq 推诿; **to ～ out of sth./doing sth.** 逃避某事物/做某事

weasel-faced /ˈwiːzlfeɪst/ *adj* 尖嘴猴腮的

weaselly /ˈwiːzəli/ *adj* **1** lit (weasel-like) 像鼬的 ‹*face, appearance*› **2** fig (deceitful) 推诿的 ‹*argument, language*›; 滑头的 ‹*person*›

weasel words *npl* 推诿话

weather /ˈweðə(r)/

A *n* [u] **1** (meteorological conditions) 天气; **good** *or* **fine ～** 好天气; **windy/rainy ～** 刮风天/下雨天; **sunny/cloudy ～** 晴天/阴天; **～ permitting** 天气好的话; **in all ～s** Brit 不论天气好坏; **whatever the ～** 无论如何; **under the ～** colloq 略有不适; **to make heavy ～ of sth.** 对某事小题大作; **students make such heavy ～ of this question** 学生们把这个问题弄得太复杂了; **～ conditions, the ～ situation** 天气状况 **2** (adverse meteorological conditions) 恶劣天气; **to be exposed to the ～** 经受日晒雨淋 **3** colloq (forecast) **the ～** 天气预报

B *vt* **1** (undergo or cause to undergo change) 使受日晒雨淋; **buildings ～ed by the soot and grime of the industrial revolution** 遭受工业革命的煤烟和污垢侵蚀的建筑物; **her face has been ～ed by the sun** 她的脸晒黑了 **2** (withstand) 经受住 ‹*gale, upheaval, crisis*›; **to ～ the storm** «*ship*» 经受住风暴的袭击; fig «*company, government*» 平安渡过危机

C *vi* «*rock, timber, paintwork*» 遭受日晒雨淋

weather: ～ balloon *n* 气象气球; **～-beaten** *adj* 受风雨侵蚀的 ‹*brick, cliff*›; 饱经风霜的 ‹*face, person*›; **～board** *n* esp Brit **1** [c] (on door) 风雨板; (on wall) 封檐板; **2** [u] (material) 封檐板板材; **a ～board house** 装有封檐板的房子; **～boarding** *n* [u] 封檐板; **～ centre** Brit, **～ bureau** Amer *n* 气象局; **～ chart** *n* = **～ map**; **～cock** *n* 风向标

weathered /ˈweðəd/ *adj* 风化的 ‹*rock*›; 风干的 ‹*timber*›; 日晒雨淋后褪色的 ‹*paintwork*›; 受日晒雨淋侵蚀的 ‹*hills*›; 饱经风霜的 ‹*face*›

weather: ～ eye *n* **to keep a ～ eye on sth./sb.** 密切注视某事物/某人; **to keep a** *or* **one's ～ eye open** 保持警惕; **～ forecast** *n* 天气预报; **～ forecaster** ▸**p. 409** *n* (presenter) 天气预报员; (meteorologist) 气象专家; **～girl** *n* colloq 女天气预报员; **～man** /-mæn/ *n* 男天气预报员; **～ map** *n* 天气图

weatherproof /ˈweðəpruːf/

A *adj* 防风雨的 ‹*garment, shelter, coating*›

B *vt* 对…进行防风雨处理

weather: ～ report *n* = **～ forecast**; **～ satellite** *n* 气象卫星; **～ ship** *n* 气象观测船; **～ station** *n* 气象站; **～strip** *n* [门窗的] 挡风雨条; **～vane** *n* 风向标

weave /wiːv/

A *vt* **1** (*pt* **wove,** *pp* **woven**) Tex (interlace) 织 ‹*wool, silk, cloth, tapestry*›; **some thick mohairs can be difficult to ～** 有些粗马海毛很难织; **to ～ sth. together** 将某物织在一起 **2** (*pt* **wove,** *pp* **woven**) (intertwine) 编 ‹*basket, garland*›; **to ～ sth. from** *or* **out of sth.** 用某物编织某物 **3** (*pt* **wove,** *pp* **woven**) Zool (spin) «*spider*» 结 ‹*web*› **4** (*pt* **wove,** *pp* **woven**) (create from interconnected elements) 编造 ‹*plot, pattern*›; **to ～ one's magic** *or* **a spell (on** *or* **over sb./sth.)** esp Brit (对某人/某物) 施展魔力; **they're hoping the new manager will be able to ～ his magic on the team** 他们希望新经理能给球队带来奇迹 **5** (*pt* **wove,** *pp* **woven**) (put together) 编排 ‹*facts, events*›; **the biography ～s together the various strands of Einstein's life** 这部传记汇集了爱因斯坦的多条人生轨迹 **6** (*pt, pp* **～d**) (pursue) 沿…迂回前行 ‹*course*›; **the river ～s its way across the plain** 河流蜿蜒流过平原; **she ～d a path towards him through the crowd** 她迂回地穿过人群向他走去

B *vi* **1** (*pt* **wove,** *pp* **woven**) Tex 织布 **2** (*pt, pp* **～d**) (pursue twisting course) «*driver, vehicle, river*» 迂回前行; **to ～ in and out** 穿进穿出; **the road ～s through a range of hills** 这条路在丘陵间绕来绕去; **to ～ to and fro** 来回穿梭; **to get weaving** Brit dated colloq 立刻动手; **come on, let's get weaving, or we'll be late** 快点，我们马上动身吧，要不就晚了 **3** (*pt, pp* **～d**) (sway) «*drunk*» 摇摇晃晃; (dodge) «*boxer*» 闪避

C *n* [c and u] 织法; **open** *or* **loose/fine** *or* **close ～** 针孔稀疏/细密的织法

weaver /ˈwiːvə(r)/ ▸**p. 409** *n* 织布工

weaving /ˈwiːvɪŋ/ *n* [u] 织布; **a ～ machine** 织布机

web /web/ *n* **1** Zool **(spider's) ～** 蜘蛛网 **2** fig (complex system) 错综复杂的事物; **a tangled ～ of ropes** 缠结的绳网; **a ～ of lies** 连篇谎话; **a ～ of social/business contacts** 社交网/业务联系网 **3** Zool (membrane) 蹼 **4** Print (roll of paper) 卷筒纸 **5** Ind (wire mesh) [出纸机里的] 铁丝网 **6** **the ～** *or* **Web** Comput 互联网

web: ～ authoring *n* [u] 网页制作; **～-based** *adj* 基于网络的; **～-based course/technology** 网络课程/技术

webbed /webd/ *adj* **1** Zool 有蹼的; **～ feet** 蹼足 **2** Med 蹼状的; **～ fingers/toes** 蹼指/趾 **3** (made from webbing) 网状的 ‹*belt, strap*›

webbing /ˈwebɪŋ/ *n* [u] **1** (fabric) 带状织物; **rucksack ～** 背包带 **2** Mil 武装背负带 **3** Zool (of aquatic animal, swimming bird) 蹼

web: ～ browser *n* 网络浏览器; **～cam** *n* 网络摄像机; **～cast** *n* 网络直播; **～chat** *n* [c and u] 网络聊天; **～ commerce** *n* [u] 网络商务; **～ content provider** *n* 网络内容供应商; **～ crawler** *n* 网络爬虫 [网络搜索软件]; **～ designer** ▸**p. 409** *n* 网页设计师; **～ email** *n* [u] = **～mail**; **～-enable** *vt* 使…能联网 ‹*application, process*›; **～-enabled** *adj* 能上网的; **a ～-enabled mobile phone** 可上网移动电话; **～-fed** *adj* 卷筒纸给纸的 ‹*machine, printing*›; **～ foot** *n* 蹼足; **～ hosting** *n* [u] 网页寄存

webify /ˈwebɪfaɪ/ *vt* colloq (change to web format) 将…转换成网络格式 ‹*text, file*›; (make available on the Internet) 使…网络化 ‹*business, service*›

webinar /ˈwebɪnɑː(r)/ *n* 网上研讨会

W

web link *n* 网络链接

webliography /ˌweblɪˈɒgrəfi/ *n* colloq 网络书目

web: ~log *n* 博客; **~mail** *n* [u] 网络邮件服务; **~master** *n* 网络管理员; **~ offset** *n* [u] 卷筒纸胶印; **~ page** *n* 网页; **~phone** *n* 网络电话; **~ presence** *n* 网络存在[指通过网络建立的个人或公司等的信息]; **~ press** *n* 卷筒纸印刷机; **~ ring** *n* 网盟 [相互链接的相同主题内容的网站集合]; **~ search** *n* 网络信息搜索; **~ server** *n* 互联网服务器; **~ site** *n* 网址; **~space** *n* [u] 网站空间; **~ spider** *n* = **~ crawler**

webzine /ˈwebziːn/ *n* 网络杂志

wed /wed/

A *vt* (*pres p* **-dd-**; *pt, pp* **~ded** *or* **wed**) **1** esp formal or archaic (get married to) 与…结婚 **2** esp formal or archaic (join in marriage) «*clergy, registrar*» 使…结婚 ‹*couple*› **3** esp formal or archaic (give in marriage) «*father, guardian*» 嫁出 ‹*daughter*› **4** fig (unite closely) 融汇 ‹*qualities, virtues*›; **the design ~s elegance with a sense of space** 这一设计将优雅与空间感融为一体

B *vi* (*pres p etc.* **-dd-**) «*couple*» 结婚

Wed. ▸**p. 182** *abbr* = **Wednesday**

we'd /wiːd/ colloq **1** = **we had** ▸**have** **2** = **we should** ▸**should** **3** = **we would** ▸**would**

wedded /ˈwedɪd/ *adj* **1** esp formal or archaic (married) 已婚的 ‹*couple*›; 婚姻的 ‹*bliss*› **2** (devoted) **to be ~ to sth.** 一心扑到…上 ‹*work, career*›; 执著于 ‹*belief, system, tradition*›

wedding /ˈwedɪŋ/ *n* 婚礼; **a church ~** 在教堂举行的婚礼; **a ~ cake/present** 婚礼蛋糕/结婚礼物

wedding: ~ anniversary *n* 结婚纪念日; **~ band** *n* esp Amer **= ~ ring**; **~ bells** *npl* 婚礼钟声; **you two are looking very radiant these days; do I hear ~ bells?** 你们俩这些日子看上去喜气洋洋; 是不是要结婚了?; **~ breakfast** *n* Brit 婚宴; **~ day** *n* (day of wedding) 结婚日; (anniversary of wedding) 结婚纪念日; **~ dress, ~ gown** *ns* 婚纱; **~ guest** *n* 婚礼来宾; **~ invitation** *n* 结婚请柬; **~ march** *n* 婚礼进行曲; **~ night** *n* 新婚之夜; **~ reception** *n* 婚宴; **~ ring** *n* 结婚戒指; **~ vows** *npl* 婚誓

wedge /wedʒ/

A *n* **1** (block for separating) 楔子; **to drive a ~ between A and B** (separate) 将某人/某物分开; fig (cause disagreement between) 在某人/某物之间挑起不和; **a ~ shape** 楔形; ▸**thin A2** **2** (piece) 楔形物; **a big ~ of cake** 一大角蛋糕 **3** **~** (formation) 楔形队形 **4** (golf club) 楔形铁头球杆 **5** (shoe) **~s, ~ shoes** 坡跟鞋 **6** (heel) 坡跟; **shoes with ~ heels** 坡跟鞋 **7** (in rock climbing) 岩石楔 **8** Meteorol 高压楔; **a ~ of high pressure** 高压楔

B *vt* **1** (secure) 把…楔住 ‹*door, window*›; **to ~ sth. shut/open** 用楔子卡住某物让它开着/关着 **2** (force) 楔入; **to ~ sb./sth. against sth.** 将某人/某物抵在某物上; **the boat was ~d between the rocks** 船卡在了岩石之间; **the salesman ~d his foot in the door to prevent me closing it** 推销员伸出脚把门卡住不让我关

C *v refl* **to ~ oneself** 强行挤入; **she ~d herself into the passenger seat** 她挤进了乘客座椅; **to get oneself ~d** 被夹住

Phrasal verb

- **wedge in** *vt* [**~ sb./sth. in, ~ in sb./sth.**] 楔入; **I can't get this cork out: it's ~d firmly in** 我取不出这个软木塞, 它塞得太紧了

wedge: ~-heeled, ~-soled *adjs* 坡跟的; **~-shaped** *adj* 楔形的

wedlock /ˈwedlɒk/ *n* [u] formal 婚姻; **to enter into ~** 结婚; **out of ~** 婚外的; **to have a child out of ~** 有私生子

Wednesday /ˈwenzdeɪ, -di/ ▸**p. 182** *n* 星期三; **on ~** 在星期三; **on ~s/every ~** 每周星期三; **~ morning/afternoon/night** 星期三早晨/下午/晚上; **this/last/next ~** 本周/上周/下周三

wee¹ /wiː/ *adj* esp Scot 很小的 ‹*baby, drop*›; **a ~ bit** 一点点; **in the ~ small hours** 在凌晨一两点钟

wee² esp child lang

A *vi* 尿尿

B *n* **1** [u] (urine) 尿 **2** [c] (act) 尿尿; **to have** *or* **do a ~** 尿尿

weed /wiːd/

A *n* **1** [c] (wild plant) 野草; **overgrown with ~s** 杂草丛生的; **to pull up ~s** 拔除杂草 **2** [u] (water plant) 水草 **3** [c] Brit colloq (weakling) (lanky, delicate-looking person) 瘦弱的人; (person lacking stamina) 懦弱的人; **don't be such a ~!** 别这么娇滴滴的! **4** [u] colloq (marijuana) 大麻 **5** [u] colloq (tobacco) **the ~** 香烟

B *vt* 给…除杂草 ‹*garden, vegetable plot*›

C *vi* «*gardener*» 除草

Phrasal verb

- **weed out** *vt* [**~ sb./sth. out, ~ out sb./sth.**] 淘汰 ‹*troublemakers, applicants*›; 删去 ‹*errors*›

weeding /ˈwiːdɪŋ/ *n* [u] 除草

weedkiller /ˈwiːdkɪlə(r)/ *n* [c and u] 除草剂

weedy /ˈwiːdi/ *adj* **1** (full of or covered with weeds) 杂草丛生的 **2** Brit colloq pej (feeble) 瘦弱的 ‹*youth*›; 体弱的 ‹*appearance*›

week /wiːk/ ▸**p. 182** *n* **1** (Sunday to Saturday or Monday to Sunday) 星期; **this/last/next ~** 本/上/下星期; **the end of the ~** 周末; **~ in, ~ out** 每个星期都; **to not know what day of the ~ it is** 稀里糊涂; **to knock sb. into the middle of next ~** dated colloq 打得某人分不清东西南北 **2** (seven-day period) 一周; **for six ~s** 达六周; **in a ~** 一周之内; **a ~ today** Brit, **today ~** Brit, **a ~ from today** Amer 一周后的今天; **Monday ~** Brit 一周后的星期一; **a ~ tomorrow** Brit, **tomorrow ~** Brit, **a ~ from tomorrow** Amer 一周后的明天; **~s ago** 几个星期以前; **~s ahead** 提前几周; **a ~'s holiday** 一周的假期; **~s and ~s, ~ after ~** 一周接一周 **3** (Monday to Friday) [与周末相对的] 工作周; **in the ~** Brit 在工作周期间 **4** (working time) [周一到周五的] 工作时间; **a 35-hour ~** 35 小时的周工作时间

weekday /ˈwiːkdeɪ/ ▸**p. 182** *n* 周日 [指星期一至星期五的任何一天]; **on ~s** 在周一至周五; **~ working hours** 工作日上班时间; **a ~ programme** 周日节目

weekend /ˌwiːkˈend, Amer ˈwiːk-/

A *n* 周末; **at** Brit *or* **on** Amer **the ~** 在周末; **a long ~** 长周末; **a ~ break/visit** 周末休假/拜访; **a ~ cottage/retreat** 周末度假小别墅/胜地

B *vi* 度周末

weekender /ˌwiːkˈendə(r), Amer ˈwiːk-/ *n* 周末游客 [尤指到乡下住宅度周末的人]

weekend warrior *n* Amer colloq 周末战士 [指仅在业余时间参加活动的人]

weekly /ˈwiːkli/

A *adj* **1** (once a week) 每周一次的 ‹*visit, flight*›; **a ~ magazine/newspaper** 周刊/周报 **2** (calculated by the week) 按周计算的 ‹*income, contract*›

B *adv* 每周; **twice ~** 一周两次

C *n* (newspaper) 周报; (magazine) 周刊

week-old *adj* 一周大的 ‹*baby, chick*›; 一周前的 ‹*newspaper, food*›

weenie /ˈwiːni/ *n* Amer colloq = **wiener**

weeny /ˈwiːni/ *adj* colloq 极小的 ‹*amount, object*›; **a ~ bit** 一点儿

weep /wiːp/

A *vi* (*pt, pp* **wept**) **1** (cry) 哭泣; **they wept with relief** 他们欣慰地哭了; **to ~ for sb./sth.** 为某人/某事物哭泣 **2** (ooze) «*wound, blister*» 流脓; «*pipe, joint*» 渗出液体

B *vt* (*pt, pp* **wept**) 流下 ‹*tears*›; **to ~ one's eyes out** 大哭

C *n* 哭泣; **to have a ~** 哭一场

weepie /ˈwiːpi/ *n* colloq (film) 伤感电影; (book) 伤感作品; (song) 伤感歌曲

weeping /ˈwiːpɪŋ/

A *n* [u] 哭泣

B *adj* **1** (crying) 哭泣的 **2** (oozing) 流脓的 ‹*wound, blister*›

weeping willow *n* 垂柳

weepy /ˈwiːpi/

A *adj* colloq **1** (tearful) 泪汪汪的 ‹*child*›; **a ~ voice** 哭腔 **2** (sentimental) 赚人泪水的 ‹*book, film*›

B *n* colloq = **weepie**

weevil /ˈwiːvɪl/ *n* 象鼻虫

wee-wee /ˈwiːwiː/ *n, vi* esp Brit child lang = **wee²**

weft /weft/ *n* **the ~** 纬纱; **the warp and ~ of the fabric** 织物的经纬线

weigh /weɪ/

A *vt* **1** (have weight of) «*person, object*» 有…重 ‹*ounce, stone, kilo*›; **what** *or* **how much do you ~?** 你体重多少? **2** (measure weight of) 称…的重量 ‹*baby, object*›; **to ~ one's suitcase on the scales** 在磅秤上称手提箱的重量 **3** (balance in hands) 掂…的重量 ‹*object*› **4** (consider carefully) 权衡 ‹*factors, advantages, cost*›; **to ~ one's words** 斟酌词句; **to ~ the benefits against the risks** 权衡利益和风险 **5** Naut **to ~ anchor** 起锚

B *vi* **1** (be burdensome) «*fear, memory*» 重压; **the guilt ~ed heavily** 心里感到深深的内疚; **to ~ on sb.'s conscience** 使某人良心不安 **2** (have influence) «*argument, evidence*» 有影响; **to ~ heavily/very little with sb.** 对某人影响很大/很小; **to ~ in sb.'s/sth.'s favour** 对某人/某事物有利

Phrasal verbs

- **weigh down** *vt* [**~ sb./sth. down, ~ down sb./sth.**] **1** (be heavy on) 压得…难以移动 ‹*person, vehicle, boat*›; 压弯 ‹*branch, tree*› **2** (oppress) «*debt, work*» 使…心情沉重 ‹*person*›; **to be ~ed down with anxiety** 忧心忡忡
- **weigh in** *vi* **1** Sport «*jockey, boxer*» 赛前称体重; **he ~ed in at 60kg** 他在赛前所称的体重为60公斤 **2** colloq (intervene with opinion) 发表有分量的意见; **to ~ in with sth.** 发表 ‹*opinion*›; 提出 ‹*suggestion, criticism*› **3** colloq (contribute with help) 参与帮助; **to ~ in with** 提供 ‹*money, aid*›
- **weigh out** *vt* [**~ sth. out, ~ out sth.**] 称出 ‹*ingredients, quantity*›
- **weigh up** *vt* [**~ sb./sth. up, ~ up sb./sth.**] 掂量 ‹*opponent, prospects*›; **after ~ing things up, I decided to hand in my resignation** 经过仔细权衡, 我决定递交辞呈

weigh: ~bridge *n* 地磅; **~-in** *n* 赛前称体重

weighing machine /ˈweɪɪŋ məˌʃiːn/ *n* (for people) 体重计; (for luggage, freight) 磅秤

weight /weɪt/

A *n* **1** [c and u] (measure of heaviness) (of person) 体重; (of objects) 重量; **to be the same ~** 重量相同; **by ~** 按重量; ▸**gold A1** **2** [u] (heaviness) 重; **under the ~ (of sb./sth.)** 在 (某人/某物的) 重压之下; **to take the ~ off one's feet** colloq 坐下歇歇脚 **3** [c] (heavy object) 重物; **what a ~!** 好重的东西! **4** [c] (immobilizing object) [起推动或固定作用的] 重体; **~s on a fishing line** 钓线上的坠; **to stop the machine and adjust its ~s** 把机器停下来调整一下压铁 **5** [c] (burden) 负担; **to be a ~ off one's mind** *or* **shoulders** 如释重负 **6** [u] (influence) 影响; **to carry ~ (with sb./sth.)** (对某人/某事物) 有影响; **what she says carries ~** 她所说的话有分量; **to add** *or* **give** *or* **lend ~ to sth.** 增加某事物的影响力;

W

to throw *or* **put one's ～ behind sb./sth.** 鼎力支持某人/某事物 **7** [u] (importance) 重要性; (preponderance) 分量; **to give** *or* **attach ～ to sth.** 重视某事物; **the ～ of evidence against her is overwhelming** 对她不利的证据无可辩驳; **the sheer ～ of medical opinion** 医生意见的绝对重要性; **(sheer) ～ of numbers** (纯粹的) 人多势众 **8** [c] (unit for weighing) 重量单位; **～s and measures** 度量衡 **9** [u] (system for weighing) 衡制; **imperial/metric ～** 英制/公制重量 **10** [c] (piece of metal for weighing) 砝码; **a set of ～s** 一组砝码 **11** [c] (used in exercising) (dumbbell) 哑铃; (barbell) 杠铃; (disc) 杠铃片; **to lift ～s** (dumbbells) 举哑铃; (barbells) 举杠铃 **12** [c] Sport (in shot-put) 铅球

B *vt* **1** (make heavier) 增加…的重量 ‹*line, dart, hem*›; **the fishing nets are ～ed with lead** 渔网是用铅坠下沉的 **2** (give importance to) 使…加权 ‹*factor, index, variable*›; **a ～ed vote** 加权选票; **a ～ed grade** Amer 加权分数 **3** (bias) 使…有倾向 ‹*evidence, argument*›; **to ～ sth. against/in favour of** *or* **towards sb./sth.** 使某事物对某人/某事物不利/有利

Phrasal verb

• **weight down** *vt* [～ **sb./sth. down, ～ down sb./sth.**] 用重物压住 ‹*groundsheet, tarpaulin, covering*›

weight gain *n* [u and c] 体重增加

weightiness /ˈweɪtɪnɪs/ *n* [u] 重要性

weighting /ˈweɪtɪŋ/ *n* [u and c] (of index, variable) 加权值; Sch (of marks) 分值; Brit (of salary scale) 额外津贴; **to give due ～ to quality** 对于质量给予应有的重视

weightless /ˈweɪtlɪs/ *adj* 失重的 ‹*environment, state*›; fig 似无重量的 ‹*body, object*›; 飘逸的 ‹*movement, grace*›

weightlessness /ˈweɪtlɪsnɪs/ *n* [u] 失重; fig 飘逸

weight: ～lifter *n* 举重运动员; **～lifting** ▸**p. 307** *n* [u] 举重; **～ limit** *n* 限重; **～ loss** *n* [u] 体重下降; **～ machine** *n* 举重训练机; **～ problem** *n* [体重] 超重; **～-train** *vi* 进行举重锻炼; **～ training** ▸**p. 307** *n* [u] 举重锻练; **～ watcher** *n* 节食减肥者

weighty /ˈweɪtɪ/ *adj* **1** (heavy) 重的 ‹*object, person*›; fig 沉重的 ‹*responsibility, burden*› **2** (serious) 重要的 ‹*decision, matter*›; **a ～ article** 很有分量的文章

weir /wɪə(r)/ *n* **1** (dam) 拦河坝 **2** Fishg 鱼梁

weird /wɪəd/ *adj* **1** (eerie) 怪异的 **2** colloq (odd) 古怪的; **a ～ and wonderful idea/story/invention** 稀奇古怪的念头/诡谲的故事/奇妙的发明

weirdly /ˈwɪədlɪ/ *adj* **1** (eerily) 诡异地 **2** colloq (oddly) 古怪地

weirdness /ˈwɪədnɪs/ *n* [u] **1** (eeriness) 怪诞 **2** colloq (oddness of person, behaviour) 古怪

weirdo /ˈwɪədəʊ/ *n* colloq 怪人

welcome /ˈwelkəm/

A *n* **1** [c and u] (greeting) 欢迎; **to give sb. a warm ～** 热烈欢迎某人; **to bid sb. ～, to extend a ～ to sb.** formal 向某人表示欢迎; **a ～ speech** 欢迎辞 **2** [c] (reaction) 反响; **they gave the news a guarded ～** 他们对那条新闻反应谨慎

B *adj* **1** (much appreciated) 受欢迎的 ‹*news, guest, gift*›; **the fine weather made a ～ change** 天气转好，令人心旷神怡; **to make sb. feel ～** 使某人感到受欢迎 **2** esp Amer (acknowledging thanks) **you're ～** 不用谢 **3** colloq (free) 可随意的; **you're ～ to use the phone** 你可以随意使用电话 **4** colloq (allowed to have) 尽管…好了; **if you want to finish my fries, you're ～ to them** 如果你想吃完我的炸薯条，你尽管吃好了

C *excl* 欢迎; **～ on board** *or* **aboard!** (on boat) 欢迎上船! ; (on plane) 欢迎登机! ; **～ to the Town Hall!** 欢迎来到市政厅!

D *vt* **1** (greet) 欢迎 ‹*visitor, guest*›; **to ～ sb. to sth.** 欢迎某人到某处; **to ～ sb. with open arms** 热情地欢迎某人 **2** (appreciate) 乐于接受 ‹*criticism, donation, application*›; **I'd ～ a hot drink** 我想来一杯热饮 **3** (approve of) 赞同 ‹*decision, change*›

Phrasal verbs

• **welcome back** *vt* [～ **sb. back, ～ back sb.**] 欢迎…回来

• **welcome in** *vt* [～ **sb. in, ～ in sb.**] 欢迎…进来

welcome mat *n* 门毯; **to lay** *or* **put** *or* **roll out the ～ (for sb.)** esp Amer (warmly welcome) 热烈欢迎 (某人) ; (try to attract) 设法吸引 (某人)

welcoming /ˈwelkəmɪŋ/ *adj* **1** (greeting formally) 欢迎的 ‹*ceremony, party, speech*› **2** (warm) 热情的 ‹*smile, embrace*›

weld /weld/

A *vt* 焊接 ‹*metal, join, part*›; 熔接 ‹*plastic, seam*›; **to ～ into a unified whole** fig 统一 ‹*nation*›; 整合 ‹*workforce*›; 使…团结 ‹*ideas*›

B *n* (in metal) 焊接点; (in plastic) 熔接处

Phrasal verb

• **weld on** *vt* [～ **sth. on, ～ on sth.**] 焊接上

welded /ˈweldɪd/ *adj* 焊接的 ‹*unit, join, metal*›

welder /ˈweldə(r)/ ▸**p. 409** *n* **1** (person) 焊工 **2** (tool) 焊机

welding /ˈweldɪŋ/ *n* [u] **1** (joining) (of metal) 焊接; (of plastic) 熔接; **a ～ torch** 焊枪 **2** (result) 焊接件 **3** fig (fusion) (of ideas) 整合; (of people, group) 团结

welfare /ˈwelfeə(r)/ *n* [u] **1** (well-being) 福祉; **to be concerned about/responsible for sb.'s ～** 关心某人的幸福/对某人的幸福负责 **2** (state assistance) 福利; **to receive/go on ～** 接受福利救济/靠福利救济生活; **a ～ centre** 福利中心

welfare: ～ assistant ▸**p. 409** *n* Brit 学生生活助理; **～ benefit** *n* [u and c] 福利救济金; **～ department** *n* 福利部门; **～ mother** *n* Amer 接受福利救济的母亲; **～ officer** ▸**p. 409** *n* Amer 福利事务官员; Brit 学校后勤人员; **～ payment** *n* = **～ benefit**; **～ recipient** *n* 福利金接受者; **～ rights adviser** ▸**p. 409** *n* Brit 福利权利咨询员; **～ services** *npl* 福利服务; **～ state** *n* **1** (system) **the ～ state** 福利制度; **a ～ state mentality** pej 福利制度依赖心理; **2** (country) 福利国家; **～ work** *n* [u] 福利工作; **～ worker** ▸**p. 409** *n* 福利工作者

welfarism /ˈwelfeərɪzəm/ *n* [u] 福利主义

welfarist /ˈwelfeərɪst/

A *adj* 福利主义的 ‹*state, policy*›

B *n* 福利主义者

ℹ Weights

■ Both the metric system and the traditional Chinese system of weights are commonly used in China.

Metric system

1 tonne 公吨
= 1,000 kilograms 千克 / 公斤

1 kilogram (kg) 千克 / 公斤
= 1,000 grams 克

1 gram (g) 克
= 1,000 milligrams 毫克

Chinese weights system

1 qian 钱
= 0.1 liang 两
= 5 grams 克

1 liang 两
= 10 qian 钱
= 0.1 jin 斤
= 50 grams 克

1 jin 斤
= 10 liang 两
= 500 grams 克
= 0.5 kilogram 千克 / 公斤

Avoirdupois system

ounce (oz)	盎司
pound (lb)	磅
stone (st)	英石
quarter	夸特
hundredweight (cwt)	英担
ton	吨
short ton	短吨 (美吨)
long ton	长吨 (英吨)

People

What's his weight?
= 他的体重是多少?

How much does he weigh?
= 他有多重?

He weighs 11 stone
= 他重 11 英石

His weight is 70 kilograms
= 他的体重是 70 公斤

Things

How heavy is the luggage?
= 行李多重?

How much does the box weigh?
= 箱子有多重?

It weighs about 11 kilograms
= 大约重 11 公斤

It is exactly 15 pounds
= 刚好重 15 磅

A weighs more than B
or ***A is heavier than B***
= A 比 B 重

A weighs less than B
or ***A is lighter than B***
= A 比 B 轻

A is as heavy as B
or ***A is the same weight as B***
or ***A and B are the same weight***
= A 和 B 一样重

It is sold by the pound
= 这是按磅卖的

■ Note the translation of these examples:

5 kilos of rice
= 5 公斤米

300 grams of strawberries
= 300 克草莓

a 7-ounce orange
= 一个 7 盎司的橘子

a 20-kilo pack of rice
= 一袋 20 公斤重的米

a pack of noodles, 2 jin in weight
= 一袋面条，重 2 斤

well¹ /wel/

A *adj* (*comp* **better,** *superl* **best**) *usu pred* **1** (in good health) 健康的; **are you ~?** 你身体好吗？; **how is he? — as ~ as can be expected** 他好吗？——好极了; **to be ~ again** 康复; **to get ~** 身体好起来; **get ~ soon!** 愿早日康复！; **he didn't look (at all) ~** 他看上去身体（很）不好; **he's not a ~ man** 他这人身体不好 **2** (in satisfactory state) 好的; **all is ~** 一切都好; **I hope all is ~ with you** 我希望你万事如意; **all being ~** 如果一切顺利; **all being ~, I'll be home by six** 如果一切顺利，我6点钟之前可以到家; **that's all very ~, but ...** 那当然很好，但是…; **it's all very ~ to laugh/go on strike, but ...** 笑起来/罢工倒很容易，可是…; **(all) ~ and good** 挺好; **if you think you can do it, that's ~ and good** 如果你认为你自己能处理，那也好; **all's ~ that ends well** Prov 结果好就一切都好 **3** (advisable) 可取的; **it would be just as ~ (for sb.) to do sth.** （某人）最好还是做某事; **it would be just as ~ to check** 最好还是核实一下; **it might be just as ~ (for sb.) to do sth.** （某人）还是做某事的好; **it might be just as ~ to telephone** 不妨打个电话 **4** (fortunate) 幸运的; **it's just as ~ (for sb.) (that ...)** （对某人来说）幸好（…）; **it was just as ~ for him that the shops were still open** 他还算幸运，商店还开着; **it's just as ~ you're not hungry, because ...** 幸好你不饿，因为…; **the flight was delayed, which was just as ~** 幸亏航班推迟了

B *adv* (*comp* **better,** *superl* **best**) **1** (satisfactorily) 好; **to work/sleep ~** 工作好/睡得好; **he isn't eating very ~** 他胃口不好; **these scissors cut ~** 这把剪刀好使; **a ~-organized conference** 组织良好的会议; **to be doing ~** (in good health) 身体健康; (recovering) 正在康复; **mother and baby are both doing ~** (after birth) 母子平安; **to leave or let ~ alone** 不管闲事; **~ done!** 干得好！; **~ played!** 好球！ **2** (successfully) 顺利地; **to go ~** «*situation, event*» 进展顺利; **if all goes ~ ...** 如果一切顺利…; **to work ~** «*system*» 运行顺利; **to do ~** «*person*» 做得好; **to do ~ at school/in an exam** 在学校里学习/考试成绩好; **he will do ~** 他会有出息的; **to be ~ out of sth.** Brit colloq 幸亏未卷入某事; **it's a risky business; you're ~ out of it** 这是个危险的行当，幸好你脱身了 **3** (profitably) 有利地; **to do (quite) ~ out of sth.** 从某事物中获益（丰厚）; **to do quite ~ out of the war** 大发战争财; **to do ~ for oneself** (get rich) 致富; **to do oneself ~** 养尊处优 **4** (appropriately) 合适地; **to be ~ judged/matched** 判断很准确/很相配; **to do ~ to do sth.** 做某事很明智; **he would do ~ to remember that ...** 他最好记住… **5** (kindly) 善意地; **to treat sb. ~** 对某人友善; **to do ~ by sb.** dated (treat generously) 对某人很慷慨 **6** (favourably) 赞成地; **to speak/think ~ of sb./sth.** 对某人/某事说好话/评价高; **to be ~ received/regarded** 受到好评/赞赏 **7** (with equanimity) 平静地; **to take sth. ~** 平静地接受某事物; **to respond ~ to sth.** 对某事物反应平静 **8** (completely) 完全地; **to mix ~** 充分搅拌; **'shake ~'** (on bottle label) "摇匀" **9** (to high degree) 彻底地; **to know sth./sb. ~** 十分了解某事物/某人; **he's ~ able to take care of himself** 他完全能够自理; **to be ~ worth seeing** 很值得一看; **~ and truly** Brit colloq 完全; **to be ~ and truly lost** 完全迷路了; **to be ~ up in sth.** Brit colloq 非常熟悉某事物 **10** (by a large amount) 远远地; **to be ~ above/below average** 远远高于/低于平均数; **to be ~ over thirty/100 years old** 远不止30/100岁; **to be ~ back from the road** 远离公路; **temperatures are ~ up in the twenties** 温度飙升到了20多度; **to go on ~ into the night** 一直持续到深夜; **to remain cold ~ into May** 寒冷一直持续到5月; **to be active ~ into one's eighties** 一直活跃到80多岁 **11** (probably) 很可能; **you may (very) ~ be right** 你很可能是对的; **it may ~ be that ...** 很可能… **12** (easily) 轻易地; **she can ~ afford to pay for it** 她完全买得起; **I can ~ believe it!** 这事我并不觉得意外！ **13** (with good reason) 应该; **I can't very ~ leave now** 我现在离开不太合适; **she looked shocked, as ~ she might** 她看上去很震惊，这是理所当然的; **how did he get in? — you may ~ ask!** 他是怎么进去的？——你问得好！ **14** (as best course of action) [表示最好做某事]; **we may as ~ go home** 我们还是回家的好; **we might just as ~ have stayed at home** 我们当初还不如待在家里; **shall I shut the door? — you might as ~** 我把门关上好吗？——你不妨关上吧 **15** Brit colloq (very) 非常; **it was ~ good** or **~ bad!** 太好了！

C *excl* **1** (expressing surprise, anger) 啊 [表示惊奇、愤怒]; **~, really!** 啊，真是的！; **~, who would have thought it!** 哎呀，谁会想到那儿去呢！; **~ I never, look who's here!** 天哪，看看谁在这儿呀！; **~, ~, ~, what have we here?** 哎呀，呀，呀，这是什么呀？; **~, ~, ~, if it isn't my old friend John!** 哟，哟，哟，那不正是我的老朋友约翰吗！ **2** (expressing relief, resignation) 好啦 [表示宽慰、让步]; **~, thank goodness that's over!** 好啦，谢天谢地，这事总算过去了！; **~, that's too bad** 唉，太倒霉了; **oh ~, there's nothing I can do about it** 算啦，我对此事毫无办法 **3** (expressing uncertainty, dismissiveness) 哦 [表示不肯定、不感兴趣]; **~, I think so** 哦，我想是吧; **she called me a fool — ~, so what?** 她叫我傻子——哦，那又怎么样？ **4** (expressing reluctant agreement) 好吧 [表示勉强同意]; **~, you may be right** 好吧，可能你是对的; **~, you have a point, but ...** 是啊，你有道理，但是… **5** (after pause, continuing thought, in conclusion) 那么 [表示停顿]; **~, as I was saying, ...** 嗯，正如我刚才说的，…; **he said he'd kill himself — ~, did he?** 他说他要自杀——那么他自杀了吗？; **~ then, what's the problem?** 那么，问题出在什么地方呢？ **6** (modifying statement) 对了 [表示更正刚说过的话]; **she is four, ~, four and a half to be precise** 她4个月，对了，准确地说，是4个半月大 **7** (marking end) 就这样 [表示结束交谈]; **~, I'd better be going now** 就这样，我现在该走了

D **as well** *adv phr* 也; **is he coming as ~?** 他也来吗？; **you know as ~ as I do ...** 你和我一样清楚…; **he already had four dogs, and now he has two cats as ~** 他已经有4条狗了，现在又有了两只猫

E **as well as** *prep phr, conj phr* 除…之外; **to work on Saturday as ~ as on Sunday** 星期天和星期六都工作; **you know as ~ as I do** 你我都知道; **by day as ~ as by night** 在白天和黑夜; **as ~ as doing sth.** 除做某事之外; **to run a business as ~ as bringing up four children** 不仅抚养4个孩子，而且还经营一家公司

well²

A *n* **1** (for water) 水井; **to dig/drill/sink a ~** 挖井/钻井/掘井 **2** (for oil) 油井; (for gas) 气井 **3** (for lift) 升降机井 **4** (for stairs) 楼梯通风井 **5** (for light, air) 通风采光井 **6** Brit Jur 工作人员席 **7** (for ink) 墨水槽 **8** (depression) 凹槽 **9** fig (source) 源泉; **to be a ~ of information about sth.** 对某事如数家珍

B *vi* **1** = **well up** **2** = **well out**

Phrasal verbs

- **well out** *vi* «*water, blood*» 涌出
- **well up** *vi* **1** lit «*water*» 冒出; **tears ~ed up in my eyes** 我热泪盈眶 **2** fig «*emotion, frustration*» 进发; **when he heard the news, joy ~ed up within him** 他听到这个消息后内心充满喜悦

we'll /wɪəl/ colloq **1** = **we shall** ▸**shall** **2** = **we will** ▸**will¹**

well-appointed *adj* 陈设讲究的 ‹*building, room*›

well-attended *adj* 有许多人出席的

well-behaved *adj* 行为端正的 ‹*person*›; 守秩序的 ‹*audience*›; 听话的 ‹*child, animal*›

well-being *n* [u] 康乐; **one's mental/physical/financial ~** 心理健康/身体健康/经济宽裕

well-built *adj* (well-constructed) 坚固的 ‹*building*›; 制造精良的 ‹*car, table*›; (sturdy) 强健的 ‹*person, body*›

well-chosen *adj* 精心挑选的 ‹*example, illustration*›; **a few ~ words** 几句仔细斟酌过的话

well-developed *adj* **1** (fully grown) 发育良好的 ‹*organism, organ*›; (shapely) 丰满匀称的 ‹*breasts*›; **~ muscles** 发达的肌肉 **2** (well thought out, devised) 完善的 ‹*plan, theory, system*›; 结构完整的 ‹*plot, story*›; **a ~ character** 刻画完美的人物 **3** (acute) 敏锐的 ‹*instinct, sense*›; (advanced) 高超的 ‹*skill*› **4** Econ 发达的 ‹*country*›; 健全的 ‹*industry, firm*›

well-disciplined *adj* 训练有素的 ‹*person, army, team*›

well-dressed *adj* 穿着讲究的

well-earned *adj* 应有的 ‹*rest*›; 当之无愧的 ‹*reputation, victory*›

well-educated *adj* 有教养的

well-fed *adj* 吃得好的

well-formed *adj* **1** (well-proportioned) 匀称的; **a ~ jaw-line** 线条优美的下颌轮廓 **2** Ling 符合语法规则的 ‹*sentence, phrase*› **3** Comput 格式正确的 ‹*document*›

well-founded *adj* 有根据的 ‹*suspicion, rumour, criticism*›; 有理由的 ‹*fear*›

wellhead /ˈwelhed/ *n* **1** (of spring) 泉源; (of stream) 水源 **2** (structure) [尤指油井或气井的] 井楼

well-heeled *adj* colloq 有钱的

well-hung *adj* colloq hum 阳具粗大的 ‹*man*›

well-informed *adj* 见多识广的 ‹*person*›; 有见识的 ‹*judgement, decision*›; **~ sources** 消息灵通人士

Wellington /ˈwelɪŋtən/ *pr n* 惠灵顿

wellington /ˈwelɪŋtən/ *n* Brit 威灵顿长筒靴; **a pair of ~s** or **~ boots** 一双长筒靴

well-intentioned *adj* 善意的 ‹*person*›; 出于好意的 ‹*actions, advice*›

well-judged *adj* 得当的 ‹*statement, speech, performance*›; 明智的 ‹*decision, choice*›; **the fielder made a ~ catch** 外场手准确扑到了球

well-kept *adj* **1** (well-maintained) 悉心照管的 ‹*garden, house*› **2** (undisclosed) 严守的 ‹*secret*›

well-known *adj* **1** (famous) 著名的 **2** (widely accepted) 众所周知的; **it is well known that ...** 众所周知，…

well-liked *adj* 深受喜爱的 ‹*person*›

well-made *adj* (well constructed) 制作精良的 ‹*product*›; 做工考究的 ‹*clothes*›; (skilfully made) 构思巧妙的 ‹*film*›; **a ~ road/house** 修建得很好的路/房子

well-meaning *adj* 善意的 ‹*person*›; 出于好心的 ‹*attempt, gesture*›

well-meant *adj* 善意的 ‹*advice, attempt*›

wellness /ˈwelnɪs/ *n* [u] 健康; **a ~ programme** 健身计划

wellness centre *n* 健身中心

well-nigh *adj* liter or archaic 几乎; **~ impossible** 几乎不可能的

well-off

A *adj* **1** (wealthy) 富裕的 **2** *pred* (fortunate) 境遇好的; **they were well off without her** 没有她，他们过得很好 **3** *pred* (well provided) **to be well off for sth.** 有充裕的某物

B *n + v pl* **the ~** 富人

well-organized *adj* 有条理的 ‹*person, group*›; 组织良好的 ‹*system, layout*›
well-paid *adj* 报酬优厚的; **a ~ job** 高薪工作
well-prepared *adj* 准备就绪的
well-qualified *adj* 完全有资格的; **to be well qualified to do sth.** 完全有能力做某事
well-read /ˌwelˈred/ *adj* (widely-read) 博览群书的; (well-informed) 通晓的
well-respected *adj* 深受尊重的 ‹*person*›
well-set *adj* **1** (solid) 牢固的 ‹*structure*› **2** (strongly built) 健壮的 ‹*person*› **3** (firmly established) 得到公认的 ‹*method, practice*›
well-spoken *adj* 谈吐文雅的
wellspring /ˈwelsprɪŋ/ *n* **1** liter (place) = **wellhead 1** **2** fig (source) 源泉; **a ~ of ideas/creativity** 丰富的思想/创造力
well-thought-of *adj* 受到好评的
well-thought-out *adj* 经过深思熟虑的
well-timed *adj* 适时的; **a ~ right hook** 打得正是时候的一记右钩拳
well-to-do *adj* 富裕的
well-trodden *adj* **1** lit 常有人走的 ‹*path, ground*› **2** fig (used repeatedly) 俗套的; **to take a ~ path** 走老路
well-wisher /ˈwelwɪʃə(r)/ *n* 表示祝愿者
well-woman clinic *n* Brit 妇女保健所
well-worn *adj* **1** lit 破旧的 ‹*chair, rug, jacket, shoes*›; **a ~ path** 老路线 **2** fig (overused) 陈腐的 ‹*cliché, joke*›; **the ~ formula of romantic comedies** 浪漫喜剧的窠臼
welly /ˈweli/ *n* Brit colloq **1** [c] = **wellington** **2** [u] (vigour) 活力; **to give it some ~** (use effort) 用力; (accelerate) 加速
Welsh /welʃ/ ▸**p. 503, p. 426**
A *adj* (of Wales) 威尔士的; (of the people) 威尔士人的; (of the language) 威尔士语的
B *n* [u] 威尔士语
C *npl* **the ~** (people) 威尔士人
welsh /welʃ/ *vi* **to ~ on sb./sth.** 对…耍赖皮 ‹*person*›; 赖 ‹*debt*›; 不遵守 ‹*agreement*›; **I never ~ on a promise** 我从不食言

> **Welsh**
> 威尔士语。属于凯尔特语族（Celtic），与英语同为威尔士官方语言。威尔士的法律文书、路标等都同时以两种语言出现。电台和电视台也有威尔士语节目。威尔士所有学校都教授威尔士语，有些学校还用威尔士语教授其他科目。主要通行于威尔士北部和西部地区，目前以其为母语者已不足威尔士总人口的五分之一。

Welsh: ~ Assembly *n* **the ~** 威尔士国民议会; **~ dresser** *n* Brit 威尔士餐具柜; **~ harp** ▸**p. 395** *n* 威尔士式竖琴; **~man** /-mən/ *n* 威尔士男子; **~ Office** *n* **the ~ Office** [英国政府的] 威尔士事务部; **~ rarebit, ~ rabbit** *ns* [u] 威尔士干酪吐司; **~ Secretary** *n* **the ~ Secretary** [英国的] 威尔士事务大臣; **~woman** *n* 威尔士女子
welt /welt/ *n* **1** (on shoe) 沿条 **2** (on skin) 红肿
welter /ˈweltə(r)/ *n sing* (of objects, papers, weeds, etc.) 杂乱的一堆; fig (of words, problems, detail, emotion, etc.) 混乱无序; **a ~ of blood/mud** 一滩血/泥
welterweight /ˈweltəweɪt/ *n* (weight) 次中量级; (person) 次中量级选手; **a ~ boxer/wrestler** 次中量级拳击手/摔跤手
wench /wentʃ/ *n* archaic or hum [尤指风骚的] 少妇
wend /wend/ *vt* liter **to ~ one's way home/toward sth.** 朝家/朝某处走去
Wendy house /ˈwendɪ haʊs/ *n* Brit [供孩子们玩耍的] 温迪屋
went /went/ *pt* ▸**go A, B**
wept /wept/ *pt, pp* ▸**weep A, B**
were /wɜː(r), wə(r)/ *pt* ▸**be**
we're /wɪə(r)/ colloq = **we are** ▸**be**
weren't /wɜːnt/ colloq = **were not** ▸**be**
werewolf /ˈwɪəwʊlf/ *n* (*pl* **werewolves** /ˈwɪəwʊlvz/) [北欧神话中的] 狼人
Wesleyan /ˈwezlɪən/
A *adj* 卫斯理的; **the ~ Church** 卫斯理宗教会
B *n* 卫斯理宗教徒
west /west/ ▸**p. 142**
A *n* [u] **1** (direction) 西; (position or location) 西方; (western part) 西部 **2** Pol, Geog **the W~** 西方国家 **3** Hist (western Europe) **the W~** 西欧 **4** Geog (western USA) **the W~** 美国西部地区; **out W~** 在遥远的西方 **5** Geog (western Britain) **the W~** 英国西部地区 **6** Hist (west Berlin) **the W~** 西柏林; (west Germany) 西德 **7** Games 坐在西首位置的人
B *adj* **1** (western) 西边的; **on the ~ side of the island** 在岛屿的西侧 **2** *attrib* (from the west) 来自西边的; **a ~ wind** 西风
C *adv* **1** (to the west, on the western side) 在西边; **~ of sth.** 在某物的西边 **2** (towards the west) 向西; **due ~** 向正西; **to go ~** colloq Brit (be killed) 被杀死; (be lost) 丢失; (meet with disaster) 遭殃
West Africa *pr n* 西非
West African
A *adj* 西非的
B *n* 西非人

> **the West Coast**
> （美国）西海岸，指美国西部太平洋沿岸各州，包括加利福尼亚（California）、俄勒冈（Oregon）和华盛顿州（Washington），尤指加利福尼亚。对许多人而言，西海岸会让人想起充足的阳光以及悠闲而时尚的生活。

west: W~ Bank *pr n* **the W~ Bank** (约旦河) 西岸; **~bound** *adj* **1** (travelling west) 西行的 ‹*traffic, train, passenger*›; **2** (leading west) 向西的 ‹*road, line, platform*›; **W~ Country** *pr n* Brit **the W~ Country** 英格兰西南诸郡; **W~ End** *pr n* Brit **the W~ End** 伦敦西区; **W~ End prices/theatre** 西区的价格/剧院

> **the West End**
> 伦敦西区。伦敦金融城（▸**the City**）的西部地区。以高档商店、剧院和宾馆等著称。区内有唐人街（Chinatown）、皮卡迪利圆形广场（Piccadilly Circus）、摄政大街（Regent Street）以及繁华的商业大街牛津街（Oxford Street）。西区剧院（West End theatre）和纽约的百老汇（▸**Broadway**）齐名，代表了英语世界商业性戏剧的最高水平。

westerly /ˈwestəli/ ▸**p. 142**
A *adj* **1** (in a westward position) 西方的 ‹*point, area*› **2** (in a westward direction) 向西的 ‹*aspect, course, journey*› **3** (from a westward direction) 从西方吹来的; **a ~ wind** 西风
B *n* 西风
western /ˈwestən/ ▸**p. 142**
A *adj attrib* **1** (of or in the west) 西方的; **~ France** 法国西部 **2** (facing west) 向西的; (going towards west) 西行的 **3** (*also* **Western**) Pol, Geog 西方的
B *n* [尤指19世纪和20世纪之交描写美国西北部牛仔的] 西部作品
Western Australia *pr n* 西澳大利亚州
westerner /ˈwestənə(r)/ *n* 西方人
Western: ~ Europe *pr n* 西欧; **~ European Time** *n* 西欧时间 [同格林尼治平均时]; **~ Isles** *pr npl* **the ~ Isles** 赫布里底群岛
westernization /ˌwestənaɪˈzeɪʃn, Amer -nɪˈz-/ *n* [u] 西方化
westernize /ˈwestənaɪz/ *vt usu passive* 使…西方化 ‹*culture, attitude*›; **a ~d country** 西化了的国家
westernmost /ˈwestənməʊst/ *adj* (furthest west) 最西的; (in or on the (most) westerm part) 在最西部的
west-facing *adj* 朝西的
West German ▸**p. 503** Hist
A *adj* (of West Germany) 西德的; (of the people) 西德人的
B *n* 西德人
West Germany *pr n* Hist 西德 [原德意志联邦共和国]
West Indian ▸**p. 503**
A *adj* (of the West Indies) 西印度群岛的; (of the people) 西印度群岛人的
B *n* 西印度群岛人
West Indies /ˌwest ˈɪndiːz/ *pr npl* **the ~** 西印度群岛
West Midlands /ˌwest ˈmɪdləndz/ *pr n + v sing* **the ~** 西米德兰兹郡
Westminster /ˈwestmɪnstə(r)/ *n* Brit 威斯敏斯特 [尤指英国下议院]

> **Westminster**
> 威斯敏斯特，英国伦敦自治市（borough）。白金汉宫、唐宁街、白厅街、圣詹姆斯公园（St James's Park）等都位于区内。亦指议会大厦（▸**the Houses of Parliament**）。因其旧时为英国王宫，现亦称威斯敏斯特宫（Westminster Palace），威斯敏斯特因此也用于指代英国政界。议会大厦西面的威斯敏斯特教堂（Westminster Abbey，亦称西敏寺）是英国最著名的建筑之一。自1066年以来，英国的每位国王都是在此加冕。教堂内有无名战士墓（Tomb of the Unknown Soldier）和诗人角（Poets' Corner），乔叟（Geoffrey Chaucer）、哈代（Thomas Hardy）等长眠于此。

west-north-west ▸**p. 142**
A *n* 西西北
B *adj* **1** (in direction) 西西北的 ‹*position*› **2** (from direction) 从西西北吹来的 ‹*wind*›
C *adv* (to direction) 向西西北; (in direction) 在西西北
west-south-west
A *n* 西西南
B *adj* **1** (in direction) 西西南的 ‹*position*› **2** (from direction) 从西西南吹来的 ‹*wind*›
C *adv* (to direction) 向西西南; (in direction) 在西西南
West Sussex /ˌwest ˈsʌsɪks/ *pr n* 西萨塞克斯郡
West Virginia /ˌwest vəˈdʒɪnɪə/ *pr n* 西弗吉尼亚州
westward /ˈwestwəd/ ▸**p. 142**
A *adj* 向西的
B *adv* (*also* **westwards**) 向西
West Yorkshire /ˌwest ˈjɔːkʃə(r)/ *pr n* 西约克郡
wet /wet/
A *adj* **1** (covered or soaked with liquid, esp water) 湿的; **you'll get ~ if you go out now** 你现在出去会被淋湿的; **her face was ~ with tears** 她泪流满面; **to get sth. ~** 把…弄湿 ‹*floor, towel*›; **to be or get ~ through** 湿透; **to be all ~** Amer colloq «*person, theory*» 大错特错; ▸**ear** **2** (rainy) 有雨的; **~ weather/day** 多雨的天气/下雨天; **tomorrow, the North will be ~** 明天北部有雨 **3** (freshly applied) 未干的 ‹*varnish, cement, ink*›; **'~ paint'** "油漆未干" **4** (soaked with urine) 尿湿的 ‹*bottom, nappy*› **5** Brit colloq pej (wimpish) 窝囊的 **6** Brit Pol colloq pej 保守中庸的 ‹*minister*› **7** colloq (allowing sale of alcohol) 不禁酒的 ‹*state, country*›
B *vt* (*pres p* **-tt-**; *pt, pp* **wet** *or* **~ted**) **1** (soak with liquid) 把…弄湿; **the shower was barely sufficient to ~ the pavement** 那场阵雨连人行道都没淋湿 **2** (soak with urine) 尿湿 ‹*nappy*›; **to ~ the bed** 尿床; **to ~ one's pants** 尿裤子
C *v refl* (*pres p* **-tt-**; *pt, pp* **wet** *or* **~ted**) **to ~ oneself** 尿裤子

W

D *n* **1** [u] (rainy weather) **the ~** 雨天; **in the ~** 在雨天; **don't go out in the ~** 雨天别出门 **2** [u] (liquid) 液体 [尤指水] **3** [c] Brit colloq pej (wimp) 窝囊废 pej **4** [c] Brit dated colloq pej (politician) 保守中庸的政客

wet: ~back *n* Amer colloq pej 湿背人 [指居住在美国的墨西哥人，尤指非法移民]; **~ blanket** *n* colloq pej 扫兴的人; **~ cell** *n* **~ cell (battery)** 湿电池; **~ dock** *n* 湿船坞; **~ dream** *n* colloq 梦遗; **~ fish** *n* [u] Brit 鲜鱼

wether /'weðə(r)/ *n* 阉羊

wet: ~land /-lənd/ *n* [u and c] (*also* **~lands**) 湿地; **~land birds/plants** 湿地鸟类/植物; **~ look** *n* (fabric) 光亮; (hair) 湿润亮泽

wetness /'wetnɪs/ *n* [u] 潮湿

wet nurse /'wetnɜːs/

A *n* 奶妈

B **wet-nurse** *vt* **1** lit 做…的奶妈 ‹*baby*› **2** fig colloq pej (mollycoddle) 从头到脚地伺候 ‹*person*›

wet: ~ rot *n* [u] **1** (decay) 湿腐; **2** **~ rot (fungus)** 湿腐菌; **~suit** *n* 潜水服

wetting /'wetɪŋ/ *n* 润湿; **to give sb./sth. a ~** 弄湿某人/某物

wetting agent *n* 润湿剂

wet-weather *adj attrib* 雨天的; **~ clothing/shoes** 雨衣/雨鞋; **~ driving skills** 雨天驾驶技能

we've /wiːv/ colloq **= we have** ▸**have**

whack /wæk, Amer hwæk/

A *n* **1** (blow) 重击; **to give sth./sb. a ~** 重击某物/某人; **he fell and landed with a ~** 他咚的一下摔倒了 **2** Brit colloq (share) 份; **to get one's (fair) ~** 得到自己（合理）的一份; **to do one's ~** 干自己份内的事 **3** colloq (try) 尝试; **to have a ~ at sth./doing sth.** 试一试某事/做某事; **to be out of ~** Amer (not working) 不正常; (not aligned) 未放齐; **my leg was put out of ~** 我的腿有点儿不听使唤

B *vt* **1** (hit) 重击 ‹*person, ball*› **2** colloq (defeat) 打败 ‹*opponent, enemy*› **3** (put roughly) 草草放下; **to ~ sth. on the table** 把某物丢在桌子上; **to ~ £10 off (the price)** colloq （将价格）砍掉 10 英镑 **4** colloq **= whack out**

C *vi* **to ~ at sth.** 用力打某物

D *excl* 砰

Phrasal verb

- **whack out** *vt* [**~ sb. out, ~ out sb.**] *usu passive* Brit colloq «*activity*» 使…筋疲力尽 ‹*person*›; **I'm ~ed out** 我累坏了

whacked /wækt, Amer hwækt/ *adj pred* colloq **1** Brit (exhausted) 筋疲力尽的; **to be ~** 累垮 **2** (defeated) 被打败的

whacking /'wækɪŋ, Amer 'hwæk-/ colloq

A *n* **1** (beating) 殴打; **to give sb./get a ~** 揍某人一顿/挨打 **2** Mil, Sport (defeat) 打败; **to get a ~** 被打得溃不成军

B *adj* Brit colloq 巨大的 ‹*object, animal*›

C *adv* Brit colloq 极其 ‹*great*›; **a ~ big parcel** 超大包裹

whacko /'wækəʊ, Amer 'hwæk-/ *adj* colloq **= wacko**

whacky /'wæki, Amer 'hwæki/ *adj* colloq **= wacky**

whale¹ /weɪl, Amer hweɪl/ *n* **1** (*pl* **~** *or* **~s**) Zool 鲸; **a school of ~s** 一群鲸 **2** *sing* fig colloq (large, fine example of sth.) 出众的事物; **a ~ of a party/story** 很棒的聚会/故事; **to have a ~ of a time** 玩得特过瘾

whale² *vt* esp Amer colloq 猛揍

whale: ~bone *n* [u] 鲸骨; **a ~bone comb/knife** 鲸骨梳/刀; **~ oil** *n* [u] 鲸油

whaler /'weɪlə(r), Amer 'hweɪlər/ *n* **1** (vessel) 捕鲸船 **2** ▸**p. 409** (person) 捕鲸人

whaling /'weɪlɪŋ, Amer 'hweɪlɪŋ/ *n* [u] 捕鲸; **a ~ vessel** 捕鲸船

whaling: ~ ship *n* 捕鲸船; **~ station** *n* 鲸油提炼站

wham /wæm, Amer hwæm/ colloq

A *excl* 砰

B *vt* (*pres p etc.* **-mm-**) 猛击 ‹*person, object*›; 撞击 ‹*vehicle*›; **to ~ one's fist into sth.** 冲某物砸一拳; **to ~ the door shut** 把门摔上

C *vi* (*pres p etc.* **-mm-**) **to ~ into sb./sth.** «*person*» 猛揍某人/猛砸某物; **the cars ~med into the wall/each other** 车砰的一声撞上了墙/撞在了一起

D *n* 重击

whammy /'wæmi, Amer 'hwæmi/ *n* colloq 打击; ▸**double whammy**

whang /wæŋ, Amer hwæŋ/ colloq

A *vt* 嘭嘭地敲 ‹*surface, table*›

B *vi* 敲出嘭嘭声; **to ~ on sth.** 嘭嘭地敲 ‹*tambourine*›

C *n* 嘭嘭声

Phrasal verb

- **whang down** *vt* [**~ sth. down, ~ down sth.**] colloq 砰地放下

wharf /wɔːf, Amer hwɔːf/ *n* (*pl* **wharves** *or* **~s**) 码头

wharfage /'wɔːfɪdʒ, Amer 'hwɔːfɪdʒ/ *n* [u] **1** (accommodation) 码头使用 **2** (fee) 码头费

wharves /wɔːvz, Amer hwɔːvz/ *pl* ▸**wharf**

what /wɒt, Amer hwɒt/

A *pron* **1** (in direct and indirect questions) 什么; **~ is happening?** 出什么事了？; **ask ~ he wants** 问问他想要什么; **~'s up** *or* **wrong** *or* **the matter?** 怎么回事？; **~ is to be done?** 怎么办呢？; **with/about ~ ...?** 用/关于什么？; **and ~ else?** 还有呢？; **~'s that, ~ did you say?** 你说什么？; **~ do six and four add up to** *or* **make?** 6 加 4 等于几？; **~'s this called in Flemish?, ~'s the Flemish for this?** 这个用佛兰芒语怎么说？; **~ did it cost?** 这东西花了多少钱？; **~'s with sb./sth.?** colloq 某人/某事怎么啦？; **~ do you think I am?** colloq 你把我看成什么人了？; **~'s it to you?** colloq 关你什么事？; **~'s the use?** 这有什么用？; **~'s life without love?** 没有爱的生活算什么生活？; **he earns/did ~?** 他赚了/做了什么？; **that's George — George ~?** 那是乔治——姓什么？; **I asked her to marry me — you ~?** colloq 我向她求婚了——你说什么？; **is he stupid or ~?** colloq 他真是傻透了; **are we going or ~?** colloq 我们走还是不走？; **he's going after all — well, ~ do you know?** colloq iron 他终于要走了——噢，真的吗？ **2** (asking what sb. wants) 什么事; **mummy! — ~?** 妈咪！——什么事？ **3** (in clauses) (thing) …那样的事物; (person) …那样的人; **and ~'s worse/better** 更糟糕/更好的是; **~ we need is ...** 我们需要的是…; **~'s surprising is that ...** 令人吃惊的是…; **you know ~ he is!** 你知道他那种人！; **she's not ~ she was** 她已经不是原来的她了; **it's good value for ~ it is** 这东西物有所值; **I** *or* **I'll tell you ~** 我来告诉你吧; **to know ~'s ~** colloq 知道轻重缓急 **4** (whatever) 无论什么; **do ~ you want/have to** 做你想做/必须做的事; **and ~ not, and ~ have you** colloq 以及诸如此类的东西; **toys, books, and ~ not** 玩具、书籍等等; **a hammer, a drill, and I don't know ~** 锤子、钻头之类的东西 **5** (in exclamations) 多么; **and ~ it must have cost!** 它肯定花了很多钱！

B *det* **1** (which) 哪个; **do you know ~ train he took?** 你知道他乘坐的是哪班火车吗？; **~ magazines do you read?** 你看哪些杂志？; **~ time is it?** 现在几点钟？ **2** (in exclamations) 多么; **~ a nice dress!** 多么漂亮的连衣裙啊！; **~ awful weather!** 天气太糟糕了！; **~ a strange thing** 咄咄怪事; **~ use is that?** 那有什么用？; fig 那有什么意义？ **3** (whatever) 无论多少; **~ money he earns he spends** 他挣多少花多少; **~ few friends she had** 她仅有的几个朋友

C *adv* **1** (how much) 多少; **~ does it matter?** 那有什么关系？ **2** colloq (in guesses) [表示估计]; **it'll cost, ~, £50** 这要花大约 50 英镑 **3** Brit dated (as question tag) **a good dinner, ~?** 很丰盛的一顿饭，是吧？

D **what about** *phr* **1** (in question) …怎么样; **~ about the children?** 孩子们怎么样？; **~ about a meal out?** 出去吃顿饭好吗？ **2** (in reply) [请求澄清问题]; **~ about your sister? — ~ about her?** 那么你姐姐呢？——什么意思？

E **what for** *phr* colloq 为什么; **~ did you do that for?** 你为什么做那事？; **I need to see a doctor — ~ for?** 我得去看医生——你怎么了？; **~'s that for?** 那是干什么用的？; **to give sb. ~ for** Brit dated colloq (punish) 严惩某人; (criticize) 训斥某人

F **what if** *phr* **1** (what will happen?) 要是…会怎么样; **~ if the train is late?** 火车要是晚点会怎么样呢？ **2** (does it matter?) 即使…又有什么关系; **~ if our house is a mess?** 我们的房子一片狼藉又有什么关系呢？ **3** (how about) …怎么样; **~ if I bring the dessert?** 我拿甜点来好吗？

G **what of** *phr* **1** (in question) …怎么样; **~ of Shakespeare?** 那么莎士比亚呢？ **2** colloq (in retort) …有什么关系; **~ of it!** 那又怎么样！

H **what with** *phr* 因为; **~ with one thing and another** 由于这样那样的事情; **~ with the recession and unemployment** 由于经济衰退和失业

I *excl* 什么; **~! I don't believe it!** 竟然有这种事！我不相信！

what-d'yer-call-it /'wɒtdjəˌkɔːlɪt/ *n* colloq 叫它什么来着

whatever /wɒt'evə(r), Amer hwɒt-/

A *pron* **1** (anything that) 任何事物; **~ you say** 随你怎么说; **~ he says goes** 他说了算; **to do ~ is required** 做一切按要求的做; **to do ~ one likes** 喜欢做什么就做什么 **2** (no matter what) 无论什么; **~ happens** 不管发生什么; **~ the reasons** 无论理由如何; **~ I do, it's wrong** 我无论做什么都是错的; **~ it costs, it doesn't matter** 无论花多少钱都不要紧; **~ you do** (as warning) 无论如何; **don't tell him, ~ you do!** 无论如何都不要告诉他！ **3** (what on earth) 到底是什么; **~ do you mean?** 你到底什么意思？; **~'s the matter?** 究竟是怎么回事？; **let's go — ~ for?** 咱们走吧——究竟为什么？; **~ next?** 接下来到底还有什么？ **4** colloq (the like) 诸如此类的东西; **you add it or subtract it or ~** 你把它加上或减去或别的什么; **go to the cinema or ~** 去电影院或类似的地方; **curtains, cushions, and ~** (in series) 窗帘、垫子等等 **5** colloq (expressing no preference) 什么都可以; **I'll call you — ~** 我给你打电话——随你的便; **what do you want to do? — ~** 你想做什么呢？——无所谓

B *det* **1** (any) 任何的; **~ hope he once had** 他曾经有过的任何希望; **they eat ~ food they can get** 他们找到什么食物就吃什么 **2** (no matter what) 无论什么的; **for ~ reason** 无论出于什么原因; **~ decision he makes** 无论他做出什么决定 **3** (what/who on earth) 究竟什么的; **~ idiot forgot the key?** 究竟哪个傻瓜把钥匙给忘了？

C *adv* **1** (at all) 丝毫; **nothing ~** 什么都没有; **there's no evidence ~** 什么证据都没有; **to have no doubt ~** 毫不怀疑; **is there any possibility ~ that you can come?** 你究竟有没有一丝可能会来？; **any chance? — none ~** 有机会吗？——丝毫没有 **2** colloq (no matter what) 无论如何; **we'd back him ~** 我们无论如何都会支持他

whatnot /'wɒtnɒt, Amer 'hwɒt-/ *n* **1** [u and c] colloq (unspecified thing) 诸如此类的东西; **sheets, towels, and ~** 床单、毛巾等等 **2** [c] (stand) 陈设架

what's-her-name /'wɒtsəneɪm, Amer 'hwɒt-/ *n* colloq 那个谁 [指想不起名字的女人]

what's-his-name /'wɒtsɪzneɪm, Amer 'hwɒt-/ *n* colloq 那个谁 [指想不起名字的男人]

whatsit /'wɒtsɪt, Amer 'hwɒt-/ *n* colloq 某个; **Mr ~** 某先生

W

what's-its-name /ˈwɒtsɪtsneɪm, Amer ˈhwɒt-/ *n* colloq 那个什么 [指叫不上来名字的东西]

whatsoever /ˌwɒtsəʊˈevə(r), Amer ˈhwɒt-/
A *pron* **1** formal (anything that) 任何事物; (no matter what) 无论什么; ～ **the circumstances** 不管情况如何; **to do** ～ **the occasion demands** 见机行事 **2** colloq (the like) 诸如此类的东西; **religion, science, or** ～ 宗教、科学等等
B *adv* = **whatever C1**
C *adj* formal (any) 任何的; (no matter what) 无论什么的; ～ **pretext** 任何借口; **for** ～ **reason** 无论什么原因

wheat /wiːt, Amer hwiːt/ *n* [u] **1** (crop) 小麦; **to grow/harvest** ～ 种植/收割小麦; **a** ～ **field** 小麦田 **2** (grain) 麦粒; **to separate the** ～ **from the chaff** fig 去芜存菁

wheaten /ˈwiːtn, Amer ˈhwiːtn/ *adj* 小麦粉制成的; ～ **bread** 小麦粉面包

wheat: ～ flour *n* [u] 小麦粉; **～germ** *n* [u] 麦芽; **～meal** *n* [u] 全麦面粉

wheedle /ˈwiːdl, Amer ˈhwiːdl/ *vt* **1** (coax) 哄 ‹*person*›; **to** ～ **sb. into doing sth.** 哄某人做某事 **2** (obtain) 骗得 ‹*favour, information*›; **to** ～ **sth. out of sb.** 从某人那里哄骗到某物; **to** ～ **one's way into a place/sb.'s heart** 花言巧语混进一个地方/骗得某人的芳心

wheedling /ˈwiːdlɪŋ, Amer ˈhwiːdlɪŋ/
A *adj* 哄人的 ‹*voice, charm, person*›
B *n* [u] 哄骗

wheel /wiːl, Amer hwiːl/
A *n* **1** (on vehicle, bicycle, cart, etc.) 车轮; (on roller skate, furniture) 轮子; **a front/rear** *or* **back** ～ 前轮/后轮; **to reinvent the** ～ 重新发明轮子 [指无谓地重复]; **a journey on** ～**s** (by car) 开车出行; (by bicycle) 骑车出行 **2** (for steering) Aut 方向盘; Naut 舵轮; **to be at** *or* **behind the** ～ 在驾驶; **to fall asleep at the** ～ 开车时睡着; **to take the** ～ 开车 **3** Ind (for spinning) 纺车; (for pottery making) 陶轮; (as part of machine) 机轮; (in watch, mechanism) 飞轮; **gear** ～**s** 齿轮; **the** ～**s of government** 复杂的政府机构; **to set the** ～**s in motion** fig 启动; **to keep the** ～**s turning** fig 保持运转; ～**s within** ～**s** 盘根错节; **to oil** *or* **grease the** ～**s (of sth.)** fig 使某事物顺利运行 **4** Hist (instrument of torture) 轮式刑车; **to break sb. on the** ～ 判处某人车裂之刑 **5** (for roulette) 轮盘 **6** fig (cycle, process) [不可抗拒的] 轮转; **the** ～**(s) of fate** 命运之轮 **7** (act of turning) 急转弯 **8** (disc) 轮状物 [尤指浅圆形奶酪] **9** Amer colloq (important person) 大亨 **10** ～**s** *pl* colloq 汽车; **to be on** ～**s** 开车; **are these your new** ～**s?** 这是你的新车吗?
B *vt* **1** (push on wheels) 推动 ‹*bicycle, wheelbarrow*› **2** (carry on wheels) 用车推 ‹*baby, invalid*›
C *vi* **1** (move in circle) «*bird, aircraft*» 盘旋; **to** ～ **and deal** colloq 玩弄手段 **2** Mil (turn sharply) «*soldier, regiment*» 急转; **to** ～ **to the right** 向右急转
D -wheeled *combining form* 有…轮子的; **a three/four～ed vehicle** 三/四轮车

Phrasal verbs

- **wheel in** *vt* [～ **sb./sth. in,** ～ **in sb./sth.**]
1 lit (push or carry on wheels) 把…推进去 ‹*bicycle, wheelchair*›; 用车把…推进去 ‹*patient*› **2** fig colloq (introduce) 挥手请进 ‹*interviewee, contestant*›
- **wheel out** *vt* [～ **sb./sth. out,** ～ **out sb./sth.**]
1 (push or carry on wheels) 把…推出去 ‹*bicycle, wheelchair*›; 用车把…推出去 ‹*patient*› **2** fig colloq (bring out) 重复提出 ‹*idea, project*›; 一成不变地推出 ‹*new model*›; **they always** ～ **him out to deal with the press** 他们总是把他推出去应付新闻界
- **wheel round** *vi* 急转

wheel: ～ alignment *n* 车轮定位; **～barrow** *n* 独轮车; **～base** *n* 轴距

wheelchair /ˈwiːltʃeə(r), Amer ˈhwiːl-/ *n* 轮椅

wheelchair: ～ access *n* [u] 轮椅通道; **～ accessible** *adj* 轮椅可进入的; **～-bound** *adj* 离不开轮椅的

wheel clamp Brit
A *n* 车轮夹锁
B *vt* 用车轮夹锁锁上 ‹*vehicle*›

wheeled /wiːld, Amer hwiːld/ *adj* 有轮的 ‹*vehicle, cart, suitcase*›

-wheeler /ˈwiːlə(r), Amer ˈhwiːlər/ *combining form* …轮的车; **a four/three～** 四轮/三轮车

wheeler dealer *n* colloq pej [商界或政界] 要手腕的人

wheelhouse /ˈwiːlhaʊs, Amer ˈhwiː/ *n* 操舵室

wheelie /ˈwiːli/ *n* 后轮支撑特技; **to do a** ～ 表演后轮平衡特技

wheelie bin /ˈwiːli bɪn/ *n* Brit colloq 带轮大垃圾箱

wheeling and dealing *n* [u] colloq [尤指商业或政治性质的] 投机取巧的交易

wheel reflector *n* [自行车的] 辐条反光片

wheelwright /ˈwiːlraɪt, Amer ˈhwiːl-/ ▸ **p. 409** *n* 木轮修造工

wheely bin /ˈwiːli bɪn/ *n* Brit colloq = **wheelie bin**

wheeze /wiːz, Amer hwiːz/
A *n* **1** (sound) 喘息声 **2** Brit colloq (scheme) 花招
B *vi* «*person, animal*» 喘息; fig «*engine, pump, organ*» 呼哧呼哧作响
C *vt* **to** ～ **(out) sth.** «*speaker*» 气喘吁吁地说出 ‹*words*›; «*organ*» 呼哧呼哧地弹出 ‹*tune*›

wheezy /ˈwiːzi, Amer ˈhwiːzi/ *adj* 气喘的 ‹*person, chest, animal*›; fig 呼哧呼哧作响的 ‹*engine, organ, notes*›; **a** ～ **cough** 喘息性咳嗽

whelk /welk, Amer hwelk/ *n* 蛾螺

whelp /welp, Amer hwelp/
A *n* **1** (puppy) 狗崽; (wolf cub) 狼崽 **2** fig (youth) 小畜生
B *vi* «*dog, wolf*» 产仔

when /wen, Amer hwen/
A *adv* **1** (at what time, how soon) 什么时候; ～ **can I see you?** 我什么时候可以见你?; **ask him** ～ **he wrote the letter** 问问他是什么时候写的那封信; **I don't know** ～ **he will arrive** 我不知道他多会儿到; **I forget** ～ 我把时间给忘了; **there is some disagreement as to** ～ **...** 关于何时…有一些分歧; **tell me** *or* **say** ～ (pouring drink) 够了请说一声 **2** (in what circumstances) 在什么情况下; **to know** ～ **to seek help** 知道在什么情况下寻求帮助; ～ **would such a rule be justifiable?** 这样的规定适用于什么情况? **3** (at or on which) 在…的时候; **the week** ～ **it all happened** 发生这一切的那个星期; **Sunday is the only day** ～ **I can relax** 星期日是我唯一可以休息的日子; **at the time** ～ (moment of) 就在…的时候; (in same period) 在…期间; **there are times** ～ **...** 有时候…; **on those occasions** ～ **...** 在…的时候; **it's times like that** ～ **you need a friend** 正是那种需要朋友的时候; **on Monday,** ～ **I was on my way to work** 在星期一我去上班的路上; **in 1993,** ～ **she was nine** 在1993 年她 9 岁时 **4** (which time) 那时; **..., by** ～ **we will have received the information** …, 到那个时候我们就已得到消息了; **..., since** ～ **he has worked in publishing** …, 打那以后他一直在出版业工作; **..., until** ～ **we must stay calm** …, 在那之前我们必须保持冷静
B *pron* **1** (what time) 什么时候; **by** ～**?** 到什么时候?; **from** ～ **until** ～**?** 从什么时候到什么时候?; **since** ～**?** lit 从什么时候开始?; iron 何曾?; **since** ～ **has that been allowed?** 那种事何曾允许过? **2** (the time that) …的时候; **that was** ～ **it all went wrong** 那时一切都乱了套; **that's** ～ **I was born** (day) 那是我出生的那天; (year) 那是我出生的那年; **now is** ～ **we must act** 我们现在必须行动了
C *conj* **1** (at the time that) 在…时; ～ **he got home** 他到家时; **I was in the bath** ～ **the phone rang** 我洗澡时电话铃响了; ～ **doing sth.** 正在做某事时; **to have an accident** ～ **driving home** 开车回家时出车祸 **2** (during the time that) 在…期间; ～ **you're in your teens** 在你的少年时期; ～ **sailing, always wear a life jacket** 驾帆船航行时一定要穿救生衣 **3** (as soon as) 一…(就); ～ **he arrives, I'll tell him** 他一到我就会告诉他的 **4** (just after which) 刚…(就); **I had just sat down** ～ **he arrived** 我刚坐下来他就到了 **5** (after) 在…之后; ～ **completed, the centre will be the largest of its kind** 该中心竣工后将是同类中最大的 **6** (once) 从…以后; ～ **you've been to Scotland, you'll want to go again** 去过苏格兰, 还会想再去 **7** (whenever) 每当…时; ～ **I sunbathe, I get freckles** 我每次日光浴都长雀斑; ～ **(it is) necessary/possible** 一有必要/可能; ～ **doing sth.** 每当做某事时; ～ **making decisions, be objective** 作决定时要客观 **8** (given that) 既然; **why buy their products** ～ **ours are cheaper?** 既然我们的产品更便宜, 为什么要买他们的呢? **9** (whereas) 可是; **you say he's stupid** ～ **in fact he's rather bright** 你说他傻, 可实际上他相当聪明

whence /wens, Amer hwens/ formal or archaic
A *adv* 从何处
B *conj* 由此; ～**, it may safely be assumed that ...** 据此, 可以有把握地假设…

whenever /wenˈevə(r), Amer hwen-/
A *conj* **1** (at whatever time) 无论何时; ～ **he does it, it won't matter** 他什么时候做都没关系; **I'll come** ～ **it's convenient** 方便时我随时可以过来 **2** (every time that) 每当; ～ **I see a black cat, I make a wish** 我每次看到黑猫都会许个愿; ～ **(it is) necessary/possible** 一有必要/可能 **3** (expressing doubt) 谁知道什么时候; **she promised to come as soon as she could,** ～ **that might be!** 她答应会尽早来, 谁知道要到猴年马月!
B *adv* **1** (when on earth) 究竟什么时候; ～ **will he arrive?** 他到底什么时候到? **2** colloq (whatever time) 无论何时; **or** ～ 或其他任何时候; **how long are you staying? — till** ～ 你要待多长时间? ——到什么时候都行

whensoever /ˌwensəʊˈevə(r)/ *conj* formal = **whenever A**

where /weə(r), Amer hweər/
A *adv* **1** (in what place) 在哪里; ～ **is my coat?** 我的外套在哪里?; ～ **did you read that?** 你在哪儿读到这个的?; **I forget** ～ **it is** 我忘了在什么地方; **I told him** ～ **he could put it** 我告诉过他可以把它放在哪里; fig sl 我让他收起那一套 **2** (to what place, to what point or situation) 到哪里; ～ **has he got to?** 他到哪里了?; ～ **are you going (to)?** 你要去哪里?; **ask him** ～ **he's headed** 问问他去了哪儿; **just** ～ **is all this leading us?** 这一切到底要将我们引向何处?; ～ **have you got to in your book?** 你那本书看到哪了?; **to know** ～ **one is going** fig 知道自己的目标 **3** (at what point) 在哪一点上; ～ **would I be if ...?** 如果…, 我会怎么样呢?; ～ **does he figure in all this?** 他在这一切中起什么作用呢?; ～**'s the harm?** 有什么害处呢?; ～**'s the problem?** 问题出在哪里呢?; **I want to know** ～ **I stand** 我想知道我的境况 **4** (in the place in which) 在…地方; (to the place in which) 到…地方; ～ **the path divides** 在路分叉的地方; **the village** ～ **we live** 我们生活的村庄; **come** ～ **I can see you** 到我能看到你的地方; **it's cold** ～ **we live** 我们住的地方很冷; **it's not** ～ **you said** (not there) 它不在你说的地方; (found elsewhere) 它在别的地方 **5** (at or to the point at which) 到…情况; **I'm** ～ **I want to be in my life** 我实现了我的人生追求; **this thought brings me back to** ～ **I started** 这股思绪让我回想起刚起步的时候; **you don't get to** ～ **he is now without ...** 如果不…你就不会取得他现在的地位

W

6 (at which point) 在…的情况下; **to reach the stage ~ ...** 达到…的阶段; **to lead to a situation ~ ...** 导致…的情况; **in several cases ~ ...** 在几种…的情况下 7 (in whichever place) 在任何地方; (to whichever place) 到任何地方; **put it ~ you want** 你想放在哪儿就放在哪儿 8 (in which place) 在那里; (to which place) 到那里; **in London, ~ my brother lives** 在伦敦，我哥哥住的地方; **he lives in Canada, ~ he emigrated to when he was a boy** 他住在加拿大，他小时候就移居到了那里

B *pron* 1 (what place) 哪里; **from ~?** 从哪里？; **near ~?** 在哪附近？ 2 (the place that) …的地方; **this is ~ it happened** 这就是事发地; **France is ~ you'll find good wine** 法国是个出产好葡萄酒的地方 3 (the point that) …的一点; (the stage that) …的阶段; **that is ~ he's mistaken** 那就是他的错误所在; **here's ~ we learn the truth** 我们就是从这一点得知真相的; **from ~ I stand** 从我的角度看

C *conj* 1 (in which situation) 在…的情况下; **~ possible/appropriate** 在可能/合适的情况下; **~ necessary** 必要时; **~ children are at risk** 当孩子们处于危险时; **~ there's a scandal, there's a reporter** 哪里有丑闻哪里就有记者 2 (whereas) 然而; **she likes dogs, ~ I prefer cats** 她喜欢狗，可我更喜欢猫

whereabouts

A /ˈweərəbaʊts, Amer ˈhweər-/ *npl* 下落; **his ~ are** *or* **is still unknown** 他仍然下落不明

B /ˌweərəˈbaʊts/ *adv* 1 (in what place) [大约] 在哪里; **they live in London — ~?** 他们住在伦敦——靠近什么地方？; **I wonder ~ it is** 我不知道它在哪里 2 (to what place) [大约] 去哪里; **~ in France are you going?** 你要去法国的什么地方？

whereas /ˌweərˈæz, Amer ˌhweər-/ *conj* 1 (in contrast) 然而; **she likes dogs, ~ I prefer cats** 她喜欢狗，而我喜欢猫 2 Jur (it being the case that) 鉴于

whereat /ˌweərˈæt, Amer ˌhweər-/ *conj* archaic or formal = **whereupon**

whereby /weəˈbaɪ, Amer ˌhweər-/ formal

A *adv* 凭此; **a system ~ people could vote by telephone** 可供人们电话投票的系统

B *conj* 因此

where'er /ˌweərˈeə(r), Amer ˌhweər-/ *conj* liter = **wherever**

wherefore /ˈweəfɔː(r), Amer ˈhweər-/ *n* 理由; **the whys and ~s (of sth.)** （某事的）来龙去脉

wherein /ˌweərˈɪn, Amer ˌhweər-/ *adv* formal 1 (in which part or respect) 在哪里; **~ lies the difficulty?** 困难出在哪里？ 2 (in which place or thing) 在那里; **the cave ~ they dwelt** 他们居住的洞穴

whereof /ˌweərˈɒv, Amer ˌhweər-/ *adv* formal 关于什么; **I know ~ I speak** 我知道自己在说什么

wheresoever /ˌweəsəʊˈevə(r), Amer ˌhweər-/ *adv* archaic 1 (everywhere) = **wherever 2** 2 (anywhere) = **wherever 3**

whereupon /ˌweərəˈpɒn, Amer ˌhweər-/ *conj* formal 于是; **he made new demands, ~ they refused to sign** 他提出了新的要求，于是他们拒绝签字

wherever /ˌweərˈevə(r), Amer ˌhweər-/ *adv* 1 (in what place) 究竟在哪里; (to what place) 究竟到哪里; **~ did you put them?** 你究竟把它们放哪里了？; **~ did she get that from?** 她究竟从什么地方得到那个的呢？; **~ can he have got to?** 他究竟到哪儿去了呢？ 2 (in every place) 在各处; (to every place) 到各处; **~ there's an oasis, there's a settlement** 有绿洲就有人居住; **he's popular ~ he goes** 他每到一处都受到欢迎 3 (in any place) 在任何地方; (to any place) 到任何地方; **~ you put the painting, it won't look right** 这幅画无论放在哪儿看上去都不对劲; **we'll meet ~'s convenient for you** 哪儿对你方便，我们就在哪儿见; **you can go ~ you like** 你爱去哪儿就去哪儿 4 colloq (somewhere) 某个地方; **or ~** 或别的什么地方 5 (whenever) 在任何情况下; **~ possible/necessary** 只要有可能/有必要 6 (expressing doubt) **she's from Mullumbimby, ~ that is!** 她来自马伦宾比，不知这是什么地方！

wherewithal /ˈweəwɪðɔːl, Amer ˈhweə-/ *n* (resources) 必要的资源; (money, means) 必要的财力; **he hasn't the ~ to buy it** 他没钱买那个

whet /wet, Amer hwet/ *vt* (*pres p etc.* **-tt-**) 1 lit (sharpen) 磨 ‹*knife, chisel, scythe*› 2 fig (stimulate) 《*remark, event*》刺激 ‹*curiosity, desire*›; **to ~ the** *or* **one's appetite** 刺激食欲

whether /ˈweðə(r), Amer ˈhweðər/ *conj* 1 (if) 是否; **I wonder ~ it's true** 我不知道这是否是真的; **the question is ~ anyone is interested** 问题是有没有人感兴趣; **ask him ~ he did it himself or ~ someone helped him** 问问他这是他自己做的还是有人帮他; **~ or not sb./sth. does sth., ~ sb./sth. does sth. or not** 某人/某物是否做某事; **I can't tell ~ she's joking or not** 我搞不清楚她是不是在开玩笑; **~ to do sth., ~ or not to do sth., ~ to do sth. or not** 是否做某事; **I don't know ~ or not to buy it** 我不知道买还是不买它; **they can't decide ~ to buy or rent** 他们无法决定是买还是租 2 (no matter if) 无论; **~ or not sb./sth. does sth., ~ sb./sth. does sth. or not** 某人/某物无论是否做某事; **you're going ~ you like it or not!** 不管喜欢与否，你都要去！; **~ or not people are happy is of little importance** 人们高兴与否无关紧要; **~ ... or ...** 无论…还是…; **everyone, ~ students or townspeople, celebrated** 无论是学生还是市民，人人都在庆祝; **they need an adult ~ it be a parent or teacher** 他们需要一个成年人，父母或老师均可

whetstone /ˈwetstəʊn, Amer ˈhwet-/ *n* 磨刀石

whew /fjuː/ *excl* 吁 [表示宽慰、仰慕、惊奇或疲劳等]; **~, this is hot work!** 哟，热死了！; **~, that was a lucky escape!** 嘘，能逃掉真幸运！; **~, what a great view!** 哇，好美的景色！

whey /weɪ, Amer hweɪ/ *n* [u] 乳清

whey-faced /ˈweɪfeɪst, Amer ˈhweɪ-/ *adj* 脸色煞白的 ‹*person*›

which /wɪtʃ, Amer hwɪtʃ/

A *pron* 1 **~ (one)** (what one) 哪一个 (what ones) 哪一些; **I know ~ ones you'd like** 我知道你想要哪一些; **~ is the shortest route?** 哪条路最近？; **~ do you want, the red one or the blue one?** 你想要哪一个，红的还是蓝的？; **~ of you did this?** 你们谁干的？; **~ is ~?** (thing) 哪个是哪个？; (person) 谁是谁？ 2 (specifying preceding noun) …的那个; **the painting ~ hangs in the sitting room** 挂在客厅里的那幅画; **the contract ~ he's spoken about** *or* **about ~ he's spoken** 他谈到的那份合同 3 (adding to preceding clause) 这个; **..., ~ reminds me ...** 这使我想起…; **we'll be moving, before ~ we need to ...** 我们要搬迁了，在这之前我们需要…; **his movie, ~ won several awards, is based on real life events** 他的影片是根据真实事件拍摄的，获过数个奖项; **he said he hadn't done it, ~ he can't prove** 他说他没干那事，但他没法证明

B *det* 1 (in questions) (referring to one) 哪个; (referring to several) 哪些; **~ way is the wind blowing?** 风是朝哪个方向刮的？; **~ books?** 哪些书？; **~ one of the children?** 哪个孩子？ 2 (in relative clauses) 那个; **in ~ case** 在那种情况下; **he left, during ~ time no one spoke** 他离开了，其间没有一个人说话; **he failed to apologize, for ~ mistake he paid dearly** formal 他没有道歉，因为这个过失他付出了沉重的代价

whichever /wɪtʃˈevə(r), Amer ˌhwɪtʃ-/

A *pron* 1 (the one that) …的那个; (the ones that) …的那些; **which restaurant? — ~ is nearest** 哪个餐馆？——最近的那个; **take ~ ones you like** 你喜欢哪些就拿哪些; **~ of you gets here first will get the prize** 你们谁第一个到达这儿谁就获奖 2 (no matter which one) 无论哪个; (no matter which ones) 无论哪些; **both courses are worthwhile, ~ you choose** 两门课程都值得选，你挑哪一门都行; **do you want the big piece or the small piece? — ~** 你想要大块还是小块？——哪块都行; **~ of the two parties forms the next government ...** 这两个政党中无论哪一个组建下届政府… 3 (which on earth) 究竟哪个; **~ did he choose?** 他到底选了哪一个？; **~ of them did he marry?** 他到底娶的是她们中的哪一个？

B *det* 1 (the one that) 那个…的; (the ones that) 那些…的; **go to ~ station is nearest** 去最近的那个车站; **underline ~ answer you consider correct** 在你认为正确的答案下画线; **take ~ ones you like** 你可以拿你喜欢的那些 2 (no matter which) 无论哪个; **~ way you look at it** 无论从哪一方面看这件事; **I'll be happy ~ horse wins** 哪匹马赢了我都高兴 3 (which on earth) 究竟是哪个; **~ one do you mean?** 你到底指的是哪个？

whiff /wɪf, Amer hwɪf/ *n* 1 (scent) 一股气味; **to get** *or* **catch a ~ of sth.** 闻到一股某种气味 2 *sing* fig (hint) 一丝; **a ~ of danger/suspicion** 一点点危险/些许怀疑 3 (inhalation) 一吸; **to take a ~ of sth.** 吸一下某物

whiffy /ˈwɪfi, Amer ˈhwɪfi/ *adj* Brit colloq pej 发臭的

Whig /wɪg, Amer hwɪg/ Brit Pol Hist

A *n* (politician) 辉格党党员; (voter) 辉格党支持者

B *modif* 辉格党的 ‹*policies, politician*›; **the ~ party** 辉格党

while /waɪl, Amer hwaɪl/

A *conj* 1 (during the time that) 在…期间; **he came ~ I was on the phone** 我打电话时他来了; **~ in Spain I visited Madrid** 我在西班牙时去了马德里; **~ doing sth.** 在做某事时; **to collapse ~ mowing the lawn** 在修剪草坪时晕倒 2 (at the same time as) 与…同时; **wait ~ I speak to him** 我和他说会儿话，你等一下; **'heels repaired ~ you wait'** "修鞋跟，立等可取"; **to eliminate draughts ~ allowing air to circulate** 在让空气流通的同时避免穿堂风; **close the door ~ you're at it** 你顺手关上门吧 3 (as long as) 只要; **~ there's life there's hope** Prov 有生命就有希望 4 (whereas) 然而; (but) 可是; **one person wants to go, ~ the other wants to stay** 一个人想走，而另一个却想留下; **it's cold here, ~ in Scotland it's even colder** 这里很冷，可苏格兰天气更冷 5 (although) 尽管; **~ the house is big, it is not in a very good state** 尽管房子大，但状况不是很好; **the peaches, ~ ripe, didn't taste of much** 这些桃子虽然熟了，但没有什么味道

B *n* 一段时间; **a ~ ago** *or* **back** colloq 不久前; **a good** *or* **long ~ ago/later** 很久以前/以后; **a short** *or* **little ~ ago/later** 不久前/以后; **a short** *or* **little ~ longer** 再一会儿; **to talk for a ~ longer** 又谈一会儿; **to chat for a (short) ~** 聊一（小）会儿; **after a ~** 过了一会儿; **in a ~** 一些时间以后; **all the ~** *or* **the whole ~, he was cheating on her** 他一直对她不忠; **to be a ~ (doing sth.)** （做某事）花相当长的时间; **to take a ~ (to do sth.)** （做某事）要花相当长的时间; **(every) once in a ~** 偶尔; **in between ~s** 间或

Phrasal verb

- **while away** *vt* [~ **sth. away**, ~ **away sth.**] 消磨 ‹*day, evening, hours*›; **to ~ away the time/morning/afternoon reading and playing cards** 靠看书和玩纸牌消磨时间/这个早上/这个下午

whilst /waɪlst, Amer hwaɪlst/ *conj* esp Brit formal = **while A**

whim /wɪm, Amer hwɪm/ *n* 突发奇想; **the ~ to do sth.** 做某事的冲动; **(to do sth.) on a ~** 心血来潮（做某事）; **to do sth. at sb.'s ~** 随某人的兴致做某事

whimper /'wɪmpə(r), Amer 'hwɪm-/
A *n* 呜咽; **to give a ~** 抽泣一声; **without a ~** 一声不哭地; **to end not with a bang but a ~** 结果是雷声大雨点小
B *vi* 呜咽
C *vt* 抽抽搭搭地说出 ‹*reply, request*›

whimpering /'wɪmpərɪŋ, Amer 'hwɪm-/
A *n* 呜咽声
B *adj attrib* 呜咽的 ‹*voice, sound*›

whimsical /'wɪmzɪkl, Amer 'hwɪm-/ *adj* 古怪的 ‹*person, behaviour, sense of humour, notion, smile, idea*›; 离奇的 ‹*story, film*›; 心血来潮的 ‹*decision*›

whimsicality /ˌwɪmzɪ'kæləti, Amer ˌhwɪm-/ *n* 1 [u] (quality) 古怪; **the ~ of the plot** 情节的离奇 2 [c] *usu pl* (action) 古怪的行为; (idea) 古怪的想法

whimsically /'wɪmzɪkli, Amer 'hwɪm-/ *adv* 心血来潮地 ‹*act, decide*›; 怪异地 ‹*smile, dress, decorate, write*›

whimsy /'wɪmzi, Amer 'hwɪm-/ *n* 1 [u] (humour, fantasy) 稀奇古怪 2 [c] (fanciful thing) 稀奇古怪的东西

whine /waɪn, Amer hwaɪn/
A *n* 1 (cry) (of person) 哭喊声; (of animal) 哀叫声 2 (noise) (of machine, motor, saw) 嘎嘎声; (of bullets) 嗖嗖声; **a nasal ~** 鼻息 3 pej (complaining tone) 抱怨的语调; **in** *or* **with a ~** 哼哼唧唧地
B *vi* 1 (cry) «*person*» 哭喊; «*animal*» 哀叫; **the dogs ~d to go out** 那几条狗呜呜叫着要出去 2 (make noise) «*machine, motor, saw*» 嘎嘎响; «*bullet*» 嗖嗖响 3 pej (complain) 哼哼唧唧地抱怨; **to ~ about sth.** 嘟囔某事
C *vt* pej 哼哼唧唧地诉说 ‹*complaint, reply*›; **'what about me?' he ~d** "那我呢？"他嘟囔着说

whinge /wɪndʒ, Amer hwɪndʒ/ esp Brit colloq
A *vi* (*pres p* **~ing**) 絮絮叨叨地抱怨
B *vt* (*pres p* **~ing**) 絮絮叨叨地嘟囔 ‹*complaint, feeling*›
C *n* 絮絮叨叨的抱怨; **to have a ~ (about sth.)** 嘟囔（某事）

whingeing /'wɪndʒɪŋ, Amer 'hwɪn-/ esp Brit colloq
A *n* [u] 絮絮叨叨的抱怨
B *adj* 絮絮叨叨抱怨的 ‹*person, voice*›

whining /'waɪnɪŋ, Amer 'hwaɪn-/
A *n* [u] 1 (act of crying) 哀叫; (sound of crying) 哀叫声 2 (sound) (of machine, motor, saw) 嘎嘎声; (of bullet) 嗖嗖声 3 pej (complaining) 嘟囔
B *adj attrib* 1 (high-pitched) 尖锐的 ‹*voice*›; 嘎嘎作响的 ‹*motor, saw*›; 嗖嗖响的 ‹*bullet*› 2 pej (complaining, crying) 嘟嘟囔囔的 ‹*person*›; 哭哭啼啼的 ‹*child*›; 呜呜叫的 ‹*dog*›

whinny /'wɪni, Amer 'hwɪni/
A *vi* «*horse*» 轻声嘶鸣
B *n* [马的] 轻声嘶鸣

whinnying /'wɪnɪɪŋ, Amer 'hwɪnɪɪŋ/ *n* [u] (action) 轻声嘶鸣; (sound) 嘶鸣声

whip /wɪp, Amer hwɪp/
A *n* 1 [c] (implement) 鞭子; **to strike** *or* **lash sb. with a ~** 用鞭子抽打某人 2 [c] Pol (official) 组织秘书 [亦称党鞭] 3 [c] Brit Pol (request to attend vote) （出席投票）书面通知; **the ~** 执政党议员资格; **to resign the party ~** 退出执政党; **a one-line/two-line/three-line ~** 紧急/十分紧急/特急出席通知 4 [c and u] Culin 搅打奶油甜食
B *vt* (*pres p etc.* **-pp-**) 1 (lash) 抽打; **to ~ sb. to death** 把某人抽打致死; **the wind ~ped the flames higher and higher** 风把火焰越吹越高 2 Culin (beat) 搅打 ‹*batter, cream*› 3 fig (stir) 煽动; **he ~ped his audience into a frenzy** 他把观众的情绪煽动得狂热起来 4 fig colloq (defeat) 把…打得一败涂地 ‹*opponent, group*› 5 colloq (remove quickly) 猛地挪动; **she ~ped the plates off the table** 她一下子把盘子从桌上拿走了; **I ~ped the key out of his hand** 我从他手中一把抢过钥匙 6 Brit colloq (steal) 偷走 7 (stop from fraying) (with twine) 缠在…的梢上 ‹*rope*›; (with overcast stitches) 锁…的边 ‹*fabric, seam*›
C *vi* (*pres p etc.* **-pp-**) 1 (lash) «*rope, tail*» 挥动; **the branches were ~ping in the wind** 枝条在风中摇曳; **the wind ~ped across the open spaces** 风呼呼地吹过空旷之处 2 colloq (move fast) «*person*» 快速移动; **I'll just ~ over** *or* **round to my sister's** 我正要赶到我姐姐家去; **to ~ round** 猛地转身; **to ~ through sth.**; 匆匆做 ‹*work*›; 匆匆浏览 ‹*book*›

Phrasal verbs

- **whip away** *vt* [**~ sth. away, ~ away sth.**] 一下子移走 ‹*plate, book*›; **the wind ~ped my hat away** 风猛地吹走了我的帽子
- **whip back**
A *vi* «*branch, rope*» 弹回来
B *vt* [**~ sth. back, ~ back sth.**] colloq 一把抢回
- **whip off** *vt* [**~ sth. off, ~ off sth.**] colloq 一把脱下 ‹*garment*›
- **whip on** *vt* [**~ sth. on, ~ on sth.**] 1 (urge on) 用鞭子催促 ‹*horse, team*› 2 colloq (put on quickly) 匆忙穿戴好
- **whip out** colloq
A *vi* 急冲出去
B *vt* [**~ sth. out, ~ out sth.**] 迅速拿出; **the man ~ped out a knife** 那个男子嗖地掏出一把刀; **he ~ped the gun out from its holster** 他嗖地从枪套中拔出枪
- **whip up**
A [**~ sth. up, ~ up sth.**] *vt* 1 Culin 搅打…成糊状 ‹*eggs, batter*› 2 colloq (produce quickly) 匆匆做 ‹*meal, snack*›; 匆匆作 ‹*report*› 3 (incite) 激起 ‹*enthusiasm, hatred, unrest*› 4 (cause to rise up and blow around) «*wind*» 卷起 ‹*dust, sand*›
B [**~ sb. up, ~ up sb.**] *vt* 煽动; **his speech ~ped the crowd up into a frenzy** 他的演讲把人群煽动得狂热起来

> **three-line whip**
>
> 三道杠出席令，亦称特急出席通知。英国议会中的各个政党都会任命一名议员担任组织秘书（whip），主要负责维护党的纪律，确保本党议员参加辩论，并遵照指定立场投票。组织秘书每星期会向议员们发送通报（亦称 whip），告知未来一个星期的议事日程。辩论的事项按重要程度在下面画一至三道横杠。三道杠的通报称 three-line whip，表示必须出席，而且必须按照指定立场投票。违纪者会受到严厉处分。

whipcord /'wɪpkɔːd, Amer 'hwɪp-/ *n* 1 [u and c] (cord) 鞭绳 2 [u] Tex 马裤呢; **~ trousers** 马裤呢裤子

whip hand *n* **the ~** 支配地位; **to have the ~ over sb.** 掌控某人

whiplash /'wɪplæʃ, Amer 'hwɪp-/ *n* 1 [c] (part of whip) 鞭索 2 [c] (stroke) 鞭打; **the ~ of sb.'s tongue** 某人话语的鞭笞 3 [u and c] Med **= whiplash injury**

whiplash injury *n* [u and c] [尤指车祸中颈椎过度屈伸形成的] 鞭抽伤

whipped cream *n* [u] 掼奶油

whipper-in /ˌwɪpər'ɪn, Amer ˌhwɪp-/ *n* (*pl* **whippers-in**) 专管猎狗的副手

whippersnapper /'wɪpəsnæpə(r), Amer 'hwɪpə-/ *n* colloq 狂妄小子; **a cheeky young ~** 放肆狂妄的年轻小子

whippet /'wɪpɪt, Amer 'hwɪpɪt/ *n* 小灵狗

whipping /'wɪpɪŋ, Amer 'hwɪp-/ *n* 1 [c] (beating) 鞭打; **to give sb. a ~** 鞭打某人 2 [u] (twine) 绑扎绳索 3 [u] (stitching on rug, fabric) 拷边

whipping: ~ boy *n* 替罪羊; **~ cream** *n* [u] 搅打奶油; **~ post** *n* [捆绑罪犯的] 鞭笞柱; **~ top** *n* 鞭抽陀螺

whippoorwill /'wɪpʊəwɪl, Amer 'hwɪp-/ *n* 三声夜鹰

whip-round *n* Brit colloq 凑份子; **to have** *or* **do a ~ for sb./sth.** 为某人/某事凑份子

whir /wɜː(r), Amer hwɜːr/ *n, vi* **= whirr**

whirl /wɜːl, Amer hwɜːl/
A *n* 1 (spinning or swirling movement) 旋转 2 (spiral motif) 旋涡式图案 3 fig (frantic activity) 繁忙; **the social ~** 纷繁的社交活动; **to be all in a ~ about sth.** 为某事都忙得晕头转向; **her head is in a ~** 她的脑子乱成一团; **to give sth. a ~** colloq 试一试某事
B *vi* 1 (spin, swirl) «*person, leaves, water, propeller*» 旋转; **my mind** *or* **head is** *or* **my thoughts are ~ing** 我的脑子里乱糟糟的 2 (rush) **to ~ past/along** «*vehicle*» 急驰过/向前疾驰; «*person*» 飞跑过/向前飞跑
C *vt* 1 (spin, swirl) «*wind, water*» 使…旋转 ‹*leaves, sand*› 2 (rush) 催促 ‹*person*›

Phrasal verb

- **whirl round**
A *vi* «*person, blade*» 快速旋转
B *vt* [**~ sth./sb. round, ~ round sth./sb.**] 快速转动 ‹*sword, rope*›; **to ~ one's partner round** 带着舞伴旋转

whirligig /'wɜːlɪgɪg, Amer 'hwɜːl-/ *n* 1 (merry-go-round) 旋转木马 2 (toy) 陀螺

whirligig beetle *n* 豉虫

whirlpool /'wɜːlpuːl, Amer 'hwɜːl-/ *n* 旋涡

whirlpool bath *n* 涡流按摩浴缸

whirlwind /'wɜːlwɪnd, Amer 'hwɜːl-/ *n* 1 Meteorol 旋风 2 fig (frantic situation) 忙乱; **a ~ of activity** 一阵忙乱的活动; **a ~ tour/romance** 马不停蹄的旅程/闪电式恋爱

whirlybird /'wɜːlɪbɜːd, Amer 'hwɜːl-/ *n* esp Amer colloq 直升机

whirr /wɜː(r), Amer hwɜːr/
A *n* (of wings of insect or bird) 呼呼声; (of propellor, motor, fan, toy) 嗡嗡声
B *vi* «*wings of insect or bird*» 呼呼作响; «*helicopter, fan, camera*» 嗡嗡作响

whisk /wɪsk, Amer hwɪsk/
A *vt* 1 Culin 搅打 ‹*sauce*›; **~ the eggs and margarine together** 把鸡蛋和人造奶油搅打在一起 2 (transport, move quickly) 迅速移动; **they ~ed me into the operating theatre** 他们匆匆把我推进了手术室
B *n* 1 Culin 搅拌器; **a hand/a mechanical/an electric ~** 手工/机械/电动搅拌器 2 (brush) 掸帚 3 (movement) 掸; **with a ~ of its tail** 用它的尾巴一扫; **a quick ~ round** colloq 匆匆打扫

Phrasal verbs

- **whisk away** *vt* [**~ sth. away, ~ away sth.**] 匆匆带走 ‹*object, garment, person*›
- **whisk off**
A *vt* [**~ sb./sth. off, ~ off sb./sth.**] 一把拧开 ‹*lid*›; 匆匆脱下 ‹*garment*›; 匆匆摘下 ‹*hat*›; 匆匆带走 ‹*person*›
B *vi* 轻快地走开
- **whisk up** *vt* [**~ sth. up, ~ up sth.**] 1 Culin 彻底搅打 2 (pick up quickly) 一把抓起

whisker /'wɪskə(r), Amer 'hwɪs-/
A *n* 1 *usu pl* Zool [老鼠、猫等的] 须 2 fig (small margin) 一点儿; **by a ~** 差一点儿; **to lose the race by a ~** 以毫厘之差输掉赛跑; **to come within a ~ of winning** 几近获胜
B **whiskers** *npl* (sideburns) 连鬓胡子; (beard, moustache) 胡须

whiskered /'wɪskəd, Amer 'hwɪs-/ *adj* 长络腮胡子的 ‹*face, man*›

whisky Brit, **whiskey** Amer, Ir /'wɪski, Amer 'hwɪs-/ *n* (*pl* **whiskies** Brit, **whiskeys** Amer, Ir) 1 [u and c] (spirit) 威士忌; **~ glasses** 威士忌酒杯 2 [c] (serving) 一杯威士忌

whisky mac *n* [u and c] 威士忌姜酒

whisper /'wɪspə(r), Amer 'hwɪs-/
A *vi* 1 (speak quietly) «*person, voices*» 低语; **stop ~ing to your friend** 别跟你朋友嘀咕了

W

2 fig (rustle) «*leaves, trees, grass*» 沙沙作响; «*wind*» 发出飒飒声

B *vt* **1** (say) 低声说 ‹*comment*›; **to ~ a word in sb.'s ear** 在某人耳边窃窃私语; **to ~ sweet nothings** 喃喃地说甜言蜜语 **2** (spread rumour) 私下传播; **it was ~ed that ...** 据说…

C *n* **1** (of person, voices) 低语; **to speak** *or* **say sth. in a ~** 低声说某事; **to drop** *or* **sink to a ~** «*voice*» 压低到耳语; **not a ~!** 别出声! **2** (rumour) 谣传; **there is a ~ (going round) that ...** 人们纷纷传言说… **3** fig (rustling) (of leaves, trees, grass) 沙沙声; (of wind) 飒飒声

whispering /ˈwɪspərɪŋ, Amer ˈhwɪs-/

A *n* **1** [u] (sound of whisper) 低语 **2** [u and c] (rumour) 传言 **3** [u] fig (rustling) (of leaves, trees, grass) 沙沙声; (of wind) 飒飒声

B *adj attrib* **1** (speaking in whisper) 低语的 ‹*person*›; 耳语的 ‹*voice*› **2** fig (rustling) 沙沙响的 ‹*leaves, trees, grass*›; 飒飒响的 ‹*wind*›

whispering: ~ campaign *n* 造谣中伤; **~ gallery** *n* 回音廊

whist /wɪst, Amer hwɪst/ ▸**p. 307** *n* [u] 惠斯特纸牌戏

whist drive *n* 惠斯特牌比赛

whistle /ˈwɪsl, Amer ˈhwɪsl/

A *n* **1** (sound) (by person through lips, device, musical instrument) 哨声; (by animal, kettle, bird) 鸣叫声; (of train, siren) 汽笛; (of wind) 呼啸声; **to emit** *or* **let out** *or* **give a ~** 发出哨音; **a piercing ~** 刺耳的哨声; **boos and ~s** 嘘声和口哨声; **(as) clean as a ~** 干干净净的; **the house was as clean as a ~** 这房子一尘不染 **2** (instrument, device) 哨子; **a blast of the ~** 一阵响亮的哨声; **the sound of the factory ~** 工厂的汽笛声; **to blow the ~ on sb./sth.** fig 检举某人/某事物; **to wet one's ~** colloq 喝酒

B *vi* **1** (make noise) «*person*» 吹口哨; «*animal, kettle, bird*» 鸣叫; «*train, siren*» 鸣笛; «*wind*» 呼啸; **to ~ at sb.** 朝某人吹口哨; **he ~d at** *or* **for us to follow him** 他对我们吹了声口哨, 示意我们跟着他; **to ~ to sb./sth.** 吹口哨召唤某人/某物; **he ~d to his dogs** 他吹口哨唤狗; **to ~ for sth.** 吹口哨召唤某物; **you can ~ for it!** 你休想得到!; **to ~ in the dark** fig 借吹口哨壮胆 **2** (move fast) «*vehicle*» 呼啸而行; **to ~ by** *or* **past** «*bullet, arrow*» 嗖地飞过

C *vt* 用口哨吹 ‹*tune, melody*›

Phrasal verb

- **whistle up** *vt* **1** (summon) 吹哨召唤 ‹*dog, person*› **2** colloq (provide at short notice) 短时间内做好 ‹*item, meal*›; **I'll see if I can ~ up a few cups of coffee** 我看看能不能马上弄几杯咖啡

whistle-blower /ˈwɪslbləʊə(r), Amer ˈhwɪsl-/ *n* 告密者

whistle-stop *n* Amer **1** (place) 无名小镇 **2** Rail 无名小站 **3** Pol [选举演讲的] 短暂停留

whistle-stop tour *n* 短暂停留的出行

whit /wɪt, Amer hwɪt/ *n sing* dated 一点儿; **not a ~** 丝毫不

white /waɪt, Amer hwaɪt/ ▸**p. 134**

A *adj* **1** (in colour) 白的; **a ~ chess piece** 白棋子; **the horse was almost pure ~ in colour** 这匹马几乎是纯白色的; **a crisp ~ shirt** 挺括的白衬衫; **a set of perfect ~ teeth** 一口洁白的牙齿; **bright** *or* **brilliant ~** 亮白色的; **as ~ as snow** 洁白如雪; **~r than ~** (of person's image) 清白无瑕; **to wash ~r than ~** 洗得白上加白; **the men in ~ coats** hum 穿白大褂的人 [指医生] **2** *pred* (pale) 苍白的 ‹*face, cheek*›; 脸色苍白的 ‹*person*›; **he turned** *or* **went ~ with shock** 他惊得脸色苍白; **her face was ~ with fear** 她吓得脸色煞白; **his hair turned ~ with shock** 由于受到惊吓, 他的头发变白了; **to go** *or* **turn as ~ as a sheet** *or* **ghost** 变得面如白纸 **3** **White** (with light skin) 白肤色的 ‹*person*›; 白人的 ‹*area, culture, prejudice*›; **the W~ races** 白人种族

B *n* **1** [c and u] (colour) 白色; (pigment) 白颜料; **in ~** 白色的; **dressed in ~** 穿白色衣服的; **he would swear black was ~** 他会颠倒黑白; **two blacks don't make a ~** 以牙还牙行不通 **2** [c] (white part) (gen) 白色部分; (of cooked egg) 蛋白; (of raw egg) 蛋清; **the ~(s) of sb.'s eye(s)** 某人的眼白 **3** [c] (in snooker, billiards, pool) 白球; **to hit/miss the ~** 击中/未击中白球; **to pot the ~** 击打白球入袋 **4** **White** [c] (person) 白人; **'W~s only'** Hist "白人专用" **5** [u and c] (wine) 白葡萄酒 **6** **White** [u] (in chess, draughts) 白方

C **whites** *npl* (white clothes) 白色衣服; (worn by cricketer etc.) 白色运动服; (worn as naval uniform) 白色海军制服; (for washing) 白色洗涤物

whitebait /ˈwaɪtbeɪt, Amer ˈhwaɪt-/ *npl + v sing or pl* 小鲱鱼

white: ~beam *n* 白面子树; **~ blood cell** *n* 白细胞; **~board** *n* **1** (for writing) 白色书写板; **2** Comput 白板; **~ book** *n* 白皮书; **~ bread** *n* [u] 白面包; **~-bread** *adj* Amer colloq 迎合白人中产阶级口味的 ‹*culture, institution*›; **~ cedar** *n* **1** [c] (tree) 白扁柏; **2** [u] (wood) 白扁柏木; **W~ Christmas** *n* 白色圣诞节 [指下雪]; **~ coffee** *n* [u and c] 加牛奶的咖啡

white-collar *adj* 白领的

white-collar: ~ crime *n* [u and c] 白领犯罪; **~ job** 白领工作; **~ union** *n* 白领工会; **~ worker** *n* 白领工作者

white: ~-coloured *adj* 白色的; **~ currant** *n* **1** (fruit) 红茶藨子果; **2** (bush) 红茶藨子; **~ dwarf** *n* 白矮星

white elephant *n* **1** (possession) 无用的累赘 **2** (public project) 公共白象 [指耗资巨大而不实用的工程]

white elephant stall *n* [义卖会的] 闲置物品出售摊位

white: ~ ensign *n* 英国皇家海军旗; **~-faced** *adj* 脸色苍白的; **~-faced with rage** 气得脸色发青; **~ fish** *n* [u] 白鲑; **~ flag** *n* [表示投降的] 白旗; **to raise the ~ flag** 举白旗投降; **~fly** *n* (*pl* **~fly** *or* **~flies**) 粉虱; **~ gold** *n* [u] 白金; **a ~-gold ring** 白金戒指; **~ goods** *npl* 白色家电 [指洗衣机、电冰箱等]; **~-haired** *adj* 白发苍苍的 ‹*person*›

Whitehall *pr n* Brit **1** (street) 白厅街 **2** (government) 白厅 [指英国政府]

> **Whitehall**
>
> 白厅街, 位于英国伦敦威斯敏斯特自治市, 北临特拉法加广场 (Trafalgar Square), 南至议会大厦 (▸**the Houses of Parliament**)。街名源自白厅宫 (Whitehall Palace), 自亨利八世 (Henry VIII) 起为英国皇宫, 1698 年毁于大火, 今仅存宴会厅 (Banqueting Hall)。白厅街上集中了英国主要的政府部门, 故亦用来指代英国政府。

white: ~-headed *adj* 白发的 ‹*person*›; 白头的 ‹*bird, animal*›; **~ heat** *n* **1** [u] Phys 白炽; **2** [c] *sing* fig (frenzy) 白热化; **a ~ heat of indignation** 激愤; **~ hope** *n* **1** 被寄予厚望的人; **2** **the great ~ hope of British boxing** 英国有希望与黑人拳手争夺拳击冠军的白人; **~ horses** *npl* 白浪; **~ hot** *adj* 白热的 ‹*metal*›; fig 白热化的 ‹*passion, intensity*›; **W~ House** *pr n* **the W~ House** (residence) 白宫 [美国总统官邸]; (government) 白宫 [指美国总统或政府]; **a W~ House aide/spokesperson** 白宫助理/发言人; **~ knight** *n* **1** (rescuer) 拯救者; **2** Fin 白衣骑士 [指向面临恶意收购的公司提出可接受的收购计划者]; **~-knuckle ride** *n* colloq 紧张刺激的游乐设施乘坐; fig 紧张刺激的经历; **~ lead** /led/ *n* [u] 铅白; **~ lie** *n* 善意的谎言; **to tell (sb.) a ~ lie** (对某人) 撒个小谎; **~ light** *n* [u] 白光

> **the White House**
>
> 白宫, 美国总统官邸和办公室。位于华盛顿特区宾夕法尼亚大街 1600 号。设计者为爱尔兰裔建筑师詹姆斯·霍本 (James Hoban)。1792 年奠基, 1800 年建成。1814 年被英军烧毁, 后重建。因建筑用的砂岩被刷成白色而得名。1901 年正式命名为白宫, 部分区域对公众开放。现已成为美国政府的代名词。

white line

A *n* **1** (on road) [车行道的] 中间白线 **2** Sport [球场的] 界线

B **white-line** *vt* «*worker, machine*» 给…标上白线 ‹*road*›; «*groundsman*» 给…标上白色界线 ‹*field, court*›

white: ~-lipped /ˌwaɪtˈlɪpt, Amer ˌhwaɪt-/ *adj* 嘴唇发白的 ‹*person*›; 白唇的 ‹*animal*›; **~ list** colloq 白名单 [与黑名单相对]; **~ magic** *n* [u] 白法术 [指用于行善的法术]; **~ meat** *n* [u] 白肉 [如鸡肉、火鸡肉等]; **~ metal** *n* [u] 白合金

whiten /ˈwaɪtn, Amer ˈhwaɪtn/

A *vt* 使变白

B *vi* 变白

whitener /ˈwaɪtnə(r), Amer ˈhwaɪt-/ *n* [u and c] (for clothes, shoes) 漂白剂; (for coffee) 咖啡伴侣; (for tea) 茶伴侣; (for teeth) 增白粉

whiteness /ˈwaɪtnɪs, Amer ˈhwaɪt-/ *n* [u] 白; **the ~ of the snow** 雪的洁白; **the ~ of sb.'s face** 某人面部的苍白

White Nile ▸**p. 663** *pr n* **the ~** 白尼罗河

whitening /ˈwaɪtnɪŋ, Amer ˈhwaɪt-/ *n* [u] **1** (making white) 弄白; **~ of walls** 墙的粉刷 **2** (becoming white) 变白 **3** (substance) 白垩粉

white: ~ noise *n* [u] 白噪声; **~-out** *n* (snow) 暴风雪; (fog) 浓雾; **W~ Paper** *n* Brit 白皮书; **~ pepper** *n* [u] 白胡椒; **~ pine** *n* 五针松; **~ room** *n* 无尘室; **~ Russia** *pr n* dated = **Belarus**

White Russian dated

A *adj* (of Belarus) 白俄的; (of the people) 白俄罗斯人的

B *n* 白俄罗斯人

white: ~ sale *n* 家用织物减价出售; **~ sauce** *n* [u] [用牛奶、黄油和面粉等调制的] 白沙司; **W~ Sea** *n* **the W~ Sea** 白海 [位于俄罗斯西北岸]; **~ shark** *n* **(great) ~ shark** (大) 白鲨; **~-skinned** *adj* 白皮肤的 ‹*person*›; 白人的 ‹*race*›; **~-skinned people** 白种人; **~ slave** *n* dated [尤指在国外] 沦为娼妓的欧洲女性; **the ~ slave trade** 欧洲妓女非法买卖; **~ slaver** *n* dated 诱迫欧洲女性为娼者; **~ slavery** *n* [u] dated [欧洲女性] 沦为娼妓; **W~s-only** *adj* 白人专用的 ‹*club, school*›; **~ spirit** *n* [u] Brit 石油溶剂油; **~ stick** *n* [盲人使用的] 白色手杖; **~ supremacist** *n* 白人至上主义者; **~ supremacist ideologies** 白人至上主义意识形态; **~ supremacy** *n* [u] 白人至上; **~ tea** *n* **1** [u and c] (tea with milk) 奶茶; **2** [u] (type of tea) 白茶; **~thorn** *n* [u and c] = **hawthorn**; **~ tie** *n* **1** [c] (tie) [正式晚礼服上系的] 白领结; **2** [u] (formal dress) 正式晚礼服; **a white-tie dinner** 须着晚礼服的晚宴; **~ trash** *n + v sing or pl* Amer pej [尤指美国南部的] 白穷鬼; **~ van man** Brit colloq [鲁莽疯狂的] 白色货车司机; **~wall tyre** *n* 白圈轮胎

whitewash /ˈwaɪtwɒʃ, Amer ˈhwaɪt-/

A *n* **1** [u] (for walls) 白涂料 **2** [c] *sing* fig (cover-up) 掩饰; **the investigation was a ~ job** 这次调查是为了掩人耳目 **3** [c] Sport colloq [尤指在系列比赛中的] 剃光头

B *vt* **1** (cover with whitewash) 粉刷 ‹*wall, building*› **2** fig pej (conceal) «*person, report*» 粉饰 ‹*character, decision*›; **to ~ sth. over, to ~ over sth.** 掩饰某事 **3** Sport colloq [尤指在系列比赛的每一场] 剃…的光头 ‹*opponent, team*›

white: ~ water *n* [u] [岩石周围的] 白色激流; **~-water rafting** *n* [u] 激流漂筏; **to go**

W

~-water rafting 去激流漂筏; ~ **wedding** *n* 白色婚礼 [指新娘穿白婚纱的传统婚礼]; ~ **whale** *n* 白鲸; ~ **wine** *n* 白葡萄酒; ~ **witch** *n* 行善女巫; ~**wood** *n* 1 [u] (wood) 白木; 2 [c] esp Amer (tree) 白木树 [尤指银杉树、椴木和郁金香树]

whitey /'waɪti, Amer 'hwaɪti/ colloq
A *n* pej 白鬼 [黑人对白人的蔑称]
B *adj* 略带白色的 ‹*blue, grey*›

whither /'wɪðə(r), Amer 'hwɪðər/ *adv* 1 archaic or liter (where) 往何处; ~ **goest thou?** 尔往何处去? 2 archaic or liter (to which) 往那边 3 Journ (what is the future of) 何种结果

whiting[1] /'waɪtɪŋ, Amer 'hwaɪt-/ *n* (*pl* **whiting**) Zool 牙鳕

whiting[2] *n* [u and c] (whitener) 白垩粉

whitish /'waɪtɪʃ, Amer 'hwaɪt-/ *adj* 发白的 ‹*hue, substance*›; 浅淡的 ‹*green, yellow*›

whitlow /'wɪtləʊ, Amer 'hwɪt-/ *n* 甲沟炎

Whitsun /'wɪtsn, Amer 'hwɪtsn/ *n* 圣灵降临节 [复活节后第七个星期日及其后几天]; **the ~ holiday** 圣灵降临节

Whit Sunday /ˌwɪt 'sʌndeɪ, Amer ˌhwɪt 'sʌndeɪ/ *n* 圣灵降临节

whittle /'wɪtl, Amer 'hwɪtl/ *vt* 1 (cut) 削 ‹*piece of wood, stick*› 2 (create) 削成 ‹*peg, walking stick*›

Phrasal verbs

• **whittle away**
A *vt* [~ **sth. away,** ~ **away sth.**]
1 (reduce by whittling) 削短 ‹*piece of wood, stick*› 2 fig (diminish) 削减 ‹*finances, savings*›; 削弱 ‹*confidence*›
B *vi* 1 (keep whittling) 不断地削; **to ~ away at** 不停地削 ‹*piece of wood, stick*› 2 fig (keep reducing) 不断削减; **to ~ away at sth.** 持续减少 ‹*savings*›; 持续削弱 ‹*confidence*›

• **whittle down** *vt* [~ **sth. down,** ~ **down sth.**]
1 = **whittle away A** 2 fig (reduce in number) 减少 ‹*applicants, number*›; **to ~ the number of candidates down to three** 将候选人数减少到三个

whiz /wɪz, Amer hwɪz/ *n, vi, vt* = **whizz**

whiz-bang *n* esp Amer colloq 巨大的成功

whizz /wɪz, Amer hwɪz/
A *vi* 1 (move noisily) **to ~ past** *or* **by** «*arrow, missile*» 飕飕飞过; «*car, bike*» 飕飕开过; **the bullet ~ed though the air** 子弹嗖的一声划过空气; **cars ~ed along the road** 汽车呼啸着沿路驶过 2 (move quickly) «*person*» 快速移动; **to ~ into the bank** 冲进银行; **the weeks ~ed by** 几个星期一晃而过; **to ~ through sth.** 麻利地完成 ‹*task*›
B *vt* colloq 赶快转交; **to ~ sth. over** 把…扔过去 ‹*object, letter*›; **to ~ sth. round** 马上交付某物
C *n* 1 *usu sing* (sound) 飕飕声 2 colloq (expert) 行家; **to be a ~ at sth.** 对某事很在行

whizz: ~-bang *n* esp Amer colloq = **whiz-bang**; ~**-kid** *n* colloq (in organization) 有为青年; (child prodigy) 神童

whizzo /'wɪzəʊ, Amer 'hwɪz-/ *excl* Brit colloq dated 很棒的 ‹*idea, gadget*›

WHO *abbr* = **World Health Organization**

who /hu:/ *pron* 1 (in direct or indirect questions) 谁; ~ **is that woman?** 那个女人是谁?; ~'**s this present for?** colloq 这礼物是给谁的?; **I sold it — ~ to?** 我把它给卖了——卖给谁了?; ~ **do you think you are?** 你以为你是什么人?; ~ **are you to tell me I can't park here?** 你是谁呀, 凭什么不让我在这儿停车?; ~'**s ~** 谁是谁; **do you know ~'s ~?** 你知道这些人的身份吗? 2 (asking for name) [用于让人说出全名]; **John's here — John ~?** 约翰来了——哪个约翰? 3 (specifying preceding noun) …的人; **people ~ like cats** 喜欢猫的人; **it's science teachers ~ are so scarce** 非常缺乏的是理科老师; **that's the man ~ I gave it to** colloq 我把东西就交给了那个男人; **he ~ hesitates is lost** Prov 犹豫不决者错失良机 4 (adding to preceding noun) [进一步提供先行词的信息]; **my mother, ~ was an architect, died last year** 我母亲是去年去世的, 她是一名建筑师; **I gave the money to Laura, ~ put it in the safe** colloq 我把钱给了劳拉, 她将它放在了保险柜里 5 (whoever) 无论谁; **give it to ~ you like** 你愿意给谁就给谁; **he ~ dares wins** 谁胆大谁就赢

whoa /wəʊ/ *excl* 1 (stop) ~, **boy** (to horse) 吁, 小家伙; ~, **that's plenty!** (to person) 好了, 足够了! 2 colloq (in surprise) 哇; ~, **that's huge!** 哇! 真大呀!

who'd /hu:d/ colloq 1 = **who had** ▸**have** 2 = **who would** ▸**would**

whodunnit Brit, **whodunit** Amer /ˌhu:'dʌnɪt/ *n* colloq (story) 侦探小说; (play) 侦探戏剧

whoe'er /hu:'eə(r)/ *pron* liter = **whoever**

whoever /hu:'evə(r)/ *pron* 1 (the one or ones who) …的人; ~ **says that is a liar** 说那话的人是个骗子; **ask ~ she gave the original to to let you have a copy** 她把原件给了谁, 你就向谁要复印件 2 (anyone who) 任何…的人; **show it to ~ you want** 你爱给谁看就给谁看 3 (all who) …的每一个人; **tell ~ you know** 告诉你认识的每一个人; **to provide food for ~ comes** 给所有来的人提供食物 4 (no matter who, expressing doubt) 无论谁; **I don't want to see them, ~ they are** 无论他们是谁, 我都不想见; **a letter for George Jones, ~ that may be** 给乔治·琼斯的一封信, 不管他是谁 5 colloq (anyone similar) **or ~** 或类似的人; **pay the manager or ~** 把钱付给经理之类的人 6 (who on earth) 究竟是谁; ~ **can that be?** 那个人究竟会是谁呢?; ~ **heard of such a thing?** colloq 居然有这样的事?; **I gave it away — ~ to?** 我把它送人了——究竟给谁了呢?

whole /həʊl/
A *adj* 1 *attrib* (entire) 全部的 ‹*contents, attention, membership*›; 整个的 ‹*group, cake, area, period*›; **a ~ sentence** 完整的句子; **he has spent his ~ life helping others** 他一辈子都在帮助别人; **we've got three ~ weeks holiday!** 我们有整整三周的假期!; **she ate a ~ bag of sweets all by herself!** 她一个人把整整一包糖全吃光了!; ~ **cities were devastated** 整座整座的城市遭到了毁坏; **she wasn't telling the ~ truth** 她没有说出全部真相; **his ~ body ached** 他浑身疼痛; **she made the ~ thing up** 整个事情都是她编造的; **this doesn't give the ~ picture** 这没有给出事情的全貌; **the ~ country/school/class** 全国/全校/全班; **the ~ (wide) world** 全世界; **you should be aware of the ~ person** 你应该了解一个人的方方面面; **with one's ~ heart** 全心全意地 2 *attrib* (emphatic use) [用于强调]; **a ~ range of issues** 一系列问题; **he's eaten the ~ lot by himself!** 他自己吃了个一干二净!; **that goes for the ~ lot of you!** 这对你们个个都适用!; **a ~ lot of money** 许多许多的钱; **you don't like him a ~ lot, do you?** colloq 你不怎么喜欢他, 是吗?; **I'm feeling a ~ lot better now** 我现在感觉好多了; **the ~ point (of sth.)** (某事的) 全部意义; **you can't leave whenever you feel like it! that's the ~ point!** 你不能想离开就离开! 这是关键!; **that's the ~ point of the exercise** 这项练习的全部意义就在于此 3 (intact) 完整的; **after the party there wasn't a single glass left ~** 聚会结束后, 一个完好的杯子都没有剩下; **you're very lucky to have got out ~** *or* **with your skin ~** 你毫发无损, 真是幸运; **to swallow/cook/roast sth. ~** 将某物囫囵吞下/整个烹煮/整个烘烤
B *adv* colloq 完全; **a ~ new era/way of life** 全新的时代/生活方式
C *n* 1 (total unit) 整体; **the ~ is greater than any of its parts** 整体大于部分; **a complete/undivided ~** 完整的/不可分割的整体; **as a ~** (not in separate parts) 作为整体; (overall) 总体上; **this will benefit society as a ~** 这将造福整个社会; **on the ~** 大体上 2 (all) 全部; **the ~ of sth.** 某物的全部; **we spent the ~ of August/the school holidays abroad** 我们整个八月/学校假期都在国外度过; **there wasn't a grain of truth in the ~ of his account** 他的全部陈述中没有一句是真实的; **the ~ of London is talking about it!** 全伦敦都在谈论这件事!; **in ~ or in part** 全部地或者部分地

whole: ~ blood *n* [u] 全血; ~ **cloth** [u] 整幅布; **out of (the) ~ cloth** Amer fig colloq 凭空捏造的

wholefood *n* [u and c] 全天然食物; **a ~ diet** 全天然食谱

wholefood shop *n* Brit 全天然食品店

whole: ~grain *adj* 全谷物制作的 ‹*flour*›; ~**grain cereal/bread/rice** 整粒麦片/全麦面包/糙米; ~**hearted** *adj* 全心全意的 ‹*approval, support*›; **to be in ~hearted agreement (with sb.)** 完全同意 (某人); ~**heartedly** *adv* 全心全意地 ‹*approve, support*›; ~**-life** *adj* 终身的 ‹*policy, insurance*›

wholemeal /'həʊlmi:l/
A *adj* 全麦的; ~ **bread/pasta** 全麦面包/意大利面
B *n* [u] (flour) 全麦粉; (bread) 全麦面包

whole milk *n* [u] 全脂牛奶

whole: ~ note *n* Amer = **semibreve**; ~ **number** *n* 整数

wholesale /'həʊlseɪl/
A *n* [u] 批发; **at ~** 以批发价; ~ **market/dealer/price** 批发市场/批发商/批发价
B *adj attrib* 大规模的 ‹*slaughter, destruction, increase*›
C *adv* 1 Comm 以批发形式 ‹*trade, sell*›; **to get sth. ~** 以批发价买到某物 2 (on large scale) 大规模地 ‹*slaughter, reduce, reject*›
D *vt* 批发 ‹*goods*›
E *vi* 批发出售; **to ~ at £10** 以 10 英镑的价格批发出售

wholesale price index *n* 批发价指数

wholesaler /'həʊlseɪlə(r)/ *n* 批发商; **a wine ~** 葡萄酒批发商

wholesome /'həʊlsəm/ *adj* 1 (good for health) 有益健康的 ‹*diet, air*› 2 (healthy) 健康的 ‹*appearance*›; **good, ~ fun** 健康有益的玩乐 3 (good for well-being) 有益身心健康的 ‹*activity, relationship, environment*›; **a ~ young man** 朝气蓬勃的小伙子

whole: ~ tone *n* 全音; ~**wheat** *n* [u] 全麦; ~ **pasta/bread/flour** 全麦意大利面/面包/面粉

wholism /'hɒlɪzəm, 'həʊl-/ *n* [u] = **holism**

wholistic /hɒ'lɪstɪk, 'həʊl-/ *adj* = **holistic**

who'll /hu:l/ colloq = **who will** ▸**will**[1]

wholly /'həʊlli/ *adv* 完全 ‹*wrong, convinced, inadequate, dependent, unnecessary*›; 全面地 ‹*successful*›; ~ **owned** 完全拥有的

wholly-owned subsidiary /ˌhəʊllɪˌəʊnd səb'sɪdɪəri/ *n* 全资子公司

whom /hu:m/ *pron* formal 1 (in direct questions) 谁; ~ **do you wish to see?** 你想见谁?; **next to ~?** 居于谁之后?; ~ **shall I say is calling?** (on phone) 请问您是哪位? 2 (specifying preceding noun) …的人; **the girl ~ I saw** 我见过的那个姑娘; **he was the person of ~ I spoke** 他就是我说的那个人 3 (adding to preceding noun) [进一步提供先行词的信息]; **she pointed to the boys, one of ~ was laughing** 她指着那些男孩, 其中一个在笑; **her mother, ~ he had met the previous day, had been very taken with him** 她母亲已被他深深地迷住了, 他是前一天遇到她的 4 (whoever) 任何人; **you may invite ~ you wish** 你愿意邀请谁就邀请谁

whomever /ˌhuːmˈevə(r)/ *pron* formal or liter **1** (the one or ones who) …的人; **he agreed to serve under ~ the party chose** 他同意在该党派选出来的人手下供职; **the report should be submitted to ~ they entrust the inquiry to** 报告应该交给他们委托调查的人 **2** (anyone who) …的任何人; **you are free to contract with ~ you please** 你愿意找谁签约就找谁; **he was free to marry ~ he chose** 他相中了谁就可以和谁结婚 **3** (everyone who) …的每一个人; **tell ~ you know** 告诉你认识的每一个人 **4** (no matter who) 无论谁; **~ he told, nothing would change** 无论他告诉了谁，一切都不会发生变化; **whatever the letter, and to ~, it is a marketing letter** 不管信的内容是什么，也不管是写给谁的，这都是一封促销信

whomp /wɒmp, Amer hwɒmp/ *vt* colloq **1** (thump) 重击 **2** (defeat) 大败

whomsoever /ˌhuːmsəʊˈevə(r)/ *pron* formal **= whomever**

whoop /huːp, wuːp, Amer hwuːp/
A *n* **1** (shout) 高呼; **a ~ of joy/triumph** 喜悦的/胜利的喊叫 **2** Med 咳喘
B *vi* **1** (shout) 高呼; **to ~ with joy** 高兴地呼喊; **to ~ it up** colloq 狂欢 **2** Med 咳喘

whoopee /ˈwʊpiː, Amer ˈhwʊ-/
A *excl* 哈哈［表示快乐或胜利］; **~! I've won** 哈哈！我赢了
B *n* [u] colloq dated **to make ~** (have fun) 狂欢; (make love) 做爱

whoopee cushion *n* 放屁坐垫［人坐上去会发出放屁声，用于恶作剧］

whooper swan /ˌhuːpə ˈswɒn/ *n* 大天鹅

whooping /ˈhuːpɪŋ/: **~ cough** ▸**p. 377** *n* [u] 百日咳; **~ crane** *n* 美洲鹤

whoops /wʊps, Amer hwʊps/ *excl* **1** (on narrowly avoiding accident) 哎哟 **2** (on making mistake) 唉

whoosh /wʊʃ, Amer hwʊʃ/
A *n* 呼呼声; **the ~ of water/wind** 流水的哗哗声/风的呼呼声; **the ~ of a car going by** 驶过的汽车的飕飕声
B *vi* «*water*» 哗哗地流; «*wind*» 呼呼地吹; **to ~ by** *or* **past** «*car, train*» 嗖的一声开过
C *excl* 嗖

whop /wɒp, Amer hwɒp/ *vt* (*pres p etc.* **-pp-**) colloq **1** (hit) 打 ‹*person, insect*›; 击 ‹*ball*› **2** (defeat) 打败

whopper /ˈwɒpə(r), Amer ˈhwɒp-/ *n* colloq **1** (large thing) 硕大的东西; **to catch a ~** (fish) 捕到一条特大的鱼; **his latest novel is a ~** 他最新的小说部头很大; **our bill is a ~** 我们的账单数目惊人 **2** (lie) 谎话; **to tell a ~** 说谎

whopping /ˈwɒpɪŋ, Amer ˈhwɒpɪŋ/ colloq
A *adj usu attrib* 巨大的; **a ~ prize/salary/mistake** 大奖/高薪/天大的错误
B *adv* 极其 ‹*big*›; **a ~ great lie** 弥天大谎
C *n* 殴打; **to get a ~** 挨揍

whore /hɔː(r)/ *n* pej (prostitute) 娼妓; (loose woman) 破鞋

who're /ˈhuːə(r)/ colloq **= who are** ▸**be**

whorehouse /ˈhɔːhaʊs/ *n* colloq 窑子

whorish /ˈhɔːrɪʃ/ *adj* pej 娼妓的

whorl /wɜːl, Amer hwɜːl/ *n* **1** Zool (of snail) 螺线; (of whelk) 螺层 **2** Bot (on stem) 轮 **3** Bot (in flower) 轮生体 **4** (in fingerprint) 指纹涡 **5** Culin 螺旋状奶油球

whortleberry /ˈwɜːtlberi, Amer ˈhwɜːrtl-/ *n* **= bilberry**

who's /huːz/ colloq **= who is** ▸**be**

whose /huːz/
A *pron* 谁的; **~ is that?** 那个是谁的？; **I'm not sure ~ he'll prefer** 我拿不准他会喜欢谁的
B *adj* **1** (in direct or indirect questions) 谁的; **~ side are you on?** 你赞成谁的观点？; **it doesn't matter ~ fault it is** 这是谁的错无关紧要 **2** (of that person) 那个人的; (of those people) 那些人的; (of that thing) 那一个的; (of those things) 那一些的; **the ones ~ names are drawn first** 最先抽到名字的那些人; **the house ~ door is painted red** 那所门被刷成红色的房子; **Internet sites ~ content is not suitable for children** 那些含儿童不宜内容的互联网站 **3** (adding to preceding noun) [进一步提供先行词的信息]; **Isobel, ~ brother he was, …** 伊索贝尔，就是他的兄弟，…

whosever /ˌhuːzˈevə(r)/
A *pron* 无论谁的; **the choice, ~ it is, is interesting** 这个选择很有意思，不管是谁的
B *adj* 无论谁的; **~ book you use, you must take care of it** 无论用谁的书都必须爱惜

whosoever /ˌhuːsəʊˈevə(r)/ *pron* formal **1** (the one or ones who) …的人; **~ the task is given to must …** 承担这个任务的人必须… **2** (anyone who) …的任何人; **to associate with ~ one pleases** 与自己想交往的任何人交往; **~ thinks that …** 任何有…想法的人 **3** (everyone who) …的每一个人; **to offer food and shelter to ~ comes** 为来的每个人提供食宿 **4** (no matter who) 无论谁; **we condemn the attacks, ~ was responsible for them** 我们谴责这些袭击，不论是谁干的

who's who *pr n* 名人录

who've /huːv/ colloq **= who have** ▸**have**

why /waɪ, Amer hwaɪ/
A *adv* **1** (in direct or indirect questions) 为什么; **~ do you ask?** 你为什么问呢？; **I'm annoyed — ~ is that?** 我很恼火——为什么呢？; **~ me?** 为什么是我呢？; **~ not?** 为什么不呢？; **I wonder ~ she said that** 我不明白她为什么说那样的话 **2** (making suggestion) [用于提建议]; **~ not sell the car?** 何不把汽车卖了呢？; **~ don't I give you a lift?** 搭我的车吧; **let's eat out — ~ not?** 咱们到外边吃吧——好哇; **I don't see ~ not** 可以呀 **3** (expressing lack of necessity) 何必; **~ get upset?** 何必生气呢？ **4** (expressing surprise, irritation, defiance) [表示惊讶、不耐烦或反抗]; **~ didn't you tell me before?** 你为什么不早告诉我？; **sit down — ~ should I?** 坐下——我为什么要坐下？; **~ can't you be quiet?** 你难道不能安静一点吗？; **~ ever not?** Brit 究竟为什么不呢？ **5** (the reason for which) [用于说明原因]; **one of the reasons ~ he left** 他离开的原因之一; **to know the reason ~** 知道原因; **that's not ~ I asked** 那不是我问的理由; **so that's ~!** 原来如此！; **why? — because you're stubborn: that's ~!** 为什么？——因为你太倔，就是因为这个！
B *n* 原因; **the ~ and how of sth.** 某事的原因和方法; **the ~s and (the) wherefores (of sth.)** (某事的) 前因后果; **the ~s and the wherefores of the situation** 这一情况的来龙去脉
C *excl* Amer colloq dated [表示惊讶、不耐烦等]; **~, we've only walked a mile!** 嗨，我们才走了1英里！; **you think so? — ~, yes!** 你是这么想的吗？——呃，是的！

WI *abbr* **1** Brit **= Women's Institute** **2** **= West Indies** **3** **= Wisconsin**

wibbly-wobbly /ˌwɪblɪˈwɒbli/ *adj* child lang **= wobbly A1**

wick /wɪk/ *n* (of candle) 烛芯; (of oil lamp) 灯芯; (of lighter) 火芯; **to get on sb.'s ~** Brit colloq 惹火某人

wicked /ˈwɪkɪd/
A *adj* **1** (evil) 恶毒的 ‹*person, deed, intention*›; **to be ~ to sb.** 恶毒地对待某人; **sb.'s ~ ways** 某人邪恶的做法; **(there's) no peace** *or* **rest for the ~** hum 恶人永无宁日啊 [工作太多时说的话] **2** (vicious) 有害的 ‹*weapon, wound*›; 乖戾的 ‹*temper*›; 刻毒的 ‹*tongue*›; (deplorable) 极端的 ‹*waste, shame*› **3** (mischievous) 顽皮的 ‹*grin, child*›; 恶作剧的 ‹*remark*› **4** colloq (excellent) 很棒的 ‹*person, event, food*›; **he's a ~ tennis player, he plays a ~ game of tennis** 他的网球打得棒极了
B *excl* sl 酷毙了

wickedly /ˈwɪkɪdli/ *adv* **1** (evilly) 恶毒地 **2** (mischievously) 顽皮地 **3** colloq (cleverly) 绝妙地 **4** (viciously) 危险地 ‹*bounce, curve*›; **a ~ strong coffee** 浓得对身体有害的咖啡 **5** colloq (exceedingly) 极其 ‹*delicious, beautiful, eloquent*›

wickedness /ˈwɪkɪdnɪs/ *n* **1** [u] (evil, wrong) 恶毒 **2** [u] (viciousness) (of weapon, wound) 危害; (of temper) 乖戾; (of tongue) 刻毒 **3** [u] (mischievousness) (of grin, child, etc.) 顽皮; (of remark) 恶作剧 **4** [c] (evil act) 恶行

wicker /ˈwɪkə(r)/ *n* [u] 柳条; **~ chair/basket** 柳条椅/柳条筐

wickerwork /ˈwɪkəwɜːk/ *n* [u] **1** **= wicker** **2** (wicker items) 柳条编制品

wicket /ˈwɪkɪt/ *n* **1** (gate, door) 小门; **a ~ gate** *or* **door** 小门 **2** Amer (in bank, ticket office) 窗口 **3** (in cricket) (structure) 三柱门; (ground) 三柱门之间的草地; (dismissal) 出局; **to be on a sticky ~** 处境不利

wicket keeper *n* [板球运动的] 三柱门守门员

wide /waɪd/ ▸**p. 436**
A *adj* **1** (broad) 宽阔的 ‹*river, space*›; 宽松的 ‹*skirt, trousers*›; **a ~ grin** 满面的笑容; **her ~ mouth/nose/shoulders** 她的大嘴/宽鼻子/宽肩膀; **they are making the street ~r** 他们正在拓宽街道; **how ~ is your garden?** 你的花园有多宽？; **'~ load'** "超宽货物"; **is the gap ~ enough for my car to pass through?** 这个空档儿够我的车通过吗？; **eyes ~ with amazement** 惊异得睁得大大的眼睛 **2** (immense) 广阔的 ‹*ocean, plain, sky*› **3** fig (considerable) 很大的 ‹*difference*›; **a ~ margin** 很大的差距; **there are ~ variations in prices** 价格变动很大 **4** fig (extensive, varied) 广泛的; **he has a ~ circle of friends** 他的朋友圈子很广; **to enjoy ~ support** 获得广泛支持; **a manager with ~ experience in the industry** 业界一位经验丰富的经理; **the newspaper with the ~st circulation** 发行量最大的报纸; **~r debate on this subject is essential** 对这个话题必须进行更加广泛的辩论; **there is ~ agreement among academics that …** 学术界有广泛的共识，认为…; **~ publicity** 广泛宣传; **in the ~r context** 在更广的背景下; **~r issues/concerns** 更广泛的问题/更普遍的关切; **in the ~st sense of the word** 广义而言 **5** (off target) 远离目标的 ‹*shot, arrow*› fig 离谱的 ‹*guess*›; **the ball is ~** 球打飞了; **to be ~ of sth.** 远离某事物 **6** Sport (outside) 边线的 ‹*position, player*›
B *adv* **1** (to or at a distance) 分得很开; **the door was open ~** 门敞开着; **to open one's eyes/mouth ~** 睁大眼睛/张大嘴巴; **he stood with his feet ~ apart** 他双脚大幅跨开站在那里; **open ~!** 张大嘴! **2** (off target) 偏离目标地 ‹*shoot, aim*›; **to be ~ of sth.** 偏离某物 **3** Sport (in outside position) 在边线 ‹*play, run*›
C *n* (in cricket) [板球] 歪球
D **-wide** *combining form* 全…范围的; **a country~ search** 全国范围的搜索; **city~ celebrations** 全城庆祝活动

wide: **~-angle** *n* 广角; **a ~-angle lens/shot** 广角透镜/镜头; **~ area network** *n* 广域网; **~ awake** *adj* **1** (fully awake) 完全醒来的; **2** (alert) 十分警觉的; **~body, ~-bodied** *adjs* 机身宽大的 ‹*aircraft*›; **~ boy** *n* Brit colloq pej **1** (petty criminal) [尤指黑市上的] 骗子; **2** (dishonest businessman) 奸商; **~-eyed** *adj* 睁大眼睛的 ‹*fear, amazement*›; **to be ~-eyed with fear/excitement** 恐惧地/激动地睁大眼睛

widely /ˈwaɪdli/ *adv* **1** (extensively) 范围广地 ‹*range, spread*›; **she has travelled ~** *or* **is ~ travelled** 她游历甚广; **they forage ~ in**

W

search of food 他们到处搜寻食物; ～ scattered farms 稀稀拉拉散布的农场; she reads ～ on a number of topics 她涉猎多个学科，博览群书; the event was ～ publicized 这一事件被广泛报道 2 (at a distance) 相距远地 ‹planted›; ～ spaced huts 间距很远的小屋 3 fig (significantly) 显著地 ‹different›; our beliefs differ ～ 我们的信仰迥异 4 (commonly) 普遍地 ‹acknowledged, held›; it is ～ accepted/believed that ... 人们普遍认可/认为…; she is ～ regarded as an expert in the field 她被普遍认为是这一领域的专家; this product is now ～ available 该产品现在大量供应; to be ～ known for sth. 因为某事物而广为人知; mosquitoes are ～ known to transmit malaria 众所周知，蚊子传播疟疾

widely-read /ˌwaɪdlɪˈred/ *adj* 1 (read by many) 有众多读者的 ‹author, book, column› 2 (well-read) 博览群书的 ‹person›

widen /ˈwaɪdn/
A *vt* 1 (make wider) 使…变宽 ‹gap, road, room›; to ～ a skirt 把裙子加宽 2 fig (extend) 扩展 ‹scope, experience, knowledge›; to ～ one's lead «athlete, racehorse, political party» 拉大领先距离
B *vi* 1 (become wider) ～ (out) «river, road, trousers» 变宽; his eyes ～ed 他瞪大了眼睛 2 fig (increase) «lead, experience» 增加; the gap is ～ing between the rich and the poor 贫富差距正在拉大

wide: ～ open *adj* 1 (fully open) 敞开的 ‹window, door›; 睁大的 ‹eyes›; 2 (not yet won) 胜负难料的 ‹race, game›; 3 *pred* (exposed) 无保护的; to be ～ open to sth. 易受某物攻击; to lay *or* leave oneself/sb. ～ open to sth. 使自己/某人易受某物攻击; 4 (not enclosed) 开阔的 ‹space, field›; 5 (accessible) 开放的; to be ～ open for young people 向年轻人开放; **～-ranging** /-ˈreɪndʒɪŋ/ *adj* 广泛的 ‹discussion, influence, interests›

wide screen
A *n* 1 [c] (screen) 宽屏 2 [u] (format) 宽屏模式
B **wide-screen** *adj attrib* 1 (offering wide field of vision) 宽屏的; a ～ TV 宽屏电视 2 (in wide format) 宽屏模式的; a ～ film/digital image 宽银幕电影/宽屏式数字影像

widespread /ˈwaɪdspred/ *adj* 分布广的 ‹famine, epidemic, infection›; 普遍的 ‹problem, belief›; 广泛的 ‹support, devastation›; drug use is ～ 毒品服用十分普遍

widget /ˈwɪdʒɪt/ *n* colloq [不知名的] 小玩意儿

widow /ˈwɪdəʊ/
A *n* 寡妇
B *vt* «tragedy, illness» 使…成为寡妇 ‹woman›; to be ～ed 成为寡妇

widower /ˈwɪdəʊə(r)/ *n* 鳏夫

widowhood /ˈwɪdəʊhʊd/ *n* [u] (state) 寡居; (period) 寡居期

widow: ～'s mite *n* [圣经用语，指穷人的] 少量捐助; **～'s pension** *n* 寡妇救济金; **～'s walk** *n* Amer [尤指新英格兰滨海房屋的] 屋顶平台; **～'s weeds** *npl* dated [寡妇穿的] 黑丧服

width /wɪdθ, wɪtθ/ ▸p. 436 *n* 1 [u] Meas 宽度 2 [c] Tex 幅宽 3 [c] (of swimming pool) 池宽 4 [u] (breadth) 宽广; a sufficient ～ of knowledge 足够宽广的知识面; a ～ of experience 丰富的阅历

widthways /ˈwɪdθweɪz, ˈwɪtθ-/, **widthwise** /ˈwɪdθwaɪz, ˈwɪtθ-/ *advs* 横向地

wield /wiːld/ *vt* 1 lit (hold and use) 挥舞 ‹weapon, tool›; 挥 ‹brush› 2 fig (exercise) 行使 ‹authority›; 施加 ‹influence›; to ～ power over sb. 对某人行使权力

wiener /ˈwiːnə(r)/ *n* Amer 法兰克福香肠

wiener schnitzel /ˌviːnə ˈʃnɪtsl/ *n* [u and c] 维也纳炸小牛排

wienie /ˈwiːni/ *n* Amer colloq = **wiener**

wife /waɪf/ ▸p. 419 *n* (*pl* **wives**) 妻子; the ～ colloq 老婆; ex-～ 前妻; lawful wedded ～ formal 结发之妻; to be ～ to sb. formal 是某人的夫人; to take sb. as one's ～ formal 娶某人为妻; child ～ 少妻

wifely /ˈwaɪfli/ *adj* 妻子的 ‹virtues, duties, affection›

wife: ～-swapper *n* 换妻的男人; **～-swapping** *n* [u] colloq 换妻; ～-swapping party 换妻派对

wi-fi, Wi-Fi, wifi /ˈwaɪfaɪ/ *n* 无线传输系统; ～ connection/access 无线传输连接/接入

wig /wɪɡ/ *n* 假发; to wear a ～ 戴假发

wigging /ˈwɪɡɪŋ/ *n* Brit colloq dated 呵斥; to get *or* receive a ～ 遭到呵斥; a stiff ～ 怒斥; to give sb. a ～ 训斥某人

wiggle /ˈwɪɡl/
A *vt* 摇动 ‹toe, ear, tail, tooth›; 转动 ‹handle, lever, screw›; to ～ one's hips 扭屁股
B *vi* 1 (move back and forth) «tail» 摇动; «screw, nail, handle» 转动; my tooth ～s about 我的牙松动了 2 (bend) «road, river» 蜿蜒前行
C *n* 1 (of toe, tail, ear) 摇动; (of handle, screw) 转动; to walk with a ～ 一扭一扭地走路 2 (of road, river) 蜿蜒处

wiggle room *n* [u] colloq 回旋余地

wiggly /ˈwɪɡli/ *adj* 扭动的 ‹worm, snake›; 波浪形的 ‹line›; 摇动的 ‹tail›; 蜿蜒的 ‹road›

wigwam /ˈwɪɡwæm, Amer -wɑːm/ *n* [旧时北美印第安人建的] 圆顶棚屋

wiki /ˈwɪki/ *n* 维基 [由用户群共同维护、允许所有用户添加或修改内容的网站或数据库]

wilco /ˈwɪlkəʊ/ *excl* 照办 [无线电用语，I will comply的缩略形式]

wild /waɪld/
A *adj* 1 (not domesticated) 野生的 ‹animal, plant, forest›; ～ horses/flowers 野马/野花; a ～ beast lit, fig 野兽 2 pej (uncivilized) 未开化的 ‹people›; the ～ tribes of the Amazon Basin 亚马孙盆地的原始部落; ～ and woolly 粗野的 3 (desolate) 荒凉的 ‹area, scenery› 4 (turbulent) 暴风雨的 ‹night›; 狂暴的 ‹weather, storm, sea› 5 (undisciplined) 放荡的 ‹youth, party›; 胡乱的 ‹aim, shot›; ～ disorder 极度混乱; he led a ～ life in his youth 他年轻时生活放荡; there was a lot of ～ play in the first ten minutes of the game 比赛的最初10分钟时间里，球员们的动作很粗野; to take a ～ swing (at sb.) (朝某人) 胡乱挥拳; to walk on the ～ side 桀骜不驯; ～ (locks of) hair (几绺) 乱蓬蓬的头发 6 (unrestrained) 无节制的; ～ laughter 纵声大笑; ～ anger/enthusiasm/delight 狂怒/狂热/狂喜; a ～ imagination 信马由缰的想象; to be ～ with grief 悲痛欲绝 7 *pred* colloq (furious) 狂怒的; to make *or* drive sb. ～ 使某人发狂; to go ～ 大发雷霆 8 *pred* colloq (enthusiastic) to be ～ about sb./sth. 热衷于某人/某事物; the children have gone ～ about these new computer games 孩子们对这些新电脑游戏非常痴迷 9 (outlandish) 轻率的 ‹talk, promise›; 无根据的 ‹idea, accusation›; ～ rumours 捕风捉影的谣言; a ～ guess 瞎猜 10 colloq (excellent) 极棒的 ‹event, experience›; (exciting) 令人激动的; we had a ～ time in New York 我们在纽约玩得开心极了 11 Games 百搭的 ‹playing card›
B *adv* 疯狂地 ‹grow›; to run ～ «garden» 变得荒芜; «child» 撒起欢儿来; to let one's imagination run ～ 让想象力自由驰骋
C *n* the ～ (state) 野生; (habitat) 野生环境; in the ～ 在野生环境中; the call of the ～ 荒野的召唤
D *npl* the ～s 偏远地区; (to live) out in the ～s (生活) 在偏僻地区

wild: ～ boar *n* 1 [c] Zool 野猪; 2 [u] Culin 野猪肉; **～ card** *n* 1 Games 百搭牌; 2 Comput 通配符; 3 Sport (opportunity) [没有参加资格赛而进入赛事的] 外卡参赛机会; 4 Sport (player) 外卡参赛选手; 5 (unpredictable element) 未知因素

wildcat /ˈwaɪldkæt/
A *n* 1 (any big cat) 野猫; (lynx, caracal) 猞猁; Amer (bobcat) 短尾猫 2 fig colloq (woman) 悍妇
B *adj* 1 Ind 自发的 ‹strike, action› 2 Comm, Fin 冒险的 ‹venture, operation, financing›

wild: ～ cherry *n* 1 (tree) 野樱桃树; 2 (fruit) 野樱桃; **～ dog** *n* = **dingo**

wildebeest /ˈwɪldɪbiːst/ *n* (*pl* ～ *or* ～s) 牛羚

wilderness /ˈwɪldənɪs/ *n* 1 (wild land) 荒野; to be in the ～ 在野外; fig 在野; to be a voice (crying) in the ～ 建议无人搭理 2 (neglected area) 疏于管理的地方; a ～ of rubbish 垃圾遍地的地方

wild: ～-eyed *adj* (angry) 怒目而视的; (frightened) 目光惊恐的; to stare in ～-eyed fright 吓得两眼发直; **～fire** *n* [u] 烈火; to spread like ～fire «news, rumour, disease» 以燎原之势迅速蔓延; **～ flower** *n* 野花; **～fowl** *npl* 野禽; **～fowling** *n* [u] 猎野禽; **～-goose chase** *n usu sing* colloq 徒劳的寻找; to send sb. on a ～-goose chase 让某人白跑一趟

wildlife /ˈwaɪldlaɪf/ *n* [u] (animals, birds, insects) 野生动物; (fauna and flora) 野生动植物; a ～ sanctuary 野生动物保护区

wildlife: ～ conservation *n* [u] 野生动植物保护; **～ park, ～ reserve** *ns* 野生动物园

wildly /ˈwaɪldli/ *adv* 1 (recklessly) 失控地 ‹act›; the troops had panicked and were shooting ～ 士兵们惊慌失措，胡乱射击; to look/stare ～ 直勾勾地看/盯着; he lashed out ～ at his attacker 他发狂般地对攻击他的人大打出手 2 (violently, energetically) 猛烈地 ‹wave, fluctuate›; 热烈地 ‹applaud›; her heart was beating ～ 她的心狂跳不已; the wind was gusting ～ 风猛烈地刮着 3 (extremely) 极其; to be ～ exaggerated 被过分夸大; to not be ～ pleased/enthusiastic 不太满意/热情

wildness /ˈwaɪldnɪs/ *n* [u] 1 (lack of discipline) (of person, life, party) 狂放不羁; (of play) 粗野; (of blow, shot, aim) 胡乱; he got sent off for the ～ of his tackle on the striker 他因为以粗野动作踢铲对方前锋被罚下场 2 (lack of restraint) (of laughter, emotions) 无节制; I was alarmed by the ～ in his eyes 他那狂野的眼神吓了我一跳 3 (turbulence) (of night, weather) 狂风暴雨; (of wind, waves) 狂暴 4 (desolateness) 荒凉 5 (extravagance) (of idea, imagination) 异想天开; (of guess) 无根据 6 (of animals, plants) 野生; in a state of ～ 处于野生状态 7 (lack of civilization) 未开化

wild rose *n* 野玫瑰

wild water *n* [u] = **white water**

wild-water rafting ▸p. 307 *n* [u] = **white-water rafting**

Wild West *n* the ～ 西大荒; a ～ film 西部片

> **the Wild West**
>
> 西大荒。19世纪后半期的美国西部。其时西大荒虽有人定居，但政府尚未实现有效的管理，因此暴力犯罪活动十分猖獗。比利小子（Billy the Kid）即为当时著名的亡命之徒。以西大荒为背景讲述西部牛仔（cowboy）故事的小说或电影被称为西部片（western），常将西大荒蒙上一层浪漫的色彩，不尽符合事实。

Wild West show *n* Amer [描写西大荒生活的] 牛仔戏

wildwood /ˈwaɪldwʊd/ *n* liter 天然林

wiles /waɪlz/ *npl* 诡计

wilful /ˈwɪlfl/ *adj* 1 (headstrong) 任性的 2 (deliberate) 蓄意的

wilfully /ˈwɪlfəli/ *adv* 1 (in headstrong way) 任性地 2 (deliberately) 蓄意地

W

wilfulness /ˈwɪlflnɪs/ *n* [u] **1** (headstrong nature) 任性 **2** (deliberate nature) 蓄意

wiliness /ˈwaɪlmɪs/ *n* [u] 诡计多端

will¹ /wɪl, əl/ *modal aux* (*short form* colloq **'ll**; *negative pres* **will not** *or* colloq **won't**; *pt* **would**; *negative pt* **would not** *or* colloq **wouldn't**) **1** (expressing future) 将 [用于谈及将来]; **the results ~ be announced on Monday** 结果将在星期一宣布; **she'll help you** 她会帮你的; **she'll have finished by now** 她现在应该完成了; **he said he'd be leaving soon** 他说他快要离开了 **2** (expressing willingness) 想要 [表示意愿]; **~ you or won't you?** 你愿意还是不愿意？; **he won't cooperate** 他不愿合作; **I won't have it!** 不行！; **~ do!** colloq 好的！ **3** (in requests, offers, invitations) 愿意 [用于请求、提议或邀请]; **open the door, ~ you?** 请你把门打开好吗？; **~ you come at ten?** 你 10 点钟来好吗？; **I'll check for you, if you want** 如果你愿意，我替你检查 **4** (in commands) 必须 [表示命令]; **~ you be quiet!** 安静点儿！; **you'll do it this minute!** 你必须马上做！ **5** (in conjecture) 可能 [表示推测]; **that ~ be my sister** 那应该是我的姐姐; **he'll be about 30 now** 他现在大概 30 岁了吧 **6** (stating general truth) 总是 [用于陈述一般事实]; **oil ~ float on water** 油浮于水; **these things ~ happen** 这些事情终究要发生的; **teachers ~ tell you that ...** 老师都会告诉你… **7** (expressing ability, capacity) 能够 [表示能力或容量]; **the lift ~ take 12** 这部电梯可载 12 人; **the car ~ do 120 km/h** 这辆汽车每小时能跑 120 公里; **the door won't open!** 门打不开！ **8** (describing habit) 经常 [表示习惯]; **she'll listen to music for hours** 她听音乐总是一听就是几个小时; **he would spend hours on the phone** 他电话一打就是好几个小时 **9** (in exasperation) 老是 [重读will或would，表示对习惯性行为感到恼火]; **she ~ run the dishwasher at midnight** 她总爱在半夜开洗碗机; **he would have to go there!** 他居然去了那里！ **10** formal (like) 愿意; **ask who you ~** 你想问谁就问谁; **call it what you ~, it's still a problem** 不管你怎么说，这仍然是个问题

will² /wɪl/

A *n* **1** [u and c] (mental power) 意志; **to have a strong/weak ~** 意志坚强/薄弱; **by an effort of ~** 用意志力; **to have a ~ of one's own** 固执己见 **2** [u] (determination) 毅力; **great strength of ~** 巨大的毅力 **3** [u and c] (desire, intention) 意愿; **to do sth. with a ~** 乐意做某事; **to do sth. against one's ~** 违背意愿做某事; **to lose the ~ to live** 丧失活下去的意欲; **the ~ of the people** 人民的意愿; **a battle of ~s** 意气之争; **where there's a ~, there's a way** Prov 有志者事竟成 **4** [c] Jur 遗嘱; **to make a/one's ~** 立遗嘱; **to leave a ~** 留下遗嘱; **he left me the house in his ~** 他在遗嘱中把房子赠给了我; **sb.'s last ~ and testament** 某人的临终遗嘱

B **at will** *adv phr* 自由地; **to come and go at ~** 来去自由; **to fire at ~** 随意开枪

C *vt* (*pt, pp* **~ed**) **1** (urge mentally) 以意志力驱使; **to ~ sb./sth. to do sth.** 以意志力促使某人/某物做某事; **to ~ sb.'s downfall** 强烈希望某人垮台; **she ~ed him to live** 她决心一定要让他活下去; **to ~ one's eyes to stay open** 努力睁着眼睛 **2** (wish, intend) 想要; **if God ~s it** 如果这是上帝的旨意; **fate ~ed it so** 命运如此 **3** Jur 遗赠; **to ~ sth. to sb.** 将某物遗赠给某人

D *v refl* (*pt, pp* **~ed**) **to ~ oneself to do sth.** 决意做某事; **to ~ oneself to stand up** 竭力站起来; **she ~ed herself to finish the race** 她竭尽全力跑完了比赛

Phrasal verb

- **will on** *vt* [**~ sb./sth. on, ~ on sb./sth.**] 以意志力驱使…进步

willful /ˈwɪlfl/ *adj* Amer = **wilful**

willfully /ˈwɪlfəli/ *adv* Amer = **wilfully**

willfulness /ˈwɪlflnɪs/ *n* [u] Amer = **wilfulness**

William the Conqueror *pr n* Brit Hist 征服者威廉 [1066年入侵英国的诺曼公爵]

willie /ˈwɪli/

A *n* Brit colloq or child lang = **willy**

B **willies** *npl* colloq **to get the ~s** 害怕; **to give sb. the ~s** 让某人害怕

willing /ˈwɪlɪŋ/ *adj* **1** *usu pred* (prepared) 乐意的; **to be (more than) ~ to do sth.** （很）愿意做某事; **~ and able** 愿意并且有能力的; ▸ **ready A1** **2** (eager) 热心的 ‹*friend, helper*›; 热切的 ‹*accomplice, victim*›; **to be very ~** 很积极; **~ hands** 热心帮忙的人 **3** *attrib* (voluntary) 志愿的 ‹*help, donation, sacrifice*›

willingly /ˈwɪlɪŋli/ *adv* 自愿地; **to go ~ to one's death** 义无反顾地献出生命

willingness /ˈwɪlɪŋnɪs/ *n* [u] 乐意; **~ to do sth.** 情愿做某事

will-o'-the-wisp /ˌwɪləðəˈwɪsp/ *n* 鬼火; **to chase a ~** fig 追求虚无之物

willow /ˈwɪləʊ/ *n* **1** [c] Bot **~ (tree)** 柳树; **~ leaves** 柳叶 **2** [u] (wood) 柳木 **3** [u] (for weaving) 柳条; **a ~ basket/cradle** 柳条筐/摇篮

willow pattern

A *n* [陶瓷器上蓝白相间的] 垂柳图案

B **willow-pattern** *modif* 有垂柳图案的 ‹*plate, design*›

willow warbler *n* 柳莺

willowy /ˈwɪləʊi/ *adj* 婀娜多姿的 ‹*figure, person*›

will power *n* [u] 意志力

willy /ˈwɪli/ *n* Brit colloq or child lang 小鸡鸡 [指阴茎]

willy-nilly /ˌwɪlɪˈnɪli/ *adv* colloq **1** (regardless of choice) 不管愿意与否 ‹*act, be led*›; **to be forced do sth. ~** 被迫无奈做某事 **2** (haphazardly) 随意地 ‹*scatter, give out*›

wilt /wɪlt/

A *vi* **1** (droop) «*plant, flower*» 枯萎 **2** fig (from heat, fatigue) «*person, audience*» 变得无精打采 **3** fig (at daunting prospect) «*person*» 畏缩; «*enthusiasm, courage*» 消退; **to ~ at sth.** 在…前退缩 ‹*defeat, prospect*›

B *vt* «*heat, drought, disease*» 使…枯萎 ‹*plant*›

C *n* [u] 萎蔫病

Wilts. /wɪlts/ *abbr* Brit = **Wiltshire**

Wiltshire /ˈwɪltʃə(r)/ *pr n* 威尔特郡

wily /ˈwaɪli/ *adj* 诡计多端的 ‹*person, plot*›; **as ~ as a fox** 像狐狸一样狡猾的

wimp /wɪmp/ *n* colloq pej 窝囊废

Phrasal verb

- **wimp out** *vi* colloq pej 畏缩不前

wimpish /ˈwɪmpɪʃ/ *adj* colloq pej 懦弱的 ‹*character, act*›

wimple /ˈwɪmpl/ *n* [中世纪妇女和现代一些修女戴的] 温帕尔头巾

wimpy /ˈwɪmpi/ *adj* colloq pej 懦弱的

win /wɪn/

A *vi* (*pres p* **-nn-**; *pt, pp* **won**) 获胜; **who is ~ning?** 现在谁占上风？; **to ~ at cards/chess/golf** 在纸牌/国际象棋/高尔夫比赛中获胜; **to ~ against sb./sth.** 战胜某人/某事物; **to ~ by a length** 以一个身位获胜; **to ~ by a whisker** 险胜; **you ~!** 你赢了！; **you (just) can't ~** 一点辙都没有; **~ or lose** 不管输赢; **it's a ~ or lose situation** 这是一个非赢即输的状况; **to play to ~** 志在必得; **to ~, place, and show** Amer [赛马骑师] 悠着点

B *vt* (*pres p* **-nn-**; *pt, pp* **won**) **1** (gain victory in) 在…中获胜 ‹*war, match, argument, bet*›; **I expect to ~ the race** 我想这次比赛我能赢; **you can't ~ them all** colloq 鱼和熊掌不能兼得; **(you) ~ some, (you) lose some** colloq 有所得就有所失 **2** (obtain by victory) 赢得 ‹*prize, medal, scholarship, votes*›; 夺取 ‹*city, area*›; **the army failed to ~ the ridge** 军队没能拿下这座山脊; **to ~ sth. from sb.** 从某人处赢取某物; **they won the election from the Conservatives** 他们击败保守党，赢得了选举; **she won £25 off me at cards** 她打牌赢了我 25 英镑; **you've won yourself a trip to New York** 你赢得了一次去纽约的旅行 **3** (acquire) 获得 ‹*approval, sympathy, admiration, promotion*›; **we won support from all sides** 我们获得了各个方面的支持; **to ~ sb.'s love/affection** 获得某人的爱; **to ~ sb.'s hand** dated 向某女子求婚成功; **to ~ sb.'s heart** 赢得某人的心; **to ~ the day** 得胜

C *n* **1** (victory) 胜利; **to have a ~ against** *or* **over sb. (in sth.)** （在某事上）赢某人; **to have a ~ on the horses** 赌马获胜; **to back sth. for a ~** 赌某物获胜 **2** (amount won) 奖金; **a £30,000 ~ in the lottery** 在乐透彩中赢得的 3 万英镑奖金

Phrasal verbs

- **win back** *vt* [**~ sb./sth. back, ~ back sb./sth.**] 重新获得 ‹*support, respect*›; **will you be able to ~ the money back from him?** 你能够从他那里把钱赢回来吗？; **they won back the territory from the invaders** 他们从入侵者手中夺回了这片领土
- **win out** *vi* 胜出; **we'll ~ out in the end** 我们将最终获胜; **to ~ out over adversity** 战胜逆境
- **win over, win round** *vt* [**~ sb. over, ~ over sb.**] 说服; **to ~ sb. over to sth./doing sth.** 说服某人同意某事/做某事
- **win through** *vi* 摆脱困境

wince /wɪns/

A *vi* (in pain) 龇牙咧嘴; (in disgust) 皱眉蹙额; **to ~ with** *or* **in pain/disgust** 疼得龇牙咧嘴/厌恶得皱眉头

B *n usu sing* (in pain) 龇牙咧嘴; (in disgust) 皱眉蹙额

winch /wɪntʃ/

A *n* 绞车

B *vt* 用绞车吊起; **to ~ sth./sb. out of** *or* **from sth.** 把某物/某人从某处吊起

Phrasal verbs

- **winch down** *vt* [**~ sth./sb. down, ~ down sth./sb.**] 把…吊到低处
- **winch up** *vt* [**~ sth./sb. up, ~ up sth./sb.**] 把…吊上来

Winchester /ˈwɪntʃɪstə(r)/ *n* **1** Comput **~ (disk** *or* **drive)** 温切斯特磁盘 **2** (gun) **~ (rifle)®** 温切斯特连发步枪

wind¹ /wɪnd/

A *n* **1** [c and u] Meteorol 风; **a high/following/prevailing/bitter ~** 大风/顺风/盛行风/刺骨的风; **a North/South ~** 北风/南风; **which way is the ~ blowing?** 风往哪个方向吹？; **to have the ~ at one's back** *or* **behind one** 顺风; **to have the ~ in one's face** *or* **against one** 顶风; **to the four ~s** 向四面八方; **gusts of ~** 一阵阵风; **without a breath of ~** 没有一丝风; **there is not much ~ today** 今天没什么风; **to go** *or* **run like the ~** 飞奔; **a fair ~** Naut 顺风; **to sail** *or* **run before the ~** 顺风航行; **to sail into the ~** 逆风航行; **to see which way the ~ blows** 观望形势 **2** [c] fig (current) 趋势; (influence) 影响; **the ~ of change** 改革之风; **the cold ~(s) of the recession** 经济衰退的寒流; **there is something in the ~** 有事情要发生; **to test the ~** 试探公众的反应 **3** [u] (breath) 呼吸; **to get** *or* **regain one's ~** 恢复正常呼吸; **wait until I get my ~ back** 等我喘口气再说; **one's second ~** 恢复过来的呼吸; fig 恢复的精力; **to get the ~ up** colloq 害怕起来; **to put the ~ up sb.** colloq 使某人感到害怕; **to knock the ~ out of sb.** (interrupt breathing of) 把某人打得背过气去; (reduce overconfidence of) 灭某人的威风; (shock) 使某人震惊 **4** [u] Brit (in the stomach) 胃气; (in the intestines) 肠气; **to have** *or* **suffer from ~** 肠胃气胀; **to get ~** 胀气; **to break ~** 放屁; **to bring up ~** 打嗝; **that's a lot of ~!** fig 那是

一派胡言！; **it's all ~ or nothing but ~** fig pej 都是瞎扯 **5** [u] Mus 管乐器; **a composition for ~ and strings** 管弦乐作品; **the ~** 管乐器组; **a ~ player** 管乐器演奏者 **6** [u] Hunt, Zool (scent) **to get ~ of sth.** 闻到某动物的气味; **the hounds got ~ of the fox** 猎犬闻到了狐狸的气味; **the employees got ~ of the fact that there were going to be redundancies** 雇员们听到了将要裁员的风声

B *vt* **1** (make breathless) «*blow, fall, exertion*» 使喘不上气 **2** Brit (cause to burp) 使…打嗝 ‹*baby*› **3** Hunt, Zool (scent) 嗅出…的气味 ‹*prey, fox, hunter*›

wind[2] /waɪnd/

A *vt* (*pt, pp* **wound** /waʊnd/) **1** (coil) 绕 ‹*string, rope*›; **he wound the scarf round his neck** 他把围巾围在脖子上; **monkeys ~ their tails around branches** 猴子把尾巴缠绕在树枝上; **I wound my arms around his neck** 我张开双臂搂着他的脖子; **to ~ thread on a bobbin** 把线绕到线轴上; **to ~ wool** 把毛线绕成团 **2** (set in motion) 给…上发条 ‹*watch, clock, clockwork toy*›; **the clock needs ~ing** 这只钟需要上发条 **3** (turn) 转动 ‹*handle, lever*›

B *vi* (*pt, pp* **wound** /waʊnd/) «*river, road, queue, staircase*» 蜿蜒; **the procession wound along the road** 游行队伍沿着道路蜿蜒行进; **to ~ one's way** 蜿蜒行进; **he wound his way home** 他东游西逛地走回家; **to ~ its way** «*river, road*» 蜿蜒延伸

C *n* **1** (bend) 弯曲; **the gentle ~ of the river** 河道的缓弯 **2** (movement) (of watch, clock) 一圈; (of handle, lever) 一转; **I'll give the clock a ~** 我要给钟上一下发条

Phrasal verbs

- **wind back**

A *vt* [**~ sth. back, ~ back sth.**] 把…倒回去 ‹*tape, film*›

B *vi* «*tape*» 倒带; «*film*» 倒胶卷; **I missed that bit — could you ~ back?** 我没听到那一点——你能倒一下带吗？

- **wind down**

A *vi* **1** (end, diminish) «*business, factory, organization, activity*» 逐步停顿 **2** (lose power) «*clock, mechanism*» 渐次停下 **3** fig (relax) 放松; **he ~s down by listening to music** 他通过听音乐来放松

B *vt* [**~ sth. down, ~ down sth.**] **1** (lower) 把…摇下 ‹*weight, load*›; **please ~ down the window** 请把窗户摇下来 **2** (prepare for closure) 使…停顿 ‹*business, factory, organization, activity*›

- **wind forward**

A *vt* [**~ sth. forward**] 把…向后倒 ‹*tape, film*›

B *vi* «*tape*» 向后绕带; «*film*» 向后卷胶片

- **wind in** *vt* [**~ sth. in, ~ in sth.**] 转动曲柄收回 ‹*fish, line*›
- **wind on** *vt, vi* = **wind forward**
- **wind out** *vt* [**~ sth. out, ~ out sth.**] 转动曲柄放出 ‹*line, net*›
- **wind up**

A [**~ sth. up, ~ up sth.**] *vt*

1 (cause to operate) 给…上发条 ‹*watch, mechanism*› **2** (raise) 把…摇起 ‹*window, shutter*›; **I wound up the car window** 我把车窗摇上去了 **3** (terminate) 使…结束 ‹*business, meeting, discussion, project*›; 结清 ‹*account*›; 搞定 ‹*affairs*›

B [**~ sb. up, ~ up sb.**] *vt*

1 colloq (make tense) 使紧张; (annoy) 惹…生气; **to be wound up about sth.** 对某事物感到气恼 **2** Brit colloq (tease) 戏弄

C *vi* **1** (finish) «*meeting, debate*» 结束; **to ~ up for sb./sth.** (make concluding remarks) 代表某人/某一方作总结发言 **2** colloq (end up) 以…告终; **the car wound up in the ditch** 汽车结果陷在了沟里; **to ~ up doing sth.** 以做某事告终; **I wound up sleeping in the car** 我最后睡在了车里; **she wound up as a dancer in Tokyo** 她最后在东京做了舞蹈演员; **you'll ~ up with a black eye** 你会落个乌眼青 **3** (operate by winding) «*clock, mechanism*» 上发条

wind /wɪnd/: **~bag** *n* colloq pej 话匣子; **~bells** *npl* = ~ chimes; **~blown** *adj* 随风飘的 ‹*dust, seeds*›; 被风吹乱的 ‹*hair*›; 被风吹起的 ‹*waves*›; **~borne** *adj* 随风飘散的 ‹*dust, spray, pollution*›; **~break** *n* (natural) 风障; (constructed) 挡风建筑; (portable) 挡风屏; **~breaker®** *n* Amer = **~cheater**; **~burn** *n* [u] 风吹性皮炎; **~cheater** *n* Brit 风衣; **~-chill factor** *n* 风寒指数; **~chimes** *npl* 风铃; **~ cone** *n* = **~sock**; **~ deflector** *n* 挡风板; **~ energy** *n* [u] 风能

winder /'waɪndə(r)/ *n* **1** (mechanism) (in clock, camera, alarm) 发条; (for car window) 摇手; (reel or spool for wire, line, yarn) 卷筒 **2** Ind (person) 卷线工

windfall /'wɪndfɔːl/ *n* **1** (fruit) 风吹落的果实; **a ~ apple** 风吹落的苹果 **2** fig (money) 意外之财

windfall profit *n* 意外利润

wind /wɪnd/: **~ farm** *n* 风力发电厂; **~flower** *n* 银莲花; **~ gauge** *n* 风速计; **~ generator** *n* 风力发电机

Windhoek /'wɪnthʊk/ *pr n* 温得和克

winding /'waɪndɪŋ/

A *adj usu attrib* 蜿蜒的 ‹*road, river, valley*›; 弯曲的 ‹*course, staircase*›

B *n* **1** [u] (action) 卷绕 **2** [c] Elec 线圈

winding /'waɪndɪŋ/: **~ gear** *n* [u] 升降机; **~ sheet** *n* 裹尸布; **~-up** *n* 结束; **~-up proceedings** 清盘程序

wind /wɪnd/: **~ instrument** ▸**p. 395** *n* 管乐器; **~jammer** /'wɪnddʒæmə(r)/ *n* **1** Naut, Hist 大型商船; **2** Amer = **~cheater**

windlass /'wɪndləs/ *n* 卷扬机

windless /'wɪndləs/ *adj* 无风的; **~ heat** 闷热; **~ calm** 风平浪静

wind /wɪnd/: **~ machine** *n* 造风机; **~mill** *n* **1** (for grinding) 风车; **to tilt at ~mills** fig 同假想敌战斗; **2** (for electricity, water) 风力机; **3** Brit (toy) 玩具风车

window /'wɪndəʊ/ *n* **1** (opening in wall, vehicle etc.) 窗; (glass in opening) 窗玻璃; (area behind opening) 窗口; (in roof) 天窗; **to look through a ~** 透过窗户看; **to lean out of a ~** 探出窗外; **to throw sth. out of the ~** 把某物扔出窗外; **the explosion shattered ~s all along the street** 爆炸把沿街所有的窗户都震碎了; **he sat at** or **by the ~** 他坐在窗边; **I'd like a seat by the ~** (on aeroplane) 我想要个靠窗的座位; **the ~ looks out on** or **over sth.** 窗子面对某物; **to go** or **fly out (of) the ~** colloq (disappear) 化为乌有; (be rejected) 被抛弃 **2** (in shop, commercial building) (exterior glass) 橱窗玻璃; (area behind) 橱窗; **a shop/restaurant ~** 商店/饭店橱窗; **to put sth. in the ~** 把某物放到橱窗里; **to get sth. out of the ~** 把某物从橱窗里拿出来; **at the back/front of the ~** 在橱窗后部/前部 **3** (for serving customers) 服务窗口; **a post office/ticket ~** 邮局/售票窗口 **4** Comput 视窗; **to open/close a ~** 打开/关闭窗口 **5** (in envelope) 透明纸窗 **6** fig (opportunity) 短暂时机; **a ~ in my diary (for a meeting with Mr Jones)** 我的日程安排中的一个（可与琼斯先生会晤的）空档; **we've missed our ~** 我们错过了时机; **a launch ~** 发射窗; **a ~ of opportunity** 一丝机会

window: **~ blind** *n* 百叶窗; **~ box** *n* 窗口花坛; **~ cleaner** *n* **1** ▸**p. 409** [c] (person) 窗户清洁工; **2** [u and c] (product) 窗户清洗液; **~ cleaning** [u] (for living) 擦窗工作; (as domestic task) 擦窗; **a ~-cleaning business** 擦窗业; **~ display** *n* 橱窗陈列; **~ dresser** ▸**p. 409** *n* 橱窗装饰人; **~ dressing** *n* [u] **1** lit (activity, result) 橱窗布置; **2** fig pej (favourable presentation) 装点门面; **~ envelope** *n* 透明窗口信封; **~ frame** *n* 窗框; **~ glass** *n* [u] 门窗玻璃; **~ ledge** *n* = **~sill**; **~ lock** *n* 窗锁; **~pane** *n* 窗玻璃; **~ seat** *n* **1** (in room) 窗座; **2** (in train, bus, aircraft) 靠窗的座位; **~-shop** *vi* 浏览橱窗; **~-shopper** *n* 浏览橱窗的人; **~-shopping** *n* [u] 浏览橱窗; **~ sill** *n* 窗沿; **~ winder** *n* 车窗摇手

wind /wɪnd/: **~pipe** *n* 气管; **~-pollinated** *adj* 风媒传粉的; **~ power** *n* [u] 风力; **~-powered** *adj* 风力的; **a ~-powered generator/pump** 风力发电机/水泵

windproof /'wɪndpruːf/

A *adj* 防风的

B *vt* 使防风

windscreen /'wɪndskriːn/ *n* Brit 挡风玻璃

windscreen: **~ washer** *n* Brit 挡风玻璃清洗装置; **~ wiper** *n* Brit 雨刮器

wind /wɪnd/: **~ section** *n* 管乐组; **~ shear** *n* [u] 风切变; **~shield** *n* Amer = **windscreen**; **~sock** *n* 风向袋

wind speed /'wɪndspiːd/ *n* [u and c] 风速

wind-speed indicator *n* 风速指示仪

wind /wɪnd/: **~storm** *n* esp Amer 风暴; **~surf** *vi* 帆板冲浪; **~surfer** *n* **1** (person) 帆板运动者; **2** (board) 帆板; **~surfing** ▸**p. 307** *n* [u] 帆板运动; **~swept** *adj* **1** (exposed) 当风的 ‹*hill, beach*›; **2** (bent by wind) 大风吹弯的 ‹*tree, grasses*›; **3** (untidy) 被风吹得乱糟糟的 ‹*hair, look*›; **~ tunnel** *n* [测试气流对物体作用的] 风洞; **~ turbine** *n* 风力涡轮机

windward /'wɪndwəd/

A *adj* 向风的 ‹*side, slope, face*›

B *adv* 向风 «*face, look, turn*»

C *n* [u] 向风面; **to sail to ~** 迎风航行; **to (the) ~ of sth.** 向某物的迎风面

windy /'wɪndi/ *adj* **1** (with high winds) 多风的 ‹*climate, plateau, desert*›; 风大的 ‹*weather, day*› **2** colloq pej (verbose) 夸夸其谈的 ‹*person*›; 空洞无物的 ‹*speech*› **3** Brit colloq (nervous) 害怕的; **to be/get ~ about sth.** 担心/开始担心某事

Windy City /ˌwɪndi 'sɪti/ *pr n* Amer **the ~** 风城 [美国芝加哥市的别称]

wine /waɪn/

A *n* **1** [u and c] (from grapes) 葡萄酒; **red/white/rosé ~** 红/白/玫瑰红葡萄酒; **sweet/dry ~** 甜/干葡萄酒; **~, women, and song** 声色犬马; **the ~ trade** 葡萄酒贸易 **2** [u and c] (from other fruits or plants) 酒; **blackberry/ginger ~** 黑莓酒/姜酒

B *vt* **to ~ and dine sb.** 用酒宴款待某人

C *vi* 喝很多酒; **to ~ and dine** 大吃大喝

wine: **~ bar** *n* [以供应葡萄酒为主的] 酒吧; **~ bin** *n* 葡萄酒柜; **~ box** *n* [带旋塞的] 盒装葡萄酒; **~ cellar** *n* **1** (place) 酒窖; **2** (stock) 一窖酒; **~ cooler** *n* 镇酒冰壶; **~ glass** *n* 葡萄酒玻璃杯; **~grower** ▸**p. 409** *n* [酿酒用] 葡萄种植者; **~growing** *n* [u] [酿酒用] 葡萄种植; **a ~growing region** or **area** 葡萄种植区; **~ gum** *n* 果味胶糖; **~ lake** *n* 葡萄酒湖 [尤指欧盟大量积存或过剩的葡萄酒]; **~ list** *n* 酒水单; **~ merchant** ▸**p. 409** *n* 酒商; **~ press** ▸**p. 409** *n* [酿酒用] 葡萄压榨机; **~ producer** ▸**p. 409** *n* = **~grower**; **~ rack** *n* 葡萄酒瓶分隔架

winery /'waɪnəri/ *n* esp Amer 葡萄酒厂

wine: **~ shop** *n* 售酒店; **~skin** *n* 酒囊; **~ taster** ▸**p. 409** *n* **1** (person) 品酒人; **2** (cup) 品酒用杯; **~ tasting** *n* **1** [u] (activity) 品酒; **a ~ tasting competition** 品酒竞赛; **2** [c] (occasion) 品酒会; **~ vinegar** *n* [u] 酒醋; **~ waiter** ▸**p. 409** *n* Brit 酒侍

wing /wɪŋ/

A *n* **1** (of bird, bat, insect) 翅膀; **on the ~** 飞行中的; **to catch insects on the ~** 捕捉飞虫; **on a ~ and a prayer** 成功的机会微乎其微; **to take sb. under one's ~** 呵护某人; **to be under sb.'s ~** 在某人的保护之下; **to clip sb.'s ~s** 限制某人的自由; **to give sb./sth.**

~s liter 给某人/某物插上翅膀; **to spread one's ~s** 充分发挥才能; **to take ~** liter 飞走 **2** Aviat 机翼 **3** Archit 房屋侧翼部; **the east ~** 东厢房; **the maternity ~ at the hospital** 医院的妇产科部门 **4** Pol 派系; **the left/right ~** 左翼/右翼 **5** Sport (position) 边路; (player) 边锋 **6** Mil (flank) 侧翼 **7** Brit Aut 挡泥板 **8** (of armchair) 翼部 **9** Mil (unit) 侧翼部队 **10** (on sanitary towel) [卫生巾的] 护翼

B **wings** *npl* **1** Theat **the ~s** 侧面; **to wait in the ~s** 在舞台侧面候场; fig 时刻准备着 **2** Aviat (pilot's certificate) 飞行胸章; **to earn** *or* **get one's ~s** 获得飞行资格

C *vt* **1** (injure on wing) 弄伤…的翅膀 ‹*bird*›; fig (wound slightly on the arm) «*bullet, shot*» 擦伤…的手臂 ‹*person*›; (wound slightly on the shoulder) «*bullet, shot*» 擦伤…的肩膀 ‹*person*› **2** (make fly) 使飞速行进; **he ~ed an arrow towards the target** 他朝靶子射出了一支箭 **3** (fly) **to ~ its way** «*bird, plane*» 飞; **the prize will be ~ing its way to you soon** 奖品很快就会送到你的手中; **to ~ it** colloq (improvise) 即兴而为

wing: ~beat *n* [翅膀的] 一扑闪; **~ case** *n* 翅鞘; **~ chair** *n* 翼状扶手椅; **~ collar** *n* [男士正式服装的] 翼领; **~ commander** *n* 空军中校

wingding /ˈwɪŋdɪŋ/ *n* esp Amer colloq 狂欢聚会; **a ~ party/celebration/outing** 狂欢聚会/庆典/远足活动

winged /wɪŋd/ *adj* 有翼的 ‹*creature, insect*›; 翼状的 ‹*sandals*›; **a blue-~ bird** 蓝翅的鸟

winger /ˈwɪŋə(r)/ *n* 边锋队员

wing: ~ flap *n* 副翼; **~ forward** *n* 边锋; **~ half** *n* dated 边前卫; **~less** *adj* 无翅的 ‹*insect, bird*›; **~-like** *adj* 翼状的 ‹*structure, limb, flap*›; **~man** /-mæn/ *n* **1** Aviat 僚机飞行员; **2** Sport = **winger**; **~ mirror** *n* 侧翼后视镜; **~ nut** *n* 翼形螺母; **~span, ~spread** *ns* 翼展; **~ tip** *n* **1** (of aircraft) 翼尖; **2** (of bird) 翅膀末梢

wink /wɪŋk/

A *vi* **1** (with eye) 眨眼; **to ~ at sb.** 向某人眨眼示意; **to ~ at dishonesty/bribery/corruption** 对欺骗/贿赂/腐败行为视而不见 **2** (flash) «*light, beacon, star*» 闪烁

B *n* **1** (with eye) 眨眼; **to give (sb.) a ~** (向某人) 眨眼示意; **with a ~** 眨一下眼地; **as quick as a ~** 一眨眼的功夫; **in a ~, in the ~ of an eye** 转瞬间; **to not get a ~ of sleep, to not sleep a ~** 没合一下眼; **to tip sb. the ~** 暗示某人; **a nod is as good as a ~ to a blind horse** Prov 心领神会 **2** (flash) 一闪

C *vt* 眨; **to ~ one's eye** 眨眼; **to ~ one's eye at sb.** 向某人使眼色

winker /ˈwɪŋkə(r)/ *n* Brit colloq 频闪信号灯

winking /ˈwɪŋkɪŋ/

A *n* [u] **1** (with eye) 眨眼; **as easy as ~** colloq 易如反掌; **in the ~ of an eye** liter 一眨眼的功夫 **2** (of light, beacon, star) 闪烁

B *adj attrib* 闪烁的 ‹*light, beacon, star*›

winkle /ˈwɪŋkl/ *n* 滨螺

Phrasal verb

- **winkle out** *vt* [~ sb./sth. out, ~ out sb./sth.] colloq **1** (physically) 拽出 ‹*object, person*›; **to ~ sth./sb. out of sth.** 从某处拽出某物/某人 **2** (obtain) **to ~ sth. out (of sb.)** (从某人口中) 套出 ‹*truth, information, confession*›

winkle-picker *n* Brit colloq [流行于20世纪50年代的] 长尖头鞋

winnable /ˈwɪnəbəl/ *adj* 可赢得的

Winnebago /ˌwɪnəˈbeɪɡoʊ/ *n* (*pl* ~ *or* ~s) **1** [c] (person) 温内贝戈人 **2** [u] (language) 温内贝戈语 **3** [c] **Winnebago®** Amer (recreational vehicle) 温内贝戈房车

winner /ˈwɪnə(r)/ *n* **1** [c] (victor) 获胜者; **to be the ~/~s** 是获胜者; **to be on to a ~** (in betting) 押对赌注; fig 有望获胜; **to back the ~** 押对赌注; **to pick** *or* **spot the ~** Horse racing 选对马; **~ takes all** 赢者通吃 **2** [c] colloq (successful person) 成功者; (successful thing) 成功的事物 **3** [u] (goal, shot) 制胜的一记进球

winning /ˈwɪnɪŋ/

A *adj attrib* **1** (victorious) 获胜的; **the ~ goal/team** 制胜的一记入球/获胜的队 **2** (charming) 迷人的 ‹*smile, expression, manner*›; **despite her ~ ways, I mistrust her** 尽管她很可爱，我却不相信她

B *n* [u] 获胜

C **winnings** *npl* 赌赢的财物

winningly /ˈwɪnɪŋli/ *adv* 迷人地 ‹*smile, look, speak*›

winning: ~ post *n* 终点柱; **~ streak** *n* 接二连三的好运气; **to be on** *or* **have a ~ streak** 赶上点顺的时候

winnow /ˈwɪnəʊ/ *vt* **1** Agric (separate from chaff) 簸 ‹*corn, crop, grain*› **2** Agric (remove) 扬去 ‹*chaff*› **3** fig (identify) 辨识 ‹*truth, facts, sense*›; **to ~ sth. from sth.** 把某物从某物中筛选出来

Phrasal verb

- **winnow out** *vt* [~ sb./sth. out, ~ out sb./sth.] 剔除 ‹*applicants, errors*›

winnower /ˈwɪnəʊə(r)/ *n* **1** (person) 扬谷者 **2** (machine) 扬谷机

wino /ˈwaɪnəʊ/ *n* (*pl* ~s) colloq pej [尤指无家可归的] 酒鬼

winsome /ˈwɪnsəm/ *adj* 楚楚动人的 ‹*person, manner, expression*›; 惹人喜爱的 ‹*kitten, puppy*›; **a ~ smile** 莞尔一笑

winsomely /ˈwɪnsəmli/ *adv* 楚楚动人地 ‹*smile, look, gaze*›; 惹人怜爱地 ‹*plead, speak*›

winter /ˈwɪntə(r)/ ▸ p. 692

A *n* **1** (season) 冬天; **a mild/severe ~** 暖冬/严冬; **in the ~** 在冬天; **the ~ holiday/season** 寒假/冬季 **2** fig liter (decline) 衰落期; **in the ~ of his life** 在他暮年时

B *vi* «*person, animal, bird*» 过冬

C *vt* 使…度过冬天 ‹*animal, livestock, herd*›

winter: ~ feed *n* [u and c] [家畜的] 越冬饲料; **~ garden** *n* (outdoor) 冬园 [种有冬季繁茂的常青植物的花园]; (indoor) 温室; **~green** *n* **1** [u and c] Bot 冬青树; **2** [u] **(oil of) ~green** 冬青油; **~green ointment** 冬青油膏

winterize /ˈwɪntəraɪz/ *vt* esp Amer 给…安装御寒设备 ‹*house, garden*›; 使…适合冬季使用 ‹*vehicle*›

winter: ~ jasmine *n* [u and c] 迎春花; **W~ Olympics** *npl* **the W~ Olympics** 冬季奥运会; **~ quarters** *npl* 冬季营房; **~ sleep** *n* 冬眠; **~ solstice** *n* 冬至; **~ sports** *npl* 冬季运动; **~time** *n* 冬季; **~ wheat** *n* [u and c] 冬小麦

wintry /ˈwɪntri/, **wintery** /ˈwɪntəri, ˈwɪntri/ *adjs* **1** lit (cold) 冬天的 ‹*weather, temperature, landscape*›; **~ conditions** 冬季环境 **2** fig (unfeeling) 冷淡的 ‹*smile, welcome*›

win-win situation *n* 双赢状况

wipe /waɪp/

A *vt* **1** (clean) 擦; **I'll ~ the table** 我来抹桌子; **she ~d her feet on the mat** 她在垫子上蹭了蹭脚; **he ~d his plate clean with a piece of bread** 他用一片面包擦干净了盘子; **to ~ the floor with sb.** colloq (defeat) 彻底击败某人; (reprimand) 严厉批评某人 **2** (remove) 擦去; **he ~d the sweat from his brow** 他抹去了额头上的汗水; **I tried to ~ the whole episode from my mind** 我努力想把那整段经历从头脑里彻底抹去; **the crash ~d 24% off stock prices** 崩盘使股价跌了24%; **to ~ the smile** *or* **grin off sb.'s face** 使某人得意不起来; **you can ~ that grin off your face!** 你别傻笑了! **3** (erase) 抹掉 ‹*image, recording*›; 擦掉 ‹*data, memory*› **4** (spread) 涂上 ‹*liquid, lotion*› **5** (pass) 用…擦 ‹*cloth, sponge*›; **he ~d the handkerchief across his forehead** 他用手帕擦了擦前额

B *n* **1** (act of wiping) 擦拭; **to give sth. a ~** 擦拭某物 **2** (disposable cloth) 湿纸巾; **an antiseptic ~** 消毒纸巾; **a hand ~** 手帕纸; **a surface ~** 抹布 **3** Cin 划变

Phrasal verbs

- **wipe away** *vt* [~ sth. away, ~ away sth.] 擦去 ‹*tears, dirt*›
- **wipe down** *vt* [~ sth. down, ~ down sth.] 把…上下擦拭干净 ‹*wall, furniture*›
- **wipe off** *vt* [~ sth. off, ~ off sth.] **1** (remove) 擦掉 ‹*mark, stain*›; **she ~d her make-up off** 她卸了妆 **2** (erase) 清除
- **wipe out**

A [~ sth. out, ~ out sth.] *vt* **1** (clean) 把…的里面擦干净 ‹*cup, cupboard*› **2** (erase) 清除 **3** (cancel, obliterate) 擦去 ‹*mistake, mark*›; 勾销 ‹*debt*›; 抹掉 ‹*memory*›; **their life savings were ~d out** 他们一生的积蓄被吞噬了

B [~ sb./sth. out, ~ out sb./sth.] *vt* (defeat utterly) 彻底打败 ‹*enemy, opposition*›; (destroy) 消灭 ‹*enemy, population*›; (kill) 干掉; **our patrol ~d out the enemy gun position** 我们的巡逻兵摧毁了敌人的炮位; **to be ~d out** colloq (exhausted) 精疲力竭

- **wipe up**

A *vt* [~ sth. up, ~ up sth.] **1** (remove) 擦去 ‹*stain, spill*› **2** (dry) 把…擦干 ‹*dishes, cutlery*›

B *vi* 擦干餐具

wipe: ~-clean *adj* 一擦就干净的 ‹*surface, flooring, fabric*›; **~-down** *n* 擦干净; **~out** *n* [c] colloq **1** esp Mil (destruction) 彻底消灭; **a nuclear ~out** 核毁灭; **2** Sport (defeat) 彻底失败

wiper /ˈwaɪpə(r)/ *n* **1** Aut 雨刮器 **2** (cloth) 抹布

wiper: ~ arm *n* 雨刮臂; **~ blade** *n* 雨刮片; **~ motor** *n* 雨刮电机

WIPO *abbr* = **World Intellectual Property Organization** 世界知识产权组织

wire /ˈwaɪə(r)/

A *n* **1** [u and c] (thin metal rod or thread) 金属丝; (telephone wire) 电话线; (electricity wire) 电线; **a length/coil of ~** 一段/一卷金属丝; **copper/gold ~** 铜丝/金丝; **~ for fencing** 篱笆用铁丝; **to get one's ~s crossed** colloq 相互误解; **to pull ~s** esp Amer 暗中施加影响; **to escape by crawling under the ~** 从铁丝网下爬出逃脱; **a ~ fence** 铁丝栅栏 **2** esp Amer colloq (telegram) 电报; **to send/receive a ~** 发/收电报 **3** Amer Horse racing 终点线; **to go down to the ~** colloq 到最后一刻; **the race went down to the ~** 比赛直到最后一刻才见分晓; **to get in under the ~** colloq 勉强按时完成

B *vt* **1** (install, connect) 给…安电线 ‹*house, building, equipment*›; **it's ~d for television in every room** 每个房间都安装了电视线; **to ~ sth. to sth.** 用电线将某物连接到某物上 **2** (fix with wire) 给…安装铁丝网 ‹*fence*›; 用金属丝固定 ‹*flower, jaw*›; 用金属丝串 ‹*necklace*›; **to ~ sth. to sth.** 用金属丝将某物连在某物上 **3** (send by telegram) 用电报传送 ‹*message, acceptance, refusal*›; **to ~ that ...** 致电说…; **to ~ money to sb.** 给某人电汇钱款 **4** esp Amer Telecom (send message to) 给…发电报 ‹*person*›; **to ~ sb. with sth.** 打电报通知某人某事

Phrasal verbs

- **wire in** *vt* [~ sth. in., ~ in sth.] 给…接通电源 ‹*device, socket*›
- **wire together** *vt* [~ sth. together, ~ together sth.] **1** Elec 给…接通导线 ‹*components, devices*› **2** (join by wire) 用金属丝连接 ‹*objects, parts*›
- **wire up** *vt* [~ sth. up, ~ up sth.] 给…安装电线 ‹*house, lamp, circuit*›; **to ~ sth./sb. up for sth.** 给…安装某物; **to ~ up a room for sound** 给房间安装扩音器

wire: ~ brush *n* 钢丝刷; **~ cutters** *npl* 钢丝钳

wired /'waɪəd/ *adj* colloq 1 Comput 联网的 2 Elec 有线的 3 (tense, nervous) 紧张的

wire: ~-drawer *n* 1 (person) 拉丝工; 2 (machine) 拉丝机; **~ entanglement** *n* 铁丝网; **~frame** *n* 三维线框; **a ~frame model** 线框模型; **~ gauge** *n* 1 (device) 线规; 2 (size) 线材标号; **~ gauze** *n* [u] 金属细网纱; **~ glass** *n* [u] 夹丝玻璃; **~-haired** *adj* 粗毛的 ‹*dog*›

wireless /'waɪəlɪs/

A *adj* 1 (without wires) 无线的; **~ network/connection/broadband** 无线网络/连接/宽带 2 *attrib* esp Brit Radio dated 无线电的; **~ broadcast/programme/waves** 无线电广播/广播节目/波

B *n* esp Brit dated 1 (radio communication) 无线电通讯; **to communicate/send a message by ~** 通过无线电交流/用无线电报发送信息 2 esp Brit dated (radio) **~ (set)** (receive signals) 无线电收音机; (transmit and receive signals) 无线电收发机; **over** *or* **on the ~** 从收音机; **to speak to sb.** *or* **get sb. on the ~** 用无线电和某人通话

wireless: ~ device *n* 无线装置; **~-enabled** *adj* 可无线传输数据的 ‹*device*›; 可无线上网的 ‹*computer, laptop*›; **~ message** *n* esp Brit dated 无线电报; **~ operator** ▸ **p. 409** *n* esp Brit dated 无线电发报员

wire: ~man /-mæn/ ▸ **p. 409** *n* esp Amer 1 (installer) 架线工; 2 (repairer) 电线维修工; **~ mesh** *n* [u] 电线网; **~ netting** *n* [u] 金属丝网; **~puller** *n* Amer colloq 幕后操纵者; **~pulling** *n* [u] Amer colloq 幕后操纵; **~ rope** *n* 钢索; **~ service** *n* esp Amer 电讯社; **~ stripper** *n* 剥线钳

wiretap /'waɪətæp/

A *vt* (*pres p etc.* **-pp-**) 搭线窃听 ‹*person, room, conversation, telephone line*›; **the suspect was ~ped for two weeks** 嫌疑人被监听了两个星期

B *vi* (*pres p etc.* **-pp-**) «*person, police, government*» 搭线窃听

C *n* 1 (device) 搭线窃听装置 2 (occurrence) 搭线窃听

wire: ~tapping *n* [u] 搭线窃听; **~ wheel** *n* [赛车等的] 辐条轮; **~ wool** *n* [u] Brit 钢丝球; **~work** *n* [u] 金属丝制品

wiring /'waɪərɪŋ/ *n* [u] 1 (installation) 线路安装; **to do/redo the ~** 接/重接线路 2 (system) 线路

wiry /'waɪəri/ *adj* 1 (sinewy) 精瘦的 ‹*person, figure*› 2 (rough) 粗硬的 ‹*hair, grass, texture*›; **to have a ~ coat** 毛皮很硬

Wisconsin /wɪ'skɒnsɪn/ *pr n* 威斯康星州

wisdom /'wɪzdəm/ *n* [u] 1 (of person) 智慧; **a man/woman of great ~** 才子/才女; **the ~ to do sth.** 做某事的智慧; **in sb.'s ~** iron 自以为聪明地; **with the ~ of hindsight** 事后聪明地; **the ~ of Solomon** 所罗门之智慧 [解决难题的大智慧] 2 (of action, decision) 明智; **to doubt** *or* **question the ~ of sth./doing sth.** 怀疑某事物/做某事是否明智 3 (body of knowledge) 知识; **folk/conventional** *or* **received ~** 民间智慧/生活常识; **ancient/Eastern ~** 古老的/东方的学问

wisdom tooth *n* 智齿; **to have a ~ out** *or* **extracted** 拔掉一颗智齿; **to cut one's ~** fig 到了懂事的年龄

wise /waɪz/ *adj* 1 (having good judgement) 聪明的; **to be sadder and ~r** 吃过苦头而变聪明; **a word to the ~** 明白人不用细说; **a ~ old owl** hum 老狐狸; **as ~ as an owl** 非常精明的 2 (prudent) 明智的 ‹*choice, action*›; **to be ~ of sb. (to do sth.)** 某人（做某事）是明智的; **the ~st thing (to do) would be ...** （要做的）最明智的事情是… 3 (learned) 博学的 ‹*scholar*›; (well-informed) 有见地的 ‹*article, discussion*›; **to be ~ after the event** 事后聪明; **not to be any the ~r, to be none the ~r, to be no ~r** (not understand) 仍不明白; (in the dark) 仍不知情; **the village ~ woman/man** 乡村巫婆/巫师; **the Three W~ Men** Relig 东方三博士 4 colloq (aware) 知情的; **to be** *or* **get ~ to sb./sth.** 认清某人/某事物; **to put sb. ~ about** *or* **to sth./sb.** 让某人知道某事物/某人

Phrasal verb

• **wise up** colloq

A *vi* (be informed) 了解; (find out) 察觉; **to ~ up to** *or* **on sth.** 了解某事

B *vt* [**~ sb. up, ~ up sb.**] 告知; **to ~ sb. up on sth.** 告知某人某事; **to get ~d up about sth.** 了解某事

-wise /waɪz/ *combining form* 1 (manner) 以…方式; (direction) 朝…方向 2 colloq (with regard to) 在…方面; **security~, there are a few problems** 安全方面，有几个问题; **he is doing OK health~** 他的健康状况良好

wiseacre /'waɪzeɪkə(r)/ *n* 自以为无所不知的人

wisecrack /'waɪzkræk/ colloq

A *n* 俏皮话; **to make a ~** 说俏皮话

B *vi* 说俏皮话

wise guy *n* colloq 1 esp Amer pej (know-all) 万事通 2 Amer (Mafioso) 黑手党成员

wisely /'waɪzli/ *adv* 明智地; **to choose one's words ~** 谨慎地说话

wish /wɪʃ/

A *vi* 1 (desire, want) 希望; **to ~ for sb./sth.** 想要某人/某物; **it's no use ~ing for things one cannot have** 企求得不到的东西是没有用的; **the people ~ for an end to war and terrorism** 人民盼望结束战争和恐怖活动; **(just) as you ~** 悉听尊便; **spend it as you ~** 你想怎么花就怎么花; **you'll have finished by tomorrow — I ~!** 到明天你就会完成了——但愿如此！ 2 (pray) 祈求; **if you ~ really hard, maybe you'll get what you want** 心诚则灵; **to ~ for sb./sth.** 祈望得到某人/某物

B *vt* 1 (expressing longing) 但愿; **to ~ that ...** 但愿…; **I ~ I were** *or* Brit **was taller/rich** 我要是个头高些/有钱就好了; **he ~es his mother would phone** 他真希望他妈妈会打电话来; **where is he now? — I only ~ I knew!** 他现在在哪儿？——我要是知道就好了！; **to ~ sb./sth. on** *or* **upon sb.** 十分希望某人遭遇某人/某事物; **I wouldn't ~ it on my worst enemy!** 即便是我的死对头，我也不想他遭遇这种事！ 2 formal (demand) 希望; (want) 想要; **that was what your father would have ~ed** 你父亲也会这么希望的; **you can stay until tomorrow if you ~** 如果你愿意，你可以待到明天; **we ~ nothing but peace** 我们只要和平; **the ambassador ~es an audience with the foreign minister** 大使希望拜见外交部长; **to ~ to do sth.** 想要做某事; **she ~es to be alone** 她想要一个人待着; **I do not ~ to be rude, but ...** 我不想显得无礼，可是…; **I ~ it to be clear that the decision is final** 我想要明确这一点：这是最终决定 3 (expressing hope) 祝愿 ‹*happiness, joy*›; **I ~ you every success!** 我祝你万事成功！; **to ~ sb. no ill** *or* **harm** 不希望某人倒霉; **to ~ sb. good luck/the best of luck** 祝某人好运/鸿运当头; **to ~ sb. well** 祝某人走运; **to ~ sb. joy of sth.** 向某人贺某事之喜 4 (expressing greetings) 祝愿; **to ~ sb. happy birthday/goodbye** 祝某人生日快乐/向某人道别; **to ~ sb. good morning/night** 向某人道早安/晚安; **to ~ sb. many happy returns of the day** 祝某人福寿绵长

C *n* 1 (desire) 愿望; **her ~ came true!** 她的愿望实现啦！; **the fairy gave her three ~es** 仙女让她许三个愿; **a ~ for sth.** 对某事的愿望; **to have/express/cherish/nurture a ~** 有/表达/怀有/心怀一个愿望; **to make a ~** 许愿; **to grant sb.'s ~** 答应某人的愿望; **to carry out sb.'s ~** 实现某人的愿望; **against sb.'s ~(es)** 违背某人的愿望; **at sb.'s ~** 按照某人的意愿; **the ~ is father to the thought** Prov 愿望是信念之父; **your ~ is my command** formal or hum 听凭阁下吩咐 2 (desired thing) 想要的东西

D **wishes** *npl* 祝愿; **good/best ~es** 美好/最好的祝愿; **to offer/send good ~es (to sb./for sth.)** （向某人/某事物）致以/送上美好的祝愿

Phrasal verb

• **wish away** *vt* [**~ sth. away, ~ away sth.**] 希望…不存在 ‹*problem*›

wishbone /'wɪʃbəʊn/ *n* 1 Culin 叉骨 2 Aut, Aviat 叉形臂; **~ suspension** 叉形臂悬架

wishful /'wɪʃfəl/ *adj* 渴望的 ‹*look, thought*›

wish-fulfilment *n* [u] [弗洛伊德心理学中的] 非直接的愿望满足

wishful thinking *n* [u] 一厢情愿; **that's ~** 那是剃头挑子一头热

wishing well *n* 许愿井

wish list *n* 愿望清单

wishy-washy /'wɪʃɪwɒʃi/ *adj* colloq pej 1 (feeble) 空泛的 ‹*idea, plan, design*›; 软弱无力的 ‹*attitude, character, approach*›; 不坚定的 ‹*liberalism*› 2 (watery) 淡而无味的 ‹*drink, food*› 3 (pale) 浅的 ‹*blue, green, colour*›

wisp /wɪsp/ *n* (of hair, beard) 一绺; (of smoke, mist) 一缕; **a ~ of straw** 一束稻草; **a ~ of a girl** 纤弱的女孩

wispy /'wɪspi/ *adj* 一绺绺的 ‹*hair, beard*›; 一缕缕的 ‹*smoke, mist*›

wisteria /wɪ'stɪərɪə/ *n* [u and c] 紫藤属植物

wistful /'wɪstfl/ *adj* 伤感的

wistfully /'wɪstfəli/ *adv* 伤感地

wistfulness /'wɪstflnɪs/ *n* [u] 伤感

wit[1] /wɪt/

A *n* 1 [u and c] (humour) (personal) 风趣; (spoken, written) 风趣的话语; **(to have a) quick** *or* **ready** *or* **sharp ~** （有）敏捷的才思; **caustic/dry ~** 刻薄的/冷面的幽默; **~ and wisdom** 机智和智慧 2 [c] (humorous person) 说话风趣的人 3 [u] (intelligence, good sense) 智力; **to have the ~ to do sth.** 知道该做某事

B **wits** *npl* 颖悟力; **he needed all his ~s to find the way back** 他需要绞尽脑汁才能找到回去的路; **to have** *or* **keep one's ~s about one** 保持头脑冷静; **to collect** *or* **gather one's ~s** 冷静思考; **to live by one's ~s** 靠耍小聪明赚钱过日子; **to be at one's ~s' end** 智穷才尽; **a battle of ~s** 斗智

wit[2] *vi* **to ~** formal 即

witch /wɪtʃ/ *n* 1 (in stories) 女巫 2 Relig 巫师 3 colloq pej (nasty woman) 丑老太婆 4 (bewitching woman) 迷人的女子

witch: ~craft *n* [u] 1 (in stories) 魔法; 2 Relig 巫术; **~ doctor** *n* 巫医

witchery /'wɪtʃəri/ *n* [u] 1 (magic) 巫术; **to perform ~** 施魔法 2 (allure) 魔力

witch: ~es' brew /ˌwɪtʃɪz 'bruː/ *n* 1 (drink, liquid) 有毒液体; 2 fig (mixture) 骇人的大杂烩; **~es' sabbath** /ˌwɪtʃɪz 'sæbəθ/ *n* 信魔者的夜半集会

witch: ~ hazel *n* 1 [u and c] Bot 金缕梅; 2 [u] Med 金缕梅酊剂; **~-hunt** *n* fig pej 政治迫害; **~-hunter** *n* fig pej 政治迫害者

witching hour *n* 1 liter 夜半巫师出没的时刻 2 fig hum **the ~** 三更半夜

witchlike /'wɪtʃlaɪk/ *adj* 女巫般的

with /wɪð, wɪθ/ *prep* 1 (accompanying) 和…一起; **to travel ~ sb.** 和某人一起旅行; **to mix sth. ~ sth.** 将某物与某物混合; **I haven't got any cash ~ me** 我没带现金; **I'll be ~ you in a second** 我一会儿就来; **~ it** colloq (fashionable) 时髦的; (in the know) 识时务的 2 (having) 拥有; (wearing) 穿戴着; (carrying) 带着; **a girl ~ black hair** 黑发女郎; **a man ~ glasses** 戴眼镜的男人; **passengers ~ tickets** 持票的乘客; **to arrive ~ some flowers** 到达时捧着一些花; **animals ~ young** 怀孕的动物 3 (using, indicating manner) 以 [表示所用的工具、物质、手段、方式或态度];

to cut sth. ~ a knife 用刀子切开某物; **to walk ~ a stick** 拄着手杖走路; **to buy sth. ~ one's savings** 用积蓄买某物; **~ a CV** Brit *or* **resumé** Amer **like yours, you're sure to find a job** 以你那样的履历定能找到工作; **~ pleasure/gratitude** 愉快/感激地; **to look at sb. ~ hate in one's eyes** 以憎恨的目光看着某人; **to do sth. ~ skill** 娴熟地做某事; **'OK,' he said ~ a sigh** "好吧,"他叹了口气说 **4** (as filling, covering) 被 [表示填充或覆盖]; **to be stuffed ~ clothes** 塞满衣服; **to be wet ~ dew** 被露水打湿; **the floor is covered ~ mud** 地板上全是泥 **5** (against, across from) 与 [表示相对]; **to play tennis ~ sb.** 和某人打网球; **to have an argument ~ sb.** 与某人争论; **a conversation/meeting ~ sb.** 与某人的谈话/见面; **to discuss sth. ~ sb.** 与某人讨论某事 **6** (indicating support) 赞同; **to vote ~ sb.** 投票支持某人; **to be ~ sb. (on sth.)** (在某事上) 与某人站在一起; **I'm ~ you 100%** *or* **all the way** 我完全支持你 **7** (in relation to, as regards) [表示关系]; **the frontier ~ Mexico** 与墨西哥接壤的边境; **risks associated ~ mining** 采矿的风险; **it's a habit ~ her** colloq 这是她的习惯 **8** (including) 包括; **~ wine, the meal is £30 a head** 算上酒水这顿饭每人 30 英镑; **it cost £50 ~ VAT** 加上增值税要花 50 英镑 **9** (towards) 对于; **to be gentle/patient ~ sb.** 对某人温和/耐心; **to be satisfied ~ sb.'s work** 对某人的工作满意 **10** (under conditions of) [表示伴随情况]; **to sleep ~ the window open** 开着窗户睡觉; **to see better ~ one's glasses on** 戴眼镜看得更清楚 **11** (in proportion to, along with) 随着; **to increase ~ age** 随着年龄的增长而增长; **temperature goes down ~ the altitude** 温度随着海拔的增高而下降; **skill comes ~ practice** 熟能生巧; **~ the approach of spring ...** 随着春天的到来…; **~ that** 随后; **he muttered a few words, and ~ that he left** 他嘟哝了几句就离开了 **12** (indicating amount left) [表示剩余的量]; **~ only two days to go before the election, ...** 离选举只有 2 天了, …; **he pulled out of the race ~ 100 metres to go** 他在还剩下 100 米时退出了比赛 **13** (due to) 由于; **I can't go out ~ all this work to do** 有这么多工作要做, 我没办法出去; **to tremble/be white ~ fear** 吓得发抖/脸色发白 **14** (affected by) 患; **people ~ Aids** 艾滋病患者; **patients ~ leukaemia** 白血病人; **to be in bed ~ chickenpox** 因患水痘卧床 **15** (in same direction as) 顺着; **to sail ~ the wind** 顺风航行; **to be swept along ~ the crowd** 被人流挟裹着前行 **16** (under the care of) 由…掌管; **to be ~ sb./sth.** 由某人/某物负责; **to leave sth. ~ sb.** 把某物交给某人照管; **the keys are ~ reception** 钥匙在服务台 **17** (employed by) 受雇于; **she's ~ the Inland Revenue** 她受雇于国内税务局; **a reporter ~ the Mirror** 一名《镜报》记者; **he's ~ the UN** 他在联合国工作 **18** (customer of) [表示使用某服务机构]; **I bank ~ the Halifax** 我的钱存在哈利法克斯银行 **19** (indicating separation) [表示分离]; **a break ~ tradition** 与传统的决裂; **to dispense ~ formalities** 免去客套 **20** (despite) 尽管; **~ all her faults I still love her** 尽管她有种种缺点, 我依然爱她 **21** (starring) 由…主演; **Casablanca ~ Humphrey Bogart** 由亨弗莱·鲍嘉主演的《卡萨布兰卡》 **22** colloq (following mentally) 跟得上; **to be ~ sb.** 能理解某人讲的话; **I'm not ~ you** 我不明白你的意思; **to be** *or* **get ~ it** 明白情况; **you don't seem very ~ it today** 你今天脑瓜子似乎不太管用; **get ~ it!** (face reality) 面对现实吧!; (be more up to date or fashionable) 别太落伍了! **23** (in exclamations) [与副词连用表示感叹]; **down ~ sb./sth.** 打倒某人/取缔某物; **on ~ the dance!** 继续跳舞吧!; **away ~ you!** 滚开!

withdraw /wɪð'drɔː, wɪθ'd-/ (*pt* **withdrew**, *pp* **withdrawn**)

A *vt* **1** (remove) 取回 ‹*book, object, key*›; **to ~ sth. from sth.** 从某处取回某物; **she withdrew her hand from his** 她把手从他手中抽回 **2** Fin 提取 ‹*amount, savings*›; **to ~ money from one's account** 从账户取钱 **3** (recall) 撤回 ‹*troops, forces*›; 召回 ‹*ambassador, diplomat*›; 停止销售 ‹*drug, product*›; 使…停止流通 ‹*banknote, coin*›; **to ~ sb. from somewhere** 把某人从某地召回 **4** (rescind) 收回 ‹*permission, statement*›; 撤回 ‹*application, claim*›; 撤销 ‹*accusation, motion, charge*›; **to ~ one's labour** Brit 罢工

B *vi* **1** (leave) 离开; **to ~ from sth.** 离开某处; **to ~ to somewhere** 离开到某处去; **the tortoise withdrew into its shell** 乌龟缩回壳里了; **to ~ into oneself** 自闭 **2** (cease to participate) 退出; **to ~ from the competition/debate** 退出比赛/争论

withdrawal /wɪð'drɔːəl, wɪθ'd-/ *n* **1** [u] (removal) 取回 **2** [u and c] Fin 提款; **to make a ~ (from an account)** (从账户上) 取钱 **3** [u] (recall) (of troops, forces) 撤回; (of ambassador, diplomat) 召回; (of drug, product) 停止销售; (of banknote, coin) 停止流通 **4** [u] (rescinding) (of permission, statement) 收回; (of application, claim) 撤回; (of accusation, motion, charge) 撤销; **~ of labour** Brit 罢工 **5** [u] (ceasing to participate) 退出 **6** [u] Psych 自闭 **7** [u] Med 戒毒过程

withdrawal: ~ slip *n* 取款凭条; **~ symptoms** *npl* 脱瘾症状

withdrawn /wɪð'drɔːn, wɪθ'd-/

A *pp* ▸**withdraw**

B *adj* 内向的

withdrew /wɪð'druː/ *pt* ▸**withdraw**

wither /'wɪðə(r)/

A *vi* **1** Bot 枯萎 **2** fig (fall into decline) «*hopes, dreams*» 破灭; «*culture*» 衰落; «*determination*» 消退 **3** (atrophy) «*limb*» 干瘪; «*person*» 衰老憔悴

B *vt* 使枯萎

Phrasal verb

- **wither away** *vi* **1** (atrophy) «*limb*» 慢慢干瘪 **2** (decline) «*culture, society*» 衰落; «*hopes, dreams*» 破灭

withered /'wɪðəd/ *adj* **1** Bot 枯萎的 **2** (fallen into decline) 破灭的 ‹*hope, dreams*›; 消退的 ‹*determination, belief*› **3** (atrophied) 干瘪的 ‹*limb*›; 衰老憔悴的 ‹*person*›

withering /'wɪðərɪŋ/ *adj* 讥讽的 ‹*remark*›; 尖刻的 ‹*condemnation*›; 使人难堪的 ‹*sarcasm, contempt*›; 轻蔑的 ‹*look, glance*›

witheringly /'wɪðərɪŋli/ *adv* 讥讽地 ‹*say, speak*›; 使人难堪地 ‹*sarcastic, contemptuous*›; 轻蔑地 ‹*look, glare*›

withers /'wɪðəz/ *npl* 鬐甲 [马肩胛骨间隆起部分]

withhold /wɪð'həʊld/ *vt* (*pt, pp* **withheld** /wɪð'held/) 拒付 ‹*money, payment, rent, tax*›; 不予 ‹*consent, permission*›; 隐瞒 ‹*information, details, name*›; **to ~ sth. from sb.** 向某人隐瞒某事

withholding tax *n* Amer [雇主从员工收入中扣除并直接上交政府的] 代扣所得税

within /wɪ'ðɪn/

A *prep* **1** (enclosed in) 在…里面; **~ the city walls** 在城墙里面; **conditions ~ the prison** 监狱里的条件; **the spread of fire ~ the building** 火在大楼里的蔓延; **a play ~ a play** 一场戏中戏 **2** (inside organization) 在…内部; **infighting ~ the party** 党内的斗争; **countries ~ the EU** 欧盟国家 **3** (inside self) 在…内心; **anger surged up ~ me** 我怒火中烧 **4** (in expressions of time) 在…内; **~ the hour** 一小时内; **to die ~ a week of each other** 在一周内相继去世; **to finish ~ the time limit** 在规定的时间内完成; **to live ~ minutes of the station** 住在离车站几分钟路程的地方 **5** (inside range or scope of) 在…范围内; **~ a 2 km radius** 在方圆 2 公里的范围内; **~ this price range** 在这个价格范围内; **to be accurate to ~ a millimetre** 误差不超过一毫米; **to keep ~ the speed limit** 不超速; **sth. is ~ sight/range** 某物在视线/范围内; **to write ~ the Victorian tradition** 遵循维多利亚时代传统写作 **6** (inside limit of) 在…的限度内; **~ the limitations of the treaty** 符合条约规定; **to be ~ one's rights to refuse** 有权拒绝; **~ the law** 合法; **to live ~ one's income** *or* **means** 量入为出

B *adv* **1** (in inner part) 在里面; **from ~** 从里面; **no sound came from ~** 里面未传出任何声音; **~ and without** 里里外外; **'enquire ~'** "请入内询洽" **2** (inside area, organization) 在内部; **to come from ~ the city/country** 来自城内/国内; **to promote people from ~** 提拔自己人 **3** (inside self) 在内心; **beauty coming from ~** 内在美

without /wɪ'ðaʊt/

A *prep* **1** (not having) 没有; **a chair ~ arms** 没有扶手的椅子; **how will I manage ~ the car?** 没有汽车我怎么应付得了呢?; **to be completely ~ shame** 毫无羞耻 **2** (not using) 不用; (not carrying) 不带; (not wearing) 不穿; **I can't open it ~ the key** 没有钥匙我无法把它打开; **can you see ~ your glasses?** 你不戴眼镜能看见吗?; **he went out ~ his coat** 他没穿外套就出去了; **she left ~ her briefcase** 她没带公文包就离开了 **3** (unaccompanied by) 无…相伴; **she went ~ me** 她没和我一起, 一个人走了 **4** (not doing the action mentioned) 不; **to leave ~ saying goodbye** 不辞而别; **it goes ~ saying that ...** …是不言而喻的; **to do sth. ~ sb. noticing** 做某事不为某人注意; **~ asking permission** 没有征得同意; ▸**much B2**

B *adv* **1** (not having sth.) 没有; **do you want a room with a bath or one ~?** 你要带浴室还是不带浴室的房间?; **I'll manage ~** 我能将就 **2** (on the outside) 在外面; **from ~** 从外面; **invaders from ~** 外来侵略者 **3** (outside organization, self) 在外部; **competition both from within the industry and from ~** 来自行业内外的竞争; **change coming from ~** 来自外界的变化

with-profits /wɪð'prɒfɪts/ *adj* Brit 能分红的 ‹*policy, investment, bond holder*›

withstand /wɪð'stænd/ *vt* (*pt, pp* **withstood** /wɪð'stʊd/) 承受住 ‹*earthquake, high winds, physical pressure*›; 经受住 ‹*attack, recession, psychological pressure, abuse, criticism*›

witless /'wɪtlɪs/ *adj* 愚蠢的; **to be scared/bored ~** 被吓破了胆/乏味得要命

witness /'wɪtnɪs/

A *n* **1** [c] (onlooker) 目击者; **to be (a) ~ to sth.** 是…的目击者 ‹*event, crime*›; **we have been ~es to great changes in society** 我们见证了社会的巨大变化 **2** [c] Jur (sb. who testifies) 证人; **a prosecution/defence ~** 原告/被告证人; **to call a ~** 传唤证人出庭作证; **to call sb. as a ~** 请某人作证人; **to produce a ~** 提供一位证人 **3** [c] Jur (signatory) 见证人; **to act as (a) ~** 充当见证人; **in the presence of a ~** 当着见证人的面; **a ~ to an agreement/a will/sb.'s signature** 合约/遗嘱/某人签名的连署人; **a ~ at a wedding** 证婚人 **4** [u] formal (testimony) 证明; **to be** *or* **bear ~ to sth.** «*appearance, state*» (prove) 证明某事物; (indicate) 表明某事物; **to give ~ on behalf of sb.** 为某人作证; **to bear false ~** Jur 作伪证; **in ~ of sth.** 作为某事的证明; **in ~ thereof, ...** 兹证明, … **5** [u] Relig 见证

B *vt* **1** (see) 目睹 ‹*accident, event*› **2** Jur (authenticate) 为…作证 ‹*signature*›; 为…的签署作证 ‹*document, agreement*›; 作…的见证人 ‹*marriage*› **3** formal (be evidence for) 见证; (be a sign of) 表明; **his hard work has paid off, (as) ~ his exam results** 他的努力获得了回报, 他的考试成绩就是明证 **4** fig (experience) «*person, society, place*» 经历 ‹*change*›; **the last decade has ~ed tremendous advances in technology** 过去的 10 年在技术方面有了巨大进步; **this house has ~ed many**

historic events 这栋房子里发生过许多历史事件

C *vi* 证明; **to ~ to sth.** 证明某事物; **his writings ~ to an inner toughness** 从他的文章中可以看出内心的坚强

witness box Brit, **witness stand** Amer *ns* 证人席; **in the ~** 在证人席上

witter /ˈwɪtə(r)/ *vi* Brit colloq 唠叨; **to ~ about sth.** 唠叨某事; **to ~ on (about sth.)** 不停地唠叨（某事）

witticism /ˈwɪtɪsɪzəm/ *n* [u] 妙语; **full of little ~s** 妙语连珠的

wittily /ˈwɪtɪli/ *adv* 机智地 ‹*deal with, treat*›; 诙谐地 ‹*describe, remark, write*›

wittiness /ˈwɪtinɪs/ *n* [u] 机智

wittingly /ˈwɪtɪŋli/ *adv* 蓄意地 ‹*destroy, damage, offend*›; 有意地 ‹*upset, prevent*›

witty /ˈwɪti/ *adj* 风趣的 ‹*person, speech, remark*›; 妙趣横生的 ‹*article, play*›

wives /waɪvz/ *pl* ▸**wife**

wiz /wɪz/ *n* colloq = **whizz C2**

wizard /ˈwɪzəd/

A *n* **1** (magician) 男巫 **2** (expert) 行家; **to be a ~ with sth.** 是某方面的行家; **to be a ~ at sth./doing sth.** 擅长某事/做某事 **3** Comput 向导程序

B *adj* Brit colloq dated 极好的

wizardry /ˈwɪzədri/ *n* [u] **1** (magic) 巫术; **Harry Potter uses his powers of ~ for good** 哈利·波特用他的魔力行善 **2** (skill) 非凡的才能; **his ~ with a tennis racquet/on the guitar** 他在网球/吉他方面的杰出才能 **3** (product of skill) 奇异事物; **technical/high-tech ~** 神奇的技术/高科技产品

wizened /ˈwɪznd/ *adj* 干瘪的 ‹*person, body*›; 皱缩的 ‹*face, fruit*›

wk *abbr* = **week**

WMD *abbr* = **weapon of mass destruction**

WML *abbr* = **Wireless Mark-up Language** 无线标记语言

WO *abbr* = **warrant officer**

woad /wəʊd/ *n* [u] **1** (dye) 靛蓝 **2** Bot 菘蓝

wobble /ˈwɒbl/

A *vi* **1** (move from side to side) 摇晃; **to ~ about** 四下晃动 **2** (quaver) «*voice*» 颤抖 **3** fig (vacillate) «*person, government*» 摇摆不定

B *vt* 使摇晃

C *n* **1** (movement) 摇晃; **wheel ~** 车轮摇摆 **2** (quaver) [声音的] 颤抖 **3** fig (vacillation) 动摇

wobbly /ˈwɒbli/

A *adj* **1** (unsteady) 摇晃的 ‹*table, jelly, legs, cyclist*›; 歪斜的 ‹*handwriting, line*›; **a ~ tooth** 松动的牙齿 **2** (quavering) 颤抖的 ‹*voice, singing*›; 站不稳的 ‹*person*› **3** fig (uncertain) 摇摆不定的 ‹*theory, plot, beginning*›

B *n* Brit colloq 怒气; **to throw a ~** 发脾气

wodge /wɒdʒ/ *n* Brit colloq **1** (piece) 一大块; **a ~ of cake/pie/bread** 一大块蛋糕/馅饼/面包; **a ~ of banknotes** 厚厚一沓钞票 **2** (amount) 大量; **a ~ of information/data** 大量的信息/数据

woe /wəʊ/

A *n* liter 痛苦; **a tale of ~** hum 悲惨的故事; **~ betide sb. if ...** hum 如果…某人就要倒霉; **~ betide the person who ...** hum 谁若是…就要倒霉

B **woes** *npl* (troubles) 麻烦; (problems) 问题; **to add to his ~s** 使他更麻烦的是

C *excl* archaic or liter 唉哟 [表示悲伤、灾难等]; **~ is me!** 我好苦啊!

woebegone /ˈwəʊbɪɡɒn, Amer -ɡɔːn/ *adj* 愁眉苦脸的 ‹*person*›; 悲伤的 ‹*expression, face*›

woeful /ˈwəʊfl/ *adj* **1** (mournful) 悲伤的 ‹*person, cry, look, expression, face*›; 悲惨的 ‹*story, tale, sight*› **2** (deplorable) 严重的 ‹*lack, inadequacy*›; 糟糕的 ‹*condition, state*›; 可悲的 ‹*ignorance*›

woefully /ˈwəʊfəli/ *adv* **1** (mournfully) 悲伤地 ‹*cry, look, gaze*› **2** (deplorably) 严重地 ‹*lacking, inadequate, underfunded*›; 糟糕地 ‹*equipped*›; 可悲地 ‹*ignorant*›

wog /wɒɡ/ *n* Brit colloq offensive 外国佬 [尤指有色人种]

wok /wɒk/ *n* 中式炒菜锅

woke /wəʊk/ *pt* ▸**wake A, B**

woken /ˈwəʊkən/ *pp* ▸**wake A, B**

wolf /wʊlf/ *n* (*pl* **wolves**) **1** Zool 狼; **a pack of wolves** 一群狼; **the big bad ~** 大灰狼; **she-~** 母狼; **to keep the ~ from the door** 勉强度日; **a ~ in sheep's clothing** 披着羊皮的狼; **to throw sb. to the wolves** 弃某人于险境而不顾; **to cry ~** 喊"狼来了" [发假警报]; **a lone ~** fig 喜欢独自行动的人; **a ~ pack** 狼群 **2** colloq fig (person) 色狼

Phrasal verb

- **wolf down** *vt* [**~ down sth., ~ sth. down**] 狼吞虎咽地吃 ‹*food, meal*›

wolf: ~ cub *n* **1** Zool 狼崽; **2** **W~ Cub** esp Brit Hist 童子军; **~ dog** Amer, **~hound** Brit *ns* 猎狼犬

wolfish /ˈwʊlfɪʃ/ *adj* 狼一般的 ‹*instinct, howl, fang*›; 凶残的 ‹*smile*›; **a ~ appetite** 填不饱的胃口

wolfram /ˈwʊlfrəm/ *n* [u] **1** (metal) 钨 **2** (ore) 钨矿

wolf whistle

A *n* 挑逗口哨

B **wolf-whistle** *vi* 吹挑逗口哨; **to wolf-whistle at sb.** 向某人吹挑逗口哨

wolverine /ˈwʊlvəriːn/ *n* 狼獾

wolves /wʊlvz/ *pl* ▸**wolf**

woman /ˈwʊmən/ *n* (*pl* **women** /ˈwɪmɪn/) **1** [c] (adult female) 成年女子; (as representative) 女人; **a single/married ~** 单身/已婚女人; **the working** *or* **a career ~** 职业女性; **an old ~** 老太太; **a six-~ team** 6 个女人的小组; **to talk ~ to ~** 女人间坦诚地交谈; **to be one's own ~** 独立自主; **the house lacked a ~'s touch** 这个家缺少女人气息; **a ~'s work is never done** Prov 女人的事情总是干不完; **a ~'s place is in the home** Prov 女人的位置在家里; **a ~ of letters** (scholar) 女学者; (author) 女作家 **2** [c] (particularized) 某种女子; **that dog/presenter ~ on the television** 电视上的那名养狗女子/女主持人 **3** [c] colloq pej (emphatic) 那个女人; **it's that wretched ~ again!** 又是那个讨厌的女人! **4** [c] colloq offensive or hum (as form of address) 娘儿们; **young ~!** 小妞儿!; **my good ~** Brit dated 大姐 **5** [c] (wife) 妻子; (lover) 情人; (girlfriend) 女朋友; **the other ~** 第三者; **the little ~** dated hum (sb.'s wife) 老婆 **6** [u] (the female sex) 女性; **history's portrayal of ~** 历史上对于女性的描述; **a ~ doctor/friend** 女医生/女性朋友 **7** [u] (feminine quality) **the ~ in sb.** 某人的女人气质; **she's all ~!** 她真有女人味儿啊!

woman-hater /ˈwʊmənheɪtə(r)/ *n* 厌恶女人的人

womanhood /ˈwʊmənhʊd/ *n* [u] **1** (adulthood) 成年女子状态; **to reach ~** (女性) 成年 **2** (femininity) 女子气质 **3** (women) 女性

womanish /ˈwʊmənɪʃ/ *adj* pej **1** (weak) 柔弱的 ‹*attitude, behaviour, tears*› **2** (effeminate) 女人气的 ‹*man, appearance, dress*›; **dressed in a ~ manner** 打扮得像女人的

womanize /ˈwʊmənaɪz/ *vi* pej 玩女人

womanizer /ˈwʊmənaɪzə(r)/ *n* pej 色鬼

womanizing /ˈwʊmənaɪzɪŋ/ *n* [u] pej 玩弄女性

womankind /ˌwʊmənˈkaɪnd/ *n* [u] 女人

womanly /ˈwʊmənli/ *adj* 女人的 ‹*figure, curve, voice, duty*›; 女子特有的 ‹*virtue, way*›

woman police constable *n* Brit 女警察

womb /wuːm/ *n* 子宫

wombat /ˈwɒmbæt/ *n* 毛鼻袋鼠

women /ˈwɪmɪn/ *pl* ▸**woman**

womenfolk /ˈwɪmɪnfəʊk/ *npl* [一个家庭或群体的] 女人们

womenkind /ˌwɪmɪnˈkaɪnd/ *n* [u] = **womankind**

women: ~'s group *n* [讨论或提高女性利益的] 妇女团体; **W~'s Institute** *pr n* Brit [尤指农村地区的] 妇女协会; **~'s libber** /ˈlɪbə(r)/ *n* colloq pej 支持妇女解放的人; **~'s liberation movement** *n* 妇女解放运动; **~'s magazine** *n* 妇女杂志; **~'s movement** *n* 妇女运动; **~'s page** *n* 女性版; **~'s prison** *n* 女子监狱; **~'s refuge** *n* [躲避家庭暴力的] 妇女避难所; **~'s rights** *npl* 妇女权利; **~'s shelter** *n* = **~'s refuge**; **~'s studies** *npl + v sing* 妇女研究; **~'s suffrage** *n* [u] 妇女选举权

won /wʌn/ *pt, pp* ▸**win A, B**

wonder /ˈwʌndə(r)/

A *n* **1** [u] (amazement) 惊奇; **a sense** *or* **feeling of ~** 惊奇感; **in ~** 惊奇地; **lost in ~** 惊叹不已地 **2** [c] (miracle) 奇迹; (spectacle) 奇观; **she's a ~!** 她是一位奇才!; **a boy/girl ~** 神童/女神童; **the ~s of medicine/the modern world** 医学/现代世界的奇迹; **to be a ~ with children/dogs** 非常擅长对付孩子/狗; **to be a ~ with computers/a paintbrush** 精通电脑/非常擅长作画; **to work** *or* **do ~s (for sb./sth.)** (对某人/某事物) 产生奇效; **it's a ~ (to me) that/how ...** (我) 真想不到…/如何…; **it's a ~ to me how they manage to survive in such cold conditions** 我真想不到他们是如何在这么寒冷的条件下生存下来的; **~s will never cease** iron 真是无奇不有; ▸**seven B1** **3** [u] (quality) 奇妙; **the ~ of poetry** 诗歌的奇妙; **no** *or* **small** *or* **little ~** 不足为奇; **(it's) no ~ that ...** 难怪…

B *adj attrib* 神奇的 ‹*cure*›; **a new ~ drug** 一种新的特效药

C *vi* **1** (think) 思忖; **to ~ about sth./doing sth.** 琢磨某事物/做某事; **why do you want to know? — no particular reason, I was just ~ing** 你为什么想知道？——没什么特别原因，我只是在琢磨; **it makes you ~** iron 这让人感到纳闷 **2** (marvel) 感到惊奇; **to ~ at sth./sb.** 对某事/某人感到惊讶 **3** (feel doubt) 感到疑惑; **to ~ about sth.** 对某事感到不解

D *vt* **1** (ask oneself) 想知道; **who is it, I ~?** 我想知道那会是谁呢?; **to ~ what/why/how ...** 想知道什么/为什么/如何…; **'how did it happen?' she ~ed** "是怎么发生的呢?" 她自忖道; **to ~ if** *or* **whether ...** 不知道是否…; **I ~ if it is going to rain** 我寻思会不会下雨; **I ~ if you can help me?** 不知你是否能帮我? **2** (be amazed) 对…感到惊讶; **to ~ that** 很奇怪…; **I shouldn't ~** colloq 我并不感到吃惊

wonderful /ˈwʌndəfl/ *adj* **1** (impressive) 令人赞叹的 ‹*experience, sight*› **2** (skilled) 了不起的 ‹*memory, achievement, musician*›; **to be ~ with sth.** 在某方面很娴熟 **3** (excellent) 绝妙的 ‹*book, music, film*›; 非常好的 ‹*person, house, restaurant, place*›; 使人愉快的 ‹*experience, situation, weather, journey*›; **you look ~** (healthy) 你看上去气色不错; (attractive) 你真漂亮

wonderfully /ˈwʌndəfəli/ *adv* **1** (very) 极其 ‹*funny, clever, exciting*› **2** (splendidly) 出色地 ‹*cope, play, behave*›

wondering /ˈwʌndərɪŋ/ *adj attrib* **1** (full of wonder) 惊讶的 ‹*look, expression*› **2** (puzzled) 疑惑的 ‹*look, expression*›

wonderingly /ˈwʌndərɪŋli/ *adv* **1** (in wonder) 惊讶地 ‹*gaze, stare, look*› **2** (in puzzlement) 疑惑地 ‹*say, stare, look*›

wonderland /ˈwʌndəlænd/ *n* 仙境

wonderment /ˈwʌndəmənt/ *n* [u] **1** (wonder) 惊讶; **in ~** 惊奇地 **2** (puzzlement) 疑惑

wonderstruck /ˈwʌndəstrʌk/ *adj* 惊讶万分的

wondrous /ˈwʌndrəs/ *adj* liter 奇妙的 ‹*sight, moment*›; 令人惊叹的 ‹*place, event, effect*›

wondrously /ˈwʌndrəsli/ *adv* liter 出奇地 ‹*beautiful, peaceful, complex, strange*›; 了不起地 ‹*talented, crafted*›

wonk /wɒŋk/ *n* Amer colloq pej 1 (swot) 一味苦干的人 2 (theorist) 死抠政策枝节的人; **a computer/policy ～** 只会玩电脑的呆子/政策专家

wonky /ˈwɒŋki/ *adj* colloq 1 (unsteady) 摇晃的 ‹*chair, table*›; 颤巍巍的 ‹*person, legs*› 2 (crooked) 歪斜的 ‹*hat, line, picture, shelves*› 3 (faulty) 有毛病的; **to go ～** «*machine, appliance, computer*» 出毛病

wont /wəʊnt, Amer wɔːnt/

A *adj* liter 习惯的; **to be ～ to do sth.** 惯于做某事; **as he is ～ to do** 如他通常的做法

B *n* [u] formal or hum 惯常做法; **one's ～** 习惯; **as is his ～** 如他所习惯的

won't /wəʊnt/ colloq = **will not** ▸**will**[1]

woo /wuː/ *vt* 1 (pursue for marriage) 追求 ‹*woman*› 2 fig (curry favour with) 争取…的支持 ‹*person, voters*›; 寻求 ‹*fame, success*›

wood /wʊd/

A *n* 1 [u and c] (material) 木头; **made of** *or* **from ～** 木制的; **to chop ～** 劈木材; **a piece of ～** 一块木头; **to touch ～** Brit, **to knock on ～** Amer 用手碰木头 [表示希望继续走好运]; **aged in the ～** «*wine*» 在木桶中酿制多年的 2 **～(s** *pl*) (forest) 树林; **in the wood/woods** 在树林里; **to be out of the ～(s)** 脱离困境 3 [c] (in golf) (club) 木头球棒; (shot) 用球棒击球 4 [c] Sport (bowl) 木瓶

B *modif* 1 (wooden) 木制的; **a ～ floor/door/beam** 木地板/木门/木梁 2 (derived from wood) 木头的; **～ shavings/fire** 木刨花/柴火

wood: ～ alcohol *n* [u] 木醇; **～ anemone** *n* 五叶银莲花; **～ ant** *n* 红褐林蚁

woodbine /ˈwʊdbaɪn/ *n* [u and c] 1 Brit (honeysuckle) 忍冬 2 Amer (Virginia creeper) 五叶地锦

woodblock /ˈwʊdblɒk/ *n* 1 (for flooring) 木地板块 2 (for woodcut print) 木刻印版

woodblock floor *n* 木条地板

wood: ～-burning stove *n* = **～ stove**; **～ carver** ▸**p. 409** *n* 木雕工; **～carving** *n* 1 [u] (action, skill) 木雕; 2 [c] (object) 木雕品; **～chuck** *n* 美洲旱獭; **～cock** *n* (*pl* **～cock**) 丘鹬; **～craft** *n* [u] esp Amer 1 (knowledge of woodland) 丛林生活技能; 2 (woodwork) 木工技术; **～cut** *n* 1 (print) 木版画; 2 (block) 木刻印版; **～cutter** ▸**p. 409** *n* 1 (feller of trees) 伐木工; 2 Art 木刻家; **～cutting** *n* [u] 1 (felling of trees) 伐木; 2 Art 木刻

wooded /ˈwʊdɪd/ *adj* 树木覆盖的 ‹*valley, area*›; **heavily** *or* **thickly ～** 树木茂密的

wooden /ˈwʊdn/ *adj* 1 (made of wood) 木制的 ‹*furniture, toy*›; **a ～ floor** 木地板 2 (wood-like) 木头似的 ‹*feel, appearance*› 3 fig (stilted) 笨拙的 ‹*performance*›; 呆板的 ‹*actor, expression, smile*›

wood engraving *n* 1 [c] (print) 木刻画 2 [u] (technique) 木刻 3 [c] (block) 木刻印版

wooden: ～-headed *adj* pej 榆木脑袋的 ‹*person*›; **～ horse** *n* 1 Literat 特洛伊木马; 2 fig 潜伏到内部搞破坏者; **～ spoon** *n* 1 Culin 木匙; 2 Brit fig (booby prize) 末名奖

woodland /ˈwʊdlənd/

A *n* [u] 树林; **～ plant/animal/scenery** 林地植物/林地动物/林区景色

B **woodlands** *npl* 林区

wood: ～lark *n* 森林云雀; **～louse** *n* (*pl* **～lice**) 鼠妇; **～man** /-mən/ ▸**p. 409** *n* (forester) 护林人; (woodcutter) 伐木人; **～pecker** *n* 啄木鸟; **～ pigeon** *n* 斑尾林鸽; **～pile** *n* 木柴堆; **～ pulp** *n* [u] 木浆; **～screw** *n* 木螺钉; **～ shavings** *npl* 刨花; **～shed** *n* 木料间; **～sman** /-mən/ ▸**p. 409** *n* 1 = **～man**; 2 esp Amer (person skilled in woodcraft) 具备森林生活技能者; **～ stove** *n* 柴火炉

woodsy /ˈwʊdzɪ/ *adj* Amer 树林的 ‹*smell, colour, flavour, atmosphere*›; 树林覆盖的 ‹*area, landscape*›; **he was homespun and ～** 他朴实而又像来自偏远地区的人

wood trim *n* [u and c] 木镶边

woodwind /ˈwʊdwɪnd/ *n* + *v sing or pl* 1 (instruments) 木管乐器; **a ～ instrument** 木管乐器; **～ section** 木管乐器组 2 (players) 木管乐器组

wood: ～ wool *n* [u] Brit 木绒; **～work** *n* [u] 1 (wooden parts) 木构件; **to come** *or* **crawl out of the ～work** colloq (be revealed) 纷纷现身; 2 Brit (activity, skill) 木工活; **a ～work teacher/class** 木工师傅/木工班; 3 Sport colloq **the ～work** 球门框; **～worm** *n* 1 [c] (larva) 木蛀虫; 2 [u] (condition) 木蛀虫害; **to have ～worm** 被木蛀虫蛀坏

woody /ˈwʊdi/ *adj* 1 (covered with trees) 树木茂盛的 ‹*area, hillside, valley*› 2 (wood-like) 木本的 ‹*stem*›; 木质的 ‹*growth, core, tissue, material*›; 像木头的 ‹*smell*›

woof[1] /wʊf/

A *n* (bark) 吠声

B *excl* 汪汪

C *vi* «*dog*» 汪汪叫

woof[2] /wuːf/ *n* Tex **the ～** 纬纱

woofer /ˈwʊfə(r)/ *n* 低音喇叭

wool /wʊl/ *n* 1 [u] (hair) 羊毛; **made of** *or* **from ～** 羊毛制的; **～ garment/coat/carpet** 羊毛衣服/外套/地毯; **～ trade/merchant/shop** 羊毛贸易/商/商店 2 [u and c] (yarn) 毛线; **to pull the ～ over sb.'s eyes** 蒙骗某人 3 [u and c] (fabric) 羊毛织物

woolen /ˈwʊlən/ *adj* Amer = **woollen**

wool: ～-gathering *n* [u] 1 (daydreaming) 胡思乱想; 2 (absent-mindedness) 心不在焉; **～grower** ▸**p. 409** *n* 羊毛生产者

wooliness /ˈwʊlɪnɪs/ *n* Amer = **woolliness**

woollen /ˈwʊlən/

A *adj* 1 (made of wool) 羊毛制的; **～ blanket/scarf/garment** 羊毛毯/围巾/衣服 2 (relating to wool) 羊毛的; **the ～ industry** 毛纺业; **～ trade/manufacturer** 羊毛贸易/生产商

B **woollens** *npl* 毛衣

woollen mill *n* 毛纺厂

woolliness /ˈwʊlɪnɪs/ *n* [u] 1 (of hair) 皮毛厚度 2 (of fabric) 含毛量 3 fig (vagueness) 模糊

woolly /ˈwʊli/

A *adj* 1 (made of wool) 羊毛制的; **～ blanket/scarf** 羊毛毯/围巾 2 (wool-like) 毛茸茸的 ‹*animal, animal's coat*›; **～ wisps of cloud** 缕缕卷毛云 3 fig (vague) 不清晰的 ‹*thinking, idea, suggestion*›; 混乱的 ‹*essay, debate*›; 糊涂的 ‹*person*›

B *n* esp Brit colloq 套头毛衫

woolly-headed /ˌwʊlɪˈhedɪd/, **woolly-minded** /ˌwʊlɪˈmaɪndɪd/ *adjs* 糊里糊涂的 ‹*person*›; 懵懂的 ‹*thinking, idea*›; 含混的 ‹*suggestion*›

wool: W～sack *n* Brit **the W～sack** 上议院议长职位; **～shed** *n* esp Austral 剪羊毛房

wooly /ˈwʊli/ *adj, n* Amer = **woolly**

woozy /ˈwuːzi/ *adj* colloq 眩晕的 ‹*person, head*›; **to feel ～** 感觉头昏脑胀

wop /wɒp/ *n* colloq offensive 1 (Italian) 意大利佬 pej 2 (other southern European) 南欧佬 pej

Worcester sauce /ˌwʊstə ˈsɔːs/, **Worcestershire sauce** /ˌwʊstəʃə ˈsɔːs/ *ns* [u] 伍斯特沙司 [含酱油和醋的辣味酱]

Worcestershire /ˈwʊstəʃaɪə(r)/ *pr n* 伍斯特郡

Worcs. *abbr* Brit = **Worcestershire**

word /wɜːd/ ▸**p. 111**

A *n* 1 [c] (unit of meaning) 单词; **the spoken/written ～** 口语/书面语用词; **an essay in 120 ～s** 一篇 120 个单词的短文; **'aunt' isn't the right ～** "aunt" 这个词不合适; **what's the ～ for 'wine' in Japanese?** "wine" 用日语怎么说? ; **long ～s** 长单词; **a big ～** colloq 大词 [指长或复杂的词]; **a bad/rude** *or* **four-letter ～** colloq 粗话/下流话; **sb.'s first/last ～s** 某人的第一句/最后一句话; **sb.'s very ～s** 某人的原话; **to put one's feelings/thoughts into ～s** 说出情感/想法; **I mean every ～ of it** 我说话算话; **～ for ～** 逐字地; **'slow' isn't the ～ for it** colloq "slow" 这个词不恰当; **there's no such ～ as 'can't'** 不存在 "不能" 这样的说法 2 [u and c] (utterance, talk) 话; **a ～ of warning/advice** 警告/劝告的话; **in ～ and deed** 在言行上; **to say a ～ or two** 说几句话; **in a ～** (briefly) 简言之; **to have a ～ (with sb.) (about sth.)** (就某事物) (和某人) 谈一谈; **to put a (good) ～ in for sb., to put in a (good) ～ for sb.** 为某人说句 (好) 话; **to get a ～ in** 插话; ▸**edgeways; the last ～ (on sth.)** (对某事的) 定论; **to say one's last ～ (on sth.)** 发表 (对某事的) 最后意见; **to get** *or* **have the last ～** lit, fig 最后说了算; **the last ～ (in sth.)** (latest trend) (某方面的) 最新潮流; **not to say a ～ (about sth.) (to sb.)** (关于某事) (对某人) 什么都不说; **I didn't say a ～ (about it)** (对此) 我什么也没说; **not a ～ to her about what I said!** 我说的话不要向她吐露一个字! ; **to not believe/hear/understand a ～ (of sth.)** (关于某事) 一句话也不信/听不到/不懂; **he left without (saying) a ～** 他一句话也没说就走了; **I can't get a ～ out of her** 我从她那里一句话也套不出; **I won't hear/say a ～ against her** 她的坏话我一句也不想听/说; **not to have a good ～ to say about sb./sth.** 从不说某人/某事的好话; ▸**mouth A1** 3 [c] *sing* (promise, assurance) 诺言; **to give sb. one's ～ (that ...)** 向某人保证 (…) ; **to keep/break one's ～** 遵守/违背诺言; **to go back on one's ～** 食言; **to hold sb. to his** *or* **her ～** 使某人遵守诺言; **to doubt** *or* **question sb.'s ～** 质疑某人的话; **to take sb. at his** *or* **her ～** 相信某人的话; **to take sb.'s ～ for it (that ...)** 相信某人 (…) 的话; **to have sb.'s ～ for it (that ...)** 得到某人的保证 (…) ; **you have my ～ for it** 对此我向你保证; **a woman of her ～** 守信的女人; **it's his ～ against mine** 就只有他和我的口头对质; **to be as good as one's ～** 守信用; **to be better than one's ～** 比答应的还要好; **my ～!** 哎呀! ; **upon my ～ of honour** archaic 我郑重承诺 4 [u] (information, news) 消息; **to have (no) ～ of** *or* **about sb./sth.** (没) 有关于某人/某事物的消息; **～ came that ...** 消息传来…; **～ as to how/what/who** *etc.* 关于如何/什么/谁等的消息; **to bring ～ of sth.** 捎来某事物的消息; **to leave/send ～ (that ...)** 留言/捎信 (说…) 5 [c] *sing* (rumour) 传言; **the ～ has got around that ...** 有传言说…; **～ got round** *or* **around that ...** 谣传…; **～ has it that he is a millionaire** 据传他是百万富翁 6 [c] *sing* (command) 命令; **to give the ～ (for sth.** *or* **to do sth.)** 下令 (做某事) ; **just say the ～** colloq 只要吩咐一下; **at the ～ (of command)** Mil 按照命令; **his ～ is law** 他的话就是法律 7 [c] *sing* (key word, slogan) **the ～** 口号 8 [c] *sing* Relig **the W～ (of God)** 圣经; **to preach the W～** 布道 9 [c] Comput 字 [基本数据单位]

B **words** *npl* 1 (speech, talk) 话; **deeds not ～s** 行动而不是言语; **harsh/kind ～s** 严厉/友好的话; **fighting ～s** 好斗的言语; **fine ～s** 华丽辞藻; **a man of few/many ～s** 寡言少语的/健谈的男子; **a flood** *or* **torrent of ～s** 一大堆话; **to say a few ～s** 讲几句话; **to exchange a few ～s of greeting** 互相问候几句; **to exchange (angry** *or* **heated) ～s** (激烈) 争吵; **to have ～s (with sb.) (about sth.)** (为某事) (和某人) 争吵; **to have no ～s to express** *or* **for sth.** 难以用语言形容某事物; **to find the ～s** 找到恰当

W

的话语; to swallow one's ~s 承认说错话; in sb.'s ~s, in the ~s of sb. 用某人的话来讲; in one's own ~s 用自己的话来说; in other ~s 换句话说; (not) in so many ~s （并非）一字不差地; in so many ~s, he apologized 他明确地道歉了; too funny/shocking for ~s 滑稽/震惊得令人无话可说; to take the ~s (right) out of sb.'s mouth 说出某人正要说的话; don't put ~s in my mouth! 别硬说这是我说过的话！ **2** Theat 台词 **3** Mus 歌词; to set the ~s to music 给歌词配曲

C *vt usu passive* 用言辞表达 ‹*advice, document*›; strongly *or* sharply ~ed 措词强硬的; a carefully ~ed letter 一封措词谨慎的信

word: ~ association *n* [u] 词语联想; **~ blindness** *n* [u] = dyslexia; **~book** *n* [带释义和其他相关信息的] 词汇手册; **~ break** *n* 断字; **~ class** *n* 词类; **~ count** *n* 字数统计; **~ deafness** *n* [u] 辨语聋

word-for-word

A *adj* 照原话一字不变的 ‹*account, repetition*›; 逐字的 ‹*translation*›

B word for word *adv* 照原话一字不变地 ‹*relate, repeat*›; 逐字 ‹*translate*›

word game *n* 猜字游戏

wordiness /'wɜːdɪnɪs/ *n* [u] **1** (of person) 喋喋不休 **2** (of text) 冗长

wording /'wɜːdɪŋ/ *n* [u and c] 措词; the standard form of ~ for a contract letter 合同函件用词的标准格式

wordless /'wɜːdlɪs/ *adj* 默默无语的

wordlessly /'wɜːdlɪsli/ *adj* 默默无语地

word list *n* 词汇表

word of mouth

A *n* [u] 口头传播; by ~ 口头地

B word-of-mouth *modif* 口头的 ‹*recommendation, advertising, referral*›

word: ~ order *n* [u and c] 词序; **~-perfect** *adj* 背得一字不差的; **~ picture** *n* [尤指栩栩如生的] 口头描述; **~play** *n* [u] 双关语; **~ processing** *n* [u] 文字处理; **~ processor** *n* 文字处理机; **~ recognition** *n* [u] 字词辨识; ~ recognition skills 字词辨识技能; **~search** *n* 文字搜索游戏; **~smith** *n* 词语大师; **~ square** *n* 四方连词; **~ stress** *n* [u] 词重音; **~ wrap, ~ wrapping** *ns* [u] 字词绕回

wordy /'wɜːdi/ *adj pej* 啰唆的 ‹*writer, speaker*›; 冗长的 ‹*document, description, speech*›

wore /wɔː(r)/ *pt* ▸**wear A, B**

work /wɜːk/

A *n* **1** [u] (activities, tasks) 工作; (labour) 劳动; research ~ 研究工作; the ~ of the Red Cross 红十字会的工作; ~ done by machines 机器干的工作; manual/intellectual ~ 手工/脑力劳动; light/heavy ~ 轻/重活儿; to go to *or* get to ~ 开始工作; to go to *or* get (down) to *or* set to ~ on sth./doing sth. 着手某事/做某事; to put sb. to ~ (on sth./doing sth.) 安排某人做（某）工作; to make ~ for sb. 给某人找麻烦; to put ~ into sth. 在某事物上花功夫; the house needs a lot of ~ doing Brit *or* done Amer to it 这房子得好好收拾一番; to be at ~ (on sth.) 忙着（做某事）; secret forces were at ~ 秘密势力在作祟; ~ in hand 手头的工作; ▸**cut out A1, devil 1, play C1** **2** [u] (employment) 职业; full-time/part-time ~ 全职/兼职工作; to be out of ~ 失业; to stop ~ (for the day) 收工; (retire) 退休; ~ clothes 工作服 **3** [u] (place of employment) 工作场所; to go to/leave ~ 上班/下班; to leave for ~ 去上班; to be off ~ 没上班; to arrive at *or* get to ~ 到达工作场所; don't ring me at ~ 我工作的时候别给我打电话; I left my bag at ~ 我把包落在上班的地方了 **4** [u] (materials, papers) 工作材料; to take one's ~ into the garden 把活儿带到花园里做; to bring ~ home from the office 把办公室的事情带回家做; to take up/put down one's ~ 拿起/放下手头的活计 **5** [u] (achievements) 工作成果; (products) 产品; sb.'s life's ~ 某人一生的成果; the ~ of craftsmen 手艺人做的活计; is this all your own ~? 这全是你一个人做的吗？; to mark students' ~ 给学生的作业打分 **6** [c] (piece of art) 作品; sb.'s latest/last/early ~ 某人的最新/最后/早期作品; the ~s of Schubert 舒伯特的作品; a ~ of genius/fiction 天才/虚构的作品; a ~ of reference 参考书; a new ~ on Elizabethan poetry 有关伊丽莎白时代诗歌的一部新作 **7** [u] (what is done by sb.) 作为; he will be remembered for his ~ 他将因其作为而名留青史; I hope you're pleased with your ~ iron 我希望你对自己的所作所为感到满意; good ~! 干得漂亮！; the ~ of sb. 某人的手笔 **8** [u] Phys 功

B works *npl* **1** + *v sing* esp Brit (factory) 工厂; ~s canteen 工厂食堂 **2** (building work) 工程; public ~s 公共工程 **3** Mil (defence) ~s （防御）工事 **4** Relig good ~s 善行 **5** the (full *or* whole) ~s colloq (everything) 全套物品

C *vi* **1** (engage in activity, occupation, task) 工作; to ~ at the hospital 在医院工作; to ~ 8 hours a day 一天工作8小时; to ~ full-time/part-time 做全职/兼职工作; to ~ as sth. 在某岗位工作; to ~ at *or* on sth. 致力于某事物; he's ~ing at his essay 他在忙着写论文; to ~ on one's lecture 准备讲座; police are ~ing on the case 警方正在查办这个案子; to ~ on a problem 着手处理某问题; to ~ for sb./a company 受雇于某人/某公司; to ~ for a living 为谋生工作; to ~ under/with sb. 在某人手下/和某人一起工作; to ~ in publishing/TV 从事出版/电视工作; to ~ on the principle that ... 根据…的原则行事; to ~ to rule esp Brit 按章工作 **2** (strive) 努力; to ~ at *or* doing sth. 努力做某事; to ~ against/for sth. 努力反对/争取某事物; to ~ against corruption 与腐败作斗争; to ~ on sb. colloq 努力说服某人; to ~ towards sth. 努力争取 ‹*solution*› **3** (function) «*institution, system*» 运转; to ~ on electricity/gas 利用电力/燃气运行; the machine ~s by electricity 这台机器是电动的; the lift doesn't ~ 电梯坏了; the bell isn't ~ing properly 电铃有故障; my brain is not ~ing colloq 我的脑子不好使 **4** (act, operate) «*person, situation, action*» 起作用; to ~ both ways 产生两方面的作用; to ~ in sb.'s favour *or* to sb.'s advantage 对某人有利; to ~ against sb. *or* to sb.'s disadvantage 对某人不利; it doesn't *or* things don't ~ like that 情况并不是那样 **5** (be successful) «*plan, treatment, spell, persuasion*» 奏效; these pills aren't ~ing 这些药片不管用; the adaptation really ~s 改编得很成功; to ~ on sb./sth. 对某人/某事物有效; his charm doesn't ~ on me 他的魅力对我不起作用; such arguments don't ~ on most people 这样的论点不会打动大多数民众 **6** (move) 逐渐移动; vibration caused the safety valve to ~ loose 震动使安全阀松掉了 **7** (twitch) «*features, lips*» 抽搐; his face ~ed with *or* in anger 他气得面部抽搐

D *vt* **1** (drive) 使…工作 ‹*person, staff*›; to ~ sb. hard/to death 使某人劳累/累得要死 **2** (labour) 工作于; to ~ nights *or* the night shift 上夜班; to ~ an area «*salesperson*» 在某地推销; «*sex worker*» 在某地卖淫; «*beggar*» 在某地行乞; I ~ed a few clubs 我在几家俱乐部工作过; to ~ one's way up 逐步升迁; to ~ one's way through sth. 勤工俭学读完 ‹*college*›; to ~ one's way through a book/an exam 费力读完书/考完试; to ~ one's way through two hamburgers colloq 吃掉两只汉堡包; to ~ one's fingers to the bone 拼命干 **3** (operate) 操作 ‹*equipment*›; to ~ a lathe 操作车床; the machine is ~ed by electricity 这台机器是电动的 **4** (exploit, use) 开采 ‹*mine, oil field*›; to ~ the land 种地; to ~ the system colloq 利用体制牟利; to ~ it *or* things colloq 想办法 **5** (*pt, pp* ~ed *or* liter wrought) (bring about) 产生 ‹*change, wonders*›; 实现 ‹*cure*›; to ~ miracles 创造奇迹; the landscape ~ed its magic on me 这景色令我着迷; the changes wrought by sth. 由某事引起的变化 **6** (fashion) «*craftsman*» 加工 ‹*gold, iron*›; to ~ clay/dough 制陶/揉面团; to ~ sth. into shape/a finished piece 把某物加工成型/加工成成品 **7** (rouse) «*speaker, singer*» 使…激动 ‹*crowd*›; to ~ listeners into a patriotic fervour 激起听众的爱国热情 **8** (sew) 缝制; (embroider) 绣制; (weave) 编织; to ~ a design/pattern on sth. 在某物上绣图案/花样 **9** (manoeuvre) 慢慢转动 ‹*object*›; to ~ a ring off one's finger 把戒指从手指上慢慢松脱下来; to ~ a few jokes into one's speech 设法在讲话中添加几个笑话; to ~ its way into the bloodstream/food chain «*substance*» 慢慢进入血液/食物链; to ~ one's way along sth. 沿着…慢慢移动 ‹*ledge*›; to ~ one's way through a crowd 慢慢挤过人群 **10** (move) «*person, vibration*» 使…移动 ‹*person, object*›; to ~ sth. up and down/from side to side 上下/来回扳动 ‹*lever, stick*›; to ~ sth. clear 把…移开 ‹*object*›; it ~ed its way loose 它松开了; to ~ one's hands free 挣脱双手 **11** (exercise) 锻炼 ‹*muscles*›

E *v refl* **1** (labour) to ~ oneself (too) hard 干得（太）辛苦; to ~ oneself to death fig colloq 把自己累死累活 **2** (rouse) to ~ oneself into a rage 变得暴跳如雷; to ~ oneself into a frenzy (of angry) 变得狂怒; (of hysterics) 变得狂躁不安 **3** (move) to ~ oneself

ℹ Word order

The word order in Chinese phrases is sometimes different from that in English. This is shown in the examples below:

art and literature	文艺	*long and thin*	细长
the bride and bridegroom	新郎和新娘	*north-east*	东北
back and forth	前后	*north-west*	西北
flesh and blood	血肉	*old and new*	新旧
food and clothing	衣食	*rich and poor*	贫富
food and drink	饮食	*short and long*	长短
hard and soft	软硬	*small and medium-sized*	中小型
here and now	此时此地	*sooner or later*	迟早
heavy and light	轻重	*south-east*	东南
hot and cold	冷热	*south-west*	西南
iron and steel	钢铁	*track and field*	田径
land and water	水陆		

loose *or* free 挣脱; **the screw had ~ed itself loose** 螺丝钉松了

Phrasal verbs

- **work around** *vi* = **work round**
- **work away** *vi* (continuously) 不停工作; (diligently) 勤奋工作
- **work down** *vi* «*garment*» 渐渐滑落
- **work in** *vt* [**~ sth. in, ~ in sth.**] **1** (incorporate) 把…安排进去 ‹*task*›; 把…穿插进去 ‹*joke, reference*› **2** Culin 掺入 ‹*ingredient*›
- **work off** *vt* [**~ sth. off, ~ off sth.**] **1** (pay off by working) 挣钱偿还 ‹*loan, debt*› **2** (get rid of) 去除 ‹*body fat, energy, anger*›; **to ~ off some excess weight** 减掉多余的体重; **to ~ sth. off on sb.** 在某人身上发泄 ‹*emotion, frustration*›; **don't ~ off your bad temper on me!** 别拿我撒气! **3** (remove) 使…松脱 ‹*lid, ring*›
- **work out**

A *vi* **1** (exercise) 锻炼 **2** (develop in a successful way) «*events, situation*» 有进展; **their marriage didn't ~ out** 他们的婚姻不美满; **sometimes things just ~ out that way** 有时候事情的结果就是那样; **I hope things ~ out for him** 我希望他顺利 **3** (be solvable) «*problem*» 被解决; **I can't get this equation to ~ out** 我无法解出这个方程 **4** (be calculated) «*total, figures*» 被算出; **to ~ out at** *or* Amer **to sth.** 总数为某数 **5** (come out) «*piece, plug*» 脱出

B [**~ sth. out, ~ out sth.**] *vt* **1** (calculate) 算出 ‹*figure, average, wages*›; **to ~ sth. out at** *or* Amer **to sth.** 算出某物为某数 **2** (solve) 解决 ‹*problem*›; 解开 ‹*riddle, clue*›; 破译 ‹*code*› **3** (deduce) 弄懂 ‹*answer, reason, meaning*›; **to ~ out who/what/where** *etc.* **...** 确定谁/什么/哪里等… **4** (devise) 制订 ‹*plan*›; **the details still have to be ~ed out** 细节仍有待确定 **5** *usu passive* (exhaust) 把…开采光 ‹*land, mine*›; **a ~ed-out silver mine** 采尽的银矿 **6** Admin 持续工作到 ‹*period of time*›; **to ~ out one's notice** 工作到期满

C [**~ sb. out, ~ out sb.**] *vt* colloq 了解…的性格; **I can't ~ her out** 我摸不透她的脾气

D *v refl* **to ~ itself out** «*problem, situation*» 逐步自行解决; **things will ~ themselves out** 事情终将自动了结

- **work over** *vt* [**~ over sb., ~ sb. over**] colloq 拷打
- **work round** *vi* **to ~ round to sth.** 渐渐讲到 ‹*topic, question*›; **to ~ round to doing sth.** 渐渐讲到做某事; **to ~ round to asking a question** 慢慢绕到提问上
- **work up**

A *vi* **1** (progress) **to ~ up to sth.** 逐渐讲到 ‹*confession*›; 逐步发展到 ‹*fight, argument*›; **to ~ up to a climax** «*music, scene*» 逐步进入高潮 **2** (ride up) «*garment*» 缩上去

B *vt* **1** [**~ up sth.**] (develop) 激起 ‹*appetite, enthusiasm*›; 逐步增强 ‹*support*›; **to ~ up a sweat** 弄出一身汗; **to ~ up the courage to confront sb.** 鼓起勇气去面对某人 **2** [**~ sth. up, ~ up sth.**] (expand) 使…完整 ‹*sketch*›; **to ~ one's notes up into a report** 把笔记扩充成报告 **3** [**~ sb. up**] (excite) 使激动; **to ~ sb. up into a frenzy/rage** 使某人变得疯狂/暴怒

C *v refl* **to ~ oneself up into a state/frenzy** 使自己大动肝火/疯狂起来; **to get (oneself) all ~ed up (over** *or* **about sth.)** (因某事物) 激动起来

workable /ˈwɜːkəbl/ *adj* **1** (feasible) 可行的 ‹*idea, plan, solution, suggestion*› **2** (usable) 可耕种的 ‹*land, soil*›; 可开采的 ‹*mine, coal seam, oil well*› **3** (capable of being mixed, kneaded, or fashioned) 可加工成型的 ‹*cement, dough, metal*›

workaday /ˈwɜːkədeɪ/ *adj attrib* 平凡的 ‹*world, life*›; 日常的 ‹*matter, clothes*›

workaholic /ˌwɜːkəˈhɒlɪk/ *n* colloq 工作狂

workaround /ˈwɜːkəraʊnd/ *n* 变通办法

work: ~ basket, ~ bag *ns* 针线筐; **~bench** *n* 工作台; **~book** *n* **1** Sch, Univ 练习册; **2** (book of instructions) 操作手册; **3** Admin 工作日志; **4** Comput 工作簿; **~box** *n* 工具盒 [如针线盒等]; **~ camp** *n* **1** (for volunteers) 劳动营; **2** (for prisoners) 劳改营; **~day** *n* **1** (day for working on) 工作日; **2** (weekday) [非周末或假期的] 平日; **~desk** *n* 办公桌

worker /ˈwɜːkə(r)/ *n* **1** (person who works) 工作者; **a domestic ~** 家政人员 **2** (person working in specified way) 干活…的人; **a quick/slow ~** 做事麻利/慢的人; **a fast ~** 闪电恋爱的人 **3** colloq (industrious person) 努力工作的人 **4** (employee) 工人 **5** (proletarian) 无产者; **~s of the world unite!** 全世界无产者联合起来! **6** (achiever) 取得成就的人; **a ~ of miracles** 奇迹创造者 **7** Zool 职虫 [如工蜂、工蚁等]; **the ~s pollinate crops** 工蜂为庄稼传粉

worker: ~ ant *n* 工蚁; **~ bee** *n* 工蜂; **~ director** *n* 工人董事; **~ participation** *n* [u] 工人参与管理; **~ priest** *n* 工人教士; **~s' control** *n* [u] 工人控制 [指工人完全参与管理的制度]

work: ~ ethic *n* 职业道德; **~ experience** *n* [u] 短期工作经历 [尤指学生实习]; **to be on ~ experience** 参加工作实习; **~fare** *n* [u] 工作福利制; **~flow** *n* 工作流程; **~force** *n* **1** + *v sing or pl* (total number of workers employed) 全体员工; **2** (total number of people available for work) 劳动力; **~ group** *n* **1** (employees) 工作小组; **2** (work party) 协作小组; **~-hardening** *n* [u] 加工硬化; **~horse** *n* **1** Agric 耕马; **2** fig (person) 吃苦耐劳的人; (machine) 重负荷的机器; **~house** *n* **1** Brit Hist [教区中的] 劳动救济所; **2** Amer (prison) 劳教所; **~-in** *n* [工厂面临关闭时的] 劳方接管

working /ˈwɜːkɪŋ/

A *adj attrib* **1** (in profession) 有工作的; (in manual job) 从事体力劳动的; **a ~ mother** 在职母亲; **the ~ population of the country** 这个国家的劳动人口 **2** (involving employment or in employed time) 工作上的; **~ conditions/relationship** 工作条件/关系; **a ~ lunch** 工作午餐; **during** *or* **in ~ hours** 在上班时间; **a ~ holiday** 打零工的假期 **3** (functioning) 运行中的 ‹*model, farm, mine*›; 操纵用的 ‹*part*›; **in (full) ~ order** 运行正常地; **to have a ~ knowledge of sth.** 有某方面基本够用的知识 **4** (provisional) 初步的 ‹*definition, hypothesis, theory*› **5** Fin 营运的 ‹*assets, expenses*›

B *n* **1** [u] (making) 制作; (tooling, shaping) 加工; **the ~ of** 对…的加工 ‹*iron, wood, leather*›; **the ~ of a bowl from a piece of clay** *or* **of a piece of clay into a bowl** 用黏土做成碗的加工过程 **2** [u] esp Sch (draft, notes) 解题思路 **3** [c] Transp 运行线路

C **workings** *npl* **1** (operation) 运转; **the ~s of a machine/an organization/a system** 机器/机构/系统的运转; **the ~s of the human mind** fig 人脑活动 **2** (of mine) 工作区; (of quarry) 采石场

working: ~ agreement *n* [冲突双方达成的] 和平共处协议; **~ capital** *n* [u] 流动资本

working class

A *n* + *v sing or pl* 工人阶级

B **working-class** *adj* 工人阶级的 ‹*background, life, culture*›

working: ~ dog *n* 役犬 [如牧羊犬]; **~ drawing** *n* 施工图; **~ girl** *n* colloq **1** (girl with job) 职业女子; **2** euph (prostitute) 妓女; **~ group** *n* 研究小组; **~ majority** *n* Brit [使政府赢得议会投票制定新法律的] 足够多数; **~ man** *n* 工人; **~-over** *n* colloq 殴打; **to give sb. a ~-over** 殴打某人; **~ party** *n* **1** Brit Admin 调查委员会; **2** Mil [执行特殊任务的] 作业队; **~ storage** *n* [u] 暂时存储器; **~ tax credit** *n* [c and u] Brit 低收入者所得税减免; **~ week** *n* 工作周; **a five-day ~ week** 5 天的工作周

work: ~-in-progress *n* 半成品; **~-in-progress canvases** 尚未完成的油画; **~-life balance** *n* [u] 工作与生活的平衡; **~load** *n* 工作量; **to have a light/heavy ~load** 工作负担轻/重; **to reduce/increase sb.'s ~load** 减轻/增加某人的工作量

workman /ˈwɜːkmən/ *n* **1** (manual worker) 男性工人 **2** (person working in a specified way) 工作…的人; **a skilled/an unskilled ~** 熟练/非熟练工; **a bad ~ (always) blames his tools** Prov 拙匠总怪工具差

workmanlike /ˈwɜːkmənlaɪk/ *adj* 精工细作的 ‹*manner, approach, attitude, product*›; 技术娴熟的 ‹*job*›

workmanship /ˈwɜːkmənʃɪp/ *n* [u] **1** (skill) 手艺 **2** (result) 工艺; **a fine piece of ~** 做工精巧的产品

work: ~mate *n* 工友; **~ of art** *n* **1** 艺术品; **2** fig 令人赏心悦目的事物; **he's certainly no ~ of art!** 他长得的确让人不敢恭维!; **~out** *n* **1** (exercise) 锻炼; **2** (training) 训练; **~pack** *n* 工作包; **a student ~pack** 学生作业包; **~people** *npl* Brit 劳工阶层; **~ permit** *n* 工作许可证; **~piece** *n* 工件; **~place** *n* 工作场所; **~ prospects** *npl* 工作机会; **~-related** *adj* 与工作有关的 ‹*matter*›; 工作引起的 ‹*illness, stress, accident*›; **~-related training** 岗位培训; **a ~-related injury** 工伤; **~room** *n* 工作间; **~-shadowing** *n* [u] [学徒近距离观察有经验员工的] 跟随培训; **~-sharing** *n* [u] 轮岗制; **~sheet** *n* **1** Sch, Univ 活页练习; **2** Admin 工作记录单; **3** Comput 工作表; **~shop** *n* **1** Ind 车间; **2** (training session) 研讨班; **a poetry/drama ~shop** 诗歌讲习班/戏剧研讨班; **~-shy** *adj* (not inclined to work) 不愿工作的; (lazy) 懒惰的; **~s manager** ▸p. 409 *n* 生产部经理; **~space** *n* **1** [c and u] (space in which to work) 工作空间; **2** [c] Comput 工作区; **~ station** *n* **1** Comput 工作站; **2** Ind 工作台; **~ study** *n* [u] 工作效率研究; **~ surface** *n* = **~top**; **~ table** *n* **1** (table for working at) 工作台; **2** (table with sewing materials) 缝纫用品台; **~top** *n* Brit [尤指厨房的] 操作台; **~-to-rule** *n* 按章工作 [故意严守规章以降低工作效率]; **~ unit** *n* 工作单位; **~wear** *n* [u] 工作服; **~ week** *n* Amer = **working week**; **~-worn** *adj* 因工作而憔悴的 ‹*face, person*›; 因工作而磨破的 ‹*hands, garment*›

world /wɜːld/ *n* **1** (earth, universe) **the ~** 世界; **the ~ is round** 地球是圆的; **all over the ~, (all) the ~ over** 全世界; **to travel the ~** 周游世界; **to be on top of the ~** lit 在世界之巅; fig 欢天喜地; **to set the ~ on fire** colloq 引起轰动; **it's not the end of the ~** colloq 这不是世界末日 [没什么大不了]; **how/what/when/where/why in the ~ ...?** colloq 究竟如何/是什么/何时/哪里/为什么…?; **more than anything in the ~** colloq 胜过世间一切; **no one in the ~** colloq 没有任何人; **the ~'s worst X, the worst X in the ~** colloq 最最糟糕的某事物; **with the best will in the ~** 尽管已竭尽全力; ▸**seven B1** **2** (section of earth) [世界的] 某一地区; **the Western/ancient/developed ~** 西方世界/古代社会/发达国家; **the Arab ~** 阿拉伯世界; **the Roman ~** 古罗马王国 **3** (everything) 万物; (everybody) **(all) the ~** 世人; **for all the ~ to see** 在世人面前; **to be** *or* **mean all the ~ to sb.** colloq 是某人的一切; **to think the ~ of sb.** colloq 非常喜爱某人; **I would give the ~ to do that** colloq 我非常想做那件事; **(not) for (all) the ~** colloq 无论如何 (都不); **I won't go, not for all the ~!** 我不去, 坚决不去!; **to have the ~ at one's feet** 前途无量 **4** (human existence) 人世; **this ~** 今世; **the ~ to come** Relig 来世; **not to be long for this ~** 不久于人世; **to bring sb. into the ~** «*midwife*» 接某人出生; «*mother*» 生下某人;

to come into the ~ «*baby*» 降生; **the John Smiths of this ~** colloq 像约翰·史密斯这类人; **out of this ~** colloq 非常棒的 **5** *sing* (human affairs, life) **the ~** 世情; **the ways of the ~** 人情世故; **a man/woman of the ~** 老于世故的男人/女人; **to know the ~** 见多识广; **in the real ~** 在现实生活中; **to make one's (own) way in the ~** 独立谋生; **what's the ~ coming to?** 这个世道是怎么了? **6** (society, other people) **the ~** 社会; **to go out into the ~** 进入社会; **in the eyes of the ~** 在别人眼中; **to come up/go down in the ~** 发迹/落泊; **to watch the ~ go by** 闲看人来人往 **7** (heavenly body) 天体; **~s apart** (distant) 相距甚远; (different) 天壤之别; **a ~ away from sth.** colloq 和某事物有天壤之别; **a ~ of difference/good** colloq 巨大的差异/好处; **to have/want the best of both ~s** colloq 两头受益/想要两全其美 **8** *sing* Relig (the secular) **the ~** 世俗; **to renounce the ~** 弃绝尘世; **the ~, the flesh, and the devil** 尘世的种种诱惑 **9** (group, sphere) 界; **the arts/business/medical ~** 艺术界/商界/医学界; **the natural/mineral ~** 自然界/矿物界; **the ~ of politics/business/the arts** 政界/商界/艺术界 **10** (personal realm) 生活圈子; **sb.'s ~** 某人的生活天地; **the ~ of the child** 儿童的世界; **(to be** *or* **live) in a ~ of one's own** *or* **one's own ~** (生活) 在自己的小天地里

world: W~ Bank *n* **the W~ Bank** 世界银行; **~-beater** *n* (person) 天下无双的人; (thing) 天下无双的事物; **~-beating** *adj* 天下无双的; **~ champion** *n* 世界冠军; **the heavyweight/chess ~ champion** 重量级/国际象棋世界冠军; **~ championship** *n* 冠军头衔; **the heavyweight/athletics ~ championship(s)** 重量级/田径冠军称号; **~-class** *adj* 世界一流的; **to be ~-class at sth.** 在某方面是世界级的; **W~ Council of Churches** *n* **the W~ Council of Churches** 世界基督教协进会; **W~ Cup** *n* **the W~ Cup** 世界杯足球赛; **~ English** *n* **1** [u] (all varieties collectively) 世界英语; **2** [c] (single variety) 世界英语变体; **~ fair** *n* 世界博览会; **~-famous** *adj* 举世闻名的; **W~ Health Organization** *n* **the W~ Health Organization** 世界卫生组织; **W~ Heritage Site** *n* 世界文化遗址; **~ language** *n* **1** (widely used language) 世界通用语; **2** (artificial language) 世界语; **~ leader** *n* **1** Pol 世界强国领导人; **2** (best in the world) (person) 世界顶尖级人物; (thing) 世界顶尖级事物

worldliness /ˈwɜːdlɪnɪs/ *n* [u] **1** (lack of spirituality, materialism) 世俗 **2** (sophistication) 世故

worldly /ˈwɜːldli/ *adj* **1** (unspiritual, material) 世俗的; **~ wisdom/success/pleasure/goods** 处世的精明/世俗的成就/尘世的欢乐/个人物品 **2** (sophisticated) 世故的 ‹*person*›

worldly-wise *adj* 善于处世的

world: ~ music *n* [u] 世界音乐; **~ power** *n* 世界强国; **~ record** *n* 世界纪录; **W~ Series** *n* **the W~ Series** [美国职业棒球联盟优胜队之间在赛季末举行的] 世界系列赛; **W~ Service** *n* **the W~ Service** [英国广播公司的] 对外广播; **~-shaking** *adj* 震惊世界的; **W~ Trade Organization** *n* **the W~ Trade Organization** 世界贸易组织; **~ view** *n* 世界观; **~ war** *n* 世界大战; **the First W~ War, W~ War I** 第一次世界大战; **the Second W~ War, W~ War II** 第二次世界大战; **~-weariness** *n* [u] 厌世; **~-weary** *adj* 厌世的

worldwide /ˌwɜːldˈwaɪd/

A *adj* 世界范围的 ‹*attention, recognition*›; 全球的 ‹*market, pollution, network, trend, movement, epidemic*›

B *adv* 在全世界 ‹*spread, sell, produce, travel*›

World Wide Web *n* **the ~** 万维网

worm /wɜːm/

A *n* **1** (invertebrate) 蠕虫 [尤指蚯蚓]; **the ~ will turn** fig 老实人被逼急了也会反抗 **2** (insect larva) 幼虫; **this apple is full of ~s** 这个苹果里满是蛀虫 **3** colloq (wretch) 懦夫 **4** *usu sing* Tech (endless screw) 蜗杆; (coiled pipe) 螺旋管 **5** *usu sing* Comput (virus) 蠕虫病毒

B **worms** *npl* Vet, Med 肠虫; **to have/get ~s** 有/生肠虫

C *vt* **1** (wriggle) **to ~ one's way** 蠕动; **to ~ one's way into sb.'s heart/confidence** fig 慢慢赢得某人的心/信任 **2** (extract) 刺探; **to ~ a secret/the truth out of sb.** 从某人嘴里套出秘密/实情 **3** Vet 给…除肠虫 ‹*animal*›

worm: ~ cast *n* 蚯蚓粪; **~-eaten** *adj* **1** (full of wormholes) 满是蛀洞的 ‹*wood, fruit, book, fabric*›; **2** (eaten by worms) 虫咬的 ‹*corpse, tissue*›; **~ gear** *n* 涡轮传动装置; **~hole** *n* **1** (made by worm, insect larva) 蛀洞; **2** Phys 蠕虫洞; **~'s-eye view** *n* (physical) 仰视景象; (hierarchical) 下层视角; **~wood** *n* **1** [u and c] Bot 蒿; **2** [u] (preparation) 黄花蒿素

worn /wɔːn/

A *pp* ▸**wear A, B**

B *adj* **1** (damaged) 破旧的 ‹*carpet, clothing, shoes, tyre*›; 风蚀的 ‹*facade, stone*› **2** (tired) 疲惫的 ‹*person, face, expression*›

worn-out *adj* **1** (exhausted) 疲惫不堪的 ‹*person, face, appearance*› **2** (unusable) 破旧的 ‹*carpet, clothing, shoes, tyre*›; 破烂不堪的 ‹*engine, equipment, road, surface*› **3** (overused) 陈腐的 ‹*phrase, idea, policy*›; **~ clichés** 陈词滥调

worried /ˈwʌrɪd/ *adj* **1** (feeling concern) 发愁的; **to be ~ about sth./sb.** 为某事物/某人担心; **to be ~ about doing sth.** 担心做某事; **to be ~ that ...** 担心…; **to be ~ sick** *or* **to death** 担心得要死 **2** (expressing concern) 关心的 ‹*expression, look*›; 表示关心的 ‹*letter*›

worrier /ˈwʌrɪə(r)/ *n* 发愁的人; **don't be such a ~!** 别老这么操心!

worrisome /ˈwʌrɪsəm/ *adj* esp Amer 令人担心的

worry /ˈwʌri/

A *vi* 担心; **to ~ about sb./sth./doing sth.** 担心某人/某事物/做某事; **to ~ for sth.** 为某事物担心; **don't ~ (about me/the car)** 别(为我/为汽车) 担心; **there's nothing to ~ about** 没什么好担心的; **not to ~** 没事儿; **don't you ~!** 你尽管放心!

B *vt* **1** (be anxious about) **to ~ that ...** 担心…; **to ~ whether** *or* **if ...** 担心是否… **2** (make anxious) «*situation, event, person*» 使…担心 ‹*person*›; **it worries me that ...** 使我发愁的是…; **I don't want to ~ you but ...** 我不想让你担心, 可是… **3** (bother) «*situation, state of affairs*» 烦扰 ‹*person*›; **it wouldn't ~ me if we didn't have a TV** 我们就算没有电视机, 我也不在乎 **4** (chase) «*dog*» 追逐 ‹*livestock*› **5** (toss about) «*dog*» 撕咬 ‹*object, bone*›

C *v refl* **to ~ oneself about sth./sb.** 担忧某事物/某人; **to ~ oneself sick over sth.** 为某事物愁得生病

D *n* **1** [u] (anxiety) 忧虑; **to cause sb. a lot of ~** 使某人非常焦虑; **a life free from ~** 无忧无虑的生活 **2** [c] (trouble, problem) 令人担忧的事物; **financial worries** 财务上的烦恼; **sb.'s only/main ~ is (that) ...** 某人唯一/主要的担心是…; **to be the least of sb.'s worries** 是某人最不担心的; **to be a ~ to sb.** 让某人发愁; **no worries!** Austral, NZ colloq 没什么!

Phrasal verb

- **worry at** *vt* [**~ at sth.**] **1** (toss about) «*dog*» 撕咬 ‹*toy, bone*› **2** (fiddle with) 拉扯 ‹*ring, hair*›; **he began to ~ at the knot in the cord** 他开始解绳子上的结

worry beads *npl* 安神念珠

worrying /ˈwʌrɪɪŋ/

A *adj* 令人担心的; **the ~ thing is that ...** 令人担忧的是…

B *n* [u] 担心; **what's with all the ~?** 你干吗这么忧心忡忡的?

worry: ~ line *n* 忧虑的皱纹; **~wart** *n* Amer colloq 爱发愁的人

worse /wɜːs/ ▸**p. 140**

A *adj* (*comp of* **bad**) **1** (more unpleasant, unsatisfactory) 更坏的; **there's nothing ~ than ...** 没有比…更糟糕的了; **I've been to far ~ places** 我去过糟糕得多的地方; **to look/taste/sound/smell ~** 更难看/更难吃/更难听/更难闻; **~ luck!** Brit colloq 真倒霉! colloq **2** (lower in standard, competence) 更差的 ‹*performance, result*›; **the film is ~ than the book** 电影比书还要差; **I'm not a good swimmer, but she's even ~ than me** 我游泳游得不好, 但她甚至比我还差; **she's ~ than her predecessor** 她不如她的前任 **3** (more serious, severe) 更严重的; **and to make matters ~, ...** 更严重的是, …; **there are ~ things in life than ...** 生活中还有比…更严重的事; **to get ~ and ~** «*crisis, illness*» 越来越严重; «*noise*» 越来越响; **my desperation grew ~** 我更加绝望了; **to go from bad to ~** «*situation, health*» 每况愈下; **the war was going from bad to ~** 战争越来越惨烈 **4** *pred* (more unwell) 健康状况更差的; **he's getting/feeling ~** 他健康状况/感觉更糟了; **he's ~ than he was yesterday** 他的病情比昨天更严重了; **my back's ~ today** 今天我的背更痛了 **5** *pred* (more unhappy) 更不高兴的; **his death made me feel ~** 他的去世使我很难过; **to be none the ~ for it/the experience** 丝毫没有因此/因这件事心情更坏 **6** (more inappropriate) 更不合适的; **the decision couldn't have come at a ~ time** 这个时候作决定是最不恰当的

B *adv* (*comp of* **badly**) **1** (more unfavourably) 更糟糕地; **the interview could not have gone ~** 那次面谈糟透了; **to think ~ of sb./sth.** 对某人/某事物评价更低; **this skirt fits ~ than the other** 这条裙子比那条更不合身; **you could do ~ than take early retirement** 你倒不如早点退休 **2** (at lower level) 更差地; **to do ~** 干得更差; **he sings ~ than you** 他唱得比你还差; **she's doing/feeling ~ today** (in health) 她今天情况/感觉更差 **3** (more intensely or seriously) 更严重地 ‹*cough, bleed*›; **it's raining ~ than ever** 雨下得比以往都大; **to hurt ~ than yesterday** 疼得比昨天还厉害; **~ still, ...** 更糟糕的是… **4** (more inappropriately) 更不合适地 ‹*timed, placed*›; **he could hardly be ~ suited for this job** 他最不适合做这项工作

C *n* **1** [c] **the ~** (less desirable one) 较差者; **the ~ of the two novels** 两本小说中较差的一本 **2** [u and c] (less desirable state) 更糟的情况; **there is ~ to come** 更糟的还在后头; **prison or ~** 牢狱或者更糟的地方; **a change** *or* **turn for the ~** 变为更差的情况; **to change for the ~** «*situation*» 恶化; «*weather*» 变更恶劣

worsen /ˈwɜːsn/

A *vi* 变得更糟

B *vt* 使变得更糟

worse off *adj* **1** (in less advantageous position) 处境更加不利的; (less fortunate) 更不幸的; **to be no ~ without sth.** 没有某物不会更糟糕 **2** (less wealthy) 更贫困的; **to be ~ (than ...)** (比…) 更贫困; **to end up ~** 结果更穷

worship /ˈwɜːʃɪp/

A *n* [u] **1** Relig (veneration) 敬神; **nature/ancestor ~** 对自然/祖先的崇拜 **2** (religious practice) 敬神活动; **an act/a place of ~** 礼拜/礼拜场所; **hours of ~** 敬拜时间; **morning/evening ~** 早晨/晚上的礼拜 **3** (admiration, devotion) 崇拜; **a person/object of ~** 崇敬的人/热爱的物品 **4** **Worship** esp Brit (as title) 阁下; **Your/His/Her W~** 阁下

B *vt* (*pres p etc.* **-pp-**, Amer **-p-**) **1** Relig (venerate) 敬奉 **2** (admire, devote oneself to) 崇拜 ‹*person, animal, money, fame*›

C *vi* (*pres p etc.* **-pp-**, Amer **-p-**) 做礼拜; **to ~ at the altar of love/fame/money** 崇拜爱情/名誉/金钱

worshipful /ˈwɜːʃɪpfl/ *adj* **1** (reverential) 敬重的; ~ **admiration/respect/fans** 敬佩/敬重/虔诚的仰慕者 **2** **Worshipful** Brit (in titles) 尊敬的 ‹*Company, Society, Mayor, Master*›

worshipper /ˈwɜːʃɪpə(r)/ *n* **1** Relig 敬神者; **a nature** ~ 热爱自然的人; **a** ~ **at the altar of sth.** 某物的敬拜者 **2** (admirer, devotee) 崇拜者; ~**s of fame and fortune** 名誉和财富的崇拜者

worst /wɜːst/

A *adj* (*superl of* **bad**) **1** *usu attrib* (most unpleasant, unfavourable) 最坏的; **the** ~ **years of the Depression** 大萧条时期最糟的年头; **hypocrites of the** ~ **kind** 最卑鄙的伪君子 **2** (of the lowest standard or quality) 最差的; **the** ~ **dentist in the town** 城里最差劲的牙医; **the** ~ **thing about the film is ...** 这部影片最差的是…; **to be** ~ **at sth.** 在…方面最差 ‹*subject, sport*›; **she was** ~ **at dealing with customers** 她最不擅长与顾客打交道 **3** *usu attrib* (most serious, severe) 最严重的 ‹*disaster, mistake*›; **my** ~ **fears** 我最担心的事 **4** (most inappropriate) 最不合适的; **at the** ~ **possible time** 在最不合适的时候; **the** ~ **person for the job** 最不适合干这项工作的人 **5** (most harmful) 最有害的; **fats are** ~ **for you** 脂肪对你最有害

B *adv* (*superl of* **badly**) **1** (most unpleasantly, unfavourably) 最坏地; **to fit** ~ **of all** 最不合身; **your feet smell the** ~ 你的脚最臭; **the** ~**-equipped school in the city** 市内设施最简陋的学校; ~ **of all** 最糟糕的是 **2** (most incompetently) 最差地; **I sang the** ~ 我唱得最差; **to do** ~ 表现最差 **3** (most severely) 最严重地; **to be** ~ **affected by sth.** 受某事物的影响最严重; **the children suffered (the)** ~ 孩子们是最受罪的

C *n* **1** (most unpleasant thing) 最坏的事物; (most unpleasant person) 最糟的人; **to look/sound/taste/smell the** ~ 最难看/最难听/最难吃/最难闻; **to look one's** ~ 显得最难看; **wasps are the** ~ **of all** 黄蜂是最讨厌的; **to think the** ~ **of sb.** 把某人往最坏处想; **at (the)** ~ 往最坏处说 **2** (thing of lowest standard) 最差的事物; (person of lowest standard) 最差的人; **the** ~ **of her books** 她写的最差的一本书; **the** ~ **of its type** *or* **kind** 同类型中最差的; **the** ~ **of the bunch** *or* **lot** 一批中最差的; **I was the** ~ **at maths in the class** 我是班上数学最差的; **as doctors go, she's the** ~ 作为医生她是最差的 **3** (most incompetent state) 最差状态; **to be at one's** ~ 处于最差状态; **I'm at my** ~ **in the mornings** 我在上午精神最差 **4** (most serious, severe state) 最严重的情况; **the storm was one of the** ~ **in recent years** 这是近年来最严重的暴风雨之一; **to be at its** ~ «*pain, situation*» 最严重; **at (the)** ~ 至多; **at the** ~ **she can only refuse** 充其量她只能拒绝; **if (the)** ~ **comes to (the)** ~ 如果情况坏到极点 **5** (greatest harm) 最大的损害; **to do one's** ~ 进行最大的破坏; **let them do their** ~! 让他们拿出最坏的招数吧! **6** (most negative trait) 最坏的品质; **to exploit the** ~ **in sb.** 利用某人最坏的品质; **to bring out the** ~ **in sb.** 使某人原形毕露 **7** (least advantageous) 最不利的方面; **the** ~ **thing about being freelance is ...** 自由职业的最大坏处是…; **to get the** ~ **of a deal/argument** 在交易中吃大亏/在争论中彻底败下阵来; **to get the** ~ **of it** 遭遇失败; **the** ~ **of both** *or* **all worlds** 各种情况的所有不利因素 **8** (least appropriate) 最不合适的情况; **to turn up at the** ~ **of times** 在最不恰当的时候出现

D *vt usu passive* formal 击败; **to be** ~**ed by government forces** 被政府军打败

worst-case scenario *n* (worst possible foreseeable circumstances) 可预期的最坏情况; (worst possible outcome) 可能出现的最坏结果; **in a** *or* **the** ~ **...** 在最坏的情况下…

worsted /ˈwʊstɪd/

A *n* [u and c] **1** (fabric) 精纺毛料 **2** (yarn) 精纺毛线

B *modif* 精纺的 ‹*suit, trousers, jacket, skirt*›

worst off *adj* **1** (in least advantageous position) (least fortunate) 最糟糕的 **2** (least wealthy) 最贫困的

worth /wɜːθ/

A *adj pred* **1** (of specified financial value) **to be** ~ **sth.** 值某金额; **the land is** ~ **millions** 这块地价值数百万; **this picture isn't** ~ **very much** 这幅画不值多少钱; **he is** ~ **millions** 他身家数百万; **how much** *or* **what is it** ~ **(to you) (to do it)?** (对你来说)(做这事)需要多少钱?; ▸**gold A1** **2** (of specified abstract value) **to be** ~ **sth.** 值某物; **two hours' work is** ~ **a day's discussion** 两小时的工作顶得上一天的讨论; **not to be** ~ **a damn** *or* **the paper it's written on** colloq 毫无价值; **to be** ~ **sth. to sb.** 对于某人来说值某物; **it's more than my life's** ~ **to tell you** hum 告诉你的话我就没命了; **for all one is** ~ colloq 拼命地; **for what it's** ~ 不论好坏; **to be** ~ **it** 值得; **the holiday cost a lot, but it was** ~ **it** 度假花了不少钱, 但是很值; **to be (well)** ~ **sb.'s while** 对某人(大)有好处 **3** (deserving of) 值得…的 ‹*mention, trying*›; **to be** ~ **doing sth.** 值得做某事; **this book is** ~ **reading** 这本书值得一读; **that idea is** ~ **considering** 这主意值得考虑; **the museum is** ~ **a visit** 这个博物馆值得参观; **to make life** ~ **living** 使生活过得有价值; **it is/isn't** ~ **doing** 这值得/不值得做; **it wasn't** ~ **the time and effort** 这不值得费时费力; **if a job's** ~ **doing, it's** ~ **doing well** Prov 如果一件事值得去做, 就要尽力把它做好

B *n* [u] **1** (amount) [相当于一定金额或时间等的数量]; **£10's** ~ **of petrol** 10英镑的汽油; **a week's** ~ **of supplies** 一周的补给品; **a pound's** ~ **of sugar** 1磅重的糖 **2** (value) 价值; **to prove one's** ~ 证明自己的价值; **to show one's inner** ~ 展示自己的内在价值; **of great/little/no** ~ 有重大价值/没什么价值/毫无价值的; **his contribution was of great** ~ 他贡献巨大; **what is its** ~ **in pounds?** 这东西值多少英镑?; **to see the** ~ **of sth.** 看到某事物的价值

worthiness /ˈwɜːðɪnɪs/ *n* [u] 值得尊敬

worthless /ˈwɜːθlɪs/ *adj* **1** (useless) 无价值的 ‹*object, agreement, currency, theory*›; 没用的 ‹*advice, promise*› **2** (having no good qualities) 不中用的 ‹*person*›; 卑劣的 ‹*liar, rogue*›

worthlessness /ˈwɜːθlɪsnɪs/ *n* **1** (of object, agreement, theory, coin) 无价值; (of advice, promise) 无用 **2** (of person) 无能; (of character) 卑劣

worthwhile /wɜːθˈwaɪl/ *adj* 值得的; **to be** ~ **doing sth.** 某事值得一做; **to find sth.** ~ 觉得某事值得; **a** ~ **career/discussion** 有前途的职业/有价值的讨论

worthy /ˈwɜːði/

A *adj* **1** *pred* (deserving) 值得的; **to be** ~ **of mention/attention/note** 值得一提/关注/注意; **to be** ~ **of doing** *or* **to do sth.** 某事值得做; **a** ~ **effort/person** 值得的努力/相配的人 **2** (admirable, honourable) 值得尊敬的 ‹*person, winner, opponent*›; 崇高的 ‹*cause*›; 值得重视的 ‹*record*› **3** *pred* (appropriate) **to be** ~ **of sth.** 适合某事物; **a speech** ~ **of the occasion** 适合这个场合的演讲 **4** *pred* (typical) **to be** ~ **of sb./sth.** 具有某人/某事物的典型特征; **patience** ~ **of a saint** 圣人特有的耐心

B *n* esp hum 大人物

wot /wɒt/ *excl* Brit colloq = **what**

wotcha, wotcher /ˈwɒtʃə(r)/ *excl* Brit colloq 你好

would /wʊd, wəd/ ▸**p. 147** *modal aux* (colloq *short form* colloq **'d**, *negative* **would not** *or* colloq **wouldn't**) **1** (in sequence of past tenses, reported speech) 将 [在过去时及间接引语中指将来的动作]; **he said he** ~ **come** 他说他要来; **I thought I** ~ **be late** 我以为要迟到了 **2** (indicating result in conditionals) [在条件句中表示结果]; **it** ~ **be wonderful if they came** 要是他们来的话, 那就太好了; **she'd be a fool to accept it** 她如果接受, 那她就是个傻瓜; **she'd look better with shorter hair** 她留短发会好看些 **3** (indicating intent in conditionals) 就会 [在条件句中表示意愿]; **I** ~ **have done it if I had had time** 要是我有时间的话, 我早就做了这事; **it's what he** ~ **have wanted** 这正是他本来想要的 **4** (expressing purpose) [说明动机]; **she burned the letters so that her husband** ~ **never read them** 她把信都烧了, 这样她丈夫就永远看不到了 **5** (expressing wish) 会 [表达愿望]; **I wish it** ~ **rain** 要是下雨就好了; **I wish he'd leave** 我希望他走开; ~ **(that) ...** liter 要是…就好了; ~ **that it were true!** 这要是真的就好了! **6** (expressing willingness) [表示意愿]; **who** ~ **live there?** 谁愿意住在那儿?; **she just wouldn't listen** 她就是不肯听 **7** (expressing desire) [表示渴望]; **I** ~ **love to go** 我很想去; **I'd like a coffee** 我想喝杯咖啡 **8** (in requests, offers) [表示客气的请求、提议或邀请]; ~ **you like something to eat?** 你想吃点什么吗?; ~ **you open the door for me, please?** 请你帮我开门好吗?; **switch off the radio,** ~ **you?** 请把收音机关掉行吗? **9** (when giving advice) [用于提出建议]; **I** ~ **check first** 我会先查一下; **I wouldn't do that if I were you** 如果我是你的话, 就不会做那事 **10** (used to soften statements) [用以缓和语气]; **I** ~ **have thought (that) ...** 我的想法是…; **it** ~ **seem that you're right** 看来你是对的; **so it** ~ **seem** 看来是这样 **11** (used to) 总是 [用于谈论过去经常发生的事]; **he'd always be the first to help** 他总是第一个来帮忙; **every winter the fields** ~ **be flooded** 每年冬季这些田地都会遭水淹 **12** (expressing ability, capacity) [表示特定条件下会出现的情况或可能性]; **the window wouldn't open** 这窗子就是打不开; **our last car** ~ **hold six** 我们最后一辆汽车坐得下6个人 **13** (expressing annoyance) [表示恼火]; **they** ~ **have to be early** 他们非要提前不可; **you** ~ **contradict him!** 你当然会跟他抬嘴! **14** (expressing conjecture, assumption) [表示推测或设想]; **what time** ~ **that be?** 那会是什么时候?; **being so young, you wouldn't remember the war** 你那时太小, 不可能记得那场战争

would-be

A *adj attrib* **1** (wanting to be) 想要成为的; ~ **intellectuals** 未来的知识分子 **2** pej (having intended to be) 本来打算的; **a** ~ **assassin/thief/fraudster** 暗杀/偷窃/诈骗未遂者

B *n* colloq 一心想当…的人

wouldn't /ˈwʊdnt/ colloq = **would not** ▸**would**

would've /ˈwʊdəv/ colloq = **would have** ▸**would**

wound[1] /wuːnd/

A *n* **1** (physical injury) 伤; **a** ~ **to** *or* **in the head** 头上的伤口; **to die from** *or* **of one's** ~**s** 受伤而死; **an open** ~ 开放性伤口; **to clean/dress/suture/swab a** ~ 清洗/包扎/缝合/擦拭伤口 **2** fig (mental injury) 创伤; **a** ~ **to sb.'s pride** 对某人自尊心的伤害

B *vt* **1** (injure physically) 使受伤; **to** ~ **sb. in the leg/stomach** 弄伤某人的腿/肚子 **2** fig (injure mentally) 伤害; **her self-esteem was** ~**ed** 她的自尊心受到了伤害

wound[2] /waʊnd/ *pt, pp* ▸**wind**[2] **A, B**

wounded /ˈwuːndɪd/

A *adj* 受伤的; ~ **in the arm** 胳膊受伤的; ~ **in action** 在战斗中受伤的

B *npl* **the** ~ 伤员

wounding /ˈwuːndɪŋ/ *adj* 伤感情的; **to be** ~ **to sb.** 伤某人的感情

wove /wəʊv/ *pt* ▸**weave A, B**

woven /ˈwəʊvn/
A *pp* ▸**weave A, B**
B *adj* 1 Tex 织的 ‹*thread, cloth, rug*› 2 (intertwined) 编结用的 ‹*cane, reeds, flowers*› 3 (made by intertwining) 编制的 ‹*basket, chair*›

wow¹ /waʊ/ colloq
A *excl* (expression of astonishment or admiration) 哇 [表示惊讶或钦佩]
B *n* [c] 巨大成功; **that band's new song is a ~** 那个乐队的新歌一炮走红
C *vt* 使…喝彩 ‹*person, audience, critics*›

wow² *n* [u] Audio 失真

wow factor *n* colloq 令人叫好的因素; **the ~ of this property is the panoramic view of the sea** 这处房产的绝妙之处是一览无余的海景

WP *abbr* = **word processing**

WPC *abbr* Brit = **woman police constable**

wpm *abbr* = **words per minute** 每分钟字数; **60 ~** 每分钟 60 个字

WRAC *abbr* Brit Hist = **Women's Royal Army Corps** 皇家陆军妇女队

wrack¹ /ræk/ *vt* = **rack¹ B1**

wrack² *n* [u and c] Bot 海藻类植物

WRAF *abbr* Brit Hist = **Women's Royal Air Force** 皇家空军妇女队

wraith /reɪθ/ *n* [临终前后显现的] 活人灵魂; **heart attacks had reduced his mother to a ~** 心脏病把他母亲折磨得形容枯槁

wraithlike /ˈreɪθlaɪk/ *adj* 幽灵般的 ‹*figure, silhouette, shadow*›; 瘦骨嶙峋的 ‹*girl*›

wrangle /ˈræŋgl/
A *n* 争吵; **we had a bit of a ~ over it** 我们为这事争吵了一阵
B *vi* 争吵; **to ~ about** *or* **over sth. (with sb.)** 为某事物（与某人）争吵
C *vt* Amer 1 (herd) 放牧 ‹*horses*› 2 (take charge of) 看管 ‹*livestock, cattle*›

wrangler /ˈræŋglə(r)/ *n* 1 Amer (herder) 牧人; (cowboy) 牛仔 2 (arguer) 争吵者

wrangling /ˈræŋglɪŋ/ *n* [u] 争吵

wrap /ræp/
A *vt* (*pres p etc.* **-pp-**) 1 (enclose) 包 ‹*present, food, parcel*›; **to ~ sb. in one's arms** 把某人搂在怀里; **to be ~ped in sth.** 被…包裹 ‹*paper*›; fig 被笼罩在…中 ‹*darkness, silence*›; 专心致志于 ‹*thoughts*›; **a baby ~ped (up) in a blanket** 裹在毯子里的婴儿; **the hills were ~ped in mist** 山峦笼罩在薄雾之中; **an affair still ~ped in mystery** 一个仍然扑朔迷离的事件 2 (swathe) (for decoration, protection) 用…包 ‹*paper, foil*›; (to keep warm) 用…裹 ‹*blanket, shawl*›; (to keep clean) 用…包扎 ‹*bandage*›; **to ~ paper/foil round** *or* **around sth.** 用纸/箔片包住某物; **to ~ a blanket around sb.** 用毯子裹住某人身体; **to ~ a handkerchief round one's finger** 用手帕包住手指; **to ~ one's arms round sb.** 搂住某人; **to ~ an arm around sb.'s waist** 用一只胳膊搂着某人的腰; **he ~ped his legs round mine** 他的腿缠着我的腿; **to ~ the car round a lamppost** colloq 开车撞上路灯柱 3 Comput 使…自动换行 ‹*word, text*›
B *vi* (*pres p etc.* **-pp-**) «*word, text*» 自动换行
C *v refl* (*pres p etc.* **-pp-**) 1 (pull on) **to ~ oneself (in a blanket)** （用毯子）裹住身体; **to ~ oneself in an air of mystery** 把自己搞得很神秘 2 Amer colloq **to ~ oneself around sth.** (eat) 啃某食物
D *n* 1 [c] (coat) 外衣; (shawl) 披肩; (scarf) 围巾; (blanket) 毯子 2 [c] Culin 墨西哥卷 [薄饼裹凉馅制成] 3 [c] *sing* (end of session) Cin 停机; Audio 录音完成; **it's a ~** Cin 就拍到这里 4 [u and c] (packaging) 包装材料
E **wraps** *npl* **to be under ~s** 处于保密状态; **to keep sth. under ~s** 对某事保密; **to take the ~s off sth.** 揭开某事的内幕

Phrasal verb

• **wrap up**
A *vt* [**~ sth./sb. up, ~ up sth./sb.**] 1 (enclose, swathe) 把…包起来 ‹*object, parcel, person*›; **~ the children up warm(ly)** 给孩子们穿得暖和点 2 colloq (conclude) 结束 ‹*project, event, talks*›; 完成 ‹*deal*›; 赢得 ‹*title, victory*›; **let's get the whole thing ~ped up** 我们来把这一切都了结了吧; **the team ~ped up the series 4:0** 该队以 4:0 的比分获得该项系列赛的胜利; **to ~ up the evening's news** esp Amer 总结夜间新闻 3 fig colloq (involve) **to be ~ped up in sb./sth.** 注意力集中在某人身上/某事物上; **to be totally ~ped up in one's work** 完全沉浸在工作中; **there is a lot of money ~ped up in the project** 有许多钱投入到了这个项目中; **to be ~ped up in oneself** 自闭
B *vi* 1 (dress) 穿得暖和; **~ up well** *or* **warm(ly)!** 穿得暖和点儿! 2 Brit colloq (shut up) **~ up!** 住嘴!
C *v refl* **to ~ oneself up (well** *or* **warm(ly))** 穿得暖和

wrap-around *adj attrib* 1 全框架的 ‹*window, windscreen*› 2 裹襟的 ‹*garment*›

wrap-around sunglasses *npl* 面罩型太阳镜

wrap-over *adj* 裹襟的 ‹*skirt, dress*›

wrapper /ˈræpə(r)/ *n* 1 (cover) 包装材料; **sweet/package ~s** 糖果包装纸/包装材料 2 Publg 书封套 3 Amer (loose negligee) 宽松女晨衣

wrapping /ˈræpɪŋ/ *n* 1 [c] (cover) (made of paper) 包装纸; (made of plastic) 包装塑料 2 [u] (material) 包装材料

wrapping paper *n* [u and c] 包装纸

wrap: ~ top *n* 裹襟上衣; **~-up** *n* Amer 新闻提要; **a ~-up session** 新闻简报

wrath /rɒθ, Amer ræθ/ *n* [u] liter 盛怒; **sb.'s ~ knows no bounds** 某人愤怒无比

wrathful /ˈrɒθfl, Amer ˈræθ-/ *adj* liter 愤怒的

wreak /riːk/ *vt* 1 (inflict) 发泄 ‹*fury*›; **to ~ revenge** *or* **vengeance on sb.** 对某人施行报复 2 (cause) 造成; **to ~ havoc** *or* **damage on sth.** 对某事物造成破坏

wreath /riːθ/ *n* 1 (for grave, memorial) 花圈; **to lay a ~** 献花圈; **a funeral ~** 殡仪花圈 2 (for victor) (round the head) 花冠; (round the neck) 花环 3 (coil of smoke, cloud etc.) 缭绕

wreathe /riːð/
A *vt* 1 (cover) 笼罩 ‹*hilltop*›; 环绕 ‹*sun, head*›; **sb.'s face is ~d in smiles** 某人笑容满面 2 liter (entwine) 使缠绕; **to ~ sth. around** *or* **about sth.** 将某物缠绕在某物上; **to ~ flowers into sb.'s hair** 把花编到某人的头发上 3 liter (form) 编成 ‹*garland*›; **to ~ flowers into a garland/leaves into a laurel crown** 把花儿编成花环/把树叶编成桂冠
B *vi* liter «*smoke, steam*» 缭绕; **to ~ upwards** 盘旋上升

wreath-laying /ˈriːθleɪɪŋ/ *n* **~ (ceremony)** 献花圈（仪式）

wreck /rek/
A *n* 1 Naut (event) 失事 2 (ship) 沉船 3 (car) 撞毁的汽车 4 (plane) 撞毁的飞机 5 (person) 受到严重损伤的人; **a human ~** 废人
B *vt* 1 (destroy, damage) 毁坏; **to be ~ed by fire/by an explosion/in a crash** 被烧毁/炸毁/撞毁; **to be ~ed** «*ship*» 失事; «*person*» 遇难 2 fig (spoil) 彻底毁灭; **you've ~ed my whole life/future!** 你毁了我的一生/前程!

wreckage /ˈrekɪdʒ/ *n* [u] 1 (of vehicle, structure) 残骸; (of building) 废墟; **to pull sb./sth. from the ~** 把某人/某物从废墟中拉出来 2 fig (surviving parts) 残留; **the ~ of sb.'s hopes/plans/prospects** 残存的一丝希望/一点计划/一点机会

wrecked /rekt/ *adj* 1 (damaged) 失事损毁的 ‹*ship, car, aircraft*›; 毁坏的 ‹*structure, building, machinery, furniture*› 2 fig (spoilt) 破灭的 ‹*plans, hopes, ambitions*›; 破裂的 ‹*friendship, marriage, relationship, talks*›; 毁了的 ‹*career, health*› 3 Brit colloq (drunk) 喝得烂醉的 4 colloq (exhausted) 精疲力竭的

wrecker /ˈrekə(r)/ *n* 1 (destroyer) 破坏者 2 esp Amer (demolition or salvage worker) 救援人 3 esp Amer (vehicle recycler) 拆卸废旧汽车者 4 Amer (recovery vehicle) 救险车

wrecking /ˈrekɪŋ/ *n* [u] 1 (damaging) 毁坏 2 fig (spoiling) 破灭; **the ~ of sb.'s hopes/prospects/marriage** 某人希望的破灭/前程的幻灭/婚姻的破裂 3 esp Amer (demolition) 房屋拆除

wrecking ball *n* 落锤 [悬挂于吊车上，供拆除建筑物用]

Wren /ren/ *n* Brit Hist 皇家海军妇女服务队队员

wren /ren/ *n* 鹪鹩

wrench /rentʃ/
A *n* 1 esp Amer (tool) 扳手; **to throw a ~ in(to) the works** Amer 阻挠 2 (violent twist) 猛扭; (violent pull) 猛拉; **to give one's ankle a ~** 扭伤脚踝 3 fig (pang) [尤指离别时的] 痛苦; **it is a real ~ leaving** 这是十分痛苦的离别
B *vt* 1 (twist or pull) 猛扭 ‹*handle, object*›; 猛拉 ‹*door, nail*›; **to ~ sth. from** *or* **out of sth.** 把某物从某物中猛拉出来; **to ~ sb./sth. round** 猛然拉转某人/某物; **to ~ sth. away** *or* **off** 猛然拉开某物 2 (injure) 扭伤 ‹*ankle, knee*›
C *vi* 猛扭; **to ~ at sth.** 猛扭某物
D *v refl* **to ~ oneself away** *or* **free** 挣脱

wrest /rest/ *vt* 1 (pull) 抢夺 ‹*object, weapon, file*› 2 (obtain) 费力取得 ‹*control*›; **to ~ a living from the soil/land** 靠土地辛苦谋生; **to ~ a confession from sb.** 千方百计使某人坦白

wrestle /ˈresl/
A *vi* 1 (in earnest) 扭打; **to ~ with sb.** 与某人搏斗 2 (as sport) 摔跤 3 fig (struggle to deal with) 奋力对付; **to ~ with a problem** 全力解决问题; **to ~ to do sth.** 努力做某事
B *vt* **to ~ the keys from sb.** 奋力夺下某人的钥匙; **to ~ sb. to the ground** 把某人摔到地上; **they ~d the table through the door** 他们好不容易把桌子弄出了门
C *n* 1 (in earnest) 扭打; **a ~ to the death** 拼死的扭打 2 (as sport) 摔跤 3 fig (struggle) 艰苦的斗争; **a ~ with sth.** 与某事的搏斗; **a ~ to do sth.** 做某事的努力

wrestler /ˈreslə(r)/ *n* 摔跤运动员

wrestling /ˈreslɪŋ/ ▸**p. 307** *n* [u] 摔跤; **a ~ champion/fan/match** 摔跤冠军/迷/比赛

wrestling hold *n* 锁臂 [摔跤的一种握法]

wretch /retʃ/ *n* 1 (miserable person) 不幸的人; **those poor ~es!** 那些可怜的人! 2 pej (contemptible person) 恶棍 3 colloq hum (rascal) 淘气鬼; **come here, you ~!** 过来，你这家伙!

wretched /ˈretʃɪd/ *adj* 1 (miserable) 悲惨的 ‹*victim, peasant, inhabitant*›; **to feel ~ (about sth.)** （为某事物）感到难过 2 (poor) 极差的 ‹*life, fate, hotel, slum*›; 破旧的 ‹*clothes*›; 恶劣的 ‹*conditions, weather*›; 少得可怜的 ‹*amount*›; **~ existence/poverty/misery** 艰难的生活/极端贫穷/极其悲惨; **it was ~ of him to do that** 他那么做很糟糕 3 *attrib* colloq (damned) 该死的 ‹*person, child, animal*›; 烦人的 ‹*car, device, machine*›

wretchedly /ˈretʃɪdli/ *adv* 1 (miserably) 苦恼地 ‹*look, gaze*›; 难受地 ‹*say, weep*› 2 (poorly) 破破烂烂地 ‹*clothed*›; 极差地 ‹*furnished, treat, behave*›; **~ small/feeble/bad** 小得可怜的/极其虚弱的/极其糟糕的

wretchedness /ˈretʃɪdnɪs/ *n* [u] 1 (misery) 痛苦 2 (poverty) 糟糕

wriggle /ˈrɪgl/
A *vi* 1 (squirm) «*worm, reptile*» 蠕动; «*person, animal, fish*» 扭动; **to ~ with embarrassment** 尴尬地扭动身体 2 (move) **to ~ along (sth.)** «*worm, animal, person*» （沿着某物）蜿

蜒行进; **to ～ under (sth.)** 在（某物）下面徐徐爬行; **to ～ down/up (sth.)** 蜿蜒爬下/爬上（某物）; **to ～ through (sth.)** 扭动着穿过（某物）; **to ～ free/away** 扭动着挣脱/逃脱; **to ～ off the hook** «*fish*» 扭动身体摆脱钩子; **to ～ into one's trousers** 扭动身体穿上裤子

B *vt* [1] (twist and turn) 扭动; **to ～ one's toes/fingers** 扭动脚趾/手指 [2] **to ～ one's way into/out of sth.** (move) 扭动着进入某处/从某处出来; **to ～ its way out of the trap** «*animal*» 扭动着钻出陷阱; **to ～ one's way out of a messy situation** colloq 逃脱困境

C *v refl* **to ～ oneself (through sth.)** 扭动身子（穿过某处）; **he managed to ～ himself free** 他设法扭动着挣脱了

D *n* (of worm) 蠕动; (of person) 扭动; **to give a ～ of pleasure** 高兴地一扭身子

Phrasal verbs

- **wriggle about, wriggle around** *vi* «*worm*» 不停地蠕动; «*person, animal, fish*» 不停地扭动
- **wriggle out** *vi* [1] (get out) 扭动着逃脱; **to ～ out through the bars** 扭动着钻过栅栏; **to ～ out of sth.** 扭动着从某物里出来; **to ～ out of one's clothes** 扭动着脱下衣服 [2] **to ～ out of sth.** colloq (avoid) 耍滑摆脱某物; **she'll ～ out of it somehow** 她总会摆脱它的

wriggler /ˈrɪɡlə(r)/ *n* 扭来扭去的人

wriggly /ˈrɪɡli/ *adj* 蠕动的 ‹*worm, animal*›; 扭动的 ‹*child, person*›

wring /rɪŋ/

A *vt* (*pt, pp* **wrung**) [1] (squeeze) 拧 ‹*cloth, towel, shirts*›; **'do not ～'** (on label) "不可拧绞" [2] (extract) 拧出 ‹*liquid, water*›; **to ～ sth. from** *or* **out of sth.** 把某物从某物中拧出; **to ～ information/money/a confession out of** *or* **from sb.** fig 从某人处费力地弄到情报/强行向某人索取钱财/迫使某人坦白 [3] (break) 扭断; **to ～ sb.'s neck** lit 扭断某人的脖子; fig 掐死某人 [4] (clasp) 攥紧; **to ～ sb.'s hand** 握紧某人的手; **to ～ one's hands** fig 扭绞双手 [表示焦虑、悲伤或绝望] [5] (affect deeply) **to ～ sb.'s heart** 使某人心碎

B *n* 绞拧; **to give sth. a ～** 拧一下某物

Phrasal verb

- **wring out** *vt* [**～ sth. out, ～ out sth.**] [1] (remove water from) 拧干 ‹*cloth, towel, garment*›; **to be wrung out** fig colloq 筋疲力尽 [2] (extract) 拧出 ‹*liquid, water*›

wringer /ˈrɪŋə(r)/ *n* 甩干机; **to put sb. through the ～** fig colloq 使某人受尽磨难

wringing /ˈrɪŋɪŋ/

A *adj* 湿得能拧出水的; **to be ～ with sweat** fig 汗流浃背

B *adv* 能拧出水地 ‹*wet*›

wrinkle /ˈrɪŋkl/

A *n* [1] (on skin) 皱纹 [2] (in fabric) 皱褶; **to iron out the ～s** lit 熨平皱痕; fig colloq 解决小问题

B *vt* [1] (crease) 使…起皱 ‹*skin, material, paper, fabric*› [2] (furrow, draw together) 皱起 ‹*nose, forehead, brow*›

C *vi* «*nose, forehead, brow*» 皱起; «*skin, material, paper, fabric*» 起皱

wrinkled /ˈrɪŋkld/ *adj* 有皱纹的

wrinkly /ˈrɪŋkli/

A *adj* [1] (lined) 有皱纹的 ‹*face, skin, person*› [2] (creased) 皱巴巴的 ‹*material, paper, fabric*›

B *n* Brit colloq 老人家

wrist /rɪst/ ▸**p. 71** *n* [1] Anat 腕关节; **to break/sprain one's ～** 弄断/扭伤腕关节; **to get a slap on the ～** lit, fig 受到轻微批评 [2] (cuff) 袖口

wrist: ～band *n* [1] (bracelet) 手镯; (for sport) 腕套; (for identity) 手牌; (on watch) 表带; [2] (cuff) 袖口; **～ guard** *n* 护腕; **～ joint** *n* 腕关节

wristlet /ˈrɪstlɪt/ (to protect the wrist) 护腕; (as ornament) 手镯

wrist: ～ rest *n* 腕枕; **～watch** *n* 手表

writ[1] /rɪt/ *n* 令状; **to issue a ～ against sb., to serve a ～ on sb., to serve sb. with a ～** 传讯某人; **～ of execution** 处决令

writ[2] *pt, pp* archaic ▸**write; to be ～ large** fig 被夸大

writable /ˈraɪtəbl/ *adj* 可写入的 ‹*disk, drive*›

write /raɪt/ (*pt* **wrote,** *pp* **written**)

A *vt* [1] (mark, pen) 写 ‹*answer, name, book, essay, report, article*›; (compose) 谱写 ‹*piece of music*›; **to ～ sth. into a contract** 把某事写入合同; **who wrote the words to this song?** 这首歌的歌词是谁写的？; **to ～ sb. (a letter)** Amer 给某人写信; **to have guilt written all over one's face** 满脸愧疚; **he had 'policeman' written all over him** 他活脱脱一副警察模样 [2] (fill in) 写满 ‹*page*›; 开 ‹*cheque, prescription*› [3] Comput 编写 ‹*program, software*›; **to ～ data (on) to sth.** 把数据写入某物 [4] Radio, TV **to ～ sb. into/out of a series/episode** 在某系列剧/某集中加入/删去某角色

B *vi* [1] (form words) 写; **to learn to read and ～** 学习读书写字; **she doesn't ～ very neatly** 她字写得不大整洁; **give me something to ～ on/with** 给我些写字的纸; **to ～ in pen** 用钢笔写; **to ～ on both sides of the paper** 在纸的正反两面书写 [2] (make marks) «*pencil*» 能写; **this pen doesn't ～/doesn't ～ properly** 这支钢笔写不出来/不好写 [3] (pen, compose) 写作; **to ～ about** *or* **on sth.** 就某主题写作; **to ～ under a pseudonym** 用笔名写作 [4] (send letter) 写信; **to ～ to sb.** 给某人写信

Phrasal verbs

- **write away** *vi* = **write off B**
- **write back**

A *vi* 回信

B *vt* [**～ sth. back, ～ back sth.**] 回 ‹*letter*›; **to ～ back that ...** 回信说…

- **write down** *vt* [**～ sth. down, ～ down sth.**]

[1] (note, record) 写下 [2] Fin (reduce nominal value of) 减记 ‹*asset, stock*›

- **write in**

A *vt* [1] [**～ sth. in, ～ in sth.**] (insert) 把…写进去 ‹*sentence, word*› [2] [**～ sb./sth. in**] Amer Pol 在选票上加写 ‹*candidate, name*› [3] [**～ sb. in**] Radio, TV 添加 ‹*character*›

B *vi* (give opinion) 致函; (to order sth.) 写信索取

- **write off**

A *vt* [**～ sth. off, ～ off sth.**]

[1] Brit (damage beyond repair) 毁掉 ‹*vehicle, boat*›; (consider beyond repair) «*insurer*» 把…报废 ‹*vehicle, boat*› [2] (cancel, deduct) 勾销 ‹*debt, loss, amount*› [3] colloq (dismiss) [**～ sb./sth. off, ～ off sb./sth.**] 不把…放在眼里 ‹*player, performer, attempt, venture*›; **to ～ sb. off as an academic failure** 认为某人在学术上一无是处; **the project was written off as a failure** 这个项目已被认定为是不成功的

B *vi* **to ～ off for sth.** (request) 致函索取 ‹*catalogue, information*›; (order) 函购 ‹*product*›

- **write out**

A [**～ sth. out, ～ out sth.**] *vt*

[1] (put to paper) 写下 ‹*address, list*›; 写出 ‹*report*›; 开 ‹*cheque, prescription*› [2] esp Sch (copy) 抄写 ‹*words, sentence*›

B [**～ sb. out**] *vt* Radio, TV 删去 ‹*character*›

- **write up** *vt* [**～ sth. up, ～ up sth.**]

[1] (report) 详细记录 ‹*events, experiment, findings*› [2] (praise) «*reviewer*» 撰文赞扬 ‹*play, concert, acting*› [3] Fin (increase nominal value of) 增记 ‹*asset, stock*›

write: ～ head *n* 写磁头; **～-in** *n* Amer [1] (vote) 投给非候选人的票; [2] (candidate) 名字写入选票的非候选人; **～-off** *n* [1] Brit Insur [汽车等] 报废物; [2] Brit (person) 无用的人; (thing) 无用的事物; **the whole holiday was a ～-off** 整个假期都是一场灾难; [3] Fin [呆坏账等的] 注销; **～ once read many disk** *n* 一次写入型光盘

write-protect *vt* 对…进行写保护 ‹*disk, CD, file*›

write-protected *adj* 写保护的

write protection *n* [u] 写保护

writer /ˈraɪtə(r)/ ▸**p. 409** *n* [1] (author) 作者 [2] (professional author) 作家; **a freelance/professional ～** 自由撰稿人/职业作家 [3] (person of particular handwriting style) 书写者; **a neat/messy ～** 字迹工整/潦草的人 [4] Comput 刻录机

writer: ～'s block *n* [u] 写作屏障; **～'s cramp** *n* [u] 书写痉挛

write-up *n* [1] (review) 报刊评论 [2] (account) 书面报道

writhe /raɪð/ *vi* [1] (twist about) 扭动; **to ～ in agony** 痛苦地扭动身体; **to ～ with embarrassment** 尴尬得如坐针毡 [2] fig (suffer emotionally) 极度痛苦

Phrasal verb

- **writhe about, writhe around** *vi* 扭动身体; **to ～ about in agony** 痛苦地扭动身体

writing /ˈraɪtɪŋ/

A *n* [u] [1] (skill) 书写 [2] (words and letters) 文字; **in ～** 以书面形式; **the ～ is on the wall** fig 显然厄运临头了 [3] (handwriting) 笔迹; **his ～ is poor/good** 他的字写得差/好 [4] (authorship) 写作 [5] (literary style) 写作风格 [6] (literature) 文学作品

B **writings** *npl* 作品

writing: ～ case *n* 文具盒; **～ desk** *n* 书桌; **～ lesson** *n* 书写课; **～ materials** *npl* 书写用品; **～ pad** *n* 便笺簿; **～ paper** *n* [u] 信纸; **～ table** *n* 写字台

written /ˈrɪtn/

A *pp* ▸**write**

B *adj* [1] (in writing) 书面的 ‹*agreement, record, inquiry*›; **～ evidence** *or* **proof** 书面证词; **a ～ question/reply** Brit Pol 书面提问/回答; **in ～ form** 以书面形式 [2] (involving writing) 书写的; **～ work/exam** 笔头作业/考试

WRNS *abbr* Brit Hist = **Women's Royal Naval Service** 皇家海军妇女服务队

wrong /rɒŋ, Amer rɔːŋ/

A *adj* [1] (incorrect, inaccurate) 错的 ‹*answer, guess, number*›; **the clock is ～** 这只钟不准; **to hit** *or* **strike the ～ note** Mus 弹错音符; fig «*action*» 不得当; «*words*» 不得体 [2] *usu attrib* (inappropriate, ill-chosen) 不合适的 ‹*decision, job*›; 错误的 ‹*time, number, place*›; **the ～ man/person (for the job/to do sth.)** 不适合（这个工作/做某事）的人; **to take the ～ train** 搭错火车; **to go the ～ way, to take the ～ road** 走错路; **to do/say the ～ thing** 做错事/说错话; **to get** *or* **have the ～ number** 拨错号码; **to be in the ～ place at the ～ time** 在错误的时间去了错误的地方; **to be on the ～ track** fig 想法不对路; **to live on the ～ side of town** colloq 住在城市贫民区; **to get on the ～ side of sb.** colloq 惹某人生气; **to get into the ～ hands** «*information, object*» 落入坏人之手; **to go down the ～ way** «*food*» 呛入气管; ▸**stick**[1] **A1** [3] *pred* (mistaken) 弄错的; **I may be ～** 我也许弄错了; **that's where you're ～** 你错就错在这里; **to be ～ about sb./sth.** 弄错某人/某事物; **I was ～ about her** 我误会她了; **to be ～ in doing sth.** 做某事是错误的; **to be not far ～** colloq 差不离 [4] *usu pred* (immoral) 不道德的; (improper) 不正当的; (unfair) 不公平的; **to be ～ to do sth.** 做某事不正当; **you were ～ to open her letters** 你不该拆她的信; **it is ～ that ...** …是不公平的; **to do something/nothing ～** 做坏事/没做任何坏事; **to be ～ of sb. (to do sth.)** 某人（做某事）是不对的; **to be ～ for sb. (to have to do sth.)** 对某人来说（不得不做某事）是不公平的; **there's nothing ～ in** *or* **with that!** 这没什么不对！; **there's nothing ～ in** *or* **with (me) doing that!** （我）做这件事没什么不对！; **(so) what's ～ with**

that? （那么）这有什么错？；**what's ～ with saying what I think?** 说出我的想法有什么错？ **5▸** *pred* (amiss) 有毛病的; (malfunctioning) 不正常的; **to be ～ with sb./sth.** 某人/某事物出了问题; **there's something ～ with my eye/this computer** 我的眼睛/这台电脑出了问题; **there's something/nothing ～** 有/没问题; **the wording is all ～** 措词完全错了; **what's ～ with him/his leg?** 他/他的腿怎么了？；**to be ～ in the head** colloq 发疯

B *n* **1▸** [u] (evil) 邪恶; **to do no ～** 不做坏事; **in his eyes, she could do no ～** 在他看来，她不可能做坏事; **to have no sense of ～** 根本不知道什么是恶 **2▸** [c] (injustice) 不公正; **to do sb. ～ (in doing sth.)** （做某事）亏待某人; **two ～s don't make a right** 以牙还牙行不通 **3▸** [u] (position of blame) **to be in the ～** 有错; **to put sb. in the ～** 归罪于某人 **4▸** [c] Jur 侵权行为; **a private/public ～** 个人/公共侵权行为

C *vt* **1▸** (treat unfairly) 冤枉; (maltreat) 虐待; **a ～ed wife** 受委屈的妻子 **2▸** formal (judge unfairly) 误解 ‹*person*›; **you ～ed him in making such a suggestion** 你作这样的暗示是误解他了

D *adv* 错误地; **to do sth. ～** 做错某事; **to get sth. ～** 弄错某事; **to get the calculations ～** 计算有误; **to get sb. (all) ～** colloq （完全）误解某人; **to go ～** (err) 犯错; (go awry) 出现问题; (break down) 出故障; **you can't go ～!** 你绝对不会出错的！；**he started to go ～ at college** 他上大学时开始走上歧途; **you won't go (far) ～ if you ...** 如果你…，你不会有什么（大）问题的; **to get in ～ with sb.** colloq 惹得某人讨厌

wrong: ～doer *n* 做坏事的人; **～doing** *n* **1▸** [u] (behaviour) 恶行; **2▸** [c] (act) 作恶; **～-foot** *vt* Brit **1▸** Sport 使措手不及; **2▸** fig (catch off guard) 使仓皇失措

wrongful /ˈrɒŋfl, Amer ˈrɔːŋ-/ *adj* 错误的 ‹*conviction, imprisonment, dismissal, arrest, accusation*›

wrongfully /ˈrɒŋfəli, Amer ˈrɔːŋ-/ *adv* 错误地 ‹*convict, imprison, dismiss, arrest, accuse*›

wrong-headed /ˌrɒŋˈhedɪd, Amer ˌrɔːŋ-/ *adj* 执迷不悟的 ‹*person, action*›; 固执己见的 ‹*opinion, advice, decision, policy*›

wrongly /ˈrɒŋli, Amer ˈrɔːŋ-/ *adv* (incorrectly) 错误地 ‹*act, state, position*›; (unfairly) 不公正地 ‹*accuse, treat*›; **he assumed, ～, that ...** 他误以为…

wrongness /ˈrɒŋnɪs, Amer ˈrɔːŋnɪs/ *n* [u] (incorrectness) 错误; (unfairness) 不公正

wrote /rəʊt/ *pt* ▸**write**

wrought[1] /rɔːt/ *pt, pp* liter ▸**work D5**

wrought[2] *adj* **1▸** *attrib* (beaten) 锻的 ‹*metal*›; **～ silver** 锻银 **2▸** (devised) **well/finely ～** 制作精良的 ‹*music*›; 精心构思的 ‹*plot, essay*›

wrought iron

A *n* [u] 锻铁

B wrought-iron *modif* 锻铁制的 ‹*bedstead, gate, railings*›

wrought ironwork *n* [u] 锻铁制品

wrought up *adj pred* 激动的 ‹*person*›

wrung /rʌŋ/ *pt, pp* ▸**wring A**

WRVS *abbr* Brit **= Women's Royal Volunteer Service** 皇家妇女志愿服务队

wry /raɪ/ *adj* **1▸** (ironic) 挖苦的 ‹*comment*›; 讽刺的 ‹*grin, smile*›; **a ～ sense of humour** 冷嘲式幽默感 **2▸** (displeased) 扭曲的 ‹*expression*›; **to make a ～ face** 露出一副怪相

wryly /ˈraɪli/ *adv* **1▸** (with irony) 挖苦地 ‹*say, comment*›; 讽刺地 ‹*smile, grin*› **2▸** (with displeasure) 面部扭曲地 ‹*look, glance, react*›

wt *abbr* **= weight A**

WTO *abbr* **= World Trade Organization**

wuss /wʊs/ *n* colloq 脓包

WV *n* Amer **= West Virginia**

WWI *abbr* **= World War I** ▸**world war**

WWII *abbr* **= World War II** ▸**world war**

WWW *abbr* **= World Wide Web**

WY *abbr* Amer **= Wyoming**

wych hazel /ˈwɪtʃ ˌheɪzl/ *n* **= witch hazel**

Wyoming /ˌwaɪˈəʊmɪŋ/ *pr n* 怀俄明州

WYSIWYG /ˈwɪzɪwɪɡ/ *adj* **= what you see is what you get** 所见即所得的 ‹*page*›; 所见即所得页面编辑的 ‹*program, editor*›

X, x /eks/

A *n* (*pl* **Xs** *or* **X's**) **1** (letter) [英语字母表的第24个字母] **2** (Roman number) [罗马数字] 10 **3** Math 第一未知量 **4** (unspecified number) 未知数 **5** (anonymous person) 未知的人; (unspecified thing) 未知事物; **Ms X** 某女士 **6** (cross-shaped symbol) X 号; (on map) [标示方位的] X 记号; (at end of letter) [表示亲吻的] X 符号; (beside answer) [标示错误答案的] 叉号; (in voting) [表示选票上投票的] X 号; (as signature) [不会写字者的] 画押
B *vt* (*pt, pp* **x-ed**) 叉掉 ‹*letter*›

Phrasal verb

- **x out** *vt* [**～ sth. out, ～ out sth.**] 画掉 ‹*letter, word*›

xenograft /'zenəgrɑːft, Amer -græft/ *n* 异种移植物

xenon /'ziːnɒn/ *n* [u] 氙

xenophobe /'zenəfəʊb/ *n* (person who hates foreigners) 仇外者; (person who fears foreigners) 惧外者

xenophobia /ˌzenə'fəʊbɪə/ *n* [u] (hate towards foreigners) 仇外; (fear of foreigners) 惧外

xenophobic /ˌzenə'fəʊbɪk/ *adj* (hating foreigners) 仇外的; (fearing foreigners) 惧外的

xenotransplantation /ˌzenəʊˌtrænsplɑːn'teɪʃn, Amer -plæn-/ *n* 异种移植

xerography /ˌzɪə'rɒgrəfi/ *n* [u] 静电印刷术

Xerox® /'zɪərɒks/

A *n* **1** [c] (machine) 静电复印机 **2** [u] (process) 静电复印法 **3** [c] (copy) 静电复印件
B *vt* 静电复印 ‹*document*›

Xinhua /ˌʃɪn'hwɑː/ *pr n* 新华社; **the ～ News Agency** 新华社

Xinjiang /ˌʃɪn'dʒjæŋ/ ►**p. 604** *pr n* **～ (Uighur Autonomous Region)** 新疆（维吾尔自治区）

XL *abbr* **= extra large** 特大号

Xmas /'eksməs/ *n* **= Christmas** colloq 圣诞节

XML *abbr* **= Extensible Markup Language** 可扩展标记语言

X-rated /'eksreɪtɪd/ *adj* **1** Cin, Hist X 级的 [即只供成年人观看的] ‹*film*› **2** (indecent, obscene) 黄色的 ‹*humour, show*›

X-rating *n* Cin Hist X级

X-ray /'eksreɪ/

A *n* **1** [c] Phys X 射线 **2** [c] (image) X 光照片 **3** [c and u] (process) X 光检查; **to have an ～** 做 X 光检查; **to give sb. an ～** 给某人做 X 光检查
B *modif* X 光的 ‹*photography, image, therapy, examination*›
C *vt* 用 X 光检查

X-ray: ～ eyes *npl* X 光眼 [指敏锐的洞察力]; **～ machine** *n* X 光机; **～ radiation** *n* [u] X 光辐射; **～ unit** *n* **1** (department) X 光室; **2** (machine) X 光机

XXL = extra extra large 特特大号

xylophone /'zaɪləfəʊn/ *n* 木琴

xylophonist /zaɪ'lɒfənɪst/ *n* 木琴演奏者 ►**p. 395, p. 409**

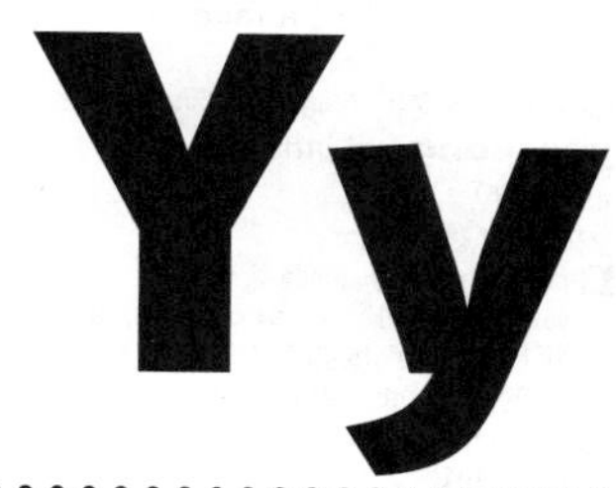

y, Y /waɪ/ *n* (*pl* **Ys** *or* **Y's**) **1** (letter) [英语字母表的第25个字母] **2** **y** Math 第二未知量 **3** (unspecified person or thing) 第二个未知者

Y2K /ˌwaɪtuːˈkeɪ/ *abbr* = **year two thousand** 2000 年 [指计算机千年虫]

yacht /jɒt/
A *n* **1** (sailing boat) 帆船 **2** (pleasure cruiser) 游艇
B *vi* (cruise) 乘游艇; (race) 驾帆船比赛

yachting /ˈjɒtɪŋ/ *n* [u] (cruising) 乘游艇; (racing) 帆船运动; **to go ～** 去乘游艇

yachtsman /ˈjɒtsmən/ *n* (cruising) 游艇驾驶员; (racing) 帆船运动员

yachtswoman /ˈjɒtswʊmən/ *n* (cruising) 女游艇驾驶员; (racing) 女帆船运动员

yack /jæk/, **yackety-yak** /ˌjækəti ˈjæk/ colloq pej
A *vi* 喋喋不休; **to ～ (away** *or* **on) for hours** 东拉西扯地谈几个小时; **to ～ at sth.** 喋喋不休地说某事
B *n* 闲谈; **to have a ～** 闲扯

yah /jɑː/ *excl* colloq **1** (expressing derision) 啧 [表示嘲笑或蔑视] **2** Brit (yes) 是 [英国上流社会用语]

yahoo[1] /jəˈhuː/ *excl* 哇哈 [表示欣喜或激动]

yahoo[2] /ˈjɑːhuː/ *n* colloq pej (coarse person) 粗人

yak[1] /jæk/ *n* Zool 牦牛

yak[2] *vi, n* colloq = **yack**

yakka /ˈjækə/ *n* [u] Austral, NZ colloq 活儿; **hard ～** 辛苦的力气活儿

Yale® /jeɪl/ *n* **～ (lock)** 耶尔锁 [一种圆柱形销栓锁，钥匙呈扁平锯齿状]

y'all /jɔːl/ *pron* Amer colloq = **you-all**

yam /jæm/ *n* **1** (tropical) (tuber) 山药; (plant) 薯蓣 **2** Amer (sweet potato) 甘薯

yammer /ˈjæmə(r)/ *vi* colloq 叽里呱啦地说话; **to ～ (on) about sth.** 哇啦哇啦地说某事

yang /jæŋ/ *n* [u] 阳 [中国古代哲学术语]

Yangtze /ˈjæŋtsiː/ ▶**p. 663** *pr n* **the ～ (River)** 长江

Yank /jæŋk/ *n* colloq pej 美国佬

yank /jæŋk/
A *n* 猛拉; **to give sth. a ～** 猛拽一下某物
B *vt* 猛拉 ‹*rope, handle, person*›; **to ～ the cork from** *or* **out of the bottle** 猛地把瓶塞拔出来
C *vi* 猛拉; **to ～ at sth.** 猛拉某物

Phrasal verbs

- **yank off** *vt* [**～ sth. off, ～ off sth.**] 猛地扯下 ‹*tie, scarf, picture*›; 猛地掀开 ‹*blanket, cover*›; 猛地拔出 ‹*hook*›
- **yank out** *vt* [**～ sth. out, ～ out sth.**] 猛地拔出 ‹*tooth, cork, gun*›

Yankee /ˈjæŋki/
A *n* **1** colloq usu pej 美国佬 **2** Amer (inhabitant of Northern states) 美国北方人; (inhabitant of New England) 新英格兰人 **3** Hist (soldier) [美国南北战争时的] 联邦军队士兵
B *modif* colloq usu pej 美国佬的 ‹*ways, custom, hospitality*›

Yankee doodle *n* 扬基歌 [美国独立战争时期流行的歌曲，现被视为美国民族之歌]

yap /jæp/ *vi* (*pres p etc.* **-pp-**) **1** (bark) «*dog, animal*» 吠叫; **to ～ at sb.** 冲某人汪汪叫 **2** colloq pej (talk) «*person*» 哇哩哇啦地说; **she's been ～ping away at me all day** 她冲我哇哩哇啦地说了一整天

yapping /ˈjæpɪŋ/
A *adj attrib* **1** (barking) 吠叫的 ‹*animal, dog*› **2** colloq pej (talkative) 哇哩哇啦的
B *n* [u] **1** (barking) 狂吠 **2** colloq pej (talking) 说话哇哩哇啦

yard[1] /jɑːd/ *n* **1** Meas 码; **the material is sold by the ～** 这种材料是论码卖的; **the 100-～ sprint/dash** 100 码短跑/冲刺 **2** **yards** fig (substantial distance) 很长的距离; (substantial extent) 巨大的范围; **～s of room/poetry** 足够大的空间/大量的诗 **3** Naut 帆桁

yard[2]
A *n* **1** (of house, farm, hospital) 庭院; (of prison) 放风场; (of school) 操场 **2** (for storage) 堆场; (for construction) 工场; (for sales) 大卖场; (for rolling stock) 调车场; (for livestock) 圈栏 **3** Amer (garden) 花园
B **Yard** *pr n* Brit colloq **the ～ = Scotland Yard**

yardage /ˈjɑːdɪdʒ/ *n* [u and c] 码数

yard: ～arm *n* 帆桁端; **～bird** *n* Amer colloq **1** sl (soldier) 新兵蛋子 [尤指勤务兵]; **2** (prisoner) 囚犯

Yardie /ˈjɑːdi/ *pr n* colloq **1** (Jamaican) 牙买加同胞 **2** Brit (gang member) 亚迪 [牙买加或西印度群岛犯罪团伙成员]

yard: ～ sale *n* Amer [卖旧家什的] 庭院售卖会; **～stick** *n* **1** (measuring rod) 码尺; **2** fig (standard) 衡量标准

yarn /jɑːn/
A *n* **1** [u] Tex 纱线; **wool/cotton/nylon ～** 羊毛线/棉纱/尼龙线 **2** [c] colloq (tale) 离奇故事; **to spin a ～** 编造离奇故事
B *vi* colloq 讲离奇故事

yarrow /ˈjærəʊ/ *n* [u and c] 蓍草

yashmak /ˈjæʃmæk/ *n* [伊斯兰教妇女戴的] 面纱

yaw /jɔː/
A *vi* «*aircraft, ship*» 偏航
B *n* [u] 偏航

yawl /jɔːl/ *n* (sailing boat) 双桅小帆船; (ship's boat) 舰载小艇; (fishing boat) 小渔船

yawn /jɔːn/
A *vi* **1** (open mouth) 打哈欠 **2** fig (gape) «*chasm, abyss, crater, gap*» 裂开
B *vt* 打着哈欠说
C *n* **1** (action) 哈欠; **to give a ～** 打哈欠 **2** fig (bore) 乏味的事情; **the meeting was a ～** 这个会议无聊透顶

yawning /ˈjɔːnɪŋ/
A *adj* **1** (with tiredness, boredom) 打哈欠的 **2** fig (gaping) 开裂的 ‹*chasm, abyss, depths*›; **a ～ gap in the market/law** 市场/法律中的巨大空白; **the ～ gap between …** …之间的鸿沟
B *n* [u] 哈欠

yawp /jɔːp/
A *n* **1** [c] lit (squawk) 嘎嘎叫声 **2** [u] Amer colloq (foolish talk) 蠢话; (noisy talk) 吵嚷
B *vi* **1** (squawk) 嘎嘎叫 **2** Amer colloq (talk foolishly) 扯淡; (talk noisily) 吵嚷

yd = **yard(s)** 码

ye[1] /jiː/ *pron* archaic (you) 你们

ye[2] *det* [the 的拟古形式，用于商店、酒馆等的招牌]

yea /jeɪ/
A *adv* archaic or formal **1** (yes) 是 **2** (indeed) 更确切地说
B *n* **1** (answer) 是 **2** (vote) 赞成票; **the ～s and the nays** 赞成票和反对票

yeah /jeə/ *adv* colloq 是的 [yes 的非正式发音]; **oh ～?** 哦，是吗?

year /jɪə(r), jɜː(r)/ ▶**p. 181**
A *n* **1** (period of time) 年; (measured from any point) 年度; **the academic** *or* **school ～** 学年; **secretary of the ～ award** 年度秘书奖; **the pre-war/post-war ～s** 战前/战后年代; **this/next/last ～** 今年/明年/去年; **the coming/current/past ～** 来年/本年/去年; **the ～ before last/after next** 前年/后年; **every other ～** 每年/每隔一年; **three ～s ago/later** 3 年前/后; **for six ～s running** 连续 6 年; **in future ～s** *or* **～s to come** 在未来的日子里; **I shall retire in two ～s** *or* **two ～s' time** 再过两年我就退休了; **～ after ～** 年年; **～ in, ～ out** 年复一年; **～ by ～** 一年一年地; **a ～-on-～ spending increase** 开销的逐年增长; **all (the) ～ round** 一年到头; **over the ～s** 多年来; **£60,000 a** *or* **per ～ (income)** 每年（收入）6 万英镑; **it'll be a ～ in** *or* **next January since she died** 到一月份，她就去世有一年了; **it was a ～ ago last October that I heard the news** 我是去年十月听到那个消息的; **it's over a ～ since I saw him last** 自从我上次见到他已经过去一年多了; **she got five ～s** colloq 她被判刑 5 年; **it has taken ～s off me** *or* **my life!** 这使我显得年轻了好几岁!; **the job has put ～s on me!** 这工作使我显得老了不少!; **I gave you the best ～s of my life** 我把一生中最好的年华给了你; **the ～s had not been kind to her** 岁月无情，她苍老了很多 **2** *sing* (particular period) 日历年; **in the ～ 1953** 在 1953 年; **in the ～ of Our Lord 1527** archaic 在公元 1527 年; **what ～ is the wine?** 这是什么年份的葡萄酒? **3** (indicating age) 岁; **she is 19 ～s old** *or* **of age** 她 19 岁; **a two-～-old child** 两岁的孩子; **he was in his fortieth ～** 他当时 40 岁 **4** Sch, Univ (year of study, level) 年级; **to be in one's third ～ (at Oxford)** （在牛津）读大三; **a first-～ student** Brit 一年级学生; **to be in (the) third ～** 是三年级的学生; **he was in my ～ at college** 他读大学时和我同届 **5** Brit (pupil) [某年级的] 学生; **to teach the second ～s** 教二年级的学生
B **years** *npl* **1** (age) 岁数; **from her earliest ～s** 从她的早年; **he's well on in ～s now** 他现在已经一大把年纪了; **to grow in ～s** liter 年事渐高 **2** colloq (a long time) 很久; **that would take ～s!** 那要花很长时间!; **it's (been) ～s since we last met!** 我们已经多年没有见面了!; **the worst film I've seen in ～s** 我多年来看过的最糟糕的影片; **he gave up smoking ～s ago** 他老早就戒烟了

year: ～ book *n* **1** (directory) 年鉴; **2** Amer (of school, university) 年刊; **～-end** *n* 年终; **～-end reports/profits/figures** 年终报告/利润/报表; **～ head** *n* Brit 学年主任

yearling /ˈjɪəlɪŋ, ˈjɜː-/
A *n* 一两岁的幼崽; **a race for ~s** 一岁赛马的比赛
B *adj* 一两岁的 ‹*calf, sheep, horse*›

year-long *adj attrib* 持续一年的 ‹*tour, visit, course*›

yearly /ˈjɪəli, ˈjɜː-/
A *adj attrib* **1** (once a year) 一年一次的; (every year) 每年的; **~ accounts/report/meeting** 年度账目/年度报告/年会 **2** (for one year) 一年的 ‹*income, subscription*›
B *adv* (once a year) 一年一次地; (every year) 每年; **the interest is paid ~** 利息按年支付; **twice ~** 每年两次

yearn /jɜːn/ *vi* 渴望; **to ~ for sb./sth.** 渴望某人/某事物; **to ~ to do sth.** 渴望做某事

yearning /ˈjɜːnɪŋ/
A *n* [u and c] 渴望; **a ~ for sb./sth.** 对某人/某事物的渴望; **a ~ to do sth.** 对做某事的渴望
B *adj* 渴望的 ‹*gaze, expression*›; **one's ~ desire/hope/need** 某人的迫切愿望/期盼/需求

year: ~-on-~ *adj* 与上年同期数字相比的 ‹*figures*›; 与上年同期相比的 ‹*growth, increase, decline*›; **~ out** *n* [中学毕业到上大学之前所休的] 间隔年; **to take a ~ out** (中学毕业后) 暂不直接上大学

year-round
A *adj* 全年的 ‹*use, activity, sport*›
B *adv* 一年到头地 ‹*work, play, be available*›

yeast /jiːst/ *n* [u and c] **1** Biol 酵母菌; **a ~ infection** 念珠菌阴道炎 **2** Culin, Ind 酵母; **baker's/brewer's ~** 面包/啤酒酵母

yeasty /ˈjiːsti/ *adj* 酵母味的 ‹*cake, wine*›; **a ~ taste/smell** 发酵的味道/气味

yech, yecch /jek, jʊk/ *excl* colloq = **yuck**

yell /jel/
A *n* 叫喊; **to give** *or* **let out a ~ of delight/pain** 发出高兴/疼痛的叫喊
B *vi* **1** (shout) 叫喊; **to ~ out** 高声喊叫; **to ~ at** *or* **to sb.** 冲某人大喊大叫; **to ~ for sb./sth.** 呼唤某人/大喊要求某物; **to ~ for help** 大喊救命 **2** colloq (sob, cry) 哭喊
C *vt* 叫喊着说; **to ~ abuse** *or* **insults at sb.** 对某人破口大骂; **to ~ that ...** 喊着说…; **to ~ encouragement/warning at sb.** 冲某人大声叫喊鼓劲儿/大声警告某人; **we ~ed ourselves hoarse** 我们嗓子都喊哑了; **to ~ one's head off** colloq (scream loudly) 尖叫; (sob loudly) 号啕大哭

yellow /ˈjeləʊ/ ▸**p. 134**
A *adj* **1** (colour) 黄色的; **to go** *or* **turn ~** 变黄; **to make** *or* **turn sth. ~** 使某物变黄; **~ rain** [东南亚部分地区的] 黄雨 **2** colloq (cowardly) 胆小的 ‹*person*›; **to have a ~ streak** 胆小怕事
B *n* **1** [u and c] (colour) 黄色; **dressed in ~** 穿黄衣服的 **2** [c] (snooker ball) 黄色球
C *vt* liter 使…变黄 ‹*paper, leaves, paint*›
D *vi* «*paper, leaves, paint*» 变黄

yellow: ~-belly *n* colloq 胆小鬼; **~ brick road** *n* 黄砖路 [源于《绿野仙踪》, 指通往财富、成功、无忧生活等的道路]; **~ card** *n* Sport 黄牌; **to show sb. the ~ card** 向某人亮黄牌; **~ fever** ▸**p. 377** *n* [u] 黄热病; **~ flag** *n* **1** Naut 黄色检疫旗; **2** Motor racing [表示前方有险情的] 黄色信号旗

yellowish /ˈjeləʊɪʃ/ ▸**p. 134** *adj* 淡黄的 ‹*colour, decor, effect*›; 发黄的 ‹*shade, light, teeth*›

yellow: ~ jacket *n* Amer colloq 小黄蜂; **~ jersey** *n* [自行车赛各赛段总成绩领先者穿的] 黄色领骑衫; **~ line** *n* [英国路边限制停车的] 黄线; **~ metal** *n* [u] 黄铜

yellowness /ˈjeləʊnɪs/ *n* [u] **1** (of colour) 黄色 **2** colloq (cowardice) 懦弱

yellow: Y~ Pages *pr npl* 黄页 [分类商业电话号码簿]; **~ press** *n* **the ~ press** (newspapers) [进行夸张或耸人听闻报道的] 黄色报刊; (writers of newspaper articles) 黄色报刊文章作者; **Y~ River** ▸**p. 663** *pr n* **the Y~ River** 黄河; **Y~ Sea** *pr n* **the Y~ Sea** 黄海; **~-skinned** *adj* offensive dated 黄皮肤的 ‹*race, person*›

yellowy /ˈjeləʊwi/ ▸**p. 134** *adj* 淡黄的

yelp /jelp/
A *n* (in pain, fear, pleasure, etc.) 尖叫声; (of dog) 吠声
B *vi* (with pain, fear, pleasure, etc.) 尖叫; «*dog*» 吠叫; **to ~ at sb.** 冲某人吠叫

Yemen /ˈjemən/ *pr n* 也门

Yemeni /ˈjeməni/ ▸**p. 503**
A *adj* 也门的
B *n* 也门人

yen¹ /jen/ ▸**p. 174** *n* Fin 日元

yen² colloq
A *n* (strong desire or longing) 瘾; **~ to do sth.** 做某事物的渴望; **~ for sb./sth.** 对某人/某事物的渴望
B *vi* (*pres p etc.* **-nn-**) 渴望; **to ~ for sb./sth.** 渴望某人/某事物; **to ~ to do sth.** 渴望做某事

yeoman /ˈjəʊmən/ *n* (*pl* **yeomen**) Brit Hist **1** **~ (farmer)** (freeholder) 自耕农 **2** (cavalry) 义勇骑兵

yeoman of the guard *n* Brit 王室警卫

yeomanry /ˈjəʊmənri/ *n* [u] Brit Hist **1** (freeholders (collectively)) 自耕农 **2** (cavalry) 义勇骑兵队

yeoman service *n* [u] 长期优良的服务; **to do ~** 提供长期优良的服务

yep /jep/ *excl* Amer colloq 是 [yes的非标准变体]

Yerevan /ˈjerɪvæn/ *pr n* 耶烈万

yes /jes/
A *particle* **1** (giving affirmative response) 是 [表示肯定的答复]; **is this your car? — ~ (it is)** 这是你的汽车吗?——是的; **are you coming? ~ or no?** 你来吗? 来还是不来?; **~ and no** 既是又不是; **are you enjoying it? — ~ and no** 你喜欢它吗?——说不准; **I enjoyed her latest novel — ~, me too** 我喜欢她的新小说——对, 我也是; **report to me tomorrow, corporal! — ~, sir!** 明天向我汇报, 下士! ——是, 长官! **2** (inviting agreement) 是吧 [用于句末表示期待对方肯定回答]; **you'll be there, ~?** 你会在那儿的, 对吧? **3** (contradicting) 不 [用于反驳否定陈述]; **I've never met her before — ~, you have** 我以前从来没有见过她——不对, 你见过; **you don't want to go — ~, I do** 你不想去——不, 我想去 **4** (accepting offer, giving permission) 好的 [表示接受建议或给予许可]; **would you like a drink? — ~, please** 你想喝一杯吗?——好的, 请给我来点儿; **to say ~ to sb./sth.** 同意某人/某事; **she always says ~ to everything** 她总是对什么事情都说"行"; **dad, can I borrow the car? — ~, but be careful** 爸爸, 我可以借用一下汽车吗?——可以, 不过小心点 **5** (asking sb. what they want, responding to an address) [用于询问某人的需求或应答对方的招呼]; **~? how can I help you?** 有什么事吗? 我能帮你什么忙?; **waiter! — ~, sir?** 服务员! ——什么事, 先生?; **oh, Mr Lawrence — ~, what is it?** 哦, 劳伦斯先生——嗯, 什么事? **6** (expressing doubt, encouragement) [表示怀疑对方所说的话或鼓励对方说下去]; **sorry I'm late: the bus didn't come — oh ~?** 对不起, 我迟到了, 公交车没来——哦, 真的吗?; **I'm going to Paris this weekend — ~?** 我周末要去巴黎——嗯? **7** (remembering sth.) 对了 [表示刚想起某事]; **where did I put the keys? oh ~, in my pocket!** 我把钥匙放在哪儿了呢? 哦, 对了, 在我的口袋里! **8** (expressing emphasis, excitement) 真的 [表示强调或表达兴奋激动之情]; **Mrs Smith has just won £2 million — ~! — £2 million!** 史密斯夫人刚刚赢了 200 万英镑——真的! 整整 200 万英镑!; **they've scored another goal — ~!** 他们又进了一个球——好极了! **9** (expressing annoyance) 行了 [表示不耐烦或气恼]; **hurry up: it's late — ~, ~, I'm coming** 快点儿, 要迟到了——行了, 行了, 我就来
B *n* (*pl* **~ses** *or* **~es**) **1** (answer) 同意; **can't you give me a straight ~ or no?** 你就不能直截了当地告诉我同意还是不同意?; **when we took a vote, there were nine ~es and 3 noes** 我们进行了一次投票, 有 9 票赞成, 3 票反对 **2** (person) 赞成的人; **I'll put you down as a ~** 我把你看作赞同者; **the ~es and the noes** 赞成者和反对者

yes-man *n* (*pl* **yes-men**) colloq pej 应声虫

yes-no question *n* 是非问句 [指一般疑问句]

yesterday /ˈjestədeɪ, -di/ ▸**p. 182**
A *n* **1** lit 昨天; **the day before ~** 前天; **~ was the third/Monday** 昨天是 3 号/星期一; **what was ~'s date?** 昨天是几号?; **~'s Times** 昨天的《泰晤士报》; **~'s news** 过时新闻 **2** fig (the past) 不久前; **~'s fashions** 前一阵流行的款式; **~'s man** pej 昨日之星; **all our ~s** liter 我们的往昔岁月; **tales of ~** 旧时传说
B *adv* **1** lit 在昨天; **all (day) ~** 昨天全天; **~ morning/afternoon/evening/night** 昨天上午/下午/傍晚/晚上; **early/late ~** 昨天早些/晚些时候; **it snowed ~** 昨天下雪了; **I saw her only ~** 我昨天才见到她; **a week ago ~** 一个星期前的昨天; **it was ~ week** *or* **a week ~** 是在一周前的昨天; **to remember sth. as if it were ~** 记得某事就像是昨天刚发生似的 **2** fig (in the past) 在不久前; **everything seems to have been built only ~** 一切似乎是昨天才建成的

yesteryear /ˈjestəjɪə(r)/ *n* [u] liter 昔日; **the fashions of ~** 过时的款式

yes-vote *n* 赞成票

yet /jet/
A *adv* **1** (by now, by then) 还; **the children were not ~ in bed** 孩子们还没有上床睡觉; **has he arrived ~?** 他已经到了吗?; **as ~** (up to now) 到目前为止; (up to then) 到那时为止; **he is as ~ unmarried** 他至今未婚; **it was an as ~ unexplored island** 那是一座当时仍无人涉足的岛屿 **2** (immediately) 即刻; **don't go ~** 先别走; **we don't need to start ~** 我们没有必要马上就开始; **they won't come just ~** 他们现在还来不了 **3** (indicating remaining possibility, time, or amount) 仍然; **she may win ~, she may ~ win** 她仍然可能赢; **you're young ~** 你还年轻; **we have ~ to decide what action to take** 我们尚需决定采取什么行动; **there's a year to go ~** 还有一年的时间 **4** (with superlatives) (up till now) 到目前为止; (up till then) 到那时为止; **it's the best ~** 这是迄今为止最好的; **it was the highest building ~ constructed** 这是当时建成的最高建筑 **5** (even, still) 甚至; **more surprising ~** *or* **~ more surprising was her reaction** 她的反应甚至更加令人吃惊; **the noise grew ~ louder** 噪音甚至变得更大 **6** (indicating increase) 再; **prices were cut ~ again** 价格再一次降低; **she made ~ another excuse** 她又找了个借口; **~ another diet book** 又一本关于节食的书; **snow, snow, and ~ more snow** 雪啊雪, 没完没了的雪 **7** (in spite of that) 不过; **so strong and ~ so gentle** 如此强壮却又如此温和
B *conj* 然而; **it's a small apartment, ~ it's surprisingly spacious** 这是一套小公寓房, 却宽敞得出奇

yeti /ˈjeti/ *n* 雪人 [据传生活在喜马拉雅山的巨型长毛动物]

yew /juː/ *n* **1** [c and u] **~ (tree)** 紫杉 **2** [u] (wood) 紫杉木

Y-fronts /ˈwaɪfrʌnts/ *npl* Brit 前缝呈倒 Y 形的男内裤

YHA *abbr* Brit = **Youth Hostels Association** 青年旅舍协会

Yid /jɪd/ *n* colloq offensive 犹太佬

Yiddish /ˈjɪdɪʃ/ ▸**p. 426**
A *adj* 意第绪语的
B *n* [u] 意第绪语

yield /jiːld/
A *vt* **1** (produce) «*land, sea*» 出产 ‹*crop, harvest*›; «*cow, mine*» 产 ‹*milk, coal*›; **trees that no**

longer ~ fruit 不再结果实的树 **2** Fin (return) «*investment, business*» 产生 ‹*interest, profit*›; **shares ~ed 8%** 股票收益 8%; **to ~ millions in taxes** 带来数百万的税收 **3** (provide) «*talks, experiment, method*» 产出 ‹*results, benefit*›; **to ~ new insights into genetics** 对遗传学提供新见解 **4** (surrender) 让出 ‹*town, territory, land, right*›; 缴出 ‹*weapon*›; **to ~ the floor to sb.** 允许某人插话; **to ~ the right of way (to sb./sth.)** Aut （给某人/某物）让行; **to ~ ground** 放弃阵地 **5** formal (reveal) «*universe, investigations*» 泄露 ‹*information, secret, facts*›; **a close examination ~ed valuable clues to the police** 经过仔细检查，警方获得了宝贵线索

B *vi* **1** (give in) «*person, government*» 屈服; **to ~ to pressure/persuasion/temptation** 屈服于压力/听从劝说/经不住诱惑; **to ~ to entreaties** 答应恳求; **I ~ to your expertise in this matter** 在这方面我要靠你的专业知识; **to ~ to no one** 对谁都不示弱 **2** (break, bend under pressure) «*lock, door*» 被弄开; «*bridge*» 倒塌; «*beam, cable*» 变形 **3** (be superseded) «*technology, practice, farmland*» 被取代 **4** (produce) «*land, sea, mine, cow*» 产; **to ~ well/poorly** 产量高/产量低 **5** esp Amer Aut «*driver, vehicle*» 让路; **'~'** (on sign) "让车"

C *n* **1** [u and c] (amount produced) 产量; **the annual milk ~** 年产奶量; **a low/high ~ (of sth.)** （某物的）低产/高产; **a high-~ variety** 高产品种 **2** [c] (return on shares, investments) 收益率; **a ~ of 10%** 10% 的利润; **a high-~ bond** 高收益率债券 **3** [c] Chem 收获率; **a 75% ~** 75% 的收获率

Phrasal verb

• **yield up**

A *vt* [**~ sth. up, ~ up sth.**] 泄露 ‹*secret, treasure*›

B *v refl* **to ~ oneself up to sth.** 屈从于某事物; **to ~ oneself up to the pleasures of the moment** 沉湎于一时的欢娱

yield curve *n* 收益曲线

yielding /ˈjiːldɪŋ/ *adj* **1** (pliable) 柔性的 ‹*material*› **2** (compliant) 顺从的 ‹*person*›

yield: ~ point *n* [弹性材料的] 屈服点; **~ stress** *n* 屈服应力; **~ to maturity** *n* [债券的] 到期收益

yin /jɪn/ *n* [u] 阴 [中国古代哲学术语]; **~ (and) yang** 阴阳

yip /jɪp/ *n, vi* Amer colloq **= yelp**

yippee /ˈjɪpiː/ *excl* colloq 咦 [表示十分高兴或兴奋，通常为儿童用语]

YMCA *abbr* **1** **= Young Men's Christian Association** 基督教青年会 **2** [c] (hostel) 基督教青年会旅舍

yob /jɒb/, **yobbo** /ˈjɒbəʊ/ *ns* Brit colloq pej 小无赖

yodel /ˈjəʊdl/

A *vi* (*pres p etc.* **-ll-**) 用约德尔唱法唱 [指用瑞士传统的真假嗓音交替演唱法唱歌]

B *n* (cry) 约德尔唱腔; (song) 约德尔歌曲

yoga /ˈjəʊɡə/ *n* [u] 瑜伽修行法; **to take up ~** 开始修练瑜伽功; **to do ~** 练瑜伽; *modif* 瑜伽的 ‹*class, teacher, exercise*›

yoghurt, yoghourt, yogurt /ˈjɒɡət, Amer ˈjəʊɡərt/ *n* **1** [u] (food) 酸奶; **natural ~** 原味酸奶 **2** [c] (tub) 一盒酸奶

yogi /ˈjəʊɡi/ *n* 瑜伽修行者

yoke /jəʊk/

A *n* **1** [c] (for oxen) 轭 **2** [c] (*pl* **~** *or* **~s**) (pair of oxen) 同轭的一对牛 **3** [c] (for person) 轭形扁担 **4** [u] fig liter (oppression) 奴役; **the tyrant's ~** 暴君的统治 **5** [c] (on garment) 抵肩

B *vt* **1** (harness together) 用轭把…套在一起 ‹*oxen, horses*› **2** (harness to another) 用轭套; **to ~ an ox/horse (up) to sth.** 用轭把牛/马套在某物上 **3** **to ~ (together)** (join together) 使…连在一起 ‹*people, machines*› **4** (join to another) 连接; **to ~ sth. to sth.** 将某物连接到某物上

yokel /ˈjəʊkl/ *n* pej 乡巴佬 pej

yolk /jəʊk/ *n* 蛋黄

yomp /jɒmp/ *vi, n* Brit 负重越野行军

yon /jɒn/ *adj* liter or dial **= yonder B**

yonder /ˈjɒndə(r)/

A *adv* archaic or dial 那边; **up/over/down ~** 在那边

B *adj attrib* archaic or dial 那边的 ‹*object, tree, house*›

C *n* [u] **to disappear** *or* **fly off into the wide blue ~** colloq 消失得无影无踪

yonks /jɒŋks/ *npl* Brit colloq 很长时间; **for ~** 很久; **~ ago** 很久以前

yoof /juːf/ *n* [u] esp Brit colloq hum (youth, young people) 年轻人; **~ culture/TV** 青年人的文化/电视节目

yoo-hoo /ˈjuːhuː/ *excl* 喂; **~! I'm over here!** 喂！我在这里！

yore /jɔː(r)/ *n* [u] liter **of ~** 很久以前的; **in days of ~** 在很久以前

Yorks. *abbr* Brit **= Yorkshire**

Yorkshire /ˈjɔːkʃə(r)/ *pr n* 约克郡

Yorkshire: ~man /-mən/ *n* 约克郡男子; **~ pudding** *n* [u and c] Brit 约克郡布丁 [由面粉、蛋、牛奶烘焙而成，常与烤牛肉同食]; **~ terrier** *n* 约克夏㹴; **~woman** *n* 约克郡女子

you /juː, jʊ/ *pron* **1** (person addressed) 你; **are ~ busy?** 你忙吗？; **don't ~ talk to me like that!** 不许你那样对我说话！; **I don't think that hairstyle is (very) ~** colloq 我觉得这种发型不（太）适合你; **there's a manager for ~!** colloq iron 你多像个经理啊！; **~ there! come over here!** 喂，你！过来！; **~ idiot!** 你这个白痴！ **2** (people addressed) 你们; **~ two** 你们俩; **all of ~, ~ all** 你们大家; **those of ~ who ...** 你们当中…的那些人; **so ~ both left at ten?** 那你们俩都是 10 点离开的吗？; **we're very different from ~ English/~ people** 我们与你们英国人/你们这些人很不一样; **~ girls, stop talking!** 你们这些女孩子，别说话了！ **3** (people in general) [泛指任何人]; **~ never know!** 事情很难说！; **~ can't beat Italian shoes** 意大利鞋质量没说的; **they say sweets give ~ spots** 听说吃糖长痘痘

you-all *pron* Amer colloq 你们

you'd /juːd/ colloq **1** **= you had** ▸**have** **2** **= you would** ▸**would**

you: ~-know-what *pron* colloq [不需或不便言明的] 那个东西; **~-know-who** *pron* colloq [不需指名的] 那个人

you'll /juːl/ colloq **1** **= you shall** ▸**shall** **2** **= you will** ▸**will**[1]

young /jʌŋ/ ▸**p. 15**

A *adj* **1** (not old) 年轻的 ‹*person, nation, organization*›; 幼小的 ‹*animal, plant*›; 幼年的 ‹*mountain range, rock*›; **children as ~ as five years of age** 年仅 5 岁的幼童; **they have a ~ family** 他们家的孩子还小; **her ~ man** 她的男朋友 [年长者用语]; **a ~ audience** 青少年观众; **to be ~ at heart** 人老心不老; **to be ~ for one's age** 比实际年龄显得小; **he's a ~ forty** 他长得年轻，不像 40 岁的人; **to marry/die ~** 结婚/去世得早; **you're only ~ once** 青春只有一次; **I'm not so ~ as I was** *or* **used to be** 我已经不年轻了; **she is two years ~er than him** *or* **than he is** 她比他小两岁; **the two ~er/~est children** 这两个年龄较小的/最小的孩子; **my ~er brother** 我的弟弟; **my ~est sister** 我的幺妹; **the ~er generation** 年轻的一代; **in my ~er days** 在我年轻的时候; **we're not getting any ~er** 岁数不饶人啊; **Mr Smith the ~er** 小史密斯先生; **a ~ wine** 新酿的葡萄酒 **2** (near beginning stages) 刚开始的 ‹*evening, project*›; 初期的 ‹*institution*›; **the ~ moon** 新月; **the night is ~** 夜幕初垂 **3** (of young people) 年轻人的 ‹*love, look, fashion*›

B *npl* **1** (young people) **the ~** 青年人; **~ and old (alike)** （不分）老少 **2** (offspring) (of animal) 幼兽; (of bird) 幼禽; **to be with ~** 怀胎

young blood *n* [c and u] 新鲜血液 [指组织中的新成员、新生力量]

youngish /ˈjʌŋɪʃ/ *adj* 颇年轻的

young-looking /ˈjʌŋlʊkɪŋ/ *adj* 看上去年轻的

young offender *n* Brit 少年犯

young offenders' institution *n* Brit 少年犯管教所

young professional *n* 年轻的专业人士

youngster /ˈjʌŋstə(r)/ *n* **1** (child) 儿童 **2** (young person) 少年; **today's ~s** 如今的小青年

Young Turk *n* 少壮派激进分子

your /jɔː(r), jʊə(r)/ ▸**p. 487** *det* **1** (of person addressed) 你的; **what is ~ name?** 你叫什么名字？; **you've got a dirty mark on ~ face** 你脸上有一块污迹; **you and ~ bright ideas!** iron 你的主意真高明啊！ iron **2** (of people addressed) 你们的; **have you all washed ~ hands?** 你们都洗过手了吗？; **you can wipe those smirks off ~ faces!** 你们别一脸傻笑了！ **3** (one's) [泛指] 大家的; **dentists advise you to have ~ teeth checked every six months** 牙医建议每 6 个月要作一次牙齿检查; **the sight is enough to break ~ heart** 这种景象足以令人心碎; **you have to buy ~ tickets at the door** 得在门口买票 **4** colloq (well known, often talked about) [用来表示某人或某事物很有名或常被提及]; **this is ~ typical English pub** 这就是典型的英国酒馆; **~ average student can't afford to live in places like this** 所谓的普通学生住不起这样的地方 **5** **Your** (in titles) [用于头衔]; **Y~ Majesty/Excellency** 陛下/阁下

you're /jʊə(r), jɔː(r)/ colloq **= you are** ▸**be**

yours /jɔːz, Amer jʊərz/ ▸**p. 487** *pron* **1** (of person addressed) 你的; **is that book ~?** 那本书是你的吗？; **he's a colleague of ~** 他是你的一位同事; **~ was not an easy task** 你的任务不轻松 **2** (of people addressed) 你们的; **our room is slightly smaller than ~** 我们的房间比你们的稍小一点儿; **this is my copy: ~ are on the table** 这是我的复印件，你们的在桌子上 **3** **Yours** (in letters) 你的 [信函末尾署名前使用]; **Y~, Nick** 你的尼克; **Y~ ever** 永远是你的

yourself /jɔːˈself, Amer jʊərˈself/ *pron* **1** (reflexive) 你自己; **have you hurt ~?** 你伤着自己了吗？; **help ~** 请随便用; **(all) by ~** (alone) （完全）独自地; (unaided) （完全）独立地; **do you live by ~?** 你是独自生活吗？; **are you sure you did this exercise by ~?** 这个练习的确是你独立完成的吗？; **(all) to ~** （完全）独有; **I'm going to be away next week, so you'll have the office to ~** 我下周要离开，所以办公室就归你一个人了 **2** (emphatic) 你本人 [表示强调]; **you ~ said that ...** 你亲口说过…; **I gave you ~ the report** 我把报告交给了你本人 **3** (in normal state) 正常状态; **you're not ~ today** 你今天不大对劲儿; **you don't seem quite ~ today** 今天你好像不太舒服; **do you feel ~ today?** 你今天感觉好吗？ **4** (acting naturally) 行为自然; **don't act sophisticated: just be ~** 不要故作高深，自然点儿吧 **5** colloq (you) 你; **and ~? how are you?** 你呢？你好吗？

yourselves /jɔːˈselvz, Amer jʊərˈ-/ *pron* **1** (reflexive) 你们自己; **did you hurt ~?** 你们伤着自己了吗？; **help ~!** 你们随便用！; **what have you been doing with ~?** 你们自己是怎么打发时间的啊？; **(all) by ~** (alone) （完全）独自地; (unaided) （完全）独立地; **are you going by ~?** 就你们自己去吗？; **(all) to ~** 独有; **I'm sure you'd like to have the house to ~ for once** 我肯定你们希望独自享用一次这所房子 **2** (emphatic) 你们本人 [表示强调]; **didn't they ask you ~ to be there?** 他们请过你们本人去那儿吗？;

this must be obvious to you ~ 这一点你们自己一定很清楚 **3** (in normal state) 正常状态; **you weren't ~ last night: what was wrong?** 你们昨天晚上不大对劲儿，是怎么回事?; **you don't seem ~: is something the matter?** 你们似乎不太舒服，有什么事吗?; **are you really feeling ~ today?** 你们今天真的感觉好吗? **4** (acting naturally) 行为自然; **just be ~ and have a good time** 你们放开好好玩吧 **5** colloq (you) 你们; **is it just ~?** 就是你们吗?

youth /juːθ/ *n* **1** [u] (period of being young) 青年时期 [尤指成年以前]; **in (the days of) my ~** 在我年轻时; **in early ~** 在少年时期 **2** [u] (state of being young) 年轻; **because of/despite his ~** 因为/尽管他年轻; **full of ~ and vitality** 充满青春活力的; **~ will have its way** *or* **its fling** Prov 年轻人不会受约束 **3** [c] (*pl* **~s** /juːðz/) (young man) 青年男子; **a gang of ~s** 一帮小伙子 **4** + *v sing or pl* (young people) 青年人; **the voice of ~** 年轻人的呼声

youth culture *n* [u] 青年文化

youthful /ˈjuːθfl/ *adj* **1** (young) 年轻的 ‹*person*›; (young-looking) 显得年轻的 ‹*appearance*› **2** (typical of youth) 年轻人的 ‹*quality*›; 青春的 ‹*enthusiasm*›

youthfulness /ˈjuːθflnɪs/ *n* [u] 年轻

youth: ~ hostel *n* 青年旅社; **~ hostelling** *n* [u] 到处住青年旅社; **~ leader** ▸**p. 409** *n* [青年中心等机构的] 青年活动领导人; **~ work** *n* [u] 青年工作; **~ worker** ▸**p. 409** *n* 青年工作者

you've /juːv/ colloq **= you have** ▸**have**

yowl /jaʊl/

A *n* (of cat, dog) 嚎叫; (of baby, person) 号哭

B *vi* «*dog, cat*» 嚎叫; «*baby, person*» 号哭

yo-yo® /ˈjəʊjəʊ/

A *n* Brit 悠悠球 [一种玩具]

B *modif* 无规律的 ‹*dieter*›; 波动的 ‹*market, inflation*›

C *vi* colloq «*person*» 犹豫不决; «*prices, inflation*» 上下波动

yo-yo: ~ dieting *n* [u] 时有时无的节食; **~ effect** *n* [不断脱离和进入某状态的] 悠悠球效应

yr *abbr* **= year A**

Y-shaped /ˈwaɪʃeɪpt/ *adj* Y形的

ytterbium /ɪˈtɜːbɪəm/ *n* [u] 镱

yttrium /ˈɪtrɪəm/ *n* [u] 钇

yuan /jʊˈɑːn/ ▸**p. 174** *n* (*pl* **yuan**) 元 [中国货币单位]

yucca /ˈjʌkə/ *n* 丝兰 [龙舌兰科植物]

yuck /jʌk/ *excl* Brit colloq 呸

yucky /ˈjʌki/ *adj* Brit colloq 难以下咽的 ‹*meal*›; 难闻的 ‹*smell*›; 令人厌恶的 ‹*film, play*›; 肮脏的 ‹*mess*›

Yugoslav /ˈjuːɡəʊslɑːv/ ▸**p. 503, p. 426** Hist

A *adj* (of Yugoslavia) 南斯拉夫的 ‹*republic, government, army*›; (of the people) 南斯拉夫人的 ‹*tradition, custom, languages*›

B *n* 南斯拉夫人

Yugoslavia /ˌjuːɡəʊˈslɑːvɪə/ *pr n* Hist 南斯拉夫; **the former Republic of ~** 前南斯拉夫共和国

Yugoslavian /ˌjuːɡəʊˈslɑːvɪən/ *adj, n* Hist **= Yugoslav**

yuk *excl* Brit colloq **= yuck**

yukky /ˈjʌki/ *adj* Brit colloq **= yucky**

Yukon /ˈjuːkɒn/ *pr n* **1** (river) **the ~ (River)** 育空河 **2** (territory) **the ~** 育空地区

Yukon Territory *pr n* **the ~** 育空地区

Yule /juːl/ *n* [u] dated 圣诞节

Yule log *n* **1** (log) [传统上在圣诞节放入炉中燃烧的] 圣诞节原木 **2** (cake) 圣诞节原木形大蛋糕

Yuletide /ˈjuːltaɪd/ *n* [u] dated 圣诞期间; **~ greetings** 圣诞祝词

yum /jʌm/ *excl* colloq **= yummy A**

yummy /ˈjʌmi/ colloq

A *excl* 味道好极了

B *adj* **1** (delicious) 好吃的 ‹*food, meal*› **2** (attractive) 性感的 ‹*person*›

yummy mummy *n* colloq hum 年轻漂亮的妈妈

yum-yum *excl* colloq **= yummy A**

Yunnan /ˌjuːnˈnæn/ ▸**p. 604** *pr n* **~ (Province)** 云南（省）

yup /jʌp/ *excl* Amer colloq **= yep**

yuppie /ˈjʌpi/ colloq pej *n* 雅皮士

> **yuppie**
>
> 雅皮士，亦作 yuppy。指城市中受过良好教育、收入水平很高的职业人士。该名称出现于 20 世纪 80 年代，为 young urban professional（年轻的都市职业人士）或 young upwardly-mobile professional（社会地位上升的年轻职业人士）的首字母缩拼。雅皮士追求个人享受、爱炫富，不似嬉皮士（▸**hippie**）那样关心社会问题。

yuppie flu ▸**p. 377** *n* [u] colloq pej 雅皮士流感 [指肌痛性脑脊髓炎]

yuppified /ˈjʌpɪfaɪd/ *adj* colloq pej 雅皮士化的 ‹*area, lifestyle*›

yuppify /ˈjʌpɪfaɪ/ *vt* colloq pej 使…雅皮士化 ‹*area*›

yuppy /ˈjʌpi/ *n* colloq pej **= yuppie**

yurt /jɜːt/ *n* 蒙古包

YWCA *abbr* **1** **= Young Women's Christian Association** 基督教女青年会 **2** (hostel) 基督教女青年会旅社

y

Zz

Z, z /zed, Amer ziː/ *n* (*pl* **Zs** *or* **Z's**) 1 (letter) [英语字母表的第26个字母] 2 Math 第三未知量 3 (unspecified person or thing) 第三个未知者

Zagreb /ˈzɑːgreb/ *pr n* 萨格勒布

Zaire /zɑːˈɪə(r)/ *pr n* 扎伊尔

Zairean, Zairian /zɑːˈɪən, zɑːˈɪərɪən/ ▸p. 503
A *adj* 扎伊尔的
B *n* 扎伊尔人

Zambezi /ˌzæmˈbiːzi/ ▸p. 663 *pr n* **the ~** 赞比西河

Zambia /ˈzæmbɪə/ *pr n* 赞比亚

Zambian /ˈzæmbɪən/ ▸p. 503
A *adj* 赞比亚的
B *n* 赞比亚人

zany /ˈzeɪni/ *adj* 滑稽可笑的 ‹*person, play*›; 古怪的 ‹*humour*›

Zanzibar /ˌzænzɪˈbɑː(r)/ *pr n* 桑给巴尔岛

zap /zæp/ colloq
A *excl* 嚓 [表示动作突然或迅速]; **you just pull the lever, and ~! the whole thing explodes** 只要拉一下控制杆，然后轰的一声，整个东西就会炸开
B *vt* (*pres p etc.* **-pp-**) 1 (destroy) 杀死 ‹*person*›; 摧毁 ‹*town, building*›; **to ~ the enemy's artillery** 消灭敌人的炮兵部队 2 (strike) 猛击; **~ him one!** 揍他！ 3 (treat) [用激光辐射等] 消除; **to ~ a tumour with a laser** 用激光杀死肿瘤
C *vi* (*pres p etc.* **-pp-**) 1 (move quickly) 快速移动; **to ~ into town** 快速进入城区 2 (use remote control) 快速变换频道; **to ~ from channel to channel** 快速调台
D *n* 1 [u] (energy) 精力; **she's so full of ~, she never stops!** 她精力旺盛，永远闲不住！ 2 [c] (burst) 震击

zapper /ˈzæpə(r)/ *n* colloq 遥控器

zappy /ˈzæpi/ *adj* colloq 活泼的

Z-bed *n* esp Brit 折叠床

Z-bend *n* Z形弯道

zeal /ziːl/ *n* (religious fanaticism) 狂热; (enthusiasm) 热情; **revolutionary/religious ~** 革命/宗教热情; **~ to do sth.** 做某事的激情

zealot /ˈzelət/ *n* often pej 狂热者; **a religious ~** 宗教狂热分子

zealotry /ˈzelətri/ *n* [u] often pej 狂热; **religious ~** 宗教狂热

zealous /ˈzeləs/ *adj* 热情的 ‹*person, missionary*›; 狂热的 ‹*follower, disciple*›; 积极的 ‹*determination*›; **to be ~ about** *or* **in sth.** 对某事物充满激情

zealously /ˈzeləsli/ *adv* 热情地

zebra /ˈzebrə, ˈziː-/ *n* (*pl* **~** *or* **~s**) 斑马

zebra: ~ crossing *n* Brit 斑马线; **~ stripes** *npl* 斑马纹

zebu /ˈziːbuː/ *n* 瘤牛

zed /zed/ *n* Brit 字母Z

zee /ziː/ *n* Amer 字母Z

Zen /zen/ *n* [u] [日本的] 禅宗

zenith /ˈzenɪθ/ *n* 1 Astron 天顶 [天体到达的最高点] 2 fig (high point) 顶峰; **to reach the ~ of one's career** 达到事业的顶峰; **the British Empire was at its ~** 大英帝国当时处于鼎盛时期

Zeppelin /ˈzepəlɪn/ *n* 齐柏林飞艇 [德国在一战中使用的一种大型飞艇]

zero /ˈzɪərəʊ/ ▸p. 521
A *n* (*pl* **~s**) 1 [u and c] Math 零; **five, four, three, two, one, ~** 五、四、三、二、一、零 [用于倒计时] 2 [u] (nil) 全无; **prospects of success were put at ~** 成功无望; **I rated my chances as ~** 我觉得自己根本没有机会 3 ▸p. 814 [u] Meteorol (point on scale) 零度; **above/below ~** 零度以上/以下; **absolute ~** 绝对零度 4 [c] colloq (insignificant person) 无足轻重的人; **her husband's a real ~** 她丈夫是个十足的废物; **to go from hero to ~** 从英雄沦落到无名小卒
B *modif* 零的; **to show ~ interest in sth.** 对某事物一点儿兴趣也没有; **a period of ~ growth** 零增长期
C *vt* 把…归零 ‹*instrument, scales*›

Phrasal verb

- **zero in** *vi* 1 Mil 瞄准某物/某人; **to ~ in on sth./sb.** 瞄准 2 (focus) 集中注意力; **to ~ in on sth./sb.** 全神贯注于; **to ~ in on the key issues** 集中讨论关键问题

zero: ~-based *adj* 从零开始的; **~-based budgeting** *n* 零基预算; **~-emission vehicle** *n* 零排放车辆; **~ gravity** *n* [u] 零重力; **~ hour** *n* [u] 1 Mil [发动进攻的] 零时; 2 fig (critical time) 关键时刻; **~ option** *n* 零选择裁军建议; **~ point** *n* [u] 最低点; **~-rated** *adj* Brit 免付增值税的 ‹*goods*›; **~ rating** *n* [c and u] Brit 免付增值税; **~ sum** *n* [一方得益与另一方受损相当的] 零和; **a ~-sum game** 零和游戏; **~ tolerance** *n* [u] 零容忍

> **zero tolerance**
>
> 零容忍。20 世纪 90 年代纽约警察局采取的一种政策，即严格执法，即使对初犯和轻微犯罪者也要拘捕并起诉，以预防更为严重的犯罪。政策实施后，纽约犯罪率迅速降低。同一时期，英国也曾采取类似的政策。

zest /zest/ *n* [u] 1 (enthusiasm) 热情; **a ~ for sth.** 对某事物的热情 2 (added interest, flavour) 趣味; **to add ~ to sth.** 为某事物添加趣味 3 Culin 柑橘皮

zester /ˈzestə(r)/ *n* 果皮刮刀

zestful /ˈzestfʊl/ *adj* 热情的 ‹*person, participation*›; 高涨的 ‹*enthusiasm*›; 热烈的 ‹*performance, commitment*›

Zhejiang /ˌdʒɜːˈdʒjæŋ/ ▸p. 604 *pr n* **~ (Province)** 浙江（省）

zigzag /ˈzɪgzæg/
A *n* 曲折线条; **there are ~s in the road** 道路蜿蜒曲折
B *adj attrib* 弯弯曲曲的 ‹*road, pattern*›
C *adv* 弯弯曲曲地 ‹*go, move*›
D *vi* (*pres p etc.* **-gg-**) «*road, river*» 蜿蜒; «*person, vehicle*» 曲折前进

zilch /zɪltʃ/ *n* colloq 1 [u] (nothing) 没有; **they paid me ~** 他们一个子儿也没付给我 2 [c] (insignificant person) 废物

zillion /ˈzɪlɪən/ colloq
A *adj* 不计其数的; **a ~ times** 无数次
B *n* 巨大数量; **~s of things** 不计其数的东西

Zimbabwe /zɪmˈbɑːbwi, -weɪ/ *pr n* 津巴布韦

Zimbabwean /zɪmˈbɑːbwɪən/ ▸p. 503
A *adj* (of Zimbabwe) 津巴布韦的; (of the people) 津巴布韦人的
B *n* 津巴布韦人

Zimmer® /ˈzɪmə(r)/ *n* **~ (frame)** 齐默助行架

zinc /zɪŋk/ *n* [u] 1 Chem 锌; **the ~ industry** 锌产业 2 (galvanized iron or steel) 镀锌物; **a ~ coating** 镀锌层

zinc: ~ blende /ˈzɪŋk blend/ *n* [u] 闪锌矿; **~ ointment** *n* [u] 氧化锌软膏; **~ white** *n* [u] 锌白

zing /zɪŋ/ colloq
A *n* 1 [c] (sound) 飕飕声 2 [u] (energy) 活力
B *vi* «*bullet, car*» 呼啸而过
C *vt* Amer 斥责

zingy /ˈzɪŋi/ *adj* colloq 充满活力的

Zion /ˈzaɪən/ *pr n* 1 Geog (hill) 锡安山; (city) 耶路撒冷 2 Relig (kingdom of heaven) 天国 3 Relig (Christian Church) 基督教会

Zionism /ˈzaɪənɪzəm/ *n* [u] 犹太复国运动

Zionist /ˈzaɪənɪst/
A *n* 犹太复国主义者
B *adj* 犹太复国的

zip /zɪp/
A *n* 1 [c] esp Brit (zipper) 拉链; **the ~ is stuck** 拉链卡住了; **to do up/undo a ~** 拉上/拉开拉链 2 [c] *sing* colloq (sound) 飕飕声; **the ~ of a bullet** 子弹的呼啸声 3 [u] colloq (energy) 活力; **she doesn't have much ~ these days** 这些天她有些萎靡不振 4 [c] Amer Post = **zip code** 5 [u] Amer colloq (nothing) 零; **to know ~ about computers** 对电脑一窍不通
B *vt* (*pres p etc.* **-pp-**) 1 (fasten) 拉…的拉链; **to ~ one's bag open/shut** 拉开/拉上袋子的拉链; **she ~ped herself into her dress** 她穿上连衣裙，拉好拉链 2 Comput 压缩 ‹*file*› 3 (send quickly) 使快速移动; **to ~ a pass out to the receiver** 嗖地把球传给接球手
C *vi* (*pres p etc.* **-pp-**) 1 (fasten) «*skirt, bag*» 拉上拉链; **the dress ~s at the back** 这条连衣裙的拉链在背后 2 (move quickly) 快速移动; **to ~ along** 快速向前; **a car ~ped past us** 一辆车从我们身边呼啸而过; **to ~ through one's work** 快速干完工作; **the morning ~ped by** 上午一下子就过去了

Phrasal verbs

- **zip on**
A *vt* [**~ sth. on, ~ on sth.**] 用拉链装上; **to ~ the hood on** 用拉链把风帽装上; **to ~ on a jacket** 穿上夹克，拉好拉链
B *vi* 用拉链装上; **the hood ~s on like this** 风帽是这样用拉链装上去的

- **zip up**
A *vt* 1 [**~ sth. up, ~ up sth.**] (fasten) 拉上…的拉链 ‹*dress, bag*› 2 [**~ sb. up, ~ up sb.**] (fasten zip for) 给…拉上拉链; **can you ~ me up please?** 请帮我拉上拉链好吗？
B *vi* «*dress, bag*» 拉上拉链; **the jacket ~s up right to the neck** 这件夹克的拉链可以一直拉到脖颈处

zip: ~ **code** *n* Amer 邮政编码; ~ **disk** *n* 极碟; ~ **drive** *n* ZIP驱动器; ~ **fastener** *n* = **zip A1**; ~ **file** *n* 压缩文件; ~ **gun** *n* Amer colloq 自制手枪; **~-in, ~-on** *adjs* 有暗拉链的 ‹*collar, sleeves*›

zipper /ˈzɪpə(r)/ *n* esp Amer = **zip A1**

zippered /ˈzɪpəd/ *adj* esp Amer 带拉链的 ‹*jacket, pocket*›

zip pocket *n* 拉链口袋

zippy /ˈzɪpi/ *adj* colloq 充满活力的 ‹*player, performance*›; 速度快的 ‹*car*›

zip-up *adj* 拉链的 ‹*jacket, case*›

zircon /ˈzɜːkɒn/ *n* [u] 锆石

zirconium /zəˈkəʊnɪəm/ *n* [u] 锆

zit /zɪt/ *n* colloq 痘

zither /ˈzɪðə(r)/ *n* 齐特琴

zloty /ˈzlɒti/ **▸p. 174** *n* (*pl* ~, **~s** *or* **zloties**) 兹罗提 [波兰货币单位]

zodiac /ˈzəʊdɪæk/ *n* **1** (belt of the heavens) 黄道带; **the signs of the** ~ 黄道十二宫 **2** (diagram) 黄道十二宫图

zombie /ˈzɒmbi/ *n* **1** (corpse brought to life) [靠巫术] 起死回生的僵尸 **2** fig colloq (dull, lifeless person) 木讷呆板的人 **3** Comput [被黑客控制的] 僵尸电脑

zombified /ˈzɒmbɪfaɪd/ *adj* colloq 无精打采的

zonal /ˈzəʊnl/ *adj* 区域的

zone /zəʊn/

A *n* **1** (area, section) 地带; **industrial/residential/pedestrian** ~ 工业区/住宅区/步行区; **a no-parking** ~ 禁止停车区; **United are still in the relegation** ~ 联队仍在降级区徘徊 **2** Mil, Pol 分区; **a demilitarized** ~ 非军事区 **3** Admin (for charging) 区段; **a ticket that covers all ~s** 全程票 **4** Amer Post 邮区

B *vt* **1** (divide) 将…分成区 ‹*town, territory*› **2** (assign) 将…划作特殊区域 ‹*area*›; **to be ~d for enterprise/housing** 被划作经济开发区/住宅区

zoning /ˈzəʊnɪŋ/ *n* [u] 分区制

zonk /zɒnk/ *vt* colloq 打; **he really ~ed me** 他把我打惨了

Phrasal verb

- **zonk out** colloq

A *vi* **1** (fall asleep) 倒头沉睡; **I ~ed out until after mid-day** 我倒下便睡，午后才醒来 **2** (lose consciousness) 昏过去

B *vt* [~ **sb. out**] (cause to fall asleep) 使入睡; (cause to lose consciousness) 使昏过去

zonked, zonked out /zɒŋkt/ *adjs* colloq **1** (intoxicated) (by alcohol) 醉酒的; (by drugs) 麻醉的 **2** (exhausted) 筋疲力尽的

zoo /zuː/ *n* (*pl* **~s**) **1** (for animals) 动物园 **2** fig (confused situation) 混乱; **it's a complete ~ in the lobby** 大堂里一片混乱

zoo keeper **▸p. 409** *n* (animal attendant) 动物园饲养员; (owner) 动物园主; (director) 动物园管理员

zoological /ˌzuːəˈlɒdʒɪkl, ˌzəʊə-/ *adj* 动物学的

zoological garden *n* 动物园

zoologist /zuːˈɒlədʒɪst, zəʊˈɒl-/ **▸p. 409** *n* 动物学家

zoology /zuːˈɒlədʒi, zəʊˈɒl-/ *n* [u] 动物学

zoom /zuːm/

A *vi* colloq **1** (move quickly) 疾行; **to ~ around the streets** 在街上飚车; **I saw you ~ing past** 我看见你飞驰而过 **2** fig (rise sharply) «*prices, profits*» 急剧上升

B *n* **1** Phot, Cin = **zoom lens** **2** Cin (camera shot) 变焦摄影

Phrasal verbs

- **zoom in** *vi* «*camera*» 拉近; «*photographer*» 拉近镜头; **the camera ~ed in on the podium** 镜头将指挥台拉近了
- **zoom out** *vi* «*camera*» 拉远; «*photographer*» 拉远镜头

zoom lens *n* 变焦距镜头

zoomorphic /ˌzuːəˈmɔːfɪk, ˌzəʊə-/ *adj* (having animal forms) 动物形的; (having gods of animal form) 动物形神祇的

zooplankton /ˈzuːəʊˌplæŋktən, ˈzəʊəʊ-/ *n* [u] 浮游动物

Z-shaped *adj* Z形的 ‹*bend*›

zucchini /zuːˈkiːni/ *n* [u and c] (*pl* ~ *or* **~s**) Amer = **courgette**

Zulu /ˈzuːluː/

A *n* (*pl* ~ *or* **~s**) **1** [c] (person) 祖鲁人 **2** [u] (language) 祖鲁语

B *adj* 祖鲁的; (of the people) 祖鲁人的; (of the language) 祖鲁语的

Zurich /ˈzjʊərɪk/ *pr n* 苏黎世

zygote /ˈzaɪgəʊt/ *n* 受精卵

English irregular verbs
英语不规则动词表

Infinitive 不定式	Past tense 过去式	Past participle 过去分词
arise	arose	arisen
awake	awoke	awoken
babysit	babysat	babysat
be	*was/were	been
bear	bore	borne
beat	beat	beaten
become	became	become
befall	befell	befallen
beget	begot, *archaic* begat	begotten
begin	began	begun
behold	beheld	beheld
bend	bent	bent
beseech	besought, beseeched	besought, beseeched
beset	beset	beset
bespeak	bespoke	bespoken
bet	bet	bet
bid[1]	bid	bid
bid[2]	*bid, bade	*bid, bidden
bind	bound	bound
bite	bit	bitten
bleed	bled	bled
blow	blew	blown
break	broke	broken
breastfeed	breastfed	breastfed
breed	bred	bred
bring	brought	brought
broadcast	broadcast, broadcasted	broadcast, broadcasted
browbeat	browbeat	browbeaten
build	built	built
burn[1]	burnt, burned	burnt, burned
burst	burst	burst
bust[1]	bust, busted	bust, busted
buy	bought	bought
cast	cast	cast
catch	caught	caught
choose	chose	chosen
cleave[1]	cleaved, clove	cleaved, cleft
cling	clung	clung
come	came	come
cost	*cost, costed	*cost, costed
countersink	countersunk	countersunk
creep	crept	crept
crow[2]	crowed, crew	crowed
cut	cut	cut
deal[1]	dealt	dealt
dig	dug	dug
dive	dived, *Amer* dove	dived
do[1]	did	done
draw	drew	drawn

Infinitive 不定式	Past tense 过去式	Past participle 过去分词
dream	dreamed, dreamt	dreamed, dreamt
drink	drank	drunk
drive	drove	driven
dwell	dwelt, dwelled	dwelt, dwelled
eat	ate	eaten
fall	fell	fallen
feed	fed	fed
feel	felt	felt
fight	fought	fought
find	found	found
fit	fitted, *Amer* fit	fitted, *Amer* fit
flee	fled	fled
fling	flung	flung
floodlight	floodlit	floodlit
fly[1]	flew	flown
forbear	forbore	forborne
forbid	forbade, forbad	forbidden
forecast	forecast, forecasted	forecast, forecasted
foresee	foresaw	foreseen
foretell	foretold	foretold
forget	forgot	forgotten
forgive	forgave	forgiven
forgo	forwent	forgone
forsake	forsook	forsaken
forswear	forswore	forsworn
freeze	froze	frozen
gainsay	gainsaid	gainsaid
get	got	got, *Amer* gotten
gird	girded, girt	girded, girt
give	gave	given
go	went	gone
grind	ground	ground
grow	grew	grown
hamstring	hamstrung	hamstrung
hang	*hung, hanged	*hung, hanged
have	had	had
hear	heard	heard
heave	*heaved, hove	*heaved, hove
hew	hewed	hewed, hewn
hide[1]	hid	hidden
hit	hit	hit
hold	held	held
hurt	hurt	hurt
inlay	inlaid	inlaid
input	input, inputted	input, inputted
inset	inset	inset
interweave	interwove	interwoven
keep	kept	kept
ken *Scot*	kent, kenned	kent, kenned

English irregular verbs 英语不规则动词表

Infinitive 不定式	Past tense 过去式	Past participle 过去分词
kneel	knelt, *esp Amer* kneeled	knelt, *esp Amer* kneeled
knit	knitted, knit	knitted, knit
know	knew	known
lay[1]	laid	laid
lead[1]	led	led
lean[2]	leaned, *Brit* leant	leaned, *Brit* leant
leap	leaped, *Brit* leapt	leaped, *Brit* leapt
learn	learned, *Brit* learnt	learned, *Brit* learnt
leave	left	left
lend	lent	lent
let[1]	let	let
lie[1]	lay	lain
light[1]	lit, lighted	lit, lighted
lose	lost	lost
make	made	made
mean[1]	meant	meant
meet	met	met
miscast	miscast	miscast
misdeal	misdealt	misdealt
mishear	misheard	misheard
mishit	mishit	mishit
mislay	mislaid	mislaid
mislead	misled	misled
misread /mɪs'riːd/	misread /mɪs'red/	misread /mɪs'red/
misspell	misspelled, *esp Brit* misspelt	misspelled, *esp Brit* misspelt
misspend	misspent	misspent
mistake	mistook	mistaken
misunderstand	misunderstood	misunderstood
mow	mowed	mowed, mown
offset	offset	offset
outbid	outbid	outbid
outdo	outdid	outdone
outgrow	outgrew	outgrown
output	output	output
outrun	outran	outrun
outsell	outsold	outsold
outshine	outshone	outshone
overbid	overbid	overbid
overcome	overcame	overcome
overdo	overdid	overdone
overdraw	overdrew	overdrawn
overeat	overate	overeaten
overfeed	overfed	overfed
overfly	overflew	overflown
overhang	overhung	overhung
overhear	overheard	overheard
overlay	overlaid	overlaid
overlie	overlay	overlain
overpay	overpaid	overpaid
override	overrode	overridden
overrun	overran	overrun
oversee	oversaw	overseen
oversell	oversold	oversold

Infinitive 不定式	Past tense 过去式	Past participle 过去分词
oversew	oversewed	oversewn
overshoot	overshot	overshot
oversleep	overslept	overslept
overspend	overspent	overspent
overtake	overtook	overtaken
overthrow	overthrew	overthrown
overwrite	overwrote	overwritten
partake	partook	partaken
pay	paid	paid
plead	pleaded, *Amer* pled	pleaded, *Amer* pled
preset	preset	preset
proofread	proofread /'pruːfred/	proofread /'pruːfred/
prove	proved	proved, proven
put	put	put
quit	quit	quit
read /riːd/	read /red/	read /red/
rebuild	rebuilt	rebuilt
recast	recast	recast
redo	redid	redone
redraw	redrew	redrawn
rehear	reheard	reheard
remake	remade	remade
rend	rent	rent
repay	repaid	repaid
reread /-riːd/	reread /-red/	reread /-red/
rerun	reran	rerun
resell	resold	resold
reset	reset	reset
resit	resat	resat
retake	retook	retaken
retell	retold	retold
rethink	rethought	rethought
rewind	rewound /ˌriː'waʊnd/	rewound /ˌriː'waʊnd/
rewrite	rewrote	rewritten
rid	rid	rid
ride	rode	ridden
ring[2]	rang	rung
rise	rose	risen
run	ran	run
saw[2]	sawed	sawn *esp Brit*, sawed *esp Amer*
say	said	said
see[1]	saw	seen
seek	sought	sought
sell	sold	sold
send	sent	sent
set	set	set
sew	sewed	sewed, sewn
shake	shook	shaken
shear	sheared	sheared, shorn
shed[2]	shed	shed
shine	*shone, shined	*shone, shined
shit	shitted, shit, shat	shitted, shit, shat
shoe	shod	shod
shoot	shot	shot

English irregular verbs 英语不规则动词表

Infinitive 不定式	Past tense 过去式	Past participle 过去分词
show	showed	shown, showed
shrink	shrank	shrunk, shrunken
shut	shut	shut
simulcast	simulcast	simulcast
sing	sang	sung
sink	sank	sunk
sit	sat	sat
slay	slew	slain
sleep	slept	slept
slide	slid	slid
sling	slung	slung
slink	slunk	slunk
slit	slit	slit
smell	smelled, *esp Brit* smelt	smelled, *esp Brit* smelt
smite	smote	smitten
sow[2]	sowed	sown, sowed
speak	spoke	spoken
speed	*sped, speeded	*sped, speeded
spell[3]	spelled, *esp Brit* spelt	spelled, *esp Brit* spelt
spend	spent	spent
spill[1]	spilt, spilled	spilt, spilled
spin	spun	spun
spit[1]	spat, *esp Amer* spit	spat, *esp Amer* spit
split	split	split
spoil	spoiled, *Brit* spoilt	spoiled, *Brit* spoilt
spotlight	spotlighted, spotlit	spotlighted, spotlit
spread	spread	spread
spring	sprang, *esp Amer* sprung	sprung
stand	stood	stood
stave	*staved, stove	*staved, stove
steal	stole	stolen
stick[2]	stuck	stuck
sting	stung	stung
stink	stank, stunk	stunk
strew	strewed	strewed, strewn
stride	strode	stridden
strike	struck	struck
string	strung	strung
strive	strove, strived	striven, strived
sublet	sublet	sublet
swear	swore	sworn
sweep	swept	swept
swell	swelled	swollen, swelled
swim	swam	swum
swing	swung	swung
take	took	taken
teach	taught	taught
tear[1]	tore	torn
telecast	telecast	telecast
tell	told	told
think	thought	thought
thrive	throve, thrived	thriven, thrived
throw	threw	thrown
thrust	thrust	thrust
tread	trod	trodden, trod
typecast	typecast	typecast
typeset	typeset	typeset
unbend	unbent	unbent
underbid	underbid	underbid
undercut	undercut	undercut
undergo	underwent	undergone
underlie	underlay	underlain
underpay	underpaid	underpaid
undersell	undersold	undersold
understand	understood	understood
undertake	undertook	undertaken
underwrite	underwrote	underwritten
undo	undid	undone
unfreeze	unfroze	unfrozen
unlearn	unlearned, *Brit* unlearnt	unlearned, *Brit* unlearnt
unstick	unstuck	unstuck
unwind /ʌn'waɪnd/	unwound /ʌn'waʊnd/	unwound /ʌn'waʊnd/
uphold	upheld	upheld
upset	upset	upset
wake	woke	woken
waylay	waylaid	waylaid
wear	wore	worn
weave	wove	woven
wed	wedded, wed	wedded, wed
weep	wept	wept
wet	wet, wetted	wet, wetted
win	won	won
wind[2] /waɪnd/	wound /waʊnd/	wound /waʊnd/
withdraw	withdrew	withdrawn
withhold	withheld	withheld
withstand	withstood	withstood
work	*worked, *liter* wrought	*worked, *liter* wrought
wring	wrung	wrung
write	wrote	written

* used according to context 用何种形式按上下文而定

信函范例

A. 假日及旅游

明信片

16.8.2010 [1]

Dear John [2],

Greetings from Beijing! Got* here a couple of days ago, but already quite charmed with the place (despite the traffic). Today we visited the Forbidden City. What a sense of grandeur and history!

Then* on to beautiful Beihai Park. We have been eating so well. Last night* Mongolian hotpot. We are here till Monday, then on to Shanghai for a few days, before heading home. Hope* your mother is now fully recovered.

See you soon [3],

Mark and Juliet

STAMP

Mr J. Roberts [4]
The Willows
49 North Terrace
Kings Barton
Nottinghamshire
NG8 4LQ
United Kingdom [5]

[1] 为节省空间，通常不写发信人的地址。日期通常以数字书写。注意美式英语中的日期书写顺序为月、日、年，如例中应为 8.16.2010。

[2] 写明信片时，对收信人的称呼通常先用 Dear，然后加收信人的名。这是英语非正式通信中的常见写法。

[3] 其他非正式的结束语还用 All the best 或 Best wishes。若发信人与收信人关系亲密，也可使用 Love 或 Love from。

[4] 地址中可用正式的方式书写收信人的姓名，前面可冠以 Mr、Ms、Mrs 或 Miss。

[5] 注意英语中地址的书写顺序为：收信人姓名、（房屋名、）房屋号码及街道名、村镇、地区、国家，与中国的习惯写法不同。

* 注意：明信片为非正式信件，为节省空间，通常在意思明了的情况下，可省略句中的主语与动词。

预订酒店房间

5 Prince Edward Road
Oxford OX7 3AA
Tel: 01865 3224XX
Email: all@fairhurst.demon.co.uk

23 April 2010

The Manager
Torbay Hotel
Dawlish
Devon EX37 2LR

Dear Sir or Madam

I saw your hotel listed in the ***Inns of Devon*** [1] guide for last year, and wish to reserve a double room with shower [2] in a quiet position for the period 6th–15th August (nine nights), as well as a single room for our son.

If you have anything suitable for this period, please let me know the price and whether you require a deposit.

Yours faithfully [3]

Charles Fairhurst

Charles Fairhurst

[1] 如果在某出版物或网站上得到这家酒店的信息，通常需指明。

[2] 也可以说 with bath 或 with en suite bathroom。

[3] 如果收信人为未具名者（即 Sir 或 Madam），英式英语通常使用的正式结束语为 Yours faithfully，而美式英语中则为 Sincerely。

取消预订酒店房间

Flat 18, 9/F, Peony Building
76 Park Road
Wan Chai
Hong Kong, China

July 20th 2010

Mrs J. Warrington
Downlands
Steyning
West Sussex
BN44 6LZ

Dear Mrs Warrington,

Unfortunately I have to cancel my/our reservation for the week of August 14th [1]. Owing to unforeseen circumstances [2], I/we have had to abandon my/our holiday plans.

I very much regret having to cancel [at such a late stage] and hope it does not cause you too much inconvenience.

Yours sincerely [3],

Joy Chan

Joy Chan

[1] 也可以说 for the period 14th-20th August。

[2] 也可以作具体说明，如 owing to my father's sudden death/my husband's illness（由于家父突然辞世/由于外子罹患疾病）。

[3] 注意，若收信人为具名者（即某先生、某女士等），英美的正式结束语都为 Yours sincerely。

Model letters

A. Holidays and travel plans

Holiday postcard [1]

1 0 0 0 8 0

中国邮政明信片
Postcard
People's Republic of China

邮票

尊敬的赵先生:

我和丹妮已于中秋节前夕抵达杭州。这是我们来北京工作后的首次旅行。杭州的风景实在太迷人了，尤其是西湖美景，更让人流连忘返。杭州的美食也让我们大快朵颐。我们将如期返京。即颂

金安!

约翰·劳斯
2010/09/28 [2]

杭州西湖 Hangzhou China

中国北京市海淀区

中山路12号109室

赵强先生

邮政编码310000

[1] The address on a postcard has a fixed format: the recipient's post code is written in the upper-left corner, followed by the recipient's address and name written on the right side of the card. The sender's post code is written in the bottom-right corner.

[2] The date is written on a new line after the signature. Note that in Chinese the date is written in the following order: year/month/day.

Booking a hotel room

桂林山水大酒店
尊敬的经理先生:

我们一家三口，拟于9月29日至10月3日赴桂林旅游。从朋友处得知[1]贵酒店环境幽雅，设备良好，价格公道。我们想在贵酒店预订双人标准房和单人房各一间，请予安排为盼。如无问题，请来函告知具体房号、价格[2]。谢谢！此致

敬礼

钱京生
2010/09/10

来信地址、邮编见信封

[1] It is usual to mention how you know about the hotel when booking a room or other facilities.

[2] You may request from the hotel a reply confirming your booking.

Cancelling a hotel booking

桂林山水大酒店
尊敬的经理先生:

我们十分抱歉地[1]通知您，因接紧急任务不能脱身，桂林之旅无法践行[2]，无奈不得不取消原先预订的房间（时间9月29日至10月3日，房号301、302），请予见谅。如果因此而给贵酒店造成经济损失，我们愿给予一定的经济补偿。再次表示歉意！此致

敬礼

钱京生 谨启
2010/09/22

[1] Words such as 抱歉 or 遗憾 are polite expressions of regret.

[2] Provide good reasons for cancelling your booking.

A. 假日及旅游

致函索取旅游小册子

The Stone House
15 Hill Street
Kendal
Cumbria LA9 4ND

3 March 2010

Bounding Out
112 Piccadilly
London W1J 9ES

Dear Sir/Madam

Please could you send me your brochure 'Trekking Holidays in Southern Europe'[1], as advertised on your website.

I am looking to find a one- or two-week organized trek, ideally in the Pyrenees, in May or June this year.

In addition, I would be grateful if you could send me your 'Weekend City Breaks'[2] brochure for 2010.

If you have anything suitable for this period, please let me know the price and whether you require a deposit.

Thank you for your assistance.

Yours faithfully

SARAH THOMAS

Sarah Thomas

1 假日跟团进行户外体育活动，是与亲友旅游之外的另一选择。
2 周末长假可选择旅行社包括机票和酒店在内的全包旅游。

投诉旅行社

674 Chestnut Street
Philadelphia, PA 19098

August 21, 2010[1]

The Director
SunFun Co.
251 Walnut Street
Philadelphia, PA 19029

Dear Sir/Madam

This July my husband and I spent a week, from July 15 to July 22[1], in your SunFun "luxury hotel" in Miami. Our room was hardly luxurious. The shower did not work and was not repaired until the last day of our vacation, despite persistent complaints. The room was directly above the kitchen, so we were unable to sleep at night because of the noise, and there was a heavy smell of cooking at all times. The hotel was not, as your brochure described, 5 minutes' walk from the sea, but nearly 30 minutes.

Our tour representative refused to move us to another room, and would not even listen to our complaints. I wish to claim $250 (half the cost of the vacation[2]), which I am sure you will agree is fair compensation[3] for our ruined vacation. I await your prompt reply.

Sincerely yours[4],

R. Divine

Mrs R. Divine

1 注意美式的日期书写方式。如果提及年份，则需在日期与年份间加逗号。
2 美式英语中 vacation 较为常用，英式英语中则多用 holiday 。
3 应当明示索赔金额，可使协商更为简单明了。
4 Sincerely yours 是美式英语中常用的正式信函结束语。

提议换房暂住

4 LONGSIDE DRIVE
CAMBRIDGE, MA 02142

May 13, 2010

Dear Mr and Mrs Candiwell

We found your names listed in the 2010 *Owners to Owners* handbook and would like to know if you are still participating in the property-exchange[1] program.

Our three-bedroomed house is located in a quiet village only ten minutes' drive from Cambridge center. We have one boy aged twelve. If you are interested, and if three weeks in July or August would suit you, we will be happy to exchange references.

We look forward to hearing from you.

Sincerely yours

Li Gang and Wu Heping

1 换房暂住是欧美盛行的一种家庭旅行方式。

确认换房暂住

Trout Villa
Burnpeat Road
Cheyenne, WY 82044
(613) 34565XX

February 5, 2010

Dear Mr and Mrs Tamberley,

As per our phone call, this is to confirm our arrangement to exchange houses from August 8th to August 22nd inclusive. We enclose various leaflets about our area[1].

As we mentioned on the phone, you will be able to pick up the keys from our neighbors, the Brownes, at 'Whitley House' (see enclosed plan).

We look forward to an enjoyable exchange.

Sincerely yours,

Shirley Dankworth

1 换房暂住需签署正式合约，合约通常订立于未曾谋面的人之间，但双方通常互通信息，如介绍当地的设施等。

A. Holidays and travel plans

Request for travel brochure[1]

上海市春秋旅行社:

暑假将至，我和几个朋友想去澳门旅游。澳门是我们向往已久的地方，但我们对澳门的旅游景点、住宿、交通等情况知之甚少。希望贵旅行社能寄来一份澳门旅游指南之类的小册子，以便我们了解澳门，做好旅游安排。有劳贵旅行社了，谢谢！
此致
敬礼！

蒋希文
2010.6.2

联系地址：无锡市解放路76号　邮编：214100

[1] Travel information is usually given free of charge.

Complaining about a travel agent

上海市消费者协会:

今年5月1日至5日，我们随本市青年旅行社组织的旅行团去香港旅游。根据旅行合同，旅行团在港期间应住四星级酒店标准房，游览香港海洋公园、迪士尼乐园、太平山、维多利亚港和大屿山五处景点。但旅行团到港后，我们住的是三星级酒店标准房，也没能去大屿山观光（旅行社的解释是因天气原因），而是硬拉我们去一家珠宝店购物。我们认为青年旅行社没有全面履行旅行合同。旅行团回沪后，我们向旅行社提出每人赔付五百元（包括住宿费差价和一观光点的损失费），但旅行社坚持只能赔付二百元。虽几经交涉，意见不能统一。无奈之下，我们只能向你们投诉，请你们出面调解，希望能得到一个满意的结果。此致
敬礼

旅行团成员 王建国、苏阿根、汪为民等
2010年6月20日

联系电话：654400XX

Inviting a friend to go on a trip

大鹏学兄:

春回大地，百花争妍，到处是一派生机蓬勃的景象。我已约好三位老同学去苏州踏青旅游。你素喜游山玩水，摄影技艺又特别高超，有你同行，此行定会尽兴。我们决定于4月2日上午8时在我家集合出发，希望你能准时到来。万一你因事不能成行，请给我一个回信，以免大家空喜一场。祝
安好！

弟 志伟上
3月28日

B. 社交

祝贺圣诞/新年

64 Argyle Gardens
London SE7 5FL

19 December 2010 1

Dear Shirley and Brian,

Merry Christmas and all the best for the New Year! I hope you're both well and that Brian is enjoying his new job.

This year seems to have flown by—I don't know where all the time has gone! The kids 2 have countless activities. Sandra is still doing her swimming, and Paul is now playing drums in a band! Mick and I can't keep up! Over the summer we all went to Greece for a holiday. It was absolutely wonderful!

Next time you're in London, you must get in touch and come over for dinner. You know you're always welcome.

All the very best to you both,

Julie

1 在非正式信件中，通常不写收信人的地址。
2 kids 是对孩子们的非正式叫法。

礼物致谢函

35 Winchester Drive
Stoke Gifford
Bristol
BS34 8PD

Dear Aunt Carol and Uncle Pete 1,

Thank you very much for your Christmas present. Mum and Dad gave me the first book in the series for my birthday, and I could not wait to get the second! I spent the whole of Boxing Day reading.

I am really looking forward to seeing you in Shropshire.

Love from, 2

Bert

1 这是在信件中对叔婶的常见称呼。
2 Love from 是亲戚间通常使用的结束语。

生日聚会邀请函

You are cordially invited to Yunling's
35th birthday party.

The festivities will commence
at 8pm on 26th June
at 15 Stirling Avenue.

Please bring a bottle. 1

RSVP 2 07658 5692XX

1 朋友间的非正式聚会中，客人通常自带酒水。请柬上注明 Please bring a bottle 或 PBAB 。
2 RSVP 源于法语习语 Répondez s'il vous plaît，意为“敬请赐复”。

婚礼邀请函

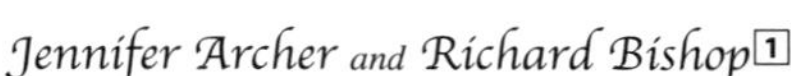

Jennifer Archer and Richard Bishop 1

request the pleasure of your company to celebrate their marriage

at St John's Church, Boughton-on-the-Green

on Saturday 7 August 2010 at 2 o'clock

and afterwards at the

Kensington Golf Club, Harrietsham 2

RSVP by 1 July:

64 Hatters Lane
Boughton-on-the-Green
Cambridge
CB19 2XJ

1 这是较为现代的婚礼请柬，新婚夫妇直接邀请客人。注意，新娘的姓名写在新郎之前。更为传统的做法是由新娘的双亲发出请柬。
2 婚礼通常分为两部分。首先是婚礼本身，通常在教堂或户籍登记处举行。然后是喜筵，通常包括餐宴、舞会和发言。美式婚礼还包括由新郎双亲于婚礼前夜举办的小型预婚宴。

B. Social correspondence

Christmas and New Year greetings[1]

李志明先生:

值此新年来临之际，谨向您致以节日的问候和良好的祝愿!

衷心希望在新的一年里，能进一步拓展我们之间的友好合作。恭祝新年快乐，万事如意! [2]

乔一民 敬启
12月20日

[1] Such kind of ceremonial greetings are usually put in short messages. In this example, the greeting is addressed to a business partner.

[2] A short greeting at Christmas might be 圣诞快乐. 新年快乐 is the greeting given at New Year.

Thanking for a present

亲爱的舅舅:

在我即将踏进大学校门之际，您送给我一台笔记本电脑，此刻，我实在无法用语言来表达我的感激之情。我知道，这不只是您对我的关爱，更寄托着殷切的期望。我一定会努力学习，发愤图强，以优异的成绩回报您对我的厚望。恭祝大安!

甥 志强[1] 敬上[2]
2010年8月20日

[1] If you are an older relative of the recipient you do not need to sign your name at the end of the letter. It is enough just to indicate your kinship, for example 父字, 姑姑 or 二叔.

[2] It is usual to sign your name using the form of address used by the recipient, for example 学生 XXX 敬上 or 儿 XX 敬上.

Invitation to a birthday party

芳芳:

5月25日是我的18岁生日。光阴荏苒，转眼间我已长大成人。我和父母商定，在生日那天晚上，在家里举行生日派对，邀请亲朋好友欢聚一堂，热闹一番。你是我最要好的朋友，特函请你参加。届时恭候光临

文佩 敬请
2010年5月15日

Wedding invitation

建民好友[1]:

兹定于2010年8月18日假紫薇大酒店举行结婚典礼，敬治喜筵，届时恭候光临

陈尔东
李珊珊 鞠躬

地址: 红星路335号紫薇大酒店二楼白玉兰厅
时间: 下午7时入席

[1] Wedding invitations today include the name of the recipient, unlike traditional Chinese wedding invitations which did not.

B. 社交

接受婚礼邀请回复函

32b Well Street
Cambridge
CB1 7UA

15 May 2010

Dear Jenny and Rick,

Thank you very much for your wedding invitation. And many congratulations again! Xiao Gu and I would be delighted to attend.

Do you have a wedding list[1], I wonder? We would be glad to know.

We are both looking forward to celebrating with you.

Best wishes,

Zhang Jiyang

[1] 受邀参加婚礼的客人通常要送给新婚夫妇礼物，以日常家居用品居多，英美的新婚夫妇通常会列出他们想要的礼物。通常礼品在某一家百货商店选定，列表可以在网上找到。

结婚礼物致谢函

64 Hatters Lane
Boughton-on-the-Green
Cambridge
CB19 2XJ

22 August 2010

Dear Zhang Jiyang and Gu Chang

I am writing to thank you for your wedding present. Whenever Rick and I use the tablecloth, we will think of you both!

We were so pleased you were able to attend the wedding. To have so many good friends present made it a special event for us.

Our honeymoon[1] in Cyprus was wonderfully relaxing. We are now back settling in to the reality of married life! We look forward to seeing you before too long.

Best wishes

Jenny

[1] 新婚夫妇一般会在新婚后外出度蜜月。

获邀出席晚宴后的致谢函

79A Westgate
Wakefield
Yorks

25/09/10

Dear Caroline and John,

This is a brief note to thank you for your invitation to dinner last night.

It was a very pleasant occasion. I thoroughly enjoyed meeting your friends, and relished John's delicious Pavlova. I appreciate your thoughtfulness in helping me make the transition to Wakefield.

I hope to be able to return the invitation soon.

Best wishes

Peter

不能出席晚宴致歉函

14 Primula Close
Chester-le-Street, DH3 3QZ

2 May 2010

Dear Mr and Mrs Bates

Thank you for your invitation to dinner on Friday 14 May to celebrate your daughter Yvonne's birthday.

I regret that I will be unable to attend, owing to a prior engagement[1]. I am actually performing in the school play that evening.

Again, I appreciate your kind invitation and will be sorry not to be there. I very much hope you all enjoy the evening.

Yours sincerely

Terry Ackerman

[1] 拒绝邀请时，通常使用 prior engagement 这一套语。

B. Social correspondence

Accepting a wedding invitation[1]

尔东好友：

顷接二位的婚礼请柬，十分高兴。你和珊珊自小青梅竹马，感情甚笃，如今喜结同心，真乃天作之合。届时我一定偕夫人一同前往祝贺。祝你们新婚快乐，幸福美满！

建民

8月15日

[1] A reply is expected to a wedding invitation. Gifts are presented to the newlyweds before the wedding ceremony begins.

Thanking for a wedding present

为民挚友：

在我和玉华结婚前夕，收到你寄来的珍贵礼物，在此表示衷心的感谢！如今你远在他乡，不能参加我们的婚礼，十分遗憾。今随信寄去我们的婚照一张，留作纪念。他日返回故里，我们定当补备菲酌，畅叙别情。祈望多加保重。祝

一切顺利！

弟 希文 谨启

2010年10月5日

Thanking for a dinner

郑念祖先生：

十分荣幸能应邀出席前晚在香山饭店举行的报业同仁迎春晚宴。在晚宴上，我不仅认识了许多业界德高望重的前辈，也结识了不少风华正茂的新锐。特别是您在晚宴上的致辞，更让我得益匪浅，让我看到了报业的光辉前景，使我明白了肩负的重任。作为业界的一名后生，自当奋发有为，敬业敬岗，为振兴报业多做贡献。

再次感谢您的盛情邀请！即颂

时绥

学生 黄思齐 敬上

2010年1月20日

Declining a dinner invitation

郑念祖先生：

首先要感谢先生的盛情邀请。我知道，这个报业同仁迎春晚宴，是一次业界的群英会。我原拟欣然前往，不料家父突发心肌梗塞，紧急住院，实在无法脱身[1]，错失了这次与业界朋友相聚的机会。今特函表示歉意，请予见谅。

此致

敬礼！[2]

钱卫平 谨启

2010年1月16日

[1] This kind of letter is intended to express both thanks and regret. You must give a good reason for declining an invitation.

[2] The most frequently used closing words are 此致　敬礼. According to different times of year, you may also use 即颂　春安/夏安/秋安/冬安. 祝　新春/圣诞/生日快乐 are used at festivals and 祝您　早日康复 is used when writing to someone who is ill.

B. 社交

B. Social correspondence

吊唁信

Larch House
Hughes Lane
Sylvan Hill
Sussex

22 June 2010

Dear Mrs Robinson,

I would like to send you my deepest sympathies[1] on your sad loss[2]. It came as a great shock to hear of Dr Robinson's illness. He will be greatly missed, I am sure, by everyone who knew him, particularly those who, like me, had the good fortune to have him as a tutor. He was an inspiring teacher, and a friend I am proud to have had. I can only guess at your feelings. If there is anything I can do, please do not hesitate to let me know.

With best wishes,
Yours sincerely,

Malcolm Cohn

[1] 给亡者亲友写吊唁信时，通常使用 send/express my [deepest] sympathies 这一套语。

[2] sad loss 意指亲友的去世。

Letter of condolence

杨老师[1]：

惊悉师母不幸仙逝，悲痛不已，今专函深致哀悼，祈望老师节哀顺变，善自珍重[2]。师母一生致力于教育事业，桃李满天下；勤于笔耕，著作等身。学生为有这样一位德高望重的师母而感到骄傲，老师也可为有这样一位成绩斐然的夫人而感到欣慰。伤感良多，不能一一。

即颂

安康!

学生 李冰 敬上

2010年10月25日

[1] Note the form of appellation at the beginning of the letter, which will be the appellation you usually use for the addressee, for example 王老师, 李主任, etc..

[2] 节哀顺变 and 善自珍重 are among the most frequently used expressions in letters of condolence.

C. 职场

C. The world of work

求职信一

Flat 5255, Weiming Gongyu
334 Tianwen Xilu, Zhongguancun
Haidian District, Beijing 100004
People's Republic of China

13 February 2010

The Personnel Manager
Patterson Software Plc
Milton Estate
London E3 4EQ

Dear Sir or Madam

I am writing to apply for the position of programmer at Patterson Software, advertised in *Computing International* on 12 February.[1]

As indicated in my enclosed curriculum vitae[2], I am currently working for Ruanruan Company in Beijing. My programming experience is extensive, with a focus on graphics, as stipulated in your advertisement. Please also note my qualification in Information Technology and my excellent command of English.[3]

From 6 March, I will be visiting the United Kingdom, and available to attend an interview at your convenience. I will be contactable at the following address:

c/o Lewis
51 Dexter Road
London N7 6BW
Tel: 020 7607 55XX

I look forward to hearing from you.

Yours faithfully

Wang Tao

[1] 求职者通常在求职信中说明自己在何处得知招聘信息。

[2] 除非需填写具体的求职表格，否则招聘者通常要求求职者提交简历（curriculum vitae 或 CV）。求职者通常在求职信中明确地谈及简历。

[3] 在求职信中简要说明简历中的要点是很有帮助的，如“大量的编程经验”、“主攻绘图”、“信息工程专业学历”、“英语能力出众”。这些可使忙碌的雇主迅速了解你的特长。

Job application 1[1]

蓝天幼儿园冯园长：

我叫史小燕，女，27岁。2004年毕业于北京师范大学学前教育系。毕业后应聘到市直机关幼儿园当教师，三年后调至市人大办公室工作。两年多来，所用非所学，深感苦恼。我喜欢孩子，热爱幼儿教育事业；我擅长音乐、舞蹈，已有三年多的幼教工作经验。我渴望能重新回到我的专业岗位，发挥自己的专长，做一名优秀的幼儿教师。今悉贵园在招聘幼教教师，现不揣冒昧，致函园长，希望能到贵园工作。我一定会兢兢业业，倍加珍惜这份工作，努力为幼儿教育事业多做贡献，恳请园长能许于成全。谨候回音。此致

敬礼！

求职者 史小燕

2010年9月10日

附件[2]：

1、本人学历证书复印件
2、本人任职资格证书复印件
3、本人履历表
4、本人联系方式

[1] A job application usually includes a brief self-introduction, reference to the position you are applying for, qualifications, and your expectations of the job.

[2] Supporting documents will usually be included in a job application.

C. 职场

C. The world of work

求职信二

Flat 2511, Bibo Huayuan Gongyu
20 Zhongshan Lu,Yinzhou District
Ningbo City, Zhejiang Province, 315000
P. R. China
tangzongwei@yahoo.com.cn

27th February 2010

Alexander Farrell
Head Teacher, Westmoor Language College
Leeds LS17 4YP
UK

Dear Mr Farrell

I am writing to express an interest in the vacancy for a Chinese teacher at your college advertised on Interlanguages.com.

I have over ten years experience of teaching Chinese to foreign students at various universities across China, and I would now like to teach in the UK. My work has given me insights into a variety of cultures, which I feel will help me rise to the challenge of working in a foreign country. You can find full details of my work history in the enclosed CV.

I am available for telephone interview [1] at any time, and could travel to the UK for a face-to-face interview from 8th March.

I look forward to hearing from you soon.

Yours sincerely

Tang Zongwei

[1] 当面面试不易达成时，电话面试是有效评价求职者的第一步。

Job application 2

加拿大
温哥华孔子学院
尊敬的[1]乔治·费尔德先生：

我的一位加拿大朋友告诉我，近期贵院正在招聘中文教师，我对此职位很感兴趣，并自信具备相应条件，故按招聘启事的要求，向贵院提交中文求职信函应征。

我先后在中国三所大学从事对外汉语教学工作，有二十多年的教学经验，发表对外汉语教学论文多篇，并出版有这方面的专著。我对中国文化和中外文化比较也有一定研究。我愿为传播中国文化和中外文化交流作出贡献。

我可以在每周二、四的任何时间接受贵院的电话面试，也可以去加拿大直接面谈。恭候佳音。此致
敬礼

李在春 谨启
2010/09/15

附：个人简历

[1] Modifiers may be used before or after the name and title. For example, 尊敬的 or 亲爱的 will be used according to the level of intimacy or hierarchy existing between the sender and the recipient. If the relationship is formal, males may be addressed as 先生 and females as 小姐 or 女士.

履历[1]

Name: WANG Tao (female)[2]
Address: Flat 5255, Weiming Gongyu
334 Tianwen Xilu
Zhongguancun, Haidian District
Beijing 100004, China
Telephone: + 86 10 6601 11XX
Nationality: Chinese
Date of birth: 11 March 1981

Education:
2001-2002 Diploma in Business at University of Essex Business School
1997-2001 BSc in Information Technology at Peking University
1992-1997 Shenyang No. 3 Middle School, Liaoning Province

Employment:
2003-present Program development engineer with Ruanruan Company, Zhongguancun, Beijing, specializing in computer graphics
2002-2003 Trainee programmer with Yinghua Company, Beijing[3]

Further skills:
Languages: Mandarin Chinese (mother tongue), English (fluent spoken and written), Spanish (good)
Interests: Chess, tennis, ballroom dancing[4]

References:

Mr QIU Pi
Engineering Director, Ruanruan Company
Zhongguancun Software Park
Beijing 100014, China

Dr Margaret McIntosh
Director of Studies
University of Essex Business School
Colchester CR3 5SA, United Kingdom

[Since my current employer is currently unaware of this application, please inform me before contacting him] [5],[6]

FURTHER DETAILS

Programming experience

In my current role at Ruanruan Company, I have responsibility for programming for two major projects. One of these is a commercial website with complex graphic elements including real-time 3D representation. The second entails digital imaging for medical applications.

Prior to this, at Yinghua Company, I worked as a member of a team developing websites for organizations in Beijing. There I honed my programming skills for the Internet, and gained greater experience of graphics applications.

In the course of my degree I gained an all-round understanding of computer science. My interests focused on software engineering (including object-oriented theory), information systems, database technology, and computer graphics. I worked in the following programming languages: C++, Java, Perl, SQL, and HTML. I became familiar with various operating systems, notably UNIX, Windows NT, and Windows XP.

Graphics skills

Both in work and during my degrees the graphic design element has been a common thread. I feel that this aspect of programming offers me the opportunity to combine my analytic and visual skills in creative ways. My experience in computer graphics extends from static to dynamic, from functional to design-oriented, and from abstract to representational. In all these contexts, my passion is for pleasing design that works to fulfil a business objective.

I have solid experience of a variety of graphics applications, notably Adobe Photoshop, Illustrator, and Fireworks. For 3D work, I use Blender and Cinema 4D.

Business and people skills

In my current role, I represent the programming team in attending company-wide strategy meetings, contributing the IT and graphics perspective in relation to corporate decision-making. Both at Ruanruan and Yinghua, I have always worked closely with other departments, notably sales and marketing, with a common purpose of making projects run as effectively as possible.

During my diploma in Business, I gained greater understanding of the international commercial environment. Modules included: Business Organization, Marketing, Business Finance, Computing for Business, and Project Management.

Examples of work:http://www.meirenzhan.com.cn/maozi http://www.shentihao.org.cn/

[1] "履历"在英式英语中常使用 curriculum vitae 或 CV 的说法，美式英语中则为 résumé。

[2] 性别并不是简历的必需内容。但若可能引起未来雇主的混淆，礼貌起见需特别注明。

[3] "求学经历"中通常需按由近及远的时间顺序列举就读的学院或学校及相关学历。"工作经历"中以同样的方式列举工作职位及单位。注意需涵盖所有年份，以便未来的雇主对你在任何时段的工作情况都毫无疑问。

[4] 通常简历会在工作情况之外列举个人兴趣爱好，以给人性格完整平衡的印象。

[5] 若雇主对求职者有意，一般会询问前雇主或在校老师。通常在简历中列出至少两名可联系到的推荐人。

[6] 简历不应长于两页。第一页应如例所示，涵盖基本情况，第二页应分门别类细述个人特长，如"编程经验"、"绘图技能"、"商业及人际技能"。

C. 职场

求职推荐函

UNIVERSITY OF ESSEX BUSINESS SCHOOL

5 April 2010

Matthew Patterson, Managing Director
Patterson Software Plc, Milton Estate
London E3 4EQ

Dear Mr Patterson

I am writing in response to your request for a reference for Wang Tao in her application for the position of programmer at Patterson Software.

Wang Tao was a student in Business at the University of Essex in 2001/2002. As her tutor at Essex, I can confirm that Wang Tao was a high-achieving all-rounder. Not only were her course marks outstanding, but she is also extremely personable, with a sympathetic and engaging manner.

At Essex, Wang Tao demonstrated first-class computing skills, a gift for graphic design, and excellent business and interpersonal instincts. She was awarded a merit for her work as leader in the group project module.

I recommend Wang Tao unreservedly for the position at Patterson Software. At many levels (implementation, interpersonal, etc.), she would be an asset and credit to any technology-oriented organization.

Yours sincerely

Margaret McIntosh

(Dr) Margaret McIntosh

感谢咨询人

51 Dexter Road
London N7 6BW

15 April 2010

Dr Margaret McIntosh
Director of Studies
University of Essex Business School
Colchester CR3 5SA, United Kingdom

Dear Dr McIntosh

I would like to thank you for writing a reference [1] to support my recent application for the position of programmer at Patterson Software in East London.

You may be pleased to know that I was offered the job and will be starting work next month. I am very excited about it.

Again, many thanks for the trouble you have taken on my behalf.

Yours sincerely

Wang Tao

Wang Tao

[1] 推荐信常常是推荐人和雇主之间的私下行为。若推荐信发挥了作用，给推荐人写感谢信是较为礼貌的做法。

求职面试邀请函

Patterson Software
Milton Estate, London E3 4EQ
Tel: 020 8988 20XX, Fax: 020 8988 34XX

8 March 2010

Wang Tao
51 Dexter Road
London N7 6BW

Dear Wang Tao

Thank you for your application for the role of programmer at Patterson Software. I am pleased to inform you that we would like to invite you to interview for the position.

We are seeing candidates during the week beginning 22 March. Would you be able to attend interview at our Milton Estate offices on Tuesday 23 March at 10 am? Please note that we do have some alternative slots, if that date and time do not suit.

You will meet Matthew Patterson, managing director, and Chris Strong, head of programming. The interview will last for about an hour, and will be followed by a brief review of some of our in-house systems.

Attached please find a map and directions for finding Milton Estate. I look forward to hearing from you. Please do let us know if you have any queries at this stage.

Yours sincerely

Kara Jones
Personal Assistant to Matthew Patterson

接受求职面试邀请

51 Dexter Road
London N7 6BW

10 March 2010

Kara Jones, Personal Assistant
Patterson Software Plc, Milton Estate
London E3 4EQ

Dear Ms Jones

Thank you for your letter inviting me to interview for the position of programmer at Patterson Software. This is to confirm that I am able to attend on Tuesday 23 March at 10 am as suggested.

I look forward to meeting Matthew Patterson and Chris Strong. Please can you advise whether or not it would be appropriate for me to bring a portfolio showcasing my graphics work?

Yours sincerely

Wang Tao

Wang Tao

C. The world of work

Curriculum vitae

姓名　李在春
性别　男
出生日期　1962年5月10日
国籍　中国
地址　上海市普陀区中山西路522号1212室　邮编 200062
电话　86 21 654125XX
电子邮件　zaichunli@yahoo.com.cn

求学经历
1972—1975 上海市杨浦高级中学
1975—1979 北京大学中文系汉语言文学专业毕业，学士学位
1979—1981 北京大学中文系现代汉语硕士研究生，硕士学位

工作经历
1981—1990 北京大学对外汉语教学，讲师
1990—1999 北京语言文化大学对外汉语教学，副教授
1999—现在 上海华东师范大学对外汉语学院，教授

科研成果
论文：《对外汉语教学的教材编写问题》、《对外汉语教学中的口语训练》、《语言教学与文化差异》、《汉语、汉字与汉民族文化》等十余篇
专著：《对外汉语教学论丛》

语言技能
汉语普通话（母语），英语（听说读写流利），法语（四级）

附：
学位证书和任职资格证书复印件

Reference letter

国风影视学院人事处负责同志：

今悉贵院拟招聘两名动漫创作研究人员，现推荐我院博士吴华同志赴你处待聘，望予接纳任用为幸。

吴华同志，男，现年32岁。1998年北京影视学院影视创作专业毕业，获学士学位。2003年本院影视编剧专业硕士研究生毕业，同年录取为本院动漫创作博士研究生，2006年获博士学位。吴华同志已发表过论文数篇，并先后与我合作出版过两部专著[1]。

吴华同志知识面宽，专业功底扎实，有较强的研究能力，勇于开拓创新，有广阔的发展前途。我相信他完全可以胜任贵院的工作，故乐意推荐。

如果你们需要吴华同志更详细的材料，我随时可以提供。

切盼尽快答复！此致

敬礼！

北京风华影视学院博士生导师[2]
史伟良
2010年8月2日

[1] Introduce the person you are recommending, highlighting his or her educational background, professional qualifications and achievements.

[2] It is important to specify the referee's status and position.

Invitation to a job interview

张克强先生：

我公司人事部在审阅了你的求职信和个人简历后，决定邀请你来公司面试。

时间：本月20日上午九时
地址：华阳路45号天宇大厦1215室

逾期不候。

天利公司人事部
2010年7月10日

Accepting an invitation to a job interview

天利公司人事部：

顷接来函，相邀于本月20日上午九时去贵公司人事部参加面试，十分高兴。我定当按时前往，接受面试。谢谢！

专此奉复。

张克强 谨启
2010年7月13日

C. 职场

接受某工作职位

51 Dexter Road
London N7 6BW

15 April 2010

Matthew Patterson, Managing Director
Patterson Software Plc
Milton Estate
London E3 4EQ

Dear Mr Patterson

Further to my interview with you last month, I am delighted to have received your letter offering me the post of programmer at Patterson Software. I am very pleased to accept the offer.

I confirm that I will be able to start work on 17 May, as discussed. Can you please inform me where and when I should report that day? I very much look forward to becoming a member of your programming and graphics team.

Yours sincerely

Wang Tao

Wang Tao

婉拒某工作职位

Flat 2511, Bibo Huayuan Gongyu
20 Zhongshan Lu,Yinzhou District
Ningbo City, Zhejiang Province, 315000
P. R. China

20th April 2010

Alexander Farrell
Head Teacher, Westmoor Language College
Leeds LS17 4YP
UK

Dear Mr Farrell

I am very grateful to you for offering me the position of Chinese teacher. Regretfully, however, I shall have to decline, since I have just agreed to take up a similar position at a college in Bath.

It was a pleasure to talk with you and your team, and I feel sorry not to be able to take on the role. I am afraid I felt obliged to act swiftly in respect of accepting the earlier offer.

Please accept my apologies for any inconvenience caused[1].

Yours sincerely

Tang Zongwei

Tang Zongwei

[1] 若写信人认为收信人也许会因为得知某事而带来麻烦时，常使用 apologies for any inconvenience caused 这一套语。此短语体现礼貌与尊敬，并不意味着写信人有过错。

辞职信

3 Norton Gardens
BRADFORD
BD7 4AU

8 May 2010

Regional Sales Manager
Nortex and Co.
Cooper St
LEEDS
LS5 2FH

Dear Mr Perrin,

I am writing to inform you of my decision to resign from my post of Sales Administrator in the Bradford office with effect from 28 June 2010. I am giving one month's (four weeks') notice as set out in my conditions of employment. I have for some time been considering a change of role and have been offered a post with a market research organization, which I believe will meet my career aspirations.

I would like to take this opportunity to say how much I value the training and professional support that I have received in my three years with Nortex and Co.

Yours sincerely,

Melinda MacPhee

Melinda MacPhee

III 难检字笔画索引

Index of Characters with Radicals Difficult to Classify

（字右边的数字指《汉英词典》正文部分的页码，带圆括号的字是繁体字或异体字）
(The number to the right of each character indicates the page number in the Chinese-English Dictionary. Characters in parentheses are the complex forms or variant forms)

Aa

ā

吖 ā

【吖啶】ādìng〈名〉［化学］acridine
【吖啶黄】ādìnghuáng〈名〉［药学］acriflavine
【吖嗪】āqín〈名〉［化学］azine

阿 ā〈前缀〉〈方〉1（用于姓、名或排行前）[used before surnames, childhood names and birth-order numbers to form terms of endearment]: ～大 eldest son 2（用于亲属称谓前）[used before terms of relatives]: ▸～爹, ～妈, ～婆
▸à, ē
【阿爸】ābà〈名〉〈方〉dad
【阿鼻地狱】ābí dìyù〈名〉［佛教］*Avici* [the lowest level of the Buddhist 'hell' realm]
【阿波罗】Ābōluó〈名〉Apollo: ～飞船 Apollo spaceship
【阿伯丁郡】Ābódīngjùn〈名〉Aberdeenshire
【阿布贾】Ābùjiǎ〈名〉Abuja
【阿布扎比】Ābùzhābǐ〈名〉Abu Dhabi
【阿昌语】Āchāngyǔ ▸**p. 918**〈名〉Achang language
【阿昌族】Āchāngzú〈名〉Achang ethnic group
【阿的平】ādìpíng〈名〉［药学］Quinacrine
【阿爹】ādiē〈名〉〈方〉dad
【阿斗】Ādǒu〈名〉1〈本〉A Dou [infant name of Liu Shan (刘禅, 207-271), last emperor of Shu Han (蜀汉), during China's Three Kingdoms period, notorious for his incompetence] 2〈喻〉weakling: 扶不起的～ good-for-nothing
【阿尔巴尼亚】Ā'ěrbāníyà〈名〉Albania: ～共和国 Republic of Albania ‖ ～人 Albanian ‖ ～语 Albanian
【阿尔卑斯山】Ā'ěrbēisīshān〈名〉Alps
【阿尔法】ā'ěrfǎ〈名〉alpha (α): ～放射性 alpha radiation ‖ ～粒子 alpha particle ‖ ～射线 alpha ray
【阿尔及尔】Ā'ěrjí'ěr〈名〉Algiers
【阿尔及利亚】Ā'ěrjílìyà〈名〉Algeria: ～民主人民共和国 Democratic People's Republic of Algeria ‖ ～人 Algerian
【阿尔泰山】Ā'ěrtàishān〈名〉Altai Mountains
【阿尔泰语】Ā'ěrtàiyǔ ▸**p. 918**〈名〉Altai language
【阿飞】āfēi〈名〉〈旧〉young hooligan
【阿伏伽德罗常量】Āfújiādéluó chángliàng〈名〉［化学］Avogadro's constant
【阿富汗】Āfùhàn〈名〉Afghanistan: ～人 Afghan ‖ ～伊斯兰国 Islamic State of Afghanistan ‖ ～语 Afghan language
【阿盖尔郡】Āgài'ěrjùn〈名〉Argyllshire
【阿哥】āgē〈名〉1（有亲属关系）elder brother: 大～ eldest brother 2（无亲属关系）big brother [used affectionately to address a man of one's own age]
▸àge
【阿根廷】Āgēntíng〈名〉Argentina: ～共和国 Republic of Argentina ‖ ～人 Argentine
【阿公】āgōng〈名〉〈方〉1（公公）husband's father 2（祖父）grandfather 3〈尊〉（老年男子）grandpa
【阿訇】āhōng〈名〉［伊斯兰教］imam
【阿基米德原理】Ājīmǐdé yuánlǐ〈名〉［物理］Archimedes' principle
【阿肯色州】Ākěnsèzhōu〈名〉Arkansas
【阿拉】ālā〈代〉〈方〉1（我）（作主语）I;（作宾语）me;（我的）my: ～姆妈 my mum 2（我们）（作主语）we;（作宾语）us;（我们的）our
【阿拉伯】Ālābó〈名〉Arabia: ～人 Arab ‖ ～语 Arabic ‖ ～世界 Arab world
【阿拉伯埃及共和国】Ālābó Āijí Gònghéguó〈名〉Arab Republic of Egypt
【阿拉伯半岛】Ālābó Bàndǎo〈名〉Arabian Peninsula
【阿拉伯国家联盟】Ālābó Guójiā Liánméng〈名〉League of Arab States
【阿拉伯联合酋长国】Ālābó Liánhé Qiúzhǎngguó〈名〉United Arab Emirates (UAE)
【阿拉伯酋长】Ālābó qiúzhǎng〈名〉Arab sheikh
【阿拉伯石油输出国组织】Ālābó Shíyóu Shūchūguó Zǔzhī〈名〉Organization of Arab Petroleum Exporting Countries (OAPEC)
【阿拉伯数字】Ālābó shùzì ▸**p. 691**〈名〉Arabic numerals
【阿拉伯湾】Ālābówān〈名〉Arabian Gulf
【阿拉伯叙利亚共和国】Ālābó Xùlìyà Gònghéguó〈名〉Syrian Arab Republic
【阿拉伯也门共和国】Ālābó Yěmén Gònghéguó〈名〉Yemen Arab Republic
【阿拉伯字母】Ālābó zìmǔ〈名〉Arabic alphabet
【阿拉斯加州】Ālāsījiāzhōu〈名〉Alaska
【阿里山】Ālǐshān〈名〉Ali Mountain
【阿联酋】Āliánqiú〈简称〉= 阿拉伯联合酋长国
【阿留申群岛】Āliúshēn Qúndǎo〈名〉Aleutian Islands
【阿留申人】Āliúshēnrén ▸**p. 279**〈名〉Aleut
【阿罗汉】āluóhàn〈名〉［佛教］arhat
【阿妈】āmā〈名〉〈方〉mum
▸àma
【阿马郡】Āmǎjùn〈名〉Armagh
【阿曼】Āmàn〈名〉Oman: ～人 Omani ‖ ～苏丹国 Sultanate of Oman
【阿猫阿狗】āmāo-āgǒu〈俗〉〈方〉〈贬〉any person, Tom, Dick or Harry
【阿妹】āmèi〈名〉〈方〉1（妹妹）younger sister 2（女孩）sister
【阿门】āmén〈名〉［宗教］amen
【阿盟】Āméng〈简称〉= 阿拉伯国家联盟
【阿米巴】āmǐbā〈名〉［医学］amoeba: ～病 amoebiasis ‖ ～痢疾 amoebic dysentery
【阿莫西林】āmòxīlín〈名〉［药学］amoxicillin
【阿姆哈拉语】Āmǔhālāyǔ ▸**p. 918**〈名〉Amharic
【阿姆斯特丹】Āmǔsītèdān〈名〉Amsterdam
【阿木林】āmùlín〈名〉〈方〉idiot
【阿片】āpiàn〈名〉［药学］opium: ～制剂 opiate
【阿婆】āpó〈名〉〈方〉1（婆婆）mother-in-law 2（祖母）grandmother 3〈尊〉（老年女子）granny
【阿Q】Ā Qiū〈名〉1〈本〉Ah Q [character created by Lu Xun in *The True Story of Ah Q*] 2〈喻〉person who takes comfort in interpreting their defeats as moral victories
【阿Q精神】Ā Qiū jīngshén〈名〉Ah Q mentality [Dutch comfort]
【阿塞拜疆】Āsàibàijiāng〈名〉Azerbaijan: ～共和国 Republic of Azerbaijan ‖ ～人 Azerbaijani ‖ ～语 Azerbaijani
【阿什哈巴德】Āshíhābādé〈名〉Ashkhabad [the capital and cultural heart of Turkmenistan]
【阿是穴】āshìxué〈名〉［中医］*ashi* point [any nerve point on the affected part of the body other than those specified for acupuncture and moxibustion]
【阿司匹林】āsīpǐlín〈名〉［药学］aspirin
【阿斯塔纳】Āsītǎnà〈名〉Astana
【阿斯旺大坝】Āsīwàng Dàbà〈名〉Aswan Dam
【阿嚏】ātì〈拟〉atishoo
【阿托品】ātuōpǐn〈名〉［药学］atropine
【阿姨】āyí〈名〉1〈方〉（有亲属关系）aunt 2〈尊〉（无亲属关系）auntie: 李～ Auntie Li 3（保姆）nanny
【阿扎尼亚】Āzāníyà〈名〉Azania [alternative name for South Africa]: ～人 Azanian
【阿诈里】āzhàlǐ〈名〉〈方〉swindler: ～的手段花样翻新。The fraudsters put new spins on old tricks.
【阿兹特克文化】Āzītèkè wénhuà〈名〉Aztec civilization

啊 ā〈叹〉ah: ～，打雷了! Oh, it's thundering! ‖ ～，是小王，快进来。Ah, Xiao Wang. Come in!
▸á, ǎ, à, a
【啊哈】āhā〈叹〉1（表惊奇、得意或恍然大悟）aha: ～，我找到你了! Ha, there you are! ‖ ～，你又捉弄我了! Aha, so you're teasing me again. 2（表赞叹）wow: ～，多精彩呀! Oh, how wonderful!
【啊呀】āyā〈叹〉1（表诧异）aha: ～，他跑得真快! Wow, he runs really fast! 2（表责备或懊悔）oh: ～，怎么满地是

a

水! Oh no! How come there is water all over the floor? ‖ ～，这事可不好办! Oh, this is no easy matter!

【啊哟】āyō〈叹〉 oh: ～，你踩着我的脚了! Ouch! You're stepping on my foot! ‖ ～，头疼死了! Ow, my headache is killing me!

锕（錒） ā〈名〉［化学］ actinium (Ac)

【锕铅】āqiān〈名〉［化学］ actinium lead (AcD)

【锕系元素】āxì yuánsù〈名〉［化学］ actinides

【锕铀】āyóu〈名〉［化学］ actinouranium (AcU)

腌 ā
►yān

【腌臜】āza〈方〉 **A**〈形〉 **1**（肮脏） filthy **2**（不顺心） unsettled **B**〈动〉 embarrass: 别～人了。 Don't be disgusting.

á

啊 á〈叹〉 **1**（表追问） well: 你倒是同意不同意呀，～? So, do you agree or not? **2**（要求对方重复） eh: ～? 你说什么? Eh? What did you say?
►ā, ǎ, à, a

ǎ

啊 ǎ〈叹〉 eh: ～? 他还没来啊! What! He still hasn't come yet?
►ā, á, à, a

à

阿 à
►ā, ē

【阿哥】àge〈名〉 **1**（儿子） son [Manchu term of address] **2**（特指皇子） *Age* [title of a Manchu emperor's son not yet of age]
►āgē

【阿妈】àma〈名〉 father [Manchu term of address]
►āmā

啊 à〈叹〉 **1**（表赞许） ah: ～，好吧。 Well, OK. **2**（表恍然大悟） aha: ～，我现在明白了。 Oh, I understand now. **3**（表惊叹） oh: ～，多漂亮的礼物! Oh, what a lovely gift!
►ā, á, ǎ, a

a

啊 a〈助〉 **1**（表感叹） [used at the end of a sentence to express appreciation]: 多好的天儿～! What a fine day! **2**（表强调） [used at the end of a sentence to express agreement, defensiveness, urge, etc.]: 快去～! Hurry up! ‖ 你可要小心～! Do be careful! ‖ 我没有去是因为我有事～。 I didn't go because I had some other arrangement. **3**（表疑问） [used at the end of a sentence to express doubt]: 你吃不吃～? Are you going to eat or not? ‖ 你这说的是真的～? Is that so? **4**（表停顿） [used to indicate a pause to draw attention]: 这些年～，我们的日子越过越好啦! Over the past few years, things have been getting better and better for us. **5**（表列举） [used in enumerating items]: 书～，杂志～，摆满了书架。 The bookshelf is filled with all sorts of books, magazines, etc.
►ā, á, ǎ, à

āi

哎 āi〈叹〉 **1**（表惊讶） oh: ～! 是老李啊! Why, it's Lao Li! ‖ ～! 真是想不到的事! Ah, this is really unexpected! **2**（表责难） well: ～! 你怎么能这么说呢! No, how can you say this? **3**（用以引人注意） hey: ～，小王，你出去能给我捎张报纸吗? Oh, Xiao Wang, would you get me a paper while you are out? ‖ ～，小心脚下! Mind your step!
►ái, ǎi, ài

【哎呀】āiyā〈叹〉 **1**（表惊讶） wow: ～! 这西瓜长得好大呀! Wow! This watermelon is really big! **2**（表责难） oh: ～，你怎么来这么晚呢? Oh, why are you so late? ‖ ～，我又忘带钥匙了。 Damn, I've forgotten my keys again.

【哎哟】āiyō〈叹〉 oh: ～! 我肚子好疼! Ouch, my stomach hurts! ‖ ～，咱们怎么没有想到他呀! Damn it! How come we never thought of him?

哀 āi
A〈动〉 **1**（同情） sympathize with: ～其不幸 feel sorry for sb.'s misfortune ►～怜 **2**（感到悲伤） mourn: ►～悼, 默～
B〈形〉 sorrowful: ►～歌, ～婉, 悲～
C〈名〉 grief: ►致～

【哀兵必胜】āibīng-bìshèng〈成〉 an indignant army under heavy pressure is bound to win

【哀愁】āichóu〈形〉 sorrowful: 无限～ be extremely grieved

【哀辞】āicí〈名〉〈书〉 elegy

【哀悼】āidào〈动〉 mourn: ～烈士 mourn the martyrs ‖ 我们对受害者家属表示～。 We grieve for the families of the victims.

【哀悼日】āidàorì〈名〉 day of mourning

【哀而不伤】āi'érbùshāng〈成〉 **1**（指人） be mournful but not distressed **2**（指作品） be melancholy but not depressing

【哀告】āigào〈动〉 entreat: 四处～ beg for help from all quarters

【哀歌】āigē **A**〈名〉 elegy **B**〈动〉 sing mournfully

【哀号】āiháo〈动〉 wail: 隔壁有人在～。 Someone is wailing next door. ‖〈喻〉 风在～。 The wind is wailing.

【哀嚎】āiháo〈动〉 **1**（指野兽） howl **2** = 哀号 āiháo

【哀鸿遍野】āihóng-biànyě〈成〉 the land is swarming with wailing disaster victims

【哀家】āijiā〈名〉〈旧〉 [term of address used by widowed empress]（作主语） I;（作宾语） me

【哀怜】āilián〈动〉 pity

【哀悯】āimǐn〈动〉 commiserate with

【哀鸣】āimíng〈动〉 moan: 寒鸦～。 Jackdaws cried sorrowfully.

【哀莫大于心死】āi mòdàyú xīnsǐ〈成〉 there is nothing worse than the death of the mind

【哀戚】āiqī〈形〉〈书〉 grievous

【哀启】āiqǐ〈名〉〈旧〉 biographical sketch of a deceased person

【哀泣】āiqì〈动〉 weep in grief: 掩面～ cover one's face and weep sadly

【哀切】āiqiè〈形〉 sad and wretched: 神情～ have a mournful look

【哀求】āiqiú〈动〉 entreat: ～开恩 beg sb. for mercy ‖ 含泪～ implore with tears

【哀伤】āishāng〈形〉 grieved: 无限～ be grief-stricken

【哀思】āisī〈名〉 sorrow and grief: 寄托～ give expression to one's grief

【哀叹】āitàn〈动〉 bemoan: ～自己的不幸 lament one's misfortune

【哀恸】āitòng〈形〉 grief-stricken

【哀痛】āitòng〈形〉 sorrowful: ～欲绝 be grief-stricken

【哀婉】āiwǎn〈形〉 bitter-sweet: ～的歌声 sad, sweet song

【哀艳】āiyàn〈形〉 plaintively touching

【哀怨】āiyuàn〈形〉 resentful

【哀乐】āiyuè〈名〉 dirge: 奏～ play funeral music

埃¹ āi〈名〉 fine dust: ►尘～

埃² āi〈量〉［物理］ angstrom

【埃博拉】āibólā ►**p. 50**〈名〉［医学］ Ebola

【埃菲尔铁塔】Āifēi'ěr Tiětǎ〈名〉 Eiffel Tower

【埃及】Āijí〈名〉 Egypt: ～人 Egyptian

【埃米尔】āimǐ'ěr〈名〉 emir

【埃塞俄比亚】Āisài'ébǐyà〈名〉 Ethiopia: ～联邦民主共和国 Federal Democratic Republic of Ethiopia ‖ ～人 Ethiopian

【埃塞克斯郡】Āisàikèsījùn〈名〉 Essex

挨 āi〈动〉 **1**（紧接着） be close to: ～墙站着 stand by the wall ‖ ～窗子的座位 seat next to the window ‖ 我们两家紧～着。 We are next-door neighbours. ‖ 学生一个～一个地走进教室。 The students filed into the classroom. **2**（靠近） approach: 你的手太脏了，别～我。 Your hands are so dirty. Don't touch me! **3**（依次） take turns doing sth.: ►～家～户
►ái

【挨边】āibiān **A**〈动〉 **1**（靠着边缘） keep to the edge: 上了大路，请～走。 Please keep to the side when you get onto the main road. **2**（接近） be close (to): 我爸都八十～了。 My father is getting on for eighty. **B**〈形〉 relevant: 你说的一点也不～儿。 What you said is completely irrelevant.

【挨次】āicì〈副〉 in turn: ～入场 enter one after another

【挨个儿】āigèr〈副〉〈口〉 one by one

【挨家挨户】āijiā-āihù〈副〉 from house to house: ～搜查 make a house-to-house search

【挨肩】āijiān〈副〉 shoulder to shoulder: 和某人～坐 sit next to sb.

【挨肩儿】āijiānr〈动〉〈口〉 be next in birth order and close in age: 这姐儿俩～，只差一岁。 The two sisters are close in age. There's just a year between them.

【挨近】āijìn〈动〉 be near to: 她家～机场。 Her home is close to the airport. ‖ ～我一点儿。 Get a bit closer to me.

【挨门逐户】āimén-zhúhù = 挨家挨户 āijiā-āihù

唉 āi
A〈叹〉 hey: ～，我在这儿。 Yes, I am here. ‖ ～，我知道了。 All right, now I know.
B〈拟〉 ah: 他双手抱着头，～～直叹气。 He held his head in his hands and kept sighing.

▸ài

【唉声叹气】āishēng-tànqì〈成〉moan and groan: 整天～ sigh away one's days

欸 āi = 唉 āi
▸ǎi

嗳（噯） āi = 哎 āi
▸ǎi, ài

锿（鎄） āi〈名〉［化学］einsteinium (Es)

ái

哎 ái〈叹〉Oh: ～，你怎么一直不说话？ Well, why haven't you said anything? ‖ ～，我想起来了。 Aha, I remember now.
▸āi, ǎi, ài

挨（捱） ái〈动〉**1**（遭受）suffer: ～了一记耳光 get a slap in the face ‖ ～批评 be criticized ▸～冻，～骂，～揍 **2**（度过）struggle to pull through: ～时日 play for time ‖ 她总算～过来了。 In the end she pulled through. **3**（拖延）delay: 今天的事不要～到明天做。 Never put off until tomorrow what you can do today. ▸延～
▸āi

【挨板子】áibǎnzi〈动〉take a beating

【挨打】áidǎ〈动〉**1**（被打）suffer a beating **2**〈喻〉（遭受攻击）come under attack: 落后就要～。 A weak country is vulnerable to attack.

【挨冻】áidòng〈动〉suffer from cold

【挨饿】ái'è〈动〉starve

【挨剋】áikēi〈口〉**1**（被骂）be told off: 他没完成作业而挨了剋。 He got a talking-to for not finishing his homework. **2**（被打）take a beating

【挨淋】áilín〈动〉get caught in the rain

【挨骂】áimà〈动〉get told off: 挨一顿臭骂 receive a good dressing-down

【挨批】áipī〈动〉be criticized

【挨整】áizhěng〈动〉be the target of criticism

【挨揍】áizòu〈口〉= 挨打 áidǎ 1

骙（騃） ái〈形〉〈书〉stupid: ▸痴～

皑（皚） ái〈形〉〈书〉pure white

【皑皑】ái'ái〈形〉〈书〉pure white: 白雪～ vast expanse of white snow ‖ ～的雪山 snow-capped mountains

癌 ái ▸**p. 50**〈名〉cancer: 皮肤～ skin cancer ‖ 抗～药 anti-cancer drug ‖ 致～物 carcinogen ▸～症，肺～，乳腺～

【癌变】áibiàn〈动〉become cancerous: 萎缩性胃炎往往是～的先兆。 Atrophic gastritis is often a precursor of cancer.

【癌扩散】áikuòsàn〈名〉spread of cancer

【癌切除术】áiqiēchúshù〈名〉［医学］surgical removal of a cancer

【癌细胞】áixìbāo〈名〉cancerous cell: 防止～扩散 prevent cancer cells from spreading

【癌症】áizhèng ▸**p. 50**〈名〉cancer: 得/患～ get/be ill with cancer ‖ ～患者 cancer patient

【癌转移】áizhuǎnyí〈名〉metastasis of cancer

ǎi

哎 ǎi〈叹〉ugh: ～，话可不能那样说。 Oh, no, you can't say that.
▸āi, ái, ài

欸 ǎi
▸āi

【欸乃】ǎinǎi〈拟〉〈书〉**1**（划船声）creak **2**（歌声）sound of a boat song

嗳（噯） ǎi = 哎 ǎi
▸āi, ài

【嗳气】ǎiqì〈动〉belch

【嗳酸】ǎisuān〈动〉have an acid burp

矮 ǎi〈形〉**1**（身材短）short: 个子～ be short ‖ 她比他～一厘米。 She is one centimetre shorter than him. ▸～小 **2** ▸**p. 82**（高度小）low: ～凳/墙 low stool/wall **3**（级别低）low in rank: 他比我～一级。 He is a grade lower than me. ‖ 在他面前我觉得～了一截。 I felt dwarfed beside him.

【矮墩墩】ǎidūndūn〈形〉stumpy

【矮杆品种】ǎigǎn pǐnzhǒng〈名〉［农业］short-stalked variety

【矮个儿】ǎigèr **A**〈形〉short **B**〈名〉short person

【矮个子】ǎigèzi = 矮个儿 ǎigèr B

【矮化】ǎihuà〈动〉**1**［植物］stunt: ～果树 dwarf fruit tree ‖ ～小麦 dwarf wheat **2**（贬低）degrade

【矮林】ǎilín〈名〉coppice

【矮胖】ǎipàng〈形〉short and stout: 他又矮又胖。 He is dumpy.

【矮人看戏】ǎirén-kànxì〈俗〉follow the crowd

【矮生】ǎishēng〈形〉dwarf

【矮生植被】ǎishēng zhíbèi〈名〉low-growing vegetation

【矮小】ǎixiǎo〈形〉short and small

【矮星】ǎixīng〈名〉［天文］dwarf star

【矮种马】ǎizhǒngmǎ〈名〉pony

【矮子】ǎizi〈名〉short person: 语言的巨人，行动的～ talk the talk but not walk the walk

【矮子看戏】ǎizi-kànxì = 矮人看戏 ǎirén-kànxì

【矮子里拔将军】ǎizili bá jiāngjun〈俗〉pick the best out of a mediocre bunch

蔼[1]（藹） ǎi〈形〉friendly: ▸和～

蔼[2]（藹） ǎi〈形〉〈书〉exuberant

【蔼蔼】ǎi'ǎi〈形〉〈书〉**1**（茂盛）lush: 草木～ lush vegetation **2**（昏暗）dim

【蔼然】ǎirán〈形〉〈书〉genial: ～可亲 kindly

霭 ǎi〈名〉〈书〉mist: ▸暮～，雾～，烟～

ài

艾[1] ài〈名〉［植物］Chinese mugwort

艾[2] ài〈形〉〈书〉old

艾[3] ài〈动〉〈书〉cease: ▸方兴未～

艾[4] ài〈形〉〈书〉handsome
▸yì

【艾奥瓦州】Ài'àowǎzhōu〈名〉Iowa

【艾尔郡】Ài'ěrjùn〈名〉Ayrshire

【艾蒿】àihāo = 艾[1] ài

【艾虎】àihǔ〈名〉**1**［动物］fitch **2**（艾制品）Chinese mugwort tiger [a tiny cloth tiger filled with Chinese mugwort, worn on the head of a child on the Dragon Boat Festival to ward off evil]

【艾灸】àijiǔ〈名〉［中医］moxibustion

【艾美奖】Àiměijiǎng〈名〉Emmy Award

【艾绒】àiróng〈名〉［中药］moxa

【艾窝窝】àiwōwo〈名〉steamed bun made of glutinous rice with sweet filling

【艾鼬】àiyòu〈名〉［动物］polecat

【艾炷】àizhù〈名〉moxa cone

【艾炷灸】àizhùjiǔ〈名〉［中医］moxa-cone moxibustion

【艾滋病】àizībìng ▸**p. 50**〈名〉acquired immune deficiency syndrome (AIDS): ～患者 AIDS patient ‖ 他～检查呈阳性。 He tested positive for AIDS.

【艾滋病病毒】àizībìng bìngdú〈名〉human immunodeficiency virus (HIV): 感染～ be infected with the AIDS virus ‖ ～携带者 HIV carrier

哎 ài〈叹〉**1**（表伤感、惋惜）alas: ～，谁叫我不把它当回事呢! Well, I shouldn't have taken it so casually! **2**（表赞许）OK: ～，走吧! All right, go!
▸āi, ái, ǎi

砹 ài〈名〉［化学］astatine (At)

唉 ài〈叹〉alas: ～，我真拿他没办法! Oh well, I really don't know what to do with him.
▸āi

爱（愛） ài〈动〉**1**（指感情深）love: ～孩子/父母 love one's children/parents ‖ 真诚的～ genuine affection ‖ 他对她～得死去活来的。 He is head over heels in love with her. ▸宠～，恋～，相～ **2**（珍惜）cherish: ▸～面子，～惜 **3**（喜欢）like: ～吃辣 love spicy food ‖ ～出风头 enjoy the limelight ‖ 不～吃海鲜 not like seafood **4**（易于）be apt to: ～发脾气 be apt to lose one's temper ‖ ～感冒 be prone to getting colds ‖ 不～说话 not like talking

【爱不释手】àibùshìshǒu〈成〉love sth. too much to part with it: 这本书他～。 He loves this book so much that he cannot stop reading it.

【爱财如命】àicái-rúmìng〈成〉love money as if it were one's own life

【爱巢】àicháo〈名〉〈喻〉love nest

【爱称】àichēng〈名〉term of endearment

【爱答不理】àidā-bùlǐ〈成〉stand-offish

【爱达荷州】Àidáhézhōu〈名〉Idaho

【爱戴】àidài〈动〉love and support: 深受民众～ stand high in public love and esteem

【爱丁堡】Àidīngbǎo〈名〉Edinburgh

【爱尔兰】Ài'ěrlán〈名〉Ireland: ～共和国 Republic of Ireland ‖ ～人 Irishman ‖ ～语 Irish

【爱抚】àifǔ〈动〉have tender affection for: 母亲～的眼神 loving eyes of a mother

a

【爱岗敬业】àigǎng-jìngyè〈惯〉 love one's job and be dedicated to one's profession
【爱国】àiguó〈动〉 love one's country: ～热情 patriotic enthusiasm ‖ ～志士 dedicated patriot ‖ ～华侨 patriotic overseas Chinese
【爱国统一战线】àiguó tǒngyī zhànxiàn〈名〉 patriotic united front
【爱国卫生运动委员会】Àiguó Wèishēng Yùndòng Wěiyuánhuì〈名〉 Patriotic Public Health Campaign Committee
【爱国者】àiguózhě〈名〉 patriot: ～导弹 Patriot missile
【爱国主义】àiguózhǔyì〈名〉 patriotism: ～教育 education in patriotism ‖ 大力弘扬～ vigorously promote patriotism
【爱好】àihào **A**〈动〉 **1**（有兴趣） be keen on: ～摄影 be interested in photography ‖ ～体育 love sports **2**（热爱） love: ～和平的国家/人民 peace-loving nation/people **B**〈名〉 hobby: ～广泛 have a wide variety of hobbies ‖ 根据个人～选择职业 follow one's interests in choosing one's occupation ‖ 音乐是他生活中的一大～。 Music is one of the great loves of his life.
【爱好者】àihàozhě〈名〉 enthusiast: 集邮～ stamp collector ‖ 文学～ literature buff ‖ 足球～ football fan
【爱河】àihé〈名〉〈喻〉 river of love: 堕入～ fall in love
【爱护】àihù〈动〉 take good care of: ～公物 show respect for public property ‖ ～年轻一代 care for the younger generation ‖ 相互关心，相互～ care for and about each other
【爱克斯光】àikèsīguāng〈名〉 X-ray: ～机 X-ray apparatus ‖ ～照片 radiograph
【爱克斯射线】àikèsī shèxiàn〈名〉［物理］ X-ray: ～探伤器 X-ray flaw detector ‖ ～微量分析仪 X-ray microanalyser
【爱理不理】àilǐ-bùlǐ = 爱答不理 àidā-bùlǐ
【爱丽舍宫】Àilìshěgōng〈名〉 Élysée Palace
【爱怜】àilián〈动〉 show tender affection for
【爱恋】àiliàn〈动〉 be in love with: ～之情 loving feelings ‖ 他深深～着养育过自己的故土。 He is deeply attached to the place where he was brought up.
【爱侣】àilǚ〈名〉 lovers
【爱美】àiměi〈动〉 **1**（指打扮） be particular about one's appearance **2**（指事物） love beautiful things
【爱美之心，人皆有之】àiměizhīxīn, rénjiēyǒuzhī〈成〉 it is only human to love beauty
【爱面子】ài miànzi〈惯〉 be concerned about one's reputation: 她死～，喜欢穷摆阔。 She is very concerned with appearance and likes to put on a show of wealth.
【爱民如子】àimín-rúzǐ〈成〉 love one's subordinates as one loves one's children
【爱莫能助】àimònéngzhù〈成〉 be willing to help but unable to do so
【爱慕】àimù〈动〉 **1**（向往） love and envy: ～虚荣 be given to vanity **2**（倾慕） admire: 向某人表达～之情 express one's admiration for sb.
【爱女】àinǚ〈名〉 beloved daughter
【爱妻】àiqī〈名〉 beloved wife
【爱琴海】Àiqínhǎi〈名〉 Aegean Sea
【爱琴群岛】Àiqín qúndǎo〈名〉 Aegean Islands
【爱情】àiqíng〈名〉 love: 纯洁的～ pure love ‖ ～不能强求。 Love cannot be forced.
【爱人】àirén〈名〉 **1**（配偶） spouse: 她的～是医生。 Her husband is a doctor. **2**（恋人） sweetheart
【爱沙尼亚】Àishāníyà〈名〉 Estonia: ～共和国 Republic of Estonia ‖ ～人 Estonian ‖ ～语 Estonian
【爱神】àishén〈名〉 Cupid
【爱斯基摩人】Àisījīmórén〈名〉 Eskimo
【爱卫会】Àiwèihuì〈简称〉= 爱国卫生运动委员会
【爱窝窝】àiwōwo = 艾窝窝 àiwōwo
【爱屋及乌】àiwū-jíwū〈成〉 love one thing on account of another
【爱惜】àixī〈动〉 **1**（珍惜） treasure: ～劳动果实 cherish the fruits of one's labour ‖ ～时间 make the best use of one's time **2**（疼爱） be very fond of
【爱惜羽毛】àixī-yǔmáo〈惯〉 cherish one's reputation as birds cherish their feathers and beasts their hair
【爱心】àixīn〈名〉 compassion: 献～ extend compassion ‖ 充满～的父母 parents full of love
【爱因斯坦相对论】Àiyīnsītǎn xiāngduìlùn〈名〉［物理］ Einstein's principle of relativity
【爱乐乐团】àiyuè yuètuán〈名〉 philharmonic orchestra: 皇家～ Royal Philharmonic Orchestra
【爱悦】àiyuè〈动〉 be attached to
【爱憎分明】àizēng-fēnmíng〈成〉 be clear about what or who to love or hate
【爱重】àizhòng〈动〉〈书〉 love and respect
【爱子】àizǐ〈名〉 beloved son

僾（僾） ài〈形〉〈书〉 **1**（仿佛） seeming: ～然 seemingly **2**（气息不畅） breathing with difficulty

隘 ài
A〈形〉 narrow: ▸狭～
B〈名〉 strategically located pass: ▸险～，关～
【隘口】àikǒu〈名〉 mountain pass
【隘路】àilù〈名〉 narrow passage

碍（礙） ài〈动〉 obstruct: 有～健康 harmful to one's health ‖ ～于情面 for fear of hurting sb.'s feelings ▸～手～脚，～眼，妨～
【碍口】àikǒu〈形〉 too embarrassing to mention: 借钱的事，说起来总是～。 To borrow money is always an embarrassing thing to do.
【碍面子】ài miànzi〈动〉 be afraid of hurting others' feelings: 我碍于面子不好拒绝他。 I didn't refuse him for fear of embarrassing him.
【碍难】àinán〈动〉〈书〉 find it difficult to do sth.: 我～从命。 I found it difficult to comply with it.
【碍事】àishì **A**〈动〉 be in the way: 桌子放在这儿太～，咱们把它搬到那边去。 The table is in the way here. Let's move it over there. **B**〈形〉 [usu used in the negative] serious: 只是感冒了，不～。 It's just a cold, nothing serious.
【碍手碍脚】àishǒu-àijiǎo〈成〉 be in the way: 别在这儿～! Get out of the way!
【碍眼】àiyǎn〈形〉 **1**（看着别扭） offensive: 门前那堆垃圾实在太～。 The garbage heap in front of the house is really an eyesore. **2**（妨碍） obstructive: 我在这儿不～吗? Am I in your way here?

嗳（噯） ài〈叹〉 oh: ～，早知如此，我们就不去了。 Gosh, if we'd known this beforehand, we wouldn't have gone there.
▸āi, ǎi

嫒（嬡） ài ▸令嫒 lìng'ài

叆（靉） ài
【叆叇】àidài〈形〉〈书〉 dense: 暮云～。 Evening clouds blocked out the sun.

暧（曖） ài
【暧昧】àimèi〈形〉 **1**（指态度） unclear: 态度～ ambiguous attitude **2**（指行为） dubious: 关系～ shady relations

ān

厂 ān = 庵 ān 1
▸chǎng

广 ān = 庵 ān 1
▸guǎng

安[1] ān
A〈形〉 **1**（平安） safe: ～抵目的地 reach a destination safely ▸～全，～然无恙，平～ **2**（安静） calm: ～坐 sit quietly ▸～定，～静，坐立不～ **3**（舒适） comfortable: ▸～居乐业，～闲，～逸
B〈动〉 **1**（使稳定） calm: ▸～邦定国，～抚，～慰 **2**（满足） feel satisfied (with): ▸～于现状，～之若素 **3**（安置） find a place for: ～炸弹 plant a bomb ▸～插，～顿，～家落户 **4**（安装） fit: ～玻璃 put in glass ‖ ～电灯 install electric lights ▸～装 **5**（怀有） cherish: 没～好心 harbour evil intentions ‖ 你～的什么心? What are you up to? **6**（加上） bestow: 给某人～个头衔 confer a title on sb. ‖ 给某人～罪名 put the blame on sb.

安[2] ān〈书〉
A〈代〉 where: 而今～在? Where is it now?
B〈副〉 how

安[3] ān = 安培 ānpéi
【安邦定国】ānbāng-dìngguó〈成〉 bring peace and stability to the country
【安不忘危】ānbùwàngwēi〈成〉 be mindful of potential danger during times of peace
【安步当车】ānbù-dàngchē〈成〉 go on foot instead of by car: 反正路也不远，我们还是～吧。 Anyway it's not far away so we might as well walk over.
【安瓿】ānbù〈名〉［药学］ ampoule
【安插】ānchā〈动〉 **1**（指人） put sb. in a certain place: 将亲信～在政府内部 install one's trusted followers in the government ‖ 这么多人叫我往哪儿～? Where can I find jobs for so many people? **2**（指物） insert: 这是作者精心～的一个倒叙。 This is a flashback carefully inserted by the author.
【安常处顺】āncháng-chǔshùn〈成〉 take things as they are
【安达曼海】Āndámànhǎi〈名〉 Andaman Sea
【安打】āndǎ〈动〉［体育］ bunt (for a base hit): 一记高质量的～ an excellent bunt

【安道尔】Āndào'ěr〈名〉 Andorra: ～人 Andorran ‖ ～公国 Principality of Andorra
【安道尔城】Āndào'ěrchéng〈名〉 Andorra la Vella
【安第斯山脉】Āndìsī shānmài〈名〉 Andes
【安定】āndìng **A**〈形〉 stable: ～团结 stability and unity ‖ 社会～ have social stability ‖ 生活～ live a settled life **B**〈动〉 stabilize: ～情绪 steady one's nerves ‖ ～人心 set people's minds at rest **C**〈名〉［药学］ diazepam: ～剂 tranquillizer
【安度】āndù〈动〉 spend peacefully: ～晚年 live out one's final years in peace
【安顿】āndùn **A**〈动〉 make proper arrangements: ～一家老小 arrange for one's family ‖ 家里都～好了吗? Have you got everything settled at home? **B**〈形〉 peaceful: 睡不～ sleep fitfully ‖ 只有把事情干完我心里才～。 I can't have peace of mind until the job is done.
【安放】ānfàng〈动〉 put in a proper place: 把仪器～好 put the instruments in their proper places ‖ 灵堂里～着花圈。 Wreaths were laid in the mourning hall.
【安分】ānfèn〈形〉 knowing one's place: 这孩子一点儿也不～。 The child is really badly behaved.
【安分守己】ānfèn-shǒujǐ〈成〉 know one's place
【安抚】ānfǔ〈动〉 appease: ～人心 reassure the public ‖ ～伤员 aid and comfort the wounded ‖ ～死者亲属 console the relatives of the dead
【安富尊荣】ānfù-zūnróng〈成〉 enjoy wealth and honour
【安哥拉】Āngēlā〈名〉 Angola: ～共和国 Republic of Angola ‖ ～人 Angolan
【安格尔西郡】Āngé'ěrxījùn〈名〉 Anglesey
【安格斯郡】Āngésījùn〈名〉 Angus
【安好】ānhǎo〈形〉 safe and sound: 我们一切～, 请勿挂念。 We are all very well. Please don't worry.
【安徽】Ānhuī ▸**p. 661**〈名〉 Anhui Province
【安魂曲】ānhúnqǔ〈名〉［宗教］ requiem
【安家】ānjiā〈动〉 **1**（定居） settle down: 在北京～ make one's home in Beijing **2**（结婚） get married: 他都三十好几了, 还没～。 He is well over thirty but he's still not married.
【安家费】ānjiāfèi〈名〉 **1**（定居费） settling-in allowance **2**（家庭津贴） family allowance
【安家立业】ānjiā-lìyè〈成〉 start a family and a career
【安家落户】ānjiā-luòhù〈成〉 **1**（指人） set up home: 退休后在农村～ settle in the countryside after one's retirement **2**（指植物） grow as well after being transplanted as before **3**（指动物） live and reproduce as before in a new area
【安检】ānjiǎn〈简称〉= 安全检查
【安检口】ānjiǎnkǒu〈名〉 security checkpoint
【安检门】ānjiǎnmén〈名〉 metal detector gate: 顺利通过机场～ pass through the airport metal detector gate
【安检员】ānjiǎnyuán ▸**p. 966**〈名〉 security personnel: 机场～ airport security
【安静】ānjìng〈形〉 **1**（不嘈杂） quiet: 病人需要～。 The patients need peace and quiet. ‖ 老师一来, 教室里立即～下来。 The class quieted down as soon as the teacher came. ‖ 请保持～。 Please keep quiet. **2**（安稳平静） calm: 过几年～的生活 live a peaceful life for several years ‖ 孩子睡得很～。 The child is sleeping peacefully.
【安居】ānjū〈动〉 live in peace and comfort
【安居房】ānjūfáng〈名〉 apartment for low-income families
【安居乐业】ānjū-lèyè〈成〉 live a peaceful life and enjoy one's work
【安卡拉】Ānkǎlā〈名〉 Ankara
【安康】ānkāng〈形〉 safe and sound: 祝二老～。 [to one's parents] The very best to both of you.
【安澜】ānlán〈形〉〈书〉 **1**（指江河） calm **2**（指社会） peaceful and tranquil: 天下～。 The country enjoys peace and stability.
【安乐】ānlè〈形〉 peaceful and happy: 生活～ live in peace and happiness
【安乐死】ānlèsǐ〈名〉 euthanasia
【安乐窝】ānlèwō〈名〉 cosy nest: 营造自己的～ build a snug little nest for oneself
【安乐椅】ānlèyǐ〈名〉 easy chair
【安理会】Ānlǐhuì〈简称〉= 安全理事会
【安良除暴】ānliáng-chúbào〈成〉 pacify the good and do away with the bullies
【安曼】Ānmàn〈名〉 Amman
【安谧】ānmì〈形〉〈书〉 tranquil
【安眠】ānmián〈动〉 **1**（指睡觉） sleep peacefully: 彻夜不能～ have a sleepless night **2** ▸**p. 772**〈婉〉（指死亡） die: ～地下 be dead and buried
【安眠酮】ānmiántóng〈名〉［药学］ methaqualone
【安眠药】ānmiányào〈名〉 sleeping pill
【安民】ānmín〈动〉 reassure the people: 兴邦～ bring peace to the people and prosperity to the country ‖ ～政策 policy of appeasement
【安民告示】ānmín gàoshì〈名〉 **1**（用于安定民心） notice to reassure the public **2**（用于提前公告） advance notice
【安乃近】ānnǎijìn〈名〉［药学］ analgin
【安宁】ānníng〈形〉 **1**（指秩序） peaceful: 社会～ social tranquillity **2**（指心绪） calm: 心里很不～ feel very unsettled ‖ 这孩子让我不得～。 The child gave me no peace.
【安排】ānpái **A**〈动〉 arrange: ～本周工作 map out the week's work ‖ ～考试日程 put together an examination schedule ‖ ～食宿 arrange accommodations ‖ 统筹～ make overall arrangements **B**〈名〉 arrangement: 今晚有什么～吗? Do you have any plans for tonight?
【安培】ānpéi〈名〉［电气］ ampere
【安培表】ānpéibiǎo = 安培计 ānpéijì
【安培计】ānpéijì〈名〉［电气］ amperemeter
【安贫乐道】ānpín-lèdào〈成〉 be happy to live a simple and virtuous life
【安琪儿】ānqí'ér〈名〉 angel
【安寝】ānqǐn〈动〉〈书〉 sleep peacefully: 夜不～ be unable to sleep well at night
【安全】ānquán〈形〉 safe: 保证～ guarantee sb.'s safety ‖ 感到～ feel secure ‖ 威胁他人～ be a menace to the safety of others ‖ ～保障措施 safety precautions ‖ 交通～ road safety ‖ 人身～ personal security ‖ ～第一 safety first
【安全报警装置】ānquán bàojǐng zhuāngzhì〈名〉 safety alarm
【安全部】ānquánbù〈名〉 ministry of security: 国家～ Ministry of National Security
【安全操作】ānquán cāozuò〈名〉 safe operation: ～规程 safety rules
【安全措施】ānquán cuòshī〈名〉 security arrangements: 执行～ observe safety precautions
【安全带】ānquándài〈名〉 safety belt: 请系上～。 Please put on your seat belt.
【安全岛】ānquándǎo〈名〉［交通］ pedestrian island
【安全灯】ānquándēng〈名〉 **1**［矿业］ safety lamp **2**［摄影］ safe light
【安全阀】ānquánfá〈名〉 safety valve: 〈喻〉 心理上的～ psychological safety valve ‖〈喻〉 政治上的～ political safety valve
【安全感】ānquángǎn〈名〉 sense of security: 她没有～。 She feels insecure.
【安全检查】ānquán jiǎnchá〈名〉 security check
【安全理事会】Ānquán Lǐshìhuì〈名〉Security Council of the United Nations: ～常任理事国 permanent member of the Security Council
【安全帽】ānquánmào〈名〉 safety helmet
【安全门】ānquánmén = 太平门 tàipíngmén
【安全期】ānquánqī〈名〉［生理］ safe period: ～避孕法 rhythm method
【安全生产】ānquán shēngchǎn〈名〉 safe production: 保证～ ensure safety in production
【安全套】ānquántào〈名〉 condom
【安全剃刀】ānquán tìdāo〈名〉 safety razor
【安全通道】ānquán tōngdào〈名〉 safe passage
【安全系数】ānquán xìshù〈名〉 safety margin
【安全意识】ānquán yìshí〈名〉 safety awareness
【安全装置】ānquán zhuāngzhì〈名〉 security apparatus
【安然】ānrán〈形〉 **1**（安全） safe: ～脱险 escape unscathed **2**（无顾虑） at ease: ～入睡 go to sleep peacefully
【安然无恙】ānrán-wúyàng〈成〉 unscathed: 她在那次事故中～。 She came out of that accident without a scratch.
【安如磐石】ānrú-pánshí〈成〉be as solid as a rock
【安如泰山】ānrú-Tàishān〈成〉 be as solid as a rock
【安莎社】Ānshāshè〈简称〉= 安莎通迅社
【安莎通迅社】Ānshā Tōngxùnshè〈名〉 Agenzia Nazionale Stampa Associata (ANSA)
【安设】ānshè〈动〉 install: ～报警系统 install a warning system ‖ ～气象站 set up a weather station
【安身】ānshēn〈动〉 make one's home: 无处～ have no place to call one's home
【安身立命】ānshēn-lìmìng〈成〉 settle down and get on with one's life
【安神】ānshén〈动〉 **1**（使心神安宁） calm the nerves: 安下神来 steady one's nerves **2**［中医］ relieve the uneasiness of body and mind
【安生】ānshēng〈形〉 **1**（安定） stable: 过～日子 live a stable life **2**（不受干扰） untroubled: 睡个～觉 have an undisturbed sleep **3**（不生事） quiet: 这孩子一会儿也不～。 The kid won't keep still even for a single moment.
【安史之乱】Ān-Shǐ Zhī Luàn〈名〉 The An-Shi Rebellion [armed rebellion led by An Lushan (安禄山) and Shi Siming (史思明) in 755 in the Tang Dynasty]
【安适】ānshì〈形〉〈书〉 quiet and comfortable: 生活～ live in peace and comfort
【安睡】ānshuì〈动〉〈书〉 sleep peacefully
【安泰】āntài〈形〉〈书〉 well: 阖家～。 All is well with the family.
【安特里姆郡】Āntèlǐmǔjùn〈名〉 Antrim

a

【安提瓜和巴布达】 Āntíguā hé Bābùdá〈名〉Antigua and Barbuda
【安恬】āntián〈形〉〈书〉peaceful
【安土重迁】āntǔ-zhòngqiān〈成〉hate to leave one's native land
【安妥】āntuǒ〈形〉safe and handled in a proper way: 货已～发出。The goods have been sent out as required.
【安危】ānwēi〈名〉safety: 不顾个人～ be heedless of one's personal safety ‖ 无视工人的～ ignore the safety of the workers
【安慰】ānwèi **A**〈动〉comfort: 自我～ console oneself ‖ ～的话 mollifying remarks **B**〈形〉comforting: 得到～ be comforted **C**〈名〉comfort: 你的信给了我很大的～。Your letter is a great comfort to me.
【安慰奖】ānwèijiǎng〈名〉consolation prize
【安慰赛】ānwèisài〈名〉［体育］consolation game
【安稳】ānwěn〈形〉**1**（平稳）smooth and steady: 这只船大，即使刮风，也很～。The boat is big and steady even in the wind. **2**（安定）undisturbed: 过～日子 live a peaceful life ‖ 睡个～觉 sleep a peaceful sleep **3**（指举止）calm and poised
【安息】ānxī〈动〉**1**（休息）rest: 一路劳顿，早点～吧。It's been a tiring journey. You'd better have an early night. **2** ▸p. 772（悼念用语）rest in peace
【安息日】ānxīrì〈名〉Sabbath: 不守～ break the Sabbath
【安息香】ānxīxiāng〈名〉benzoin
【安闲】ānxián〈形〉peaceful and carefree: ～自在 be leisurely and carefree ‖ 过～的生活 enjoy a life of leisure
【安详】ānxiáng〈形〉calm: 举止～ behave with composure ‖ ～地死去 die with serenity ‖ ～的面容 unruffled expression
【安享】ānxiǎng〈动〉enjoy in peace: ～太平 enjoy peaceful times ‖ ～晚年 enjoy one's old age in peace
【安歇】ānxiē〈动〉**1**（睡觉）retire for the night: 他到半夜才～。He didn't go to bed until midnight. **2**（休息）take a rest: 找个地方～ find a place to have a rest
【安心】ānxīn **A**〈动〉harbour an intention: ～不善 harbour evil intentions ‖ 谁知道他安的什么心! God knows what he is up to! **B**〈形〉free from worries: ～工作 keep one's mind on one's work ‖ 听到这消息，爸爸就～了。Dad was relieved at the news.
【安逸】ānyì〈形〉easy and comfortable: 生活～ lead a life of ease and comfort
【安营】ānyíng〈动〉set up camp
【安营扎寨】ānyíng-zhāzhài〈成〉pitch camp
【安于】ānyú〈动〉be satisfied with
【安于现状】ānyú xiànzhuàng〈成〉be content with things as they are
【安葬】ānzàng〈动〉bury: ～烈士遗骨 bury the remains of the martyrs
【安枕】ānzhěn〈动〉**1**〈本〉sleep comfortably **2**〈喻〉be free from worry: ～无忧 be free from worry
【安之若素】ānzhī-ruòsù〈成〉**1**（指行为）bear with equanimity **2**（指态度）regard with indifference
【安置】ānzhì〈动〉**1**（指物）put in a proper place: ～行李 put one's luggage in a proper place **2**（指人）find a suitable position for sb.: 妥善～失业人员 make proper arrangements for the placement of unemployed workers ‖ ～费 settlement allowance
【安置房】ānzhìfáng〈名〉resettlement housing: 加快落实动迁户的～ speed up the resettlement of relocated households ‖ 灾民急需过渡～。The disaster victims are in urgent need of transitional resettlement housing.
【安装】ānzhuāng〈动〉fix: ～玻璃 put in a pane of glass ‖ ～电话 install a telephone ‖ ～门窗 fit the doors and windows ‖ 把相机～在三脚架上 mount a camera on a tripod
【安装程序】ānzhuāng chéngxù〈名〉installation procedure
【安装队】ānzhuāngduì〈名〉installation team
【安装费】ānzhuāngfèi〈名〉installation cost
【安装工】ānzhuānggōng〈名〉installer
【安装工程】ānzhuāng gōngchéng〈名〉installation work
【安装盘】ānzhuāngpán〈名〉［计算机］installation disc
【安装手册】ānzhuāng shǒucè〈名〉installation manual
【安装调试】ānzhuāng tiáoshì〈名〉installation and trial run

桉
ān〈名〉［植物］eucalyptus: ～油 eucalyptus oil ‖ ～油精 cajeputol

氨
ān〈名〉［化学］ammonia: 合成～ synthetic ammonia
【氨苯磺胺】ānběn huáng'àn〈名〉［药学］sulfanilamide
【氨茶碱】ānchájiǎn〈名〉［药学］aminophylline
【氨基】ānjī〈名〉［化学］amino
【氨基酸】ānjīsuān〈名〉［生化］amino acid
【氨纶】ānlún〈名〉［纺织］spandex
【氨气】ānqì〈名〉ammonia: ～塔 ammonia still
【氨水】ānshuǐ〈名〉ammonia solution

庵（菴）
ān〈名〉**1**〈书〉（草屋）hut: 茅～ thatched hut **2**（寺院）nunnery
【庵堂】āntáng〈名〉nunnery

谙（諳）
ān〈动〉〈书〉be well versed in: 不～世事 not know the ways of the world ‖ 深～水性 be a very good swimmer
【谙达】āndá〈动〉〈书〉know well: ～世情 be worldly-wise
【谙练】ānliàn〈书〉**A**〈动〉know well: ～骑射 be proficient in horsemanship and archery **B**〈形〉experienced: 骑术～ ride with experience and skill
【谙事】ānshì〈动〉be sensible: 孩子小，还不～。He's still very young and doesn't have much sense.
【谙熟】ānshú〈动〉be well versed in: ～中国历史 be conversant with Chinese history

鹌（鵪）
ān
【鹌鹑】ānchun〈名〉quail

鲅（鮟）
ān
【鲅鱇】ānkāng〈名〉［鱼类］goosefish

鞍
ān〈名〉saddle: ▸马～
【鞍鼻】ānbí〈名〉［医学］saddle nose
【鞍部】ānbù〈名〉saddle (of a mountain)
【鞍鞯】ānchàn〈名〉saddle and saddle blanket
【鞍工】āngōng〈名〉saddler
【鞍马】ānmǎ〈名〉**1** ▸p. 909［体育］pommelled horse **2**〈书〉（鞍子和马）saddle and horse: ～生活 life on horseback
【鞍马劳顿】ānmǎ-láodùn〈成〉be travel-worn
【鞍前马后】ānqián-mǎhòu〈成〉〈喻〉follow closely and wait upon sb. carefully
【鞍桥】ānqiáo〈名〉pommel and cantle
【鞍式】ānshì〈名〉saddle: ～函数 saddle function
【鞍形】ānxíng〈名〉saddle: ～键 saddle key ‖ ～接头 saddle joint
【鞍子】ānzi〈名〉saddle

ǎn

俺
ǎn〈代〉〈方〉**1**（我）（作主语）I;（作宾语）me;（我的）my: ～爹 my dad **2**（我们）（作主语）we;（作宾语）us;（我们的）our: ～村 our village ‖ ～都愿意去。All of us are willing to go.
【俺们】ǎnmen〈代〉〈方〉（作主语）we;（作宾语）us;（我们的）our

埯（垵）
ǎn
A〈名〉hole for dibbling seeds
B〈动〉dibble: ～豆 dibble in the beans
C〈量〉[for crops planted by dibbling]: 一～儿花生 a cluster of peanut seedlings
【埯子】ǎnzi〈名〉hole for dibbling seeds: 挖～ dibble a hole

唵[1]
ǎn〈动〉〈方〉put into one's mouth: ～了两口雪 take two mouthfuls of snow

唵[2]
ǎn〈叹〉〈方〉well: ～，东西都收拾好了吗? So, have you got things ready?

铵（銨）
ǎn〈名〉［化学］ammonium: ▸硫酸～
【铵根】ǎngēn = 铵 ǎn

揞
ǎn〈动〉apply medicinal powder to: 伤口上～上点儿消炎粉。Apply some antiphlogistic powder to the cut.

àn

犴
àn ▸狴犴 bì'àn

岸
àn
A〈名〉bank: 上～ go ashore ‖ 在河对～ on the other side of the river ‖ 两～绿柳成荫。Willow trees lined the river banks. ▸彼～, 海～, 沿～
B〈形〉**1**（高大）tall and big: ▸魁～, 伟～ **2**（高傲）lofty: ▸傲～
【岸标】ànbiāo〈名〉shore beacon
【岸炮】ànpào〈名〉coastal artillery
【岸然】ànrán〈形〉〈书〉in a solemn manner: ▸道貌～

按[1]
àn〈动〉**1**（压）push down: ～电钮/开关 press a button/switch ‖ ～键 press a key ‖ ～喇叭 sound a horn ‖ 有人～门

铃。 Someone is ringing the doorbell. 2（搁置） put aside: 我们先～下此事不说。 Let's put this aside for a while. 3（抑制） restrain: ～不住心头怒火 be unable to control one's anger ▸～捺, ～压

按² àn

A〈动〉 1〈书〉（核对） check: 有原文可～ have the original to check against 2（加按语） make comments: 编者～ editor's note

B〈介〉 according to: ～成本出售 sell at cost ‖ ～计划进行 proceed as planned ‖ ～制度办事 act in accordance with rules and regulations ‖ ～字母顺序排列 arrange alphabetically ▸～劳分配, ～图索骥

【按比例】 ànbǐlì〈副〉 in proportion

【按兵不动】 ànbīng-bùdòng 〈成〉 1〈本〉 hold one's troops where they are 2〈喻〉 take no action: 大家都在复习迎考，你怎么还～呢? Everyone is preparing for the exams. How come you still haven't got yourself in gear?

【按部就班】 ànbù-jiùbān〈成〉 1〈本〉 in good order: 学习科学知识应该～，循序渐进。 Scientific knowledge should be pursued in an orderly and progressive manner. 2〈喻〉 keep to conventional ways

【按次】 àncì〈副〉 in sequence: ～进入 enter in proper order

【按键】 ànjiàn〈名〉 button: 录音～ record button

【按键式电话】 ànjiànshì diànhuà 〈名〉 touch-tone telephone

【按键通话系统】 ànjiàn tōnghuà xìtǒng〈名〉 press-talk system

【按揭】 ànjiē〈名〉 mortgage: ～贷款 mortgage loan ‖ ～购房 purchase a house with a loan ‖ 银行提供六成～。 The bank provided a 60% mortgage.

【按金】 ànjīn 〈名〉 〈方〉 1（押金） deposit 2（租金） rent: 交纳～ pay rent

【按扣儿】 ànkòur〈名〉〈口〉 snap fastener

【按劳分配】 ànláo-fēnpèi〈成〉 distribution according to labour

【按理】 ànlǐ〈副〉 by rights: ～你这事是不能办的。 I cannot do this for you on principle. ‖ 这种事～是不会发生的。 Such things would not take place in the ordinary course of events.

【按例】 ànlì〈副〉 according to convention: ～这里的书不出借。 According to our practice, the books here are not to be loaned.

【按脉】 ànmài〈动〉 take a pulse

【按摩】 ànmó〈动〉 massage: 给某人做面部/头部～ give sb. a facial/scalp massage

【按摩器】 ànmóqì〈名〉 massager

【按摩师】 ànmóshī ▸p. 966〈名〉（男） masseur;（女） masseuse

【按摩仪】 ànmóyí〈名〉 massage machine

【按摩院】 ànmóyuàn〈名〉 massage parlour

【按捺】 ànnà〈动〉 restrain: ～不住心头的怒火 be unable to suppress one's anger

【按钮】 ànniǔ〈名〉 button: ～拨号盘 push-button dialling pad ‖ 复位～ reset button

【按钮开关】 ànniǔ kāiguān 〈名〉 push-button switch

【按钮控制】 ànniǔ kòngzhì 〈名〉 push-button control

【按钮式】 ànniǔshì〈形〉 push-button: ～电话 push-button phone

【按期】 ànqī〈副〉 on time: ～举行 take place as scheduled ‖ 生产计划～完成了。 The production was fulfilled on schedule.

【按时】 ànshí〈副〉 on time: ～吃药 take medicine on time ‖ ～上下班 keep good working hours

【按说】 ànshuō〈副〉 ordinarily: ～他应该五点前回来。 Normally, he should be back by five. ‖ 他这么大的孩子，～该懂事了。 Normally, a child of his age should show good sense.

【按图索骥】 àntú-suǒjì〈成〉〈喻〉 try to find sth. by following up a clue

【按下葫芦浮起瓢】 ànxià húlu fúqǐ piáo〈俗〉〈喻〉 if it's not one damned thing, it's another

【按需分配】 ànxū-fēnpèi〈成〉 distribution according to need

【按压】 ànyā〈动〉 1（用手压住） press down with one's hand: 我将他～在地上，一顿好打。 I pushed him down to the ground and gave him a good beating. 2（压抑） suppress: ～心中的仇恨 hold back the bitterness in one's heart

【按语】 ànyǔ〈名〉 note: 编者～ editor's note

【按照】 ànzhào〈介〉 according to: ～惯例 according to the accepted practice ‖ ～情节轻重 depending on the seriousness of the case ‖ ～实际情况决定工作方针 determine working policies in the light of actual conditions ‖ ～贡献大小，分别给予奖励。 Each person was rewarded according to his contribution.

【按质论价】 ànzhì-lùnjià〈成〉 fix a price against quality

胺 àn〈名〉［化学］ amine

案¹ àn〈名〉 1（木盘） wooden tray: ▸举～齐眉 2（桌子） long, narrow table or desk: ▸伏～, 拍～而起, 书～ 3（木板） long board [propped up to serve as a table or counter]: 肉～ meat counter ▸～板, 白～, 红～

案² àn

A〈名〉 1（案件） case: 强奸/诈骗～ rape/fraud case ‖ 该～即将由法院审理。 The case will go to trial. ▸～件, 惨～, 破～ 2（文书） record: ▸～卷, 备～, 有～可查 3（文件） plan: ▸草～, 教～, 提～

B = 按² àn A

【案板】 ànbǎn〈名〉 chopping board: 木制/塑料～ wooden/plastic board

【案秤】 ànchèng〈名〉 counter scale

【案底】 àndǐ〈名〉〈方〉 criminal record: 有～的嫌疑人 suspect with a record

【案牍】 àndú〈名〉〈旧〉 official documents

【案发】 ànfā〈动〉 [of a crime] take place: ～当日，嫌疑人不在现场。 On the day of the crime, the suspect was not at the crime scene.

【案犯】 ànfàn〈名〉 the accused: 抓获～ capture the offenders

【案件】 ànjiàn〈名〉 case: 办理～ work on a case ‖ 民事/刑事～ civil/criminal case

【案卷】 ànjuàn〈名〉 files

【案例】 ànlì〈名〉 case: ～分析 case analysis

【案情】 ànqíng〈名〉 specifics of a case: 分析/研究～ analyse/study a case ‖ ～复杂。 The case is complicated.

【案头】 àntóu〈名〉 1（桌子） desk 2 = 案头工作 àntóu gōngzuò

【案头工作】 àntóu gōngzuò〈名〉 1（文字准备） notes written before a performance 2（文字工作） desk work: 我还有些～要做。 I still have some desk work to do.

【案由】 ànyóu〈名〉 brief summary

【案语】 ànyǔ = 按语 ànyǔ

【案值】 ànzhí 〈名〉 amount of money involved in a legal case: 这起诈骗案～八百万元人民币。 This fraud case involved 8 million *yuan*.

【案子】 ànzi 〈名〉 1〈方〉（桌子） long, narrow table: 乒乓球～ ping-pong table ‖ 肉～ meat counter 2〈口〉（案件） case: 法院不受理这个～。 The court will not hear this case.

暗 àn

A〈形〉 1（黑暗） dark: 天色渐渐～下来。 The sky gradually darkened. ‖ 屋里光线太～。 The room is too dimly lit. ▸～室, ～无天日, 阴～ 2〈书〉（糊涂） muddled: ▸～昧, 兼听则明，偏信则～ 3（隐秘） hidden: ▸～堡, ～号, ～语

B〈副〉（暗中） secretly: ▸～喜, 明争～斗

【暗暗】 àn'àn 〈副〉 to oneself: ～称奇 marvel at sth. secretly ‖ ～发誓 vow to oneself

【暗坝】 ànbà〈名〉 submerged dam

【暗堡】 ànbǎo〈名〉［军事］ bunker

【暗补】 ànbǔ〈名〉 covert subsidy

【暗藏】 àncáng〈动〉 hide: ～凶器 illegally possess murder weapons ‖ 口袋里～着一把刀 conceal a knife in one's pocket

【暗娼】 ànchāng〈名〉 unlicensed prostitute

【暗场】 ànchǎng〈名〉 plot not acted out on stage but understood through dialogue or monologue

【暗潮】 àncháo〈名〉 undercurrent

【暗处】 ànchù 〈名〉 1（指光线不足） dark place: 躲在～ hide in the dark 2（指隐蔽） secret place: 在～活动 act under cover

【暗袋】 àndài〈名〉［摄影］ camera bag

【暗淡】 àndàn〈形〉 bleak: 色彩～ dull colour ‖ 房间里灯光～。 The room was dimly lit. ‖〈喻〉 公司前景～。 The company's prospects are gloomy.

【暗道】 àndào〈名〉 secret passage

【暗地里】 àndìli = 暗中 ànzhōng 2

【暗兜】 àndōu〈名〉 inside pocket

【暗度陈仓】 àndù-Chéncāng 〈成〉 do something in secret: ▸明修栈道，～

【暗房】 ànfáng = 暗室 ànshì 1

【暗访】 ànfǎng〈动〉 make secret enquiries: ～民情 conduct a private investigation into people's real conditions ▸明察～

【暗缝】 ànfèng〈名〉 false hem: ～缝纫机 blind stitch sewing machine

【暗沟】 àngōu〈名〉 underground drain: ～排水 subdrainage

【暗管】 ànguǎn〈名〉 concealed piping

【暗害】 ànhài〈动〉 kill secretly: 险遭～ narrowly escape murder

【暗含】 ànhán〈动〉 imply: ～不满 imply resentment

【暗号】 ànhào〈名〉 secret signal: 破译～ break a code ‖ 联络～ contact password

【暗合】 ànhé〈动〉 be in complete agreement without prior consultation: 母亲的话正与他的心意～。 What his mother said was just what he had in mind.

【暗河】 ànhé〈名〉 underground river

【暗盒】 ànhé〈名〉［摄影］ cartridge

【暗花】 ànhuā〈名〉 faint patterns

【暗火】 ànhuǒ〈名〉 smouldering fire

【暗疾】 ànjí〈名〉 1（潜伏的） latent disease 2（说不出口的） unmentionable disease

【暗记】 ànjì A〈名〉 secret mark B〈动〉 commit to memory

【暗间】 ànjiān〈名〉 inner room

a

【暗箭】ànjiàn〈名〉〈喻〉a stab in the back: 放～ attack by underhand means ‖ ～伤人 stab sb. in the back

【暗箭难防】ànjiàn nánfáng〈成〉arrows shot from a hiding place are difficult to guard against: ▸明枪易躲，～

【暗礁】ànjiāo〈名〉1〈本〉submerged rock: 触～沉没 be wrecked on a hidden reef 2〈喻〉latent danger: 前进道路上的～ hidden obstacles to progress

【暗经】ànjīng ▸p. 50〈名〉［医学］latent menstruation

【暗井】ànjǐng〈名〉［矿业］blind shaft

【暗扣】ànkòu〈名〉1（扣子）covered button 2（折扣）hidden discount

【暗亏】ànkuī〈名〉hidden loss

【暗里】ànli = 暗中 ànzhōng 2

【暗恋】ànliàn〈动〉love secretly: 他～着她。He is her secret admirer.

【暗流】ànliú〈名〉undercurrent: ～急湍。The subterranean flow is rapid. ‖〈喻〉不满的～ undercurrent of resentment

【暗码】ànmǎ〈名〉1（密码）secret code: ～电报 coded message 2〈旧〉（符号）secret sign

【暗昧】ànmèi〈形〉1（暧昧）ambiguous 2（愚昧）dim: ～无知 be stupid and ignorant

【暗盘】ànpán〈名〉price secretly agreed upon between buyer and seller

【暗泣】ànqì〈动〉〈书〉shed tears in secret

【暗器】ànqì〈名〉〈旧〉hidden weapons

【暗渠】ànqú〈名〉1（指水道）underground stream 2［建筑］culvert

【暗弱】ànruò〈形〉1（指光线）dim 2〈书〉（指人）ignorant and weak: 昏庸～ be stupid and weak

【暗色】ànsè〈名〉dark colour

【暗杀】ànshā〈动〉assassinate: 实施～ carry out an assassination ‖ ～未遂 attempted assassination

【暗沙】ànshā〈名〉submerged sandbank

【暗伤】ànshāng〈名〉1（指人）internal injury 2（指物体）indiscernible damage

【暗哨】ànshào〈名〉hidden sentry post

【暗射】ànshè〈动〉insinuate

【暗射地图】ànshè dìtú〈名〉blank map

【暗示】ànshì A〈动〉drop a hint: 得到～ take a hint ‖ 巧妙的～ subtle hint ‖ 他没有懂我的～。He didn't take my hint. B〈名〉suggestion

【暗事】ànshì〈名〉underhand actions: ▸明人不做～

【暗室】ànshì〈名〉1［摄影］darkroom 2〈书〉（黑暗之处）dark place: ▸不欺～

【暗送秋波】ànsòng-qiūbō〈成〉1（眉目传情）give sb. the eye 2〈贬〉（献媚取宠）curry favour with sb. secretly

【暗算】ànsuàn〈动〉plot in secret: 险遭～ almost fall a prey to a dark scheme

【暗锁】ànsuǒ〈名〉built-in lock

【暗滩】àntān〈名〉hidden shoal

【暗探】àntàn A〈名〉undercover agent B〈动〉spy: ～军机 spy out military secrets

【暗通关节】àntōngguānjié〈成〉make secret deals: 他与那家公司的管理人员～。He's established secret contact with the management of that company.

【暗无天日】ànwútiānrì〈成〉total lack of justice

【暗物质】ànwùzhì〈名〉［物理］dark matter: 宇宙中的～ the universe's dark matter

【暗喜】ànxǐ〈动〉feel secretly delighted: 心中～ feel secretly pleased

【暗下里】ànxiàli〈副〉secretly

【暗线】ànxiàn〈名〉1（指文章线索）foreshadowing 2（指线人）mole 3（指电线）concealed wiring

【暗线箱】ànxiànxiāng〈名〉wall box

【暗香疏影】ànxiāng-shūyǐng〈成〉1（指香味和倒影）faint fragrance and dappled shadows 2（指梅花）Chinese plum blossoms

【暗箱】ànxiāng〈名〉［摄影］dark box

【暗箱操作】ànxiāng cāozuò〈名〉manipulation behind the scenes

【暗想】ànxiǎng〈动〉think to oneself

【暗笑】ànxiào〈动〉1（指高兴）laugh to oneself: 看到对手着急的样子，他不禁心里～。He couldn't help laughing to himself at his opponent's anxiety. 2（指讥笑）sneer secretly at

【暗星】ànxīng〈名〉［天文］dark star

【暗影】ànyǐng〈名〉1（阴影）shadow 2［天文］umbra

【暗语】ànyǔ〈名〉code word

【暗喻】ànyù = 隐喻 yǐnyù

【暗针】ànzhēn〈名〉slip stitch

【暗中】ànzhōng〈副〉1（黑暗中）in the dark: ～摸索 feel one's way in the dark 2（私下里）secretly: ～监听 listen in secret ‖ ～打听 make secret enquiries ‖ ～监视 watch in secret

【暗转】ànzhuǎn〈名〉［戏剧］blackout

【暗自】ànzì〈副〉to oneself: ～发笑 laugh to oneself ‖ ～落泪 shed private tears ‖ ～盘算 think to oneself

黯 àn〈形〉1（昏暗）dark 2（沮丧）gloomy: ▸～然销魂

【黯淡】àndàn = 暗淡 àndàn

【黯黑】ànhēi〈形〉1（指肤色）pitch-black: 肤色～ be dark-skinned 2（指天色）dark: ～的夜晚 dark night ‖ 天色已经～了。It's already dark.

【黯然】ànrán〈形〉1（黯淡无光）dark-looking: 夜色～ dark night ▸～失色 2（沮丧）dejected: ～泪下 shed melancholy tears

【黯然神伤】ànrán-shénshāng〈惯〉feel depressed

【黯然失色】ànrán-shīsè〈成〉pale into insignificance: 她的歌声使对手们～。Her singing put her rivals to shame.

【黯然销魂】ànrán-xiāohún〈成〉be extremely sad and depressed

āng

肮（骯） āng

【肮脏】āngzāng〈形〉1（不干净）dirty: ～的地方 squalid place ‖ ～的屋子 filthy room 2（卑鄙）vile: 灵魂～ have a dark soul ‖ ～的交易 dirty deal ‖ 干～的勾当 do dark deeds

áng

昂 áng

A〈动〉raise: ～起头 lift up one's head ▸～首

B〈形〉1（价高）expensive: ▸～贵 2（情绪高）high-spirited: ▸～奋，激～，轩～

【昂藏】ángcáng〈形〉〈书〉impressive: 气宇～ have imposing looks

【昂奋】ángfèn〈形〉excited: 心情～ be high-spirited

【昂贵】ángguì〈形〉〈书〉expensive: ～的仪器 expensive instrument ‖ 造价～。Production costs are high.

【昂然】ángrán〈形〉〈书〉proud and bold: ～屹立 stand proudly

【昂首】ángshǒu〈动〉〈书〉hold one's head high: ～挺立 stand proudly, head erect

【昂首阔步】ángshǒu-kuòbù〈成〉walk with one's head high

【昂首挺胸】ángshǒu-tǐngxiōng〈成〉hold up one's head and throw out one's chest

【昂扬】ángyáng〈形〉〈书〉excited: 歌声～ spirited singing ‖ 斗志～ have a high morale

àng

盎[1] àng〈名〉ancient vessel with a big belly and a small mouth

盎[2] àng〈形〉〈书〉abundant: ～～ full of vigour ▸～然

【盎格鲁－撒克逊人】Ànggélǔ-Sākèxùnrén〈名〉Anglo-Saxon

【盎然】àngrán〈形〉〈书〉abundant: 趣味～ be full of interest

【盎司】àngsī ▸p. 978〈量〉ounce (oz): 一磅等于十六～。There are 16 ounces to the pound.

āo

凹 āo〈形〉concave: 路面～下去了。The road surface caved in. ▸～凸不平 ▸wā

【凹版】āobǎn〈名〉［印刷］gravure: ～印刷 intaglio printing

【凹槽】āocáo〈名〉1［建筑］rabbet 2［地质］trough

【凹地】āodì〈名〉hollow

【凹度】āodù〈名〉concavity

【凹痕】āohén〈名〉dent: 把车门撞出～ put a dent in the car door

【凹镜】āojìng = 凹面镜 āomiànjìng

【凹口】āokǒu〈名〉notch

【凹面】āomiàn〈名〉concave surface

【凹面镜】āomiànjìng〈名〉concave mirror

【凹面体】āomiàntǐ〈名〉concavity

【凹模】āomú〈名〉cavity die

【凹透镜】āotòujìng〈名〉concave lens

【凹凸不平】āotū-bùpíng〈形〉uneven: ～的路面 bumpy road

【凹凸印刷】āotū yìnshuā〈名〉embossing: ～机 embossing press

【凹凸纸】āotūzhǐ〈名〉embossed paper

【凹纹】āowén〈名〉design in intaglio

【凹陷】āoxiàn〈动〉indent: 两颊～ have sunken cheeks ‖ 地面～。The ground caved in.

【凹形】āoxíng〈名〉concavity

【凹印】āoyìn〈名〉gravure

熬 āo〈动〉stew in water: ～白菜 stewed cabbage ‖ ～豆腐 stewed bean curd ▸áo

【熬心】āoxīn〈形〉〈方〉moody

爊 āo〈动〉〈书〉（文火煮）cook on a slow fire

áo

敖 áo〈古〉= 遨 áo

【敖包】áobāo〈名〉*aobao* [sacred pile of stones, earth, grass, etc. used by Mongolians as a place of worship or road or boundary sign]

遨 áo〈动〉tour

【遨游】áoyóu〈动〉〈书〉 travel: ～世界 tour the world ‖ ～太空 travel through space

嗷 áo

【嗷嗷】áo'áo〈拟〉 ouch: 痛得～叫 howl with pain

【嗷嗷待哺】áo'áo-dàibǔ〈成〉 howl for food

廒 áo〈名〉〈古〉granary: ▸仓～

獒 áo〈名〉［动物］mastiff

熬 áo〈动〉 1（烹煮） cook on a soft fire: ～粥 cook porridge ‖ 让汤多～一会儿。 Leave the soup to simmer for a while. 2（提炼） extract by heating for a long time: ～盐 make salt by boiling sea water ‖ ～油 extract oil by heating 3（忍耐） endure: ～苦日子 endure hard times ‖ ～过冬天 live through the winter ‖ 他～红了眼睛。 His eyes are bloodshot as a result of staying up late.
▸āo

【熬煎】áojiān〈动〉 torment: 受尽～ endure all sorts of hardships ‖ 疾病时时～着她。 She frequently suffered from illness.

【熬磨】áomó〈动〉〈方〉 1（挨日子） go through painfully 2（纠缠） harass: 这孩子很听话，从不～人。 He is a well-behaved boy and never pesters people.

【熬头儿】áotour〈名〉〈方〉 hope for a better life after enduring hardships: 没个～ see no light at the end of the tunnel

【熬夜】áoyè〈动〉 stay up all night: 熬了一夜 sit up all through the night ‖ ～看书 stay up reading ‖ 经常～会伤身体的。 Staying up late often is harmful to one's health.

聱 áo

【聱牙】áoyá〈形〉〈书〉 tough-going: ▸佶屈～

螯 áo〈名〉pincers

【螯合】áohé〈动〉［化学］ chelate: ～剂 chelating agent

【螯虾】áoxiā〈名〉crayfish

【螯肢】áozhī〈名〉 chelicera: ～动物 cheliceral creature

【螯足】áozú〈名〉cheliped

翱（翺） áo〈动〉〈书〉take wing

【翱翔】áoxiáng〈动〉〈书〉 soar: 展翅～ soar on the wings ‖ 在高空～ hover high in the sky

鳌（鰲、鼇） áo〈名〉 huge legendary green sea-turtle

【鳌山】áoshān〈名〉〈旧〉 turtle-shaped mountain [made up of colourful lanterns for celebration of the Lantern Festival]

【鳌头】áotóu〈名〉 1〈本〉 turtle head [carved on a stone block in front of the imperial palace and reserved for the scholar who came first in the highest imperial examination to step on] 2〈喻〉 champion: ▸独占～

鏖 áo〈动〉〈书〉 engage in fierce battle

【鏖兵】áobīng〈动〉〈书〉 battle hard

【鏖战】áozhàn〈动〉 engage in fierce battle: 双方经过两小时的～才决出胜负。 It took two hours' fierce contest to decide which side was the stronger.

ǎo

拗（抝） ǎo〈动〉〈方〉 cause to bend or break: 啪的一声把树枝～断 snap a branch
▸ào, niù

袄（襖） ǎo〈名〉 lined Chinese-style coat: ▸棉～

媪 ǎo〈名〉〈书〉 old woman: 翁～ old man and woman

【媪妪】ǎoyù〈名〉〈书〉 old woman

ào

岙（嶴） ào〈名〉 flat land in a mountain

坳 ào〈名〉 col: 山～ mountain col

拗（抝） ào〈动〉 disobey: ▸～口, 违～
▸ǎo, niù

【拗口】àokǒu〈形〉 hard to pronounce: 这几句话读着有点～。 These sentences do not read very well.

【拗口令】àokǒulìng = 绕口令 ràokǒulìng

傲 ào

A〈形〉 1（自大） arrogant: ▸～慢, 倨～ 2（不屈） proud and unyielding: ▸～骨, ～然
B〈动〉 look down on: ▸～物

【傲岸】ào'àn〈形〉〈书〉 haughty: ～不群 be haughty and aloof

【傲骨】àogǔ〈名〉〈喻〉 proud and unyielding character

【傲慢】àomàn〈形〉 arrogant: 态度～ put on airs ‖ ～无礼 insolent and rude

【傲气】àoqì〈名〉 conceit: 打掉某人的～ knock all the conceit out of sb.

【傲然】àorán〈形〉〈书〉 unyielding

【傲世】àoshì〈动〉〈书〉 look down on the world

【傲视】àoshì〈动〉〈书〉 regard with disdain: ～万物 treat everything with disdain

【傲物】àowù〈动〉〈书〉 be supercilious: ▸恃才～

奥 ào

A〈名〉〈古〉 innermost part of a house: ▸堂～
B〈形〉 1〈书〉（里面） inner 2（精深） abstruse: ▸～妙, ～旨, 深～

【奥博】àobó〈形〉〈书〉 1（含义深广） extensive and profound: 文辞～。 The language is profound. 2（知识丰富） knowledgeable: 学问～ be erudite

【奥地利】Àodìlì〈名〉 Austria: ～共和国 Republic of Austria ‖ ～人 Austrian

【奥克兰】Àokèlán〈名〉 Auckland

【奥克尼群岛郡】Àokèníqúndǎojùn〈名〉 Orkney Islands

【奥林匹克】Àolínpǐkè〈形〉 Olympic

【奥林匹克村】Āolínpǐkècūn〈名〉 Olympic Village

【奥林匹克火炬】Àolínpǐkè huǒjù〈名〉 Olympic torch

【奥林匹克精神】Àolínpǐkè jīngshén〈名〉 Olympic spirit: 发扬～ promote the Olympic spirit

【奥林匹克申办委员会】Àolínpǐkè Shēnbàn Wěiyuánhuì〈名〉 Olympic Games Bid Committee

【奥林匹克圣火】Àolínpǐkè shènghuǒ〈名〉 Olympic flame: 传递/点燃～ pass/light the Olympic flame

【奥林匹克委员会】Àolínpǐkè Wěiyuánhuì〈名〉 Olympic Committee: 国际～ International Olympic Committee (IOC) ‖ 国际～官员/委员 IOC official/member

【奥林匹克运动会】Àolínpǐkè Yùndònghuì ▸p. 909〈名〉 Olympic Games: 参加～ take part in the Olympic Games ‖ 主办/举办～ host the Olympics

【奥林匹斯山】Àolínpǐsīshān〈名〉 (Mount) Olympus

【奥林匹亚】Àolínpǐyà〈名〉 Olympia

【奥纶】àolún〈名〉［纺织］Orlon

【奥秘】àomì〈名〉 mystery: 探索太空～ probe space mysteries ‖ 成功的～ the secret of success ‖ 大自然的～ the mystery of nature

【奥妙】àomiào A〈名〉 profundity: 不知其中～ not know the subtleties ‖ 其中必有～。 There must be more to it than meets the eye. B〈形〉 profound

【奥塞梯】Àosàití〈名〉 Ossetia

【奥申委】Àoshēnwěi〈简称〉= 奥林匹克申办委员会

【奥数】àoshù〈名〉 Olympic Mathematics

【奥斯卡奖】Àosīkǎjiǎng〈名〉 Oscar (Academy Award): 获得～ win an Oscar ‖ ～获得者 Oscar winner

【奥斯卡金像奖】Àosīkǎ jīnxiàngjiǎng = 奥斯卡奖 Àosīkǎjiǎng

【奥斯陆】Àosīlù〈名〉 Oslo

【奥斯曼帝国】Àosīmàn Dìguó〈名〉 Ottoman Empire [1290-1922]

【奥陶纪】Àotáojì〈名〉［地质］ Ordovician Period

【奥陶系】Àotáoxì〈名〉［地质］Ordovician System

【奥委会】Àowěihuì〈简称〉= 奥林匹克委员会

【奥匈帝国】Ào-Xiōng Dìguó〈名〉 Austro-Hungarian Empire [1867-1918]

【奥运】Àoyùn〈简称〉= 奥林匹克运动会

【奥运村】Àoyùncūn = 奥林匹克村 Āolínpǐkècūn

【奥运会】Àoyùnhuì〈简称〉= 奥林匹克运动会

【奥运精神】Àoyùn jīngshén = 奥林匹克精神 Àolínpǐkè jīngshén

【奥运旗】Àoyùnqí = 五环旗 Wǔhuánqí

【奥运圣火】Àoyùn shènghuǒ = 奥林匹克圣火 Àolínpǐkè shènghuǒ

【奥运选手】Àoyùn xuǎnshǒu〈名〉 Olympian

【奥旨】àozhǐ〈名〉〈书〉 profound implication

骜（驁）ào

A〈名〉〈书〉（骏马） steed
B = 傲 ào

澳 ào

〈名〉 **1**（海湾） bay: 三都～ Sandu Bay **2** ▸**p. 661** Ào（澳门） Macao

【澳大利亚】Àodàlìyà〈名〉 Australia: ～人 Australian ‖ ～土著居民 Australoid

【澳大利亚联邦】Àodàlìyà Liánbāng〈名〉 Commonwealth of Australia

【澳抗】àokàng〈名〉 Australia antigen

【澳联社】Àoliánshè〈名〉 Australian Associated Press

【澳毛】àomáo〈名〉 Australian wool

【澳门】Àomén ▸**p. 661**〈名〉 Macao: ～特别行政区 Macao Special Administrative Region (MSAR) ‖ ～元 pataca

【澳元】Àoyuán ▸**p. 328**〈名〉 Australian dollar (AUD)

【澳洲】Àozhōu〈名〉 Australia

懊 ào

〈动〉（烦恼）be annoyed;（悔恨）be regretful: ▸～悔, ～恼

【懊恨】àohèn〈动〉 regret: ～不已 be very remorseful

【懊悔】àohuǐ〈动〉 regret: 她对当教师并不～。 She has no regrets about being a teacher.

【懊侬】àonáo〈动〉〈书〉 deeply regret

【懊恼】àonǎo〈动〉 fret: 考试没通过，他很～。 He was very upset about failing the test. ‖ 你不必为这种小事～。You mustn't fret yourself about such trivial things.

【懊丧】àosàng〈形〉 depressed: 神情～ look dejected

鏊 ào

【鏊子】àozi〈名〉〈方〉 griddle

Bb

bā

八 bā ▸**p. 691**〈数〉 eight: ～点钟 eight o'clock ‖ ～频道 Channel 8 ‖ 一式～份 in eight duplicate copies

【八拜之交】 bābàizhījiāo 〈成〉 sworn brotherhood: ～的朋友 sworn brothers

【八宝】 bābǎo 〈名〉 eight treasures [assorted ingredients for certain special dishes]: ～菜 eight-treasure pickle ‖ ～饭 eight-treasure rice pudding

【八宝山】 Bābǎoshān〈名〉 Babao Hill [site of a cemetery with attached crematorium in Beijing]: ～革命公墓 Babaoshan Revolutionary Cemetery

【八宝粥】 bābǎozhōu 〈名〉 eight-treasure rice porridge

【八辈子】 bābèizi〈名〉〈口〉 very long time: 我真是倒了～霉了。 What a long run of bad luck I've had! ‖ 那都是～以前的事了。 That was a million years ago.

【八边形】 bābiānxíng〈名〉 octagon

【八成】 bāchéng **A**〈数量〉 eighty per cent: ～新 practically new ‖ 你拿～, 我拿两成。 You take eighty per cent and I twenty per cent. **B**〈副〉 most likely: 他～儿不在家。 Most probably he is not at home.

【八度】 bādù〈名〉［音乐］ octave: 降低一个～ fall one octave

【八方】 bāfāng〈名〉 all directions: ～来客 guests from various places ▸四面～

【八哥】 bāge〈名〉［鸟类］ mynah bird

【八股】 bāgǔ 〈名〉 **1**〈旧〉（指科举文体） eight-part essay form **2**〈喻〉（空洞死板的文章） stereotyped article: ▸党～

【八股文】 bāgǔwén〈名〉 eight-part essay

> **八股文**
>
> A literary exercise forming part of Ming and Qing imperial examinations. Candidates were expected to write an eight-part essay using a set number of characters. Each part adhered to a strict form and structure that included parallel sentences, tonal patterns and rhyme schemes. The essay became obsolete following the abolition of the imperial examination system in the early 20th century.

【八卦】 bāguà〈名〉 **1**（指符号） Eight Trigrams **2**（指传闻） gossip: ～网 gossip web ‖ 娱乐～ entertainment gossip

【八卦教】 Bāguàjiào = 天理教 Tiānlǐjiào

【八卦图】 bāguàtú〈名〉 Eight Trigrams arranged in an octagon

【八卦阵】 bāguàzhèn 〈名〉 Eight-Trigram military formation:〈喻〉 摆～ bring into a mystifying situation

【八国集团】 Bāguó Jítuán〈名〉 Group of Eight (G8)

> **八卦**
>
> Arrangement of lines in the *I Ching* (▸《易经》) used for divination. Each Trigram contains a combination of three broken or unbroken lines (a trigram), the broken line representing *yin* and the unbroken line representing *yang*. The variation between the opposites represented by the broken and the unbroken lines symbolizes the changing nature of matter. The concept has had a profound influence on Chinese philosophy.

【八国联军】 Bāguó Liánjūn 〈名〉 Eight-Power Allied Forces [foreign troops sent in 1900 to suppress the Boxer Rebellion]

【八级考试】 bājí kǎoshì〈名〉 Band Eight Examination [test for those studying for a degree in English]

【八角】 bājiǎo 〈名〉 **1**（指角） eight angles: ～帽 octagonal cap **2**（指植物） star anise **3**（指果实） aniseed

【八角形】 bājiǎoxíng〈名〉 octagon

【八节】 bājié〈名〉 eight solar terms: 四时～ four seasons and eight solar terms

【八九不离十】 bā jiǔ bùlí shí〈惯〉 not far off: 猜个～ make a very close guess

【八开】 bākāi〈名〉［印刷］ octavo, 8vo

【八路】 Bālù〈名〉 **1** = 八路军 Bālùjūn **2**（指人） Eighth Route Army man

【八路军】 Bālùjūn〈名〉 Eighth Route Army [led by the Chinese Communist Party during the War of Resistance Against Japan]

【八面见光】 bāmiànjiànguāng = 八面玲珑 bāmiàn-línglóng

【八面玲珑】 bāmiàn-línglóng 〈成〉 be smooth and slick: 他是个～的人。 He is a bit of a smoothie.

【八面威风】 bāmiàn-wēifēng 〈成〉 have a commanding presence

【八旗】 bāqí〈名〉 'Eight Banners'

> **八旗**
>
> The Manchu administrative, social and military system established in 1601 by the Manchu leader Nurhachi (努尔哈赤). Named after eight coloured flags, banner companies became instrumental in the establishment of the Qing Dynasty in 1644. However, at the end of the Qing Dynasty the banners declined as an effective fighting force, with the next generation degenerating into privileged good-for-nothings.

【八旗子弟】 bāqízǐdì〈名〉〈喻〉 idle and wasteful children of privileged families

【八强】 bāqiáng〈名〉［体育］ final eight: 进入～ make the final eight

【八荣八耻】 bāróng-bāchǐ〈名〉 Eight Honours and Eight Disgraces

【八抬大轿】 bātái-dàjiào〈名〉〈旧〉 eight-bearer sedan chair

【八仙】 bāxiān ▸**p. 274** 〈名〉 Eight Immortals [in Taoist mythology]

【八仙过海，各显神通】 bāxiān-guòhǎi, gèxiǎn shéntōng〈成〉 **1**〈本〉 cross the sea like the Eight Immortals, each showing their prowess **2**〈喻〉 rely on one's own strengths to prove one's worth

> **八仙**
>
> Legendary beings of Chinese mythology. Li Tieguai has an iron staff and gourd; Han Zhongli has a palm-leaf fan; Zhang Guolao has a paper donkey; Lü Dongbin has a precious sword; He Xiangu has a lotus flower; Han Xiangzi has a bamboo flute; Cao Guojiu has an official tablet, and Lan Caihe has a flower basket. 'Cross the sea like the Eight Immortals, each showing his prowess' is a well-known proverb, meaning that it is up to each person to demonstrate his or her own special strength.

【八仙桌】 bāxiānzhuō〈名〉 old-style square table for eight people

【八一建军节】 Bā-Yī Jiànjūnjié〈名〉 Army Day [August 1]

【八一南昌起义】 Bā-Yī Nánchāng Qǐyì〈名〉 August 1 Nanchang Uprising [1927]

【八音盒】 bāyīnhé〈名〉 musical box〈英〉, music box〈美〉

【八月】 bāyuè ▸**p. 928**〈名〉 **1**（阳历） August **2**（阴历） eighth month of the lunar year

【八月份】 bāyuèfèn = 八月 bāyuè

【八月节】 Bāyuèjié = 中秋节 Zhōngqiūjié

【八字】 bāzì〈名〉 Eight Characters [in four pairs denoting the time, date, month and year of a person's birth, each pair consisting of one Heavenly Stem and one Earthly Branch, used in fortune-telling]: ▸生辰～

【八字步】 bāzìbù〈名〉 measured gait with toes turned outwards: 踱着～ walk splay-footed

【八字胡】 bāzìhú〈名〉 droopy moustache

【八字没一撇】 bā zì méi yī piě〈惯〉〈喻〉 things are not even beginning to take shape yet

【八字帖】 bāzìtiě 〈名〉 〈旧〉 eight-character paper exchanged at betrothal ceremonies in arranged marriages [stating birth information of the betrothed boy or girl expressed in eight Chinese characters]

巴[1] Bā〈名〉 **1**（古国名） ancient state in the eastern part of present-day Sichuan Province and Chongqing **2**（四川、重庆一带） eastern part of Sichuan Province and Chongqing

巴[2] bā

A〈动〉 **1**（盼望） expect anxiously: ▸～不得, ～望 **2**（紧贴） cling to: 葡萄蔓～在支架上。 The grape vine clings to its support. **3**（粘住） stick to: 粥～了锅, 铲不下来。 The porridge has stuck to the pot and won't come off. **4**〈方〉（邻近） be close to

B〈名〉 crust: ▸锅～

b

巴[3] bā

A〈名〉bus: 大～ bus ‖ 中～ minibus ‖ 小～ minivan ▸～士
B〈量〉bar: 毫～ millibar ‖ 微～ microbar
【巴巴】bābā〈后缀〉very: 干～ very dry ‖ 他可怜～的。He looks very miserable.
【巴巴多斯】Bābāduōsī〈名〉Barbados: ～人 Barbadian
【巴巴结结】bāba-jiējiē〈形〉〈方〉**1**（勉强）succeed only after making great efforts: 他只能～读懂英文报纸。He could barely make sense of English newspapers. **2**（艰难）with difficulty: 老人～地走到客厅。The old man managed to walk to the drawing room with great difficulty. **3**（不流利）blundering: 他吓得说话～的。He was stammering with fright.
【巴巴儿地】bābārde〈副〉〈方〉**1**（迫切）anxiously: 他～等着小伙伴。He is waiting anxiously for his young companions. **2**（特地）especially
【巴比伦】Bābǐlún〈名〉Babylon: ～王国 Babylonia
【巴比妥】bābǐtuǒ〈名〉［药学］barbitone: ～中毒 barbiturism
【巴别塔】Bābiétǎ〈名〉Tower of Babel
【巴布亚新几内亚】Bābùyà Xīnjǐnèiyà〈名〉Papua New Guinea: ～人 Papua New Guinean
【巴不得】bābude〈动〉〈口〉be only too eager to: 他～马上见到妻子。He can't wait to see his wife. ‖ 我～有个念大学的机会。I wish I could have a chance to study at the university.
【巴豆】bādòu〈名〉［植物］Purging Croton
【巴尔干】Bā'ěrgàn〈名〉Balkan: ～半岛 the Balkan Peninsula ‖ ～国家 the Balkans ‖ ～人 Balkan
【巴格达】Bāgédá〈名〉Baghdad
【巴哈马】Bāhāmǎ〈名〉Bahamas: ～联邦 Commonwealth of the Bahamas ‖ ～人 Bahamian
【巴基斯坦】Bājīsītǎn〈名〉Pakistan: ～联合通讯社 Associated Press of Pakistan (APP) ‖ ～人 Pakistani ‖ ～伊斯兰共和国 Islamic Republic of Pakistan
【巴解组织】Bājiě Zǔzhī〈简称〉= 巴勒斯坦解放组织
【巴结】bājie **A**〈动〉fawn on: ～上司 curry favour with one's superiors ‖ ～有权势的人 be obsequious to people in power **B**〈形〉〈方〉diligent: 他学习英语很～。He works very hard at English.
【巴库】Bākù〈名〉Baku
【巴拉圭】Bālāguī〈名〉Paraguay: ～共和国 Republic of Paraguay ‖ ～人 Paraguayan
【巴勒斯坦】Bālèsītǎn〈名〉Palestine: ～国 State of Palestine ‖ ～人 Palestinian
【巴勒斯坦解放组织】Bālèsītǎn Jiěfàng Zǔzhī〈名〉Palestine Liberation Organization (PLO)
【巴厘】Bālí〈名〉Bali: ～人 Balinese ‖ ～语 Balinese
【巴厘岛】Bālídǎo〈名〉Bali Island
【巴黎】Bālí〈名〉Paris
【巴黎公社】Bālí Gōngshè〈名〉Paris Commune [established by French workers in 1871]
【巴黎和会】Bālí Héhuì〈名〉**1**（1919年）Paris Peace Conference **2**（1946年）Paris Conference
【巴黎圣母院】Bālí Shèngmǔyuàn〈名〉Notre-Dame de Paris
【巴里纱】bālǐshā〈名〉［纺织］voile
【巴林】Bālín〈名〉Bahrain: ～国 State of Bahrain ‖ ～人 Bahraini
【巴罗克】Bāluókè〈名〉baroque: ～风格 baroque style ‖ ～艺术 baroque art
【巴马科】Bāmǎkē〈名〉Bamako
【巴拿马】Bānámǎ〈名〉Panama: ～共和国 Republic of Panama ‖ ～人 Panamanian
【巴拿马城】Bānámǎchéng〈名〉Panama City
【巴拿马运河】Bānámǎ Yùnhé ▸**p. 294**〈名〉Panama Canal
【巴儿狗】bārgǒu〈名〉**1**（指狗）Pekinese **2**〈喻〉〈粗〉（指人）sycophant: 那条～总是巴结老板。That wretched toady is always sucking up to the boss.
【巴塞罗那】Bāsàiluónà〈名〉Barcelona
【巴山蜀水】Bāshān-Shǔshuǐ〈名〉mountains and rivers of Sichuan Province
【巴士】bāshì〈名〉〈方〉bus: 乘～ take a bus
【巴士底狱】bāshìdǐyù〈名〉Bastille
【巴斯克人】Bāsīkèrén ▸**p. 279**〈名〉the Basques
【巴斯克语】Bāsīkèyǔ ▸**p. 918**〈名〉the Basque language
【巴松管】bāsōngguǎn ▸**p. 929**〈名〉［音乐］bassoon
【巴头探脑】bātóu-tànnǎo〈成〉pop in one's head and look around
【巴望】bāwàng **A**〈动〉hope anxiously (for): 我～着你来信。I'm looking forward to hearing from you. **B**〈名〉good prospect: 事情有～了。Things are beginning to look up.
【巴乌】bāwū ▸**p. 929**〈名〉［音乐］bamboo flute
【巴西】Bāxī〈名〉Brazil: ～联邦共和国 Federative Republic of Brazil ‖ ～人 Brazilian
【巴西利亚】Bāxīlìyà〈名〉Brasilia
【巴掌】bāzhang〈名〉palm: 挨一～ get a slap ‖ 拍～ clap one's hands ‖ ～大的地方 tiny place ▸一个～拍不响

扒 bā

〈动〉**1**（紧紧把住）cling to: ～住栏杆 cling to the balustrade **2**（拆）dig up: ～房 pull down a house ‖ ～坟 dig up a tomb **3**（拨开）push aside: ～开杂草 push the weeds aside ▸～拉 **4**（剥）strip off: ～羊皮 skin a goat ‖ ～光衣服 strip naked ‖〈喻〉～掉伪装 strip off sb.'s mask
▸pá
【扒车】bāchē〈动〉climb onto a moving train or bus
【扒拉】bāla〈动〉〈口〉**1**（拨动）nudge: ～开人群 push one's way through a crowd ‖ ～算盘 flick the beads of the abacus **2**（去除）remove from office or list: 他的职务被～掉了。He was stripped of his post.
【扒皮】bāpí〈动〉**1**〈本〉skin: 你再干这种混账事，小心我扒了你的皮！If you dare try something like that again, be careful — I'll skin you alive! **2**〈喻〉exploit: 钱一经他的手，少不了要被扒掉一层皮。Any money he handles is sure to get skimmed.
【扒头儿】bātour〈名〉〈方〉handrail: 墙上连个～都没有，叫人怎么爬上去？How can one climb the wall without anything to hold on to?

叭 bā

= 吧 bā
【叭儿狗】bārgǒu = 巴儿狗 bārgǒu

芭 bā

【芭蕉】bājiāo〈名〉plantain
【芭蕉扇】bājiāoshàn〈名〉palm-leaf fan
【芭蕾舞】bālěiwǔ〈名〉ballet: 跳～ dance the ballet ‖ 古典～ classical ballet ‖ ～演员 ballet dancer

吧 bā

A〈拟〉crack: ～的一声，带子断了。The tape broke with a snap.
B〈动〉〈方〉puff on one's pipe: ～一口烟 take a puff at one's pipe
C〈名〉bar: ▸酒～，网～
▸ba
【吧嗒】bādā〈拟〉click: 锁～一声锁上了。The lock snapped shut. ‖ 雨点～～地落在屋顶上。Raindrops were pattering on the roof.
【吧嗒】bāda〈动〉**1**（指嘴唇）smack one's lips: ～一下嘴 smack one's lips **2**〈方〉（特指抽烟）inhale loudly: 他坐在那里～～地抽着烟。He sat there puffing his pipe.
【吧唧】bājī〈拟〉squelch: 她穿着雨靴～～地在泥泞的路上走着。She squelched along the muddy road in her wellington boots.
【吧唧】bāji = 吧嗒 bāda
【吧女】bānǚ〈名〉bar girl
【吧台】bātái〈名〉bar: 坐在～前 sit at the bar

疤 bā

〈名〉scar: 额头上有道～ have a scar across one's forehead ‖ 伤口已结了～。A scar has formed over the wound.
▸伤～
【疤痕】bāhén〈名〉scar: 留下～ leave a scar
【疤拉】bāla = 疤瘌 bāla
【疤瘌】bāla〈名〉scar
【疤瘌眼儿】bālayǎnr〈名〉**1**（指眼睛）eye with a scar on the eyelid **2**（指人）person with a scar over one eye

捌 bā

▸**p. 691**〈数〉eight [used for the numeral 八 on cheques, etc. to avoid alterations or mistakes]

笆 bā

〈名〉basketry: ▸篱～
【笆斗】bādǒu〈名〉bamboo basket with a round bottom
【笆篓】bālǒu〈名〉basket carried on the back

粑 bā

〈名〉〈方〉coarse-grained cake: 糖～ sweet cake ▸糍～
【粑粑】bāba〈名〉〈方〉coarse-grained cake: 玉米～ corn cake

玔 bā

〈名〉〈书〉［动物］sow

鲃（鲃）bā

【鲃鱼】bāyú〈名〉［鱼类］barbel

bá

拔 bá

〈动〉**1**（拽出）pull out: ～草 weed ‖ ～掉插头 pull the plug out ‖ ～枪威胁 draw a pistol and threaten to shoot ‖ 我最近太忙，～不开身。I've been very busy lately and can't get away. ▸～苗助长，一毛不～ **2**（超出）stand out among others: ▸～尖儿，出类～萃 **3**（挑选）choose: ▸提～，选～ **4**（攻取）seize: 一夜～掉敌军三个营寨 capture three enemy

camps in one night ⑤（吸出） suck out: ～毒 draw out poison ⑥〈方〉（使变凉） cool by immersing in cold water: 把面放在凉水里～一～。 Cool the noodles in cold water. ⑦（调高） lift: ～嗓子 raise the pitch of one's voice ▸～高

【拔除】báchú〈动〉 remove: ～敌军据点 wipe out an enemy stronghold ‖ ～杂草 pull up weeds

【拔刀相助】bádāo-xiāngzhù〈成〉 draw one's sword to help: 路见不平，～ be ready to lend a hand at the sight of an injustice

【拔地而起】bádì'érqǐ〈成〉 rise steeply from the ground: 高楼大厦～。 High-rise buildings and mansions are springing up.

【拔钉子】bá dīngzi〈动〉〈喻〉 get rid of a difficult obstacle

【拔毒】bádú〈动〉［中医］ draw out a poison

【拔高】bágāo〈动〉①（提高） raise: ～嗓门大喊 shout at the top of one's voice ②（抬高地位） overrate: ～自己，贬低别人 blow one's own trumpet, while putting others down ‖ 剧中的这个人物显然被～了。 The character in the play is obviously larger than life.

【拔罐子】bá guànzi〈动〉［中医］ cup: 给病人～ cup a patient

【拔河】báhé〈名〉［体育］ tug-of-war

【拔火罐儿】bá huǒguànr **A**〈名〉 removable stove chimney **B** = 拔罐子 bá guànzi

【拔火筒】báhuǒtǒng = 拔火罐儿 bá huǒguànr A

【拔尖儿】bájiānr〈形〉 top-notch: 他在我们班是～的学生。 He is head and shoulders above the other students in our class.

【拔脚】bájiǎo = 拔腿 bátuǐ

【拔节】bájié〈动〉［农业］ grow fast

【拔锚】bámáo〈动〉 weigh anchor

【拔苗助长】bámiáo-zhùzhǎng〈成〉 help something to grow by artificial means, and in doing so do it great harm

【拔取】báqǔ〈动〉 employ by selection: ～人才 select and employ talented people

【拔山扛鼎】báshān-kángdǐng〈成〉 be impossibly strong

【拔丝】básī〈动〉①（指金属材料） draw wire: ～机 wire drawing machine ②（指烹调方法） caramelize: ～苹果 toffee apple

【拔俗】bású〈形〉〈书〉 refined

【拔腿】bátuǐ〈动〉①（抬腿） take a step: ～就跑 take to one's heels ②（脱身） get away: 我工作忙，拔不开腿。 I'm so busy with work that I can't get away.

【拔牙】báyá〈动〉 take out a tooth: 拔掉一颗牙 have a tooth pulled out

【拔牙钳】báyáqián〈名〉 dental forceps

【拔秧】báyāng〈动〉 [of rice planting] pull up seedlings

【拔营】báyíng〈动〉［军事］ decamp

【拔擢】bázhuó〈动〉〈书〉 select and promote: ～贤能 select and promote talented people of integrity

菝 bá

【菝葜】báqiā〈名〉［植物］ chinaroot greenbrier

跋[1] bá〈动〉 walk in the mountains: ▸～山涉水, ～涉

跋[2] bá〈名〉 epilogue: 写一篇～ write an afterword ▸题～, 序～

【跋扈】báhù〈形〉 bossy: ▸飞扬～

【跋前疐后】báqián-zhìhòu〈成〉 be caught between a rock and a hard place

【跋山涉水】báshān-shèshuǐ〈成〉 trek through difficult terrain and rivers

【跋涉】báshè〈动〉 trek: 长途～ long-distance trek

【跋文】báwén ▸**p. 918**〈名〉 epilogue

【跋语】báyǔ〈名〉 postscript

魃 bá ▸旱魃 hànbá

bǎ

把[1] bǎ

A〈动〉①（握住） hold: 用一只手～方向盘 steer with one hand ②（控制） monopolize: ～着公司的大权 keep the power of the company in one's own hands ▸～持 ③（守卫） guard: ～住这个胡同口。 Keep watch at this end of the alley. ▸～关, ～门, ～守 ④（固定） chain: 用角铁～住椅子腿 hold the chair leg in place with an angle iron ⑤〈方〉（靠近） be close to: ～门站着 stand at the door ‖ ～着巷口有个小酒馆。 There is a pub at the entrance of the lane. ⑥（托着孩子让其大小便） hold a baby while it relieves itself: 给孩子～尿 hold a baby to let it pee

B〈名〉①（把手） handle: 车～ bicycle handlebars ②（小捆物品） bundle: 草～ a bundle of straw ▸火～

C〈量〉①（用于有柄或把手的物体） [for sth. in a bunch, with its legs parted, or with a handle]: 一～尺子/钥匙 a ruler/key ‖ 一～伞 an umbrella ②（用于某些抽象事物） [for some abstract ideas]: 加～劲 make an extra effort ‖ 一～年纪的人 elderly person ③（用于与手有关的动作） [for sth. done with hand]: 擦～汗 wipe your sweat away ‖ 一～鼻涕一～泪 tearful and snivelling ‖ 要我帮一～吗? Can I give you a hand?

把[2] bǎ〈介〉①（表示处置） [used to advance the object of a verb to the position before it]: ～话题引开 steer the conversation away from a topic ‖ ～门关上 close the door ‖ ～双手伸出来 hold one's hands out ②（表示致使） [used to introduce a 'subject + verb + complement' structure]: ～孩子们乐坏了。 The children were overjoyed. ‖ 快～他累死了。 He was so tired he could have dropped. ③（表示不好的结果） [used to introduce a 'doer + action' structure expressing an unhappy outcome]: 要犁地的时候我偏偏～牛丢了。 I was just about to start ploughing when the ox went missing.

把[3] bǎ〈助〉 [used after some numerals or measure words to express approximation] approximately: 百～里 about fifty kilometres ‖ 个～月 a month or so ▸bà

【把柄】bǎbǐng〈名〉①〈本〉 handle: 锄头～ handle of a hoe ②〈喻〉 handle: 给人以～ give sb. leverage ‖ 小心别让他抓住你什么～。 Be careful not to let him get anything on you.

【把持】bǎchí〈动〉①（独占） dominate: ～财权 have the monopoly of financial authority ‖ ～公司内一切重要职位 occupy all the key positions in the corporation ②（控制） control: ～不住自己 lose control over oneself

【把舵】bǎduò〈动〉 take the helm

【把风】bǎfēng〈动〉 keep watch

【把关】bǎguān〈动〉①（守卫关卡） guard a pass ②〈喻〉 make stringent checks: 严格～ make strict checks ‖ 把好产品质量关 keep a check on and guarantee the quality of a product

【把家】bǎjiā〈动〉〈方〉 keep house: 她是个～好手。 She is good at housekeeping.

【把酒】bǎjiǔ〈动〉〈书〉 raise one's wine cup: ～敬客 raise one's glass and propose a toast to the guest

【把揽】bǎlǎn = 把持 bǎchí 1

【把牢】bǎláo〈形〉〈方〉 reliable: 她办事不～。 She is not dependable when it comes to managing things.

【把脉】bǎmài〈动〉［中医］ take sb.'s pulse

【把门】bǎmén〈动〉①（指门户） guard a gate: 这门把得很严。 The gate was closely guarded. ‖ 〈喻〉他说话嘴上缺个～儿的。 He often comes out with inappropriate remarks. ②（指球门） keep goal

【把式】bǎshi = 把势 bǎshi

【把势】bǎshi〈名〉①（武术） martial arts: 耍～ do martial arts ②（指人） master: 车～ cart driver ③〈方〉（技艺） skill

【把守】bǎshǒu〈动〉 guard

【把手】bǎshou〈名〉① = 拉手 lāshou ②（把儿） grip

【把水搅浑】bǎ shuǐ jiǎohún〈惯〉〈喻〉 muddy the waters

【把头】bǎtou〈名〉 foreman

【把玩】bǎwán〈动〉 hold and play with: 老人在～玉器。 The old man lovingly handled his piece of jade.

【把握】bǎwò **A**〈动〉①（掌控） grasp: ～方向盘 hold the steering wheel ②（抓住） grasp: ～机会 seize an opportunity **B**〈名〉 assurance: 有必胜的～ be sure of winning ‖ 他有～按时完成任务。 He is confident of completing the task in time.

【把戏】bǎxì〈名〉①（杂耍） circus tricks: 变～ perform magic ‖ 耍～的人 juggler ②（花招） cheap tricks: 他又在玩什么鬼～? What cheap trick is he up to this time?

【把兄弟】bǎxiōngdì〈名〉〈旧〉 blood brother

【把盏】bǎzhǎn〈动〉〈书〉 raise a wine cup

【把捉】bǎzhuō〈动〉 grasp: ～事物本质 grasp the essence of a matter ‖ ～文件的精神实质 get the gist of the document

【把子】bǎzi **A**〈名〉①（捆） bundle: 韭菜～ a bundle of leeks ②（武器） stage weapons ③（打斗动作） mock fighting ④ = 把兄弟 bǎxiōngdì **B**〈量〉 **a**〈贬〉（伙） gang: 一～小偷 a gang of thieves **b**（捆） bundle: 一～蒜苗 a bundle of garlic bolts **c**（用于某些抽象事物） [for sth. abstract]: 加～劲儿 make an extra effort ▸bàzi

屉 bǎ〈方〉

A〈名〉 excrement

B〈动〉 defecate

【屉屉】bǎba〈名〉〈口〉 poo poo

钯（鈀） bǎ〈名〉［化学］ palladium (Pd)

靶 bǎ〈名〉 target: 打～ shoot at a target ‖ 中～ hit the target ▸箭～子

【靶标】bǎbiāo〈名〉 target

【靶场】bǎchǎng〈名〉 shooting range

【靶船】bǎchuán〈名〉 target vessel

【靶机】bǎjī〈名〉 target drone

【靶台】bǎtái〈名〉 shooting platform

【靶心】bǎxīn〈名〉 bull's-eye: 击中～ hit the bull's-eye

【靶子】bǎzi〈名〉 target: 命中～ hit the target ‖ ～学说 target theory

bà

坝（壩） bà〈名〉 1（用于拦水）dam: 筑～ build a dam ‖ 筑～拦河 dam a river ‖ 洪水冲垮了堤～。The floodwater burst the dam. 2（用于巩固堤防）embankment: ▸丁～ 3〈方〉（沙滩）sandbank 4（坝子）plain

【坝基】bàjī〈名〉 dam foundation

【坝塘】bàtáng〈名〉〈方〉 small reservoir

【坝田】bàtián〈名〉 patch of fields surrounded by hills

【坝子】bàzi〈名〉 1（用于拦水） dam 2（平原） plain: 川西～ West Sichuan Plain

把 bà〈名〉 1（器具把手） handle: 壶～儿 pot handle 2（花、果柄） stem: 花～儿 pedicel ‖ 梨～儿 pear stem
▸bǎ

【把子】bàzi〈名〉handle: 刀～ knife handle
▸bǎzi

爸 bà〈名〉〈口〉 dad

【爸爸】bàba ▸**p. 588**〈名〉 dad

耙 bà

A〈名〉 harrow: 拉～ draw a harrow ▸钉齿～

B〈动〉 harrow: 那块地已经～过，可以下种了。The field has been harrowed for sowing.
▸pá

【耙齿】bàchǐ〈名〉 harrow spikes

【耙片】bàpiàn〈名〉 harrow disc

罢（罷） bà〈动〉 1（停止） stop: ▸～工，～手 2（免除） dismiss: ～掉她的官 remove her from her office ▸～免 3（结束） finish: 她吃～晚饭就走了。She left after finishing supper.

【罢笔】bàbǐ〈动〉 stop writing

【罢黜】bàchù〈动〉〈书〉 1（免除） dismiss 2（废除） ban: ～百家，独尊儒术 proscribe all non-Confucian schools of thought and espouse Confucianism as the orthodox state ideology

【罢工】bàgōng〈动〉 go on strike: 参加～ take part in a strike ‖ 举行～ go on a strike ‖ 为提高工资～ strike for a pay rise

【罢官】bàguān〈动〉 dismiss

【罢教】bàjiào〈动〉 go on a teaching strike

【罢考】bàkǎo〈动〉 boycott an examination

【罢课】bàkè〈动〉 boycott class

【罢了】bàle〈助〉 [used at the end of a declarative sentence] that's all: 我不过做了自己应该做的事～。I just did what I should, nothing more.

【罢了】bàliǎo〈动〉 let pass: 他不领情也就～，反倒怪起我来。His ingratitude was one thing, but then he went on to lay the blame on me.

【罢论】bàlùn〈名〉〈书〉 abandoned idea: 此事已做～。This idea has already been dropped.

【罢免】bàmiǎn〈动〉 remove from office: 他的主席职务被～了。He was ousted from his position as chairman.

【罢免权】bàmiǎnquán〈名〉 recall

【罢赛】bàsài〈动〉 boycott a game

【罢市】bàshì〈动〉 protest by suspending business

【罢手】bàshǒu〈动〉 throw in the towel: 不成功，我们决不～。We'll never give up until we have succeeded.

【罢讼】bàsòng = 罢诉 bàsù

【罢诉】bàsù〈动〉 withdraw a lawsuit

【罢休】bàxiū〈动〉 give up: 不达目的，决不～。We'll not stop until we reach our goal.

【罢演】bàyǎn〈动〉 boycott a performance

【罢战】bàzhàn〈动〉 end a war

【罢职】bàzhí〈动〉 dismiss

鲅（鮁） bà〈名〉［鱼类］ Spanish mackerel

霸（覇） bà

A〈名〉 1（联盟首领） overlord: 春秋五～ five overlords of the Spring and Autumn Period 2（恶人） tyrant: 他是当地一～。He is a local bully. ▸恶～，渔～ 3（霸权） hegemony: 反～斗争 struggle against local despots ▸争～

B〈动〉 dominate: 军阀割据，各～一方。The country was ruled by warlords, each dominating a region. ▸～占，独～一方

【霸持】bàchí〈动〉 forcibly occupy: ～他人产业 snatch and hold other people's property ‖ ～文坛 dominate literary circles

【霸道】bàdào A〈名〉 way of might B〈形〉 domineering: 她很～。She has an overbearing manner. ▸横行～

【霸道】bàdao〈形〉 potent: 这酒很～，喝一点就醉。This alcohol is strong. You only need to drink a little and you are drunk.

【霸气】bàqì A〈形〉 domineering: ～十足的统治者 completely tyrannical ruler B〈名〉 imperiousness: 他一身～。He has an overbearing manner.

【霸权】bàquán〈名〉 supremacy: 争夺～ contend for hegemony

【霸权主义】bàquán zhǔyì〈名〉 hegemonism

【霸王】bàwáng〈名〉 1（指项羽） the Conqueror [title assumed by Xiang Yu (232-202 BC)] 2〈喻〉（霸道的人） tyrant: 土～ local tyrant

【霸王鞭】bàwángbiān〈名〉 1（指民间舞蹈） rattle stick dance 2（指短棍） rattle stick 3［植物］ crab cactus

【霸王龙】bàwánglóng〈名〉 tyrannosaurux rex

【霸业】bàyè〈名〉enterprise of maintaining hegemony: 建立～ build up a hegemony

【霸占】bàzhàn〈动〉 take by force: ～别国领土 annex the territory of another country ‖ ～财产 occupy property by force

【霸主】bàzhǔ〈名〉 1（特指诸侯） powerful chief of feudal lords 2（指人或集团） overlord: 取得～地位 obtain hegemony

ba

吧 ba〈助〉 1（用于舒缓语气） [used at the end of an imperative sentence to soften the tone]: 快走～! Please hurry up! ‖ 那就下周～。OK. Let's make it next week. 2（表示疑问） [used at the end of a question]: 你就是小李～? You are Xiao Li, aren't you? ‖ 大家都完成工作了～? Have all of you finished the job? 3（表示揣测、估计） [used at the end of a declarative sentence to indicate uncertainty]: 大概是前天～。It was probably the day before yesterday. ‖ 他大概不会来了～。He will not be coming, I suppose. 4（表示停顿） [used before a pause after each one of a pair of opposite suppositions to imply a dilemma]: 去～，不好；不去～，也不好。Going will not do, but neither will not going.
▸bā

bāi

刮 bāi

【刮划】bāihua〈动〉〈方〉 1（安排） arrange 2（修理） repair: 玩具叫他给～坏了。He damaged the toy with his tinkering.

掰 bāi〈动〉 1（指用手） break off with one's hands: ～着手指数数 count on one's fingers ‖〈喻〉 一分钱～成两半花 watch every penny ‖ 他把巧克力～成了两半。He broke the bar of chocolate into two. 2〈方〉（破裂） break up: 他俩的交情早就～了。The two of them broke up ages ago.

【掰手腕】bāi shǒuwàn = 掰腕子 bāi wànzi

【掰腕子】bāi wànzi〈名〉 arm wrestling: 我～掰不过他。There's no way I can beat him in an arm wrestle.

bái

白[1] bái ▸**p. 863**

A〈形〉 1（指颜色） white: 皮肤～ fair-skinned ‖ 她的头发已经～了。Her hair has turned grey. ▸黑～分明 2（纯洁） pure: ▸清～ 3（明亮） bright: 大～天 broad daylight ‖ 东方发～。Day was dawning in the east. 4（清楚） clear: ▸不～之冤，真相大～ 5（空白） plain: ～开水 plain boiled water ‖ ～纸 blank paper ▸～手起家

B〈动〉 1（解释） explain: ▸表～，自～ 2（冷眼看） stare at coldly: ～了某人一眼 cast a disdainful glance at sb.

C〈名〉 1（念白） spoken part: ▸独～，对～ 2（白话） the vernacular: 文～杂陈 mixture of classical and vernacular Chinese 3（丧事） funeral: ▸红～喜事 4（白色部分） white: ▸蛋～，眼～ 5（食用茎） stalk: ▸葱～，茭～ 6（反动） White [signifying counter-revolutionary political alignment]: ▸～区，～色恐怖 7（方言） dialect: 苏～ Suzhou dialect

D〈副〉 1（徒然） in vain: ～跑一趟 make a fruitless trip ‖ ～辛苦 one's efforts have been to no avail 2（无代价） free of charge: ～吃～拿 eat and help oneself for free ‖ ～给 give for free

白[2] bái〈形〉 misspelt: 写～字 write a wrong character

【白皑皑】bái'ái'ái〈形〉 snow-white: ～的山峰 snow-covered mountain peak

【白矮星】bái'ǎixīng〈名〉［天文］ white dwarf

【白案】bái'àn〈名〉 flour or rice cooking

【白白】báibái〈副〉 in vain: ～送死 die in vain ‖ 这简直是～浪费精力。This is quite simply a waste of energy.

【白班】báibān〈名〉 day shift: 上～ work the day shift

【白斑】báibān〈名〉［医学］ leukoplakia: ～病 vitiligo

【白板】báibǎn〈名〉1（指木板）unpainted plank 2（指麻将）white dragon
【白版】báibǎn〈名〉blank space
【白报纸】báibàozhǐ〈名〉newsprint
【白璧微瑕】báibì-wēixiá〈成〉small blemish
【白璧无瑕】báibì-wúxiá〈成〉impeccable moral integrity
【白醭】báibú〈名〉white mould
【白布】báibù〈名〉calico
【白菜】báicài〈名〉Chinese cabbage
【白茬】báichá〈形〉1（指土地）unplanted 2（指家具）unpainted: ～大门 unpainted gate
【白吃】báichī〈动〉have a free meal: 这顿饭不能让他～了。We can't let him have the meal for free.
【白痴】báichī〈名〉1（指病症）idiocy 2（指病人）idiot: 天生的～ born idiot ‖〈喻〉他们简直把我当～了。They must think I'm an idiot.
【白炽灯】báichìdēng〈名〉incandescent lamp
【白唇鹿】báichúnlù〈名〉white-lipped deer
【白醋】báicù〈名〉white vinegar
【白搭】báidā〈动〉〈口〉be of no use: 你说也～，他不会同意的。It's no use talking to him. He won't give his consent.
【白大褂】báidàguà〈名〉〈口〉1（指衣服）doctor's white coat 2〈喻〉（医务人员）doctor or nurse
【白带】báidài〈名〉［生理］leucorrhoea
【白蛋白】báidànbái〈名〉［生化］albumin
【白道】báidào〈名〉1（月球轨道）moon's orbit 2〈喻〉（合法谋生途径）circle of officials: 他黑道～都有联系。He has connections both in the government and in the underworld.
【白地】báidì〈名〉1（空地）unsown field: 我们留了一块～种棉花。We left a plot for cotton. 2（荒地）barren land: 村子被烧成一片～。The village was reduced to waste land by fire. 3（白色底面）white base: ～薄板 plate with white base
【白癜风】báidiànfēng ▸p. 50〈名〉［医学］vitiligo
【白丁】báidīng〈名〉〈旧〉commoner
【白俄】Bái É〈名〉expatriate Russian [one who fled Russia after 1917]
【白俄罗斯】Bái'éluósī〈名〉Belarus: ～共和国 Republic of Belarus ‖ ～人 Belarusian ‖ ～语 Belarusian
【白垩】bái'è〈名〉［地质］chalk: ～纪 Cretaceous Period ‖ ～系 Cretaceous System
【白发苍苍】báifà-cāngcāng〈形〉grey-haired
【白矾】báifán〈名〉［化学］alum
【白饭】báifàn〈名〉1（米饭）boiled rice 2 = 白食 báishí
【白费】báifèi〈动〉waste: ～力气 waste one's energy ‖ ～口舌 waste one's breath ‖ ～心思 rack one's brains in vain ‖ 一切辛苦全～了。All that hard work was for nothing.
【白费蜡】báifèilà〈惯〉waste one's time and energy
【白粉】báifěn〈名〉1（化妆粉）white face powder 2〈口〉（刷墙粉）chalk 3〈口〉（海洛因）heroin: 吸～ do heroin
【白粉病】báifěnbìng〈名〉［植物］powdery mildew
【白干儿】báigānr〈名〉strong, colourless alcoholic drink
【白宫】Báigōng〈名〉White House
【白骨】báigǔ〈名〉white bones of the dead
【白骨精】báigǔjīng〈名〉1〈本〉White Bone Demon [in the novel *Journey to the West*《西游记》] 2〈喻〉sly and ruthless woman
【白瓜子】báiguāzǐ〈名〉pumpkin seed
【白果】báiguǒ〈名〉［植物］gingko
【白鹤】báihè〈名〉white crane
【白喉】báihóu ▸p. 50〈名〉［医学］diphtheria
【白狐】báihú〈名〉arctic fox
【白虎星】báihǔxīng〈名〉1（指星辰）White Tiger Star 2（带来恶运的人）jinx
【白花花】báihuāhuā〈形〉shining white: ～的银元 gleaming silver dollars
【白化病】báihuàbìng〈名〉albinism: ～人 albino
【白话】báihuà〈名〉1（空话）empty promise: 空口说～ make empty promises 2（指语言形式）the vernacular: ～小说 novels in the vernacular
【白话诗】báihuàshī〈名〉free verse in vernacular Chinese
【白话文】báihuàwén〈名〉writings in vernacular Chinese: ～运动 Vernacular Movement [1917-1919]

> 白话文
>
> *Baihuawen* (or so-called vernacular Chinese) refers to the style of written language based on vernacular Mandarin Chinese (白话), in contrast to classical Chinese, the traditional form of written Chinese based on classical texts. *Baihuawen* became widely used in vernacular Chinese literature after the May 4th Movement of 1919, gradually replacing the classical style of writing.

【白桦】báihuà〈名〉［植物］white birch
【白晃晃】báihuǎnghuǎng〈形〉gleaming: ～的照明弹 dazzling flare
【白灰】báihuī = 石灰 shíhuī
【白芨】báijī〈名〉［中药］hyacinth bletilla
【白鳖豚】báijìtún = 白鳍豚 báiqítún
【白金】báijīn〈名〉1（铂）platinum 2（银）silver
【白金汉宫】Báijīnhàngōng〈名〉Buckingham Palace
【白金汉郡】Báijīnhànjùn〈名〉Buckinghamshire
【白净】báijìng〈形〉fair and clear: ～的皮肤 fair complexion
【白酒】báijiǔ〈名〉〈口〉liquor
【白驹过隙】báijū-guòxì〈成〉in the twinkling of an eye: 人生如～。Life is fleeting.
【白卷】báijuàn〈名〉〈口〉blank examination paper: 交～ have nothing to show for oneself
【白开水】báikāishuǐ〈名〉plain boiled water
【白口】báikǒu〈名〉1（指戏曲）spoken parts 2（指线装书）white fore-edge
【白口铁】báikǒutiě〈名〉white iron
【白蜡】báilà〈名〉insect wax
【白蜡虫】báilàchóng〈名〉wax insect
【白蜡树】báilàshù〈名〉Chinese ash
【白兰地】báilándì〈名〉brandy
【白兰瓜】báilánguā〈名〉honeydew melon
【白兰花】báilánhuā〈名〉gardenia
【白莲教】Báiliánjiào〈名〉White Lotus Society [a religious sect in the Yuan, Ming, and Qing dynasties]
【白鲢】báilián〈名〉［鱼类］silver carp
【白脸】báiliǎn〈名〉1（指脸谱）white face in Beijing opera: 扮演～ play the villain ▸唱～ 2（指男子）handsome young man: 他只不过是个小～。He is merely a pretty face.
【白蔹】báiliǎn〈名〉［植物］radix ampelopsis
【白磷】báilín〈名〉white phosphorus
【白蛉】báilíng〈名〉sandfly
【白领】báilǐng〈名〉white collar: ～阶层 white-collar class
【白令海】Báilìnghǎi〈名〉Bering Sea: ～峡 Bering Strait
【白鹭】báilù〈名〉egret
【白露】Báilù〈名〉White Dew [beginning of the 15th of the 24 solar terms]
【白马王子】báimǎ wángzǐ〈名〉Prince Charming, knight in shining armour: 梦中的～ the man of one's dreams
【白茫茫】báimángmáng〈形〉vast expanse of whiteness: 田野被大雪覆盖着，～一眼望不到边。Covered with snow, the fields were an endless expanse of whiteness.
【白茅】báimáo〈名〉［植物］cogongrass: ～根 cogongrass rhizome
【白霉素】báiméisù〈名〉［药学］albomycin
【白蒙蒙】báiméngméng〈形〉hazy: ～的晨雾 a haze of morning mist
【白米】báimǐ〈名〉〈口〉husked rice: ～饭 cooked rice
【白面】báimiàn〈名〉〈口〉white flour
【白面儿】báimiànr〈名〉〈口〉heroin
【白面书生】báimiàn shūshēng〈名〉1（年轻的读书人）young scholar 2（面孔白净的读书人）fair-complexioned scholar
【白描】báimiáo〈名〉1（指画法）sketch 2（指写作手法）sketch: 用～手法刻画人物性格 portray a person's character in a sketch
【白沫】báimò〈名〉1（指泡沫）foam 2（指唾沫）frothy saliva: 口吐～ foam at the mouth
【白木耳】báimù'ěr〈名〉edible white fungus
【白内障】báinèizhàng ▸p. 50〈名〉［医学］cataract
【白嫩】báinèn〈形〉（指皮肤）soft and delicate
【白皮书】báipíshū〈名〉white paper
【白票】báipiào〈名〉blank ballot: 一张～ a blank ballot paper
【白旗】báiqí〈名〉white flag: 挂～ fly the white flag
【白鳍豚】báiqítún〈名〉Chinese river dolphin
【白切鸡】báiqiējī = 白斩鸡 báizhǎnjī
【白区】báiqū〈名〉White Areas [esp the Kuomintang-controlled areas during the Second Revolutionary War, 1927-1937]
【白饶】báiráo〈动〉1（白给）give sth. extra free of charge 2〈方〉（白搭）be useless: 我们昨天干的全算～。What we did yesterday turned out to be completely useless.
【白热】báirè〈名〉white heat: 在战斗的～阶段 in the heat of the battle
【白热化】báirèhuà〈动〉incandesce: 竞争趋于～。Competition is becoming white-hot.
【白人】Báirén〈名〉white person
【白刃】báirèn〈名〉naked blade
【白刃战】báirènzhàn〈名〉bayonet fighting
【白日】báirì〈名〉1（太阳）sun 2（白天）daytime
【白日见鬼】báirì-jiànguǐ〈成〉sheer fantasy
【白日梦】báirìmèng〈名〉pipe dream: 做～ have a daydream
【白日做梦】báirì-zuòmèng〈成〉daydream
【白肉】báiròu〈名〉〈口〉1（指猪肉）unseasoned boiled pork 2（指鸡肉、鱼等）white meat

b

【白润】báirùn〈形〉fair and delicate

【白色】báisè ▸p. 863 A〈名〉white B〈形〉〈喻〉reactionary: ▸～恐怖，～政权

【白色金属】báisè jīnshǔ〈名〉white metal

【白色恐怖】báisè kǒngbù〈名〉White terror

【白色人种】báisè rénzhǒng〈名〉white race

【白色收入】báisè shōurù〈名〉legal income

【白色污染】báisè wūrǎn〈名〉pollution from plastic bags, etc.

【白色政权】báisè zhèngquán〈名〉reactionary regime

【白山黑水】báishān-hēishuǐ〈名〉the Changbai Mountains and Heilongjiang River of Northeast China

【白鳝】báishàn〈名〉white eel

【白芍】báisháo〈名〉［中药］root of herbaceous peony

【白食】báishí〈名〉free meal: 吃～ have meals free of charge

【白事】báishì〈名〉funeral: 办～ conduct a funeral

【白手起家】báishǒu-qǐjiā〈成〉start from scratch: ～的企业家 self-made entrepreneur

【白首】báishǒu〈名〉〈书〉grey hairs: ～老人 grey-haired old man

【白薯】báishǔ〈名〉sweet potato

【白水】báishuǐ〈名〉1（白开水） plain boiled water 2〈书〉（明净的水） clear water

【白说】báishuō〈动〉waste one's breath: 这事就算我～了。Well, just ignore what I have said. ‖ 说了也～。It would be useless to speak out.

【白苏】báisū〈名〉［植物］common perilla

【白汤】báitāng〈名〉clear soup

【白糖】báitáng〈名〉white sugar

【白体】báitǐ〈名〉［印刷］lean type

【白天】báitiān〈名〉daytime: 不分～黑夜地干活 work day and night

【白天不做亏心事，夜里不怕鬼敲门】báitiān bùzuò kuīxīnshì, yèlǐ bùpà guǐ qiāomén〈俗〉a clear conscience sleeps in the midst of thunder

【白田】báitián〈名〉uncultivated plot

【白条】báitiáo〈名〉1（指禽、畜） slaughtered poultry or animal: ～鸡 processed chicken ‖ ～猪 pork 2（指收据） unofficial receipt 3（欠条） IOU: ▸打～

【白铁】báitiě〈名〉galvanized iron

【白铁皮】báitiěpí〈名〉galvanized iron sheet

【白厅】Báitīng〈名〉Whitehall

【白铜】báitóng〈名〉white brass

【白头】báitóu〈名〉1 = 白首 báishǒu 2（无署名或印章） anonymous: ～材料 unsigned document

【白头翁】báitóuwēng〈名〉1（指人） white-haired old man 2［鸟类］grey starling 3［中药］root of the Chinese pulsatilla

【白头偕老】báitóu-xiélǎo〈成〉live in conjugal bliss to a ripe old age

【白脱】báituō〈名〉〈方〉butter

【白玩儿】báiwánr〈动〉1（无代价） have fun without paying: 这次旅游是公司出的钱，我们是～。The trip was paid for by the company and we just enjoyed ourselves for free. 2（不费力） do with ease: 这件事让她去做那是～。It would be as easy as pie for her to do the job.

【白文】báiwén〈名〉1（古书注解本正文） text: 读完～再读注解。Read the text first and then the notes. 2（古书无注解本） unannotated edition of a book 3（印章的阴文） intagliated characters

【白皙】báixī = 白净 báijing

【白细胞】báixìbāo〈名〉white blood cell

【白鹇】báixián〈名〉［鸟类］silver pheasant

【白相】báixiàng〈动〉〈方〉enjoy oneself

【白熊】báixióng〈名〉polar bear

【白血病】báixuèbìng ▸p. 50〈名〉leukemia: ～患者 leukaemic

【白血球】báixuèqiú〈旧〉= 白细胞 báixìbāo

【白眼】báiyǎn〈名〉disdainful look: 遭人～ be held in disdain ‖ ～看人 look at sb. with contempt ▸翻～

【白眼儿狼】báiyǎnrláng〈名〉〈口〉ingrate

【白眼珠】báiyǎnzhū〈名〉〈口〉white of the eye

【白羊座】Báiyángzuò〈名〉［天文］Aries

【白杨】báiyáng〈名〉white poplar

【白药】báiyào〈名〉*baiyao* [a white medicinal powder for treating wounds, bruises, etc.]

【白页】báiyè〈名〉White Pages [the white part of a telephone directory in China containing the phone numbers of organizations or institutions]

【白夜】báiyè〈名〉white night

【白衣苍狗】báiyī-cānggǒu〈成〉life is full of the unexplained

【白衣天使】báiyī tiānshǐ〈名〉hospital staff

【白衣战士】báiyī zhànshì〈名〉medical worker

【白蚁】báiyǐ〈名〉［昆虫］termite

【白翳】báiyì〈名〉［中医］slight corneal opacity

【白银】báiyín〈名〉silver

【白玉】báiyù〈名〉white jade

【白玉兰】báiyùlán〈名〉［植物］gardenia

【白云苍狗】báiyún-cānggǒu = 白衣苍狗 báiyī-cānggǒu

【白云石】báiyúnshí〈名〉［地质］dolomite

【白斩鸡】báizhǎnjī〈名〉tender boiled chicken

【白纸】báizhǐ〈名〉1（指颜色） white paper 2（指没有写或画过） blank paper

【白纸黑字】báizhǐ-hēizì〈成〉written in black and white: 这是～，赖是赖不掉的。There's no point in denying it when it's down in black and white.

【白种】báizhǒng〈名〉white race: ～人 white people

【白昼】báizhòu〈名〉daytime

【白术】báizhú〈名〉［中药］rhizome of large-headed atractylodes

【白字】báizì〈名〉wrongly written or mispronounced character: 他老念～。He tends to mispronounce words. ‖ 这封信～连篇。The letter is full of wrong characters.

【白族】Báizú〈名〉Bai ethnic group

bǎi

百 bǎi ▸p. 691〈数〉1（指数目） hundred: ～分之一 a hundredth 2（表示很多） all kinds of: ～花盛开 numerous flowers in full bloom ▸～货，千方～计

【百般】bǎibān A〈副〉by all means: ～抵赖 persist in one's denial ‖ ～纠缠 pester endlessly ‖ ～阻挠 obstruct by all means possible B〈数〉in a hundred and one ways: 遭受～屈辱 be humiliated in every possible way

【百宝箱】bǎibǎoxiāng〈名〉treasure box

【百倍】bǎibèi ▸p. 31〈数〉hundredfold: ～偿还 repay a hundredfold ‖ 精神～ in renewed high spirits ▸身价～

【百病】bǎibìng〈名〉all kinds of diseases and ailments: ～缠身 be disease-ridden ‖ 包治～ guaranteed to cure every single disease

【百步穿杨】bǎibù-chuānyáng〈成〉be a crack shot

【百尺竿头，更进一步】bǎi chǐ gāntóu, gèng jìn yī bù〈成〉improve on one's achievements

【百出】bǎichū〈动〉〈贬〉be full of: 矛盾～ be full of contradictions

【百川归海】bǎichuān-guīhǎi〈成〉〈喻〉all things tend to go in the same direction

【百端待举】bǎiduān-dàijǔ〈成〉a hundred things remain to be done

【百读不厌】bǎidú-bùyàn〈成〉worth reading a hundred times: ～的好书 best-loved book

【百儿八十】bǎi'er-bāshí〈惯〉about a hundred

【百发百中】bǎifā-bǎizhòng〈成〉1〈本〉shoot with unfailing accuracy: 他打靶时总是～。He never missed the bull's eye in target practice. 2〈喻〉surely succeed: 照他的话做，包你～。Do as he tells you, and you'll make every shot tell.

【百废俱兴】bǎifèi-jùxīng〈成〉all that was left undone is now being restarted

【百分比】bǎifēnbǐ ▸p. 691〈名〉percentage

【百分表】bǎifēnbiǎo〈名〉gauge

【百分尺】bǎifēnchǐ〈名〉micrometer

【百分点】bǎifēndiǎn〈名〉percentage point: 增长了五个～ rise by five percentage points

【百分号】bǎifēnhào〈名〉percentage sign (%)

【百分率】bǎifēnlǜ〈名〉percentage

【百分数】bǎifēnshù ▸p. 691〈名〉percentage

【百分之百】bǎifēnzhībǎi〈副〉one hundred per cent: 有～的把握 be absolutely sure ‖ ～的纯羊绒 hundred per cent pure cashmere

【百分制】bǎifēnzhì〈名〉hundred-point system

【百感交集】bǎigǎn-jiāojí〈成〉experience a whole range of emotions

【百合】bǎihé〈名〉lily

【百花齐放】bǎihuā-qífàng〈成〉1〈本〉all flowers are in bloom 2〈喻〉flourishing art and literature

【百花齐放，百家争鸣】bǎihuā qífàng, bǎijiā zhēngmíng〈成〉let a hundred flowers bloom and a hundred schools of thought contend

【百花争妍】bǎihuā-zhēngyán = 百花争艳 bǎihuā-zhēngyàn

【百花争艳】bǎihuā-zhēngyàn〈成〉flowers are blooming in all their beauty

【百喙莫辩】bǎihuì-mòbiàn = 百口莫辩 bǎikǒu-mòbiàn

【百货】bǎihuò〈名〉general merchandise: 日用～ daily necessities ‖ ～商店 store〈英〉, department store〈美〉

【百家姓】Bǎijiāxìng〈名〉Book of Family Names

【百家争鸣】bǎijiā-zhēngmíng〈成〉1〈本〉contention and flourishing of numerous schools of thought [during the Spring and Autumn and the Warring States periods, 770-221 BC] 2 = 百花齐放，百家争鸣 bǎihuā qífàng, bǎijiā zhēngmíng

【百洁布】bǎijiébù〈名〉scouring pad

【百科】bǎikē〈名〉all subjects: ～词典

encyclopaedic dictionary ‖ ～知识 encyclopaedic knowledge
【百科全书】bǎikē quánshū〈名〉encyclopaedia:《不列颠～》*Encyclopaedia Britannica*
【百孔千疮】bǎikǒng-qiānchuāng〈成〉**1**（受损严重）be badly damaged **2**（问题很多）be full of problems
【百口莫辩】bǎikǒu-mòbiàn〈成〉no one can explain it away
【百老汇】Bǎilǎohuì〈名〉Broadway
【百里挑一】bǎilǐ-tiāoyī〈成〉one in a thousand: ～的美丽女子 exceptionally beautiful woman
【百炼成钢】bǎiliàn-chénggāng〈成〉be forged through repeated struggle: 在艰苦环境里～ be steeled in hardship
【百灵鸟】bǎilíngniǎo〈名〉lark
【百忙】bǎimáng〈名〉busy schedule: ～中 in the midst of pressing affairs ‖ 谢谢您在～之中抽出时间接待我。Thank you for taking time out from your busy schedule to see me.
【百慕大】Bǎimùdà〈名〉Bermuda: ～人 Bermudan
【百衲本】bǎinàběn〈名〉anthology
【百衲衣】bǎinàyī〈名〉**1** = 袈裟 jiāshā **2**（补丁多）heavily-patched garment
【百年】bǎinián〈数量〉**1**（一百年）hundred years: ～华诞 celebration of one's hundredth birthday ‖ ～庆典 centenary celebration **2**（一生）lifetime: 祝你们～好合。I wish the two of you life-long happiness and perfect harmony. ▸～之后
【百年不遇】bǎinián-bùyù〈成〉not seen in a hundred years: ～的洪水 worst flooding in a century
【百年大计】bǎinián-dàjì〈成〉project of vital and lasting importance: ～，质量第一。The first priority in a long-term project is quality.
【百年纪念】bǎinián jìniàn〈名〉centenary, centennial
【百年树人】bǎinián-shùrén〈成〉it takes a hundred years for education to bear fruit
【百年之好】bǎinián-zhīhǎo〈成〉lasting harmony: 结成～ get married
【百年之后】bǎiniánzhīhòu〈成〉after sb. passes away
【百日咳】bǎirìké〈名〉[医学] whooping cough: ～疫苗 pertussis vaccine
【百日维新】Bǎirì Wéixīn〈名〉Hundred Days Reform [in 1898]
【百十】bǎishí ▸**p. 927**〈数〉about a hundred: ～来块钱 about one hundred *yuan* ‖ 这个村子有～口人。There are around a hundred people in the village.
【百世】bǎishì〈名〉〈书〉many generations: ▸流芳～
【百事可乐】Bǎishì Kělè〈名〉Pepsi-Cola
【百事通】bǎishìtōng〈名〉〈贬〉**1**（知道一切）know-it-all **2**（指人）Mr know-it-all
【百兽之王】bǎishòuzhīwáng〈名〉king of the beasts [tiger or lion]
【百思不得其解】bǎisī bùdé qí jiě = 百思不解 bǎisī-bùjiě
【百思不解】bǎisī-bùjiě〈成〉still unable to solve a problem after much thought: 让人～ beyond all comprehension
【百岁老人】bǎisuì lǎorén〈名〉centenarian
【百听不厌】bǎitīng-bùyàn〈成〉it is never boring to listen to
【百团大战】Bǎituán Dàzhàn〈名〉Hundred-Regiment Campaign [1940]
【百万】bǎiwàn ▸**p. 691**〈数〉**1**（一百万）million **2**（非常多）extremely large number: ～雄师 mighty army of some million-odd soldiers ‖ ～富翁 millionaire
【百位】bǎiwèi〈名〉[数学] hundred: ～数 three-digit figure
【百闻不如一见】bǎi wén bùrú yī jiàn〈成〉seeing is believing
【百无禁忌】bǎiwújìnjì〈成〉without any restraint
【百无聊赖】bǎiwúliáolài〈成〉be bored stiff
【百无一失】bǎiwúyīshī〈成〉perfectly safe
【百无一是】bǎiwúyīshì〈成〉having no redeeming features: 他有缺点，但并不是～。He is not perfect, but nor is he completely worthless.
【百物】bǎiwù〈名〉〈书〉all kinds of things: ～昂贵。Everything is expensive.
【百姓】bǎixìng〈名〉common people: 平民～ commoner
【百业】bǎiyè〈名〉〈书〉all professions
【百业待举】bǎiyè-dàijǔ〈成〉all sectors of the economy need to be revived
【百叶】bǎiyè〈名〉〈方〉**1** = 千张 qiānzhang **2**（牛羊等的胃）certain part of tripe
【百叶窗】bǎiyèchuāng〈名〉**1**（指窗扇）blind〈英〉; shade〈美〉: 放下～ pull down the blinds ‖ ～帘 Venetian blind **2**（指机械设备装置）shutter
【百依百顺】bǎiyī-bǎishùn〈成〉be obedient in all things: 他对妻子～。He's completely under his wife's thumb.
【百战百胜】bǎizhàn-bǎishèng〈成〉be invincible
【百战不殆】bǎizhàn-bùdài〈成〉never lose a single battle: 知己知彼，～。Know the enemy, know yourself, and victory is guaranteed in every battle.
【百折不回】bǎizhé-bùhuí = 百折不挠 bǎizhé-bùnáo
【百折不挠】bǎizhé-bùnáo〈成〉keep on fighting despite repeated setbacks: ～的精神 relentless spirit ‖ ～的勇气 unflinching courage
【百褶裙】bǎizhěqún〈名〉pleated skirt
【百足之虫，死而不僵】bǎi zú zhī chóng, sǐ ér bù jiāng〈成〉old institutions die hard

伯 bǎi ▸大伯子 dàbǎizi
▸bó

佰 bǎi ▸**p. 691**〈数〉hundred [used for 百 on cheques, receipt, etc. to avoid mistakes or alterations]

柏 bǎi〈名〉cypress
▸bó, bò
【柏树】bǎishù〈名〉cypress
【柏油】bǎiyóu〈名〉asphalt
【柏油路】bǎiyóulù〈名〉tarmacked road

捭 bǎi〈动〉〈书〉divide
【捭阖】bǎihé〈动〉〈书〉manoeuvre to divide or unite: ▸纵横～

摆¹（擺）bǎi〈动〉**1**（放置）place: ～水果摊 run a fruit stall ‖ ～正自己的位置 know one's own place ‖ 面前～着重要任务 be confronted with an important task **2**（罗列）list: ▸～事实，讲道理 **3**〈方〉（陈述）state clearly: ～家常 make small talk ‖ ～明立场/观点 lay out one's position/views clearly **4**（显示）show: ～老资格 parade one's seniority ‖ ～排场 do sth. in style ▸～架子

摆²（擺）bǎi
A〈动〉sway: ～尾巴 wag the tail ‖ 她离开时～了～手。She waved as she left. ▸摇头～尾
B〈名〉oscillating device: ▸单～，钟～

摆³（襬）bǎi〈名〉skirt: ～宽 skirt width ▸下～，衣～
【摆布】bǎibu〈动〉**1**（布置）put in order: 房子～得很高雅。The house is decorated in excellent taste. **2**（操纵）order about: 任人～ be subject to the whim of others
【摆荡】bǎidàng〈动〉sway: 随风～ sway in the wind
【摆动】bǎidòng〈动〉sway: 树在风中～。Trees swayed in the wind. ‖ 他走路时～着手臂。He swung his arms as he walked.
【摆渡】bǎidù **A**〈动〉ferry: ～过河 ferry across the river **B**〈名〉ferry: ～汽船 ferry steamer
【摆放】bǎifàng〈动〉arrange: 把鲜花～在墓前 lay fresh flowers at sb.'s grave ‖ 把这些东西～好 arrange these things in good order
【摆份儿】bǎifènr〈动〉〈方〉put on airs
【摆幅】bǎifú〈名〉swing
【摆功】bǎigōng〈动〉exaggerate one's contribution
【摆好】bǎihǎo〈动〉put in a good word for sb.: 他老在我的面前摆他媳妇的好。He is always singing his wife's praises to me. ▸评功～
【摆花架子】bǎi huājiàzi〈惯〉put up an impressive front
【摆划】bǎihua〈动〉〈方〉**1**（摆弄）fiddle with **2**（处理）deal with: 这件事真不好～! This is really a hard thing to manage! **3**（修理）fix: 他不知怎么就把收音机给～好了。He has somehow got the radio working again.
【摆架子】bǎi jiàzi〈动〉put on airs: 摆臭架子 reek of affectation ‖ 她在下级面前～。She lorded it over her subordinates.
【摆件】bǎijiàn〈名〉ornaments
【摆阔】bǎikuò〈动〉〈口〉flash one's cash: 在朋友面前～ flash one's cash in front of one's friends
【摆阔气】bǎi kuòqi = 摆阔 bǎikuò
【摆擂台】bǎi lèitái〈惯〉take on all challengers
【摆列】bǎiliè〈动〉place: 展品～有序。The exhibits are arranged in good order.
【摆龙门阵】bǎi lóngménzhèn〈惯〉〈方〉chat
【摆轮】bǎilún〈名〉[机械] balance wheel
【摆门面】bǎi ménmiàn〈惯〉be ostentatious
【摆迷魂阵】bǎi míhúnzhèn〈惯〉confuse
【摆弄】bǎinòng〈动〉**1**（玩弄）play with: ～铅笔 toy with a pencil ‖ ～枪支 fiddle with a gun **2**（操控）order about: 受人～ be at sb.'s mercy **3**〈方〉（操作或修理）work with: 坏收音机终于给他～好了。The broken radio was finally fixed by him.
【摆平】bǎipíng〈动〉**1**（公正）treat fairly: 我们两边要～。We should be fair to both sides. **2**〈方〉（收拾）punish: 我去把他～。I'm going to lay him flat.
【摆谱儿】bǎipǔr〈动〉〈方〉**1** = 摆门面 bǎi ménmiàn **2** = 摆架子 bǎi jiàzi
【摆设】bǎishè〈动〉furnish and decorate: 他家～得很考究。His house is elaborately furnished.
【摆设】bǎishe〈名〉ornament: 小～ knick-knacks ‖ 书是供人读的，不是拿来当～

的。Books are intended for reading rather than for show.

【摆事实，讲道理】bǎi shìshí, jiǎng dàoli〈俗〉present facts and reason things out

【摆手】bǎishǒu〈动〉① (摇手) shake one's hand in disapproval ② (用手示意) gesture: 警察～示意车辆通行。The policeman waved the traffic on.

【摆摊儿】bǎi tānr〈动〉set up a stall: ～为生 live by running a stall

【摆摊子】bǎi tānzi〈动〉①〈本〉set up a stall ②〈喻〉(做准备) make plans for a project: 摊子不能摆得太大。Don't be too ambitious and employ too many people. ③〈贬〉(铺张) be ostentatious

【摆脱】bǎituō〈动〉cast off: ～纠缠 shake sb. off ‖ ～贫困 shake off poverty ‖ ～追踪者 escape one's pursuers ‖ 帮助企业～长期面临的困难 help enterprises to shake off long-term problems

【摆乌龙】bǎi wūlóng〈动〉[体育] score an own goal: 门将自～。The goalkeeper scored an own goal.

【摆钟】bǎizhōng〈名〉pendulum clock

【摆桌】bǎizhuō〈动〉〈口〉throw a dinner party

【摆子】bǎizi〈名〉〈方〉malaria: ▸打～

bài

呗 bài ▸梵呗 fànbài ▸bei

败(敗) bài

A〈动〉① (搞砸) tarnish: 事情可能就～在他的手里。He may spoil the whole show. ▸～坏, 身～名裂 ② (失败) fail: 不计成～ be indifferent about success or failure ▸反～为胜, 功～垂成 ③ (被挫败) lose: 惨～ be heavily defeated ‖ 他～给了民主党候选人。He lost to the Democratic candidate. ④ (击败) defeat: 大～敌军 trounce the enemy ⑤ (损害) ruin: ▸～家子, ～胃 ⑥ (消除) counteract: ▸～毒, ～火 **B**〈形〉① (腐烂) rotten: ～肉 rotten meat ▸～絮, 腐～ ② (凋谢) faded: ～叶 withered leaves ③ (破旧) worn-out

【败北】bàiběi〈动〉suffer defeat: 主队以一比三～。The home team lost 1 to 3.

【败笔】bàibǐ〈名〉① (指书法) faulty stroke ② (指绘画) bad part ③ (指写作) faulty wording: 故事的结尾是个～。The ending of the story is flawed.

【败兵】bàibīng〈名〉defeated troops

【败草残花】bàicǎo-cánhuā〈成〉withered grass and wilted flowers

【败毒】bàidú〈动〉① (祛火) relieve internal heat ② (解毒) detoxify

【败坏】bàihuài **A**〈动〉ruin: ～名声 defame ‖ ～门楣 disgrace one's family ‖ ～社会风气 corrupt public morality **B**〈形〉badly corrupted: 道德～ morally corrupted

【败火】bàihuǒ〈动〉relieve internal heat: 据说绿茶能～。It is said that green tea relieves internal heat.

【败绩】bàijì〈书〉**A**〈动〉be utterly defeated **B**〈名〉defeat: 无一～ have a completely unbroken record ‖ 屡遭～ suffer repeated defeats

【败家】bàijiā〈动〉squander a family fortune: 投机能起家，也能～。Speculation can lead either to sudden wealth or to downfall.

【败家子】bàijiāzǐ〈名〉squanderer

【败将】bàijiàng〈名〉① (指将领) defeated general ②〈喻〉(指失利者) loser: ▸手下～

【败局】bàijú〈名〉lost game: 扭转～ turn the tables ‖ ～已定。The game is as good as lost.

【败军】bàijūn〈名〉defeated troops: ～之将 defeated general

【败类】bàilèi〈名〉degenerate: 民族～ traitor to the nation

【败露】bàilù〈动〉come to light: 事情已经～。The game is up. ‖ 阴谋～了。The conspiracy has been exposed.

【败落】bàiluò〈动〉decline: 后来，那个商人家道～了。Later, the merchant's fortunes took a downward plunge.

【败诉】bàisù〈动〉lose a lawsuit: 法官判决原告～。The judge found against the plaintiff.

【败退】bàituì〈动〉retreat in defeat: 节节～ lose ground in successive defeats

【败亡】bàiwáng〈动〉〈书〉perish on defeat

【败胃】bàiwèi〈动〉spoil one's appetite

【败象】bàixiàng〈名〉scales of defeat

【败谢】bàixiè〈动〉wither away: 那盆花已～了。The pot plant has already wilted.

【败兴】bàixìng〈动〉put a dampener on things: ～而归 go back disappointed

【败絮】bàixù〈名〉worn cotton wool: ▸金玉其外，～其中

【败血病】bàixuèbìng = 败血症 bàixuèzhèng

【败血症】bàixuèzhèng ▸p. 50〈名〉septicaemia

【败叶】bàiyè〈名〉withered leaves

【败仗】bàizhàng〈名〉defeat: 吃～ suffer a defeat ‖ 打～ lose a battle

【败阵】bàizhèn〈动〉be defeated on the battle field: 由于状态不佳，他败下阵来。He was off form so he was beaten.

【败子】bàizǐ = 败家子 bàijiāzǐ

【败走】bàizǒu〈动〉flee in defeat: ～麦城 suffer a major defeat

拜 bài〈动〉① (行礼) make obeisance: ▸回～, 叩～ ② (尊崇) respect: ▸～物教, 崇～ ③ (会见) pay a visit: ～岳父母 pay a visit to one's parents-in-law ④〈书〉(授予) appoint to an official post: ～为大将 appoint (sb.) as general ⑤ (恭贺) congratulate: ▸～年, ～寿 ⑥ (用作敬词) [used before a verb to show respect]: ～读 have the pleasure of reading ▸～谢 ⑦ (结成某种关系) establish a particular relationship: ～某人为师 formally take sb. as one's master

【拜把子】bài bǎzi〈动〉become sworn brothers

【拜拜】bàibài〈动〉〈口〉bye-bye

【拜别】bàibié = 拜辞 bàicí

【拜辞】bàicí〈动〉〈敬〉bid farewell: ～朋友 take leave of one's friends ‖ 走得仓促，未及～。I didn't say goodbye as I left in a hurry.

【拜倒】bàidǎo〈动〉〈贬〉prostrate oneself: ～在她的石榴裙下 grovel at her feet

【拜读】bàidú〈动〉〈敬〉have the honour to read: 期盼早日～大作。I'm looking forward to reading your great work.

【拜访】bàifǎng〈动〉pay a visit: 登门～ call at sb.'s house ‖ 专程～ pay a special visit (to)

【拜佛】bàifó〈动〉worship Buddha: 烧香～ burn incense and worship Buddha

【拜服】bàifú〈动〉revere: 他的学识令同事们～。His learning is highly respected by his colleagues.

【拜贺】bàihè〈动〉congratulate: ～新年 give greetings to sb. on the New Year

【拜会】bàihuì〈动〉pay a formal call: 礼节性～ pay a courtesy call

【拜火教】Bàihuǒjiào〈名〉Zoroastrianism

【拜见】bàijiàn〈动〉〈敬〉pay a courtesy call: ～恩师 call on one's beloved teacher

【拜金】bàijīn〈动〉be money-minded: ～主义 money worship

【拜客】bàikè〈动〉pay a visit: 他出门～去了。He went out on a visit.

【拜领】bàilǐng〈动〉〈书〉〈敬〉accept with thanks

【拜盟】bàiméng = 拜把子 bài bǎzi

【拜年】bàinián〈动〉extend New Year greetings: 给老师～ pay a New Year's call on one's teachers

【拜认】bàirèn〈动〉formally acknowledge sb. as: ～义父 acknowledge sb. as one's adoptive father

【拜扫】bàisǎo〈动〉〈书〉offer sacrifices at a tomb: ～烈士墓 pay respects at the martyrs' tomb

【拜师】bàishī〈动〉be formally apprenticed to

【拜识】bàishí〈动〉〈书〉have the honour to acquaint oneself with: 闻名已久，无缘～。Though I've known of you for a long time, I have never had the opportunity to meet you.

【拜寿】bàishòu〈动〉extend birthday congratulations

【拜堂】bàitáng〈动〉〈旧〉pay ceremonial obeisances

【拜天地】bài tiāndì = 拜堂 bàitáng

【拜托】bàituō〈动〉〈敬〉request: ～您给打听打听。May I trouble you to ask around? ‖ 我可以把孩子～给您吗? May I leave my children in your care?

【拜望】bàiwàng〈动〉〈敬〉visit: ～老师 call on one's teacher

【拜物教】bàiwùjiào〈名〉fetishism

【拜谢】bàixiè〈动〉extend one's gratitude: 登门～ call at sb.'s house to express one's thanks

【拜谒】bàiyè〈动〉〈书〉① (拜访) pay a formal visit: ～市长 visit the mayor ② (瞻仰) pay one's respects: ～黄帝陵 pay homage at the Mausoleum of the Yellow Emperor

【拜占庭】Bàizhàntíng〈名〉Byzantium: ～帝国 Byzantine Empire [395-1453]

稗 bài

A〈名〉barnyard grass **B**〈形〉insignificant: ▸～史

【稗官野史】bàiguān-yěshǐ〈成〉anecdotal history

【稗史】bàishǐ〈名〉unofficial history

【稗子】bàizi〈名〉① (指植物) barnyard grass ② (指种子) seed of barnyard grass

bai

呗 bai = 呗 bei

bān

扳 bān〈动〉① (拉动) pull: ～手腕 do arm wrestling ‖ ～着指头算 count on one's fingers ② (扭转) win back: ～成平

局 level the score ‖ ～回一局 win back a game

【扳本】bānběn〈动〉〈口〉 win back lost money

【扳不倒儿】bānbudǎor〈名〉 **1**〈方〉〈本〉 roly-poly **2**〈喻〉 official who always makes a comeback

【扳道】bāndào〈动〉 switch: ～工 pointsman

【扳机】bānjī〈名〉 trigger: 扣动～ pull the trigger

【扳平】bānpíng〈动〉 draw: ～比分 equalize the score

【扳手】bānshou〈名〉 **1**（指工具） spanner〈英〉; wrench〈美〉: 活动～ adjustable spanner **2**（指器具的一部分） machine lever

【扳指儿】bānzhir〈名〉 thumb ring

【扳子】bānzi = 扳手 bānshou 1

班 bān

A〈名〉 **1**（班级） class;（班组） group: 英语～ English class ‖ 07 级毕业～ class of 2007 ‖ 一年级有六个～。 There are six classes in Grade One. ▸补习～ **2**（轮班） shift: 三～倒 work in three shifts ‖ 值夜～ work the night shift ▸白～, 换～, 上～ **3**（指军队） squad: 一个排由三个～组成。 Three squads make up a platoon. **4**〈旧〉（戏班子） troupe of performers: 搭～ set up a troupe
B〈形〉 regular: ▸～车, ～机, ～轮
C〈量〉 **1**（指人） [used to denote a group of people]: 这～年轻人干劲十足。 These young people work with great enthusiasm. **2**（指交通工具） [used for scheduled forms of transportation]: 乘下一～飞机 take the next plane
D〈动〉〈书〉 withdraw

【班巴拉语】Bānbālāyǔ ▸**p. 918**〈名〉 Bambara

【班辈】bānbèi〈名〉 seniority: 他的～比我高。 He ranks as my senior.

【班禅】bānchán〈名〉 Panchen: ～喇嘛 Panchen Lama

【班车】bānchē〈名〉 scheduled bus

【班次】bāncì〈名〉 **1**（年级） order of classes: 在学校时，他比我～高。 At school, he was in a higher class than me. **2**（次数） number of journeys: 增加航班～ increase the number of flights

【班底】bāndǐ〈名〉 **1**〈旧〉（指戏班子） regular members of a theatrical troupe **2**（泛指组织） core members of a group

【班房】bānfáng〈名〉〈口〉 jail: 因贿赂罪坐～ be imprisoned for bribery

【班夫郡】Bānfūjùn〈名〉 Banffshire

【班会】bānhuì〈名〉 class meeting: 开～ have a class meeting

【班机】bānjī〈名〉 scheduled flight

【班吉】Bānjí〈名〉 Bangui

【班级】bānjí〈名〉 classes

【班轮】bānlún〈名〉 regular passenger or cargo ship

【班门弄斧】Bānmén-nòngfǔ〈成〉〈喻〉 show off one's skill before an expert

【班期】bānqī〈名〉 scheduled time: 轮船客运～ passenger ship timetable ‖ 信件投递～ delivery schedule

【班师】bānshī〈动〉〈书〉 **1**（调回） withdraw troops **2**（得胜归来） return in triumph: ～回朝 move the troops back to the imperial court

【班图语】Bāntúyǔ ▸**p. 918**〈名〉 Bantu language

【班线】bānxiàn〈名〉 schedules and routes: 新增多条城际客运～ add several new intercity passenger buses and transport routes

【班长】bānzhǎng〈名〉 **1**（指班级） class monitor **2**（指军队） squad leader **3**（指小组） team leader

【班珠尔】Bānzhū'ěr〈名〉 Banjul

【班主】bānzhǔ〈名〉〈旧〉 head of a theatrical troupe

【班主任】bānzhǔrèn〈名〉 teacher in charge of a class

【班子】bānzi〈名〉 **1**（戏班） troupe: ▸戏～ **2**（专门组织） team in charge of an organization: 领导～ leadership

【班组】bānzǔ〈名〉 working group: 优秀～ model team

般 bān

A〈量〉 type: 十八～武艺 all kinds of martial arts
B〈助〉 like: 闪电～冲刺 dash like lightning ▸bō

【般配】bānpèi〈形〉 well-matched: 挺～的一对儿 well-matched couple ‖ 他俩很～。 They are a good match.

颁（頒） bān〈动〉 issue

【颁布】bānbù〈动〉 proclaim: ～命令 issue an order ‖ ～宪法 promulgate a constitution

【颁发】bānfā〈动〉 **1**（发布） proclaim: ～嘉奖令 issue an order of commendation ‖ ～营业执照 issue a business licence **2**（授予） award: ～奖金 award a bonus ‖ ～奖章 bestow a medal

【颁奖】bānjiǎng〈动〉 bestow a prize: 为劳动模范～ award prizes to model workers ‖ ～典礼 prize-giving ceremony

【颁行】bānxíng〈动〉 promulgate for enforcement

斑 bān

A〈名〉 spot: 胎～ Mongolian macula ▸雀～
B〈形〉 speckled: ▸～鸠, ～马

【斑白】bānbái〈形〉〈书〉 grizzled: 两鬓～ have grey hair at the temples

【斑斑】bānbān〈形〉 full of stains and spots: 墨迹～ ink-spotted ‖ 血迹～ blood-stained

【斑驳】bānbó〈形〉〈书〉 mottled: ～的阳光照在她的脸上。 The dappled sunlight fell across her face.

【斑驳陆离】bānbó-lùlí〈成〉 multicoloured

【斑点】bāndiǎn〈名〉 spot

【斑痕】bānhén〈名〉 stain: 铁锈的～ rusty mark

【斑鸠】bānjiū〈名〉 turtledove

【斑斓】bānlán〈形〉〈书〉 brightly-coloured: 色彩～ a riot of colour

【斑羚】bānlíng〈名〉 goral

【斑马】bānmǎ〈名〉 zebra

【斑马线】bānmǎxiàn〈名〉 zebra crossing〈英〉; crosswalk〈美〉

【斑蝥】bānmáo〈名〉［昆虫］Chinese blister beetle

【斑秃】bāntū ▸**p. 50**〈名〉［医学］ alopecia areata

【斑纹】bānwén〈名〉 streak

【斑疹伤寒】bānzhěn shānghán〈名〉 typhus fever

【斑竹】bānzhú〈名〉 mottled bamboo

搬 bān

〈动〉 **1**（移动） move: 把桌子～出去 move the table out ‖ 没人帮忙，我可～不动这架钢琴。 I can't move the piano without help. **2**（迁移） move: ～往新居 move to a new house ‖ 我们三年～了四次家。 We've had four moves within three years. **3**（呈现） adapt and show: ～上银幕 adapt for the screen ‖ 那部小说去年被～上了舞台。 The novel was dramatized last year. **4**（套用） copy indiscriminately: 盲目机械地照～别人的东西 copy sth. from sb. blindly and mechanically ▸生～硬套

【搬兵】bānbīng〈动〉 **1**〈本〉 call for reinforcements **2**〈喻〉（求助） ask for help

【搬家】bānjiā〈动〉 **1**（换住址） move house: 我们下周～。 We're moving next week. **2**（迁移） relocate: 那工厂已经～了。 The factory has already relocated.

【搬家公司】bānjiā gōngsī〈名〉 removal firm

【搬弄】bānnòng〈动〉 **1**（摆弄） fiddle with: ～步枪枪栓 fiddle with the bolt of a rifle **2**（卖弄） flaunt: ～学问 show off one's knowledge **3**（挑拨） stir up

【搬弄是非】bānnòng-shìfēi〈成〉 make mischief

【搬起石头砸自己的脚】bānqǐ shítou zá zìjǐde jiǎo〈俗〉 fall into a pit of one's own digging

【搬迁】bānqiān〈动〉 move: ～户 family to be relocated ‖ ～到住宅区 move to a residential area ‖ 工厂将要～。 The factory is going to be moved.

【搬演】bānyǎn〈动〉 perform a cover version: ～外国经典剧目 a show featuring covers of foreign classics

【搬移】bānyí〈动〉 **1**（挪动） move: ～家具 move furniture **2** = 搬迁 bānqiān

【搬用】bānyòng〈动〉 adopt indiscriminately: 机械地～别国的模式 copy foreign models mechanically

【搬运】bānyùn〈动〉 transport: ～货物 transport goods ‖ ～行李 carry luggage

【搬运费】bānyùnfèi〈名〉 portage

【搬运工】bānyùngōng〈名〉 porter

瘢 bān〈名〉 scar: 刀～ scar of a knife-cut

【瘢痕】bānhén〈名〉 scar: 伤口虽已痊愈，却留下一个～。 The wound has healed but it has left a scar.

癍 bān〈名〉 skin rash

bǎn

坂 bǎn〈名〉〈书〉 slope: 如丸走～ as fast as a ball rolling down a slope

【坂上走丸】bǎnshàng-zǒuwán〈成〉 moving at high speed

板[1] bǎn

A〈名〉 **1**（片状物） board: 木～ wooden board ‖ 护墙～ weather board ‖ 钢～ steel sheet ▸～壁, 菜～, 铺～ **2**（响板） clappers: ▸快～儿书, 檀～ **3**（节奏） accented beat: ▸慢～, 散～, 走～ **4**（门板） shutter: 上～儿 put up the shutters **5**（黑板） blackboard: ▸～报, ～书
B〈形〉 **1**（呆板） stiff: 你还要那样就显得太～了。 You would appear very inflexible if you carried on like that. **2**（硬） hardened: 地～了，没法犁。 The field is too hard to plough.
C〈动〉 look serious: ～着面孔 have a stern look
D〈量〉 [used for a sheet of buttons, etc.]: 一～按扣 a sheet of snap fasteners

板²（闆） bǎn ▸老板 lǎobǎn

【板板六十四】bǎnbǎn liùshísì〈俗〉stubborn

【板报】bǎnbào = 黑板报 hēibǎnbào

【板壁】bǎnbì〈名〉wooden partition

【板擦ル】bǎncār〈名〉blackboard eraser

【板材】bǎncái〈名〉plate material

【板车】bǎnchē = 平板车 píngbǎnchē

【板锉】bǎncuò〈名〉flat file

【板荡】bǎndàng〈名〉〈书〉turmoil

【板凳】bǎndèng〈名〉wooden bench: 小～ stool ‖ ～队员 reserve player

【板斧】bǎnfǔ〈名〉broad axe

【板鼓】bǎngǔ ▸p. 929〈名〉small drum used for marking time in Chinese orchestra

【板胡】bǎnhú ▸p. 929〈名〉*banhu* fiddle

【板结】bǎnjié〈动〉harden: 这块地已经～了。The field has hardened over.

【板块】bǎnkuài〈名〉**1**［地质］plate: 欧亚～ Eurasian plate ‖ ～运动 plate movement **2**〈喻〉（组成部分）main parts: 高科技～ high-tech sector ‖ 这档节目分两个～。This show is divided into two parts.

【板块构造】bǎnkuài gòuzào〈名〉［地质］plate tectonics: ～学说 plate tectonics theory

【板栗】bǎnlì〈名〉［植物］Chinese chestnut

【板球】bǎnqiú ▸p. 909〈名〉cricket: ～运动员 cricketer

【板上钉钉】bǎnshàng-dìngdīng〈成〉that clinches it: 计划已是～，不能更改了。The plan is already finalized and cannot be altered.

【板式】bǎnshì〈名〉[in Chinese opera and music] beat modes

【板书】bǎnshū **A**〈动〉write on a blackboard **B**〈名〉words/characters written on a blackboard: 漂亮的～ beautiful blackboard handwriting

【板刷】bǎnshuā〈名〉**1**（刷子）brush **2**（黑板擦）eraser

【板鸭】bǎnyā〈名〉dried salted duck

【板烟】bǎnyān〈名〉cavendish

【板眼】bǎnyǎn〈名〉**1**（节拍）[in traditional Chinese music] accented and unaccented beats：一板一眼 one accented and one unaccented beat **2**（条理）orderliness: ▸有板有眼

【板油】bǎnyóu〈名〉leaf fat

【板障】bǎnzhàng〈名〉obstacle board

【板正】bǎnzhèng〈形〉**1**（整齐）tidy and regular: 这些书装订得板板正正。The books are well bound. **2**（庄重认真）serious: 样貌～ look severe

【板滞】bǎnzhì〈形〉〈书〉stiff: ～的神情 stiff look ‖ 两眼～ with glazed eyes

【板子】bǎnzi〈名〉**1**（片状硬物）board **2**（刑具）cane: 打～ flog with a birch

版 bǎn

A〈名〉**1**（底版）printing block: 拼～ make up a page of type ▸胶～，排～，铜～ **2**（版本）version: 原～ original version ‖ 英文/中文～ English/Chinese edition ▸盗～ **3**（版面）section: 体育～ sports section ‖ 头～新闻 front-page news **4**（夹板）board frame: ▸～筑

B〈量〉edition: 初/再～ first/second edition ‖ 第一～ first edition

【版本】bǎnběn〈名〉edition: 最新～ latest edition ‖ ～学 bibliology

【版次】bǎncì〈名〉edition

【版画】bǎnhuà〈名〉engraving

【版刻】bǎnkè〈名〉carving

【版面】bǎnmiàn〈名〉**1**（一整面）page space: 一个～ a page **2** = 版心 bǎnxīn **3**（编排形式）layout: ～调整 copy fitting

【版面费】bǎnmiànfèi〈名〉page charge: 文章一旦被录用，就要付～，否则不予发表。When an article is selected, page charges must be paid or it will not get published.

【版权】bǎnquán〈名〉copyright: 购买～ buy the copyright ‖ ～所有，翻印必究。All rights reserved. Piracy in any form will be prosecuted.

【版权法】bǎnquánfǎ〈名〉copyright law

【版权所有人】bǎnquán suǒyǒurén〈名〉copyright owner

【版权页】bǎnquányè〈名〉imprint

【版式】bǎnshì〈名〉format

【版税】bǎnshuì〈名〉royalty

【版图】bǎntú〈名〉territory: 中国～辽阔。China has a vast territory.

【版心】bǎnxīn〈名〉type area

【版主】bǎnzhǔ〈名〉webmaster

【版筑】bǎnzhù〈名〉**1**（指工具）board frames and ram **2**（土木营造）civil engineering project

钣（鈑） bǎn〈名〉metal plate: 钢～ steel plate ‖ 铝～ aluminium plate

【钣金工】bǎnjīngōng〈名〉panel beater

舨 bǎn ▸舢舨 shānbǎn

bàn

办（辦） bàn

A〈动〉**1**（办理）do: ～护照 apply for a passport ‖ ～手续 go through procedures ‖ 把好事～成了坏事 make a mess of an otherwise good thing ‖ 这是他经～的。He was in charge of this. ▸～法，～公，～理 **2**（置备）get sth. ready: ～嫁妆 prepare sb.'s dowry ‖ ～酒席 prepare a feast ▸备～，置～ **3**（惩罚）bring to justice: 首恶必～。The chief culprit must be brought to justice. ▸惩～，法～ **4**（经营）run: ～合资企业 set up a joint venture ‖ ～农场 run a farm ‖ 出资～学 sponsor a school

B〈名〉office: 党～ Party committee office ‖ 房改～ housing reform office ▸外～

【办案】bàn'àn〈动〉handle a case: 依法～ use legal means to crack a case

【办法】bànfǎ〈名〉way: 用尽一切～ employ every means ‖ 老/新～ old/new solutions ‖ 他～多。He is a resourceful guy. ‖ 这不是解决问题的～。This is no solution to the problem.

【办公】bàngōng〈动〉deal with official business: 现场～ carry out one's duties on the ground ‖ ～场所 office space ‖ ～时间 office/business hours

【办公会议】bàngōng huìyì〈名〉working meeting

【办公楼】bàngōnglóu〈名〉office block

【办公室】bàngōngshì〈名〉office

【办公厅】bàngōngtīng〈名〉general office: 国务院～ General Office of the State Council

【办公用品】bàngōng yòngpǐn〈名〉office appliance

【办公桌】bàngōngzhuō〈名〉(executive) desk

【办公自动化】bàngōng zìdònghuà〈名〉office automation

【办货】bànhuò〈动〉make purchases: 办年货 shop for the Spring Festival

【办理】bànlǐ〈动〉handle: ～登机手续 go through check-in procedures ‖ 请酌情～! Please handle it as you see fit.

【办事】bànshì〈动〉handle affairs: ～公道 be fair and just ‖ 按政策～ act according to policy ‖ ～员 office clerk ‖ 人多好～。Many hands make light work.

【办事处】bànshìchù〈名〉office: 设立～ set up an office ‖ 街道～ community office ‖ 驻东京～ office in Tokyo

【办事机构】bànshì jīgòu〈名〉administrative office

【办学】bànxué〈动〉run a school: ～条件 conditions for setting up a school

【办罪】bànzuì〈动〉punish for a crime

半 bàn

A ▸p. 691〈数〉**1**（二分之一）half: ～杯咖啡 half a cup of coffee ‖ ～小时 half an hour ‖ 前/后～部分 first/second half **2**（很少）very little: 一星～点ル面粉都没有 have no flour at all ‖ 他连～句话都没说。He didn't breathe a word.

B〈形〉**1**（在中间）halfway: ～夜时分 in the middle of the night ‖ 上到～山腰 climb halfway up the hill **2**（半数）half: ▸～壁江山，～边天

C〈副〉partially: ～躺着 recline ‖ 把门～开着 leave the door ajar ‖ ～饥饿 semi-starved ‖ ～熟的鸡蛋 parboiled egg

【半百】bànbǎi ▸p. 691〈数〉fifty years of age: 年近～ approach fifty

【半辈子】bànbèizi〈名〉half of one's life: 大～ the greater part of one's life

【半壁江山】bànbì-jiāngshān〈成〉half of the country: ～已落入敌手。Half the country has already fallen into enemy hands.

【半边】bànbiān〈名〉one part: 这块地东～ル种着土豆，西～ル种着玉米。Potatoes are grown on the east side of the plot and corn on the west.

【半边天】bànbiāntiān〈名〉**1**〈本〉half the sky: 晚霞映红了～。Half of the sky shone red with the glow of the sunset. **2**〈喻〉women

【半场】bànchǎng〈名〉half of a game: 下～，双方交换了场地。At half-time the teams changed ends.

【半成品】bànchéngpǐn〈名〉semi-finished product

【半大不小】bàndà-bùxiǎo〈形〉between adulthood and childhood

【半导体】bàndǎotǐ〈名〉**1**（指物质）semiconductor **2**（指收音机）transistor radio

【半岛】bàndǎo〈名〉peninsula: 朝鲜～ Korean Peninsula

【半道ル】bàndàor = 半路 bànlù

【半点】bàndiǎn〈数量〉very little: 这是个科学问题，来不得～虚假。This is a scientific matter and as such no fakery is admissible.

【半吊子】bàndiàozi〈名〉**1**（不稳重的人）impulsive person **2**（一知半解的人）dabbler **3**（未完成的事）something unfinished

【半封建】bànfēngjiàn〈形〉semi-feudal: ～半殖民地社会 semi-feudal and semi-colonial society

【半工半读】bàngōng-bàndú〈动〉work one's way through one's education

【半公开】bàngōngkāi〈形〉more or less open

【半挂车】bànguàchē〈名〉articulated lorry

【半官方】bànguānfāng〈形〉semi-official:

～机构/刊物 semi-official institution/publication
【半昏迷】bànhūnmí **A** ▸**p. 50**〈名〉［医学］semi-coma **B**〈形〉semiconscious
【半价】bànjià〈名〉half price: ～销售 sell at half price
【半截】bànjié〈数量〉half: ～粉笔 half a piece of chalk ‖ 听到不幸的消息，她的心一下子凉了～。 Her heart sank at the sad news.
【半截入土】bànjié rùtǔ〈成〉with one foot in the grave
【半斤八两】bànjīn-bāliǎng〈成〉six of one and half a dozen of the other: 他俩～，都不是好东西。 Those two are equally bad.
【半径】bànjìng〈名〉radius
【半决赛】bànjuésài〈名〉semi-final: 进入～ get to the semi-final
【半空】bànkōng〈名〉mid-air: 柳絮在～飘荡。 Willow catkins are flying in the air.
【半拉】bànlǎ〈数量〉〈口〉half: ～梨 half a pear ‖ 过了～月 half a month later
【半劳动力】bànláodònglì〈名〉semi-able-bodied labourer
【半劳力】bànláolì = 半劳动力 bànláodònglì
【半老徐娘】bànlǎo-xúniáng〈成〉woman of fading charms
【半流体】bànliútǐ〈名〉semi-liquid
【半流质饮食】bànliúzhì yǐnshí〈名〉semi-fluid diet
【半路】bànlù〈名〉**1**（指路程）halfway point: ～相遇 meet halfway ‖ 公共汽车在～上抛锚了。 The bus broke down on the way. **2**〈喻〉（指进程）the middle: 他看电视入了神，不愿意～走开。 Absorbed in the TV programme, he was reluctant to leave before the end.
【半路出家】bànlù-chūjiā〈成〉**1**〈本〉become a monk/nun late in life **2**〈喻〉switch to a job one is not trained for
【半路杀出个程咬金】bànlù shāchū gè Chéng Yǎojīn〈俗〉an unexpected opponent appears halfway
【半票】bànpiào〈名〉half fare
【半瓶醋】bànpíngcù〈名〉〈喻〉dabbler: 他在绘画上是个～。 He is just a dabbler at drawing.
【半坡遗址】Bànpō yízhǐ〈名〉Banpo Site [Chinese archaeological site dating from approximately 4,500 BC]
【半旗】bànqí〈名〉half-mast: 下～致哀 fly at half-mast to express mourning
【半球】bànqiú〈名〉**1**（指球体）hemisphere: 大脑～ cerebral hemisphere ▸东～, 西～ **2**（特指地球）semi-globe
【半晌】bànshǎng〈数量〉〈方〉quite a long time: 前～ morning ‖ 休息了～才缓过劲 recover one's strength after a long rest
【半身】bànshēn〈名〉**1**（左、右侧）one side of the body: ～不遂 hemiplegia **2**（上、下身）half of the body: ▸上～, 下～
【半身像】bànshēnxiàng〈名〉**1**（指平面像）half-length portrait **2**（指雕像）bust
【半生】bànshēng **A**〈名〉half a lifetime: 操劳大～ work hard for much of one's life **B**〈形〉half cooked: ▸～不熟
【半生不熟】bànshēng-bùshú〈成〉**1**（指烹饪）half cooked **2**（不熟练）unskilled: 用～的英语解释 manage to explain things in half-baked English
【半世】bànshì = 半生 bànshēng A
【半数】bànshù ▸**p. 691**〈名〉half: 不足～ less than half the number ‖ 超过～的选票 a majority of the votes
【半衰期】bànshuāiqī〈名〉［物理］half life period
【半死】bànsǐ〈形〉half-dead: 饿得～ be half-dead with hunger
【半死不活】bànsǐ-bùhuó〈成〉**1**（指生理状态）be more dead than alive **2**（指精神状态）sluggish
【半天】bàntiān〈数量〉**1**（指白天）half day: ～休假 half-day holiday **2**（很久）quite a while: 我们等了～他才来。 We waited for a long time before he arrived.
【半途】bàntú〈名〉〈书〉midway point
【半途而废】bàntú'érfèi〈成〉give up halfway: ～的人 quitter
【半推半就】bàntuī-bànjiù〈成〉yield but with a show of reluctance
【半脱产】bàntuōchǎn〈动〉be given partial release from one's regular work
【半文盲】bànwénmáng〈名〉semi-literacy
【半夏】bànxià〈名〉［中药］tuber of pinellia
【半仙】bànxiān〈名〉demigod
【半心半意】bànxīn-bànyì〈成〉be half-hearted: 为人民服务要全心全意，不能～。 We must serve the people wholeheartedly, not half-heartedly.
【半新不旧】bànxīn-bùjiù〈成〉no longer new: 衣服～，但他舍不得扔。 Even though the clothes were no longer new, he couldn't bear to throw them away.
【半信半疑】bànxìn-bànyí〈成〉not quite convinced: 我对她的话～。 I'm rather dubious about what she says.
【半休】bànxiū〈动〉work for half the day, rest for the other half: 手术后他～了一年。 He worked half-time for a year after the operation.
【半宿】bànxiǔ〈名〉half a night: 他们谈了～。 They talked for half the night.
【半夜】bànyè〈名〉**1**（一夜的一半）half of a night: 前/后～ first/second half of the night **2**（午夜）midnight: ～时分 at the stroke of midnight ▸深更～
【半夜三更】bànyè-sāngēng〈成〉late at night: ～了，不要大声说话。 It's very late now. Don't speak loudly.
【半音】bànyīn〈名〉semitone〈英〉, half-tone〈美〉: ～符 minim〈英〉, half note〈美〉
【半元音】bànyuányīn〈名〉semivowel
【半圆】bànyuán〈名〉semicircle
【半月刊】bànyuèkān〈名〉fortnightly
【半载】bànzǎi〈名〉half a year: 这工程不是一年～能完成的。 The project will not be completed within the space of a year.
【半殖民地】bànzhímíndì〈名〉semi-colony: ～半封建的旧中国 semi-colonial, semi-feudal old China
【半中间】bànzhōngjiān〈名〉the middle: ～退出比赛 give up the match halfway ‖ 他小说写到～就病倒了。 He fell ill in the middle of working on his novel.
【半子】bànzǐ〈名〉〈书〉son-in-law
【半自动】bànzìdòng〈形〉semi-automatic: ～步枪 semi-automatic rifle

扮 bàn

〈动〉**1**（装扮）play: ～哈姆雷特 act the part of Hamlet ‖ ～成保安人员 disguise oneself as a security guard ▸女～男装 **2**（指面部表情）put on an expression: ▸～鬼脸
【扮鬼脸】bàn guǐliǎn〈动〉make faces: 对婴儿～ make a face at the baby
【扮酷】bànkù〈动〉pretend to be cool
【扮相】bànxiàng〈名〉appearance: 她～好。 She cuts a good figure when in costume and makeup. ‖ 我现在这～能见客人吗? How can I receive guests looking like this?
【扮演】bànyǎn〈动〉play the part of: ～坏蛋 play the villain ‖ ～主角 play the main part ‖〈喻〉～不光彩的角色 play a dishonourable role ‖ 这个角色他～得不错。 He was very good in the part.
【扮装】bànzhuāng〈动〉do one's make-up: 快～吧，下一场就该你上了。 Get your make-up on quick. You are on in the next scene.
【扮作】bànzuò〈动〉disguise as: 侦察员～小贩混进了城。 The scout stole into the town disguised as a peddler.

伴 bàn

A〈名〉companion: 结～同行 join sb. on a trip ‖ 找他做～ turn to him for company ▸～侣, 伙～, 旅～
B〈动〉**1**（陪着）accompany: ▸～随, ～同, 陪～ **2**（伴有）accompany: 雷声～着闪电。 Thunder accompanied the lightning. ‖ 轻度感染常～有高烧。 A high fever often accompanies a mild infection. **3**（配合）accompany: ▸～唱, ～舞, ～奏
【伴唱】bànchàng〈动〉sing an accompaniment to: 为一名歌手～ accompany a singer ‖ 很多地方戏剧都有～的特点。 Vocal accompaniment is a feature of many local operas.
【伴读】bàndú〈动〉accompany sb. in their studies
【伴君如伴虎】bàn jūn rú bàn hǔ〈成〉kings and bears often worry their keepers
【伴郎】bànláng〈名〉best man
【伴侣】bànlǚ〈名〉mate: 生活～ life partner ‖ 终身～ lifelong companion
【伴娘】bànniáng〈名〉bridesmaid
【伴生】bànshēng〈动〉accompany: ～矿物 associated mineral
【伴送】bànsòng〈动〉accompany: ～到路口 see sb. to the street corner
【伴随】bànsuí〈动〉follow: ～左右，形影不离 follow around
【伴同】bàntóng〈动〉accompany: ～朋友游览西安名胜 take a friend around the sights of Xi'an
【伴舞】bànwǔ **A**〈动〉**1**（陪人跳舞）dance with **2**（为配合演唱）back-up dance **B**〈名〉accompanying dancer
【伴星】bànxīng〈名〉［天文］companion star
【伴音】bànyīn〈名〉accompanying audio
【伴游】bànyóu **A**〈动〉accompany sb. on a journey **B**〈名〉travelling companion
【伴奏】bànzòu **A**〈动〉accompany: 用钢琴～ accompany on the piano **B**〈名〉musical accompaniment

拌 bàn

〈动〉**1**（搅和）mix: ～饲料 mix the fodder ‖ 凉～黄瓜 cucumber salad **2**（争吵）bicker
【拌和】bànhuò〈动〉blend
【拌面】bànmiàn〈名〉noodles served with soy sauce, sesame butter, etc.
【拌种】bànzhǒng〈动〉mix seeds with fertilizer, pesticide, etc.
【拌种机】bànzhǒngjī〈名〉seed dresser
【拌嘴】bànzuǐ〈动〉bicker: 那小两口总是～。 The young couple are forever squabbling.

绊（絆）bàn

A〈动〉trip: 被绳索/树枝～倒 trip over a

rope/branch ‖ 在石头上～了一跤 stumble on a stone ‖〈喻〉让琐事～住了手脚 get oneself bogged down with trifles

B〈名〉**1**（使人跌倒） tripping: 使～ル trip (sb.) up **2**〈喻〉（害人手段） trap: 在暗地里使～ル set a trap for sb.

【绊脚石】bànjiǎoshí〈名〉〈喻〉stumbling block: 旧思想是社会进步的～。Old ideologies are an obstacle to social progress.

【绊ル】bànr = 绊子 bànzi

【绊手绊脚】bànshǒu-bànjiǎo = 碍手碍脚 àishǒu-àijiǎo

【绊子】bànzi〈名〉**1**（指摔跤） tripping: ▸使～ **2**〈喻〉（害人的手段） tripwire

b

瓣 bàn

A〈名〉**1**（指花） petal: ▸花～ **2**（指蒜） clove;（指水果） segment: 蒜～ル cloves of garlic ‖ 橘子～ル orange segments **3**（指物品） piece: 碗摔成了好几～。The bowl broke into several pieces. **4**（瓣膜） lamella: ▸三尖～

B〈量〉section: 一～橘子 a slice of orange ‖ 一～蒜 a clove of garlic

【瓣膜】bànmó〈名〉［生理］ valve: 她的心脏～有毛病。She has problems with a heart valve.

bāng

邦 bāng〈名〉

nation: 兴～安民 bring prosperity to the country and peace to the people ▸联～, 邻～, 友～

【邦交】bāngjiāo〈名〉diplomatic relations: 断绝～ sever diplomatic relations

【邦联】bānglián〈名〉confederation: 美国南部～ Confederate States of America

帮（幫）bāng

A〈动〉**1**（协助） help: ～他管理企业 aid him in managing the enterprise ‖ ～她复习功课 help her with her revision ‖ 你～了我大忙。You've been a great help to me. **2**（从事） be hired as a labourer: ～短工 take a seasonal job

B〈名〉**1**（物体的构成部分） side: 车～ side of a cart ▸船～, 鞋～ **2**〈贬〉（帮派） clique: 四人～ Gang of Four ▸匪～, 拉～结伙 **3**（指黑社会） secret society: 青～ Green Gang **4**（指蔬菜） outer leaf: 白菜～ outer leaves of Chinese cabbage

C〈量〉group: 一～孩子 a bunch of children ‖ 一～土匪/强盗 a gang of bandits /robbers

【帮办】bāngbàn **A**〈动〉assist in management: ～税务 assist in handling taxation **B**〈名〉assistant

【帮补】bāngbǔ〈动〉give financial aid: ～家用 help support the family

【帮衬】bāngchèn〈动〉**1**〈方〉（帮忙） help: ～照料菜摊子 help with minding the vegetable stand **2** = 帮补 bāngbǔ

【帮厨】bāngchú〈动〉be a kitchen help

【帮凑】bāngcòu〈动〉club together to help sb. out: 同事们为他住院～了不少钱。His colleagues clubbed together and collected quite a lot of money for his stay in hospital.

【帮倒忙】bāng dàománg〈惯〉do more harm than good: 他们是在给我～。They've been more of a hindrance to me than a help.

【帮扶】bāngfú〈动〉assist: 相互～ help each other

【帮工】bānggōng **A**〈动〉help with work

B〈名〉help: 雇用临时～ hire temporary hands

【帮会】bānghuì〈名〉underground gang

【帮教】bāngjiào〈动〉help and educate: ～对象 target of help and education

【帮困】bāngkùn〈动〉help the needy

【帮忙】bāngmáng〈动〉help: 答应～ promise to lend a hand ‖ ～干家务 help about the house ‖ 你要～吗? Do you need any help? ‖ 我能帮您什么忙吗? Can I be of any assistance? ‖ 我想请你帮个忙。I'd like to ask you for help.

【帮派】bāngpài〈名〉clique: 分裂成几个～ break into several factions ‖ ～活动 factionalism ‖ ～头子 faction leader

【帮腔】bāngqiāng〈动〉**1**（指戏曲演出） sing an accompaniment to **2**（支持） speak in support of sb.: 为某人～ take up sb.'s cause

【帮手】bāngshou〈名〉assistant: 找个～ find help

【帮套】bāngtào〈名〉**1**（牲口套） harness **2**（牲口） pack animal

【帮闲】bāngxián **A**〈动〉serve the rich and powerful as a literary hack **B**〈名〉literary hack

【帮凶】bāngxiōng **A**〈动〉abet **B**〈名〉accomplice: 谋杀案的～ accessory to a murder

【帮佣】bāngyōng **A**〈动〉work as a hired labourer **B**〈名〉hired labourer

【帮主】bāngzhǔ〈名〉gang master

【帮助】bāngzhù〈动〉help: ～孤寡老人 help old people who live alone ‖ 请求～ ask for assistance ‖ ～母亲干家务活 help one's mother with housework ‖ 你的一番话对我大有～。What you said helped me enormously.

【帮子】bāngzi **A**〈名〉**1**（菜帮） outer leaf **2**（鞋帮） upper: 鞋～ shoe upper **B**〈量〉band: 来了一～年轻人。Here come a group of young people.

哪 bāng〈拟〉

rat-a-tat

【哪哪】bānglāng〈拟〉bang: 门～一声关上了。The door banged shut.

梆 bāng

A〈拟〉rat-a-tat: ～～～敲门 give a rat-a-tat on the door

B〈名〉**1**（用于打更） night watchman's clapper **2** ▸p. 929［音乐］ clappers

【梆子】bāngzi〈名〉**1**（用于打更） night watchman's clapper **2** ▸p. 929［音乐］ wooden clappers: 敲～ play clappers **3** = 梆子腔 bāngziqiāng

【梆子腔】bāngziqiāng〈名〉**1**（指曲调） music of clapper operas **2**（指剧种） clapper opera

浜 bāng〈名〉〈方〉

creek: 小河～ little stream

bǎng

绑（綁）bǎng〈动〉

tie: 把行李～起来 tie up the luggage ‖ 手被反～着 with one's arms bound behind one's back

【绑匪】bǎngfěi〈名〉kidnapper

【绑缚】bǎngfù〈动〉bind: ～罪犯 tie up a criminal

【绑架】bǎngjià〈动〉kidnap: ～事件 abduction

【绑票】bǎngpiào〈动〉kidnap for ransom

【绑腿】bǎngtuǐ〈名〉gaiter: 扎着～ wear puttees

【绑扎】bǎngzā〈动〉**1**（捆） tie up **2**（包扎） bind up: ～伤口 dress a wound

榜 bǎng〈名〉

1（名单） list: 选民～ list of eligible voters ▸光荣～, 排行～ **2**（文告） announcement: 张～招贤 post up a notice to attract talented people **3**（匾额） horizontal inscribed board: ▸～额, ～书

【榜额】bǎng'é〈名〉horizontal inscribed board

【榜首】bǎngshǒu〈名〉first place: 高居～ top the list ‖ 名列～ rank first

【榜书】bǎngshū〈名〉large Chinese character calligraphy

【榜尾】bǎngwěi〈名〉last place: 该队最终名列～。The team came in last.

【榜眼】bǎngyǎn〈名〉*bangyan* [a title for the scholar placed second in the highest imperial examination in the Ming and Qing dynasties]

【榜样】bǎngyàng〈名〉example: 树立～ set an example ‖ 孩子们的好～ good role model for children

膀 bǎng〈名〉

1（肩） shoulder: ▸肩～ **2**（上臂） upper arm;（胳膊） arm: ▸臂～ **3**（翅膀） wing: ▸翅～ ▸bàng, pāng, páng

【膀臂】bǎngbì〈名〉〈喻〉trusty assistant: ▸左膀右臂

【膀大腰圆】bǎngdà-yāoyuán〈成〉beefy: ～的小伙子 hefty young man

【膀爷】bǎngyé〈名〉〈方〉bare-chested man: 几个～聚在树荫里下棋。Some bare-chested men gathered in the shade of the trees to play chess.

【膀子】bǎngzi〈名〉**1**（上臂） upper arm;（胳膊） arm: 光着～ bare to the waist **2**〈方〉（翅膀） wing: 老鹰受伤的～ the injured wing of the eagle

bàng

蚌 bàng〈名〉

clam: ▸鹬～相争，渔人得利

【蚌壳】bàngké〈名〉clamshell

棒 bàng

A〈名〉**1**（棍棒） stick: 棒球～ baseball bat ‖ 高尔夫球～ golf club ‖ 木～ wooden stick ▸～槌, 棍～ **2**（指接力赛） leg of a relay race: 跑第一～ run the first leg

B〈形〉**1**〈口〉（优秀） terrific: 功课～ excellent in study ‖ 你的字写得真～! Your calligraphy is really fantastic! **2**（健康） hefty: ～小伙子 strong young man

【棒冰】bàngbīng〈名〉〈方〉ice lolly〈英〉; popsicle〈美〉

【棒操】bàngcāo〈名〉club exercise

【棒槌】bàngchui〈名〉**1**〈本〉wooden club **2**〈喻〉layman

【棒喝】bànghè〈动〉〈喻〉give a sharp warning: ▸当头～

【棒球】bàngqiú ▸p. 909〈名〉baseball: 打～ play baseball ‖ ～场 baseball field

【棒ル糖】bàngrtáng〈名〉lollipop

【棒ル香】bàngrxiāng〈名〉bamboo-wick incense

【棒针】bàngzhēn〈名〉heavy-gauge knitting needle: ～衫 bulky sweater

【棒子】bàngzi〈名〉**1**（棍子） stick

2〈方〉（玉米） maize: ～面 corn flour
3（玉米穗轴） corncob

傍 bàng〈动〉**1**（依附） approach: ～大款 be kept by a sugar daddy **2**（靠近） near: 依山～水 near hills and water ▸～晚

【傍黑儿】bànghēir〈名〉〈方〉 nightfall

【傍角儿】bàngjuér〈方〉 **A**〈动〉 play a supporting role **B**〈名〉 supporting actor/actress/role

【傍人门户】bàngrén-ménhù〈成〉 depend on sb. for a living

【傍晚】bàngwǎn〈名〉 nightfall: ～时分 at dusk

【傍午】bàngwǔ〈名〉 about noon

【傍依】bàngyī〈动〉 be close to: 小区～西湖。 The residential area is located near the West Lake.

谤（謗） bàng〈动〉〈书〉defame: ▸诽～, 毁～

【谤议】bàngyì〈动〉〈书〉 slander

塝 bàng〈名〉 side of a canal or ridge in a field

蒡 bàng ▸ 牛蒡 niúbàng

稖 bàng

【稖头】bàngtóu〈名〉〈方〉 maize

膀 bàng ▸ 吊膀子 diào bàngzi
▸bǎng, pāng, páng

磅[1] bàng

A ▸**p. 978**〈量〉 pound (lb): 重40～ weigh 40 lb
B〈名〉scales: 用～称一下 weigh with scales
C〈动〉 weigh with scales: ～一下你的体重 weigh yourself

磅[2] bàng〈名〉 point: 五～字 5-point type
▸páng

【磅秤】bàngchèng〈名〉 platform scale

镑（鎊） bàng〈量〉pound: ▸英～

bāo

包 bāo

A〈动〉**1**（裹） wrap: ～饺子 make *jiaozi* ‖ 用薄纸把瓷器～起来 pack china in tissue paper **2**（总括） include: ▸～含, ～括 **3**（藏有） cover: ▸～藏祸心 **4**（全面负责） take on everything: 把工程～给一家建筑公司 contract a project out to a building company ‖ 这事～在我身上。 Just leave it all to me. ▸～产, 承～ **5**（担保） assure: ～你满意。 Satisfaction guaranteed. ‖ 商品～退。 All goods are sold with a refund guarantee. ▸打～票 **6**（专用） charter: ～一条船/一架飞机 charter a ship/plane **7**（围拢） surround: ▸～围
B〈名〉**1**（包裹） package: 软件～ software package ▸红～, 邮～, 炸药～ **2**（袋子） bag: 把～寄存起来 check in one's bag ‖ 塑料～ plastic bag ▸麻～, 书～ **3**（肿块） swelling: 额头上有个～ have a bump on one's forehead ‖ 头上撞个～ get a bump on the head **4**（帐篷） yurt: ▸蒙古～
C〈量〉 packet: 两～大米 two sacks of rice ‖ 一～饼干 a packet of biscuits ‖ 他一天抽一～烟。 He smokes a pack of cigarettes a day.

【包办】bāobàn〈动〉**1**（全部承担） take on everything oneself and refuse to let others take part: 那件事他～了。 He promised to do the whole job himself. **2**（自做主张） monopolize: ～婚姻 arranged marriage ‖ 父母不应～子女婚事。 Parents should not arrange marriages for their children.

【包庇】bāobì〈动〉 shield: ～罪犯 shield a criminal ‖ 相互～ shield each other ‖ ～罪 offence of shielding an offender

【包藏】bāocáng〈动〉 conceal: 他的话里～着讥讽。 There was hidden sarcasm in his remarks.

【包藏祸心】bāocáng-huòxīn〈成〉harbour evil intentions

【包产】bāochǎn〈动〉 make a production contract: ～到户 contract with each household for production quotas

【包场】bāochǎng〈动〉 make a block booking of a show

【包抄】bāochāo〈动〉 envelop: 从两侧～匪徒 outflank the bandits from both sides

【包车】bāochē **A**〈动〉 charter a vehicle: 包了八辆车 charter eight coaches **B**〈名〉 chartered vehicle

【包乘】bāochéng〈动〉 charter: ～一架飞机 charter a plane

【包乘制】bāochéngzhì〈名〉transportation contract system

【包吃包住】bāochī-bāozhù〈动〉 provide full board

【包打天下】bāodǎ-tiānxià〈成〉run things all by oneself without consulting others: 一人不能～。 One man cannot win a game all by himself.

【包打听】bāodǎtīng〈名〉**1**〈旧〉（侦探） detective **2**〈贬〉（探人隐私的人） snoop

【包二奶】bāo'èrnǎi〈动〉 keep a mistress

【包饭】bāofàn **A**〈动〉 get meals at a fixed rate: 按月～ board by the month **B**〈名〉 meal at a mutually agreed-upon monthly rate: 吃～ have meals at a mutually agreed monthly rate

【包房】bāofáng〈名〉**1**（指火车包厢） compartment **2**（指房间） lodgings

【包袱】bāofu〈名〉**1**（布片） cloth-wrap **2**（布包） cloth package: 背着大～ shoulder a load **3**〈喻〉（负担） burden: 成为父母的～ become a burden to one's parents ‖ 放下思想～ cast off the burdens on one's mind **4**（笑料） punch line: 抖～ crack a joke

【包袱底儿】bāofudǐr〈名〉〈方〉**1**（指钱物） valuable family property **2**〈喻〉（隐私） private secrets: 抖～ expose sb.'s secrets **3**〈喻〉（本领） unique skill: 抖搂～ show off one's skills

【包袱皮儿】bāofupír〈名〉 cloth wrapping

【包干儿】bāogānr〈动〉 take full responsibility for a task: 分组～ divide up the work among groups ‖ 经费实行～。 Each unit assumes responsibility for balancing surpluses and deficits.

【包工】bāogōng〈动〉 work on contract: ～建造房屋 contract to build a house ‖ ～包料 contract for labour and materials in a lump sum

【包工头】bāogōngtóu〈名〉 labour contractor

【包公】Bāogōng〈名〉 Lord Bao [Bao Zheng (包拯), an official in the Song Dynasty idolized in legends as a model of honesty and justice]

【包谷】bāogǔ〈名〉〈方〉 maize

【包管】bāoguǎn〈动〉 assure: ～你不受损失。 We assure you against loss. ‖ ～让你睡一宿好觉。 I guarantee you a good night's sleep.

【包裹】bāoguǒ **A**〈动〉 wrap: ～伤口 dress a wound ‖ 把婴儿～起来 wrap up the baby **B**〈名〉 package; parcel〈英〉: 寄～ post a parcel ‖ 把～用快件寄出 send a parcel by express mail

【包裹单】bāoguǒdān〈名〉 parcel notification form: 填写～ fill in a parcel form

【包含】bāohán〈动〉 contain: 权利～着义务。 Rights imply duties. ‖ 这句话～三层意思。 The meaning of the sentence is three-fold.

【包涵】bāohan ▸**p. 156**〈动〉〈套〉 excuse: 招待不周，请多多～。The service was below par. Please accept my apologies.

【包伙】bāohuǒ = 包饭 bāofàn

【包机】bāojī **A**〈动〉 charter a plane: 开展～业务 offer charter flight service **B**〈名〉 chartered flight

【包间】bāojiān〈名〉（指餐馆）booth;（指火车） compartment;（指船） cabin: 订一个～ book a room

【包金】bāojīn〈名〉 gilding: ～项链 gilded necklace

【包茎】bāojīng〈名〉［医学］ phimosis

【包举】bāojǔ〈动〉〈书〉 embrace all: ～无遗 all-inclusive

【包括】bāokuò〈动〉 include: ～一切费用 all charges included ‖ 每月租金1,500元，～水电费。 The monthly rent is 1,500 *yuan*, inclusive of electricity and water.

【包揽】bāolǎn〈动〉**1**（指做事） undertake the whole thing: ～一切 take on everything **2**（指获奖） pocket: ～全部四枚金牌 sweep all four gold medals

【包罗】bāoluó〈动〉 cover: 他们的研究几乎～所有的学科。 Their research practically covered every subject.

【包罗万象】bāoluó-wànxiàng〈成〉 be all-inclusive

【包米】bāomǐ〈名〉〈方〉 maize

【包赔】bāopéi〈动〉 guarantee to compensate: ～损失 guarantee to pay for the loss

【包皮】bāopí〈名〉**1**（外皮） wrapper **2**［解剖］ foreskin: ～过长 redundant prepuce

【包票】bāopiào〈名〉**1**（保单） guarantee **2**（许诺） assurance: ▸打～

【包青天】Bāoqīngtiān = 包公 Bāogōng

【包容】bāoróng〈动〉**1**（见谅） pardon: 如有差错，请多多～。 Please forgive me if I make any mistakes. **2**（容纳） hold: 这个礼堂能～很多观众。 The auditorium can seat a large audience.

【包身工】bāoshēngōng〈名〉〈旧〉 **1**（指制度） indentured labour system **2**（指人） indentured labourer

【包探】bāotàn〈名〉〈旧〉 police detective

【包头】bāotóu〈名〉**1**（指布）head-dress **2**（指皮子） toecap: 鞋带的金属～ metal tip of a shoelace **3** Bāotóu（指城市） Baotou

【包头巾】bāotóujīn〈名〉 turban

【包土栽培】bāotǔzāipéi〈名〉 ball planting

【包围】bāowéi〈动〉**1**（围住） surround: ～敌人 surround the enemy ‖ 被～ be hemmed in ‖ 农村～城市 the countryside encircles the city **2**（包抄） outflank

【包围圈】bāowéiquān〈名〉 ring of encirclement: 冲出～ break through the encirclement ‖ 缩小～ narrow the ring

【包席】bāoxí **A**〈动〉 book a table for a group at a restaurant: 包五桌席 book five tables **B**〈名〉 group table at a restaurant

b

【包厢】bāoxiāng〈名〉box
【包销】bāoxiāo〈动〉have exclusive sales rights: ～该厂全部产品 make exclusive sales of a factory's entire stock
【包心菜】bāoxīncài〈名〉〈方〉cabbage
【包养】bāoyǎng〈动〉buy sb. off
【包银】bāoyín〈名〉〈旧〉artist's wage
【包圆儿】bāoyuánr〈动〉〈口〉1（全部买下）buy everything left: 给我打八折，我～了。Give me a 20% discount, and I'll buy the whole lot. 2（全部承担）finish off: 这半瓶酒我～。I'll finish off the half bottle of wine.
【包月】bāoyuè〈动〉pay monthly
【包孕】bāoyùn = 包蕴 bāoyùn
【包蕴】bāoyùn〈动〉contain: 他短短几句话，却～着深刻的哲理。His remarks, though brief, contained profound truths.
【包扎】bāozā〈动〉1（指伤口）dress: ～伤口 bandage a wound 2（指物品）bind: 书已～好，准备寄出。The books have been packed up for posting.
【包装】bāozhuāng A〈动〉pack: ～精美 be attractively packaged ‖ ～成本 packing cost ‖ 真空～ vacuum pack ‖〈喻〉被～为高端产品 be packaged as a high-end product ‖〈喻〉～年轻女歌星 package a young female singer B〈名〉package: ～新颖美观 fashionable and attractive packaging
【包装材料】bāozhuāng cáiliào〈名〉packaging
【包装车间】bāozhuāng chējiān〈名〉packing department
【包装箱】bāozhuāngxiāng〈名〉packing box
【包装纸】bāozhuāngzhǐ〈名〉wrapping paper
【包子】bāozi〈名〉steamed stuffed bun: 肉/菜～ steamed bun with meat/vegetable stuffing
【包租】bāozū〈动〉1（指转租）block rent 2（指专用）charter: ～合同 charter contract ‖ 这辆汽车可以～。This car is available for hire.

苞[1] bāo〈名〉bud: 花～ flower buds

苞[2] bāo〈形〉〈书〉luxuriant

【苞谷】bāogǔ = 包谷 bāogǔ
【苞米】bāomǐ = 包米 bāomǐ

孢 bāo

【孢子】bāozǐ〈名〉［生物］spore
【孢子植物】bāozǐ zhíwù〈名〉spore-producing plant

枹 bāo

【枹树】bāoshù〈名〉Japanese silkworm oak

胞 bāo〈名〉1（胞衣）afterbirth 2（嫡亲）siblings: ～弟 younger brother by blood 3（同胞）compatriot: 海外侨～ overseas compatriots ‖ 台～ compatriots in Taiwan

【胞衣】bāoyī〈名〉［医学］afterbirth

炮 bāo〈动〉1（烹调）sauté: ～牛肉 quick-fried beef 2〈方〉（烘烤）dry by heat: 湿衣服放在暖气片上很快就～干了。Damp clothes will dry very soon on the radiator.
▸páo, pào

剥（剝）bāo〈动〉〈口〉hull: ～花生 shell peanuts ‖ ～光衣服 strip to the skin ‖ ～去树皮 strip the bark off a tree
▸bō

【剥皮】bāopí〈动〉peel: ～花生 shelled peanuts

龅（齙）bāo

【龅牙】bāoyá〈名〉bucktooth

煲 bāo〈方〉

A〈名〉deep cooking pot: 电饭～ electric rice cooker ‖ 瓦～ earthenware pot
B〈动〉stew: ～粥 make porridge in a cooker

褒（襃）bāo〈动〉praise: ▸～贬

【褒贬】bāobiǎn〈动〉pass judgement on: ～不一 pass different judgements (on sb./sth.) ‖ 妄加～ make presumptuous comments on the merits and demerits
【褒贬】bāobian〈动〉speak ill of: 别在背地里～人。Don't bad-mouth other people behind their backs.
【褒词】bāocí〈名〉1（表扬的话）words of praise 2 = 褒义词 bāoyìcí
【褒奖】bāojiǎng〈动〉praise and award: ～有功人员 commend and honour meritorious personnel
【褒扬】bāoyáng〈动〉praise: ～先进工作者 commend model workers
【褒义】bāoyì〈名〉commendatory sense
【褒义词】bāoyìcí〈名〉commendatory term

báo

雹 báo〈名〉hail

【雹灾】báozāi〈名〉disaster caused by hail
【雹子】báozi〈名〉hail

薄 báo〈形〉1（厚度小）thin: 像纸一样～ be paper-thin ‖ ～～地抹上一层黄油 spread butter thinly ‖ 面包切得太～了。The bread has been cut too thin. ‖〈喻〉家底～ have no substantial resources ‖〈喻〉脸皮～ be thin-skinned 2（贫瘠）infertile: 变～地为肥田 turn poor land into fertile field 3（冷淡）cold: 待他不～ treat him quite well ‖ 你待我不～。You have been most kind to me. 4（淡）weak: ～酒 light liquor
▸bó, bò

【薄板】báobǎn〈名〉sheet metal
【薄饼】báobǐng〈名〉thin pancake
【薄脆】báocuì〈名〉crisp fritter
【薄片】báopiàn〈名〉thin slice
【薄田】báotián〈名〉barren land

bǎo

饱（飽）bǎo

A〈形〉1（不饿）full: 吃～喝足 eat and drink one's fill ‖ 解决人民的温～问题 solve the problem of providing sufficient food and clothing for the people 2（充足）full: ～览美景 feast one's eyes on the beautiful scenery ‖ ～受虫害的庄稼 insect-ridden crops 3（丰满）plump: 米粒很～。The grains of rice are plump.
B〈动〉1（满足）satisfy: 大～眼福 feast one's eyes (on) ‖ 一～口福 satisfy one's appetite for good food ▸～餐 2（装满）embezzle: 公～私囊 feather one's nest with public money

【饱餐】bǎocān〈动〉eat one's fill: ～一顿 eat a big meal
【饱尝】bǎocháng〈动〉1（指品尝）fully appreciate: ～美味 fully appreciate good food 2（指体验）endure: ～艰辛 experience hardship
【饱读】bǎodú〈动〉be well read: ～诗书 be well read in the classics
【饱嗝儿】bǎogér〈名〉burp: 打～ belch
【饱含】bǎohán〈动〉be filled with: ～热泪 welling with hot tears
【饱汉不知饿汉饥】bǎohàn bù zhī èhàn jī〈俗〉those who have not known hunger can never imagine how it feels
【饱和】bǎohé〈动〉saturate: 达到～ reach saturation point
【饱和色】bǎohésè〈名〉saturated colour
【饱经沧桑】bǎojīng-cāngsāng〈成〉have gone through a great many changes in one's life: 他这一辈子～。His life was full of ups and downs.
【饱经风霜】bǎojīng-fēngshuāng〈成〉have experienced the hardships of life: ～的一生 a stormy life
【饱满】bǎomǎn〈形〉1（丰满）full: ～的种子 plump seeds 2（充沛）full of vigour: 精神～ in high spirits
【饱暖】bǎonuǎn A〈名〉material comforts: ～思淫欲。Wealth and lust go hand in hand. B〈形〉well fed and warmly clad
【饱食终日，无所用心】bǎo shí zhōngrì, wú suǒ yòng xīn〈成〉feed the stomach and starve the mind
【饱受】bǎoshòu〈动〉suffer a lot from: ～贫穷之苦 suffer a great deal from poverty
【饱学】bǎoxué〈形〉erudite: ～之士 man of learning
【饱以老拳】bǎoyǐlǎoquán〈成〉give sb. a good pummelling

宝（寶）bǎo

A〈名〉1（珍品）treasure: 无价之～ priceless treasure ▸财～, 国～, 文房四～ 2（指货币）coins: ▸元～ 3（指孩子）baby: ▸～～ 4〈贬〉（指人）good-for-nothing: ▸活～ 5〈旧〉（指赌具）gambling tool: ▸压～
B〈形〉1（珍贵）precious: ▸～刀, ～贵 2〈敬〉（你的）your: ▸～地, ～眷

【宝宝】bǎobao〈名〉baby
【宝贝】bǎobèi A〈名〉1（珍宝）treasure 2 = 宝宝 bǎobao 3（昵称）darling 4（怪人）odd fish: 他可是个～。He is really an odd fellow. B〈动〉love dearly: 两位老人可～外孙了。The old couple dote on their grandson.
【宝贝疙瘩】bǎobèi gēda〈名〉〈方〉cherished person or thing: 他是父母的～。He is the apple of his parents' eye.
【宝刹】bǎochà〈名〉1（佛塔）temple pagoda: ～古寺 ancient temples 2〈敬〉（寺庙）your splendid temple
【宝刀】bǎodāo〈名〉precious sword
【宝刀不老】bǎodāo-bùlǎo〈成〉〈喻〉still maintain one's skills at an advanced age
【宝岛】bǎodǎo〈名〉1（指岛屿）precious island 2（指台湾岛）Taiwan Island
【宝地】bǎodì〈名〉1（好地方）blessed land: 风水～ land with very auspicious *feng shui* 2〈套〉（你的地方）your place: 我们想借贵方～暂住几天。Could you oblige us with accommodation in your house for a few days?
【宝典】bǎodiǎn〈名〉treasured book

【宝贵】bǎoguì **A**〈形〉valuable: ～的时间 precious time **B**〈动〉treasure: 这是极可～的经验。This is valuable experience to be treasured.

【宝号】bǎohào〈名〉〈敬〉**1**（指公司）your company **2**（指名字）your name

【宝货】bǎohuò〈名〉**1**（指物品）precious objects **2** = 活宝 huóbǎo

【宝剑】bǎojiàn〈名〉sword: ▸上方～

【宝眷】bǎojuàn〈名〉〈敬〉your wife and children

【宝库】bǎokù〈名〉treasury: 艺术～ treasure house of fine arts ‖ 知识～ treasury of knowledge

【宝蓝】bǎolán〈形〉sapphire blue

【宝瓶座】Bǎopíngzuò〈名〉［天文］Aquarius

【宝山空回】bǎoshān-kōnghuí〈成〉gain nothing from a rare opportunity

【宝石】bǎoshí〈名〉precious stone: ～镶嵌 mounted with gemstones ▸红～, 蓝～

【宝石婚】bǎoshíhūn〈名〉sapphire wedding

【宝塔】bǎotǎ〈名〉pagoda: ～形 tower-shaped

【宝玩】bǎowán〈名〉precious knick-knacks

【宝物】bǎowù〈名〉treasure

【宝藏】bǎozàng〈名〉precious mineral deposits: 发掘地下～ tap mineral resources

【宝重】bǎozhòng〈动〉treasure: 他的书法作品一度不为世人所～。His calligraphic works were not valued very highly at one time.

【宝座】bǎozuò〈名〉throne: 登上冠军～ take winning place

保 bǎo

A〈动〉**1**（养育）raise: ▸～姆, ～育 **2**（保护）protect: ～和平 safeguard peace ▸～护, ～健, ～障 **3**（保持）maintain: ～暖 keep warm ‖ ～住（经理的）位子 keep one's position (as manager) ▸～存, ～密, ～墒 **4**（保证）guarantee: ～质～量 guarantee both quality and quantity ‖ ～您满意。Satisfaction guaranteed. ▸～送, 旱涝～收 **5**（担保）bail: 他被～出去了。He was out on bail. ▸～释, 取～
B〈名〉**1**（担保人）guarantor: ▸交～, 作～ **2**〈旧〉（指户籍编制）*bao* [a unit of an old administrative system, consisting of some 100 households]: ▸～甲制度

【保安】bǎo'ān **A**〈动〉**1**（指社会治安）ensure public security: ～措施/条例 security measures/rules ‖ 做好社会～工作 do a good job in maintaining law and order **2**（指生产安全）ensure safety: ～规程 safety regulations **B** = 保安人员 bǎo'ān rényuán

【保安人员】bǎo'ān rényuán **▸p. 966**〈名〉security guard: 招聘～ recruit security personnel

【保安族】Bǎo'ānzú〈名〉Bonan ethnic group

【保本】bǎoběn〈动〉break even: ～价 break-even price ‖ ～销售 sell at cost

【保膘】bǎobiāo〈动〉keep fat

【保镖】bǎobiāo〈名〉**1**〈旧〉（指工作）guard for persons/goods in long-distance transit **2**（指人）bodyguard: 当～ serve as a hired bodyguard

【保不定】bǎobuding = 保不住 bǎobuzhù A

【保不住】bǎobuzhù **A**〈副〉〈口〉most probably: 他～已经回家了。He may well have gone home. **B**〈动〉be unable to maintain: 雨这么大，这块地的收成～了。The yield of this plot of land will be badly affected by the heavy rain.

【保藏】bǎocáng〈动〉preserve: ～种子 preserve seeds ‖ 鱼子酱不易～。Caviar does not keep well.

【保持】bǎochí〈动〉maintain: ～警惕 maintain vigilance ‖ ～距离 keep a distance ‖ ～冷静 keep calm ‖ ～世界记录 hold the world record ‖ ～中立 maintain neutrality ‖ ～力 retention ▸水土～

【保存】bǎocún〈动〉preserve: ～实力 preserve one's strength ‖ ～完好 be in safe keeping

【保存期】bǎocúnqī〈名〉shelf life

【保单】bǎodān〈名〉**1**〈旧〉（担保的字据）guarantee **2**（质保单）warranty **3**（保险单）insurance policy: ～持有人 policy holder

【保底】bǎodǐ〈动〉**1**（保本）keep above the bottom line **2**（保证最低数额）guarantee a minimum sum: 上不封顶，下不～ impose no ceiling or floor

【保费】bǎofèi = 保险费 bǎoxiǎnfèi

【保管】bǎoguǎn **A**〈动〉take care of: ～行李 store luggage ‖ 交由某人～ entrust to sb.'s care ‖ 将贵重物品妥善～ leave one's valuables in safekeeping **B** = 保管员 bǎoguǎnyuán **C**〈副〉surely: 只要努力，～你成功。If you work hard, then success is sure to follow.

【保管费】bǎoguǎnfèi〈名〉storage fee

【保管员】bǎoguǎnyuán **▸p. 966**〈名〉storekeeper

【保户】bǎohù〈名〉insured party

【保护】bǎohù〈动〉protect: ～妇女儿童的合法权益 defend the legal rights and interests of women and children ‖ ～生态环境 preserve the eco-environment ‖ ～现场 keep the scene intact ‖ ～珍稀和濒危物种 preserve rare and endangered species ‖ 受警方～ be under police protection

【保护层】bǎohùcéng〈名〉protective layer: 在皮肤上形成～ form a protective layer over the skin

【保护关税】bǎohù guānshuì〈名〉protective tariff

【保护国】bǎohùguó〈名〉protectorate

【保护价】bǎohùjià〈名〉protective price

【保护开关】bǎohù kāiguān〈名〉protection switch

【保护膜】bǎohùmó〈名〉protective film

【保护区】bǎohùqū〈名〉conservation area: 自然～ nature reserve ‖ 野生动植物～ wildlife reserve

【保护伞】bǎohùsǎn〈名〉〈贬〉protective cover: 为不法分子提供～ shield unlawful elements

【保护色】bǎohùsè〈名〉protective colouring

【保护网】bǎohùwǎng〈名〉protective net

【保护主义】bǎohù zhǔyì〈名〉protectionism: 地方～ local protectionism

【保皇】bǎohuáng〈动〉be loyal to the monarchy: ～党 royalist ‖ ～派 royalist

【保级】bǎojí〈动〉［足球］avoid relegation: 球队在～战中失利，降级已成定局。The team lost the relegation battle, so demotion is inevitable.

【保家卫国】bǎojiā-wèiguó〈成〉protect our homes and defend our country

【保加利亚】Bǎojiālìyà〈名〉Bulgaria: ～共和国 Republic of Bulgaria ‖ ～人 Bulgarian ‖ ～语 Bulgarian

【保甲制度】bǎojiǎ zhìdù〈名〉〈旧〉*Baojia* system [an old administrative system organized on the basis of households]

【保价】bǎojià〈动〉insure: ～邮件 insured postal item ‖ ～包裹 insured parcel

【保驾】bǎojià〈动〉**1**〈旧〉（护卫皇帝）escort and guard the emperor **2**（保卫）protect: 为经济建设～护航 safeguard economic construction ‖ 别害怕，我们俩为你～。Don't be afraid. The two of us will escort you there.

【保荐】bǎojiàn〈动〉recommend with a guarantee: ～贤能 recommend men of integrity and ability

【保健】bǎojiàn〈动〉maintain health: 全民～工作 public health work ‖ ～饮料 health drinks ‖ 妇幼～医院 health clinic for women and children

【保健操】bǎojiàncāo〈名〉callisthenics

【保健品】bǎojiànpǐn〈名〉health care products

【保健食品】bǎojiànshípǐn〈名〉health food

【保健站】bǎojiànzhàn〈名〉health care centre

【保教】bǎojiào〈名〉child care and education: ～人员 personnel for child care and education

【保洁】bǎojié〈动〉keep clean: ～工作 cleaning work ‖ ～公司 cleaning company

【保洁工】bǎojiégōng〈名〉cleaner

【保举】bǎojǔ〈动〉recommend sb. for a post with a personal guarantee

【保龄球】bǎolíngqiú〈名〉**1** **▸p. 909**（指运动）bowling: ～道 bowling alley **2**（指球）bowling ball: 红色/蓝色～ red/blue bowling ball

【保留】bǎoliú〈动〉**1**（留着）retain: ～工资 retain one's previous salary ‖ ～国籍 retain citizenship **2**（搁置）lay aside: 议案暂时～，以后再议。Let's table the bill for later discussion. **3**（不同意）disagree: 持～意见 have one's reservations **4**（保存）keep back: ～座位 reserve a seat ‖ 图书馆将为你把这本书～到周末。The library will keep the book for you till the weekend.

【保留剧目】bǎoliú jùmù〈名〉stock play: 《哈姆雷特》是该剧院的～。*Hamlet* is in the repertory of the theatre.

【保媒】bǎoméi〈动〉〈旧〉act as matchmaker

【保密】bǎomì〈动〉keep secret: 对某人～ keep a secret from sb. ‖ 我一定给你～。Your secret is safe with me.

【保密文件】bǎomì wénjiàn〈名〉classified document

【保苗】bǎomiáo〈动〉save seedlings from dying off

【保命】bǎomìng〈动〉save one's life: 为了～ for the sake of survival

【保姆】bǎomǔ〈名〉**1**（家政服务员）domestic help: 雇～ hire a maid **2**（照料小孩者）nanny

【保暖】bǎonuǎn〈动〉keep warm: ～防风 warm and windproof ‖ ～内衣 thermal underwear

【保票】bǎopiào = 包票 bāopiào

【保全】bǎoquán〈动〉**1**（保住）preserve: ～面子 save one's face ‖ ～性命 save one's life **2**（维护）keep in good condition: ～工 maintenance worker

【保人】bǎorén〈名〉guarantor

【保墒】bǎoshāng〈动〉［农业］preserve soil moisture

【保湿】bǎoshī〈动〉retain moisture

【保释】bǎoshì〈动〉release on bail: ～出狱 bail sb. out of prison ‖ ～金 bail money

【保守】bǎoshǒu **A**〈动〉guard: ～国家机密 guard state secrets ‖ ～秘密 keep sth. under one's hat **B**〈形〉conservative: ～思想 conservative ideas ‖ ～的估计 conservative estimates ‖ 她的衣着太～。She is too conventional in her attire.

b

【保守党】Bǎoshǒudǎng〈名〉Conservative Party
【保守疗法】bǎoshǒu liáofǎ〈名〉conservative therapy
【保守派】bǎoshǒupài〈名〉conservatives
【保守主义】bǎoshǒu zhǔyì〈名〉conservatism
【保税区】bǎoshuìqū〈名〉bonded area
【保送】bǎosòng〈动〉guarantee sb. for admission to school: ～读研 recommend sb. for admission to a graduate school ‖ ～生 student recommended for further education
【保胎】bǎotāi〈动〉prevent a miscarriage
【保外就医】bǎowài-jiùyī〈动〉be freed on medical parole
【保卫】bǎowèi〈动〉defend: ～国家主权和领土完整 safeguard state sovereignty and territorial integrity ‖ ～祖国 defend one's country ‖ ～工作 security work ‖ ～科 security division
【保温】bǎowēn〈动〉preserve heat: ～性能 thermal insulation property
【保温杯】bǎowēnbēi〈名〉Thermos cup
【保温瓶】bǎowēnpíng〈名〉Thermos; (vacuum) flask〈英〉
【保鲜】bǎoxiān〈动〉keep fresh: ～技术 preservation techniques ‖ ～膜 cling film ‖ ～袋 plastic food bag
【保险】bǎoxiǎn **A**〈名〉**1**（指商业行为）insurance: 人寿～ life insurance ‖ 旅游～ travel insurance ‖ 人身～ personal insurance ‖ 失业～ unemployment insurance ‖ 养老～ pension **2**〈口〉（指枪械装置）safety catch **B**〈形〉safe: 买股票可不～。It's not safe to invest in stocks. ‖ 为～起见，我多带了几节电池。I took along a few extra batteries for safety's sake. **C**〈动〉be sure: 房价～还会继续上涨。It's a safe bet that house prices will continue to rise. ‖ 我敢～这消息绝对可靠。I dare assure you of the reliability of the news.
【保险带】bǎoxiǎndài〈名〉safety belt
【保险单】bǎoxiǎndān〈名〉insurance policy
【保险法】bǎoxiǎnfǎ〈名〉insurance law
【保险费】bǎoxiǎnfèi〈名〉premium
【保险杠】bǎoxiǎngàng〈名〉[of a car] bumper
【保险公司】bǎoxiǎn gōngsī〈名〉insurance company
【保险柜】bǎoxiǎnguì〈名〉safe
【保险金】bǎoxiǎnjīn〈名〉insurance
【保险丝】bǎoxiǎnsī〈名〉fuse
【保险索赔】bǎoxiǎnsuǒpéi〈名〉insurance claim
【保险箱】bǎoxiǎnxiāng〈名〉safe
【保险总额】bǎoxiǎn zǒng'é〈名〉coverage
【保修】bǎoxiū〈动〉**1**（免费修理）guarantee: ～条款 warranty terms ‖ 这个钟～一年。The clock comes with a year's guarantee. **2**（维护）maintain: ～任务 maintenance task ‖ 设备～ equipment maintenance
【保修单】bǎoxiūdān〈名〉warranty
【保修期】bǎoxiūqī〈名〉warranty period: ～内 under warranty ‖ ～为三年 three-year guarantee
【保养】bǎoyǎng〈动〉**1**（保护调养）take care of one's health: 皮肤～ skin care ‖ 他很会～身体。He certainly knows how to take care of his health. **2**（维护修理）keep in good repair: ～道路 maintain the roads ‖ 车辆/机器～ vehicle/machine maintenance ‖ 这条路～得很好。The road has been well-maintained.
【保有】bǎoyǒu〈动〉own: ～大量房地产 own a large number of properties ‖ ～修订的权利 have the right to revision
【保佑】bǎoyòu〈动〉bless: 上帝～你。God bless you.
【保育】bǎoyù〈动〉rear: ～工作者 child-care worker
【保育员】bǎoyùyuán ▸**p. 966**〈名〉child-care worker
【保育院】bǎoyùyuàn〈名〉nursery
【保障】bǎozhàng **A**〈动〉safeguard: ～安全 ensure safety ‖ ～劳动者的合法权益 protect the rights and interests of the workers **B**〈名〉safeguard: 经济建设的～ safeguarding of economic construction ‖ 社会～体系 social security system
【保真】bǎozhēn〈名〉high fidelity: 高～ hi-fi
【保证】bǎozhèng **A**〈动〉guarantee: ～不再发生类似事件 guarantee against the occurrence of similar incidents ‖ ～完成任务 guarantee to accomplish a task ‖ 他～一年内还清借款。He promised that he would pay off the loan within a year. **B**〈名〉assurance: 书面～ written pledge ‖ 质量～ quality assurance ‖ 他们得到了安全～。They got guarantees for their safety.
【保证金】bǎozhèngjīn〈名〉**1**（为保证履行义务）deposit: 交纳～ pay a deposit ‖ 收取～ collect a deposit **2**〈旧〉［法律］bail
【保证人】bǎozhèngrén〈名〉**1**（立保证书者）bondsman **2**（提供保释金者）sponsor **3**（担保人）guarantor
【保证书】bǎozhèngshū〈名〉letter of guarantee
【保值】bǎozhí〈动〉preserve the value
【保值利率】bǎozhí lìlǜ〈名〉index-linked interest rate
【保质】bǎozhì〈动〉guarantee quality: ～保量 guarantee both quality and quantity
【保质期】bǎozhìqī〈名〉best-before date
【保重】bǎozhòng〈动〉take care of oneself: ～身体 take good care of one's health ‖ 多多～! Take good care of yourself!
【保准】bǎozhǔn〈口〉**A**〈形〉dependable: 他这人不～。He is not trustworthy. **B**〈动〉assure: 我～不迟到。I assure you that I will not be late.

鸨（鴇）bǎo〈名〉**1**［鸟类］bustard **2**〈旧〉（妓院老板）procuress: ▸老～

【鸨母】bǎomǔ〈名〉〈旧〉procuress

葆 bǎo〈书〉

A〈动〉preserve: 永～青春 preserve one's youthful looks
B〈形〉luxuriant

堡 bǎo〈名〉fortress: 炸掉暗～ blow up a bunker ▸城～, 碉～, 桥头～ ▸bǔ, pù

【堡礁】bǎojiāo〈名〉barrier reef: ～岛 barrier island
【堡垒】bǎolěi〈名〉**1**〈本〉fortress: 撤离～ evacuate a fortress ‖ 炮轰～ bombard a fort **2**〈喻〉（坚固的事物）stronghold: 封建～ stronghold of feudalism ‖ 坚强的战斗～ powerful fighting force
【堡垒战】bǎolěizhàn〈名〉fortress warfare
【堡寨】bǎozhài〈名〉walled village

褓 bǎo ▸襁褓 qiǎngbǎo

bào

报（報）bào

A〈动〉**1**（告知）report: ～火警 report a fire ‖ ～失 report the loss of sth. ▸～案, ～告, 汇～ **2**（上报）submit a report: 把统计表～上来 submit the statistics to an upper level organ **3**（答复）reply: ～以热烈的掌声 respond with warm applause **4**（回报）repay: ▸～答, ～国, ～效 **5**（报复）retaliate: ▸～仇, ～复
B〈名〉**1**（报纸）newspaper: 看～ read a newspaper ▸日～, 晚～, 周～ **2**（期刊）periodical: ▸画～, 学～ **3**（告示）report: ▸海～, 喜～ **4**（电报）telegram: ▸电～, 发～

【报案】bào'àn〈动〉report a crime: 向警方～ report a case to the police
【报表】bàobiǎo〈名〉statement: 进度～ progress statement ‖ 年度～ annual report
【报偿】bàocháng〈动〉recompense: 你好好工作就是对父母的最好～。Working hard is the best way to repay your parents.
【报呈】bàochéng〈动〉submit an official report: ～上级批准 submit to a higher authority for approval
【报仇】bàochóu〈动〉revenge: 报私仇 settle personal scores ‖ 伺机～ seek vengeance
【报仇雪耻】bàochóu-xuěchǐ〈成〉take revenge for an insult
【报仇雪恨】bàochóu-xuěhèn〈成〉take revenge
【报酬】bàochou〈名〉remuneration: 不计～ be unconcerned about pay ‖ 付给～ pay a reward ‖ 劳动～ reward for one's labours ‖ 这个职业～不高。This profession doesn't pay very well.
【报春花】bàochūnhuā〈名〉［植物］primrose
【报答】bàodá〈动〉repay: ～恩情 reward debt of gratitude ‖ ～父母的养育之恩 reward one's parents for their care and upbringing
【报单】bàodān〈名〉declaration form: 进口/出口～ import/export declaration
【报导】bàodǎo = 报道 bàodào
【报到】bàodào〈动〉report for duty: 到新岗位～ report for duty at a new post ‖ 向大会报到处～ register at the conference registration desk
【报道】bàodào **A**〈动〉report: ～奥运会的最新消息 give an update on the Olympics ‖ 电视现场～ be on live TV ‖ 据～ it is reported (that) **B**〈名〉news report: 独家～ exclusive coverage ‖ 实况～ live coverage ‖ 追踪～ follow-up report
【报德】bàodé〈动〉repay kindness: 以德～ reward kindness with kindness ▸以怨～
【报端】bàoduān〈名〉〈书〉newspaper: 他的文章已见诸～。His article has appeared in the paper.
【报恩】bào'ēn〈动〉repay a debt of gratitude: 以恩～ requite a favour with a favour
【报贩】bàofàn〈名〉newspaper hawker
【报废】bàofèi〈动〉**1**（指过程）report sth. as worthless: 那部车～了。The car was written off. **2**（指结果）discard as useless: ～设备 rejected equipment
【报复】bàofù〈动〉get back at sb.: 采取～行动 take retaliatory actions ‖ 进行～ wreak vengeance on ‖ ～性关税 retaliatory tariffs ‖ ～心理 sheer vindictiveness
【报告】bàogào **A**〈动〉report: ～护照被窃 report the theft of one's passport ‖ 向

警方～ tip off the police **B**〈名〉 report: 做～ make a speech ‖ 口头/书面～ oral/written report ‖ 实验～ laboratory report

【报告会】bàogàohuì〈名〉 talk: 学术～ symposium

【报告文学】bàogào wénxué〈名〉 reportage

【报关】bàoguān〈动〉 declare goods: ～手续 customs procedures ‖ ～单 customs declaration

【报馆】bàoguǎn〈名〉〈旧〉 newspaper agency

【报国】bàoguó〈动〉 dedicate oneself to the service of one's country: ～无门 have no opportunity to serve the country ‖ 以身～ lay down one's life for one's country ▸精忠～

【报花】bàohuā〈名〉 newspaper imagery

【报户口】bào hùkǒu〈动〉 apply for residence

【报话机】bàohuàjī〈名〉 walkie-talkie

【报话员】bàohuàyuán ▸**p. 966**〈名〉 radio operator

【报夹】bàojiā〈名〉 newspaper clip

【报价】bàojià **A**〈动〉 quote: ～低于对手 quote lower than one's opponent **B**〈名〉 quoted price: ～单 quotation ‖ 最后～ final quotation

【报架】bàojià〈名〉 newspaper rack

【报检】bàojiǎn〈动〉 apply for quarantine inspection: 生猪出栏～ apply for quarantine inspection of live pigs for slaughter

【报捷】bàojié〈动〉 announce a victory

【报界】bàojiè〈名〉 the press: ～同仁 colleagues of the press ‖ 向～宣布 announce to the press

【报警】bàojǐng〈动〉 **1**（告知警方） report to the police: 报火警 report a fire ‖ 车丢了，你～了吗？ Have you reported the car theft? **2**（发出警报） sound an alarm: 鸣钟～ sound the alarm bell ‖ ～电话 emergency call ‖ ～器 alarm

【报刊】bàokān〈名〉 newspapers and periodicals: 订阅～ subscribe to newspapers and periodicals ‖ ～发行量 circulation of newspapers and periodicals ‖ ～杂志 newspapers and magazines

【报刊亭】bàokāntíng〈名〉 news stand

【报考】bàokǎo〈动〉 register for an examination: ～大学 register for university matriculation ‖ ～条件 application conditions

【报料】bàoliào **A**〈动〉 leak information: 据业内人士～ according to leaks by an insider **B**〈名〉 leak: 记者接到～后，迅速赶赴现场采访。 After receiving the tip-off, journalists rushed to the scene to get interviews.

【报名】bàomíng〈动〉 sign up: ～参加考试 put one's name down to take an examination ‖ ～参赛 sign up for a match

【报幕】bàomù〈动〉 announce the programme: ～员 announcer

【报盘】bàopán〈动〉［经济］ offer

【报批】bàopī〈动〉 submit to higher authorities for approval: 逐级～ seek the approval of the relevant authorities at the level up

【报请】bàoqǐng〈动〉 submit a written request: 这件事必须～上级批准。 This has to be reported to the higher authorities for approval.

【报人】bàorén〈名〉 newspaperman

【报丧】bàosāng〈动〉 announce sb.'s death: 向亲友～ inform relatives and friends of sb.'s death

【报社】bàoshè〈名〉 newspaper office

【报审】bàoshěn〈动〉 report to higher authorities for an examination

【报失】bàoshī〈动〉 report a loss: 已向有关银行～。 The loss has been reported to the bank concerned.

【报时】bàoshí〈动〉 sound the correct time

【报数】bàoshù〈动〉 number off: ～! Count off!

【报税】bàoshuì〈动〉 declare goods for duty

【报摊】bàotān〈名〉 news-stand

【报亭】bàotíng〈名〉 newspaper kiosk

【报童】bàotóng〈名〉 newspaper delivery boy

【报头】bàotóu〈名〉 masthead

【报务员】bàowùyuán ▸**p. 966**〈名〉 **1**（指电报） telegraph operator **2**（指广播） radio operator

【报喜】bàoxǐ〈动〉 announce good news: ～不报忧 report the good news but not the bad ‖ 我来给你报个喜。 I have come to give you some good news.

【报销】bàoxiāo〈动〉 **1**（销账） submit one's expenses: ～差旅费 reimburse travelling expenses ‖ 凭发票～ submit one's receipts for reimbursement **2**（报废） report as unusable: 这部车应该～了。 This car must be taken off the roads. **3**（诙）（除去） wipe out: ～了好几个匪徒 kill off a number of bandits

【报晓】bàoxiǎo〈动〉 herald the dawn: ～的钟声 the sound of bells calling in the day

【报效】bàoxiào〈动〉 render a service to repay a kindness: 以实际行动～祖国 repay one's country with real actions

【报信】bàoxìn〈动〉 inform: 如果发生意外，请及时给我报个信儿。 If anything goes wrong, please let me know as soon as possible. ▸通风～

【报修】bàoxiū〈动〉 report for repairs

【报业】bàoyè〈名〉 newspaper industry: ～巨头 press baron

【报应】bàoyìng〈名〉［佛教］ divine retribution: 因果～ punitive justice ‖ 总有一天会遭到～的。 There will be a day of retribution.

【报怨】bàoyuàn〈动〉 avenge a grievance: 以德～ requite injustice with kindness

【报站】bàozhàn〈动〉 announce a stop

【报章】bàozhāng〈名〉 the press: ～杂志 newspapers and magazines

【报账】bàozhàng〈动〉 apply for reimbursement: 车费可以～。 Travel expenses can be claimed.

【报纸】bàozhǐ〈名〉 **1**（指刊物） newspaper: 订阅～ subscribe to a newspaper ‖ 地方/全国性～ local/national newspaper **2**（指纸） newsprint

刨（鉋） bào

A〈名〉 **1**（指工具） plane **2**（指机床） planing machine: ▸～床

B〈动〉 shave: 把桌面～光 plane a table smooth ‖ ～好的木材 dressed timber ▸páo

【刨冰】bàobīng〈名〉 ice shavings

【刨床】bàochuáng〈名〉 **1**（指机床） planing machine **2**（指部件） plane stock

【刨刀】bàodāo〈名〉 **1**（指工具） planer tool **2**（指部件） plane iron

【刨工】bàogōng〈名〉［机械］ **1**（指工种） planing **2**（指工人） planer

【刨花】bàohuā〈名〉 wood shavings

【刨花板】bàohuābǎn〈名〉 chipboard

【刨子】bàozi〈名〉 plane

抱 bào

A〈名〉〈书〉 bosom: ▸怀～

B〈动〉 **1**（心存） hold: ～有成见 be prejudiced ‖ ～有希望 cherish a hope ‖ 不～幻想 have no illusions ‖ ～乐观/悲观态度 be optimistic/pessimistic ▸～负，～恨 **2**（患） be in poor health: ▸～病 **3**（怀抱） carry in the arms: ～着孩子 hold a baby in one's arms ‖ ～着一大堆书 hug a pile of books ‖ ～膝而坐 sit with one's arms around one's knees ▸搂～，拥～ **4**（初次得到） have one's first child/grandchild: 听说她～上孙子啦。 I hear she has become a grandmother. **5**（收养） adopt: 他是她～的孩子。 He's her adopted son. ▸～养 **6**〈口〉（团结） hang together: 大家～成团儿准能成功。 If everybody clubs together, we are bound to be successful. **7**（孵） hatch: ～小鸡 hatch chickens

C〈量〉 armful: 一～鲜花 an armful of fresh flowers ‖ 这树有两～粗。 It would take two people with their arms outstretched to reach around the tree.

【抱病】bàobìng〈动〉 be in poor health: ～工作 work even when one is ill

【抱不平】bào bùpíng〈惯〉 be outraged about an injustice and speak out against it: 他替她～。 He felt outraged at the wrong she had suffered and intervened. ▸打～

【抱残守缺】bàocán-shǒuquē〈成〉 be conservative: ～的人 sentimental conservative

【抱粗腿】bào cūtuǐ〈惯〉〈口〉 curry favour with sb. powerful

【抱佛脚】bào fójiǎo〈惯〉 make a last-minute effort: 为应付考试～ cram for a test

【抱负】bàofù〈名〉 ambition: 怀有当作家的～ have an ambition to become a writer ‖ 实现～ realize one's ambition

【抱憾】bàohàn〈动〉 regret: ～终生 live a life of remorse

【抱恨】bàohèn〈动〉 be bitterly regretful: ～终生 harbour an eternal regret

【抱愧】bàokuì〈动〉 feel ashamed

【抱歉】bàoqiàn ▸**p. 156**〈动〉 be sorry: 深感～ much to one's regret ‖ 真～，打扰了。 Sorry to have disturbed you.

【抱屈】bàoqū〈动〉 feel wronged

【抱拳】bàoquán〈动〉 salute or congratulate by cupping one hand in the fist of the other and holding both to one's chest

【抱厦】bàoshà〈名〉 **1**（指门廊） porch **2**（指小房子） lean-to at the back of a house

【抱头鼠窜】bàotóu-shǔcuàn〈成〉 scurry off like a frightened rat

【抱团儿】bàotuánr〈动〉〈口〉 stick together

【抱委屈】bào wěiqu = 抱屈 bàoqū

【抱窝】bàowō〈动〉 hatch

【抱薪救火】bàoxīn-jiùhuǒ〈成〉 pour oil onto the fire

【抱养】bàoyǎng〈动〉 adopt: ～孩子 adopt a child

【抱冤】bàoyuān〈动〉 nurse a grievance

【抱怨】bàoyuàn〈动〉 complain: ～吃得不好 grumble about one's food ‖ 无休止地～ complain incessantly

趵 bào〈动〉〈书〉 leap

▸bō

【趵突泉】Bàotūquán〈名〉 Baotu Spring

b

豹 bào〈名〉 leopard: ▸金钱～, 猎～, 雪～

【豹猫】bàomāo〈名〉leopard cat

【豹死留皮，人死留名】bàosǐ-liúpí, rénsǐ-liúmíng〈俗〉 when a leopard dies, it leaves its skin; when a man dies, he leaves his reputation

【豹子】bàozi〈名〉leopard

鲍（鮑）bào〈名〉 1〈书〉（咸鱼） salted fish 2（指海鲜） abalone

【鲍鱼】bàoyú〈名〉 1（指海鲜） abalone 2〈书〉（咸鱼） salted fish

暴¹ bào〈动〉expose: ▸～露

暴² bào

A〈形〉 1（突然而猛烈） sudden and violent: ～洪 flash flood ▸～病 2（残忍） cruel: ▸～行, 残～ 3（暴躁） quick-tempered: 脾气～ have a short temper ▸～躁

B〈动〉〈书〉spoil: ▸自～自弃

暴³ bào〈动〉bulge: 气得头上青筋都～起来了 be so angry that the veins on one's forehead stand out

【暴病】bàobìng〈名〉 sudden illness: ～身亡 die of a sudden illness

【暴跌】bàodiē〈动〉 fall steeply: 物价～。Prices dropped sharply.

【暴动】bàodòng〈动〉 rebel: 发动武装～ launch an armed revolt ‖ 镇压～ suppress an uprising

【暴发】bàofā〈动〉 1〈贬〉（指发财） make a quick fortune: ▸～户 2（指得势） suddenly make it big 3（指发作） break out: ～流感 an outbreak of flu ‖ 山洪～。A mountain torrent burst forth.

【暴发户】bàofāhù〈名〉upstart

【暴风】bàofēng〈名〉 1（大风） gale: ～的呼啸 roar of a tempest 2（飓风） hurricane

【暴风雪】bàofēngxuě〈名〉 snowstorm: 遇到西伯利亚的～ encounter the blizzards of Siberia

【暴风雨】bàofēngyǔ〈名〉 rainstorm: 遭到～的袭击 be overtaken by a storm ‖ ～般的掌声 thunderous applause

【暴风骤雨】bàofēng-zhòuyǔ〈成〉 violent storm: 在斗争的～中 in the storm and stress of struggle

【暴富】bàofù〈动〉 suddenly come into money: 一夜～ get rich overnight

【暴光】bàoguāng = 曝光 bàoguāng

【暴虎冯河】bàohǔ-pínghé〈成〉 take great risks but with reckless courage

【暴君】bàojūn〈名〉 despot

【暴库】bàokù〈动〉 have a packed store: 这种产品严重～。The stockroom is bursting with the products.

【暴雷】bàoléi〈名〉 thunderclap

【暴力】bàolì〈名〉 violence: 使用～ use violence ‖ 诉诸～ resort to violence ‖ ～冲突 violent conflict

【暴利】bàolì〈名〉 sudden huge profits: 牟取～ seek colossal profits

【暴戾】bàolì〈形〉 ruthless and tyrannical

【暴戾恣睢】bàolì-zìsuī〈成〉 be extremely cruel and despotic

【暴烈】bàoliè〈形〉 1（暴躁刚烈） violent: 性情～ have a fiery temper 2（暴猛） ferocious: ～的行动 ferocious action

【暴露】bàolù〈动〉 expose: ～目标 reveal one's position ‖ ～身份 reveal one's identity ‖ ～真面目 show one's true colours ‖ ～在光天化日之下 be exposed to the light of day ‖ 罪行～了。The crime was brought to light.

【暴露文学】bàolù wénxué〈名〉 literature exposing the dark side of society

【暴露无遗】bàolù-wúyí〈成〉be completely exposed: 他的险恶用心终于～。His evil intentions finally came out into the open.

【暴乱】bàoluàn〈动〉 riot: 发动～ stage a riot ‖ 平息～ quell a revolt

【暴民】bàomín〈名〉 mob

【暴怒】bàonù〈动〉 be in a violent rage

【暴虐】bàonüè A〈形〉 tyrannical: ～无道的政权 heavy-handed regime B〈动〉〈书〉 treat brutally: ～无辜 commit atrocities against innocent people

【暴晒】bàoshài〈动〉 be exposed to strong sunlight: 丝绸衣服不宜～。Silk clothing should not be exposed to the sun.

【暴尸】bàoshī〈动〉 die and not be buried: ～街头 die in the street

【暴食】bàoshí〈动〉 gorge oneself: ▸暴饮～

【暴死】bàosǐ〈动〉 die a sudden death

【暴殄天物】bàotiǎn-tiānwù〈成〉recklessly waste natural resources

【暴跳如雷】bàotiào-rúléi〈成〉 fly into a rage: 他经常为一丁点小事就～。He often flies off the handle at the slightest cause.

【暴突】bàotū〈动〉 bulge: 他气得两眼～。His eyes bulged with fury.

【暴徒】bàotú〈名〉 thug

【暴行】bàoxíng〈名〉 act of violence: 犯下～ commit atrocities ‖ 野蛮的～ savage brutality

【暴饮暴食】bàoyǐn-bàoshí〈成〉 eat and drink excessively

【暴雨】bàoyǔ〈名〉 torrential rain: 下～ bucket down ‖ ～成灾。Torrential rains brought on severe flooding. ‖ ～倾盆。There was a heavy downpour.

【暴躁】bàozào〈形〉 fiery: ～的脾气 hot temper ‖ 性子～的人 fiery character

【暴增】bàozēng〈动〉 boom: 小汽车销量～。Car sales are booming.

【暴涨】bàozhǎng〈动〉 1（指水） rise suddenly: 河水～。The river suddenly rose. 2（指价格） rise steeply: 物价～60%。The prices jumped by 60%.

【暴政】bàozhèng〈名〉 despotism: 施行～ tyrannize ‖ 在～统治下 under a despotic regime

【暴卒】bàozú〈动〉〈书〉 die of a sudden disease

曝 bào

▸pù

【曝光】bàoguāng〈动〉 1［摄影］ expose: ～不足 underexposure ‖ 曝了光的胶卷 exposed films 2（披露） make public: 他的受贿行为被媒体～。His bribe-taking was widely exposed by the media.

爆 bào〈动〉 1（猛然迸裂） burst: 车胎～了。A tyre burst. ▸～破, 引～ 2（突然发生） break out: ▸～发 3（指烹饪方法） quick-cook: 葱～腰花 quick-fried kidneys with scallions

【爆肚儿】bàodǔr〈名〉［食品］ quick-fried tripe

【爆发】bàofā〈动〉 1（指火山） erupt: 火山～。A volcano erupted. 2（突然发生） burst out: 城里～了骚乱。Disturbances erupted in the city. ‖ 人群中～出一阵掌声。The crowd burst into applause.

【爆发力】bàofālì〈名〉［体育］ explosive force

【爆冷】bàolěng = 爆冷门 bào lěngmén

【爆冷门】bào lěngmén〈惯〉 turn out an unexpected result: 世乒赛上连连～，种子选手纷纷落马。The World Table Tennis Championships produce unexpected winners time and time again, with seeded players getting knocked out one after the other.

【爆料】bàoliào〈动〉 reveal: 据记者～，明星吸毒并不少见。According to revelations by journalists, quite a few celebrities take drugs.

【爆裂】bàoliè〈动〉 burst: ～的水管 burst water pipe

【爆满】bàomǎn〈动〉 be filled to capacity: 电影院观众～。The theatre is packed out. ‖ 那节目演出时场场～。The show played to a series of packed houses.

【爆米花】bàomǐhuā〈名〉 1（指大米） puffed rice 2（指玉米） pop corn

【爆棚】bàopéng = 爆满 bàomǎn

【爆破】bàopò〈动〉 blow up: ～英雄 demolition hero ‖ ～专家 explosives expert

【爆破手】bàopòshǒu〈名〉demolition man

【爆破筒】bàopòtǒng〈名〉 Bangalore torpedo

【爆胎】bàotāi〈动〉 have a burst tyre: 我的车～了。My car has a burst tyre.

【爆笑】bàoxiào〈动〉 roar with laughter: ～爱情喜剧 a hilarious romantic comedy ‖ 滑稽表演令人～。People roared with laughter at the comedy.

【爆炸】bàozhà〈动〉 1〈本〉 blow up: ～原子弹 detonate an atomic device ‖ ～装置 explosive device ‖ 核～ nuclear explosion ‖ 炸弹～了。The bomb went off. 2〈喻〉 explode: 人口～ population explosion ‖ 知识～ knowledge explosion

【爆炸力】bàozhàlì〈名〉 explosive force

【爆炸式】bàozhàshì〈形〉 1（指增长） explosive: ～增长 explosive increase 2（指发型） spiky: ～发型 spiky hairstyle

【爆炸性】bàozhàxìng〈名〉 explosive quality: ～化学混合物 explosive mixture of chemicals ‖ ～新闻 explosive news

【爆仗】bàozhang = 爆竹 bàozhú

【爆竹】bàozhú〈名〉 firecrackers

> 爆竹
> ▸鞭炮

bēi

陂 bēi〈名〉〈书〉 1（池塘） pond: ～池 pond 2（水边） bank 3（山坡） hill slope

▸pō

杯（盃）bēi

A〈名〉 1（杯子） glass: 瓷～ china cup ‖ 啤酒～ beer mug ▸茶～, 干～ 2（奖杯） trophy: 争夺世界～ compete for the World Cup ▸冠军～, 奖～

B〈量〉 cup: 一～咖啡 a cup of coffee ‖ 两～酒下肚，他的话就多了起来。He became talkative after two drinks.

【杯葛】bēigé〈动〉〈方〉 boycott

【杯弓蛇影】bēigōng-shéyǐng〈成〉〈喻〉 be beset with imaginary fears: 你这不是～么？ Aren't you a bit overly suspicious?

【杯酒言欢】bēijiǔ-yánhuān〈成〉 drink happily together

【杯盘狼藉】bēipán-lángjí〈成〉 wine cups and dishes all over the place

【杯赛】bēisài〈名〉Cup: 参加～ play in the Cup
【杯水车薪】bēishuǐ-chēxīn〈成〉〈喻〉utterly inadequate measure: 那时对地震灾民的援助不过是～。Aid to the earthquake victims at that time was completely inadequate.
【杯中物】bēizhōngwù〈名〉〈书〉alcohol: 酷爱～ be rather too fond of a drink
【杯子】bēizi〈名〉glass

卑 bēi〈形〉**1**〈书〉(低洼) low: 地势～湿 low-lying and damp ▸～微 **2** (地位低下) low: 位～ low in position **3** (低劣) inferior: ▸～鄙, ～劣 **4**〈书〉(谦恭) humble: ▸不～不亢, 谦～
【卑鄙】bēibǐ〈形〉base: ～的勾当 dirty deal ‖ ～的目的 mean intentions ‖ ～的手段 dirty tricks
【卑鄙龌龊】bēibǐ-wòchuò〈成〉foul: 此事～至极。The whole scheme stinks to high heaven.
【卑鄙无耻】bēibǐ-wúchǐ〈成〉base and shameless: ～之徒 person with no sense of shame
【卑不足道】bēibùzúdào〈成〉too trivial to be worth mentioning: ～的人 a nobody
【卑恭】bēigōng〈形〉servile
【卑躬屈节】bēigōng-qūjié = 卑躬屈膝 bēigōng-qūxī
【卑躬屈膝】bēigōng-qūxī〈成〉bow and scrape: 对老板～ crawl to the boss
【卑贱】bēijiàn〈形〉**1** (指地位或出生) humble: 出身～ be of low birth **2** (指品性) mean and low: 行为～ behave pitifully
【卑劣】bēiliè〈形〉base: ～手段 mean trick ‖ ～行径 base conduct
【卑怯】bēiqiè〈形〉abject: ～的姑娘 shy self-effacing girl
【卑微】bēiwēi〈形〉petty and low: 出身～ of humble origins
【卑污】bēiwū〈形〉foul
【卑下】bēixià〈形〉**1** (低劣) base: 品质～ of low character **2** (低下) humble: 地位～ have low social status
【卑职】bēizhí〈名〉**1**〈书〉(指职位) low position **2**〈旧〉(用于自称) I

背 (揹) bēi〈动〉**1** (用背驮) carry on the back: ～孩子 carry a child on one's back ‖ ～我走! Give me a piggyback! **2** (承担) shoulder: ～了一屁股债 be up to one's ears in debt ‖ 替别人～恶名 take the blame for somebody else
▸bèi
【背包】bēibāo〈名〉**1**〈本〉backpack; rucksack〈英〉: ～上有可调节的背带。The rucksack has adjustable straps. **2** [军事] blanket roll
【背包袱】bēi bāofu〈动〉〈口〉have a weight on one's mind: 批评使他背上了思想包袱。The weight of the criticism lingered on his mind.
【背带】bēidài〈名〉**1** (指服装上的) braces〈英〉; suspenders〈美〉**2** (指枪上的) sling; (指背包上的) strap
【背负】bēifù〈动〉**1** (用背驮) carry on the back **2** (承担) bear: ～重任 have a heavy responsibility on one's shoulder
【背黑锅】bēi hēiguō〈动〉〈口〉carry the can: 让人～ leave sb. holding the bag ‖ 替老板～ take the rap for one's boss
【背篓】bēilǒu〈名〉〈方〉pannier
【背头】bēitóu〈名〉swept-back hair
【背债】bēizhài〈动〉be in debt: 不～ be debt-free ‖ 背了一身债 be heavily in debt
【背子】bēizi = 背篓 bēilǒu

悲 bēi
A〈形〉sad: ▸～伤, ～痛, 乐极生～
B〈动〉pity: ▸～天悯人
【悲哀】bēi'āi〈形〉mournful: 感到～ feel sad ‖ 为朋友之死而～ be grieved over the death of one's friend ‖ 他英年早逝, 令人～。It is tragic that he died so young.
【悲不自胜】bēibù-zìshèng〈成〉be overcome with grief
【悲惨】bēicǎn〈形〉wretched: 过着～的生活 live a miserable life ‖ ～的结局 tragic ending ‖ ～的命运 heavy fate
【悲愁】bēichóu〈形〉sad and worried: 一脸～ look dolefully worried
【悲楚】bēichǔ〈形〉〈书〉sorrowful
【悲怆】bēichuàng〈形〉〈书〉sorrowful: ～的曲调 melancholy music
【悲悼】bēidào〈动〉mourn: ～亡友 grieve over a friend who has passed away
【悲愤】bēifèn〈形〉grievous and indignant: ～交集 be overcome with grief and indignation
【悲愤填膺】bēifèn-tiányīng〈成〉be seized by grief and indignation
【悲歌】bēigē **A**〈动〉sing with solemn fervour: ～一曲 sing a sad song with deep emotion **B**〈名〉sad melody
【悲观】bēiguān〈形〉pessimistic: 表现出～情绪 display pessimism ‖ 持～看法 be pessimistic ‖ ～失望 be disheartened
【悲观厌世】bēiguān-yànshì〈成〉be pessimistic and world-weary
【悲观主义】bēiguān zhǔyì〈名〉pessimism: ～观点 pessimistic view
【悲号】bēiháo〈动〉wail with grief
【悲欢离合】bēihuān-líhé〈成〉ups and downs of life
【悲剧】bēijù〈名〉tragedy: 古典～ classical tragedy ‖ 酿成～ cause a tragedy ‖ 爱情～ tragic love ‖ 家庭～ domestic tragedy
【悲苦】bēikǔ〈形〉wretched: 排遣胸中的～ dispel one's sorrow ‖ ～的神情 miserable look
【悲凉】bēiliáng〈形〉desolate: 曲调～。The tunes are doleful and melancholic.
【悲悯】bēimǐn〈动〉feel sympathy for
【悲鸣】bēimíng〈动〉wail
【悲凄】bēiqī〈形〉mournful
【悲戚】bēiqī〈形〉mournful: ～的神情 mournful look
【悲泣】bēiqì〈动〉weep with grief
【悲切】bēiqiè〈形〉grieved
【悲情】bēiqíng **A**〈名〉pathos **B**〈形〉sad: ～故事 sad story ‖ ～戏 tragedy
【悲伤】bēishāng〈形〉sad: ～不已 be greatly distressed ‖ ～成疾 be ill with grief
【悲酸】bēisuān〈形〉sad and bitter: 阵阵～涌上心头。She was overwhelmed by bitter sorrow.
【悲叹】bēitàn〈动〉bemoan: ～自己的不幸 lament one's misfortunes
【悲天悯人】bēitiān-mǐnrén〈成〉bemoan the hard times and the misery of the people
【悲恸】bēitòng〈动〉wail with grief: ～不已 be overcome with grief
【悲痛】bēitòng〈形〉grieved: 深感～ feel profound sorrow ‖ ～万分 be in extreme grief ‖ 化～为力量 turn sorrow into strength
【悲痛欲绝】bēitòng-yùjué〈成〉be grief-stricken: 劝慰～的亲属 console grief-stricken relatives
【悲喜交集】bēixǐ-jiāojí〈成〉have mixed feelings: ～的泪水 tears of joy and grief
【悲喜剧】bēixǐjù〈名〉tragicomedy
【悲咽】bēiyè〈动〉〈书〉sob sadly
【悲壮】bēizhuàng〈形〉tragic and soul-stirring: ～的诗篇 sad yet stirring poetry

碑 bēi〈名〉stele: 立～纪念 erect a tablet to the memory (of) ▸～文, 界～, 树～立传
【碑额】bēi'é〈名〉head of a stele
【碑记】bēijì〈名〉tablet inscription
【碑碣】bēijié〈名〉〈书〉stele
【碑刻】bēikè〈名〉tablet inscription
【碑林】bēilín〈名〉forest of steles: 西安～ Forest of Steles in Xi'an
【碑铭】bēimíng = 碑文 bēiwén
【碑拓】bēità〈名〉rubbings from tablets
【碑帖】bēitiè〈名〉stone rubbing
【碑亭】bēitíng〈名〉pavilion sheltering a stone tablet
【碑文】bēiwén〈名〉inscription on monument or tablet
【碑志】bēizhì = 碑记 bēijì
【碑座】bēizuò〈名〉tablet base

鹎 (鵯) bēi〈名〉[鸟类] bulbul

běi

北 běi
A ▸**p. 205**〈名〉north: 向～航行/行驶 sail/drive north ‖ 朝～的阳台/房间 north-facing balcony/room ‖ 黄河以～ to the north of the Yellow River
B〈动〉be defeated: 追奔逐～ pursue the defeated enemy ▸败～
【北爱尔兰】Běi'ài'ěrlán〈名〉Northern Ireland: ～问题 Northern Ireland issue
【北安普敦郡】Běi'ānpǔdūnjùn〈名〉Northamptonshire
【北半球】běibànqiú〈名〉Northern Hemisphere
【北边】běibian ▸**p. 205**〈名〉north: 蒙古在中国的～。Mongolia lies to the north of China.
【北冰洋】Běibīngyáng〈名〉Arctic Ocean
【北部】běibù ▸**p. 205**〈名〉northern part: 中国～ northern China
【北朝】Běicháo〈名〉Northern Dynasties period [386-581]
【北辰】Běichén〈名〉〈旧〉Polaris
【北达科他州】Běidákētāzhōu〈名〉North Dakota
【北大荒】Běidàhuāng〈名〉[in North-east China] Great Northern Wilderness
【北大西洋公约组织】Běi Dàxīyáng Gōngyuē Zǔzhī〈名〉North Atlantic Treaty Organization (NATO)
【北斗星】Běidǒuxīng〈名〉Plough〈英〉; Big Dipper〈美〉
【北豆腐】běidòufu〈名〉northern-style tofu
【北伐】Běifá〈简称〉= 北伐战争
【北伐战争】Běifá Zhànzhēng〈名〉Northern Expedition [1926-1927]
【北方】běifāng ▸**p. 205**〈名〉north: ～人 northerner ‖ ～地区 northern region ‖ ～的生活费用比南方低。It is less expensive to live in the north than in the south.
【北方话】běifānghuà ▸**p. 918**〈名〉northern dialect
【北非】Běi Fēi〈名〉North Africa
【北风】běifēng〈名〉northerly wind: ～呼啸。The wind comes howling from the north.

b

【北国】bĕiguó〈名〉〈书〉the north: ～风光 northern scenery
【北海】Bĕihăi〈名〉North Sea: ～油田 North Sea oilfield
【北海道】Bĕihăidào〈名〉Hokkaido
【北寒带】bĕihándài〈名〉north frigid zone
【北回归线】bĕihuíguīxiàn〈名〉Tropic of Cancer
【北货】bĕihuò〈名〉delicacies from northern China
【北极】bĕijí〈名〉**1**（指地球）North Pole **2**（指磁场）north pole
【北极光】bĕijíguāng〈名〉northern lights
【北极圈】Bĕijíquān〈名〉Arctic Circle
【北极星】Bĕijíxīng〈名〉North Star, Pole Star: ～序 north polar sequence ‖ 没有指南针，他只能依靠～来航行。Without a compass, he had to navigate by the North Star.
【北极熊】bĕijíxióng〈名〉polar bear
【北京】Bĕijīng ▸**p. 661**〈名〉Beijing
【北京大学】Bĕijīng Dàxué〈名〉Peking University
【北京烤鸭】Bĕijīng kăoyā〈名〉roast Peking duck
【北京人】Bĕijīngrén〈名〉**1**（指居民）native of Beijing **2** = 北京猿人 Bĕijīng yuánrén
【北京时间】Bĕijīng Shíjiān〈名〉Beijing Time
【北京猿人】Bĕijīng yuánrén〈名〉Peking Man
【北卡罗莱纳州】Bĕikăluóláinàzhōu〈名〉North Carolina
【北马里亚纳】Bĕimălĭyànà〈名〉Northern Mariana Islands: ～联邦 Commonwealth of the Northern Mariana Islands
【北美】Bĕi Mĕi〈简称〉= 北美洲
【北美洲】Bĕi Mĕizhōu〈名〉North America
【北美自由贸易区】Bĕi Mĕi Zìyóu Màoyìqū〈名〉North American Free Trade Area (NAFTA)
【北面】bĕimiàn ▸**p. 205**〈名〉north: 俄罗斯在中国的～。Russia lies to the north of China.
【北欧】Bĕi Ōu〈名〉Northern Europe
【北漂】bĕipiāo〈名〉drifters in Beijing: 北京有几万"～"长期居留。There are tens of thousands of drifters living long-term in Beijing.
【北齐】Bĕi Qí〈名〉Northern Qi Dynasty
【北曲】bĕiqŭ〈名〉**1**（指元宋时期）northern tunes **2**（指金元时代）northern operas
【北山羊】bĕishānyáng〈名〉ibex
【北上】bĕishàng〈动〉go north: ～车辆 northbound traffic
【北宋】Bĕi Sòng〈名〉Northern Song Dynasty
【北纬】bĕiwĕi〈名〉northern latitude
【北魏】Bĕi Wèi〈名〉Northern Wei Dynasty
【北温带】bĕiwēndài〈名〉north temperate zone
【北洋】Bĕiyáng〈名〉northern coastal region in the Qing Dynasty
【北洋军阀】Bĕiyáng Jūnfá〈名〉Northern Warlords [1912-1927]
【北洋水师】Bĕiyáng Shŭishī〈名〉Northern Fleet (of the Qing Dynasty)
【北约】Bĕiyuē〈简称〉= 北大西洋公约组织
【北约克郡】Bĕiyuēkèjùn〈名〉North Yorkshire
【北岳】Bĕiyuè〈名〉Northern Sacred Mountain [Hengshan Mountain (恒山) in Shanxi Province]
【北周】Bĕi Zhōu〈名〉Northern Zhou Dynasty

bèi

贝（貝）bèi

〈名〉**1**（指生物）shellfish **2**（指货币）cowry
【贝德福德郡】Bèidéfúdéjùn〈名〉Bedfordshire
【贝雕】bèidiāo〈名〉shell carving
【贝尔法斯特】Bèi'ĕrfăsītè〈名〉Belfast
【贝尔莫潘】Bèi'ĕrmòpān〈名〉Belmopan
【贝尔格莱德】Bèi'ĕrgéláidé〈名〉Belgrade
【贝加尔湖】Bèijiā'ĕrhú ▸**p. 305**〈名〉Lake Baikal
【贝壳】bèiké〈名〉shell
【贝劳】Bèiláo〈名〉Palau: ～共和国 Republic of Palau
【贝勒】bèile〈名〉*beile* [a rank of the Manchu nobility below that of prince]
【贝雷帽】bèiléimào〈名〉beret
【贝类】bèilèi〈名〉shellfish
【贝里克郡】Bèilĭkèjùn〈名〉Berwickshire
【贝鲁特】Bèilŭtè〈名〉Beirut
【贝母】bèimŭ〈名〉[中药] **1**（指植物）fritillary **2**（指鳞茎）bulb of the fritillary
【贝宁】Bèiníng〈名〉Benin: ～共和国 Republic of Benin ‖ ～人 Beninese
【贝塔】bèită〈名〉beta (β): ～射线 beta ray
【贝叶树】bèiyèshù〈名〉[植物] talipot
【贝子】bèizĭ〈名〉*beizi* [a rank of the Manchu nobility below that of *beile* (贝勒)]

狈（狽）bèi ▸狼狈 lángbèi

备（備）bèi

A〈形〉complete: ▸齐～, 求全责～
B〈动〉**1**（具有）possess: ～有样品。Samples are readily available. ▸德才兼～ **2**（准备）prepare: ～饭 prepare a meal ‖ ～马 saddle and bridle the horse ▸～料, 筹～ **3**（防备）take precautions against: 以～不时之需 for unexpected future use ▸防～, 攻其不～, 警～
C〈名〉equipment: ▸军～, 设～, 装～
D〈副〉fully: ～受欢迎 be met with warm welcome ‖ ～受尊敬 enjoy great respect
【备案】bèi'àn〈动〉put on record: ～存查 file on record for reference ‖ 此事已报主管部门～。This has been reported to the relevant department for their records.
【备办】bèibàn〈动〉prepare for: ～嫁妆 get together a trousseau ‖ ～年货 make purchases for the Spring Festival
【备不住】bèibuzhù〈副〉〈方〉maybe: ～已经有人告诉她了。She has probably been told about it already.
【备查】bèichá〈动〉keep for future reference: 存档～ keep on file for reference
【备尝艰辛】bèicháng-jiānxīn〈成〉suffer untold hardships
【备而不用】bèi'érbùyòng〈成〉save sth. for possible future use
【备份】bèifèn **A**〈名〉backup: ▸～文件 **B**〈动〉copy: ～大量数据 back up huge amounts of data
【备份文件】bèifèn wénjiàn〈名〉[计算机] backup file
【备耕】bèigēng〈动〉prepare for ploughing and sowing
【备荒】bèihuāng〈动〉prepare against natural disasters
【备货】bèihuò〈动〉stock up
【备件】bèijiàn〈名〉spare part
【备考】bèikăo **A**〈动〉prepare for examinations: 学生们正在～。The students are preparing for their examinations. **B**〈名〉reference
【备课】bèikè〈动〉prepare lessons
【备料】bèiliào〈动〉**1**（为生产）prepare materials: 他上班前就备好了料。He got the materials ready before the shift started. **2**（为力畜）prepare feed
【备品】bèipĭn〈名〉spare parts
【备取】bèiqŭ〈动〉be on the waiting list: ～生 student on the waiting list for admission
【备述】bèishù〈动〉〈书〉tell in detail: ～其事 describe sth. down to the smallest detail
【备忘录】bèiwànglù〈名〉**1**（指外交文书）memorandum: 谅解～ memorandum of understanding **2**（指笔记）memo pad: 办公室～ office memo
【备用】bèiyòng〈动〉keep back: 安排一架直升飞机～ keep a helicopter on standby ‖ 留些钱～ hold some money in reserve ‖ ～物资 reserve goods and materials
【备用机场】bèiyòng jīchăng〈名〉alternate airport
【备战】bèizhàn〈动〉prepare for war: 扩军～ armaments expansion and war preparations ‖〈喻〉～奥运会 train for the Olympic Games
【备至】bèizhì〈形〉〈书〉supreme: 关心～ show extreme care
【备置】bèizhì〈动〉acquire
【备注】bèizhù〈名〉**1**（指文字说明）remarks **2**（指表格栏）comments: ～栏 comments

背 bèi

A〈名〉**1**（背部）back: ～靠着墙 lean one's back against the wall ‖ 腰酸～痛 have backache ▸～脊, 汗流浃～, 马～ **2**（反面）back of an object: 手～ back of the hand
B〈动〉**1**（背对着）back on to: ～山面水 backing on to a mountain and facing a river **2**（违反）act contrary to: ～着良心做事 act against one's conscience ▸～信弃义 **3**（离开）leave: ▸～井离乡 **4**（瞒着）do sth. behind sb.'s back: ～着妻子买了一栋别墅 buy a villa behind one's wife's back ‖ 说话不～人 speak without noticing who's listening **5**（背诵）recite: ～书/台词 learn the text/one's lines by heart **6**（指手或手臂）have one's hands crossed or tied behind: ～着手来回踱步 walk back and forth with one's hands clasped behind one **7**（掉转）turn away: 她厌恶地～过脸去。She turned on her heel in disgust.
C〈形〉**1**〈口〉（不走运）unlucky: 今天打麻将，我手气很～。I'm not having much luck at mah-jong today. **2**（听觉不灵）hard of hearing: 他耳朵很～。He is very hard of hearing. **3**（偏僻）out-of-the-way: 那条街很～。That is a very out-of-the-way street.
▸bēi
【背部】bèibù〈名〉back: ～受伤 have a back injury
【背城借一】bèichéng-jièyī〈成〉put up a last desperate struggle
【背城一战】bèichéng-yīzhàn = 背城借一 bèichéng-jièyī
【背道而驰】bèidào'érchí〈成〉go against: 与奥运会宗旨～ run counter to the Olympic ideal
【背地里】bèidìli〈副〉on the sly: ～说他坏话 speak ill of him behind his back

b

【背对背】bèiduìbèi = 背靠背 bèikàobèi
【背飞】bèifēi〈动〉［排球］ make a backward flight
【背风】bèifēng〈形〉 leeward: 在～处晒晒太阳 enjoy the sunshine protected from the wind
【背光】bèiguāng〈形〉 **1**（光线不好） badly-lit **2**（背后照明） backlit: 他～站着。He stood with his back to the light.
【背后】bèihòu〈名〉 **1**（后面） behind: 在门～ behind the door **2**（背地里） behind sb.'s back: ～捣鬼 scheme behind the scenes ‖ ～下毒手 stab sb. in the back
【背货】bèihuò〈名〉 slow-selling goods
【背脊】bèijǐ〈名〉 back
【背剪】bèijiǎn〈动〉 **1**（放在身后） have one's hands clasped behind one's back: 他～双手，在一边看热闹。 He stood on the side and watched the excitement with his hands behind his back. **2**（被捆在身后） have one's hands tied at the back: 那小偷双手～给抓走了。 The thief was taken away with his hands trussed behind him.
【背井离乡】bèijǐng-líxiāng〈成〉 leave one's home: 成千上万的人们因战争而～。 Thousands of people have been displaced by the war.
【背景】bèijǐng〈名〉 **1**（布景） backdrop: 舞台～ stage background ‖ 照片的～ background to the photograph **2**（环境） background: 家庭～ family background ‖ 历史/社会～ historical/social context **3**（权势） powerful connections: 这个官司有～，不可掉以轻心。 This lawsuit has a history, and should not be dismissed lightly.
【背景音乐】bèijǐng yīnyuè〈名〉 background music
【背静】bèijing〈形〉 quiet and secluded: 走～的小巷 take a quiet back lane
【背靠背】bèikàobèi〈动〉 be back to back: ～站着 stand back to back
【背离】bèilí〈动〉 **1**（离开） leave: ～故土 leave one's native land **2**（违背） deviate from: ～传统 depart from tradition ‖ ～原则 stray from the principle
【背理】bèilǐ〈形〉 unreasonable: 这件事她做得有点～。 It was unreasonable of her to do it.
【背面】bèimiàn〈名〉 **1**（后面） back: 在支票的～签字 sign the back of a cheque ‖ 信封～ the back of an envelope **2**（背部） back
【背叛】bèipàn〈动〉 betray: ～革命 betray the revolution ‖ ～妻子 forsake one's wife ‖ ～祖国 turn one's back on one's country
【背鳍】bèiqí〈名〉［鱼类］ dorsal fin
【背气】bèiqì〈动〉 stop breathing temporarily: 他气得差点儿背过气去。 He nearly choked with rage.
【背弃】bèiqì〈动〉 abandon: ～诺言 go back on one's word ‖ ～信仰 renounce one's faith
【背人】bèirén〈动〉 **1**（避开别人） be private: 咱们找个～的地方谈一谈。 Let's find a private place where we can talk. **2**（不让人知道） be unmentionable: ～的交易 shady deal ‖ 她没什么～的事。 She had nothing to hide from anyone.
【背时】bèishí〈形〉 **1**（过时） outdated: ～服装 unfashionable dress **2**（不走运） unlucky: 这些天我真～。 I've been really unlucky recently.
【背书】bèishū **A**〈动〉 **1**（指背诵） recite a text **2**（指签字） endorse: ～单据 back a bill ‖ ～支票 endorse a cheque **B**〈名〉 endorsement: 记名～ endorsement in full ‖ 无/不记名～ blank endorsement
【背水一战】bèishuǐ-yīzhàn〈成〉 fight to the death
【背诵】bèisòng〈动〉 recite: ～课文 recite a text
【背心】bèixīn〈名〉 **1**（指内衣） vest〈英〉; undershirt〈美〉 **2**（指外穿的） waistcoat〈英〉; vest〈美〉: 防弹～ bullet-proof vest
【背信弃义】bèixìn-qìyì〈成〉 betray a trust: ～的行为 act of treachery
【背兴】bèixìng〈形〉〈方〉 unlucky
【背眼】bèiyǎn〈形〉 inconspicuous: 在～的地方卿卿我我 whisper sweet nothings in out-of-the-way places
【背阴】bèiyīn〈形〉 shady: ～处 shade ‖ 楼后～的地方还有积雪。 Some snow still remained in the shade of the building.
【背影】bèiyǐng〈名〉 view of sb.'s back: 他噙着泪水，凝望着父亲远去的～。 He gazed at his father's receding figure with tearful eyes.
【背约】bèiyuē〈动〉 break one's promise
【背越式】bèiyuèshì〈名〉［体育］ Fosbury flop: ～跳高 Fosbury-flop high jump
【背运】bèiyùn **A**〈名〉 bad luck: 走～ have a streak of bad luck **B**〈形〉 unlucky: 玩牌老～ always be unlucky at cards

钡（鋇） bèi〈名〉［化学］ barium (Ba)

【钡餐】bèicān〈名〉［药学］ barium meal

倍 bèi

A〈动〉 double: ▸加～，事半功～
B〈量〉 time: 四～ four-fold ‖ 15 是 5 的 3～。 Fifteen is three times as much as five.
C〈副〉 exceptionally: ～感亲切 feel particularly affectionate
【倍加】bèijiā〈副〉〈口〉 extremely: ～小心 be doubly careful ‖ 和平来之不易，应当～珍惜。 Peace has not come easily and should be especially cherished.
【倍率】bèilǜ〈名〉 magnifying power
【倍式】bèishì〈名〉 duplication formula
【倍数】bèishù〈名〉 **1**［数学］ multiple: 21 是 3 和 7 的～。 Twenty-one is the multiple of 3 and 7. ▸最小公～ **2**［经济］ multiplier: ～效应 multiplier effect
【倍增】bèizēng〈动〉 redouble: 信心/勇气～ with doubled confidence/courage

ℹ 倍数

■ 汉语用"A 的大小是 B 的…倍"及"A 比 B 大…倍"，而英语可用更多句型来表达:

A 的大小（宽度、长度、重量…）是 B 的 X 倍 或 A 比 B 大（宽、长、重…）X–1 倍
= A is X times as big (wide, long, heavy ...) as B
或 The size (width/breadth, length, weight ...) of A is X times that of B
或 A is X times the size (width/breadth, length, weight...) of B
或 A is X-1 times bigger (wider, longer, heavier ...) than B

■ 英语里表示几倍的时候，一般是用阿拉伯数字或用英语的基数词加上 time(s)。两倍通常说 twice，三倍可用 three times、triple 或 treble，四倍可用 four times 或 quadruple:

这条河的宽度是另一条的 3 倍
= This river is three times as wide as the other one
或 The width of this river is three times/triple/treble that of the other one
或 This river is three times/triple/treble the width of the other one

我的新大衣正好比她的贵 3 倍
= My new coat is exactly three times more expensive than hers
或 My new coat is exactly four times as expensive as hers
或 The price of my new coat is four times/quadruple that of hers
或 My new coat is four times/quadruple the price of hers

黑箱子的重量是红箱子的 6 倍
= The black box is six times as heavy as the red one
或 The black box is six times the weight of the red one
或 The weight of the black box is six times that of the red one
或 The black box is five times heavier than the red one

■ 注意下面 double、treble/triple、quadruple 做动词的用法:

房地产的价格在最近 10 年里几乎上涨了 1 倍
= The price of property has almost doubled in the last ten years

从去年以来我们公司的利润增加了两倍
= The profit of our company has trebled/tripled since last year

这所学校的学生数目增加到了 5 年前的 4 倍
= The number of students of the school has quadrupled as compared with five years ago

其他短语

我们的客厅只有他们的一半大
= Our living room is only half the size of theirs

她的身高是我的两倍
= She is twice my height

我母亲的年龄是我的 3 倍
= My mother is triple my age

我以 5 倍于往常的价格买到了这张票
= I paid five times the usual price for the ticket

从去年以来失业率增加了 20%
= The rate of unemployment has increased by 20% since last year

学电脑的人数增加到了 6 年前的 5 倍
或 学电脑的人数比 6 年前增加了 4 倍
= The number of computer learners has increased (to) four times as compared with six years ago

从 2000 年以来互联网的使用人数增加了 8 倍
= The number of Internet users has increased by a factor of 8 since the year 2000

b

悖 bèi〈书〉

A〈动〉run contrary to: 并行不～ be mutually compatible ‖ 有～常理 be against common sense

B〈形〉unreasonable: ▸～谬

【悖理】bèilǐ = 背理 bèilǐ

【悖论】bèilùn〈名〉paradox

【悖谬】bèimiù〈形〉〈书〉absurd

【悖逆】bènì〈形〉〈书〉disloyal

【悖入悖出】bèirù-bèichū〈成〉ill-gotten, ill-spent

被 bèi

A〈名〉quilt: 新棉～ a new quilt ▸～面, 毛巾～

B〈动〉**1**（覆盖）cover: ▸～覆 **2**（遭受）suffer: ～屈含冤 be wronged ▸～灾

C〈助〉[used in the passive voice when the doer of the action is not mentioned]: ～拘留 be taken into custody ‖ ～免职 be stripped of one's post

D〈介〉[used in the passive voice to introduce the doer of the action or the action if the doer is not mentioned] by: ～经理解雇 be dismissed by the manager ‖ ～压迫民族 oppressed nation ‖ ～剥削者 the exploited

【被捕】bèibǔ〈动〉be arrested: 他因虚报账目而～。He was arrested for falsifying accounts.

【被袋】bèidài〈名〉bedding bag

【被单】bèidān〈名〉**1**（铺床用）sheet **2**（人盖用）double-layered sheet

【被动】bèidòng〈形〉**1**（受外力迫使）passive: ～挨打 be on the defensive ‖ 工作要主动，不要～。We should be active, not passive in our work. **2**（处于不利地位）unfavourable: 陷入～ be thrown into an unfavourable situation

【被动式】bèidòngshì〈名〉[语言] the passive

【被动吸烟】bèidòng xīyān〈名〉passive smoking: ～者 passive smoker

【被动语态】bèidòng yǔtài〈名〉[语言] passive voice

【被服】bèifú〈名〉bedding and clothing: ～厂 bedding and clothing factory

【被俘】bèifú〈动〉be taken prisoner: ～士兵 prisoners of war (POW)

【被覆】bèifù **A**〈动〉cover: 山上～着苍翠的树木。The mountain is mantled by verdant trees. **B**〈名〉plant cover: 滥伐森林，严重破坏了地面～。Severe deforestation has destroyed the ground cover.

【被告】bèigào〈名〉defendant: ～席 dock ‖ 为～辩护 defend the accused ‖ ～被宣告无罪。The defendant was acquitted of the charge.

【被害人】bèihàirén〈名〉victim

【被减数】bèijiǎnshù〈名〉minuend

【被叫】bèijiào〈名〉[通信] called party

【被控】bèikòng〈动〉be accused of: ～犯谋杀罪/受贿罪 be charged with murder/bribery

【被里】bèilǐ〈名〉quilt lining

【被面】bèimiàn〈名〉quilt cover: 软缎～ satin quilt cover

【被难】bèinàn〈动〉**1**（指丧生）be killed in a disaster: 飞机失事，乘客全部～。All the passengers died in the air crash. **2**（指遭灾）suffer from a natural disaster: ～的渔民 disaster-stricken fishermen

【被迫】bèipò〈动〉be forced: ～投降 surrender under compulsion ‖ ～卖淫 be forced into prostitution

【被褥】bèirù〈名〉bedding: 晾晒～ sun and air the bedclothes

【被套】bèitào〈名〉**1**（指袋子）bedding bag **2** = 被罩 bèizhào **3**（棉胎）cotton wadding for a quilt

【被头】bèitóu〈名〉cover on the top edge of a quilt

【被窝儿】bèiwōr〈名〉〈口〉quilt: 躺在～里 lie under one's quilt

【被卧】bèiwo〈名〉quilt: 一床～ a quilt

【被絮】bèixù〈名〉cotton padding of a quilt

【被选举权】bèixuǎnjǔquán〈名〉right to be elected

【被灾】bèizāi〈动〉suffer disaster

【被罩】bèizhào〈名〉quilt cover

【被子植物】bèizǐ zhíwù〈名〉angiosperm

【被子】bèizi〈名〉quilt: 叠～ fold up a quilt ‖ 把～盖好! Cover yourself with the quilt.

棓 bèi ▸五倍子 wǔbèizǐ

辈（輩）bèi

〈名〉**1**（人）people of a certain kind: 我～ people like me ‖ 无能之～ incompetent people **2**（代）generation: 老一～ older generation ‖ 他们同～。They are of the same generation. ▸老前～, 晚～, 祖～ **3**（一生）lifetime: ▸～子

【辈出】bèichū〈动〉come forth in large numbers: 英雄～的时代 age of heroes ‖ 歌坛新人～。Many new singers are emerging. ▸人才～

【辈分】bèifen〈名〉position in the family hierarchy: 我的～比他高。I rank as his senior in the family hierarchy.

【辈行】bèiháng = 辈分 bèifen

【辈数儿】bèishùr = 辈分 bèifen

【辈子】bèizi〈名〉lifetime: 后/前半～ second/first half of one's life ‖ 他当了一～教师。He has been a teacher all his life.

惫（憊）bèi

〈形〉worn out: ▸疲～

焙 bèi

〈动〉bake over a slow fire: ～辣椒 dry chillies over a slow fire ▸烘～

【焙烤】bèikǎo〈动〉bake: ～食品 bakery item

【焙烧】bèishāo〈动〉bake: ～膨胀 calcining expansion

蓓 bèi

【蓓蕾】bèilěi〈名〉bud: 枝头出现～。Buds appeared on the branches.

褙 bèi

〈动〉stick one piece of cloth or paper onto the back of another: ▸裱～

【褙子】bèizi〈名〉〈方〉pieces of used cloth or rags pasted layer upon layer

鞴 bèi

〈动〉saddle and bridle: ～马 saddle and bridle a horse

鐾 bèi

〈动〉sharpen: 在皮带上～剃刀 sharpen a razor on the strap

【鐾刀】bèidāo〈动〉sharpen a knife: ～布 sharpening strap

bei

呗（唄）bei

〈助〉〈口〉**1**（表示理所当然）[indicating that sth. is obvious]: 不会就学～。You can't? Well, learn to. ‖ 被老板炒了，回家～。Now that we have been fired by the boss, let's go home. **2**（表示勉强同意）[expressing resignation]: 要买就买～。Well, buy it if you want to. ‖ 你不同意，那就算了～。Since you disagree, that's the end of it.

▸bài

臂 bei ▸胳臂 gēbei

▸bì

bēn

奔 bēn

〈动〉**1**（跑）rush: 匆匆～向学校 dash to school ‖ 她伸开双臂朝他～去。She ran towards him with arms outspread. ‖〈喻〉～向未来 march on to the future ▸～驰 **2**（逃跑）flee: ▸出～, 东～西窜, 逃～ **3**（私奔）elope: ▸私～ **4**（赶忙去做）hurry: ▸～命, ～丧

▸bèn

【奔波】bēnbō〈动〉rush about: ～于两个城市之间 shuttle back and forth between the two cities ‖ 四处～ be always on the go ‖ 为儿子的婚事～ be rushed off one's feet for one's son's wedding

【奔驰】bēnchí〈动〉tear along: ～而过 speed by ‖ 骏马在辽阔的原野上～。Fine horses are galloping in the open country.

【奔窜】bēncuàn〈动〉flee in disorder: 四处～ flee in all directions

【奔放】bēnfàng〈形〉bold and unrestrained: 热情～ in an outburst of enthusiasm ‖ ～的舞蹈 wild and passionate dancing

【奔赴】bēnfù〈动〉rush to (a place): ～前线 hurry to the front ‖ ～战场 rush to the battle-field

【奔劳】bēnláo〈动〉be busy rushing about: 日夜～ be rushed off one's feet day and night

【奔流】bēnliú〈动〉flow at great speed: ～不息 flow ceaselessly ‖ 大河～入海。The great river gushes into the sea.

【奔忙】bēnmáng〈动〉be busy rushing about: 为解决这些问题～了好几天 rush about for several days solving these problems

【奔命】bēnmìng〈动〉rush about on errands: ▸疲于～

▸bènmìng

【奔跑】bēnpǎo〈动〉run quickly: 一路～ run all the way ‖ 孩子们在沙滩上四处～。Children were tearing about on the sand.

【奔丧】bēnsāng〈动〉rush to attend a family funeral

【奔驶】bēnshǐ〈动〉speed along: 汽车～在高速公路上。Cars sped along the expressway.

【奔逝】bēnshì〈动〉**1**（指时间）fly past **2**（指江水）rush by: 岁月～。Time is flying by.

【奔逃】bēntáo〈动〉flee: 狼狈～ flee helter-skelter ‖ 四散～ scatter and fly in all directions

【奔腾】bēnténg〈动〉**1**（指马匹）gallop: 万马～ ten thousand horses galloping **2**（指水流）surge forward: 大江～不息。The river rushes on and on. ‖ 洪水～着冲下山谷。The floods surged down the valley.

【奔突】bēntū〈动〉run amok: ～向前 rush wildly ahead ‖ 四下～ run in all directions

【奔袭】bēnxí〈动〉make a surprise long-range raid: ～敌营 make a shock long-distance attack upon the enemy's camp

【奔泻】bēnxiè〈动〉 pour down: 瀑布～而下。The waterfall rushes down.

【奔涌】bēnyǒng〈动〉 surge: ～向前 surge ahead ‖ 泪水～ tears gushing from one's eyes

【奔逐】bēnzhú〈动〉 run after: 孩子们在海滩上～嬉戏。The children are chasing each other and having fun on the beach.

【奔走】bēnzǒu〈动〉 **1**（跑） run: ▸～相告 **2**（四处活动） dash about: 为某事四处～ rush about all over the place to get sth. done ‖ 他～了几天，事情还没有个结果。He ran around in vain for several days.

【奔走呼号】bēnzǒu-hūháo〈成〉 go around campaigning for a cause: 为慈善募捐活动～ go collecting for a charitable cause

【奔走相告】bēnzǒu-xiānggào〈成〉 rush about spreading the news

贲（賁） bēn

〈动〉〈书〉run: 狼～ run like a wolf

【贲门】bēnmén〈名〉［生理］ cardia

锛（錛） bēn

A〈名〉 adze

B〈动〉 **1**（砍削） cut with an adze: ～木头 cut wood with an adze **2**〈口〉（指刀刃豁口） be dented: 刀刃～了。The blade of the knife was broken.

【锛子】bēnzi〈名〉 adze

běn

本 běn

A〈名〉 **1**（根） root: 木有～，水有源。A tree has its roots, just as a river has its source. **2**（根本） basis: 胜利之～ foundation of victory ▸～末倒置，忘～ **3**（册子） book: ▸笔记～，日记～，账～ **4**（版本） edition: 简装/精装～ paperback/hardback edition ‖ 影印～ facsimile ▸抄～，选～，译～ **5**（脚本） script: ▸唱～，剧～ **6**（奏章） memorial to the emperor: 参某人一～ present a memorial to impeach sb. **7**（本金） capital: ～小利大 make big profits with little capital ‖ 无～生意 deal not requiring any input of capital ▸股～，资～，够～ **8**（费用） cost: ▸成～，工～

B〈形〉 **1**（固有） original: ▸～能，～性，～质 **2**（中心） principal: ▸～部，～题

C〈副〉 originally: 我～想提醒他，只是没有机会。I had wanted to remind him but I didn't get the chance. ▸～来

D〈代〉 **1**（自己方面的） one's own: ～单位 one's own department ‖ ～校 our school ▸～地，～国，～人 **2**（这） this: ～案被告 defendant in this case ‖ ～合同 the present contract ‖ ～星期 this week

E〈介〉 according to: ～着章程办事 act in accordance with the rules and regulations

F〈量〉 [used for books, plays or films]: 三～书 three books ‖ 两～账 two accounts ‖ 头～戏 first play ‖ 这部电影有八～。This is an eight-reel film.

【本本】běnběn〈名〉 printed documents

【本本主义】běnběnzhǔyì〈名〉 pedantry

【本币】běnbì〈简称〉= 本位货币

【本部】běnbù〈名〉 headquarters: 校～ main campus

【本埠】běnbù〈名〉 this town: ～信件/邮件 local letter/mail

【本草】běncǎo〈名〉 Chinese herbal medicine: 《～纲目》 *Compendium of Materia Medica*

> 《本草纲目》
>
> *Compendium of Materia Medica*, the most comprehensive medical text in the history of Chinese medicine, compiled in the Ming Dynasty by Li Shizhen (李时珍), and first published in 1593. It comprises 52 volumes containing thousands of detailed descriptions of herbs and their properties, illustrations, and prescriptions for the cure of common illnesses. Using substantial scientific data, the work corrected the errors of earlier books and proposed a relatively scientific classification of medicines.

【本初子午线】běnchū zǐwǔxiàn〈名〉 prime meridian

【本岛】běndǎo〈名〉 main island: 台湾～ the main island of Taiwan

【本地】běndì〈名〉 this locality: ～风俗 local customs ‖ ～居民 indigenous people ‖ ～新闻 local news ‖ ～邮件 local mail

【本地人】běndìrén〈名〉 native

【本分】běnfèn **A**〈名〉 one's duty: 尽自己的～ do one's bit **B**〈形〉 content: 守～ know one's place ‖ 为人～ behave properly ‖ ～人 honest person

【本该】běngāi〈副〉〈口〉 ought to have done

【本固枝荣】běngù-zhīróng〈成〉〈喻〉 things will develop only when the foundation is sound

【本国】běnguó〈名〉 one's native country: 发展～经济 develop the domestic economy ‖ ～制造 domestically manufactured

【本国语】běnguóyǔ〈名〉 mother tongue

【本行】běnháng〈名〉 **1**（指专业） one's trade: 干老～ follow one's old profession ‖ 画画本不是他的～。Painting was not his original occupation. **2**（工作） one's present job: 熟悉～业务 know one's stuff ▸三句话不离～

【本纪】běnjì〈名〉 basic annals

【本家】běnjiā〈名〉 member of the same family: ～兄弟 brothers of the same clan

【本届】běnjiè〈形〉 current: ～毕业生 this year's graduates ‖ ～年会 this year's annual conference

【本金】běnjīn〈名〉 **1**（指存款） principal: 这笔～的利息会相当可观。The interest on this principal will be quite impressive. **2**（指投资） capital: 做生意就得有～。You need capital to start any business.

【本科】běnkē〈名〉 undergraduate course: 大学～ university undergraduate programme ‖ ～毕业生 university graduate

【本来】běnlái **A**〈形〉 original: ～的想法 original idea ‖ ～的颜色 natural colours **B**〈副〉 **1**（最初） originally: 他～想在沿海城市工作。At first he intended to work in a coastal city. ‖ 这篇文章～没打算发表。This article was not intended for publication. **2**（表示理应如此） in the first place: ～就不该提拔他当首席财务官。It goes without saying that he should never have been promoted to chief financial officer.

【本来面目】běnlái miànmù〈成〉 true colours: 恢复历史的～ restore historical facts ‖ 认清他们的～ see them in their true colours

【本垒】běnlěi〈名〉［体育］ home base: ～打 home run

【本利】běnlì〈名〉 principal and interest: ▸连本带利

【本领】běnlǐng〈名〉 ability: 苦练～ train hard to improve one's skills ‖ 过硬的～ first-rate capabilities

【本名】běnmíng〈名〉 **1**（原来的名字） original name **2**（本人的名字） first name

【本命年】běnmìngnián〈名〉 zodiac year [every 12th year from the year one was born]

【本末】běnmò〈名〉〈喻〉 **1**（完整的经过） ins and outs: 详述～ tell the whole story **2**（主次） the fundamental and the incidental: 分清～ distinguish between what is essential and what is trivial

【本末倒置】běnmò-dàozhì〈成〉 put the cart before the horse: 只管工作，不顾身体，是～。To work at the expense of one's health is to get one's priorities mixed up.

【本能】běnnéng〈名〉 instinct: ～反应 instinctive reaction ‖ 动物～ animal instinct ‖ 求生的～ instinct for survival

【本票】běnpiào〈名〉 **1**（支票） banker's cheque **2**（期票） promissory note

【本期】běnqī〈名〉［会计］ current period

【本钱】běnqian〈名〉 capital: 我们～少。We have only a small amount of capital. ‖〈喻〉 身体是一切的～。Health is the prerequisite for everything else.

【本人】běnrén〈代〉 **1**（我） I: 这是～的亲身经历。This is my own experience. ‖ 我～愿意跟他见面。For my part I will be ready to meet him. **2**（用于复指） oneself: 你必须～来取。You must come in person for it. ‖ 主任～没到会。The dean himself failed to show up at the meeting.

【本嗓】běnsǎng〈名〉 one's natural voice

【本色】běnsè〈名〉 inherent qualities: 保持劳动人民的～ retain the true character of the working people ‖ 英雄～ true qualities of a hero

【本色】běnshǎi〈名〉 natural colour

【本身】běnshēn〈代〉 itself: 设计～存在的缺点 inherent weakness in the design ‖ 生活～就是复杂多样的。Life itself is extremely diverse. ▸打铁先得～硬

【本事】běnshì〈名〉 original story: 电影～ synopsis of the film

【本事】běnshi〈名〉 capability: 年纪小，～可不小 be young but skilful ‖ 真正有～的人 people of genuine ability

【本题】běntí〈名〉 subject under discussion: 脱离～ beside the point ‖ 这与～无关。This is irrelevant.

【本体】běntǐ〈名〉 **1**［哲学］（自身） thing-in-itself: ～论 ontology **2**（主体） main part

【本土】běntǔ〈名〉 **1**（指生长地） native land: ▸本乡～ **2**（指国家） metropolitan territory: 英国的～并不大。England's metropolitan territory is actually quite small.

【本位】běnwèi〈名〉 **1**（标准） standard: ▸金～ **2**（指岗位或单位） one's own department: ～工作 one's own job

【本位货币】běnwèi huòbì〈名〉 standard currency

【本位主义】běnwèizhǔyì〈名〉 sectionalism

【本文】běnwén〈名〉 **1**（这篇文章） this text **2**（原文） source text

【本息】běnxī〈名〉 principal and interest: 偿还～ pay back the principal and interest

【本乡本土】běnxiāng běntǔ〈名〉 native place: 都～的，还客气什么。We're all natives of this place, so no need to stand on ceremony.

【本相】běnxiàng〈名〉 true features: ～毕露 show one's true colours

【本心】běnxīn〈名〉 original intent: 出于～ out of one's true will

【本性】běnxìng〈名〉 natural disposition: ～善良 be intrinsically good ‖ 侵略～ aggressive nature

【本性难移】běnxìng-nányí〈成〉 you can't expect a leopard to change its spots

【本业】běnyè〈名〉 **1**（指职业） one's own profession: 安于～ be satisfied with one's

b

own occupation 2〈旧〉（农业） agriculture

【本义】běnyì〈名〉 original meaning: 这个词的～ the literal meaning of the word

【本意】běnyì〈名〉 original idea: 他的～是好的。 He meant well. ‖ 你的诠释使我了解了话语的～。 Your interpretation helped me to understand the true intent of the discourse.

【本原】běnyuán〈名〉［哲学］ principle: 万物之～ first principle of all things

【本源】běnyuán〈名〉 origin: 事物的～ origin of things

【本愿】běnyuàn〈名〉original intention: 找到特洛伊古城的遗址是他的～。 His original wish was to find the ruins of ancient Troy.

【本着】běnzhe〈介〉 in line with: ～人道主义的精神 in the spirit of humanitarianism

【本真】běnzhēn A〈名〉 1（本来面目） original nature 2（本性） true nature: 难以看清其～。 It is difficult to see its true nature clearly. B〈形〉 true to one's original nature: 为人～ be true to one's nature in dealing with people

【本职】běnzhí〈名〉 one's job: 做好～工作 do one's own job well

【本旨】běnzhǐ〈名〉〈书〉 1（原意） original meaning 2（主要意图） main purpose

【本质】běnzhì〈名〉 nature: 透过现象看～ see through appearances to the real essence ‖ 抓住问题的～ grasp the essentials of a problem ‖ ～特征 intrinsic characteristics

【本州】Běnzhōu〈名〉 Honshu

【本主儿】běnzhǔr〈名〉 1（当事人） person concerned: 等～到了再谈。 Let's wait until the person concerned arrives before we discuss this further. 2（原主） owner of lost property

【本子】běnzi〈名〉 1（册子） notebook: 改～ correct students' assignments ‖ 练习～ exercise book 2（版本） edition: 我读过两种～的《红楼梦》。 I have read two versions of *A Dream of Red Mansions*. 3（证件） certificate: 没～不能驾车。 One can't drive without a licence.

【本族语】běnzúyǔ〈名〉 native language

苯 běn〈名〉［化学］ benzene

【苯胺】běn'àn〈名〉 aniline

【苯甲基】běnjiǎjī〈名〉 benzyl

【苯乙烯】běnyǐxī〈名〉 styrene

畚 běn = 簸箕 bòji 1, 2

【畚箕】běnjī〈方〉= 簸箕 bòji

bèn

夯 bèn〈形〉 clumsy
▸hāng

坌 bèn〈书〉
A〈名〉 dust: 尘～ dust
B〈动〉 1（撒粉末） scatter fine powder 2（聚集） bring together: ～集 gather together

奔 bèn
A〈动〉 1（径直走） go straight towards: 直～医院 head straight for the hospital ‖ ～小康 strive for a comfortable life ▸投～ 2〈口〉（四处奔走） rush about for: 为村民～谷物种子 be busy purchasing corn seed for the villagers 3（接近） approach: 他是～古稀的人了。 He is getting on for seventy.
B〈介〉〈口〉 in the direction of: ～南跑 run south ‖ ～左拐 turn to the left
▸bēn

【奔命】bènmìng〈动〉 1（指赶路） be in a desperate hurry 2（指做事） toil hard to survive
▸bēnmìng

【奔头儿】bèntour〈名〉〈口〉 prospect: 大有～ have great prospects ‖ 没～ have no future

笨 bèn〈形〉 1（傻） stupid: 脑子～ slow-witted ‖ 我觉得自己很～。 I felt such a fool. 2（不灵巧） clumsy: 手～ be all thumbs ‖ 嘴～ be slow of speech 3（笨重） awkward: 这床太～了，搬不动。 The bed is too bulky to move.

【笨伯】bènbó〈名〉〈书〉 stupid man

【笨蛋】bèndàn〈名〉〈粗〉 idiot: 为什么干那事，你这个～? Why did you do that, you cretin?

【笨活儿】bènhuór〈名〉〈口〉 heavy manual labour

【笨货】bènhuò〈名〉〈粗〉 fool, idiot: 真是个～，竟然犯那样的错误。 It was clumsy of you to make a mistake like that.

【笨口拙舌】bènkǒu-zhuōshé〈成〉 be awkward in speech

【笨鸟先飞】bènniǎo-xiānfēi〈成〉〈喻〉 the slow need to start early

【笨手笨脚】bènshǒu-bènjiǎo〈成〉 be all fingers and thumbs: 他干什么都～的。 He is awkward in everything he does.

【笨头笨脑】bèntóu-bènnǎo〈成〉 1（傻） slow: 他～的。 He is completely thick. 2（笨重） clumsy: 这家具～的，我一点也不喜欢。 This furniture looks clumsy. I don't like it at all.

【笨重】bènzhòng〈形〉 1（不灵巧） cumbersome: ～的家具 cumbersome furniture 2（繁重） heavy: ～的体力劳动 heavy manual labour

【笨拙】bènzhuō〈形〉 clumsy: 动作～ awkward in movement

【笨嘴拙舌】bènzuǐ-zhuōshé = 笨口拙舌 bènkǒu-zhuōshé

bēng

崩 bēng〈动〉 1（倒塌） collapse: ▸山～地裂, 雪～ 2（爆裂） burst: 炸～ blow up ‖ 气球～了。 The balloon burst. ‖ 左后车胎～了。 The left rear tyre blew out. ▸分～离析 3（不成功） break: 生意谈～了。 The business negotiations broke down. 4（垮掉） fall apart: ▸～溃 5（炸） blast: ～山开路 blast a road through a hill 6（击中） hit: 一块炸弹碎片～伤了他的腿。 A piece of the exploded bomb left a wound in his leg. 7〈方〉（枪毙） shoot dead: 一枪～了他。 He was killed by a single shot. 8〈旧〉（死亡） die: ▸驾～

【崩溃】bēngkuì〈动〉 collapse: 处于～的边缘 be on the brink of collapse ‖ 精神～ suffer a nervous breakdown

【崩裂】bēngliè〈动〉 burst into pieces: 飞机尾部在飞行中～了。 The plane's tail burst apart in mid-flight.

【崩龙族】Bēnglóngzú〈旧〉 = 德昂族 Dé'ángzú

【崩漏】bēnglòu ▸**p. 50**〈名〉［医学］ uterine bleeding

【崩盘】bēngpán〈动〉［金融］ crash

【崩塌】bēngtā〈动〉 collapse: 山洞～了。 The cave fell in.

【崩坍】bēngtān〈动〉 collapse: 隧道顶部～了。 The roof of the tunnel caved in.

绷（繃、綳） bēng
A〈动〉 1（拉紧） strain: 把电线/绳子～紧 strain the wire/rope ‖ 绳子～断了。 The rope snapped. ‖ 这夹克太小了，～在身上不舒服。 This jacket is too small and is uncomfortably tight. 2（弹起） spring up: 弹簧～飞了。 The spring sprung up. 3（固定） pin: ～被头 tack a cover to the top of a quilt ‖ ～臂章 pin an armband on a sleeve
B〈名〉 1（绷子） embroidery frame: 竹～ bamboo tambour 2（床屉子） bed frame [strung with strips of rattan]
▸běng, bèng

【绷带】bēngdài〈名〉 bandage: 用～包扎伤口 bandage the wound

【绷弓子】bēnggōngzi〈名〉 1（门上弹簧） return spring 2〈方〉（弹弓） catapult

【绷簧】bēnghuáng〈名〉〈方〉 spring

【绷子】bēngzi〈名〉 embroidery frame

嘣 bēng〈拟〉 1（指心跳） thump: 我听见我的心～～直跳。 I could hear my heart thumping. 2（指爆炸声） bang: 气球～的一声破了。 The balloon burst with a bang. ‖ 隔壁房间里传来～的一声爆炸声。 The thud of an explosion was heard from the next room.

béng

甭 béng〈副〉〈口〉 needn't: 这事你～管了，我们会处理的。 There is no need to concern yourself with this matter. We'll deal with it.

běng

绷（繃、綳） běng〈动〉
1（指表情） pull a long face: ▸～脸
2（用力支撑） strain oneself: ▸～劲
▸bēng, bèng

【绷劲】běngjìn〈动〉 strain one's muscles: 绷住劲 strain one's muscles ‖ 他一～，把重物举了起来。 He tightened his muscles and lifted the heavy weight.

【绷脸】běngliǎn〈动〉 pull a long face: 他绷着脸，一句话都没说。 Pulling a long face, he remained absolutely quiet.

bèng

泵 bèng
A〈名〉 pump: 排水～ drainage pump ▸离心～, 水～, 气～
B〈动〉 pump: ～油/水 pump oil/water

【泵房】bèngfáng〈名〉 pump house

【泵站】bèngzhàn〈名〉 pumping station

迸 bèng〈动〉 1（溅射） spurt: ～出火花 emit sparks ‖ 燃烧的木头火星四～。 The burning wood threw off sparks. ▸～裂 2（突然发出） burst out: 她当时怎么突然～出这句话? What made her blurt out such a remark? ▸～发

【迸发】bèngfā〈动〉 burst out: ～出一阵掌

声 burst into applause ‖ 烟花～出阵阵火花雨。 The fireworks burst into showers of sparks.

【迸溅】bèngjiàn〈动〉 fly in all directions: 火花～。 Sparks were flying in all directions.

【迸裂】bèngliè〈动〉 burst into pieces: 一声轰鸣，巨石～。 With a boom, the huge rocks flew off into pieces.

【迸流】bèngliú〈动〉 spurt: 手上鲜血～。 Blood spurted from the hand.

绷（繃、綳）bèng

A〈动〉crack: 西瓜～成了两半。The watermelon split into two.

B〈副〉 very: ～脆 very crisp ‖ ～硬 hard as a rock ‖ ～亮 shining bright ▸bēng, běng

【绷瓷】bèngcí〈名〉 crackled glaze chinaware

甏 bèng〈名〉〈方〉 earthen jar: 酒～ wine jar

镚（鏰）bèng

【镚儿】bèngr = 镚子 bèngzi

【镚子】bèngzi〈名〉 small coin

蹦 bèng〈动〉 **1**（跳） jump: 东～西跳 bounce around ‖ 一路连～带跳 hop and skip all the way **2**（出现） appear suddenly: 好长时间不见，他突然在兰州～了出来。 After a long absence he suddenly popped up in Lanzhou. ▸活～乱跳

【蹦蹦儿戏】bèngbèngrxì〈名〉〈旧〉 predecessor for *pingju* (评剧)

【蹦床】bèngchuáng〈名〉 trampoline

【蹦跶】 bèngda〈动〉〈方〉〈喻〉 battle desperately

【蹦迪】bèngdí〈动〉〈口〉 to go disco dancing

【蹦极】bèngjí〈名〉 bungee jumping: ～起源于新西兰。 Bungee originated in New Zealand.

【蹦跳】bèngtiào〈动〉skip: 小羊在田里蹦来跳去。 The lambs were frolicking in the fields.

bī

屄 bī〈名〉〈粗〉 cunt〈粗〉

逼 bī

A〈动〉 **1**（迫近） press upon: ～敌人后退 force the enemy troops back ‖ 全场紧～ full court press ▸～近, ～真 **2**（强迫） force: ～她说出真相 wring the truth out of her ‖ ～上绝路 drive sb. to an impasse ‖ 房东～她搬家。 The landlord is pressing her to get out. ▸～迫, ～人 **3**（强行索要） press for: ▸～供, ～债

B〈形〉〈书〉 narrow: ▸～仄

【逼宫】bīgōng〈动〉 **1**〈旧〉（针对帝王） force an abdication **2**（针对政府首脑） oust

【逼供】bīgòng〈动〉 force confessions: 刑讯～ use torture to extract a confession

【逼供信】bī-gòng-xìn〈惯〉 obtain confessions by forceful means and give them credence: 严禁～。 It is strictly forbidden to give credence to confessions extracted through torture.

【逼和】bīhé〈动〉［体育］ force a draw: ～主队 fight the home team to a draw

【逼婚】bīhūn〈动〉 force into a marriage

【逼近】bījìn〈动〉 close in on: ～岸边 approach the bank ‖ 从后面～敌军 press in on the enemy troops from the rear

【逼良为娼】 bīliáng-wéichāng 〈成〉 **1**〈本〉 force a woman into prostitution **2**〈喻〉 force an honest person to commit crimes

【逼命】bīmìng〈动〉 **1**（用武力） threaten with violence **2**（催促过紧） press hard: 别太～了。工人们要罢工抗议了。 Don't push too hard. The workers are planning to walk out in protest.

【逼迫】bīpò〈动〉 force: ～让步 force a concession ‖ 在环境的～下 under the pressure of circumstances

【逼人】bīrén〈形〉 pressing: ～太甚 put too much pressure on sb. ‖ 形势～。 The situation is pressing.

【逼上梁山】 bīshàng-Liángshān 〈成〉〈喻〉 be driven to revolt

【逼视】bīshì〈动〉 stare hard at: 在众人的～下，她显得局促不安。 The stares of the crowd made her appear uneasy.

【逼问】bīwèn〈动〉 **1**（强迫作答） force sb. to answer **2**（仔细盘问） question closely: 在我们的一再～下，他才说了实话。 He told the truth only after we questioned him persistently.

【逼肖】bīxiào〈动〉〈书〉 bear a close resemblance to: 他与父亲长相～。 He bore a striking resemblance to his father.

【逼仄】 bīzè〈形〉〈书〉 cramped: 居室～。 The room is rather cramped.

【逼债】bīzhài〈动〉 hound a debtor: 她一直在向我～。 She keeps pressing me for the debt.

【逼真】bīzhēn〈形〉 **1**（极相似） lifelike: 形象～的画像 lifelike portrait **2**（清楚） clear: 听得～ hear distinctly ‖ 看得～ have a clear view

【逼租】bīzū〈动〉 hound sb. for rent

鳊（鯿）bī〈名〉［鱼类］ ponyfish

bí

荸 bí

【荸荠】bíqí〈名〉 **1**（指植物）water chestnut **2**（指地下茎） water chestnut tuber

鼻 bí

A〈名〉 **1**（鼻子） nose: ▸～孔, ～音 **2**（鼻状物） nose-like object: ▸门～儿, 印～

B〈形〉 initial: ▸～祖

【鼻翅儿】bíchìr = 鼻翼 bíyì

【鼻出血】bíchūxiě ▸**p. 50**〈名〉［医学］ nosebleed

【鼻窦】bídòu〈名〉［生理］ paranasal sinus

【鼻窦炎】bídòuyán ▸**p. 50**〈名〉［医学］ nasosinusitis

【鼻尖】bíjiān〈名〉 tip of the nose

【鼻疽】bíjū〈名〉［畜牧］ glanders

【鼻孔】bíkǒng〈名〉 nostril: 挖～ pick one's nose

【鼻梁】bíliáng〈名〉 ridge of the nose: 高～ big nose

【鼻黏膜】 bíniánmó〈名〉［生理］ nasal mucous membrane

【鼻腔】bíqiāng〈名〉 nasal cavity

【鼻青脸肿】bíqīng-liǎnzhǒng〈成〉 with a bloody nose and swollen face: 他被打得～。 He was beaten black and blue in the face.

【鼻圈】bíquān〈名〉 nose ring

【鼻儿】bír〈名〉 little hole: ▸门～, 针～

【鼻塞】bísè〈名〉 nasal congestion

【鼻饲】bísì〈名〉［医学］ nasal feeding

【鼻酸】bísuān〈形〉 having a twinge in the nose: 她鼻子一酸，就流下泪来。 She felt a twinge in her nose and started weeping.

【鼻涕】bítì〈名〉 snot: 流～ have a runny nose

【鼻涕虫】bítìchóng〈名〉 slug

【鼻息】bíxī〈名〉 **1**（气息） breath: ～均匀 regular and even breathing **2**（鼾声） snore: ～如雷 snore like thunder ▸仰人～

【鼻烟】bíyān〈名〉 snuff: ～壶 snuff bottle

【鼻咽】bíyān〈名〉［生理］ nasopharynx: ～癌 nasal pharyngeal cancer

【鼻炎】bíyán ▸**p. 50**〈名〉［医学］ rhinitis

【鼻翼】bíyì〈名〉 nose wing

【鼻音】bíyīn〈名〉 nasal sound

【鼻韵母】bíyùnmǔ〈名〉 [in Chinese pronunciation] vowel followed by a nasal consonant [eg an, en, in, un, ang, ing etc.]

【鼻子】bízi〈名〉 nose: 捂住～ hold one's nose ‖ 哭～ snivel ‖〈喻〉 牵着～走 lead by the nose ▸蒜头～, 鹰钩～

【鼻子眼儿】bíziyǎnr〈名〉〈口〉 nostril

【鼻祖】bízǔ〈名〉〈书〉 **1**（始祖） forefather: 中华民族的～ forefather of the Chinese nation **2**（创始人） initiator: 天体物理学的～ forefather of celestial physics

bǐ

匕 bǐ〈名〉 **1**〈旧〉（匙子） spoon **2**〈书〉（匕首） dagger: ▸图穷～现

【匕首】bǐshǒu〈名〉 dagger

比 bǐ

A〈动〉 **1**（挨着） stand close together: ～肩而立 stand shoulder to shoulder ▸～邻, ～翼双飞 **2**（依附） collude with: ▸朋～为奸 **3**（较量） compete with: ～奉献 strive to outdo each other in making contributions ‖ ～力气 rival sb. else in strength ▸～武, 对～ **4**（比较） compare: 和去年相～ in contrast with last year ‖ 不～不知道，一～吓一跳。 Comparison makes one keenly aware of one's limitations. **5**（相当） match: 两者根本没法～。 There is no comparison between the two. ‖ 说起容貌，我～不上她。 I can't rival her in looks. ▸今非昔～ **6**［数学］ be the ratio of: 3～5 three to five **7**（指得分） be against: 我们以二～一获胜。 We won the match by two to one. **8**（依照） emulate: ～着旧衣裁新衣 pattern a new garment on an old one ▸将心～心 **9**（比划） gesticulate: 连说带～ gesticulate as one talks **10**（类推） draw an analogy: 莎士比亚把世界～作舞台。 Shakespeare compared the world to a stage.

B〈介〉 than: ～去年上升2% two per cent up on last year ‖ 生活一天～一天好。 Life is getting better and better. ‖ 我弟弟～我小三岁。 My brother is three years my junior.

C〈名〉 ratio: 该校将改善师生～。 The school is trying to improve its pupil-teacher ratio. ▸～例, ～率

【比比皆是】 bǐbǐ-jiēshì〈成〉 be great in number: 这种例子～。 Such examples can be found everywhere.

【比对】bǐduì〈动〉 compare

b

【比方】bǐfang **A**〈动〉**1**（比喻）draw an analogy (with): 用常青的松树~人坚贞的品格 draw an analogy between evergreen pine trees and steadfast loyal people **2**（例如）take for example: ~说"白领犯罪"问题。Take, for example, the question of 'white-collar crime'. **B**〈名〉analogy: 打~ make an analogy **C**〈连〉supposing: ~说你有一百万元，你怎么花呢? Say you had a million *yuan*, how would you spend it?
【比分】bǐfēn〈名〉score: ~接近 with close scores ‖ ~交替上升。The score seesawed.
【比附】bǐfù〈动〉〈书〉make a far-fetched comparison
【比号】bǐhào〈名〉sign of ratio
【比画】bǐhua〈动〉**1**（做手势）gesticulate: 用手~ gesture with one's hands **2**（比武）practise fighting
【比划】bǐhua = 比画 bǐhua
【比基尼】bǐjīní〈名〉bikini: 身穿~的女孩 a girl in a bikini
【比及】bǐjí〈连〉〈书〉by the time: ~医生赶到，为时已晚。It was too late by the time the doctor arrived.
【比价】bǐjià〈名〉**1**（指价格）price ratio: 进出口~ terms of trade **2**（指币值）exchange rate: 美元与欧元的~ exchange rate of the euro against the US dollar
【比肩】bǐjiān〈动〉〈书〉**1**（肩并肩）shoulder to shoulder: ~而立/作战 stand/fight shoulder to shoulder **2**〈喻〉（地位同等）match
【比肩继踵】bǐjiān-jìzhǒng = 摩肩接踵 mójiān-jiēzhǒng
【比肩接踵】bǐjiān-jiēzhǒng = 摩肩接踵 mójiān-jiēzhǒng
【比较】bǐjiào **A**〈动〉compare: ~两种译文 compare the two translations ‖ ~分析 contrastive analysis ‖ 把两本账一~，发现有许多出入。Comparison of the two accounts revealed numerous disparities. **B**〈介〉in contrast to: 他的学习成绩~上学期有很大提高。His scores are far better than last term. **C**〈副〉relatively: ~困难/容易 relatively difficult/easy ‖ 腐败问题~严重。Corruption is quite serious.
【比较级】bǐjiàojí〈名〉［语言］comparative degree: ~形式 comparative form
【比较价格】bǐjiào jiàgé = 不变价格 bùbiàn jiàgé
【比较文学】bǐjiào wénxué〈名〉comparative literature
【比较语言学】bǐjiào yǔyánxué〈名〉comparative linguistics
【比来】bǐlái〈副〉〈书〉recently
【比勒陀利亚】Bǐlètuólìyà〈名〉Pretoria
【比利时】Bǐlìshí〈名〉Belgium: ~王国 Kingdom of Belgium ‖ ~人 Belgian
【比例】bǐlì〈名〉**1**［数学］proportion: 4比8与6比12的~相等。4 is to 8 as 6 is to 12. ▸反~，正~ **2**（倍数关系）proportion: 进出口~ proportion of imports to exports ‖ 男女~ proportion of men to women ‖ ~失调 be out of proportion **3** = 比重 bǐzhòng 2 **4**［测绘］scale: 按~绘制地图 draw a map to scale ‖ 百万分之一~的地图 map on the scale of one-millionth
【比例尺】bǐlìchǐ〈名〉**1** = 比例 bǐlì 4 **2**（指工具）architect's scale
【比例税】bǐlìshuì〈名〉proportional tax: ~率 flat rate ‖ ~制 proportional taxation
【比量】bǐliang〈动〉**1**（大致测量）take rough measurements **2**（比划）make gestures
【比邻】bǐlín **A**〈名〉〈书〉next-door neighbour **B**〈动〉be next to: 跟学校~的农场 farm adjoining the campus ‖ 我们两家~而居。Their house is next door to ours.
【比率】bǐlǜ〈名〉ratio: 以每年百分之三的~增长 increase at the yearly rate of 3% ‖ 人口中老年人的~很高。The population contains a high percentage of old people.
【比美】bǐměi〈动〉compare favourably with: 日落可以和日出~。The sunset can rival the sunrise in beauty.
【比目鱼】bǐmùyú〈名〉flatfish
【比拟】bǐnǐ **A**〈动〉compare: 无可~ incomparable **B**〈名〉analogy
【比年】bǐnián〈名〉〈书〉**1**（近几年）recent years: ~以来，他一直缠绵病榻。Over the last few years, he has been confined to bed by sickness. **2**（每年）every year
【比配】bǐpèi〈动〉go with: 这丝带和帽子不~。These ribbons do not go with your hat.
【比拼】bǐpīn〈动〉compete fiercely: 经过激烈~ after a heated competition ‖ 艺术片与商业片~票房。Art-house films and commercial films are competing at the box office.
【比丘】bǐqiū〈名〉［佛教］Buddhist monk
【比丘尼】bǐqiūní〈名〉［佛教］Buddhist nun
【比热】bǐrè〈名〉［物理］specific heat
【比如】bǐrú〈动〉take for example: ~说 for instance
【比萨饼】bǐsàbǐng〈名〉pizza
【比萨斜塔】Bǐsà Xiétǎ〈名〉Leaning Tower of Pisa
【比赛】bǐsài **A**〈动〉have a contest: ~篮球/排球 have a basketball/volleyball match ‖ 他骑自行车与汽车~。He raced his bicycle against the motorcar. **B**〈名〉game; match〈英〉: 观看~ watch a game ‖ 中断~ suspend a match ‖ 篮球/网球~ basketball/tennis match ‖ ~以平局结束。The contest ended in a tie.
【比赛场馆】bǐsài chǎngguǎn〈名〉competition venues
【比赛服】bǐsàifú〈名〉competition clothes
【比赛规则】bǐsài guīzé〈名〉rules of a contest
【比赛项目】bǐsài xiàngmù〈名〉event: 参加~ enter for an event
【比色】bǐsè〈形〉colorimetric
【比色法】bǐsèfǎ〈名〉［化学］colorimetry
【比色计】bǐsèjì〈名〉［化学］colorimeter
【比上不足，比下有余】bǐ shàng bù zú, bǐ xià yǒu yú〈成〉fall short of the best but be better than the worst
【比试】bǐshi〈动〉**1**（较量）compete: 咱们~一下，看谁跳得高。Let's have a competition and see who jumps higher. **2**（比划）make gestures
【比手画脚】bǐshǒu-huàjiǎo〈成〉illustrate with the help of gestures
【比索】bǐsuǒ ▸**p. 328**〈名〉peso
【比特】bǐtè〈量〉［计算机］bit: ~率 bit rate
【比特郡】Bǐtèjùn〈名〉Bute
【比武】bǐwǔ〈动〉contest in martial arts skill: 参加~ take part in a martial arts contest ‖〈喻〉技术大~ skills competition
【比翼】bǐyì〈动〉fly side by side
【比翼鸟】bǐyìniǎo〈名〉〈喻〉devoted couple
【比翼齐飞】bǐyì-qífēi = 比翼双飞 bǐyì-shuāngfēi
【比翼双飞】bǐyì-shuāngfēi〈成〉fly side by side
【比喻】bǐyù **A**〈名〉metaphor **B**〈动〉liken to: 诗歌中常用玫瑰花~爱情。In poetry the rose is often a metaphor for love.
【比喻义】bǐyùyì〈名〉figurative meaning
【比照】bǐzhào〈动〉**1**（依据）be according to: 我们可以~别国的经验制定自己的环保条例。We can establish our regulations for environmental protection in the light of the experience of other countries. **2**（对比）contrast: 两相~，差异明显。When the two are contrasted, the differences are obvious.
【比值】bǐzhí〈名〉ratio: ~相等 be in the same ratio
【比重】bǐzhòng〈名〉**1**［物理］relative density **2**（比例）proportion: 第三产业在国民经济中的~逐年增加。The proportion of tertiary industry in the national economy has increased annually.
【比重计】bǐzhòngjì〈名〉gravimeter
【比作】bǐzuò〈动〉compare (to): 把死亡~睡眠 compare death to sleep

吡 bǐ
▸pǐ
【吡啶】bǐdìng〈名〉［化学］pyridine
【吡咯】bǐluò〈名〉［化学］pyrrole

妣 bǐ〈名〉〈旧〉one's deceased mother: ▸如丧考~，先~

彼 bǐ〈代〉**1**（那个）that;（另一个）another: ▸~此，顾此失~ **2**（对方）other party: ▸知~知己，百战不殆
【彼岸】bǐ'àn〈名〉**1**（对岸）opposite bank: 大洋~的中华学子 Chinese students and scholars on the other side of the Pacific Ocean **2**［佛教］life beyond **3**〈喻〉（指境界）dreamland: 走向幸福的~ enter a dreamland of happiness
【彼此】bǐcǐ〈代〉**1**（相互）each other, one another: ~帮助 help each other ‖ 消除委员~间的误会 clear up misunderstandings between the committee members **2**〈套〉（差不多）[used in reduplication as a reply] you too: 您受累啦！——~~。You must have had a hard time! — So must you.
【彼一时，此一时】bǐ yīshí, cǐ yīshí = 此一时，彼一时 cǐ yīshí, bǐ yīshí

秕 bǐ
A〈形〉shrivelled: ~粒 blighted grains
B〈名〉blighted grain: ▸~糠
【秕谷】bǐgǔ〈名〉blighted millet
【秕糠】bǐkāng〈名〉**1**〈本〉blighted grains and chaff **2**〈喻〉worthless stuff
【秕子】bǐzi〈名〉blighted grain

笔（筆）bǐ
A〈名〉**1**（书写工具）pen: 毛~ writing brush ‖ 自来水~ fountain pen ‖ 这支~书写流畅。This pen writes smoothly. ▸画~，下~ **2**（技巧）technique: 用锋利的~抨击 wield an incisive pen ▸~法，文~ **3**（笔画）stroke: 寥寥几~就绘成一幅画 dash off a picture with a few strokes ▸~顺，起~，一~勾销 **4**（笔迹）handwriting: ▸~迹，绝~
B〈动〉write: ▸代~，亲~
C〈量〉**1**（用于款项）[for sums of money]: 一~钱 a sum of money ‖ 一~生意 a business deal ‖ 一~债 a debt **2**（用于书画）[for writing or drawing]: 写一~好字 write well **3**（用于笔画）[for strokes]: "凸"字有5~。The character 凸 has five strokes.

【笔触】bǐchù〈名〉style of drawing or writing: 以灵巧的～赋予画面以生气 bring a picture to life with a deft touch of the brush
【笔答】bǐdá〈动〉answer questions in writing: ～试题 written test questions
【笔底生花】bǐdǐ-shēnghuā〈成〉have an elegant writing style
【笔底下】bǐdǐxia〈名〉writing ability: ～不错 write well
【笔调】bǐdiào〈名〉style: 讽刺的～ satirical tone ‖ 清新的～ lucid style
【笔端】bǐduān〈名〉〈书〉style of writing: 他的思旧之情见于～。His writings exude nostalgia.
【笔伐】bǐfá〈动〉denounce in writing: ▸口诛～
【笔法】bǐfǎ〈名〉pen-craft: ▸春秋～
【笔锋】bǐfēng〈名〉1（尖端）tip of the writing brush 2（指文章）vigour of literary style;（指书画）vigour of brushwork: ～犀利 wield an incisive pen
【笔杆儿】bǐgǎnr = 笔杆子 bǐgǎnzi 1, 2
【笔杆子】bǐgǎnzi〈名〉1（指物）shaft of a writing brush 2（指写作能力）ability to write: 要～ wield the pen ‖ 他～比我强。He is a better writer than I am. 3（指人）person entrusted with writing: 她是我们这里的～。She is the best writer here.
【笔耕】bǐgēng〈动〉engage in writing: ～不辍 keep writing as a profession ‖ 伏案～ write at one's desk
【笔供】bǐgòng〈名〉written confession
【笔管】bǐguǎn〈名〉barrel of a pen
【笔管条直】bǐguǎn-tiáozhí〈成〉bolt upright: ～地站着 stand erect
【笔画】bǐhuà〈名〉1（指汉字组成）strokes 2（笔画数）number of strokes: 按姓氏～排列 arrange in the order of the number of strokes in a surname ‖ ～索引 stroke index
【笔会】bǐhuì〈名〉1（指活动）discussion through articles 2（指组织）writers' association: 国际～ PEN (International Association of Poets, Playwrights, Editors, Essayists and Novelists)
【笔记】bǐjì A〈动〉jot down B〈名〉1（记录）notes: 记～ take notes ‖ 课堂～ classroom notes 2（指体裁）jottings
【笔记本】bǐjìběn〈名〉notebook: 记在～上 jot down in a notebook
【笔记本电脑】bǐjìběn diànnǎo〈名〉laptop
【笔记小说】bǐjì xiǎoshuō〈名〉literary sketches
【笔迹】bǐjì〈名〉handwriting: 辨认～ identify the handwriting ‖ ～鉴定 handwriting verification
【笔架】bǐjià〈名〉pen holder
【笔尖】bǐjiān〈名〉1（笔端）tip 2（特指钢笔尖）nib: 换个～ change the nib of a pen
【笔据】bǐjù〈名〉written pledge
【笔力】bǐlì〈名〉1（指力量）power of literary style: ～遒劲/雄健 firm/forceful style 2（指能力）ability to write articles: 从这篇文章可以看出作者的～。This article reveals the writing ability of its author.
【笔立】bǐlì〈动〉stand upright: ～的山峰 sharply-angled peaks
【笔录】bǐlù A〈动〉put down in writing B〈名〉written record: 供词～ written record of a person's confession
【笔路】bǐlù〈名〉1 = 笔法 bǐfǎ 2（思路）train of thought
【笔帽】bǐmào〈名〉pen cap
【笔名】bǐmíng〈名〉pen name: 用～发表作品 write under a pseudonym
【笔墨】bǐmò〈名〉writing: ～生涯 literary career ‖ 非～所能形容。It's beyond description.
【笔墨官司】bǐmò-guānsi〈成〉written polemic: 打～ engage in written polemic
【笔墨纸砚】bǐmòzhǐyàn〈名〉writing brush, ink stick, paper and ink-stone
【笔润】bǐrùn = 润笔 rùnbǐ
【笔势】bǐshì〈名〉1（指书画）style of brushwork 2（指文学作品）vigour of literary style 3（思路）trend of thought shown in a piece of writing
【笔试】bǐshì A〈动〉test in writing B〈名〉written examination
【笔受】bǐshòu〈动〉〈书〉take down what is dictated
【笔顺】bǐshùn〈名〉order of strokes of each word observed in calligraphy
【笔算】bǐsuàn A〈动〉calculate in writing B〈名〉written calculation
【笔谈】bǐtán A〈动〉1（指交流）exchange ideas through writing 2（指表达意见）comment in writing B〈名〉notes: 《梦溪～》*Dream Pool Essays*
【笔套】bǐtào〈名〉1 = 笔帽 bǐmào 2（袋子）pen sheath
【笔体】bǐtǐ〈名〉handwriting: 认出～ recognize sb.'s handwriting
【笔挺】bǐtǐng〈形〉1（直而挺）erect: ～地站着 stand upright 2（平整）well-ironed: ～的西装 well-pressed suit
【笔筒】bǐtǒng〈名〉pen pot
【笔头】bǐtóu〈名〉1（笔尖）nib 2〈喻〉（写作能力）writing skill: 他～快。He writes very well.
【笔误】bǐwù A〈动〉make a clerical error B〈名〉slip of the pen
【笔洗】bǐxǐ〈名〉dish or flat bowl for washing a writing brush
【笔下】bǐxià〈名〉1 = 笔底下 bǐdǐxia 2（用意）wording and meaning of one's writings
【笔下超生】bǐxià-chāoshēng〈成〉show leniency by not committing someone's bad behaviour to paper
【笔下留情】bǐxià-liúqíng〈成〉be charitable in criticism: 身为记者，他在揭露社会阴暗面时从不～。As a journalist, he's never been shy to expose the dark side of society.
【笔下生花】bǐxià-shēnghuā = 笔底生花 bǐdǐ-shēnghuā
【笔心】bǐxīn = 笔芯 bǐxīn
【笔芯】bǐxīn〈名〉1（指铅笔）pencil lead 2（指水笔或圆珠笔）refill
【笔形】bǐxíng〈名〉form of a stroke or combination of strokes
【笔译】bǐyì〈名〉written translation
【笔意】bǐyì〈名〉〈书〉artistic conception: ～清新 fresh imagery
【笔友】bǐyǒu〈名〉pen pal〈美〉; pen-friend〈英〉
【笔札】bǐzhá〈名〉〈书〉1（笔和纸）stationery 2（文章）articles 3（信）letters
【笔债】bǐzhài〈名〉literary commission
【笔战】bǐzhàn〈动〉fight a battle of words: 打～ engage in a paper war
【笔者】bǐzhě〈名〉the author
【笔直】bǐzhí〈形〉perfectly straight: 身子挺得～ draw oneself up to one's full height ‖ ～的道路 straight road
【笔致】bǐzhì〈名〉〈书〉style of literary work or drawing
【笔走龙蛇】bǐzǒu-lóngshé〈成〉make vigorous and graceful strokes

俾 bǐ〈动〉〈书〉cause: ～众周知 for everyone's information

鄙 bǐ
A〈形〉1（品格低下）low;（言行粗俗）vulgar: ▸～俗, 卑～ 2〈谦〉（我）（作主语）I;（作宾语）me;（所有格）my: ▸～见, ～人, ～意
B〈动〉〈书〉despise
C〈名〉〈书〉out-of-the-way place: ▸边～
【鄙薄】bǐbó A〈动〉have contempt for: ～势利小人 despise snobs ‖ 他脸上露出～的神情。A contemptuous look crept into his face. B〈形〉〈谦〉〈书〉ignorant and shallow: ～之志 my petty wish
【鄙称】bǐchēng A〈动〉despise B〈名〉derogatory appellation
【鄙见】bǐjiàn〈名〉〈谦〉my humble opinion: ～以为 in my humble opinion
【鄙陋】bǐlòu〈形〉shallow: ～无知的人 person of superficial knowledge ‖ ～平庸 shallow and mediocre
【鄙弃】bǐqì〈动〉feel contempt for: ～官僚主义作风 loathe bureaucracy ‖ ～懦夫 scorn a coward
【鄙人】bǐrén〈名〉〈旧〉〈谦〉your humble servant: ～以为 in my poor opinion ‖ ～不敢。I don't dare.
【鄙视】bǐshì〈动〉look down upon: ～他的吝啬/虚伪 despise his meanness/hypocrisy ‖ 受到～ be held in contempt
【鄙俗】bǐsú〈形〉vulgar: ～的言词 vulgar remarks
【鄙夷】bǐyí〈动〉〈书〉despise: ～的神情 contemptuous look
【鄙意】bǐyì〈名〉〈谦〉my humble opinion

bì

币（幣） bì〈名〉money: ▸港～, 货～
【币市】bìshì〈名〉coin market
【币值】bìzhí〈名〉currency value
【币制】bìzhì〈名〉monetary system

必 bì〈副〉1（一定）definitely: ～胜 be sure to win ‖ 经济改革～将促进社会进步。Economic reform will necessarily promote social progress. ▸骄兵～败 2（必须）must: 你不～为我担心。You needn't worry about me. ‖ 他言～有据。He invariably bases his remarks on facts. ▸～不可少, 事～躬亲
【必备】bìbèi〈动〉must have
【必不可少】bìbùkěshǎo〈惯〉indispensable
【必得】bìděi〈副〉must : 你～亲自去一趟。You must go yourself.
【必定】bìdìng〈副〉1（无疑）undoubtedly: ～成功 be sure to succeed ‖ 他～会来的。He is sure to come. 2（有决心）determinedly: 她说她～要见经理。She said she must see the manager.
【必读书】bìdúshū〈名〉must-read book
【必恭必敬】bìgōng-bìjìng = 毕恭毕敬 bìgōng-bìjìng
【必然】bìrán A〈形〉inevitable: ～结果 inevitable outcome ‖ ～联系 necessary connection ‖ 侵略者～失败。The invaders are bound to fail. B〈名〉［哲学］necessity
【必然王国】bìrán wángguó〈名〉［哲学］realm of necessity
【必然性】bìránxìng〈名〉certainty

【必修】bìxiū〈形〉mandatory

【必修课】bìxiūkè〈名〉compulsory course

【必须】bìxū〈副〉must: ～照办 must do as one was told ‖ 报考者～有中学毕业文凭。For applicants, a high school diploma is a must. ‖ 你明天～来。You must come tomorrow. ‖ 一切开支～入账。All expenditures must be entered in the accounts.

【必需】bìxū〈动〉be essential to: 煤和铁是发展现代工业所～的原料。Coal and iron are essential to the development of modern industry.

【必需品】bìxūpǐn〈名〉essentials: 日用～ daily necessities ‖ 生活～ essentials of life

【必要】bìyào〈形〉necessary: ～的时候 when the need arises ‖ ～的准备 necessary preparations

【必要产品】bìyào chǎnpǐn〈名〉necessary product

【必要劳动】bìyào láodòng〈名〉necessary labour: ～时间 necessary labour time

【必要前提】bìyào qiántí〈名〉prerequisite

【必要条件】bìyào tiáojiàn〈名〉prerequisite

【必要性】bìyàoxìng〈名〉necessity

【必由之路】bìyóuzhīlù〈成〉only way: 经济发展的～ only road to economic development

毕（畢） bì

A〈动〉finish: 礼～! Salute over! ▸～业, 完～

B〈形〉〈书〉complete: ▸原形～露

C〈名〉one of the 28 constellations in ancient Chinese astronomy

【毕恭毕敬】bìgōng-bìjìng〈成〉be extremely deferential: ～地鞠躬 bow in humble reverence

【毕竟】bìjìng〈副〉after all: 尽管迟到了，但他～还是来了。Even though he was late, at least he made it in the end. ‖ 他～是孩子，还不懂这种事儿。He is after all a child and too young to understand such things.

【毕露】bìlù〈动〉come to light: ▸锋芒～, 原形～

【毕命】bìmìng〈动〉〈书〉meet with sudden death: 饮弹～ be killed by a bullet

【毕其功于一役】bì qí gōng yú yī yì〈成〉accomplish the whole task in one go

【毕生】bìshēng〈名〉lifetime: 她把自己的～精力都献给了慈善事业。She devoted all her life to charity.

【毕肖】bìxiào〈动〉〈书〉resemble closely: 神态～ resemble in manner

【毕业】bìyè〈动〉finish school: 大学～ graduate from college ‖ ～典礼 graduation

【毕业论文】bìyè lùnwén〈名〉graduation thesis

【毕业设计】bìyè shèjì〈名〉graduation project

【毕业生】bìyèshēng〈名〉graduate: 法学专业～ law graduate

【毕业证书】bìyèzhèngshū〈名〉diploma: 授予～ grant a diploma

闭（閉） bì〈动〉**1**（闭合）close: ～上眼睛/嘴 close one's eyes/mouth ▸～关自守, 夜不～户 **2**（憋住）stop up: ▸～气 **3**（结束）end: ▸～会, ～幕

【闭关】bìguān〈动〉**1**（紧闭关口）block the passage **2**（指僧人静修）meditate in seclusion

【闭关锁国】bìguān-suǒguó〈成〉close a country to external contact

【闭关自守】bìguān-zìshǒu〈成〉close a country to the outside world: 废除～的政策 abandon the closed-door policy ‖ ～的经济 closed economy

【闭馆】bìguǎn〈动〉[of a library or exhibition] be closed to the public: 今日～。Closed today.

【闭合】bìhé **A**〈动〉close: ～开关 turn off a switch **B**〈形〉closed: ～曲线 closed curve

【闭会】bìhuì〈动〉close a meeting: 国会～期间 when parliament is in recess

【闭架】bìjià〈动〉deny access to shelves: ～售书 sell books using a system that denies access to the book shelves

【闭经】bìjīng ▸**p. 50**〈名〉［医学］amenorrhoea

【闭卷】bìjuàn〈动〉keep a book closed: ～考试 closed-book examination

【闭口】bìkǒu〈动〉remain tight-lipped: ～不谈 keep mum

【闭路电视】bìlù diànshì〈名〉closed-circuit television

【闭门】bìmén〈动〉close the door

【闭门读书】bìmén-dúshū〈成〉study behind closed doors

【闭门羹】bìméngēng〈名〉denial of entrance: ▸吃～

【闭门思过】bìmén-sīguò〈成〉shut oneself away to reflect on one's mistakes

【闭门谢客】bìmén-xièkè〈成〉close one's door to visitors

【闭门造车】bìmén-zàochē〈成〉work without any knowledge of the actual process

【闭目】bìmù〈动〉close one's eyes: ～养神 close one's eyes in repose

【闭目塞听】bìmù-sètīng〈成〉turn a deaf ear and a blind eye to reality

【闭幕】bìmù〈动〉**1**〈本〉fall **2**〈喻〉（结束）conclude: 致～词 give a closing address ‖ 我现在宣布会议～。I now declare the meeting closed.

【闭幕式】bìmùshì〈名〉closing ceremony

【闭气】bìqì〈动〉**1**（无法呼吸）stop breathing involuntarily: 挨了那一拳，他差点闭住了气。After he took the blow, he almost stopped breathing. **2**（屏息）hold one's breath: 他闭住气听完了这消息。He heard the news with bated breath.

【闭塞】bìsè **A**〈动〉block: 鼻孔～ have a blocked nose **B**〈形〉**1**（偏僻）out of the way: 这个小镇太～。This little town is too much of a backwater. **2**（消息不灵通）ill-informed: 消息～ be ill-informed

【闭市】bìshì〈动〉[of a market or shop] close: 这里冬天～早。The shops here close up early in winter.

【闭锁】bìsuǒ **A**〈动〉block: ～电路 exclusive circuit ‖ ～电阻 blocked resistance ‖ ～装置 blocking device **B**〈名〉［医学］atresia: 处女膜～ imperforate hymen ‖ 肛门～ anal atresia

【闭月羞花】bìyuè-xiūhuā〈成〉be bewitchingly beautiful: 有～之容 be of bewitching beauty

庇 bì〈动〉shelter: ▸～护, 包～

【庇护】bìhù〈动〉provide shelter: ～通缉犯 shelter the wanted ‖ 要求～ claim sanctuary ‖ 在某人的～下 under sb.'s wing

【庇护权】bìhùquán〈名〉right of asylum

【庇护所】bìhùsuǒ〈名〉shelter

【庇荫】bìyìn〈书〉**A**〈动〉shade **B**〈名〉shelter

【庇佑】bìyòu〈动〉〈书〉bless and protect: 乞求神灵～ seek the blessings and protection of gods

畀 bì〈动〉〈书〉confer: ～以重任 appoint sb. to an important post

荜（蓽） bì

【荜路蓝缕】bìlù-lánlǚ = 筚路蓝缕 bìlù-lánlǚ

毖 bì〈动〉〈书〉guard against: ▸惩前～后

哔（嗶） bì

【哔叽】bìjī〈名〉［纺织］serge

陛 bì〈名〉〈书〉flight of steps to the hall of audience in the imperial palace

【陛下】bìxià〈名〉〈尊〉**1**（用于直呼）Your Majesty **2**（用于转述）His/Her Majesty

毙（斃） bì〈动〉**1**（死亡）die: ▸～命, 倒～, 束手待～ **2**（枪毙）shoot dead: 她由于从事间谍活动给～了。She was executed for spying. **3**〈书〉（灭亡）perish: ▸多行不义必自～

【毙命】bìmìng〈动〉〈贬〉get killed: 逃犯当场～。The escaped prisoner was killed on the spot.

【毙伤】bìshāng〈动〉kill and wound: 他们～敌军 100 名。They killed and wounded 100 enemy soldiers.

铋（鉍） bì〈名〉bismuth (Bi)

秘（祕） bì
▸mì

【秘鲁】Bìlǔ〈名〉Peru: ～共和国 Republic of Peru ‖ ～人 Peruvian

狴 bì

【狴犴】bì'àn〈名〉〈古〉**1**〈本〉legendary tiger-like beast whose image used to be painted on prison doors **2**〈喻〉（监狱）prison

敝 bì〈形〉**1**〈书〉（破烂）worn-out: ～衣 worn-out clothes ▸～帚自珍, 舌～唇焦 **2**〈书〉（衰败）declining: ▸凋～, 疲～ **3**〈谦〉（我的）my;（我们的）our: ～公司 my company ‖ ～校 our school ‖ ～姓 my surname

【敝人】bìrén〈名〉〈旧〉〈谦〉I

【敝屣】bìxǐ〈名〉〈书〉〈喻〉worthless thing

【敝帚千金】bìzhǒu-qiānjīn = 敝帚自珍 bìzhǒu-zìzhēn

【敝帚自珍】bìzhǒu-zìzhēn〈成〉〈喻〉cherish one's own possessions even though they may be of little value

婢 bì〈名〉maidservant: ▸奴～, 奴颜～膝

【婢女】bìnǚ〈名〉servant girl

赑（贔） bì

【赑屃】bìxì〈名〉〈古〉legendary giant turtle-shaped animal

筚（篳） bì〈名〉〈书〉bamboo fence

【筚篥】bìlì〈名〉〈古〉ancient bamboo pipe with a reed mouth piece

【筚路蓝缕】bìlù-lánlǚ〈成〉 endure great hardships in starting up a project

愎 bì〈形〉 stubborn: ▸刚～自用

弼 bì〈动〉〈书〉 aid: ▸辅～

蓖 bì

【蓖麻】bìmá〈名〉［植物］ castor-oil plant: ～油 castor oil ‖ ～子 castor bean

【蓖麻蚕】bìmácán〈名〉 castor silkworm

【蓖麻毒】bìmádú〈名〉 ricin

跸（蹕） bì〈动〉〈书〉 clear the road for the emperor: ▸驻～

痹（痺） bì 〈名〉 rheumatism: ▸麻～

【痹症】bìzhèng〈名〉［中医］ rheumatism

滗（潷） bì 〈动〉 strain: ～汤药 strain the decoction ‖ 把水～掉 strain off the water ‖ 把汤～到碗里 decant the soup into the bowl ‖ 把渣子～出去 sieve out the sediment

裨 bì〈名〉 benefit: 无～于事 be of no use ▸pí

【裨益】bìyì〈书〉 **A**〈名〉 benefit: 大有～ be very beneficial **B**〈动〉 benefit: 保护环境将～子孙后代。 Environmental protection will benefit future generations.

辟[1] bì

A〈名〉〈书〉 monarch: ▸复～

B〈动〉 summon and appoint

辟[2] bì〈动〉〈书〉 ward off: ▸～邪 ▸pì

【辟谷】bìgǔ〈动〉 refuse to eat grain

【辟邪】bìxié〈动〉 exorcize evil spirits: ～之物 talisman

【辟易】bìyì〈动〉〈书〉 back away in fear: ～道侧 withdraw to the side of the road

碧 bì

A〈名〉 green jade

B〈形〉 bluish green: ～草 verdant grass ‖ ～瓦 green, glazed tile ▸金～辉煌

【碧波】bìbō〈名〉 bluish/green waves: ～万顷 vast stretch of blue water ‖ ～荡漾 rippling with green wavelets ‖ ～草如茵 a carpet of green grass

【碧空】bìkōng〈名〉 clear blue sky: ～如洗 cloudless blue sky

【碧蓝】bìlán〈形〉deep blue: ～的天空 blue sky

【碧绿】bìlǜ〈形〉 dark green: ～的田野 green fields

【碧螺春】bìluóchūn〈名〉 *Bi Luo Chun* [a type of Chinese green tea]

【碧血丹心】bìxuè-dānxīn〈成〉 absolute loyalty and supreme courage

【碧油油】bìyōuyōu〈形〉 bright green: ～的麦田 bright green wheat fields

【碧玉】bìyù〈名〉 jasper

蔽 bì〈动〉 **1**（躲藏） cover: ～雨 shelter from the rain ▸掩～, 一叶～目, 不见泰山, 隐～ **2**（概括） sum up: ▸一言以～之

【蔽芾】bìfèi〈形〉〈书〉[of trees, etc.] young and small

【蔽匿】bìnì〈动〉〈书〉 hide: ～罪证 conceal the evidence of a crime ‖ 不可～ cannot be concealed

【蔽障】bìzhàng **A**〈动〉 block: 浓雾～了视线。 Heavy fog blocked the view. **B**〈名〉 obstacle: 清除～ remove obstacles

箅 bì

【箅子】bìzi〈名〉 grate: ▸炉～

弊 bì〈名〉 **1**（害处） disadvantage: ～多利少。 The disadvantages outweigh the advantages. ‖ 利远大于～。 The benefits far outweigh the drawbacks. ▸～端, 时～ **2**（欺诈） corrupt practice: ▸营私舞～, 作～

【弊病】bìbìng〈名〉 **1**（不良现象） ills: 社会～ social evils **2**（缺点） disadvantage: 这个方案～很多。The plan has many drawbacks.

【弊端】bìduān〈名〉 corrupt practice: 根除～ wipe out abuses ‖ 体制中的～ pitfalls of the system

【弊害】bìhài〈名〉 harm

【弊绝风清】bìjué-fēngqīng〈成〉 completely free from corruption

【弊政】bìzhèng〈名〉〈书〉 misrule: 革除～ abolish corrupt politics ‖ 抨击～ denounce misgovernment

薜 bì

【薜荔】bìlì〈名〉［植物］ climbing fig

篦 bì

A〈名〉 double-edged fine-toothed comb

B〈动〉 using a double-edged fine-toothed comb

【篦子】bìzi〈名〉 double-edged fine-toothed comb

壁 bì〈名〉 **1**（墙壁） wall: ▸～灯, ～画, 残垣断～ **2**（悬崖） cliff: ▸绝～, 峭～ **3**（防御工事） rampart: ▸～垒, 坚～清野 **4**（壁状物） sth. resembling a wall: 肠～ intestinal wall ‖ 炉～ wall of a furnace ‖ 内/外～ inside/outside wall **5**（指星宿） one of the 28 constellations in ancient Chinese astronomy

【壁板】bìbǎn〈名〉 wainscotting

【壁报】bìbào〈名〉 wall newspaper: 办～ edit and put up a wall newspaper

【壁橱】bìchú〈名〉 built-in wardrobe

【壁灯】bìdēng〈名〉 wall lamp

【壁挂】bìguà〈名〉 wall hanging: 刺绣～ embroidered hangings ‖ 毛织～ wool tapestry

【壁柜】bìguì = 壁橱 bìchú

【壁虎】bìhǔ〈名〉［动物］ gecko

【壁画】bìhuà〈名〉 mural: 敦煌～ Dunhuang frescoes

【壁龛】bìkān〈名〉 niche

【壁垒】bìlěi〈名〉 **1**〈古〉（障碍）barrier: 设置关税～ erect tariff barriers ‖ 贸易～ trade barrier **2**（对立阵营） line of demarcation: 哲学上的两大～ two diametrically opposed philosophical theories

【壁垒森严】bìlěi-sēnyán〈成〉 **1**（指防御） heavily guarded: ～的总部 heavily-guarded headquarters **2**（指界限）sharply divided

【壁立】bìlì〈形〉 sheer: ～的崖面 perpendicular cliff-face

【壁炉】bìlú〈名〉 fireplace

【壁球】bìqiú ▸**p. 909**〈名〉 squash

【壁上观】bìshàngguān = 作壁上观 zuòbìshàngguān

【壁虱】bìshī〈名〉 **1**（蜱） tick **2**〈方〉（臭虫） bug

【壁饰】bìshì〈名〉 wall decoration

【壁毯】bìtǎn〈名〉 tapestry

【壁障】bìzhàng〈名〉obstacle: 消除影响双方关系的～ remove the obstacles influencing relations between both parties

【壁纸】bìzhǐ〈名〉 wallpaper

【壁钟】bìzhōng〈名〉 wall clock

【壁柱】bìzhù〈名〉［建筑］ pilaster

避 bì〈动〉 **1**（逃避） avoid: ～雨 shelter from the rain ‖ ～而不谈 evade a point ▸～难, 回～, 逃～ **2**（避免） keep away: ▸～孕

【避车道】bìchēdào〈名〉lay-by〈英〉; pull-off〈美〉

【避弹坑】bìdànkēng〈名〉［军事］foxhole

【避风】bìfēng〈动〉 **1**〈本〉 take shelter from the wind: ～处 shelter from the wind **2**〈喻〉 stay away from trouble: 他到国外去了，想避一避风。 He went abroad in order to lie low for a while.

【避风港】bìfēnggǎng〈名〉 sanctuary

【避风头】bì fēngtou = 避风 bìfēng 2

【避峰】bìfēng〈动〉 avoid extremes: ～出游 travel outside of peak times ‖ ～用电 use electricity at off-peak hours

【避讳】bìhuì〈动〉 observe a taboo

【避讳】bìhui〈动〉 **1**（指忌讳） avoid a taboo **2**（回避） evade: ～政治问题 evade political issues

【避忌】bìjì = 避讳 bìhui

【避开】bìkāi〈动〉 keep away from: ～目光 shy away from sb.'s gaze ‖ ～诱惑 shun temptation

【避坑落井】bìkēng-luòjǐng〈成〉〈喻〉 out of the frying pan into the fire

【避雷器】bìléiqì〈名〉 lightning protector

【避雷针】bìléizhēn〈名〉 lightning conductor: 安装～ install a lightning rod

【避乱】bìluàn〈动〉 seek refuge from war

【避免】bìmiǎn〈动〉 avoid: ～冲突 avert a conflict ‖ ～重复 avoid repetition ‖ ～事态恶化 prevent the worsening of the situation ‖ 不可～的战争 inevitable war

【避难就易】bìnán-jiùyì〈成〉 evade what is difficult and do what is easy

【避难】bìnàn〈动〉 take refuge: 寻求～ seek asylum ‖ 政治～ political asylum

【避难所】bìnànsuǒ〈名〉 sanctuary

【避让】bìràng〈动〉 **1**（避免） avoid **2**（让路） make way: ～道旁 retreat to the roadside ‖ ～不及 unable to step aside

【避实击虚】bìshí-jīxū〈成〉 evade the enemy's main force and strike his weak points

【避世】bìshì〈动〉 live as a recluse

【避暑】bìshǔ〈动〉 **1**（指盛夏） avoid summer heat: ～胜地 summer retreat **2**（指中暑） prevent sunstroke: ～药 medicine for preventing sunstroke

【避税】bìshuì〈动〉 avoid a tax

【避蚊剂】bìwénjì〈名〉 mosquito repellent

【避嫌】bìxián〈动〉 avoid suspicion: 应该～。 You should avoid being suspected.

【避邪】bìxié〈动〉 exorcize evil spirits

【避孕】bìyùn〈动〉 prevent pregnancy: ～措施 contraception measures ‖ ～用品 contraceptives

【避孕环】bìyùnhuán〈名〉 contraceptive ring

【避孕套】bìyùntào〈名〉 condom

【避孕药】bìyùnyào〈名〉 contraceptive pill

b

【避重就轻】bìzhòng-jiùqīng〈成〉**1**（指难易程度） always take the easy way out **2**（指重要程度） evade major issues by engaging in trivial ones

嬖 bì〈书〉

A〈动〉**1**（宠爱） take as favourite: ～爱 make a pet of **2**（宠幸） be in high favour: ～妾 favourite concubine
B〈名〉 favourite

髀 bì〈名〉**1**（大腿） thigh: 抚～长叹 rest one's hands on one's thighs and utter a deep sigh **2**（大腿骨） thighbone

【髀肉复生】bìròu-fùshēng〈成〉 remain idle in comfort and ease while yearning for active service: 退休之后，他常有～之叹。He often regretted being out of the action after his retirement.

臂 bì〈名〉**1**（胳膊） arm: 张开双～ open one's arms ‖ 右/左～ right/left arm ‖ ～戴黑纱 wear a black armband ▸～膀, 手～ **2**（上臂） upper arm: ▸长～猿 **3**（臂状物） arm: ～式吊车 boom hoist
▸bei

【臂膀】bìbǎng〈名〉**1**（胳膊） arm;（上臂） upper arm **2**〈喻〉（帮手） assistant
【臂力】bìlì〈名〉 strength of one's arm
【臂纱】bìshā〈名〉 (black) armband: 戴～ wear a black armband
【臂弯】bìwān〈名〉 crook of the arm
【臂章】bìzhāng〈名〉 armband

璧 bì〈名〉 round flat piece of jade with a hole in the centre

【璧还】bìhuán〈动〉〈书〉 return sth. borrowed in good shape and with thanks
【璧谢】bìxiè〈动〉〈书〉 decline with thanks

襞 bì〈名〉**1**〈书〉（指衣服） folds in a garment **2**［生理］ folds: 胃～ stomach fold

biān

边（邊） biān

A〈名〉**1**（边缘） edge: 街道两～ both sides of the street ‖ 海～ seaside ‖ 湖～ edge of a lake **2**（附近） side: ▸旁～, 身～, 手～ **3**（方面） side: 双/多～会谈 bilateral/multilateral talks ‖ 这件事上，我站在你一～。I am with you on this issue. ▸一～倒 **4**（边境） border: ▸～防, 戍～ **5**（指装饰） border: 金～ gold border ▸花～ **6**（指线段） side: 三角形有三条～。A triangle has three sides. ▸四～形 **7**（边界） limit: 一眼望不到～的大草原 a prairie so broad that the eye cannot take it all in ‖ 这话可太没～了。That's a tall tale if ever I heard one. ▸～际
B〈副〉 simultaneously: ～喝茶～聊天 have a chat over tea ‖ ～乘车～看书会伤眼睛的。It's bad for your eyes to read in a moving vehicle.
▸bian

【边岸】biān'àn〈名〉 shore
【边鄙】biānbǐ〈名〉〈书〉 remote border district
【边材】biāncái〈名〉 sapwood
【边裁】biāncái〈名〉［体育］ linesman
【边城】biānchéng〈名〉 border town
【边陲】biānchuí〈名〉〈书〉 border area: ～重镇 key town on the frontier
【边地】biāndì〈名〉 border area
【边防】biānfáng〈名〉 frontier defence: ～哨卡 border post ‖ ～部队 frontier army ‖ ～站 frontier station ‖ ～哨所 frontier post
【边锋】biānfēng〈名〉［体育］ wing: 左/右～ left/right wing
【边幅】biānfú〈名〉**1**（边缘） edges, fringes **2**（外表） appearance: ▸不修～
【边关】biānguān〈名〉 frontier pass: 镇守～ guard a frontier pass
【边际】biānjì〈名〉 boundary: 他说话不着～。He talked quite off the point.
【边际效应】biānjì xiàoyìng〈名〉 edge effect
【边疆】biānjiāng〈名〉 border area: 守卫～ guard the frontier ‖ ～城镇 frontier towns
【边角料】biānjiǎoliào〈名〉 leftover material
【边界】biānjiè〈名〉 border: 划定～ establish a border ‖ 开放～ open the border ‖ 越过～ cross a border ‖ ～线 border line ‖ ～争端 boundary dispute
【边境】biānjìng〈名〉 frontier: 开放～ open the border ‖ 偷越～ slip through the border ‖ ～地区 border area ‖ ～线 border line
【边境口岸】biānjìng kǒu'àn〈名〉 frontier port
【边境贸易】biānjìng màoyì〈名〉 border trade: 扩大～ expand the frontier trade
【边框】biānkuàng〈名〉 frame
【边贸】biānmào〈简称〉= 边境贸易
【边门】biānmén〈名〉 side door
【边民】biānmín〈名〉 inhabitants of a border area
【边卡】biānqiǎ〈名〉 border checkpoint
【边区】biānqū〈名〉 border area: 陕甘宁～ Shaanxi-Gansu-Ningxia Border Region
【边塞】biānsài〈名〉 frontier fort
【边务】biānwù〈名〉 border affairs
【边线】biānxiàn〈名〉［体育］ sideline
【边沿】biānyán〈名〉 edge: 在泳池～ on the edge of the pool
【边音】biānyīn〈名〉［语言］ lateral
【边缘】biānyuán **A**〈名〉 edge: ～地区 border district ‖ 峡谷的～ rim of a canyon ‖ 在死亡的～ on the brink of death **B**〈形〉 marginal: ～学科 marginal subject
【边缘化】biānyuánhuà〈动〉 marginalize: 在重大国际事务中，一些发展中国家被～了。In major international affairs, some developing countries are marginalized.
【边缘科学】biānyuán kēxué〈名〉 frontier science
【边缘政策】biānyuán zhèngcè〈名〉 brinkmanship
【边远】biānyuǎn〈形〉 outlying: ～地区 outlying area ‖ ～省份 remote border province
【边寨】biānzhài〈名〉 borderland village
【边注】biānzhù〈名〉 marginal

砭 biān

A〈动〉**1**（用石针） perform acupuncture with a stone needle **2**（批评） criticize severely: 痛～时弊 lash out at social ills with caustic criticism
B〈名〉 stone acupuncture needle

【砭骨】biāngǔ〈动〉〈书〉 chill one to the bone: 朔风～。The biting north wind cuts to the bone.
【砭石】biānshí〈名〉［中医］ stone acupuncture needle

编（編） biān

A〈动〉**1**（编织） weave: ～辫子 plait one's hair ‖ ～席 weave a mat ‖ 用柳条～个篮子 weave a basket from willow twigs **2**（组织） organize: ～目录 make a catalogue ‖ ～班/组 group into classes/teams ▸～号, ～码 **3**（编辑） edit: ～词典/教材 compile a dictionary/textbook ‖ ～书 edit a book **4**（写作） write: ～剧本 write a play ‖ ～计算机程序 program **5**（编造） fabricate: ～故事 make up a story
B〈名〉**1**（指书） volume: 上～ Book I ▸简～, 续～ **2**（人员名额） size of an establishment: ▸超～, 缺～, 在～

【编程】biānchéng〈动〉［计算机］ program
【编创】biānchuàng〈动〉 create: 电视剧～人员 creator of TV series
【编次】biāncì〈动〉 put into correct order
【编凑】biāncòu〈动〉 fabricate
【编导】biāndǎo **A**〈动〉 write and direct: ～电影 write the script and direct a film **B**〈名〉 writer and director: 影视～ scenarist-director
【编订】biāndìng〈动〉 compile and collate
【编队】biānduì **A**〈动〉 organize into teams **B**〈名〉 formation: 作战～ battle formation
【编队飞行】biānduì fēixíng〈名〉 formation flight
【编发】biānfā〈动〉 edit and release
【编号】biānhào **A**〈动〉 number: 给书～ number the books **B**〈名〉 serial number
【编后】biānhòu〈名〉 editorial afterword
【编辑】biānjí **A**〈动〉 edit: ～方针 editorial policies ‖ ～工作 editorial work **B**〈名〉 editor: 报纸～ newspaper editor ‖ 责任～ managing editor ▸总～
【编辑部】biānjíbù〈名〉 editorial department
【编辑室】biānjíshì〈名〉 editorial office: 新闻～ newsroom
【编校】biānjiào〈动〉 edit and proofread
【编结】biānjié〈动〉 weave: ～鱼网 weave a net
【编剧】biānjù **A**〈动〉 write a play **B**〈名〉 playwright
【编列】biānliè〈动〉**1**（编辑） compile: 把文章～成书 compile articles into a book **2**（制订） draw up: ～计划 work out a plan
【编录】biānlù〈动〉 compile: ～诗集 compile a book of poetry
【编码】biānmǎ **A**〈动〉 code: ～方案 code scheme ‖ ～程序 code program **B**〈名〉 code: 邮政～ post code〈英〉; zip code〈美〉
【编目】biānmù **A**〈动〉 catalogue: 对图书按字母顺序进行～ catalogue books alphabetically **B**〈名〉 catalogue: 图书～ book catalogue
【编年】biānnián〈动〉 arrange in chronological order
【编年史】biānniánshǐ〈名〉 annals
【编年体】biānniántǐ〈名〉 chronological style
【编排】biānpái〈动〉**1**（排列） arrange: ～图片和文章 lay out the pictures and articles ‖ 按科目～ organize by subject **2**（编剧并演出） arrange and rehearse: ～一出新戏 put together a new play
【编派】biānpai〈动〉〈方〉 make fun of sb. with made-up stories: 别在背后～人! Don't make up nasty stories about people behind their backs!
【编遣】biānqiǎn〈动〉 reorganize a unit

and discharge surplus personnel
【编磬】biānqìng ▸p. 929〈名〉［音乐］stone/jade chimes
【编审】biānshěn **A**〈动〉read and edit **B**〈名〉senior editor
【编外】biānwài〈名〉personnel not on regular staff: ～人员 non-staff personnel
【编务】biānwù〈名〉editorial work: ～繁忙 be busy with editorial work
【编写】biānxiě〈动〉**1**（汇编）compile: ～讲义 compile materials for lectures **2**（写作）write: ～剧本 write a play ‖ ～计算机程序 write a computer program
【编选】biānxuǎn〈动〉compile: ～出版有关论文 compile and publish related theses
【编演】biānyǎn〈动〉write and produce on stage: ～文艺节目 write and stage performances
【编译】biānyì **A**〈动〉edit and translate **B**〈名〉editor-translator
【编余】biānyú〈名〉redundant staff: 分流～人员 relocate surplus personnel
【编造】biānzào〈动〉**1**（汇集）draw up: ～统计表 compile a statistical table ‖ ～预算 prepare a budget **2**（虚构）invent: ～情节 weave a plot **3**（捏造）fabricate: ～谎言 make up lies ‖ ～罪名 trump up charges
【编者】biānzhě〈名〉editor: ～按 editor's note
【编织】biānzhī〈动〉**1**（编）weave: ～草帽 weave a straw hat **2**（织）knit: ～毛衣 knit a sweater
【编制】biānzhì **A**〈动〉**1**（编织）weave: ～藤席 weave rattan sleeping mats **2**（编写）compile: ～程序 program ‖ ～教学计划 draw up a curriculum ‖ ～预算 prepare a budget **B**〈名〉authorized staff: 扩大/缩小～ enlarge/reduce the staff ‖ 符合～规定的人数 be at full strength
【编钟】biānzhōng ▸p. 929〈名〉［音乐］chimes
【编著】biānzhù〈动〉compile
【编撰】biānzhuàn〈动〉compose: ～报告 compile a report
【编组】biānzǔ〈动〉organize into groups: ～站 marshalling station ‖ 按能力/年龄/性别～ group according to ability/age/sex
【编纂】biānzuǎn〈动〉compile: ～百科全书 compile an encyclopedia ‖ ～词典 compile a dictionary

煸 biān〈动〉sauté: ～豆角 stir-fried beans

蝙 biān
【蝙蝠】biānfú〈名〉［动物］bat
【蝙蝠衫】biānfúshān〈名〉batwing jacket

鳊（鯿） biān
【鳊鱼】biānyú〈名〉bream

鞭 biān
A〈名〉**1**（鞭子）whip: 挥～ wield a whip ‖ 皮～ leather whip ▸快马加～ **2**（指兵器）staff: 九节～ nine-joint staff ‖ 竹节～ bamboo whip **3**（小爆竹）a string of firecrackers: 一挂～ a string of firecrackers ▸～炮 **4**（鞭状物）whip-like object: ▸教～ **5**（生殖器）[of certain animals] penis : 牛～ ox's penis
B〈动〉〈书〉lash: ～马 flog a horse
【鞭策】biāncè〈动〉spur on: ～某人努力 spur sb. on to effort
【鞭长莫及】biāncháng-mòjí〈成〉beyond one's grasp: ～，爱莫能助。It's beyond my ability to help, though I am willing to do so.
【鞭笞】biānchī〈动〉〈书〉flog
【鞭虫】biānchóng〈名〉whipworm
【鞭打】biāndǎ〈动〉flog: 被～致死 be flogged to death
【鞭打快牛】biāndǎ-kuàiniú〈成〉〈喻〉ask too much of sb. who is already doing a great job
【鞭毛】biānmáo〈名〉［生物］flagellum: ～虫 flagellate
【鞭炮】biānpào〈名〉firecrackers: 一挂～ a string of firecrackers ‖ 放～ let off firecrackers

> **鞭炮**
>
> Fireworks (*yanhua*, 烟花) and firecrackers (*baozhu*, 爆竹 or *bianpao*, 鞭炮) are let off at important Chinese festivals and celebrations. In ancient times, bamboo was burnt during celebrations, and the explosive noise produced when it split in the heat was believed to drive away evil spirits and disease. This is why firecrackers are known as 'exploding bamboo' (*baozhu*). From the Song Dynasty, firecrackers were made out of gunpowder wrapped in auspicious red paper, but the name *baozhu* continued to be used. Long, fused strings of individually wrapped firecrackers make a tremendous noise when lit. Firecrackers are also used to see out the old year and welcome in the new — in the words of an old verse: 'the blast of firecrackers bids farewell to the passing year' (爆竹声中一岁除).

【鞭辟入里】biānpì-rùlǐ〈成〉[of criticism] penetrating: ～的讽刺 piercing sarcasm
【鞭挞】biāntà〈动〉〈书〉castigate: ～腐败现象 castigate corrupt practices ‖ 无情地～了家庭暴力 lash out mercilessly at domestic violence
【鞭子】biānzi〈名〉whip: 挥舞～ wield a whip

biǎn

贬（貶） biǎn〈动〉**1**（指价值）reduce in value: ～价 reduce the price ▸～值 **2**〈书〉（指职位）demote: ～为庶民 be degraded to commoner status ‖ 因失职而遭～ be demoted for failing to fulfil one's duties ▸～官, ～谪 **3**（贬低）disparage: 被报界～得一文不值 be maligned in the press as worthless
【贬斥】biǎnchì〈动〉**1**〈书〉（降职）demote: 累遭～ be demoted again and again **2**（斥责）denounce: 互相～ denounce each other
【贬黜】biǎnchù〈动〉〈书〉dismiss
【贬词】biǎncí = 贬义词 biǎnyìcí
【贬低】biǎndī〈动〉degrade: ～别人，抬高自己 put other people down in order to make oneself appear superior ‖ ～某人的才能 depreciate sb.'s ability
【贬官】biǎnguān〈动〉demote
【贬毁】biǎnhuǐ〈动〉disparage and defame
【贬价】biǎnjià〈动〉reduce in price: ～出售 sell at a reduced price
【贬损】biǎnsǔn〈动〉disparage: 他的话极大地～了某些同事。His statements were very derogatory towards some of his colleagues.
【贬义】biǎnyì〈名〉derogatory sense: 带有～ be derogatory in tone
【贬义词】biǎnyìcí〈名〉derogatory term
【贬抑】biǎnyì〈动〉belittle: ～之词 depreciatory remarks
【贬责】biǎnzé〈动〉reproach
【贬谪】biǎnzhé〈动〉banish from the court: 屡遭～ be frequently banished
【贬值】biǎnzhí〈动〉**1**（指货币）devalue: 使美元～ devalue the US dollar ‖ 货币～ currency devaluation **2**（指物资）depreciate: ～商品 depreciated goods ‖ 这笔投资肯定要～。The investment was certain to fall in value.
【贬职】biǎnzhí〈动〉〈书〉demote

扁 biǎn〈形〉flat: 压～ flatten by pressing ‖ ～鼻子 snub nose ‖〈喻〉别把人看～了。Don't underestimate others.
▸piān
【扁柏】biǎnbǎi〈名〉［植物］false cypress
【扁担】biǎndan〈名〉shoulder pole
【扁担星】Biǎndanxīng〈名〉［天文］Altair
【扁豆】biǎndòu〈名〉haricot bean
【扁率】biǎnlǜ〈名〉［天文］flatness: 地球的～ flatness of the earth
【扁平】biǎnpíng〈形〉flat
【扁平足】biǎnpíngzú〈名〉flatfoot
【扁桃】biǎntáo〈名〉**1**［植物］（指树）almond tree **2**（指果实）almond **3**〈口〉（蟠桃）flat peach
【扁桃体】biǎntáotǐ〈名〉［生理］tonsil
【扁桃腺】biǎntáoxiàn = 扁桃体 biǎntáotǐ
【扁形动物】biǎnxíng dòngwù〈名〉flatworm
【扁圆】biǎnyuán〈形〉〈口〉oval

匾 biǎn〈名〉**1**（木制横牌）horizontal inscribed board: 门上挂着一块～。There is a board with writing on it hanging over the door. **2**（丝制横牌）silk banner embroidered with words of praise: 绣金～ embroidered silk banner with words in gold **3**（竹制器皿）big, round shallow basket made from bamboo strips
【匾额】biǎn'é〈名〉= 匾 biǎn 1
【匾文】biǎnwén〈名〉inscription on a horizontal board

萹 biǎn
【萹豆】biǎndòu = 扁豆 biǎndòu

褊 biǎn〈形〉〈书〉narrow
【褊狭】biǎnxiá〈形〉narrow: 气量～ be narrow-minded ‖ ～的办公室 cramped office
【褊窄】biǎnzhǎi〈形〉narrow: ～的楼梯 narrow flight of stairs

碥 biǎn〈名〉**1**（指水边）rock sticking out obliquely at the side of a river **2**（指崖岸边）stone steps along dangerous parts of a cliff

biàn

卞 biàn〈形〉〈书〉short-tempered: ～急 testy

弁 biàn
A〈名〉**1**〈古〉（男帽）man's cap: 皮～ man's leather cap **2**〈旧〉（武官）low-ranking military officer: 将～ low-ranking officer **3**〈旧〉（军中差役）orderly: ▸马～
B〈形〉anterior: ▸～言
【弁言】biànyán〈名〉〈书〉foreword

b

苄 biàn

【苄基】biànjī〈名〉［化学］benzyl

汴 Biàn

〈名〉Bian [another name for Kaifeng (开封)]

忭 biàn

〈形〉〈书〉delighted: 不胜欣～ be overjoyed ‖ 欢～ joyful

变（變）biàn

A〈动〉**1**（改变）change: 风向～了。The wind has changed. ‖ 他～坏了。He has turned bad. ‖ 天气～冷/热了。It's getting cold/warm. ‖ 头发一夜之间就～白了。His hair turned grey overnight. ►～心，改～，瞬息万～ **2**（成为）become: 后进～先进。The backward has become the advanced. **3**（改造）transform: ～废为宝 turn waste materials into useful things ‖ 魔术师把手帕～成了一只鸽子。The magician turned the handkerchief into a dove. **4**（不确定）be changeable: ►～量，～数 **5**（变卖）sell off: ►～产
B〈名〉**1**（突发事件）unexpected turn of events: ►～乱，兵～，事～ **2** = 变文 biànwén

【变本加厉】biànběn-jiālì〈成〉be further intensified: ～地扩军备战 step up arms build-up and war preparations

【变产】biànchǎn〈动〉sell off one's property

【变成】biànchéng〈动〉become: 把水力～电力 transform water power into electrical power ‖ 梦想～了现实。The dream became a reality.

【变蛋】biàndàn〈方〉= 松花蛋 sōnghuādàn

【变电站】biàndiànzhàn〈名〉transformer substation

【变调】biàndiào **A**〈名〉tonal modification **B** = 转调 zhuǎndiào

【变动】biàndòng〈动〉change: 人事～ personnel change ‖ 计划有所～。There is some alteration in the plan.

【变法】biànfǎ〈动〉introduce institutional reforms

【变法儿】biànfǎr〈动〉〈口〉try different ways: 变着法儿骗人 try every means possible to cheat others

【变革】biàngé〈动〉transform: ～旧制度 transform the old system ‖ 实行～ carry out changes ‖ 经济/社会/政治～ economic/social/political transformation

【变更】biàngēng〈动〉change: ～地址 change one's address ‖ 做出重大～ make major changes

【变故】biàngù〈名〉mishap: 如果发生～怎么办? What if anything unexpected happens?

【变卦】biànguà〈动〉go back on one's word: 别人一说，他就～。He changes his mind according to what other people say. ‖ 已经答应的事，怎么能～呢? How can we break our promise on what has already been agreed?

【变花样】biànhuāyàng〈动〉do conjuring tricks

【变化】biànhuà〈动〉change: 化学～ chemical change ‖ 可喜的～ welcome change ‖ 形势～很快。The situation is changing fast. ‖ 这个城市发生了显著的～。The city has undergone a marked transformation.

【变化无常】biànhuà-wúcháng〈成〉constantly changing: ～的人/天气 changeable person/weather

【变幻】biànhuàn〈动〉fluctuate: 风云～ constant change of events

【变幻莫测】biànhuàn-mòcè〈成〉changeable

【变换】biànhuàn〈动〉alter: ～发球方式 change one's serve ‖ ～手法 vary one's tactics

【变节】biànjié〈动〉betray: ～行为 treacherous acts ‖ ～分子 turncoat

【变局】biànjú〈名〉emergency: 应付～ cope with an emergency

【变口】biànkǒu〈名〉［曲艺］use of various dialects in *quyi*, a form of folk art

【变脸】biànliǎn〈动〉**1**（指脸色）suddenly turn: 受到我的批评，她就跟我～了。After hearing my criticisms she suddenly turned on me. **2**［戏曲］change facial expression rapidly

【变量】biànliàng〈名〉variable

【变流器】biànliúqì〈名〉［电气］current transformer

【变乱】biànluàn〈名〉turmoil

【变卖】biànmài〈动〉auction off: ～家产 sell off one's family property

【变频】biànpín〈名〉frequency conversion: ～空调 variable frequency air conditioner

【变迁】biànqiān〈动〉change: 历史～ historical changes ‖ 故乡的～ changes in the home country

【变色】biànsè〈动〉**1**（指颜色）change colour: 吸烟会使牙齿～。Smoking discolours the teeth. **2**（指脸色）change one's countenance

【变色镜】biànsèjìng〈名〉light-sensitive glasses

【变色龙】biànsèlóng〈名〉**1**［动物］chameleon **2**〈喻〉（多变的人）chameleon

【变色眼镜】biànsè yǎnjìng = 变色镜 biànsèjìng

【变生肘腋】biànshēng-zhǒuyè〈成〉trouble is brewing close at hand

【变声】biànshēng〈动〉experience one's voice breaking

【变数】biànshù〈名〉**1**［数学］variable: 常数与～ constants and variables **2**（不确定因素）variable factor: 由于～很多，成本很难准确估算。With so many variables, the exact cost is difficult to estimate.

【变速】biànsù〈动〉change speed

【变速器】biànsùqì〈名〉transmission; gearbox〈英〉: 手动～ manual transmission

【变速运动】biànsù yùndòng〈名〉［物理］variable motion

【变态】biàntài〈动〉**1**［生物］metamorphose: ～叶 metamorphosed leaf **2**（不正常）be abnormal: ～行为 abnormal act ‖ 心理～ psychopathy ‖ ～反应 allergic reaction

【变体】biàntǐ〈名〉variation

【变天】biàntiān〈动〉**1**〈本〉change: 今晚也许要～。Perhaps the weather will break tonight. **2**〈喻〉（指政权更替）stage a comeback: 妄想～ dream of staging a comeback

【变通】biàntōng〈动〉be flexible: 根据具体情况做适当的～ make appropriate changes in the light of specific conditions

【变味】biànwèi〈动〉**1**〈本〉go bad: 肉～了，不能吃了。The meat has gone bad, it's unfit to eat. **2**（指内涵改变）make a departure: 和原文对比一下，我发现译文有点～了。Reading the translation against the original text, I found in it a slight departure in tone.

【变温动物】biànwēn dòngwù〈名〉cold-blooded animal

【变文】biànwén〈名〉a form of religious narrative literature widely popular at Buddhist services during and after the Tang Dynasty

【变戏法】biàn xìfǎ〈惯〉**1**〈本〉perform conjuring tricks **2**〈喻〉（玩花招）play tricks: ～变不出水坝，水坝要靠艰苦的劳动去创造。You can't conjure up a dam, you can create one by hard work.

【变相】biànxiàng〈形〉covert: ～剥削 covert exploitation ‖ ～贪污 embezzlement in disguised form ‖ ～体罚 corporal punishment in disguise ‖ ～涨价 disguised price hike

【变心】biànxīn〈动〉have a change of heart: 海枯石烂，永不～。One's loyalty will remain unchanged even if the seas dry up and the rocks crumble.

【变星】biànxīng〈名〉［天文］variable (star)

【变形】biànxíng〈动〉**1**（指外形）change shape: 脊柱～ have a deformed spine ‖ 车轮压得～了。The wheel was crushed out of shape. **2**（指魔法）transfigure

【变形虫】biànxíngchóng〈名〉amoeba

【变形金刚】biànxíng jīngāng〈名〉transformer

【变型】biànxíng〈动〉change category or type: 处于～期的社会 society in transition

【变性】biànxìng〈动〉**1**［化学］denature **2**［医学］degenerate: ～反应 reaction of degeneration **3**（改变性别）change sex: 女子～而成的男子 female-to-male transsexual ‖ ～人 transgender person ►～手术

【变性手术】biànxìng shǒushù〈名〉transgender surgery

【变压器】biànyāqì〈名〉transformer

【变样】biànyàng〈动〉become different: 经济改革以来，这个村子大～了。The village has changed a great deal since the economic reform. ‖ 他完全变了样。He has changed completely.

【变异】biànyì〈名〉［生物］variation: 遗传～ genetic abnormality

【变易】biànyì〈动〉modify: ～规章制度 alter the rules and regulations

【变质】biànzhì〈动〉go bad: 蜕化～ become morally degenerate ‖ 闻闻这肉，有没有～? Take a smell of the meat. Is it off? ‖ 这牛奶～了。The milk has gone bad.

【变种】biànzhǒng〈名〉**1**［生物］mutation: 这株植物是通常类型的～。This plant is a variant of the common type. **2**〈喻〉variety: 虚无主义的～ variation on nihilism

【变奏】biànzòu〈名〉［音乐］variation

【变奏曲】biànzòuqǔ〈名〉variation

便 biàn

A〈形〉**1**（适宜）suitable: 此事不～公开。It's not appropriate to make this public. ►未～ **2**（方便）convenient: ～于携带 be portable ‖ 行走不～ have difficulty walking ►轻～ **3**（非正式）informal: ►～饭，～函，～衣
B〈名〉**1**（方便）convenience: ►～车，顺～ **2**（排泄物）excrement or urine: ►～盆，粪～，排～
C〈动〉relieve oneself: ►～血，大～，小～
D〈副〉**1**（表时间顺承）soon afterwards: 转身～走 turn and leave ‖ 新政策一实行～受到了普遍欢迎。The new policy was

well-received as soon as it came into effect. **2**（表条件）then: 他吃饭很简单：不是面条～是米饭。 He eats simple meals: if it's not noodles, then it's rice. ‖ 你要回家～回吧。 You may go home if you want to.

E〈连〉[often used as 即便] even if: 即～再穷，我也要送小孩上学。 Even if I were very poor, I would want my child to go to school.

▸pián

【便步】biànbù〈名〉［军事］route step: ～行军 route march

【便餐】biàncān〈名〉informal meal: 吃顿～ have a simple meal

【便车】biànchē〈名〉passing vehicle: 咱们搭～可以节省费用。 If we hitch a ride it will keep the costs down.

【便池】biànchí〈名〉urinal

【便当】biàndang〈形〉〈方〉convenient: 从这里坐汽车去城里很～。 By bus it's easy to get to town from here.

【便道】biàndào〈名〉**1**（近道）short cut: 走～ take a short cut **2**（人行道）pavement〈英〉; sidewalk〈美〉: 禁止车辆上～! No vehicles on the pavement! ‖ 行人请走～。 Pedestrians please walk on the pavement only. **3**（临时通道）makeshift road

【便殿】biàndiàn〈名〉palace hall for the emperor to rest or feast

【便饭】biànfàn **A**〈名〉simple meal: ▸家常～ **B**〈动〉have a light meal: 明晚来舍下～吧。 Come over and eat something simple with us tomorrow evening.

【便服】biànfú〈名〉**1**（非正式服装）casual wear: 穿～的军官 officer in mufti **2**（中式服装）traditional Chinese clothes

【便函】biànhán〈名〉informal letter

【便壶】biànhú〈名〉chamber pot

【便笺】biànjiān〈名〉**1**（便条）note **2**（便条纸）notepaper: 一张～ a sheet of notepaper

【便捷】biànjié〈形〉**1**（方便）convenient: ～的方法 convenient method **2**（快捷）quick: 行动～ act nimbly

【便览】biànlǎn〈名〉brief guide: 交通～ road book ‖ 邮政～ postal guide

【便利】biànlì **A**〈形〉convenient: 交通～ have good transport facilities ‖ 提供～条件 provide favourable conditions **B**〈动〉facilitate: 为了～群众 for the convenience of the masses

【便利店】biànlìdiàn〈名〉convenience store

【便路】biànlù〈名〉short cut

【便帽】biànmào〈名〉informal cap

【便门】biànmén〈名〉side door: 走～ go through the side door

【便秘】biànmì ▸**p. 50**〈名〉［医学］constipation

【便民】biànmín〈形〉convenient: ～措施 convenient measures ‖ ～商店 convenience store

【便溺】biànniào **A**〈动〉relieve oneself **B**〈名〉urine and excrement

【便盆】biànpén〈名〉bedpan

【便桥】biànqiáo〈名〉temporary bridge

【便士】biànshì ▸**p. 328**〈名〉penny

【便所】biànsuǒ〈名〉WC, public convenience

【便条】biàntiáo〈名〉note: 留～ leave a note

【便桶】biàntǒng〈名〉chamber pot

【便携式】biànxiéshì〈形〉portable: ～电视摄像机 portable TV camera

【便鞋】biànxié〈名〉slippers

【便血】biànxiě〈动〉have blood in one's stool

【便宴】biànyàn〈名〉informal dinner: 设～招待 treat sb. to an informal dinner

【便衣】biànyī〈名〉**1**（指衣服）plain clothes: ～警察 plain-clothes policeman **2**（指人）plain-clothed man

【便宜】biànyí〈形〉〈书〉convenient ▸piányi

【便宜从事】biànyí-cóngshì = 便宜行事 biànyí-xíngshì

【便宜行事】biànyí-xíngshì〈成〉act on one's initiative without having to seek approval from a higher level: 你～吧! Use your discretion!

【便于】biànyú〈动〉be convenient for: ～携带 be easy to carry ‖ 为了～查阅 for ease of reference

【便中】biànzhōng〈副〉〈书〉at one's convenience: ～请通知他。 Please inform him of it at your convenience.

【便装】biànzhuāng = 便服 biànfú 1

遍 biàn

A〈动〉be everywhere: ～游名山 travel to all the famous mountains ‖ 消息传～了全镇。 The news spread all over the town. ‖ 我们的朋友～天下。 We have friends all around the world. ▸～布, ～地

B〈量〉once through, one time: 好几～ several times ‖ 请再来一～! Once more/again, please!

【遍布】biànbù〈动〉spread all over: ～全球 can be found all over the world

【遍地】biàndì〈名〉all over the place, everywhere: ～皆是 be thick on the ground

【遍地开花】biàndì-kāihuā〈成〉〈喻〉spring up all over the place: 乡镇企业～。 Township enterprises sprang up all over the country.

【遍及】biànjí〈动〉reach everywhere: 探矿者的足迹～全岛。 Prospectors have been to all corners of the island.

【遍体鳞伤】biàntǐ-línshāng〈成〉be covered with cuts and bruises: 被打得～ be beaten black and blue

【遍野】biànyě〈动〉spread all over the open country

缏（緶）biàn

▸pián

【缏子】biànzi = 草帽缏 cǎomàobiàn

辨 biàn

〈动〉differentiate: ▸～别, ～认, 明～是非

【辨别】biànbié〈动〉distinguish: ～方向 take one's bearings ‖ ～是非 know right from wrong ‖ ～真伪 tell the true from the false ‖ ～能力 discriminating power

【辨惑】biànhuò〈动〉straighten out confusing points

【辨明】biànmíng〈动〉clarify: ～是非 make a clear distinction between right and wrong

【辨认】biànrèn〈动〉identify: ～罪犯/尸体 identify a criminal/corpse ‖ 指纹～ fingerprint identification ‖ 你能根据这个人的照片～出他吗? Can you identify the man by his picture?

【辨识】biànshí〈动〉distinguish: ～足迹 identify footprints

【辨析】biànxī〈动〉differentiate and analyse: 同义词～ synonym discrimination

【辨正】biànzhèng〈动〉identify and rectify

【辨证】biànzhèng〈动〉distinguish symptoms of diseases

【辨证论治】biànzhèng lùnzhì = 辨证施治 biànzhèng shīzhì

【辨证施治】biànzhèng shīzhì〈名〉［中医］treatment based on an overall analysis of the patient's condition

辩（辯）biàn

〈动〉argue: 真理愈～愈明。 The truth emerges more clearly through debate. ▸～驳, 雄～, 争～

【辩白】biànbái〈动〉offer an explanation: 你不必～了，大家没有责怪你的意思。 You don't have to explain. We have no intention of blaming you.

【辩驳】biànbó〈动〉dispute: 无可～ beyond dispute ‖ 无可～的论据 irrefutable argument

【辩才】biàncái〈名〉eloquence: 他颇有～。 He is quite good at arguing his point.

【辩词】biàncí = 辩辞 biàncí

【辩辞】biàncí〈名〉argument

【辩护】biànhù〈动〉**1**（辩解）defend: 为内阁的外交政策～ speak in defence of the cabinet's foreign policy **2**［法律］defend: 请律师为自己的案子～ hire a lawyer to plead one's case ‖ 被告未作任何～。 The accused made no defence.

【辩护词】biànhùcí〈名〉defence

【辩护律师】biànhù lǜshī〈名〉lawyer/counsel for the defence

【辩护权】biànhùquán〈名〉right to defence

【辩护人】biànhùrén〈名〉defender: 被告～ advocate for the defence

【辩护士】biànhùshì〈名〉defender

【辩解】biànjiě〈动〉explain away: 为自己的错误～ be on the defensive about one's mistakes ‖ 她～说，当时并没有"禁止停车"的标志。 She defended herself, saying that there wasn't a 'No Parking' sign.

【辩论】biànlùn〈动〉argue: ～政治问题 argue about politics ‖ 引起～ provoke a debate ‖ 公开～ public debate ‖ 展开激烈～ hotly debate

【辩明】biànmíng〈动〉argue out: ～事理 reason out

【辩难】biànnàn〈动〉〈书〉retort with challenging questions: 相互～ exchange sharp retorts

【辩士】biànshì〈名〉debater

【辩手】biànshǒu〈名〉debater: 最佳～ most skilled debater

【辩说】biànshuō〈动〉argue

【辩诉】biànsù〈动〉［法律］conduct one's own defence

【辩诬】biànwū〈动〉defend against false accusation

【辩证】biànzhèng **A**〈动〉investigate and verify: 反复～ repeated authentication **B**〈形〉dialectical: ～关系 dialectical relationship ‖ ～的观点 dialectical point of view ‖ ～统一 dialectical unity

【辩证法】biànzhèngfǎ〈名〉［哲学］**1**（泛指）dialectics: 自然～ dialectics of nature **2**（唯物辩证法）materialist dialectics

【辩证逻辑】biànzhèng luójí〈名〉dialectical logic

【辩证唯物主义】biànzhèng wéiwùzhǔyì〈名〉dialectical materialism: ～认识论 dialectical materialist theory of knowledge

辫（辮）biàn

〈名〉**1**（指头发）plait: 梳着两条长～ wear one's hair in two long braids **2**（辫状物）braid: 草帽～ straw braid

b

【辫子】biànzi〈名〉 1 (指头发) plait〈英〉; braid〈美〉: 梳/扎～ plait one's hair 2 (辫状物) braid: 蒜～ braid of garlic 3 〈喻〉(把柄) handle: ▸揪～

bian

边（邊） bian〈后缀〉 [indicating locality]: 北～ north
▸biān

biāo

标（標） biāo
A〈名〉 1 〈书〉(末端) treetop: ～端 treetop 2 (表面) outward sign: 治～而不治本 treat the symptoms of a disease rather than its root cause ▸～本兼治 3 (奖品) prize: ▸夺～, 锦～ 4 (标记) marker: 界～ boundary marker ▸～志, 航～, 商～ 5 (标准) standard: ▸～准, 达～ 6 (条件) quota 7 (目标) target: ▸指～ 8 (出价) bid: 开～ open bids ▸～底, 招～, 中～
B〈动〉 mark: ～上记号 put a mark on ‖ 瓶子上～有"有毒"字样。 The bottle is marked 'poisonous'. ▸～价, ～签, ～题
C〈量〉 group: 一～人马赫然出现在前方。 A group of soldiers suddenly loomed large ahead.
【标榜】biāobǎng〈动〉〈贬〉 1 (宣扬) parade: ～自由和民主 flaunt the banner of liberty and democracy 2 (吹嘘) excessively praise: 极力～ praise to the skies ‖ 自我～ blow one's own trumpet
【标本】biāoběn〈名〉 1 (表面和本质) root cause and symptoms: ▸～兼治 2 [生物] specimen: 采集～ collect specimens ‖ 把昆虫制成～ make a specimen of an insect 3 (代表) example: 苏州园林是中国园林的～。 The gardens in Suzhou are characteristic of Chinese gardens. 4 [医学] sample: 唾液～ saliva sample ‖ 血液～ blood sample
【标本兼治】biāoběn-jiānzhì〈成〉 1 (指疾病) treat both the outward symptoms and root causes of an illness 2 (指问题) strike at the root of a problem as well as its effect
【标兵】biāobīng〈名〉 1 (指士兵) pacesetter 2 (榜样) example: 树立～ set sb. up as an example
【标尺】biāochǐ〈名〉 1 [测绘] surveyor's rod 2 [水利] staff gauge 3 [军事] rear sight
【标灯】biāodēng〈名〉 1 (灯塔) beacon 2 (信号灯) marker light
【标底】biāodǐ〈名〉 bottom price of a bid
【标的】biāodì〈名〉 1 (箭靶) target: 命中～ hit the target 2 (目标) aim 3 (所指对象) common objective
【标点】biāodiǎn A〈名〉 punctuation mark B〈动〉 punctuate
【标点符号】biāodiǎn fúhào〈名〉 punctuation mark
【标度】biāodù〈名〉[数学] scale
【标杆】biāogān〈名〉 1 (指测量用具) surveyor's pole 2 = 样板 yàngbǎn 3
【标高】biāogāo〈名〉[测绘] elevation
【标号】biāohào〈名〉 1 (指数字) grade: 水泥～ grade of cement 2 (指符号) signs and symbols
【标记】biāojì〈名〉 mark: 做～ mark ‖ 识别～ distinguishing mark
【标价】biāojià A〈动〉 price: ～50元 be priced at 50 *yuan* ▸明码～ B〈名〉 marked price: 所售商品均有～。 All goods for sale have marked prices.
【标金】biāojīn〈名〉 1 (指押金) deposit for bidding 2 (指金条) standard gold
【标量】biāoliàng〈名〉[物理] scalar
【标卖】biāomài〈动〉 1 (标价出售) sell at a marked price 2 (招标出售) sell by tender
【标煤】biāoméi〈名〉 standard coal: 节约～5,000吨 save 5,000 tonnes of standard coal
【标明】biāomíng〈动〉 mark: ～价格 mark the price ‖ ～每座山峰的高度 indicate the elevation of each mountain peak ‖ 用星号～ mark with an asterisk
【标牌】biāopái〈名〉 1 (牌匾) sign: 门边的～ plaque beside the door 2 (产品标识) logo
【标签】biāoqiān〈名〉 label: 货运～ shipping tag ‖ 价格～ price tag ‖ 评论文学作品要客观，不要乱贴～。 One must be objective in appraising literary works, and not attach arbitrary labels to them.
【标枪】biāoqiāng〈名〉[体育] javelin: ～投手 javelin thrower
【标石】biāoshí〈名〉 stone marker
【标示】biāoshì〈动〉 indicate: ～牌 sign post
【标书】biāoshū〈名〉 1 (投标书) tender 2 (招标书) invitation to bidding
【标题】biāotí〈名〉 heading: 通栏大字～ banner ‖ 文章的～ title of an essay
【标题新闻】biāotí xīnwén〈名〉 title news
【标题音乐】biāotí yīnyuè〈名〉 programme music
【标图】biāotú〈动〉 mark on a chart/map
【标王】biāowáng〈名〉 highest bid
【标新立异】biāoxīn-lìyì〈成〉 try to impress by appearing novel and unique
【标音】biāoyīn〈动〉 transcribe: 宽式/严式～ broad/narrow transcription
【标语】biāoyǔ〈名〉 slogan: 宣传～ campaign slogan ‖ ～牌 placard
【标志】biāozhì A〈名〉 symbol: 识别地图上的～ read the marks on the map ‖ ～性建筑 landmark structure ‖ 成功的～ mark of success ‖ 交通/停车～ traffic/stop signs B〈动〉 indicate: ～一个时代的结束/开始 mark the end/beginning of an era ‖ 这些数字～着一个国家经济发展的程度。 These figures indicate the level of economic development of a country.
【标识】biāozhì = 标志 biāozhì
【标识牌】biāozhìpái〈名〉 information sign: 道路～ road information sign
【标致】biāozhì〈形〉 beautiful: 长得很～ look very pretty
【标注】biāozhù〈动〉 mark: ～声调 mark the tones
【标准】biāozhǔn A〈名〉 standard: 合乎～ comply with the criteria ‖ 双重～ double standard ‖ 质量～ quality criterion ‖ 实践是检验真理的唯一～。 The only way of getting to the truth is through trial and error. B〈形〉 standard: ～发音 standard pronunciation ‖ ～格式 standard form ‖ 发音很～。 The pronunciation is standard.
【标准大气压】biāozhǔn dàqìyā〈名〉[气象] standard atmosphere
【标准粉】biāozhǔnfěn〈名〉 standard wheat flour
【标准杆】biāozhǔngān〈名〉[体育] par
【标准化】biāozhǔnhuà〈动〉 standardize: ～考试 standardized test
【标准间】biāozhǔnjiān〈名〉 standard room
【标准件】biāozhǔnjiàn〈名〉 standard part
【标准时】biāozhǔnshí〈名〉 standard time: 格林尼治～ Greenwich Mean Time (GMT)
【标准时区】biāozhǔn shíqū〈名〉 time zone
【标准像】biāozhǔnxiàng〈名〉 official portrait
【标准音】biāozhǔnyīn〈名〉 standard pronunciation
【标准语】biāozhǔnyǔ ▸p. 918〈名〉 standard language/speech

飑（颮） biāo〈名〉[气象] squall

彪 biāo
A〈名〉 1 〈书〉(斑纹) tiger stripes 2 (小老虎) young tiger
B〈形〉〈书〉 brilliant: ▸～炳
【彪炳】biāobǐng〈动〉〈书〉 shine: ～青史 shine in history
【彪炳千古】biāobǐng-qiāngǔ〈成〉 shine through the ages
【彪悍】biāohàn〈形〉 valiant
【彪形大汉】biāoxíng dàhàn〈名〉 strapping fellow
【彪壮】biāozhuàng〈形〉 hefty

摽 biāo〈动〉〈书〉 1 (挥去) wave off 2 (抛弃) abandon
▸biào

骠（驃） biāo ▸黄骠马 huángbiāomǎ
▸piào

膘 biāo〈名〉 [of livestock] fat: ～肥体壮 brawny and sturdy ‖ 这块肉～很厚。 This piece of meat has got lots of fat on it. ▸跌～, 蹲～
【膘情】biāoqíng〈名〉 condition of fattening: ～良好 be fattening well
【膘实】biāoshi〈形〉 [of domestic animals] plump

飙（飆、飇） biāo〈名〉〈书〉 whirlwind: ▸狂～
【飙车】biāochē〈动〉〈方〉 drive at high speed
【飙升】biāoshēng〈动〉 skyrocket: 汽车产量～。 Auto production skyrocketed.
【飙涨】biāozhǎng〈动〉 skyrocket: 股价/房价～。 Share prices/house prices are skyrocketing.

镖（鏢） biāo〈名〉 1 (指暗器) dart-like weapon: ▸飞～ 2 (指财物) property convoyed for others: ▸保～
【镖局】biāojú〈名〉〈旧〉 professional establishment providing armed escort for treasures sent over long distances

> **镖局**
> An agency that provided highly skilled military escorts as protection for travelling merchants or their property. Such escorts flourished in the Qing Dynasty but declined in the early part of the 20th century.

【镖客】biāokè〈名〉〈旧〉 armed escort
【镖师】biāoshī = 镖客 biāokè

瘭 biāo
【瘭疽】biāojū〈名〉[中医] pyogenic infection of the pad of a finger or toe

藨 biāo

【藨草】biāocǎo〈名〉［植物］bulrush

镳（鑣）biāo〈名〉〈书〉bit (of a bridle): ▸分道扬～

biǎo

表[1] biǎo

A〈名〉**1**（外表）surface: ▸～面，地～，外～ **2**（表格）form: 填～ fill in a form ‖ 造～ make up a table for submission to higher levels ‖ 申请～ application form ▸制～，时间～ **3**（奏章）memorial: 上～ submit a memorial **4**（指亲戚关系）relationship between the children of a brother and a sister or of sisters: ▸～哥，～亲 **5**（柱子）ceremonial columns: ▸华～ **6**（计时木杆）gnomon: ▸圭～ **7**（计数器）meter: 煤气～ gas meter ▸水～，温度～ **8**（榜样）model: ▸～率
B〈动〉**1**（表示）express: ～决心 express one's determination ‖ 深～同情 show deep sympathy **2**［中医］cure a cold with medicine: ▸～汗

表[2]（錶）biǎo〈名〉watch: 石英～ quartz watch ‖ 我的～一天快/慢半分钟。My watch gains/loses half a minute a day. ▸手～，秒～

【表白】biǎobái〈动〉profess: ～爱情 declare one's love ‖ 一再～ explain oneself repeatedly ‖ 真诚的～ sincere profession
【表册】biǎocè〈名〉statistical forms
【表层】biǎocéng〈名〉surface: 皮肤的～ surface of the skin
【表层结构】biǎocéng jiégòu〈名〉［语言］surface structure
【表尺】biǎochǐ〈名〉［军事］rear sight
【表达】biǎodá〈动〉express: ～方式 way of expression ‖ ～能力 expressive power ‖ 我难以～我的感激之情。I can hardly express my gratitude. ‖ 语言是用来～思想的。Language is used to convey ideas.
【表带】biǎodài〈名〉watch strap
【表弟】biǎodì〈名〉younger male cousin
【表哥】biǎogē〈名〉older male cousin
【表格】biǎogé〈名〉form
【表功】biǎogōng〈动〉brag about one's contribution: 他这人好～。He tends to boast of his own meritorious deeds.
【表汗】biǎohàn〈动〉［中医］induce perspiration
【表姐】biǎojiě〈名〉older female cousin
【表决】biǎojué〈动〉vote: 举手～ take a show of hands ‖ ～结果 voting result
【表决程序】biǎojué chéngxù〈名〉voting procedure
【表决权】biǎojuéquán〈名〉right to vote: 拥有～ have the right to vote
【表壳】biǎoké〈名〉watchcase
【表里】biǎolǐ〈名〉external and internal
【表里不一】biǎolǐ-bùyī〈成〉think one way and act another: ～的人 double dealer
【表里如一】biǎolǐ-rúyī〈成〉think and act in one and the same way
【表链】biǎoliàn〈名〉watch chain
【表露】biǎolù〈动〉reveal: ～出不安 show one's anxiety ‖ ～感情 display one's emotions
【表妹】biǎomèi〈名〉younger female cousin
【表蒙子】biǎoméngzi〈名〉watch glass
【表面】biǎomiàn〈名〉**1**（指物体）surface: ～损伤 superficial damage ‖ 粗糙/光滑～ rough/smooth surface ‖ 地球～ surface of the earth **2**（指现象）appearance: 被～现象迷惑 be misled by appearances ‖ 他～文静，其实脾气火暴。Beneath that ostensible calmness is a man of fierce temper. ‖ 她只是～客气。She's just feigning politeness.
【表面处理】biǎomiàn chǔlǐ〈名〉surface treatment
【表面化】biǎomiànhuà〈动〉come to the surface: 矛盾又～了。The contradictions have surfaced again.
【表面文章】biǎomiàn wénzhāng〈名〉〈喻〉ostentation: 他喜欢做～。He cares only for show.
【表面现象】biǎomiàn xiànxiàng〈名〉superficial phenomenon
【表面张力】biǎomiàn zhānglì〈名〉［物理］surface tension
【表面积】biǎomiànjī〈名〉surface area
【表明】biǎomíng〈动〉make clear: ～立场 declare one's stand ‖ ～身份 reveal one's identity ‖ ～态度 make one's attitude clear ‖ 所有证据都～，他就是杀人凶手。All evidence pointed to him as the murderer.
【表盘】biǎopán〈名〉dial
【表皮】biǎopí〈名〉［生物］epidermis
【表亲】biǎoqīn〈名〉cousin: 我们是～。We are cousins.
【表情】biǎoqíng **A**〈动〉show one's emotions **B**〈名〉expression: 毫无～ be expressionless ‖ 面部～ facial expression ‖ 她脸上闪现出愤怒的～。A look of rage flashed across her face.
【表示】biǎoshì **A**〈动〉**1**（表达）express: ～感谢 express one's thanks ‖ ～歉意 extend an apology ‖ ～祝贺 convey one's congratulations ‖ 他点头～同意。He nodded his consent. **2**（意为）mean: 红灯～车辆不得通行。A red light means stop. **B**〈名〉expression: 感激的～ expression of gratitude
【表述】biǎoshù〈动〉formulate: ～己见 state one's views ‖ ～不清 be inarticulate
【表率】biǎoshuài〈名〉example: 以他为～ follow his example ‖ 起～作用 play an exemplary role
【表态】biǎotài〈动〉make known one's position: 明确～ make one's position clear ‖ 他对这一问题没有～。He didn't reveal his stand on the issue.
【表土】biǎotǔ〈名〉［农业］topsoil
【表现】biǎoxiàn **A**〈动〉**1**（显示）display: ～出高度的责任感 demonstrate a high sense of responsibility ‖ 那出戏充分～了被压迫人民的大无畏精神。The play gives the fullest expression to the dauntless spirit of the oppressed people. **2**〈贬〉（炫耀）show off: 好～ love to show off **B**〈名〉behaviour: ～不佳 acquit oneself poorly ‖ 她在学校～很好。She is doing well at the school.
【表现力】biǎoxiànlì〈名〉power of expression: 艺术～ artistic expressions
【表现手法】biǎoxiàn shǒufǎ〈名〉artistic approach
【表现形式】biǎoxiàn xíngshì〈名〉form of expression: 文学的～ form of literary expression
【表现主义】biǎoxiànzhǔyì〈名〉［语言］expressionism
【表象】biǎoxiàng〈名〉**1**［心理］presentation **2**［哲学］representation
【表形文字】biǎoxíng wénzì〈名〉［语言］pictograph
【表兄】biǎoxiōng = 表哥 biǎogē
【表演】biǎoyǎn〈动〉**1**（演出）perform: ～节目 put on a performance ‖ ～魔术 perform conjuring tricks ‖ ～过火 overact ‖ 军事～ military display **2**（演示）demonstrate: ～机器的操作方法 demonstrate how to run a machine
【表演唱】biǎoyǎnchàng〈名〉singing with actions
【表演赛】biǎoyǎnsài〈名〉exhibition match
【表扬】biǎoyáng〈动〉praise: ～先进集体和个人 commend advanced collectives and individuals ‖ 受到～ be given a commendation ‖ ～信 letter of commendation
【表意文字】biǎoyì wénzì〈名〉［语言］ideogram
【表音文字】biǎoyīn wénzì〈名〉［语言］phonography
【表语】biǎoyǔ〈名〉［语言］predicative
【表彰】biǎozhāng〈动〉commend: ～劳动模范 commend model workers ‖ 受到～ receive a commendation
【表针】biǎozhēn〈名〉watch hand
【表征】biǎozhēng〈名〉**1**（征候）symptom **2**［心理］representation
【表侄】biǎozhí〈名〉maternal nephew
【表侄女】biǎozhínǚ〈名〉maternal niece
【表字】biǎozì〈名〉〈旧〉second name: 诸葛亮～孔明。Zhuge Liang was also known as Zhuge Kongming.

婊 biǎo

【婊子】biǎozi〈名〉〈粗〉whore〈粗〉

裱 biǎo〈动〉**1**（指画）mount: 我想把这幅画～一下。I'd like to have this painting mounted. ▸～褙 **2**（裱糊）paper: ～墙 paper the wall

【裱褙】biǎobèi〈动〉mount
【裱糊】biǎohú〈动〉paper: ～房间 paper a room

biào

摽 biào〈动〉**1**（捆紧）fasten together **2**（紧挽胳膊）be arm in arm **3**（频繁接触）attach to **4**（比着干）compete in doing sth.: ▸～劲儿
▸biāo

【摽劲儿】biàojìnr〈动〉〈方〉compete in doing sth.: 两个小组在摽着劲儿干。The two teams are competing with each other.

鳔（鰾）biào〈名〉**1**（鱼鳔）air bladder **2** = 鳔胶 biàojiāo

【鳔胶】biàojiāo〈名〉fish glue

biē

瘪（癟）biē
▸biě

【瘪三】biēsān〈名〉〈方〉bum

憋 biē

A〈动〉suppress: ～着一肚子气 bottle up one's anger ‖ ～足了劲 be bursting with energy ‖ 我实在～不住了。I'm bursting. **B**〈形〉oppressed: 我～得要死，打开窗户吧。I'm stifling in here; let's open the window. ‖ 他心里～得慌。He felt totally suffocated. ▸～闷，～气

【憋闷】biēmen〈形〉suffocated: 胸部感到

～ feel tight in the chest ‖ 他心里很～。 He felt very depressed.
【憋气】biēqì〈动〉1（呼吸不畅） feel suffocated 2（无处发泄） choke with resentment: 那事听了真让人～。 That really made us feel hurt and resentful.
【憋屈】biēqu〈形〉 aggrieved: 感到～ feel aggrieved

b

鳖（鱉、鼈） biē〈名〉［动物］ soft-shelled turtle
【鳖甲】biējiǎ〈名〉［中药］ turtle shell
【鳖裙】biēqún〈名〉 calipash

bié

别¹ bié
A〈动〉1（分开） leave: 久～重逢 reunite after a long separation ‖ 洒泪而～ take one's tearful leave ▸～离, 告～ 2（区分） distinguish: ▸分门～类, 识～, 区～ 3〈方〉（转） turn: ～过身子 turn away ‖ 他的态度一时～不过来。 It's hard for him to change his attitude so quickly.
B〈名〉1（差别） distinction: ▸内外有～, 天壤之～ 2（类别） group: ▸级～, 类～
C〈代〉 other: ～国的模式 foreign models ‖ ～无他法 have no alternative ▸～处, ～名, ～人
D〈形〉1（特殊） unique: ▸～致, 特～ 2（错误） misspelled: ▸～字

别² bié〈动〉1（固定） clip: ～上胸针 pin the brooch on ‖ 胸前～着一朵大红花 have a big red flower pinned to one's chest 2（插着） stick in: 腰里～着一把枪 with a pistol stuck in one's belt ‖ 把门～上。 Bolt the door. 3（绊倒） trip: ～某人一脚 trip sb. 4（阻碍） stop: 他用自行车～我。 He swerved his bike to stop me.

别³ bié〈副〉1（不要） had better not: ～费口舌了! Save your breath! ‖ ～哭了! Stop crying! ‖ ～装腔作势了! Stop posing! 2（表猜测） [used with 是 after it to express supposition]: 你脸色不好，～是病了? You don't look well. Are you ill?
▸biè
【别称】biéchēng〈名〉 another name: 晋是山西的～。 Jin is another name for Shanxi.
【别出心裁】biéchū-xīncái〈成〉 try to be different: 这座建筑的设计～。 The design of this building is out of ordinary.
【别处】biéchù〈名〉 elsewhere: 你去～看看就知道我们的价格最便宜。 Shop around and you'll find our price the best.
【别动队】biédòngduì〈名〉〈旧〉 special detachment
【别管】biéguǎn〈口〉**A**〈连〉（指人） no matter who;（指事） no matter what: ～是谁，违犯法律就要受到惩罚。 Whoever violates the law will be punished. **B**〈动〉1（别在乎） not care about: ～我! 你走吧! Go! Don't worry about me. 2（别干涉） do not interfere: ～闲事! Mind your own business!
【别号】biéhào〈名〉 alias: 苏轼字子瞻，～东坡。 Su Shi, whose courtesy name was Zizhan, was also known as Dongpo.
【别集】biéjí〈名〉 collection of some of an author's works
【别家】biéjiā〈名〉 other households (enterprises, shops, etc.): 除了我们，～商店都关门了。 All shops are closed except ours.
【别价】biéjie〈副〉〈方〉 [used in dissuading] don't: ～，等雨停了再走。 Don't go out until it has stopped raining.
【别具匠心】biéjù-jiàngxīn〈成〉= 独具匠心 dújù-jiàngxīn
【别具一格】biéjù-yīgé〈成〉 have a unique style
【别具只眼】biéjù-zhīyǎn〈成〉 have a unique insight: 作者对人性～。 The author has a unique insight into human nature.
【别开生面】biékāi-shēngmiàn〈成〉 break fresh ground: ～的学术报告会 entirely new sort of symposium
【别来无恙】biélái-wúyàng〈成〉 you have been well, I trust, since we parted
【别离】biélí〈动〉 take leave of: ～家园 leave one's home
【别论】biélùn〈名〉 different matter: 另当～ should then be regarded as a different matter
【别名】biémíng〈名〉 alias: 用～ use an alias
【别情】biéqíng〈名〉〈书〉 sorrow of separation
【别人】biérén〈代〉 someone else: 家里就我一个人，没有～。 I'm home alone. There's no one else.
【别人】biéren〈代〉 other people: ～都同意，就你一个人反对。 Everyone agrees except you. ‖ 她只想到自己，从来不考虑～。 She thinks only of herself and doesn't care about other people.
【别史】biéshǐ〈名〉 privately compiled history
【别树一帜】biéshù-yīzhì〈成〉 have a distinct style of one's own
【别墅】biéshù〈名〉 villa
【别说】biéshuō〈连〉 to say nothing of: ～是一万元，就是一千元我也出不起。 I can't afford to pay 1,000 *yuan*, let alone 10,000 *yuan*.
【别提】biétí〈动〉 you can well imagine: 那里的天气～有多冷了! It is indescribably cold there!
【别无长物】biéwúchángwù〈成〉 have nothing except: 他除了身上穿的，～。 He has nothing but the clothes on his back.
【别无二致】biéwú'èrzhì〈成〉 be identical: 这里的情形和我们那儿～。 The situation here is exactly the same as in our place.
【别绪】biéxù〈名〉〈书〉 sorrow of separation: ▸离情～
【别样】biéyàng **A**〈形〉 different **B**〈名〉 different style
【别有洞天】biéyǒu-dòngtiān〈成〉 place of unique beauty
【别有风味】biéyǒu-fēngwèi〈成〉 have a distinctive flavour: 小镇别有一番风味。 The small town has a distinctive charm of its own.
【别有天地】biéyǒu-tiāndì = 别有洞天 biéyǒu-dòngtiān
【别有用心】biéyǒu-yòngxīn〈成〉 have a hidden agenda: ～的人 someone with an axe to grind
【别针】biézhēn〈名〉1（用于固定） safety pin 2（用于装饰） brooch
【别致】biézhì〈形〉 unique: 这手表样子很～。 The watch has an unconventional design.
【别传】biézhuàn〈名〉 anecdotal biography
【别字】biézì〈名〉1（错字） incorrectly written or mispronounced character 2 = 别号 biéhào

蹩 bié〈动〉〈方〉 sprain: 训练时～了脚 sprain one's ankle in training
【蹩脚】biéjiǎo〈形〉〈方〉 shoddy: ～医生 quack doctor ‖ 他说的英语很～。 He speaks very poor English.

biě

瘪（癟） biě〈形〉 shrivelled: ～谷 blighted grain ‖ 轮胎～了。 The tyre is flat.
▸biē

biè

别（彆） biè〈动〉〈方〉 dissuade
▸bié
【别扭】bièniu〈形〉1（不舒畅） uncomfortable: 心里～ feel bad 2（脾气不好） disagreeable: 脾气～ be of uncertain temper ‖ 他挺～，不好打交道。 He is difficult to deal with. 3（不和睦） not getting along well: 他与妻子老是闹～。 He and his wife are always at loggerheads. 4（不顺畅） awkward: 这篇文章读起来很～。 This article reads awkwardly.
【别嘴】bièzuǐ〈形〉〈方〉 awkward: 这段文字读起来很～。 This passage is awkward to read.

bīn

玢 bīn〈名〉〈古〉 a kind of jade
▸fēn

宾（賓） bīn〈名〉 guest: ▸嘉～, 外～
【宾白】bīnbái〈名〉［戏曲］ spoken parts
【宾格】bīngé〈名〉［语言］ objective case
【宾馆】bīnguǎn〈名〉 hotel
【宾客】bīnkè〈名〉 guests: ～盈门 house full of visitors
【宾朋】bīnpéng〈名〉〈书〉 visitors: 他家常常～满座。 He often has a houseful of guests.
【宾夕法尼亚州】Bīnxīfǎníyàzhōu〈名〉 Pennsylvania
【宾语】bīnyǔ〈名〉［语言］ object
【宾至如归】bīnzhì-rúguī〈成〉 home from home〈英〉; home away from home〈美〉
【宾主】bīnzhǔ〈名〉 host and guest

彬 bīn
【彬彬】bīnbīn〈形〉〈书〉 refined: ▸文质～
【彬彬有礼】bīnbīn-yǒulǐ〈成〉 well-mannered: 对客人～ behave courteously to guests

傧（儐） bīn
【傧相】bīnxiàng〈名〉1〈旧〉（司仪） usher 2（伴娘） bridesmaid 3（伴郎） best man

斌 bīn = 彬 bīn

滨（濱） bīn
A〈名〉 shore: 汉水之～ bank of the Hanshui River ▸海～, 湖～

B〈动〉 border: ～海地区 coastal region ‖ ～江路 road along the river

缤（繽） bīn
【缤纷】bīnfēn〈形〉〈书〉 vivid and colourful: ～天地 colourful world ▸五彩～

槟（檳） bīn
▸bīng
【槟子】bīnzi〈名〉 ❶（指树） binzi tree [species of apple tree] ❷（指果实） binzi fruit

镔（鑌） bīn
【镔铁】bīntiě〈名〉 wrought iron

濒（瀕） bīn〈动〉 ❶（靠近） be close to: 东～大海 border the sea to the east ❷（面临） be on the brink of: ▸～危
【濒近】bīnjìng〈形〉 close to
【濒临】bīnlín〈动〉 ❶（紧靠） border on: ～太平洋 border on the Pacific ❷（面临） be on the brink of: ～灭绝 be on the verge of extinction ‖ ～破产 be close to bankruptcy
【濒死】bīnsǐ〈动〉 be close to death: ～状态 state of impending death
【濒危】bīnwēi〈动〉 ❶（指动植物） be endangered: ～植物 endangered plant ‖ 大熊猫被列为世界～动物。 The giant panda has been listed as one of the endangered animals of the world. ❷（指人） be terminally ill: ～病人 critically ill person
【濒于】bīnyú〈动〉 be on the brink of: ～灭亡 be near extinction ‖ ～破产 be on the brink of bankruptcy

bìn

摈（擯） bìn〈动〉〈书〉 abandon: ～诸门外 shut out ‖ 为众人所～ be rejected by the people
【摈斥】bìnchì〈动〉 dismiss: ～异己 get rid of people who hold dissenting opinions
【摈除】bìnchú〈动〉 dispense with: ～陈规陋习 get rid of outworn conventions and vulgar practices ‖ ～糟粕 discard the dross
【摈弃】bìnqì〈动〉 abandon: ～旧观念 abandon outdated notions ‖ ～陋习 shed outmoded practices

殡（殯） bìn〈动〉 ❶（停放灵柩） lay a coffin in a memorial hall ❷（运送灵柩） carry the body to the burial place or crematorium: ▸～车, 出～
【殡车】bìnchē〈名〉 hearse
【殡殓】bìnliàn〈名〉 place a corpse in a coffin and bring it to the burial place
【殡仪馆】bìnyíguǎn〈名〉 funeral parlour
【殡葬】bìnzàng **A**〈动〉 bury **B**〈名〉 burial ceremony

膑（臏） bìn = 髌 bìn

髌（髕） bìn
A〈名〉 kneecap
B〈动〉〈古〉 chop off the kneecaps as a punishment
【髌骨】bìngǔ〈名〉 kneecap

鬓（鬢） bìn〈名〉 temples: 两～斑白 be going grey at the temples
【鬓发】bìnfà〈名〉 hair on the temples
【鬓角】bìnjiǎo〈名〉 ❶（指部位） temples ❷（指毛发） sideburns; sideboards〈英〉
【鬓脚】bìnjiǎo = 鬓角 bìnjiǎo

bīng

冰 bīng
A〈名〉 ❶〈本〉 ice: ～融化了。 The ice has melted. ‖ 河水结～了。 The river froze over. ▸～天雪地 ❷（冰状物） ice-like object: ▸～糖, 干～
B〈动〉 ❶（使人感到冷） feel cold: 这水～手。 The water feels cold. ❷（使物体变冷） ice: 把饮料～上。 Ice the drinks. ▸～镇
【冰棒】bīngbàng〈方〉= 冰棍儿 bīnggùnr
【冰雹】bīngbáo〈名〉 hail
【冰茶】bīngchá〈名〉 iced tea
【冰碴儿】bīngchár〈名〉〈口〉 ❶（碎冰） small pieces of ice ❷（薄冰） thin coat of ice
【冰场】bīngchǎng〈名〉 ice rink: ▸旱～
【冰川】bīngchuān〈名〉 glacier: ～退缩 glacial recession
【冰川期】bīngchuānqī〈名〉 ice age
【冰床】bīngchuáng〈名〉 sled, sledge, sleigh
【冰镩】bīngcuān〈名〉 ice chisel
【冰袋】bīngdài〈名〉［医学］ ice pack
【冰刀】bīngdāo〈名〉 ice skates
【冰岛】Bīngdǎo〈名〉 Iceland: ～共和国 Republic of Iceland ‖ ～人 Icelander ‖ ～语 Icelandic
【冰灯】bīngdēng〈名〉 ice lantern: ～展 ice lantern show
【冰点】bīngdiǎn〈名〉［物理］ freezing point
【冰雕】bīngdiāo〈名〉 ❶（指艺术） ice carving: ～艺术 art of ice carving ❷（指作品） ice sculpture: ～展 ice sculpture exhibition
【冰冻】bīngdòng〈动〉 freeze: ～季节 freezing season
【冰冻三尺, 非一日之寒】bīng dòng sān chǐ, fēi yī rì zhī hán〈成〉 Rome wasn't built in a day
【冰毒】bīngdú〈名〉 methamphetamine
【冰帆】bīngfān〈名〉 iceboat
【冰封】bīngfēng〈动〉 [of rivers, lakes, ponds, etc.] freeze over
【冰峰】bīngfēng〈名〉 icy peak
【冰盖】bīnggài〈名〉 ice cap
【冰镐】bīnggǎo〈名〉 ice pick
【冰挂】bīngguà〈名〉 glaze ice
【冰柜】bīngguì = 电冰柜 diànbīngguì
【冰棍儿】bīnggùnr〈名〉 ice lolly〈英〉; popsicle〈美〉
【冰花】bīnghuā〈名〉 ❶（薄冰） frost: 窗子上结满了～。 The windows were covered with frost. ❷（指艺术品） iced object of art ❸（雾凇） rime
【冰肌玉骨】bīngjī-yùgǔ〈成〉〈喻〉 ❶（指美女） beautifully pale, pure-looking lady ❷（高洁） noble and unsullied
【冰激凌】bīngjīlíng〈名〉 ice cream: ～蛋卷 ice-cream cone
【冰窖】bīngjiào〈名〉 ice cellar
【冰晶】bīngjīng〈名〉 ice crystal
【冰库】bīngkù〈名〉 freezer
【冰块儿】bīngkuàir〈名〉 ice cube: 要～吗? Would you like some ice cubes?
【冰冷】bīnglěng〈形〉 ice-cold: ～的表情 frosty look ‖ 他手脚～。 His hands and feet are as cold as ice.
【冰凉】bīngliáng〈形〉 ice-cold: 她的手～。 Her hands were like ice.
【冰凌】bīnglíng〈名〉 ice
【冰溜】bīngliù = 冰锥 bīngzhuī
【冰排】bīngpái〈名〉 ice raft
【冰片】bīngpiàn〈名〉［中药］ borneol
【冰期】bīngqī〈名〉 ice age
【冰淇淋】bīngqílín = 冰激凌 bīngjīlíng
【冰碛】bīngqì〈名〉［地质］ moraine: ～湖 morainal lake ‖ ～岩 tillite
【冰橇】bīngqiāo〈名〉 sled
【冰清玉洁】bīngqīng-yùjié = 玉洁冰清 yùjié-bīngqīng
【冰球】bīngqiú〈名〉［体育］ ❶ ▸p. 909（指运动） ice hockey: ～场 hockey rink ❷（指球） puck
【冰山】bīngshān〈名〉 ❶（指山） ice-covered mountain ❷（指巨冰） iceberg ❸〈喻〉（靠山） political backer that cannot be relied on for long
【冰山一角】bīngshān yījiǎo〈成〉 part of the picture
【冰上舞蹈】bīngshàng wǔdǎo〈名〉 ice dance
【冰上运动】bīngshàng yùndòng ▸p. 909〈名〉 ice sports
【冰释】bīngshì〈动〉〈书〉 dissolve: ～前嫌 discard unpleasant memories ‖ 涣然～ be instantly dispelled
【冰霜】bīngshuāng〈名〉 ❶〈本〉 ice and frost ❷〈喻〉（指节操） moral integrity ❸〈喻〉（指神情、态度） austerity: ▸冷若～
【冰坛】bīngtán〈名〉［体育］ the world of ice-sports
【冰炭】bīng-tàn〈名〉〈喻〉 mutually exclusive things
【冰炭不相容】bīng-tàn bù xiāngróng〈成〉 as incompatible as ice and hot coals
【冰糖】bīngtáng〈名〉 crystal rock sugar
【冰糖葫芦】bīngtáng húlu〈名〉 fruit pieces on a stick covered with a layer of caramelized sugar
【冰天雪地】bīngtiān-xuědì〈成〉 world of ice and snow
【冰坨】bīngtuó〈名〉 block of ice
【冰箱】bīngxiāng = 电冰箱 diànbīngxiāng
【冰消瓦解】bīngxiāo-wǎjiě〈成〉〈喻〉 disintegrate
【冰鞋】bīngxié〈名〉 ice skates
【冰雪聪明】bīngxuě-cōngmíng〈成〉 [esp of girls] extremely intelligent
【冰镇】bīngzhèn〈动〉 ice: ～啤酒 iced beer ‖ ～西瓜 iced melon
【冰柱】bīngzhù = 冰锥 bīngzhuī
【冰砖】bīngzhuān〈名〉 ice-cream brick
【冰锥】bīngzhuī〈名〉 icicle

并 Bīng〈名〉 Bing [another name for Taiyuan (太原)]
▸bìng

兵 bīng〈名〉 ❶（武器） weapons: ▸短～相接 ❷（军队） army: 派～ dispatch troops ‖ 散～ stray/disbanded troops ▸调～遣将, 精～, 炮～ ❸（军人） soldier: 当～打仗 join the army and go to war ‖ 招～ recruit ‖ 新～ new recruit ▸～员, 官～, 征～ ❹（军事） warfare: ▸～法, ～书, 纸上谈～ ❺（指棋子） pawn
【兵败如山倒】bīng bài rú shān dǎo〈成〉 an army in flight is like a landslide
【兵变】bīngbiàn〈名〉 mutiny: 发动～ launch a mutiny
【兵不血刃】bīngbùxuèrèn〈成〉 win a military victory without shedding blood

【兵不厌诈】bīngbùyànzhà〈成〉all's fair in love and war
【兵部】Bīngbù〈名〉［历史］War Ministry
【兵车】bīngchē〈名〉1（古）（战车）war chariot 2（军用车）military vehicle
【兵多将广】bīngduō-jiàngguǎng〈成〉have powerful military forces
【兵法】bīngfǎ〈名〉warcraft:《孙子～》*Art of War by Sun Zi*
【兵分两路】bīngfēn-liǎnglù〈成〉the army is separated into two divisions, each taking a different route
【兵符】bīngfú〈名〉〈旧〉1（指凭证）commander's tally 2 = 兵书 bīngshū
【兵戈】bīnggē〈名〉〈书〉1（武器）arms: 诉诸～ resort to war 2（战争）war: ～四起。Wars broke out across the land.
【兵革】bīnggé〈名〉〈书〉1（武器和盔甲）weapons and armour 2（战争）war: ～未息 be still at war
【兵工】bīnggōng〈名〉military industry: ～企业 munitions plant
【兵工厂】bīnggōngchǎng〈名〉munitions factory
【兵贵神速】bīngguìshénsù〈成〉speed is essential in war
【兵荒马乱】bīnghuāng-mǎluàn〈成〉turmoil and chaos of war
【兵火】bīnghuǒ〈名〉〈书〉flames of war: ～连天 flames of war raging rampant ‖ 书稿毁于～。The manuscripts were destroyed in the war.
【兵祸】bīnghuò〈名〉〈书〉scourge of war: ～连年 successive years of disastrous war
【兵家】bīngjiā〈名〉1（古）（指专家）military strategist 2〈书〉（指统帅）military commander: ～必争之地 strategic point
【兵舰】bīngjiàn〈名〉warship
【兵谏】bīngjiàn〈动〉〈旧〉coerce a ruler by force of arms into accepting one's exhortations: 发动～ present an exhortation to the ruler and back it by force
【兵精粮足】bīngjīng-liángzú〈成〉have well-trained troops and abundant supplies
【兵来将挡，水来土掩】bīng lái jiàng dǎng, shuǐ lái tǔ yǎn〈成〉〈喻〉take appropriate measures as the situation calls for
【兵力】bīnglì〈名〉military strength: 部署～ deploy troops ‖ 集中优势～ concentrate superior forces ‖ ～分散 spread one's forces too thinly
【兵连祸结】bīnglián-huòjié〈成〉war-torn
【兵临城下】bīnglínchéngxià〈成〉the city is under siege
【兵乱】bīngluàn〈名〉〈书〉disaster of war: 屡遭～ be war-torn
【兵马】bīngmǎ〈名〉military forces
【兵马未动，粮草先行】bīngmǎ wèidòng, liángcǎo xiānxíng〈成〉food and fodder should go before troops and horses
【兵马俑】bīngmǎyǒng〈名〉terracotta warriors and horses
【兵痞】bīngpǐ〈名〉〈旧〉army ruffian
【兵棋】bīngqí〈名〉formation model
【兵器】bīngqì〈名〉arms: ～工业 weapons industry
【兵强马壮】bīngqiáng-mǎzhuàng〈成〉well-trained and powerful troops
【兵权】bīngquán〈名〉military power: 掌握～ wield military power
【兵戎】bīngróng〈名〉〈书〉arms
【兵戎相见】bīngróng-xiāngjiàn〈成〉meet on the battlefield

> **兵马俑**
>
> Terracotta models of soldiers and cavalry buried in the tomb of the Emperor Qin Shihuang (▸秦始皇), located in Xi'an, Shaanxi Province. Construction of the tomb started in about 221 BC, at the beginning of the Qin Dynasty. The Terracotta Warriors were discovered in 1974. To date, four massive sites have been excavated. The biggest pit is 12,600 sq m in area and contains 6,000 life-size warriors including chariots, charioteers, cavalry soldiers, foot soldiers, and archers arranged in rows in a rectangular military formation. The warriors are moulded extremely realistically, each with unique features.

【兵士】bīngshì〈名〉private
【兵书】bīngshū〈名〉book on the art of war
【兵团】bīngtuán〈名〉1（指军事单位）corps: 陆军第六～ Sixth Army Corps 2（指部队）large military unit: 野战～ field army ‖ 主力～ main force
【兵饷】bīngxiǎng〈名〉〈旧〉soldier's pay and provisions
【兵械】bīngxiè〈名〉armament
【兵蚁】bīngyǐ〈名〉［昆虫］soldier ant
【兵役】bīngyì〈名〉military service: 服～ serve in the army ‖ ～登记 military service register
【兵役法】bīngyìfǎ〈名〉military service law
【兵役制】bīngyìzhì〈名〉conscription: 恢复～ bring back conscription
【兵营】bīngyíng〈名〉military camp
【兵油子】bīngyóuzi〈名〉〈口〉army ruffian
【兵员】bīngyuán〈名〉soldiers: 招募～ conscript soldiers
【兵源】bīngyuán〈名〉military manpower resources: ～充足/不足 sufficient/insufficient military manpower resources
【兵灾】bīngzāi〈名〉〈旧〉war disaster
【兵站】bīngzhàn〈名〉military depot
【兵种】bīngzhǒng〈名〉arm of the services
【兵卒】bīngzú〈名〉〈旧〉soldier

槟（檳）bīng

▸bīn

【槟榔】bīnglang〈名〉1（指树）betel palm 2（指果实）betel nut

bǐng

丙 bǐng

〈名〉1（指天干）third of the ten Heavenly Stems (天干) 2（第三）third
【丙丁】bǐngdīng〈名〉〈书〉fire: 阅后付～ burn a message after reading it
【丙二醇】bǐng'èrchún〈名〉［化学］propylene glycol
【丙肝】bǐnggān〈简称〉= 丙型肝炎
【丙纶】bǐnglún〈名〉［纺织］polypropylene fibre
【丙型肝炎】bǐngxíng gānyán ▸p. 50〈名〉［医学］hepatitis C
【丙种维生素】bǐngzhǒng wéishēngsù〈名〉vitamin C

邴 Bǐng

〈名〉Bing [surname]

秉 bǐng

A〈动〉1〈书〉（握着）grasp: ～笔 hold a writing brush ▸～烛 2〈书〉（掌管）preside over: 共～国事 take concerted charge of state affairs 3（依从）act in accordance with: 一～善意，履行义务 fulfil in good faith all one's obligations ▸～公
B〈量〉bing [an ancient capacity unit in China]
【秉笔直书】bǐngbǐ-zhíshū〈成〉write impartially
【秉承】bǐngchéng〈动〉〈书〉take orders: ～上级指示行事 act according to the instructions of one's superior ‖ ～他人旨意 act on the orders of sb. else
【秉持】bǐngchí〈动〉〈书〉uphold: ～公心 uphold justice
【秉公】bǐnggōng〈副〉impartially: ～办理 handle a matter impartially ‖ ～执法 be impartial in dispensing justice
【秉性】bǐngxìng〈名〉natural disposition: 她～善良。It is her nature to be kind to people. ‖ ～各异。Each has a different disposition.
【秉正】bǐngzhèng〈动〉〈书〉be upright: ～无私 be unbiased and selfless
【秉政】bǐngzhèng〈动〉〈旧〉hold political power: ～经年 be in power for years
【秉烛】bǐngzhú〈动〉〈书〉sit by a lighted candle
【秉烛夜游】bǐngzhú-yèyóu〈成〉〈喻〉make merry while one can

柄 bǐng

A〈名〉1（把儿）handle: 斧/勺～ handle of an axe/a ladle ‖ 剑～ sword hilt 2〈书〉（权力）authority: 国～ state power 3（把柄）handle: ▸把～, 话～, 笑～ 4（指植物）stem: 叶～ leaf stalk
B〈动〉〈书〉control: ▸～权
C〈量〉〈方〉[for objects with handles]: 两～锄头 two hoes
【柄权】bǐngquán〈动〉〈书〉be in power

饼（餅）bǐng

〈名〉1〈本〉round flat cake: 薄～ flat cake ‖ 肉馅～ meat pie ‖ 玉米～ corn cake ▸烧～, 油～ 2（饼状物）sth. in the shape of a cake: ▸柿～, 铁～
【饼铛】bǐngchēng〈名〉baking pan
【饼肥】bǐngféi〈名〉fertilizer cake
【饼干】bǐnggān〈名〉biscuit〈英〉; cookie〈美〉
【饼子】bǐngzi〈名〉pancake

炳 bǐng〈书〉

A〈形〉shining: ～如日月 as bright as the sun and the moon
B〈动〉shine down on: 日月～天。The sun and the moon shine in the sky. ▸彪～

屏 bǐng

〈动〉1（放弃）discard: ▸～弃 2（抑止）hold (one's breath): ～住呼吸 hold one's breath
▸píng
【屏除】bǐngchú〈动〉get rid of: ～恶习 get rid of bad habits ‖ ～私心 dismiss all selfish considerations
【屏迹】bǐngjì〈动〉〈书〉1（收敛行踪）go into hiding: ～海外 lie low abroad 2（归隐）retire from the world: ～山村 retire to a mountain village
【屏绝】bǐngjué〈动〉〈书〉brush aside: ～交际 isolate oneself from social activities ‖ ～往来 break off social intercourse
【屏气】bǐngqì〈动〉hold one's breath
【屏气凝神】bǐngqì-níngshén〈成〉hold one's breath with concentration
【屏弃】bǐngqì〈动〉abandon: ～前嫌 discard previous animosity ‖ ～杂念 brush aside distracting thoughts

【屏退】bǐngtuì〈动〉〈书〉**1**（使离开）force sb. to retire: ～左右 order the attendants to retire **2**〈书〉（隐退）retire from public life: ～乡间 retire to the country

【屏息】bǐngxī〈动〉hold one's breath: ～静听 listen with bated breath

禀¹（稟） bǐng〈动〉〈书〉**1**（赐予）endow (sb. with sth.): ▸～赋 **2**（承受）take: ▸～承

禀²（稟） bǐng

A〈动〉〈书〉report: 待我～过家父，再来告知。I'll let you know after I've consulted my father.

B〈名〉〈旧〉official report: 具～详报 report in great detail

【禀报】bǐngbào〈动〉〈书〉report to one's superior: 据实～ report the truth

【禀呈】bǐngchéng〈动〉〈书〉submit: ～上级 submit a report to higher authorities

【禀承】bǐngchéng = 秉承 bǐngchéng

【禀赋】bǐngfù〈名〉gift: ～聪颖 be endowed with great intelligence ‖ ～很高 be gifted with rare intelligence ‖ 他没有音乐的～。He doesn't have a gift for music.

【禀告】bǐnggào〈动〉〈书〉report to one's superior: ～官署 report to the government agency in charge

【禀明】bǐngmíng〈动〉〈书〉explain to one's superior: ～原委 tell the whole story

【禀受】bǐngshòu〈动〉〈书〉be endowed with: 他～了母亲的善良和父亲的慷慨。He inherited his mother's kind-heartedness and his father's generosity.

【禀性】bǐngxìng〈名〉nature: ～仁慈 have a merciful disposition ‖ ～善良 be kind by nature ‖ 江山易改，～难移。A leopard cannot change its spots.

bìng

并¹（併） bìng〈动〉combine: 把两张桌子～在一起 put the two desks together ▸～力, 合～, 兼～

并²（並） bìng

A〈动〉be side by side: ～排坐 sit side by side ‖ 肩～肩 shoulder to shoulder ▸～蒂莲, ～驾齐驱

B〈副〉**1**（同时）simultaneously: 数罪～罚 concurrent punishment of several crimes ▸～进, ～举, 相提～论 **2**（都）together: 举国～受其害。The whole country fell victim to it. **3**（用于加强否定语气）actually: 翻译～不比创作容易。Translation is in no way easier than creative writing. ‖ 我～不想难为你。I have no intention of embarrassing you.

C〈连〉and: 大会讨论～通过了董事会的工作报告。The meeting discussed and approved the report on the work of the board of directors.

▸Bìng

【并案】bìng'àn〈动〉combine two or more related cases: ～审理 combine cases and try together

【并存】bìngcún〈动〉coexist: 机遇和挑战～。The opportunity and the challenge go hand in hand. ‖ 两种体制～是一个伟大的构想。The coexistence of the two systems is a great conception.

【并蒂莲】bìngdìlián〈名〉〈喻〉devoted couple

【并发】bìngfā〈动〉erupt simultaneously: ～肺炎 be complicated by pneumonia

【并发症】bìngfāzhèng〈名〉complication: 引起～ cause complications

【并非】bìngfēi〈动〉〈书〉be actually not: 事实～如此。That's not actually the case.

【并购】bìnggòu〈名〉mergers and acquisitions

【并轨】bìngguǐ〈动〉integrate

【并驾齐驱】bìngjià-qíqū〈成〉advance at equal pace: 两匹马～冲过终点。The two horses were neck and neck at the finish.

【并肩】bìngjiān **A**〈动〉be side by side: ～而行 walk side by side **B**〈副〉closely: ～作战 fight side by side

【并进】bìngjìn〈动〉advance side by side: 与时代～ keep up with the times ▸齐头～

【并举】bìngjǔ〈动〉develop simultaneously: 工农业～ develop agriculture and industry at the same time

【并力】bìnglì〈动〉〈书〉join forces: ～坚守阵地 hold the ground with joint efforts

【并立】bìnglì〈动〉coexist: 战国时期，七雄～。Seven powerful states existed simultaneously in the Warring States Period.

【并联】bìnglián **A**〈动〉connect in parallel **B**〈名〉parallel connection: ～装置 parallel arrangement ‖ ～电路 parallel circuit

【并列】bìngliè〈动〉stand side by side: ～榜首 be side by side at the top of the successful candidates list ‖ ～第一 tie for first place

【并拢】bìnglǒng〈动〉join together: 两腿要～。Keep your legs together.

【并茂】bìngmào〈形〉〈书〉both being remarkable: ▸声情～, 图文～

【并排】bìngpái〈动〉be side by side: ～行驶 run side by side ‖ 四人～坐着 sit four abreast

【并且】bìngqiě〈连〉**1**（表示并列）and: 讨论～通过一项计划 discuss and approve a plan **2**（表示递进）besides: 租金合理，～地段极佳。The rent is reasonable and furthermore the location is excellent.

【并吞】bìngtūn〈动〉swallow up

【并网】bìngwǎng〈动〉［电气］［通信］synchronize a network: ～发电 be connected to a power grid

【并行】bìngxíng〈动〉**1**（并排行进）walk side by side: 携手～ go hand in hand ‖ 他俩骑车～。They cycled next to one another. **2**（同时进行）carry on simultaneously: ～领土管辖权 practise concurrent territorial jurisdiction

【并行不悖】bìngxíng-bùbèi〈成〉run parallel without coming into conflict: 两种政策可以～。These two policies may both be carried out without one conflicting with the other.

【并用】bìngyòng〈动〉use simultaneously: 手脚～ use both hands and feet

【并重】bìngzhòng〈动〉attach equal importance to: 预防与治疗～ place equal emphasis on prevention and cure

病 bìng **p. 50**

A〈名〉**1**（疾病）disease: 常见～ common disease ‖ 血液～ blood disease ‖ 他的～治好了。He is cured of his disease. ▸～情, ～症, 职业～ **2**（弊端）evil: ▸弊～ **3**（错误）fault: ▸语～

B〈动〉fall ill: ～得不轻 be seriously ill ‖ ～死 die of a disease ‖ 突然～了 be taken ill suddenly

【病案】bìng'àn〈名〉medical record

【病包儿】bìngbāor〈名〉〈口〉chronic invalid

【病变】bìngbiàn〈名〉pathological change: 引起～ bring about pathological changes

【病病歪歪】bìngbing-wāiwāi〈形〉sickly-looking: 瞧他～的样子，一天还总不闲着。He looked very feeble but he never took a rest all day.

【病残】bìngcán〈名〉**1**（指状态）illness and disability **2**（指人）the sick and the disabled: ～救济金 invalidity benefit ▸老弱～

【病程】bìngchéng〈名〉course of a disease

【病虫害】bìngchónghài〈名〉plant diseases and insect pests: 防治～ control plant diseases and insect pests

【病床】bìngchuáng〈名〉sickbed: 守在～旁 keep by sb.'s sickbed

【病从口入，祸从口出】bìngcóngkǒurù, huòcóngkǒuchū〈俗〉disease enters through the mouth and trouble comes out of it

【病毒】bìngdú〈名〉virus: 感染～ be infected with a virus ‖ 清除～ eradicate the virus ‖ ～抗体 viral antibody ‖ 艾滋病～ AIDS virus ▸计算机～

【病毒携带者】bìngdú xiédàizhě〈名〉virus carrier: 艾滋病～ AIDS carrier

【病毒性】bìngdúxìng〈形〉viral: ～流感 flu

【病笃】bìngdǔ〈形〉〈书〉critically ill

【病房】bìngfáng〈名〉ward

【病夫】bìngfū〈名〉〈书〉sick person

【病根】bìnggēn〈名〉**1**（指疾病）old complaint: 这是坐月子落下的～。This is her old childbearing complaint. **2**〈喻〉（指灾祸、挫折等）cause of trouble: 企业亏损的～ cause of the loss in the enterprise

【病故】bìnggù〈动〉die of illness

【病害】bìnghài〈名〉plant disease: 棉花易受各种～。Various diseases attack the cotton plant.

【病号】bìnghào〈名〉sick person: 老～ chronic invalid

【病号饭】bìnghàofàn〈名〉patient's diet

【病候】bìnghòu〈名〉symptoms of illness

【病患】bìnghuàn〈名〉**1**（疾病）disease **2**（病人）sick person: 救治～ bring a patient out of danger

【病急乱投医】bìng jí luàn tóu yī〈俗〉〈喻〉desperate people will try anything

【病家】bìngjiā〈名〉patient and his/her family

【病假】bìngjià〈名〉sick leave: 请三天～ ask for three days' sick leave ‖ 休～ be on sick leave ‖ ～工资 sick-pay ‖ ～条 sick note

【病句】bìngjù〈名〉faulty sentence: 修改～ correct a wrong sentence

【病菌】bìngjūn〈名〉germ

【病况】bìngkuàng〈名〉patient's condition

【病来如山倒，病去如抽丝】bìng lái rú shān dǎo, bìng qù rú chōu sī〈俗〉diseases come like an avalanche but it takes time for them to go away

【病理】bìnglǐ〈名〉pathology: ～生理学 pathological physiology

【病历】bìnglì〈名〉medical record

【病例】bìnglì〈名〉medical case: ～报告 case report

【病魔】bìngmó〈名〉serious illness: ～缠身 be afflicted with a chronic disease

【病情】bìngqíng〈名〉patient's condition: ～恶化 exacerbation of the disease ‖ 他的～加重了。He has taken a turn for the worse. ‖ ～有所好转。The patient's on the mend.

【病区】bìngqū〈名〉sick ward

【病人】bìngrén〈名〉sick person

b

病痛

哪儿痛?

■ 汉语用“疼”或“痛”，而英语有不同的词或短语:

哪儿疼?
= Where does it hurt?

告诉我哪里痛
= Tell me where it hurts

我眼痛
= My eyes hurt
或 My eyes are hurting me
或 My eyes are sore
或 I have sore eyes

我耳朵疼
= My ear aches
或 I have earache

我浑身痛
= I'm aching all over

我背部有点痛
= I've got a slight ache in my back

我感到腿部一阵剧痛
= I felt a sharp pain in my leg

我有各种疼痛
= I have various aches and pains

事故

小王伤了背
= Xiao Wang hurt his back

王励车祸中受了轻伤
= Wang Li was slightly injured in the car crash

他在事故中多处受伤
= He sustained multiple injuries in the accident

他在火灾中严重烧伤
= He was badly burnt in the fire

她断了左臂
= She broke her left arm

她扭伤了手腕
= She sprained her wrist

扭伤很重
= It was a bad sprain

慢性病

他心脏弱
= He has a weak heart

他胃不好
= He has a weak stomach

他背老痛
= He has a bad back

他有蛀牙
= He has bad teeth

他有肾病
= He has kidney trouble

生病

■ 注意 ill 和 sick 的用法:

他病了
= He is ill

他生病了
= He has fallen ill

照顾生病的孩子
= to look after a sick child

感到恶心
= to feel sick

■ 英语动词 have 几乎可以和所有表示疼痛或疾病的词搭配，表示患有某种病:

患皮肤癌
= to have skin cancer

腹泻／拉肚子
= to have diarrhoea

有支气管炎
= to have bronchitis

患风湿
= to have rheumatism

发高烧
= to have a high fever

■ 汉语里表达得、患、感染上或传染上某种病时，英语常用 catch、get、develop 或 contract:

得肺炎
= to catch pneumonia

患疟疾
= to catch malaria

食物中毒
= to get food poisoning

患流感
= to get flu

感染艾滋病
= to contract Aids
或 to get Aids

患麻疹
= to develop measles
或 to get measles

■ 英语里有些表示病痛的名词既是可数的，又是不可数的:

牙痛
= to have a toothache
或 to have toothache

背痛
= to have a backache
或 to have backache

肚子痛
= to have a stomach ache
或 to have stomach ache

■ 英语里有些表示病痛的名词是可数的，但一般用单数形式，前面加不定冠词:

患感冒
= to catch a cold

患头痛
= to have a headache

患皮肤感染
= to get an inflammation of the skin

■ 汉语表达疾病突发时，用“一阵”、“发作”等，而英语常用 bout、attack 或 fit 等:

突发流感
= to have a bout of flu

突发神经紧张
= to have a bout of nerves

哮喘病发作
= to have an attack of asthma

心脏病发作
= to have a heart attack

一阵咳嗽
= to have a coughing fit

癫痫发作
= to have an epileptic fit

治疗

他正接受心脏病的治疗
= He is being treated for heart trouble

他吃了些咳嗽药
= He took some cough medicine
或 He took some cough medicine

我给开了感冒药片
= I have been prescribed tablets for flu

这种药有处方时才卖
= This medicine is only available on prescription

医生正在为他做手术
= The surgeon is operating on him

他左腿动过手术
= He had an operation on his left leg

我接种过水痘
= I was vaccinated/immunized against chickenpox
或 I received/had a vaccination against chickenpox
或 I had a chickenpox vaccination

他打了感冒针
= He had flu injections

护士给他打了感冒针
= The nurse gave him flu injections

感冒胶囊
= capsules for colds
或 cold relief capsules

流感冲剂
= sachets of powder for flu
或 sachets of flu powder

维生素片
= vitamin pills
或 vitamin tablets

晕车药
= travel sickness tablets

眼药水
= eye drops

止咳糖浆
= cough syrup

针灸疗法
= acupuncture therapy

喉咙喷剂
= throat spray

烧伤药膏
= burn treatment cream

【病容】bìngróng〈名〉sickly look: 她一脸～。She looks ill.
【病入膏肓】bìngrùgāohuāng〈成〉be beyond recovery
【病史】bìngshǐ〈名〉medical history
【病势】bìngshì〈名〉patient's condition: ～加重/减轻 one's condition is worsening /improving
【病逝】bìngshì〈动〉〈书〉die of illness
【病榻】bìngtà〈名〉〈书〉sickbed: 守候在母亲的～前 keep watch at one's mother's sickbed
【病态】bìngtài〈名〉1〈本〉sickly appearance: 故作～ pretend to be ill 2〈喻〉morbid state: ～经济 sick economy ‖ ～社会 diseased society ‖ ～心理 morbid mentality
【病体】bìngtǐ〈名〉sick body
【病痛】bìngtòng〈名〉slight illness: 减轻～ alleviate the ailment
【病退】bìngtuì〈动〉retire on account of illness
【病危】bìngwēi〈形〉dangerously ill
【病危通知】bìngwēi tōngzhī〈名〉critical condition notice to the patient's family: 下～ issue a critical condition notice about a patient
【病象】bìngxiàng〈名〉symptom
【病休】bìngxiū〈动〉be on sick leave
【病秧子】bìngyāngzi = 病包儿 bìngbāor
【病疫】bìngyì〈名〉epidemic disease
【病因】bìngyīn〈名〉pathogeny: ～仍然无法确定。The cause of the disease is still in doubt.
【病友】bìngyǒu〈名〉fellow patient
【病愈】bìngyù〈动〉get over an illness: ～出院 recover and leave hospital
【病员】bìngyuán〈名〉sick person
【病原】bìngyuán〈名〉pathogeny
【病原虫】bìngyuánchóng〈名〉protozoon
【病原体】bìngyuántǐ〈名〉pathogen
【病源】bìngyuán〈名〉cause of a disease
【病院】bìngyuàn〈名〉specialized hospital: 结核/精神～ tuberculosis/mental hospital
【病灶】bìngzào〈名〉focus of infection
【病征】bìngzhēng〈名〉symptom
【病症】bìngzhèng〈名〉disease, illness: 疑难～ difficult and complicated cases
【病株】bìngzhū〈名〉diseased plant
【病状】bìngzhuàng〈名〉symptom: 早期～ early symptoms

摒 bìng〈动〉get rid of

【摒除】bìngchú〈动〉get rid of: ～杂念 brush aside random thoughts
【摒挡】bìngdàng〈动〉〈书〉put in order: ～日常事务 deal with daily routines
【摒绝】bìngjué〈动〉brush aside: ～一切应酬 decline all social activities
【摒弃】bìngqì〈动〉abandon: ～前嫌 let bygones be bygones

bō

拨（撥）bō

A〈动〉1（号码）dial: ～打电话 make a phone call 2（火）poke: ～火 stir up the fire 3（频道）change over to 4（钟表）set: 把表～到七点钟 set the watch to 7 o'clock 5（琴弦）pluck: ～动琴弦 pluck the strings 6（配给）assign: ～款 earmark some cash ‖ 给急救中心～五个护士 assign five nurses to the emergency centre 7（调转）turn round: 他～头便走。He turned round and went off. B〈量〉（指人）group;（指物）batch: 分两～儿干活 work in two groups ‖ 轮～儿休息 rest by turns
【拨备】bōbèi〈动〉［金融］make provisions
【拨发】bōfā〈动〉allocate and distribute: ～救灾物资 allocate and distribute disaster relief
【拨付】bōfù〈动〉allocate money: ～研究经费 earmark and pay out a sum of money for research
【拨号】bōhào〈动〉dial a number: ～键 dialling key ‖ ～网络 dial-up network
【拨火棍】bōhuǒgùn〈名〉poker
【拨开乌云见青天】bōkāi wūyún jiàn qīngtiān〈俗〉〈喻〉dispel misrule and restore social justice
【拨款】bōkuǎn A〈动〉allocate money: ～救灾 allocate money to help fight the disaster ‖ 政府大量～，发展山区教育。The government has allocated a large sum of money for promoting education in mountain areas. B〈名〉money allocated: 减少/增加～ reduce/increase appropriations ‖ 财政～ financial allocations ‖ 国家～ state appropriation
【拨拉】bōla〈动〉move: ～算盘珠子 move the beads on the abacus ‖ 把锅里的肉～两下。Stir the meat in the pan.
【拨浪鼓】bōlanggǔ〈名〉rattle-drum
【拨乱反正】bōluàn-fǎnzhèng〈成〉bring order out of chaos
【拨弄】bōnong〈动〉1（指用手）fiddle with: ～琴弦 pluck the strings 2（操控）order about: 别想～他们! Don't try to order them around! 3（挑拨）stir up: ～是非 stir things up
【拨冗】bōrǒng〈动〉〈书〉〈套〉squeeze out some time from a busy schedule of routine trivialities: 如蒙～相助，本人将不胜感激。If you can spare a little time to help me, I should take it as an extraordinary kindness.
【拨云见日】bōyún-jiànrì〈成〉〈喻〉1（指公正）restore the rule of justice 2（指教学）be enlightened by sb.'s teaching
【拨子】bōzi A〈名〉［音乐］pick, plectrum B〈量〉group: 一～人马 a group of people

波 bō

〈名〉1（水纹）wave: ▸～涛, 水～ 2〈喻〉（风波）unexpected turn of events: 一～未平，一～又起。One trouble follows closely on the heels of the next. 3（眼神）wink: ▸秋～, 眼～ 4［物理］wave: ▸冲击～, 电磁～, 声～
【波长】bōcháng〈名〉［物理］wavelength
【波荡】bōdàng〈动〉rise and fall: 船随着海浪～。The ship heaved with the sea waves.
【波导】bōdǎo〈名〉［物理］wave guide
【波动】bōdòng〈动〉fluctuate: 价格～ price fluctuation ‖ 情绪～ experience mood swings ‖ 这一决定在证券市场上引起了一阵阵～。The decision caused ripples in the stock market.
【波段】bōduàn〈名〉wave band: 中波～ medium wave band
【波多黎各】Bōduōlígè〈名〉Puerto Rico: ～人 Puerto Rican ‖ ～自由联邦 Commonwealth of Puerto Rico
【波多诺伏】Bōduōnuòfú〈名〉Porto Novo
【波恩】Bō'ēn〈名〉Bonn
【波尔卡】bō'ěrkǎ〈名〉polka
【波峰】bōfēng〈名〉［物理］wave crest
【波幅】bōfú〈名〉［物理］amplitude
【波哥大】Bōgēdà〈名〉Bogotá
【波谷】bōgǔ〈名〉［物理］trough
【波黑】Bō-Hēi〈名〉Bosnia-Herzegovina: ～共和国 Republic of Bosnia-Herzegovina
【波及】bōjí〈动〉spread to: 骚乱已经～全岛。The rioting has already affected the whole island.
【波谲云诡】bōjué-yúnguǐ = 云谲波诡 yúnjué-bōguǐ
【波兰】Bōlán〈名〉Poland: ～共和国 Republic of Poland ‖ ～人 Pole ‖ ～语 Polish
【波澜】bōlán〈名〉〈书〉billows: 激起感情上的～ stir up a surge of emotion ‖ ～起伏 one cliffhanger after another
【波澜壮阔】bōlán-zhuàngkuò〈成〉surging forward with great momentum: ～的群众运动 surging mass movement
【波浪】bōlàng〈名〉wave: ～起伏。Waves rise and fall. ‖ ～拍打着海岸。The waves lapped the seashore.
【波利尼西亚】Bōlìníxīyà〈名〉Polynesia: ～人 Polynesian ‖ ～语 Polynesian
【波罗的海】Bōluódìhǎi〈名〉Baltic Sea
【波罗蜜】bōluómì〈名〉1［佛教］Paramita 2 = 菠萝蜜 bōluómì
【波罗蜜多】bōluómìduō = 波罗蜜 bōluómì 1
【波洛奈兹舞】bōluònàizīwǔ〈名〉polonaise
【波普文化】bōpǔ wénhuà〈名〉pop culture
【波普艺术】bōpǔ yìshù〈名〉pop art
【波谱】bōpǔ〈名〉［物理］spectrum: ～仪 spectrometer
【波士顿】Bōshìdùn〈名〉Boston
【波束】bōshù〈名〉［物理］beam
【波斯】Bōsī〈名〉Persia: ～人 Persian ‖ ～语 Persian
【波斯猫】bōsīmāo〈名〉Persian cat
【波斯尼亚和黑塞哥维那共和国】Bōsīníyà hé Hēisàigēwéinà Gònghéguó〈名〉Republic of Bosnia and Herzegovina
【波斯湾】Bōsīwān〈名〉Persian Gulf
【波涛】bōtāo〈名〉billows: 掀起～ raise waves ‖ ～滚滚。The waves rolled on. ‖ ～汹涌。The sea billows.
【波纹】bōwén〈名〉ripple: 卷发上的～ waves in one's hair
【波伊斯郡】Bōyīsījùn〈名〉Powys
【波音】bōyīn〈名〉Boeing: 一架～747飞机 a Boeing 747 aircraft
【波源】bōyuán〈名〉［物理］wave source
【波折】bōzhé〈名〉twists and turns: 几经～ experience many ups and downs ‖ 事情出现了～。The event took an unexpected turn.

玻 bō

【玻壳】bōké〈名〉(TV tube) bulb
【玻利维亚】Bōlìwéiyà〈名〉Bolivia: ～共和国 Republic of Bolivia ‖ ～人 Bolivian
【玻璃】bōli〈名〉1〈本〉glass: ～瓶 glass bottle ‖ 防弹～ bulletproof glass ‖ 安全～ safety glass 2（玻璃状物）plastic: ▸～丝, ～纸, 有机～
【玻璃板】bōlibǎn〈名〉glass pane
【玻璃厂】bōlichǎng〈名〉glassworks
【玻璃钢】bōligāng〈名〉glassed steel
【玻璃幕墙】bōli mùqiáng〈名〉glass wall
【玻璃纱】bōlishā〈名〉［纺织］organdie
【玻璃丝】bōlisī〈名〉glass fibre
【玻璃体】bōlitǐ〈名〉［解剖］crystalline lens
【玻璃纤维】bōli xiānwéi〈名〉fibre glass
【玻璃纸】bōlizhǐ〈名〉cellophane

b

【玻璃砖】bōlizhuān〈名〉1（指玻璃制品）plate glass 2（厚玻璃）glass block

趵 bō〈动〉〈书〉kick
▸bào

【趵趵】bōbō〈拟〉〈书〉sound of stamping feet

钵（鉢、缽） bō〈名〉1（陶碗）earthen bowl: 饭～ big rice bowl 2（僧人的碗具）alms bowl: ▸衣～

般 bō
▸bān

【般若】bōrě〈名〉［佛教］highest wisdom

饽（餑） bō

【饽饽】bōbo〈名〉〈方〉1（特指面点）cake: 棒子面～ maize cake 2（糕点）pastry

剥（剝） bō = 剥 bāo
▸bāo

【剥夺】bōduó〈动〉divest: ～某人的财产 strip sb. of his property ‖ ～某人的人身自由 deprive sb. of his personal liberty ‖ ～某人的政治权利终身 deprive sb. of his political rights for life

【剥茧抽丝】bōjiǎn-chōusī〈成〉〈喻〉make a painstaking investigation or examination

【剥离】bōlí〈动〉come off: 表土～ topsoil stripping ‖ 胎盘～ placental abruption

【剥落】bōluò〈动〉peel off: 灰泥从墙上～。The plaster is coming off the wall. ‖ 油漆开始～。The paint is beginning to flake off.

【剥蚀】bōshí〈动〉1（侵蚀）erode: 被风雨～ be worn away by the weather ‖ 峭壁表面遭到～。The face of the cliff had suffered erosion. 2（盗用）embezzle bit by bit

【剥削】bōxuē〈动〉exploit: 被～阶级 exploited classes ‖ 残酷～ ruthless exploitation

【剥削阶级】bōxuē jiējí〈名〉exploiting class

菠 bō

【菠菜】bōcài〈名〉spinach

【菠薐菜】bōléngcài〈方〉= 菠菜 bōcài

【菠萝】bōluó〈名〉pineapple

【菠萝蜜】bōluómì〈名〉jackfruit

铍（鈹） bō〈名〉［化学］bohrium (Bh)

播 bō〈动〉1（播种）sow: ～小麦 sow wheat ‖ 春～ spring seeding ‖ ～下仇恨的种子 sow the seeds of hatred ▸～种, 条～ 2（广播）broadcast: ～新闻 broadcast news ‖ 现场直～ live report from the scene ▸～送, ～音, 广～ 3〈书〉（迁移）migrate: ～迁 migrate

【播报】bōbào〈动〉broadcast: ～新闻 broadcast the news

【播出】bōchū〈动〉broadcast: 在电视上～ be broadcast on the TV ‖ 这档节目在中午～。This programme is on air at noon.

【播发】bōfā〈动〉broadcast: 全文～总统的国情咨文 broadcast the entire State of the Union Message of the president

【播放】bōfàng〈动〉1（放映）play on air: ～电影插曲 play some hits from movie soundtracks ‖ ～广告 air an advertisement ‖ ～激光唱片 play a CD ‖ DVD～器 DVD player 2（电视转播）televise: 向全国～比赛实况 televise a match live nationwide

【播放器】bōfàngqì〈名〉audio player: MP3～ MP3 player

【播讲】bōjiǎng〈动〉present over radio/on TV: ～科学知识 give a radio/TV talk on science ‖ ～英语 teach English

【播客】bōkè〈名〉podcast: ～发布 podcasting ‖ ～发布者 podcaster

【播弄】bōnong〈动〉manipulate

【播弄是非】bōnong-shìfēi〈成〉spread rumours and sow dissension

【播撒】bōsǎ〈动〉scatter: ～农药 dust crops with a pesticide ‖ 飞机～树种 broadcast seeds of trees by plane

【播送】bōsòng〈动〉transmit: 向全世界～节目 broadcast programmes all over the world

【播音】bōyīn〈动〉transmit: 开始/停止～ go on/off the air ‖ ～室 broadcasting studio ‖ ～员 announcer ‖ ～到此结束。That concludes our programme for this transmission.

【播映】bōyìng〈动〉televise: ～国产故事片 televise a domestically made feature film

【播云】bōyún〈名〉［气象］cloud seeding

【播种】bōzhǒng〈动〉sow seeds: ～机 sowing machine ‖ 他在～。He is sowing seeds.

【播种】bōzhòng〈动〉grow by sowing seeds: ～冬小麦 sow the field with winter wheat ‖ 最佳～时间 best time to sow

bó

孛 bó〈书〉= 勃 bó

伯¹ bó〈名〉1（伯父）uncle 2（长兄）eldest among brothers: ～兄 eldest brother 3〈套〉（父辈年长的男子）uncle: 世～ uncle

伯² bó〈名〉earl, count: ▸～爵
▸bǎi

【伯伯】bóbo〈名〉1（伯父）uncle 2（父辈年长的男子）uncle: 王～ Uncle Wang

【伯尔尼】Bó'ěrní〈名〉Berne

【伯父】bófù〈名〉1 ▸**p. 588**（父亲的哥哥）uncle 2〈套〉（父辈年长的男子）uncle

【伯爵】bójué〈名〉（在不列颠）earl;（在欧洲大陆）count: ～夫人 countess

【伯克郡】Bókèjùn〈名〉Berkshire

【伯劳】bóláo〈名〉［鸟类］shrike

【伯乐】Bólè〈名〉〈喻〉good judge of talent

【伯利兹】Bólìzī〈名〉Belize

【伯母】bómǔ ▸**p. 588**〈名〉aunt

【伯仲】bózhòng〈名〉〈书〉match: 不分～ be on a par ‖ ～之间 about the same

【伯仲叔季】bó-zhòng-shū-jì〈名〉sequence of brothers

【伯祖】bózǔ ▸**p. 588**〈名〉great-uncle

【伯祖母】bózǔmǔ ▸**p. 588**〈名〉great-aunt

驳¹（駁） bó〈动〉refute: 我～得他无话可说。My rebuttal left him speechless. ▸～论, 反～, 批～

驳²（駁） bó〈形〉〈书〉1（颜色杂）variegated: ▸斑～ 2（混杂）mixed: ▸～杂

驳³（駁） bó
A〈动〉transport by barge: ▸～运
B〈名〉barge: 铁～ iron barge

【驳岸】bó'àn〈名〉low stone wall protecting an embankment from erosion by water

【驳斥】bóchì〈动〉refute: ～对方 contradict an opponent ‖ ～谬论 refute a fallacy

【驳船】bóchuán〈名〉barge

【驳倒】bódǎo〈动〉demolish sb.'s argument: 用事实～对方 refute one's opponent using facts ‖ 真理是驳不倒的。Truth is irrefutable.

【驳回】bóhuí〈动〉1（不批准）reject: ～请求 turn down a request ‖ ～专利申请 reject a patent application 2［法律］overrule: ～上诉，维持原判 reject an appeal and uphold the original verdict ‖ 判决被最高法院～。The judgement was overruled by the Supreme Court.

【驳价】bójià〈动〉haggle over prices: 他从不～。He never bargains over prices.

【驳壳枪】bókéqiāng〈名〉Mauser pistol

【驳论】bólùn〈动〉〈书〉explain one's views by refuting opposite views

【驳面子】bó miànzi〈动〉offend sb.'s sensibilities: 我只是说了句实话，并不是有意驳他的面子。I had no intention of hurting his feelings; I just told the truth.

【驳难】bónàn〈动〉〈书〉condemn as false

【驳议】bóyì〈名〉〈书〉rebuttal

【驳运】bóyùn〈动〉transport by lighter

【驳杂】bózá〈形〉mixed: 品种～ be heterogeneous in variety

【驳正】bózhèng〈动〉〈书〉criticize and correct

帛 bó〈名〉〈书〉silk: 布～ clothing ▸玉～

【帛画】bóhuà〈名〉〈古〉painting on silk

【帛书】bóshū〈名〉〈古〉book copied on silk

泊¹ bó〈动〉1（停靠）anchor: 把船～在海湾 anchor a boat in a bay ▸停～ 2（停留）stay for a time: ▸漂～ 3（停放）park: ～车 park a car

泊² bó〈形〉indifferent to fame and gain: ▸淡～
▸pō

【泊车】bóchē〈动〉park a vehicle

【泊地】bódì〈名〉［交通］mooring

【泊位】bówèi〈名〉［交通］1（指船只）berth 2（指车辆）parking place: 深水～ deep-water berth ‖ 汽车～ car park place

柏 bó
▸bǎi, bò

【柏忌】bójì〈名〉［体育］bogey: 双～ double-bogey

【柏拉图】Bólātú〈名〉Plato

【柏林】Bólín〈名〉Berlin

勃 bó〈形〉〈书〉exuberant: ▸蓬～

【勃勃】bóbó〈形〉thriving: 生机～ full of life ▸生气～, 兴致～, 野心～

【勃发】bófā〈动〉1（旺盛）thrive: 生机～ be dynamic ‖ 诗兴～ be seized with a

sudden desire to write poetry ‖ 英姿～ dashing and spirited **2**（爆发） break out: ～事件 sudden incidents

【勃郎宁】bólángníng〈名〉Browning pistol: ～自动步枪 Browning automatic rifle

【勃然】 bórán 〈形〉〈书〉 **1**（旺盛） thriving: 乡镇企业～而兴。 Township and village enterprises quickly began to flourish. **2**（愤然） agitated: ～不悦 be obviously unhappy ‖ ～大怒 fly into a rage

【勃兴】bóxīng〈动〉〈书〉 flourish quickly: 高科技开发区的～ vigorous growth of the hi-tech development zones

钹（鈸） bó〈名〉 cymbals

铂（鉑） bó 〈名〉［化学］ platinum (Pt)

舶 bó〈名〉 big boat: 船～ ships

【舶来品】bóláipǐn〈名〉〈旧〉 imports

脖 bó〈名〉 **1** ▸**p. 614** （颈） neck **2**（颈状物） sth. in the shape of a neck: 烟囱拐～儿 neck of a stovepipe

【脖颈儿】bógěngr〈名〉 nape

【脖梗儿】bógěngr = 脖颈儿 bógěngr

【脖领儿】bólǐngr〈名〉〈方〉 coat collar

【脖子】bózi〈名〉 neck: 伸长～ crane one's neck

博[1] bó

A〈形〉 **1**（丰富） abundant: ▸地大物～, 渊～ **2**（宽阔） vast **3**（广泛） extensive

B〈动〉 be well-informed: ▸～古通今

博[2] bó〈动〉 win: 以～欢心 just to win sb.'s favour

博[3] bó〈动〉 **1**（下棋） play: ～弈 play chess **2**（赌博） gamble

【博爱】bó'ài〈动〉 show universal love: ～众生 universally love all living things

【博采众长】 bócǎi-zhòngcháng 〈成〉 discover and make use of the strong points of all others

【博彩】bócǎi ▸**p. 772**〈动〉〈婉〉 gamble

【博茨瓦纳】Bócíwǎnà〈名〉 Botswana: ～共和国 Republic of Botswana ‖ ～人 Botswanan

【博大】bódà〈形〉 **1**（宽广） broad: 胸怀～ be broad-minded **2**（丰富） abundant: ▸～精深

【博大精深】bódà-jīngshēn〈成〉 extensive and profound: 他的学问～。 He has extensive and profound knowledge.

【博导】bódǎo〈简称〉= 博士生导师

【博得】bódé〈动〉 win: ～满场喝彩 bring down the house ‖ ～同情 win sympathy ‖ 他逐渐～她的欢心。 He wormed himself into her favour.

【博古】bógǔ〈动〉 be conversant in things of the past: ～多识 be well-informed about history

【博古通今】 bógǔ-tōngjīn 〈成〉 be conversant in both ancient and modern affairs

【博客】bókè〈名〉 blog: 写～ write a blog

【博览】bólǎn〈动〉 read extensively: ～群书 be well-read

【博览会】bólǎnhuì〈名〉 exposition: 举办～ run an exhibition ‖ 世界～ world fair ‖ 世界园艺～ International Horticultural Exposition

【博洽】bóqià〈形〉〈书〉 well-informed: ～多闻 learned and well-informed

【博取】bóqǔ〈动〉 court: ～欢心 curry favour ‖ ～同情 seek sb.'s sympathy

【博施济众】bóshī-jìzhòng〈成〉provide liberal relief to the poor

【博识】bóshí〈形〉 erudite

【博识洽闻】 bóshí-qiàwén 〈成〉 learned and well-informed

【博士】bóshì〈名〉 **1**（指学位） doctor: ～生 doctoral candidate ‖ 文学～ Doctor of Literature **2**〈旧〉（专家） expert: ▸茶～

【博士后】bóshìhòu〈名〉 post-doc: ～流动站 mobile centre for post-doctoral research

【博士生】 bóshìshēng 〈名〉 doctoral student

【博士生导师】 bóshìshēng dǎoshī 〈名〉 doctoral tutor

【博士学位】bóshì xuéwèi〈名〉 doctorate: 获得经济学～ take one's doctorate in economics

【博闻强记】 bówén-qiángjì 〈成〉 have encyclopaedic knowledge and extraordinary powers of retention

【博闻强识】 bówén-qiángzhì = 博闻强记 bówén-qiángjì

【博物】bówù〈名〉〈旧〉 natural science

【博物馆】bówùguǎn〈名〉 museum: 历史～ museum of history ‖ ～馆长 museum curator

【博物院】bówùyuàn〈名〉 museum: 故宫～ Palace Museum

【博学】bóxué〈形〉 learned: ～多才 learned and versatile ‖ ～之士 learned scholar

【博雅】bóyǎ〈形〉〈书〉 erudite: ～之士 erudite scholar

【博弈】bóyì〈动〉 **1**（下棋） play chess **2**（较量） test one's strength

【博弈论】bóyìlùn〈名〉 game theory

【博引】bóyǐn〈动〉〈书〉 quote extensively: ▸旁征～

【博主】bózhǔ〈名〉 blogger: ～的真实身份 the blogger's true identity

鹁（鵓） bó

【鹁鸽】bógē〈名〉［鸟类］ pigeon

【鹁鸪】bógū〈名〉［鸟类］ wood-pigeon

渤 Bó

【渤海】Bóhǎi〈名〉 Bohai Sea: ～湾 Bohai Bay

搏 bó〈动〉 **1**（拼搏） struggle: 人生能有几回～! Few are the important struggles in one's life! ▸～斗, 拼～, 肉～ **2**（跳动） beat: ▸脉～ **3**（突袭） pounce on: 如猛虎～羊 like a tiger pouncing upon a goat

【搏动】bódòng〈动〉 beat rhythmically: 心脏～正常。 The heart beat is normal.

【搏斗】bódòu〈动〉 wrestle: 进行殊死～ make a desperate fight ‖ 同歹徒顽强～ put up a stubborn fight against the ruffian ‖ 与死神～ fight against death

【搏击】bójī **A**〈动〉 strike against: ～风浪 battle against winds and waves **B**〈名〉［体育］ boxing

【搏杀】bóshā〈动〉 **1**（指格斗） fight with a weapon **2**（指游戏或下棋） be locked in a fierce contest

【搏战】bózhàn〈动〉 struggle

鲌（鮊） bó〈名〉［鱼类］ Spanish mackerel

僰 Bó〈名〉 ancient ethnic group living in south-west China

箔 bó〈名〉 **1**（苇或秫编织物） matting: 苇～ reed matting ▸席～ **2**（蚕箔） bamboo tray: ▸蚕～ **3**（金属薄片） foil: ▸金～, 银～ **4**（指纸） paper tinsel: ▸锡～

【箔材】bócái〈名〉［冶金］ foil

魄 bó ▸落魄 luòbó

▸pò, tuò

膊 bó〈名〉 upper arm: ▸赤～, 胳～

踣 bó〈动〉〈书〉 fall down

薄[1] bó〈动〉 approach: ▸～暮, 日～西山

薄[2] bó

A〈形〉 **1**（不厚） thin: 像纸一样～ be as thin as paper ‖ ～～地抹上一层黄油 thinly spread with butter ‖ 湖面上结了一层～冰。 A layer of thin ice had formed on the lake. **2**（少） slight: ～施粉黛 wear a little make-up ‖ 这份礼显得太～了。 The gift seems too meagre. ▸～技, ～利多销, 微～ **3**（不仁慈） ungenerous: 你待我不～, 我却无以回报。 I regret not having the opportunity to reciprocate your generosity. **4**（轻佻） frivolous: ▸轻～ **5**（苛刻） harsh: ▸刻～

B〈动〉 **1**（减轻） reduce: ～赋税 reduce the tax **2**（轻视） belittle: 虽不喜欢也不能～待了他。 We mustn't do him down even though we don't like him. ▸鄙～, 厚此～彼, 厚今～古

▸báo, bò

【薄产】bóchǎn〈名〉〈书〉 meagre family property

【薄待】bódài〈动〉 treat ungenerously

【薄地】bódì〈名〉 unfertile land

【薄技】bójì〈名〉〈书〉〈谦〉 slight skill: 家产万贯, 不如～在身。 A little skill is better than a great fortune.

【薄酒】bójiǔ〈名〉〈谦〉 light wine: ～一杯, 略表敬意。 This small cup of wine is just a token of my respect.

【薄礼】bólǐ〈名〉〈谦〉 modest gift: 些许～, 敬请笑纳。 Please accept my humble gift.

【薄利】bólì〈名〉 thin margin: 获～ make meagre profits ‖ 这是一家～商店。 This is a shop operating on a small profit margin.

【薄利多销】bólì-duōxiāo〈成〉 small profits but quick returns

【薄面】bómiàn〈名〉〈谦〉 for my sake: 看在我～上, 原谅他这一次吧。 For my sake, please forgive him this time.

【薄命】bómìng〈形〉 ill-fated: 自古红颜多～。 Since ancient times beautiful women have often been unlucky.

【薄膜】bómó〈名〉 film: ～覆盖栽培 plastic-sheet-covered cultivation ▸塑料～

【薄暮】bómù〈名〉〈书〉 dusk: ～时分 at twilight

【薄情】bóqíng〈形〉 fickle: ～郎 fickle man

【薄弱】bóruò〈形〉 weak: ～环节 weak links ‖ 技术力量～ lack qualified technical personnel ‖ 意志～ weak-willed

【薄田】bótián〈名〉 infertile land

【薄物细故】bówù-xìgù〈成〉 trifles

【薄雾】bówù〈名〉 mist: ～笼罩着山丘。 A thin haze veiled the hills.

【薄晓】bóxiǎo〈名〉〈书〉 daybreak

【薄行】bóxíng〈书〉 **A**〈名〉 frivolous conduct **B**〈形〉 frivolous

【薄幸】bóxìng〈形〉〈书〉capricious: ～之人 fickle lover
【薄葬】bózàng〈动〉make a simple burial for the dead: 提倡厚养～ advocate providing generously for one's parents during their lifetime and a simple burial for when they die

b

髆 bó〈名〉〈书〉shoulder

礴 bó ▸磅礴 pángbó

bǒ

跛 bǒ〈形〉lame: 脚有点～ have a slight limp
【跛鳖千里】bǒbiē-qiānlǐ〈成〉〈喻〉persistence ensures success
【跛脚】bǒjiǎo **A**〈名〉lame foot **B**〈动〉limp: 士兵因受伤而～。The soldier is limping from a wound.
【跛脚鸭】bǒjiǎoyā〈名〉lame duck
【跛行】bǒxíng〈动〉walk with a limp
【跛子】bǒzi〈名〉lame person: 变成～ go lame

簸 bǒ〈动〉winnow: ～麦子 winnow the chaff away
▸bò
【簸荡】bǒdàng〈动〉bump and sway: 小船在大海上～。The boat was tossed at sea.
【簸动】bǒdòng〈动〉shake
【簸箩】bǒluo〈名〉shallow basket
【簸弄】bǒnong〈动〉**1**（用手）fiddle **2**（挑拨）stir up: ～是非 stir up trouble
【簸扬】bǒyáng〈动〉winnow: ～机 winnower

bò

柏 bò ▸黄柏 huángbò
▸bǎi, bó

薄 bò
▸báo, bó
【薄荷】bòhe〈名〉mint: ～糖 mint ‖ ～油 peppermint oil

檗 bò ▸黄檗 huángbò

擘 bò〈名〉〈书〉thumb: ▸巨～
【擘划】bòhuà = 擘画 bòhuà
【擘画】bòhuà〈动〉〈书〉arrange
【擘肌分理】bòjī-fēnlǐ〈成〉make a detailed analysis

簸 bò
▸bǒ
【簸箕】bòji〈名〉**1**（用于簸粮食）winnowing pan **2**（用于撮垃圾）dustpan **3**（指指纹）loop

bo

卜（蔔） bo ▸萝卜 luóbo
▸bǔ

啵 bo〈助〉〈方〉[denoting consultation, request and command]: 你的主意多，给咱们想个办法，行～? You are a man of ideas. Try and think of a strategy for us, won't you?

bū

逋 bū〈动〉〈书〉**1**（逃亡）flee: ▸～逃 **2**（拖欠）fall into arrears: ▸～欠
【逋客】būkè〈名〉〈书〉**1**（逃亡者）fugitive **2**（隐士）recluse
【逋留】būliú〈动〉〈书〉stop: ～国外数载 stay abroad for many years
【逋欠】būqiàn〈动〉〈书〉be in arrears: ～贷款 default on a loan
【逋逃】būtáo〈书〉**A**〈动〉flee **B**〈名〉fugitive

晡 bū〈名〉〈书〉late afternoon

bú

醭 bú〈名〉whitish mould: 这瓶酱油长了一层～。This bottle of soy sauce is covered with a film of whitish mould.

bǔ

卜 bǔ〈动〉**1**（卜卦）divine: 求神问～ pray to gods and consult the oracle ▸～卦，求签问～ **2**〈书〉（挑选）choose: ～宅 choose a site for one's house **3**（知道）foretell: 吉凶未～。It is hard to predict whether a lucky or an evil fate is awaiting us. ‖ 胜败未～。It is still a toss-up whether they will win or not.
▸bo
【卜辞】bǔcí〈名〉oracle inscriptions of the Shang Dynasty on tortoise shells or animal bones
【卜卦】bǔguà〈动〉practise divination
【卜居】bǔjū〈动〉〈书〉choose a dwelling place: ～郊野 make one's home in the country
【卜课】bǔkè〈动〉practise divination
【卜筮】bǔshì〈动〉practise divination using tortoise shell or straws

补（補） bǔ
A〈动〉**1**（修）repair: ～车胎 fix a puncture ‖ ～衣服 patch clothes ‖ 小修小～ make petty repairs ▸修～ **2**（补偿）make up for: ～交税款 pay taxes in arrears **3**（增添）supplement: 缺什么～什么 supply whatever is needed ▸～缺，～足 **4**（补养）nourish: ～元气 help restore vitality ‖ 你刚出院，得～～身体。You should build up your health with tonics after your discharge from hospital. ▸～药，滋～
B〈名〉〈书〉benefit: ▸～益，于事无～
【补白】bǔbái **A**〈名〉filler: ～图案 tailpiece ‖ 明天报上仍需两篇～。We still need two more fillers for tomorrow's newspaper. **B**〈动〉give further explanation: 这件事我来～几句。I'd like to add a few words on the matter.
【补办】bǔbàn〈动〉make up for sth.: ～工作证 apply for a work permit after the fact ‖ ～住院手续 complete the formalities for admitting a patient to hospital after he has been put in a ward
【补报】bǔbào〈动〉**1**（报告）make a report after the event **2**（回报）repay: ～父母养育之恩 repay one's parents for their loving care **3**（注册）register after the fact: 过期不予～。Late registration is not accepted.
【补差】bǔchā **A**〈动〉grant the margin **B**〈名〉supplementary pension
【补偿】bǔcháng〈动〉compensate: ～损失 offset the damage ‖ 得到～ get compensation ‖ 额外～ extra compensation
【补偿金】bǔchángjīn〈名〉compensation amounts
【补偿贸易】bǔcháng màoyì〈名〉counter trade
【补充】bǔchōng〈动〉**1**（填补不足）supplement: ～人力 supplement manpower ‖ ～新鲜血液 infuse new blood ‖ ～营养 supplement one's diet ‖ 作为社会主义经济的～ serve as a complement to the socialist economy **2**（追加）add: ～规定 additional regulations ‖ ～说明 additional remarks ‖ ～条款 supplementary clauses
【补跌】bǔdiē〈动〉[金融] fall for a second time: 高科技股进入～状态。High technology shares are falling again.
【补丁】bǔding〈名〉patch: 一块～ a patch ‖ 打～ patch up
【补钉】bǔdīng = 补丁 bǔding
【补过】bǔguò〈动〉make up for one's mistakes: ▸将功～
【补给】bǔjǐ **A**〈动〉supply: 靠打针～营养 give supplementary nutrition by injection **B**〈名〉[军事] provision: ～不足 run short of supplies
【补给品】bǔjǐpǐn〈名〉supplies: 医药～ medical supplies
【补给线】bǔjǐxiàn〈名〉[军事] supply line
【补剂】bǔjì〈名〉tonic: 人参～ ginseng tonic
【补假】bǔjià〈动〉**1**（指假期）take delayed holidays **2**（指手续）carry out retroactive procedures for leave
【补角】bǔjiǎo〈名〉[数学] supplementary angle
【补救】bǔjiù〈动〉remedy: 采取～措施 take remedial action ‖ 用尽一切～办法 exhaust all remedies
【补苴罅漏】bǔjū-xiàlòu〈成〉make up for deficiencies
【补考】bǔkǎo〈动〉resit an exam
【补课】bǔkè〈动〉**1**（指上课）make up missed lessons: 帮助学生～ help students make up for lessons missed **2**〈喻〉（指重做）make good a job badly done: 工作不合格的要～。Any inferior work must be brought up to standard.
【补漏】bǔlòu〈动〉**1**（指漏洞）repair a leak **2**（指疏忽）stop up a leak: ～纠偏 close up loopholes and rectify deviations
【补苗】bǔmiáo〈动〉[农业] fill the gaps with seedlings
【补偏救弊】bǔpiān-jiùbì〈成〉remedy deviations and rectify errors
【补票】bǔpiào〈动〉buy a ticket after the normal time
【补品】bǔpǐn〈名〉tonic
【补缺】bǔquē〈动〉**1**（指职位）fill a vacancy **2**（指缺漏）make up for deficiencies: ～堵漏 make up for deficiencies and plug up loopholes
【补缺选举】bǔquē xuǎnjǔ〈名〉by-election
【补色】bǔsè〈名〉complementary colour
【补射】bǔshè〈动〉tap in: 一脚～，球应声入门。One tap and the ball flew into the goal.

【补时】bǔshí〈动〉［体育］have extra time: ▸伤停～

【补水】bǔshuǐ〈动〉 provide supplementary water: 水库负责在枯水期向漓江～。 In the dry season the reservoir provides supplementary water to Lijiang.

【补台】bǔtái〈动〉 help sb. out

【补贴】bǔtiē **A**〈动〉 subsidize: ～家用 supplement the family income **B**〈名〉 subsidy: 出口/贸易～ export/trade subsidy ‖ 伙食～ food subsidies ‖ 交通～ traffic allowance ‖ 住房～ housing subsidy ‖ 他们依靠政府～维持生存。 They depend on government subsidies for their survival.

【补习】bǔxí〈动〉 take extra classes

【补习班】bǔxíbān〈名〉 remedial class

【补休】bǔxiū〈动〉 take deferred holidays

【补选】bǔxuǎn〈名〉 by-election: ～人大代表 hold a by-election for a deputy to the People's Congress

【补血】bǔxuè〈动〉 nourish the blood: ～药 haematinic

【补牙】bǔyá **A**〈动〉 fill a tooth cavity **B**〈名〉 tooth filling

【补养】bǔyǎng〈动〉 take nourishing food to build up one's health

【补药】bǔyào〈名〉 tonic

【补液】bǔyè **A**〈动〉 give fluid infusion **B**〈名〉 liquid tonic: 营养～ liquid tonic

【补遗】bǔyí〈名〉 addendum: 这本词典的新版本附有长达 50 页的～。 The new edition of the dictionary includes a 50-page addendum.

【补益】bǔyì〈书〉**A**〈名〉 benefit: 大有～ be of great help **B**〈动〉 benefit: ～国家 benefit the nation

【补语】bǔyǔ〈名〉［语言］complement

【补涨】bǔzhǎng〈动〉 rise in price accordingly: 粮价上涨后，肉禽也开始～。 After the price of grain went up, the price of poultry started to rise accordingly. ‖ 不少个股出现～。 A large number of individual shares have risen in price accordingly.

【补正】bǔzhèng〈动〉 supplement and correct: ～如下 make the following corrections and improvements

【补助】bǔzhù **A**〈动〉 subsidize: ～困难学生 subsidize needy students **B**〈名〉 subsidy: 困难～ hardship grant ‖ 失业～ unemployment benefit ‖ 医疗～ medical benefit

【补助金】bǔzhùjīn〈名〉 grant: 临时就业～ temporary employment subsidy ‖ 伤残～ disability pension

【补缀】bǔzhuì〈动〉 mend: 她把新布～在他的旧上衣上。 She patched his old coat with a new piece of cloth.

【补妆】bǔzhuāng〈动〉 touch up one's make-up

【补足】bǔzú〈动〉 make up for a deficiency: ～亏空 make up for the deficit

捕 bǔ

〈动〉 catch: ～鱼 catch fish ‖ 凶手已被～。 The murderer has already been arrested. ▸～获，追～

【捕风捉影】bǔfēng-zhuōyǐng〈成〉〈喻〉 spread rumours or act on unsubstantiated evidence

【捕获】bǔhuò〈动〉 catch: ～猎物 capture one's prey ‖ ～逃犯 seize an escaped convict

【捕集】bǔjí〈动〉（获取） capture;（收集） collect: 我国的碳～技术处于世界领先地位。 China's carbon capture technology is a world leader.

【捕鲸】bǔjīng〈动〉 whale: ～船 whaling ship

【捕快】bǔkuài〈名〉〈旧〉 captor in a *yamen*

【捕捞】bǔlāo〈动〉 catch: ～鱼虾 catch fish and shrimps ‖ ～季节 catching season ‖ ～许可证 fishing licence

【捕猎】bǔliè〈动〉 hunt: 这种动物被～得快要灭绝了。 The game is being hunted to the verge of extinction.

【捕拿】bǔná〈动〉 arrest: ～逃犯 arrest escaped prisoners

【捕杀】bǔshā〈动〉 catch and kill: 严禁～濒危动物。 It is strictly forbidden to hunt endangered species.

【捕食】bǔshí〈动〉 **1**（捕捉） hunt for food: 狼又出来～了。 The wolf reappeared in search of food. **2**（猎获并食用） hunt and eat: 鹿被狮子～了。 The deer fell prey to the lion.

【捕鼠器】bǔshǔqì〈名〉 mousetrap

【捕捉】bǔzhuō〈动〉 **1**（捉） catch: ～海龟 fish for turtles ‖ ～老鼠/昆虫 catch mice/insects **2**〈喻〉（抓住） grasp: ～镜头 take a candid shot ‖ ～战机 seize the right moment to attack

哺 bǔ

A〈动〉 nurse
B〈名〉 food being chewed in one's mouth: 吐～ spit out chewed food

【哺乳】bǔrǔ〈动〉 breast-feed: 给孩子～ nurse one's baby ‖ ～期 lactation period

【哺乳动物】bǔrǔ dòngwù〈名〉 mammal: ～学 mammalogy

【哺养】bǔyǎng〈动〉〈书〉 feed: 把婴儿交给她～ give the baby to her to feed

【哺育】bǔyù〈动〉 **1**（喂养） feed: ～婴儿 feed the baby **2**〈喻〉（培养） raise: 国家～了我们。 The country has nurtured us.

堡 bǔ

▸bǎo, pù

【堡子】bǔzi〈名〉〈方〉 **1**（指小城镇） town or village surrounded with protective earthen walls **2**（村落） village

bù

不 bù ▸p. 221

〈副〉 **1**（表否定） not: ～参加选举 stay out of an election ‖ ～符合标准 not up to standard ‖ ～愿意 be unwilling ‖ ～知道 not know ‖ ～法 unlawful ‖ ～轨 conspiracy ‖ ～规则 irregular ‖ 我～想去。 I don't want to go. **2**（表不在乎或不相干） no matter: 不管喜欢～喜欢，你都得干。 Like it or not, you will have to do it. ‖ 信～信由你。 Believe it or not. **3**（表否定回答） no: 他是学生吗？——～，他不是。 Is he a student? — No, he isn't. ‖ 再来杯茶吧？——～了，谢谢。 How about another cup of tea? — No more, thanks. **4**〈口〉（表疑问） [used to indicate question]: 这本书他喜欢～？ Does he like the book? ‖ 你去看电影～？ Are you going to the cinema? ‖ 他走～走？ Is he leaving? ‖ 我漂亮～漂亮？ Am I beautiful? **5**（表无法实现） [used to indicate that sth. is not achieved]: 吃～饱，穿～暖 badly fed and clothed ‖ 他什么事都做～好。 He can do nothing right. **6**（表选择） either ... or ...: 他～是上课就是在写论文。 If he's not in class then he's writing his thesis.

【不安】bù'ān〈形〉 **1**（指环境） unstable: ▸动荡～ **2**（指心情） uneasy: 内心～ be inwardly disturbed ‖ 她良心～。 Her conscience pricks her. ‖ 调查结果令人～。 The findings are disturbing. ▸坐立～ **3**〈套〉（抱歉） sorry: 给你添了这么多麻烦，真是～。 I'm sorry to have caused you so much trouble.

【不安本分】bù'ān-běnfèn〈成〉 be dissatisfied with one's post

【不谙世故】bù'ān-shìgù〈成〉 know little of the world: 他不谙人情世故。 He has seen little of life.

【不白之冤】bùbáizhīyuān〈成〉 unredressed grievance: 蒙受～ suffer from a gross injustice

【不败之地】bùbàizhīdì〈成〉 invincible position: 立于～ put oneself in an invincible position

【不卑不亢】bùbēi-bùkàng〈成〉 be neither haughty nor humble: 对上司～ be neither supercilious nor obsequious to one's superiors

【不备】bùbèi〈形〉 unprepared: 乘其～ catch sb. off guard ▸攻其～

【不比】bùbǐ〈动〉 **1**（比不上） be inferior to: 他在班里～任何人差。 He's second to none in the class. **2**（不同于） be unlike: 学习～玩耍，得下苦功夫。 Unlike playing, study requires painstaking efforts.

【不比不知道，一比吓一跳】bùbǐ bù zhīdào, yī bǐ xià yī tiào〈俗〉 if you don't make comparisons then you don't know, but once you do, prepare for a shock

【不必】bùbì〈副〉 not necessarily: ～着急 there's no hurry ‖ 你～介意。 You don't have to care at all. ‖ 咱俩就～拘礼了。 Let's dispense with formalities.

【不避艰险】bùbì-jiānxiǎn〈成〉 flinch from no difficulty or danger

【不变】bùbiàn〈动〉 be unchanged: 以～应万变 counter numerous changes with the same unchanged stance

【不变价格】bùbiàn jiàgé〈名〉 fixed price

【不便】bùbiàn **A**〈形〉 inconvenient: 交通～ have poor transport facilities ‖ 行动～ move with difficulty **B**〈动〉 be short of cash: 手头～就吭声。 Do give me a call if you're strapped for cash.

【不辨菽麦】bùbiàn-shūmài〈成〉 lack the least bit of common knowledge

【不才】bùcái〈书〉 **A**〈代〉〈谦〉 I: 恐怕～难当此任。 I'm afraid I am not up to the job. **B**〈形〉 talentless: 我虽～，但愿为您效劳。 I may have little talent, but I will be glad to offer you my services.

【不测】bùcè ▸p. 772 **A**〈形〉 unexpected: 应付～事件 cope with unexpected events ▸天有～风云 **B**〈名〉 accident: 险遭～ have a narrow escape ‖ 提高警惕，以防～ sharpen one's vigilance against possible contingency

【不曾】bùcéng〈副〉 never: 我～受过这样的善待。 Never before have I been treated so well. ‖ 我一生中～如此伤心过。 I have never felt so unhappy in all my life.

【不成】bùchéng **A**〈动〉 **1** = 不行 bùxíng A1 **2**（不足） fall short of: ～比例 be out of proportion ‖ ～敬意。 This can hardly express my respect to you. **B** = 不行 bùxíng B1, B2 **C**〈助〉 [used at the end of a rhetorical question beginning with 难道 or 莫非]: 难道我们就放弃～？ Are we just going to give it up? ‖ 莫非他被错判了～？ Has he been wrongly sentenced after all?

【不成功，便成仁】bù chénggōng, biàn chéngrén〈成〉 fight to win or die in the process

【不成体统】bùchéng-tǐtǒng〈成〉 most

b

improper: 正式晚会上穿短裤，～。Shorts are inappropriate at a formal party.

【不成文】bùchéngwén〈形〉unwritten: ～的规矩 unwritten conventions

【不成文法】bùchéngwénfǎ〈名〉［法律］unwritten law

【不承认主义】bùchéngrènzhǔyì〈名〉policy of non-recognition

【不逞之徒】bùchěngzhītú〈成〉reckless ruffian

【不齿】bùchǐ〈动〉〈书〉hold in contempt: 为世人所～ be despised by the people

【不耻下问】bùchǐ-xiàwèn〈成〉not feel ashamed to consult one's subordinates

【不啻】bùchì〈动〉〈书〉**1**（不止）be not less than: 所需资金，～百万。This requires a fund totalling no less than a million *yuan*. **2**（如同）be like: 这消息对她～晴天霹雳。The news came to her like a bolt from the blue.

【不出所料】bùchū-suǒliào〈成〉as expected: ～，公牛队卫冕成功。As expected, the Bulls succeeded in defending the championship.

【不揣冒昧】bùchuǎi-màomèi〈成〉venture: ～，陈述管见 take the liberty of stating one's humble opinion

【不辞】bùcí〈动〉**1**（不告别）not say goodbye: ～而别 leave without saying goodbye **2**（不顾）not shrink from: ～辛劳 not shrink from the toil and hardship

【不错】bùcuò〈形〉**1**（正确）right: 你说的～。You are right. ‖ ～，他是昨天来的。Yes, he did come yesterday. **2**（好）pretty good: 他身体还～。He is still in pretty good health. ‖ 这部电影～。The film is not bad.

【不打不成器】bù dǎ bù chéngqì〈俗〉spare the rod and spoil the child

【不打不相识】bù dǎ bù xiāngshí〈俗〉out of blows friendship grows

【不打自招】bùdǎ-zìzhāo〈成〉confess without being tortured

【不丹】Bùdān〈名〉Bhutan: ～人 Bhutanese ‖ ～王国 Kingdom of Bhutan ‖ ～语 Bhutanese

【不单】bùdān **A**〈副〉not the only one: 有这种想法的～是我一个人。I'm not the only one to have this idea. **B**〈连〉not only: 他～人好，而且能干。He is not only kind but also capable.

【不但】bùdàn〈连〉not only: 黑猩猩～会使用工具，而且在某种程度上还会制造工具。Chimpanzees can not only use tools but to a certain extent they can also make them. ‖ 那样～解决不了现存问题，反而会引出新问题。Instead of solving any existing problems, it will only create new ones.

【不惮】bùdàn〈动〉〈书〉not fear: ～其烦 not mind taking the trouble

【不当】bùdàng〈形〉inappropriate: ～行为 improper behaviour ‖ 处理～ be not properly handled

【不倒翁】bùdǎowēng〈名〉tumbler: 政坛～ durable politician

【不到长城非好汉】bù dào Chángchéng fēi hǎohàn〈俗〉**1**〈本〉one who fails to reach the Great Wall is not a hero **2**〈喻〉one should not give up until one succeeds

【不到黄河心不死】bù dào Huánghé xīn bù sǐ〈俗〉**1**（指心态）not stop until all hope is gone **2**（指行为）not stop until one achieves one's goal

【不道德】bù dàodé〈形〉immoral: ～的生活 life of immorality ‖ ～的行为 unethical conduct ‖ 剽窃是～的。It is not ethical to plagiarize.

【不到家】bùdàojiā〈惯〉〈喻〉not up to scratch: 技术还～ skills that do not measure up

【不得】bùdé〈动〉not be allowed: ～上诉 not subject to appeal ‖ ～有误 let there be no mistake

【不得】bude〈助〉（不可以）must not;（不能够）cannot: 动弹～ cannot move ‖ 奈何～ there is nothing to be done ‖ 批评～ will not stand any criticism ‖ 这个问题轻视～。This is no small matter. ▸哭笑～

【不得不】bùdébù〈惯〉have no choice but to: ～承认 admit grudgingly ‖ ～服从 cannot but obey ‖ 在事实面前，他～认罪。The facts compelled him to plead guilty.

【不得而知】bùdé'érzhī〈成〉be unable to find out: 结果如何，尚～。The result is still unknown.

【不得劲】bùdéjìn〈形〉〈口〉**1**（用不上劲）awkward: 这锹把子太直，使着～。The shovel handle is too straight to be used with ease. **2**（不舒服）unwell: 我感冒了，浑身～。I caught a cold and felt out of sorts all over.

【不得了】bùdéliǎo〈形〉〈口〉**1**（情况严重）terrible: 万一出了岔子可～。It will be disastrous if there is the least blunder. ‖ 如果让他这样下去，那可～。If nothing is done about him, there'll be no end of trouble. **2**（程度深）extremely: 急得～ desperately anxious ‖ 热得～。It's awfully hot.

【不得人心】bùdé-rénxīn〈成〉not enjoy popular support: 他说话刻薄，很～。He was unpopular because of his scathing tongue.

【不得要领】bùdé-yàolǐng〈成〉fail to get the point: ～的演讲 pointless talk

【不得已】bùdéyǐ〈形〉imperative: 她～才接受那份工作。She had no choice but to accept the job.

【不得已而求其次】bùdéyǐ ér qiú qí cì〈成〉have to be content with the second best

【不登大雅之堂】bù dēng dàyǎ zhī táng〈成〉not appeal to refined tastes: 我厌恶这种～的幽默。I hate this kind of coarse humour.

【不等】bùděng〈形〉different: 长短/大小～ differ in length/size ‖ 各人工资～。The salary varies from person to person.

【不等号】bùděnghào〈名〉［数学］unequal sign

【不等式】bùděngshì〈名〉［数学］inequality

【不迭】bùdié〈动〉**1**（急忙）hurry: 忙～ hasten to do sth. **2**（来不及）be too late to do sth.: 后悔～ be too late for regrets **3**（不断）be endless: 叫苦～ complain incessantly

【不丁点儿】bùdīngdiǎnr〈形〉very little

【不顶事】bùdǐngshì〈动〉〈口〉be useless

【不定】bùdìng **A**〈副〉not necessarily: 这次总统选举还～谁胜出呢。The outcome of the presidential election is still far from certain. ‖ 我还～报不报名呢。I'm still in two minds about whether to enter my name. **B**〈形〉unsteady: 漂泊～ drift from place to place ‖ 心神～ be restless

【不定冠词】bùdìng guàncí ▸p. 411〈名〉［语言］indefinite article

【不动产】bùdòngchǎn〈名〉real estate

【不动声色】bùdòng-shēngsè〈成〉maintain one's composure: 别人都慌了神，他却～。While all the others were thrown into a panic, he remained calm.

【不冻港】bùdònggǎng〈名〉ice-free port

【不独】bùdú〈连〉〈书〉not only: 改革～需要勇气，还需要能力。Reform requires not only courage but also ability.

【不端】bùduān〈形〉improper: 行为～ be badly behaved

【不断】bùduàn **A**〈动〉not stop: 连绵～的山脉 range upon range **B**〈副〉constantly: ～努力 make unceasing efforts ‖ 新事物～涌现。New things keep emerging.

【不对】bùduì〈形〉**1**（错）wrong: 是她～。She is in the wrong. ‖ 这没有什么～的。There is nothing wrong with it. **2**（反常）odd: 你今天脸色有些～。You don't look quite your usual self today. **3**（不和谐）inharmonious: 她俩素来～。The two of them have always been at odds.

【不对茬儿】bùduìchár〈惯〉〈方〉not fit for the occasion

【不对劲】bùduìjìn〈形〉〈口〉**1**（不顺手）awkward: 他用毛笔觉得～。He never felt handy with a brush. **2**（不和睦）at odds: 我觉得他们之间有点～。I sensed that things weren't quite right between them. **3**（反常）abnormal: 这机器听着～。The machine sounds odd. ‖ 她觉得身体有点～。She's feeling a bit under the weather.

【不对头】bùduìtóu = 不对劲 bùduìjìn

【不二法门】bù'èr-fǎmén〈成〉one and only way

【不二价】bù'èrjià〈名〉fixed price

【不发达】bùfādá〈形〉underdeveloped: ～地区 underdeveloped areas ‖ ～国家 underdeveloped country

【不乏】bùfá〈动〉〈书〉have no lack: ～先例 there's no lack of precedents

【不乏其人】bùfá-qírén〈成〉there's no lack of such people

【不法】bùfǎ〈形〉illegal: ～分子 lawbreaker ‖ ～商人 lawbreaking merchant ‖ ～之徒 unprincipled fellow

【不凡】bùfán〈形〉out of the ordinary: ▸出手～, 自命～

【不妨】bùfáng〈副〉might as well: ～问一问。There's no harm in asking. ‖ 你～试一试。You might as well have a try.

【不费吹灰之力】bùfèi chuīhuīzhīlì〈成〉without the slightest effort

【不分青红皂白】bùfēn qīnghóng-zàobái〈成〉make no distinction between right and wrong: ～地责难 condemn indiscriminately ‖ ～的攻击 indiscriminate attack

【不分胜负】bùfēn-shèngfù〈成〉tie: 辩论最终～。The debate ended in a tie.

【不忿】bùfèn〈动〉〈书〉take offence

【不孚众望】bùfú-zhòngwàng〈成〉not inspire popular confidence

【不服】bùfú〈动〉**1**（不信服）defy: ～裁判 refuse to accept the referee's decision ‖ ～判决，提出上诉 appeal a conviction **2**（不习惯）not be accustomed to: 水土～ be unaccustomed to the feel of a new place

【不服气】bùfúqì〈口〉= 不服 bùfú 1

【不符】bùfú〈动〉not tally with: 与时代精神～ be inconsistent with the spirit of the time ‖ 与事实～ go against the facts

【不复】bùfù〈副〉〈书〉no more: ～存在 no longer exist

【不负众望】bùfù-zhòngwàng〈成〉live up to popular expectations

【不干胶】bùgānjiāo〈名〉**1**（指不会凝固）non-drying adhesive **2**（指不失去黏

性）post-it note: ～标签 stick-on labels

【不甘】bùgān〈动〉 not reconcile oneself: ～失败 refuse to resign oneself to defeat ‖ ～人后 not be slow in coming forward ‖ ～落后 not reconcile oneself to lagging behind ‖ ～寂寞 hate to be neglected

【不甘示弱】bùgān-shìruò〈成〉 refuse to be outdone

【不甘心】bù gānxīn〈动〉 not be resigned to: ～失败 refuse to resign oneself to defeat

【不尴不尬】bùgān-bùgà〈成〉 be caught in a fix

【不敢】bùgǎn〈动〉 **1**（没胆量）not dare: ～得罪人 dare not offend anybody **2** = 不敢当 bùgǎndāng

【不敢当】bùgǎndāng〈惯〉〈谦〉 I really don't deserve this: 您学识渊博，简直可以做我的老师。——～。 You are learned enough to be my teacher. — It's too much of a compliment.

【不敢苟同】bùgǎn-gǒutóng〈成〉 beg to differ: 这种说法我～。 I can't agree with that statement.

【不敢越雷池一步】bùgǎn yuè Léichí yī bù〈成〉 keep cautiously within bounds

【不公】bùgōng〈形〉 unfair: 办事～ act unfairly ‖ 分配～ unjust distribution

【不攻自破】bùgōng-zìpò〈成〉 collapse of itself: 谣言在事实面前～。 The facts dispelled the rumour.

【不共戴天】bùgòng-dàitiān〈成〉 absolutely irreconcilable: ～的敌人 sworn enemy

【不苟】bùgǒu〈形〉 careful: ►一丝～

【不苟言笑】bùgǒu-yánxiào〈成〉 be of a serious disposition: 他一向～。 He is always reserved.

【不够】bùgòu **A**〈动〉 be insufficient: 钱～用。 Money is lacking. ‖ 他～朋友。 He is not much of a friend. ‖ 我们资金～。 We are short of funds. **B**〈副〉 insufficiently: ～好 not good enough ‖ 分析～透彻。 The analysis lacks depth.

【不顾】bùgù〈动〉 **1**（不照顾） not care: ～别人 show no concern for others ►不管～ **2**（不考虑） disregard: ～大局 disregard the general interests ‖ ～个人安危 be heedless of personal safety ‖ ～后果 be regardless of consequences ‖ ～事实 fly in the face of facts

【不关】bùguān〈动〉 have nothing to do with: 那～你的事。 That's no concern of yours.

【不关痛痒】bùguān-tòngyǎng〈成〉 be of no consequence

【不管】bùguǎn〈连〉 regardless of: ～怎么说 whatever you say ‖ ～天晴下雨，我明天都会来。 I shall come tomorrow, rain or shine.

【不管不顾】bùguǎn-bùgù **A**〈动〉 take no care of: 他对店里的事～。 He does not care a bit about what's happening in the shop. **B**〈副〉 recklessly: 他～地扑上去就打司机。 He threw himself upon the driver and beat him recklessly.

【不管部长】bùguǎn bùzhǎng〈名〉 minister without portfolio

【不管三七二十一】bùguǎn sān qī èrshíyī〈俗〉 throw caution to the wind: 经理～，一进门就开始训斥我们。 Upon entering the office, the manager began reprimanding us indiscriminately.

【不光】bùguāng **A**〈副〉 not the only one: 捐款的～是他一个人。 He is not the only one to have donated. **B**〈连〉 not only: 词典～提供词义，还提供词的用法。 A dictionary provides not only the meaning but also the usage of a word.

【不规则】bùguīzé〈形〉 random: ～分布 irregular distribution ‖ ～菱形 irregular rhombus

【不规则动词】bùguīzé dòngcí〈名〉［语言］ irregular verb

【不轨】bùguǐ〈形〉 against the law: 行为～ act against the law ‖ ～行为 lawless behaviour ►图谋～

【不过】bùguò **A**〈副〉 **1**（非常） exceedingly: 乖巧～的孩子 the cutest kid ‖ 那就再好～了！ That would be perfect! **2**（只） merely: 我～随便问问罢了。 I was just asking. ‖ 我猜她～三十岁。 I guess she is at most 30 years old. **B**〈连〉 however: 他受了伤，～情绪还好。 He was injured, but his mood was not bad.

【不过尔尔】bùguò-ěr'ěr〈成〉 just so-so

【不过意】bùguòyì ►**p. 156**〈形〉 sorry: 叫您破费了，很～。 I am very sorry to have put you to such expense.

【不寒而栗】bùhán'érlì〈成〉 tremble with fear: 使人～ give sb. the creeps

【不好意思】bùhǎoyìsi〈惯〉 **1**（害羞） be embarrassed: ～求助 be shy of asking for help ‖ 他受到了表扬，反而～起来。 He felt embarrassed when he was praised. **2**（不便） find it embarrassing: ～拒绝 find it rude to refuse ‖ ～再问 hesitate to ask again **3** ►**p. 156**〈套〉 excuse me: ～，请让一下。 Excuse me, please let me pass.

【不合】bùhé〈动〉 not conform to: ～标准 not up to standard ‖ ～口味 not to one's taste ‖ ～情理 unreasonable

【不合时宜】bùhé-shíyí〈成〉 ill-timed: 他说了些～的话。 He said something out of turn with the occasion.

【不和】bùhé〈形〉 at odds: 夫妻～ marital discord ‖ 家庭～ family discord

【不哼不哈】bùhēng-bùhā〈动〉 remain silent: 他平时意见挺多的，今儿个怎么～了？ He has often complained about things, so why is he silent today?

【不怀好意】bùhuái-hǎoyì〈成〉 have evil designs: 他～地笑了笑。 He laughed maliciously.

【不欢而散】bùhuān'érsàn〈成〉 part on bad terms: 他们性格不合，最终～。 Their personalities were incompatible and they finally broke up on bad terms.

【不慌不忙】bùhuāng-bùmáng〈成〉 leisurely: 讲话～ speak in a deliberate manner ‖ ～地回答 reply with composure

【不讳】bùhuì〈动〉〈书〉 **1**（无忌讳） not conceal anything: ►直言～ **2** ►**p. 772**〈婉〉（死亡） die

【不惑】bùhuò〈形〉〈书〉 free of confusion: ～之年 age of forty

【不积跬步，无以至千里】bù jī kuǐbù, wú yǐ zhì qiānlǐ〈成〉 learning has to be acquired gradually

【不羁】bùjī〈形〉〈书〉 unruly: ►放荡～

【不及】bùjí **A**〈动〉 **1**（比不上） be not so good as: 她的心灵远～相貌那样美。 Her heart is no way as beautiful as her appearance. **2**（达不到） be beyond one's reach: 力所～ be beyond one's power **3**（来不及） not be quick enough **B**〈形〉 too late: ►过犹～, 有过之无～

【不及物动词】bùjíwù dòngcí〈名〉［语言］ intransitive verb

【不即不离】bùjí-bùlí〈成〉 keep sb. at arm's length: 与过去的朋友保持～的关系 keep a discreet distance from one's former friends

【不计】bùjì〈动〉 disregard: ～报酬 irrespective of pay ‖ ～个人得失 disregard one's personal gain or loss

【不计其数】bùjìqíshù〈成〉 countless: 战斗非常激烈，死伤～。 The fighting was fierce and casualties were innumerable.

【不计前嫌】bùjì-qiánxián〈成〉 disregard past grudges

【不济】bùjì〈形〉〈口〉 insufficient: 眼力～ have failing eyesight ‖ 精力～ one's energy is failing

【不假思索】bùjiǎ-sīsuǒ〈成〉 without hesitation: ～，一挥而就 finish writing without seeming to think

【不见不散】bùjiàn-bùsàn〈惯〉 not leave without seeing each other: 咱们老地方见，～。 Let's meet at the old place. Be sure to be there!

【不见得】bùjiàndé〈副〉 not necessarily: 他说的～就对。 What he says is not necessarily right.

【不见棺材不落泪】bùjiàn guāncái bù luòlèi〈俗〉〈喻〉 remain unconvinced until faced with grim reality

【不见经传】bùjiàn-jīngzhuàn〈成〉 not to be found in the classics: ～的小人物 nonentity

【不讲道理】bùjiǎng dàolǐ〈动〉 be unreasonable

【不讲情面】bùjiǎng qíngmiàn〈动〉 not spare sensibilities

【不骄不躁】bùjiāo-bùzào〈成〉 be neither conceited nor rash

【不结盟】bùjiéméng〈形〉 non-aligned: ～国家 non-aligned countries

【不解】bùjiě〈动〉 **1**（不理解） fail to understand: ～其意 fail to grasp sb.'s point ‖ 迷惑～ feel baffled **2**（不可化解） be irreconcilable: ～之仇 irreconcilable enmity

【不解之缘】bùjiězhīyuán〈成〉 unbreakable bond: 和音乐结下～ have a strong attachment to music

【不介意】bùjièyì〈动〉 not mind: 我抽支烟您～吧？ Do you mind if I smoke?

【不禁】bùjīn〈副〉 cannot help doing: ～暗暗发笑 cannot help laughing to oneself ‖ ～要问 cannot but ask

【不仅】bùjǐn **A**〈副〉 not the only one: 这～是我一个人的爱好。 I'm not the only one who loves to do this. **B**〈连〉 not only: ～方法对头，而且措施得力 adopt not only the correct approach but also effective measures

【不尽】bùjìn〈形〉 **1**（不完全） incomplete: ～合理 not completely reasonable ‖ ～正确 not quite right ►～然 **2**（无尽头） endless: 感激～ be filled with immense gratitude

【不尽然】bùjìnrán〈形〉〈书〉 not necessarily so

【不近人情】bùjìn-rénqíng〈成〉 be devoid of human feeling

【不进则退】bùjìn-zétuì〈成〉 move forward, or you'll fall behind

【不经之谈】bùjīngzhītán〈成〉 cock-and-bull story

【不经一事，不长一智】bùjīng-yīshì, bùzhǎng-yīzhì〈俗〉 wisdom comes from experience

【不经意】bùjīngyì〈动〉 be thoughtless: 稍～，就会出错。 Even slight absentmindedness can result in a blunder.

【不景气】bùjǐngqì〈形〉 depressed: 经济～ depressed economy ‖ 目前生意相当～。 Business is quite slack at the moment. ‖ 当地的房地产市场～。 The local property market was in a slump.

b

【不胫而走】bùjìng'érzǒu〈成〉 spread like wildfire: 谣言～。 The rumour spread like wildfire.

【不久】bùjiǔ〈形〉 1（指未来） soon: ～就要过春节了。 The Spring Festival is just around the corner. ‖ 他身患重病，将～于人世。 He is terminally ill and will soon be gone. 2（指过去） soon after: 书出版后～，他就得了诺贝尔文学奖。 He was awarded the Nobel Prize for literature soon after the book was published.

【不拘】bùjū A〈动〉 not confine oneself to: ～礼节 without protocol ‖ 长短～。 No particular limit is set on the length. B〈连〉 no matter: ～是谁救了那孩子，都应该受到表扬。 Whoever rescued the child should be commended.

【不拘小节】bùjū-xiǎojié〈成〉 not care about small things

【不拘一格】bùjū-yīgé〈成〉 not stick to one pattern: ～选拔人才 select talents of all kinds

【不绝如缕】bùjué-rúlǚ〈成〉 1（指形势） hanging by a thread: 他家几代单传，～。 There has been only one son in his family for generations, making the family line precarious. 2（指声音） linger faintly: 他们的歌声～，回荡在山谷中。 Their singing lingered faintly in the valley.

【不堪】bùkān A〈动〉 1（无法忍受） cannot bear: ～其苦 cannot endure hardships ‖ ～忍受 cannot stand ►～一击 2（不能） be unable: ►～入耳，～设想 B〈形〉 utter: 疲惫～ dog-tired ‖ 痛苦～ extremely sad ►狼狈～

【不堪回首】bùkān-huíshǒu〈成〉 cannot bear to look back at the past: 往事～ cannot bear to recall past events

【不堪入耳】bùkān-rù'ěr〈成〉 offensive to the ear: ～的话 disgusting language

【不堪入目】bùkān-rùmù〈成〉 offensive to the eye

【不堪设想】bùkān-shèxiǎng〈成〉 too dreadful to contemplate: 后果将～。 The consequences will be disastrous.

【不堪一击】bùkān-yījī〈成〉 cannot withstand a single blow

【不堪造就】bùkān-zàojiù〈成〉 with no prospects: 这孩子并非～。 The child is not beyond educating.

【不看僧面看佛面】bùkàn sēngmiàn kàn fómiàn〈俗〉 do sth. for sb. out of reverence for sb. else of greater importance

【不亢不卑】bùkàng-bùbēi = 不卑不亢 bùbēi-bùkàng

【不可】bùkě A〈动〉 cannot: ～更改的决定 irrevocable decision ‖ 做事～半途而废。 Never do things by halves. B〈助〉 must: 非去～ must go ‖ 这事非他～。 Only he can manage it.

【不可多得】bùkě-duōdé〈成〉 hard to come by: ～的人才 rare talent

【不可告人】bùkě-gàorén〈成〉 not to be divulged: ～的勾当 sinister intrigues ‖ ～的目的 ulterior motive

【不可估量】bùkě-gūliàng〈成〉 inestimable: ～的损失 immeasurable loss

【不可或缺】bùkě-huòquē〈成〉 indispensable: ～的条件 necessary condition ‖ 氧气是生命所～的。 Oxygen is indispensable to life.

【不可救药】bùkě-jiùyào〈成〉 be incurable: 认为某人～ consider sb. to be beyond redemption ‖〈喻〉 有些腐败官员已经～了。 Some corrupt officials are beyond redemption.

【不可开交】bùkě-kāijiāo〈成〉 be tied up: 忙得～ have one's hands full

【不可抗拒】bùkě-kàngjù〈成〉 inexorable

【不可抗力】bùkěkànglì〈名〉 force majeure

【不可理喻】bùkě-lǐyù〈成〉 defy reason: 他蛮横到了极点，简直～。 He is so coarse as to defy reason.

【不可名状】bùkě-míngzhuàng〈成〉 defy description: 其罪行～。 His crimes are beyond description.

【不可磨灭】bùkě-mómiè〈成〉 indelible: ～的丰功伟绩 ineffaceable meritorious deeds

【不可偏废】bùkě-piānfèi〈成〉 not over-emphasize one thing to the exclusion of the other: 健康和工作二者～。 Neither health nor work should be over-emphasized one over the other.

【不可企及】bùkě-qǐjí〈成〉 matchless

【不可收拾】bùkě-shōushi〈成〉 unmanageable: 那里的情况一团糟，已经到了～的地步。 Things are in a mess there and are getting out of control.

【不可思议】bùkě-sīyì〈成〉 be inconceivable: ～的事件 inconceivable occurrence

【不可同日而语】bùkě tóngrì ér yǔ〈成〉 cannot be mentioned in the same breath

【不可向迩】bùkě-xiàng'ěr〈成〉 unreachable

【不可一世】bùkě-yīshì〈成〉 be high and mighty: 摆出一副～的架势 put on an air of extreme arrogance

【不可知论】bùkězhīlùn〈名〉［哲学］ agnosticism

【不客气】bù kèqi A〈形〉 1（不礼貌） impolite: ～的拒绝 curt refusal ‖ ～地说 to put it bluntly ‖ 如果你再这样没脸没皮的，别怪我～。 You'll get the rough side of my tongue if you're cheeky again. 2（不拘礼） straightforward: 我们之间就～了。 Let's dispense with formalities. B〈动〉〈套〉 1（不用谢） you're welcome: 谢谢。——～。 Thanks. — My pleasure. 2〈套〉（表示婉拒） no, thanks: 再给你来杯茶吧？——～，我自己来。 Would you care for another cup of tea? — Don't bother, please. I'll help myself.

【不快】bùkuài〈形〉 1（不高兴） unhappy: 感到心中～ feel unhappy 2（不舒服） under the weather: 身子略感～ be out of sorts

【不愧】bùkuì〈副〉 deserving the title of: 岳飞～为民族英雄。 Yue Fei deserves to be revered as a national hero.

【不扩散核武器条约】Bù Kuòsàn Héwǔqì Tiáoyuē〈名〉 Treaty on the Non-Proliferation of Nuclear Weapons (NPT)

【不赖】bùlài〈形〉〈方〉 not bad: 他的菜炒得还～。 He is a fairly good cook.

【不郎不秀】bùláng-bùxiù〈成〉 good for nothing

【不劳而获】bùláo'érhuò〈成〉 live off the toil of other people

【不力】bùlì〈形〉 ineffective: 办事～ lack efficiency in one's work ‖ 领导～ not exercise effective leadership

【不利】bùlì〈形〉 1（无益处） unfavourable: ～于经济发展 be unfavourable to economic growth ‖ 处于～地位 be at a disadvantage ‖ 这对我们双方都～。 It will be harmful to both of us. 2（不顺利） unsuccessful: 首战～ lose the first battle

【不良】bùliáng〈形〉 1（不好） bad: 存心～ harbour evil intent ‖ ～倾向 unhealthy trend 2（不完全） defective: 接触～ loose contact

【不良贷款】bùliáng dàikuǎn〈名〉 non-performing loan

【不良率】bùliánglǜ〈名〉 1（指贷款） default rate: 国家助学贷款的～较低。 The default rate for national student loans is pretty low. 2（指视力等） fraction defective: 学生视力的～居高不下。 There is a high rate of poor eyesight among students.

【不列颠】Bùlièdiān〈名〉 Britain: ～人 Briton ‖ ～群岛 British Isles

【不列颠百科全书】Bùlièdiān Bǎikē Quánshū〈名〉 Encyclopaedia Britannica

【不了】bùliǎo〈动〉 be without end: 哭个～ keep crying ‖ 整天忙个～ be busy all day long

【不了了之】bùliǎo-liǎozhī〈成〉 end inconclusively: 事情就这样～了。 The matter was left unsettled.

【不料】bùliào〈动〉 be contrary to expectations: 他去海滨游泳，～被淹死了。 He went to the seaside for a swim. Who could have guessed he would drown?

【不吝】bùlìn〈动〉〈书〉〈套〉 be generous with: ～指教 not stint with comments or criticism

【不露锋芒】bùlù-fēngmáng〈成〉not show off one's talents

【不露声色】bùlù-shēngsè〈成〉 not show one's emotions: 他心里很慌，却～，别人并没有觉察出来。 He felt very uneasy at heart but managed not to show it, so that no one realized anything was wrong.

【不伦不类】bùlún-bùlèi〈成〉 neither fish nor fowl: ～的比喻 far-fetched analogy

【不论】bùlùn A〈连〉 regardless of: ～成败 sink or swim ‖ ～职务高低 no matter what posts they hold ‖ 国家～大小都有权决定自己的政策。 Every state, large or small, has the right to decide its own policies. B〈动〉 not talk about: ～人过 not discuss sb. else's faults ‖ 存而～ put sth. on file but not discuss it

【不落窠臼】bùluò-kējiù〈成〉 not follow the beaten track: 他的作品～，使人耳目一新。 His works are fresh and original.

【不落俗套】bùluò-sútào〈成〉 depart from convention: ～的批评家 unconventional critic ‖ ～的幽默感 off-beat sense of humour

【不买账】bùmǎizhàng〈动〉〈口〉 pay no heed to: 他那些主意选民～。 The voters won't buy his ideas. ‖ 这个建议我提过两次，可董事会就是～。 I submitted this proposal twice, but the board won't go for it.

【不满】bùmǎn A〈形〉 resentful: 表示强烈～ express one's great displeasure ‖ 心怀～ nurse a grievance ‖ 我对那事很～。 I'm very unhappy about that. B〈动〉 1（不满意） be discontent with: ～现状 not be contented with things as they are 2（未达到） be less than: 毕业～一年 be out of school for less than a year ‖ 他～三十岁。 He is on the right side of thirty.

【不蔓不枝】bùmàn-bùzhī〈成〉〈喻〉 succinct and to the point: 这篇论文～，写得很精彩。 This essay is concise and well written.

【不毛之地】bùmáozhīdì〈成〉 barren land: 谁能想到十年前这果园还是～呢! Who would have thought that this orchard used to be wasteland ten years ago!

【不免】bùmiǎn〈副〉 unavoidably: 回到故乡，～想起儿时的事。 The visit to my hometown naturally brought back childhood memories.

【不妙】bùmiào〈形〉not encouraging: 情况～。Things look bleak.

【不名一文】bùmíng-yīwén〈成〉not have a penny to one's name

【不名誉】bùmíngyù〈形〉disgraceful: 他一时糊涂，做下～的蠢事。He made the dishonourable blunder in a muddle-headed moment.

【不明】bùmíng A〈动〉fail to understand: ～是非 confuse right and wrong ▸～事理，～真相 B〈形〉unknown: ～国籍的商人 merchant of unidentified nationality ‖ 逃犯依然下落～。The escaped prisoner's whereabouts are still unknown.

【不明不白】bùmíng-bùbái〈成〉without any clear reason: 死得～ die a mysterious death

【不明飞行物】bùmíng fēixíngwù〈名〉unidentified flying object (UFO)

【不明事理】bùmíng-shìlǐ〈成〉lack common sense

【不明真相】bùmíng-zhēnxiàng〈成〉be unaware of the facts

【不鸣则已，一鸣惊人】bù míng zéyǐ, yī míng jīngrén〈成〉it may not have cried out yet, but once it does, it will startle everyone

【不谋而合】bùmóu'érhé〈成〉happen to share the same view: 他的想法与我～。His idea coincides with mine.

【不能不】bùnéngbù〈助〉have to: ～去 have to go

【不能自拔】bùnéng-zìbá〈成〉be in an inextricable situation: 堕入情网，～ fall inextricably in love

【不能自已】bùnéng-zìyǐ〈成〉cannot control oneself: 接到被聘用的通知，她兴奋得～。When she received notice that she'd got the job, she was beside herself with excitement.

【不念旧恶】bùniàn-jiù'è〈成〉let bygones be bygones

【不佞】bùnìng A〈名〉〈旧〉〈谦〉I B〈形〉〈书〉not capable

【不怕不识货，就怕货比货】bù pà bù shíhuò, jiù pà huò bǐ huò〈俗〉drawing comparisons reveals something's true worth

【不怕官，只怕管】bù pà guān, zhǐ pà guǎn〈俗〉it is not the official but the person in direct control, however low his position, who is to be feared

【不怕一万，就怕万一】bù pà yīwàn, jiù pà wànyī〈俗〉be prepared for all eventualities

【不配】bùpèi〈形〉1（不匹配）mismatched: 这袜子的颜色和鞋～。The colour of the socks does not match the shoes. 2（无资格）be unworthy of: ～当母亲 be unfit to be a mother ‖ ～为人师表 be unworthy of being a teacher

【不偏不倚】bùpiān-bùyǐ〈成〉be even-handed: 办案～ show complete impartiality in handling a case

【不平】bùpíng A〈形〉1（不平整）uneven: 道路～ rough road ‖ 表面～。The surface is not level. ‖ 地面～。The ground is uneven. 2（不公平）unfair: ～的事情 injustices 3（不满）resentful: 愤愤～ feel indignant B〈名〉1（不公正）injustice: 路见～，拔刀相助 come to the rescue of a stranger who has suffered an injustice ▸打抱～ 2（不满）resentment: 消除心中的～ vent one's resentment

【不平则鸣】bùpíngzémíng〈成〉where there is injustice, there will be protest

【不平等】bùpíngděng〈形〉unequal: ～待遇 unequal treatment ‖ ～条件 discriminatory conditions

【不平等条约】bùpíngděng tiáoyuē〈名〉unjust treaty: 废除一切～ nullify all unequal treaties

【不破不立】bùpò-bùlì〈成〉without destruction there can be no construction

【不欺暗室】bùqī-ànshì〈成〉be scrupulously honest even if there is no witness around

【不期而遇】bùqī'éryù〈成〉bump into: 我在机场与一位朋友～。I ran into a friend at the airport.

【不起眼儿】bùqǐyǎnr〈形〉nondescript: ～的小人物 small potato

【不切实际】bùqiè-shíjì〈形〉impracticable: ～的计划 impractical plans ‖ 抱～的幻想 cherish fanciful ideas

【不情之请】bùqíngzhīqǐng〈成〉〈套〉my presumptuous request

【不求甚解】bùqiú-shènjiě〈成〉not seek deep understanding: 他读书颇多，但～。He reads extensively though superficially.

【不求有功，但求无过】bùqiú yǒugōng, dànqiú wúguò〈成〉be more concerned with avoiding blame or mistakes than gaining praise

【不屈】bùqū〈动〉be unyielding: 英勇～ demonstrate unyielding heroism ▸宁死～

【不屈不挠】bùqū-bùnáo〈成〉dauntless: ～，前赴后继 dauntlessly step into the breach as others fall

【不然】bùrán A〈形〉not so: 其实～。Actually that's not the case. ‖ ～，情况不像他说的那样严重。No, it's not as serious as he described. B〈连〉or: 快点走吧！～就要迟到了。Hurry up, or we'll be late.

【不人道】bùréndào〈形〉inhuman: ～的做法 inhuman practice

【不仁】bùrén〈形〉1（不仁慈）malevolent: 为富～ rich and heartless 2〈喻〉（无知觉）numb: ▸麻木～

【不忍】bùrěn〈动〉cannot bear: 我～看着他破产。I cannot endure seeing him go broke. ▸于心～

【不日】bùrì〈副〉〈书〉in a few days: 代表团～抵京。The delegation is to arrive in Beijing within the next few days.

【不容】bùróng〈动〉not tolerate: ～辩解 not allow any excuse ‖ ～忽视 must not be ignored ‖ ～怀疑 be beyond doubt

【不容分说】bùróng-fēnshuō = 不由分说 bùyóu-fēnshuō

【不容置喙】bùróng-zhìhuì〈成〉not allow others to put in a word

【不容置疑】bùróng-zhìyí〈成〉leave no room for doubt: 她的诚恳～。There's no question about her sincerity.

【不如】bùrú A〈动〉be inferior to: 药补～食补。Nourishing food is better than tonics. ‖ 论技术我～你。I can't match you in skill. B〈副〉it would be better: 租房～买房。It would be better to buy a house than to rent one.

【不辱使命】bùrǔ-shǐmìng〈成〉bring one's mission to fruition

【不入虎穴，焉得虎子】bù rù hǔxué, yān dé hǔzǐ〈成〉nothing ventured, nothing gained

【不三不四】bùsān-bùsì〈成〉1（指人）shady: 交～的朋友 make friends with dubious characters 2（指言词）neither one thing nor the other: 说些～的话 make frivolous remarks

【不善】bùshàn A〈形〉bad: 管理～ mismanagement ‖ 来者～ come with ill intent B〈动〉not be good at: ～交际 be inexperienced in socializing ‖ ～言谈 be slow of speech

【不上不下】bùshàng-bùxià〈成〉be suspended in mid air

【不甚了了】bùshèn-liǎoliǎo〈成〉not know much (about): 对此我～。I am not clear about it.

【不声不响】bùshēng-bùxiǎng〈成〉hold one's peace

【不胜】bùshèng A〈动〉1（经不住）not be up to: ～重荷 sink beneath one's burden ▸～其烦 2（做不到）[used to indicate difficulty in performing or completing an action]: 拼写错误太多，改～改。There are too many spelling mistakes to correct. ▸防～防，数～数 B〈副〉extremely: ～感激 be deeply grateful ‖ ～荣幸 be greatly honoured

【不胜枚举】bùshèng-méijǔ〈成〉too many to list: 他著述颇丰，～。He has written too many books to list here. ‖ 这种案件～。Such cases defy enumeration.

【不胜其烦】bùshèng-qífán〈成〉cannot bear the irritation: 所有这些问题逐渐使我～。All these questions are beginning to tax my patience.

【不失时机】bùshī-shíjī〈成〉seize the opportune moment

【不失为】bùshīwéi〈动〉may after all be regarded as: 在目前情况下，这～一种好办法。Under the current circumstances, this may after all be a good way out.

【不识好歹】bùshí-hǎodǎi〈成〉cannot tell good from bad: 他～，把我的话当成恶意了。He doesn't know good from bad and decided that what I said carried ill intent.

【不识庐山真面目】bùshí Lúshān zhēnmiànmù〈成〉fail to see the truth of the matter

【不识时务】bùshí-shíwù〈成〉lack understanding of the state of affairs

【不识抬举】bùshí-táijǔ〈成〉fail to appreciate sb.'s kindness

【不识相】bù shíxiàng〈动〉〈口〉have no sense of what is right for the situation

【不时】bùshí〈副〉1（常常）frequently 2（随时）any time: ▸～之需

【不时之需】bùshízhīxū〈成〉possible future need : 以备～ provide for a rainy day

【不食人间烟火】bù shí rénjiān yānhuǒ〈成〉above secular desires

【不是玩儿的】bùshì wánrde〈惯〉it's no joke: 枪万一走火可～。If the gun goes off accidentally, it's no joke.

【不是玩意儿】bùshì wányìr〈惯〉be a despicable person: 他到处说别人的坏话，真～。He is really rotten, speaking ill of others all over the place.

【不是味儿】bùshìwèir〈惯〉1（不好吃）not quite the right taste: 这鸡做得～。The chicken doesn't taste quite right. 2（不标准）odd: 他的英语说得～。His English is a bit off. ‖ 他一听她的话～，转身就走了。Finding her words strange, he turned and went away. 3（不舒坦）upset: 因受到怠慢心里觉得～ feel bad about being slighted

【不是冤家不聚头】bù shì yuānjiā bù jù tóu〈俗〉it is fate that throws enemies or lovers together

【不适】bùshì〈形〉1（不合适）unsuitable 2（不舒服）out of sorts: 感到非常～ feel very unwell ‖ 略感～ feel off colour

【不是】bùshi〈名〉fault: 我给打了圆场反倒落个～。Though it was I who saved the

situation, I was the one who got the blame in the end.

【不爽】bùshuǎng〈形〉**1**（指身体） not well;（指心情） out of sorts: 近来她心情～。She has been in a bad mood recently. **2**（没差错） accurate: ▸屡试～

【不俗】bùsú〈形〉 outstanding: 表现～ outstanding performance ‖ 战绩～ extraordinary military exploits

【不速之客】bùsùzhīkè〈成〉 uninvited guest: 做～ crash a party

【不遂】bùsuì〈动〉〈书〉**1**（不成功） fail **2**（不如愿） go against one's own will: 他稍有～，就大发脾气。Anything unsatisfactory would provoke him into a rage.

【不通】bùtōng **A**〈动〉 be impassable: 鼻子～ have a stuffed nose ‖ 此路～。This is not a through road. **B**〈形〉 making no sense: 这篇文章文理～。The article lacks coherence and logic.

【不同凡响】bùtóng-fánxiǎng〈成〉 out of the ordinary: 他的新作～，轰动一时。His new work was unique and was an instant hit.

【不痛不痒】bùtòng-bùyǎng〈成〉〈喻〉 superficial: 说些～的话 make some perfunctory remarks

【不妥】bùtuǒ〈形〉 improper: 处理～ be mishandled ‖ 讲话～ speak out of turn ‖ 以上建议如有～之处，请予指正。If there is anything inappropriate in my proposal, please point it out.

【不外】bùwài〈动〉 be nothing more than: 常来的～是我的几个老朋友。The frequent callers are nothing more than a few old friends of mine. ‖ 原因～有三。There are only these three reasons.

【不外乎】bùwàihū = 不外 bùwài

【不为已甚】bùwéi-yǐshèn〈成〉 not go too far

【不惟】bùwéi〈连〉〈书〉 not only: 此举～无益，反而有害。Not only is this useless, it is very harmful.

【不韪】bùwěi〈名〉 big mistake: ▸冒天下之大～

【不畏艰险】bùwèi-jiānxiǎn〈成〉defy hardship and danger

【不谓】bùwèi〈动〉〈书〉**1**（不能说） cannot be regarded as: 任务～不重。It's really a hard task. **2**（没料到） not expect: ～今日能再相见! What a surprise to see you again today!

【不闻不问】bùwén-bùwèn〈成〉 be indifferent to: 对孩子的学习～ show no interest in the child's study

【不问】bùwèn〈动〉 pay no attention to: ～是非曲直 make no distinction between right and wrong

【不无】bùwú〈动〉 be somewhat: ～裨益 be of some benefit ‖ ～关系 be related in some way ‖ 这话～道理。What was said was not without reason.

【不无小补】bùwú-xiǎobǔ〈成〉 of some use

【不务正业】bùwù-zhèngyè〈成〉**1**（无正当职业） not engage in honest work: 游手好闲，～ just idle around and do no decent work **2**（不恪尽职守） not attend to one's duties

【不惜】bùxī〈动〉**1**（不吝惜） not stint: ～一切代价 at any cost **2**（不犹豫） not hesitate: 为了人民的利益～牺牲自己的生命 not hesitate to lay down one's life for the interests of the people ▸在所～

【不惜工本】bùxī-gōngběn〈成〉 spare no expense

【不暇】bùxiá〈动〉〈书〉 be too busy: ～他顾 have no time for other matters ▸应接～，自顾～

【不下】bùxià〈动〉**1** = 不下于 bùxiàyú 2 **2**（无法了结） stop: 放心～ feel anxious ‖ 争执～ dispute without coming to an agreement ▸相持～

【不下于】bùxiàyú〈动〉**1**（不次于） be as good as: 他虽没有任何文凭，但知识水平～工商管理硕士。In terms of knowledge, he is on a par with an MBA holder, though he has no diploma. **2**（不少于） be as many as: 报名参加马拉松赛的运动员～五千人。As many as 5,000 runners entered for the marathon race.

【不相干】bùxiānggān〈动〉 have nothing to do with

【不相上下】bùxiāng-shàngxià〈成〉 roughly the same: 能力～ equally capable

【不详】bùxiáng〈形〉**1**（不清楚） unknown: 地址～ unknown address ‖ 他生平～。Little is known about his life. **2**（不详细） unspecified

【不祥】bùxiáng〈形〉 inauspicious: ～的预感 ominous premonition ‖ ～之兆 evil omen

【不想】bùxiǎng〈动〉 not expect: ～计划竟会如此成功。To our surprise, the plan turned out to be a great success.

【不像话】bù xiànghuà〈形〉〈口〉**1**（不合常理） unreasonable: 整天闲转，太～了。It is absurd to idle around all day. ‖ 单方面撕毁合同，太～。One party tearing up the contract was completely inappropriate. **2**（过分） outrageous: 店员竟敢骂顾客，太～了。It is scandalous for a shop assistant to call a customer names. ‖ 这条路的状况实在～。The state of this road is a crying shame.

【不像样】bù xiàngyàng〈形〉〈口〉**1**（变形） out of shape, unpresentable: 箱子压得～了。The box was crushed out of shape. **2**（糟糕） beyond description: 屋子乱得～。The house was in a complete mess.

【不消】bùxiāo〈动〉 not need: ～说 needless to say ‖ 我们连房都买不起，更～说买汽车了。We cannot afford a house, let alone a car. ‖ 我～几日就回来。I'll be back in a few days.

【不孝】bùxiào〈动〉 violate filial obligations: 对父母～ lack of filial piety to one's parents

【不肖】bùxiào〈形〉〈书〉 unworthy: ～之子 unworthy son ‖ ～子孙 unworthy descendants

【不屑】bùxiè〈动〉**1**（认为不值得） disdain: ～与他为伍 feel shame at being in his company **2**（轻视） be scornful: ～的神情 scornful looks

【不屑一顾】bùxiè-yīgù〈成〉 regard as beneath one: 对建议～ pour scorn on a suggestion ‖ 他对行政上的琐事～。He regarded all these administrative details as beneath him.

【不屑于】bùxièyú = 不屑 bùxiè 1

【不懈】bùxiè〈形〉 untiring: ～的努力 relentless efforts ‖ ～追求 unremitting pursuit ▸坚持～

【不信邪】bùxìnxié〈惯〉 be sceptical of heretical beliefs

【不兴】bùxīng〈动〉**1**（不接受） not go in for: 我们这儿～这一套。We don't go in for such practice. **2**（不流行） be out of date: 现在～留刘海了。Fringes are out of fashion now. **3**（不允许） not allow: ～欺负人。Stop bullying. ‖ 大人说话，小孩～插嘴。Children are not allowed to interrupt when adults are talking. **4**（不能） can't: 老让我做作业，就～玩会儿吗? You are always after me about my homework. Can't I play for a while?

【不行】bùxíng **A**〈动〉**1**（不允许） not allow: 你这样下去～。You can't go on like this. **2**（无法忍受） be unbearable: 累得～ be terribly tired ‖ 热得～ be unbearably hot **B**〈形〉**1**（不好） poor: 身体～ be in poor health ‖ 哪里领导～，哪里的生产就上不去。Incompetent leadership results in poor productivity. ‖ 他搞工程设计～。He is no good at engineering design. **2**（行不通） unworkable: 这种化学疗法恐怕～。I'm afraid that this kind of chemotherapy will not work. **3** ▸**p. 772**（垂危） dying: 老太太病重，怕是～了。The old lady is fatally ill. I'm afraid we're losing her. ‖ 她的视力～了。Her eyesight is fading.

【不省人事】bùxǐng-rénshì〈成〉 become unconscious: 经过急救，仍～ remain unconscious after emergency treatment ‖ 醉得～ be so drunk that one passes out

【不幸】bùxìng **A**〈形〉 unlucky: ～身亡 die to our great sorrow ‖ 他～摔断了腿。It's unfortunate that he broke his leg. **B** ▸**p. 772**〈名〉 misfortune: 惨遭～ meet with a tragic death

【不幸之幸】bùxìngzhīxìng〈成〉 a stroke of good luck in a stretch of bad

【不休】bùxiū〈动〉 never stop: 纠缠～ keep nagging ‖ 争吵～ quarrel incessantly ▸喋喋～

【不修边幅】bùxiū-biānfú〈成〉 be careless about one's appearance

【不朽】bùxiǔ〈形〉 immortal: ～的业绩 monumental achievements ▸永垂～

【不锈钢】bùxiùgāng〈名〉 stainless steel

【不虚此行】bùxū-cǐxíng〈成〉 the journey has not been made in vain

【不许】bùxǔ〈动〉**1**（不允许） not allow: ～随地吐痰! No spitting! ‖ 这里～抽烟。No smoking here. **2**〈口〉（不能） can't: 你就～自己想办法吗? Can't you manage by yourself?

【不宣而战】bùxuān'érzhàn〈成〉 start an undeclared war

【不学无术】bùxué-wúshù〈成〉 have neither learning nor skill: ～的人 ignoramus

【不徇私情】bùxùn-sīqíng〈成〉 free from favouritism of any kind

【不逊】bùxùn〈形〉〈书〉 impertinent: ▸出言～

【不亚于】bùyàyú〈动〉 not inferior to: ～进口名牌产品 not inferior to imported branded products

【不言而喻】bùyán'éryù〈成〉 it goes without saying

【不厌】bùyàn〈动〉**1**（不满足） not be tired of **2**（不排斥） not object to: ▸兵～诈

【不厌其烦】bùyàn-qífán〈成〉 spare no trouble

【不厌其详】bùyàn-qíxiáng〈成〉 not be sparing in the details

【不要紧】bù yàojǐn〈动〉**1**（不严重） be not serious: ～，她只是感冒了。It's nothing serious. She just has a cold. ‖ 对不起，踩了您的脚。——～。Sorry to have stepped on your foot. — It doesn't matter. **2**（表面上虽无大碍） seem all right, but: 你这一走～，可把你妈急坏了。You may not see anything wrong in leaving home like this, but it makes your mother very anxious.

【不要脸】bùyàoliǎn〈动〉〈口〉be shameless: 只有~的人才会做出~的事。Only shameless people would do such shameful things.

【不一】bùyī〈形〉different: 长短~ of varying lengths ‖ 大小~ vary in size ‖ 人们对此反应~。People have mixed reactions to this.

【不一而足】bùyī'érzú〈成〉not the only case: 凡此种种，~。Such cases are numerous.

【不依】bùyī〈动〉**1**（不依从）disobey: 她对孩子的要求没有~的。She complied with her child's every wish. **2**（不允许）not let sb. off: 你要再迟到，我可~。If you are late again, I won't let you off so easily.

【不依不饶】bùyī-bùráo〈成〉wouldn't let sb. off

【不宜】bùyí〈动〉〈书〉not be suitable: ~操之过急。It's no good being too hasty. ‖ 病人非常虚弱，~立即手术。The patient is too weak to risk an immediate operation.

【不遗余力】bùyí-yúlì〈成〉go all out: ~地提供帮助 be unstinting in one's efforts to help

【不已】bùyǐ〈副〉to a great extent: 后悔~ feel deep regret ‖ 赞叹~ praise again and again

【不以成败论英雄】bù yǐ chéngbài lùn yīngxióng〈成〉not judge whether a person is a hero on the basis of whether he is successful or not

【不以规矩，不能成方圆】bù yǐ guīju, bùnéng chéng fāngyuán〈成〉nothing can be accomplished without the necessary tools

【不以为然】bùyǐwéirán〈成〉take exception to: ~地摇摇头 shake one's head in disapproval ‖ 他嘴上没说什么，心里却~。He thought otherwise although he said nothing against it.

【不以为意】bùyǐwéiyì〈成〉take no notice: 屡遭挫折却~ suffer repeated frustrations but never care

【不义之财】bùyìzhīcái〈成〉dirty money

【不亦乐乎】bùyìlèhū〈成〉**1**〈本〉isn't it a pleasure?: 有朋自远方来，~? Is it not a pleasure to have friends come from afar? **2**（非常）extremely: 他整天忙得~。He is extremely busy rushing about all day long.

【不易之论】bùyìzhīlùn〈成〉sound statement

【不意】bùyì〈动〉〈书〉not expect: 他们~丢失证件，只好半途返回。The unexpected loss of their papers forced them to return before they reached their destination. ▸出其~

【不翼而飞】bùyì'érfēi〈成〉**1**（丢失）vanish into thin air: 我抽屉里的钱~了。The money I had in the drawer disappeared without trace. **2**（传播得快）spread like wildfire: 消息~，很快便家喻户晓了。The news spread like wildfire from household to household.

【不用】bùyòng〈副〉need not: ~介绍了，我们认识。No need for introductions. We know each other. ‖ ~客气，我们自己来。Don't stand on ceremony. We'll help ourselves.

【不由得】bùyóude **A**〈动〉be a natural consequence: 他态度十分诚恳，~你不信。He was so sincere that you could not possibly refuse to believe him. **B**〈副〉can't help: 他看到那些蚂蟥，~身上发麻。Seeing those leeches, he couldn't help breaking out in goose bumps.

【不由分说】bùyóu-fēnshuō〈成〉allow no explanation: 老人~把儿子训了一顿。The old man gave his son a good dressing-down without giving him the opportunity to explain himself.

【不由自主】bùyóu-zìzhǔ〈成〉involuntarily: 一听见音乐，她就~地脚下打起拍子来。Listening to the music, she couldn't help tapping her feet.

【不渝】bùyú〈动〉〈书〉remain faithful: ▸坚贞~, 忠贞~

【不虞】bùyú〈书〉**A**〈动〉**1**（没料到）not expect: ~之患 unexpected trouble **2**（不担心）not worry about: ~匮乏 fear no shortage of supplies **B**〈名〉contingency: 以备~ be prepared for any contingency

【不虞之备】bùyúzhībèi〈成〉spare parts

【不虞之誉】bùyúzhīyù〈成〉unexpected praise

【不育症】bùyùzhèng〈名〉infertility

【不约而同】bùyuē'értóng〈成〉take the same view or action without previous consultation: 他们~地提出了同样的解决办法。They happened to come up with the same solution.

【不在】bùzài〈动〉**1**〈本〉be out: ~国内 be out of the country **2** ▸**p. 772**〈婉〉be dead: 他去年就~了。He died last year.

【不在话下】bùzài-huàxià〈成〉**1**（理所当然）it goes without saying: 好课本有助于学习，这自然~。It goes without saying that a good textbook is a great study aid. **2**（没问题）be easy: 击败主队应该~。Beating the home team should be a piece of cake.

【不在其位，不谋其政】bù zài qí wèi, bù móu qí zhèng〈成〉if it's not your job, don't worry about it

【不在乎】bùzàihu〈动〉not care: 满~ not care a bit ‖ 只要他好好工作，我倒~他挣多少钱回家。So long as he works hard, I don't really mind how much money he brings home.

【不在意】bùzàiyì〈动〉pay no attention to

【不赞一词】bùzàn-yīcí〈成〉not utter a word

【不择手段】bùzé-shǒuduàn〈成〉by hook or by crook: ~向上爬 try to get promoted by hook or by crook ‖ 为达目的~ stop at nothing to get what one wants

【不怎么样】bù zěnmeyàng〈惯〉ordinary: 他游泳~。He isn't much of a swimmer. ‖ 这产品销路~。This product doesn't sell well.

【不粘锅】bùzhānguō〈名〉non-stick cooker

【不战而胜】bùzhàn'érshèng〈成〉win a victory without striking a blow

【不折不扣】bùzhé-bùkòu〈成〉**1**（完全）thoroughly: ~地履行合同 fully respect a contract **2**（十足）out-and-out: ~的大傻瓜 fool through and through

【不振】bùzhèn〈形〉dispirited: 精神~ be in low spirits ‖ 食欲~ have no appetite ▸萎靡~, 一蹶~

【不争】bùzhēng〈形〉unquestionable: 这是~的事实。This is an indisputable fact.

【不争气】bù zhēngqì〈动〉be disappointing

【不正当竞争】bùzhèngdàng jìngzhēn〈名〉unequal competition

【不正之风】bùzhèngzhīfēng〈成〉dishonest practices: 纠正~ correct unhealthy tendencies

【不支】bùzhī〈动〉cannot bear: 体力~ be physically not up to it

【不知不觉】bùzhī-bùjué〈成〉unconsciously: 人~就老了。Old age creeps up on you before you realize it.

【不知好歹】bùzhī-hǎodǎi〈成〉not know good from bad

【不知进退】bùzhī-jìntuì〈成〉have no sense of propriety: 我~，有时难免冒犯别人。I am not a tactful person and tend to offend people sometimes.

【不知就里】bùzhī-jiùlǐ〈成〉not know the inside story: 我当时~，错怪了你。I was in the dark at the time and made the mistake of blaming you.

【不知所措】bùzhī-suǒcuò〈成〉be at a loss: 一时~ not know what to do for a moment

【不知所云】bùzhī-suǒyún〈成〉not know what sb. is driving at: 这篇文章我看了好几遍，还是~。After several readings, I still cannot make head or tail of this article.

【不知天高地厚】bù zhī tiān gāo dì hòu〈成〉not know one's own limitations

【不织布】bùzhībù〈名〉［纺织］unwoven fabric

【不值】bùzhí〈动〉not worth: ~一谈 not worth mentioning ‖ 为这点小事吵架，~。It makes no sense to quarrel over such a trifle.

【不值一文】bùzhí-yīwén〈成〉not worth a penny

【不止】bùzhǐ〈动〉**1**（不停）not stop: 血流~ keep bleeding ‖ 生命不息，战斗~ keep on fighting till death **2**（超过）exceed: ~一次 more than once ‖ 她~四十了吧。She is probably over forty.

【不只】bùzhǐ〈连〉not just: ~我，另外还有三个目击者。Apart from me there were three other eye-witnesses.

【不至于】bùzhìyú〈动〉be unlikely: 他~糊涂到干这种事。He knows better than to do such a thing. ‖ 我相信她~连这点道理都不懂。I believe she has more sense than that.

【不治之症】bùzhìzhīzhèng〈成〉incurable disease

【不致】bùzhì〈动〉be unlikely: 早点出发就~迟到。Set off early and you won't be late.

【不置可否】bùzhì-kěfǒu〈成〉decline to comment: ~的答复 non-committal reply

【不周】bùzhōu〈形〉insufficiently complete: 计划~ not well-planned ‖ 照顾~，请多包涵。Please excuse any shortcomings in our service.

【不着边际】bùzhuó-biānjì〈成〉wide of the mark: 她越说越~。The more she talked, the further she strayed from the point.

【不自量】bùzìliàng〈惯〉overestimate one's abilities: 此人很~，常以专家自居。He far overestimated his own abilities, often rating himself as an expert.

【不自量力】bùzìliànglì〈成〉overrate one's abilities: 这么大的工程你能拿下来？我看你有点~。Can you cope with such a huge project? I'm afraid you may be a bit beyond yourself here.

【不足】bùzú **A**〈形〉insufficient: 经费~ be short of funds ‖ 人手~ be understaffed ‖ 证据~ lack of evidence ‖ 准备~ not well-prepared ▸先天~ **B**〈动〉**1**（不到）be less than: ~三年 less than three years **2**（不值得）not deserve: ~称道 not worth commending ▸~挂齿, ~为奇 **3**（不能）cannot: 不杀~以平民愤。Nothing less than the death sentence can

b

assuage public indignation. ‖ 道听途说～为信。 Hearsay cannot be taken seriously.

【不足挂齿】bùzú-guàchǐ〈成〉 nothing to speak of: 区区小事，～。 My paltry efforts are nothing to speak of.

【不足为凭】bùzú-wéipíng〈成〉 cannot be taken as evidence

【不足为奇】bùzú-wéiqí〈成〉 not at all surprising

【不足为训】bùzú-wéixùn〈成〉 not to be taken as authoritative

【不做声】bù zuòshēng〈动〉 keep silent: 他坐在那里～。 He sat there without saying a word.

【不作为】bùzuòwéi **A**〈名〉［法律］ negligence **B**〈动〉 [of officials] be inactive: 主管部门的～ inaction of the departments responsible

布[1] bù〈名〉 **1**（指织物） cloth: 一匹～ a bolt of cloth ‖ 织～ weave cloth ▸～料，棉～ **2**（布状物） cloth-like object: 塑料～ plastic cloth **3**（指货币） ancient coin

布[2]（**佈**） bù〈动〉 **1**（遍布） spread: 阴云密～ be covered with dark clouds ‖ 她的双眼～满了血丝。 Her eyes were netted with little veins. ▸遍～，分～，散～ **2**（设置） deploy: ～好阵势 deploy troops in battle formation ‖ ～下天罗地网 cast an escape-proof net ▸～局，～雷，～置 **3**（宣告） announce: ▸～告，发～，宣～

【布帛】bùbó〈名〉 cotton and silk

【布帛菽粟】bùbó-shūsù〈成〉 food and clothing

【布达拉宫】Bùdálāgōng〈名〉 Potala Palace

> 布达拉宫
>
> Historically, the chief residence of the Dalai Lama. The Potala is situated on top of the Red Mountain in Lhasa, Tibet. The first palace on this site was built in the 7th century for King Songsten Gampo (松赞干布). It was expanded in the 17th century by the 5th Dalai Lama. The Potala contains more than a thousand rooms and many thousands of shrines and statues. In the east part of the Potala is the White Palace, housing the living quarters. The central part of the Potala is the Red Palace, used for prayer and religious study.

【布达佩斯】Bùdápèisī〈名〉 Budapest

【布道】bùdào〈动〉［基督教］ preach

【布丁】bùdīng〈名〉 pudding

【布尔什维克】Bù'ěrshíwéikè〈名〉 Bolshevik

【布防】bùfáng〈动〉 organize a defence: 沿江～ deploy troops along the river for defence

【布告】bùgào **A**〈名〉 notice: 张贴～ put up a notice **B**〈动〉 proclaim: ～天下 proclaim to the whole country ‖ 特此～ It is hereby announced that ...

【布告栏】bùgàolán〈名〉 notice board

【布谷】bùgǔ〈名〉［鸟类］ cuckoo

【布基纳法索】Bùjīnàfǎsuǒ〈名〉 Burkina Faso

【布加勒斯特】Bùjiālèsītè〈名〉 Bucharest

【布景】bùjǐng〈名〉 **1**（指画） composition **2**（指舞台） scenery: 更换～ change the scenes ‖ 舞台～ stage setting

【布局】bùjú〈动〉 **1**（规划） overall arrangement: 对称的～ symmetrical arrangement ‖ 促进经济合理～ foster rational economic distribution **2**（画面安排） composition: 画面～雅致。 This painting has a graceful composition.

【布控】bùkòng〈动〉 station to supervise: 对嫌疑犯实施～ put the suspects under surveillance

【布拉柴维尔】Bùlācháiwéi'ěr〈名〉 Brazzaville

【布拉迪斯拉发】Bùlādísīlāfā〈名〉 Bratislava

【布拉格】Bùlāgé〈名〉 Prague

【布拉吉】bùlājí〈名〉 catsuit

【布朗族】Bùlǎngzú〈名〉 Blang ethnic group, Bulong ethnic group

【布雷】bùléi〈动〉 set mines: 在入港处～ mine the entrance to a habour

【布雷肯郡】Bùléikěnjùn〈名〉 Breconshire, Brecknockshire

【布里奇敦】Bùlǐqídūn〈名〉 Bridgetown

【布料】bùliào〈名〉 cloth

【布隆迪】Bùlóngdí〈名〉 Burundi: ～共和国 Republic of Burundi ‖ ～人 Burundian

【布鲁塞尔】Bùlǔsài'ěr〈名〉 Brussels

【布鲁斯】bùlǔsī〈名〉 the blues

【布嫩族】Bùnènzú〈名〉 Bunun ethnic group

【布匹】bùpǐ〈名〉 piece goods

【布琼布拉】Bùqióngbùlā〈名〉 Bujumbura

【布设】bùshè〈动〉 set: ～地雷 set mines ‖ ～警戒线 throw a cordon around

【布施】bùshī **A**〈动〉 donate **B**〈名〉〈书〉 almsgiving: 他太高傲，不会接受～。 He is too proud to accept charity.

【布头】bùtóu〈名〉 **1**（指零头） leftovers **2**（指剩料） scraps of cloth

【布娃娃】bùwáwa〈名〉 cloth doll

【布纹纸】bùwénzhǐ〈名〉［摄影］ wove paper

【布鞋】bùxié〈名〉 cloth shoes

【布衣】bùyī〈名〉 **1**〈本〉 clothes made of common cloth **2**〈旧〉（平民） commoner: ～出身 be the son of a commoner

【布衣蔬食】bùyī-shūshí〈成〉 coarse clothes and simple fare

【布依族】Bùyīzú〈名〉 Bouyei ethnic group

【布宜诺斯艾利斯】Bùyínuòsī'àilìsī〈名〉 Buenos Aires

【布艺】bùyì〈名〉 cloth art: ～沙发 cloth-art sofa

【布展】bùzhǎn〈动〉 set up an exhibit

【布阵】bùzhèn〈动〉 deploy troops in rank for battle: ～排兵 deploy troops for battle

【布置】bùzhì〈动〉 **1**（摆设） arrange: ～会场 fix up a place for a meeting ‖ ～新房 decorate the bridal chamber ‖ 房间～得很漂亮。 The room is done up beautifully. **2**（分派任务） make arrangements for: ～任务/家庭作业 assign tasks/homework

步 bù

A〈动〉 **1**（步行） walk: ～入宴会厅 walk into the banquet hall ‖ 徒～旅行 travel on foot ▸～行，安～当车，散～ **2**〈书〉（跟随） follow: ～母亲之后尘 follow in one's mother's footsteps ▸～人后尘 **3**（用脚步测量） measure by paces: ～一～这块地的宽度 pace out the width of the field

B〈名〉 **1**（脚步） step: 后退/前进一～ take a step back/forward ‖ 跑～走! At the double, quick march! ‖ 我一～也走不动了。 I couldn't move a step further. ▸疾～，舞～ **2**（环节） step: 迈向成功的第一～ first step on the path to success ‖ 下一～怎么办? What's the next step? ▸～骤，逐～ **3**（处境） situation: 落到这一～ fall into this state ▸地～

【步兵】bùbīng〈名〉 **1**（指兵种） infantry **2**（指士兵） foot soldier

【步步为营】bùbù-wéiyíng〈成〉 advance and consolidate at every step

【步调】bùdiào〈名〉 step: 采取统一的～ take concerted action ‖ ～一致 act in unison

【步伐】bùfá〈名〉 pace: 跟上时代的～ keep pace with the times ‖ 加快～ quicken one's pace

【步法】bùfǎ〈名〉 footwork: ～别致的舞蹈 dance with exquisite steps

【步话机】bùhuàjī〈名〉 walkie-talkie

【步犁】bùlí〈名〉 walking plough

【步履】bùlǚ〈名〉〈书〉 walk: ～轻盈 walk in light steps ‖ ～维艰 walk with difficulty

【步枪】bùqiāng〈名〉 rifle

【步人后尘】bùrénhòuchén〈成〉 follow sb.'s footsteps: 不要总是～，要有所创造。 Don't just follow other people's lead. Be creative.

【步入】bùrù〈动〉 step into: ～会场 walk into the meeting room ‖ ～老年/中年 approach old/middle age

【步态】bùtài〈名〉 gait: ～蹒跚 walk with unsteady steps ‖ ～轻盈 walk with light cheerful steps

【步行】bùxíng〈动〉 go on foot: ～上班/上学 walk to work/school

【步行街】bùxíngjiē〈名〉 pedestrian shopping street

【步韵】bùyùn〈动〉 follow an established rhyme sequence

【步骤】bùzhòu〈名〉 step: 具体～ concrete measures ‖ 有计划、有～地开展工作 carry out the work step by step in a well-planned way

【步子】bùzi〈名〉 footstep: 放慢/加快～ slacken/quicken one's pace

怖 bù〈动〉 fear: ▸恐～

钚（**鈈**） bù〈名〉［化学］ plutonium (Pu)

部 bù

A〈名〉 **1**（部分） part: 南～ southern part ‖ 腿～受伤 be wounded in the leg ▸腹～，局～，外～ **2**（部队） troops: 率～起义 lead one's troops in an uprising **3**（种类） category: ▸～类 **4**（政府机构） ministry: 农业/文化～ Ministry of Agriculture/Culture **5**（部门） department: 邮购～ mail order department ▸编辑～

B〈量〉 **1**（用于书籍、影片） [used for books, films, etc.]: 一～词典/电影 a dictionary/film **2**（用于机器、车辆等） [used for machines, vehicles, etc.]: 两～电话 two telephones ‖ 一～机器 a machine **3**（用于演奏、唱歌） part: 管乐器～ wind part ‖ 三～合唱 chorus in three parts

【部队】bùduì〈名〉 army: 部署～ deploy an army ‖ 集结～ mass troops ‖ 率领～ command an army ‖ 导弹～ missile forces ‖ 野战～ field army units ‖ 后勤～ rear-service unit

【部分】bùfen〈名〉 part: 承担～责任 take part of the blame ‖ 不可分割的一～ an integral part ‖ 绝大～ best part ‖ 身体各～ various parts of the body

【部件】bùjiàn〈名〉 parts: 备用～ spare parts ‖ 汽车～一般都是统一规格的。 Car parts are usually standardized.

【部将】bùjiàng〈名〉〈旧〉 military officers under one's command

【部类】bùlèi〈名〉 category: 展品共分十大～。 Exhibits fall into ten major categories.

【部落】bùluò〈名〉 clan: ～首领 tribal chief ‖ 原始～ primitive tribe

【部门】bùmén〈名〉 department: 国民经济的重要～ important sectors of the national economy ‖ 有关～ departments concerned ‖ 政府～ government agencies ‖ 主管～ department in charge

【部首】bùshǒu〈名〉［语言］ radicals

【部属】bùshǔ **A** = 部下 bùxià **B**〈动〉 be attached to a particular ministry: 司法部的～院校 universities and colleges affiliated to the Ministry of Justice

【部署】bùshǔ〈动〉 lay out: ～军队 deploy troops ‖ 战斗～ battle disposition ‖ 战略～ strategic deployment ‖ 在建筑物周围～警察 set policemen around the building

【部头】bùtóu〈名〉 size (of written works): 大～作品 voluminous works

【部委】bùwěi〈名〉 ministries and commissions: 国务院（所属）各～ ministries and commissions under the State Council

【部位】bùwèi〈名〉 part: 发音～ point of articulation ‖ 注意不要碰着他的受伤～。Take care not to touch his wound.

【部下】bùxià〈名〉 **1**（指部队） troops under one's command **2**（下属） subordinate: 他对～很好。 He treats his subordinates very well.

【部长】bùzhǎng〈名〉 minister: 财政～ minister of finance ‖ 外交～ minister of foreign affairs

【部长会议】bùzhǎng huìyì〈名〉 Council of Ministers

【部族】bùzú〈名〉 tribe

埠 bù〈名〉 **1**（码头） wharf: ▸～头, 船～ **2**（港口城市） port: ▸本～, 商～, 外～ **3**（旧）（与外国通商的城市） commercial port: 开～ open a commercial port

【埠头】bùtóu〈名〉〈方〉 wharf

簿 bù〈名〉 notebook: 练习～ exercise-book ‖ 支票～ book of cheques ▸账～

【簿册】bùcè〈名〉 **1**（笔记本） notebook **2**（账本） account book

【簿籍】bùjí〈名〉 account books

【簿记】bùjì〈名〉 bookkeeping

【簿子】bùzi〈名〉 notebook

cā

拆 cā
▸chāi

【拆烂污】 cā lànwū 〈惯〉〈方〉〈喻〉 botch up

擦 cā 〈动〉 1▸(摩擦) rub: ～火柴 strike a match ▸摩～, 摩拳～掌 2▸(挨着) touch lightly: ～着墙根往西走 edge one's way west along the wall ▸～黑儿, ～肩而过 3▸(抹) wipe: ～窗玻璃 clean a windowpane ‖ ～皮鞋 shine shoes ‖ ～干眼泪 wipe one's tears away ▸～亮 4▸(涂) spread: ～碘酒 apply iodine ▸～粉 5▸(使成细条) shred: ～胡萝卜丝/土豆丝 shred carrots/potatoes

【擦背】 cābèi 〈动〉 rub one's back

【擦边球】 cābiānqiú 〈名〉〈喻〉 limits of acceptance: 打～ play close to the edge

【擦粉】 cāfěn 〈动〉 powder: 给脸上～ powder one's face

【擦黑儿】 cāhēir 〈名〉〈方〉 sunset: 赶到家时, 天已～了。 We did not get home until sunset.

【擦痕】 cāhén 〈名〉 scratch: 他发现自己的新车上有一道～。 He found a scratch on his new car.

【擦肩而过】 cājiān'érguò 〈成〉 brush past sb.: 他与我～, 但没有看见我。 He brushed past me without seeing me.

【擦亮】 cāliàng 〈动〉 polish: ～银器 polish the silver

【擦亮眼睛】 cāliàng yǎnjing 〈惯〉〈喻〉 sharpen one's vigilance: ～, 谨防上当。 Sharpen your vigilance against deception.

【擦屁股】 cā pìgu 〈惯〉〈喻〉 clear up the mess

【擦伤】 cāshāng **A** 〈动〉 scrape: ～皮肤 graze the skin ‖ 她只是～了一点儿皮。 She received a mere scratch. **B** 〈名〉 abrasion: 多处～ suffer multiple abrasions ‖ 皮肤上有几处～ have a few scrapes on the skin

【擦拭】 cāshì 〈动〉 wipe: ～家具 wipe the furniture ‖ ～枪支 clean firearms

【擦网球】 cāwǎngqiú 〈名〉［体育］ netball

【擦洗】 cāxǐ 〈动〉 scrub: ～车床 clean the lathe ‖ 油漆不容易～掉。 The paint doesn't scrub off easily.

【擦鞋器】 cāxiéqì 〈名〉 shoe polisher

【擦音】 cāyīn 〈名〉［语言］ fricative

【擦澡】 cāzǎo 〈动〉 rub oneself down with a wet towel

【擦子】 cāzi 〈名〉 eraser

嚓 cā 〈拟〉 swish: 用镰刀～～地割草 swish off the weeds with a sickle ‖ 我听到～～的脚步声。 I heard the scrape of footsteps.
▸chā

cǎ

礤 cǎ

【礤床儿】 cǎchuángr 〈名〉 vegetable shredder

cāi

猜 cāi 〈动〉 1▸(怀疑) suspect: 我～是他偷了我的车。 I suspect he stole my car. ▸～忌, ～疑, 两小无～ 2▸(猜测) guess: ～谜语 guess a riddle ‖ ～出心思 guess sb.'s thoughts ‖ 你～对了! You've got it!

【猜测】 cāicè 〈动〉 guess: ～心思 guess sb.'s thoughts ‖ 妄加～ make a random guess ‖ 我们的～已完全得到证实。 Our suppositions were fully confirmed.

【猜度】 cāiduó 〈动〉 surmise: 他反复～她说这话的用意。 He kept wondering what she really meant by saying that.

【猜忌】 cāijì 〈动〉 be suspicious and jealous: 他俩貌合神离, 互相～。 Though they may be friends in name, they are suspicious and jealous of each other.

【猜料】 cāiliào 〈动〉 guess: 会发生什么事, 还很难～。 What will happen is anybody's guess.

【猜谜】 cāimí 〈动〉 1▸〈本〉 guess a riddle 2▸〈喻〉 work out: 直说吧, 我可不想～。 Tell me straight; I don't want to have to suss it out.

【猜摸】 cāimo 〈动〉 speculate: 没人能～得透他的心思。 Nobody can work out what's on his mind.

【猜破】 cāipò 〈动〉 guess right

【猜拳】 cāiquán = 划拳 huáquán

【猜想】 cāixiǎng 〈动〉 guess: 凭空～ make empty guesses ‖ 我～他几年之内不会回来。 I suppose he won't be back within the next few years.

【猜哑谜】 cāi yǎmí 〈动〉 guess at the real meaning of sth.

【猜疑】 cāiyí 〈动〉 harbour suspicions: 互相～ be suspicious of each other ‖ 毫无理由地～ have groundless suspicions

【猜中】 cāizhòng 〈动〉 guess correctly: ～谜语 solve a riddle ‖ 你～了。 You have guessed right.

cái

才[1] cái 〈名〉 1▸(才能) ability: 诗～ gift for writing poetry ‖ 这人很有～。 That man has a real talent. ▸～华, 多～多艺, 口～ 2▸(人才) talent: ▸奇～, 全～, 人～, 天～

才[2] cái 〈副〉 1▸(表前提条件) not until: 我看了报纸, ～了解到事情的真相。 I didn't know the truth until I read the newspaper. ‖ 狼只有饥饿时～攻击人。 A wolf will only attack a human being when it is hungry. 2▸(刚刚) only just: 电影～开始。 The movie has just started. ‖ 我刚刚～到。 I've only just arrived. 3▸(只有) only: 他到美国～一个月, 就可以同当地人交流了。 He was able to communicate with the locals only one month after his arrival in the US. ‖ 我开始踢球的时候～五岁。 I started playing football when I was just five. 4▸(表强调) actually: 他～不傻呢。 He is no fool. ‖ 她～不想一辈子呆在那儿呢。 She has not the least desire to stay there forever. 5▸(表时间晚) not until: 你怎么这么晚～来上课? Why are you so late for class? ‖ 我到半夜一两点～睡觉。 I didn't go to bed until the small hours.

【才出虎口, 又入狼窝】 cái chū hǔkǒu, yòu rù lángwō 〈俗〉 out of the frying pan into the fire

【才分】 cáifèn 〈名〉 talent: 他～过人。 He was of above average intelligence.

【才干】 cáigàn 〈名〉 ability: 显示～ show one's ability ‖ 有～ be capable ‖ 增长～ develop one's abilities ‖ 他在这项研究中充分地发挥出了～。 His abilities were on full display during the course of the research.

【才高八斗】 cáigāo-bādǒu 〈成〉 be endowed with great talents

【才华】 cáihuá 〈名〉 talent: 在服装设计方面很有～ be very talented at fashion design ‖ ～出众 have outstanding talent ‖ ～横溢 overflow with talent

【才具】 cáijù 〈名〉〈书〉 ability: ～有限 be of limited capacity

【才力】 cáilì 〈名〉 ability: ～超群 be endowed with outstanding ability

【才略】 cáilüè 〈名〉 ability and sagacity: ～过人 be of exceptional wit and sagacity

【才貌】 cáimào 〈名〉 wit and charm: ～出众 be of remarkable talent and good looks

【才貌双全】 cáimào-shuāngquán 〈成〉 be endowed with both beauty and talent: 她～, 让我佩服得五体投地。 I was swept off my feet by her wit and charm.

【才能】 cáinéng 〈名〉 ability: 展示～ demonstrate one's ability ‖ 文学～ talent for literature ‖ 行政管理～ administrative ability ‖ 艺术～ artistic talent

【才女】 cáinǚ 〈名〉 talented female scholar

【才气】 cáiqì 〈名〉 literary or artistic talent: 很有～的作家 gifted writer

【才情】 cáiqíng 〈名〉 literary or artistic talent: 卖弄～ show off one's literary or

artistic talent

【才人】cáirén〈名〉1（旧）（宫女）gifted lady-in-waiting 2（有才华的人）talented scholar

【才识】cáishí〈名〉ability and insight: ～过人 be gifted with extraordinary talent and insight

【才疏学浅】cáishū-xuéqiǎn〈成〉〈谦〉be unlearned and of little talent: 本人～，恐不堪当此重任。I'm afraid that I may not be up to this important task because I lack knowledge and skills.

【才疏志大】cáishū-zhìdà = 志大才疏 zhìdà-cáishū

【才思】cáisī〈名〉literary creativeness and imaginative power: ～敏捷 be of keen intellect

【才学】cáixué〈名〉talent and learning: ～过人 be exceptionally learned

【才艺】cáiyì〈名〉talent and skill: ～出众 be of unusual talent and skill

【才智】cáizhì〈名〉ability and wisdom: 充分发挥聪明～ give full play to one's wisdom and intelligence

【才子】cáizǐ〈名〉talented scholar

【才子佳人】cáizǐ-jiārén〈成〉gifted scholar and fair lady: 又是一个老掉牙的～的故事。It's just another old story about a talented man and a beautiful woman.

材 cái〈名〉1（木料）timber: 用～林 timber forest ▸木～ 2（材料）material: ▸～料，钢～，就地取～，药～ 3（资料）data: ▸教～，素～，题～ 4（才能）ability: ▸因～施教 5（指某种人）person of a certain type: 蠢～ fool ‖ 庸～ man of mediocre talents 6（棺材）coffin: ▸棺～，寿～

【材料】cáiliào〈名〉1（原料）material: 防火～ fire-resistant material ‖ 劣质～ poor-quality material ‖ 这点～不够做一套衣服。There is not enough material to make a suit. ▸建筑～，原～ 2（资料）data: 收集～ collect data ‖ 学习～ study materials 3（参考内容）reference material: 档案～ archival material ‖ 人事～ personnel file 4〈喻〉（人才）material: 我弟弟个子矮，不是跳高的～。My brother is short. He's not high jump material. ‖ 他绝对是个当领导的～。Without doubt, he has the makings of a leader.

【材树】cáishù〈名〉timber tree

【材质】cáizhì〈名〉texture of wood: ～细密 be fine-textured ‖ 不同～的门窗 doors and windows of different materials

【材种】cáizhǒng〈名〉wood assortment

财（財） cái〈名〉money: 爱～ love money ‖ 君子爱～，取之有道。A righteous man makes money in righteous ways. ▸～产，～政，理～

【财报】cáibào〈简称〉= 财务报告

【财宝】cáibǎo〈名〉valuables: 金银～ gold and silver treasures

【财帛】cáibó〈名〉〈旧〉riches

【财产】cáichǎn〈名〉property: 保护国家～ protect state property ‖ 继承～ inherit property ‖ 家庭～ family possessions

【财产保险】cáichǎn bǎoxiǎn〈名〉property insurance: 家庭～ family property insurance

【财产法】cáichǎnfǎ〈名〉property law

【财产分配】cáichǎn fēnpèi〈名〉asset distribution

【财产继承权】cáichǎn jìchéngquán〈名〉property inheritance rights

【财产权】cáichǎnquán〈名〉property rights

【财产税】cáichǎnshuì〈名〉property tax

【财产所有权】cáichǎn suǒyǒuquán〈名〉property rights

【财产所有人】cáichǎn suǒyǒurén〈名〉property owner

【财产转让】cáichǎn zhuǎnràng〈名〉transfer of property

【财大气粗】cáidà-qìcū〈成〉money carries weight

【财东】cáidōng〈名〉man of means

【财阀】cáifá〈名〉tycoon

【财富】cáifù〈名〉wealth: 创造～ create wealth ‖ 精神～ spiritual wealth ‖ 物质～ material possessions ‖ 健康是一大～。Good health is a great asset.

【财经】cáijīng〈名〉finance and economy: ～报道 business report ‖ ～体制 financial and economic system

【财会】cáikuài〈名〉finance and accounting: ～档案 financial and accounting archives ‖ ～人员 accountant

【财礼】cáilǐ = 彩礼 cǎilǐ

【财力】cáilì〈名〉financial resources: ～雄厚/有限 have abundant/limited financial resources

【财路】cáilù〈名〉means of making money: 广开～ exploit all possible avenues for wealth

【财贸】cáimào〈名〉finance and trade: ～工作 work in the field of finance and trade ‖ ～系统 field of finance and trade

【财迷】cáimí〈名〉miser: 老～ old miser ‖ 她真是个～。She really is a miser.

【财迷心窍】cáimí-xīnqiào〈成〉be obsessed with money: 他～，六亲不认。He's so mad for money that he forgets his family.

【财气】cáiqì〈名〉luck in making money

【财权】cáiquán〈名〉1（指所有权）property rights: 继承～ inherit property rights 2（指控制权）economic power: 掌握～ hold the purse strings

【财神】cáishén ▸p. 274〈名〉1（指神仙）God of Wealth 2（指人）person who brings money to sb.

> **财神**
>
> Also 财神爷, the god of wealth, also known as Zhao Gongming (赵公明). He has a black face, a thick beard, and wears an iron cap. In his hand he carries an iron whip and he rides a black tiger. At each Spring Festival people used to put up images of the god and make offerings to him. Zhao Gongming is sometimes called the martial god of wealth, while the civil god of wealth is Fan Li (范蠡), a politician-turned-merchant in the late Spring and Autumn period. Lord Guan (▸关帝庙) is also regarded as the God of Wealth.

【财势】cáishì〈名〉wealth and power: 依仗～ count on sb.'s wealth and influence ‖ 以～压人 exert pressure upon others with wealth and power

【财税】cáishuì〈名〉finance and taxation: ～制度 financial and taxation system

【财团】cáituán〈名〉consortium: 金融～ financial consortium

【财务】cáiwù〈名〉1（指事务）financial affairs: 主管～ be in charge of financial affairs ‖ ～公开 keep the public informed of financial affairs 2（指人）person in charge of financial affairs

【财务报表】cáiwù bàobiǎo〈名〉financial statement

【财务报告】cáiwù bàogào〈名〉financial report

【财务处】cáiwùchù〈名〉office of financial affairs

【财务官】cáiwùguān ▸p. 966〈名〉finance officer: 公司首席～ chief finance officer of the company

【财务监督】cáiwù jiāndū〈名〉financial supervision

【财务结算】cáiwù jiésuàn〈名〉financial settlement

【财务开支】cáiwù kāizhī〈名〉financial expense

【财务科】cáiwùkē〈名〉finance section

【财务会计学】cáiwù kuàijìxué〈名〉financial accounting

【财务审计】cáiwù shěnjì〈名〉financial audit

【财务支出】cáiwù zhīchū〈名〉fiscal expenditure

【财务总监】cáiwù zǒngjiān〈名〉Chief Financial Officer (CFO)

【财物】cáiwù〈名〉property: 爱护公共～ take good care of public property

【财险】cáixiǎn〈名〉property insurance

【财雄势大】cáixióng-shìdà〈成〉be of great wealth and influence

【财源】cáiyuán〈名〉financial resources: 广开～ explore all possible sources of revenue ‖ ～茂盛 have abundant financial resources ‖ ～滚滚。Fortune floods in from all sides.

【财运】cáiyùn〈名〉luck in making money: ～亨通 be overwhelmingly fortunate in making money

【财政】cáizhèng〈名〉finance: ～管理 financial management ‖ ～专家 finance expert ‖ ～状况 financial situation ‖ 解决～问题 resolve fiscal problems

【财政包干制】cáizhèng bāogānzhì〈名〉fiscal responsibility system

【财政拨款】cáizhèng bōkuǎn〈名〉financial allocation

【财政补贴】cáizhèng bǔtiē〈名〉financial subsidy

【财政部】cáizhèngbù〈名〉ministry of finance: ～长 finance minister

【财政赤字】cáizhèng chìzì〈名〉budgetary deficits: 消灭～ erase a budget deficit

【财政大臣】cáizhèng dàchén〈名〉Chancellor of the Exchequer

【财政局】cáizhèngjú〈名〉bureau of finance

【财政年度】cáizhèng niándù〈名〉fiscal year

【财政厅】cáizhèngtīng〈名〉provincial department of finance

【财主】cáizhu〈名〉wealthy man

裁 cái

A〈动〉1（剪切）cut into parts: ～衣服 cut out a garment ‖ 这块布能～两件上衣。This piece of cloth will cut into two coats. ▸～纸 2（解雇）cut down: 她让经理给～了。She was dismissed by the manager. ▸～减，～军，～员 3（控制）control: ▸独～，制～ 4（判断）judge: ▸～定，～判，仲～ 5（安排取舍）select and plan: ▸别出心～

B〈名〉form of writing: ▸体～

C〈量〉[division of standard-size printing paper]: 八～报纸 newspaper in octavo ‖ 对～纸 folio

【裁并】cáibìng〈动〉cut down and merge

【裁撤】cáichè〈动〉dissolve: 今年改革的重点就是～不必要的机构。This year's reform focuses on dissolving unnecessary agencies.

【裁处】cáichǔ〈动〉judge and take action: 这件事完全由你～。The matter is completely over to you.

【裁定】cáidìng **A**〈动〉［法律］adjudicate: 依法～ adjudicate according to law ‖ 陪审团～他无罪。The jury ruled that he was innocent of all charges. **B**〈名〉ruling: 司法～ judicial verdict ‖ 对～提出上诉 appeal a decision
【裁定书】cáidìngshū〈名〉written verdict
【裁断】cáiduàn〈动〉consider and judge: 证据不足，很难～。Lack of evidence makes it difficult to reach a final decision.
【裁夺】cáiduó〈动〉consider and decide: 此事如何处置，报请上级～。Submit this matter to the higher authorities for a decision. ‖ 文稿采用与否，由主编～。It's up to the chief editor to decide whether to use this contribution or not.
【裁度】cáiduó〈动〉〈书〉deduce: 妄加～ make a rushed inference
【裁缝】cáiféng〈动〉tailor: ～得体 be well tailored
【裁缝】cáifeng〈名〉tailor: ～店 the tailor's
【裁减】cáijiǎn〈动〉reduce: ～机构 cut down the number of institutions ‖ ～军备 reduce armaments ‖ ～员工 cut staff
【裁剪】cáijiǎn〈动〉tailor: 按纸样～衣料 trim material to a pattern ‖ 这套西装～得很合适。The suit is well tailored.
【裁决】cáijué〈动〉rule: 做出～ reach a verdict ‖ 此事请当地主管部门～。This affair should be dealt with by the local authorities concerned. ‖ 这场争论由他来～。Decisions on the dispute are up to him.
【裁决书】cáijuéshū〈名〉arbitral award
【裁军】cáijūn〈动〉reduce armaments: ～谈判 disarmament talks ‖ 分阶段～ phased disarmament
【裁量权】cáiliàngquán〈名〉power of discretion: ～在法院。The court has the power of discretion.
【裁判】cáipàn **A**〈动〉**1**［法律］adjudicate: 做出～ reach a verdict ‖ 缺席～ judgement by default **2**［体育］referee **B** ▸p. 966〈名〉［体育］（排球、乒乓球、羽毛球等）umpire;（篮球、足球、拳击）referee: 国际/国家～ international/national referee ‖ 主～ chief judge
【裁判员】cáipànyuán = 裁判 cáipàn B
【裁判长】cáipànzhǎng〈名〉［体育］head referee
【裁员】cáiyuán〈动〉cut jobs: ～百分之十 reduce staff by 10% ‖ ～减薪 reduce staff and salary
【裁纸】cáizhǐ〈动〉cut paper
【裁纸刀】cáizhǐdāo〈名〉paper cutter
【裁纸机】cáizhǐjī〈名〉paper cutter
【裁酌】cáizhuó〈动〉〈书〉consider and decide: 处理是否妥当，敬请～。Your consideration as to whether or not this matter has been handled correctly is cordially requested.

cǎi

采¹（採） cǎi〈动〉**1**（摘）pick: ～花 pick flowers ‖ ～蘑菇 pick mushrooms ‖ ～橡胶 tap a rubber tree ‖ ～药 gather medicinal herbs ‖ 潜水～珠 dive for pearls ‖ ～茶 pick tea **2**（选）select: ▸～取，～用，博～众长 **3**（采集）gather: ～标本 collect specimens ‖ ～水样 collect water samples ▸～访，～风，～集 **4**（开采）dig for: ～金 extract gold ▸～掘，～矿

采² cǎi〈名〉facial expression: ▸风～，无精打～ ▸cài

【采办】cǎibàn〈动〉buy in bulk: ～军需品 procure military supplies ‖ ～年货 make purchases for the Spring Festival
【采编】cǎibiān〈动〉gather and edit: ～人员 reporters and editors
【采茶戏】cǎicháxì〈名〉tea-picking opera
【采伐】cǎifá〈动〉fell: ～树木 fell trees ‖ 非法～ lumber illegally ‖ ～工 logger
【采访】cǎifǎng〈动〉interview: ～新闻 cover a story ‖ 接受～ grant an interview ‖ 电话～ telephone interview ‖ 现场～ on-the-spot interview
【采风】cǎifēng〈动〉collect folk songs or rhymes: 西部～ collect folk songs and rhymes in western China
【采购】cǎigòu **A**〈动〉purchase: ～药品 purchase medicine ‖ 大量～ buy in bulk **B**〈名〉buyer
【采光】cǎiguāng〈名〉natural light: ～不好 have poor light
【采集】cǎijí〈动〉collect: ～标本 collect specimens ‖ ～民谣 collect ballads
【采景】cǎijǐng〈动〉find locations (for shooting a film)
【采掘】cǎijué〈动〉excavate: ～金矿 mine for gold ‖ ～设备 excavation equipment
【采矿】cǎikuàng〈动〉mine: 地下～ underground mining ‖ 露天～ open-pit mining
【采矿工】cǎikuànggōng〈名〉miner
【采矿业】cǎikuàngyè〈名〉mining industry
【采莲船】cǎiliánchuán = 跑旱船 pǎo hànchuán
【采料场】cǎiliàochǎng〈名〉borrow-area
【采录】cǎilù〈动〉**1**（收集录制）collect and record: ～民间歌曲 collect and record folk songs **2**（采访录制）interview and record
【采买】cǎimǎi〈动〉select and purchase: ～副食品 purchase non-staple food
【采煤】cǎiméi〈动〉mine for coal: 露天～ opencast coal mining
【采煤工】cǎiméigōng〈名〉coal miner
【采煤机】cǎiméijī〈名〉coal-mining machine
【采蜜】cǎimì〈动〉[of bees] collect nectar
【采棉机】cǎimiánjī〈名〉cotton picker
【采纳】cǎinà〈动〉adopt: ～建议 take sb.'s advice ‖ 他的方案被～了。His plan was approved.
【采暖】cǎinuǎn〈动〉enjoy heating: 集中～ central heating
【采暖费】cǎinuǎnfèi〈名〉heating charges
【采取】cǎiqǔ〈动〉adopt: ～措施 take measures ‖ ～书信形式 use letter format ‖ ～行动 take action ‖ ～一切办法 adopt all kinds of methods
【采石】cǎishí〈动〉quarry: ～场 quarry
【采收】cǎishōu〈动〉pick: ～葡萄/种子 pick grapes/seeds
【采撷】cǎixié〈动〉〈书〉**1**（摘）pluck: ～花果 pick flowers and fruit **2**（收集）collect: ～植物标本 collect botanical specimens
【采写】cǎixiě〈动〉interview and write up: ～百姓关注的话题 write about the concerns of the public
【采血】cǎixiě〈动〉［医学］take blood: ～站 blood-collection centre
【采信】cǎixìn〈动〉［法律］accept: 他的证言未被法庭～。His testimony was not accepted by the court.
【采盐场】cǎiyánchǎng〈名〉salt pit
【采样】cǎiyàng〈动〉take a sample: ～检查 take a sample to inspect ‖ 随机～ random sampling ‖ ～器 sampler
【采用】cǎiyòng〈动〉use: ～稿件 use sb.'s contribution ‖ ～武力 resort to force ‖ ～先进技术 adopt advanced technology
【采油】cǎiyóu〈动〉extract oil
【采择】cǎizé〈动〉choose: ～最佳方案 choose the best plan
【采摘】cǎizhāi〈动〉pick: ～花朵 pick flowers ‖ ～棉花/苹果 pick cotton/apples ‖ ～桑叶 gather mulberry leaves ‖ ～野果充饥 pluck wild fruits to ease one's hunger ‖ ～季节 picking season
【采制】cǎizhì〈动〉**1**（采集加工）collect and process: ～标本 collect and process specimens ‖ ～春茶 pick and process spring tea **2**（采访录制）interview, record and produce: ～电视新闻 conduct an interview and record it for TV news
【采种】cǎizhǒng〈动〉collect seeds
【采珠】cǎizhū〈动〉fish for pearls

彩¹ cǎi〈名〉**1**（色彩）colour: ▸～笔，～旗 **2**（变化）variety: ▸丰富多～ **3**（博彩）winnings: 摸～ draw a lottery ticket ▸～票，～头，中～ **4**（喝彩）applause: 博得满堂～ bring the house down ▸喝～，倒～ **5**（血）blood from a wound: ▸～号，挂～

彩²（綵） cǎi〈名〉（彩带）variegated silk: ▸剪～，张灯结～

【彩笔】cǎibǐ〈名〉colour pencil
【彩超】cǎichāo〈名〉colour ultrasound
【彩车】cǎichē〈名〉**1**（游行车）float **2**（婚车）bridal car
【彩绸】cǎichóu〈名〉coloured silk
【彩带】cǎidài〈名〉streamer
【彩旦】cǎidàn〈名〉［戏曲］[in traditional operas] female comedian
【彩蛋】cǎidàn〈名〉［美术］painted eggshell
【彩灯】cǎidēng〈名〉coloured light
【彩电】cǎidiàn〈简称〉= 彩色电视
【彩调】cǎidiào〈名〉［戏曲］local opera of the Guangxi Zhuang Autonomous Region
【彩管】cǎiguǎn〈简称〉= 彩色显像管
【彩号】cǎihào〈名〉wounded soldier
【彩虹】cǎihóng〈名〉rainbow
【彩绘】cǎihuì **A**〈名〉coloured pattern: ～瓷器 porcelain decorated with coloured patterns **B**〈动〉paint: 古建筑已～一新。The ancient building was painted like new.
【彩轿】cǎijiào〈名〉〈旧〉bridal sedan chair
【彩卷】cǎijuǎn〈简称〉= 彩色胶卷
【彩扩】cǎikuò〈简称〉= 彩色扩印
【彩礼】cǎilǐ〈名〉betrothal gifts
【彩练】cǎiliàn〈名〉streamer
【彩铃】cǎilíng〈名〉Colour Ring Back Tone (CRBT): 手机～业务 mobile ringtone business
【彩迷】cǎimí〈名〉lottery enthusiast
【彩民】cǎimín〈名〉lottery player
【彩墨画】cǎimòhuà〈名〉painting in ink and colour
【彩排】cǎipái〈名〉dress rehearsal: 演出的前一晚，演员们又进行了一次～。The night before the performance, the actors had another dress rehearsal.
【彩牌楼】cǎipáilou〈名〉decorated archway
【彩棚】cǎipéng〈名〉decorated tent: 搭～ pitch a decorated tent
【彩票】cǎipiào〈名〉lottery ticket: 买～ play the lottery ‖ ～销售点 lottery ticket

outlet ‖ 福利～ welfare lottery ticket ‖ 体育～ sports lottery ticket

【彩旗】cǎiqí〈名〉 coloured banner: 道路两旁挂满了欢迎的～。 Welcome banners hung on both sides of the street.

【彩球】cǎiqiú〈名〉 coloured ball

【彩券】cǎiquàn〈名〉 lottery ticket

【彩色】cǎisè ▸**p. 863**〈名〉 colour: ～插图 colour illustrations

【彩色玻璃】cǎisè bōli〈名〉 stained glass

【彩色打印机】cǎisè dǎyìnjī〈名〉 colour printer

【彩色电视】cǎisè diànshì〈名〉colour television

【彩色电视机】cǎisè diànshìjī〈名〉 colour TV set

【彩色胶卷】cǎisè jiāojuǎn〈名〉colour film

【彩色扩印】cǎisè kuòyìn〈名〉 enlargements of colour prints

【彩色片】cǎisèpiàn〈名〉 colour film

【彩色显像管】cǎisè xiǎnxiàngguǎn〈名〉［电子］ colour (television) picture tube

【彩色印刷】cǎisè yìnshuā〈名〉 colour printing: ～机 colour printer

【彩色照片】cǎisè zhàopiàn〈名〉 colour photo

【彩饰】cǎishì〈名〉 coloured decoration: ～陶器 polychrome pottery

【彩塑】cǎisù〈名〉 painted sculpture: ～泥人 painted clay figurine

【彩陶】cǎitáo〈名〉 coloured pottery: ～文化 painted pottery culture

【彩头】cǎitóu〈名〉 **1**（指征兆） good omen: 讨个好～ ask for a happy omen **2**（指财物） profits gained in a lottery, gambling, etc.

【彩霞】cǎixiá〈名〉 rosy clouds: ～满天。 The sky was glowing with rosy clouds.

【彩信】cǎixìn〈名〉 multimedia message service (MMS): ～手机 an MMS mobile phone

【彩绣】cǎixiù〈名〉 coloured embroidery

【彩页】cǎiyè〈名〉 colour page

【彩印】cǎiyìn〈简称〉 **1** = 彩色印刷 **2** = 彩色扩印

【彩釉】cǎiyòu〈名〉 coloured ceramic glaze: ～陶 glazed coloured pottery

【彩云】cǎiyún〈名〉 rosy clouds

【彩照】cǎizhào〈简称〉= 彩色照片

【彩纸】cǎizhǐ〈名〉 **1**（彩色的纸） colour paper **2**［摄影］ colour photographic paper

睬 cǎi〈动〉 pay attention to: 对人不理不～ take absolutely no notice of anyone ‖ 别～他。 Ignore him. ▸理～

踩 cǎi〈动〉 **1**（脚踏） step on: ～出一条小径 tread a narrow path ‖ ～刹车 step on the brake ‖ ～油门 step on the gas ‖ ～在脚下 trample under foot **2**〈喻〉（贬低） demean: 他惯于～着别人的肩膀向上爬。 He's always putting other people down for his personal advancement.

【踩道】cǎidào〈动〉 case the joint

【踩点】cǎidiǎn〈动〉 **1** = 踩道 cǎidào **2**（指跳舞） dance to the beat

【踩高跷】cǎi gāoqiāo〈动〉 walk on stilts

【踩水】cǎishuǐ〈动〉 tread water

【踩踏】cǎità〈动〉 step on: 请勿～! Keep off! ‖ 请勿～草地。 Please keep off the grass.

【踩线】cǎixiàn〈动〉［体育］ make a foot-fault

【踩闸】cǎizhá〈动〉 step on the brake

cài

采 cài
▸cǎi

【采地】càidì〈名〉 fief

【采邑】càiyì = 采地 càidì

菜 cài〈名〉 **1**（蔬菜） vegetable: 择/种～ trim/grow vegetables ‖ 时令～ vegetables in season ▸～农, 泡～ **2**（油菜） rape: ▸～油 **3**（菜肴） dish: 四川/家常～ Sichuan/home cooking ‖ 中国～种类繁多。 Chinese dishes cover a wide spectrum. ▸点～, 荤～, 素～

【菜案】cài'àn〈名〉 cooking dishes: ～师 chef

【菜板】càibǎn〈名〉 chopping board

【菜帮子】càibāngzi〈名〉 outer leaves (of a cabbage, etc.)

【菜场】càichǎng = 菜市 càishì

【菜单】càidān〈名〉 menu: 今天～上有什么菜? What's on the menu today? ‖〈喻〉～栏/窗口 menu bar/window

【菜刀】càidāo〈名〉 kitchen knife

【菜点】càidiǎn〈名〉 main courses and desserts

【菜豆】càidòu〈名〉 kidney bean

【菜墩子】càidūnzi〈名〉 chopping block

【菜贩子】càifànzi〈名〉〈贬〉 greengrocer

【菜粉蝶】càifěndié〈名〉 cabbage butterfly

【菜瓜】càiguā〈名〉 cucumber

【菜馆】càiguǎn〈名〉〈方〉 restaurant

【菜花】càihuā〈名〉 **1**（花椰菜） cauliflower **2**（油菜花） rape flower

【菜窖】càijiào〈名〉 vegetable cellar

【菜金】càijīn〈名〉 food expense

【菜篮子】càilánzi〈名〉 **1**〈本〉 shopping basket **2**（副食品供应） non-staple food supply

【菜篮子工程】càilánzi gōngchéng〈名〉 non-staple food supply project

【菜鸟】càiniǎo〈名〉〈口〉 rookie: 棒球～ baseball rookie

【菜牛】càiniú〈名〉 beef cattle

【菜农】càinóng〈名〉 vegetable grower

【菜圃】càipǔ〈名〉 vegetable garden

【菜谱】càipǔ〈名〉 **1**（菜单） menu **2**（指书） cookery book〈英〉; cookbook〈美〉

【菜畦】càiqí〈名〉 vegetable bed

【菜青】càiqīng〈形〉 dark greyish green

【菜青虫】càiqīngchóng〈名〉 cabbage caterpillar

【菜色】càisè〈名〉 famished look: 面有～ have a sallow complexion

【菜市】càishì〈名〉 food market: ～场 food market

【菜蔬】càishū〈名〉 **1**（蔬菜） vegetables: 瓜果～ fruit and vegetables **2**（菜肴） dishes

【菜薹】càitái〈名〉 slender stalk

【菜摊】càitān〈名〉 vegetable stall: 马路～ roadside vegetable stands

【菜汤】càitāng〈名〉 vegetable soup

【菜系】càixì〈名〉 cuisine: 鲁菜是中国四大～之一。 Shandong cuisine is one of China's four great cuisines.

【菜心】càixīn〈名〉 heart (of a cabbage, etc.)

【菜肴】càiyáo〈名〉 cooked dish: 美味～ appetizing dishes ‖ 中式/欧式～ Chinese/European food

【菜油】càiyóu〈名〉 rapeseed oil

【菜园】càiyuán〈名〉 vegetable garden

【菜园子】càiyuánzi = 菜园 càiyuán

【菜子】càizǐ〈名〉 **1**（蔬菜种子） vegetable seed **2**（油菜籽） rapeseed

【菜子油】càizǐyóu = 菜油 càiyóu

蔡 Cài〈名〉 Cai [state in the Zhou Dynasty]

cān

参[1]（參） cān〈动〉 **1**（加入） enter: ▸～加, ～军 **2**（参考） consult: ▸～看, ～阅, ～照

参[2]（參） cān〈动〉 **1**（拜见） call to pay one's respects to: ▸～谒, ～拜 **2**〈旧〉（检举） impeach an official before an emperor: ～一本 impeach an official in a memorial to the emperor ▸～劾

参[3]（參） cān〈动〉〈书〉 investigate and understand: ▸～禅, ～透
▸cēn, shēn

【参拜】cānbài〈动〉 pay homage (to): ～孔庙 pay homage to a Confucian Temple

【参半】cānbàn〈动〉 be fifty-fifty: 疑信～ half believing, half doubting ‖ 悲喜～ feel happy and sad in equal measure ▸毁誉～

【参禅】cānchán〈动〉 [of Buddhists] practise meditation

【参订】cāndìng〈动〉 proofread and correct

【参股】cāngǔ〈动〉 purchase shares in businesses: 这个商业巨头在这家新公司～48%。 The tycoon purchased 48% of the shares in this new corporation.

【参观】cānguān〈动〉 visit: ～博物馆 visit museums ‖ 组织～ organize a visit ‖ ～团 visiting group ‖ ～者 visitor ‖ 谢绝～。 Not open to visitors.

【参合】cānhé〈动〉〈书〉consult and summarize

【参劾】cānhé〈动〉〈书〉 impeach

【参加】cānjiā〈动〉 **1**（加入） join;（参与） take part in: ～工会 join the labour union ‖ ～会谈 take part in talks ‖ ～竞赛 enter a competition ‖ ～社会活动 participate in social activities **2**（提出） give one's opinion: 这件事，请你也～点意见。 Please give us your opinion on this matter.

【参见】cānjiàn〈动〉 **1** = 参看 cānkàn 2 **2**（拜见） pay one's respects to: ～国王 pay respects to the King

【参校】cānjiào〈动〉 **1**（校订） proofread **2**（订正）check one book against another

【参军】cānjūn〈动〉 join the army: 报名～ sign up for the army

【参看】cānkàn〈动〉 **1**（参阅） consult: ～其他出处 refer to other sources ‖ 他～了许多书刊。 He consulted many books and journals. **2**（参见） refer also to: ～下面注释 see notes below ‖ 详细资料请～263 页。 For more information, see page 263.

【参考】cānkǎo〈动〉 **1**（参阅） refer to: ～历史文献 consult historical records ‖ ～价格 price indication ‖ ～手册 reference manual ‖ ～依据 frame of reference ‖ ～意见 advisory opinion ‖ 仅供～。 For reference only. **2** = 参看 cānkàn 2

【参考书】cānkǎoshū〈名〉 reference book: 查阅～ consult reference books

【参考书目】cānkǎo shūmù〈名〉 bibliography

【参考文献】cānkǎo wénxiàn〈名〉 reference

【参考系】cānkǎoxì〈名〉［物理］ frame of reference

【参考资料】cānkǎo zīliào〈名〉 reference material: 查阅～ consult reference material
【参量】cānliàng〈名〉［数学］parameter
【参谋】cānmóu **A**〈名〉 **1**［军事］ staff officer: ～部 general office ▸～长 **2**（顾问）adviser **B**〈动〉 advise: 这事儿让我来给你～～。Let me give you some advice on this matter.
【参谋长】cānmóuzhǎng〈名〉 chief of staff
【参拍】cānpāi〈动〉 **1**（指拍摄） participate in filming: 她～的是一部惊悚片。The film she worked on was a thriller. **2**（指拍卖） participate in an auction: 有数十件名画～。There are dozens of famous paintings up for auction.
【参评】cānpíng〈动〉 be entered for competitive appraisal: ～作品 works entered for competitive appraisal
【参赛】cānsài〈动〉 enter a competition: ～选手 contestant ‖ ～资格 qualifications for participation in a competition
【参事】cānshì〈名〉 adviser: 国务院～ consultant to the State Council
【参数】cānshù〈名〉［数学］parameter
【参天】cāntiān〈动〉 [of trees] tower: ～大树 towering trees
【参透】cāntòu〈动〉 fully comprehend: ～玄机 come to a thorough understanding of the mysterious truth ‖ ～诗的微妙含义 fully comprehend the subtleties of a poem
【参悟】cānwù〈动〉 comprehend
【参详】cānxiáng〈动〉〈书〉 carefully observe and study: 我把草拟的计划摆出来，请诸位～。I'd like to present the draft plan for your consideration.
【参选】cānxuǎn〈动〉 **1**（指人） stand for election **2**（指事物） enter a contest for competitive selection
【参验】cānyàn〈动〉 investigate and verify
【参谒】cānyè〈动〉 pay respects: ～黄帝陵 pay homage at the Yellow Emperor's Mausoleum
【参议】cānyì **A**〈动〉〈书〉 counsel **B**〈名〉 adviser
【参议员】cānyìyuán〈名〉 senator
【参议院】cānyìyuàn〈名〉 Senate: 美国～ US Senate
【参与】cānyù〈动〉 take part in: ～决策 participate in decision-making ‖ 积极～ take an active part in ‖ ～此事 have a hand in the matter
【参院】cānyuàn〈简称〉= 参议院
【参阅】cānyuè〈动〉 refer to: 请～本书第六页。See page 6.
【参杂】cānzá〈动〉 mix
【参赞】cānzàn **A**〈名〉 counsellor: 政务～ political attaché ▸商务～, 文化～ **B**〈动〉〈书〉 act as an adviser: ～朝政 take part in state affairs
【参展】cānzhǎn〈动〉 take part in an exhibition: ～单位 participants in an exhibition ‖ ～作品 exhibits
【参战】cānzhàn〈动〉 go to war: ～部队 combat troops ‖ ～国 belligerent state
【参照】cānzhào〈动〉 consult and follow: ～国际市场价格 base sth. on international market prices ‖ ～执行 act accordingly
【参照物】cānzhàowù〈名〉 object of reference
【参照系】cānzhàoxì = 参考系 cānkǎoxì
【参政】cānzhèng〈动〉 participate in government: ～党 participating party
【参政议政】cānzhèng-yìzhèng〈动〉 participate in the administration and discussion of state affairs
【参酌】cānzhuó〈动〉 consider in the light of actual conditions: ～具体情况，制定工作计划。Working plans will be made in view of concrete conditions.

餐 cān
A〈动〉 eat: 饱～一顿 eat one's fill ▸～具, 会～, 野～
B〈名〉 meal: 用～ eat ‖ 工作午～ working lunch ‖ 主～ main meal of the day ▸进～, 就～
C〈量〉 [for meals]: 一日三～ three meals a day
【餐叉】cānchā〈名〉 fork
【餐车】cānchē〈名〉 dining car; restaurant car〈英〉
【餐刀】cāndāo〈名〉 knife
【餐点】cāndiǎn〈名〉 **1**（点心） refreshments **2**（营业点） food establishments
【餐碟】cāndié〈名〉 dish, plate
【餐风宿露】cānfēng-sùlù = 风餐露宿 fēngcān-lùsù
【餐馆】cānguǎn〈名〉 restaurant: 开～ open a restaurant ‖ 西/中～ western-style/ Chinese restaurant
【餐盒】cānhé〈名〉 food box: 一次性～ disposable food box
【餐会】cānhuì〈名〉 dinner party
【餐巾】cānjīn〈名〉 serviette
【餐巾纸】cānjīnzhǐ〈名〉 paper towel
【餐具】cānjù〈名〉 tableware
【餐券】cānquàn〈名〉 meal ticket
【餐室】cānshì〈名〉 dining room
【餐厅】cāntīng〈名〉 **1**（饭厅） dining room **2**（饭馆） restaurant: 清真～ Muslim restaurant ‖ 旋转～ revolving restaurant ‖ 自助～ cafeteria
【餐位】cānwèi〈名〉 seat in a restaurant
【餐饮】cānyǐn〈名〉 food and beverage: 提供～服务 provide food service ‖ ～业 catering business
【餐桌】cānzhuō〈名〉 dining table

cán

残（殘）cán
A〈动〉 **1**（伤害） damage: ▸～害, ～杀, 摧～ **2**（受损） be incomplete: ～指 finger stub ‖ 身～志不～ be defective physically but not spiritually ‖ 这套书～了。This set of books is incomplete. ▸～破, ～缺
B〈形〉 **1**（残忍） cruel: ▸～暴, ～忍, 凶～ **2**（剩余） remaining: ～秋 waning autumn days ‖ ～烛 dying candle ▸～冬, ～阳, ～余, 风卷～云
【残奥会】Cán'àohuì〈简称〉= 残疾人奥运会
【残败】cánbài〈形〉 dilapidated: ～的景象 scene of dilapidation ‖ 这幢建筑～不堪。The building has gone to ruin.
【残暴】cánbào〈形〉 brutal: ～的侵略者 barbarous invaders ‖ 老虎生性～。Tigers are cruel by nature.
【残本】cánběn〈名〉 incomplete copy
【残编断简】cánbiān-duànjiǎn = 断编残简 duànbiān-cánjiǎn
【残兵】cánbīng〈名〉 remnants of an army
【残兵败将】cánbīng-bàijiàng〈成〉 remnants of a defeated army: 收拾～ muster the remnants of one's troops
【残部】cánbù〈名〉 remnants of a defeated army: 收罗～ rake up the remains of one's defeated troops
【残春】cánchūn ▸p. 345〈名〉〈书〉 end of spring
【残次】cáncì〈形〉 defective: ～品 shoddy goods
【残存】cáncún〈动〉 remain: ～的封建思想 remaining feudal ideology ‖ 深秋，树上还～着一些枯叶。Some withered leaves still hang on trees in late autumn.
【残敌】cándí〈名〉 remnants of enemy troops: 肃清～ wipe out remaining enemy troops
【残冬】cándōng ▸p. 345〈名〉〈书〉 end of winter
【残毒】cándú〈名〉 residue of hazardous chemicals: 农药的～会在土壤中积淀。Residues of pesticides will build up in the soil.
【残匪】cánfěi〈名〉 remaining bandits
【残废】cánfèi〈贬〉 **A**〈动〉 be disabled: 终身～ be permanently disabled ‖ 车祸使他～了。The traffic accident left him disabled. **B**〈名〉 the disabled
【残羹冷炙】cángēng-lěngzhì〈成〉 leftovers
【残骸】cánhái〈名〉 remains: 发掘～ dig up relics ‖ 失事船只的～ wreck of a ship
【残害】cánhài〈动〉 slaughter: ～无辜 slaughter innocent people ‖ ～忠良 persecute loyal and righteous people
【残花败柳】cánhuā-bàiliǔ〈成〉 faded beauty
【残货】cánhuò〈名〉 substandard merchandise
【残疾】cánjí〈名〉 physical disability: 腿上落下了～ have a disability in the leg ‖ ～儿童 disabled child ‖ ～人 disabled person
【残疾人奥运会】Cánjírén Àoyùnhuì〈名〉 Paralympics
【残疾人联合会】Cánjírén Liánhéhuì〈名〉 Disabled Persons' Federation
【残迹】cánjì〈名〉 relic: 如今只能看到昔日巍峨宫殿的～。Today we can only see the remains of the once imposing palace.
【残局】cánjú〈名〉 **1**（指棋局） end game **2**〈喻〉 aftermath: 收拾～ pick up the pieces
【残卷】cánjuàn〈名〉 torn and incomplete manuscript
【残军败将】cánjūn-bàijiàng = 残兵败将 cánbīng-bàijiàng
【残酷】cánkù〈形〉 cruel: 遭受～的剥削和压迫 suffer ruthless exploitation and oppression ‖ ～镇压叛乱 quell a rebellion with brutal force ‖ ～的现实 harsh reality ‖ ～无情 be cruel and merciless
【残联】Cánlián〈简称〉= 残疾人联合会
【残留】cánliú〈动〉 remain: ～物 residue ‖ 她脸上还～着油彩。There were still traces of grease paint on her face.
【残年】cánnián〈名〉 **1**（晚年） twilight years: ～暮景 evening of life ▸风烛～ **2**（岁末） end of the year: ～将尽。The year will soon be out.
【残虐】cánnüè〈书〉 **A**〈形〉 cruel and tyrannical **B**〈动〉 ill-treat: 囚犯曾被～。The prisoners have been physically maltreated.
【残篇断简】cánpiān-duànjiǎn = 断编残简 duànbiān-cánjiǎn
【残品】cánpǐn〈名〉 defective goods
【残破】cánpò〈形〉 dilapidated: 家园～ dilapidated home ‖ 房子已～不堪。The house was in a sorry state.
【残棋】cánqí〈名〉 end game
【残缺】cánquē〈形〉 fragmentary: ～的石碑 broken stone tablets ‖ ～的账本 incomplete account books
【残缺不全】cánquē-bùquán〈成〉 fragmented: ～的记忆 fragmented memories
【残忍】cánrěn〈形〉 brutal: ～地杀害 kill

sb. in cold blood ‖ ～的杀手 ruthless murderer
【残杀】 cánshā〈动〉 slaughter: ～无辜 slaughter the innocent ▸自相～
【残山剩水】cánshān-shèngshuǐ〈成〉 ravaged land
【残生】cánshēng〈名〉1（晚年）remaining years: 安度～ live out one's latter years in peace ‖ 了此～ end one's final days 2（指生命） one's wretched life
【残损】cánsǔn〈形〉 broken: ～货品 damaged goods ‖ 瓷器很容易～。 China breaks easily.
【残效】 cánxiào 〈名〉 residual effect (of insecticide)
【残雪】cánxuě〈名〉melting snow
【残阳】cányáng〈名〉 setting sun: ～余辉 sunset glow ‖ ～如血。 The setting sun is as red as blood.
【残余】cányú A〈动〉 be left over: ～势力 remaining forces ‖ ～杂质 residual impurities B〈名〉〈喻〉 dregs: 封建～ vestiges of feudalism
【残垣断壁】cányuán-duànbì〈成〉desolate scene
【残月】cányuè〈名〉 1（亏月） waning moon: ～如弓 waning crescent moon 2（快落的月亮） setting moon: 晓风～ dawn breeze and fading moon
【残渣】cánzhā〈名〉 residue: 火山～ slag ‖ 咖啡～ coffee dregs
【残渣余孽】 cánzhā-yúniè 〈成〉〈喻〉 dregs of the old society
【残障】cánzhàng〈名〉 physical disability: ～人士 handicapped people
【残照】cánzhào〈名〉 evening glow: 西风～。 The sun was setting and the west wind was blowing.
【残枝落叶】 cánzhī-luòyè 〈成〉 broken branches and fallen leaves
【残肢】cánzhī〈名〉 stump
【残株】cánzhū〈名〉 stubble
【残砖破瓦】cánzhuān-pòwǎ〈成〉 broken bricks and cracked tiles

蚕（蠶） cán〈名〉silkworm: 养～ sericulture ▸～豆, ～茧, ～食
【蚕宝宝】 cánbǎobǎo 〈名〉〈方〉 silkworm
【蚕箔】cánbó〈名〉 bamboo tray for raising silkworms
【蚕床】cánchuáng〈名〉 silkworm-rearing shelf
【蚕蔟】cáncù〈名〉 bundle of straw for silkworms to spin cocoons on
【蚕豆】cándòu〈名〉 broad bean
【蚕蛾】cán'é〈名〉silk moth
【蚕房】 cánfáng 〈名〉 building for silkworms
【蚕茧】cánjiǎn〈名〉 silkworm cocoon
【蚕眠】cánmián〈名〉 inactive state of the silkworm before it sheds its skin
【蚕农】cánnóng〈名〉 sericulturist
【蚕桑】cánsāng〈名〉 silkworm breeding and mulberry growing
【蚕沙】cánshā〈名〉silkworm excrement
【蚕山】cánshān〈方〉= 蚕蔟 cáncù
【蚕食】cánshí〈动〉〈喻〉 encroach upon: ～别国领土 encroach on another country's territory ‖ ～政策 policy of piecemeal encroachment ‖ 他们的领土被～。 Their land was gradually eaten away.
【蚕食鲸吞】 cánshí-jīngtūn 〈成〉〈喻〉 seize another country's territory by piecemeal encroachment or wholesale annexation
【蚕室】cánshì〈名〉 silkworm nursery
【蚕丝】cánsī〈名〉 natural silk
【蚕蚁】cányǐ〈名〉newly-hatched silkworm
【蚕蛹】cányǒng〈名〉 silkworm chrysalis
【蚕月】cányuè〈名〉 silkworm season
【蚕纸】cánzhǐ〈名〉 silkworm egg sheet
【蚕子】cánzǐ〈名〉 silkworm egg

惭（慚） cán〈动〉 feel ashamed
【惭愧】cánkuì〈形〉 ashamed: 感到～ feel ashamed ‖ ～不已 feel mortified ‖ ～地低下了头 hang one's head in shame
【惭赧】 cánnǎn 〈动〉〈书〉 blush with shame
【惭色】cánsè〈名〉〈书〉 ashamed expression: 面有～ look ashamed
【惭颜】 cányán 〈名〉〈书〉 ashamed expression
【惭怍】cánzuò〈动〉〈书〉 feel ashamed

cǎn

惨（慘） cǎn 〈形〉 1（狠毒） cruel: ▸～无人道 2（惨重） severe: 饿～了 be famished ‖ 输～了 suffer a crushing defeat ▸～败 3（凄惨） wretched: ～遭折磨 be brutally tortured ‖ 死得很～ die a tragic death 4（暗淡） gloomy: ▸～淡
【惨案】cǎn'àn〈名〉 1（指屠杀） massacre: 流血～ bloody massacre 2（指悲惨事件） tragedy: 火车相撞的～ tragic collision of two trains ‖ 这起～骇人听闻。 The murder case sounds horrifying.
【惨白】cǎnbái〈形〉 1（指景色） dismal: ～的月光 dim moonlight 2（指脸色） deathly pale: 脸色～ be as white as a sheet
【惨败】cǎnbài〈动〉suffer a crushing defeat: 以～告终 end in disaster ‖ 在足球赛中屡遭～ be continuously thrashed at football
【惨变】cǎnbiàn A〈名〉 tragic turn of events: 家庭的～令人心碎。 The family's disastrous change in fortune was heartbreaking. B〈动〉 turn pale: 他吓得脸色～。 He turned deathly pale with fear.
【惨不忍睹】cǎnbùrěndǔ〈成〉 be too horrible to look at: 她的凄凉处境～。 The sight of her wretchedness is hard to bear.
【惨怛】 cǎndá 〈形〉〈书〉 grief-stricken: 形容～ look deeply grieved
【惨淡】cǎndàn〈形〉 1（暗淡） gloomy: 天色～ sombre sky ‖ ～的灯光 dim light ‖ 寒冬～的阳光 pale sunlight of cold winter 2（凄凉） desolate: 神情～ sad expression 3（萧条） bleak: 生意～ slack business 4（尽心竭力） painstaking: ▸～经营
【惨淡经营】cǎndàn-jīngyíng〈成〉 1（指诗文创作） struggle to put together the plot of a story or the composition of a painting 2（指经营事业） take great pains to carry on one's work under difficult circumstances: 他～的公司终于开始盈利了。 The company that he had struggled so hard to keep above water eventually began to make a profit.
【惨跌】cǎndiē〈动〉 fall heavily: 上周股市～。 Stocks fell sharply last week.
【惨毒】cǎndú〈形〉 merciless: ～的高压政策 brutal high-handed policy
【惨祸】cǎnhuò〈名〉terrible tragedy: 酒后开车，酿成～。 Drunk driving caused the tragic accident.
【惨叫】cǎnjiào〈动〉 give a blood-curdling scream
【惨景】cǎnjǐng〈名〉 tragic sight
【惨境】cǎnjìng〈名〉 dire straits
【惨剧】cǎnjù〈名〉 tragedy: 一幕人间～ a human tragedy ‖ ～发生了。 A disaster occurred.
【惨绝人寰】 cǎnjué-rénhuán 〈成〉 be extremely tragic: ～的大屠杀 massacre of unparalleled savagery
【惨苦】cǎnkǔ〈形〉 wretched: 生活～ miserable life
【惨况】cǎnkuàng〈名〉 misery: 贫民窟的～ misery of the slums
【惨厉】cǎnlì〈形〉 mournful: ～的哭叫声 heart-rending cry ‖ 风声～。 The wind wailed mournfully.
【惨烈】cǎnliè〈形〉 1（凄惨） extremely tragic: ～的景象 wretched sight 2（壮烈） heroic, brave: ～牺牲 die a martyr's death 3（剧烈） fierce: ～的战斗 fierce fighting
【惨然】cǎnrán〈形〉 grieved: 神色～ look grieved ‖ ～落泪 shed tears of grief
【惨杀】 cǎnshā 〈动〉 slaughter: ～无辜 slaughter the innocent ‖ 遭到～ be murdered in cold blood
【惨伤】cǎnshāng〈形〉 deeply sorrowful
【惨死】cǎnsǐ〈动〉 die a tragic death: 每年有几千人～于车祸。 Thousands of people die every year on the roads.
【惨痛】cǎntòng〈形〉 agonizing: ～的教训 bitter lesson
【惨无人道】 cǎnwúréndào 〈成〉 cold-blooded: ～的行径 inhuman act
【惨象】cǎnxiàng〈名〉 tragic scene
【惨笑】cǎnxiào〈动〉 force a bitter smile
【惨重】cǎnzhòng〈形〉 catastrophic: 伤亡～ suffer heavy casualties ‖ 损失～ suffer grievous losses
【惨状】cǎnzhuàng〈名〉 pitiful sight: 失事现场的～令人目不忍睹。 The tragic sight of the crash was horrible.

黪（黲） cǎn〈形〉〈书〉 1（浅青黑色） dark: ～发 dark hair 2（昏暗） bleak

càn

灿（燦） càn〈形〉 resplendent: 黄～～的油菜花 bright yellow rape flowers ▸～烂
【灿烂】cànlàn〈形〉 resplendent: ～的东方文化 splendid oriental culture ‖ ～辉煌 resplendent ‖ 笑得那么～ smile a dazzling smile ‖ 阳光～。 The sun is shining brightly.
【灿然】cànrán〈形〉〈书〉brilliant: ～一笑 break into a wide smile ‖ ～一新 take on a completely new look ‖ 大厅里灯火～。 The hall is brightly lit.

掺（摻） càn〈名〉〈古〉 a kind of drum music
▸chān, shǎn

孱 càn
▸chán
【孱头】càntou〈名〉〈方〉〈粗〉 weakling

粲 càn〈书〉〈形〉 luminous: 云轻星～ floating clouds and glittering stars
【粲然】cànrán〈形〉〈书〉 1（光亮的样子） beaming: 星光～。 The stars are shining. 2（显著的样子） obvious: 成绩～可见 have made marked achievements

3（笑时露牙的样子） beaming: ～一笑 give a beaming smile

璨 càn
A〈名〉〈古〉1（指玉） fine jade 2（指光泽） the lustre of fine jade
B〈形〉〈书〉 brilliant: ～若明星 bright as stars ▸璀～

cāng

仓（倉） cāng〈名〉1（指地方） storehouse: ▸～库，粮～，清～ 2（指证券） holding: ▸平～
【仓廒】cāng'áo〈名〉 granary
【仓储】cāngchǔ〈动〉 store in a warehouse: ～费 storage charge
【仓储式超市】 cāngchǔshì chāoshì〈名〉 warehouse-type supermarket
【仓促】cāngcù〈形〉 hurried: 时间～ be pressed for time ‖ ～决定 rush into a decision ‖ 走得太～ leave in too much of a hurry
【仓猝】cāngcù = 仓促 cāngcù
【仓房】cāngfáng〈名〉 storehouse
【仓皇】cānghuáng〈形〉 in a flurry: ～撤退 beat a hasty retreat ‖ ～应战 put up a flurry of resistance ‖ ～逃窜 flee in panic
【仓皇失措】cānghuáng-shīcuò〈成〉 be all a fluster: 他常因意想不到的困难而～。He often gets into a panic when he meets unexpected difficulties.
【仓库】cāngkù〈名〉 storehouse: 货品/家具～ freight/furniture warehouse ‖ 粮食储存在～里。 The grain was stored in the warehouse.
【仓库保管员】 cāngkù bǎoguǎnyuán ▸**p. 966**〈名〉 storeman
【仓廪】cānglǐn〈名〉〈旧〉 granary
【仓容】cāngróng〈名〉 storage capacity
【仓鼠】cāngshǔ〈名〉［动物］ hamster
【仓位】cāngwèi〈名〉 1（指仓库） hold 2（指证券） holding
【仓租】cāngzū〈名〉 warehouse storage charge

伧（傖） cāng〈形〉〈书〉 vulgar ▸chen
【伧俗】cāngsú〈形〉〈书〉 coarse: 言语～ speak with vulgarity

苍（蒼） cāng ▸**p. 863**
A〈形〉1（青色） dark green: ～山 green mountains ▸～松，～天 2（灰白） ash white: ～髯 grey beard ▸～白
B〈名〉〈书〉 sky: ▸上～
【苍白】cāngbái ▸**p. 863**〈形〉 1（指颜色） colourless: 她吓得脸色～。She turned pale with fear. 2（指文辞或艺术形象） flat: 论据～无力 feeble argument ‖ 人物形象～无力。 The images are rather colourless.
【苍苍】cāngcāng ▸**p. 863**〈形〉 1（指头发） ash white: 白发～ be grey-haired 2（指植物） dark green: ～松柏 green pines and cypresses 3（指天空或群山） vast and hazy: ～莽莽 vast and lush ‖ 山色～。 The mountains looked vast and misty.
【苍翠】cāngcuì ▸**p. 863**〈形〉 dark green: ～葱茏 verdant ‖ 山峦～。 The hills are lush and green.
【苍翠欲滴】cāngcuì-yùdī〈成〉 juicy and verdant
【苍耳】 cāng'ěr〈名〉［植物］ Siberian cocklebur
【苍黄】cānghuáng ▸**p. 863**〈形〉 1（暗黄） greenish yellow: 面色～ have a sallow complexion ‖ ～的天空 gloomy sky 2〈书〉〈喻〉（多变） changeable 3 = 仓皇 cānghuáng
【苍劲】cāngjìng〈形〉 1（指树） old and strong: ～的松树 tall and sturdy pines 2（指书法） vigorous: 笔法～ forceful and bold brush strokes
【苍老】cānglǎo〈形〉 1（衰老） hoary: 过度劳累使她显得过早～。 Overwork made her look older than her age. 2（苍劲） vigorous
【苍凉】cāngliáng〈形〉 desolate: 一片～景色 a desolate scene ‖ 满目～。 A scene of desolation filled the eyes.
【苍龙】cānglóng〈名〉 1（指东方七宿） Green Dragon 2（指马） black horse: 驾～ ride a black horse 3（指恶魔） fiend
【苍鹭】cānglù〈名〉［鸟类］ heron
【苍茫】cāngmáng〈形〉 1（辽阔） vast: ～大海 vast seas 2（迷茫） indistinct: 云水～的天际 blurred horizon between clouds and water
【苍莽】cāngmǎng〈形〉〈书〉 boundless
【苍穹】cāngqióng〈名〉〈书〉 heavens
【苍生】 cāngshēng〈名〉〈书〉 common people: 拯救～ save the common people ‖ 天下～ people under heaven
【苍松】cāngsōng〈名〉 green pines: ～翠柏 green pines and verdant cypresses
【苍天】cāngtiān〈名〉 Heaven: ～保佑。May Heaven bless us. ‖ ～不容。God forbid.
【苍鹰】cāngyīng〈名〉［鸟类］ goshawk
【苍蝇】cāngying〈名〉 fly: ～拍 fly swatter
【苍蝇不叮无缝的蛋】cāngying bù dīng wú fèng de dàn〈俗〉〈喻〉 bad people can influence only those who are vulnerable
【苍郁】cāngyù〈形〉〈书〉 verdant: 草木～ lush vegetation
【苍术】cāngzhú〈名〉1［植物］ Chinese atractylodes 2［中药］ rhizome of Chinese atractylodes

沧（滄） cāng〈形〉 deep green
【沧海】cānghǎi〈名〉 deep blue sea: ▸曾经～
【沧海横流】cānghǎi-héngliú〈成〉〈喻〉 country in chaos
【沧海桑田】cānghǎi-sāngtián〈成〉〈喻〉 time brings drastic changes to the world
【沧海一粟】cānghǎi-yīsù〈成〉 a drop in the ocean: 个人再伟大，也不过是～。However great an individual may be, he is but a drop in the ocean.
【沧海遗珠】cānghǎi-yízhū〈成〉〈喻〉 undiscovered talent
【沧桑】cāngsāng〈名〉 vicissitudes of life: 历尽～ have experienced all that life has to offer ‖ ～巨变 earth-shattering change ▸饱经～

舱（艙） cāng〈名〉 cabin: 航天器～ capsule ‖ 头等～的设备非常豪华。The first-class cabins are fitted out luxuriously. ▸船～，货～，驾驶～
【舱壁】cāngbì〈名〉 (ship) bulkhead
【舱房】cāngfáng〈名〉 cabin
【舱口】cāngkǒu〈名〉 hatchway
【舱面】 cāngmiàn〈名〉 deck: ～作业 on-deck operation
【舱室】cāngshì〈名〉 cabin
【舱位】cāngwèi〈名〉 1（指客运） cabin berth: 预订～ reserve a bunk on a ship 2（指货运） shipping space: ～包租 berth charter

cáng

藏 cáng
A〈动〉1（躲藏） conceal: ～在门后/床下 hide behind the door/under the bed ‖ 她心里～不住事儿。 She can never keep anything to herself. ▸～匿，隐～ 2（储藏） store: 他在家里～了些古玩。 He stored some antiques in his home. ▸～书，冷～，收～
B〈名〉 reserve: ▸矿～
▸zàng
【藏躲】cángduǒ〈动〉 go into hiding: 四处～ hide hither and thither
【藏锋守拙】cángfēng-shǒuzhuō〈成〉 conceal one's brilliance and behave humbly
【藏富】cángfù〈动〉 conceal one's wealth
【藏奸】cángjiān〈动〉 1（心怀恶意）bear ill will: 笑里～ hide one's evil intentions behind one's smiles 2〈方〉（耍滑） be reluctant to exert oneself in work or helping others: ～耍滑 be calculating
【藏经阁】 cángjīnggé〈名〉 depository of Buddhist scriptures
【藏酒窖】cángjiǔjiào〈名〉 wine cellar
【藏龙卧虎】 cánglóng-wòhǔ〈成〉 undiscovered talent: ～之地 place where talents are to be found
【藏猫猫】 cángmāomāo〈动〉〈口〉 play hide-and-seek
【藏匿】cángnì〈动〉 hide: ～匕首 conceal a dagger ‖ 他越狱后在山洞里～了几天。 After breaking out of jail, he hid in a cave for a few days.
【藏品】cángpǐn〈名〉 object of value: ～丰富 rich collection of valuable objects
【藏身】cángshēn〈动〉 go into hiding: 无处～ have no place to hide ‖ ～之处 hide-out
【藏书】cángshū A〈动〉 collect books B〈名〉 book collection: 积累大量～ accumulate a vast library of books ‖ 该馆～逾百万。 The library boasts a collection of over one million books.
【藏书票】 cángshūpiào〈名〉 book-collector's stamp
【藏头露尾】 cángtóu-lùwěi〈成〉 divulge part but not all: 实话实说，别这样～的。Talk straight, don't be so evasive.
【藏污纳垢】cángwū-nàgòu〈成〉 shelter evil people and countenance evil practices: ～之地 den of iniquity
【藏掖】cángyē〈动〉〈书〉 try to conceal: ～躲闪 dodge and hide ‖ 他很正直，行事从不～。 He is an upright person and his actions have always been open and above board.
【藏拙】cángzhuō〈动〉 hide one's weaknesses by keeping quiet
【藏踪】cángzōng〈动〉 go into hiding

cāo

操 cāo
A〈动〉1（拿） hold;（掌握） grasp: ～生杀大权 have absolute power ‖ 警察～起警棍将歹徒打昏在地。 The policeman grabbed a baton and knocked the criminal down. ▸～刀，～纵，稳～胜券 2（从事） do: ▸～持，～劳，重～旧业 3（弹奏） play: ▸～琴 4（说） speak: ～英语 speak English ‖ 这个外国人～着一口流利的汉语。 This foreigner speaks fluent Chinese. 5（操练） exercise: ▸～练，出～

[B]〈名〉[1]（体育活动） exercise: ▸健美～, 课间～, 体～ [2]（品德） conduct: ▸～守, 贞～

【操办】cāobàn〈动〉 make arrangements: ～婚礼 make preparations for the wedding

【操场】cāochǎng〈名〉 playground

【操持】cāochí〈动〉[1]（料理） take care of: ～家务 attend to household chores [2]（筹划） make preparations

【操刀】cāodāo〈动〉[1]（做手术） hold the reins: 手术由主任医师～。 The chief physician will perform the operation. [2]（主管） be in charge

【操典】cāodiǎn〈名〉［军事］ drill regulations: 步兵/炮兵～ infantry/artillery drill manual

【操舵】cāoduò〈动〉 steer

【操戈】cāogē〈动〉〈书〉 take up arms: ▸同室～

【操课】cāokè〈名〉［军事］ military drill

【操控】cāokòng〈动〉 control

【操劳】cāoláo〈动〉[1]（劳作） work hard: ～过度 overwork oneself ‖ 她常年为子女～。 She labours for her children all the year round. [2]（操心） attend to: ～公务 attend to official business

【操练】cāoliàn〈动〉 be on manoeuvres: 军事～ military exercise ‖ ～刺杀 drill with bayonets

【操盘】cāopán〈动〉［金融］ trade: 股票～手 stock trader ‖ 有丰富的～经验 have a lot of experience in speculating

【操切】cāoqiè〈形〉〈书〉 rash: ～从事 handle with undue haste ‖ 父母不希望他把婚事办得太～了。 His parents didn't want him to rush the wedding.

【操琴】cāoqín〈动〉 play the *huqin*

【操神】cāoshén〈动〉 bother: 父母因孩子淘气没少～。 The parents were very troubled by their child's naughtiness.

【操守】cāoshǒu〈名〉 integrity

【操心】cāoxīn〈动〉 be concerned about: 这辈子让我～的事可太多了。 I've got so much to worry about in my life.

【操行】cāoxíng〈名〉 behaviour: 他在校～良好。 His conduct at school is good.

【操行评语】cāoxíng píngyǔ〈名〉 remarks on a student's conduct

【操演】cāoyǎn〈动〉 exercise: 新兵正在～。 The new recruits are going through the drills.

【操之过急】cāozhī-guòjí〈成〉 be hasty: 千万不能～。 Don't be too rash.

【操纵】cāozòng〈动〉[1]（操作） operate: ～机器 operate machines ‖ ～自如 handle with skill ‖ 无线电～ radio control [2]〈贬〉（暗中控制） manipulate: ～市场 manipulate the market ‖ ～选举 rig an election ‖ 幕后～ pull strings

【操纵舵】cāozòngduò〈名〉［航空］ control vane

【操纵杆】cāozònggǎn〈名〉 operating lever

【操纵室】cāozòngshì〈名〉 control cabin

【操纵台】cāozòngtái〈名〉 console

【操纵者】cāozòngzhě〈名〉 manipulator

【操作】cāozuò〈动〉 operate: 易于～ easy to operate ‖ ～方法 method of operation ‖ 手工～ manual operation

【操作程序】cāozuò chéngxù〈名〉 operating procedure

【操作规程】cāozuò guīchéng〈名〉 operating instructions

【操作手册】cāozuò shǒucè〈名〉 operating manual

【操作系统】cāozuò xìtǒng〈名〉［计算机］ operating system

【操作性能】cāozuò xìngnéng〈名〉［机械］ serviceability

【操作员】cāozuòyuán ▸**p. 966**〈名〉 operator

【操作指令】cāozuò zhǐlìng〈名〉 operational order

糙 cāo〈形〉 coarse: 她干粗活，手变得很～。 Her hands became rough with hard work. ‖ 他的活总是干得很～。 He is always slovenly in his work. ▸～米, 粗～, 毛～

【糙粮】cāoliáng〈名〉〈方〉 coarse grain

【糙米】cāomǐ〈名〉 brown rice

【糙皮病】cāopíbìng ▸**p. 50**〈名〉［医学］ pellagra

cáo

曹[1] cáo〈名〉〈书〉 people of the same kind: 吾～ all of us ▸尔～

曹[2] Cáo〈名〉 Cao [state in the Zhou Dynasty]

嘈 cáo〈形〉 noisy

【嘈杂】cáozá〈形〉 noisy: 人声～ hubbub of voices

漕 cáo〈动〉〈古〉 transport grain by water

【漕船】cáochuán〈名〉 boat for transporting grain

【漕渡】cáodù〈动〉［军事］ cross a river in boats or on rafts

【漕河】cáohé〈名〉 waterway for transporting grain

【漕粮】cáoliáng〈名〉〈古〉 grain transported by water

【漕运】cáoyùn〈动〉〈古〉 transport grain by water to meet demands

槽 cáo〈名〉[1]（食槽） manger;（水槽） trough: 酒～ wine trough ‖ 马～ manger ‖ 水～ gutter ▸～头, 跳～ [2]（沟） ditch: 挖～ dig a trench ‖ 河～ channel ▸渡～ [3]（凹槽） groove

【槽床】cáochuáng〈名〉 trough stand

【槽坊】cáofang〈名〉〈旧〉[1]（用于酿酒） distillery [2]（用于造纸） paper mill

【槽钢】cáogāng〈名〉［冶金］ channel iron

【槽罐车】cáoguànchē〈名〉 tanker

【槽口】cáokǒu〈名〉［机械］ notch

【槽头】cáotóu〈名〉 manger: ～兴旺 manger full of sturdy livestock

【槽牙】cáoyá〈名〉 molar: 掉了一颗～ have a molar missing

【槽子】cáozi = 槽 cáo

螬 cáo ▸蛴螬 qícáo

艚 cáo〈名〉〈旧〉 a kind of wooden boat

【艚子】cáozi〈名〉 big wooden cargo boat with a cabin before the helm

cǎo

草[1] cǎo

[A]〈名〉[1]（指植物） grass: 枯～ withered grass ▸～地, ～原, 青～ [2]（指材料） straw: ▸～帽, ～鞋, 稻～ [3]（山野民间） wilderness: ▸～寇, ～贼

[B]〈形〉[1]（卑贱） lowly: ▸～民 2 [2]〈口〉（雌性） female: ▸～驴

草[2] cǎo

[A]〈形〉[1]（潦草） careless: 他的字太～不容易辨认。 His handwriting is too sloppy to be intelligible. ▸～率, 潦～ [2]（未确定） draft: ▸～案, ～稿, ～图

[B]〈名〉[1] [a]（草书） cursive style of writing in Chinese calligraphy: ▸～书, 狂～, 章～ [b]（手写体） handwritten form of a phonetic alphabet [2]（草稿） rough draft: ▸起～

[C]〈动〉[1]（创始） initiate: ▸～创 [2]〈书〉（写初稿） draft: ▸～拟

【草案】cǎo'àn〈名〉 draft: 计划/决议～ draft plan/resolution ‖ ～已经修订。 The draft has been amended.

【草包】cǎobāo〈名〉[1]〈本〉 straw bag [2]〈喻〉 good-for-nothing: 他是个～。 He is a layabout.

【草本】cǎoběn [A]〈形〉 herbal [B]〈名〉 original draft

【草本植物】cǎoběn zhíwù〈名〉 herb

【草编】cǎobiān〈名〉 straw weaving: ～制品 straw-woven ware

【草标】cǎobiāo〈名〉〈古〉 wisp of straw attached to an article for sale

【草草】cǎocǎo〈副〉 carelessly: ～结束辩论 hastily close a debate ‖ ～了事 do sth. rashly ‖ ～收场 rashly bring sth. to a close

【草测】cǎocè〈动〉 make a preliminary survey

【草叉】cǎochā〈名〉 pitch fork

【草场】cǎochǎng〈名〉 grassland: 肥沃的～ fertile pasture ‖ ～退化 grassland degeneration

【草虫】cǎochóng〈名〉[1]（指虫子） grass insect [2]［美术］ grass-and-insect painting

【草创】cǎochuàng〈动〉 initiate: ～阶段 initial stage

【草丛】cǎocóng〈名〉 thick growth of grass

【草底儿】cǎodǐr〈名〉〈口〉 draft: 打～ make a draft

【草地】cǎodì〈名〉[1]（草坪） lawn: 请勿践踏～。 Please keep off the grass. [2]（草原） grassland: 这片～不适合放牧。 This grassland is not suitable for grazing. [3]（沼泽地） grassy marshland

【草甸子】cǎodiànzi〈名〉〈方〉 grassy marshland

【草垫子】cǎodiànzi〈名〉 straw mat

【草垛】cǎoduò〈名〉 haystack: 堆～ heap up a haystack ‖ 麦～ stack of wheat straw

【草房】cǎofáng〈名〉 thatched cottage

【草稿】cǎogǎo〈名〉 draft: 打～ make a draft ‖ 提出宣言的～ bring out a draft declaration

【草根】cǎogēn〈名〉[1]〈本〉 grass root [2]（平民） grassroots: ～运动/民主 grassroots movement/ democracy

【草菇】cǎogū〈名〉 straw mushroom: ～蒸鸡 steamed chicken with straw mushrooms

【草荒】cǎohuāng〈名〉 neglected farmland

【草灰】cǎohuī ▸**p. 863**〈名〉[1]（指灰） plant ash [2]（指颜色） ash grey: ～的套装 ash grey suit

【草鸡】cǎojī〈方〉[A]〈名〉[1]（母鸡） hen [2]（土鸡） local small-bodied chicken [B]〈形〉 cowardly

【草菅人命】cǎojiān-rénmìng〈成〉 treat human life as if it were worthless

【草荐】cǎojiàn〈名〉 straw mat

【草芥】cǎojiè〈名〉〈喻〉 trifle: 他视名利

如～。 He treats fame and gain as worthless.

【草寇】cǎokòu〈名〉〈旧〉bandit

【草库伦】cǎokùlún〈名〉fenced-in pasture

【草笠】cǎolì〈名〉straw hat

【草帘子】cǎoliánzi〈名〉straw screen or mat

【草料】cǎoliào〈名〉fodder

【草驴】cǎolǘ〈名〉female donkey

【草履虫】cǎolǚchóng〈名〉paramecium

【草绿】cǎolǜ〈名〉grass green

【草莽】cǎomǎng〈名〉**1**（草丛）thick growth of grass **2**（荒地）wilderness **3**〈旧〉（民间）common people: ～英雄 hero of the bush

【草帽】cǎomào〈名〉straw hat

【草帽缏】cǎomàobiàn〈名〉plaited straw

【草帽辫】cǎomàobiàn = 草帽缏 cǎomàobiàn

【草莓】cǎoméi〈名〉strawberry: ～酱 strawberry jam

【草棉】cǎomián〈名〉cotton plant

【草民】cǎomín〈名〉〈旧〉**1**（百姓）common people **2**〈谦〉（作主语）I;（作宾语）me

【草木】cǎomù〈名〉vegetation: ～茂盛 lush vegetation ‖ 人非～，孰能无情？Unlike plants, don't humans have feelings of all kinds?

【草木灰】cǎomùhuī〈名〉plant ash

【草木皆兵】cǎomù-jiēbīng〈成〉be highly suspicious of everything: 市民人心惶惶，～。 The whole city was in a state of extreme panic.

【草拟】cǎonǐ〈动〉draft: ～城市规划 draw up a city plan ‖ ～合同/协议书 draw up a contract/an agreement ‖ 文件尚在～中。 The document is still in draft form.

【草棚】cǎopéng〈名〉thatched shack

【草皮】cǎopí〈名〉turf: 铺～ turf

【草坪】cǎopíng〈名〉lawn: 绿茵茵的～ verdant lawn ‖ 在～上嬉戏 play games on the lawn

【草签】cǎoqiān **A** = 草标 cǎobiāo **B**〈动〉initial: 他和这家公司～了两年的合同。 He initialled a two-year contract with this company.

【草裙舞】cǎoqúnwǔ〈名〉hula

【草人】cǎorén〈名〉scarecrow

【草苫子】cǎoshānzi〈名〉straw mat

【草珊瑚】cǎoshānhú〈名〉［植物］Sarcandra glabra

【草绳】cǎoshéng〈名〉straw rope

【草食】cǎoshí〈形〉herbivorous: ～动物 herbivore

【草书】cǎoshū〈名〉［书法］cursive script

【草率】cǎoshuài〈形〉careless: ～的决定 hasty decision ‖ ～从事 do perfunctorily

【草酸】cǎosuān〈名〉［化学］oxalic acid

【草台班子】cǎotái bānzi〈名〉〈旧〉small, poorly-equipped travelling troupe

【草滩】cǎotān〈名〉grassy expanse of ground near water

【草炭】cǎotàn〈名〉peat

【草堂】cǎotáng〈名〉cottage

【草体】cǎotǐ〈名〉**1** = 草书 cǎoshū **2**（手写体）cursive hand of a phonetic alphabet

【草田轮作】cǎotián lúnzuò〈名〉［农业］rotation of grass and crops

【草头王】cǎotóuwáng〈名〉〈旧〉bandit chief

【草图】cǎotú〈名〉draft

【草屋】cǎowū〈名〉thatched hut

【草席】cǎoxí〈名〉straw mat

【草鞋】cǎoxié〈名〉straw sandals

【草鞋没样，边打边像】cǎoxié méi yàng, biān dǎ biān xiàng〈俗〉〈喻〉work things out as you go along

【草写】cǎoxiě = 草体 cǎotǐ

【草样】cǎoyàng〈名〉draft design

【草药】cǎoyào〈名〉［中医］herbal medicine

【草野】cǎoyě〈名〉〈旧〉〈喻〉common people: 身居～ live among the common people ‖ ～之人 man in the street

【草鱼】cǎoyú〈名〉grass carp

【草原】cǎoyuán〈名〉grassland: 辽阔的～ vast expanse of grassland ‖ ～退化 grassland deterioration

【草约】cǎoyuē〈名〉draft agreement: 经济合作～ draft treaty of economic cooperation

【草泽】cǎozé〈名〉**1**（指洼地）swamp: 蚊虫滋生的～ mosquito-infested swamp **2**〈旧〉（指民间）common people

【草贼】cǎozéi〈名〉bandit

【草纸】cǎozhǐ〈名〉**1**（粗糙的纸）coarse paper **2**（卫生纸）toilet paper

【草字】cǎozì〈名〉**1** ▸**p. 999**（草书）Chinese character written in cursive hand **2**〈旧〉〈谦〉（表字）my humble name

cào

肏 cào〈动〉〈粗〉fuck〈粗〉

cè

册 cè

A〈名〉**1**（册子）volume: 装订成～ be bound into book form ▸～子，画～，纪念～ **2**〈书〉（指命令）imperial edict to confer nobility titles: ▸～封，～立

B〈量〉volume: 这套百科全书一共二十六～。 The encyclopedia consists of 26 volumes. ‖ 发行量达十万～。 Circulation runs to 100,000 copies.

【册封】cèfēng〈动〉〈旧〉bestow a title on sb.: ～皇后 crown as empress

【册立】cèlì〈动〉〈旧〉appoint sb. as empress or crown prince

【册页】cèyè〈名〉album of painting or calligraphy

【册子】cèzi〈名〉book: ▸小～

厕[1]**（厠、廁）** cè〈名〉toilet: 男～ men's (toilet) ‖ 女～ women's (toilet) ▸～所，公～，茅～

厕[2]**（厠、廁）** cè〈动〉〈书〉participate in: ▸～身

【厕身】cèshēn〈动〉〈书〉〈谦〉occupy a humble place: ～其间 occupy a place among them ‖ ～于政界 mix in political circles

【厕所】cèsuǒ〈名〉toilet: ▸公共～

【厕足】cèzú〈动〉〈书〉participate in: ～其间 get involved

侧（側） cè

A〈名〉side: 左/右～ left/right side ‖ 大道两～ both sides of the street ▸～门，～面，～影

B〈动〉lean to one side: ～着身子睡 sleep on one's side ▸～耳，～目，～身 ▸zhāi

【侧柏】cèbǎi〈名〉［植物］oriental arborvitae

【侧耳】cè'ěr〈动〉prick up one's ears: ～倾听 be all ears

【侧翻】cèfān〈动〉［体育］turn on one's side

【侧光】cèguāng〈名〉［摄影］sidelight

【侧滑】cèhuá〈动〉［交通］skid sideways: 车辆向外～撞上护栏后翻倒。 The car skidded sideways, hit the guard rail, and then rolled.

【侧击】cèjī〈动〉make a flank attack: 从左边/右边～ attack the left/right flank ▸旁敲～

【侧记】cèjì〈名〉sidelights: 《国际博览会～》 *Sidelights on the International Fair*

【侧近】cèjìn〈形〉near: ～有一个报刊亭。 There is a news-stand nearby.

【侧力】cèlì〈名〉lateral force

【侧立】cèlì〈动〉stand motionless and side-on to show one's respect or awe

【侧门】cèmén〈名〉side door: 罪犯从～逃跑了。 The criminal fled by the side door.

【侧面】cèmiàn〈名〉profile: 从～了解 find out from indirect sources ‖ 她从～看很美。 She has a beautiful profile. ‖ 这部电影反映了社会的一个～。 The film reflects one aspect of the society.

【侧面像】cèmiànxiàng〈名〉profile

【侧目】cèmù〈动〉cast sb. a sidelong glance

【侧目而视】cèmù'érshì〈成〉cast a sidelong glance (at sb./sth.): 老百姓对贪官污吏总是～。 The common people can't bear the sight of corrupt officials.

【侧身】cèshēn〈动〉**1**（斜着身子）move sideways: ～挤进大厅 edge one's way into the hall **2** = 厕身 cèshēn

【侧视】cèshì〈动〉look sideways

【侧视图】cèshìtú〈名〉side view

【侧室】cèshì〈名〉**1**（指房间）side room **2**〈旧〉（妾）concubine: ～而出 be born of a concubine

【侧手翻】cèshǒufān〈名〉［体育］cartwheel

【侧卧】cèwò〈动〉lie on one's side

【侧线】cèxiàn〈名〉**1**［鱼类］lateral line: ～鳞 lateral-line scale ‖ ～器官 lateral-line organ **2**［铁路］side line

【侧旋】cèxuán〈名〉［体育］sidespin

【侧翼】cèyì〈名〉［军事］flank: 从～包抄敌人 outflank the enemy

【侧影】cèyǐng〈名〉silhouette

【侧泳】cèyǒng〈名〉［体育］sidestroke

【侧枝】cèzhī〈名〉［植物］side branch

【侧重】cèzhòng〈动〉lay special emphasis on: ～于 pay more attention to ‖ 工作的～点是调整经济结构。 The focus of the work is on restructuring the economy.

【侧足】cèzú〈动〉**1**〈书〉（双脚斜着站立）stand motionless and side-on: ～而立 have a frightened stance **2** = 厕足 cèzú

测（測） cè〈动〉**1**（测量）measure: ～风向 determine the wind direction ‖ ～高度 gauge the height ‖ ～体温 take sb.'s temperature ▸～绘，深不可～ **2**（料想）conjecture: ▸～度，猜～，变幻莫～

【测报】cèbào〈动〉measure and report: 气象～ weather forecast

【测标】cèbiāo〈名〉surveying rod

【测查】cèchá〈动〉**1**（检查）test and examine **2**（勘查）survey: ～地形 survey the terrain ‖ 实地～ make an on-the-spot investigation

【测程仪】cèchéngyí〈名〉mileage meter

【测电笔】cèdiànbǐ〈名〉［电气］test pencil

【测定】cèdìng〈动〉determine: ～船只方

位 take a ship's bearings ‖ ～高度 measure the height ‖ 风力～ anemometry ‖ 听力～ audiometry
【测度】cèdù〈名〉［数学］ measure: ～函数 measure function
【测度】cèduó〈动〉 conjecture: 他的～没有充分根据。 His speculation is not well founded. ‖ 有关其他星球上有生命的说法只是～而已。 It's only speculation that there is life on other planets.
【测风仪】cèfēngyí〈名〉 anemometer
【测杆】cègān〈名〉 surveying rod
【测估】cègū〈动〉 estimate
【测光表】cèguāngbiǎo〈名〉 photometric meter
【测候】cèhòu〈动〉［气象］ make astronomical and meteorological observations
【测谎器】cèhuǎngqì〈名〉 lie detector
【测绘】cèhuì〈动〉 map out: 地形/地质～ topographical/geological survey ‖ ～员 cartographer
【测绘局】cèhuìjú〈名〉 bureau of surveying and mapping
【测距】cèjù〈动〉 measure distance: 光学～ optical measurement of distance ‖ ～仪 rangefinder
【测控】cèkòng〈动〉 observe and control: 卫星～中心 satellite observation and control centre
【测量】cèliáng〈动〉 measure: ～高度/速度 measure height/speed ‖ ～仪器 measuring device ‖ ～员 surveyor ‖ ～标志 survey mark
【测漏】cèlòu〈动〉 track down a leak
【测评】cèpíng〈动〉 test and appraise
【测深仪】cèshēnyí〈名〉 Fathometer
【测声计】cèshēngjì〈名〉 phonometer
【测试】cèshì〈动〉 test: 通过/未通过～ pass/fail a test ‖ ～成绩 test result ‖ 水平～ proficiency test ‖ ～电路/电压 test circuits/voltage ‖ 性能～ service test
【测试赛】cèshìsài〈名〉［体育］ athletics trials: 奥运～ Olympic trials
【测算】cèsuàn〈动〉 measure and calculate: 这只是一个粗略的～。 This is a rough calculation.
【测探】cètàn〈动〉 1▸（测量和勘探） survey and explore: ～金矿 prospect for gold 2▸〈喻〉（推测） probe: ～动机 probe sb.'s motives ‖ ～意图 fathom sb.'s intentions
【测温仪】cèwēnyí〈名〉 thermometer: 红外线/电子～ infrared/electronic thermometer
【测向仪】cèxiàngyí〈名〉 direction finder
【测验】cèyàn〈动〉 test: ～机器的性能 test the performance of a machine ‖ ～成绩 test result ‖ 文化水平～ literacy test ‖ 智力～ intelligence test ‖ 英语写作～ English composition test
【测震】cèzhèn〈动〉 measure an earthquake: ～仪 seismograph
【测字】cèzì〈动〉 tell sb.'s fortune by analysing the component parts of a Chinese character: ～先生 fortune-teller
【测醉器】cèzuìqì〈名〉 breath-testing device

恻（惻） cè〈形〉〈书〉 sad: ▸～隐之心, 凄～
【恻然】cèrán〈形〉〈书〉 sad: 每当回想起年轻时的痛苦经历，她不禁～。 Whenever she recalled the painful experiences of her youth, she could not help feeling sad.
【恻隐】cèyǐn〈动〉〈书〉 feel compassion
【恻隐之心】cèyǐn-zhīxīn〈成〉 compassion: 他对苦难的人们总是充满～。 He is always filled with sympathy for those in difficulty.

策[1] cè〈书〉
A〈名〉 riding crop: 执～ hold a riding crop
B〈动〉 1▸（驱赶） whip with a crop: ▸鞭～ 2▸（督促） urge: ▸～励, ～勉

策[2] cè
A〈名〉 1▸〈旧〉（指书写工具） bamboo or wooden slips: 简～ bamboo slips 2▸〈旧〉（指文体） expository writing required in imperial examinations: ▸～论 3▸〈旧〉（指计算工具） bamboo slips used as chips: 筹～ chips 4▸（谋略） plan: ▸计～, 决～
B〈动〉〈书〉 plan: ▸～动, ～划
【策动】cèdòng〈动〉 stir up: ～兵变/政变 plot to stage a mutiny/coup d'état
【策反】cèfǎn〈动〉 instigate a rebellion
【策划】cèhuà〈动〉 plan: ～计谋 devise a stratagem ‖ 幕后～ plot behind the scenes ‖ ～并参与一项犯罪活动 plot and take part in a criminal activity ‖ 精心～ elaborate plot
【策划人】cèhuàrén〈名〉 1▸（指阴谋） plotter: 阴谋的～ architect of the plot 2▸（指项目等） planner
【策划师】cèhuàshī ▸p. 966〈名〉 planner: 注册～ registered planner
【策励】cèlì〈动〉〈书〉 spur on: ～自己更加努力 spur oneself on to greater efforts
【策略】cèlüè A〈名〉 tactics: 改变～ change one's tack ‖ 斗争～ tactics of struggle ‖ 政治～ political strategy ‖ 军事～ military policy B〈形〉 tactful: 你说这话不够～。 It was tactless of you to say that.
【策论】cèlùn〈名〉〈旧〉 political treatise
【策马】cèmǎ〈动〉 urge on a horse: ～前进 flog a horse along
【策勉】cèmiǎn〈动〉〈书〉 spur on
【策士】cèshì〈名〉〈旧〉 tactician: ～谋臣 counsellors and strategists
【策应】cèyìng〈动〉［军事］ support by taking coordinated action
【策源地】cèyuándì〈名〉 place of origin: 革命运动的～ cradle of revolutionary movements ‖ 战争～ hotbed of war

cèi

瓻 cèi〈动〉〈口〉 shatter: 玻璃杯～得粉碎。 The glass shattered to pieces. ‖ 盘子掉到地上～了。 The plate dropped onto the ground and smashed.

cēn

参（參） cēn
▸cān, shēn
【参差】cēncī〈形〉 uneven
【参差不齐】cēncī-bùqí〈成〉 not uniform: 学生的英语水平～。 The students' level of English is variable.

cén

岑 cén〈名〉〈书〉 1▸（山） high hill 2▸（崖岸） shore
【岑寂】cénjì〈形〉〈书〉 quiet and still: ～的夜晚 still night

涔 cén〈书〉
A〈名〉 puddle
B〈形〉 rainy
【涔涔】céncén〈形〉〈书〉 1▸（形容泪、汗、血、雨等） dripping: 汗水～ dripping with sweat ‖ 听到这个不幸的消息，他泪水～。 When he heard the bad news, tears streamed down his cheeks. 2▸（形容天色） gloomy: 雪花纷扬，天色～。 The sky was overcast and it had begun to snow.

C

cēng

噌 cēng〈拟〉 swish: ～的一下他划着了火柴。 He struck the match with a swish.
▸chēng

céng

层（層） céng
A〈动〉〈书〉 tier: ▸～峦叠嶂, ～出不穷
B〈名〉 1▸（重叠物） thing made up of layers: ▸大气～, 云～ 2▸（层次） layer: 底/顶～ bottom/top layer ‖ 高～领导 high-ranking leaders ▸～次, 表～, 对流～
C〈量〉 1▸（指建筑物） storey: 五～楼 five-storey building ‖ 高～建筑 high buildings ‖ 三～蛋糕 three-tiered cake 2▸（指含义） layer: 多了一～顾虑 add to sb.'s worry ‖ 这段话有好几～意思。 This paragraph has several layers of meaning. 3▸（指覆盖物） layer: 铺一～砾石 lay a layer of gravel ‖ 上两～漆 apply two coats of paint
【层报】céngbào〈动〉 report to the higher authorities level by level
【层层】céngcéng〈副〉 layer upon layer: ～把关 check at all levels ‖ ～动员 mobilize level by level ‖ ～包围 surround ring upon ring
【层出不穷】céngchū-bùqióng〈成〉 appear one after another: 新鲜事物～。 A succession of new things have emerged.
【层出叠见】céngchū-diéxiàn ＝ 层见叠出 céngxiàn-diéchū
【层次】céngcì〈名〉 1▸（条理） arrangement of ideas: 他说话～不清。 He doesn't put his ideas together very well. 2▸（等级） administrative level: 各～的行政机关都应招贤纳士。 The administrative organs at all levels should employ talented people. 3▸（差别） level: 多～服务 service at all levels ‖ 年龄～ age bracket
【层次分明】céngcì-fēnmíng〈成〉 have distinct gradation
【层叠】céngdié〈动〉 pile on top of another: ～的雪峰 range upon range of snow-capped mountains
【层高】cénggāo〈名〉 storey height
【层积云】céngjīyún〈名〉［气象］ stratocumulus
【层级】céngjí〈名〉 levels and ranks: 不同～ of different levels and ranks
【层林】cénglín〈名〉〈书〉 row upon row of trees: 深秋时节，～尽染，景色宜人。 In late autumn, the deeply coloured dense woods presented a beautiful view.
【层峦】céngluán〈名〉 range upon range of hills: ～叠翠 range upon range of green hills ‖ ～起伏 range upon range of undulating hills
【层峦叠嶂】céngluán-diézhàng〈成〉 range upon range of hills
【层面】céngmiàn〈名〉 1▸（范围） scope

of a certain level **2**（方面） aspect: 经济～ economic field ‖ 多～的交流 communication at all levels **3**［地质］ bedding: ～构造 bedding plane structure

【层见叠出】 céngxiàn-diéchū 〈成〉 occur repeatedly

【层压玻璃】 céngyā bōli 〈名〉 laminated glass

【层云】 céngyún 〈名〉［气象］ stratus

曾 céng 〈副〉 once: 我～去过那里。 I went there once. ▸～几何时, 不～, 未～ ▸zēng

【曾几何时】 céngjǐhéshí 〈成〉〈书〉 before long: ～，该市发生了巨变。 It was not long before drastic changes took place in this city.

【曾经】 céngjīng 〈副〉 once: 我～见过他。 I have seen him before. ‖ 这部影片～轰动一时。 The film once caused a great sensation.

【曾经沧海】 céngjīng-cānghǎi 〈成〉〈喻〉 have seen a lot of life

【曾用名】 céngyòngmíng 〈名〉 previous name

嶒 céng ▸崚嶒 léngcéng

cèng

蹭 cèng 〈动〉 **1**（摩擦） rub: ～破手上的皮 graze one's hand **2**（沾上） get stained: ～一身泥 get mud all over oneself ‖ 油漆未干，小心别～着。 Mind the wet paint. **3**〈口〉（无偿得到） scrounge: 他想在我这儿～吃～喝。He tried to scrounge meals and drinks off me. ‖ 下班后我想～汤姆的车回家。I want to cadge a lift home from Tom after work. **4**（挪动） shuffle: 他一步一步慢慢往前～。 He inched his way forward. **5**（磨蹭） dawdle: 别～时间，赶快干。 Don't dillydally; just get on with it. ▸磨～

【蹭蹬】 cèngdèng 〈动〉〈书〉 be down on one's luck

chā

叉 chā

A〈名〉 **1**（指器具） fork: 一把～子 a fork ‖ 钢/木～ steel/wooden fork ▸餐～, 刀～, 鱼～ **2**（指符号） cross: 他的试卷上满是～。 His test paper was full of crosses.

B〈动〉 **1**（用叉子） fork: ～肉 fork some meat ‖ ～鱼 spear a fish ‖ 他～起一些腌肉放在面包上。 He forked some bacon onto a piece of bread. **2**（交错） criss-cross: ▸交～, 三～神经 ▸chá, chǎ, chà

【叉车】 chāchē = 铲车 chǎnchē

【叉角羚】 chājiǎolíng 〈名〉［动物］ pronghorn

【叉烧】 chāshāo **A**〈动〉 grill: ～肉 grilled pork **B**〈名〉 grilled pork

【叉烧包】 chāshāobāo 〈名〉 steamed bun stuffed with grilled pork

【叉腰】 chāyāo 〈动〉 rest one's hands on one's hips: 他双手～，怒视着闯入者。 He stood with arms akimbo, glaring at the intruders.

【叉子】 chāzi 〈名〉 **1**（指器具） fork **2**（指符号） cross

杈 chā 〈名〉 wooden fork ▸chà

差 chā

A〈形〉 different: ▸～别, ～距, ～异, 时～

B〈名〉 **1**（错误） mistake: ▸～错, 误～, 一念之～ **2**［数学］ difference: 五和二的～是三。 The difference between five and two is three.

C〈副〉〈书〉 barely: ▸～可, ～强人意 ▸chà, chāi, cī

【差别】 chābié 〈名〉 difference: 缩小城乡～ narrow the gap between town and country ‖ 年龄～ difference in age ‖ 质量与数量上的～ qualitative and quantitative differences ‖ 你去不去没什么～。 It makes little difference whether you go or not.

【差别关税】 chābié guānshuì 〈名〉 differential rates of duty

【差池】 chāchí 〈名〉〈书〉 **1**（错误） error **2**（意外） mishap

【差错】 chācuò 〈名〉 **1**（错误） mistake: 出～ make a mistake ‖ 减少～ reduce errors ‖ 国家大事的决策，容不得半点～。 In making decisions about state affairs, there can be no error whatsoever. **2**（意外） accident: 避免出现任何～。 Any accident should be avoided.

【差额】 chā'é 〈名〉 difference: 补足～ make up the balance ‖ 进出口～ gap between imports and exports ‖ 贸易～ balance of trade

【差额选举】 chā'é xuǎnjǔ 〈名〉 multi-candidate election: ～制 differential voting system

【差价】 chājià 〈名〉 price difference: 地区/季节～ regional/seasonal price differences ‖ 批零～ disparity between wholesale and retail prices

【差距】 chājù 〈名〉 gap: 拉大～ widen the gap ‖ 缩小～ narrow the gap ‖ 贫富～ rich-poor divide

【差可】 chākě 〈形〉〈书〉 barely passable: 成绩～ barely passable results

【差强人意】 chāqiáng-rényì 〈成〉 just passable: 一幅～的作品 a passable piece of work

【差失】 chāshī 〈名〉 mistake

【差数】 chāshù 〈名〉［数学］ difference

【差误】 chāwù 〈名〉〈书〉 mistake

【差以毫厘，失之千里】 chā yǐ háolí, shī zhī qiānlǐ = 差之毫厘，谬以千里 chā zhī háolí, miù yǐ qiānlǐ

【差异】 chāyì 〈名〉 difference: 气候～ difference in climate ‖ 文化～ cultural diversity ‖ 看法上的～ difference of opinion

【差之毫厘，谬以千里】 chā zhī háolí, miù yǐ qiānlǐ 〈成〉 small discrepancies lead to great errors

插 chā 〈动〉 insert: 把门～上 bolt the door ‖ ～上电源 plug in ‖ 在花瓶中～一束鲜花 put a bunch of fresh flowers into the vase ‖ 双峰直～云霄。 The two peaks towered into the clouds. ‖ 我可以～一两句话吗? May I put in a word or two? ▸～翅难飞, ～销, ～秧

【插班】 chābān 〈动〉 join a class in the middle of a course or school year: ～生 student joining midway through

【插板】 chābǎn 〈名〉 connecting block

【插播】 chābō 〈动〉 insert in a radio or TV programme: ～的广告 commercial insertion

【插翅难飞】 chāchì-nánfēi 〈成〉 be unable to escape even with wings: 监狱戒备森严，犯人～。 The prison is so heavily guarded that prisoners would be unable to escape even if they had wings.

【插翅难逃】 chāchì-nántáo = 插翅难飞 chāchì-nánfēi

【插戴】 chādài 〈名〉 woman's head ornament

【插断】 chāduàn 〈动〉 interrupt

【插队】 chāduì 〈动〉 **1**（指排队） jump the queue **2**（指下乡运动） go to live and work in the countryside as a member of a rural production team: ～落户 go to the countryside and settle in the communes ‖ ～知青 school graduate sent to live and work in the countryside as a member of a rural production team

【插杠子】 chā gàngzi 〈惯〉〈贬〉〈喻〉 stick one's nose into: 事情本来进行得挺好，你非得插一杠子。 Things were going really well until you came meddling.

【插管】 chāguǎn 〈动〉［医学］ intubate

【插花】 chāhuā 〈动〉 **1**（搭配花卉） arrange flowers: ～艺术 art of flower arrangement **2**（夹杂） intercrop: 玉米地里还～着种大豆。 Soybeans are intercropped with maize.

【插话】 chāhuà **A**〈动〉 interject: 大人说话时，孩子别～。 When adults are talking, children should not interrupt them. ‖ 她不断～发表意见。 She kept butting in with her own opinions. ‖ 我可以插句话吗? May I cut in? **B**〈名〉 **1**（指话语） interjection: 编者的～ editorial interjection **2**（指事件） digression: 一段～ a digression

【插画】 chāhuà 〈名〉 illustration: 有～的书 illustrated book

【插架】 chājià 〈动〉 put on shelf

【插件】 chājiàn 〈名〉 plug-in unit

【插脚】 chājiǎo **A**〈动〉 **1**（落脚） set foot in: 大礼堂非常拥挤，我无法～。The auditorium is so crowded that I can't get in. **2**〈喻〉（参与） take part in: 他们自己组织这些活动，你最好别～。They organize these activities themselves so you'd better leave them to it. **B**〈名〉［电子］ prong

【插科打诨】 chākē-dǎhùn 〈成〉 crack jokes and play the fool

【插孔】 chākǒng 〈名〉 socket: 电器～ sockets for electrical appliances

【插空】 chākòng 〈动〉 find time: 他是个音乐爱好者，再忙都要～去听音乐会。 As a music lover, however busy he is, he always manages to find time to attend a concert.

【插口】 chākǒu **A**〈动〉 interrupt: 人家说话时别～。 Don't butt in when someone is speaking. **B**〈名〉 socket: 电器～ socket for electrical appliances

【插屏】 chāpíng 〈名〉［美术］ table plaque

【插瓶】 chāpíng 〈名〉 vase

【插曲】 chāqǔ 〈名〉 **1**［音乐］ interlude **2**（指歌曲） song in a film or play **3**〈喻〉（指事件） episode: 这段经历是他一生难忘的～。 This experience is an unforgettable interlude in his life.

【插入】 chārù 〈动〉 **1**（插进去） insert: 把插头～插座 put a plug in the socket ‖ 派遣侦察队～敌人心脏。 Scouting troops are to be dispatched to infiltrate the enemy forces. **2**（加入） join: 你女儿可以～三年级。Your daughter can join Grade Three.

【插入符号】 chārù fúhào 〈名〉 insertion mark

【插入语】 chārùyǔ 〈名〉［语法］ parenthesis

【插身】chāshēn〈动〉1（挤入）squeeze in: 体育场挤满了观众，很难～。The stadium is so thronged with spectators that it is difficult to get in. 2（参与）get involved in: 他不愿意～这场纠纷。He is unwilling to involve himself in this dispute.
【插手】chāshǒu〈动〉1（帮助）lend a hand: 无需～ need no help ‖ 她想帮妈妈干家务，可又插不上手。She wanted to help her mother with the household chores, but didn't know how. 2（参与）get involved in: 这件事让他们去做，你不要～。Let them do it. You don't need to get involved. 3（干涉）interfere in: 明智的父母不会～儿女的婚事。Wise parents will not interfere with their children's marriages. ‖ 在任何情况下，我们都不能让别国～我国内政。Under no circumstances will we allow other nations to interfere in our internal affairs.
【插穗】chāsuì［植物］A〈动〉transplant a cutting B〈名〉cutting
【插条】chātiáo = 插穗 chāsuì
【插头】chātóu〈名〉［电气］plug
【插图】chātú〈名〉illustration: 彩色～ colour illustration ‖ ～本 illustrated edition
【插销】chāxiāo〈名〉bolt: 门上的～插好了吗？Is the bolt on the door properly fastened?
【插叙】chāxù〈名〉［语言］narration interspersed with flashbacks
【插秧】chāyāng〈动〉transplant rice seedlings or shoots: ～机 rice transplanter
【插页】chāyè〈名〉insert
【插一杠子】chā yī gàngzi〈惯〉get involved at a wrong time
【插枝】chāzhī = 插穗 chāsuì
【插足】chāzú〈动〉1（落脚）set foot in: 道路又脏又泥泞，没有～的地方。The road is dirty and muddy. There's nowhere to put one's feet. 2〈喻〉（介入）get involved in: 由于第三者～，离婚率逐年上升。The divorce rate is going up year by year as a result of third party involvement. ‖ 你不应～此事。You shouldn't get involved with this.
【插嘴】chāzuǐ〈动〉interrupt: 插不上嘴 cannot get a word in ‖ 我们谈话时她老是～。She kept cutting in on our conversation.
【插座】chāzuò〈名〉socket; power point〈英〉

喳 chā
▸zhā
【喳喳】chāchā〈拟〉whisper: ▸喊喊～
【喳喳】chācha〈动〉whisper: 她在我耳边～了几句，然后就消失了。She whispered a few words in my ear and then disappeared.

馇（餷）chā
〈动〉1（煮饲料）cook and stir: ～猪食 cook and stir feed for pigs 2〈方〉（煮粥）cook (into porridge): ～粥 cook porridge
▸zha

碴 chā
▸胡子拉碴 húzilāchā
▸chá

锸（鍤）chā
〈名〉〈书〉shovel

嚓 chā
▸咔嚓 kāchā, 啪嚓 pāchā
▸cā

chá

叉 chá
〈动〉〈方〉block up: 事故把道路～了两个小时。The accident jammed the road for two hours.
▸chā, chǎ, chà

垞 chá
〈名〉small mound

茬 chá
A〈名〉1（指茎和秆）stubble: 谷/麦～ paddy/wheat stubble 2（指须发）stubble: 发～ stubble ‖ 胡～ beard stubble 3（指话语）something just said: 接～ take a cue ▸话～儿
B〈量〉1（指作物）batch: 换～ change of crops ‖ 在中国南方，水稻可一年熟两～。In South China paddies can yield two crops a year. 2（指人）generation: 一～新干部 a new generation of cadres ‖ 部队又招募了一～新兵。The army has conscripted another batch of new recruits.
【茬口】chákǒu〈名〉1（指作物）crops for rotation: 一年之中，农民要选好～进行轮作。The farmers should select the right crops and rotate them during the year. 2（指土壤）soil on which a crop has been planted and harvested: 中国北方的农民总是借着小麦的～种玉米。Farmers in North China always grow maize on soil where a crop of wheat has been harvested. 3〈方〉（时机）chance: 趁着股票下跌的～，赶快买进。With stocks going down, you shouldn't miss the opportunity to buy in.
【茬子】cházi〈名〉stubble: 刨～ dig out the stubble ‖ ～地 stubble field

茶 chá
〈名〉1（茶叶）tea: 采～ pick tea ▸绿～, 普洱～, ～树, ～叶 2（茶饮）tea: 给客人上～ serve tea to guests ‖ 喝～ drink tea ‖ 品～ taste tea 3〈旧〉（聘礼）betrothal gift: 下～ send betrothal gifts to a bride ▸～礼 4（饮料）certain kind of drink or liquid food: 杏仁～ almond paste ▸奶～, 油～ 5（茶色）dark brown colour: ▸～镜, ～色 6（油茶树）tea-oil tree: ▸～油 7（山茶）camellia: ▸～花

> **茶**
>
> Tea originated in China, and tradition has it that the use of tea leaves was invented by Shen Nong (神农), the father of Chinese agriculture. In earliest times, tea had a medicinal use, later becoming a popular beverage. The main area of tea cultivation is central, south-east and south-west China. Different methods of processing produce green tea, black tea, oolong tea and fragrant tea. The world's first monograph on tea, the *Classic of Tea* (《茶经》), appeared in the Tang Dynasty. The purple-clay teapots of Yixing in Jiangsu Province are particularly famous.

【茶吧】chábā〈名〉tea house
【茶杯】chábēi〈名〉teacup
【茶博士】chábóshì〈名〉〈旧〉waiter in a tea house
【茶场】cháchǎng〈名〉tea plantation
【茶匙】cháchí〈名〉teaspoon
【茶炊】cháchuī〈名〉tea urn
【茶道】chádào〈名〉tea ceremony: ～大师 tea master
【茶底儿】chádǐr〈名〉tea dregs
【茶点】chádiǎn〈名〉refreshments: 供应～ provide refreshments
【茶碟儿】chádiér〈名〉saucer
【茶饭】cháfàn〈名〉food and drink: ～不进 neither drink nor eat
【茶坊】cháfāng〈名〉tea house
【茶房】cháfáng〈名〉〈旧〉attendant
【茶缸】chágāng〈名〉mug
【茶馆】cháguǎn〈名〉tea house
【茶褐色】cháhèsè ▸p. 863〈名〉dark brown
【茶壶】cháhú〈名〉teapot: 一把～ a teapot
【茶花】cháhuā〈名〉camellia
【茶话会】cháhuàhuì〈名〉tea party
【茶会】cháhuì = 茶话会 cháhuàhuì
【茶几】chájī〈名〉coffee table
【茶鸡蛋】chájīdàn〈名〉tea egg
【茶碱】chájiǎn〈名〉［化学］theophylline
【茶巾】chájīn〈名〉tea cloth
【茶晶】chájīng〈名〉citrine
【茶镜】chájìng〈名〉glasses with brown lenses
【茶具】chájù〈名〉tea set
【茶客】chákè〈名〉customer of a tea house
【茶礼】chálǐ〈名〉〈旧〉betrothal gifts [sent by a man to a woman]
【茶寮】cháliáo〈名〉〈方〉tea house
【茶楼】chálóu〈名〉tea house
【茶炉】chálú〈名〉1（烧水炉）water boiler 2（供开水处）hot water shop
【茶卤】chálǔ〈名〉strong tea
【茶末】chámò〈名〉tea dust
【茶农】chánóng〈名〉tea grower
【茶盘】chápán〈名〉tea tray
【茶钱】cháqián〈名〉1（茶资）payment for tea 2〈旧〉（小费）tip
【茶青】cháqīng ▸p. 863〈名〉brownish green
【茶色】chásè ▸p. 863〈名〉dark brown: ～玻璃 brown glass
【茶社】cháshè〈名〉tea house
【茶室】cháshì〈名〉tea room
【茶食】cháshi〈名〉cakes and sweetmeats
【茶寿】cháshòu〈名〉108th birthday
【茶树】cháshù〈名〉tea tree
【茶水】cháshuǐ〈名〉1（茶）tea: 供应～ supply tea and boiled water 2（水）boiled water
【茶肆】chásì〈名〉〈书〉tea house
【茶摊】chátān〈名〉tea stall
【茶汤】chátāng〈名〉gruel of millet flour and sugar
【茶亭】chátíng〈名〉tea-booth
【茶托】chátuō〈名〉saucer
【茶碗】cháwǎn〈名〉handleless teacup
【茶文化】cháwénhuà〈名〉tea culture
【茶锈】cháxiù〈名〉tea stain
【茶叶】cháyè〈名〉tea leaves: ～罐 tea caddy
【茶叶蛋】cháyèdàn = 茶鸡蛋 chájīdàn
【茶艺】cháyì〈名〉tea ceremony
【茶油】cháyóu〈名〉tea-seed oil
【茶余饭后】cháyú-fànhòu〈成〉at one's leisure: 这本畅销书成为人们～的话题。This best-seller has become a hot topic for leisure-time discussion.
【茶园】cháyuán〈名〉1（指茶林）tea plantation 2〈旧〉（戏院）theatre
【茶盅】cházhōng〈名〉handleless teacup
【茶砖】cházhuān〈名〉tea brick
【茶庄】cházhuāng〈名〉tea store
【茶资】cházī〈名〉payment for tea
【茶籽饼】cházǐbǐng〈名〉pulp made with oil extracted from seeds of tea-oil bushes
【茶座】cházuò〈名〉1（指茶馆）tea house: 音乐～ music saloon 2（指座位）seats in a tea house: 茶馆有三十几个～。There are over thirty seats in the tea house.

C

查 chá〈动〉**1**（检查）check: ～电表/煤气表 read the electricity/gas meter ‖ ～票 check tickets ‖ ～卫生 make a public health and sanitation check ▸～户口, ～账 **2**（调查）investigate: ～出秘密 uncover a secret ‖ ～事故起因 look into the cause of the accident ‖ 这件贿赂案一定要彻底～一～。This bribery should be investigated thoroughly. ▸～访, ～考, ～证 **3**（查阅）consult: ～档案 check sb.'s record ‖ ～资料 consult reference materials ‖ ～字典 look up a word in the dictionary
▸Zhā

【查案】chá'àn〈动〉investigate a case

【查办】chábàn〈动〉investigate and deal with accordingly: ～一起案子 investigate a case ‖ 他被撤职～。He was dismissed and investigated.

【查抄】cháchāo〈动〉make an inventory of a criminal's possessions and confiscate them: 海关官员～了走私物品。The customs officer confiscated the smuggled goods.

【查处】cháchǔ〈动〉investigate and prosecute: ～各类违纪案件 investigate all kinds of cases that violate discipline and punish those involved ‖ 依法～ investigate and handle in accordance with law

【查点】chádiǎn〈动〉make an inventory: ～库存 make an inventory of the goods in stock ‖ ～人数 check the number of people

【查对】cháduì〈动〉check: ～数据 verify the statistics ‖ ～原文 check the original text ‖ ～账目 verify accounts

【查房】cháfáng〈动〉do a ward round

【查访】cháfǎng〈动〉make enquiries: 暗中～ engage in secret investigations

【查封】cháfēng〈动〉seal up: ～财产 seal up and confiscate sb.'s property

【查岗】chágǎng〈动〉**1** = 查哨 cháshào **2**（指工作人员）check that sb. is on duty

【查号台】cháhàotái〈名〉directory enquiries

【查核】cháhé〈动〉examine: ～账目 check accounts

【查户口】chá hùkǒu〈动〉check residence cards

【查获】cháhuò〈动〉track down: ～大批毒品 track down and seize a large amount of drugs

【查缉】chájī〈动〉**1**（搜寻）search for: ～走私物品 search for smuggled goods **2**（搜捕）hunt down and arrest: ～逃犯 track down an escaped convict

【查检】chájiǎn〈动〉**1**（查阅检索）consult **2**（检查）examine: 登机以前，行李需经～。Before boarding a plane, passengers should have their luggage checked.

【查缴】chájiǎo〈动〉track down: ～违禁物品 track down contraband goods

【查禁】chájìn〈动〉ban: ～赌博 prohibit gambling ‖ ～黄色书刊 ban pornographic books and magazines

【查究】chájiū〈动〉look into and find out: ～责任 find out who should be held responsible ‖ 对群众举报的腐败分子要认真～。The corrupt elements reported by the public must be thoroughly investigated and prosecuted.

【查勘】chákān〈动〉survey: ～地形 survey the terrain ‖ ～石油矿藏 prospect for oil deposits

【查看】chákàn〈动〉inspect: ～工程质量 examine the quality of the construction ‖ ～身份证 check sb.'s identity card

【查考】chákǎo〈动〉investigate: ～文物的年代 try to ascertain the date of a relic

【查扣】chákòu〈动〉track down: ～走私香烟 track down smuggled cigarettes

【查明】chámíng〈动〉ascertain: ～事情的真相 get to the truth of a matter ‖ 车祸起因现已～。The cause of the traffic accident has been established.

【查票】chápiào〈动〉check tickets

【查铺】chápù〈动〉make a bed check

【查清】cháqīng〈动〉make a thorough investigation of

【查哨】cháshào〈动〉［军事］do the rounds of guard posts

【查实】cháshí〈动〉check and verify: 经～，凶案系一惯犯所为。It was confirmed that the murder had been committed by a habitual offender.

【查收】cháshōu〈动〉check and accept: 寄去词典一部，请～。Please find a dictionary enclosed herewith.

【查问】cháwèn〈动〉**1**（寻问）enquire about: ～电话号码 enquire about a telephone number ‖ ～火车发车时间 ask about train departure times **2**（盘查）cross-examine: ～来往车辆 question passing vehicles ‖ ～目击证人 interrogate an eyewitness

【查无实据】cháwúshíjù〈成〉investigation reveals no evidence

【查寻】cháxún〈动〉search for: ～被拐卖的妇女 search for abducted women ‖ 他到邮局～挂号信。He went to the post office to enquire about his registered letter.

【查巡】cháxún〈动〉go on a tour of inspection

【查询】cháxún〈动〉make enquiries: ～地址/电话号码 ask for sb.'s address/telephone number ‖ 电话～ telephone enquiries

【查验】cháyàn〈动〉inspect: ～护照 examine a passport ‖ ～身份证 check sb.'s identity card

【查夜】cháyè〈动〉do the rounds at night

【查阅】cháyuè〈动〉consult: ～历史文献 consult historical documents ‖ ～资料 refer to data

【查账】cházhàng〈动〉audit

【查找】cházhǎo〈动〉seek: ～失主 try to find the owner of the lost property ‖ ～资料 gather data

【查照】cházhào〈动〉〈旧〉please note: 望～办理。Please pay attention and take appropriate action.

【查证】cházhèng〈动〉validate: ～属实 be verified ‖ 证人的证词仍需～。The testimony of the witness still needs to be confirmed.

搽 chá〈动〉apply: ～口红 apply lipstick ‖ 给伤口～药 apply medication to the wound

猹 chá〈名〉badger-like wild animal

楂 chá = 茬 chá
▸zhā

槎[1] chá〈名〉〈书〉raft: 乘～ take a raft ‖ 浮～ floating raft

槎[2] chá = 茬 chá

碴 chá
A〈名〉**1**（裂口）sharp edge: 碗～儿 sharp edge of a broken bowl **2**（碎块）fragments: 冰～儿 shards of ice ‖ 玻璃～儿 fragments of glass
B〈动〉〈方〉cut: 他在海滩上玩儿时，被碎玻璃～了右脚。While he was playing in the sand, his right foot was cut by broken glass.
▸chā

【碴口】chákǒu〈名〉cut

【碴儿】chár〈名〉**1**（碎块）broken pieces **2**（裂口）sharp edge of broken glass, china, etc.: 碗～刮破了他的上嘴唇。The sharp edge of the bowl cut his upper lip. **3**（不和）rift: 他们从前有～，现在和好了。There was a rift between them, but now they have made it up. ‖ 他不时地找～和经理吵架。He would occasionally pick a quarrel with his manager.

察 chá〈动〉**1**（细看）examine: ▸～看, ～言观色, 观～ **2**（调查）investigate: ▸勘～, 考～

【察访】cháfǎng〈动〉go and find out: ～民情 obtain first-hand information on people's situation ‖ 实地～ make an on-the-spot investigation

【察觉】chájué〈动〉perceive: ～到对手的敌意 sense the hostility of the enemy ‖ 你有没有～到你儿子的心事? Were you aware of what was going on for your son?

【察勘】chákān〈动〉survey: ～沙漠 carry out a survey of the desert

【察看】chákàn〈动〉observe: ～工程进度 check the progress of the construction ‖ ～灾情 observe a natural calamity

【察其言，观其行】chá qí yán, guān qí xíng〈成〉check what a person says against what he does

【察言观色】cháyán-guānsè〈成〉observe sb. closely

【察验】cháyàn〈动〉check: ～新设备 check the new equipment

楂 chá

【楂子】cházi〈名〉〈方〉coarsely ground maize

chǎ

叉 chǎ〈动〉fork: ～着腿站着 stand with legs apart
▸chā, chá, chà

衩 chǎ ▸裤衩 kùchǎ
▸chà

蹅 chǎ〈动〉〈口〉tramp: ～着深雪回家 trudge home through deep snow

镲（鑔） chǎ ▸p. 929〈名〉［音乐］small cymbals

chà

叉 chà ▸劈叉 pǐchà
▸chā, chá, chǎ

汊 chà〈名〉tributary: 河的西～ west branch of the river ▸～子

【汊港】chàgǎng〈名〉tributary

【汊流】chàliú = 岔流 chàliú

【汊子】chàzi〈名〉tributary

杈 chà〈名〉branch of a tree: ▸树～, 枝～
▸chā
【杈子】chàzi〈名〉branch of a tree: 打～ trim branches off a tree ‖ 树～ tree branches

岔 chà
A〈名〉1（分支）branch: 河～ branch of a river ‖ 三～路口 junction of three roads ▸～道儿, ～口 2（差错）trouble: 把钱交给她，出不了～儿。You won't have any problems if you give her money. ▸～子 2
B〈动〉1（偏离方向）turn off: 他的车～到右边路上了。His car turned right. 2（转移话题）change the topic of conversation: ▸打～
【岔道儿】chàdàor = 岔路 chàlù
【岔开】chàkāi〈动〉1（转移）diverge: 他有意～话题。He intentionally changed the topic of conversation. 2（使错开）stagger: ～访问时间 space out visits ‖ 把护士值班时间～ stagger the nurses' shifts
【岔口】chàkǒu〈名〉fork: 我们在～分手。We parted at the fork in the road.
【岔流】chàliú〈名〉tributary
【岔路】chàlù〈名〉side road: ～口 fork in the road ‖ 大路向左分出一条～。The main road branches off to the left.
【岔气】chàqì〈动〉feel a pain in the chest when breathing
【岔子】chàzi〈名〉1（岔路）side road 2（差错）trouble: 她从未出过～。She has never had an accident. ‖ 他很认真，出不了～。He's very careful. Nothing will go wrong.

刹 chà〈名〉［佛教］Buddhist temple: 古～ ancient Buddhist temple
▸shā
【刹那】chànà〈名〉instant: 一～ in a flash ‖ ～间，会场变得鸦雀无声。The conference room fell silent instantly.

衩 chà〈名〉slit: 这条裙子两边都有～。The skirt has slits on both sides. ▸开～
▸chǎ

诧（詫）chà〈形〉astonished: ▸～异, 惊～
【诧愕】chà'è〈形〉〈书〉astounded
【诧然】chàrán〈形〉〈书〉surprised
【诧异】chàyì〈形〉astonished: 大家都用～的眼光看着他。Everyone looked at him with astonishment.

差 chà
A〈动〉1（有差别）differ from: 结果与期望～得很远。The results fell far short of expectations. ‖ 两位作家的风格相～甚远。The two writers are completely different in style. ▸～不多 2（欠缺）be short of: ～五分九点 five minutes to nine ‖ 还～多少钱？How much more money do we need? ‖ 两个电话号码只～一个数字。The two telephone numbers are just one digit different.
B〈形〉1（不对）wrong: 此言～矣。This remark is wrong. 2（不好）inferior: 产品质量太～。Product quality is very poor. ‖ 土质很～，不适合耕作。The soil is substandard and not suitable for growing crops.
▸chā, chāi, cī
【差不多】chàbuduō A〈形〉1（相似）roughly the same: 他俩长得～。The two of them look very much alike. 2（大多数）most: ～的家务活她都会干。She can do a wide range of housework. 3（还可以）not bad: 这套音响的效果还～。The sound on this stereo is not too bad. B〈副〉nearly: 他俩～同岁。The two of them are roughly the same age. ‖ 我们在那儿呆了～两个星期。We stayed there for almost two weeks.
【差不离】chàbulí = 差不多 chàbuduō A1, A2
【差点儿】chàdiǎnr A〈形〉slightly inferior: 她挺能干，就是经验～。She is very capable, but a bit short of experience. B〈副〉nearly: ～射中目标 miss the target by a hair ‖ 她～淹死。She very nearly drowned. ‖ 我们～撞上了那辆车。We narrowly missed crashing into that car.
【差劲】chàjìn〈形〉poor: 这电影够～的。The film isn't any good. ‖ 他这人没有时间观念，真～。It doesn't occur to him to be on time. It's really bad.
【差生】chàshēng〈名〉poor student: 帮助～补习功课 help the poor students with their lessons
【差事】chàshì〈形〉〈口〉not up to standard: 这瓷器太～了，一碰就破。This piece of porcelain is so shoddy. One knock and it will break.
▸chāishi

姹 chà〈形〉〈书〉beautiful
【姹紫嫣红】chàzǐ-yānhóng〈成〉beautiful flowers: 春天里百花盛开，～。In spring when all the flowers come out there is a riot of deep purples and bright reds.

chāi

拆 chāi〈动〉1（打开）tear open: ～机器 disassemble a machine ‖ ～信 rip open a letter ‖ 这件毛衣该～了。This old sweater needs to be taken apart. ▸～封, ～洗, ～卸 2（拆毁）demolish: ～建筑物 demolish buildings ‖ ～脚手架 take down scaffolding ▸～除
▸cā
【拆白党】chāibáidǎng〈名〉〈方〉〈旧〉swindlers
【拆除】chāichú〈动〉pull down: ～旧房 knock down old houses ‖ ～路障 remove a barricade ‖ 为开辟新道路，～了几栋房屋。Several houses were demolished to make way for the new road.
【拆穿】chāichuān〈动〉expose: ～谎言 uncover a lie ‖ ～骗局 expose a fraud ‖ ～西洋镜 expose sb.'s tricks
【拆东墙，补西墙】chāi dōngqiáng, bǔ xīqiáng〈俗〉〈喻〉rob Peter to pay Paul
【拆兑】chāiduì〈动〉〈方〉borrow: ～应急 borrow money for urgent use
【拆封】chāifēng〈动〉break a seal: 信还没有～。The letter is still sealed.
【拆股】chāigǔ〈动〉dissolve a partnership: ～分息 dissolve the partnership and divide up the dividends
【拆股发行】chāigǔ fāxíng〈名〉［经济］scrip issue
【拆毁】chāihuǐ〈动〉demolish: ～房屋 demolish houses
【拆伙】chāihuǒ〈动〉dissolve
【拆建】chāijiàn〈动〉tear down and rebuild
【拆借】chāijiè〈动〉make a short term loan
【拆开】chāikāi〈动〉take apart
【拆零】chāilíng〈动〉sell by the piece
【拆卖】chāimài〈动〉sell by the piece: 这套瓷器可～。This set of china can be sold by the piece.
【拆迁】chāiqiān〈动〉pull down old houses and relocate the residents: ～工程 resettlement project ‖ ～补偿 compensation for demolition ‖ ～户 household to be relocated
【拆墙脚】chāi qiángjiǎo〈惯〉〈喻〉undermine: 拆民主进程的墙脚 subvert the democratic process
【拆散】chāisǎn〈动〉break apart: 别把新玩具～了。Don't break the new toys.
【拆散】chāisàn〈动〉break up: ～婚姻 break up a marriage ‖ 丈夫吸毒～了这个家庭。The family was torn apart by the husband's drug use.
【拆台】chāitái〈动〉pull the rug from under sb.'s feet: 互相～ counteract each other's efforts
【拆息】chāixī〈名〉daily interest rate
【拆洗】chāixǐ〈动〉1（棉被、棉衣等）take apart and wash: ～被褥 unpick and wash bedding 2（机器）take apart for cleaning: ～机器 disassemble and clean the machine
【拆线】chāixiàn〈动〉［医学］remove stitches
【拆卸】chāixiè〈动〉disassemble: ～机器 dismantle a machine
【拆账】chāizhàng〈动〉pay wages in proportion to takings
【拆装】chāizhuāng〈动〉disassemble and assemble
【拆字】chāizì = 测字 cèzì

钗（釵）chāi〈名〉hairpin: 金/玉～ gold/jade hairpin

差 chāi
A〈动〉dispatch: ～某人去某地 send sb. over to a place ‖ 一位记者被～往中东报道战事。A reporter was dispatched to the Middle East to cover the war. ▸～遣, 鬼使神～
B〈名〉1（指差事）errand: 肥～ cushy job ▸出～, 交～ 2（指人）runner: ▸听～, 信～
▸chā, chà, cī
【差旅费】chāilǚfèi〈名〉business travel expenses: 报销～ claim reimbursement for travel expenses
【差遣】chāiqiǎn〈动〉send on an errand: 听候～ be at sb.'s disposal
【差使】chāishǐ〈动〉dispatch: 他整天受老板～。He spends his days being ordered about by his boss.
【差使】chāishi〈名〉〈旧〉official post
【差事】chāishi〈名〉assignment: 苦～ thankless task
▸chàshì
【差役】chāiyì〈名〉1（指劳动）corvée: 服～ serve one's corvée 2〈旧〉（指人）bailiff in a *yamen*: 衙门里的～ bailiff in a *yamen*

chái

侪（儕）chái〈名〉〈书〉peers: 吾～ people like us
【侪辈】cháibèi〈名〉〈书〉peers

C

C

柴 chái

A〈名〉 firewood: 砍/劈～ cut/chop firewood ▸～火，火～，木～

B〈形〉〈方〉 **1**（形容人） bony: 老人病得很重，人都变～了。 The old man has been critically ill and is reduced to a skeleton. ▸骨瘦如～ **2**（形容食物） tough: 老芹菜～得很。 Old celery is too tough. ‖ 牛排做得太老，嚼起来很～。 The steak is overdone and it is tough. **3**（形容质量、能力） shoddy: 这种灯泡这么快就坏，质量太～了。 This bulb broke quickly because it was of very poor quality.

【柴草】 cháicǎo〈名〉 firewood: 用～生火 build a fire with sticks

【柴达木盆地】 Cháidámù Péndì〈名〉 Qaidam Basin

【柴刀】 cháidāo〈名〉 firewood chopper

【柴扉】 cháifēi〈名〉〈书〉 brushwood door

【柴胡】 cháihú〈名〉 **1**［植物］ Chinese thorowax **2**［中药］ root of Chinese thorowax

【柴火】 cháihuo〈名〉 firewood: 拾～ pick up firewood

【柴郡】 Cháijùn〈名〉 Cheshire

【柴门】 cháimén〈名〉〈喻〉 poverty-stricken family: 出身～ be born into a poor family

【柴米】 cháimǐ〈名〉 daily necessities: 不当家不知～贵。 No one knows the difficulty of running a household except for those that do.

【柴米油盐】 chái-mǐ-yóu-yán〈成〉 main daily necessities

【柴油】 cháiyóu〈名〉 diesel oil

【柴油机】 cháiyóujī〈名〉 diesel

豺 chái〈名〉 jackal

【豺狼】 cháiláng〈名〉〈喻〉 cruel and evil people: ～成性 be rapacious and ruthless ‖ ～当道 the cruel and the wicked hold sway

chǎi

踳 chǎi〈名〉 ground beans or maize: 豆～儿 ground beans

chài

虿（蠆） chài〈名〉〈古〉 scorpion-like insect

瘥 chài〈动〉〈书〉 recuperate: 久病初～ have just recovered from a long illness ▸cuó

chān

觇（覘） chān〈动〉〈书〉 observe

【觇标】 chānbiāo〈名〉［测绘］ surveyor's beacon

掺（摻） chān〈动〉 mix: 往牛奶里～水 mix the milk with water ‖ 水和油～不到一起。 Water and oil do not mix. ▸～兑，～杂 ▸càn, shǎn

【掺兑】 chānduì〈动〉 mix: 用水～酒精 mix water with alcohol

【掺和】 chānhuo〈动〉 **1**（混杂） mix: 把鸡蛋、面粉和水～在一起做面条 to mix eggs, flour and water to make noodles **2**（相处） mix: 他和同事～不到一起去。 He doesn't mix well with his colleagues. **3**（介入） meddle: 别跟我瞎～，我要工作。 Stop harassing me, will you? I've got work to do.

【掺假】 chānjiǎ〈动〉 adulterate: ～的酒 adulterated liquor

【掺杂】 chānzá〈动〉 mix: 这部电视连续剧史实之中～着虚构。 This TV series jumbles up historical facts with fantasy.

搀[1]（攙） chān = 掺 chān

搀[2]（攙） chān〈动〉 help sb. by the arm: 把老人～上公共汽车 take the old man's arm and help him board the bus ▸～扶

【搀扶】 chānfú〈动〉 help sb. by the arm: ～着老人过马路 hold the old man by the arm and help him across the street

chán

单（單） chán ▸dān, Shàn

【单于】 chányú〈名〉〈古〉 *chanyu* [title of the chief of the *Xiongnu* (匈奴)]

谗（讒） chán

A〈动〉 slander: 君子不～人。 A gentleman doesn't speak ill of others. ▸～害，～言

B〈名〉 slanderous remarks: 进～ make false accusations against sb. to one's superior ‖ 信～ believe false accusations

【谗害】 chánhài〈动〉 frame sb.: ～忠良 persecute the loyal and the righteous by defaming them

【谗佞】 chánnìng〈名〉〈书〉 slanderer and sycophant

【谗言】 chányán〈名〉 slander: 听信～ believe false accusations

婵（嬋） chán

【婵娟】 chánjuān〈书〉 **A**〈形〉 fair: 体态～ graceful bearing **B**〈名〉 moon: 但愿人长久，千里共～。 May we all live long and share moonlight even when far apart.

【婵媛】 chányuán〈形〉〈书〉 **1** = 婵娟 chánjuān A **2**（相连） joined

馋（饞） chán〈形〉 **1**（想吃） greedy: 嘴～ be greedy ‖ ～得流口水 be so ravenous that one's mouth waters **2**（羡慕） hunger for: 看见别人打麻将，他就～得手发痒。 His fingers get itchy whenever he sees others playing mah-jong. ▸眼～

【馋鬼】 chánguǐ〈名〉 glutton

【馋痨】 chánláo〈名〉 greed

【馋猫】 chánmāo〈名〉〈喻〉 greedy-guts

【馋涎欲滴】 chánxián-yùdī〈成〉 drool with desire

【馋嘴】 chánzuǐ **A**〈形〉 greedy **B**〈名〉 glutton: 他是个～。 He is a voracious eater.

禅（禪） chán〈名〉 **1**［佛教］ deep meditation: ～定 lost in Buddhist meditation ▸参～，坐～ **2**（指佛事） anything relating to Buddhism: ▸～房，～机 ▸shàn

【禅床】 chánchuáng〈名〉 bed for meditation

【禅房】 chánfáng〈名〉 **1**（指房舍） Buddhist monks' living quarters **2**（指寺院） Buddhist temple

【禅机】 chánjī〈名〉 Buddhist allegory

【禅理】 chánlǐ〈名〉 Buddhism doctrines

【禅林】 chánlín〈名〉 Buddhist temple

【禅门】 chánmén〈名〉 Buddhism

【禅师】 chánshī〈名〉〈尊〉 Zen master

【禅寺】 chánsì = 禅林 chánlín

【禅堂】 chántáng〈名〉 meditation hall

【禅悟】 chánwù〈名〉 realization of truth through meditation

【禅学】 chánxué〈名〉 doctrines of Zen Buddhism

【禅院】 chányuàn = 禅林 chánlín

【禅杖】 chánzhàng〈名〉 Buddhist monk's staff

【禅宗】 chánzōng〈名〉［佛教］ Zen Buddhism

孱 chán〈形〉 frail ▸càn

【孱弱】 chánruò〈形〉〈书〉 **1**（体弱） frail: 体质～ have a delicate constitution **2**（软弱无能） weak and incompetent **3**（力量薄弱） insubstantial: 军力～ weak military capability

缠（纏） chán〈动〉 **1**（绕） wind: ～着绷带 be bandaged ‖ 鸟被金属网～住。 The bird got entangled in the wire netting. ‖ 把线～在线轴上。 Wind the thread around the reel. ▸～绕 **2**（纠缠） harass: ～着不放 stick to like a leech ‖ 乞丐一直～着我们要钱。 Beggars kept pestering us for money. ▸纠～ **3**〈方〉（应付） deal with: 这人真难～。 This guy was really difficult to deal with.

【缠绑】 chánbǎng〈动〉 tie up: 他手上～着纱布，不能洗衣服。 He cannot wash his clothes because of his bandaged hand.

【缠绵】 chánmián〈形〉 **1**（指疾病或感情） lingering: ～于病榻 be bedridden with a lingering disease ‖ ～于感情的旋涡之中 be caught up in the whirlwind of love **2**（指乐曲） melodious and moving: ～的旋律 sweet and touching melody

【缠绵悱恻】 chánmián-fěicè〈成〉 exceedingly sentimental: 她被这～的电影打动了。 She was moved by the mushy film.

【缠磨】 chánmo〈动〉〈口〉 pester: 推销商～我买他的产品。 The salesman pestered me to buy his products.

【缠扰】 chánrǎo〈动〉 bother: 被杂事～ be bothered by lots of little things

【缠绕】 chánrào〈动〉 **1**（盘绕） wind: 风筝～在树枝上。 The kite was entwined on the branch. **2**（纠缠） pester: 她想摆脱他的～，可他却不放过她。 She tried to get rid of him, but he stuck to her like a burr.

【缠身】 chánshēn〈动〉 be bogged down with: 病魔～ be bogged down with illness ‖ 公务～ be occupied with business

【缠手】 chánshǒu〈形〉 **1**（难脱身） difficult to free oneself from: 我不能出差，孩子还小，太～。 I cannot go away on business. My child is too young for me to get away. **2**（难办） troublesome: 这件案子有些～。 The case was quite hard to deal with.

【缠足】 chánzú〈动〉〈旧〉 bind a woman's feet

缠足

The custom of binding female feet. At around the age of seven a girl's feet would be bent double and bound tight with strips of cloth to make them narrow and pointed. The resulting tiny foot was considered to be beautiful and erotic. A bound foot was known as a 'three inch gold lotus'（三寸金莲） or 'lily foot', an expression believed to have originated with a tenth-century imperial concubine who danced on gold lotus flowers on bound feet only three inches long. The practice of foot-binding gradually died out during the early 20th century.

蝉（蟬） chán〈名〉cicada
【蝉联】chánlián〈动〉continue to hold a title: ～冠军 retain the championship
【蝉蜕】chántuì **A**〈名〉cicada slough **B**〈动〉〈书〉〈喻〉extricate oneself
【蝉衣】chányī〈名〉［中药］cicada slough
【蝉翼】chányì〈名〉cicada's wings: 薄如～ be as thin as a cicada's wings ‖ ～纱 organdie

廛 chán〈名〉**1**〈古〉（住房） commoner's house **2**〈书〉（店铺） shop: 市～ marketplace

潺 chán
【潺潺】chánchán〈拟〉murmur: ～小溪 gurgling brook
【潺湲】chányuán〈形〉〈书〉flowing slowly: 山间溪水～。The brook flows gently through the mountain.

蟾 chán〈名〉**1**（癞蛤蟆）toad **2**（月亮） moon: ▸～宫, ～光
【蟾蜍】chánchú〈名〉**1**（癞蛤蟆） toad **2**（月亮） moon
【蟾宫】chángōng〈名〉〈书〉moon
【蟾宫折桂】chángōng-zhéguì〈成〉〈喻〉obtain a *jinshi* (进士) degree
【蟾光】chánguāng〈名〉〈书〉moonlight
【蟾酥】chánsū〈名〉［中药］toad cake

巉 chán〈形〉〈书〉dangerously steep
【巉峻】chánjùn〈形〉〈书〉precipitous: 山势～，无法攀登。The mountain was too steep to climb.
【巉岩】chányán〈名〉〈书〉precipitous rock: ～绝壁 precipitous cliff

chǎn

产（產） chǎn
A〈动〉**1**（生下） give birth to: ～下一对男婴 give birth to twin boys ‖ ～卵 lay eggs ▸～妇, 顺～, 死～, 早～ **2**（出产） produce: ～橡胶 produce rubber ‖ ～小麦 produce wheat ‖ 高～ high yield ▸～奶, 丰～, 盛～ **3**（生产） make: ～钢铁/汽车 produce steel/cars ‖ 突尼斯～ be made in Tunisia ▸～销, 国～, 增～
B〈名〉**1**（产品） product: ▸矿～, 水～ **2**（产业） property: 家～ family wealth ‖ 房～ property ▸～权, 动～, 资～
【产成品】chǎnchéngpǐn〈名〉finished goods
【产程】chǎnchéng〈名〉［医学］childbirth
【产出】chǎnchū〈动〉output: ～投入比率 output-input ratio
【产地】chǎndì〈名〉place of production: 柑橘～ orange-producing region ‖ 原～ native place of origin
【产儿】chǎn'ér〈名〉**1**（婴儿） newborn: ▸早～ **2**（产物） product: 市场经济是改革的～。A market economy is a product of the reform.
【产房】chǎnfáng〈名〉delivery room
【产妇】chǎnfù〈名〉woman in labour: 给～接生 deliver a baby for a woman in labour ‖ 高危～ high risk puerpera
【产羔】chǎngāo〈动〉［畜牧］lamb: ～期 lambing period
【产供销】chǎn-gōng-xiāo〈名〉［经济］production, supply and marketing: 形成～一条龙 form an integrated system for production, supply and marketing
【产后出血】chǎnhòu chūxuè〈名〉postpartum haemorrhage
【产后期】chǎnhòuqī〈名〉puerperium
【产后热】chǎnhòurè〈名〉puerperal fever
【产后抑郁】chǎnhòu yìyù〈名〉puerperal depression
【产假】chǎnjià〈名〉maternity leave: 休～ be on maternity leave
【产驹】chǎnjū〈动〉［畜牧］foal: ～率 foaling rate
【产科】chǎnkē〈名〉obstetrics department: ～病房 obstetrics ward ‖ ～医院 maternity hospital
【产量】chǎnliàng〈名〉output: 提高/增加～ step up/increase output ‖ 单位面积～ yield per unit area
【产卵】chǎnluǎn〈动〉（指鸟禽类） lay eggs;（指鱼、蛙） spawn;（指昆虫） oviposit: ～洄游 spawning migration ‖ ～季节 egg-laying season
【产奶】chǎnnǎi〈动〉produce milk
【产品】chǎnpǐn〈名〉product: 推销～ promote a product ‖ ～抽样检验 production sampling test ‖ 畅销～ fast-selling products ‖ 名优～ superior product ▸副～, 农～
【产品附加值】chǎnpǐn fùjiāzhí〈名〉added value of product
【产品开发】chǎnpǐn kāifā〈名〉product development
【产品说明】chǎnpǐn shuōmíng〈名〉description of product
【产品性能】chǎnpǐn xìngnéng〈名〉properties of product
【产品质量】chǎnpǐn zhìliàng〈名〉product quality
【产婆】chǎnpó〈名〉〈旧〉midwife
【产前】chǎnqián〈名〉antenatal period: 定期的～检查 regular antenatal examination
【产钳】chǎnqián〈名〉obstetrical forceps
【产区】chǎnqū〈名〉producing region: 粮食～ grain-producing area ‖ 小麦丰～ area rich in wheat production
【产权】chǎnquán〈名〉property rights: 保护/拥有～ protect property rights ‖ 知识～ intellectual property rights
【产权变更】chǎnquán biàngēng〈名〉change of title
【产权登记】chǎnquán dēngjì〈名〉registration of property rights
【产权交易】chǎnquán jiāoyì〈名〉property rights exchange
【产权转让】chǎnquán zhuǎnràng〈名〉transfer of property rights
【产褥】chǎnrù〈名〉［医学］confinement: ～感染 puerperal infection ‖ ～期 confinement
【产生】chǎnshēng〈动〉produce: ～错觉 create an illusion ‖ 对绘画～兴趣 develop an interest in painting ‖ ～影响 exert influence ‖ 两人～了感情。The two of them formed an attachment to each other. ‖ 所有官员必须通过选举～。All the office holders must be elected.
【产物】chǎnwù〈名〉outcome: 集体智慧的～ product of collective wisdom ‖ 计算机是二十世纪科学发展的～。The computer is the product of 20th century scientific development.
【产销】chǎnxiāo〈名〉production and marketing: ～对路 production based on marketing ‖ ～直接挂钩 establish direct contact between the production and marketing departments ‖ ～两旺。Both production and marketing are prospering.
【产需】chǎnxū〈名〉production and marketing
【产业】chǎnyè〈名〉**1**（财产） property: 变卖～ sell one's property ‖ 继承～ inherit a property ‖ 个人/私有～ individual/private property **2**（行业） industry: 劳动密集型/知识密集型～ labour-intensive/knowledge-intensive industries ‖ 朝阳～ sunrise industry ‖ 支柱～ pillar industry ▸第一～ **3**（工业） industry
【产业革命】chǎnyè gémìng = 工业革命 Gōngyè Gémìng
【产业工人】chǎnyè gōngrén〈名〉industrial worker
【产业后备军】chǎnyè hòubèijūn〈名〉industrial reserve army
【产业化】chǎnyèhuà〈动〉industrialize
【产业结构】chǎnyè jiégòu〈名〉［经济］industrial set-up: 优化～ optimize the structure of production
【产业链】chǎnyèliàn〈名〉industrial chain: 形成完整的～ form a complete industrial chain
【产业区】chǎnyèqū〈名〉industrial area: 高新技术～ high-tech industrial area ‖ 临港～ industrial area near the harbour
【产院】chǎnyuàn〈名〉maternity hospital
【产崽】chǎnzǎi〈动〉[of an animal] give birth: 猫一胎通常～四至六只。A cat usually bears four to six kittens per litter. ‖ 这头母猪几时～? When will the sow farrow?
【产值】chǎnzhí〈名〉output value: 工农业总～ gross value of industrial and agricultural production ‖ 国民经济总～ gross national product (GNP) ‖ 国内总～ gross domestic product (GDP) ▸净～, 总～

刬 chǎn = 铲 chǎn ▸chàn

谄（諂） chǎn〈动〉flatter: ▸～媚
【谄媚】chǎnmèi〈动〉〈贬〉suck up to: ～上司 ingratiate oneself with one's boss ‖ 羞于～ feel ashamed to fawn on sb. ‖ ～的话 grovelling remarks
【谄上欺下】chǎnshàng-qīxià〈成〉be servile to one's superiors and tyrannical with one's subordinates
【谄笑】chǎnxiào〈动〉smile obsequiously: ▸胁肩～
【谄谀】chǎnyú〈动〉〈书〉toady: ～求荣 flatter sb. in pursuit of glory

铲（鏟） chǎn
A〈名〉shovel: 铁～ iron shovel ‖ 园艺～ garden spade ▸～子, 锅～, 煤～
B〈动〉shovel: ～草 weed with a spade ‖ 把地～平 level the ground with a spade ▸～除, ～土机, ～运机
【铲车】chǎnchē = 叉车 chāchē
【铲除】chǎnchú〈动〉root out: ～杂草 dig out weeds ‖ ～积雪/垃圾 shovel away the

snow/rubbish ‖ ～腐败 root out corruption ‖ 连根～ pull out by the root
【铲斗】chǎndǒu〈名〉［机械］basket: ～挖泥船 dipper dredger
【铲球】chǎnqiú〈名〉［足球］slide
【铲土机】chǎntǔjī〈名〉hauling scraper
【铲运机】chǎnyùnjī = 铲土机 chǎntǔjī
【铲子】chǎnzi = 铲 chǎn A

阐（闡） chǎn〈动〉expound: ▸～明, ～述
【阐发】chǎnfā〈动〉clarify: ～论点 clarify one's argument ‖ ～诗歌 explain a poem ‖ 该文深刻地～了那首诗的意义。The article elucidated the meaning of the poem in depth.
【阐明】chǎnmíng〈动〉clarify: ～观点/看法 expound one's views ‖ ～立场 define one's position ‖ 用事实～ illustrate/elucidate through facts
【阐释】chǎnshì〈动〉explain: ～法律 interpret a law ‖ 你的～缺乏说服力。Your interpretation is not persuasive.
【阐述】chǎnshù〈动〉set forth: ～观点/见解/看法 expound one's views ‖ ～计划/理由 set forth a plan/one's reasons ‖ 详加～ give a detailed explanation
【阐扬】chǎnyáng〈动〉expound and propagate: ～教义 expound and propagate religious doctrines ‖ ～真理 advocate the truth

chàn

忏（懺） chàn〈动〉repent
【忏悔】chànhuǐ〈动〉1（悔过）repent: ～罪行 repent one's crimes ‖ 表示～ express remorse 2［宗教］confess (one's sins): ～罪过你就会获得宽恕。Repent of your sins and you will be forgiven. ‖ 他临死前向牧师做了～。He confessed to the priest before he died.
【忏悔者】chànhuǐzhě〈名〉penitent
【忏悔自新】chànhuǐ-zìxīn〈成〉confess one's sins and make a fresh start

刬（剗） chàn ▸一刬 yīchàn ▸chǎn

颤（顫） chàn〈动〉quiver: 冻得直～ shiver with cold ‖ 他气得声音发～。His voice trembled with anger. ▸～抖, 发～ ▸zhàn
【颤搐】chànchù ▸p. 50〈名〉［医学］twitch
【颤动】chàndòng〈动〉quiver: 声带～ vibration of the vocal cords ‖ 大地在我们脚下～。The ground quaked beneath our feet.
【颤抖】chàndǒu〈动〉tremble: 嗓音～ trembling voice ‖ 浑身～ shiver all over ‖〈喻〉树叶在寒风中～。The leaves quivered in the cold wind.
【颤巍巍】chànwēiwēi〈形〉doddery: 老妇人～地走下楼梯。The old lady tottered down the stairs.
【颤音】chànyīn〈名〉1［语言］trill 2［音乐］vibrato
【颤悠】chànyou〈动〉quiver: ～的烛光 flickering light of the candle ‖ 湖面倒影～不已。Reflections flicker in the water of the lake. ‖ 人走过时吊桥颤颤悠悠。The suspension bridge shakes when people walk on it.

羼 chàn〈动〉mix: ～了水的牛奶 milk mixed with water ‖ 在酒里～入水 blend wine with water
【羼杂】chànzá = 掺杂 chānzá

韂 chàn〈名〉saddle blanket: ▸鞍～

chāng

伥（倀） chāng〈名〉ghost of one devoured by a tiger, who helps the tiger to entice other people for food: ▸为虎作～
【伥鬼】chāngguǐ = 伥 chāng

昌 chāng〈形〉1（兴旺）thriving: ▸～明, ～盛 2〈书〉（正当）proper: ▸～言
【昌隆】chānglóng〈形〉thriving: 生意～。The business is thriving.
【昌明】chāngmíng〈书〉A〈形〉flourishing: 国策～。The national policy is advanced. ‖ 科学技术～。Science and technology are flourishing. B〈动〉make flourish: ～大义 advocate righteousness ‖ ～文化 promote culture
【昌盛】chāngshèng〈形〉thriving and prosperous: 繁荣～的国家 prosperous country ‖ 日益～ be ever-more prosperous
【昌言】chāngyán〈书〉A〈名〉valuable remarks: 善纳～ follow good advice readily B〈动〉speak frankly: ～无忌 not mince one's words

倡 chāng〈名〉〈书〉1（指歌者）singer;（指舞者）dancer;（指乐器演奏者）musician: ▸～优 2〈书〉= 娼 chāng ▸chàng
【倡优】chāngyōu〈名〉1〈古〉（伶人）entertainers 2〈书〉（娼妓和优伶）prostitutes and actors or actresses

菖 chāng
【菖蒲】chāngpú〈名〉［植物］calamus

猖 chāng〈形〉rampant: ▸～獗, ～狂
【猖獗】chāngjué〈形〉〈贬〉rampant: ～一时 run wild for a time ‖ 扒手～的城市 city infested with pickpockets
【猖狂】chāngkuáng〈形〉〈贬〉savage: ～进攻 make a savage attack ‖ ～一时 run wild for a brief period ‖ ～挑衅 recklessly provoke ‖ 击退～的敌人 defeat the savage enemy

阊（閶） chāng
【阊阖】chānghé〈名〉〈书〉1（天门）gate of Heaven 2（宫门）gate of a palace

娼 chāng〈名〉prostitute: 逼良为～ force a girl of good family into prostitution ‖ 沦落为～ be reduced to prostitution
【娼妇】chāngfù〈名〉〈粗〉whore〈粗〉
【娼妓】chāngjì〈名〉prostitute: 沦为～ be forced into prostitution
【娼寮】chāngliáo〈名〉brothel
【娼门】chāngmén〈名〉〈旧〉brothel

鲳（鯧） chāng
【鲳鱼】chāngyú〈名〉butterfish

cháng

长（長） cháng
A〈形〉long: ～发 long hair ‖ ～时间地工作 work long hours ‖ 很～时间 a long time ‖ 前方的路仍然很～。The road ahead is still very long. ▸～途, ～征, ～期, 漫～, 与世～辞
B〈名〉1（长度）length: 这条高速公路全～166公里。The expressway covers a distance of 166 kilometres. ‖ 这条隧道有多～? How long is this tunnel? ▸身～, 周～ 2（长处）strength: 取人之～, 补己之短 overcome one's shortcomings by learning from other's strengths ‖ 人各有所～。Everyone has his own strong points. ▸特～, 扬～避短
C〈动〉be good at: ▸～技, 擅～ ▸zhǎng
【长安】Cháng'ān〈名〉Chang'an [ancient capital of China]
【长白山】Chángbáishān〈名〉Changbai Mountain
【长鼻猴】chángbíhóu〈名〉proboscis monkey
【长臂猿】chángbìyuán〈名〉gibbon
【长编】chángbiān〈名〉draft
【长别】chángbié〈动〉〈书〉1（久别）part for a long time: ～后，思乡切 be nostalgic for home after a long absence 2（永别）part forever
【长波】chángbō〈名〉［通信］long wave (LW): ～波段 long-wave band ‖ ～通信 long-wave communication
【长策】chángcè〈名〉long-term plan: 这只是权宜之计，决非～。It's just an expedient measure, not a long-term plan.
【长长短短】chángcháng-duǎnduǎn〈形〉of uneven lengths
【长城】Chángchéng〈名〉1〈本〉Great Wall: 万里～世界闻名。The 10 thousand-*li* Great Wall is world famous. 2〈喻〉insurmountable barrier: 解放军是保卫祖国的钢铁～。The PLA is a Great Wall of steel guarding our country.

> **长城**
> An ancient military defence structure, made up of strategic passes, walls, and beacon towers. Walls were already built for defence purposes in the Spring and Autumn and Warring States periods. Parts of the wall were consolidated during the Qin Dynasty to prevent invasion from the Xiongnu (匈奴) from the north. There were constant consolidations and additions by later generations, particularly during the Ming Dynasty, and most of what remains dates from this period. Today, the wall stretches from Jiayuguan (嘉峪关) in Gansu Province to Shanhaiguan (山海关) in Hebei Province, an overall length of over 6,000 kms. For visitors, the most famous part of the wall is at Badaling (八达岭) in the north-west part of Beijing. The wall is often referred to as the 'ten-thousand-*li* Great Wall, and a common saying has it that 'you are not a man unless you've climbed the Great Wall' (不到长城非好汉). The Great Wall was designated a UNESCO World Heritage site in 1987.

【长虫】chángchong〈名〉〈方〉snake
【长抽短吊】chángchōu-duǎndiào〈名〉［体育］[in table tennis, badminton, etc.] long drives combined with drop shots
【长处】chángchu〈名〉strength: 充分发挥～ bring out the best in sb. ‖ 每个人都有自己的～和短处。Everyone has his own

strengths and weaknesses.

【长传】chángchuán〈动〉［体育］ make a long pass

【长春】Chángchūn ▸**p. 661**〈名〉 Changchun [capital of Jilin Province (吉林)]

【长蝽】chángchūn〈名〉［昆虫］ chinch bug

【长辞】chángcí〈动〉〈书〉 die: 与世～ pass away

【长此以往】chángcǐyǐwǎng〈成〉 if things go on like this: 孩子整天泡网吧，～，怎么得了？ Children are spending the whole day in Internet cafes. If nothing is done to change this, what will become of them?

【长存】chángcún〈动〉 be everlasting: 他的英名将与世～。 His heroic name will be remembered forever. ‖ 友谊～。 Friendship will live forever.

【长岛】Chángdǎo〈名〉 Long Island

【长凳】chángdèng〈名〉 backless bench

【长笛】chángdí ▸**p. 929**〈名〉［音乐］ flute

【长度】chángdù ▸**p. 82**〈名〉 extent: ～相等 be of equal length ‖ ～单位 unit of length ‖ 这张木板床～为三米。 The bed is 3 metres long.

【长短】chángduǎn〈名〉 **1**（长度） length: ～正合适 be just the right length **2**（意外） mishap: 万一他有个～，我怎么向他父母交代？ If anything happened to him, how could I face his parents? **3**（是非） ins and outs: 背地里不要议论别人的～。 Don't gossip about others behind their backs.

【长短句】chángduǎnjù = 词 cí 3

【长吨】chángdūn ▸**p. 978**〈量〉 long ton (L/T) [= 1016.15kg]

【长法】chángfǎ〈名〉〈口〉 long-term solution: 总这么忍下去不是～儿。 It won't work if we keep putting up with everything like this.

【长方体】chángfāngtǐ〈名〉 cuboid

【长方形】chángfāngxíng〈名〉 rectangle

【长风破浪】chángfēng-pòlàng〈成〉 ride the wind and cleave the waves

【长歌当哭】chánggē-dàngkū〈成〉 sing to vent one's grief or indignation

【长庚】Chánggēng〈名〉〈古〉［天文］ Venus

【长工】chánggōng〈名〉〈旧〉 long-term hired hand

【长骨】chánggǔ〈名〉［生理］ long bone

【长鼓】chánggǔ ▸**p. 929**〈名〉［音乐］ long drum

【长鼓舞】chánggǔwǔ〈名〉 drum dance of Yao or Korean ethnic groups

【长跪】chángguì〈动〉 kneel down with a straight back

【长号】chánghào ▸**p. 929**〈名〉［音乐］ trombone: ～手 trombonist

【长河】chánghé〈名〉〈喻〉 long process: 历史的～ long process of history

【长虹】chánghóng〈名〉 rainbow: ▸气贯～

【长话】chánghuà〈名〉 **1**（指话语） long explanation: ▸～短说 **2** = 长途电话 chángtú diànhuà

【长话短说】chánghuà-duǎnshuō〈成〉 cut a long story short

【长技】chángjì〈名〉 proficiency in a particular field

【长假】chángjià〈名〉**1**（指节假日） long leave of absence: 放～ have a long holiday ‖ 休～ be on a long leave **2**（指请假） resignation: 请～ resign from office

【长江】Chángjiāng ▸**p. 294**〈名〉 Yangtze River: ～大桥 Yangtze River Bridge

【长江后浪推前浪】Chángjiāng hòulàng tuī qiánlàng〈俗〉〈喻〉 it is a general trend that the later generations surpass former ages

【长江流域】Chángjiāng Liúyù〈名〉 Yangtze Valley

【长江三角洲】Chángjiāng Sānjiǎozhōu〈名〉 Yangtze River Delta

【长江三峡】Chángjiāng Sānxiá〈名〉 Yangtze Gorges

【长焦距】chángjiāojù〈名〉［摄影］ long-focus

【长角羚】chángjiǎolíng〈名〉 gemsbok

【长颈鹿】chángjǐnglù〈名〉 giraffe

【长镜头】chángjìngtóu〈名〉［摄影］ full-length shot

【长久】chángjiǔ〈形〉 long-term: ～打算 plan long-term ‖ ～之计 long-term plan

【长卷】chángjuàn〈名〉 long scrolls of paintings or calligraphy

【长空】chángkōng〈名〉〈书〉 vast sky: 万里～ vast expanse of sky ‖ 一道闪电划破～。 A flash of lightning split the sky.

【长裤】chángkù〈名〉 trousers〈英〉; pants〈美〉

【长款】chángkuǎn〈名〉 **1**［会计］ surplus cash **2**（指衣服） long style: ～羊绒大衣 long-style cashmere coat

【长廊】chángláng〈名〉 long walkway

【长链】chángliàn〈形〉［化学］ long-chain

【长龙】chánglóng〈名〉〈喻〉 long queue: 售票窗口前排起了～。 A long queue of people formed in front of the ticket-office window.

【长毛绒】chángmáoróng〈名〉［纺织］ plush

【长矛】chángmáo〈名〉 long spear

【长眠】chángmián ▸**p. 772**〈动〉〈婉〉 die: ～地下 be dead and buried

【长明灯】chángmíngdēng〈名〉 altar lamp that burns day and night

【长命百岁】chángmìng-bǎisuì〈成〉 [used as a blessing] enjoy a long life: 祝（您）～。 Many happy returns.

【长命锁】chángmìngsuǒ〈名〉 [ornamental pendant] long-life lock

【长年】chángnián〈名〉 **1**（整年） whole year: 地质工程师们～在野外工作。 Geological engineers work in the field all year round. **2**（多年） many years **3**〈书〉（长寿） longevity: 富贵～ wealth, position and long life

【长年累月】chángnián-lěiyuè〈成〉 year in, year out: 我们～做这项单调的工作。 We do this monotonous job year in, year out.

【长袍】chángpáo〈名〉 robe: ～马褂 long gown and mandarin jacket

【长跑】chángpǎo ▸**p. 909**〈名〉［体育］ long-distance running: ～运动员 long-distance runner

【长篇】chángpiān **A**〈形〉 full-length: ～传记 full-length biography ▸～大论, ～小说 **B**〈名〉 long literary piece: 他创作了一部～。 He wrote a full-length novel.

【长篇大论】chángpiān-dàlùn〈成〉 long-winded argument: 要简明、扼要，不要～。 Be concise and to the point, and avoid verbosity.

【长篇累牍】chángpiān-lěidú〈成〉 long and tedious article

【长篇小说】chángpiān xiǎoshuō〈名〉 full-length novel: ～连载 instalment of a serialized novel

【长期】chángqī〈名〉 long period of time: ～存在的问题 chronic problem ‖ ～合作 long-term cooperation ‖ ～目标 long-term goal ‖ ～贷款/债券 long-term loan/bond ‖ ～失业 chronic unemployment ‖ ～以来 for a long time

【长期共存】chángqī gòngcún〈名〉 long-term coexistence: ～、互相监督、肝胆相照、荣辱与共 long-term coexistence, mutual supervision, sincere treatment of each other and the sharing of weal and woe

【长崎】Chángqí〈名〉 Nagasaki

【长枪】chángqiāng〈名〉 **1**（指矛） spear **2**（指枪） long-barrelled gun

【长驱】chángqū〈动〉 make a long-distance raid: ～千里 push on for one thousand *li*

【长驱直入】chángqū-zhírù〈成〉 drive straight in: 我军～。 Our troops drove deep.

【长拳】chángquán〈名〉［武术］ Northern boxing

【长裙】chángqún〈名〉 long skirt

【长绒棉】chángróngmián〈名〉［纺织］ long-staple cotton

【长三角】chángsānjiǎo〈简称〉 = 长江三角洲

【长沙】Chángshā ▸**p. 661**〈名〉 Changsha [capital of Hunan Province (湖南)]

【长衫】chángshān〈名〉 unlined long gown

【长舌】chángshé〈形〉〈喻〉 fond of gossip: ～妇 gossipy woman

【长蛇阵】chángshézhèn〈名〉〈喻〉 single-line battle array: 排成一字～ deploy the troops in a long line

【长蛇座】Chángshézuò〈名〉［天文］ Hydra

【长生不老】chángshēngbùlǎo〈成〉 enjoy eternal youth

【长生果】chángshēngguǒ〈名〉〈方〉 peanut

【长石】chángshí〈名〉［矿业］ feldspar

【长时记忆】chángshí jìyì〈名〉［心理］ long-term memory

【长逝】chángshì〈动〉〈书〉 die

【长寿】chángshòu〈形〉 long-lived: ～之道 art of prolonging life ‖ ～面 longevity noodles ‖ 祝您健康～。 I wish you a long and healthy life.

【长谈】chángtán〈动〉 have a long talk: 促膝～ sit close together for a long talk

【长叹】chángtàn〈动〉 let out a deep sigh: 一声～ heave a deep sigh ‖ 仰天～ look up to heaven and sigh deeply

【长天】chángtiān〈名〉〈书〉 vast sky: 仰望～ look up at the vast sky

【长条校样】chángtiáo jiàoyàng〈名〉［印刷］ galley proof

【长挑】chángtiao〈形〉〈口〉 tall and slender

【长亭】chángtíng〈名〉 roadside pavilion: ～话别 bid sb. farewell at a travellers' pavilion ‖ 十里～ travellers' pavilions at ten-*li* intervals

【长统胶鞋】chángtǒng jiāoxié〈名〉 wellingtons

【长统袜】chángtǒngwà〈名〉 stockings

【长统靴】chángtǒngxuē〈名〉 high boots

【长痛不如短痛】chángtòng bùrú duǎntòng〈俗〉 would rather suffer acute pain for a short while than mild pain for a long time: ～，还是早点动手术吧。 To avoid long-term suffering, you'd better have the operation as soon as possible.

【长途】chángtú **A**〈形〉 long-distance: ～运输 transport over a long distance ‖ ～行军 make a long march ▸～电话, ～旅行, ～汽车 **B**〈简称〉 **1** = 长途电话 **2** = 长途汽车

【长途跋涉】chángtú-báshè〈成〉 make a long trek

【长途电话】chángtú diànhuà〈名〉 long-distance call: 打～ call sb. up long-distance ‖ 接～ receive a long-distance call

【长途旅行】chángtú lǚxíng〈名〉 long journey

【长途汽车】chángtú qìchē〈名〉 long-distance bus: 坐～ take a long-distance bus ‖ ～站 long-distance bus station

【长途台】 chángtútái〈名〉[通信] toll exchange

【长途运输】 chángtú yùnshū〈名〉 long-distance transport

【长袜】 chángwà〈名〉 stockings

【长尾猴】 chángwěihóu〈名〉[动物] guenon

【长尾雉】 chángwěizhì〈名〉[鸟类] long-tailed pheasant

【长物】 chángwù〈名〉〈书〉 valuable thing: 别无～ have nothing else of value

【长线】 chángxiàn〈形〉 over-quota: ～产品 goods in excessive supply

【长项】 chángxiàng〈名〉 strength: 数字不是我的～。 I am not good at figures.

【长销】 chángxiāo〈动〉 sell all year round: 这款产品供不应求，～不衰。 The supply of this product falls short of demand, and sales are never waning.

【长效】 chángxiào〈形〉 of lasting effect: ～肥料 slow-release fertilizer ‖ ～机制 slow-release mechanism

【长效避孕药】 chángxiào bìyùnyào〈名〉 long-lasting contraceptive

【长啸】 chángxiào〈动〉〈书〉 let out a long and loud cry: 仰天～ look up to the sky and let out a long and mournful cry

【长袖善舞】 chángxiù-shànwǔ〈成〉〈喻〉 have tricks up one's sleeve and be likely to succeed

【长吁短叹】 chángxū-duǎntàn〈成〉 moan and groan

【长须鲸】 chángxūjīng〈名〉[动物] fin-back

【长夜】 chángyè **A**〈名〉 long night: 漫漫～ long, long night **B**〈副〉 whole night:

C

ℹ 长度、宽度及高度

■ 说汉语的国家和地区一般使用公制，如厘米、米、公里等，而在美国和英国多使用英制，如英寸、码、英里等：

1 公里 (kilometre/km)
= 1,000 米 (metres)
= 0.621 英里 (mile)

1 米 (metre/m)
= 100 厘米 (centimetres)
= 1.094 码 (yards)

1 厘米／公分 (centimetre/cm)
= 10 毫米 (millimetres)
= 0.394 英寸 (inch)

1 英寸 (inch/in)
= 2.54 厘米 (centimetres)

1 英尺 (foot/ft)
= 12 英寸 (inches)
= 30.48 厘米 (centimetres)

1 码 (yard/yd)
= 3 英尺 (feet)
= 0.914 米 (metre)

1 英里 (mile/ml)
= 1,760 码 (yards)
= 1.609 公里 (kilometres)

长度

这根电线有多长?
= How long is the wire?

有 5 米长
= It is five metres long

电线是按米卖的
= Wires are sold by the metre

我需要 1 根 6 米长的电线
= I need a wire six metres long

A 比 B 长
= A is longer than B

A 比 B 长两英尺
= A is two feet longer than B

A 长了两英尺
= A is two feet too long

A 比 B 短
= A is shorter than B

A 比 B 短 10 英寸
= A is ten inches shorter than B

A 短了 10 英寸
= A is ten inches too short

A 和 B 一样长
= A is as long as B
或 A is the same length as B
或 A and B are the same length
或 A and B are equal in length

A 没有 B 长
= A is not as long as B

A 和 B 长度不同
= A and B are not the same length
或 A and B are different lengths

■ 注意下面英语的翻译：

1 根 4 米长的绳子
= a rope four metres long
或 a four-metre-long rope

1 座长 1,000 米的桥
= a bridge 1,000 metres long

宽度

床有多宽?
= What width is the bed?
或 How wide is the bed?

有一米五宽
= It is 1.5 metres wide
或 It is one and a half metres wide

A 比 B 宽
= A is wider than B

A 比 B 宽两厘米
= A is two centimetres wider than B

A 宽了两厘米
= A is two centimetres too wide

A 比 B 窄
= A is narrower than B

A 和 B 一样宽
= A is as wide as B
或 A is the same width as B
或 A and B are the same width
或 A and B are equal in width

A 没有 B 宽
= A is not as wide as B

A 和 B 不一样宽
= A and B are not the same width
或 A and B are different widths

■ 注意下面英语的翻译：

1 条 3 米宽的小巷
= a lane 3 metres wide

1 个 20 厘米宽的画框
= a picture frame twenty centimetres in width

高度

■ 英语用 tall 和 small/short 来形容人的高矮。说某人身材矮小时，用 small 比用 short 更显礼貌些。形容女士小巧玲珑可用 petite。形容物件用 high 和 low：

她有多高?
= How tall is she?

张伟个子很高
= Zhang Wei is very tall

李先生个子矮小
= Mr. Li is a small man

梅小姐小巧玲珑
= Miss Mei is petite

她身高一米五八
= She's 1m58cm/1.58m
或 She's 1 metre 58 centimetres

她大约 5 英尺高
= She's about 5 foot/feet tall

他身高为 6 英尺 3 英寸
= He is 6' 3" tall
或 He is 6' 3"
或 He's six foot/feet 3
或 He's six foot/feet 3 inches

一位 5 英尺高的姑娘
= a five-foot-tall girl

一个身高大约一米八的男人
= a man about 1 metre 8 in height

这棵树有多高? —— 8 米多高
= How high is the tree?
— It's over 8 metres high

这张椅子 80 公分高
= The chair is 80cm high

一座 200 米高的建筑物
= a 200-metre-high building

一座大约 300 米高的铁塔
= an iron tower about 300 metres high

A 比 B 高
= A is taller/higher than B

B 比 A 矮／低
= B is shorter/smaller/lower than A

B 没有 A 高
= B is not as tall/high as A

A 和 B 同样高
= A is as tall/high as B
或 A is the same height as B
或 A and B are the same height

长度、宽度及高度

这张床长 2 米，宽 1.2 米
= The bed is 1.2 metres (wide) by 2 metres (long)
或 The bed is 1.2 metres wide and 2 metres long
或 The bed is 1.2 metres in width and 2 metres in length

这张餐桌长 2 米，宽 1.5 米，高 1.2 米
= The dining table is two metres long, 1.5 metres wide and 1.2 metres high

～不眠 lie awake all night
【长椅】chángyǐ〈名〉settee
【长音阶】chángyīnjiē〈名〉［音乐］major scale
【长缨】chángyīng〈名〉〈书〉long rope
【长于】chángyú〈动〉be good at: ～绘画 be good at painting ‖ ～社交 be adroit at social activities
【长元音】chángyuányīn〈名〉［语言］long vowel
【长圆】chángyuán〈名〉oval: ～脸 oval face
【长远】chángyuǎn〈形〉long-term: ～利益 far-reaching benefits ‖ ～之计 long-term plan ‖ 从～来看 in the long run ‖ 做～打算 take a long view
【长斋】chángzhāi〈名〉permanent abstention from meat: 吃～ practise permanent abstinence from meat
【长针】chángzhēn〈名〉［中医］long needle
【长征】chángzhēng **A**〈动〉make a long journey **B** Chángzhēng〈名〉Long March: 二万五千里～ 25,000-*li* Long March
【长治久安】chángzhì-jiǔ'ān〈成〉long-term peace and stability: 维持国家的～ maintain the long-term stability of the country
【长住】chángzhù〈动〉settle: 我不打算在这里～。I'm not going to live here for long.
【长足】chángzú〈形〉〈书〉rapid: ～的进步 marked progress

场（場）cháng

A〈名〉**1**（用于晒粮或脱粒）level open space: 翻～ turn the crops over on the threshing ground ‖ 扬～ do winnowing on the threshing ground ▸～院, 打～, 晒～ **2**〈方〉（集市）market: ▸赶～
B〈量〉spell: 大干一～ go all out to do sth. ‖ 害了一～病 be ill for a while ‖ 一～大雪/大雨 a heavy fall of snow/rain ‖ 一～风波 a disturbance/turmoil
▸chǎng
【场屋】chángwū〈名〉shed on threshing ground
【场院】chángyuàn〈名〉sunning ground: 农家～ farmyard

肠（腸）cháng

〈名〉**1**（指器官）intestines: ▸～子, 大～, 直～ **2**（心思）heart: ▸愁～, 衷～ **3**（指食品）sausage: ▸腊～, 香～
【肠癌】cháng'ái ▸**p. 50**〈名〉bowel cancer
【肠成形术】chángchéngxíngshù〈名〉［医学］enteroplasty
【肠穿孔】chángchuānkǒng ▸**p. 50**〈名〉［医学］intestinal perforation
【肠道】chángdào〈名〉intestinal tract: ～传染病 enteric infection
【肠肥脑满】chángféi-nǎomǎn = 脑满肠肥 nǎomǎn-chángféi
【肠梗阻】chánggěngzǔ ▸**p. 50**〈名〉［医学］intestinal obstruction: 患～ have a blockage in one's intestines
【肠绞痛】chángjiǎotòng ▸**p. 50**〈名〉［医学］intestinal colic
【肠粘膜】chángniánmó〈名〉［医学］intestinal mucosa
【肠套叠】chángtàodié ▸**p. 50**〈名〉［医学］intussusception
【肠胃】chángwèi〈名〉digestive system: ～不舒服 have an upset stomach ‖ ～病 stomach trouble
【肠炎】chángyán ▸**p. 50**〈名〉［医学］enteritis
【肠衣】chángyī〈名〉sausage casing
【肠粘连】chángzhānlián ▸**p. 50**〈名〉［医学］intestinal adhesion
【肠子】chángzi〈名〉intestines: 消化大部分是在～里进行的。Most digestion takes place in the intestines. ‖〈喻〉他一肚子花花～。He is full of sly schemes.

尝¹（嘗、嚐）cháng〈动〉

1（品尝）taste: ～～蛋糕 try some cake ‖ 你可以先～后买。You may taste before you buy. ▸～鲜, 品～ **2**（尝试）try: ▸～试, 浅～辄止 **3**（感受）experience: ～到甜头 become aware of the benefits ‖ 备～人生的辛酸 taste all the bitterness of life

尝²（嘗）cháng〈副〉ever: ▸何～, 未～

【尝鼎一脔】chángdǐng-yīluán〈成〉〈喻〉get to know the flavour of sth. by sampling a part
【尝试】chángshì〈动〉try: ～各种方法 try every method ‖ 大胆～ make bold attempts
【尝受】chángshòu〈动〉have an experience of (hardship, misery, etc.): ～生活的艰辛 experience the arduousness of life
【尝鲜】chángxiān〈动〉have a taste of what has just arrived on the market
【尝新】chángxīn〈动〉have a taste of what is new

倘 cháng

▸tǎng
【倘佯】chángyáng = 徜徉 chángyáng

常 cháng

A〈名〉**1**〈书〉（纲纪）law and order: ▸伦～, 三纲五～ **2**（规律）law: ▸～规 **3**（平常的事）common thing: ▸家～, 习以为～
B〈形〉**1**（平常）common: ▸～态, 人之～情, 失～ **2**（固定不变）constant: ▸～量, ～任
C〈副〉frequently: ～去某个地方 often go to a place ‖ 不～见面 hardly ever meet up ▸经～, 通～
【常备】chángbèi〈动〉be always on the alert: ～商品 stock merchandise ‖ ～药 common medicine
【常备不懈】chángbèi-bùxiè〈成〉be constantly on the alert: 要～地抓好防火工作。We should always watch out for fires.
【常备军】chángbèijūn〈名〉standing troops
【常备无患】chángbèi-wúhuàn〈成〉preparedness averts peril
【常常】chángcháng〈副〉often: 他～邀请朋友参加聚会。He frequently invites friends to parties. ‖ 他俩下班后～去酒吧喝两杯。The two of them often went to a bar for a couple of drinks after work.
【常春藤】chángchūnténg〈名〉Chinese ivy: 爬满～的墙壁 ivied wall
【常服】chángfú〈名〉everyday clothes: 居家～ daily wear
【常规】chángguī **A**〈名〉**1**（规矩）common practice: 打破～ break with convention ‖ 符合～ conform to conventions ‖ 按照～ according to conventional practice ‖ 有～必有例外。There is no rule without an exception. **2**［医学］routine: 化验血/尿～ have a routine blood/urine test **B**〈形〉routine: ～弹头 conventional warhead ‖ ～检查 routine examination
【常规部队】chángguī bùduì〈名〉conventional forces
【常规赛】chángguīsài〈名〉［篮球］regular season
【常规武器】chángguī wǔqì〈名〉conventional weapons: 使用～ use conventional weapons ‖ 非～ unconventional weapons
【常规战争】chángguī zhànzhēng〈名〉conventional warfare: 使～升级 escalate a conventional war
【常规治疗】chángguī zhìliáo〈名〉［医学］routine treatment: 给予/接受～ give/take routine treatment
【常轨】chángguǐ〈名〉normal practice: 遵循～解决问题 go through the usual procedures to solve problems
【常衡】chánghéng〈名〉avoirdupois
【常会】chánghuì〈名〉regular meeting: 一年举行两次～。Two regular meetings are held annually.
【常见】chángjiàn〈动〉be common: ～错误 common mistake ‖ ～症状 common symptom ‖ 冬天这里下雪不～。Snow is rarely seen here in winter.
【常见病】chángjiànbìng ▸**p. 50**〈名〉common ailment: 关节炎是矿工的一种～。Arthritis is common among miners.
【常见问题】chángjiàn wèntí〈名〉frequently asked question (FAQ)
【常客】chángkè〈名〉regular visitor: 剧院的～ regular theatre-goer
【常来常往】chánglái-chángwǎng〈成〉frequently visit one another
【常礼】chánglǐ〈名〉common courtesy
【常理】chánglǐ〈名〉convention: 按～他明天应回访李先生。According to convention, he ought to pay Mr Li a return visit tomorrow.
【常例】chánglì〈名〉common practice: 沿用～ follow convention
【常量】chángliàng〈名〉［物理］constant: ～与变量 constants and variables
【常流河】chángliúhé〈名〉［水文］perennial stream
【常旅客】chánglǚkè〈名〉［航空］frequent flyer
【常绿】chánglǜ〈形〉evergreen: 四季～ evergreen
【常绿灌木】chánglǜ guànmù〈名〉evergreen shrub
【常年】chángnián **A**〈副〉perennially: ～不化的积雪 constant snow ‖ 他～在野外工作。He works in the wild year in, year out. **B**〈名〉average year: ～亩产量 per *mu* yield for an average year ‖ 该地区～雨量为 600-800 毫米。In this area the rainfall averages 600-800 millimetres a year.
【常青】chángqīng〈形〉evergreen: 四季～ evergreen
【常青树】chángqīngshù〈名〉**1**〈本〉evergreen: 松柏都是～。Pines and cypresses are both evergreens. **2**〈喻〉old-timer
【常情】chángqíng〈名〉reason: 不合～ contrary to reason ‖ 按～, 如果我们不邀请他, 他是不会来的。It stands to reason that he won't come if we don't invite him. ▸人之～
【常染色体】chángrǎnsètǐ〈名〉［生物］autosome
【常人】chángrén〈名〉common people: 她所遭受的苦痛是～无法理解的。Her sufferings are beyond the understanding of ordinary people.
【常任】chángrèn〈形〉permanent: 联合国安理会的～理事国 permanent member of the UN Security Council
【常任理事】chángrèn lǐshì〈名〉permanent council member

C

C

【常设】chángshè〈形〉[of an organization] permanent: ～机构 standing body
【常胜将军】chángshèng-jiāngjūn〈成〉unbeatable general
【常识】chángshí〈名〉**1**（知识）general knowledge: 安全～ elementary safety knowledge ‖ 保健～ ABC of health care **2**（常理）common sense: 靠～判断 judge using common sense
【常事】chángshì〈名〉common occurrence: 这是日常生活中的～。It's a common occurrence in daily life.
【常数】chángshù〈名〉［数学］constant
【常态】chángtài〈名〉normalcy: 保持～ keep the normal state ‖ 恢复～ return to normal ‖ 一反～ contrary to sb.'s normal behaviour
【常态化】chángtàihuà〈动〉normalize: 两岸直航～ the normalization of cross-straits direct flights ‖ ～管理 normalized management
【常谈】chángtán〈名〉platitude: ▸老生～
【常套】chángtào〈名〉convention: 摆脱～ break away from the usual pattern
【常委】chángwěi〈简称〉**1** = 常务委员会 **2** = 常务委员
【常委会】chángwěihuì〈简称〉= 常务委员会
【常温】chángwēn〈名〉normal temperature
【常温动物】chángwēn dòngwù〈名〉homoiotherm
【常务】chángwù〈形〉executive: ～副部长 executive vice minister
【常务理事】chángwù lǐshì〈名〉executive director
【常务委员】chángwù wěiyuán〈名〉member of the standing committee: 担任～ act as a member of the standing committee
【常务委员会】chángwù wěiyuánhuì〈名〉standing committee: ～委员 member of the standing committee ‖ 人大～ Standing Committee of the National People's Congress
【常性】chángxìng〈名〉**1**（持久性）perseverance: 缺乏～ lack perseverance ‖ 她做事没有～。She has no tenacity, whatever she does. **2**〈书〉（习性）habit
【常压】chángyā〈名〉**1**［化学］atmospheric pressure **2**［物理］constant pressure
【常言】chángyán〈名〉proverb: ～道 as the saying goes ‖ ～说得好 as the saying appropriately puts it
【常用】chángyòng〈形〉commonly used: ～词 common words ‖ ～药 commonly used remedy ‖ 不～ be rarely used
【常用对数】chángyòng duìshù〈名〉［数学］common logarithm
【常住】chángzhù〈动〉permanently reside: ～居民 permanent resident ‖ ～人口 permanent population ‖ ～户口 permanent residence
【常驻】chángzhù〈动〉be resident: ～国外 be resident abroad ‖ ～国外机构 permanent establishment abroad ‖ ～代表 permanent representative

偿（償）cháng

A〈动〉**1**（归还）repay;（抵补）compensate for: 补～损失 compensate sb. for the loss ▸～还, 赔～ **2**（满足）be fulfilled: 得～夙愿 fulfil a long-cherished wish ▸如愿以～
B〈名〉payment: ▸无～, 有～
【偿付】chángfù〈动〉pay back: ～债务 repay a debt ‖ 到期应～的债券 bonds due for repayment ‖ ～能力 solvency
【偿还】chánghuán〈动〉pay back: ～贷款 repay a loan ‖ ～血债 pay a debt of blood ‖ 分期～ pay back in instalments ‖ 连本带利～ repay with interest
【偿还能力】chánghuán nénglì〈名〉［经济］debt paying ability
【偿还期】chánghuánqī〈名〉［经济］maturity
【偿还期限】chánghuán qīxiàn〈名〉［经济］term of redemption
【偿命】chángmìng〈动〉pay a life for a life: 杀人～, 欠债还钱 get what one is due
【偿清】chángqīng〈动〉clear: ～抵押借款 pay off a mortgage
【偿债】chángzhài〈动〉clear a debt
【偿债能力】chángzhài nénglì〈名〉［经济］solvency

徜 cháng

【徜徉】chángyáng〈动〉〈书〉stroll: ～河畔 roam a riverbank ‖ 在林中～ roam among the trees

裳 cháng〈名〉〈旧〉skirt

▸shang

嫦 cháng

【嫦娥】Cháng'é ▸**p. 274**〈名〉Chang'e [Goddess of the Moon]

> **嫦娥**
>
> The Goddess of the Moon, and wife of Hou Yi (后羿), a mythical archer who shot down nine superfluous suns which were scorching the earth. When Chang'e secretly ate a pill of immortality given to Hou Yi by the Queen Mother of the West, her body became light and she floated up to moon, where she took up residence in the Guanghan Gong Palace (广寒宫). In former times, Chang'e was worshipped at the Mid-Autumn Festival.

chǎng

厂（廠）chǎng

〈名〉**1**（场所）yard: 煤～ coal yard ‖ 木材～ timber yard **2**（工厂）factory: 办～ run a factory ‖ 玻璃～ glass factory ‖ 电机/机床～ electrical machinery/machine tool plant ‖ 纺织/水泥/造纸/轧钢～ textile/cement/paper/steel mill ‖ ～办学校 factory-run school ‖ ～校挂钩 link schools with factories ▸～家, 工～
▸ān
【厂标】chǎngbiāo〈名〉factory logo
【厂部】chǎngbù〈名〉factory headquarters
【厂方】chǎngfāng〈名〉factory
【厂房】chǎngfáng〈名〉**1**（指房屋）factory building: 建～ construct factory buildings **2**（指车间）factory workshop: 扩建～ enlarge workshops ‖ ～与设备 plant and equipment
【厂规】chǎngguī〈名〉factory rules and regulations
【厂纪】chǎngjì〈名〉factory discipline: 违反/遵守～ violate/observe factory discipline
【厂家】chǎngjiā〈名〉factory: 生产～ manufacturing plant
【厂价】chǎngjià〈名〉price at factory
【厂矿】chǎngkuàng〈名〉factories and mines
【厂礼拜】chǎnglǐbài ▸**p. 836**〈名〉weekly day of rest for factory workers
【厂龄】chǎnglíng〈名〉length of a worker's service in a factory
【厂区】chǎngqū〈名〉factory yard
【厂商】chǎngshāng〈名〉**1**（厂家）manufacturer: 承包～ contractor **2**（厂家和商家）industrial and commercial firms
【厂休】chǎngxiū = 厂礼拜 chǎnglǐbài
【厂长】chǎngzhǎng〈名〉factory director
【厂址】chǎngzhǐ〈名〉location of a factory
【厂子】chǎngzi〈名〉〈口〉factory: 关闭～ shut down a factory

场（場）chǎng

A〈名〉**1**（场所）venue: 斗牛～ bullring ‖ 火箭发射～ rocket launching site ‖ 垃圾～ rubbish dump ‖ 足球～ football pitch ‖ 高尔夫球～ golf course ▸靶～, 操～ **2**（地点）site: 犯罪现～ scene of the crime ‖ 施工现～ construction site ▸当～, 逢～作戏 **3**（舞台）stage;（赛场）sports ground: 运动员入～。Athletes enter the sports field. ▸出～, 登～, 上～ **4**（表演过程）show;（比赛过程）match: ▸开～, 终～ **5**（生产场所）farm: ▸牧～, 农～, 渔～ **6**［物理］field: 静电～ static electrical field ‖ 引力～ gravitational field ▸磁～, 电～
B〈量〉**1**（指比赛、电影、音乐会等）[used for sports and recreation]: 一～电影 a film showing ‖ 一～球赛 a ball game ‖ 一～音乐会 a concert **2**［戏剧］scene: 第二幕第一～ Act II, Scene I
▸cháng
【场次】chǎngcì〈名〉performance: 增加演出～ increase the number of performances of a play
【场地】chǎngdì〈名〉site: 比赛～ competition ground ‖ 核试验～ nuclear test site ‖ 施工～ construction site ‖ 比赛进行到一半时, 双方交换～。At half-time the teams change ends.
【场地赛】chǎngdìsài〈名〉track racing: 由拉力赛转为～ move from rally to track racing
【场馆】chǎngguǎn〈名〉venue: 奥运～ Olympic venues ‖ 体育～ sports venues
【场合】chǎnghé〈名〉occasion: 公开/社交～ public/social event ‖ 说话要注意～。Tailor your words to the occasion.
【场记】chǎngjì〈名〉**1**（指记录）log **2**（指人）log keeper
【场景】chǎngjǐng〈名〉scene: 拍摄～ shoot a scene ‖ 可笑的～ funny sight ‖ 壮观的～ magnificent spectacle
【场论】chǎnglùn〈名〉［物理］field theory
【场面】chǎngmiàn〈名〉**1**（指戏剧、电影等）scene: 描写～ depict a scene ‖ 剧中感人的～ touching scene in a play **2**（指传统戏曲）accompanying musical instruments and their performers **3**（情景）spectacle: 目睹可怕的～ witness a horrifying scene ‖ ～壮观 magnificent spectacle ‖ 欢乐的～ joyous occasion **4**（排场）show: ▸撑～
【场面话】chǎngmiànhuà〈名〉polite remarks
【场面人】chǎngmiànrén〈名〉**1**（善于交际者）sociable person **2**（有地位者）person of prestige
【场面上】chǎngmiànshang〈名〉social event: 他和那些～的人混得很熟。He was on pretty good terms with those people of prestige.
【场内交易】chǎngnèi jiāoyì〈名〉［经济］transaction on exchange
【场所】chǎngsuǒ〈名〉arena: 公共～ public place ‖ 学习～ place for study ‖ 娱乐～ entertainment venue

【场外交易】chǎngwài jiāoyì〈名〉［经济］over-the-counter transaction
【场外指导】chǎngwài zhǐdǎo〈名〉［体育］sideline coaching
【场长】chǎngzhǎng〈名〉head of a farm, dairy, fishery, nursery, etc.
【场子】chǎngzi〈名〉〈口〉venue: 这个～能容纳一千多观众。The place can accommodate more than 1,000 spectators.

昶 chǎng〈形〉〈书〉**1**（日长）[of the day] long **2**（舒畅）relaxed

惝 chǎng
【惝恍】chǎnghuǎng〈形〉〈书〉**1**（失意）disheartened **2**（模糊不清）muddled

敞 chǎng
A〈形〉spacious: ▸～车, ～亮, 宽～
B〈动〉be open: ～着大门 leave the gate open ‖ 窗户大～着。The window was wide open. ▸～怀, ～开
【敞车】chǎngchē〈名〉**1**（指货运列车）railway flatcar **2**（敞篷车）open wagon **3**（指卡车）truck without an awning
【敞怀】chǎnghuái〈动〉have one's shirt unbuttoned
【敞开】chǎngkāi **A**〈动〉open wide: ～大门 open the gate wide ‖〈喻〉～思想 get things off one's chest ‖〈喻〉～胸怀 speak one's mind **B**〈副〉freely: ～肚皮吃 eat to one's heart's content ‖ ～供应 have an unlimited supply (of sth.) ‖ 有不同意见就～说。Don't hesitate to voice your disagreement, if any.
【敞快】chǎngkuài〈形〉straightforward: 他为人处事向来很～。He is straight in his handling of people and business.
【敞亮】chǎngliàng〈形〉**1**（宽敞明亮）bright and spacious: ～的教室 light and roomy classroom **2**〈喻〉（舒展开朗）open and clear: 关于该政策的思想豁然～了。All doubts or apprehensions about the policy cleared up.
【敞露】chǎnglù〈动〉bare: ～胸脯 bare one's chest
【敞篷车】chǎngpéngchē〈名〉convertible
【敞胸露怀】chǎngxiōng-lòuhuái〈成〉bare one's chest

氅 chǎng〈名〉〈旧〉cloak: ▸大～

chàng

怅（悵） chàng〈形〉disappointed: ▸～然, ～惘, 惆～
【怅怅】chàngchàng〈形〉〈书〉frustrated and dissatisfied: ～离去 depart despondently ‖ ～不乐 be depressed
【怅恨】chànghèn〈动〉〈书〉be disappointed and resentful
【怅然】chàngrán〈形〉〈书〉unhappy: ～而返 return in dejection ‖ ～离去 walk away despondently
【怅然若失】chàngrán-ruòshī〈成〉feel lost
【怅惋】chàngwǎn〈动〉〈书〉sigh with regret: 这位杰出科学家的去世令世人～。The whole world is grieved to hear of the prominent scientist's death.
【怅惘】chàngwǎng〈形〉〈书〉anxious and in low spirits

畅（暢） chàng〈形〉**1**（无阻碍）unimpeded: ▸～通, ～销, 流～ **2**（尽情）uninhibited: ▸～所欲言, ～饮, 欢～
【畅达】chàngdá〈形〉smooth: 车辆往来～ smooth flow of traffic ‖ 论文文字～, 观点明确。The thesis reads smoothly and has a clear argument.
【畅怀】chànghuái〈动〉do as much as one likes: ～大笑 laugh to one's heart's content ‖ ～痛饮 drink as much as one likes
【畅快】chàngkuài〈形〉carefree: 心情～ be carefree and cheerful
【畅抒】chàngshū〈动〉freely express: ～胸怀 freely express one's mind
【畅顺】chàngshùn = 顺畅 shùnchàng
【畅所欲言】chàngsuǒyùyán〈成〉speak one's mind freely: 与会者都能～。Everybody at the meeting spoke open and freely.
【畅谈】chàngtán〈动〉talk freely: ～理想 talk freely about one's hopes and dreams ‖ ～天下大事 speak without restraint about world events
【畅通】chàngtōng〈动〉proceed without hindrance: ～无阻 be free from obstacles ‖ 道路～。The roads are clear.
【畅想】chàngxiǎng〈动〉〈书〉give free rein to one's imagination: ～未来 give one's imagination free rein when thinking about the future
【畅销】chàngxiāo〈动〉sell well: ～国内外市场 sell well on home and foreign markets ‖ ～书 best seller
【畅行无阻】chàngxíng-wúzǔ〈成〉proceed without obstruction: 眼下道路～。The road is now open.
【畅叙】chàngxù〈动〉talk to one's heart's content: ～友情 speak at length about an old friendship
【畅饮】chàngyǐn〈动〉drink all one wants: 开怀～ drink to one's heart's content
【畅游】chàngyóu〈动〉**1**（指游览）enjoy a sightseeing tour: ～名胜古迹 enjoy a trip to places of historic interest **2**（指游泳）have a good swim

倡 chàng〈动〉**1**〈书〉（领唱）lead the singing: ▸一～百和 **2**（带头）initiate: ▸～导, ～议, 首～, 提～
▸chāng
【倡办】chàngbàn〈动〉initiate: ～国际文化交流中心 initiate the establishment of an international cultural exchange centre ‖ ～文学社 found a literary society
【倡导】chàngdǎo〈动〉initiate: ～计划生育 advocate family planning ‖ 积极～ zealously advocate ‖ ～者 advocate
【倡廉】chànglián〈动〉applaud honesty and integrity to a government official: 反腐～ oppose corruption and advocate integrity
【倡始】chàngshǐ〈动〉initiate
【倡始人】chàngshǐrén〈名〉initiator
【倡首】chàngshǒu〈动〉〈书〉take the lead
【倡言】chàngyán〈动〉〈书〉propose: ～全面的社会改革 initiate sweeping social reform
【倡议】chàngyì **A**〈动〉propose: 在某人的～下 at sb.'s suggestion ‖ ～书 proposal ‖ ～者 sponsor **B**〈名〉initiative: 响应～ respond to a proposal ‖ 和平～ peace initiative

唱 chàng
A〈动〉**1**（唱歌）sing: ～国歌 sing the national anthem ‖ ～赞歌 sing the praises of sth. ‖ 同声合～ sing in unison ▸～歌, ～腔 **2**（大声叫）call: 鸡～三遍。The cock has crowed for the third time. ▸～付, ～票, ～收
B〈名〉song: 这出戏里我的～儿不多。I don't have many singing parts in the opera. ▸～本
【唱白脸】chàng báiliǎn〈惯〉〈喻〉play the villain: 一个唱红脸, 一个～。One plays the hero and the other the villain.
【唱本】chàngběn〈名〉libretto of a ballad-singer
【唱词】chàngcí〈名〉lyrics: 音乐还好, 但～较差。The music was fine, but the libretto was only second-rate.
【唱碟】chàngdié〈方〉= 唱片 chàngpiàn
【唱独角戏】chàng dújiǎoxì〈惯〉〈喻〉put on a one-man show
【唱段】chàngduàn〈名〉aria: 京剧～ an aria from a Peking opera
【唱对台戏】chàng duìtáixì〈惯〉stage a rival show
【唱反调】chàng fǎndiào〈惯〉sing a different tune
【唱付】chàngfù〈动〉call out the amount of change returned to a customer
【唱高调】chàng gāodiào〈惯〉affect a high moral tone: 别～了。Get off your high horse, will you?
【唱歌】chànggē〈动〉sing: 教/练习～ teach/practise singing
【唱工】chànggōng = 唱功 chànggōng
【唱功】chànggōng〈名〉［戏曲］singing
【唱和】chànghè〈动〉**1**（指写作）write and reply in poems, using the same rhyming sequence **2**（指唱歌）sing a song with others joining in the chorus: 此唱彼和。One sings and the others join in.
【唱红脸】chàng hóngliǎn〈惯〉〈喻〉play the hero
【唱机】chàngjī〈名〉record player: 激光～ compact disc (CD) player
【唱空城计】chàng kōngchéngjì〈成〉〈喻〉present a powerful front to conceal a weak defence
【唱老调】chàng lǎodiào〈惯〉sing the same old tune
【唱名】chàngmíng **A**〈动〉roll-call: ～表决 roll-call vote **B**〈名〉［音乐］sol-fa syllables [do, re, mi, fa, sol, la, and ti]
【唱念做打】chàng-niàn-zuò-dǎ〈成〉［戏曲］singing, recitation, acting and acrobatics: ～俱佳 excel in singing, recitation, acting and acrobatics
【唱盘】chàngpán = 唱片 chàngpiàn
【唱片】chàngpiàn〈名〉record: 录制～ make a record ‖ 激光～ compact disc (CD)
【唱片集】chàngpiànjí〈名〉album: 发行～ release an album
【唱票】chàngpiào〈动〉call out the votes: ～人 teller
【唱腔】chàngqiāng〈名〉［音乐］aria
【唱曲】chàngqǔ〈动〉sing a song
【唱喏】chàngrě〈动〉〈方〉〈古〉exchange pleasantries while making a slight bow with hands folded and extended in front
【唱诗班】chàngshībān〈名〉choir
【唱收】chàngshōu〈动〉[of a salesperson] call out the amount of money paid by a customer
【唱双簧】chàng shuānghuáng〈动〉**1**〈本〉give a two-man comic show **2**〈喻〉collaborate in a scheme or show
【唱戏】chàngxì〈动〉〈口〉sing and act in a Chinese opera: 唱京戏 sing a Beijing opera
【唱针】chàngzhēn〈名〉needle (of a gramophone)

【唱主角】chàng zhǔjué〈惯〉〈喻〉play the leading role

chāo

抄¹ chāo〈动〉**1**（抄写）copy: ～笔记/稿子/文件 copy notes/drafts/documents ‖ ～书 copy from a book ‖ ～两遍 make two copies ▸～本, ～写, 传～, 照～ **2**（抄袭）copy: ～别人的答案 copy other people's answers ‖ 这篇文章是从一本书上～来的。This article has been lifted from a book. ▸～袭

抄² chāo〈动〉**1**（搜查并没收）search for and confiscate: ～家产 confiscate sb.'s property ‖ ～犯罪窝点 raid the criminals' dens and confiscate evidence ▸～获, ～家, 查～ **2**（走近道）take a shortcut: ～近道走 walk a shorter route ▸～后路, 包～ **3**（插入袖筒）fold one's arms: 他～着手站在一边，一点忙儿也不愿帮。He stood by with folded arms, unwilling to offer any help. ▸～手 A

抄³ chāo = 绰 chāo 1

【抄本】chāoběn〈名〉handwritten copy: ▸手～

【抄查】chāochá = 查抄 cháchāo

【抄道】chāodào **A**〈动〉take a shortcut: 时间不够了，咱们还是～走吧。We're running out of time — let's take the shortcut. **B**〈名〉〈方〉shortcut: 走～ take a shortcut

【抄底】chāodǐ〈动〉［金融］buy at the bottom: ～获利 make profits by buying at the bottom of the market

【抄后路】chāo hòulù〈动〉outflank and attack from the rear: ～包围敌军 outflank and surround the enemy troops

【抄获】chāohuò〈动〉ferret out: ～窃贼的赃物 ferret out stolen goods

【抄家】chāojiā〈动〉〈旧〉search sb.'s house and confiscate his property

【抄件】chāojiàn〈名〉copy

【抄近儿】chāojìnr〈动〉〈口〉take a shortcut: 他们总是～走小道。They always take the shortcut along the path.

【抄录】chāolù〈动〉copy: ～名言 copy quotations

【抄没】chāomò〈动〉ransack and confiscate: ～财产 confiscate sb.'s property

【抄身】chāoshēn〈动〉search a person

【抄收】chāoshōu〈动〉receive and take down

【抄手】chāoshǒu **A**〈动〉fold one's arms: ～站在一旁 stand by with folded arms ‖ ～掌柜 ineffectual boss **B**〈名〉**1**（指人）copyist **2**〈方〉= 馄饨 húntun

【抄送】chāosòng〈动〉copy in: 将文件～各部门 send a copy of the document to all departments

【抄网】chāowǎng〈名〉dip net

【抄袭】chāoxí〈动〉**1**（剽窃）plagiarize: ～答案 copy answers ‖ ～他人作品 crib other people's work **2**（照搬）copy indiscriminately: 机械/盲目～ copy mechanically/blindly **3**（突袭）outflank and attack from behind

【抄写】chāoxiě〈动〉transcribe: ～员 copyist ‖ 你用不着把整篇文章都～下来。Don't bother to copy out the whole article.

【抄用】chāoyòng〈动〉copy indiscriminately: ～别国/他人经验 apply another country's/other people's experience without discrimination

【抄斩】chāozhǎn〈动〉〈古〉confiscate sb.'s property and behead him: 满门～ confiscate sb.'s property and exterminate his family

吵 chāo
▸chǎo

【吵吵】chāochao〈动〉〈方〉make a noise: 别～了，听人家讲话! Be quiet and listen to the speaker! ‖ 外面在～什么? Why is there so much noise outside?

钞（鈔） chāo〈名〉banknote: 现～ cash ‖ 美～ US dollar ▸～票, 假～, 验～机

【钞票】chāopiào〈名〉banknote; bill〈美〉

绰（綽） chāo〈动〉**1**（抓）seize: ～起大棒 grab a club ‖ ～起活儿就干 plunge right into the job **2** = 焯 chāo
▸chuò

超 chāo〈动〉**1**（超过）exceed: ～到某人前面 get ahead of sb. ‖ ～世界先进水平 surpass advanced world levels ‖ ～了半小时 overrun the time limit by a half hour ▸～车, ～过, ～编, ～额 **2**（超出）be more than usual: ～豪华 super-luxurious ▸～高温, ～级, ～人 **3**（不受限制）go beyond: ▸～现实主义, ～俗, ～自然

【超拔】chāobá〈书〉**A**〈形〉outstanding: 技艺～ outstanding skill **B**〈动〉**1**（提拔）promote: ～擢用 promote sb. to a post ahead of time **2**（摆脱）free oneself from: 恶习一旦养成，则难以～。Once formed, bad habits are difficult to break.

【超薄】chāobáo〈形〉ultra-thin: ～镜片 ultra-thin lens

【超编】chāobiān〈动〉be overstaffed: ～人员 excess personnel ‖ 人员～ overstaff

【超标】chāobiāo〈动〉exceed the set standard: 因排污～被罚款 be fined for exceeding sewage drainage standards

【超产】chāochǎn〈动〉surpass a production target: ～百分之十 exceed the production quota by 10%

【超常】chāocháng〈形〉well above average: 智力～ be of extraordinary intelligence ‖ ～发挥 surpass oneself

【超车】chāochē〈动〉overtake: 试图～抢道 try to cut into a lane ‖ 违章～ overtake other vehicles against traffic regulations

【超车道】chāochēdào〈名〉overtaking lane

【超尘拔俗】chāochén-bású〈成〉rise above the ordinary

【超尘出俗】chāochén-chūsú = 超尘拔俗 chāochén-bású

【超出】chāochū〈动〉go beyond: ～范围 overstep the limits ‖ ～权限 overstep one's authority ‖ ～预算 overrun a budget

【超大规模集成电路】chāodàguīmó jíchéng diànlù〈名〉very large-scale integrated circuit

【超导】chāodǎo〈形〉［物理］superconductive

【超导材料】chāodǎo cáiliào〈名〉［物理］superconducting material

【超导体】chāodǎotǐ〈名〉［物理］superconductor

【超导性】chāodǎoxìng〈名〉［物理］superconductivity

【超等】chāoděng〈形〉first-rate: ～质量 extra good quality

【超低价】chāodījià〈名〉super low price: ～折扣机票 super cheap discount ticket

【超低空飞行】chāodīkōng fēixíng〈名〉minimum altitude flying

【超低频】chāodīpín〈名〉ultra-low frequency (ULF)

【超低温】chāodīwēn〈名〉ultra-low temperature

【超跌】chāodiē〈动〉［金融］oversell: 购进几只～股 buy a few oversold stocks

【超跌反弹】chāodiē fǎntán〈动〉［金融］rebound: 出现～迹象 show indications of rebounding

【超度】chāodù〈动〉［宗教］expiate the sins of the dead: ～亡魂 save the souls of the deceased from hell ‖ ～众生 save mankind from eternal misery

【超短波】chāoduǎnbō〈名〉ultrashort wave (USW)

【超短裙】chāoduǎnqún〈名〉miniskirt

【超额】chāo'é〈动〉exceed the quota: ～20% exceed the quota by 20% ‖ ～利润 surplus profit ‖ ～完成任务 surpass a task

【超凡】chāofán〈动〉**1**（超出常人）transcend the worldly: 追求～的生活 pursue a transcendental life ▸～入圣 **2**（超出平常水平）be extraordinary: 具有～的力量 have superhuman strength

【超凡入圣】chāofán-rùshèng〈成〉transcend worldliness and attain sainthood

【超凡脱俗】chāofán-tuōsú〈成〉rise above the ordinary

【超负荷】chāofùhè〈动〉overburden: ～运转 operate at an overload

【超高空】chāogāokōng〈名〉［物理］super altitude

【超高能】chāogāonéng〈名〉extra-high energy

【超高频】chāogāopín〈名〉［电子］ultra-high frequency: ～信号 ultra-high frequency signal

【超高温】chāogāowēn〈名〉ultra-high temperature: ～耐火材料 extreme temperature refractory

【超高压】chāogāoyā〈名〉**1**［物理］super high pressure **2**［电气］ultra-high voltage: ～线路带电作业 working on live extra-high tension power lines

【超固态】chāogùtài〈名〉state of ultra-solidity

【超广角镜头】chāoguǎngjiǎo jìngtóu〈名〉fish-eye lens

【超过】chāoguò〈动〉outdo (sb. at sth.): ～历史最高水平 top all previous records ‖ ～期限 miss a deadline ‖ 在数量上～ outnumber ‖ 投资～5千万美元 invest in excess of 50 million US dollars ‖ 进口～了出口。Imports exceeded exports.

【超乎寻常】chāohūxúncháng〈成〉be extraordinary

【超级】chāojí〈形〉super: ～公路 super-highway ‖ ～明星 superstar

【超级杯】chāojíbēi〈名〉［足球］Super Cup

【超级大国】chāojídàguó〈名〉superpower: 经济～ economic superpower

【超级稻】chāojídào〈名〉super rice: 推广种植～ promote the planting of super rice

【超级模特】chāojí mótè〈名〉supermodel

【超假】chāojià〈动〉overstay one's leave: ～两天 overstay one's leave by two days

【超巨星】chāojùxīng〈名〉［天文］super-giant star

【超绝】chāojué〈形〉extraordinary: 技艺～ unparalleled skill

【超龄】chāolíng〈动〉be overage

【超伦】chāolún〈形〉〈书〉outstanding

【超卖】chāomài〈动〉［金融］oversell: 大盘连续下跌，技术上处于～状态。In the declining market, stocks are technically oversold.
【超敏反应】chāomǐn fǎnyìng〈名〉［医学］hypersensitivity reaction
【超模】chāomó〈简称〉= 超级模特
【超浓缩】chāonóngsuō〈形〉hyper-concentrated: ～洗涤剂 hyperconcentrated detergent
【超女】chāonǚ〈名〉super girl: ～大赛 Super Girl Contest
【超平彩电】chāopíng cǎidiàn〈名〉hyperplane colour TV
【超期】chāoqī〈动〉exceed the time limit: ～服役 extended army service
【超前】chāoqián **A**〈形〉ahead: ～意识 sense of looking forward and being ahead of one's time **B**〈动〉surpass one's predecessors
【超前绝后】chāoqián-juéhòu〈成〉unique
【超前消费】chāoqián xiāofèi〈名〉deficit spending
【超群】chāoqún〈动〉be pre-eminent: 技艺～ incomparable skill ‖ 他医术～。He is a much better medical doctor than all the others.
【超群出众】chāoqún-chūzhòng〈成〉be above the rank and file: 武艺～ exceptional martial arts skills
【超群绝伦】chāoqún-juélún〈成〉be without comparison: 作为大提琴表演艺术家，他是～的。He is second to none as a concert cellist.
【超然】chāorán〈形〉aloof: ～的态度 aloof attitude
【超然不群】chāorán-bùqún〈成〉stand apart from the crowd
【超然物外】chāorán-wùwài〈成〉**1**（置身事外）be above worldly considerations **2**（超脱于社会）shun social disputes
【超热】chāorè〈形〉［物理］epithermal: ～材料 hyperthermal material
【超人】chāorén **A**〈动〉be extraordinary: 才智～ far surpass others in ability and wisdom ‖ ～的记忆力 exceptionally good memory **B**〈名〉superman: ～哲学 philosophy of the superman ‖ 女～ superwoman
【超人气】chāorénqì〈名〉enormous popularity: ～演艺明星 hugely popular performer ‖ ～概念车 best-loved concept car
【超升】chāoshēng〈动〉［佛教］[of a dead person's soul] rise to the Western Paradise
【超生】chāoshēng〈动〉**1**［佛教］be reincarnated **2**（宽容）be merciful: ▸笔下～ **3**（指生育）exceed the stipulated family planning limit
【超声波】chāoshēngbō〈名〉［物理］ultrasonic: ～探测器 ultrasonic detector ‖ ～疗法 ultrasonic therapy ‖ ～发生器 ultrasonic generator
【超声洁牙器】chāoshēng jiéyáqì〈名〉［医学］ultrasonic teeth cleaner
【超声速】chāoshēngsù = 超音速 chāoyīnsù
【超声探伤仪】chāoshēng tànshāngyí〈名〉ultrasonic flaw detector
【超声心动图】chāoshēng xīndòngtú〈名〉［医学］ultrasonic cardiogram
【超时】chāoshí〈动〉overrun: ～工作 work overtime ‖ ～报酬/补贴 overtime payment/allowance
【超市】chāoshì〈名〉supermarket
【超收】chāoshōu **A**〈动〉earn more than planned or allowed **B**〈名〉earnings in excess of what is allowed
【超水平】chāoshuǐpíng〈形〉surpassing one's normal level: ～发挥 outperform oneself
【超俗】chāosú〈动〉transcend worldliness
【超俗绝世】chāosú juéshì〈成〉out of the ordinary
【超速】chāosù〈动〉speed: 因～被罚款 be fined for speeding ‖ ～检测器 police speed trap
【超脱】chāotuō **A**〈形〉unconventional: 见解～ unconventional view ‖ 想法～ original idea **B**〈动〉**1**（超越）be detached: ～尘世 be detached from this world ‖ ～现实 detach oneself from reality **2**（解脱）absolve sb.
【超微波】chāowēibō〈名〉［物理］ultra microwave
【超文本】chāowénběn〈名〉hypertext
【超文本标记语言】chāowénběn biāojì yǔyán〈名〉［计算机］hypertext markup language (HTML)
【超我】chāowǒ〈名〉［心理］superego
【超现实主义】chāoxiànshízhǔyì〈名〉surrealism: ～画家 surrealist painter ‖ ～者 surrealist
【超小型】chāoxiǎoxíng〈形〉subminiature
【超新星】chāoxīnxīng〈名〉［天文］supernova
【超星体】chāoxīngtǐ〈名〉［天文］superstar
【超星系】chāoxīngxì〈名〉［天文］supergalaxy
【超压】chāoyā〈名〉overpressure
【超验】chāoyàn〈形〉［哲学］transcendental
【超验主义】chāoyàn zhǔyì〈名〉transcendentalism: ～者 transcendentalist
【超一流】chāoyīliú〈形〉superb: ～的演员 first-rate actor/actress
【超逸】chāoyì〈形〉graceful and refined: ～不俗 unconventionally elegant ‖ 举止～ graceful demeanour
【超意识】chāoyìshí〈名〉［心理］superconsciousness
【超音速】chāoyīnsù〈名〉supersonic speed: ～客机 supersonic airliner
【超音速飞机】chāoyīnsù fēijī〈名〉supersonic aircraft
【超音速战斗机】chāoyīnsù zhàndòujī〈名〉supersonic fighter
【超员】chāoyuán〈动〉**1**（指编制）be overstaffed: 该部门严重～。The department is terribly overstaffed. **2**（指载人数）be overloaded: 节假日期间，火车常常～。Trains are often overcrowded during holidays.
【超越】chāoyuè〈动〉surpass: ～对手 outdo one's rivals ‖ ～极限 exceed the limit ‖ ～权限 act outside of one's jurisdiction ‖ ～自我 excel oneself
【超载】chāozài〈动〉overburden: 严禁～ no overloading ‖ ～的车辆 overloaded vehicle ‖ ～过牧 overgraze
【超支】chāozhī **A**〈名〉overspend **B**〈动〉overspend: 他每月都～。Every month his expenditure exceeds his income.
【超值】chāozhí〈动〉exceed the real value of a commodity
【超重】chāozhòng〈动〉**1**（指负载）be overloaded: 这卡车～了。The truck was overloaded. **2**（指重量）be overweight: ～信件 overweight letter ‖ 行李～需额外付费。If your luggage is overweight, you'll have to pay extra.
【超重行李】chāozhòng xíngli〈名〉overweight luggage
【超重量级】chāozhòngliàngjí〈名〉［体育］super-heavyweight
【超卓】chāozhuó〈形〉superb
【超擢】chāozhuó〈动〉〈书〉promote sb. ahead of time
【超子】chāozǐ〈名〉［物理］hyperon
【超自然】chāozìrán〈形〉supernatural: ～主义 supernaturalism

焯 chāo〈动〉scald: ～芹菜 blanch the celery
▸zhuō

剿（勦） chāo〈动〉〈书〉plagiarize: ▸～袭
▸jiǎo
【剿说】chāoshuō〈动〉〈书〉plagiarize
【剿袭】chāoxí〈书〉= 抄袭 chāoxí 1, 2

C

cháo

晁 Cháo〈名〉Chao [surname]

巢 cháo〈名〉nest: 筑～ build a nest ‖ 鸟～ bird's nest ‖ 蜂～ wasps' nest ▸鹊～鸠占, 匪～, 老～, 倾～出动
【巢居】cháojū〈动〉live in trees
【巢窟】cháokū = 巢穴 cháoxué
【巢穴】cháoxué〈名〉nest: 捣毁～ destroy one's nest ‖ 蜷缩在～里 curl up in a hideout ‖〈喻〉强盗的～ den of thieves

朝 cháo
A〈动〉**1**（朝拜）（指臣子）have an audience with;（指信徒）make a pilgrimage to: ▸～拜, ～见, ～贡, ～圣 **2**（正对着）face: ～北/东/南/西 face north/east/south/west ‖ 坐北～南 face south ‖ 这扇窗～着大海。The window faces the sea.
B〈名〉**1**（朝廷）imperial court: 临～听政 hold court ‖ 在～党 ruling party ▸～野, 上～, 早～ **2**（朝代）dynasty: 六～古都 ancient capital of six dynasties ‖ 唐/宋/清～ Tang/Song/Qing Dynasty ▸改～换代, 三～元老
C〈介〉towards: ～东走 go east ‖ ～前看 look ahead ‖ 这门～里/外开。The door opens inwards/outwards.
▸zhāo
【朝拜】cháobài〈动〉**1**（指臣子）pay respects to: ～天子 pay respects to the emperor **2**（指信徒）make a pilgrimage: ～神佛 worship gods and the Buddha ‖ ～圣地 worship at the shrine
【朝臣】cháochén〈名〉courtier
【朝代】cháodài〈名〉dynasty: ～更迭 dynastic succession
【朝顶】cháodǐng〈动〉make a pilgrimage to a temple on a mountain top
【朝服】cháofú〈名〉〈古〉formal dress for imperial audiences
【朝纲】cháogāng〈名〉court discipline: ～不振 the imperial court is weakening ‖ 重振～ reinforce imperial rule
【朝贡】cháogòng〈动〉pay tribute
【朝贺】cháohè〈动〉pay one's respects (to the sovereign) and extend one's good wishes
【朝见】cháojiàn〈动〉have an audience with a sovereign: 获准～国王 be granted an audience with the king
【朝觐】cháojìn〈动〉**1**〈书〉（指臣子）be presented at court **2**（指信徒）worship: ～圣地 worship at the shrine
【朝山进香】cháoshān jìnxiāng〈成〉go on a pilgrimage to offer incense at a temple on a famous mountain

【朝圣】cháoshèng〈动〉**1**（指宗教圣地）make a pilgrimage: 前往麦加/耶路撒冷～ go on a pilgrimage to Mecca/Jerusalem ‖ ～者 pilgrim **2**（指儒家圣地） make a pilgrimage to the birthplace of Confucius
【朝廷】cháotíng〈名〉**1**（指场所） imperial court **2**（指机构） imperial government: ～命官 official of the imperial government
【朝鲜】Cháoxiǎn〈名〉 Korea: ～民主主义人民共和国 Democratic People's Republic of Korea (DPRK) ‖ ～人 Korean ‖ ～语 Korean
【朝鲜泡菜】Cháoxiǎn pàocài〈名〉 kimchi
【朝鲜战争】 Cháoxiǎn Zhànzhēng 〈名〉 Korean War
【朝鲜族】Cháoxiǎnzú〈名〉 **1**（在中国） Korean ethnic group **2**（在朝韩） Koreans
【朝向】 cháoxiàng 〈名〉［建筑］ orientation
【朝阳】cháoyáng〈动〉 have a southern exposure: 我的卧室～。 My bedroom faces south.
▸zhāoyáng
【朝阳花】cháoyánghuā = 向日葵 xiàngrìkuí
【朝野】cháoyě〈名〉 **1**〈旧〉（朝廷和民间） the court and the common people: ～震惊。 Both the rulers and the people were shocked. **2**（执政和在野双方） the government and the opposition: ～各党派 all political parties
【朝政】cháozhèng〈名〉〈书〉〈旧〉 state power: 把持～ monopolize state power ‖ 议论～ discuss state affairs
【朝中有人好做官】cháozhōng yǒu rén hǎo zuòguān〈俗〉 it is easy to be an official if you have connections at court
【朝珠】cháozhū〈名〉 string of coral beads [worn by court officials in the Qing Dynasty]

嘲 cháo
〈动〉 mock: ▸～笑, 冷～热讽
▸zhāo
【嘲讽】 cháofěng 〈动〉 taunt: 辛辣的～ biting ridicule
【嘲弄】cháonòng〈动〉mock: ～别人 mock others ‖ 受到～ be held up to ridicule ‖ 对司法的～ a mockery of justice
【嘲笑】cháoxiào〈动〉 laugh at: 惹人～ incur ridicule ‖ 当面～ laugh in sb.'s face ‖ 不要～别人的生理缺陷。 Don't taunt people about their physiological defects.
【嘲谑】cháoxuè〈动〉 tease: 以～的口气说 speak in a bantering tone of voice

潮[1] cháo
A〈名〉 tide: 早/晚～ morning/evening tide ‖ ～涨～落 flood and low tide ‖ 难民～ stream of refugees ‖ 人流如～ the crowd is surging like a tide ▸～水, 高～, 寒～, 思～, 心～
B〈形〉 moist: 发～ get damp ‖ 粮食受～了。 The grain has got damp. ‖ 夏天这里气候很～。 It is very humid here in summer. ‖ 这屋子又冷又～。 The house is cold and damp. ▸～湿

潮[2] cháo
〈形〉〈方〉 inferior: 金银成色～ low content of gold and silver ‖ 手艺～ have inferior skill

潮[3] Cháo
〈名〉 Chao [short for Chaozhou (潮州), Guangdong Province]
【潮波】cháobō〈名〉［海洋］ tidal wave
【潮差】cháochā〈名〉［海洋］ tidal range
【潮高】cháogāo〈名〉［海洋］ height of tide
【潮红】 cháohóng 〈名〉 blush: 两颊～ be flushed in the cheeks ‖ 他因发高烧而脸色～。 The fever gave him a flush about the face.
【潮乎乎】cháohūhū〈形〉〈口〉 dank: 被褥摸起来～的。 The bedding feels damp.
【潮呼呼】cháohūhū = 潮乎乎 cháohūhū
【潮解】cháojiě〈动〉［化学］ deliquesce
【潮剧】cháojù〈名〉 Chao opera
【潮流】cháoliú〈名〉 **1**（指海水） tide: 汹涌的～ surging tide **2**〈喻〉（指趋势） trend: 反/违背～ go against the tide ‖ 赶～ go with the tide ‖ 领导～ lead the trend ‖ 顺应～ go with the tide ‖ 历史～ historical trend ‖ 时代～ current of the times
【潮气】 cháoqì 〈名〉 humidity: 吸收～ absorb moisture ‖ 今天～很大。 It's very clammy today.
【潮热】cháorè〈名〉［生理］ hot flush
【潮人】cháorén〈名〉 fashionable person
【潮润】 cháorùn 〈形〉 **1**（指土地、空气等） good and moist: ～的空气/泥土 moist air/earth **2**（指眼睛） moist with tears: 他双眼～。 His eyes moistened with tears.
【潮湿】cháoshī〈形〉 moist: 空气～ damp atmosphere ‖ 气候～ damp climate
【潮水】cháoshuǐ〈名〉［海洋］ tidal water: 汹涌的～ surging tides ‖ ～在上涨。 The tide is coming in.
【潮位】cháowèi〈名〉［海洋］ tidemark
【潮汐】cháoxī〈名〉［海洋］ tide: ～的涨落 rise and fall of the tide ‖ ～发电 tidal power generation ‖ ～资源 tidal energy resource
【潮信】 cháoxìn 〈名〉 **1**（潮水） tide **2** ▸p. 772〈书〉〈婉〉（月经） menstruation
【潮绣】cháoxiù〈名〉Chaozhou embroidery
【潮汛】cháoxùn〈名〉 high tides
【潮涌】 cháoyǒng 〈动〉 surge: 人流～而来。 A great tidal wave of people came surging forward. ‖ 孤独感～而来。 A sense of loneliness flooded in.
【潮沼】cháozhǎo〈名〉［地理］tidal marsh

chǎo

吵 chǎo
A〈形〉 noisy: 隔壁太～了，叫人睡不着觉。 It was so noisy next door that I couldn't sleep.
B〈动〉 **1**（发出噪音） make a noise: 大～大嚷 make a horrendous racket ‖ 轻点儿，别把孩子～醒了。 Be quiet! Don't wake the child. **2**（争吵） quarrel: ～着～着就打了起来 squabble and then come to blows ‖ 为琐碎小事而～ quibble over trivial matters ▸～架, 争～
▸chāo
【吵吵闹闹】chǎochǎo-nàonào〈成〉raise a racket
【吵架】chǎojià〈动〉 have a row: 为小事～ quarrel over little things
【吵闹】chǎonào **A**〈动〉 **1**（争吵） have a row: ～不休 keep quarrelling ‖ 为小事～ make a fuss over little things **2**（烦扰） bother: 他在工作，不要去～他。 He's working. Don't disturb him. **B**〈形〉 clamorous: 人声～ hubbub of voices
【吵嚷】chǎorǎng〈动〉 make a racket: ～的人群 noisy crowd ‖ 一片～声 a complete racket
【吵扰】chǎorǎo〈动〉 disturb: ～人 disturb others
【吵人】chǎorén〈形〉 terribly noisy: 室外的噪音真～。 The noise outside the room was deafening.
【吵嘴】chǎozuǐ〈动〉 quarrel: 兄弟之间经常～。 There is constant bickering among the brothers.

炒 chǎo
〈动〉 **1**（指饭菜） stir-fry: ～鸡蛋 scramble eggs ‖ ～鸡丁 fry diced chicken ▸～菜 **2**（指炒货） fry while stirring: ～花生 pan-fried peanuts ‖ 糖～栗子 chestnuts pan-fried with brown sugar ▸～货 **3**（投机） speculate: ～外汇 speculate in foreign exchange ▸～地皮, ～股 **4**（指传闻） give repeated exposure to: 皇室丑闻被传媒大～。 The royal scandal was getting a lot of exposure. **5**（解雇） dismiss: ▸～鱿鱼
【炒菜】chǎocài **A**〈动〉 cook food: 今天我炒了两个菜。 I made two dishes today. **B**〈名〉 stir-fried dish: 午饭我要了两个～和一杯啤酒。 I ordered two dishes and a glass of beer for lunch.
【炒地皮】chǎo dìpí〈动〉 speculate in real estate
【炒饭】chǎofàn〈名〉 fried rice: 蛋～ egg-fried rice
【炒房】chǎofáng〈动〉 speculate in real estate: 温州～团 Wenzhou housing speculators
【炒更】chǎogēng〈动〉〈方〉 moonlight
【炒股】chǎogǔ〈动〉 speculate on the stock market: 他～赚了很多钱。 He played the market and made a lot of money.
【炒锅】chǎoguō〈名〉 wok
【炒汇】chǎohuì〈动〉 speculate in foreign exchange
【炒货】chǎohuò〈名〉 pan-fried seeds and nuts
【炒家】chǎojiā〈名〉 speculator
【炒冷饭】chǎo lěngfàn〈惯〉〈喻〉dish up the same old stuff
【炒买炒卖】chǎomǎi-chǎomài〈俗〉 buy quick and sell quick
【炒米】chǎomǐ〈名〉 **1**（指米） parched rice **2**（指蒙古食品） millet stir-fried in butter
【炒米花】chǎomǐhuā〈名〉 puffed rice
【炒面】chǎomiàn〈名〉 **1**（指面条） *chow mein* [stir-fried noodles with shredded meat and vegetables] **2**（指面粉） parched wheat flour
【炒勺】 chǎosháo 〈名〉 round-bottomed frying pan
【炒鱿鱼】chǎo yóuyú〈惯〉〈喻〉 give sb. the sack: 被～ get the sack ‖ 他炒了老板的鱿鱼。 He upped and resigned on the boss.
【炒作】chǎozuò〈动〉 sensationalize: 恶意～ publicize sth. maliciously

chào

耖 chào
A〈名〉 harrow-like implement for pulverizing soil
B〈动〉 level the ground with a harrow-like implement

chē

车（車）chē
A〈名〉 **1**（交通工具） vehicle: 驾～ drive a car ‖ 派～接人 send a car for sb. ‖ 机动～ motor vehicle ‖ 旅游～ sightseeing bus

‖ 首班/末班～ first/last bus ▸～祸, ～辆, 乘～ **2**（带轮装置） wheeled instrument: 滑～ pulley ▸～床, 纺～ **3**（机器） machine: ▸～间, 试～
B〈动〉 **1**（指汲水） lift water using a waterwheel: ～水 lift water by waterwheel **2**（指用车床） shape on a lathe: ～机器零件 shape a machine part on a lathe **3**〈方〉（侧转） turn: ～过头来 turn one's head ‖ 他迅速～过身去。He turned around quickly. **4**〈方〉（用车拉） carry in a cart: 把垃圾～走 cart away the rubbish **5**〈方〉（指用缝纫机）make clothes with a sewing machine: ～衣服 make clothes with a sewing machine
▸jū

【车把】chēbǎ〈名〉 handlebar

【车把式】chēbǎshi〈名〉 coachman

【车把势】chēbǎshi = 车把式 chēbǎshi

【车帮】chēbāng〈名〉 sideboard of a cart or truck

【车场】chēchǎng〈名〉 car park: 多层～ multi-storey car park ▸停～

【车臣】Chēchén〈名〉 Chechnya: ～共和国 Republic of Chechnya ‖ ～人 Chechen ‖ ～语 Chechen

【车程】chēchéng〈名〉 drive: 两小时的～ a two-hour journey

【车床】chēchuáng〈名〉［机械］ lathe: 半自动/自动～ semi-automatic/automatic lathe

【车次】chēcì〈名〉 **1**（指火车） train number **2**（指长途汽车） coach number

【车带】chēdài〈名〉〈口〉 tyre: ～爆了 have a blowout

【车贷】chēdài〈名〉 vehicle-purchasing loan: 办理～业务 manage a car loan business

【车刀】chēdāo〈名〉 lathe tool

【车到山前必有路】chē dào shānqián bì yǒu lù〈俗〉〈喻〉 things will eventually sort themselves out

【车道】chēdào〈名〉 lane: 单/双～ single/double lane ‖ 六～公路 six-lane highway

【车灯】chēdēng〈名〉 vehicle light: 打亮～ put one's lights on

【车顶】chēdǐng〈名〉 roof: ～天窗 sunshine roof

【车队】chēduì〈名〉 **1**（指队伍） motorcade: 总统～ presidential motorcade **2**（指组织单位） convoy: 六～ convoy number six

【车匪路霸】chēfěi-lùbà〈名〉 highwayman

【车费】chēfèi〈名〉 fare

【车份儿】chēfènr〈名〉〈方〉〈旧〉vehicle rent

【车夫】chēfū〈名〉〈旧〉 driver: 人力～ rickshaw boy ‖ 三轮～ pedicab driver

【车工】chēgōng〈名〉 **1**（指工种） lathe work: ～车间 turning shop **2**（指工人） lathe operator

【车公里】chēgōnglǐ〈量〉vehicle kilometre

【车轱辘】chēgūlu〈名〉〈口〉 wheel (of a vehicle):〈喻〉～话 repetitious talk

【车行】chēháng〈名〉 **1**（指租车） car company **2**（指售车） vehicle dealer's shop **3**（指修车） garage

【车祸】chēhuò〈名〉 traffic accident: 死于～ die in a road accident ‖ 发生了一起～。A car accident occurred.

【车技】chējì〈名〉 **1**［杂技］ trick-cycling **2**（指开车） driving skill: 你的～还不错。You're pretty good at driving.

【车架】chējià〈名〉 frame (of a car, bicycle, etc.)

【车间】chējiān〈名〉 workshop: 锻工～ blacksmith's ‖ 印刷～ printing shop ‖ 装配～ assembly shop ‖ ～主任 workshop manager

【车检】chējiǎn〈动〉 inspect a vehicle: ～中心 vehicle inspection centre

【车距】chējù〈名〉 distance between vehicles: 请保持～。 Please keep your distance.

【车库】chēkù〈名〉 garage

【车筐】chēkuāng〈名〉 bicycle basket

【车况】chēkuàng〈名〉 condition of a vehicle: ～良好。The car is in good condition.

【车链】chēliàn〈名〉 bicycle chain

【车辆】chēliàng〈名〉 vehicle: ～厂 carriage/wagon works ‖ 禁止～通行。 No through road.

【车裂】chēliè〈动〉〈古〉 tear a person apart with five chariots

【车铃】chēlíng〈名〉 bicycle bell

【车流】chēliú〈名〉 traffic flow: ～量 traffic flow

【车轮】chēlún〈名〉 wheel: ～打滑 wheel slips ‖ 备用～ spare tyre ‖〈喻〉 历史的～ wheel of history

【车轮战】chēlúnzhàn〈名〉〈喻〉 tactic of fighting an enemy by turns to wear him down

【车马费】chēmǎfèi〈名〉 travel allowance

【车马盈门】chēmǎ-yíngmén〈成〉 the house receives a host of distinguished guests

【车门】chēmén〈名〉 car door: 打开～ open the door

【车牌】chēpái〈名〉 number plate〈英〉; license plate〈美〉: ～号码 licence number

【车棚】chēpéng〈名〉 shed for vehicles: 自行车～ bicycle shed

【车篷】chēpéng〈名〉 awning of a vehicle

【车皮】chēpí〈名〉 railway carriage

【车票】chēpiào〈名〉 ticket

【车前草】chēqiáncǎo〈名〉［植物］Asiatic plantain

【车钱】chēqián〈名〉 fare

【车圈】chēquān〈名〉 wheel rim

【车身】chēshēn〈名〉 body of a vehicle: ～长度 length of a vehicle

【车市】chēshì〈名〉 car market

【车手】chēshǒu〈名〉 racing driver

【车水马龙】chēshuǐ-mǎlóng〈成〉 heavy traffic

【车速】chēsù〈名〉 **1**（指车辆） vehicle speed: 每小时一百公里的～ a speed of 100 kilometres per hour **2**（指车床） speed of a lathe

【车胎】chētāi〈名〉 tyre: ～瘪了 have a flat tyre ‖ ～防滑链 tyre chain

【车条】chētiáo〈名〉〈口〉 spoke

【车贴】chētiē〈名〉 travel allowance

【车头】chētóu〈名〉 **1**（指汽车） front of a vehicle **2**（指火车） engine: ▸火～

【车尾】chēwěi〈名〉 rear of a vehicle

【车尾行李箱】chēwěi xínglixiāng〈名〉 boot〈英〉; trunk〈美〉

【车位】chēwèi〈动〉 parking space

【车险】chēxiǎn〈名〉 car insurance

【车厢】chēxiāng〈名〉 **1**（用于载人） carriage〈英〉; car〈美〉: 卧铺～ sleeping car ‖ 我的座位在第三～。 My seat is in car No 3. **2**（用于载货） cargo body

【车削】chēxiāo〈名〉［机械］ turning

【车型】chēxíng〈名〉 make and model

【车载电话】chēzài diànhuà〈名〉vehicular telephone

【车载电台】chēzài diàntái〈名〉 vehicle radio station

【车载斗量】chēzài-dǒuliáng〈成〉 be common and numerous

【车闸】chēzhá〈名〉 brake

【车展】chēzhǎn〈名〉 car exhibition

【车站】chēzhàn〈名〉 **1**（停靠点） stop **2**（总站） station: ～候车室 station waiting room ‖ ～站长 station master

【车照】chēzhào〈名〉 driving licence: 出示～ show a driver's licence ‖ 申请/吊销～ apply for/revoke a driving licence

【车辙】chēzhé〈名〉 track: 深深的～ deep ruts

【车轴】chēzhóu〈名〉 axle

【车主】chēzhǔ〈名〉 vehicle owner

【车资】chēzī〈名〉 (passenger's) fare

【车子】chēzi〈名〉〈口〉 small vehicle

【车组】chēzǔ〈名〉 **1**（指人员） crew: ～人员 crew member ‖ 公共汽车/列车～ bus/train crew **2**（指车辆） motorcade

【车座】chēzuò〈名〉（指汽车） car seat;（指自行车） saddle

砗（硨）chē

【砗磲】chēqú〈名〉［动物］ giant clam

chě

尺 chě〈名〉［音乐］ note on the *gongche* (工尺) scale, corresponding to 2 in *jianpu* (简谱) numbered musical notation
▸chǐ

扯 chě〈动〉 **1**（拉）pull: ～袖子 tug at sb.'s sleeve ‖ ～住不放 grab onto and not let go ‖ 用力一～ give sth. a good tug ‖〈喻〉～着嗓门喊 shout at the top of one's voice ‖〈喻〉别把正事和娱乐～在一起。 Don't mix business with pleasure. ▸～后腿, 牵～ **2**（撕） rip: ～成两半 tear sth. in half ‖ 这种纸一～就破。 This paper tears easily. **3**（聊） chat: ～闲话 have a chat ‖ 他的话～得太长了。 He dragged on and on. ▸～淡, 东拉西～, 胡～, 闲～

【扯淡】chědàn〈动〉〈方〉 talk nonsense: 别瞎～。 Stop that nonsense.

【扯后腿】chě hòutuǐ〈惯〉〈贬〉 hold sb. back

【扯谎】chěhuǎng〈动〉 tell a lie: 当面～ tell a bare-faced lie

【扯家常】chějiācháng〈动〉 chit-chat

【扯皮】chěpí〈动〉〈贬〉 pass the buck: 互相～ push responsibility onto each other ‖ 你是负责这份工作的人，不要同他人～。 You are the one who took on this job. Don't try to get out of it.

【扯平】chěpíng〈动〉 even things up: 你付车钱我买门票,我们就～了。 You pay the ride, I'll pay for the tickets. Then we'll be even. ‖ 第四季度公司收支勉强～。 In the fourth quarter the firm barely broke even.

【扯谈】chětán〈动〉 chat

【扯闲篇】chě xiánpiān〈惯〉 chat about mindless things

chè

彻（徹）chè

〈动〉 pierce: 冷～骨髓。 The cold cuts one to the bone. ‖ 胜利的歌声响～四方。 Songs of victory are ringing out far and wide. ▸～底, 贯～, 透～

【彻查】chèchá〈动〉 investigate thoroughly: ～飞机失事原因 launch a thorough investigation into the cause of the air crash

【彻底】chèdǐ〈形〉 complete: ～摧毁 destroy sth. completely ‖ ～解决 settle sth. once and for all ‖ ～坦白 make a total

C

confession ‖ ～完蛋 be completely finished ‖ ～消灭 totally eradicate

【彻骨】chègǔ〈动〉 be chilled to the bone: 寒风～。The wind is piercingly cold.

【彻头彻尾】chètóu-chèwěi〈成〉〈贬〉 out-and-out: ～的谎言 out-and-out lie ‖ ～的骗局 deception from beginning to end

【彻悟】chèwù〈动〉 come to a complete awakening

【彻夜】chèyè〈副〉 all night: ～未眠 not sleep a wink all night ‖ ～工作/学习 work/study all night

C

坼 chè〈动〉〈书〉 split open: 天旱地～。The land cracked in the drought.

【坼裂】chèliè〈动〉〈书〉 split open

掣 chè〈动〉 1（拽） pull: ▸～肘, 牵～ 2（闪过） flash past: ▸风驰电～ 3（抽） draw: ～签 draw lots ‖ 把手～回去 withdraw one's hand

【掣肘】chèzhǒu〈动〉〈喻〉 prevent sb. from doing something

撤 chè〈动〉 1（取消） remove;（拿走） clear away: ～碗碟/茶具 clear away the dishes/tea set ‖ ～去冷盘，上热菜 remove the cold dishes and bring out the hot ones ‖ ～去职务 remove sb. from office ▸～销, ～职 2（退出） retreat: ～到安全地带 withdraw to a safe area ‖ 军队～走了。The troops pulled out. ▸～兵, ～退

【撤编】chèbiān〈动〉 close down an establishment

【撤兵】chèbīng〈动〉 withdraw troops

【撤并】chèbìng〈动〉 dissolve and merge: ～子公司 dissolve and merge subsidiary companies

【撤出】chèchū〈动〉withdraw: ～军队 pull troops out ‖ ～危险地带 evacuate a danger zone

【撤除】chèchú〈动〉 remove: ～军事基地 remove a military base ‖ ～路障 demolish a barricade

【撤防】chèfáng〈动〉 withdraw a garrison: 部队～ withdraw troops from fortified positions

【撤岗】chègǎng〈动〉 withdraw a sentry

【撤柜】chèguì〈动〉 take off the shelves: 问题奶粉已全部～，停止销售。The problem milk powder has been taken off the shelves and is no longer being sold.

【撤换】chèhuàn〈动〉 dismiss and replace: ～旧桌椅 replace the old desks and chairs ‖ ～内阁成员 reshuffle cabinet ministers ‖ 他们要求～市长。They called for the dismissal of the mayor.

【撤回】chèhuí〈动〉 1（指军队） withdraw;（指外派人员） recall: ～大使/代表 recall an ambassador/a representative ‖ ～军队 recall troops 2（收回） revoke: ～辞呈 withdraw one's resignation ‖ ～起诉 drop a charge ‖ ～申请 withdraw one's application

【撤架】chèjià〈动〉 take off the shelves: 该商品已全部～，停止销售。This product has been taken off the shelves and is no longer being sold.

【撤军】chèjūn〈动〉 recall troops: 单方面～ unilaterally withdraw troops ‖ 无条件～ unconditional withdrawal of the troops

【撤离】chèlí〈动〉 evacuate: ～危险地带 evacuate a danger zone ‖ ～现场 vacate the scene

【撤诉】chèsù〈动〉 drop a charge

【撤退】chètuì〈动〉 retreat: 下令～ order a withdrawal ‖ 掩护～ cover sb.'s retreat

【撤席】chèxí〈动〉 clear the table (after a feast)

【撤消】chèxiāo = 撤销 chèxiāo

【撤销】chèxiāo〈动〉revoke: ～处分 revoke a penalty ‖ ～订单 withdraw an order (for goods) ‖ ～原计划 abandon the original plan ‖ ～职务 remove sb. from office

【撤职】chèzhí〈动〉 dismiss sb. from their post: ～处分 punishment by dismissal ‖ ～查办 discharge sb. from office and put them on trial

【撤资】chèzī〈动〉 withdraw investment

【撤走】chèzǒu〈动〉 withdraw: ～军队 recall troops ‖ ～专家 withdraw experts

澈 chè〈形〉 clear: ▸澄～, 明～, 清～

【澈底】chèdǐ = 彻底 chèdǐ

chēn

抻 chēn〈动〉〈口〉stretch: ～长 lengthen by stretching ‖ ～着脖子看 stretch out one's neck to look

【抻面】chēnmiàn〈名〉 hand-pulled/hand-stretched noodles

琛 chēn〈名〉〈书〉 treasure

嗔 chēn〈动〉 1（怒） get angry: 转～为喜 go from anger to happiness ▸～怒 2（对人不满） blame: ▸～怪

【嗔怪】chēnguài〈动〉 rebuke: 招待不周，请勿～。Please excuse me if I've been a poor host.

【嗔怒】chēnnù〈动〉 get angry

【嗔色】chēnsè〈名〉 sullen look

【嗔怨】chēnyuàn〈动〉 complain

瞋 chēn〈动〉〈书〉 glare at

【瞋目而视】chēnmù'érshì〈成〉 stare angrily: 两人～。The two men glared angrily at each other.

chén

臣 chén〈名〉 1（指官吏） official under a feudal ruler: 君～ monarch and his subjects ▸～民, 乱～贼子, 忠～ 2（官吏自称） your servant: ▸～妾 3〈书〉〈旧〉〈谦〉（古人自称） I

【臣服】chénfú〈动〉〈书〉 acknowledge allegiance to: 无须～于大国。There is no need to submit to the rule of a superpower.

【臣僚】chénliáo〈名〉 body of civil and military officials in feudal times

【臣民】chénmín〈名〉 officials and subjects of a feudal ruler: 君主及其～ monarch and his subjects

【臣妾】chénqiè〈名〉〈旧〉 [a form of self-address] your servant woman

【臣子】chénzǐ〈名〉 feudal official

尘（塵） chén〈名〉 1（灰尘） dust: 除～ dust ‖ 防～网 dust gauze ‖ 吸～器 vacuum cleaner ▸～土, 一～不染 2（尘世） this world: ▸～世, 红～ 3〈书〉（踪迹） track: ▸步人后～, 前～

【尘埃】chén'āi〈名〉 dust: 拂去～ flick off dust

【尘埃落定】chén'āi luòdìng〈成〉〈喻〉all done and dusted

【尘暴】chénbào〈名〉［气象］ dust storm

【尘凡】chénfán〈名〉 this secular world

【尘肺】chénfèi ▸p. 50〈名〉［医学］ pneumoconiosis

【尘封】chénfēng〈动〉〈书〉 be covered with dust: 这些书籍被～达十年之久。These books were covered with dust for ten long years. ‖〈喻〉～的往事 the dusty past

【尘垢】chéngòu〈名〉 dust and dirt

【尘寰】chénhuán〈名〉［佛教］this mortal world: 撒手～ let go of this mortal life

【尘芥】chénjiè〈名〉〈喻〉 trivialities: 他视名利如～。He regards fame and gain as nothing.

【尘粒】chénlì〈名〉［工程］ dust particle

【尘虑】chénlǜ = 尘念 chénniàn

【尘念】chénniàn〈名〉 worldly desires: ～俱消 be completely free of worldly thoughts

【尘世】chénshì〈名〉［宗教］ this mortal life: 弃绝～ forsake the world

【尘事】chénshì〈名〉 secular affairs: 不问～ pay no attention to worldly affairs

【尘俗】chénsú〈名〉 1（世俗） the world 2〈书〉（尘世） this mortal life

【尘土】chéntǔ〈名〉 dust: ～飞扬 dust swirls in the air ‖ ～蔽日。Clouds of dust obscured the sky. ‖ 汽车飞驰而过，扬起一片～。The car raced past, leaving a trail of dust.

【尘雾】chénwù〈名〉 1（尘土） cloud of dust: 一片～ a cloud of dust 2（云雾） dust fog

【尘嚣】chénxiāo〈名〉〈书〉 hubbub: 远离～ keep away from a noisy place

【尘烟】chényān〈名〉 1（尘土） cloud of dust: ～滚滚 clouds of dust churning 2（尘土和烟雾） smoke and dust: ～弥漫 be heavy with smoke and dust

【尘缘】chényuán〈名〉［宗教］ worldly desires: ～未断 have not broken free from the bonds of this world

辰[1] chén〈名〉 fifth of the twelve Earthly Branches (地支)

辰[2] chén〈名〉 1（众星） celestial bodies: ▸星～ 2（时间） time: ▸诞～, 良～美景 3（计时单位） any of the traditional twelve two-hour periods of the day: ▸时～

【辰光】chénguāng〈名〉〈方〉 time: ～还早。It's early yet.

【辰砂】chénshā〈名〉［矿业］ cinnabar

【辰时】chénshí〈名〉〈旧〉 period of the day from 7 am to 9 am

【辰星】chénxīng〈名〉〈旧〉［天文］ Mercury

沈 chén = 沉 chén ▸shěn

沉[1] chén〈形〉 1（指程度） deep: 睡得很～ sleep very soundly ▸～迷, ～思, ～痛 2（指颜色） dark;〈喻〉 glum: 他脸色阴～。He looks very gloomy. 3（指重量） heavy: 这桌子真～。The table is heavy. ▸～甸甸, ～重 4（指感觉） heavy: 腿发～ heavy legs ‖ 眼皮～ heavy eyelids ▸昏～

沉[2] chén

A〈动〉 1（指在水中） sink: ～入水中 be submerged in water ▸～淀, ～积, 石～大

海 2 (下降) fall: 地基下～。 The foundations have subsided. ‖ 月落星～。 The moon is down and the stars are out. ▶～降, ～陷 3 (使下沉) keep down: ～下心来工作 get down to work ‖ 他一听这话就～下了脸。 His face froze at the remark. ▶～鱼落雁, 破釜～舟 4 (沦落) sink into a certain condition: ～于酒色 indulge in wine and women ▶～沦, ～湎
B 〈形〉 low-spirited: ▶～郁, 低～, 消～
【沉沉】 chénchén 〈形〉 1 (重) heavy 2 (程度深) deep: ～入睡 sink/fall into a deep/sound sleep ‖ 暮霭～。 Dusk is falling. ▶死气～
【沉船】 chénchuán 〈名〉 sunken ship
【沉甸甸】 chéndiàndiàn 〈形〉 heavy: ～的包裹 heavy parcel ‖ 〈喻〉 女儿的病使他心里～的。 His daughter's illness weighed heavily on his mind.
【沉淀】 chéndiàn A 〈动〉 1 (指溶液) deposit: 咖啡渣会～下去的。 The coffee grounds will settle. 2 〈喻〉 (凝聚) amass: 文化～ cultural growth ‖ 资金～ accumulation of capital B 〈名〉 sediment: ～池 sedimentation tank
【沉淀物】 chéndiànwù 〈名〉 sediment: 有～的葡萄酒 wine with a sediment
【沉放】 chénfàng 〈动〉 submerge: 把过江钢管～水底。 Submerge the steel pipe that crosses the river.
【沉浮】 chénfú 〈动〉 〈喻〉 rise and fall: 宦海～ the ups and downs of an official career
【沉痼】 chéngù 〈名〉 〈书〉 1 (疾病) chronic disease 2 〈喻〉 (恶习) incurable bad habit: 他有小偷小摸的～。 He is an inveterate pilferer.
【沉酣】 chénhān 〈动〉 〈书〉 be deeply immersed: ～经史 be deeply immersed in the study of classical works ‖ 睡梦～ be submerged in sleep
【沉缓】 chénhuǎn 〈形〉 heavy and slow
【沉积】 chénjī 〈动〉 1 (指物体) deposit: 河口～了淤泥。 The river deposited silt at its mouth. 2 [地质] [化学] sedimentation: 血管里的钙～ calcium deposits in the blood vessels ▶～岩 3 〈喻〉 (沉淀、积聚) accumulate: 历史/文化～ accretion of history/culture
【沉积构造】 chénjī gòuzào 〈名〉 [地质] sedimentary structure
【沉积物】 chénjīwù 〈名〉 [地质] sediment
【沉积岩】 chénjīyán 〈名〉 [地质] sedimentary rock: 石灰岩是～。 Limestone is a sedimentary rock.
【沉寂】 chénjì 〈形〉 1 (寂静) quiet: ～的山谷 hushed valley ‖ 死一般的～ unearthly silence 2 (无音信) without news: 他走后, 音信～。 We have not heard from him since he left.
【沉降】 chénjiàng 〈动〉 subside: 地面～ earth subsidence
【沉降带】 chénjiàngdài 〈名〉 zone of subsidence
【沉浸】 chénjìn 〈动〉 be immersed: ～在悲痛中 be buried in grief ‖ 大家都～在节日的气氛里。 Everyone was enveloped by the festive mood.
【沉井】 chénjǐng 〈名〉 [建筑] open caisson
【沉静】 chénjìng 〈形〉 1 (安静) calm: 打破～ shatter the calm ‖ 夜晚的～ still of the night 2 (沉稳) serene: 神色～ wear a serene look ‖ 性情～ placid temper
【沉疴】 chénkē 〈名〉 〈书〉 chronic illness: ～缠身 be plagued with constant illness
【沉雷】 chénléi 〈名〉 muffled thunder
【沉沦】 chénlún 〈动〉 fall into: 不甘～ refuse to sink into degradation ‖ 赌博酗酒使他彻底～了。 Gambling and drinking completely sank him.
【沉落】 chénluò 〈动〉 1 (下降) sink: ～水中 sink into water ‖ 太阳向西山～。 The sun is setting behind the mountains in the west. 2 (败落) decline: 家道～。 The family fortunes declined.
【沉闷】 chénmèn 〈形〉 1 (指天气、气氛) oppressive: 气氛～ stuffy atmosphere ‖ 天气～ depressing weather 2 (指人) depressed: 陷入～之中 lapse into dreary depression ‖ 心情～ feel depressed 3 (指性格) undemonstrative: 性格～be reserved by nature
【沉迷】 chénmí 〈动〉 indulge in: ～于吃喝玩乐 indulge in eating, drinking, and merrymaking ‖ ～于幻想 be given to fantasies/illusions/reveries ‖ ～不醒 be deeply infatuated
【沉眠】 chénmián 〈动〉 be sound asleep
【沉绵】 chénmián 〈形〉 〈书〉 suffering from a lingering illness: ～枕席 be bedridden with a lingering disease
【沉湎】 chénmiǎn 〈动〉 〈书〉 abandon oneself to: ～于赌博 indulge in gambling ‖ ～于酒色 overindulge in wine and women
【沉没】 chénmò 〈动〉 sink: 轮船在风暴中～。 The ship went down in the storm. ‖ 这艘船触礁～了。 The ship hit a rock and sank.
【沉默】 chénmò A 〈形〉 taciturn: 安静～ be quiet and uncommunicative ▶～寡言 B 〈动〉 be silent: 保持～ keep quiet ‖ ～良久 remain silent for a long time ‖ ～就是认可。 Silence counts as consent.
【沉默寡言】 chénmòguǎyán 〈成〉 be of few words: ～的人 man of few words
【沉溺】 chénnì 〈动〉 indulge in: ～于电脑游戏 indulge in computer games ‖ ～于酒色 be given to wine and women
【沉潜】 chénqián A 〈动〉 1 (沉于水中) stay under water: ～于海底 submerge at the bottom of the sea 2 (潜心于) concentrate one's mind: ～在工作里 devote oneself to one's work B 〈形〉 〈书〉 reserved: ～好学 quiet and studious
【沉睡】 chénshuì 〈动〉 be fast asleep: ～不醒 be sound asleep ‖ 从～中醒来 awake from a sound sleep
【沉思】 chénsī 〈动〉 contemplate: 陷入～ be lost in thought ‖ ～许久 ponder for quite some time ‖ ～默想 ponder in silence
【沉痛】 chéntòng 〈形〉 1 (极其悲痛) deeply grieved: ～哀悼 express profound sorrow over ‖ 怀着～的心情 with a heavy heart 2 (深刻而痛心) bitter: 接受～的教训 learn a lesson from bitter experience
【沉稳】 chénwěn 〈形〉 1 (沉着稳重) steady: ～可靠的人 steady and reliable person 2 (安稳踏实) untroubled: 睡得～ be sound asleep
【沉陷】 chénxiàn 〈动〉 1 (下沉) sink: 地基～了。 The foundations have subsided. 2 (陷入) get stuck: 轮子～进了泥沼。 The wheels got stuck in the mud. 3 〈喻〉 (沉湎) indulge: ～于往事的回忆中 allow oneself to wallow in the past
【沉香】 chénxiāng 〈名〉 [植物] eaglewood
【沉箱】 chénxiāng 〈名〉 [建筑] caisson
【沉毅】 chényì 〈形〉 steady and strong: 行动～果敢 act with fortitude and resolve
【沉吟】 chényín 〈动〉 1 (低声吟咏) recite in a low voice 2 (自言自语) mutter to oneself 3 (犹豫不决) be unable to make up one's mind: ～良久 think for a long time ‖ ～不决 be undecided
【沉勇】 chényǒng 〈形〉 calm, steady and courageous
【沉鱼落雁】 chényú-luòyàn 〈成〉 [of feminine beauty] be extremely beautiful
【沉郁】 chényù 〈形〉 depressed: 心情～ feel depressed
【沉冤】 chényuān 〈名〉 long-term injustice: 百年～终得昭雪。 The century-old grievance was finally redressed.
【沉冤莫白】 chényuān-mòbái 〈成〉 a long-standing injustice that cannot be righted
【沉渣】 chénzhā 〈名〉 1 (渣滓) dregs: 清洗茶壶里的～ rinse the dregs out of the teapot 2 〈喻〉 dregs of society: ～泛起 the surfacing of the dregs of society
【沉滞】 chénzhì 〈形〉 〈书〉 stagnant
【沉重】 chénzhòng 〈形〉 1 (重) heavy: 心情～ be heavy-hearted ‖ ～的代价 heavy price ‖ ～的负担 heavy burden ‖ ～的打击 hard blow 2 (严重) serious: 病情～ be critically ill
【沉住气】 chénzhùqì 〈动〉 keep cool: 沉不住气 lose one's composure ‖ 沉得住气 be able to keep calm ‖ ～! Steady on!
【沉着】 chénzhuó 〈形〉 composed: ～应付 deal with sth. calmly ‖ ～冷静 be steady and calm ‖ 勇敢～ be brave and composed
【沉醉】 chénzuì 〈动〉 1 (大醉) be very drunk 2 〈喻〉 become intoxicated: ～于成功之中 revel in one's success ‖ ～在节日的欢乐里 be intoxicated with the joyous spirit of the festival

忱 chén 〈名〉 〈书〉 sincerity: ▶热～, 谢～

陈[1] (陳) chén

A 〈动〉 1 (排列) display: ▶～列, ～设 2 (描述) explain: 详～ explain in detail ▶～述, ～诉
B 〈形〉 old: ▶～旧, 推～出新, 新～代谢

陈[2] (陳) Chén 〈名〉 1 (指国名) Chen [state in the Zhou Dynasty] 2 (南朝之一) Chen Dynasty

【陈兵】 chénbīng 〈动〉 deploy troops: ～百万 deploy a million soldiers ‖ ～边境 mass troops along the border
【陈陈相因】 chénchén-xiāngyīn 〈成〉 〈喻〉 stay in the same old routine
【陈词】 chéncí A 〈动〉 state one's opinion: 慷慨～ express oneself passionately and articulately ‖ 冒昧～ venture an opinion B 〈名〉 clichés: ▶～滥调
【陈词滥调】 chéncí-làndiào 〈成〉 clichés: 满纸～ writing full of platitudes
【陈醋】 chéncù 〈名〉 mature vinegar
【陈放】 chénfàng 〈动〉 put on display: ～展品 display exhibits
【陈腐】 chénfǔ 〈形〉 〈贬〉 hackneyed: 观念～ old-fashioned concept ‖ ～之见 hackneyed opinion
【陈谷子烂芝麻】 chén gǔzi làn zhīma 〈俗〉 〈喻〉 petty remarks about old issues
【陈规】 chénguī 〈名〉 outdated convention: 打破～ break old routines ‖ 墨守～ stick to old convention
【陈规陋习】 chénguī-lòuxí 〈成〉 outworn customs and objectionable habits: 为～所拘囿 limit oneself to outdated customs and habits
【陈货】 chénhuò 〈名〉 old stock
【陈迹】 chénjì 〈名〉 thing of the past: 历史～ historical site
【陈酒】 chénjiǔ 〈名〉 1 (陈年的酒) mellow wine 2 〈方〉 (黄酒) yellow rice wine

C

【陈旧】chénjiù〈形〉 antiquated: 观念～ old-fashioned notion ‖ 设备～ out-of-date equipment ‖ 思想～ have old-fashioned ideas
【陈粮】chénliáng〈名〉 grain stocked for many years
【陈列】chénliè〈动〉display: ～馆/室 exhibition hall ‖ 家具/汽车～室 furniture/car showroom ‖ 请勿触摸～品。 Please do not touch the exhibits. ‖ 这里～着各式服装。 A range of different styles of clothes is exhibited here.
【陈年】chénnián〈形〉 aged: ～佳酿 good vintage ‖ ～老酒 wine preserved for a long time ‖ ～旧帐 long-standing debts
【陈酿】chénniàng〈名〉 mature wine
【陈皮】chénpí〈名〉［中药］ dried orange peel
【陈皮梅】chénpíméi〈名〉 preserved plums
【陈情】chénqíng〈动〉〈书〉 give a full account: 恳切～ state sincerely
【陈请】chénqǐng〈动〉 state and plead: ～上级批准 petition the higher authorities for approval
【陈设】chénshè **A**〈动〉 display **B**〈名〉 furnishings: ～大方 be furnished in good taste ‖ ～豪华 be luxuriously furnished ‖ ～朴素/雅致 be modestly/tastefully furnished ‖ 没有～的房间 bare room
【陈世美】Chén Shìměi〈名〉 man who deserts his wife after securing a high position
【陈述】chénshù〈动〉 state: ～案情 state a case ‖ ～理由 state one's reasons ‖ ～事实 state the facts ‖ 做出～ make a statement (of sth.) ‖ 做十分钟的～ make a 10-minute presentation ‖ 如实地～ give a faithful account
【陈述句】chénshùjù〈名〉［语言］ declarative statement
【陈述语气】chénshù yǔqì〈名〉［语言］ indicative mood
【陈说】chénshuō **A**〈动〉 explain: ～事件的经过 give an account of an incident **B** = 陈言 chényán B
【陈诉】chénsù〈动〉 relate: ～委屈 state one's grievances
【陈言】chényán **A**〈动〉 air one's views: 率直～ openly declare one's views **B**〈名〉〈书〉 hackneyed words and expressions: ▸～务去
【陈言务去】chényánwùqù〈成〉 obsolete words and hackneyed expressions must be eliminated
【陈账】chénzhàng〈名〉 **1**（老账） old debt: 清还～ pay off old debts **2**（旧事） something that happened a long time ago
【陈芝麻烂谷子】chén zhīma làn gǔzi = 陈谷子烂芝麻 chén gǔzi làn zhīma

宸 chén〈名〉〈书〉 **1**（大房屋） great mansion **2**（皇宫） imperial palace: ～扉 gate of the imperial palace **3**（皇位） throne;（帝王） emperor: ～衷 wishes of an emperor

梣 chén〈名〉［植物］ Bunge's ash

晨 chén〈名〉 morning: ▸～星, 清～, 早～
【晨报】chénbào〈名〉 morning newspaper
【晨炊】chénchuī〈名〉〈书〉morning cooking
【晨祷】chéndǎo〈名〉［宗教］ morning prayer
【晨光】chénguāng〈名〉 first light of day: ～悄悄地穿过百叶窗。 The morning light was stealing through the shutters.
【晨光熹微】chénguāng-xīwēi〈成〉 first faint rays of dawn
【晨昏】chénhūn〈名〉〈书〉dawn and dusk
【晨练】chénliàn〈名〉 morning exercise: 进行～ exercise in the morning
【晨雾】chénwù〈名〉 morning mist: ～笼罩着河面。 Morning fog veiled the river.
【晨夕】chénxī〈名〉 morning and evening
【晨曦】chénxī〈名〉〈书〉 light of the early morning sun
【晨星】chénxīng〈名〉 **1**（早晨的星星） morning stars: 寥若～ few and far between **2**［天文］ morning star
【晨钟暮鼓】chénzhōng-mùgǔ = 暮鼓晨钟 mùgǔ-chénzhōng

谌（諶） chén〈书〉
A〈动〉 have faith
B〈副〉 truly

chěn

碜 chěn〈形〉 **1**（指外貌） ugly: ▸寒～ **2**〈口〉（指食物） gritty: ▸牙～

chèn

衬（襯） chèn
A〈形〉 close to the skin: ▸～布, ～裤, ～衫
B〈名〉 lining: 钢～ steel liner ‖ 领/衣～ collar/coat lining
C〈动〉 **1**（加衬里） line: ～一层布 put a piece of cloth underneath ‖ 一双～着毛皮的手套 a pair of fur-lined gloves **2**（衬托） contrast with: 红花有绿叶～着，显得更加鲜艳夺目。 The red flowers stood out in bold relief against a background of green leaves. ▸～托, 反～, 陪～
【衬布】chènbù〈名〉 lining cloth
【衬垫】chèndiàn〈名〉［机械］ liner: 接合～ joint liner
【衬裤】chènkù〈名〉 underpants
【衬里】chènlǐ〈名〉 lining
【衬料】chènliào〈名〉 lining
【衬领】chènlǐng〈名〉 detachable collar
【衬袍】chènpáo〈名〉 undergown
【衬裙】chènqún〈名〉 petticoat
【衬衫】chènshān〈名〉 shirt
【衬套】chèntào〈名〉 bush
【衬托】chèntuō〈动〉 set off: 黑色的丝绒～出钻石的璀璨。 The black velvet set off the brilliance of the diamond.
【衬页】chènyè〈名〉［印刷］ flyleaf
【衬衣】chènyī〈名〉 shirt
【衬映】chènyìng〈动〉 set off: 蓝天～着白色的山巅。 The white peak contrasts with the azure sky.
【衬纸】chènzhǐ〈名〉 slip sheet
【衬字】chènzì〈名〉 word inserted into a line of verse or the lyrics of a song for balance

称（稱） chèn
A〈动〉 match: 他的讲话和晚会的气氛不相～。 His speech doesn't fit the mood of the party. ▸～心如意, ～职, 相～
B〈形〉 suitable: ▸对～, 匀～
▸chēng
【称身】chènshēn〈动〉 fit: 她这条裙子极～。 The skirt fits her perfectly.
【称心】chènxīn〈形〉 satisfactory: ～的工作 satisfactory job ‖ 日子过得很～ live in contentment
【称心如意】chènxīn-rúyì〈成〉 have sth. as one wishes: 她找到了一份～的工作。 She found a job that was perfect for her.
【称愿】chènyuàn〈动〉 be gratified
【称职】chènzhí〈形〉 fully qualified: ～的教师 qualified teacher ‖ 不～ be unequal to the task

趁 chèn〈介〉 taking advantage of: ～热吃 eat while it's hot ‖ ～你有空的时候多看些书。 Do read more books when you have the time. ‖ ～此机会我发表了自己的观点。 I took this opportunity to venture my views. ▸～便, ～势, ～早
【趁便】chènbiàn〈副〉 when it is convenient: 回家的路上我～去看了一位朋友。 I called on a friend of mine on my way home.
【趁火打劫】chènhuǒ-dǎjié〈成〉 try to profit from other's misfortune
【趁机】chènjī〈副〉 opportunistically: ～报复 exploit the situation to take revenge ‖ ～逃走 seize the chance to escape
【趁空】chènkòng〈副〉 at one's leisure: ～合一下眼 catch a few winks while there is time
【趁钱】chènqián〈动〉〈方〉 be wealthy
【趁热打铁】chènrè-dǎtiě〈成〉strike while the iron is hot
【趁人之危】chènrénzhīwēi = 乘人之危 chéng-rénzhīwēi
【趁墒】chènshāng〈副〉 while there is sufficient moisture in the soil: ～播种 sow while the soil is not too dry
【趁势】chènshì〈副〉 taking advantage of a situation: ～前进 press forward while the situation allows
【趁手】chènshǒu〈副〉〈方〉 in passing: 请～把门带上。 Please shut the door as you go.
【趁早】chènzǎo〈副〉 while there is still time: ～动身 get going as soon as possible

榇（櫬） chèn〈名〉〈书〉 coffin: 灵～ coffin

谶（讖） chèn〈名〉〈书〉 prophecy: ▸～语
【谶纬】chènwěi〈名〉 divination combined with mystical Confucianist or Taoist belief
【谶语】chènyǔ〈名〉 prophecy believed to have been fulfilled

chen

伧（傖） chen ▸寒伧 hánchen
▸cāng

chēng

柽（檉） chēng
【柽柳】chēngliǔ〈名〉［植物］ Chinese tamarisk

琤（琤） chēng
【琤琤】chēngchēng〈拟〉〈书〉 **1**（玉器声） jingle **2**（琴声） twang **3**（流水声） gurgle
【琤瑽】chēngcōng〈拟〉〈书〉 **1**（玉器声） jingle **2**（流水声） gurgle: 溪流～ babbling brook

称¹（稱） chēng〈动〉 weigh: ～体重 weigh sb. ‖ 用秤～ weigh sth. on scales

称²（稱） chēng
A〈动〉 **1**〈书〉（赞扬）praise: ▸～道, ～颂, ～赞 **2**（说） state: 连连～好 keep praising ‖ 据～ according to sb. ▸～谢, ～快, 声～, 宣～ **3**（叫做） call: 通常～之为… it is commonly called ... ‖ 他～得起是一位英雄。 He deserves to be called a hero. ‖ ▸～兄道弟, 自～ **4**（自立为） rely on one's power or influence and proclaim oneself (to be) sb.: ▸～霸, ～雄
B〈名〉 name: 代～ substitutive designation ‖ 俗～ popular name ‖ 苏州有"东方威尼斯"之～。 Suzhou is known as the 'Venice of the East'. ▸～号, 别～

称³（稱） chēng〈动〉〈书〉raise: ▸～兵, ～觞
▸chèn

【称霸】chēngbà〈动〉 dominate: ～世界 dominate the world ‖ ～一方 hold sway over a region ▸称王～
【称便】chēngbiàn〈动〉 hail sth. as a great service to the public: 修筑了这条公路，当地群众无不～。 The local people all applauded the new road as a great service to the public.
【称兵】chēngbīng〈动〉〈书〉 take up arms: ～作乱 take up arms and stage a rebellion
【称病】chēngbìng〈动〉 plead illness: ～不出 claim to be ill and stay at home ‖ ～谢绝邀请 feign sickness and decline an invitation
【称臣】chēngchén〈动〉 submit to a ruler
【称大】chēngdà〈动〉 pull one's weight about
【称道】chēngdào〈动〉 praise: 无足～ be not worth mentioning ‖ 值得～ be worthy of praise
【称孤道寡】chēnggū-dàoguǎ〈成〉 style oneself king
【称号】chēnghào〈名〉 title: 获得～ earn the title (of) ‖ 荣誉～ honorary title
【称贺】chēnghè〈动〉〈书〉 congratulate: 登门～ call at sb.'s house and extend congratulations to him
【称呼】chēnghu **A**〈动〉 address: 用小名～ call sb. by their pet name ‖ 我该怎么～你呢? How would you like to be addressed? **B**〈名〉 form of address
【称斤掂两】chēngjīn-diānliǎng〈成〉 calculate carefully
【称快】chēngkuài〈动〉 express one's happiness: 拍手～ clap and cheer
【称量】chēngliáng〈动〉 measure the weight (of sth.)
【称名道姓】chēngmíng-dàoxìng〈成〉 deign to call sb. by his name
【称奇】chēngqí〈动〉 express one's wonder: 众人对此发现啧啧～。 The general public expressed their amazement at the discovery.
【称觞】chēngshāng〈动〉 raise one's cup and propose a toast
【称赏】chēngshǎng〈动〉 speak highly of: 无人不～他的慷慨。 His generosity was widely acknowledged.
【称述】chēngshù〈动〉〈书〉 relate: 事情太复杂，无法详细～。 The matter is too complicated to be reported in detail.
【称说】chēngshuō〈动〉 name: 他一一～景点。 He named the scenic places one by one.
【称颂】chēngsòng〈动〉 praise: 值得～ be praiseworthy ‖ 宽恕是值得～的美德。 Forgiveness is a virtue worth praising.
【称叹】chēngtàn〈动〉 praise highly: 连连～ keep praising
【称王称霸】chēngwáng-chēngbà〈成〉 act the bully
【称为】chēngwéi〈动〉 be known as: 狮子被～百兽之王。 The lion is known as the king of beasts.
【称谓】chēngwèi〈名〉 title
【称羡】chēngxiàn〈动〉 admire: ～不已 express profuse admiration ‖ 人人都～她惊人的勇气。 Everyone admires her for her amazing courage.
【称谢】chēngxiè〈动〉 express one's thanks: 连声～ thank profusely
【称兄道弟】chēngxiōng-dàodì〈成〉 be on intimate terms
【称雄】chēngxióng〈动〉 reign supreme: 割据～ set up a separatist regime ‖ 该队现已～全国。 The team now reigns supreme as the finest in the country.
【称许】chēngxǔ〈动〉 commend (sb. on/for sth.): 博得～ win much praise
【称扬】chēngyáng〈动〉〈书〉 commend
【称引】chēngyǐn〈动〉〈书〉 quote
【称誉】chēngyù〈动〉 praise: 交口～ praise unanimously
【称赞】chēngzàn〈动〉 praise: 大加～ shower praises ‖ 老人助人为乐，受到人们的～。 The old man was acclaimed for his generous help to others. ‖ 老师的～使他很受鼓舞。 He was much encouraged by the teacher's praise.

蛏（蟶） chēng〈名〉［动物］ razor clam
【蛏干】chēnggān〈名〉 dried razor clam
【蛏田】chēngtián〈名〉 razor clam farm
【蛏子】chēngzi〈名〉 razor clam

铛（鐺） chēng〈名〉griddle: 饼～ pan
▸dāng

赪（赬） chēng〈形〉〈书〉 red

撑（撐） chēng〈动〉 **1**（抵住） support: 用双手～着下巴 rest one's chin in one's hands ‖ 这个八角形屋顶由八根圆柱～着。 The octagonal roof rested on eight columns. ▸支～ **2**（船、筏等） punt: ～船 move a boat using a pole ▸～篙 **3**（坚持） sustain: 冻得～不住了 so cold that one can no longer stand it ‖ 他实在～不住，辞职不干了。 He really couldn't endure it any longer and so he resigned. ▸～场面, ～持, ～腰 **4**（张开） unfurl: ～伞 open an umbrella ‖ 把塑料袋～开 hold open a plastic bag **5**（胀） fill to the point of bursting: 孩子们吃得肚皮都要～破了。 The children ate until they were almost bursting.
【撑场面】chēng chǎngmiàn〈惯〉 keep up appearances
【撑持】chēngchí〈动〉 sustain: 真不知道他们还能～多久。 I wonder how long they can keep going. ‖ 他一病，家里全靠妻子～。 After he fell ill, his wife took care of everything for the family.
【撑竿跳高】chēnggān tiàogāo ▸p. 909〈名〉［体育］ pole-vault: 进行～比赛 compete in the pole-vault ‖ ～运动员 pole-vaulter
【撑篙】chēnggāo〈名〉 punt-pole
【撑门面】chēng ménmian = 撑场面 chēng chǎngmiàn
【撑死】chēngsǐ〈副〉〈方〉 at most: 他～只有三十岁。 He is thirty at most.
【撑腰】chēngyāo〈动〉〈喻〉 back: 有人～ be backed by sb. ‖ 干吧，有大家给你～。 Just do it. We are all behind you.
【撑腰打气】chēngyāo-dǎqì〈成〉 support and encourage
【撑住】chēngzhù〈动〉 **1**（指承重） support: 撑不住 be unable to support ‖ 撑得住 be strong enough to support **2**（坚持） keep going: 撑不住 be unable to put up with ‖ 撑得住 be able to sustain ‖ 那里很艰苦，你撑得住吗? Can you bear the hardships there?

噌 chēng
▸cēng
【噌吰】chēnghóng〈拟〉〈书〉 [of a bell or a drum boom]

瞠 chēng〈动〉〈书〉 stare
【瞠乎其后】chēnghūqíhòu〈成〉 be left far behind without any hope of catching up
【瞠目】chēngmù〈动〉〈书〉 gape at: ～相视 stare at each other with eyes agog
【瞠目结舌】chēngmù-jiéshé〈成〉 stare stunned and speechless
【瞠视】chēngshì〈动〉 stare at

chéng

成¹ chéng
A〈动〉 **1**（成功） accomplish: ～不了大事 cannot achieve great deeds ‖ 事～之后 when it is done ‖ 他是个能～大事的人。 He is a great achiever. ▸～功, 大功告～, 一事无～ **2**（成全） help to achieve: ▸～全, ～人之美 **3**（长大） grow: ▸～熟, ～长 **4**（成为） become: ～了明星/英雄 become a star/hero ‖ 两个对手竟～了朋友。 The two adversaries unexpectedly became friends. ▸～为, 变～, 弄假～真 **5**（指数量） amount to: ▸～倍, ～年, ～批 **6**（表同意） be all right: ～! 就这么办。 OK! Go ahead. ‖ 没有你可不～。 We cannot do it without you. **7**（表有能力） be capable: 他可真～，与谁都能合作。 He is really accommodating and can work with anyone.
B〈形〉 **1**（现成） fixed: ～衣 ready-made clothes ▸～规, ～品, 现～ **2**（成年） fully grown: ▸～虫, ～人
C〈名〉 achievement: ▸～果, ～绩, 坐享其～

成² chéng〈名〉 one-tenth: 增产三～ 30 per cent increase in output ‖ 上座率有九～。 The auditorium was at 90% capacity.
【成案】chéng'àn〈名〉 precedent: 无～可循。 There is no precedent to follow.
【成败】chéngbài〈名〉 success or failure: 不以～论英雄 one should not judge a person by his successes or failures ‖ ～在此一举。 Success or failure hinges on this one action.
【成倍】chéngbèi ▸p. 31〈动〉 increase several times: 产量～增长。 The output has increased several times over.
【成本】chéngběn〈名〉 cost: 降低～ lower the cost ‖ 收回～ recover the cost ‖ 生产～ cost of production ‖ 运输～ transportation cost ‖ ～管理 cost control ‖ ～核算 costing

【成本会计】chéngběn kuàijì〈名〉cost accounting
【成比例】chéng bǐlì〈动〉be proportionate (to sth.): 不～ be out of proportion ‖ 成反/正比例 be inversely/directly proportional to sth. ‖ 工资的提高跟物价的上涨要～。The wage increases should be proportionate to the increases in prices.
【成才】chéngcái〈动〉become a talented person: 自学～ become talented through self-study
【成材】chéngcái〈动〉**1**（指树木）grow to full size: 这些树还未～就被砍伐了。These trees were cut down before they had reached their full size. ▸～林 **2**（喻）（指人）become a useful person
【成材林】chéngcáilín〈名〉［林业］mature timber
【成虫】chéngchóng〈名〉［昆虫］adult insect
【成仇】chéngchóu〈动〉become enemies: ▸反目～
【成丁】chéngdīng〈动〉[of a boy] come of age
【成都】Chéngdū ▸**p. 661**〈名〉Chengdu [capital of Sichuan Province (四川)]
【成堆】chéngduī〈动〉pile up: 问题～。Problems are piling up. ‖ 西瓜～地摆在地上。The watermelons were stacked in heaps on the ground.
【成对】chéngduì〈动〉form a pair: ▸成双～
【成法】chéngfǎ〈名〉**1**（指法律、法规）set rules **2**（指方法）tried methods
【成方】chéngfāng〈名〉［中医］set prescription
【成分】chéngfèn〈名〉**1**（构成因素）component part: 化学～ chemical composition ‖ 主要～ principal ingredients **2**（出身）one's class status: 个人～ one's class status ‖ 家庭～ class status of one's family ▸阶级～
【成分股】chéngfèngǔ〈名〉［金融］constituent stock: 恒生指数的～ Hang Seng Index Constituent Stocks
【成份】chéngfèn = 成分 chéngfèn
【成风】chéngfēng〈动〉become popular: ▸蔚然～
【成佛】chéngfó〈动〉become a Buddha
【成服】chéngfú = 成衣 chéngyī
【成功】chénggōng **A**〈动〉succeed: 获得～ achieve success ‖ ～的奥秘 secret of success ‖ 巨大的～ great success ‖ 良好的开端是～的一半。Make a good start and you're half the way to success. ‖ 失败是～之母。Failure is the mother of success. ‖ 我的最后一次尝试～了。I was successful in my last attempt. **B**〈形〉successful: 演出很～ The performance was a great success. ‖ ～地完成了新产品的开发 successfully complete the development of a new product
【成功率】chénggōnglǜ〈名〉success rate
【成规】chéngguī〈名〉established convention: 打破～ break established conventions ‖ 因袭～ follow convention
【成果】chéngguǒ〈名〉fruition: 结出丰硕的～ yield a bumper harvest ‖ 取得～ achieve a positive result ‖ ～转让 results transfer ‖ 科研～ achievement in scientific research ‖ 劳动～ fruition of labour ‖ 研究～ fruit of one's research
【成婚】chénghūn〈动〉get married: 他四十岁了还没～。He is 40 and still single.
【成活】chénghuó〈动〉survive: ～率 survival rate ‖ 去年栽的树全都～了。The trees planted last year have all survived.
【成绩】chéngjì〈名〉achievement: 肯定～ affirm sb.'s achievement ‖ 取得好～ obtain a good result ‖ ～显著 remarkable achievements ‖ 考试～ examination results ‖ 学业～ school records ‖ ～单 academic report
【成家】chéngjiā〈动〉**1**（结婚）get married: 他还没～。He is still single. ▸～立业 **2**（成为专家）become a recognized authority: ▸成名～
【成家立业】chéngjiā-lìyè〈成〉get married and start a career
【成见】chéngjiàn〈名〉**1**（偏见）prejudice: 抱有～ have a prejudice ‖ 没有～ have an open mind ‖ ～很深 have deep-rooted prejudices **2**（个人见解）personal opinion: 没有～ have no definite opinion ‖ 他凡事都有个～。He has his own opinion about things.
【成交】chéngjiāo〈动〉strike a deal: 拍板～ strike a bargain ‖ ～额 turnover ‖ ～量 volume of business ‖ 这桩买卖～了。The deal was closed.
【成教】chéngjiào〈简称〉= 成人教育
【成就】chéngjiù **A**〈名〉achievement: 超过前人的所有～ surpass all previous achievements ‖ 取得重大～ make a real achievement ‖ 学术～ academic achievement ‖ ～感 sense of accomplishment ‖ 重大～ substantial achievement **B**〈动〉achieve: 你终于～了这件大事。You have at last accomplished this great thing.
【成句】chéngjù〈动〉form a complete sentence
【成矿】chéngkuàng〈动〉［矿业］mineralize
【成立】chénglì〈动〉**1**（建立）found: ～公司 set up a company ‖ ～专门委员会 form a special committee ‖ 中华人民共和国～于 1949 年 10 月 1 日。The People's Republic of China was founded on October 1, 1949. **2**（站得住脚）be sound: 理由不能～。The excuse doesn't stand up.
【成例】chénglì〈名〉precedent: 援引～ cite a precedent ‖ 无～可循 there is no precedent to follow
【成殓】chéngliàn〈动〉〈书〉place a body in a coffin
【成林】chénglín〈动〉grow into a wood
【成龙】chénglóng〈动〉〈喻〉become somebody: ▸望子～
【成龙配套】chénglóng-pèitào〈成〉link up the parts to form a whole: 使生产和销售～ form a complete system of production and marketing
【成寐】chéngmèi〈动〉〈书〉go to sleep: 夜不～ lie awake all night
【成眠】chéngmián〈动〉〈书〉fall asleep: 辗转不能～ toss and turn without getting a wink of sleep ‖ 夜不～ pass a sleepless night
【成名】chéngmíng〈动〉make a name for oneself: 一举～ achieve instant fame ‖ 一夜～ become famous overnight
【成名成家】chéngmíng-chéngjiā〈成〉establish one's reputation as an authority
【成名曲】chéngmíngqǔ〈名〉signature song
【成名作】chéngmíngzuò〈名〉work by which sb.'s reputation was made: 这本小说是我的～。This is the novel that made me famous.
【成命】chéngmìng〈名〉order already issued: 收回～ revoke a command
【成年】chéngnián **A**〈动〉come of age: ～人 adult ‖ 尚未～ be under age ‖ 长到十八岁就算～了。At the age of 18 you are considered an adult. ▸～人, 未～人 **B**〈副〉〈口〉all year round: ～在外出差 be away on business all year round ▸～累月
【成年人】chéngniánrén〈名〉adult
【成年累月】chéngnián-lěiyuè〈成〉year in, year out
【成批】chéngpī〈副〉in batches: ～出售 sell in bulk ‖ ～生产 produce in batches
【成品】chéngpǐn〈名〉finished product: ～车间 finishing room ‖ ～服装 ready-made clothes ‖ ～销路 sale of final products ▸半～
【成品钢】chéngpǐngāng〈名〉［冶金］finished steel
【成品粮】chéngpǐnliáng〈名〉processed grain
【成气候】chéng qìhòu〈惯〉〈喻〉be promising: 成不了气候 will not get anywhere ‖ 像他那样不～的人，什么事也干不成。An unpromising person like him will not get anywhere.
【成器】chéngqì〈动〉grow up to be something: 你这不～的东西！You good-for-nothing!
【成千上万】chéngqiān-shàngwàn〈成〉thousands upon thousands
【成亲】chéngqīn〈动〉get married: 他都四十了，还没～。He is still unmarried at the age of 40.
【成趣】chéngqù〈动〉be interesting: 相映～ contrast pleasingly with one another
【成全】chéngquán〈动〉help sb. succeed: 多亏你～，我才找到了工作。Thanks to you, I got a job.
【成群】chéngqún〈动〉form groups: 汇聚～ assemble in large numbers ‖ ～的牛羊 herds of cattle and flocks of sheep ‖ 学生们～地聚集在老师周围。The students crowded around the teacher. ▸三五～
【成群结队】chéngqún-jiéduì〈成〉gather in groups
【成人】chéngrén **A**〈动〉grow up: 长大～ come to adulthood **B**〈名〉adult: ～电影 adult movie
【成人高考】chéngrén gāokǎo〈名〉entrance examination to institutions of higher learning for adults
【成人高校】chéngrén gāoxiào〈名〉institution of higher learning for adults
【成人教育】chéngrén jiàoyù〈名〉adult education
【成人之美】chéngrénzhīměi〈成〉help sb. achieve his goal
【成仁】chéngrén〈动〉〈书〉die for a just cause: ▸杀身～
【成仁取义】chéngrén-qǔyì〈成〉die for a just cause
【成日】chéngrì〈副〉all day long: ～不在家 be out all the time ‖ 他～无所事事。He does nothing all day long.
【成日成夜】chéngrì-chéngyè〈成〉day and night
【成色】chéngsè〈名〉**1**（纯度）purity of gold/silver: 这枚金戒指～极好。This gold ring is of high purity. **2**（质量）quality: 看～定价钱 fix prices according to the quality
【成事】chéngshì〈动〉make it: 你很固执，成不了事。Your stubbornness will get you nowhere.
【成事不足，败事有余】chéng shì bùzú, bài shì yǒuyú〈成〉be unable to help accomplish anything but liable to spoil everything
【成书】chéngshū **A**〈动〉be written: 这本书～于清代。This book was written in the Qing Dynasty. **B**〈名〉book already in circulation

【成熟】chéngshú **A**〈动〉 mature: 思想～ be mature in mind ‖ ～的果实 ripe fruit ‖ 她身体已发育～。 Her body is already fully developed. **B**〈形〉〈喻〉 mature: 考虑～ consider sth. well ‖ ～的市场 mature market ‖ 计划逐渐酝酿～。 The plans gradually matured. ‖ 行动的时机尚未～。 The time is not yet ripe for action.

【成熟儿】chéngshú'ér〈名〉［医学］ mature infant

【成熟期】chéngshúqī〈名〉 maturity

【成数】chéngshù〈名〉 **1**（整数） round number **2**（比例） rate

【成双成对】chéngshuāng-chéngduì ＝ 成双作对 chéngshuāng-zuòduì

【成双作对】chéngshuāng-zuòduì〈成〉 form a pair: 情侣们～，沿着小路散步。 Lovers strolled two by two along the path.

【成说】chéngshuō〈名〉 accepted view: 不拘于～ not stick to the accepted theory

【成诵】chéngsòng〈动〉〈书〉 be able to recite: 熟读～ learn by rote ▸过目～

【成算】chéngsuàn〈名〉〈书〉 preconceived idea: 心有～ have a preconceived plan in mind

【成套】chéngtào〈动〉 form a complete set: ～家具 complete sets of furniture ‖ ～设备 complete sets of equipment

【成体】chéngtǐ〈名〉［动物］ adult

【成天】chéngtiān〈口〉＝ 成日 chéngrì

【成为】chéngwéi〈动〉 become: ～热门话题 turn into a hot topic of conversation ‖ ～歌唱家/作家 become a singer/writer ‖ ～笑柄 become a laughing stock ‖ ～泡影 go up in smoke

【成文】chéngwén **A**〈名〉 **1**（指文章） existing writings: 抄袭～ plagiarize existing writings **2**〈喻〉（指老一套） set pattern **B**〈动〉 be written down: 不～的规矩 unwritten rule ▸～法

【成文法】chéngwénfǎ〈名〉 statutory law: ～典 code of written law

【成问题】chéng wèntí〈惯〉 be a problem: 这家酒店的卫生状况～。 The sanitary conditions in this hotel are questionable.

【成仙】chéngxiān〈动〉 become an immortal

【成像】chéngxiàng〈名〉［物理］ imaging

【成效】chéngxiào〈名〉 effect: 初见～ begin to show results ‖ 卓有～ be highly effective ‖ ～显著 achieve remarkable success

【成心】chéngxīn〈副〉 purposely: ～与某人过不去 deliberately make things difficult for sb. ‖ 他不是～要伤害你。 He did not mean to hurt you.

【成行】chéngxíng〈动〉〈书〉 embark on a planned journey: 因天气恶劣，我们未能～。 Because of the bad weather, we didn't leave as planned.

【成形】chéngxíng〈动〉 **1**（指形状） take shape: 敲打～ beat into shape ‖ 新房子开始～了。 The new house is beginning to take shape. **2**［医学］（指修复） correct a disfigurement: ▸～外科 **3**［医学］（指正常形状） be solid: ～粪便 solid motions

【成形外科】chéngxíng wàikē〈名〉［医学］ plastic surgery: ～医生 plastic surgeon

【成型】chéngxíng〈动〉 take a desired shape: 使塑料～ shape the plastic ‖ ～模 shaping die

【成性】chéngxìng〈动〉 become second nature: 嗜赌/酗酒～ be a habitual gambler/drunkard

【成宿】chéngxiǔ〈副〉〈口〉 all night long: ～睡不着觉 lie awake all night

【成药】chéngyào〈名〉 medicine prepared by pharmacist

【成也萧何，败也萧何】chéng yě Xiāo Hé, bài yě Xiāo Hé〈成〉 whether success or failure, they were both caused by the same person

【成夜】chéngyè〈副〉 all night long: ～不睡觉 stay up all night

【成衣】chéngyī〈名〉 ready-made clothes: 一套～ a ready-made suit ‖ 买～ buy clothes off the peg

【成衣店】chéngyīdiàn〈名〉 tailor's shop

【成因】chéngyīn〈名〉 cause: 癌症～ origins of cancer ‖ 事故～ cause of an accident

【成荫】chéngyīn〈动〉 provide a leafy shade: 绿树～。 The trees give welcome shade.

【成瘾】chéngyǐn〈动〉 be addicted: 赌博～ become addicted to gambling ‖ 吸毒～ be addicted to drugs

【成语】chéngyǔ〈名〉 idiom: ～典故 proverbs and allusions

> **四字成语**
>
> Idiomatic expression usually made up of four characters, and containing, within one sentence, a single, complete meaning. Most four-character expressions have ancient origins, and their language is often very different from modern Chinese. Four-character expressions are similar to idioms and proverbs, but whereas these come from vernacular speech, four-character expressions have literary origins. Some of the meanings can be understood literally. Others can be understood only in their original context.

【成员】chéngyuán〈名〉 member: 内阁～ cabinet member ‖ 家庭～ family member

【成员国】chéngyuánguó〈名〉 member state: 联合国～ United Nations member ‖ 世界贸易组织～ member of the World Trade Organization

【成约】chéngyuē〈名〉 signed agreement: 违背～ break an agreement

【成灾】chéngzāi〈动〉 cause disaster

【成则为王，败则为寇】chéng zé wéi wáng, bài zé wéi kòu〈俗〉 losers are always in the wrong, nothing succeeds like success

【成章】chéngzhāng〈动〉 **1**（成为文章） make a good piece of writing: ▸出口～ **2**（形成条理） be logical: ▸顺理～

【成长】chéngzhǎng〈动〉（指状态） mature;（指过程） grow: ～壮大 grow in strength ‖ 健康～ grow healthily ‖ 该国工业正在迅速～。 The country's industry is developing rapidly.

【成竹在胸】chéngzhú-zàixiōng ＝ 胸有成竹 xiōngyǒuchéngzhú

丞 chéng〈名〉〈古〉 deputy officer: 县～ county magistrate's deputy

【丞相】chéngxiàng〈名〉〈古〉 prime minister

呈 chéng

A〈动〉 **1**（递交） present: ～上名片 present one's business card ▸～递，～献，面～ **2**（显现） appear: ～某种颜色 assume the colour of ‖ 检查～阳性/阴性 test positive/negative ▸～露，～现，～祥

B〈名〉 petition: ▸辞～，签～

【呈报】chéngbào〈动〉 present a report: ～上级机关审批 submit a report to higher authorities for approval

【呈递】chéngdì〈动〉 submit: ～报告 submit a report (to) ‖ ～辞职书 hand in one's resignation ‖ ～国书 present one's letters of credentials ‖ 你必须向委员会～你的申请。 You must submit your request to the committee.

【呈览】chénglǎn〈动〉〈书〉 submit (a report, etc.) to a superior for scrutiny

【呈露】chénglù〈动〉 emerge: 退潮后，沙滩～出来。 When the tide went out, the beach was exposed.

【呈请】chéngqǐng〈动〉 request official approval: ～上级审批 apply to the higher authorities for approval ‖ 将计划～委员会批准 submit a plan to the council for approval

【呈送】chéngsòng〈动〉 respectfully submit: ～公函/公文 submit an official letter/document ‖ ～礼品 present gifts

【呈文】chéngwén〈书〉 **A**〈名〉 document submitted to a superior: 转送～ forward a document **B**〈动〉 petition

【呈现】chéngxiàn〈动〉 appear: ～节日气氛 take on a festive air ‖ 这座城市～出一派繁荣景象。 The city presents an appearance of prosperity.

【呈献】chéngxiàn〈动〉 respectfully present: ～花圈 lay a wreath with due formality

【呈祥】chéngxiáng〈动〉 bring good luck: 龙凤～。 The dragon and phoenix are harbingers of prosperity.

【呈阅】chéngyuè〈动〉〈书〉 submit to higher authorities for perusal

【呈正】chéngzhèng〈动〉〈书〉〈敬〉 present one's work for criticism

【呈子】chéngzi〈名〉〈旧〉 petition: 递～ submit a petition

枨（棖） chéng〈动〉〈书〉 move sb.: ▸～触

【枨触】chéngchù〈动〉〈书〉 **1**（触动） touch **2**（感到） be moved

诚（誠） chéng

A〈形〉 sincere: ▸～恳，忠～

B〈副〉〈书〉 indeed: ～非易事。 It is by no means easy. ‖ ～有此事。 There really was such a thing. ▸～惶～恐，～然 A

C〈连〉〈书〉 if: ～如所说，则… supposing what you say is true, ...

【诚笃】chéngdǔ〈形〉 honest: ～君子 sincere gentleman ‖ ～的友情 sincere friendship

【诚服】chéngfú〈动〉 submit oneself willingly: ▸心悦～

【诚惶诚恐】chénghuáng-chéngkǒng〈成〉 with reverence and awe

【诚恳】chéngkěn ▸**p. 156**〈形〉 sincere: ～地道歉 express one's heartfelt apologies ‖ ～的态度 sincere attitude

【诚聘】chéngpìn〈动〉 hire in good faith

【诚朴】chéngpǔ〈形〉 sincere and straightforward

【诚然】chéngrán〈书〉 **A**〈副〉 truly: 人人都爱那个小宝宝，她也～可爱。 Everyone likes the baby; she is really adorable. **B**〈连〉［used correlatively with 但是］ no doubt: ～他很聪明，但是不诚实。 He is smart to be sure, but he's not honest.

【诚如】chéngrú〈动〉 be very similar

【诚实】chéngshí〈形〉 honest: ～可靠 be trustworthy

【诚心】chéngxīn **A**〈名〉 sincerity: 一片～ in all sincerity **B**〈形〉 sincere and earnest: 她对人很～。 She is sincere to others.

【诚心诚意】chéngxīn-chéngyì〈成〉 wholeheartedly

【诚心实意】chéngxīn-shíyì ＝ 诚心诚意 chéngxīn-chéngyì

【诚信】chéngxìn〈形〉 honest: 做生意要

讲～。 In business dealings you must be honest.

【诚意】chéngyì〈名〉good faith: 毫无～ be completely insincere ‖ 缺乏～ lack sincerity

【诚招】chéngzhāo〈动〉hire in good faith

【诚挚】chéngzhì〈形〉sincere: 致以最～的谢意 extend heartfelt thanks ‖ 谈判在～友好的气氛中进行。 The talks were held in a sincere and friendly atmosphere.

承 chéng

A〈动〉**1**（托着） bear: ▸～载, ～重 **2**（承担） undertake: ～制西服 undertake the tailoring of suits ▸～办, ～包 **3**（书）〈套〉（承蒙） be indebted: ～您关照，不胜感激。 I feel indebted to you for taking care of me. ▸～恩, ～蒙, ～情 **4**（继承） continue: 子～父业。 The son kept on his father's profession. ▸～上启下, 继～ **5**（接受） receive: ～命 take orders ▸秉～

B〈名〉bearer: ▸轴～

【承办】chéngbàn〈动〉undertake: ～奥运会 host the Olympic Games ‖ ～单位 undertaking agent ‖ 无人愿意～此事。 Nobody was willing to handle the affair.

【承包】chéngbāo〈动〉undertake a contract: ～工程 undertake a contracted project ‖ ～施工项目 contract (for) construction projects ‖ ～单位 contracting unit ‖ ～合同 contract

【承包期】chéngbāoqī〈名〉contract period

【承包人】chéngbāorén〈名〉contractor

【承包商】chéngbāoshāng〈名〉contractor

【承包责任制】chéngbāo zérènzhì〈名〉system of contracted responsibility

【承保】chéngbǎo〈动〉undertake to provide insurance: ～火险 provide fire insurance ‖ ～通知书 cover note ‖ 公司为工人～意外保险。 The company provides accident insurance for its workers.

【承保单】chéngbǎodān〈名〉cover note

【承保人】chéngbǎorén〈名〉insurer

【承担】chéngdān〈动〉bear: ～法律责任 bear the legal liability ‖ ～风险 run a risk ‖ ～后果 take the consequences (for sth.) ‖ ～任务 undertake a task ‖ ～责任 assume the responsibility (for sb./sth.) ‖ 经济上我可～不起。 Financially speaking, I can't take it on.

【承当】chéngdāng〈动〉bear: ～全部责任 take full responsibility ‖ ～任务 undertake a task

【承兑】chéngduì〈动〉［经济］ accept to pay: ～汇票 accept a bill of exchange ‖ ～票据 accept a note ‖ ～交单 documents against acceptance ‖ ～人 acceptor ‖ ～债务 acceptance liability

【承兑信用证】chéngduì xìnyòngzhèng〈名〉acceptance credit

【承兑银行】chéngduì yínháng〈名〉accepting bank

【承恩】chéng'ēn〈动〉〈书〉receive a favour

【承付】chéngfù〈动〉［经济］ undertake to pay: ～贷款 undertake to pay a loan ‖ ～人 acceptor

【承购】chénggòu〈动〉undertake to purchase: ～债券 undertake to purchase bonds

【承管】chéngguǎn〈动〉take full charge and bear full responsibility: 这件事由你～。 The matter will be left in your charge.

【承欢】chénghuān〈动〉〈旧〉**1**（侍奉父母） please one's parents: ～膝下 take good care of one's parents and make them happy **2**（迎合奉承） cater to sb.'s desires: ～献媚 pander to sb.'s desires

【承继】chéngjì〈动〉**1**（被过继） be adopted as heir to one's paternal uncle **2**（收养） adopt one's brother's son as heir **3**（继承） inherit: ～王位 succeed to the throne ‖ ～遗产 receive an inheritance ‖ 他死后，财产由其遗孀～。 Upon his death, the estate fell to his widow.

【承建】chéngjiàn〈动〉undertake a construction project: ～饭店/桥梁 undertake the construction of a hotel/bridge

【承教】chéngjiào〈动〉〈书〉〈套〉thanks for your advice

【承接】chéngjiē〈动〉**1**（接住） hold out a vessel to have liquid poured into it: 用水桶～屋顶流下的雨水 use buckets to catch rainwater from the roof **2**（承担） undertake: ～书刊印刷 undertake the printing of books and magazines **3**（衔接） continue: ～上文/上页 continued from the preceding paragraph/page

【承揽】chénglǎn〈动〉undertake: ～车辆维修 contract for auto maintenance ‖ ～工程 undertake a project

【承蒙】chéngméng〈动〉〈套〉be indebted: ～关照，不胜感激。 I feel indebted to you for your considerable care of me. ‖ ～惠顾。 Thank you for your custom. ‖ ～指教，十分感谢。 I am most grateful to you for your advice.

【承诺】chéngnuò〈动〉agree to do sth.: 履行～ fulfil one's promise ‖ 信守～ keep to one's word ‖ 两国～互不干涉内政。 Both countries promised not to meddle with each other's internal affairs.

【承诺书】chéngnuòshū〈名〉letter of commitment

【承平】chéngpíng〈形〉〈旧〉peaceful: ～年代 peacetime ‖ ～盛世 prosperous times of peace

【承前启后】chéngqián-qǐhòu = 承先启后 chéngxiān-qǐhòu

【承情】chéngqíng〈动〉〈套〉owe sb. a debt of gratitude: ～款待，十分感激。 Thank you so much for your hospitality. I am indebted to you.

【承认】chéngrèn〈动〉**1**（指个人） admit: ～错误 acknowledge one's mistake ‖ ～事实 admit the truth ‖ 公开～ openly acknowledge **2**（指国家） recognize: ～新国家/政府/政权 recognize a new state/government/regime ‖ 正式～其为该国的合法政府 officially recognize it as the lawful government of the country

【承上启下】chéngshàng-qǐxià〈成〉form a connecting link between the preceding and the following

【承受】chéngshòu〈动〉**1**（经受） bear: ～考验 endure a trial ‖ ～压力 stand the pressure ‖ ～重量 bear the weight (of sth.) **2**（继承） inherit: ～财产/遗产 inherit a property/legacy

【承受力】chéngshòulì〈名〉endurance: 心理～ psychological endurance ‖ 超过人们的～ be beyond people's endurance

【承望】chéngwàng〈动〉[usu used in the negative] expect: 不～您亲自来指导，谢谢。 Thank you for coming unexpectedly to give us instructions.

【承袭】chéngxí〈动〉**1**（指遵循） follow: ～传统 follow tradition ‖ ～旧制 observe the old system **2**（指拥有） inherit: ～王位 succeed to the throne

【承先启后】chéngxiān-qǐhòu〈成〉carry on the past and usher in the future

【承想】chéngxiǎng〈动〉[usu used in the negative] expect: 没～结果会如此! Who would have thought it would come to this!

【承销】chéngxiāo〈动〉consign: ～货物 consigned goods ‖ ～商 underwriter ‖ ～店 consignment store

【承修】chéngxiū〈动〉undertake to repair

【承印】chéngyìn〈动〉undertake printing: ～书刊 undertake the printing of books and periodicals

【承应】chéngyìng〈动〉〈书〉agree to do

【承允】chéngyǔn〈动〉〈书〉promise

【承运】chéngyùn〈动〉undertake transportation: ～原材料 undertake the transportation of raw materials ‖ ～人 freighter

【承载】chéngzài〈动〉bear the weight: ～能力 load capacity ‖ 这辆卡车～重量为2吨。 The truck has a load capacity of two tons.

【承造】chéngzào〈动〉undertake to manufacture

【承重】chéngzhòng〈动〉bear the weight: ～能力 weight capacity ‖ ～墙 bearing wall

【承转】chéngzhuǎn〈动〉forward: 及时～ promptly forward

【承租】chéngzū〈动〉rent: ～人 leaseholder

【承做】chéngzuò〈动〉undertake to make: ～各式时装 accept orders for all manner of fashionable clothes

城 chéng

〈名〉**1**（城墙） wall: ～外 outside the city ▸～墙, 兵临～下, 长～ **2**（城区） city: 东～ eastern part of the city ▸～区, 内～, 紫禁～ **3**（城市） town: 大学～ university town ‖ 古～ ancient city ‖ 全～ entire city ▸～乡, ～镇, 卫星～ **4**（大型商场） large shop: 服装～ garment city ‖ 美食～ gourmet restaurant

【城邦】chéngbāng〈名〉city-state

【城堡】chéngbǎo〈名〉castle: 温莎～ Windsor Castle

【城池】chéngchí〈名〉〈书〉city: 攻克/占领～ capture/take a city ‖ ～失守。 The city fell.

【城垛】chéngduǒ〈名〉**1**（城墙外突部分） rampart **2**（城墙） battlements

【城防】chéngfáng〈名〉city defence: ～部队 city garrison ‖ ～工事 defence works of a city

【城府】chéngfǔ〈名〉〈书〉mind that is hard to read: 他是个～很深的人。 He's a deep one. ▸胸无～

【城根】chénggēn〈名〉areas of a city close to the city wall

【城关】chéngguān〈名〉area just outside a city gate

【城管】chéngguǎn〈名〉**1** = 城市管理 chéngshì guǎnlǐ **2**（指管理人员） urban management officer

【城郭】chéngguō〈名〉city walls

【城壕】chéngháo〈名〉city moat

【城狐社鼠】chénghú-shèshǔ〈成〉〈喻〉evil-doers with influential backing

【城隍】chénghuáng〈名〉**1**〈古〉（护城河） (city) moat **2**（指神） guardian deity of a city

【城隍庙】chénghuángmiào〈名〉town god's temple

【城际】chéngjì〈形〉intercity: ～快车 intercity express

【城建】chéngjiàn〈简称〉= 城市建设

【城郊】chéngjiāo〈名〉outskirts: ～农业 suburban agriculture ‖ ～住宅区 suburban residential area ‖ 在～ on the outskirts

【城里人】chénglǐrén〈名〉townsman

【城楼】chénglóu〈名〉city gate tower: 天

安门～ Tian'anmen Gate Tower
【城门】chéngmén〈名〉city gate
【城门失火，殃及池鱼】chéngmén shīhuǒ, yāng jí chí yú〈成〉〈喻〉get caught in the crossfire
【城墙】chéngqiáng〈名〉city wall
【城区】chéngqū〈名〉city proper: 北京～ Beijing proper ‖ 老～ old town ‖ ～和郊区 urban and suburban areas
【城阙】chéngquè〈名〉〈书〉1（望楼）watch tower on either side of a city gate 2（宫阙）imperial palace
【城市】chéngshì〈名〉city: ～生活 urban life ‖ 消费～ consumer city ‖ 中等～ medium-sized city
【城市改造】chéngshì gǎizào〈名〉urban renewal
【城市管理】chéngshì guǎnlǐ〈名〉city management
【城市规划】chéngshì guīhuà〈名〉city planning
【城市国家】chéngshì guójiā〈名〉city-state
【城市化】chéngshìhuà〈动〉urbanize: 加快～步伐 accelerate the pace of urbanization
【城市建设】chéngshì jiànshè〈名〉urban construction
【城市交通】chéngshì jiāotōng〈名〉urban traffic: ～管制 urban traffic control
【城市居民】chéngshì jūmín〈名〉urban residents
【城市垃圾】chéngshì lājī〈名〉urban rubbish〈英〉; urban garbage〈美〉
【城市贫民】chéngshì pínmín〈名〉urban poor
【城市圈】chéngshìquān〈名〉area of a city: 发挥～促进就业的功能 develop the metropolitan regions to promote employment
【城市热岛】chéngshì rèdǎo〈名〉［气象］urban heat island
【城市人口】chéngshì rénkǒu〈名〉urban population
【城市运动会】chéngshì yùndònghuì〈名〉city games
【城头】chéngtóu〈名〉1（城墙上）top of the city wall 2（城门）gate tower
【城下之盟】chéngxiàzhīméng〈成〉treaty signed under coercion: 订立～ sign a treaty under coercion
【城乡】chéngxiāng〈名〉town and country: ～差别 urban-rural disparity
【城乡信用社】chéngxiāng xìnyòngshè〈名〉credit cooperatives serving both urban and rural areas
【城厢】chéngxiāng〈名〉city proper and the surrounding area
【城垣】chéngyuán〈名〉〈书〉city wall
【城镇】chéngzhèn〈名〉cities and towns: 边境～ frontier town ‖ ～户籍 urban residence registration
【城镇化】chéngzhènhuà〈动〉urbanize: 积极稳妥推进～ actively and steadily promote urbanization
【城中村】chéngzhōngcūn〈名〉urban village: ～改造 transforming urban villages

埕[1]

chéng〈名〉〈方〉wine jar: 酒～ wine jar

埕[2]

chéng〈名〉razor clam farm

乘 chéng

A〈动〉1 ▸p. 781（乘坐）travel by: ～船 take a boat ride ‖ ～电梯 take the lift ‖ ～飞机 fly ‖ ～公交车 take a bus ‖ ～火车 take a train ▸～车, ～客, 搭～ 2［数学］multiply: 四～三等于十二。Four times three is twelve.
B〈介〉taking advantage of: ～敌不备 take the enemy unawares ▸～人之危, ～虚而入
C〈名〉Buddhist teachings: ▸大～, 小～
▸shèng
【乘便】chéngbiàn〈副〉on one's way: 请你～把这封信替我寄了。Please post the letter for me at your convenience.
【乘车】chéngchē〈动〉take a bus: 免费～ get a free ride
【乘除】chéngchú〈名〉［数学］multiplication and division
【乘法】chéngfǎ〈名〉［数学］multiplication
【乘法表】chéngfǎbiǎo〈名〉multiplication table
【乘法运算】chéngfǎ yùnsuàn〈名〉multiplication
【乘方】chéngfāng〈名〉［数学］1（指运算）involution 2（指积）power
【乘风破浪】chéngfēng-pòlàng〈成〉brave the wind and battle the waves
【乘号】chénghào〈名〉［数学］multiplication sign (×)
【乘机】chéngjī A〈动〉fly: ～前往北京 fly to Beijing B〈副〉seizing the opportunity: ～报复 exploit a situation to take revenge ‖ ～逃脱 seize a chance to escape
【乘积】chéngjī〈名〉［数学］product
【乘警】chéngjǐng〈名〉on-board police
【乘客】chéngkè〈名〉passenger
【乘凉】chéngliáng〈动〉relax and enjoy the cool: 大树底下好～。With a powerful protector, one need never fear.
【乘龙快婿】chénglóng-kuàixù〈成〉ideal son-in-law [usu of high social rank or fast-rising official]
【乘幂】chéngmì = 乘方 chéngfāng 2
【乘骑】chéngqí〈名〉mount
【乘人不备】chéngrénbùbèi〈成〉catch sb. unprepared
【乘人之危】chéngrénzhīwēi〈成〉take advantage of others' misfortunes
【乘胜】chéngshèng〈副〉on the back of a victory: ～追击 give chase to enemy troops
【乘时】chéngshí〈副〉〈书〉seize an opportunity: ～而起 emerge at a favourable moment
【乘式】chéngshì〈名〉［数学］multiplier
【乘势】chéngshì A〈副〉availing oneself of a favourable situation: ～扩大战果 take an opportunity to build on one's success B〈动〉〈书〉rely on one's power: ～欺人 bully others on the strength of one's power
【乘数】chéngshù〈名〉［数学］multiplier: ～法则 multiplier rule
【乘务】chéngwù〈名〉on-board service
【乘务员】chéngwùyuán ▸**p. 966**〈名〉（飞机和船上）steward;（火车和汽车上）conductor
【乘务组】chéngwùzǔ〈名〉crew: 列车～ train crew
【乘隙】chéngxì〈副〉opportunistically: ～而入 seize an opportunity to step in ‖ ～突围 seize the chance to break through a siege
【乘兴】chéngxìng〈副〉when in high spirits: ～作诗 improvise a poem while in a joyful mood ‖ ～而来，败兴而归 go with great enthusiasm and return disappointed
【乘虚】chéngxū〈副〉when sb. is off guard: ～出击 attack where the enemy is weak
【乘虚而入】chéngxū'érrù〈成〉act when sb. is off guard: 安全防卫不严使小偷～。Lax security allowed the thieves to enter.
【乘员】chéngyuán〈名〉passenger
【乘坐】chéngzuò〈动〉take: 我经常～国航的客机。I often fly Air China.

盛

chéng〈动〉1（装）put in a container: 用盘子～菜 serve food on plates ‖ ～饭 fill a bowl with rice ‖ ～汤 ladle out soup 2（容纳）hold: 货物太多，仓库里～不下了。The warehouse is spilling over with so many goods.
▸shèng
【盛殓】chéngliàn〈动〉〈书〉place in a coffin
【盛器】chéngqì〈名〉container

程 chéng

A〈名〉1（规则）regulation: ▸～式, 规～, 章～ 2（距离）distance: ▸航～, 射～, 行～ 3（路程）journey: 送一～ accompany sb. part of the way ▸起～, 前～, 征～ 4（经过）process: ▸～序, 过～, 疗～
B〈动〉〈书〉assess: ▸计日～功
【程度】chéngdù〈名〉degree: 达到很高的～ reach a high level ‖ 文化～ educational level ‖ 准确～ degree of accuracy ‖ 在很大～上 to a great extent ‖ 你的英语熟练～已经很高了。You have achieved a high degree of proficiency in English.
【程控】chéngkòng〈形〉programme-controlled
【程控电话】chéngkòng diànhuà〈名〉programmed telephone
【程控交换台】chéngkòng jiāohuàntái〈名〉program-controlled switchboard
【程式】chéngshì〈名〉form: 公文～ forms and formulas of official documents ‖ 京剧表演～ style of Beijing opera
【程式化】chéngshìhuà〈动〉stylize
【程序】chéngxù〈名〉1（过程）order: 简化～ simplify a process ‖ 报关～ customs procedure ‖ 司法～ judicial process ‖ 按照法律～ according to legal procedures 2［计算机］program: 计算机～ computer program ▸～控制, ～语言
【程序编制】chéngxù biānzhì〈名〉(computer) programming
【程序法】chéngxùfǎ〈名〉［法律］procedural law: ～规则 procedural rule
【程序控制】chéngxù kòngzhì〈名〉program control: ～器 program controller
【程序设计】chéngxù shèjì〈名〉programming
【程序维护】chéngxù wéihù〈名〉program maintenance
【程序文件】chéngxù wénjiàn〈名〉program file
【程序系统】chéngxù xìtǒng〈名〉program system
【程序语言】chéngxù yǔyán〈名〉program language
【程序员】chéngxùyuán ▸**p. 966**〈名〉programmer
【程序运行】chéngxù yùnxíng〈名〉program run
【程序执行】chéngxù zhíxíng〈名〉program execution

惩（懲）

chéng〈动〉1〈书〉（警戒）give a warning: ▸～前毖后 2（处罚）punish: ▸～罚, ～治, 奖～
【惩办】chéngbàn〈动〉punish: 严加～ punish severely ‖ 依法～ punish sb. in accordance with the law

C

【惩处】 chéngchǔ 〈动〉 punish: ～罪犯 punish a criminal ‖ 依法～ punish according to law

【惩恶劝善】 chéng'è-quànshàn 〈成〉 punish wickedness and encourage virtue

【惩恶扬善】 chéng'è-yángshàn 〈成〉 punish the evil and praise the good

【惩罚】 chéngfá 〈动〉 punish: 受到～ be punished ‖ 经济～ financial penalty

【惩罚性】 chéngfáxìng 〈形〉 punitive: ～反倾销税 punitive anti-dumping duties ‖ ～(进口)关税 punitive (import) tariff

【惩戒】 chéngjiè 〈动〉 discipline sb. as a warning: 吊销执照，以示～ revoke sb.'s licence as a punishment

【惩前毖后】 chéngqián-bìhòu 〈成〉 learn from past errors to avoid future ones

【惩一儆百】 chéngyī-jǐngbǎi 〈成〉 punish one person as a warning to others

【惩一警百】 chéngyī-jǐngbǎi = 惩一儆百 chéngyī-jǐngbǎi

【惩治】 chéngzhì 〈动〉 punish: ～腐败 crack down on corruption ‖ 依法～ bring to justice

裎 chéng 〈动〉〈书〉 be naked: 裸～ be naked
▸chěng

塍(堘) chéng 〈名〉〈方〉 path between fields: ▸田～

酲 chéng 〈形〉〈书〉 drunk

澄 chéng
A 〈形〉 clear: ▸～碧, ～澈, ～空
B 〈动〉 clarify, purify: ▸～清 B
▸dèng

【澄碧】 chéngbì 〈形〉 clear blue: 海天～ azure sky and sea

【澄澈】 chéngchè 〈形〉〈书〉 crystal-clear: ～的水 clear water ‖ ～见底 be so clear that one can see the bottom

【澄净】 chéngjìng 〈形〉 clear and clean: 空气～ clean and fresh air

【澄静】 chéngjìng 〈形〉 clear and calm: ～的湖水 clear and calm lake

【澄空】 chéngkōng 〈名〉 cloudless sky

【澄明】 chéngmíng 〈形〉 clear and bright

【澄清】 chéngqīng **A** 〈形〉 clear: ～的江水 clear river **B** 〈动〉 **1**(使纯净) purify **2**(使明朗) clarify: ～事实 get the facts straight ‖ ～误会/疑点 clear up a misunderstanding/doubt ‖ 得到～ be clarified
▸dèngqīng

【澄清度】 chéngqīngdù 〈名〉[化工] clarity

【澄清剂】 chéngqīngjì 〈名〉[食品] clarifying agent

【澄莹】 chéngyíng 〈形〉〈书〉 clear

橙 chéng ▸**p. 863**
A 〈名〉 orange: 甜～ sweet orange ‖ ～树 orange tree ▸～汁, ～子, 脐～
B 〈形〉 orange: ▸～红, ～黄, ～色

【橙红】 chénghóng ▸**p. 863** 〈形〉 orange red

【橙黄】 chénghuáng ▸**p. 863** 〈形〉 orange

【橙皮】 chéngpí 〈名〉 orange peel

【橙色】 chéngsè ▸**p. 863** 〈名〉 orange: ～颜料 orange pigment

【橙汁】 chéngzhī 〈名〉 orange juice: 鲜～ fresh orange juice ‖ 榨～ squeeze the juice out of an orange

【橙汁饮料】 chéngzhī yǐnliào 〈名〉 orangeade

【橙子】 chéngzi 〈名〉 orange

chěng

逞 chěng 〈动〉 **1**(炫耀) show off: ～阔 parade one's wealth ‖ ～威风 show off one's strength ‖ ～英雄 play the hero ▸～能, ～强 **2**(实现) carry out: ▸得～ **3**(放纵) indulge in: ▸～性

【逞能】 chěngnéng 〈动〉 display one's ability: ～好强 like to show off and be anxious to do everything well

【逞强】 chěngqiáng 〈动〉 flaunt one's superiority: ～好胜 parade one's superiority and strive to put others down

【逞性】 chěngxìng 〈动〉 be wilful: ～妄为 act wilfully

【逞性子】 chěngxìngzi = 逞性 chěngxìng

【逞凶】 chěngxiōng 〈动〉 act violently: ～霸道 throw one's weight about and act violently

骋(騁) chěng 〈动〉 **1**(奔跑) gallop: ▸驰～ **2**〈书〉(放任) give free rein to: ▸～怀, ～目

【骋怀】 chěnghuái 〈动〉〈书〉 give free rein to one's thoughts and feelings

【骋目】 chěngmù 〈动〉〈书〉 look into the distance: ～远眺 look towards the distant horizon

裎 chěng 〈名〉〈书〉 traditional Chinese-style jacket with buttons down the front
▸chéng

chèng

秤 chèng 〈名〉 scales: 过～ weigh on scales ▸磅～, ～锤, 过～, 弹簧～

【秤不离锤，锤不离秤】 chèng bù lí chuí, chuí bù lí chèng 〈俗〉 be inseparable from one another

【秤锤】 chèngchuí 〈名〉 weight

【秤杆】 chènggǎn 〈名〉 balance arm

【秤钩】 chènggōu 〈名〉 steelyard hook

【秤毫】 chèngháo 〈名〉 lifting cord of a steelyard

【秤纽】 chèngniǔ = 秤毫 chèngháo

【秤盘】 chèngpán 〈名〉 balance scale

【秤砣】 chèngtuó = 秤锤 chèngchuí

【秤星】 chèngxīng 〈名〉 gradations marked on the beam of a steelyard

牚 chèng 〈名〉 **1**(斜柱) tilted pillar used as a prop **2**(横木) rung

chī

吃[1] chī ▸口吃 kǒuchī

吃[2] chī 〈动〉 **1**(吞咽) eat: ～火锅 eat hot pot ‖ ～面 eat noodles ‖ ～午饭/早饭 have lunch/breakfast ‖ ～药 take medicine ▸～素, 省～俭用 **2**(就餐) have one's meals at: ～食堂 have one's meals in the cafeteria ▸～馆子, ～小灶 **3**(吸收) absorb: ～墨 absorb ink ‖ ～水分 soak up moisture **4**(消灭) wipe out: ～掉敌人一个师 annihilate an enemy division ‖ ～掉对方的王棋 take an opponent's king **5**(耗费) exhaust: ▸～劲B1, ～力 **6**(遭受) suffer: ～败仗 suffer a defeat ‖ ～批评 be criticized ▸～官司, ～惊, ～亏 **7**(依靠) live off: ～养老金 live on one's pension ▸～老本, 靠山～山, 靠水～水 **8**(理解) fully understand: ▸～不准, ～透 **9**(接受) accept: 新部长可不～他阿谀奉承的那一套。 His flattery does not work with the new minister. ▸～软不～硬

【吃白饭】 chī báifàn 〈惯〉 **1**(没有菜) eat nothing but plain cooked rice **2**(不付钱) eat without paying **3**(无贡献) live off others: 他在家～。 He lived off his family.

【吃白食】 chī báishí 〈惯〉〈方〉 live off others: ～的人 sponger ‖ 他不工作，光～。 He sponges off others without earning an honest living of his own.

【吃百家饭】 chī bǎijiāfàn 〈惯〉 eat from the communal pot: ～长大的 be brought up by one's neighbours

【吃饱了撑的】 chībǎole chēngde 〈俗〉〈方〉 meddle

【吃闭门羹】 chī bìméngēng 〈惯〉 be refused entrance at the door

【吃瘪】 chībiě 〈动〉〈方〉 be humiliated

【吃不饱】 chībubǎo 〈动〉 **1**〈本〉 not have enough to eat: ～, 穿不暖 not have enough food and clothing **2**〈喻〉(指工作、学习) operate under capacity because of a lack of orders, materials, etc.

【吃不开】 chībukāi 〈形〉 unpopular: 没有学历的人在学校～。People without a good academic background are unpopular at school.

【吃不来】 chībulái 〈动〉 not be used to certain food: 他～姜蒜。 He does not eat ginger and garlic. ‖ 我～素食。 I am not used to a vegetarian diet.

【吃不了，兜着走】 chībuliǎo, dōuzhezǒu 〈俗〉 bear all the consequences: 谁敢捣乱，我叫他～。 If anyone ventures to make trouble, I will make him feel sorry for it.

【吃不上】 chībushàng 〈动〉 not have enough to eat: ～一顿饱饭 be unable to get a square meal

【吃不消】 chībuxiāo 〈动〉 be unable to stand: 痛得我～。 I cannot bear the pain.

【吃不住】 chībuzhù 〈动〉 be unable to support: 箱子太重，这个架子～。 The stand is not strong enough to hold this heavy trunk.

【吃不准】 chībuzhǔn 〈动〉 not quite understand

【吃长斋】 chī chángzhāi 〈动〉 practise abstinence from meat and fish all the year round

【吃吃喝喝】 chīchi-hēhē 〈成〉 wine and dine

【吃穿】 chī-chuān 〈名〉 food and clothing: ～不愁 not have to worry about food and clothing

【吃醋】 chīcù 〈动〉 be jealous: 爱～的丈夫/妻子/情人 jealous husband/wife/lover

【吃错药】 chīcuòyào 〈惯〉〈喻〉 do sth. out of character

【吃大锅饭】 chī dàguōfàn 〈惯〉〈喻〉 get the same reward regardless of one's performance in work

【吃大户】 chī dàhù 〈动〉〈旧〉 go uninvited into the homes of landlords and eat the food

【吃刀】 chīdāo 〈动〉[机械] penetrate a certain depth: ～深度 depth of cut

【吃得开】chīdekāi〈形〉 popular: 她在村里很～。She is quite popular in the village.

【吃得苦中苦，方为人上人】 chīde kǔ zhōng kǔ, fāng wéi rén shàng rén〈俗〉 no pain, no gain

【吃得来】chīdelái〈动〉 be able to eat: 我爱吃米饭，但面条也～。 I am fond of rice, but I don't mind noodles either.

【吃得消】chīdexiāo〈动〉 be able to bear: 天气虽冷，我还～。 It's very cold, but I can bear it.

【吃得住】chīdezhù〈动〉 be able to bear: 那个木箱～你的重量吗？Can that wooden box support your weight?

【吃定心丸】chī dìngxīnwán〈惯〉 receive assurance

【吃豆腐】chī dòufu〈动〉〈方〉 **1**（调戏） flirt with a woman **2**（调侃） make fun of **3**（指吊丧） visit the newly bereaved to offer one's condolences

【吃豆腐饭】chī dòufufàn = 吃豆腐 chī dòufu 3

【吃独食】chī dúshí〈动〉 **1**〈本〉 have food all to oneself **2**〈喻〉（独占） not share profit with others

【吃饭】chīfàn〈动〉 **1**（进食） eat: 请客～ ask sb. to dinner **2**（生存） make do: 靠打零工～ earn one's keep by doing odd jobs ‖ 靠父母/工资～ live off one's parents/wages

【吃饭防噎，走路防跌】chīfàn fáng yē, zǒulù fáng diē〈俗〉〈喻〉 be highly cautious at all times

【吃粉笔灰】chī fěnbǐhuī〈惯〉〈诙〉 be a teacher

【吃干饭】chī gānfàn〈惯〉 **1**（不干事） do not work to earn one's keep **2**（没本事） lack ability

【吃官司】chī guānsi〈惯〉〈口〉 get into trouble with the law: 让人～ take sb. to court

【吃馆子】chī guǎnzi〈动〉〈口〉 eat out: 从她上次～到现在已有一段时间了。 It's a long time since she last ate out.

【吃惯】chīguàn〈动〉 be used to certain food: 吃得惯 be used to certain food ‖ 他吃不惯西餐。 He is not accustomed to western cuisine. ‖ 我～了当地的饭食。I'm used to the local food. ‖ 你能～这里的素食吗？ Are you used to the vegetarian food here?

【吃光】chīguāng〈动〉 finish up

【吃喝】chīhē〈名〉〈口〉 food and drink: 不愁～ have enough to eat and drink ‖ 禁止公款～ ban wining and dining on public funds ‖ ～风 the habit of wining and dining at public expense

【吃喝嫖赌】chī-hē-piáo-dǔ〈成〉 lead a dissipated life

【吃喝玩乐】chī-hē-wán-lè〈成〉 indulge in gluttony and pleasure-seeking

【吃红牌】chī hóngpái〈动〉［体育］ get a red card

【吃后悔药】chī hòuhuǐyào〈惯〉 regret: ～没用。It's no use crying over spilt milk.

【吃皇粮】chī huángliáng〈惯〉〈喻〉 live off a government salary: 他是～的。 He is a government employee.

【吃黄牌】chī huángpái〈动〉［体育］ get a yellow card

【吃回扣】chī huíkòu〈动〉 draw a commission

【吃荤】chīhūn〈动〉 not be a vegetarian; eat meat

【吃紧】chījǐn〈形〉 **1**（严重） critical: 病人情况～。 The patient was in a critical condition. ‖ 形势～。 The situation was tense. **2**（重要） important: 不管他会怎么想都不～，反正我不去。 It makes no difference to me whatever he may think. I'm not going.

【吃进】chījìn〈动〉〈口〉 buy in: ～货物 buy in goods ‖ ～美元，抛出欧元 buy US dollars and sell Euros

【吃劲】chījìn **A**〈动〉（承重） bear weight: 这根柱子不大～。 This pillar doesn't bear much weight. **B**〈形〉 **1**（费力） strenuous: 他一天走八十里地并不～。 He can walk 80 *li* a day without difficulty. **2**〈方〉（重要） important: 这电影，看不看不～。 It's not important whether you see the film or not.

【吃惊】chījīng〈动〉 be surprised: 令人～ give sb. a shock ‖ 大为～ be greatly surprised

【吃开口饭】chī kāikǒufàn〈惯〉〈旧〉 earn a living as an entertainer

【吃空额】chī kòng'é〈动〉 embezzle by doctoring the payroll

【吃空饷】chī kòngxiǎng = 吃空额 chī kòng'é

【吃苦】chīkǔ〈动〉 bear hardships: 不怕～ fear no hardships

【吃苦耐劳】chīkǔ-nàiláo〈成〉 endure hardships and work hard

【吃苦头】chī kǔtou〈动〉 suffer: 吃尽苦头 endure untold sufferings

【吃亏】chīkuī〈动〉 **1**（遭受损失） come to grief: 怕～ be unwilling to be taken advantage of ‖ 吃小亏占大便宜 suffer a little in order to gain a lot **2**（不利） be at a disadvantage: 和年龄大的孩子竞争他就太～了。 Competing with older children put him at a great disadvantage.

【吃老本】chī lǎoběn〈惯〉 rest on one's laurels

【吃了豹子胆】 chīle bàozidǎn〈惯〉 be brazen

【吃里扒外】chīlǐ-páwài = 吃里爬外 chīlǐ-páwài

【吃里爬外】chīlǐ-páwài〈成〉 live off one person while secretly helping another

【吃力】chīlì〈形〉 **1**（费劲儿） strenuous: 工作～ feel the strain of work **2**〈方〉（劳累） worn out: 走了一段路我感到很～。 After walking some way, I felt exhausted.

【吃力不讨好】chīlì bù tǎohǎo〈俗〉 do a hard but thankless task: ～的工作 thankless task

【吃奶】chīnǎi〈动〉 suck the breast: 给孩子～ give suck to a baby

【吃派饭】chī pàifàn〈动〉 board with different peasant families

【吃偏饭】chī piānfàn〈惯〉 **1**〈本〉 eat too much of what one likes **2**〈喻〉 enjoy special favour

【吃偏食】chī piānshí = 吃偏饭 chī piānfàn

【吃枪药】chī qiāngyào〈惯〉 be irritable: 你今天是～了还是怎么的？ Why are you so irritable today?

【吃青】chīqīng〈动〉 harvest and consume grain before it grows ripe

【吃请】chīqǐng〈动〉 accept an invitation to dinner: 禁止干部在执行公务中～ prohibit officials from accepting dinner invitations during the course of their work

【吃人不吐骨头】chīrén bù tǔ gǔtou〈俗〉 be ruthless and cruel to people

【吃软不吃硬】chīruǎn bù chīyìng〈俗〉 be open to persuasion, but not to coercion

【吃软饭】 chī ruǎnfàn〈惯〉 live off a woman

【吃伤】chīshāng〈动〉 be tired of eating a particular food: 小时候爱吃巧克力，把我～了。 Eating too much chocolate during childhood turned me off it.

【吃食】chīshí〈动〉 feed: 母牛在草地上～。 The cows were feeding in the meadows.

【吃食】chīshi〈名〉〈口〉 food: 我们带着一篮子～去野餐。 We went for a picnic with a hamper of food.

【吃水】chīshuǐ **A**〈动〉 **1**（指水分） absorb water: 沙质土壤～很快。The sandy soil soaks up water very quickly. ‖ 这块地不～。 This plot does not absorb water properly. **2**（指饮用水） get drinking water: 高山地区～困难。 It is difficult to get drinking water in alpine areas. **B**〈名〉［航海］ draught: ～浅/深 have a shallow/deep draught ‖ ～20英尺的船 ship with a 20 feet draught ‖ 空载/载重～线 light/heavy waterline

【吃水深度】chīshuǐ shēndù〈名〉 draught (of water)

【吃素】chīsù〈动〉 **1**（吃素食） live on a vegetarian diet **2**〈喻〉（不杀伤） not effective: 我的手枪不是～的。 My handgun isn't just for show.

【吃透】chītòu〈动〉 have a thorough understanding: ～文件精神 have a thorough grasp of a document

【吃席】chīxí〈动〉 attend a feast

【吃闲饭】chī xiánfàn〈惯〉 lead an idle life

【吃现成饭】chī xiànchéngfàn〈惯〉〈喻〉 enjoy the fruits of others' work

【吃香】chīxiāng〈形〉〈口〉 well-liked: 这种产品在市场上很～。 This kind of product commands a ready sale in the market.

【吃香的，喝辣的】chī xiāngde, hē làde〈俗〉 eat and drink well

【吃相】chīxiàng〈名〉 table manners: ～难看 bad table manners

【吃小灶】 chī xiǎozào〈动〉〈喻〉 enjoy special treatment

【吃鸭蛋】chī yādàn〈俗〉〈喻〉 score a duck

【吃哑巴亏】chī yǎbakuī〈俗〉 be unable to speak out about one's grievances

【吃眼前亏】chī yǎnqiánkuī〈俗〉 deal with a difficult situation on the spot: 好汉不～。 Great men will wait until the time is right to deal with a tricky situation.

【吃一堑，长一智】chī yī qiàn, zhǎng yī zhì〈成〉 wisdom grows out of experience

【吃硬不吃软】chīyìng bù chīruǎn〈俗〉 be open to coercion, but not to persuasion

【吃斋】chīzhāi〈动〉 **1**（吃素） be a vegetarian for religious reasons **2**（僧尼吃饭） eat **3**（俗家人在寺院吃饭） be treated to meals by monks or nuns in the temple or nunnery

【吃着碗里，瞧着锅里】 chīzhe wǎnli, qiáozhe guōli〈俗〉〈口〉 never feel content with what one has

【吃重】chīzhòng **A**〈形〉 arduous: 左后卫有点～。 The left rear guard had to bear the brunt of the attack. **B**〈动〉 have a load capacity (of): 这辆新卡车～5吨。 The new truck has a load capacity of 5 tons.

【吃准】chīzhǔn〈动〉〈口〉 be sure: 他～会在那儿遇见她。 He was certain that he would meet her there. ‖ 他是什么意思我吃不准。 I was not quite sure what he was driving at.

【吃罪】chīzuì〈动〉 take the blame: ～不起 cannot take the blame

郗 Chī〈名〉 Chi [surname]

▸Xī

C

哧 chī〈拟〉titter: ～～地笑 chuckle ‖ ～的一声撕开信封 rip open an envelope

【哧溜】chīliū〈拟〉[sound of slithering or slipping]: 他踩在香蕉皮上，～一声滑倒了。He stepped on a banana peel and slipped and fell.

鸱（鴟） chī〈名〉〈古〉sparrow hawk

【鸱尾】chīwěi〈名〉owl-like pottery figure at either end of a roof ridge

【鸱吻】chīwěn = 鸱尾 chīwěi

【鸱鸮】chīxiāo〈名〉［鸟类］owls and similar birds

蚩 chī〈形〉〈书〉stupid

【蚩拙】chīzhuō〈形〉〈书〉stupid and clumsy

眵 chī〈名〉eye secretion: ▸眼～

笞 chī〈动〉〈书〉flog: ～刑 flogging as a punishment

嗤 chī〈动〉〈书〉ridicule: ▸～笑，～之以鼻

【嗤笑】chīxiào〈动〉sneer at: 让人～ be sneered at

【嗤之以鼻】chīzhīyǐbí〈成〉pooh-pooh: 对这样的好主意他却～。He turned up his nose at what was really a good suggestion.

痴（癡） chī

A〈形〉**1**（傻）stupid: ▸～呆，～人说梦，如醉如～ **2**（着迷）obsessed: ▸～迷，～情，～心

B〈名〉crazed person: ▸情～，书～

【痴骇】chī'ái〈形〉foolish: 一副～的样子 look like an idiot

【痴呆】chīdāi〈形〉**1**（呆滞）stupid: 眼神～ have glassy eyes ‖ 样子～ look like an idiot **2**（傻）insane

【痴呆症】chīdāizhèng ▸**p. 50**〈名〉［医学］dementia: 老年～ senile dementia

【痴狂】chīkuáng〈形〉**1**（精神错乱）idiotic **2**（着迷）infatuated

【痴愣】chīlèng〈动〉be in a daze

【痴恋】chīliàn〈动〉be crazy about

【痴梦】chīmèng〈名〉daydream: 别做～了，那是不可能的。Stop daydreaming! That's impossible.

【痴迷】chīmí〈形〉infatuated: ～不悟 be so infatuated as to be unable to rid one's mind ‖ 他对那个姑娘很～。He was really crazy about the girl.

【痴男怨女】chīnán-yuànnǚ〈成〉pining lovers

【痴情】chīqíng **A**〈名〉blind passion: 辜负她的一片～ be unworthy of her passionate love **B**〈形〉infatuated: 她对文学很～。She was crazy about literature.

【痴人说梦】chīrén-shuōmèng〈成〉〈喻〉talk fantastic nonsense

【痴想】chīxiǎng **A**〈动〉daydream **B**〈名〉wishful thinking

【痴笑】chīxiào〈动〉giggle: 一阵～ a fit of giggles

【痴心】chīxīn **A**〈名〉infatuation: 一片～ sheer infatuation **B**〈形〉infatuated: ～的倾慕者 crazed admirer

【痴心女子负心汉】chīxīn nǚzǐ fùxīnhàn〈俗〉an innocent girl is ready to be infatuated with a heartless man

【痴心妄想】chīxīn-wàngxiǎng〈成〉labour under a delusion: 他～有一天能暴富。He has wild dreams of making a fortune some day.

【痴长】chīzhǎng〈动〉〈谦〉be older but not wiser: 我～你两岁，但学识不如你。Although I am two years your senior, I'm not as knowledgeable as you.

【痴子】chīzi〈名〉〈方〉**1**（傻子）idiot **2**（疯子）lunatic

【痴醉】chīzuì〈动〉be captivated: 大提琴演奏家精湛的表演令他～。He was captivated by the cellist's excellent performance.

媸 chī〈形〉〈书〉ugly: ～妍莫辨 cannot distinguish between the ugly and the beautiful

螭 chī〈名〉**1**（指龙）legendary hornless dragon **2** = 魑 chī

魑 chī

【魑魅】chīmèi〈名〉〈古〉legendary maneating monster in mountains and forests

【魑魅魍魉】chīmèi-wǎngliǎng〈成〉**1** ▸**p. 274**（妖怪）demons and devils **2**〈喻〉（坏人）all sorts of evil persons

chí

池 chí〈名〉**1**（水塘）pond: 荷花～ lotus pond ‖ 一～春水 a pond of spring water ▸喷水～，游泳～ **2**〈书〉（护城河）moat: ▸城～，金城汤～ **3**（类池处）enclosed space with raised sides: ▸舞～，乐～ **4**（剧场前厅）stalls: ▸～座

【池汤】chítāng〈名〉common bathing pool: 洗～ bathe in a bathing pool

【池堂】chítáng = 池汤 chítāng

【池塘】chítáng〈名〉**1**（水池）pond: 挖～ dig a pond ‖ ～养殖 aquaculture **2** = 池汤 chítāng

【池盐】chíyán〈名〉lake salt

【池鱼之祸】chíyúzhīhuò = 池鱼之殃 chíyúzhīyāng

【池鱼之殃】chíyúzhīyāng〈成〉〈喻〉injury to an innocent bystander: 遭受～ be implicated in a disaster

【池浴】chíyù〈动〉bathe in a common bathing pool

【池沼】chízhǎo〈名〉pool

【池中物】chízhōngwù〈成〉〈喻〉people living in a small place and with no great ambitions: 此人绝非～。He is far from being mediocre and will go a long way.

【池子】chízi〈名〉〈口〉**1**（池塘）pond **2**（浴池）big bathhouse pool **3**（舞池）dance floor **4**〈旧〉（指剧场）front stalls

【池座】chízuò〈名〉stalls (in a theatre)

弛 chí〈动〉**1**（放松）loosen: ▸～缓，松～ **2**（废除）remove: ▸～禁，废～

【弛缓】chíhuǎn **A**〈动〉calm down: 世界紧张局势已趋～。World tension has eased off. ‖ 紧张的心情渐渐～下来。The feelings of nervousness gradually subsided. **B**〈形〉lax

【弛禁】chíjìn〈动〉〈书〉lift a ban

【弛懈】chíxiè〈动〉〈书〉slacken

驰（馳） chí〈动〉**1**（指车、马等）race: 飞～ go like the wind ▸～骋，奔～，风～电掣 **2**（指人）speed: ▸～马 **3**（指心神）turn eagerly towards: ▸～念，心～神往 **4**〈书〉（指名声）spread: 名～天下 be known all over the world ▸～名，～誉

【驰骋】chíchěng〈动〉〈书〉gallop: ～疆场 gallop across the battlefield ‖〈喻〉～文坛 make a noise in the literary world

【驰电】chídiàn〈动〉wire a quick message: ～求援 quickly cable for assistance

【驰马】chímǎ〈动〉gallop: 骑手～穿过田野。The rider galloped through the field.

【驰名】chímíng〈动〉be well-known: ～中外 win fame at home and abroad ‖ ～商标 famous trademark

【驰目】chímù〈动〉〈书〉look as far as the eyes can see: ～远眺 gaze far into the distance

【驰慕】chímù〈动〉yearn for

【驰念】chíniàn〈动〉〈书〉think longingly of sb. far away

【驰驱】chíqū〈动〉〈书〉**1**（策马奔驰）gallop: ～疆场 gallop across the battlefield **2**（为人奔走）try to be of service: 供人～ be at sb.'s beck and call

【驰书】chíshū〈动〉〈书〉lose no time and send a letter: ～告急 send an emergency letter requesting help

【驰突】chítū〈动〉〈书〉charge: 往来～ charge back and forth

【驰行】chíxíng〈动〉speed: 小船在水上～。The boat sped over the water.

【驰誉】chíyù〈动〉be widely known: ～全球 be known the world over

【驰援】chíyuán〈动〉rush to the rescue: 星夜～ set out by starlight and rush to sb.'s rescue

【驰骤】chízhòu〈动〉〈书〉gallop: 纵横～ gallop about freely

迟（遲） chí〈形〉**1**（慢）slow: ▸～缓，姗姗来～，事不宜～ **2**（晚）late: 睡得～ stay up late ‖ 对不起，我来～了。I am sorry I'm late. ‖ 宜早不宜～。It is better to be early than late. ▸～到，～早

【迟迟】chíchí〈副〉slowly: ～不做答复 hold off answering ‖ 冬天～不去。Winter was reluctant to go.

【迟到】chídào〈动〉arrive late: 上学/上班～ be late for school/work ‖ 因交通拥挤而～ be delayed by traffic ‖ ～者 latecomer

【迟钝】chídùn〈形〉slow: 反应/听觉～ be slow in reacting/hearing ‖ 过度悲伤使她变得～。Extreme grief blunted her senses.

【迟缓】chíhuǎn〈形〉slow: 行动～ be slow to act ‖ 工作进展～。The work is plodding ahead.

【迟留】chíliú〈动〉linger on: ～数日 stay on for a few more days

【迟慢】chímàn〈形〉slow: 行动～ be slow-footed

【迟暮】chímù〈名〉**1**（傍晚）twilight: 我们在乡间散步，直到～。We walked in the country till almost nightfall. **2**〈书〉（晚年）one's later years: 进入～之年 be in the twilight of one's life

【迟误】chíwù〈动〉delay: 不得～ allow no delay ‖ 她赴约从未～过。She was never late for appointments.

【迟延】chíyán〈动〉delay: ～付款 defer payment ‖ 毫不～地执行命令 carry out the orders without delay

【迟疑】chíyí〈动〉hesitate: 毫不～ without the slightest hesitation

【迟疑不决】chíyí-bùjué〈成〉be unable to make up one's mind: 在两种意见之间～ vacillate between two opinions

【迟早】chízǎo〈副〉sooner or later: 你～会

明白这一切。 In time you'll learn everything. ‖ 问题～会解决的。 Problems are always resolved in time.

【迟滞】chízhì **A**〈形〉**1**（缓慢） sluggish: 道路施工导致交通～。 Construction on the road slowed up traffic. **2**（呆滞） dull: 目光～ have glassy eyes **B**〈动〉 delay: ～敌人的行动 check the movement of the enemy ‖ ～至今 be held up until now

持 chí

〈动〉**1**（握住） hold: ～币抢购 panic buy ‖ ～美国护照 hold an American passport ‖ 手～鲜花 have a bunch of flowers in one's hand ▸～法, ～枪 **2**（抱有） hold: ～保留态度 have reservations ‖ ～不同意见 have different opinions ‖ ～观望态度 take a wait-and-see attitude ▸～之有故, 各～己见 **3**（掌管） manage: ▸～家, 操～, 主～ **4**（支持） support: ▸～久, 支～ **5**（对抗） oppose: ▸僵～, 争～ **6**（控制） control: ▸劫～, 挟～

【持币】chíbì〈动〉 have cash in hand: ～待购 be ready to buy with cash in one's hand ‖ ～观望 hold out for the price to go down

【持不同政见者】chíbùtóngzhèngjiànzhě〈名〉 political dissident

【持仓】chícāng〈动〉［经济］ hold a position

【持筹】chíchóu〈动〉 hold stocks

【持刀】chídāo〈动〉 hold a knife: ～抢劫 robbery at knife point

【持法】chífǎ〈动〉 administer justice: ～公正 enforce laws fairly and impartially

【持股】chígǔ〈动〉 hold shares: ～公司 holding company

【持家】chíjiā〈动〉 keep house: ～有方 run a household effectively ‖ 勤俭～ be industrious and thrifty in running one's household

【持节】chíjié〈动〉〈古〉 serve as a diplomatic envoy

【持久】chíjiǔ〈形〉 lasting: 维护～的和平 maintain lasting peace ‖ 做～打算 make a long-term plan ‖ ～力 endurance

【持久性】chíjiǔxìng〈名〉 endurance: ～有机污染物 persistent organic pollutant

【持久战】chíjiǔzhàn〈名〉 protracted war: 打～ undertake a protracted war

【持论】chílùn〈动〉〈书〉 state one's case: ～公允 make impartial statements ‖ ～有据 put forward a well-grounded argument

【持平】chípíng **A**〈形〉 impartial: ～之道 even-handed policy **B**〈动〉 match: 使进出口～ equate exports and imports ‖ 使预算与增长率～ balance the budget with the growth rate

【持平之论】chípíngzhīlùn〈成〉 impartial statement

【持枪】chíqiāng〈动〉 hold a gun: 行～礼 salute with a gun

【持球】chíqiú〈名〉［体育］ holding

【持身】chíshēn〈动〉〈书〉 make demands on oneself: ～高尚 conduct oneself nobly

【持续】chíxù〈动〉 last: ～降雨 persistent rainfall ‖ 使国民经济～稳定增长 bring about a sustained, stable growth in the national economy ‖ 好天气将～下去。 The good weather will hold for a while. ‖ 物价～上涨。 Prices kept rising.

【持有】chíyǒu〈动〉 hold: ～不同意见 have different opinions ‖ ～大学文凭 have a bachelor degree ‖ ～股票/债券 hold stock/bonds

【持斋】chízhāi〈动〉 be on a vegetarian diet for religious reasons

【持正】chízhèng〈书〉 **A**〈动〉 be fair and just: ～不阿 be impartial and above flattery **B**〈形〉 fair

【持之以恒】chízhīyǐhéng〈成〉 persevere: 刻苦学习，～ study hard and with perseverance ‖ 锻炼身体要～。 Exercise requires unremitting effort.

【持之有故】chízhīyǒugù〈成〉 have sufficient grounds for one's views

【持重】chízhòng〈形〉 discreet: 个性～ be cautious by nature ‖ ～待机 be prudent and bide one's time

匙 chí

〈名〉 spoon: ▸茶～, 羹～, 汤～ ▸shi

【匙子】chízi〈名〉 spoon

踟 chí

【踟躇】chíchú = 踟蹰 chíchú

【踟蹰】chíchú〈动〉 hesitate: ～不前 hesitate to move forward

篪 chí

〈名〉〈古〉 bamboo flute

chǐ

尺 chǐ

A〈量〉 *chi* [unit of length, equal to 0.333 metre]: ▸得寸进～, 咫～

B〈名〉**1**（指量具） ruler: 板～ measure board ‖ 卷～ tape measure ▸～子, 皮～, 折～ **2**（尺状物） ruler-shaped instrument: ▸计算～, 戒～ **3**（制图工具） instrument for drawing graphs: 制图～ drafting scale ▸比例～ **4**［中医］ *chi* pulse ▸chě

【尺寸之功】chǐcùnzhīgōng〈成〉 little contribution: 无～ without the least contribution

【尺寸】chǐcun〈名〉**1**（长短、大小） measurement: 量～ take sb.'s measurements ‖ 依照～定制 be made to measure **2**〈口〉（分寸） sense of propriety: 办事得掌握～。 We must know what to do and what not to do.

【尺牍】chǐdú〈名〉〈旧〉 correspondence

【尺度】chǐdù〈名〉 yardstick: 放宽～ relax the requirements ‖ 检验真理的～ yardstick of truth

【尺短寸长】chǐduǎn-cùncháng〈成〉〈喻〉 everybody has his strengths and weaknesses

【尺幅千里】chǐfú-qiānlǐ〈成〉 rich in meaning though limited in scope

【尺骨】chǐgǔ〈名〉［生理］ ulna

【尺蠖】chǐhuò〈名〉［昆虫］ looper: ～蛾 geometrid moth

【尺码】chǐmǎ〈名〉**1**（大小号码） size: 你要多大的～? What size do you want? ‖ 这双鞋的～还差不多。 These shoes are about the right size. **2**（标准） yardstick: 两件事性质不同，不能用一个～衡量。 We can't apply the same yardstick to two different things.

【尺素】chǐsù〈名〉〈旧〉 correspondence

【尺页】chǐyè〈名〉 page of painting or calligraphy that is one-*chi* -square

【尺有所短，寸有所长】chǐ yǒu suǒ duǎn, cùn yǒu suǒ cháng = 尺短寸长 chǐduǎn-cùncháng

【尺子】chǐzi〈名〉 rule: 用～量 measure with a ruler

呎 chǐ

〈旧〉= 英尺 yīngchǐ

齿（齒） chǐ

A〈名〉**1**（牙齿） tooth: 笑不露～ smile a tight-lipped smile ▸恒～, 牙～, 智～ **2**（齿状物） tooth-like part of anything: 梳/耙～ teeth of a comb/rake ▸～轮, 锯～ **3**〈书〉（年龄） age: ▸年～, 序～

B〈动〉〈书〉**1**（并列） rank: ～列 rank among ‖ 不～于人类 be ineligible to rank among the human race **2**（提到） speak of: ▸～数, 不足挂～

【齿根】chǐgēn〈名〉 root (of a tooth)

【齿垢】chǐgòu〈名〉 tartar (on the teeth)

【齿冠】chǐguān〈名〉 crown

【齿及】chǐjí〈动〉〈书〉 mention: 区区小事，何足～。 Such a trivial matter is not worth mentioning.

【齿鲸】chǐjīng〈名〉 toothed whale

【齿冷】chǐlěng〈动〉〈书〉 laugh at

【齿轮】chǐlún〈名〉 gear: 变速～ variable gear

【齿腔】chǐqiāng〈名〉 dental cavity

【齿数】chǐshǔ〈动〉〈书〉 mention: 不足～ deserve no mention

【齿髓】chǐsuǐ〈名〉［生理］ dental pulp

【齿系】chǐxì〈名〉 dentition

【齿音】chǐyīn〈名〉［语言］ dental sound

【齿龈】chǐyín = 牙龈 yáyín

【齿状】chǐzhuàng〈形〉 dentate

侈 chǐ

〈形〉**1**（浪费） extravagant: ▸～靡, 奢～ **2**〈书〉（夸大）exaggerated: ▸～论, ～谈

【侈论】chǐlùn〈名〉〈书〉 gross exaggerations

【侈糜】chǐmí = 侈靡 chǐmí

【侈靡】chǐmí〈形〉〈书〉 extravagant and wasteful: ～成风令人担忧。 Extravagance and waste has become a disturbing trend.

【侈谈】chǐtán **A**〈动〉 brag: ～民主/世界和平 shoot one's mouth off about democracy/world peace **B**〈名〉 bragging

耻（恥） chǐ

A〈动〉 feel ashamed: ～与为伍 feel ashamed to associate with sb. ▸可～, 无～

B〈名〉 shame: 不以为～，反以为荣 take shame as honour ‖ 引以为～ regard it as a disgrace ▸国～, 奇～大辱, 雪～

【耻骨】chǐgǔ〈名〉［生理］ pubic bone

【耻骂】chǐmà〈动〉 abuse

【耻辱】chǐrǔ〈名〉 disgrace: 蒙受～ be humiliated ‖ 洗雪～ avenge an insult ‖ 国家的～ disgrace to the nation

【耻笑】chǐxiào〈动〉 mock: 为人～ be an object of ridicule

豉 chǐ

▸豆豉 dòuchǐ

褫 chǐ

〈动〉〈书〉 deprive

【褫夺】chǐduó〈动〉〈书〉 dispossess: ～公民权 deprive sb. of civil rights ‖ ～继承权 disinherit sb.

【褫革】chǐgé〈动〉〈书〉 remove sb. from office

【褫职】chǐzhí〈动〉〈书〉 deprive sb. of their post

chì

彳 chì

【彳亍】chìchù〈动〉〈书〉 walk in fits and starts: 独自在河边～ take a solitary walk along a river

C

叱 chì〈动〉〈书〉reproach loudly: 怒～ angrily rebuke ▸～骂, ～问, ～责

【叱呵】chìhē〈动〉 yell at: ～部下 give one's subordinates a dressing-down ‖ 厉声～ shout angrily at

【叱喝】chìhè〈动〉 yell at: 厉声～ shout angrily at

【叱令】chìlìng〈动〉 shout an order: ～匪徒放下武器 shout orders for the bandits to lay down their weapons ‖ 他～我坐下。He snapped at me to sit down.

【叱骂】chìmà〈动〉curse: 遭人～ be cursed by others

【叱问】chìwèn〈动〉 call sb. to account

【叱责】chìzé〈动〉 scold: 她从不当着客人的面～孩子。She never tells her children off in front of guests.

【叱咤】chìzhà〈动〉〈书〉yell

【叱咤风云】chìzhà-fēngyún〈成〉 be all-powerful

斥 chì〈动〉 1〈书〉(开拓) open up: ▸～地 2〈书〉(侦察) reconnoitre: ▸～候 3 (使离开) oust: 同极相～。Like poles repel. ▸贬～, 排～ 4 (责备) scold: 痛～ bitterly denounce ▸～骂, ～责, 驳～ 5〈书〉(支付) fund: ▸～资

【斥地】chìdì〈动〉〈书〉 expand territory: ～千里 expand one's territory by one thousand *li*

【斥革】chìgé〈动〉〈书〉 dismiss: ～功名 strip sb. of his titles and honours

【斥候】chìhòu〈旧〉 A〈动〉 reconnoitre B〈名〉 scout

【斥力】chìlì〈名〉［物理］ repulsion

【斥骂】chìmà〈动〉 reproach: 受到～ receive a good dressing-down

【斥卖】chìmài〈动〉〈书〉 sell up: ～房产 sell off one's property

【斥退】chìtuì〈动〉 1〈旧〉(免职) fire: 他被上司～。He was dismissed by his boss. 2〈旧〉(使退学) expel a student: 他因犯罪而被学校～。He was expelled from school for his crimes. 3 (命令退出) order sb. out: ～左右 dismiss the servants in waiting

【斥责】chìzé〈动〉 scold: 因失职而受～ be reprimanded for neglect of duty ‖ 大声～ reproach loudly

【斥逐】chìzhú〈动〉〈书〉 repel: ～入侵之敌 repel invaders

【斥资】chìzī〈动〉 fund: ～创建学校 provide funds for setting up schools ‖ 为一家企业～百万 invest a million dollars in a business

赤 chì ▸**p. 863**

A〈形〉 1 (红) red: ～色 red ▸面红耳～ 2 (纯真) loyal: ▸～诚, ～金, ～心 3 (空) empty: ▸～地, ～贫, ～手空拳 4 (革命) revolutionary: ～色革命 red revolution ▸～卫队

B〈动〉 be naked: ～着脚 be barefoot ▸～膊, ～裸, ～条条

C〈名〉 pure gold: 金无足～。There is no such thing as a hundred per cent pure gold.

【赤背】chìbèi〈动〉 be stripped to the waist

【赤膊】chìbó〈动〉 be naked to the waist: 打～ be stripped to the waist

【赤膊上阵】chìbó-shàngzhèn〈成〉〈喻〉 throw away all disguise

【赤潮】chìcháo〈名〉 algal bloom

【赤忱】chìchén〈书〉 A〈形〉 absolutely sincere: ～相待 treat each other with absolute sincerity B〈名〉 absolute sincerity: 我被她的一片～深深打动。I was very touched by her unqualified sincerity.

【赤诚】chìchéng〈形〉 absolutely sincere: ～之心 loyal devotion

【赤带】chìdài〈名〉［中医］ leucorrhoea with blood discharge

【赤胆忠心】chìdǎn-zhōngxīn〈成〉 utter devotion: 他对组织的～不容置疑。His devotion to the organization is unquestionable.

【赤道】chìdào〈名〉 1 (指地球) equator: ～气候 equatorial climate 2［天文］ celestial equator

【赤道非洲】Chìdào Fēizhōu〈名〉 Equatorial Africa

【赤道几内亚】Chìdào Jǐnèiyà〈名〉 Equatorial Guinea: ～人 Equatorial Guinean

【赤地】chìdì〈名〉〈书〉 barren land

【赤地千里】chìdì-qiānlǐ〈成〉 scene of utter desolation

【赤豆】chìdòu〈名〉〈方〉 red bean

【赤褐色】chìhèsè ▸**p. 863**〈名〉 russet

【赤红】chìhóng ▸**p. 863**〈形〉 crimson: ～脸 ruddy complexion

【赤狐】chìhú〈名〉［动物］ red fox

【赤脚】chìjiǎo A〈动〉 be barefoot: 打～ go barefoot ‖ ～走路 walk barefoot B〈名〉 bare feet

【赤脚医生】chìjiǎo yīshēng〈名〉 barefoot doctor

【赤金】chìjīn〈名〉 pure gold

【赤口毒舌】chìkǒu-dúshé〈成〉 venomous tongue

【赤佬】chìlǎo〈名〉〈方〉〈粗〉 scoundrel

【赤练蛇】chìliànshé〈名〉［动物］ red-banded odd-tooth snake

【赤磷】chìlín〈名〉 red phosphorus

【赤露】chìlù〈动〉 bare: ～着上身 be naked to the waist

【赤裸】chìluǒ〈动〉 1 (光着身子) be naked: ～着双腿 be bare-legged ‖ 全身～ be stark-naked 2〈喻〉(无遮盖) be undisguised: ～的山坡 bare hillside ‖ ～的原野 barren land

【赤裸裸】chìluǒluǒ〈形〉 1 (光着身子) stark-naked: ～一丝不挂 be stark-naked 2〈喻〉 naked: ～的强盗行径 plain robbery

【赤霉素】chìméisù〈名〉［生化］ gibberellin

【赤贫】chìpín〈形〉 utterly destitute: ～如洗 in extreme poverty ‖ 短短三年他就从～一跃而成巨富。He went from rags to riches in only three years.

【赤日】chìrì〈名〉〈书〉 scorching sun: ～炎炎 blazing heat ‖ ～当空。A blazing sun is hanging in the sky.

【赤身】chìshēn〈形〉 naked: ▸～露体

【赤身露体】chìshēn-lùtǐ〈成〉 be stark-naked: 这儿的海滩上不允许～。You can't go naked on this beach.

【赤身裸体】chìshēn-luǒtǐ ＝ 赤身露体 chìshēn-lùtǐ

【赤手空拳】chìshǒu-kōngquán〈成〉 be unarmed: ～的示威者 unarmed demonstrators

【赤陶】chìtáo〈名〉 terracotta

【赤条条】chìtiáotiáo〈形〉 stark-naked

【赤铁矿】chìtiěkuàng〈名〉 hematite

【赤卫队】chìwèiduì〈名〉 Red Guards [Chinese Communist militias from 1927 to 1937]

【赤县】Chìxiàn〈简称〉＝ 赤县神州

【赤县神州】Chìxiàn-Shénzhōu〈名〉〈喻〉 China

【赤小豆】chìxiǎodòu〈名〉 red bean

【赤心】chìxīn〈名〉 genuine sincerity: ～相待 treat sb. with absolute sincerity ‖ 他们对祖国的一片～从未动摇。Their loyalty to the motherland never wavered.

【赤眼蜂】chìyǎnfēng〈名〉［昆虫］ trichogramma

【赤子】chìzǐ〈名〉 1 (指婴儿) newborn: ～般的真诚 as honest as a newborn baby ▸～之心 2〈书〉(指成人) person cherishing true love for his native land: 海外～ overseas compatriot

【赤子之心】chìzǐzhīxīn〈成〉 whole-hearted devotion

【赤字】chìzì〈名〉 deficit: 减少～ reduce a deficit ‖ 财政～ financial deficit ‖ 贸易～ trade deficit ‖ 预算～ budget deficit

【赤足】chìzú〈动〉 be barefoot

饬（飭） chì

A〈书〉〈动〉 1 (整顿) put in order: ▸整～ 2 (命令) order: 严～ issue strict orders ▸～令

B〈形〉 cautious and respectful: ▸谨～

【饬令】chìlìng〈动〉 issue an order: ～查办 order to investigate and prosecute

炽（熾） chì〈形〉 1 (指火) ablaze 2 (热烈) vigorous: ▸～烈, ～热

【炽烈】chìliè〈形〉 blazing: 感情～ be aflame with passion ‖ 篝火在～地燃烧。The campfire is burning furiously.

【炽情】chìqíng〈名〉 passion: 满腔～ with whole-hearted enthusiasm

【炽热】chìrè〈形〉 1 (极热) red-hot: ～的钢水 red-hot molten steel ‖ ～的阳光 blazing sun 2 (热烈) passionate: 感情～ passionate feelings ‖ ～的爱国心 vehement patriotism

【炽盛】chìshèng〈形〉〈书〉 ablaze: 火势～。The fire is blazing.

【炽燥】chìzào〈形〉 hot and dry

【炽灼】chìzhuó〈形〉〈书〉 1 (指火) blazing 2 (指权势) powerful

翅 chì〈名〉 1 (翅膀) wing: 鸡～ chicken wing ‖ 鸟儿展～飞翔。The bird spread its wings to fly. ▸～膀, ～幅 2 (鳍) fin: ▸鱼～ 3 (翅膀状物) wing-like thing: 纱帽～ wing-like flaps of a black gauze cap ▸～果

【翅膀】chìbǎng〈名〉 wing: 拍动～ flap one's wings ‖ 飞机～ wings of an aeroplane

【翅膀硬了】chìbǎng yìngle〈惯〉〈喻〉 grown up enough to live an independent life

【翅幅】chìfú〈名〉 wingspread

【翅果】chìguǒ〈名〉［植物］ winged fruit

【翅脉】chìmài〈名〉［昆虫］ nervure

【翅子】chìzi〈名〉 1 (鱼翅) shark's fin 2〈方〉(翅膀) wing

敕（勅） chì〈名〉〈书〉 imperial decree: ▸～封, ～命

【敕封】chìfēng〈动〉 confer a title or territory by imperial edict

【敕建】chìjiàn〈动〉 construct by imperial order

【敕令】chìlìng A〈动〉 [of an emperor] issue an order B〈名〉 imperial order

【敕命】chìmìng〈名〉 imperial order

【敕书】chìshū〈名〉 imperial edict

【敕造】chìzào〈动〉 construct on imperial order

啻 chì〈副〉〈书〉 merely: ▸不～, 何～

chōng

冲[1]（衝）chōng

A〈名〉**1**（交通要道）thoroughfare: ▸首当其～，要～ **2**［天文］opposition: ▸大～

B〈动〉**1**（猛闯）dash: ～过防线 crash through the defence ‖ ～进房间 burst into a room ‖ ～向敌人 charge at the enemy ▸～刺，～锋，～口而出 **2**（上升）soar: 火箭直～云霄。The rocket shoots skyward. ▸～天，怒发～冠 **3**（碰撞）clash: ▸～突，～撞

冲[2]（沖）chōng

〈动〉**1**（冲洗）rinse: 便后～水。Flush the toilet after use. ‖ 洪水～走了整个村子。The flood washed away the whole village. ▸～刷，～洗 **2**（沏）pour boiling water on: ～奶粉 prepare milk by adding hot water to milk powder **3**（相抵）offset: ▸～喜，～账

冲[3]（沖）chōng

〈名〉〈方〉stretch of flatland in a hilly area

▸chòng

【冲程】chōngchéng〈名〉［机械］stroke

【冲冲】chōngchōng〈形〉excited: 怒气～ in a burning fury ‖ 兴～ in high spirits

【冲刺】chōngcì〈动〉**1**［体育］sprint: 向终点线～ sprint to the finish line ‖ 赛跑运动员全力～越过终点。The runners sprinted down the finishing straight. **2**（指最后努力）make final efforts for success: 申办工作已进入～阶段。The bidding for a successful outcome has entered its final stage.

【冲淡】chōngdàn〈动〉**1**（指浓度）dilute: 加水把茶～ weaken the tea by adding water ‖ 加水把酒～ thin the wine with water **2**（指效果）play down: ～了戏剧性效果 weaken the dramatic effect ‖ 故事的生动性被～了。The vividness of the story has been watered down.

【冲荡】chōngdàng〈动〉wash away

【冲抵】chōngdǐ〈动〉［会计］charge against: ～账目 counterbalance accounts

【冲顶】chōngdǐng〈动〉**1**（指登山）make a final spurt to the top of a mountain **2**（指足球运动）score a header

【冲动】chōngdòng **A**〈名〉impulse: 创作～ creative impulse ‖ 性～ sexual urge **B**〈动〉be impulsive: 一时～ act out of a sudden impulse ‖ 他容易～。He is often impulsive.

【冲犯】chōngfàn〈动〉offend: 这出戏可能会～一些人。The play is liable to offend some people.

【冲锋】chōngfēng〈动〉assault: 打退敌人的～ fight off the enemy's assault ‖ 发起～ mount a charge against ‖ 在科技发展的道路上，他们～在前。They are in the vanguard of the technological advance.

【冲锋号】chōngfēnghào〈名〉charge: 吹～ sound the charge

【冲锋枪】chōngfēngqiāng〈名〉sub-machine gun

【冲锋陷阵】chōngfēng-xiànzhèn〈成〉**1**（指打仗）charge the enemy line: 冒着枪林弹雨～ charge under heavy fire **2**（指奋斗）fight valiantly for a just cause

【冲服】chōngfú〈动〉take (medicine) after dissolving it: 用水～药丸 wash down a pill with water

【冲关】chōngguān〈动〉**1**（指车辆）charge a checkpoint: 一辆卡车企图～逃费。A truck tried to charge through the checkpoint to avoid the toll. **2**［金融］break through a barrier: 银行股几度～均未果。Bank shares were unsuccessful in breaking through the barriers.

【冲毁】chōnghuǐ〈动〉destroy: 堤岸被暴风雨～。The embankment was washed out by the storm. ‖ 河水～了大坝。The river burst the dam.

【冲昏头脑】chōnghūn-tóunǎo〈惯〉go to sb.'s head: 被胜利～ get carried away by one's success

【冲击】chōngjī〈动〉**1**（猛撞）pound: 海浪～着悬崖。The surf pounded against the cliff. **2**（冲锋）assault: 打退敌人的～ repel the enemy's charge ‖ 向敌人阵地发起～ make a pass at the enemy's position **3**（干扰）shock: 受到～ experience a shock ‖ 罢工的浪潮～着该国。Waves of strikes hit that country.

【冲击波】chōngjībō〈名〉［物理］shock wave:〈喻〉股市暴跌，～遍及金融界。The stock-market crash sent shock waves through the financial community.

【冲击力】chōngjīlì〈名〉impact: 爆炸的～震碎了窗户。The force of the explosion broke the windows.

【冲积】chōngjī〈名〉［地质］alluviation: ～层 alluvium ‖ ～平原 alluvial plain ‖ ～土 alluvial soil

【冲剂】chōngjì〈名〉［中药］powdered medicine to be taken after being mixed with liquid

【冲决】chōngjué〈动〉smash: ～堤防 burst the dykes ‖ ～罗网 throw off one's chains

【冲口而出】chōngkǒu'érchū〈成〉blurt out: 她来不及考虑后果，话已～。She blurted out the words before she could consider the consequences.

【冲垮】chōngkuǎ〈动〉burst: ～堤防 burst the dyke ‖ ～敌军防线 shatter the enemy line

【冲扩】chōngkuò〈动〉develop and enlarge: ～彩卷 develop and enlarge a roll of colour film

【冲浪】chōnglàng **A**〈名〉［体育］surfing: ～板 surfboard **B**〈动〉surf: 在网上～ surf the net

【冲浪浴】chōnglàngyù〈名〉surfing bath

【冲力】chōnglì〈名〉momentum: 下落水流的～使水轮转动。The force of the falling water turns the waterwheel.

【冲凉】chōngliáng〈动〉〈方〉take a cool shower

【冲量】chōngliàng〈名〉［物理］impulse

【冲破】chōngpò〈动〉breach: ～敌军防御工事 burst through the enemy defences ‖ ～封锁 break through a blockade ‖ ～传统束缚 smash the shackles of convention

【冲散】chōngsàn〈动〉scatter: ～人群 break up a crowd

【冲杀】chōngshā〈动〉charge: 在枪林弹雨中～ charge head-on against a hail of bullets

【冲沙闸】chōngshāzhá〈名〉［水利］scouring sluice

【冲晒】chōngshài〈动〉［摄影］develop and print

【冲绳岛】Chōngshéngdǎo〈名〉Okinawa

【冲蚀】chōngshí〈动〉erode: 海水～岩石。The sea is wearing away the rocks. ‖ 洪水～出一条深谷。Floods carved out a deep gorge.

【冲刷】chōngshuā〈动〉wash down: ～汽车 wash down the car ‖ 急流沿山坡而下，～出一条水沟。The torrents scoured a channel down the hillside.

【冲塌】chōngtā〈动〉[of floods] destroy: 桥被洪水～了。The bridge was swept away by the floods.

【冲腾】chōngténg〈动〉rise up

【冲天】chōngtiān〈动〉soar skyward: 干劲～ work with soaring enthusiasm ‖ 怒气～ with towering rage

【冲突】chōngtū〈动〉**1**（不一致）conflict: 相互～ conflict with each other ‖ 他们的意见总是～。Their opinions always clash. **2**（有矛盾）clash: 边界～ border conflict ‖ 军事～ military conflict ‖ 劳资～ labour conflict ‖ 流血～ bloody clash ‖ 正面～ head-on collision ‖ 利益～ a collision of interests

【冲洗】chōngxǐ〈动〉**1**（洗刷）rinse: ～厕所 flush the lavatory ‖ ～地板 wash the floor ‖ 用消毒药水～伤口 wash a wound with a disinfectant **2**［摄影］develop: ～放大 develop and enlarge ‖ 我想把这些照片～出来。I would like to have these pictures developed.

【冲洗液】chōngxǐyè〈名〉flushing liquid

【冲喜】chōngxǐ〈动〉arrange a wedding to ward off illness

【冲线】chōngxiàn〈动〉［体育］breast the tape

【冲销】chōngxiāo〈动〉［会计］charge against: ～坏账 write off an uncollectible account

【冲泻】chōngxiè〈动〉rush down in torrents

【冲要】chōngyào〈名〉〈书〉**1**（指地点）strategically important place: 水陆～ important water and land communication centre **2**（指职位）prominent position: 位居～ be in a key position

【冲印】chōngyìn〈动〉develop and print: ～快照 develop and print a snapshot

【冲澡】chōngzǎo〈动〉〈口〉take a shower: 冲个凉水澡 have a cold bath

【冲账】chōngzhàng〈动〉［会计］**1**（指账目）balance out **2**（指款项）write off

【冲撞】chōngzhuàng〈动〉**1**（猛撞）collide: 海浪～着山崖。The waves dashed upon the cliff. ‖ 两列火车发生～，多人丧生。Many people were killed when the two trains collided. **2**（冒犯）offend: 我的一句玩笑话～了她。My joking remarks offended her. **3**［足球］charge: ～守门员 run at the goalie

充 chōng

A〈形〉full: ▸～分，～其量

B〈动〉**1**（使满）fill: ▸～电，～耳不闻，填～ **2**（补足）make up a deficiency: ▸～数 **3**（当作）act as: 一个本地人～作我们的导游。A local man acted as our guide. ‖ 这箱子可～凳子用。The box can serve as a seat. ▸～当，～任 **4**（冒充）pose as: ～内行 pose as an expert ‖ 以次～好 pass off shoddy products as the real thing ▸冒～，打肿脸～胖子

【充畅】chōngchàng〈形〉**1**（指货物）free and smooth: 货源～ sufficient and prompt supply of commodities **2**（指写作）smooth and fluent

【充斥】chōngchì〈动〉〈贬〉flood: 假货～市场。Fake products flooded the market.

【充磁】chōngcí〈动〉magnetize

【充当】chōngdāng〈动〉act as: ～中间人 act as go-between ‖ 她～来宾的翻译。She served as interpreter for the guests.

【充电】chōngdiàn〈动〉**1**（指电池）charge: 给蓄电池～ charge a storage battery ‖ 给手机～ recharge a cell phone ‖

～器 charger 2〈喻〉（指知识）brush up: 在技术方面充一下电 brush up on technology

【充电电池】chōngdiàn diànchí〈名〉rechargeable battery

【充耳不闻】chōng'ěr-bùwén〈成〉turn a deaf ear to: 上司对我的恳求～。My boss turned a deaf ear to my entreaties.

【充分】chōngfèn〈形〉1（充足）abundant: 理由～ have sufficient reasons ‖ ～证明 bear ample testimony (to sth.) ‖ ～准备 make adequate preparation ‖ 我们为旅行做好了～准备。We are fully prepared for the journey. ‖ 我有～的理由相信他是诚实的。I have every reason to believe that he is honest. 2（尽量）full: ～发挥才能 display one's abilities to the full ‖ ～利用 make full use of

C

【充分就业】chōngfèn jiùyè〈名〉［经济］full employment

【充公】chōnggōng〈动〉confiscate: 非法收入被～。The illegal income was confiscated.

【充饥】chōngjī〈动〉appease one's hunger: 吃一块巧克力～ allay one's hunger with a bar of chocolate ‖ 以饼干～ relieve one's hunger with biscuits ▸画饼～

【充军】chōngjūn〈动〉〈古〉be exiled into the military

【充满】chōngmǎn〈动〉be brimming with: ～爱国热情 be imbued with patriotism ‖ ～同情心 brim over with sympathy ‖ 对未来～信心 brim with confidence about one's future ‖ 空气中～浓浓的玫瑰花香。The air was heavy with the strong scent of roses. ‖ 他的好客让我心里～了感激。His hospitality filled my heart with gratitude. ‖ 女孩两眼～了泪水。The girl's eyes were brimming with tears.

【充沛】chōngpèi〈形〉abundant: 精力～ be full of life ‖ 雨水～ with abundant rainfall

【充其量】chōngqíliàng〈副〉at the outside: 那块手表～值五十块钱。That watch will cost 50 *yuan* at most.

【充气】chōngqì〈动〉inflate: 给轮胎～ pump up a tyre ‖ 给气球～ inflate a balloon

【充气床垫】chōngqì chuángdiàn〈名〉air bed

【充气机】chōngqìjī〈名〉inflator

【充气救生衣】chōngqì jiùshēngyī〈名〉air jacket

【充气艇】chōngqìtǐng〈名〉inflatable boat

【充气玩具】chōngqì wánjù〈名〉inflatable toy

【充任】chōngrèn〈动〉fill a post: ～外交职务 fill a diplomatic post

【充塞】chōngsè〈动〉fill: ～市场 congest the market

【充实】chōngshí A〈形〉substantial: 内容～ be substantial in content ‖ 生活～ live a full life B〈动〉substantiate: ～基层 strengthen grass roots organizations ‖ ～内容 enrich the content ‖ ～师资力量 augment the teaching staff ‖ ～文化生活 enrich one's cultural life ‖ 用知识～头脑 enrich the mind with knowledge

【充数】chōngshù〈动〉make up the numbers: 以次品～ make up the amount with defective products ‖ 我来只是充个数。I am here to make up the numbers. ▸滥竽～

【充填】chōngtián〈动〉fill up

【充填物】chōngtiánwù〈名〉filling

【充血】chōngxuè ▸**p. 50**〈动〉［医学］be congested: 脑～ cerebral congestion ‖ 他眼球～了。His eyeballs are congested.

【充溢】chōngyì〈动〉〈书〉overflow with: ～着欢乐 with an exuberance of joy ‖ 她脸上～着喜悦的微笑。She beamed radiantly with joy.

【充盈】chōngyíng〈形〉1（充足）plentiful: 仓廪～。The granaries are full. 2〈书〉（丰满）full and round: 肌体～ well-developed body ‖ 体态～ full figure

【充裕】chōngyù〈形〉abundant: 时间～ have plenty of time ‖ 资金～ have sufficient funds ‖ 粮食～。Food provisions are plentiful.

【充值】chōngzhí〈动〉top up: 交通一卡通可以随时～。A metro pass can be topped up at any time.

【充值卡】chōngzhíkǎ〈名〉top-up card

【充足】chōngzú〈形〉abundant: 供应～ have an abundant supply ‖ 光线～ have ample light ‖ 资金/理由～ have sufficient funds/reason ‖ 睡眠～ get enough sleep

忡 chōng〈形〉〈书〉worried

【忡忡】chōngchōng〈形〉laden with anxiety: ▸忧心～

涌 chōng〈名〉〈方〉branch of a river

▸yǒng

舂 chōng〈动〉pound in a mortar: ～米 husk rice with a mortar and pestle ‖ ～药 pound medicinal herbs into powder in a mortar

憧 chōng

【憧憧】chōngchōng〈形〉flickering: 灯影～ flickering shadows of the light ‖ 人影～ shadows of people moving about

【憧憬】chōngjǐng〈动〉long for: ～幸福的明天 long for the happy days to come ‖ 她～着一种平静安宁的生活。She craves a life of peace and quiet.

艟 chōng ▸艨艟 méngchōng

chóng

虫（蟲）chóng〈名〉1（虫子）insect: 杀～剂 insecticide ▸～害，～子 2〈喻〉〈贬〉（指人）person with a certain kind of undesirable quality: ▸害人～，糊涂～，可怜～

【虫草】chóngcǎo〈简称〉= 冬虫夏草

【虫害】chónghài〈名〉insect attack: 闹～ be infested with insects ‖ ～防治 pest control

【虫胶】chóngjiāo〈名〉shellac

【虫媒花】chóngméihuā〈名〉［植物］entomophilous flower

【虫情】chóngqíng〈名〉pest situation: ～严重 serious pest situation ‖ ～预报 forecast of pest outbreak

【虫牙】chóngyá〈名〉〈口〉decayed tooth

【虫眼】chóngyǎn〈名〉wormhole

【虫灾】chóngzāi〈名〉plague of insects

【虫豸】chóngzhì〈名〉〈书〉insect

【虫蛀】chóngzhù〈动〉be worm-eaten: ～的木材 worm-eaten timber ‖ ～的苹果 wormy apple

【虫子】chóngzi〈名〉worm

种 Chóng〈名〉Chong [surname]

▸zhǒng, zhòng

重 chóng

A〈动〉1（重复）repeat: 书买～了。Two copies of the same book have been bought by mistake. ‖ 这两道练习题出～了。These two exercises duplicate one another. 2（重叠）overlap: 把两张纸～在一起 put one piece of paper on top of the other B〈副〉again: ～抄 copy again ‖ 这一页必须～排。This page will have to be redone. ▸～逢，～归于好 C〈量〉layer: 多～性格 multiple personality

▸zhòng

【重版】chóngbǎn〈动〉republish: 这本书～过无数次。The book went through countless editions.

【重播】chóngbō〈动〉1（指播放）rerun: ～节目 repeat a programme 2（指播种）resow: 因受蝗灾，不少田地必须～种子。Quite a few fields had to be seeded for a second time due to the plague of locusts.

【重操旧业】chóngcāo-jiùyè〈成〉return to one's former trade

【重茬】chóngchá = 连作 liánzuò

【重唱】chóngchàng〈名〉［音乐］ensemble of two or more singers, each singing one part: ▸二～，四～

【重重】chóngchóng〈形〉layer upon layer: 克服～困难 surmount numerous difficulties ‖ 陷入～包围 be heavily besieged ‖ 顾虑～ have no end of worries ‖ 心事～ be laden with anxiety

【重出】chóngchū〈动〉reappear: ～江湖 reappear in public life

【重打锣鼓另开张】chóng dǎ luógǔ lìng kāizhāng〈俗〉begin anew: 公司破产后，他决定～。After the failure of his company, he decided to start from scratch all over again.

【重蹈覆辙】chóngdǎo-fùzhé〈成〉follow the same old road to ruin: 你必须从过去的错误中吸取教训，不能～。You must learn from past mistakes so as not to fall into the same old trap again.

【重叠】chóngdié〈动〉overlap: 山峦～ hill upon hill ‖ 行政机构～ overlapping administrative organizations ‖ ～的影像 superimposed image

【重读】chóngdú〈动〉1（指朗读）read again 2（留级）repeat a year: ～生 repeater ‖ 他两门考试不及格，必须～五年级。He had to repeat the fifth grade because he failed two exams.

▸zhòngdú

【重发球】chóngfāqiú〈名〉［体育］let service

【重返】chóngfǎn〈动〉return: ～工作岗位 return to work ‖ ～家园 return to one's homeland ‖ ～舞台 be back on the stage ‖ ～校园 resume one's interrupted studies at school ‖ ～政治舞台 return to political stage

【重犯】chóngfàn〈动〉relapse: 避免～错误 avoid making the same mistake

【重放】chóngfàng〈动〉rerun: ～录像 run replays of sth. ‖ 以慢镜头～ replay in slow motion

【重逢】chóngféng〈动〉meet again: 久别～ meet again after a long separation ‖ 朋友别后～ reunion of parted friends

【重复】chóngfù〈动〉1（指出现）recur: 历史不会～。History cannot repeat itself. 2（指说话或做事）duplicate: ～抽样 repeated sampling ‖ ～引进 introduction of redundant items

【重复建设】chóngfù jiànshè〈名〉redundant construction

【重构】chónggòu〈名〉reconstruction
【重光】chóngguāng〈动〉**1**（重见光明）recover one's sight **2**（光复）recover: ～河山 recover lost territory
【重归于好】chóngguīyúhǎo〈成〉be reconciled
【重合】chónghé〈动〉［数学］coincide: 两个三角形完全～。The two triangles coincide exactly.
【重婚】chónghūn〈动〉［法律］commit bigamy: ～罪 bigamy
【重茧】chóngjiǎn = 重趼 chóngjiǎn
【重趼】chóngjiǎn〈名〉callus
【重见光明】chóngjiàn-guāngmíng〈惯〉recover one's sight
【重见天日】chóngjiàn-tiānrì〈成〉〈喻〉regain one's freedom
【重建】chóngjiàn〈动〉reconstruct: ～家园 rebuild one's land ‖ 战后～工作 post-war reconstruction
【重九】Chóngjiǔ = 重阳 Chóngyáng
【重聚】chóngjù〈动〉reunite
【重考】chóngkǎo〈动〉retake an exam
【重峦叠嶂】chóngluán-diézhàng〈成〉range upon range of hills
【重码】chóngmǎ〈名〉coincident code
【重名】chóngmíng〈动〉have the same name: ～重姓 have the same first name and the same surname ‖ 她与我～。She is my namesake.
【重拍】chóngpāi〈动〉re-photograph: ～一个镜头 retake a scene
【重启】chóngqǐ〈动〉restart: ～计算机 reboot a computer ‖ ～六方会谈 resume six-party talks
【重起炉灶】chóngqǐ-lúzào = 另起炉灶 lìngqǐ-lúzào
【重庆】Chóngqìng ▸**p. 661**〈名〉Chongqing
【重山叠岭】chóngshān-diélǐng〈成〉range upon range of hills
【重申】chóngshēn〈动〉reaffirm: ～观点 reiterate one's views ‖ ～立场 reaffirm one's stand
【重审】chóngshěn〈动〉［法律］retry: ～案件 rehear a case
【重生】chóngshēng〈动〉**1**（死而复生）come back to life: 人死不能～。Those who have died cannot be revived. **2**（再生长）grow again: 剪去的指甲会～。Cut finger nails will grow again.
【重生父母】chóngshēng-fùmǔ = 再生父母 zàishēng-fùmǔ
【重孙】chóngsūn〈名〉great grandson: ～女 great granddaughter
【重沓】chóngtà〈形〉〈书〉repetitious: 句子～ redundant sentences
【重弹老调】chóngtánlǎodiào = 老调重弹 lǎodiào-chóngtán
【重提】chóngtí〈动〉bring up again: 旧事～ rake up the past
【重围】chóngwéi〈名〉rings of encirclement: 杀出～ break through a tight encirclement ‖ 陷入～ be under siege
【重温】chóngwēn〈动〉review: ～旧情 rekindle old affections ‖ ～往事 review the past
【重温旧梦】chóngwēn-jiùmèng〈成〉revive an old dream
【重文】chóngwén〈名〉［语言］variant form of a Chinese character
【重午】Chóngwǔ〈名〉〈旧〉Dragon Boat Festival
【重现】chóngxiàn〈动〉reappear: ～在脑海里 recur in one's mind ‖ 他的回忆录～了战争场面。His memoirs revive the battle scenes.
【重霄】chóngxiāo〈名〉〈书〉empyrean
【重写】chóngxiě〈动〉rewrite: ～历史 rewrite history
【重新】chóngxīn〈副〉again: ～部署 rearrange ‖ ～恢复职务 be reinstated in one's post ‖ ～考虑 reconsider ‖ ～上台 come back to power ‖ ～审理案件 rehear a case ‖ ～调整 readjust ‖ ～开始 start all over again
【重新做人】chóngxīn-zuòrén〈成〉turn over a new leaf: 痛改前非，～ repair the past and make a fresh start
【重修】chóngxiū〈动〉**1**（指翻修）renovate: ～校舍 renovate an old school building **2**（指修订）revise: ～宪法 revise the constitution **3**（指学习）retake a course after failing an examination
【重修旧好】chóngxiū-jiùhǎo〈成〉bury the hatchet
【重言】chóngyán〈名〉［语言］tautology
【重演】chóngyǎn〈动〉**1**（指表演）repeat a performance **2**（指出现）replay: 历史的悲剧决不会～。The tragedies of history must not be repeated.
【重阳】Chóngyáng〈名〉Double Ninth Festival

> **重阳节**
>
> The ninth day of the ninth month of the lunar calendar, also known as Dogwood Day (茱萸节). The custom at this time is to ascend to a high place, drink chrysanthemum wine, wear dogwood, and eat double-nine cakes (重阳糕). Today, Double Ninth Festival is also China's Day of the Elderly (老人节).

【重洋】chóngyáng〈名〉〈书〉seas and oceans: 远涉～ travel across the oceans ‖ 远隔～ be separated by vast oceans
【重样】chóngyàng〈动〉be the same: 这些画不～。These pictures are different from each other.
【重译】chóngyì〈动〉**1**（再次翻译）retranslate: ～文学名著 retranslate a literary masterpiece **2**（转译）translate from a translation: ～本 retranslation
【重印】chóngyìn〈动〉reprint: ～本 reprint ‖ 该书已是第四次～。This book is now in its 4th reprint.
【重影】chóngyǐng〈名〉double image
【重映】chóngyìng〈动〉reshow (a film)
【重游】chóngyóu〈动〉revisit: 旧地～ revisit a once familiar place
【重振】chóngzhèn〈动〉revitalize: ～精神 rejuvenate one's spirits ‖ ～军威 restore the prestige of the army
【重整旗鼓】chóngzhěng-qígǔ〈成〉rally forces after a setback
【重置】chóngzhì〈动〉replace
【重奏】chóngzòu〈名〉［音乐］ensemble of two or more instrumentalists, each playing one part: 弦/器乐四～ string/instrumental quartet ▸二～
【重足而立】chóngzú'érlì〈成〉be panic-stricken
【重组】chóngzǔ〈动〉restructure: ～内阁 reshuffle the cabinet ‖ 资产～ reorganization of assets

崇 chóng

A〈形〉lofty: ▸～高, ～山峻岭
B〈动〉esteem: ▸～奉, ～尚, 推～
【崇拜】chóngbài〈动〉worship: ～权力/金钱 worship power/money ‖ 个人～ personality cult ‖ ～者 admirer ‖ 她～的政治家是林肯。Her political idol was Lincoln.
【崇本务实】chóngběn-wùshí〈成〉do things in a down-to-earth manner
【崇奉】chóngfèng〈动〉believe in: ～礼教 follow Confucian teaching ‖ 每个宗教都有自己～的神明。Each religion has a different God to worship.
【崇高】chónggāo〈形〉lofty: ～的理想 lofty ideal ‖ ～的目标 noble aim ‖ ～的威望 high prestige ‖ ～的自我牺牲精神 noble spirit of self-sacrifice
【崇敬】chóngjìng〈动〉esteem: 令人～ command respect ‖ 他们怀着～之情缅怀那位老人。They cherish the memory of the old man.
【崇山峻岭】chóngshān-jùnlǐng〈成〉precipitous mountains
【崇尚】chóngshàng〈动〉uphold: ～科学 advocate science ‖ 那是一个～英雄的年代。That was an age of hero worship.
【崇洋】chóngyáng〈动〉worship foreign things: 盲目～ worship foreign things blindly
【崇洋媚外】chóngyáng-mèiwài〈成〉worship foreign things and toady to foreign powers
【崇仰】chóngyǎng〈动〉worship: ～真理 have faith in the truth

chǒng

宠（寵）chǒng〈动〉dote on: 父亲太～她了。Her father overindulged her. ‖ 这孩子给～坏了。The child is very spoilt. ▸～信, 失～

【宠爱】chǒng'ài〈动〉dote on: 那个孩子深受父母～。That child is spoiled by his parents. ‖ 他～最小的儿子。He dotes on his youngest son.
【宠儿】chǒng'ér〈名〉pet: 家庭的～ pet of the family ‖ 时代的～ darling of the day
【宠坏】chǒnghuài〈动〉spoil
【宠溺】chǒngnì〈动〉spoil
【宠辱不惊】chǒngrǔ-bùjīng〈成〉be unmoved by honour or disgrace
【宠物】chǒngwù〈名〉pet: ～店 pet shop ‖ ～食品 pet food ‖ ～医院 pet hospital
【宠信】chǒngxìn〈动〉〈贬〉particularly favour and trust: ～奸佞 show undue favour to wily sycophants ‖ 赢得皇上的～ win imperial favour
【宠幸】chǒngxìng〈动〉favour
【宠用】chǒngyòng〈动〉favour and put sb. in important position: ～亲信 trust and put one's followers in key positions

chòng

冲[1]（衝）chòng〈形〉〈口〉

1（指水流）relentless: 雨下得很～。It's raining hard. **2**（指劲头）vigorous: 说话～ speak bluntly **3**（指气味）pungent: 这药味儿～。The medicine has a strong smell.

冲[2]（衝）chòng〈动〉punch: 在钢板上～一个孔 punch a hole in a steel plate ▸～床, ～模

冲[3]（衝）chòng〈口〉

A〈动〉face: 窗户～着南面。The window faces south. ‖ 房子～着大海。The house fronts onto the sea.
B〈介〉**1**（朝着）towards: 那话是～他说的。That remark was directed at him. ‖ 有气别～我撒呀! Don't vent your anger on me! **2**（凭借）on the basis of: ～着他们

C

这股子干劲儿，没有克服不了的困难。With such drive, there's no difficulty they cannot overcome. ‖ ～着咱们的老交情，我答应这么做。 For old times' sake, I promise to do it.
▸chōng

【冲床】chòngchuáng〈名〉［机械］punching machine

【冲劲儿】chòngjìnr〈名〉1（劲头） vim and vigour: 他干什么都有一股子～。Whatever he does he does with pizzazz. ‖ 她到终点时仍～十足。She still had a lot left in her at the finish. 2（刺激性） strength: 这酒～大。This wine has quite a kick.

【冲模】chòngmú〈名〉［机械］die

【冲头】chòngtóu〈名〉［机械］punching pin

【冲压】chòngyā〈动〉［机械］stamp: ～汽车车身 punch out car bodies ‖ 这台机器一天能～两万枚硬币。This machine can stamp out 20,000 coins a day.

【冲子】chòngzi〈名〉［机械］drill

铳（銃） chòng〈名〉blunderbuss: 鸟～ fowling musket

chōu

抽[1] chōu〈动〉1（指从两物间） draw: 从书架上～出一本书 pull a book out of the shelf ‖ 从信封里～出信来 take a letter out of the envelope ▸～签，～身 2（指从总体中） take: ～时间看病 find time to see a doctor ‖ 把他～出来 release him from his job ▸～查，～调，～样 3（长出） put forth: ▸～穗，～枝 4（缩小） contract: 这件衣服一洗给～了。The garment has shrunk in the wash. ▸～搐，～筋 5（吸） take in: ～雪茄 smoke cigars ‖ 把湖水～干 pump out lake water ‖ 他一天要～一包烟。He smokes up to a pack of cigarettes a day.

抽[2] chōu〈动〉1（打） whip: ～陀螺 spin a top ‖ 他向马～了一鞭子。He whipped the horse. 2［体育］drive: 把球～过去 drive the ball over the net ‖ 正手～ forehand drive ▸～球

【抽测】chōucè〈动〉make a spot check: ～水污染情况 spot check water pollution levels

【抽查】chōuchá〈动〉make spot checks: ～合格 pass a spot check ‖ 经～发现，这些是假钞。On random inspection, these notes proved to be forgeries.

【抽成】chōuchéng〈动〉deduct a percentage: 每人有 25% 的红利～。Everyone will take 25% of the dividend.

【抽抽】chōuchou〈动〉〈口〉1（缩水） shrink: 这块布一洗就～。This cloth shrinks in the wash. 2（萎缩） wither: 树叶经烈日一晒就～。The tree leaves will shrivel up in the hot sun.

【抽搐】chōuchù〈动〉twitch: 不由自主地～ twitch involuntarily ‖ 他的身体一阵阵地～。His body was jerking in quick spasms.

【抽打】chōudǎ〈动〉whip: 用鞭子～某人 flog sb. with a whip

【抽打】chōuda〈动〉get dust out through beating: 把地毯好好～一下。Give the carpet a good beating.

【抽搭】chōuda〈动〉〈口〉sob: 她抽抽搭搭地哭了起来。She broke into sobs.

【抽调】chōudiào〈动〉transfer: ～年轻人担任要职 move young people into key posts

【抽丁】chōudīng〈动〉〈旧〉press-gang: 强行～ press-gang conscripts

【抽动】chōudòng〈动〉twitch: 她哭得身子都～起来了。Sobs shook her body.

【抽斗】chōudǒu〈名〉〈方〉drawer

【抽肥补瘦】chōuféi-bǔshòu〈成〉take from those that have and give to those that have not

【抽风】chōufēng〈动〉1▸p. 50［医学］convulse 2〈口〉〈喻〉（发神经） lose the plot: 你抽什么风，半夜三更了还唱歌? Are you crazy, singing in the dead of night? 3（抽空气） pump air: ～机 air pump

【抽功夫】chōu gōngfu = 抽空 chōukòng

【抽换】chōuhuàn〈动〉replace part of a whole

【抽检】chōujiǎn〈动〉make spot checks: ～一批液态奶 carry out a spot check on a batch of milk

【抽奖】chōujiǎng〈动〉draw for a prize: ～仪式 lottery drawing ceremony ‖ 她参加～得了辆汽车。She won a car in the lucky dip.

【抽筋】chōujīn〈动〉〈口〉develop a cramp: 他腿～了。He got a cramp in his leg.

【抽考】chōukǎo〈动〉make sample tests

【抽空】chōukòng〈动〉find time: 抽不出空来 be unable to find time to do sth. ‖ ～陪孩子出来玩玩 find time to go out and play with the kids

【抽气机】chōuqìjī〈名〉air exhauster

【抽泣】chōuqì〈动〉sob: 独自～ sob to oneself

【抽签】chōuqiān〈动〉draw lots: ～决定比赛次序 draw lots to decide who goes first in the competition ‖ 陪审团名单通过～决定。The jury was selected by drawing lots.

【抽青】chōuqīng〈动〉bud: 老树正在～。The old tree is going green.

【抽球】chōuqiú〈动〉［体育］drive

【抽取】chōuqǔ〈动〉draw: ～10%的佣金 take a 10% commission ‖ ～地下水 pump water from underground ‖ ～蛇毒 extract snake venom

【抽杀】chōushā〈动〉［体育］smash

【抽纱】chōushā〈名〉1［美术］drawn work 2（指工艺品） material made by drawn work

【抽梢】chōushāo〈动〉branch out: 树木开始～。The trees began to branch out.

【抽身】chōushēn〈动〉absent oneself: 及早～ seize the first chance to get away ‖ 他工作忙得抽不出身来照顾孩子。He was tied down to his job and unable to take care of his children. ‖ 一有机会，她便～走了。She took the first opportunity to leave.

【抽身引退】chōushēn yǐntuì〈成〉retire from active public life

【抽水】chōushuǐ〈动〉1（汲水） pump water: 从河里～ pump water from a river 2（缩水） shrink: 这种布～得厉害。The cloth shrinks considerably in the wash.

【抽水机】chōushuǐjī〈名〉pump

【抽水马桶】chōushuǐ mǎtǒng〈名〉flush toilet

【抽水站】chōushuǐzhàn〈名〉water-pumping station

【抽税】chōushuì〈动〉tax

【抽丝】chōusī〈动〉1（指丝线） reel off raw silk from cocoons: ▸病来如山倒，病去如～ 2（指丝袜） ladder〈英〉; run〈美〉: 丝织长统袜容易～。Silk stockings run easily.

【抽丝剥茧】chōusī-bōjiǎn = 剥茧抽丝 bōjiǎn-chōusī

【抽穗】chōusuì〈动〉［of cereal plants］ear: 玉米正在～。The maize is in ear.

【抽缩】chōusuō〈动〉shrink

【抽薹】chōutái〈动〉sprout: 大蒜～了。The garlic has sprouted.

【抽逃】chōutáo〈动〉secretly withdraw funds

【抽屉】chōuti〈名〉drawer

【抽头】chōutóu〈动〉1（指设赌局者） take a cut of the winnings 2（指经纪人） get commissions as brokers

【抽闲】chōuxián〈动〉manage to find time: ～做家务 find time to do housework

【抽象】chōuxiàng A〈动〉form a general idea from particular circumstances: 人们从所有绿色物体中～出绿的概念。People abstract the idea of greenness from the colour of all green objects. B〈形〉abstract: 说得太～ speak in an overly abstract way ‖ 不要这样～地谈问题。Don't speak in such abstract terms.

【抽象概念】chōuxiàng gàiniàn〈名〉abstract concept: 美是一个～。Beauty is an abstract concept.

【抽象画】chōuxiànghuà〈名〉abstract painting

【抽象劳动】chōuxiàng láodòng〈名〉［经济］abstract labour

【抽象名词】chōuxiàng míngcí ▸p. 411〈名〉［语法］abstract noun

【抽象派】chōuxiàngpài〈名〉abstractionist school: ～艺术 abstractionist art ‖ ～艺术家 abstractionist

【抽象思维】chōuxiàng sīwéi〈名〉abstract thought

【抽象艺术】chōuxiàng yìshù〈名〉abstract art

【抽象主义】chōuxiàngzhǔyì〈名〉abstractionism

【抽血】chōuxiě〈动〉draw blood (for a test or transfusion)

【抽薪止沸】chōuxīn-zhǐfèi〈成〉〈喻〉strike at the root of the trouble

【抽选】chōuxuǎn〈动〉select

【抽芽】chōuyá〈动〉bud: 树木正在～。The trees are producing their buds.

【抽烟】chōuyān〈动〉smoke: ～有害健康。Smoking is hazardous to health.

【抽验】chōuyàn〈动〉make a spot-check

【抽样】chōuyàng〈动〉take a sample: ～验收 approve after sample-testing ‖ ～调查 sample survey ‖ 随机～ random sampling

【抽样检验】chōuyàng jiǎnyàn〈名〉sampling test

【抽噎】chōuyē〈动〉sob

【抽咽】chōuyè〈动〉sob

【抽绎】chōuyì = 䌷绎 chōuyì

【抽印】chōuyìn〈动〉offprint: ～本 offprint ‖ 把这本杂志里的头篇文章～一百份。Offprint 100 copies of the first article of the magazine.

【抽油泵】chōuyóubèng〈名〉［石油］oil-well pump

【抽油烟机】chōuyóuyānjī〈名〉grease pump

【抽枝】chōuzhī〈动〉sprout: 树木在雨后～了。After the rain trees sprouted.

【抽壮丁】chōu zhuàngdīng = 抽丁 chōudīng

挡（搊） chōu〈动〉1〈书〉（弹奏） play 2〈方〉（扶起） lift up by applying force from underneath: 小孩摔倒

了，快把他～起来。 The child has fallen down. Hurry and help him to his feet.

䌷（紬） chōu〈动〉〈书〉 draw out
【䌷绎】chōuyì〈动〉 expound

瘳 chōu〈书〉
A〈形〉 cured
B〈动〉 harm

chóu

仇（雠、讐） chóu〈名〉 1▸（仇敌） enemy: ▸～敌, 疾恶如～, 同～敌忾 2▸（仇恨） animosity: 这～一定要报。 This wrong must be avenged. ‖ 他俩之间有～。 There is enmity between the two of them. ▸报～, 世～, 血海深～ ▸Qiú
【仇雠】chóuchóu〈名〉〈书〉 foe
【仇敌】chóudí〈名〉 enemy: 杀掉～ kill an enemy ‖ 家族的～ clan enemy
【仇恨】chóuhèn A〈动〉 hate: ～他人 hate others B〈名〉 hatred: 充满～ be consumed with hatred ‖ 怀有～ feel hatred (towards) ‖ 阶级～ class hatred ‖ 刻骨～ bitter enmity ‖ 种族～ racial animosity
【仇家】chóujiā〈名〉 enemy
【仇人】chóurén〈名〉 foe: 不共戴天的～ sworn enemy
【仇人相见，分外眼红】 chóurén xiāngjiàn, fènwài yǎnhóng〈俗〉 enemies see red the moment they meet
【仇杀】chóushā〈动〉 kill in revenge
【仇视】chóushì〈动〉 view sb./sth. with hostility: ～敌人/侵略者 be hostile to enemies /invaders
【仇外】chóuwài〈动〉 be anti-foreign: ～心理 anti-foreign mentality
【仇冤】chóuyuān〈名〉 enmity
【仇怨】chóuyuàn〈名〉 grudge: 两家的～很深。 The feud between the two families is deep-seated.

俦（儔） chóu〈名〉〈书〉 1▸（伴侣） companion 2▸（同辈） peers
【俦类】chóulèi〈名〉〈书〉 peers
【俦侣】chóulǚ〈名〉〈书〉 companion

帱（幬） chóu〈名〉〈书〉 1▸（帐子） bed curtain 2▸（车帷） carriage curtain

惆 chóu〈形〉〈书〉 grieved
【惆怅】chóuchàng〈形〉 melancholy: 莫名的～ nameless sadness ‖ ～若失 be in a despondent mood

绸（綢） chóu〈名〉 silk
【绸带】chóudài〈名〉 ribbon: 把～打成蝴蝶结 tie a ribbon in a bow
【绸缎】chóuduàn〈名〉 silk goods
【绸缪】chóumóu A〈书〉〈形〉 affectionate: 情意～ be head over heels in love B〈动〉 repair: ▸未雨～
【绸子】chóuzi〈名〉 silk fabric

畴（疇） chóu〈名〉〈书〉 1▸（田地） field: ▸平～, 田～ 2▸（种类） type: ▸范～
【畴昔】chóuxī〈名〉〈书〉 bygone days

酬 chóu
A〈动〉 1▸〈书〉（敬酒） propose a toast: ▸～酢 2▸（回报） reciprocate: ▸～报, ～谢 3▸（实现） realize: ▸壮志未～ 4▸（交往） socialize with: ▸应～
B〈名〉 remuneration: ▸报～, 稿～, 同工同～
【酬报】chóubào A〈动〉 recompense: 无以～ no way to repay ‖ 他们拿钱来～他的辛劳。 They gave him money as a reward for his effort. B〈名〉 remuneration: 不计～ not be concerned about pay
【酬宾】chóubīn〈动〉 sell at a discount price: ～活动 bargain sales ‖ 所有商品以八折～。 All the goods are sold at a 20% discount.
【酬唱】chóuchàng〈动〉 converse in poetry
【酬答】chóudá〈动〉 1▸（酬谢） thank with a gift: 我已充分～了他对我的好意。 I have thanked him fully for his kindness. 2▸（应答） respond
【酬对】chóuduì〈动〉 respond: 善于～ always be ready with an answer
【酬和】chóuhè〈动〉 respond in verse
【酬金】chóujīn〈名〉 monetary reward: 付给～ remunerate sb. ‖ ～优厚 handsome reward
【酬劳】chóuláo A〈动〉 reward: 他们用鲜花和水果～胜利者。 They rewarded the winners with gifts of fruit and flowers. B〈名〉 reward: 不要～ unwilling to take payment ‖ 他们不计～地工作。 They work with no thought of reward.
【酬谢】chóuxiè〈动〉 thank sb. with a gift: ～某人 recompense sb. ‖ 公司赠送他一张支票，～他为公司服务四十年。 He was presented with a cheque in recognition of his forty years' service to the company.
【酬应】chóuyìng〈动〉 1▸（交往） socialize with 2▸〈书〉（应答） respond: ～如流 come up with quick response
【酬酢】chóuzuò〈动〉〈书〉 1▸（敬酒） exchange toasts 2▸（应酬） socialize with

稠 chóu〈形〉 1▸（稠密） dense: 地窄人～ small in area but dense in population 2▸（浓） thick: 肉汁/粥太～。 The gravy/porridge is too thick.
【稠密】chóumì〈形〉 dense: 人口～ densely populated ‖ 枝叶～的树 trees thick with leaves
【稠人广众】chóurén-guǎngzhòng〈成〉big gathering

愁 chóu
A〈动〉worry: 不～吃，不～穿 have enough to eat and wear ‖ 他会～出病来的。 He'll get sick with worry.
B〈名〉 sadness: ▸哀～, 多～善感, 借酒浇～
【愁肠】chóucháng〈名〉 pent-up sadness
【愁肠百结】 chóucháng-bǎijié 〈成〉 be overwhelmed with sorrow and longing
【愁肠寸断】chóucháng-cùnduàn〈成〉feel gut-wrenching sadness
【愁城】 chóuchéng〈名〉〈书〉 worrying situation: 陷入～ fall into a sea of worries
【愁楚】chóuchǔ〈名〉〈书〉 worries and pains: 满腹～ be deeply worried and grieved
【愁怀】 chóuhuái〈名〉〈书〉 anxiety and distress
【愁苦】chóukǔ〈形〉 anxious and distressed: ～的面容 forlorn look
【愁眉】chóuméi〈名〉 knitted brows: ～紧锁/不展 with knitted brows
【愁眉苦脸】chóuméi-kǔliǎn〈成〉 look miserable: 别这样～的。 Don't be so doleful. ‖ 什么事让你这么～的? What are you looking so distressed about?
【愁眉锁眼】chóuméi-suǒyǎn〈成〉 with a worried frown
【愁闷】chóumèn〈形〉glum: 他心里很～。 He is very downcast.
【愁容】chóuróng〈名〉 worried look: 面带～ wear an anxious expression
【愁思】chóusī〈名〉 deep longing: 陷入无限～ sink into a state of profound melancholy ‖ ～百结 be overwhelmed with sorrow
【愁绪】chóuxù〈名〉〈书〉 gloomy mood: ～全消 sadness vanishes ‖ ～满怀 have the weight of the world on one's shoulders
【愁云】chóuyún〈名〉 gloom: 他脸上～顿现。 A heavy cloud came over him.
【愁云惨雾】chóuyún-cǎnwù〈成〉 gloomy scene

筹（籌） chóu
A〈名〉 1▸（小棍儿） chip: 酒～ chips used in drinking games ‖ 竹～ bamboo chip ▸～码 2▸（计策） strategy: ▸一～莫展, 运～帷幄
B〈动〉 plan: ▸～备, 统～
【筹办】chóubàn〈动〉 make arrangements for: ～晚会 make preparations for an evening party ‖ ～婚礼 make arrangements for a wedding ‖ ～学校 plan to set up a school
【筹备】 chóubèi〈动〉 prepare: ～会议 arrange a meeting ‖ 做大量～工作 do extensive preparation work
【筹备会】 chóubèihuì〈名〉 preparatory meeting
【筹备委员会】chóubèi wěiyuánhuì〈名〉 preparatory committee
【筹措】 chóucuò〈动〉 raise: ～旅费 raise money for travelling expenses ‖ ～资金 raise funds
【筹划】 chóuhuà〈动〉 1▸（规划） plan and prepare: ～未来 plan for the future ‖ 这里正在～造核电站。 Plans are being drawn up to build a nuclear power plant here. 2▸（筹措） raise: ～资金 raise funds
【筹集】chóují〈动〉 collect: ～资金 raise funds ‖ 通过募捐～五十万美元 raise half a million US dollars in donations
【筹建】chóujiàn〈动〉 prepare to establish: ～学校 make preparations for the establishment of a school ‖ 公司开始～。 Preparations have kicked off for setting up the company.
【筹借】chóujiè〈动〉 try to get a loan: ～到大笔款项 be granted a big loan
【筹款】chóukuǎn〈动〉 raise money: 通过发行股票的方式～ flotation involving the issue of shares
【筹略】chóulüè〈名〉 strategy
【筹码】chóumǎ〈名〉 counter: 把～换成现钱 cash in one's chips ‖〈喻〉 用作政治交易的～ use as bargaining chips in political deals
【筹谋】chóumóu〈动〉 devise strategies: ～解决问题的途径 work out a strategy
【筹募】chóumù〈动〉 collect: ～福利基金 organize the collection of welfare funds
【筹拍】chóupāi〈动〉 plan to shoot: ～电影 plan to shoot a film
【筹商】chóushāng〈动〉 discuss: ～对策 discuss what countermeasures to take
【筹算】chóusuàn〈动〉 1▸（计算） calculate with chips 2▸（谋划） calculate: 精明地～ calculate shrewdly ‖ 不经～贸然行

事 do things without thinking them through
【筹委会】chóuwěihuì〈简称〉= 筹备委员会
【筹资】chóuzī〈动〉raise funds: ～办学 raise money for schools
【筹组】chóuzǔ〈动〉prepare and form: ～工作班子 prepare for setting up a work-team

踌（躊）chóu
【踌躇】chóuchú〈形〉1（犹豫）hesitant: 毫不～ without a moment's hesitation ‖ ～不决 dither ‖ 别再～了，下决心吧! Stop dithering and make up your mind. 2〈书〉（得意）smug: ▸～满志
【踌躇不前】chóuchú-bùqián〈成〉hang back
【踌躇满志】chóuchú-mǎnzhì〈成〉be puffed up with pride: 一副～的样子 utter complacency

雠（讎、讐）chóu
A〈名〉〈书〉foe: ▸仇～
B〈动〉collate: ▸校～

chǒu

丑[1] chǒu〈名〉1（指地支）second of the twelve Earthly Branches 2［戏曲］*chou* [the comic role, one of the four main roles in traditional Chinese opera]: 小～ clown

丑[2]（醜）chǒu
A〈形〉1（难看）ugly: 长得～ be ugly ▸～八怪, ～陋 2（令人厌恶）disgraceful: ▸～恶, ～态百出 3〈方〉（坏）bad: ～脾气 be bad-tempered
B〈名〉disgrace: ▸出～, 家～
【丑八怪】chǒubāguài〈名〉〈口〉monster: 童话里的巫婆都是些～。In fairy tales, witches are ugly creatures.
【丑旦】chǒudàn = 彩旦 cǎidàn
【丑恶】chǒu'è〈形〉ugly: ～灵魂/嘴脸 ugly soul/features ‖ ～现象 vile practice ‖ ～行为 disgusting behaviour
【丑化】chǒuhuà〈动〉vilify: ～劳动人民形象 smear the reputation of the working people ‖ 被～成逆来顺受的可怜虫 be lampooned as a doormat
【丑话】chǒuhuà〈名〉1（粗话）foul language 2（不中听的话）offensive words: 我把～说在前头。Do not be offended by my frankness.
【丑剧】chǒujù〈名〉farce: 形同一幕～ make a complete mockery.
【丑角】chǒujué〈名〉1（指戏曲角色）comic character: 扮～ act the clown ‖ 马戏团～ circus clown 2（不光彩的人）clown
【丑类】chǒulèi〈名〉villains
【丑陋】chǒulòu〈形〉ugly: 相貌～ have ugly features
【丑婆子】chǒupózi〈名〉［戏曲］old comedienne
【丑时】chǒushí〈名〉〈旧〉period of the day from 1 am to 3 am
【丑史】chǒushǐ〈名〉ignominious past
【丑事】chǒushì〈名〉scandal: 掩盖～ hush up a scandal
【丑态】chǒutài〈名〉buffoonery: 官场～ the buffoonery of officialdom
【丑态百出】chǒutài-bǎichū〈成〉act like a buffoon
【丑态毕露】chǒutài-bìlù〈成〉act shamelessly
【丑闻】chǒuwén〈名〉scandal: 卷入～ be embroiled in a scandal ‖ 政治～ political scandal
【丑媳妇总要见公婆】chǒuxífu zǒng yào jiàn gōngpó〈俗〉〈喻〉one cannot hide one's shortcomings forever
【丑星】chǒuxīng〈名〉clown star
【丑行】chǒuxíng〈名〉disgraceful behaviour

瞅 chǒu〈动〉〈方〉look at: ～一眼 sneak a peep ‖ 你～～这个。Take a look at this.
【瞅见】chǒujiàn〈动〉〈方〉see: 你～了没有? Did you see it?
【瞅空】chǒukòng〈动〉〈方〉watch for an opportunity: ～去他家坐坐。Try to find time to drop in on him.

chòu

臭 chòu
A〈形〉1（难闻）smelly: ～鸡蛋 rotten egg ‖ 真～! What a stink! ▸～豆腐, ～气, 腥～ 2（令人厌恶）disgusting: ～名声 infamy ▸～架子 3〈口〉（拙劣）poor: 这一着真～! What a lousy move! ▸～棋, ～球 4〈口〉（失效）dud: ～子儿 dud ▸～弹
B〈副〉unrelentingly: 挨了一顿～揍 get a good beating ▸～骂
▸xiù
【臭不可闻】chòubùkěwén〈成〉1（指气味）give off an unbearable stench 2（指名声）be infamous
【臭虫】chòuchóng〈名〉bedbug
【臭椿】chòuchūn〈名〉［植物］tree of heaven
【臭大姐】chòudàjiě〈名〉［昆虫］stink bug
【臭弹】chòudàn〈名〉dud
【臭豆腐】chòudòufu〈名〉strong-smelling preserved fermented bean curd
【臭烘烘】chòuhōnghōng〈形〉stinking: ～的袜子 smelly socks
【臭乎乎】chòuhūhū〈形〉〈口〉smelly: 这条鱼～的，最好别吃了。This fish is a bit smelly. Better not eat it.
【臭架子】chòujiàzi〈名〉nauseating airs: 摆～ put on airs
【臭老九】chòulǎojiǔ〈名〉〈贬〉stinking ninth grader [a label given to intellectuals]
【臭骂】chòumà〈动〉give sb. a dressing down: 挨一顿～ get a good dressing down
【臭美】chòuměi〈动〉〈口〉〈贬〉show off: 你有什么可～的! You've got nothing to be smug about! ‖ 人家都说他～。Everyone says he is a show-off.
【臭名】chòumíng〈名〉infamy: ～远扬 be infamous
【臭名昭著】chòumíng-zhāozhù〈成〉be notorious: 他是个～的政客。He is a notorious politician.
【臭皮囊】chòupínáng〈名〉［佛教］mortal flesh
【臭棋】chòuqí〈名〉〈口〉stupid move: 走了一着～ make a lousy move
【臭气】chòuqì〈名〉foul smell: 散发～ give off a bad odour ‖ ～熏天 stink to high heaven
【臭球】chòuqiú〈名〉〈口〉［体育］lousy pass
【臭水沟】chòushuǐgōu〈名〉sewage ditch
【臭味相投】chòuwèi-xiāngtóu〈成〉〈贬〉be two of a kind: 他俩～。They are birds of a feather.
【臭腺】chòuxiàn〈名〉［动物］scent gland
【臭氧】chòuyǎng〈名〉［化学］ozone: ～发生器 ozonizer ‖ ～消耗 ozone depletion
【臭氧层】chòuyǎngcéng〈名〉ozone layer
【臭鼬】chòuyòu〈名〉［动物］skunk

chū

出[1] chū〈动〉1（出去）go out: ～火车站 come out of the railway station ‖ 进进～～的，干什么呀? What's this coming and going all about? 2（出现）appear: 语～《老子》。The quotations are from *Laozi*. ▸～丑，水落石～ 3（来到）show up: ▸～场, ～席 4（给出）offer: ～考题 set an examination paper ‖ ～主意 offer advice ‖ 有钱的～钱，有力的～力。The rich will contribute money; the strong, labour. 5（支出）pay out: ▸～纳, 入不敷～, 岁～ 6（离开）leave: ▸～发, ～家, ～局 7（超过）exceed: 不～三天，他准回来。He is sure to be back within three days. ‖ 球～了边线。The ball was out. ▸～格, ～乎意料, ～界 8（长出）put forth: ▸～苗, ～芽 9（生产、产生）produce: ～成果 produce results ‖ 实践～真知。Genuine knowledge comes from practice. ‖ 四川～橘子。Sichuan Province produces oranges. ▸～活, 人才辈～ 10（发生）happen: ～问题/毛病 go wrong/amiss 11（出版）publish: 这种杂志每月～一期。This magazine comes out monthly. 12（发出）vent: ▸～汗, ～花儿, ～疹子 13（显得量多）grow in volume: ▸～饭, ～数儿 14〈方〉（趋向）go out [used with 往 indicating an outward direction]: 电影散场了，大家都往～走。The movie was over and the audience came out. 15（表动作趋向）[used after a verb to indicate an outward direction or a completed action]: 拿～证件 show one's papers ‖ 掏～钱包 draw out one's purse ‖ 我看～了他的心事。I've read his mind. 16（表比较）be in excess: 多～两把椅子。There are two more chairs than needed. ‖ 新办法实施后，效率高～一倍。The new programme raised efficiency two-fold.

出[2]（齣）chū〈量〉[for operas, plays, etc.]: 一～戏 a performance
【出版】chūbǎn〈动〉publish: ～新书 publish a new book ‖ 自费～ self-publish ‖ ～计划 publication schedule ‖ ～自由 freedom of the press ‖ 她的新书～了。Her new book is out.
【出版发行】chūbǎn fāxíng〈名〉publication and distribution
【出版界】chūbǎnjiè〈名〉the press
【出版权】chūbǎnquán〈名〉right of publication
【出版商】chūbǎnshāng〈名〉publisher
【出版社】chūbǎnshè〈名〉publishing house
【出版物】chūbǎnwù〈名〉publication: 非法～ illegal publication
【出版许可证】chūbǎn xǔkězhèng〈名〉imprimatur
【出榜】chūbǎng〈动〉1（指名单）publish a list of successful candidates: 考试后三日～。The examination results will be out in three days. 2〈旧〉（指文告）put up a notice: ～招贤 advertise for qualified people
【出奔】chūbēn〈动〉flee: 离家～ run away from home ‖ 仓促～ flee in a hurry

【出殡】chūbìn〈动〉 hold a funeral procession

【出兵】chūbīng〈动〉 dispatch troops: ～边疆 send troops to border areas ‖ ～御敌 dispatch troops to resist the enemy

【出材量】chūcáiliàng〈名〉［林业］ mill turn

【出材率】chūcáilǜ〈名〉［林业］ turnout percentage

【出彩】chūcǎi〈动〉 1〈旧〉（指戏曲表演） apply red to sb. to indicate bleeding 2〈诙〉（出丑） make a fool of oneself 3（显得精彩） perform outstandingly: 表演很～ give an excellent performance

【出操】chūcāo〈动〉 go out to do exercises: 新兵每天～两小时。 New recruits have two hours' drill time every day.

【出岔子】chū chàzi〈惯〉 go awry: 一定是～了。 Something must have gone wrong.

【出差】chūchāi〈动〉 go away on business: 去东京～ go on a business trip to Tokyo ‖ ～费 allowance for a business trip

【出产】chūchǎn A〈动〉 produce: 本地～ be locally manufactured ‖ 这里～的丝绸畅销世界各地。 The silk manufactured here sells well all over the world. B〈名〉 product: 当地的～ local produce

【出厂】chūchǎng〈动〉 [of products] be dispatched from the factory: ～检验 routine test ‖ ～价 factory price ‖ ～日期 date of production ‖ 不合格产品不能～。 Substandard products are not to leave the factory.

【出场】chūchǎng〈动〉 1（上台表演） enter the stage: ～费 appearance fee ‖ 她要到第二幕才～。 She doesn't go on till Act II. 2（参加比赛） enter the arena: ～运动员名单 list of players for the match

【出超】chūchāo〈名〉［经济］ trade surplus

【出车】chūchē〈动〉 1（指车辆） dispatch a vehicle: 公共汽车早上六点～。 Bus services start at 6 am. 2（指人） be out driving a vehicle: ～送人去机场 drive sb. to the airport

【出乘】chūchéng〈动〉 be on duty as a member of the crew

【出丑】chūchǒu〈动〉 make a spectacle of oneself: 使某人～ score a point over sb. ‖ 当众～ be publicly humiliated

【出处】chūchù〈名〉 source: 查明引文～ find out the source of a quotation

【出错】chūcuò〈动〉 make a mistake

【出道】chūdào〈动〉 serve out one's apprenticeship and start one's career: 他～早。 He had an early start in his career.

【出典】chūdiǎn A〈名〉 source: 这句成语的～见《圣经》。 This idiom is an allusion to the *Bible*. B〈动〉〈旧〉 mortgage: ～房屋 mortgage one's house

【出点子】chū diǎnzi〈动〉〈口〉 make suggestions: 大家一起～，或许能想出办法。 Let's brainstorm, and we may work out a solution.

【出动】chūdòng〈动〉 1（外出活动） set out: 待命～ await orders to go into action 2（派出） dispatch: ～军队镇压叛乱 dispatch troops to stamp out a rebellion 3（行动起来） go into action: 全村人～寻找失踪的孩子。 The whole village turned out to search for the missing child.

【出尔反尔】chū'ěr-fǎn'ěr〈成〉 go back on one's word: 你不能总是～。 You cannot be always chopping and changing.

【出发】chūfā〈动〉 1（指行为） set out: 按时～ depart on schedule ‖ 准备～ get ready to leave ‖ 我们几时～? When shall we set out? 2（指想法、观点） take a perspective: 从长远的观点～ from a long-term point of view ‖ 从全局～ in view of the overall situation

【出发点】chūfādiǎn〈名〉 1（指旅程） starting point 2（动机） purpose: 全心全意为人民服务是我们的基本～。 Our basic aim is to serve the people wholeheartedly.

【出饭】chūfàn〈动〉〈口〉 [of rice,millet,etc.] swell a lot during cooking: 这种米很～。 This kind of rice swells up a lot when it's cooked.

【出访】chūfǎng〈动〉 visit a foreign country: ～俄罗斯 go to Russia for a visit

【出份子】chū fènzi〈动〉〈口〉 1（指凑钱送礼） club together: ～买礼物 club together to buy sb. a gift 2（指参加喜丧活动） present a gift

【出风头】chū fēngtou〈惯〉 court publicity: 爱～ be fond of the limelight ‖ 大～ cut a dashing figure

【出伏】chūfú〈动〉 come to the end of the hottest days of the year: 今天～。 The hottest days are over today.

【出港】chūgǎng〈动〉 clear a port

【出阁】chūgé〈动〉〈旧〉 [of a girl] get married: 他的两个女儿都已～。 Both of his daughters are married.

【出格】chūgé〈形〉 1（出众） outstanding: 她在班里是～的。 She's head and shoulders above her classmates. 2（过分） excessive: 你的玩笑开得太～了。 You've carried this joke too far. ‖ 她做得有点～。 She's going a bit too far.

【出工】chūgōng〈动〉 show up for work: ～不出力 show up for the work but do not exert oneself ‖ 他昨天没～。 He was absent from work yesterday.

【出恭】chūgōng〈动〉〈书〉 go to the lavatory

【出乖露丑】chūguāi-lùchǒu〈成〉 expose one's weak points

【出轨】chūguǐ〈动〉 1（脱轨）be derailed: 火车突然～。 The train suddenly jumped the rails. 2（指行为言语过分） overstep the bounds: 对女士讲这样的话太～了。 It is overstepping the mark to say that to a lady. 3〈喻〉（有婚外情） have an extramarital affair

【出国】chūguó〈动〉 go abroad: ～访问 go abroad for a visit ‖ ～留学 study abroad ‖ ～旅行 travel abroad ‖ ～深造 go abroad for advanced studies ‖ ～热 craze for going abroad

【出海】chūhǎi〈动〉 be out at sea: ～捕鱼 go fishing at sea ‖ ～口 access to the sea

【出汗】chūhàn〈动〉 sweat: 出冷汗 break into a cold sweat ‖ 出一身汗 sweat all over

【出航】chūháng〈动〉 1（指飞机） take off 2（指船） set sail: 船准时～。 The ship set sail on schedule.

【出号】chūhào〈形〉 extra-large: 那家店里有～的鞋卖。 That store sells extra-large shoes.

【出乎意料】chūhū-yìliào〈成〉beyond one's expectations: ～的好消息 good news beyond all expectations

【出花儿】chūhuār〈动〉 have smallpox

【出活】chūhuó〈动〉 1（有成果） get sth. done: 他干了老半天，却没～。He worked for ages but got nothing done. 2（有效率） be efficient: 改进后的工具既轻巧又～。 The improved tools are efficient as well as handy to use.

【出货】chūhuò〈动〉 1（生产出） manufacture 2（出仓库） take goods out of the warehouse: ～单 delivery order

【出货量】chūhuòliàng〈名〉 shipment volume: 水产海鲜市场～大增。 There has been a surge in the shipping volume of seafood products.

【出击】chūjī〈动〉 launch an attack: 频频向敌人～ strike at the enemy repeatedly ‖ 重兵～ launch a mighty army against ‖ 主动～ be on the attack

【出继】chūjì〈动〉 be adopted as a son: 他一出生就～给了伯父。 He was adopted by his uncle immediately after his birth.

【出家】chūjiā〈动〉 become a monk or nun: ～修行 enter religious practice

【出家人】chūjiārén〈名〉（和尚） monk;（尼姑） nun

【出价】chūjià〈动〉 make an offer: 最高～ highest bid ‖ 有人～十万元买这房子。 Someone has offered 100,000 *yuan* for the house.

【出嫁】chūjià〈动〉 [of a girl] get married

【出将入相】chūjiàng-rùxiàng〈成〉 have both civil and military abilities

【出界】chūjiè〈动〉［体育］ be out: 球～了吗? Did the ball cross the line?

【出借】chūjiè〈动〉 loan: ～录像带/图书 lend video tapes/books

【出境】chūjìng〈动〉 1（指国家） leave the country: 办理～手续 go through exit formalities ‖ 驱逐～ deport ‖ ～旅游 outbound travel 2（指地区） leave a certain region

【出境签证】chūjìng qiānzhèng〈名〉 exit visa

【出境许可证】chūjìng xǔkězhèng〈名〉 exit permit

【出境游】chūjìngyóu〈名〉 outbound tourism: 东南亚是中国公民～的热门路线。 Southeast Asia is a popular destination for outbound Chinese tourists.

【出镜】chūjìng〈动〉［影视］ appear on screen: ～率 number of screen appearances

【出九】chūjiǔ〈动〉 come to the end of the coldest days of the year: 出了九，天气会慢慢暖和起来。 Now that the coldest days are over, the weather will be getting warmer.

【出局】chūjú〈动〉 be eliminated: 淘汰～ be eliminated from competition ‖ 裁判宣布击球员～。 The umpire gave the batsman out.

【出具】chūjù〈动〉 produce: ～介绍信/健康证明 write out a letter of introduction/a health certificate

【出圈】chūjuàn〈方〉= 起圈 qǐjuàn

【出科】chūkē〈动〉〈旧〉 graduate from a traditional opera school

【出口】chūkǒu A〈动〉 1（说出来） utter: 这话我怎么能说～? How could I let those words come out of my mouth? ►～成章, ～伤人 2（离开港口） leave port 3（输出国外） export: ～技术/小麦 export techniques/wheat ‖ 禁止～ ban exports ‖ ～创汇 earn foreign exchange through export ►～商品 B〈名〉 exit: 安全～ fire escape ‖ 地铁～ subway exit ‖ 紧急～ emergency exit

【出口成章】chūkǒu-chéngzhāng〈成〉talk poetically

【出口关税】chūkǒu guānshuì〈名〉export tariff

【出口检疫】chūkǒu jiǎnyì〈名〉 export quarantine

【出口量】chūkǒuliàng〈名〉 export volume

【出口贸易】chūkǒu màoyì〈名〉 export trade

【出口配额】chūkǒu pèi'é〈名〉export quota
【出口伤人】chūkǒu-shāngrén〈成〉offend with rude remarks: 她这人尖酸刻薄，总是～。She has an acid tongue, and offends people every time she opens her mouth.
【出口商品】chūkǒu shāngpǐn〈名〉export goods
【出口退税】chūkǒu tuìshuì〈名〉export tax rebate: ～政策 policy of tax refunds on export goods
【出口许可证】chūkǒu xǔkězhèng〈名〉export permit: ～制度 export licence system
【出口转内销】chūkǒu zhuǎn nèixiāo〈动〉sell exports on the home market
【出来】chūlái〈动〉**1**（到外面）come out: 快～，外面有人找。Come out quickly. Someone wants to see you. ‖ 全家人都～迎接客人。The whole family turned out to greet the guest. **2**（出现）emerge: 问题又～了。Another problem cropped up. ‖ 选举结果～了。The election results are out. **3**（表随动作由里到外）be out: 那人刚从监狱里放～。That man has just been released from prison. **4**（完成）complete: 报告写～没有? Have you finished writing the report? **5**（表由隐蔽到显露）[used after a verb indicating revealing]: 看不～她有那么大年纪。She doesn't look her age. ‖ 你能听～他的弦外之音吗? Can you make out what he meant?
【出栏】chūlán〈动〉[of livestock] become full-grown and ready for slaughter
【出栏率】chūlánlǜ〈名〉number of animals for sale
【出类拔萃】chūlèi-bácuì〈成〉outstanding: 他是个～的演说家。He excels as an orator.
【出力】chūlì〈动〉exert oneself: 大家都很～。Everyone went all out.
【出列】chūliè〈动〉［军事］fall out
【出猎】chūliè〈动〉go hunting
【出溜】chūliu〈动〉〈方〉slide: 脚下一～，差点儿摔倒 slip and almost fall over ‖ 从沙堆上～下来 slide down the sand dune ‖ 她的学习成绩在往下～。Her school record is slipping.
【出笼】chūlóng〈动〉**1**（指馒头等）come out of the steamer: 刚～的馒头 steamed bread just out of the steamer **2**〈喻〉（指钞票、货物）put forth in large quantities **3**〈喻〉〈贬〉（指伪劣商品等）appear
【出娄子】chūlóuzi〈动〉go wrong
【出炉】chūlú〈动〉**1**〈本〉take out from an oven: 刚～的芝麻烧饼 baked sesame cakes straight out of the oven **2**〈喻〉（产生）produce: 十佳运动员名单今日～。The names of the ten best athletes will be announced today.
【出路】chūlù〈名〉**1**（机会）way out: 另谋～ seek other employment opportunities ‖ 不改革就没有～。There is no other solution than reform. ‖ 坚持错误是没有～的。You will get nowhere if you cling to your mistakes. **2**（销路）sales outlet: 为产品找～ find outlets for products
【出乱子】chū luànzi〈惯〉get into trouble: 这样做会～的。If you do it like this, you'll get yourself into trouble.
【出落】chūluo〈动〉bloom: 几年没见，那姑娘～得更漂亮了。That girl has grown prettier in the years since I last saw her.
【出马】chūmǎ〈动〉go into action: 亲自～ take personal charge of a matter ▸老将～，一个顶俩
【出卖】chūmài〈动〉**1**（出售）sell: ～房产 sell one's house ‖ 高价～ sell at a high price **2**〈贬〉（背叛）sell out: ～民族利益 betray the interests of the nation ‖ ～朋友 sell out one's friends ‖ 她觉得被人～了。She felt betrayed.
【出毛病】chū máobìng〈惯〉break down: 机器～了。The machine is out of order.
【出梅】chūméi〈动〉come to the end of the rainy season
【出门】chūmén〈动〉**1**（外出）go out: 她最近不大～。She doesn't go out much these days. **2**（到外地）be away from home: ～在外，自己保重。Take care of yourself while you are away from home. ‖ 在家千日好，～一时难。There is no place like home.
【出门子】chū ménzi〈动〉〈方〉[of a girl] get married
【出面】chūmiàn〈动〉do personally: ～交涉 negotiate on sb.'s behalf ‖ 亲自～ handle the matter oneself ‖ 政府～干预。The government stepped in.
【出苗】chūmiáo = 露苗 lòumiáo
【出名】chūmíng **A**〈形〉famous: ～的人物 famous personality ‖ 她已相当～。She has gained considerable repute. **B**〈动〉lend one's name (to an occasion or enterprise): 他们将～组织慈善拍卖。They will lend their names to an auction for charity.
【出没】chūmò〈动〉come and go: 这里有老虎～。This area is a tiger haunt.
【出没无常】chūmò-wúcháng〈成〉appear and disappear unpredictably
【出谋划策】chūmóu-huàcè〈成〉give advice and suggestions from behind the scenes: 她经常为女儿～。She frequently schemed on her daughter's behalf.
【出纳】chūnà **A**〈动〉**1**（指钱）receive and pay out money **2**（指物）give out and receive objects **B**〈名〉cashier〈英〉; teller〈美〉
【出纳员】chūnàyuán〈名〉cashier〈英〉; teller〈美〉
【出票】chūpiào〈动〉issue a ticket: 当日～ issue tickets on the same day ‖ ～口 ticket slot
【出票率】chūpiàolǜ〈名〉ratio of tickets sold: 两场演出～都在95%以上。The ratio of tickets sold for the two performances is over 95%.
【出品】chūpǐn **A**〈动〉produce **B**〈名〉product: 新～ new product
【出聘】chūpìn〈动〉〈旧〉[of a woman] get married: 她的女儿上个月～了。Her daughter got married last month.
【出圃】chūpǔ〈动〉transplant mature seedlings from a nursery
【出其不意】chūqíbùyì〈成〉take sb. by surprise: ～地对某人下手 catch sb. with his pants down
【出奇】chūqí〈形〉extraordinary: 笨得～ extraordinarily stupid ‖ 冷得～ unusually cold
【出奇制胜】chūqí-zhìshèng〈成〉seize victory through a surprise attack: ～的战术 shock tactics
【出气】chūqì〈动〉vent one's spleen: 别拿我～。Don't take it out on me.
【出气筒】chūqìtǒng〈名〉〈喻〉punch bag: 秘书成了他的～。His secretary had to bear the brunt of his temper.
【出勤】chūqín〈动〉**1**（指上班）show up for work: 一周没～ be absent from work for a whole week ‖ ～奖 attendance bonus ‖ ～率 attendance **2**（指外出）go out on business
【出去】chūqù〈动〉**1**（外出）go out: ～散步 go out for a walk **2**（离开）be out: 搬/拿～ move/take sth. out ‖ 说～ let sth. out ‖ 滚～! Piss off!
【出缺】chūquē〈动〉fall vacant: 局长病故～，由副局长替代。The director's illness and death created a vacancy in the office, and the vice-director filled in.
【出让】chūràng〈动〉sell for oneself: 廉价～ sell at a reduced price
【出人命】chū rénmìng〈动〉cause loss of life: 警方接报，超市～了。The police were informed that there had been a death at the supermarket.
【出人头地】chūréntóudì〈成〉be a cut above the rest
【出人意表】chūrényìbiǎo = 出人意料 chūrényìliào
【出人意料】chūrényìliào〈成〉exceed all expectations: 他的回答～。His answer came as a surprise.
【出任】chūrèn〈动〉take up a post: ～要职 hold a key position ‖ 他～驻中国大使。He was made ambassador to China.
【出入】chūrù **A**〈动〉come in and go out: ～请下车! Cyclists please dismount at the gate! ‖ 东西堆在过道，～不方便。The corridor is jammed up with stuff, causing a lot of inconvenience. **B**〈名〉discrepancy: 两种说法有很大～。There is considerable discrepancy between the two versions. ‖ 她说的与事实有～。What she said is inconsistent with the facts.
【出入证】chūrùzhèng〈名〉pass
【出丧】chūsāng〈动〉hold a funeral procession
【出色】chūsè〈形〉outstanding: 表演～ perform perfectly on the stage ‖ ～地完成任务 accomplish a task with flying colours ‖ 她干得非常～。She is brilliant at her job.
【出山】chūshān〈动〉〈喻〉take up an official post: 再度～ resume an old activity
【出身】chūshēn **A**〈动〉be descended from: ～低微 be of humble stock ‖ ～名门 come from noble ancestry ‖ ～于农民家庭 come from peasant stock **B**〈名〉one's background: 行伍～ rise from the ranks ‖ 演员～的政治家 actor-turned politician
【出神】chūshén〈动〉be lost in thought: 听得～ listen with rapt attention ‖ 他坐在那里～。He sat there, lost in thought.
【出神入化】chūshén-rùhuà〈成〉reach the acme of perfection: 他的演技已经达到～的境界。His performance has reached outstanding heights.
【出生】chūshēng〈动〉be born: ～日期 date of birth ‖ ～地 birthplace ‖ 这个婴儿～时重 8 磅。The baby weighed eight pounds at birth.
【出生率】chūshēnglǜ〈名〉birth rate: ～激增/骤减 baby boom/bust
【出生入死】chūshēng-rùsǐ〈成〉untold dangers: 他为了国家的独立～。He risked death for the independence of his country.
【出生证】chūshēngzhèng〈名〉birth certificate
【出声】chūshēng〈动〉utter a sound: 读～ read out ‖ 别～! Hush!
【出师】chūshī〈动〉**1**（指学徒）serve out one's apprenticeship: 他～了。He is through with his apprenticeship. **2**〈书〉（指军队）dispatch troops: ～前线 send troops to the front
【出师不利】chūshībùlì〈成〉start off on the wrong foot
【出使】chūshǐ〈动〉be sent on a diplomatic

mission: ～外国 be accredited to a foreign country

【出示】chūshì〈动〉 show: ～证件 produce one's papers ‖ ～证据 present evidence ‖ 请～月票。 Please show your monthly ticket.

【出世】chūshì〈动〉 **1**（出生） be born: 她那时还没～呢。 She was not yet born then. **2**（产生） come into being **3**（超脱人世） withdraw from the world

【出仕】chūshì〈动〉〈旧〉 assume an official post

【出事】chūshì〈动〉 have an accident: ～地点 site of an accident ‖ 飞机～了。 There was a plane crash.

【出手】chūshǒu **A**〈动〉 **1**（卖出） sell: 家具已全部～。 All the furniture has been sold. **2**（花钱） give out: ～阔绰 spend money freely **3**（打人） come to blows **B**〈名〉 **1**（袖长） sleeve length **2**（本领） skill displayed in making opening moves

【出手不凡】chūshǒu-bùfán〈成〉 make a skilful opening move

【出首】chūshǒu〈动〉〈书〉 **1**（告发） denounce sb. as a criminal **2**（自首） give oneself up to the police

【出售】chūshòu〈动〉 sell: 禁止～ sales are prohibited ‖ 按市场价格～ sell at the market price ‖ 高价～ sell at a high price ‖ 亏本～ sell at a loss

【出书】chūshū〈动〉 publish/produce a book

【出数儿】chūshùr〈动〉〈口〉 [of rice] rise well with cooking

【出双入对】chūshuāng-rùduì〈成〉 go everywhere in pairs

【出水】chūshuǐ〈动〉 **1**（从水中出来） appear above water: ～才见两腿泥。 It is the end that counts most. **2**（水向外流） spurt water: 那眼泉又～了。 The spring is flowing again. ‖ 我们的井～了! Our well is producing water!

【出水芙蓉】chūshuǐ-fúróng〈成〉 **1**〈本〉（指花） lotus flower just appearing above the water **2**〈喻〉（指物） beautiful work of art **3**〈喻〉（指人） beautiful woman

【出水管】chūshuǐguǎn〈名〉 discharging tube

【出水口】chūshuǐkǒu〈名〉 water outlet

【出台】chūtái〈动〉 **1**（指演出） enter the stage: 她 15 岁就开始～演出。 She went on the stage at 15. **2**〈喻〉（指政策、措施） come out: ～改革方案 set forth a programme of reforms

【出摊】chūtān〈动〉 set up a stall

【出逃】chūtáo〈动〉 flee: 仓皇～ flee in confusion ‖ 携巨款～ run off with a large sum of money

【出题】chūtí〈动〉 **1**（出题目） assign a topic: 出作文题 set a topic for a composition **2**（出试卷） set an exam paper: 出偏题 raise out-of-the-way questions

【出挑】chūtiāo〈动〉 bloom

【出粜】chūtiào〈动〉 sell (grain)

【出铁】chūtiě〈动〉 tap molten iron

【出庭】chūtíng〈动〉 appear before the court: ～辩护 defend a case in court ‖ ～作证 testify before a court

【出头】chūtóu〈动〉 **1**（脱离困境） free oneself: 还完债后，他觉得自己有了～的日子。 When he had paid off his debts, he felt himself liberated. **2**（露出顶部） be exposed: ▸～的椽子先烂 **3**（领头） come forward: 她有实权，但从不～。 She has a lot of power, but always remains in the background. **4** ▸**p. 526**（超出） exceed: 二十～的姑娘 girl in her early twenties ‖ 她四十～。 She is a little over 40.

【出头的椽子先烂】chūtóude chuánzi xiān làn〈俗〉〈喻〉 he who comes forward first is the first to suffer

【出头露面】chūtóu-lòumiàn〈成〉 be in the limelight: 她不喜欢～。 She never seeks the limelight.

【出头鸟】chūtóuniǎo〈名〉〈喻〉 one who stands out from the crowd: ▸枪打～

【出徒】chūtú〈动〉 complete one's apprenticeship

【出土】chūtǔ〈动〉 **1**（指文物） be unearthed: ～文物 unearthed relic **2**（指植物） come up out of the ground

【出脱】chūtuō〈动〉 **1**（卖出） manage to sell **2**（出落） bloom **3**（开脱） acquit: ～罪孽 absolve sb. from sin

【出外】chūwài〈动〉 go away from home: ～打工 leave home and do casual work ‖ ～谋生 leave home and make a living elsewhere

【出亡】chūwáng〈动〉〈书〉 flee one's home: ～他乡 flee one's country into exile

【出位】chūwèi〈动〉 be out of the ordinary: 衣着～ dress outlandishly ‖ 大胆～的表演 a bold, unusual performance

【出污泥而不染】chū wūní ér bù rǎn〈成〉 **1**〈本〉 [of lotus] rise unsullied from mud **2**〈喻〉 remain unaffected in spite of general corruption

【出席】chūxí〈动〉 be present: ～会议 attend a meeting

【出席人数】chūxí rénshù〈名〉 attendance

【出息】chūxi **A**〈名〉 promise: 没有～ good-for-nothing ‖ 有～的年轻人 promising young man **B**〈动〉 make progress: 她儿子比去年～多了。 Her son is doing much better than last year.

【出险】chūxiǎn〈动〉 **1**（脱离危险） get out of danger: 救人～ go to sb.'s rescue **2**（出现险情） be in danger: 河堤一旦～，士兵们将立即赶去抢修。 Once the dyke is threatened, the soldiers will immediately rush to repair it.

【出现】chūxiàn〈动〉 appear: ～感冒症状 develop signs of a cold ‖ 期待～奇迹 hope for a miracle ‖ 新事物不断～。 New things are constantly emerging.

【出线】chūxiàn〈动〉［体育］ qualify for the next round: 我队已～进入半决赛。 Our team has qualified for the semi-final.

【出线权】chūxiànquán〈名〉 qualification: 获得～ be qualified for the next round ‖ 该队取得了～。 The team passed the qualifying competition.

【出项】chūxiàng〈名〉 expense: 修房、度假及其他～几乎花光了他的存款。 House repairs, holidays and other expenses reduced his savings to almost nothing.

【出血】chūxiě〈动〉〈方〉〈喻〉 spend money: 让某人～ bleed sb. ▸chūxuè

【出新】chūxīn〈动〉 bring forth sth. new: 文艺创作要不断～。 We must keep producing creative new literary works.

【出行】chūxíng〈动〉 embark on a journey: 乘火车～ go on a train journey ‖ 这次～我跑了不少地方。 This journey took me to quite a few places.

【出血】chūxuè〈动〉 bleed: 大～ massive haemorrhage ‖ 胃～ gastric haemorrhage ▸chūxiě

【出血热】chūxuèrè〈名〉 haemorrhagic fever

【出巡】chūxún〈动〉 make a tour of inspection: ～江南 make an inspection tour to the areas south of the Yangtze River

【出牙】chūyá〈动〉 cut teeth

【出芽】chūyá〈动〉 sprout

【出言】chūyán〈动〉 speak: ～谨慎 choose one's words carefully

【出言不逊】chūyán-bùxùn〈成〉 make impertinent remarks: 他～。 His remarks were impertinent.

【出演】chūyǎn〈动〉 **1**（表演） perform: 每天～三场 give three performances a day **2**（扮演） play the part: 他～哈姆雷特。 He played the part of Hamlet.

【出洋】chūyáng〈动〉 go abroad: ～考察 go abroad on a study tour ‖ ～留学 study abroad

【出洋相】chū yángxiàng〈惯〉 make a spectacle of oneself: 那女人又踢又叫，出尽了洋相。 The woman kicked and screamed and made a real fool of herself. ‖ 他使我在朋友面前大～。 He made a monkey of me before my friends.

【出迎】chūyíng〈动〉 go out to greet

【出油】chūyóu〈动〉［石油］ produce oil: ～井 producing well

【出游】chūyóu〈动〉 go sightseeing: 结伴～ pair up on a tour

【出于】chūyú〈介〉 out of: ～不可告人的目的 actuated by ulterior motives ‖ ～好心 out of kindness ‖ ～好奇/同情 out of curiosity/sympathy ‖ ～无奈 there being no alternative

【出语】chūyǔ〈动〉 speak: ～不俗 speak in an uncommon way ‖ ～惊人 make shocking remarks

【出狱】chūyù〈动〉 be released from prison: 刑满～ be freed after serving out one's sentence

【出院】chūyuàn〈动〉 leave hospital: 病愈～ be discharged from hospital when one is better

【出月】chūyuè〈动〉 be after the end of this month: 铁路要～才完工。 The railway won't be completed until after the end of this month.

【出月子】chū yuèzi〈动〉 [for women after child birth] complete one's month of confinement

【出展】chūzhǎn〈动〉 **1**（到外地展览） be on a loan exhibition: 她的画曾两次～欧洲。 Her paintings have been exhibited in Europe on loan twice. **2**（展出） be exhibited: 新出土的陶俑正在国家博物馆～。 The newly unearthed pottery figurines are now being exhibited at the national museum.

【出战】chūzhàn〈动〉 go to war: 伺机～ watch for a chance to attack ‖ 巴西将派出一支劲旅～世界杯赛。 Brazil is fielding a strong team for the World Cup.

【出账】chūzhàng **A**〈动〉 enter an item of expenditure in the accounts: 他的招待费可作为业务开支～。 His entertaining could be entered as a business expense. **B**〈名〉〈方〉 expense: 这个月～太多。 We have had huge expenses this month.

【出招】chūzhāo〈动〉 come up with ideas: 请他帮你～。 Ask him to help you come up with some ideas. ‖ 专家为节能～。 The experts came up with ideas for saving energy.

【出蛰】chūzhé〈动〉 come out of hibernation

【出诊】chūzhěn〈动〉 visit a patient at home: 医生～去了。 The doctor went off on a home visit.

【出疹子】chū zhěnzi〈动〉 come out in a rash

【出阵】chūzhèn〈动〉1（指打仗）go into battle: 司令员亲自～。The general went in person to the front line. 2〈喻〉（指竞争）take part in: 主力齐～，我队一定能取胜。If the key players take part, our team can definitely win.

【出征】chūzhēng〈动〉go on an expedition: 率兵～ command an expedition

【出众】chūzhòng〈形〉outstanding: 才华～ have exceptional talent ‖ 她美貌～。Her beauty set her apart from all the others.

【出资】chūzī〈动〉fund: ～兴建 provide funds for the construction ‖ 工程由当地几家公司联合～。The project is jointly funded by several local companies.

【出走】chūzǒu〈动〉flee: 离家～ run away from home

【出租】chūzū〈动〉rent out: 开展～业务 provide rental service ‖ 房屋～ rooms to let

【出租车】chūzūchē〈名〉taxi: 在路边叫～ hail a cab on the street ‖ 打电话叫～ call for a taxi

初 chū

A〈形〉1（起初）initial: 唐朝～年 in the early years of the Tang Dynasty ▸～创, ～冬, ～期 2（原来）original: 和好如～ be on good terms again ▸～心, ～衷 3（第一个）first: 正月～一/二 first/second day of the first lunar month ▸～伏, ～稿 4（最低等）elementary: ▸～等, ～级, ～小

B〈名〉beginning: 二十世纪～ beginning of the 20th century ▸年～, 月～

C〈副〉initially: ～见成效 achieve initial success ‖ 雪后～晴 clear up just after a fall of snow ▸～出茅庐, ～犯, 如梦～醒

【初版】chūbǎn **A**〈动〉be first published: 本书～于1956年。This book was first published in 1956. **B**〈名〉first edition

【初步】chūbù〈形〉initial: ～估计 preliminary estimates ‖ ～方案 tentative programme ‖ 取得～成功 gain initial success

【初产】chūchǎn〈名〉［医学］primiparity

【初产妇】chūchǎnfù〈名〉primiparous woman

【初潮】chūcháo〈名〉［生理］first menstruation

【初出茅庐】chūchū-máolú〈成〉〈喻〉be wet behind the ears: ～的报社记者 fledgling newspaper reporter

【初创】chūchuàng〈动〉be newly established: ～阶段 early stage of establishment

【初春】chūchūn ▸**p. 345**〈名〉early spring

【初次】chūcì〈名〉first time: ～参加社交活动 make one's debut in society ‖ ～登台演出 make a stage debut ‖ ～见面 meet sb. for the first time ‖ ～露面 make one's first appearance

【初等】chūděng〈形〉elementary: ～代数/几何/数学 elementary algebra/geometry/mathematics

【初等教育】chūděng jiàoyù〈名〉primary education

【初冬】chūdōng ▸**p. 345**〈名〉early winter

【初度】chūdù〈名〉〈书〉birthday: 五十～ 50th birthday

【初犯】chūfàn **A**〈动〉commit a crime for the first time: 他因是～而被原谅。He was forgiven his first offence. **B**〈名〉first offender: 对～从轻判处 impose a light sentence on a first offender

【初伏】chūfú〈名〉1（头伏）first of the three ten-day hottest periods of summer 2（头伏第一天）first day of the first of the three ten-day hottest periods of summer

【初稿】chūgǎo〈名〉first draft: 写出～ write out the first draft

【初会】chūhuì〈动〉meet for the first time: 我与她的～非常短暂。My first encounter with her was quite brief.

【初婚】chūhūn〈动〉1（第一次结婚）get married for the first time: 她的～结局不幸。Her first marriage ended unhappily. 2（新婚）be newly married: 他们仍像～时那样恩爱。They are still as much attached to each other as they were when they were newly married.

【初级】chūjí〈形〉primary: ～班 elementary course ‖ ～读本 primer

【初级产品】chūjí chǎnpǐn〈名〉primary product: ～出口国/生产国 primary exporter/producer

【初级法院】chūjí fǎyuàn〈名〉lower court

【初级阶段】chūjí jiēduàn〈名〉initial stage: 社会主义～ initial stage of socialism

【初级小学】chūjí xiǎoxué〈名〉lower primary school

【初级职称】chūjí zhíchēng〈名〉junior academic title

【初级中学】chūjí zhōngxué〈名〉junior high school

【初加工】chūjiāgōng〈名〉［机械］preliminary working

【初见】chūjiàn〈动〉1（指遇见）meet for the first time 2（指显示）appear for the first time: ～成效 show initial results

【初交】chūjiāo〈名〉new acquaintance

【初亏】chūkuī〈名〉［天文］first contact

【初来乍到】chūlái-zhàdào〈成〉be a newcomer: ～，不周之处请多包涵。Since I am a newcomer here, please excuse me for any mistakes.

【初恋】chūliàn〈名〉first love: 他的～是甜蜜而难忘的。His first love was sweet and unforgettable.

【初露锋芒】chūlù-fēngmáng〈成〉show one's talent for the first time: 他大学一毕业就在商界～。He showed his hand in business soon after he left university.

【初露头角】chūlù-tóujiǎo〈成〉begin to display one's talent: ～的作家 budding writer

【初民】chūmín〈名〉primitive people

【初年】chūnián ▸**p. 618**〈名〉early years: 唐朝～ in the early years of the Tang Dynasty

【初评】chūpíng〈名〉preliminary assessment: 进行～ make a preliminary appraisal

【初期】chūqī ▸**p. 618**〈名〉early stage: ～症状 first symptoms ‖ 20世纪90年代～ early 1990s

【初秋】chūqiū ▸**p. 345**〈名〉early autumn

【初赛】chūsài〈名〉preliminary: 在～中就被淘汰出局 be eliminated in the qualifying rounds

【初审】chūshěn〈动〉1（指评审）undergo a preliminary examination: ～合格 go through a preliminary evaluation 2［法律］be on trial of first instance: ～裁决 ruling of first instance

【初生牛犊不怕虎】chūshēng niúdú bù pà hǔ〈俗〉〈喻〉the young are fearless

【初生之犊】chūshēngzhīdú〈成〉〈喻〉the young and inexperienced

【初始】chūshǐ〈形〉initial: ～价格 initial price ‖ ～速度 initial velocity

【初试】chūshì〈名〉1（指试机）first try 2（指考试）qualifying examination: ～通过者有资格参加复试。Those who have passed the preliminary examination are qualified for the final.

【初霜】chūshuāng〈名〉first frost

【初速度】chūsùdù〈名〉［物理］initial velocity

【初岁】chūsuì ▸**p. 618**〈名〉〈书〉beginning of a year

【初探】chūtàn〈名〉[often used in the title of a book or an article] primary research: 《大陆架成因～》*An Initial Survey of the Formation of the Continental Shelf*

【初夏】chūxià ▸**p. 345**〈名〉early summer

【初小】chūxiǎo〈简称〉= 初级小学

【初心】chūxīn〈名〉〈书〉one's original intention: ～不改 have one's first desire unchanged

【初选】chūxuǎn **A**〈动〉elect for the first time **B**〈名〉primary election

【初学】chūxué〈动〉be a beginner: ～画画/英语 be a beginner at painting/English ‖ ～者 beginner

【初旬】chūxún ▸**p. 618**〈名〉first ten days of a month: 一月～ first ten days of January

【初叶】chūyè ▸**p. 618**〈名〉early years of a historical period: 20世纪～ in the early 20th century ‖ 宋朝～ in the early years of the Song Dynasty

【初夜】chūyè〈名〉1（初更）early evening 2（新婚之夜）wedding night

【初愿】chūyuàn〈名〉one's original intention: 经商并非我的～。Going into business was not my original intention.

【初月】chūyuè〈名〉new moon

【初战】chūzhàn〈名〉first battle: ～告捷 win the first battle

【初诊】chūzhěn〈动〉pay one's first visit to a doctor

【初中】chūzhōng〈简称〉= 初级中学

【初衷】chūzhōng〈名〉one's original intention: 不改～ not change one's original intention ‖ 有违～ go against one's original intention

樗 chū〈名〉［植物］tree of heaven

【樗蒲】chūpú〈名〉ancient game like dice-throwing

chú

刍（芻）chú〈书〉

A〈动〉cut grass: ▸～荛

B〈名〉hay: ▸～秣, 反～

C〈形〉〈谦〉my: ～见 my humble opinion ▸～议

【刍粮】chúliáng〈名〉fodder and food

【刍秣】chúmò〈名〉〈书〉hay

【刍荛】chúráo〈书〉**A**〈动〉cut grass and firewood **B**〈名〉1（打柴人）woodcutter 2〈谦〉（用于自称）I: ～之言 my humble remarks

【刍议】chúyì〈名〉〈书〉〈谦〉my humble opinion

除 chú

A〈名〉doorsteps: ▸庭～

B〈动〉1〈书〉（授予）appoint sb. to office: ～忠州刺史 appoint sb. as the prefectural governor of Zhongzhou 2（清除）get rid of: ～草 dig up weeds 3［数学］divide: 15～以3得5。Fifteen divided by three equals five. ‖ 4～28等于7。Four into twenty-eight is seven.

C〈介〉except: ～此之外，我想让你答应我一件事。Apart from this, I want you to promise me one thing. ▸～外

【除暴安良】chúbào-ānliáng〈成〉eradicate the bad elements and support the good

C

【除弊】chúbì〈动〉 eradicate a social problem: 兴利～ promote what is beneficial and abolish what is harmful

【除冰】chúbīng〈动〉 remove ice: ～设备 de-icing equipment

【除草】chúcǎo〈动〉 weed: ～机 weeder ‖ ～剂 weed-killer

【除尘】chúchén〈动〉 dust: ～器 vacuum cleaner

【除虫】chúchóng〈动〉 kill off insects: ～剂 insecticide

【除虫菊】chúchóngjú〈名〉［植物］ pyrethrum

【除臭】chúchòu〈动〉［化工］ deodorize: ～剂 deodorant

【除恶务尽】chú'è-wùjìn〈成〉 evil must be completely eradicated

【除法】chúfǎ〈名〉［数学］ division

【除非】chúfēi **A**〈连〉 only if: ～医生允许，否则病人不可下床走动。 The patient is only allowed to get out of bed once the doctor has given permission. ‖ 要想人不知，～己莫为。 Better not do it if you don't want others to know. **B**〈介〉 except: 那台机床～他没人会开。 No one can operate that machine tool but him.

【除根】chúgēn〈动〉 root out: 肝炎这种病不太容易～。 Hepatitis is not easily eradicated. ▸斩草～

【除垢】chúgòu〈动〉 descale: ～剂 clearing agent

【除号】chúhào〈名〉 division sign (÷)

【除旧布新】chújiù-bùxīn〈成〉 demolish the old and establish the new

【除旧迎新】chújiù-yíngxīn〈成〉 ring out the old (year) and ring in the new

【除菌】chújūn〈动〉 degerm: ～剂 disinfectant

【除开】chúkāi = 除了 chúle

【除了】chúle〈介〉 **1**（表排除） except: ～他，所有人都到会了。 Everyone except him was present at the meeting. **2**（表包含） besides: ～钱，盗贼还偷了什么? Did the burglar steal anything apart from your money? **3**（表选择） either ... or ...: 他～看电视，就是睡觉。 He was either glued to the TV or sleeping.

【除名】chúmíng〈动〉 dismiss: 他被学校～了。 He was expelled from school.

【除去】chúqù **A**〈动〉 get rid of: ～污渍 remove stains ‖ ～水分 extract moisture ‖ ～炸弹的引信 defuse a bomb ‖ 把名字从名单上～ remove a name from the list **B**〈介〉 except: ～他，还有三人没到。 Apart from him there are three others who also haven't arrived.

【除权】chúquán〈动〉［金融］ exclude rights: ～日 ex-rights date

【除湿】chúshī〈动〉 dehumidify: ～器 dehumidifier

【除数】chúshù〈名〉［数学］ divisor

【除霜】chúshuāng〈动〉 defrost: 给冰箱～ defrost a refrigerator ‖ 自动～ auto-defrosting

【除四害】chúsìhài〈动〉 eliminate the four pests [usu referring to rats, bedbugs, flies and mosquitoes]

【除外】chúwài〈动〉 exclude: 午餐每人 5 元，饮料～。 Lunch costs five *yuan* per person excluding drinks.

【除夕】chúxī〈名〉 Chinese New Year's Eve: ～之夜 the night of New Year's Eve

【除息】chúxī〈动〉［金融］ exclude dividend: ～日 ex-dividend date

【除锈】chúxiù〈动〉 remove rust: ～剂 rust inhibitor

【除夜】chúyè〈名〉〈书〉 Chinese New Year's Eve

【除皱】chúzhòu〈动〉 get rid of wrinkles: ～治疗 anti-wrinkle treatment

厨（廚）chú

厨（廚） chú〈名〉 **1**（厨房） kitchen: 下～ go to the kitchen to cook ▸～房 **2**（厨师） cook: 名～ famous chef

【厨房】chúfáng〈名〉 kitchen

【厨娘】chúniáng〈名〉 woman cook

【厨具】chújù〈名〉 kitchen utensil

【厨师】chúshī ▸**p. 966**〈名〉 cook: 当～ work as a cook ‖ ～长 head chef ‖ 助理～ assistant chef

【厨艺】chúyì〈名〉 cooking skill: ～高超 be good at cooking

【厨子】chúzi〈名〉〈口〉 cook

锄（鋤）chú

A〈名〉 hoe: 鹤嘴～ mattock ▸～头

B〈动〉 **1**（除草松土） hoe: ～草 hoe up weeds ▸～地 **2**（铲除） uproot: ▸～奸

【锄地】chúdì〈动〉 do hoeing

【锄奸】chújiān〈动〉 ferret out and get rid of traitors

【锄强扶弱】chúqiáng-fúruò〈成〉 eliminate the bullies and support the weak

【锄头】chútou〈名〉 **1**（镐状农具） pickaxe **2**〈方〉（松土、除草用的农具） hoe

蜍 chú

蜍 chú ▸蟾蜍 chánchú

雏（雛）chú

A〈名〉 young bird: ～鸭 duckling

B〈形〉 young: ～燕 young swallow

【雏凤】chúfèng〈名〉〈喻〉 talented young man: ～清于老凤声。 The young will surpass the old.

【雏鸡】chújī〈名〉 chick

【雏妓】chújì〈名〉 child prostitute

【雏菊】chújú〈名〉 daisy

【雏鸟】chúniǎo〈名〉 fledgling

【雏儿】chúr〈名〉 **1**（指鸟、禽） young bird: 鸭～ duckling **2**〈喻〉（指人） fledgling

【雏形】chúxíng〈名〉 **1**（指形式） embryonic form: 她的计划还只是个～。 Her plan was still in embryonic state. **2**（指模型） miniature: 建筑物的～ model of a building

橱（櫥）chú

橱（櫥） chú〈名〉 cabinet: ▸～柜, 壁～, 书～

【橱窗】chúchuāng〈名〉 display window: 布置～ window-dressing ‖ 浏览商店～ window-shop

【橱柜】chúguì〈名〉 **1**（餐具柜） sideboard **2**（矮柜） low cupboard that also serves as a table

躇 chú

躇 chú ▸踌躇 chóuchú

蹰（躕）chú

蹰（躕） chú ▸踟蹰 chíchú

chǔ

处（處）chǔ

处（處） chǔ〈动〉 **1**〈书〉（居住） reside: ▸穴居野～ **2**（位于） be situated in: 地～平原/山区 be situated on the plain/in the mountains ‖ 我厂正～在发展阶段。 Our factory is going through a phase of development. ▸设身～地 **3**（相处） get along: ～得来/不来 get along well/badly ‖ 他已和新邻居～熟了。 He has already become familiar with his new neighbour. ‖ 她和新上司～得如何? How did she get on with her new boss? **4**（处理） manage: ▸～理, ～事, ～置 **5**（处罚） punish: ～以枪决 condemn to be shot

▸chù

【处变不惊】chǔbiàn-bùjīng〈成〉 be calm in the face of a crisis

【处罚】chǔfá〈动〉 punish: 减轻～ mitigate a punishment ‖ 受到～ be punished ‖ 从轻～ punish leniently

【处方】chǔfāng **A**〈动〉 prescribe: ～权 right to prescribe **B**〈名〉 prescription: 开～ write out a prescription ‖ 按～配药 make up a prescription

【处方药】chǔfāngyào〈名〉 prescription medicine: 非～ over the counter medicine

【处分】chǔfèn **A**〈动〉 take disciplinary action: 严肃～违纪人员 take serious disciplinary action against those who have broken the rules ‖ 免于～ exempt sb. from punishment ‖ 行政～ administrative disciplinary measure ‖ 按情节轻重予以～。 The punishment should fit the crime. **B**〈名〉 punishment: 给予警告～ give sb. a warning

【处境】chǔjìng〈名〉 predicament: ～困难 in a real predicament ‖ ～危险 in a dangerous situation ‖ 我理解你的～。 I understand your situation.

【处决】chǔjué〈动〉 **1**（执行死刑） put to death: ～杀人犯 execute a murderer ‖ 依法～ execute in accordance with the law **2**（处理决定） handle and decide: 大会休会期间，一切事项均由常委会～。 The standing committee is in full charge between sessions.

【处理】chǔlǐ〈动〉 **1**（安排） handle: ～国事 manage state affairs ‖ ～日常事务 deal with routine matters ‖ 亲自～ take sth. into one's own hands ‖ 交由某人～ leave the matter in sb.'s hands **2**（惩处） punish: 从宽～ punish leniently ‖ 严肃～ punish severely **3**（低价出售） sell at reduced prices: ～积压商品 sell old stock at reduced prices **4**（按要求加工、对待） treat using a special process: ～伤口 treat a wound ‖ 数据～ data processing ‖ 污水～ sewage disposal

【处理品】chǔlǐpǐn〈名〉 (shop-soiled or substandard) goods sold at reduced prices

【处理器】chǔlǐqì〈名〉 processor: 数据/文字～ data/word processor

【处女】chǔnǚ **A**〈名〉 virgin: ▸～膜 **B**〈形〉〈喻〉 maiden: ▸～航, ～作

【处女地】chǔnǚdì〈名〉 virgin soil

【处女峰】chǔnǚfēng〈名〉 unscaled peak

【处女航】chǔnǚháng〈名〉（指船） maiden voyage;（指飞机） first flight

【处女膜】chǔnǚmó〈名〉［生理］ hymen

【处女秀】chǔnǚxiù〈名〉 debut: 美国女排的～令人惊讶。 The debut of the U.S. women's volleyball team was a real stunner.

【处女作】chǔnǚzuò〈名〉 first effort: 那位年轻女演员的舞台～是《华伦夫人的职业》。 The young actress made her stage debut in *Mrs Warren's Profession*.

【处女座】Chǔnǚzuò〈名〉［天文］ Virgo

【处身】chǔshēn〈动〉 place oneself: ～险境 place oneself amid great dangers

【处士】chǔshì〈名〉〈旧〉 recluse

【处世】chǔshì〈动〉 conduct oneself in society: ～经验 worldly experience ‖ ～之道 way of the world ‖ 立身～ start in life

【处事】chǔshì〈动〉 handle affairs: ～公正 deal with things fairly ‖ ～精明 have a good head for business

【处暑】Chǔshǔ〈名〉End of Heat [beginning of the 14th of the 24 solar terms]
【处死】chǔsǐ〈动〉put to death: 他因谋杀罪被～。He was executed for murder.
【处心积虑】chǔxīn-jīlǜ〈成〉〈贬〉scheme incessantly: ～想搞垮对手 plot and scheme against one's rival
【处刑】chǔxíng〈动〉［法律］sentence: ～适当 sentence appropriately ‖ 处以极刑 sentence to death
【处于】chǔyú〈动〉be: ～昏迷状态 be in a coma ‖ ～劣势 be at a disadvantage ‖ ～逆境 be in adverse circumstances ‖ ～水深火热之中 be in a living hell ‖ ～有利地位 be in an advantageous position ‖ ～最佳状态 be at one's best
【处之泰然】chǔzhī-tàirán〈成〉not bat an eyelid
【处治】chǔzhì〈动〉punish: 严加～ punish severely
【处置】chǔzhì〈动〉1（处理）handle: ～得当 handle properly ‖ ～失当 mismanage ‖ 任由某人～ leave to sb.'s discretion ‖ 安全～核废料 the safe disposal of nuclear waste ‖ ～权 disposal 2（惩处）punish: 依法～ punish according to law
【处子】chǔzǐ〈名〉〈书〉virgin
【处子秀】chǔzǐxiù〈名〉sporting debut: 姚明在 NBA 的～中表现出色。Yao Ming's NBA debut was outstanding.

杵 chǔ

A〈名〉1（用于捣碎）pestle 2（用于洗衣）club-shaped paddle: 砧～ block and club ▸～臼

B〈动〉1（捣）pound with a pestle: ～药 pound medicinal herbs 2（捅）poke: 用伞～了他一下 give him a prod with an umbrella ‖ 在麻袋上～两个洞 poke two holes in the sack
【杵臼】chǔjiù〈名〉mortar and pestle
【杵舞】chǔwǔ = 杵乐 chǔyuè
【杵乐】chǔyuè〈名〉pestle dance [an indigenous dance of the Gaoshan people of Taiwan]

础（礎）chǔ

〈名〉plinth: 月晕而风，～润而雨。The lunar halo presages wind; a moist plinth indicates rain. ▸基～
【础石】chǔshí〈名〉〈书〉1（指石头）plinth 2（基础）foundation: 人民是社会的～。The people are the cornerstone of society.

楮 chǔ

〈名〉1（指树）paper mulberry 2〈书〉（指纸）paper

储（儲）chǔ

A〈动〉store up: ～粮备荒 store grain in case of famine ‖ ～煤过冬 store up coal for the winter

B〈名〉heir to the throne: 废～ depose a crown prince ‖ 立～ make sb. crown prince
【储备】chǔbèi A〈动〉stockpile: ～大量食物 keep great reserves of food ‖ ～过冬饲料 stock up on fodder for the winter ‖ ～粮食 build up grain supplies ‖ ～石油 reserve oil B〈名〉reserve: 动用～ draw on reserves ‖ 黄金/石油～ gold/oil reserve ‖ 外汇～ foreign exchange reserve
【储备基金】chǔbèi jījīn〈名〉reserve funds
【储备金】chǔbèijīn〈名〉reserved money
【储备粮】chǔbèiliáng〈名〉grain reserves
【储备银行】chǔbèi yínháng〈名〉reserve bank: 联邦～ Federal Reserve Bank
【储藏】chǔcáng〈动〉1（保藏）store: ～必需品 hoard essential goods ‖ 货物～在仓库里。The goods were stored in the warehouse. ▸～室 2（蕴藏）reserve: ～量 reserves ‖ 我国铁矿～丰富。Our country is rich in iron ore deposits.
【储藏室】chǔcángshì〈名〉storeroom
【储存】chǔcún〈动〉stockpile: ～信息 store information ‖ ～一点儿钱以备急需 lay aside a little money for emergencies ‖ ～战略物资 stockpile strategic materials
【储户】chǔhù〈名〉depositor
【储积】chǔjī A〈动〉save: 他每月把一部分工资～起来。He sets aside part of his wages each month. B〈名〉savings: 粮食～ grain stocks
【储集】chǔjí〈动〉store up
【储君】chǔjūn〈名〉crown prince: 立/废～ designate/depose a crown prince
【储量】chǔliàng〈名〉［矿业］reserves: 煤炭～ coal reserves ‖ 探明～ proved reserves ‖ 日渐减少的石油～ dwindling oil reserves
【储气】chǔqì〈动〉store gas: ～罐 gas tank
【储蓄】chǔxù A〈动〉save: 为买房每月～一笔钱 save money every month in order to buy a house B〈名〉savings: 动用～ dip into one's savings ‖ 定期～ fixed deposit ‖ 邮政～ postal savings
【储蓄存款】chǔxù cúnkuǎn〈名〉saving deposit
【储蓄额】chǔxù'é〈名〉total savings deposits
【储蓄罐】chǔxùguàn〈名〉piggy bank
【储蓄所】chǔxùsuǒ〈名〉savings bank
【储蓄银行】chǔxù yínháng〈名〉savings bank
【储蓄账户】chǔxù zhànghù〈名〉savings account
【储油】chǔyóu〈动〉［石油］store oil: ～罐 oil tank
【储运】chǔyùn〈动〉store up and transport
【储值卡】chǔzhíkǎ〈名〉top-up card

楚[1] chǔ

〈形〉1（痛苦）painful: ▸苦～，凄～，酸～ 2（清晰）neat: ▸齐～，清～，衣冠～～

楚[2] Chǔ

〈名〉1（指国名）Chu [state in the Zhou period]: ▸四面～歌，朝秦暮～ 2（指地区）Chu [name for the region of Hubei and Hunan, mainly Hubei]: ▸～剧
【楚材晋用】Chǔcái-Jìnyòng〈成〉〈喻〉brain drain
【楚楚】chǔchǔ〈形〉1（整洁）tidy: ▸衣冠～ 2（娇柔）dainty: ～动人 delicate and charming
【楚楚可怜】chǔchǔ-kělián〈成〉[of young women] delicate and charming
【楚辞】Chǔcí〈名〉*Songs of Chu*

> 《楚辞》
>
> An anthology of poetry written in a new literary form by the scholar Qu Yuan (屈原) and other poets who lived in the State of Chu during the Warring States period. *Li Sao* (《离骚》), thought to have been written by Qu Yuan, is the most representative work of the *Songs of Chu*.

【楚风】Chǔfēng〈名〉songs of Chu
【楚河汉界】Chǔhé-Hànjiè〈成〉〈喻〉border of two opposing powers
【楚剧】chǔjù〈名〉Chu opera
【楚瓦什人】Chǔwǎshírén〈名〉Chuvash

褚 Chǔ

〈名〉Chu [surname]
▸zhǔ

chù

亍 chù

▸彳亍 chìchù

处（處）chù

〈名〉1（地方）place: 停车～ parking spot ‖ 心灵深～ in one's heart of hearts ▸～所，暗～，去～ 2（方面）part: ▸长～，短～，坏～ 3（部门）department: 工商管理～ business administration office ‖ 科研～ scientific research department ▸办事～，联络～
▸chǔ
【处处】chùchù〈名〉everywhere: ～碰壁 run into obstacles at every turn ‖ ～严格要求自己 make all kinds of strict demands of oneself
【处所】chùsuǒ〈名〉place: 暂住的好～ good place to stay for a while ‖ 避雨的～ shelter from rain

怵 chù

〈动〉dread: 我们有理，不～他。With justice on our side, we do not fear him. ▸～目惊心，发～
【怵场】chùchǎng = 憷场 chùchǎng
【怵目惊心】chùmù-jīngxīn = 触目惊心 chùmù-jīngxīn
【怵头】chùtóu = 憷头 chùtóu

绌（絀）chù

〈形〉insufficient: ▸相形见～，左支右～

畜 chù

〈名〉domestic animal: ▸～生，耕～，家～
▸xù
【畜肥】chùféi〈名〉animal droppings
【畜圈】chùjuàn〈名〉pen
【畜栏】chùlán〈名〉corral
【畜类】chùlèi〈名〉domestic animals
【畜力】chùlì〈名〉livestock power: 有些山区还得用～运输。The use of animal power for transport is still common in some mountain areas.
【畜生】chùsheng〈名〉1（家畜）domestic animal 2〈粗〉（恶人）beast: 她骂他～。She called him a beast.
【畜疫】chùyì〈名〉epidemic among domestic animals

搐 chù

〈动〉twitch: ▸～动，抽～
【搐动】chùdòng〈动〉twitch: 她默默地抽泣，双肩不停地～。She wept silently, her shoulders shaking.
【搐搦】chùnuò〈书〉= 抽搐 chōuchù

触（觸）chù

〈动〉1（碰到）touch: ～雷 set off a mine accidentally ‖ 柳枝低垂，～到了水面。The willow branches hung down and brushed the water. ▸～电，一～即发 2（触动）touch: ～起前情 stir up memories of the past ▸～怒，感～
【触底】chùdǐ〈动〉touch bottom
【触电】chùdiàn〈动〉1（指强电流）get an electric shock: ～身亡 die from an electric shock ‖ 小心～! Danger! Electricity! 2〈喻〉（指影视工作）make one's debut
【触动】chùdòng〈动〉1（触碰）touch sth. and move it slightly: 切勿～电闸! Don't touch the electric brake! 2（侵犯）go against: ～某些人的既得权益 affect some

people's vested interests ‖ 谁说老规矩～不得? Who says you can't touch age-old practices? 3（打动） move: ～心弦 tug at sb.'s heart strings ‖ 对某人～很大 greatly touch sb.
【触发】chùfā〈动〉 trigger: ～暴乱 trigger a riot ‖ ～乡情 stir up sb.'s nostalgic feelings
【触发地雷】chùfā dìléi〈名〉 contact mine
【触犯】chùfàn〈动〉 go against: ～法律 break the law ‖ ～公众利益 work against the public interest
【触击】chùjī〈动〉 1（碰） strike 2［体育］ bunt
【触及】chùjí〈动〉 touch: ～本质 get to the essence of sth. ‖ ～灵魂 touch sb. very deeply ‖ ～痛处 touch a nerve ‖ 没有～争论的焦点 not touch on the key point
【触礁】chùjiāo〈动〉 1（指礁石） hit a rock: 船～沉没。 The ship struck a rock and sank. 2〈喻〉（指障碍） run into difficulty: 他们的婚姻～了。 Their marriage is on the rocks.
【触角】chùjiǎo〈名〉［动物］ tentacle
【触景生情】chùjǐng-shēngqíng〈成〉 recall old memories at the sight of familiar places
【触觉】chùjué〈名〉［生理］ sense of touch: 单凭～, 你能知道这是什么东西吗? Just by feeling, can you make out what this object is?
【触觉器官】chùjué qìguān〈名〉 tactile organ
【触类旁通】chùlèi-pángtōng〈成〉 reason by analogy
【触霉头】chù méitóu〈惯〉〈方〉 have a stroke of bad luck
【触摸】chùmō〈动〉 touch: 轻轻～ touch gently ‖ 请勿～。 Hands off!
【触摸屏】chùmōpíng〈名〉［计算机］ touch screen
【触目】chùmù A〈动〉 be eye-catching: ▸～皆是 B〈形〉 eye-catching: ～的红色滑雪服 striking red ski outfit
【触目皆是】chùmù-jiēshì〈成〉 catch one's eye wherever one goes
【触目惊心】chùmù-jīngxīn〈成〉 startling: 空难的新闻令人～。 The news of the air crash was shocking.
【触怒】chùnù〈动〉 enrage: ～舆论 offend public opinion ‖ 他的话～了老板。 His remarks infuriated the boss.
【触杀】chùshā〈动〉 kill by contact: ～剂 contact insecticide
【触手】chùshǒu〈名〉［动物］ tentacle
【触痛】chùtòng〈动〉 strike a nerve
【触网】chùwǎng〈动〉［体育］ touch net
【触须】chùxū〈名〉［动物］ cirrus
【触诊】chùzhěn〈动〉［中医］ examine by touch

憷 chù〈动〉 fear: 这孩子～见生人。 The child is timid with strangers. ▸发～
【憷场】chùchǎng〈动〉 suffer from stage fright: 考试～ seize up during exams
【憷头】chùtóu〈形〉〈方〉 timid: 他遇到危险从不～。 He never shrinks from danger.

黜 chù〈动〉〈书〉 dismiss: ～退 dismiss sb. from office ▸罢～, 废～
【黜免】chùmiǎn〈动〉〈书〉 dismiss

矗 chù〈形〉 towering: ～入云霄 tower into the clouds
【矗立】chùlì〈动〉 tower: 灯塔～在港口。 The lighthouse towers above the harbour.

chuā

欻 chuā〈拟〉 [indicating a short quick sound]: ～的一声撕开信 rip open a letter with a swish
▸xū
【欻拉】chuālā〈拟〉 [indicating a sharp noise]: ～一声，芹菜倒进了滚烫的油锅。 The celery fell into the hot oil with a spatter.

chuāi

揣 chuāi〈动〉 hide in one's clothes: ～在怀里 tuck into one's bosom ‖ ～在口袋里 tuck into one's pocket ▸～手儿
▸chuǎi, chuài
【揣手儿】chuāishǒur〈动〉 tuck one's hands into the sleeves of one's opposite arms

搋 chuāi〈动〉 1（揉搓） rub: ～面 knead dough ‖ 这些衣服太脏，要好好～一～。 The clothes are too dirty and must be given a good scrub. 2（疏通） unblock a drain with a suction pump: 浴缸的下水道堵了，你去～～吧。 The bathtub drain is clogged. Will you give it a pump?
【搋子】chuāizi〈名〉 suction pump

chuǎi

揣 chuǎi〈动〉 conjecture: ▸～测, ～摩, 不～冒昧
▸chuāi, chuài
【揣测】chuǎicè〈动〉 guess: ～老板的心绪 gauge the boss's mood ‖ 无法～ no way of guessing
【揣度】chuǎiduó〈动〉〈书〉 surmise: 他善于～别人的心思。 He is good at reading people's thoughts. ‖ 我～她的本意是好的。 I guessed that she had meant well.
【揣摩】chuǎimó〈动〉 try to work out: 我始终～不透他下一步要干什么。 I can never figure out what he will do next.
【揣想】chuǎixiǎng〈动〉 conjecture: 他默默～着她为什么这么生气。 He is brooding over what has made her so angry.

chuài

啜 Chuài〈名〉 Chuai [surname]
▸chuò

揣 chuài
A ▸囊揣 nāngchuài
B ▸挣揣 zhèngchuài
▸chuāi, chuǎi

嘬 chuài〈动〉〈书〉 bite
▸zuō

踹 chuài〈动〉 1（踢） kick: 把门～开 kick the door open 2（踩） step in: 一脚～在水坑里 step in a puddle of water

膗 chuài ▸囊膗 nāngchuài

chuān

川 chuān〈名〉 1 ▸p. 294（河流） river: ▸～流不息, 河～ 2 ▸p. 661 Chuān（四川） Sichuan: ▸～菜, ～剧 3（平地） plain: ▸米粮～, 一马平～
【川贝】chuānbèi〈名〉［中药］ Sichuanese tendril-leaved fritillary bulb
【川菜】chuāncài〈名〉 Sichuan cuisine: ～馆 Sichuan restaurant
【川剧】chuānjù〈名〉 Sichuan opera
【川军】chuānjūn〈名〉［中药］ Chinese rhubarb
【川流不息】chuānliú-bùxī〈成〉 flow continuously: 干道上车辆～。 The cars flowed in steady stream along the main road.
【川崎】Chuānqí〈名〉 Kawasaki
【川芎】chuānxiōng〈名〉［中药］ rhizome of *Chuanxiong*
【川资】chuānzī〈名〉〈书〉 travelling expenses: ～不足 be short of travelling expenses

氚 chuān〈名〉［化学］tritium (T or ^{3}H)

穿 chuān
A〈动〉 1（刺孔） penetrate: ～耳朵眼儿 have one's ears pierced ‖ 钉子～透了木头。 The nail went all the way through the wood. ▸～刺, ～孔, 水滴石～ 2 ▸p. 781（通过） pass through: ～过村庄 pass through a village ‖ ～街走巷 tread streets and alleys ‖ 横～马路时要小心。 Be careful crossing the street. 3（串联） string: ～一挂珠子 thread beads on a string ‖ ～一条珍珠项链 string pearls into a necklace 4（套在身上） wear: ～便服 be in civilian dress ‖ 你的套头毛衣前后～反了。 You've got your sweater on back to front. ‖ 鞋越～越松。 The shoes will stretch with wear.
B〈形〉 complete [used after some verbs]: 磨～ be worn through ‖ 看～他的伪装 see through his disguise ▸拆～, 揭～
【穿帮】chuānbāng〈动〉〈口〉 let sth. slip: ～镜头 slip into view ‖ 这件事～了。 The matter slipped out into the open.
【穿插】chuānchā A〈动〉 1（交替） alternate: 大会全体会议和小组讨论～进行。 The plenary session of the assembly alternates with group discussions. ‖ 晚会上歌曲、舞蹈、戏曲、相声～演出。 The evening show alternated between singing, dancing, traditional opera and comic dialogues. 2（插进） intersperse: 在讲话中～几个笑话 work a few jokes into one's speech 3［军事］ penetrate deep into enemy forces: ～到敌人后方 attack deep into the enemy's rear guard B〈名〉 subplot
【穿刺】chuāncì〈动〉［医学］ puncture: 腰椎～ lumbar puncture
【穿戴】chuāndài A〈动〉 be dressed: ～齐整 be fully dressed B〈名〉 dress: 讲究～ be particular about one's clothes ‖ ～入时 be fashionably dressed
【穿甲弹】chuānjiǎdàn〈名〉［军事］ armour-piercing bullet
【穿孔】chuānkǒng〈动〉 1［医学］ perforate: 十二指肠壁～ perforated duodenal wall ▸肠～, 胃～ 2（打孔） perforate: ～机 punch
【穿廊】chuānláng〈名〉 [of a Chinese courtyard] covered corridor
【穿连裆裤】chuān liándāngkù〈惯〉〈喻〉 collude: 封建势力和宗教势力～，共同压

迫人民。 The feudal and religious forces collaborated to oppress the people.

【穿山甲】chuānshānjiǎ〈名〉 1▸［动物］pangolin 2▸［中药］ pangolin scales

【穿梭】chuānsuō〈动〉 shuttle back and forth: ～往来 shuttle to and fro ‖ 在两个城市之间～ shuttle between two cities

【穿梭外交】chuānsuō wàijiāo〈名〉 shuttle diplomacy

【穿堂风】chuāntángfēng〈名〉 draught

【穿堂门】chuāntángmén〈名〉 gate at either end of a small alley which connects two lanes

【穿透】chuāntòu〈动〉 penetrate

【穿线】chuānxiàn〈动〉 1▸〈本〉 thread a needle 2▸〈喻〉 act as a go-between: 为生产商与买主～搭桥 marry the manufacturers with the buyers

【穿小鞋】chuān xiǎoxié〈惯〉〈喻〉 make things hard for sb.: 上司给他～。 The boss has been making things difficult for him.

【穿孝】chuānxiào〈动〉 be in mourning

【穿心莲】chuānxīnlián〈名〉［中药］ Andrographis paniculata Nees

【穿新鞋，走老路】chuān xīnxié, zǒu lǎolù〈俗〉〈喻〉 make no real change

【穿行】chuānxíng〈动〉 pass through: 在人群中～ weave one's way through a crowd ‖ 火车在隧道中～。 The train is going through a tunnel.

【穿靴戴帽】chuānxuē-dàimào〈惯〉〈喻〉 use clichés

【穿一条裤子】chuān yītiáo kùzi〈俗〉〈贬〉〈喻〉 collude

【穿衣镜】chuānyījìng〈名〉 full-length mirror

【穿越】chuānyuè〈动〉 cross: ～边境 cross the border ‖ ～沙漠 cross a desert ‖ 飞速～隧道 shoot through a tunnel

【穿云裂石】chuānyún-lièshí〈成〉 [of music] piercingly resonant

【穿凿】chuānzáo〈动〉 give a far-fetched interpretation

【穿凿附会】chuānzáo-fùhuì〈成〉draw far-fetched analogies

【穿针引线】chuānzhēn-yǐnxiàn〈成〉 1▸〈本〉 pass a thread through the eye of a needle 2▸〈喻〉 act as a go-between between different parties in order to promote their cooperation

【穿着】chuānzhuó〈名〉 dress: ～朴素/优雅 be plainly/elegantly turned out ‖ 不讲究～ not be particular about what one wears

chuán

传（傳） chuán〈动〉 1▸（交给） pass: ～给后代 hand down for posterity ‖ 把球～给边锋 pass the ball to the wing ‖ 优良传统代代～ pass down fine traditions from generations to generation 2▸（传授） pass on: 把手艺～给徒弟 pass on one's skills to an apprentice ▸～授, 祖～ 3▸（散布） spread: ～口信 pass on a message ‖ ～谣 spread rumours ‖ 坏事～千里。 Bad news travels fast. ‖ 这件事不能～出去。 This affair must be hushed up. ▸～播, 宣～, 以讹～讹 4▸（传唤） summon: ～被告/证人 summon a defendant/witness ‖ ～某人到庭作证 call sb. to testify ▸～票, ～讯 5▸（表达） convey: ▸～情, ～神 6▸（传导） transmit: ～热 conduct heat ‖ 一股暖流～遍他全身。 A feeling of warmth ran through his body. ▸～导 7▸（传染） infect: ▸～染 ▸zhuàn

【传帮带】chuán-bāng-dài〈惯〉 teach, help, and lead

【传播】chuánbō〈动〉 spread: ～奥运精神 spread the Olympic spirit ‖ ～疾病 transmit a disease ‖ ～谣言 circulate rumours ‖ ～知识 spread knowledge

【传播学】chuánbōxué〈名〉 media studies

【传布】chuánbù〈动〉 disseminate: ～消息 spread news ‖ ～新思想 propagate new ideas

【传唱】chuánchàng〈动〉 be circulated and sung: 这首歌在青少年中广为～。 This song is very popular with teenagers.

【传抄】chuánchāo〈动〉 make private copies: ～本 hand-written copy

【传承】chuánchéng A〈动〉 impart and inherit: 这项工艺经历代～，至今已有几千年的历史。 The skill has been passed down from generation to generation for thousands of years. B〈名〉 inheritance: 文化～ cultural inheritance

【传达】chuándá A〈动〉 1▸（告知） pass on: ～命令 pass on an order ‖ ～上级指示 convey instructions from a higher authority 2▸（接待） receive and register visitors: ～室 janitor's room B〈名〉 caretaker

【传代】chuándài〈动〉 pass on from generation to generation

【传单】chuándān〈名〉 flyer: 空投～ airdrop leaflets ‖ 散发～ hand out leaflets

【传导】chuándǎo〈动〉［物理］［生理］ transmit: 神经纤维是刺激的～体。 A nerve fibre is a conductor that transmits a stimulus.

【传道】chuándào〈动〉 1▸［宗教］ preach: ～士 preacher 2▸〈旧〉（指圣贤之道） propagate doctrines of ancient sages: 师者，所以～、授业、解惑也。 It takes a teacher to transmit wisdom, impart knowledge and resolve doubts.

【传递】chuándì〈动〉 deliver: ～信件 deliver mail ‖ ～信息 pass on information

【传动】chuándòng〈动〉［机械］ drive: 皮带/齿轮/链条～ belt/gear/chain drive ‖ 动力～系统 driveline ‖ ～装置 transmission

【传动带】chuándòngdài〈名〉 drive belt

【传粉】chuánfěn〈动〉［植物］ pollinate: ～昆虫 insect pollinator

【传感器】chuángǎnqì〈名〉［电气］ sensor: 激光/红外线～ laser/infrared sensor

【传告】chuángào〈动〉 pass on: 奔走～ go about spreading the news ‖ 把喜讯～给其他同事 relay the good news to other members of staff

【传观】chuánguān = 传看 chuánkàn

【传呼】chuánhū〈动〉 1▸（指电话） notify sb. of a phone call: ▸～电话 2▸（寻呼） page: ～台 paging station

【传呼电话】chuánhū diànhuà〈名〉 neighbourhood telephone service

【传呼机】chuánhūjī〈名〉 pager

【传话】chuánhuà〈动〉 pass on a message: ～传错了。 The message was incorrectly relayed. ‖ 有事给我传个话。 Send me a message if you need me for anything.

【传唤】chuánhuàn〈动〉［法律］subpoena: ～被告/证人 summon a defendant/witness ‖ 被～ be under a subpoena

【传家】chuánjiā〈动〉 pass down from generation to generation

【传家宝】chuánjiābǎo〈名〉 1▸〈本〉 family heirloom: 留给后代的～ heirloom for one's descendants 2▸〈喻〉 cherished tradition

【传见】chuánjiàn〈动〉 summon: 听候～ wait to be summoned

【传教】chuánjiào〈动〉［宗教］ preach

【传教士】chuánjiàoshì〈名〉［宗教］ missionary: 天主教/基督教/新教～ Catholic/Christian/Protestant missionary

【传戒】chuánjiè〈动〉［佛教］ 1▸（指和尚） initiate sb. into monkhood 2▸（指尼姑） initiate sb. into nunhood

【传经】chuánjīng〈动〉 pass on one's valuable experience

【传经送宝】chuánjīng-sòngbǎo〈成〉 pass on one's valuable experience

【传看】chuánkàn〈动〉 pass sth. round

【传令】chuánlìng〈动〉 dispatch orders: ～嘉奖 cite sb. in a dispatch

【传令兵】chuánlìngbīng〈名〉 orderly

【传媒】chuánméi〈名〉 1▸（大众媒体） media: 这桩丑闻被～炒得很热。 The scandal was getting a lot of media attention. 2▸（媒介） means of transmission: 猴子是多种疾病的～。 Monkeys transmit a number of diseases.

【传票】chuánpiào〈名〉 1▸［法律］ subpoena: 发出～ issue a summons ‖ 接到～ receive a summons ‖ 法院的～ court summons 2▸［会计］ voucher for establishing the truth of accounts

【传奇】chuánqí A〈名〉1▸（指唐宋小说体裁） short stories [of the Tang and Song dynasties] 2▸（指明清长篇戏曲） long poetic dramas [of the Ming and Qing dynasties] 3▸（指欧洲中世纪骑士文学） romance B〈形〉 legendary: ～人物 legendary figure ‖ ～故事 cock-and-bull story

【传切】chuánqiē〈动〉［篮球］ give and go: 默契的～配合 well-coordinated give-and-go move

【传情】chuánqíng〈动〉express one's amorous feelings: 眉目～ cast amorous glances at sb.

【传球】chuánqiú〈动〉［体育］ pass the ball: ～失误 misplaced pass

【传染】chuánrǎn〈动〉 be contagious: 接触～ contagion ‖ 母婴～ mother to child transmission ‖ 你把感冒～给我了。 You've given me your cold. ‖〈喻〉 他把恐慌～给了她。 He infected her with his panic.

【传染病】chuánrǎnbìng〈名〉 infectious disease: ～医院 isolation hospital

【传染性】chuánrǎnxìng〈名〉 infectiousness: ～肝炎 infectious hepatitis

【传染源】chuánrǎnyuán〈名〉 source of infection

【传人】chuánrén A〈动〉 1▸（传授） pass on a special skill: 他的绝技从不～。 He never passed on his unique skill. 2▸（传染） be infectious: 肝炎容易～。 Hepatitis is highly contagious. B〈名〉 successor: 龙的～ descendant of the dragon [the Chinese]

【传神】chuánshén〈形〉 lifelike: ～之笔 vivid touch (in writing or painting) ‖ 这些画很～。 The pictures are very lifelike.

【传声】chuánshēng〈动〉 transmit sound

【传声器】chuánshēngqì〈名〉 microphone

【传声筒】chuánshēngtǒng〈名〉 1▸〈本〉 loudspeaker 2▸〈喻〉 mouthpiece

【传世】chuánshì〈动〉 be handed down from ancient times: ～珍宝 treasure handed down from ancient times ‖ ～之作 work handed down from generation to generation

【传授】chuánshòu〈动〉 pass on: ～技能 impart skills ‖ ～知识 pass on one's knowledge

【传输】chuánshū〈动〉 transmit: 图文～ relaying of text and pictures

【传输线】chuánshūxiàn〈名〉 transmission line

【传说】chuánshuō **A**〈动〉 it is said: ～这一风俗起源于唐代。 Legend has it that this custom goes back to the Tang Dynasty. **B**〈名〉 legend: 古老的～ ancient legend
【传送】chuánsòng〈动〉 transmit: ～信息 relay a message ‖ ～带 conveyor belt
【传诵】chuánsòng〈动〉 be on everyone's lips: 千古～的名篇佳作 famous writings widely read throughout the ages
【传颂】chuánsòng〈动〉 be praised far and wide: 到处～着他的英雄事迹。 Accounts of his heroism resound throughout the land.
【传统】chuántǒng〈名〉 tradition: 保持艰苦朴素的优良～ keep up the fine tradition of simple living and hard work ‖ ～观念/思想 traditional concept/idea ‖ ～剧目 traditional repertoire ‖ 文化～ cultural heritage
【传为佳话】 chuánwéi-jiāhuà 〈成〉 be talked about with approval by everyone
【传为美谈】 chuánwéi-měitán 〈成〉 be talked about with approval by everyone
【传闻】chuánwén **A**〈动〉 rumour has it that: ～可能要爆发战争。 There is talk of possible war. **B**〈名〉 hearsay: 别信，那不过是～而已。 Don't believe it; it's mere hearsay.
【传习】chuánxí〈动〉 impart and learn: ～气功疗法 teach and learn *qigong* therapy
【传销】chuánxiāo〈名〉 pyramid sales: 打击～ crack down pyramid sales ‖ ～活动在中国是非法的。 Pyramid selling is illegal in China.
【传心术】chuánxīnshù〈名〉 telepathy
【传讯】chuánxùn〈动〉［法律］ summon for interrogation
【传言】chuányán **A**〈名〉 rumour: 那不过是～而已。 That's nothing but hearsay. **B**〈动〉 pass on a message: ～送语 act as a messenger
【传扬】chuányáng〈动〉 spread: 他的美名～四方。 His fame spread far and wide.
【传艺】chuányì〈动〉 impart a skill: 收徒～ offer apprenticeships and pass on one's skills
【传译】chuányì〈动〉 interpret: 同声～ simultaneous interpretation
【传阅】chuányuè〈动〉 circulate: ～文件 circulate a document
【传真】chuánzhēn **A**〈名〉 fax: 发～ send sb. a fax ‖ 收到～ receive a fax **B**〈动〉 fax: 把文件～过去 fax a document through
【传真机】chuánzhēnjī〈名〉 fax machine
【传旨】chuánzhǐ〈动〉〈旧〉 pass on an imperial decree
【传中】chuánzhōng〈动〉［足球］ pass to the centre: 将左路～球顶入对方球门 head a pass from the left wing into the opposite team's goal
【传种】chuánzhǒng〈动〉 breed: 挑选优良品种来～ choose the best species to breed from
【传宗接代】 chuánzōng-jiēdài 〈成〉 produce a male heir to carry on the family line

船 chuán〈名〉 boat: 划～ row a boat ‖ 上～ embark ‖ 下～ disembark ‖ 卸～ offload a ship ‖ 造～ build a ship ‖ 装～ load a ship
【船板】chuánbǎn〈名〉 deck of a boat
【船帮】chuánbāng〈名〉 **1**（船侧） side of a ship **2**（船队） merchant fleet
【船舶】chuánbó〈名〉 shipping: ～设计师 marine architect
【船埠】chuánbù〈名〉 wharf
【船舱】chuáncāng〈名〉 **1**（用于装货） ship's hold **2**（用于载客） cabin
【船厂】chuánchǎng〈名〉 shipyard
【船到江心补漏迟】chuán dào jiāngxīn bǔ lòu chí〈俗〉〈喻〉 prevention is the best cure
【船到桥头自然直】 chuán dào qiáotóu zìrán zhí〈俗〉 cross a bridge when you come to it
【船底】chuándǐ〈名〉 bottom of a vessel
【船东】chuándōng〈名〉 shipowner
【船队】chuánduì〈名〉 fleet
【船夫】chuánfū〈名〉 boatman: ～曲 boatman's song
【船工】chuángōng = 船夫 chuánfū
【船棺葬】chuánguānzàng〈名〉［考古］ boat-coffin burial
【船户】chuánhù〈名〉 **1**（以船为家者） boat dweller **2**〈方〉（船夫） boatman
【船级】chuánjí〈名〉 ship's classification
【船籍】chuánjí〈名〉 ship's registry
【船家】chuánjiā〈名〉〈旧〉 boatman
【船具】chuánjù〈名〉 marine supplies
【船老大】chuánlǎodà〈名〉〈方〉 **1**（船长） chief crewman of a wooden boat **2**（船夫） boatman
【船民】chuánmín〈名〉 people who live on boats
【船篷】chuánpéng〈名〉 **1**（篷子） awning **2**（船帆） sail
【船票】chuánpiào〈名〉 boat ticket
【船期】chuánqī〈名〉 sailing date
【船艄】chuánshāo〈名〉 stern
【船身】chuánshēn〈名〉 hull
【船首】chuánshǒu = 船头 chuántóu
【船台】chuántái〈名〉 berth
【船体】chuántǐ〈名〉 hull
【船头】chuántóu〈名〉 bow: 调转～ wind a ship
【船王】chuánwáng〈名〉 shipping magnate
【船桅】chuánwéi〈名〉 mast
【船尾】chuánwěi〈名〉 stern
【船尾楼】chuánwěilóu〈名〉 poop
【船坞】chuánwù〈名〉 dock
【船舷】chuánxián〈名〉 ship's side
【船员】chuányuán ▸**p. 966**〈名〉 crew
【船运】chuányùn〈动〉 ship
【船闸】chuánzhá〈名〉 ship lock
【船长】chuánzhǎng〈名〉 captain: ～室 captain's cabin
【船只】chuánzhī〈名〉 vessels: 往来～ shipping traffic ‖ 每天都有各类～进港。 Vessels of all kinds come into this harbour every day.
【船主】chuánzhǔ〈名〉 **1**（指拥有者） shipowner **2**（船长） captain

遄 chuán〈形〉〈书〉 swift: ～归 return speedily

椽 chuán
【椽子】chuánzi〈名〉 rafter

chuǎn

舛 chuǎn〈书〉
A〈动〉 run counter to: 他的性格和我相～。 His character is completely different from mine. ▸～驰
B〈名〉 mistake: ▸～错, 乖～
C〈形〉 unfortunate: ▸命途多～
【舛驰】chuǎnchí〈动〉〈书〉 run in the opposite direction
【舛错】chuǎncuò〈名〉〈书〉 **1**（错误） error: 避免～ avoid a mistake **2**（意外） accident: 不会有什么～。 There won't be any mishaps.
【舛讹】chuǎn'é〈名〉〈书〉 falsehood
【舛误】chuǎnwù〈名〉〈书〉 error: 此书～甚多。 There are many errors in this book.

喘 chuǎn
A〈动〉 puff and pant: 气～吁吁 be out of breath ‖ 累得直～ pant from one's exertions ‖ 吓得直～ gasp in horror ▸～气, ～息, 苟延残～
B ▸**p. 50**〈名〉［医学］ asthma
【喘咳】chuǎnké〈动〉 pant and cough
【喘气】chuǎnqì〈动〉 **1**（指呼吸） gasp: 喘不过气来 be out of breath ‖ 喘粗气 puff and pant ‖ 马喘着粗气。 The horse panted heavily. **2**（指休息） take a breather: 干了很久了，我们喘口气吧。 We've been working for a long time; let's take a break.
【喘息】chuǎnxī〈动〉 **1**（指呼吸） puff and pant: ～不已 gasp/pant for breath **2**（指休息） breathe: ～未定 before one has a chance to catch one's breath ‖ 不给敌人任何～的机会 not allow the enemy any breathing space
【喘吁吁】 chuǎnxūxū 〈形〉 puffing and panting
【喘嘘嘘】chuǎnxūxū = 喘吁吁 chuǎnxūxū

chuàn

串 chuàn
A〈动〉 **1**（连成串） string together: 把珍珠/珠子～起来 string pearls/beads together ▸～讲, 贯～ **2**（勾结） gang up: ▸～供, ～通 **3**（表演） act: ▸～戏, 反～ **4**（走动） go here and there: ～街 wander through the streets ‖ 到处乱～ roam about aimlessly ▸～门 **5**（连接错误） get things mixed up: 收音机～台 get two or more radio stations at once ▸～行, ～线 **6**（混杂） get mixed together: ▸～花, ～味, ～秧儿
B〈名〉 string of things: ▸钱～子, 羊肉～
C〈量〉 cluster: 一～钥匙 a bunch of keys ‖ 一～珍珠 a string of pearls ‖ 我问了他一～问题。 I asked him a series of questions.
【串案】chuàn'àn〈名〉 linked cases
【串场】chuànchǎng〈名〉 interlude: 杂技小丑的～给人们带来笑声和欢乐。 The clown's interludes amused everyone.
【串灯】chuàndēng〈名〉 string of lights: 建筑物上挂着～。 The buildings were decorated with strings of lights.
【串供】chuàngòng〈动〉 collude to make each other's confessions tally: 他们相互～，企图推翻原供词。 They were in cahoots and attempted to retract their testimony.
【串行】chuànháng〈动〉 **1**（指阅读）skip a line: 奶奶老眼昏花，看书经常～。 My grandmother's eyesight has deteriorated and she often skips lines when she reads. **2**［计算机］ serial: ～输出/输入 serial output/input
【串花】chuànhuā〈动〉 cross-breed
【串话】chuànhuà〈名〉［通信］ cross-talk
【串换】chuànhuàn〈动〉 swap: ～座位 change seats
【串讲】chuànjiǎng〈动〉 **1**（逐字逐句讲解） explain a text word by word and sentence by sentence **2**（扼要概括） give a summary of a text by reviewing it: ～课文 link up and narrate the main ideas of a text
【串联】chuànlián〈动〉 **1**（联系） link up:

他～几户农民经营养鸡场。He linked up several farmers to run a chicken farm. **2**［电气］series: ～的两个晶体管 two transistors connected in series ‖ ～电路 series circuit

【串联式】chuànliánshì〈形〉［电气］serial-type: ～稳压电路 serial regulating circuit

【串铃】chuànlíng〈名〉string of bells

【串门】chuànmén〈动〉〈口〉drop in on sb.: ～聊天 drop in for a chat ‖ 他答应来我这儿～。He promised to drop round.

【串门子】chuàn ménzi = 串门 chuànmén

【串骗】chuànpiàn〈动〉collaborate to swindle

【串气】chuànqì〈动〉gang up: 暗中～ be in secret collusion

【串亲戚】chuàn qīnqi〈动〉go visiting one's relatives

【串儿红】chuànrhóng〈名〉［植物］scarlet sage

【串烧】chuànshāo〈动〉［音乐］perform in a series: 经典情歌大～ a medley of classic love songs ‖ 土风舞～ a sequence of folk dances

【串通】chuàntōng〈动〉**1**（勾结）gang up: ～舞弊 act in complicity ‖ 与敌人～ collude with the enemy ‖ 他们～起来欺骗我。They are conspiring to deceive me. ▸～一气 **2**（联络）contact

【串通一气】chuàntōng-yīqì〈成〉collude with each other: 他俩～，诱人上当。The two of them are colluding to lure people into a trap.

【串味】chuànwèi〈动〉absorb the smell of sth. else: 不要把茶叶和化妆品放在一起，以防～。Don't put tea together with cosmetics in case the taste gets spoiled.

【串戏】chuànxì〈动〉**1**（演戏）act in a play **2**（特指票友）play a part in a professional performance

【串线】chuànxiàn〈动〉cross: 电话～了。The telephone lines are crossed.

【串演】chuànyǎn〈动〉act the role of: ～角色 play a role ‖ ～罗密欧 play Romeo

【串秧儿】chuànyāngr〈动〉〈口〉cross-breed

【串游】chuànyou〈动〉roam

【串珠】chuànzhū〈名〉string of beads

【串子】chuànzi〈名〉string: 钱～ string of coins

钏（釧）chuàn〈名〉〈旧〉bracelet: 金/玉～ gold/jade bracelet

chuāng

创（創）chuāng

A〈名〉wound: 刀/剑/枪～ knife/sword/bullet wound ▸～痕，～伤

B〈动〉inflict losses: 脚部受～ receive a wound in one's foot ‖ 重～敌军 inflict heavy casualties on the enemy ▸重～

▸chuàng

【创痕】chuānghén〈名〉scar: 没有留下～ leave no scar ‖ ～累累 be covered with scars

【创巨痛深】chuāngjù-tòngshēn〈成〉suffer from severe wounds and acute pains

【创可贴】chuāngkětiē〈名〉plaster〈英〉; Band-Aid〈美〉

【创口】chuāngkǒu〈名〉wound: 包扎～ dress a wound ‖ 缝合～ stitch a wound ‖ ～愈合。The wound healed over.

【创面】chuāngmiàn〈名〉surface of a wound

【创伤】chuāngshāng〈名〉wound: 留下～ leave a scar ‖ 医治～ heal wounds ‖〈喻〉感情～ emotional trauma ‖〈喻〉精神～ mental scar ‖〈喻〉心理～ psychological wound ‖〈喻〉战争～ scars of war

【创伤外科】chuāngshāng wàikē〈名〉［医学］department of traumatology

【创伤学】chuāngshāngxué〈名〉［医学］traumatology

【创痛】chuāngtòng〈名〉pain from an injury: 忍受～ endure wounds

疮（瘡）chuāng〈名〉**1**〈书〉（伤口）wound: 刀/剑/枪～ knife/sword/bullet wound ▸百孔千～，金～ **2**（疾病）sore: 生～ have a boil ‖ 恶～ malignant sore ▸冻～，疥～，痔～

【疮疤】chuāngbā〈名〉**1**〈本〉scar: 留下～ leave scars **2**〈喻〉（短处）sore: 揭～ touch sb.'s sore spot

【疮痕】chuānghén〈名〉scar

【疮痂】chuāngjiā〈名〉［医学］scab

【疮口】chuāngkǒu〈名〉wound: 清洗～ clean a sore ‖ 给～消毒 disinfect a sore

【疮痍】chuāngyí〈名〉〈书〉〈喻〉devastation

【疮痍满目】chuāngyí-mǎnmù〈成〉destruction can be seen everywhere

窗 chuāng〈名〉window: 开～ open a window ‖ 玻璃～ glass window ‖〈喻〉世界之～ window on the world ▸～户，～口，～明几净

【窗玻璃】chuāngbōli〈名〉windowpane

【窗洞】chuāngdòng〈名〉opening in a wall

【窗扉】chuāngfēi〈名〉casement

【窗风撑】chuāngfēngchēng〈名〉casement stay

【窗格子】chuānggézi〈名〉window lattice

【窗户】chuānghu〈名〉window: 关上～ close a window ‖ ～打不开/闩不上。The window won't open/close. ‖ 眼睛是心灵的～。Eyes are the windows of the soul.

【窗户纸】chuānghuzhǐ〈名〉window paper

【窗花】chuānghuā〈名〉paper cut-out for window decoration

【窗孔】chuāngkǒng〈名〉［解剖］iris

【窗口】chuāngkǒu〈名〉window: ～遮阳篷 window shade ‖ 坐在～ sit by the window ‖ 售票～ ticket window ‖ 非活动/活动～ inactive/active window ‖ 经济特区在对外开放中发挥着～作用。Special economic zones are serving as windows to the outside world.

【窗口行业】chuāngkǒu hángyè〈名〉window trades

【窗框】chuāngkuàng〈名〉window frame

【窗帘】chuānglián〈名〉curtain: 卷起～ draw a curtain ‖ 拉开～ pull open the curtains ‖ 拉上～ pull curtains

【窗帘布】chuāngliánbù〈名〉casement cloth

【窗帘盒】chuāngliánhé〈名〉pelmet

【窗棂】chuānglíng〈名〉window lattice

【窗幔】chuāngmàn〈名〉window curtain

【窗明几净】chuāngmíng-jījìng〈成〉bright and clean: 学校里每间教室都～。Every classroom in the school is bright and clean.

【窗纱】chuāngshā〈名〉window gauze: 安装～ screen a window

【窗扇】chuāngshàn〈名〉window sash

【窗式空调】chuāngshì kōngtiáo〈名〉window air conditioner

【窗台】chuāngtái〈名〉window ledge

【窗帷】chuāngwéi〈名〉window curtain

【窗沿】chuāngyán〈名〉window sill

【窗子】chuāngzi〈名〉window

chuáng

床（牀）chuáng

A〈名〉**1**（指卧具）bed: 铺～ make a bed ‖ 躺在～上 lie in bed ‖ 木板～ plank bed ‖ 双层～ bunk bed ▸～单，～铺，卧～ **2**（指床状物）bed-shaped support: ▸～子，车～，牙～ **3**（指地面）bed: 花/岩～ flower/rock bed ▸河～，矿～，苗～

B〈量〉[of quilt, bedding, etc.]: 两～铺盖 two sets of bedding ‖ 一～被子 one quilt

【床板】chuángbǎn〈名〉bed plank

【床单】chuángdān〈名〉bed sheet: 更换～ change the sheets

【床单布】chuángdānbù〈名〉sheeting

【床垫】chuángdiàn〈名〉mattress: 弹簧～ spring mattress

【床架】chuángjià〈名〉bedstead

【床铺】chuángpù〈名〉bed and bedding: 整理～ tidy up a bed

【床褥】chuángrù〈名〉bedding

【床上戏】chuángshàngxì〈名〉bedroom scene

【床上用品】chuángshàng yòngpǐn〈名〉bedding

【床虱】chuángshī〈名〉bedbug

【床榻】chuángtà〈名〉bed: 卧病～ be bed-ridden

【床头柜】chuángtóuguì〈名〉bedside table

【床腿】chuángtuǐ〈名〉foot post

【床帏】chuángwéi〈名〉〈书〉**1**〈本〉bed cover **2**〈喻〉（性关系）love affairs

【床位】chuángwèi〈名〉berth: 卧铺～ sleeping berth ‖ 有 400 张～的医院 400-bed hospital

【床戏】chuángxì〈名〉［影视］bedroom scene

【床沿】chuángyán〈名〉bedside: 坐在～儿上 sit on the edge of a bed

【床罩】chuángzhào〈名〉bedspread

【床笫】chuángzǐ〈名〉〈书〉**1**（床铺）bed and bed mat **2**（闺房）place of conjugal intimacies: ～之言 pillow talk

【床子】chuángzi〈名〉［机械］lathe

噇 chuáng〈动〉〈方〉eat and drink extravagantly

幢 chuáng〈名〉**1**（指旗子）pennant or streamer used in ancient China **2**（指石柱）stone pillar inscribed with Buddha's name or Buddhist scriptures

▸zhuàng

【幢幢】chuángchuáng〈形〉〈书〉flickering: 灯影～ flickering shadows of a lamp ‖ 人影～ shadows of people moving about

chuǎng

闯（闖）chuǎng〈动〉**1**（猛冲）charge: ～进去 burst in ‖ 向前～ rush forward **2**（开拓）temper oneself: ～新路 blaze a new trail ‖ 敢～敢干 dare to break through and act ‖ 年轻人应该到社会上去～一～。Young people should temper themselves in society. ▸～将，～劲，～练 **3**（四处奔走）rush about: ▸～江湖，走南～北 **4**（招致）invite: ▸～祸

【闯荡】chuǎngdàng〈动〉make a living

away from home: ～江湖 make a living wandering from place to place

【闯关】chuǎngguān〈动〉break through a barrier: 该队连闯几关，进入决赛。 The team advanced to the finals after beating several rival teams.

【闯关东】chuǎng Guāndōng〈惯〉〈旧〉seek a living in the north-east [formerly of poor people from Hebei and Shandong who sought a better life in the north-east of China]

【闯红灯】chuǎng hóngdēng〈惯〉jump a red light

【闯祸】chuǎnghuò〈动〉get into trouble: 他闯下了大祸。 He has brought serious trouble on himself.

【闯江湖】chuǎng jiānghú〈惯〉〈旧〉make an itinerant living

【闯将】chuǎngjiàng〈名〉path-breaker

【闯劲】chuǎngjìn〈名〉pioneering spirit: 缺乏～ lack pizzazz ‖ ～十足的年轻人 spirited young man

【闯练】chuǎngliàn〈动〉leave home to temper oneself: 鼓励年轻人到社会上去～ encourage young people to temper themselves in society

【闯入】chuǎngrù〈动〉burst in: ～别人的地盘 intrude into others' territory ‖ ～大楼 break into a building ‖ ～房间 barge into the room ‖ ～决赛 force one's way into the finals

【闯世界】chuǎng shìjiè〈惯〉make a living away from home

chuàng

创（創）chuàng

A〈动〉**1**（创造）create: ～历史最高纪录 hit an all-time high ‖ ～奇迹 work miracles ‖ ～新高 hit new highs ▸～办, ～纪录, ～刊 **2**（获取）make profits: ▸～汇, ～利, ～收

B〈形〉original: ▸～见, ～举, ～议

▸chuāng

【创办】chuàngbàn〈动〉set up: ～工厂 set up a factory ‖ ～机构 establish an organization ‖ ～刊物/杂志 start a publication/magazine ‖ ～学校 found a school

【创办人】chuàngbànrén〈名〉founder

【创编】chuàngbiān〈动〉（指文字）compose;（指动作）choreograph: ～剧本 write a play

【创导】chuàngdǎo〈动〉initiate: ～者 pioneer

【创汇】chuànghuì〈动〉earn foreign exchange: 出口～ export to earn foreign exchange ‖ ～产品 foreign-exchange-earning product

【创获】chuànghuò〈名〉new discovery: 很多技术员都有～。 Lots of technicians have made new discoveries.

【创纪录】chuàng jìlù〈动〉set a record

【创见】chuàngjiàn〈名〉original idea: 富有～ highly original ‖ 这个计划是他的～。 This plan is his own creation.

【创建】chuàngjiàn〈动〉set up: ～公司 start a company ‖ ～全国先进卫生城市 build a nationally advanced clean city ‖ ～政党 found a political party

【创举】chuàngjǔ〈名〉unprecedented undertaking: 前无古人的～ pioneering undertaking unparalleled in history ‖ 伟大的～ great beginning

【创刊】chuàngkān〈动〉start publication: 该报～于 1956 年 12 月 1 日。 The newspaper was launched on Dec 1, 1956.

【创刊词】chuàngkāncí〈名〉inaugural statement

【创刊号】chuàngkānhào〈名〉first issue

【创立】chuànglì〈动〉establish: ～基金 set up a fund ‖ ～通讯社 create a news agency ‖ ～学派 found an academic school

【创利】chuànglì〈动〉generate profits: 这家工厂～一百多万元。 The factory made a profit of over one million *yuan*.

【创牌子】chuàng páizi〈惯〉establish a brand

【创设】chuàngshè〈动〉**1**（设立）set up: ～委员会 set up a committee **2**（创造）create: ～有利条件 create favourable conditions

【创始】chuàngshǐ〈动〉initiate: ～阶段 initial stage

【创始人】chuàngshǐrén〈名〉founder

【创世纪】Chuàngshìjì〈名〉［基督教］Genesis

【创世主】Chuàngshìzhǔ〈名〉［基督教］Creator

【创收】chuàngshōu〈动〉generate income by providing paid services: 他们在忙着搞～。 They are busy creating extra income.

【创税】chuàngshuì〈动〉generate taxes: 该企业去年为国家～三百多万元。 The business paid over three million *yuan* in taxes last year.

【创新】chuàngxīn〈动〉break fresh ground: 大胆～ be bold in blazing new trails ‖ ～能力 ability to innovate ‖ ～精神 pioneering spirit ‖ 艺术上要不断～。 We should be generating new ideas in the arts all the time.

【创业】chuàngyè〈动〉break new ground: ～精神 pioneering spirit ‖ 艰苦～ strive to build a career ‖ ～史 history of an undertaking

【创业板】chuàngyèbǎn〈名〉［金融］Growth Enterprise Market (GEM): 中国的～在深圳上市。 China's GEM is listed in Shenzhen. ‖ 投资者看好～。 Investors are hopeful for the GEM.

【创议】chuàngyì **A**〈动〉propose: ～开展劳动竞赛 propose launching an emulation campaign **B**〈名〉proposal: 大家对这项～反应热烈。 Everybody responded enthusiastically to this proposal.

【创意】chuàngyì **A**〈动〉initiate an idea **B**〈名〉original idea: 颇有～ be very creative

【创优】chuàngyōu〈动〉strive to be the best: 争先～ strive to be the best and the most advanced ‖ ～活动 activities encouraging excellence

【创造】chuàngzào〈动〉bring about: ～财富 create wealth ‖ ～机会 create opportunities ‖ ～奇迹 work miracles ‖ ～条件 set the stage for sth.

【创造力】chuàngzàolì〈名〉creativity: 表现出～ demonstrate one's creative power ‖ 富有～ rich with creativity

【创造性】chuàngzàoxìng〈名〉creativity: 缺乏～ lack originality ‖ ～的工作 creative work

【创制】chuàngzhì〈动〉formulate: ～拼音文字 create an alphabetic system of writing

【创作】chuàngzuò **A**〈动〉create: ～歌剧/歌曲 compose an opera/a song ‖ ～艺术作品 produce works of art ‖ ～技巧 craftsmanship ‖ ～思想 ideas of guiding artistic/literary creation ‖ ～源泉 source of creation **B**〈名〉literary or artistic work: 文学～ literary work

怆（愴）chuàng

〈形〉〈书〉sorrowful: ▸～然, 悲～

【怆然】chuàngrán〈形〉〈书〉sorrowful: ～泪下 burst into sorrowful tears

【怆痛】chuàngtòng〈形〉distressed

chuī

吹 chuī

〈动〉**1**（吹气）blow: ～蜡烛 blow at a candle ‖ ～气球 blow up a balloon ‖ ～灭/熄 blow out ▸～灯 1, ～口哨 **2**（演奏）play: ～笛子 play the flute ‖ ～号角/喇叭 blow the horn/trumpet ▸～号, ～奏 **3**（夸张）boast: ～过头 blow out of proportion ▸～牛, ～嘘, 自～自擂 **4**〈口〉（失败）fall apart: 我和男朋友～了。 I have broken up with my boyfriend. ‖ 整个计划都～了。 The whole plan fell through. ▸～台, 告～ **5**（奉承）compliment: 他们把他～上了天。 They praised him to the skies. ▸～捧 **6**（空气流动）blow: 风～雨打 the wind blowing and the rain beating down ▸～风机

【吹吹拍拍】chuīchuī-pāipāi〈成〉fawn on

【吹打】chuīdǎ〈动〉**1**（指乐器）play wind and percussion instruments: ～乐 ensemble of Chinese wind and percussion instruments **2**（指风雨）beat

【吹灯】chuīdēng〈动〉**1**（吹熄灯火）blow out a lamp **2**〈喻〉〈方〉（死亡）die **3**〈喻〉〈方〉（失败）fall through

【吹灯拔蜡】chuīdēng-bálà〈成〉〈方〉〈喻〉**1**（死亡）kick the bucket **2**（失败）be finished

【吹风】chuīfēng〈动〉**1**（让风吹）get a blast of air: 你感冒了，不要～。 You've got a cold. Don't go getting yourself caught in a dranght. **2**（吹头发）blow-dry one's hair: ▸～机 **3**〈口〉〈喻〉（透露消息）drop a hint: 下次会议要讨论什么，你给我们吹吹风吧。 Will you give us some idea of what will be taken up at the next meeting? ▸～会

【吹风会】chuīfēnghuì〈名〉briefing: 外交部～ Foreign Ministry briefing

【吹风机】chuīfēngjī〈名〉hair drier

【吹拂】chuīfú〈动〉swish: 微风～着树枝。 A breeze was swaying the branches.

【吹鼓手】chuīgǔshǒu〈名〉**1**〈旧〉（吹奏者）trumpeter and drummer **2**〈喻〉〈贬〉eulogist

【吹管】chuīguǎn〈名〉［机械］blowpipe: 氢氧～ oxyhydrogen blowpipe

【吹号】chuīhào〈动〉blow the bugle

【吹胡子瞪眼】chuīhúzi-dèngyǎn〈俗〉froth at the mouth and glare with rage: 他对我～。 He fumed with rage at me.

【吹灰之力】chuīhuīzhīlì〈成〉just a small effort: 不费～ a piece of cake

【吹火筒】chuīhuǒtǒng〈名〉blowpipe

【吹口哨】chuī kǒushào〈动〉whistle

【吹拉弹唱】chuī-lā-tán-chàng〈惯〉**1**〈本〉blow, pull, pluck and sing **2**〈喻〉be musically versatile

【吹喇叭】chuī lǎba〈惯〉〈喻〉lavish praises on sb.

【吹喇叭，抬轿子】chuī lǎba, tái jiàozi〈俗〉〈喻〉flatter those in power

【吹擂】chuīléi〈动〉boast

【吹冷风】chuī lěngfēng〈惯〉〈喻〉pour cold water on

【吹毛求疵】chuīmáo-qiúcī〈成〉nit-pick: 对别人的建议～。 It's easy to pick holes in other people's proposals.

【吹牛】chuīniú〈动〉 talk big: 爱～ like to boast ‖ ～大王 windbag
【吹牛拍马】chuīniú-pāimǎ〈成〉 brag and tout
【吹牛皮】chuī niúpí = 吹牛 chuīniú
【吹拍】chuīpāi〈动〉 toady to
【吹捧】chuīpěng〈动〉 flatter: 互相～ flatter each other ‖ 把某人～上天 praise sb. to the skies
【吹气】chuīqì〈动〉 blow
【吹塑】chuīsù〈名〉 blow moulding
【吹台】chuītái〈动〉〈口〉 fall through: 整件事情都～了。 The whole thing's fallen through.
【吹嘘】chuīxū〈动〉 boast: ～自己富有 boast of one's wealth ‖ 自我～ self-praise
【吹氧】chuīyǎng〈名〉［冶金］ oxygen blast: ～转炉 oxygen-blown converter
【吹制】chuīzhì〈动〉 blow: ～的玻璃制品 blow-moulded glass
【吹奏】chuīzòu〈动〉 play: ～横笛 play the flute ‖ ～乐器 wind instruments
【吹奏乐】chuīzòuyuè〈名〉 wind music

炊 chuī〈动〉 cook a meal: ▸～具, 断～, 野～
【炊具】chuījù〈名〉 cooking utensils
【炊事】chuīshì〈名〉 cooking: 干～工作 do kitchen work ‖ ～班 kitchen team ‖ ～兵 mess cook ‖ ～员 kitchen staff
【炊烟】chuīyān〈名〉 cooking smoke: ～袅袅。 Cooking smoke curls up.
【炊帚】chuīzhou〈名〉 scourer

C

chuí

垂 chuí
A〈动〉 **1**（垂落） hang down: ～发 have one's hair down ‖ 羞愧地～下头 hang one's head in shame ▸～钓, ～柳, ～首帖耳 **2**（流下） drip: ▸～涎三尺 **3**〈书〉（留传） bequeath: 功～千秋 one's achievements will be remembered forever ▸名～青史, 永～不朽 **4**〈书〉〈敬〉（指长辈或上级） condescend: ▸～爱, ～念, ～问
B〈副〉〈书〉 on the verge of: ▸～暮, ～死, 功败～成
【垂爱】chuí'ài〈动〉〈书〉〈敬〉 provide tender care (for me): 承蒙～ be grateful for your concern
【垂成】chuíchéng〈动〉〈书〉 approach completion: 功败～ suffer defeat on the verge of success
【垂垂】chuíchuí〈副〉〈书〉 gradually: ～老矣 be slowly getting old
【垂钓】chuídiào〈动〉 go angling: 在岸边/船上～ angle from the bank/a boat
【垂范】chuífàn〈动〉〈书〉 set an example: 领导率先～。 The leaders took charge in setting an example.
【垂范后世】chuífàn-hòushì〈成〉〈书〉 set an example for posterity
【垂挂】chuíguà〈动〉 hang from above: 窗户上～着深绿色的窗帘。 The window was hung with dark green curtains.
【垂花门】chuíhuāmén〈名〉［建筑］ festoon gate
【垂帘听政】chuílián-tīngzhèng〈成〉 hold court from behind a screen
【垂柳】chuíliǔ〈名〉 weeping willow: ～依依。 The weeping willows sway gently in the breeze.
【垂落】chuíluò〈动〉 fall: 汗水从他的额头～下来。 Sweat dropped from his forehead. ‖ 夜幕～。 Night fell.

【垂暮】chuímù〈动〉 **1**〈书〉（指时间） approach sunset **2**（指人生） be in the twilight of one's life: ～之年 in the twilight of one's years
【垂念】chuíniàn〈动〉〈书〉〈敬〉 show kind concern for (me)
【垂青】chuíqīng〈动〉〈书〉 look upon sb. with favour: 深得～ stand high in sb.'s favour
【垂手】chuíshǒu〈动〉 **1**（表示容易） be extremely easy: ▸～可得 **2**（表示恭敬） let one's hands hang by one's sides: ～侍立 stand respectfully in attendance
【垂手可得】chuíshǒu-kědé〈成〉 be within easy reach
【垂首】chuíshǒu〈动〉 hang one's head: ～默哀 bow one's head in silent tribute ‖ ～叹息 hang one's head and heave a sigh
【垂首帖耳】chuíshǒu-tiē'ěr〈成〉〈贬〉 be docile and obedient
【垂死】chuísǐ〈形〉 dying: ～的人 dying man
【垂死挣扎】chuísǐ-zhēngzhá〈成〉 put up a last-ditch struggle
【垂体】chuítǐ〈名〉［生理］ pituitary gland
【垂髫】chuítiáo〈名〉〈书〉 early childhood: ～之年 during young childhood
【垂头丧气】chuítóu-sàngqì〈成〉 hang one's head in dismay: ～的样子 look crestfallen
【垂危】chuíwēi〈形〉 **1**（指人） critically ill: 生命～ nearing one's end **2**（指国家） in great peril
【垂问】chuíwèn〈动〉〈书〉〈敬〉 [of one's elders or superiors] deign to ask sb. about sth.
【垂涎】chuíxián〈动〉 covet: ～已久 have hankered for sth. for a long time
【垂涎三尺】chuíxián-sānchǐ〈成〉 drool with envy
【垂涎欲滴】chuíxián-yùdī〈成〉 **1**（形容嘴馋） lick one's chops over sth. **2**〈贬〉（形容眼红） hanker for sth.
【垂询】chuíxún〈动〉〈书〉〈敬〉 deign to enquire into sth.: 欢迎～。 Your enquiry is welcome.
【垂杨柳】chuíyángliǔ〈名〉 weeping willow
【垂直】chuízhí〈动〉 **1**（成90度角） be perpendicular: ～降落 vertical landing ‖ 标杆与地面～。 The post is perpendicular to the ground. **2**［数学］ be at right angles to: 线段AB和线段CD～。 The line AB is at right angles to the line CD.
【垂直传播】chuízhí chuánbō〈名〉［医学］ vertical transmission
【垂直度】chuízhídù〈名〉 verticality
【垂直高度】chuízhí gāodù〈名〉 perpendicular height
【垂直距离】chuízhí jùlí〈名〉 vertical distance

陲 chuí〈名〉〈书〉 frontier: ▸边～

捶（搥） chuí〈动〉 thump: ～背 pound sb.'s back ‖ ～鼓 beat a drum ▸～床捣枕, ～打, ～胸顿足
【捶床捣枕】chuíchuáng-dǎozhěn〈成〉 turn uneasily on one's bed
【捶打】chuídǎ〈动〉 beat: 用拳头～桌子 pound the table with one's fist
【捶胸顿足】chuíxiōng-dùnzú〈成〉 thump one's chest and stamp one's feet

棰 chuí〈书〉
A〈名〉 **1**（短木棍） cudgel **2** = 槌 chuí
B〈动〉 beat with a stick

椎 chuí
A = 槌 chuí
B = 捶 chuí
▸zhuī
【椎心泣血】chuíxīn-qìxuè〈成〉 be deeply grieved

槌 chuí〈名〉 mallet: ▸棒～, 鼓～

锤（鎚、鎚） chuí
A〈名〉 **1**（秤砣） weight: 平衡～ balance weight ▸秤～ **2**（秤锤状物） weight-shaped thing: ▸纺～ **3**（指兵器） weapon with a heavy head and a handle or chain **4**（榔头） hammer: 用～敲打 strike sth. with a hammer ‖ 铁～ iron hammer ▸钉～, 汽～
B〈动〉 hammer into shape: 把金子～成金箔 beat gold into foil ▸～打, ～炼
【锤打】chuídǎ〈动〉 strike with a hammer: 把金属～成一只碗 hammer a bowl out of metal
【锤骨】chuígǔ〈名〉［生理］ malleus
【锤炼】chuíliàn〈动〉 **1**（磨炼） temper: 在艰苦的环境中～自己 temper oneself in difficult circumstances ‖ 长跑是一项～意志的运动。 Long-distance running is the kind of exercise that can steel people's will. **2**（推敲） hammer out: ～字句 refine the wording and phrasing
【锤子】chuízi〈名〉 hammer

chūn

春 chūn〈名〉 **1** ▸p. 345（春天） spring: 温暖如～ be as warm as spring ‖ ～回大地。 Spring is here again. ▸～风, ～季, ～游 **2**〈书〉（年） year: 至今已历八～。 It has been eight years since then. **3**〈喻〉（生命） life: ▸妙手回～ **4**（情欲） love: ▸～心, ～药, 怀～
【春饼】chūnbǐng〈名〉 spring pancake
【春播】chūnbō〈动〉 sow in spring: ～季节 spring sowing season ‖ ～作物 spring crops
【春蚕】chūncán〈名〉 spring silkworm
【春茶】chūnchá〈名〉 spring tea
【春潮】chūncháo〈名〉 **1**［海洋］ spring tide **2**（潮流） tide
【春城】chūnchéng〈名〉 spring city [referring to Kunming (昆明)]
【春分】Chūnfēn〈名〉 Spring Equinox [beginning of the 4th of the 24 solar terms]
【春风】chūnfēng〈名〉 **1**〈本〉 spring breeze: ～拂面。 Spring breeze caressed the cheeks. ‖ ～送暖。 Spring breezes carry warmth. **2**〈书〉〈喻〉（指情感） favour **3**〈喻〉（指神色） kindly and pleasant countenance: ▸～满面
【春风得意】chūnfēng-déyì〈成〉 be flushed with success: ～时 in one's palmy days
【春风化雨】chūnfēng-huàyǔ〈成〉 **1**〈本〉 life-giving spring breeze and rain **2**〈喻〉 beneficial influence of education
【春风满面】chūnfēng-mǎnmiàn〈成〉 beaming with satisfaction: 你看上去真是～! You look absolutely radiant!
【春耕】chūngēng〈动〉 plough a field before the spring sowing: ～大忙季节 busy spring ploughing season
【春耕夏耘】chūngēng-xiàyún〈成〉 plough the field in spring and till it in summer
【春宫】chūngōng〈名〉 **1**（指宫室） crown prince's palace **2**（指图画） pornographic picture

【春灌】chūnguàn〈动〉［农业］ spring irrigation

【春光】chūnguāng〈名〉 sights and sounds of spring

【春光明媚】chūnguāng-míngmèi〈成〉 spring in all its brightness and charm

【春寒】chūnhán〈名〉 spring chill: 倒～ the return of the spring chill

【春寒料峭】chūnhán-liàoqiào〈成〉 there is a chill in the air in spring

【春旱】chūnhàn〈名〉 spring drought

【春花秋月】chūnhuā-qiūyuè〈成〉 1〈本〉 spring flowers and autumn moon 2〈喻〉 happy days

【春华秋实】chūnhuá-qiūshí〈成〉〈喻〉 literary talent and moral integrity

【春荒】chūnhuāng〈名〉 springtime grain shortage

【春晖】chūnhuī〈名〉〈书〉 1（春日阳光） spring sunshine 2〈喻〉（父母关爱） parental love and care: ▸寸草～

【春季】chūnjì ▸p. 345〈名〉 spring

【春假】chūnjià〈名〉 spring holiday

【春节】Chūnjié〈名〉 Spring Festival: 欢度～ celebrate Spring Festival

> **春节**
>
> The first day of the lunar New Year, the most important festival in the Chinese calendar and also the nine days that follow. Celebrations begin a week before the eve of the New Year. The 24th day of the 12th month of the year (or the 23rd in northern China) is celebrated as the 'small year' (小年). This is the day on which the Kitchen God (灶王爷) returns to heaven to report on the family activities. New Year's Eve (除夕) is often known as the 'big year' (大年三十), the time when the family reunites for a celebratory meal (▸年夜饭). The 15th day of the new lunar month is the Lantern Festival (▸元宵节), and is the concluding period of the Spring Festival activities.

【春节联欢晚会】chūnjié liánhuān wǎnhuì〈名〉 Spring Festival Gala: 在央视～上亮相 appear in the CCTV Spring Festival Gala

【春卷】chūnjuǎn〈名〉 spring roll

【春困】chūnkùn〈名〉 spring fever

【春困秋乏】chūnkùn-qiūfá〈俗〉 one feels sleepy in spring and fatigued in autumn

【春兰秋菊】chūnlán-qiūjú〈成〉 1〈本〉 orchids in spring and chrysanthemums in autumn 2〈喻〉 each has its own strong points

【春雷】chūnléi〈名〉 spring thunder: ～作响。Spring thunder came crashing.

【春联】chūnlián〈名〉 Spring Festival couplets: 贴～ paste up Spring Festival couplets

【春令】chūnlìng〈名〉 1（指季节） spring 2（指气候） spring weather: 冬行～ mild winter

【春梦】chūnmèng〈名〉〈喻〉 1（指短暂） transient joy 2（指无法实现） pipe dream

【春牛】chūnniú〈名〉〈旧〉 Spring Ox made of clay to usher in spring

【春暖花开】chūnnuǎn-huākāi〈成〉 spring has come and flowers are in bloom

【春情】chūnqíng〈名〉 amorous feelings

【春秋】chūnqiū〈名〉 1（年） year: 他在狱中已度过了十几个～。 He has spent over 10 years in prison. 2〈书〉（年龄） age: ～已高 be advanced in years ▸～鼎盛, ～正富 3（指史书） chronicle: 《春秋》 *The Spring and Autumn Annals* 4 Chūnqiū（指时代） Spring and Autumn Period

【春秋笔法】chūnqiū bǐfǎ〈成〉 style of the *Spring and Autumn Annals* in which subtle and guarded words are used in criticism

【春秋鼎盛】chūnqiū-dǐngshèng〈成〉 in the prime of life

【春秋衫】chūnqiūshān〈名〉 spring and autumn jacket

【春秋正富】chūnqiū-zhèngfù〈成〉 in the prime of life

【春去秋来】chūnqù-qiūlái〈成〉 1〈本〉 spring is gone and autumn has come 2〈喻〉（指时间） passage of time

【春日】chūnrì〈名〉 spring days

【春色】chūnsè〈名〉 1（指景色） spring scenery: ～撩人 teasing scenes of spring ▸～满园 2（指神情） joyful look: 面有～ with a cheerful look

【春色满园】chūnsè-mǎnyuán〈成〉 the garden is filled with the beauty of spring

【春色宜人】chūnsè-yírén〈惯〉 pleasant spring scenery

【春上】chūnshang〈名〉〈口〉 spring: 今年～天气比往年冷。 This spring is colder than in previous years.

【春笋】chūnsǔn〈名〉 spring bamboo shoot: ▸雨后～

【春天】chūntiān〈名〉 1 ▸p. 345（指季节） spring: ～里百花盛开。 Flowers come out in spring. 2〈喻〉（指氛围） right environment: 迎来繁荣文艺创作的～ entire an environment conducive to literary creativity

【春晚】chūnwǎn〈简称〉= 春节联欢晚会

【春捂秋冻】chūnwǔ-qiūdòng〈俗〉 take care not to change one's clothes too quickly with the change of seasons

【春宵】chūnxiāo〈名〉 1（春夜） spring night 2〈喻〉（指男女欢爱） night of sexual bliss: ～苦短。 Nights of loving are always too short.

【春宵一刻值千金】chūnxiāo yīkè zhí qiānjīn〈俗〉 every minute of the wedding night is precious

【春小麦】chūnxiǎomài〈名〉 spring wheat

【春心】chūnxīn〈名〉 amorous feelings: ～荡漾 surging of lustful desire

【春汛】chūnxùn〈名〉［水利］ spring flood

【春药】chūnyào〈名〉 aphrodisiac

【春意】chūnyì〈名〉 1（指气息） spring: 这花儿给屋子增添了几分～。 The flower touched the room with spring. ▸～盎然, ～阑珊 2（春心） amorous feelings

【春意盎然】chūnyì-àngrán〈成〉 spring is very much in the air

【春意阑珊】chūnyì-lánshān〈成〉 spring is on the wane

【春游】chūnyóu〈动〉 go on a spring excursion

【春雨贵如油】chūnyǔ guì rú yóu〈俗〉 spring rain is as precious as oil

【春运】chūnyùn〈名〉 passenger transport during or around the Spring Festival: ～高峰 peak time Spring Festival traffic

【春种】chūnzhòng〈动〉 sow in spring

【春装】chūnzhuāng〈名〉 spring clothes

椿 chūn

〈名〉［植物］ Chinese toon: ▸香～, 臭～

【椿象】chūnxiàng〈名〉［昆虫］ stink bug

【椿萱】chūnxuān〈名〉〈书〉 father and mother

蝽 chūn

= 椿象 chūnxiàng

chún

纯（純）chún

A〈形〉 1（无杂质） pure: ～而不杂 be pure and unadulterated ‖ ～学术研究 pure academic research ‖ ～赢利 pure profit ▸～洁, ～净, ～水 2（熟练） skilful: 功夫不～ not be skilled enough ▸～熟, 炉火～青

B〈副〉 purely: ▸～属

【纯粹】chúncuì A〈形〉 pure: 他是～的法国人。 He is pure French. B〈副〉 purely: ～是浪费时间 be a sheer waste of time ‖ 这～是个骗局。 It is fraud pure and simple.

【纯度】chúndù〈名〉 purity: 高～ be of high purity ‖ 金/银的～ fineness of gold/silver

【纯钢】chúngāng〈名〉［冶金］ clean steel

【纯化】chúnhuà〈动〉 purify: ～过程 purging process

【纯化剂】chúnhuàjì〈名〉 purifying agent

【纯碱】chúnjiǎn〈名〉［化学］ sodium carbonate

【纯洁】chúnjié A〈形〉 pure: 思想～ be pure in thought ‖ ～的心灵 simple heart ‖ ～无私 pure and unselfish B〈动〉 purify: ～心灵 cleanse one's spirit ‖ ～组织 purify an organization

【纯洁度】chúnjiédù〈名〉 clarity

【纯洁性】chúnjiéxìng〈名〉 purity: 保持组织的～ keep the purity of an organization

【纯金】chúnjīn〈名〉 solid gold

【纯金属】chúnjīnshǔ〈名〉 pure metal: ～结晶 pure metal crystal

【纯净】chúnjìng A〈形〉 pure: ～的空气 pure air B〈动〉 purify: ～灵魂 cleanse the soul ‖ ～心灵 cleanse the heart

【纯净水】chúnjìngshuǐ〈名〉 purified water

【纯利】chúnlì〈名〉［经济］ net profit: 获～ have a net profit

【纯利润】chúnlìrùn = 纯利 chúnlì

【纯良】chúnliáng〈形〉 kind and honest: 她是个心地～的女人。 She is a woman of purity and honesty.

【纯毛】chúnmáo〈名〉 pure wool

【纯美】chúnměi〈形〉 pure and fine: 音色～ have a pure and sweet resonance

【纯棉】chúnmián〈名〉 pure cotton: ～T恤 100% cotton T-shirt

【纯平彩电】chúnpíng cǎidiàn〈名〉 flat screen colour TV

【纯朴】chúnpǔ = 淳朴 chúnpǔ

【纯情】chúnqíng〈名〉 pure love: ～少女 girl of innocent love

【纯然】chúnrán〈书〉 A〈形〉 pure: ～一色 be of solid colour B〈副〉 purely: 我帮他～是出于友谊。 I helped him purely out of friendship.

【纯色】chúnsè〈名〉 one colour: ～制服 uniforms of one colour

【纯收入】chúnshōurù〈名〉 net income

【纯熟】chúnshú〈形〉 skilled: 技术/技艺～ be highly skilled

【纯属】chúnshǔ〈副〉 completely: ～猜测 be pure guesswork ‖ ～虚构 be a pure fabrication ‖ ～巧合 by pure coincidence ‖ ～意外 be a pure accident

【纯水】chúnshuǐ〈名〉 pure water

【纯天然】chúntiānrán〈形〉 all-natural

【纯文学】chúnwénxué〈名〉 belles-lettres

【纯物质】chúnwùzhì〈名〉 pure substance

【纯血统】chúnxuètǒng〈名〉 pure blood

【纯一】chúnyī〈形〉 simple: 目标～ single-mindedness

【纯艺术】chúnyìshù〈名〉 pure art

【纯音】chúnyīn〈名〉［物理］ pure tone

【纯音乐】chúnyīnyuè〈名〉 absolute music

【纯银】chúnyín〈名〉［冶金］ pure silver

【纯育】chúnyù〈名〉 pure breeding

C

【纯贞】chúnzhēn〈形〉 pure and faithful: ～的爱情 pure and faithful love
【纯真】chúnzhēn〈形〉 pure: ～无邪 pure and innocent ‖ ～的爱情 pure and sincere love
【纯正】chúnzhèng〈形〉 **1**（纯粹） pure: 颜色～ pure colour ‖ 说一口～的英语 speak pure English **2**（正派） upright: 动机～ have pure motives
【纯挚】chúnzhì〈形〉 pure and sincere: ～的感情 pure and sincere feelings
【纯种】chúnzhǒng〈形〉 thoroughbred: ～马 pure-bred horse ‖ ～繁育 pedigree breeding

C

莼（蒓）chún
【莼菜】chúncài〈名〉［植物］ water shield

唇（脣）chún〈名〉 **1**（嘴唇） lip: 紧闭双～ press one's lips together ‖ 上～ upper lip ‖ 下～ lower lip ▸～齿相依, ～膏, ～舌 **2**（唇状物） lip-shaped thing: ▸阴～
【唇齿】chúnchǐ〈名〉〈喻〉 be closely related and mutually dependent
【唇齿相依】chúnchǐ-xiāngyī〈成〉 be closely related and mutually dependent: 友好邻邦～。 Friendly neighbouring countries are closely related and mutually dependent.
【唇读】chúndú〈动〉 lip-read
【唇膏】chúngāo〈名〉 lipstick
【唇红齿白】chúnhóng-chǐbái〈成〉 be good-looking
【唇焦舌敝】chúnjiāo-shébì〈成〉 talk till one's tongue and lips are parched: 说得～ talk until one's mouth is dry
【唇裂】chúnliè ▸**p. 50**〈名〉［医学］ cleft lip
【唇枪舌剑】chúnqiāng-shéjiàn〈成〉 have a heated verbal exchange: 双方～。 The two sides engaged in a battle of words.
【唇舌】chúnshé〈名〉 debate: 徒费～ waste one's breath
【唇亡齿寒】chúnwáng-chǐhán〈成〉〈喻〉 share a common fate
【唇吻】chúnwěn **1**〈书〉（嘴唇） lips **2**〈喻〉（言语） words
【唇线】chúnxiàn〈名〉 lipline
【唇音】chúnyīn〈名〉［语言］ labial (sound)
【唇印】chúnyìn〈名〉 lip print
【唇语】chúnyǔ〈名〉 lip language

淳 chún〈形〉〈书〉 pure: ▸～厚, ～朴
【淳厚】chúnhòu〈形〉 pure and honest
【淳美】chúnměi〈形〉 pure and sweet: 嗓音～ have a pure and sweet voice
【淳朴】chúnpǔ〈形〉 honest: ～善良 honest and kind-hearted ‖ ～的人 simple man

鹑（鶉）chún〈名〉 **1** = 鹌鹑 ānchun **2**〈书〉（指衣服） ragged clothes: ▸～衣百结
【鹑衣】chúnyī〈名〉〈书〉 ragged and patched clothes
【鹑衣百结】chúnyī-bǎijié〈成〉 be in rags and tatters

醇 chún
A〈形〉〈书〉 **1**（指酒味） rich: ▸～酒, 清～ **2**（指味道） pure: ▸～厚, ～美, ～正
B〈名〉［化学］ alcohol: 低/高～酒 wine with a low/high alcoholic content ▸～解, 胆固～, 甲～
【醇和】chúnhé〈形〉 pure and mild
【醇厚】chúnhòu〈形〉 **1**（指酒味） rich: ～的酒 full-bodied wine ‖ 这酒酒味儿～。 The wine tastes mellow. **2** = 淳厚 chúnhòu
【醇化】chúnhuà〈动〉 **1**（使更完美） refine **2**［化学］ alcoholize: ～物 alcoholate
【醇解】chúnjiě〈名〉［化学］ alcoholysis
【醇酒】chúnjiǔ〈名〉 full-bodied wine
【醇醪】chúnláo〈名〉〈书〉 strong wine
【醇酶】chúnméi〈名〉［生化］ alcoholase
【醇美】chúnměi〈形〉 pure and sweet: 嗓音～ have a pure and sweet voice
【醇酸】chúnsuān〈名〉［化学］ alcohol acid
【醇香】chúnxiāng〈形〉 aromatic
【醇正】chúnzhèng〈形〉 pure and rich
【醇中毒】chúnzhòngdú〈名〉 alcoholism

chǔn

蠢[1] chǔn〈动〉〈书〉 squirm: ▸～动

蠢[2] chǔn〈形〉 **1**（愚笨） stupid: ～头～脑 stupid-looking ‖ 你真是～透了! You are such an idiot! ▸～货, ～事, 愚～ **2**（笨拙） clumsy: 这家具的样子真～! The furniture looks really awkward! ▸～笨
【蠢笨】chǔnbèn〈形〉 clumsy: ～如牛 be as clumsy as an ox
【蠢材】chǔncái〈名〉 idiot
【蠢蠢】chǔnchǔn〈形〉〈书〉 **1**（指虫子爬动） wriggling **2**（动荡不安） restless
【蠢蠢欲动】chǔnchǔn-yùdòng〈成〉 be ready to make trouble: 敌人～, 准备进攻。 The enemy was busy preparing for an attack.
【蠢动】chǔndòng〈动〉 **1**（蠕动） wriggle **2**（行动） stir up trouble
【蠢话】chǔnhuà〈名〉 stupid remark: 别讲～。 Don't make stupid remarks.
【蠢货】chǔnhuò〈名〉〈贬〉 fool: 你这～。 You stupid thing.
【蠢驴】chǔnlǘ〈名〉〈粗〉 idiot
【蠢人】chǔnrén〈名〉 fool
【蠢事】chǔnshì〈名〉 folly: 干～ do something stupid
【蠢猪】chǔnzhū〈名〉〈粗〉 idiot

chuō

踔 chuō〈动〉〈书〉 **1**（跳跃） jump **2**（超越） go beyond
【踔厉】chuōlì〈形〉〈书〉 vigorous and high-spirited

戳 chuō
A〈动〉 **1**（捅） jab: 一～就破 break at the slightest touch ‖ 把眼睛～了可不是好玩儿的。 It is no joking matter to have your eye poked. ▸～穿 **2**〈口〉（刺伤） get injured: 打球时～了手腕 sprain one's wrist while playing a ball game ‖ 钢笔掉在地上, 把笔尖儿～了。 The pen dropped onto the ground and the nib was blunted. **3**〈方〉（竖起） erect: ～起一面大旗 hoist a huge banner ‖ 别像根木头一样～在那儿。 Don't stand there like a lump of wood.
B〈名〉〈口〉 stamp: 橡皮～ rubber stamp ‖ 盖过～的邮票 used stamp ▸～记, 手～, 邮～
【戳穿】chuōchuān〈动〉 **1**（捅透） pierce: 用刺刀～敌人的胸膛 pierce the enemy's chest with a bayonet ‖ 钉子把他的鞋底～了。 The nail punctured the sole of his shoe. **2**（揭穿） explode: ～谎言 expose a lie ‖ ～骗局 uncover a fraud ‖ ～阴谋 unmask a conspiracy
【戳穿西洋镜】chuōchuān-xīyángjìng〈惯〉 expose sb.'s tricks
【戳脊梁骨】chuō jǐlianggǔ〈惯〉 speak ill of sb. behind his back
【戳记】chuōjì〈名〉 seal: 在瓶盖上盖上～ place a seal over the cap of a bottle
【戳子】chuōzi〈名〉〈口〉 stamp: 在文件上盖～ affix a seal to a document

chuò

啜 chuò〈动〉〈书〉 **1**（喝） sip: ～酒 sip wine ▸～饮 **2**（抽泣） sob: ▸～泣 ▸Chuài
【啜泣】chuòqì〈动〉 sob: 暗自～ sob to oneself ‖ 她忍不住～起来。 She broke into sobs.
【啜饮】chuòyǐn〈动〉 sip: ～美酒 sip good wine

惙 chuò〈形〉〈书〉 **1**（忧愁） worried: ▸～～ **2**（疲乏） fatigued **3**（弱） feeble
【惙惙】chuòchuò〈形〉〈书〉 troubled: 忧心～ have a troubled heart

绰（綽）chuò〈形〉 **1**（宽绰） ample: ▸宽～, 阔～ **2**〈书〉（体态柔美） graceful: ▸～约 ▸chāo
【绰绰有余】chuòchuò-yǒuyú〈成〉 ample: 时间～ have all the time in the world
【绰号】chuòhào〈名〉 nickname: 他的～叫胖子。 He is nicknamed 'fatty'. ‖ 我不喜欢别人叫我的～。 I don't like to be called by my nickname.
【绰约】chuòyuē〈形〉〈书〉 [of a girl] elegant: 丰姿～ have a graceful bearing ‖ ～多姿 be charmingly delicate

辍（輟）chuò〈动〉〈书〉 stop halfway: 时作时～ in fits and starts ▸～笔, ～学, 中～
【辍笔】chuòbǐ〈动〉 stop in the middle of writing or painting: 画才画了一半, 他就～不干了。 He stopped when the painting was only half done.
【辍学】chuòxué〈动〉 discontinue one's studies: 因病～ drop out of school on account of illness
【辍学率】chuòxuélǜ〈名〉 dropout rate
【辍止】chuòzhǐ〈动〉 cease

龊（齪）chuò ▸龌龊 wòchuò

cī

刺 cī〈拟〉 [ripping/tearing/scratching sound]: 烟火～～地冒着火花。 The fireworks ripped alight. ‖ 汽车～地刹住了。 The car screeched to a halt. ▸cì
【刺啦】cīlā〈拟〉 [ripping/tearing/scratching sound]: ～一声划着火柴 strike a match with a scratching sound ‖ ～一声, 他撕下一块布。 He ripped off a piece of cloth.
【刺棱】cīlēng〈拟〉 [sound of a quick/swift

movement]: 老鼠～一下钻进洞里。 The mouse scampered into its hole.
【刺溜】cīliū〈拟〉[slipping/sliding sound]: 他～一下滑倒了。He slipped and fell.

呲 cī〈动〉〈口〉give (sb.) a talking-to: 挨了一顿～儿 get a good talking-to

差 cī ▸参差 cēncī
▸chā, chà, chāi

疵 cī〈名〉flaw: ▸吹毛求～, 瑕～
【疵布】cībù〈名〉defective cloth
【疵点】cīdiǎn〈名〉flaw: 布上的～ imperfections in the cloth
【疵品】cīpǐn〈名〉defective product
【疵瑕】cīxiá〈名〉flaw

粢 cī
▸zī
【粢饭】cīfàn〈名〉〈方〉steamed rice ball

跐 cī〈动〉slip
【跐溜】cīliū〈动〉slip: 他脚下一～, 滑倒了。He slipped and fell.

cí

词（詞） cí ▸p. 999〈名〉**1**（词语）word: 旧～新用 new uses of old terms ‖ 组～造句 put words together in sentences ▸～典, ～语, 褒义～ **2**（言辞）statement: 没～儿了 be speechless ▸～不达意, 台～, 义正～严 **3**（指文体）*ci* [a form of classical Chinese poetry]: ▸～牌, ～谱, 填～ **4**（歌词）lyrics **5**（歌剧的歌词）libretto: ▸唱～, 歌～
【词不达意】cíbùdáyì = 辞不达意 cíbùdáyì
【词典】cídiǎn〈名〉dictionary: 查～ look sth. up in the dictionary
【词典学】cídiǎnxué〈名〉lexicography
【词调】cídiào〈名〉tonal patterns and rhyme schemes of *ci* poetry
【词法】cífǎ〈名〉［语言］morphology
【词锋】cífēng〈名〉incisiveness of a piece of writing: 他～犀利。His writings are sharp and incisive.
【词干】cígàn〈名〉［语言］stem
【词根】cígēn〈名〉［语言］root: 动词的～ verb root
【词根语】cígēnyǔ〈名〉［语言］root language
【词话】cíhuà〈名〉**1**（指评论）notes and comments on *ci* poetry **2**（指说唱艺术）storytelling interspersed with songs and ballads
【词汇】cíhuì〈名〉vocabulary: 常用～ words in everyday use ‖ 基本～ basic vocabulary ‖ ～表 vocabulary
【词汇空缺】cíhuì kòngquē〈名〉［语言］lexical gap
【词汇量】cíhuìliàng〈名〉wordage: 丰富～ enrich one's vocabulary
【词汇学】cíhuìxué〈名〉lexicology
【词句】cíjù〈名〉words and phrases: 删掉多余的～ delete unnecessary words ‖ 斟酌～ measure one's words
【词库】cíkù〈名〉lexicon
【词类】cílèi〈名〉［语言］word class
【词牌】cípái〈名〉names of tunes to which *ci* poems are composed
【词频】cípín〈名〉word frequency
【词谱】cípǔ〈名〉collection of tunes of *ci* poems
【词曲】cíqǔ〈名〉**1**（词和曲）general term for *ci* and *qu* poetry **2**（歌词和歌曲）words and music of a song
【词人】círén〈名〉*ci* master
【词素】císù〈名〉［语言］morpheme
【词条】cítiáo〈名〉entry: 这部汉英词典收录约十万～。This Chinese-English dictionary contains about 100,000 entries.
【词头】cítóu = 前缀 qiánzhuì
【词尾】cíwěi = 后缀 hòuzhuì
【词形】cíxíng〈名〉［语言］morphology: ～变化 inflection
【词性】cíxìng〈名〉［语言］part of speech: ～标注 part-of-speech label
【词序】cíxù〈名〉［语言］word order
【词义】cíyì〈名〉［语言］lexical meaning: ～辨析 meaning discrimination
【词语】cíyǔ〈名〉words and expressions: ～解释 explain terms ‖ 外来～ loan words ‖ ～汇编 glossary
【词源】cíyuán〈名〉［语言］etymology: 追溯～ trace a word to its origin ‖ ～词典 etymological dictionary ‖ ～研究者 etymologist
【词韵】cíyùn〈名〉**1**（指韵）*ci* poem rhyming scheme **2**（指韵书）rhyming dictionary (of *ci* poems)
【词藻】cízǎo = 辞藻 cízǎo
【词缀】cízhuì〈名〉［语言］affix
【词组】cízǔ〈名〉［语言］phrase: 固定～ set phrase

茈 cí ▸凫茈 fúcí
▸zǐ

茨 cí〈书〉
A〈动〉thatch
B〈名〉［植物］puncture vine
【茨冈人】Cígāngrén〈名〉Gypsy
【茨菰】cígu = 慈姑 cígu

兹 cí ▸龟兹 Qiūcí
▸zī

祠 cí〈名〉ancestral hall: ▸～堂, 宗～
【祠堂】cítáng〈名〉ancestral temple

瓷 cí〈名〉porcelain: 细～ fine china ‖ 釉面～ glazed tile ▸～器, ～砖, 青～, 搪～
【瓷雕】cídiāo〈名〉［美术］porcelain carving
【瓷公鸡，一毛不拔】cígōngjī, yīmáobùbá〈歇后〉〈喻〉miser
【瓷瓶】cípíng〈名〉**1**（指瓶子）china vase **2** = 绝缘子 juéyuánzǐ
【瓷漆】cíqī = 磁漆 cíqī
【瓷器】cíqì〈名〉porcelain: 一套～ a set of china ‖ 家用～ household china

> **瓷器**
> Porcelain is believed to have originated in China, and has a history that can be traced back to the Shang Dynasty. There are three main types of porcelain: celadon, white, and coloured. Jingdezhen in Jiangxi Province is known as the capital of Chinese porcelain.

【瓷实】císhi〈形〉〈方〉solid: 他长得很～。He is solidly built. ‖ 这房子地基特别～。The house has exceptionally solid foundations.
【瓷胎】cítāi〈名〉unbaked porcelain
【瓷土】cítǔ〈名〉porcelain clay
【瓷牙】cíyá〈名〉porcelain tooth
【瓷窑】cíyáo〈名〉china kiln
【瓷釉】cíyòu〈名〉ceramic glaze
【瓷砖】cízhuān〈名〉glazed tile: 用～铺地 cover a floor with tiles

辞[1]（辭） cí〈名〉**1**（文辞）phraseology: 赞美之～ words of admiration ▸～不达意, ～令, ～藻, 修～ **2**（指古典文学体裁）*ci* [a type of classical Chinese literature]: 《楚～》 *Songs of Chu* ▸～赋 **3**（指古体诗）a form of classical Chinese poetry: 《木兰～》 *The Ballad of Mulan*

辞[2]（辭） cí〈动〉**1**（推托）shrink from: ▸～谢, 推～, 万死不～ **2**（辞职）resign: 她已～了工作。She's quit her job. ▸～呈, ～职 **3**（辞退）dismiss: 他因酗酒被～。He was fired because of his drinking. ▸～工 1, ～退 **4**（告别）part from: ▸～旧迎新, 告～
【辞别】cíbié〈动〉say goodbye: ～朋友/双亲 say goodbye to one's friends/parents
【辞不达意】cíbùdáyì〈惯〉the words fail to convey the meaning
【辞呈】cíchéng〈名〉resignation: 提交～ hand in one's resignation
【辞典】cídiǎn = 词典 cídiǎn
【辞赋】cífù〈名〉literary form like *fu*, descriptive prose interspersed with verse
【辞格】cígé〈名〉［语言］figure of speech
【辞工】cígōng〈动〉**1**（指老板）dismiss:

ℹ 词序

有时候汉英词序完全不同，如汉语说南北，英语说 north and south（北南）。下面的这些固定表达在翻成英语时顺序都是颠倒过来的：

文艺	art and literature	细长	long and thin
新郎和新娘	the bride and bridegroom	东北	north-east
前后	back and forth	西北	north-west
血肉	flesh and blood	新旧	old and new
衣食	food and clothing	贫富	rich and poor
饮食	food and drink	长短	short and long
软硬	hard and soft	中小型	small and medium-sized
此时此地	here and now	迟早	sooner or later
轻重	heavy and light	东南	south-east
冷热	hot and cold	西南	south-west
钢铁	iron and steel	田径	track and field
水陆	land and water		

老板辞了他的工。The boss fired him. 2（指雇员）resign one's post: ～跳槽 leave one's job and go to another
【辞活】cíhuó = 辞工 cígōng 2
【辞旧迎新】cíjiù-yíngxīn〈成〉ring out the old, ring in the new
【辞令】cílìng〈名〉language appropriate to the occasion: 善于～ be gifted with a silver tongue ‖ 外交～ diplomatic language
【辞聘】cípìn〈动〉1（指拒绝）turn down a job 2（指解除）remove from office
【辞却】cíquè〈动〉〈书〉1（辞掉）resign 2（推掉）decline
【辞让】círàng〈动〉decline politely: 他～了一番，最后还是答应出任公司顾问。He declined at first but finally agreed to serve as adviser for the company.
【辞色】císè〈名〉〈书〉utterance and facial expression: 假以～ look at sb. encouragingly
【辞世】císhì ▸p. 772〈动〉〈婉〉pass away: 她的双亲均已～。Both her parents are deceased.
【辞书】císhū〈名〉dictionary
【辞岁】císuì〈动〉see the old year out
【辞退】cítuì〈动〉1（解雇）fire: ～员工 lay off staff members ‖ 被～ get the sack 2（辞谢）decline with thanks: ～礼物 decline a gift
【辞谢】cíxiè〈动〉decline with thanks: ～邀请 decline sb.'s invitation
【辞行】cíxíng〈动〉bid farewell: 他匆匆向朋友～。He bade his friends a hurried farewell.
【辞藻】cízǎo〈名〉flowery language: 堆砌～ string together ornate phrases ‖ ～华丽 flowery rhetoric
【辞灶】cízào〈动〉〈旧〉see off the kitchen god to Heaven
【辞章】cízhāng〈名〉1（诗文）poetry and prose 2（写作技巧）art of writing
【辞职】cízhí〈动〉resign: 提出～ submit one's resignation ‖ 准予～ accept sb.'s resignation ‖ 因病～ resign for health reasons ‖ 引咎～ take the blame and resign ‖ 集体～ collective resignation
【辞职信】cízhíxìn〈名〉letter of resignation

慈 cí

A〈动〉〈书〉have affection for: 敬老～幼 respect the old and love the young ▸～幼养老
B〈形〉loving: 心～ be kind-hearted ▸～悲, ～母, 仁～
C〈名〉〈书〉mother: ▸～训, 家～
【慈蔼】cí'ǎi〈形〉kindly and amiable
【慈爱】cí'ài〈形〉loving: ～的母亲 loving mother ‖ ～的目光 fond glance
【慈悲】cíbēi〈形〉merciful: ～之心 charitable heart ‖ 发发～吧! For pity's sake!
【慈父】cífù〈名〉loving father
【慈姑】cígu〈名〉［植物］arrowhead
【慈航】cíháng〈名〉［佛教］journey of salvation
【慈和】cíhé〈形〉〈书〉kindly and amiable: 面容～ have a benign look
【慈眉善目】címéi-shànmù〈成〉have a kindly look
【慈母】címǔ〈名〉loving mother: ～之心 mother's loving kindness
【慈善】císhàn〈形〉benevolent: 参与～活动 participate in philanthropic activities ‖ ～捐赠 charitable donations ‖ ～机构 charitable institution
【慈善家】císhànjiā〈名〉philanthropist
【慈善事业】císhàn shìyè〈名〉charities: 献身～ be devoted to charity
【慈善箱】císhànxiāng〈名〉poor box [esp in church]
【慈善学校】císhàn xuéxiào〈名〉charity school
【慈善医院】císhàn yīyuàn〈名〉charity hospital
【慈祥】cíxiáng〈形〉kindly: ～的面容 benign face
【慈心】cíxīn〈名〉kind heart
【慈训】cíxùn〈名〉〈书〉maternal teachings
【慈幼养老】cíyòu-yǎnglǎo〈成〉be kind to the young and care for the old

磁 cí

〈名〉1［物理］magnetism: 消～ demagnetize ▸～场, ～石, 地～ 2〈旧〉= 瓷 cí
【磁棒】cíbàng〈名〉［物理］magnetic bar
【磁棒存储器】cíbàng cúnchǔqì〈名〉［计算机］magnetic rod storage
【磁暴】cíbào〈名〉［天文］magnetic storm
【磁北】cíběi〈名〉［物理］magnetic north
【磁场】cíchǎng〈名〉［物理］magnetic field: 地球～ earth's magnetic field ‖ 磁铁周围有～。A magnet has a field around it.
【磁场强度】cíchǎng qiángdù〈名〉magnetic field intensity
【磁带】cídài〈名〉tape: 听/放～ listen to/play a tape ‖ 盒式～ cassette tape ‖ 空白～ blank tape ‖ ～录像机 video recorder ‖ ～录音机 tape recorder
【磁带盒】cídàihé〈名〉cassette
【磁导】cídǎo〈名〉［物理］permeance
【磁电效应】cídiàn xiàoyìng〈名〉magneto-electric effect
【磁电学】cídiànxué〈名〉［物理］magnetoelectricity
【磁粉】cífěn〈名〉［电气］magnetic powder
【磁浮】cífú〈名〉magnetic suspension: ～列车 maglev train
【磁感应】cígǎnyìng〈名〉［物理］magnetic induction: ～传感器 magnetic induction sensor
【磁钢】cígāng〈名〉［冶金］magnetic steel
【磁鼓】cígǔ〈名〉［计算机］magnetic drum
【磁光】cíguāng〈形〉［物理］magneto-optic
【磁化】cíhuà〈动〉magnetize: ～杯 magnetizing cup ‖ ～水 magnetized water
【磁极】cíjí〈名〉［物理］magnetic pole
【磁卡】cíkǎ〈名〉magnetic card: ～阅读机 magnetic card reader
【磁卡电话】cíkǎ diànhuà〈名〉card telephone
【磁控】cíkòng〈名〉［电子］magnetic control
【磁力】cílì〈名〉［物理］magnetic force
【磁力线】cílìxiàn〈名〉［物理］magnetic lines of force
【磁疗】cíliáo〈名〉magnetic therapy
【磁罗盘】cíluópán〈名〉［航海］magnetic compass
【磁南】cínán〈名〉［物理］magnetic south
【磁能】cínéng〈名〉［电气］magnetic energy
【磁盘】cípán〈名〉［计算机］disk: 复制～ make a copy of a disk ‖ ～备份 back-up disk
【磁盘操作系统】cípán cāozuò xìtǒng〈名〉disk operating system (DOS)
【磁盘存储器】cípán cúnchǔqì〈名〉magnetic disk memory
【磁盘格式化】cípán géshìhuà〈名〉disk formatting
【磁盘驱动器】cípán qūdòngqì〈名〉［计算机］disk drive
【磁偏角】cípiānjiǎo〈名〉［物理］magnetic declination
【磁漆】cíqī〈名〉enamel
【磁强】cíqiáng〈名〉magnetic strength
【磁石】císhí〈名〉1 = 磁铁 cítiě 2（指矿石）magnetite: ～检波器 magneto detector
【磁体】cítǐ〈名〉［物理］magnet
【磁条】cítiáo〈名〉magnetic strip
【磁铁】cítiě〈名〉magnet: 马蹄形～ horseshoe magnet ‖ ～矿 magnetite
【磁通量】cítōngliàng〈名〉［物理］magnetic flux
【磁头】cítóu〈名〉［物理］magnetic head: ～清洁带 head cleaner for video-cassette recorders
【磁效应】cíxiàoyìng〈名〉magnetic effect
【磁心】cíxīn〈名〉［计算机］magnetic core
【磁心存储器】cíxīn cúnchǔqì〈名〉［计算机］magnetic core memory
【磁性】cíxìng〈名〉［物理］magnetism: ～金属 magnetic metal ‖ 抗～ diamagnetism ‖ ～水雷 magnetic mine
【磁悬浮】cíxuánfú = 磁浮 cífú
【磁学】cíxué〈名〉［物理］magnetics
【磁针】cízhēn〈名〉［物理］magnetic needle: ～方位 magnetic bearings ‖ ～罗盘 magnetic compass

雌 cí

〈形〉female: ～兔 female rabbit ▸～花, ～激素, ～性
【雌伏】cífú〈动〉〈书〉1（屈居下位）submit to others' control 2（退步藏身）lie low: ～待机 hide and bide one's time
【雌狐】cíhú〈名〉vixen
【雌虎】cíhǔ〈名〉tigress
【雌花】cíhuā〈名〉［植物］female flower
【雌黄】cíhuáng A〈名〉［矿业］orpiment B〈动〉〈贬〉tamper with: 信口～ make irresponsible remarks
【雌激素】cíjīsù〈名〉［生化］oestrogen
【雌老虎】cílǎohǔ〈名〉1〈本〉tigress 2〈喻〉bad-tempered woman, shrew
【雌鹿】cílù〈名〉doe
【雌蕊】círuǐ〈名〉［植物］pistil: 退化～ pistillode
【雌狮】císhī〈名〉lioness
【雌威】cíwēi〈名〉tantrum: 发～ throw a tantrum
【雌性】cíxìng〈名〉female sex: ～动物 female animals ‖ ～激素 oestrogen
【雌雄】cí-xióng〈名〉1（指性别）male and female: ～莫辨 be unable to distinguish the male from the female ▸～同体, ～异体 2（胜负）victory and defeat: ▸决一～
【雌雄同体】cí-xióng tóngtǐ〈名〉［生物］hermaphrodite: ～性 hermaphroditism
【雌雄同株】cí-xióng tóngzhū〈名〉［植物］monoecism: ～植物 monoecious plants
【雌雄异体】cí-xióng yìtǐ〈名〉［动物］dioecism
【雌雄异株】cí-xióng yìzhū〈名〉［植物］dioecism
【雌蚁】cíyǐ〈名〉［昆虫］female ant

鹚（鷀、鶿）cí ▸鸬鹚 lúcí

糍（餈）cí

【糍粑】cíbā〈名〉glutinous rice cake

cǐ

此 cǐ〈代〉 1（这个） this: ～人 this person ►～地, ～起彼伏, 厚～薄彼 2（现在） now;（这里） here: 由～往西 go west from here ‖ 到～为止。 That's the end of it. ►～后, 从～, 就～ 3（这样） such: ►长～以往

【此岸】cǐ'àn〈名〉［佛教］ temporality

【此辈】cǐbèi〈名〉 people of this type

【此处】cǐchù〈名〉 this place

【此次】cǐcì〈名〉〈书〉 this time: ～访问 this visit

【此道】cǐdào〈名〉 things like this: 精于～ be good at such things

【此等】cǐděng〈名〉 this kind

【此地】cǐdì〈名〉 this place

【此地无银三百两】cǐdì wú yín sānbǎi liǎng〈成〉〈喻〉 clumsy denial resulting in self-exposure

【此番】cǐfān〈名〉〈书〉 this time

【此后】cǐhòu〈名〉 from now on: 他于1984年去了北京，～一直住在那里。 He went to Beijing in 1984 and has lived there ever since. ‖ ～一切都十分顺利。 Afterwards everything went really well.

【此呼彼应】cǐhū-bǐyìng〈成〉 respond to each other

【此间】cǐjiān〈名〉〈书〉 this place: ～官方人士 official sources here ‖ ～物产丰富。 This place is rich in natural resources.

【此举】cǐjǔ〈名〉〈书〉 this move: ～定能成功。 This move will surely succeed.

【此刻】cǐkè〈名〉 this moment: ～他该到了。 He should have arrived by now.

【此路不通】cǐlù-bùtōng〈成〉 1〈本〉 this road is blocked 2〈喻〉 there is no way out

【此起彼伏】cǐqǐ-bǐfú〈成〉 rise one after another: 欢呼声～。 Recurrent cheers broke out.

【此前】cǐqián〈名〉 before this: ～我在休假。 Before that I was on holiday.

【此生】cǐshēng〈名〉 this life

【此时】cǐshí〈名〉 this moment: ～此刻 at this very moment

【此外】cǐwài〈连〉 besides: ～，我想求你给我办件事。 Besides, I want to ask a favour of you.

【此行】cǐxíng〈名〉〈书〉 this journey: 不虚～ worthwhile journey

【此一时，彼一时】cǐ yīshí, bǐ yīshí〈成〉 things are now different from what they were

【此致敬礼】cǐzhì jìnglǐ〈套〉 with best regards

cì

次 cì

A〈动〉〈书〉 come next in order: ►～之

B〈形〉 1（第二） next: ～年 next year ‖ ～子 second son ►～日 2（差等） second-rate: ～棉 poor quality cotton ‖ 质量～ inferior in quality ►～等, ～品

C〈名〉 1（顺序） order: 顺～排列 arrange in order ‖ 依～入座 take seats one by one ►～序, 名～, 座～ 2〈书〉（旅途中停留处） rest stop: ►旅～, 途～ 3〈书〉（中间） middle: ►胸～

D〈量〉 time: 去过一/两～ have been to a place once/twice ‖ 第一/二～ the first/second time ‖ 最后一～ the last time ►首～

【次大陆】cìdàlù〈名〉［地理］ subcontinent

【次贷危机】cìdài wēijī〈名〉subprime crisis

【次等】cìděng〈形〉 second-grade

【次第】cìdì A〈名〉 order B〈副〉 in turn: ～就座 take seats one after another ‖ ～入场 enter in turn

【次货】cìhuò〈名〉 shoddy goods

【次级】cìjí〈形〉 secondary: ～市场 secondary market

【次级抵押】cìjí dǐyā〈名〉［经济］ subprime mortgage

【次级债】cìjízhài〈名〉［金融］ subprime mortgage: 美国～危机 the U.S. subprime crisis

【次品】cìpǐn〈名〉 shoddy goods

【次轻量级】cìqīngliàngjí〈名〉［体育］ featherweight

【次区域】cìqūyù〈名〉 sub-region

【次日】cìrì〈名〉 next day

【次生】cìshēng〈形〉 secondary

【次生林】cìshēnglín〈名〉［林业］ second growth: ～改造 secondary forest conversion

【次生灾害】cìshēng zāihài〈名〉 secondary disaster

【次声】cìshēng〈名〉［物理］ infrasonic sound

【次声波】cìshēngbō〈名〉 infrasonic wave

【次声武器】cìshēng wǔqì〈名〉 infrasonic weapon

【次数】cìshù〈名〉 frequency: 减少/增加～ decrease/increase the number of times ‖ ～不多 not very often ‖ 他脉搏跳动～正常。 His pulse was normal.

【次席】cìxí〈名〉 seat next to the guest of honour

【次序】cìxù〈名〉 sequence: ～颠倒 be in reverse order ‖ 按年代先后～ in chronological order

【次要】cìyào〈形〉 minor: ～人物 minor character ‖ ～原因 subsidiary reason ‖ 这是我们的主要目的，其他都是～的。 This is our main aim; all the others are of secondary importance.

【次要矛盾】cìyào máodùn〈名〉 secondary contradiction: 区别主要矛盾与～ distinguish between the principal and secondary contradictions

【次优】cìyōu〈形〉 second best: ～方案 second best solution

【次于】cìyú〈动〉 be inferior to: 印度人口仅～中国。 India is second only to China in population.

【次韵】cìyùn〈动〉use the rhythm sequence of a poem

【次长】cìzhǎng〈名〉 deputy-minister

【次之】cìzhī〈动〉 come second: 该省的自然资源以煤最多，石油～。 Among the natural resources of the province, coal occupies first place and oil comes second.

【次重量级】cìzhòngliàngjí〈名〉［体育］ middle heavyweight

【次最轻量级】cìzuìqīngliàngjí〈名〉［体育］ flyweight

伺 cì

►sì

【伺候】cìhou〈动〉 serve: ～病人 wait on the sick ‖ 难～ be hard to please

刺 cì

A〈动〉 1（扎入） stab: ～入心脏 stab sth. into sb.'s heart ‖ 用匕首/刺刀～人 stab sb. with a dagger/bayonet ►～刀, ～骨, ～绣 2（刺杀） assassinate: 被～ be assassinated ►～客, 行～, 遇～ 3（讽刺） mock: ►讽～, 讥～ 4（侦察） pry into: ►～探 5（刺激） stimulate: ►～鼻, ～耳, ～激

B〈名〉 1（针状物） thorn: 被～扎疼 be pricked by thorns ‖ 手指上扎了一根～ get one's finger pricked by a thorn ‖ 他话里带～。 There is a sting in his words. ►～槐, ～猬, 马～ 2（凸起物） sharp small raised spot on the skin or surface of sth.: ►粉～, 毛～ 3〈书〉（名片） visiting card: ►名～

►cī

【刺柏】cìbǎi = 桧 guì

【刺鼻】cìbí〈形〉 pungent: ～的气味 pungent odour

【刺刺不休】cìcì-bùxiū〈成〉 chatter on and on

【刺丛】cìcóng〈名〉 prickly bushes

【刺刀】cìdāo〈名〉 bayonet: 上～! Fix bayonets!

【刺耳】cì'ěr〈形〉 ear-piercing: ～的话 caustic remarks ‖ ～的汽笛声 penetrating whistle

【刺骨】cìgǔ〈形〉 piercing: 寒风～。 The icy wind cuts one to the bone.

【刺槐】cìhuái〈名〉［植物］ locust tree

【刺激】cìjī〈动〉 1（激发） stimulate: ～神经 stimulate a nerve ‖ ～食欲 whet one's appetite ‖ ～消费和经济增长 stimulate consumption and economic growth ‖ 受到～ receive a stimulus ‖ 经济～ economic incentive 2（强烈影响） provoke: 别～他了。 Don't provoke him. ‖ 这一不幸的消息对她～很大。 She was very upset by the sad news.

【刺激反应】cìjī fǎnyìng〈名〉 stimulus-response

【刺激物】cìjīwù〈名〉 excitant

【刺激性】cìjīxìng〈形〉 irritant: ～毒气 irritant gas

【刺客】cìkè〈名〉 assassin

【刺毛】cìmáo〈名〉［生物］ seta

【刺目】cìmù = 刺眼 cìyǎn

【刺挠】cìnao〈形〉〈方〉 itching

【刺配】cìpèi〈动〉〈古〉 tattoo the face of a criminal and send him into exile: ～他乡 tattoo sb.'s face and send him into exile

【刺儿话】cìrhuà〈名〉〈口〉 biting remarks

【刺儿头】cìrtóu〈名〉〈方〉 difficult person

【刺杀】cìshā〈动〉 1（暗杀） assassinate: 密谋～ plot sb.'s assassination ‖ 执行～任务 carry out an assassination 2［军事］ charge at sb. with bayonets: 练～ practise bayonet fighting ‖ ～训练 bayonet drill

【刺参】cìshēn〈名〉［动物］ species of sea cucumber

【刺史】cìshǐ〈名〉〈古〉 feudal prefectural governor

【刺探】cìtàn〈动〉 make secret enquiries: ～军情 spy out military secrets ‖ ～隐私 pry into sb.'s privacy

【刺痛】cìtòng〈动〉 prick: 一阵～ have a tingle ‖ 深深～某人的心 hurt sb. deeply

【刺猬】cìwei〈名〉 hedgehog

【刺五加】cìwǔjiā〈名〉［中药］ Acanthopanax

【刺绣】cìxiù A〈动〉 embroider: 用金线/银线～ embroider in gold/silver thread B〈名〉 embroidery: 擅长～ be good at needlework ‖ ～技艺 skill in embroidery

【刺眼】cìyǎn〈形〉 1（指光） dazzling: 亮得～ be dazzlingly bright ‖ ～的阳光 glaring sunlight 2（指形象） harsh on the eye: 打扮得～ be loudly dressed

【刺痒】cìyang〈形〉 itchy: 我浑身～。 I itched all over.

> **刺绣**
>
> A traditional Chinese handicraft using silk thread to stitch designs on fabric. The word 刺绣 is also used for the embroidered article itself. Chinese embroidery has a history dating back thousands of years. The four major styles are Suzhou, Hunan, Sichuan and Guangdong embroidery. There are two types of embroidery: that used for everyday articles such as clothes and domestic items, and that used for decoration such as on scrolls and screens.

C

【刺针】cìzhēn〈名〉［动物］ aculeus
【刺字】cìzì〈动〉〈古〉 tattoo characters [on the face of a convict]

赐（賜）cì

A〈动〉**1**（给予） grant: ～衔 confer a title ▸～予, 恩～, 赏～ **2**〈敬〉（指称行为） grant: ▸～复, ～教
B〈名〉〈敬〉 favour: 厚～受之有愧。 I feel unworthy of the precious gift you have bestowed on me.
【赐福】cìfú **A**〈动〉 bless: 上帝～于你们。 God bless you. **B**〈名〉 blessing: 这是上天的～。 This is a blessing from Heaven.
【赐复】cìfù〈动〉〈套〉 be kind enough to grant me a reply: 请早日～。 Please favour me with an early reply.
【赐教】cìjiào〈动〉〈套〉 condescend to teach: 请不吝～。 Please enlighten me with your advice.
【赐予】cìyǔ〈动〉 grant : ～头衔 confer a title on sb. ‖ 上天～他一副好体格。 God favoured him with a sound constitution.

cōng

匆（悤）cōng〈形〉 hasty: ▸～促, ～忙

【匆匆】cōngcōng〈形〉 hurried: ～离去 hurry off ‖ 来去～ come and go in haste ‖ 行色～ be in a hurry to set out ‖ ～过客 hurrying passers-by
【匆匆忙忙】cōngcōng-mángmáng〈成〉 hurried: ～地工作 rush one's work
【匆卒】cōngcù = 匆猝 cōngcù
【匆促】cōngcù〈形〉 hurried: ～起程 set out hastily ‖ 时间～ be pressed for time
【匆猝】cōngcù〈形〉 hasty
【匆忙】cōngmáng〈形〉 hurried: ～成交 snap up a bargain ‖ ～回答 hastily reply ‖ ～决定 make a hasty decision ‖ ～下结论 rush to a conclusion ‖ 不必这么～。 There is no need to hurry.

苁（蓯）cōng

【苁蓉】cōngróng〈名〉［植物］ desert cistanche

囱 cōng ▸烟囱 yāncōng

玜（瑽）cōng

【玜琮】cōngróng〈拟〉〈书〉 (of jade pendants) jingle

枞（樅）cōng = 冷杉 lěngshān

【枞树】cōngshù〈名〉［植物］ fir

葱（蔥）cōng

A〈形〉 pale green: ▸～绿, ～郁
B〈名〉［植物］ onion: ▸～花, 洋～
【葱白】cōngbái〈形〉 bluish white
【葱白儿】cōngbáir〈名〉 spring onion bulb
【葱葱】cōngcōng〈形〉 luxuriantly green: 松柏～ lush pines and cypresses
【葱翠】cōngcuì〈形〉 luxuriantly green: ～的草地 lush green meadows ‖ ～的竹林 green bamboo grove
【葱花】cōnghuā〈名〉 spring onion: ～饼 spring onion pancake
【葱黄】cōnghuáng〈形〉 greenish yellow
【葱茏】cōnglóng〈形〉 luxuriantly green: 草木～ lush vegetation
【葱绿】cōnglǜ〈形〉 fresh and green: ～的草地 lush meadows ‖ 麦苗一片～。 The wheat shoots are a lush green.
【葱茂】cōngmào〈形〉 verdant and luxuriant
【葱头】cōngtóu〈名〉 onion
【葱郁】cōngyù〈形〉 luxuriantly green: ～的牧场 lush pasture

聪（聰）cōng

A〈名〉〈书〉 hearing: 两耳失～ become deaf in both ears
B〈形〉 **1**（听觉敏锐） having a keen sense of hearing: ▸耳～目明 **2**（聪明） clever: ▸～慧, ～明
【聪慧】cōnghuì〈形〉 intelligent
【聪敏】cōngmǐn〈形〉 intelligent and quick-witted: ～好学 be intelligent and enjoy studying
【聪明】cōngming〈形〉 clever: ～绝顶 be extremely intelligent ‖ ～伶俐 be clever and quick-witted ‖ ～能干 be bright and capable ‖ 充分发挥～才智 display to the full one's talent and wisdom
【聪明反被聪明误】cōngming fǎn bèi cōngming wù〈俗〉 clever people may fall victim to their own cleverness
【聪明一世，糊涂一时】cōngming yīshì, hútu yīshí〈俗〉 a lifetime of cleverness can be interrupted by moments of stupidity
【聪悟】cōngwù〈形〉〈书〉 clever
【聪颖】cōngyǐng〈形〉〈书〉 intelligent: ～过人 be exceptionally bright

cóng

从（從）cóng

A〈动〉 **1**（跟从） follow: 师～ be an apprentice to sb. ▸～师, ～众, 盲～ **2**（听从） listen to: ▸～命, 顺～, 力不～心 **3**（依照） adopt a certain attitude: ～宽/严处理 be lenient/heavy-handed ‖ ～轻/重处罚 punish leniently/severely ▸～长计议, ～简, ～速 **4**（参加） join: ▸～军, ～事, 投笔～戎
B〈名〉 follower: ▸仆～, 侍～, 随～
C〈形〉 **1**（次要） secondary: 区别主～ distinguish the principal from the subordinate ▸～犯, ～句 **2**（同宗） [relationship between cousins, etc.] of the same paternal grandfather or great-grandfather: ～父 (paternal) uncle
D〈介〉 **1**（自） from: ～北京出发 set off from Beijing ‖ ～第一天起 from the first day ‖ ～古到今 from ancient times to the present ‖ ～零开始 start from scratch ‖ ～现在起 from now on ‖ ～心坎里 from the bottom of one's heart ‖ ～这儿往北/东 go north/east from here ▸～始至终 **2**（通过） through: ～后门进来 come in through the back door ‖ ～门前经过 pass the gate ‖ 小偷是～窗户进来的。 The thief came in through the window. **3**（根据） from: ～本质上讲 by nature ‖ ～长远看 in the long run ‖ ～实际出发 be realistic
E〈副〉 ever: ～没听说过 have never heard of ▸～未
【从不】cóngbù ▸**p. 221**〈副〉 never: ～叫苦 never complain of hardship
【从长计议】cóngcháng-jìyì〈成〉 take one's time to reach a decision: 这事应～，不宜操之过急。 We must take our time with this. It's no good being overhasty.
【从此】cóngcǐ〈副〉 henceforth: ～以后 from then on
【从动】cóngdòng〈形〉［机械］ driven
【从动齿轮】cóngdòng chǐlún〈名〉［机械］ driven gear
【从动轮】cóngdònglún〈名〉［机械］ driven wheel
【从而】cóng'ér〈连〉 thus: 罢工使全市交通瘫痪，～影响了人们的正常生活。 The strike paralyzed the traffic in the city, thereby adversely affecting the lives of the people.
【从犯】cóngfàn〈名〉［法律］ accessory: 他被指控为作案～。 He was accused as an accessory to the crime.
【从缓】cónghuǎn〈动〉 postpone: ～处理 put off dealing with sth.
【从简】cóngjiǎn〈动〉 be simple: 婚礼/丧事～ have a simple wedding/funeral ‖ 手续～ simplify formalities
【从谏如流】cóngjiàn-rúliú〈成〉 follow good advice readily
【从教】cóngjiào〈动〉 go into teaching: 他～三十年，桃李满天下。 With thirty years of teaching under his belt, he had scores of former pupils all over the world.
【从今往后】cóngjīn-wǎnghòu〈成〉 from now on: ～，你就要靠自己了。 From now on, you have to look after yourself.
【从井救人】cóngjǐng-jiùrén〈成〉 compromise one's own interests without doing others any good
【从句】cóngjù〈名〉 subordinate clause: 表语/宾语/定语～ predicative/objective/attributive clause
【从军】cóngjūn〈动〉 join the army: 战争爆发，他志愿～。 When war broke out, he volunteered for service in the army.
【从宽】cóngkuān〈动〉 treat with leniency: ～处理 treat leniently
【从来】cónglái〈副〉 always: ～没去过上海 have never been to Shanghai ‖ 她的话我～不信。 I never believe what she says.
【从良】cóngliáng〈动〉 cease to be a prostitute by getting married: ～成家 reform and get married
【从略】cónglüè〈动〉 be omitted: 此处引文～。 The quotation is omitted here.
【从命】cóngmìng〈动〉 obey an order: 欣然～ gladly comply with sb.'s wish ▸恭敬不如～, 恕难～
【从前】cóngqián〈名〉 the past: ～的同事/校友 former colleague/schoolmate ‖ 我～看过那部电影。 I have seen the film before.
【从轻】cóngqīng〈动〉 inflict a relatively light punishment: ～发落 deal with an offender leniently
【从戎】cóngróng〈动〉〈书〉 enlist: ▸投笔～
【从容】cóngróng〈形〉 **1**（镇静） calm: 举止～ carry oneself with ease ‖ ～自在 be calm and at ease ▸～不迫 **2**（充足） abundant: 时间～ there is plenty of time ‖ 手头不～ be strapped for cash
【从容不迫】cóngróng-bùpò〈成〉 leisurely
【从容就义】cóngróng-jiùyì〈成〉 meet one's death like a hero
【从容自若】cóngróng-zìruò〈成〉 be calm

and composed

【从善如流】cóngshàn-rúliú〈成〉follow good advice readily

【从商】cóngshāng〈动〉do business: 弃政～ forsake politics for business

【从师】cóngshī〈动〉learn from a master: ～学艺 follow a master and learn his craft

【从实】cóngshí〈副〉in the light of the fact: ～交代 make a clean breast of things

【从始至终】cóngshǐ-zhìzhōng〈成〉from start to finish

【从事】cóngshì〈动〉**1** ▸p. 966（参与）undertake: ～法律工作 follow a legal career ‖ ～文学创作 be engaged in literary work **2**（处置）deal with: 草率～ act rashly ‖ 军法～ handle according to military law

【从属】cóngshǔ〈动〉subordinate: ～单位 subsidiary unit ‖ ～关系 subordinate relationship

【从俗】cóngsú〈动〉follow the general custom

【从速】cóngsù〈动〉do sth. as quickly as possible: ～办理 deal with the matter as soon as possible ‖ 欲购～。Buy now, while stocks last.

【从天而降】cóngtiān'érjiàng〈成〉appear from nowhere: 厄运/灾祸～ misfortune/disaster comes out of nowhere

【从头】cóngtóu〈副〉**1**（从最初）from the beginning: ～做起 start from the very beginning ▸～到尾 **2**（重新）afresh: ～再来 begin anew ‖ 这项工作还得～做。The job will have to be done all over again.

【从头到脚】cóngtóu-dàojiǎo〈成〉from head to foot: ～打量一番 look sb. up and down

【从头到尾】cóngtóu-dàowěi〈成〉from beginning to end: 这本小说～都很有趣。The novel was interesting from start to finish.

【从未】cóngwèi〈副〉never: ～听说 have never heard about ‖ ～有过 be unprecedented

【从小】cóngxiǎo〈副〉since childhood: 他们～就是好朋友。They have been good friends since childhood. ‖ 我～就热爱音乐。I have loved music ever since I was a child.

【从心所欲】cóngxīnsuǒyù〈成〉do as one pleases

【从新】cóngxīn〈副〉again: ～安排 rearrange ‖ ～做人 turn over a new leaf ‖ 让我们～开始吧。Let's start all over again.

【从刑】cóngxíng〈名〉［法律］accessory punishment

【从严】cóngyán〈动〉deal with strictly: ～打击走私活动 crack down hard on smuggling ‖ ～治军 be strict with the army

【从业】cóngyè〈动〉obtain employment: ～人员 the employed

【从一而终】cóngyī'érzhōng〈成〉be loyal to one's husband

【从艺】cóngyì〈动〉take up the stage as one's career

【从影】cóngyǐng〈动〉work in films

【从优】cóngyōu〈动〉give as generously as possible: 待遇～ give preferential treatment ‖ 有相关工作经验者～录用。Candidates with relevant working experience will be given preferential treatment.

【从者】cóngzhě〈名〉follower

【从者如云】cóngzhě-rúyún〈成〉have a huge following

【从征】cóngzhēng〈动〉〈书〉go on a military expedition

【从政】cóngzhèng ▸p. 966〈动〉enter politics: 弃文～ forsake letters for politics

【从中】cóngzhōng〈副〉from among: ～牟利 profit from ‖ ～受益 benefit from ‖ ～斡旋 mediate between ‖ ～吸取教训 draw a lesson from ‖ ～作梗 block obstacles in the way

【从众】cóngzhòng〈动〉follow the crowd: ～心理 group psychology

【从重】cóngzhòng〈动〉deal with severely: ～处罚 punish heavily

丛（叢）cóng

A〈动〉grow together: ▸～集, ～林, ～生 **B**〈名〉**1**（指草木）thicket: ▸草～, 灌木～, 树～ **2**（指人或物）collection: 刀～ collection of bayonets ▸论～

【丛脞】cóngcuǒ〈形〉〈书〉trifling: 杂事～ have trivial bits and pieces

【丛集】cóngjí **A**〈动〉crowd together: 债务～ with debts piling up **B**〈名〉collected writings: 研究生论文～ collection of essays by graduate students

【丛刊】cóngkān〈名〉collection

【丛刻】cóngkè〈名〉block-printed book series

【丛林】cónglín〈名〉**1**（指树林）forest: 进入～ go into the forest ‖ 热带～ tropical forests **2**［宗教］temple

【丛林法则】cónglín fǎzé〈名〉jungle law

【丛林战】cónglínzhàn〈名〉［军事］jungle warfare

【丛莽】cóngmǎng〈名〉luxuriant grass: 山林～ wooded hills with luxuriant grass

【丛密】cóngmì〈形〉dense: 野草～ thick weeds

【丛山】cóngshān〈名〉ranges of mountains

【丛生】cóngshēng〈动〉**1**（指植物）grow in clumps: 荆棘～ thorns grow in clumps ‖ 杂草～ be overgrown with weeds **2**（指疾病等）break out in profusion: 百病～ all kinds of diseases and ailments breaking out

【丛书】cóngshū〈名〉series

【丛谈】cóngtán〈名〉collected writings

【丛杂】cóngzá〈形〉〈书〉miscellaneous: 事务～, 难以脱身 be tied down to numerous different things

【丛葬】cóngzàng〈动〉bury a large number of corpses in one common grave

【丛冢】cóngzhǒng〈名〉〈书〉mass of graves

淙 cóng

【淙淙】cóngcóng〈拟〉gurgle: ～流水声 gurgling sound of a brook ‖ ～泉水 murmuring spring

琮 cóng

〈名〉rectangular-sided jade piece with a round hole in the centre

【琮琤】cóngchēng〈拟〉**1**（指玉佩）jingle: 她的耳环随着头部的摆动～作响。Her earrings jingled with each movement of her head. **2**（指溪水）gurgle: 溪水～。The brook gurgles along.

còu

凑（湊）còu

〈动〉**1**（聚合）gather together: ～人数 assemble enough people ‖ ～在一起 clump together ‖ 临时～成的队伍 scratch team ▸～份子, ～钱, ～数 **2**（靠近）move close: ～到耳边低语 come to whisper in one's ear ▸～近, ～拢 **3**（遇着）happen by chance: 正～上个晴天。It happened to be a sunny day. ▸～巧, ～热闹

【凑份子】còu fènzi〈动〉**1**（凑钱）club together: ～买礼物 club together to buy (sb.) a present **2**〈方〉（添乱）add to the trouble: 别在这里～了。Don't add to our trouble.

【凑合】còuhe〈动〉**1**（聚在一起）assemble: 这里～了一大堆人。A crowd of people assembled here. **2**（拼凑）knock together: 把从报纸上搜集来的事实～成一个故事 make up a story by piecing together facts gathered from the papers **3**（将就）make do: ～过日子 keep one's head above water ‖ 停电时就用蜡烛～一下 make do with candles when there is a power failure ‖ 我这件棉袄～着还能穿一冬。I can make this cotton-padded jacket do for another winter. **4**（还可以）be passable: 她的日语还～。Her Japanese is not bad.

【凑集】còují〈动〉gather together: ～一笔钱 scrape some money together ‖ ～一大群人 assemble a large crowd of people

【凑近】còujìn〈动〉approach: 把耳朵～仪器 press one's ear to the instrument ‖ ～点儿。Come a bit closer.

【凑拢】còulǒng〈动〉〈方〉move closer: ～点, 我告诉你一个秘密。Come closer. I will tell you a secret.

【凑钱】còuqián〈动〉club together: ～买辆汽车 club together to buy a car

【凑巧】còuqiǎo〈副〉as chance would have it: 她来时, 我～不在家。I happened to be out when she came. ‖ 真不～, 她出去了。Unfortunately, she's out.

【凑趣儿】còuqùr〈动〉**1**（迎合）take part in order to please others **2**（逗笑取乐）tease: 别拿我～。Don't make fun of me.

【凑热闹】còu rènao〈惯〉**1**（指一起热闹）join in the fun: 我来唱支歌, 凑凑热闹。Let me sing a song to add to the fun. **2**（添乱）add to the trouble: 我已经够烦了, 别再～了。I'm annoyed enough as it is; don't give me any more trouble.

【凑手】còushǒu〈形〉handy: 钱不～, 下次再买吧。I don't have much money on me; let's buy it next time. ‖ 这把钳子很～。The pliers are very handy.

【凑数】còushù〈动〉**1**（凑足数额）make up the numbers: 我们还需要几个才能凑够这个数。We still need some more to make up the numbers. **2**（充数）serve as a stopgap: 我在这球队里只是凑凑数而已。I am only in the team as a sort of filler.

【凑整儿】còuzhěngr〈动〉make up a round number: 我这里有97元, 你再给我3元, 凑个整儿好吗? I have ninety-seven *yuan*. Will you give me three more to make up a round number?

【凑足】còuzú〈动〉make up a deficiency: ～人数 gather together enough people

辏（輳）còu

〈动〉〈书〉converge: ▸辐～

cū

粗 cū

A〈形〉**1**（粗糙）coarse: 摸上去很～ be rough to the touch ‖ ～制木器 crude carpentry ▸～布, ～茶淡饭 **2**（不仔细）careless: ▸～心 **3**（颗粒大）coarse: ～粉 coarse powder ▸～沙, ～盐 **4**（直径大）wide: 腰～ have a large waist ‖ ～电线/绳/树干 thick wire/rope/trunk **5**（指宽度）

thick: ～笔画 thick strokes ▸～眉大眼, ～线条 **6**（形容声音）gruff: ～嗓子 husky voice ‖ ～声大气 deep, gruff voice **7**（粗鲁）rude: 说话很～ use coarse language ▸～话, ～人, ～俗
B〈副〉roughly: ▸～略, ～通
【粗暴】cūbào〈形〉rough: 态度～ have a rude attitude ‖ ～的行为 coarse behaviour
【粗笨】cūbèn〈形〉**1**（不灵巧）clumsy: 动作～ be clumsy ‖ 手脚～ be all thumbs **2**（笨重）unwieldy: ～的家具 bulky furniture
【粗鄙】cūbǐ〈形〉vulgar: 行为～ behave in a vulgar way ‖ 言语～ use coarse language
【粗布】cūbù〈名〉**1**（粗棉布）coarse cloth: ～军装 uniform made of coarse cloth **2**（土布）hand-woven cloth
【粗糙】cūcāo〈形〉**1**（不光滑）coarse: 皮肤～ have rough skin ‖ ～的表面 harsh surface **2**（不精巧）crudely made: 做工～ be of poor workmanship ‖ ～的仿制品 coarse imitation ‖ ～草率 work in a slipshod manner ‖ 表面～ roughness of the surface
【粗茶淡饭】cūchá-dànfàn〈成〉simple fare
【粗大】cūdà〈形〉**1**（指人体或物体）bulky: ～的辫子 fat braids ‖ ～的胳膊 strong and powerful arms **2**（指声音）husky: ～的嗓门 husky voice
【粗放】cūfàng〈形〉**1**［农业］extensive: ▸～耕作, ～经营 **2**（粗疏）careless: ～生产 crude production **3**（粗犷豪放）free and easy: ～的笔触 free and easy style
【粗放耕作】cūfàng gēngzuò〈名〉extensive cultivation
【粗放经营】cūfàng jīngyíng〈名〉extensive management: 由～向集约经营转变 change from extensive to intensive economy management
【粗钢】cūgāng〈名〉crude steel
【粗工】cūgōng〈名〉**1**（指工作）rough work **2**（指人）unskilled workman
【粗估】cūgū〈名〉rough estimation
【粗犷】cūguǎng〈形〉**1**（粗野）rough **2**（有气魄）straightforward and uninhibited: ～率直 be straightforward and candid ‖ 性格～ be of straightforward, unsophisticated character
【粗汉】cūhàn〈名〉rough fellow
【粗豪】cūháo〈形〉**1**（粗犷豪放）forthright **2**（粗壮豪迈）strident: ～的汽笛声 shrill whistling
【粗花呢】cūhuāní〈名〉［纺织］tweed
【粗话】cūhuà〈名〉coarse language: 他爱讲～。He has a foul mouth.
【粗活】cūhuó〈名〉heavy manual labour: 她干～，手变得很粗糙。Her hands became rough with hard work.
【粗加工】cūjiāgōng〈名〉［机械］rough machining
【粗具规模】cūjù-guīmó〈成〉be roughly in shape
【粗狂】cūkuáng〈形〉crude and bold
【粗砺】cūlì〈形〉gruff
【粗粝】cūlì **A**〈名〉〈书〉coarse rice **B**〈形〉coarse: ～的饭食 coarse food
【粗粒盐】cūlìyán〈名〉sea salt
【粗粮】cūliáng〈名〉coarse grains [such as maize, sorghum and millet]: ～细做 make delicacies out of coarse grain
【粗劣】cūliè〈形〉shoddy: 做工～ be of poor workmanship ‖ ～的产品 shoddy products
【粗陋】cūlòu〈形〉**1**（简陋）coarse and crude: 陈设～ be crudely furnished **2**（丑陋）crude and ugly: 面貌～ look vulgar and ugly
【粗卤】cūlǔ = 粗鲁 cūlǔ
【粗鲁】cūlǔ〈形〉crude: 说话～ be coarse in speech ‖ 行为～ rude behaviour
【粗略】cūlüè〈形〉rough: ～估计 make a rough calculation ‖ ～一看 give sth. a cursory glance
【粗麻布】cūmábù〈名〉sacking
【粗莽】cūmǎng〈形〉rash: 性格～ be rash in disposition ‖ ～的人 unrefined person
【粗毛】cūmáo〈名〉coarse wool
【粗眉大眼】cūméi-dàyǎn〈成〉heavy features
【粗呢】cūní〈名〉［纺织］coarse tweed
【粗浅】cūqiǎn〈形〉elementary: ～的道理 simple truth ‖ ～的体会 superficial understanding
【粗人】cūrén〈名〉**1**（粗心的人）rough fellow **2**〈谦〉（没修养的人）ill-bred person: 我是个～，说话直来直去，你可别见怪。I'm a bit of a boor. I hope you won't mind if I speak bluntly.
【粗沙】cūshā〈名〉coarse sand
【粗纱】cūshā〈名〉［纺织］low count yarn: ～机 roving frame
【粗砂】cūshā〈名〉grit: ～轮 coarse wheel
【粗声粗气】cūshēng-cūqì〈成〉deep and gruff voice: ～地说 talk in a raspy voice
【粗实】cūshi〈形〉stout: ～的手臂 sinewy arms ‖ ～的树干 thick tree trunk
【粗手笨脚】cūshǒu-bènjiǎo〈成〉be all thumbs: 做事～ do things in a heavy-handed manner
【粗疏】cūshū〈形〉**1**（马虎）careless: 办事～ be careless in work **2**（粗而稀疏）[of hair] coarse and thin
【粗率】cūshuài〈形〉rough and careless: ～的举动 foolhardy act ‖ ～的决定 rash decision
【粗饲料】cūsìliào〈名〉coarse fodder
【粗俗】cūsú〈形〉vulgar: 举止～ uncouth behaviour ‖ 说话～ use coarse language ‖ 他言语～。His language is vulgar.
【粗算】cūsuàn〈名〉rough calculation
【粗体】cūtǐ〈名〉［印刷］boldface: ～字 boldface font
【粗通】cūtōng〈动〉have a rough idea: ～文墨 be just able to read and write ‖ ～英语 know a little English
【粗细】cūxì〈名〉**1**（指尺寸）thickness: 碗口～的钢管 steel tubes as big as the mouth of a bowl ‖ 这样～的沙子最合用。This sand is just the right fineness. **2**（精致程度）quality of work: 工资多少要跟活儿的～挂钩。Pay must be in line with the quality of the work done.
【粗纤维】cūxiānwéi〈名〉coarse fibre
【粗线条】cūxiàntiáo **A**〈名〉rough outline: ～的描写 rough sketch **B**〈形〉rough-and-ready: ～的作风 rough and ready style
【粗心】cūxīn〈形〉careless: ～的孩子 careless child ‖ 是我～，考虑不周。It was thoughtless of me not to have considered it.
【粗心大意】cūxīn-dàyì〈成〉careless: 他忘了付账，真是～。It was remiss of him to forget to pay the bill.
【粗选】cūxuǎn〈名〉［矿业］roughing
【粗哑】cūyǎ〈形〉gruff: 嗓子～ have a husky voice
【粗盐】cūyán〈名〉crude salt
【粗野】cūyě〈形〉rough: 动作～ play rough ‖ 说话～ use coarse language ‖ ～的人 uncouth person
【粗枝大叶】cūzhī-dàyè〈成〉crude and careless: 我们干任何工作都不能～。We mustn't be sloppy with any of the work we do.
【粗制滥造】cūzhì-lànzào〈成〉be crudely made: 应当注意保证质量，不要～。Care should be taken to maintain quality and not to turn out shoddy products.
【粗制品】cūzhìpǐn〈名〉semi-finished product
【粗中有细】cūzhōng-yǒuxì〈成〉be crude in most matters, but sharp in some
【粗重】cūzhòng〈形〉**1**（指声音）gruff: ～的嗓音 gruff voice ‖ 他～的鼾声影响了我们的睡眠。His thunderous snoring disturbed our sleep. **2**（指器物）unwieldy: ～的家具 bulky furniture **3**（指条状物）thick and heavy: 眉毛浓黑～ have bushy black eyebrows **4**（指工作）hard: ～的体力活儿 strenuous manual work
【粗壮】cūzhuàng〈形〉**1**（指人体）heavy-set: 体格～ be of sturdy build ‖ ～的汉子 stocky man **2**（指物体）thick and strong: ～的树枝 thick branch **3**（指声音）deep and resonant: 声音～ have a deep, resonant voice

cú

徂 cú〈动〉〈书〉**1**（到）get to: 自春～夏 from spring to summer **2**（过去）pass: ～年 past years **3**（开始）begin: 六月～暑。Summer begins in June. **4** = 殂 cú

殂 cú〈动〉〈书〉die
【殂谢】cúxiè〈动〉〈书〉die

cù

卒 cù〈副〉abruptly
▸zú
【卒中】cùzhòng = 中风 zhòngfēng

促 cù
A〈形〉hurried: ▸仓～, 短～, 急～
B〈动〉**1**〈书〉（靠近）be close to: ～膝 sit close together **2**（催促）urge: ▸～成, 催～, 督～
【促成】cùchéng〈动〉facilitate: ～各派政治和解 bring about political reconciliation between factions ‖ ～双方达成协议 help to bring about an agreement between the two parties ‖ 大力～ make great efforts to bring sth. to fruition
【促进】cùjìn〈动〉boost: ～健康 promote health ‖ ～经济发展 fuel economic growth ‖ ～全球经济一体化 foster integration with the global economy ‖ ～相互了解 promote mutual understanding ‖ 化肥会～植物生长。Fertilizer will accelerate the growth of plants.
【促进派】cùjìnpài〈名〉promoter of progress
【促请】cùqǐng〈动〉urge and demand: ～注意 draw sb.'s attention
【促使】cùshǐ〈动〉urge: ～问题得到解决 precipitate the settlement of an issue ‖ 他的话～我作出决定。His remark precipitated my decision.
【促膝谈心】cùxī-tánxīn〈成〉have a heart-to-heart talk
【促销】cùxiāo〈动〉promote sales: 从事～活动 be engaged in sales promotion ‖ ～产品 product on promotion ‖ ～价 promotion price
【促织】cùzhī = 蟋蟀 xīshuài

猝 cù〈副〉〈书〉 all of a sudden: ▸～不及防, ～然, ～死
【猝不及防】cùbùjífáng〈成〉 be caught off guard
【猝倒】cùdǎo ▸**p. 50**〈名〉［医学］ cataplexy
【猝尔】cù'ěr〈副〉〈书〉 suddenly
【猝发】cùfā〈动〉 break out: 心脏病～ have a sudden heart attack
【猝然】cùrán〈副〉 all of a sudden: ～加速/离去 suddenly accelerate/depart ‖ ～决定 make a sudden decision
【猝死】cùsǐ ▸**p. 50**〈名〉［医学］ sudden death: 婴儿～综合征 sudden infant death syndrome (SIDS)

酢 cù〈名〉**1**〈古〉= 醋 cù **2** = 酢浆草 cùjiāngcǎo
▸zuò
【酢浆草】cùjiāngcǎo〈名〉［植物］ creeping oxalis

蔟 cù ▸蚕蔟 cáncù

醋 cù〈名〉**1**（指调料） vinegar: ▸陈～, 米～ **2**（指情感） jealousy: ▸～坛子, ～意, 吃～
【醋罐子】cùguànzi = 醋坛子 cùtánzi
【醋劲儿】cùjìnr〈名〉〈口〉 jealousy: ～大的情人 jealous lover
【醋精】cùjīng〈名〉［化学］ acetin
【醋酸】cùsuān〈名〉［化学］ acetic acid: ～盐 acetate
【醋坛子】cùtánzi〈名〉〈喻〉 jealous person
【醋意】cùyì〈名〉 jealousy: ～大发 outbreak of jealousy

簇 cù
A〈动〉〈书〉 cluster together: ▸～居, ～生, ～拥
B〈名〉 cluster: 花～ flower cluster ▸花团锦～
C〈量〉 cluster: 一～鲜花 a bunch of flowers
D〈副〉 completely: ▸～新
【簇居】cùjū〈动〉 live in a compact community: 少数民族～区 regions where people of minority ethnic groups live in compact communities
【簇聚】cùjù〈动〉 gather in clusters
【簇生】cùshēng〈动〉 grow in clusters: ～的草 tufted grass
【簇新】cùxīn〈形〉 brand-new: ～的大衣 brand-new overcoat
【簇拥】cùyōng〈动〉 cluster: 前后～着一大群人 be surrounded by large crowds ‖ 孩子们～着老师走进教室。 The children crowded round the teacher as they went into the classroom.

蹙 cù〈书〉
A〈动〉 knit (one's brows): 双眉紧～ with one's brows tightly knitted ▸～额, ～眉
B〈形〉 urgent: 穷～ urgent
【蹙额】cù'é〈动〉〈书〉 frown
【蹙眉】cùméi〈动〉 frown: ～思索 knit one's brows in thought

蹴 cù〈动〉**1**（踏） tread: ▸一～而就 **2**〈书〉（踢） kick: ▸～鞠
【蹴鞠】cùjū〈动〉〈古〉 kick a ball

cuān

汆 cuān
A〈动〉 **1**（用水煮） quick-boil: ～丸子 quick-boiled meatballs in soup **2**〈口〉（用汆子烧水） boil water in a metal pot
B〈名〉 small, cylindrical metal pot which can be thrust into a fire to boil water quickly
【汆子】cuānzi〈名〉 small, cylindrical metal pot which can be thrust into a fire to boil water quickly

撺（攛） cuān〈动〉**1**〈口〉（怂恿） egg sb. on: ▸～掇, ～弄 **2**〈方〉（发怒） fly into a rage: 他～儿了。 He flared up. **3**〈方〉（匆忙地做） do sth. in a hurry: 临时现～ rush things at the last moment
【撺掇】cuānduo〈动〉〈口〉 egg sb. on: 别～他去打架。 Don't encourage him to fight.
【撺弄】cuānnong = 撺掇 cuānduo

镩（鑹） cuān
A〈名〉 ice pick: ▸冰～
B〈动〉 break with an ice pick: ～冰 break ice with an ice pick
【镩子】cuānzi〈名〉 ice pick

蹿（躥） cuān〈动〉 **1**（跳跃） leap: ～墙而过 jump over a wall ‖ ～上房 leap onto the roof ‖ 火舌～上层层楼面。 Flames were leaping from floor to floor. ▸～房越脊 **2**〈口〉（喷射） spurt: 伤口～血。 Blood spouted from the wound.
【蹿蹦】cuānbèng〈动〉 leap
【蹿房越脊】cuānfáng-yuèjǐ〈成〉 leap over house-tops and roofs
【蹿个儿】cuāngèr〈动〉〈口〉 shoot up: 我的孩子～了, 原来的衣服都穿不上了。 My child has shot up and outgrown his clothes.
【蹿红】cuānhóng〈动〉 become popular in a short space of time
【蹿火】cuānhuǒ〈动〉〈方〉 burn with anger: 有话好好说, 别～。 Let's try to talk calmly. Don't get angry.
【蹿升】cuānshēng〈动〉 rise fast

cuán

攒（攢） cuán〈动〉 put together: ～钱聚餐 get together for a dinner party ‖ 买零件～一台电脑 buy the parts to assemble a computer ▸～动, ～聚
▸zǎn
【攒动】cuándòng〈动〉 crowd together and move back and forth: ▸人头～
【攒盒】cuánhé〈名〉 multi-layered container for holding food
【攒集】cuánjí = 攒聚 cuánjù
【攒聚】cuánjù〈动〉 crowd together: 布告栏前～了许多学生。 The students huddled together in front of the bulletin board.
【攒眉】cuánméi〈动〉 knit one's brows: ～蹙额 furrow one's brows
【攒三聚五】cuánsān-jùwǔ〈成〉 gather in small groups: 他们～站在那儿。 They are standing there in small groups.
【攒射】cuánshè〈动〉 fire a volley

cuàn

窜（竄） cuàn〈动〉 **1**〈贬〉（乱跑） flee: 仓皇逃～ flee in panic ‖ 东逃西～ flee in all directions ▸～犯, 抱头鼠～, 流～ **2**（改动） make changes in wording: ▸～定, ～改
【窜定】cuàndìng〈动〉 finalize a draft
【窜犯】cuànfàn〈动〉 raid: ～边境 invade the border areas ‖ ～某国 invade a country
【窜改】cuàngǎi〈动〉 doctor: ～文件 tamper with a document ‖ ～原文 alter the original text ‖ 任意～ doctor as one wishes
【窜踞】cuànjù〈动〉 flee to and occupy (a place)
【窜扰】cuànrǎo〈动〉 harass: ～边境 harass the border areas ‖ ～活动 harassment
【窜逃】cuàntáo〈动〉 scurry off

篡 cuàn〈动〉**1**（夺取） usurp: ▸～夺, ～权, ～位 **2**（歪曲） distort: ▸～改
【篡党夺权】cuàndǎng-duóquán〈成〉 usurp Party leadership and seize state power
【篡夺】cuànduó〈动〉 usurp: ～领导权 usurp the leadership ‖ ～王位 seize the throne
【篡改】cuàngǎi〈动〉 doctor: ～历史 distort history ‖ ～统计资料 cook the statistics ‖ ～遗嘱 falsify a will
【篡国】cuànguó〈动〉 usurp state power
【篡权】cuànquán〈动〉 seize power: 阴谋～ scheme for power
【篡位】cuànwèi〈动〉 seize the throne: 阴谋～ plot to supplant the king

cuī

衰 cuī〈动〉〈书〉 decrease in order and degree
▸shuāi

崔 cuī〈形〉〈书〉 lofty: ▸～嵬
【崔巍】cuīwēi = 崔嵬 cuīwéi
【崔嵬】cuīwéi〈形〉〈书〉 lofty: 山峰～ towering mountain peaks

催 cuī〈动〉**1**（催促） urge: ～孩子们睡觉 hurry the children off to bed ‖ ～他们快一点。 Hurry them up a bit. ‖ 银行～他们偿还贷款。 The bank is pressing them for repayment of the loan. ▸～办, ～促, ～人泪下 **2**（加快） speed up: 钟表的滴答声～我入睡。 The ticking of the clock lulled me to sleep. ▸～眠, ～生
【催办】cuībàn〈动〉 press sb. into doing (sth.): ～手续 urge sb. to go through the formalities
【催逼】cuībī〈动〉 press sb.: ～偿还债务 press sb. to repay a debt
【催产】cuīchǎn〈动〉［医学］ induce labour
【催产素】cuīchǎnsù〈名〉［药学］ oxytocin
【催促】cuīcù〈动〉 press: ～付款 press sb. for payment ‖ ～作出决定 hurry sb. into a decision
【催肥】cuīféi〈动〉［畜牧］ fatten
【催化】cuīhuà〈动〉［化学］ catalyse: ～反应 catalytic reaction ‖ ～剂 catalyst
【催缴】cuījiǎo〈动〉 press sb. for payment: ～税款 press sb. to pay an overdue tax

【催款单】 cuīkuǎndān 〈名〉［经济］ prompt-note
【催泪弹】 cuīlèidàn〈名〉 tear-gas grenade
【催泪毒气】 cuīlèi dúqì〈名〉 tear gas: 他们向示威者释放了～。 They tear-gassed the demonstrators.
【催泪瓦斯】 cuīlèi wǎsī = 催泪毒气 cuīlèi dúqì
【催眠】 cuīmián〈动〉 hypnotize
【催眠曲】 cuīmiánqǔ〈名〉 lullaby: 唱/哼～ sing/hum a lullaby
【催眠术】 cuīmiánshù〈名〉 hypnotism
【催眠药】 cuīmiányào〈名〉［药学］ soporific
【催命】 cuīmìng〈动〉 **1**（催促死亡） put a nail in sb.'s coffin **2**〈喻〉（催促） keep pressing sb. to do sth.
【催命鬼】 cuīmìngguǐ〈名〉〈喻〉 person who keeps pressing another
【催奶】 cuīnǎi〈口〉= 催乳 cuīrǔ
【催迫】 cuīpò〈动〉 press
【催青】 cuīqīng〈动〉［农业］ hasten the hatching of silkworms
【催情】 cuīqíng〈动〉［畜牧］ induce oestrus
【催人泪下】 cuīrén-lèixià〈成〉 move sb. to tears: ～的电影 heart-rendering film
【催乳】 cuīrǔ〈动〉 promote lactation
【催生】 cuīshēng = 催产 cuīchǎn
【催收】 cuīshōu〈动〉 press sb. for payment
【催熟】 cuīshú〈动〉［农业］ speed up the ripening: ～果实 accelerate the ripening of fruit ‖ ～剂 maturing agent
【催讨】 cuītǎo〈动〉 press sb. for payment: ～债务 press sb. for payment of a debt
【催吐剂】 cuītùjì〈名〉［药学］ emetic
【催债】 cuīzhài〈动〉 press sb. for a debt
【催租】 cuīzū〈动〉 press sb. for payment of rent

摧 cuī
〈动〉 break: ▸～毁, ～折, 坚不可～
【摧残】 cuīcán〈动〉 wreck: ～身体/心灵 ruin one's body/mind ‖ ～致死 torture to death ‖ 身心受到极大～ be physically and spiritually tortured
【摧毁】 cuīhuǐ〈动〉 demolish: ～堡垒 demolish a fortress ‖ ～防御工事 smash the defences
【摧枯拉朽】 cuīkū-lāxiǔ〈成〉〈喻〉 easily overcome: 中国人民解放军以～之势于1949年4月23日一举解放了南京。 The PLA took Nanjing on April 23, 1949 as easily as breaking up dead wood.
【摧眉折腰】 cuīméi-zhéyāo〈成〉 bow and scrape
【摧折】 cuīzhé〈动〉 **1**（折断） break **2**（挫折） setback

cuǐ

璀 cuǐ
【璀璨】 cuǐcàn〈形〉 radiant: ～的明星 bright star ‖ ～的明珠 lustrous pearl
【璀璨夺目】 cuǐcàn-duómù〈成〉 dazzling: 一颗～的钻石 a dazzling diamond

cuì

倅 cuì
〈形〉〈书〉 secondary

脆 cuì
〈形〉 **1**（易破碎） fragile: 变～ embrittle ‖ ～而不坚 brittle and easily breakable ‖ 蛋壳很～。 Egg-shells are very brittle. ‖ 这种纸又薄又～。 This kind of paper is thin and fragile. **2**（指情感） delicate: ▸～弱 **3**（指食物） crisp: 香～可口 crisp, fragrant and pleasant to the taste ‖ 这种苹果吃起来又～又甜。 This kind of apple is crisp and sweet to eat. ▸～枣 **4**（指声音） clear: 嗓音又～又甜。 The voice is sweet and crisp. ▸～亮, 清～ **5**（干脆） neat
【脆薄】 cuìbáo〈形〉 thin and brittle
【脆骨】 cuìgǔ〈名〉 gristle
【脆亮】 cuìliàng〈形〉 sharp and clear: ～的嗓子 ringing voice
【脆嫩】 cuìnèn〈形〉 crisp and tender
【脆弱】 cuìruò〈形〉 fragile: 神经～ be of weak disposition ‖ 性格～ be of weak character ‖ 感情～ be easily upset
【脆生生】 cuìshēngshēng = 脆生 cuìsheng
【脆生】 cuìsheng〈形〉〈方〉 **1**（指食物） crisp: ～爽口 be crisp and refreshing ‖ ～的蔬菜/水果 crisp vegetables/fruit **2**（指声音） clear and crisp
【脆爽】 cuìshuǎng〈形〉 [of food] crisp and refreshing
【脆性】 cuìxìng〈名〉 brittleness: ～材料 fragile material
【脆枣】 cuìzǎo〈方〉= 焦枣 jiāozǎo

萃 cuì
〈书〉
A〈动〉 gather together: ▸荟～
B〈名〉（指人） gathering of people;（指物） collection of things: ▸出类拔～
【萃萃蝇】 cuìcuìyíng〈名〉［昆虫］ tsetse fly
【萃集】 cuìjí = 萃聚 cuìjù
【萃聚】 cuìjù〈动〉〈书〉 assemble: 群英～之地 place where heroes gather together
【萃取】 cuìqǔ〈名〉［化学］ extraction: ～车间 extraction plant

啐 cuì
A〈叹〉 [a way to express contempt, reproach, disgust, etc.]: ～! 休得胡言乱语。 Tut-tut! Don't talk nonsense.
B〈动〉 spit: ～痰 spit phlegm ‖ ～唾沫 spit saliva

淬 cuì
〈动〉 quench: ▸～火
【淬火】 cuìhuǒ〈动〉 quench: ～硬化 quench hardening
【淬砺】 cuìlì〈动〉〈书〉 temper oneself: ～意志 steel one's will
【淬硬钢】 cuìyìnggāng〈名〉［冶金］ quenched steel

悴 cuì
▸憔悴 qiáocuì

毳 cuì
〈名〉〈书〉 fine hair or down on birds or animals
【毳毛】 cuìmáo〈名〉［医学］ fine hair on the human body

瘁 cuì
〈形〉〈书〉 overworked: ▸鞠躬尽～, 心力交～

粹 cuì
〈书〉
A〈形〉 pure: ～而不杂 pure and unadulterated ▸～白, 纯～
B〈名〉 essence: ▸国～, 精～
【粹白】 cuìbái〈形〉〈书〉 **1**（纯粹） pure and unadulterated **2**（纯白） pure white
【粹美】 cuìměi〈形〉〈书〉 flawless

翠 cuì
A〈名〉 **1**（翠鸟） kingfisher: 点～ handicraft using kingfisher's feathers for ornament **2**（翡翠） jadeite: ▸～花, 珠～
B〈形〉 green: ～竹 green bamboo ▸～菊, ～绿, ～玉
【翠柏】 cuìbǎi〈名〉 bluish green cypress: 苍松～ green pines and verdant cypresses
【翠花】 cuìhuā〈名〉 flower-shaped ornaments inlaid with jadeite
【翠菊】 cuìjú〈名〉［植物］ China aster
【翠柳】 cuìliǔ〈名〉 green willow: ～依依。 The willows swing gently in the breeze.
【翠绿】 cuìlǜ〈形〉 emerald green: ～的稻田/松树 green paddy field/pine trees
【翠鸟】 cuìniǎo〈名〉 kingfisher
【翠生生】 cuìshēngshēng〈形〉 fresh and green: ～的青菜 fresh greens
【翠微】 cuìwēi〈名〉〈书〉 **1**（指山色） hazy blue mountain scenery **2**（指青山） blue mountains
【翠玉】 cuìyù〈名〉 blue jade

cūn

村 cūn
A〈名〉 **1**（村庄） village: ～办企业 village industry ‖ 邻～ neighbouring village ▸～寨, ～庄, 乡～ **2**（居住区） populated place or area: 华侨新～ new housing estate for overseas Chinese
B〈形〉 rustic: ▸～话, ～野
【村村通】 cūncūntōng〈名〉 project wiring and connecting up villages: "～"工程 a construction project connecting up every village
【村夫俗子】 cūnfū-súzǐ〈成〉 uncouth and ill-educated person
【村妇】 cūnfù〈名〉 country woman
【村姑】 cūngū〈名〉 country lass
【村话】 cūnhuà〈名〉 coarse language
【村口】 cūnkǒu〈名〉 village entrance
【村落】 cūnluò〈名〉 village: ～环境 village environment ‖ 偏僻～ remote village
【村民】 cūnmín〈名〉 villager
【村民委员会】 cūnmín wěiyuánhuì〈名〉 villagers' committee
【村舍】 cūnshè〈名〉 cottage
【村史】 cūnshǐ〈名〉 village history
【村塾】 cūnshú〈名〉〈旧〉 village private school
【村俗】 cūnsú **A**〈名〉 village customs **B**〈形〉 coarse: 谈吐～ vulgar in speech
【村头】 cūntóu = 村口 cūnkǒu
【村委会】 cūnwěihuì〈简称〉= 村民委员会
【村务】 cūnwù〈名〉 village affairs: ～公开 publicize village affairs
【村圩】 cūnxū〈名〉〈方〉 village fair
【村学】 cūnxué = 村塾 cūnshú
【村野】 cūnyě **A**〈名〉 countryside **B**〈形〉 rustic: 尽说些～难听的话 come out with nothing but vulgarities
【村寨】 cūnzhài〈名〉 village
【村长】 cūnzhǎng〈名〉 village head
【村镇】 cūnzhèn〈名〉 villages and towns
【村庄】 cūnzhuāng〈名〉 village
【村子】 cūnzi〈名〉 village

皴 cūn
A〈动〉 be chapped: ～了的脸/手 chapped face/hands
B〈名〉 **1**〈方〉（泥垢） grime: 要用肥皂和水才能洗掉你脖子上的～。 It would take soap as well as water to remove the

grime on your neck. 2▸［美术］ interior brush texturing

【皴法】cūnfǎ〈名〉［美术］ techniques of brush texturing

【皴裂】cūnliè〈动〉 be chapped from the cold: 手足～ have chapped hands and feet

cún

存 cún

A〈动〉1▸（存在） exist: 父母俱～。 Both parents are still alive. ▸～亡，残～，生～ 2▸（安顿） take shelter: ▸～身 3▸（蓄积） keep: ～粮备荒 store up grain against famine ‖ 把货～起来 keep the goods in storage ▸～食，保～，积～ 4▸（储蓄） deposit: 把钱～入银行 make a bank deposit ▸～户，～款，～折 5▸（寄放） check: ～行李 check in one's baggage ‖ ～自行车 leave one's bicycle in a bicycle park ▸～车，寄～ 6▸（怀有） bear: 不～幻想 be under no illusion ‖ 心～怀疑 harbour suspicions ▸～心 7▸（保留） retain: 他心直口快，肚子里～不住话。 He is outspoken and can't hold anything back. ▸～档，～根，求同～异

B〈名〉 goods in stock: 收支相抵，净～2,000元。 The accounts show a surplus of 2,000 *yuan*. ▸结～，库～

【存案】cún'àn〈动〉 officially register: ～备查 keep on file for future reference

【存查】cúnchá〈动〉 keep on file for future reference

【存车】cúnchē〈动〉 park: ～处 parking spot

【存储】cúnchǔ〈动〉1▸（储备） stockpile: ～粮食 store up grain ‖ ～战争物资 stockpile war materials 2▸［计算机］ store: ～数据/信息 store data/information ‖ ～系统 storage system

【存储器】cúnchǔqì〈名〉［计算机］ memory: ～容量 memory capacity ‖ 磁盘～ disc memory

【存单】cúndān〈名〉 deposit receipt: 定期～ time certificate

【存档】cúndàng〈动〉1▸（归档） place on file: ～备查 file for future reference ‖ 把文件～ keep a document on file 2▸［计算机］ save a file

【存底】cúndǐ A〈名〉copy on file B〈动〉 keep the original draft

【存而不论】cún'érbùlùn〈成〉 put aside and not discuss for the time being

【存放】cúnfàng〈动〉1▸（储存） store: 把货物～在仓库 store goods in a warehouse ‖ 把行李～在旅馆 deposit one's luggage at the hotel 2▸（储蓄） deposit: 我把所有的钱都～在银行了。 I have deposited all my money in the bank.

【存根】cúngēn〈名〉 counterfoil: 保单～ policy copy ‖ 票据～ ticket stubs ‖ ～簿 cheque-stub book

【存户】cúnhù〈名〉 depositor

【存活】cúnhuó〈动〉 survive: 有80%的～机会 have an 80% chance of survival ‖ 在这次地震中他～了下来。 He survived the earthquake. ‖ 很少生物能够在沙漠里～。 Very few creatures can survive in the desert.

【存活率】cúnhuólǜ〈名〉［生物］ survival rate

【存货】cúnhuò A〈动〉 stock up B〈名〉 goods in stock: 备有～ be in stock ‖ 清点～ take an inventory of stock ‖ 我们手头上有一批～。 We have a supply on hand.

【存款】cúnkuǎn A〈动〉 deposit: 简化～手续 simplify depositing procedures ‖ ～凭证 deposit slip B〈名〉 savings: 提取～ withdraw one's savings ‖ ～余额 balance held on deposit ‖ 储蓄～ savings deposit ‖ 定期～ fixed deposit ‖ 我账上有多少～? How much do I have in credit?

【存款保险】cúnkuǎn bǎoxiǎn〈名〉 deposit insurance

【存款单】cúnkuǎndān〈名〉 deposit slip

【存款利率】cúnkuǎn lìlǜ〈名〉 savings rate

【存款利息】cúnkuǎn lìxī〈名〉 deposit interest

【存款人】cúnkuǎnrén〈名〉 depositor

【存款银行】cúnkuǎn yínháng〈名〉 depository bank

【存款账户】cúnkuǎn zhànghù〈名〉 savings account

【存栏】cúnlán〈动〉［畜牧］ raise livestock on farms: ～总头数 total number of livestock

【存量】cúnliàng〈名〉 amount in storage

【存留】cúnliú〈动〉 persist: 这一风俗～至今。 The custom still survives to this day.

【存念】cúnniàn〈动〉 keep sth. as a memento: 王教授～。 To Professor Wang as a memento.

【存盘】cúnpán〈动〉［计算机］ save

【存钱】cúnqián〈动〉 save money

【存钱罐】cúnqiánguàn〈名〉 piggy bank

【存取】cúnqǔ〈动〉1▸（存入和取出） deposit or withdraw: ～自由 deposit or withdraw as one wishes 2▸［计算机］ access: 随机～ random access

【存入】cúnrù〈动〉 put in: 把钱～银行 put one's money in a bank

【存身】cúnshēn〈动〉 put down roots: 无处～ have no place to call one's home

【存食】cúnshí ▸p. 50〈动〉［医学］ suffer from indigestion

【存世量】cúnshìliàng〈名〉 number in existence: 藏品的～越少价值越昂贵。 The fewer the number of a valuable object, the higher its price.

【存亡】cúnwáng〈动〉 live or die: ～与共 share a common destiny ‖ ～未卜 life and death cannot be predicted ‖ 与阵地共～ defend a position to the death

【存亡绝续】cúnwáng-juéxù〈成〉 survive or perish: ～的关头 at the most critical moment

【存问】cúnwèn〈动〉〈书〉 pass on one's regards

【存物处】cúnwùchù〈名〉 cloakroom

【存息】cúnxī〈名〉［经济］ credit interest

【存项】cúnxiàng〈名〉 balance

【存心】cúnxīn A〈动〉 harbour intentions: ～欺诈 with intent to defraud ‖ ～不良 harbour evil intentions ‖ 谁知道他存的什么心! God knows what he is up to! B〈副〉 intentionally: ～刁难 deliberately make things difficult (for sb.) ‖ ～找碴儿 purposely pick faults

【存休】cúnxiū〈名〉 accumulated holidays

【存恤】cúnxù〈动〉〈书〉 express sympathy for and provide relief to

【存续】cúnxù〈动〉 exist and keep going

【存续期】cúnxùqī〈名〉 duration: 该基金规模为一千万，～为五年。 The fund has 10 million, with a duration of five years.

【存蓄】cúnxù A〈动〉 store: ～淡水 store fresh water B〈名〉 reserves

【存衣处】cúnyīchù〈名〉 cloakroom

【存疑】cúnyí〈动〉 leave a question open: 这件事只好暂时～。 We have to put this matter aside for the time being.

【存余】cúnyú〈名〉 surplus

【存在】cúnzài A〈动〉 exist: 客观/实际～ exist objectively/in reality B〈名〉［哲学］ existence: ～决定意识。 One's being determines one's consciousness.

【存在主义】cúnzàizhǔyì〈名〉［哲学］ existentialism

【存照】cúnzhào A〈动〉 keep for future reference B〈名〉 document on file

【存折】cúnzhé〈名〉 deposit book: 活期储蓄～ current deposit book

【存正】cúnzhèng〈动〉〈套〉 please take my work and point out whatever inadequacies you find in it: 这是我的新诗集，敬请～。 This is my new collection of poetry. I'd really appreciate your valuable comments.

【存执】cúnzhí〈名〉 counterfoil: 汇款～ remittance stub

【存贮】cúnzhù〈动〉 store

蹲 cún〈动〉〈方〉 injure one's leg as a result of a heavy fall: 他从墙上跳下时～了腿。 He injured his leg jumping down from a wall.

▸dūn

cǔn

忖 cǔn〈动〉 ponder: ▸～量，思～

【忖度】cǔnduó〈动〉 speculate: ～人心 speculate on what another person is thinking ‖ 我～他今天不会来了。 I presume he won't come today.

【忖量】cǔnliàng〈动〉1▸（揣度） guess: 我～不出她的来意。 I couldn't figure out what she had come for. 2▸（思量） ponder: 他经过反复～。 He turned the matter over and over in his mind for a long time.

【忖摸】cǔnmo〈动〉 reckon: 我～他下周回来。 I reckon he will be back next week.

cùn

寸 cùn

A〈量〉 *cun* [unit of length, equal to 3.333 centimetres]: ▸英～

B〈形〉 very little: ▸～步难行，～土，手无～铁

C〈名〉 *cunkou* pulse: ▸～关尺，～口

【寸步】cùnbù〈名〉 single step: ～不让 refuse to budge an inch

【寸步不离】cùnbù-bùlí〈成〉 keep close to sb.

【寸步难行】cùnbù-nánxíng〈成〉 find it difficult to move even a step: 脱离了群众，我们就～。 If we separate ourselves from the general population, we will find ourselves in a very difficult situation.

【寸步难移】cùnbù-nányí ＝ 寸步难行 cùnbù-nánxíng

【寸草】cùncǎo〈名〉 blade of grass: ～不生 be barren

【寸草不留】cùncǎo-bùliú〈成〉 leave not so much as a blade of grass

【寸草春晖】cùncǎo-chūnhuī〈成〉〈喻〉 one can never repay the love and care one has received from one's parents

【寸长】cùncháng〈名〉〈书〉 small merit

【寸地】cùndì〈名〉 tiny piece of land: ～千金。 An inch of land is worth a thousand taels of gold.

【寸断】cùnduàn〈动〉〈书〉 be torn to small pieces: 她肝肠～。 Her heart was torn apart with grief.

【寸功】cùngōng〈名〉〈书〉 humble achievement: ～未立 haven't made the

smallest contribution ‖ 身无～ have achieved nothing at all
【寸关尺】cùn-guān-chǐ〈名〉［中医］*cun*, *guan* and *chi* [three places on the wrist where the pulse is usually taken]
【寸金难买寸光阴】cùn jīn nán mǎi cùn guāngyīn〈俗〉time is more precious than gold
【寸进】cùnjìn〈名〉〈书〉little progress: 略有～ have made very little progress
【寸楷】cùnkǎi〈名〉［书法］regular script in characters of one-*cun* size
【寸刻】cùnkè〈名〉very short time
【寸口】cùnkǒu〈名〉［中医］*cunkou* pulse
【寸铁】cùntiě〈名〉small weapon: 手无～ be unarmed
【寸头】cùntóu〈名〉crew cut: 理～ have a crew cut ‖ 留～ have a crew cut
【寸土】cùntǔ〈名〉small piece of land: ～不让 not yield an inch of territory
【寸土必争】cùntǔ-bìzhēng〈成〉fight for every inch of one's land
【寸心】cùnxīn〈名〉〈书〉1（内心）heart: ～如割 be heart-broken 2（心意）feelings: 聊表～ as a token of my appreciation
【寸阴】cùnyīn〈名〉〈书〉very short time
【寸有所长】cùn yǒu suǒ cháng〈成〉〈喻〉every man has his strong points
【寸有所长，尺有所短】cùn yǒu suǒ cháng, chǐ yǒu suǒ duǎn = 尺有所短，寸有所长 chǐ yǒu suǒ duǎn, cùn yǒu suǒ cháng

cuō

搓 cuō〈动〉1（摩擦）rub with one's hands: ～衬衣/袜子 scrub the shirt/socks ‖ ～手掌 rub one's palms ▸～板，～澡 2（来回揉）twist with one's hands: ～麻绳 make hemp rope by twisting fibres in one's hands ‖ 把面～成小球 roll the dough into small balls ▸揉～
【搓板】cuōbǎn〈名〉scrubbing board: ～棱 corrugated surface of a washboard
【搓背】cuōbèi〈动〉scrub one's back
【搓麻将】cuō májiàng〈动〉play mah-jong
【搓弄】cuōnòng〈动〉knead
【搓球】cuōqiú〈动〉［体育］chop: 他一板把球搓过去。He returned the shot with a chop.
【搓揉】cuōróu〈动〉knead: 他把纸～成一团。He crumpled the paper into a ball.
【搓绳】cuōshéng〈动〉make a rope by twisting the strands together
【搓手顿脚】cuōshǒu-dùnjiǎo〈成〉get anxious and impatient
【搓手顿足】cuōshǒu-dùnzú = 搓手顿脚 cuōshǒu-dùnjiǎo
【搓洗】cuōxǐ〈动〉scrub
【搓澡】cuōzǎo〈动〉scrub and wash

磋 cuō〈动〉1〈书〉（磨光）grind and polish 2（研讨）consult: ▸～商
【磋磨】cuōmó〈动〉〈书〉learn from each other by comparing notes
【磋商】cuōshāng〈动〉hold a discussion: 进行～ have consultations ‖ 经过～，双方达成停火协议。After some negotiations, the two sides agreed on a ceasefire.

蹉 cuō
【蹉跌】cuōdiē〈动〉〈书〉1（跌倒）slip and fall 2〈喻〉（失误）make a slip
【蹉跎】cuōtuó〈动〉waste time: ～自误 throw away one's opportunities
【蹉跎岁月】cuōtuó-suìyuè〈成〉waste one's time

撮 cuō
A〈动〉1〈方〉（捏取）hold with one's fingers: ～点儿盐 take a pinch of salt 2（摘取）summarize: ▸～要 3〈书〉（聚拢）assemble: ▸～合 4（指用簸箕）scoop up: ～起一簸箕土 scoop up a dustpan of dirt 5〈方〉（吃）eat: 上馆子～一顿 eat at a restaurant
B〈量〉〈方〉pinch: 一～鼻烟 a pinch of snuff ‖〈喻〉一小～匪徒 a handful of bandits
▸zuǒ
【撮合】cuōhe〈动〉act as go-between: 从中～ bring people together
【撮箕】cuōjī〈名〉〈方〉dustpan
【撮弄】cuōnòng〈动〉1（戏弄）tease: 别～他了。Don't make fun of him. 2（教唆）incite: ～别人做坏事 incite others to do something bad
【撮要】cuōyào A〈动〉make a summary: 把工作情况～汇报 submit an outline report on one's work B〈名〉abstract: 论文～ abstract of a thesis

cuó

嵯 cuó
【嵯峨】cuó'é〈形〉〈书〉precipitous

矬 cuó〈方〉
A〈形〉short: ～个ㄦ dwarf ▸～子
B〈动〉lower one's body: 身子一～就钻过去了 lower one's body to get through
【矬子】cuózi〈名〉〈方〉short person

痤 cuó
【痤疮】cuóchuāng ▸p. 50〈名〉［医学］acne: 他脸上生了～。He's got acne on his face.

瘥 cuó〈名〉〈书〉disease
▸chài

cuǒ

脞 cuǒ〈形〉〈书〉trivial: ▸丛～
【脞谈】cuǒtán〈名〉〈书〉trivial talk

cuò

挫 cuò〈动〉1（受挫折）suffer a setback: ▸～折，受～ 2（压下去）subdue: ～其锋芒 blunt the edge of sb.'s advance ‖ ～其锐气 dampen sb.'s spirits ▸～败，抑扬顿～
【挫败】cuòbài A〈名〉setback: 遭到严重～ suffer a serious defeat ‖ 一连串～ a series of frustrations B〈动〉thwart: ～敌人的进攻 foil the enemy's attack ‖ ～阴谋 foil a plot
【挫伤】cuòshāng A ▸p. 50〈名〉［医学］wound: 满身的肿块和～ be covered in bumps and bruises B〈动〉1（指皮肉）bruise: 我跌倒时～了脚踝。I fell and bruised my ankle. 2（指热情等）dampen: ～积极性 dampen sb.'s enthusiasm ‖ ～自尊心 injure sb.'s pride
【挫折】cuòzhé〈动〉1（阻碍）dampen: ～群众的积极性 dampen the enthusiasm of the public 2（失利）suffer a setback: 从～中振作起来 rebound from a setback ‖ 在恋爱上受到～ be crossed in love

厝 cuò
A〈动〉〈书〉1（放置）place: ▸～火积薪 2（停放灵柩）place a coffin in a temporary shelter pending burial: ▸浮～
B〈名〉〈方〉building: ～后边跑出一条狗。A dog ran out from behind the house.
【厝火积薪】cuòhuǒ-jīxīn〈成〉〈喻〉latent danger

措 cuò〈动〉1（处理）manage: ▸～置，不知所～，失～ 2（筹划）make plans: 筹～款项 raise funds ▸～施，举～
【措办】cuòbàn〈动〉plan and handle
【措词】cuòcí〈动〉word: ～不当 use bad diction ‖ ～得体 be appropriately worded ‖ ～严厉 be couched in harsh terms ‖ 这篇讲话～谨严。The wording of the address was carefully chosen.
【措辞】cuòcí = 措词 cuòcí
【措施】cuòshī〈名〉measure: 采取～ take measures ‖ 补救～ remedial measures ‖ 防盗～ precautions against burglary ‖ 应急～ emergency measures ‖ 行政～ administrative action
【措手】cuòshǒu〈动〉set one's hand to: 无从～ not know what to do
【措手不及】cuòshǒu-bùjí〈成〉be caught unawares: 打他个～ make a surprise attack on sb. ‖ 你弄得我～。You've caught me unawares.
【措意】cuòyì〈动〉〈书〉pay attention to: 不甚～ not pay much attention to
【措置】cuòzhì〈动〉manage: ～得当 handle properly ‖ ～失当 mismanage
【措置裕如】cuòzhì-yùrú〈成〉manage very well

锉（銼） cuò
A〈名〉file: 三角～ triangular file ‖ 用～锉去棱角 file away the edges and corners with a rasp ▸～刀
B〈动〉file: ～锯齿 file the teeth of a saw ‖ ～指甲 file one's nails
【锉床】cuòchuáng〈名〉［机械］filing machine
【锉刀】cuòdāo〈名〉［机械］file: ～硬度 file hardness
【锉工】cuògōng〈名〉filer
【锉屑】cuòxiè〈名〉filings

错[1]（錯） cuò
A〈名〉〈书〉grindstone for polishing jade: 他山之石，可以为～。Advice from others may help one to overcome one's shortcomings.
B〈动〉1〈书〉（打磨玉石）polish jade: ▸攻～ 2（摩擦）grind: ～牙 grind one's teeth

错[2]（錯） cuò
A〈动〉1〈书〉（镶）inlay [with gold, silver, etc.];（涂）plate [with gold, silver, etc.]: ▸～金，～银 2（交错）be interlocked and jagged: 一团密集交～的电缆 a mess of cables ▸盘根～节，犬牙交～ 3（失去）miss: ～过机会 miss the opportunity ▸～车 4（避开）stagger: 把两个会的时间～一下 stagger the two meetings
B〈形〉1（复杂）complex: ▸～乱，～杂 2（不对）wrong: 猜/答～ guess/answer

wrong ‖ 读～ mispronounce ‖ 念～ misread ‖ 认～人 mistake sb. for sb. else ‖ 走～路 take the wrong road ►～怪, ～觉, 大～特～ **3**（差） bad: 电影不～。 The film is not bad. ‖ 他们关系不～。 They are on good terms.

C〈名〉 mistake: 犯～ make a mistake ‖ 没～ without a mistake ►出～, 认～, 阴差阳～

【错爱】 cuò'ài〈动〉〈谦〉 do not deserve sb.'s kindness: 承蒙～。 I am really grateful for your kindness.

【错案】 cuò'àn〈名〉［法律］ misjudged case: 纠正～ redress a mishandled case

【错别字】 cuòbiézì〈名〉（指读错） mispronounced character;（指写错） wrongly written character

【错层】 cuòcéng〈名〉 split level

【错车】 cuòchē〈动〉 cede right of way: ～道 lay-by

【错处】 cuòchu〈名〉 fault: 你的报告上有很多～。 There are many errors in your report.

【错待】 cuòdài〈动〉 treat unfairly

【错讹】 cuò'é〈名〉 error

【错愕】 cuò'è〈形〉〈书〉 dumbfounded

【错峰】 cuòfēng〈动〉 miss the peak demand period

【错怪】 cuòguài〈动〉 blame sb. unjustly: ～了人 blame the wrong person

【错过】 cuòguò〈动〉 miss: ～机会 miss an opportunity ‖ 赶快，要不就～末班车了。 Hurry up, or we'll miss the last bus.

【错话】 cuòhuà〈名〉 improper remarks

【错会】 cuòhuì〈动〉 misunderstand: 你～了我的话。 You have misconstrued my words.

【错角】 cuòjiǎo〈名〉［数学］ alternate angle

【错解】 cuòjiě〈动〉 misinterpret

【错金】 cuòjīn〈动〉［美术］ inlay with gold: ～器皿 gold-inlaid ware

【错觉】 cuòjué〈名〉 misconception: 产生～ have a wrong impression ‖ 引起～ cause an illusion

【错开】 cuòkāi〈动〉 stagger: ～休假 stagger vacations ‖ ～上班时间 stagger office hours

【错漏】 cuòlòu〈名〉 [of language] mistakes and omissions

【错乱】 cuòluàn〈形〉 deranged: 颠倒～ be topsy-turvy ‖ 精神～ be mentally deranged

【错落】 cuòluò〈形〉 disorderly: ～有致 be in picturesque disorder ‖ 绿树鲜花～其间 dotted with green trees and fresh flowers

【错谬】 cuòmiù〈名〉 mistake

【错失】 cuòshī〈动〉 miss: ～良机 let slip a golden opportunity

【错时】 cuòshí〈动〉 stagger time: ～上下班 stagger office hours

【错位】 cuòwèi〈动〉 **1**［医学］ dislocate: 脚踝～ dislocation of the ankle **2**（失去常态） turn upside down: 管理体制上下～。 There are vertical dislocations within the management system.

【错误】 cuòwù **A**〈形〉 wrong: ～答案 wrong answer ‖ ～决定/结论 wrong decision/conclusion ‖ ～言论 incorrect statement **B**〈名〉 mistake: 承认～ acknowledge one's mistake ‖ 犯～ make a mistake ‖ 改正～ right a wrong ‖ ～百出 be full of mistakes

【错译】 cuòyì〈动〉 mistranslate

【错银】 cuòyín〈动〉［美术］ inlay with silver

【错杂】 cuòzá〈形〉 mixed

【错诊】 cuòzhěn〈名〉［医学］ wrong diagnosis

【错字】 cuòzì〈名〉 misprinted character: ～连篇 pages and pages of wrongly written characters

【错综复杂】 cuòzōng-fùzá〈成〉 complex: 情节～的小说 novel with an intricate plot

Dd

d

dā

耷 dā〈名〉〈书〉big ear

【耷拉】dāla〈动〉hang down: ～着脸 pull a long face ‖ ～着脑袋 hang one's head ‖ 小狗～着尾巴跑了。The little dog ran off with its tail hanging down.

哒（噠） dā = 嗒 dā

【哒嗪】dāqín〈名〉［化学］diazine

搭 dā〈动〉**1**（挂）hang over: 肩膀上～着一条毛巾 hang a towel over one's shoulder ‖ 他把手～在我肩上。He rested his hand on my shoulder. **2**（乘坐）travel by: ～轮船到上海 arrive in Shanghai by ship ‖ 我能～你的车进城吗？Could you give me a lift to town? **3**（搭建）put up: ～浮桥 construct a pontoon bridge ‖ ～帐篷 pitch a tent ‖ ～桥 build a bridge ‖ 喜鹊在树上～了个窝。The magpies nested in the tree. ▸～架子，手～凉棚 **4**（连接）touch: 千万别让两根电线～上了。Make sure that the two wires are not touching. ▸～帮，～伙 **5**（附加）add to: 差点儿把命～上 nearly lose one's life ‖ 买五～一。For every five you buy, you will receive one extra. **6**（搭配）combine: 粗粮和细粮～着吃有利于健康。It is good for your health if you combine coarse grain with fine grain foods. **7**（抬）lift together: 书柜太沉，两个人～不动。The bookcase is too heavy for two people to carry.

【搭班】dābān〈动〉**1**〈旧〉（指艺人）temporarily join a theatrical troupe: ～唱戏 temporarily join an operatic troupe **2**〈口〉（临时合作）team up temporarily: 他与杨博士～搞科研。He teamed up with Dr Yang on a research project.

【搭班子】dā bānzi〈惯〉**1** = 搭班 dābān **2**（建立班子）organize a team to do a job: 公司正在～。The company is choosing its leadership.

【搭伴】dābàn〈动〉join sb. on a trip: 他们～旅游。They were travelling companions.

【搭帮】dābāng〈动〉〈方〉join company with: ～结伙 in groups ‖ 我跟他们～走。I joined company with them.

【搭便】dābiàn〈副〉incidentally: 我是出差～来看看大家。I am just dropping in while on business.

【搭补】dābǔ〈动〉subsidize: ～家用 help out with family expenses

【搭茬儿】dāchár〈动〉〈方〉respond: 他说了半天，但没人～。He went on and on but no one responded. ‖ 这事儿跟你无关，别～。It's none of your business, so don't say a word.

【搭碴儿】dāchár = 搭茬儿 dāchár

【搭车】dāchē〈动〉**1**（乘坐）take: 搭直达列车 take a through train **2**（指顺风车）get a lift: 我也去城里，你搭我的车吧。I'm going to town, too. I can give you a ride. **3**〈喻〉（指机会、便利）take an opportunity: 利用调整物价之机～涨价 take advantage of price regulations to raise prices

【搭乘】dāchéng〈动〉travel by: 他～七点钟的航班去纽约。He took the 7 o'clock flight to New York.

【搭当】dādàng = 搭档 dādàng

【搭档】dādàng **A**〈动〉pair up: 我们两个人～吧。Let's work as a team. ‖ 他跟我～打桥牌。He is partnering me at bridge. **B**〈名〉partner: 老～ old workmate

【搭话】dāhuà〈动〉**1**（回答）answer: 我问了他几遍，他就是不～。I asked him several times, but he just didn't respond. **2**（搭讪）make conversation: 他不爱跟别人～。He doesn't like to talk with others.

【搭伙】dāhuǒ〈动〉**1**（合作）team up: 他们～一起做买卖。They have teamed up to do business together. **2**（一起吃饭）eat regularly: 在食堂～ take one's meals at a canteen

【搭架子】dā jiàzi〈动〉**1**（构建）build a framework: 动笔之前先要搭好架子。Make an outline before you start writing. **2**〈方〉〈喻〉（摆架子）assume airs: 他没啥了不起的，却爱～。There's really nothing to him, but he likes to assume airs.

【搭肩】dājiān〈动〉**1**（帮忙抬）help to shoulder sth. **2**（站在他人肩上）stand on another's shoulders

【搭建】dājiàn〈动〉**1**（盖建）put up: 临时～帐篷 rig up a tent **2**（组织）set up: ～领导班子 organize a leading group

【搭脚儿】dājiǎor〈动〉〈方〉hitch-hike

【搭界】dājiè〈动〉**1**（交界）have a common border: 这里是两国～的地方。This is where the border is between the two countries. ‖ 中国的北部与俄罗斯和蒙古～。China borders Russia and Mongolia to the north. **2**〈方〉（有关系）have something to do with: 这两件事根本不～。There is no connection whatsoever between these two things.

【搭救】dājiù〈动〉come to the rescue: ～溺水儿童 rescue a drowning child

【搭客】dākè〈动〉〈方〉pick up passengers: 这是辆专用车，不～。This is a special bus and it does not pick up passengers.

【搭扣】dākòu〈名〉hasp

【搭拉】dāla = 耷拉 dāla

【搭理】dāli = 答理 dāli

【搭卖】dāmài = 搭售 dāshòu

【搭配】dāpèi **A**〈动〉**1**（安排分配）combine proportionally: 合理～ arrange in proper proportions ‖ 这两个词不～。The two words don't go together. **2**（配合）cooperate: 两位选手～得十分默契。The two players make a perfect team. **B**〈形〉matched: 这两种颜色不～。These two colours don't go. **C**〈名〉collocation: ～词典 dictionary of collocations

【搭腔】dāqiāng〈动〉respond: 我跟他说话，但他没有～。I spoke to him, but he made no response.

【搭桥】dāqiáo〈动〉**1**（架桥）build a bridge: 逢山开路，遇水～ cut paths through mountains and build bridges over rivers **2**（撮合）act as a matchmaker: 牵线～ act as a go-between **3**［医学］perform a bypass surgery: 心脏～手术 heart bypass surgery

【搭讪】dāshàn〈动〉try to strike up a conversation: 他想跟我～，我没理他。I ignored him when he tried to talk to me.

【搭赸】dāshàn = 搭讪 dāshàn

【搭手】dāshǒu〈动〉lend a hand: 搭把手 give sb. a hand ‖ 搭不上手 cannot be of any help

【搭售】dāshòu〈名〉tie-in sale

【搭头】dātou〈名〉〈方〉gift: 我买了台电视机，这部收音机是～。I bought a TV set and this radio came free.

【搭载】dāzài〈动〉**1**（顺便装载）pick up **2**（指用卫星）load on a satellite

嗒 dā〈拟〉clatter: ～～的马蹄声 clatter of horses' hoofs ‖ 雨点～～地打在树叶上。Raindrops fell pattering upon the leaves.
▸tà

答 dā = 答 dá [only used in phrases like 答理，答应，etc.]
▸dá

【答茬儿】dāchár = 搭茬儿 dāchár

【答碴儿】dāchár = 搭茬儿 dāchár

【答理】dāli〈动〉**1**（回应）respond: 我向他问好，他没～我。I greeted him but he didn't respond. **2**（理睬）pay attention to: 她不太爱～人。She is a bit standoffish. ‖ 他俩谁也不～谁。They are not on speaking terms.

【答腔】dāqiāng = 搭腔 dāqiāng

【答讪】dāshàn = 搭讪 dāshàn

【答言】dāyán〈动〉respond: 这不关你的事，你答什么言! This is none of your business, so why waste your breath?

【答应】dāying〈动〉**1**（回答）reply: 问你呢，你怎么不～。I'm asking you a question. Why don't you answer? **2**（允诺）promise: ～保守秘密 promise to keep it a secret **3**（同意）comply with: 他妈不～这门亲事。His mother didn't approve of the marriage.

褡 dā

【褡包】dābāo〈名〉long, broad girdle

【褡裢】dālian〈名〉1（指口袋）long, rectangular bag 2（指上衣）[worn by wrestlers] multi-layered cloth jacket

dá

打 dá〈量〉dozen: 论～出售 sell by the dozen ‖ 一～铅笔 a dozen pencils ‖ 整整一～ a round dozen
▸dǎ

达（達）dá

A〈动〉1（通往）extend: 这条高速公路直～北京。This expressway leads straight to Beijing. ▸四通八～ 2（达到）reach: 不～目的，决不罢休 refuse to give up until one has reached one's objective ‖ 死亡人数已～三百。The death toll has reached 300. ▸到～，欲速则不～ 3（通达）understand fully: ▸通情～理，通权～变 4（表示）convey: ▸传～，辞不～意 B〈形〉1（开放）broad-minded: ▸～观，豁～ 2（显达）eminent: ▸～官贵人，飞黄腾～

【达标】dábiāo〈动〉be up to standard: 质量～。The quality is up to standard.

【达成】dáchéng〈动〉reach: ～共识 come to a consensus ‖ ～交易 clinch a deal ‖ ～协议 reach an agreement

【达旦】dádàn〈动〉〈书〉be approaching dawn: ～不寐 have a sleepless night ▸通宵～

【达到】dádào〈动〉reach: ～标准 be up to standard ‖ ～国际先进水平 reach advanced international standards ‖ ～目的 achieve one's purpose

【达尔文进化论】Dá'ěrwén jìnhuàlùn〈名〉Darwinian evolution theory

【达费德郡】Dáfèidéjùn〈名〉Dyfed

【达观】dáguān〈形〉philosophical: 遇事要～些，不要愁坏了身体。Be optimistic. Don't worry yourself sick.

【达官贵人】dáguān-guìrén〈成〉high dignitary

【达吉斯坦】Dájísītǎn〈名〉Dagestan

【达喀尔】Dákā'ěr〈名〉Dakar

【达卡】Dákǎ〈名〉Dhaka

【达赖喇嘛】Dálài Lǎma〈名〉Dalai Lama

【达勒姆郡】Dálèmǔjùn〈名〉Durham

【达人】dárén〈名〉expert: 游戏～ gaming expert ‖ 时尚～ fashion expert

【达斡尔族】Dáwò'ěrzú〈名〉Daur ethnic group

【达意】dáyì〈动〉express one's idea: 抒情～ express one's ideas and feelings ▸辞不～

【达因】dáyīn〈量〉［物理］dyne: ～计 dyne meter

沓 dá〈量〉pile: 一～纸 a pad of paper ‖ 一～报纸 a pile of newspapers
▸tà

【沓子】dázi〈名〉〈口〉pile: 一～钞票 a wad of bank notes

怛 dá〈书〉

A〈形〉grieved: ～伤 sad ‖ 惨～ miserable and sad
B〈动〉dread

荙（薘）dá ▸莙荙菜 jūndácài

鍅（鐽）dá〈名〉Darmstadtium (Ds)

笪 dá〈名〉1〈方〉（竹席）bamboo-strip mat [for airing grain on] 2〈书〉（绳索）bamboo tow rope

答 dá〈动〉1（回答）answer: 你问我～。You ask and I'll answer. ‖ 他笑而不～。He smiled but gave no reply. 2（回报）repay: ▸～谢，报～
▸dā

【答案】dá'àn〈名〉answer: 寻求/找～ search for an answer ‖ 请在答题纸上写上～。Please write your answers on the answer sheet.

【答拜】dábài〈动〉repay a visit

【答辩】dábiàn〈动〉（指被告）answer a charge;（指原告）respond to a plea: 出庭～ defend a case in court

【答词】dácí〈名〉answering speech: 致～ give a speech in reply

【答对】dáduì〈动〉answer: ～得体 answer appropriately

【答非所问】dáfēisuǒwèn〈成〉give an irrelevant answer

【答复】dáfù〈动〉reply: 及时/正式～ prompt/formal reply ‖ 口头/书面～ oral/written answer ‖ 敬请～。Please reply.

【答话】dáhuà〈动〉respond: 人家问你，你怎么不～? When asked, why do you not respond?

【答卷】dájuàn A〈动〉answer the questions B〈名〉answering sheet, test paper: 收～ collect the completed examination papers ‖〈喻〉用自己的实际行动交一份很好的～ allow one's actions to speak for themselves

【答礼】dálǐ〈动〉return a salute

【答数】dáshù〈名〉solution

【答题】dátí〈动〉answer questions

【答谢】dáxiè〈动〉express appreciation: ～宴会 reciprocal banquet

【答疑】dáyí〈动〉answer questions: ～解惑 answer by setting straight

靼 dá ▸鞑靼人 Dádárén

瘩 dá

【瘩背】dábèi〈名〉［中医］carbuncle on the back

鞑（韃）dá

【鞑靼人】Dádárén〈名〉1（指古代民族）Tartar 2（指俄联邦）Tatar

【鞑靼斯坦共和国】Dádásītǎn Gònghéguó〈名〉The Republic of Tatarstan

dǎ

打[1] dǎ〈动〉1（击打）beat: 浪～海岸 waves beating against the seashore ‖ ～门 knock at the door ‖ 敲锣～鼓 beat drums and gongs ‖ 在鼻子上～一拳 give sb. a punch on the nose ‖ 雨～在窗子上。The rain spattered against the window. ‖ 他经常～老婆。He often beats his wife. 2（打碎）break: 花瓶～了。The vase smashed. ▸鸡飞蛋～ 3（攻击）attack: ～一仗 wage a war ‖ 他和那伙人～了起来。He got into a punch-up with that gang. ▸～架，～援 4（捕猎）catch: ～鱼 catch fish ‖ ～野味 hunt wild game 5（收集）collect: ～柴 gather firewood ‖ 每亩地可～1,000斤粮食。One *mu* of land can yield 1,000 *jin* of grain. 6（汲取）draw: 从井里～水 draw water from a well 7（搅拌）mix: 把蛋清～匀 beat the egg white well ‖ 往锅里～两个鸡蛋 crack two eggs into a pan 8（修筑）build: ～坝 construct a dam ‖ ～墙 build a wall 9（制造）make: ～镰刀 forge a sickle ‖ ～家具 make furniture 10（挖掘）dig: ～井 dig a well ‖ ～眼儿 drill a hole 11（编织）knit: ～草帽儿 weave a straw hat ‖ ～毛衣 knit a sweater 12（标记号）draw: ～个问号 insert a question mark ‖ ～格子 draw squares 13（提或举）hold up: ～灯笼 carry a lantern ‖ ～伞 use an umbrella ‖ ～手电 flash a torch ‖〈喻〉～起精神 cheer up 14（收拾捆好）tie up: ～包裹 wrap up a package ‖ ～铺盖卷儿 pack up one's bedclothes 15（进行）do: ▸～禅，～埋伏 16（买）buy: ～醋 buy vinegar ‖ ～车票 buy a bus ticket 17（玩）play: ～扑克 play cards ‖ ～球 play ball games 18（写）write: ～报告 write a report ‖ ～底稿 make a draft 19（扣结）tie: ▸～结 20（去除）get rid of: ～蛔虫 cure sb. of intestinal worms ▸～尖，～胎 21（发出）fire: ～枪 fire a gun ‖ ～电话 make a phone call ▸～雷 22（加进）inject: ▸～点滴，～气 23（指说话方式）adopt a certain manner: ▸～官腔，～马虎眼 24（预算）estimate: 酒水～五十元 estimate the expenses for beverages at 50 *yuan* 25（想）design: ▸～算盘，～主意 26（办理）deal with: ▸～离婚 file for divorce ▸～官司，～交道 27（表动作发生）go through: ～踉跄 stagger ‖ ▸～手势 make gestures ▸～嗝儿，～滚 28（错定为）label sb. as: 他曾被～成现行反革命。He was labelled as an active counter-revolutionary. 29（指折扣）give a discount: ～九五折 give a discount of 5% 30（与及物动词连用）[used with another transitive verb to form a compound verb]: ▸～扮，～捞，～听 31（与不及物动词连用）[used with an intransitive verb to form a new verb]: ▸～败，～倒 32（表状态）[used with an adjective to form a compound word indicating a state]: ▸～蔫儿 33（脱粒）thresh: ～稻子 husk rice ‖ ～麦子 thresh wheat ▸～场

打[2] dǎ〈介〉〈口〉from: ～猫眼往外看 look out through a spyhole ‖ ～三月起，我再也没有抽过烟。I haven't smoked since March.
▸dá

【打熬】dǎ'áo〈动〉endure: 他在贫困山区～了三年。He scraped by in a poor mountainous area for three years.

【打把式】dǎ bǎshi = 打把势 dǎ bǎshi

【打把势】dǎ bǎshi〈动〉1（练武术）do *wushu* exercises 2（手舞足蹈）dance for joy

【打靶】dǎbǎ〈动〉shoot at a target: 练习～ practise target shooting ‖ ～场 shooting range

【打白条】dǎ báitiáo〈动〉1（指收据）write out a non-standard receipt 2（指欠条）make an IOU: 购买农民粮食不～ not deal with IOUs when purchasing grain from farmers

【打摆子】dǎ bǎizi〈动〉〈方〉contract malaria

【打败】dǎbài〈动〉1（战胜）beat: ～侵略者 defeat the invaders ‖ 甲队以3比1～了乙队。Team A beat Team B 3 to 1. 2（失败）be defeated: 这场比赛如果你们～了，就失去了决赛资格。If you lose

this match, then you won't be able to take part in the finals.

【打板子】dǎ bǎnzi〈惯〉 1〈本〉 flog 2〈喻〉(严惩) punish: 这件事我没办好，该～。 I should be punished for not doing the job well.

【打扮】dǎban A〈动〉 get dressed up: 把孩子们～得漂漂亮亮 get the children looking nice ‖ ～成知识分子模样 dress oneself up as an intellectual ‖ 节日的首都～得格外壮观。 The capital was magnificently decked out for the holiday. B〈名〉 way of dressing: 农民～ be dressed like a peasant ‖ 看他的～，像是城里来的。 He's from the city, by the looks of him.

【打榜】dǎbǎng〈动〉 enter the charts: ～歌曲 song in the charts

【打包】dǎbāo〈动〉 1(包装起来) pack: ～装箱 pack and crate ‖ ～机 packaging machine 2(指饭菜) put leftovers in a doggy bag

【打包票】dǎ bāopiào = 打保票 dǎ bǎopiào

【打苞】dǎbāo〈动〉［植物］ grow ears

【打保票】dǎ bǎopiào〈惯〉 vouch for: 我敢～，他不是干那种事的人。 I guarantee that he is not the type of person who would do such a thing.

【打抱不平】dǎ bàobùpíng〈惯〉 speak up for the interests of the oppressed

【打比】dǎbǐ〈动〉 1(比喻) draw an analogy: 讲话～容易使人理解。 You can make yourself better understood by drawing analogies. 2〈方〉(比较) compare: 他只不过是个小孩，怎能跟大人～呢？ He is only a child, so how can you compare him with an adult?

【打比方】dǎ bǐfāng = 打比 dǎbǐ 1

【打边鼓】dǎ biāngǔ = 敲边鼓 qiāo biāngǔ

【打表】dǎbiǎo〈动〉 start the taxi meter: 出租车司机必须～载客。 Taxi drivers must use the meter when taking passengers.

【打擦边球】dǎ cābiānqiú〈惯〉〈喻〉 hover on the fringes

【打不住】dǎbuzhù〈动〉 1(多于) be more than: 这台电脑五千元～。 This computer is worth more than 5,000 *yuan*. 2(无法停止) cannot stop

【打草】dǎcǎo〈动〉 cut grass

【打草惊蛇】dǎcǎo-jīngshé〈成〉〈喻〉 act rashly and alert the enemy: 秘密调查疑犯以免～ make a secret investigation so as not to alert the suspect

【打杈】dǎchà〈动〉 prune: 给西红柿～ prune the tomatoes

【打岔】dǎchà〈动〉 butt in: 别人说话时别～。 Don't butt in when other people are talking. ‖ 我工作的时候不喜欢别人～。 I don't like to be interrupted when I'm working.

【打禅】dǎchán〈动〉 [of a monk] sit in meditation

【打场】dǎcháng〈动〉 thresh grain

【打场子】dǎ chǎngzi〈动〉 attract an audience and form them into a circle

【打成一片】dǎchéngyīpiàn〈成〉 become one with: 跟群众～ be at one with the masses

【打赤膊】dǎ chìbó〈动〉 be naked to the waist: ～干活 do one's work stripped to the waist

【打冲锋】dǎ chōngfēng〈动〉 1(指战斗) make a charge: 这次战斗哪个连～？ Which company will charge the enemy in the battle? 2〈喻〉(指行动) be in the vanguard: 青年人应该在现代化建设中～。 Young people should be in the vanguard in the modernization drive.

【打憷】dǎchù〈动〉 flinch: 遇到困难就～ tend to flinch from any difficulty

【打春】dǎchūn〈口〉= 立春 lìchūn

【打从】dǎcóng〈介〉 1(自从) since: ～小时侯起，他就爱唱歌。 He has loved singing since childhood. 2(经过) by: ～他家门前经过 pass by his house

【打打闹闹】dǎdǎ-nàonào〈动〉 fight in jest or for fun

【打蛋器】dǎdànqì〈名〉 egg-whisk

【打倒】dǎdǎo〈动〉 1(击倒) floor: ～在地 knock flat ‖ 他在第一个回合就把对手～了。 He floored his opponent in the first round. 2(推翻) topple: ～霸权主义！ Down with hegemony! ‖ 他被～了。 He was overthrown.

【打道】dǎdào〈动〉 clear the way: ～回府 go back home

【打得火热】dǎde huǒrè〈惯〉 1(指关系) be as thick as thieves 2(指爱情) be madly in love with each other

【打的】dǎdī〈动〉〈方〉 take a taxi: ～回家 take a taxi home

【打底子】dǎ dǐzi 1(起草) sketch: 写文章之前先打个底子。 Before you write an article, you should sketch it out first. 2(垫底) put sth. at the bottom: 地面用三合土～ put a layer of lime, sand and clay at the bottom of the floor 3(打基础) lay a foundation: 不论学什么都要先打好底子。 Whatever you learn, you must lay good foundations first.

【打点滴】dǎ diǎndī〈动〉 put sb. on a drip

【打点】dǎdian〈动〉 1(收拾) prepare: ～行装 pack one's belongings 2(送人钱财) bribe for a favour: 上下～ bribe for favours at all levels

【打叠】dǎdié〈动〉 get ready: ～行李 pack one's luggage

【打动】dǎdòng〈动〉 move: ～观众的心弦 touch the heartstrings of the audience ‖ 他的话深深地～了我。 His words moved me deeply.

【打洞机】dǎdòngjī〈名〉 perforator

【打斗】dǎdòu〈动〉 fight: 影片中的～场面扣人心弦。 The fight scenes in the film were breathtaking.

【打嘟噜】dǎ dūlu〈动〉 speak with a lisp

【打赌】dǎdǔ〈动〉 make a bet: 我敢～他明天不会来。 I bet he won't come tomorrow.

【打短工】dǎ duǎngōng〈动〉 work as a casual labourer

【打断】dǎduàn〈动〉 1(使断) break: ～脊梁 break the backbone 2(使中断) interrupt: ～思路 interrupt a train of thought ‖ 别～他的话。 Don't cut him short.

【打断骨头连着筋】dǎduàn gǔtou liánzhe jīn〈俗〉 maintain a strong bond despite some hiccups

【打盹儿】dǎdǔnr〈动〉 have a nap: 打个盹儿 have a nap ‖ 他白天老是～。 He kept dozing off during the day.

【打趸儿】dǎdǔnr〈副〉〈口〉 1(成批) wholesale: 这箱肥皂是我们～买来的。 We bought this box of soap wholesale. 2(归总) altogether: 所有人的加班费请～领去。 Please collect up everybody's overtime payments.

【打顿】dǎdùn〈动〉 pause: 他讲话老～。 He made too many pauses in his speech.

【打耳光】dǎ ěrguāng〈动〉 box sb.'s ears: 自己打自己的耳光 box one's own ears

【打发】dǎfa〈动〉 1(派) dispatch sb. on an errand: ～人去叫医生 send for a doctor 2(使离去) dismiss: 老板～掉了几名懒散的员工。 The boss dismissed several sluggish workers. 3(消磨) kill time: 他靠读小说来～时间。 He whiled away his time reading novels. 4(安排) make arrangements: ～客人住下 arrange accommodation for a guest

【打翻身仗】dǎ fānshēnzhàng〈惯〉〈喻〉 work hard for a change for the better

【打非】dǎfēi〈动〉 combat illegal publication and marketing: 扫黄～ clamp down on pornography and illegal publications

【打榧子】dǎ fěizi〈动〉 snap one's fingers

【打分】dǎfēn〈动〉 give a mark: 给试卷～ mark examination papers

【打嗝儿】dǎgér〈动〉 1(指冷嗝) hiccup 2(指饱嗝) burp

【打更】dǎgēng〈动〉 sound the night watches

【打埂】dǎgěng〈动〉［农业］ ridge

【打工】dǎgōng ▸p. 966〈动〉 do temporary work: ～妹 female worker ‖ ～仔 labourer

【打躬作揖】dǎgōng-zuòyī〈成〉 bow and scrape

【打钩】dǎgōu〈动〉 tick: 对的～，错的划叉 put a tick against the correct ones and a cross against the wrong ones

【打谷场】dǎgǔchǎng〈名〉 threshing ground

【打鼓】dǎgǔ〈动〉〈喻〉 feel uncertain: 不知道能不能及格，我心里直～。 I am very nervous about whether or not I will pass.

【打卦】dǎguà〈动〉 practise divination by casting lots on the ground

【打拐】dǎguǎi〈动〉 crack down on abduction and people trafficking

【打官腔】dǎ guānqiāng〈惯〉 talk like a bureaucrat: 他爱～。 He always speaks like an official.

【打官司】dǎ guānsi〈动〉 bring a case to court

【打光棍儿】dǎ guānggùnr〈动〉 remain a bachelor

【打鬼】dǎguǐ = 跳布扎 tiào bùzhá

【打滚】dǎgǔn〈动〉 1(滚动) roll about: 疼得直～ writhe in agony ‖ 连连～ roll over and over 2〈喻〉(生活) live somewhere for a long time: 他从小在农村～长大。 He was born and brought up in the countryside.

【打棍子】dǎ gùnzi〈惯〉〈喻〉 criticize or accuse without foundation

【打哈哈】dǎ hāha〈惯〉 joke: 别跟我～。 Don't make fun of me. ‖ 这是正经事，你可别～。 This is a serious matter. You'd better not joke about it.

【打哈欠】dǎ hāqian〈动〉 yawn

【打鼾】dǎhān〈动〉 snore

【打寒战】dǎ hánzhàn〈动〉 shiver with cold

【打寒颤】dǎ hánzhàn = 打寒战 dǎ hánzhàn

【打夯】dǎhāng〈动〉 ram: ～机 ramming machine

【打黑】dǎhēi〈动〉 combat underworld gangs: 扫黄～ clamp down on pornography and underworld gangs

【打横】dǎhéng〈动〉 take the least important seat at a square table during a formal dinner

【打横炮】dǎ héngpào〈惯〉〈喻〉 deliberately complicate matters

【打呼】dǎhū = 打呼噜 dǎ hūlu

【打呼噜】dǎ hūlu〈动〉 snore

【打滑】dǎhuá〈动〉 1(指车轮或皮带轮) skid: 防止～ forestall skidding 2〈方〉(指路面) slip: 两脚在冰上直～ one's feet

keep slipping on the ice

【打晃儿】dǎhuàngr〈动〉stagger: 孩子刚一岁，走路还有点～。The child has just turned one and still can't walk steadily.

【打诨】dǎhùn〈动〉[of a clown in traditional Chinese opera] make a joke: ▸插科～

【打火】dǎhuǒ〈动〉produce a flame

【打火机】dǎhuǒjī〈名〉cigarette lighter

【打火枪】dǎhuǒqiāng〈名〉lighter

【打火石】dǎhuǒshí〈名〉flint

【打伙儿】dǎhuǒr〈动〉〈口〉team up: 上个星期天他们几个人～去农贸市场买菜。They went to the farmers' market together last Sunday to buy vegetables.

【打击】dǎjī〈动〉**1**（敲打）strike: ▸～乐器 **2**（攻击）attack: ～报复 take revenge ‖ ～犯罪活动 fight crime ‖ 对违法事件～不力 impose insufficient punishment for illegal activities ‖ 给侵略者以毁灭性的～ deal the invaders/aggressors a crushing blow ‖ 严厉～ launch a tough crackdown **3**（使受挫）put down: ～群众的积极性 dampen the enthusiasm of the masses

【打击乐器】dǎjī yuèqì〈名〉percussion instruments: 鼓、铃鼓和铙钹都属于～。Drums, tambourines and cymbals are all percussion instruments.

【打饥荒】dǎ jīhuang〈惯〉〈喻〉be in financial difficulties

【打家劫舍】dǎjiā-jiéshè〈成〉rob houses

【打假】dǎjiǎ〈动〉crack down on counterfeits: ～活动 anti-fakery activity

【打价】dǎjià〈动〉〈口〉bargain: 不～儿! No bargaining!

【打架】dǎjià〈动〉have a fight: 为点小事跟人～ fight with sb. over something trivial

【打尖】dǎjiān〈动〉**1**（停留）make a brief refreshment stop **2**［农业］remove the top: 给棉花～ top the cotton plants

【打江山】dǎ jiāngshān〈动〉fight for control of the country

【打交道】dǎ jiāodao〈惯〉have dealings with: 要学会跟各种各样的人～。One must learn to mix with all sorts of people.

【打脚】dǎjiǎo〈动〉〈方〉pinch: 这双鞋～。These shoes pinch.

【打搅】dǎjiǎo〈动〉**1**（扰乱）disturb: 他在睡觉，别去～了。He's sleeping. Don't disturb him. **2** ▸**p. 156**〈婉〉（麻烦）[used to show one's thanks for sb.'s hospitality]: ～您了，再见。Sorry to have troubled you. See you later.

【打醮】dǎjiào〈动〉［道教］perform a Taoist ritual

【打劫】dǎjié〈动〉pillage: ▸趁火～

【打结】dǎjié〈动〉tie a knot

【打紧】dǎjǐn〈形〉〈方〉serious: 缺一个人不～。It makes no difference with one person absent.

【打救】dǎjiù〈动〉rescue

【打卡】dǎkǎ〈动〉punch a card: 上下班～ punch in and out ‖ ～机 card punch

【打开】dǎkāi〈动〉**1**（使开）open: ～包裹 open up a package ‖ ～窗子/书本 open a window/book ‖ 保险柜打不开。The safe won't open. **2**（接通）turn on: ～电视机/煤气/水龙头 turn on the TV/gas/tap **3**（使扩展）bring about a new situation: ～局面 open up new prospects ‖ ～思路 broaden one's mind ‖ ～销路 develop new markets

【打开天窗说亮话】dǎkāi tiānchuāng shuō liànghuà〈俗〉put all one's cards on the table

【打瞌睡】dǎ kēshuì〈动〉nod off: 上课～ doze off in class

【打孔机】dǎkǒngjī〈名〉puncher

【打垮】dǎkuǎ〈动〉thrash: ～敌人的精锐师团 destroy the enemy's crack division

【打蜡】dǎlà〈动〉wax: 给地板～ wax the floor

【打捞】dǎlāo〈动〉recover: ～沉船 salvage a sunken boat ‖ ～船 rescue ship

【打雷】dǎléi〈动〉thunder: 外面在～。It's thundering outside.

【打擂台】dǎ lèitái〈惯〉take up a challenge in a contest

【打冷枪】dǎ lěngqiāng〈惯〉**1**（指开枪）shoot at individuals from a concealed position **2**〈喻〉（暗算）stab sb. in the back: 向前任～ snipe at one's predecessor

【打冷战】dǎ lěngzhan〈动〉shiver with cold or fear

【打冷颤】dǎ lěngzhan = 打冷战 dǎ lěngzhan

【打愣】dǎlèng〈动〉〈方〉be in a daze

【打理】dǎlǐ〈动〉arrange: ～公司业务 manage company business ‖ ～家务 take care of domestic affairs

【打量】dǎliang〈动〉**1**（观察）look sb. up and down: 他们两个相互～着。The two of them were sizing each other up. ‖ 她转过身来～着他。She turned and looked him up and down. **2**（以为）suppose: 你还想瞒着我，～我不知道？So you still want to keep me in the dark, thinking that I know nothing about it?

【打猎】dǎliè〈动〉go hunting: 禁止～ ban hunting

【打零】dǎlíng〈动〉〈方〉**1**（做零工）do odd jobs: ～的花匠 jobbing gardener **2**（孤单一人）be alone

【打零工】dǎ línggōng = 打零 dǎlíng 1

【打乱】dǎluàn〈动〉disrupt: ～计划 mess up a plan ‖ 暴风雪～了我们的节日安排。The snowstorm played havoc with our holiday plans.

【打落水狗】dǎ luòshuǐgǒu〈惯〉destroy a defeated enemy

【打麻将】dǎ májiàng〈动〉play mah-jong

【打马虎眼】dǎ mǎhuyǎn〈惯〉act dumb

【打埋伏】dǎ máifu〈动〉**1**（伏击）lie in ambush **2**〈喻〉（隐瞒）hold back: 实话实说，别跟我～。I want the truth, so don't hold anything back from me.

【打闷棍】dǎ mèngùn〈惯〉**1**（指抢劫）rob sb. by beating him unconscious with a club **2**〈喻〉（指打击）give sb. a stunning blow

【打鸣儿】dǎmíngr〈动〉〈口〉crow: 公鸡～。Roosters crow.

【打磨】dǎmó〈动〉polish: ～铜制门把 polish a brass doorknob

【打闹】dǎnào〈动〉**1**（玩耍）play in a boisterous way **2**（争斗）quarrel and fight

【打蔫儿】dǎniānr〈动〉〈口〉**1**（指植物）wilt **2**（指人）be listless: 天热得人直～。The heat is making people listless.

【打牌】dǎpái〈动〉**1**（指娱乐）play cards or mah-jong: 打一局桥牌 have a round of bridge **2**〈喻〉（指利用）make use of sth. to attain one's objective: 打中国牌 play the China card

【打泡】dǎpào〈动〉get a blister: 手上～ get blisters on one's hand

【打屁股】dǎ pìgu〈动〉〈喻〉take sb. to task

【打拼】dǎpīn〈动〉go all out

【打平】dǎpíng〈动〉draw: 甲队和乙队以二比二～。Team A and Team B drew 2:2.

【打平手】dǎ píngshǒu〈动〉draw: 甲乙两队打了个平手。It was a draw between Team A and Team B.

【打破】dǎpò〈动〉**1**（打碎）break into pieces: ～花瓶 smash a vase **2**（突破）put an end to: ～地区壁垒 break regional barriers ‖ ～常规 break conventions ‖ ～记录 break a record ‖ ～僵局 break a deadlock

【打破砂锅问到底】dǎpò shāguō wèn dàodǐ〈俗〉〈喻〉insist on getting to the bottom of sth.

【打气】dǎqì〈动〉**1**（充气）pump up: 给篮球～ pump up a basketball ‖ 给轮胎～ pump up a tyre **2**（加油）cheer up: 人们叫喊着为球员们～。The crowd yelled encouragement at the players.

【打气筒】dǎqìtǒng〈名〉pump

【打千】dǎqiān〈动〉〈旧〉salute

【打钎】dǎqiān〈动〉drill with a hammer and a rock drill

【打前失】dǎ qiánshi〈动〉[of a horse, donkey etc.] stumble

【打前站】dǎ qiánzhàn〈动〉make advance arrangements: 为总理的访问～ make advance preparations for the Premier's visit

【打枪】dǎqiāng〈动〉**1**（指枪弹）fire a shot **2** = 枪替 qiāngtì

【打情骂俏】dǎqíng-màqiào〈成〉flirt

【打秋风】dǎ qiūfēng〈惯〉extort money under false pretences

【打趣】dǎqù〈动〉joke about: 拿小孩～ tease a kid

【打圈子】dǎ quānzi = 兜圈子 dōu quānzi

【打拳】dǎquán〈动〉do shadow-boxing

【打群架】dǎ qúnjià〈动〉engage in gang fighting

【打扰】dǎrǎo〈动〉**1**（扰乱）disturb: 请勿～。Please do not disturb. **2** ▸**p. 156**〈婉〉（麻烦）bother: ～多日，非常感谢! Thanks for going to so much trouble for me the last few days. ‖ 我希望没有～你。I hope I am not intruding.

【打入】dǎrù〈动〉**1**（关入）throw into: ～地牢 be thrown into a dungeon ‖ ～闷葫芦 throw into bewilderment ‖ ～十八层地狱 condemn to eternal damnation ▸～冷宫 **2**（进入）get access to: ～决赛 make it to the finals ‖ ～国际市场 break into the world market

【打入冷宫】dǎrù lěnggōng〈惯〉**1**（指嫔妃）banish (a disfavoured empress or imperial concubine) to a deserted place **2**〈喻〉（不予理睬）leave sb. out in the cold

【打扫】dǎsǎo〈动〉sweep: ～院子 sweep the yard ‖ ～战场 clean up the battlefield

【打闪】dǎshǎn〈动〉flash: 天上又打雷又～。Thunder roared and lightning flashed across the sky.

【打扇】dǎshàn〈动〉fan

【打食】dǎshí〈动〉**1**（指鸟兽）search for food **2**（指人）aid bowel movement

【打手】dǎshou〈名〉hatchet man

【打水漂】dǎ shuǐpiāo〈惯〉**1**（本）play ducks and drakes: 用石块在水池上～ skim a stone across the pond ‖ 石块在湖面上～。The stone skipped across the lake. **2**〈喻〉（指钱）squander: 他把钱打了水漂。He played loose with his money.

【打私】dǎsī〈动〉crack down on smuggling and the sale of contraband

【打死老虎】dǎ sǐlǎohǔ〈惯〉〈喻〉attack those who are no longer in power

【打算】dǎsuàn **A**〈动〉plan: ～去北京一游 plan on going to Beijing for a visit ‖ 他真～跟她结婚吗? Does he have any intention of marrying her? **B**〈名〉plan: 长远

～ long-term plan ‖ 另有～ intend otherwise ‖ 你对将来有什么～? What's your plan for the future?

【打算盘】dǎ suànpán〈动〉**1**〈本〉use an abacus **2**〈合计〉calculate: 爱打小算盘的人 person of calculating mind ‖ 打错算盘 miscalculate ‖ 打如意算盘 hatch a crazy plan ‖ 打小算盘 show petty shrewdness

【打胎】dǎtāi〈动〉〈口〉have an abortion

【打太极拳】dǎ tàijíquán〈动〉**1**〈本〉practise tai chi **2**〈喻〉dodge and shirk

【打探】dǎtàn〈动〉look into: ～别人的秘密 pry into other people's secrets

【打天下】dǎ tiānxià **1**〈指政权〉seize state power by armed force **2**〈喻〉〈指事业〉establish an enterprise

【打铁】dǎtiě〈动〉〈口〉forge iron

【打铁先得本身硬】dǎtiě xiān děi běnshēn yìng〈俗〉〈喻〉to do a job well, one must be highly competent

【打挺儿】dǎtǐngr〈动〉〈方〉bend backwards

【打听】dǎting〈动〉enquire about: ～别人的秘密 pry into other people's secrets ‖ ～消息 ask for information ‖ 四处～ ask around

【打通】dǎtōng〈动〉**1**〈使无隔断〉make an opening: 把两间屋子～ knock down a wall between two rooms **2**〈喻〉〈使无障碍〉get through barriers: ～关节 persuade key people ‖ ～思想 talk sb. round

【打头】dǎtóu **A**〈动〉take the lead: 在各项工作中～ take the lead in doing everything ‖ 谁来打个头? Who'd like to be the first? **B**〈副〉〈方〉from the beginning: ～重来吧。Let's start afresh.

【打头炮】dǎ tóupào〈惯〉〈喻〉be the first to act or speak

【打头阵】dǎ tóuzhèn〈惯〉fight in the van: 青年人应该在现代化建设中～。Young people should spearhead the modernization drive.

【打退堂鼓】dǎ tuìtánggǔ〈惯〉**1**〈指击鼓〉beat the drum before the magistrate withdraws from the court **2**〈喻〉〈退缩〉beat a retreat: 遇到困难就～ back away from a problem ‖ 现在～为时已晚。It is too late to back out now.

【打围】dǎwéi〈动〉**1**〈围捕野兽〉encircle and hunt down animals **2**〈打猎〉go hunting

【打问】dǎwèn〈动〉ask about sth./sb.: 把事情的前因后果～清楚 uncover the ins and outs of a matter

【打问号】dǎ wènhào〈惯〉raise a question about: 我们对对方的诚意打了个问号。We had doubts about the sincerity of the other party.

【打戏】dǎxì〈名〉martial arts drama

【打下手】dǎ xiàshǒu〈动〉assist: 我来给你～。I'll be your assistant.

【打先锋】dǎ xiānfēng〈动〉**1**〈指战争〉be the vanguard **2**〈喻〉〈带头奋进〉take the lead: 在经济改革中～ spearhead the economic reform

【打响】dǎxiǎng〈动〉**1**〈开火〉begin shooting: 战斗于午夜～。Fighting started at midnight. **2**〈初步成功〉win initial success: ～春耕第一炮 make a good start in the spring ploughing ‖ 一炮～ make an instantaneous hit

【打响指】dǎ xiǎngzhǐ〈动〉snap one's fingers

【打消】dǎxiāo〈动〉dismiss: ～顾虑 dismiss one's misgivings ‖ ～念头 abandon an idea

【打小报告】dǎ xiǎobàogào〈动〉rat on sb.

【打旋】dǎxuán〈动〉spin

【打雪仗】dǎ xuězhàng〈动〉have a snowball fight

【打压】dǎyā〈动〉combat and suppress

【打鸭子上架】dǎ yāzi shàng jià = 赶鸭子上架 gǎn yāzi shàng jià

【打牙祭】dǎ yájì〈动〉〈方〉have a square meal occasionally

【打哑谜】dǎ yǎmí〈动〉speak in riddles

【打掩护】dǎ yǎnhù〈动〉**1**〈指作战〉shield: 你们留在这儿～。You stay here to provide cover for us. **2**〈喻〉〈遮掩〉cover up: 实情我们都知道了，你用不着～。We've found out the truth. It's no use trying to cover it up any more.

【打眼】dǎyǎn **A**〈动〉**1**〈钻孔〉make a hole **2**〈方〉〈快速一瞥〉cast a glance at: 他～一看，果然是他丢失的那块表。He glanced at it and found it was the very watch he had lost. **3**〈方〉〈上当〉fail to detect the flaw in the goods one buys **B**〈形〉〈方〉eye-catching: 你的新衣服挺～。Your new dress is quite eye-catching.

【打样】dǎyàng〈动〉**1**〈指设计图样〉draw a design **2**［印刷］make a proof

【打烊】dǎyàng〈动〉〈方〉close for the night: ～时间 closing time ‖ 那家杂货店晚上九点～。The general store closes at 9 o'clock in the evening.

【打噎】dǎyē〈动〉**1**〈打嗝〉belch **2**〈哽住〉choke

【打印】dǎyìn〈动〉**1**〈盖章〉put a seal on **2**〈打字印刷〉cut a stencil and mimeograph **3**〈用打印机〉print: ～文件 print documents ‖ 激光～ laser-print

【打印机】dǎyìnjī〈名〉printer: 激光～ laser printer ‖ 喷墨～ ink-jet printer ‖ 远程～ remote printer

【打油诗】dǎyóushī〈名〉doggerel

【打游击】dǎ yóujī〈惯〉**1**〈指打仗〉engage in guerrilla warfare **2**〈诙〉〈指工作或活动〉live or eat at no fixed abode

【打预防针】dǎyùfángzhēn〈惯〉〈喻〉caution against

【打圆场】dǎ yuánchǎng〈动〉mediate a dispute: 他很会替人～。He is a good mediator.

【打援】dǎyuán〈动〉attack enemy reinforcements: 围城～ besiege a city so as to strike at the enemy reinforcements

【打杂儿】dǎzár〈动〉do odd jobs: ～的 odd jobs man

【打早】dǎzǎo〈副〉**1**〈很久以前〉long ago **2**〈尽早〉as early as possible

【打造】dǎzào〈动〉make: ～农具 make farm tools ‖ ～中国的硅谷 build China's Silicon Valley

【打战】dǎzhàn〈动〉tremble: 他冷得牙齿直～。He was so cold his teeth were chattering.

【打颤】dǎzhàn = 打战 dǎzhàn

【打仗】dǎzhàng〈动〉go to war: 打败仗 lose a battle ‖ 打胜仗 win a battle ‖〈喻〉在生产战线上打个漂亮仗 make remarkable achievements in production

【打招呼】dǎ zhāohu〈动〉**1**〈问候〉greet: 在回家路上跟熟人～ say hello to an acquaintance on the road home **2**〈通知〉forewarn: 你来也不事先打个招呼。You should have let me know about your arrival beforehand.

【打照面儿】dǎ zhàomiànr〈动〉**1**〈相遇〉have a face-to-face encounter **2**〈露面〉make a brief appearance: 他打了个照面儿就走了。He just showed his face and then left.

【打折】dǎzhé〈动〉give a discount: 按货价打八折 allow a discount of 20% on the prices of goods

【打折扣】dǎ zhékòu〈动〉**1**〈指价格〉give a discount: 要是付现金，可以～吗? Do you allow any discount for cash? **2**〈喻〉〈指行为做事〉detract from the desired quality: 执法不能～。We must enforce the law properly.

【打褶】dǎzhě〈动〉pleat: 给围裙～ pleat an apron

【打针】dǎzhēn〈动〉**1**〈指医生〉give an injection **2**〈指病人〉have an injection: 打流感针 be injected against flu

【打肿脸充胖子】dǎzhǒng liǎn chōng pàngzi〈俗〉puff oneself up: 人家都知道我们快要破产了，何必还～。There's no point in keeping up appearances when everyone knows we're nearly bankrupt.

【打中】dǎzhòng〈动〉hit the mark: ～要害 hit the vital spot

【打皱】dǎzhòu〈动〉crease: 脸上～ have wrinkles on one's face ‖ 这种布容易～。This cloth crumples easily.

【打主意】dǎ zhǔyi〈动〉devise a plan: 打定主意 make up one's mind ‖ 你另～吧。You'd better try and find other ways.

【打住】dǎzhù〈动〉come to a halt: 他讲了半截突然～了。He stopped short in the middle of his story.

【打转】dǎzhuàn〈动〉**1**〈旋转〉spin: 陀螺在地上～。The top is spinning on the ground. **2**〈喻〉〈绕圈子〉go round: 别老在家里～，出去找点活儿干吧。Don't just hang about the house. Go out and find some work to do.

【打桩】dǎzhuāng〈动〉pile: ～机 pile driver

【打字】dǎzì〈动〉type: ～机 typewriter ‖ ～员 typist

【打总儿】dǎzǒngr〈动〉〈口〉deal with at one go: ～买 buy wholesale ‖ ～算账 settle accounts once and for all

【打嘴】dǎzuǐ〈动〉**1**〈打嘴巴〉slap sb. on the cheek **2**〈方〉〈出丑〉make a fool of oneself by boasting

【打嘴仗】dǎ zuǐzhàng〈动〉quarrel

【打坐】dǎzuò〈动〉[of a monk] sit in meditation

dà

大[1] dà

A〈形〉**1**〈指体积、数量、面积〉big: ～地震 massive earthquake ‖ ～发展 great development ‖ ～工程 large project ‖ 风越刮越～。The wind is getting up. **2**〈指排行〉eldest: ▸～哥，老～ **3**〈敬〉〈指对方〉your: 尊姓～名 your name ▸～作 **4**〈表强调〉[used before words indicating time or festival for emphasis]: ～清早 very early in the morning ▸～白天，～年三十

B〈名〉**1**〈指大小程度〉size: 那间房子有多～? How big is that room? **2**〈指年纪〉age: 你的女儿现在多～了? How old is your daughter? **3**〈成年人〉adult: 一家～小 whole family

C〈副〉very: ～不相同 be very different ‖ 不～舒服 not be very well ‖ 天～亮了。It is already broad daylight. ▸～吃一惊，～失所望

大[2] dà〈名〉〈方〉**1**〈父亲〉father: 俺～ my dad **2**〈叔伯〉uncle: 二～ father's second younger brother ▸dài

【大安】dà'ān〈形〉1 (有秩序) quite orderly 2 (健康) very healthy: 顺颂～ wishing you well
【大巴】dàbā〈名〉〈方〉bus
【大白】dàbái A〈名〉〈方〉whiting B〈动〉become known: ～于天下 become known to all ‖ 真相已经～。The truth has come out.
【大白菜】dàbáicài〈名〉Chinese cabbage
【大白话】dàbáihuà〈名〉colloquial speech
【大白天】dàbáitiān〈名〉daytime
【大白天说梦话】dàbáitiān shuō mènghuà〈俗〉daydream talk
【大伯子】dàbǎizi〈名〉〈方〉brother-in-law [husband's elder brother]
【大败】dàbài〈动〉1 (打败) defeat utterly: 甲队～乙队。Team A smashed Team B. 2 (被打败) suffer a crushing hefty defeat
【大班】dàbān〈名〉1〈旧〉〈方〉(经理) taipan [foreign head of a business in China] 2 (指幼儿园) top class

> **大班**
> A term originally used in the 19th century for foreign businessmen working on the Chinese Mainland and Hong Kong. Today it is still used in Hong Kong to describe the manager or head of a company.

【大阪】Dàbǎn〈名〉Osaka
【大板车】dàbǎnchē〈名〉large flatbed tricycle
【大半】dàbàn A ▸p. 927〈数〉more than half: ～年 better part of a year ‖ 这家工厂里～是妇女。Most of the workers in this factory are women. B〈副〉most probably: 她～不来了。Most likely she won't come.
【大饱眼福】dàbǎoyǎnfú〈成〉feast one's eyes (on sth.): 下周的电影节可以让影迷们～。Next week's film festival should be a real feast for cinema-goers.
【大鸨】dàbǎo〈名〉［鸟类］great bustard
【大暴雨】dàbàoyǔ〈名〉heavy downpour
【大本营】dàběnyíng〈名〉1 (指军队) supreme headquarters 2 (指活动) base camp
【大便】dàbiàn A〈名〉faeces B〈动〉defecate
【大兵】dàbīng〈名〉1〈贬〉(指士兵) soldier 2 (指部队) powerful army
【大兵团】dàbīngtuán〈名〉large troop formation: ～作战 large formation warfare
【大伯】dàbó〈名〉〈口〉uncle
【大不敬】dàbùjìng〈形〉〈旧〉disrespectful: 你这是对父母的～。You are showing disrespect to your parents by doing this.
【大不列颠】Dàbùlièdiān〈名〉Great Britain: ～及北爱尔兰联合王国 United Kingdom of Great Britain and Northern Ireland (UK)
【大不了】dàbuliǎo A〈副〉at worst: 怕什么? ～不当官就是了。What's there to be afraid of? At the worst, I will be dismissed from my post. B〈形〉terrible, serious: 这件事没什么～，别担心。Don't worry. It's nothing serious.
【大步流星】dàbù-liúxīng〈成〉walk with big strides
【大部分】dàbùfen〈名〉majority: ～地区 most of the regions ‖ 一年的～时间 the best part of a year
【大部头】dàbùtóu〈名〉tome
【大材小用】dàcái-xiǎoyòng〈成〉〈喻〉make little use of a great talent: 让你当打字员是～。The job of a typist is beneath you.
【大菜】dàcài〈名〉1 (主菜) main course 2 (西餐) Western-style food
【大餐】dàcān〈名〉1 (指饭食) square meal:〈喻〉音乐～ musical feast 2 (指西餐) Western-style food: 圣诞～ Christmas dinner
【大肠】dàcháng〈名〉［生理］large intestine
【大肠杆菌】dàcháng gǎnjūn〈名〉colon bacillus
【大氅】dàchǎng〈名〉〈旧〉overcoat: 披个～ wear a cloak
【大钞】dàchāo〈名〉large denomination banknote
【大潮】dàcháo〈名〉1 (指潮水) high tide 2〈喻〉(指潮流) social trend: 改革～ megatrend of reform
【大车】dàchē〈名〉1 (指车) cart: 赶～ drive a cart ‖ ～店 inn for carters 2〈尊〉(指人) (火车上) train driver; (船上) ship driver
【大彻大悟】dàchè-dàwù〈成〉attain supreme enlightenment
【大臣】dàchén〈名〉cabinet minister
【大乘】dàchéng〈名〉［佛教］Mahayana
【大吃大喝】dàchī-dàhē〈成〉indulge oneself in drinking and dining
【大吃一惊】dàchī-yījīng〈成〉be dumbfounded: 这消息让他们～。They were speechless at the news.
【大冲】dàchōng〈名〉［天文］favourable opposition
【大虫】dàchóng〈名〉〈方〉tiger
【大出血】dàchūxuè〈名〉massive haemorrhage
【大处落墨】dàchù-luòmò〈成〉focus on key points
【大处着眼，小处着手】dàchù zhuóyǎn, xiǎochù zhuóshǒu〈成〉keep the ultimate goal in mind whilst tackling the day-to-day
【大吹大擂】dàchuī-dàléi〈成〉talk big
【大吹法螺】dàchuī-fǎluó〈成〉talk big
【大锤】dàchuí〈名〉sledgehammer
【大春】dàchūn〈名〉〈方〉1 (指季节) spring 2 (指作物) spring-sown crop
【大春作物】dàchūn zuòwù = 大春 dàchūn 2
【大醇小疵】dàchún-xiǎocī〈成〉be sound as a whole but flawed in details
【大慈大悲】dàcí-dàbēi〈成〉be infinitely compassionate and merciful
【大葱】dàcōng〈名〉spring onion〈英〉; scallion〈美〉
【大错特错】dàcuò-tècuò〈成〉be as wrong as wrong can be: 你～了，她不是我爱人。You've got it all wrong! She is not my wife.
【大打出手】dàdǎ-chūshǒu〈成〉come to blows: 他们因为裁判的判决而～。They came to blows over the referee's ruling.
【大大】dàdà〈副〉greatly: 开支～超过了收入。The spending vastly exceeded the income.
【大大】dàda〈名〉〈方〉1 (伯父) uncle [one's father's older brother] 2 (父亲) dad
【大大咧咧】dàda-liēliē〈形〉casual: 他总是～的样子，但做事可不含糊。He is casual in manner, but he does everything in great earnest.
【大袋鼠】dàdàishǔ〈名〉［动物］kangaroo
【大胆】dàdǎn〈形〉bold: ～创新 dare to innovate ‖ ～的计划 plan of great daring
【大刀】dàdāo〈名〉broadsword
【大刀阔斧】dàdāo-kuòfǔ〈成〉〈喻〉bold and resolute: ～地改组政府 drastically reshuffle the government
【大道】dàdào〈名〉1 (指道路) main road 2 (指理想) way of virtue and justice
【大道理】dàdàolǐ〈名〉general principle: 小道理服从～。Minor principles are subordinated to major ones.
【大灯】dàdēng〈名〉headlight (of a car)
【大堤】dàdī〈名〉dyke
【大敌】dàdí〈名〉arch rival: 他的粗心是他的～。His carelessness is his worst enemy. ‖〈喻〉腐败是经济建设的～。Corruption is disastrous to economic construction. ▸如临～
【大敌当前】dàdí-dāngqián〈成〉be faced with a dangerous enemy
【大抵】dàdǐ〈副〉approximately: ～如此 more or less like this ‖ ～相同 approximately the same
【大地】dàdì〈名〉earth: ～回春。Spring is back again.
【大地原点】dàdì yuándiǎn〈名〉geodetic origin
【大典】dàdiǎn〈名〉1 (典礼) grand ceremony: 开国～ grand founding ceremony 2〈书〉(典籍) tome of classical writings: 《永乐～》*Yongle Canon* 3〈书〉(法令) state institutions
【大殿】dàdiàn〈名〉1 (旧时官府中) audience hall 2 (寺庙中) main hall of a Buddhist temple
【大调】dàdiào〈名〉［音乐］major: A～ A major ‖ C～音阶 scale of C major
【大动干戈】dàdòng-gāngē〈成〉1 (指战争) get into a fight 2〈喻〉(指做事) do sth. in a big way
【大动肝火】dàdòng-gānhuǒ〈成〉fly into a rage
【大动脉】dàdòngmài〈名〉1［生理］aorta 2〈喻〉(干道) artery: 交通～ artery of communications
【大豆】dàdòu〈名〉soya bean
【大都】dàdū〈副〉mostly: 这儿的学生～来自农村。Most of the students here come from the countryside.
【大都市】dàdūshì〈名〉metropolis: ～人 metropolitan ‖ ～的夜生活 night life of the metropolis
【大肚子】dàdùzi〈名〉〈口〉1 (指肚子大) potbelly 2 (指饭量大) heavy eater 3 (指怀孕) pregnant woman
【大度】dàdù〈形〉〈书〉magnanimous: ～之举 generous gesture ‖ 他很～。He has a big heart. ▸豁达～
【大端】dàduān〈名〉〈书〉main features: 举其～ point out the main features
【大队】dàduì〈名〉1 (指部队组织) brigade: 飞行～ aviation brigade 2 (指生产组织) brigade: 生产～ production brigade 3 (指队伍) large group: ～人马 a large contingent of troops
【大多】dàduō〈副〉mostly: 他们～不同意我的意见。Most of them disagreed with me.
【大多数】dàduōshù〈名〉vast majority: ～城市人口 majority of the urban population ‖ ～人赞成这个方案。The majority supported the plan.
【大额】dà'é〈形〉large in sum: ～存单 certificate of a large deposit ‖ ～现金 large amounts of cash
【大恩大德】dà'ēn-dàdé〈成〉great kindness: 受某人的～ owe sb. a vast debt of gratitude
【大而化之】dà'érhuàzhī〈成〉casually
【大而无当】dà'érwúdàng〈成〉be big but impractical
【大发雷霆】dàfā-léitíng〈成〉be furious: 他～。He boiled over with rage.
【大法】dàfǎ〈名〉1 (宪法) constitution 2〈书〉(重要法律) major statute
【大法官】dàfǎguān〈名〉chief justice
【大凡】dàfán〈副〉generally speaking: ～自私的人，最终往往要吃亏。In most cases, selfish people will suffer in the end.

【大方】dàfāng〈名〉〈书〉expert: ▸贻笑～

【大放厥词】dàfàng-juécí〈成〉〈贬〉talk drivel

【大方】dàfang〈形〉**1**（不小气）generous: 出手～ be generous with money **2**（不做作）easy: 举止～ have an easy manner **3**（不俗气）tasteful: 她的房间陈设～。Her house is furnished in good taste.

【大粪】dàfèn〈名〉faeces

【大风】dàfēng〈名〉gale: ～警报 gale warning ‖ 刮～了。It is blowing a gale.

【大风大浪】dàfēng-dàlàng〈成〉〈喻〉great upheavals and changes

【大夫】dàfū〈名〉〈旧〉*dafu* [senior state official in feudal China] ▸dàifu

【大幅】dàfú = 大幅度 dàfúdù

【大幅度】dàfúdù〈副〉substantially: ～裁员 cut staff drastically ‖ ～降价 make massive price reductions ‖ ～削减预算 make major cuts in budget ‖ ～增产 increase production by a large margin

【大副】dàfù〈名〉［航海］first mate

【大腹便便】dàfù-piánpián〈成〉〈贬〉potbellied

【大盖帽】dàgàimào〈名〉**1**（指帽子）peaked cap **2**（指人）person with a peaked cap [esp policemen and tax collectors]

【大概】dàgài **A**〈名〉broad outline: 这事他只给我说了个～。He just gave me a general idea of the story. **B**〈形〉approximate: ～的估计 rough estimate ‖ ～的数字 approximate figure **C**〈副〉**1**（表估计）approximately: 去那里～需要半小时。It will take approximately half an hour to get there. **2**（表猜测）probably: 这几天我一直没见他，～是出差去了吧。I haven't seen him in the past few days. He may have gone on a business trip. ‖ 我先走一步，你～不会介意吧。Presumably, you won't mind if I leave a little earlier.

【大干】dàgàn〈动〉go all out: ～一场 make a good go of things ‖ ～快上 go all out to make quick advances

【大纲】dàgāng〈名〉outline: 草拟～ draft an outline ‖ 教学～ teaching syllabus

【大哥】dàgē〈名〉**1**（有血缘关系）eldest brother **2**（无血缘关系）big brother [a polite form of address for a man about one's own age]

【大哥大】dàgēdà〈名〉〈口〉**1**（指人）boss **2**（指物）mobile phone

【大革命】dàgémìng〈名〉**1**（泛指）great revolution: 法国～ French Revolution **2**（特指中国）Great Revolution in China [referring to the First Revolutionary Civil War during 1924-1927]

【大个儿】dàgèr **A**〈名〉〈口〉tall man: 他是个～。He is tall. **B**〈形〉big: 挑～的吃 choose big ones to eat

【大公】dàgōng〈名〉grand duke

【大公国】dàgōngguó〈名〉grand duchy

【大公无私】dàgōng-wúsī〈成〉**1**（不自私）be selfless **2**（公正）be totally impartial

【大功】dàgōng〈名〉great achievement: 立～ perform extraordinary deeds

【大功告成】dàgōng-gàochéng〈成〉be brought to a successful completion

【大姑娘】dàgūniang〈名〉**1**（指未婚）unmarried young woman: 她已出落成一个漂亮的～了。She has bloomed into a pretty young lady. **2**（大女儿）eldest daughter

【大姑子】dàgūzi〈名〉〈口〉husband's elder sister

【大鼓】dàgǔ〈名〉**1** ▸**p. 929**［音乐］bass drum **2**［曲艺］*dagu*: 山东～ Shandong clapper ballad

【大关】dàguān〈名〉**1**（指关口）strategic pass **2**（指界限）new high: 突破百万～ have reached a new high of one million

【大观】dàguān〈名〉magnificent spectacle: ▸蔚为～

【大管】dàguǎn ▸**p. 929**〈名〉［音乐］bassoon

【大褂儿】dàguàr〈名〉Chinese long gown

【大规模】dàguīmó〈形〉large-scale: ～营救行动 large-scale rescue operation ‖ ～集成电路 large-scale integration

【大规模杀伤性武器】dàguīmó shāshāngxìng wǔqì〈名〉weapons of mass destruction

【大锅饭】dàguōfàn〈名〉**1**（指饭食）mess **2**（指分配方式）meal from a big pot: 吃～ share the same pot ‖ 打破～ break away from indiscriminate egalitarianism

【大国】dàguó〈名〉great power: 经济～ economic giant ▸超级～，核～

【大国沙文主义】dàguó shāwénzhǔyì〈名〉great-nation chauvinism

【大过】dàguò〈名〉**1**（指过错）serious mistake: 这不是什么～。This is not a serious mistake. **2**（指处分）major demerit: 记～一次 record a major demerit

【大海捞针】dàhǎi-lāozhēn = 海底捞针 hǎidǐ-lāozhēn

【大韩民国】Dàhán Mínguó〈名〉Republic of Korea

【大寒】Dàhán〈名〉Great Cold [beginning of the last of the 24 solar terms]

【大喊大叫】dàhǎn-dàjiào〈成〉make a hullabaloo

【大汉】dàhàn〈名〉hefty man: ▸彪形～

【大汗淋漓】dàhàn-línlí〈成〉perspire profusely

【大旱逢甘霖】dàhàn féng gānlín〈成〉〈喻〉timely relief from distress

【大旱望云霓】dàhàn wàng yúnní〈成〉〈喻〉look forward to relief from distress

【大好】dàhǎo〈形〉**1**（很好）excellent: ～时光 golden years ‖ 形势～。The situation is excellent. **2**（痊愈）fully recovered

【大好河山】dàhǎo-héshān〈成〉beautiful country

【大号】dàhào〈名〉**1**（指型号）large size: ～皮鞋 large-size leather shoes ‖ 特～ extra large **2**（指名字）[used in a polite form of question to ask the name of the person addressed to] your name **3** ▸**p. 929**［音乐］tuba

【大合唱】dàhéchàng〈名〉cantata: 《黄河～》*The Yellow River Cantata*

【大和民族】Dàhé Mínzú〈名〉Japanese nation

【大河有水小河满，大河无水小河干】dàhé yǒu shuǐ xiǎohé mǎn, dàhé wú shuǐ xiǎohé gān〈俗〉〈喻〉individual well-being depends on general prosperity

【大亨】dàhēng〈名〉bigwig: 金融～ financial tycoon ‖ 影业～ movie mogul

【大轰大嗡】dàhōng-dàwēng〈成〉create a big storm

【大红】dàhóng〈名〉bright red

【大红大绿】dàhóng-dàlǜ〈成〉be gaudy and showy

【大红大紫】dàhóng-dàzǐ〈成〉be at the height of popularity: 主演了这部电影之后，她一下子～了。Once she'd starred in the film, she shot to immediate fame.

【大红人】dàhóngrén〈名〉great favourite: 他是部长的～。He is a big favourite with the minister. ‖ 他现在成了～。He is now a hot commodity.

【大后方】dàhòufāng〈名〉vast rear area [areas under KMT rule during China's War of Resistance against Japan]

【大后年】dàhòunián ▸**p. 618**〈名〉three years from now

【大后天】dàhòutiān ▸**p. 618**〈名〉three days from now

【大胡子】dàhúzi〈名〉**1**（指胡须）bushy beard **2**（指人）bushy-bearded man

【大户】dàhù〈名〉**1**（表有权势）wealthy and influential family **2**（表人多）large family: 王姓是村里的～。The Wangs are a big clan in the village. **3**（表所占比重大）（指用户）major consumer;（指生产者）major producer: 电视机生产～ big TV set producer ‖ 用水～ big water consumer ‖ 纳税～ big tax payer

【大花脸】dàhuāliǎn〈名〉**1**［戏曲］character with painted face, specializing in singing **2**（表脸脏）dirty face

【大哗】dàhuá〈形〉〈书〉clamorous: 舆论～。There was a public outcry.

【大话】dàhuà〈名〉tall talk: 说～ talk big

【大环境】dàhuánjìng〈名〉overall situation

【大黄】dàhuáng〈名〉［植物］Chinese rhubarb

【大黄蜂】dàhuángfēng〈名〉［昆虫］hornet

【大回环】dàhuíhuán〈名〉［体育］giant circle: 单臂～ single-arm circle ‖ 向后～ swing backwards

【大会】dàhuì〈名〉**1**（全体会议）plenary session: 人民代表～ People's Congress ‖ 联合国～ UN General Assembly **2**（群众会议）mass meeting: 动员～ mobilization meeting

【大伙儿】dàhuǒr〈代〉〈口〉all of us: ～都到了，现在开会。Since all of us are here, let's start our meeting.

【大祸临头】dàhuò-líntóu〈成〉be faced with imminent disaster

【大惑不解】dàhuò-bùjiě〈成〉be greatly puzzled: 令人～ profoundly confuse sb.

【大吉】dàjí〈形〉**1**（很吉利）extremely lucky: ▸万事～ **2**（表诙谐）[used humorously after a verb or verbal phrase]: 溜之～ beat a hasty retreat ▸关门～

【大吉大利】dàjí-dàlì〈成〉good luck and great prosperity

【大几】dàjǐ ▸**p. 927**〈数〉〈口〉[used after 20 or 30, usu referring to age] over: 二十～的人了，怎么还跟个小孩似的? You're over twenty. How can you still behave like a child?

【大计】dàjì〈名〉matter of fundamental importance: 共商～ discuss together matters of vital importance ▸百年～

【大忌】dàjì〈名〉**1**（指忌讳）absolute taboo: 犯～ break the absolute taboo **2**（指祭日）anniversary of an emperor's/empress's death

【大家】dàjiā〈名〉**1**（众人）everybody: ～的事～办。It's everybody's business and everybody's responsibility. ‖ 请～安静! May I have everyone's attention, please? **2**（有名望的人）famous expert: ～手笔 handwriting of a great calligrapher ‖ ～风范 noble air **3**（指家族）wealthy and influential family of long standing

【大家闺秀】dàjiā-guīxiù〈成〉girl from a wealthy and influential family

【大家伙儿】dàjiāhuǒr = 大伙儿 dàhuǒr

【大家庭】dàjiātíng〈名〉**1**（指家庭）extended family **2**〈喻〉（指集体）harmonious community: 民族～ big family of nationalities

【大驾】dàjià〈名〉**1**〈敬〉（指对方）you: 恭候～ await you respectfully ‖ 有劳～了。Would you do me a favour? **2**（指皇

帝） emperor 3▸（指车驾） imperial carriage

【大件】dàjiàn〈名〉 1▸（指贵重） big item 2▸（指体积大） bulky piece: ～商品 major durable consumer goods ‖ ～行李 bulky luggage

【大建】dàjiàn〈名〉 lunar month of 30 days

【大江】dàjiāng〈名〉 1▸（泛指大河） large river 2▸（特指长江） Yangtze River

【大奖】dàjiǎng〈名〉 grand prize: 获～ win a grand prize

【大奖赛】dàjiǎngsài〈名〉 grand prize contest: 电视～ TV grand prix

【大将】dàjiàng〈名〉 1▸（指军衔） senior general: ～风度 bearing of a general 2▸（泛指高级将领） high-ranking officer 3▸〈喻〉（指骨干） key figure: 她是我们篮球队里的～。 She is a key player in our basketball team.

【大蕉】dàjiāo〈名〉［植物］ plantain

【大教堂】dàjiàotáng〈名〉 cathedral: 圣保罗～ St Paul's Cathedral

【大街】dàjiē〈名〉 high street〈英〉; main street〈美〉: 逛～ stroll down a street

【大街小巷】dàjiē-xiǎoxiàng〈成〉 streets and lanes

【大节】dàjié〈名〉 1▸（指节日） major event 2▸（指节操） political integrity

【大捷】dàjié〈名〉 resounding victory: 取得～ win a resounding victory

【大姐】dàjiě〈名〉 1▸（有血缘关系） eldest sister 2▸（无血缘关系） elder sister [a polite form of address for a woman about one's own age]

【大姐大】dàjiědà〈名〉 woman of power

【大解】dàjiě〈动〉 empty one's bowels

【大襟】dàjīn〈名〉 front of a Chinese garment with buttons on one side

【大惊失色】dàjīng-shīsè〈成〉 turn pale with fright: 他听到那消息后～。 He paled with shock at the news.

【大惊小怪】dàjīng-xiǎoguài〈成〉 make a fuss about something very trivial: 没什么好～的。There's nothing to be alarmed about.

【大舅】dàjiù〈名〉 oldest maternal uncle

【大舅子】dàjiùzi〈名〉〈口〉 wife's elder brother

【大局】dàjú〈名〉 overall situation: 维护～ safeguard general interests ‖ 无关～ of little account ‖ ～已定。 The die is cast. ▸顾全～

【大局观】dàjúguān〈名〉 overview: 增强干部的～ improve cadres' ability to see the bigger picture

【大举】dàjǔ A〈副〉 on a large scale: ～进攻 launch a large-scale attack B〈名〉〈书〉 major step: 共商～ discuss what major steps to take next

【大军】dàjūn〈名〉 1▸（指军队） main army: 百万～ an army one million strong ‖ ～压境。 The army is bearing down in force. 2▸（指人员） large contingent: 产业～ large contingent of industrial workers ‖ 失业～ large numbers of laid-off workers

【大卡】dàkǎ〈名〉 kilocalorie

【大开方便之门】dà kāi fāngbiàn zhī mén〈惯〉 open the floodgates

【大楷】dàkǎi〈名〉 1▸［书法］ big Chinese characters in regular script 2▸（大写印刷体） block letters

【大考】dàkǎo〈名〉 final exam

【大可不必】dàkěbùbì〈成〉 be entirely unnecessary

【大客车】dàkèchē〈名〉 bus

【大课】dàkè〈名〉 big class

【大快人心】dàkuài-rénxīn〈成〉 to the great satisfaction of the people: ～的消息 heartening news

【大块头】dàkuàitóu〈名〉 person of heavy build

【大款】dàkuǎn〈名〉 moneybags: 傍～ live off a moneybags

【大括弧】dàkuòhú〈名〉 brace ({ })

【大牢】dàláo〈名〉 prison: 坐～ serve one's term of imprisonment

【大佬】dàlǎo〈名〉〈方〉 boss: 房地产～ real estate magnate

【大老粗】dàlǎocū〈名〉〈口〉 rough guy

【大老婆】dàlǎopo〈名〉〈旧〉 official wife

【大老远】dàlǎoyuǎn〈形〉 very far away: ～跑来 come all the way

【大礼拜】dàlǐbài ▸**p. 836**〈名〉 1▸（指休息天） day off every ten days 2▸（指周末） long weekend: 过～ have a long weekend 3▸（指星期） week with a long weekend

【大礼堂】dàlǐtáng〈名〉 auditorium

【大理石】dàlǐshí〈名〉 marble

【大力】dàlì A〈名〉 great efforts: 出～ make great efforts B〈副〉 energetically: ～弘扬爱国主义 vigorously promote patriotism ‖ ～推荐 give unqualified recommendation

【大力神】dàlìshén ▸**p. 274**〈名〉 Hercules

【大力士】dàlìshì〈名〉 man of unusual strength

【大丽花】dàlìhuā〈名〉［植物］ dahlia

【大殓】dàliàn〈动〉 place the deceased in a coffin

【大梁】dàliáng〈名〉 1▸［建筑］ girder 2▸（指人） mainstay: 挑～ shoulder the main responsibility

【大量】dàliàng〈形〉 1▸（指数量） many, much: ～出售 launch a massive sale ‖ ～事实 a host of facts ‖ ～资金 large funds 2▸（指度量） broad-minded: ▸宽宏～

【大料】dàliào = 八角 bājiǎo 3

【大龄】dàlíng〈形〉 relatively old: ～青年 single young person past the usual age for marriage

【大羚羊】dàlíngyáng〈名〉［动物］ oryx

【大溜】dàliù〈名〉〈口〉 mainstream: 随～ follow the crowd

【大楼】dàlóu〈名〉 multi-storey building: 摩天～ skyscraper

【大陆】dàlù〈名〉 1▸（指陆地） continent: ～国家 continental state ‖ 亚洲～ Asian continent 2▸（中国大陆） mainland China: 台湾同胞回～探亲。 Taiwanese compatriots return to the mainland to visit relatives.

【大陆岛】dàlùdǎo〈名〉 continental island

【大陆架】dàlùjià〈名〉［地质］ continental shelf

【大陆桥】dàlùqiáo〈名〉［地质］ land bridge

【大陆性气候】dàlùxìng qìhòu〈名〉 continental climate

【大路】dàlù A〈名〉 main road B〈形〉 popular: ～菜 common vegetables ‖ ～活 run-of-the-mill product

【大路货】dàlùhuò〈名〉 popular goods of average quality

【大略】dàlüè A〈名〉 1▸（概要） gist: 知道个～ have a general idea ‖ 你能告诉我个～吗? Can you give me the gist of it? 2▸（谋略） great vision: ▸雄才～ B〈副〉 briefly: 时间有限，我就～说说我的想法吧。 Time is limited, so I'll just tell you briefly what I have in mind.

【大伦敦郡】Dàlúndūnjùn〈名〉 Greater London

【大妈】dàmā〈名〉 1▸（有亲属关系） aunt [wife of father's elder brother] 2▸（无亲属关系） auntie [a polite form of address for an elderly woman]

【大麻】dàmá〈名〉 1▸［植物］ hemp: ～织物 hemp cloth 2▸（指毒品） marijuana: 吸食～ use marijuana

【大麻哈鱼】dàmáhǎyú〈名〉 chum salmon

【大麻子】dàmázǐ〈名〉 1▸（蓖麻籽） hempseed: ～油 hempseed oil 2▸［植物］ castor oil plant 3▸（指籽） castor bean

【大马哈鱼】dàmǎhǎyú = 大麻哈鱼 dàmáhǎyú

【大马趴】dàmǎpā〈动〉〈口〉 fall flat on one's face: 摔了个～ fall flat on one's face

【大马士革】Dàmǎshìgé〈名〉 Damascus

【大麦】dàmài〈名〉 1▸（指植物） barley: ～穗 spikes of barley 2▸（指籽实） barley grain: ～茶 barley water

【大曼彻斯特郡】Dàmànchèsītèjùn〈名〉 Greater Manchester

【大忙】dàmáng〈形〉 very busy: ～季节 high season

【大猫熊】dàmāoxióng〈名〉 giant panda

【大毛】dàmáo〈名〉 long-haired pelt

【大帽子】dàmàozi〈名〉〈喻〉 political label: 不要给人乱扣～。 Don't try to pin random political labels on people.

d

【大门】dàmén〈名〉 main gate: 关～ close the gate

【大米】dàmǐ〈名〉 rice: ～饭 cooked rice

【大面儿】dàmiànr〈名〉〈方〉 1▸（表面上） appearance: 他的作文～上还过得去。 His composition looks OK. 2▸（面子上） face: 顾全～ save one's face

【大民族主义】dàmínzúzhǔyì〈名〉 big-nationality chauvinism

【大名】dàmíng〈名〉 1▸（指名字） formal name: 他的小名叫丫子，～叫王华。 His nickname is Yazi and his formal name is Wang Hua. 2▸（指名声） your reputed name: ▸久闻～

【大名鼎鼎】dàmíng-dǐngdǐng〈成〉 very famous: ～的人物 big-name figure

【大鸣大放】dàmíng-dàfàng〈成〉 speak out freely

【大谬不然】dàmiù-bùrán〈成〉 be grossly mistaken

【大漠】dàmò〈名〉 vast desert

【大模大样】dàmú-dàyàng〈成〉 be defiant and arrogant: ～地走出去 walk out with a swagger

【大拇哥】dàmǔgē〈名〉〈方〉 thumb

【大拇指】dàmǔzhǐ〈名〉〈口〉 thumb

【大拿】dàná〈名〉〈方〉 1▸（掌权人） boss: 他是我们单位的～。 He is in charge in our unit. 2▸（权威） authority: 技术～ technical expert

【大男】dànán〈名〉 1▸（男子） man 2▸（特指未婚） ageing bachelor 3▸（长子） eldest son

【大男大女】dànán-dànǚ〈名〉 unmarried man and woman well past the average marrying age

【大男子主义】dànánzǐzhǔyì〈名〉 male chauvinism

【大难不死，必有后福】dànàn bù sǐ, bì yǒu hòufú〈俗〉 good fortune awaits the survivor of a great disaster

【大难临头】dànàn-líntóu〈成〉 disaster is looming

【大脑】dànǎo〈名〉 cerebrum: ～发育不全 cerebral agenesia

【大脑皮质】dànǎo pízhì〈名〉 cerebral cortex

【大内】dànèi〈名〉〈旧〉 imperial palace

【大鲵】dàní〈名〉［动物］ giant salamander

【大逆不道】dànì-bùdào〈成〉 treason

【大年】dànián〈名〉 1▸（丰年） bumper year 2▸（指年头） lunar year with a 30-day December 3▸（春节） Spring Festival: 欢欢喜喜过～ happily celebrate Spring Festival

【大年初一】dànián chūyī〈名〉 lunar New Year's Day
【大年三十】dànián sānshí〈名〉lunar New Year's Eve
【大年夜】dàniányè〈名〉〈方〉 lunar New Year's Eve
【大娘】dàniáng〈名〉〈方〉 1（有亲属关系） aunt [wife of father's elder brother] 2（无亲属关系） auntie [a polite form of address for an elderly woman]
【大排档】dàpáidàng〈名〉(street) food stall
【大排行】dàpáiháng〈名〉 rank of cousins in an extended family in birth order
【大牌】dàpái A〈名〉 celebrity B〈形〉 famous: ～歌星 famous pop singer
【大盘】dàpán〈名〉［金融］ large cap
【大炮】dàpào〈名〉 1（指武器） cannon 2〈喻〉（指人） braggart
【大鹏】dàpéng〈名〉 roc
【大篷车】dàpéngchē〈名〉 delivery truck
【大批】dàpī〈形〉 many: ～出口产品 large batches of export products ‖ ～追随者 a legion of followers
【大辟】dàpì〈名〉〈旧〉 capital punishment
【大片儿】dàpiānr〈名〉 blockbuster
【大票】dàpiào〈名〉 bill of large denomination
【大起大落】dàqǐ-dàluò〈成〉 great ups and downs: 该队本赛季一直～。 The team has been very up and down this season.
【大气】dàqì A〈名〉 1（指空气） air 2（指喘息） heavy breathing: 喘～ breathe heavily ‖ 吓得～不敢出 be scared breathless B〈形〉 magnanimous: 为人～ keep an open mind with people
【大气层】dàqìcéng〈名〉 atmosphere: 重返～ re-enter the earth's atmosphere
【大气候】dàqìhòu〈名〉 1（指气候） macroclimate 2（指形势或思潮） overall situation
【大气磅礴】dàqì-pángbó〈成〉 be grand and magnificent: ～的绘画 magnificent painting
【大气污染】dàqì wūrǎn〈名〉 air pollution: ～物 air pollutant
【大气压】dàqìyā A〈名〉 atmospheric pressure B〈量〉［物理］ atmosphere
【大器】dàqì〈名〉〈喻〉 great talent: 他老说儿子成不了～。 He has said repeatedly that his son won't amount to anything.
【大器晚成】dàqì-wǎnchéng〈成〉 gain success late in life: ～的学者 late-blooming scholar
【大千世界】dàqiān-shìjiè〈成〉 boundless universe: ～，无奇不有。 In this boundless world of ours, we are not lacking in the unusual.
【大前年】dàqiánnián ▸p. 618〈名〉 three years ago
【大前提】dàqiántí〈名〉［逻辑］ major premise
【大前天】dàqiántiān ▸p. 618〈名〉 three days ago
【大钱】dàqián〈名〉 1（钱） money: 不值一个～ be not worth a penny 2（很多钱） big money: 赚～ earn big money
【大庆】dàqìng〈名〉 1（指庆典） grand celebration 2（指生日庆贺） birthday of an elderly person
【大秋】dàqiū〈名〉 1（指季节） autumn harvest season 2（指收成） autumn harvest: ～作物 autumn crops
【大球】dàqiú〈名〉 big ball sports [basketball, football, and volleyball]: 中国的三～水平还不高。 China is not strong in the three big ball sports.
【大曲】dàqū〈名〉 1（指发酵剂） yeast for making spirits 2（指白酒） spirits made with such yeast
【大全】dàquán〈名〉complete works:《中国戏曲～》*Encyclopedia of Chinese Drama*
【大权】dàquán〈名〉 great power: ～在握 be in charge
【大权独揽】dàquán-dúlǎn〈成〉 have sole power
【大权旁落】dàquán-pángluò〈成〉 lose one's power to one's subordinates
【大热天】dàrètiān〈名〉 sizzling hot day
【大人】dàrén〈名〉〈敬〉 [a respectful salutation for one's parents, elder people, seniors, etc., usu used in letters]: 父亲/母亲～ Dear Father/Mother
【大人不记小人过】dàrén bù jì xiǎorén guò〈俗〉 a great man does not bear petty grudges
【大人物】dàrénwù〈名〉 important person
【大人】dàren〈名〉 1（成年人） adult: ～的事，小孩不要管! Children should not meddle in adults' business! 2〈旧〉（官员） Your Honour
【大肉】dàròu〈名〉 pork: ～排骨 pork chops
【大儒】dàrú〈名〉 erudite and virtuous scholar
【大赛】dàsài〈名〉 major contest: 足球～ major football tournament ‖ 全国青年歌手～ national contest for young singers
【大扫除】dàsǎochú〈动〉 have a clean-up: 进行～ do some spring-cleaning
【大嫂】dàsǎo〈名〉 1（有亲属关系） sister-in-law [elder brother's wife] 2（无亲属关系） big sister [a polite form of address for married women older than oneself]
【大杀风景】dàshā-fēngjǐng〈成〉 be a wet blanket
【大煞风景】dàshā-fēngjǐng = 大杀风景 dàshā-fēngjǐng
【大厦】dàshà〈名〉 mansion: 友谊～ Friendship Mansion
【大厦将倾】dàshà-jiāngqīng〈成〉〈喻〉 the situation is hopeless: ～，一木难支 a hopeless situation that no one can save
【大少爷】dàshàoye〈名〉 1〈旧〉（指少主人） eldest son of one's master 2（指青年男子） dandy: ～作风 extravagant ways
【大舌头】dàshétou〈口〉 A〈形〉 big-tongued: 他说话有点～。 His words are slightly slurred. B〈名〉 thick-tongued person: 他是个～。 He has a thick tongue.
【大赦】dàshè〈动〉 grant amnesty to: ～犯人 grant amnesty to criminals ‖ 宣布～ announce a general pardon ‖ ～令 order of amnesty
【大赦国际】Dàshè Guójì〈名〉 Amnesty International
【大婶儿】dàshěnr〈名〉〈口〉 1（有亲属关系） aunt [wife of father's eldest younger brother] 2（无亲属关系） aunt [a polite form of address for women younger than one's mother]
【大声疾呼】dàshēng-jíhū〈成〉 appeal loudly
【大牲口】dàshēngkou〈名〉 draught animal
【大圣】dàshèng〈名〉 1（指人） great sage 2（指佛） Buddha 3（指皇帝） emperor 4（指神仙） immortal
【大胜】dàshèng〈动〉 win a great victory: 甲队～乙队。 Team A crushed Team B.
【大失所望】dàshī-suǒwàng〈成〉 be greatly disappointed: 令人～ fall far short of expectations
【大师】dàshī〈名〉 1（指有造诣） grand master: 喜剧/艺术～ grand master of comedy/art 2（指等级称号） great master 3（指僧人） Great Master
【大师班】dàshībān〈名〉 master class: 歌剧艺术～ master class in opera
【大师傅】dàshīfu〈名〉〈口〉 1 = 大师 dàshī 3 2（指厨师） chef
【大使】dàshǐ〈名〉 ambassador: 互派～ exchange ambassadors ‖ 中国驻联合国～ Chinese ambassador to the United Nations ‖ ～会谈 talks at ambassadorial level
【大使馆】dàshǐguǎn〈名〉 embassy: 设立～ set up an embassy
【大事】dàshì A〈名〉 matter of great importance: 成就～ accomplish great deeds ‖ 误～ mess up something really important ‖ 国家～ state affairs ▸～记，终身～ B〈副〉 in a big way: ～渲染 play up
【大事化小，小事化了】dàshì huà xiǎo, xiǎoshì huà liǎo〈俗〉 minimize the problems
【大事记】dàshìjì〈名〉 record of important events
【大势所趋】dàshì-suǒqū〈成〉 the prevailing trend: 和平是～。 The tendency of events is toward peace.
【大势已去】dàshì-yǐqù〈成〉 the game is as good as lost
【大是大非】dàshì-dàfēi〈成〉 major issue of principle: ～面前立场坚定 stand firm over key issues of principle
【大手笔】dàshǒubǐ〈名〉 1（指人） great artist 2（指作品） work of great artist 3〈喻〉（指举措） great work
【大手大脚】dàshǒu-dàjiǎo〈成〉 be extravagant: 花钱～ be extravagant with money
【大寿】dàshòu〈名〉 important birthday: 庆贺父亲的九十～ celebrate father's 90th birthday
【大书特书】dàshū-tèshū〈成〉 write elaborately on
【大叔】dàshū〈名〉 uncle [a respectful term of address]
【大暑】Dàshǔ〈名〉 Great Heat [beginning of the 12th of the 24 solar terms]
【大树底下好乘凉】dàshù dǐxia hǎo chéngliáng〈俗〉〈喻〉 an influential person provides good protection
【大帅】dàshuài〈名〉〈书〉 commander-in-chief
【大率】dàshuài〈副〉〈书〉 more or less: ～如此 more or less so
【大肆】dàsì〈副〉 wantonly: ～吹嘘 boast wantonly ‖ ～掠夺 plunder without restraint ‖ ～渲染 blow sth. out of proportion
【大蒜】dàsuàn〈名〉 garlic: ～味 garlic taste
【大踏步】dàtàbù〈副〉 in big strides: ～前进 make progress in leaps and bounds
【大谈】dàtán〈动〉 prate on
【大堂】dàtáng〈名〉 1〈旧〉（公堂） court room in a *yamen* 2（大厅） lobby: ～经理 lobby manager
【大提琴】dàtíqín ▸p. 929〈名〉 cello
【大体】dàtǐ A〈名〉 general principle: 识～，顾大局 understand the basic principles and take into consideration the overall situation B〈副〉 more or less: 我们的想法～一致。 We share pretty much the same view.
【大体上】dàtǐshàng〈副〉 in the main: 这个计划～可以接受。 The plan is acceptable in principle.
【大天白日】dàtiān-báirì〈成〉 broad daylight: ～的，你怎么能干出这种事来? How could you have done such a thing in broad daylight?
【大田】dàtián〈名〉 large field
【大田作物】dàtián zuòwù〈名〉 field crop
【大厅】dàtīng〈名〉main hall: 宾馆～ hotel lobby ‖ 候机～ airport terminal

【大庭广众】 dàtíng-guǎngzhòng 〈成〉 public place with a large crowd: 这是她第一次在～下唱歌。 It was the first time that she had sung in public.

【大同】dàtóng **A**〈名〉 Great Harmony **B**〈动〉 share common ground over major issues: ▸～小异

【大同乡】dàtóngxiāng〈名〉 fellow provincial

【大同小异】 dàtóng-xiǎoyì 〈成〉 be very similar

【大头】dàtóu〈名〉 **1**（指假面具） head mask **2**（指银币） silver coin **3**（大部分） main part: 取～ take the lion's share ‖ 抓～儿 focus on the major problem **4**（冤大头） squanderer: 拿～ dupe sb.

【大头菜】 dàtóucài 〈名〉 swede 〈英〉; rutabaga 〈美〉

【大头针】dàtóuzhēn〈名〉 pin

【大屠杀】dàtúshā〈名〉 holocaust

【大团圆】dàtuányuán〈动〉 **1**（指家庭） be reunited with one's family **2**（指结局） [of a movie, novel, play, etc.] have a happy ending

【大腿】dàtuǐ〈名〉 thigh: ～肌肉拉伤 thigh strain ‖〈喻〉 胳膊拧不过～。 The weak cannot challenge the strong.

【大碗儿茶】dàwǎnrchá〈名〉 tea served in a big cup

【大腕】dàwàn〈名〉 big shot

【大王】dàwáng〈名〉 **1**（巨头） magnate: 石油～ oil baron ‖ 报刊/钢铁～ press/steel baron **2**（有造诣的人） highly skilled person: 足球～ football hero ‖ 爆破～ ace dynamiter ‖ 吹牛～ first-class boaster

【大为】dàwéi〈副〉〈书〉 greatly: ～改观 changed a great deal ‖ ～失望 be very disappointed ‖ ～震惊 be in total shock

【大尉】dàwèi〈名〉［军事］ senior captain

【大我】dàwǒ〈名〉 the collective: 小我服从～。 Put collective interests above individual interests.

【大无畏】dàwúwèi〈形〉 fearless: ～的精神 dauntless spirit ‖ ～的勇气 indomitable courage

【大西洋】Dàxīyáng〈名〉 Atlantic Ocean

【大喜】 dàxǐ 〈名〉 **1**（非常高兴） great happiness: ～若狂 be wild with joy **2**（结婚） wedding: 哪天是你们～的日子? When is your wedding day?

【大喜过望】dàxǐ-guòwàng〈成〉 be overjoyed: 一场及时雨使农民们～。 Farmers were overjoyed at the timely rain.

【大戏】dàxì〈名〉**1**（大型戏剧）full-scale traditional opera: 看～ watch a full-scale opera **2**〈方〉（京剧） Beijing opera

【大显身手】dàxiǎn-shēnshǒu〈成〉 display one's skill to the fullest: 这是你～的好机会。 This is a good opportunity for you to show what you can do.

【大显神通】dàxiǎn-shéntōng〈成〉 display one's prowess to the full: 高科技在农业生产中～。 Technology plays a very important and effective role in farming.

【大限】dàxiàn〈名〉 hour of one's death: ～已到。 One's death is approaching.

【大相径庭】dàxiāng-jìngtíng〈成〉 be poles apart: 两种～、格格不入的文化 two distant warring cultures ‖ 在许多问题上，她与我的看法～。 Her views are completely different to mine on many issues. ‖ 结果与我们的期望～。 The result is a world away from what we expected.

【大小】dàxiǎo **A**〈名〉 **1**（指尺寸） size: 把苹果按～分开 sort the apples according to size ‖ 试穿一下鞋子看～合不合适 try the shoes on for size **2**（指辈分） seniority: 不分～ make no distinction between the old and the young ‖ 没大没小 show no respect to one's elders **3**（大人和小孩） old and young: ～平安。 All's well in the family. **B**〈副〉 at any rate: ～是个官 be an official at any rate ‖ ～是笔生意。 It's a deal anyway. **C**〈形〉 big and small: 国家不分～，一律平等。 All countries, big or small, are equal. ‖ 这条街上～商店有几十家。 There are dozens of shops, big and small, on this street.

【大小非】dàxiǎofēi〈名〉［金融］large and small-sized non-tradable share: ～减持 sale of non-tradable shares

【大小姐】 dàxiǎojiě 〈名〉 **1**〈旧〉（长女） eldest daughter of one's master **2**（指年轻女子） pampered girl

【大校】dàxiào〈名〉 senior colonel

【大写】dàxiě **A**〈名〉 elaborate form of Chinese numerals: ～金额 amount in words **B**〈动〉 write in capitals: ～字母 capital letter ‖ 英语中每句话的首字母都要～。 The first letter of each English sentence should be capitalized.

【大写特写】dàxiě-tèxiě = 大书特书 dàshū-tèshū

【大兴】dàxīng〈动〉 go in for sth. in a big way: ～调查研究之风 energetically undertake research and studies ‖ ～水利 large-scale building of water conservancy projects

【大兴土木】dàxīng-tǔmù〈成〉 launch an enormous construction project

【大猩猩】dàxīngxing〈名〉 gorilla

【大刑】dàxíng〈名〉 cruel torture: 动/用～ cruelly penalize

【大型】dàxíng〈形〉 large-scale: ～变电站 large-scale substation ‖ ～水库 large reservoir ‖ ～超市 hypermarket

【大姓】dàxìng〈名〉 **1**（指家族） big reputable family **2**（指姓氏） popular surname

【大雄宝殿】Dàxióng Bǎodiàn〈名〉 Hall of Sakyamuni

【大熊猫】dàxióngmāo〈名〉 giant panda

【大熊座】Dàxióngzuò〈名〉［天文］ Great Bear

【大修】dàxiū〈动〉 overhaul: 进行～ carry out big repairs ‖ 需要～ be in a bad state of repair

【大选】dàxuǎn〈动〉 general election: 举行～ hold a general election

【大学】dàxué〈名〉 university: ～毕业生 university graduate ‖ 名牌～ elite university

【大学生】dàxuéshēng〈名〉 university student

【大雪】 dàxuě 〈名〉 **1** Dàxuě（指节气） Great Snow [beginning of the 21st of the 24 solar terms] **2**（指雪） heavy snow: 一场～ a heavy fall of snow

【大循环】 dàxúnhuán 〈名〉［生理］ systemic circulation

【大牙】 dàyá 〈名〉 **1**（槽牙） molar **2**（门牙） front tooth: ▸笑掉～

【大雅】dàyǎ〈形〉〈书〉 elegant: ▸不登～之堂, 无伤～

【大烟】dàyān〈名〉 opium

【大言不惭】 dàyán-bùcán 〈成〉 boast shamelessly

【大盐】dàyán〈名〉 crude salt

【大眼瞪小眼】dàyǎn dèng xiǎoyǎn〈俗〉 look at one other helplessly

【大雁】dàyàn〈名〉 wild goose

【大洋】dàyáng〈名〉 **1**（海洋） ocean: 横越～ get across an ocean ‖ 四～ the four oceans **2**〈旧〉（银元） silver dollar: 五块～ five silver dollars

【大洋洲】Dàyángzhōu〈名〉 Oceania

【大样】dàyàng〈名〉 **1**［印刷］ full-page proof **2**［建筑］ detail drawing

【大摇大摆】dàyáo-dàbǎi〈成〉 haughtily: ～地闯了进去 went in with a strut

【大要】dàyào〈名〉 gist: 论文的～ abstract of a thesis

【大爷】dàyé〈名〉 idle and wayward man: ～作风 wayward habits of an idle man

【大爷】dàye〈名〉 **1**（有亲属关系） uncle [father's elder brother] **2**（无亲属关系） uncle [respectful form of address for an elderly man]

【大业】dàyè〈名〉 great cause: 国家统一～ great cause of national reunification

【大衣】dàyī〈名〉 overcoat: 军～ army coat ‖ 皮～ fur coat

【大姨】dàyí〈名〉 aunt [mother's eldest sister]

【大姨子】 dàyízi 〈名〉〈口〉 sister-in-law [wife's elder sister]

【大义】dàyì〈名〉 righteousness: 深明～ have a profound understanding of what is righteous

【大义凛然】dàyì-lǐnrán〈成〉 be staunchly righteous

【大义灭亲】dàyì-mièqīn〈成〉 place righteousness above family loyalty

【大异其趣】dàyì-qíqù〈成〉 have very different tastes and interests

【大意】dàyì〈名〉 general idea: 段落～ gist of a paragraph ‖ 歌词～ main idea of a song

【大意】dàyi〈形〉 careless: ～不得 can't afford to be careless

【大意失荆州】 dàyi shī Jīngzhōu 〈成〉〈喻〉 suffer a major setback as a result of negligence

【大印】dàyìn〈名〉 seal of power

【大英百科全书】Dàyīng Bǎikē Quánshū〈名〉 *Encyclopedia Britannica*

【大油】dàyóu〈名〉〈口〉 lard

【大有可为】 dàyǒu-kěwéi 〈成〉 be very promising

【大有人在】dàyǒurénzài〈成〉 such people are by no means rare

【大有文章】dàyǒu-wénzhāng〈成〉〈喻〉 there is more to it than meets the eye

【大有作为】dàyǒu-zuòwéi〈成〉 be able to develop one's ability to the fullest

【大鱼吃小鱼】 dàyú chī xiǎoyú 〈俗〉〈喻〉 law of the jungle

【大雨滂沱】dàyǔ-pāngtuó〈成〉 the rain is falling in sheets

【大雨倾盆】dàyǔ-qīngpén〈成〉it's raining heavily

【大雨如注】dàyǔ-rúzhù 〈成〉 it's pelting with rain

【大狱】dàyù〈名〉 **1**（重案） major case **2**（监狱） prison

【大元帅】dàyuánshuài〈名〉［军事］ generalissimo

【大员】 dàyuán 〈名〉〈旧〉 high-ranking official

【大院】 dàyuàn 〈名〉 courtyard: 办公～ office compound ‖ 使馆～ embassy compound ▸深宅～

【大约】dàyuē〈副〉 **1** ▸**p. 927**（表约数） approximately: 他～有五十开外了。 He is around fifty or so. **2**（表猜测） probably: 她～是回家去了。 She has probably gone home.

【大月】dàyuè〈名〉 month

【大跃进】 Dàyuèjìn 〈名〉 Great Leap Forward

【大运河】Dàyùnhé ▸**p. 294**〈名〉 Grand Canal

【大杂烩】dàzáhuì〈名〉 hotchpotch〈英〉; hodgepodge〈美〉: 这台节目是个～。The programme was a bit of a mixture.

【大杂院儿】 dàzáyuànr 〈名〉 multi-household compound

d

大跃进

A plan launched in 1958 by the Chinese Communist Party. The aim was to bring about sweeping economic and social reforms, with a view to transforming China into a modern, industrialized Communist state. The party hoped that within 15 years or less China would catch up with or overtake Great Britain in industrial production. People's communes were set up, and a mass movement was launched to smelt steel and boost grain production. The policy was abandoned in 1960, and today it is considered both in China and abroad as having caused major economic collapse, as well as a humanitarian disaster in which many millions of people died of famine.

d

【大藏经】 Dàzàngjīng〈名〉［佛教］ Tripitaka
【大枣】 dàzǎo〈名〉 jujube
【大灶】 dàzào〈名〉 1（指灶头）big stove 2（指食堂） ordinary meals at a canteen: 吃～ take meals from a canteen
【大札】 dàzhá〈名〉〈书〉〈敬〉your letter
【大展宏图】 dàzhǎn-hóngtú〈成〉 realize one's ambition: 我们可以在改革中～。We can spread our wings in the reform.
【大战】 dàzhàn A〈名〉1（指战争）large-scale war: 世界～ world war 2〈喻〉（指比赛） major sporting event: 足球～ major football match B〈动〉 fight a fierce battle: ～三天 fight fierce battles for three consecutive days
【大站】 dàzhàn〈名〉 1（指火车站） major station 2（指汽车站） major bus stop
【大张旗鼓】 dàzhāng-qígǔ〈成〉 in a big way: ～地宣传 widely publicize
【大丈夫】 dàzhàngfu〈名〉 real man: ～能屈能伸。 A great man knows when to yield and when not to.
【大政】 dàzhèng〈名〉 state affairs: ～方针 fundamental policy
【大旨】 dàzhǐ〈名〉〈书〉 main idea: 了解～ get the gist
【大志】 dàzhì〈名〉 great ambition: 胸无～ be devoid of ambition
【大治】 dàzhì〈形〉〈书〉 orderly and prosperous: 天下～。 There is great order and prosperity throughout the country.
【大致】 dàzhì A〈形〉 general: ～说来 generally speaking ‖ ～相似 be similar in substance B〈副〉 approximately: 对费用的～估计 approximate estimate of the cost ‖ 时间～是十点钟。 It's about 10 o'clock.
【大智若愚】 dàzhì-ruòyú〈成〉 great wisdom has the look of folly
【大众】 dàzhòng〈名〉 general public: 劳苦～ toiling masses ‖ ～传媒 mass media
【大众化】 dàzhònghuà〈动〉 popularize: 使科学～ popularize science ‖ ～语言 language of the ordinary people
【大主教】 dàzhǔjiào〈名〉 archbishop
【大专】 dàzhuān〈名〉 1（大学和高等专科）institutions of higher education 2（大学专科） junior college for professional training
【大专院校】 dàzhuān yuànxiào = 大专 dàzhuān 1
【大篆】 dàzhuàn〈名〉［书法］ big seal character
【大字报】 dàzìbào〈名〉 big-character poster
【大自然】 dàzìrán〈名〉 nature: 回归～ get back to nature ‖ ～的造化 fundamental forces of nature
【大宗】 dàzōng A〈形〉 large: ～货物 bulky goods ‖ ～买卖 bulk sale ‖ ～交易 volume trading B〈名〉 staple: ～商品/产品 staple commodities/products ‖ 本地出产以棉花为～。 Cotton is the staple product here.
【大总统】 dàzǒngtǒng〈名〉〈旧〉 president: 临时～ interim president
【大族】 dàzú〈名〉 famous and influential clan
【大作】 dàzuò A〈名〉〈敬〉 your work: 拜读～ have the honour of perusing your work B〈动〉 erupt: 狂风～。 A stiff wind broke out. ‖ 雷声～。 There erupted peals of thunder.
【大做文章】 dàzuò-wénzhāng〈成〉〈喻〉 1（指努力） make painstaking efforts: 在产品质量上～ concentrate one's efforts on the quality of the products 2（指借题发挥） make a big issue about

da

跶（躂） da ▸蹦跶 bèngda, 蹓跶 liūda

dāi

呆（獃） dāi
A〈形〉 1（笨） slow-minded: ▸～子 2（死板） blank: 吓～ be scared stiff ▸发～
B〈动〉 stay: ～一宿 stay for a night ‖ ～在家里 stay at home
【呆板】 dāibǎn〈形〉 inflexible: 方法～ be inflexible in one's methods ‖ 他的文章太～。 His article is trite and dull. ‖ 他这个人太～。 He is so stubborn.
【呆笨】 dāibèn〈形〉 stupid
【呆若木鸡】 dāiruòmùjī〈成〉 be dumbstruck
【呆头呆脑】 dāitóu-dāinǎo〈成〉 be stupid-looking
【呆小症】 dāixiǎozhèng ▸**p. 50**〈名〉［医学］ cretinism: ～患者 cretin
【呆账】 dāizhàng〈名〉 bad debt
【呆滞】 dāizhì〈形〉 1（迟钝） dull: 他的两眼～无神。 His eyes glazed over. 2（流通不畅） idle: ～资本 idle capital ‖ ～资产 bad assets 3（不活跃） sluggish: 市场～ inactive market ‖ 市面～ sluggish market
【呆子】 dāizi〈名〉 idiot: ▸书～

呔 dāi〈叹〉 hey

待 dāi〈动〉 stay: ～一个晚上 stay one night
▸dài
【待会儿】 dāihuir〈动〉〈口〉 wait a minute: 让他～。 Tell him to wait a minute.

dǎi

歹 dǎi〈形〉 bad: ▸～徒, 为非作～
【歹毒】 dǎidú〈形〉 malicious: 心肠～ be malicious ‖ 用心～ have sinister motives
【歹人】 dǎirén〈名〉 villain
【歹徒】 dǎitú〈名〉 scoundrel: 抓获～ capture a gangster
【歹心】 dǎixīn〈名〉 malice: 存～ have bad intentions ‖ 起～ brew malice
【歹意】 dǎiyì = 歹心 dǎixīn

逮 dǎi〈动〉〈口〉 capture: ～小偷 catch a thief ‖ ～老鼠 catch mice
▸dài

傣 Dǎi = 傣族 Dǎizú
【傣剧】 dǎijù〈名〉 Dai opera
【傣族】 Dǎizú〈名〉 Dai ethnic group

dài

大 dài
▸dà
【大夫】 dàifu〈名〉〈口〉 doctor
▸dàfū
【大王】 dàiwang〈名〉〈旧〉 king: 山～ chief of mountain bandits
▸dàwáng

代 dài
A〈动〉 1（代替） act for: 请～我向她问好。 Please say hello to her for me. ▸～笔, ～人受过, 取～ 2（代理） act as: ～总理 acting premier
B〈名〉 1（时期） historical period: ▸当～, 历～, 时～ 2（朝代） dynasty: 唐～ Tang Dynasty ▸改朝换～ 3（辈） generation: 老一～领导人 older generation leaders ‖ 开发西部需要几～人的艰苦努力。 Everyone must work hard to develop China's western regions. ▸传宗接～ 4［地质］ era: ▸古生～, 新生～
【代办】 dàibàn A〈动〉 do sth. for sb.: ～托运 under commissions for shipments ‖ 邮政～所 postal agency ‖ 此事就请你～吧。 Will you act on my behalf? B〈名〉 1（外交代表） diplomatic representative 2（临时负责人） chargé d'affaires: 本任～ chargé d'affaires en titre
【代办处】 dàibànchù〈名〉 office of the Chargé d'Affaires
【代办所】 dàibànsuǒ〈名〉 agency: 储蓄～ savings agency
【代笔】 dàibǐ〈动〉 write on sb.'s behalf: ～遗嘱 dictated will
【代币券】 dàibìquàn〈名〉voucher: 企业不得发放～。 Companies may not issue vouchers.
【代表】 dàibiǎo A〈动〉 1（指代替他人或集体） represent: ～地区/国家/政府 represent one's district/country/government ‖ ～人民的利益 represent the interests of the people ‖ 这个符号～什么? What does this symbol stand for? 2（表示） embody: ～时代精神 embody the spirit of the era B〈名〉 1（指由选举产生） representative: 选举～ elect an representative ‖ 商务～ commercial representative ‖ 中国驻联合国～ China's representative to the United Nations ▸全权～ 2（指受委托或指派） delegate: 列席～ non-voting delegate ‖ 人大～ deputy to the National People's Congress ‖ 正式～ official delegate
【代表大会】 dàibiǎo dàhuì〈名〉 congress: 职工～ workers' conference ▸人民～
【代表队】 dàibiǎoduì〈名〉 representative team: 体育～ athletic team
【代表人物】 dàibiǎo rénwù〈名〉 typical representative
【代表团】 dàibiǎotuán〈名〉 delegation: ～团长 leader of a delegation ‖ 贸易～ trade mission ‖ 政府～ governmental mission
【代表性】 dàibiǎoxìng〈名〉 representativeness: 这种看法很有～。 This view is representative.

【代表资格】dàibiǎo zīgé〈名〉qualifications of a representative: ～审查委员会 deputies' credentials committee

【代表作】dàibiǎozuò〈名〉representative work: 贝多芬的～ Beethoven's masterpiece

【代步】dàibù〈书〉**A**〈动〉ride instead of walking: ～工具 riding tools **B**〈名〉vehicle, horse, etc. used to ride instead of walking

【代偿】dàicháng〈名〉［医学］compensation

【代称】dàichēng〈名〉another name

【代词】dàicí〈名〉［语言］pronoun: 人称～ personal pronoun ‖ 指示～ demonstrative pronoun

【代代花】dàidàihuā〈名〉［植物］bitter orange flower

【代代相传】dàidài-xiāngchuán〈成〉hand down from generation to generation

【代耕】dàigēng〈动〉**1**（指非农职业）make a living by means other than farming: 以笔～ earn one's living by writing **2**（替人耕种）do farm work for sb.

【代沟】dàigōu〈名〉generation gap

【代购】dàigòu〈动〉buy on sb.'s behalf

【代管】dàiguǎn〈动〉manage on behalf of another person

【代号】dàihào〈名〉code name: 识别～ identification code

【代价】dàijià〈名〉price: 付出沉重～ pay a heavy price ‖ 不惜任何～ at any cost

【代金】dàijīn〈名〉allowance: ～券 coupon

【代课】dàikè〈动〉act as a substitute teacher

【代劳】dàiláo〈动〉do sth. for sb.: 这件事你能～吗？ I wonder if you could do this for me?

【代理】dàilǐ〈动〉**1**（指临时）act for: ～厂长 acting director of a factory ‖ 在我外出期间，副主任将～我的工作。 In my absence, the vice chairman will act for me. **2**（指受委托）act as agent: ～出口 act as agent for export ‖ 独家～ sole agent ‖ 全权～ universal agency

【代理处】dàilǐchù〈名〉agency: 商务～ trade agency

【代理点】dàilǐdiǎn〈名〉agency: 机票、火车票～ airline and train ticket agency

【代理人】dàilǐrén〈名〉**1**（表委托关系）agent: 指定～ appoint an agent ‖ 销售～ sales agent **2**（表服务关系）procurator

【代理商】dàilǐshāng〈名〉agent: 出口～ export agent

【代码】dàimǎ〈名〉code: 输入～ input code

【代名词】dàimíngcí〈名〉**1**（同义词）synonym: 市场经济并不是资本主义的～。 Market economy isn't a synonym for capitalism. **2** = 代词 dàicí

【代庖】dàipáo〈动〉act in sb.'s place: ▸越俎～

【代培】dàipéi〈动〉train on contract: 为兄弟院校～教师 train teachers for other colleges and universities on contract

【代人受过】dàirén-shòuguò〈成〉be made a scapegoat

【代乳粉】dàirǔfěn〈名〉dairy milk powder substitute

【代售】dàishòu〈动〉be commissioned to sell sth.: ～机票 be commissioned to sell air tickets

【代数】dàishù〈名〉algebra

【代替】dàitì〈动〉substitute for: ～王老师上课 substitute for Mr Wang ‖ 用蜂蜜～食糖 substitute honey for sugar

【代为】dàiwéi〈动〉act for: ～说情 intercede on sb.'s behalf ‖ 请～问候。 Please say hello to him for me.

【代销】dàixiāo〈动〉sell on consignment: ～店 commission agent ‖ ～商 sales agent

【代谢】dàixiè〈动〉replace: 新旧～。 The new replaces the old.

【代行】dàixíng〈动〉act on sb.'s behalf: ～职权 function in an acting capacity

【代序】dàixù〈名〉replacement introduction

【代言费】dàiyánfèi〈名〉endorsement fee: 品牌～高得惊人。 Endorsement fees for brand names are shockingly high.

【代言人】dàiyánrén〈名〉spokesman

【代议制】dàiyìzhì〈名〉parliamentarism

【代用】dàiyòng〈动〉substitute: ～燃料 replacement fuel ‖ ～品 substitute

【代远年湮】dàiyuǎn-niányān〈成〉remote in past years

【代职】dàizhí〈动〉act for: 我不在的时候，由他～。 In my absence he will act for me.

【代字号】dàizìhào〈名〉swung dash（～）

轪（軑） dài〈名〉〈古〉**1**（指铁帽）iron cap on the axis of a wheel **2**（指车轮）wheel

甙 dài〈名〉［化学］glucoside

岱 Dài〈名〉Dai [another name for Mount Tai (泰山)]

【岱岳】Dàiyuè = 泰山 Tàishān

【岱宗】Dàizōng = 泰山 Tàishān

d

迨 dài〈介〉〈书〉when

绐（紿） dài〈动〉〈书〉cheat

骀（駘） dài

【骀荡】dàidàng〈形〉〈书〉**1**（指春风）refreshing: 春风～ refreshing spring breeze **2**（指人）loose

玳（瑇） dài

【玳瑁】dàimào〈名〉［动物］hawksbill turtle

带（帶） dài

A〈名〉**1**（区域）belt: 地震～ seismic belt ▸皮～ **2**（轮胎）tyre: 自行车～ bicycle tyre ‖ 汽车外～ truck tyre **3**［生理］leucorrhoea: ▸～下

B〈动〉**1**（携带）carry: ～把伞 take an umbrella ‖ 你～钱了吗？ Do you have any money on you? ‖ 请你给她～个口信好吗？ Would you mind taking a message to her? ‖ 她旅游时总是～着照相机。 She always carries a camera when she travels. ▸携～ **2**（带领）lead: ▸～队，～路

ℹ“带来”和“拿走”、“来”和“走/去”

“带来”和“拿走”

■ 在使用 bring 和 take 时很容易混淆。应该注意的是：使用时要参照说话者和听者所处的位置。

■ bring（带来／拿来／带去）指把某人或某物从某个地方带到说话者或听者所处的地方：

我能带我丈夫去参加你的聚会吗？
= Can I bring my husband to your party?

她会给我们带来新思想
= She will bring us new ideas

他给我们带来了一些蛋糕
= He brought us some cakes

请把你们的法语课本带到学校来
= Please bring your French textbooks to school

你能给我拿杯水吗？
= Can you bring me a glass of water, please?

■ take（带去／拿去／拿走）指把某人或某物从说话者或听者所处的地方带到另外一个地方去：

是汤姆拿了
= It's Tom who took it

有人把电脑拿走了
= Someone has taken the computer away

考卷不在这儿了，已经拿到考场去
= The exam papers are not here any more — they have been taken to the exam room

请不要把孩子带走
= Please don't take the children away with you

探望你母亲时，务必带上一束鲜花
= Do take your mum a bunch of flowers when visiting her

你能把猫带到兽医那儿吗？
= Can you take the cat to the vet?

“来”和“走/去”

■ come（来）和 go（走／去）的区分与 bring 和 take 相似。

■ come（来）指从某个地方来到说话者或听者的地方：

学生们还没来
= The students haven't come yet

你能来我家吗？
= Can you come to my house?

他们从伦敦到这儿来工作
= They came from London to work here

■ go（去／走）指离开说话者或听者所处的地方到另外一个地方去，也可指离开一个地方到另外一个地方：

我得走了
= I have to go now

他们昨天去了公园
= They went to the park yesterday

你乘飞机去那儿吗？
= Are you going there by plane?

火车开走了
= The train has gone

3 ▸p. 145（捎带）do sth. incidentally: 上街～包茶叶来。 Get me a bag of tea when you go shopping. ‖ 请随手把门～上。 Close the door behind you, please. 4（呈现）have: 面～笑容 with a smile on one's face 5（含有）carry: ～偏见的报道 biased report ‖ 这黄瓜～点儿苦味儿。 This cucumber is a bit bitter to the taste. 6（带动）drive: 先进～后进。 The more advanced spur on the less advanced. 7（同时发生）happen simultaneously: 连说～笑 talking and laughing 8（看管）raise: 你的孩子现在谁～着呢? Who is looking after your child?

【带班】dàibān〈动〉1（指值班）lead a group of people on duty: 带夜班 head up a night shift 2（指管班级）be in charge of the student affairs of a class: 她既要上课，又要～。 She teaches and is responsible for a class.

【带操】dàicāo〈名〉［体育］gymnastics with ribbons

【带刺儿】dàicìr〈动〉1（指物品）be prickly: ～的叶子 prickly leaves ‖ ～的玫瑰 thorny rose 2〈喻〉（指话语）be sarcastic: ～的话 sarcastic remarks ‖ 说话别～嘛。 Don't be sarcastic.

【带电】dàidiàn〈动〉be charged: ～作业 live-wire job

【带动】dàidòng〈动〉1（指运动）drive: 拖拉机～拖车。 The trailer is driven by a tractor. 2（引导）spur on: 在他的～下，大家都积极参加义务劳动。 His example spurred all others to participate in voluntary labour.

【带队】dàiduì〈动〉lead a group: 你来亲自～吧。 You'd better lead the team yourself.

【带钢】dàigāng〈名〉［冶金］strip steel

【带好儿】dàihǎor〈动〉give regards to: 请你给王教授带个好儿。 Please give my best regards to Professor Wang.

【带话】dàihuà〈名〉take a message: 给带个话儿 give sb. a message

【带劲】dàijìn〈形〉〈口〉1（有劲头）energetic: 干得挺～ work energetically ‖ 她的文章很～。 Her article was very forceful. 2（有乐趣）exciting: 骑摩托车兜风真～! It's great fun to take a spin on a motorcycle.

【带菌】dàijūn〈动〉carry bacteria: ～食物 food carrying germs ‖ ～者 carrier

【带宽】dàikuān〈名〉［通信］bandwidth: 视频～ video bandwidth

【带累】dàilěi〈动〉trouble: 我再也不想～你了。 I don't want to trouble you any more.

【带领】dàilǐng〈动〉lead: ～游客参观博物馆 take visitors around a museum ‖ 他～病人去医院。 He led the patient to the hospital. ‖ 班长～大家去爬山。 The monitor took his classmates to climb the mountain.

【带路】dàilù〈动〉lead the way: 你来～，我跟着走。 You lead on and I'll follow. ‖ 导游～，游客尾随。 Guides lead the way and visitors follow.

【带路人】dàilùrén〈名〉guide

【带球】dàiqiú〈动〉［足球］［篮球］dribble: ～突破防线 dribble past the defence

【带身子】dàishēnzi〈动〉〈口〉be in the family way

【带式】dàishì〈形〉belt-type: ～输送机 belt conveyor

【带头】dàitóu〈动〉take the lead: ～冲锋 lead the charge ‖ ～闹事者 riot leader ‖ 谁来～? Who will take the lead?

【带头人】dàitóurén〈名〉leader: 学术～ academic leader

【带头羊】dàitóuyáng〈名〉bellwether

【带下】dàixià ▸p. 50〈名〉［中医］morbid leucorrhoea

【带孝】dàixiào = 戴孝 dàixiào

【带薪】dàixīn〈动〉be paid: ～休假 paid vacation

【带信儿】dàixìnr〈动〉give a message

【带音】dàiyīn〈动〉[of vocal chords] vibrate

【带引】dàiyǐn〈动〉guide

【带有】dàiyǒu〈动〉have: ～讽刺意味 have satirical meaning ‖ ～民族色彩 have a national flavour

【带鱼】dàiyú〈名〉ribbon fish

【带职】dàizhí〈动〉be in service

【带状】dàizhuàng〈形〉zonal: ～分布 zonal distribution ▸～疱疹

【带状疱疹】dàizhuàng pàozhěn ▸p. 50〈名〉［医学］herpes zoster

【带子】dàizi〈名〉1（条状物）belt 2〈口〉（录像带）tape;（录音带）cassette tape

殆 dài〈书〉

A〈形〉dangerous: ▸知彼知己，百战不～

B〈副〉nearly: 敌人伤亡～尽。 The enemy was practically wiped out.

贷（貸）dài

A〈动〉1（借）lend: 向银行～款 solicit a loan from a bank 2（推卸）shirk: ▸责无旁～ 3（宽恕）pardon: ▸严惩不～

B〈名〉loan: ▸信～，高利～

【贷方】dàifāng〈名〉1［会计］credit: ～金额 amount of credit ‖ ～余额 balance due 2（指人）creditor: ～催款。 The creditor is pressing for the repayment of a loan.

【贷款】dàikuǎn A〈动〉grant a loan: 向银行～五十万元 obtain a loan of half a million *yuan* from a bank B〈名〉loan: 偿还～ redeem a loan ‖ 发放～ issue credits ‖ 低息～ low-interest loan

【贷学金】dàixuéjīn〈名〉student loan

待[1] dài〈动〉

1（等待）wait for: 尚～解决 await a solution ‖ 岁月不～人。 Time and tide wait for no man. ▸～命，期～，守株～兔 2（需要）need: 尚～说明 need to be explained ‖ 有～改善 need to be improved ▸自不～言 3（想要）be about to: ～说不说 hold back what one is about to say ▸～答不理

待[2] dài〈动〉

1（对待）treat: ～人和气 treat people kindly ‖ 你～我太好了。 You have been very kind to me. ▸亏～，优～ 2（招待）entertain: ～客 treat a guest to dinner ▸款～

▸dāi

【待查】dàichá〈动〉need checking

【待产】dàichǎn〈动〉be in labour

【待答不理】dàidā-bùlǐ〈俗〉be lukewarm towards sb.

【待岗】dàigǎng〈动〉be unemployed: ～人员 unemployed personnel

【待机】dàijī〈动〉1（指机会）wait for an opportunity: ～而动 wait for the right moment to move ‖ ～行事 wait for an opportune moment to act 2（指状态）put on standby

【待机时间】dàijī shíjiān〈名〉standby time

【待价而沽】dàijià'érgū〈成〉wait for the highest bid: 囤积居奇，～ store up commodities in short supply and sell them only at highest prices

【待考】dàikǎo〈动〉〈书〉remain to be verified

【待理不理】dàilǐ-bùlǐ〈成〉be stand-offish: 人家跟你说话，你怎么～的? Why are you so indifferent to what I am saying?

【待令】dàilìng〈动〉await orders

【待命】dàimìng〈动〉await orders: 原地～ stand by to await orders ‖ 整装～ get things ready and wait for orders

【待聘】dàipìn〈动〉wait for an appointment or a job: ～人员 applicant awaiting engagement

【待人处世】dàirén-chǔshì〈成〉way one treats others and conducts oneself in society

【待人接物】dàirén-jiēwù〈成〉way one conducts oneself in relation to others

【待售】dàishòu〈动〉be offered for purchase: 此房～。 This house is up for sale.

【待续】dàixù〈动〉to be continued

【待业】dàiyè ▸p. 966〈动〉be unemployed: ～青年 unemployed youth

【待遇】dàiyù〈名〉1（对待）treatment: ～不公 unfair treatment ‖ 政治～ political treatment 2（指权利、地位、报酬等）remuneration: ～优厚 attractive remuneration ‖ 提高知识分子～ raise pay and benefits for intellectuals

【待字】dàizì〈动〉〈书〉[of a young girl] still be single

【待字闺中】dàizì-guīzhōng〈成〉wait in the boudoir to be betrothed

怠 dài〈形〉

1（懒惰）slack: ▸～工，懈～ 2（轻慢）disrespectful: ▸～慢

【怠惰】dàiduò〈形〉idle

【怠工】dàigōng〈动〉go slow

【怠慢】dàimàn〈动〉1（轻慢）snub: 受到～ get the cold shoulder 2〈套〉（表歉意）neglect: ～之处，请多包涵。 Pardon me for any oversight.

袋 dài

A〈名〉bag: 表～ watch pocket ‖ 购物～ shopping bag ‖ 塑料～ plastic bag ▸旅行～

B〈量〉1（指袋装物）bag: 一～米 a bag of rice ‖ 一～面粉 a sack of flour 2（指水烟、旱烟）pouch: 一～烟 a pouch of tobacco ‖ 一～烟的工夫 a short while

【袋狸鼠】dàilíshǔ〈名〉bandicoot rat

【袋泡茶】dàipàochá〈名〉1（指茶包）tea bag 2（指茶）tea in bags

【袋鼠】dàishǔ〈名〉kangaroo

【袋熊】dàixióng〈名〉wombat

【袋装】dàizhuāng〈形〉bagged: ～面粉 bagged flour ‖ ～奶粉 milk powder in packets

【袋子】dàizi〈名〉bag: 米～ rice sack

逮[1] dài〈动〉〈书〉

reach: 力有未～ beyond one's power

逮[2] dài〈动〉

capture ▸～捕

▸dǎi

【逮捕】dàibǔ〈动〉arrest: ～某人 place sb. under arrest ‖ 实施～ conduct an arrest ‖ ～证 arrest warrant

戴 dài〈动〉

1（穿戴）wear: ～花 wear a flower ‖ ～红领巾 wear a red scarf 2（尊奉）respect: ▸爱～，拥～

【戴高帽子】dài gāomàozi〈惯〉lay it on thick: 爱～ be fond of flattering

【戴绿帽子】dài lǜmàozi〈惯〉be made a cuckold

【戴帽子】 dài màozi〈动〉〈喻〉 brand: 他被戴上自由主义者的帽子。 He was labelled a liberalist.
【戴胜】 dàishèng〈名〉［鸟类］ hoopoe
【戴孝】 dàixiào〈动〉 go into mourning
【戴月披星】 dàiyuè-pīxīng = 披星戴月 pīxīng-dàiyuè
【戴罪立功】 dàizuì-lìgōng〈成〉 atone for one's crimes by doing good deeds

黛 dài〈名〉 black pigment
【黛绿】 dàilǜ〈名〉 dark green

dān

丹 dān

A〈形〉 red: ▸～顶鹤, ～心
B〈名〉 pellet: ▸灵～妙药
【丹顶鹤】 dāndǐnghè〈名〉 red-crested crane
【丹毒】 dāndú ▸**p. 50**〈名〉［医学］ erysipelas
【丹凤眼】 dānfèngyǎn〈名〉 slanting eyes
【丹佛】 Dānfó〈名〉 Denver
【丹桂】 dānguì〈名〉［植物］ orange osmanthus
【丹麦】 Dānmài〈名〉 Denmark: ～人 Dane ‖ ～王国 kingdom of Denmark ‖ ～语 Danish
【丹青】 dānqīng〈名〉 **1**（指颜料） red and green paints **2**（指绘画） painting **3**（指史册） historical records
【丹青妙笔】 dānqīng-miàobǐ〈成〉 superb artistry in painting
【丹砂】 dānshā〈名〉 cinnabar
【丹参】 dānshēn〈名〉［中药］ root of red-rooted salvia
【丹田】 dāntián〈名〉 pubic region
【丹心】 dānxīn〈名〉 loyal heart: 一片～ a loyal heart

担（擔） dān

〈动〉 **1**（用肩挑） carry on a shoulder pole: ～水 carry water **2**（担负） shoulder: ～风险 run a risk ‖ ～责任 shoulder the responsibility
▸dàn
【担保】 dānbǎo〈动〉 guarantee: 用名誉～ give one's word ‖ 提供～ offer security ‖ ～人 guarantor ‖ 我（敢）以性命～。 I bet my life on it.
【担不是】 dān bùshi〈动〉 take the blame: 你们用不着担心，出了问题我来～。 You needn't worry. I'll take the blame if anything goes wrong.
【担承】 dānchéng〈动〉 bear
【担待】 dāndài〈动〉 **1**（包涵） excuse: 他还是个孩子，不懂事，您多～。 Please forgive him. He is a kid after all. **2**（承担） bear responsibility: 出了事由谁～? Should anything go wrong, who will bear the responsibility?
【担当】 dāndāng〈动〉 take on: ～重任 shoulder great responsibility
【担负】 dānfù〈动〉 bear: ～责任 shoulder the responsibility ‖ ～重任 have heavy responsibilities
【担纲】 dāngāng〈动〉 play the leading role: 该片由几位新秀～。 Several promising young actors and actresses star in the film.
【担架】 dānjià〈名〉 stretcher: 抬～ bear a stretcher
【担惊受怕】 dānjīng-shòupà〈成〉 be in fear: 一天到晚～ be in constant fear
【担名】 dānmíng〈动〉 assume a nominal status: 让你当顾问只不过是担个名儿，其实不用做什么具体工作。 Your position as consultant is only nominal; you don't have to do any specific work.
【担任】 dānrèn〈动〉 take charge of: ～领导职务 assume the leadership ‖ ～指挥 act as a conductor
【担险】 dānxiǎn〈动〉 run a risk
【担心】 dānxīn〈动〉 worry: ～他的安全 be concerned for his safety ‖ ～她的健康 worry about her health ‖ 消除人们的～ ease people's concerns
【担忧】 dānyōu〈动〉 be concerned about: 为前程～ be exercised about one's future ‖ 儿行千里母～。 Wherever her children are, a mother will always worry. ‖ 我们对此深感～。 It's a big concern to us.

单（單） dān

A〈形〉 **1**（不成双） single: ～排扣上衣 single-breasted coat ‖ ～扇窗户 single leaf window ▸～打, ～独, ～身 **2**（微弱） thin: ▸～薄, 势～力薄 **3**（不复杂） simple: ▸～纯, 简～ **4**（指衣物） unlined: ▸～裤, ～衣 **5**（指单数） odd: ▸～日, ～数
B〈名〉 **1**（指布） cover: ▸床～ **2**（列表） list: 工资～ pay slip ▸菜～, 账～, 传～
C〈副〉 only: ～凭经验 judging by experience alone
D ▸**p. 448**〈连〉 and: 一百～八将 one hundred and eight officers
▸chán, Shàn
【单摆】 dānbǎi〈名〉 simple pendulum
【单帮】 dānbāng〈名〉〈旧〉 solo travelling trader: 跑～ travel around trading on one's own
【单倍体】 dānbèitǐ〈名〉［生物］ haploid: ～育种 haploid breeding ‖ ～植株 haplobiont
【单笔】 dānbǐ〈名〉 single sum: ～贷款/投资不得超过10万元。 A single loan/investment cannot exceed 100,000 yuan.
【单边】 dānbiān〈名〉［经济］ one side: ～贸易 unilateral trade
【单兵】 dānbīng〈名〉 individual soldier
【单薄】 dānbó〈形〉 **1**（指衣物） thin: 穿着～ be thinly clad **2**（指人） thin and frail: 她身体很～。 She is thin and frail. **3**（指力量） insubstantial: 兵力～ be short of men ‖ 力量～ be feeble in strength
【单产】 dānchǎn〈名〉 unit production
【单车】 dānchē〈名〉〈方〉 bicycle
【单程】 dānchéng〈名〉 one way: ～票 single ticket〈英〉, one-way ticket〈美〉
【单传】 dānchuán〈动〉 **1**（指后代） have only one son for several generations in a row **2**〈旧〉（指传授） pass on a skill from one single master
【单纯】 dānchún〈形〉 **1**（纯真） simple: 思想～ be unsophisticated **2**（单一） pure: ～追求利润/速度 seek profit/speed alone
【单纯词】 dānchúncí〈名〉［语言］ single-morpheme word
【单词】 dāncí ▸**p. 999**〈名〉 word: 记～ memorize words
【单打】 dāndǎ〈名〉 singles: 男子/女子～ men's/women's singles
【单打独斗】 dāndǎ-dúdòu〈成〉 fight one-on-one
【单打一】 dāndǎyī〈惯〉 have a one-track mind
【单单】 dāndān〈副〉 only: ～他不同意。 He alone disagrees. ‖ 别人都知道，～我不知道。 Everybody knows it except me.
【单刀】 dāndāo〈名〉［武术］ **1**（指兵器） short-hilted broadsword **2**（指武术项目） single-sword event
【单刀直入】 dāndāo-zhírù〈成〉 speak in a straightforward way: 他提意见总是～，不拐弯抹角。 He is always straightforward when he airs his views and never beats about the bush.
【单调】 dāndiào〈形〉 monotonous: ～的工作/生活 dull work/life ‖ 色彩～ drab colouring
【单独】 dāndú〈副〉 by oneself: ～核算 independent accounting ‖ ～行动 act alone ‖ 我想～跟你谈一谈。 I'd like a word with you on your own.
【单发】 dānfā〈动〉［体育］ make a single-shot
【单方】 dānfāng〈名〉 **1**（指药方） home remedy **2**（单方面） one side: ～承诺 unilateral undertaking ‖ ～行动 act alone
【单方面】 dānfāngmiàn〈名〉 unilateralism: ～裁军/停火 unilateral disarmament/ceasefire
【单放机】 dānfàngjī〈名〉 tape player
【单飞】 dānfēi〈动〉［航空］ fly solo
【单峰驼】 dānfēngtuó〈名〉 dromedary
【单幅】 dānfú〈名〉 single width: ～布 single-width cloth
【单干】 dāngàn〈动〉 go it alone: ～户 one-man-band ‖ 他不爱跟人合伙做事，喜欢～。 He doesn't go in for partnerships, preferring to work alone.
【单杠】 dāngàng〈名〉 horizontal bar
【单个儿】 dāngèr **A**〈副〉 by oneself: 我～能完成这项任务。 I can complete this task by myself. **B**〈形〉 separate: 这套茶具～卖吗? Is this tea set sold by the piece?
【单根独苗】 dāngēn-dúmiáo〈成〉 only child
【单轨】 dānguǐ〈名〉 monorail
【单果】 dānguǒ〈名〉 simple fruit
【单过】 dānguò〈动〉 live independently: 儿女大了，现在都～了。 All my children are grown-up and live independently now.
【单号】 dānhào〈名〉 odd numbers: ～座 odd-numbered seat
【单耗】 dānhào〈名〉 unit consumption: 用电～达到国际先进水平。 Unit consumption of power has reached advanced international levels.
【单花果】 dānhuāguǒ = 单果 dānguǒ
【单铧犁】 dānhuálí〈名〉 single-furrow plough
【单簧管】 dānhuángguǎn ▸**p. 929**〈名〉 clarinet
【单季稻】 dānjìdào〈名〉 single-crop rice
【单价】 dānjià〈名〉 unit price: ～指数 unit value index
【单间】 dānjiān〈名〉 **1**（用于居住） single room **2**（供顾客使用） one-bay: ～铺面 one-bay shopfront
【单键】 dānjiàn〈名〉［化学］ single bond
【单晶】 dānjīng〈名〉 monocrystal
【单晶硅】 dānjīngguī〈名〉［电子］ monocrystalline silicon
【单晶体】 dānjīngtǐ〈名〉［物理］ monocrystal
【单句】 dānjù〈名〉［语言］ simple sentence
【单据】 dānjù〈名〉 document: 凭～报销 be reimbursed against receipts
【单孔目】 dānkǒngmù〈名〉［动物］ Monotremata: ～动物 monotreme
【单口相声】 dānkǒu xiàngsheng〈名〉 solo *xiangsheng*
【单裤】 dānkù〈名〉 unlined trousers
【单跨】 dānkuà〈形〉 single-span: ～桥 single-span bridge

【单利】dānlì〈名〉［经济］simple interest
【单恋】dānliàn〈动〉have one-sided love for sb.
【单列】dānliè〈动〉list as an independent unit: ▸计划～市
【单面】dānmiàn〈名〉single side: ～复制 single-sided copying
【单名】dānmíng〈名〉one-character name
【单宁酸】dānníngsuān〈名〉［化学］tannic acid
【单偶婚】dān'ǒuhūn〈名〉monogamy
【单皮鼓】dānpígǔ ▸**p. 929**〈名〉small drum
【单片】dānpiàn **A**〈名〉monochip: ～结构 single chip architecture **B**〈形〉monolithic: ～集成电路 monolithic integrated circuit
【单枪匹马】dānqiāng-pǐmǎ〈成〉single-handed: 他～打入黑社会团伙。He single-handedly infiltrated an underworld gang.
【单亲】dānqīn〈名〉single parent: ～家庭 single-parent family
【单曲】dānqǔ〈名〉single song: ～排行榜 singles chart
【单染色体】dānrǎnsètǐ〈名〉［生物］monosome
【单人】dānrén〈名〉single person: ～被单 single sheet
【单人床】dānrénchuáng〈名〉single bed
【单人划艇】dānrén huátǐng〈名〉［体育］Canadian single
【单人间】dānrénjiān〈名〉single room: 在酒店订个～ book sb. into a single room at a hotel
【单人皮艇】dānrén pítǐng〈名〉［体育］single kayak
【单人舞】dānrénwǔ〈名〉solo dance
【单日】dānrì〈名〉odd-numbered day
【单弱】dānruò〈形〉**1**（指身体）thin and weak: 身体～ fragile construction **2**（指力量）weak: 兵力～ be short of forces
【单色】dānsè〈名〉monocolour
【单身】dānshēn〈名〉**1**（指未婚）unmarried person: ▸～汉 **2**（指独自生活）living alone: ～在外 live alone away from home
【单身汉】dānshēnhàn〈名〉bachelor: ～生活 bachelor's life
【单声道】dānshēngdào〈名〉［物理］single track
【单式】dānshì〈名〉［经济］single entry
【单数】dānshù〈名〉**1** ▸**p. 691**（正奇数）odd number **2** ▸**p. 411**［语法］singular
【单丝不成线，独木不成林】dānsī bù chéng xiàn, dúmù bù chéng lín〈俗〉one single strand of silk doesn't make a thread, nor one solitary tree a forest
【单糖】dāntáng〈名〉［化学］monosaccharide
【单体】dāntǐ〈名〉**1**［化学］monomer **2**［植物］monosome: ～生物 monosomic
【单位】dānwèi〈名〉**1**（度量）unit: 长度～ unit of length ‖ 时间～ unit of time ‖ 体积～ unit of volume ‖ ～面积 unit area ▸货币～ **2**（机构）unit: 经济～ economic unit ‖ 生产～ production unit ‖ 基层～ grass-roots unit ▸工作～
【单位制】dānwèizhì〈名〉system of units
【单弦儿】dānxiánr〈名〉**1**（指乐器）*danxianr* [single-stringed instrument held in front of the body and plucked with a plectrum] **2**（指曲艺形式）*danxianr* [story-telling to musical accompaniment]
【单线】dānxiàn〈名〉**1**（指线）singleline: ～缝纫机 single-thread sewing machine ‖ ～天线 single-wire antenna **2**（指联系）one-way contact: 过去他和我是～联系。He had been my only contact. **3**（指轨道）single track: ▸～铁路
【单线铁路】dānxiàn tiělù〈名〉single-track railway
【单相思】dānxiāngsī〈动〉develop an unrequited love: 只怕你对她只是～。I'm afraid your love for her is unrequited.
【单向】dānxiàng〈形〉one-way: ～电路 one-way circuit ‖ ～行驶 one-way driving
【单项】dānxiàng〈名〉**1**（指项目）individual event: ～奖 individual event prize ▸～比赛 **2**（指方面）single item: ～奖金 bonuses for separate items
【单项比赛】dānxiàng bǐsài〈名〉individual competition
【单项式】dānxiàngshì〈名〉［数学］monomial
【单相】dānxiàng〈形〉［电气］single-phase
【单行】dānxíng **A**〈形〉**1**（专项）special: ▸～法规，～条例 **2**（指行驶方向）one-way: ▸～线 **B**〈动〉**1**（指发生）happen singly: ▸祸不～ **2**（指著作）publish separately: ▸～本
【单行本】dānxíngběn〈名〉**1**（指版本）separate edition **2**（指书）offprint
【单行道】dānxíngdào = 单行线 dānxíngxiàn
【单行法规】dānxíng fǎguī〈名〉separate regulations
【单行条例】dānxíng tiáolì〈名〉specific regulations
【单行线】dānxíngxiàn〈名〉one-way street
【单姓】dānxìng〈名〉single-character surname
【单性】dānxìng〈形〉**1**（无性别区分）unisex: ▸～花 **2**（孤雌）parthenogenetic
【单性花】dānxìnghuā〈名〉unisex flower
【单性生殖】dānxìng shēngzhí〈名〉parthenogenesis
【单眼】dānyǎn〈名〉［动物］simple eye
【单眼皮】dānyǎnpí〈名〉single-edged eyelid
【单叶】dānyè〈名〉［植物］simple leaf
【单一】dānyī〈形〉single: 产品结构～ monotonous product mix ‖ ～的分配制度 single distribution system
【单一性】dānyīxìng〈名〉monotony
【单衣】dānyī〈名〉unlined garment
【单义词】dānyìcí〈名〉［语言］monosemic word
【单翼机】dānyìjī〈名〉monoplane
【单音词】dānyīncí〈名〉［语言］monosyllable
【单引号】dānyǐnhào〈名〉single quotation mark
【单元】dānyuán〈名〉unit: 课本前三个～ first three units in a textbook ‖ 五号楼三～312室 No 312, Entrance 3, Building 5
【单元楼】dānyuánlóu〈名〉apartment building
【单元音】dānyuányīn〈名〉［语言］monophthong
【单质】dānzhì〈名〉［化学］simple substance
【单字】dānzì〈名〉**1**（指汉字）individual character **2**（指其他语言）individual word
【单子】dānzi〈名〉**1**（大幅布）sheet: 床～ bed sheet **2**（用于分项记事）list;（账单）bill;（表格）form: 要买些什么，请开个～。Please make a list of what you want to buy.
【单作】dānzuò〈名〉［农业］monoculture

眈 dān

【眈眈】dāndān〈形〉glaring: ▸虎视～

耽[1] dān〈动〉〈书〉abandon oneself to: ～于恶习/幻想 indulge in bad habits/illusions ‖ ～于酒色 be given to sensual pleasures

耽[2]（躭）dān〈动〉delay: ▸～搁，～误

【耽搁】dānge〈动〉**1**（停留）stop over: 要尽快回来，别在那里～太久。Come back as quickly as possible; don't stay there for too long. ‖ 去北京途中，我要在西安～一下。I may have a stopover in Xi'an on my way to Beijing. **2**（拖延）delay: ～时间 waste time ‖ 这件事不能再～了。This cannot be delayed any more. **3**（错过）miss a chance to do sth.: 你来得太晚了，把机会～了。You have come too late and missed the chance.
【耽溺】dānnì〈动〉〈书〉abandon oneself to: ～酒色 be given to sensual pleasures ‖ ～于寻欢作乐 abandon oneself to pleasure
【耽误】dānwu〈动〉delay: 塌方～了整个工程。The collapse has held up the whole project.

殚（殫）dān〈动〉〈书〉exhaust

【殚精竭虑】dānjīng-jiélǜ〈成〉devote one's entire energy and thought to

箪（簞）dān〈名〉round food container made of bamboo

【箪食壶浆】dānsì-hújiāng〈成〉welcome troops with food and drinks

dǎn

胆（膽）dǎn〈名〉**1**（胆囊）gall bladder: ▸～囊，肝～，卧薪尝～ **2**（胆子）guts: ▸～大妄为，～略，大～ **3**（内胆）inner container: ▸瓶～，球～

【胆大包天】dǎndà-bāotiān〈成〉be extremely audacious: ～的罪行 outrageous crime
【胆大妄为】dǎndà-wàngwéi〈成〉act brazenly and recklessly: ～之徒 daredevil
【胆大心细】dǎndà-xīnxì〈成〉be bold but cautious
【胆道】dǎndào = 胆管 dǎnguǎn
【胆道结石】dǎndào jiéshí ▸**p. 50**〈名〉［医学］biliary lithiasis
【胆敢】dǎngǎn〈动〉dare: 敌人～来犯，就叫他们完蛋。If the enemy dare to invade, we will wipe them out.
【胆固醇】dǎngùchún〈名〉cholesterol
【胆管】dǎnguǎn〈名〉biliary duct
【胆寒】dǎnhán〈形〉terrified: 令敌人～ strike terror into the enemy's heart
【胆结石】dǎnjiéshí = 胆囊结石 dǎnnáng jiéshí
【胆力】dǎnlì〈名〉courage: ～过人 have extraordinary courage
【胆量】dǎnliàng〈名〉guts: 有～ have the guts ‖ 那个男孩～大。That boy has got real guts.
【胆略】dǎnlüè〈名〉courage and resourcefulness: ～超群 have unusual courage and resourcefulness
【胆囊】dǎnnáng〈名〉gall bladder: ～收缩

素 cholecystokinin
【胆囊结石】dǎnnáng jiéshí ▸**p. 50**〈名〉［医学］gall bladder stone
【胆囊炎】dǎnnángyán ▸**p. 50**〈名〉［医学］cholecystitis
【胆气】dǎnqì〈名〉guts
【胆怯】dǎnqiè〈形〉cowardly: 他～了。His courage failed.
【胆识】dǎnshí〈名〉courage and insight: 很有～ be blessed with courage and insight
【胆小鬼】dǎnxiǎoguǐ〈名〉coward
【胆小如鼠】dǎnxiǎo-rúshǔ〈成〉be as timid as a mouse
【胆虚】dǎnxū〈形〉diffident
【胆战心惊】dǎnzhàn-xīnjīng〈成〉be terror-stricken
【胆汁】dǎnzhī〈名〉［生理］bile
【胆壮】dǎnzhuàng〈形〉plucky
【胆子】dǎnzi〈名〉guts: ～大 have great courage ‖ 好大的～! What a nerve!

疸 dǎn ▸黄疸 huángdǎn

掸（撣） dǎn〈动〉dust: ～掉衣服上的灰尘 flick the dust off one's coat ‖ ～去身上的雪 brush the snow off one's clothes
▸Shàn
【掸子】dǎnzi〈名〉duster: 鸡毛～ feather duster

赕（賧） dǎn〈动〉〈书〉offer as a tribute to
【赕佛】dǎnfó〈动〉make offerings to the Buddha to ward off calamities and receive blessings

亶 dǎn〈形〉〈书〉honest and dependable
▸dàn

dàn

石 dàn〈量〉*dan* [unit of dry measure for grain, equal to 100 litres]
▸shí

旦[1] dàn〈名〉〈书〉**1**（早晨）dawn: ▸～夕, 通宵达～ **2**（某一天）day: ▸毁于一～, 元～

旦[2] dàn〈名〉［戏曲］*dan* [the female role, one of the four main roles in traditional Chinese opera]: ▸花～
【旦旦】dàndàn〈形〉〈书〉sincere: ▸信誓～
【旦角】dànjué = 旦[2] dàn
【旦暮】dànmù〈名〉〈书〉brief span of time
【旦夕】dànxī〈名〉〈书〉**1**（早晨和晚上）morning and evening **2**（短时间）short time: 命在～。Death is nearing. ▸危在～
【旦夕之间】dànxīzhījiān〈成〉in a short time

但 dàn
A〈副〉only: 不求有功，～求无过 seek no glory, merely try to avoid blame
B〈连〉yet: 一般如此，～也有例外。This is true in general, but there are exceptions.
【但凡】dànfán〈副〉without exception: ～该他干的事，他总会干得很好。Whatever job he is assigned to do, he will do it perfectly. ‖ ～认识他的人，对他都很鄙视。Everyone who knows him holds him in contempt.
【但是】dànshì〈连〉but: 她年龄小，～很懂事。She is young but quite sensible. ‖ 他说要来的，～根本就没有露面。He said he would come, yet he did not show up at all.
【但书】dànshū〈名〉［法律］proviso
【但愿】dànyuàn〈动〉I wish: ～如此 I hope so

担（擔） dàn
A〈名〉carrying pole with loads on both ends: ▸货郎～, 重～
B〈量〉**1** ▸**p. 978**（100斤）*dan* [unit of weight, equal to 50 kilograms] **2**（成担的东西）[used for things carried on a shoulder pole] load: 一～水 two buckets of water carried on a shoulder pole
▸dān
【担担面】dàndanmiàn〈名〉〈方〉*dandan* noodles
【担子】dànzi〈名〉**1**（指物）shoulder pole with loads on both ends **2**〈喻〉（指工作和责任）responsibility: 你身上的～不轻啊! You have got such a heavy responsibility! ▸挑～

诞[1]（誕） dàn〈形〉absurd: ▸怪～, 荒～

诞[2]（誕） dàn
A〈动〉be born: ▸～辰, ～生
B〈名〉birthday: ▸华～, 圣～, 寿～
【诞辰】dànchén〈名〉birthday (of a respected person or senior)
【诞生】dànshēng〈动〉be born: 1949年10月1日，中华人民共和国～了。The People's Republic of China was founded on October 1, 1949.

啖（啗） dàn〈动〉〈书〉**1**（吃）eat: ～饭 have a meal **2**（喂）feed: ～虎狼以肉 feed meat to tigers and wolves ‖ 以枣～之 feed with dates **3**（诱惑）lure with huge profits: ～以重金 entice with huge amounts of money ‖ 以私利～之 lure with personal gains

淡 dàn〈形〉**1** ▸**p. 863**（指味道、气味、颜色等）light: ～咖啡 weak coffee ‖ ～～的香气 light fragrance ‖ ～蓝色 pale blue ‖ ～绿 light green ▸轻描～写, ～墨 **2**（淡漠）indifferent: ▸～然, 冷～ **3**（不咸）not salty: 这道菜有点儿～。The dish is a little bland. **4**（不兴旺）slack: ▸～季, ～市 **5**（无关紧要）trivial: ▸扯～
【淡泊】dànbó〈动〉〈书〉be indifferent to fame and fortune: ～名利 be indifferent to fame and profit
【淡泊明志】dànbó-míngzhì〈成〉show one's aspirations by leading a simple life
【淡薄】dànbó〈形〉**1**（不浓密）thin: 雾渐渐～了。The mist gradually thinned. **2**（不强烈）weak: 酒味～。The wine tastes weak. **3**（不深刻）indifferent: 法制观念～ lack awareness of law and discipline ‖ 人情～。People are indifferent to each other. **4**（不清晰）faint: 我对这件事的记忆很～。I have only a dim recollection of the event.
【淡菜】dàncài〈名〉dried mussels
【淡出】dànchū〈动〉**1**［影视］fade out **2**〈喻〉（退出）gradually retreat: ～演艺圈 gradually distance oneself from theatrical circles
【淡而无味】dàn'érwúwèi〈成〉**1**（指味道）be tasteless **2**〈喻〉（平淡）be insipid: ～的话 insipid remarks
【淡化】dànhuà〈动〉**1**（减少盐分）desalinate: ～海水/咸水 desalinate sea/salt water **2**（淡薄）become weaker: 家族观念～了。The concept of family is becoming less important. **3**（减弱）play down: ～个人的作用 dilute the role of individuals ‖ ～这一事件 play down the event
【淡季】dànjì〈名〉off season: 旅游～ slow tourist season ‖ ～票价便宜得多。Off-season tickets are a lot cheaper.
【淡漠】dànmò〈形〉**1**（冷淡）indifferent: 态度～ indifferent attitude **2**（不真切）vague: 这件事在我的记忆里已经～了。The event has become hazy in my mind.
【淡墨】dànmò〈名〉light ink
【淡然】dànrán〈形〉〈书〉detached: ～一笑 smile drily ‖ ～处之 treat with indifference
【淡入】dànrù〈动〉**1**［影视］fade in **2**〈喻〉（进入）gradually enter
【淡市】dànshì〈名〉sluggish market
【淡水】dànshuǐ〈名〉fresh water: ～游泳池 freshwater swimming pool ‖ ～鱼 freshwater fish
【淡水湖】dànshuǐhú〈名〉freshwater lake
【淡忘】dànwàng〈动〉fade from one's memory: 我已把他～了。He has faded from my memory.
【淡雅】dànyǎ〈形〉simple but in good taste: 陈设～ be simply but elegantly furnished ‖ 衣着～ be dressed in a simple but tasteful style
【淡月】dànyuè〈名〉slack month
【淡竹】dànzhú〈名〉［植物］Henon Bamboo
【淡妆】dànzhuāng〈名〉light make-up: 她喜欢施～。She likes to wear light make-up.
【淡妆浓抹】dànzhuāng-nóngmǒ〈成〉in light or heavy make-up: ～总相宜。In light or heavy make-up, either way she always looks attractive.

惮（憚） dàn〈动〉〈书〉fear: ～烦 fear being bothered ▸肆无忌～

弹（彈） dàn〈名〉**1**（用于弹弓）pellet: 泥～ mud ball ▸～丸 **2**（爆炸物）bomb: ▸～片, 中～, 子～
▸tán
【弹道】dàndào〈名〉trajectory
【弹道导弹】dàndào dǎodàn〈名〉ballistic missile
【弹弓】dàngōng〈名〉catapult
【弹痕】dànhén〈名〉shot mark: ～累累 be riddled with bullets
【弹尽粮绝】dànjìn-liángjué〈成〉run out of ammunition and provisions
【弹壳】dànké〈名〉**1**（指炮弹）shell case **2**（指枪弹）cartridge case
【弹坑】dànkēng〈名〉shell crater
【弹孔】dànkǒng〈名〉bullet hole
【弹盘】dànpán〈名〉magazine
【弹片】dànpiàn〈名〉shell fragment
【弹膛】dàntáng〈名〉cylinder
【弹头】dàntóu〈名〉bullet: ▸核～
【弹丸】dànwán〈名〉**1**（用于弹弓）shot **2**（指枪弹）shot **3**（指地方）tiny place: ～之地 tiny place

d

【弹无虚发】dànwúxūfā〈成〉 every bullet finds its target
【弹匣】dànxiá〈名〉 1（指部件） magazine 2（指盒子） cartridge box
【弹药】dànyào〈名〉 ammunition: 运送～ transport ammunition ‖ ～库 ammunition depot
【弹着点】dànzhuódiǎn〈名〉 point of impact
【弹子】dànzǐ〈名〉 1（用于弹弓） pellet shot 2〈方〉= 台球 táiqiú 1 3〈方〉（玻璃小球） marble: ～游戏 game of marbles
【弹子锁】dànzisuǒ〈方〉= 撞锁 zhuàngsuǒ

蛋

蛋 dàn〈名〉 1（卵） egg: 炒/煎/煮～ scrambled/fried/boiled eggs ‖ 孵～ hatch eggs ‖ 下～ lay eggs 2（蛋状物） egg-shaped thing: ▸脸～儿, 山药～ 3〈贬〉（指人） person of certain characteristics: ▸笨～, 混～, 穷光～
【蛋白】dànbái〈名〉 1（指蛋的一部分） egg white 2［生化］ protein: 高～食品 food rich in protein
【蛋白胨】dànbáidòng〈名〉［化学］ peptone
【蛋白酶】dànbáiméi〈名〉［生化］ proteinase
【蛋白质】dànbáizhì〈名〉［生化］ protein
【蛋彩画】dàncǎihuà〈名〉 tempera painting
【蛋粉】dànfěn〈名〉 egg powder
【蛋糕】dàngāo〈名〉 cake: 生日～ birthday cake
【蛋羹】dàngēng〈名〉 egg custard
【蛋花汤】dànhuātāng〈名〉 egg drop soup
【蛋黄】dànhuáng〈名〉 yolk: ～月饼 yolk moon cake
【蛋黄酱】dànhuángjiàng〈名〉mayonnaise
【蛋鸡】dànjī〈名〉 laying hen
【蛋卷】dànjuǎn〈名〉 egg roll
【蛋卷冰激凌】dànjuǎn bīngjilíng〈名〉 ice-cream cone
【蛋壳】dànké〈名〉 eggshell
【蛋品】dànpǐn〈名〉 egg product
【蛋青】dànqīng〈名〉 pale blue
【蛋清】dànqīng = 蛋白 dànbái 1
【蛋松】dànsōng〈名〉 dried egg floss
【蛋用鸡】dànyòngjī = 蛋鸡 dànjī

氮

氮 dàn〈名〉［化学］ nitrogen (N): 含～量 nitrogen content
【氮肥】dànféi〈名〉［化学］ nitrogenous fertilizer
【氮化】dànhuà〈动〉 nitride: ～铝 aluminium nitride ‖ ～钢 nitriding steel
【氮气】dànqì〈名〉 nitrogen

亶

亶 dàn = 但 dàn
▸dǎn

瘅（癉）

瘅（癉） dàn〈书〉
A〈名〉 illness from overwork
B〈动〉 loathe: ▸彰善～恶

赕（賧）

赕（賧） dàn〈书〉
A〈动〉 advance money
B〈名〉 top of a scroll or back of a thread-bound book

澹

澹 dàn〈形〉〈书〉 peaceful
【澹泊】dànbó = 淡泊 dànbó
【澹然】dànrán = 淡然 dànrán

dāng

当[1]（當） dāng

A〈动〉 1（等于） be equal: ▸门～户对, 相～ 2（掌管） be in charge: ▸～家, ～权, 独～一面 3（承担） accept: 不敢～。 I just don't deserve it. ‖ 一人做事一人～。 One must be accountable for what one does. ▸敢作敢～ 4（阻拦） block: ▸螳臂～车 5（担任） serve as: ～第一把手 play first fiddle ‖ ～秘书 work as a secretary ‖ 既～爸又～妈 have the role of both father and mother 6（对着） face: ▸首～其冲 7（应该） should: 理～如此。 That's the way it should be. ‖ ～买的就买，不～买的就不买。 Buy what you must but not what you shouldn't.
B〈介〉 when: ～我上床时，已经是十二点了。 It was already 12 o'clock when I went to bed. ▸～初, ～前
C〈名〉 1（空隙） space: ▸空～2 2（指顶部） end: ▸瓦～

当[2]（噹） dāng

当[2]（噹） dāng〈拟〉 jingle: ～～敲铃 jingle a bell ‖ 铃声～～。 The bell clanged.
▸dàng
【当班】dāngbān〈动〉 be on duty: ～护士 nurse on shift ‖ 今天我～。 I am on duty today.
【当兵】dāngbīng〈动〉 serve in the army: 他18岁那年当了兵。 He joined the army when he was 18.
【当差】dāngchāi〈旧〉 A〈动〉 run errands for officials and employers B〈名〉 male servant
【当场】dāngchǎng〈副〉 on the spot: ～被捕 be caught in the act ‖ ～成交 clinch a deal then and there
【当初】dāngchū〈名〉 beginning: ～这里是一个小渔村。 It used to be a small fishing village. ‖ 早知今日，何必～。 Knowing the score, how could things come to this?
【当代】dāngdài ▸**p. 618**〈名〉 present age: ～文学 contemporary literature ‖ ～作家 contemporary writer
【当道】dāngdào A〈动〉〈贬〉 be in power: 恶人～，好人受气。 When villains are in power, good people suffer. B〈名〉 middle of the road: 别～站着。 Don't stand in the way.
【当地】dāngdì〈名〉 locality: ～居民 local residents ‖ ～人 native ‖ 我不是～人。 I'm not local here.
【当断不断，反受其乱】dāngduàn-bùduàn, fǎnshòu-qíluàn〈成〉 he who hesitates is lost
【当归】dāngguī〈名〉［中药］ Chinese angelica
【当行出色】dānghàng-chūsè〈成〉 excel in one's own field
【当红】dānghóng〈形〉 popular: ～歌手 singer in vogue
【当机立断】dāngjī-lìduàn〈成〉 make a prompt decision: 事情紧迫，必须～。 The circumstances call for a quick decision.
【当即】dāngjí〈副〉 immediately: 接到命令，～出发 set out at once upon receiving the order
【当家】dāngjiā A〈动〉 1（说了算） be the head of the family: 他家是妻子～。 It is his wife who calls the shots in the house. 2（主持家务） keep house: 我的妻子很会～。 My wife is a very good housekeeper. B〈形〉 special: 这是本店的～菜。 This is the speciality of the restaurant.
【当家的】dāngjiāde〈名〉 1（指家） head of a family 2（指寺庙） head monk of a Buddhist temple 3〈方〉（丈夫） husband
【当家作主】dāngjiā-zuòzhǔ〈成〉 rule the roost: 在我们村里是村民～。 The villagers are the masters of our village.
【当间儿】dāngjiànr〈名〉〈方〉 middle: 正～ right in the centre ‖ 屋子～放着一张矮桌子。 In the middle of the room, there was a low table.
【当街】dāngjiē A〈动〉 face a street: 他家～开了个小店铺。 His family runs a small shop in the street. B〈名〉〈方〉 street: ～站了好多人。 Many people are standing in the street.
【当今】dāngjīn ▸**p. 618**〈名〉 1（现在） today: ～社会 present-day society ‖ ～世界 the world today 2〈旧〉（皇帝） reigning emperor
【当紧】dāngjǐn〈形〉〈方〉 important: 这事很～，须抓紧办理。 This is an urgent matter that calls for immediate attention.
【当局】dāngjú〈名〉 authorities: 向～申诉 file a complaint with the authorities ‖ 地方～ local authorities ‖ 政府～ government authorities
【当局者迷，旁观者清】dāngjúzhě mí, pángguānzhě qīng〈成〉 outsiders sometimes have a clearer view than those on the inside
【当空】dāngkōng〈动〉 be in the sky: 皓月～。 A bright moon is shining in the sky. ‖ 烈日～。 The sun is blazing right overhead in the sky.
【当口儿】dāngkour〈名〉〈口〉 this very moment: 正在这～，停电了。 The power went out at that very moment.
【当啷】dānglāng〈拟〉 clank: 铁门～一声关上了。 The iron gate clanked shut.
【当量】dāngliàng〈名〉［化学］equivalent: 化学～ chemical equivalent ‖ 梯恩梯～ TNT equivalent
【当令】dānglìng〈动〉 be in season: 现在草莓正～。 Strawberries are in season just now.
【当面】dāngmiàn〈副〉 face-to-face: ～道歉 make a face-to-face apology ‖ ～点清 check on the spot ‖ ～撒谎 lie to sb.'s face
【当面锣，对面鼓】dāngmiàn luó, duìmiàn gǔ〈俗〉 argue face-to-face: 咱们～，把事情说清楚。 Let's argue things out face-to-face.
【当面是人，背后是鬼】dāngmiàn shì rén, bèihòu shì guǐ〈俗〉 be two-faced
【当面一套，背后一套】dāngmiàn yītào, bèihòu yītào〈俗〉 be two-faced
【当年】dāngnián A〈名〉 those days: 不减～ not less than before ‖ 她～挺能干的。 She was once quite capable. B〈动〉 be in the prime of life: 男人四十正～。 A forty-year-old man is in his prime.
▸dàngnián
【当前】dāngqián A〈动〉 be confronted with: 大敌～ face a formidable enemy B〈名〉 the present: ～任务 present task ‖ ～形势对我们有利。 The present situation is favourable to us.
【当枪使】dāngqiāngshǐ〈惯〉〈喻〉use sb. as a weapon: 我可不愿意被人～。 I don't want to be anyone's weapon.
【当权】dāngquán〈动〉 hold power: ～派 people in power
【当然】dāngrán A〈副〉 of course: 这～是最好的解决办法。 This is certainly the best solution. B〈形〉 1（应该如此） natural: ▸理所～ 2（指职务） ex officio:

～会员 member as of right ‖ 总统是该委员会的～成员。 The president is an ex officio member of the committee.
【当仁不让】 dāngrén-bùràng 〈成〉 not decline to accept what one deserves: 既然选上了，就～。 Since you have been voted into the chair, don't hesitate to take it.
【当日】 dāngrì 〈名〉 that time
▸dàngrì
【当时】 dāngshí 〈名〉 that time: 她～的确是这么说的。 That was exactly what she said then.
▸dàngshí
【当事人】 dāngshìrén 〈名〉 **1**（指与案件有关） party: 讯问～ question the party ‖ ～陈述 statements of the parties **2**（指与事实有关） person involved: 我是～之一。 I was one of the people involved.
【当庭】 dāngtíng 〈副〉 in court: ～释放 be released by the court
【当头】 dāngtóu **A** 〈副〉 overhead: 烈日～。 The fierce sun was shining overhead. ▸～棒喝 **B** 〈动〉 **1**（在眼前） be faced with: 国难～ be faced with a national crisis **2**（放在首位） put in first place: 不能遇事钱～。 You can't put money above everything else.
▸dàngtou
【当头棒喝】 dāngtóu-bànghè 〈成〉〈喻〉 sharp warning
【当头一棒】 dāngtóu-yībàng 〈成〉〈喻〉 **1**（指警告） sharp warning **2**（指打击） surprise attack
【当务之急】 dāngwùzhījí 〈成〉 urgent matter: 保护环境是～。 Environmental protection is of paramount importance.
【当下】 dāngxià 〈副〉 that very moment: 他～就被吓昏了。 He was so scared that he fainted right away.
【当先】 dāngxiān 〈动〉 be in the van: ▸一马～
【当心】 dāngxīn **A** 〈动〉 be careful: ～脚下! Mind your step! ‖ ～扒手! Beware of pickpockets! ‖ ～别踩了草坪! Keep off the grass! **B** 〈名〉 **1**（胸口） centre of the chest: ～一拳 punch right in the centre of the chest **2**（正中央） centre: 旗杆竖立在操场～。 The flagpole stands at the centre of the playground.
【当选】 dāngxuǎn 〈动〉 be elected: 他在这次大会上～为主席。 He was elected president at the congress.
【当选总统】 dāngxuǎn zǒngtǒng 〈名〉 president-elect
【当腰】 dāngyāo 〈名〉 middle: ～折断 break right in the middle
【当一天和尚撞一天钟】 dāng yī tiān héshang zhuàng yī tiān zhōng = 做一天和尚撞一天钟 zuò yī tiān héshang zhuàng yī tiān zhōng
【当院】 dāngyuàn 〈名〉〈方〉 courtyard interior
【当政】 dāngzhèng 〈动〉 be in power
【当之无愧】 dāngzhī-wúkuì 〈成〉 be worthy of: 这个荣誉你～。 You fully deserve the honour.
【当值】 dāngzhí 〈动〉 be on duty
【当中】 dāngzhōng 〈名〉 **1**（中间） middle: 人民英雄纪念碑坐落在天安门广场～。 The Monument to the People's Heroes stands in the middle of Tian'anmen Square. **2**（之中） among: 在所有选手～，他是最有希望的。 Of all the players, he is the most promising one.
【当中间儿】 dāngzhōngjiànr 〈名〉〈口〉 middle: 孩子睡在大床的～。 The baby lay sleeping right in the middle of the big bed.
【当众】 dāngzhòng 〈副〉 in public: ～表态 make one's position known to the public ‖ ～侮辱 publicly affront sb. ‖ ～宣布 declare in public ‖ ～出丑 make a spectacle of oneself in public

珰（璫） dāng 〈名〉〈书〉 **1**（耳饰） earring **2**（宦官） eunuch

铛（鐺） dāng 〈拟〉 clang
▸chēng

裆（襠） dāng 〈名〉 crotch: 这条裤子～有点儿紧。 The crotch of the trousers is a bit tight. ▸裤～

dǎng

挡（擋） dǎng
A 〈动〉 **1**（阻挡） obstruct: ～住敌人进攻 ward off an enemy attack ‖ ～住视线 obstruct the view ▸兵来将～，水来土掩 **2**（遮挡） ward off: ～风/雨 shelter from the wind/rain ‖ 穿上这件大衣～～寒气吧。 Put on this coat to keep off the cold. ▸遮～
B 〈名〉 **1**（遮挡物） fender: 炉～儿 fire screen **2**（挡位） gear: 低速～ bottom gear ‖ 挂一/二～ to be in first/second gear ‖ 汽车未挂～。 The car is not in gear. ▸倒～，换～，空～
▸dàng
【挡板】 dǎngbǎn 〈名〉 guard
【挡车】 dǎngchē 〈动〉 operate fly frames: ～工 loom tender
【挡风】 dǎngfēng 〈动〉 shelter from the wind: ～玻璃 windscreen 〈英〉, windshield 〈美〉
【挡风墙】 dǎngfēngqiáng 〈名〉〈喻〉 protector
【挡横儿】 dǎnghèngr 〈动〉〈方〉 get in the way: 不干你的事儿，你挡什么横儿。 It's none of your business. Why are you getting in the way?
【挡驾】 dǎngjià 〈动〉 turn away a visitor with an excuse: 凡说情者一律～ turn away each and every intercessor
【挡箭牌】 dǎngjiànpái 〈名〉 **1**（本） shield **2**〈喻〉（借口） excuse: 有错误就改，不要找～。 Correct any mistake you make. Don't come up with excuses.
【挡泥板】 dǎngníbǎn 〈名〉 **1**（指自行车） mudguard 〈英〉; fender 〈美〉 **2**（指汽车） wing (of car) 〈英〉; fender 〈美〉

党（黨） dǎng
A 〈名〉 **1**（派别） faction: ▸～羽，结～营私，死～ **2**〈书〉（亲族） kinsfolk **3**（政党） political party: ▸～派 **4**（中国共产党） Communist Party of China: 从严治～ tighten Party discipline ‖ ～的全国代表大会 national congress of the Party
B 〈动〉〈书〉 be partial to: ▸～同伐异
【党八股】 dǎngbāgǔ 〈名〉 Party jargon
【党报】 dǎngbào 〈名〉 party newspaper
【党代表】 dǎngdàibiǎo 〈名〉 Party representative
【党代会】 dǎngdàihuì 〈名〉 Party congress
【党阀】 dǎngfá 〈名〉 despotic leader of a political party
【党费】 dǎngfèi 〈名〉 party membership fees: 交～ pay party membership fees
【党风】 dǎngfēng 〈名〉 Party conduct: ～不正 unhealthy Party conduct ‖ ～建设 improve the Party's style of work
【党纲】 dǎnggāng 〈名〉 party programme
【党规】 dǎngguī 〈名〉 party rules
【党棍】 dǎnggùn 〈名〉 dirty party official
【党国】 dǎngguó 〈名〉 the party and the state [used by the KMT]
【党徽】 dǎnghuī 〈名〉 party emblem
【党籍】 dǎngjí 〈名〉 party membership: 保留～ retain one's party membership ‖ 开除～ expel from the party
【党纪】 dǎngjì 〈名〉 party discipline
【党纪国法】 dǎngjì guófǎ 〈成〉 party discipline and state law
【党建】 dǎngjiàn 〈名〉 Party building
【党课】 dǎngkè 〈名〉 Party lecture: 上～ attend a Party lecture
【党魁】 dǎngkuí 〈名〉〈贬〉 party chief
【党龄】 dǎnglíng 〈名〉 party standing: 有20年～ have been a party member for 20 years
【党派】 dǎngpài 〈名〉 political parties and groups: ▸民主～
【党票】 dǎngpiào 〈名〉〈贬〉 Party membership: 捞～ grab party membership
【党旗】 dǎngqí 〈名〉 party flag
【党群关系】 dǎngqún guānxì 〈名〉 relations between the Party and the masses: 密切～ enhance ties between the Party and the masses
【党参】 dǎngshēn 〈名〉［中药］ Pilose Asiabell Root
【党同伐异】 dǎngtóng-fáyì 〈成〉 defend those with whom one shares similar views and attack those with whom one doesn't
【党徒】 dǎngtú 〈名〉〈贬〉 member of a political faction
【党团】 dǎngtuán 〈名〉 **1**（党派和团体） political parties and groups **2**（特指中国共产党和共青团） Chinese Communist Party and Chinese Communist Youth League **3**（指议员集体） parliamentary group of a political party
【党团员】 dǎngtuányuán 〈名〉 Party and League members
【党委】 dǎngwěi 〈名〉 Party committee
【党务】 dǎngwù 〈名〉 party affairs
【党小组】 dǎngxiǎozǔ 〈名〉 Party group (under a Party branch)
【党校】 dǎngxiào 〈名〉 Party school
【党性】 dǎngxìng 〈名〉 Party spirit: ～强 have a strong sense of Party principles and interests
【党羽】 dǎngyǔ 〈名〉〈贬〉 members of a gang
【党员】 dǎngyuán 〈名〉 party member: 接纳新～ admit a new party member ▸预备～
【党章】 dǎngzhāng 〈名〉 party constitution
【党证】 dǎngzhèng 〈名〉 party membership card
【党政】 dǎngzhèng 〈名〉 Party and government: ～机关 Party and government departments
【党支部】 dǎngzhībù 〈名〉 Party branch: ～书记 Party branch secretary
【党中央】 Dǎngzhōngyāng 〈名〉 Central Committee of the Party
【党总支】 dǎngzǒngzhī 〈名〉 general Party branch
【党组】 dǎngzǔ 〈名〉 leading Party members' group
【党组织】 dǎngzǔzhī 〈名〉 Party organization: 各级～ Party organizations at various levels

谠（讜） dǎng 〈形〉〈书〉 upright: ～论 unbiased criticism

dàng

氹 dàng = 凼 dàng

当（當） dàng
A〈形〉 appropriate: 处理不～ be mishandled ▸得～，妥～
B〈动〉 **1**（等于） be equal to: 他一个人能～两个人用。 He can do as much work as two people. **2**（当作） regard as: 你把他～朋友吗？ Do you regard him as a friend? ▸安步～车 **3**（以为） think: 我～是谁呢，原来是你啊。 I was wondering who it could be. **4**（典当） pawn: 他～了结婚戒指。 He pawned his wedding ring. ▸典～
C〈名〉 pledge: ▸赎～
D〈介〉 at/in/on: ▸～年，～日
▸dāng

【当成】dàngchéng〈动〉 regard as: 不要把别人都～傻瓜。 Don't treat others as if they were all fools.
【当当】dàngdàng〈动〉 pawn things
【当年】dàngnián〈名〉 current year: ～还本付息 repay principal and interest within the current year ‖ ～兴建，～投产 be built and put into production in the same year
▸dāngnián
【当票】dàngpiào〈名〉 pawn ticket
【当铺】dàngpù〈名〉 pawnshop
【当日】dàngrì〈名〉 same day: ～返回 return on the same day ‖ ～有效 good for the date of issue only
▸dāngrì
【当时】dàngshí〈名〉 that very moment: 收到你的信，我～就回了信。 I wrote back to you as soon as I received your letter.
▸dāngshí
【当天】dàngtiān〈名〉 same day
【当头】dàngtou〈名〉〈口〉 pledge
▸dāngtóu
【当晚】dàngwǎn〈名〉 same evening
【当夜】dàngyè〈名〉 same night
【当月】dàngyuè〈名〉 same month
【当真】dàngzhēn **A**〈动〉 take seriously: 我在开玩笑呢，你可别～。 I was just kidding. Don't take it seriously. **B**〈形〉 real: 此话～? Are you serious? **C**〈副〉 sure enough: 天气预报说今天有雨，现在～下起来了。 The weather forecast said it would rain today, and sure enough it's beginning to rain now.
【当做】dàngzuò〈动〉 regard as: 我把他～知心朋友。 I count him among my close friends.

凼 dàng〈名〉〈方〉 water hole: 粪～ cesspool ‖ 水～ water pit
【凼肥】dàngféi〈名〉 wet compost

宕 dàng〈书〉
A〈形〉 unrestrained: ▸跌～
B〈动〉 procrastinate: ▸推～，延～

垱（壋） dàng〈名〉〈方〉 earth embankment in a river or paddy field

挡（擋） dàng ▸摒挡 bìngdàng
▸dǎng

荡¹（盪、蕩） dàng〈动〉
1（冲洗） wash away: ▸～涤 **2**（晃动） swing: ～秋千 play on a swing ▸动～ **3**（闲逛） loaf around: ▸闲～，游～ **4**（清除） get rid of: ▸倾家～产，扫～

荡²（蕩） dàng
A〈形〉 **1**（坦荡） vast: ▸坦～ **2**（不检点） loose in morals: ▸～妇，淫～
B〈名〉 **1**（浅水湖） shallow lake: 芦苇～ shallow lake filled with reeds **2** = 凼 dàng

【荡除】dàngchú〈动〉 get rid of: ～积习 get rid of old habits
【荡船】dàngchuán〈名〉 swingboat
【荡涤】dàngdí〈动〉〈书〉 cleanse: ～灵魂的罪恶 cleanse the soul of sin ‖ ～污泥浊水 clean up the filth
【荡妇】dàngfù〈名〉 loose woman
【荡平】dàngpíng〈动〉 quell
【荡气回肠】dàngqì-huícháng = 回肠荡气 huícháng-dàngqì
【荡然】dàngrán〈形〉〈书〉 completely lost: 资财～。 One's assets are all gone.
【荡然无存】dàngrán-wúcún〈成〉 all gone: 原作的讽刺意味在电影中似乎已～。 The sarcasm of the original novel seems to be completely lost in the film.
【荡漾】dàngyàng〈动〉 ripple: 春心～ one's heart is filled with thoughts of love ‖ 歌声～。 Songs filled the air.

档（檔） dàng
A〈名〉 **1**（细柱） crosspiece: ▸横～ **2**（指橱柜） shelves for files: ▸存～，归～ **3**（指文件、材料） files: ▸～案，调～ **4**（等级） grade: ▸高～ **5**〈方〉（摊位） stand: 鱼～ fish stall ▸大排～
B〈量〉 [used for events, etc.]: 几～子事凑在一起了。 Several things happened at once.

【档案】dàng'àn〈名〉 files: 查阅～ consult the archives ‖ 个人～ personal file ‖ ～馆 archives ‖ ～局 record office ▸人事～
【档次】dàngcì〈名〉 grade: 拉开收入～ widen the difference between income brackets
【档期】dàngqī〈名〉 [of films or television programmes] slot
【档子】dàngzi〈量〉〈方〉 [used for events, etc.]: 这～事你就交给别人去管吧。 Leave this matter to someone else.

菪 dàng ▸莨菪 làngdàng

dāo

刀 dāo
A〈名〉 **1**（指工具） knife: ▸菜～，铣～，铡～ **2**（刀状物） knife-shaped thing: 双～电闸 double-point switch ▸冰～
B〈量〉 a hundred sheets: 一～纸 a hundred sheets of paper

【刀把儿】dāobàr〈名〉 **1**（刀柄） handle of a knife **2**〈喻〉（权柄） power: 掌握～ hold power **3**〈方〉〈喻〉（把柄） handle
【刀把子】dāobàzi = 刀把儿 dāobàr
【刀背】dāobèi〈名〉 back of a knife blade
【刀笔】dāobǐ〈名〉 writing of indictments, appeals, etc.: ～老手 old hand in pettifoggery
【刀笔吏】dāobǐlì〈名〉 pettifogger
【刀兵】dāobīng〈名〉 **1**（武器） weapons: ～相见 take up arms against one other **2**（战争） war: ～之灾 disaster of war
【刀柄】dāobǐng〈名〉 hilt
【刀叉】dāochā〈名〉 knife and fork
【刀豆】dāodòu〈名〉 sword bean
【刀法】dāofǎ〈名〉 **1**（指厨艺） cutting skill **2**（指雕刻） carving skill or style **3**（指武功） swordsmanship
【刀锋】dāofēng〈名〉 knife edge
【刀斧手】dāofǔshǒu〈名〉〈旧〉 headsman
【刀耕火种】dāogēng-huǒzhòng〈成〉 slash-and-burn cultivation
【刀功】dāogōng〈名〉 **1**（指厨艺） cutting and slicing skill **2**（指武功） swordsmanship
【刀光剑影】dāoguāng-jiànyǐng〈成〉 glint and flash of knives and swords
【刀架】dāojià〈名〉 knife rest
【刀具】dāojù〈名〉［机械］ cutter
【刀口】dāokǒu〈名〉 **1**（刀锋） blade: ～锋利。 The knife has a sharp blade. **2**〈喻〉（关键处） crucial point: 把力量用在～上 direct one's efforts to the right spot **3**（伤口） cut: ～尚未愈合。 The cut has not healed yet.
【刀马旦】dāomǎdàn〈名〉［戏曲］ sword-and-horse *dan* [a female role in traditional Chinese opera]
【刀片】dāopiàn〈名〉 **1**［机械］ blade **2**（用于刮胡须） razor blade
【刀枪】dāoqiāng〈名〉 **1**（刀和枪） sword and spear **2**（武器） weapons
【刀枪不入】dāoqiāng-bùrù〈成〉 proof against sharp weapons
【刀枪入库，马放南山】dāoqiāng rùkù, mǎ fàng nánshān〈俗〉 put the weapons back in the arsenal and graze the war horses on the hillside
【刀鞘】dāoqiào〈名〉 sheath
【刀儿】dāor〈名〉 small knife: 铅笔～ pencil sharpener
【刀刃】dāorèn〈名〉 **1**（刀锋） blade **2**（关键处） crucial spot: 好钢用在～上 make the best use of the best material
【刀山火海】dāoshān-huǒhǎi〈成〉〈喻〉 severest trials
【刀伤】dāoshāng〈名〉 gash
【刀削面】dāoxiāomiàn〈名〉 pared noodles
【刀鱼】dāoyú〈名〉 long-tailed anchovy
【刀子】dāozi〈名〉 small knife
【刀子嘴，豆腐心】dāozizuǐ, dòufuxīn〈俗〉 be sharp-tongued but tender-hearted
【刀俎】dāozǔ〈名〉 **1**〈本〉 butcher's knife and chopping block **2**〈喻〉 persecutor or oppressor: ▸人为～，我为鱼肉

叨 dāo
▸dáo, tāo

【叨叨】dāodao〈动〉 chatter away: 瞎～ talk nonsense ‖ 别再～这件事了。 Stop jabbering on about this.
【叨唠】dāolao〈动〉 talk on and on
【叨念】dāoniàn = 念叨 niàndao

氘 dāo〈名〉［化学］ deuterium (D)

dáo

叨 dáo
▸dāo, tāo

【叨咕】dáogu〈动〉〈方〉 mutter: 他们在～什么？ What are they whispering about?

捯 dáo〈动〉〈方〉 **1**（回拉） wind back: 把风筝～下来。 Wind down the kite. **2**（快步走） walk step by step: 小腿～快点儿跟上我。 Move your young legs a bit faster and keep up with me. **3**（追究） investigate: ～老账 rake up old scores

【捯饬】dáochi〈动〉〈方〉smarten up
【捯根儿】dáogēnr〈动〉〈方〉get to the bottom of sth.
【捯气儿】dáoqìr〈动〉〈方〉1（指临死前）gasp for breath on one's deathbed 2（指上气不接下气）be out of breath

dǎo

导（導）dǎo

A〈动〉1（引领）guide: ～淮入海 channel the Huai River into the sea ▸～游, 先～, 因势利～ 2（开导）instruct: ▸开～, 指～ 3（传导）conduct: 铜～电。Copper conducts electricity. ▸～热, ～体 4（导演）direct: ～戏 direct a play ‖ 执～ serve as a director
B〈名〉director: 赵～ Director Zhao
【导板】dǎobǎn = 倒板 dǎobǎn
【导报】dǎobào〈名〉guide
【导标】dǎobiāo〈名〉beacon
【导播】dǎobō A〈动〉organize and direct a programme for broadcast B〈名〉programme director
【导出】dǎochū〈动〉derive, induce: ～单位 derived unit
【导弹】dǎodàn〈名〉missile: ～发射场 missile launch site
【导电】dǎodiàn〈动〉conduct electricity: ～体 electric conductor
【导读】dǎodú〈动〉provide guidance for reading: 世界名著～ guide to world literary masterpieces
【导发】dǎofā〈动〉lead to: 由于疏忽～了事故。It was carelessness that caused the accident.
【导购】dǎogòu〈动〉serve as a shopping guide: ～小姐 female shopping guide
【导管】dǎoguǎn〈名〉1［机械］duct: 金属～ metal conduit 2（指动植物）duct 3［医学］catheter
【导轨】dǎoguǐ〈名〉［机械］slideway: 滑门～ sliding door guide
【导航】dǎoháng〈动〉pilot: 为船只～ navigate a ship ‖ ～台 guidance station ‖ ～员 navigator
【导火索】dǎohuǒsuǒ = 导火线 dǎohuǒxiàn
【导火线】dǎohuǒxiàn〈名〉1（用于引爆）fuse: 点燃～ ignite a fuse ‖ 定时～ time fuse 2〈喻〉（起因）immediate cause: 海湾战争的～是什么？What is the immediate cause of the Gulf War?
【导流】dǎoliú〈名〉［水利］diversion: ～渠 water diversion canal
【导轮】dǎolún〈名〉［机械］guide pulley
【导论】dǎolùn〈名〉introduction
【导盲犬】dǎomángquǎn〈名〉guide dog
【导尿】dǎoniào〈名〉［医学］catheterization: ～管 catheter
【导热】dǎorè〈动〉conduct heat
【导师】dǎoshī〈名〉1（教师）tutor: 博士生～ supervisor of a PhD candidate 2（指引导者）guru
【导师制】dǎoshīzhì〈名〉tutorial system
【导视】dǎoshì〈名〉programme guide: 电视节目～ TV programme guide
【导体】dǎotǐ〈名〉［物理］conductor: 超～ superconductor ▸半～
【导线】dǎoxiàn〈名〉［电气］lead
【导向】dǎoxiàng A〈动〉1（指发展）lead to: 这次争论～双边关系的恶化。This dispute led to the deterioration of the bilateral relations. 2（指运动）guide: 这种雷达的～性能良好。This radar has very good guidance quality. B〈名〉guidance: 舆论～ guidance of public opinion ‖ 产品结构的调整应以市场为～。The adjustment of a product mix should be guided by the market.
【导言】dǎoyán〈名〉introduction
【导演】dǎoyǎn A〈动〉direct B〈名〉director: 名～ big-name director
【导引】dǎoyǐn〈动〉lead
【导游】dǎoyóu A〈动〉conduct a sightseeing tour B〈名〉tour guide: ～小姐 female tour guide
【导语】dǎoyǔ〈名〉prologue
【导源】dǎoyuán〈动〉1（指河流）have its source in: 黄河～于青海。The Yellow River originates in Qinghai Province. 2（来源）come from: 认识～于实践。Knowledge derives from practice.
【导致】dǎozhì〈动〉lead to: ～心脏病发作 trigger a heart attack ‖ 吸烟会～肺癌。Smoking can lead to lung cancer.

岛（島）dǎo ▸p. 164〈名〉island: ▸安全～, 半～

【岛国】dǎoguó〈名〉island country
【岛弧】dǎohú〈名〉island arc
【岛民】dǎomín〈名〉islander
【岛屿】dǎoyǔ〈名〉islands and islets

捣（搗）dǎo

〈动〉1（捶打）crush: ～蒜 pound garlic into paste ‖ ～衣 beat clothes while washing 2（攻打）charge: 直～敌营 make a swift assault on the enemy camp ▸～毁 3（扰乱）disturb: ▸～乱
【捣蛋】dǎodàn〈动〉make trouble: 调皮～ be mischievous
【捣蛋鬼】dǎodàngui〈名〉mischief
【捣鼓】dǎogu〈动〉〈方〉1（摆弄）fiddle with: 他钻在房里～他的集邮册。He was fiddling about in the room with his stamp collection. 2（经营）trade in: ～股票 deal in stocks ‖ ～点儿小买卖 do some small business
【捣鬼】dǎoguǐ〈动〉play tricks: 你在捣什么鬼? What mischief are you up to?
【捣毁】dǎohuǐ〈动〉destroy: ～一家地下工厂 destroy an underground workshop
【捣乱】dǎoluàn〈动〉1（破坏）make trouble: ～分子 troublemaker 2（干扰）disturb
【捣麻烦】dǎo máfan〈动〉〈口〉make trouble
【捣腾】dǎoteng = 倒腾 dǎoteng

倒[1]

dǎo〈动〉1（横躺）fall: ～在他的怀里 fall into his arms ‖ 飓风把大树刮～了。A hurricane toppled the big tree. ▸～塌, 卧～ 2（垮台）collapse: ▸～闭, ～台 3（使垮台）bring down: ▸～阁 4（被损坏）malfunction: 吃了酸苹果，我的牙～了。The sour apple set my teeth on edge. ‖ 他的嗓子～了，不再登台。He has lost his voice and no longer performs on the stage. ▸～胃口

倒[2]

dǎo〈动〉1（转换）change: ～座位 change seats ▸～班, ～车 2（调转）move around: 地方小，～不开身儿。There is no room to move around. 3（出售）sell up: 存货全都～出去了。The stock was sold up. 4（投机倒把）buy and resell at a profit: ～水果 deal in fruit 5〈口〉（震惊）be astonished ▸dào
【倒班】dǎobān〈动〉work in shifts: 昼夜～ work in shifts round the clock ‖ 两班倒 work in two shifts
【倒板】dǎobǎn〈名〉［戏曲］*daoban* [beat pattern used in traditional Chinese opera]
【倒闭】dǎobì〈动〉go out of business: 工厂～了。The factory has gone bankrupt.
【倒毙】dǎobì〈动〉drop dead: ～街头 drop dead in the street
【倒仓】dǎocāng〈动〉1（拿出晾晒）take grain out of a granary to air 2（换仓）transfer grain from one granary to another 3［戏曲］[of a young singer's voice] break
【倒茬】dǎochá = 轮作 lúnzuò
【倒车】dǎochē〈动〉change trains/buses: 去沈阳用不着在中途～。You don't have to change trains on your way to Shenyang. ▸dàochē
【倒伏】dǎofú〈动〉[of crops] lodge: 抗～品种 lodging-resistant strain
【倒戈】dǎogē〈动〉transfer one's allegiance
【倒阁】dǎogé〈动〉bring down a government
【倒海翻江】dǎohǎi-fānjiāng = 翻江倒海 fānjiāng-dǎohǎi
【倒换】dǎohuàn〈动〉1（轮流）take turns: 几种作物～着种 rotate several crops 2（掉换）exchange: ～次序 change the order ‖ ～麦种 exchange wheat seeds
【倒汇】dǎohuì〈动〉speculate in foreign exchange
【倒嚼】dǎojiào〈动〉〈口〉ruminate
【倒买倒卖】dǎomǎi-dǎomài〈成〉buy and resell at a profit
【倒卖】dǎomài〈动〉resell at a profit: ～紧俏商品 speculate in goods in short supply ‖ 转手～ sell what one has bought at a profit
【倒楣】dǎoméi = 倒霉 dǎoméi
【倒霉】dǎoméi〈动〉be down on one's luck: 总有一天他会～的。He will come to a bad end one of these days.
【倒弄】dǎonong〈动〉〈口〉buy and sell
【倒牌子】dǎo páizi〈惯〉lose credibility
【倒儿爷】dǎoryé = 倒爷 dǎoyé
【倒嗓】dǎosǎng〈动〉[of one's voice] go hoarse
【倒手】dǎoshǒu〈动〉1（换只手）shift from one hand to the other: 他把箱子倒了个手。He shifted the box from one hand to the other. 2（指货物买卖）change hands: ～买卖 engage in round transaction
【倒塌】dǎotā〈动〉collapse: 那座房子～了。The house collapsed.
【倒台】dǎotái〈动〉fall from power: 政府的～ fall of the government
【倒腾】dǎoteng〈动〉〈口〉1（移动）move: 把花盆～出去晒晒。Move the flower pots out into the sun. 2（调配）deploy: 人手少，～不开 not have enough hands for so many jobs 3（贩卖）trade in: ～牲口 deal in cattle
【倒替】dǎotì〈动〉take turns: 两个人～着看护病人。The two took turns in looking after the patient.
【倒头】dǎotóu〈动〉lie down: ～便睡 fall asleep as soon as one's head touches the pillow
【倒胃口】dǎo wèikou〈惯〉1（指食欲）spoil one's appetite: 再好的美味吃多了也～。Even the best food can taste sour when you eat too much of it. 2〈喻〉（反感）get fed up: 这种书看了让人～。Such books are disgusting.
【倒休】dǎoxiū〈动〉change one's working hours and off hours

【倒牙】dǎoyá〈动〉〈方〉 set one's teeth on edge
【倒爷】dǎoyé〈名〉〈贬〉 profiteer
【倒运】dǎoyùn〈动〉 1 = 倒霉 dǎoméi 2（指贩卖） profiteer by buying at one place and selling at another 3（指转运） transport goods
【倒账】dǎozhàng A〈动〉 repudiate a debt B〈名〉 bad debt

祷（禱）

dǎo〈动〉 1（祷告） pray: ▸～告，祈～ 2〈旧〉（请求） beg: 盼～ hope earnestly
【祷告】dǎogào〈动〉 say one's prayers
【祷念】dǎoniàn〈动〉 say a prayer and wish for sth.
【祷文】dǎowén〈名〉 prayer
【祷祝】dǎozhù〈动〉 pray for

蹈

dǎo〈动〉 1〈书〉（踏） tread: ▸重～覆辙 2（跳） trip: ▸手舞足～ 3（遵循） obey: ▸～袭，循规～矩
【蹈常袭故】dǎocháng-xígù〈成〉 follow a set routine
【蹈海】dǎohǎi〈动〉〈书〉 drown oneself in the sea: ～自尽 commit suicide by drowning oneself in the sea
【蹈袭】dǎoxí〈动〉 mimic: ～前人 slavishly follow one's predecessors

dào

到

dào
A〈动〉 1（抵达） arrive: ～京 arrive in Beijing ‖ ～目前为止 so far ‖ ～站 arrive at a station ▸～会，～期，迟～ 2（前往） go to: ～城里去 go to town ‖ ～群众中去 join the masses 3（达成） [used as a verb complement to indicate the result of an action]: 做得～ can be done ‖ 看～ catch sight of ‖ 来信收～了。I have received your letter. ▸说～做～
B〈形〉 considerate: 有不～的地方请原谅。Please excuse me if I have been inconsiderate in any way.
【到岸价格】dào'àn jiàgé〈名〉 landed cost
【到案】dào'àn〈动〉［法律］ appear in court
【到场】dàochǎng〈动〉 be present: ～祝贺 be present to extend one's congratulations ‖ ～作证 attend as a witness
【到处】dàochù〈副〉 everywhere: ～流浪 roam from place to place ‖ ～碰壁 run into a brick wall at all turns ‖ ～树敌 make enemies everywhere
【到达】dàodá〈动〉 arrive: ～港 port of arrival ‖ 火车正点～。The train arrived on time. ‖ 救济物资终于～灾民的手里。The supplies finally reached the disaster victims.
【到底】dàodǐ A〈动〉 do sth. to its end: 将改革进行～ carry the reform through to its end B〈副〉 1（终于） in the end: 我想了很久，～明白了。I thought it over for a long time and finally came to understand. ‖ 实验～成功了。At long last the experiment succeeded. 2（究竟） [used in questions for emphasis]: 你～想干什么？ What on earth are you up to? ‖ 火星上～有没有生命？ Is there actually any form of life on Mars? 3（毕竟） after all: ～是年轻人干劲大。After all, young people are more energetic.
【到点】dàodiǎn〈动〉 it is time: 快～了，咱们赶紧进去吧。It's about time. Let's go in quickly. ‖ 商店一～就开门。The shop opens on time.
【到顶】dàodǐng〈动〉 reach the highest point: 要破除增产～的思想。We must get rid of the idea that the maximum output has been reached.
【到访】dàofǎng〈动〉 make a visit
【到会】dàohuì〈动〉 be present at a meeting
【到家】dàojiā〈形〉 satisfactory: 他的表演还不～。His performance could be better.
【到来】dàolái〈动〉 arrive: 春天～前 before the advent of spring ‖ 在雨季～前做好防汛准备 get ready for flood control before the rainy season sets in
【到了儿】dàoliǎor〈副〉〈方〉 at long last: 我～也没盼到他来。I have been longing for his arrival, but all in vain.
【到期】dàoqī〈动〉 become due: 我的护照～了。My passport's run out. ‖ 租约何时～? When does the lease expire?
【到任】dàorèn〈动〉 assume a post
【到手】dàoshǒu〈动〉 come into one's possession: 眼看～的粮食，决不能让洪水冲走。We mustn't allow the flood to wash away the grain that is almost ours.
【到庭】dàotíng〈动〉 appear in court: ～作证 appear in court as a witness
【到头】dàotóu〈动〉 reach the end: 顺这条路走～再左拐 walk straight to the end of the road and turn left
【到头来】dàotóulái〈副〉 [usu used in a negative sense] in the long run: 坏人～是不会有好下场的。Bad people are bound to suffer in the end.
【到位】dàowèi A〈动〉 be in place: 资金已经～。The funds are already in place. B〈形〉 satisfactory: 表演非常～。The performance was very satisfactory.
【到职】dàozhí = 到任 dàorèn

倒[1]

dào
A〈动〉 1（颠倒） turn upside down: 你可以把次序～过来。You can reverse the order. 2（后退） move backwards: 把时钟～拨 turn the clock back ‖ 他把车～进了停车场。He backed the car into the parking space. ▸～车，～退 3（倾倒） pour: ～茶/水 pour tea/water ‖ ～垃圾 dump rubbish
B〈形〉 upside down: 广告画贴～了。The poster was upside down. ▸～彩，本末～置

倒[2]

dào〈副〉 1（反而） [contrary to expectation]: 本想省事，～费了事。Instead of saving trouble, it created more trouble for us. ‖ 没想到最懒的人～起来得这么早。We had not expected that out of everyone the laziest person would have got up so early. 2（但是） [indicating contrast] but: 屋子并不宽绰，收拾得～还干净。The room is not spacious at all, but really quite clean and tidy. ‖ 你有什么高见，我～想听听。I'd like to hear what you've got to say though. 3（表责怪） [contrary to the fact, used after a 'verb + 得' structure, implying blame]: 说得～容易，你来试试。You say it's easy, you come and have a try then. ‖ 想得～美，根本没有那回事。Nothing of the sort; that's just wishful thinking. 4（表让步） [used in the subordinate clause at the beginning of a sentence, indicating concession]: 她人～挺好的，就是有时粗心点。Nice as she is, she is careless sometimes. ‖ 质量～不错，就是价钱贵了点。The quality is quite good, but the price is a bit too high. 5（表追问） [used in an imperative sentence or question, indicating impatience]: 你～说呀！Out with it, please! ‖ 你～去不去呀？ Don't you want to go, after all? 6（用以舒缓语气） [used to soften the tone]: 那～不至于。That might just not happen.
▸dǎo
【倒背如流】dàobèi-rúliú〈成〉 know sth. inside out
【倒不如】dàobùrú〈连〉 it would be better to ...
【倒彩】dàocǎi〈名〉 catcall: 喝～ make catcalls
【倒插门】dàochāmén〈惯〉〈口〉 [of a man] marry into and live with the wife's family: ～女婿 live-in son-in-law
【倒查】dàochá〈动〉 investigate after the fact: ～管理部门的责任 look into where management might have been responsible
【倒车】dàochē〈动〉 reverse a car: 正在～。The car is reversing.
▸dǎochē
【倒车灯】dàochēdēng〈名〉 reversing lights〈英〉; backup lights〈美〉
【倒春寒】dàochūnhán〈名〉 unseasonably cold early spring weather
【倒刺】dàocì〈名〉 1（指钩） barb 2（指手指甲根部的表皮） hangnail
【倒打一耙】dàodǎ-yīpá〈成〉 make groundless counter charges
【倒挡】dàodǎng〈名〉 reverse gear
【倒读数】dàodúshù〈动〉 count down: 为航天飞机的发射开始～ begin the countdown for the launch of a space shuttle
【倒飞】dàofēi〈名〉［航空］ inverted flight
【倒钩】dàogōu〈名〉〈方〉 launch a sting operation
【倒挂】dàoguà〈动〉 1（指位置） hang upside down: 崖壁上古松～ old pine trees hanging upside down from the precipice 2（指价格） be reversed: 购销价格～ purchasing prices higher than selling prices ‖ 脑体～ brain workers earning less than manual workers
【倒挂金钟】dàoguà jīnzhōng〈名〉［植物］ fuchsia
【倒灌】dàoguàn〈动〉 1（指水） flow from a lower to a higher place: 海水～ sea water encroachment 2（指烟） pour in down a chimney
【倒果为因】dàoguǒwéiyīn〈成〉 reverse cause and effect
【倒好儿】dàohǎor〈名〉 catcall: 喊～ shout catcalls
【倒计时】dàojìshí〈动〉 count down: 奥运会～已到最后一天。The countdown to the Olympic Games is now in its final day.
【倒剪】dàojiǎn〈动〉 hold one's hands behind one's back
【倒睫】dàojié〈名〉 trichiasis
【倒立】dàolì〈动〉 1（指物） stand upside down: 水中映现出～的塔影。The pagoda is reflected upside down in the water. 2（指人） do a handstand
【倒流】dàoliú〈动〉 1（指水流） flow upstream 2〈喻〉（指事物） flow backwards: 商品～ backward flow of goods ‖ 时光不会～。Time never flows backwards.
【倒赔】dàopéi〈动〉 lose sth. instead of making sth.: 经营不善，～了两万元。Mismanagement has resulted in a loss of 20 thousand *yuan*.
【倒片】dàopiàn〈动〉 rewind (a film)
【倒是】dàoshì〈副〉 1（反而） [contrary to common sense]: 该说的不说，不该说的～说个没完。While little has been said of what should have been said, too much has

been said of what shouldn't have been said. ❷（表责怪） [contrary to the fact, implying blame]: 他说得～不错，可就是不兑现。 He promised a lot but did nothing. ❸（表吃惊） [indicating unexpectedness]: 哦，你还有什么理由，我～想听一听。 Well, what else have you got to say? I'd like to hear it. ❹（表让步） [indicating concession]: 东西～好东西，就是价钱太贵。 It's good stuff; it's just that it's too expensive. ❺（表转折） [indicating a transition]: 屋子不大，布置得～挺有品味。 The room is not big, but it's tastefully furnished. ❻（用于缓和语气） [indicating a polite offer]: 如果你愿意，我～可以帮忙。 If you like, I'm willing to help. ❼（表催促） [indicating eagerness to know]: 你～快说呀! Out with it!

【倒数】dàoshǔ〈动〉 count backwards: ～第二 second from last

【倒数】dàoshù〈名〉［数学］ reciprocal

【倒锁】dàosuǒ〈动〉（锁在内） lock sb. in;（锁在外） lock oneself out

【倒贴】dàotiē〈动〉 pay instead of getting paid: 这东西别说卖钱，就是～白送都没人要。 You will never sell this for money. No one will take it even if they get it free.

【倒退】dàotuì〈动〉 go backwards: 历史的～ retrogression of history ‖ 他吓得～了好几步。 He was so scared that he took a few steps back.

【倒行逆施】dàoxíng-nìshī〈成〉 go against the trend of the times

【倒序】dàoxù = 逆序 nìxù

【倒叙】dàoxù〈名〉［语言］ flashback

【倒悬】dàoxuán〈动〉 ❶（倒挂） be hung by the feet ❷〈喻〉（表处境） be in dire straits: 解民于～ save the people from their dire plight

【倒烟】dàoyān〈名〉 smoke blowing in through the chimney

【倒影】dàoyǐng〈名〉 inverted image: 水中～ reflections in the water

【倒映】dàoyìng〈动〉 reflect: 一轮满月～在湖面上。 A full moon is reflected in the lake.

【倒栽葱】dàozāicōng〈惯〉 fall headfirst: 风筝断了线，来了个～。 The kite fell headlong after its string was broken.

【倒找】dàozhǎo〈动〉 [of a seller] pay the buyer instead of being paid

【倒置】dàozhì〈动〉 place upside down: 请勿～。 This way up. ▸本末～, 轻重～

【倒转】dàozhuǎn A〈动〉 be the other way round: ～来说，道理也是一样。 The same is true the other way round. B〈副〉 on the contrary: 你把地址写错了，～来怪我。 You got the address wrong and then you put the blame on me.

【倒转】dàozhuàn〈动〉 reverse: 时运～ one's luck has turned ‖ ～乾坤 turn back the course of events ‖ 前进的车轮不能～。 The march of progress cannot be reversed.

【倒装句】dàozhuāngjù〈名〉 inverted sentence

【倒座儿】dàozuòr〈名〉 ❶（指房屋） house opposite to the main house in a quadrangle ❷（指座位） seat facing the back of the vehicle

盗（盜）dào

A〈动〉 steal: 被～ be stolen ▸～窃, 偷～

B〈名〉 thief: ▸～贼, 海～

【盗版】dàobǎn A〈动〉 pirate: ～碟 pirated disc ‖ 加大打击～活动的力度 intensify the campaign against piracy B〈名〉 pirated edition

【盗伐】dàofá〈动〉 fell trees illegally

【盗匪】dàofěi〈名〉 bandits

【盗汗】dàohàn〈动〉 night sweat

【盗劫】dàojié〈动〉 steal and plunder: ～文物 plunder cultural relics

【盗寇】dàokòu〈名〉 robber

【盗猎】dàoliè〈动〉 poach

【盗卖】dàomài〈动〉 steal and sell: ～枪支弹药 rob and sell arms and ammunition

【盗墓】dàomù〈动〉 rob a grave

【盗窃】dàoqiè〈动〉 steal: ～公物 steal public property ‖ ～案 case of theft ‖ ～犯 thief

【盗取】dàoqǔ〈动〉 steal

【盗印】dàoyìn〈动〉 pirate

【盗用】dàoyòng〈动〉 appropriate: ～公款 misappropriate public funds ‖ ～他人名义 use the name of another person fraudulently

【盗贼】dàozéi〈名〉 robbers

悼 dào〈动〉 mourn

【悼词】dàocí〈名〉 funeral oration: 致～ deliver a memorial speech

【悼辞】dàocí = 悼词 dàocí

【悼念】dàoniàn〈动〉 mourn: ～亡友 mourn for a dead friend ‖ 集会～死者 gather to mourn for the dead

【悼念仪式】dàoniàn yíshì〈名〉 memorial service

【悼亡】dàowáng〈动〉〈书〉 ❶（悼念亡妻） mourn for one's deceased wife ❷（妻子亡故） lose one's wife

【悼唁】dàoyàn〈动〉〈书〉 express one's condolences: 致电～ send a telegram of condolences

道[1] dào〈名〉

❶（道路） road: 抄近～ take a short cut ▸～路, 人行～ ❷（航道） course: 黄河故～ old course of the Yellow River ‖ 主航～ main channel ▸河～, 下水～ ❸（方法） way: 治国之～ way to run a country ▸～理, 门～ ❹（道德） morals: ▸～义, 古～热肠 ❺（指思想体系） teachings: ▸传～, 尊师重～ ❻（道士） Taoist: 一僧一～ a monk and a Taoist ▸～士, ～院 ❼（技艺） skill: ▸棋～, 医～ ❽（指组织） superstitious sect: ▸会～门 ❾（线条） line: 画两条横～儿，一条斜～儿 draw two horizontal lines and one slanting line ❿（指历史行政区域名称） an administrative division in ancient China

道[2] dào〈动〉

❶（表达） speak: ▸能说会～ ❷（表示） express in words: ▸～歉, ～喜 ❸（说） [used in the early vernacular] say ❹（以为） think: 我～是谁呢，原来是你。 So it's you. I was wondering who it could be.

道[3] dào〈量〉

❶（指细长物） [for long and narrow objects]: 一～河 a river ‖ 万～霞光 streams of sunshine ❷（指门、墙） [for doors, walls, etc.]: 两～门 two doors ‖ 三～防线 three defence lines ❸（指命令、问题） [for orders, questions, etc.]: 十五～题 fifteen questions ‖ 一～命令 an order ❹（指菜肴、步骤） [for courses in a meal, stages in a procedure, etc.]: 吃四～菜 have four courses ‖ 省一～手续 save one step in the process

【道白】dàobái〈名〉［戏曲］ spoken part

【道班】dàobān〈名〉 maintenance team (for road or railway)

【道别】dàobié〈动〉 ❶（分别） part: 握手～ part with a handshake ❷（辞行） say good bye to: 起程前他到邻居家一一～。 Before his departure, he went from door to door to say good-bye to his neighbours.

【道不同，不相为谋】dào bùtóng, bù xiāng wéi móu〈成〉 people following different ways won't consult each other

【道岔】dàochà〈名〉 ❶（指道路） side road ❷（指铁路） points〈英〉; switch〈美〉: 扳～ pull railway switches

【道场】dàochǎng〈名〉 ❶（指法事） Buddhist or Taoist rites to appease and pray for the dead: 做～ conduct Buddhist or Taoist rites ❷（指场所） site where Buddhist or Taoist rites are performed

【道道儿】dàodaor〈名〉〈口〉 ❶（线条） line: 电视屏幕上有一条亮～。 There's a bright line on the TV screen. ❷（方法） way: 只要肯动脑筋，就能想出尽快完成任务的～来。 As long as we use our brains, we can surely find ways to fulfil our tasks in the shortest possible time. ❸（门道） knack: 这事你得说出个～来。 You have to come up with an explanation for it. ‖ 你不懂这方面的～，就别乱发议论。 You don't understand this kind of thing, so don't go shooting your mouth off about it.

d

【道德】dàodé A〈名〉 morality: ～败坏 be morally degenerate ‖ 公共～ public morals ‖ 职业～ professional ethics B〈形〉 moral: 这种做法不～。 This is unethical.

【道德风尚】dàodé fēngshàng〈名〉 prevailing moral practices

【道德观】dàodéguān〈名〉 moral outlook

【道德品质】dàodé pǐnzhì〈名〉 moral character: ～高尚的人 person of high moral character

【道地】dàodì = 地道 dìdao 1, 2

【道钉】dàodīng〈名〉 ❶［铁路］ spike ❷（猫眼道钉） cat's eye

【道乏】dàofá〈动〉 thank sb. for taking the trouble: 你帮了他大忙了，他要亲自来给你～呢。 You have been a great help to him and he will come to thank you in person.

【道高一尺，魔高一丈】dào gāo yī chǐ, mó gāo yī zhàng〈成〉〈喻〉 ❶（指修行） one's religious attainments are always challenged by greater evil influences ❷（指正邪消长） the greater one's accomplishments, the greater the obstacles ❸（正必胜邪） justice will eventually prevail over evil

【道姑】dàogū〈名〉 Taoist nun

【道观】dàoguàn〈名〉 Taoist temple

【道号】dàohào〈名〉 Taoist name

【道贺】dàohè〈动〉 congratulate

【道行】dàohéng〈名〉〈口〉 ❶（指修行） religious attainments (of a monk or Taoist priest) ❷（指本领） technical skill: ～深 be highly skilled

【道教】Dàojiào〈名〉 Taoism

> **道教**
>
> A Chinese philosophy and religion which holds that the 'Tao' (the 'Way') is the origin of all things in the universe. Taoism was founded in the Eastern Han Dynasty by Zhang Daoling (张道陵), whom followers regard as a master. A central figure in Taoism is the philosopher Lao Zi (老子), honoured as Taishang Laojun (太上老君). The main Taoist classic is Lao Zi's *Tao Te Ching* (《道德经》).

【道具】dàojù〈名〉 prop: 舞台～ stage prop

【道口】〈名〉 ❶（指公路） road junction ❷（指铁路） level railway crossing

【道理】dàolǐ〈名〉 ❶（法则） principle: 发展是硬～。 Development is of paramount importance. ‖ 你的话有点～。

There is some measure of truth in your remarks. **2**（根据） reason: 他讲的话毫无～。What he said made no sense. ‖ 摆事实，讲～。 Enumerate the facts and reason things out. **3**（打算） way: 怎么办，我自有～。 I have a way to solve the problem.

【道林纸】dàolínzhǐ〈名〉 glazed printing paper

【道路】dàolù〈名〉 **1**（指地面上） road: 修筑～ build a road ‖ 走上富裕的～ embark on the road to prosperity ‖ 人生～ one's path through life ‖ 前途是光明的，～是曲折的。 The future is bright but the road ahead has twists and turns. **2**（通道） passage

【道貌岸然】dàomào-ànrán〈成〉 be sanctimonious

【道袍】dàopáo〈名〉 Taoist robe

【道破】dàopò〈动〉 lay bare: 他不愿～其中的秘密。 He didn't want to expose the secret. ▸一语～

【道歉】dàoqiàn〈动〉 apologize: 当面～ apologize to sb. in person ‖ 公开～ make a public apology

【道情】dàoqíng〈名〉［曲艺］ folk tales sung to a bamboo percussion instrument

【道-琼斯指数】Dào-Qióngsī zhǐshù〈名〉 Dow-Jones index (DJI)

【道人】dàoren〈名〉 **1**〈旧〉〈敬〉（道士） Taoist priest **2**〈古〉（佛教徒） Buddhist follower **3**〈方〉（打杂的人） odd-job person in a Buddhist temple

【道士】dàoshi〈名〉 Taoist priest

【道听途说】dàotīng-túshuō〈成〉 hearsay

【道统】dàotǒng〈名〉 Confucian orthodoxy

【道喜】dàoxǐ〈动〉 congratulate sb. on a happy occasion

【道谢】dàoxiè〈动〉 thank: 说几句～的话 say a few words of thanks

【道学】dàoxué **A** = 理学 lǐxué **B**〈形〉 pedantic: ～气 pedantry ‖ ～先生 pedant

【道牙】dàoyá〈名〉 curb

【道义】dàoyì〈名〉morality: 给予～上的支持 give moral support

【道院】dàoyuàn〈名〉 **1**（道观） Taoist residence or temple **2**（修道院） monastery

【道藏】dàozàng〈名〉 Taoist Canon

【道砟】dàozhǎ〈名〉［铁路］ ballast

【道子】dàozi〈名〉〈口〉 line: 画一条～ draw a line

稻 dào〈名〉 rice: ▸旱～，晚～

【稻苞虫】dàobāochóng〈名〉［昆虫］rice-plant skipper

【稻草】dàocǎo〈名〉 rice straw

【稻草人】dàocǎorén〈名〉 scarecrow

【稻谷】dàogǔ〈名〉 paddy

【稻糠】dàokāng〈名〉 rice chaff

【稻壳】dàoké〈名〉 rice husk

【稻米】dàomǐ〈名〉 rice

【稻螟虫】dàomíngchóng〈名〉 rice borer

【稻穗】dàosuì〈名〉 ear of rice

【稻田】dàotián〈名〉 paddy field: ～养鱼 paddy-field fish culture

【稻秧】dàoyāng〈名〉 rice seedlings

【稻种】dàozhǒng〈名〉 rice seeds

【稻子】dàozi〈名〉 paddy: 收割～ harvest rice

dē

嘚 dē〈拟〉 clip clop

dé

得 dé〈动〉 **1**（获得） get: ～冠军 win the championship ‖ ～满分 get full marks ▸～胜，取～ **2**（患上） contract: ～腮腺炎 come down with mumps ‖ ～痔疮 have piles ▸～病 **3**（允许） [used before verbs to express permission or possibility, usu in the negative]: 不～随地吐痰! No spitting! ‖ 这笔钱未经批准不～擅自动用。 No one is allowed to draw on this sum of money without approval. **4**（适合） suit: ▸～当，～体，～用 **5**〈书〉（满足） be satisfied: ▸～意扬扬 **6**〈口〉（完成） be ready: 饭～了。Dinner is ready. ‖ 衣服还没有做～。The garment is not ready yet. **7**〈口〉（表无需再说） [expressing approval or prohibition]: ～，就这么办。 All right, that's decided. ‖ ～了，别说了。 Come, that's enough. **8**〈口〉（表只好如此） [expressing helplessness or frustration]: ～，钥匙又丢了。 Oh, no! I've lost my key again. **9**（结果为） result in: 二三～六。 Two times three is six. ‖ 五减一～四。 Five minus one is four.

▸de, děi

【得便】débiàn〈动〉 be convenient: 这几样东西，请您～捎给她。Please take these things to her when it's convenient for you.

【得病】débìng〈动〉 fall ill: 不讲卫生，容易～。 If you disrespect personal hygiene, it's easy to get ill.

【得不偿失】débùchángshī〈成〉 the loss outweighs the gain

【得逞】déchěng〈动〉〈贬〉 have one's way: 阴谋未能～。 The plot fell through.

【得宠】déchǒng〈动〉〈贬〉 find favour with sb.: 极为～ be high in sb.'s favour

【得出】déchū〈动〉 arrive at: 你是怎样～这一结论的? What led you to this conclusion?

【得寸进尺】décùn-jìnchǐ〈成〉〈喻〉 give him an inch and he'll take a mile

【得当】dédàng〈形〉 appropriate: 处理～ be properly handled ‖ 措词～ appropriate wording ‖ 详略～ be detailed without being superfluous

【得到】dédào〈动〉 obtain: ～补偿 receive compensations ‖ ～满足 achieve contentment ‖ ～支持 win support ‖ 反对党～议会中1/3的席位。The opposition secured

ℹ 道歉

■ 在英語里，如果打扰了别人或做错了什么，场合不同一般要用不同的道歉方式。

■ 在书面语或较正式的场合中，如会议上、同事间、上下级间等，英语可用下面的句型：

我必须为我做的事道歉
= I must apologize for what I have done

我真诚地为我说的话道歉
= I apologize unreservedly for what I said

我要向你道歉，并收回我说的话
= I owe you an apology, and take back all I said

是我把事情弄糟了，请允许我表达最真诚的歉意
= May I offer you my sincerest apologies for the mess that I made

我不能赴约，为此非常遗憾
= I very much regret that I am unable to keep the appointment
或 I am very sorry that I am unable to keep the appointment

给你添麻烦了，实在对不起
= I am truly sorry for the trouble I have caused to you

让你失望了，我实在对不起
= I'm terribly sorry I disappointed you

请原谅我的过错
= I must ask you to excuse my mistake

我希望你能原谅我的粗心
= I hope you will pardon me for my carelessness

我失信了，请原谅
= Please forgive me for not having kept my promise

■ 在非正式的日常口语交流中，如在朋友间、熟人间，最常见的句型有：

对不起
= Sorry

对不起，我迟到了
= Sorry I'm late
或 Sorry for being late

对不起，打扰你了
= Sorry to bother you
或 Sorry to disturb you

对不起，打断一下
= Sorry to interrupt

真对不起，我得走了
= I'm very sorry, but I have to go

对不起，我不是那意思
= I'm sorry. I didn't mean that

那是我的错
= It was my fault

对那件事，我真的很难过
= I really feel bad about that

■ 如果不小心碰到别人或挡了别人的路，可以说：

对不起
= Sorry（英）
或 Excuse me（美）

■ 如果想引起别人的注意，可以说：

请问几点了?
= Excuse me, (but) what time is it?

劳驾，我用一下你的笔可以吗?
= Excuse me, do you mind if I use your pen?

■ 如果在办公室打喷嚏、咳嗽等，可以说：

不好意思
= Excuse me

■ 如果在与别人的谈话中不得不离开片刻，可以说：

对不起，我要离开一会儿
或 **对不起，失陪一下**
= Excuse me (for) a second
或 Excuse me (for) a moment

one third of the seats in the parliament.

【得道多助，失道寡助】dédào duō zhù, shīdào guǎ zhù〈成〉 a just cause enjoys abundant support while an unjust cause finds little

【得法】défǎ〈形〉 doing sth. the right way: 管理～，效益就好。 Proper management ensures better economic returns.

【得分】défēn **A**〈动〉 score: ～最多 score the most points ‖ ～手 scorer ‖ 到目前为止双方均未～。 No goals have been scored by either side so far. **B**〈名〉 score

【得过且过】déguò-qiěguò〈成〉 muddle along: 工作～ muddle through one's work

【得计】déjì〈动〉 succeed in one's scheme: 上了当还自以为～ be taken in but still think one has got the better of the other party

【得奖】déjiǎng〈动〉 win a prize: ～电影 prize-winning film ‖ ～人 prize winner

【得劲】déjìn〈形〉 **1**（舒服） well: 我这两天感冒了，浑身不～。 I've been suffering from a cold and feeling unwell all over for the past few days. **2**（顺手） handy: 改进后的工具用起来很～。 The improved tools work very well. ‖ 新车开起来很～。 The new car handles very well.

【得救】déjiù〈动〉 be rescued: 落水儿童～了。 The drowning child was saved.

【得克萨斯州】Dékèsàsīzhōu〈名〉 Texas

【得空】dékòng〈动〉 have spare time: ～来串门。 Drop in when you have time.

【得了】déle **A**〈动〉 [expressing approval or prohibition] be enough: ～，别说了。 That's enough. No need to discuss it further. **B**〈助〉 [used in declarative sentences to indicate affirmation]: 你走～，不用挂念家里的事。 You just go, and don't worry about us at home.
▸ déliǎo

【得力】délì **A**〈动〉 benefit from: ～于平时的勤学苦练 benefit from diligent study and constant practice **B**〈形〉 **1**（能干） capable: 办事～ do things efficiently ‖ ～助手 right-hand man **2**（强有力） strong: 领导～ powerful leadership

【得脸】déliǎn〈动〉 gain favour

【得了】déliǎo〈形〉〈口〉 [used in rhetorical questions or negative forms]: 这还～吗? Isn't that terrible? ‖ 不～了，出事故啦! It's awful! There has been an accident.
▸ déle

【得陇望蜀】déLǒng-wàngShǔ〈成〉〈喻〉 the more one gets, the more one wants

【得其所哉】déqísuǒzāi〈成〉 find one's right place

【得人心】dé rénxīn〈动〉 have the support of the people: 不～ lose popular support ‖ 新政策大～。 The new policy is very popular with the people.

【得色】désè〈名〉complacent: 面有～ look smug

【得胜】déshèng〈动〉 score a victory: ～归来 return in triumph ▸ 旗开～

【得胜回朝】déshèng-huícháo〈成〉 return to the imperial court a victor

【得失】déshī〈名〉 **1**（得与失） gain and loss: 不计个人～ regardless of personal gains or losses ‖ ～参半 gains balance losses **2**（利弊） advantages and disadvantages: 两种办法各有～。 Each of the two approaches has its own advantages and disadvantages.

【得时】déshí〈动〉 have good luck

【得势】déshì〈动〉〈贬〉 be in power: 小人～ small man in power

【得手】déshǒu〈动〉 **1**（达到目的） come off: 屡屡～ succeed time and again ‖ 进攻～。 The attack was successful. **2**（顺手） be handy: 怎么～就怎么干。 Do it the way that best suits you.

【得体】détǐ〈形〉 appropriate: 穿着～ be suitably attired ‖ 说话不～ make inappropriate remarks ‖ 事事办得很～。 Everything was done correctly.

【得天独厚】détiān-dúhòu〈成〉 enjoy exceptional natural advantages: ～的条件 exceptionally good conditions

【得悉】déxī〈动〉〈书〉 hear of: ～你学业有成，不胜欣慰。 I rejoice to hear of your academic success.

【得闲】déxián = 得空 dékòng

【得心应手】déxīn-yìngshǒu〈成〉 **1**（指技艺纯熟） work with great skill: 他打起乒乓球来真是～。 He plays table tennis with great skill. **2**（顺手） be fit for use: 这支笔用起来～。 This pen writes quite well.

【得宜】déyí〈形〉〈书〉 proper: 裁剪～ be well tailored ‖ 措置～ be properly handled

【得以】déyǐ〈动〉 can, may: ～实现 can be realized ‖ 他～晋升，全靠自己的实绩。 He won his promotion by virtue of his own merits.

【得益】déyì〈动〉 profit from: ～不少 have benefited quite a lot

【得意】déyì〈动〉 be proud of oneself: 因成功而～ be smug with success ‖ ～之作 one's favourite work ‖ ～门生 favourite pupil ▸ 自鸣～

【得意忘形】déyì-wàngxíng〈成〉 be carried away by one's success: 近来的成功使她～。 Her recent success has completely gone to her head.

【得意扬扬】déyì-yángyáng〈成〉be puffed up

【得意洋洋】déyì-yángyáng = 得意扬扬 déyì-yángyáng

【得用】déyòng〈形〉 fit for use: 这把剪刀不～。 These scissors don't cut very well.

【得鱼忘筌】déyú-wàngquán〈成〉〈喻〉 discard the means by which one's end is achieved

【得知】dézhī〈动〉 get to know: ～你的船平安返港，非常高兴。 I am very happy to hear that your ship has returned to the port safe and sound.

【得志】dézhì〈动〉 achieve one's ambition: 少年～ enjoy success when young ‖ 郁郁不～ feel depressed about one's unsuccessful career

【得主】dézhǔ〈名〉 winner: 金牌～ gold medallist

【得罪】dézuì〈动〉 offend: 多有～。 Sorry to have offended you. ‖ 不要～他。 Don't offend him.

锝（鍀） dé〈名〉［化学］ technetium (Tc)

德 dé〈名〉 **1**（道德） morals: ～智体全面发展 be highly moral, intellectual and physical ▸～才兼备，积～，品～ **2**（信念） mind: ▸同心同～ **3**（恩惠） kindness: ▸恩～ **4** ▸德昂族 Dé'ángzú

【德昂族】Dé'ángzú〈名〉 De'ang ethnic group, Deang ethnic group

【德比】débǐ〈名〉 local derby

【德比郡】Débǐjùn〈名〉 Derbyshire

【德才兼备】décái-jiānbèi〈成〉 have both ability and integrity: 她～。 She possesses both integrity and ability.

【德高望重】dégāo-wàngzhòng〈成〉enjoy high prestige and command universal respect: 他～。 He enjoys high public regard.

【德国】Déguó〈名〉Germany: ～人 German

【德黑兰】Déhēilán〈名〉 Tehran

【德里】Délǐ〈名〉 Delhi

【德望】déwàng〈名〉〈书〉 moral prestige

【德文】Déwén ▸**p. 918**〈名〉 German (language)

【德文郡】Déwénjùn〈名〉 Devon

【德行】déxíng〈名〉 morality and virtuous conduct

【德行】déxing〈名〉〈口〉 disgraceful behaviour: 瞧他那～! What a disgusting fellow he is!

【德性】déxing = 德行 déxing

【德艺双馨】déyì shuāngxīn〈动〉 be known for one's moral character and artistic achievements

【德意志】Déyìzhì〈名〉 Germany: ～联邦共和国 Federal Republic of Germany ‖ ～民主共和国 German Democratic Republic

【德意志新闻社】Déyìzhì Xīnwénshè〈名〉 Deutsche Presse-Agentur

【德语】Déyǔ ▸**p. 918**〈名〉 German (language)

【德育】déyù〈名〉 moral education: 加强和改进～工作 strengthen and improve work in moral education

【德政】dézhèng〈名〉 benevolent rule

【德治】dézhì〈名〉 rule of virtue

de

地 de〈助〉 [used with an adverb or adverbial phrase]: 合理～安排和使用劳动力 dispose of available manpower rationally ‖ 应该历史～评价一个人。 We should judge a person from the historical point of view.
▸ dì

的[1] de ▸**p. 843**; ▸**p. 487** in English-Chinese dictionary〈助〉 **1**（表限定） [used with an adjective or attribute phrase] **a**（表修饰） [indicating a modifying and modified relationship]: 美好～未来 bright future ‖ 铁～纪律 iron discipline **b**（表所属） [indicating a possessive relationship]: 人民～公仆 servant of the people ‖ 我～父亲 my father **c**（表职务或身份） [indicating a relationship of a person and his title or capacity]: 今天是我～东。 It's my treat today. ‖ 谁～介绍人? Who is the matchmaker? **d**（表行为指向） [indicating the receiver of an action]: 别开我～玩笑。 Don't make fun of me. ‖ 你净扫大家～兴。 You are just getting us all down. **2**（用于名词化） [used after a noun, pronoun, verb, or an adjective to form a noun phrase without a head noun] **a**（替代上文所指） [indicating sb./sth. already mentioned]: 这铺是我～，那才是你～。 This bunk is mine, and that is yours. ‖ 玫瑰花开了，有红～，有黄～。 The roses are in bloom; some are red and some yellow. **b**（表类别） [indicating a certain type of person or thing]: 男～ male ‖ 我爱吃甜～。 I like sweet food. **c**（表状态） [indicating a condition or situation]: 大热天～，你还来看我。 It's very kind of you to come and see me on such a hot day. ‖ 无缘无故～，他瞪你干什么? Why on earth did he glare at you? There's got to be a reason. **d**（表不相干） [indicating a subject that has nothing to do with what is going on]: 我能行，你忙你～去吧。 I can manage. You just get on with your work. **e**（表不同） [indicating diversity]:

推～推，拉～拉。 Some are pushing and some are pulling. ‖ 说～说，笑～笑。 Some are talking and some laughing. **3**（表强调） [used after the predicative verb to emphasize the doer, the time, the place, etc.]: 谁说～? Who said that? ‖ 他是昨天发～烧。 It was yesterday that he had a fever. **4**（表肯定） [used at the end of a declarative sentence to give a positive tone to the statement]: 这件事我知道～。 That I know. ‖ 是他！我认识～。 It's him. I know him. **5**（表"之类"） [used after two things of the same kind to imply 'and so on' or 'and the like']: 废铜烂铁～，他拣了一大筐。 He collected a basketful of scrap metals, iron, copper, and so on. ‖ 他们又唱又跳～，高兴极了。 They were overjoyed, singing and dancing. **6**（用于两个数量词之间） [used between two numerals] **a**（指相乘） [indicating multiplication]: 这间教室是三米～六米，合十八平方米。 This classroom is three metres by six, with a total floor space of eighteen square metres. **b**（指相加） [indicating addition]: 四块～五块，一共九块。 Four *yuan* plus five *yuan* is nine *yuan*.

的² de = 得 de 2, 3
▸dī, dí, dì

【的话】dehuà〈助〉 [used at the end of a conditional clause]: 如果我不来～，你代我主持一下会议。 Will you please chair the meeting on my behalf if I don't come?

底 de〈助〉〈旧〉 [indicating a possessive relationship]: 我～书 my book
▸dǐ

得 de〈助〉 **1**（表可以） [used after a verb to express possibility]: 她去～，我也去～。 If she can go, I can, too. ‖ 这孩子说不～也骂不～。 This child cannot be reasoned with. **2**（表可能） [used between a verb and its complement to express possibility or capability]: 办～到 can be done ‖ 买～起 can afford it ‖ 这女人说～到做～到。 She is a woman of her word. **3**（用于连接补语） [used between a verb or an adjective and its complement to indicate the result or degree]: 干～很好 very well-done ‖ 漂亮～很 very beautiful **4**（表动作完成） [used after a verb in earlier vernacular Chinese to indicate the completion of an action]: 回～家来 after coming home
▸dé, děi

děi

得 děi
A〈动〉 **1**（需要） need: 这条铁路～两年才能完工。 This railway will take two years to complete. ‖ 买这么豪华的别墅～多少钱啊! I wonder how much money such a luxurious villa would cost! **2**（将要） certainly will: 快八点了，你再不走，就～迟到了。 It's nearing eight o'clock. If you don't set out, you'll certainly be late.
B〈副〉〈口〉 must: 咱们～把工程赶上去，绝不能落后。 We have to speed up our project; we must not fall behind. ‖ 时间不早了，我～走了。 It's getting late. I must be going.
▸dé, de

dèn

扽 dèn〈动〉〈方〉 **1**（用力拉） tug: 小心点儿，别把灯绳～断了。 Be careful not to break the lamp cord. **2**（拉紧） pull taut: ～住绳子往上爬。 Pull the rope taut and climb up.

dēng

灯（燈） dēng〈名〉 **1**（用于照明） light: 开～ turn on a light ‖ 熄～ put out the light ‖ 床头～ bedside lamp ▸闪光～，指示～ **2**（用于加热） burner: ▸酒精～，喷～

【灯标】dēngbiāo〈名〉 **1**（指航标） beacon **2**（指标牌） light sign: 夜市～ lights at the night market
【灯彩】dēngcǎi〈名〉 coloured lanterns
【灯草】dēngcǎo〈名〉 rush [used as wick]
【灯蛾扑火】dēng'é-pūhuǒ〈成〉 **1**〈本〉 moths throwing themselves into lamp flames **2**〈喻〉 suicidal act
【灯管】dēngguǎn〈名〉 fluorescent lamp: 日光灯～ fluorescent tube
【灯光】dēngguāng〈名〉 **1**（指光亮） lamplight: ～明亮/昏暗 be brightly/dimly lit **2**（指设备） lighting: 舞台～ stage lighting
【灯光球场】dēngguāng qiúchǎng〈名〉 floodlit field
【灯红酒绿】dēnghóng-jiǔlǜ〈成〉 scene of feasting and pleasure-seeking
【灯花】dēnghuā〈名〉 snuff
【灯会】dēnghuì〈名〉 lantern festival
【灯火】dēnghuǒ〈名〉 lights: ～管制 blackout ▸万家～
【灯火辉煌】dēnghuǒ huīhuáng〈成〉 be brightly lit: 节日之夜，大街上～。 On the evening of the festival, the main street is ablaze with lights.
【灯节】Dēngjié〈名〉 Lantern Festival
【灯具】dēngjù〈名〉 lamps and lanterns
【灯笼】dēnglong〈名〉 lantern: 挂～ hang a lantern
【灯笼椒】dēnglongjiāo〈名〉 bell pepper
【灯笼裤】dēnglongkù〈名〉 knickerbockers
【灯谜】dēngmí〈名〉 riddle pasted on a lantern: 猜～ guess riddles pasted on lanterns

> **灯谜**
> Also known as *denghu* (灯虎), these are riddles pasted onto lanterns, and sometimes also onto walls or lengths of string. Lanterns are traditionally seen at the Lantern Festival (▸元宵节). The custom of pasting riddles on lanterns for passers-by to guess at probably began in the Song Dynasty.

【灯苗】dēngmiáo〈名〉 lamp flame
【灯捻】dēngniǎn〈名〉 lamp wick
【灯泡】dēngpào〈名〉 bulb: 卡口～ bayonet-socket bulb ‖ 螺口～ screw socket bulb
【灯伞】dēngsǎn〈名〉 umbrella lampshade
【灯市】dēngshì〈名〉 lantern fair
【灯饰】dēngshì〈名〉 decorative lamp
【灯丝】dēngsī〈名〉 filament
【灯塔】dēngtǎ〈名〉 lighthouse
【灯台】dēngtái〈名〉 lamp stand
【灯头】dēngtóu〈名〉 **1**（灯口） electric light socket: 卡口～ bayonet-socket ‖ 螺口～ screw-socket **2**（指煤油灯装置） lamp holder/base **3**（电灯） electric light: 五个～ five electric lights
【灯箱】dēngxiāng〈名〉 light box: ～广告 advertising light box
【灯心】dēngxīn = 灯芯 dēngxīn
【灯芯】dēngxīn〈名〉 wick
【灯芯草】dēngxīncǎo〈名〉［植物］ rush
【灯芯绒】dēngxīnróng〈名〉 corduroy: ～裤子 cord trousers
【灯油】dēngyóu〈名〉 lamp-oil
【灯语】dēngyǔ〈名〉 lamp signal
【灯盏】dēngzhǎn〈名〉 oil lamp
【灯罩】dēngzhào〈名〉 **1**（用于电灯） lampshade **2**（用于油灯） (oil) lamp chimney
【灯柱】dēngzhù〈名〉 lamp post
【灯座】dēngzuò〈名〉 lamp stand

登 dēng〈动〉 **1**（攀爬） climb: ～上顶峰 reach the summit of a mountain ‖ ～上王位 ascend to the throne ▸～山，一步～天 **2**（刊登） publish: ～广告 run an advertisement ‖ 报上～了一条消息。 The newspaper carried a news story. ‖ 那篇文章～出来了。 The article was published. ▸～账 **3**〈旧〉（中科举） succeed in imperial exams: ▸～第，～科 **4**（成熟） ripen: ▸五谷丰～

【登岸】dēng'àn〈动〉 go ashore
【登报】dēngbào〈动〉 publish in the newspaper
【登比郡】Dēngbǐjùn〈名〉 Denbighshire
【登场】dēngcháng〈动〉 [of gathered crops] be taken to the threshing ground
【登场】dēngchǎng〈动〉 go on stage: ～亮相 make one's entrance on the stage ▸粉墨～
【登程】dēngchéng〈动〉〈书〉 hit the road
【登第】dēngdì〈动〉〈旧〉 pass the imperial examination and win the title of *jinshi* (进士)
【登峰造极】dēngfēng-zàojí〈成〉 reach the pinnacle: 他的医术已是～了。 He possesses the finest medical skills.
【登高】dēnggāo〈动〉 **1**（上到高处） ascend a height: ～望远 climb a height to view distant places **2**（重阳节登山） climb hills on the Double Ninth Festival
【登革热】dēnggérè ▸**p. 50**〈名〉［医学］ dengue fever
【登机】dēngjī〈动〉 board a plane: ～牌/口 boarding pass/gate
【登基】dēngjī〈动〉〈旧〉 ascend the throne
【登极】dēngjí = 登基 dēngjī
【登记】dēngjì〈动〉 register: ～户籍 register one's residence ‖ 在酒店～住宿 check in at a hotel ‖ ～簿 registry
【登科】dēngkē〈动〉〈旧〉 pass the imperial civil service examination and win a title
【登临】dēnglín〈动〉〈书〉 climb and visit: ～名山大川，饱览壮丽景色 visit famous mountains and large rivers and enjoy their beauty
【登龙门】dēng lóngmén〈动〉〈喻〉 rise to fame
【登陆】dēnglù〈动〉 **1**（指军队、台风） go ashore: ～作战 landing operations ‖ 台风很快将在这附近～。 The typhoon will soon come ashore near here. **2**（指产品） enter the local market
【登陆场】dēnglùchǎng〈名〉 beachhead
【登陆舰】dēnglùjiàn〈名〉 landing ship
【登陆艇】dēnglùtǐng〈名〉 landing craft
【登录】dēnglù〈动〉 **1**（登记） enter **2**［计算机］ log in
【登门】dēngmén〈动〉 call at sb.'s house:

～拜访 call on sb. ‖ ～道谢 call on sb. to express gratitude ‖ ～吊唁 go to sb.'s home to offer one's condolences ‖ ～求教 go to sb. for advice

【登攀】dēngpān〈动〉ascend

【登山】dēngshān〈动〉**1**（爬山）go up a mountain: ～观景 climb a hill for a view **2**［体育］mountaineer: ～队/服 mountaineering party/clothes

【登时】dēngshí〈副〉at once: 注射后，他～恢复了知觉。 After the injection, he immediately came to.

【登台】dēngtái〈动〉**1**（演出）go on the stage: ～表演 perform on stage **2**〈喻〉（从政）enter the political arena

【登堂入室】dēngtáng-rùshì = 升堂入室 shēngtáng-rùshì

【登徒子】dēngtúzǐ〈名〉lecher

【登月】dēngyuè〈动〉land on the moon

【登月舱】dēngyuècāng〈名〉lunar module (LM)

【登载】dēngzǎi〈动〉publish: 各大报纸都～了这条消息。 All major newspapers carried the news.

【登账】dēngzhàng〈动〉enter a transaction

噔 dēng〈拟〉thud: ～～～的脚步声 sound of heavy footsteps ‖ 他～～～地上了楼。 He thumped upstairs.

蹬 dēng〈动〉**1**（用力踏）press down with the foot: ～三轮车 pedal a tricycle **2**（踩）step on: ～在桌子上贴画儿 step onto the table to put up a picture **3**（穿）put on: 脚～长筒靴 wear high boots **4**（甩）give sb. the brush-off: 他把女朋友～了。 He dumped his girlfriend.
▸dèng

【蹬技】dēngjì〈名〉acrobatic juggling with the feet

【蹬腿】dēngtuǐ〈动〉**1**（伸腿）kick one's legs: 他一～坐起身。 He sat up with a kick of his legs. **2** ▸**p. 772**〈口〉（死亡）kick the bucket

děng

等¹ děng

A〈形〉equal: 大小不～ vary in size ▸～于，相～

B〈量〉**1**（档次）grade: 共分三～ be classified into three grades ‖ 二/三～品 second-class/third-class goods ▸同～，优～ **2** = 戥 děng **3**（类）kind: 天下竟然有这～事? I just can't believe such a thing could ever have happened!

C〈助〉**1**〈书〉（表复数）[used after a personal pronoun or a personal name to indicate plurality]: 尔～ you ‖ 我～ we **2**（表列举未尽）and so on: 北京、西安～地 Beijing, Xi'an and some other places ‖ 衣服、鞋袜～～ clothes, shoes, socks, and so on **3**（表列举煞尾）[indicating the end of an enumeration]: 北京、天津、上海、重庆～四个直辖市 the four municipalities directly under the Central Government – Beijing, Tianjin, Shanghai and Chongqing

等² děng

A〈动〉wait: ～火车 wait for a train ‖ 请稍～一会儿。 Just a moment, please.

B〈连〉until: ～雨停了再走。 Stay till the rain stops.

【等边三角形】děngbiān sānjiǎoxíng〈名〉equilateral triangle

【等次】děngcì〈名〉grade: 产品应按质量划分～。 The products should be ranked according to quality.

【等待】děngdài〈动〉wait for: ～审议/审批 await deliberation/approval ‖ ～时机 wait for an opportunity

【等到】děngdào〈连〉by the time: ～我们赶到，他们已经走了。 They had left by the time we arrived.

【等额选举】děng'é xuǎnjǔ〈名〉single-candidate election

【等而下之】děng'érxiàzhī〈成〉from that grade down

【等分】děngfēn〈动〉divide into equal parts

【等份】děngfèn〈名〉equal division: 把甜瓜分成四～ divide a melon into four equal portions

【等高线】děnggāoxiàn〈名〉［地质］contour line: ～地形图 hypsographic map

【等号】děnghào〈名〉［数学］equal sign: 画～ draw an equal sign

【等候】děnghòu〈动〉await: ～进一步通知 wait until further notice ‖ ～命令 await orders

【等候区】děnghòuqū〈名〉waiting area

【等级】děngjí〈名〉rank: 按大小/质量分～ be graded according to size/quality ‖ ～证书 grade certificate ‖ ～制度 hierarchy ‖ 工资～ wage scale ‖ ～社会/制度 hierarchical society/system ‖ 封建社会～森严。 Feudal society was rigidly stratified.

【等价】děngjià〈动〉be equal in value: ～交换 equal exchange

【等价物】děngjiàwù〈名〉［经济］equivalent: 货币是体现各种商品价值的一般～。 Currency is the equivalent that reflects the values of commodities.

【等距离】děngjùlí〈形〉equidistant: ～外交 equidistant diplomacy

【等离子】děnglízǐ〈名〉plasma: ～电视机 plasma TV

【等量齐观】děngliàng-qíguān〈成〉equate with: 不能把他的绘画和书法～。 We cannot equate his paintings with his calligraphy.

【等米下锅】děngmǐ-xiàguō〈成〉be waiting for the final piece of the jigsaw

【等内】děngnèi〈形〉[of goods] up to standard

【等身】děngshēn〈动〉be life-sized: 著作～ be prolific in writing

【等式】děngshì〈名〉［数学］equation

【等速度】děngsùdù〈名〉uniform velocity

【等速运动】děngsù yùndòng = 匀速运动 yúnsù yùndòng

【等同】děngtóng〈动〉equate with: 金钱和幸福不能～。 Money cannot be equated with happiness.

【等外】děngwài〈形〉substandard: ～品 substandard goods

【等温】děngwēn〈形〉isothermal

【等闲】děngxián〈书〉**A**〈形〉ordinary: 红军不怕远征难，万水千山只～。 The Red Army fears not the trials of the Long March, deeming all hardships as ordinary. ▸～之辈 **B**〈副〉**1**（轻易）aimlessly: 年轻人不可～度日。 Young people should not fritter away their time. **2**（无端）for no reason: ～平地起波澜 make trouble out of nothing

【等闲视之】děngxiánshìzhī〈成〉regard as unimportant: 这种错误不可～。 These kind of mistakes can never be treated lightly.

【等闲之辈】děngxiánzhībèi〈成〉nobody

【等腰三角形】děngyāo sānjiǎoxíng〈名〉isosceles triangle

【等因奉此】děngyīn-fèngcǐ〈成〉〈喻〉bureaucratic language

【等于】děngyú〈动〉**1**（结果为）be equal to: 四加四～八。 Four and four is eight. **2**（等同于）be tantamount to: 你的回答～拒绝。 Your answer is tantamount to a refusal. ‖ 这事～解决了。The matter is as good as settled.

【等于零】děngyú líng〈动〉be of no use: 我说的话你不听，～。 What I say amounts to nothing if you do not listen.

【等着瞧】děngzheqiáo〈动〉wait and see: 采取～的态度 adopt a wait-and-see attitude

戥 děng

A ▸戥子 děngzi

B〈动〉weigh with a small steelyard

【戥子】děngzi〈名〉small steelyard-like device: 用～戥一戥就知道它的重量了。 We can only know how heavy it is by weighing it with a device.

d

dèng

邓（鄧） Dèng

【邓巴顿郡】Dèngbādùnjùn〈名〉Dunbartonshire

【邓弗里斯郡】Dèngfúlǐsījùn〈名〉Dumfriesshire

【邓小平理论】Dèng Xiǎopíng Lǐlùn〈名〉Deng Xiaoping Theory

凳 dèng〈名〉stool: 方～ square stool ▸板～

【凳子】dèngzi〈名〉stool

澄 dèng〈动〉**1**（澄清）settle: ▸～清 **2**〈方〉（滤出）strain: 把汤～出来。 Strain the soup.
▸chéng

【澄清】dèngqīng〈动〉settle: 等水～了再用。 Don't use the water until it becomes clear.
▸chéngqīng

【澄沙】dèngshā〈名〉sweetened bean paste: ～馅儿汤圆 glutinous flour dumplings stuffed with sweetened bean paste filling

磴 dèng

A〈名〉〈书〉stone steps

B〈量〉step: 爬11～楼梯/梯子 climb a staircase of 11 steps/a ladder of 11 rungs

瞪 dèng〈动〉**1**（用力睁大）open one's eyes wide: 他惊恐得～大了眼睛。 His eyes popped with terror. **2**（表不满）glare at: 她生气地～了他一眼。 She threw him an angry glance.

【瞪羚】dènglíng〈名〉［动物］gazelle

【瞪眼】dèngyǎn〈动〉**1**（眼看着）stare: 干～ look on in despair **2**（发脾气）glower at sb.: 又不是我的错，你干吗跟我～? It is not my fault. Why are you scowling at me?

镫（鐙） dèng〈名〉stirrup: ▸马～

【镫子】dèngzi〈名〉〈口〉stirrup

蹬 dèng ▸蹭蹬 cèngdèng
▸dēng

dī

氐 dī〈名〉**1**（指民族） Di [ancient ethnic group] **2**（指星宿） one of the 28 constellations in ancient Chinese astronomy
▸dǐ

低 dī
A〈形〉 **1** ▸**p. 82**（指高度） low: ～飞 fly low ▸～矮，～空 **2**（指地势） low-lying: 水往～处流。 Water finds its own level. ▸～地，～洼 **3**（指水平） below average: ～收入 low income ‖ 生活水平～ low living standards ‖ 河水水位～于往年。 The river is lower than in previous years. ▸～音，眼高手～ **4**（指级别） lower in grade: ～年级学生 students in lower grades
B〈动〉 lower: 他惭愧得～下头。 He hung his head in shame.

【低矮】dī'ǎi〈形〉low: ～的房屋 low houses
【低保】dībǎo〈名〉 minimum social security benefits: ～户 household receiving minimum social security benefits ‖ ～金 minimum social security grant
【低倍】dībèi〈形〉 low-power: ～放大镜 low-power magnifier
【低层】dīcéng **A**〈名〉 lower floor: 我一直住在～。 I have been living on one of the lower floors. **B**〈形〉 low-grade: ～会议 low-level meeting ‖ ～职员 low-ranking office worker
【低产】dīchǎn〈形〉 low-yield: ～田 low-yield farmland ‖ ～油田 low-output oil field ‖ ～作物 low-yielding crop
【低潮】dīcháo〈名〉 low tide: ～时岩石露了出来。 The rocks are exposed at low tide. ‖〈喻〉 住房市场现处于～。 The housing market is in the doldrums. ‖〈喻〉 当时革命正处于～。 The revolution was at a low ebb at that time.
【低沉】dīchén〈形〉 **1**（指天色） overcast: ～的天空 overcast sky **2**（指声音） low and deep: ～的音调 deep note ‖ 他声音～。 He has a deep voice. **3**（指情绪） downcast: 情绪～ be in low spirits ‖ 士气～ sagging morale
【低垂】dīchuí〈动〉 droop: ～着头 with one's head hanging low
【低档】dīdàng〈形〉low-grade: ～产品 low-grade product
【低等】dīděng〈形〉 low-grade: ～动物 lower animal ‖ ～植物 lower plant
【低地】dīdì〈名〉 lowland
【低调】dīdiào〈名〉**1**（指声音）low pitch **2**（不张扬） low key: ～讲话 low-key speech ‖ 他们对这一问题保持～。 They remain low-key about the matter.
【低端】dīduān〈形〉 low-end
【低估】dīgū〈动〉 underestimate: ～困难 underestimate a difficulty ‖ ～问题的复杂性 underestimate the complexity of an issue
【低谷】dīgǔ〈名〉 **1**（指谷地） low-lying valley **2**〈喻〉（指状态） all-time low: 事业～ slump in one's career ‖ 经济开始走出～。 The economy is coming out of a slump.
【低耗】dīhào〈形〉 low-cost
【低缓】dīhuǎn〈形〉 **1**（指声音） deep and slow: 他～的歌声悦耳动听。 His deep and unhurried singing is quite pleasant to the ear. **2**（指地势） low and gently sloping: 地势～ low and gently sloping terrain
【低回】dīhuí〈动〉〈书〉 **1**（徘徊） be reluctant to leave: 使人～不忍离去 make one reluctant to leave **2**（萦回） undulate: 思绪～ undulating train of thought ‖ ～婉转的音乐 undulating and plaintive music
【低级】dījí〈形〉 **1**（简单） elementary: ～哺乳动物 lower mammal ‖ ～生物 low form of life **2**（指品味） coarse: ～趣味 bad taste ‖ ～报刊 yellow press ‖ ～表演 cheap performance **3**（指级别） low-grade: ～茶叶 poor grade of tea ‖ ～公职人员 lower-level public employee
【低价】dījià〈名〉 low price: ～贱卖 undersell ‖ ～住房 low-cost housing
【低贱】dījiàn〈形〉 **1**（指地位） lowly: 出身～ of humble origin **2**（指价格） cheap: ～的粮价 low grain price
【低空】dīkōng〈名〉 low altitude: ～飞行 fly at a low altitude
【低栏】dīlán〈名〉［体育］ low hurdles
【低廉】dīlián〈形〉 cheap: 价格～ low in price ‖ 租金～ low rent
【低劣】dīliè〈形〉 inferior: ～产品 products of inferior quality ‖ 品质～ poor quality
【低龄】dīlíng〈形〉 juvenile: ～犯罪 juvenile delinquency
【低落】dīluò〈形〉 low: 情绪～ feel down ‖ 士气～ low morale
【低眉顺眼】dīméi-shùnyǎn〈成〉 be submissive and servile
【低迷】dīmí〈形〉 **1**（迷离） indistinct: ～的天空 hazy sky **2**（不景气） sluggish: 股市～ depressed stock market ‖ 市场～ sluggish market
【低能】dīnéng〈形〉 idiotic: ～班级 class of low intelligence ▸～儿
【低能儿】dīnéng'ér〈名〉〈旧〉 child with learning difficulties
【低频】dīpín〈名〉 low frequency
【低气压】dīqìyā〈名〉［气象］low pressure
【低热】dīrè = 低烧 dīshāo
【低人一等】dīrényīděng〈成〉 be inferior to others: 干服务行业的并不～。 Those working in the service sector are in no way inferior to others.
【低三下四】dīsān-xiàsì〈成〉 obsequious: 不要向老板～。 Do not go crawling to the boss.
【低烧】dīshāo ▸**p. 50**〈名〉［医学］ slight fever: 发～ run a low fever
【低声下气】dīshēng-xiàqì〈成〉 speak humbly and under one's breath: 不要在别人面前～。 Don't humble yourself before others.
【低首下心】dīshǒu-xiàxīn〈成〉 be submissive
【低俗】dīsú〈形〉 vulgar: 穿着～ be vulgarly dressed ‖ ～的作品 vulgar writings
【低碳钢】dītàngāng〈名〉［冶金］ mild steel
【低碳经济】dītàn jīngjì〈名〉 low-carbon economy: 促进～的发展 promote the development of low-carbon economies
【低糖】dītáng〈形〉 low in sugar: ～糕点 low-sugar cake
【低头】dītóu〈动〉 **1**（垂下头） bow one's head: ～沉思 bow one's head in meditation **2**（屈服） yield to: 不向压力～ not bow to pressure
【低头认罪】dītóu-rènzuì〈成〉 hang one's head and admit one's guilt
【低洼】dīwā〈形〉 low-lying: ～地区 low-lying area
【低微】dīwēi〈形〉 **1**（指声音） low: ～的呼吸声 low breathing sound **2**（微薄） meagre: 待遇～ low pay ‖ 收入～ meagre income **3**（指身份） humble: 出身～ be of humble origin
【低温】dīwēn〈名〉 low temperature: ～处理 low-temperature treatment ‖ ～阴雨 low temperature and wet weather
【低息】dīxī〈名〉 low interest: ～贷款 low-interest loan
【低下】dīxià〈形〉 **1**（差） below average: 社会地位～ be low in social standing ‖ 生产水平～ low production level **2**（低级） vulgar: 情趣～ vulgar taste
【低陷】dīxiàn〈形〉 sunken: 双颊～ hollow-cheeked
【低血糖】dīxuètáng ▸**p. 50**〈名〉［医学］ hypoglycaemia: ～休克 hypoglycaemic shock
【低血压】dīxuèyā ▸**p. 50**〈名〉 hypotension
【低压】dīyā〈名〉 **1**［物理］ low pressure **2**［电气］ low voltage: ～电器 low voltage electric appliances **3**［医学］ diastolic pressure **4**［气象］ depression: ～槽 trough
【低音】dīyīn〈名〉 bass: 男～ bass ‖ 女～ alto ‖ 他在合唱队里唱～。 He sings bass in the chorus.
【低音管】dīyīnguǎn ▸**p. 929**〈名〉 bassoon
【低音提琴】dīyīn tíqín ▸**p. 929**〈名〉 double bass
【低语】dīyǔ〈动〉 whisper: 他在奶奶耳边～了几句。 He whispered several words in his granny's ear.
【低云】dīyún〈名〉［气象］ low cloud

的 dī〈名〉〈口〉 taxi: ▸打～
▸de, dí, dì

【的哥】dīgē ▸**p. 966**〈名〉 male taxi driver
【的士】dīshì〈名〉 taxi

羝 dī〈名〉〈书〉 ram

堤（隄） dī〈名〉 embankment

【堤岸】dī'àn〈名〉 embankment: 修补～ repair an embankment
【堤坝】dībà〈名〉 dykes and dams: 在河上修筑～ build a dam across a river
【堤防】dīfáng〈名〉 dyke: 加固～ strengthen the dyke
【堤围】dīwéi〈名〉 dyke
【堤堰】dīyàn〈名〉 dykes and dams

提 dī
▸tí

【提防】dīfang〈动〉 beware of: ～扒手! Watch out for pickpockets!
【提溜】dīliu〈动〉〈方〉 carry sth. in one's hand: 手里～着书包 carry a schoolbag in one's hand
【提溜着心】dīliuzhexīn〈俗〉〈口〉be worried

嘀 dī
▸dí

【嘀嗒】dīdā = 滴答 dīdā
【嘀嗒】dīda = 滴答 dīda
【嘀里嘟噜】dīlidūlū〈形〉〈口〉 jabbering: 他～的，谁也不知道他在说什么。 He was jabbering, and no one could understand a word he said.

滴 dī
A〈动〉 **1**（液体落下） drip: ～水的龙头 dripping tap ‖ 屋顶在～水。 Water is dripping from the roof. **2**（使液体落下） let drops of a liquid fall: ～眼药水 drip eye drops into one's eyes
B〈名〉 drop: 汗～ beads of sweat ‖ 泪～ teardrop ‖ 雨～ raindrop
C〈量〉 drop: 两～眼泪 two teardrops ‖ 一～血 a drop of blood

【滴虫】 dīchóng〈名〉 trichomonad: ～病 trichomoniasis
【滴答】 dīdā〈拟〉 tick: ～～的钟声 tick-tock of a clock
【滴答】 dīda〈动〉 drip: 水龙头～着水。The tap is dripping water.
【滴滴涕】 dīdītì〈名〉 DDT (dichloro-diphenyl-trichloroethane)
【滴定】 dīdìng〈名〉［化学］ titration: ～管 burette
【滴管】 dīguǎn〈名〉 dropper
【滴灌】 dīguàn〈名〉［农业］drip irrigation
【滴沥】 dīlì〈拟〉 dripping sound of water: 雨水～。 The rain kept pattering.
【滴溜溜】 dīliūliū〈形〉 round and round: ～转 spin round ‖ 项链断了，珍珠～滚了一地。 The necklace broke and the pearls rolled all over the floor.
【滴溜儿】 dīliūr〈形〉〈口〉 **1**（很圆） perfectly round: ～滚圆 perfectly round **2**（转得飞快） turning quickly: 陀螺在地上～转动。 The top is spinning fast on the ground.
【滴漏】 dīlòu〈名〉 hourglass: 铜壶～ water clock of brass water containers
【滴水不漏】 dīshuǐ-bùlòu〈成〉 watertight: ～的安全措施 watertight security measures ‖ ～的论点 flawless argument
【滴水成冰】 dīshuǐ-chéngbīng〈成〉 be freezing cold: 今天的天气～。 It is freezing cold today.
【滴水穿石】 dīshuǐ-chuānshí ＝ 水滴石穿 shuǐdī-shíchuān
【滴水瓦】 dīshuǐwǎ〈名〉 drip tile [placed at either end of eaves]

镝（鏑） dī〈名〉［化学］ dysprosium (Dy)
▸dí

dí

狄 Dí〈名〉 ancient name for ethnic groups in north China

迪 dí〈动〉〈书〉 enlighten: ▸启～
【迪拉姆】 dílāmǔ ▸**p. 328**〈名〉 dirham
【迪斯科】 dísikē〈名〉 disco: 跳～ dance disco ‖ ～舞厅 discotheque
【迪厅】 dítīng〈名〉 discotheque
【迪士尼乐园】 Díshìní Lèyuán〈名〉 Disneyland

的 dí〈副〉〈书〉 true: ～证 reliable evidence
▸de, dī, dì
【的当】 dídàng〈形〉 suitable: 他的评价十分～。 His appraisal is very appropriate.
【的黎波里】 Dílíbōlǐ〈名〉 Tripoli
【的确】 díquè〈副〉 indeed: 他～是个好心人。 He is indeed kind-hearted. ‖ 我～不知道。 Honestly, I don't know.
【的确良】 díquèliáng〈名〉［纺织］ dacron

籴（糴） dí〈动〉 buy in: ～米 buy rice

荻 dí〈名〉 a kind of reed

敌（敵） dí
A〈名〉 enemy: 分清～我 draw a clear line between the enemy and ourselves ‖〈喻〉懒惰是纪律的大～。 Idleness is the enemy to discipline. ▸～人, 情～, 无～
B〈形〉 **1**（敌对） hostile: ▸～对, ～国 **2**（相当） equal: ▸匹～, 势均力～
C〈动〉 resist: ～不过 be no match for ‖ ～不住金钱的诱惑 cannot resist the temptation of money ▸寡不～众
【敌百虫】 díbǎichóng〈名〉［农业］ dipterex
【敌敌畏】 dídíwèi〈名〉 DDVP (dimethyl-dichlorovinyl-phosphate)
【敌对】 díduì〈形〉 hostile: ～双方 opposing sides ‖ ～态度 antagonism
【敌方】 dífāng〈名〉 enemy
【敌国】 díguó〈名〉 enemy state
【敌后】 díhòu〈名〉 enemy's rear area: 深入～ penetrate the enemy's rear ‖ ～根据地 base areas behind enemy lines
【敌军】 díjūn〈名〉 enemy troops
【敌寇】 díkòu〈名〉 enemy
【敌情】 díqíng〈名〉 enemy activities: 侦察～ make a reconnaissance of the enemy's situation ‖ 有～。 There are signs of enemy activity.
【敌情观念】 díqíng guānniàn〈名〉 alertness to the presence of the enemy
【敌酋】 díqiú〈名〉〈旧〉 enemy chief: 活捉～ capture the enemy chief alive
【敌人】 dírén〈名〉 enemy: 打败～ defeat an enemy ‖ 战胜～ vanquish the enemy
【敌视】 díshì〈动〉 be hostile to: ～他国 be hostile towards other countries ‖ ～态度 hostile attitude
【敌手】 díshǒu〈名〉 **1**（对手） opponent: 比技术，咱们几个都不是他的～。 In terms of technical skill, none of us can rival him. ▸棋逢～ **2**（敌人） enemy hands: 落入～ fall into enemy hands
【敌台】 dítái〈名〉 enemy broadcasting station
【敌探】 dítàn〈名〉 enemy spy
【敌特】 dítè〈名〉 enemy spy
【敌伪】 díwěi〈名〉 enemy and the puppet regime [during the War of Resistance against Japan]: ～时期 period of Japanese occupation
【敌我】 dí-wǒ〈名〉 the enemy and ourselves: ～不分 fail to differentiate between the enemy and ourselves
【敌我矛盾】 dí-wǒ máodùn〈名〉 contradiction between ourselves and the enemy
【敌焰】 díyàn〈名〉〈书〉 arrogance of the enemy: ～嚣张。 The enemy is puffed up with arrogance.
【敌意】 díyì〈名〉 enmity: 怀有～ be hostile to ‖ 没有～ feel no hostility
【敌占区】 dízhànqū〈名〉 enemy-occupied territory
【敌阵】 dízhèn〈名〉 enemy's position: 包围～ have the enemy's position surrounded

涤（滌） dí
A〈动〉 cleanse: ▸荡～, 洗～
B ＝ 涤纶 dílún
【涤除】 díchú〈动〉〈书〉 do away with: ～旧习 eliminate an old habit ‖ ～污垢 wash away the dirt
【涤荡】 dídàng〈动〉〈书〉 wash away: ～污泥浊水 clean up the mud and dirty water
【涤卡】 díkǎ〈名〉 Terylene drill
【涤纶】 dílún〈名〉 polyester fibre
【涤瑕荡垢】 díxiá-dànggòu〈成〉 get rid of all bad practices

笛 dí〈名〉 **1**（指乐器） flute: ▸短～ **2**（指发音器） whistle: 鸣～ sound a siren ▸警～, 汽～
【笛膜】 dímó〈名〉 membrane covering holes in flute
【笛子】 dízi〈名〉 flute: 吹～ play the flute

觌（覿） dí〈动〉〈书〉 meet: ～面 meet each other

嘀 dí
▸dī
【嘀咕】 dígu〈动〉 **1**（小声说话） whisper: 他俩一见面就～上了。 They started whispering to each other as soon as they met. **2**（犹豫） have doubts/misgivings about sth.: 心里直犯～ cannot help doubting

嫡 dí〈名〉 **1**〈旧〉（正妻） legal wife: ～长子 legal wife's eldest son ▸～子 **2**（指亲属） relative of lineal descent: ▸～亲, ～堂 **3**（正宗） legal connections: ▸～派, ～系
【嫡出】 díchū〈动〉 be born of the legal wife
【嫡传】 díchuán〈动〉 be handed down directly from the master to the disciple or his official heir
【嫡母】 dímǔ〈名〉[concubine's children's term of address for their father's primary wife] direct line mother
【嫡派】 dípài〈名〉 **1** ＝ 嫡系 díxì **2**（指传授派别） disciples personally instructed by the master
【嫡亲】 díqīn〈形〉 related by blood: ～弟兄/姐妹 full brothers/sisters
【嫡堂】 dítáng〈形〉 related by blood [between cousins of the same surname and grandfather]: ～兄弟/姐妹 male/female cousins of the same surname and grandfather
【嫡系】 díxì〈名〉 **1**（指家族） direct line of descent: ～后裔 descendants of the direct line of descent **2**（指派系） being under the direct control of a faction: ～部队 troops under the direct control of a faction
【嫡子】 dízǐ〈名〉 son by the legal wife

翟 dí〈名〉〈古〉 **1**（野鸡） long-tailed pheasant **2**（野鸡毛） pheasant feather
▸Zhái

樀 dí〈名〉〈书〉 eaves

镝（鏑） dí〈名〉〈书〉 arrow
▸dī

dǐ

氐 dǐ〈名〉〈书〉 foundation
▸dī

邸 dǐ〈名〉 residence of a high official: ▸官～
【邸宅】 dǐzhái〈名〉 mansion

诋（詆） dǐ〈动〉〈书〉 slander
【诋毁】 dǐhuǐ〈动〉 slander: ～他人人格 blacken sb.'s character ‖ 极尽～之能事 exert one's mud-slinging abilities to the full

抵[1] dǐ
A〈动〉 **1**（支撑） support: 他用手～住下巴。 He supported his chin in his hand. ‖ 请～住门，别让风刮开。 Please prop something against the door so that it will not be blown open. **2**（抵挡） resist: ～不住 be unable to resist ▸～挡, ～御 **3**（相

d

当） be equal to: 一个～两个。 One is the equivalent of two. 4 （抵消） balance: 收支相～。 The accounts are balanced. 5 （抵偿） compensate for: ▸～命, ～债
B 〈名〉 mortgage: 用房屋做～ get a mortgage on a house

抵[2]（牴） dǐ〈动〉 oppose: ▸～触, ～牾

抵[3] dǐ〈动〉〈书〉 reach: 当日～沪 reach Shanghai on the same day

【抵补】dǐbǔ〈动〉 compensate for: ～损失 make up for the losses
【抵偿】dǐcháng〈动〉 compensate for: ～损失 make good a loss ‖ 拿实物做～ repay in kind ‖ ～贸易 compensation trade
【抵触】dǐchù〈动〉 conflict: 相互～ contradict each other ‖ ～情绪 resistance
【抵达】dǐdá〈动〉 reach: ～港口 reach the harbour ‖ ～目的地 get to the destination
【抵挡】dǐdǎng〈动〉 resist: ～洪水 keep the flood in check ‖ ～严寒 keep out the severe cold ‖ 攻势太猛，难以～。 The attack is too fierce to withstand.
【抵还】dǐhuán〈动〉 repay
【抵换】dǐhuàn〈动〉 take the place of
【抵抗】dǐkàng〈动〉 resist: ～侵略 resist aggression ‖ 顽强～ put up a stubborn resistance ‖ ～力 power of resistance
【抵赖】dǐlài〈动〉 disavow: ～所犯罪行 deny one's guilt ‖ 铁证如山，不容～。 The evidence is rock-solid and cannot be denied.
【抵命】dǐmìng〈动〉 pay with one's life: 杀人～。 Life should be paid for with life.
【抵塞】dǐsāi〈动〉 1 （拖住） stall sb. off 2 （敷衍） do sth. perfunctorily
【抵事】dǐshì〈动〉 do: 谁说人少了不～? Who says that it will not do with only a few people?
【抵数】dǐshù〈动〉 make up the number
【抵死】dǐsǐ〈副〉 till death: ～不承认 persistently deny
【抵牾】dǐwǔ〈动〉〈书〉 conflict with
【抵消】dǐxiāo〈动〉 counteract: 互相～ cancel each other out ‖ 今年的亏损～了去年的利润。 This year's losses cancelled out last year's gains.
【抵押】dǐyā〈动〉 mortgage: 以房子做～ take out a mortgage on a house
【抵押贷款】dǐyā dàikuǎn〈名〉 mortgage loan: 用～购房 buy a house with a mortgage
【抵押品】dǐyāpǐn〈名〉 security
【抵御】dǐyù〈动〉 resist: ～风沙侵袭 resist sand storms ‖ ～寒冷 keep out the cold
【抵债】dǐzhài〈动〉 pay a debt in kind: 用实物～ pay one's debt in kind
【抵账】dǐzhàng〈动〉 repay a debt in kind
【抵制】dǐzhì〈动〉 resist: ～不正之风 resist unhealthy practices ‖ 受到～ meet with resistance
【抵罪】dǐzuì〈动〉 atone for a crime: 将功～ do good deeds to atone for one's crimes

底 dǐ〈名〉 1 （底部） bottom: 锅～ bottom of a pan ‖ 箱～ bottom of a chest ‖ 战斗到～ fight to the end ▸～边, ～肥, 鞋～ 2 （衬底） ground: 白～红花 red flowers on white ground 3 （内情） ins and outs: 不摸～ not know the real situation ‖ 心里没～ feel uncertain about ▸～细, 交～, 刨根问～ 4 （底稿） master copy: 留个～儿 keep a copy on file ▸～稿 5 （末尾） end of a year or month: 将近年～ towards the end of a year ‖ 十月～ end of October 6 （最后部分） remnants: 仓～儿 remnants of grain in the stores ‖ 货～儿 remnants of stock
▸de

【底版】dǐbǎn = 底片 dǐpiàn
【底本】dǐběn〈名〉 master copy
【底边】dǐbiān〈名〉 1 （指几何图形） base (of a triangle, etc.) 2 （指页面） bottom (of a page)
【底册】dǐcè〈名〉 bound copy of a document kept on file: 请抄两份，一份上报，一份留作～。 Please make two copies, one for the leadership, the other to be kept on file.
【底层】dǐcéng〈名〉 1 （指楼层） ground floor: 大楼的～有家商店。 There is a shop on the ground floor of the building. 2 （指阶层） lowest rung: 生活在社会最～ live at the bottom of society
【底肥】dǐféi〈名〉 base fertilizer: 施～ apply base fertilizer
【底稿】dǐgǎo〈名〉 original manuscript: 打～ make a draft
【底功】dǐgōng〈名〉 basic skill: ～扎实 have solid basic training
【底火】dǐhuǒ〈名〉 1 （指火） fire in the stove before refuelling 2 ［军事］ primer
【底价】dǐjià〈名〉 minimum price: 规定～ establish a floor
【底里】dǐlǐ〈名〉〈书〉 inside story: 不知～ not know the ins and outs ‖ 探听～ try to find out the ins and outs of a matter
【底码】dǐmǎ〈名〉 bottom price
【底牌】dǐpái〈名〉 1 （指扑克牌） hand: 亮～ show one's hand 2 〈喻〉（底细） inside story: 摸清对方的～，再考虑如何行动。 Let's find out the real situation on the other side before we act. 3 〈喻〉（撒手锏） last resort: 不到万不得已，别打这张～。 Do not resort to doing this unless you have exhausted all other possibilities.
【底盘】dǐpán〈名〉 1 （指汽车等） chassis: ～高度 chassis height 2 （指安装板） board on which most components are fixed in an electronic apparatus 3 〈方〉（指底座） base
【底片】dǐpiàn〈名〉 negative
【底漆】dǐqī〈名〉primer: 给家具上～ apply an undercoat on a piece of furniture
【底气】dǐqì〈名〉 1 （呼吸量） breath: 他～不足，爬到第三层就气喘了。He didn't have enough breath and was panting as he climbed up to the third floor. 2 （信心） drive: 教师们的～更足了。 The teachers are feeling more energetic in their work.
【底色】dǐsè〈名〉 1 （指颜色） undercoat 2 ［纺织］ bottom
【底墒】dǐshāng〈名〉 soil moisture
【底数】dǐshù〈名〉 1 ［数学］ base number 2 （底细） truth of a matter: 心中有～ know how the matter stands
【底特律】Dǐtèlǜ〈名〉 Detroit
【底细】dǐxì〈名〉 ins and outs: 他不了解这件事的～。 He had no idea about the ins and outs of the matter.
【底下】dǐxia〈名〉 1 （下面） beneath: 树～ under the tree ‖ 桌子～ under the table ‖ 笔～不错 write well ‖ 手～一帮人 a number of people under sb. 2 （后面） afterwards: 他们～说的话我就听不清了。 I did not catch what they said next.
【底下人】dǐxiarén〈名〉 1 〈旧〉（仆人） servant 2 （下手） subordinate: 上边没说话，～不好做主。 Without the instruction of their superiors, underlings do not dare to take action.
【底限】dǐxiàn〈名〉 minimum
【底线】dǐxiàn〈名〉 1 ［体育］ base line: ～球战术 baseline game 2 （内线） planted agent: 要是没有～，他们是不会成功的。 They could not have succeeded without their stooges. 3 （最低限度） bottom line: 谈判的～ bottom line for negotiations
【底薪】dǐxīn〈名〉 basic salary
【底蕴】dǐyùn〈名〉〈书〉 inside story: 不知其中～ not know the ins and outs of the matter
【底止】dǐzhǐ〈名〉〈书〉 limit: 永无～。 There will never be an end to it.
【底子】dǐzi〈名〉 1 （底部） base: 鞋～ sole of a shoe 2 （底细） ins and outs: 把～搞清楚 get to the root of the matter 3 （基础） foundation: 数学～薄 have a poor grounding in maths ‖ 我乡的经济～薄。 Our township has a poor economic foundation. 4 （草稿） rough draft: 画画前得先在画布上打个炭笔～。 Make a rough sketch on the canvas with a crayon before you start to paint. 5 （最后部分） remnant: 货～ remnants of stock ‖ 粮食～ remnants of grain 6 （衬底） background: 白～小紫花的衬衫 white shirt printed with small violet flowers
【底座】dǐzuò〈名〉 base: 雕塑～ base of a sculpture ‖ 台灯～ stand of a reading lamp

柢 dǐ〈名〉〈书〉 main root of a tree

砥 dǐ〈名〉〈书〉 whetstone

【砥砺】dǐlì〈书〉 A〈名〉 whetstone B〈动〉 1 （磨炼） temper: ～意志力 temper one's willpower 2 （勉励） encourage: 互相～ encourage each other
【砥柱中流】dǐzhù-zhōngliú = 中流砥柱 zhōngliú-dǐzhù

骶 dǐ

【骶骨】dǐgǔ〈名〉［解剖］ sacrum

dì

地 dì〈名〉 1 （大地） earth: 天～ heaven and earth ▸～震, ～质 2 （陆地） land: ▸盆～, 山～ 3 （田地） fields: 下～干活 go and work in the fields ▸耕～, 荒～ 4 （地面） ground: 扫～ sweep the floor ‖ 水泥～ cement floor ▸席～ 5 （领地） territory: ▸领～, 殖民～ 6 （地区） area: 世界各～ all parts of the world ▸内～, 外～ 7 （地方） location: 两～分居 live apart in different places ▸场～, 胜～ 8 （处境） position: ▸～步, 境～ 9 （状态） mental state: ▸见～, 心～ 10 （指行政区域） prefecture: ～县两级干部 cadres from the prefecture and the county 11 （区域） administrative areas under the central government: ～税局 local tax bureau 12 （空间） space: 这占不了多少～儿。 This won't take up much space. 13 （距离） distance: 二十里～ distance of 20 *li* ‖ 两站～远 two bus stops away 14 （背景） background: 白字黑～的木牌 board with white characters on a black background
▸de

【地板】dìbǎn〈名〉 floorboard: 擦洗～ scrub the floor ‖ 给～打蜡 wax the floor ‖ 镶木～ parquet flooring
【地板革】dìbǎngé〈名〉 vinyl flooring
【地堡】dìbǎo〈名〉［军事］ bunker
【地标】dìbiāo〈名〉 landmark

【地表】dìbiǎo〈名〉earth's surface: ～温度 surface temperature
【地鳖】dìbiē〈名〉［昆虫］ground beetle
【地波】dìbō〈名〉ground wave: ～传播 propagation of ground waves
【地步】dìbù〈名〉1（境地）predicament: 真没想到他会落到这个～。I never expected he would find himself in such a predicament. 2（程度）extent: 到了背水一战的～ have one's back to the wall ‖ 劳资纠纷已发展到不可收拾的～。The industrial dispute has got out of hand. 3（余地）leeway: 留有回旋的～ leave room for manoeuvre
【地层】dìcéng〈名〉layer: ～沉裂 subsidence break
【地产】dìchǎn〈名〉real estate: 他做～生意。He is engaged in the real estate business.
【地秤】dìchèng〈名〉bathroom scales
【地磁】dìcí〈名〉［物理］geomagnetism: ～感应 earth induction ‖ ～仪 magnetometer
【地大物博】dìdà-wùbó〈成〉vast territory and abundant natural resources: 加拿大～，人口稀少。Canada is a big country abounding in natural resources and with a sparse population.
【地带】dìdài〈名〉region: 草原～ grasslands region ‖ 丘陵～ hilly land ‖ 危险～ danger zone
【地道】dìdào〈名〉tunnel: 挖～ dig a tunnel
【地道战】dìdàozhàn〈名〉tunnel warfare
【地道】dìdao〈形〉1（正宗）genuine: ～药材 genuine herbal medicines ‖ ～的山东烟台苹果 genuine Yantai apples from Shandong Province 2（纯正）pure: 他的普通话说得真～。He speaks perfect *putonghua*. 3（够标准）excellent: 他干的活儿真～。He has done an excellent job.
【地地道道】dìdi-dàodào〈形〉out-and-out: 他是个～的吝啬鬼。He is a miser to the core.
【地点】dìdiǎn〈名〉site: 犯罪～ crime scene ‖ 开会～是在大礼堂。The meeting will be held in the auditorium.
【地动山摇】dìdòng-shānyáo〈成〉the earth shakes and mountains move
【地动仪】dìdòngyí〈名〉seismograph
【地洞】dìdòng〈名〉hole in the ground: 掘～ dig a hole in the ground
【地段】dìduàn〈名〉site: 繁华～ prosperous area ‖ 黄金～ prime site
【地对地导弹】dìduìdì dǎodàn〈名〉surface-to-surface missile
【地对空导弹】dìduìkōng dǎodàn〈名〉surface-to-air missile
【地方】dìfāng〈名〉1（地方政府）local government: ～工业 local industries ‖ 充分发挥中央和～两个积极性。Give full play to the initiatives of both central and local authorities. 2（本地）locality: 他在农村的时侯，常给～上的群众治病。When he was in the countryside, he often gave medical treatment to the local people. ‖ 这～有什么娱乐设施？What kind of leisure facilities are there in the locality? 3（非军队）civilian
【地方保护主义】dìfāng bǎohùzhǔyì〈名〉local protectionism: 打破～ break up local protectionism
【地方病】dìfāngbìng〈名〉endemic disease: ～防治 prevention and cure of endemic diseases
【地方各级人民代表大会】dìfāng gèjí rénmíndàibiǎodàhuì〈名〉local People's Congresses at various levels
【地方观念】dìfāng guānniàn〈名〉localism
【地方国营】dìfāng guóyíng〈形〉state-owned but locally administered: ～企业 locally administered state enterprise
【地方民族主义】dìfāng mínzúzhǔyì〈名〉local nationalism
【地方戏】dìfāngxì〈名〉local opera
【地方政府】dìfāng zhèngfǔ〈名〉local government
【地方志】dìfāngzhì〈名〉local annals
【地方主义】dìfāngzhǔyì〈名〉localism
【地方】dìfang〈名〉1（区域）place: 把洗的衣服挂在通风的～ hang the washing in an airy place ‖ 你是什么～人？Where are you from? 2（空间）space: ～狭窄 cramped place ‖ 屋子太小，没有～加床。The room is too small and there is no space for another bed. 3（部分）part: 你的话有对的～，也有不对的～。What you said is partly right and partly wrong. ‖ 这本书有的～写得夸张不实。Parts of the book are too exaggerated to be true.
【地府】dìfǔ〈名〉nether world
【地覆天翻】dìfù-tiānfān = 天翻地覆 tiānfān-dìfù
【地埂】dìgěng〈名〉field embankment
【地宫】dìgōng〈名〉1（地下陵墓）tomb chamber 2（地下藏经室）underground shrine housing Buddhist relics
【地沟】dìgōu〈名〉underground irrigation canal
【地瓜】dìguā〈名〉〈方〉1（甘薯）sweet potato 2（豆薯）yam bean
【地光】dìguāng〈名〉earthquake lightning
【地广人稀】dìguǎng-rénxī〈成〉vast but sparsely populated
【地滚球】dìgǔnqiú〈名〉1（指棒球）grounder 2 = 保龄球 bǎolíngqiú
【地核】dìhé〈名〉［地质］core of the earth
【地黄】dìhuáng〈名〉［中药］glutinous rehmannia [Chinese foxglove]
【地积】dìjī〈名〉area
【地基】dìjī〈名〉1（地皮）ground 2（房基）foundation: 打～ lay the foundations of a building ‖ 这间房子～牢固。The house stands on a firm foundation.
【地极】dìjí〈名〉［地质］terrestrial pole
【地价】dìjià〈名〉land price
【地角】dìjiǎo〈名〉ends of the earth
【地脚】dìjiǎo〈名〉1（页脚）foot margin 2〈方〉（地基）foundation
【地窖】dìjiào〈名〉cellar
【地界】dìjiè〈名〉1（指界限）land demarcation 2〈方〉（地区）area
【地久天长】dìjiǔ-tiāncháng = 天长地久 tiāncháng-dìjiǔ
【地块】dìkuài〈名〉1（指耕地）plot of land 2［地质］massif
【地牢】dìláo〈名〉dungeon
【地老虎】dìlǎohǔ〈名〉〈口〉cutworm
【地老天荒】dìlǎo-tiānhuāng〈成〉outlast even heaven and earth
【地雷】dìléi〈名〉mine: 埋设～ lay mines ‖ 引爆～ detonate a mine
【地理】dìlǐ ▸p. 164〈名〉1（指学科）geography: ～知识 geographical information ‖ 经济～ economic geography ▸自然～ 2（指地貌）geographical features of a place
【地栗】dìlì〈名〉〈方〉water chestnut
【地力】dìlì〈名〉soil fertility: 多施底肥，增加～。Apply more base fertilizer to enhance soil fertility.
【地利】dìlì〈名〉1（地理优势）geographical advantages: 天时～ opportune time and geographical advantages 2（指土地条件）land productivity: 充分发挥～优势，适合种什么就种什么。Make full use of the potential of the land and grow whatever is suitable.
【地量】dìliàng〈名〉lowest amount
【地灵人杰】dìlíng-rénjié = 人杰地灵 rénjié-dìlíng
【地龙】dìlóng〈名〉［中药］earthworm
【地垄】dìlǒng〈名〉1（指土埂）bank of earth between fields 2（指土地）long strips of arable land between banks of earth 3（地道）tunnel
【地漏】dìlòu〈名〉［建筑］floor drain
【地脉】dìmài〈名〉veins of the earth
【地幔】dìmàn〈名〉［地理］mantle
【地貌】dìmào〈名〉topography: ～图 geomorphological map
【地面】dìmiàn〈名〉1（地表）earth's surface: 高出～五尺 five *chi* above ground level ‖ ～沉降 surface subsidence 2［建筑］floor: 瓷砖～ ceramic tile floor ‖ 水磨石～ terrazzo floor 3〈口〉（区域）territory: 这里已经进入缅甸～。We are now in Myanmar territory. 4〈口〉（当地）locality: 他在～儿上有势力。He pulls great weight in the locality.
【地面部队】dìmiàn bùduì〈名〉ground forces
【地面砖】dìmiànzhuān〈名〉floor tile
【地名】dìmíng〈名〉place name
【地名学】dìmíngxué〈名〉toponymy
【地膜】dìmó〈名〉mulch film
【地亩】dìmǔ〈名〉farmland: 丈量～ measure farmland
【地盘】dìpán〈名〉domain: 扩大～ expand one's spheres of influence ‖ 争夺～ compete for spheres of influence
【地皮】dìpí〈名〉1（地面）ground: 下雨以后，～还没有干。The ground is still wet after the rain. 2（建筑用地）building lot: 城市里～很紧张。Land is very scarce in cities.
【地痞】dìpǐ〈名〉local riff-raff: ～流氓 local bullies and loafers
【地平线】dìpíngxiàn〈名〉horizon: 太阳从～上升起。The sun is coming out from behind the horizon.
【地铺】dìpù〈名〉mattress on the floor: 睡～ sleep on a makeshift bed on the floor
【地气】dìqì〈名〉1（指潮气）ground vapour: 不要躺在地上，～太阴，会着凉的。If you lie on the ground, you'll catch cold from the damp. 2（指温度）temperature
【地契】dìqì〈名〉title deed for land
【地壳】dìqiào〈名〉earth's crust: ～运动 crustal movement
【地勤】dìqín〈名〉［航空］ground service: ～人员 ground personnel
【地球】dìqiú〈名〉earth
【地球村】dìqiúcūn〈名〉global village
【地球化学】dìqiú huàxué〈名〉geochemistry
【地球科学】dìqiú kēxué〈名〉geoscience
【地球人】dìqiúrén〈名〉earth person
【地球日】dìqiúrì〈名〉1（保护地球活动日）Earth Day 2（天）earth day
【地球同步轨道】dìqiú tóngbù guǐdào〈名〉geosynchronous orbit
【地球同步卫星】dìqiú tóngbù wèixīng〈名〉geostationary satellite
【地球卫星】dìqiú wèixīng〈名〉earth satellite
【地球物理学】dìqiú wùlǐxué〈名〉geophysics

d

【地球仪】dìqiúyí〈名〉terrestrial globe
【地球引力】dìqiú yǐnlì〈名〉gravity
【地球中心说】dìqiú zhōngxīnshuō〈名〉geocentrism
【地区】dìqū〈名〉1（区域）area: 边缘～ marginal area ‖ 贫困～ impoverished area 2（指行政区域）prefecture: 陕西省咸阳～ Xianyang prefecture of Shaanxi Province 3（指殖民地、托管地）trust or mandated territory
【地区冲突】dìqū chōngtū〈名〉regional conflict/clash
【地权】dìquán〈名〉land rights
【地儿】dìr〈名〉〈口〉place: 腾个～ make room ‖ 没～去 have nowhere to go
【地热】dìrè〈名〉geothermal energy: ～资源 geothermal resources
【地上茎】dìshàngjīng〈名〉［植物］aerial stem
【地势】dìshì〈名〉topography: ～险要 strategically important terrain that is difficult of access ‖ ～平坦 smooth terrain
【地税】dìshuì〈名〉1（土地税）land tax 2（地方税）local tax
【地摊】dìtān〈名〉roadside stall: 摆～ set up a stand on the street
【地坛】dìtán〈名〉Altar of the Earth
【地毯】dìtǎn〈名〉carpet
【地毯式轰炸】dìtǎnshì hōngzhà〈名〉carpet bombing
【地铁】dìtiě〈名〉underground〈英〉; subway〈美〉: 乘～ take the subway
【地头】dìtóu〈名〉1（田地两端）edge of a field: 请大家在～休息一会儿。Please have a rest at the edge of the field. 2〈方〉（地方）this place: ▶～蛇
【地头蛇】dìtóushé〈名〉〈喻〉local villain: ▶强龙难压～
【地图】dìtú〈名〉map: 旅游～ tourist map ‖ 世界～ map of the world ‖ 最新～ up-to-date map
【地图册】dìtúcè〈名〉atlas
【地推子】dìtuīzi〈名〉〈口〉wheeled push broom
【地王】dìwáng〈名〉land contractor who has succeeded in bidding for the most expensive land in a certain area
【地委】dìwěi〈名〉prefectural Party committee
【地位】dìwèi〈名〉position: 有很高的～ hold a very high rank ‖ 国际～ international standing ‖ 学术～ academic position ‖ 政治～ political standing
【地温】dìwēn〈名〉［气象］ground temperature
【地物】dìwù〈名〉surface features
【地峡】dìxiá〈名〉［地质］isthmus
【地下】dìxià A〈名〉underground: ～核试验 underground nuclear testing ‖ ～通道 underground passage ▶～水 B〈形〉underground: ～工作 underground activities ‖ 工作转入～。The work has gone underground.
【地下党】dìxiàdǎng〈名〉underground party: ～组织 underground party organization
【地下工厂】dìxià gōngchǎng〈名〉underground workshop
【地下茎】dìxiàjīng〈名〉［植物］subterranean stem
【地下室】dìxiàshì〈名〉basement
【地下水】dìxiàshuǐ〈名〉groundwater: ～采掘 groundwater mining
【地下】dìxia〈名〉ground
【地线】dìxiàn〈名〉［电气］earth wire〈英〉; ground (wire)〈美〉
【地心】dìxīn〈名〉earth's core
【地心说】dìxīnshuō〈名〉geocentrism
【地心引力】dìxīn yǐnlì〈名〉earth's gravity
【地形】dìxíng〈名〉terrain: 占据有利～ gain vantage ground ‖ ～图 topographic map
【地形雨】dìxíngyǔ〈名〉［气象］orographic rain
【地学】dìxué〈名〉geoscience
【地衣】dìyī〈名〉［植物］lichen
【地窨子】dìyìnzi〈名〉〈口〉1（地下室）basement 2（地窖）cellar
【地狱】dìyù〈名〉1〈本〉hell 2〈喻〉hell on earth: ～般的待遇 hellish treatment ▶人间～
【地域】dìyù〈名〉1（区域）region: ～辽阔 vast in territory 2（当地）locality: ～观念 localism
【地缘】dìyuán〈名〉relations formed through geographical links: ～经济 geoeconomics ‖ ～政治 geopolitics
【地震】dìzhèn〈名〉earthquake: 强烈～ powerful earthquake
【地震波】dìzhènbō〈名〉seismic wave
【地震带】dìzhèndài〈名〉seismic belt
【地震监测站】dìzhèn jiāncèzhàn〈名〉earthquake monitoring station
【地震烈度】dìzhèn lièdù〈名〉seismic intensity
【地震仪】dìzhènyí〈名〉seismograph
【地震震级】dìzhèn zhènjí〈名〉earthquake

ℹ 地理名称

不使用定冠词

■ 一般来讲，英语里表示地名的名词（包括英语的地名及翻译成英语的汉语地名）前面都不用定冠词：

北京
= Beijing

中国
= China

伦敦
= London

法国
= France

解放路
= Jiefang Road

天安门广场
= Tiananmen Square

特拉法尔加广场
= Trafalgar Square

越秀公园
= Yuexiu Park

海德公园
= Hyde Park

洞庭湖
= Dongting Lake

密歇根湖
= Lake Michigan

维多利亚站
= Victoria Station

白云机场
= Baiyun Airport

广州火车站
= Guangzhou Railway Station

纳皮尔大学
= Napier University

北京大学
= Beijing University
或 Peking University

使用定冠词

■ 江河海洋、山脉群岛、海峡海湾、沙漠等地理名称前一般要用定冠词：

长江
= the Changjiang
或 the Yangtze

印度洋
= the Indian Ocean

密西西比河
= the Mississippi River

台湾海峡
= the Taiwan Straits

红海
= the Red Sea

墨西哥湾
= the Gulf of Mexico

好望角
= the Cape of Good Hope

索罗门群岛
= the Solomon Islands

菲律宾群岛
= the Philippine Islands

阿尔卑斯山
= the Alps

喜马拉雅山脉
= the Himalayas

天山山脉
= the Tianshan Mountains

撒哈拉沙漠
= the Sahara

阿拉伯沙漠
= the Arabian Desert

■ 由两个或两个以上的名词组成的国名前一般用定冠词；有些国名（单个名词）、城市及地区名称前也要加定冠词：

美利坚合众国
= the United States of America

中国人民共和国
= the People's Republic of China

荷兰
= the Netherlands

海牙
= the Hague

北极
= the North Pole

中东
= the Middle East

加勒比海地区
= the Caribbean

magnitude
【地政】dìzhèng〈名〉geopolitics
【地支】dìzhī〈名〉Earthly Branches
【地址】dìzhǐ〈名〉address: 办公/家庭～ business/home address ‖ 网络～ website
【地志学】dìzhìxué〈名〉topology
【地质】dìzhì〈名〉geology: ～学家 geologist
【地质勘探】dìzhì kāntàn〈名〉geological prospecting
【地中海】Dìzhōnghǎi〈名〉Mediterranean Sea
【地轴】dìzhóu〈名〉earth's axis
【地主】dìzhǔ〈名〉**1**（有土地的人）landlord **2**（本地人）host: 尽～之谊 perform the duties of a host
【地砖】dìzhuān〈名〉floor tile
【地租】dìzū〈名〉ground rent

弟 dì

〈名〉**1**（有血缘关系）younger brother: 二～ second younger brother ‖ 小～ little brother **2**（有亲缘关系）younger brother-in-law or male cousin: ▸表～, 妻～, 堂～ **3**（谦）（指男性朋友）（主格）I;（宾格）me
【弟弟】dìdi ▸**p. 588**〈名〉younger brother
【弟妇】dìfù = 弟媳 dìxí
【弟妹】dìmèi ▸**p. 588**〈名〉**1**（弟弟和妹妹）younger brothers and sisters **2**（弟媳妇）younger brother's wife
【弟媳】dìxí ▸**p. 588**〈名〉one's younger brother's wife
【弟兄】dìxiong〈名〉brothers: 他没有～。He has no brothers. ‖ 他们～俩是双胞胎。They are twin brothers.
【弟子】dìzǐ〈名〉follower: 佛门～ Buddhist disciple

的 dì

〈名〉target: ▸目～, 众矢之～ ▸de, dī, dí

帝 dì

〈名〉**1**（天神）God: ▸玉皇大～, 上～, 天～ **2**（君主）emperor **3**（帝国主义）imperialism: 反～斗争 anti-imperialist struggle
【帝俄】Dì'É〈名〉Tsarist Russia
【帝国】dìguó〈名〉empire: ～大厦 Empire State Building ‖ 神圣罗马～ Holy Roman Empire
【帝国主义】dìguózhǔyì〈名〉imperialism: ～列强 imperialist powers
【帝君】dìjūn〈名〉title of reverence added to the names of gods: 文昌～ God of Literature
【帝企鹅】dìqǐ'é〈名〉emperor penguin
【帝王】dìwáng〈名〉emperor
【帝位】dìwèi〈名〉throne
【帝汶岛】Dìwèndǎo〈名〉Timor
【帝制】dìzhì〈名〉monarchy: 推翻～ overthrow the monarchy

递（遞）dì

A〈动〉hand over: 请把报～给我。Please pass me the newspaper. ▸～眼色, 投～
B〈副〉successively: ～升 increase progressively ▸～减, ～增
【递补】dìbǔ〈动〉fill vacancies in the proper order: 委员出缺，由候补委员～。Any vacancies in the committee should be filled by the alternate members in a proper order.
【递加】dìjiā〈动〉increase by degrees
【递减】dìjiǎn〈动〉decrease by degrees: 劳动生产率逐步提高，产品的成本也随之～。The cost of the product decreases accordingly with the gradual rise of productivity.
【递降】dìjiàng〈动〉fall progressively: 改进工艺，使原材料消耗逐月～。Reduce the consumption of raw materials month after month by improving craftsmanship.
【递交】dìjiāo〈动〉submit: ～辞呈 tender one's resignation ‖ ～国书 present the credentials
【递解】dìjiè〈动〉escort (a prisoner) from one place to another: ～还乡 send a criminal to his native place under escort
【递进】dìjìn〈动〉go forward one by one
【递升】dìshēng〈动〉promote to the next rank
【递送】dìsòng〈动〉send: ～情报 send out information ‖ 按快件～ send by express mail
【递眼色】dì yǎnsè〈动〉wink at: 他给我递了个眼色，让我保持沉默。He gave me a wink as a sign for me to keep silent.
【递增】dìzēng〈动〉increase progressively: 收入逐年～。The income grows year by year.

娣 dì

〈名〉〈古〉**1**（指弟妻）wife of one's husband's younger brother **2**（指妹妹）little sister

第 dì

A〈名〉**1**（次序）sequence: ▸次～ **2**（大宅子）residence of a high official: ▸府～, 宅～ **3**（书）（科第）placement in imperial examinations: ▸及～, 落～
B〈前缀〉[marker of ordinal numerals]: ～四届世界妇女大会 Fourth World Conference on Women ▸～一
【第二产业】dì-èr chǎnyè〈名〉［经济］secondary industry: 调整～ readjust the secondary industry
【第二次国内革命战争】Dì-èr Cì Guónèi Gémìng Zhànzhēng〈名〉Second Revolutionary Civil War [1927-1937]
【第二次世界大战】Dì-èr Cì Shìjiè Dàzhàn〈名〉Second World War, World War II [1939-1945]
【第二次鸦片战争】Dì-èr Cì Yāpiàn Zhànzhēng〈名〉Second Opium War [1856-1860]
【第二国际】Dì-èr Guójì〈名〉Second International
【第二课堂】dì-èr kètáng〈名〉**1**（指课外实践）extramural teaching/learning activity **2**（指职业教育）vocational education
【第二人称】dì-èr rénchēng〈名〉［语法］second person
【第二审】dì'èrshěn〈名〉［法律］second instance: ～法院 court of second instance
【第二世界】dì-èr shìjiè〈名〉Second World
【第二梯队】dì-èr tīduì〈名〉second echelon [middle-aged leaders]
【第二外语】dì-èr wàiyǔ〈名〉second foreign language
【第二现场】dì-èr xiànchǎng〈名〉［法律］secondary scene
【第二信号系统】dì-èr xìnhào xìtǒng〈名〉［生理］second signal system
【第二宇宙速度】dì-èr yǔzhòu sùdù〈名〉second cosmic velocity
【第二职业】dì-èr zhíyè〈名〉second job
【第六感觉】dì-liù gǎnjué〈名〉sixth sense: 我的～如此告诉我。My gut told me so.
【第纳尔】Dìnà'ěr ▸**p. 328**〈名〉Dinar
【第三部门】dì-sān bùmén〈名〉third sector
【第三产业】dì-sān chǎnyè〈名〉［经济］tertiary industry: 积极发展～ vigorously develop tertiary industries
【第三次国内革命战争】Dì-sān Cì Guónèi Gémìng Zhànzhēng〈名〉Third Revolutionary Civil War [1945-1949]
【第三人称】dì-sān rénchēng〈名〉［语法］third person
【第三世界】dì-sān shìjiè〈名〉Third World: ～国家 Third World countries
【第三梯队】dì-sān tīduì〈名〉third echelon [young cadres]
【第三宇宙速度】dì-sān yǔzhòu sùdù〈名〉third cosmic velocity
【第三者】dìsānzhě〈名〉**1**（第三方）third party: ～利益 third party interests **2**（特指男女关系）the other man/woman: 由于～插足，他们离婚了。They divorced because there was a third party.
【第三状态】dì-sān zhuàngtài〈名〉third state
【第四宇宙速度】dì-sì yǔzhòu sùdù〈名〉fourth cosmic velocity
【第五纵队】dì-wǔ zòngduì〈名〉fifth column [enemy agents]
【第一】dì-yī ▸**p. 691**〈数〉**1**（指名次）first: 一百米跑～ finish first in the 100-metre dash **2**（指重要程度）foremost: 百年大计，质量～。Quality should be given top priority as it is a matter of primary importance for generations to come.
【第一把手】dì-yībǎshǒu〈名〉first in command: 当～ play the first fiddle
【第一产业】dì-yī chǎnyè〈名〉［经济］primary industry: 加强～ strengthen the primary industry
【第一次国内革命战争】Dì-yī Cì Guónèi Gémìng Zhànzhēng〈名〉First Revolutionary Civil War [1924-1927]
【第一次世界大战】Dì-yī Cì Shìjiè Dàzhàn〈名〉First World War, World War I [1914-1918]
【第一次鸦片战争】Dì-yī Cì Yāpiàn Zhànzhēng〈名〉First Opium War [1840-1842]
【第一夫人】dì-yī fūrén〈名〉First Lady
【第一国际】Dì-yī Guójì〈名〉First International
【第一人称】dì-yī rénchēng〈名〉［语法］first person
【第一生产力】dì-yī shēngchǎnlì〈名〉primary productive force: 科学技术是～。Science and technology are the primary productive force.
【第一世界】dì-yī shìjiè〈名〉First World
【第一手】dìyīshǒu〈形〉first-hand: ～材料 first-hand material
【第一桶金】dìyītǒng jīn〈名〉first earnings: 做家教是他大学生涯挣得的～。He made his first university earnings as a tutor.
【第一现场】dì-yī xiànchǎng〈名〉［法律］primary scene
【第一线】dìyīxiàn〈名〉front line: 把年轻干部放在农村～ place young cadres in prominent positions in the countryside ‖ 从教学～退下来 step down from the front line of teaching ‖ 生产～ front line of production
【第一信号系统】dì-yī xìnhào xìtǒng〈名〉［生理］first signal system
【第一宇宙速度】dì-yī yǔzhòu sùdù〈名〉first cosmic velocity

谛（諦）dì

〈书〉
A〈形〉careful: ～观 watch carefully ‖ ～听 listen attentively
B〈名〉(Buddhism) truth: 妙～ fine truth ▸真～

d

蒂 dì〈名〉1（指植物） stem: ▸并～莲 2（末端） end: ▸烟～

【蒂龙郡】Dìlóngjùn〈名〉 Tyrone

棣[1] dì = 棣棠 dìtáng

棣[2] dì 〈名〉〈书〉 younger brother: ▸棠～

【棣棠】dìtáng〈名〉［植物］ kerria

睇 dì〈动〉〈书〉 look askance

缔（締） dì〈动〉 1（结合） form a tie: ▸～盟 2（订立） conclude: ▸～约 3（建立） found: ▸～造

【缔交】dìjiāo〈动〉 1〈书〉（指个人友谊） form a friendship 2（指邦交） establish diplomatic relations: 两国～以后，关系一直正常。 The relations between these two countries have been normal ever since they established diplomatic ties.

【缔结】dìjié〈动〉 conclude: ～和约 conclude a peace treaty ‖ ～贸易协定 conclude a trade agreement

【缔盟】dìméng〈动〉 form an alliance

【缔约】dìyuē〈动〉 sign a treaty: ～方 contracting party

【缔约国】dìyuēguó〈名〉 signatory

【缔造】dìzào〈动〉 found: ～新国家 found a nation ‖ 中华人民共和国的～者 founders of the People's Republic of China

碲 dì〈名〉［化学］ tellurium (Te)

蝃（蝃） dì

【蝃蝀】dìdōng〈名〉〈书〉 rainbow

diǎ

嗲 diǎ〈形〉〈方〉 1（指撒娇） coquettish: ▸～声～气 2（优异） good: 味道～ taste good

【嗲声嗲气】diǎshēng-diǎqì〈形〉〈方〉 coquettish

diān

掂 diān〈动〉 weigh in the hand: 你～一～这块铁有多重。 Please weigh this piece of iron in your hand.

【掂掇】diānduo〈动〉〈口〉 1（斟酌） consider: 你～着办吧。 Just do it as you see fit. 2（估计） reckon: 我～着这么办能行。 I reckon it can be done like this.

【掂斤播两】diānjīn-bōliǎng〈成〉 fuss over mere trifles

【掂量】diānliang〈动〉 1（掂重量） weigh in the hand: 他～了一下西瓜，说有八斤来重。 He weighed the watermelon in his hand and said it was about eight *jin*. ‖〈喻〉 你好好～～老师说的话。 You'd better weigh up the teacher's words carefully. 2（斟酌） consider: 事情就是这样，各组～着办吧。 That's how things stand. Each group can act at its own discretion.

【掂算】diānsuàn〈动〉 estimate: ～成本与收益 weigh the costs against the benefits

滇 Diān ▸**p. 661**〈名〉 Dian [another name for Yunnan Province (云南)]: 川～公路 Sichuan-Yunnan highway

【滇池】Diānchí ▸**p. 305**〈名〉 Dianchi Lake

【滇红】diānhóng〈名〉 Yunnan black tea

【滇剧】diānjù〈名〉 Yunnan opera

颠[1]**（顛）** diān〈名〉 1〈书〉（头顶） crown: 华～ grey-haired 2（顶部） top: 山～ mountain top ‖ 塔～ top of a pagoda

颠[2]**（顛）** diān〈动〉 1（颠簸） jolt: 路不平，车～得厉害。 The car jolted badly over the rough road. 2（跌落） fall: ▸～覆，～扑不破 3〈方〉（跳着跑） run while jumping: 整天跑跑～～的 be on the move all day long

【颠簸】diānbǒ〈动〉 jolt: 气流造成飞机～的现象较为普遍。 It is a common phenomenon for aircraft to be jolted about by air turbulence.

【颠倒】diāndǎo〈动〉 1（反过来） turn upside down: ～事实 stand facts on their heads ‖ ～顺序 reverse the order ‖ 这一面朝上，别放～了。 This side should face up. Don't turn it upside down. 2（错乱） be confused: ▸神魂～

【颠倒黑白】diāndǎo-hēibái〈成〉 confuse right and wrong: ～，造谣生事 confuse black with white and stir up trouble by spreading rumours

【颠倒是非】diāndǎo-shìfēi〈成〉 stand facts on their heads: ～，认敌为友 confound right with wrong and take enemies for friends

【颠覆】diānfù〈动〉 1（翻倒） turn over: 防止列车～ prevent the train from overturning 2（推翻政权） subvert: ～政府 topple the government

【颠来倒去】diānlái-dǎoqù〈成〉 over and over: ～地想 turn sth. over in one's mind

【颠连】diānlián〈形〉〈书〉 1（困苦） hard: ～无告 untold hardship 2（连绵） continuous: 群山～起伏 rolling mountains

【颠沛流离】diānpèi-liúlí〈成〉 lead a life of vagrancy

【颠扑不破】diānpū-bùpò〈成〉 be indisputable: ～的真理 irrefutable truth

【颠茄】diānqié〈名〉［药学］ belladonna: ～酊 tincture of belladonna

【颠三倒四】diānsān-dǎosì〈成〉 be topsy-turvy: 说话～ speak words that do not hang together

巅（巔） diān〈名〉 peak: 泰山之～ peak of Mount Tai

【巅峰】diānfēng〈名〉 peak: 他的事业达到了～。 He reached the pinnacle of his career. ‖ 作为职业运动员，他已过了～期。 He is past it as a professional athlete.

【巅峰期】diānfēngqī〈名〉 peak period

癫（癲） diān〈形〉 insane: ▸疯～

【癫狂】diānkuáng〈形〉 1（精神错乱） insane 2（言行轻浮） frivolous and arrogant

【癫痫】diānxián ▸**p. 50**〈名〉［医学］ epilepsy: ～病患者 epileptic

【癫子】diānzi〈名〉〈方〉 madman

diǎn

典[1] diǎn

A〈名〉 1（书籍） standard work of scholarship: ▸～籍，经～ 2（标准） standard: ▸～范，～章 3〈书〉（法规） statute: 国～ state code of law 4（仪式） ceremony: 开国大～ founding ceremony of a state ▸盛～，庆～ 5（典故） allusion: 用～ quote an allusion ‖ 出～ origin of an allusion

B〈动〉〈书〉 be in charge of: ～试 preside over a test ▸～狱

典[2] diǎn〈动〉 mortgage: 把房子～出去 mortgage a house ▸～押

【典藏】diǎncáng〈动〉 collect: 值得～ be worth collecting ‖ 用以～或馈赠亲友 for collecting or presenting to friends and family

【典当】diǎndàng〈动〉 pawn: ～手表 pawn a watch ‖ ～品 pawned item

【典范】diǎnfàn〈名〉 model: ～作品 model work ‖ 爱国主义的～ paragon of patriotism ‖ 杰出～ outstanding example

【典故】diǎngù〈名〉 allusion: 出自《圣经》的～ allusion to the *Bible*

【典籍】diǎnjí〈名〉 ancient classics

【典礼】diǎnlǐ〈名〉 ceremony: 国庆～ National Day celebration ‖ 结婚～ wedding ceremony ‖ 在毕业～上 at the graduation ceremony

【典卖】diǎnmài〈动〉 mortgage

【典型】diǎnxíng A〈名〉 1（代表人物或事件） example: 树立～ set an example ‖ 用～示范的方法推广先进经验 popularize advanced experience through demonstrations with typical examples 2（特指艺术形象） model personalities B〈形〉 typical: ～的美国人 typical American ‖ ～的热带气候 typical tropical weather

【典型性】diǎnxíngxìng〈名〉 representativeness

【典押】diǎnyā = 典当 diǎndàng

【典雅】diǎnyǎ〈形〉 elegant: 风格～ elegant style ‖ 谈吐～ be refined in speech ‖ 客厅布置得很～。 The drawing room is elegantly decorated.

【典狱】diǎnyù〈动〉 be in charge of a prison: ～长 prison warden

【典章】diǎnzhāng〈名〉〈旧〉 decrees and regulations

点[1]**（點）** diǎn

A〈名〉 1（斑痕） spot: 墨～儿 ink spots ‖ 泥～儿 mud stain ‖ 她买了条带白～儿的蓝裙子。 She bought a blue skirt with white spots. 2（指笔画） [in Chinese characters] dot stroke: 这个字缺一～。 There is a dot stroke missing in this character. 3（小滴液体） drop: 雨～儿 raindrops 4（金属响器） iron device sounded to tell time in ancient times 5（节奏） beat: 步～儿 step ▸鼓～ 6（规定的时间） appointed time: ▸误～，正～ 7［数学］ point: 两～成一直线。 Connecting two points forms a line. ▸交～ 8（特定之处） certain point: 语法～ grammar point ▸沸～，起～ 9（方面） aspect: ▸缺～，特～ 10（小数点） decimal point: 百分之五～七 five point seven per cent 11（指股市） point: 上升100～ gain 100 points ‖ 下跌30～ drop 30 points

B〈动〉 1（加点） dot: 读书时圈圈～～ mark the text with circles and dots while reading ▸画龙～睛 2（装饰） decorate: ▸～染，～缀，装～ 3（指定） select: 乐队演奏听众～的乐曲。 The orchestra played numbers on request. ▸～播，～菜，～歌 4（清点） check one by one: ～钱 count money ‖ ～人数 count heads ▸盘～，清～ 5（轻触） skim: 蜻蜓～水。 Dragonflies

skim the water. ▸～穴 6（点头） nod: ▸～头 7（指着） point: 用手指～ point with one's hand 8（指点） hint: ▸～拨, 指～ 9（点燃） light: ～烟 light a cigarette ‖〈喻〉 ～燃他心中的怒火 ignite anger in him ▸～火 10 = 踮 diǎn 11（使滴下） drip: ～眼药水 put eyedrops in one's eyes 12（播种） dibble: ～花生 dibble peanuts

C〈量〉 1（用于夜间计时） 1/25 of a night 2（小时） hour: 十～ 10 o'clock 3（用于事项） [for items]: 两～意见 two suggestions 4（表少量） a bit: 一～儿小事 some minor matters ‖ 吃～儿东西再走。 Why don't you eat something before you leave?

点² (點) diǎn〈名〉 refreshments: ▸茶～, 早～

【点播】 diǎnbō〈动〉 1（指播种） dibble: ～蚕豆 dibble broad beans 2（选定） request a programme from a radio/TV station: ～节目 request a programme

【点拨】 diǎnbo〈口〉 = 指点 zhǐdiǎn 1

【点补】 diǎnbu〈动〉〈口〉 snack: 先吃片面包～一下。 Kill your hunger with a piece of bread.

【点菜】 diǎncài〈动〉 order: 你们是吃份饭还是要～? Would you like the table d'hôte or à la carte?

【点唱】 diǎnchàng〈动〉 [of an audience] request a number (for performer to sing)

【点穿】 diǎnchuān = 点破 diǎnpò

【点滴】 diǎndī A〈形〉 bit: ～经验 bits of experience ‖ 知识是点点滴滴积累起来的。 Knowledge is accumulated bit by bit. B〈名〉 1（小事） tidbit: 奥运会～ tidbits of the Olympic Games 2（静脉滴注） intravenous drip: ▸打～

【点发】 diǎnfā = 点射 diǎnshè

【点歌】 diǎngē〈动〉 request a song to be played

【点焊】 diǎnhàn〈名〉 spot welding

【点化】 diǎnhuà〈动〉 enlighten

【点火】 diǎnhuǒ〈动〉 1（点着） light a fire: 用木柴～ use wood to light a fire 2（引燃） ignite: 电子～ electronic ignition 3（挑起是非） stir up trouble: ▸煽风～

【点货】 diǎnhuò〈动〉 take stock

【点击】 diǎnjī〈动〉［计算机］ click: ～率 click rate

【点击量】 diǎnjīliàng〈名〉 number of hits: 新华网新闻网页每天的～ the daily volume of hits for the Xinhua News webpage

【点击数】 diǎnjīshù = 点击量 diǎnjīliàng

【点饥】 diǎnjī〈动〉 snack to stave off hunger: 买些水果在旅途中～ buy some fruit to stave off hunger on the journey

【点将】 diǎnjiàng〈动〉 1〈旧〉（指军队） call the officer roll and assign fighting tasks 2（派遣） name sb. for a particular job: 经理是集团总经理亲自点的将。 The sales department manager was personally appointed by the general manager.

【点交】 diǎnjiāo〈动〉 hand over item by item

【点卯】 diǎnmǎo〈动〉〈旧〉 call the roll in the morning

【点名】 diǎnmíng〈动〉 1（点到） take a roll call: 集合士兵～ muster the soldiers for roll call 2（指名） refer to sb. by name: ～批评 criticize by name ‖ 没想到他会～让我当他的助手。 I had not expected him to name me as his assistant.

【点明】 diǎnmíng〈动〉 point out: ～问题所在 put one's finger on what is wrong ‖ ～主题 make clear the theme

【点评】 diǎnpíng A〈动〉 comment: ～一场辩论赛 comment on a debate B〈名〉 comment

【点破】 diǎnpò〈动〉 lay bare: ～意图 reveal sb.'s real intention

【点球】 diǎnqiú〈名〉 penalty kick: 判给主队一个～ give the host team a penalty ‖ ～大战 penalty shoot-out

【点燃】 diǎnrán〈动〉 light: ～蜡烛 light a candle ‖ ～炉火 ignite a stove

【点染】 diǎnrǎn〈动〉〈书〉 touch up: 此画尚需稍加～。 The painting still wants a few finishing touches. ‖ 此文略加～, 即可刊出。 This essay can be published after some polishing.

【点射】 diǎnshè〈动〉［军事］ fire in bursts

【点石成金】 diǎnshí-chéngjīn〈成〉 work wonders

【点收】 diǎnshōu〈动〉 check and accept: 现款请当面～。 Please count the cash before you leave.

【点数】 diǎnshù A〈动〉 count and check the number B〈名〉［体育］ point: 在～上领先 lead in points

【点题】 diǎntí〈动〉 bring out the theme

【点铁成金】 diǎntiě-chéngjīn = 点石成金 diǎnshí-chéngjīn

【点头】 diǎntóu〈动〉 1〈本〉 nod: ～称是 nod and praise ‖ ～同意 nod one's agreement ‖ ～致意 greet with a nod 2〈喻〉（同意） give one's consent: 主任已经～了。 The director has already okayed it.

【点头哈腰】 diǎntóu-hāyāo〈成〉 bow and scrape

【点头之交】 diǎntóuzhījiāo〈成〉 nodding acquaintance

【点心】 diǎnxin〈名〉 dessert, dim sum: ～铺 snack bar

【点穴】 diǎnxué〈动〉 attack sb.'s vital point

【点验】 diǎnyàn〈动〉 examine item by item

【点映】 diǎnyìng〈动〉 hold a film showing in a particular place: 影片发行将采用社区～方式预热。 The film will be hyped during scheduled film showings.

【点阵】 diǎnzhèn〈名〉 1［物理］ lattice 2［计算机］ dot matrix: ～字符 dot matrix character

【点种】 diǎnzhòng = 点播 diǎnbō 1

【点缀】 diǎnzhuì〈动〉 1（装饰） adorn: ～有红玫瑰的白帽子 white hat embellished with red roses ‖ 购买装饰品～圣诞树 buy ornaments for the Christmas trees ‖ 夜空～着明亮的星星。 The night sky was set with bright stars. 2（应景） garnish

【点子】 diǎnzi〈名〉 1（指液体） drop: 雨～ raindrops 2（指痕迹） spot: 泥～ mud stain 3（节拍） beat 4（关键） key point: 你这话算是说到～上了。 Your remarks are to the point. 5（主意） idea: 出～ contribute ideas ‖ ～多 be full of ideas

碘 diǎn〈名〉［化学］ iodine: 加～食盐 iodized salt ‖ ～中毒 iodine intoxication

【碘酊】 diǎndīng〈名〉［药学］ tincture of iodine

【碘化银】 diǎnhuàyín〈名〉 silver iodide

【碘酒】 diǎnjiǔ = 碘酊 diǎndīng

【碘盐】 diǎnyán〈名〉 iodized salt

踮 diǎn〈动〉 be on tiptoe: ～起脚走 walk on tiptoe ‖ 他们～起脚, 想看得更清楚。 They stood on tiptoe to get a better look.

diàn

电 (電) diàn

A〈名〉 1（闪电） lightning: 雷～交加 lightning accompanied by peals of thunders ‖ ～闪雷鸣。 The lightning flashed and the thunder roared. 2（电能） electricity: 断～ cut off the power ‖ 我们已经三天没有～了。 We have been out of power for three days. ▸充～, 静～ 3（电报） telegram: 致～ send a telegram ‖ 急～ express telegram

B〈动〉 1（触电） give/get an electric shock: 被～了一下 get an electric shock 2（用电报、电传等） cable a message: ▸～贺, ～复

【电霸】 diànbà〈名〉 overlord of electricity

【电棒】 diànbàng〈名〉〈方〉 1（手电筒） (electric) torch 2（灯管） fluorescent lamp

【电报】 diànbào A〈名〉 telegram: 打/发～ send a telegram ‖ 加急～ urgent cable ‖ 密码～ coded telegram B〈动〉 telegraph: ～总部 wire head office

【电报挂号】 diànbào guàhào〈名〉 cable/telegraphic address

【电报局】 diànbàojú〈名〉 telegraph office

【电笔】 diànbǐ = 测电笔 cèdiànbǐ

【电表】 diànbiǎo〈名〉 1（安培计） ammeter 2（电度表） electric meter

【电冰柜】 diànbīngguì〈名〉 refrigerator

【电冰箱】 diànbīngxiāng〈名〉 refrigerator

【电波】 diànbō〈名〉 electric wave

【电厂】 diànchǎng〈名〉 power plant

【电场】 diànchǎng〈名〉 electric field

【电唱机】 diànchàngjī〈名〉 record player

【电唱头】 diànchàngtóu〈名〉 pickup

【电车】 diànchē〈名〉 1（有轨电车） tram〈英〉; streetcar〈美〉 2（无轨电车） trolley bus: ▸无轨～

【电陈】 diànchén〈动〉 declare by telegraph

【电池】 diànchí〈名〉 battery: 充电～ rechargeable battery ‖ 碱性～ alkaline cell ‖ ～充电器 battery charger

【电传】 diànchuán A〈名〉 telex: 国际～ overseas telex B〈动〉 send a telex

【电吹风】 diànchuīfēng〈名〉 electric hair dryer

【电瓷】 diàncí〈名〉 electroceramics

【电磁】 diàncí〈名〉 electromagnetism

【电磁波】 diàncíbō〈名〉 electromagnetic wave

【电磁场】 diàncíchǎng〈名〉 electromagnetic field

【电磁炉】 diàncílú〈名〉 electromagnetic oven

【电磁炮】 diàncípào〈名〉 electromagnetic artillery

【电磁铁】 diàncítiě〈名〉 electromagnet

【电磁灶】 diàncízào = 电磁炉 diàncílú

【电大】 diàndà〈简称〉= 电视大学

【电导】 diàndǎo〈名〉 conductivity

【电灯】 diàndēng〈名〉 electric light

【电灯泡】 diàndēngpào〈名〉 1〈本〉 bulb 2〈口〉〈喻〉 gooseberry: 我可不想当～。 I don't want to play gooseberry.

【电动】 diàndòng〈形〉 power-operated: ～剃须刀 electric shaver ‖ ～玩具 electric toy

【电动机】 diàndòngjī〈名〉 motor: ～功率 motor power

【电动势】 diàndòngshì〈名〉 electromotive force

【电度表】 diàndùbiǎo = 电表 diànbiǎo 2

【电镀】 diàndù〈动〉 electroplate

【电饭煲】 diànfànbāo = 电饭锅 diànfànguō

d

【电饭锅】diànfànguō〈名〉electric rice cooker
【电费】diànfèi〈名〉electric bill: 付～ pay for electricity
【电风扇】diànfēngshàn = 电扇 diànshàn
【电复】diànfù〈动〉reply by telegraph
【电告】diàngào〈动〉inform by telegraph
【电工】diàngōng〈名〉**1**（电力工程）electrical engineering: ～手册 electric engineering handbook ►～学 **2**（电力工人）electrician
【电工学】diàngōngxué〈名〉electrical engineering
【电功率】diàngōnglǜ〈名〉［电气］electric power
【电灌】diànguàn〈动〉irrigate by electric pumping: ～站 electric pumping station
【电光】diànguāng〈名〉**1**（指光）electric light: ～源 electric light source **2**（指光泽）lightning
【电焊】diànhàn〈名〉electric welding: ～工 electric welder
【电贺】diànhè〈动〉send a telegram of congratulations
【电荷】diànhè〈名〉electric charge
【电弧】diànhú〈名〉electric arc: ～焊接 arc welding ‖ ～切割机 arc cutting machine
【电化】diànhuà〈名〉electrical audio-visual aids
【电化教学】diànhuà jiàoxué〈名〉audio-visual aided instruction: ～设备 electrical audio-visual aids
【电化教育】diànhuà jiàoyù〈名〉audio-visual instruction
【电话】diànhuà〈名〉**1**（电话机）telephone: 安装～ have a phone put in ‖ 拨号～ dial phone ►磁卡～, 可视～, 智能～ **2**（指话语）call: 打～ make a phone call ‖ 接听～ answer the phone ‖ 长途～ long-distance phone call ‖ 骚扰～ nuisance call ‖ 有你的～。You are wanted on the phone.
【电话簿】diànhuàbù〈名〉phone directory
【电话费】diànhuàfèi〈名〉telephone charge
【电话分机】diànhuà fēnjī〈名〉telephone extension
【电话号码】diànhuà hàomǎ〈名〉phone number
【电话会议】diànhuà huìyì〈名〉conference call: 召开～ hold a telephone conference
【电话机】diànhuàjī〈名〉telephone: 老式～ old-fashioned phone
【电话交换台】diànhuà jiāohuàntái〈名〉telephone exchange
【电话接线员】diànhuà jiēxiànyuán ►p. 966〈名〉telephone operator
【电话卡】diànhuàkǎ〈名〉phone card
【电话区号】diànhuà qūhào〈名〉area code
【电话亭】diànhuàtíng〈名〉phone booth; telephone box〈英〉
【电话总机】diànhuà zǒngjī〈名〉central exchange
【电汇】diànhuì **A**〈动〉remit by telegram **B**〈名〉telegraphic transfer
【电火花】diànhuǒhuā〈名〉electric spark
【电击】diànjī〈名〉electric shock: ～危险 shock hazard
【电机】diànjī〈名〉electric machinery
【电吉他】diànjítā ►p. 929〈名〉electric guitar
【电极】diànjí〈名〉electrode: 阳～ anode ‖ 阴～ cathode
【电教】diànjiào〈简称〉= 电化教育
【电解】diànjiě〈动〉［化学］electrolyse
【电解质】diànjiězhì〈名〉electrolyte
【电介质】diànjièzhì〈名〉［化学］dielectric
【电锯】diànjù〈名〉electric saw
【电烤箱】diànkǎoxiāng〈名〉electric grill
【电缆】diànlǎn〈名〉electric cable: 光纤～ optical fibre cable
【电老虎】diànlǎohǔ〈名〉〈喻〉**1** = 电霸 diànbà **2**（指耗电量大）big power consumer
【电烙铁】diànlàotie〈名〉electric soldering iron
【电离】diànlí〈动〉ionize
【电离层】diànlícéng〈名〉ionosphere
【电力】diànlì〈名〉electric power: ～变电站 electric power substation
【电力网】diànlìwǎng = 电网 diànwǎng 2
【电力线】diànlìxiàn〈名〉power line: ～载波通信 power line carrier communications
【电疗】diànliáo〈名〉electrotherapy: 超短波～ ultrashort-wave therapy
【电料】diànliào〈名〉electrical materials and appliances: ～行 electrical materials and appliances shop
【电铃】diànlíng〈名〉electric bell
【电令】diànlìng **A**〈动〉send an order by telegram **B**〈名〉order transmitted by telegram
【电流】diànliú〈名〉electric current: 高压～ high-voltage current
【电流表】diànliúbiǎo = 安培计 ānpéijì
【电炉】diànlú〈名〉**1**（家用）electric cooker **2**［冶金］electric furnace: ～炼钢 electric furnace steel making
【电路】diànlù〈名〉electric circuit: 集成～ integrated circuit
【电路板】diànlùbǎn〈名〉circuit board: 印刷～ printed circuit board
【电路图】diànlùtú〈名〉circuit diagram
【电码】diànmǎ〈名〉code: 摩尔斯～ Morse code
【电脉冲】diànmàichōng〈名〉electric pulse
【电门】diànmén〈名〉switch
【电木】diànmù〈名〉［化学］Bakelite
【电脑】diànnǎo〈名〉computer: 个人～ personal computer (PC) ‖ ～程序 computer program ‖ ～应用软件 computer applications
【电脑病毒】diànnǎo bìngdú〈名〉computer virus
【电能】diànnéng〈名〉electric energy
【电钮】diànniǔ〈名〉button
【电瓶】diànpíng〈名〉storage battery
【电瓶车】diànpíngchē〈名〉electric car
【电气】diànqì〈名〉electric: ～开关 electric switch ‖ ～机车 electric locomotive
【电气化】diànqìhuà〈动〉electrify: ～铁路 electric railway
【电器】diànqì〈名〉electrical appliance: 家用～ household electrical appliances
【电热】diànrè〈形〉electrothermal
【电热杯】diànrèbēi〈名〉electric Thermos jug
【电热毯】diànrètǎn〈名〉electric blanket
【电容】diànróng〈名〉electric capacity
【电容器】diànróngqì〈名〉condenser: ～纸 condenser paper
【电扇】diànshàn〈名〉electric fan
【电石】diànshí〈名〉［化学］calcium carbide
【电示】diànshì〈动〉notify by telegraph
【电势】diànshì〈名〉electrical potential
【电势差】diànshìchā〈名〉electrical potential difference
【电视】diànshì〈名〉**1**（电视机）television set (TV): 高清晰度～ high definition television (HDTV) **2**（指节目）television programme: 看～ watch TV ‖ ～节目 TV programme ►闭路～, 有线～
【电视大学】diànshì dàxué〈名〉TV university
【电视电话】diànshì diànhuà〈名〉videophone: ～电话会议 teleconference
【电视会议】diànshì huìyì〈名〉videoconference
【电视机】diànshìjī〈名〉television set (TV)
【电视剧】diànshìjù〈名〉television drama: ～剧本 TV drama script ‖ 五集电视连续剧 5-part TV serial
【电视片】diànshìpiàn〈名〉TV film
【电视屏幕】diànshì píngmù〈名〉television screen
【电视收视率】diànshì shōushìlǜ〈名〉TV ratings
【电视塔】diànshìtǎ〈名〉television tower
【电视台】diànshìtái〈名〉television station: 中国中央～ China Central Television Station (CCTV)
【电视转播】diànshì zhuǎnbō〈动〉telecast: ～车 television truck
【电台】diàntái〈名〉**1**（无线电台）transmitter-receiver **2**（广播电台）radio station
【电烫】diàntàng〈动〉have one's hair permed
【电梯】diàntī〈名〉**1**（升降式）lift〈英〉; elevator〈美〉: 自动升降～ automatic elevator **2**（扶式）escalator
【电筒】diàntǒng〈名〉electric torch
【电头】diàntóu〈名〉dateline
【电网】diànwǎng〈名〉**1**（用于阻隔）electric fence: 高压～ high voltage fence **2**（用于输电）power grid
【电位】diànwèi〈名〉［电气］potential
【电文】diànwén〈名〉text of a telegram
【电线】diànxiàn〈名〉power line: 高压/低压～ high/low voltage line ‖ ～杆 wire pole
【电信】diànxìn〈名〉telecommunications
【电信局】diànxìnjú〈名〉telecommunications bureau
【电信卡】diànxìnkǎ〈名〉telephone card: ～充值服务 telephone card top-up service ‖ ～余额 telephone card balance
【电刑】diànxíng〈名〉**1**（指刑讯）electric torture **2**（指死刑）electrocution
【电学】diànxué〈名〉electricity
【电讯】diànxùn〈名〉**1**（无线电信息）telegraphic dispatch: 发～ send a dispatch **2**（电信）telecommunications: 国际～联盟 International Telecommunications Union ‖ ～中断 telecommunications breakdown
【电压】diànyā〈名〉voltage: ～稳压器 voltage stabilizer ‖ ～不足 undervoltage ‖ 民用～为220伏。The civil electricity stands at 220 volts.
【电压表】diànyābiǎo〈名〉voltage meter
【电眼】diànyǎn〈名〉**1**（电子眼）electric eye **2**（光电器）phototube
【电唁】diànyàn〈动〉cable a message of condolence
【电业】diànyè〈名〉electric power industry: ～管理局 power administration
【电椅】diànyǐ〈名〉electric chair
【电影】diànyǐng〈名〉film〈英〉; movie〈美〉: 放映～ show a film ‖ 拍（摄）～ shoot a film ►立体～
【电影编剧】diànyǐng biānjù〈名〉scenarist
【电影放映队】diànyǐng fàngyìngduì〈名〉film projection team
【电影放映机】diànyǐng fàngyìngjī〈名〉cinematograph
【电影分镜头剧本】diànyǐng fēnjìngtóu

jùběn〈名〉 shooting script
【电影节】diànyǐngjié〈名〉 film festival: 戛纳～ Cannes Film Festival
【电影剧本】diànyǐng jùběn〈名〉 screenplay
【电影摄影】diànyǐng shèyǐng〈名〉 cinematography: ～机 film camera ‖ ～师 cinematographer
【电影演员】diànyǐng yǎnyuán ▸**p. 966**〈名〉 film actor/actress
【电影译制厂】diànyǐng yìzhìchǎng〈名〉 film dubbing studio
【电影院】diànyǐngyuàn〈名〉 cinema; movie theater〈美〉
【电影制片厂】diànyǐng zhìpiànchǎng〈名〉 film studio: 西安～ Xi'an Film Studio
【电影周】diànyǐngzhōu〈名〉 film week
【电邮】diànyóu〈名〉 email: 手机也可收发～。 Mobile phones can also send and receive e-mails.
【电源】diànyuán〈名〉 power supply: 接通～ turn on the power ‖ 切断～ cut off the electricity supply
【电熨斗】diànyùndǒu〈名〉 electric iron
【电闸】diànzhá〈名〉 electric brake
【电站】diànzhàn〈名〉 electric power station
【电纸书】diànzhǐshū〈名〉 electronic book: 亚马逊～ Amazon electronic reader
【电钟】diànzhōng〈名〉 electric clock
【电珠】diànzhū〈名〉 small bulb
【电子】diànzǐ〈名〉 electron: ▸正～
【电子版】diànzǐbǎn〈名〉 electronic version: 《牛津英语大词典》～ *Oxford English Dictionary* in electronic form
【电子表】diànzǐbiǎo = 电子手表 diànzǐ shǒubiǎo
【电子秤】diànzǐchèng〈名〉 electronic scale
【电子出版物】diànzǐ chūbǎnwù〈名〉 electronic publication
【电子词典】diànzǐ cídiǎn〈名〉 electronic dictionary
【电子动画】diànzǐ dònghuà〈名〉 animatronics
【电子公告栏】diànzǐ gōnggàolán〈名〉 bulletin board system (BBS)
【电子管】diànzǐguǎn〈名〉 electronic tube: ～收音机 valve radio set
【电子货币】diànzǐ huòbì〈名〉 electronic money
【电子计算机】diànzǐ jìsuànjī〈名〉 computer
【电子流】diànzǐliú〈名〉 electron current
【电子枪】diànzǐqiāng〈名〉 electronic gun
【电子琴】diànzǐqín ▸**p. 929**〈名〉 electronic keyboard
【电子商务】diànzǐ shāngwù〈名〉 E-commerce
【电子手表】diànzǐ shǒubiǎo〈名〉 electronic watch
【电子书目】diànzǐ shūmù〈名〉 webliography
【电子束】diànzǐshù〈名〉 electron beam: ～炉 electron beam furnace ‖ ～切割 electron beam cutting
【电子图书】diànzǐ túshū〈名〉 electronic book
【电子显微镜】diànzǐ xiǎnwēijìng〈名〉 electron microscope
【电子信箱】diànzǐ xìnxiāng〈名〉 email (account): 申请～ apply for an email account
【电子眼】diànzǐyǎn〈名〉 surveillance camera: 主要交通路口都安装了～。 The main traffic junctions have been equipped with surveillance cameras.
【电子音乐】diànzǐ yīnyuè〈名〉 electronic music
【电子营销】diànzǐ yíngxiāo〈名〉 e-marketing
【电子邮件】diànzǐ yóujiàn〈名〉 email
【电子邮箱】diànzǐ yóuxiāng〈名〉 email (account)
【电子游戏】diànzǐ yóuxì〈名〉 video game: ～机 video game player
【电子战】diànzǐzhàn〈名〉 electronic warfare
【电子追踪】diànzǐ zhuīzōng〈名〉 electronic tagging
【电阻】diànzǔ〈名〉 electric resistance
【电阻器】diànzǔqì〈名〉 resistor
【电钻】diànzuàn〈名〉 electric drill

佃 diàn〈动〉 rent land
▸tián
【佃户】diànhù〈名〉 tenant (farmer)
【佃农】diànnóng〈名〉 tenant farmer
【佃租】diànzū〈名〉 land rent

甸 diàn〈名〉〈古〉 outskirts
【甸子】diànzi〈名〉〈方〉 pastureland

阽 diàn〈动〉〈书〉 be close to: ～于死亡 be at death's door

店 diàn〈名〉 **1**（店铺） shop: ▸～主, 夫妻～, 粮～, 书～, 杂货～ **2**（小旅馆） inn: 住～ stop at an inn
【店东】diàndōng〈名〉〈旧〉 shopkeeper
【店家】diànjiā〈名〉〈方〉 shopkeeper
【店客】diànkè〈名〉 customer
【店面】diànmiàn〈名〉 shop front: 装潢～ decorate the shop front
【店铺】diànpù〈名〉 shop〈英〉; store〈美〉: 临街～ store facing the street
【店堂】diàntáng〈名〉 business area of a shop
【店小二】diànxiǎo'èr〈名〉〈旧〉 attendant
【店员】diànyuán ▸**p. 966**〈名〉 shop assistant〈英〉; sales clerk〈美〉: 男～ salesman ‖ 女～ saleswoman
【店主】diànzhǔ〈名〉 shopkeeper〈英〉; storekeeper〈美〉

玷 diàn
A〈名〉 flaw in a piece of jade
B〈动〉 blemish: ▸～污
【玷辱】diànrǔ〈动〉 bring disgrace on: ～门楣 bring disgrace upon one's family
【玷污】diànwū〈动〉 **1**（弄脏） stain: ～名声 tarnish sb.'s reputation **2** ▸**p. 772**〈婉〉（强奸） rape

垫（墊） diàn
A〈动〉 **1**（支撑） cushion;（铺衬） pad;（填充） fill up: 烫衣服时最好在上面～块布。 You'd better put a piece of cloth on top of the garment before you iron it. ‖ 睡觉时枕头不能～得太高。 You shouldn't have the pillows too high when you sleep. **2**（临时填补） fill in a gap: 正戏开演前，他们先～了几出折子戏。 Before the performance began, they filled things out with some operatic numbers. **3**（垫付） advance money: ▸～付
B〈名〉 cushion: 给椅子上铺个～儿 put a cushion on the chair ▸床～, 靠～, 鞋～, 坐～
【垫背】diànbèi **A**〈动〉 take the blame for sb.: 别想拿我做～。 Don't expect to make me a scapegoat. ‖ 我可不想给别人～。 I certainly do not want to bear the blame for others. **B**〈名〉 scapegoat
【垫补】diànbu〈动〉 **1**（指付钱） make up for a financial deficiency by appropriating money from elsewhere **2**（指吃东西） have a snack: 开饭时间还不到，咱们先吃点什么～～吧。 It's not mealtime yet. Let's have a snack first.
【垫底儿】diàndǐr〈动〉 **1**（放在底部） put at the bottom: 箱子里铺些棉花～。 Put some cotton at the bottom of the box. **2**（指吃东西） have sth. to eat while waiting for one's meal **3**（打基础） lay the foundation **4**（居末位） be bottom: 他在班上是～的。 He's bottom of the class. ‖ 在去年的锦标赛中我们队垫了底儿。 Our team finished bottom of the championship last year.
【垫付】diànfù〈动〉 advance some money
【垫话】diànhuà **A**〈动〉〈方〉 send word to sb. of sth. in advance: 明天开会，请给有关人员垫个话。 We'll have a meeting tomorrow. Please send word to those concerned. **B**〈名〉 prologue
【垫肩】diànjiān〈名〉 **1**（为了美观） shoulder pad: 带～的外套 shoulder-padded jacket **2**（用于保护） pad for protecting the shoulder
【垫脚石】diànjiǎoshí〈名〉 stepping stone: 甘愿当～ be willing to act as a stepping stone
【垫片】diànpiàn〈名〉［机械］ **1**（用于间隔） spacer: 绝缘～ insulation spacer **2**（用于填补） shim: 轴承～ bearing shim
【垫平】diànpíng〈动〉 level up
【垫圈】diànquān〈名〉［机械］ washer
【垫支】diànzhī = 垫付 diànfù
【垫子】diànzi〈名〉 pad: 茶杯～ teacup mat ‖ 弹簧～ spring mattress ‖ 沙发～ sofa cushion

钿（鈿） diàn〈名〉mother-of-pearl inlay
▸tián

淀[1]（澱） diàn〈动〉 form sediment: ▸～粉, 沉～

淀[2] diàn〈名〉 shallow lake
【淀粉】diànfěn〈名〉 starch

惦 diàn〈动〉 keep thinking about: 心里一直～着你 keep thinking about you
【惦记】diànji〈动〉 keep thinking about
【惦念】diànniàn〈动〉 be anxious about

奠 diàn〈动〉 **1**（建立） establish: ▸～定, ～基 **2**（祭奠） make offerings to the dead: ▸祭～
【奠定】diàndìng〈动〉 establish: 这些实验为太空旅行～了基础。 The experiments prepared the ground for space travel.
【奠都】diàndū〈动〉 found a capital
【奠基】diànjī〈动〉 lay the foundation: ～典礼 cornerstone-laying ceremony
【奠基人】diànjīrén〈名〉 founder
【奠基石】diànjīshí〈名〉 cornerstone
【奠酒】diànjiǔ〈动〉 offer libation
【奠仪】diànyí〈名〉〈旧〉 condolence money

殿 diàn
A〈名〉 hall: ▸宫～
B〈动〉 bring up the rear: ▸～后, ～军
【殿后】diànhòu〈动〉 bring up the rear

【殿军】diànjūn〈名〉 1▸（指部队） rear-guard 2▸（指排名）last among the winners
【殿试】diànshì〈名〉〈古〉 final imperial examination
【殿堂】diàntáng〈名〉 palace: 艺术～ palace of art ‖ 音乐～ palace of music
【殿下】diànxià〈名〉〈尊〉 Your/His/Her (Royal) Highness

靛 diàn
A〈名〉 indigo: ▸～蓝
B〈形〉 indigo-blue: ▸～青
【靛蓝】diànlán〈名〉 indigo
【靛青】diànqīng〈形〉 indigo-blue

簟 diàn〈名〉〈方〉 bamboo mat

癜 diàn〈名〉 piebald skin disease: 紫～ purpura ▸白～风

d

diāo

刁 diāo〈形〉 1▸（刁蛮） crafty: ▸～钻，放～ 2▸〈方〉（挑剔） picky: ▸嘴～
【刁悍】diāohàn〈形〉 cunning and fierce
【刁横】diāohèng〈形〉 crafty and rude
【刁滑】diāohuá〈形〉 cunning
【刁民】diāomín〈名〉〈旧〉 unruly people
【刁难】diāonàn〈动〉 make things difficult for: 百般～ put up innumerable obstacles ‖ 故意～ deliberately make things difficult for others
【刁顽】diāowán〈形〉 cunning and stubborn
【刁钻】diāozuān〈形〉 cunning: 发球～ tricky service
【刁钻古怪】diāozuān-gǔguài〈成〉 sly and capricious

叼 diāo〈动〉 hold in the mouth: 嘴里～着一支香烟 with a cigarette dangling from one's lips

凋 diāo
A〈动〉 wither: ▸～落，～谢
B〈形〉 hard: ▸～敝
【凋败】diāobài〈动〉 wither away
【凋敝】diāobì〈形〉 1▸（指生活） hard: 民生～ impoverishment 2▸（指事业） depressed: 经济～ economic slump
【凋残】diāocán〈动〉 wither and fall
【凋零】diāolíng A〈动〉 wither and fall B〈形〉 declining: 百业～。 All business languished.
【凋落】diāoluò〈动〉 wither and fall
【凋萎】diāowěi〈动〉 wither
【凋谢】diāoxiè〈动〉 1▸（指草木） wither and fall: 玫瑰花三天以后～了。 The roses withered and died after three days. 2▸〈喻〉（指人） die

貂 diāo〈名〉［动物］ marten
【貂皮】diāopí〈名〉 mink: ～大衣 mink coat
【貂裘】diāoqiú〈名〉 marten coat
【貂熊】diāoxióng〈名〉 glutton

碉 diāo
【碉堡】diāobǎo〈名〉 pillbox
【碉楼】diāolóu〈名〉 watchtower

雕[1]（鵰） diāo〈名〉 eagle

雕[2]（彫） diāo
A〈动〉 1▸（刻） engrave: 在木块上～像 carve a figure out of wood ▸～花，～刻 2▸〈书〉（雕饰） decorate with patterns and colourful paintings: ▸～梁画栋
B〈名〉 carving: ▸浮～，根～，木～
【雕版】diāobǎn〈名〉 wood block for printing: ～印刷 block printing
【雕虫小技】diāochóng-xiǎojì〈成〉 meagre literary skill: ～，难登大雅之堂。 The meagre skills of a scribe do not appeal to refined tastes.
【雕花】diāohuā A〈动〉 carve patterns or designs on woodwork B〈名〉 carving
【雕花玻璃】diāohuā bōli〈名〉 cut glass
【雕镌】diāojuān〈书〉= 雕刻 diāokè
【雕刻】diāokè A〈动〉 carve, engrave: ～大理石像 cut a figure in marble ‖ 用木头/石头～ carve sth. out of wood/stone B〈名〉 carving
【雕栏玉砌】diāolán-yùqì〈成〉 magnificent palace
【雕梁画栋】diāoliáng-huàdòng〈成〉 1▸（指梁） carved beams and painted rafters 2▸（指建筑） richly ornamented building
【雕漆】diāoqī〈名〉 carved lacquerware
【雕砌】diāoqì〈动〉 write in a laboured and ornate style
【雕饰】diāoshì A〈动〉 1▸（雕琢） carve 2▸（刻意修饰） over-decorate B〈名〉 carvings
【雕塑】diāosù A〈动〉 sculpt: 用大理石～ carve sth. out of a block of marble ‖ ～家 sculptor B〈名〉 sculpture: ～公园 sculpture garden ‖ 抽象～ abstract sculpture
【雕像】diāoxiàng〈名〉 statue: 维纳斯的～ sculpture of Venus
【雕琢】diāozhuó〈动〉 1▸（指雕刻） cut and polish: ～钻石 cut a diamond 2▸（指写文章） write in an ornate style

鲷（鯛） diāo〈名〉［鱼类］ porgy

diǎo

鸟（鳥） diǎo〈名〉〈粗〉 cock〈粗〉: 你们这些～人! You fuckers! ▸niǎo

屌 diǎo〈名〉〈粗〉 penis

diào

吊[1]（弔） diào〈动〉 1▸（追悼） condole: ▸～丧，～唁 2▸（安慰） console: ▸～民伐罪 3▸（追怀） reminisce: ▸凭～

吊[2] diào
A〈动〉 1▸（悬挂） hang: 天花板上～着两盏灯。 Two lamps hung from the ceiling. ▸～灯，～桥 2▸（指用绳子） lift up with a rope: 用起重机～起建筑材料 use a crane to lift up building materials ▸～车，～装 3▸（收回） revoke: ▸～销 4▸（加面子或里子） put in a fur lining: ～皮袄 line a coat with fur 5▸（指打球） spin the ball
B〈量〉 string of 1,000 copper coins
【吊膀子】diào bàngzi〈动〉〈方〉 flirt
【吊车】diàochē〈名〉 crane: 龙门～ gantry crane
【吊窗】diàochuāng〈名〉 window hinged on top
【吊床】diàochuáng〈名〉 hammock
【吊带】diàodài〈名〉 braces
【吊灯】diàodēng〈名〉 pendent lamp: 枝形～ chandelier
【吊顶】diàodǐng〈名〉 suspended ceiling
【吊斗】diàodǒu〈名〉 cableway bucket
【吊儿郎当】diào'erlángdāng〈成〉 slapdash: 工作～ be sloppy about one's work
【吊杠】diàogàng〈名〉［体育］ trapeze
【吊古】diàogǔ〈动〉 visit a historical site and muse over the past
【吊环】diàohuán〈名〉 1▸［体育］ rings 2▸（指器械） strap
【吊祭】diàojì = 祭奠 jìdiàn
【吊脚楼】diàojiǎolóu = 吊楼 diàolóu 1
【吊卷】diàojuàn = 调卷 diàojuàn
【吊扣】diàokòu〈动〉 suspend: ～驾照 suspend sb.'s driving licence
【吊兰】diàolán〈名〉［植物］ spider plant
【吊楼】diàolóu〈名〉 1▸（水上房屋） house projecting over the water 2▸（竹板房或竹房子） house propped up by wooden supports with ladders leading up
【吊民伐罪】diàomín-fázuì〈成〉 console the suffering and punish the wicked
【吊铺】diàopù〈名〉 hanging bed
【吊桥】diàoqiáo〈名〉 1▸（悬索桥） suspension bridge 2▸（可吊起、放下的桥） drawbridge: 河上有座～。 There is a drawbridge across the river.
【吊球】diàoqiú〈名〉（指排球） fake hit;（指网球、羽毛球） drop shot
【吊丧】diàosāng〈动〉 pay a condolence call
【吊嗓子】diào sǎngzi〈动〉 train one's voice
【吊扇】diàoshàn〈名〉 ceiling fan
【吊死鬼】diàosǐguǐ〈名〉 ghost of a person who has hanged himself
【吊索】diàosuǒ〈名〉 sling
【吊桶】diàotǒng〈名〉 well-bucket
【吊胃口】diào wèikǒu〈动〉 1▸〈本〉 whet the appetite 2▸〈喻〉 hold in suspense: 别吊人胃口了，快说谁得了第一名。 Don't keep us in suspense. Tell us who won the first prize.
【吊慰】diàowèi〈动〉〈书〉 offer condolences
【吊线】diàoxiàn〈动〉 plumb-line
【吊销】diàoxiāo〈动〉 revoke: ～驾驶执照 rescind a driver's licence ‖ 这家公司的营业执照已被～。 The business licence of this firm has been withdrawn.
【吊孝】diàoxiào = 吊丧 diàosāng
【吊唁】diàoyàn〈动〉 offer one's condolences
【吊影】diàoyǐng〈动〉〈书〉 be extremely lonely
【吊钟花】diàozhōnghuā = 倒挂金钟 dàoguà jīnzhōng
【吊装】diàozhuāng〈动〉［建筑］ assemble prefabricated parts
【吊子】diàozi = 铫子 diàozi

钓（釣） diào〈动〉 1▸（用钩捕捉） fish: ～起一条大鱼 hook up a big fish ▸垂～ 2▸〈喻〉（猎取） go after: ▸沽名～誉
【钓饵】diào'ěr〈名〉 bait: 用虫子作～ use worms as bait
【钓竿】diàogān〈名〉 fishing rod: 伸缩～ telescopic rod
【钓钩】diàogōu〈名〉 1▸（鱼钩） fish hook 2▸〈喻〉（圈套） trap
【钓具】diàojù〈名〉 fishing tackle

【钓鱼】diàoyú〈动〉 fish: ～比赛 angling contest
【钓鱼岛】Diàoyúdǎo〈名〉 Diaoyu Islands
【钓鱼台】diàoyútái〈名〉 fishing terrace

调[1]（調）diào〈动〉 ①（调动） transfer: ～工作/单位 transfer to another post/unit ‖ ～军队 move troops ▸～任, 借～ ②（调查） investigate: ▸～查, ～研, 函～ ③（调取） ask for: ▸～档, ～卷

调[2]（調）diào〈名〉 ①［音乐］ key: B/C～ key of B/C ②（曲调） tune: 这首歌的～儿很美。 This song has a lovely tune. ③（口音） accent: ▸南腔北～ ④（观点） opinion: ▸唱高～, 老～重弹 ⑤（风格） style: ▸格～, 情～ ⑥［语言］ tone: ▸～值, 降～, 升～
▸tiáo
【调包】diàobāo = 掉包 diàobāo
【调兵遣将】diàobīng-qiǎnjiàng〈成〉 ①（指作战） deploy forces: 双方都在～, 准备决一死战。 Both warring sides were moving troops for a decisive battle. ②（调配人力） muster and organize manpower: 对重点工程必须～, 保证如期完成。 We must muster all necessary manpower to ensure timely completion of key projects.
【调拨】diàobō〈动〉 ①（调配拨付） transfer and allocate: ～物资 allocate supplies ‖ ～资金 allocate and transfer funds ② = 调遣 diàoqiǎn
【调查】diàochá〈动〉 investigate: 进行～ carry out an investigation ‖ 法庭～ judicial inquiry ‖ 市场～ market survey ‖ 事故原因正在～之中。 The cause of the accident is under investigation.
【调查报告】diàochá bàogào〈名〉 research report
【调查研究】diàochá yánjiū〈动〉 investigate and research
【调查组】diàocházǔ〈名〉 investigation team
【调档】diàodàng〈动〉 ①（调阅） ask for sb.'s dossier ②（调入） transfer sb.'s files
【调动】diàodòng〈动〉 ①（变动） transfer: ～工作 transfer to a different job ②（动员） mobilize: ～一切积极因素 bring all positive factors into play ‖ 充分～中央和地方的积极性 give full play to the initiatives of both the central and the local authorities ③（调用） move: ～部队 deploy troops
【调度】diàodù Ａ〈动〉 ①（调遣） dispatch: ～车辆 dispatch vehicles ②（管理） manage: 生产～ production management Ｂ〈名〉 dispatcher: ～室 dispatcher's office ‖ ～员 controller
【调防】diàofáng〈动〉［军事］ transfer a garrison: 他所在的部队马上就要～。 His army unit will soon be transferred.
【调函】diàohán〈名〉 letter of transfer
【调号】diàohào〈名〉 ①［语言］ tone mark ②［音乐］ key signature
【调虎离山】diàohǔ-líshān〈成〉〈喻〉 lure sb. away from their base
【调换】diàohuàn〈动〉 ①（对换） exchange: ～房子 swap apartments ‖ ～位置 change positions ②（更换） change: 我想～一下工作。 I'd like to change to another job.
【调回】diàohuí〈动〉 transfer back
【调集】diàojí〈动〉 assemble: ～兵力 assemble forces
【调卷】diàojuàn〈动〉 ask for files for examination
【调类】diàolèi〈名〉［语言］ tone category
【调离】diàolí〈动〉 be transferred from: 他已～这家公司。 He has already been transferred from this company.
【调令】diàolìng〈名〉 transfer order
【调门儿】diàoménr〈名〉〈口〉 ①（音调） pitch: ～定得太高 pitch a tune too high ②（观点） view
【调派】diàopài〈动〉 assign: ～干部帮助农民脱贫致富 assign cadres to help lift farmers out of poverty
【调配】diàopèi〈动〉 allocate: 合理～人力 rational deployment of human resources
▸tiáopèi
【调遣】diàoqiǎn〈动〉 dispatch: ～援军 bring up reinforcements ‖ 听从～ be ready to accept an assignment
【调任】diàorèn〈动〉 transfer to another post: ～校长 be transferred to the post of headmaster
【调式】diàoshì〈名〉［音乐］ scale
【调研】diàoyán〈简称〉= 调查研究
【调演】diàoyǎn〈动〉 organize joint performances
【调用】diàoyòng〈动〉 transfer and allocate: ～抗洪物资 transfer flood-control materials ‖ ～资金 allocate funds
【调阅】diàoyuè〈动〉 call for consultation: ～案卷 send for files for inspection
【调运】diàoyùn〈动〉 allocate and transport: 往灾区～粮食 allocate and transport grains to the disaster area
【调值】diàozhí〈名〉［语言］ tone pitch
【调职】diàozhí〈动〉 be transferred to another post: 原主任～到省里去工作了。 Our former director has been transferred to a post in the provincial government.
【调转】diàozhuǎn〈动〉 ①（调动） transfer: 我的～手续办好了。 I have gone through all the transfer formalities. ② = 掉转 diàozhuǎn
【调子】diàozi〈名〉 ①（曲调） tune: 定～ set the tone ②（基调） tone: 降低批评的～ tone down the criticism ‖ ～低沉的演说 low-key speech ③（观点） view: 他改变了～。 He changed his point of view.

掉 diào〈动〉 ①（落下） fall: ～头发 lose hair ‖ ～眼泪 shed tears ‖ ～雨点儿 start to rain ‖ ～进海里 fall into the sea ‖ 我衬衫上的一颗钮扣～了。 One of the buttons on my shirt has come off. ②（丢失） be missing: 你～什么东西了没有? Have you lost anything? ‖ 文章里～了几个字。 Some words are missing from the article. ③（落后） lag behind: 一些士兵因疲劳而～队。 Fatigued, some of the soldiers fell behind. ④（转） turn: 请把桌子～过来。 Please turn the desk round. ‖ 她～过脸去暗自流泪。 She turned her head away and shed silent tears. ⑤（减少） drop: ▸～膘, ～价 ⑥ａ（表除去） [used after transitive verbs to indicate removal]: 擦～ wipe off ‖ 扔～ throw away ‖ 洪水冲～了整个村庄。 The flood washed away a whole village. ｂ（表离开） [used after intransitive verbs to indicate departure]: 飞～ fly away ‖ 跑～ run away ⑦（调换） exchange: ～座 swap seats ⑧（卖弄） show off: ▸～书袋 ⑨（回转） swing: ～臂而去 walk out on someone
【掉包】diàobāo〈动〉 stealthily substitute one thing for another: ～计 scheme to substitute one thing for another
【掉膘】diàobiāo〈动〉 [of livestock] lose weight
【掉队】diàoduì〈动〉 fall behind: 别～。 Don't go falling behind.
【掉过儿】diàoguòr〈动〉 swap places with sb.
【掉换】diàohuàn = 调换 diàohuàn
【掉魂】diàohún〈动〉 lose one's wits
【掉价】diàojià〈动〉 ①（价格下降） drop in price: 电视机～了。 The price of TV sets fell. ②（降低身份） cheapen: 教授干那种事太～了。 It was so degrading for a professor to have done such a thing.
【掉脑袋】diào nǎodai〈动〉〈口〉 be beheaded: 干这种事是要～的。 It would cost your head if you did such things.
【掉期】diàoqī〈动〉［金融］ swap: 外汇～交易 foreign exchange swap transaction
【掉色】diàoshǎi〈动〉 fade: 掉了色的蓝衬衫 faded blue shirt
【掉书袋】diào shūdài〈惯〉〈贬〉 embellish one's speech or writing with quotations and allusions
【掉头】diàotóu〈动〉 ①（指人） turn one's head away: ～逃跑 turn tail and run ②（指车船） make a U-turn: 不许～! No U-turns!
【掉以轻心】diàoyǐqīngxīn〈成〉 lower one's guard: 决不能～。 You should never let your guard down.
【掉转】diàozhuǎn〈动〉 turn back: ～身子 turn around ‖ ～船头 turn a boat round ‖ ～枪口 turn one's gun against sb.

铫（銚）diào
【铫子】diàozi〈名〉 vessel for decocting medicinal herbs

diē

爹 diē ▸**p. 588**〈名〉〈口〉 father
【爹爹】diēdie〈名〉〈方〉 daddy

跌 diē〈动〉 ①（摔） fall: ～了一跤 have a fall ‖ ～入河中 fall into a river ▸～倒 ②（下降） drop: ～至第二位 fall into second place ‖ 物价猛～。 Prices fell sharply. ‖ 金价～了2%。 The price of gold went down two per cent. ▸下～ ③（落下） drop: ▸～水
【跌膘】diēbiāo〈动〉 [of livestock] lose weight
【跌宕】diēdàng〈形〉〈书〉 ①（指性格） free and easy: ～不羁 be free and unrestrained ②（指音乐） flowing rhythmically: 歌声～ sing in cadence ③（指文章） varied: 故事情节～起伏。 The plot of the story is full of twists and turns.
【跌荡】diēdàng = 跌宕 diēdàng
【跌倒】diēdǎo〈动〉 stumble and fall
【跌跌撞撞】diēdie-zhuàngzhuàng〈形〉 doddering: 那醉汉～地在街上走。 The drunkard stumbled down the street.
【跌幅】diēfú〈名〉 margin of decrease: ～榜 table showing the price drop range ‖ 银行股～最大。 The sharpest decline is in bank stocks.
【跌价】diējià〈动〉 go down in price
【跌跤】diējiāo〈动〉 ①（摔跌） trip and fall: 他跌了一跤。 He tripped and fell. ②〈喻〉（受挫折） suffer a setback: 在工作中少不了要～。 One inevitably encounters obstacles in one's work.
【跌落】diēluò〈动〉 ①（掉落） fall off: ～马下 fall off a horse ②（下跌） go down: 油价大幅～。 Oil prices went down sharply.
【跌势】diēshì〈名〉 bearishness
【跌水】diēshuǐ〈名〉 ①［水利］ hydraulic drop ②（人工瀑布） waterfall

【跌停板】diētíngbǎn〈名〉［金融］limit down

【跌眼镜】diē yǎnjing〈惯〉come as a surprise: 令不少行家大～ come as a total surprise to many specialists

【跌足】diēzú〈动〉〈书〉stamp one's foot

【跌足捶胸】diēzú-chuíxiōng〈成〉stamp one's foot and beat one's chest in bitterness

dié

迭 dié

A〈动〉1（轮流）alternate: ▸更～ 2（赶上）be in time for: 后悔不～ be too late for regrets

B〈副〉repeatedly: ～有发现。Discoveries have been made one after the other. ▸～出, ～起

【迭出】diéchū〈动〉keep coming forth: 精品～ produce excellent works one after the other ‖ 新人～。New people keep emerging.

【迭次】diécì〈副〉〈书〉again and again: ～交涉 make repeated representations ‖ ～谈判，了无结果 hold successive talks but with no result

【迭起】diéqǐ〈动〉occur repeatedly: 比赛高潮～。The match reached one climax after another.

垤 dié〈名〉〈书〉small mound: 丘～ hillock ‖ 蚁～ anthill

眣 dié〈动〉〈书〉[of the sun] move towards the west

▸yì

谍（諜） dié

A〈名〉spy: ▸间～

B〈动〉spy

【谍报】diébào〈名〉intelligence report: 一份～ an intelligence report ‖ ～员 spy

堞 dié〈名〉battlements: ▸雉～

耋 dié〈形〉〈书〉1（七八十岁）aged 70 to 80 2（年纪大）elderly: ▸耄～

喋 dié

【喋喋不休】diédiébùxiū〈成〉rattle on: 她喜欢～地诉说自己孩子的事。She likes to rattle on about her kids.

【喋血】diéxuè〈动〉〈书〉shed lots of blood

牒 dié〈名〉1（书籍）record: 史～ history book 2（公文）official document: ▸度～, 通～

叠（疊） dié〈动〉1（累积）pile up: ▸重～ 2（折叠）fold: ～衣裳 fold up one's clothes ‖ 把信～好 fold a letter

▸折～

【叠床架屋】diéchuáng-jiàwū〈成〉〈喻〉needless duplication

【叠翠】diécuì〈形〉〈书〉green (of groves of trees): 峰峦～。Green trees cover range upon range of ridges and peaks.

【叠句】diéjù〈名〉［语言］reiterative sentence

【叠罗汉】dié luóhàn〈名〉［杂技］pyramid

【叠印】diéyìn〈动〉［摄影］double exposure

【叠韵】diéyùn〈名〉［语言］rhyming compound

【叠嶂】diézhàng〈名〉rows of mountains: ▸重峦～

【叠字】diézì〈名〉［语言］reiterative locution

碟 dié〈名〉small dish: 搪瓷～儿 enamel dish ‖ 一～黄瓜片 a dish of sliced cucumber ▸～片, 光～

【碟机】diéjī〈名〉disc player: 高清晰～ high definition disc player ‖ ～生产商 disc player manufacturer

【碟片】diépiàn〈名〉disc

【碟子】diézi〈名〉small dish

蝶 dié〈名〉butterfly

【蝶泳】diéyǒng〈名〉butterfly stroke

蹀 dié〈动〉〈书〉stamp one's foot

【蹀躞】diéxiè〈动〉〈书〉1（小步走）walk in small steps 2（徘徊）pace about

【蹀血】diéxuè = 喋血 diéxuè

鲽（鰈） dié〈名〉［鱼类］flatfish

dīng

丁[1] dīng〈名〉1（指天干）fourth of the ten Heavenly Stems (天干) 2（第四）fourth: ～班 fourth class

丁[2] dīng〈名〉1（成年男子）man: ▸成～, 壮～ 2（从事某种职业的人）person engaged in certain types of manual work: ▸园～ 3（人口）population: ▸人～, 添～

丁[3] dīng〈动〉〈书〉encounter: ▸～忧

丁[4] dīng〈名〉little cube: 把黄瓜切成～ cut a cucumber into cubes ‖ 炒鸡～ fried chicken cubes

▸zhēng

【丁坝】dīngbà〈名〉groyne

【丁村人】Dīngcūnrén〈名〉Dingcun Man [mid-Palaeolithic homo sapiens, whose fossils were found in Dingcun, Shanxi Province]

【丁当】dīngdāng = 叮当 dīngdāng

【丁点儿】dīngdiǎnr〈量〉〈口〉tiny bit: 人不可能一～毛病都没有。No man is flawless. ‖ 不要为～事就睡不着觉。Don't lose sleep over such a small matter.

【丁丁当当】dīngdīng-dāngdāng〈拟〉ding dong

【丁冬】dīngdōng = 叮咚 dīngdōng

【丁鲹】dīngguì〈名〉［鱼类］tench

【丁克】dīngkè〈名〉dinky (double income, no kids): ～家庭 dinky family

【丁零】dīnglíng〈拟〉jingle: 铃声～。The bell chimes.

【丁零当啷】dīngling-dānglāng〈拟〉jingle-jangle: 把钥匙弄得～直响 jingle the keys

【丁宁】dīngníng = 叮咛 dīngníng

【丁是丁，卯是卯】dīng shì dīng, mǎo shì mǎo〈俗〉be conscientious and meticulous

【丁香】dīngxiāng〈名〉1（落叶灌木）lilac 2（常绿植物）clove: ～油 clove oil

【丁忧】dīngyōu〈动〉〈书〉be in mourning for one's parent

【丁字尺】dīngzìchǐ〈名〉T-square

【丁字钢】dīngzìgāng〈名〉T-steel

【丁字街】dīngzìjiē〈名〉T-junction

仃 dīng ▸伶仃 língdīng

叮 dīng〈动〉1（叮咬）sting: 他被黄蜂～了一下。He was stung by a wasp. 2（嘱咐）repeat what one says to make sure: ▸～咛, ～嘱 3（追问）question closely

【叮当】dīngdāng〈拟〉ding dong: ～的铃声 the tinkling sound of a bell ‖ 铃儿发出欢快的～声。Bells jingled merrily.

【叮咚】dīngdōng〈拟〉tinkle

【叮咛】dīngníng〈动〉warn: 千～万嘱咐 exhort repeatedly

【叮问】dīngwèn〈动〉question closely

【叮嘱】dīngzhǔ〈动〉exhort: 老师～学生用功学习。The teacher urged the students to be diligent.

玎 dīng

【玎珰】dīngdāng = 叮当 dīngdāng

【玎玲】dīnglíng〈拟〉jingle

盯 dīng〈动〉stare at: ～着海外市场 eye overseas markets ‖ ～着那个家伙 keep a close watch on that guy

【盯防】dīngfáng〈名〉close-marking defence

【盯人】dīngrén〈动〉［体育］mark an opponent: 全场～ full-court press ‖ ～防守 close-marking defence

【盯梢】dīngshāo〈动〉shadow: 派人～ put a tail on sb. ‖ 他发觉一辆警车在盯他们的梢。He noticed a police car shadowing them.

钉（釘） dīng

A〈名〉nail: ▸螺丝～, 图～

B〈动〉1（紧随）tail: ～住对方 watch the other side closely 2（督促）urge: ～着孩子做作业 urge one's child to do their homework

▸dìng

【钉齿耙】dīngchǐbà〈名〉spike-tooth harrow

【钉锤】dīngchuí〈名〉nail hammer

【钉螺】dīngluó〈名〉［动物］snail

【钉帽】dīngmào〈名〉head of a nail

【钉耙】dīngpá〈名〉spiked rake

【钉是钉，铆是铆】dīng shì dīng, mǎo shì mǎo = 丁是丁，卯是卯 dīng shì dīng, mǎo shì mǎo

【钉鞋】dīngxié〈名〉1（防滑雨鞋）old-fashioned rainproof shoes 2（运动鞋）spikes

【钉子】dīngzi〈名〉1〈本〉nail 2〈喻〉（难对付的事物）something that is hard to deal with: ▸～户 3〈喻〉（指人）saboteur: 安插～ plant a saboteur 4〈喻〉（障碍）snag: 到处碰～ run up against a wall in every direction

【钉子户】dīngzihù〈名〉household which refuses to relocate to make way for a construction project

疔 dīng〈名〉［中医］boil

【疔疮】dīngchuāng〈名〉［中医］furuncle

耵 dīng

【耵聍】dīngníng〈名〉〈书〉earwax

酊 dīng ▸碘酊 diǎndīng ▸dǐng

【酊剂】dīngjì〈名〉tincture

耵 dīng〈动〉resole a shoe: ～鞋底 resole a shoe

dǐng

顶（頂） dǐng

A〈名〉**1**（头顶）crown: 头～ top of the head ▸秃～ **2**（顶部）peak: ▸山～, 屋～ **3**（上限）limit: 奖金不封～ place no ceiling on bonuses

B〈副〉exceedingly: ～管用 very useful ‖ ～大 largest

C〈量〉[used of sth. that has a top]: 一～花轿 a bridal sedan chair ‖ 一～帽子 a hat ‖ 一～蚊帐 a mosquito net

D〈动〉**1**（用头支撑）carry on the head: 头上～着一罐水 carry a pitcher of water on one's head ▸～天立地, ～碗 **2**（拱起）prop up: 用木杠子把门～上 prop open the door with a wooden stick **3**（撑起）cope with: 妇女～起半边天。Women hold up half the sky. ‖ 这活儿一个人～不下来。One person alone cannot handle this job. **4**（相当）be equivalent to: 三个臭皮匠，～个诸葛亮。Two heads are better than one. ‖ 他干活一个～两个。He can do the work of two people. **5**（承受）bear: ～得住严寒 be able to cope with the severe winter ‖ 这根柱子～不住这么大的重量。This pillar cannot bear such great weight. **6**（代替）substitute: 我不在时，她～我上课。She taught in my place during my absence. **7**（转让）transfer ownership: 这房子已经～给别人了。This house has been made over to someone else. ▸～盘 **8**（撞或支撑）butt: ～入空门 head the ball into an open goal ‖ 用枪～住她的腰 dig the gun into her waist **9**（迎着）brave: ～风雪 face blizzards ▸～风冒雨 **10**（顶撞）retort: 他不听我的话，还～了我几句。He wouldn't listen to me and even hit back with a retort. ▸～嘴 **11**〈口〉（支持）support

【顶班】dǐngbān〈动〉**1**（替班）work as substitute: 他爸如果病了，儿子就去～。When the father was ill, the son worked in his place. **2**（指干整时段的活儿）work regular shifts: 厂长经常～劳动。The director often works regular shifts.

【顶板】dǐngbǎn〈名〉**1**［矿业］roof: ～陷落 roof caving ‖ ～岩石 roof stone **2**（屋顶）ceiling

【顶层】dǐngcéng〈名〉top floor

【顶灯】dǐngdēng〈名〉**1**（指车顶）overhead light **2**（指屋顶）ceiling light

【顶点】dǐngdiǎn〈名〉**1**（最高点）pinnacle: 达到事业的～ reach the pinnacle of one's career **2**［数学］apex: 三角形的～ apex of a triangle

【顶端】dǐngduān〈名〉top: 站在电视塔的～俯瞰古城 have a bird's-eye view of the ancient city from the top of the TV tower

【顶多】dǐngduō〈副〉at (the) most

【顶风】dǐngfēng **A**〈动〉**1**（逆着风）go against the wind: ～跑/骑车 run/cycle against the wind ‖ ～站立 stand upwind ▸～冒雨 **2**〈喻〉（公然对抗）flagrantly flout a decree, law or policy that is being vigorously implemented: ～违纪 violate discipline while discipline is being tightened ‖ ～作案 commit an offence in defiance of an ongoing crackdown on crimes **B**〈名〉headwind

【顶风冒雨】dǐngfēng-màoyǔ〈成〉brave wind and rain

【顶峰】dǐngfēng〈名〉peak: 达到～ reach the climax ‖ 攀登科学～ scale the heights of science

【顶缸】dǐnggāng〈动〉〈喻〉take the blame for somebody else

【顶岗】dǐnggǎng = 顶班 dǐngbān

【顶杠】dǐnggàng〈动〉bicker

【顶格】dǐnggé〈动〉be set flush with the top margin

【顶刮刮】dǐngguāguā = 顶呱呱 dǐngguāguā

【顶呱呱】dǐngguāguā〈形〉〈口〉tip-top: 他在教学上是～的。He is a first-rate teacher.

【顶级】dǐngjí〈形〉first-class: ～科学家 top-notch scientist ‖ ～球员 top-class player

【顶尖】dǐngjiān **A**〈名〉top: 打掉棉花～ remove the top of a cotton plant ‖ 镀金塔的～在阳光下闪闪发光。The gilded tower top is shining in the sun. **B**〈形〉first-class: ～大学 first-rate university ‖ ～学生 top-notch student

【顶角】dǐngjiǎo〈名〉［数学］apex angle

【顶礼膜拜】dǐnglǐ-móbài〈成〉〈贬〉bow down and worship

【顶梁柱】dǐngliángzhù〈名〉**1**〈本〉key pillar that supports the beam of a building **2**〈喻〉pillar: 家里的～ the pillar of one's family

【顶楼】dǐnglóu〈名〉top floor

【顶命】dǐngmìng〈动〉give a life for a life

【顶牛儿】dǐngniúr〈动〉wrangle: 双方仍然为此事～。The two parties are still at loggerheads over the matter.

【顶盘】dǐngpán〈动〉take over a business

【顶棚】dǐngpéng〈名〉ceiling

【顶事】dǐngshì〈形〉useful: 我吃药了，但不～。I've taken the medicine, but don't feel any better. ‖ 这些人很～。These people are a great help.

【顶数】dǐngshù **A**〈动〉make up the numbers: 我干不了多少事，只能顶个数。I can't do much; I'm here just to make up the numbers. **B**〈形〉[usu used in the negative] having effect: 你说了不～。What you said carries no weight.

【顶替】dǐngtì〈动〉take sb.'s place: 我～她做编辑。I am taking over from her as editor. ‖ 她走了谁来～? Who will be her replacement after her departure? ▸冒名

【顶天立地】dǐngtiān-lìdì〈成〉be a force to be reckoned with: ～的英雄 dauntless hero

【顶头】dǐngtóu〈动〉meet head-on: 两辆汽车～相撞。The two cars had a head-to-head collision.

【顶头上司】dǐngtóu shàngsi〈名〉one's immediate superior

【顶碗】dǐngwǎn〈名〉［杂技］pagoda of bowls: 表演～ perform with a pagoda of bowls

【顶芽】dǐngyá〈名〉［植物］terminal bud

【顶叶】dǐngyè〈名〉［植物］terminal leaf

【顶用】dǐngyòng = 顶事 dǐngshì

【顶账】dǐngzhàng = 抵账 dǐzhàng

【顶针】dǐngzhen〈名〉thimble: 一只～ a thimble

【顶真】dǐngzhēn **A**〈形〉〈方〉earnest: 他干什么事都很～。He takes everything he does very seriously. **B**〈名〉［语言］[known also as 顶针, 联珠] a rhetorical device which requires a sentence to begin with the word or phrase at the end of the previous sentence

【顶撞】dǐngzhuàng〈动〉**1**（用头撞）butt sb.: 用头～某人的腹部 give sb. a butt in the stomach **2**（反驳）contradict one's superior: ～上司 argue head-on with one's boss ‖ 他不想～父亲。He did not want to contradict his father outright.

【顶嘴】dǐngzuǐ〈动〉answer back: 别跟爸爸～，那样不礼貌。Don't answer your father back; it's not polite.

【顶罪】dǐngzuì〈动〉**1**（替人受过）bear the blame for sb. else **2**（抵罪）be equal to the crime: 罚不～。The punishment does not match the crime.

酊 dǐng ▸酩酊 mǐngdǐng ▸dīng

鼎 dǐng

A〈名〉**1**（古炊器）ancient vessel with two loop handles and three or four legs: 铜～ bronze tripod ‖ 三足～ tripod **2**〈书〉（王权）throne: ▸问～ **3**〈喻〉（并立三方）tripartite balance of forces **4**〈方〉（锅）wok

B〈形〉great: ▸～力, 一言九～

C〈副〉〈书〉meanwhile: ▸～盛

> **鼎**
>
> Ancient vessels, usually made of bronze, and dating from the Shang and Zhou dynasties. They were used mainly at ancestral shrines in sacrificial ceremonies, or were buried in tombs. Nine *ding* were said to have been cast by Yu (禹), the founder of the Xia Dynasty, and these were handed down to succeeding dynasties as national treasures, becoming associated with the power of the state and the emperor's throne. The Simuwu *ding* excavated at the Shang Dynasty ruins in Anyang, Henan Province, weighs over 800 kg, and stands as the heaviest bronze object ever discovered.

【鼎鼎】dǐngdǐng〈形〉magnificent: 大名～ well-known

【鼎鼎大名】dǐngdǐng dàmíng〈成〉be famous

【鼎沸】dǐngfèi〈形〉tumultuous: 名声～ be at the height of one's popularity ‖ 会上群情～。Passions were running high at the meeting. ▸人声～

【鼎革】dǐnggé〈动〉〈书〉abolish the old and introduce the new: ～时期 time of dynastic change ‖ 天地～ succession of the old by the new

【鼎力】dǐnglì〈名〉〈书〉〈敬〉great effort: ～相助 give generous assistance

【鼎立】dǐnglì〈动〉〈喻〉[of three forces] confront each other like the three legs of a tripod

【鼎盛】dǐngshèng〈形〉**1**（昌盛）flourishing: 在帝国的～时期 at the height of the empire ‖ 他的事业现处于～时期。His career is at its peak now. **2**（强壮）prime: ～之年 in one's prime ▸春秋～

【鼎新】dǐngxīn〈动〉〈书〉innovate: ▸革故～

【鼎峙】dǐngzhì〈动〉〈书〉be in a tripartite confrontation

【鼎足】dǐngzú〈名〉**1**〈本〉three legs of a tripod **2**〈喻〉（三方对峙）tripartite confrontation

【鼎足之势】dǐngzúzhīshì〈成〉tripartite confrontation

d

dìng

订（訂） dìng〈动〉**1**（订立）conclude: ～合同 conclude a contract ‖ ～计划 agree upon a plan ‖ ～生产指标 set a production target **2**（改正）revise: ▸～正, 校～ **3**（订阅）order: ～报纸 subscribe to a newspaper ‖ ～房间 book a room ‖ ～三桌酒席 reserve three tables for a feast ▸～购, ～户 **4**（装订）staple: 把所有文件～在一起。Staple all the documents together. ▸～书机, 装～

【订单】dìngdān〈名〉order: 接受～ accept an order ‖ ～源源而来。Orders are pouring in.

【订购】dìnggòu〈动〉order: 网上～ order online

【订户】dìnghù〈名〉subscriber

【订婚】dìnghūn〈动〉be engaged: ～礼物 engagement present ‖ ～戒指 engagement ring

【订货】dìnghuò **A**〈动〉order goods: 凭样～ order by sample ‖ ～单 goods order **B**〈名〉order: 交付～ complete an order ‖ 大宗～ quantity order

【订货会】dìnghuòhuì〈名〉order-placing meeting

【订交】dìngjiāo〈动〉〈旧〉establish friendly relations

【订金】dìngjīn〈名〉deposit: 付～ pay a deposit ‖ 买房付～ make a down payment on a house

【订立】dìnglì〈动〉agree on: ～合同 enter into a contract ‖ ～攻守同盟 form an offensive and defensive alliance ‖ ～条约/协议 conclude a treaty/an agreement

【订票】dìngpiào〈动〉book a ticket: 订三张机票 book three air tickets

【订书钉】dìngshūdīng〈名〉staple

【订书机】dìngshūjī〈名〉stapler

【订阅】dìngyuè〈动〉subscribe: ～报纸/杂志 subscribe to a newspaper/magazine

【订正】dìngzhèng〈动〉make corrections: ～印刷错误 amend printing errors

钉（釘） dìng〈动〉**1**（用钉子固定）nail: ～钉子 drive in a nail ‖ ～马掌 nail on horseshoes ‖ 把画～到墙上 nail a picture on the wall **2**（缝缀）sew on: ～扣子 sew a button on ▸dīng

定 dìng
A〈形〉**1**（安稳）calm: ▸安～, 心神不～ **2**（固定）fixed: ▸～量, ～期
B〈动〉**1**（固定）fix: ▸～睛, ～影 **2**（决定）decide: ～几条规矩 set a few rules ‖ 比赛～于下星期举行。The match is scheduled for next week. ▸～价 **3**（确定）establish: 她的命运已～。Her fate is sealed. ▸～局, ～论 **4**（预订）order: ～两桌菜 order dishes for two tables ▸～金
C〈副〉〈书〉surely: ～能成功 be sure to succeed

【定案】dìng'àn **A**〈动〉reach a verdict: ～证据 substantial evidence **B**〈名〉verdict: 推翻～ reverse a verdict ‖ 已成～, 不能更改。This is the final decision and it cannot be changed.

【定本】dìngběn〈名〉definitive edition

【定编】dìngbiān〈动〉determine the size of the staff: ～定岗 limit the number of positions and fill each with qualified personnel

【定产】dìngchǎn〈名〉fixed production

【定场白】dìngchǎngbái〈名〉[in traditional Chinese opera] monologue

【定场诗】dìngchǎngshī〈名〉four-line poem that opens a traditional opera

【定单】dìngdān = 订单 dìngdān

【定点】dìngdiǎn **A**〈动〉designate a certain place: ～供应 direct supply of material at fixed locations ‖ ～轰炸 pinpoint bombing **B**〈形〉**1**（指定）designated: 国家～企业 state-designated enterprises ‖ ～厂 designated factory **2**（规定时间）fixed-time: ～作业 operation at fixed time

【定调子】dìng diàozi〈动〉set the tone: 领导一～, 大家就不好说话了。Once the leadership has set the tone, people will hesitate to speak out.

【定都】dìngdū〈动〉fix a site for the capital

【定夺】dìngduó〈动〉make a final decision: 这事由你～。It is up to you to decide.

【定额】dìng'é **A**〈动〉set a quota **B**〈名〉quota: 完成～ fill the quota ‖ 生产～ production quota ‖ ～包干 be held responsible for an enterprise's own finance after handing in a fixed sum to the authorities

【定岗】dìnggǎng〈动〉fix jobs and responsibilities

【定稿】dìnggǎo **A**〈动〉finalize a manuscript: 这本词典由主编～。The dictionary is finalized by the editor-in-chief. **B**〈名〉final version: ～即将付印。The final text will soon go to press.

【定格】dìnggé **A**〈名〉hard and fast rule: 写小说并无～。There is no set rule for novel-writing. **B**〈动〉[影视] freeze-frame: 影片在此～。The film was freeze-framed here.

【定购】dìnggòu **A**〈名〉fixed quota for purchasing: ～粮 grain quota **B** = 订购 dìnggòu

【定冠词】dìngguàncí ▸**p. 411**〈名〉[语法] definite article

【定规】dìngguī **A**〈名〉established practice: 无～可循。There are no hard and fast rules to go by. ‖ 这种做法已成～。This has become the established practice. **B**〈副〉〈方〉firmly

【定户】dìnghù = 订户 dìnghù

【定滑轮】dìnghuálún〈名〉fixed pulley

【定婚】dìnghūn = 订婚 dìnghūn

【定货】dìnghuò = 订货 dìnghuò

【定级】dìngjí〈动〉grade: 给粮食/棉花～ grade the grain/cotton ‖ 给某人～ rank sb.

【定计】dìngjì〈动〉contrive a stratagem

【定价】dìngjià **A**〈动〉set a price: 按质～ fix the price according to the quality ‖ 统一～ price on a uniform basis ‖ ～过高 overpriced **B**〈名〉fixed price: 按～销售商品 sell commodities at fixed prices ‖ 政府～ government set prices

【定价权】dìngjiàquán〈名〉costing power: 铁路运输的～主要在铁道部。The costing of the railroads lies predominantly with the Ministry of Railways.

【定见】dìngjiàn〈名〉set idea: 他对此事已有～。He has very fixed ideas on the matter.

【定金】dìngjīn = 订金 dìngjīn

【定睛】dìngjīng〈动〉fix one's eyes upon: 她～一看, 原来是她的男朋友。She had a good, hard look, and it turned out it was her boyfriend.

【定居】dìngjū〈动〉take up residence: ～新疆 settle in Xinjiang ‖ 在香港～ make one's home in Hong Kong

【定居点】dìngjūdiǎn〈名〉settlement

【定局】dìngjú〈名〉foregone conclusion: 主队失败已成～。The host team's defeat was a foregone conclusion.

【定礼】dìnglǐ = 彩礼 cǎilǐ

【定理】dìnglǐ〈名〉theorem: 基本～ fundamental theorem

【定力】dìnglì〈名〉strong willpower: 多一些～, 少一些浮躁 a little more perseverance and a little less impetuosity

【定例】dìnglì〈名〉usual practice: 每周游泳一次, 已成了我们家的～。It has become a routine in our family to go swimming once a week.

【定量】dìngliàng **A**〈动〉**1**（指测定）determine the amount of the components of a substance: ～分析 quantitative analysis **2**（指规定）fix the amount: ～供应 rationing **B**〈名〉fixed quantity

【定律】dìnglǜ〈名〉law

【定论】dìnglùn〈名〉foregone conclusion: 飞机失事原因尚无～。There is still no conclusive explanation for the air crash.

【定名】dìngmíng〈动〉name

【定盘星】dìngpánxīng〈名〉**1**（杆秤上起算点）first mark on a steelyard arm **2**〈喻〉（准主意）definite view

【定评】dìngpíng〈名〉accepted opinion: 此事早有～。There has long been an accepted opinion about it.

【定期】dìngqī **A**〈动〉set a time **B**〈形〉**1**（指周期）regular: ～举行记者招待会 hold regular press conferences **2**（指期限）time-bound: ～存款 fixed deposit ‖ ～航班 scheduled flight

【定期债券】dìngqī zhàiquàn〈名〉term bonds

【定钱】dìngqian = 定金 dìngjīn

【定亲】dìngqīn〈动〉be betrothed

【定情】dìngqíng〈动〉pledge one's love: ～物 pledge of love

【定然】dìngrán〈副〉〈书〉certainly: 你～错了。You are definitely wrong.

【定神】dìngshén〈动〉**1**（指心神）steady one's nerves: 坐下来定定神 sit down to steady one's nerves **2**（指注意力）focus one's attention: 他～一看, 来客原来是他的大学同学。He had a good look at the visitor and realized that it was one of his former college classmates.

【定时】dìngshí **A**〈名〉set time **B**〈动〉be at fixed time: ～吃饭 eat at regular hours ‖ ～上下课。The classes begin and end at fixed times.

【定时器】dìngshíqì〈名〉timer

【定时炸弹】dìngshí zhàdàn〈名〉time bomb

【定式】dìngshì〈名〉fixed pattern: 思维～ set way of thinking

【定势】dìngshì〈名〉mind-set: 心理～ mind-set

【定数】dìngshù〈名〉**1**（指数额）fixed number: 心中已有～ already have a fixed number in mind **2**（命数）destiny: 凡事都有～。Everything is predestined.

【定说】dìngshuō〈名〉accepted argument: 玛雅文化消失的原因尚无～。Why the Mayan civilization disappeared still remains a matter of dispute.

【定投】dìngtóu〈动〉[金融] invest on a fixed investment basis: 坚持长期～成长型基金 stick to a long-term fixed investment growth fund

【定位】dìngwèi **A**〈动〉position: 卫星～系统 GPS **B**〈名〉**1**（指位置）location: 听觉～ auditory localization **2**（指人生追求）niche: 找到人生～ find one's niche in life ‖ 市场～ market niche

【定位球】dìngwèiqiú〈名〉[足球] place kick: 主罚～ kick a place kick ‖ 赛前重点训练～ focus on practising place kicks

before the game

【定息】dìngxī〈名〉fixed rate of interest

【定弦】dìngxián〈动〉**1**〈本〉tune a stringed instrument **2**〈方〉〈喻〉（拿定主意）make up one's mind: 毕业以后干什么，我还没～呢。 I haven't made up my mind about what to do after graduation.

【定向】dìngxiàng〈动〉orientate: ～爆破 directional blasting ‖ ～培养 conduct target training

【定向招生】dìngxiàng zhāoshēng **A**〈动〉enrol students who are assigned to specific posts or areas **B**〈名〉directional recruitment of students

【定心】dìngxīn〈动〉reassure

【定心丸】dìngxīnwán〈名〉〈喻〉assurance: 吃了～ be reassured

【定刑】dìngxíng〈动〉sentence

【定型】dìngxíng〈动〉finalize a design: ～产品 approved product ‖ 这种轿车尚未～。 The design for this make of car has yet to be finalized.

【定性】dìngxìng〈动〉**1**（指问题的性质）determine the nature of: 那次事件早已～。 The nature of the incident has long been decided. **2**（指化学特性）determine the chemical composition of a substance

【定义】dìngyì〈名〉definition: 下～ define

【定音鼓】dìngyīngǔ ►**p. 929**〈名〉［音乐］kettledrum

【定影】dìngyǐng〈动〉［摄影］fix: ～液 fixer

【定于一尊】dìngyúyīzūn〈成〉look up to the supreme authority as the only standard

【定语】dìngyǔ〈名〉［语法］attribute

【定语从句】dìngyǔ cóngjù〈名〉［语法］attributive clause

【定员】dìngyuán **A**〈动〉fix the number of people **B**〈名〉personnel quota: 车厢的～ seating capacity of a car

【定则】dìngzé〈名〉［物理］rule

【定址】dìngzhǐ〈动〉**1**（指工程地址）fix a site: 新工厂已经～了。 The site of the new factory has been determined. **2**（指居住地址）fixed residence

【定准】dìngzhǔn **A**〈名〉established standard **B**〈副〉surely: 他～来。 I'm sure he will come.

【定子】dìngzǐ〈名〉［电子］stator

【定罪】dìngzuì〈动〉convict sb. of a crime: 量刑～ mete out penalties in accordance with the crime

【定做】dìngzuò〈动〉have sth. made to order: ～的鞋 custom-made shoes

啶 dìng ►吡啶 bǐdìng

铤（鋌） dìng〈名〉〈书〉copper and iron that has not been smelted or cast ►tǐng

腚 dìng〈名〉〈方〉buttocks

碇（椗） dìng〈名〉heavy stone to anchor a boat to: 起～ weigh anchor ‖ 下～ cast anchor

锭（錠） dìng

A〈名〉**1**（铸块）ingot: ►钢～，银～ **2**［纺织］spindle: 压～ reduce spindles ►纱～

B〈量〉ingot-shaped tablet: 一～墨 a slab of Chinese ink ‖ 一～银子 a silver ingot

【锭剂】dìngjì〈名〉［药学］lozenge

【锭子】dìngzi〈名〉［纺织］spindle

diū

丢 diū〈动〉**1**（丢失）lose: 钱包～了。 The wallet is lost. ‖ 我的行李～了。 I have mislaid my baggage. **2**（扔）throw: 不要随地乱～纸屑。 Don't throw paper all over the place. ‖ 优良传统不能～。 Fine traditions should not be discarded. **3**（放下）put aside: ～下手里的活儿 put aside what one is doing

【丢丑】diūchǒu〈动〉be disgraced: 给家人～ bring disgrace upon the family ‖ 当众～ make a fool of oneself in public

【丢掉】diūdiào〈动〉**1**（失去）lose:〈喻〉～饭碗 lose one's job **2**（抛弃）cast away: ～幻想 cast off illusions ‖ ～旧衣服 cast aside old clothes

【丢份儿】diūfènr〈动〉〈方〉lose face: 他不觉得清扫厕所就～。 He doesn't think it demeaning to clean the toilet.

【丢官】diūguān〈动〉lose one's official post

【丢车保帅】diūjū-bǎoshuài〈成〉〈喻〉sacrifice minor things to save major ones

【丢盔弃甲】diūkuī-qìjiǎ〈成〉be badly defeated

【丢脸】diūliǎn〈动〉lose face: 在公众面前～ lose face with the public

【丢面子】diū miànzi〈惯〉lose face

【丢弃】diūqì〈动〉abandon: ～旧鞋 discard old shoes

【丢人】diūrén〈动〉lose face: 贫穷并没有什么可～的。 There's no disgrace in being poor.

【丢人现眼】diūrén-xiànyǎn〈成〉make a fool of oneself

【丢三落四】diūsān-làsì〈惯〉be scatter-brained

【丢失】diūshī〈动〉lose: 我的身份证～了。 I have lost my identity card.

【丢手】diūshǒu〈动〉wash one's hands of: 他～不干了。 He washed his hands of the matter.

【丢眼色】diū yǎnsè〈惯〉tip sb. the wink: 他们相互～。 They sent eye signals to each other.

【丢卒保车】diūzú-bǎojū〈成〉〈喻〉sacrifice minor things to save major ones

铥（銩） diū〈名〉［化学］thulium (Tm)

dōng

东（東） dōng〈名〉**1** ►**p. 205**（指方向）east: ～临大海 face the sea to the east ‖ ～郊 eastern suburbs ►～边，～风 **2**（东道主）host: ►～道主，做～ **3**（主人）owner: ►～家，股～

【东半球】dōngbànqiú〈名〉Eastern Hemisphere

【东北】dōngběi〈名〉**1** ►**p. 205**（指方向）north-east: ～风 north-easterly wind **2** Dōngběi（特指中国东北地区）north-east China: ～平原 North-east Plain

【东北虎】dōngběihǔ〈名〉Manchurian tiger

【东奔西窜】dōngbēn-xīcuàn〈成〉flee in all directions

【东奔西跑】dōngbēn-xīpǎo〈成〉rush about: ～找工作 run around looking for a job

【东奔西走】dōngbēn-xīzǒu = 东奔西跑 dōngbēn-xīpǎo

【东边】dōngbian ►**p. 205**〈名〉east: ～日出西边雨。 It rained in the west but was sunny in the east.

【东边不亮西边亮】dōngbian bù liàng xībian liàng〈俗〉there's always plenty of room for manoeuvre

【东部】dōngbù ►**p. 205**〈名〉eastern part: 中国位于亚洲～。 China is in the east of Asia.

【东窗事发】dōngchuāng-shìfā〈成〉[of conspiracy, secret plot, etc.] be exposed

【东床】dōngchuáng〈名〉son-in-law: ～快婿 good son-in-law

【东倒西歪】dōngdǎo-xīwāi〈成〉**1**（不稳）unsteady: 走路～ stagger **2**（凌乱歪斜）dilapidated: ～的桌椅 rickety desks and chairs

【东道】dōngdào〈名〉host

【东道国】dōngdàoguó〈名〉host country: ～法国 host country France

【东道主】dōngdàozhǔ〈名〉host: 这个队将与～比赛。 This team will play the host.

【东帝汶】Dōng Dìwèn〈名〉East Timor

【东躲西藏】dōngduǒ-xīcáng〈成〉flee here and there

【东方】dōngfāng〈名〉**1** ►**p. 205**（指方向）east: 太阳从～升起。 The sun rises in the east. **2**（亚洲）East: ～文化 Oriental culture

【东非】Dōng Fēi〈名〉East Africa

【东风】dōngfēng〈名〉easterly wind: 正在刮～。 The wind is blowing in an easterly direction. ►万事俱备，只欠～

【东风吹马耳】dōngfēng chuī mǎ'ěr〈成〉〈喻〉fall on deaf ears

【东格拉摩根郡】Dōnggélāmógēnjùn〈名〉East Glamorgan

【东宫】dōnggōng〈名〉〈旧〉**1**（指宫殿）Eastern Palace **2**（皇太子）crown prince

【东郭先生】Dōngguō xiānsheng〈成〉gullible softie

【东海】Dōnghǎi〈名〉East China Sea

【东汉】Dōng Hàn〈名〉Eastern Han Dynasty

【东家长，西家短】dōng jiā cháng, xī jiā duǎn〈惯〉gossip about various people

【东家】dōngjia〈名〉master

【东晋】Dōng Jìn〈名〉Eastern Jin Dynasty

【东京】Dōngjīng〈名〉Tokyo: ～都 Greater Tokyo ‖ ～湾 Gulf of Tonkin

【东经】dōngjīng〈名〉east longitude: 北京位于～116度，北纬40度。 Beijing is located at 40° N and 116° E.

【东拉西扯】dōnglā-xīchě〈成〉beat about the bush: 别～，有话直说。 Stop beating about the bush. What exactly have you got to say?

【东鳞西爪】dōnglín-xīzhǎo = 一鳞半爪 yīlín-bànzhǎo

【东洛锡安郡】Dōngluòxī'ānjùn〈名〉East Lothian

【东盟】Dōngméng〈简称〉= 东南亚国家联盟

【东面】dōngmiàn ►**p. 205**〈名〉east: 面朝～ face east

【东南】dōngnán〈名〉**1** ►**p. 205**（指方向）south-east **2** Dōngnán（特指中国东南地区）south-east China

【东南亚】Dōngnán Yà〈名〉South-east Asia: ～金融危机 South-east Asian financial crisis

【东南亚国家联盟】Dōngnán Yà Guójiā Liánméng〈名〉Association of South-east Asian Nations (ASEAN)

【东欧】Dōng Ōu〈名〉East Europe: ～国家 Eastern European countries

d

【东拼西凑】dōngpīn-xīcòu〈成〉scrape together: ～的报告 scraped-together report
【东萨塞克斯郡】Dōngsàsàikèsījùn〈名〉East Sussex
【东三省】Dōngsānshěng〈名〉Three North-east Provinces [China's Liaoning, Jilin, and Heilongjiang provinces]
【东沙群岛】Dōngshā Qúndǎo〈名〉Dongsha Islands
【东山再起】Dōngshān-zàiqǐ〈成〉make a comeback: 前首相～。 The former prime minister staged a comeback.
【东施效颦】Dōngshī-xiàopín〈成〉copy blindly and in doing so make a fool of oneself
【东突】dōngtū〈名〉East Turkestan: 打击"～"恐怖势力 crack down on East Turkestani terrorist forces
【东魏】Dōng Wèi〈名〉Eastern Wei Dynasty
【东西】dōng-xī ▸p. 205〈名〉**1**（东方和西方）east and west: ～向的大街 street running east to west **2**（从东到西）distance from east to west: 这座城～约六公里，南北约八公里。 The city is about 6 kilometres from east to west and 8 kilometres from north to south.
【东西】dōngxi〈名〉thing: 想不想吃点～? Do you want to eat something? ‖ 你手里拿着什么～? What's that in your hand? ‖ 可爱的小～ little darling ‖ 那家伙不是个好～。 That guy is bad.
【东乡族】Dōngxiāngzú〈名〉Dongxiang ethnic group
【东亚】Dōng Yà〈名〉East Asia: ～运动会 East Asian Games
【东洋】Dōngyáng〈名〉〈旧〉Japan: ～货 Japanese goods ‖ ～人 Japanese
【东一榔头，西一棒子】dōng yī lángtou, xī yī bàngzi〈成〉act or speak haphazardly
【东瀛】Dōngyíng〈名〉〈旧〉**1**（东海）East China Sea **2**（日本）Japan: 留学～ study in Japan
【东岳】dōngyuè〈名〉Eastern Sacred Mountain [Taishan Mountain (泰山) in Shandong Province]
【东张西望】dōngzhāng-xīwàng〈成〉look around
【东正教】Dōngzhèngjiào〈名〉Orthodox Eastern Church
【东周】Dōng Zhōu〈名〉Eastern Zhou Dynasty

冬[1] dōng ▸p. 345〈名〉winter: 严～ severe winter ‖ ～去春来。 After winter comes spring. ▸～眠，隆～

冬[2]（咚、鼕）dōng〈拟〉rat-a-tat
【冬奥会】dōng'ào huì〈简称〉= 冬季奥运会 Dōngjì Àoyùnhuì
【冬不拉】dōngbùlā ▸p. 929〈名〉tamboura
【冬菜】dōngcài〈名〉**1**（腌菜）preserved cabbage or mustard greens **2**（冬令菜）winter vegetables
【冬虫夏草】dōngchóng-xiàcǎo〈名〉Chinese caterpillar fungus
【冬储】dōngchǔ〈动〉store for winter use: ～大白菜 store Chinese cabbages for the winter
【冬耕】dōnggēng〈名〉winter ploughing
【冬菇】dōnggū〈名〉dried mushrooms
【冬瓜】dōngguā〈名〉white gourd
【冬灌】dōngguàn〈名〉winter irrigation
【冬烘】dōnghōng〈形〉pedantic: ～先生 pedant
【冬季】dōngjì ▸p. 345〈名〉winter
【冬季奥运会】Dōngjì Àoyùnhuì〈名〉Winter Olympic Games
【冬节】Dōngjié = 冬至 Dōngzhì
【冬令】dōnglìng〈名〉**1**（指季节）winter **2**〈书〉（指气候）winter weather: 春行～ wintry weather in spring
【冬眠】dōngmián〈名〉hibernation: 进入～ go into hibernation
【冬青】dōngqīng〈名〉[植物] Chinese holly
【冬日】dōngrì〈名〉**1**（指季节）winter days **2**（指太阳）winter sun
【冬笋】dōngsǔn〈名〉winter bamboo shoots
【冬天】dōngtiān ▸p. 345〈名〉winter: ～来了，春天还会远吗? When Winter comes, can Spring be far behind?
【冬闲】dōngxián〈名〉slack winter season
【冬小麦】dōngxiǎomài〈名〉winter wheat
【冬歇期】dōngxiēqī〈名〉[足球] winter break
【冬训】dōngxùn〈名〉winter training
【冬衣】dōngyī〈名〉winter clothes
【冬泳】dōngyǒng〈名〉winter outdoor swimming: ～爱好者 winter swimming enthusiasts
【冬月】dōngyuè〈名〉eleventh month
【冬运】dōngyùn〈名〉winter transportation
【冬蛰】dōngzhé = 冬眠 dōngmián
【冬至】Dōngzhì〈名〉Winter Solstice [beginning of the 22nd of the 24 solar terms]: ～点 Winter Solstice point

> **冬至**
>
> The Winter Solstice is one of the 24 solar terms, and falls each year around the 22nd December. The shortest day of the year, it is the first day of a series of nine nine-day periods (known as 九九) that make up the season of winter. The third period of nine days (三九) is the coldest period. The Winter Solstice is a traditional Chinese festival. In north China people celebrate by eating *jiaozi* (▸饺子) and *wonton* (▸馄饨), while in the south, people eat glutinous rice balls (▸汤圆) and meat.

【冬装】dōngzhuāng〈名〉winter clothes

咚 dōng = 冬[2] dōng

氡 dōng〈名〉[化学] radon (Rn)

鸫（鶇） dōng〈名〉[鸟类] thrush

蝀（蝀） dōng ▸蝃蝀 dìdōng

dǒng

董 dǒng
A〈动〉〈书〉supervise: ～其成 supervise the project until its completion
B〈名〉director: 商～ member of the board of directors of a company
【董事】dǒngshì〈名〉director
【董事会】dǒngshìhuì〈名〉board of directors
【董事长】dǒngshìzhǎng〈名〉chairman of the board: 副～ deputy chairman

懂 dǒng〈动〉understand: ～礼貌 have good manners ‖ 不～就问。 If you don't understand, just ask. ‖ 你能听～我的话吗? Can you follow me?
【懂得】dǒngde〈动〉understand: 我当然～他的意思。 I could, of course, grasp his meaning.
【懂行】dǒngháng〈动〉know the ropes
【懂事】dǒngshì〈形〉sensible: 他是个～的孩子。 He is a sensible child.

dòng

动（動） dòng
A〈动〉**1**（移动）move: 他一～不～，假装睡着了。 He didn't move, pretending to be asleep. ‖ 微风吹～了树叶。 A soft breeze stirred the leaves. ▸风吹草～，纹丝不～ **2**（挪动）change the position of sth.: 别～我的东西。 Don't move my things. ▸挪～，兴师～众 **3**（行动）act: 咱们～起来吧。 Let's get things moving. ▸～工，轻举妄～ **4**（使用）use: ～筷子 start eating ▸～笔，～脑筋，大～干戈 **5**（触动）touch: ～感情 be carried away with emotion ‖ 不为金钱所～ not to be excited by money ▸～情，～人 **6**（可变动）be movable: ▸～产，～态
B〈副〉easily: 他～不～就发火。 He loses his temper easily. ▸～辄得咎
【动笔】dòngbǐ〈动〉set pen to paper
【动兵】dòngbīng〈动〉dispatch troops
【动不动】dòngbudòng〈副〉easily: ～就发脾气 flare up easily ‖ 他～就跟人吵架。 He was ready to quarrel at the drop of a hat.
【动产】dòngchǎn〈名〉movables: ～和不动产 movable and immovable property ‖ ～抵押 chattel mortgage
【动车】dòngchē〈名〉CRH train [a multiple unit train in China]
【动车组】dòngchēzǔ〈名〉China Railway Highspeed (CRH)
【动词】dòngcí〈名〉verb: ～短语 verbal phrase ‖ 不规则～ irregular verb ▸及物～，情态～，助～
【动粗】dòngcū〈动〉come to blows
【动荡】dòngdàng **A**〈动〉undulate: 湖水～ rippling lake **B**〈形〉turbulent: ～的局势 unstable situations ‖ 政治～ political unrest
【动荡不安】dòngdàng-bù'ān〈成〉be tumultuous
【动肝火】dòng gānhuǒ〈惯〉lose one's temper: 别为这点小事～。 Don't work yourself up about such a trivial thing.
【动感】dònggǎn〈名〉vividness: 这座雕塑极富～。 The sculpture is very lifelike.
【动工】dònggōng〈动〉**1**（开工）start construction work: 破土～ break the ground and start construction **2**（施工）construct
【动画片】dònghuàpiàn〈名〉cartoon
【动火】dònghuǒ〈动〉lose one's temper: 因误会而～ flare up over a misunderstanding
【动机】dòngjī〈名〉motive: ～不纯 have mixed motives ‖ 作案～ motive for committing a crime
【动静】dòngjing〈名〉**1**（声响）noise: 屋里一点～也没有。 The room is completely quiet. **2**（情况）activity: 查看敌方的～ find out what is going on on the enemy side
【动力】dònglì〈名〉impetus: ～不足 shortage of power ‖ ～车间 power house ‖ 精神～ ideological motivating power ‖ 社会

发展的～ impetus of social development
【动力学】dònglìxué〈名〉 dynamics
【动量】dòngliàng〈名〉 momentum: ～守恒定律 law of conservation of momentum
【动乱】dòngluàn〈名〉 turmoil: ～年代 tumultuous years ‖ 社会～ social unrest ‖ 制造～ stir up social chaos
【动脉】dòngmài〈名〉 artery: 冠状～ coronary arteries ‖ 主～ aorta
【动脉硬化】dòngmài yìnghuà ▸p. 50〈名〉［医学］ arteriosclerosis
【动脉粥样硬化】dòngmài zhōuyàng yìnghuà ▸p. 50〈名〉［医学］ atherosclerosis
【动漫】dòngmàn〈名〉 animation and cartoon
【动脑筋】dòng nǎojīn〈动〉 exercise one's brains
【动能】dòngnéng〈名〉 kinetic energy
【动怒】dòngnù〈动〉 lose one's temper
【动气】dòngqì〈动〉 get angry
【动迁】dòngqiān〈动〉 relocate: ～户 relocated household
【动情】dòngqíng〈动〉 1（指情绪） get worked up 2（指爱慕之情） have one's passions aroused
【动人】dòngrén〈形〉 moving: ～的场面 touching scene ‖ ～的故事 moving story
【动人心魄】dòngrénxīnpò〈成〉 be soul-stirring: ～的音乐 soul-stirring music
【动人心弦】dòngrénxīnxián〈成〉 be deeply moving: 歌声嘹亮，～。 The resounding songs touch everyone's heart.
【动容】dòngróng〈动〉〈书〉 be visibly moved: 观者无不为之～。 Every viewer was visibly moved.
【动身】dòngshēn〈动〉 set out: ～去机场 set out for the airport ‖ 及早～ start early ‖ 看样子要下雨了，早点～吧。 It looks like rain. We'd better get going now.
【动手】dòngshǒu〈动〉 1（开始做） get to work: 咱们～干吧。 Let's get started. 2（触碰） touch: 请勿～。 Please do not touch. 3（打架） strike: 君子动口不～。 A gentleman argues but never raises his fist. ‖ 不知怎的，两人说着说着就动起手来了。 The two were talking when somehow they came to blows.
【动手动脚】dòngshǒu-dòngjiǎo〈成〉 1（举止轻浮） make sexual advances: 相识不久就想～ want to get physical early in a relationship 2（打人） make motions to start a fight
【动态】dòngtài A〈名〉 1（发展趋势） trends: ～平衡 dynamic equilibrium ‖ 科技新～ recent developments in science and technology ‖ 思想～ trends of thought 2（指艺术形象） bearing: 武士～各异，栩栩如生。 Each of the warriors has a different stance and is very lifelike. B〈形〉 dynamic: ▸～分析
【动态分析】dòngtài fēnxī〈名〉 dynamic analysis
【动态口令】dòngtài kǒulìng〈名〉 dynamic password
【动弹】dòngtan〈动〉 move: 站着别～! Stand still!
【动听】dòngtīng〈形〉 easy on the ear: ▸娓娓～
【动土】dòngtǔ〈动〉 break ground
【动问】dòngwèn〈动〉〈套〉 may I ask: 不敢～，您是比利时人吗? Excuse me, but are you from Belgium?
【动窝】dòngwō〈动〉〈口〉 make a move: 我们想动动窝。We're thinking of moving.
【动武】dòngwǔ〈动〉 start a fight
【动物】dòngwù〈名〉 animal: ～保护区 fauna reserve ‖ ～化石 zoolite ▸冷血～
【动物学】dòngwùxué〈名〉 zoology
【动物园】dòngwùyuán〈名〉 zoo
【动向】dòngxiàng〈名〉 trend: 侦察敌军～ scope out the movements of enemy troops ‖ 市场～ market trend ‖ 新～ new movement
【动心】dòngxīn〈动〉 one's mind is persuaded: 他不为花言巧语的广告～。 He was not swayed by the fine words in the advertisements. ‖ 姑娘的才智使他动了心。 He was attracted by the girl's intelligence.
【动刑】dòngxíng〈动〉 subject sb. to torture
【动摇】dòngyáo〈动〉 1（犹豫） waver: 在困难面前毫不～ hold fast in the face of difficulties ‖ 她对丈夫的忠诚从未～过。 She never wavered in her loyalty to her husband. 2（使不稳） shake: ～军心 shake the morale of the army ‖ 困难和挫折并没有～我们的决心。 Difficulties and frustrations failed to weaken our determination.
【动议】dòngyì〈名〉 motion: 提出～ propose a motion ‖ 紧急～ urgent motion ‖ ～仅以一票之差被否决。 The motion was defeated by a single vote.
【动因】dòngyīn〈名〉 motive: 创作～ creative motivation
【动用】dòngyòng〈动〉 employ: ～库存 draw on stocks ‖ ～武力 use force
【动员】dòngyuán〈动〉 mobilize: ～群众/军队 mobilize the masses/army ‖ 总～ full mobilization ‖ ～大会 mobilization meeting
【动员令】dòngyuánlìng〈名〉 order of mobilization
【动辄】dòngzhé〈副〉 easily: ～发怒 fly into a rage at the slightest provocation
【动辄得咎】dòngzhé-déjiù〈成〉 be blamed for whatever one does
【动真格的】dòng zhēngéde〈动〉〈口〉 do sth. with all one's heart: 反腐要～ fight corruption in earnest
【动嘴】dòngzuǐ〈动〉 talk: 别光～。 Don't just pay lip service. ‖ 他只～，不行动。 He is all talk and no action.
【动作】dòngzuò A〈名〉 action: ～敏捷 be quick in one's movements ‖ 体操～ gymnastic movement ‖ 用话语、表情和～表达思想 express oneself through a combination of words, facial expressions and movements B〈动〉 act: 我们早就该～了。 We should have acted much earlier.
【动作片】dòngzuòpiàn〈名〉 action movie

冻（凍）dòng

A〈动〉 1（结冰） freeze: 不～港 ice-free port 2（感到冷） feel freezing: ～僵 be frozen stiff ‖ 我的手～坏了。 My hands have been frostbitten.
B〈名〉 1（结冰现象） freezing: ▸解～, 霜～ 2（胶状食品） jelly: 肉皮～ pigskin jelly ▸果～
【冻冰】dòngbīng〈动〉 freeze
【冻疮】dòngchuāng〈名〉 chilblain: 生～ have chilblains
【冻豆腐】dòngdòufu〈名〉 frozen bean curd
【冻结】dòngjié〈动〉 1〈本〉［of water］ freeze: 水在0°C～成冰。 Water freezes at 0°C. 2〈喻〉 freeze: ～存款 freeze deposits ‖ ～经济和军事援助 freeze economic and military aid
【冻馁】dòngněi〈动〉〈书〉 be cold and hungry: ～而死 die of cold and hunger
【冻肉】dòngròu〈名〉 frozen meat: 冻牛肉 chilled beef
【冻伤】dòngshāng ▸p. 50〈名〉 frostbite
【冻土】dòngtǔ〈名〉 frozen soil: ～带 tundra
【冻雨】dòngyǔ〈名〉 sleet

侗 Dòng

▸tóng
【侗剧】dòngjù〈名〉 Dong opera
【侗族】Dòngzú〈名〉 Dong ethnic group

栋（棟）dòng

A〈名〉〈书〉 1（正梁） ridge pole: ▸～梁, 雕梁画～ 2（房屋） house: ▸汗牛充～
B〈量〉［used for housing］: 一～房子/楼 a house/building
【栋梁】dòngliáng〈名〉 1〈本〉 ridge pole and beam 2〈喻〉 person of great ability: 国家的～ pillar of the state ‖ ～之材 person of tremendous talent

峒 dòng〈名〉 cave

胨（腖）dòng〈名〉［生化］ peptone

洞 dòng

A〈名〉（孔） hole;（穴） cavity: 戳一个～ poke a hole ‖ 挖～ dig a hole ‖ 钻～ bore a hole ‖ ～口 mouth of a cave ▸～穴, 漏～
B〈形〉 penetrating: ▸～察, ～若观火
C ▸p. 691〈数〉 zero［used for the numeral '0' when speaking of figures］
【洞察】dòngchá〈动〉 have an insight into: ～民情 have a thorough grasp of popular feeling ‖ ～是非 see clearly the rights and wrongs of the case ‖ ～力 insight
【洞彻】dòngchè〈动〉 understand thoroughly: ～事理 be very sensible
【洞穿】dòngchuān〈动〉 pierce: 子弹～头部而亡。 The bullet penetrated his skull and he died.
【洞达】dòngdá〈动〉〈书〉 understand thoroughly: ～事理 be sensible
【洞房】dòngfáng〈名〉 bridal chamber: 入～ enter the bridal chamber
【洞房花烛】dòngfáng-huāzhú〈成〉 wedding festivities: ～夜 wedding night
【洞府】dòngfǔ〈名〉 cave dwelling
【洞见】dòngjiàn〈动〉〈书〉 see clearly: ～症结 get to the heart of a matter
【洞鉴】dòngjiàn〈动〉〈书〉 see clearly: ～古今 have an insight into history and the present world
【洞开】dòngkāi〈动〉［of doors, windows, etc.］ be wide open: 门户～。 The doors are wide open.
【洞窟】dòngkū〈名〉 cave
【洞若观火】dòngruòguānhuǒ〈成〉 understand sth. thoroughly at a glance
【洞天】dòngtiān〈名〉 1（指有神仙居住） heavenly abode 2（指风景优美） scenic spot of exceptional beauty: 别有～ full of exceptional beauty and charm
【洞天福地】dòngtiān-fúdì〈成〉 1（神仙居住地） blessed spot 2（名山胜地） picturesque places
【洞庭湖】Dòngtínghú ▸p. 305〈名〉 Dongting Lake
【洞悉】dòngxī〈动〉〈书〉 know sth. inside out: ～内情 have a thorough grasp of the inside information
【洞箫】dòngxiāo〈名〉 Chinese vertical bamboo flute
【洞晓】dòngxiǎo〈动〉〈书〉 know clearly: ～音律 have a good understanding of music
【洞熊】dòngxióng〈名〉 cave bear
【洞穴】dòngxué〈名〉 grotto

【洞眼】dòngyǎn〈名〉small hole
【洞烛其奸】dòngzhú-qíjiān〈成〉see through sb.'s treacherous tricks

恫 dòng〈动〉〈书〉1（使恐惧）intimidate 2（恐惧）fear
▸tōng
【恫吓】dònghè〈动〉intimidate: 受到～ be intimidated ‖ 武力～ threaten with force

胴 dòng〈名〉torso
【胴体】dòngtǐ〈名〉1（指牲畜）trunk 2（指人）torso

硐 dòng〈名〉cave

dōu

都 dōu〈副〉1（两者以上）all: 我们三个人～要来。All three of us will come. ‖ 一切～准备好了。Everything is ready. 2（两者）both: 他们俩那时～还年轻。They were both young at that time. ‖ 你今天或明天来～行。You can come either today or tomorrow. 3（表理由）[used before 是 to indicate the cause]: ～是那场雨，把他给淋病了。He was caught in the rain and that made him ill. ‖ ～是我不好，让你受苦了。It was all my fault that you had to suffer. 4（甚至）even: 连小孩～知道这个道理。Even children know this. ‖ 他自己～不着急，你着急个啥？If he is not worried, why should you be? 5（已经）already: ～六月了，天还这么凉。It's already June, but it's still so cool. ‖ ～十一点了，你还不睡？It is already eleven o'clock. Aren't you sleepy at all? 6（表强调）[used in the negative with 一点儿 to show emphasis]: 我一点儿～不饿。I am not at all hungry. ‖ 这事我一点儿～不知道。I don't have the faintest idea about it.
▸dū

兜 dōu
A〈名〉pocket: 他把一只手放在衣～里。He put his hand in his coat pocket. ‖ 她把门锁好，钥匙装在～里。She locked the door and pocketed the key. ▸裤～, 网～
B〈动〉1（拢住）wrap up and let hang in a piece of cloth, etc.: 你手绢里～着什么？What have you got in your handkerchief? 2（绕）move round: 咱们开车去街上～一圈，好吗？Let's go for a ride in town, shall we? 3（招揽）solicit: ▸～生意, ～销 4（承担）take complete responsibility for: 有问题我～着。If anything goes wrong, I'll take the responsibility. ▸吃不了, ～着走 5（曝光）reveal: 他的丑事全被～出来了。His scandal was completely exposed.
【兜抄】dōuchāo〈动〉round up: ～逃犯 close in on the escaped criminal
【兜底】dōudǐ〈动〉reveal all: 你的同伙都兜了底。Your partner has confessed everything. ‖ 你不该兜他的底。You shouldn't have dragged the skeleton out of his closet.
【兜兜】dōudou = 兜肚 dōudu
【兜兜裤儿】dōudoukùr〈名〉sunsuit
【兜肚】dōudu〈名〉diamond-shaped undergarment covering the abdomen and chest
【兜翻】dōufan〈动〉1（翻弄）rummage: 她在包里～着找汽车钥匙。She rummaged in her bag for the car key. 2（重提）rake up: 过去的事就不要再～了。Don't go raking up old stuff. 3（揭穿）expose: 他们走私汽车牟取暴利的事被～出来了。Their highly profitable dealings in smuggled cars were brought to light.
【兜风】dōufēng〈动〉1（挡住风）catch the wind 2（游逛）go for a drive: 他们喜欢晚饭后开着车去～。They like taking the car for a spin after supper.
【兜揽】dōulǎn〈动〉1（招引）canvass: ～生意 drum up business ‖ ～游客 canvass for tourists 2（包揽）take things on: 别～那么多的事。Don't take too many things upon yourself.
【兜帽】dōumào〈名〉hood
【兜圈子】dōu quānzi〈动〉1〈本〉go around in circles 2〈喻〉beat about the bush: 别跟我～，有话直说。Don't beat about the bush. If you've got something to say, tell it to me straight.
【兜生意】dōu shēngyi〈动〉solicit business
【兜售】dōushòu〈动〉peddle: 上门～化妆品 go from door to door selling cosmetics
【兜头盖脸】dōutóu-gàiliǎn〈成〉right to one's face
【兜销】dōuxiāo〈动〉= 兜售 dōushòu
【兜子】dōuzi〈名〉pocket

蔸 dōu
A〈名〉root and stump of a plant
B〈量〉clump: 一～草 a clump of grass ‖ 两～白菜 two cabbages

篼 dōu〈名〉container made of bamboo, rattan, etc.: 背～ bamboo basket carried on the back
【篼子】dōuzi〈名〉〈方〉mountain sedan chair

dǒu

斗 dǒu
A〈名〉1〈古〉（指酒具）wine vessel 2［天文］（北斗）Big Dipper 3［天文］（南斗）Southern Dipper 4〈旧〉（指粮食量器）*dou* 5（指星宿）one of the 28 constellations in ancient Chinese astronomy 6（斗状物）object shaped like a cup or dipper: ▸漏～, 烟～ 7（指指纹）whorls of a fingerprint
B〈量〉*dou* [unit of dry measure for grain, equal to 10 litres]
C〈形〉*dou*-sized: ▸～胆, ～室
▸dòu
【斗笔】dǒubǐ〈名〉big writing brush
【斗车】dǒuchē〈名〉mining truck
【斗胆】dǒudǎn〈副〉boldly: 恕我～说一句，这事你也有错。I venture to say that you are also to blame for this.
【斗拱】dǒugǒng〈名〉［建筑］corbel bracket
【斗箕】dǒuji〈名〉fingerprint
【斗笠】dǒulì〈名〉cone-shaped bamboo hat
【斗篷】dǒupeng〈名〉cape
【斗渠】dǒuqú〈名〉lateral canal
【斗室】dǒushì〈名〉〈书〉small room
【斗烟丝】dǒuyānsī〈名〉pipe tobacco
【斗转星移】dǒuzhuǎn-xīngyí〈成〉passage of time
【斗子】dǒuzi〈名〉1（运煤器具）coal bucket 2（盛物器具）container made of tree branches, planks, etc.

抖 dǒu〈动〉1（颤动）tremble: 全身发～ tremble all over 2（甩动）shake: ～掉尘土/雪花 shake the dust/snow off ‖ ～开床单 shake out a sheet 3（振作）rouse: ～起精神 pluck up one's spirits 4 = 抖搂 dǒulou 2 5（得意）be pleased with oneself: ～威风 throw one's weight about ‖ 他如今当了官，～起来了。Now that he's an official, he's started taking on airs.
【抖颤】dǒuchàn = 颤抖 chàndǒu
【抖动】dǒudòng〈动〉shake: 他笑得身子直～。He was shaking with laughter.
【抖搂】dǒulou〈动〉〈方〉1（抖动）shake off: 把衣服上的尘土～干净 shake off the dust from one's clothes 2（披露）expose: 他的腐败行为被～了出来。His corrupt behaviour was brought to light. 3（耗费）waste: 他把父亲留给他的钱～个精光，沦为乞丐。He squandered all the money his father left him and became a beggar.
【抖擞】dǒusǒu〈动〉stir up: ～精神 pull oneself together

陡 dǒu
A〈形〉steep: 山很～。The mountain is very steep. ▸～立, ～坡, ～峭
B〈副〉〈书〉suddenly: 风波～起。Disturbances suddenly erupted. ▸～变
【陡壁】dǒubì〈名〉steep cliff: 悬崖～ cliffs and precipices
【陡壁悬崖】dǒubì-xuányá〈成〉steep cliffs and crags
【陡变】dǒubiàn〈动〉〈书〉change suddenly: 他脸色～。His expression suddenly turned. ‖ 形势～。The situation changed all of a sudden.
【陡峻】dǒujùn〈形〉tall and precipitous
【陡立】dǒulì〈动〉[of mountains, building, etc.] rise steeply: 山峰～。Mountains rise steeply.
【陡坡】dǒupō〈名〉steep slope: 爬上～ climb a steep hillside
【陡峭】dǒuqiào〈形〉precipitous: ～的山峰 steep mountain
【陡然】dǒurán〈副〉〈书〉suddenly: 局势～严峻起来。The situation became grim all of a sudden.
【陡直】dǒuzhí〈形〉sheer

蚪 dǒu ▸蝌蚪 kēdǒu

dòu

斗（鬥） dòu〈动〉1（对打）fight: ▸～争, 搏～, 械～ 2（批斗）accuse and denounce at a meeting: ～恶霸 subject the local despot to a 'struggle meeting' 3（使争斗）make animals fight: ～蛐蛐 hold a cricket fight ▸～鸡, ～牛 4（竞争）contend with: ▸～智, ～嘴 5（凑在一起）piece together: ～榫儿 dovetail ▸～眼
▸dǒu
【斗法】dòufǎ〈动〉1（指法术）match in magic powers 2（指计谋）plot secretly and scheme against each other
【斗鸡】dòujī〈动〉1（指公鸡）have a cock fight 2（指游戏）play the rooster game [a hopping and bumping game]
【斗鸡眼】dòujīyǎn〈名〉lazy eye
【斗鸡走狗】dòujī-zǒugǒu〈成〉idle away one's time in cock fighting and dog racing
【斗口】dòu kǒu〈方〉= 斗嘴 dòuzuǐ
【斗牛】dòuniú〈名〉bullfight: ～士 matador
【斗殴】dòu'ōu〈动〉scuffle: 聚众～ mob fight
【斗牌】dòupái〈动〉play cards
【斗气】dòuqì〈动〉quarrel with sb. on

account of a personal grudge

【斗士】dòushì〈名〉fighter

【斗心眼儿】dòu xīnyǎnr〈动〉〈贬〉fight a battle of wits

【斗眼】dòuyǎn = 斗鸡眼 dòujīyǎn

【斗艳】dòuyàn〈动〉〈书〉vie in glamour: ▸争奇～

【斗勇】dòuyǒng〈动〉contend in valour

【斗争】dòuzhēng〈动〉❶（抗争）struggle: 与恐怖主义～ fight terrorism ‖ 对敌～ struggle against the enemy ‖ 你死我活的～ life-and-death struggle ▸阶级～ ❷（打击）accuse and denounce at a meeting: ～地主 denounce a landlord at a meeting ❸（奋斗）strive for: 为独立而～ fight for independence ‖ 为正义事业而～ struggle for a just cause

【斗志】dòuzhì〈名〉fighting spirit: 激励群众～ ignite the fighting spirit of the masses ‖ 丧失～ lose the will to fight ‖ 瓦解敌军～ take the fight out of the enemy troops ‖ ～昂扬 be full of fighting spirit ‖ ～旺盛 have plenty of fight in one

【斗智】dòuzhì〈动〉engage in a battle of wits

【斗嘴】dòuzuǐ〈动〉❶（争吵）bicker: 夫妻间～ tiff between husband and wife ‖ 不要为小事～。Don't bicker over trivialities. ❷（耍贫嘴）banter

豆[1] dòu〈名〉ancient stemmed bowl

豆[2] dòu〈名〉❶（豆子）bean: ▸黄～, 豌～ ❷（豆状物）bean-shaped things: 花生～ peanut ‖ 咖啡～ coffee bean

【豆瓣儿】dòubànr〈名〉segments of a bean

【豆瓣儿酱】dòubànrjiàng〈名〉fermented bean sauce

【豆包】dòubāo〈名〉steamed bun stuffed with sweetened bean paste

【豆饼】dòubǐng〈名〉［农业］soya bean cake

【豆豉】dòuchǐ〈名〉fermented soya beans

【豆腐】dòufu〈名〉bean curd, tofu: 冻～ frozen bean curd

【豆腐饭】dòufufàn〈名〉〈方〉dinner for friends and relatives attending a funeral

【豆腐干】dòufugān〈名〉dried bean curd

【豆腐脑儿】dòufunǎor〈名〉jellied bean curd

【豆腐皮】dòufupí〈名〉thin sheets of dried bean curd

【豆腐乳】dòufurǔ〈名〉fermented bean curd

【豆腐渣】dòufuzhā〈名〉bean dregs:〈喻〉～工程 jerry-built project

> **豆腐**
>
> Chinese bean curd has a history of 2,000 years. It is usually made from soya beans. The beans are first soaked in water, then mashed, and the bean residue strained away. The bean water is then boiled, and bittern (salt residue) or gypsum is added. After the mixture has set, the water is strained off, leaving the bean curd. Bean curd made with bittern is known as 'northern bean curd', and is relatively solid. Bean curd made with gypsum is called 'southern bean curd', and is white and soft. Soya milk made with gypsum, and not completely set, is known as 'jellied bean curd' (豆腐脑儿). Bean curd may be cut into squares and fermented or preserved.

【豆花儿】dòuhuār〈名〉〈方〉bean jelly

【豆荚】dòujiá〈名〉pod

【豆浆】dòujiāng〈名〉soya milk

【豆角儿】dòujiǎor〈名〉fresh kidney beans in pod

【豆秸】dòujiē〈名〉bean stalk

【豆蔻】dòukòu〈名〉cardamom

【豆蔻年华】dòukòu-niánhuá〈成〉[of girls] aged thirteen to fourteen

【豆绿】dòulǜ〈名〉pea green

【豆苗】dòumiáo〈名〉pea shoot

【豆奶】dòunǎi〈名〉soya milk

【豆萁】dòuqí〈名〉beanstalk

【豆青】dòuqīng = 豆绿 dòulǜ

【豆蓉】dòuróng〈名〉fine bean mash: ～包子 steamed bun with fine bean mash stuffing

【豆沙】dòushā〈名〉bean paste: ～包 steamed bun stuffed with sweetened bean paste

【豆象】dòuxiàng〈名〉［昆虫］bean weevil

【豆芽儿】dòuyár〈名〉bean sprouts

【豆芽儿菜】dòuyárcài = 豆芽儿 dòuyár

【豆油】dòuyóu〈名〉soya bean oil

【豆渣】dòuzhā = 豆腐渣 dòufuzhā

【豆汁】dòuzhī〈名〉❶（指北京小吃）fermented drink made from ground beans ❷〈口〉= 豆浆 dòujiāng

【豆制品】dòuzhìpǐn〈名〉bean products

【豆猪】dòuzhū〈名〉pig with parasitic cysticercus

【豆子】dòuzi〈名〉❶（指作物）pod-bearing plant ❷（指籽粒）beans

逗[1] dòu〈动〉❶（停留）stop: ▸～留 ❷ = 读 dòu

逗[2] dòu

A〈动〉❶（引逗）tease: ～孩子玩 play with a child ‖ 别～了! No kidding! ▸～乐儿, 挑～, 引～ ❷（招引）induce: 姑娘那双大眼睛实在～人喜爱。The girl's big eyes are really charming.

B〈形〉amusing: 他真～。He is funny.

【逗点】dòudiǎn = 逗号 dòuhào

【逗哏】dòugén〈动〉［曲艺］crack jokes

【逗号】dòuhào〈名〉comma

【逗乐儿】dòulèr〈动〉act the fool

【逗留】dòuliú〈动〉stop: 在火奴鲁鲁～几天 stop for a few days in Honolulu

【逗闷子】dòu mènzi〈动〉〈方〉crack jokes

【逗弄】dòunong〈动〉❶（引逗）tease: 男孩在～那只狗。The boy was teasing the dog. ❷（取笑）make fun of: 别～我了。Don't make fun of me.

【逗趣儿】dòuqùr〈动〉amuse

【逗笑儿】dòuxiàor〈动〉make people laugh

【逗引】dòuyǐn〈动〉tease: 孩子被～哭了。The child was teased to tears.

饾（飣） dòu

【饾饤】dòudìng **A**〈名〉〈古〉display food **B**〈动〉〈书〉fill one's writing with fancy phrases

读（讀） dòu〈名〉slight pause in reading to mark the end of a phrase, clause, or sentence: ▸句～

▸dú

痘 dòu〈名〉❶（天花）smallpox ❷（痘苗）vaccine: ▸牛～, 种～ ❸（豆状疱疹）pox: ▸水～ ❹（粉刺）pimple

【痘苗】dòumiáo〈名〉vaccine

窦（竇） dòu〈名〉❶（洞）hole: ▸情～初开, 疑～ ❷（指人体器官）sinus: ▸鼻～

【窦性心动过缓】dòuxìng xīndòng guòhuǎn ▸**p. 50**〈名〉［医学］nodal bradycardia

【窦性心动过速】dòuxìng xīndòng guòsù ▸**p. 50**〈名〉［医学］nodal tachycardia

【窦炎】dòuyán ▸**p. 50**〈名〉［医学］sinusitis: ▸鼻～

dū

㕇 dū〈动〉touch or tap lightly: ～一个点儿 reinforce a point by making a light touch ‖ 点～ add a few touches to a painting

都 dū〈名〉❶（首府）capital: 古～ ancient capital ▸～城, 建～, 首～ ❷（都市）big city: ▸～会, ～市 ❸（特色城市）city noted for a certain product: 景德镇是中国的瓷～。Jingdezhen is the porcelain capital of China.

▸dōu

【都柏林】Dūbólín〈名〉Dublin

【都城】dūchéng〈名〉capital (city)

【都督】dūdu〈名〉〈旧〉❶（指古代）military commander ❷（指民国时期）governor of a province in charge of both military and civil administration

【都会】dūhuì〈名〉big city

【都江堰】Dūjiāngyàn〈名〉Dujiang Weirs [water conservation and flood prevention project in Sichuan Province]

【都市】dūshì〈名〉big city

阇（闍） dū〈名〉〈书〉platform over a city gate

▸shé

督 dū〈动〉❶（察看）oversee: ▸～察, 监～ ❷（督导）superintend and direct: ▸～办, ～战

【督办】dūbàn **A**〈动〉supervise and manage: ～粮草 oversee the supply of food and fodder ‖ 此事交你～。I'll leave the matter in your hands. **B**〈名〉〈旧〉supervisor

【督察】dūchá **A**〈动〉supervise **B**〈名〉supervisor

【督促】dūcù〈动〉supervise and urge: ～大家归还图书 urge everybody to return the books

【督导】dūdǎo〈书〉**A**〈动〉supervise and direct **B**〈名〉supervisor

【督军】dūjūn〈名〉〈旧〉provincial military governor

【督励】dūlì〈名〉〈书〉urge and encourage

【督率】dūshuài〈动〉lead

【督学】dūxué〈名〉〈旧〉school inspector

【督造】dūzào〈动〉supervise the manufacture

【督战】dūzhàn〈动〉〈旧〉supervise military operations

嘟[1] dū〈动〉〈方〉pout

嘟[2] dū〈拟〉toot: 摩托车～～地响着。The motorcycle vroomed.

【嘟噜】dūlu **A**〈动〉❶（发颤音）trill: 姑娘～着用俄语应了一声。The girl trilled a reply in Russian. ❷（下垂）hang down in a bunch **B**〈量〉bunch: 一大～香蕉/钥匙 a big bunch of bananas/keys

【嘟囔】dūnang〈动〉mutter to oneself: 我们听见老人走开时嘴里～着什么。We

d

heard the old man muttering something as he walked away.

dú

毒 dú

A〈名〉**1**（毒物）poison: 投～ administer (a) poison ▸病～, 中～, 以～攻～ **2**（有害影响）poisonous influence: ▸流～, 余～ **3**（毒品）narcotics: 吸～ take narcotics ▸贩～

B〈形〉**1**（有毒）poisonous: ～箭 poisoned arrow ‖ ～烟 toxic smoke ‖ ～蜘蛛 poisonous spider ▸～气, ～蛇, ～药 **2**（残酷）cruel: 心肠～ cruel-hearted **3**（猛烈）fierce: 太阳很～。The sun was glaring down fiercely. ▸～计, 狠～

C〈动〉poison: 用药～老鼠 poison rats ▸～死

【毒案】dú'àn〈名〉drug case

【毒草】dúcǎo〈名〉**1**〈本〉poisonous weed **2**〈喻〉harmful writing

【毒疮】dúchuāng〈名〉noxious sore

【毒打】dúdǎ〈动〉beat up: 他被流氓～。He was beaten up by the hoodlums.

【毒饵】dú'ěr〈名〉poison bait

【毒犯】dúfàn〈名〉drug offender

【毒贩】dúfàn〈名〉drug dealer

【毒害】dúhài **A**〈动〉〈喻〉corrupt: ～青少年 corrupt young people ‖ 坏书会～年轻人的思想。Bad books will poison the young mind. **B**〈名〉poison: 清除～ get rid of poisonous influences

【毒化】dúhuà〈动〉poison: ～空气 poison the air ‖ ～社会风气 debase social morality ‖ 妒忌～了许多人际关系。The venom of jealousy has poisoned many a relationship.

【毒计】dújì〈名〉wicked scheme: 设下～ devise wicked schemes

【毒剂】dújì〈名〉poison

【毒辣】dúlà〈形〉sinister: 心肠～ harbour murderous intent ‖ 阴险～ be cunning and sinister

【毒瘤】dúliú ▸**p. 50**〈名〉malignant tumour

【毒谋】dúmóu〈名〉malicious plot

【毒品】dúpǐn〈名〉drugs

【毒气】dúqì〈名〉noxious gas: ～弹 gas bomb ‖ ～室 gas chamber

【毒杀】dúshā〈动〉poison: 有人试图～那只狗。Someone tried to poison the dog.

【毒蛇】dúshé〈名〉venomous snake

【毒手】dúshǒu〈名〉murderous scheme: ▸下～

【毒鼠强】dúshǔqiáng〈名〉tetramine

【毒死】dúsǐ〈动〉kill with poison: 那个罪犯～了许多人。The criminal poisoned many people to death.

【毒素】dúsù〈名〉**1**〈本〉［生化］toxin: 分泌～ excrete toxins ‖ 中和～ a neutralized toxin **2**〈喻〉pernicious influence: 封建主义～ pernicious ideas of feudalism

【毒腺】dúxiàn〈名〉venom gland

【毒枭】dúxiāo〈名〉drug baron

【毒刑】dúxíng〈名〉cruel punishment

【毒性】dúxìng〈名〉toxicity: ～大 be highly poisonous

【毒药】dúyào〈名〉poisonous drug

【毒液】dúyè〈名〉venom

【毒瘾】dúyǐn〈名〉drug addiction

【毒瘾婴】dúyǐnyīng〈名〉crack baby

【毒资】dúzī〈名〉**1**（买毒品的钱）money for drugs **2**（指获利）drug money

独（獨）dú

A〈形〉**1**（单一）only: ▸～木桥, ～身, ～子 **2**〈口〉（不能容人）intolerant: 这女孩有点～, 不许别人动她的东西。The girl is intolerant of others touching her things.

B〈名〉childless person: ▸鳏寡孤～

C〈副〉**1**（单独）alone: ～居 lead a solitary existence ‖ ～坐 sit alone ▸～霸, ～当一面, ～立 **2**（只有）only: ～有斯诺先生还没来。Mr Snow is the only one who has not shown up. **3**（特别）uniquely: ▸～创, ～具慧眼

【独霸】dúbà〈动〉monopolize: ～市场 monopolize the market ‖ ～全球 dominate the world

【独霸一方】dúbà yīfāng〈成〉tyrannize a region

【独白】dúbái〈名〉soliloquy

【独步】dúbù〈动〉be unrivalled: ～当时 be unrivalled in one's time ‖ ～一时 reign supreme for a time

【独裁】dúcái〈名〉dictatorship: ～政府 dictatorial government ‖ ～统治 autocratic rule ‖ ～者 dictator

【独唱】dúchàng〈动〉sing a solo: 男/女高音～ tenor/soprano solo ‖ ～会 recital

【独出心裁】dúchū-xīncái〈成〉create new styles

【独处】dúchǔ〈动〉live alone: 喜欢～ like to be by oneself

【独创】dúchuàng〈动〉original creation: ～精神 creative spirit

【独创性】dúchuàngxìng〈名〉originality: 具有～ show originality

【独创一格】dúchuàng-yīgé〈成〉develop a manner of one's own

【独当一面】dúdāng-yīmiàn〈成〉take charge of sth. on one's own: 她能～。She is able to take care of things by herself.

【独到】dúdào〈形〉original: ～的见解 original ideas ‖ 有～之处 have unique qualities

【独董】dúdǒng〈简称〉= 独立董事

【独断】dúduàn〈动〉**1**（独自决断）make decisions on one's own **2**（专断）be arbitrary

【独断独行】dúduàn-dúxíng〈成〉decide and act alone

【独断专行】dúduàn-zhuānxíng〈成〉act arbitrarily

【独夫民贼】dúfū-mínzéi〈成〉autocrat and traitor to the people

【独根】dúgēn〈名〉only son and heir

【独家】dújiā **A**〈名〉only one **B**〈形〉sole: ～代理 exclusive agent ‖ ～经营 sole agency ‖ ～新闻 exclusive

【独角戏】dújiǎoxì〈名〉**1**〈本〉monodrama **2**〈喻〉（指无帮手）one-man show: 唱～ go it alone **3** = 滑稽 huájī B

【独居】dújū〈动〉live in solitude: ～老人 reclusive old person

【独具慧眼】dújù-huìyǎn = 独具只眼 dújù-zhīyǎn

【独具匠心】dújù-jiàngxīn〈成〉show great ingenuity

【独具只眼】dújù-zhīyǎn〈成〉be able to see what others cannot

【独来独往】dúlái-dúwǎng = 独往独来 dúwǎng-dúlái

【独揽】dúlǎn〈动〉monopolize: ～大权 wield absolute power

【独力】dúlì〈副〉on one's own: ～经营 run a business on one's own

【独立】dúlì〈动〉**1**（独自站立）stand alone: ～寒秋 stand alone in the cold autumn **2**（指国家）be independent: 宣布～ declare independence ‖ 要求～ demand independence ‖ 民族～ national independence **3**（指部队）be independent: ～师/团 independent division/regiment **4**（独自）be on one's own: ～生活 live on one's own ‖ ～思考 think independently **5**（指部门）become independent: 该部门已经从原单位～出去了。This department has already split from the original work unit.

【独立成分】dúlì chéngfèn〈名〉［语言］independent element

【独立董事】dúlì dǒngshì ▸**p. 966**〈名〉independent director

【独立核算】dúlì hésuàn〈动〉keep separate accounts: ～单位/企业 independent accounting unit/enterprise

【独立王国】dúlì wángguó〈名〉independent kingdom

【独立性】dúlìxìng〈名〉independence

【独立自主】dúlì-zìzhǔ〈成〉act independently and of one's own initiative: ～的和平外交政策 independent foreign policy of peace

【独联体】Dúliántǐ〈名〉Commonwealth of Independent States: ～成员国 Commonwealth of Independent States member nation

【独领风骚】dúlǐng-fēngsāo〈成〉command one's field: 加利福尼亚在计算机行业～。California is a leading power in the computer industry.

【独龙族】Dúlóngzú〈名〉Derung ethnic group, Drung ethnic group

【独轮车】dúlúnchē〈名〉wheelbarrow: 独轮脚踏车 unicycle

【独门】dúmén〈名〉**1**（指院门）door for one single family: ～独院 courtyard with a single entrance for one family **2**（指独有）special individual skill

【独苗】dúmiáo〈名〉only child

【独木不成林】dúmù bù chéng lín〈俗〉〈喻〉one person alone cannot accomplish much

【独木难支】dúmù-nánzhī〈成〉〈喻〉one person alone cannot save the situation

【独木桥】dúmùqiáo〈名〉**1**〈本〉single-plank foot bridge **2**〈喻〉difficult route

【独木舟】dúmùzhōu〈名〉dugout canoe

【独幕剧】dúmùjù〈名〉one-act play

【独辟蹊径】dúpì-xījìng〈成〉〈喻〉blaze a new trail

【独善其身】dúshàn-qíshēn〈成〉**1**（修身养性）maintain personal integrity **2**（只顾自己）be concerned only for oneself

【独身】dúshēn〈形〉**1**（独自一人）away from one's family: ～一人 be living alone or away from one's family ‖ ～在外 be away from one's home and one's family **2**（未婚）unmarried: 她仍然是～。She's still single.

【独身主义】dúshēnzhǔyì〈名〉celibacy

【独生女】dúshēngnǚ〈名〉only daughter

【独生子】dúshēngzǐ〈名〉only son

【独生子女】dúshēng zǐnǚ〈名〉only child: ～政策 one child policy

【独树一帜】dúshù-yīzhì〈成〉develop one's own unique style

【独特】dútè〈形〉unique: ～的风格 unique style ‖ ～的经历 unique experience

【独体字】dútǐzì〈名〉single-element Chinese character

【独吞】dútūn〈动〉keep sth. all to oneself: ～利润 pocket all the profits ‖ ～遗产 take all the inheritance for oneself

【独往独来】dúwǎng-dúlái〈成〉**1**（指没

同伴）travel back and forth without company **2**（不爱社交）be unsociable
【独舞】dúwǔ〈名〉solo dance
【独弦琴】dúxiánqín ▸**p. 929**〈名〉monochord
【独行】dúxíng **A**〈动〉**1**（独自行走）walk alone **2**（指做事）go one's own way **B**〈名〉〈书〉unique behaviour
【独行其是】dúxíng-qíshì〈成〉do what one thinks is right, without considering others' opinions
【独秀】dúxiù〈形〉〈书〉outstanding: 一枝～ outstanding talent
【独眼龙】dúyǎnlóng〈名〉〈贬〉person blind in one eye
【独一无二】dúyī-wú'èr〈成〉unparalleled: 历史上～的事件 event without parallel in history
【独院】dúyuàn〈名〉one-family courtyard
【独占】dúzhàn〈动〉have sth. all to oneself: ～市场 monopolize the market
【独占鳌头】dúzhàn-áotóu〈成〉〈喻〉come out first
【独资】dúzī〈名〉exclusive investment: ～企业 individual ownership enterprise
【独子】dúzǐ = 独生子 dúshēngzǐ
【独自】dúzì〈副〉by oneself: ～料理 manage everything by oneself ‖ ～生活 live alone
【独奏】dúzòu **A**〈名〉solo **B**〈动〉play a solo: 小提琴～ violin solo

顿（頓）dú ▸冒顿 Mòdú ▸dùn

读（讀）dú〈动〉**1**（念出声）read aloud: 请跟我～。Please read after me. ▸朗～, 宣～ **2**（阅读）read: 这篇文章值得一～。This article is worth reading. ▸～者, 默～ **3**（指上学）study: ～大学 attend university ‖ ～文学专业 study literature ▸工～, 走～ **4**（读音）be pronounced in a certain way: 这个字～去声。This character is pronounced in the fourth tone.
▸dòu
【读本】dúběn〈名〉reader: 法语～ French reader ‖ 经济学～ readings in economics
【读后感】dúhòugǎn〈名〉thoughts on reading something
【读经】dújīng〈动〉**1**（指儒家经典）read Confucian classics **2**［宗教］read scriptures
【读卡机】dúkǎjī〈名〉card reader
【读秒】dúmiǎo〈动〉countdown: 新春倒计时开始～。The countdown to Chinese New Year has started. ‖ 裁判开始～。The referee began the countdown.
【读破】dúpò〈动〉［语言］pronounce a character differently when it has a meaning or function different to its usual one [eg when the character 好 in 喜好 (xǐhào) (like/love) is pronounced as (hào) instead of its usual pronunciation (hǎo)]
【读书】dúshū〈动〉**1**（看书）read: 埋头～ be absorbed in one's book ‖ ～笔记 reading notes **2**（学习）study: 认真～ study in earnest ‖ 他～很用功。He works very hard at his studies. **3**（上学）attend school: 他只读过两年书。He attended school for only two years.
【读书人】dúshūrén〈名〉scholar
【读数】dúshù〈名〉reading: 温度计～ readings on the thermometer
【读物】dúwù〈名〉reading material: 儿童～ reading material for children ‖ 科普～ popular science books ‖ 课外～ collateral readings
【读音】dúyīn〈名〉pronunciation
【读者】dúzhě〈名〉reader: 青少年～ juvenile reader ‖ ～来信 readers' letters

渎¹（瀆）dú〈名〉〈书〉ditch: ▸沟～

渎²（瀆）dú〈动〉〈书〉show contempt: ▸～职, 亵～
【渎职】dúzhí〈动〉neglect one's duty: ～罪 offence of dereliction of duty

椟（櫝）dú〈名〉〈书〉casket: ▸买～还珠

犊（犢）dú〈名〉calf: ▸牛～

牍（牘）dú〈名〉**1**（指木片）wooden tablets for writing **2**（文件）documents: ▸案～, 文～

黩（黷）dú〈动〉〈书〉act rashly
【黩武】dúwǔ〈形〉militaristic: ▸穷兵～

髑 dú
【髑髅】dúlóu〈名〉〈书〉skull of a dead person

dǔ

肚 dǔ〈名〉tripe: 羊～儿 sheep tripe ‖ 拌～丝儿 sliced tripe and cucumber in soy sauce
▸dù
【肚子】dǔzi〈名〉tripe
▸dùzi

笃（篤）dǔ
A〈形〉**1**（忠实）sincere: 爱情甚～ be deeply in love ‖ 友谊甚～ be devoted in friendship ▸～信, ～志 **2**（严重）critical: ▸～病, 危～
B〈副〉〈书〉extremely: ▸～爱
【笃爱】dǔ'ài〈动〉love deeply: ～自己的职业 be devoted to one's job
【笃诚】dǔchéng〈形〉〈书〉sincere and earnest
【笃定】dǔdìng〈方〉**A**〈副〉certainly: ～办好 be sure to succeed **B**〈形〉calm
【笃厚】dǔhòu〈形〉sincere and magnanimous
【笃实】dǔshí〈形〉**1**（忠实）honest and sincere: ～可靠 honest and reliable **2**（实在）solid: 学问～ sound scholarship
【笃守】dǔshǒu〈动〉be faithful to: ～诺言 be faithful to one's promise
【笃信】dǔxìn〈动〉sincerely believe in: ～宗教的人 profoundly religious person
【笃学】dǔxué〈动〉〈书〉study diligently
【笃志】dǔzhì〈动〉〈书〉devote oneself to: ～学习 devote oneself to study

堵 dǔ
A〈动〉block: 把窟窿～上 stop up a hole ‖ 主干道被～了三个小时。The trunk road was jammed tight for three hours.
B〈形〉stifled: 心里～得慌 feel suffocated ▸～心
C〈量〉[of walls]: 一～墙 a wall
【堵车】dǔchē〈动〉be jammed: 高峰时段这里经常～。It's often very congested here during rush hour.
【堵点】dǔdiǎn〈名〉［交通］traffic congestion point
【堵击】dǔjī〈动〉intercept and attack
【堵截】dǔjié〈动〉intercept: ～敌人的援军 intercept the enemy's reinforcements ‖ 警察在火车站～逃犯。The police caught up with the escaped criminal at the railway station.
【堵塞】dǔsè〈动〉block: ～漏洞 plug a hole ‖ 每逢节假日，车辆便～了几乎所有的道路。On holidays, almost all the roads were blocked with heavy traffic. ‖〈喻〉～法律漏洞 plug legal loopholes
【堵心】dǔxīn〈形〉frustrated: 这事真让人～。This is really frustrating.
【堵嘴】dǔzuǐ〈动〉silence sb.: 用贿赂堵住某人的嘴 gag sb. with bribes

赌（賭）dǔ〈动〉**1**（赌博）gamble: 禁～ ban gambling ‖ 嗜～ be fond of gambling ‖ ～到倾家荡产 gamble oneself out of house and home **2**（争输赢）bet: ▸～东道, 打～
【赌本】dǔběn〈名〉**1**（赌资）money to gamble with **2**〈喻〉（资本）resources for risky ventures
【赌博】dǔbó〈动〉gamble: 沉溺于～ indulge in gambling ‖ ～成瘾 be given to gambling ‖ 用扑克/纸牌～ gamble at poker/cards ‖ 我们不能拿千百万人民的生命～。We mustn't gamble with the lives of millions of people.
【赌场】dǔchǎng〈名〉casino: 经营～ run a casino ‖ ～得意，情场失意 lucky at cards, unlucky in love
【赌东道】dǔ dōngdào〈动〉bet on sth. for which the loser has to stand a treat
【赌风】dǔfēng〈名〉penchant for gambling: 刹住～ crack down on gambling ‖ ～盛行。Gambling is widespread.
【赌鬼】dǔguǐ〈名〉inveterate gambler
【赌棍】dǔgùn〈名〉hardened gambler
【赌局】dǔjú〈名〉gambling party: 开～ hold a gambling party
【赌具】dǔjù〈名〉gambling device
【赌窟】dǔkū〈名〉gambling den
【赌马】dǔmǎ〈动〉bet on horses
【赌气】dǔqì〈动〉act rashly out of spite: 他一～辞职不干了。He resigned in a rage.
【赌钱】dǔqián〈动〉gamble
【赌球】dǔqiú〈动〉gamble on ball games
【赌徒】dǔtú〈名〉gambler
【赌债】dǔzhài〈名〉gambling debt: 借钱还～ borrow money to pay off one's gambling debts
【赌咒】dǔzhòu〈动〉take an oath
【赌注】dǔzhù〈名〉wager: 下～ make a bet
【赌资】dǔzī〈名〉money to gamble with

睹 dǔ〈动〉witness: ▸目～, 熟视无～
【睹物伤情】dǔwù-shāngqíng〈成〉feel sad on seeing sth.
【睹物思人】dǔwù-sīrén〈成〉seeing sth. reminds one of sb.

dù

杜¹ dù〈名〉birch-leaf pear

杜² dù〈动〉stop: ▸～绝, 防微～渐
【杜衡】dùhéng〈名〉［植物］wild ginger
【杜蘅】dùhéng = 杜衡 dùhéng

【杜鹃】dùjuān〈名〉**1**［鸟类］cuckoo **2**［植物］azalea
【杜绝】dùjué〈动〉stop: ～弊端 stop all corrupt practices ‖ ～铺张浪费 put an end to extravagance and waste ‖ ～言路 block all channels of criticisms and suggestions ‖ ～走后门 stop 'backdoorism'
【杜康】dùkāng〈名〉〈书〉alcoholic drinks: 何以解忧？惟有～。To allay these worries of mine, there is nothing but wine.
【杜梨】dùlí〈名〉birch-leaf pear
【杜门】dùmén〈动〉〈书〉close the door: ～谢客 close one's door to visitors
【杜松子酒】dùsōngzǐjiǔ〈名〉gin
【杜仲】dùzhòng〈名〉［中药］bark of Eucommia
【杜撰】dùzhuàn〈动〉〈贬〉fabricate: ～编造 draw on one's imagination ‖ 新闻报道应该真实，不能～。News reports should be true, not made up.

d

肚 dù〈名〉belly
▸dǔ
【肚肠】dúcháng〈名〉**1**〈本〉intestines and stomach **2**〈喻〉（心思）heart
【肚带】dùdài〈名〉girth
【肚量】dùliàng〈名〉**1**（度量）magnanimity: 他一点～都没有。He is not remotely generous. **2**（饭量）appetite
【肚皮】dùpí〈名〉〈方〉belly: 笑破～ laugh till one's sides split
【肚皮舞】dùpíwǔ〈名〉belly dance
【肚脐】dùqí〈名〉navel
【肚脐眼儿】dùqíyǎnr〈名〉〈口〉belly button
【肚子】dùzi〈名〉**1**（腹部）belly: 饿～ go hungry **2**（肚状物）sth. like a belly: ▸腿～
▸dǔzi

妒 dù〈动〉envy: 因～生恨。Hatred is bred from envy. ▸～忌，嫉～
【妒火】dùhuǒ〈名〉agony of jealousy: ～中烧 be burning with jealousy
【妒忌】dùjì〈动〉be jealous of: ～他人的成功/成就 envy sb. for his success/achievements ‖ 出于～ out of envy
【妒贤嫉能】dùxián-jínéng〈成〉be jealous of the talented and able

度 dù
A〈名〉**1**（计量长短）linear measure: ▸～量衡 **2**（法则）rules: ▸尺～，制～ **3**（限度）limit: 劳累过～ be overworked ‖ 烟酒无～ smoke and drink without restraint ▸挥霍无～，适～ **4**（考虑）consideration: 把生死置之～外 give no thought to personal safety **5**（程度）extent: ▸长～，透明～，知名～ **6**（容忍度）magnanimity: ▸～量，气～ **7**（风度）manner: ▸风～，态～ **8**（指时间或空间）limited time or space: ▸国～，年～
B〈量〉**1**（指温度、角度）degree: 零下30多～ more than 30 degrees below zero ‖ 45～角 angle of 45 degrees ‖ 北京位于东经116～，北纬40～。Beijing is located at 40° N and 116° E. **2**（指电量）kilowatt-hour: 30～电 30 kilowatts **3**（指程度标识）degree of intensity: 60～的酒 60% proof alcohol ‖ 三～烧伤 third-degree burn **4**（指次数）occasion: 一年一～ once a year ‖ 再～声明 restate
C〈动〉**1**〈书〉（越过）go beyond **2**（度过）spend: ～蜜月 spend the honeymoon ‖ 欢～春节 have a happy Spring Festival ▸～日如年，虚～年华 **3**（指佛教或道教）preach: ▸超～，剃～
▸duó
【度牒】dùdié〈名〉〈古〉government-issued certificates for monks/nuns who have taken the ceremony of ordination
【度过】dùguò〈动〉pass: ～手术这一关 come through an operation ‖ ～晚年 spend one's remaining years
【度假】dùjià〈动〉go on holiday: 在海滨～ holiday at the seaside ‖ ～目的地 vacation destination ‖ ～胜地 holiday resort
【度假村】dùjiàcūn〈名〉holiday village
【度冷丁】dùlěngdīng〈名〉［药学］Dolantin
【度量】dùliàng〈名〉tolerance: ～大 be broad-minded ‖ ～小 be narrow-minded
【度量衡】dùliànghéng〈名〉weights and measures
【度命】dùmìng〈动〉eke out an existence
【度日】dùrì〈动〉eke out an existence: 靠救济～ live off donations
【度日如年】dùrì-rúnián〈成〉one day seems like a year
【度数】dùshu〈名〉degree: ～很深的镜片/眼镜 strong lens/glasses
【度汛】dùxùn〈动〉pass through the flood season

钍（釷）dù〈名〉［化学］dubnium (Db)

渡 dù
A〈动〉**1**（通过）cross (a body of water): ～河 cross a river ‖ 远～重洋 travel across the oceans **2**（度过）pull through: ～过难关 pull through difficult times **3**（载运过河）ferry across: 用船～某人过河 ferry sb. across a river ▸～船
B〈名〉ferry crossing: 古～ ancient ferry crossing
【渡槽】dùcáo〈名〉aqueduct
【渡船】dùchuán〈名〉ferry: 乘～过河 get a ferry across a river
【渡过】dùguò〈动〉tide over: ～困境 weather a crunch ‖ ～危机 pull through a crisis
【渡口】dùkǒu〈名〉ferry crossing
【渡轮】dùlún〈名〉ferry: 乘～ go by ferry
【渡桥】dùqiáo〈名〉makeshift bridge: 架设～ build a temporary bridge
【渡头】dùtóu〈名〉ferry station

镀（鍍）dù〈动〉plate: ▸～金，电～
【镀层】dùcéng〈名〉film
【镀铬】dùgè〈动〉chrome-plate
【镀金】dùjīn〈动〉**1**〈本〉gild: ～首饰 gold-plated jewellery **2**〈喻〉（博取虚名）enhance one's social status through an activity or a course of study: 出国～ study abroad in order to improve one's social status
【镀锡】dùxī〈动〉tin-plate
【镀锌】dùxīn〈动〉galvanize
【镀银】dùyín **A**〈名〉silver-plating **B**〈动〉silver-plate

蠹 dù
A〈名〉moth: 书～ bookworm
B〈动〉be worm-eaten: ▸户枢不～
【蠹弊】dùbì〈书〉= 弊病 bìbìng 1
【蠹虫】dùchóng〈名〉**1**（指虫子）moth **2**〈喻〉（指人）vermin
【蠹害】dùhài〈名〉harm
【蠹鱼】dùyú = 衣鱼 yīyú
【蠹蛀】dùzhù〈动〉be moth-eaten

duān

端¹ duān〈形〉**1**（直）erect: ～坐 sit upright ‖ 字写得～～正正 neat and regular handwriting **2**（正派）proper: ▸品行不～

端² duān〈名〉**1**（一头）end: 笔～ tip of a pen ‖ 两～ two ends ‖ 该市坐落在半岛的西北～。The city lies at the north western tip of the peninsula. ▸顶～，尖～ **2**（开头）beginning: ▸发～，祸～，开～ **3**（起因）cause: ▸借～，无～，争～ **4**（事情）unhappy event: ▸弊～ **5**（方面）point: 举其一～ to mention one example ▸～倪，诡计多～

端³ duān〈动〉**1**（平举）hold sth. level with both hands: ～茶 serve tea ‖ ～一盆水来 bring in a basin of water ‖ 双手～着碗 hold a bowl with both hands **2**（扫除）wipe out: ～掉匪巢 destroy the bandits' lair
【端端正正】duānduān-zhèngzhèng〈形〉straight: 纸上～地写着几个字。Several words were carefully and regularly written on the paper.
【端方】duānfāng〈形〉〈书〉righteous: 他品行～。He is a man of integrity.
【端架子】duān jiàzi〈动〉put on airs
【端节】Duānjié = 端午节 Duānwǔjié
【端口】duānkǒu〈名〉［计算机］port: 视频～ video port
【端丽】duānlì〈形〉〈书〉neat and graceful: 姿容～ comely face ‖ 字体～ neat and beautiful handwriting
【端量】duānliang〈动〉look sb. up and down: 他把来人仔细～了一番。He looked the new arrival up and down.
【端倪】duānní **A**〈名〉inkling: 渐显～ begin to take shape ‖ 初见～ start to have an inkling **B**〈动〉〈书〉predict: 事件的发展无从～。There is no way to predict how this event will unfold.
【端午节】Duānwǔjié〈名〉Dragon Boat Festival

> **端午节**
>
> Dragon Boat Festival, a traditional Chinese festival taking place on the fifth day of the fifth month of the lunar year. Legend has it that on this day the poet of the State of Chu, Qu Yuan (屈原), drowned himself in the river. From this day forth, the festival has commemorated his memory. On this day, people eat glutinous rice dumplings (▸粽子) and hold dragon-boat races.

【端线】duānxiàn〈名〉［体育］（指棒球）end line;（指网球）base line
【端详】duānxiáng **A**〈名〉〈书〉details: 听～ listen to the whole story ‖ 请听我细说～。Please listen to my story in detail. **B**〈动〉scrutinize: 他把我～了半天。He looked at me for a long time. **C**〈形〉dignified and serene: 举止～ dignified and serene bearing
【端绪】duānxù〈名〉〈书〉inkling: 事情毫无～。I haven't got a clue how things will work out.
【端砚】duānyàn〈名〉Duanxi ink stone
【端阳】Duānyáng = 端午节 Duānwǔjié
【端由】duānyóu〈名〉〈书〉reason: 把事情的～说一下。Tell me all about it.

【端正】duānzhèng **A**〈形〉 **1**（不歪斜）straight:（协调匀称） regular: 五官～ have regular features ‖ ～的字体 words written in neat and regular forms **2**（正派） correct: 品行～ conduct properly ‖ 态度～ have the right attitude **B**〈动〉 correct: ～党风 rectify the Party's style of work ‖ ～态度 correct attitude

【端庄】duānzhuāng〈形〉 dignified: 举止～ conduct oneself in a dignified manner ‖ 神情～ with a dignified and graceful expression

【端子】duānzi〈名〉 terminal: 接线～ terminal block

【端坐】duānzuò〈动〉 sit straight

duǎn

短 duǎn

A〈形〉 **1** ▸**p. 82**（指长度） short: ～大衣 short overcoat ‖ ～头发 short hair **2**（指时间） brief: 昼长夜～。 The days are long and the nights are short. ▸～期 **3**（浅薄） shallow: ▸～见, ～浅

B〈动〉 be short of: 别人都来了，就～他一个。 All the others have arrived except him. ‖ 我～你三块钱。 I owe you three *yuan*. ▸理～, 缺斤～两

C〈名〉 shortcoming: ▸护～, 揭～, 取长补～

【短板】duǎnbǎn〈名〉〈喻〉 weakness: 有些地区的文化单位存在"小、散、滥"等～。 Cultural units in some areas are weak in terms of their small size, indiscipline, excesses and so on.

【短兵相接】 duǎnbīng-xiāngjiē 〈成〉 engage in close combat

【短波】duǎnbō〈名〉 short wave: ～收音机 short-wave receiver

【短不了】 duǎnbuliǎo 〈口〉 **A**〈动〉 cannot do without: 动物～空气。 Animals cannot do without air. ‖ 建设国家～人才。 Educated people are indispensable in building our country. **B**〈副〉 inevitably: 双方～要有一番激烈的争论。 There will inevitably be a heated debate between the two parties.

【短长】 duǎncháng 〈名〉 strengths and weaknesses: 议论他人～ gossip about other people

【短程】duǎnchéng〈形〉 short-range: ～弹道导弹 short-range ballistic missiles ‖ ～运输 short distance transportation

【短秤】duǎnchèng〈动〉 give short measure: 卖东西不应该～。 You mustn't sell customers short.

【短绌】duǎnchù〈动〉 fall short

【短处】duǎnchu〈名〉 shortcoming: 每个人都有自己的长处和～。 Everyone has his own strengths and weaknesses.

【短促】duǎncù〈形〉 very brief: 呼吸～ be short of breath ‖ ～的访问 quick visit ‖ 时间～。 Time is pressing.

【短打】duǎndǎ〈名〉 **1**［戏曲］ hand-to-hand fighting wearing jacket and trousers **2** = 短装 duǎnzhuāng

【短道速滑】 duǎndào sùhuá ▸**p. 909**〈名〉［体育］ short-track speed skating

【短笛】duǎndí ▸**p. 929**〈名〉［音乐］ piccolo

【短工】duǎngōng〈名〉 temporary work: 打～ temp ‖ 雇～ hire a temp

【短号】duǎnhào ▸**p. 929** 〈名〉［音乐］ cornet

【短划线】duǎnhuàxiàn〈名〉 en rule

【短见】 duǎnjiàn 〈名〉 **1** （指见识） shallow view **2**（自杀） suicide: 寻～ commit suicide

【短剑】duǎnjiàn〈名〉 dirk

【短斤缺两】duǎnjīn-quēliǎng = 缺斤短两 quējīn-duǎnliǎng

【短剧】duǎnjù〈名〉 short programme: 音乐～ a short musical

【短裤】duǎnkù〈名〉 shorts

【短路】duǎnlù〈动〉［电气］ short-circuit: 电路～了。 There was a short circuit.

【短命】duǎnmìng〈动〉 be short-lived: ～的国会 short-lived parliament

【短跑】duǎnpǎo ▸**p. 909**〈名〉 sprint: ～运动员 sprinter

【短篇小说】duǎnpiān xiǎoshuō〈名〉 short story

【短片】duǎnpiàn〈名〉 short film

【短平快】duǎn-píng-kuài **A**〈名〉［排球］ rapid spike **B**〈形〉 fast and effective: ～产品 instant-effective product

【短评】duǎnpíng〈名〉 brief commentary

【短期】duǎnqī〈名〉 short time: ～计划/目标 short-term plan/goal ‖ ～贷款 short-term loan ‖ 这项巨大工程很难在～内完成。 It's very difficult to complete this huge project in a short space of time.

【短浅】duǎnqiǎn〈形〉 narrow and shallow: 见识～ lack knowledge and experience ‖ 目光～ have short-sighted views

【短欠】duǎnqiàn〈动〉 **1**（亏欠） owe: ～着联合国的会费 be in arrears in membership dues to the United Nations **2**（缺乏） be in need of: 她物质上什么也不～。 She wants for nothing materially.

【短枪】duǎnqiāng〈名〉 handgun

【短球】duǎnqiú〈名〉［体育］[in tennis, etc.] drop shot

【短拳】duǎnquán〈名〉 [a style of Chinese boxing] short jab

【短缺】duǎnquē〈动〉 be short of: 人手～ be short-staffed ‖ 资金～ be short of funds ‖ 师资～ teacher shortage

【短少】 duǎnshǎo 〈动〉 lack: 保存的东西，一件也不～。 None of the things put in safekeeping is missing.

【短视】 duǎnshì 〈形〉 **1**（近视） near-sighted **2**〈喻〉（目光短浅） short-sighted: ～观点 short-sighted view

【短寿】duǎnshòu〈动〉 be short-lived: ～种子 short-lived seed

【短统靴】duǎntǒngxuē〈名〉 ankle boots

【短途】duǎntú〈形〉 short: ～旅行 short trip ‖ ～运输 short haul

【短袜】duǎnwà〈名〉 socks

【短尾猴】 duǎnwěihóu 〈名〉 stump-tailed monkey

【短线】duǎnxiàn 〈形〉 **1**（指产品、专业等） in short supply **2**（短期） short-term: ～投资 short-term investment

【短项】duǎnxiàng〈名〉 weak point

【短小】duǎnxiǎo〈形〉 **1**（指事物） short and small: 篇幅～ be short in length **2**（指身材） short: 身材～ be short

【短小精悍】 duǎnxiǎo-jīnghàn 〈成〉 **1**（指人） not of imposing stature but strong and capable **2**（指文章） short and pithy

【短信】duǎnxìn〈名〉 text message: 一有消息我就发～给你。 I will text you as soon as I get the news.

【短训班】duǎnxùnbān〈名〉 crash course

【短语】duǎnyǔ〈名〉 phrase

【短暂】 duǎnzàn 〈形〉 brief: ～的访问 flying visit ‖ ～的停留 brief stay

【短装】duǎnzhuāng〈名〉 short clothes

duàn

段 duàn

A〈量〉 **1**（指长条东西） [used of a section or segment of sth. that is long]: 两～木头 two logs ‖ 一～铁路 a section of railway **2**（表距离） [used of distance or time]: 一～路 a length of road ‖ 一～时间 a period of time **3**（指事物一部分） [used of writing, speech, etc.]: 一～文章 a paragraph ‖ 一～音乐 a passage of music

B〈名〉 **1**（部分） stage: 路～ section of a road ▸地～, 阶～ **2**（指机构） administrative unit: 机务～ locomotive department ▸工～ **3**（段位） grade: 九～棋手 9th-grade *weiqi* master

【段落】duànluò〈名〉 **1**（指文章） paragraph: 划分～ divide into paragraphs ‖ ～大意 gist of a paragraph **2**（阶段） stage: 告一～ come to an end for the time being

【段位】duànwèi〈名〉［体育］ grade

【段子】duànzi〈名〉［曲艺］ short performance: 评书～ story-telling number ‖ 相声～ cross talk number

断（斷） duàn

A〈动〉 **1**（断裂） break: 棍子～成了两截。 The stick broke in two. ‖ 他的腿～了。 His leg was broken. ▸割～, 柔肠寸～ **2**（断绝） cut off: ～水 cut off the water supply ‖ ～了音讯 break off contact ▸～电, ～交, 间～ **3**（戒掉） give up: ～酒 give up alcohol ‖ ～烟 quit smoking **4**（拦截） intercept: ～球 intercept a pass **5**（判断） judge: ▸～案, 当机立～ **6**（干涸） dry up: ▸～流

B〈副〉〈书〉 [usu found in negative sentences] absolutely: ～不可行 be totally out of the question ‖ ～无此理 be completely unreasonable

【断案】duàn'àn〈动〉 settle a case: 秉公～ settle a lawsuit impartially

【断背】duànbèi ▸**p. 772** 〈名〉〈婉〉 homosexuality

【断壁残垣】duànbì-cányuán = 残垣断壁 cányuán-duànbì

【断编残简】duànbiān-cánjiǎn 〈成〉 stray fragments of text

【断层】duàncéng〈名〉 **1**［地质］ fault: ～带 fault zone ‖ ～移动 fault displacement **2**〈喻〉（中断） break in the continuity of personnel structure: 教师～ shortage of teachers of a certain generation

【断肠】duàncháng〈动〉 be heart-broken: ～人 heartbroken person

【断炊】duànchuī〈动〉 run out of food and fuel

【断代】duàndài〈动〉 **1** = 断后 duànhòu 1 **2**（后继无人） have no successors **3**（划分朝代） divide history into periods

【断代史】duàndàishǐ〈名〉 dynastic history

【断档】duàndàng〈动〉 be out of stock: 汽油～了。 We're out of petrol.

【断电】duàndiàn〈动〉 cut off electricity

【断定】duàndìng〈动〉 decide: ～人质已被杀死 conclude that the hostage has been killed ‖ 无法～嫌疑人是否有罪 be unable to decide whether the suspect is guilty or not

【断断】duànduàn〈副〉 [usu used in the negative] absolutely: ～使不得 will never do ‖ 我们～不能走回头路。 We must never go back to the old ways.

【断断续续】 duànduàn-xùxù 〈成〉 intermittent: ～地下雨 rain on and off ‖ 远处

d

传来～的歌声。 Intermittent singing could be heard from afar.

【断顿】duàndùn〈动〉 run out of food

【断根】duàngēn〈动〉 1 = 断后 duànhòu 1 2（彻底去除） eradicate: 恶习难以～。 Bad habits are hard to get rid of.

【断供】duàngōng〈动〉 1（指供应） have a supply failure: 加油站曾一度～。 There was a supply failure at the petrol station for a while. 2（指按揭） halt mortgage payments

【断后】duànhòu〈动〉 1（无后代） have no heirs 2（在后掩护） shield a retreat

【断乎】duànhū〈副〉〈书〉 [usu used in the negative] absolutely: ～不可加入 absolutely cannot join

【断魂】duànhún〈动〉 be overwhelmed with sorrow

【断简残编】duànjiǎn-cánbiān = 断编残简 duànbiān-cánjiǎn

d

【断交】duànjiāo〈动〉 break off relations: 与朋友～ sever ties with a friend ‖ 两国因边界冲突而～。The two countries broke off diplomatic relations after a border conflict.

【断井颓垣】duànjǐng-tuíyuán〈成〉scene of devastation

【断句】duànjù〈动〉 punctuate: 给古文～ punctuate an ancient text

【断绝】duànjué〈动〉 cut off: ～邦交/外交关系 cut off diplomatic relations ‖ ～联系 sever ties

【断粮】duànliáng〈动〉 run out of food

【断裂】duànliè〈动〉 fracture

【断流】duànliú〈动〉 dry up: 这条河旱季经常～。 The river often dries up in the dry season.

【断路】duànlù〈名〉［电气］broken circuit: ～继电器 shut-down relay

【断面】duànmiàn〈名〉［测绘］section: 横～ cross section

【断奶】duànnǎi〈动〉wean: 给孩子～ wean a baby ‖ 婴儿六个月时就断了奶。 The baby was weaned at six months.

【断念】duànniàn〈动〉 abandon an idea

【断片】duànpiàn〈名〉 part

【断七】duànqī〈名〉 seventh period of seven days after a person's death

【断气】duànqì〈动〉 breathe one's last: 老人快～了。 The old man was close to his last.

【断球】duànqiú〈动〉 intercept the ball

【断然】duànrán A〈形〉 drastic: 采取～措施 adopt drastic measures ‖ ～处置 deal with sth. resolutely ‖ ～否认 vehemently deny B〈副〉 absolutely: 二者～不同。 The two are completely different. ‖ 此事～不可。 You absolutely cannot do that.

【断水】duànshuǐ〈动〉 1（停水） cut off water supply 2（断流） dry up: 小河～了。The stream has dried up.

【断送】duànsòng〈动〉 ruin: ～前程 wreck one's career ‖ 吸毒～了他年轻的生命。 Drugs claimed his life at a young age.

【断头台】duàntóutái〈名〉 guillotine: 把某人送上～ send sb. to the guillotine

【断弦】duànxián〈动〉〈书〉 lose one's wife: ～之痛 grief over the death of one's wife ‖ ～再续 marry again after the death of one's wife

【断线风筝】duànxiàn fēngzheng〈成〉〈喻〉 person or thing that is gone beyond recall

【断想】duànxiǎng〈名〉 [often in titles of articles] brief comments: 观剧～ some thoughts after watching a play

【断言】duànyán A〈动〉 assert categorically: 可以～，公司的前途是十分光明的。 It can be safely said that the corporation has a very bright future. ‖ 我敢～，他不会来开会了。 I dare say he won't come to the meeting. B〈名〉 assertion: 不可妄加～ cannot be said lightly

【断语】duànyǔ〈名〉 verdict: 妄下～ jump to a rash conclusion

【断狱】duànyù〈动〉〈书〉 hear the facts and decide on a verdict: ～不公 pass unjust judgement

【断垣残壁】duànyuán-cánbì = 残垣断壁 cányuán-duànbì

【断章取义】duànzhāng-qǔyì〈成〉 quote out of context: 不要～。 Don't quote out of context.

【断种】duànzhǒng〈动〉 have no heir

【断子绝孙】duànzǐ-juésūn〈成〉〈粗〉 die without heir

【断奏】duànzòu〈名〉［音乐］ staccato

缎（緞） duàn〈名〉 satin: ▸绸～，花～

【缎带】duàndài〈名〉 satin ribbon

【缎子】duànzi〈名〉 satin: ～被面 satin quilt cover

椴 duàn〈名〉［植物］ Chinese linden

煅 duàn〈动〉 1（指中药制法） calcine 2 = 锻 duàn

【煅烧】duànshāo〈动〉 calcine

锻（鍛） duàn〈动〉 hammer: ▸～工

【锻锤】duànchuí〈名〉 forge hammer

【锻工】duàngōng〈名〉 1（指工种） forging 2（指工人） blacksmith

【锻件】duànjiàn〈名〉 forging

【锻炼】duànliàn〈动〉 1（锻造冶炼） forge and smelt 2（指强身健体） take exercise: 缺乏～ lack exercise ‖ ～身体 take some exercise 3（磨砺） toughen: ～意志 temper one's will power ‖ 他在战争的熔炉中～过。 He had been steeled in the furnace of war.

【锻铁】duàntiě〈名〉 wrought iron

【锻压】duànyā〈动〉 forge and press

【锻冶】duànyě〈动〉 forge and smelt

【锻造】duànzào〈动〉 forge

duī

堆 duī

A〈名〉 1（土墩） mound: 马王～ Mawangdui [archaeological site located in Changsha, Huan Province] ‖ 双～集 Shuangduiji [major campaign fought between the nationalists and the communists during the Chinese Civil War after World War II] 2（堆积物） pile: 草～ hay stack ‖ 沙～ pile of sand ▸垃圾～, 原子核反应～
B〈动〉 pile: ～干草 stack hay ‖ ～雪人 build a snowman ‖ 仓里～满了粮食。 The barn was heaped with grain.
C〈量〉 pile: 一～人 a bunch of people ‖ 一～生锈的机器 a heap of rusty machinery ‖ 一～石头 a pile of stones

【堆存】duīcún〈动〉 store up

【堆叠】duīdié〈动〉 pile up: 把椅子～起来 stack the chairs ‖ 桌子上～着许多书。 The desk is piled high with books.

【堆放】duīfàng〈动〉 pile up: 不要随处～垃圾。 Do not heap rubbish everywhere. ‖ 桌上～着碗碟。 The table was stacked with plates and bowls.

【堆肥】duīféi〈名〉［农业］ compost

【堆积】duījī〈动〉 amass: ～如山 be piled mountain-high ‖ 把落叶～起来 heap up fallen leaves

【堆集】duījí〈动〉 pile up: 桌上～着许多本字典。 Many dictionaries are piled on the table.

【堆砌】duīqì〈动〉 1〈本〉 pile up sth. to build sth.: ～围墙 build brick or rock fences 2〈喻〉（罗列） fill one's writing with florid and fancy phrases: ～词藻 string together ornate phrases

【堆笑】duīxiào〈动〉 wear a smile: 满脸～ be all smiles

【堆绣】duīxiù〈名〉 appliqué embroidery

【堆栈】duīzhàn〈名〉 storehouse

duì

队（隊） duì

A〈名〉 1（行列） queue〈英〉; line〈美〉: 列～ form a queue ‖ 排～ queue up ▸横～，纵～ 2（指集体） team: ▸～友, 球～, 游击～ 3（少先队） Young Pioneers: ▸～礼，～日
B〈量〉 line: 一～保镖 a row of bodyguards ‖ 一～小学生 a line of pupils

【队部】duìbù〈名〉 headquarters office

【队礼】duìlǐ〈名〉 salute of the Chinese Young Pioneers

【队列】duìliè〈名〉 1（行列） queue〈英〉; line〈美〉 2（队伍） formation: ～整齐 be in neat formation ‖ ～训练 formation drill

【队旗】duìqí〈名〉 team flag: 互换～ exchange team banners ‖ 少先队～ flag of the Young Pioneers

【队日】duìrì〈名〉 day for Young Pioneer activity

【队伍】duìwu〈名〉 1（指军队） troops: 从～上转业 be discharged from the army and assigned a civilian job 2（指集体） ranks: 参加革命～ join the revolutionary ranks ‖ 师资～ teaching staff ‖ 游行～ procession

【队形】duìxíng〈名〉 formation: 保持～ preserve the formation ‖ 飞行～ flying formation ‖ ～变换 change of formation

【队友】duìyǒu〈名〉 teammate

【队员】duìyuán〈名〉 team member: 防守～ defensive player ‖ 主力～ key player

【队长】duìzhǎng〈名〉 1［体育］ captain: 女排～ captain of a women's volleyball team 2（负责人） team leader: 工作队～ leader of a work team

对（對） duì

A〈动〉 1〈书〉（切合） fit: ▸文不～题 2（回答） reply: ▸～白，～答，应～ 3（对付） take on: 一～一 on a one-to-one basis ‖ 第二轮中甲队～乙队。 Team A faces team B in the second round. 4（朝向） face: 窗户～着大街。 The window faces the street. ‖ 这些话是针～我的。 These words are directed at me. 5（核对） bring two things into contact: ～暗号 check the password 6（符合） suit: ～胃口 agree with sb. 7（比较） check: ～笔迹 identify the handwriting ‖ ～答案 check the answers 8（调整） adjust: ～表 set watches ‖ ～焦距 adjust the focus 9（掺和） mix: 稀饭里～点儿水 add some water to the porridge 10（平分成两份） halve: ▸～半

B〈形〉**1**（对面）opposite: ▸～面 **2**（正确）correct: 这是你的吗？——～。Is this yours? — Yes. ‖ 你这种态度是不～的。Yours is not the proper attitude.
C〈名〉couplet: 喜～ wedding couplet ▸～联, ～子
D〈量〉couple: 一～新人 a newly married couple ‖ 一～选手 a couple of players
E〈介〉to: ～我有用 be useful to me ‖ ～华政策 policy towards China

【对岸】duì'àn〈名〉opposite bank: 游到河～ swim to the other side of the river

【对案】duì'àn〈名〉counter proposal

【对白】duìbái〈名〉dialogue: 电影～ film dialogue

【对半】duìbàn〈动〉go halves: ～分 go halves

【对比】duìbǐ **A**〈动〉contrast: ～今昔 contrast the present with the past **B**〈名〉ratio: 双方力量的～ balance of forces between the two sides ‖ 鲜明的～ sharp contrast ‖ 我们班男女生人数～是一比三。The ratio of boys to girls in our class is one to three.

【对比度】duìbǐdù〈名〉contrast: ～失真 contrast distortion

【对比色】duìbǐsè〈名〉contrast colour

【对簿公堂】duìbùgōngtáng〈成〉go to court: 他俩要～。They will see each other in court.

【对不起】duìbuqǐ〈动〉**1** ▸**p. 156**〈套〉（表歉意）sorry: ～，我把咖啡洒在你的桌布上了。Sorry, I've spilt coffee on your tablecloth. **2**（辜负）let sb. down: 你这样做是～他的。Doing that is unfair to him. ‖ 努力学习，不要～父母。Study hard; don't let your parents down.

【对不住】duìbuzhù = 对不起 duìbuqǐ 2

【对策】duìcè〈名〉countermeasure: 上有政策，下有～。The government has its policies and the people have their ways of getting around them.

【对茬儿】duìchár〈动〉〈方〉tally: 她说的总数跟记录上的数字对不上茬儿。The amount she mentioned did not tally with the figure shown in the records.

【对唱】duìchàng〈名〉operatic dialogue sung in antiphonal style

【对称】duìchèn〈形〉symmetric: ～美 symmetrical beauty

【对冲】duìchōng〈名〉［金融］hedging: ～基金 hedge fund

【对词】duìcí〈动〉practise lines together

【对答】duìdá〈动〉answer: 我不知如何～。I don't know how to respond.

【对答如流】duìdá-rúliú〈成〉answer fluently

【对打】duìdǎ〈动〉**1**（交手开打）come to blows **2**［武术］［戏曲］duel

【对待】duìdài〈动〉treat: 认真～ treat seriously ‖ 正确～群众的批评 adopt a correct attitude towards the criticism of the masses ‖ 别再把我当孩子～了。Don't treat me like a child any more.

【对得起】duìdeqǐ〈动〉be worthy of: 你这样做～你的妻子吗？Are these actions of yours worthy of your wife?

【对得住】duìdezhù = 对得起 duìdeqǐ

【对等】duìděng〈形〉reciprocal

【对调】duìdiào〈动〉swap: ～工作 exchange jobs ‖ 我们能～一下座位吗？Can we swap seats?

【对方】duìfāng〈名〉other party: 尊重～ respect the other party ‖ ～付费电话 reverse charge call〈英〉; collect call〈美〉

【对方场地】duìfāng chǎngdì〈名〉［体育］opponents' court

【对方队员】duìfāng duìyuán〈名〉［体育］opposing players

【对付】duìfu〈动〉**1**（处理）deal with: ～复杂局势 deal with a complicated situation ‖ 你走吧，我能～。You can leave now. I can manage. ‖ 他这个人难～。He is hard to deal with. **2**（凑合）make do: 经济困难，只好～着过。In difficult times you just have to make do.

【对歌】duìgē〈动〉sing in antiphonal style

【对光】duìguāng〈动〉**1**［摄影］focus a camera **2**（调节光线）adjust the power of microscope, spectacles, etc.

【对过】duìguò〈名〉opposite side: 街～ the opposite side of the street ‖ 商店就在～。The shop is across the road.

【对号】duìhào〈动〉**1**（查对号码）check the number: ▸～入座 **2**（相符合）match: 考生和相片对不上号。The examinee doesn't match the photo. ‖ 你的账和我的对不上号。Your account did not tally with mine.

【对号入座】duìhào-rùzuò〈成〉**1**〈本〉seat oneself according to one's ticket number **2**〈喻〉match: 本剧纯属虚构，请勿～。It's purely fictional. Please don't apply it to your own life.

【对话】duìhuà **A**〈名〉dialogue: 劳资～ dialogue between labour and management ‖ 政治～ political dialogue ‖ ～比对抗好。Dialogue is better than confrontation. ▸人机～ **B**〈动〉hold a dialogue: 双方应尽早开始～。The two sides should start a dialogue as soon as possible.

【对话框】duìhuàkuàng〈名〉［计算机］dialogue box: 关闭～ close the dialogue box

【对换】duìhuàn〈动〉exchange: ～工作/位置 swap jobs/places ‖ 我愿意用这张激光唱片～你的影视光盘。I will swap my CD for your video disc.

【对火】duìhuǒ〈动〉use another person's lighted cigarette to light one's own

【对家】duìjiā〈名〉**1**（指打牌）opposite party **2**（指说亲）other party

【对讲机】duìjiǎngjī〈名〉intercom

【对奖】duìjiǎng〈动〉check to see if one has the winning ticket

【对焦】duìjiāo〈动〉bring into focus

【对角】duìjiǎo〈名〉opposite angles

【对角线】duìjiǎoxiàn〈名〉［数学］diagonal

【对接】duìjiē〈动〉［航天］dock: 两艘宇宙飞船～成功。The two spaceships successfully docked.

【对接会】duìjiēhuì〈名〉matchmaking symposium: 举办银行和企业～ hold a matchmaking symposium for banks and enterprises

【对襟】duìjīn〈名〉Chinese-style jacket with a buttoned opening straight down the front: ～毛衣 Chinese-style cardigan

【对劲儿】duìjìnr〈形〉〈口〉**1**（合适）right: 我今天有点不～。I feel a bit strange today. ‖ 这只鞋穿上不～。This shoe doesn't fit well. **2**（相投）compatible: 我俩一向很～。We've always got along well.

【对局】duìjú〈动〉play a game: 甲队和乙队将在第二轮比赛中～。Team A and Team B will play each other in the second round.

【对局室】duìjúshì〈名〉indoor venue for 'go' tournaments

【对决】duìjué〈动〉fight to the finish

【对开】duìkāi **A**〈动〉**1**（指交通工具）run from opposite directions **2**（对半分配）halve: ～利润 halve the profits **B**〈名〉［印刷］folio: ～本 folio volume

【对抗】duìkàng〈动〉**1**（相持不下）oppose: ～上司 oppose one's boss **2**（抵抗）confront: ～情绪 hostile feeling ‖ 军事～ military confrontation

【对抗赛】duìkàngsài〈名〉［体育］dual meet

【对抗性矛盾】duìkàngxìng máodùn〈名〉antagonistic contradiction

【对口】duìkǒu〈形〉**1**（指演员）alternate **2**（指内容和性质）suitable: 专业～ job suited to one's training **3**（指口味）be to one's taste

【对口疮】duìkǒuchuāng〈名〉［医学］boil on the nape of the neck

【对口词】duìkǒucí〈名〉rhymed dialogue

【对口会谈】duìkǒu huìtán〈名〉counterpart talks

【对口快板儿】duìkǒu kuàibǎnr〈名〉rhymed dialogue between two performers using clappers

【对口相声】duìkǒu xiàngsheng〈名〉cross-talk

【对口型】duìkǒuxíng〈动〉lip-sync

【对口援助】duìkǒu yuánzhù〈名〉unit-to-unit aid program

【对垒】duìlěi〈动〉be pitted against each other: 甲队将和乙队～。Team A will play Team B.

【对立】duìlì〈动〉be in opposition to: ～情绪 antagonistic sentiments ‖ ～双方 opposing sides ‖ 善与恶相～。Good is in opposition to evil.

【对立面】duìlìmiàn〈名〉antithesis: 骄傲是谦虚的～。Conceit is the antithesis of modesty.

> **对联**
>
> An antithetical couplet pasted or hung on doors, pillars or walls. The couplet is written vertically, and conventions are observed regarding the number of characters it contains, as well as the tonal pattern used. Couplets, known as *chunlian* (春联), are most commonly seen at Spring Festival. Elegiac couplets mourn the dead. Couplets can also be found at famous beauty spots.

【对立统一】duìlì tǒngyī〈名〉［哲学］unity of opposites: ～规律 law of unity of opposites

【对联】duìlián〈名〉antithetical couplet

【对流】duìliú〈动〉［物理］convect

【对流层】duìliúcéng〈名〉［气象］troposphere

【对路】duìlù〈形〉〈口〉**1**（合乎需求）appropriate: ～产品 products in great demand **2**（称心合意）agreeable: 他觉得新找的工作很～。He was pretty happy with the new job.

【对门】duìmén **A**〈动〉[of two houses] face each other: 她家和我家～。Her flat and mine are facing each other. **B**〈名〉building opposite: ～那家养了一只狗。The house opposite ours has a dog.

【对面】duìmiàn **A**〈名〉**1** = 对过 duìguò **2**（正前方）front: ～来了一辆公交车。There is a bus coming from the opposite direction. **B**〈形〉face-to-face: ～谈 talk face-to-face

【对内】duìnèi〈形〉internal

【对牛弹琴】duìniú-tánqín〈成〉cast pearls before swine: 跟他谈茶道等于～。Talking to him about tea culture is like casting pearls before swine.

【对偶】duì'ǒu〈名〉［语言］antithesis

【对生】duìshēng〈形〉［植物］opposite: ～叶 opposite leaf

【对手】duìshǒu〈名〉**1**（指比赛）opponent: 战胜～ defeat one's rival ‖ 击倒～

knock down one's opponent ‖ 竞争～ competitor **2**（指技能） equal: 他根本不是我的～。He is no match for me. ▸棋逢～
【对手戏】duìshǒuxì〈名〉 two-hander
【对数】duìshù〈名〉［数学］ logarithmic: ～表 logarithmic table
【对台戏】duìtáixì〈名〉 rival show: ▸唱～
【对头】duìtóu〈形〉〈口〉 **1**（正确） correct: 思想～，工作就能做好。 If our thinking is on the right track, we can make a success of what we are doing. **2**（正常） right: 你的脸色不大～，是不是病了？ You're not looking very well. Are you ill? **3**（合得来） compatible: 两个人过去有点不～，现在和好了。 They didn't get along very well in the past, but they have made it up.
【对头】duìtou〈名〉 **1**（仇人） enemy: ▸死～ **2**（竞争对手） rival
【对外】duìwài〈形〉 external: ～保密 keep sth. secret from outsiders ‖ ～关系 foreign relations
【对外开放】duìwài kāifàng〈动〉 open up to the outside world: 必须实行～。 We must pursue the policy of opening up to the outside world.
【对外贸易】duìwài màoyì〈名〉 foreign trade: ～部 ministry of foreign trade ‖ ～顺差 foreign trade surplus ‖ ～政策 foreign trade policy
【对味儿】duìwèir〈形〉〈口〉 **1**（指口味） to one's taste: 这鱼很对我的味儿。 This fish course is very much to my taste. **2**（指想法）[usu used in the negative] all right: 我觉得他刚才说的话不大～。What he said just now didn't sound quite right to me.
【对虾】duìxiā〈名〉 prawn
【对象】duìxiàng〈名〉 **1**（指目标） object: 崇拜的～ object of worship ‖ 调查的～ target of an investigation ‖ 这本书的～是儿童。 The book is aimed at children. **2**（指人）（男） boyfriend;（女） girlfriend: 介绍～ introduce a boy/girlfriend to sb. ‖ 找～ look for a boy/girlfriend ‖ 他已经有～了。 He has a girlfriend already.
【对象国】duìxiàngguó〈名〉 target country
【对消】duìxiāo〈动〉 balance out: 这样收益和损失就～了。 In this way the gains would cancel out the losses.
【对销贸易】duìxiāo màoyì〈名〉 counter trade
【对眼】duìyǎn **A**〈名〉 eye with a squint **B**〈形〉 satisfactory: 这些衣服看着都不～。 None of these clothes look good to me.
【对弈】duìyì〈动〉〈书〉 play chess
【对应】duìyìng **A**〈动〉 match: ～措施 reciprocal measure ‖ ～关系 corresponding relationship ‖ 汉语里的"桌子"和英语里的"table"～吗？ Does the Chinese word '桌子' correspond to the English word 'table'? **B**〈形〉 corresponding: ～方式 corresponding measures
【对应词】duìyìngcí〈名〉［语言］ equivalent
【对于】duìyú〈介〉 with regard to: ～我来说，这是个沉重的打击。 This is a heavy blow to me. ‖ ～自己的个人生活，他只字不提。 He refrained from saying anything about his private life.
【对仗】duìzhàng〈名〉 verbal parallelism
【对照】duìzhào〈动〉 **1**（参照） check sth. against sth. else: ～原文检查译文 check the translation against the original ‖ 英汉～读本 English-Chinese bilingual textbook **2**（对比） compare: 形成鲜明的～ bring out a striking contrast
【对折】duìzhé〈名〉 50% discount: ～出售 sell at a 50% discount
【对着干】duìzhegàn〈动〉〈口〉 **1**（指对立） work in opposition to: 他老和我～。 He always acts in opposition to me. **2**（指竞赛） compete with sb. in doing sth.: 咱俩～，看谁打字快。 Let's have a competition to see who types faster.
【对阵】duìzhèn〈动〉 **1**（指军队） be poised for combat: 两军～。 The two armies are pitted against each other on the battlefield. **2**（指运动队） play against: 甲队和乙队～。 Team A is playing Team B.
【对证】duìzhèng〈动〉 verify: ～笔迹 identify the handwriting ‖ ～事实 verify facts ▸死无～
【对症下药】duìzhèng-xiàyào〈成〉 **1**〈本〉 prescribe the right medicine for an illness **2**〈喻〉（采取措施） take the correct actions to solve a problem
【对质】duìzhì〈动〉 establish the truth: 让犯人与原告～ confront a prisoner with his accusers
【对峙】duìzhì〈动〉 **1**（相对耸立） face each other: 两山隔江～。 The two mountains face each other across the river. **2**（对抗） engage in a stand-off: 两军～。 The two armies are locked in confrontation.
【对撞机】duìzhuàngjī〈名〉［物理］ collider
【对准】duìzhǔn〈动〉 aim at: ～靶子 aim at the target ‖ 将大炮～敌舰 train a gun on an enemy warship
【对酌】duìzhuó〈动〉〈书〉 drink together
【对子】duìzi〈名〉 **1**（指语句） pair of antithetical phrases: 对～ supply an antithetical phrase to a given phrase **2**（指对联） antithetical couplet **3**（指人） pair: 结成互帮互学的～ form a pair that can learn from each other and help each other

兑[1] duì
〈名〉 one of the Eight Trigrams, symbolizing 'lake'

兑[2] duì
〈动〉 **1**（交换） exchange: ～成现金 convert to cash and pay ▸～换 **2**（取现） cash: ▸～付, 汇～ **3**（掺和） add to: 往酒中～水 water down the wine ‖ 奶里～了水。 The milk has been watered down.
【兑付】duìfù〈动〉 cash and pay (check, money order, etc.)
【兑换】duìhuàn〈动〉 convert: 把美元～成人民币 convert US dollars into *Renminbi*
【兑奖】duìjiǎng〈动〉 cash in a lottery ticket
【兑现】duìxiàn〈动〉 **1**（换取现金） cash: ～支票 cash a cheque ‖ 支票尚未～。 The cheque hasn't cleared yet. **2**〈喻〉（实现承诺） make good: ～承诺 honour one's pledge

敦 duì
〈名〉〈古〉 grain container ▸dūn

碓 duì
〈名〉 husking device
【碓臼】duìjiù〈名〉 mortar

dūn

吨（噸） dūn
▸p. 978 〈量〉 **1**（公制单位） metric ton (= 1,000 kilograms) **2**（英制单位） ton **3**（指登记吨） registered ton
【吨公里】dūn-gōnglǐ〈量〉 tonne kilometre (tkm)
【吨海里】dūn-hǎilǐ〈量〉 nautical mile
【吨位】dūnwèi〈名〉 tonnage
【吨英里】dūn-yīnglǐ〈量〉 ton mile

惇 dūn
〈形〉〈书〉 sincere

敦 dūn
〈形〉 sincere: ▸～促, ～聘 ▸duì
【敦促】dūncù〈动〉 urge: ～双方保持冷静 urge the two sides to remain calm ‖ ～做出解释 press for an explanation
【敦厚】dūnhòu〈形〉 honest and sincere: ～朴实 be simple and sincere ‖ 温柔～ be gentle and honest
【敦煌】Dūnhuáng〈名〉 Dunhuang: ～壁画 Dunhuang murals ‖ ～石窟 Dunhuang Grottoes

> **敦煌石窟**
>
> Buddhist grottoes in the Dunhuang region of Gansu Province, and, more specifically, the Mogao Grottoes, located on Mingsha Mountain to the south-east of the city of Dunhuang, a strategic point along the ancient Silk Road (▸丝绸之路). Dating from 366, today's Mogao grottoes include 492 caves, containing over 3,000 painted statues and murals. The grottoes cover an area of 450 sq m. The murals depict images of Buddha, stories from Buddhist scriptures, and Buddhist historical events and myths. In 1900, a sealed cave was opened up, and it was found to contain a vast number of scriptures, secular texts, and other historical objects.

【敦睦】dūnmù〈动〉〈书〉 promote friendly relations: ～邦交 promote friendly ties between two countries
【敦聘】dūnpìn〈动〉〈书〉 cordially invite sb. to take up a post
【敦请】dūnqǐng〈动〉 cordially invite sb.
【敦劝】dūnquàn〈动〉 plead with
【敦实】dūnshi〈形〉 stocky: ～的小伙子 stocky young man

墩 dūn
A〈名〉 **1**（土堆） mound: 土～ mound **2**（指石头） block of stone;（指木头） block of wood: 石～ stone block used as a seat ▸树～ **3**（指坐具） stool in the shape of a block
B〈动〉 mop
C〈量〉 clump: 一～草 a clump of grass
【墩布】dūnbù〈名〉 mop
【墩子】dūnzi〈名〉 block: 菜～ chopping board ‖ 草～ stool made of tightly wound ropes of straw

撴 dūn
〈动〉〈方〉 seize: 死死～住他的手 seize his hand and hold it tight

骟（驐） dūn
〈动〉〈方〉 castrate: ～鸡/牛 castrate a rooster/bull

礅 dūn
〈名〉 big and heavy stone: 石～ stone block

镦（鐓） dūn
〈动〉 **1**（使变粗短） upset: 冷/热～ upset by the cold/heat **2** = 骟 dūn

蹾 dūn
〈动〉〈方〉 put down with great force: 玻璃杯易碎，请别用力～。 The glasses are fragile. Please handle them with care.

蹲 dūn
〈动〉 **1**（指姿势） squat: ～在墙边晒太阳 squat next to the wall to take in some sun ‖ 他让孩子们在他四周～个

半圆形。 He told the children to squat in a semicircle around him. **2**（停留） linger: 不要老～在家里。 Don't just lie around at home.
▸cún

【蹲班】dūnbān〈动〉 repeat a year
【蹲班房】dūn bānfáng〈动〉〈口〉 serve time in jail
【蹲膘】dūnbiāo〈动〉 **1**（指家畜） fatten in the shed: 大豆是给猪～的好饲料。 Soya is excellent for fattening pigs. **2**（指人） remain idle and grow fat
【蹲点】dūndiǎn〈动〉 work and gain experience in a grass-roots unit for a period of time: 去农村～ go to work with a chosen grass-roots unit in the countryside to gain first-hand experience
【蹲坑】dūnkēng〈动〉 squat over a pit to relieve oneself
【蹲苗】dūnmiáo〈动〉［农业］ restrain the growth of seedlings in order to encourage root growth
【蹲守】dūnshǒu〈动〉 be undercover

dǔn

盹 dǔn〈名〉 nap: ▸打～儿

趸（躉） dǔn
A〈形〉 wholesale
B〈动〉 buy wholesale: ～苹果 buy apples wholesale ‖ 现～现卖 buy wholesale and sell immediately
【趸船】dǔnchuán〈名〉 pontoon
【趸买】dǔnmǎi〈动〉 buy wholesale
【趸卖】dǔnmài〈动〉 sell wholesale
【趸批】dǔnpī〈名〉 wholesale

dùn

囤 dùn〈名〉 bin: 粮食～ bin for storing grain
▸tún

沌 dùn ▸混沌 hùndùn

炖（燉） dùn〈动〉 **1**（用小火煮） stew: ～牛肉 stewed beef **2**（使变热） warm sth. in a container of boiling water: ～酒 warm up wine ‖ ～药 simmer herbal medicine

砘 dùn〈动〉 roll field with a stone roller after sowing
【砘子】dùnzi〈名〉 roller

盾[1] dùn〈名〉 **1**（指兵器） shield: ▸～牌 **2**（盾状物） shield-shaped object: ～状火山 shield volcano ‖ 金～ gold shield

盾[2] dùn ▸**p. 328**〈名〉（荷兰盾） guilder;（越南盾） dong;（印尼盾） rupiah
【盾构】dùngòu〈名〉 scutal suture
【盾构机】dùngòujī〈名〉［机械］ tunnel-boring machine
【盾牌】dùnpái〈名〉 **1**（指兵器） shield **2**〈喻〉（借口） excuse

钝（鈍） dùn〈形〉 **1**（不锋利） blunt: ～刀 blunt knife **2**（笨） stupid: ▸迟～
【钝角】dùnjiǎo〈名〉［数学］ obtuse angle: ～三角形 obtuse triangle
【钝器】dùnqì〈名〉 blunt instrument
【钝滞】dùnzhì〈形〉 blunt: 目光～ glassy eyes

顿（頓） dùn
A〈动〉 **1**（以头触地） kowtow: ▸～首 **2**（跺地） stamp: ▸捶胸～足 **3**（稍停） pause: 他～了一下又接着说下去。 He continued after a pause. ▸～号 **4**（处理） put in order: ▸安～, 整～ **5**（指书写法） pause with force and let the brush mark become thicker at the beginning or end of a stroke
B〈量〉 time: 吃了上～没下～ not know where the next meal is coming from ‖ 大骂/痛打一～ give sb. a good dressing-down/beating
C〈副〉〈书〉 suddenly: ～感羞愧 feel ashamed of oneself all of a sudden ‖ 他～生邪念。 An evil thought suddenly sprung into his mind.
D〈形〉 tired: ▸困～, 劳～
▸dú
【顿挫】dùncuò〈动〉 [in rhythm, intonation, musical notes, etc.] pause and turn
【顿号】dùnhào〈名〉 slight pause mark (、)
【顿开茅塞】dùnkāi-máosè = 茅塞顿开 máosè-dùnkāi
【顿然】dùnrán〈副〉〈书〉 suddenly: ～领悟 suddenly realize
【顿时】dùnshí〈副〉 suddenly: 她～大哭起来。 She suddenly burst out crying.
【顿首】dùnshǒu〈动〉〈书〉 kowtow [used at the end of a letter]
【顿悟】dùnwù〈动〉 come to a sudden realization
【顿足捶胸】dùnzú-chuíxiōng = 捶胸顿足 chuíxiōng-dùnzú

遁 dùn〈动〉 **1**（逃走） escape: ▸～逃 **2**（隐藏） hide: ▸～迹
【遁词】dùncí〈名〉 pretext
【遁辞】dùncí = 遁词 dùncí
【遁迹】dùnjì〈动〉〈书〉 live in seclusion: ～深山 live reclusively in remote mountains
【遁入空门】dùnrù kōngmén〈成〉 become a monk/nun
【遁世】dùnshì〈动〉〈书〉 live in seclusion
【遁逃】dùntáo〈动〉 escape: 仓惶～ flee in panic

楯 dùn〈书〉= 盾[1] dùn
▸shǔn

duō

多[1] duō
A〈形〉 **1**（数量大） many: 朋友～ have many friends ‖ 钱～ have a lot of money ‖ ～吃蔬菜少吃肉 eat more vegetables and less meat ‖ 今年雨水很～。 There is plenty of rain this year. ▸～才～艺, ～云 **2**（过分） excessive: ▸～疑, ～余 **3**（相差大） much more: 我感觉好～了。 I feel much better now. ‖ 她比她弟弟勤快～了。 She is far more industrious than her brother.
B〈动〉 be greater in quantity than intended: ～呆些时间 lengthen one's stay ‖ ～收五块钱 overcharge by five *yuan*
C ▸**p. 927**〈数〉 [used after numerals] odd: 二百～页 200-odd pages ‖ 他六十～岁了。 He is over sixty.

多[2] duō〈副〉 **1**（询问程度） [used in questions] how: 你的宝宝～大了？ How old is your baby? ‖ 死海有～深？ How deep is the Dead Sea? **2**（表程度深） [used in exclamations] how: ～可爱的小狗啊！ What a lovely puppy! ‖ 他心里～高兴啊！ How happy he was! **3**（指某种程度） to an unspecified extent: 要～坏有～坏 be as bad as can be ‖ 不管你走～远，我都会去看你的。 I will go to visit you no matter how far away you are.
【多半】duōbàn **A** ▸**p. 927**〈数〉 most: 我们车间～是女工。 Most of the workers in our workshop are women. **B**〈副〉 most probably: 他～生气了。 Most probably he was angry.
【多胞胎】duōbāotāi〈名〉 multiple birth
【多宝槅】duōbǎogé〈名〉 curio shelves
【多宝架】duōbǎojià = 多宝槅 duōbǎogé
【多宝鱼】duōbǎoyú〈名〉［鱼类］ turbot
【多倍体】duōbèitǐ〈名〉［生理］ polyploid: ～植物 polyploid plant
【多边】duōbiān〈形〉 multilateral: ～协商 plurilateral consultations ‖ ～会谈 multilateral talks
【多边贸易】duōbiān màoyì〈名〉 multilateral trade: ～谈判 multilateral trade negotiation
【多边外交】duōbiān wàijiāo〈名〉 multilateral diplomacy: ～活动 multilateral diplomatic activities
【多边形】duōbiānxíng〈名〉［数学］ polygon
【多变】duōbiàn〈动〉 be changeable: ～的天气 changeable weather
【多才多艺】duōcái-duōyì〈成〉 be versatile: ～的作家 versatile writer
【多彩多姿】duōcǎi-duōzī = 多姿多彩 duōzī-duōcǎi
【多层】duōcéng〈形〉 multi-storeyed: ～建筑 multi-storey building
【多层住宅】duōcéng zhùzhái〈名〉 multi-storey housing
【多产】duōchǎn〈形〉 **1**（指产量） productive: ～的果树 fertile fruit tree ‖ ～作家 prolific writer **2**［医学］ multiparous: ～妇 multiparous woman
【多吃多占】duōchī-duōzhàn〈惯〉 eat or take more than one is entitled to
【多重】duōchóng〈形〉 multiple: ～关税 multiple tariff ‖ ～人格 multiple personality
【多愁善感】duōchóu-shàngǎn〈成〉 be emotional: 她是个～的人。 She's the kind of person who feels things very deeply.
【多此一举】duōcǐyījǔ〈成〉 take unnecessary action: 真是～。 This is really unnecessary.
【多党】duōdǎng〈形〉 multi-party: ～联合政府 multiparty government
【多党合作】duōdǎng hézuò〈名〉 multi-party cooperation
【多党制】duōdǎngzhì〈名〉 multi-party system
【多动症】duōdòngzhèng ▸**p. 50**〈名〉［医学］ hyperkinesia
【多端】duōduān〈形〉 varied: 变化～ be changeable ‖ 诡计～ have a whole bag of sinister tricks ‖ 他作恶～。 He has done all kinds of evil things.
【多多】duōduō〈副〉 a great deal: ～保重！ Take care!
【多多益善】duōduō-yìshàn〈成〉 the more the better
【多发】duōfā〈形〉 frequent: 事故～地段 accident hot spot

【多发病】duōfābìng〈名〉frequently occurring disease
【多方】duōfāng〈副〉1（指方法）in many ways: ～援助 help in many ways ‖ ～阻挠 hinder by various means 2（指方面）multi-party: ～会谈 multi-party talks ‖ ～努力 multi-pronged efforts
【多佛】Duōfó〈名〉Dover
【多哥】Duōgē〈名〉Togo: ～共和国 Republic of Togo ‖ ～人 Togolese
【多功能】duōgōngnéng〈形〉multi-purpose: ～会议中心 multifunctional convention centre ‖ ～厅 multi-purpose hall
【多寡】duōguǎ〈名〉number: 各班人数～不等。The number of students varies from class to class.
【多国】duōguó〈形〉multinational: ～维和部队 multinational peace-keeping forces
【多国公司】duōguó gōngsī〈名〉multinational company
【多哈】Duōhā〈名〉Doha
【多会儿】duōhuir〈代〉〈方〉1（什么时候）when: 你～才能有空? When can you be free? 2（任何时候）whenever: 你～想走就～走。You can leave whenever you want to.
【多级】duōjí〈形〉multilevel: ～火箭 staged rocket
【多极管】duōjíguǎn〈名〉［电子］multi-electrode tube
【多极化】duōjíhuà〈动〉multi-polarize: 世界开始走向～。The world is moving towards multi-polarization.
【多价】duōjià〈形〉［化学］［生物］polyvalent: ～染色体 multivalent chromosome
【多角形】duōjiǎoxíng = 多边形 duōbiānxíng
【多节材】duōjiécái〈名〉knotty wood
【多晶体】duōjīngtǐ〈名〉polycrystal
【多空】duōkōng〈名〉［金融］long-short: ～量能此消彼涨。The long and short trading volume decreases and increases alternately.
【多口相声】duōkǒu xiàngsheng〈名〉cross talk [performed by three or more persons]
【多快好省】duō-kuài-hǎo-shěng〈惯〉more, faster, better and cheaper
【多亏】duōkuī〈动〉owe sth. to sb.: ～你，我才没有出洋相。Thanks to you, I was saved from making a fool of myself. ‖ ～你的帮助，我才得以成功。But for your help, I wouldn't have succeeded.
【多劳多得】duōláo-duōdé〈惯〉more work, more pay
【多棱镜】duōléngjìng〈名〉prism
【多利羊】duōlìyáng〈名〉Dolly [the world's first cloned sheep]
【多裂叶】duōlièyè〈名〉［植物］multifid leaf
【多路】duōlù〈形〉multichannel: ～传输 multiplex transmission
【多虑】duōlǜ〈动〉be overanxious
【多伦多】Duōlúnduō〈名〉Toronto
【多么】duōme〈副〉1（表疑问）[used in questions enquiring degree] how: 你知道天有～高吗? Do you know how high the sky is? 2（表感叹）[used in exclamations] how: 这孩子～聪明啊! This child is so clever! ‖ 我们～幸运啊! How lucky we are! ‖ ～美丽的景色啊! What a beautiful scene! 3（表程度深）[indicating a far extent or a high degree] no matter how: 不论下～大的雨我都要来。I will come no matter how hard it rains.
【多媒体】duōméitǐ〈名〉［计算机］multimedia: ～教具 multimedia kits for teachers
【多米尼加】Duōmǐníjiā〈名〉Dominica: ～共和国 Dominican Republic ‖ ～人 Dominican
【多米诺骨牌】duōmǐnuò gǔpái〈名〉domino: ～效应 domino effect
【多面手】duōmiànshǒu〈名〉versatile person: 他是个既喜欢网球、板球，又喜欢游泳的～。He is an all-rounder who likes tennis, cricket and swimming.
【多面体】duōmiàntǐ〈名〉［数学］polyhedron: ～结构 polyhedral structure
【多民族】duōmínzú〈形〉multi-ethnic: ～国家 multi-ethnic country
【多谋善断】duōmóu-shànduàn〈成〉wise and determined
【多幕剧】duōmùjù〈名〉play of many acts
【多难兴邦】duōnàn-xīngbāng〈成〉much distress helps regenerate a nation
【多瑙河】Duōnǎohé ▸p. 294〈名〉Danube: 蓝色～ Blue Danube
【多年生】duōniánshēng〈形〉［植物］perennial: ～植物 perennial plant
【多尿症】duōniàozhèng〈名〉polyuria
【多普勒效应】Duōpǔlè xiàoyìng〈名〉［物理］Doppler effect
【多妻制】duōqīzhì〈名〉polygamy
【多情】duōqíng〈形〉affectionate: 她很～。She is very affectionate. ▸自作～
【多如牛毛】duōrúniúmáo〈成〉countless
【多塞特郡】Duōsàitèjùn〈名〉Dorset
【多少】duōshǎo A〈名〉amount: ～不等 vary in number B〈副〉1（或多或少）somewhat: ～有点儿贵 be somewhat expensive ‖ 他～有些骄傲。He is proud to a degree. 2（稍微）slightly: 我～有点儿害怕。I'm a little afraid.
【多少】duōshao〈代〉1（询问数量）（指可数）how many;（指不可数）how much;（指时间）how long: 这本书～钱? How much does this book cost? 2（指不定的数量）[expressing an unspecified number or amount]: 能记～记～ try to remember whatever you can ‖ 能说～就说～ say whatever you can
【多神教】duōshénjiào〈名〉polytheism
【多声道】duōshēngdào〈形〉multitrack: ～录音 multitrack recording
【多时】duōshí〈名〉〈书〉long time: 等候～ have waited for a long time
【多事】duōshì〈动〉1（做多余的事）do unnecessary things: 她的父母会照顾她的，你就不用～了。Her parents will look after her, so you don't need to worry about this. 2（多管闲事）be nosy: 本性～ be nosy by nature ‖ ～的邻居 interfering neighbour
【多事之秋】duōshìzhīqiū〈成〉troubled times
【多数】duōshù〈名〉majority: 占～ be in the majority ‖ 绝大～ overwhelming majority ‖ 压倒～ overwhelming majority ‖ 以微弱～通过一项法案 pass an act by a narrow majority
【多数党】duōshùdǎng〈名〉majority (party)
【多糖】duōtáng〈名〉［化学］polysaccharide
【多厅影院】duōtīng yǐngyuàn〈名〉cineplex
【多头】duōtóu〈名〉1（指证券交易）bull 2（多方面）many sides
【多头市场】duōtóu shìchǎng〈名〉bull market
【多头政治】duōtóu zhèngzhì〈名〉polyarchy
【多退少补】duōtuì-shǎobǔ〈惯〉refund for any overpayment or a supplemental payment for any deficiency
【多维】duōwéi〈形〉multidimensional: ～空间 multidimensional space
【多项】duōxiàng〈形〉multiple: ～方程式 polynomial equation ‖ ～选择题 multiple-choice question
【多相】duōxiàng〈形〉［电气］multiphase: ～电路 polyphase circuit
【多谢】duōxiè ▸p. 236〈动〉〈套〉thank you very much
【多心】duōxīn〈动〉be oversensitive: 他这个人爱～。He tends to be oversensitive.
【多行不义必自毙】duō xíng bùyì bì zì bì〈成〉the wicked are brought down by their own wickedness
【多样】duōyàng〈形〉various
【多样化】duōyànghuà〈形〉diverse: ～的风格 diverse style ‖ ～经济 diverse economy ‖ ～社会 highly diverse society
【多样性】duōyàngxìng〈名〉diversity
【多一半】duōyībàn = 多半 duōbàn
【多一事不如少一事】duō yī shì bùrú shǎo yī shì〈俗〉let sleeping dogs lie
【多疑】duōyí〈形〉overly suspicious: 不必～。Don't be paranoid.
【多义词】duōyìcí〈名〉［语言］polyseme
【多音字】duōyīnzì〈形〉［语言］polyphonic character
【多余】duōyú A〈动〉be surplus: ～出的粮食 surplus grain B〈形〉superfluous: ～的话 uncalled-for remarks ‖ 她觉得自己是～的。She felt she was superfluous to requirements.
【多语】duōyǔ〈形〉multilingual: ～词典 multilingual dictionary
【多语种】duōyǔzhǒng〈形〉multilingual: ～对照版本 polyglot edition ‖ ～广播 multilingual broadcast
【多元】duōyuán〈形〉pluralistic: ～文化 pluralistic culture
【多元化】duōyuánhuà〈动〉become pluralistic: 开拓～国际市场 open up a multi-outlet international market ‖ 世界更加～。The world is becoming more pluralistic.
【多云】duōyún〈名〉cloud: ～间晴天 mixture of cloud and sunshine ‖ ～的天气 cloudy day
【多灾多难】duōzāi-duōnàn〈成〉be dogged by bad luck: 那年他家～。His family was hit with a lot of bad luck that year.
【多制式】duōzhìshì〈名〉multisystem
【多种】duōzhǒng〈形〉various: 我们的对外开放采取～形式。We have adopted many different ways of implementing the policy of opening China to the outside world.
【多种多样】duōzhǒng-duōyàng〈成〉varied: ～的生活方式 varied lifestyle ‖ 她的作品～。Her works cover many differing genres.
【多种经营】duōzhǒng jīngyíng diversified economy: 因地制宜，～ diversify the economy in accordance with local conditions
【多姿】duōzī〈形〉of various postures: ▸婀娜～
【多姿多彩】duōzī-duōcǎi〈成〉varied and graceful
【多子多福】duōzǐ-duōfú〈成〉more sons, more blessings
【多嘴】duōzuǐ〈动〉shoot one's mouth off: 不干你的事，别～! It's none of your business; keep your mouth shut!
【多嘴多舌】duōzuǐ-duōshé〈成〉be gossipy

咄 duō

【咄咄】duōduō〈叹〉〈旧〉tut-tut
【咄咄逼人】duōduō-bīrén〈成〉overbearing: 他～，野心勃勃。He is overbearing

and ambitious.
【咄咄怪事】duōduō-guàishì〈成〉absurdity: 真是～! How ridiculous!

哆 duō
【哆嗦】duōsuo〈动〉 tremble: 吓得直～ tremble with fear

剟 duō〈动〉〈书〉 1（击打） strike 2（删除） delete 3（割取） cut

掇 duō〈动〉 1 ▸拾掇 shíduo 2 ▸撺掇 cuānduo 3 ▸掂掇 diānduo

裰 duō
A〈动〉 patch
B ▸直裰 zhíduō

duó

夺（奪） duó〈动〉 1（摆脱） force one's way: 眼泪～眶而出 tears gush from one's eyes ▸～门而出 2（强拿） take by force: ～过暴徒的刀 seize the knife from the ruffian ▸～权, 掠～ 3（争先取得） contend for: ～丰收 strive for a bumper harvest ‖ ～奖牌 compete for a medal ▸～标, ～魁 4（胜过） prevail over: ▸巧～天工, 先声～人 5（剥夺） deprive: ～人饭碗 take another person's job ▸剥～ 6〈书〉（错过） lose: 勿～农时。 Don't miss the right season for each farming job. 7〈书〉（决定） decide: ▸裁～, 定～ 8〈书〉（失去） be missing: ▸讹～
【夺杯】duóbēi〈动〉 win the cup
【夺标】duóbiāo〈动〉 1（夺冠） win the championship 2（中标） have one's tender accepted
【夺冠】duóguàn〈动〉 win the title
【夺眶而出】duókuàng'érchū〈成〉[of tears] gush from one's eyes
【夺魁】duókuí〈动〉 win the title
【夺门而出】duómén'érchū〈动〉 get to the door and force one's way out
【夺目】duómù〈形〉〈书〉 dazzling: ▸鲜艳～
【夺取】duóqǔ〈动〉 1（强取） seize: ～阵地 capture a position ‖ ～政权 seize power 2（争取） strive for: ～新的胜利 strive for new victories
【夺权】duóquán〈动〉 seize power

度 duó〈动〉〈书〉 surmise: ▸审时～势, 以己～人
▸dù
【度德量力】duódé-liànglì〈成〉 appraise oneself by standards of morality and ability

铎（鐸） duó〈名〉〈古〉 large bell usu with deep, dull sound: 振～ strike a bell ‖ 木～ wooden bell

踱 duó〈动〉 pace: ～方步 walk with measured steps ‖ ～来～去 pace up and down

duǒ

朵（朶） duǒ〈量〉[of flowers, clouds, etc.]: 一～玫瑰花 a rose ‖ 蓝天上飘着～～白云。 White clouds drifted high in the blue sky. ▸花～
【朵颐】duǒyí〈形〉〈书〉 relishing: 大快～ eat with great relish

垛（垜） duǒ
A〈名〉 battlements: ▸城～
B〈量〉[used of a wall]: 一～矮石墙 a low stone wall
▸duò
【垛堞】duǒdié = 垛口 duǒkǒu
【垛口】duǒkǒu〈名〉 battlement
【垛子】duǒzi〈名〉 battlement
▸duòzi

哚 duǒ ▸吲哚 yǐnduǒ

躲（躱） duǒ〈动〉 1（避开） avoid: ～风/雨 shelter from the wind/rain ‖ ～到一旁 dodge aside ‖ 他从前的朋友都～着他。 His former friends all shun him. ▸～债, 明枪易～, 暗箭难防 2（隐藏） take cover: ～起来 go into hiding ‖ ～在门背后 hide behind the door ‖ ～在树林中 hide in the trees
【躲避】duǒbì〈动〉 1（隐避） hide: 他该不是在有意～我吧? He can't be trying to hide from me, can he? 2（避开） avoid: ～暴风雨 shelter from the storm ‖ ～洪水 seek refuge from floods ‖ ～困难 avoid difficulties
【躲藏】duǒcáng〈动〉 go into hiding: ～在废墟间 conceal oneself among the ruins ‖ 无处～。 There was nowhere to hide.
【躲得过初一，躲不过十五】duǒdeguò chūyī, duǒbuguò shíwǔ〈俗〉 you can run, but you cannot hide
【躲躲闪闪】duǒduo-shǎnshǎn〈成〉 evasive: 别～的，回答"是"还是"不是"。 Answer 'yes' or 'no'. Stop being evasive.
【躲懒】duǒlǎn〈动〉 shirk a task: 她勤恳工作，从不～。 She worked hard, never shirking.
【躲让】duǒràng〈动〉 make way for
【躲闪】duǒshǎn〈动〉 dodge: ～到一旁 dodge aside ‖ 左右～ dodge right and left
【躲债】duǒzhài〈动〉 avoid a debt

duò

驮（馱） duò
▸tuó
【驮子】duòzi A〈名〉 pack B〈量〉[for goods carried by a pack animal]: 五～货 five packs of goods

剁（剁） duò〈动〉 chop: ～肉 mince meat ‖ 请把洋葱～碎。 Please chop the onions up into pieces.

垛（垜） duò
A〈动〉 stack: 把柴火～起来 pile up the firewood
B〈名〉 pile: 草～ stack of hay ‖ 麦～ grain stack
C〈量〉 stack: 一～柴火 a stack of firewood
▸duǒ
【垛子】duòzi〈名〉 heap: 稻草～ straw stack
▸duǒzi

柁 duò〈古〉= 舵 duò
▸tuó

舵 duò〈名〉 rudder: 方向～ rudder ‖ 转右～! Starboard the helm!
【舵工】duògōng〈名〉 helmsman
【舵轮】duòlún〈名〉 steering wheel
【舵盘】duòpán = 舵轮 duòlún
【舵手】duòshǒu〈名〉 1（掌舵的人） helmsman 2〈喻〉（领袖） leader

堕（墮） duò〈动〉 fall: ～入水中 fall into the water
【堕落】duòluò〈动〉 1（变坏） degenerate: ～成罪犯 sink to the level of criminal ‖ 腐化～ become corrupt and degenerate ‖ 我不明白他怎么会～到这个地步。 I do not understand how he could sink to such depths. 2（沦落） come down in the world: ～风尘 be driven to prostitution
【堕马】duòmǎ〈动〉〈书〉 fall off a horse
【堕胎】duòtāi〈动〉 induce an abortion

惰 duò〈形〉 lazy: ▸怠～, 懒～
【惰性】duòxìng〈名〉 inertia: 虽然我答应参加聚会，但出于～没有去。 Though I had promised to go to the party, I was lazy and didn't go. ▸～气体
【惰性气体】duòxìng qìtǐ〈名〉 inert gas
【惰性元素】duòxìng yuánsù〈名〉 inert element

跺（跥） duò〈动〉 stamp: ～地板 stamp the floor
【跺脚】duòjiǎo〈动〉 stamp one's foot: 气得直～ stamp one's foot in anger

Ee

ē

阿[1] ē
A 〈动〉 play up to: 刚直不～ be upright and tenacious ▸～附, ～谀
B 〈名〉 1 (指丘陵) big mound 2 (弯曲处) winding area: 山～ mountain bend

阿[2] Ē transliteration, used in 阿弥陀佛
▸ā, à

【阿附】ēfù 〈动〉 toady to: ～权贵 toady to high officials ‖ ～上司 curry favour with one's superior
【阿胶】ējiāo 〈名〉 [中药] E-gelatin
【阿弥陀佛】Ēmítuófó 〈名〉 [佛教] 1 (指佛) Amitabha 2 (指口头念诵的佛号) [used as an exclamation] merciful Buddha
【阿其所好】ēqísuǒhào 〈成〉 pander to sb.'s whims
【阿谀】ēyú 〈动〉 flatter
【阿谀逢迎】ēyú-féngyíng 〈成〉 butter up
【阿谀奉承】ēyú-fèngchéng = 阿谀逢迎 ēyú-féngyíng

屙 ē 〈动〉 〈方〉 discharge: ～屎 excrete excrement ‖ ～尿 urinate

婀 ē
【婀娜】ēnuó 〈形〉 〈书〉 lithe and graceful: 体态～ have a supple, graceful carriage
【婀娜多姿】ēnuó-duōzī 〈成〉 be lissom and graceful

é

讹（訛） é
A 〈形〉 erroneous: ～字 wrong character ▸以～传～
B 〈动〉 blackmail: ～钱 extort money ‖ 你想～我，没门儿！ There's no way you can blackmail me!
【讹传】échuán 〈名〉 false rumour: 纯系～，切勿轻信。 It's sheer rumour. Don't be taken in.
【讹夺】éduó 〈书〉 = 讹脱 étuō
【讹谬】émiù 〈名〉 error
【讹脱】étuō 〈名〉 〈书〉 error
【讹误】éwù 〈名〉 error
【讹言】éyán 〈名〉 rumour
【讹诈】ézhà 〈动〉 1 (为财物) blackmail: ～钱财 extort money 2 (威胁、恫吓) coerce: 核～ nuclear blackmail ‖ 政治～ political blackmail

俄[1] é 〈副〉 〈书〉 presently: ▸～而, ～顷

俄[2] É 〈名〉 Russia
【俄而】é'ér 〈副〉 before long
【俄尔】é'ěr = 俄而 é'ér
【俄国】Éguó 〈名〉 Russia
【俄亥俄州】Éhài'ézhōu 〈名〉 Ohio
【俄克拉何马州】Ékèlāhémǎzhōu 〈名〉 Oklahoma
【俄勒冈州】Élègāngzhōu 〈名〉 Oregon
【俄罗斯】Éluósī 〈名〉 Russia: ～联邦 Russian Federation ‖ ～人 Russian ‖ ～语 Russian
【俄罗斯族】Éluósīzú 〈名〉 1 (中国境内) Russian ethnic group 2 (俄罗斯境内) Russians
【俄顷】éqǐng 〈副〉 〈书〉 presently: ～，云消雨霁。 All of a sudden, the rain let up and the clouds melted.
【俄通-塔斯社】Étōng-Tǎsīshè 〈名〉 Itar-Tass
【俄延】éyán 〈动〉 〈书〉 delay
【俄语】Éyǔ ▸p. 918 〈名〉 Russian

哦 é 〈动〉 〈书〉 chant softly: ▸吟～
▸ó, ò

峨 é 〈形〉 〈书〉 high: ▸嵯～, 巍～
【峨冠博带】éguān-bódài 〈成〉 high hat and broad waistband
【峨嵋山】Éméishān 〈名〉 Mount Emei

娥 é 〈书〉
A 〈形〉 beautiful: ▸～眉
B 〈名〉 beauty: ▸嫦～, 宫～, 姮～
【娥眉】éméi 〈名〉 1 (指眉毛) beautiful brows 2 (指美女) beautiful woman

锇（鋨） é 〈名〉 [化学] osmium (Os)

鹅（鵝） é 〈名〉 goose: ▸企～, 天～
【鹅蛋】édàn 〈名〉 goose's egg
【鹅蛋脸】édànliǎn 〈名〉 oval face
【鹅黄】éhuáng 〈名〉 light yellow
【鹅卵石】éluǎnshí 〈名〉 cobblestone
【鹅毛】émáo 〈名〉 goose feather: ～扇 goose feather fan ‖ ～大雪 large snowflakes ▸千里送～
【鹅绒】éróng 〈名〉 goose down
【鹅行鸭步】éxíng-yābù 〈成〉 waddle like ducks and geese
【鹅掌风】ézhǎngfēng 〈名〉 [中医] tinea manuum [fungal infection of the hand]

蛾 é 〈名〉 moth: 飞～ flying moth ‖ 螟～ snout moth
▸yǐ
【蛾眉】éméi = 娥眉 éméi
【蛾子】ézi 〈名〉 moth

额（額） é 〈名〉 1 ▸p. 614 (前额) forehead: ▸焦头烂～, 前～ 2 (顶部) top part: 门～ lintel ▸碑～ 3 (匾额) horizontal inscribed board: 横～ horizontal hanging placard ▸匾～ 4 (指数目) amount: 全～火险 full cover against fire ▸～外, 定～, 数～
【额定】édìng 〈形〉 rated: ～产量 rated capacity ‖ ～负荷 rated load
【额窦炎】édòuyán ▸p. 50 〈名〉 [医学] frontal sinusitis
【额度】édù 〈名〉 quota: 贷款～ loan limit ‖ 融资～ financing limit ‖ 信贷～ credit line
【额骨】égǔ 〈名〉 [解剖] frontal bone
【额角】éjiǎo 〈名〉 [解剖] frontal eminence
【额手称庆】éshǒu-chēngqìng 〈成〉 throw one's arms in the air with joy
【额数】éshù 〈名〉 specified amount
【额头】étóu 〈名〉 forehead
【额外】éwài 〈形〉 additional: ～报酬 premium payment ‖ ～负担 additional burden ‖ ～收入 extraneous income

ě

恶（噁） ě
▸è, wū, wù
【恶心】ěxin A 〈形〉 feel sick: 感到～ feel nauseous ‖ 一见到血就～ be sickened at the sight of blood ‖ 使人～的气味 nauseating smell B 〈动〉 1 (感到厌恶) sicken: 他的行为让人～。 His conduct was sickening. 2 (使人难堪) embarrass: 得找个机会～他一下。 Let's find an opportunity to embarrass him.

è

厄[1] è 〈书〉
A 〈形〉 difficult: ▸困～
B 〈名〉 adversity: 遭～ meet adversities ▸～境, ～运
C 〈动〉 be stranded: ～于风暴 be caught in a storm

厄[2] **（阨）** è 〈名〉 strategic point: 险～ strategic pass
【厄尔尼诺】è'ěrnínuò 〈名〉 El Niño: ～现象 El Niño phenomenon
【厄瓜多尔】Èguāduō'ěr 〈名〉 Ecuador: ～共和国 Republic of Ecuador ‖ ～人 Ecuadorian
【厄境】èjìng 〈名〉 difficult situation: 身处～ be in dire straits
【厄立特里亚】Èlìtèlǐyà 〈名〉 Eritrea
【厄难】ènàn 〈名〉 distress

【厄运】 èyùn〈名〉 misfortune: 连遭～ encounter one misfortune after another ‖ 同～斗争 struggle against adversity

扼 è〈动〉 1（掐） grip: ▸～杀 2（把守） guard: ▸～守

【扼杀】 èshā〈动〉 1（掐死） strangle: 她在床上被人～了。 She was strangled in bed. 2〈喻〉（摧残） wreck: ～和平进程 kill the peace process ‖ ～在萌芽状态 nip in the bud

【扼守】 èshǒu〈动〉 guard: ～关口 guard a strategic pass

【扼腕】 èwàn〈动〉〈书〉 wring one's hands: ～叹息 wring one's hands and sigh

【扼要】 èyào〈形〉 brief and to the point: 简明～ be brief and to the point ‖ 他～说明了将来的打算。 He outlined his plans for the future.

【扼制】 èzhì〈动〉 control: ～通货膨胀 check inflation

呃 è〈动〉 hiccup ▸e

【呃逆】 ènì ▸**p. 50**〈动〉［医学］ hiccup

轭（軛） è〈名〉 yoke

垩（堊） è

A〈名〉 chalk

B〈动〉〈书〉 whitewash: ～壁 whitewash a wall

恶（惡） è

A〈名〉 evil: 作～ do evil ‖ 不念旧～ forgive and forget ‖ 善～不分 make no distinction between good and evil ▸惩～劝善，邪～，罪～

B〈形〉 1（凶猛） fierce: ～狗 ferocious dog ‖ ～骂 vicious abuse ‖ ～战 fierce battle ▸～霸 2（坏） bad: ～名 unsavoury reputation ‖ ～势力 evil force ▸～习，～意 ▸ě, wū, wù

【恶霸】 èbà〈名〉 local tyrant: ～地主 despotic landlord

【恶报】 èbào〈名〉 misfortune as retribution for evil-doing: ▸善有善报，恶有～

【恶变】 èbiàn〈动〉［医学］ become cancerous

【恶补】 èbǔ〈动〉 engage in intensive practice

【恶炒】 èchǎo〈动〉 spread malicious rumours: 媒体的～ vicious media speculation ‖ ～新股 speculate maliciously on new share issues

【恶臭】 èchòu〈名〉 stench

【恶斗】 èdòu〈动〉 fight fiercely

【恶毒】 èdú〈形〉 vicious: ～诽谤 venomous slander ‖ ～攻击 attack viciously ‖ 用心～ harbour ill intent ‖ 手段～ take vicious measures

【恶感】 ègǎn〈名〉 ill feeling: 他俩互抱～，总是争斗不休。 There is bad blood between them and they are always fighting.

【恶搞】 ègǎo〈动〉 parody: 对那部大片的～ make a spoof of a blockbuster movie ‖ 有些明星屡遭网民～。 Some celebrities have suffered the ridicule of the internet community.

【恶贯满盈】 èguàn-mǎnyíng〈成〉 be guilty of countless crimes and deserve damnation

【恶鬼】 èguǐ〈名〉 evil spirit

【恶棍】 ègùn〈名〉 scoundrel

【恶果】 èguǒ〈名〉 disastrous result: 带来～ entail pernicious consequences

【恶狠狠】 èhěnhěn〈形〉 vicious: ～地踢一脚 give sb. a vicious kick ‖ 他～地看了我一眼。 He gave me a poisonous look.

【恶化】 èhuà〈动〉 deteriorate: 日益～的健康状况 deteriorating health ‖ 病情在～。 The condition is worsening. ‖ 事态急剧～。 Events took a drastic turn for the worse.

【恶疾】 èjí〈名〉 nasty disease

【恶迹】 èjì〈名〉 misdeed

【恶浪】 èlàng〈名〉 1（巨浪） ferocious waves: 滔天～ ferocious waves leaping skywards 2〈喻〉（恶势力） evil forces

【恶劣】 èliè〈形〉 abominable: 品行～ abominable conduct ‖ 影响～ have a bad influence ‖ ～的天气 adverse weather ‖ ～的自然条件 harsh natural conditions

【恶露】 èlù〈名〉［医学］ lochia

【恶梦】 èmèng = 噩梦 èmèng

【恶名】 èmíng〈名〉 unsavoury reputation: ～在外 have a bad public reputation

【恶魔】 èmó〈名〉 demon

【恶念】 èniàn〈名〉 evil intent: 心存～ harbour evil intent

【恶癖】 èpǐ〈名〉 pernicious habit

【恶气】 èqì〈名〉 1（指气味） foul smell 2（怒气） outrage 3（怨气） resentment: 出～ vent one's grievance

【恶人】 èrén〈名〉 evil person

【恶人先告状】 èrén xiān gàozhuàng〈俗〉 the villain sues his victim before he himself can be prosecuted

【恶煞】 èshà〈名〉 1（凶神） devil 2〈喻〉（恶人） fiendish person

【恶少】 èshào〈名〉 young ruffian

【恶声】 èshēng〈名〉 1（指言语） abusive language: ～对骂 hurl insults at one another 2（指声音） angry voice: ▸～恶气 3〈书〉（指名声） bad reputation

【恶声恶气】 èshēng-èqì〈成〉 speak angrily

【恶事】 èshì〈名〉 evil deed: ～传千里 scandal spreads apace

【恶俗】 èsú A〈形〉 ugly and vulgar B〈名〉 evil practices

【恶习】 èxí〈名〉 evil practice: 沾染～ fall into a bad habit ‖ ～难改 bad habits die hard

【恶性】 èxìng〈形〉 pernicious: ～事故 calamitous accident

【恶性竞争】 èxìng jìngzhēng〈名〉 cut-throat competition: 家电行业大打价格战，这种～愈演愈烈。The domestic appliance industry is conducting a fierce price war. The competition is cut-throat and is escalating in intensity.

【恶性循环】 èxìng xúnhuán〈名〉 vicious circle

【恶性肿瘤】 èxìng zhǒngliú ▸**p. 50**〈名〉 malignant tumour

【恶言】 èyán〈名〉 abusive language: 口出～ have a wicked tongue ‖ ～相向 hurl insults at one another

【恶言恶语】 èyán-èyǔ〈成〉 abusive language

【恶意】 èyì〈名〉 malice: 心怀～ harbour malice ‖ ～中伤 viciously slander

【恶有恶报】 è yǒu èbào〈成〉 evil is rewarded with evil

【恶语】 èyǔ〈名〉 rude language: ～伤人 hurt sb. with vicious remarks

【恶运】 èyùn〈名〉 bad luck

【恶战】 èzhàn A〈名〉 fierce fighting B〈动〉 battle fiercely: ～一场 have a fierce battle

【恶兆】 èzhào〈名〉 evil omen

【恶浊】 èzhuó〈形〉 foul: ～的空气 foul air

【恶作剧】 èzuòjù〈名〉 monkey business: 搞～ play practical jokes

饿（餓） è

A〈形〉 hungry: 挨～ go hungry ‖ 又累又～ be tired and hungry

B〈动〉 starve: ～死 starve to death ‖ 别～着肚子去上班。 Don't go out to work on an empty stomach.

【饿饭】 èfàn〈动〉 go hungry

【饿鬼】 èguǐ〈名〉〈喻〉 piggish eater

【饿虎扑食】 èhǔ-pūshí〈成〉 a hungry tiger pouncing on its prey

【饿殍遍野】 èpiǎo-biànyě〈成〉 the fields were strewn with corpses of the starved

鄂 È ▸**p. 661**〈名〉 E [another name for Hubei Province (湖北)]

【鄂伦春族】 Èlúnchūnzú〈名〉 Oroqen ethnic group

【鄂温克族】 Èwēnkèzú〈名〉 Ewenki ethnic group, Evenk ethnic group

阏（閼） è〈书〉

A〈动〉 block

B〈名〉 sluice ▸yān

谔（諤） è

【谔谔】 è'è〈形〉〈书〉 outspoken

萼 è〈名〉［植物］ calyx: ▸～片，花～

【萼片】 èpiàn〈名〉［植物］ sepal

遏 è〈动〉 check

【遏抑】 èyì〈动〉 restrain: ～不住胸中的怒火 cannot suppress one's anger

【遏止】 èzhǐ〈动〉 check: 改革的潮流不可～。 The tide of reform is unstoppable.

【遏制】 èzhì〈动〉 contain: ～流行病的蔓延 contain an epidemic ‖ ～通货膨胀 check inflation ‖ ～政策 policy of containment

愕 è〈形〉 astonished: ▸惊～

【愕然】 èrán〈形〉〈书〉 astounded: 为之～ be astonished at sth.

【愕视】 èshì〈动〉〈书〉 stare in astonishment

噁（噁） è ▸二噁英 èr'èyīng

腭 è〈名〉 palate: ▸软～，硬～

【腭裂】 èliè ▸**p. 50**〈名〉［医学］ cleft palate

颚（顎） è〈名〉 1（指器官） mandibles: ▸上～，下～ 2 = 腭 è

【颚骨】 ègǔ〈名〉 jawbone

噩 è〈形〉 shocking

【噩耗】 èhào〈名〉 news of the death of a beloved: 传来～ news came of the death of somebody dear

【噩梦】 èmèng〈名〉 nightmare: 做～ have a nightmare

【噩运】 èyùn〈名〉 bad luck

【噩兆】 èzhào〈名〉 evil omen

鳄（鱷） è〈名〉 crocodile: ▸扬子～

【鳄鱼】 èyú〈名〉 crocodile: 掉～眼泪 shed crocodile tears

e

呃 e〈助〉[used at the end of a sentence to express admiration or wonder]: 他真是个了不起的人～! Oh, he is really a great guy! ‖ 这学期过得真快～! The term simply flew by!
▸è

ēn

恩 ēn〈名〉**1**（恩惠） favour: 他对我有～。 I owe him a favour. ▸报～, 忘～负义 **2**（恩爱） affection: 一日夫妻百日～。 One day of married life fosters enduring affections.
【恩爱】ēn'ài〈形〉 affectionate: ～夫妻 devoted couple
【恩宠】ēnchǒng〈名〉 imperial favour: 深受～ be in high favour
【恩赐】ēncì〈动〉 bestow imperial favours: 要自力更生，不能靠别人～。 Rely on yourself and never count on others' charity.
【恩德】ēndé〈名〉 benevolence: 大恩大德 great kindness
【恩典】ēndiǎn **A**〈名〉 favour **B**〈动〉 bestow
【恩断义绝】ēnduàn-yìjué〈成〉 love is lost
【恩恩爱爱】ēnēn'ài'ài〈形〉 intimate
【恩格尔系数】Ēngé'ěr xìshù〈名〉［统计］ Engel coefficient
【恩惠】ēnhuì〈名〉 favour: 得到～ receive a favour
【恩将仇报】ēnjiāngchóubào〈成〉 bite the hand that feeds one
【恩情】ēnqíng〈名〉 loving kindness
【恩人】ēnrén〈名〉 benefactor
【恩深义重】ēnshēn-yìzhòng〈成〉 huge debt of gratitude
【恩师】ēnshī〈名〉 my kind and respected teacher
【恩同再造】ēntóngzàizào〈成〉 favour that is as good as giving one a new life
【恩威并施】ēnwēi-bìngshī〈成〉 temper justice with mercy
【恩威并行】ēnwēi-bìngxíng = 恩威并施 ēnwēi-bìngshī
【恩威并用】ēnwēi-bìngyòng = 恩威并施 ēnwēi-bìngshī
【恩怨】ēnyuàn〈名〉 gratitude and grudges: ～分明 make a clear distinction between kindnesses and wrongs ‖ 不计较个人～ not to allow oneself to be swayed by personal resentment
【恩泽】ēnzé〈名〉 favour bestowed by a superior
【恩重如山】ēnzhòng-rúshān〈成〉 tremendous kindness
【恩准】ēnzhǔn〈动〉 graciously grant: 得到君主的～ get the gracious approval of a monarch

蒽 ēn〈名〉［化学］ anthracene

èn

摁 èn〈动〉 press: ～电铃 ring an electric bell ‖ ～快门 press the shutter ‖ ～手印 register one's fingerprint ‖ 他们把他～在地上。 They pinned him to the ground.
【摁钉儿】èndīngr〈名〉 drawing pin
【摁扣儿】ènkòur〈名〉 snap fastener

ér

儿[1]（兒） ér
A〈名〉 **1**（孩子） child: 新生～ newborn ▸～童, 婴～ **2**（儿子） son: 有一～一女 have a son and a daughter ▸～媳, ～子 **3**（年轻人） youngster: ▸健～, 男～
B〈形〉 male: ▸～马

儿[2]（兒） ér〈后缀〉[transcribed as r] **1**（表示小） [added to nouns to indicate littleness, intimacy, etc.]: 鸟儿 birdie ‖ 小孩儿 little child **2**（表词意改变） [added to a noun to form a new one with a different meaning]: ▸白面儿, 头儿 **3**（表名词化） [added to verbs, adjectives or measure words to form nouns]: 盖儿 lid ‖ 错儿 mistake ‖ 片儿 piece **4**（动词后缀） [added to certain verbs]: 火儿了 flare up ‖ 喜欢玩儿 love to play **5**（形容词叠词后缀） [added to adjectives consisting of the same two Chinese characters]: 乖乖儿 be obedient ▸好好儿
【儿歌】érgē〈名〉 nursery rhyme
【儿化】érhuà〈名〉［语言］ r-ending retroflexion
【儿皇帝】érhuángdì〈名〉 puppet emperor
【儿科】érkē〈名〉 paediatrics: ～医生 paediatrician
【儿郎】érláng〈名〉〈书〉 man: 好～，上战场 Good men go to the battlefield.
【儿马】érmǎ〈名〉〈口〉 stallion
【儿男】érnán〈名〉 man
【儿女】érnǚ〈名〉 **1**（儿子和女儿） children: 养育～ raise children ‖ 中华～ sons and daughters of the Chinese nation **2**（男人和女人） men and women: ▸～情长
【儿女情长】érnǚ-qíngcháng〈成〉 be indulged in love: ～，英雄气短。 Indulgence in love weakens a person's will.
【儿女亲家】érnǚ qìngjiā〈名〉 parents-in-law of one's son/daughter
【儿孙】érsūn〈名〉 descendants: ～满堂 have children and grandchildren in the household
【儿童】értóng〈名〉 children: 关心～ care for children ‖ 虐待～ ill-treat a child ‖ ～福利 child welfare ‖ 学龄～ children of school age
【儿童节】Értóngjié〈名〉 Children's Day
【儿童团】értóngtuán〈名〉 Children's Corps
【儿童文学】értóng wénxué〈名〉 children's literature
【儿童游乐园】értóng yóulèyuán〈名〉 children's playground
【儿媳】érxí〈名〉 daughter-in-law
【儿媳妇】érxífu = 儿媳 érxí
【儿戏】érxì〈名〉 trifling matter: 视同～ regard as a mere trifle ‖ 别拿人命当～。 Don't trifle with human life.
【儿行千里母担忧】ér xíng qiānlǐ mǔ dānyōu〈俗〉 a mother's thoughts follow her son wherever he goes
【儿子】érzi〈名〉 son: 人民的好～ worthy son of the people

而 ér〈连〉 **1**（表并列） and: 长期～复杂的问题 long-standing and complex problems ‖ 年轻～有才华 young and talented ‖ 战～胜之 fight and defeat it **2**（表转折） but: 出力～不讨好 be a fool for one's pains ‖ 我认为这一点很重要，～他却不以为然。 I think this very important but he doesn't. **3**（表假设） if: 人民公仆～不为人民办事，就不配叫人民公仆。 If a public servant does not serve the interests of the people, he does not deserve to be called a public servant. **4**（至） to: 从上～下 from top to bottom ‖ 由南～北 from south to north **5**（表原因） [used between an adverbial element of purpose, cause, manner, etc. and a verb to be modified]: 为自由～斗争 fight for freedom ‖ 因生病～缺席 be absent because of illness
【而后】érhòu〈副〉 after that: 我们去喝一杯，～回家。 Let's go for a drink and then go home. ‖ 我们开车去西安，～乘飞机到北京。 We drove to Xi'an and thence flew to Beijing.
【而今】érjīn〈副〉 nowadays
【而况】érkuàng〈连〉 let alone: 小孩连走都不会，～跑呢。 The baby can't even walk, let alone run.
【而立】érlì〈名〉〈书〉 thirty years of age: ～之年 the age of thirty ‖ 年届～ turn thirty
【而且】érqiě〈连〉 **1**（表并列） and: 这屋子很宽敞，～光线充足。 The room is spacious and bright. **2**（表递进） but also: 我们不但战胜了自然灾害，～获得了丰收。 We not only came through the natural calamity, but also had a bumper harvest.
【而外】érwài〈助〉 besides
【而已】éryǐ〈助〉 that is all: 如此～，岂有他哉。 That's all there is to it! ‖ 这不是真品，不过是复制品～。 This is not real. It's just a reproduction.

鸸（鴯） ér
【鸸鹋】érmiáo〈名〉［鸟类］ emu

ěr

尔（爾） ěr〈书〉
A〈代〉 **1**（你） thou: 非～之过。 It's not your fault. ▸～曹, ～虞我诈 **2**（那） that: ～日 that day ‖ ～时 at that time
B〈副〉 so: 果～ if so ▸不过～～, 乃～
C〈助〉 merely: 无他，但手熟～。 It is just that I am an old hand at it.
D〈后缀〉 [used after adjective or adverb]: ▸率～, 莞～
【尔曹】ěrcáo〈代〉〈书〉〈贬〉 you people
【尔代节】Ěrdàijié = 开斋节 Kāizhāijié
【尔尔】ěr'ěr〈代〉 average: 不过～ be run-of-the-mill
【尔后】ěrhòu〈连〉〈书〉 thereafter: 2000年我们初次相识，～就经常见面。 We first met in 2000 and I saw him quite often thereafter.
【尔虞我诈】ěryú-wǒzhà〈成〉 each trying to cheat the other: 各派勾心斗角，～。 All the factions intrigued against each other, resorting to deception and fraud.

耳 ěr〈名〉 **1** ▸p. 614（耳朵） ear: ▸～闻目睹, 内～, 外～, 中～ **2**（耳状物） ear-like thing: ▸木～, 银～ **3**（两侧） both sides: ▸～房, ～门
【耳报神】ěrbàoshén〈名〉〈旧〉 informant
【耳背】ěrbèi ▸p. 772〈形〉 hard of hearing: 老人身体还硬朗，就是有点～。 The old man is still going strong except for being slightly hard of hearing.
【耳鼻喉科】ěr-bí-hóukē〈名〉［医学］ ear-nose-throat (ENT) department
【耳边风】ěrbiānfēng〈名〉〈喻〉 unheeded advice: 不要把我的警告当～。 Don't turn a deaf ear to my warning.
【耳标】ěrbiāo〈名〉 ear tag: 每头生猪都挂有～。 Each of the pigs has an ear tag.

e

【耳鬓厮磨】ěrbìn-sīmó〈成〉[of a boy and a girl] have a close childhood friendship
【耳沉】ěrchén ▸**p. 772**〈形〉〈书〉hard of hearing
【耳垂】ěrchuí〈名〉ear lobe
【耳聪目明】ěrcōng-mùmíng〈成〉**1**〈本〉have good eyes and ears **2**〈喻〉(敏锐) have a thorough grasp of the situation
【耳朵】ěrduo〈名〉ear
【耳朵软】ěrduoruǎn〈惯〉be easily influenced: 她～，容易受骗。She was too credulous and so was susceptible to fraud.
【耳朵眼儿】ěrduoyǎnr〈名〉**1**(外耳门) earhole **2**(耳垂上的洞) hole in the ear lobe for earrings: 扎～ have one's ears pierced
【耳房】ěrfáng〈名〉**1**(侧房) side rooms **2**(小屋) small annex
【耳福】ěrfú〈名〉good fortune of hearing sth. rare or beautiful: 一饱～ enjoy every bit of what one hears
【耳根】ěrgēn〈名〉**1**(耳朵根部) root of the ear **2**〈方〉(耳朵) ear: ～清净 hear no idle gossip
【耳垢】ěrgòu〈名〉earwax
【耳鼓】ěrgǔ〈名〉eardrum
【耳刮子】ěrguāzi〈口〉= 耳光 ěrguāng
【耳掴子】ěrguāizi〈口〉= 耳光 ěrguāng
【耳光】ěrguāng〈名〉**1**(打脸) box on the ears: 打～ box sb. about the ears **2**(打击) blow: 事实给了造谣的人一记响亮的～。The facts were a real slap in the face for the rumour-monger.
【耳郭】ěrguō〈名〉outer ear
【耳环】ěrhuán〈名〉earring: 戴～ wear earrings
【耳机】ěrjī〈名〉earphone
【耳际】ěrjì〈名〉〈书〉one's ears: 在～回响 reverberate in one's ears
【耳尖】ěrjiān〈形〉sharp of hearing
【耳镜】ěrjìng〈名〉[医学] otoscope
【耳科】ěrkē〈名〉[医学] otological department: ～医生 ear specialist
【耳孔】ěrkǒng〈名〉earhole: 穿～ have one's ears pierced
【耳廓】ěrkuò = 耳郭 ěrguō
【耳力】ěrlì〈名〉〈书〉hearing: ～不济 have poor hearing
【耳聋】ěrlóng〈形〉deaf
【耳轮】ěrlún〈名〉[解剖] helix
【耳麦】ěrmài〈名〉ear microphone
【耳门】ěrmén〈名〉**1**(指耳朵) opening of the ear **2**(指门) side door
【耳鸣】ěrmíng ▸**p. 50**〈名〉[医学] tinnitus: 神经性～ nervous tinnitus
【耳膜】ěrmó〈名〉eardrum
【耳目】ěrmù〈名〉**1**(耳朵和眼睛) ears and eyes: ▸掩人～ **2**(见闻) information: ～不广 be poorly informed **3**〈喻〉(指人) spies: ～众多 have eyes and ears everywhere
【耳目闭塞】ěrmù-bìsè〈成〉be ill-informed
【耳目所及】ěrmù-suǒjí〈成〉from what one sees and hears
【耳目一新】ěrmù-yīxīn〈成〉find everything fresh and new
【耳旁风】ěrpángfēng = 耳边风 ěrbiānfēng
【耳热】ěrrè〈形〉**1**(耳朵发热) hot in the ear: 酒后～ one's ears burning under the influence of alcohol **2**(兴奋) extremely excited; (害臊) embarrassed: 一提起他，她就脸红～。Whenever his name was mentioned, her cheeks reddened and her ears burned.
【耳濡目染】ěrrú-mùrǎn〈成〉be imperceptibly influenced by what one sees and hears
【耳软心活】ěrruǎn-xīnhuó〈成〉be credulous and flexible
【耳塞】ěrsāi〈名〉**1**(指塞子) earplug **2**(指受话器) earpiece: 通过～听传译。Interpretation is heard through an earpiece.
【耳生】ěrshēng〈形〉unfamiliar to the ear: 多年不见了，可你说话的声音倒不～。We haven't seen each other for years, but your voice is still familiar.
【耳屎】ěrshǐ〈名〉〈口〉earwax
【耳饰】ěrshì〈名〉ear drop
【耳熟】ěrshú〈形〉familiar to the ear: 他的名字有点～。His name rings a bell.
【耳熟能详】ěrshú-néngxiáng〈成〉what is frequently heard can be repeated in detail
【耳顺】ěrshùn **A**〈名〉〈书〉sixty years of age: ～之年 sixty years of age ‖ 年逾～ over sixty **B**〈形〉pleasing to the ear: 我听京剧越来越～了。I am starting to really enjoy Beijing opera.
【耳套】ěrtào〈名〉ear muff(s)
【耳提面命】ěrtí-miànmìng〈成〉give earnest instructions in person
【耳听八方】ěrtīngbāfāng〈成〉be extremely alert
【耳听是虚，眼见为实】ěrtīng shì xū, yǎnjiàn wéi shí〈俗〉seeing is believing
【耳挖子】ěrwāzi〈名〉ear pick
【耳闻】ěrwén〈动〉〈书〉hear about: 这件事我有所～。I've heard about this.
【耳闻不如目见】ěrwén bùrú mùjiàn〈成〉seeing for oneself is better than hearing from others
【耳闻目睹】ěrwén-mùdǔ〈成〉hear with one's own ears and see with one's own eyes
【耳蜗】ěrwō〈名〉cochlea
【耳穴】ěrxué〈名〉ear acupuncture point
【耳炎】ěryán ▸**p. 50**〈名〉[医学] otitis: 内～ otitis interna ‖ 中～ otitis media
【耳语】ěryǔ〈动〉whisper in sb.'s ear
【耳针】ěrzhēn〈名〉ear acupuncture: ～疗法 ear acupuncture therapy
【耳坠】ěrzhuì〈名〉earring
【耳子】ěrzi〈名〉side handle

迩（邇）ěr〈形〉〈书〉close: ▸遐～

【迩来】ěrlái〈名〉〈书〉lately

饵（餌）ěr

A〈名〉**1**(诱饵) bait: ▸钓～，诱～ **2**(糕饼) cakes: ▸果～
B〈动〉〈书〉entice: ～以重利 entice with huge profits
【饵料】ěrliào〈名〉**1**(鱼食) fish feed **2**(鱼饵) fishing bait **3**(有毒诱饵) poison bait
【饵子】ěrzi〈名〉(fishing) bait

珥 ěr〈名〉〈古〉jade or pearl earrings

铒（鉺）ěr〈名〉[化学] erbium (Er)

èr

二 èr

A ▸**p. 691**〈数〉two: ～哥 second elder brother ‖ ～路公共汽车 No 2 bus ‖ 第～遍 the second time
B〈形〉**1**(不专) inconstant: ▸～心，三心～意 **2**(不同) different: 不～价! No bargaining! ▸～话
【二八】èrbā〈数〉〈旧〉sixteen: 年方～ be only sixteen years of age
【二把刀】èrbǎdāo〈口〉**A**〈形〉incompetent: 说实话，我讲日语可是～。To be frank, I only speak a smattering of Japanese. **B**〈名〉dabbler
【二把手】èrbǎshǒu〈名〉second in command: 当～ play second fiddle
【二百五】èrbǎiwǔ〈名〉〈口〉half-wit: 他是个～。He's not all there.
【二板】èrbǎn〈名〉[金融] second board: ～市场 second board market
【二倍体】èrbèitǐ〈名〉[生物] diploid
【二部制】èrbùzhì〈名〉two-shift system
【二重】èrchóng〈形〉double
【二重唱】èrchóngchàng〈名〉[音乐] (vocal) duet
【二重性】èrchóngxìng〈名〉duality
【二重奏】èrchóngzòu〈名〉[音乐] (instrumental) duet
【二传手】èrchuánshǒu〈名〉[排球] setter
【二次】èrcì〈形〉second
【二次方】èrcìfāng〈名〉[数学] square
【二次方程】èrcì fāngchéng〈名〉[数学] quadratic equation
【二次幂】èrcìmì〈名〉[数学] second power
【二次能源】èrcì néngyuán〈名〉secondary energy source
【二次污染】èrcì wūrǎn〈名〉secondary pollution
【二代证】èrdàizhèng〈名〉second-generation ID card: 办～ get a second-generation ID card
【二道贩子】èrdào fànzi〈名〉scalper
【二等】èrděng〈形〉second-class
【二等兵】èrděngbīng〈名〉**1**(英美陆军及美国海军陆战队) private **2**(美国空军) airman second class; (英国空军) leading aircraftman **3**(英国海军陆战队) marine second class
【二等分】èrděngfēn〈动〉bisect
【二等公民】èrděng gōngmín〈名〉second-class citizen
【二叠纪】Èrdiéjì〈名〉[地质] Permian Period
【二噁英】èr'èyīng〈名〉dioxin
【二房】èrfáng〈名〉**1**(指家族排行) second male branch of an extended family **2**(小老婆) concubine
【二房东】èrfángdōng〈名〉sub-lessor
【二分法】èrfēnfǎ〈名〉**1**[逻辑] dichotomy **2**[哲学] theory of one dividing into two
【二分音符】èrfēn yīnfú〈名〉[音乐] minim〈英〉; half note〈美〉
【二伏】èrfú = 中伏 zhōngfú
【二副】èrfù〈名〉second mate
【二鬼子】èrguǐzi〈名〉〈口〉traitor
【二锅头】èrguōtóu〈名〉*erguotou* [twice-distilled liquor usu from sorghum]
【二胡】èrhú ▸**p. 929**〈名〉*erhu* [two-stringed bowed instrument]: ～独奏 *erhu* solo
【二虎相争，必有一伤】èr hǔ xiāng zhēng, bì yǒu yī shāng = 两虎相斗，必有一伤 liǎng hǔ xiāng dòu, bì yǒu yī shāng
【二花脸】èrhuāliǎn〈名〉*erhualian* [flowery-faced male role in Beijing opera]
【二话】èrhuà〈名〉objection: ～不说 without demur ‖ 尽管干吧，我决无～。Do as you please. I won't raise any objections.
【二黄】èrhuáng〈名〉*erhuang* [one of the two chief types of music in traditional Chinese opera]
【二婚】èrhūn〈名〉remarriage

【二级】èrjí〈形〉 secondary
【二级市场】èrjí shìchǎng〈名〉 secondary market
【二极管】èrjíguǎn〈名〉［电子］ diode
【二价】èrjià〈名〉［化学］ bivalence
【二尖瓣】èrjiānbàn〈名〉［生理］ mitral valve
【二甲苯】èrjiǎběn〈名〉［化学］ xylene
【二进宫】èrjìngōng〈动〉〈口〉 be jailed a second time
【二进制】èrjìnzhì〈名〉 binary system
【二郎腿】èrlángtuǐ〈名〉 crossed legs: 翘着～ sit cross-legged
【二老】èrlǎo〈名〉 parents
【二愣子】èrlèngzi〈名〉〈口〉 hothead
【二流子】èrliúzi〈名〉 idler
【二路】èrlù〈形〉〈口〉 second-rate: ～货 inferior goods
【二律背反】èrlǜbèifǎn〈名〉［哲学］ antinomy
【二门】èrmén〈名〉 inner gate
【二米饭】èrmǐfàn〈名〉 (cooked) rice and millet mix
【二秘】èrmì〈名〉 second secretary
【二拇指】èrmuzhǐ〈名〉〈口〉 forefinger
【二奶】èrnǎi〈名〉 kept woman: ▸包～
【二年生】èrniánshēng〈形〉［植物］ biennial: ～植物 biennial plant
【二炮】Èrpào〈名〉 Strategic Missile Force
【二人同心，其利断金】èr rén tóngxīn, qí lì duàn jīn〈成〉 unity is strength
【二人世界】èrrén shìjiè〈名〉 world of two people: 享受～ enjoy the two people's world
【二人台】èrréntái〈名〉［曲艺］ *errentai* [song-and-dance duet popular in Inner Mongolia]
【二人转】èrrénzhuàn〈名〉［曲艺］ *errenzhuan* [two-character song-and-dance performance popular in the north-east of China]
【二审】èrshěn〈名〉［法律］ second instance: ～裁定 second instance order
【二十八宿】èrshíbāxiù〈名〉 the twenty-eight lunar mansions
【二十四节气】èrshísì jiéqì〈名〉 the twenty-four solar terms

> **二十四节气**
>
> The solar terms mark 24 evenly-spaced points in the Chinese solar calendar. Starting from the Spring Equinox (at 0° longitude, when the sun is directly above the equator), each 15° advance of the sun along the ecliptic marks a solar term. Solar terms are traditionally used to help farmers determine when to plant and harvest crops according to changes in the weather. For example, the 6th solar term, Grain Rain (谷雨), marks the time in the year that rain starts to fall. The dates of the terms are fixed. The Beginning of Spring (立春), for example, always occurs between the 3rd and the 5th of February. The 24 solar terms are, in order: 立春, 雨水, 惊蛰, 春分, 清明, 谷雨, 立夏, 小满, 芒种, 夏至, 小暑, 大暑, 立秋, 处暑,白露, 秋分, 寒露, 霜降, 立冬, 小雪, 大雪, 冬至, 小寒, 大寒.

【二十四史】èrshísìshǐ〈名〉 Twenty-Four Books of History
【二手】èrshǒu〈形〉 second-hand: ～材料 second-hand materials ‖ ～车 second hand car ‖ ～房 house that has had a previous owner
【二踢脚】èrtījiǎo〈名〉 double-kick firecracker
【二头肌】èrtóujī〈名〉［解剖］ biceps
【二维】èrwéi〈形〉 two-dimensional: ～空间 two-dimensional space
【二五眼】èrwuyǎn〈方〉 **A**〈形〉 inferior **B**〈名〉 incompetent person
【二线】èrxiàn〈名〉 **1**（指防线） secondary defence line **2**〈喻〉（指工作岗位） secondary-line post: 退居～ retire to a secondary-line post
【二项式】èrxiàngshì〈名〉［数学］ binomial (formula)
【二心】èrxīn〈名〉 duplicity: 怀有～ harbour disloyalty
【二氧化硫】èryǎnghuàliú〈名〉［化学］ sulphur dioxide (SO_2)
【二氧化碳】èryǎnghuàtàn〈名〉［化学］ carbon dioxide (CO_2)
【二一添作五】èryī tiānzuòwǔ〈惯〉 go halves
【二元】èryuán **A**〈名〉［数学］ binary: ～方程 equation with two unknowns **B**〈形〉［化学］ binary
【二元论】èryuánlùn〈名〉［哲学］ dualism
【二月】èryuè ▸**p. 928**〈名〉 **1**（阳历） February **2**（阴历） second month of the lunar year
【二战】Èrzhàn〈名〉 Second World War
【二者必居其一】èrzhě bì jū qí yī〈俗〉 either one or the other
【二致】èrzhì〈形〉 different: 殊无～ there is no difference whatsoever

弍 èr〈书〉= 二 èr

刵 èr〈动〉〈古〉 cut off sb.'s ear

贰（貳） èr
A ▸**p. 691**〈数〉 two [used for the numeral 二 on cheques, etc. to avoid alterations or mistakes]
B〈动〉〈书〉 defect: ▸～臣

Ff

fā

发（發）fā

A〈动〉**1**（发射）launch: ～导弹 launch a missile ‖ ～炮 fire a cannon ‖ 一枪未～ without firing a shot ▸百～百中，弹无虚～ **2**（产生）produce: ～芽 sprout ▸～电，～声 **3**（引发）trigger: ▸～动，～奋，启～ **4**（显现出）become: ～黄的照片 yellowing photo ‖ 气得脸色～青 turn purple with rage ‖ 她的嘴唇冻得～青。 Her lips were blue from the cold. ▸～胖 **5**（指感情）show one's feelings: ～慈悲 show mercy ▸～愁，～怒，～笑 **6**（感到）feel: ～痒 itch ‖ 他两腿～软。 His legs felt weak. ‖ 我嘴里～苦。 I have a bitter taste in my mouth. ▸～晕 **7**（财势兴旺）flourish: ～一笔横财 have a financial windfall ‖ 他炒股票～了。 He has made a fortune speculating in shares. ▸～财，～家，暴～户 **8**（扩大）expand: ▸～达，～扬，～展 **9**（生长）grow: ▸～育 **10**（指食物）rise: ～豆芽 raise bean sprouts ‖ 我的蛋糕做坏了，面没～起来。 My cake is a disaster. It hasn't risen. **11**（出发）set out: 夕～朝至 start out in the evening and arrive in the morning **12**（来自）send off: ～自伦敦的报道 news dispatched from London ▸～兵，～配，打～ **13**（揭露）expose: ▸～掘，揭～ **14**（散开）disperse: ▸蒸～ **15**（发送）give out: ～传单 distribute leaflets ‖ ～电子邮件 send an email ‖ ～工资 pay out wages ‖ ～贺电 send a congratulatory telegram **16**（表示）express: ▸～牢骚

B〈量〉[used for ammunition]: 三～炮弹 three shells ‖ 三～子弹 three bullets

▸fà

【发案】fā'àn〈动〉[of a criminal case] occur: ～现场 scene of a crime

【发榜】fābǎng〈动〉publish a list of successful candidates: 录取新生明日～。 The admission list will come out tomorrow.

【发包】fābāo〈动〉contract out: ～工程 contract a project out

【发报】fābào〈动〉send a telegram: ～机 telegraph

【发标】fābiāo〈动〉advertise tenders

【发飙】fābiāo〈动〉**1**（发狂）go crazy **2**（发威）show one's prowess: 小将突然～，击败了上届冠军。 The youngster suddenly came of age and defeated the defending champion.

【发表】fābiǎo〈动〉**1**（表达）issue: ～看法 voice one's opinion ‖ ～联合公报 issue a joint communiqué ‖ ～声明 make a statement ‖ ～演说 deliver a speech ‖ ～意见 express one's opinion **2**（刊登）publish: ～论文 publish a thesis ‖ ～社论 carry an editorial

【发兵】fābīng〈动〉dispatch troops: ～增援 send reinforcements

【发病】fābìng〈动〉[of a disease] flare up: ～率 incidence of a disease ‖ 他突然～。 He fell ill suddenly.

【发布】fābù〈动〉issue: ～命令 issue an order ‖ ～通缉令 issue a wanted circular ‖ ～信息 release information ‖ 新闻～会 press conference

【发财】fācái〈动〉**1**（获得大量钱财）get rich: 发横财 have a windfall ‖ ～致富 get rich ‖ 发国难财 exploit the national crisis for profiteering purposes ‖ 恭喜～! I wish you prosperity! **2**〈套〉（工作）work: 您在哪儿～? Where do you work?

【发颤】fāchàn〈动〉tremble: 浑身～ tremble all over ‖ 他兴奋得声音有点～。 There was a slight quiver of delight in his voice.

【发车】fāchē〈动〉[of a vehicle] depart: ～信号 departure signal ‖ D82 次火车四点半～。 The train D82 leaves at 4:30.

【发痴】fāchī〈动〉go mad

【发愁】fāchóu〈动〉worry: 不为吃穿～ have no worries about food and clothing ‖ 老为钱～ have constant money worries

【发出】fāchū〈动〉**1**（发生）send out: ～警报 sound the alarm ‖ ～一声尖叫 give a scream **2**（发布）issue: ～号召 issue a call ‖ ～警告 issue a warning (to) ‖ ～指示 issue a directive ‖ ～最后通牒 give an ultimatum **3**（送出）send out: ～传票 issue a summons ‖ ～通知 dispatch a notice ‖ ～邀请 send out invitations

【发怵】fāchù = 发憷 fāchù

【发憷】fāchù〈动〉feel timid: 对明天的考试我有些～。 I'm apprehensive about tomorrow's examination.

【发达】fādá〈形〉developed: 肌肉～ well-developed muscle ‖ 经济～ advanced economically ‖ 交通～ have advanced communications

【发达国家】fādá guójiā〈名〉developed country: 欠～ underdeveloped country

【发呆】fādāi〈动〉stare blankly: 坐在那儿～ sit there in a trance ‖ ～的神态 air of abstraction ‖ 他眼神～。 His eyes glazed over.

【发嗲】fādiǎ〈动〉speak or act coquettishly

【发电】fādiàn〈动〉generate electricity: 利用太阳能/风力～ generate electricity by harnessing solar energy/wind power ‖ ～厂 power plant ‖ ～站 power station

【发电车】fādiànchē〈名〉generator car

【发电机】fādiànjī〈名〉generator

【发动】fādòng〈动〉**1**（使开始）launch: ～政变 stage a coup d'état ‖ ～攻势 mount an offensive ‖ ～战争 wage a war **2**（动员）mobilize: ～全班同学 get the whole class into action ‖ ～群众 mobilize the masses **3**（使发动）start: ～机器/引擎 start a machine/an engine ‖ 汽车～不起来。 The car won't start.

【发动机】fādòngjī〈名〉engine

【发抖】fādǒu〈动〉tremble: 冻得/气得～ tremble with cold/rage ‖ 浑身～ tremble all over ‖ 他激动得声音～。 His voice trembled with excitement.

【发堵】fādǔ〈动〉feel oppressed: 我的心里一阵～。 I was overcome by a sudden feeling of oppression.

【发端】fāduān〈名〉〈书〉outset: 冷战的～ inception of the Cold War ‖ ～于 beginning in

【发凡】fāfán〈名〉〈书〉introduction: ～起例 introduction and guide ‖ 《修辞学～》 *An Introduction to Rhetoric*

【发放】fāfàng〈动〉**1**（签发）grant: ～贷款 grant credit ‖ ～经营许可证 issue a business licence ‖ ～救灾物资 hand out relief **2**（发出）send out: ～信号弹 send up a signal flare **3**（分发）distribute

【发奋】fāfèn〈动〉**1**（奋发）exert oneself: ～工作 go all out in one's work **2** = 发愤 fāfèn

【发愤】fāfèn〈动〉resolve: ～学习 resolve to study hard ‖ ～进取，才能成功。 Success is gained through resolve to win.

【发愤图强】fāfèn-túqiáng〈成〉make determined efforts to better oneself

【发疯】fāfēng〈动〉go mad: 被拐小孩的母亲急得～了。 The mother of the kidnapped child was crazy with worry. ‖ 他简直～了，竟然打自己的母亲。 He must have been out of his mind to beat his own mother. ‖ 她觉得自己简直要～了。 She felt as if she was sliding into madness.

【发福】fāfú〈动〉〈套〉put on weight: 您～了。 You've put on weight.

【发糕】fāgāo〈名〉steamed sponge cake

【发稿】fāgǎo〈动〉**1**（指电讯稿）distribute news dispatches: ～时间 release date **2**（指文字稿）send manuscripts to press: ～付印 send a manuscript for printing ‖ 到～时为止 at press time

【发功】fāgōng〈动〉[of a *qigong* master] emit energy

【发光】fāguāng **A**〈动〉give out light: ～的不一定都是金子。 All that glitters is not gold. **B**〈形〉luminescent: ～体 luminous body

【发汗】fāhàn〈动〉induce perspiration: ～可以治感冒。 A good sweat cures a cold.

【发号施令】fāhào-shīlìng〈成〉issue orders: 你有什么权力对我～? What right have you got to order me about?

【发狠】fāhěn〈动〉**1**（下狠心）make a determined effort: ～戒烟 make a determined effort to give up smoking ‖ 他为买一部车而～工作。 He is working like crazy in order to buy a car. **2**（发怒）get angry: 别以为你一～就把他们吓跑了。 Don't assume that your anger will frighten them off.

【发横】fāhèng〈动〉 behave unreasonably: 她老在母亲面前～。 She is always harsh and rude to her mother.

【发花】fāhuā〈动〉 become hazy: 她饿得两眼～。 She was so hungry that her vision blurred.

【发话】fāhuà〈动〉 give instructions: 我们下一步该怎么办，你得～。 You must tell us what to do next. ‖ 人家早～啦，不许咱再到这里来。 They warned us long ago that we should not come here again.

【发还】fāhuán〈动〉 return: ～失物 return lost property ‖ 把试卷～给学生 give the test papers back to the students

【发慌】fāhuāng〈动〉 get flustered: 心中～ feel nervous ‖ 站在讲台上，我有点儿～。 I felt a bit nervous on the podium. ‖ 镇静，别～! Keep calm! Don't get into a panic.

【发挥】fāhuī〈动〉 1（指表现潜能） bring into play: ～才能 give play to one's talent ‖ ～积极性 exercise one's initiative ‖ ～想象力 give free rein to one's imagination ‖ ～专长 give full play to one's expertise ‖ 他在考试中没～出自己的水平。 He didn't do himself justice in the exam. 2（指表达） elaborate: 借题～ seize a pretext to air one's view ‖ 这一点我不想多加～。 I don't want to elaborate on this.

【发昏】fāhūn〈动〉 1（神志不清） feel dizzy: 饿得～ feel faint with hunger 2（失去理智） lose one's head: 你是不是～了，怎么能做这种事情? Have you lost your mind? How could you do something like this?

【发火】fāhuǒ〈动〉 1（点燃） catch fire: ～装置 ignition 2（爆炸） detonate: 炮弹没有～。 The shell did not go off. 3（生气） fly into a rage: 冲某人～ vent one's anger on sb. ‖ 动不动就～ flare up easily

【发货】fāhuò〈动〉 dispatch goods: 按期～ dispatch goods on schedule ‖ ～单/通知书 consignment note

【发急】fājí〈动〉 get/become impatient: 他一输就～。 He became agitated every time he lost a game. ‖ 发现儿子走失，她～了。 She became anxious when she found out her son was missing.

【发迹】fājì〈动〉 gain fame and fortune: 靠走私军火～ make one's fortune smuggling munitions

【发家】fājiā〈动〉 build up a family fortune: ～致富 build up family wealth

【发贱】fājiàn〈动〉 demean oneself: 你巴结他，真是～! Your sucking up to him is so cheap!

【发酵】fājiào〈动〉 ferment: ～饲料 fermented feed

【发酵粉】fājiàofěn〈名〉 baking powder: 用～发面 leaven the dough with yeast powder

【发酵酒】fājiàojiǔ〈名〉 fermented wine

【发紧】fājǐn〈动〉 1（指紧绷） [of the chest muscles] become taut 2（指紧张） feel nervous

【发窘】fājiǒng〈动〉 feel uneasy: 令人～的场合 embarrassing occasion ‖ 这个问题让她～。 The question embarrassed her.

【发酒疯】fā jiǔfēng〈动〉 get drunk and out of control: 才喝了两杯就大～ got roaring drunk on only two drinks

【发觉】fājué〈动〉 find: 他埋头读书，有人进来他都没有～。 He was so absorbed in reading that he was not aware someone had come in. ‖ 我～他在撒谎。 I found that he was lying.

【发掘】fājué〈动〉 excavate: ～古墓 excavate an ancient tomb ‖ 进行考古～ carry out archaeological excavations ‖ ～历史遗迹 dig up historical ruins ‖〈喻〉 ～潜力 tap potential ‖〈喻〉 ～人才 seek talented people ‖〈喻〉 ～中医药学遗产 explore the legacy of traditional Chinese medicine

【发刊词】fākāncí〈名〉 foreword to a new periodical

【发苦】fākǔ〈动〉 become bitter: 不加糖的咖啡喝后嘴里～。 Black coffee leaves a bitter taste in the mouth.

【发狂】fākuáng〈动〉 go crazy: 爱得～ be madly in love ‖ 被逼得～ be driven crazy

【发困】fākùn〈动〉〈口〉 feel sleepy: 午饭后～ feel sleepy after lunch ‖ 这些药让人～。 These tablets make you drowsy.

【发懒】fālǎn〈动〉 feel lethargic: 炎热的天气使人直～。 The hot weather makes me feel lethargic.

【发牢骚】fā láosao〈动〉 let off steam: 大～ pour out one's grievances ‖ 你老～，真让人受不了。 Your constant whining is driving me to distraction.

【发冷】fālěng〈动〉 feel cold: 我浑身～。 I feel chilly all over.

【发愣】fālèng〈动〉 be in a daze: 他站在那儿～。 He stood there in a numbed daze.

【发亮】fāliàng〈动〉 shine: 把机器擦得闪闪～ polish the machine till it shines ‖ 在阳光下闪闪～ shine in the sun ‖ 她兴奋得两眼～。 Her eyes twinkled with excitement.

【发令】fālìng〈动〉 issue an order: ～开火 give an order to fire

【发令枪】fālìngqiāng〈名〉［体育］ starting pistol

【发聋振聩】fālóng-zhènkuì = 振聋发聩 zhènlóng-fākuì

【发落】fāluò〈动〉 deal with: 从轻～ deal with sb. leniently ‖ 罪犯在等候～。 The criminal is awaiting the judge's sentence.

【发麻】fāmá〈动〉 feel numb: 手～ feel numb in the hand ‖ 我两腿～。 I have pins and needles in my legs.

【发毛】fāmáo〈动〉 be panicky: 他每次考试前都～。 He gets scared before each exam.

【发霉】fāméi〈动〉 go mouldy: ～的面包 mouldy bread

【发闷】fāmēn〈动〉 1（闷气） go stuffy: 今天天气～。 It's stuffy today. 2（指声音） be muffled: ～的雷声 muffle of thunder

【发闷】fāmèn〈形〉 depressed: 独自在角落里～ be sulking alone in a corner

【发蒙】fāmēng〈动〉 get into a muddle: 头脑～ feel muddled ‖ 你越讲我越～。 The more you talk, the more you confuse me.

【发蒙】fāméng〈动〉〈旧〉 teach a child to read and write: ～读物 elementary reader

【发面】fāmiàn A〈动〉 leaven dough: 用酵母～ leaven the dough with yeast B〈名〉 leavened dough: ～饼 leavened pancake

【发明】fāmíng A〈动〉 invent: ～一种新型晶体管 devise a new type of transistor ‖ 贝尔于1876年～了电话。 Bell invented the telephone in 1876. B〈名〉 invention: 已获专利的～ patented invention ‖ 中国古代四大～ four great inventions in ancient China

【发木】fāmù〈动〉 go numb: ～的手指 numb fingers ‖ 我的脚趾冻得～了。 My toes have gone numb with cold.

【发奶】fānǎi〈动〉 promote lactation: 喝鱼汤可以～。 Fish soup is good for inducing lactation.

【发难】fānàn〈动〉 1（指反抗或叛乱） launch a revolt: 公开～ launch an open attack 2〈书〉（问难） raise difficult questions for discussion

【发腻】fānì〈动〉 1（厌烦） be sickening: 令人～的讲座 nasty lecture 2（指油腻） be greasy: 这道菜让人嘴里～。 The dish tastes unpleasantly greasy.

【发蔫】fāniān〈动〉 1（指庄稼、花草） wither: 几天没浇水，花都开始～了。 Having gone several days without water, the flowers are beginning to droop. 2（指精神） be listless: 她最近有点～。 She has been a bit listless recently.

【发怒】fānù〈动〉 get angry: 动辄～ get angry easily ‖ 无端～ fly into a rage for no reason

【发排】fāpái〈动〉［印刷］ send a manuscript for typesetting: 你的论文已经～。 Your thesis has been sent for typesetting.

【发胖】fāpàng〈动〉 put on weight: 如果不多运动，身体就会～。 If you don't take more exercise, you'll get fat.

【发泡】fāpào〈动〉 froth: ～塑料 plastic foam

【发配】fāpèi〈动〉〈旧〉 banish sb. into exile: ～边疆 be exiled to the borderlands

【发脾气】fā píqi〈动〉 lose one's temper: 为一点小事大～ fly into a rage over a trivial matter

【发飘】fāpiāo〈动〉 feel weak: 他病刚好，脚底下还～。 He has just recuperated from the illness and is still a bit shaky.

【发票】fāpiào〈名〉 invoice: 开～ issue an invoice ‖ 增值税～ VAT invoice ‖ 凭～报销 reimburse one's expenses against receipts

【发起】fāqǐ〈动〉 1（倡导） initiate 2（发动） start: ～冲锋 charge forward ‖ ～宣传攻势 launch a press campaign ‖ ～国 sponsor nation

【发情】fāqíng〈动〉［动物］ be in heat: ～期 heat period

【发球】fāqiú〈动〉 serve: ～得分 win one's service ‖ ～抢攻 smash after service ‖ 换～ change of service

【发热】fārè〈动〉 1（温度升高） generate heat: 长时间的攀爬使他浑身～。 He was warmed up by the long climb. ‖ 如果割草机～，就把它关掉。 If the lawn mower gets hot, turn it off. 2（发烧） run a temperature: 不明原因的～ fever of undetermined origin 3〈喻〉（不冷静） be impetuous: 别头脑～! Don't be impetuous!

【发人深思】fārénshēnsī〈成〉 thought-provoking: ～的问题 thought-provoking question

【发人深省】fārénshēnxǐng〈成〉 be thought-provoking: 他话虽不多，却～。 His words, though few, really make us think.

【发轫】fārèn〈动〉〈书〉 commence: ～之作 maiden work

【发散】fāsàn〈动〉 1（指光线、热量等） diffuse: ～光 divergent light ‖〈喻〉 ～式思维 divergent thinking 2［中医］（指内热） sweat out

【发丧】fāsāng〈动〉 1（指死讯） announce a death 2（指丧事） arrange a funeral

【发涩】fāsè A〈形〉 1（不润滑） hard-going: 轴～，该上油了。 The axle doesn't work smoothly and needs oiling. 2（有涩味） bitter: 这柿子有点～。 This persimmon tastes a bit astringent. B〈动〉 itch: 眼睛～ eyes itch

【发痧】fāshā〈动〉〈方〉have heatstroke
【发傻】fāshǎ〈动〉 1（目瞪口呆） be dumbfounded: 听到这个消息，他一下子～了。He was stupefied at the news. 2（犯糊涂） act foolishly
【发善心】fāshànxīn〈动〉show kindness of heart
【发烧】fāshāo〈动〉 run a fever: 发高烧 run a high fever ‖ ～说胡话 run a fever and babble deliriously
【发烧友】fāshāoyǒu〈名〉fan
【发射】fāshè〈动〉 1（指物体） launch: ～火箭/鱼雷/导弹/卫星 launch a rocket/torpedo/missile/satellite ‖ ～炮弹 fire artillery shells 2（指信号） emit: ～无线电波 send out radio waves ‖ ～功率 transmitting power
【发射场】fāshèchǎng〈名〉launch site
【发射架】fāshèjià〈名〉 launcher: 导弹～ missile launcher
【发身】fāshēn〈动〉go through puberty: ～期 puberty
【发神经】fā shénjīng〈动〉〈口〉 go mad: 把枪放下！你是～还是怎么了？ Put that gun down! Are you crazy or something?
【发生】fāshēng〈动〉 happen: ～交通事故 have a traffic accident ‖ ～兴趣 develop an interest ‖ 机器～了故障。The machine broke down. ‖ 中国～了巨大变化。Great changes have taken place in China.
【发生额】fāshēng'é〈名〉［金融］ amount incurred: 资金往来～ amount of fund transfer incurred ‖ 民间借贷的～ amount incurred in private lending
【发声】fāshēng〈动〉 make a sound: 练习～ practise vocalization ‖ ～技巧 vocalism ‖ ～器官 vocal organ
【发市】fāshì〈动〉 make the first successful deal: 半天还没有～呢! There hasn't been a single deal so far!
【发事】fāshì〈动〉 have an accident: ～地点 site of an accident
【发誓】fāshì〈动〉 make an oath: ～绝对保密 swear absolute secrecy ‖ 手按《圣经》～ swear on the *Bible*
【发售】fāshòu〈动〉 sell: 按成本～ sell at cost price ‖ 公开～ put on public sale
【发水】fāshuǐ〈动〉flood: 这条河一下雨就～。The river floods whenever there is rain.
【发送】fāsòng〈动〉 1（指信号） transmit by radio: ～电信稿 send a dispatch ‖ ～无线电信号 send radio signals 2（指物或人） dispatch: ～货物 dispatch goods ‖ ～旅客 dispatch travellers
【发送】fāsong〈动〉handle funeral arrangements
【发酸】fāsuān〈动〉 1（指食物） go sour: 牛奶～了。The milk's gone sour. ‖ 面包有点～。The bread tastes a bit off. 2（指眼鼻） feel a tingle in one's eyes/nose: 我一听到那不幸的消息，就鼻子～。I felt a prickle in my nose when I heard the sad news. 3（指肢体） ache: 我累得浑身～。I am aching all over with fatigue.
【发条】fātiáo〈名〉［机械］ spring: 给手表上～ wind up the watch
【发帖】fātiě〈动〉 post: 在网站上海量～ submit a large number of posts on a website
【发威】fāwēi〈动〉 display one's prowess: 下半场开始～ start to display one's prowess during the second half ‖ 在众人面前～ assume an air of importance in public
【发文】fāwén A〈动〉 issue a document: 联合～ issue a joint document B〈名〉 outgoing message
【发问】fāwèn〈动〉 ask a question: 连续～ keep firing questions
【发现】fāxiàn A〈动〉 discover: ～病毒 detect viruses ‖ ～人才 find talented people ‖ ～问题 identify problems ‖ ～险情 spot a danger ‖ 哥伦布于 1492 年～了美洲。Columbus discovered America in 1492. ‖ 我～你经常跟那个女孩出去。I've noticed that you often go out with that girl. ‖ 嫌疑人被警方～。The suspect was spotted by the police. B〈名〉 find: 取得重大～ make an important find ‖ 震撼世界的～ earth-shattering discovery ‖ 考古～ archaeological finds
【发祥】fāxiáng〈动〉〈书〉 1（出现） happen 2（起源） appear and grow prosperous: 中国古代文明～于黄河流域。China's ancient civilization arose first in the Yellow River valley.
【发祥地】fāxiángdì〈名〉 place of origin: 人类的～ cradle of humanity ‖ 中国古代文化的～ birthplace of the ancient Chinese culture
【发笑】fāxiào〈动〉 burst into laughter: 忍不住～ burst out laughing ‖ 引人～ raise a laugh
【发泄】fāxiè〈动〉 give vent (to): ～不满 air one's grievances ‖ 他向工人～怒气。He unleashed his anger on the workmen.
【发薪】fāxīn〈动〉 pay wages or salary: ～日 pay day
【发信】fāxìn〈动〉 post a letter
【发行】fāxíng〈动〉 circulate: ～报纸 publish a newspaper ‖ ～彩票 distribute lottery tickets ‖ ～债券 issue bonds ‖ ～影片 release a film ‖ 通过邮局～ circulate through the post office ‖ ～量 circulation
【发行价】fāxíngjià〈名〉 issue price: 跌破～ fall below the issue price
【发行权】fāxíngquán〈名〉 distribution rights: 海外～ overseas distribution rights
【发虚】fāxū〈动〉 1（感到心虚） feel apprehensive: 面对如此多的观众，他真有些～。He was really diffident before so large an audience. 2（感到虚弱）be feeble: 病愈后，他感到～。Infirmity began to catch up with him after his recovery.
【发芽】fāyá〈动〉 sprout: 使种子在温室里～ germinate seeds in a greenhouse
【发言】fāyán A〈动〉 make a speech: 要求～ demand the floor ‖ 每位～限三分钟 limit the length of each speech to three minutes ‖ 请您～。The floor is yours. B〈名〉 speech: 不用稿子的～ unscripted speech ‖ 精彩的～ brilliant speech
【发言权】fāyánquán〈名〉 right to speak: 他对该事最有～。He is best qualified to speak on this matter. ‖ 没有调查，就没有～。No investigation, no say.
【发言人】fāyánrén〈名〉 spokesperson: 外交部～ spokesman of the foreign ministry ‖ 新闻～ press spokesperson
【发炎】fāyán A〈动〉 get inflamed: 引起皮肤～ cause a skin irritation ‖ 伤口有点～。The wound has become a bit inflamed. B ▸**p. 50**〈名〉 inflammation
【发扬】fāyáng〈动〉 carry on: ～艰苦奋斗的精神 carry on the spirit of plain living and hard struggle ‖ ～民主 promote democracy ‖ ～优良传统 carry forward the fine tradition
【发扬光大】fāyáng-guāngdà〈成〉 carry forward: 奥林匹克精神会～。The Olympic spirit will prevail.
【发疟子】fā yàozi〈动〉suffer from malaria
【发音】fāyīn A〈动〉 pronounce: ～方法 method of articulation ‖ 这个词怎么～? How do you pronounce this word? B〈名〉 pronunciation: 纠正～ correct sb.'s pronunciation ‖ 标准～ standard pronunciation ‖ 清楚的/不清楚的～ clear/poor pronunciation
【发育】fāyù〈动〉 grow: ～成熟 grow to maturity ‖ 影响儿童～ affect the development of children ‖ 婴儿～良好。The baby is coming along well.
【发源】fāyuán〈动〉 originate in: 黄河～于青海。The Yellow River rises in Qinghai Province.
【发源地】fāyuándì〈名〉 place of origin: 美国是棒球的～。America is the home of baseball.
【发愿】fāyuàn〈动〉 make one's wishes heard: 起誓～ vow to speak one's mind
【发晕】fāyūn〈动〉 feel dizzy: 她高兴得～了。She felt giddy with happiness. ‖ 他的头～。His head is swimming.
【发运】fāyùn〈动〉 ship: 由铁路～ be consigned by rail
【发展】fāzhǎn〈动〉 1（指演变） develop: ～国民经济 develop the national economy ‖ ～生产力 expand the productive forces ‖ ～壮大 grow from strength to strength ‖ 促进经济～ promote economic development ‖ 德、智、体、美全面～ develop morally, intellectually, physically and aesthetically ‖ 可持续～ sustainable development ‖ ～是硬道理。Development is a hard truth. ‖ 两国关系稳步～。Relations between the two countries are developing steadily. 2（招募） admit: ～新成员 recruit new members ‖ ～新会员国 add new member states
【发展期】fāzhǎnqī〈名〉 development period: 文化产业进入一个黄金～。The cultural industries are entering a golden period of development.
【发展中国家】fāzhǎnzhōng guójiā〈名〉 developing country
【发怔】fāzhèng〈动〉 be stupefied
【发作】fāzuò〈动〉 1（突然暴发） break out: 心脏病再度～ have another heart attack ‖ 周期性～ periodic attacks ‖ 毒性/药性～了。The poison/medicine took effect. 2（发怒） lose one's temper: 她很生气，但当着学生的面又不好～。She was very angry, but in the presence of her students she had to refrain from losing her temper.

fá

乏 fá

A〈动〉 lack: 不～经验/勇气 be not short of experience/courage ▸～味, 缺～
B〈形〉 1（累） tired: 干～了 be done in from working ‖ 走～了 be tired out with walking ▸疲～, 人困马～ 2〈方〉（无用） worn-out: 车胎～得不能用了。The tyre is completely worn out.
【乏困】fákùn〈形〉 tired
【乏力】fálì〈形〉 1（没力气） worn-out 2（没能力） incapable: 回天～ be unable to save the situation
【乏术】fáshù〈动〉〈书〉 be unable to do sth.: 破门～ have no way to score
【乏味】fáwèi〈形〉 boring: ～的读物 tedious reading ‖ 他感到生活很～。Life seems flat to him.

伐[1]

fá〈动〉 1（砍倒） cut down: ～树 fell trees ▸～木, 砍～ 2（攻击） attack: ▸讨～, 口诛笔～

伐[2] fá〈动〉〈书〉 boast: 不矜不～ not be conceited ▸～善

【伐木】fámù〈动〉 fell timber: ～工人 lumberjack ‖ ～许可证 felling licence

【伐善】fáshàn〈动〉〈书〉brag about one's strengths

罚（罰） fá〈动〉 punish: ～点球 have a penalty kick ‖ 施以/处以重～ impose tough penalties (on) ‖ 受～ be penalized ▸～款, 赏～分明, 体～

【罚不当罪】fábùdāngzuì〈成〉be punished too severely

【罚出场】fá chūchǎng〈动〉［体育］ send off (for a foul)

【罚单】 fádān〈名〉 ticket: 交通违规～ ticket

【罚金】fájīn〈名〉 fine: 处以～ impose a fine ‖ 交纳～ pay a forfeit

【罚酒】fájiǔ〈动〉 make sb. drink as a forfeit: 我因迟到被～三杯。 Because I was late I was forced to drink three glasses of wine.

【罚款】fákuǎn **A**〈动〉 fine: 处以～ fine sb. ‖ 对酒后驾驶～很重 impose a heavy fine on sb. for drunk driving **B**〈名〉 fine: 交～ pay a penalty ‖ 免除～ remit a fine

【罚没】fámò〈动〉 fine and confiscate: 拍卖～的物品 sell off confiscated goods

【罚球】fáqiú〈动〉（指篮球） take a free throw;（指冰球） take a penalty shot;（指足球） take a penalty kick: 罚点球 take a spot kick ‖ ～命中/得分 score a penalty

【罚息】fáxī〈动〉 be charged interest: 信用卡客户透支几元、几十元就要被～。 Credit card customers who go overdrawn by a few will be charged interest.

【罚一儆百】fáyī-jǐngbǎi〈成〉 punish one as a deterrent to others

【罚则】fázé〈名〉 penalty provisions

垡 fá〈方〉

A〈动〉 turn up soil

B〈名〉 upturned soil: 深耕晒～ plough and aerate the soil

阀[1]**（閥）** fá〈名〉 **1**（指物）meritorious: ▸门～ **2**（指人） powerful person or group: ▸财～, 军～

阀[2]**（閥）** fá〈名〉［机械］ valve: ▸安全～, 减压～

【阀门】fámén〈名〉［机械］ valve: 打开/关闭～ open/close a valve

筏 fá〈名〉 raft: 橡皮～ rubber raft ▸木～, 竹～

【筏道】fádào〈名〉 log chute

【筏子】fázi〈名〉 raft: 羊皮～ sheepskin raft

fǎ

法 fǎ

A〈名〉 **1**（法律） law: 依～治国 rule the state by law ‖ 宪～ constitution ‖ 移民～ immigration law ▸婚姻～, 立～, 民～ **2**（标准） standard: ▸～帖 **3**（方法） method: 表达～ mode of expression ‖ 做～ way of doing ▸教学～, 如～炮制, 土～, 用～ **4**［佛教］ dharma: ▸佛～ **5**（法术） magic: 作～ do magic ‖ 斗～ exercise magic powers against each other **B**〈动〉 follow: ～其遗志 pursue sb.'s unfulfilled wish ▸效～

【法案】fǎ'àn〈名〉 bill: 提交～ present a bill ‖ 制定～ formulate an act ‖《人权～》*Bill of Rights*

【法办】fǎbàn〈动〉 bring to justice: 将罪犯逮捕～ have criminals arrested and brought to justice

【法宝】 fǎbǎo〈名〉 **1**［佛教］ Sutras **2**（特效方法） talisman: 群众路线是我们工作的～。 Relying on the masses is the most effective method in our work.

【法币】fǎbì ▸**p. 328**〈名〉〈旧〉 *fabi* [paper currency issued by the KMT government from 1935 to 1948]

【法不责众】fǎbùzézhòng〈成〉 laws fail if too many people disrespect them

【法场】fǎchǎng〈名〉 **1** = 道场 dàochǎng **2**〈旧〉（刑场） execution ground: 劫～ raid an execution ground to rescue the condemned ‖ 押赴～ take sb. under escort to the execution ground

【法槌】fǎchuí〈名〉 gavel: 法官一敲～，喊道：“肃静!” The judge banged his gavel and said, 'Silence in court!'

【法典】fǎdiǎn〈名〉 code: 制定～ formulate the laws

【法定】 fǎdìng〈形〉 legal: ～计量单位 legal unit of measurement ‖ ～退休年龄 mandatory retirement age ‖ ～义务 legal obligation ‖ ～程序 legal proceeding ‖ ～继承人 legitimate heir ‖ ～假日 official holiday ‖ ～年龄 lawful age ‖ 达到～人数 reach a quorum

【法度】fǎdù〈名〉 **1**（法律和制度） law **2**（准则） norm: 行为不合～ against norms of conduct

【法夫郡】Fǎfūjùn〈名〉 Fife

【法官】fǎguān〈名〉 judge

【法规】fǎguī〈名〉 laws and regulations: 交通安全～ traffic safety code ‖ 行政～ administrative rules and regulations ‖ 新～下月实施。 The new law comes into force next month.

【法国】Fǎguó〈名〉 France: ～人 French person

【法国梧桐】Fǎguó wútóng〈名〉 plane tree

【法国新闻社】 Fǎguó Xīnwénshè〈名〉 Agence France-Presse (AFP)

【法号】fǎhào〈名〉 Buddhist monastic title

【法纪】fǎjì〈名〉 law and discipline: 目无/遵守～ flout/observe law and discipline

【法家】Fǎjiā〈名〉 Legalist school

【法警】fǎjǐng〈名〉 bailiff

【法拉】fǎlā〈量〉［物理］ farad

【法拉第定律】Fǎlādì dìnglǜ〈名〉Faraday's law

【法兰克福】Fǎlánkèfú〈名〉 Frankfurt

【法兰绒】fǎlánróng〈名〉［纺织］ flannel

【法兰西共和国】 Fǎlánxī Gònghéguó〈名〉 Republic of France

【法郎】fǎláng ▸**p. 328**〈名〉〈旧〉 franc: 法国/瑞士～ French/Swiss franc

【法老】fǎlǎo〈名〉 Pharaoh

【法理】fǎlǐ〈名〉 **1**（法学理论）legal principle: 合乎～ be in conformity with legal principles ‖ ～依据 legal basis **2**〈书〉（法则） law: 自然～ law of nature **3**（佛法义理） Buddhist doctrine

【法力】fǎlì〈名〉 **1**［佛教］ dharma power: ～无边。 The dharma is omnipotent. **2**（神奇的力量） magic power: 使～ exercise one's magic power

【法令】fǎlìng〈名〉 decree: 颁布～ issue a decree

【法律】fǎlǜ〈名〉 law: 触犯～ break the law ‖ 遵守～ observe the law ‖ ～手段 legal means ‖ ～面前人人平等。 Everyone is equal in the eyes of the law.

【法律事务所】fǎlǜ shìwùsuǒ〈名〉law firm

【法律援助】fǎlǜ yuánzhù〈名〉 legal aid: 提供～ offer legal aid

【法律制裁】fǎlǜ zhìcái〈名〉 legal sanction: 给予～ punish according to law

【法螺】 fǎluó〈名〉 **1**（指动物） triton **2**（指号角） conch

【法盲】fǎmáng〈名〉 legal illiterate

【法门】fǎmén〈名〉 **1**［佛教］ door to enlightenment **2**（方法） way: ▸不二～

【法名】fǎmíng〈名〉 religious name: 为某人取～ bestow a religious name upon sb.

【法袍】fǎpáo〈名〉 judicial robe

【法器】fǎqì〈名〉 religious musical instruments

【法权】fǎquán〈名〉 right: ▸治外～

【法人】fǎrén〈名〉 legal entity: 企业～ legal body of an enterprise ‖ ～代表 legal representative ‖ ～团体 body corporate

【法人股】fǎréngǔ〈名〉 corporate shares

【法师】fǎshī〈名〉〈尊〉 Master

【法式】fǎshì **A**〈名〉 method **B**〈形〉 French: ～面包 French bread

【法事】fǎshì〈名〉 religious services

【法属波利尼西亚】Fǎshǔbōlìníxīyà〈名〉 French Polynesia

【法术】fǎshù〈名〉 magic arts

【法帖】fǎtiè〈名〉 model calligraphy: 临摹～ copy model calligraphy

【法庭】fǎtíng〈名〉 tribunal: 特别～ special tribunal ‖ ～调查 court investigation ‖ 国际～ international tribunal ▸军事～

【法统】fǎtǒng〈名〉 legal convention

【法网】fǎwǎng〈名〉 net of justice: 落入～ be brought to justice ‖ ～恢恢，疏而不漏。 Loose as it seems, the omnipresent net of justice allows no criminal to go unpunished.

【法西斯】fǎxīsī〈名〉 fascist: ～专政 fascist dictatorship ‖ ～主义 fascism ‖ ～主义者 fascist

【法新社】Fǎxīnshè〈简称〉= 法国新闻社

【法学】fǎxué〈名〉 science of law: ～博士 doctor of laws ‖ ～家 jurist

【法眼】fǎyǎn〈名〉 **1**［佛教］mind which perceives both past and future **2**（洞察力） insight

【法衣】fǎyī〈名〉 Buddhist master's robe

【法医】fǎyī〈名〉 forensic scientist: ～鉴定 medico-legal expertise

【法医学】fǎyīxué〈名〉 forensic medicine

【法语】Fǎyǔ ▸**p. 918**〈名〉 French

【法院】fǎyuàn〈名〉 court of law: 中级～ intermediate court ‖ 最高～ Supreme Court

【法则】fǎzé〈名〉law: 自然～ law of nature

【法旨】fǎzhǐ〈名〉〈书〉 divine will

【法制】fǎzhì〈名〉 legal system: 加强～教育 promote legal education ‖ 完善～体系 perfect the legal system ‖ ～观念 legal sense ‖ ～建设 improve the legal system

【法治】fǎzhì〈动〉 govern by law: ～国家 country under the rule of law ‖ 我们推行的是～而不是人治。 We have a government of law, not of man.

【法子】fǎzi〈名〉〈口〉 way: 没～ have no way out ‖ 想～解决问题 find a solution to the problem

砝 fǎ

【砝码】fǎmǎ〈名〉weight: 五公斤的～ five-kilo weight ‖ 为谈判增添～ weigh in favour of negotiation

f

fà

发（髮） fà ▸**p. 614**〈名〉hair: 染～ dye one's hair ‖ 白～ grey hair ▸假～, 卷～, 理～
▸fā

【发辫】fàbiàn〈名〉plait: 留～ wear one's hair in braids

【发菜】fàcài〈名〉[植物] long thread moss

【发际】fàjì〈名〉hairline

【发髻】fàjì〈名〉hair worn in a bun: 梳个～ comb a knot out of one's hair

【发夹】fàjiā〈名〉hairclip

【发胶】fàjiāo〈名〉hair spray

【发蜡】fàlà〈名〉pomade

【发廊】fàláng〈名〉**1**（理发处）hairdresser's: 去～理发 go to the barber's for a haircut **2**（美容处）beauty salon: 开～ open a beauty parlour

【发妻】fàqī〈名〉〈书〉first wife

【发卡】fàqiǎ〈名〉hairpin

【发式】fàshì = 发型 fàxíng

【发网】fàwǎng〈名〉hairnet

【发屋】fàwū = 发廊 fàláng

【发型】fàxíng〈名〉hairstyle: 改变～ change one's hairstyle ‖ 流行～ stylish coiffure ‖ ～设计师 hairstylist

【发型师】fàxíngshī ▸**p. 966**〈名〉hair stylist

【发指】fàzhǐ〈动〉〈书〉bristle with anger: 敌军的暴行令人～。The enemy troops' atrocities made one's blood boil.

珐（琺） fà

【珐琅】fàláng〈名〉enamel: ～制品 enamelware

fān

帆 fān〈名〉**1**（指布篷）sail: 扬～ set sail ▸一～风顺 **2**〈书〉（指船）sailing boat: 黄浦江上，千～竞发。Thousands of sailboats are racing along the Huangpu River.

【帆板】fānbǎn〈名〉[体育] windsurfer: ～运动 windsurfing

【帆布】fānbù〈名〉canvas: ～篷 canvas roof ‖ ～椅 hammock seat ‖ ～包 canvas bag

【帆布床】fānbùchuáng〈名〉camp bed〈英〉; cot〈美〉

【帆船】fānchuán〈名〉sailing boat〈英〉; sailboat〈美〉: 进行～比赛 sail a race

【帆樯】fānqiáng〈名〉〈书〉mast: ～林立 forest of sails and masts

番[1] fān〈形〉foreign: ▸～邦, ～茄, ～薯

番[2] fān
A〈动〉do in turns: ▸轮～
B〈量〉**1**（指行为）[for actions, deeds, etc.]: 一～好意 a show of hospitality ‖ 花了一～心血 make painstaking efforts ‖ 说服他真让人费了一～口舌。It really took a lot of talking to convince him of it. ▸三～五次 **2**（指倍数）-fold, times: 翻一～ increase twofold ‖ 产量三年内翻了两～。The output quadrupled in three years. **3**（指种类）kind: 别有一～风味 be an altogether different flavour

【番邦】fānbāng〈名〉〈旧〉barbarian land

【番号】fānhào〈名〉designation of a military unit

【番茄】fānqié〈名〉tomato: ～汤 tomato soup ‖ ～酱 tomato sauce ‖ ～汁 tomato juice

【番薯】fānshǔ〈方〉= 甘薯 gānshǔ

蕃 fān = 番[1] fān
▸fán

幡 fān〈名〉**1**（指旗子）streamer: ～杆 streamer pole **2**〈旧〉（招魂幡）funeral streamer

【幡儿】fānr〈名〉funeral streamer: 打～ carry a funeral streamer

【幡然】fānrán〈副〉〈书〉quickly and completely

【幡然悔悟】fānrán-huǐwù〈成〉wake up to one's error

藩 fān〈名〉**1**（篱笆）fence: ▸～篱 **2**〈书〉（屏障）screen: ▸屏～ **3**〈旧〉（属地）vassal: 外～ vassal states ▸～国

【藩国】fānguó〈名〉〈旧〉vassal state

【藩篱】fānlí〈名〉fence: 突破～ break through the barrier

【藩属】fānshǔ〈名〉〈旧〉vassal state

【藩镇】fānzhèn〈名〉〈旧〉military governorship of outlying prefectures

翻 fān〈动〉**1**（翻转）reverse: 把唱片～个面 flip a record ‖ ～到另一页 turn to a fresh page ‖ 小船～了。The little boat capsized. ▸～跟头 **2**（翻找）look through: ～查记录 rummage around among the records ‖ 那帮盗匪把屋子～了个底朝天。The burglars turned the house upside down. ‖ 他～遍了所有的口袋才找到了钥匙。He searched all his pockets before he found the key. ▸～箱倒柜 **3**（变换）change: ▸花样～新 **4**（翻译）translate: ～成英语/汉语 translate sth. into English/Chinese ‖ 这首诗～得不错。This poem is well translated. **5**（不和）fall out: 为遗产与同胞手足闹～了 fall out with siblings over an inheritance ‖ 他俩因意见分歧而～了脸。The two of them fell out over differences in opinion. **6**（推翻）overturn: ▸～案, ～供 **7** ▸**p. 31**（成倍增加）multiply: ～两番 quadruple **8**（越过）cross: ～过篱笆 climb over a hedge ‖ ～过山头 cross a mountain

【翻案】fān'àn〈动〉**1**（指判决）reverse a verdict **2**（指处分、评价等）reverse: ～文章 article reversing the original verdict

【翻白眼】fān báiyǎn〈动〉**1**（指生理现象）show the whites of one's eyes **2**（指神态）glare at sb.

【翻版】fānbǎn〈名〉**1**（指版本）reprint: ～书比原版书便宜。Reprints are less expensive than original editions. **2**（指文章、观点）reproduction

【翻本】fānběn〈动〉recoup one's losses

【翻场】fāncháng〈动〉turn over crops or grain on the threshing ground

【翻唱】fānchàng〈动〉sing a cover song: ～20世纪30年代的经典歌曲 sing a cover of a classic 1930s tune

【翻车】fānchē〈动〉[of a car] overturn

【翻船】fānchuán〈动〉**1**〈本〉capsize **2**〈喻〉（失败）fall through: 阴沟里～ capsize in a ditch

【翻地】fāndì〈动〉turn up soil: ～筑垄 ridge the land

【翻动】fāndòng〈动〉turn and move: 她一晚上睡不着觉，不停地～身子。She tossed and turned all night and could not fall asleep.

【翻斗】fāndǒu〈名〉skip bucket: ～车 dump truck

【翻番】fānfān ▸**p. 31**〈动〉double: 五年实现国民生产总值～ achieve a doubling of the GNP in five years

【翻飞】fānfēi〈动〉**1**（飞舞）fly up and down: 鸟儿在树林里上下～。Birds are flying up and down in the woods. **2**（飘扬）flutter in the wind

【翻覆】fānfù **A**〈动〉**1**（颠倒）overturn: 卡车滑下路面～了。The truck skidded off the road and overturned. **2**（翻动身体）toss and turn: 她彻夜～，不能入眠。She tossed and turned in bed the whole night. **B**〈名〉cataclysmic change: 天地～ earth-shaking changes

【翻改】fāngǎi〈动〉alter and remake: ～大衣 remake an overcoat

【翻盖】fāngài〈动〉rebuild: ～房屋 renovate a house

【翻盖式手机】fāngàishì shǒujī〈名〉flip phone

【翻个儿】fāngèr〈动〉do the other way round: 把杯子～放着。Put the cup upside down.

【翻跟头】fān gēntou〈动〉**1**（指动作）turn a somersault: 杂技演员在台上～。The acrobats tumbled over the stage. **2**（受挫）suffer setbacks

【翻供】fāngòng〈名〉withdraw one's confession: 他～并申辩无罪。He retracted his confession and pleaded not guilty.

【翻滚】fāngǔn〈动〉**1**（翻腾）churn: 天上乌云～。The black clouds rolled about in the sky. ‖ 海浪～。The sea churned. **2**（滚动）roll about: 痛得在地上直～ writhe on the ground in agony ‖ 那辆车～下了山坡。The car tumbled down the mountainside.

【翻悔】fānhuǐ〈动〉back out: 同意了又～ renege on one's agreement ‖ 一旦答应，就别～。Once you've agreed, don't try to back out.

【翻检】fānjiǎn〈动〉thumb through: ～词典 thumb through a dictionary ‖ ～资料 leaf through reference materials

【翻建】fānjiàn〈动〉rebuild: ～危房 repair a dilapidated house

【翻江倒海】fānjiāng-dǎohǎi〈成〉overwhelming: 以～之势 with an overwhelming momentum

【翻浆】fānjiāng〈动〉[of ground or road surfaces] break up and turn muddy when a spring thaw sets in

【翻筋斗】fān jīndǒu = 翻跟头 fān gēntou 1

【翻旧账】fān jiùzhàng = 翻老账 fān lǎozhàng

【翻卷】fānjuǎn〈动〉flutter: 船尾～起层层浪花。The ship left a wake of waves. ‖ 红旗在风中～。Red flags fluttered in the wind.

【翻刻】fānkè〈动〉**1**［印刷］carve a new plate: ～重印 carve a new plate and reprint **2**（制光盘）copy: 怎样才能防止光盘被～? How can I prevent the disc from being copied?

【翻来覆去】fānlái-fùqù〈成〉**1**（指身体）toss and turn: 我整夜在床上～睡不着。I kept tossing and turning in bed all night, unable to sleep. **2**（反复）again and again: ～想了好几天后 after several days deliberation

【翻老账】fān lǎozhàng〈动〉rake up old scores: 咱们不要～了。Let's let bygones be bygones.

【翻脸】fānliǎn〈动〉fall out: 为小事而～

fall out over small things ‖ 他从来没和人翻过脸。 He never falls out with anyone.
【翻脸不认人】fānliǎn bù rèn rén〈俗〉turn one's back on an old friend
【翻脸无情】fānliǎn-wúqíng〈成〉turn against sb. and show no mercy
【翻领】fānlǐng〈名〉turndown collar: ～衬衣 shirt with a turndown collar
【翻录】fānlù〈动〉duplicate: ～磁带 pirate a tape ‖ 版权所有，～必究。 All rights reserved. Unauthorized reproduction may result in prosecution.
【翻毛】fānmáo〈形〉1（指毛皮） furry: ～大衣 fur coat 2（指皮革） suede: ～皮鞋 suede shoes
【翻弄】fānnòng〈动〉turn back and forth: 他心不在焉地～着报纸。 He skipped absent-mindedly through the newspaper.
【翻拍】fānpāi〈动〉［摄影］reproduce: ～照片 reproduce a photograph
【翻盘】fānpán〈动〉〈喻〉turn the tables
【翻然】fānrán = 幡然 fānrán
【翻砂】fānshā［机械］A〈名〉founding: ～车间 foundry shop B〈动〉mould
【翻晒】fānshài〈动〉dry in the sun: ～粮食/被褥 air the grain/bedding in the sun
【翻山越岭】fānshān-yuèlǐng〈成〉trek over mountains
【翻身】fānshēn〈动〉1（指身体） turn over 2〈喻〉（指身份） free oneself: ～农奴 emancipated serf ‖ ～做主 stand up and be master of one's own fate 3〈喻〉（指处境） take a favourable turn: 今年要打个～仗，实现扭亏为盈。 This year we must turn things around by turning losses into profits.
【翻绳儿】fānshéngr〈名〉cat's cradle
【翻腾】fānténg〈名〉［体育］tuck: 向后～三周半 backward tuck with three-and-a-half somersaults
【翻腾】fānteng〈动〉1（翻滚） churn: 波浪～ surging waves ‖〈喻〉一股怒火在我心中～。 I seethed with a secret rage. 2（翻动） rummage: 在床下～ poke around under the bed ‖〈喻〉过去的事儿，不去～也好。 It is advisable not to rake up the past.
【翻天】fāntiān〈动〉1（指吵闹） be wild: 因薪水问题与资方吵翻了天 kick up a big fuss with the management over pay ‖ 那些捣蛋的孩子在教室闹～了。 The naughty children threw the classroom into turmoil. 2〈喻〉（指造反） overthrow the government: 想～不成? Are you wanting to stage a rebellion?
【翻天覆地】fāntiān-fùdì〈成〉earth-shattering: 城市里发生了～的变化。 Tremendous changes have taken place in the city.
【翻胃】fānwèi = 反胃 fānwèi
【翻箱倒柜】fānxiāng-dǎoguì〈成〉ransack: 侦探在屋子里～，寻找证据。 The detective ransacked the house for evidence.
【翻新】fānxīn〈动〉1（改造） renovate: ～衣服 refashion clothes 2（创新） innovate: ▸花样～
【翻修】fānxiū〈动〉renovate: ～店面 give the shop a face-lift ‖ ～房屋 renovate a house
【翻译】fānyì A〈动〉translate: 口头～ oral interpretation ‖ 诗歌不容易～。 Poetry doesn't translate easily. ‖ 他不懂英语，得靠女儿为他～。 He doesn't speak English, and relies on his daughter to interpret for him. B〈名〉translator: 担任～ act as interpreter ‖ 高级～ senior interpreter/translator ‖ 英语～ English interpreter
【翻译片】fānyìpiàn〈名〉dubbed film
【翻印】fānyìn〈动〉reprint: 版权所有，～必究。 All rights reserved. Unauthorized reproduction in any form may result in prosecution.
【翻涌】fānyǒng〈动〉〈书〉churn: 波涛～，漫过岩石。 The waves surged over the rocks. ‖〈喻〉仇恨在他胸中～。 Hatred surged in him.
【翻阅】fānyuè〈动〉leaf through: ～报刊 thumb through newspapers and magazines ‖ ～参考书 scan reference books
【翻越】fānyuè〈动〉traverse: ～障碍物 surmount an obstacle
【翻云覆雨】fānyún-fùyǔ〈成〉blow hot and cold about
【翻造】fānzào〈动〉rebuild
【翻转】fānzhuǎn〈动〉flip over: 跳水运动员～动作优美。 The diver executed a graceful flip.

fán

凡[1] fán
A〈名〉1〈书〉（概要） abstract: ▸发～ 2（尘世） this mortal world
B〈副〉1〈书〉（总共） altogether: 全书～十八卷。 The book comes to 18 volumes. 2（凡是） all: ～此种种，不一而足 and so on and so forth ‖ ～年满十八岁的公民，都有选举权。 Every citizen aged 18 and over has the right to vote.
C〈形〉commonplace: ▸非～, 自命不～
【凡尘】fánchén〈名〉this mortal world: 超脱～ transcend the mortal world
【凡尔赛】Fán'ěrsài〈名〉Versailles
【凡夫俗子】fánfū-súzǐ〈成〉common people
【凡例】fánlì〈名〉editorial guide
【凡人】fánrén〈名〉ordinary people: ～琐事 ordinary people and daily trivialities
【凡士林】fánshìlín〈名〉petroleum jelly
【凡是】fánshì〈副〉any: ～犯法者，都应受到惩罚。 Anyone who breaks the law should be punished.
【凡俗】fánsú〈名〉ordinariness: 不同～ be out of the ordinary
【凡响】fánxiǎng〈名〉〈喻〉mediocre: 非同～ out of the ordinary
【凡心】fánxīn〈名〉worldly desires: 动了～ develop a desire for the secular life
【凡庸】fányōng〈形〉ordinary: ～之辈 common herd

凡[2] fán〈名〉［音乐］note on the *gongche* (工尺) scale, corresponding to 4 in *jianpu* (简谱) numbered musical notation

矾（礬） fán〈名〉［化学］vitriol: ▸明～
【矾土】fántǔ〈名〉［化学］alumina

钒（釩） fán〈名〉［化学］vanadium (V)

烦（煩） fán
A〈形〉1（心情不畅） restless: 心里很～ feel fidgety ‖ 这几天我～得很。 I have been feeling restless the last few days. ▸心～意乱 2（厌烦） fed up: 她唠唠叨叨我都听～了。 I'm fed up with her nagging. ‖ 我～透了洗碗。 I am sick and tired of washing dishes. ‖ 这饭我都吃～了。 I am tired of this dish. 3（多而杂乱） numerous and confusing: ▸要言不～
B〈动〉1（烦扰） annoy: 别～我了! Lay off! ‖ 孩子们要这要那，不停地～我。 The children irritate me with their constant demands. 2〈套〉（麻烦） trouble: 有事相～ bother sb. with sth. ‖ 能不能～你捎个口信? May I trouble you to pass on a message?
【烦劳】fánláo〈动〉〈敬〉trouble: ～您帮个忙。 Would you please do me a favour?
【烦闷】fánmèn〈形〉moody: 她因被解雇而～。 She was down about the dismissal.
【烦恼】fánnǎo〈形〉annoyed: 因经济拮据而～ worry about the financial situation ‖ 别自寻～! Don't worry your head about it!
【烦扰】fánrǎo A〈动〉disturb: 她要是睡了，就别～她。 If she's asleep, don't disturb her. ‖ 我不再～你了。 I won't bug you any more. B〈形〉annoyed: 因其他事而～ be disturbed by other matters
【烦人】fánrén〈形〉annoying: 那孩子真～，老是没完没了地提问题。 That child's a real pest; he's continually asking questions.
【烦冗】fánrǒng = 繁冗 fánrǒng
【烦神】fánshén A〈动〉take pains: 这事你就不要～了。 Don't bother about it. B〈形〉energy-exhausting: ～的事 mind-bending affair
【烦琐】fánsuǒ = 繁琐 fánsuǒ
【烦琐哲学】fánsuǒ zhéxué〈名〉1（经院哲学） scholasticism 2〈喻〉（指作风或文风） hair-splitting
【烦嚣】fánxiāo〈形〉〈书〉noisy and annoying: ～的集市 bustling market
【烦心】fánxīn A〈形〉annoying: 别谈这些～的事。 Don't talk about these irritating things. B〈动〉〈方〉worry about: 你有啥～的? What's bothering you? ‖ 那男孩太淘气，真让人～。 That boy is really naughty. It worries me a lot.
【烦言】fányán〈名〉〈书〉1（抱怨） complaint: 口无～ make no complaints whatsoever ‖ 啧有～ be full of complaints 2（烦琐的话） tedious talk: ～碎辞 verbosity
【烦忧】fányōu〈形〉fretful: 令人～的政局 unsettling political situation
【烦躁】fánzào〈形〉fidgety: 感到莫名其妙的～ feel unaccountably agitated ‖ ～不安 be restless

蕃 fán〈书〉
A〈形〉luxuriant: ▸～茂
B〈动〉proliferate
▸fān
【蕃茂】fánmào〈形〉luxuriant: ～的森林 luxuriant forest
【蕃息】fánxī〈动〉〈书〉multiply: 万物～。 All creatures multiply.
【蕃衍】fányǎn = 繁衍 fányǎn

樊 fán〈名〉1〈书〉（篱笆） fence 2（笼子） cage: ▸～笼
【樊篱】fánlí〈名〉1（篱笆） fence 2〈喻〉（束缚） barriers: 冲破封建～的束缚 cast off the shackles of feudalism
【樊笼】fánlóng〈名〉1（笼子） cage 2〈喻〉（指境地） prison

璠 fán〈名〉〈书〉jade

燔 fán〈动〉〈书〉1（烧） burn 2（烤） bake

f

繁 fán

A〈形〉**1**（多）numerous: ～星 swarms of stars ▸～多, 频～ **2**（茂盛）luxuriant: 枝～叶茂的树 luxuriant trees ▸～华, ～荣 **3**（复杂）complicated: ▸删～就简
B〈动〉multiply: ▸～衍, ～育
▸Pó

【繁本】fánběn〈名〉unabridged version
【繁博】fánbó〈形〉extensive: 引证～ extensive quotations
【繁多】fánduō〈形〉various: 种类～ have a wide variety
【繁复】fánfù〈形〉heavy and complicated: ～的计算 complicated calculation ‖ ～的手续 bureaucratic procedure
【繁花似锦】fánhuā-sìjǐn〈成〉flowers in full bloom
【繁华】fánhuá〈形〉thriving: ～的商业区 busy commercial district ‖ 整条街道～热闹。The whole street is a scene of bustling activity.
【繁丽】fánlì〈形〉rich and flowery: 词藻～ flowery language
【繁乱】fánluàn〈形〉entangled: 思绪～ have a convoluted train of thought
【繁忙】fánmáng〈形〉busy: 工作～ be busily engaged ‖ 事务～，无法分身。I have so much work. I can't get away.
【繁茂】fánmào〈形〉lush: ～的枝叶 luxuriant foliage
【繁密】fánmì〈形〉dense: 林木～ be densely wooded ‖ 人口～ be densely populated
【繁难】fánnán〈形〉complicated: ～的数学题 complicated mathematical problem ‖ 遇到～的事 get entangled in a web of difficulties
【繁闹】fánnào〈形〉bustling: ～的集市 busy market
【繁荣】fánróng **A**〈形〉flourishing: 促进经济～ promote economic prosperity ‖ ～兴旺的景象 scene of boom and prosperity **B**〈动〉prosper: ～文艺 boost literature and art ‖ 利用外资～本国经济 use foreign capital to boost the country's economy
【繁荣昌盛】fánróng-chāngshèng〈成〉thriving and prosperous: 国家～。The country prospered.
【繁冗】fánrǒng〈形〉**1**（指事务）diverse and complicated **2**（指文章）lengthy and tedious: ～的引言 tortuous introduction
【繁缛】fánrù〈形〉〈书〉over-elaborate: ～的礼仪 over-elaborate protocols
【繁盛】fánshèng〈形〉**1**（繁荣）flourishing: ～的小镇 prosperous little town **2**（繁茂）luxuriant: 那里草木～。The flora there is luxuriant.
【繁琐】fánsuǒ〈形〉complicated and overloaded: ～的手续 tedious formalities ‖ ～的办事程序 tedious handling procedures
【繁体】fántǐ〈名〉**1**（指汉字形体）unsimplified form **2** = 繁体字 fántǐzì
【繁体字】fántǐzì〈名〉［语言］complex form of character
【繁文缛节】fánwén-rùjié〈成〉red tape: 不受～的限制 be unhampered by red tape
【繁芜】fánwú〈形〉〈书〉wordy: 删除～ delete unnecessary words ‖ 文笔～ long-winded writing style
【繁星】fánxīng〈名〉〈书〉swarms of stars: 满天～ starry sky
【繁衍】fányǎn〈动〉multiply: 人类的～ human reproduction
【繁育】fányù〈动〉breed: ～优良品种 breed good strains
【繁杂】fánzá〈形〉miscellaneous: ～的家务劳动 miscellaneous household chores
【繁征博引】fánzhēng-bóyǐn〈成〉quote extensively
【繁殖】fánzhí〈动〉breed: 近亲～ close breeding ‖ 无性/有性～ asexual/sexual reproduction ‖ 细菌～迅速。Bacteria reproduce quickly.
【繁重】fánzhòng〈形〉heavy: 任务～ onerous task ‖ ～的体力劳动 strenuous manual labour

蹯 fán〈名〉〈书〉paw

fǎn

反 fǎn

A〈动〉**1**（翻转）turn over: ▸物极必～, 易如～掌 **2**（回）return, counter: ▸～击, ～问 **3**（反抗）oppose: ～战宣言 anti-war proclamation ‖ ～政府示威 anti-government demonstration ‖ ～走私 combat smuggling ▸～腐 **4**（背叛）rebel (against): ～贼 rebels **5**（类推）generalize: ▸举一～三 **6**（不符）breach: ▸～常
B〈形〉reverse: 正～两面穿的夹克 reversible jacket ‖ 他把毛衣穿～了。He wore his sweater inside out. ▸～话, ～面, ～锁
C〈副〉on the contrary: 害人～害己 be hoist with one's own petard ‖ 他不但不做自我批评，～怪罪别人。Not only did he not take the blame himself but on the contrary he laid it elsewhere.
D〈名〉**1** reactionary: 镇～ suppress the counter-revolutionaries **2** ▸反切 fǎnqiè

【反霸】fǎnbà〈动〉**1**（指霸权主义）oppose hegemony: ～斗争的浪潮 surge of anti-hegemony struggles **2**（指恶霸）oppose local despots
【反败为胜】fǎnbài-wéishèng〈成〉convert defeat into victory: 客队最终～。The guest team turned the tables (on the home team) and finally won the game.
【反绑】fǎnbǎng〈动〉tie sb.'s hands behind their back
【反比】fǎnbǐ〈名〉inverse ratio: 成～ be in reverse ratio ‖ ～关系 inverse proportion
【反比例】fǎnbǐlì〈名〉［数学］inverse ratio
【反驳】fǎnbó〈动〉refute: ～对手 refute an opponent ‖ ～论点 refute an argument ‖ 有力的～ powerful retort
【反哺】fǎnbǔ〈动〉**1**（指鸟）feed mother bird in return when grown up **2**〈喻〉（指人）look after one's parents in return: ～之情 filial piety **3**〈喻〉（指产业）repay
【反差】fǎnchā〈名〉contrast: 形成～ pose a contrast ‖ 今昔对比，～强烈。The present poses a striking contrast with the past.
【反常】fǎncháng〈形〉abnormal: 态度～ unusual attitude ‖ 天气/气候～ unusual weather/climate ‖ ～现象 abnormal phenomenon ‖ 他今天有点～。He is a bit off today.
【反超】fǎnchāo〈动〉turn the tables
【反衬】fǎnchèn〈动〉serve as a foil: 对英雄的赞美就～着对懦夫的嘲讽。The praise of the hero is a foil to the mocking of the coward.
【反冲力】fǎnchōnglì〈名〉［物理］backlash
【反刍】fǎnchú〈动〉**1**（指动物）chew the cud: ～动物 ruminant **2**〈喻〉（指人）ruminate
【反串】fǎnchuàn〈动〉[in traditional opera] play a role one is not trained for
【反唇相讥】fǎnchún-xiāngjī〈成〉answer back sarcastically
【反弹道导弹】fǎndàndào dǎodàn〈名〉anti-ballistic missile
【反导】fǎndǎo〈简称〉= 反弹道导弹
【反倒】fǎndào〈副〉on the contrary: 雇的人多了，干的活～少了。More workers were hired but less work was done. ‖ 好心帮忙，～落下不是。Kind help was met only with complaints.
【反帝】fǎndì〈动〉be anti-imperialist: ～斗争 anti-imperialist struggle
【反调】fǎndiào〈名〉opposite view: 唱～ sing a different tune
【反动】fǎndòng **A**〈形〉reactionary: ～势力 reactionary forces **B**〈名〉reaction: 滥用文言文，是对推广普通话的一种～。The indiscriminate use of classical Chinese runs counter to the popularization of *putonghua*.
【反动派】fǎndòngpài〈名〉reactionaries
【反对】fǎnduì〈动〉oppose: ～霸权主义/官僚主义 combat hegemonism/bureaucracy ‖ ～不正之风 combat unhealthy trends ‖ ～种族/性别歧视 oppose racial/sexual discrimination ‖ 二十票赞成，十八票～。There are 20 for and 18 against.
【反对党】fǎnduìdǎng〈名〉opposition party: ～领袖 opposition leader
【反对派】fǎnduìpài〈名〉opposition faction
【反而】fǎn'ér〈副〉conversely: 你的溺爱～会害了小孩。Doting on your children can actually do them harm. ‖ 他非但没有生气，～请我们喝酒。He didn't get angry. On the contrary, he bought us a drink.
【反方】fǎnfāng〈名〉opposing side: ～获胜。The opposing side won.
【反封建】fǎn fēngjiàn〈动〉oppose feudalism
【反讽】fǎnfěng〈动〉make a sarcastic retort
【反腐】fǎnfǔ〈动〉combat corruption: ～倡廉 combat corruption and advocate clean politics
【反复】fǎnfù **A**〈副〉repeatedly: ～解释 explain over and over again ‖ ～思考 turn sth. over in one's mind ‖ 经过无数次的～ after numerous repetitions **B**〈动〉back out: 我决不～。I'll never go back on my word. **C**〈名〉reversal: 有很多曲折～ be full of reversals and zigzags
【反复无常】fǎnfù-wúcháng〈成〉blow hot and cold: 情绪～ variable mood ‖ 天气～ changeable weather ‖ 这人～，很不可靠。This fellow is unreliable; he is always chopping and changing.
【反感】fǎngǎn **A**〈形〉disgusted: 极为～ have a deep repugnance ‖ 他的模样令人～。His appearance was repellent. **B**〈名〉disgust: 感到～ feel repulsion ‖ 引起～ arouse disgust
【反戈一击】fǎngē-yījī〈成〉turn against one's own side
【反革命】fǎngémìng **A**〈形〉counter-revolutionary: ～集团 counter-revolutionary clique ‖ ～活动 counter-revolutionary activity **B**〈名〉counter-revolution: 打成～ be labelled as counter-revolutionary
【反攻】fǎngōng〈动〉counter-attack: 发起～ launch a counteroffensive ‖ 大举～ mount a large-scale counteroffensive
【反攻倒算】fǎngōng-dàosuàn〈成〉launch a revenge counter-attack
【反躬自省】fǎngōng-zìxǐng = 反躬自问 fǎngōng-zìwèn
【反躬自问】fǎngōng-zìwèn〈成〉examine one's own conscience
【反骨】fǎngǔ〈名〉〈旧〉renegade nature

【反顾】fǎngù〈动〉〈书〉 1 (回头看) look back 2 (翻悔) go back on one's word: ▸义无～
【反观】fǎnguān〈动〉 observe from an opposite angle
【反光】fǎnguāng A〈动〉 reflect light: 镜子把光反到墙上。 The mirror reflected light on the wall. B〈名〉 reflected light: 雪地上的～让我睁不开眼。 My eyes were dazzled by the sunlight on the snow.
【反光灯】fǎnguāngdēng〈名〉 reflector lamp
【反光镜】fǎnguāngjìng〈名〉 reflector
【反过来】fǎnguolai〈副〉 in reverse order
【反话】fǎnhuà〈名〉 irony: 故意说～ say with deliberate irony
【反悔】fǎnhuǐ〈动〉 go back on one's word: 一经承诺，决不～。 Once you've made your promise there's no going back on it.
【反击】fǎnjī〈动〉 counter-attack: ～侵略者 deliver a counterblow against the aggressor
【反季节】fǎnjìjié〈形〉 out of season: ～蔬菜 out-of-season vegetables ‖ ～销售 off-season sale
【反剪】fǎnjiǎn〈动〉 1 (放在背后) cross one's hands behind one's back: 他～着双手，大模大样地进来了。 He swaggered in, holding his hands behind his back. 2 (绑在背后) have one's hands tied behind one's back: 被～双臂押上法庭 be frog-marched into the court
【反间计】fǎnjiànjì〈名〉 discord-sowing stratagem: 中了敌人的～ fall victim to the enemy's scheme of sowing discord
【反诘】fǎnjié〈动〉〈书〉 ask in retort: ～句 rhetorical question
【反抗】fǎnkàng〈动〉 resist, revolt: ～侵略 resist aggression ‖ 奋起～ rise in revolt ‖ 武力～ resist by force ‖ 消极～ passive resistance
【反客为主】fǎnkè-wéizhǔ〈成〉〈喻〉 gain the advantage: 客队～，最终获胜。 The guest team turned the tables and finally pulled off a victory.
【反恐】fǎnkǒng〈名〉 anti-terrorism: ～斗争 anti-terrorist struggle ‖ ～战争 war on terrorism
【反口】fǎnkǒu〈动〉 deny what one has said: 话已说出，不能～。 What's said cannot be unsaid.
【反馈】fǎnkuì A〈名〉［电子］ feedback: 正/负～ positive/negative feedback B〈动〉 feed back: 信息～ feedback of information
【反粒子】fǎnlìzǐ〈名〉［物理］ antiparticle
【反垄断法】fǎnlǒngduànfǎ〈名〉 anti-trust law
【反面】fǎnmiàn A〈名〉 1 (指物体) back: 布料的～ back of the cloth ‖ 硬币的～ reverse of a coin 2 (指问题、观点等) reverse: 既看到事物的正面，也看到其～ see the reverse as well as the normal side of things B〈形〉 negative: ～经验 negative experience ‖ ～意见 adverse opinion
【反面教材】fǎnmiàn jiàocái〈名〉 negative example
【反面人物】fǎnmiàn rénwù〈名〉 villain
【反目】fǎnmù〈动〉 fall out: 夫妻～。 The couple fell out.
【反目成仇】fǎnmù-chéngchóu〈成〉 fall out and become enemies
【反扒】fǎnpá〈动〉 fight pick-pocketing
【反派】fǎnpài〈名〉 villain: 他过去常演～人物。 He used to play the villain.
【反叛】fǎnpàn〈动〉 revolt: ～封建礼教 rebel against feudal ethics ‖ ～者 rebel ‖ ～活动 rebellious activities
【反叛】fǎnpan〈名〉〈口〉 revolt
【反批评】fǎnpīpíng〈名〉 counter-criticism
【反扑】fǎnpū〈动〉 (指猎物、人等) pounce upon sb. after being beaten off; (指敌军) launch a counteroffensive: 敌人猖狂的～ the enemy's savage counter-attack
【反其道而行之】fǎn qí dào ér xíng zhī〈成〉 do exactly the opposite
【反潜】fǎnqián〈形〉 anti-submarine: ～鱼雷 anti-submarine torpedo
【反切】fǎnqiè〈名〉［语言］ a method of demonstrating the pronunciation of a Chinese character by using two other Chinese characters, the first with the same initial consonant and the other with the same final vowel as the character in question [for example, the pronunciation of 塑 is described as 桑故切]
【反倾销】fǎn qīngxiāo〈动〉 engage in anti-dumping: ～调查 anti-dumping investigation ‖ ～税 anti-dumping duty
【反射】fǎnshè〈动〉 1 (指光、波等) reflect: ～望远镜 reflecting telescope ‖ 声音～ reflection of sound ‖ 月亮靠～发光。 The moon shines with reflected light. 2［生理］ reflex: ～作用使瞳孔在受光刺激时收缩。 A reflex causes the contraction of the pupils when exposed to light.
【反身】fǎnshēn A〈动〉 turn around: 我见他～要走，就把他拦住了。 I stopped him when I found him turning to leave. B〈形〉［语言］ reflexive
【反身代词】fǎnshēn dàicí〈名〉［语法］ reflexive pronoun
【反式脂肪】fǎnshì zhīfáng〈名〉 trans fat: 降低餐品中的～含量 reduce trans fats in food products
【反手】fǎnshǒu A〈名〉［体育］ backhand: ～抽球 backhand shot ‖ 他～击球很棒。 He has a good backhand. B〈动〉 1 (背手) put one's hand behind one's back: 他进屋后，～把门关上。 He came in and closed the door behind him. 2 = 反掌 fǎnzhǎng
【反守为攻】fǎnshǒu-wéigōng〈成〉 turn defence into offence
【反水】fǎnshuǐ〈动〉〈方〉 defect
【反思】fǎnsī〈动〉 reflect over: ～过去，是为了未来。 Reflecting on the past is a nod to the future.
【反诉】fǎnsù〈名〉［法律］ countercharge
【反锁】fǎnsuǒ〈动〉 be locked in or out: 他被～在里面。 He was locked in.
【反贪】fǎntān〈动〉 combat graft
【反弹】fǎntán〈动〉 rebound: ～入网 be deflected into the net ‖ 球从墙上～了回来。 The ball bounced off the wall. ‖〈喻〉 股市迅速～。 The stock market rebounded.
【反坦克】fǎntǎnkè〈动〉 be anti-tank: ～炮 anti-tank gun
【反托拉斯法】fǎntuōlāsīfǎ〈名〉 anti-trust law
【反胃】fǎnwèi〈动〉 feel queasy: 我～想吐。 My stomach churned and I felt sick. ‖ 他消化不良，老是～。 He has indigestion. He keeps regurgitating.
【反问】fǎnwèn〈动〉 1 (指提问) ask a question in reply 2［语法］ rhetorical question
【反诬】fǎnwū〈动〉 make up a false countercharge
【反物质】fǎnwùzhì〈名〉［物理］ antimatter
【反响】fǎnxiǎng〈名〉 repercussion: 总统遇刺在全国引起强烈～。 The assassination of the president had strong repercussions throughout the country.
【反向】fǎnxiàng〈动〉 go in the opposite direction: ～行驶 go in reverse
【反兴奋剂】fǎnxīngfènjì〈动〉 be anti-doping: ～机构 anti-doping agency
【反省】fǎnxǐng〈动〉 do some soul-searching: ～自己的错误 reflect on one's mistakes ‖ 深刻～ do some deep soul-searching
【反咬】fǎnyǎo〈动〉 make a false countercharge against one's accuser: 他还想～我。 He's still trying to shift the blame onto me.
【反咬一口】fǎnyǎo-yīkǒu〈惯〉 make a false countercharge against one's accuser
【反义词】fǎnyìcí〈名〉［语法］ antonym
【反应】fǎnyìng A〈动〉 react: ～灵敏的运动员 athlete with swift reflexes ‖ 做出～ make a response ‖ ～不一 reactions vary ‖ ～良好 respond favourably ‖ 她～迟钝。 She is slow to respond. B〈名〉［生理］［医学］［物理］［化学］ reaction: 过敏～ allergic reaction ‖ 碱性/酸性～ alkaline/acid reaction ‖ 她对青霉素有不良～。 She has a bad reaction to penicillin. ▸核～, 化学～
【反应堆】fǎnyìngduī = 原子核反应堆 yuánzǐhé fǎnyìngduī
【反映】fǎnyìng〈动〉 1 (体现) reflect: ～时代的特点 reflect the features of the age ‖ 真实地～生活 hold up a mirror to life ‖ 眼神能～出内心的思想。 The eyes can mirror one's thought. 2 (报告) make known: ～真实情况 inform sb. of the real situation ‖ 向主管部门～ report to the department in charge
【反映论】fǎnyìnglùn〈名〉［哲学］ theory of reflection: 辩证唯物主义的～ dialectical materialist theory of reflection
【反犹太复国主义】fǎnyóutàifùguózhǔyì〈名〉 anti-Zionism
【反语】fǎnyǔ〈名〉 irony
【反掌】fǎnzhǎng〈动〉 turn one's hand over: ～一击 turn over one's palm and hit ▸易如～
【反正】fǎnzhèng〈动〉 1 (回到正道) set right: ▸拨乱～ 2 (军队投诚) come over from the enemy side
【反正】fǎnzheng〈副〉 1 (表示结果都一样) anyway: 不管发生什么事，～我们都得活下去。 Come what may, we've all got to get through things. ‖ 去不去～都一样。 Whether we go or not makes no difference. 2 (强调理由充分) as: 你别着急，～不是什么要紧事。 Don't worry. It's not that important. ‖ 这没有多大关系，～我们要迟到了。 It doesn't make much difference as we are going to be late anyway.
【反证】fǎnzhèng〈名〉 1 (指证据) proof to the contrary: 对指控提出～ produce evidence in rebuttal of the charge 2 = 反证法 fǎnzhèngfǎ
【反证法】fǎnzhèngfǎ〈名〉 reduction to absurdity
【反之】fǎnzhī〈连〉〈书〉 conversely: ～亦然 vice versa
【反转片】fǎnzhuǎnpiàn〈名〉 reversal film
【反作用】fǎnzuòyòng〈名〉 1 (指力) counteraction: 作用与～定律 law of action and reaction 2 (指效果) negative effect: 他们本想阻止反抗，结果却起了～。 Their attempt to prevent opposition was self-defeating, however.
【反坐】fǎnzuò〈动〉〈古〉［法律］ sentence the accuser to the punishment facing the person he falsely accused

f

返 fǎn〈动〉 return: ～乡 return to one's hometown ‖ 重～拳坛 make one's return to the ring

【返场】fǎnchǎng〈动〉 give an encore: 那位女演员四次～。The actress returned for four encores.

【返潮】fǎncháo〈动〉 get damp: 盐容易～。Salt gets damp easily.

【返程】fǎnchéng〈名〉 return journey: ～票 ticket for the return journey

【返岗】fǎngǎng〈动〉 [of laid-off employees] return to one's original job

【返工】fǎngōng〈动〉 redo sth. poorly done: 这项工程必须～。This project has to be redone.

【返归】fǎnguī〈动〉 return: ～自然/故里 return to nature/one's hometown

【返航】fǎnháng〈动〉 return to base: 飞机在～途中出现机械故障。There was some mechanical trouble on the plane on its way back. ‖ 那艘船在暴风雨中安然～。The ship came safely home through the storm.

【返还】fǎnhuán〈动〉 pay back: ～订金 repay a down payment ‖ ～公物 return public property ‖ 申请费不再～。The application fee is non-refundable.

【返回】fǎnhuí〈动〉 return: ～地球 return to earth ‖ ～工作岗位 return to one's post ‖ 原路～ retrace one's steps

【返老还童】fǎnlǎo-huántóng〈成〉 recover one's youthful vigour

【返利】fǎnlì **A**〈动〉 give back some of the profit **B**〈名〉 return on profit

【返贫】fǎnpín〈动〉 slide back into poverty

【返聘】fǎnpìn〈动〉 re-employ the retired: ～人员 re-employed personnel

【返璞归真】fǎnpú-guīzhēn = 归真返璞 guīzhēn-fǎnpú

【返青】fǎnqīng〈动〉 resume growth

【返券】fǎnquàn〈动〉 redeem a voucher: 打折、～、抽奖等都是商家的促销手段。Discounts, vouchers, and prize draws are all promotion techniques used by the stores.

【返俗】fǎnsú〈动〉 resume secular life

【返销】fǎnxiāo〈动〉 sell back: ▸～粮

【返销粮】fǎnxiāoliáng〈名〉 resold grain: 吃～ live on resold grain

【返校】fǎnxiào〈动〉 return to school: 学生已经～。The students are already back at school.

【返修】fǎnxiū〈动〉 remake: ～率 sent-back percentage ‖ 这些产品需要～。These products need reprocessing.

【返照】fǎnzhào〈动〉 reflect light: 夕阳～ reflection of the sunset ▸回光～

【返祖现象】fǎnzǔ xiànxiàng〈名〉［生物］ reversion

fàn

犯 fàn

A〈动〉 **1**（得罪） go against: ▸～上，冒～ **2**（侵犯） attack: 人不～我，我不～人。We will not attack unless we are attacked. ▸进～，侵～ **3**（违犯） violate: ～行规 break the business rule ‖ ～忌讳 break a taboo ▸～禁 **4**（做出） commit: ～错误 make an error ‖ ～谋杀罪/偷窃罪 commit murder/theft ▸～罪 **5**（复发） suffer recurrence;（重复） revert to: 为这事～愁 be concerned about this matter ‖ 他心脏病又～了。He suffered another heart attack. ‖ 老毛病又～了。The old habits resurfaced again.

B〈名〉 criminal: ▸惯～，杀人～，战～

【犯案】fàn'àn〈动〉 be found out and brought to justice: 他又～了。He was caught and once again brought to justice.

【犯病】fànbìng〈动〉 suffer recurrence of an illness: 三天两头～ get ill too often ‖ 他又～了。His illness recurred.

【犯不上】fànbushàng = 犯不着 fànbuzháo

【犯不着】fànbuzháo〈动〉〈口〉 not be worth the effort: ～为这些小事着急。It's not worth worrying about such small things.

【犯愁】fànchóu〈动〉 worry: 不再为吃饭穿衣～ have no more worries about food and clothing ‖ 她为儿子的不求上进～。She is getting worried about her son's lack of ambition.

【犯憷】fànchù〈动〉〈方〉 feel apprehensive: 面对主考官，他有点儿～。Looking at the examiner, he felt nervous.

【犯得上】fàndeshàng = 犯得着 fàndezháo

【犯得着】fàndezháo〈动〉〈口〉 [usu used in rhetorical questions] be worthwhile: 为这么点小事对孩子发脾气，～吗? Is it worthwhile losing your temper with the kid over such a small thing?

【犯嘀咕】fàn dígu〈动〉 have misgivings

【犯法】fànfǎ〈动〉 break the law: 知法～ break the law deliberately ‖ ～行为 offences against the law

【犯规】fànguī〈动〉［体育］ foul: 故意～ intentional foul ‖ 技术～ technical foul ‖ 因手球～而被罚 be penalized for handling the ball

【犯浑】fànhún〈动〉 be unreasonable: 他犯起浑来，谁的话也不听。He refuses to listen to anyone when he is being difficult.

【犯忌】fànjì〈动〉 violate a taboo: 人们认为在船上提"翻"字是～。People think that mentioning the word 'capsize' on a boat is taboo.

【犯贱】fànjiàn〈动〉 demean oneself: 别～! Don't be so pathetic!

【犯节气】fàn jiéqi〈动〉 suffer a seasonal illness

【犯戒】fànjiè〈动〉 break a commandment

【犯禁】fànjìn〈动〉 violate a ban

【犯困】fànkùn〈动〉 feel sleepy: 午饭后～ feel sleepy after lunch ‖ 让人～的天气 drowsy weather

【犯赖】fànlài〈动〉 act shamelessly

【犯难】fànnán〈动〉 get into an embarrassing situation: 让人～ put sb. in an awkward position

【犯人】fànrén〈名〉 prisoner: 提审～ bring charges against a prisoner ‖ 追捕～ track down a criminal

【犯傻】fànshǎ〈动〉〈方〉 **1**（装糊涂） play the fool: 其实他啥都知道，他是在～呢。Actually, he knows everything. He is just playing the fool. **2**（干傻事） do something foolish: 你说那样的话，准是～了。You must be mad to say that. ‖ 他才不会～干那样的蠢事呢。He knows better than to make such a blunder. **3**（发呆） be in a daze: 大家都走了，他还坐那儿～。He was still sitting there in a daze when everybody had left.

【犯上】fànshàng〈动〉 **1**（指长辈） defy one's elders **2**（指上级） defy one's superiors

【犯上作乱】fànshàng-zuòluàn〈成〉 rebel

【犯事】fànshì〈动〉 commit a crime

【犯颜】fànyán〈动〉〈书〉 defy authorities: ～直谏 criticize the emperor to his face

【犯疑】fànyí〈动〉 suspect

【犯罪】fànzuì〈动〉 commit a crime: 打击～活动 crack down on crime ‖ 走上～道路 turn to crime ‖ ～分子 criminal

【犯罪嫌疑人】fànzuì xiányírén〈名〉 criminal suspect

饭（飯） fàn〈名〉 **1**（熟食） cooked cereals: ▸干～ **2**（米饭） cooked rice: 吃～吃面都行。Either rice or noodles will do. **3**（食物） meal: ～前/后 before/after the meal ‖ 他每顿～都在家里吃。He eats all his meals at home. ▸晚～，做～

【饭菜】fàncài〈名〉 **1**（饭和菜） meal: 可口的～ delicious meal ‖ ～凉了。The food's getting cold. **2**（下饭的菜） dishes

【饭店】fàndiàn〈名〉 **1**（旅馆） hotel: 下榻于豪华～ stay at a luxury hotel ‖ 五星级～ five-star hotel **2**（餐馆） restaurant

【饭馆】fànguǎn〈名〉 small restaurant: 下～ eat in a restaurant ‖ ～老板 restaurant proprietor

【饭盒】fànhé〈名〉 lunch box

【饭局】fànjú〈名〉 dinner party, banquet: 我今晚有～。I've been invited to dinner this evening.

【饭来张口，衣来伸手】fàn lái zhāngkǒu, yī lái shēnshǒu〈俗〉 be waited on hand and foot

【饭粒】fànlì〈名〉 grain of cooked rice

【饭量】fànliàng〈名〉 appetite: ～大 have a huge appetite ‖ ～小 have not got much of an appetite

【饭囊】fànnáng〈名〉〈喻〉 good-for-nothing: 他是个～衣架。He is a good-for-nothing.

【饭票】fànpiào〈名〉 meal ticket

【饭铺】fànpù〈名〉〈方〉 small restaurant

【饭食】fànshi〈名〉 food: 学校餐厅～不错。The food at the school cafeteria isn't bad.

【饭堂】fàntáng〈方〉= 食堂 shítáng

【饭厅】fàntīng〈名〉 dining room: 在～吃饭 eat in the dining room

【饭桶】fàntǒng〈名〉 **1**〈本〉 food bucket **2**〈喻〉 good-for-nothing: 你这个～! You good-for-nothing!

【饭碗】fànwǎn〈名〉 **1**〈本〉 rice bowl **2**〈喻〉 job: 丢～ lose one's job ‖ 找～ look for a job ‖ 你不要自己砸自己的～。Take care not to get yourself fired. ▸铁～

【饭庄】fànzhuāng〈名〉 restaurant

【饭桌】fànzhuō〈名〉 dining table

泛 fàn

A〈动〉 **1**〈书〉（漂浮） float: ～舟湖上 go boating on the lake **2**（透出） be suffused with: 她脸上～出红晕。Her cheeks were suffused with blushes. **3**（溢出） flood: ▸～滥

B〈形〉 **1**（广泛） general: ▸～指，宽～ **2**（不深入） superficial: ▸空～

【泛称】fànchēng **A**〈名〉 general term **B**〈动〉 be known generally as

【泛读】fàndú **A**〈动〉 read extensively **B**〈名〉 extensive reading: ～课文 texts for extensive reading

【泛泛】fànfàn〈形〉 **1**（不深入） general: ～而谈 generalize ‖ 这个问题她只是～地提了一下。She merely touched upon the subject. **2**（寻常） common: ～之才 mediocre person

【泛光灯】fànguāngdēng〈名〉 floodlight

【泛蓝】fànlán〈名〉 Pan-Blue Coalition [political alliance in Taiwan, consisting of the Kuomintang, the People First Party, and the New Party]: ～阵营 the Pan-Blue Camp ‖ 团结～的民众促进两岸和平发展。Those in

f

the Pan-Blue Coalition promote peaceful development of cross-Strait relations.
【泛滥】fànlàn〈动〉1（指水灾）flood: 河水～。The river has flooded. 2〈喻〉run rampant: 吸毒～ explosion of drug abuse ‖ 自由化～会造成严重的后果。The rampancy of liberalization may have grave consequences.
【泛滥成灾】fànlàn-chéngzāi〈成〉1（指水灾）flood: 黄河决堤，～。The Yellow River overflowed its banks and there was massive flooding. 2〈喻〉spread unchecked: 市场上盗版光盘～。There is a flood of pirated CDs on the market.
【泛论】fànlùn A〈动〉speak in general terms B〈名〉general discussion
【泛绿】fànlǜ〈名〉Pan-Green Coalition: ～阵营 Pan-Green Camp
【泛美】Fàn-Měi〈形〉Pan-American: ～航空公司 Pan-American Airways
【泛神论】fànshénlùn〈名〉［哲学］pantheism
【泛酸】fànsuān〈动〉regurgitate acid
【泛溢】fànyì〈动〉overflow
【泛指】fànzhǐ〈动〉refer in general
【泛舟】fànzhōu〈动〉〈书〉go boating: ～西湖 go boating on the West Lake

范（範）fàn

A〈名〉1〈书〉（模子）mould: 铁～ iron mould 2（榜样）model: ▸典～，规～ 3（界限）boundary: ▸～畴，就～
B〈动〉〈书〉control: ▸防～
【范本】fànběn〈名〉model: 习字～ model for calligraphy
【范畴】fànchóu〈名〉1（基本概念）category: 政治经济学～ the category of political economics 2（范围）scope: 汉字属于表意文字的～。Chinese characters belong in the category of ideographs.
【范例】fànlì〈名〉example: 典型～ typical example ‖ 英文书信～ example of English letter-writing
【范围】fànwéi〈名〉scope: 超出～ be beyond the scope of ‖ 涉及～很广 cover a wide range ‖ 活动～ range of activities ‖ 职权～ terms of reference
【范文】fànwén〈名〉model essay: 熟读～ learn model essays by heart

贩（販）fàn

A〈名〉trader: 报～ newsvendor ▸商～，摊～
B〈动〉buy to resell: ～药材 buy and sell Chinese herbs
【贩毒】fàndú〈动〉traffic in drugs: ～分子 drug trafficker
【贩夫】fànfū〈名〉〈旧〉vendor
【贩黄】fànhuáng〈动〉sell obscene publications
【贩卖】fànmài〈动〉traffic: ～儿童 traffic in children ‖ ～军火 traffic in arms
【贩私】fànsī〈动〉smuggle: 打击～活动 crack down on smuggling
【贩运】fànyùn〈动〉transport goods for sale: 长途～ long-distance freight
【贩子】fànzi〈名〉〈贬〉dealer: 毒品～ drug dealer ‖ 牲口～ cattle trader ▸票～，人～，战争～

畈 fàn

A〈名〉[used in place names] land
B〈量〉〈方〉tract: 一～稻田 a tract of paddy field

梵 fàn

〈名〉1（指古代印度）ancient India: ▸～语 2（指佛教）Buddhist: ▸～刹
【梵呗】fànbài〈名〉eulogy to the Buddha
【梵刹】fànchà〈名〉Buddhist temple
【梵蒂冈】Fàndìgāng〈名〉Vatican
【梵文】Fànwén ▸p. 918〈名〉Sanskrit
【梵语】Fànyǔ ▸p. 918〈名〉Sanskrit

fāng

方 fāng

A〈形〉1（指形状）square: ～脸 square face ‖ ～头皮鞋 square-toed leather shoes ‖ 六米见～的地毯 carpet six metres square 2（正直）upright: 品格端～ be honest and fair
B〈名〉1（地方）place: 何～人氏? Where are you from? ▸～言，远～ 2（方向）direction: ▸八～，南～ 3（方面）side: 甲/乙～ Party A/B ▸女～，双～ 4（方法）way: 引导有～ give wise guidance ▸千～百计 5（方术）magic arts 6（药方）prescription: 按～配药 make up a prescription ▸处～，偏～ 7［数学］power: 三的五次～ three to the power of five ‖ 十的三次～是一千。Ten to the power of three is a thousand. ▸立～，平～
C〈量〉1（指方形物体）[for square things]: 几～石碑 several stone tablets ‖ 两～图章 two seals 2（平方米）square metre 3（立方米）cubic metre: 三～木材/沙子 three cubic metres of lumber/sand
D〈副〉〈书〉1（正）just when: ▸～兴未艾，来日～长 2（才）just, only: 她年～十八。She is just eighteen years of age.
【方案】fāng'àn〈名〉1（计划）plan: 提出初步～ propose a preliminary plan ‖ 制定～ draw up a plan ‖ 施工～ construction project 2（规则）rule: 汉语拼音～ Chinese *Pinyin* system
【方便】fāngbiàn A〈形〉1（便利）convenient: 交通～ have a good transport service ‖ 在～的时候 at one's convenience 2（合适）appropriate: ～时 as occasion serves ‖ 这儿说话不～。This isn't the right place to talk about it. B〈动〉1（使便利）facilitate: ～乘客/群众 make things convenient for passengers/the general public 2〈婉〉（有余钱）have money to spare: 你～的话，借我 100 元。Can you spare me 100 *yuan*? 3 ▸p. 772〈婉〉（解手）go to the toilet: 请等一会儿，他～去了。Please wait a moment; he has just gone to excuse himself.
【方便面】fāngbiànmiàn〈名〉instant noodles
【方便食品】fāngbiàn shípǐn〈名〉convenience food
【方便之门】fāngbiànzhīmén〈成〉convenience: 大开～ offer every convenience
【方步】fāngbù〈名〉measured steps: 迈着～离去 go off with measured steps
【方才】fāngcái A〈名〉just now: 你晚了，火车～开走。You are too late; the train's just left. ‖ 他～还在车间里。He was in the workshop only a moment ago. B〈副〉not until: 到了年底，她～拿到工资。She was not paid until the end of the year.
【方材】fāngcái〈名〉hewn timber
【方策】fāngcè〈名〉〈书〉strategy
【方差】fāngchā〈名〉［统计］variance
【方程】fāngchéng〈名〉［数学］equation: 微分～ differential equation
【方程式】fāngchéngshì = 方程 fāngchéng
【方程式赛车】fāngchéngshì sàichē〈名〉formula car racing: 一级方程式世界锦标赛 Formula One World Championship
【方尺】fāngchǐ A〈名〉a square of a *chi* B〈量〉square *chi* [= 1/9 square metre]
【方寸】fāngcùn A〈名〉1（指正方形）a square of a *cun*: ～之地 heart 2〈书〉（心思）state of mind: 乱了～ be at a loss ‖ ～未定 be undecided what to do ‖ ～大乱 be completely lost B〈量〉square *cun* [= 1/9 square decimetre]
【方队】fāngduì〈名〉phalanx: 排成密集～ form a solid phalanx
【方法】fāngfǎ〈名〉way: 传统～ traditional method ‖ 思想～ way of thinking ‖ 学习～ study method ‖ 一套新的教学～ new teaching methodology
【方法论】fāngfǎlùn〈名〉［哲学］methodology: 辩证唯物主义的～ methodology of dialectical materialism
【方方面面】fāngfāng-miànmiàn〈成〉every respect: 要办好一件事，须考虑～的问题。The successful accomplishment of a task requires consideration of every aspect.
【方格】fānggé〈名〉check, chequer, pattern of squares: ～裙子 check skirt ‖ ～纸 graph/squared paper
【方根】fānggēn〈名〉［数学］root: ▸立～，平～
【方剂】fāngjì〈名〉［中医］prescription
【方家】fāngjiā〈名〉〈旧〉expert: 为～所笑 incur the ridicule of experts
【方解石】fāngjiěshí〈名〉［矿业］calcite
【方巾气】fāngjīnqì〈名〉pedantry: ～十足 sheer pedantry
【方今】fāngjīn〈名〉now
【方块】fāngkuài〈名〉[in cards] diamond: ～十 the ten of diamonds
【方块字】fāngkuàizì〈名〉Chinese characters
【方框】fāngkuàng〈名〉square frame
【方括号】fāngkuòhào〈名〉square brackets ([ ])
【方里】fānglǐ A〈名〉a square of a *li* B〈量〉square *li* [a quarter of a square kilometre]
【方略】fānglüè〈名〉overall strategy: 作战～ military strategy
【方面】fāngmiàn〈名〉respect: 矛盾的主要/次要～ principal/secondary aspect of a contradiction ‖ 来自各～的意见 opinions from different quarters ‖ 她在许多～与众不同。She is different from others in many respects. ‖ 我们应该从正反两～看这个问题。We should look at the problem from both sides.
【方面军】fāngmiànjūn〈名〉front army: 中国工农红军第四～ Fourth Front Army of the Chinese Workers' and Peasants' Red Army
【方枘圆凿】fāngruì-yuánzáo〈成〉completely incompatible
【方始】fāngshǐ〈书〉= 方才 fāngcái B
【方士】fāngshì〈名〉1（指占星、相面、卜卦等）diviner 2（指求仙、炼丹）alchemist
【方式】fāngshì〈名〉way: 付款～ method of payment ‖ 工作～ work pattern ‖ 经营～ mode of operation ‖ 思维～ way of thinking ‖ 用和平谈判的～解决问题 solve a problem by peaceful means
【方术】fāngshù〈名〉〈旧〉mystic arts
【方糖】fāngtáng〈名〉sugar cube
【方外】fāngwài〈名〉1〈书〉（域外）foreign land 2（世俗之外）place beyond the secular world: ～之人 Buddhist or Taoist priest

【方位】fāngwèi〈名〉1（方向）points of the compass: 四个基本～ four cardinal points of the compass 2（方向和位置）bearing: 在地图上找出～ locate sth. on the map ‖ 目标～ target bearing ‖ 全～的改革 all-round reforms

【方位词】fāngwèicí〈名〉［语法］ noun of locality

【方位角】fāngwèijiǎo〈名〉［天文］ azimuth

【方向】fāngxiàng〈名〉direction: 辨别～ get one's bearings ‖ 迷失～ lose one's bearings ‖ 指明～ point the direction for ‖ 政治～ political orientation ‖ 她把车朝北京～开去。 She drove in the direction of Beijing.

【方向舵】fāngxiàngduò〈名〉aeroplane rudder

【方向盘】fāngxiàngpán〈名〉steering wheel: 握着～ hold the wheel

【方兴未艾】fāngxīng-wèi'ài〈成〉be in the ascendant: ～的汽车市场 fledgling automobile market ‖ 房地产业～。 The real estate industry is on the ascendant.

【方言】fāngyán〈名〉dialect: 本地～ native dialect

【方言学】fāngyánxué〈名〉dialectology

【方药】fāngyào〈名〉herbs on prescription

【方音】fāngyīn〈名〉pronunciation of a dialect

【方圆】fāngyuán〈名〉1（周围）vicinity: ～六英里以内 within a six-mile radius 2（指长度）circumference: ～两百公里的湖 lake about 200 kilometres in circumference 3（方形和圆形）rectangle and circle: 没有规矩，不成～。 If you don't follow the rules, you can't do the right thing.

> **中国方言**
>
> There are generally considered to be seven main Chinese dialects: Mandarin (as spoken in northern China), Wu (as spoken in Shanghai, south-east Jiangsu and Zhejiang), Yue (Cantonese, as spoken in Guangdong and Hong Kong), Xiang (as spoken in Hunan), Hakka (as spoken in southern China and by the Chinese diaspora), Min (as spoken in Fujian), and Gan (as spoken in Jiangxi). Mandarin is the most widely distributed, and is spoken by over 70% of the Chinese population. Today's Mandarin ('putonghua' or standard Chinese) has its origins in the Beijing dialect. It is known in Taiwan as *guoyu* (国语).

【方丈】fāngzhàng A〈名〉 a square of a *zhang* B〈量〉 square *zhang* [= 11.11 square metres]

【方丈】fāngzhang〈名〉1（指人）abbot 2（指房间）abbot's quarters

【方针】fāngzhēn〈名〉guiding principle: 坚持党的基本～ adhere to the Party's fundamental policy ‖ ～政策 general and specific policy ‖ 教育～ guiding principles for education

【方阵】fāngzhèn〈名〉phalanx: 布设～ form a phalanx ‖ 排成～的士兵 soldiers drawn up in square formation

【方正】fāngzhèng〈形〉1（不偏不倚）upright and square: ～的脸膛 square face ‖ 他字写得方方正正。 His handwriting is square and upright. 2〈书〉（正直）upright: ～之士 man of integrity ‖ 他～不阿。 He is upright and above flattery.

【方志】fāngzhì〈名〉local records

【方舟】fāngzhōu〈名〉Noah's ark

【方桌】fāngzhuō〈名〉square table

【方子】fāngzi〈名〉1 = 方材 fāngcái 2（处方）prescription: 按～抓药 make up a prescription ‖ 治咳嗽的～ prescription for cough 3（配方）directions for mixing

坊 fāng

〈名〉1（胡同）alley [usu used as part of the name of a street or lane]: 安仁～ Anren Lane 2（牌坊）memorial archway: 贞节～ chastity arch ►牌～ ►fáng

【坊本】fāngběn〈名〉〈旧〉block-printed edition prepared by a printing house

【坊间】fāngjiān〈名〉1（街市上）street stall 2〈旧〉（书店）bookshop

芳 fāng

A〈形〉1（香）fragrant: ►～香，芬～ 2（美好）beautiful: ►～名，～心 3〈书〉〈敬〉（你的）your: ►～邻 B〈名〉1（美德）virtue: ►流～百世 2（花卉）flower: 群～ all the flowers

【芳草】fāngcǎo〈名〉green grass: ～如茵 carpet of green grass

【芳菲】fāngfēi〈书〉A〈形〉fragrant: 春草～ fresh spring grass B〈名〉flowers and plants: ～满园。 The garden is full of flowers.

【芳邻】fānglín〈名〉〈书〉1（好邻居）good neighbour 2〈敬〉（你的邻居）your neighbour

【芳龄】fānglíng〈名〉〈旧〉age of a girl:

f

ℹ 方位

■ 基本方位:

东	east	南	south
西	west	北	north

注意：方位顺序的表达在汉英里是不同的。汉语说东南西北，而英语说 north、south、east、west。

■ 汉语说"东北"、"西北"等，英语说 north-east、north-west 等，和汉语的顺序相反:

东北	north-east	西北	north-west
东南	south-east	西南	south-west

■ 英语方位词可做名词、形容词及副词，而汉语的方位词只做名词。本注释中的例子体现了英语方位词三种词性的用法。

介词和英语方位名词

■ 表达在某个地方之内的某个方位时，英语用 in；指在某个地方之外的某个方位时，英语用 to。英语的方位词前要用定冠词 the:

广州在中国南部
= Guangzhou is in the south of China

我住在中国西部
= I live in the west of China

日本在中国的东边
= Japan lies to the east of China

河南省在湖北省的北边
或 河南省在湖北省以北
= Henan Province is located to the north of Hubei Province

■ 以下是其他介词的用法（注意下面例子特指说话者和听话者都知道的一个范围）。注意英语定冠词的用法:

她来自北方
= She comes from the north

西南部明天将有暴风雨
= There will be storms in the south-west tomorrow

英语方位形容词

■ 英语的方位词 north、south 等本身也可做形容词:

南极
= the South Pole

北美洲
= North America

中国东部海岸
= the east coast of China

欧洲西南部
= South-west Europe

东门
= the east exit

东北风
= a north-east wind

■ 以 south 为例，其他表方位的英语形容词还有 southern、southerly、southernmost 及 southward。其他方位词 north、east 及 west 的用法和 south 相同:

南部城市
= southern cities

三亚是中国最南部的海滨城市
= Sanya is the most southerly seaside city of China

海南省是中国最南部的省份
= Hainan is the southernmost province of China

火车朝南开走了
= The train moved off in a southward direction

其他短语

朝北的房子
= a north-facing house

朝北去的火车
= a northbound train

窗户朝东
= The window faces east

博物馆在往南几英里处
= The museum is located a few miles south

电影院在从这向西大约 3 英里处
= The cinema is about three miles to the west of here

■ 汉语说"朝"、"向"某个方向时，英语用下面几种表达法。在这里以 east 为例加以说明，其他方位词的用法相同:

他朝东开走了
= He drove off in an eastward direction
或 He drove off eastwards
或 He drove off in an easterly direction
或 He drove off towards the east
或 He drove off east（east 做副词）

二八～ aged 16 ‖ ～几何? May I know your age?
【芳名】fāngmíng〈名〉1（指名字） name of a young girl: 请问～? [to a girl] May I have your name? 2（指名声） good name: ～远扬 be known far and wide ‖ 她将～永垂。 Her name will be remembered forever.
【芳年】fāngnián〈名〉〈书〉 prime of life: 正值～ in one's prime
【芳容】fāngróng〈名〉〈书〉 good looks of a young woman
【芳香】fāngxiāng A〈名〉 fragrance: ～扑鼻 the fragrance assails one's nostrils ‖ ～四溢 sweet fragrance all around ‖ 花的～ scent of flowers B〈形〉 fragrant: 茉莉花气味～。 Jasmine has a fragrant aroma.
【芳香剂】fāngxiāngjì〈名〉 aromatic
【芳心】fāngxīn〈名〉〈书〉heart of a young girl: 赢得～ win the heart of a girl
【芳泽】fāngzé〈名〉1（指润发油） scented hair oil used by women in old times 2（香气） fragrance 3〈书〉（指仪容） woman's looks

枋

枋 fāng〈名〉1（指树） tree used as timber for vehicles 2（指木材） hewn timber
【枋子】fāngzi〈名〉 1（指木材） hewn timber 2〈方〉（棺材） coffin

钫¹（鈁）

钫[1]（鈁） fāng〈名〉［化学］francium (Fr)

钫²（鈁）

钫[2]（鈁） fāng〈名〉〈古〉 1（指酒器） bronze wine vessel 2（指锅） pot

fáng

防

防 fáng
A〈名〉 1（堤坝） dam: ▸堤～ 2（防务） defence: ▸边～, 国～
B〈动〉 1（预防） prevent: ～癌 prevent cancer ‖ 建墙以～外人闯入 build a wall to keep out intruders ‖ 谨～假冒! Beware of bogus imitations! ▸～腐, 预～ 2（防御） defend: ▸～卫, ～务
【防暴】fángbào〈动〉 be anti-riot: ～武器 anti-riot weapons ‖ ～任务 anti-riot duty ‖ ～警察 riot police
【防爆】fángbào〈动〉 be explosion-proof: ～材料 explosion-proof material ‖ ～玻璃 explosion-proof glass
【防备】fángbèi〈动〉 guard against: ～敌人的空袭 guard against enemy air raids ‖ 有所/没有～ be on/off one's guard
【防波堤】fángbōdī〈名〉 groyne
【防不胜防】fángbùshèngfáng〈成〉 hard to guard against
【防潮】fángcháo〈动〉 1（指潮湿） be damp-proof: ～包装 damp-proof packaging ‖ ～剂 drying agent 2（指潮水） protect against the tide: ～闸门 tidal gate
【防尘】fángchén〈动〉 be dust-proof: ～面罩 dust mask
【防除】fángchú〈动〉 prevent and kill off: ～苍蝇 prevent and kill off flies
【防磁】fángcí〈动〉［物理］ be anti-magnetic: ～手表 anti-magnetic watch
【防弹】fángdàn〈动〉 be bulletproof: ～背心 bulletproof vest ‖ ～玻璃 bulletproof glass
【防盗】fángdào〈动〉 guard against theft: ～措施严密 be strongly guarded against thieves
【防盗门】fángdàomén〈名〉 theft-proof door: 安装～ install a burglar-proof door
【防地】fángdì〈名〉［军事］ station
【防冻】fángdòng〈动〉 1（指冻害） prevent frostbite: ～药品 anti-frostbite medication 2（指冻结） be freeze-proof: ～剂 anti-freeze
【防毒】fángdú〈动〉 protect against poisonous gases
【防毒面具】fángdú miànjù〈名〉 gas mask
【防范】fángfàn〈动〉 be on guard: ～措施 precautionary measures ‖ 对于走私活动要严加～。 Take strict precautions against smuggling.
【防风】fángfēng〈动〉 protect against the wind
【防风林】fángfēnglín〈名〉 windbreak: ～带 shelter belt
【防辐射】fángfúshè〈动〉 shield from radiation
【防腐】fángfǔ〈动〉 be antiseptic: ～材料 anti-rot material
【防腐剂】fángfǔjì〈名〉 preservative
【防腐蚀】fángfǔshí〈动〉 be anticorrosive
【防寒】fánghán〈动〉 protect against the cold: 穿件厚大衣～ wear a thick overcoat as protection against the bitter cold
【防旱】fánghàn〈动〉 take precautions against drought
【防洪】fánghóng〈动〉 prevent flooding: ～大堤 flood dyke ‖ ～闸 floodgate ‖ ～能力 flood control capacity
【防护】fánghù〈动〉 protect: 人体～ physical protection ‖ ～罩 guard ‖ ～堤 protection embankment
【防护林】fánghùlín〈名〉 shelter forest: 三北～ shelter forests in northern, north-western and north-eastern China
【防滑】fánghuá〈动〉 be non-slip: ～地板 non-slip floor ‖ ～链 tyre chain
【防滑漆】fánghuáqī〈名〉 non-slip paint
【防滑鞋】fánghuáxié〈名〉 non-slip shoes
【防化兵】fánghuàbīng〈名〉［军事］ anti-chemical warfare corps
【防化服】fánghuàfú〈名〉 chemical protection suit
【防患未然】fánghuàn-wèirán〈成〉 take preventive measures: 对这个问题我们要～。 Let's nip this problem in the bud before it gets out of hand.
【防火】fánghuǒ〈动〉 prevent fires: 提高民众的～意识 raise people's awareness of fire prevention ‖ ～材料 fireproof material ‖ 森林～ prevention of forest fires
【防火墙】fánghuǒqiáng〈名〉 1（用于阻燃） firewall 2［计算机］ firewall
【防空】fángkōng〈动〉 take precautions in defence of an enemy aircraft: ～警报 air-raid siren ‖ ～部队 air defence forces
【防空洞】fángkōngdòng〈名〉 1〈本〉 bomb shelter 2〈喻〉（用以掩护） hide-away
【防空壕】fángkōngháo〈名〉 air-raid dugout
【防恐】fángkǒng〈动〉 prevent terrorist attacks: ～演习/警报 terrorism prevention exercise/alarm
【防控】fángkòng〈动〉 prevent and control: 做好甲流的～工作 do effective H1N1 prevention and control work
【防老】fánglǎo〈动〉 prepare for one's old age: 养儿～。 Boys are brought up to take care of their elderly parents.
【防老化】fánglǎohuà〈动〉 be anti-ageing
【防涝】fánglào〈动〉 prevent waterlogging
【防凌】fánglíng〈动〉 prevent an ice run
【防区】fángqū〈名〉 garrison area
【防沙】fángshā〈动〉 prevent sand from spreading
【防沙林】fángshālín〈名〉 sand-break
【防沙治沙】fángshā-zhìshā〈动〉 control desertification: ～生态工程 control desertification through ecological engineering ‖ 植树造林，～ reforestation and control of desertification
【防晒霜】fángshàishuāng〈名〉 suncream
【防身】fángshēn〈动〉 protect oneself: ～招数 self-protection techniques ‖ ～术 art of self-defence
【防守】fángshǒu〈动〉defend: ～边境 keep guard on the frontier ‖ 加强～ strengthen the defence ‖ 人盯人～ close-marking defence ‖ 上半场我们～不好。Our defence wasn't very good in the first half.
【防暑】fángshǔ〈动〉 prevent heatstroke: 喝绿茶能～。 Drinking green tea can help to prevent sunstroke.
【防霜冻】fángshuāngdòng〈动〉 resist frost
【防水】fángshuǐ〈动〉 be waterproof: ～手表 waterproof watch
【防特】fángtè〈动〉 guard against enemy spies
【防微杜渐】fángwēi-dùjiàn〈成〉nip in the bud
【防伪】fángwěi〈动〉 prevent counterfeiting: ～标记 anti-counterfeiting mark
【防卫】fángwèi〈动〉 defend: ～能力 defence capabilities ▸正当～
【防卫过当】fángwèi guòdàng〈名〉［法律］ excessive self-defence
【防务】fángwù〈名〉 defence: ～条约 defence pact
【防线】fángxiàn〈名〉 line of defence: 突破～ break through the line of defence
【防锈】fángxiù〈动〉 be rustproof: ～漆 anti-rust paint
【防汛】fángxùn〈动〉 prevent flooding: ～抗旱 control flooding and combat drought ‖ ～器材 flood-relief equipment ‖ ～指挥部 flood-control headquarters
【防疫】fángyì〈动〉 prevent epidemics: ～针 inoculation
【防疫站】fángyìzhàn〈名〉 epidemic prevention station
【防御】fángyù〈动〉 guard against: ～外来侵略 guard against external aggression ‖ 由～转入进攻 go from the defensive to the offensive ‖ 积极～ active defence ‖ ～工事 defences
【防灾】fángzāi〈动〉 take precautions against natural calamities: ～减灾 take precautions against natural calamities in order to minimize damage
【防震】fángzhèn〈动〉 1（指震动） be shockproof: ～表 shockproof watch 2（指地震） take precautions against earthquakes: ～措施 anti-quake measures ‖ ～棚 earthquake shelter
【防止】fángzhǐ〈动〉 prevent: ～国有资产流失 prevent state-asset drain ‖ ～核扩散 non-proliferation of nuclear weapons ‖ ～疾病蔓延 prevent the spread of a disease ‖ ～交通事故 prevent traffic accidents
【防治】fángzhì〈动〉 provide prevention and cure: ～病虫害 prevent and control plant diseases and eliminate pests ‖ ～环境污染 prevent and remedy environmental pollution
【防皱】fángzhòu〈动〉 be wrinkle-proof
【防蛀】fángzhù〈动〉 be mothproof

坊 fáng〈名〉workshop: 染～ dye-works ▸作～ ▸fāng

妨 fáng〈动〉obstruct: 不～事。It doesn't matter.

【妨碍】fáng'ài〈动〉hinder: ～交通 block traffic ‖ ～视线 obstruct the view ‖ ～工作 hinder sb.'s work ‖ ～执行公务 interfere with a public function

【妨害】fánghài〈动〉harm: ～社会秩序 disturb social order ‖ 吸烟～健康。Smoking is harmful to health.

【妨害公务罪】fánghài gōngwùzuì〈名〉crime of interference with public function

肪 fáng ▸脂肪 zhīfáng

房 fáng

A〈名〉**1**（房屋）house: 建～ build a house ‖ 租～ rent a house ▸～改，平～，危～ **2**（房间）room: 两间～ two rooms ▸客～ **3**（房状物）house-like structure: ▸蜂～，心～ **4**（指家族）branch of an extended family: 三～ third son and his family ▸远～，长～ **5**（妻子）wife: ▸填～，正～ **6**（指星宿）one of the 28 constellations in ancient Chinese astronomy

B〈量〉〈旧〉[for daughters-in-law and concubines]: 他有三～儿媳妇。He has three daughters-in-law.

【房舱】fángcāng〈名〉cabin

【房产】fángchǎn〈名〉property: 继承～ inherit property ‖ ～抵押 property loan ‖ ～证 property title certificate

【房产主】fángchǎnzhǔ〈名〉property owner

【房车】fángchē〈名〉caravan〈英〉; trailer〈美〉

【房贷】fángdài〈名〉housing loan

【房地产】fángdìchǎn〈名〉real property〈英〉; real estate〈美〉: ～市场 real property market

【房顶】fángdǐng〈名〉roof

【房东】fángdōng〈名〉（男）landlord;（女）landlady

【房改】fánggǎi〈动〉housing reform: ～方案 housing reform plan

【房管】fángguǎn〈名〉real property management: ～所 real property management office ‖ ～局 housing management department

【房基】fángjī〈名〉foundation of a building: 打～ lay the foundation of a building

【房间】fángjiān〈名〉room: 布置～ furnish a room ‖ 预订～ book a room

【房客】fángkè〈名〉tenant

【房奴】fángnú〈名〉mortgage slave : 不少贷款购房者成了～。Many people who take out loans to buy a house become mortgage slaves.

【房契】fángqì〈名〉title deed

【房钱】fángqián〈名〉house rental

【房市】fángshì〈名〉property market

【房事】fángshì ▸**p. 772**〈名〉〈婉〉sexual intercourse: 行～ make love

【房屋】fángwū〈名〉house: 建造～ build a house

【房型】fángxíng〈名〉type of a house

【房源】fángyuán〈名〉houses for rent or sale: ～紧缺，房价上升。Housing is tight, so prices have gone up.

【房檐】fángyán〈名〉eaves

【房展】fángzhǎn〈名〉housing exhibition: 看～ visit a housing exhibition

【房展会】fángzhǎnhuì〈名〉real estate expo: ～上，新楼盘纷纷亮相。Many new flats were unveiled at the real estate expo.

【房主】fángzhǔ〈名〉house owner

【房子】fángzi〈名〉house

【房租】fángzū〈名〉rent: 付～ pay the rent ‖ 拖欠～ fall behind with the rent

鲂（魴） fáng〈名〉[鱼类] triangular bream

fǎng

仿[1] fǎng

A〈动〉**1**（像）resemble: ▸相～ **2**（仿照）imitate: ～原样做一个 make one after the original ‖ ～羊皮纸 imitation parchment ▸～效，模～

B〈名〉characters written after a calligraphy model: ▸～纸

仿[2]（**彷**）fǎng ▸仿佛 fǎngfú，仿若 fǎngruò

【仿办】fǎngbàn〈动〉〈书〉follow the example of: 依例～ follow a precedent ‖ 这种做法各省可以～。Other provinces may well follow the practice.

【仿单】fǎngdān〈名〉directions for use

【仿佛】fǎngfú **A**〈副〉seemingly: ～在哪儿见过他 seem to have met him somewhere ‖ 她的眼睛～会说话。Her eyes seem to speak. ‖ 问题～没完没了。It seemed as if there were no end to the problems. **B**〈动〉be similar: 姐妹几个模样相～。The sisters look very much alike.

【仿古】fǎnggǔ〈动〉be modelled after an antique: ～建筑 pseudo-classic architecture ‖ ～陶器 archaistic pottery

【仿冒】fǎngmào〈动〉counterfeit: ～产品 counterfeit goods ‖ ～名牌 counterfeit of a well-known brand

【仿皮】fǎngpí〈名〉fake leather: ～公文包 leather-style briefcase

【仿若】fǎngruò〈书〉= 仿佛 fǎngfú A

【仿生学】fǎngshēngxué〈名〉bionics: ～家 bionics expert

【仿宋体】fǎngsòngtǐ〈名〉[印刷] imitation Song Dynasty-style typeface

【仿效】fǎngxiào〈动〉imitate: ～电影明星 emulate a movie star

【仿影】fǎngyǐng〈名〉[书法] model characters

【仿造】fǎngzào〈动〉copy: ～古董 fake curio

【仿照】fǎngzhào〈动〉follow: ～办理 follow suit ‖ ～苏州园林建造花园 create a garden in the style of Suzhou gardens

【仿真】fǎngzhēn **A**〈动〉simulate **B**〈形〉simulated: ～手枪 simulated pistol

【仿纸】fǎngzhǐ〈名〉checked paper for calligraphy practice

【仿制】fǎngzhì〈动〉copy: ～的家具 reproduction furniture ‖ ～品 imitation

访（訪） fǎng〈动〉**1**（咨询）consult **2**（探寻）enquire into: ▸～查，采～ **3**（拜访）visit: ～友 call on a friend ‖ 我有客来～。I have a visitor. ▸互～

【访查】fǎngchá〈动〉investigate

【访古】fǎnggǔ〈动〉search for ancient relics

【访旧】fǎngjiù〈动〉**1**（指人）visit an old friend **2**（指地方）visit an old haunt

【访贫问苦】fǎngpín-wènkǔ〈成〉visit the impoverished and the wretched

【访求】fǎngqiú〈动〉seek: ～名医 seek and consult a reputed/reputable doctor

【访谈】fǎngtán〈动〉interview

【访谈录】fǎngtánlù〈名〉interview

【访问】fǎngwèn〈动〉visit: ～巴黎 visit Paris ‖ ～亲友 call on relatives and friends ‖ 进行国事～ make a state visit ‖ ～学者 visiting scholar

【访寻】fǎngxún〈动〉seek: ～失散的女儿 look for one's missing daughter

纺（紡） fǎng

A〈动〉spin: 把棉花～成线 spin cotton into thread ▸混～，棉～

B〈名〉thin silk cloth: 杭～ Hangzhou silk

【纺车】fǎngchē〈名〉spinning wheel

【纺绸】fǎngchóu〈名〉soft plain-weave silk fabric

【纺锤】fǎngchuí〈名〉spindle

【纺锭】fǎngdìng = 纱锭 shādìng

【纺纱】fǎngshā〈名〉spinning: ～机 spinning machine

【纺织】fǎngzhī〈动〉spin and weave: ～工业 textile industry ‖ ～机械 textile machinery ‖ ～女工 woman textile worker ‖ ～厂 textile mill

【纺织娘】fǎngzhīniáng〈名〉[昆虫] long-horned grasshopper

【纺织品】fǎngzhīpǐn〈名〉textile

舫 fǎng〈名〉boat: ▸画～，石～

fàng

放 fàng〈动〉**1**（不加拘束）give way to: 她～声笑了。She burst into laughter. ▸～任，豪～ **2**（放逐）send into exile: ▸～逐，流～ **3**（使自由）let go: ～他一马 let him through ‖ ～点热水洗个澡 run a hot bath ‖ ～开我！Let go of me! ‖ 交了赎金，就能～你走。You will be set free when the ransom is paid. **4**（放牧）put out to feed: ～牛/羊 graze cattle/sheep **5**（开始或停止）let out: ▸～假，～学 **6**（使爆炸）set off: ～爆竹 set off firecrackers ‖ ～枪 let off a gun ‖ ～烟火 set off rockets **7**（发出）give off: ～风筝 fly a kite ‖ ～光/热 give off light/heat **8**（点燃）light: ▸～荒，～火 **9**（分发）hand out: ▸发～ **10**（借出）loan: ～高利贷 lend out money at an exorbitant rate of interest ▸～债 **11**（开放）bloom: ▸百花齐～ **12**（放大）enlarge: ～照片 blow up a photo ‖ 把裙子～长 let out the hemline of a skirt **13**（摆放）put: ～下武器 lay down one's weapon ‖ 把壶～在炉子上 put the kettle on the stove ‖ 把花瓶～在桌子上 put a vase on the table ‖ 把人民的利益～在首位 give priority to the interests of the people ‖ 别把他那些话～在心上。Don't take his remarks to heart. **14**（搁置）lay aside: 这事不要紧，先～一～。This isn't urgent. Let's leave it for later consideration. **15**（弄倒）cause to fall down: ～树 cut down trees ▸～倒 **16**（加进去）put in: 菜里少～点盐。Don't put too much salt in the dish. **17**（控制）conduct oneself: ～慢脚步/速度 slacken one's pace/speed ‖ ～聪明点儿! Be smart! ‖ ～老实点! Behave yourself! **18**（播放）show: ～电影 screen a film ‖ ～录像 play a videotape **19**（扩展）extend: ～大 amplify

【放榜】fàngbǎng = 发榜 fābǎng

f

【放包袱】fàng bāofu = 放下包袱 fàngxià bāofu

【放长线，钓大鱼】fàng chángxiàn, diào dàyú〈俗〉〈喻〉adopt a long-term vision to achieve a bigger goal

【放黜】fàngchù〈动〉〈书〉banish

【放达】fàngdá〈形〉〈书〉unrestrained

【放大】fàngdà〈动〉enlarge: ～照片 enlarge a photograph ‖ 把标本/细菌～1,000 倍 magnify the sample/bacteria by a thousand times

【放大镜】fàngdàjìng〈名〉magnifying glass

【放大器】fàngdàqì〈名〉1（用于放大信号）amplifier: 视频～ video amplifier ‖ 音频～ audio-frequency amplifier 2（用于制图）pantograph

【放大炮】fàng dàpào〈惯〉〈喻〉1（说空话）boast: 他就会吹牛皮～。Boasting is about the only thing he's any good at. 2（言语激烈）shoot one's mouth off

【放贷】fàngdài〈动〉loan: 违规～ loaning malpractice

【放胆】fàngdǎn〈动〉act boldly: 她～摸着黑上了楼。She plucked up courage and went upstairs in the dark.

【放诞】fàngdàn〈形〉unruly: 生性～ be unruly by nature

【放荡】fàngdàng〈形〉1（不检点）loose: 生活～ live a life of debauchery 2（放纵）unconventional

【放荡不羁】fàngdàng-bùjī〈成〉unconventional and unrestrained: 他年轻时～。He was quite Bohemian in his youth.

【放倒】fàngdǎo〈动〉〈口〉knock down: 把对手～ knock one's opponent down

【放电】fàngdiàn〈动〉［物理］1（电荷消失）discharge electricity: 闪电是由云团～造成的。Lightning is caused by clouds discharging electricity. 2（释放电能）discharge electricity

【放刁】fàngdiāo〈动〉act perversely

【放毒】fàngdú〈动〉1（指毒药）poison 2〈喻〉（指言论）spread poisonous ideas: 向青少年～ corrupt young people with evil ideas

【放飞】fàngfēi〈动〉1（指飞机）permit a plane to take off 2（指鸟）set free: ～鸽子 release a pigeon 3（指风筝）fly: ～风筝 fly a kite

【放风】fàngfēng〈动〉1（指囚犯）let prisoners out for exercise: ～场地 exercise yard ‖ 囚犯每天可以～一小时。The prisoner got an hour of exercise in the prison yard each day. 2（散布消息）let out: 他～要报仇。He let it be known that he would take revenge. 3〈方〉（望风）keep watch

【放歌】fànggē〈动〉〈书〉sing passionately: ～一曲 sing a song heartily

【放工】fànggōng〈动〉leave work: 今天咱们早点～。Let's knock off a bit earlier today.

【放过】fàngguò〈动〉let off: 老师连一点小错都不肯～。The teacher would not let the least little mistake pass.

【放虎归山】fànghǔ-guīshān = 纵虎归山 zònghǔ-guīshān

【放话】fànghuà〈动〉divulge information

【放怀】fànghuái〈动〉1（尽情）do sth. to one's heart's content: ～大笑 laugh heartily ‖ ～高歌 sing to one's heart's content 2（放心）feel relieved: 听了那不幸的消息，他难以～。It was difficult to find peace of mind after hearing the bad news.

【放还】fànghuán〈动〉1（释放）release: ～人质 release a hostage ‖ 交保～ release on bail 2（放回）put back: 把书～原处。Put the book back.

【放荒】fànghuāng〈动〉set fire to wild bushes and weeds

【放火】fànghuǒ〈动〉1（纵火）set on fire: ～烧房 set fire to a house ‖ ～犯 arsonist 2〈喻〉（煽风点火）create a disturbance

【放假】fàngjià〈动〉have a holiday: 给学生放三天假 let students have three days off ‖ 学校已经～。The school has broken up for the holidays.

【放开】fàngkāi〈动〉let go: ～搞活 open up and enliven the economy ‖ ～粮食价格 lift control over grain prices ‖ ～手脚 give a free hand

【放空】fàngkōng〈动〉1（错失目标）miss the target 2（指交通工具）run without goods: 调度工作搞得好就可以避免车辆～。Good dispatch can help avoid vehicles travelling without freight.

【放空炮】fàng kōngpào〈惯〉〈喻〉spout hot air: 再别～了! No more of your empty talk!

【放空气】fàng kōngqì〈惯〉〈贬〉1（指舆论）spread word 2〈喻〉（指气氛）give a false impression

【放宽】fàngkuān〈动〉relax: ～录取条件 relax admission requirements ‖ ～期限 extend a time limit ‖ 进一步～政策 adopt a more flexible policy

【放款】fàngkuǎn〈动〉grant a loan: ～限度 loan ceiling ‖ 银行向购房者～越来越多。Banks are putting up more and more money for people buying houses.

【放浪】fànglàng〈形〉〈书〉1（放纵）unrestrained 2（放荡）dissolute

【放浪形骸】fànglàng-xínghái〈成〉be unconventional and unrestrained

【放冷风】fàng lěngfēng〈惯〉〈喻〉spread rumours

【放冷箭】fàng lěngjiàn〈惯〉〈喻〉stab in the back

【放量】fàngliàng〈动〉1（指数量）increase in number: 今天股市～了。The stock market surged today. 2（尽量）do sth. to one's heart's content: 难得相聚，咱们～喝。Let's drink to our heart's content in celebration of this rare get-together.

【放疗】fàngliáo〈动〉treat with radiation therapy: 接受～ have radiation therapy

【放马后炮】fàng mǎhòupào〈惯〉〈喻〉second-guess: 他老爱～。He is always second-guessing.

【放牧】fàngmù〈动〉graze: 在山坡上～牛羊 graze cattle and sheep on the slope

【放牛娃】fàngniúwá〈名〉child cowherd

【放排】fàngpái〈动〉set a raft going downstream

【放盘】fàngpán〈动〉sell at reduced prices or purchase at raised prices

【放炮】fàngpào〈动〉1（指大炮）fire a cannon 2（指爆竹）set off firecrackers 3（指火药）blast: ～开凿隧道 blast a tunnel 4（爆胎）burst: 后胎～了。The rear tyre burst. 5〈喻〉（指言语）shoot one's mouth off: 发言要慎重，不要乱～! Be prudent and try not to shoot your mouth off.

【放屁】fàngpì〈动〉1（指生理现象）break wind 2〈粗〉（指骂人话）shit〈粗〉: ～! Rubbish!

【放弃】fàngqì〈动〉abandon: ～财产 relinquish one's possessions ‖ ～出国的打算 give up the idea of going abroad ‖ ～继承权 waive one's inheritance ‖ ～原则 forsake a principle

【放青】fàngqīng〈动〉graze

【放情】fàngqíng〈动〉do sth. to one's heart's content: ～山水 enjoy oneself in the embrace of nature

【放晴】fàngqíng〈动〉clear up: 下午天将～。It will clear up this afternoon.

【放权】fàngquán〈动〉delegate powers: 提倡～ encourage devolution of power

【放任】fàngrèn〈动〉give free reign to: 采取～的态度 take a laissez-faire attitude

【放任自流】fàngrèn-zìliú〈成〉take things as they come

【放散】fàngsàn〈动〉waft in all directions

【放哨】fàngshào〈动〉keep sentry: 站岗～ stand sentry

【放射】fàngshè〈动〉radiate: 太阳既～可见光，也～紫外线。The sun radiates both visible and ultraviolet light.

【放射病】fàngshèbìng〈名〉radiation sickness

【放射疗法】fàngshè liáofǎ〈名〉radiotherapy: 有些癌症可用～治疗。Some cancers can be treated by radiation therapy.

【放射线】fàngshèxiàn〈名〉radioactive rays

【放射形】fàngshèxíng〈名〉radiating formation

【放射性】fàngshèxìng〈名〉［物理］radioactivity: ～污染 radioactive pollution ‖ ～物质 radioactive material ‖ ～元素 radioactive element

【放射源】fàngshèyuán〈名〉radioactive source

【放生】fàngshēng〈动〉release captive animals back into the wild

【放声】fàngshēng〈动〉shout at the top of one's voice: ～大笑 roar with laughter ‖ 我真想～大哭一场。I want a good cry.

【放手】fàngshǒu〈动〉1（松手）lose one's grip: 抓紧，别～! Hold tight, don't let go! 2〈喻〉（解除思想束缚）have a free hand: ～发动群众 go all out to mobilize the masses 3（罢休）hand over control: 你要干不好就～吧，让别人去干。If you are not up to it, hand it over to someone else.

【放肆】fàngsì〈形〉wanton: 说话别那么～! Don't give me any of your lip! ‖ 他对这位姑娘太～了。His behaviour with the girl was too familiar.

【放松】fàngsōng〈动〉relax: ～对孩子的管教 relax one's grip on the children ‖ ～肌肉 relax one's muscles ‖ ～警惕 lower one's guard

【放送】fàngsòng〈动〉broadcast: ～一首歌 broadcast a song

【放卫星】fàng wèixīng〈动〉1（发射卫星）launch a satellite 2〈口〉（说大话）talk up 3（有大突破）make a breakthrough

【放下】fàngxià〈动〉lay down

【放下包袱】fàngxià bāofu〈惯〉〈喻〉take a load off one's mind: 放下思想包袱 free oneself of one's mental burden

【放下屠刀，立地成佛】fàngxià túdāo, lìdì chéng fó〈成〉attain salvation through repentance

【放像机】fàngxiàngjī〈名〉video cassette player

【放血】fàngxiě〈动〉1［医学］let blood 2〈口〉（伤害）make sb. bleed 3〈口〉〈喻〉（损失钱财）pay money: 让他放点血。Let him pay for it.

【放心】fàngxīn〈动〉feel at ease: 让母亲～ set one's mother's mind at rest ‖ 请～，我们一定能找到你的儿子。Rest assured! We'll find your son for you. ‖ 我确实对他不大～。I do have little confidence in him.

【放心菜】fàngxīncài〈名〉quality-assured vegetables
【放心肉】fàngxīnròu〈名〉quality-assured meat
【放行】fàngxíng〈动〉allow to pass: 免税～ tax-free clearance
【放学】fàngxué〈动〉let children out of school: ～提前了15分钟。School was out 15 minutes ahead of schedule.
【放眼】fàngyǎn〈动〉take a broad view: ～未来 look towards the future ‖ ～世界 have the whole world in view
【放羊】fàngyáng〈动〉**1**〈本〉graze sheep: 在河边～ graze sheep by a river **2**〈喻〉set free: 老师没来上课，学生就放羊了。The teacher did not come to class and so the pupils were left unattended.
【放养】fàngyǎng〈动〉breed in a suitable place: ～海带 cultured kelp ‖ 在池塘里～鱼虾 breed fish and shrimps in a pond
【放音机】fàngyīnjī〈名〉cassette player
【放映】fàngyìng〈动〉show: ～电影 show a film ‖ ～机 projector ‖ ～员 projectionist ‖ ～室 projection room ‖ 这部电影已连续～了一个月。The film has been running for a month.
【放淤】fàngyū〈动〉［农业］warp
【放债】fàngzhài〈动〉lend money at interest: 以高利～ lend money at usury
【放账】fàngzhàng = 放债 fàngzhài
【放赈】fàngzhèn〈动〉〈书〉dispense charity: ～救济灾民 distribute relief to disaster victims
【放之四海而皆准】fàng zhī sìhǎi ér jiē zhǔn〈成〉be universally applicable: ～的真理 universally applicable truth
【放置】fàngzhì〈动〉place: 把花圈～在墓前 place a wreath at a tomb ‖ 设备长期～不用。The equipment was put aside and not used for a long time.
【放逐】fàngzhú〈动〉exile: 被～到一个荒岛上 be banished to a desert island
【放纵】fàngzòng **A**〈动〉indulge: 不要太～孩子。Don't indulge your children too much. **B**〈形〉self-indulgent: 行为～ intemperate conduct ‖ ～不羁 uninhibited indulgence

fēi

飞(飛) fēi

A〈动〉**1**（指鸟、虫等）fly: 蝴蝶在花丛中～来～去。The butterfly fluttered about among the flowers. ‖ 小麻雀～走了。The little sparrows flew off. **2**（指自然物体）float: ～云 floating clouds **3**（指飞行器）fly: 飞机从纽约～往巴黎。The plane flew from New York to Paris. ‖ 我明天直～伦敦。I will fly non-stop to London tomorrow. ▸～行，起～ **4**（快速运动）move swiftly: ～身扑球 dive at full tilt to get the ball ‖ 火车从她眼前～过。The train flew past her. **5**（挥发）volatilize: 盖上瓶子吧，免得香味～了。Put the top on the bottle to prevent the aroma from evaporating.
B〈形〉**1**（意外）unexpected: ▸～来横祸 **2**（无根据）groundless: ▸流言～语
【飞白】fēibái〈名〉style of calligraphy characterized by hollow strokes, as if done with a half-dry brush
【飞奔】fēibēn〈动〉dash: ～上楼 dash upstairs ‖ 骑马～而去 ride off at a gallop
【飞镖】fēibiāo ▸**p. 411**〈名〉**1**（指武器）dart: 投掷～ throw a dart **2**（指游戏）darts: 玩～ play darts
【飞播】fēibō〈动〉sow by a plane: ～造林 forestation by aerial sowing
【飞车】fēichē **A**〈动〉drive at lightning speed **B**〈名〉speeding vehicle: 开～是造成交通事故的主要原因之一。Reckless speeding is one of the major causes of traffic accidents.
【飞车走壁】fēichē zǒubì〈名〉［杂技］stunt cycling
【飞驰】fēichí〈动〉speed: 火车～而过。The train flew past.
【飞虫】fēichóng〈名〉winged insect
【飞船】fēichuán〈名〉spaceship: 宇宙～ spacecraft
【飞弹】fēidàn〈名〉**1**（导弹）missile **2**（流弹）stray bullet
【飞地】fēidì〈名〉enclave: ～工业 enclave industry
【飞碟】fēidié〈名〉**1**（不明飞行物）unidentified flying object (UFO) **2**（指射击的靶）frisbee: ～射击 skeet
【飞短流长】fēiduǎn-liúcháng〈成〉tell tales
【飞蛾扑火】fēi'é-pūhuǒ = 飞蛾投火 fēi'é-tóuhuǒ
【飞蛾投火】fēi'é-tóuhuǒ〈成〉bring destruction upon oneself: ～，自取灭亡 seek one's own doom like moths flying into flames
【飞红】fēihóng **A**〈形〉crimson: 她羞得满脸～。She flushed with embarrassment. **B**〈动〉blush suddenly
【飞鸿】fēihóng〈名〉〈书〉**1**（鸿雁）swan goose **2**（书信）letter
【飞狐】fēihú〈名〉flying fox
【飞黄腾达】fēihuáng-téngdá〈成〉enjoy a meteoric rise: 他已经～了。He's risen high in the world.
【飞蝗】fēihuáng〈名〉migratory locust
【飞机】fēijī〈名〉aeroplane〈英〉; airplane〈美〉: ～场 airport ‖ ～跑道 runway ▸航天～
【飞溅】fēijiàn〈动〉spray: 泉水～了我一身。The water from the spring splashed all over me.
【飞快】fēikuài〈形〉**1**（很快）speedy: ～跑向远处 sprint off into the distance ‖ 火车～地驶过车站。The train rushed through the station. **2**（很锋利）razor-sharp
【飞来横祸】fēilái-hénghuò〈成〉unexpected disaster
【飞掠】fēilüè〈动〉fly past
【飞轮】fēilún〈名〉**1**［机械］flywheel **2**（指齿轮）free wheel
【飞毛腿】fēimáotuǐ〈名〉fleet-footed runner
【飞毛腿导弹】fēimáotuǐ dǎodàn〈名〉Scud missile
【飞沫传染】fēimò chuánrǎn ▸**p. 50**〈名〉［医学］droplet infection
【飞盘】fēipán〈名〉frisbee: 玩～ throw a frisbee
【飞跑】fēipǎo〈动〉run very fast
【飞禽】fēiqín〈名〉birds: ～走兽 birds and beasts
【飞泉】fēiquán〈名〉**1**（指泉水）cliff-side spring **2**（喷泉）fountain
【飞人】fēirén〈名〉**1**［杂技］aerialist **2**（指运动员）best athlete: 女～ best female athlete
【飞散】fēisàn〈动〉**1**（指烟、雾等）disperse: 一团浓烟在空中～。A cloud of heavy smoke wafted in the air. **2**（指鸟）fly away in all directions: 听到枪声，鸟儿四处～。The birds flew off at the sound of the gun.
【飞沙走石】fēishā-zǒushí〈成〉sand flying and pebbles rolling
【飞身】fēishēn〈动〉vault: ～上马 leap into the saddle ‖ 他们毫不费力地～越过墙头。They vaulted effortlessly over the wall.
【飞驶】fēishǐ〈动〉race: 一辆吉普车～而过。A jeep raced past.
【飞逝】fēishì〈动〉fly: 如流星～ fly past like a shooting star ‖ 时光～。Time flies.
【飞鼠】fēishǔ〈名〉**1**（指哺乳动物）flying squirrel **2**〈书〉（蝙蝠）bat
【飞速】fēisù〈副〉rapidly: ～前进 gallop ahead ‖ 经济～发展。The economy developed fast.
【飞腾】fēiténg〈动〉soar: 烈焰～。Furious flames flew into the air.
【飞天】fēitiān〈名〉［佛教］flying Apsaras
【飞艇】fēitǐng〈名〉airship
【飞吻】fēiwěn〈动〉blow a kiss
【飞舞】fēiwǔ〈动〉flutter: 一只蝴蝶在花间～。A butterfly fluttered from flower to flower. ‖ 柳絮在空中～。Willow catkins are dancing in the breeze.
【飞翔】fēixiáng〈动〉hover: 展翅～ on the wing
【飞行】fēixíng〈动〉fly: 低空～ low-altitude flying ‖ 特技～ stunt flight
【飞行器】fēixíngqì〈名〉aircraft
【飞行员】fēixíngyuán ▸**p. 966**〈名〉pilot
【飞絮】fēixù〈名〉floating catkins
【飞旋】fēixuán〈动〉fly in circles: 雄鹰在天空中～。An eagle was circling in the sky.
【飞檐】fēiyán〈名〉［建筑］upturned eaves
【飞檐走壁】fēiyán-zǒubì〈成〉leap onto roofs and vault over walls
【飞眼】fēiyǎn〈动〉make eyes at sb.
【飞扬】fēiyáng **A**〈动〉rise: 彩旗～。Flags of various colours are fluttering in the wind. **B**〈形〉radiant: ▸神采～
【飞扬跋扈】fēiyáng-báhù〈成〉be arrogant and domineering: 他们都不喜欢他的～。They did not appreciate his arrogant behaviour.
【飞鱼】fēiyú〈名〉flying fish
【飞跃】fēiyuè **A**〈名〉［哲学］leap: 认识的～ knowledge leap ‖ 质的～ change in essence **B**〈动〉**1**（突飞猛进）make great strides: 实现历史性～ achieve a historic leap **2**（腾空跳跃）leap: 他纵身～墙头。He leapt over the wall.
【飞越】fēiyuè〈动〉fly across: ～大西洋 fly across the Atlantic ‖ 成功地～喜马拉雅山 make a successful flight over the Himalayas
【飞灾横祸】fēizāi-hènghuò = 飞来横祸 fēilái-hènghuò
【飞贼】fēizéi〈名〉**1**（指贼）cat burglar **2**（指敌人）intruder from the air
【飞涨】fēizhǎng〈动〉soar: 物价～。Prices are rising sharply.
【飞针走线】fēizhēn-zǒuxiàn〈成〉do skilful needlework
【飞舟】fēizhōu〈名〉speed boat: ～竞渡。The speed boats are racing.

妃 fēi

〈名〉〈旧〉**1**（指皇帝的妾）imperial concubine **2**（王侯的妻子）wife of a prince
【妃红】fēihóng〈名〉light pink
【妃嫔】fēipín〈名〉〈旧〉imperial concubine
【妃子】fēizi〈名〉〈旧〉imperial concubine

非[1] fēi

A〈动〉 **1**（违背） run counter to: ▸～法, ～礼 **2**（指责） blame: ▸～难, ～议 **3**（不是） be not: ～笔墨所能形容 beyond description ‖ ～司机不能开车。 No one can drive except the driver.
B〈名〉 wrong: ▸是～, 痛改前～
C〈前缀〉 non-, un-, in-: ～公有制经济 non-public sectors of the economy ‖ ～营利机构 non-profit institution ‖ ～种子选手 unseeded player
D〈副〉 **1**（不） not: ▸～常, ～同小可 **2**（一定） must: 你不让我去，我～去。 You won't let me go, but I'll go anyway. ‖ 要成功，～下苦功夫不可。 Success requires painstaking efforts.

非[2] Fēi〈名〉 Africa

【非暴力】fēibàolì〈名〉 non-violence
【非比寻常】fēibǐxúncháng〈成〉 unusual: 这事～。 This is rather out of the ordinary.
【非标】fēibiāo〈形〉 non-standard: ～汽油/管道 non-standard petrol/pipeline
【非常】fēicháng **A**〈形〉 extraordinary: ～事件 extraordinary event ‖ ～时期 time of emergency **B**〈副〉 extremely: ～抱歉 terribly sorry ‖ ～必要 highly necessary ‖ ～精彩 simply marvellous ‖ ～珍贵 of great rarity ‖ 她身体～虚弱。 Her health is seriously debilitated.
【非常任理事国】fēichángrèn lǐshìguó〈名〉 non-permanent member
【非处方药】fēichǔfāngyào〈名〉 over-the-counter medicine
【非此即彼】fēicǐ-jíbǐ〈成〉 one or the other
【非但】fēidàn〈连〉 not only: ～我不知道，他也不知道。 Not only do I not know, but he doesn't know either.
【非导体】fēidǎotǐ〈名〉［物理］ non-conductor
【非得】fēiděi〈副〉 have to: 学好外语～下功夫不行。 The mastery of a foreign language involves painstaking effort.
【非典】fēidiǎn〈简称〉= 非典型肺炎
【非典型肺炎】fēidiǎnxíng fèiyán ▸p. 50〈名〉 Severe Acute Respiratory Syndrome (SARS)
【非独】fēidú〈连〉〈书〉 not merely: ～无害，而且有益。 It is not only harmless but also very useful.
【非法】fēifǎ〈形〉 illegal: ～出版物 illegal publications ‖ ～活动 unlawful activities ‖ ～所得 illicit gains
【非凡】fēifán〈形〉 outstanding: ～的勇气 outstanding courage ‖ 市场上热闹～。 The market is bustling with activity.
【非分】fēifèn〈形〉 **1**（不守本分） presumptuous: ～的要求 presumptuous demands **2**（不是自己分内的） not one's own: ～之财 money not honestly earned
【非分之想】fēifènzhīxiǎng〈成〉 inordinate ambition
【非公莫入】fēigōng-mòrù〈成〉 no admittance except on business
【非公有制】fēigōngyǒuzhì〈形〉 non-state: ～经济/企业 non-state economy/enterprise
【非官方】fēiguānfāng〈形〉 unofficial: ～组织 non-governmental organization (NGO)
【非婚生子女】fēihūnshēng zǐnǚ〈名〉 illegitimate child
【非金属】fēijīnshǔ〈名〉 non-metal
【非晶体】fēijīngtǐ〈名〉 amorphous body
【非军事】fēijūnshì〈形〉 non-military: ～区 demilitarized zone
【非军事化】fēijūnshìhuà〈动〉 demilitarize
【非礼】fēilǐ **A**〈形〉 impolite: ～举动 improper behaviour **B**〈动〉 harass sexually: 欲行～ attempt to sexually harass
【非驴非马】fēilǘ-fēimǎ〈成〉 neither fish nor foul
【非卖品】fēimàipǐn〈名〉 article not for sale
【非命】fēimìng〈名〉 unnatural death: 死于～ die a violent death
【非难】fēinàn〈动〉 reproach: 受到～ be met with censure ‖ 无可～ above criticism
【非农化】fēinónghuà〈动〉 de-agriculturalize: 农村劳动力～转移 de-agriculturalization of the rural labour force
【非亲非故】fēiqīn-fēigù〈成〉 neither relative nor friend: 我跟他～的。 He is neither a relative nor a friend of mine.
【非人】fēirén〈形〉 inhuman: 过着～的生活 live a sub-human life
【非条件反射】fēitiáojiàn fǎnshè〈名〉［生理］ unconditioned reflex
【非同小可】fēitóngxiǎokě〈成〉 no trivial matter: 这事～，我们必须认真对待。 This is by no means insignificant. We must be serious about it.
【非同寻常】fēitóngxúncháng〈成〉 extraordinary: 他是个～的人，过着～的生活。 He is no ordinary man and he lives an extra ordinary life.
【非徒】fēitú〈连〉〈书〉 not only ... (but)
【非我莫属】fēiwǒmòshǔ〈成〉 belong exclusively to me
【非物质文化遗产】fēiwùzhìwénhuà yíchǎn〈名〉 Intangible Cultural Heritage: 国家～名录 National Intangible Cultural Heritage Directory
【非刑】fēixíng〈名〉〈书〉 brutal torture: 受尽～折磨 suffer all kinds of cruel punishments
【非刑拷打】fēixíng kǎodǎ〈动〉 torture sb. brutally
【非遗】fēiyí〈简称〉= 非物质文化遗产
【非议】fēiyì〈动〉 reproach: 引起～ incur disapproval ‖ 遭人～ be subject to reproach ▸无可～
【非营利性】fēiyínglìxìng〈形〉 non-profit-making
【非营业性】fēiyíngyèxìng〈形〉 non-operating: ～收入/支出 non-operating income
【非再生资源】fēizàishēng zīyuán〈名〉 unrenewable resource
【非政府组织】fēizhèngfǔ zǔzhī〈名〉 non-governmental organization (NGO)
【非正规军】fēizhèngguījūn〈名〉 irregular troops
【非正式】fēizhèngshì〈形〉 informal: ～访问 unofficial visit ‖ ～会晤 informal meeting
【非洲】Fēizhōu〈名〉 Africa: ～国家首脑会议 Conference of the Heads of African States
【非洲统一组织】Fēizhōu Tǒngyī Zǔzhī〈名〉 Organization of African Unity (OAU)

菲[1] fēi〈形〉 luxuriant and fragrant: ▸芳～

菲[2] fēi〈名〉［化学］ phenanthrene ▸fěi

【菲菲】fēifēi〈形〉〈书〉 **1**（花草茂盛） exuberant **2**（香气浓郁） fragrant: 芳草～。 The grass gives off a sweet fragrance.
【菲林】fēilín〈名〉〈旧〉 roll of film
【菲律宾】Fēilǜbīn〈名〉 the Philippines: ～共和国 Republic of the Philippines ‖ ～人 Filipino

啡 fēi ▸咖啡 kāfēi, 吗啡 mǎfēi

绯（緋） fēi〈形〉 red: 深～ dark red

【绯红】fēihóng〈形〉 bright red: ～的朝阳 deep red rising sun ‖ 两颊～ bright red cheeks
【绯闻】fēiwén〈名〉 sex scandal

扉 fēi〈名〉〈书〉 door leaf: 柴～ wicker gate ▸心～

【扉画】fēihuà〈名〉 flyleaf picture
【扉页】fēiyè〈名〉［印刷］ flyleaf

蜚 fēi = 飞 fēi

【蜚短流长】fēiduǎn-liúcháng = 飞短流长 fēiduǎn-liúcháng
【蜚声】fēishēng〈动〉〈书〉 become well-known: ～海内外 make a name for oneself both at home and abroad ‖ ～文坛 be famous in literary circles
【蜚语】fēiyǔ = 飞语 fēiyǔ

霏 fēi〈书〉

A〈形〉（指雨雪） thick and fast;（指云雾） heavy
B〈动〉 drift in the air

【霏霏】fēifēi〈形〉〈书〉（指雨雪） thick and fast;（指云雾） heavy: 雨雪～。 It is snowing thick and fast.

鲱（鯡） fēi〈名〉［鱼类］ Pacific herring

féi

肥 féi

A〈形〉 **1**（含脂肪多） fat: ～猪 fat pig ‖ 减～药 slimming medicine ‖ 马无夜草不～。 Horses cannot get fat without being fed at night. **2**（肥沃） fertile **3**（富）［usu with a derogatory sense］ rich **4**（收入多） fat: ▸～差, ～缺 **5**（宽大） loose: 这裤腰太～了。 The waist of the trousers is too loose.
B〈动〉 **1**（使肥沃） fertilize: ▸～田 **2**（变富） get rich by illegal means: ～私囊 line one's pockets ▸损公～私
C〈名〉 **1**（肥料） fertilizer: 缺～ be in need of fertilizer ‖ 给小麦上～ manure the wheat ▸化～, 积～ **2**（好处） gain: ▸分～

【肥差】féichāi〈名〉 lucrative job
【肥肠】féicháng〈名〉 pork intestines: 熘～ sautéed intestines
【肥大】féidà〈形〉 **1**（宽大） loose: ～的短裤 baggy shorts ‖ ～的鞋 roomy shoes **2**（粗大壮实） plump: 笨拙～的身体 clumsy and corpulent figure **3**（指病态） hypertrophied: 扁桃体/心脏～ hypertrophy of the tonsils/heart
【肥分】féifèn〈名〉［农业］ fertilizer nutriment
【肥厚】féihòu〈形〉 **1**（厚实） fleshy: ～的嘴唇 full lips **2**（指病态） hypertrophied: 右心室～ hypertrophy of ventriculus dexter **3**（指土壤） thick and fertile: 表土～ thick and fertile topsoil **4**（优厚） lucrative: ～的利润 fat profit
【肥己损人】féijǐ-sǔnrén〈成〉 enrich oneself at the expense of others
【肥力】féilì〈名〉［农业］ fertility: 提高土壤～ increase soil fertility

【肥料】féiliào〈名〉 fertilizer: 无机/有机～ inorganic/organic fertilizer

【肥美】féiměi〈形〉 [1]（肥沃） fertile: ～的牧场 rich pasture ‖ ～的土地 fertile land [2]（肥壮） plump: ～的牛羊 plump cattle and sheep [3]（肥而味美） fleshy and delicious: ～的羊肉 delicious mutton

【肥胖】féipàng〈形〉 fat: ～症 obesity

【肥缺】féiquē〈名〉 plum job

【肥肉】féiròu〈名〉 fat meat: 这火腿～太多。 This ham has too much fat on it.

【肥实】féishi〈形〉 [1]（肥胖） stout: ～的黑马 stout black horse [2]（脂肪多） fatty: ～的肉 fatty meat [3]（富足） wealthy: 日子过得挺～ live in affluence

【肥瘦】féishòu〈名〉 [1]（指衣服、鞋） width of clothing: 试一试，看这鞋的～怎么样。 Try on the shoes and see if they are a good fit. [2]〈方〉（指肉） half-lean meat: 来二斤～! One kilo of half-lean meat, please!

【肥水】féishuǐ〈名〉 [1]（指肥料） nutrient-rich water: ～灌溉 manuring irrigation [2]〈喻〉（利益） profit

【肥水不流外人田】féishuǐ bù liú wàirén tián〈俗〉〈喻〉 benefits are to be shared exclusively among one's own people

【肥硕】féishuò〈形〉 [1]（指果实） big and fleshy [2]（指肢体） plump

【肥田】féitián [A]〈名〉 fertile land [B]〈动〉 enrich the soil: ～粉 ammonium sulphate ‖ 粪可以～。 Manure may be used to fertilize the soil.

【肥头大耳】féitóu-dà'ěr〈成〉 fat and bulky

【肥沃】féiwò〈形〉 fertile: ～的田地 rich and fertile field ‖ 土壤～。 The soil is fertile.

【肥效】féixiào〈名〉［农业］ fertilizer efficiency: ～持久 long-lasting fertilizing effect

【肥腴】féiyú〈形〉〈书〉 [1]（肥沃） fertile [2]（肥胖） plump

【肥育】féiyù〈动〉［畜牧］ fatten

【肥皂】féizào〈名〉 soap: ～泡 soap bubble ‖ ～水 soapsuds

【肥皂剧】féizàojù〈名〉 soap opera

【肥壮】féizhuàng〈形〉 stout and strong: 禾苗～ healthy and strong seedlings ‖ 牲口～ thriving herds of cattle

腓 féi〈名〉（腿肚子） calf (of a leg)

【腓尼基语】Féiníjīyǔ ▸p. 918〈名〉 Phoenician

fěi

匪[1] fěi〈副〉〈书〉 not: ▸～夷所思，获益～浅

匪[2] fěi〈名〉 bandit: ▸～巢，土～

【匪帮】fěibāng〈名〉 bandit gang

【匪巢】fěicháo〈名〉 bandits' lair

【匪盗】fěidào〈名〉 robber: ～猖獗 rampant robbery

【匪患】fěihuàn〈名〉 banditry: 清除～ eliminate bandits

【匪祸】fěihuò〈名〉 banditry

【匪窟】fěikū〈名〉 bandits' lair: 直捣～ storm the bandits' lair

【匪首】fěishǒu〈名〉 bandit chief: ～已经落网。 The bandit chief has been captured.

【匪徒】fěitú〈名〉 [1]（盗匪） bandit: 蒙面～ masked bandit [2]（盗匪似的人） reactionaries

【匪穴】fěixué〈名〉 bandits' lair

【匪夷所思】fěiyísuǒsī〈成〉 fantastical: 他们的严格～。 They are fantastically strict.

诽（誹） fěi〈动〉 slander

【诽谤】fěibàng〈动〉 slander: 造谣～ cook up a story to slander sb. ‖ 恶毒的～ vicious slander ‖ ～是要负法律责任的。 Libel is subject to legal charge.

【诽谤罪】fěibàngzuì〈名〉 calumny: 犯～ commit libel

菲 fěi〈形〉〈书〉〈谦〉 humble: ～礼 my humble gift
▸fēi

【菲薄】fěibó [A]〈形〉 humble: 薪水～ be poorly-paid ‖ ～的收入 meagre income [B]〈动〉 belittle: ～前人 belittle the predecessors ▸妄自～

【菲仪】fěiyí〈名〉〈书〉〈谦〉 my humble gift

【菲酌】fěizhuó〈名〉〈书〉〈谦〉 simple meal with wine

悱 fěi〈形〉〈书〉 speechless

【悱恻】fěicè〈形〉〈书〉 grief-stricken: ▸缠绵～

斐 fěi〈形〉〈书〉 rich in literary grace

【斐济】Fěijì〈名〉 Fiji: ～共和国 Republic of Fiji ‖ ～人 Fijian ‖ ～语 Fijian

【斐然】fěirán〈形〉〈书〉 [1]（有文采） brilliantly learned: ▸～成章 [2]（显著） brilliant: 成绩～ splendid results

【斐然成章】fěirán-chéngzhāng〈成〉 show striking literary talent

榧 fěi〈名〉［植物］ Chinese torreya

【榧子】fěizi〈名〉［植物］ [1]（指乔木） Chinese torreya [2]（指果实） Chinese torreya nut

翡 fěi

【翡翠】fěicuì〈名〉 [1]［鸟类］ halcyon [2]（指矿物） jadeite: ～绿 jade green

篚 fěi〈名〉〈古〉 round bamboo basket

fèi

芾 fèi ▸蔽芾 bìfèi
▸fú

吠 fèi〈动〉 bark: 狂～ bark furiously

【吠形吠声】fèixíng-fèishēng〈成〉〈喻〉 blindly follow suit

【吠影吠声】fèiyǐng-fèishēng ＝ 吠形吠声 fèixíng-fèishēng

肺 fèi〈名〉 lung

【肺癌】fèi'ái ▸p. 50〈名〉 lung cancer: 吸烟会引起～。 Smoking causes lung cancer.

【肺病】fèibìng ▸p. 50〈名〉 pulmonary tuberculosis

【肺尘病】fèichénbìng ▸p. 50〈名〉［医学］ pneumoconiosis

【肺腑】fèifǔ〈名〉 [1]（肺脏） lungs [2]（内心） bottom of one's heart: 感人～ move people deeply ‖ ～之言 words from the bottom of one's heart

【肺活量】fèihuóliàng〈名〉 lung capacity: 他的～很大。 He has a big lung capacity.

【肺结核】fèijiéhé ▸p. 50〈名〉 pulmonary tuberculosis (TB)

【肺痨】fèiláo ▸p. 50〈名〉 tuberculosis

【肺气肿】fèiqìzhǒng ▸p. 50〈名〉 pneumonectasis

【肺循环】fèixúnhuán〈名〉［生理］ pulmonary circulation

【肺炎】fèiyán ▸p. 50〈名〉 pneumonia

【肺叶】fèiyè〈名〉［生理］ pulmonary lobe

【肺鱼】fèiyú〈名〉 lungfish

【肺脏】fèizàng〈名〉 lungs

狒 fèi

【狒狒】fèifèi〈名〉［动物］ baboon

废（廢） fèi

[A]〈动〉 [1]〈书〉（倾倒） collapse: 那房屋已～。 The house has collapsed. [2]（覆灭） perish: 王朝兴～ the rise and fall of a dynasty [3]（放弃） abandon: 不因人～言 not reject an opinion because of the speaker ▸～除，半途而～ [4]〈书〉（废黜） depose: ▸～黜

[B]〈形〉 [1]（无用） useless: ～金属 scrap metal ‖ ～塑料 waste plastics ▸～话，～料 [2]（伤残） disabled: ▸残～ [3]（荒芜） deserted: ▸～墟 [4]（沮丧） disheartened: ▸颓～

[C]〈名〉 waste: 变～为宝 turn waste into valuable materials

【废弛】fèichí〈动〉〈书〉 become lax: 校纪～。 School discipline has become lax.

【废除】fèichú〈动〉 abolish: ～不平等条约 abrogate unequal treaties ‖ ～旧的规章制度 abolish old regulations

【废黜】fèichù〈动〉 [1]〈书〉（罢免） dismiss [2]（取消王位） dethrone: 女王被～后，流亡国外。 The queen went into exile after being dethroned.

【废耕】fèigēng〈动〉 be left uncultivated

【废话】fèihuà [A]〈名〉 nonsense: ～连篇 pages of nonsense ‖ 别说～! Don't talk rubbish! [B]〈动〉 talk nonsense: 别～，快干你的事去。 Stop your nonsense and get down to your business!

【废旧】fèijiù〈形〉 old and useless: ～物资 waste and old materials

【废料】fèiliào〈名〉 scrap: ～场 junk yard ‖ ～处理 waste disposal ‖ 核～ nuclear waste

【废奴主义】fèinúzhǔyì〈名〉 abolitionism

【废票】fèipiào〈名〉 [1]（指凭证） invalid ticket [2]（指选票） invalid ballot

【废品】fèipǐn〈名〉 [1]（指产品） waste product: ～率 reject rate [2]（指垃圾） scrap: ～收购站 recycling station

【废品回收】fèipǐn huíshōu〈名〉 salvage of waste material: ～站 recycling centre

【废气】fèiqì〈名〉 exhaust fumes: ～排放 waste-gas exhaust ‖ ～综合利用 multi-purpose use of waste gas

【废弃】fèiqì〈动〉 abandon: ～的建筑物 derelict building ‖ ～物 waste ‖ 这个词已经～不用。 This word has fallen into disuse.

【废寝忘食】fèiqǐn-wàngshí〈成〉 forget to eat and sleep: ～地工作 devote oneself heart and soul to one's work

【废热】fèirè〈名〉［化工］ waste heat

【废人】fèirén〈名〉 [1]（指有残疾） disabled person [2]（无用的人） good-for-nothing

【废水】fèishuǐ〈名〉 waste water: 工业～ industrial effluents ‖ ～处理 waste water treatment

【废铁】fèitiě〈名〉 scrap iron

【废铜烂铁】fèitóng-làntiě〈成〉 metal scrap

【废物】fèiwù〈名〉1〈本〉waste materials: ~回收利用 waste recycling 2〈喻〉〈贬〉good-for-nothing

【废墟】fèixū〈名〉ruins: 变成~ fall into ruin ‖ 那座古堡如今是一片~。The old castle now lies in ruins.

【废学】fèixué〈动〉drop out of school

【废液】fèiyè〈名〉waste water

【废渣】fèizhā〈名〉waste residue

【废止】fèizhǐ〈动〉annul: ~合同 revoke a contract ‖ ~协议 nullify an agreement

【废址】fèizhǐ〈名〉abandoned site

【废纸】fèizhǐ〈名〉waste-paper: 教室里不要乱扔~。Don't litter the classroom with waste-paper. ‖ 有合同不履行，等于一张~。An unfulfilled contract amounts to nothing but scrap paper.

【废纸篓】fèizhǐlǒu〈名〉waste-paper basket; wastebasket〈美〉

【废置】fèizhì〈动〉put aside as useless: 处理~设施 dispose of neglected facilities

沸 fèi

〈动〉boil: 把水煮~ bring water to the boil ‖ ~油 boiling oil ▸扬汤止~

【沸点】fèidiǎn〈名〉boiling point

【沸沸扬扬】fèifèi-yángyáng〈成〉tumultuous: 不要把这事闹得~。Don't shout it from the rooftops.

【沸热】fèirè〈形〉boiling hot: ~的阳光 scorching sun

【沸水】fèishuǐ〈名〉boiling water: ~反应堆 boiling water reactor

【沸腾】fèiténg〈动〉1 ▸p. 776（指液体）boil: 水在100℃时~。Water boils at 100 degrees centigrade. 2（指情绪）boil over with excitement: 热血~的青年 young people bubbling over with enthusiasm ‖ 人群~了。The crowd was simmering with excitement.

【沸扬】fèiyáng〈动〉seethe with excitement

费（費）fèi

A〈动〉1（花费）cost: 白~力气 labour in vain ‖ 做饭可~时间了。Cooking takes a lot of time. ▸浪~, 消~ 2（耗费）be wasteful: 空调机太~电。The air-conditioner consumes too much electricity. ‖ 我的汽车很~油。My car uses up a lot of petrol. ‖ 走山路~鞋。Shoes soon wear out on mountain paths.

B〈名〉fee: 报销交通~ reimburse transportation costs ‖ 安装~ installation charges ‖ 广告~ advertising expenses ‖ 学杂~ tuition and miscellaneous fees ‖ 医药~ medical expenses ▸差旅~, 生活~

【费城】Fèichéng〈名〉Philadelphia

【费唇舌】fèi chúnshé〈惯〉require considerable explanation: 要说服她可得~。It will take a lot of talking to win her over. ‖ 情况既然如此，我也就不多~了。With the situation as it is, I might as well save my breath.

【费改税】fèigǎishuì〈动〉transform administrative fees into taxes

【费工】fèigōng〈动〉take a lot of work

【费工夫】fèi gōngfu〈动〉be time-consuming: ~的活儿 exacting job

【费功夫】fèi gōngfu = 费工夫 fèi gōngfu

【费话】fèihuà〈动〉require considerable explanation: 咱们别~，赶快干活吧。Let's save our breath and get down to work.

【费解】fèijiě〈形〉incomprehensible: 他的话很让人~。His words are truly puzzling.

【费尽心机】fèijìn-xīnjī〈成〉rack one's brains: 他~终于赢得她的欢心。He did everything he could to gain her favour.

【费劲】fèijìn〈动〉〈口〉need great effort: 她视力不好，看书很~。Her poor eyesight makes reading hard for her. ‖ 他费了好大劲儿才找到这份工作。He put so much in to getting the job.

【费口舌】fèi kǒushé = 费唇舌 fèi chúnshé

【费力】fèilì〈动〉1（耗费力气）exert great effort: 他不用~就能举起那块石头。Lifting the stone is nothing to him. 2（吃力）be strenuous: ~的工作 arduous task ‖ 他觉得打网球太~。He finds tennis too physically demanding.

【费力不讨好】fèilì bù tǎohǎo〈俗〉do a hard but thankless job: ~的差事 hard but thankless task

【费率】fèilǜ〈名〉premium rate

【费钱】fèiqián〈动〉cost a lot

【费神】fèishén〈动〉1（耗费精神）exert great mental effort: 你不必~。You may spare yourself the trouble. ‖ 校勘工作很~。Collation is exacting. 2〈套〉（用于请托或致谢）[used in making requests or extending thanks]: 这裙子您~给放大一点，好吗？Could I trouble you to let down the skirt for me?

【费时】fèishí〈动〉take time: 这幢摩天大楼~三年才建成。It took three years to build the skyscraper.

【费事】fèishì A〈动〉involve a lot of trouble: 你用电脑来做这些计算，可以少费点事。It will be much less trouble if you do the calculations on a computer. B〈形〉time-consuming: 我喜欢这道菜，可做起来太~了。I enjoy this dish, but it's too much of a performance to cook it.

【费手脚】fèi shǒujiǎo〈动〉exert great effort: 他为展览的事很费了些手脚。He has put a great deal of effort into the exhibition.

【费心】fèixīn〈动〉take the trouble: 这孩子真让我~。The child is a weight on my mind. ‖ 他为我们这事费了不少心。He has gone to a lot of trouble helping us with it.

【费用】fèiyong〈名〉cost: 学习~ study expenses ‖ 所有~都给你报销。All expenditures will be reimbursed to you. ‖ 我无力承担这笔~。I can ill afford the expense.

剕 fèi

〈名〉〈古〉amputation of the feet

痱 fèi

【痱子】fèizi〈名〉prickly heat

【痱子粉】fèizifěn〈名〉prickly-heat powder

镄（鐨）fèi

〈名〉fermium (Fm)

fēn

分 fēn

A〈动〉1（划分）divide: ~粮/钱 divide the grain/money ‖ ~三个月付清 spread the payments over three months ‖ 把土地~成小块 separate land into small plots ▸~离, ~手 2（分配）distribute: ~到一套住房 be assigned a flat ‖ 把财产~给子女 divide one's property among one's children 3（区分）distinguish: 不~青红皂白 make no distinction between right and wrong ‖ 两队现在还难~胜负。Now it's still a toss-up between the two teams.

B〈形〉divided: ~行 bank branch ‖ ~校 branch campus ‖ ~社 publishing division ▸~部, ~支

C〈名〉1［数学］fraction: 百~之二十八 twenty-eight per cent ‖ 二~之一 a half ▸~数, 通~ 2（得分）point: 打~ award points ‖ 得满~ attain full marks

D〈量〉1（表成数）[for evaluation of something abstract]: 六~成绩，四~错误。Sixty per cent are achievements and forty per cent mistakes. ‖ 他有了几~醉意。He is already a trifle tipsy. 2 ▸p. 978（计量单位）*fen* [units of length, weight and area, respectively equal to 0.333 centimetre, 0.5 gram and 66.7 square metres] 3 ▸p. 328（指利率）[unit of interest rate] a（月利）1% monthly interest: 月利一~五 1.5% monthly interest b（年利）10% annual interest: 年利一~五 15% annual interest 4（指时间、角度、经纬度等）minute: 三点四十五~ a quarter to four, forty-five ‖ 北纬50度26~ 50 degrees 26 minutes (50°26′) north latitude ‖ 35度25~ 35 degrees 25 minutes (35°25′)

E ▸p. 691〈数〉one tenth: ▸~米

▸fèn

【分包】fēnbāo〈动〉subcontract: ~商 subcontractor

【分保】fēnbǎo = 再保险 zàibǎoxiǎn

【分贝】fēnbèi〈量〉［物理］decibel: 90~的噪声 90 decibels of noise

【分崩离析】fēnbēng-líxī〈成〉disintegrate: 战后帝国主义~。The post-war era saw the disintegration of the imperialist powers.

【分辨】fēnbiàn〈动〉distinguish: ~是非 tell right from wrong ‖ ~真假 distinguish truth from falsehood ‖ 天下着大雨，连方向也~不清了。It was hard to find the way in the heavy rain.

【分辨率】fēnbiànlǜ〈名〉［物理］resolution: 低/高~ low/high resolution

【分辩】fēnbiàn〈动〉explain oneself: 不容~ allow no explanation

【分别】fēnbié A〈动〉1（离别）part: 他们已经~多年了。They have been away from each other for many years. 2（区分）distinguish: ~善恶 distinguish good from evil ‖ ~是非 distinguish between right and wrong B〈名〉difference: 两者之间没有多大~。There isn't much difference between the two. C〈副〉1（用不同方式）differently: ~包装 be individually wrapped ‖ ~处理/对待 deal with/treat differently 2（各自）respectively: 护士和医生的工资~长了5%和7%。The nurses and the doctors got pay raises of 5% and 7% respectively.

【分兵】fēnbīng〈动〉divide forces: ~把守 divide up forces for defence ‖ 部队~三路前进。The troops advanced by three separate routes.

【分拨】fēnbō〈动〉1（调拨）allocate: ~救灾物资 allocate relief materials 2（分派）assign: 他把这工作~给了我。He assigned the job to me.

【分布】fēnbù〈动〉be distributed: ~不均 be unevenly distributed ‖ ~区域 distribution range ‖ 人口~ population distribution

【分部】fēnbù〈名〉sub-branch

【分餐】fēncān〈动〉have separate meals: 非典时期~制很流行。During SARS it was usual for people to eat separately.

【分册】fēncè〈名〉volume: 第三~ Volume Three

【分岔】fēnchà〈动〉fork: 路在这儿~。The road branches off at this point.

【分杈】fēnchà〈动〉［农业］branch

【分成】fēnchéng〈动〉divide by tenths: 二八~ divide into two shares of two tenths and eight tenths ‖ 你我按三七~。30%

f

for you, and 70% for me.

【分词】fēncí〈名〉［语法］ participle: ～短语 participial phrase ‖ 过去/现在～ past/present participle

【分寸】fēncun〈名〉 sense of propriety: 处世有～ know well how to behave ‖ 批评要掌握～，不要伤了感情。 Don't go too far in your criticism. You don't want to hurt other people's feelings.

【分担】fēndān〈动〉 share: ～费用 share the cost ‖ ～风险 share risks ‖ ～责任 share responsibility

【分道扬镳】fēndào-yángbiāo〈成〉 **1**（分道而行） jerk the reins to take separate routes **2**（指目标不同） go separate ways: 他俩～了。 The two of them went their own separate ways.

【分店】fēndiàn〈名〉 branch (of a shop): 开设～ set up a branch

【分队】fēnduì〈名〉 contingent: 通信兵～ contingent of signalmen ▸小～

【分而治之】fēn'érzhìzhī〈成〉 divide and rule

【分发】fēnfā〈动〉 distribute: ～救济品 dispense relief ‖ 把食品～给难民 issue food to refugees

【分肥】fēnféi〈动〉 divide up a booty

【分赴】fēnfù〈动〉 go in different directions: 记者～全国各地进行采访。 The journalists went to different parts of the country to do interviews.

【分割】fēngē〈动〉 carve up: ▸黄金～

【分隔】fēngé〈动〉 partition off: 把厨房～开来 partition the kitchen off ‖ 一块隔板把两个房间～开来。 A partition separated the two rooms.

【分隔带】fēngédài〈名〉［交通］ central reservation〈英〉; median strip〈美〉: 主辅路的～已完成绿化。 Plants have been planted on the central reservations of main and side roads.

【分工】fēngōng〈动〉 divide up the work: ～合作 cooperate with due division of labour ‖ 劳动～ division of labour ‖ 社会～越来越细。 Society is becoming increasingly compartmentalized. ▸社会～

【分公司】fēngōngsī〈名〉 branch office

【分管】fēnguǎn〈动〉 be put in charge of: 他～外事工作。 He is in charge of foreign affairs.

【分行】fēnháng〈名〉 branch (of a bank)

【分毫】fēnháo〈名〉 fraction: ～不差 without the slightest error ‖ 不差～ exact match

【分号】fēnhào〈名〉 **1**（指标点） semicolon **2**（分店） branch: 在巴黎开设～ open up a branch in Paris

【分红】fēnhóng〈动〉 distribute dividends: 股份～ dividends on shares ‖ 年终～ distribute bonuses at the end of the year

【分洪】fēnhóng〈动〉 divert flood: ～闸 flood-diversion sluice

【分户账】fēnhùzhàng〈名〉［会计］ ledger

【分化】fēnhuà〈动〉 **1**（分裂） break up: ▸阶级～ **2**（使分化） split up: ～敌人 split up the enemy ‖ ～瓦解敌军 split and demoralize the enemy forces ‖ ～组合 realignment and regrouping **3**［生物］ differentiate: ～作用 differentiation

【分会】fēnhuì〈名〉 branch (of a society, committee, association, etc.)

【分机】fēnjī〈名〉 extension: ～号码 extension number

【分级】fēnjí〈动〉 grade: ～核算 business accounting at different levels

【分家】fēnjiā〈动〉 **1**（指一家人） divide up family property and live apart: 他结婚后就～单过了。 After he got married he left home and started to live independently. **2**（分离） fall apart: 他的鞋底和鞋帮已经～了。 The soles and uppers of his shoes have fallen apart.

【分拣】fēnjiǎn〈动〉 sort out: ～邮件 sort the mail ‖ ～设备 sorting equipment

【分解】fēnjiě〈动〉 **1**［物理］［数学］ resolve: ～成因式 resolve into factors ‖ 力的～ resolution of force **2**［化学］ decompose: 水可以～成氢和氧。 Water can be analysed into hydrogen and oxygen. **3**（调解） mediate: 打得难分难解 be locked in a fierce fight ‖ 你去给他们～～。 Would you try and mediate between them? **4**（分化） disintegrate: 促使敌人内部～ cause the enemy to splinter **5**（讲述） explain: 欲知后事如何，且听下回～。 If you want to know what happens next, listen to the next episode.

【分界】fēnjiè **A**〈动〉 be demarcated by: 两国以河流自然～。 The two countries use the river as a natural boundary between them. **B**〈名〉 demarcation line: 两个时代的～ divide between two eras

【分界线】fēnjièxiàn〈名〉 **1**（指界限） dividing line: 划定～ draw a boundary ‖ 军事～ military demarcation line **2**（指区别） demarcation: 是非的～ demarcation of right and wrong

【分斤掰两】fēnjīn-bāiliǎng〈成〉 quibble over every penny

【分进合击】fēnjìn-héjī〈成〉 concerted attack by converging columns

【分镜头剧本】fēnjìngtóu jùběn〈名〉 shooting script

【分居】fēnjū〈动〉 **1**（因不在一起） live apart: 夫妻两地～。 The husband and wife live far away from each other. **2**（因感情不合） separate: 他跟妻子～了。 He has separated from his wife.

【分局】fēnjú〈名〉 branch: 警察～ police substation ‖ 铁路～ railway division

【分句】fēnjù〈名〉 clause

【分开】fēnkāi〈动〉 **1**（不聚在一起） part: 人群～让他通过。 The crowd parted to let him through. **2**（使分开） separate: ～两个拳击手 separate two boxers ‖ 政企～ separate government from enterprise ‖ 这两件事要～来解决。 These two issues should be dealt with separately.

【分类】fēnlèi〈动〉 classify: 按年龄/性别～ classify by age/sex ‖ 把文件～ catalogue the papers ‖ 图书/植物～ classification of books/plants ‖ ～广告 classified advertisements

【分厘】fēnlí〈名〉 very small amount, tiny bit: ～不差 without the slightest error

【分离】fēnlí〈动〉 **1**（分开） separate: 把氢从空气中～出来 separate hydrogen from air ‖ 使政教～ separate church and state **2**（别离） leave: ～多年的父子终于团聚了。 After being separated for many years, father and son were finally reunited.

【分理处】fēnlǐchù〈名〉 sub-branch

【分力】fēnlì〈名〉［物理］component force

【分列式】fēnlièshì〈名〉［军事］ march-past

【分裂】fēnliè **A**〈名〉［物理］［生物］ fission: 核～ nuclear fission ‖ 细胞～ cell division **B**〈动〉 split: ～国家 split the country ‖ 制造～ stir up division ‖ 坚持团结，反对～。 Uphold unity and oppose secession.

【分流】fēnliú **A**〈动〉**1**（指河流）branch off **2**（指人员、车辆等） divert: ～企业富余人员 reassign surplus employees ‖ 把行人和车辆～ segregate pedestrians and vehicles ‖ 资金严重～。 The funds are widely scattered. **B**〈名〉［电气］ shunt

【分馏】fēnliú〈名〉［化学］ fractional distillation: ～装置 fractionating device ‖ ～塔 fractionating tower

【分袂】fēnmèi〈动〉〈书〉take leave of one another

【分门别类】fēnmén-biélèi〈成〉 classify: 把收集的动物标本～地摆列起来 display collected animal specimens according to categories

【分米】fēnmǐ ▸**p. 82**〈量〉 decimetre

【分泌】fēnmì〈动〉［生理］ secrete: ～胃液 secrete gastric juice ‖ ～物 secretion

【分娩】fēnmiǎn〈动〉 give birth: 无痛～ painless delivery ‖ 足月～ full-term delivery ‖ 她即将～，不宜乘机旅行。 She is too near her term to travel by air.

【分秒必争】fēnmiǎo-bìzhēng〈成〉 every second counts

【分明】fēnmíng **A**〈形〉 clear: 爱憎～ know whom to love and whom to hate ‖ 黑白～ in sharp contrast ‖ 赏罚～ be fair in meting out rewards and penalties **B**〈副〉 clearly: 你～是在撒谎！ It's obvious that you're lying!

【分母】fēnmǔ〈名〉［数学］ denominator

【分蘖】fēnniè〈动〉［农业］ tiller: 麦子正在～。 The wheat is tillering.

【分派】fēnpài〈动〉 **1**（安排） assign: ～工作 distribute the work ‖ ～任务 assign sb. a task ‖ 这工作～给了我。 The job has been assigned to me. **2** = 分摊 fēntān

【分配】fēnpèi〈动〉 **1**（按规定分） distribute: ～住房 assign housing ‖ 按比例～ divide according to ratio ‖ 利润～ distribution of profits **2**（分派） assign: ～任务 assign tasks ‖ 服从～ accept the assigned job ‖ 毕业～ job assignment upon graduation **3**［经济］ distribute: 社会～ social distribution ▸按劳～, 按需～

【分批】fēnpī〈动〉 divide into batches: ～交货 deliver goods by instalments ‖ ～进入展厅 enter the exhibition hall in groups

【分片】fēnpiàn〈动〉 divide up into parts: ～包干 divide up work and assign a part to each

【分期】fēnqī〈动〉 **1**（指时间） do in stages: ～连载 appear in instalments ‖ ～实施 implement by stages **2**（指过程） segmentation: 历史～ historical segmentation

【分期付款】fēnqī fùkuǎn〈名〉 payment by instalments

【分歧】fēnqí **A**〈名〉 difference: 消除～ settle differences ‖ 法官们对这一判决意见有～。 The judges were divided on the decision. **B**〈形〉 divergent: 意见很～ have different opinions

【分清】fēnqīng〈动〉 distinguish: ～敌友 draw a distinction between friends and enemies ‖ ～是非 distinguish right from wrong ‖ ～主次 distinguish the primary and the secondary

【分散】fēnsàn **A**〈动〉 **1**（使不集中） divert: ～公众注意力 divert public attention ‖ ～精力 diffuse one's energies **2**（分发） distribute: ～传单 distribute leaflets **B**〈形〉 scattered: 山区农民住得很～。 The farmers in the mountain area live scattered all around.

【分设】fēnshè〈动〉 branch out: 该局下面～三个处。 The bureau has three departments under it.

【分身】fēnshēn〈动〉 [usu used in the negative] spare time: 我～无术。 I can't be in two places at once.

【分神】fēnshén〈动〉 distract: 有很多事～ have a lot of distractions ‖ 集中注意力学习，不要分神。Focus on your studies and don't be distracted.

【分式】fēnshì〈名〉［数学］ fraction: ～运算 fractional operation

【分手】fēnshǒu〈动〉 split up: 舍不得～ be loath to part ‖ 他跟女朋友～了。He's split up with his girlfriend.

【分数】fēnshù ▸p. 691〈名〉**1**（评分） mark: 打～ give marks ‖ 考试～ exam score **2**［数学］ fraction: ▸假～, 真～

【分数式】fēnshùshì〈名〉 fractional expression

【分数线】fēnshùxiàn〈名〉**1**（指线）fraction line **2**（指最低标准） cut-off point: 录取～ enrolment cut-off point

【分水岭】fēnshuǐlǐng〈名〉 watershed: 两条河流的～ watershed of two rivers ‖ 中国历史上两个时代的～ watershed between two eras of Chinese history

【分说】fēnshuō〈动〉 explain oneself: ▸不容～, 不由～

【分摊】fēntān〈动〉 share: ～费用 share the cost ‖ 咱俩～，一人一半。Let's share it and go halves.

【分庭抗礼】fēntíng-kànglǐ〈成〉 stand up (to sb.) as an equal

【分头】fēntóu **A**〈副〉 separately: 放学后，孩子们～回家。After school the children went their separate ways back to their homes. ‖ 大家～去准备吧。Let's prepare for it separately. **B**〈名〉 parted hair: 留～ wear one's hair parted

【分文】fēnwén〈名〉 single penny: ～不取 completely free of charge ‖ 他还清了全部债务，～不欠。He paid off all his debts to the last penny. ▸身无～

【分析】fēnxī〈动〉 analyse: ～形势 analyse a situation ‖ ～能力 analytical ability ‖ 对比～ contrastive analysis ▸光谱～, 精神～

【分析化学】fēnxī huàxué〈名〉 analytical chemistry

【分析师】fēnxīshī ▸p. 966〈名〉 analyst: 证券～ securities analyst ‖ 宏观经济～ macroeconomic analyst

【分享】fēnxiǎng〈动〉 share: ～快乐 share in the joys ‖ ～劳动成果 share in the fruits of the labour

【分销店】fēnxiāodiàn〈名〉 retail shop

【分销商】fēnxiāoshāng ▸p. 966〈名〉 distributor: 产品将通过全国各地的～出售。Products will be sold through nationwide distributors.

【分晓】fēnxiǎo **A**〈名〉 outcome: 谁是冠军，明天可见～。The champion will be known tomorrow. **B**〈动〉 understand clearly: 且看下图，便可～。A glance at the following chart will clarify your doubts.

【分校】fēnxiào〈名〉 branch campus

【分心】fēnxīn〈动〉**1**（不专心） distract: 孩子们学习时容易～。Children are easily distracted when they are studying. **2**（劳神） take trouble: 这事让您～了。This claimed a good deal of your attention.

【分野】fēnyě〈名〉 divide: 两党之间的政治～ political division between two parties ‖ 两个学派的～ the divide of the two schools of thought

【分一杯羹】fēnyībēigēng〈成〉 take a share of the spoils

【分忧】fēnyōu〈动〉 share sb.'s cares and burdens: ～解愁 relieve sb. of his daily worries ‖ 为家人～ share one's family worries

【分赃】fēnzāng〈动〉 share in the spoils: 因～不均而争吵 quarrel over uneven distribution of spoils

【分站赛】fēnzhànsài〈名〉［体育］ qualifying session: 中国女排在四个～中连连夺冠。China's women's volleyball team took all four qualifying sessions.

【分针】fēnzhēn〈名〉 minute hand

【分支】fēnzhī〈名〉 branch: 设立～机构 set up branch operations

【分子】fēnzǐ〈名〉**1**［数学］ numerator **2**［化学］ molecule: 水～含有两个氢原子和一个氧原子。A molecule of water consists of two atoms of hydrogen and one atom of oxygen.
▸fènzǐ

【分子结构】fēnzǐ jiégòu〈名〉 molecular structure

【分子量】fēnzǐliàng〈名〉 molecular weight

【分子式】fēnzǐshì〈名〉 molecular formula: 水的化学～ chemical formula for water

【分组】fēnzǔ〈动〉 divide into groups: ～讨论/学习 discuss/study in groups

【分组赛】fēnzǔsài〈名〉 heat: 中国队在～中抽得上上签。China drew the best deal in the heats.

芬 fēn〈名〉 fragrance

【芬芳】fēnfāng **A**〈形〉 fragrant: ～的花朵 fragrant flowers **B**〈名〉 fragrance: 空气中弥漫着丁香花的～。The air is filled with the sweet scent of lilacs.

【芬兰】Fēnlán〈名〉 Finland: ～共和国 Republic of Finland ‖ ～人 Finn ‖ ～语 Finnish

吩 fēn

【吩咐】fēnfu〈动〉**1**（命令） instruct **2**（嘱咐） order: 医生～我卧床。The doctor ordered me to stay in bed. ‖ 您有何～? Do you have any instructions to deliver? ‖ 有事尽管～。Don't hesitate to tell me if you need a hand.

纷（紛）fēn

A〈形〉**1**（多） numerous: ▸～飞, ～至沓来 **2**（杂乱） disorderly: ▸～杂 **B**〈名〉 dispute: 排难解～ solve disputes ▸～争, 纠～

【纷呈】fēnchéng〈动〉〈书〉 appear one after another: 流派～ have a variety of schools ‖ 色彩～ be a riot of colour

【纷繁】fēnfán〈形〉 numerous and complicated: 门类～ be of various kinds ‖ 头绪～ have too many things going on

【纷飞】fēnfēi〈动〉 fly all over the place: 大雪～。Snowflakes are falling thick and fast. ‖ 战火～。The flames of war are raging.

【纷纷】fēnfēn **A**〈形〉 numerous and confused: 落叶～。Leaves fell in profusion. ▸议论～ **B**〈副〉 one after another: 国会议员～要求发言。The members of Parliament clamoured to speak. ‖ 全国各地～捐款捐物。Donations poured in from all parts of the country.

【纷纷扬扬】fēnfēn-yángyáng〈成〉 fluttering: 雪花～，下个不停。Snow kept fluttering.

【纷乱】fēnluàn〈形〉 chaotic: ～的脚步声 hurried footsteps ‖ 他思绪～。His thoughts were in a whirl.

【纷披】fēnpī〈形〉〈书〉 spreading out in all directions: 头发～ one's hair is all over the place ‖ 枝叶～ with the branches and twigs spreading in all directions

【纷扰】fēnrǎo〈形〉 chaotic: 内心～ confused state of mind ‖ 世事～ messy worldly affairs

【纷纭】fēnyún〈形〉 diverse and confused: 头绪～ have too many irons in the fire ‖ 众说～ opinions vary

【纷杂】fēnzá〈形〉〈书〉 jumbled: 思绪～ confused state of mind

【纷争】fēnzhēng〈名〉 dispute: 调解～ mediate a dispute ‖ 引起～ cause dissension

【纷至沓来】fēnzhì-tàlái〈成〉 come thick and fast: 贺信～。Letters of congratulations flooded in.

玢 fēn ▸赛璐玢 sàilùfēn
▸bīn

氛 fēn〈名〉 atmosphere: ▸气～

【氛围】fēnwéi〈名〉 atmosphere: 创造和平宁静的～ create an atmosphere of peace and calm ‖ 在欢乐的～中 be in a joyful atmosphere

酚 fēn〈名〉［化学］ phenol

【酚酞】fēntài〈名〉［化学］ phenolphthalein

雰 fēn〈名〉〈书〉 mist

【雰雰】fēnfēn〈形〉〈书〉 heavy: 昨晚雨雪～。It was snowing heavily last night.

【雰围】fēnwéi = 氛围 fēnwéi

fén

坟（墳）fén〈名〉 grave: 上～ visit a tomb ‖ 把鲜花摆放在～前 lay fresh flowers at sb.'s grave ▸～墓, 祖～

【坟场】fénchǎng = 坟地 féndì

【坟地】féndì〈名〉 graveyard

【坟墓】fénmù〈名〉 grave: 自掘～ dig one's own grave

【坟丘】fénqiū〈名〉 grave

【坟山】fénshān〈名〉〈方〉**1**（指山） hill serving as graveyard **2**（坟地） cemetery hill **3**（指坟头） large tomb mound

【坟头】féntóu〈名〉 grave mound: 把花圈摆放在～ lay a wreath at sb.'s grave

【坟茔】fényíng〈名〉**1**（坟墓） grave: 拜谒先辈的～ visit the graves of one's forefathers **2**（坟地） graveyard

汾 fén

【汾河】Fénhé ▸p. 294〈名〉 Fenhe River

【汾酒】fénjiǔ〈名〉 Fenyang wine

棼 fén〈形〉〈书〉 confused: ▸治丝益～

焚 fén〈动〉 burn: 玉石俱～ the good goes down with the bad ▸玩火自～, 心急如～, 忧心如～

【焚膏继晷】féngāo-jìguǐ〈成〉 burn the midnight oil

【焚化】fénhuà〈动〉 cremate: ～尸体 cremate a dead body ‖ ～炉 incinerator

【焚毁】fénhuǐ〈动〉 burn down: 一场大火～了许多房屋。A fire burned many houses down.

【焚琴煮鹤】fénqín-zhǔhè = 煮鹤焚琴 zhǔhè-fénqín

【焚烧】fénshāo〈动〉 set on fire: ～枯叶/垃圾/信件 burn dead leaves/rubbish/letters

【焚尸】fénshī〈动〉 cremate a dead body: ～灭迹 destroy traces of a crime by burning the corpse

【焚书坑儒】fénshū-kēngrú〈成〉 burning books and burying Confucian scholars alive

【焚香】fénxiāng〈动〉 burn incense: ～拜佛 burn incense to worship the Buddha ‖ ～沐浴 take a bath and burn incense

鼢 fén

【鼢鼠】fénshǔ〈名〉［动物］ zokor

fěn

粉 fěn

A〈名〉 **1**（用于化妆） face powder: 给脸上搽～ powder one's face ▸爽身～ **2**（粉末） powder: 磨成～ grind into powder ‖ 发酵～ baking-powder ▸奶～, 漂白～, 洗衣～ **3**（指淀粉制品） food made from starch: ▸～皮, 凉～ **4**（指粉丝或粉条） noodles made from starch: 绿豆～ mung bean noodles ▸～条 **5**（面粉） flour: 把小麦磨成～ grind wheat into flour ‖ 标准～ standard flour ‖ 富强～ quality flour

B〈动〉 **1**（变成粉末） powder: ～煤 powdered coal ‖ 石灰放得太久, 已经～了。 The lime was exposed to the air for too long and became powder. **2**〈方〉（粉刷） whitewash: ～墙 whitewash a wall

C ▸**p. 863**〈形〉 **1**（白色） whitewashed: ▸～蝶, ～连纸 **2**（粉红色） pink: ～牡丹 pink peony ‖ ～色 pink colour

【粉笔】fěnbǐ〈名〉 chalk: 彩色～ coloured chalk ‖ ～画 chalk drawing ‖ ～灰 chalk dust

【粉饼】fěnbǐng〈名〉 powder cake

【粉彩】fěncǎi〈名〉 mixed glaze

【粉肠】fěncháng〈名〉［sausage shaped］ steamed pastry roll

【粉尘】fěnchén〈名〉 dust: ～污染 dust pollution

【粉刺】fěncì〈名〉 acne: 长～ have acne

【粉黛】fěndài〈名〉〈书〉 **1**（指颜料） face powder and eyebrow tint: 不施～ wear no cosmetics **2**（指美女） beautiful women

【粉底】fěndǐ〈名〉 foundation: 打着厚厚的～ apply heavy foundation ‖ ～霜 foundation cream

【粉蝶】fěndié〈名〉 white butterfly

【粉坊】fěnfáng〈名〉 starch-noodle shop

【粉红】fěnhóng ▸**p. 863**〈形〉 pink: 穿～色衣服的女孩 girl in pink

【粉剂】fěnjì〈名〉 powder: ～药物 powdered medicine ‖ ～农药 powdered farm chemical

【粉连纸】fěnliánzhǐ〈名〉 semi-transparent white paper

【粉末】fěnmò〈名〉 powder: 研成～ grind to powder ‖ ～金属 powdered metal ‖ ～冶金 powder metallurgy

【粉墨登场】fěnmò-dēngchǎng〈成〉〈喻〉［usu sarcastic］ make one's entry into the political arena

【粉嫩】fěnnèn〈形〉 fair and tender

【粉皮】fěnpí〈名〉［食品］ sheet jelly

【粉扑儿】fěnpūr〈名〉 powder puff

【粉芡】fěnqiàn〈名〉 starch paste

【粉墙】fěnqiáng **A**〈名〉 plaster wall **B**〈动〉 **1**（用灰泥） plaster a wall **2**（用白色涂料） whitewash a wall

【粉砂】fěnshā〈名〉［地质］ silt: ～黏土 silt soil

【粉身碎骨】fěnshēn-suìgǔ〈成〉 die a violent death: 我宁愿～也不投降。 I would rather have my body smashed into pieces than surrender.

【粉饰】fěnshì〈动〉 whitewash: ～门面 give a shop front a facelift ‖〈喻〉～现实 gloss over reality ‖〈喻〉～太平 present a false picture of peace and prosperity

【粉刷】fěnshuā〈动〉 whitewash: ～墙壁 whitewashed walls

【粉丝】fěnsī〈名〉 **1**［食品］ fine vermicelli **2**〈口〉（追星族） fans: 铁杆～ stalwart

【粉碎】fěnsuì **A**〈形〉 shattered: ～性骨折 comminuted fracture ‖ 花瓶掉到地板上摔得～。 The vase landed on the floor and smashed to pieces. **B**〈动〉 **1**（使粉碎） shatter: ～矿石 shattered ore ‖ ～机 pulverizer **2**（挫败） crush: ～敌人的进攻 crush the enemy's attack ‖ ～阴谋诡计 crush a conspiracy

【粉条】fěntiáo〈名〉 starch noodles

【粉头】fěntóu〈名〉〈旧〉 prostitute

【粉蒸肉】fěnzhēngròu〈名〉 pork steamed with ground glutinous rice

【粉装玉琢】fěnzhuāng-yùzhuó〈成〉 **1**（指雪景） silvery white: ～的世界 world of silvery white **2**（指皮肤） fair and tender

fèn

分 fèn〈名〉 **1**（成分） content: 糖/盐～ sugar/salt content ▸成～, 水～, 养～ **2**（本分） extent of one's duty or rights: ▸～内, 本～, 非～之想 **3**（情分） factor: 看在上帝的～上 for the love of Christ ▸情～, 天～, 缘～ **4** = 份 fèn A
▸fēn

【分际】fènjì〈名〉 **1**〈书〉（指界限） sense of propriety: 他做事严守～。 He always behaves with great discretion. **2**（程度） degree: 想不到他会糊涂到这等～! I never thought he could be this confused!

【分量】fènliàng〈名〉 weight: 给足～ give good measure ‖ ～足 be in good measure ‖ 他的话有～。 His words carry weight.

【分内】fènnèi〈形〉 due: 做好～的事 pull one's (own) weight ‖ 这是我～的事。 This is simply my duty.

【分外】fènwài **A**〈副〉 exceptionally: ～妖娆 especially enchanting ‖ 月到中秋～明。 The moon seems exceptionally bright at the Mid-Autumn Festival. **B**〈形〉 supplementary: ～的事他也乐意干。 He is always ready to do even what is beyond his duty.

【分子】fènzǐ〈名〉 element: 分裂～ divisive element ▸积极～, 知识～
▸fēnzǐ

份 fèn

A〈名〉 **1**（一部分） part: 分成两～ divide into two parts ‖ 股～ share **2**〈方〉（身份） status: 摆～ put on airs ‖ 他认为那个活儿让他跌～。 He thought that the job was beneath him. **3**（后缀）［used after 省、县、年、月 to form a unit］: ▸年～, 省～

B〈量〉 **1**（指成组的东西） portion: 一～儿礼物 one part of the present ‖ 吃两～儿牛排 have two portions of beefsteak **2**（指复本） copy: 本合同一式两～, 双方各执一～。 There are two copies of the contract, one for each party.

【份额】fèn'é〈名〉 share: 增加市场～ increase the share of market ‖ 占有适当的～ possess an appropriate share

【份儿】fènr〈名〉〈口〉 **1**（一部分） share: 他在促成这件事上出了大力, 但荣誉却没他的～。 He played an important role in bringing this to fruition but took no share in the credit. ‖ 这场打斗你有～吗? Did you have a hand in the fighting? **2**（地位） position: 没你说话的～。 You have no say in the matter. **3**（程度） degree: 都累到这～上了, 他还在干活儿。 He went on working even though he was that tired.

【份儿饭】fènrfàn〈名〉 set meal

【份子】fènzi〈名〉 **1**（指分摊的钱） share: 凑～买礼物 club together to buy a present **2**（指礼金） money as gift: ▸出～

奋（奮） fèn〈动〉 **1**（振作） exert oneself: ▸～斗, 勤～, 振～ **2**（举起） raise: ～臂高呼 raise one's arms and shout **3**（指鸟） spread and flutter the wings: ▸～飞

【奋笔疾书】fènbǐ-jíshū〈成〉 wield one's pen passionately

【奋不顾身】fènbùgùshēn〈成〉 dash ahead regardless of one's safety: ～的消防队员 fire-fighters working at the risk of their safety

【奋斗】fèndòu〈动〉 struggle: ～目标 goal/objective of a struggle ‖ 为实现理想而～ strive to make one's dream come true ▸艰苦～

【奋发】fènfā〈动〉 exert oneself: 鼓舞人民～努力、积极向上 inspire the people to work hard and to aim high

【奋发图强】fènfā-túqiáng〈成〉 go all out to achieve success

【奋飞】fènfēi〈动〉 fly energetically

【奋激】fènjī〈形〉〈书〉 greatly excited: 群情～ popular feeling runs high

【奋进】fènjìn〈动〉 advance courageously: 他的话语催人～。 His remarks are inspiring.

【奋力】fènlì〈动〉 go all out: ～拼搏 struggle under one's own steam ‖ ～抢救落水儿童 do all one can to rescue the drowning child

【奋袂】fènmèi〈动〉〈书〉 roll one's sleeves up for action: ～而起 work oneself up for action

【奋勉】fènmiǎn〈动〉〈书〉 make a determined effort

【奋起】fènqǐ〈动〉 **1**（振作起来） brace oneself: ～反抗 rise up to revolt ‖ ～还击 brace oneself for a counter-attack **2**（举起） raise/lift with all one's strength

【奋起直追】fènqǐ-zhízhuī〈成〉 do all one can to catch up

【奋然】fènrán〈形〉 energetic

【奋勇】fènyǒng〈动〉 summon up all one's courage: ～杀敌 fight the enemy bravely ‖ ～当先 fight courageously in the vanguard ▸自告～

【奋战】fènzhàn〈动〉 fight bravely: 浴血～ fight a bloody battle ‖ ～到底 fight it out ‖ 经过三个月的艰苦～, 大江终于截流成功。 After three months' strenuous labour, we finally succeeded in damming the great river.

忿 fèn ▸不忿 bùfèn

偾（僨） fèn〈动〉〈书〉 spoil

粪（糞） fèn

A〈名〉 excrement: 马～ horse dung ‖ 鸟～ bird droppings ‖ ～车 dung-cart

B〈动〉〈书〉 manure: ～田 manure the fields

【粪便】fènbiàn〈名〉 excrement and urine

【粪肥】fènféi〈名〉 dung: 施～ apply manure

【粪坑】fènkēng〈名〉 cesspit

【粪筐】fènkuāng〈名〉manure basket
【粪桶】fèntǒng〈名〉night-soil bucket
【粪土】fèntǔ〈名〉1（粪便和泥土）muck 2〈喻〉（无价值的东西）worthless thing: 视名利若～。Regard fame and gain as nothing.

愤（憤）fèn〈名〉anger

【愤愤】fènfèn〈形〉indignant: ～而去 leave in anger
【愤愤不平】fènfèn-bùpíng〈成〉be indignant: 她因待遇不公而～。She felt aggrieved at the unfair treatment.
【愤恨】fènhèn〈动〉detest: 无比～ completely detest ‖ 令人～ detestable
【愤激】fènjī〈形〉〈书〉roused to indignation
【愤慨】fènkǎi〈形〉indignant: 无比～ be highly resentful ‖ 我对他们的卑劣行径感到～。I was indignant at their mean actions.
【愤懑】fènmèn〈形〉〈书〉resentful: 不胜～ be very resentful
【愤怒】fènnù〈形〉angry: ～声讨 angrily denounce ‖ ～的人群 angry mob ‖ 因名声受到诋毁而～ be angered at the slander against one's reputation
【愤青】fènqīng〈名〉angry youth [extremely nationalistic young Chinese]
【愤然】fènrán〈形〉〈书〉angry: 她～离家出走。She left home in a huff. ‖ 他～退出会议。He stormed out of the meeting.
【愤世嫉俗】fènshì-jísú〈成〉be cynical

鲼（鱝）fèn〈名〉［鱼类］eagle ray

fēng

丰¹（豐）fēng〈形〉1（茂盛）lush: ▸～茂, ～美 2（丰满）well-rounded: ▸～满, ～润 3（丰富）plentiful: 他收入颇～。He has a handsome income. ▸～收, ～衣足食 4（伟大）great: ▸～碑, ～功伟绩

丰²fēng〈形〉good-looking: ▸～采, ～韵, ～姿

【丰碑】fēngbēi〈名〉1（指石碑）monument: 人民心中不朽的～ ever-lasting monument in the hearts of the people 2〈喻〉（指杰作）monumental work: 医学文献的～ monumental work in medical literature
【丰采】fēngcǎi = 风采 fēngcǎi 1
【丰产】fēngchǎn〈动〉yield a bumper crop: ～不丰收 a good harvest but poor sales ‖ ～田 high-yield land
【丰登】fēngdēng〈动〉yield a bumper harvest: ▸五谷～
【丰度】fēngdù〈名〉demeanour
【丰富】fēngfù A〈形〉plentiful: 自然资源～ be rich in natural resources ‖ ～的想象力 fertile imagination ‖ 表情～ expressive face ‖ 能源～的国家 energy-rich country B〈动〉enrich: ～业余生活 enrich one's off-work hours ‖ 通过旅游～经历 enrich one's experience through travel ‖ 博览群书以～词汇 enlarge one's vocabulary through extensive reading
【丰富多彩】fēngfù-duōcǎi〈成〉rich and colourful: 演出～的节目 present a varied and interesting programme ‖ ～的课外活动 varied and colourful extracurricular activities
【丰功伟绩】fēnggōng-wěijì〈成〉tremendous achievements
【丰厚】fēnghòu〈形〉1（厚实）thick: 绒毛～ with rich and thick fur 2（丰富）abundant: ～的礼物 generous gift ‖ ～的利润 fat profit ‖ ～的收入 liberal income
【丰满】fēngmǎn〈形〉1（充足）plentiful: ～的粮仓 full granary 2（胖得匀称）full and round: 体态～ have a well-rounded figure 3（长成）full-grown: 羽毛～ be full-fledged ‖〈喻〉～的人物形象 well-rounded portrayal of characters
【丰茂】fēngmào〈形〉luxuriant: ～的牧场 lush pastures ‖ 枝叶～的大树 large trees with luxuriant foliage
【丰美】fēngměi〈形〉lush: ～的菜肴 abundant and tasty dishes
【丰年】fēngnián〈名〉bumper year: 瑞雪兆～。A timely snow promises a good harvest.
【丰沛】fēngpèi〈形〉〈书〉plentiful: 雨水～ have plenty of rain
【丰饶】fēngráo〈形〉rich and fertile: 辽阔～的平原 vast and fertile plain ‖ 物产～ be abundant in produce
【丰乳】fēngrǔ〈动〉enlarge the breast
【丰润】fēngrùn〈形〉plump and tender: ～的两颊 plump and tender cheeks
【丰赡】fēngshàn〈形〉〈书〉plentiful: 内容～ substantial in content
【丰盛】fēngshèng〈形〉rich: ～的饭菜 solid meal ‖ ～的宴席 sumptuous banquet
【丰收】fēngshōu〈动〉reap a bumper harvest: 今年棉花～了。The cotton crop did well this year. ‖ 小麦～在望。A bumper wheat harvest is in sight. ‖〈喻〉去年科幻小说创作获得了大～。Last year saw a bumper crop of science fiction.
【丰硕】fēngshuò〈形〉substantial: 取得～成果 score great successes
【丰胸】fēngxiōng〈动〉enlarge the breast
【丰衣足食】fēngyī-zúshí〈成〉be well off: 过着～的生活 live in abundance
【丰盈】fēngyíng〈形〉1（丰满）full and round: 体态～ have a well-rounded figure 2（充足）plentiful: 衣食～ have plenty of food and clothing
【丰腴】fēngyú〈形〉〈书〉1（丰满）full and round: 体态～ have a plump figure 2（肥沃）luxuriant: ～的热带植被 lush tropical vegetation 3（丰盛）sumptuous: ～的酒席 sumptuous feast
【丰裕】fēngyù〈形〉abundant: 生活～ be comfortably off ‖ ～的家庭 wealthy family
【丰韵】fēngyùn = 风韵 fēngyùn
【丰姿】fēngzī = 风姿 fēngzī
【丰足】fēngzú〈形〉plentiful: 衣食～ enjoy ample food and clothing

风（風）fēng

A〈名〉1（指空气流动）wind: 刮～下雨。It is windy and raining. ‖ 起～了。A wind picked up. ▸北～, 逆～, 信～ 2（风气）tendency: 树新～ foster healthy tendencies ‖ 校～ spirit of a school ‖ 此～不可长。This tendency is not to be encouraged. ▸～土人情, 歪～邪气 3（姿态）bearing: ▸～采, ～范, 作～ 4（景象）scene: ▸～光, ～景 5（消息）news: 她一点～都不漏。She wouldn't drop the slightest hint. ▸通～报信, 闻～而动 6（指民歌）one of the three sections of *The Book of Songs*（《诗经》）, consisting of ballads 7（指致病因素）disease-causing element: ▸～寒, ～湿 8（指疾病）[used in certain disease names]: ▸白癜～, 鹅掌～ B〈动〉1（吹干）air: ▸～干 2（吹净）winnow: 小麦已晒干～净。The wheat has been sun-dried and winnowed. C〈形〉1（风干）air-dried: ～肉 air-dried meat 2（很快）swift as the wind: ▸～发, ～行 3（无根据）rumoured: ▸～传, ～闻, ～言～语
【风暴】fēngbào〈名〉windstorm: 遭到～袭击 be battered by a tempest ‖ 战胜～ weather the storm ‖ 热带～ tropical storm ‖ 革命～ storm of revolution ‖ 政治～ political storm ‖ 金融～ financial storm
【风泵】fēngbèng〈名〉air pump
【风标】fēngbiāo〈名〉weathercock
【风波】fēngbō〈名〉storm: 金融～ financial turmoil ‖ 政治～ political storm ‖ 平地起～。The storm rose out of nowhere.
【风伯】fēngbó〈名〉God of wind
【风采】fēngcǎi〈名〉〈书〉1（神采）graceful demeanour: 一睹女王的～ have a glimpse of the Queen's regal bearing ‖ 她～动人。She cuts quite a figure. 2（文采）literary grace
【风餐露宿】fēngcān-lùsù〈成〉live rough: 他是一名地质学家，习惯了～。He is a geologist and is used to living rough.
【风潮】fēngcháo〈名〉unrest: 闹～ create an unrest ‖ 平息～ suppress an unrest
【风车】fēngchē〈名〉1（指装置）windmill 2（指玩具）pinwheel
【风尘】fēngchén〈名〉1（指劳累）travel fatigue: 满面～ be travel-worn 2（纷乱的社会）hardships and uncertainties of an unstable society: ～知己 friend in need 3（妓女）prostitution: 沦落～ fall into prostitution ‖ ～女子 street walker
【风尘仆仆】fēngchén-púpú〈成〉be travel-worn
【风驰电掣】fēngchí-diànchè〈成〉like the wind: 列车～般驶过车站。The train flashed through the station.
【风传】fēngchuán A〈动〉[of news or rumours] get about: ～他有可能成为下一届联合国秘书长。He is being tipped as the next UN Secretary General. B〈名〉rumour
【风吹草动】fēngchuī-cǎodòng〈成〉〈喻〉rustlings of change: 一有～，就惊惶失措 fly into a panic at the mere rustle of misfortune
【风吹浪打】fēngchuī-làngdǎ〈成〉experience storms: 经受～的锻炼 be forged by hardships
【风吹日晒】fēngchuī-rìshài〈成〉be exposed to the wind and sun
【风吹雨打】fēngchuī-yǔdǎ〈成〉be buffeted by wind and rain: 经不起～ not be able to withstand the elements
【风锤】fēngchuí〈名〉pneumatic hammer
【风挡】fēngdǎng〈名〉windscreen
【风刀霜剑】fēngdāo-shuāngjiàn〈成〉〈喻〉adverse circumstances
【风灯】fēngdēng〈名〉storm lantern: 提着～ carry a storm lantern
【风笛】fēngdí ▸p. 929〈名〉bagpipes
【风洞】fēngdòng〈名〉［航空］wind tunnel
【风斗】fēngdǒu〈名〉wind scoop
【风度】fēngdù〈名〉carriage: 绅士～ gentlemanly bearing ‖ 大将～ carriage of a great general ‖ 他很有～。He has great style.
【风度翩翩】fēngdù-piānpiān〈成〉graceful bearing
【风发】fēngfā〈形〉energetic: ▸意气～
【风帆】fēngfān〈名〉sail: 扬起～ put up sail ‖〈喻〉鼓起生活的～ raise the sail of life

f

【风范】fēngfàn〈名〉air: 王者～ regal manner ‖ 艺术大家的～ air of an art master

【风风火火】fēngfēng-huǒhuǒ〈成〉❶（形容匆忙冒失） hustling and bustling: 她总是～的。 She is always hustling and bustling. ❷（指有活力） dynamic: ～的战争年代 lively war years

【风风雨雨】fēngfēng-yǔyǔ〈成〉 trials and tribulations: 三十年的～ thirty years of hardship

【风干】fēnggān〈动〉 air-dry: ～腊肉 air-dried bacon

【风镐】fēnggǎo〈名〉 pneumatic pick

【风格】fēnggé〈名〉 style: 独特的艺术～ distinctive artistic style ‖ 古典～ classical style ‖ 民族～ national style ‖ 选手们赛出了水平，赛出了～。 The athletes did well and displayed fine sportsmanship.

【风骨】fēnggǔ〈名〉 ❶（指人） integrity ❷（指诗文书画） energetic style

【风光】fēngguāng〈名〉 scenery: 田园～ pastoral scene ‖ 青山绿水好～ splendid view of green mountains and clear waters ‖ ～旖旎。 The scenery was enchanting.

【风光】fēngguang〈形〉〈方〉 grand: 把婚礼办得很～ hold a grand wedding ‖ 儿子有出息，母亲也～。 The son's achievements were a credit to his mother.

【风害】fēnghài〈名〉 damage caused by a windstorm

【风寒】fēnghán〈名〉 chill: 因受～而感冒 catch a cold from exposure ‖ 只是受了点～。 It's nothing but a chill.

【风和日丽】fēnghé-rìlì〈成〉 warm and sunny: ～的时节 time of sunshine and gentle breeze

【风戽】fēnghù〈名〉 wind-powered waterwheel

【风花雪月】fēnghuā-xuěyuè〈成〉 ❶（指诗文） effete and sentimental writings ❷（指男女情爱） love affair: 过着～的生活 live a frivolous and flirtatious life

【风华】fēnghuá〈名〉〈书〉 elegance and talent: ～绝代 unparalleled manner and deportment

【风华正茂】fēnghuá-zhèngmào〈成〉 in one's prime: 处于～时期 be in one's prime

【风化】fēnghuà Ⓐ〈名〉 ❶（风俗） decency: 这有伤～。 It is an offence against decency. ❷［化学］ efflorescence Ⓑ〈动〉［地质］ weather: 岩石已～成沙土。 The rock has weathered away into soil.

【风火墙】fēnghuǒqiáng〈名〉 fire wall

【风级】fēngjí〈名〉［气象］ wind force scale

【风纪】fēngjì〈名〉 conduct: 整顿～ straighten out discipline ‖ 军人～ soldiers' conduct

【风纪扣】fēngjìkòu〈名〉 collar hook of a uniform: 系上～ hook up one's collar

【风景】fēngjǐng〈名〉 scenery: 以～优美著称 be famous for scenic beauty ‖ 西湖～如画。 The West Lake scenery is like a painting. ▸杀～

【风景画】fēngjǐnghuà〈名〉 landscape painting

【风景林】fēngjǐnglín〈名〉 scenic forest

【风景区】fēngjǐngqū〈名〉 scenic spot

【风景线】fēngjǐngxiàn〈名〉〈喻〉 scenic vista

【风镜】fēngjìng〈名〉 goggles: 一副～ a pair of goggles

【风卷残云】fēngjuǎncányún〈成〉 make a clean sweep

【风口】fēngkǒu〈名〉 draughty spot: 不要站在～上。 Don't stand in the draught.

【风口浪尖】fēngkǒu-làngjiān〈成〉〈喻〉 the point where the going is toughest

【风浪】fēnglàng〈名〉 ❶〈本〉 stormy waves: 海上～很大。 The sea is heavy and rough. ❷〈喻〉（艰难险阻） stormy experience: 久经～ have weathered many a storm

【风雷】fēngléi〈名〉 wind and thunder: 革命的～ storm of revolution

【风力】fēnglì〈名〉 ❶（指力量） wind force ❷（指强度） wind power: ～发电 wind power generation

【风力发电机】fēnglì fādiànjī〈名〉 wind turbine

【风里来，雨里去】fēngli lái, yǔli qù〈俗〉 keep going irrespective of the hardships

【风凉】fēngliáng〈形〉 cool: 在～的地方休息 have a break in a cool place

【风凉话】fēngliánghuà〈名〉 irresponsible and sarcastic remarks: 他爱说～。 He is given to sarcasm.

【风铃】fēnglíng〈名〉 wind chime

【风流】fēngliú〈形〉 ❶（风雅洒脱） distinguished and admirable: ～儒雅 be cultured, talented and refined ❷（杰出） talented and unrestrained: ～才子 romantic talent ❸（有关男女私情） amorous: ～案 love affair ‖ ～韵事 romantic affairs ❹（放荡） loose: ～寡妇 merry widow ‖ ～女子 loose woman

【风流倜傥】fēngliú-tìtǎng〈成〉 casual and elegant bearing

【风流蕴藉】fēngliú-yùnjiè〈成〉 urbanely charming

【风马牛不相及】fēng mǎ niú bù xiāng jí〈成〉 have no relevance whatsoever to each other

【风貌】fēngmào〈名〉 ❶（指事物） style and features: 保持古城～ preserve the ancient look of the city ‖ 时代～ features of the age ❷（指人） bearing: ～娉婷 have graceful carriage ❸（风光） view: 都市新～ new look of a metropolis ‖ 远近～，历历在目。 Scenes from far and near flash before one's eyes.

【风貌区】fēngmàoqū〈名〉 scenic area: 北京什刹海～ Beijing Shichahai Scenic Area

【风媒传粉】fēngméi chuánfěn〈名〉［农业］ wind pollination

【风门】fēngmén〈名〉 ❶［矿业］ ventilation door ❷（挡风的门） storm door

【风靡】fēngmǐ〈动〉 be in fashion: ～全国 fashionable throughout the country ‖ ～一时 be all the rage for a time

【风磨】fēngmò〈名〉 windmill

【风能】fēngnéng〈名〉 wind energy

【风派】fēngpài〈名〉 time-server

【风平浪静】fēngpíng-làngjìng〈成〉 ❶〈本〉 calm and tranquil: ～的湖面 tranquil lake ❷〈喻〉（安定平静） safe and sound: ～的生活 uneventful life

【风起云涌】fēngqǐ-yúnyǒng〈成〉 roll on with great force: 近二十年来，改革大潮～。 Over the last two decades, the waves of reform have surged forward dramatically.

【风气】fēngqì〈名〉 atmosphere: 社会～ social conduct ‖ 勤俭节约已经形成～。 Thrift and industry have become a common practice.

【风琴】fēngqín ▸**p. 929**〈名〉 organ

【风情】fēngqíng〈名〉 ❶（指风向、风力） information about wind direction, wind-force, etc. ❷〈书〉（指仪表举止） demeanour ❸〈书〉（情怀） liking: 别有一番～ have unique taste ❹〈贬〉（男女情爱） flirtatious expressions: 卖弄～ flirt ❺（风土人情） local manners and customs: 南国～ customs of the South

【风趣】fēngqù Ⓐ〈形〉 humorous: 说话～的人 witty person Ⓑ〈名〉 humour

【风圈】fēngquān〈名〉（日晕） solar halo;（月晕） lunar halo

【风骚】fēngsāo Ⓐ〈名〉〈书〉 ❶（文学作品） literature ❷（文采） literary excellence: 在文坛独领～ be unrivalled in literary circles Ⓑ〈形〉 coquettish: ～女子 flirtatious woman ‖ 卖弄～ show off one's coquettishness

【风色】fēngsè〈名〉 ❶（风向和风力） condition of wind: ～对帆船比赛很重要。 Wind is very important in competitive sailing. ❷（情势） situation: 他一看～不对，拔腿就跑。 Finding things going against him, he took to his heels.

【风沙】fēngshā〈名〉 wind-borne sand: 这一带～很大。 It's windy and dusty in this region.

【风扇】fēngshàn〈名〉 electric fan: ▸电～

【风尚】fēngshàng〈名〉 prevailing custom: 开创新～ set a fashion ‖ 时代～ craze of the day

【风声】fēngshēng〈名〉 ❶（风的声音） sound of the wind ❷（消息） information: 走漏～ leak information ‖ ～越来越紧。 The situation is getting more and more tense.

【风声鹤唳】fēngshēng-hèlì〈成〉 be panic-stricken

【风湿】fēngshī ▸**p. 50**〈名〉［医学］ rheumatism: ～性关节炎 rheumatoid arthritis

【风湿病】fēngshībìng ▸**p. 50**〈名〉 rheumatism

【风蚀】fēngshí〈名〉［地质］ wind erosion

【风势】fēngshì〈名〉 ❶〈本〉 wind force: ～减弱了。 The wind has dropped. ❷〈喻〉 situation: 看～行事 size up the situation before taking any action

【风霜】fēngshuāng〈名〉〈喻〉 hardships: ～之苦 the difficulty of hardships ▸饱经～

【风水】fēngshuǐ〈名〉 feng shui: 看～ practise feng shui ‖ ～宝地 place of excellent geomantic quality ‖ ～先生 feng shui master

> 风水
>
> *Feng shui* refers to the auspicious topographical features of a particular place, with *feng* and *shui* meaning respectively 'wind' and 'water' in Chinese. Those who believe in *feng shui* believe that the physical environment of a house or cemetery — such as the way the wind blows or the water flows — can influence the fortune of the family and future generations.

【风俗】fēngsú〈名〉 custom: 尊重当地的～ respect local customs ‖ 传统/古老的～ traditional/ancient customs ‖ 社会～ social customs

【风俗画】fēngsúhuà〈名〉 genre painting

【风速】fēngsù〈名〉 wind speed

【风瘫】fēngtān〈名〉 paralysis

【风调雨顺】fēngtiáo-yǔshùn〈成〉 favourable weather

【风头】fēngtou〈名〉 ❶（情势） trend of events: 避避～ lie low until sth. blows over ‖ 看～办事 see which way the wind blows ❷〈贬〉（出头露面） publicity: 爱出～ be fond of the limelight ‖ 想出～ seek the limelight

【风土人情】fēngtǔ-rénqíng〈成〉 local customs and practices

【风味】fēngwèi〈名〉 special flavour: 地方～ local flavour ‖ ～小吃 local delicacies ‖ 这道菜～独特。 This dish has its own special flavour. ‖ 她的歌曲充满了民歌～。 Her songs had the quality of folk songs.

【风闻】fēngwén〈动〉get wind of: ～公司要倒闭了。Rumour has it that the company is closing down.

【风物】fēngwù〈名〉scenery

【风险】fēngxiǎn〈名〉risk: 承担～ take risks ‖ 冒～ run a risk ‖ 投资是有～的。All investments carry their risks.

【风箱】fēngxiāng〈名〉**1**（指装置）bellows: 拉～ pump the bellows **2**［音乐］windchest

【风向】fēngxiàng〈名〉**1**〈本〉wind direction **2**〈喻〉situation: 看～行事 size up the situation before taking any action

【风向标】fēngxiàngbiāo〈名〉weathercock

【风信子】fēngxìnzǐ〈名〉［植物］hyacinth

【风行】fēngxíng〈动〉catch on: ～全国 be popular all over the country ‖ 流行歌曲～榜 hit parade ‖ ～一时 be all the rage for a while

【风雅】fēngyǎ〈书〉**A**〈名〉literary pursuits: ▸附庸～ **B**〈形〉elegant: 举止～ have refined manners

【风言风语】fēngyán-fēngyǔ **A**〈名〉slanderous gossip: 我不喜欢听这些～。I don't like this idle gossip. **B**〈动〉spread gossip: 唧唧喳喳地～ buzz about a scandal

【风衣】fēngyī〈名〉windcheater〈英〉; windbreaker〈美〉

【风雨】fēngyǔ〈名〉**1**〈本〉wind and rain: ～无阻 come rain or come shine ‖ ～大作 the storm rages **2**〈喻〉trials and tribulations: 经～，见世面 brave the storm and face the world

【风雨交加】fēngyǔ-jiāojiā〈成〉with heavy rains and high winds

【风雨飘摇】fēngyǔ-piāoyáo〈成〉precarious situations: ～的政权 tottering regime

【风雨如晦】fēngyǔ-rúhuì〈成〉a grim and grave situation

【风雨同舟】fēngyǔ-tóngzhōu〈成〉standing together through thick and thin

【风月】fēngyuè〈名〉**1**（景色）scene: ～清幽 tranquil and exquisite scene **2**（男女情爱）romance: ～场 arena of love

【风云】fēngyún〈名〉**1**〈本〉wind and cloud: ▸天有不测～ **2**〈喻〉stormy situation: ～突变 sudden change in the situation

【风云变幻】fēngyún-biànhuàn〈成〉volatile situation: ～的时代 age of rapid change

【风云人物】fēngyún-rénwù〈名〉man of the moment: 本年度～ man of the year

【风韵】fēngyùn〈名〉charm: ～犹存 [of a woman past her prime] still look attractive

【风灾】fēngzāi〈名〉windstorm disaster

【风障】fēngzhàng〈名〉windbreak

【风疹】fēngzhěn〈名〉rubella

【风筝】fēngzheng〈名〉kite: 放～ fly a kite

【风致】fēngzhì〈名〉〈书〉**1**（指女性）good looks **2**（情致）wit

【风中之烛】fēngzhōngzhīzhú〈成〉〈喻〉person or thing that may die at any moment

【风烛残年】fēngzhú-cánnián〈成〉twilight of one's life

【风姿】fēngzī〈名〉graceful carriage: 展示女性的～ display female charm ‖ ～绰约 be charming in manner ‖ 迷人的～ charming manners

【风钻】fēngzuàn〈名〉pneumatic drill

枫（楓）fēng〈名〉［植物］maple

【枫叶】fēngyè〈名〉maple leaf: ～是加拿大的象征。The maple leaf is the Canadian national symbol.

封[1] fēng〈动〉confer a title upon: ～为伯爵 make sb. an earl ‖ ～为宰相 be appointed as First Minister ▸～地，～妻荫子

封[2] fēng

A〈动〉close: ～死排污口 block the opening to a drain ‖ ～阳台 shut off the veranda ‖ 这个罐子得～严实了。The jar must be well sealed. ▸～山，密～ **B**〈名〉envelope: 赏～ enveloped reward ▸信～ **C**〈量〉[for sth. enveloped]: 一～挂号信 a registered letter

【封笔】fēngbǐ〈动〉[of a writer, painter, etc.] lay one's pen to rest: ～之作 swansong

【封闭】fēngbì〈动〉**1**（关闭）seal off: ～港口/机场 close a port/an airport ‖ 用蜡～住瓶口 seal a bottle with wax ‖ ～性社会 closed society **2**（查封）close down: ～赌场 close down a gambling casino

【封闭疗法】fēngbì liáofǎ〈名〉［医学］block therapy

【封闭式基金】fēngbìshì jījīn〈名〉［金融］closed-end fund

【封存】fēngcún〈动〉seal up for safekeeping: ～账户 freeze an account ‖ ～的账户 blocked accounts

【封底】fēngdǐ〈名〉back cover

【封地】fēngdì〈名〉feudal estate

【封顶】fēngdǐng〈动〉**1**（指建筑物）roof: 这座楼房计划于七月～。This building was due to be roofed in July. **2**（指上限）put a ceiling on: 奖金不～ put no ceiling on bonuses

【封冻】fēngdòng〈动〉freeze: 河已～。The river has frozen over.

【封二】fēng'èr〈名〉inside front cover

【封官许愿】fēngguān-xǔyuàn〈成〉promise official posts and other favours

【封航】fēngháng〈动〉shut down a route

【封后】fēnghòu〈动〉[of a woman] be named as winner: 两次在世锦赛中～ be two-times champion at the world championships ‖ 在奥斯卡两度～ be a double Best Actress Oscar winner

【封火】fēnghuǒ〈动〉bank (up) a fire

【封建】fēngjiàn **A**〈名〉**1**（指制度）system of enfeoffment **2**（指思想或社会）feudalism: 反～ oppose feudalism **B**〈形〉feudal: ～迷信活动 feudal and superstitious activities ‖ ～意识 feudal ideology

【封建割据】fēngjiàn gējù〈名〉feudal separationist rule

【封建社会】fēngjiàn shèhuì〈名〉feudal society

【封建主义】fēngjiànzhǔyì〈名〉feudalism

【封疆】fēngjiāng〈名〉〈书〉**1**（疆界）borders **2**（指人）provincial governor: ～大吏 high provincial governor

【封禁】fēngjìn〈动〉ban: ～淫秽书刊 ban pornographic books and periodicals ‖ 那部黄色影片遭到～。That pornographic film was banned.

【封镜】fēngjìng〈动〉finish shooting: 下月～。The shooting will finish next month.

【封口】fēngkǒu〈动〉**1**（指开口）seal: 没有～的信 unsealed letter **2**（指伤口）close up: 他臂上的伤已经～了。The cut in his arm has closed up. **3**（闭口不谈）close a matter: 他没～，还可以商量。He hasn't closed the matter. It is still open to discussion.

【封口费】fēngkǒufèi〈名〉hush money: 几位记者拿到了数量不等的～。Several reporters received varying amounts of hush money.

【封里】fēnglǐ〈名〉**1**（指封二）inside front cover **2**（指封二和封三）inside front and back covers

【封门】fēngmén〈动〉**1**（封闭大门）seal up a door **2** = 封口 fēngkǒu 3

【封面】fēngmiàn〈名〉**1**（扉页）title page **2**（指封一和封底）jacket **3**（指封一）front cover: ～女郎 cover girl ‖ ～设计 cover design

【封皮】fēngpí〈名〉**1**（封面）cover **2**（护页）jacket **3**（信封）envelope **4**〈方〉（包裹用的纸）wrapper **5**〈方〉（封条）paper strip seal

【封妻荫子】fēngqī-yìnzǐ〈成〉confer titles of honour on an official's wife and hereditary ranks on his descendants

【封三】fēngsān〈名〉inside back cover

【封杀】fēngshā〈动〉smother: ～对方的大力扣球 block an opponent's powerful smash ‖〈喻〉那次丑闻之后，这位演员就被所有媒体～了。After the scandal, the actor was shut out by all media.

【封山】fēngshān〈动〉close a mountain pass: 大雪～。Heavy snow closed the mountain pass.

【封山育林】fēngshān-yùlín〈成〉close hillsides to facilitate afforestation

【封赏】fēngshǎng **A**〈动〉grant titles and territories **B**〈名〉grant: 领～ accept a reward

【封四】fēngsì = 封底 fēngdǐ

【封锁】fēngsuǒ〈动〉block off: ～边境 close the border ‖ ～所有出口 seal all the exits ‖ ～消息 block news ‖ 实行新闻～ impose a news blackout ‖ 经济～ economic blockade

【封锁线】fēngsuǒxiàn〈名〉cordon: 突破～ break through the blockade

【封套】fēngtào〈名〉big envelope: 唱片～ record jacket ‖ 书的～ slipcase

【封条】fēngtiáo〈名〉seal: 贴上～ glue a paper seal

【封网】fēngwǎng〈动〉[of volleyball] block

【封一】fēngyī = 封面 fēngmiàn 3

【封斋】fēngzhāi **A**〈动〉fast **B**〈名〉day of fasting

【封装】fēngzhuāng〈动〉seal and package

【封嘴】fēngzuǐ〈动〉**1**（闭口不谈）hush: ～钱 hush money **2**（把话说死）leave no room for further discussion: 先不要～，再考虑一下。Give it another thought before it is finalized.

砜（碸）fēng〈名〉［化学］sulphone

疯（瘋）fēng

A〈形〉**1**（神经错乱）mad: 逼～ drive sb. mad ‖ 装～ feign madness ‖ 车开这么快，简直～了！You must be crazy to drive so fast! ▸发～ **2**（指农作物）overgrown: ▸～长 **B**〈动〉play wilfully: 别～了，做作业去吧。Stop playing and get down to your homework.

【疯癫】fēngdiān〈形〉insane

【疯疯癫癫】fēngfeng-diāndiān〈形〉mentally deranged: 她有点～的。She is a bit giddy.

【疯狗】fēnggǒu〈名〉rabid dog

【疯话】fēnghuà〈名〉nonsense

【疯狂】fēngkuáng〈形〉**1**（发疯）crazy: 爱得～ be crazy for love **2**（猖狂）frenzied: ～的报复 frenzied revenge ‖ ～的反扑 desperate counter-attack ‖ ～的掠夺 unbridled plunder

【疯魔】fēngmó〈动〉**1**（精神失常）be fascinated: 他们下棋下～了。They were

f

engrossed in playing chess. **2**（使入迷）fascinate: 这场足球赛几乎令所有的观众～了。 The football game nearly drove all the fans crazy.
【疯牛病】fēngniúbìng ▸**p. 50**〈名〉mad cow disease
【疯人院】fēngrényuàn〈名〉mental asylum
【疯长】fēngzhǎng〈动〉［农业］overgrow: 防止棉花～ prevent cotton plants from overgrowing
【疯子】fēngzi〈名〉lunatic

峰（峯）fēng

A〈名〉**1** ▸**p. 164**（山尖）peak: 孤～ solitary peak ‖ 高耸于群～之上 tower above the cluster of peaks ▸～峦，洪～，山～ **2**（峰状物）hump: 双～骆驼 two-humped camel ▸驼～
B〈量〉[used of camels]: 一～骆驼 a camel
【峰巅】fēngdiān〈名〉summit: 登上～ reach the summit
【峰顶】fēngdǐng〈名〉summit: 登～一览风光 reach the summit to see the view
【峰谷】fēnggǔ〈名〉peaks and troughs: 实行～分时电价 implement electricity pricing according to time of use
【峰回路转】fēnghuí-lùzhuǎn〈成〉winding path amidst high peaks
【峰会】fēnghuì〈名〉summit meeting: 参加～ attend a summit ‖ 举行～ hold a summit
【峰峦】fēngluán〈名〉ridges and peaks: ～起伏 fluctuating ridges and peaks
【峰年】fēngnián〈名〉peak year: 地震活动的～ peak year of earthquake activity
【峰态】fēngtài〈名〉［统计］kurtosis
【峰位】fēngwèi〈名〉peak
【峰值】fēngzhí〈名〉peak value: ～电流 peak point current ‖ 产量超历史～ exceed the highest yield in history

烽 fēng〈名〉beacon

【烽火】fēnghuǒ〈名〉**1**（指烟火）beaconfire **2**（指战火）flames of war;（指战争）war: ～连天 flames of war raging everywhere
【烽火台】fēnghuǒtái〈名〉beacon tower
【烽烟】fēngyān〈名〉beacon fire: ～四起。War raged all over the country.

锋（鋒）fēng〈名〉**1**（锋口）

cutting edge: 剑～ cutting edge of a sword ▸笔～，针～相对 **2**（指人）vanguard: ▸前～，先～ **3**［气象］front: ▸冷～，暖～
【锋利】fēnglì〈形〉**1**（指工具或兵器）sharp: ～的剑 keen-edged sword ‖ 这把刀很～。The knife has a sharp edge. **2**（指言语、文笔）incisive: 目光～ have sharp eyes ‖ 谈吐～ have a sharp tongue ‖ ～泼辣的笔调 sharp and pungent style
【锋芒】fēngmáng〈名〉**1**（指刀剑）spearhead: 斗争的～ spearhead of the struggle ‖ 批评的～直指作家本人。The focus of the criticism is directed right at the writer himself. **2**（指锐气和才干）abilities: 不露～ hide one's light under a bushel ‖ 小试～ try out one's new spurs ▸～毕露
【锋芒逼人】fēngmáng-bīrén〈成〉trenchant, aggressive: ～的批评 biting criticism
【锋芒毕露】fēngmáng-bìlù〈成〉make a display of one's abilities: 他～。His manner is aggressive.
【锋面】fēngmiàn〈名〉［气象］frontal surface: ～气旋 frontal cyclone
【锋锐】fēngruì〈形〉**1**（锐利）sharp **2**（深刻）incisive

蜂 fēng〈名〉**1**（黄蜂）wasp: ～刺 bee

sting **2**（蜜蜂）bee: 养～酿蜜 keep bees for honey ▸～蜜，工～ **3**（成群）swarm: ▸～拥
【蜂巢】fēngcháo〈名〉beehive
【蜂毒】fēngdú〈名〉bee venom
【蜂房】fēngfáng〈名〉beehive
【蜂糕】fēnggāo〈名〉steamed sponge cake
【蜂集】fēngjí〈动〉= 蜂聚 fēngjù
【蜂胶】fēngjiāo〈名〉propolis
【蜂聚】fēngjù〈动〉〈书〉swarm together: 广场上万人～。Thousands of people swarmed on the square.
【蜂蜡】fēnglà〈名〉beeswax
【蜂蜜】fēngmì〈名〉honey: 采集～ gather honey
【蜂鸣器】fēngmíngqì〈名〉buzzer: ～响了。The buzzer is ringing.
【蜂鸟】fēngniǎo〈名〉hummingbird
【蜂起】fēngqǐ〈动〉rise in swarms: 义军～。Uprising forces surged in swarms.
【蜂群】fēngqún〈名〉bee colony
【蜂乳】fēngrǔ〈名〉royal jelly
【蜂王】fēngwáng〈名〉queen bee
【蜂王浆】fēngwángjiāng〈名〉royal jelly
【蜂窝】fēngwō〈名〉**1**（蜂巢）hive **2**（蜂巢状物）honeycomb: ～构造 honeycomb structure ‖ ～组织 cellular tissue
【蜂窝煤】fēngwōméi〈名〉honeycomb briquet
【蜂箱】fēngxiāng〈名〉beehive
【蜂拥】fēngyōng〈动〉swarm: ～而至 arrive in swarms ‖ 他一走出法庭，记者便～而上。Reporters swarmed around him as soon as he stepped out of the court.

酆 fēng

【酆都城】Fēngdūchéng〈名〉nether world

féng

冯（馮）Féng〈名〉Feng [surname]

▸píng

逢 féng〈动〉come upon: ～人就问/说

ask/tell whoever happens to come one's way ‖ ～单/双日开放 open on odd/even days of the month ▸每～佳节倍思亲
【逢场作戏】féngchǎng-zuòxì〈成〉**1**（指街头艺人）put on a performance when occasion arises **2**（随便应酬）play a game
【逢集】féngjí〈动〉be on market day: ～购物 go shopping on market day ‖ 这里星期日～。Sunday is market day here.
【逢年过节】féngnián-guòjié〈成〉on New Year's Day and other festivals
【逢人说项】féngrén-shuōxiàng〈成〉speak well of sb. before everybody
【逢凶化吉】féngxiōng-huàjí〈成〉turn bad luck into good: 他遇事总能～。He can always turn situations to his advantage.
【逢迎】féngyíng〈动〉curry favour with: 百般～ flatter and toady by every means possible ▸阿谀～

缝（縫）féng〈动〉sew: ～衣服

make clothes ‖ ～伤口 stitch up a wound ▸fèng
【缝补】féngbǔ〈动〉mend: ～衣服 mend clothes ‖ 她把衣服～好了。She has mended the coat.
【缝缝连连】féngfeng-liánlián〈动〉mend
【缝合】fénghé〈动〉sew up: ～伤口 sew up a wound
【缝纫】féngrèn〈动〉sew: 教孩子～ teach children sewing ‖ ～车间 tailoring workshop
【缝纫机】féngrènjī〈名〉sewing machine
【缝制】féngzhì〈动〉make: ～衬衣 make a shirt
【缝缀】féngzhuì〈动〉patch: 她把杂色布～在一起做了个坐垫套。She made a patchwork cover for the cushion.

fěng

讽（諷）fěng〈动〉**1**（讥讽）

mock: ▸讥～，冷嘲热～ **2**（劝告）remonstrate implicitly: ▸～谏，借古～今 **3**〈书〉（背诵）chant: ▸～诵
【讽嘲】fěngcháo〈动〉sneer at: ～的口吻 sarcastic tone
【讽刺】fěngcì〈动〉satirize: ～小说 satirical novel ‖ 辛辣的～ bitter satire ‖ 他的话带有强烈的～意味。His remarks are dripping with sarcasm.
【讽刺文学】fěngcì wénxué〈名〉satire
【讽谏】fěngjiàn〈动〉〈书〉remonstrate tactically
【讽诵】fěngsòng〈动〉〈书〉read aloud with intonation and expression: ～古诗 read out an ancient poem with great expression
【讽喻】fěngyù〈名〉allegory: ～诗 allegorical poem

唪 fěng〈动〉recite loudly

【唪经】fěngjīng〈动〉chant a scripture

fèng

凤（鳳）fèng〈名〉phoenix

> 凤
>
> Also known in Chinese as *fenghuang* (凤凰). In ancient times, the phoenix was known as king of the birds. The male phoenix is called *feng* and the female *huang*. The phoenix has the head of a bird, the neck of a snake, the throat of a swallow, the back of a tortoise and the tail of a fish. It has five colours and stands six feet in height. In ancient times, the phoenix was associated with the power of the emperor. Today it is still regarded as propitious and appears in many decorative designs.

【凤蝶】fèngdié〈名〉swallowtail (butterfly)
【凤冠】fèngguān〈名〉phoenix coronet
【凤凰】fènghuáng〈名〉phoenix
【凤梨】fènglí〈名〉pineapple
【凤毛麟角】fèngmáo-línjiǎo〈成〉as rare as phoenix feathers and unicorn horns: 好的电工在这一带如～。Good electricians are like gold dust round here.
【凤尾鱼】fèngwěiyú〈名〉long-tailed anchovy
【凤尾竹】fèngwěizhú〈名〉fern-leaf hedge bamboo
【凤仙花】fèngxiānhuā〈名〉garden balsam
【凤眼】fèngyǎn〈名〉upwardly slanting eyes

奉 fèng

A〈动〉**1**（献给）submit respectfully: 双

f

手～上 present with both hands **2**（接受）receive: ～命 at sb.'s command **3**（尊重）revere: ～为典范 be revered as a model ‖ 被～为权威 be looked upon as authoritative **4**（信仰）believe in: 改～基督 convert to Christianity **5**（侍候）wait on: ▸～养
B〈副〉〈敬〉honourably: ▸～告, ～陪
【奉承】fèngcheng〈动〉flatter: 爱听～话 love flattery ‖ 他讨厌别人～。He hates people trying to butter him up. ▸阿谀～
【奉达】fèngdá〈动〉〈书〉〈敬〉inform: 特此～。I hereby inform you of it.
【奉复】fèngfù〈动〉〈书〉〈敬〉reply: 谨此～。I hereby present my reply.
【奉告】fènggào〈动〉〈敬〉inform: 详情我当面～。I will give the details in person. ‖ 无可～。No comment.
【奉公】fènggōng〈动〉serve the public: ▸克己～
【奉公守法】fènggōng-shǒufǎ〈成〉follow the law when conducting public business: ～的公民 law-abiding citizens
【奉还】fènghuán〈动〉〈敬〉gratefully return: 原物～ return sth. intact
【奉令】fènglìng = 奉命 fèngmìng
【奉命】fèngmìng〈动〉follow orders: ～回国 return from abroad as ordered ‖ 奉老板之命 by order of the boss ‖ 我也只是～行事。I was just under orders to do it.
【奉陪】fèngpéi〈动〉〈敬〉keep sb. company: ～到底 keep sb. company to the very end ‖ 恕难～。I won't be able to keep you company.
【奉劝】fèngquàn〈动〉〈敬〉may I suggest: ～你少喝点酒。I suggest that you try not to drink too much. ‖ ～你少要花招。May I suggest that you stop playing tricks?
【奉若神明】fèngruòshénmíng〈成〉worship sb. as a god
【奉使】fèngshǐ〈动〉〈书〉serve as envoy by order: ～西欧 go to Western Europe as ordered
【奉送】fèngsòng〈动〉〈敬〉offer as a gift
【奉托】fèngtuō〈动〉〈书〉〈敬〉request sb. to do sth.
【奉为圭臬】fèngwéi-guīniè〈成〉hold up as a model
【奉献】fèngxiàn〈动〉offer up: 把青春～给祖国 dedicate one's youth to one's motherland ‖ 无私～ dedicate oneself selflessly
【奉行】fèngxíng〈动〉pursue: ～独立自主的外交政策 pursue an independent foreign policy
【奉养】fèngyǎng〈动〉support and attend to: ～老人是传统美德。It is regarded as a traditional virtue to take good care of one's parents.
【奉迎】fèngyíng〈动〉**1** = 逢迎 féngyíng **2**〈敬〉（迎接）have the honour of welcoming: 他是专程来～各位的。He has come here with the express purpose of welcoming all of you.
【奉赠】fèngzèng〈动〉〈书〉〈敬〉present with respect
【奉旨】fèngzhǐ〈动〉be at the emperor's order

俸 fèng〈名〉salary: 薪～ pay
【俸禄】fènglù〈名〉〈旧〉government salary

缝（縫） fèng〈名〉**1**（接合处）seam: 无～长筒袜 seamless stockings ▸无～钢管 **2**（缝隙）crack: 岩～ crevice in the rock ‖ 门开了一道～。The door opened just a crack. ▸见～插针 ▸féng
【缝隙】fèngxì〈名〉crack: 透过墙上～向里看 peep through a crack in the wall ‖ 地板有了～。There were cracks in the floorboard.
【缝子】fèngzi〈名〉〈口〉crack: 墙裂了道～。There is a crack in the wall.

fó

佛 fó〈名〉**1**（佛陀）Buddha: 拜～ worship Buddha ‖ 供～ enshrine Buddha **2**（佛教徒）Buddhist: ▸立地成～ **3**（佛教）Buddhism: 信～ believe in Buddhism ▸～经 **4**（佛像）statue of Buddha: 一尊～ a statue of Buddha ‖ 石～ stone Buddha ▸卧～ **5**（佛经）Buddhist scripture: 诵～ recite Buddhist scriptures ▸念～ ▸fú
【佛得角】Fódéjiǎo〈名〉Cape Verde: ～共和国 Republic of Cape Verde ‖ ～人 Cape Verdean
【佛典】fódiǎn = 佛经 fójīng
【佛法】fófǎ〈名〉**1**（指教义）Buddhist doctrine: 传布～ spread Buddhism **2**（指法力）power of Buddha: ～无边。The power of Buddha is unlimited.
【佛光】fóguāng〈名〉**1**（指光明）light of Buddha: ～普照 omnipresent light of Buddha **2**（指光辉）Buddhist radiance **3**［物理］anticorona
【佛号】fóhào〈名〉Amitabha: 口诵～ chant Amitabha
【佛家】Fójiā〈名〉**1**（指僧侣）Buddhist **2**（指佛教思想）Buddhism
【佛教】Fójiào〈名〉Buddhism: ～寺院 Buddhist monastery ‖ ～徒 Buddhist

> **佛教**
> Founded by Sakyamuni in the 6th century BC in ancient India (modern Nepal), Buddhism spread to China at the end of the Western Han Dynasty. It reached its height in the Sui and Tang Dynasties, developing into many sects with indigenous characteristics. The most influential of these was the *Chan* (*Zen*) sect (禅宗). People living in Tibet and Inner Mongolia followed Tibetan Buddhism (Lamaism). Monks are known as *heshang* (和尚) or *sengren* (僧人). Nuns are known as *nigu* (尼姑). Buddhism has had a marked influence on Chinese philosophy, literature, art and folk customs. Wutai, Emei, Putuo and Jiuhua mountains are the four holy mountains in China associated with Buddhism.

【佛经】fójīng〈名〉Buddhist scripture
【佛龛】fókān〈名〉niche for a statue of Buddha
【佛口蛇心】fókǒu-shéxīn〈成〉honeyed words but evil intent
【佛兰芒人】Fólánmángrén〈名〉Fleming
【佛兰芒语】Fólánmángyǔ ▸p. 918〈名〉Flemish
【佛罗里达州】Fóluólǐdázhōu〈名〉Florida
【佛门】fómén〈名〉Buddhism: 皈依～ be converted to Buddhism ‖ ～弟子 Buddhist follower ‖ ～净地 sacred Buddhist place
【佛蒙特州】Fóméngtèzhōu〈名〉Vermont
【佛事】fóshì〈名〉Buddhist ceremony: 做～ engage in a Buddhist service
【佛手】fóshǒu〈名〉［植物］Buddha's hand
【佛手瓜】fóshǒuguā〈名〉［植物］chayote
【佛寺】fósì〈名〉Buddhist temple
【佛塔】fótǎ〈名〉pagoda: 修建～ build a pagoda

> **佛塔**
> A place for worship and for storing Buddhist relics (bones of the Buddha), Buddhist images, sutras, and the remains of monks. Pagodas evolved from Indian stupas. From the end of the Han Dynasty, Chinese pagodas have consisted of a crypt, often referred to as an underground palace, a base, the body of the pagoda, and the top surmounted by a Buddhist temple made up of a pedestal, a lotus, an alms bowl, a wheel, and a precious pearl. There are usually an odd number of storeys. The underground palace, where the relics are stored, is directly under the base of the pagoda.

【佛堂】fótáng〈名〉Buddhist shrine
【佛头着粪】fótóu-zhuófèn〈成〉〈喻〉desecrate
【佛陀】Fótuó〈名〉Buddha
【佛像】fóxiàng〈名〉statue of Buddha
【佛学】fóxué〈名〉Buddhist philosophy
【佛牙】fóyá〈名〉tooth relic of Buddha
【佛爷】fóye〈名〉Buddha
【佛珠】fózhū〈名〉rosary: 手捻～ twirl one's beads
【佛祖】fózǔ〈名〉Buddhist patriarch

fǒu

缶 fǒu〈名〉**1**〈书〉（指瓦器）*fou* [ancient earthen wine vessel] **2**（指乐器）*fou* [ancient percussion instrument]: 击～ beat the *fou*

否 fǒu
A〈动〉deny: ▸～定, ～认
B〈副〉**1**〈书〉（表否定）no **2**（表疑问）[used at the end of a question] or not: 当～? Is it appropriate? ‖ 知～? Do you know it? ‖ 可～帮我一把? I wonder if you could do me a favour?
C〈助〉〈书〉[used at the end of a question]: 知其人～? Have you any knowledge of him?
▸pǐ
【否定】fǒudìng **A**〈动〉negate: ～某人的意见 go against sb.'s opinion ‖ ～一切 negate everything ‖ ～以前的判断 reverse the previous judgement **B**〈形〉negative: 作～回答 answer in the negative ‖ ～形式 negative form
【否定句】fǒudìngjù〈名〉negative sentence
【否决】fǒujué〈动〉veto: ～提案 veto a proposal ‖ 遭到～ be overruled
【否决权】fǒujuéquán〈名〉power of veto: 有～ have power of veto ‖ 行使～ exercise a veto
【否认】fǒurèn〈动〉deny: ～与抢劫案有牵连 deny any involvement in the robbery ‖ 断然～ categorically deny
【否则】fǒuzé〈连〉otherwise: 你快点走吧，～会误了火车。You'd better hurry up; otherwise you'll miss the train. ‖ 举起手来，～我要开枪了。Hands up, or I'll shoot.

fū

夫[1] fū〈名〉**1**（丈夫）husband: 有妇之～ married man ▸～妻, ～唱妇随 **2**（成年男子）man: ▸匹～, 一～当关，万～莫

开 3（体力劳动者） manual labourer: ▸农～, 渔～

夫²（伕） fū 〈名〉〈旧〉 conscripted labourer: ▸～役

▸fú

【夫唱妇随】 fūchàng-fùsuí 〈成〉 conjugal harmony

【夫妇】 fūfù 〈名〉 husband and wife: 新婚～ newly-weds

【夫妻】 fūqī 〈名〉 husband and wife: ～恩爱 conjugal affection ‖ 模范～ model couple ‖ 结为～ join in marriage ▸结发～

【夫妻店】 fūqīdiàn 〈名〉 family-run shop 〈英〉; mom-and-pop shop 〈美〉

【夫权】 fūquán 〈名〉〈旧〉 power of a husband over his wife

【夫人】 fūren 〈名〉 1（妻子） wife: 总经理及其～ general manager and his wife ‖ 请代向您的～问好。 Please remember me to your wife. 2（指称谓） Mrs: 第一～ First Lady ‖ 撒切尔～ Mrs Thatcher

【夫婿】 fūxù 〈名〉〈书〉 husband

【夫役】 fūyì 〈名〉〈旧〉 1（指服劳役） servants 2（指做杂役） coolie

【夫子】 fūzǐ 〈旧〉〈名〉 1（称学者） master: 孔～ Confucius ‖ 孟～ Mencius 2（称老师） 谨遵～教诲。 I will follow your advice to the letter. 3（称丈夫） my husband 4〈贬〉（指迂腐的人） pedant: 老～ old pedant

呋 fū

【呋喃】 fūnán 〈名〉［化学］ furan

肤（膚） fū

A 〈名〉 skin: ▸切～之痛

B 〈形〉 superficial and shallow

【肤泛】 fūfàn 〈形〉 superficial: ～之论 shallow argument

【肤皮潦草】 fūpí-liáocǎo = 浮皮潦草 fúpí-liáocǎo

【肤浅】 fūqiǎn 〈形〉 superficial: ～的认识 superficial understanding ‖ 这人很～。 He is very shallow.

【肤色】 fūsè 〈名〉 skin colour: 各种～的人 people of all colours

麸（麩） fū 〈名〉 bran

【麸皮】 fūpí 〈名〉 bran

【麸子】 fūzi 〈名〉 bran

趺 fū 〈名〉 1 = 跗 fū 2（指石座） pedestal of a stone tablet

【趺坐】 fūzuò 〈动〉 sit cross-legged in meditation

跗 fū 〈名〉［生理］ instep: ～关节 tarsal joint

【跗骨】 fūgǔ 〈名〉 tarsus

【跗蹠】 fūzhí 〈名〉 tarsometatarsus

稃 fū 〈名〉 husk

孵 fū 〈动〉 hatch: ～小鸡 hatch chicks

【孵化】 fūhuà 〈动〉 incubate: 人工～ artificial incubation

【孵化器】 fūhuàqì 〈名〉 incubator

【孵育】 fūyù 〈动〉 hatch: 刚～出来的蝌蚪/小鸡 newly-hatched tadpoles/chicks

ℹ 否定

■ 英语的 no 和 not 都可以翻译成汉语的“不”或“没/没有”，但它们的具体用法在英语里是不同的。

no 的用法

■ 用在名词前面：

没有牛奶了
= There is no milk left

我们没机会赢这场比赛
= There is no chance of our winning the match

我家里没筷子
= I have no chopsticks at home

她没有杂志读
= She has no magazines to read

■ 用于一些固定短语中：

欺侮人的人不比罪犯好到哪儿去
= Bullies are no better than criminals

不少于 20 人听了演讲
= No fewer than twenty people attended the lecture

参加聚会的不超过 10 人
= No more than 10 people came to the party

这位歌手不再受欢迎了
= The singer is no longer popular

not 的用法

■ not 用来否定谓语或谓语的一部分，包括实义动词如 like 和 go、系动词 be、助动词如 will 和 shall、情态动词如 may 和 can 等。not 的缩写形式是 n't：

我昨晚没去酒吧
= I did not go to the pub last night

这家商店不卖香烟
= The shop doesn't sell cigarettes

他们没有法语词典
= They don't have French dictionaries

李红不是演员
= Li Hong is not an actress

这花瓶不很漂亮
= The vase is not very beautiful

我明天不去看电影
= I won't go to the cinema tomorrow

会议还没开始
= The meeting has not (yet) started

他不在看电视
= He is not watching TV

我不知道她来不来
= I don't know if she is coming or not

我不会游泳
= I can't swim

你不许那样做
= You mustn't do that

■ 有些汉语惯用说法如“没学问”、“没礼貌”等，在翻译成英语时可用“am/is/are + not + 形容词”的形式：

我没钱
= I am not rich

这些小说没意思
= These novels are not interesting

这个乐队没有名气
= The band is not famous

■ 用于否定动词不定式：

老师告诉我们上课不要迟到
= The teacher told us not to be late for class

我请她不要再那样做了
= I asked her not to do that any more

■ 用于否定一句话或几个词：

我喜欢读书，不喜欢读杂志
= I like reading books but not magazines

是小梅帮了我，不是小陈
= It was Xiao Mei who helped me out, not Xiao Chen

no 和 not 用于回答疑问句

■ 当问题以肯定的形式提出时，要用 no 来表示否定的回答，汉英一致：

你把信寄出了吗？—— 没有，我忘了
= Have you posted the letter? — No, I forgot

你想喝点什么吗？—— 不用了，谢谢
= Would you like something to drink? — No, thanks

你昨天去上班了吗？—— 没有，我病了
= Did you go to work yesterday? — No, I was ill

你懂汉语吗？—— 不，我不懂
= Do you understand Chinese? — No, I don't

你会骑摩托车吗？—— 不，我不会
= Can you ride a motorbike? — No, I can't

■ 当问题以否定的形式提出时，如回答是肯定的，汉语使用“不”，英语则用 yes；如回答是否定的，汉语用“是/是的”，英语则用 no：

你不累吗？—— 不，我累
= Aren't you tired? — Yes, I'm tired

你没见过马兰吗？—— 不，我见过
= Haven't you seen Ma Lan? — Yes, I have

附近没有家电影院吗？—— 是的，没有
= Isn't there a cinema nearby? — No, there isn't

你没去过香港吗？—— 是的，没去过
= Haven't you been to Hong Kong? — No, I haven't

■ 在回答反意疑问句时，如陈述部分是肯定的，汉英都用“不”来否定陈述部分。如果陈述部分是否定的，汉英恰好相反：如回答是肯定的，汉语使用“不”，英语用 yes；如回答是否定的，汉语用“是/是的”，英语用 no：

他喜欢踢足球，不是吗？—— 不，他不喜欢
= He likes playing football, doesn't he? — No, he doesn't

这张桌子是新的，是不是？—— 是，是新的
= The table is new, isn't it? — Yes, it is

你不是马小姐，是吗？—— 不，我是
= You aren't Miss Ma, are you? — Yes, I am

这不便宜，是吗？—— 是的，不便宜
= It isn't cheap, is it? — No, it isn't

敷 fū〈动〉1（搽）apply: ～粉 apply powder ‖ 给伤口～药膏 apply ointment to the wound 2（铺开）lay out: ▸～设 3（够）suffice: 不～应用 be insufficient for use ▸入不～出

【敷陈】fūchén〈动〉〈书〉elaborate

【敷料】fūliào〈名〉［医学］dressing

【敷设】fūshè〈动〉lay: ～电缆 lay electric cables ‖ ～管道 lay pipelines ‖ ～地雷 lay mines

【敷衍】fūyǎn〈动〉1（应付）go through the motions: 采取～的态度 take a perfunctory attitude ‖ 他～了几句就走了。 He just made a few casual remarks before he left. 2（勉强维持）scarcely get by: 汤姆一家靠他那点收入只够～一周。 Tom's meagre income was barely enough for his family to get through a week.

【敷衍了事】fūyǎn-liǎoshì〈成〉muddle through one's work: ～的检讨 perfunctory self-criticism

【敷衍塞责】fūyǎn-sèzé〈成〉go through the motions of performing one's duty: 不能抱～的态度。 You shouldn't just go through the motions.

fú

夫 fú

A〈代〉〈书〉1（这）this;（那）that: ～也不语。 That man does not talk. 2（他）he: ～为其君勤也。 He just served his master.

B〈助〉1（用在句首）[used at the beginning of a sentence to introduce a subject]: ～战，勇气也。 Fighting requires courage. 2（用在句末）[used at the end of or in the middle of a sentence with an exclamatory force]: 悲～! That's too sad!

▸fū

弗 fú〈副〉〈书〉not: 自愧～如 feel ashamed of one's inferiority

【弗吉尼亚州】Fújíníyàzhōu〈名〉Virginia

【弗里敦】Fúlǐdūn〈名〉Freetown

【弗林特郡】Fúlíntèjùn〈名〉Flintshire

【弗马纳郡】Fúmǎnàjùn〈名〉Fermanagh

伏[1] fú

A〈动〉1（趴）lie prostrate: ～地 lie out on the ground 2（靠）lean over: ～在桌子上睡着了 fall asleep leaning against a table ▸～案 3（低下去）go down: 小船一起一～，随波飘荡。 The small boat bobbed up and down with the waves. ▸倒～，起～ 4（隐藏）hide: 昼～夜出 hide by day and come out at night ▸～兵，危机四～ 5（屈服）yield 6（降伏）vanquish: ▸降龙～虎

B〈名〉hot season: ▸入～，三～

伏[2] fú = 伏特 fútè

【伏安】fú'ān〈名〉［物理］volt-ampere: 千～ kilo volt-ampere

【伏案】fú'àn〈动〉bend over a table: ～读书/写作/作画 bend over one's desk to read /write/paint

【伏笔】fúbǐ〈名〉foreshadowing: 埋下～ foreshadow

【伏兵】fúbīng〈名〉ambush: 设下～ lay an ambush ‖ ～四起 with troops ambushing on all sides

【伏尔加格勒】Fú'ěrjiāgélè〈名〉Volgograd

【伏尔加河】Fú'ěrjiāhé ▸**p. 294**〈名〉Volga River

【伏法】fúfǎ〈动〉be put to death: 罪犯已于昨日～。 The criminal was executed yesterday.

【伏击】fújī〈动〉ambush: ～敌人 ambush the enemy ‖ 遭到～ get caught in an ambush ‖ ～圈 ambush ring

【伏暑】fúshǔ〈名〉dog days

【伏特】fútè〈量〉［电气］volt: 220～ 220 volts ‖ ～计 voltmeter

【伏特加】fútèjiā〈名〉vodka

【伏天】fútiān〈名〉dog days

【伏贴】fútiē〈形〉1（合适）fit perfectly: 这件夹克我穿着很～。 The jacket fits me perfectly. 2 = 服帖 fútiē 1

【伏卧】fúwò〈动〉lie on one's stomach

【伏羲】Fúxī ▸**p. 274**〈名〉fu xi [legendary ruler of great antiquity]

【伏线】fúxiàn = 伏笔 fúbǐ

【伏汛】fúxùn〈名〉summer flood: ～期 summer flood period

【伏诛】fúzhū〈动〉〈旧〉be executed

【伏罪】fúzuì = 服罪 fúzuì

凫（鳬） fú

A〈名〉wild duck

B〈动〉swim: 在湖中～水 swim in a lake

【凫茈】fúcí〈名〉〈古〉water chestnut

扶 fú〈动〉1（用手支撑）support oneself: ～着墙站起来 prop oneself up against a wall ‖ ～杖而立 support oneself with a stick 2（用手扶起）help sb. up: ～他站起来 help him up ‖ 让我～你呢，还是你自己走呢? Do you want me to support you, or can you manage to walk on your own? ▸～苗，搀～ 3（扶助）help: 大家应该互相帮～。 We should help each other. ‖ 荷花虽好，还要绿叶～。For all its beauty, the lotus needs green leaves to set it off. ▸～贫，～植，救死～伤 4（勉强支撑）try hard to do sth. despite illness: ▸～病

【扶病】fúbìng〈动〉work in spite of illness: ～工作 go on working in spite of one's illness

【扶持】fúchí〈动〉support: ～老人过马路 help an elderly man across the street ‖ ～正气 encourage healthy trends ‖ ～乡镇企业 help develop township enterprises ‖ 在政府的～下，企业有了起色。 With the help of the government, the enterprise has taken a turn for the better.

【扶乩】fújī = 扶箕 fújī

【扶箕】fújī〈名〉planchette writing

【扶老携幼】fúlǎo-xiéyòu〈成〉help the aged and lead the young

【扶鸾】fúluán = 扶箕 fújī

【扶苗】fúmiáo〈动〉straighten up seedlings

【扶贫】fúpín〈动〉aid the poor: ～工作 poverty relief work ‖ ～计划 poverty alleviation programme

【扶桑】fúsāng〈名〉1（指灌木）legendary mulberry tree in the ocean where the sun is supposed to rise 2 Fúsāng〈旧〉（日本）Japan: 东渡～ go east to Japan

【扶手】fúshǒu〈名〉1（扶杆）handrail: 楼梯～ banister 2（指椅子的）armrest: ～椅 armchair

【扶疏】fúshū〈形〉〈书〉luxuriant and well-spaced: 花木～。 The flowers are luxuriant and well-spread out.

【扶梯】fútī〈名〉staircase

【扶危济困】fúwēi-jìkùn〈成〉help those in plight or in peril

【扶养】fúyǎng〈动〉1（指长辈）support: ～孤寡老人 provide for old widows and widowers ‖ ～父母 support one's parents 2（指子女）bring up: ～孩子 support one's children ‖ 把子女～成人 bring up one's children

【扶养费】fúyǎngfèi〈名〉（指给前配偶）alimony;（指给子女）child support (payment)

【扶摇直上】fúyáo-zhíshàng〈成〉skyrocket: 他的事业～。 His career took off like a rocket.

【扶掖】fúyè〈动〉〈书〉support: ～后辈 support the younger generation

【扶正】fúzhèng〈动〉〈旧〉[of a concubine] be elevated to the status of wife

【扶正祛邪】fúzhèng-qūxié〈成〉［中医］strengthen body resistance and eliminate disease

【扶植】fúzhí〈动〉nurture: ～地方工业 foster the growth of local industries ‖ ～新生事物 foster new things ‖ ～新政权 prop up a new regime

【扶助】fúzhù〈动〉assist: ～困难户 give aid to poor families ‖ ～老弱 help the old and the weak

芙 fú

【芙蕖】fúqú〈名〉〈书〉lotus

【芙蓉】fúróng〈名〉1（木芙蓉）cotton rose hibiscus 2（荷花）lotus: ▸出水～

芾 fú〈形〉〈书〉luxuriant

▸fèi

苿 fú

【芣苢】fúyǐ〈名〉〈古〉［植物］Asiatic plantain

佛（彿） fú ▸仿佛 fǎngfú

▸fó

孚 fú〈动〉inspire confidence in: 不～众望 command no public confidence ‖ 深～众望 enjoy great popularity

拂 fú〈动〉1（轻轻擦过）touch lightly: 春风～面。 A spring breeze caresses the cheeks. 2（拂拭）flick: ～去灰尘 flick away the dust 3（甩动）fling: ▸～袖 4〈书〉（违背）go against: ～耳 grate on the ears ▸～意

【拂尘】fúchén〈名〉horsetail whisk

【拂拂】fúfú〈形〉blowing gently: 凉风～。 A cool breeze is blowing gently.

【拂逆】fúnì〈动〉〈书〉go against: ～人意 go against sb.'s wishes

【拂拭】fúshì〈动〉〈书〉wipe off: ～桌上的灰尘 dust the table

【拂晓】fúxiǎo〈名〉dawn: ～动身 set/start off at dawn ‖ ～前发起反攻 launch a counter-attack before daybreak

【拂袖】fúxiù〈动〉〈书〉shake out one's sleeves in anger: ～而起 shake out one's sleeves and get up ‖ ～而去 storm off

【拂煦】fúxù〈动〉〈书〉blow a warm pleasant breeze: 春风～。 The spring wind is blowing warm.

【拂意】fúyì〈动〉〈书〉go against sb.'s wishes: 不忍拂其意 not have the heart to turn sb. down

苻 Fú〈名〉Fu [surname]

服 fú

A〈名〉1（服装）clothes: 演出～ costumes ▸～装，便～，校～ 2（丧服）

mourning dress: 她有～在身。 She is in mourning.
B〈动〉 **1**（穿） wear: ▸～丧 **2**（服用） take: 口～ take orally ‖ 日～三次 to be taken three times a day ▸～毒, ～用 **3**（承当） serve: ～兵役 serve in the army ▸～刑, ～役 **4**（信服） obey: 不～裁判 refuse to accept the referee's ruling ‖ 不～父母管教 disobey one's parents ‖ 口～心不～ concede but without one's heart being in it ▸佩～, 心～口～ **5**（使信服） convince: 以理～人 convince by reasoning ▸说～, 征～ **6**（适应） be accustomed to: ▸水土不～
▸fù
【服从】fúcóng〈动〉 obey: ～裁判 abide by the referee's decision ‖ ～命令 obey orders ‖ 少数～多数。 The minority submits to the majority.
【服毒】fúdú〈动〉 take poison: ～自杀 commit suicide by taking poison
【服法】fúfǎ〈动〉 submit to the law: 认罪～ plead guilty and submit oneself to the law
【服老】fúlǎo〈动〉 reconcile oneself to old age: 不～ refuse to resign oneself to growing old
【服气】fúqì〈动〉 accept: 不～ be unhappy
【服软】fúruǎn〈动〉 **1**（服输） admit defeat: 他不会在困难面前～。 He will never give in in difficult situations. **2**（认错） acknowledge one's mistake **3**（听从劝说） yield to persuasion: ～不服硬 yield to persuasion but not to coercion
【服丧】fúsāng〈动〉 be in mourning: ～期满。 The mourning period has ended.
【服色】fúsè〈名〉 style and colour of clothes: 民族～ styles and colours of ethnic garments
【服式】fúshì〈名〉 style of clothes
【服饰】fúshì〈名〉 dress: ～华丽 be splendidly dressed
【服侍】fúshì〈动〉 wait on: ～父母 attend to one's parents ‖ ～病人 take care of the sick
【服输】fúshū〈动〉 acknowledge defeat: 他从不～。 He has never accepted failure.
【服帖】fútiē〈形〉 **1**（顺从） obedient: 那匹野马被驯得服服帖帖的。 The wild horse has been trained to be docile and obedient. ‖ 他对顶头上司很～。 He is obedient to his immediate superior. **2**（妥当） well-arranged: 诸事均已安排～。 Everything is properly arranged.
【服务】fúwù〈动〉 serve: ～周到 render excellent services ‖ 提供～ provide a service ‖ 上门～ doorstep service ‖ 售后～ after-sales service ‖ 她在银行～了二十年。 She served in the bank for 20 years.
【服务行业】fúwù hángyè〈名〉 service industry
【服务器】fúwùqì〈名〉［计算机］server: 局域网～ LAN server
【服务商】fúwùshāng〈名〉 service provider: 电信～ telecommunications service provider
【服务台】fúwùtái〈名〉 service desk
【服务员】fúwùyuán ▸**p. 966**〈名〉 attendant
【服刑】fúxíng〈动〉 serve a prison term: ～期满 complete one's term of imprisonment ‖ 在狱中～ serve a sentence in jail
【服药】fúyào〈动〉 take medicine: 按时～ take medicine on time
【服役】fúyì〈动〉 **1**（指兵役） be on active service: ～期间 during one's term of military service **2**〈旧〉（指劳役） do corvée labour
【服膺】fúyīng〈动〉〈书〉 **1**（牢记在心） bear in mind **2**（信服） feel truly convinced: ～真理 subject oneself to truth
【服用】fúyòng〈动〉 take: ～禁药 take drugs ‖ 空腹～ take on an empty stomach
【服装】fúzhuāng〈名〉 dress: 民族～ ethnic clothing ‖ ～款式 clothing style ‖ 儿童～ children's clothes
【服罪】fúzuì〈动〉 plead guilty: 不～ plead not guilty ‖ 低头～ bow one's head and plead guilty

怫 fú〈形〉〈书〉 glowering
【怫然】fúrán〈形〉〈书〉 glowering

绋（紼） fú〈名〉〈古〉 **1**（大绳） thick rope **2**（牵引灵柩的大绳） tow rope for a bier: ▸执～

茯 fú
【茯苓】fúlíng〈名〉［植物］ *fuling* [edible fungus]: ～饼 *fuling* cake

氟 fú〈名〉［化学］ **1**（指气体元素） fluorine: 含～牙膏 toothpaste containing fluorine **2**（氟利昂） freon: 无～冰箱 freon-free refrigerator
【氟利昂】fúlì'áng〈名〉［化学］ freon

俘 fú
A〈动〉 capture: 被～ be taken prisoner ▸～获
B〈名〉 prisoner: 遣～工作 repatriation of prisoners ▸战～
【俘获】fúhuò〈动〉 capture: ～大批敌兵 capture lots of enemy soldiers
【俘虏】fúlǔ **A**〈动〉 capture: 此战我们～了敌军一个营。 We captured an enemy battalion in the battle. **B**〈名〉 captive: 交换～ exchange captives ‖ 优待～的政策 policy of lenient treatment to prisoners of war

洑 fú〈书〉
A〈名〉 whirlpool
B〈动〉 [of water] flow underground
▸fù

莩 fú〈名〉〈书〉 **1**（指芦苇杆） white membrane inside reed stalk **2**（指种子） seed coat
▸piǎo

蚨 fú ▸青蚨 qīngfú

浮 fú
A〈动〉 **1**（指在表面） float: 使沉船～出水面 float a sunken ship ‖ 她脸上～起一丝笑容。 A faint smile played on her face. ‖ 油～在水面上。 Oil floats on water. ▸～沉, ～桥, ～云 **2**〈方〉（游） swim: 他能一口气～到对岸。 He could swim across in one breath. ▸～水 **3**（指在空中） move in the air: 天上～着几朵白云。 A few white clouds were floating in the sky. **4**（超过） exceed: ～额 surplus number ▸人～于事
B〈形〉 **1**（指在表面） superficial: ▸～雕, ～土 **2**（可移动） movable: ▸～财 **3**（暂时） temporary: ～支 provisional expenditure **4**（浮躁） frivolous: 他人太～, 不能担此重任。 He is too frivolous to take the important position. **5**（空虚） hollow: ▸～夸, ～名
【浮报】fúbào〈动〉 give inflated figures in a report: ～产量 report an inflated output figure
【浮标】fúbiāo〈名〉 buoy
【浮冰】fúbīng〈名〉 drifting ice
【浮财】fúcái〈名〉 movable property
【浮尘】fúchén〈名〉 surface dust
【浮沉】fúchén〈动〉 go up and down: 与世～ follow social trends ‖ 宦海～ ups and downs of officialdom
【浮筹】fúchóu〈名〉［金融］ floating stock
【浮出水面】fúchū shuǐmiàn〈成〉〈喻〉 become evident
【浮词】fúcí〈名〉 useless remarks: ～艳句 flowery but hollow remarks
【浮厝】fúcuò〈动〉〈旧〉 place a coffin in a temporary shelter pending burial
【浮荡】fúdàng **A**〈动〉 float: 在湖面～ float on the lake **B**〈形〉 loose: ～女子 loose woman
【浮雕】fúdiāo〈名〉 relief
【浮吊】fúdiào〈名〉［机械］ floating crane
【浮动】fúdòng〈动〉 **1**（漂浮移动） float: 树叶在湖面上～。 Leaves were floating about on the lake. **2**（不固定） fluctuate: ～汇率 floating exchange rate ‖ ～收入 fluctuating income ‖ 蔬菜价格随季节～。 The prices of vegetables fluctuate with the season. **3**（不稳定） be unstable: 物价飞涨, 人心～。 With prices soaring, there is a growing anxiety among the people.
【浮泛】fúfàn **A**〈动〉 **1**〈书〉（指在水面） float in water: 轻舟在湖面上～。 A small boat is floating on the lake. **2**（流露） reveal: 她脸上～着幸福的神情。 Her face beamed with happiness. **B**〈形〉 superficial: ～的研究 superficial study
【浮光掠影】fúguāng-lüèyǐng〈成〉 skim over the surface: ～地看一看 take a cursory look
【浮华】fúhuá〈形〉 showy: ～的生活 ostentatious lifestyle ‖ 文辞～ florid language
【浮滑】fúhuá〈形〉 slick and frivolous: ～习气 slick and frivolous habits
【浮家泛宅】fújiā-fànzhái〈成〉 live on a boat
【浮夸】fúkuā〈形〉 pompous: ～的言辞 pretentious language ‖ ～作风 tendency to boast and exaggerate
【浮力】fúlì〈名〉［物理］ buoyancy: 测试船的～ test a boat for its buoyancy ‖ 咸水的～比淡水大。 Salt water has greater buoyancy than fresh water.
【浮面】fúmiàn〈名〉 surface: 把汤～的油撇掉 skim the grease from the soup ‖ 他只是～上客气。 His politeness was only on the surface.
【浮名】fúmíng〈名〉 hollow reputation: 不慕～ seek no reputation
【浮皮】fúpí〈名〉 **1**（表皮） outer skin **2**（表面） surface
【浮皮潦草】fúpí-liáocǎo〈成〉 cursory: ～的作风 cursory style ‖ ～地检查 make a superficial inspection
【浮萍】fúpíng〈名〉 duckweed
【浮签】fúqiān〈名〉 detachable note
【浮浅】fúqiǎn〈形〉 superficial: ～的看法 superficial opinion ‖ ～的认识 superficial conception
【浮桥】fúqiáo〈名〉 pontoon bridge
【浮生】fúshēng **A**〈名〉 fleeting life: ～若梦 life is fleeting like a dream **B**〈动〉 grow floating on water: 浮萍～在水面上。 Duckweed grows floating on water.
【浮石】fúshí〈名〉 pumice stone
【浮水】fúshuǐ〈动〉〈口〉 swim
【浮筒】fútǒng〈名〉 pontoon
【浮屠】fútú〈名〉 **1**（佛陀） Buddha

2〈书〉(和尚) Buddhist monk 3〈塔〉Buddhist stupa: 救人一命，胜造七级～。There is greater merit in saving a single life than in building a seven-storeyed pagoda.
【浮土】fútǔ〈名〉1（指土）surface soil 2（指尘）surface dust: 掸掉鞋上的～ dust the shoes
【浮现】fúxiàn〈动〉1（在脑中显现）appear in one's mind: ～在脑海里 appear in one's mind ‖ 童年的往事～在他的眼前。Childhood memories floated before his eyes. 2（显露）appear: 他脸上～出笑容。His face was lit up with a smile. ‖ 陆地从大海中～出来。Land emerged from the sea.
【浮箱】fúxiāng〈名〉buoyancy tank
【浮想】fúxiǎng A〈名〉recollections: ▸～联翩 B〈动〉recollect: ～往事 recall the past
【浮想联翩】fúxiǎng-liánpiān〈成〉thoughts float through one's mind: 看了那部电影，我～。After I saw the film I had a lot going on in my head.
【浮选】fúxuǎn〈名〉［矿业］flotation
【浮游】fúyóu〈动〉1（漂浮）float: ▸～生物 2〈书〉（漫游）wander around: ～四方 swan around
【浮游生物】fúyóu shēngwù〈名〉plankton
【浮员】fúyuán〈名〉excessive staff: 裁减～ downsize
【浮云】fúyún〈名〉floating clouds
【浮云蔽日】fúyún-bìrì〈成〉〈喻〉treacherous court officials deluding the monarch
【浮躁】fúzào〈形〉flippant and impetuous
【浮肿】fúzhǒng〈名〉oedema
【浮子】fúzi〈名〉float

f

桴[1] fú〈名〉〈书〉small raft

桴[2]（枹）fú〈名〉〈书〉drumstick

【桴鼓相应】fúgǔ-xiāngyìng〈成〉〈喻〉work in perfect coordination

符 fú

A〈名〉1（符节）tally: ▸兵～，虎～ 2（标记）symbol: ▸～号，音～ 3（指图形和线条）charm: ▸～咒，护身～
B〈动〉tally with: 与事实不～ not tally with facts ‖ 两个数目相～。The two figures tally.
【符号】fúhào〈名〉1（记号）symbol: 数学～ mathematical sign ‖ 注音～ phonetic symbol ▸标点～，化学～ 2（标志）insignia
【符合】fúhé〈动〉accord with: ～标准 be up to standard ‖ ～国际惯例 be consistent with international practice ‖ ～录取条件 meet admission requirements ‖ ～事实 correspond to facts ‖ ～要求 meet the requirements
【符节】fújié〈名〉〈古〉tally
【符箓】fúlù = 符 fú A3
【符咒】fúzhòu〈名〉magic figures and incantations

匐 fú ▸匍匐 púfú

袱 fú〈名〉cloth covering: ▸包～

幅 fú

A〈名〉1（幅面）width: 宽～布 broad-width cloth ‖ 大～油画 large oil painting ▸～员，振～ 2（幅度）margin: 大～上涨 go up sharply ▸跌～
B〈量〉[of paintings, photos, cloth, etc.]: 一～画/肖像 a picture/portrait ‖ 一～布 a length of cloth
【幅度】fúdù〈名〉extent: 大～调价 readjust prices by a large margin ‖ 增长～ growth margin
【幅员】fúyuán〈名〉size of a country's territory: ～广大 be vast in territory ‖ ～辽阔 have a vast territory

辐（輻）fú〈名〉spoke

【辐辏】fúcòu〈动〉〈书〉converge like the spokes of a wheel: 车马～。Carts and horses are clustered like spokes of a wheel.
【辐射】fúshè A〈动〉radiate: 成扇形～ radiate fanuise ‖ 大多数公路从北京向周围～。Most highways radiate out from Beijing. B〈名〉［物理］radiation: 防～ shield the radiation ▸核～，热～
【辐条】fútiáo〈名〉〈口〉spoke

蜉 fú

【蜉蝣】fúyóu〈名〉［昆虫］mayfly

福[1] fú〈名〉1（幸运）good fortune: 祸～难料。It's hard to predict which way things will go. ▸造～，享～ 2（福气）good luck: 托您的～ thanks to you ‖ 无～消受 not have the luck to enjoy ▸～气，口～

福[2] Fú〈名〉Fu [another name for Fujian Province (福建)]

【福地】fúdì〈名〉1（幸福的地方）paradise 2［道教］heavenly abode: ▸洞天～
【福尔马林】fú'ěrmǎlín〈名〉［药学］formalin
【福分】fúfen〈名〉〈口〉good fortune: 有～ have good luck ‖ ～不浅 enjoy great blessings
【福建】Fújiàn ▸p. 661〈名〉Fujian Province
【福将】fújiàng〈名〉1（指将领）general of good fortune 2（指普通人）person of good fortune
【福晋】fújìn〈名〉〈旧〉wife of a Manchu prince
【福克兰群岛】Fúkèlán qúndǎo〈名〉Falkland Islands
【福利】fúlì〈名〉well-being: 关心职工的～ have the well-being of the staff at heart ‖ 为人民谋～ work for the well-being of the people ‖ ～彩票 welfare lottery
【福利院】fúlìyuàn〈名〉home: 残疾人～ sheltered accommodation for disabled people ‖ 老人～ nursing home
【福气】fúqi〈名〉good luck: 他一辈子没受过穷，真有～。He has had the good fortune to be free from poverty all his life.
【福如东海】fúrú dōnghǎi〈成〉boundless happiness: 祝您～，寿比南山。Wish you a long life and boundless happiness.
【福寿】fúshòu〈名〉felicity and longevity: ～双全 enjoy both felicity and longevity ‖ 今天是母亲的生日，我们祝愿她～绵绵。It's Mother's birthday today. We wish her many happy returns.
【福寿螺】fúshòuluó〈名〉［动物］channeled apple snail
【福娃】fúwá〈名〉Fuwa [Beijing Olympic mascot]
【福无双至，祸不单行】fú wú shuāng zhì, huò bù dān xíng〈俗〉blessings never come in pairs and misfortunes never come singly
【福相】fúxiàng〈名〉features promising good fortune
【福星】fúxīng〈名〉lucky star: ～高照 one's star is in the ascendant
【福音】fúyīn〈名〉1［基督教］Gospel 2（好消息）good tidings: 给患者带来～ bring patients good news
【福音书】Fúyīnshū〈名〉［基督教］Gospel
【福祉】fúzhǐ〈名〉〈书〉1（福气）good fortune 2（幸福）well-being: 为人民大众谋～ strive for the well-being of the people
【福至心灵】fúzhì-xīnlíng〈成〉one seems resourceful when fortune smiles upon one
【福州】Fúzhōu ▸p. 661〈名〉Fuzhou [capital of Fujian Province (福建)]

蝠 fú ▸蝙蝠 biānfú

幞 fú = 幞头 fútóu

【幞头】fútóu〈名〉〈古〉headdress for a man

fǔ

父 fǔ〈名〉〈书〉1（老年男子）[a term of respect for an elderly man]: 田～ old farmer ‖ 渔～ old fisherman 2 = 甫[1] fǔ ▸fù

抚（撫）fǔ〈动〉1（安慰）console: ～问 console ▸～恤，安～ 2（保护）nurture: ▸～养，～育 3（轻按）stroke: 用手轻～婴儿的头 run one's hand gently over a baby's head ▸～摩，～琴

【抚爱】fǔ'ài〈动〉1（照料）caress: ～婴儿 stroke a baby 2（爱护）look after: 受到父母的～ be taken care of by one's parents
【抚躬自问】fǔgōng-zìwèn = 反躬自问 fǎngōng-zìwèn
【抚今追昔】fǔjīn-zhuīxī〈成〉reflect on the past in the light of the present
【抚摸】fǔmō〈动〉stroke: ～雕像 run one's hands over a statue ‖ ～着女儿的头发 stroke one's daughter's hair
【抚摩】fǔmó = 抚摸 fǔmō
【抚弄】fǔnòng〈动〉pet: 孩子们喜欢～小狗。Children love to pet puppies.
【抚琴】fǔqín〈动〉〈书〉play the zither
【抚慰】fǔwèi〈动〉comfort: ～灾民 console the people in the disaster area ‖ 百般～ do everything one can to comfort
【抚恤】fǔxù〈动〉console and compensate: ～死难者家属 console the bereaved family
【抚恤金】fǔxùjīn〈名〉benefit payment
【抚养】fǔyǎng〈动〉bring up: ～子女 rear one's children ‖ 把孩子～成人 bring up one's children ‖ ～费 child support payment
【抚育】fǔyù〈动〉1（指孩子）nurture: ～孤儿 bring up an orphan 2（指动植物）look after: ～幼苗 nurture seedlings
【抚掌】fǔzhǎng = 拊掌 fǔzhǎng

甫[1] fǔ〈名〉〈旧〉one's courtesy name: ▸台～

甫[2] fǔ〈副〉〈书〉just: 惊魂～定 have just recovered from a fright

拊 fǔ〈动〉clap

【拊膺】fǔyīng〈动〉〈书〉beat one's chest in grief: ～长叹 beat one's chest and let out a deep sigh of grief ‖ ～顿足 beat one's chest and stamp one's feet in grief

【拊掌】fǔzhǎng〈动〉〈书〉clap hands: ～大笑 clap one's hands and laugh heartily

斧 fǔ〈名〉①（指工具）axe: ▸板～ ②（指兵器）battleaxe: ▸～钺

【斧头】fǔtóu〈名〉axe

【斧削】fǔxuē〈动〉〈书〉〈喻〉request sb.'s help in reviewing an article

【斧钺】fǔyuè〈名〉〈书〉capital punishment: 甘冒～以陈 be willing to risk capital punishment to state the facts

【斧凿】fǔzáo [A]〈名〉axe and chisel [B]〈动〉artificially embellish: ～之痕 traces of artificial embellishment

【斧正】fǔzhèng〈动〉〈书〉〈敬〉request sb.'s help in reviewing an article: 敬请～。Please make any corrections necessary.

【斧锧】fǔzhì〈名〉〈古〉executioner's block and cleaver

【斧子】fǔzi〈名〉axe

府 fǔ〈名〉①（指机构）organs of state power: ▸官～, 政～ ②〈旧〉（指储藏处）government repository: ▸～库 ③（指住处）official residence: 元首～ official residence of the head of state ▸王～, 总统～ ④〈敬〉（你的家）your residence: 贵～ your home ▸～上 ⑤（指行政区划）prefecture: 开封～ Prefecture of Kaifeng

【府城】fǔchéng〈名〉〈旧〉prefectural seat

【府绸】fǔchóu〈名〉poplin

【府邸】fǔdǐ = 府第 fǔdì

【府第】fǔdì〈名〉domicile

【府库】fǔkù〈名〉government repository

【府上】fǔshang〈名〉〈敬〉①（指家）your home: 我明日来～拜访。I'll pay a visit to your home tomorrow. ②（指老家）one's native place: 您～是西安吗? Is Xi'an your hometown?

俯 fǔ〈动〉①（头低下）bow: ▸～视, ～首帖耳 ②〈敬〉〈旧〉（称对方行动）deign: ～准 deign to grant one's consent

【俯察】fǔchá〈动〉①（向低处看）look down from above ②〈敬〉（理解）be kind enough to examine

【俯冲】fǔchōng〈动〉［航空］dive: 垂直～ nosedive ‖ ～轰炸 dive-bomb

【俯伏】fǔfú〈动〉lie prostrate: ～听命 be at sb.'s disposal

【俯角】fǔjiǎo〈名〉［测绘］angle of depression

【俯就】fǔjiù〈动〉①〈敬〉（就职）deign to accept: 经理一职，尚祈～。We sincerely hope you will accept the post of manager. ②（迁就）adapt oneself to : 他事事～。He can adapt himself to anything.

【俯瞰】fǔkàn〈动〉overlook: 从塔顶可以～全城。From the top of the tower you can see into the city.

【俯念】fǔniàn〈动〉〈书〉〈敬〉be kind enough to show concern: ～群情 be kind enough to consider the feelings of the people

【俯拍】fǔpāi〈动〉［摄影］take a crane shot

【俯身】fǔshēn〈动〉bend down: ～亲了亲摇篮中的女儿 bend down and kiss one's daughter in the cradle

【俯拾即是】fǔshí-jíshì〈成〉be extremely common: 历史上这类先例～。History has numerous precedents of this kind.

【俯视】fǔshì〈动〉overlook: 从山上～河谷 overlook a river valley from a hill

【俯首】fǔshǒu〈动〉①（低头）bow one's head: ～沉思 bend one's head in meditation ②（顺从）be obedient: ～就范 surrender without struggle

【俯首屈膝】fǔshǒu-qūxī〈成〉kneel down humbly

【俯首帖耳】fǔshǒu-tiē'ěr〈成〉be obedient

【俯首听命】fǔshǒu-tīngmìng〈成〉follow with docility

【俯顺民情】fǔshùn mínqíng〈成〉defer to popular opinion

【俯卧】fǔwò〈动〉lie face down

【俯卧撑】fǔwòchēng〈名〉［体育］press-up〈英〉; push-up〈美〉: 做～ do press-ups

【俯仰】fǔyǎng [A]〈动〉perform a simple action: ▸～由人 [B]〈名〉instant: ▸～之间

【俯仰由人】fǔyǎng-yóurén〈成〉be at others' beck and call

【俯仰之间】fǔyǎngzhījiān〈成〉in the twinkling of an eye

【俯允】fǔyǔn〈动〉〈书〉〈敬〉deign to approve: 承蒙～，不胜感激。Thank you very much for your permission.

釜 fǔ〈名〉cauldron

【釜底抽薪】fǔdǐ-chōuxīn〈成〉〈喻〉strike at the root

【釜底游鱼】fǔdǐ-yóuyú〈成〉〈喻〉a person in dire danger

【釜山】Fǔshān〈名〉Pusan

辅（輔） fǔ〈动〉assist: ▸～助, 相～相成

【辅币】fǔbì〈简称〉= 辅助货币

【辅弼】fǔbì〈动〉〈书〉assist

【辅车相依】fǔchē-xiāngyī〈成〉be cheek by jowl with

【辅导】fǔdǎo〈动〉tutor: ～材料 teaching material ‖ 课外～ extracurricular tutor ‖ 个别～ individual tutorial

【辅导员】fǔdǎoyuán ▸p. 966〈名〉instructor: 少先队～ Young Pioneers counsellor ‖ 校外～ off-campus instructor ‖ 政治～ political adviser

【辅课】fǔkè〈名〉minor course

【辅料】fǔliào〈名〉①（指工业材料）supplementary material ②（指调味品）seasoning

【辅修】fǔxiū〈动〉take selected subjects

【辅音】fǔyīn〈名〉［语言］consonant

【辅助】fǔzhù [A]〈动〉assist: 积极～ assist actively [B]〈形〉auxiliary: ～工 auxiliary worker ‖ ～疗法 supplementary treatment ‖ ～药物 adjuvant

【辅助货币】fǔzhù huòbì ▸p. 328〈名〉small denomination currency

【辅佐】fǔzuǒ〈动〉assist: ～朝政 assist the ruler with government affairs

脯 fǔ〈名〉①（肉干）dried meat: 鹿～ dried venison ②（蜜饯果干）preserved fruit: ▸果～, 杏～
▸pú

腑 fǔ ▸脏腑 zàngfǔ

腐 fǔ
[A]〈动〉go bad: ～肉 rotten meat ▸～烂, ～朽
[B]〈形〉stale: ▸～儒, 陈～
[C]〈名〉bean curd: ▸～乳, 豆～

【腐败】fǔbài [A]〈动〉rot: 肉若不冷藏容易～。Meat rots easily if it is not refrigerated. [B]〈形〉corrupt: ～分子 corrupt elements ‖ ～无能 corrupt and incompetent [C]〈名〉corruption: 根除～ stamp out corruption ‖ 政治～ political corruption

【腐臭】fǔchòu〈形〉rancid: ～味 putrid odour

【腐恶】fǔ'è [A]〈形〉corrupt and evil [B]〈名〉evil influences: 惩治～ chastise the corrupt and the evil

【腐化】fǔhuà〈动〉①（指思想行为）become corrupt: 生活～ lead a dissipated life ‖ ～堕落 degenerate ②（使堕落）corrupt: ～年青人 corrupt the youth ③（腐烂）rot: ～的鸡蛋 rotten eggs

【腐旧】fǔjiù〈形〉old-fashioned: ～的思想 outworn ideas

【腐烂】fǔlàn [A]〈动〉decompose: ～变质 deteriorate ‖ 伤口周围开始～。The flesh around the wound started to decay. [B]〈形〉rotten: ～的尸体 rotting corpse ‖ 生活～ life of debauchery

【腐儒】fǔrú〈名〉pedantic scholar

【腐乳】fǔrǔ〈名〉fermented bean curd

> **腐乳**
> Also called *doufuru* (豆腐乳) and *jiangdoufu* (酱豆腐). Used as a condiment, this is a traditional fermented and protein-rich food. Small cubes of bean curd are left to ferment for five to six days and soy sauce, salt, red colouring, cooking-wine, prickly ash, liquorice and fennel are added. (▸豆腐)

【腐生】fǔshēng〈形〉［生物］saprogenic: ～生物 saprogen

【腐蚀】fǔshí〈动〉①［化学］corrode ②〈喻〉（堕落）corrupt: 淫秽刊物会～人们的思想。pornographic magazines corrode people's minds.

【腐蚀剂】fǔshíjì〈名〉corrosive

【腐熟】fǔshú〈动〉［农业］become thoroughly decomposed

【腐朽】fǔxiǔ〈形〉①（指含纤维的物质）rotten: ～的木头 rotten wood ‖ 屋顶的梁因受潮而～了。The damp has rotted the roof beams. ②（指思想、生活、制度）degenerate: 化～为神奇 transform the rotten into the miraculous ‖ ～思想 decadent ideology ‖ ～的生活方式 corrupt lifestyle

【腐殖酸】fǔzhísuān〈名〉［化学］humic acid

【腐殖质】fǔzhízhì〈名〉［地质］humus

【腐竹】fǔzhú〈名〉dried bean curd stick

fù

父 fù〈名〉①（父亲）father: 慈～ kind father ‖ 养～ foster father ▸～辈, 生～ ②（长辈男子）male relative of a senior generation: ▸～老, 伯～, 祖～ ③（鼻祖）father: 现代心理学之～ father of modern psychology
▸fǔ

【父爱】fù'ài〈名〉paternal love: 他对女儿毫无～。He has no paternal feelings towards his daughter.

【父辈】fùbèi〈名〉relatives or friends of one's father's generation

【父本】fùběn〈名〉［植物］male parent: ～植株 paternal plant

【父老】fùlǎo〈名〉elders: ～乡亲 fellow countrymen ‖ ～兄弟 elders and brothers

【父母】fùmǔ〈名〉parents: ～双亡。One's parents are both dead.

【父母官】fùmǔguān〈名〉〈旧〉officials serving the interests of the people

【父母之命，媒妁之言】fùmǔ zhī mìng, méishuò zhī yán〈成〉order of the parents and proposal of a matchmaker: 过去很多

婚姻靠的都是～。 Many marriages in the past were arranged by parents and matchmakers.

【父亲】fùqin ▸**p. 588**〈名〉 father: 没有～的孩子 fatherless child ‖ 长得像～ take after one's father

【父亲节】Fùqinjié〈名〉 Father's Day

【父权制】fùquánzhì〈名〉 patriarchy

【父系】fùxì〈形〉 **1**（指血统） paternal: ～亲属 paternal relative **2**（父子相承） patrilineal: ～社会 patriarchal society

【父兄】fùxiōng〈名〉 **1**（父亲和哥哥） father and elder brother **2**（家长） patriarch

讣（訃）fù

A〈动〉 notify of sb.'s death

B〈名〉 obituary

【讣告】fùgào **A**〈动〉 notify of sb.'s death **B**〈名〉 obituary: 发布～ issue an obituary

【讣文】fùwén〈名〉 obituary

【讣闻】fùwén = 讣文 fùwén

付 fù

〈动〉 **1**（交给） hand over: ～诸表决 put to a vote ‖ ～诸实施 put into practice ‖ 一切努力尽～东流。 All efforts came to nothing. **2**（支付） pay: ～饭钱 pay for one's meal ‖ ～加班费 pay overtime ‖ 邮资已～ postage paid ‖ 你得～50元的押金。 You have to pay a deposit of ¥50.

【付丙】fùbǐng〈动〉〈书〉 burn: 阅后～ burn after reading

【付出】fùchū〈动〉 pay: ～沉重代价 pay heavily ‖ ～辛勤劳动 put in a lot of hard work

【付方】fùfāng〈名〉 credit

【付费】fùfèi〈动〉 be fee-paying: ～电视 pay-per-view TV

【付刊】fùkān〈动〉 put into print

【付款】fùkuǎn〈动〉 pay: 按月～ make monthly payments ‖ 货到～ cash on delivery ‖ 首期～ initial payment ▸分期～

【付款人】fùkuǎnrén〈名〉 payer

【付排】fùpái〈动〉［印刷］ send to the compositor

【付讫】fùqì〈动〉 pay in full: 现金～ paid ‖ 邮资～ postage paid

【付托】fùtuō = 托付 tuōfù

【付息】fùxī〈动〉 pay interest: 还本～ pay principal with interest

【付现】fùxiàn〈动〉 pay in cash: ～可以打折吗？ Do you allow any discount for cash?

【付型】fùxíng〈动〉［印刷］ make paper moulds

【付印】fùyìn〈动〉 **1**（准备出版） send to the press **2**（交付印刷） hand over to the printer's: 核准稿件以备～ pass for press

【付邮】fùyóu〈动〉 post: 包裹已经～。 The parcel is already in the post.

【付与】fùyǔ〈动〉 give: 将贷款～一家企业 grant a loan to a business

【付账】fùzhàng〈动〉 pay: 用支票～ pay by cheque

【付之一炬】fùzhī-yījù〈成〉 set fire to: 将大楼～ set fire to a building

【付之一笑】fùzhī-yīxiào〈成〉 laugh sth. off: 对非议～ laugh off the criticism

【付诸东流】fùzhū-dōngliú〈成〉 come to nothing: 一切辛苦都～了。 All that hard work has been in vain.

【付诸行动】fùzhū-xíngdòng〈动〉 put into practice or action: 将理想～ put one's ideals into action or practice

【付梓】fùzǐ〈动〉〈书〉 send to the press

负（負）fù

A〈动〉 **1**（背） carry on one's back: 背～ carry on one's back ▸～荆请罪 **2**（担负） shoulder: ～责任 shoulder a responsibility ‖ 身～重任 bear heavy responsibilities upon one's shoulders **3**（依仗） rely on: ～险固守 rely on one's strategic position for a stubborn defence ▸～隅顽抗 **4**（遭受） suffer: ▸～伤 **5**（享有） enjoy: 久～盛名 have long enjoyed a good reputation **6**（拖欠） owe: ▸～债 **7**（背弃） betray: 有～重望 not live up to sb.'s expectations ▸～心, 辜～, 忘恩～义 **8**（失败） lose: ～于客队 lose to the guest team ‖ 该队六胜三～。 This team has had six wins and three defeats. ▸不分胜～

B〈名〉 responsibility assumed: ▸如释重～

C〈形〉 **1**［数学］ minus: ～五 minus five ▸～增长 **2**［物理］ negative: ▸～极

【负担】fùdān **A**〈动〉 bear: ～责任 take the responsibility ‖ 搬家的一切费用由公司～。 Any moving expenses will be borne by the company. **B**〈名〉 burden: 减轻农民～ ease burdens on farmers ‖ 工作～ work load ‖ 精神～ mental burden ‖ 作业～过重 be overloaded with homework

【负电】fùdiàn〈名〉 negative electricity

【负号】fùhào〈名〉［数学］ minus sign (−)

【负荷】fùhè **A**〈动〉〈书〉 bear: 不堪～ can't bear the burden ‖ ～过重 be overloaded **B**〈名〉 load: 超～ overload ‖ 满～ full load

【负极】fùjí〈名〉 negative pole: 电池的～ negative terminal of a battery

【负笈】fùjí〈动〉〈书〉 leave home to pursue one's studies: ～东瀛 go to study in Japan

【负荆请罪】fùjīng-qǐngzuì〈成〉 offer a humble and sincere apology

【负疚】fùjiù ▸**p. 156**〈动〉 feel guilty: ～的表情 guilty look ‖ 沉重的～感 heavy load of guilt

【负累】fùlěi〈名〉 burden

【负离子】fùlízǐ〈名〉［物理］ anion

【负利率】fùlìlǜ〈名〉 negative interest rate

【负面】fùmiàn〈形〉 negative: ～效果 negative effect ‖ ～影响 negative influence

【负片】fùpiàn〈名〉［摄影］ negative

【负气】fùqì〈动〉 be angrily wilful: ～出走 storm off in a huff

【负情】fùqíng〈动〉 betray one's love

【负屈】fùqū〈动〉 suffer wrongful treatment: ～含冤 suffer injustice

【负伤】fùshāng〈动〉 receive an injury: 在战斗中～ be wounded in action ‖ 因公～ be injured at work

【负数】fùshù ▸**p. 691**〈名〉［数学］ negative number

【负心】fùxīn〈动〉 be unfaithful: ～人 heart-breaker ‖ ～汉 fickle-hearted man

【负隅顽抗】fùyú-wánkàng〈成〉 put up a desperate resistance

【负约】fùyuē〈动〉 go back on one's promise

【负载】fùzài〈名〉 load: ～容量 load capacity

【负责】fùzé **A**〈动〉 be responsible for: ～外事工作 be in charge of foreign affairs ‖ 对自己的行为～ be responsible for one's actions ‖ 概不～ acknowledge no liability **B**〈形〉 responsible: 她说这话是很不～的。 It was irresponsible of her to say this. ‖ 他做事很～。 He always conducts himself responsibly.

【负责人】fùzérén〈名〉 person in charge

【负增长】fùzēngzhǎng〈名〉 negative growth: 人口出现～。 The population appears to be in decline.

【负债】fùzhài **A**〈动〉 be in debt: ～累累 debt-ridden ‖ ～经营 operate on borrowings ‖ 他～已达10万元。 His borrowings have reached 100,000 *yuan*. **B**〈名〉 debt: 账面～ book debt

【负重】fùzhòng〈动〉 **1**（指重物） carry a heavy load **2**（指重任） shoulder a heavy task: ▸忍辱～

【负罪】fùzuì〈动〉 bear the blame: ～感 guilty conscience

妇（婦）fù

〈名〉 **1**（妇女） woman: 老～ old woman ▸～科, ～女 **2**（已婚女子） married woman: ▸寡～, 媳～ **3**（妻子） wife: ▸夫～, 夫唱～随

【妇产科】fùchǎnkē〈名〉 gynaecology and obstetrics department

【妇代会】fùdàihuì〈简称〉= 妇女代表大会

【妇道】fùdào〈名〉〈旧〉 female virtues: 不守～ not observe accepted female behaviour

【妇道】fùdao〈名〉 women: ～人家 women

【妇科】fùkē〈名〉 gynaecology: ～病 gynaecological disease ‖ ～检查 gynaecological examination

【妇联】fùlián〈简称〉= 妇女联合会

【妇女】fùnǚ〈名〉 woman: ～的社会地位 women's social status ‖ 家庭～ housewife ‖ 职业～ career woman

【妇女代表大会】fùnǚ dàibiǎo dàhuì〈名〉 women's congress: 全国～ national women's congress

【妇女节】Fùnǚjié〈名〉 International Women's Day

【妇女联合会】fùnǚ liánhéhuì〈名〉 women's federation: 中华全国～ All-China Women's Federation

【妇人】fùrén〈名〉 married woman

【妇孺】fùrú〈名〉〈书〉 women and children: ～皆知。 It is known even to women and children.

【妇婴】fùyīng〈名〉 women and infants: ～卫生 women and infant hygiene

【妇幼】fùyòu〈名〉 women and children: ～保健 health care for women and children ‖ ～保健站 health care centre for women and children

附 fù

〈动〉 **1**（附带） attach: ～有插图的词典 illustrated dictionary ‖ 随信～上我的简历。 My resume is enclosed. ▸～件, ～设 **2**（靠近） get close: ～在耳边低语 whisper in sb.'s ear ▸～近 **3**（依附） rely on: ▸～议, 魂不～体

【附白】fùbái〈动〉 add an explanation

【附笔】fùbǐ〈名〉 additional remarks

【附带】fùdài **A**〈动〉 be incidental: ～说一下 by the way ‖ 有～条件的援助 conditional aid **B**〈形〉 supplementary: ～责任 accessorial liability

【附点】fùdiǎn〈名〉［音乐］ dot

【附耳】fù'ěr〈动〉 move close to sb.'s ear: ～低语 whisper in sb.'s ear ‖ ～交谈 talk in whispers

【附凤攀龙】fùfèng-pānlóng = 攀龙附凤 pānlóng-fùfèng

【附睾】fùgāo〈名〉［生理］ epididymis

【附和】fùhè〈动〉 echo: ～他人意见 echo others' views ▸随声～

【附会】fùhuì〈动〉 make a far-fetched analogy: ▸牵强～

【附骥】fùjì〈动〉 ride on the coat-tails of a great man

【附加】fùjiā〈动〉 attach: 在合同中～一个

条款 attach a stipulation to the contract ‖ ～费用 fringe cost ‖ ～工资 supplementary wage ‖ ～议定书 additional protocol
【附加税】fùjiāshuì〈名〉surcharge: 征收～ impose a surcharge
【附加刑】fùjiāxíng = 从刑 cóngxíng
【附加值】fùjiāzhí〈名〉added value: 高～产品 product with high added value
【附件】fùjiàn〈名〉1（附属品）attachment: 以～形式发送 send as an attachment ‖ 添加～ attach a document (to email) ‖ 法律文件的～ annex to a legal document 2（指文件）enclosure 3（指零件）accessory: 汽车～ automobile accessories 4［解剖］adnexa: 子宫～ adnexa uteri ‖ ～炎 adnexitis
【附近】fùjìn A〈形〉neighbouring: ～村庄 neighbouring village ‖ ～居民 nearby residents ‖ ～商店 nearby shop B〈名〉neighbourhood: ～有没有商店? Are there any shops in the vicinity? ‖ 邮局就在～。The post office is close by.
【附丽】fùlì〈动〉〈书〉depend on: 无所～ have nothing to depend on
【附录】fùlù〈名〉appendix: 词典～ appendix to a dictionary
【附上】fùshàng〈动〉be enclosed herewith: 随信～支票一张,请查收。Enclosed please find a cheque.
【附设】fùshè〈动〉have as an attached institution: 学院～一所中学。There is a middle school attached to the college.
【附生植物】fùshēng zhíwù〈名〉epiphyte
【附属】fùshǔ A〈动〉be affiliated to: 那所学院～于这所大学。The college is affiliated to the university. B〈形〉auxiliary: ～机构 auxiliary body ‖ ～医院 affiliated hospital
【附属国】fùshǔguó〈名〉dependent state
【附属小学】fùshǔ xiǎoxué〈名〉attached primary school
【附属中学】fùshǔ zhōngxué〈名〉attached middle school
【附送】fùsòng〈动〉give as a bonus: 买咖啡两瓶～咖啡杯 buy two coffees and get a cup for free
【附小】fùxiǎo〈简称〉= 附属小学
【附言】fùyán〈名〉postscript (PS)
【附议】fùyì〈动〉second a motion: 他的提议没人～。No one seconded his motion.
【附庸】fùyōng〈名〉1（指小国）vassal state 2（指人或事物）appendage
【附庸风雅】fùyōng-fēngyǎ〈成〉pose as a cultured person among men of letters
【附载】fùzǎi〈动〉carry as appendix
【附则】fùzé〈名〉supplementary articles
【附识】fùzhì〈名〉explanatory remarks: 再版～ reprint remarks
【附中】fùzhōng〈简称〉= 附属中学
【附注】fùzhù〈名〉annotations
【附着】fùzhuó〈动〉adhere to: ～力 adhesive force ‖ 细菌能～在皮肤上。Germs cling to the skin.

阜 fù〈书〉
A〈名〉mound
B〈形〉abundant: ▸物～民丰

服 fù〈量〉dose: 一～药 a dose of medicine
▸fú

咐 fù ▸吩咐 fēnfu

驸（駙） fù〈名〉horse hitched up by the side of the shaft horse
【驸马】fùmǎ〈名〉〈古〉emperor's son-in-law

赴 fù〈动〉go to: ～美求学 go to study in the USA ‖ ～灾区演出 journey to the disaster area to give a performance
【赴敌】fùdí〈动〉〈书〉go to fight the enemy
【赴会】fùhuì〈动〉attend a meeting
【赴难】fùnàn〈动〉go to the rescue of one's nation
【赴任】fùrèn〈动〉proceed to one's post
【赴汤蹈火】fùtāng-dǎohuǒ〈成〉〈喻〉defy all difficulties and dangers: ～, 在所不辞 be willing to risk death to accomplish a task
【赴宴】fùyàn〈动〉attend a banquet
【赴约】fùyuē〈动〉keep an appointment: 他准时～。He arrived on time for his appointment.

复¹（復） fù
A〈动〉1（回）turn over 2（报复）revenge: ▸报～ 3（恢复）recover: ～国 restore a nation ▸～学, 恢～ 4（回答）reply: 盼～ await your reply ‖ 请速回～。Please reply immediately. ▸～命, ～信
B〈副〉again: 旧情～燃。The old love flared up again. ▸故态～萌, 死灰～燃

复²（複） fù
A〈名〉〈书〉lined clothes
B〈动〉（重复）repeat: ▸～写, ～制
C〈形〉compound: ～比例 compound proportion
【复本】fùběn〈名〉duplicate
【复本位制】fùběnwèizhì〈名〉［经济］bimetallism: ～货币制度 bimetallic monetary system
【复辟】fùbì〈动〉stage a comeback: ～活动 restoration activities
【复查】fùchá〈动〉re-examine: ～平反冤案 review and redress past frame-ups ‖ ～账目 check the accounts
【复仇】fùchóu〈动〉avenge: 矢志～ vow to avenge oneself ‖ 他决心为死去的父亲～。He was determined to avenge his dead father.
【复出】fùchū〈动〉stage a comeback: 危急关头他再次～。He made another comeback at the crucial moment.
【复聪】fùcōng〈动〉recover one's hearing
【复电】fùdiàn A〈动〉send a telegram in reply: 我已～。I've already sent a telegram in reply. B〈名〉telegram in reply: 拍～ cable a reply
【复读】fùdú〈动〉repeat: ～班 re-take class ‖ ～生 student doing retakes
【复读机】fùdújī〈名〉sound recorder
【复发】fùfā〈动〉recur: 心脏病～ have another heart attack ‖ 他的病已多次～。He has had several recurrences of his illness. ▸旧病～
【复返】fùfǎn〈动〉return: 他一去不～了。He has gone, never to return.
【复方】fùfāng〈名〉1［中医］prescription composed of two or more recipes of herbs: ～甘草合剂 brown mixture 2［药学］medicinal compound: ～阿司匹林 aspirin compound
【复辅音】fùfǔyīn〈名〉［语言］consonant cluster
【复岗】fùgǎng〈动〉return to one's old job
【复工】fùgōng〈动〉1（指罢工后）return to work: 设法说服工人～ try to persuade workers on strike to return to work 2（指停工后）resume construction
【复古】fùgǔ〈动〉restore ancient ways: ～倾向 tendency to idolize the ancients
【复归】fùguī〈动〉return: 暴风雨过后, 湖面～平静。The lake calmed down again after the storm.
【复果】fùguǒ〈名〉［植物］compound fruit
【复函】fùhán〈书〉A〈动〉reply to a letter: 请尽早～。Kindly favour us with an early reply. B〈名〉letter of reply
【复航】fùháng〈动〉1（指飞机）resume flight 2（指船）resume voyage
【复合】fùhé〈形〉compound: ～维生素B vitamin B complex ‖ ～材料 compound material ‖ ～肥料 compound fertilizer
【复合词】fùhécí〈名〉［语言］compound word
【复合句】fùhéjù〈名〉［语言］compound sentence, complex sentence
【复合量词】fùhé liàngcí〈名〉［语言］compound classifier
【复合元音】fùhé yuányīn〈名〉［语言］triphthong
【复核】fùhé〈动〉review: ～账目 check the accounts
【复会】fùhuì〈动〉resume a session
【复婚】fùhūn〈动〉remarry
【复活】fùhuó A〈动〉come back to life: 耶稣在死后第三天～。Jesus was resurrected from the dead on the third day after he died. B〈名〉1（重新兴盛）revival: 防止军国主义的～ guard against the revival of militarism 2［基督教］the Resurrection
【复活节】Fùhuójié〈名〉［基督教］Easter
【复活赛】fùhuósài〈名〉repêchage
【复交】fùjiāo〈动〉1（指人）resume relations: 他们多年以后才～。They didn't resume their friendship for many years. 2［外交］resume diplomatic relations
【复旧】fùjiù〈动〉revive old ways: ～如新 restore sth. to its original state
【复句】fùjù = 复合句 fùhéjù
【复刊】fùkān〈动〉resume publication
【复课】fùkè〈动〉resume classes
【复垦】fùkěn〈动〉reclaim
【复利】fùlì〈名〉［经济］compound interest
【复明】fùmíng〈动〉regain one's eyesight: 手术后白内障病人可以～。Patients may recover their eyesight after a cataract operation.
【复命】fùmìng〈动〉report upon completion of a task
【复牌】fùpái〈动〉resume transaction
【复盘】fùpán〈动〉1（指棋赛）do a post-game analysis 2（指股市）resume trading
【复权】fùquán〈动〉1［金融］adjust: ～后的股价 adjusted share price 2［法律］rehabilitate
【复赛】fùsài〈动〉［体育］compete in a semi-final: 参加～的队员 semi-finalists
【复审】fùshěn〈动〉1（再次审查）re-examine: 可行性报告被留下～。The feasibility report was kept for reconsideration. 2［法律］review: ～案件 review a case
【复生】fùshēng〈动〉come back to life: 死而～ come back to life
【复市】fùshì〈动〉resume business
【复式】fùshì〈形〉multiple
【复式教学】fùshì jiàoxué〈名〉multi-grade teaching
【复试】fùshì〈动〉1（指考试）sit for the second round of an examination 2（指面试）go for a second round interview
【复述】fùshù〈动〉1（指话语）repeat:

你能把我的要求～一遍吗? Can you repeat my requirements? **2**（指学习内容）go over: ～课文 go over a text

【复数】fùshù ▸**p. 411**〈名〉［语言］plural: ～形式 plural form

【复苏】fùsū **A**〈动〉resuscitate: 枯萎的植物雨后～了。The withered plants were resuscitated after the rain. **B**〈名〉**1**［经济］recovery: 经济～ economic recovery **2**［医学］resuscitation

【复位】fùwèi〈动〉**1**（指关节）reduce: 使脱臼～ reset a fracture ‖ ～术 reduction **2**（指仪表）reset: 使自动计程仪～ reset an odometer **3**（指权位）return to the throne

【复位键】fùwèijiàn〈名〉recall button

【复胃】fùwèi〈名〉ruminant stomach

【复习】fùxí〈动〉revise: ～功课 review one's lessons ‖ ～备考 revise for an examination

【复线】fùxiàn〈名〉multitrack: ～铁路 double line railway

【复现】fùxiàn〈动〉reappear

【复写】fùxiě〈动〉copy

【复写纸】fùxiězhǐ〈名〉carbon paper

【复信】fùxìn **A**〈动〉reply **B**〈名〉letter of reply

【复兴】fùxīng〈动〉revive: ～民族经济 rejuvenate the national economy ‖ 经济～ economic revival ▸文艺～

【复姓】fùxìng〈名〉two-character surname

【复学】fùxué〈动〉go back to school: 帮助失学儿童～ help dropouts go back to school

【复眼】fùyǎn〈名〉［动物］compound eye

【复业】fùyè〈动〉**1**（指职业）take up one's old trade **2**（指营业）reopen business: 饭店经过三个月整顿后才～。The hotel reopened after three months of rectification.

【复叶】fùyè〈名〉［植物］compound leaf

【复议】fùyì〈动〉reconsider: ～案件 reconsider a case

【复音】fùyīn〈名〉［物理］complex tone

【复音词】fùyīncí〈名〉［语言］polysyllabic word

【复印】fùyìn〈动〉copy: ～文件 photocopy a document ‖ ～设备 reprographic equipment ‖ ～件 photocopy

【复印机】fùyìnjī〈名〉photocopier

【复元】fùyuán = 复原 fùyuán 1

【复员】fùyuán〈动〉**1**（进入和平状态）return to peacetime conditions **2**（军人退役）be demobilized: ～回乡 be demobilized and return to the countryside ‖ ～军人 ex-serviceman

【复原】fùyuán〈动〉**1**（病后康复）recover from an illness: 他已病愈～。He has recovered from his illness. **2**（恢复原样）restore to former condition: 无法～的壁画 frescoes beyond restoration

【复原乳】fùyuánrǔ〈名〉［食品］reconstituted milk

【复圆】fùyuán〈动〉［天文］（指全食）come to the fourth contact;（指偏食）come to the last contact

【复杂】fùzá〈形〉complex: ～的结构 complicated structure ‖ ～的人际关系 complicated interpersonal relationship ‖ ～的心情 mixed feelings

【复杂化】fùzáhuà〈动〉complicate: 没有必要把事情～。There's no need to complicate matters.

【复杂性】fùzáxìng〈名〉complexity

【复诊】fùzhěn〈动〉seek further medical consultation

【复职】fùzhí〈动〉resume one's post

【复制】fùzhì〈动〉duplicate: ～一张CD burn a CD ‖ ～品 copy

【复制片】fùzhìpiàn〈名〉duplicated film

【复种】fùzhòng〈名〉［农业］multiple cropping

【复壮】fùzhuàng〈名〉rejuvenate: ～品种 rejuvenated seed strain

洑 fù

〈动〉swim ▸fú

【洑水】fùshuǐ〈动〉swim: ～过河 swim across a river

副[1] fù

A〈形〉**1**（辅助）assistant: ～部长 deputy minister ‖ ～校长 vice president ‖ ～省长/市长 deputy governor/mayor ‖ ～主席 vice chairman ‖ ～主编 associate editor-in-chief ‖ ～驾驶员 co-pilot **2**（附带）auxiliary: ～梁 secondary beam
B〈名〉assistant post: 团～ assistant commander ▸大～, 二～
C〈动〉correspond to: ▸名～其实

副[2] fù

〈量〉**1**（表成对）[for a pair of things]: 一～手套 a pair of gloves **2**（表成套）[for a set of things]: 一～象棋 a chess set **3**（指表情）[for facial expressions]: 一～笑脸 a smiling face

【副本】fùběn〈名〉duplicate: 文件～ duplicate of a document

【副标题】fùbiāotí〈名〉subheading

【副产品】fùchǎnpǐn〈名〉by-product: 这种新材料是航天工业的～。This new material is a by-product of the space industry.

【副词】fùcí〈名〉adverb

【副处】fùchù〈名〉deputy head of a department

【副高】fùgāo〈名〉secondary senior position

【副歌】fùgē〈名〉［音乐］refrain

【副官】fùguān〈名〉〈旧〉adjutant

【副虹】fùhóng〈名〉［气象］secondary bow

【副教授】fùjiàoshòu〈名〉associate professor

【副刊】fùkān〈名〉supplement: 文学～ literature supplement

【副科】fùkē〈名〉**1**（指课程）minor subject **2**（指职位）deputy section-chief

【副品】fùpǐn〈名〉substandard goods

【副热带】fùrèdài〈名〉subtropical belt: ～高压 subtropical high

【副食】fùshí〈名〉non-staple food: ～店 grocery ‖ ～品 non-staple food or products

【副手】fùshǒu〈名〉assistant

【副题】fùtí〈名〉subtitle

【副修】fùxiū〈动〉take as a minor: ～课程 minor courses

【副研究员】fùyánjiūyuán〈名〉associate research fellow

【副业】fùyè〈名〉side occupation: 搞～ engage in sideline production ‖ 家庭～ household sideline production

【副油箱】fùyóuxiāng〈名〉auxiliary tank

【副职】fùzhí〈名〉assistant post: 担任～ work as an assistant

【副总理】fùzǒnglǐ〈名〉vice-premier, vice-chancellor

【副总统】fùzǒngtǒng〈名〉vice president

【副作用】fùzuòyòng〈名〉side effect: 无～ free from side effects

赋[1]（賦）fù

A〈动〉bestow: ▸～予
B〈名〉natural endowment: ▸～性, 天～

赋[2]（賦）fù

A〈名〉〈旧〉land tax
B〈动〉levy: ～以重税 levy heavy tax

赋[3]（賦）fù

A〈名〉prose poem
B〈动〉compose: ～诗庆贺 compose a congratulatory poem

【赋税】fùshuì〈名〉tax

【赋闲】fùxián〈动〉〈书〉be out of a job: ～在家 sit at home doing nothing

【赋性】fùxìng〈名〉nature: ～聪颖 have natural endowments

【赋役】fùyì〈名〉taxes and corvée

【赋有】fùyǒu〈动〉be endowed with: ～才能 be gifted with talents ‖ 人类～理性。Man is endowed with reason.

【赋予】fùyǔ〈动〉entrust: ～妇女更高的社会地位 confer more social prestige on women ‖ 人民～的权力 power entrusted by the people

傅[1] fù

A〈动〉〈书〉instruct
B〈名〉instructor: ▸师～

傅[2] fù

〈动〉**1**（附着）adhere **2**（涂抹）apply: ～粉 powder ‖ ～药 apply medicine

富 fù

A〈形〉**1**（富裕）rich: 让一部分人先～起来 let some people become rich first ‖ ～户 rich family ‖ 首～ wealthiest household **2**（丰富）abundant: ～含营养 be rich in nutrition ‖ 他颇～幽默感。He has a good sense of humour. ▸丰～, 年～力强
B〈动〉enrich: ～民政策 policy to enrich the people ▸～国
C〈名〉resource: ▸～源, 财～

【富二代】fù'èrdài〈名〉the second generation rich

【富富有余】fùfù-yǒuyú〈成〉have more than enough

【富贵】fùguì〈形〉rich and powerful: ～人家 rich and powerful family ▸荣华～

【富贵病】fùguìbìng〈名〉costly chronic disease

【富国】fùguó **A**〈动〉enrich one's country: ～利民 enrich the state and benefit the people **B**〈名〉rich country

【富国强兵】fùguó-qiángbīng〈成〉make one's country rich and strong

【富豪】fùháo〈名〉person of wealth and standing

【富矿】fùkuàng〈名〉high-grade ore: 富铁矿 high-grade iron ore deposit

【富丽】fùlì〈形〉beautiful and magnificent: 陈设豪华～ beautiful and sumptuous furnishings

【富丽堂皇】fùlì-tánghuáng〈成〉sumptuous: ～的宫殿 magnificent palace

【富民】fùmín〈动〉make the people rich and prosperous: ～政策 policy of enriching the people

【富农】fùnóng〈名〉〈旧〉rich peasant

【富婆】fùpó〈名〉woman of means

【富强】fùqiáng〈形〉prosperous and powerful: 把中国建设得更加繁荣～ build China

into a more prosperous and powerful country

【富饶】fùráo〈形〉richly endowed: ～的土地 fertile land

【富商】fùshāng〈名〉rich merchant

【富实】fùshí〈形〉well-off: 家业～ have substantial family property

【富士山】Fùshìshān〈名〉Mount Fuji

【富庶】fùshù〈形〉rich and populous: ～的国家 rich and populous country

【富态】fùtai ▸**p. 772**〈形〉〈婉〉plump: 她长得很～。She is a very portly lady.

【富翁】fùwēng〈名〉man of means

【富营养化】fùyíngyǎnghuà〈动〉eutrophicate

【富有】fùyǒu **A**〈形〉rich: 非常～ extremely wealthy ‖ ～的人家 wealthy family **B**〈动〉abound in: ～成果的会谈 productive talk ‖ ～代表性 be representative ‖ ～生命力 be full of vitality ‖ ～同情心 be sympathetic

【富于】fùyú〈动〉be rich in: ～想象力的作家 imaginative writer ‖ ～自我牺牲精神 be endowed with the spirit of self-sacrifice

【富裕】fùyù **A**〈形〉affluent: 走共同～的道路 take the road of common prosperity ‖ 农民逐渐～起来。The peasants are gradually becoming better-off. **B**〈动〉enrich: 发展生产，～人民 increase production and enrich the people

【富余】fùyu〈形〉surplus: ～劳动力 redundant workers ‖ 时间还～，别着急! Take your time; there's no rush. ‖ ～的苹果我们都送人。We are giving away all our surplus apples.

【富源】fùyuán〈名〉natural resources

【富足】fùzú〈形〉abundant: 生活～ live in plenty

腹 fù〈名〉**1**（肚子）belly: ～中的婴儿 unborn baby ▸～腔，空～ **2**（内心）heart: ▸～稿，～议 **3**（指凸出部分）belly: 瓶～ belly of a bottle

【腹案】fù'àn〈名〉plan in one's mind: 他初步有了个～。He has worked out a rough plan in his mind.

【腹背受敌】fùbèi-shòudí〈成〉be caught between a rock and a hard place

【腹部】fùbù〈名〉abdomen

【腹地】fùdì〈名〉hinterland: 深入～ get far into the interior

【腹稿】fùgǎo〈名〉plan in one's mind: 打～ work out a draft in one's mind

【腹股沟】fùgǔgōu〈名〉［解剖］groin

【腹肌】fùjī〈名〉abdominal muscle

【腹面】fùmiàn〈名〉abdominal side

【腹膜】fùmó〈名〉peritoneum: ～炎 peritonitis

【腹鳍】fùqí〈名〉［鱼类］ventral fin

【腹腔】fùqiāng〈名〉abdominal cavity: ～镜 peritoneoscope

【腹水】fùshuǐ ▸**p. 50**〈名〉［医学］peritoneal dropsy

【腹痛】fùtòng ▸**p. 50**〈名〉abdominal pain

【腹泻】fùxiè ▸**p. 50**〈动〉diarrhoea: ～不止 have persistent diarrhoea

【腹心】fùxīn〈名〉**1**（要害）vital organs: ～之患 serious hidden danger **2**（指人）trusted subordinate: ～之交 bosom friend **3**〈书〉（诚心）true thoughts and feelings: ～相照 be frank with one another

【腹议】fùyì〈动〉〈书〉keep one's thoughts to oneself

【腹胀】fùzhàng ▸**p. 50**〈名〉abdominal distention

【腹足】fùzú〈名〉［动物］proleg

缚（縛） fù〈动〉tie up: 他手被～着。His hands were tied. ▸束～，作茧自～

鲋（鮒） fù〈名〉［鱼类］crucian carp

赙（賻） fù〈动〉〈书〉present a funeral gift

【赙仪】fùyí〈名〉〈书〉gift presented to a bereaved family

【赙赠】fùzèng〈动〉〈书〉present a gift to a bereaved family

蝮 fù

【蝮蛇】fùshé〈名〉Pallas pit viper

鳆（鰒） fù

【鳆鱼】fùyú〈名〉abalone

覆 fù〈动〉**1**（盖住）cover: ～上塑料薄膜 cover with plastic film ▸～盖 **2**（翻过来）overturn: ▸颠～ **3**（灭亡）perish: ～国之辱 humiliation of a conquered nation ▸～灭 **4** = 复[1] fù A1, A4

【覆被】fùbèi〈动〉cover: 森林～占该国面积的五分之一。Forests cover one fifth of the country.

【覆巢之下无完卵】fù cháo zhī xià wú wánluǎn〈成〉〈喻〉no individual can escape the disaster that befalls the group

【覆盖】fùgài **A**〈动〉cover: 大雪～了公路。Snow covered the highway. ‖ 地球表面的三分之二为海洋所～。Two thirds of the Earth is covered by sea. **B**〈名〉plant cover: 没有～，土壤容易流失。Erosion occurs easily without vegetation.

【覆盖率】fùgàilǜ〈名〉coverage rate

【覆盖面】fùgàimiàn〈名〉**1**（覆盖的面积）covering square: 森林的～日益减少。The forest cover is constantly shrinking. **2**（影响范围）coverage: 扩大法制教育的～ make legal education more widely accessible

【覆灭】fùmiè〈动〉destroy: 全军～。The whole army was destroyed.

【覆没】fùmò〈动〉**1**〈书〉（指船）capsize and sink **2**（指军队）be annihilated: ▸全军～

【覆盆之冤】fùpénzhīyuān〈成〉irremediable wrong

【覆盆子】fùpénzǐ〈名〉［植物］raspberry

【覆水难收】fùshuǐ-nánshōu〈成〉it is no use crying over spilt milk

【覆亡】fùwáng〈动〉fall: 罗马帝国的～ fall of the Roman Empire

【覆辙】fùzhé〈名〉track of an overturned cart: ▸重蹈～

馥 fù〈形〉〈书〉fragrant

【馥郁】fùyù〈形〉〈书〉strongly fragrant: ～的花香 strong scent of flowers ‖ 芬芳～ sweet and fragrant ‖ 花朵散发着～的芳香。The flower emitted a strong fragrance.

Gg

gā

夹（夾）gā
▸jiā, jiá
【夹肢窝】gāzhiwō〈名〉armpit

旮 gā
【旮旯儿】gālár〈名〉〈方〉1（角落）nook: 墙～ corner 2（偏僻处）out-of-the-way place: 住在山～ live in a remote mountain recess

伽 gā
▸jiā, qié
【伽马】gāmǎ〈名〉1（希腊字母）gamma (γ) 2［物理］gamma
【伽马刀】gāmǎdāo〈名〉［医学］gamma knife
【伽马射线】gāmǎ shèxiàn〈名〉［物理］gamma ray

呷 gā
▸xiā
【呷呷】gāgā = 嘎嘎 gāgā

咖 gā
▸kā
【咖喱】gālí〈名〉curry: ～粉 curry powder ‖ ～牛肉 beef curry

胳 gā
▸gē, gé
【胳肢窝】gāzhiwō = 夹肢窝 gāzhiwō

嘎（嘎）gā〈拟〉snap: 棍子～的一声断了。The stick broke with a snap. ‖ 汽车～的一声刹住了。The car screeched to a halt.
【嘎巴】gābā〈拟〉snap: 小树～一声被风吹断了。The young tree suddenly snapped in the wind.
【嘎巴】gāba〈动〉〈方〉crust: 剩下的粥都～在锅上了。The porridge leftovers crusted on the pot.
【嘎嘣】gābēng〈拟〉crunch: 狗把骨头啃得～响。The dog was crunching on the bone.
【嘎嘣脆】gābēngcuì〈形〉〈方〉1（很脆）crunchy: 这些苹果吃起来～。These apples are crunchy. 2（干脆）quick and efficient: 办事～ be quick and efficient about one's business
【嘎噔】gādēng〈拟〉crack: 巨大的重力～一下把金属杆压成了两段。The great weight snapped the metal bar in two.
【嘎嘎】gāgā〈拟〉（鸭子叫）quack;（乌鸦等叫）caw: 积雪在我们脚下～作响。Our feet crunched on the snow.
【嘎然】gārán〈副〉suddenly: ～而止 stop suddenly
【嘎吱】gāzhī〈拟〉crunch: ～～地嚼着胡萝卜 crunch on an carrot ‖ 门～一声开了。The door creaked open.

gá

轧（軋）gá〈动〉〈方〉1（挤）squeeze: ～车子 jostle one's way onto a bus 2（结交）associate: ～朋友 make friends 3（查对）check: ▸～账
▸yà, zhá
【轧姘头】gá pīntou〈动〉〈方〉[of a married man or woman] have an affair
【轧账】gázhàng〈动〉check the accounts

钆（釓）gá〈名〉［化学］gadolinium (Gd)

噶 gá
【噶伦】gálún〈名〉Galoin [title of a high official in Tibetan government in former times]
【噶厦】gáxià〈名〉Gaxag [Tibetan government before 1959]

gǎ

尕 gǎ〈形〉〈方〉1（乖僻）eccentric: 她爷爷脾气很～。Her grandfather is rather eccentric. 2（调皮）mischievous: ～小子 naughty boy
【尕古】gǎgu〈形〉〈方〉1（指人）bad-tempered 2（指物品）substandard
【尕子】gǎzi〈名〉〈方〉1（指孩子）naughty child 2（指人）mischievous person

尜 gǎ〈形〉〈方〉young: ～娃 little kid

gà

尬 gà ▸尴尬 gāngà

gāi

该[1]（該）gāi〈动〉1（表结果）will be: 又～期末考试了。There will be final examinations again. ‖ 明年我女儿～十八岁了。My daughter is going to be eighteen next year. 2（轮到）be one's turn: 今天～谁值班? Who is on duty today? 3（理应如此）deserve: ～! 那是他自己不好。Serves him right! It was his own fault. ▸活～ 4（应该）ought to: 你不～为此责怪他。You shouldn't blame him for it. ‖ 下一步我～怎么办? What should I do next? 5（表强调）must: 我想他现在～好了吧? I think he should be all right by now, shouldn't he? ‖ 要是雨现在停了，～有多好啊! If only the rain would stop now!

该[2]（該）gāi〈动〉〈口〉owe: 他～我二十元钱。He owes me twenty *yuan*.

该[3]（該）gāi ▸p. 968〈代〉〈书〉that: ～厂 the said factory ‖ ～项工程 the project in question
【该当】gāidāng〈动〉1（指惩罚）deserve: ～何罪? What punishment do you think you deserve? 2（应该）should be: ～别论 should be regarded as a different matter ‖ ～如此! It should be so!
【该欠】gāiqiàn〈动〉owe: ～图书馆一本书 owe the library a book
【该死】gāisǐ〈动〉〈口〉damn: ～的天气! What wretched weather! ‖ ～，我把文件落在家里了! Oh blast! I've left my documents at home!
【该账】gāizhàng〈动〉owe: ～不还 refuse to pay the money one owes
【该着】gāizháo〈动〉〈口〉be just one's luck: 他又没赶上火车，～他倒霉! He missed his train again. Just his luck!

陔 gāi〈名〉〈书〉1（指台阶下）order of steps 2（指土埂）ridges between fields

垓[1] gāi〈量〉〈古〉one hundred million

垓[2] gāi
【垓心】gāixīn〈名〉〈旧〉centre of a battlefield: 困于～ be bottled up in the centre of a battlefield

赅（賅）gāi〈书〉〈形〉comprehensive: ▸言简意～
【赅博】gāibó〈形〉〈书〉learned: 学问～ be erudite
【赅括】gāikuò〈动〉〈书〉summarize

gǎi

改 gǎi〈动〉1（改变）change: 把谷仓～为车库 convert a barn into a garage ‖ 把日期～到五月十日 change the date to May 10th ‖ 你的老习惯也该～一～了。It's time to make a break from your old habit. ▸～革，朝令夕～ 2（修改）alter: ～稿子 revise a manuscript ‖ 把裙子～短 raise the hemline of a skirt ▸～写，篡～ 3（改正）rectify: 把错字～过来 correct wrong characters ▸～过，～邪归正 4（更改）switch to: ～乘火车 switch to a train ‖ ～

学法律 switch to law
【改版】gǎibǎn〈动〉1（指版本）revise an existing edition 2（指版式）correct type-setting
【改扮】gǎibàn〈动〉disguise oneself as: 犯人～成清洁工逃跑了。The prisoner escaped disguised as a cleaner.
【改编】gǎibiān〈动〉1（指著作）adapt: 把小说～成电影/戏剧剧本 adapt a story for the screen/stage ‖ 将钢琴曲～为管弦乐 adapt piano music for orchestra 2（指编制）remodel: 把一个营～为一个加强连 remodel troops into a reinforced battalion
【改变】gǎibiàn〈动〉change: ～（对…的）看法 change one's opinion (of) ‖ ～方向 change direction ‖ ～工作作风 shift the style of work ‖ 邻里关系发生了～。Something has changed in the relations between the neighbours. ‖ 近年来中国的面貌有很大～。China has changed a lot over the past few years.
【改产】gǎichǎn〈动〉switch to the manufacture of a different product: ～消费者需要的产品 change to manufacturing products that consumers need
【改朝换代】gǎicháo-huàndài〈成〉dynastic change
【改道】gǎidào〈动〉1（指道路）divert: 车辆～行驶。Traffic is being diverted onto another road. 2（指河流）change course: 黄河在历史上曾经多次～。The Yellow River has changed its course many times throughout history. 3（指路线）change one's route: 我们～去了西安。We changed our route and went to Xi'an.
【改点】gǎidiǎn〈动〉reschedule: 所有火车都～运行。All the trains now follow a new timetable.
【改订】gǎidìng〈动〉revise: ～计划 revise a plan ‖ ～规章制度 reformulate rules and regulations
【改动】gǎidòng〈动〉change: ～不多 make few changes ‖ 文字上做必要的～ make necessary changes in wording ‖ 时间表有几处～。There have been a few alterations to the timetable.
【改恶从善】gǎi'è-cóngshàn〈成〉turn over a new leaf
【改革】gǎigé〈动〉reform: ～不合理的规章制度 overhaul unreasonable regulations ‖ 深化～ deepen the reform ‖ 出台～方案 unveil a reform package ‖ 机构～ structural reform ‖ 体制～ institutional reform
【改革开放】gǎigé-kāifàng〈动〉reform and open to the outside world: ～政策 policy of reform and opening up
【改革派】gǎigépài〈名〉reformists
【改观】gǎiguān〈动〉transform: 城市面貌大为～。The city has completely transformed.
【改过】gǎiguò〈动〉mend one's ways: 勇于～ have the courage to correct one's mistakes
【改过自新】gǎiguò-zìxīn〈成〉turn over a new leaf: 发誓要～ make a pledge to mend one's ways
【改行】gǎiháng〈动〉change one's profession: ～经商 switch over to business ‖ ～做外交工作 move into foreign relations work
【改换】gǎihuàn〈动〉change: ～包装 repack ‖ ～名称 rename ‖ ～题目 change the topic
【改换门庭】gǎihuàn-méntíng〈成〉1（指地位）raise one's social status 2（指忠心）transfer one's loyalty
【改悔】gǎihuǐ〈动〉repent and mend one's ways: 毫无～之意 be absolutely unrepentant ‖ 他没有任何～的表现。There's no sign of him mending his ways. ▸死不～
【改嫁】gǎijià〈动〉marry another man: 丈夫死后不久她就～了。She remarried soon after her husband's death.
【改建】gǎijiàn〈动〉rebuild: 把体育馆～为大剧院 transform the gymnasium into an opera house
【改进】gǎijìn〈动〉improve: ～工作作风 improve one's working style ‖ 提出～措施 propose improvement measures
【改口】gǎikǒu〈动〉1（指话语）change one's story: 发现自己说错了，他马上～。Realizing that what he had said was wrong, he immediately corrected himself. 2（指称呼）address sb. by a different name: 过去人们叫他"主任"，但现在得～叫他"主席"了。He used to be addressed as 'director', but now we have to use 'president' instead.
【改良】gǎiliáng〈动〉1（改进）improve: ～品种 improve a breed ‖ ～土壤 enrich the soil 2 = 改善 gǎishàn
【改良型】gǎiliángxíng〈名〉improved type
【改良主义】gǎiliángzhǔyì〈名〉reformism: ～运动 reformist movement
【改名】gǎimíng〈动〉rename: ～换姓 assume a new name
【改判】gǎipàn〈动〉amend a verdict: 他的死刑～为无期了。His punishment was commuted from death to life imprisonment.
【改期】gǎiqī〈动〉reschedule: 会议～举行。The meeting will be held some other time.
【改签】gǎiqiān〈动〉endorse: 乘客～了下一个航班。The passenger got his ticket endorsed for the next flight.
【改任】gǎirèn〈动〉change to a new post: 杨先生不再担任厂长，～工会主席。Mr Yang is no longer the factory manager; he has become the chairman of the trade union.
【改日】gǎirì〈副〉on another day: 咱们～再做这件事吧。Let's do it some other day.
【改色】gǎisè〈动〉change colour: 夏秋交替之际树木～。The trees change colour when summer gives way to autumn. ▸面不～
【改善】gǎishàn〈动〉improve: ～伙食 prepare better foods ‖ ～投资环境 improve the investment climate ‖ 关系没有丝毫～。There is not the slightest improvement in relations.
【改善型】gǎishànxíng〈形〉improved: ～居民住房需求旺盛。Improved residential housing is in great demand.
【改天】gǎitiān = 改日 gǎirì
【改天换地】gǎitiān-huàndì〈成〉change the world: ～的革命精神 the revolutionary spirit of changing the world
【改头换面】gǎitóu-huànmiàn〈成〉〈贬〉make superficial changes
【改土】gǎitǔ〈动〉［农业］improve the soil
【改弦更张】gǎixián-gēngzhāng〈成〉〈喻〉make a fresh start
【改弦易辙】gǎixián-yìzhé〈成〉change one's course: 是～的时候了。It is time we struck out on a new path.
【改线】gǎixiàn〈动〉change course: 由于风暴，飞机～飞行。The plane changed course to avoid the storm.
【改邪归正】gǎixié-guīzhèng〈成〉turn over a new leaf: 使某人～ draw sb. from sin to the right path
【改写】gǎixiě〈动〉1（修改）rewrite: ～剧本 revise a play ‖ 这份报告必须～。This report will have to be reworded. 2（改编）adapt: 把小说～成电影剧本 adapt a novel for the big screen ‖ 本书是根据一部英文小说～的。This book is based on an English novel.
【改型】gǎixíng〈动〉modify: 对喷气式飞机进行～，以降低噪声 modify a jetliner to make it quieter
【改选】gǎixuǎn〈动〉re-elect: ～工会主席 re-elect a union chair
【改样】gǎiyàng〈动〉alter: 几年没见，你还没～儿。You haven't changed a bit since I last saw you years ago.
【改易】gǎiyì〈动〉〈书〉alter: ～文章标题 change the title of an article
【改用】gǎiyòng〈动〉replace: 别再邮寄，～传真。Don't send it off by post again. Send it by fax instead.
【改元】gǎiyuán〈动〉change the title of an imperial reign
【改造】gǎizào〈动〉1（改进）transform: ～农村电网 upgrade the rural power grid ‖ ～盐碱地 transform saline-alkli land ‖ 技术～ technical innovation 2（使根本改变）reform: ～少年犯 rehabilitate juvenile delinquents ‖ 被送到劳改厂接受～ be sent to a labour camp for rehabilitation
【改辙】gǎizhé〈动〉strike out on a new path
【改正】gǎizhèng〈动〉correct: ～错别字 correct wrong characters ‖ ～错误 correct one's mistakes
【改正液】gǎizhèngyè〈名〉correction fluid
【改制】gǎizhì〈动〉restructure
【改装】gǎizhuāng〈动〉1（指装束）change one's outfit 2（指包装）repackage 3（指交通工具）modify: 二战后很多战舰被～供民用。After the Second World War, many warships were refitted for civil use.
【改锥】gǎizhuī〈名〉screwdriver
【改组】gǎizǔ〈动〉reorganize: ～内阁 reshuffle the cabinet ‖ ～破产公司 restructure a bankrupt company
【改嘴】gǎizuǐ = 改口 gǎikǒu

胲 gǎi〈名〉〈书〉cheek muscle
▸hǎi

gài

丐 gài〈书〉
A〈动〉beg: ～食 beg one's bread
B〈名〉beggar

芥 gài
▸jiè
【芥菜】gàicài = 盖菜 gàicài
▸jiècài
【芥蓝】gàilán〈名〉［植物］cabbage mustard

钙（鈣） gài〈名〉calcium (Ca): 补～ add calcium ‖ 缺～ calcium-deficient
【钙化】gàihuà〈动〉［医学］calcify: ～点 calcification
【钙片】gàipiàn〈名〉calcium tablet
【钙缺乏】gàiquēfá ▸**p. 50**〈名〉［医学］calcium deficiency

盖[1]（蓋） gài
A〈名〉1（指器物）lid: 茶壶～儿 teapot lid ‖ 瓶～儿 bottle top ▸～碗，锅～ 2〈书〉（伞）umbrella: ▸华～ 3（指动物甲壳）

shell: 乌龟～ tortoise shell **4**（指人的骨骼）cover-shaped part of human skeleton: 头～骨 skull ‖ 膝～骨 knee cap
B〈动〉**1**（蒙）cover: ～被子睡觉 sleep under a quilt ‖ ～上盖子 put the lid on ‖ 箱子没～好。The box is not closed properly. **2**（打上）stamp: ～钢印 affix a steel seal (to) ‖ 在信封上～邮戳 postmark a letter ▸～章 **3**（遮掩）cover (up): 想把丑闻～住 try to cover up a scandal ▸欲～弥彰, 掩～ **4**（压过）drown out: 外面的嘈杂声～过了老师的讲课声。The noise from outside drowned out the teacher's voice. **5**（建造）construct: ～房子 build a house **6**（平整土地）level land

盖²（葢）gài〈书〉
A〈副〉approximately: 死伤者～百人。About a hundred people were injured or killed.
B〈连〉because: 有所不知，～未学也。If there are things we do not know, it is because we have not learned them.
▸Gě

【盖板】gàibǎn〈名〉cover plate
【盖菜】gàicài〈名〉［植物］leaf mustard
【盖棺论定】gàiguān-lùndìng〈成〉no verdict can be made on a man until after his death
【盖浇饭】gàijiāofàn〈名〉meat-vegetables-rice combo
【盖韭】gàijiǔ〈名〉cold-bed leek
【盖了】gàile〈形〉〈方〉extremely good
【盖了帽了】gàilemàole〈方〉= 盖了 gàile
【盖帘】gàilián〈名〉straw cover
【盖洛普民意测验】Gàiluòpǔ mínyì cèyàn〈名〉Gallup poll
【盖帽儿】gàimàor **A**〈名〉（指篮球）shot blocking **B**〈形〉〈方〉superb: 在这地方度假真是～了。This is a wonderful place for a holiday.
【盖然性】gàiránxìng〈名〉［逻辑］probability
【盖世】gàishì〈动〉〈书〉be unparalleled: ～英雄 unrivalled hero
【盖世无双】gàishì-wúshuāng〈成〉unparalleled anywhere in the world
【盖世太保】Gàishìtàibǎo〈名〉Gestapo
【盖头】gàitou〈名〉red bridal veil: 揭～ uncover a red bridal veil
【盖碗】gàiwǎn〈名〉covered teacup: ～茶 tea served in a covered teacup
【盖销】gàixiāo〈动〉cancel: ～邮票 cancel a stamp ‖ ～票 stamp cancelled for collectors
【盖印】gàiyìn〈动〉affix a seal
【盖章】gàizhāng〈动〉seal: 合同不～无效。The contract is not valid unless it is sealed.
【盖子】gàizi〈名〉**1**（用于封闭）lid: 打开～ take the lid off ‖〈喻〉捂～ try to cover up the truth **2**（指甲壳）shell: 乌龟～ tortoise shell

溉 gài〈动〉irrigate: ▸灌～

概 gài
A〈名〉**1**（风度）manner: ▸气～ **2**（大略）general idea: ▸～况, 梗～ **3**（景象）scene: 胜～ beautiful scenery
B〈副〉without exception: ～不负责 have no responsibility under any circumstances ‖ 学习时间～不会客 see no visitors during study hours ‖ 本店～不赊账。This shop does not give credit.

【概不追究】gàibùzhuījiū〈成〉no further action will be taken (against sb. for his past offences)
【概而不论】gài'érbùlùn〈成〉not care at all
【概而论之】gài'érlùnzhī〈成〉generally speaking
【概观】gàiguān〈名〉general survey: 人类思想史～ general overview of human thought ‖《英国文学～》*A Survey of English Literature*
【概况】gàikuàng〈名〉general overview: 学习～ study survey ‖《英语国家～》*A Survey of English-Speaking Countries*
【概括】gàikuò **A**〈动〉summarize: 文章的标题很好地～了文章的主题。The title of the essay is an effective summary of its contents. ‖ 目前的形势可以用两句话加以～。The present situation can be summarized in two sentences. **B**〈形〉brief and to the point: ～地说 to put it briefly ‖ 说得很～ said very succinctly
【概括性】gàikuòxìng〈名〉ability to generalize
【概览】gàilǎn〈名〉outline:《西安～》*A General Overview of Xi'an*
【概率】gàilǜ〈名〉**1**（可能性）chance: 这场比赛我们队获胜的～不大。Our team stands little chance of winning the game. **2**［数学］［统计］probability
【概率分布】gàilǜ fēnbù〈名〉［数学］probability distribution
【概率论】gàilǜlùn〈名〉［数学］law of probability
【概略】gàilüè **A**〈名〉summary: 故事～ summary of the story **B**〈形〉brief: ～说明 brief explanation
【概略图】gàilüètú〈名〉sketch
【概论】gàilùn〈名〉introduction:《美国文学～》*A Compendium of American Literature*
【概貌】gàimào〈名〉outline: 中国少数民族生活～ general picture of the life of Chinese ethnic groups ‖ 地区～ general picture of a region
【概莫能外】gàimònéngwài〈成〉admit no exceptions whatsoever
【概念】gàiniàn〈名〉concept: 提出一个新～ present a new concept ‖ 形成～ form an idea ‖ 抽象～ abstract concept ‖ 深奥的～ complex notion ‖ 小孩子没有"危险"的～。Children have no concept of danger.
【概念车】gàiniànchē〈名〉concept car
【概念股】gàiniàngǔ〈名〉［金融］concept stock
【概念化】gàiniànhuà〈动〉deal with in abstract terms: 写作不应～。Written work should not be abstract.
【概述】gàishù **A**〈名〉brief account:《社会学～》*A Survey of Sociology* **B**〈动〉outline: 他～了自己的计划/理由。He outlined his plan/reasons.
【概数】gàishù〈名〉approximate number
【概说】gàishuō〈名〉survey
【概算】gàisuàn **A**〈动〉make a rough estimate: ～一下，这个礼堂可坐 1,200 多人。At a rough estimate this auditorium can seat over 1,200 people. **B**〈名〉［经济］rough estimate
【概要】gàiyào〈名〉essentials: 剧情～ synopsis of a play ‖《天文学～》*A Compendium of Astronomy* ‖ 老师只讲了故事的～。The teacher gave only the gist of the story.

gān

干¹ gān〈名〉〈古〉shield: ▸～戈

干² gān〈动〉**1**〈书〉（违犯）affront: 有～禁例 violate a prohibition ▸～犯 **2**（干扰）interrupt: ▸～扰 **3**（牵涉）be concerned with: 与他何～? What has it got to do with him? **4**〈书〉（求取）seek

干³ gān〈名〉Heavenly Stems: ▸～支, 天～

干⁴ gān〈名〉〈书〉waterfront

干⁵（乾）gān
A〈形〉**1**（不湿）dry: 把毛巾拧～ wring out a towel ‖ 擦～眼泪 dry one's tears ‖ 感到口～ feel parched ‖ 衣服在阳光下很快就～了。The clothes soon dried off in the sun. ‖ 油漆未～。Wet paint! ▸～菜, ～旱, ～燥 **2**（枯竭）dried up: 把眼泪哭～ cry oneself dry ‖ 把沼泽地里的水排～ drain the swamps ‖ 水熬～了。The water boiled away. ▸～涸, 外强中～ **3**（非血缘关系）adopted: ▸～妈, ～亲 **4**（不用水）dry: ▸～馏, ～洗 **5**（指酒料）dry: ▸～红, ～啤
B〈动〉**1**（使净尽）empty: 咱们～了这一杯! Let's empty our glasses! ▸～杯 **2**〈方〉（不理睬）leave sb. in the cold: 别把客人～在那里。Don't leave the guests in the cold.
C〈副〉**1**（白白地）vainly: 站在一旁～生气 look on vainly in fury ‖ 我不会在那儿～等。I'll not wait there for nothing. ▸～瞪眼, ～着急 **2**（不实地）without real meaning: ▸～号, ～笑
D〈名〉dried food: 杏/牛肉～ dried apricot/beef ‖ 豆腐～ dried bean curd
▸gàn

【干巴巴】gānbābā〈形〉〈口〉**1**（不湿润）dry: ～的土地 parched land **2**（不生动）dull: 他的讲话～的，听得我直打哈欠。His speech was so boring that I couldn't help yawning.
【干爸】gānbà〈名〉〈口〉nominally adoptive father
【干巴】gānba〈形〉〈口〉**1**（不湿润）dry: 有些水果长时间放置会～的。Some fruits dry up if they are kept too long. **2**（不滋润）dried-up: 人老了，皮肤就～了。When people grow old, their skin shrivels. **3**（不生动）dull: 这份报告读起来～乏味。This report makes rather dry reading.
【干白】gānbái〈名〉dry white wine
【干杯】gānbēi〈动〉drink a toast: 为两国人民的友谊～ propose a toast to the friendship of the two peoples ‖ 为成功～ drink a toast to success
【干贝】gānbèi〈名〉dried scallop
【干瘪】gānbiě〈形〉**1**（不滋润）dried-up: ～的老头 wizened old man **2**（不生动）dry: 那是我所看过的最～的文章。It's the dullest article I've ever read.
【干冰】gānbīng〈名〉［化学］dry ice
【干菜】gāncài〈名〉dried vegetable: 储存～过冬 store dried vegetables for the winter
【干草】gāncǎo〈名〉hay
【干柴烈火】gānchái-lièhuǒ〈成〉〈喻〉**1**（指情势）explosive situation **2**（指男女）burning with desire
【干醋】gāncù〈名〉jealousy about something that is none of one's business: 吃～ experience uncalled-for jealousy
【干脆】gāncuì **A**〈形〉straightforward: 做事～利索 do things in a clear and efficient manner ‖ 他说话很～。He is very straightforward. **B**〈副〉bluntly: ～回绝他们算

g

了。Just give them a straight refusal.

【干达族】Gāndázú〈名〉Ganda: ～人 Ganda people ‖ ～语 Ganda language

【干打雷，不下雨】gān dǎléi, bù xiàyǔ〈俗〉**1**〈本〉thunder without rain **2**〈喻〉all talk and no action

【干打垒】gāndǎlěi〈名〉**1**（指筑墙方式）rammed-earth construction **2**（指房）house with walls of rammed earth

【干瞪眼】gāndèngyǎn〈惯〉〈方〉look on in despair: 我没办法，只能～。I was unable to do anything but stand and watch.

【干电池】gāndiànchí〈名〉dry battery

【干爹】gāndiē〈方〉= 干爸 gānbà

【干儿子】gān'érzi〈名〉〈口〉nominally adoptive son

【干犯】gānfàn〈动〉infringe upon: ～法纪 violate law and discipline ‖ ～法律 break the law

【干饭】gānfàn〈名〉cooked rice: ▸吃～

【干粉】gānfěn〈名〉**1**（指食品）dried noodles **2**（用于灭火）dry powder: ～灭火器 dry chemical fire extinguisher

【干干净净】gāngān-jìngjìng〈成〉spotless

【干戈】gāngē〈名〉〈书〉weapons of war: 化～为玉帛 bury the hatchet ‖ ～四起。Wars broke out everywhere.

【干股】gāngǔ〈名〉gratuitous share

【干果】gānguǒ〈名〉**1**［植物］dry fruit **2**（指果品）dried fruit

【干旱】gānhàn〈形〉arid: 天气～ dry weather

【干旱期】gānhànqī〈名〉dry spell

【干号】gānháo〈动〉cry but shed no tears

【干嚎】gānháo = 干号 gānháo

【干涸】gānhé〈形〉dried-up: 那条河早就～了。That river dried up long ago.

【干红】gānhóng〈名〉dry red wine: ～葡萄酒 dry red wine

【干花】gānhuā〈名〉dried flower

【干货】gānhuò〈名〉dried food

【干急】gānjí = 干着急 gānzháojí

【干季】gānjì〈名〉［气象］dry season

【干将】gānjiàng〈名〉*Ganjiang* [treasured double-edged sword] ▸gànjiàng

【干将莫邪】gānjiàng-mòyé〈名〉*Ganjiang* and *Moye* [treasured double-edged swords]

【干结】gānjié〈形〉dry and hard: 大便～ be constipated

【干姐妹】gānjiěmèi〈名〉sworn sisters

【干净】gānjìng〈形〉**1**（不脏）clean: 爱～ be a clean person ‖ 把厨房打扫～ clean up the kitchen ‖ 把毛巾洗～ wash the towel clean ‖〈喻〉说话嘴不～ have a foul mouth ‖〈喻〉他手脚有点不～。He has itchy fingers. **2**（一点不剩）empty: 把敌人消灭～ wipe out the enemy **3**（不拖沓）clear-cut: 处理问题～利落 solve problems quickly and efficiently ‖ 他文笔～。He is very concise in his writing.

【干净利落】gānjìng-lìluo〈成〉smooth and clean

【干酒】gānjiǔ〈名〉dry wine

【干咳】gānké〈动〉have a dry cough: 发出短促的～声 emit short dry coughs

【干渴】gānkě〈形〉very thirsty: ～而死 die of thirst

【干枯】gānkū〈形〉dried-up: ～的皮肤 shrivelled skin ‖ 小树都晒～了。The young trees have shrivelled up in the sun. ‖ 小河冬天会～。The small river dries up in winter.

【干哭】gānkū〈动〉cry without tears

【干酪】gānlào〈名〉cheese

【干冷】gānlěng〈形〉crisp: ～的冬日 crisp winter day

【干礼】gānlǐ〈名〉money as a gift

【干连】gānlián = 牵连 qiānlián

【干粮】gānliang〈名〉dry provisions: 星期天郊游，请自带～。Bring your own food on Sunday's outing.

【干粮袋】gānliangdài〈名〉haversack

【干裂】gānliè〈动〉crack: ～的嘴唇 chapped lips

【干馏】gānliú〈名〉［化学］dry distillation

【干妈】gānmā〈名〉〈口〉nominally adoptive mother

【干娘】gānniáng = 干妈 gānmā

【干女儿】gānnǚ'ér〈名〉〈口〉nominally adoptive daughter

【干呕】gān'ǒu〈动〉retch

【干啤】gānpí〈名〉dry beer

【干亲】gānqīn〈名〉nominal kinship: 认～ take sb. as one's adoptive kin

【干扰】gānrǎo〈动〉**1**（扰乱）disturb: ～某人的工作 interfere with sb.'s work ‖ 排除～ overcome a disturbance ‖ 母语对外语学习的～ mother tongue interference in foreign language study **2**［物理］interfere: 电子～ electronic interference ‖ 移动电话会～电视信号吗？Does a mobile phone interfere with TV signals?

【干扰素】gānrǎosù〈名〉［生物］interferon

【干涩】gānsè〈形〉**1**（指皮肤）dry and rough: ～的皮肤 dry and coarse skin **2**（指嗓音）hoarse: 嗓音～ have a husky voice **3**（指表情、动作）stiff: ～地一笑 force a stiff smile

【干涉】gānshè〈动〉**1**（干预）interfere: ～别人私事 interfere in sb.'s private affairs ‖ ～婚姻/言论自由 interfere with the freedom of marriage/speech ‖ ～他国内政 interfere in the internal affairs of another country ‖ 武装～ military intervention **2**〈书〉（关联）relationship: 二者了无～。There is no connection between the two.

【干涉仪】gānshèyí〈名〉［物理］interferometer

【干尸】gānshī〈名〉mummified corpse

【干湿表】gānshībiǎo〈名〉［气象］psychrometer

【干瘦】gānshòu〈形〉bony: ～的老头 emaciated old man

【干爽】gānshuǎng〈形〉**1**（指气候）dry and crisp: ～的空气 crisp air **2**（指土地道路）dry: ～的地方 arid place

【干丝】gānsī〈名〉shredded dried bean curd

【干洗】gānxǐ〈动〉dry-clean: 把衣服送去～ have the clothing dry-cleaned ‖ ～机 dry-cleaner ‖ 这套西服只能～。This suit has to be dry-cleaned.

【干洗店】gānxǐdiàn〈名〉dry-cleaner's

【干洗剂】gānxǐjì〈名〉dry-cleaner

【干系】gānxì〈名〉responsibility: 逃脱不了～ cannot escape the responsibility ‖ 他不承认与这一事故有任何～。He denied any responsibility for the accident.

【干笑】gānxiào〈动〉force a smile

【干薪】gānxīn〈名〉sinecure salary

【干性】gānxìng〈形〉drying: ～油 dry oil

【干眼症】gānyǎnzhèng ▸**p. 50**〈名〉［医学］xerophthalmia

【干谒】gānyè〈动〉〈书〉seek favour

【干预】gānyù〈动〉interfere: ～他人的事 stick one's nose into other people's business ‖ ～货币市场 intervene in the currency market ‖ 行政～ administrative interference ‖ 这件事与我们无关，我们不～。It's none of our business, and we will not get involved in it.

【干燥】gānzào〈形〉dry: 气候～ dry climate ‖ ～箱 drying chest

【干燥剂】gānzàojì〈名〉［化学］drying agent

【干着急】gānzháojí〈动〉〈口〉be anxious but unable to do anything: 我对这事儿是～没办法。I was anxious, but I could do nothing about it.

【干政】gānzhèng〈动〉〈书〉meddle in state affairs

【干支】gānzhī〈名〉Heavenly Stems and Earthly Branches: ～纪年 years designated by Heavenly Stems and Earthly Branches

【干租】gānzū〈动〉dry-lease: ～协议 dry-lease agreement

甘[1] gān

A〈形〉sweet: ▸～草，～露，同～共苦

B〈副〉willingly: ～守清贫 be content to live a simple life ‖ 不～落后 be unwilling to lag behind ▸～拜下风，～心

甘[2] Gān ▸**p. 661**〈名〉Gan [another name for Gansu Province (甘肃)]

【甘氨酸】gān'ānsuān〈名〉［生化］glycine

【甘拜下风】gānbàixiàfēng〈成〉bow to sb.'s superiority

【甘草】gāncǎo〈名〉［植物］liquorice

【甘醇】gānchún〈名〉［化学］glycol

【甘当】gāndāng〈动〉**1**（指惩罚）be willing to accept: ～其罪 be willing to accept punishment **2**（指做事）be willing to act as

【甘结】gānjié〈名〉〈旧〉written pledge given to the government authorities

【甘居】gānjū〈动〉be content to be in an unfavourable state: ～人后 be willing to be outdone

【甘居中游】gānjū-zhōngyóu〈成〉rest content to stay mediocre

【甘苦】gānkǔ〈名〉**1**（欢乐和艰辛）sweetness and bitterness **2**（指困苦）hardships: 深知其中的～ know well what hardship is like

【甘苦与共】gānkǔ-yǔgòng〈成〉stick together through thick and thin

【甘蓝】gānlán〈名〉［植物］wild cabbage

【甘冽】gānliè〈形〉sweet and cool

【甘霖】gānlín〈名〉〈书〉timely rain: 一场～缓解了旱情。A timely rain eased the drought.

【甘露】gānlù〈名〉sweet dew

【甘美】gānměi〈形〉sweet and rich: ～的果汁 sweet, rich juice

【甘泉】gānquán〈名〉sweet spring (water)

【甘薯】gānshǔ〈名〉sweet potato

【甘肃】Gānsù ▸**p. 661**〈名〉Gansu Province

【甘甜】gāntián〈形〉sweet: ～可口的水果 sweet and delicious fruit

【甘托克】Gāntuōkè〈名〉Gangtok

【甘味】gānwèi〈书〉**A**〈名〉delicacy **B**〈动〉have an appetite: ▸食不～

【甘心】gānxīn〈动〉**1**（愿意）be willing: ～为人效劳 be willing to offer one's service **2**（满意）be content with: 不达目的不～ be dissatisfied unless one has reached one's goal

【甘心情愿】gānxīn-qíngyuàn〈成〉willingly and gladly: ～把机会让给别人 willingly give the opportunity to others

【甘休】gānxiū〈动〉be willing to give up:

他不会就此～。 He will not let it go at that. ▸善罢～
【甘油】gānyóu〈名〉［化学］glycerine: ～基 glyceryl
【甘油三酯】gānyóusānzhǐ〈名〉［化学］triglyceride
【甘于】gānyú〈动〉be glad to: ～为国家奉献一生 be willing to give one's whole life to the cause of one's country
【甘雨】gānyǔ〈名〉timely rain: 久旱逢～ have timely rain after a long drought
【甘愿】gānyuàn〈动〉be willing to: ～受罚 be ready to bear punishment ‖ ～牺牲个人利益 be willing to sacrifice one's personal interests
【甘蔗】gānzhe〈名〉sugar cane
【甘蔗没有两头甜】gānzhe méiyǒu liǎngtóu tián〈俗〉you cannot have your cake and eat it
【甘之如饴】gānzhī-rúyí〈成〉take adversity with a smile

忏 gān〈动〉〈书〉interfere

玕 gān ▸琅玕 lánggān

杆 gān〈名〉pole: ▸栏～, 桅～ ▸gǎn
【杆塔】gāntǎ〈名〉tower
【杆子】gānzi〈名〉pole: 电线～ wire pole

肝 gān〈名〉liver: 酗酒伤～。 Alcohol abuse damages your liver.
【肝癌】gān'ái ▸p. 50〈名〉liver cancer
【肝病】gānbìng ▸p. 50〈名〉liver disease: ～患者 person suffering from liver disease
【肝肠寸断】gāncháng-cùnduàn〈成〉be deeply grieved: 那个消息令她～。 She was heartbroken at the news.
【肝胆】gāndǎn〈名〉〈喻〉1（勇气）heroic spirit 2（真诚）sincerity
【肝胆过人】gāndǎn-guòrén〈成〉be unsurpassed in valour
【肝胆相照】gāndǎn-xiāngzhào〈成〉have utter devotion to (friends, etc.): ～, 荣辱与共 be completely devoted to one another, sharing good times and bad
【肝胆照人】gāndǎn-zhàorén〈成〉be exceedingly sincere or loyal
【肝功】gāngōng〈简称〉= 肝功能
【肝功能】gāngōngnéng〈名〉liver function: ～衰竭 liver failure
【肝坏死】gānhuàisǐ ▸p. 50〈名〉［医学］hepatic necrosis
【肝昏迷】gānhūnmí ▸p. 50〈名〉［医学］hepatic coma
【肝火】gānhuǒ〈名〉irritability: 动～ fly into a rage ‖ ～旺 be hot-tempered
【肝脑涂地】gānnǎo-túdì〈成〉die the cruellest death: ～, 也在所不惜 would not grudge anything, even one's life
【肝气】gānqì〈名〉1 ▸p. 50［中医］hepatic *qi* [a disease with such symptoms as costal pain, vomiting, diarrhoea, etc.] 2（易怒）irritability
【肝细胞】gānxìbāo〈名〉liver cell
【肝炎】gānyán ▸p. 50〈名〉hepatitis: 丙型～ hepatitis C ‖ 甲型～ hepatitis A ‖ 乙型～ hepatitis B
【肝硬化】gānyìnghuà ▸p. 50〈名〉［医学］(hepatic) cirrhosis
【肝油】gānyóu〈名〉liver oil: 鱼～ cod liver oil
【肝脏】gānzàng〈名〉liver: ～移植 liver transplant
【肝肿大】gānzhǒngdà ▸p. 50〈名〉［医学］hepatomegaly

坩 gān〈名〉〈书〉earthenware pot
【坩埚】gānguō〈名〉［化学］crucible

苷 gān ▸糖苷 tánggān

矸 gān
【矸石】gānshí〈名〉［矿业］gangue
【矸子】gānzi〈口〉= 矸石 gānshí

泔 gān〈名〉pig swill
【泔脚】gānjiǎo〈名〉〈方〉pig swill
【泔水】gānshuǐ〈名〉slops

柑 gān〈名〉mandarin orange
【柑橘】gānjú〈名〉1（橙和橘）oranges and tangerines 2（统称）citrus
【柑子】gānzi〈名〉〈方〉mandarin orange

竿 gān〈名〉bamboo pole: 爬～ climb a pole ‖ 钓鱼～ fishing rod ▸揭～而起, 立～见影
【竿子】gānzi〈名〉bamboo pole

酐 gān ▸酸酐 suāngān

疳 gān〈名〉［中医］infantile malnutrition
【疳积】gānjī = 疳 gān

尴（尷）gān
【尴尬】gāngà〈形〉1（难以处理）awkward: 处境～ be in an awkward position 2〈方〉（难为情）embarrassed: 神情～ embarrassed look ‖ 她～地笑了。 She smiled with embarrassment.

gǎn

杆（桿）gǎn
A〈名〉arm: 秤～ arm of a steelyard ‖ 枪～ barrel of a gun
B〈量〉[used for a long and thin cylindrical object]: 一～秤 a steelyard ‖ 一～枪 a gun ▸gān
【杆秤】gǎnchèng〈名〉steelyard
【杆菌】gǎnjūn〈名〉［生物］bacillus: 结核～ tubercle bacilli
【杆子】gǎnzi〈名〉shaft: ▸笔～

秆（稈）gǎn〈名〉stalk: 麻～ hemp stalk ‖ 麦～ wheat straw ‖ 玉米～ corn stalk
【秆子】gǎnzi〈名〉stalk: 高粱～ sorghum stalk

赶（趕）gǎn
A〈动〉1（追）run after: 跑步～上队伍 run to catch up with the troops ▸你追我～, 追～ 2（加快）hurry: ～火车/汽车 try to catch the train/bus ‖ ～任务 hurry through one's work ‖ ～时间 race against the clock ‖ ～到现场/医院 rush to the scene/hospital ▸～紧 3（驱走）drive away: ～苍蝇/蚊子 shoo off flies/mosquitoes ‖ 把侵略者～出去 chase the invaders away ▸～跑, ～走 4（驾）drive: ～马车 drive a carriage ‖ ～羊入栏 herd sheep into a sheepfold 5（前往参加）go to: ～庙会 go to a temple fair ▸～集, ～考 6（碰上）meet with: ～上下雨 run into rain ‖ 我到你们学校那天, 正～上你们放假。 It happened to be a holiday the day I arrived at your school. ▸～巧
B〈介〉〈口〉until: ～明儿我上街给你买一辆自行车。 I'll go and buy a bike for you tomorrow. ‖ ～他不在的时候你再来。 Come again when he is out.
【赶不及】gǎnbují〈动〉〈口〉not have enough time: 会两点开, 我们恐怕～了。 The meeting starts at two, and I'm afraid we won't be able to make it.
【赶不上】gǎnbushàng〈动〉1（指速度）be unable to keep pace with: 政治改革～经济改革的步伐。 The political reform is failing to keep up with the economic reform. 2 = 赶不及 gǎnbují 3（指机遇）be unable to meet with: ～好天气 be not lucky enough to have good weather 4（指比较）be no match: 论保暖性能, 什么也～羊毛。 Nothing can compare with wool when it comes to warmth. ‖ 我～你。 I am no match for you.
【赶场】gǎncháng〈方〉= 赶集 gǎnjí
【赶场】gǎnchǎng〈动〉[of a performer] hurry from one theatre to another
【赶超】gǎnchāo〈动〉catch up with and surpass: ～世界先进水平 catch up with and surpass advanced international standards
【赶潮流】gǎn cháoliú〈动〉follow the trend: 盲目～ blindly follow fashions
【赶车】gǎnchē〈动〉1（指搭乘）make a vehicle: 他急着～, 把行李忘在出租车上了。 In his hurry to catch the train, he left his luggage in the taxi. 2（指驾驭）drive a cart
【赶道】gǎndào = 赶路 gǎnlù
【赶得及】gǎndejí〈动〉〈口〉be in time for: 吃完饭赶火车还～。 We can still make the train if we have our meal first.
【赶得上】gǎndeshàng〈动〉1（指比较）match: 在这一方面几乎没有人能～他。 Few people can match him in this aspect. 2（指时间）be able to make it: 别担心, 我们～开会。 Don't worry. We will be in time for the meeting. 3（指机遇）be able to have: 如果～好天气, 我们的假期将过得非常好。 As long as we get good weather, it will be a successful holiday.
【赶点】gǎndiǎn〈动〉1（指交通工具）speed up in order to arrive in time 2（指时机）be just in time: 你正赶上点儿啦, 我正要人帮忙呢。 You are just in time to help me.
【赶赴】gǎnfù〈动〉hasten to: ～前线 hurry to the front line ‖ ～现场 rush to the scene
【赶工】gǎngōng〈动〉hurry through one's work: ～铺路 work fast to surface a road
【赶海】gǎnhǎi〈动〉〈方〉go to gather seafood on the beach at low tide: ～人 beach comber
【赶活儿】gǎnhuór〈动〉rush a job
【赶集】gǎnjí〈动〉go to a market
【赶脚】gǎnjiǎo〈动〉work as a porter with a mule
【赶紧】gǎnjǐn〈副〉without delay: ～穿好衣服去开门 hurriedly get dressed and open the door ‖ ～回家 hurry home ‖ 叫他～来。 Tell him to come immediately.
【赶尽杀绝】gǎnjìn-shājué〈成〉kill all
【赶考】gǎnkǎo〈动〉go and take an imperial examination: 进京～ go to the capital to sit for an imperial examination
【赶快】gǎnkuài〈副〉immediately: ～回家 hurry home ‖ ～去叫医生 hurry to get a doctor ‖ 这件事得～处理! This matter

must be dealt with immediately!

【赶浪头】gǎn làngtou〈惯〉〈贬〉 follow the trend

【赶路】gǎnlù〈动〉 hurry on one's way: 休息片刻继续～ resume one's journey after a short rest

【赶忙】gǎnmáng〈副〉 hurriedly: ～用手捂住脸 quickly cover one's face with one's hands ‖ 他意识到自己说错了，～改口。 He hastened to correct himself as soon as he realized he'd made a mistake.

【赶庙会】gǎn miàohuì〈动〉 go to a temple fair

【赶明儿】gǎnmíngr〈副〉〈口〉 one of these days: ～我再来看你。 I'll come to see you again soon. ‖ ～我再详细给你讲。 I'll tell you in detail one of these days.

【赶跑】gǎnpǎo = 赶走 gǎnzǒu

【赶前不赶后】gǎn qián bù gǎn hòu〈俗〉 better a big push at the start than a mad dash at the end

【赶巧】gǎnqiǎo〈副〉 happen to: 今天我～有空。 I just happen to be free today. ‖ 我去拜访她，～她不在。 It so happened that she was out when I went to call on her.

【赶热闹】gǎn rènao〈动〉 join in the fun

【赶上】gǎnshàng〈动〉 **1** (指水平) catch up with: ～世界先进水平 catch up with the advanced world **2** (指交通工具) be in (good) time for: 差点没～公共汽车 nearly miss the bus **3** (指时机) run into: ～坏天气 run into bad weather ‖ 我到他家时正～吃午饭时间。 It happened to be lunchtime when I got to his home. **4** (指比较) be a match (for sb./sth.): 什么衣服也赶不上棉布衣服穿着舒服。 Nothing is comparable to cotton when it comes to comfort.

【赶时髦】gǎn shímáo〈动〉 follow fashion: 她想～学外语。 She wants to keep up with the fashion for learning foreign languages.

【赶趟儿】gǎntàngr〈动〉〈方〉 be in time: 再不出发，我们就赶不上趟儿了。 We'll be late if we don't leave right now.

【赶圩】gǎnxū〈方〉= 赶集 gǎnjí

【赶鸭子上架】gǎn yāzi shàng jià〈俗〉〈喻〉 ask sb. to do sth. beyond his capacity

【赶早】gǎnzǎo〈副〉 as soon as possible: 我们明天得～走。 We must set out as early as possible tomorrow.

【赶走】gǎnzǒu〈动〉 drive away: ～侵略者 expel invaders from one's country

敢 gǎn

A〈形〉 brave: ▸勇～, 果～

B〈动〉 **1** (有勇气) dare: ～干/说/想 dare to act/speak/think ‖ 不～说半个"不"字 dare not mutter dissent ‖ 谁～不听他的! No one dares to disobey him! ‖ 他不～把真相告诉父亲。 He didn't have the guts to tell his father the truth. **2** (确信) be certain: 我～说他能活到八十岁。 I'm sure he will live to eighty.

C〈副〉〈书〉〈谦〉 boldly: ～问您贵姓? May I ask your name?

【敢保】gǎnbǎo〈动〉 be sure

【敢打敢拼】gǎndǎ-gǎnpīn〈成〉 dare to stand up to an opponent

【敢怒而不敢言】gǎn nù ér bùgǎn yán〈成〉 choke with silent fury

【敢情】gǎnqing〈副〉〈方〉 **1** (表推测) well I never: ～昨晚下雪啦。 Well I never! It snowed last night. **2** (当然) obviously: 明天会下雪? 那～好! It'll rain tomorrow? That would be wonderful!

【敢是】gǎnshi〈副〉〈方〉 perhaps: 她好久没给我写信了，～忘了我的地址? She hasn't written to me for ages; perhaps she's lost my address. ‖ ～走错了吧? I fear we may have taken the wrong road.

【敢死队】gǎnsǐduì〈名〉 death squad

【敢想敢干】gǎnxiǎng-gǎngàn〈成〉 be innovative in mind and in deed

【敢于】gǎnyú〈动〉 dare: ～承担责任 be brave enough to take on a responsibility ‖ ～挑战权威 dare to challenge authority

【敢字当头】gǎn zì dāngtóu〈成〉 put daring above all else

【敢作敢当】gǎnzuò-gǎndāng〈成〉 be bold enough to do sth. and to take responsibility for the consequences

【敢作敢为】gǎnzuò-gǎnwéi〈成〉 act with courage and determination

感 gǎn

A〈动〉 **1** (引起) move: ▸～动, ～想 **2** [中医] be affected by wind-cold: 外～发热 external contraction fever **3** (感谢) thank: ▸～恩戴德, ～谢 **4** (感到) feel: 对钓鱼～兴趣 be interested in fishing ‖ 颇～意外 be taken by surprise ‖ 深～不安 feel extremely anxious ‖ 她对你的批评深～不悦。 She was quite unhappy about your criticism. ▸～到 **5** (感应) sensitize: ▸～光

B〈名〉 feeling: 有安全～ have a sense of security ‖ 读后～ thoughts on a book ‖ 失落～ sense of loss ▸快～, 美～, 手～

【感触】gǎnchù〈名〉 thoughts and feelings: 深有～地说 say with deep feeling ‖ ～很深 be deeply moved

【感戴】gǎndài〈动〉〈书〉 show gratitude and respect: 她对导师～万分。 She is deeply grateful to her academic adviser.

【感到】gǎndào〈动〉 feel: ～恶心 be sick in the stomach ‖ ～沮丧 feel frustrated ‖ ～欣慰 be satisfied (with) ‖ 对家庭生活～厌倦 be tired of family life ‖ 母亲为自己的女儿～骄傲。 The mother took pride in her daughter.

【感动】gǎndòng〈动〉 **1** (被感动) be moved: ～得不知说什么好 be touched beyond words ‖ ～得热泪盈眶 be moved to tears ‖ 深受～ be deeply moved **2** (使人感动) move: 他的讲话深深地～了我。 His speech touched me profoundly.

【感恩】gǎn'ēn〈动〉 feel grateful: ～不尽 be extremely grateful

【感恩戴德】gǎn'ēn-dàidé〈成〉 be overwhelmed with gratitude

【感恩节】Gǎn'ēnjié〈名〉 Thanksgiving Day

【感恩图报】gǎn'ēn-túbào〈成〉 feel deeply grateful and seek ways to return the kindness

【感奋】gǎnfèn〈动〉〈书〉 be moved and inspired: 他的讲话令人～。 His speech moved everybody and inspired them to greater efforts.

【感愤】gǎnfèn〈动〉〈书〉 be indignant: 令公众～不已 arouse strong public indignation

【感官】gǎnguān〈名〉 sense organ

【感光】gǎnguāng〈动〉 sensitize

【感光材料】gǎnguāng cáiliào〈名〉 photosensitive material

【感光度】gǎnguāngdù〈名〉 sensitivity: 低/高～ lower/higher sensitivity

【感光剂】gǎnguāngjì〈名〉 sensitizer

【感光片】gǎnguāngpiàn〈名〉 light-sensitive sheet

【感光纸】gǎnguāngzhǐ〈名〉 light-sensitive paper

【感化】gǎnhuà〈动〉 help to change: ～少年犯 help juvenile delinquents to go straight

【感化院】gǎnhuàyuàn〈名〉〈旧〉 reformatory

【感怀】gǎnhuái〈动〉 recall with emotion: ～往事 recall past events with emotion ‖ 国庆～ National Day reflections

【感激】gǎnjī〈动〉 feel grateful: 不胜～ be extremely grateful ‖ 表达～之情 express one's gratitude ‖ 对某人的帮助十分～ be very grateful to sb. for their help

【感激涕零】gǎnjī-tìlíng〈成〉 shed tears of gratitude

【感觉】gǎnjué **A**〈名〉 feeling: 跟着～走 follow one's feelings ‖ 疼痛的～ painful feeling ‖ 皮肤失去了～。 The skin has lost its sensitivity. **B**〈动〉 **1** (感到) feel: ～饿/冷 feel hungry/cold ‖ ～房子在摇晃 feel the house shake ‖ ～上当受骗 feel cheated **2** (认为) be afraid (that): 我～你说的不对。 I'm afraid what you said is wrong.

【感觉迟钝】gǎnjué chídùn〈名〉[医学] unpleasant, abnormal sensation

【感觉器官】gǎnjué qìguān〈名〉 sense organ: 耳朵、眼睛、舌头、鼻子和皮肤是～。 Ears, eyes, tongue, nose and skin are sense organs.

【感觉神经】gǎnjué shénjīng〈名〉[解剖] sensory nerve

【感觉细胞】gǎnjué xìbāo〈名〉[心理] sensory cell

【感觉异常】gǎnjué yìcháng〈名〉[医学] abnormal feeling

【感觉中枢】gǎnjué zhōngshū〈名〉[生理] sensorium

【感慨】gǎnkǎi〈动〉 sigh with emotion: 非常/无限～ sigh with deep feeling

【感慨万端】gǎnkǎi-wànduān〈成〉 all sorts of feelings well up in one's mind

【感慨万千】gǎnkǎi-wànqiān = 感慨万端 gǎnkǎi-wànduān

【感慨系之】gǎnkǎixìzhī〈成〉 sigh with deep feeling

【感愧】gǎnkuì〈动〉〈书〉 feel both grateful and ashamed: ～交加 feel both grateful and ashamed

【感喟】gǎnkuì〈动〉〈书〉 heave a sigh

【感冒】gǎnmào **A** ▸**p. 50**〈名〉 cold: 流行性～ influenza flu ‖ 重～ heavy cold **B**〈动〉 **1** (得感冒) have a cold **2**〈口〉(感兴趣) [often used in the negative] be interested in: 我对这种事一概不～。 I am not at all interested in such things.

【感冒药】gǎnmàoyào〈名〉 cold medicine

【感念】gǎnniàn〈动〉 think of sb. with deep feeling: ～不忘 keep thinking of sb. with deep emotion ‖ 我非常～我的祖母。 I remember my grandmother with deep affection.

【感佩】gǎnpèi〈动〉〈书〉 be filled with gratitude and admiration: 由衷～ gratefully admire (sb.)

【感情】gǎnqíng〈名〉 **1** (情义) feeling: 表达～ express one's emotions ‖ 流露～ show one's emotions ‖ 培养～ develop feelings (for sb.) ‖ 伤～ hurt sb.'s feelings ‖ ～冲动 get carried away with one's emotions ‖ ～纠葛 emotional entanglement ‖ 复杂的～ mixed feelings ‖ 她～细腻。 She has delicacy of feeling. ‖ 他们多年来～不和。 There have been hard feelings between them for years. **2** (爱) affection: 对某人产生～ become attached to sb. ‖ 对某人怀有～ cherish a deep affection for sb. ‖ 把全部～倾注到孩子身上 devote all one's affections to one's children

【感情色彩】gǎnqíng sècǎi〈名〉sentiment
【感情投资】gǎnqíng tóuzī〈名〉emotional investment [effort made and money spent to improve human relations]
【感情用事】gǎnqíng-yòngshì〈成〉give way to one's feelings: 不要~。Don't let yourself be swayed by your own sentiments.
【感染】gǎnrǎn〈动〉**1**（指疾病）infect: ~病毒 be infected with a virus ‖ 受~ get infected ‖ 预防~ take precautions against infection ‖ 病毒~ viral infection ‖ 肺部~ lung infection ‖ 细菌~ bacterial infection ‖〈喻〉这种蠕虫病毒已经~了上万台电脑。The worm virus has affected over ten thousand computers. **2**（指情绪）imbue: 那位教师以自己的热情~了他的学生。The teacher imbued his students with his enthusiasm.
【感染力】gǎnrǎnlì〈名〉appeal: 缺乏~ lack punch ‖ 富有~的表演 performance with plenty of punch ‖ 艺术~ artistic appeal ‖ 有~的笑声 infectious laugh
【感人】gǎnrén〈形〉moving: ~的一刻 touching moment
【感人肺腑】gǎnrénfèifǔ〈成〉move sb. deeply
【感伤】gǎnshāng〈形〉sad: ~主义 sentimentalism ‖ 听到那首歌，她就有点~。She felt sad whenever she heard that song.
【感生】gǎnshēng〈动〉[电气] induce: ~电流 induced current ‖ ~电压 induced voltage/potential
【感受】gǎnshòu **A**〈动〉**1**（感到）experience: ~集体的温暖 experience the warmth of the collective ‖ 人们已经~到计算机革命所带来的巨大影响。People have already felt the tremendous influence of the computer revolution. **2**（患）catch: ~风寒 catch cold **B**〈名〉experience: 美国之行使我~很深。My visit to America made a deep impression on me.
【感叹】gǎntàn〈动〉sigh with emotion: ~悲惨的身世 sigh with sadness at one's miserable life
【感叹词】gǎntàncí〈名〉exclamation
【感叹号】gǎntànhào〈名〉exclamation mark (!); exclamation point〈美〉
【感叹句】gǎntànjù〈名〉exclamatory sentence
【感天动地】gǎntiān-dòngdì〈成〉**1**（指真诚）be 100% sincere **2**（指悲痛）be completely heart-breaking
【感同身受】gǎntóngshēnshòu〈成〉〈套〉[said when expressing gratitude on sb. else's behalf] feel as if one were experiencing something in person
【感物伤怀】gǎnwù-shānghuái〈成〉feel sad to see sth. that reminds one of the past
【感悟】gǎnwù〈动〉realize: ~到人生的真谛 come to realize the true meaning of life
【感想】gǎnxiǎng〈名〉thoughts: 谈几点~ have a few reflections to offer ‖ 你对此事有何~? What do you think of it?
【感谢】gǎnxiè〈动〉thank: ~光临 thanks for coming ‖ 表示衷心~ express one's heartfelt thanks ‖ 非常~。Many thanks. ‖ 真不知该怎样~您才好。How can I ever thank you enough?
【感谢信】gǎnxièxìn〈名〉thank-you letter
【感性】gǎnxìng〈形〉perceptive
【感性认识】gǎnxìng rènshi〈名〉perceptual knowledge: 从~到理性认识的飞跃 leap from perceptual knowledge to rational knowledge
【感言】gǎnyán〈名〉thoughts expressed in words
【感应】gǎnyìng **A**〈动〉respond: 心理~ psychological response **B**〈名〉[电气] induction: 静电~ static induction ‖ ~电动机 induction motor ‖ ~电流 induction current
【感应卡】gǎnyìngkǎ〈名〉Proximity card: ~读卡器 Proximity card reader
【感遇】gǎnyù〈动〉〈书〉be indebted for the favourable treatment received
【感召】gǎnzhào〈动〉inspire: 在政策的~下 inspired by the policy
【感召力】gǎnzhàolì〈名〉charisma
【感知】gǎnzhī **A**〈名〉[哲学] perception **B**〈动〉feel: ~自己的心跳加快 feel one's heart beating faster

橄 gǎn

【橄榄】gǎnlǎn〈名〉**1**（指果实）Chinese olive **2**［植物］olive: ~树 olive tree
【橄榄绿】gǎnlǎnlǜ〈名〉olive green
【橄榄球】gǎnlǎnqiú〈名〉**1** ▸p. 909（指运动）rugby: ~场 rugby pitch ‖ ~运动员 rugby player **2**（指球）rugby ball
【橄榄油】gǎnlǎnyóu〈名〉olive oil
【橄榄枝】gǎnlǎnzhī〈名〉olive branch: 伸出~ extend an olive branch

擀 gǎn〈动〉roll: ~饺子皮 roll out *jiaozi* wrappers ▸~面

【擀面】gǎnmiàn〈动〉make noodles with a rolling pin
【擀面杖】gǎnmiànzhàng〈名〉rolling pin
【擀面杖吹火，一窍不通】gǎnmiànzhàng chuī huǒ, yī qiào bù tōng〈歇后〉be completely ignorant of sth.

gàn

干¹（幹）gàn〈名〉**1**（主干）trunk: ▸树~ **2**（主体）body: ▸~流, ~线, 骨~ **3**（干部）cadre: 提~ promote a soldier or a worker to the rank of a cadre ▸~群

干²（幹）gàn **A**〈动〉**1**（做）do: ~工作 do a job ‖ ~实事 achieve tangible results ‖ 蛮~ act

ℹ 感谢与劳驾

表示感谢

■ 要对别人为你做的事或说的话表示感激或欣赏，在英语中有多种表达方式可供选择：

你讲的故事可真有趣，非常感谢
= Your story was really interesting. Thank you very much

谢谢你的生日礼物
= Thank you very much for the birthday presents

你今晚真漂亮 —— 谢谢
= You look really beautiful tonight — Thanks

我来接你好吗？
——不用了，但我还是要谢谢你
= Shall I pick you up?
— No, but thank you anyway

你帮了我大忙。我真是感激不尽
= You've done me a big favour. I can't thank you enough

我非常感谢你们的大力支持
= I'd like to say a big thank you for your huge support

你这么关心我，我不知如何表达我的谢意
= Words can not express my gratitude for your concern
或 I can't express how grateful I am to you for your concern

我衷心感谢你所有的帮助
= I'm sincerely grateful to you for all your help

我真的非常感谢你邀请我参加聚会
= I really appreciate you inviting me to your party

这是你的咖啡 —— 非常感谢
= Here is your coffee
— Thank you. I appreciate it

■ 注意下面汉语间接表达感谢时的英文翻译：

你想再来块蛋糕吗？ —— 那太好了
Would you like another piece of cake?
— Yes, that would be lovely

这是我给你订的机票 —— 真麻烦你了
= Here is the flight ticket I booked for you
— I've caused you so much trouble
或 I've troubled you too much

我已经把你儿子送回家了
—— 你可真是，辛苦你了
= I've taken your son home
— You shouldn't have. That was really a lot of work for you

表示劳驾

■"劳驾"表示"烦劳他人"之意，在翻译成英语时要看语境，可用多种方式表达：

这是你让我给你买的书 —— 真是劳驾你了
= Here is the book you asked me to buy for you
— I'm really grateful to you (for doing that)
或 Thank you very much for the trouble

你能把这篇文章翻译成英文吗？劳驾了
= Can you translate the article into English? Thank you in advance for the trouble

同意的，请举手。劳驾了
= Please put up your hands if you agree. Thanks

劳您大驾。不知道您能否让我搭个便车
= Can you do me a favour? I'm wondering if you could give me a lift

能否劳驾你向我推荐一本英语词典？
= Can you please recommend me an English dictionary?

劳驾了，你能告诉我他的电话号码吗？
= Sorry to bother you, but can you tell me his phone number?

■ 引起别人的注意或请别人让路时说的"劳驾"则要翻译成 excuse me:

劳驾，附近有邮局吗？
= Excuse me, is there a post office nearby?

劳驾，让我过去好吗？
= Excuse me, can I just get past?

g

recklessly ‖ 要～就～好。 If you do it, do it well. ‖ 这是他们～的。 They did it. ②（从事） work as: 教师这一行，我已～了十五年。 I have been working as a teacher for fifteen years. ③（打架） fight: 为一点小事～了起来 start a fight over something insignificant
B〈名〉 ability: ▸才～
C〈形〉 able: ▸～将，精～，精明强～
▸gān

【干部】gànbù〈名〉 ①（领导） cadre: 任免～ appoint and dismiss cadres ‖ 选拔～ select cadres ‖ 党政～ Party and Government officials ‖ 各级领导～ leading cadres at all levels ‖ 老～ veteran cadre ②（公职人员） functionary

【干部学校】gànbù xuéxiào〈名〉 cadre school

【干才】gàncái〈名〉 ①（指能力） ability: 他很有～。He is quite capable. ②（指人） capable person: 这些人都是～。 These people are all very capable.

【干道】gàndào〈名〉 main road

【干掉】gàndiào〈动〉〈口〉 do away with: ～对手 eliminate an opponent ‖ ～敌军一个哨兵 finish off an enemy sentry

【干活儿】gànhuór〈动〉 work: 下地～ go to work in the field ‖ 不～就没有工资。 A person who doesn't work won't get paid.

【干架】gànjià〈动〉〈方〉 ①（争吵） quarrel ②（打架） come to blows

【干将】gànjiàng〈名〉 capable person
▸gānjiàng

【干劲】gànjìn〈名〉 drive: 鼓足～ go all out ‖ 有头脑，有～ have brains and drive ‖ ～十足 be full of drive

【干警】gànjǐng〈名〉 ①（干部和警察） cadres and police ②（警察） police

【干练】gànliàn〈形〉 intelligent and worldly-wise: 精明～ be bright and capable

【干流】gànliú〈名〉 mainstream

【干吗】gànmá〈口〉 **A**〈动〉 what to do: 你想～? What do you want to do? ‖ 这是～用的? What's this for? **B**〈代〉 why: ～非我去? Why on earth must I go? ‖ ～不问问她? Why not ask her?

【干渠】gànqú〈名〉 main canal

【干群】gànqún〈名〉 cadres and the masses: ～关系 relations between the cadres and the masses

【干什么】gàn shénme **A**〈动〉 what to do: 你在～? What are you doing? **B**〈代〉 why: 你～老盯着她? Why are you always staring at her?

【干事】gànshi〈名〉 clerk: 文艺/宣传～ person in charge of recreational activities/publicity work

【干细胞】gànxìbāo〈名〉 stem cell: ～移植 stem cell transplantation ‖ 人类胚胎～ human embryonic stem cell

【干线】gànxiàn〈名〉 main line: 铁路～ trunk railway ‖ ～电缆 trunk cable ‖ 交通～ main lines of communication

【干线机车】gànxiàn jīchē〈名〉 mainline locomotive

【干线渠道】gànxiàn qúdào〈名〉main irrigation channel

【干校】gànxiào〈简称〉= 干部学校

【干休所】gànxiūsuǒ〈名〉 home for retired cadres

【干训班】gànxùnbān〈名〉 training class for cadres

【干仗】gànzhàng〈动〉〈方〉 come to blows

旰 gàn〈书〉〈名〉 evening: ▸宵衣～食

绀（紺） gàn〈形〉 deep purple

【绀青】gànqīng〈形〉 dark purple

骭 gàn〈名〉〈书〉 ①（小腿） lower leg ②（肋骨） rib

赣（贛） Gàn〈名〉 ① ▸**p. 294**（赣江） Ganjiang River ② ▸**p. 661**（江西） Gan [another name for Jiangxi Province (江西)]

gāng

冈（岡） gāng〈名〉 ridge: ▸山～

【冈比亚】Gāngbǐyà〈名〉 Gambia: ～共和国 Republic of Gambia ‖ ～人 Gambian

【冈底斯山】Gāngdǐsīshān〈名〉 Gandise Mountains

【冈峦】gāngluán〈名〉 series of hills: ～起伏 undulating hills

扛（摃） gāng〈动〉〈书〉 raise with both hands
▸káng

刚[1]（剛） gāng〈形〉 ①（硬） stiff: ▸～毛 ②（坚强） strong: 柔中有～ be gentle but firm ‖ 他的性格太～。 He has too strong a character. ▸～烈，～强，～毅

刚[2]（剛） gāng〈副〉 ①（才） just: ～出生的婴儿 newborn baby ‖ ～出院 be just out of hospital ‖ ～过八点。 It's just gone eight o'clock. ‖ 他们～到。 They just got here. ②（恰好） only just: 大小～合适 be just about the right size ‖ 考试～及格 squeak through an examination ③（仅仅） [at the exact point in time, space, quantity, degree, etc.] only just: ～够 just enough ‖ 我这个月的钱～够花。 I have barely enough money to last this month.

【刚愎自用】gāngbì-zìyòng〈成〉 headstrong: 他是我所见过的最～的人。 He is the most opinionated man I have ever seen.

【刚才】gāngcái〈名〉 the moment before: ～发生的事 what happened just now ‖ ～我还见过他。 I saw him just now.

【刚度】gāngdù〈名〉［物理］ stiffness

【刚刚】gānggang〈副〉 just: 考试～及格 just scrape through an examination ‖ 这个书架～能放下这些书。 This shelf is just right for these books. ‖ 太阳～出来。 The sun has just come out.

【刚果】Gāngguǒ〈名〉 Congo: ～共和国 Republic of the Congo ‖ ～民主共和国 Democratic Republic of Congo ‖ ～人 Congolese ‖ ～语 Congolese

【刚果河】Gāngguǒhé ▸**p. 294**〈名〉 Congo River

【刚好】gānghǎo〈副〉 ①（正合适） just: ～赶上公共汽车 be just in time for the bus ‖ 我们进来时～十点钟。 It was just ten o'clock when we came in. ‖ 这件大衣你穿～。 This coat fits you perfectly. ②（恰巧） happen to: ～我包里有一支钢笔。 I just happen to have a pen in my bag. ‖ 昨天我～碰见她，就告诉了她这件事。 It so happened that I saw her yesterday, and I told her about it.

【刚健】gāngjiàn〈形〉 robust: ～的步伐 firm and vigorous steps

【刚劲】gāngjìng〈形〉 ①（指形态） determined ②（指风格） vigorous: 那幅画笔法～。 The picture is painted with vigorous strokes.

【刚烈】gāngliè〈形〉 firm and morally upright: 禀性～ be firm and upright in nature ‖ ～的女子 woman of strong character and integrity

【刚毛】gāngmáo〈名〉［动物］ bristle

【刚强】gāngqiáng〈形〉 staunch: 意志～ be strong-willed ‖ ～不屈的性格 unyielding character

【刚巧】gāngqiǎo〈副〉 coincidentally: 我进来时，他～在屋里。 He just happened to be in the house when I came in.

【刚韧】gāngrèn〈形〉 firm and unyielding: 个性～ be strong and tenacious in character

【刚柔相济】gāngróu-xiāngjì〈成〉 temper force with mercy

【刚体】gāngtǐ〈名〉［物理］ rigid body

【刚性】gāngxìng **A**〈形〉 ①（坚强） strong-willed: 他这个人很～。 He has a strong will. ②（坚硬） rigid: ～材料/结构 rigid material/structure ③（不易改变） inflexible: ～工资 rigid wage ‖ ～指标 compulsory quota **B**〈名〉［物理］ rigidity

【刚需】gāngxū〈名〉 inflexible demand

【刚毅】gāngyì〈形〉 firm and resolute: 神色～ with a firm expression on one's face ‖ 性格～ have a steady and strong-willed character

【刚玉】gāngyù〈名〉［矿业］diamond spar

【刚正】gāngzhèng〈形〉 principled

【刚正不阿】gāngzhèng-bù'ē〈成〉 upright and never stooping to flattery

【刚直】gāngzhí〈形〉 staunch and upright

岗（崗） gāng = 冈 gāng
▸gǎng

肛 gāng〈名〉 anus and anal canal

【肛表】gāngbiǎo〈名〉 anal thermometer

【肛道】gāngdào〈名〉 proctodaeum

【肛管】gāngguǎn〈名〉 anal canal

【肛交】gāngjiāo〈名〉 anal sex

【肛裂】gāngliè ▸**p. 50**〈名〉［医学］ anal fissure

【肛瘘】gānglòu ▸**p. 50**〈名〉［医学］ anal fistula

【肛门】gāngmén〈名〉 anus

纲（綱） gāng〈名〉 ①（总绳） head rope of a fishing net ②〈喻〉（主体） key link: ▸～领，提～挈领 ③［生物］ class: 哺乳～ Mammalia ‖ 苔～ Hepaticae ‖ 藓～ Musci ④〈旧〉（指组织） organization for transporting certain goods in large quantities under convoy: 茶～ tea convoy

【纲常】gāngcháng〈简称〉= 三纲五常

【纲纪】gāngjì〈名〉〈书〉 social order and law: 整顿～ restore order and strengthen discipline

【纲举目张】gāngjǔ-mùzhāng〈成〉〈喻〉 once the general plan is laid out, the details are easy to arrange

【纲领】gānglǐng〈名〉 ①（奋斗目标和行动步骤） programme: 政治～ political programme ‖ 共同～ common programme ②（原则） guiding principle: ～性文件/方案 programmatic document/plan

【纲目】gāngmù〈名〉compendium: 《本草～》 *Compendium of Materia Medica*

【纲要】gāngyào〈名〉 ①（提纲） outline: 写文章之前要先拟一个～。 Make an outline before you write an essay. ②（概要）

compendium: 发展～ programme for development ‖ 《物理学～》 *A Compendium of Physics*

钢（鋼） gāng〈名〉 steel: ～是铁和碳的合金。 Steel is an alloy of iron and carbon. ▸～笔，～琴，～铁
▸gàng

【钢板】 gāngbǎn〈名〉 **1**〔冶金〕 steel plate: 薄～ sheet steel **2**〔机械〕 spring **3**（指誊写工具） stencil steel board: 刻～ cut stencils

【钢蹦儿】 gāngbèngr〈名〉〈口〉 coin

【钢笔】 gāngbǐ〈名〉 **1**（自来水笔） fountain pen **2**（蘸水钢笔） dip pen

【钢笔画】 gāngbǐhuà〈名〉 pen-and-ink drawing

【钢材】 gāngcái〈名〉 steel products

【钢厂】 gāngchǎng〈名〉 steelworks

【钢尺】 gāngchǐ〈名〉 steel rule

【钢窗】 gāngchuāng〈名〉 steel window

【钢刀】 gāngdāo〈名〉 steel knife

【钢锭】 gāngdìng〈名〉 steel ingot

【钢箍】 gānggū〈名〉 steel hoop

【钢骨水泥】 gānggǔ shuǐní〈名〉〔建筑〕 reinforced concrete

【钢鼓】 gānggǔ ▸**p. 929**〈名〉〔音乐〕 steel drum

【钢管】 gāngguǎn〈名〉 steel pipe: 无缝～ seamless steel tube

【钢管舞】 gāngguǎnwǔ〈名〉 pole dancing

【钢轨】 gāngguǐ〈名〉 railway rail

【钢号】 gānghào〈名〉〔冶金〕 steel grade

【钢花】 gānghuā〈名〉 sparks of molten steel: ～飞溅 sparks of molten steel flying in all directions

【钢化玻璃】 gānghuà bōli〈名〉 armoured glass

【钢架】 gāngjià〈名〉 steel frame: ～结构 steel frame structure ‖ ～桥 steel-framed bridge

【钢结构】 gāngjiégòu〈名〉〔建筑〕 steel structure

【钢筋】 gāngjīn〈名〉 reinforcing steel bar: ～水泥 reinforced cement ‖ ～混凝土 reinforced concrete

【钢筋铁骨】 gāngjīn-tiěgǔ〈成〉 **1**（指体格） be extremely strong **2**（指意志） be iron-willed

【钢精】 gāngjīng〈名〉 aluminium: ～锅 aluminium pan

【钢锯】 gāngjù〈名〉〔机械〕 hacksaw

【钢口】 gāngkou〈名〉 edge of a knife: 这刀～儿不错。 The knife has a nice blade.

【钢盔】 gāngkuī〈名〉 steel helmet

【钢梁】 gāngliáng〈名〉 steel girder

【钢炮】 gāngpào〈名〉 modern cannon: 小～ small calibre gun

【钢坯】 gāngpī〈名〉 steel billet

【钢瓶】 gāngpíng〈名〉 steel cylinder

【钢钎】 gāngqiān〈名〉 drill rod

【钢枪】 gāngqiāng〈名〉 rifle: 手握～ hold a rifle

【钢琴】 gāngqín ▸**p. 929**〈名〉 piano: 弹～ play the piano ‖ ～伴奏 piano accompaniment ‖ ～独奏 piano solo ‖ ～曲 piano music ‖ ～协奏 piano concerto ‖ ～家 pianist ‖ ～凳 piano stool

【钢圈】 gāngquān〈名〉 rim of a wheel

【钢水】 gāngshuǐ〈名〉 molten steel

【钢丝】 gāngsī〈名〉 steel wire: ▸走～

【钢丝床】 gāngsīchuáng〈名〉 spring bed

【钢丝锯】 gāngsījù〈名〉 wire saw

【钢丝绳】 gāngsīshéng〈名〉〔工程〕 steel cable

【钢丝刷】 gāngsīshuā〈名〉 wire brush

【钢索】 gāngsuǒ〈名〉 cable wire

【钢铁】 gāngtiě〈名〉 **1**（铁和钢） iron and steel;（钢） steel: ～厂 steelworks ‖ ～工人 steelworker ‖ ～工业 steel industry **2**〈喻〉（坚强） iron: ～意志 iron will ‖ ～战士 dauntless soldier ‖ 解放军是保卫祖国的～长城。 The PLA is a great wall of steel guarding our country.

【钢印】 gāngyìn〈名〉 **1**（指器具） steel seal: 给自行车打～ stamp the cycle registration number on a bicycle ‖ 在证书上加盖～ stamp a certificate with a steel seal **2**（指痕迹） embossed stamp

【钢渣】 gāngzhā〈名〉〔冶金〕 slag

【钢珠】 gāngzhū〈名〉 ball bearing

缸 gāng〈名〉 **1**（用于盛东西） vat: 水～ water vat ‖ 鱼～ fish tank ▸烟灰～ **2**（缸状物） pot-shaped vessel: ▸汽～ **3** = 缸瓦 gāngwǎ

【缸管】 gāngguǎn〈名〉 earthen pipe

【缸盆】 gāngpén〈名〉 glazed earthen basin

【缸瓦】 gāngwǎ〈名〉 compound of sand, clay, etc. for making earthenware

【缸砖】 gāngzhuān〈名〉 quarry tile

【缸子】 gāngzi〈名〉〈口〉 mug: 搪瓷～ enamel mug

罡 gāng

【罡风】 gāngfēng〈名〉 **1**〔道教〕 wind in the empyrean **2**（大风） gale

gǎng

岗（崗） gǎng〈名〉 **1**（坡地） hillock: 土～ earth mound **2**（凸起） ridge: 她脸上有一道肉～儿。 She has a little muscle ridge on her cheek. **3**（岗位） sentry: ▸～楼，～哨，站～ **4**〈喻〉（职位） post: ▸在～，离～ **5**（指人） sentry: 换～ relieve a guard ‖ 布/设～ post/station a sentry ‖ 交通～ traffic police post
▸gāng

【岗地】 gǎngdì〈名〉 farmland in hilly countryside that has not been irrigated

【岗警】 gǎngjǐng〈名〉 policeman on sentry duty

【岗楼】 gǎnglóu〈名〉 watchtower

【岗卡】 gǎngqiǎ〈名〉 checkpoint

【岗哨】 gǎngshào〈名〉 **1**（哨位） sentry post **2**（站岗人） sentry: 流动～ soldier on patrol duties

【岗亭】 gǎngtíng〈名〉 sentry post

【岗位】 gǎngwèi〈名〉 post: 重返工作～ return to one's work ‖ 坚守～ stick to one's post ‖ ～津贴 job allowance ‖ ～培训 job-specific training ‖ 工作～ post of duty ‖ ～责任制 job responsibility system

【岗子】 gǎngzi〈名〉 **1**（坡地） hillock: 土～ earth mound **2**（凸起） ridge

港 gǎng〈名〉 **1**（港口） harbour: 进/离～ enter/leave a port ▸军～，渔～ **2**（机场） airport: 飞机已经离～。 The plane has taken off. **3** ▸**p. 661** Gǎng（香港） Hong Kong

【港币】 gǎngbì ▸**p. 328**〈名〉 Hong Kong dollar (HK $)

【港埠】 gǎngbù〈名〉 **1**（通商港口） port: 国际～ international port **2**（码头） wharf

【港汊】 gǎngchà〈名〉 branching stream

【港督】 Gǎngdū〈名〉 governor of Hong Kong

【港府】 Gǎngfǔ〈名〉 Hong Kong government

【港客】 gǎngkè〈名〉 Hong Kong guest

【港口】 gǎngkǒu〈名〉 harbour: 驶入～ sail into a harbour ‖ 驶离～ sail away from a harbour ‖ ～城市 port city

【港口吞吐量】 gǎngkǒu tūntǔliàng〈名〉 port capacity

【港人】 Gǎngrén〈名〉 Hong Kong residents: ～治港 administration of Hong Kong by Hong Kong people

【港台】 Gǎng-Tái〈名〉 Hong Kong and Taiwan

【港湾】 gǎngwān〈名〉 harbour

【港务】 gǎngwù〈名〉 port (administrative) affairs: ～局 port authority

【港元】 gǎngyuán = 港币 gǎngbì

gàng

杠（槓） gàng

A〈名〉 **1**（粗棍） thick rod: ▸撬～ **2**（指工具） set of stout poles used to carry a coffin in a funeral procession in former times: ▸～夫 **3**〔体育〕 bar: ▸单～，高低～，双～ **4**（指零件） rod: ▸保险～ **5**（粗线） thick line: 老师在他的作业上画了很多红～～。 The teacher made scores of corrections in red on his paper. **6**〈口〉（标准） standard: 三条～儿 three criteria

B〈动〉 mark with thick lines: ～掉几个句子 cross out several sentences

【杠棒】 gàngbàng〈名〉 shoulder pole

【杠房】 gàngfáng〈名〉〈旧〉 undertaker's

【杠夫】 gàngfū〈名〉 pallbearer

【杠杆】 gànggǎn〈名〉 **1**（指机械） lever: ～效应 leverage effect ‖ 汽车制动～ brake lever of an automobile **2**〈喻〉（指人或事物） leverage: 经济～ economic leverage

【杠杠】 gànggang〈名〉〈口〉 **1**（限制） rules: 征兵有年龄～。 There are age limits for recruitment. **2**（标准） criterion: 硬～ strict criteria

【杠铃】 gànglíng〈名〉〔体育〕 barbell

【杠头】 gàngtóu〈名〉〈方〉 **1**（指领头人） pallbearer's head **2**（指爱抬杠者） argumentative person

【杠子】 gàngzi〈名〉 **1**（粗棍） thick rod **2**（指体育器械） bar: ▸盘～ **3**（粗线） thick line: 凡是不合语法的句子都画了红～。 The ungrammatical sentences are all marked with red lines.

钢（鋼） gàng〈动〉 **1**（锻） reinforce the edge of a knife by adding steel and retempering: 把钝剪刀～一～ reinforce a blunt pair of scissors **2**（磨） sharpen: 在石头上～刀 sharpen a knife on a stone ‖ ～刀布 razor strop
▸gāng

戆（戇） gàng〈形〉〈方〉 crude: ～头～脑 be slow-witted
▸zhuàng

【戆大】 gàngdà〈名〉〈方〉 blockhead

gāo

皋（臯） gāo〈名〉〈书〉 **1**（水边高地） waterside highland **2**（高地） highland

g

高 gāo ▸p. 82

A〈形〉**1**（指高度） tall: ～个子姑娘 tall girl ‖ ～山 high mountain ▸～原，～大 **2**（超出一般） above average: 评价～ have a high opinion ‖ ～年级 higher grade ‖ ～水平/速度/质量 high level/speed/quality ‖ ～收入/消费 high wages/consumption ‖ 她的体温偏～。 Her temperature is above normal. ▸～蛋白，兴～采烈 **3**（指等级） high: 少校的军衔～于上尉。 A major ranks above a captain. ▸～等，～级 **4**〈敬〉（你的） your;（他的） his;（她的） her;（他们的） their: ▸～见，～论，～寿 **5**［化学］ containing one more oxygen atom in an acid or a chemical compound: ▸～锰酸钾

B〈名〉**1**（高度） height: ～三米，长五米 three metres high and five metres long ‖ 销售额今年创新～。 Sales have reached a new high this year. **2**（高处） high place: ▸登～，居～临下 **3**［数学］ altitude: 三角形的～ altitude of a triangle

【高矮】gāo'ǎi〈名〉〈口〉 height: ～不一 vary in height

【高昂】gāo'áng **A**〈动〉 hold one's head up high: ～起头，走自己的路。 Hold your head high and go your own way. **B**〈形〉**1**（指心理） high: 斗志～ have high morale ‖ 情绪～ be in high spirits **2**（指价格） expensive: 为和平付出～代价 pay a dear price for peace

【高傲】gāo'ào〈形〉 haughty: ～自大 be self-important ‖ 摆出一副～的样子 assume a haughty air

【高帮鞋】gāobāngxié〈名〉 high-top (shoe)

【高保真】gāobǎozhēn〈形〉［电子］ hi-fi: ～音像效果 high fidelity audio-visual effects ‖ ～音像设备 hi-fi

【高爆炸弹】gāobào zhàdàn〈名〉［军事］ high-explosive bomb

【高倍】gāobèi〈形〉 high-power: ～望远镜 high-power telescope ‖ ～显微镜 high-power microscope

【高标号】gāobiāohào〈名〉 high grade

【高标准】gāobiāozhǔn〈名〉 high standard

【高不成，低不就】gāo bù chéng, dī bù jiù〈俗〉 cannot have what one desires but unwilling to settle for less

【高不可攀】gāobùkěpān〈成〉 be unapproachable: 冠军宝座并非～。 The championship is not beyond reach.

【高才生】gāocáishēng〈名〉 outstanding student

【高材生】gāocáishēng ＝ 高才生 gāocáishēng

【高参】gāocān〈名〉**1**（指军人） senior staff officer **2**（出谋划策的人） mentor

【高层】gāocéng〈形〉**1**（指高度） high-rise: ～办公楼 high-rise office building ‖ ～住宅 high-rise housing **2**（指地位） high-level: ～会谈 high-level talks

【高层建筑】gāocéng jiànzhù〈名〉 high-rise; tower block〈英〉

【高层住宅】gāocéng zhùzhái〈名〉 high-rise housing

【高产】gāochǎn **A**〈形〉 high-yield: ～稳产 high and stable yield ‖ ～作家 prolific writer **B**〈名〉 enormous yield: 创～ achieve high output ‖ 获得大豆～ reap a heavy crop of soya beans

【高唱】gāochàng〈动〉 sing loudly: ～国歌 sing the National Anthem with spirit

【高超】gāochāo〈形〉 excellent: 技艺～ superb skill ‖ 演技～ excellent acting

【高潮】gāocháo〈名〉**1**［海洋］ high tide: ▸～线 **2**〈喻〉（指阶段） high point: 社会主义建设的新～ new upsurge in socialist construction ‖ 晚会的～是女高音独唱。 The high point of the evening was a soprano solo. **3**（指情节） climax: ～迭起 reach one climax after another ‖ 戏剧/故事的～ climax of a play/story **4**［生理］ orgasm: ▸性～

【高潮线】gāocháoxiàn〈名〉 high-water line

【高程】gāochéng〈名〉［工程］ elevation

【高处不胜寒】gàochù bù shèng hán〈成〉〈喻〉 one is likely to feel desolate if one is too outstanding

【高矗】gāochù〈形〉 tall and upright

【高纯度】gāochúndù〈名〉 high purity

【高次】gāocì〈形〉［数学］ higher-degree: ～方程 equation of higher degree

【高大】gāodà〈形〉**1**（指高度） tall and big: ～的楼房 high building ‖ 身材～的男人 man of big and square frame **2**（指形象） high and noble: ～的形象 lofty image

【高蛋白】gāodànbái〈形〉 high-protein: ～食品/饮食 high-protein food/diet

【高档】gāodàng〈形〉 top-grade: ～宾馆 de luxe hotel ‖ ～商品 high-end goods

【高等】gāoděng〈形〉 higher: ～学府 institution of higher learning ▸～数学

【高等动物】gāoděng dòngwù〈名〉 higher animal: 脊椎动物是～。 Vertebrates are higher animals.

【高等法院】gāoděng fǎyuàn〈名〉 high court

【高等教育】gāoděng jiàoyù〈名〉 higher education: 受过～ have higher education

【高等数学】gāoděng shùxué〈名〉［数学］ higher mathematics

【高等学校】gāoděng xuéxiào〈名〉 institution of higher learning

【高等院校】gāoděng yuànxiào〈名〉 institutions of higher learning

【高等植物】gāoděng zhíwù〈名〉 higher plant: 开花植物是～。 Flowering plants are higher plants.

【高等职业学校】gāoděng zhíyè xuéxiào〈名〉 vocational higher education institution

【高低】gāodī **A**〈名〉**1** ▸p. 82（指高度） height;（指声音） pitch: 不论职位～ regardless of official status ‖ ～不平的路 bumpy road **2**（优劣程度） superiority or inferiority: 难分～ hard to tell which is better ‖ 一争～ vie with one other to see who is the superior **3**（利害得失） discretion: 不知～ have no sense of propriety **B**〈副〉〈方〉 just: 不管旁人怎么劝，她～不答应。 No matter how much others tried to persuade her, she just wouldn't agree.

【高低杠】gāodīgàng〈名〉［体育］ asymmetric bars

【高地】gāodì〈名〉**1**（地势高处） upland: 戈兰～ Golan Heights **2**［军事］ height: 占据战略～ hold a strategic height

【高调】gāodiào〈名〉 lofty tone: 唱～ use grandiose words

【高度】gāodù **A** ▸p. 82〈名〉 height: 测量～ measure the height ‖ 跳过 2 米 40 的～ clear a height of 2.40 metres ‖ 飞行～ flying altitude **B**〈副〉 highly: ～评价（某人） have a high opinion (of sb.) ‖ ～赞扬（某人/某事） speak highly (of sb./sth.) ‖ ～重视（某人/某事） attach great importance (to sth./sb.) ‖ 要求思想～集中 demand a high level of concentration **C**〈形〉（指汽油） high-octane;（指酒） high-proof: ～酒 high-proof liquor

【高度表】gāodùbiǎo〈名〉 altimeter

【高端】gāoduān〈形〉 high-end: ～产品 high-end product ‖ ～访问 high-end visit

【高额】gāo'é〈形〉 huge: 获得～利润 make an enormous profit

【高尔夫球】gāo'ěrfūqiú〈名〉**1** ▸p. 909（指运动） golf: ～场 golf course ‖ ～杆 golf club **2**（指球） golf ball

【高发】gāofā〈形〉 frequent: 肝炎～地区 area with a high incidence of hepatitis ‖ 交通事故～地段 stretch of road prone to traffic accidents

【高分】gāofēn〈名〉 high grade: 考试得～ get high marks in an examination

【高分辨率】gāofēnbiànlǜ〈形〉 high-resolution: ～电视机 high-resolution television

【高分子】gāofēnzǐ〈名〉［化学］high polymer

【高分子化合物】gāofēnzǐ huàhéwù〈名〉 macromolecular compound

【高分子化学】gāofēnzǐ huàxué〈名〉 (high) polymer chemistry

【高分子聚合物】gāofēnzǐ jùhéwù〈名〉 high polymers

【高分子物理】gāofēnzǐ wùlǐ〈名〉 (high) polymer physics

【高风亮节】gāofēng-liàngjié〈成〉 lofty morals and noble character

【高风险】gāofēngxiǎn〈形〉 high-risk: ～投资 high-risk investment

【高峰】gāofēng〈名〉 peak: 世界第一～ highest peak in the world ‖ 攀登科技～ scale the heights of science and technology

【高峰负荷】gāofēng fùhè〈名〉 peak load

【高峰会谈】gāofēng huìtán〈名〉 summit talk

【高峰会议】gāofēng huìyì〈名〉 summit meeting

【高峰期】gāofēngqī〈名〉 peak season: 交通～ rush hour ‖ 人口生育～ baby boom ‖ 用电～ peak load

【高干】gāogàn〈简称〉＝高级干部

【高高在上】gāogāo-zàishàng〈成〉 set oneself high above the masses

【高歌】gāogē〈动〉〈书〉 sing loudly: ～一曲 sing a song loudly ▸引吭～

【高歌猛进】gāogē-měngjìn〈成〉 advance triumphantly

【高阁】gāogé〈名〉〈书〉**1**（指建筑） tall building **2**（指橱柜） tall shelf: ▸束之～

【高个儿】gāogèr〈名〉 tall person

【高跟儿鞋】gāogēnrxié〈名〉 high heels

【高工】gāogōng〈简称〉＝高级工程师

【高估】gāogū〈形〉 overestimate

【高官】gāoguān〈名〉 senior official

【高官厚禄】gāoguān-hòulù〈成〉 high position with a high salary: 不为～所动 be distracted neither by high position nor high salary

【高管】gāoguǎn〈名〉 senior executive: 银行～ bank executive

【高贵】gāoguì〈形〉**1**（指品格） noble: ～品德 virtuous qualities ‖ 品质～的人 person of noble character **2**（指出身） high class: 出身～ be of noble birth **3**（指价格） extremely valuable

【高寒】gāohán〈形〉 arctic-alpine: ～山区 high-altitude mountain area

【高喊】gāohǎn〈动〉 shout loudly: ～口号 shout slogans loudly

【高呼】gāohū〈动〉 shout loudly: 振臂～ raise one's arm and shout ‖ ～口号 shout slogans

【高胡】gāohú ▸p. 929〈名〉 *gaohu* [high-pitch *erhu* (二胡)]

【高积云】gāojīyún〈名〉［气象］altocumulus (clouds)
【高级】gāojí〈形〉1（指人） high-level: ～代表团 high-level delegation ‖ ～经济师 senior economist 2（指物） high-grade: ～宾馆 high-class hotel ‖ ～公寓 high-grade apartment ‖ ～化妆品 de luxe cosmetics ‖ ～英语 advanced English
【高级编辑】gāojí biānjí〈名〉senior editor
【高级读本】gāojí dúběn〈名〉advanced reader
【高级法院】gāojí fǎyuàn〈名〉higher court
【高级干部】gāojí gànbù〈名〉high-level official
【高级工程师】gāojí gōngchéngshī ▸p. 966〈名〉senior engineer
【高级会议】gāojí huìyì〈名〉high-level conference
【高级讲师】gāojí jiǎngshī〈名〉senior lecturer
【高级将领】gāojí jiànglǐng〈名〉high-ranking officer
【高级教师】gāojí jiàoshī〈名〉senior teacher
【高级军官】gāojí jūnguān〈名〉high-ranking military officer
【高级人民法院】Gāojí Rénmín Fǎyuàn〈名〉Higher People's Court
【高级人民检察院】Gāojí Rénmín Jiǎncháyuàn〈名〉Higher People's Procuratorate
【高级小学】gāojí xiǎoxué〈名〉senior primary school
【高级知识分子】gāojí zhīshifènzǐ〈名〉highly qualified intellectual
【高级职称】gāojí zhíchēng〈名〉senior academic title
【高级指挥员】gāojí zhǐhuīyuán ▸p. 966〈名〉high-ranking commander
【高级中学】gāojí zhōngxué〈名〉senior middle school
【高加索】Gāojiāsuǒ〈名〉Caucasia: ～人 Caucasian people ‖ ～语 Caucasian
【高甲戏】gāojiǎxì〈名〉*Gaojia* opera [form of opera popular in Fujian Province]
【高价】gāojià〈名〉high price: 出～购买 pay a high price ‖ 低价买进，～卖出 buy low and sell high ‖ ～商品 expensive goods
【高架路】gāojiàlù〈名〉causeway
【高架桥】gāojiàqiáo〈名〉fly-over
【高检】Gāojiǎn〈简称〉= 高级人民检察院
【高见】gāojiàn〈名〉〈套〉profound opinion: 有何～? What do you think of it?
【高脚杯】gāojiǎobēi〈名〉goblet
【高教】gāojiào〈简称〉= 高等教育
【高阶】gāojiē〈名〉higher order: ～方程 equation of higher order
【高洁】gāojié〈形〉noble and unsullied: 品行～ have a noble and unsullied character
【高精度】gāojīngdù〈形〉high-precision
【高精尖】gāo-jīng-jiān〈形〉high-grade, precision and advanced: 开发～产品 develop high-grade, precision and advanced products
【高就】gāojiù〈动〉〈套〉be elevated to a higher post: 另有～ have landed a better job ‖ 请问您在哪儿～? May I ask where you work?
【高举】gāojǔ〈动〉hold high: ～爱国主义的旗帜 uphold the banner of patriotism ‖ ～红旗 hold aloft the red banner
【高踞】gāojù〈动〉〈书〉stand above
【高峻】gāojùn〈形〉high and steep
【高开低走】gāokāi-dīzǒu〈动〉［金融］open high and close low
【高看】gāokàn〈动〉1（评价高） think highly of 2（高估） overestimate
【高亢】gāokàng〈形〉〈书〉1（指声音） loud and sonorous: ～的歌声 loud and sonorous singing 2（指地势） high: ～地 high land/field 3〈书〉（指神情） haughty: 神态～ have a high and mighty look about one
【高考】gāokǎo〈名〉university entrance examination: 参加～ take the college entrance examination ‖ ～状元 student who comes out top in a college entrance examination

> **高考**
> An examination taken by high school students in their final year. It is usually divided into arts and sciences. Compulsory subjects are Chinese, mathematics and English. The examination was suspended when the Cultural Revolution began in 1966, and was restored in 1977.

【高科技】gāokējì〈名〉high tech: ～产品 high-tech product ‖ ～产业园 high-tech park ‖ ～企业 high-tech enterprise
【高空】gāokōng〈名〉high altitude: ～作业 work high above the ground ‖ ～飞行 high-altitude flight ‖ 飞机在一万三千米的～飞行。The plane was flying at an altitude of 13,000 metres.
【高栏】gāolán〈名〉［体育］high hurdles: 男子 110 米～ men's 110m high hurdles
【高丽】Gāolí〈名〉1（指古代） Koryo [Korean dynasty] 2（指现代） Korea
【高丽参】gāolíshēn〈名〉Korean ginseng
【高利】gāolì〈名〉high interest: 牟取～ reap high profits ‖ ～放债 loan money at high interest
【高利贷】gāolìdài〈名〉usury: 放～ practise usury
【高良姜】gāoliángjiāng〈名〉［植物］(lesser) galangal
【高粱】gāoliang〈名〉Chinese sorghum: ～地 sorghum field ‖ ～杆儿 sorghum stem ‖ ～酒 sorghum spirits ‖ ～米 Chinese sorghum ‖ ～饴 sorghum candy
【高龄】gāolíng A〈名〉advanced age: 活到九十～ live to the advanced age of 90 B〈形〉overage: ～孕妇 older pregnant woman
【高岭土】gāolǐngtǔ〈名〉［矿业］kaolin
【高领儿】gāolǐngr〈名〉high collar
【高楼】gāolóu〈名〉high-rise: ～大厦 high-rise ‖ ～综合征 sick building syndrome
【高卢语】Gāolúyǔ〈名〉Gaulish language
【高炉】gāolú〈名〉［冶金］blast furnace
【高论】gāolùn〈名〉〈套〉profound opinion: 愿听～。May I have your opinion about it?
【高迈】gāomài〈形〉〈书〉1（岁数大） advanced in years 2（超凡） outstanding
【高慢】gāomàn〈形〉〈书〉arrogant: 神色～ be supercilious
【高帽子】gāomàozi〈名〉〈喻〉flattery: 她总是喜欢给人戴～。She is always making flattering remarks. ▸戴～
【高门】gāomén〈名〉〈旧〉distinguished family: ～大户 distinguished family ‖ ～望族 wealthy and influential clan
【高锰酸钾】gāoměngsuānjiǎ〈名〉［化学］potassium permanganate
【高密度】gāomìdù〈形〉high-density: ～板 high-density board ‖ ～脂蛋白 high-density lipoprotein
【高棉】Gāomián〈名〉Khmer: ～人 Khmer ‖ ～语 Khmer
【高妙】gāomiào〈形〉ingenious: 医术～ consummate medical skill
【高明】gāomíng A〈形〉brilliant: 棋艺～的棋手 chess master ‖ 这个主意很～。It's a brilliant idea. B〈名〉expert: 另请～ go and find sb. better qualified
【高难】gāonán〈形〉extremely difficult: ～动作 extremely difficult movement
【高能】gāonéng〈形〉high-energy: ～电池 high-capacity battery ‖ ～燃料 high-energy fuel
【高能耗】gāonénghào〈形〉high-energy consuming
【高能物理学】gāonéng wùlǐxué〈名〉high-energy physics
【高攀】gāopān〈动〉associate with sb. of a higher social position or with better qualification: ～不上 have no way of making sb.'s acquaintance ‖ 不敢～ dare not aspire to such an honour
【高抛式发球】gāopāoshì fāqiú〈名〉［体育］high toss service
【高朋满座】gāopéng-mǎnzuò〈成〉a househould of distinguished guests
【高频】gāopín〈名〉［电子］high frequency (HF): 超～ ultra-high frequency (UHF)
【高频放大】gāopín fàngdà〈名〉［通信］high-frequency amplification: ～器 high-frequency amplifier
【高聘】gāopìn〈动〉appoint to a high position: 两名讲师被～为副教授。Two lecturers were engaged as associate professors.
【高气压】gāoqìyā〈名〉high atmospheric pressure
【高腔】gāoqiāng〈名〉*gaoqiang* [a style of singing in Chinese operas]
【高强】gāoqiáng〈形〉masterful: 武艺～ excel in martial arts
【高强度磁场】gāoqiángdù cíchǎng〈名〉［物理］high-intensity magnetic field
【高强度钢】gāoqiángdùgāng〈名〉［冶金］high-strength steel
【高跷】gāoqiāo〈名〉stilts: 踩～ walk on stilts
【高清】gāoqīng〈名〉high definition: ～电视/频道 high-definition TV/channel
【高球】gāoqiú〈名〉［体育］high ball: 放～ lob
【高热】gāorè = 高烧 gāoshāo
【高人】gāorén〈名〉1（指品格） man of noble character 2（指技艺） master
【高人一等】gāorényīděng〈成〉〈贬〉be a cut above the rest: 他自以为～。He considers himself a cut above the rest.
【高僧】gāosēng〈名〉senior monk
【高山病】gāoshānbìng ▸p. 50〈名〉［医学］altitude sickness
【高山大川】gāoshān-dàchuān〈成〉high mountains and big rivers
【高山反应】gāoshān fǎnyìng〈名〉altitude reaction/sickness
【高山滑雪】gāoshān huáxuě〈名〉［体育］alpine skiing
【高山景行】gāoshān-jǐngxíng〈成〉great nobility of character
【高山流水】gāoshān-liúshuǐ〈成〉〈喻〉1（指音乐） sublime music 2（指人） understanding friends
【高山植物】gāoshān zhíwù〈名〉alpine plant
【高山族】Gāoshānzú〈名〉Gaoshan ethnic group
【高尚】gāoshàng〈形〉1（指品格） noble: ～的品质 noble character ‖ 品质～的人 high-minded person 2（指趣味） tasteful: ～的情趣 refined taste ‖ ～的娱乐 tasteful entertainment
【高烧】gāoshāo ▸p. 50〈名〉high fever: 发～ run a high fever ‖ ～不退 have a continuous high fever
【高射机枪】gāoshè jīqiāng〈名〉［军事］anti-aircraft machine gun
【高射炮】gāoshèpào〈名〉［军事］anti-aircraft gun

g

【高射炮兵】gāoshè pàobīng〈名〉［军事］anti-aircraft artilleryman
【高深】gāoshēn〈形〉profound: ～的学问 great learning ‖ ～莫测 unfathomable
【高升】gāoshēng〈动〉get a promotion: 祝贺你～。Congratulations on your promotion.
【高士】gāoshì〈名〉〈书〉learned person with noble interests and character
【高视阔步】gāoshì-kuòbù〈成〉swagger
【高收入】gāoshōurù〈名〉high income: ～者 high-income earner
【高手】gāoshǒu〈名〉master: 棋坛～ master chess player ‖ ～如云 be full of experts
【高寿】gāoshòu **A**〈形〉long-life: 祝您～! I wish you a long life! **B**〈名〉〈套〉your venerable age: 您～? May I ask how old you are?
【高斯】gāosī〈量〉［物理］gauss
【高耸】gāosǒng〈动〉stand tall and erect: ～入云 tower into the sky
【高速】gāosù〈形〉high-speed: ～行驶 drive at a high speed ‖ ～增长 high-speed growth
【高速公路】gāosù gōnglù〈名〉motorway〈英〉; expressway〈美〉
【高速火车】gāosù huǒchē〈名〉high-speed train
【高速铁路】gāosù tiělù〈名〉high-speed railway
【高台跳水】gāotái tiàoshuǐ〈名〉［体育］high dive
【高抬贵手】gāotái-guìshǒu〈成〉let sb. off: 请您～。Please show some leniency.
【高谈阔论】gāotán-kuòlùn〈成〉give a long and pompous speech
【高碳钢】gāotàngāng〈名〉high-carbon steel
【高汤】gāotāng〈名〉**1**（指煮肉、骨的汤）soup-stock **2**（清汤）thin soup
【高堂】gāotáng〈名〉**1**（指厅堂）hall with high ceiling **2**〈书〉（父母）parents
【高挑】gāotiǎo〈形〉lanky: ～的身材 tall and thin physique
【高筒靴】gāotǒngxuē〈名〉knee-length boots
【高头大马】gāotóu-dàmǎ〈成〉**1**〈本〉horse of great stature **2**〈喻〉man of great stature: 他儿子是个～的壮小伙。His son is a tall and strong young man.
【高徒】gāotú〈名〉brilliant student: ▸严师出～
【高危】gāowēi〈形〉high-risk: ～病人 patient in a critical condition ‖ ～孕妇 high-risk pregnant woman
【高危妊娠】gāowēi rènshēn〈名〉［医学］high-risk pregnancy
【高纬度】gāowěidù〈名〉high latitude
【高位】gāowèi〈名〉**1**〈书〉（指地位）high position: 他有朋友身居～。He has friends in high places. **2**（指身体位置）upper part: ～截瘫 high paraplegia ‖ ～截肢 high amputation
【高温】gāowēn〈形〉high-temperature: 耐～ be tolerant of great heat ‖ ～消毒 high-temperature sterilization
【高温材料】gāowēn cáiliào〈名〉［材料］high-temperature material
【高温超导体】gāowēn chāodǎotǐ〈名〉［材料］high-temperature superconductor
【高卧】gāowò〈动〉**1**（高枕）sleep with one's head on a high pillow **2**（隐居）live in seclusion
【高屋建瓴】gāowū-jiànlíng〈成〉operate from a strategically advantageous position
【高下】gāoxià〈名〉superiority or inferiority: 难分～ hard to tell which is better ‖ 一争～ vie with each other to prove who is better
【高限】gāoxiàn〈名〉upper limit
【高香】gāoxiāng〈名〉top-quality incense sticks: ▸烧～
【高消费】gāoxiāofèi〈名〉high consumption
【高小】gāoxiǎo〈简称〉= 高级小学
【高校】gāoxiào〈简称〉= 高等学校
【高效】gāoxiào〈形〉high-efficiency: ～节能 energy-efficient ‖ ～杀虫剂 high-efficiency insecticide
【高新技术】gāo-xīn jìshù〈名〉high technology: ～产品 high technology product ‖ ～产业化 apply high and new technology to production
【高薪】gāoxīn〈名〉high salary: ～聘用 employ sb. at a high rate ‖ ～养廉 cultivate honesty through high pay ‖ ～阶层 high-salary class
【高兴】gāoxìng **A**〈形〉happy: ～得跳起来 jump for joy ‖ 不要～得太早。Don't rejoice too soon. **B**〈动〉be happy to: 你不～去就算了。You don't have to go if you don't want to.
【高性能】gāoxìngnéng〈形〉high-performance: ～汽车 high-performance car
【高血糖】gāoxuètáng〈名〉high blood sugar
【高血压】gāoxuèyā〈名〉hypertension: 患～ suffer from high blood pressure
【高压】gāoyā **A**〈名〉**1**［物理］high pressure **2**［电子］high voltage: ～电缆 high-tension cable **3**［气象］high atmospheric pressure **4**［医学］maximum pressure **B**〈形〉high-handed: ～政策 high-handed policy ▸～手段
【高压泵】gāoyābèng〈名〉high-pressure pump
【高压电】gāoyādiàn〈名〉high-voltage electricity
【高压锅】gāoyāguō〈名〉pressure cooker
【高压开关】gāoyā kāiguān〈名〉high-tension switch
【高压气体】gāoyā qìtǐ〈名〉compressed gas
【高压手段】gāoyā shǒuduàn〈名〉high-handed measure
【高压水龙】gāoyā shuǐlóng〈名〉pressurized hose
【高压线】gāoyāxiàn〈名〉high-tension cable
【高压氧舱】gāoyāyǎngcāng〈名〉［医学］hyperbaric oxygen cabin
【高雅】gāoyǎ〈形〉elegant: 格调～ have an elegant style ‖ 举止～ be gracious in manner ‖ ～艺术 high art
【高盐湖】gāoyánhú〈名〉［水文］salina
【高扬】gāoyáng〈动〉〈书〉**1**（高涨）raise high: 情绪～ be in high spirits **2**（发扬）develop to a high degree: ～艰苦朴素的作风 keep up the practice of plain living
【高扬程】gāoyángchéng〈名〉high lift: ～水泵 high-lift pump
【高腰裤】gāoyāokù〈名〉high-waist trousers
【高腰鞋】gāoyāoxié〈名〉ankle boots
【高音】gāoyīn〈名〉**1**［音乐］high pitch: 男～ tenor ‖ 女～ soprano **2**［物理］top: ～喇叭 tweeter
【高音符】gāoyīnfú〈名〉［音乐］high note
【高原】gāoyuán ▸**p. 164**〈名〉［地理］plateau: 黄土～ Loess Plateau ‖ ～训练 altitude training
【高原反应】gāoyuán fǎnyìng〈名〉altitude sickness
【高远】gāoyuǎn〈形〉high and far away: 志向～ have lofty aspirations
【高院】gāoyuàn〈简称〉= 高级人民法院
【高云】gāoyún〈名〉［气象］high cloud
【高瞻远瞩】gāozhān-yuǎnzhǔ〈成〉be forward-looking
【高涨】gāozhǎng **A**〈动〉rise: 物价～。Prices are surging. **B**〈形〉rising: ～的士气 surging military spirit
【高招】gāozhāo〈名〉masterstroke: 出～ come up with a brilliant idea
【高着】gāozhāo = 高招 gāozhāo
【高枕无忧】gāozhěn-wúyōu〈成〉sit back and relax: 问心无愧便能～。You can sleep easy with a clear conscience.
【高枝】gāozhī〈名〉〈喻〉high position: ▸攀～儿
【高知】gāozhī〈简称〉= 高级知识分子
【高脂肪】gāozhīfáng〈名〉high fat: ～食品 high-fat diet
【高脂血】gāozhīxuè ▸**p. 50**〈名〉［医学］hyperlipemia
【高职】gāozhí〈简称〉**1** = 高级职称 **2** = 高等职业学校
【高中】gāozhōng〈简称〉= 高级中学
【高姿态】gāozītài〈名〉lofty stance
【高足】gāozú〈名〉〈套〉brilliant student: 他是李先生的～。He is Mr Li's best student.
【高祖】gāozǔ〈名〉**1**（曾祖父的父亲）paternal great-great-grandfather **2**〈书〉（远祖）earliest ancestor
【高祖母】gāozǔmǔ〈名〉paternal great-great-grandmother

羔 gāo〈名〉kid: 羊～ lamb ‖ 鹿～ fawn
【羔皮】gāopí〈名〉lambskin: ～大衣 lambskin coat
【羔羊】gāoyáng〈名〉lamb: 迷途的～ lost lamb ‖ 替罪的～ scapegoat
【羔子】gāozi〈名〉**1**（指羊）lamb: 山羊～ kid ‖ 羊～ lamb **2**（指其他动物）kid: 鹿～ fawn **3**〈粗〉（指人）whelp: 王八～ son of a bitch〈粗〉

槔（槹）gāo ▸桔槔 jiégāo

睾 gāo〈名〉testicle
【睾囊】gāonáng〈名〉［解剖］scrotum
【睾酮】gāotóng〈名〉testosterone
【睾丸】gāowán〈名〉testicle
【睾丸酮】gāowántóng〈名〉testosterone

膏 gāo
A〈名〉**1**（肥肉）fat;（油脂）grease: 春雨如～。Spring rain is as precious as oil. ▸～粱, 民脂民～ **2**（指化妆品）cream: ▸雪花～, 洗发～ **3**（糊状物）paste: ▸软～, 牙～, 药～ **4**（心尖脂肪）fat: ▸病入～肓
B〈形〉〈书〉rich: ▸～腴
▸gào
【膏方】gāofāng〈名〉［中医］tonic prescription: 冬令进补～ prescription for a winter replenishment cream
【膏肓】gāohuāng〈名〉〈旧〉vital organs: ▸病入～
【膏剂】gāojì〈名〉medicinal extract
【膏粱】gāoliáng〈名〉〈书〉rich food
【膏粱子弟】gāoliáng zǐdì〈成〉children from wealthy families
【膏血】gāoxuè〈名〉〈喻〉the fruits of one's labour: 浪费人民的～ waste the fruits of people's labour
【膏药】gāoyao〈名〉plaster: 把～贴在患处 put a plaster on an affected part ▸狗皮～
【膏腴】gāoyú〈形〉〈书〉fertile: ～之地 rich and prosperous region

【膏泽】gāozé〈名〉〈书〉timely rainfall
【膏子】gāozi〈名〉〈口〉medicinal extract

篙 gāo〈名〉punt-pole: 竹～ bamboo punting pole
【篙子】gāozi〈名〉〈方〉1 = 篙 gāo 2（晒衣杆） pole for drying washing in the sun

糕（餻）gāo〈名〉cake: 绿豆～ green bean cake ▸～点, 蛋～, 雪～
【糕饼】gāobǐng〈方〉= 糕点 gāodiǎn
【糕点】gāodiǎn〈名〉cake: ～铺 bakery ‖ ～师 pastry cook
【糕干】gāogan〈名〉sweetened rice flour: ～粉 powdered rice-cereal

gǎo

杲 gǎo〈形〉〈书〉bright: ～日 brilliant sun
【杲杲】gǎogǎo〈形〉〈书〉[of the sun] bright: 秋阳～。The autumn sun is shining brightly.

搞 gǎo〈动〉1（进行） do: ～调查 make an investigation ‖ ～改革 carry on reforms ‖ ～科研 engage in scientific research ‖ ～小动作 play petty games ‖ ～阴谋 hatch a plot ‖ 不～特殊化 seek no personal privileges ‖ 她～行政工作。She is an administrator. 2（完成） make: ～个方案/计划 make a plan 3（建立） set up: ～培训班 start a training course ‖ 这年头～工厂不容易。It's not easy to run a factory nowadays. 4（得到） get: 设法～两张音乐会门票 manage to get two tickets for the concert 5（达到某种状态） [followed by a complement]: 把某人～臭 discredit sb. ‖ 把某事～砸 bungle sth. ‖ 把事情～得一团糟 make a mess of things 6（整人） plot: 他们在暗中～我。They are plotting against me.
【搞错】gǎocuò〈动〉get in a muddle: ～时间 get the wrong time ‖ 我把你的地址～了。I got your address wrong.
【搞掂】gǎodiàn〈动〉〈方〉be worked out: 孩子转学问题已～。The question of the child's school transfer has already been worked out.
【搞定】gǎodìng〈动〉〈方〉resolve: 你应该在走之前先把事情～。You should settle the matter before you leave.
【搞对象】gǎo duìxiàng〈动〉〈口〉date: 搞了几个对象都没搞成 go on several dates but with no success
【搞鬼】gǎoguǐ〈动〉make mischief: 背后～ make trouble behind sb.'s back ‖ 他又在～。He is making mischief again.
【搞好】gǎohǎo〈动〉do a good job (of)
【搞混】gǎohùn〈动〉confuse: 把她和她妹妹～ mix her up with her younger sister
【搞活】gǎohuó〈动〉invigorate: ～市场 liberalize the market ‖ 对内～经济 invigorate the domestic economy
【搞小动作】gǎo xiǎodòngzuò〈惯〉1（指学生） fidget 2（搞鬼） carry out petty scheming
【搞笑】gǎoxiào〈动〉amuse: ～片 comic film ‖ 他们的表演显然是为了～。Apparently their performances are meant to make people laugh.

缟（縞）gǎo〈名〉〈旧〉thin white silk: ～衣 thin white silk garment
【缟素】gǎosù〈名〉〈书〉white mourning dress: 三军～。The whole army wore mourning dress.

镐（鎬）gǎo〈名〉pickaxe: 尖～ pointed pickaxe ▸鹤嘴～
▸Hào
【镐头】gǎotou〈名〉pick

槁 gǎo〈形〉parched: ▸枯～
【槁木】gǎomù〈名〉withered tree: 形如～ be as thin as a rake
【槁木死灰】gǎomù-sǐhuī〈成〉〈喻〉complete apathy

稿 gǎo〈名〉1〈书〉（茎） crop stalks: ▸～荐 2（草稿） rough draft: 定～ finalize a draft ‖ 初/原～ first/original manuscript ‖ 手写～ hand-written manuscript ‖ 修改～ revised draft ▸草～, 腹～, 拟～ 3（诗文） contribution: 约～ commission a piece ‖ 一～多投 submit a contribution to more than one publishing outlet ▸～费, 退～, 征～
【稿本】gǎoběn〈名〉manuscript
【稿酬】gǎochóu = 稿费 gǎofèi
【稿费】gǎofèi〈名〉contribution fee
【稿件】gǎojiàn〈名〉manuscript: 录用/退回～ accept/reject a manuscript
【稿荐】gǎojiàn〈名〉straw mattress
【稿源】gǎoyuán〈名〉source of contributions
【稿约】gǎoyuē〈名〉note to contributors
【稿纸】gǎozhǐ〈名〉standard writing paper [with squares or lines]
【稿子】gǎozi〈名〉1（草稿） rough draft: 打个～ make a draft 2（诗文） manuscript: 写～ write an article 3〈喻〉（计划）plan: 下一步怎么办我心里还没个～。I have no idea what to do next.

gào

告 gào〈动〉1（汇报） report to: ▸禀～ 2（通知） inform: 请电～详情。Please phone with the particulars. ‖ 做何打算，盼～。I'm looking forward to hearing your plan. ▸～知, 奔走相～, 劝～ 3（请求） request: ▸～贷, ～假, 央～ 4（宣告） announce: ～一段落 come to the end of a phase ‖ 暂～休会 go into recess ▸～成, ～竣 5（表明） express: 不～而别 leave without saying goodbye ▸～别, 自～奋勇 6（控诉） press charges against (sb.): 到法院去～他 take him to court ▸～发, 控～, 原～
【告白】gàobái A〈名〉public announcement B〈动〉〈书〉express: 他无法～内心的悲痛之情。He could not express his feelings of sadness.
【告便】gàobiàn〈动〉ask to be excused: 对不起，我～一下。May I be excused?
【告别】gàobié〈动〉1（辞行） say goodbye to: ～祖国 bid farewell to one's country ‖ 挥泪～ say a tearful goodbye ‖ 挥手～ wave goodbye to sb. ‖ 我是来向你～的。I've come to say goodbye to you. 2（离开） leave: 我们～了西安，又赶往兰州。We left Xi'an and went on to Lanzhou. 3（诀别） pay one's last respects to the deceased: 向遗体～ pay one's last respects to the deceased
【告别词】gàobiécí〈名〉farewell speech
【告别演说】gàobié yǎnshuō〈名〉farewell address
【告别宴会】gàobié yànhuì〈名〉farewell banquet
【告禀】gàobǐng〈动〉〈书〉report (to one's superior or senior)
【告病】gàobìng〈动〉〈书〉resign on account of illness
【告成】gàochéng〈动〉be completed: 大功～ be brought to a successful completion
【告吹】gàochuī〈动〉〈口〉fall through: 整个计划～了。The whole plan fell through. ‖ 这件婚事可能要～。The wedding may be called off.
【告辞】gàocí〈动〉say goodbye: 我该～了。I have to leave now.
【告贷】gàodài〈动〉〈书〉ask for a loan: 四处～ go around begging for a loan ‖ ～无门 be unable to get a loan
【告地状】gào dìzhuàng〈动〉〈旧〉beg in the street with a placard
【告发】gàofā〈动〉inform on: ～某人 report sb. to the authorities ‖ 向经理～某人 turn sb. in to the boss ‖ 他因贩毒被人～。Someone turned him in for pushing drugs.
【告乏】gàofá〈动〉be in short supply
【告负】gàofù〈动〉〈书〉lose: 客队仅以一球之差～。The guest team lost the game by just one goal.
【告急】gàojí〈动〉1（报告情况紧急） raise an alarm 2（出现紧急情况） be in an emergency: 因敌人轰炸，大桥～。The bridge was in immediate danger because of enemy bombing.
【告假】gàojià〈动〉ask for leave: ～一天 ask for a day's leave
【告捷】gàojié〈动〉1（传来捷报） announce a victory: 前线频频～。The front line troops constantly reported victories. 2（取胜） win: 首战～ win the first battle
【告竭】gàojié〈动〉〈书〉run out: 库藏～ be out of stock
【告诫】gàojiè〈动〉warn: ～某人不要抽烟 caution sb. against smoking ‖ 再三～ warn again and again
【告借】gàojiè〈动〉ask for a loan: ～无门 be unable to get a loan
【告警】gàojǐng〈动〉1（指紧急情况） report an emergency 2（指警报） sound an alarm
【告绝】gàojué〈动〉be extinct: 那种传染病早已～。That kind of infectious disease was wiped out a long time ago.
【告竣】gàojùn〈动〉be declared completed: 那座建筑终于～。The structure was finally completed.
【告老还乡】gàolǎo-huánxiāng〈成〉retire from office at an old age and return to one's native place
【告密】gàomì〈动〉inform (against/on sb.): ～者 informer ‖ 由于叛徒～，她被捕并遭杀害。She was arrested and murdered because a renegade informed against her.
【告破】gàopò〈动〉[of a case] be cracked: 那起重大凶杀案已经～。The major murder case has already been cracked.
【告罄】gàoqìng〈动〉〈书〉run out: 库存～ be out of stock ‖ 食品～。Food supplies have run out.
【告缺】gàoquē〈动〉be short: 药品～ have a shortage of medicine
【告饶】gàoráo〈动〉beg for mercy: 跪在地上～ kneel down and beg for mercy
【告扰】gàorǎo〈动〉〈书〉sorry to disturb

or bother sb.
【告示】gàoshi〈名〉official notice: 贴～ put up a notice ‖ 安民～ official notice to reassure the public
【告示牌】gàoshipái〈名〉notice board〈英〉; bulletin board〈美〉
【告诉】gàosù〈动〉take legal action against: 撤消～ withdraw an accusation
【告诉】gàosu〈动〉tell: 谁～你的? Who told you that? ‖ 我～大家一个好消息。I'm going to tell you all some good news.
【告退】gàotuì〈动〉1（提前离开）ask to be excused: 聚会还没有结束，便有几个客人～了。Some guests left before the party was even over. 2（退出）stop doing: 今年将有两名队员挂靴～。Two players in the team will hang up their boots this year. 3〈旧〉（辞职）resign from office
【告慰】gàowèi〈动〉comfort: ～在天之灵 be a comfort to sb.'s soul in paradise
【告御状】gào yùzhuàng〈动〉report to higher authorities
【告枕头状】gào zhěntouzhuàng〈动〉complain about sth. to one's husband when in bed
【告知】gàozhī〈动〉inform: 把你的计划～总经理。Notify the general manager of your plan.
【告知书】gàozhīshū〈名〉notice: 医学观察～ medical observation chart ‖ 房屋动迁～ housing relocation notice
【告终】gàozhōng〈动〉end up: 以失败～ end up in failure ‖ 以损人开始，以害己～ start with the intention of harming others but end up by harming oneself
【告状】gàozhuàng〈动〉1（向司法机关）press charges (against sb.) 2（向上级、长辈）tell on: 向老板～ report sb. to the boss
【告罪】gàozuì〈动〉apologize

郜 Gào〈名〉Gao [surname]

诰（誥）gào
A〈动〉〈书〉admonish
B〈名〉1〈书〉（指命令）imperial mandate: ▸～封，～命 2〈旧〉（指文章）written admonition
【诰封】gàofēng〈动〉〈书〉confer an honorary title by imperial mandate
【诰命】gàomìng〈名〉1（指命令）imperial mandate 2（指妇女）titled lady

锆（鋯）gào〈名〉［化学］zirconium (Zr)

膏 gào〈动〉1（上润滑油）lubricate: 给车轴～点油 oil the axle 2（指毛笔）dip a writing brush in ink and smooth it on an ink stone before writing: ～毛笔 dip a writing brush in ink and smooth it on an ink stone before writing ‖ ～墨 dip into ink
▸gāo

gē

戈 gē〈名〉1（指兵器）dagger-axe 2（泛指武器）weapon: ▸干～，同室操～
【戈比】gēbǐ〈名〉kopek
【戈壁】gēbì〈名〉Gobi: ～滩 Gobi Desert
【戈兰高地】Gēlán Gāodì〈名〉Golan Heights

仡 gē
▸yì
【仡佬族】Gēlǎozú〈名〉Gelao ethnic group

圪 gē
【圪垯】gēda〈名〉1 = 疙瘩 gēda 2（小土丘）hillock: 长满了草的土～ grassy knoll

疙 gē
【疙疤】gēba〈方〉scab
【疙瘩】gēda〈名〉1（硬块）lump: 她脸上肿起了两个～。Two bumps appeared on her face. ▸鸡皮～ 2（块状物）knot: 毛线～ wool knot ‖ 结成～ tangle into knots ‖ 解开～ undo a knot 3（问题）misunderstanding: 解开两人间的～ remove the misunderstanding between two people ‖ 夫妻不和成了他心里的一个～。The bad blood between the couple escalated into something of a problem.
【疙瘩汤】gēdatāng〈名〉dough drop soup
【疙疙瘩瘩】gēge-dādā〈形〉bumpy: ～的石子路 bumpy cobbled street ‖ 她脸上～的。The skin on her face is rough. ‖ 这问题～的。This is a thorny problem.
【疙里疙瘩】gēligēdā = 疙疙瘩瘩 gēge-dādā

咯 gē
▸kǎ, lo, luò
【咯嗒】gēdā〈拟〉cluck: 母鸡～～叫。The hen is clucking.
【咯噔】gēdēng〈拟〉clip-clop: 穿着高跟鞋～～地走 clip-clop on high heels ‖ 听到电话中传来她的声音，我心里～了一下。When I heard her voice on the phone, my heart started thumping.
【咯咯】gēgē〈拟〉1（指笑声）giggle: 禁不住～地笑了起来 cannot help bursting into giggles 2（指鸟叫或鸡叫声）cluck: 母鸡～叫着四处觅食。The hens are clucking and scratching around. 3（指枪声）crack: 能够听见机关枪的～声 be able to hear the chatter of machine guns 4（指咬牙声）creak: 牙齿咬得～直响 grind one's teeth
【咯吱】gēzhī〈拟〉creak: 门～一声开了。The door creaked open.

饹（餎）gē
▸le
【饹馇】gēzha〈名〉flat cake made of bean powder

格 gē
▸gé
【格登】gēdēng = 咯噔 gēdēng
【格格】gēgē = 咯咯 gēgē

哥 gē〈名〉1（哥哥）elder brother: 大/二～ first/second elder brother 2（指同辈年长男子）brother: ▸表～ 3（指无亲属关系者）brother: 张大～ Brother Zhang
【哥本哈根】Gēběnhāgēn〈名〉Copenhagen
【哥德巴赫猜想】Gēdébāhè cāixiǎng〈名〉［数学］Goldbach's Conjecture
【哥德体】gēdétǐ〈名〉［印刷］Gothic
【哥哥】gēge〈名〉1 ▸**p. 588**（指同父或同母）elder brother: 亲～ elder blood brother ‖ 同父异母/同母异父～ elder half-brother ‖ 她有三个～。She has three elder brothers. 2（指同族）male cousin older than oneself: 叔伯～ first or second cousin on one's father's side ‖ 远房表～ distant cousin on one's mother's side 3（用于昵称）older brother
【哥老会】Gēlǎohuì〈名〉〈旧〉Society of Brothers
【哥伦比亚】Gēlúnbǐyà〈名〉Colombia: ～共和国 Republic of Colombia ‖ ～人 Colombian
【哥们儿】gēmenr〈名〉〈口〉1（有亲缘关系）all the brothers in a family: 他们家～三个呢。There are three boys in his family. 2（好朋友）mates: ～义气 brotherhood ‖ 他们俩是我的～。Those two are my buddies.
【哥儿】gēr〈名〉1（兄弟）brothers: 你们～几个? How many boys do you have in your family? 2（指男孩）boy of a wealthy or an influential family: ▸公子～
【哥儿们】gērmen = 哥们儿 gēmenr
【哥萨克人】Gēsàkèrén〈名〉Cossack
【哥斯达黎加】Gēsīdálíjiā〈名〉Costa Rica: ～共和国 Republic of Costa Rica ‖ ～人 Costa Rican
【哥特人】Gētèrén〈名〉Goth
【哥特式】gētèshì〈形〉Gothic: ～建筑 Gothic architecture
【哥特体】gētètǐ〈名〉［印刷］gothic type

胳 gē
▸gā, gé
【胳臂】gēbei = 胳膊 gēbo
【胳膊】gēbo ▸**p. 614**〈名〉arm
【胳膊拧不过大腿】gēbo nǐng bùguo dàtuǐ〈俗〉〈喻〉the weak cannot contend with the strong
【胳膊肘儿】gēbozhǒur〈名〉elbow
【胳膊肘儿往外拐】gēbozhǒur wǎng wài guǎi〈俗〉side with outsiders instead of one's own

g

鸽（鴿）gē〈名〉pigeon: ▸信～，和平～
【鸽巢】gēcháo〈名〉pigeonhole
【鸽笼】gēlóng〈名〉pigeon cage
【鸽派】gēpài〈名〉dove: ～观点 dovish view
【鸽哨】gēshào〈名〉pigeon whistle
【鸽子】gēzi〈名〉pigeon: 放飞～ release pigeons

袼 gē
【袼褙】gēbei〈名〉*gebei* [odd bits of cloth pasted together for making cloth shoes]: 打～ make *gebei*

搁（擱）gē〈动〉1（放）put: 把茶具～到橱柜里 put the tea things away in the cupboard ‖ 这东西该～哪? Where does this go? 2（加入）add: 汤里多～点盐。Put more salt in the soup. 3（搁置）put aside: 这事先～下，下次再谈好吗? Shall we put this aside and discuss it again next time? 4（装入）hold: 一个包～不下这些东西。One bag is not going to hold all these things.
▸gé
【搁扳】gēbǎn〈名〉shelf
【搁笔】gēbǐ〈动〉（指写作）stop writing; （指作画）stop painting: 由于年事已高，他已经～多年了。He stopped writing years ago because of his age.
【搁脚凳】gējiǎodèng〈名〉footstool
【搁浅】gēqiǎn〈动〉1（指船只）run aground: 船在沙洲～了。The ship ran aground on the sandbank. 2〈喻〉（受

阻） reach a deadlock: 和谈~了。 The peace talks reached a deadlock.

【搁置】gēzhì〈动〉shelve: 先把小事~一旁 first of all, lay aside all trivial matters

割 gē

〈动〉 **1**（切割） cut: ~草 mow the grass ‖ 风如刀~。 The wind cuts like a knife. ‖ 我要~一公斤小牛肉。 I want to buy one kilogram of veal. ▸切~, 收~ **2**（分割） divide: ▸~据, ~裂, ~让 **3**（舍弃） give up: ▸~舍

【割爱】gē'ài〈动〉 give up what one treasures

【割草机】gēcǎojī〈名〉 mower

【割除】gēchú〈动〉remove: ~肿瘤 cut out a tumour

【割地】gēdì〈动〉 cede territory: ~赔款 cede one's territory and pay indemnities

【割断】gēduàn〈动〉cut off: ~电线 cut off electric wires ‖ ~联系 sever relations ‖ ~历史 chop up history

【割胶】gējiāo〈动〉 tap a rubber tree

【割炬】gējù〈名〉［机械］ cutting torch

【割据】gējù〈动〉 divide up by force: 封建~ feudal separatist rule ‖ 军阀~ nation carved up into separate regimes by rival warlords

【割礼】gēlǐ〈名〉 circumcision

【割裂】gēliè〈动〉 separate: 两者不能~开来。 The two cannot be separated.

【割破】gēpò〈动〉 cut: ~手指 cut one's finger

【割漆】gēqī〈动〉 tap a lacquer tree

【割弃】gēqì〈动〉 abandon: ~文章中与主题无关的部分 cross out parts of the essay unrelated to the topic

【割枪】gēqiāng〈名〉［机械］cutting torch

【割让】gēràng〈动〉 cede: ~土地 cede a territory

【割肉】gēròu〈动〉〈喻〉 sell sth. at a price lower than its original price

【割舍】gēshě〈动〉 give up: 难以~ find it hard to part with

【割腕】gēwàn〈动〉 commit suicide by cutting one's wrist

【割席】gēxí〈动〉〈书〉 renounce a friendship: ~断交 break off friendly relations

歌 gē

A〈动〉 **1**（唱） sing: 放声高~ sing at the top of one's voice ‖ 能~善舞 be good at both singing and dancing ▸~手, ~咏, 载~载舞 **2**（歌颂） praise: ▸~功颂德, ~颂, 可~可泣

B〈名〉 song: 唱~ sing a song ▸~谱, 民~

【歌本】gēběn〈名〉 songbook

【歌唱】gēchàng〈动〉 **1**（唱） sing: 放声~ raise one's voice in song ‖ 尽情/纵情~ sing to one's heart's content ‖ ~家 singer **2**（歌颂） sing the praises of: ~祖国 sing the praises of one's country

【歌词】gēcí〈名〉 lyrics: 给~谱曲 set a song to music ‖ ~大意 main content of a song ‖ ~作者 songwriter

【歌带】gēdài〈名〉 song tape

【歌单儿】gēdānr〈名〉 song sheet

【歌功颂德】gēgōng-sòngdé〈成〉〈贬〉 sing the praises (of sb. or sth.)

【歌喉】gēhóu〈名〉 singing voice: 一展~ show off one's voice in a song ‖ ~婉转动听 have a beautiful voice

【歌后】gēhòu〈名〉 singing queen

【歌会】gēhuì〈名〉 singing party: 举行~ hold a sing-song

【歌集】gējí〈名〉 songbook

【歌伎】gējì〈名〉〈旧〉 sing-song girl

【歌剧】gējù〈名〉 opera: ~演员 opera singer ‖ ~团 opera troupe ‖ ~院 opera house

【歌诀】gējué〈名〉 directions put into rhyme for easy memorization

【歌迷】gēmí〈名〉fan (of a song or a singer)

【歌女】gēnǚ〈名〉 singing-girl

【歌片儿】gēpiānr〈名〉 song sheet

【歌谱】gēpǔ〈名〉 music score for a song

【歌曲】gēqǔ〈名〉 song: 流行~ popular song ‖ 校园~ campus song

【歌曲作者】gēqǔ zuòzhě ▸p. 966〈名〉 songwriter

【歌声】gēshēng〈名〉 sound of singing: 嘹亮的~ loud and clear singing

【歌手】gēshǒu〈名〉 singer: 青年~ young singer

【歌颂】gēsòng〈动〉 sing the praises (of): ~祖国 sing the praises of one's homeland

【歌坛】gētán〈名〉 singing circles: ~新秀 new singing star

【歌厅】gētīng〈名〉 karaoke hall

【歌王】gēwáng〈名〉 best singer

【歌舞】gēwǔ〈名〉 song and dance: ~节目 song-and-dance performance ‖ ~晚会 evening of song and dance ‖ ~团 song-and-dance ensemble

【歌舞伎】gēwǔjì〈名〉 kabuki [a form of traditional Japanese drama with highly stylized song, mime, and dance]

【歌舞剧】gēwǔjù〈名〉 song-and-dance drama

【歌舞升平】gēwǔ-shēngpíng〈成〉 put on a show to celebrate peace and prosperity

【歌舞厅】gēwǔtīng〈名〉 song-and-dance hall

【歌星】gēxīng〈名〉 singing star: 当红~ popular singer

【歌谣】gēyáo〈名〉 ballad: 民间~ folk song

【歌吟】gēyín〈动〉 **1**（指歌曲） sing **2**（指诗文） recite a poem in sing-song tones

【歌咏】gēyǒng〈名〉 singing: ~比赛 singing contest ‖ ~队 chorus

【歌友会】gēyǒuhuì〈名〉 fan club

【歌仔戏】gēzǎixì〈名〉 *Gezai* opera

> **歌仔戏**
>
> A genre of traditional Chinese opera, popular in Taiwan and southern Fujian. The genre originated in the early twentieth century and is based on local folk songs. Accompanying instruments include the *kezixian* (壳子弦, a two-stringed fiddle with a coconut body), the *daguangxian* (大广弦, a two-stringed fiddle), the Taiwan flute, and the *yueqin* (月琴, a four-stringed round guitar).

gé

革 gé

A〈名〉 leather: ▸皮~, 人造~, 制~

B〈动〉 **1**（改变） change: ▸变~, 改~, 沿~ **2**（开除） dismiss: ▸~职 **3**（废弃） get rid of: ▸~除

▸jí

【革出】géchū〈动〉〈书〉 expel

【革除】géchú〈动〉 **1**（废弃） get rid of: ~陋俗 abolish bad customs and irrational practices **2**（开除） dismiss: ~公职 discharge sb. from public office

【革故鼎新】gégù-dǐngxīn〈成〉 discard the old and introduce the new

【革龟】géguī〈名〉［动物］ leatherback turtle

【革履】gélǚ〈名〉 leather shoes: 西装~ be dressed in Western suit and leather shoes

【革面洗心】gémiàn-xǐxīn = 洗心革面 xǐxīn-gémiàn

【革命】gémìng **A**〈动〉 **1**（改变社会制度） start a revolution: 干~ do revolutionary work ‖ 社会主义~ socialist revolution **2**（突破性变革） totally transform: 工业/技术~ industrial/technical revolution **B**〈形〉 revolutionary: ~精神 revolutionary spirit ‖ ~英雄主义 revolutionary heroism

【革命家】gémìngjiā〈名〉 revolutionary: 伟大的无产阶级~ great proletarian revolutionary

【革命委员会】gémìng wěiyuánhuì〈名〉 revolutionary committee [a term used to indicate various levels of government and leading organizations during the Cultural Revolution]

【革命性】gémìngxìng〈名〉 revolutionary nature

【革命者】gémìngzhě〈名〉 revolutionary

【革囊】génáng〈名〉 leather case

【革委会】géwěihuì〈简称〉= 革命委员会

【革新】géxīn〈动〉 renovate: 技术~ technical innovation ‖ ~和守旧 progress and conservation ‖ ~派 reformers

【革职】gézhí〈动〉 dismiss: ~查办 discharge sb. from his post and bring him to trial ‖ ~留用 demote but retain at a post ‖ 因贪污被~ be stripped of one's post for embezzlement

【革制品】gézhìpǐn〈名〉 leather goods

阁（閣） gé

〈名〉 **1**（架子） shelf: ▸束之高~ **2**（小房间） cabin: ▸~楼 **3**〈旧〉（闺房） boudoir: 出~ get married ▸闺~ **4**（亭子） Chinese pavilion: ▸亭台楼~ **5**（内阁） cabinet: ~僚 member of cabinet ‖ 倒~ topple a cabinet ‖ 入~ become a cabinet minister ▸~员, 内~, 组~

【阁楼】gélóu〈名〉 attic

【阁下】géxià〈名〉（称呼高官） Your/His/Her Excellency;（称公爵、主教） Your/His/Her Grace;（称红衣主教） Your/His Eminence;（称法官、市长） Your/His/Her Honour: 首相/总理/总统~ Mr/Mrs Prime Minister/Mr/Mrs Premier/Mr/Mrs President ‖ 大使~到了。 His/Her Excellency the Ambassador has arrived.

【阁员】géyuán〈名〉 cabinet member

格¹ gé

A〈名〉 **1**（方框） square: 一个字写一~ write only one character in each square ▸~子, 方~, 横~纸 **2**（隔层） division: 书架最高的一~ top shelf in a bookcase **3**（格式） pattern;（标准） standard: ▸~律, 规~, 破~ **4**（品质） quality: ▸~调, 风~, 性~ **5**［语言］ case: ▸宾~, 主~

B〈动〉〈书〉 obstruct: ▸~~不入, ~于成例

格² gé

〈动〉 examine, study: ▸~物

格³ gé

〈动〉 hit, beat: ▸~斗, ~杀勿论

▸gē

【格调】gédiào〈名〉 **1**（指文艺作品） style: ~豪放 vigorous and flowing style ‖ ~清新 fresh and lucid style ‖ ~高雅 high-brow **2**〈书〉（指人） taste: 此人~不高。 This is not a man of superior taste.

【格斗】gédòu〈动〉 grapple: 徒手～ fight with bare fists

【格格不入】gégé-bùrù〈成〉 be incompatible (with): 跟我的想法～ be out of step with what I have in mind ‖ 我跟那些人～。I don't belong among those people.

【格格】gége〈名〉 gege [address for Manchu princess or daughter of a Manchu prince]

【格局】géjú〈名〉 layout: 世界多极化～ multi-polarized structure of the world ‖ 世界贸易新～ new pattern of world trade

【格里历】Gélǐlì〈名〉［天文］ Gregorian calendar

【格林纳达】Gélínnàdá〈名〉 Grenada: ～人 Grenadian

【格林尼治】Gélínnízhì〈名〉 Greenwich: ～时间 Greenwich Mean Time

【格陵兰】Gélínglán〈名〉 Greenland

【格鲁吉亚】Gélǔjíyà〈名〉 Georgia: ～共和国 Republic of Georgia ‖ ～人 Georgian ‖ ～语 Georgian

【格洛斯特郡】Géluòsītèjùn〈名〉 Gloucestershire

【格律】gélǜ〈名〉 metre (of a poem): ～诗 metrical poem

【格杀勿论】géshā-wùlùn〈成〉 execute summarily

【格式】géshì〈名〉 format: 公文～ format of an official document ‖ 书信～ layout of a letter ‖ 改变文档～ modify the format of a document

【格式化】géshìhuà〈动〉［计算机］format: 将磁盘～ format a disc ‖ ～软盘 formatted diskette

【格外】géwài〈副〉 ①（特别） unusually: ～努力 extraordinarily hard-working ‖ ～小心 be especially careful ‖ 今天天气～冷。It's unusually cold today. ②（另外） additionally: ～的负担 extra burden

【格温特郡】Géwēntèjùn〈名〉 Gwent

【格物】géwù〈动〉〈书〉 investigate the nature of things

【格物致知】géwù-zhìzhī〈成〉 investigate the nature of things in order to acquire knowledge

【格言】géyán〈名〉 maxim

【格于成例】géyúchénglì〈动〉 be limited by usual practices

【格语法】géyǔfǎ〈名〉［语言］ case grammar

【格栅】gézhà〈名〉 grid

【格致】gézhì〈名〉〈旧〉 physics

【格子】gézi〈名〉 ①（方框） square: 方～本儿 notebook with squared paper ‖ 在纸上打上方～。Draw lines on the paper to form squares. ②［建筑］ latticework: ～窗 lattice window ‖ ～花呢 tartan

胳 gé

▸gā, gē

【胳肢】gézhi〈动〉 tickle: ～人 tickle sb. under the arm ‖ 这孩子怕～。The child is ticklish.

搁（擱） gé

〈动〉〈口〉 bear: 丝绸衣服～不住洗。Silk clothes don't wash well. ‖ 这种轮胎～得住磨损。This tyre will take wear and tear.

▸gē

【搁栅】gézhà〈名〉［建筑］ joist

葛 gé

〈名〉 ①（指植物） kudzu (vine) ②（指纺织品） poplin: ▸毛～

▸Gě

【葛布】gébù〈名〉 kudzu-hemp cloth

【葛根】gégēn〈名〉 root of kudzu vine

【葛麻】gémá〈名〉 kudzu

【葛藤】géténg〈名〉〈喻〉 complicated relationships

蛤 gé

〈名〉［动物］ clam

▸há

【蛤蚧】géjiè〈名〉［动物］ gecko

【蛤蜊】gélí〈名〉［动物］ clam

隔 gé

〈动〉 ①（阻隔） separate: ～开一段距离 keep a distance ‖ ～着窗子朝外看 look out of the window ‖ 划线把栏目～开 rule off the columns ‖ 把房间～出一部分 partition off a part of a room ‖ 两批货应该～开放。The two cargo loads should be kept apart from one another. ▸～岸观火, 分～, 阻～ ②（相距） be apart from: ～两天看一次医生 go to the doctor's every three days ‖ 两座城市相～两百英里。The two cities are 200 miles apart. ‖ 每～十分钟开出一列火车。A train leaves every ten minutes.

【隔岸观火】gé'àn-guānhuǒ〈成〉 observe sb.'s trouble with indifference from a safe distance

【隔板】gébǎn〈名〉 partition

【隔壁】gébì〈名〉 next door: 住在～ live next door ‖ 我听见～有人在唱歌。I heard somebody singing next door.

【隔层】gécéng〈名〉［建筑］ interlayer

【隔代遗传】gédài yíchuán〈名〉 atavism

【隔断】géduàn〈动〉 block off: 战争～了他和家人的联系。The war cut him off from his family. ‖ 大雪～了交通。Heavy snow blocked the roads.

【隔断】géduan〈名〉［建筑］ partition

【隔房】géfáng〈形〉 of different subfamilies: ～兄弟 half-brothers

【隔行】géháng〈动〉 ①（指行业） be in different professions: ▸～如隔山 ②（指文字） be double-spaced: ～打印 type in double space ‖ ～书写 write in double space

【隔行如隔山】géháng rú géshān〈俗〉 one knows little about trades other than one's own

【隔阂】géhé〈名〉 misunderstanding: 产生～ produce feelings of estrangement ‖ 消除～ clear up misunderstandings ‖ 语言～ language barrier

【隔火墙】géhuǒqiáng〈名〉［建筑］ fire wall

【隔间】géjiān〈名〉 partition

【隔绝】géjué〈动〉 cut off: ～空气 seal off air ‖ 音信～ cut off from any news ‖ 过着与世～的生活 live in complete isolation

【隔离】gélí〈动〉 isolate: ～审查 be taken into custody and placed under investigation ‖ 将肝炎病人和其他病人～开来 isolate the patients with hepatitis from the rest ‖ ～7天 be quarantined for seven days ‖ ～病房 isolation ward ‖ 种族～ racial segregation

【隔离层】gélícéng〈名〉 separation layer

【隔离带】gélídài〈名〉 ①［农业］ isolation belt ②［交通］ dividing strip

【隔离墩】gélídūn〈名〉［交通］ partition block

【隔离服】gélífú〈名〉 protective clothing

【隔离墙】gélíqiáng〈名〉 separation wall

【隔膜】gémó Ⓐ〈名〉 estrangement: 产生/消除～ cause/end an estrangement ‖ 相互之间有～ be estranged from one another Ⓑ〈形〉 unfamiliar: 我对这种新方法实在～。I am unacquainted with the new method.

【隔年黄历】génián-huánglì〈俗〉〈喻〉 something outdated

【隔墙】géqiáng〈名〉 partition wall

【隔墙有耳】géqiáng-yǒu'ěr〈成〉 walls have ears

【隔热】gérè〈动〉 insulate against heat: ～性能 heat-proof quality ‖ ～层 thermal shroud

【隔热砖】gérèzhuān〈名〉 insulating brick

【隔日】gérì〈副〉 every other day: ～有一次航班。There is a flight every other day. ‖ 我～再来看你。I'll come and see you some other day.

【隔三岔五】gésān-chàwǔ = 隔三差五 gésān-chàwǔ

【隔三差五】gésān-chàwǔ〈成〉 now and then: 我～给妈妈买点东西。I buy my mother something every now and then.

【隔山】géshān〈形〉〈旧〉 of the same father but different mothers: ～兄弟姐妹 half-brothers and half-sisters by the same father

【隔扇】géshan〈名〉 partition board

【隔声】géshēng〈动〉［建筑］ insulate against sound

【隔声窗】géshēngchuāng〈名〉 soundproof window

【隔声门】géshēngmén〈名〉 soundproof door

【隔世】géshì〈动〉 be separated by a generation: ～之感 be confused and puzzled as if one has come from another life in the past ▸恍如～

【隔心】géxīn〈动〉 be estranged: 她再婚后，儿子和她～了。After her remarriage her son became estranged from her.

【隔靴搔痒】géxuē-sāoyǎng〈成〉〈喻〉 ①（指语言） fail to grasp the root of a matter ②（指行为） take superficial measures

【隔夜】géyè〈动〉 be from the previous night: ～茶 last night's tea ‖ 夫妻没有～仇。Bad blood between wife and husband never lasts the night.

【隔音】géyīn〈动〉 be soundproof: ～材料 soundproof material ‖ 这间屋子～不好。This room is not well soundproofed.

【隔音符号】géyīn fúhào〈名〉［语言］ syllable-dividing mark (')

【隔音墙】géyīnqiáng〈名〉［建筑］ sound-insulating wall

【隔音室】géyīnshì〈名〉 soundproof room

嗝 gé

〈名〉 ①（气嗝） hiccup: 打着～说 say sth. with a hiccup ▸打～儿 ②（饱嗝） burp: 饱～ belch

槅 gé

〈名〉 ①（指门或隔扇） lattice ②（指架子） set of latticed shelves: 多宝～ curio shelves

【槅门】gémén〈名〉 latticed door

【槅扇】géshan = 隔扇 géshan

膈 gé

〈名〉［解剖］ diaphragm

▸gè

【膈膜】gémó〈名〉 diaphragm

骼 gé

〈名〉 skeleton: ▸骨～

镉（鎘） gé

〈名〉 cadmium (Cd): ～电池 cadmium battery

【镉合金】géhéjīn〈名〉 cadmium metal

gě

个(個) gě〈代〉self: ▸自～儿
▸gè

合 gě
A〈名〉*ge* [measuring implement for grain]
B〈量〉*ge* [unit of dry measure for grain, equal to 0.1 litre]
▸hé

各 gě〈形〉〈方〉unusual: 性格有点～ be a bit odd
▸gè

舸 gě〈名〉〈书〉barge

盖(蓋) Gě〈名〉Ge [surname]
▸gài

葛 Gě〈名〉Ge [surname]
▸gé

gè

个[1](個) gè
A〈量〉**1**（后加名词）[used before a noun which does not have a fixed measure word of its own]: 三～星期 three weeks ‖ 四～钟头 four hours **2**（后加约数词）[used before an approximate number to make the sentence sound informal]: 隔～两三天你再来。Come again in a couple of days. ‖ 街上没几～人。There are few people in the street. **3**（插在动宾结构中）[used between a verb and its object]: 帮～忙 do sb. a favour ‖ 表～态 make one's position known ‖（和某人）说～话 have a word (with sb.) ‖ 洗～热水澡 take a hot bath **4**（加在补语前）[used between a verb and its complement]: 吃～痛快 eat to one's heart's content ‖ 玩～高兴 have a good time ‖ 笑～不停 keep laughing
B〈形〉individual: ▸～别, ～体, ～性
C = 个儿 gèr

个[2](個) gè〈后缀〉**1**（用于量词"些"后）[suffix to 些]: 那些～鸟不会飞。Those birds cannot fly. ‖ 我们有些～问题需要解决。We have some problems to solve. **2**〈方〉（用于时间名词后）[suffix to some nouns of time]: 今儿～ today ‖ 明儿～ tomorrow ‖ 昨儿～ yesterday
▸gě

【个案】gè'àn〈名〉case: 作～处理 handle on a case-by-case basis

【个案研究】gè'àn yánjiū〈名〉case study

【个把】gèbǎ ▸**p. 927**〈数〉〈口〉a couple: 等～小时 wait for a couple of hours ‖ 我还需要～人帮忙。I still need one or two helpers.

【个别】gèbié〈形〉**1**（单独）individual: ～谈话 speak personally (to sb.) ‖ ～辅导 instruct individually **2**（少数）very few: 只有～人缺席。Only a few people were absent. ‖ 这种情况极其～。Such instances are extremely rare.

【个别差异】gèbié chāyì〈名〉［心理］individual difference

【个唱】gèchàng〈简称〉= 个人演唱会

【个个】gègè〈代〉each and every one

【个股】gègǔ〈名〉shares of an individual company: ～行情 individual share quotations

【个例】gèlì〈名〉exceptional case

【个儿】gèr〈名〉**1**（个头）size: 挑大～的 choose bigger ones ‖ 长～ grow in stature ‖ 瘦高～ lanky ‖ 她～不高。She is small in stature. **2**（单个）individual: 挨～批评 criticize one by one ‖ 论～卖 sell by the piece

【个人】gèrén **A**〈名〉individual: 兼顾国家、集体和～的利益 take into consideration the interests of the state, the collective, and the individual ‖ ～奋斗 struggle on one's own ‖ ～爱好 personal preference ‖ ～经历 personal experiences ‖ ～意见 personal opinion **B**〈代〉oneself: 我～认为 I myself think ‖ 就我～而言，我不喜欢她。Personally, I don't like her.

【个人财产】gèrén cáichǎn〈名〉personal property

【个人崇拜】gèrén chóngbài〈名〉personality cult

【个人储蓄】gèrén chǔxù〈名〉personal savings

【个人存款】gèrén cúnkuǎn〈名〉individual deposit

【个人贷款】gèrén dàikuǎn〈名〉personal loan

【个人画展】gèrén huàzhǎn〈名〉solo exhibition of paintings

【个人计算机】gèrén jìsuànjī〈名〉personal computer (PC)

【个人简历】gèrén jiǎnlì〈名〉curriculum vitae (CV)〈英〉; résumé〈美〉

【个人利益】gèrén lìyì〈名〉personal interest

【个人迷信】gèrén míxìn〈名〉personality cult

【个人密码】gèrén mìmǎ〈名〉personal identification number (PIN)

【个人全能】gèrén quánnéng ▸**p. 909**〈名〉［体育］individual combined event

【个人所得税】gèrén suǒdéshuì〈名〉personal income tax: 缴纳/支付～ pay individual income tax ‖ 征收～ levy individual income tax ‖ ～申报表 individual income tax return

【个人卫生】gèrén wèishēng〈名〉personal hygiene

【个人问题】gèrén wèntí〈名〉personal problems [usu referring to one's marital situation]

【个人肖像权】gèrén xiàoxiàngquán〈名〉individual portrait rights

【个人演唱会】gèrén yǎnchànghuì〈名〉solo concert: 举行～ give a solo concert

【个人隐私】gèrén yǐnsī〈名〉privacy: 打探别人的～ poke one's nose into other people's affairs

【个人英雄主义】gèrén yīngxióngzhǔyì〈名〉individualistic heroism

【个人用品】gèrén yòngpǐn〈名〉personal effects

【个人游】gèrényóu〈名〉individual travel: 内地进一步放宽了赴港澳的～。The mainland has taken steps to relax restrictions on individual travel to Hong Kong and Macao.

【个人账户】gèrén zhànghù〈名〉personal account

【个人主义】gèrénzhǔyì〈名〉〈贬〉egotism

【个税】gèshuì〈简称〉= 个人所得税

【个体】gètǐ〈名〉**1**（个人）individual **2** ▸**p. 966**（个体户）individual operation: 干～ be self-employed

【个体工商户】gètǐ gōngshānghù ▸**p. 966**〈名〉**1**（指经济实体）individual business **2**（指社会阶层）self-employed business person

【个体户】gètǐhù〈简称〉= 个体工商户

【个体基因型】gètǐ jīyīnxíng〈名〉［生物］idiotype

【个体经济】gètǐ jīngjì〈名〉individual economy: 个体农业经济 individual agricultural economy

【个体经营】gètǐ jīngyíng〈名〉individual operation (of a business): ～者 self-employed person

【个体名词】gètǐ míngcí〈名〉［语法］individual noun

【个体所有制】gètǐ suǒyǒuzhì〈名〉individual ownership

【个头儿】gètóur〈名〉stature: 他～不小。He's rather tall. ‖ 这苹果～大。This is a big apple.

【个位】gèwèi〈名〉［数学］basic unit: ～数 digit

【个性】gèxìng〈名〉**1**（特性）individuality: 有～的人 person of marked individuality ‖ 这个演员缺乏～。There's nothing special about this actor. **2**［哲学］peculiarity: ～和共性 common and specific properties

【个中】gèzhōng〈名〉〈书〉therein: ～奥妙/滋味 secret/taste of sth. ‖ ～人 insider ‖ ～事 inside story

【个子】gèzi〈名〉height: 小～ short person ‖ 高～ tall person

各 gè
A〈代〉each: ～地区～部门 every locality and department ‖ ～国 every country ‖ ～位来宾 all the guests present ‖ ～族人民 people of all nationalities ‖ 由于～种原因 for various reasons
B〈副〉each: ～不相同 different from one another ‖ ～有利弊 each has its advantages and disadvantages ▸～执一词
▸gě

【各安职守】gè'ānzhíshǒu〈成〉each minds their own business

【各半】gèbàn〈动〉be fifty-fifty: 责任～ share the responsibility fifty-fifty ‖ 我们班男女～。My class is half boys, half girls.

【各奔前程】gèbèn-qiánchéng〈成〉each goes his own way

【各别】gèbié〈形〉**1**（不同）separate: 这些问题不同，应～对待。These are separate problems and have to be handled differently. **2**〈方〉（特别）unusual: 式样很～。The style is unique. **3**〈贬〉（特殊）weird: 这个人很～。This person is really strange.

【各不相让】gèbùxiāngràng〈成〉neither is willing to yield

【各持己见】gèchí-jǐjiàn〈成〉each stands their ground

【各打五十大板】gè dǎ wǔshí dàbǎn〈俗〉punish the guilty and the innocent alike

【各得其所】gèdé-qísuǒ〈成〉**1**（指人）each gets what he wants **2**（指事物）each is in its proper place

【各地】gèdì〈名〉various places

【各个】gègè **A**〈代〉each: ～部分 every part ‖ ～单位 each unit ‖ ～领域 all fields **B**〈副〉one after another

【各个击破】gègè-jīpò〈成〉defeat one by one

【各国议会联盟】Gèguó Yìhuì Liánméng〈名〉Inter-Parliamentary Union

【各行各业】gèháng-gèyè〈成〉all walks of life

【各怀鬼胎】gèhuái-guǐtāi〈成〉each has their own axe to grind
【各级】gèjí〈名〉all levels: ～领导 leaders at all levels ‖ ～人民法院 people's courts at various levels
【各界】gèjiè〈名〉all walks of life: ～代表 representatives from all walks of life ‖ ～人士 personalities from all different walks of life
【各尽所能】gèjìn-suǒnéng〈成〉from each according to their ability: ～，按劳分配 from each according to their ability, to each according to their work ‖ ～，按需分配 from each according to their ability, to each according to their needs
【各就各位】gèjiù-gèwèi〈成〉**1**［体育］on your marks **2**〈喻〉（指岗位或位置）each goes to their respective place: 请～。Go to your respective places.
【各取所需】gèqǔ-suǒxū〈成〉each takes what they need
【各人】gèrén〈代〉each one
【各人自扫门前雪，莫管他人瓦上霜】gè-rén zì sǎo mén qián xuě, mò guǎn tārén wǎ shàng shuāng〈俗〉〈喻〉everyone minds their own business
【各色】gèsè〈形〉**1**（各种）various: ～货物，一应俱全 be stocked with goods of all kinds ‖ ～人等 all kinds of people **2**〈方〉〈贬〉（古怪）weird: 他那个人很～。He is rather eccentric.
【各式各样】gèshì-gèyàng〈成〉of various kinds: ～的服装 dresses of all styles ‖ ～的用途 a wide variety of uses
【各适其所】gèshì-qísuǒ〈成〉each to their taste
【各抒己见】gèshū-jǐjiàn〈成〉each speaks their mind
【各司其事】gèsī-qíshì〈成〉each attends to their own duties
【各司其职】gèsī-qízhí = 各司其事 gèsī-qíshì
【各位】gèwèi〈代〉everyone [term of address]
【各显神通】gèxiǎn-shéntōng〈成〉each demonstrates their own skill
【各行其是】gèxíng-qíshì〈成〉each does what they believe right
【各有千秋】gèyǒu-qiānqiū〈成〉each has sth. to recommend them
【各有所长】gèyǒu-suǒcháng〈成〉each has their own strong points
【各有所好】gèyǒu-suǒhào〈成〉each has their own likes
【各执一词】gèzhí-yīcí〈成〉each sticks to their own argument
【各种各样】gèzhǒng-gèyàng〈成〉all kinds: ～的方法 a whole variety of ways
【各自】gèzì〈代〉each: 保留～的特色 preserve the distinctive identities ‖ ～回家 go separate ways home ‖ ～为战 fight independently ‖ 他们在～的领域都声名显赫。They attained distinction and eminence in their respective fields.
【各自为政】gèzì-wéizhèng〈成〉each does things in their own way

虼 gè

【虼螂】gèláng〈名〉dung beetle
【虼蚤】gèzao〈名〉〈口〉flea

硌 gè〈动〉〈口〉scratch: ～脚 hurt one's foot ‖ ～牙 hurt one's teeth
▸luò

铬（鉻）gè〈名〉chromium (Cr): 镀～的 chrome-plated

【铬镀层】gèdùcéng〈名〉chromium coating
【铬化】gèhuà〈动〉chromize: ～处理 chromizing
【铬镍合金】gènié héjīn〈名〉chromium-nickel alloy

膈 gè

▸gé
【膈应】gèying〈动〉〈方〉feel nauseous: 看到蛇心里就～ feel nauseous at the sight of snakes

gěi

给（給）gěi

A〈动〉**1**（使得到）give: 把这封信～她 hand this letter to her ‖ ～她一周假 grant her a week's leave ‖ ～我一些时间 give me some time ‖ 她～我的印象很好。She gave me a very good impression. **2**（使受苦）make sb. suffer: ～敌人以沉重打击 strike a heavy blow at the enemy ‖ ～他点颜色看看 teach him a lesson **3**（允许）let: ～我看看。Let me have a look. ‖ 他不～大家知道他病了。He didn't let it be known that he was ill.
B〈介〉**1**（被）[used in passive sentences to introduce either the doer of the action or the action if the doer is not mentioned] by: ～人捅了一刀 get stabbed by sb. ‖ 衣服～汗水湿透了。The clothes were soaked with sweat. **2**（引出接受对象）[used after a verb indicating the handing or passing over of sth.] to, with: 把球回传～守门员 pass the ball back to the goalkeeper ‖ 发～每个士兵一支枪。Each soldier was issued with a rifle. **3**（朝）[used to introduce the recipient of an action] to, for: ～孩子们讲故事 tell stories to the children ‖ ～某人道歉 apologize to someone ‖ ～你添麻烦了，不好意思。Sorry to have troubled you. **4**（后接"我"，用于加强语气）[followed by 我 in the imperative sentence for emphasis]: 快～我闭嘴。Shut up! ‖ 你～我走开。Go away!
C〈助〉[used before a verb for emphasis]: 花瓶～打了。Someone broke the vase. ‖ 她把自行车～修好了。She has had her bicycle repaired.
▸jǐ
【给出路】gěi chūlù〈动〉give sb. a way out
【给分】gěifēn〈动〉score points: 他的作文老师给了30分。His essay was awarded thirty points by the teacher.
【给脸】gěiliǎn〈动〉save sb.'s face: ～不要脸 be fool enough to reject a face-saving offer
【给面子】gěi miànzi〈动〉save sb.'s face: 他一点儿不～，让我下不了台。He showed me no respect and completely humiliated me.
【给以】gěiyǐ〈动〉〈书〉grant: ～充分重视 give ample attention ‖ ～道义支持 give moral support ‖ ～很高评价 value highly ‖ ～记过处分 give sb. a demerit

gēn

根 gēn

A〈名〉**1**（指植物）root: 生/扎～ take/strike root ‖ 树～ tree root ‖〈喻〉佛教在日本深深地扎下了～。Buddhism set down deep roots on Japanese soil. ▸～深叶茂，盘～错节 **2**（祖先）descendant: 寻～ trace one's family roots ‖ 单～独苗 sole male heir **3**（底部）foot: 发～ hair root ▸墙～，舌～，牙～ **4**（源头）source: ▸祸～，刨～问底 **5**（基础）basis **6**［数学］（方根）root: ▸平方～ **7**［数学］（解）solution of an algebraic equation **8**［化学］radical: ▸酸～
B〈副〉completely: ▸～除，～治
C〈量〉[for long, thin objects]: 一～棍子/绳子 a stick/rope ‖ 一～头发 a strand of hair
【根本】gēnběn **A**〈名〉base: 抓住问题的～ get to the root of a problem ‖ 从～上解决问题 tackle a problem at its source **B**〈形〉basic: ～变化 fundamental change ‖ ～利益 fundamental interests ‖ ～原因 root cause **C**〈副〉**1**（压根儿）at all: ～不当人看 simply not treat sb. as a human being ‖ 那～不是孩子该去的地方。That is no place for a child. ‖ 他～不是什么医生。He is no doctor in the first place. **2**（完全）totally: 问题已得到～解决。The matter has been settled once and for all. ‖ 我～就不同意。I totally disagree. **3**（从来）at all times: 他～不会做这种事。He is quite above such conduct. ‖ 我～就没见过他。I've never seen him before.
【根本法】gēnběnfǎ〈名〉**1**（指宪法）constitution **2**（基本法）fundamental law: 宪法是我国的～。The Constitution is the basic law of our country.
【根除】gēnchú〈动〉root out: ～腐败现象 root out corruption ‖ ～水患 eliminate the scourge of floods
【根底】gēndǐ〈名〉**1**（基础）foundation: 打下牢固的写作～ gain a firm foundation in writing ‖ 法语～好 have a solid foundation in French **2**（底细）cause: 追问～ enquire as to the cause of a matter ‖ 不了解一个人的～ do not know the background of a person
【根雕】gēndiāo〈名〉tree-root carving
【根腐病】gēnfǔbìng〈名〉［农业］root rot
【根管】gēnguǎn〈名〉［解剖］root canal
【根号】gēnhào〈名〉［数学］root sign (√)
【根基】gēnjī〈名〉**1**（基础）foundation: 动摇～ shake sth. to its very foundation ‖ 削弱农业的～ erode the roots of agriculture ‖ ～牢固 firm foundation **2**（地基）foundations: 这栋房子～牢固。The house stands on firm foundations. ‖〈喻〉这家新公司～浅。The new firm is still on an insecure footing. **3**（家庭背景）family wealth: ～差 be financially insecure
【根脚】gēnjiao = 根基 gēnjī 2
【根茎】gēnjīng〈名〉［植物］rootstock
【根究】gēnjiū〈动〉get to the bottom of: ～缘由 enquire into the origin of sth.
【根据】gēnjù **A**〈介〉according to: ～本条例/通知 in accordance with this regulation/notice ‖ ～同名小说改编的电影 film based on a novel of the same title ‖ ～现行中国法律处置 handle according to existing Chinese law **B**〈名〉basis: 毫无～ be utterly groundless ‖ 没有任何事实～ no basis in fact whatsoever ‖ 她的怀疑是有充分～的。There is definitely cause for her suspicion. **C**〈动〉depend on: 你～什么怀疑他的话？On what grounds do you doubt what he said? ‖ 制定目标要～自身的能力。Targets must be set according to one's individual competences.
【根据地】gēnjùdì〈名〉base: 建立～ establish a base ‖ 革命～ revolutionary base
【根绝】gēnjué〈动〉root out: ～腐败 stamp

out corruption ‖ ～血吸虫病 stamp out snail fever
【根瘤】gēnliú〈名〉［植物］root nodule: ～病 root-knot
【根毛】gēnmáo〈名〉［植物］root hair
【根苗】gēnmiáo〈名〉**1**（根和苗） roots and shoots **2**（根源） root: 细说～ explain the causes **3**（后代） offspring: 家里的唯一～ only male child in a family
【根深柢固】gēnshēn-dǐgù = 根深蒂固 gēnshēn-dìgù
【根深蒂固】gēnshēn-dìgù〈成〉〈喻〉 be deep-rooted: ～的习惯 well-seated habit ‖ 这种思想在农村～。 The idea is deeply rooted in the countryside.
【根深叶茂】gēnshēn-yèmào〈成〉〈喻〉 be well-established and flourishing
【根式】gēnshì〈名〉［数学］radical expression: ～方程 radical equation
【根系】gēnxì〈名〉［植物］root system
【根须】gēnxū〈名〉［植物］root hair
【根芽】gēnyá〈名〉［植物］root bud
【根由】gēnyóu〈名〉 origin: 追问～ probe into the cause ‖ 问题的～ root of a problem
【根源】gēnyuán **A**〈名〉 root: 消除战争～ root out the causes of war ‖ 思想～ ideological root ‖ 不注意卫生是各种疾病的～。 Lack of attention to hygiene is the cause of various diseases. **B**〈动〉 stem from: 这场战争～于意识形态的冲突。 The war originated in ideological conflict.
【根植】gēnzhí〈动〉 be rooted (in): ～于生活 be rooted in life
【根治】gēnzhì〈动〉 cure once and for all: ～虫害 bring insect pests under permanent control ‖ 目前尚无～这种病的药。 There is still no perfect cure for this disease at present.
【根子】gēnzi〈名〉〈口〉 root: 这棵树～扎得浅。 The tree has shallow roots. ‖ 贫穷的～在于教育落后。 Poverty has its roots in poor education. ▸命～

跟 gēn

A〈名〉 heel: 低～鞋 low-heeled shoes ▸后～, 脚～
B〈动〉 **1**（跟随） follow: 紧～其后 follow close on the heels of ‖ ～我读。 Read after me. ‖ 她到哪儿我～到哪儿。 I followed her wherever she went. **2**（嫁给） marry (sb.): 她最后～了一个姓王的。 She finally married someone called Wang.
C〈介〉 **a**（引出行为对象） with: ～某人告别 say good-bye to sb. ‖ 我有话要～你讲。 I want to have a word with you. **b**（表示在一起） with: ～孩子们住在一起 live with one's children ‖ ～朋友合伙做生意 carry on business in partnership with one's friend ‖ 这事～我没关系。 It has nothing to do with me. **c**（表比较） as: ～以往一样 same as before ‖ 不能～某人/某物相比 cannot be compared with sb./sth.
D ▸**p. 448**〈连〉 and: 中国～美国都是大国。 Both China and America are big countries.
【跟班】gēnbān **A**〈动〉 join a regular shift or class: ～学习 join a class **B**〈名〉〈旧〉 footman
【跟不上】gēnbushàng〈动〉 fail to keep pace with
【跟从】gēncóng〈动〉 follow: 你领头，我～你。 You take the lead and I'll follow.
【跟单】gēndān〈名〉 document attached
【跟斗】gēndou = 跟头 gēntou
【跟风】gēnfēng〈动〉 be given to fads: ～炒作 promotional hype
【跟腱】gēnjiàn〈名〉 Achilles tendon
【跟脚】gēnjiǎo〈方〉 **A**〈动〉〈口〉 tail: 这个小男孩真～。 The little boy follows his parents about all day long. **B**〈形〉 well-fitting: 我这双鞋真～。 The shoes fit me perfectly. **C**〈副〉 close on: 你先走，我们～就到。 You go ahead and we'll join you in a minute.
【跟进】gēnjìn〈动〉 **1**（跟踪进展） follow up **2**（照做） follow suit
【跟屁虫】gēnpìchóng〈名〉〈口〉〈贬〉 hanger-on: 像～一样追随某人 follow sb. around like a stalker
【跟前】gēnqián〈名〉 vicinity: 窗户～的座位 window seat
【跟前】gēnqian〈名〉 state of having children: 子女不在～，老两口儿有点孤独。 Having no children around them, the old couple feel somewhat lonely.
【跟上】gēnshang〈动〉 keep pace with: ～潮流 keep abreast of the times
【跟梢】gēnshāo = 盯梢 dīngshāo
【跟随】gēnsuí〈动〉 follow: ～左右 follow sb. wherever they go ‖ 女孩～爸爸出去了。 The girl followed his father out.
【跟趟儿】gēntàngr〈动〉〈方〉 keep up with
【跟帖】gēntiě〈名〉 follow-up post
【跟头】gēntou〈名〉 **1**（指动作） somersault: 杂技演员在舞台上翻～。 The acrobats tumbled on the stage. **2**（挫折） fall: 摔/栽～ have a fall
【跟着】gēnzhe **A**〈动〉 follow: ～感觉走 follow one's intuition ‖ 后面～一群摄影师。 A crowd of photographers followed behind. **B**〈副〉 immediately after: 我们看完电影～就去看球赛。 Immediately after watching the film, we went to watch a match.
【跟踪】gēnzōng〈动〉 shadow: ～目标 shadow a target ‖ ～追击 go in hot pursuit of ‖ ～报道 follow up on ‖ ～采访 follow-through interview ‖ ～服务 follow-up service ‖ 有人～。 Someone is on the trail.
【跟踪球】gēnzōngqiú〈名〉［计算机］ trackball
【跟踪系统】gēnzōng xìtǒng〈名〉 tracking system

gén

哏 gén

A〈形〉〈方〉 funny: 这个故事真～。 This story is intensely amusing.
B〈名〉 clowning: ▸逗～, 捧～

gěn

艮 gěn〈形〉〈方〉

1（指脾气） blunt; （指话语） forthright: 她说话真～。 She is very direct in speech. **2**（指食物） tough: 苹果太～，我没法吃。 The apple is so tough that I can't eat it.
▸gèn

gèn

亘（亙） gèn〈动〉 stretch: ▸横～, 绵～

【亘古】gèngǔ〈副〉〈书〉 from time immemorial: 世上没有～不变的东西。 There is nothing in the world that does not change.
【亘古及今】gèngǔ-jíjīn〈成〉 from time immemorial down to the present day
【亘古未有】gèngǔ-wèiyǒu〈成〉 be unprecedented

艮 gèn〈名〉 one of the Eight Trigrams, symbolizing 'mountain'

▸gěn

莨 gèn ▸毛莨 máogèn

gēng

更 gēng

A〈动〉 **1**（改换） change: ▸～改, ～新, 改弦～张 **2**〈书〉（经历） experience: 少不～事 be young and inexperienced
B〈名〉〈旧〉 watch [one of the five two-hour periods into which the night was formerly divided]: 头～ first watch ‖ 四～ fourth watch
▸gèng
【更次】gēngcì〈名〉〈旧〉 period of a night watch, about two hours: 睡一～ sleep for about two hours
【更迭】gēngdié〈动〉 change: 朝代～ dynastic change ‖ 内阁～ cabinet reshuffle
【更定】gēngdìng〈动〉〈书〉 revise: ～规章制度 revise rules and regulations ‖ ～现行法律 revise an existing law
【更动】gēngdòng〈动〉 modify: 未做任何～ no alteration whatsoever has been made ‖ 有所～ some modifications have been made
【更番】gēngfān〈副〉 alternately: ～值班 be on duty by turns
【更夫】gēngfū〈名〉〈旧〉 night watchman
【更改】gēnggǎi〈动〉 change: ～计划 change a plan
【更鼓】gēnggǔ〈名〉〈旧〉 night watchman's drum
【更换】gēnghuàn〈动〉 renew: ～电话号码 change one's telephone number ‖ ～零件/设备 replace a part/a piece of equipment ‖ ～座位 change seats ‖ 这些证件要每年～一次。 These licences need to be renewed every year.
【更阑】gēnglán〈形〉〈书〉 deep: ～人静 deep is the night and all is quiet
【更楼】gēnglóu〈名〉〈旧〉 night watch tower
【更漏】gēnglòu〈名〉 hourglass
【更名】gēngmíng〈动〉 change one's name: ～改姓 change one's name ‖ ～启事 name-changing notice
【更年期】gēngniánqī〈名〉 climacteric: 女性～ female menopause
【更年期综合征】gēngniánqī zōnghézhēng〈名〉 climacteric syndrome
【更仆难数】gēngpú-nánshǔ〈成〉 countless
【更深人静】gēngshēn-rénjìng〈成〉 deep is the night and all is quiet
【更生】gēngshēng〈动〉 **1**（再生） be reborn; （再振兴） rejuvenate: ▸自力～ **2**（再利用） regenerate: ～产品 reclaimed product ‖ 可～资源 renewable resources
【更生霉素】gēngshēng méisù〈名〉 dactinomycin
【更始】gēngshǐ〈动〉〈书〉 start afresh: 万象～ all is fresh and new again
【更替】gēngtì〈动〉 replace: 人员～ personnel replacement ‖ 季节～。 Seasons alternate.
【更新】gēngxīn〈动〉 **1**（去旧换新） renew: ～观念 change one's idea ‖ ～设备 upgrade equipment ‖ ～网页 update a web page ‖ ～知识 update one's knowledge ‖

g

产品/武器～ renewal of products/weapons ▸万象～ 2 (重新生长) rejuvenate: ～林地 regenerate forest land
【更新换代】gēngxīn-huàndài〈成〉 replace the old with the new: 这种产品需要～了。 This product needs to be updated.
【更新世】Gēngxīnshì〈名〉[地质] Pleistocene Epoch
【更衣】gēngyī〈动〉 1 (换衣服) change one's clothes 2 ▸p. 772 〈婉〉(去厕所) go to the toilet
【更衣室】gēngyīshì〈名〉 locker room
【更易】gēngyì〈动〉 alter: 这篇报告几经～。 The report has been revised several times.
【更张】gēngzhāng〈动〉〈喻〉 reform: ▸改弦～
【更正】gēngzhèng〈动〉 correct: ～文章中的错误 make corrections to articles
【更卒】gēngzú〈名〉〈旧〉 night watcher

庚 gēng〈名〉 1 (指天干) seventh of the ten Heavenly Stems 2 ▸p. 526 (指年纪) age: ▸贵～, 同～
【庚齿】gēngchǐ〈名〉〈书〉 age
【庚日】gēngrì〈名〉 any day designated by the combination of the seventh of the ten Heavenly Stems with one of the twelve Earthly Branches
【庚帖】gēngtiě = 八字帖 bāzìtiě
【庚子赔款】Gēngzǐ Péikuǎn〈名〉 Boxer Indemnity

狭 gēng〈名〉[动物] terrier: 斗牛～ bull terrier

耕（畊） gēng〈动〉 1 (耕作) plough: 备～ prepare land for ploughing and sowing ▸～畜, 春～, 男～女织 2〈喻〉(从事) take up: ▸笔～, 舌～
【耕畜】gēngchù〈名〉 farm animal
【耕地】gēngdì A〈动〉 plough: 机器～又快又好。 Machines plough fast and well. B〈名〉 cultivated land: ～面积 area under cultivation ‖ 不要随便占用～。 Don't divert arable land to other uses.
【耕读】gēngdú〈动〉 do farm work while studying/teaching: ～学校 school providing part-time study and part-time agricultural work
【耕夫】gēngfū〈名〉〈书〉 farmer
【耕稼】gēngjià〈名〉〈书〉 farming
【耕具】gēngjù〈名〉 farm tool: ～齐备 have a complete set of tilling tools
【耕牛】gēngniú〈名〉 farm cattle
【耕田】gēngtián A〈动〉 till B = 耕地 gēngdì B
【耕云播雨】gēngyún-bōyǔ〈成〉 provide favourable conditions: 为培养科技人才～ work hard to train scientific researchers
【耕耘】gēngyún〈动〉 cultivate: ～播种 plough and sow ▸一分～, 一分收获
【耕种】gēngzhòng〈动〉 till: ～田地 work the land ‖ 我爷爷当年～了 30 亩地。 My grandfather farmed 30 *mu* of land.
【耕作】gēngzuò〈动〉 farm: ～方法 farming method ‖ ～技术 farming skill ‖ 粗放型～ extensive cultivation ‖ ～制度 cropping system

赓（賡） gēng〈动〉〈书〉 continue: ▸～续
【赓续】gēngxù〈动〉 continue without stopping

缅（緪） gēng〈名〉〈方〉 thick rope
【缅索】gēngsuǒ〈名〉〈方〉 thick rope

羹 gēng〈名〉 liquid food: 豆腐～ bean curd gruel ‖ 鸡蛋～ egg custard ‖ 莲子～ custard of lotus seeds
【羹匙】gēngchí〈名〉 soup spoon
【羹汤】gēngtāng〈名〉 broth

gěng

埂 gěng〈名〉 1〈书〉(堤防) dyke: ▸～堰 2 (土丘) hillock: ▸土～ 3 (分界线) ridge between fields: ▸地～, 田～
【埂堰】gěngyàn〈名〉 ridge
【埂子】gěngzi〈名〉 ridge between fields

耿 gěng〈形〉 1〈书〉(光亮) bright 2 (正直) upright: ▸～介, ～直
【耿耿】gěnggěng〈形〉 1〈书〉(光亮) bright: ～星河 bright Milky Way 2 (忠诚) dedicated: 忠心～ be dedicated heart and soul 3 (担忧) vexed: ～不寐 lose sleep over (sth.)
【耿耿于怀】gěnggěngyúhuái〈成〉 take sth. to heart: 她对老师的批评～。 She took the teacher's criticism very badly.
【耿介】gěngjiè〈形〉〈书〉 upright: 性情～ upright character
【耿直】gěngzhí〈形〉 upright: 秉性～ honest and frank by nature ‖ 他为人～。 He is a man of frank and honest character.

哽 gěng〈动〉 1 (卡住) choke: 一根骨头～在我的喉咙里。 A bone has stuck in my throat. 2 (哽咽) choke with emotion: ～不成声 choke up and be unable to speak a word ▸～塞, ～咽
【哽塞】gěngsè〈动〉 choke: 他喉咙～了, 未能把话讲完。 He choked and couldn't finish his words.
【哽噎】gěngyē〈动〉 1 (卡住) choke: 他喉咙里被什么东西～住了。 Something caught in his throat and choked him. 2 = 哽咽 gěngyè
【哽咽】gěngyè〈动〉 choke with sobs: ～落泪 choke with tears

绠（綆） gěng〈名〉〈书〉 well rope
【绠短汲深】gěngduǎn-jíshēn〈成〉〈喻〉 out of one's depth

梗 gěng
A〈名〉 stalk: 茶叶～儿 stalk of a tea leaf ‖ 花～儿 stem of a flower
B〈动〉 1 (挺着) straighten up: ～着脖子 straighten up one's neck 2 (阻塞) obstruct: ▸～塞, ～阻
C〈形〉 upright: ▸～直
【梗概】gěnggài〈名〉 gist: 故事～ outline of a story
【梗塞】gěngsè〈动〉 block: 交通～ traffic jam ‖ 心肌～ myocardial infarction
【梗死】gěngsǐ〈动〉[医学] have myocardial infarction: ▸心肌～
【梗咽】gěngyè = 哽咽 gěngyè
【梗直】gěngzhí = 耿直 gěngzhí
【梗阻】gěngzǔ A〈动〉 1 (堵住) block: 交通～ traffic jam 2 (阻拦) block: 横加～ wilfully obstruct B〈名〉[医学] obstruction: 不完全～ partial obstruction ▸肠～

颈（頸） gěng ▸脖颈儿 bógěngr ▸jǐng

鲠（鯁） gěng
A〈名〉〈书〉 fish bone: ▸如～在喉
B〈动〉 have sth. stuck in the throat: 被鱼刺～住了 choke on a fish bone
C〈形〉 upright: ▸～直
【鲠直】gěngzhí = 耿直 gěngzhí

gèng

更 gèng〈副〉 1〈书〉(进一步) further: ～进一步 go a step further ‖ ～有甚者 what is more 2 (越发) more: ～简单 simpler ‖ ～漂亮 more beautiful ‖ 伙食不好, 服务～差。 The food is bad and the service is even worse.
▸gēng
【更加】gèngjiā〈副〉 even more: ～复杂 be even more complicated ‖ ～混乱 be even more confused ‖ 我们必须～努力。 We must double our efforts.
【更上一层楼】gèng shàng yī céng lóu〈成〉〈喻〉 scale new heights
【更胜一筹】gèngshèng-yīchóu〈成〉 be even better
【更为】gèngwéi〈书〉= 更加 gèngjiā

gōng

工[1] gōng
A〈名〉 1 (指人) worker: 合同～ contract worker ‖ 临时～ casual worker ▸技～, 矿～, 女～ 2 (指阶层) working class: ▸～农联盟 3 (工时) work: 上～ go to work ‖ 收～ stop work ▸～具, ～龄, 罢～, 加～ 4 (人工) person-day: 这活需要十个～。 The work will take ten person-days. 5 (工程) construction: 动/开～ begin/start construction ▸～地, ～期, 竣～ 6 (工业) industry: ▸化～, 军～ 7 (工程师) engineer: 王～ Engineer Wang ▸高～
B〈形〉 fine: ▸～巧, ～细, 异曲同～
C〈动〉 be good at: ～诗善话 be versed in both poetry and painting ▸～于心计

工[2] gōng〈名〉[音乐] note on the *gongche* (工尺) scale, corresponding to 3 in *jianpu* (简谱) numbered musical notation
【工本】gōngběn〈名〉 cost: 不惜～ do sth. regardless of the cost ‖ ～费 cost
【工笔】gōngbǐ〈名〉[美术] *gongbi* [traditional Chinese painting method]: ～画 fine brushwork painting
【工兵】gōngbīng〈名〉[军事] military engineer: ～部队 engineering troops ‖ ～连 engineer company
【工厂】gōngchǎng〈名〉 factory; works〈英〉: ▸兵～, 化～, 军～
【工场】gōngchǎng〈名〉 workshop
【工潮】gōngcháo〈名〉 labour movement: 闹～ go on strike
【工尺】gōngchě〈名〉[音乐] *gongche* [traditional Chinese musical scale]
【工尺谱】gōngchěpǔ〈名〉[音乐] *gongchepu* [traditional Chinese musical notation]
【工程】gōngchéng〈名〉 1 (指学科)

engineering: 土木～ civil engineering ‖ 系统～ systems engineering 2（指项目）project: 水利～ water conservancy projects ‖ 安居～ housing project ‖ 市政～ municipal works ‖ "希望～" Project Hope
【工程兵】gōngchéngbīng〈名〉［军事］military engineer
【工程队】gōngchéngduì〈名〉construction team
【工程费】gōngchéngfèi〈名〉engineering cost
【工程公司】gōngchéng gōngsī〈名〉engineering company
【工程管理】gōngchéng guǎnlǐ〈名〉engineering management
【工程技术】gōngchéng jìshù〈名〉engineering
【工程监督】gōngchéng jiāndū〈名〉project supervision
【工程师】gōngchéngshī ▶p. 966〈名〉engineer: 高级～ senior engineer ‖ 人类灵魂的～ engineer of the soul ‖ 总～ chief engineer
【工程项目】gōngchéng xiàngmù〈名〉engineering project
【工程学院】gōngchéng xuéyuàn〈名〉college of engineering
【工程验收】gōngchéng yànshōu〈名〉acceptance of works
【工程院】gōngchéngyuàn〈名〉academy of engineering: ～院士 academician of the academy of engineering
【工程造价】gōngchéng zàojià〈名〉construction cost
【工程制图】gōngchéng zhìtú〈名〉engineering drawing
【工党】Gōngdǎng〈名〉Labour Party
【工地】gōngdì〈名〉construction site: 建筑～ construction site
【工读】gōngdú A〈动〉work one's way through college: ～生 self-supporting student B〈名〉education of juvenile delinquents: ～学校 reform school
【工段】gōngduàn〈名〉section: ～长 section chief
【工房】gōngfáng〈名〉〈方〉1（指房屋）workers' living quarters 2（工作间）workshop
【工分】gōngfēn〈名〉work point: 记～ make a record of work points ‖ ～值 cash value of a work point
【工蜂】gōngfēng〈名〉worker bee
【工夫】gōngfu〈名〉1（时间）time: 一眨眼的～ in the twinkling of the eye ‖ 写书很费～。Writing a book is time-consuming. 2（空闲）free time: 没～看书 not have the time to read ‖ 有～请给我写信。Write to me when you have the time. 3（时候）moment: 我年轻那～ in my youth
【工会】gōnghuì〈名〉trade union〈英〉; labour union〈美〉: 同业～ union of same trade organizations ‖ ～会费 union membership dues ‖ ～会员 union member ‖ 中华全国总～ All-China Federation of Trade Unions
【工价】gōngjià〈名〉labour cost
【工间】gōngjiān〈名〉break during working hours: ～休息 tea break
【工间操】gōngjiāncāo〈名〉work-break exercises: 做～ do work-break exercises
【工件】gōngjiàn〈名〉workpiece
【工匠】gōngjiàng〈名〉craftsman
【工交】gōngjiāo〈名〉industry and communications: ～战线 industrial and communications sectors
【工具】gōngjù〈名〉1（器具）tool: 电动～ power tool ‖ 交通～ means of transportation ‖ 生产～ implement of production 2〈喻〉（手段）means: 被人当～使 be used as a tool ‖ 语言是表达思想的～。Language is an instrument for communication.
【工具房】gōngjùfáng〈名〉tool house
【工具架】gōngjùjià〈名〉tool rack
【工具栏】gōngjùlán〈名〉［计算机］tool bar
【工具书】gōngjùshū〈名〉reference book: 查阅～ consult a reference book
【工具箱】gōngjùxiāng〈名〉toolbox
【工卡】gōngkǎ〈名〉employee's name badge
【工楷】gōngkǎi〈名〉neat regular script: 写一手漂亮的～ write in beautiful regular script
【工科】gōngkē〈名〉engineering course: ～大学 college of engineering
【工矿】gōngkuàng〈名〉industry and mining: ～企业 industrial and mining enterprises
【工力】gōnglì〈名〉1（技术）workmanship: 颇见～ show the hand of a master 2（人力）manpower
【工力悉敌】gōnglì-xīdí〈成〉be rivals of equal skill
【工联主义】gōngliánzhǔyì〈名〉(trade) unionism
【工料】gōngliào〈名〉1（人工和材料）labour and materials: ～费 flat cost 2（材料）materials (for a project): 购买～ purchase materials (for a project)
【工龄】gōnglíng〈名〉length of service: 有二十年～的工人 worker of twenty years' standing
【工贸】gōngmào〈名〉industry and trade: ～公司 industrial and trade company
【工帽】gōngmào〈名〉work hat
【工农】gōngnóng〈名〉1（指人）workers and peasants: ～出身 be of worker or peasant origin 2（指产业）industry and agriculture: ～差别 difference between industry and agriculture
【工农兵】gōngnóngbīng〈名〉workers, peasants and soldiers
【工农联盟】gōngnóng liánméng〈名〉worker-peasant alliance
【工农业总产值】gōngnóngyè zǒngchǎnzhí〈名〉gross output value of industry and agriculture
【工棚】gōngpéng〈名〉1（用于居住）builders' temporary shed 2（用于做工）work shed: 搭～ put up a work shed
【工频】gōngpín〈名〉power frequency
【工期】gōngqī〈名〉deadline for a project: 缩短～ shorten the deadline for a project ‖ 延误～ be behind schedule for a project
【工钱】gōngqian〈名〉1（干零活收入）charge for a service: 拒付～ refuse to pay sb. for his work 2〈口〉（工资）wage: 克扣～ dock part of the worker's wage
【工巧】gōngqiǎo〈形〉[of a piece of writing, craft, etc.] fine
【工区】gōngqū〈名〉industrial work place
【工人】gōngrén〈名〉worker: 产业～ industrial worker
【工人阶级】gōngrén jiējí〈名〉working class
【工人纠察队】gōngrén jiūcháduì〈名〉workers' pickets
【工人俱乐部】gōngrén jùlèbù〈名〉workers' club
【工人文化宫】gōngrén wénhuàgōng〈名〉workers' palace of culture
【工人运动】gōngrén yùndòng〈名〉labour movement
【工日】gōngrì〈名〉person-day
【工伤】gōngshāng〈名〉occupational injury: ～保险 insurance against injury at work ‖ ～事故 work-related accident
【工商】gōngshāng〈名〉industry and commerce: ～界 business circles ‖ ～人士 industrial and commercial figures
【工商管理】gōngshāng guǎnlǐ〈名〉business administration: ～硕士 Master of Business Administration (MBA)
【工商局】gōngshāngjú〈简称〉= 工商行政管理局
【工商联】gōngshānglián〈简称〉= 工商业联合会
【工商所】gōngshāngsuǒ〈名〉administrative office of industry and commerce
【工商行政管理局】gōngshāng xíngzhèng guǎnlǐjú〈名〉administrative bureau for industry and commerce: 国家～ State Administration of Industry and Commerce
【工商业】gōngshāngyè〈名〉industry and commerce
【工商业联合会】gōngshāngyè liánhéhuì〈名〉association of industry and commerce
【工商银行】gōngshāng yínháng〈名〉industrial and commercial bank
【工时】gōngshí〈名〉person-hour: 节约百分之十的～ save ten per cent of the person-hours ‖ ～定额 person-hour quota
【工事】gōngshì〈名〉fortifications: 修筑～ build fortifications ‖ 防御～ defence works
【工头】gōngtóu〈名〉foreman
【工团主义】gōngtuánzhǔyì〈名〉syndicalism
【工稳】gōngwěn〈形〉〈书〉apt: 造句～。The words are apt and well chosen.
【工细】gōngxì〈形〉elaborate: 雕刻～ be elaborate in carving
【工效】gōngxiào〈名〉work efficiency: 提高～ increase work efficiency
【工效学】gōngxiàoxué〈名〉ergonomics
【工薪】gōngxīn〈名〉wage
【工薪阶层】gōngxīn jiēcéng〈名〉wage-earner class
【工薪族】gōngxīnzú〈名〉wage-earners
【工休】gōngxiū〈名〉1（休息日）regular holiday: ～日 day off 2（工间休息）break
【工序】gōngxù〈名〉process: 最后一道～ the final step
【工业】gōngyè〈名〉industry: 振兴～ vitalize industries ‖ 基础～ basic industry ‖ 汽车～ automobile industry
【工业博览会】gōngyè bólǎnhuì〈名〉industrial fair
【工业产权】gōngyè chǎnquán〈名〉industrial property right: ～法 industrial property law
【工业城市】gōngyè chéngshì〈名〉industrial city
【工业大学】gōngyè dàxué〈名〉institute of technology
【工业废料】gōngyè fèiliào〈名〉industrial waste
【工业废气】gōngyè fèiqì〈名〉industrial waste gas
【工业废水】gōngyè fèishuǐ〈名〉industrial sewage
【工业粉尘】gōngyè fěnchén〈名〉industrial dust
【工业革命】Gōngyè Gémìng〈名〉Industrial Revolution
【工业国】gōngyèguó〈名〉industrialized nation: 工业大国 industrial power
【工业化】gōngyèhuà〈动〉industrialize:

g

～程度高 be highly industrialized ‖ ～国家 industrialized country

【工业垃圾】gōngyè lājī〈名〉industrial refuse

【工业品】gōngyèpǐn〈名〉industrial product

【工业企业】gōngyè qǐyè〈名〉industrial enterprise

【工业区】gōngyèqū〈名〉industrial area

【工业污染】gōngyè wūrǎn〈名〉industrial pollution

【工业园区】gōngyè yuánqū〈名〉industrial park

【工蚁】gōngyǐ〈名〉worker ant

【工艺】gōngyì〈名〉**1**（技术）technology: ～复杂 sophisticated technology ‖ ～设计 technological design **2**（手艺）handicraft: ▸～美术, ～品

【工艺流程】gōngyì liúchéng〈名〉technological process: ～图 flow chart

【工艺美术】gōngyì měishù〈名〉arts and crafts: ～学校 school for arts and crafts

【工艺品】gōngyìpǐn〈名〉handiwork: 手～ artistic handicraft

【工艺水平】gōngyì shuǐpíng〈名〉technological level

【工友】gōngyǒu〈名〉**1**（指工人）fellow worker **2**（指勤杂工）handyman

【工于】gōngyú〈动〉be good at: ～弦乐器 be good at playing stringed instruments

【工于心计】gōngyú-xīnjì〈成〉be adept at scheming

【工余】gōngyú〈名〉leisure: ～时间 spare time

【工欲善其事，必先利其器】gōng yù shàn qí shì, bì xiān lì qí qì〈成〉a workman must first sharpen his tools if he is to do his work well

【工贼】gōngzéi〈名〉blackleg〈英〉; scab〈美〉

【工长】gōngzhǎng〈名〉foreman

【工整】gōngzhěng〈形〉neat: 她的字写得很～。She has very neat handwriting.

【工致】gōngzhì〈形〉[of a painting, craft, etc.] elaborate: 他的水彩画很～。He paints elaborately in water colours.

【工种】gōngzhǒng〈名〉work category

【工装】gōngzhuāng〈名〉work clothes

【工装裤】gōngzhuāngkù〈名〉overalls

【工资】gōngzī〈名〉wage: 发～ pay (out) wages ‖ 增加～ raise sb.'s salary ‖ 基本～ basic salary ‖ ～改革 wage reform ‖ ～总额 total payroll ‖ 加班～ overtime pay ‖ 实得～ take-home pay

【工资标准】gōngzī biāozhǔn〈名〉wage standard

【工资表】gōngzībiǎo〈名〉payroll

【工资级别】gōngzī jíbié〈名〉wage grade

【工字钢】gōngzìgāng〈名〉I-steel

【工字梁】gōngzìliáng〈名〉［建筑］I-beam

【工字铁】gōngzìtiě〈名〉I-iron

【工字形】gōngzìxíng〈名〉I-shape

【工作】gōngzuò **A**〈动〉work: 着手～ set about one's work ‖ 在医院～ work in a hospital ‖ 一周～四十个小时 work a forty-hour week **B**〈名〉**1** ▸**p. 966**（职业）job: 调动～ transfer sb. to another post ‖ 找～ look for work ‖ 你是干什么～的? What do you do? **2**（任务）assignment: 秘书/研究～ secretarial/research work ‖ 日常～ routine work

【工作餐】gōngzuòcān〈名〉working meal

【工作单位】gōngzuò dānwèi〈名〉work unit

【工作电路】gōngzuò diànlù〈名〉operating circuit

【工作队】gōngzuòduì〈名〉work team

【工作服】gōngzuòfú〈名〉work clothes

【工作会议】gōngzuò huìyì〈名〉working conference

【工作狂】gōngzuòkuáng〈名〉workaholic

【工作量】gōngzuòliàng〈名〉workload: ～太大 heavy workloads

【工作流程】gōngzuò liúchéng〈名〉workflow

【工作帽】gōngzuòmào〈名〉work cap

【工作面】gōngzuòmiàn〈名〉**1**［矿业］face: 采煤～ coal face **2**［机械］working surface

【工作人员】gōngzuò rényuán〈名〉working personnel: 国家机关～ state functionary

【工作日】gōngzuòrì ▸**p. 836**〈名〉**1**（指日子）working day: 把～由六天缩短为五天 shorten working days from six days to five **2**（指时间）work hours per day

【工作时间】gōngzuò shíjiān〈名〉work hours

【工作室】gōngzuòshì〈名〉**1**（指公司）studio: 影视～ film and television studio **2**［建筑］working chamber

【工作守则】gōngzuò shǒuzé〈名〉work regulations

【工作台】gōngzuòtái〈名〉workbench

【工作态度】gōngzuò tàidu〈名〉working attitude

【工作午餐】gōngzuò wǔcān〈名〉working lunch

【工作效率】gōngzuò xiàolǜ〈名〉work efficiency

【工作许可证】gōngzuò xǔkězhèng〈名〉work permit

【工作语言】gōngzuò yǔyán〈名〉working language

【工作原理】gōngzuò yuánlǐ〈名〉operating principle

【工作站】gōngzuòzhàn〈名〉work station: 征兵～ drafting centre ‖ 救灾～ disaster relief centre ‖ 计算机辅助设计～ work station for computer-aided design

【工作者】gōngzuòzhě〈名〉worker: 地下～ underground worker ‖ 教育～ educator ‖ 新闻～ journalist

【工作证】gōngzuòzhèng〈名〉employee's card: 出示～ produce one's employee's card

【工作制】gōngzuòzhì〈名〉working day: 八小时～ eight-hour day

【工作重心】gōngzuò zhòngxīn〈名〉focus of work

【工作周】gōngzuòzhōu ▸**p. 836**〈名〉workweek

【工作组】gōngzuòzǔ〈名〉working group: 派出～进行专项调查 send out a working group to conduct specialized research

【工作作风】gōngzuò zuòfēng〈名〉work style

弓 gōng

A〈名〉**1**（指兵器）bow: 拉～ draw a bow ‖ 强～ heavy bow ▸弹～, 左右开～ **2**（弓状物）anything bow-shaped: ▸～子 **3**（指量具）*gong* [bow-shaped wooden measure for land]
B〈量〉*gong* [unit of measure for land, equal to five *chi* (尺)]
C〈动〉bend: 弯腰～背 crouch over ‖ ～着身子 hunch oneself

【弓背】gōngbèi **A**〈名〉hunchback **B**〈动〉arch one's back

【弓箭】gōngjiàn〈名〉bow and arrow: ～手 archer

【弓箭步】gōngjiànbù〈名〉forward lunge

【弓弩】gōngnǔ〈名〉bow and crossbow: ～手 crossbowman

【弓身】gōngshēn〈动〉bend oneself

【弓弦】gōngxián〈名〉bowstring

【弓形梁】gōngxíngliáng〈名〉［建筑］bow beam

【弓形门】gōngxíngmén〈名〉arch

【弓腰】gōngyāo〈动〉bend over

【弓子】gōngzi〈名〉bow: 小提琴～ violin bow ‖ 弹棉花～ bow used for teasing cotton

公[1] gōng

A〈形〉**1**（非个人）public: ▸～差, ～款, ～务 **2**（共同）common: ▸～倍数, ～式 **3**（共有）universal: ▸～海 **4**（公开）open: ▸～然, ～演 **5**（公平）fair: 评判不～ partial in one's judgement ▸～道, ～平, 秉～ **6**（国际通用）metric: ▸～制
B〈动〉make public: ▸～之于世
C〈名〉**1**（公家）the state: ▸充～, 归～ **2**（公务）official duty: 因～在外 be away on official duty ‖ 非～莫入。No admittance except on business. ▸～余, 办～

公[2] gōng

A〈名〉**1**（公爵）duke: ～侯 dukes and marquises ‖ 王～ princes and dukes ▸～爵 **2**〈尊〉（用于称呼）mister (Mr) [term of address for an elderly man]: 李～ revered Mr Li **3**（公公）father-in-law: ▸～婆
B〈形〉[of an animal] male: ～猫 tomcat ‖ ～狗 male dog

【公安】gōng'ān〈名〉**1**（社会治安）public security: ～机关 public security agency ‖ ～人员 public security officer **2**（指人）public security officer: 他是个老～。He is a veteran public security officer.

【公安部】Gōng'ānbù〈名〉Ministry of Public Security

【公安部队】gōng'ān bùduì〈名〉public security troops

【公安干警】gōng'ān gànjǐng〈名〉public security police

【公安局】gōng'ānjú〈名〉public security bureau

【公安厅】gōng'āntīng〈名〉department of public security

【公案】gōng'àn〈名〉**1**（指案件）complicated legal case **2**（指事件）controversial issue

【公办】gōngbàn〈形〉state-owned: ～学校 public school

【公报】gōngbào〈名〉communiqué: 联合～ joint communiqué ‖ 新闻～ press communiqué

【公报私仇】gōngbào-sīchóu〈成〉abuse one's authority to revenge oneself on a personal enemy

【公倍数】gōngbèishù〈名〉［数学］common multiple: 最小～ lowest common multiple

【公布】gōngbù〈动〉announce: ～法令 issue a decree ‖ ～名单 publish a name list ‖ ～于众 make public

【公厕】gōngcè〈简称〉= 公共厕所

【公差】gōngchā〈名〉［数学］common difference

【公差】gōngchāi〈名〉**1**（指职责）official business: 出～ go on official business **2**〈旧〉（指人）runner or bailiff in a *yamen*

【公产】gōngchǎn〈名〉public property: 侵吞～ embezzle state property

【公车】gōngchē〈名〉**1**（公用车）public vehicle: ～私用 use a public vehicle for

private functions ‖ 公司给她配有～。 She gets a company car. 2 （公共汽车） public bus: 坐～上班 go to work by public bus

【公称】gōngchēng〈名〉 nominal dimension

【公尺】gōngchǐ〈名〉 metre (m)

【公出】gōngchū〈动〉 be away on official business: 他～去了美国。 He's been away on official business in the United States.

【公畜】gōngchù〈名〉 stud (animal)

【公担】gōngdàn〈名〉［物理］ quintal

【公道】gōngdào〈名〉justice: 讨～ demand justice ‖ 主持～ uphold justice

【公道】gōngdao〈形〉 just: 处事～ be fair in one's dealings ‖ 价钱～。 The price is reasonable.

【公德】gōngdé〈名〉 social morality: 社会～ public morals ‖ 他做生意不讲～。 There is nothing socially ethical about his business.

【公敌】gōngdí〈名〉 public enemy: 人民～ enemy of the people

【公爹】gōngdiē〈名〉〈方〉 husband's father

【公断】gōngduàn〈动〉 1 （断案） settle according to law: 这件事必须～。 This has to be settled in court. 2 （评判） arbitrate: 给两人作～ arbitrate between two people ‖ 留待后人～ await the verdict of time 3 （决断） make an impartial judgement

【公吨】gōngdūn ▸**p. 978**〈名〉 metric ton (MT)

【公而忘私】gōng'érwàngsī〈成〉 be so devoted to public service as to forget one's own interests: ～的工作作风 selfless working style

【公法】gōngfǎ〈名〉 1 （有关国家的法律） public law 2 （国际法） international law

【公房】gōngfáng〈名〉 public housing

【公费】gōngfèi〈名〉 state expense: ～留学 study abroad on a state scholarship ‖ 享受～医疗 enjoy free medical care

【公费医疗】gōngfèiyīliáo〈名〉 free health treatment

【公分】gōngfēn ▸**p. 82**〈名〉 centimetre (cm)

【公分母】gōngfēnmǔ〈名〉［数学］ common denominator

【公愤】gōngfèn〈名〉 public indignation: 激起～ arouse public indignation

【公干】gōnggàn A〈名〉 official business: 有何～? What business has brought you here? B〈动〉 attend to official duties: 外出～ be away on official business

【公告】gōnggào A〈动〉 give public notice B〈名〉 public announcement: 发布～ issue a public announcement ‖ 张贴～ put up a public notice ‖ 会议～ meeting notice ‖ 电子～牌 electronic board

【公共】gōnggòng〈形〉 public: ～场所 public place ‖ ～设施 communal facilities ‖ ～事务 public affairs ‖ ～财产 public property

【公共厕所】gōnggòng cèsuǒ〈名〉 public toilet; public restroom〈美〉

【公共道德】gōnggòng dàodé〈名〉 social morality

【公共关系】gōnggòng guānxì〈名〉 public relations (PR): 改善～ improve public relations ‖ ～学 public relations

【公共基金】gōnggòng jījīn〈名〉 public fund

【公共假日】gōnggòng jiàrì〈名〉 public holiday

【公共交通】gōnggòng jiāotōng〈名〉 public transport: 改善～ improve public transport

【公共课】gōnggòngkè〈名〉 commonly required course

【公共利益】gōnggòng lìyì〈名〉 public interest

【公共汽车】gōnggòng qìchē〈名〉 public bus

【公共秩序】gōnggòng zhìxù〈名〉 public order

【公公】gōnggong〈名〉 1 （丈夫的父亲） father-in-law 2 〈方〉（爷爷） grandfather 3 〈方〉（外公） grandfather 4 〈尊〉（指老人） grandpa: 王～ Grandpa Wang 5 〈旧〉（指太监） *gonggong* [form of address for a court eunuch]

【公关】gōngguān〈简称〉= 公共关系

【公关部】gōngguānbù〈名〉 public relations department

【公关先生】gōngguān xiānsheng〈名〉 PR man

【公关小姐】gōngguān xiǎojiě〈名〉PR lady

【公馆】gōngguǎn〈名〉〈旧〉 mansion

【公国】gōngguó〈名〉 duchy: 卢森堡大～ Grand Duchy of Luxembourg ‖ 摩纳哥～ Principality of Monaco

【公海】gōnghǎi〈名〉 high seas: ～捕鱼 fishing on the high seas

【公害】gōnghài〈名〉 1 （指对环境） pollution nuisance 2 （指对公众） public nuisance: 赌博是一大～。 Gambling is a public hazard.

【公函】gōnghán〈名〉 official correspondence

【公会】gōnghuì〈名〉 trade association

【公鸡】gōngjī〈名〉 rooster: ▸铁～

【公积金】gōngjījīn〈名〉public reserve fund

【公祭】gōngjì A〈动〉 hold a public memorial ceremony B〈名〉 public memorial ceremony

【公家】gōngjiā〈名〉〈口〉 the state: ～财产 state property

【公假】gōngjià〈名〉 leave of absence for official affairs

【公检法】gōng-jiǎn-fǎ〈名〉 public security organs, procuratorial organs and people's courts

【公交】gōngjiāo〈简称〉= 公共交通

【公交车】gōngjiāochē〈名〉 bus: 乘～回家 go home by bus

【公交卡】gōngjiāokǎ〈名〉 public transportation card: 一张～，跑遍全上海。 You can get everywhere in Shanghai with one public transportation card.

【公教人员】gōngjiào rényuán ▸**p. 966**〈名〉 government employees and teachers

【公斤】gōngjīn ▸**p. 978**〈名〉kilogram (kg)

【公举】gōngjǔ〈动〉 publicly elect: 他被与会者～为委员会主席。 He was chosen as chairman of the committee by all those present.

【公决】gōngjué〈动〉 make a collective decision: 全民～ public referendum

【公爵】gōngjué〈名〉 duke: ～夫人 duchess

【公开】gōngkāi A〈形〉 public: ～辩论 open debate ‖ ～场合 public occasion ‖ ～道歉 make a public apology ‖ ～进行 conduct publicly ‖ ～批评 open criticism ‖ ～行动 overt act ‖ ～宣判 publicly sentence B〈动〉 make public: ～秘密 disclose a secret ‖ ～内幕 divulge the inside story ‖ 这事不可～出去。 Don't make it known to the public.

【公开化】gōngkāihuà〈动〉 come out into the open: 党内的斗争不久就～了。 The struggles within the party soon came out into the open.

【公开赛】gōngkāisài〈名〉 open tournament: 澳大利亚网球～ Australian Tennis Open ‖ 男子羽毛球～ men's open badminton tournament

【公开审判】gōngkāi shěnpàn〈名〉 open trial

【公开信】gōngkāixìn〈名〉 open letter

【公开招标】gōngkāi zhāobiāo〈名〉 public bidding

【公筷】gōngkuài〈名〉 serving chopsticks

【公款】gōngkuǎn〈名〉 public money: 挪用～ misappropriate public funds ‖ 贪污～ embezzle public money ‖ 携～潜逃 run off with public money

【公厘】gōnglí〈名〉 millimetre (mm)

【公里】gōnglǐ ▸**p. 82**〈名〉 kilometre (km): 平方～ square kilometre

【公理】gōnglǐ〈名〉 1 （真理） established truth 2 ［数学］ axiom: 欧几里得～ Euclidean axiom

【公理会】Gōnglǐhuì〈名〉［基督教］ Congregational Church

【公历】gōnglì ▸**p. 618**〈名〉 Gregorian calendar

【公立】gōnglì〈形〉 public: ～学校 state school〈英〉, public school〈美〉

【公例】gōnglì〈名〉 general rule

【公粮】gōngliáng〈名〉〈旧〉 agricultural tax paid in grain: 交～ deliver tax grain to the state

【公了】gōngliǎo〈动〉 settle in court: 这事你想～还是私了? Do you prefer settle in court or out of court?

【公路】gōnglù〈名〉 road: ～货运 highway freight ‖ ～交通 road traffic ‖ ～收费站 toll station ▸高速～

【公路赛】gōnglùsài ▸**p. 909**〈名〉［体育］ road racing

【公路自行车赛】gōnglù zìxíngchēsài ▸**p. 909**〈名〉［体育］ road cycling race

【公驴】gōnglǘ〈名〉 male ass

【公论】gōnglùn〈名〉 public opinion: 是非自有～。 Right and wrong is decided by public opinion.

【公买公卖】gōngmǎi-gōngmài〈成〉 buy and sell at reasonable prices

【公民】gōngmín ▸**p. 279**〈名〉 citizen: ～义务 civic duties ‖ 中国～ Chinese citizen

【公民道德】gōngmín dàodé〈名〉 civic virtue

【公民权】gōngmínquán〈名〉 civil rights: 剥夺～ deprive a person of his civil rights

【公民身份】gōngmín shēnfen〈名〉 citizenship

【公民投票】gōngmín tóupiào〈名〉 referendum

【公民自由】gōngmín zìyóu〈名〉 civil liberties

【公亩】gōngmǔ〈名〉 are (= 100 square metres)

【公墓】gōngmù〈名〉 public cemetery

【公牛】gōngniú〈名〉 bull: 小～ bull-calf

【公派】gōngpài〈动〉 be sent by the state: ～留学 study abroad on government scholarship

【公判】gōngpàn〈动〉 publicly try: ～大会 public trial meeting

【公平】gōngpíng〈形〉 fair: ～对待 treat sb. fairly ‖ ～交易 fair deal ‖ ～竞争 fair competition ‖ ～合理 be fair and reasonable

【公平秤】gōngpíngchèng〈名〉 fair scales

【公婆】gōngpó〈名〉 1 （丈夫的父母） parents-in-law 2 〈方〉（夫妻） couple: 两～ two couples

【公仆】gōngpú〈名〉 public servant: ～意

识 attitude of a public servant ‖ 人民的～ servant of the people

【公切线】gōngqiēxiàn〈名〉［数学］ common tangent

【公勤人员】gōngqín rényuán ▸p. 966〈名〉office attendants

【公顷】gōngqǐng〈名〉hectare (ha)

【公权】gōngquán〈名〉［法律］ public rights

【公然】gōngrán〈副〉openly: ～干涉别国内政 blatantly intrude into other countries' internal affairs ‖ ～侵犯人权 flagrantly violate human rights ‖ 在光天化日之下～拦路抢劫 stage a daring daylight hold-up

【公认】gōngrèn〈动〉generally acknowledge: ～的国际法准则 generally recognized principle of international law ‖ ～的国际惯例 established international practice ‖ 这是～的事实。This is an accepted fact.

【公社】gōngshè〈名〉1（指生活组织形式） primitive commune: 原始氏族～ (primitive) clan commune 2（指政权组织形式） commune: 巴黎～ Paris Commune 3（人民公社） people's commune: ～社员 member of the people's commune

【公审】gōngshěn〈动〉conduct a public trial: ～大会 public trial meeting

【公升】gōngshēng〈名〉litre

【公使】gōngshǐ〈名〉minister: 中国驻瑞士～ Chinese envoy to Switzerland ▸特命全权～

【公使馆】gōngshǐguǎn〈名〉legation

【公示】gōngshì〈动〉make known to the public and seek opinions: ～栏 notification column ‖ 财务～ notification of financial affairs

【公示牌】gōngshìpái〈名〉public notice board: 教育收费～ public notice about school fees ‖ 文明施工承诺～ public notice encouraging commitment to proper practices in construction

【公式】gōngshì〈名〉1（指式子）formula: 数学～ mathematical formula 2（指方法） universally applicable method

【公式化】gōngshìhuà A〈形〉formulaic writing style: ～的写作方法 stereotyped writing B〈动〉solve different problems through a formulistic approach: 把马克思主义理论～ apply Marxist theories mechanically

【公事】gōngshì〈名〉official business: 这事是～还是私事? Is the matter public or private?

【公事房】gōngshìfáng〈名〉〈旧〉office

【公事公办】gōngshì gōngbàn〈成〉do official business according to official principles

【公署】gōngshǔ〈名〉government office: 地区专员～ prefectural commissioner's office ‖ 行政～ administrative office

【公说公有理，婆说婆有理】gōng shuō gōng yǒulǐ, pó shuō pó yǒulǐ〈俗〉each side claims to be in the right

【公司】gōngsī〈名〉company: 管理～ manage a company ‖ 开办～ set up a company ‖ 国有～ state corporation ‖ 跨国～ transnational corporation ‖ 贸易～ trading corporation

【公司财务】gōngsī cáiwù〈名〉corporate financing

【公司法】gōngsīfǎ〈名〉corporate law

【公私】gōngsī〈名〉public and private affairs: ～分明 draw a clear distinction between public and private interests ‖ ～兼顾 take both public and private interests into account

【公私合营】gōngsī héyíng〈名〉joint public-private operation: ～企业 joint public-private enterprise

【公诉】gōngsù〈名〉public prosecution: (对某人) 提起～ start legal proceedings (against sb.)

【公诉词】gōngsùcí〈名〉indictment

【公诉人】gōngsùrén〈名〉public prosecutor〈英〉; district attorney〈美〉

【公诉书】gōngsùshū〈名〉public indictment

【公所】gōngsuǒ〈名〉〈旧〉public office

【公摊】gōngtān〈动〉share funds: 这笔费用我们～。Let's share the expenses.

【公堂】gōngtáng〈名〉1〈旧〉(法庭) court of law: 对簿～ confront each other in court ‖ 私设～ set up a kangaroo court 2（指厅堂） ancestral hall

【公帑】gōngtǎng〈名〉〈书〉public money: 糜费～ squander public money

【公推】gōngtuī〈动〉recommend by general acclaim: 他被～为委员会主席。He was elected chairman of the committee.

【公文】gōngwén〈名〉official document: 收发～ receive and dispatch official documents ‖ 伪造～ forge an official document

【公文包】gōngwénbāo〈名〉portfolio

【公文袋】gōngwéndài〈名〉official envelope

【公文旅行】gōngwén lǚxíng〈名〉red tape

【公文纸】gōngwénzhǐ〈名〉document paper

【公务】gōngwù〈名〉official business: 履行～ perform an official duty ‖ 执行～ perform an official duty ‖ ～在身 have official duties to fulfil

【公务车】gōngwùchē〈名〉service car

【公务护照】gōngwù hùzhào〈名〉service passport

【公务卡】gōngwùkǎ〈名〉official business card: 公务消费必须使用～。Spending in the name of official business requires an official business card.

【公务签证】gōngwù qiānzhèng〈名〉service visa

【公务员】gōngwùyuán ▸p. 966〈名〉1（机关工作人员） civil servant: 政府～ government functionary 2〈旧〉(勤杂人员) orderly

【公物】gōngwù〈名〉public property: 爱护～ respect public property

【公心】gōngxīn〈名〉1（指公正） fair-mindedness 2（指关爱他人） heart set on the public good: 出于～ in the public interest

【公信力】gōngxìnlì〈名〉ability to win public trust: 提高政府部门的～ improve government departments' capacity to win public trust

【公休】gōngxiū〈名〉public holiday

【公学】gōngxué〈名〉private school; public school〈英〉

【公演】gōngyǎn〈动〉perform in public: 新戏即将～ The new play is about to be staged to the public

【公羊】gōngyáng〈名〉ram

【公议】gōngyì〈动〉have a public discussion: 自报～ self-assessment combined with public discussion

【公益】gōngyì〈名〉common good: 热心～ be public-minded ‖ ～事业 public service

【公益广告】gōngyì guǎnggào〈名〉public-service advertisement

【公益金】gōngyìjīn〈名〉public welfare fund

【公益劳动】gōngyì láodòng〈名〉labour for public good

【公因子】gōngyīnzǐ〈名〉［数学］common factor

【公营】gōngyíng〈形〉publicly-owned: ～企业 state-owned enterprise

【公映】gōngyìng〈动〉be shown to the public: 首次～ première

【公用】gōngyòng〈动〉be for public use: ～建筑 public building

【公用电话】gōngyòng diànhuà〈名〉public phone: ～亭 public telephone booth

【公用事业】gōngyòng shìyè〈名〉public utilities: ～公司 public-service corporation

【公用事业费】gōngyòng shìyèfèi〈名〉utility bill

【公有】gōngyǒu〈动〉be publicly-owned: ～财产 public property

【公有制】gōngyǒuzhì〈名〉public ownership: ～企业 publicly-owned enterprise ‖ 坚持以～为主导、各种经济成分并存的所有制 uphold an ownership structure embracing diverse economic sectors with public ownership as the main one

【公余】gōngyú〈名〉spare time: ～时间加班 do extra work in one's own time

【公寓】gōngyù〈名〉flat〈英〉; apartment〈美〉: ～大楼 apartment building ‖ 豪华～ luxury flat

【公元】gōngyuán ▸p. 618〈名〉Christian era: ～21 世纪 21st century AD

【公元前】gōngyuánqián ▸p. 618〈名〉before the birth of Christ (BC): ～221 年 221 BC

【公园】gōngyuán〈名〉park: 国家～ national park ‖ 森林～ forest park ‖ 主题～ theme park

【公约】gōngyuē〈名〉1（指条约） pact: 缔结和平～ conclude a peace treaty ‖ 禁止核武器～ treaty to outlaw nuclear weapons 2（指条款） agreed pledge: 安全～ safety regulation ‖ 文明～ civility pledge

【公约数】gōngyuēshù〈名〉［数学］ common divisor: 最大～ highest common divisor

【公允】gōngyǔn〈形〉fair and just: 持论～ be just and fair in argument ‖ 执法～ carry out the law without bias

【公债】gōngzhài〈名〉national debt: 发行～ issue public bonds

【公债券】gōngzhàiquàn〈名〉public bonds

【公章】gōngzhāng〈名〉official seal: 私刻～ counterfeit an official seal

【公正】gōngzhèng〈形〉fair: ～对待某人/某事 treat sb./sth. fairly ‖ ～地处理问题 tackle a problem in an even-handed manner ‖ 受到～的审判 get a fair trial

【公证】gōngzhèng〈动〉notarize: 对合同/契约/遗嘱进行～ notarize a contract/deed/will

【公证处】gōngzhèngchù〈名〉notary office

【公证费】gōngzhèngfèi〈名〉notarial charge

【公证人】gōngzhèngrén ▸p. 966〈名〉notary

【公证书】gōngzhèngshū〈名〉notarial deed

【公证员】gōngzhèngyuán = 公证人 gōngzhèngrén

【公之于世】gōngzhīyúshì〈成〉make public: 她不想把这事～。She didn't want to publicize the matter.

【公直】gōngzhí〈形〉fair

【公职】gōngzhí〈名〉public office: 担任～ hold public office ‖ 开除～ discharge sb. from public office

【公制】gōngzhì〈名〉metric system: 折成～ convert to the metric system

【公众】gōngzhòng〈名〉the public: ～利

益 public interest ‖ ～关注的焦点 focus of public concern

【公众人物】gōngzhòng rénwù〈名〉public figure

【公诸同好】gōngzhū-tónghào〈成〉show one's collections to the like-minded and share one's enjoyment with them

【公诸于众】gōngzhūyúzhòng = 公之于世 gōngzhīyúshì

【公猪】gōngzhū〈名〉boar

【公主】gōngzhǔ〈名〉princess

【公助】gōngzhù〈动〉1（共同资助）provide public-funded aid: 社会～ social financial aids 2（公家资助）provide government-funded aid: 民办～学校 private school subsidized by government funds

【公转】gōngzhuàn〈动〉revolve: ～周期 period of revolution ‖ 地球绕太阳～。The earth revolves around the sun.

【公子】gōngzǐ〈名〉〈旧〉1（诸侯的儿子）son of a feudal prince: 富家～ son of a wealthy family ▸花花～ 2〈尊〉（称对方的儿子）your son

【公子哥儿】gōngzǐgēr〈名〉1（富家子）pampered son of a wealthy family 2（指年轻男子）dandy

【公子王孙】gōngzǐ-wángsūn〈名〉〈旧〉sons of wealthy families

功 gōng〈名〉1（功劳）achievement: ～大于过 merits outweigh demerits ‖ 他荣立一等～。He was awarded a first-class merit. ▸居～, 立～, 战～ 2（成效）success: ▸大～告成, 徒劳无～ 3（技能）skill: ▸练～, 基本～ 4［物理］work: 把热转化为～ convert heat into work ‖ 机械～ mechanical work

【功败垂成】gōngbài-chuíchéng〈成〉suffer defeat when victory is within reach

【功不抵过】gōngbùdǐguò〈成〉one's merit cannot wipe out one's faults

【功臣】gōngchén〈名〉1〈旧〉（指大臣）official of merit 2（有功的人）hero: 以～自居 paint a heroic picture of oneself ‖ 开国～ founder of a state

【功成不居】gōngchéng-bùjū〈成〉claim no credit for one's meritorious service

【功成名就】gōngchéng-míngjiù〈成〉achieve success and win recognition

【功成身退】gōngchéng-shēntuì〈成〉retire after being covered with glories

【功成业就】gōngchéng-yèjiù〈成〉be crowned with success

【功到自然成】gōng dào zìrán chéng〈俗〉constant efforts yield sure success

【功德】gōngdé〈名〉1（功业和德行）merits and virtues 2［佛教］beneficence: ～箱 beneficence box

【功德无量】gōngdé-wúliàng〈成〉one's kindness knows no bounds

【功德圆满】gōngdé-yuánmǎn〈成〉achieve perfect virtues and merits

【功底】gōngdǐ〈名〉grounding: 为成功打下坚实～ lay solid foundations for success ‖ 文化～浅 have a weak grounding in education

【功夫】gōngfu〈名〉1（本领）workmanship: 那是真～。That's true workmanship. ‖ 艺高还需～深。Good workmanship requires long practice. 2（武术）martial arts: 中国～ Chinese martial arts 3 = 工夫 gōngfu

【功夫茶】gōngfuchá〈名〉*gong fu* tea

【功夫片儿】gōngfupiānr = 功夫片 gōngfupiàn

【功夫片】gōngfupiàn〈名〉kung fu film

> 功夫
>
> *Kung fu* is synonymous with *wushu* (武术, martial arts). *Wushu* is a physical exercise and a method of self-defence that involves a series of movements performed according to particular rules. The most splendid and best-known *wushu* school is the Shaolin school, while in works of art and literature the Wudang and the Emei schools are the most prominent. *Wushu* masters possess a strong sense of justice and a desire to help the weak. These qualities feature as important elements in martial arts novels (▸武侠小说).

【功过】gōng-guò〈名〉merits and demerits: ～自有后人评说。Accomplishments and faults will be judged by later generations.

【功绩】gōngjì〈名〉meritorious deeds: 卓越的～ outstanding feat ‖ 他的～将永载史册。His achievements will go down in history.

【功架】gōngjià〈名〉opera performer's movements and postures

【功课】gōngkè〈名〉1（家庭作业）homework: 做～ do one's homework 2（课程内容）course: 复习～ review one's lessons 3［佛教］scripture-chanting: 那些和尚在做～。Those monks are chanting Buddhist scriptures.

【功亏一篑】gōngkuīyīkuì〈成〉fall short of success for lack of a final effort

【功劳】gōngláo〈名〉credit: 你的～不小。Your contributions have been significant. ‖ 大家都有～。Everyone has put in a contribution.

【功劳簿】gōngláobù〈名〉record of merits: 我们不应躺在自己的～上。We should not rest on our laurels.

【功力】gōnglì〈名〉1（效力）efficacy 2（本领）ability: 他在书法方面有很深的～。He has a good grounding in calligraphy.

【功利】gōnglì〈名〉1（功效和利益）utility and efficacy 2（名誉、地位等）official position and material gain: 追求～ seek fame and wealth

【功利主义】gōnglìzhǔyì〈名〉utilitarianism: ～者 utilitarian

【功率】gōnglǜ〈名〉power: 输出～ output rating ‖ 大～发动机 high-power engine

【功名】gōngmíng〈名〉scholarly honour and official rank: 博取～ seek an official position

【功名利禄】gōngmíng-lìlù〈成〉official position and material gain

【功能】gōngnéng〈名〉function: 肝～ liver function ‖ 多～ multi-functional ‖ 主要～ main function

【功能词】gōngnéngcí〈名〉［语言］function word

【功能键】gōngnéngjiàn〈名〉［计算机］function key

【功能食品】gōngnéng shípǐn〈名〉functional food

【功能饮料】gōngnéng yǐnliào〈名〉functional beverage

【功能语法】gōngnéng yǔfǎ〈名〉［语言］functional grammar

【功能语言学】gōngnéng yǔyánxué〈名〉［语言］functional linguistics

【功效】gōngxiào〈名〉effectiveness: 测试药的～ measure the efficacy of a drug ‖ 立见～ have an immediate effect

【功勋】gōngxūn〈名〉feat: 建立不朽的～ perform immortal feats ‖ ～演员 accomplished performer

【功业】gōngyè〈名〉outstanding achievements

【功用】gōngyòng〈名〉function

【功罪】gōng-zuì〈名〉merits and demerits

红（紅） gōng ▸女红 nǚgōng ▸hóng

攻 gōng〈动〉1（攻打）attack: ～下战略要地 storm a strategic fortress ‖ 向守军猛～ charge the garrison ▸强～, 佯～ 2（抨击）accuse: ▸群起而～之 3（研究）specialize in: 专～社会心理学 specialize in social psychology ▸～读

【攻城略地】gōngchéng-lüèdì〈成〉take cities and seize territories

【攻错】gōngcuò〈动〉〈喻〉overcome one's weak points with others' strong points

【攻打】gōngdǎ〈动〉assault: ～敌人阵地 attack enemy positions

【攻读】gōngdú〈动〉1（钻研）study hard: ～硕士学位 study for a master's degree ‖ 刻苦～ study hard 2（主修）major in: ～生物学 study biology ‖ 在大学～法律 read law at a university

【攻防】gōngfáng〈动〉attack and defend: ～战术 strategy of offence and defence ‖ ～转换 shift between offence and defence

【攻防战】gōngfángzhàn〈名〉warfare : 城市～ urban warfare

【攻关】gōngguān〈动〉1（指关口）storm a strategic pass 2〈喻〉（指难题）tackle a key problem: ～小组 task team ‖ 联合～ jointly tackle a crucial problem

【攻击】gōngjī〈动〉attack: 发起～ launch an offensive ‖ 对敌军进行猛烈～ make a violent attack on the enemy ‖ 进行人身～ make a personal attack (on sb.) ‖ 用激烈的言辞相互～ attack each other with sharp words

【攻击波】gōngjībō〈名〉wave of attacks: 以 15:0 的～锁定胜局。Seal victory with a 15-0 wave of attacks.

【攻击队形】gōngjī duìxíng〈名〉［军事］assault formation

【攻击机】gōngjījī〈名〉［军事］attack plane

【攻击型选手】gōngjīxíng xuǎnshǒu〈名〉aggressive player

【攻歼】gōngjiān〈动〉wipe out

【攻坚】gōngjiān〈动〉1（指防御工事）attack a fortification 2（指难题）tackle a thorny problem

【攻坚战】gōngjiānzhàn〈名〉attack heavily fortified positions: 打一场～ launch an attack against heavily fortified positions

【攻讦】gōngjié〈动〉〈书〉expose sb.'s faults and then attack him

【攻克】gōngkè〈动〉seize: ～城市 capture a city ‖〈喻〉～技术难题 overcome a technical difficulty

【攻略】gōnglüè A〈动〉〈书〉attack and seize: ～要塞 seize a fortress B〈名〉tactic: 市场营销～ marketing tactics

【攻破】gōngpò〈动〉breach: ～敌人防线 break through the enemy line

【攻其不备】gōngqíbùbèi〈成〉catch sb. unawares

【攻其一点，不及其余】gōng qí yī diǎn, bù jí qí yú〈成〉attack one particular point without considering the situation in general

【攻取】gōngqǔ〈动〉attack and capture: ～要塞 capture a fortress through attack

【攻势】gōngshì〈名〉offensive: 采取～ go on the offensive ‖ 宣传～ publicity campaign ‖ 中国队～凌厉。The Chinese team is on a strong offensive.

【攻守同盟】gōngshǒu tóngméng〈名〉

1▸（指军事） offensive and defensive alliance: 三个邻国建立了～。 The three neighbouring countries signed a pact of military alliance. 2▸（指阴谋） conspiracy of silence: 订立～ reach an understanding not to betray each other
【攻丝】gōngsī〈名〉［机械］ tapping
【攻无不克】 gōngwúbùkè 〈成〉 be all-conquering: ～，战无不胜 be all-conquering and ever-victorious
【攻陷】 gōngxiàn 〈动〉 capture: ～城池 capture a city
【攻心】gōngxīn〈动〉 1▸（指意志） mount a psychological attack: ～战术 psychological tactics 2▸（指身体） be in a coma or remain in a stupor because of sorrow or hatred: 怒气～ be comatose with anger
【攻占】gōngzhàn〈动〉 attack and capture: ～山头 storm and capture a hill

供 gōng〈动〉 1▸（供给） supply: ～不起孩子上学 unable to afford tuition for one's child's schooling ‖ 她哥哥～她学费。 Her brother pays her tuition. ▸～电，～货，～暖 2▸（用于） provide certain convenience or support: 仅～参考。 For reference only. ‖ 那个旅馆可～400 位客人食宿。 The hotel accommodates 400 guests. ▸gòng
【供不应求】 gōngbùyìngqiú 〈成〉 supply falls short of demand
【供电】gōngdiàn〈动〉 supply electricity: 向工厂～ supply power to a factory
【供电局】 gōngdiànjú 〈名〉 power supply bureau
【供电设备】gōngdiàn shèbèi〈名〉 power supply equipment
【供电系统】gōngdiàn xìtǒng〈名〉 power network
【供电站】 gōngdiànzhàn 〈名〉 supply station
【供稿】gōnggǎo〈动〉 contribute: 本版文章均由自由撰稿人～。 All articles on this page are contributions from freelance writers.
【供过于求】 gōngguòyúqiú 〈成〉 supply exceeds demand
【供货】gōnghuò〈动〉 supply goods: ～商 supplier
【供给】gōngjǐ〈动〉 supply: ～不足 be in short supply ‖ 粮食～ food supply
【供给制】gōngjǐzhì〈名〉 supply system
【供楼】gōnglóu〈动〉buy property in instalments
【供暖】gōngnuǎn〈动〉 supply heat: 集中～ centralized heating
【供气】gōngqì〈动〉 supply gas
【供求】gōngqiú〈名〉 supply and demand: ～关系 relationship between supply and demand ‖ ～脱节 supply is out of line with demand
【供水】gōngshuǐ〈动〉 supply water
【供销】gōngxiāo〈名〉 supply and marketing: ～两旺。 Both supply and marketing are flourishing.
【供销合作社】 gōngxiāo hézuòshè 〈名〉 supply and marketing cooperative
【供销社】 gōngxiāoshè 〈简称〉= 供销合作社
【供需】gōngxū〈名〉 supply and demand: 解决～矛盾 redress the imbalance between supply and demand
【供血】gōngxuè〈动〉 give blood: ～不足 insufficient blood supply
【供养】 gōngyǎng 〈动〉 support: ～孤老 support the old and childless ‖ ～父母 provide for one's parents ▸gòngyǎng
【供应】 gōngyìng 〈动〉 supply: 保障～ guarantee supply ‖ ～不足 insufficient supply
【供应点】gōngyìngdiǎn〈名〉supply centre: 早餐～ breakfast spot
【供应链】gōngyìngliàn 〈名〉 supply chain: 食品～ food supply chain
【供应站】gōngyìngzhàn〈名〉 supply depot

肱 gōng〈名〉 1▸（上臂） upper arm: 曲～而枕 sleep with one's head resting on one's bent arm 2▸（手臂） arm: ▸股～
【肱二头肌】 gōng'èrtóujī 〈名〉 (brachial) biceps
【肱骨】gōnggǔ〈名〉 humerus
【肱三头肌】 gōngsāntóujī 〈名〉 triceps brachii

宫¹（宫） gōng〈名〉 1▸（宫殿） palace: ▸皇～，行～ 2▸（天宫） palace (for celestial beings in mythology): ▸龙～，月～ 3▸（庙） temple: 雍和～ Yonghe Lama Temple 4▸（指文化娱乐场所） palace: 工人文化～ Workers' Cultural Palace ▸少年～ 5▸［生理］ uterus: ▸～颈，刮～

宫²（宫） gōng 〈名〉 ［音乐］ note on the ancient Chinese pentatonic (五音) scale, corresponding to 1 in *jianpu* (简谱) numbered musical notation
【宫城】gōngchéng〈名〉 imperial capital
【宫词】gōngcí〈名〉 palace poetry
【宫灯】gōngdēng〈名〉 palace lantern
【宫殿】gōngdiàn〈名〉 palace: ～式建筑 palatial architecture
【宫调】gōngdiào〈名〉［音乐］ modes of ancient Chinese music
【宫娥】gōng'é = 宫女 gōng nǚ
【宫禁】 gōngjìn 〈名〉 1▸（指地方） emperor's living quarters 2▸（指禁令） palace prohibitions
【宫颈】gōngjǐng〈名〉 cervix: ～环 cervical ring
【宫颈糜烂】gōngjǐng mílàn〈名〉［医学］ cervical erosion
【宫颈癌】 gōngjǐng'ái ▸**p. 50** 〈名〉［医学］ cervical cancer
【宫颈炎】 gōngjǐngyán ▸**p. 50** 〈名〉［医学］ cervicitis
【宫女】gōngnǚ〈名〉 palace maid
【宫阙】 gōngquè 〈名〉〈书〉 (imperial) palace
【宫室】gōngshì〈名〉 1▸（房屋） mansion 2▸（宫殿） palace
【宫缩】gōngsuō〈名〉［医学］ uterine contraction
【宫廷】gōngtíng〈名〉 1▸（宫殿） palace: ～秘方 palace recipe 2▸（帝王和大臣） (imperial) court
【宫廷舞】gōngtíngwǔ〈名〉 imperial court dance
【宫廷政变】 gōngtíng zhèngbiàn 〈名〉 palace coup: 发动～ mount a palace coup
【宫外孕】gōngwàiyùn〈名〉［医学］ectopic pregnancy
【宫闱】gōngwéi〈名〉〈书〉palace: ～秘闻 palace secrets
【宫刑】gōngxíng〈名〉castration: 被处以～ be castrated

恭 gōng〈形〉 respectful: ▸～候，～敬，洗耳～听
【恭贺】gōnghè ▸**p. 780** 〈动〉 congratulate: ～新年 offer one's congratulations on the New Year ‖ ～新禧! Happy New Year!
【恭候】gōnghòu〈动〉〈敬〉 await respectfully: ～多时 await sb. for quite a while ‖ ～光临。 Your company is respectfully awaited.
【恭谨】gōngjǐn〈形〉respectful and cautious
【恭敬】gōngjìng〈形〉 respectful: 向某人～地鞠一躬 bow to sb. in humble reverence
【恭敬不如从命】gōngjìng bùrú cóngmìng〈成〉 it is better to do as sb. asks instead of standing on ceremony
【恭请】gōngqǐng〈动〉 invite respectfully: ～光临。 We request the honour of your presence.
【恭顺】gōngshùn〈形〉 respectful and submissive: 极其～ with profound respect and humility
【恭维】gōngwei〈动〉 compliment: ～话 flattery ‖ 不敢～ cannot bring oneself to be complimentary
【恭喜】gōngxǐ ▸**p. 780**〈动〉〈套〉 congratulate: ～发财! May you be prosperous! ‖ ～你生了个千金。 Congratulations on the birth of your daughter.
【恭迎】gōngyíng〈动〉 welcome respectfully: ～校长 welcome the president most respectfully
【恭正】 gōngzhèng 〈形〉 carefully and neatly

蚣 gōng ▸蜈蚣 wúgōng

躬 gōng
A〈名〉 1▸（身体） body: ▸鞠～ 2▸（自己） oneself: 反～自问 examine oneself
B〈副〉 personally: ～耕 till the soil ▸～行，事必～亲
C〈动〉 stoop: ▸～身
【躬逢其盛】gōngféng-qíshèng〈成〉live in times of prosperity
【躬亲】gōngqīn〈动〉〈书〉 do (sth.) personally: ～其事 attend to a matter in person ▸事必～
【躬身】gōngshēn〈动〉 bend forward: 主人～迎进客人。The host bowed his guests in.
【躬行】 gōngxíng 〈动〉〈书〉 carry out personally: ～实践 practise what one preaches

龚（龔） Gōng 〈名〉 Gong [surname]

觥 gōng〈名〉〈古〉 *gong* [drinking vessel made of bronze]
【觥筹交错】 gōngchóu-jiāocuò 〈成〉 the cups go gaily round

gǒng

巩（鞏） gǒng〈形〉 consolidated: ▸～固
【巩固】gǒnggù **A**〈动〉 consolidate: ～国防 consolidate national defence ‖ ～所学知识 consolidate one's knowledge **B**〈形〉 consolidated: 该国政权～。 The political power in this country is stable.
【巩膜】gǒngmó〈名〉［解剖］ sclera: ～炎 scleritis

汞 gǒng〈名〉 mercury (Hg)
【汞灯】gǒngdēng〈名〉 mercury lamp
【汞溴红】gǒngxiùhóng〈名〉［药学］ merbromin

【汞中毒】gǒngzhòngdú〈名〉mercury poisoning
【汞柱】gǒngzhù〈名〉mercury column

拱¹ gǒng
A〈动〉1 (两手相合) cup one hand in the other before the chest: ▸～手 2 (环绕) surround: 海水环～的小岛 island surrounded by seas ▸～抱, ～卫 3 (成弓形) arch: ～背 arch one's back
B〈形〉arch-shaped: ～式涵洞 arch culvert

拱² gǒng〈动〉1 (挤推) push with the body: 从人群中～了过去 elbow one's way through the crowd ‖ 用头把门～开 push the door open with one's head 2 (顶出) spring up from the soil
【拱坝】gǒngbà〈名〉[水利] arch dam
【拱抱】gǒngbào〈动〉surround: 群山～的山村 village surrounded by hills
【拱道】gǒngdào〈名〉[建筑] archway
【拱点】gǒngdiǎn〈名〉[天文] apsis
【拱顶】gǒngdǐng〈名〉[建筑] vault
【拱肩】gǒngjiān〈名〉[建筑] spandrel
【拱门】gǒngmén〈名〉arch
【拱棚】gǒngpéng〈名〉arched shed
【拱桥】gǒngqiáo〈名〉arch bridge: 石～ stone arch bridge
【拱让】gǒngràng〈动〉hand sth. over on a plate: 将自己的财产～他人 hand over one's personal property on a silver platter
【拱绕】gǒngrào〈动〉surround
【拱手】gǒngshǒu〈动〉cup one hand in the other before the chest in respect: ～告别 cup one's hands in a farewell gesture ‖ ～让人 surrender (sth.) in submission
【拱卫】gǒngwèi〈动〉surround and protect
【拱形】gǒngxíng〈名〉arch form
【拱形梁】gǒngxíngliáng〈名〉[建筑] arch beam

珙 gǒng〈名〉〈古〉a kind of jade
【珙桐】gǒngtóng〈名〉[植物] dove tree

gòng

共 gòng
A〈动〉share: ～患难 go through hardships together ‖ ～命运 share a common fate ▸休戚与～
B〈形〉common: ▸～识, ～性
C〈副〉1 (一同) together: ～负盈亏 jointly share profits and losses ‖ ～进午餐 have lunch together ▸和平～处, 同舟～济 2 (总计) altogether: 我们班～有十名女生。There are ten girls altogether in our class.
【共餐】gòngcān〈动〉dine together

> **中国共产党**
> The Communist Party of China, China's ruling party. With a current membership of more than 70 million, this makes it the world's largest political party. Founded in Shanghai in July 1921, it came to power with the founding of the People's Republic of China on October 1st 1949. The emblem of the CPC is a hammer and sickle and the official party newspaper is the *People's Daily* (▸《人民日报》).

【共产党】gòngchǎndǎng〈名〉Communist Party: ～人 Communist ‖ ～员 Communist Party member ‖《～宣言》*Communist Manifesto*
【共产国际】Gòngchǎn Guójì〈名〉Comintern
【共产主义】gòngchǎnzhǔyì〈名〉communism: ～者 communist ‖ ～运动 communist movement
【共产主义青年团】gòngchǎnzhǔyì qīngniántuán〈名〉Communist Youth League (of China)
【共处】gòngchǔ〈动〉coexist: 和平～ coexist peacefully
【共存】gòngcún〈动〉coexist: 机遇与挑战～。Opportunity goes hand in hand with challenge.
【共度】gòngdù〈动〉experience together: ～佳节 celebrate a festival together ‖ ～难关 be in the same boat
【共犯】gòngfàn [法律] A〈动〉collaborate in a criminal act B〈名〉accomplice: 他父亲是主犯, 他是～。He was his father's accomplice.
【共管】gòngguǎn〈动〉manage jointly: 齐抓～ take charge of and manage jointly
【共和】gònghé〈名〉republic
【共和党】Gònghédǎng〈名〉Republican Party
【共和国】gònghéguó〈名〉republic: 民主～ democratic republic
【共和制】gònghézhì〈名〉republicanism
【共计】gòngjì〈动〉amount to: ～三十位客人 a total of thirty guests ‖ ～约五十万美元 total around $500,000
【共价】gòngjià〈名〉[化学] covalence
【共价键】gòngjiàjiàn〈名〉[化学] covalent bond
【共建】gòngjiàn〈动〉jointly establish: ～文明社区 jointly establish a civilized community
【共居】gòngjū〈动〉1 (同住) cohabit: 两个同学～一室。The two students shared a room. 2 (共存) coexist: 矛盾的两个方面～于一个统一体。The two sides of a contradiction coexist in a uniform entity.
【共聚】gòngjù A〈动〉gather together: ～一堂 gather in the same hall B〈名〉[化学] copolymerization: ～物 copolymer
【共勉】gòngmiǎn〈动〉encourage each other: 与你～ mutual encouragement
【共鸣】gòngmíng〈动〉1 [物理] resonate 2 (指情感) respond sympathetically: 引起～ arouse sympathy
【共鸣器】gòngmíngqì〈名〉resonator
【共谋】gòngmóu〈名〉[法律] collusion
【共谋罪】gòngmóuzuì〈名〉crime of conspiracy
【共栖】gòngqī〈名〉[生物] commensalism
【共青团】gòngqīngtuán〈简称〉= 共产主义青年团

> **共青团**
> The full name is the Communist Youth League of China. Its predecessor, the Socialist Youth League of China, was established in 1922, and it took its present name in 1925. In 1949, its name was officially changed to the Chinese New Democracy Youth League. It reverted to the name of the Communist Youth League of China in 1957. The national congress of the Communist Youth League takes place every five years. Its national leaders are representatives of the National Congress and the Central Committee. Members are aged between 14 and 28. Its national publication is the *China Youth Daily* (《中国青年报》) and the biweekly magazine *China Youth* (《中国青年》).

【共商】gòngshāng〈动〉discuss together: ～国是 discuss important state matters together
【共生】gòngshēng〈动〉1 [地质] have intergrowth: ～矿 mineral intergrowth 2 [生物] symbiosis
【共识】gòngshí〈名〉consensus: 达成～ arrive at a common understanding
【共事】gòngshì〈动〉be colleagues: ～多年 have been colleagues for years
【共通】gòngtōng〈形〉1 (普适) universal: ～的原理 universally applicable principles 2 (共同) common: 这两个句子有一个～的错误。The two sentences have an error in common.
【共同】gòngtóng A〈形〉common: ～的敌人 common enemy ‖ ～利益 mutual interest ‖ 有许多～之处 have a lot in common ‖ ～的目标 common goal B〈副〉jointly: ～努力 make joint efforts ‖ ～战斗 fight side by side
【共同财产】gòngtóng cáichǎn〈名〉[法律] community property
【共同担保】gòngtóng dānbǎo〈名〉joint guarantee
【共同点】gòngtóngdiǎn〈名〉common ground: 我们有很多～。We have a lot in common.
【共同犯罪】gòngtóng fànzuì〈名〉[法律] joint offence
【共同纲领】gòngtóng gānglǐng〈名〉common programme
【共同市场】Gòngtóng Shìchǎng〈名〉Common Market
【共同体】gòngtóngtǐ〈名〉community: 欧洲经济～ European Economic Community (EEC)
【共同语言】gòngtóng yǔyán〈名〉〈喻〉common language: 她和丈夫缺乏～。She and her husband lack a common language.
【共享】gòngxiǎng〈动〉share: ～欢乐 share joys ‖ 信息～ share information
【共享软件】gòngxiǎng ruǎnjiàn〈名〉shareware
【共性】gòngxìng〈名〉common nature: ～与个性 generality and particularity ‖ 爱美是人的～。Human beings share a common love of beauty.
【共议】gòngyì〈动〉discuss together: ～国是 discuss state policies together
【共赢】gòngyíng〈动〉share a common victory: 合作～ cooperate and share in a victory
【共振】gòngzhèn〈名〉[物理] resonance: 核磁～ nuclear magnetic resonance
【共轴】gòngzhóu〈形〉[数学] coaxial: ～圆 coaxial circle
【共总】gòngzǒng = 总共 zǒnggòng

贡（貢）gòng
A〈动〉1 (贡献) pay tribute (to): ▸～奉, ～献 2 〈旧〉(举荐) recommend or select talents for imperial court: ▸～生, ～院
B〈名〉tribute: ▸进～, 纳～
【贡缎】gòngduàn〈名〉tribute silk
【贡奉】gòngfèng〈动〉present tribute
【贡赋】gòngfù = 贡税 gòngshuì
【贡米】gòngmǐ〈名〉tribute rice
【贡品】gòngpǐn〈名〉tribute
【贡生】gòngshēng〈名〉〈古〉tribute scholar (selected by the local government to study in the capital city)
【贡税】gòngshuì〈名〉tribute and taxes: 缴纳～ pay tribute and taxes
【贡献】gòngxiàn A〈动〉contribute: 为项目～自己的一份力量 do one's bit for the project ‖ 为国家～出自己宝贵的生命 sacrifice one's valuable life for one's country

g

B〈名〉 contribution: 为世界和平做～ contribute to world peace ‖ 他的～很大。 His contribution has been huge.

【贡院】gòngyuàn〈名〉〈旧〉 place where the provincial examination or metropolitan examination was held

供¹ gòng

A〈动〉 **1**（供奉） present incense or offerings before the image of a god or the deceased: ～佛 enshrine and worship Buddha **2**（从事） assume office: ▸～事, ～职

B〈名〉 offerings: ～果 sacrificial fruit ▸上～

供² gòng

A〈动〉 confess: 小偷～出了所有罪行。 The thief made a full confession of his wrongdoings. ▸逼～, 串～, 诱～

B〈名〉 confession: 翻～ withdraw a confession ‖ 招～ make a confession ▸口～

▸gōng

【供案】gòng'àn〈名〉 altar table

【供称】gòngchēng〈动〉 confess: 她～杀了自己的丈夫。 She confessed that she had killed her husband.

【供词】gòngcí〈名〉 confession

【供奉】gòngfèng **A**〈动〉 **1**（指对神佛） make offerings to: ～神灵 offer sacrifices to the gods **2**（供养） support and serve: ～父母 support and serve one's parents **B**〈名〉 entertainers in the imperial palace: 内廷～ inner court attendant

【供品】gòngpǐn〈名〉 offerings

【供认】gòngrèn〈动〉 make a confession: ～不讳 confess everything

【供事】gòngshì〈动〉 hold office: 在京城～ work in the capital

【供养】gòngyǎng〈动〉 offer sacrifices: ～祖先 offer sacrifices to one's ancestors ▸gōngyǎng

【供职】gòngzhí〈动〉 hold office: 在政府部门～ work in a government department

【供状】gòngzhuàng〈名〉 written confession

【供桌】gòngzhuō〈名〉 altar table

gōu

勾¹ gōu

〈动〉 **1**（标记） tick off: 把清单中的有关项目～出来 tick (off) the related items on the list ‖ 从名单中～掉某人的名字 strike sb.'s name off a list ▸～销 **2**（勾勒） sketch: 用铅笔～出面部轮廓 use a pencil to sketch the outline of sb.'s face ▸～画, ～勒 **3**（串通） collude with: ▸～搭, ～结, ～引 **4**（引起） evoke: ～起我对青年时代的回忆 evoke memories of my youth **5**（涂抹） fill up the joints: ～墙缝 point a brick wall **6**（调制） thicken: ▸～芡

勾² gōu

〈名〉［数学］ shorter leg of a right triangle: ▸～股定理

▸gòu

【勾除】gōuchú〈动〉 tick off

【勾搭】gōuda〈动〉 **1**（串通） collude with: 那男孩和一帮坏人～上了。 The boy got mixed up with a bad gang. **2**（男女私通） carry on with: 她跟老板～上了。 She is carrying on with her boss.

【勾兑】gōuduì〈动〉 blend: ～酒 blended spirit

【勾缝】gōufèng〈动〉 point a brick wall

【勾勾搭搭】gōugou-dādā〈动〉 hitch with

【勾股定理】gōugǔ dìnglǐ〈名〉［数学］ Pythagoras' theorem

【勾画】gōuhuà〈动〉 sketch: ～出房子的平面图 trace out the floor plan of a house ‖ 寥寥几笔就～出一位村姑的形象。 A few words bring out the image of a village girl.

【勾魂】gōuhún〈动〉 enchant

【勾魂摄魄】gōuhún-shèpò〈成〉 have bewitching power

【勾结】gōujié〈动〉〈贬〉 gang up with: 相互～ conspire with each other ‖ 与劫匪～ collude with robbers

【勾栏】gōulán〈名〉〈古〉 brothel: ～中人 prostitute

【勾勒】gōulè〈动〉 **1**（用线条） sketch: ～马的轮廓 sketch a horse **2**（用语言） outline: ～场面 give a brief account of a scene ‖ ～人物形象 briefly describe a figure

【勾连】gōulián〈动〉 **1**（勾结） collude with: 跟敌人～在一起 be in collaboration with the enemy **2**（牵涉） have sth. to do with: 跟他没有～ have nothing to do with him ‖ 我认为他跟黑手党有～。 I think he's got involved with the Mafia.

【勾脸】gōuliǎn〈动〉［戏曲］ paint the face

【勾留】gōuliú = 逗留 dòuliú

【勾描】gōumiáo〈动〉 sketch: 用铅笔把景物的轮廓～出来 sketch out the scenery with a pencil

【勾芡】gōuqiàn〈动〉 thicken by adding starch

【勾拳】gōuquán〈名〉 hook: 打出一记右/左～ deliver a right/left hook

【勾通】gōutōng〈动〉 collude with

【勾销】gōuxiāo〈动〉 cross out: ～一笔坏账 write off a bad debt ‖ ～债务 liquidate a debt ▸一笔～

【勾心斗角】gōuxīn-dòujiǎo = 钩心斗角 gōuxīn-dòujiǎo

【勾引】gōuyǐn〈动〉 **1**（诱惑） seduce: 用甜言蜜语～一位姑娘 seduce a girl through sweet talk **2**（引起） evoke: ～起对往事的回忆 bring back memories of the past

【勾针】gōuzhēn = 钩针 gōuzhēn

佝 gōu

【佝偻】gōulóu〈动〉 stoop

【佝偻病】gōulóubìng ▸**p. 50**〈名〉［医学］ rickets

沟（溝） gōu

〈名〉 **1**（指人工水道） ditch: 水～ drain ‖ 挖～排水 dig trenches to drain the water away ▸暗～, 阴～ **2**（指洼处） gully: 乱石～ boulder-strewn gully ▸～壑 **3**（浅槽） groove: 开～播种 make furrows for sowing ‖ 汽车从沙漠上开过，留下两道～。 The truck left two rows of tracks in the sand as it crossed the desert.

【沟播】gōubō〈名〉［农业］ trench sowing

【沟渎】gōudú〈名〉〈书〉 irrigation canal

【沟沟坎坎】gōugōu-kǎnkǎn〈成〉 setbacks one meets

【沟灌】gōuguàn〈名〉［农业］ furrow irrigation

【沟壑】gōuhè〈名〉 gully: ～纵横 be crossed with gullies

【沟堑】gōuqiàn〈名〉 ditch

【沟渠】gōuqú〈名〉 irrigation canals and ditches: 疏通～ dredge irrigation ditches

【沟通】gōutōng〈动〉 **1**（连接） link up: ～大江南北 link up northern and southern China **2**（交流） communicate: ～能力 communication skills ‖ ～思想 exchange ideas ‖ 和年轻人～交流 communicate with the younger generation

【沟沿儿】gōuyánr〈名〉 bank of a canal

枸 gōu

▸gǒu, jǔ

【枸橘】gōujú = 枳 zhǐ

钩（鈎、鉤） gōu

A〈名〉 **1**（钩子） hook: ▸秤～, 上～, 鱼～ **2**（指笔画） [in Chinese characters] hooked stroke **3**（指符号） tick〈英〉; check〈美〉: 对的打～（✓），错的打叉（×）。 Put a tick next to what is correct and a cross next to that which is incorrect.

B〈动〉 **1**（用钩子取） hook: 把掉在井里的东西～上来 fish out the things that had dropped in the well ‖ 用脚面～住钢丝倒挂着 hook one's feet on a wire and hang upside down **2**〈书〉（探求） investigate: ▸～沉, ～玄 **3**（编织） crochet: 给孩子～一件毛衣 crochet a sweater for a child **4**（缝） sew with large stitches: ～贴边 sew on an edging

【钩沉】gōuchén〈动〉〈书〉 search after lost abstruse principles

【钩秤】gōuchèng〈名〉 steelyard

【钩虫病】gōuchóngbìng ▸**p. 50**〈名〉［医学］ hookworm disease

【钩稽】gōujī〈书〉 **A**〈动〉 examine **B**〈名〉 accounting

【钩肩搭背】gōujiān-dābèi〈成〉 throw one's arm round sb.'s shoulder

【钩拳】gōuquán〈名〉 [in boxing] hook

【钩心斗角】gōuxīn-dòujiǎo〈成〉 scheme against each other: ～, 相互倾轧 scheme against each other and get locked in strife

【钩玄】gōuxuán〈动〉〈书〉 seek abstruse principles

【钩针】gōuzhēn〈名〉 crochet hook

【钩子】gōuzi〈名〉 hook: 小～ little hook ‖ 蝎子的～ sting of a scorpion

篝 gōu

〈名〉〈书〉 bamboo cage

【篝火】gōuhuǒ〈名〉 bonfire: 燃起～ light a bonfire ‖ ～晚会 bonfire party

gǒu

苟¹ gǒu

A〈形〉 careless: 不～ careful

B〈副〉 **1**（随便） casually: ▸～同 **2**（姑且） short-sightedly: ▸～安, ～活, ～延残喘

苟² gǒu

〈连〉〈书〉 if: ～无民，何以有君？ If there were no subjects, how could there be a ruler?

【苟安】gǒu'ān〈动〉 live for the moment: ～一时 seek momentary ease and comfort

【苟合】gǒuhé〈动〉 **1**（迎合） readily subscribe to sb.'s view: ～取容 echo other people's views in order to curry favour with them **2**（私通） engage in illicit sexual relations

【苟活】gǒuhuó〈动〉 live from day to day

【苟简】gǒujiǎn〈形〉〈书〉 slapdash: 做事～ do things in a slapdash way

【苟且】gǒuqiě〈形〉 **1**（草率） aimless: 因循～ follow routines and live an aimless life **2**（随便） careless: 做事不敢～ do things carefully **3**（不正当） illicit

【苟且偷安】gǒuqiě-tōu'ān〈成〉 be content with temporary ease and comfort

【苟且偷生】gǒuqiě-tōushēng〈成〉 muddle along from day to day

【苟全】gǒuquán〈动〉 live aimlessly for a time: ～性命 barely manage to survive

【苟同】 gǒutóng〈动〉〈书〉 readily subscribe to sb.'s view: 不敢～ cannot agree
【苟延残喘】 gǒuyán-cánchuǎn〈成〉 be on one's last legs

狗 gǒu〈名〉 dog: 宠物～ pet dog ‖ 看门～ guard dog ‖ 野～ wild dog ▸疯～, 猎～
【狗宝】 gǒubǎo〈名〉［中药］ stone of a dog's gall bladder, kidney or bladder
【狗吃屎】 gǒuchīshǐ〈惯〉〈诙〉 fall flat on one's face: 跌了个～ stumble and fall flat on one's face ‖ 把某人摔个～ knock sb. flat
【狗胆包天】 gǒudǎn-bāotiān〈成〉 be monstrously audacious
【狗窦】 gǒudòu〈名〉 hole in the wall for a dog to get in and out
【狗改不了吃屎】 gǒu gǎibuliǎo chī shǐ〈俗〉 a leopard can't change its spots
【狗苟蝇营】 gǒugǒu-yíngyíng ＝ 蝇营狗苟 yíngyíng-gǒugǒu
【狗獾】 gǒuhuān〈名〉 badger
【狗急跳墙】 gǒují-tiàoqiáng〈成〉 despair gives courage even to a coward
【狗链】 gǒuliàn〈名〉 leash; lead〈英〉
【狗拿耗子，多管闲事】 gǒu ná hàozi, duō guǎn xiánshì〈歇后〉 poke one's nose into other people's business
【狗皮膏药】 gǒupí gāoyao〈名〉 1（指膏药） dogskin plaster 2〈喻〉（骗人货） quack medicine
【狗屁】 gǒupì〈名〉〈粗〉 shit〈粗〉: ～文章 shitty article ‖ ～不通 unreadable rubbish
【狗屎】 gǒushǐ〈名〉〈粗〉 1〈本〉 dung 2〈喻〉 crap〈粗〉: 一堆臭～ a heap of crap
【狗屎堆】 gǒushǐduī〈名〉〈粗〉〈喻〉 bastard〈粗〉
【狗头军师】 gǒutóu-jūnshī〈成〉 villainous adviser
【狗腿子】 gǒutuǐzi〈名〉〈贬〉 henchman
【狗尾草】 gǒuwěicǎo〈名〉 foxtail grass
【狗尾续貂】 gǒuwěi-xùdiāo〈成〉 make wretched sequel to a fine work
【狗窝】 gǒuwō〈名〉 1〈本〉 doghouse 2〈喻〉〈谦〉（自己家） home: 金窝银窝，不如自己的～。 East or West, home is best.
【狗熊】 gǒuxióng〈名〉 1〈本〉 black bear 2〈喻〉〈贬〉（胆小鬼） coward
【狗血淋头】 gǒuxuè-líntóu ＝ 狗血喷头 gǒuxuè-pēntóu
【狗血喷头】 gǒuxuè-pēntóu〈成〉 pour out a torrent of abuse: 她把他骂得～。 She cursed him at full blast.
【狗眼看人低】 gǒuyǎn kàn rén dī〈俗〉〈贬〉 be a damned snob
【狗咬狗】 gǒuyǎogǒu〈惯〉〈喻〉 dog-eat-dog: ～的社会 dog-eat-dog society
【狗咬吕洞宾】 gǒu yǎo Lǚ Dòngbīn〈歇后〉 mistake a good man for a bad
【狗鱼】 gǒuyú〈名〉 pike
【狗仔】 gǒuzǎi〈名〉 paparazzo
【狗仔队】 gǒuzǎiduì〈名〉 paparazzi: 经常受到～骚扰 frequently harassed by the paparazzi
【狗崽子】 gǒuzǎizi〈名〉〈粗〉 1〈本〉 puppy 2〈喻〉 son of a bitch〈粗〉
【狗仗人势】 gǒuzhàngrénshì〈成〉〈喻〉 bully people with the backing of a powerful person
【狗嘴里吐不出象牙】 gǒuzuǐli tǔbuchū xiàngyá〈俗〉〈喻〉 you won't get anything clean out of a filthy mouth

枸 gǒu
▸gōu, jǔ
【枸杞】 gǒuqǐ〈名〉 Chinese wolfberry
【枸杞子】 gǒuqǐzǐ〈名〉［中药］ Chinese wolfberry fruit

笱 gǒu〈名〉〈方〉 basket fishing trap

gòu

勾 gòu
▸gōu
【勾当】 gòudang〈名〉〈贬〉 deal: 肮脏的～ dirty deal ‖ 不可告人的～ sinister business

构（構） gòu
A〈动〉 1（组合） form: ～屋 build a house ▸～筑 2（组织） fabricate: ▸～思, 虚～
B〈名〉 composition: 佳～ good piece of writing
【构成】 gòuchéng A〈动〉 constitute: ～犯罪 constitute a crime ‖ ～威胁 constitute a threat ‖ 太阳系由太阳及其行星～。 The solar system consists of the sun and its planets. B〈名〉 composition: 人员～不合理 the personnel structure is not rational
【构词法】 gòucífǎ〈名〉 word-formation
【构架】 gòujià A〈名〉 1［建筑］ framework: 房子的～ framework of a house 2〈喻〉（结构） structure: 小说的～ structure of a novel B〈动〉 establish: ～新理论体系 establish a new theoretical system
【构件】 gòujiàn〈名〉 component part
【构建】 gòujiàn〈动〉 construct: ～新体系/理论 construct a new system/theory ‖ ～和谐社会 build a harmonious society
【构拟】 gòunǐ〈动〉 conceive: ～城市新蓝图 design a new blueprint for the city
【构思】 gòusī〈动〉 conceive: ～故事情节 construct the plot of a story ‖ ～新颖 original in conception ‖ 这篇小说～巧妙。 The plot of the story is skilfully conceived.
【构图】 gòutú〈动〉 compose: 这幅画的～很独特。 The composition of the picture is quite unique.
【构陷】 gòuxiàn〈动〉 make a false charge against: ～忠良 make false charges against loyal officials
【构想】 gòuxiǎng A〈动〉 conceive B〈名〉 concept: "一国两制"的～ concept of 'one country, two systems'
【构型】 gòuxíng〈名〉 1［化学］ configuration: 原子～ atomic configuration 2（布局） layout: 展览馆～独特。 The layout of the exhibition hall is unique.
【构怨】 gòuyuàn〈动〉〈书〉 incur hatred
【构造】 gòuzào A〈名〉 1（结构） structure: 人体～ anatomy of the human body 2［地质］ tectonism: 地质～ geological structure B〈动〉 construct: ～房屋 construct a house
【构造板块】 gòuzào bǎnkuài〈名〉 tectonic plate
【构造地震】 gòuzào dìzhèn〈名〉 tectonic earthquake
【构筑】 gòuzhù〈动〉 construct: ～工事 build defences ‖ ～桥梁 build a bridge

购（購） gòu〈动〉 purchase: ～车 buy a car ‖ ～货 purchase goods ‖ ～票 purchase a ticket ▸～买, 订～, 收～
【购办】 gòubàn〈动〉 purchase
【购并】 gòubìng ＝ 并购 bìnggòu
【购房团】 gòufángtuán〈名〉 property purchasing group
【购货单】 gòuhuòdān〈名〉 order form
【购货券】 gòuhuòquàn〈名〉 ration coupon
【购买】 gòumǎi〈动〉 buy: ～房子 buy a house ‖ ～公债 purchase government bonds ‖ 现金～ make a cash purchase
【购买力】 gòumǎilì〈名〉 purchasing power: 提高～ raise the purchasing power
【购物】 gòuwù〈动〉 go shopping: ～车 shopping trolley〈英〉, shopping cart〈美〉 ‖ ～袋 carrier bag〈英〉, shopping bag〈美〉 ‖ ～单 shopping list ‖ ～篮 shopping basket
【购物村】 gòuwùcūn〈名〉 shopping village
【购物街】 gòuwùjiē〈名〉 shopping street: ～上人山人海。 The shopping streets were packed with shoppers.
【购物券】 gòuwùquàn〈名〉 voucher
【购物中心】 gòuwù zhōngxīn〈名〉 shopping centre
【购销】 gòu-xiāo〈名〉 buying and selling: ～合同 purchase and sale contract ‖ ～两旺 brisk buying and selling
【购置】 gòuzhì〈动〉 purchase: ～家具 buy furniture ‖ ～商品房 purchase commercial housing
【购置税】 gòuzhìshuì〈名〉 purchase tax: 车辆～ vehicle purchase tax

诟（詬） gòu〈书〉
A〈名〉 shame
B〈动〉 rebuke: ▸～病
【诟病】 gòubìng〈动〉〈书〉 denounce: 为世人～ be denounced by the public
【诟骂】 gòumà〈动〉〈书〉 revile: 当众～ revile sb. in public ‖ 互相～ trade abuses

垢 gòu
A〈形〉〈书〉 filthy: ▸蓬头～面
B〈名〉 1（脏东西） filth: ▸藏污纳～, 污～ 2〈书〉（羞辱） humiliation: ▸忍辱含～

够（夠） gòu
A〈动〉 1（达到） be enough: ～标准 be up to standard ‖ 不～资格 be unqualified ‖ 钱不～花 not have enough money ‖ 时间不～ not have enough time 2（触及） reach: 梯子～不着窗户。 The ladder won't quite reach the window.
B〈副〉 enough: 今天天气～冷。 It's pretty cold today. ‖ 说的～多了。 Enough said. ‖ 她哭了个～。 She wept her fill.
C〈形〉 tired of: 天天吃同样的饭，我真吃～了。 I'm tired of having the same kind of food every day.
【够本】 gòuběn〈动〉 break even: 他做了几笔生意，刚～。 He made several sales and just broke even.
【够不着】 gòubuzháo〈动〉 cannot reach
【够得着】 gòudezháo〈动〉 be able to reach
【够格】 gòugé〈动〉 be qualified: 不～ be unqualified ‖ 他当英语老师～。 He's qualified as a teacher of English.
【够交情】 gòu jiāoqing〈动〉 1（交情深） be on good terms 2 ＝ 够朋友 gòu péngyou
【够劲儿】 gòujìnr〈形〉〈口〉 1（指程度） potent: 这酒真～。 This alcohol is potent. 2（指负担） enough: 既要攻读学位又要带两个孩子，真～。 Studying for a degree and taking care of two kids at the same time is really too much.
【够朋友】 gòu péngyou〈动〉 be a friend

indeed: 你这样做不～。 You're no real friend to behave like this.
【够呛】gòuqiàng = 够戗 gòuqiàng
【够戗】gòuqiàng〈形〉〈方〉 1（不可能） unlikely: 午饭前能干完吗？——我看～。 Can you finish it before lunch? — Seems unlikely. 2（程度深） unbearable: 累得真～ be completely worn out ‖ 疼得～ be unbearably painful
【够瞧的】gòuqiáode〈形〉〈口〉 really awful: 今天真冷得～。 It's terribly cold today.
【够受的】gòushòude〈形〉〈口〉 hardly bearable: 累得真～ be completely worn out
【够损的】gòusǔnde〈形〉〈口〉 1（指语言） bitterly sarcastic 2（指行为） tart and mean: 他真～. He's really a mean fellow.
【够味儿】gòuwèir〈形〉〈口〉 perfect: 这菜真～。 The dish is very tasty. ‖ 他的京剧唱得～。 He sings Beijing opera absolutely perfectly.
【够意思】gòu yìsi〈形〉〈口〉 1（相当好） terrific: 这些画真～。 These paintings are really something. 2（够朋友） very generous: 你那位朋友那天真～。 That friend of yours was very kind to me that day.

遘 gòu〈动〉〈书〉 encounter: ～会 meet ‖ ～时 meet with a fine opportunity

彀 gòu〈动〉 draw a bow to the full
【彀中】gòuzhōng〈名〉〈书〉〈喻〉 trap: 入我～ fall into my trap

媾 gòu〈动〉 1〈书〉（结婚） wed: 婚～ become related by marriage 2（交好） make friends: ▸～和 3（交配） have sex: ▸交～
【媾和】gòuhé〈动〉 make peace: 单独～ negotiate peace without consulting one's allies

觏（覯） gòu〈动〉〈书〉 encounter

gū

估 gū〈动〉 estimate: 低～ underestimate ‖ 高～ overestimate ▸～计, 评～
▸gù
【估测】gūcè〈动〉 estimate: ～产量 estimate production output
【估产】gūchǎn〈动〉 estimate production output: 这块地～ 1,000 斤。 The yield of this plot is estimated at 1,000 *jin*.
【估堆儿】gūduīr〈动〉 estimate the quantity or price of goods in a heap
【估计】gūjì〈动〉 reckon: 对自己～过高 have an exaggerated opinion of oneself ‖ ～他不会来了。 I reckon he won't come. ‖ 他的财产～有七位数。 His fortune is estimated in seven figures.
【估计值】gūjìzhí〈名〉 estimated value
【估价】gūjià〈动〉 1（估计价格） evaluate: 给房子～ appraise a house ‖ 他给这幅画～太高。 His valuation of the painting is too high. 2（评价） appraise: 恰如其分地～历史人物 properly evaluate the historical role of heroes ‖ 正确～自己 have a correct estimation of oneself
【估价师】gūjiàshī ▸**p. 966**〈名〉 appraiser: 房地产～ real estate valuator
【估量】gūliáng〈动〉 evaluate: 不可～的损失 immeasurable loss
【估摸】gūmo〈动〉〈口〉 reckon: 我～着我们现在的速度是每小时 70 公里。 I estimate we are going at 70 kilometres an hour.
【估算】gūsuàn〈动〉 assess: ～地震造成的损失 assess the damage caused by an earthquake
【估值】gūzhí〈名〉 estimated value

咕 gū〈拟〉（指母鸡） cluck;（指鸽子） coo
【咕咚】gūdōng〈拟〉 plop: ～一声跳进河里 plop into the river ‖ 他拿起矿泉水，～～喝了几口。 He took a bottle of mineral water and drank it down in gulps.
【咕嘟】gūdū〈拟〉 gurgle: 锅里的水～作响。 The boiling water bubbled in the pot. ‖ 泉水～～地往外冒。 The spring kept bubbling up.
【咕嘟】gūdu〈动〉〈方〉 1（煮） boil for a long time: 把土豆～烂了再吃。 Potatoes should be thoroughly boiled before you eat them. 2（撅嘴） pout: 她不乐意，～起了嘴。 She pouted in disapproval.
【咕叽】gūjī = 咕唧 gūjī
【咕唧】gūjī〈拟〉 squelch: ～～地走过泥地 squish through the mud
【咕唧】gūji〈动〉 whisper: 她走过去，在邻居的耳边～了几句。 She walked over and whispered something in her neighbour's ear.
【咕隆】gūlōng〈拟〉 rattle: 货车在镇子里～～驶过。 Freight wagons rumbled through the town.
【咕噜】gūlū〈拟〉 rumble: ～～地漱口 gargle one's mouth ‖ 他肚子饿得～～作响。 His stomach rumbled with hunger.
【咕噜】gūlu = 咕哝 gūnong
【咕哝】gūnong〈动〉 mumble

呱 gū
▸guā, guǎ
【呱呱】gūgū〈拟〉〈书〉 [of a baby] cry: 婴儿在母亲怀里～地哭泣。 The infant is mewling in her mother's arms.
▸guāguā
【呱呱坠地】gūgū-zhuìdì〈成〉 come into the world with a cry

沽[1] gū〈动〉〈书〉 1（买） buy: ～酒 buy wine ▸～名钓誉 2（卖） sell: ▸待价而～

沽[2] Gū〈名〉 Gu [another name for Tianjin (天津)]
【沽名钓誉】gūmíng-diàoyù〈成〉 fish for fame and compliments

姑[1] gū〈名〉 1〈书〉（婆婆） mother-in-law: ▸翁～ 2（丈夫的姐妹） sister-in-law: 小～子 husband's younger sister ▸～嫂 3（姑母） aunt: 大～ eldest aunt on father's side ‖ 二～ second aunt on father's side ▸～母 4（女孩） country girl 5（指出家人） nun: ▸道～, 尼～

姑[2] gū〈副〉 for the time being: ～置勿论 leave sth. aside for the time being
【姑表】gūbiǎo〈名〉 paternal cousin: ～兄弟 male cousins from one's father's sister's family
【姑爹】gūdiē〈方〉= 姑父 gūfu
【姑夫】gūfu ▸**p. 588**〈名〉 uncle [husband of father's sister]
【姑父】gūfu = 姑夫 gūfu
【姑姑】gūgu ▸**p. 588**〈名〉〈口〉 auntie [father's sister]
【姑宽】gūkuān〈动〉 be too tolerant: 从严查处，绝不～ show no mercy whatsoever
【姑老爷】gūlǎoye ▸**p. 588**〈名〉〈口〉 1〈尊〉（指女婿） [for a man, used by members of his wife's family] son-in-law 2（指长辈） husband of one's mother's paternal aunt
【姑姥姥】gūlǎolao ▸**p. 588**〈名〉 sister of one's maternal grandfather
【姑妈】gūmā ▸**p. 588**〈名〉〈口〉 auntie [father's married sister]
【姑母】gūmǔ ▸**p. 588**〈名〉 auntie [father's sister]
【姑奶奶】gūnǎinai〈名〉〈口〉 1 ▸**p. 588**（父亲的姑母） great-aunt 2（指女儿） married daughter 3（自称） I, your great-aunt [used by a woman when quarrelling]
【姑娘】gūniáng〈名〉〈方〉 1（姑母） aunt 2（丈夫的姐妹） sister-in-law
【姑娘】gūniang〈名〉 1（女子） girl: 十八岁的～ girl of eighteen 2〈口〉（女儿） daughter: 我的两个～ my two daughters
【姑娘家】gūniangjia〈名〉 single young lady
【姑婆】gūpó〈名〉〈方〉 1（丈夫的姑母） husband's paternal aunt 2（父亲的姑母） grandfather's sister
【姑且】gūqiě〈副〉 for the time being: 你～试一试。 Give it a try.
【姑嫂】gūsǎo〈名〉 sisters-in-law: ～关系不好。 The sisters-in-law are on bad terms.
【姑妄听之】gūwàngtīngzhī〈成〉 might as well hear sb. out
【姑妄言之】gūwàngyánzhī〈成〉 tell sb. sth. for what it is worth
【姑息】gūxī〈动〉 indulge: ～迁就 indulge and yield to ‖ 决不～ absolutely won't tolerate
【姑息养奸】gūxī-yǎngjiān〈成〉 to tolerate evil is to abet it
【姑爷爷】gūyéye ▸**p. 588**〈名〉 paternal great-aunt's husband
【姑爷】gūye〈名〉〈口〉 son-in-law
【姑丈】gūzhàng = 姑夫 gūfu
【姑子】gūzi〈名〉〈口〉 Buddhist nun

孤 gū
A〈形〉 1（无父母） orphaned: ▸～儿 2（单独） alone: ▸～单, ～立, ～掌难鸣
B〈名〉 1（孤儿） orphan: ▸遗～ 2（我） [used by an emperor or a king] I: ▸称～道寡
【孤傲】gū'ào〈形〉 proud and aloof: 生性～ be proud and reserved by nature
【孤本】gūběn〈名〉 only existing copy
【孤单】gūdān〈形〉 1（无依靠） alone: 丈夫死后，她～一人过日子。 She lived all by herself after her husband's death. 2（单薄） feeble: 势力～ be weak and helpless
【孤胆】gūdǎn〈形〉 single-handed: ～英雄 lone fighter
【孤岛】gūdǎo〈名〉 desert island
【孤独】gūdú〈形〉 lonely: 过～的生活 live a solitary life ‖ ～感 loneliness
【孤独症】gūdúzhèng ▸**p. 50**〈名〉［医学］ autism
【孤儿】gū'ér〈名〉 1（丧父） fatherless child 2（无父母） orphan: 成为～ be orphaned ‖ 收养～ adopt an orphan
【孤儿寡母】gū'ér-guǎmǔ〈成〉 orphans and widows

g

【孤儿院】gū'éryuàn〈名〉orphanage
【孤芳自赏】gūfāng-zìshǎng〈成〉〈喻〉remain aloof from the world
【孤高】gūgāo〈形〉haughty and aloof: 她是个沉默寡言的女孩，冷漠而～。She is a silent girl, cold and remote.
【孤寡】gūguǎ **A**〈名〉widows and orphans **B**〈形〉heirless and without support: ～老人 heirless old person without support
【孤寂】gūjì〈形〉lonely: 感到～ feel lonely ‖ 孩子不在身边时她很～。She was very lonely while her children were not with her.
【孤家寡人】gūjiā-guǎrén〈成〉loner
【孤介】gūjiè〈形〉upright: 这个人性情～。This is a man of upright character.
【孤军】gūjūn〈名〉isolated force: ～深入 isolated force penetrating deep into enemy territory ‖ ～作战 fight a lone battle
【孤苦】gūkǔ〈形〉alone and poor
【孤苦伶仃】gūkǔ-língdīng〈成〉friendless and uncared for: 那位老人～，没人照管。The old man was left high and dry.
【孤老】gūlǎo〈名〉solitary childless old person
【孤立】gūlì **A**〈动〉isolate: ～敌人 isolate the enemy **B**〈形〉isolated: 不能～地看待这件事。You can't deal with this kind of thing in isolation. ‖ 执政党越来越～。The ruling party was becoming increasingly isolated.
【孤立无援】gūlì-wúyuán〈成〉isolated and cut off from help
【孤立主义】gūlìzhǔyì〈名〉isolationism
【孤零零】gūlínglíng〈形〉solitary: ～的一棵树 lone tree ‖ 一个人～地住在山洞里 live all by oneself in a cave
【孤陋寡闻】gūlòu-guǎwén〈成〉ignorant and ill-informed
【孤僻】gūpì〈形〉unsociable and eccentric: 他非常～，几乎没有朋友。He keeps himself to himself and has hardly any friends.
【孤身】gūshēn〈形〉alone: ～前往 go there alone ‖ ～一人生活 live all by oneself
【孤身只影】gūshēn-zhīyǐng〈成〉alone
【孤孀】gūshuāng〈名〉widow
【孤行】gūxíng〈动〉insist on one's own way: ▸一意～
【孤行己见】gūxíng-jǐjiàn〈成〉carry out one's own ideas regardless of opinions of others
【孤雄生殖】gūxióng shēngzhí〈名〉［生物］patrogenesis
【孤云野鹤】gūyún-yěhè〈成〉〈喻〉free of worldly cares
【孤掌难鸣】gūzhǎng-nánmíng〈成〉〈喻〉it is difficult to achieve anything on one's own
【孤证】gūzhèng〈名〉unique example
【孤注一掷】gūzhù-yīzhì〈成〉risk everything on a single venture

轱（軲）gū

【轱辘】gūlu **A**〈名〉〈口〉wheel **B**〈动〉roll: 石头从山上～下来。The stone rolled down the mountain.

骨 gū

▸gǔ
【骨朵儿】gūduor〈名〉〈口〉flower bud: 花～ a flower bud
【骨碌碌】gūlūlū〈形〉rolling: 小家伙的眼睛～地到处看。The child looked all around.
【骨碌】gūlu〈动〉roll: 一～从床上爬起来 roll out of bed

鸪（鴣）gū

▸鹁鸪 bógū，鹧鸪 zhègū

菇 gū

〈名〉mushroom: ▸冬～，蘑～，香～

菰 gū

〈名〉**1**（茭白）wild rice **2** = 菇 gū

蛄 gū

▸蟪蛄 huìgū，蝼蛄 lóugū
▸gǔ

菁 gū

【菁葖】gūtū〈名〉**1**［植物］follicle **2**（骨朵儿）flower bud

辜 gū

A〈名〉guilt: ▸死有余～，无～
B〈动〉let down: ▸～负
【辜负】gūfù〈动〉fail to live up to: ～某人的期望 fall short of sb.'s expectations ‖ ～人民的信任 be unworthy of people's trust ‖ ～人家的一番好意 abuse sb.'s kindness

酤 gū

〈书〉〈动〉**1**（买酒）buy wine **2**（卖酒）sell wine

觚 gū

〈名〉**1**（指酒具）wine vessel in former times **2**〈旧〉（写字板）wooden slip for writing: 操～ engage in literary composition **3**〈书〉（棱角）edge and corner

毂（轂）gū

▸gǔ
【毂辘】gūlu = 轱辘 gūlu

箍 gū

A〈动〉bind fast: ～桶 hoop a barrel ‖ 腰间～了一条宽腰带 have a broad sash round one's waist
B〈名〉hoop: 铁～ iron hoop
【箍桶匠】gūtǒngjiàng〈名〉hooper

gǔ

古 gǔ

A〈名〉**1**（指年代）ancient times: 从～到今 from time immemorial ▸～往今来，远～ **2**（指事物）antiquities: ▸怀～，考～，食～不化 **3**（指诗）ancient-style poetry [a form of pre-Tang poetry, usu having four to seven characters per line]: ▸五～，七～
B〈形〉**1**（年代久）ancient: ～建筑 ancient building ‖ ～战场 historic battlefield ▸～代，～迹，～老 **2**（质朴）simple and unadorned: ▸～道热肠，人心不～ **3**（指风格）classical: ▸～朴
【古奥】gǔ'ào〈形〉archaic and abstruse: 行文～ use abstruse language
【古巴】Gǔbā〈名〉Cuba: ～共和国 Republic of Cuba ‖ ～人 Cuban
【古板】gǔbǎn〈形〉inflexible: 为人～ be stuck in one's ways ‖ 他的思想很～。He's very rigid in his ideas.
【古币】gǔbì〈名〉ancient coin: 收藏～ collect ancient coins ‖ ～收藏家 numismatist
【古刹】gǔchà〈名〉ancient temple: ～钟声 chimes of an ancient temple
【古城】gǔchéng〈名〉ancient city: ～遗址 site of an ancient city
【古代】gǔdài〈名〉**1**（指过去）ancient times: ～历史 ancient history ‖ ～英雄 hero of ancient times **2**（指奴隶社会）age of slave society or primitive society
【古道热肠】gǔdào-rècháng〈成〉considerate and warm-hearted
【古典】gǔdiǎn **A**〈名〉classical allusion **B**〈形〉classical: ～政治经济学 classical political economics
【古典芭蕾】gǔdiǎn bālěi〈名〉classical ballet
【古典式摔跤】gǔdiǎnshì shuāijiāo〈名〉［体育］Graeco-Roman style wrestling
【古典音乐】gǔdiǎn yīnyuè〈名〉classical music
【古典主义】gǔdiǎnzhǔyì〈名〉classicism: 新～ neo-classicism
【古董】gǔdǒng〈名〉**1**（指器物）antique: 收藏～ collect curios and antiques ‖ ～鉴赏家 connoisseur of curios **2**〈喻〉（指人）old fogey: 他是个老～。He is an old fogey.
【古董商】gǔdǒngshāng〈名〉antique dealer
【古都】gǔdū〈名〉ancient capital: 南京是六朝～。Nanjing was the ancient capital of six dynasties.
【古风】gǔfēng〈名〉**1**（指风俗习惯）ancient customs: ～犹存。Ancient customs are still observed. **2** = 古体诗 gǔtǐshī
【古怪】gǔguài〈形〉bizarre: 穿着/行为～ odd dress/behaviour ‖ 性情～ eccentric character
【古国】gǔguó〈名〉country with a long history: 文明～ country with an ancient civilization
【古汉语】gǔ-Hànyǔ ▸p. 918〈名〉classical Chinese
【古话】gǔhuà〈名〉old saying
【古籍】gǔjí〈名〉ancient books: 整理～ sift through ancient books
【古迹】gǔjì〈名〉place of historic interest: 文物～ ancient records and relics
【古今中外】gǔjīn-zhōngwài〈成〉at all times and in all countries: ～，概莫能外。It is true at all times and in all countries.
【古旧】gǔjiù〈形〉antiquated: ～书店 antique bookshop
【古柯】gǔkē〈名〉［植物］coca: ～碱 cocaine
【古来】gǔlái〈副〉from time immemorial: ～少有 very little since ancient times
【古兰经】Gǔlánjīng〈名〉［伊斯兰教］Koran
【古老】gǔlǎo〈形〉ancient: ～的风俗 old customs ‖ 这首歌很～。This song is as old as the hills.
【古里古怪】gǔligǔguài〈形〉eccentric
【古历】gǔlì〈名〉lunar calendar
【古墓】gǔmù〈名〉ancient tomb: 发掘～ excavate an ancient tomb
【古朴】gǔpǔ〈形〉simple and unsophisticated: 民风～ have simple customs and traditional values
【古钱】gǔqián〈名〉ancient money
【古琴】gǔqín ▸p. 929〈名〉*guqin* [seven-stringed plucked instrument in some ways similar to the zither]
【古人】gǔrén〈名〉ancients: 前不见～，后不见来者。Looking back, I do not see the ancients, looking forward, I do not see the ones to come.
【古人类学】gǔrénlèixué〈名〉palaeoanthropology: ～家 palaeoanthropologist
【古色古香】gǔsè-gǔxiāng〈成〉quaint: ～的村舍 cottage with old quaint charm
【古生代】Gǔshēngdài〈名〉［地质］Palaeozoic Era

g

【古生物】gǔshēngwù〈名〉 ancient extinct life
【古诗】gǔshī〈名〉 1 = 古体诗 gǔtǐshī 2（古代诗歌） ancient poetry
【古书】gǔshū〈名〉 ancient book
【古体诗】gǔtǐshī〈名〉 ancient-style poetry [form of pre-Tang poetry, usu having four to seven characters per line]
【古铜色】gǔtóngsè ▸p. 863〈名〉 bronze: ～的脸庞/皮肤 bronze-coloured face/skin
【古玩】gǔwán〈名〉 antique: ～店 antique shop
【古往今来】gǔwǎng-jīnlái〈成〉 since time immemorial
【古为今用】gǔwéijīnyòng〈成〉 make the past serve the present: ～，洋为中用 make the past serve the present and foreign things serve China
【古文】gǔwén〈名〉 1（指文体） classical Chinese prose 2（指字体） pre-Qin Chinese script
【古文字】gǔwénzì〈名〉 ancient writing: ～学 palaeography
【古物】gǔwù〈名〉 antique: 收藏～ collect antiquities
【古昔】gǔxī〈名〉〈书〉 ancient times
【古稀】gǔxī〈名〉〈书〉 seventy years of age: 年逾～ past seventy years of age ‖ ～老人 a seventy-year-old
【古希腊】gǔ-Xīlà〈名〉 ancient Greece
【古训】gǔxùn〈名〉 ancient maxim
【古雅】gǔyǎ〈形〉 of classic elegance: 房间陈设～。 The room was furnished in a graceful classical style.
【古谚】gǔyàn〈名〉 ancient proverb
【古音】gǔyīn〈名〉 1（指古代） pronunciation of Chinese characters in ancient times, as opposed to their modern pronunciation 2（指周、秦时期） pronunciation of Chinese characters in the Zhou and Qin dynasties
【古英语】gǔ-Yīngyǔ ▸p. 918〈名〉 Old English
【古语】gǔyǔ〈名〉 1（指词语） archaism 2（古话） old saying
【古猿】gǔyuán〈名〉 paleolithic ape
【古远】gǔyuǎn〈形〉 very ancient
【古镇】gǔzhèn〈名〉 ancient town/village: 千年～ thousand year-old village
【古筝】gǔzhēng ▸p. 929〈名〉 *guzheng* [zither-like 21-stringed or 25-stringed plucked musical instrument]
【古装】gǔzhuāng〈名〉 ancient costume: ～戏 costume drama
【古拙】gǔzhuō〈形〉 simple and unsophisticated

谷[1] gǔ ▸p. 164〈名〉 valley: ▸～地, 河～, 山～

谷[2]（穀） gǔ〈名〉 1（谷类作物） grain: ▸五～ 2（粟） millet: ▸～穗, ～子 3〈方〉（稻谷） rice, paddy: ▸稻～
▸yù
【谷氨酸】gǔ'ānsuān〈名〉［生化］ glutamate
【谷氨酸钠】gǔ'ānsuānnà〈名〉 monosodium glutamate
【谷仓】gǔcāng〈名〉 granary
【谷草】gǔcǎo〈名〉 millet straw
【谷蛋白】gǔdànbái〈名〉［生化］ gluten: ～面包 gluten bread
【谷底】gǔdǐ〈名〉 1［地质］ valley floor 2〈喻〉（最低点） all-time low: 石油价格已跌至～。 The price of oil has reached an all-time low.
【谷地】gǔdì〈名〉 valley
【谷歌】Gǔgē〈名〉 Google
【谷贱伤农】gǔjiàn-shāngnóng〈成〉 cheap grain harms the peasants
【谷糠】gǔkāng〈名〉 rice chaff
【谷壳】gǔké〈名〉 husk of rice
【谷类作物】gǔlèi zuòwù〈名〉 cereal crop
【谷粒】gǔlì〈名〉 grain
【谷神星】Gǔshénxīng〈名〉［天文］ Ceres
【谷穗】gǔsuì〈名〉 ear of millet
【谷维素】gǔwéisù〈名〉［药学］ oryzanol
【谷物】gǔwù〈名〉 1（指籽实） cereal 2（指作物） cereal crop
【谷雨】Gǔyǔ〈名〉 Grain Rain [beginning of the 6th of the 24 solar terms]
【谷子】gǔzi〈名〉 1（指植物） millet 2（粟） unhusked millet 3〈方〉（稻） unhusked rice

汩 gǔ
【汩汩】gǔgǔ〈拟〉 gurgle: 一条小溪在岩石间～流淌。 A brook bubbles between rocks.

诂（詁） gǔ〈动〉 interpret archaic or dialectal language in current language: ▸训～

股[1] gǔ
A〈名〉 1（大腿） thigh: ▸～肱 2（指机构） section: 人事～ personnel section 3（指绳线） strand: 三～的绳子 three-strand rope 4（份） share: 把钱均分成六～ divide the money into six equal shares ▸入～ 5（股票） share: 炒～ speculate in stocks ▸～民, ～市
B〈量〉 1（指成条的东西） [for sth. long and narrow]: 一～鲜血 a stream of blood ‖ 一～线 a skein of thread 2（指气味、味道等） [for flavour, fragrance]: 一～淡淡的烟草味 a faint tincture of tobacco ‖ 空气中有一～油漆味。 The air smelt of paint. 3〈贬〉（指人） band: 一～敌军 a band of enemy soldiers

股[2] gǔ〈名〉［数学］ longer leg of a right-angled triangle: ▸勾～定理
【股本】gǔběn〈名〉 capital stock
【股东】gǔdōng〈名〉 shareholder〈英〉; stockholder〈美〉: ～大会 meeting of shareholders
【股份】gǔfèn〈名〉 shares〈英〉; stock〈美〉: 持有公司百分之四十八的～ hold 48% of a company's stock ‖ ～资本 share capital
【股份公司】gǔfèn gōngsī〈名〉 joint-stock company
【股份有限公司】gǔfèn yǒuxiàn gōngsī〈名〉 limited company (Ltd)
【股份制】gǔfènzhì〈名〉 share-holding system: ～银行 joint-equity bank
【股改】gǔgǎi〈名〉 stock market reform
【股肱】gǔgōng〈名〉〈书〉〈喻〉 right-hand man: ～之臣 most trustworthy minister
【股骨】gǔgǔ〈名〉［解剖］ thighbone
【股海】gǔhǎi〈名〉〈喻〉 fluctuating stock market: ～沉浮 rises and falls on the stock market
【股价】gǔjià〈名〉 share price: ～暴涨。 Share prices leapt.
【股金】gǔjīn〈名〉 share capital
【股利】gǔlì = 股息 gǔxī
【股民】gǔmín〈名〉 stock investor
【股票】gǔpiào〈名〉 shares〈英〉; stock〈美〉: 发行～ issue shares ‖ ～价格 share price ‖ ～经纪人 stockbroker
【股票价格指数】gǔpiào jiàgé zhǐshù〈名〉 stock market index
【股票交易所】gǔpiào jiāoyìsuǒ〈名〉 stock exchange
【股票市场】gǔpiào shìchǎng〈名〉 stock market
【股评】gǔpíng〈名〉 stock analysis: ～家 stock analyst
【股权】gǔquán〈名〉 stock ownership
【股神】gǔshén〈名〉 god of stocks: 美国人巴菲特被誉为"～"。The American man Warren Buffet is known as a god of stocks.
【股市】gǔshì〈名〉 stock market
【股息】gǔxī〈名〉 dividend: 分派～ distribute dividends ‖ ～收益 dividend yield
【股癣】gǔxuǎn ▸p. 50〈名〉［医学］ crural tinea
【股灾】gǔzāi〈名〉 stock market crash
【股指】gǔzhǐ〈简称〉= 股票价格指数

骨 gǔ〈名〉 1（骨头） bone: ▸筋～, 肋～ 2（品质） moral character: ▸～气, 傲～, 奴颜媚～ 3（骨架） skeleton: 伞～ frame of an umbrella
▸gū
【骨癌】gǔ'ái ▸p. 50〈名〉 osteocarcinoma
【骨刺】gǔcì ▸p. 50〈名〉［医学］ spur
【骨雕】gǔdiāo〈名〉 bone carving
【骨顶鸡】gǔdǐngjī〈名〉［鸟类］ coot
【骨董】gǔdǒng = 古董 gǔdǒng
【骨粉】gǔfěn〈名〉［材料］ bone meal
【骨感】gǔgǎn〈形〉 bony
【骨干】gǔgàn〈名〉 1［解剖］ diaphysis 2〈喻〉（中坚力量） backbone: 起～作用 be a mainstay ‖ ～教师 core teacher ‖ ～力量 core strength ‖ ～分子 key member
【骨骼】gǔgé〈名〉［解剖］ skeleton: 人体～ human skeleton
【骨骼肌】gǔgéjī〈名〉［解剖］ skeletal muscle
【骨鲠】gǔgěng A〈名〉 fish bone B〈形〉 upright: 秉性～ be upright and honest by nature ‖ ～之臣 upright official who does not hesitate to speak his mind
【骨鲠在喉】gǔgěng-zàihóu〈成〉 have a thought that one cannot help expressing: 如～，不吐不快 have an opinion one cannot suppress
【骨坏死】gǔhuàisǐ〈名〉 osteonecrosis
【骨灰】gǔhuī〈名〉 ashes of the dead: ～盒 casket for funerary ashes ‖ 他的～被撒进大海。 His ashes were scattered over the sea.
【骨灰瓮】gǔhuīwèng〈名〉 urn for funerary ashes
【骨架】gǔjià〈名〉 1（指骨骼） skeleton 2〈喻〉（指结构） framework: 房子/小说的～ framework of a house/novel
【骨胶】gǔjiāo〈名〉［化工］ bone glue
【骨节】gǔjié〈名〉 joint
【骨结核】gǔjiéhé ▸p. 50〈名〉［医学］ bone tuberculosis
【骨臼】gǔjiù〈名〉［医学］ bone socket
【骨科】gǔkē〈名〉 department of orthopaedics: ～医生 orthopaedist
【骨刻】gǔkè〈名〉［美术］ bone sculpture
【骨库】gǔkù〈名〉 bone storage cabinet
【骨力】gǔlì〈名〉 vigour of strokes
【骨立】gǔlì〈形〉 bony: 憔悴～ be haggard and bony
【骨龄】gǔlíng〈名〉 bone age
【骨瘤】gǔliú ▸p. 50〈名〉［医学］ osteoma
【骨膜】gǔmó〈名〉［解剖］ periosteum
【骨牌】gǔpái〈名〉 domino

g

【骨牌效应】gǔpái xiàoyìng〈名〉domino effect
【骨盆】gǔpén〈名〉[解剖] pelvis
【骨气】gǔqì〈名〉1（指人）backbone: 有～的人 person of integrity 2（指书法）vigour of strokes: 这些字写得有～。These characters were written with vigour.
【骨器】gǔqì〈名〉bone object
【骨肉】gǔròu〈名〉1〈本〉flesh and blood 2〈喻〉（指亲人）kin: ～兄弟 blood brothers 3〈喻〉（指关系）close relations: ～同胞 compatriots of the same flesh and blood ‖ 他俩情同～。There seems to be a kinship between them.
【骨殖】gǔshi〈名〉skeleton
【骨瘦如柴】gǔshòu-rúchái〈成〉bag of bones
【骨髓】gǔsuǐ〈名〉[解剖] bone marrow: 捐献～ donate marrow ‖ ～移植 bone marrow transplantation
【骨头】gǔtou〈名〉1（骨胳）bone: 啃～ gnaw at a bone 2（指品质）character: ▸懒～, 硬～
【骨头架子】gǔtou jiàzi〈名〉〈口〉1（指骨骼）skeleton: 瘦得只剩～ be all skin and bone 2（指人）walking skeleton
【骨血】gǔxuè〈名〉offspring: 这孩子是他的亲～。This child is his own flesh and blood.
【骨折】gǔzhé〈名〉fracture: 粉碎性～ comminuted fracture ‖ 他在这次车祸中多处～。He sustained multiple fractures in the car accident.
【骨质疏松】gǔzhì shūsōng ▸p. 50〈名〉[医学] osteoporosis: ～综合征 osteoporosis syndrome
【骨质增生】gǔzhì zēngshēng ▸p. 50〈名〉[医学] hyperplasia
【骨子】gǔzi〈名〉ribs: 伞～ frame of an umbrella
【骨子里】gǔzilǐ〈名〉〈喻〉in one's heart of hearts: 从～瞧不起 look down upon sb. deep in one's heart

牯 gǔ
【牯牛】gǔniú〈名〉bull

贾（賈）gǔ〈书〉
A〈动〉1（做买卖）do business 2（买）purchase: ～马 buy a horse 3（招致）incur: ▸～祸 4（卖）sell: ▸余勇可～
B〈名〉businessman: ▸商～
▸Jiǎ
【贾祸】gǔhuò〈动〉〈书〉court disaster
【贾怨】gǔyuàn〈动〉〈书〉invite resentment

钴（鈷）gǔ〈名〉[化学] cobalt
(Co): ～同位素 cobalt isotope
【钴铒】gǔmǔ〈名〉〈书〉iron

羖 gǔ〈名〉〈书〉[动物] ram

蛄 gǔ ▸蝲蛄 làgǔ, 蝲蝲蛄 làlàgǔ
▸gū

蛊（蠱）gǔ〈名〉legendary venomous worm
【蛊惑】gǔhuò〈动〉poison and bewitch: ～人心 excite the masses to violence

鹄（鵠）gǔ〈名〉〈古〉[in archery]
target: 中～ hit the target
▸hú

鼓 gǔ
A〈名〉1（指乐器）drum: 打～ beat a drum ‖ 击～为号 signal with a drum ▸～角, ～手, 腰～ 2（鼓状物）anything drum-shaped: ▸耳～ 3〈古〉（指报时）watch: 四～ fourth watch
B〈动〉1（敲）play: ～琴 play the zither ▸～掌 2（振奋）pluck up: ～起勇气 pluck up one's courage ▸～动, ～励, ～足干劲 3（扇）blow: ～风 work a pair of bellows 4（胀大）bulge: ～着腮帮子 puff out one's cheeks ‖ 口袋～了起来。The pockets are bulging. ▸～胀
【鼓板】gǔbǎn ▸p. 929〈名〉[音乐] clappers
【鼓包】gǔbāo A〈动〉bulge: 脸上鼓了个包 have a swelling on one's face B〈名〉lump: 头上碰了一个～ get a bump on one's head
【鼓吹】gǔchuī〈动〉1（宣扬）incite: ～革命 advocate revolution ‖ 大力～经济改革 vigorously agitate for economic reform 2（吹嘘）boast: 别在他人面前～自己。Don't blow your own trumpet in front of other people.
【鼓槌】gǔchuí〈名〉drumstick
【鼓捣】gǔdao〈动〉〈方〉1（摆弄）tinker with: 不要～我的手表。Don't fiddle with my watch. 2（唆使）incite: ～他去偷东西 encourage him to go and steal things
【鼓点】gǔdiǎn〈名〉1（指击鼓的节奏）drumbeat 2（指鼓板节奏）clapper beat
【鼓动】gǔdòng〈动〉1（激励）inspire: ～某人立即行动 inspire sb. to immediate action ‖ 政治～家 political agitator 2〈贬〉（唆使）incite: ～群众闹事 incite the masses to violence 3（扇动）flap: ～双翅 flap the wings
【鼓风机】gǔfēngjī〈名〉[机械] air blower
【鼓风炉】gǔfēnglú〈名〉blast furnace
【鼓鼓囊囊】gǔgu-nāngnāng〈形〉bulging: ～的钱包 bulging wallet ‖ 口袋里装得～。The pocket was full to bulging.
【鼓角】gǔjiǎo〈名〉battle drum and horn: ～齐鸣 sound the bugles and drums
【鼓劲】gǔjìn〈动〉encourage: 给某人～ give sb. encouragement ‖ 为自己的球队～加油 pull for one's team
【鼓励】gǔlì〈动〉encourage: ～某人好好学习 encourage sb. in his studies ‖ 说几句～的话 offer a few words of encouragement
【鼓励奖】gǔlìjiǎng〈名〉consolation prize
【鼓楼】gǔlóu〈名〉drum tower
【鼓膜】gǔmó〈名〉[解剖] eardrum
【鼓弄】gǔnong〈动〉〈口〉fiddle with: ～一台旧收音机 tinker with an old radio
【鼓舌】gǔshé〈动〉wag one's tongue: ▸摇唇～
【鼓舌如簧】gǔshé-rúhuáng〈成〉talk glibly: 她～, 说个不停。She jabbered on and on without stopping.
【鼓师】gǔshī〈名〉drummer
【鼓手】gǔshǒu〈名〉drummer
【鼓书】gǔshū = 大鼓 dàgǔ
【鼓舞】gǔwǔ A〈动〉encourage: ～人心 encouraging ‖ ～士气 boost the army morale ‖ 受到～ feel heartened B〈形〉encouraging: 结果令人～。The results are encouraging. ▸欢欣～
【鼓舞人心】gǔwǔ-rénxīn〈成〉inspiring
【鼓翼】gǔyì〈动〉beat wings: 鸟儿～而飞。Birds fly by flapping its wings.
【鼓乐】gǔyuè〈名〉music accompanied by drumbeats: ～喧天 great din of drums and pipes ‖ ～齐鸣。Music and drumbeats blasted out.
【鼓噪】gǔzào〈动〉clamour: ～一时 make a great commotion about sth. for a while
【鼓掌】gǔzhǎng〈动〉applaud: ～通过 clap one's hands in approval ‖ 为某人的讲话热烈～ clap sb.'s speech enthusiastically
【鼓胀】gǔzhàng〈名〉1 bulge: 手臂上～的肌肉 bulging arm muscles 2 [中医] distention of abdomen
【鼓足干劲】gǔzú gànjìn〈成〉go all out

毂（轂）gǔ〈名〉hub
▸gū
【毂盖】gǔgài〈名〉hub cap

榖 gǔ = 楮 chǔ

臌 gǔ〈名〉[中医] distention: ▸～胀
【臌胀】gǔzhàng = 鼓胀 gǔzhàng 2

瞽 gǔ〈形〉〈书〉1（眼瞎）blind: ～者 the blind 2（无识别力）lacking discernment: ～说 stupid talk

gù

估 gù
【估衣】gùyi〈名〉〈旧〉second-hand clothes for sale
▸gū

固[1] gù
A〈形〉1（结实）firm: ▸坚～, 牢～, 稳～ 2（坚硬）solid: ▸～态, ～体, 凝～ 3（顽固）stubborn: ▸～执, 顽～ 4 = 痼 gù
B〈动〉strengthen: ▸～化
C〈副〉firmly: ▸～辞, ～守

固[2] gù〈书〉
A〈副〉in the first place: 人～有一死，或重于泰山，或轻于鸿毛。Though death befalls all men alike, it may be weightier than Mount Tai or lighter than a feather.
B〈连〉no doubt: 人～不易知，知人也未易也。It is hard to know others indeed, and it is no easier to get others to know oneself.
【固步自封】gùbù-zìfēng = 故步自封 gùbù-zìfēng
【固辞】gùcí〈动〉〈书〉decline
【固氮】gùdàn〈名〉nitrogen immobilization
【固定】gùdìng A〈形〉fixed: ～模式 fixed pattern of behaviour ‖ ～职业 regular profession ‖ ～座位 regular seat B〈动〉fix: 用钉子把某物～在墙上 fix sth. to the wall with a nail
【固定靶】gùdìngbǎ〈名〉stationary target
【固定词组】gùdìng cízǔ〈名〉set phrase
【固定电话】gùdìng diànhuà〈名〉landline telephone
【固定服务卫星】gùdìng fúwù wèixīng〈名〉fixed service satellite
【固定汇率】gùdìng huìlǜ〈名〉fixed exchange rate: ～制度 fixed-exchange-rate system
【固定利率】gùdìng lìlǜ〈名〉fixed interest rate
【固定资产】gùdìng zīchǎn〈名〉fixed assets: ～流失 loss on fixed assets
【固化】gùhuà〈动〉solidify: ～剂 solidifying agent
【固话】gùhuà〈简称〉= 固定电话

g

【固件】gùjiàn〈名〉［计算机］firmware
【固陋】gùlòu〈形〉〈书〉ill-informed
【固然】gùrán〈连〉〈书〉**1**（表转折）to be sure: 她～年轻，但是很有经验。She is young, to be sure, but experienced. **2**（表承认）of course: 我能通过考试～好，通不过也不要紧。If I can pass the exam, of course that would be good, but it doesn't matter if I can't.
【固若金汤】gùruòjīntāng〈成〉be strongly fortified: 该城～，侵略者难以攻入。The city was secured from the invaders.
【固沙】gùshā〈动〉stabilize sand dunes: ～造林 dune-fixing afforestation
【固沙林】gùshālín〈名〉dune-fixing forest
【固守】gùshǒu〈动〉**1**（指守卫）defend tenaciously: 部队～阵地。The troops were strongly entrenched in their position. **2**（指遵循）stubbornly stick to: ～旧习 cling to old customs
【固态】gùtài〈名〉［物理］solid state
【固体】gùtǐ〈名〉solid
【固体酒精】gùtǐ jiǔjīng〈名〉solidified alcohol
【固体燃料】gùtǐ ránliào〈名〉solid fuel
【固体炸药】gùtǐ zhàyào〈名〉solid explosive
【固网】gùwǎng〈名〉landline: ～运营商 landline operator
【固有】gùyǒu〈形〉innate: ～观念 innatism ‖ 极性是磁铁的～性质。Polarity is inherent in a magnet.
【固执】gùzhí **A**〈形〉stubborn: ～的人总是我行我素。An obstinate person always does what he wants. ‖ 他生性有点～。There is a streak of stubbornness in his character. **B**〈动〉stick to: ▸～己见
【固执己见】gùzhí-jǐjiàn〈成〉stubbornly persist in one's own opinions: 他～，不愿听取别人的意见。He's very stubborn and unwilling to listen to other people's points of view.

故[1] gù

A〈名〉**1**（缘由）reason: 借～推辞 excuse oneself from accepting ‖ 无～缺席 be absent without cause ▸无缘无～ **2**（事故）incident: ▸变～, 事～
B〈连〉〈书〉therefore: 近日突发疾病，～未能如期返回。Having contracted a sudden illness, I was not able to get back on time.
C〈副〉intentionally: ▸明知～犯, 欲擒～纵

故[2] gù

A〈名〉**1**（指事物）sth. in the past: ▸吐～纳新, 温～知新 **2**（指人）old friend: ▸非亲非～, 一见如～
B〈形〉original: ▸～伎重演, ～态复萌, ～乡
C ▸**p. 772**〈动〉〈婉〉pass away: 病～ die of illness ▸～去, ～世, 身～
【故步自封】gùbù-zìfēng〈成〉be complacent and conservative
【故此】gùcǐ〈连〉hence
【故道】gùdào〈名〉**1**（指路）old road **2**（指河道）old course: 黄河～ old course of the Yellow River
【故地】gùdì〈名〉old haunt: ～重游 revisit an old haunt
【故都】gùdū〈名〉one-time capital
【故而】gù'ér〈连〉〈书〉hence
【故宫】gùgōng〈名〉**1**（指旧朝皇宫）imperial palace of a former dynasty **2** Gùgōng（指北京故宫）Imperial Palace [in Beijing]
【故宫博物院】Gùgōng Bówùyuàn〈名〉Palace Museum in Beijing
【故国】gùguó〈名〉**1**（指国家）ancient land **2**（祖国）native land **3**（故乡）hometown
【故伎】gùjì〈名〉old trick
【故伎重演】gùjì-chóngyǎn〈成〉be up to one's old tricks again
【故交】gùjiāo〈名〉〈书〉old friend
【故旧】gùjiù〈名〉〈书〉old friends and acquaintances
【故居】gùjū〈名〉former home: 宋庆龄～ former residence of Song Qingling
【故垒】gùlěi〈名〉former fortress
【故里】gùlǐ〈名〉native place: 荣归～ return home in glory
【故弄玄虚】gùnòng-xuánxū〈成〉deliberately mystify
【故去】gùqù ▸**p. 772**〈动〉〈婉〉pass away: 他三岁时父亲便～了。His father passed away when he was only three years old.
【故人】gùrén〈名〉**1**（老朋友）old friend: 过访～ visit an old friend **2**（死者）the deceased
【故杀】gùshā〈名〉［法律］wilful murder: 证据表明这是一起～。The evidence indicated that it had been a premeditated murder.
【故实】gùshí〈名〉**1**（指事实）instructive historical facts **2**（典故）source
【故世】gùshì ▸**p. 772**〈动〉〈婉〉[of one's elders] pass away
【故事】gùshì〈名〉old practice: 奉行～ follow the old routines
【故事】gùshi〈名〉**1**（指事情）story: 讲～ tell a story ‖ 民间～ folk story ‖ 童话～ fairy tale **2**（指情节）plot
【故事会】gùshihuì〈名〉story-telling gathering
【故事片】gùshipiàn〈名〉feature film: 拍～ shoot a feature film
【故态】gùtài〈名〉〈书〉one's old ways
【故态复萌】gùtài-fùméng〈成〉slip back into old habits
【故土】gùtǔ〈名〉hometown: 怀念～ long for home ‖ ～难离 it is hard to leave one's native land
【故我】gùwǒ〈名〉my former self: 依然～ remain true to one's former self
【故习】gùxí〈名〉old habit: 一改～ get rid of old habits once and for all
【故乡】gùxiāng〈名〉hometown: 热爱～ love one's hometown ‖ 第二～ second home
【故意】gùyì **A**〈副〉deliberately: ～刁难 place obstacles in sb.'s way ‖ ～歪曲事实 deliberately distort facts ‖ 他是～那样做的。He did it on purpose. **B**〈名〉［法律］premeditated action
【故意犯罪】gùyì fànzuì〈名〉intentional offence
【故意杀人】gùyì shārén〈名〉intentional killing
【故意伤害】gùyì shānghài〈名〉intentional injury
【故友】gùyǒu〈名〉**1**（死去的朋友）deceased friend: 悼念～ mourn one's departed friend **2**（老朋友）old friend: 亲朋～ relatives and old friends
【故园】gùyuán〈名〉native place
【故障】gùzhàng〈名〉breakdown: 排除～ fix a fault ‖ 机械～ mechanical breakdown ‖ 技术～ technical trouble ‖ 发动机出了～。The engines failed.
【故障检修】gùzhàng jiǎnxiū〈名〉trouble shooting
【故障率】gùzhànglǜ〈名〉failure rate
【故知】gùzhī〈名〉〈书〉old friend: 他乡遇～ run into an old friend far away from home
【故址】gùzhǐ〈名〉old location
【故纸堆】gùzhǐduī〈名〉large number of old books
【故作】gùzuò〈动〉pretend: ～镇静 pretend to be calm ‖ ～高深 pretend to be erudite and profound ‖ ～姿态 put on airs

顾（顧）gù

A〈动〉**1**（看）turn round and look: ▸环～, 瞻前～后, 左～右盼 **2**（拜访）call on: ▸光～, 三～茅庐 **3**（光顾）patronize: ▸～客, 惠～ **4**（顾及）attend to: 兼～国家、集体和个人利益 take the interests of the state, the collective and the individual into consideration ‖ ～大局，识大体 bear the overall situation in mind whilst putting the general interest above all else ‖ 忙得～不上吃饭 too busy to have time for a meal ‖ 你不能只～自己。You cannot think only of yourself. ▸～此失彼, 兼～ **5**（珍惜）look after: ▸奋不～身, ～恋
B〈名〉customer: ▸主～
C〈副〉〈书〉instead
D〈连〉〈书〉but
【顾此失彼】gùcǐ-shībǐ〈成〉be unable to attend everything at once
【顾及】gùjí〈动〉take into consideration: 无暇～此事 have no time to attend to it
【顾忌】gùjì〈动〉have scruples: 毫无～地撒谎 tell lies without scruple ‖ 无所～的人 man with no scruples
【顾家】gùjiā〈动〉look after one's family: 她很～。She is a real home-loving type.
【顾客】gùkè〈名〉customer: ～盈门 have a lot of customers ‖ ～就是上帝。The customer is God. ‖ ～至上。The customer comes first.
【顾怜】gùlián〈动〉care for: 我做这些全是为了～他。I did all this for his good.
【顾脸】gùliǎn〈动〉guard one's reputation closely: 不～ have no sense of shame
【顾恋】gùliàn〈动〉be concerned: ～子女 be concerned for one's children
【顾虑】gùlǜ **A**〈动〉have misgivings: 你还～什么？What is it that you've still got misgivings about? **B**〈名〉misgiving: 打消/消除～ dispel one's worries ‖ ～重重 be full of misgivings
【顾面子】gù miànzi〈动〉care about one's reputation
【顾名思义】gùmíng-sīyì〈成〉as the term suggests
【顾命】gùmìng〈名〉〈书〉dying emperor's will: ～大臣 minister-regent
【顾念】gùniàn〈动〉miss: ～妻儿 miss one's wife and children
【顾盼】gùpàn〈动〉〈书〉look around: 左右～ look right and left
【顾盼自雄】gùpàn-zìxióng〈成〉strut about looking very pleased with oneself
【顾前不顾后】gù qián bù gù hòu〈俗〉attend to the present and leave the future to itself
【顾全】gùquán〈动〉show consideration for and take care to preserve: ～面子 save sb.'s face
【顾全大局】gùquán dàjú〈成〉consider the big picture
【顾问】gùwèn ▸**p. 966**〈名〉consultant: 聘请～ employ an adviser ‖ 法律～ legal adviser ‖ 军事～ adviser on military affairs
【顾问委员会】gùwèn wěiyuánhuì〈名〉advisory committee

【顾惜】gùxī〈动〉treasure: ～身体 take good care of one's health
【顾影自怜】gùyǐng-zìlián〈成〉1（形容孤独失意）look at one's shadow and lament one's lot 2（形容自我欣赏）look at one's reflection and admire oneself
【顾主】gùzhǔ〈名〉customer
【顾左右而言他】gù zuǒyòu ér yán tā〈成〉steer clear of the crucial point

堌
gù〈名〉dyke

梏
gù〈名〉〈古〉wooden handcuffs: ▸桎～

崮
gù〈名〉mountain with a flat top and precipitous sides

牿
gù〈名〉1（用于圈养）cattle shed 2（用于牛角上）beam of wood tied across ox horns to prevent them from hurting people

雇（僱）
gù〈动〉hire: ～保姆 keep a maid ‖ ～出租车 hire a taxi ‖ 受～于一家夜总会 be hired in a nightclub ▸～农，～佣，解～
【雇工】gùgōng A〈动〉hire labour B〈名〉hired labourer: 当～ work for hire
【雇农】gùnóng〈名〉hired farmhand
【雇请】gùqǐng〈动〉hire: ～保姆 employ a babysitter ‖ ～家教 hire a family tutor
【雇佣】gùyōng〈动〉employ
【雇佣兵】gùyōngbīng〈名〉mercenary: ～役制 mercenary system
【雇佣军】gùyōngjūn〈名〉mercenaries: 当～ fight for hire
【雇佣文人】gùyōng wénrén〈名〉hack writer
【雇用】gùyòng〈动〉engage: ～临时工 hire a casual labourer
【雇员】gùyuán〈名〉employee
【雇主】gùzhǔ〈名〉employer

锢（錮）
gù〈动〉1（填塞）plug with molten metal: ▸～漏 2（禁止）hold in custody: ▸禁～
【锢漏】gùlou〈动〉plug with molten metal

痼
gù〈形〉1（指疾病）chronic: ▸～疾 2（指习惯、风俗）inveterate: ▸～弊，～习
【痼弊】gùbì〈名〉long-standing abuse
【痼疾】gùjí〈名〉chronic illness: ～患者 chronic invalid
【痼癖】gùpǐ〈名〉addiction
【痼习】gùxí〈名〉deep-rooted habit: ～难改。Deep-rooted habits are hard to give up.

guā

瓜
guā〈名〉1（指植物）melon: ▸南～，丝～ 2（瓜状物）melon-shaped thing: ▸脑～儿
【瓜分】guāfēn〈动〉divide up: 肆意～一个国家 carve up a country at will
【瓜葛】guāgé〈名〉association: 这事跟他毫无～。This has absolutely nothing to do with him. ‖ 被怀疑与杀人犯有～ be suspected of implication in a murderer
【瓜果】guāguǒ〈名〉melons and fruit
【瓜农】guānóng〈名〉melon farmer
【瓜皮帽】guāpímào〈名〉skull cap
【瓜片茶】guāpiànchá〈名〉*guapian* tea
【瓜瓤】guāráng〈名〉melon pulp
【瓜熟蒂落】guāshú-dìluò〈成〉〈喻〉everything comes easily at the right time
【瓜藤上长不出茄子】guāténgshang zhǎngbuchū qiézi〈俗〉〈喻〉one cannot make a silk purse out of a sow's ear
【瓜田李下】guātián-lǐxià〈成〉in suspicious circumstances: 瓜田不纳履，李下不正冠 don't do anything to arouse suspicion
【瓜条】guātiáo〈名〉1（指果脯）sweetened gourd slices 2（腌黄瓜条）sliced cucumber condiments
【瓜蔓】guāwàn〈名〉vine of melon
【瓜秧】guāyāng〈名〉melon seedling
【瓜子】guāzǐ〈名〉melon seed: 嗑～ crack and eat melon seeds
【瓜子脸】guāzǐliǎn〈名〉oval face

呱
guā〈拟〉（指鸭）quack;（指乌鸦、蛙类）croak
▸gū, guǎ
【呱哒】guādā〈拟〉clatter: ～～的马蹄声 clatter of hoof-beats
【呱嗒】guāda〈动〉1〈方〉（板着脸）put on a stern expression: ～着脸走来走去 go about with a straight face 2〈贬〉（说话）talk non-stop: 乱～一阵子 talk nonsense for quite a long time
【呱嗒板儿】guādabǎnr〈名〉1（竹板儿）bamboo clappers 2〈方〉（木屐）clogs
【呱呱】guāguā〈拟〉（指鸭）quack;（指蛙类）croak;（指乌鸦）caw
【呱呱叫】guāguājiào〈形〉〈口〉〈喻〉top-notch: 他做起饭来～。He is a terrific cook.
【呱唧】guāji A〈拟〉clap B〈动〉〈方〉clap one's hands: 我们给他～～。Give him a clap.

刮[1]
guā〈动〉1（使脱离）scrape: ～胡子 shave off one's beard ‖ ～鱼鳞 scale a fish 2（索取）extort: ～人钱财 extort money from sb. ▸搜～ 3（涂抹）daub: ～糨子 smear paste over cloth ‖ 先～腻子再油漆 apply wood-filler before painting

刮[2]（颳）
guā〈动〉blow: ～大风。It was blowing a gale. ‖ 树叶被风～得四处乱飞。The leaves were blown about.
【刮鼻子】guā bízi〈动〉1（指别人的鼻子）scrape sb.'s nose [as a punishment if sb. loses a game] 2（指自己的鼻子）scrape one's own nose to scorn sb.
【刮刀】guādāo〈名〉scraping knife
【刮地皮】guā dìpí〈动〉〈喻〉extort money (and property) from the people
【刮宫】guāgōng〈动〉perform dilatation and curettage (of the uterus)
【刮刮叫】guāguājiào = 呱呱叫 guāguājiào
【刮刮卡】guāguākǎ〈名〉scratch card
【刮脸】guāliǎn〈动〉shave: 他～时把脸刮破了。He cut himself shaving. ‖ ～刀 razor
【刮目】guāmù〈动〉change one's opinions completely: 令人～ make sb. change his ideas (about) ▸～相看
【刮目相待】guāmù-xiāngdài = 刮目相看 guāmù-xiāngkàn
【刮目相看】guāmù-xiāngkàn〈成〉see sb. in a new light: 现在我们要对她～。We must do a reappraisal of her now.
【刮痧】guāshā〈名〉［中医］*guasha* [a treatment that involves scraping the patient's neck, chest or back with coin, etc.]
【刮水器】guāshuǐqì〈名〉windscreen wiper
【刮削】guāxiāo〈动〉scrape: ～器 scraper

括
guā ▸挺括 tǐngguā
▸kuò

栝
guā
【栝楼】guālóu〈名〉［植物］Chinese trichosanthes

鸹（鴰）
guā ▸老鸹 lǎoguā

guǎ

呱
guǎ ▸拉呱儿 lāguǎr
▸gū, guā

剐（剮）
guǎ〈动〉1（割肉）cut into pieces: ▸千刀万～ 2（划破）scrape: 脸上～了一道深深的口子 inflict a nasty cut on the face ‖ 她的腿被石头～伤了。She scraped her leg against a stone.

寡
guǎ〈形〉1（少）few: ▸～廉鲜耻，沉默～言 2（死了丈夫）widowed: ▸～妇，～居 3〈套〉（我）I: ▸～人 4（淡而无味）tasteless: ▸清汤～水
【寡不敌众】guǎbùdízhòng〈成〉be hopelessly out-numbered
【寡淡】guǎdàn〈形〉dull: ～无味 be tasteless
【寡断】guǎduàn〈形〉indecisive
【寡恩】guǎ'ēn〈形〉ungrateful
【寡妇】guǎfu〈名〉widow: 她三十岁上就成了～。She was widowed at the age of 30.
【寡妇门前是非多】guǎfu ménqián shìfēi duō〈俗〉slander gathers round a widow's door
【寡合】guǎhé〈形〉unsociable: 落落～ be aloof in social contexts
【寡欢】guǎhuān〈形〉joyless: ▸郁郁～
【寡见鲜闻】guǎjiàn-xiǎnwén〈成〉see little of the world and be ill-informed
【寡居】guǎjū〈动〉be widowed: 她母亲已～多年。Her mother has been widowed for many years.
【寡廉鲜耻】guǎlián-xiǎnchǐ〈成〉be shameless and unscrupulous: 那家伙真是～。Nothing can embarrass that guy.
【寡母】guǎmǔ〈名〉widow with children: 孤儿～ a widow and her child
【寡情】guǎqíng〈形〉unfeeling: ～少义 be cold-hearted
【寡人】guǎrén〈代〉〈古〉[of a feudal ruler] I
【寡头】guǎtóu〈名〉magnate: 金融～ financial magnate
【寡头政治】guǎtóu zhèngzhì〈名〉oligarchy
【寡味】guǎwèi〈形〉〈书〉1（指滋味）tasteless: 饭菜～ unpalatable food 2（指意味）dull: 讲话索然～ be insipid in speech
【寡言】guǎyán〈形〉taciturn: ▸沉默～
【寡欲】guǎyù〈形〉temperate: ▸清心～

guà

卦
guà〈名〉1（指符号）divinatory symbols: 卜～ divine by the Eight Trigrams ‖ 八～ Eight Trigrams 2（指行

为）divination: 给人算～ read sb.'s fortune
【卦辞】guàcí〈名〉hexagram statement

诖（詿） guà〈动〉〈书〉 1（欺骗）deceive 2（牵累）implicate
【诖误】guàwù〈动〉〈书〉be implicated in some trouble

挂（掛） guà
A〈动〉1（悬挂）hang (up): ～蚊帐 put up a mosquito-net ‖ 墙上～着一幅油画。An oil painting was hanging on the wall. ‖ 他腰间～了一大串钥匙。A large ring of keys was hooked to his belt. 2（惦念）care for: ～在心上 have sth. on one's mind ▸～记，～念，～心 3（表面带着）be coated (with): 窗户上～了一层霜。The window was frosted over. ‖ 她脸上～着微笑。There was a smile on her face. 4（搁置）put aside: 这事先～一～，下次开会再说吧。Let's put this matter to one side until the next meeting. 5（钩住）get caught: 钉子～破了裤子。The trousers caught on a nail and tore. ‖ 另一节车厢已～上了。Another railway carriage has been hooked on. ‖ 风筝～在屋顶上了。The kite got caught on the roof. 6（结束通话）hang up: 我还没来得及回答，他便把电话～了。Before I could reply, he hung up. 7（打电话）put (sb.) through: 你的电话～通了。Your call has been put through. ‖ 她一回来就给我～了电话。She called through to me as soon as she came back. 8（登记）register: 给我～外科。I'd like to register for surgery.
B〈量〉1（指成串的东西）string: 一～鞭炮 a string of firecrackers ‖ 一～珠子 a string of pearls 2（指畜力车）[for a carriage]: 一～马车 a horse and cart
【挂碍】guà'ài〈名〉worry: 心中没有～ have no worries
【挂不住】guàbuzhù〈动〉〈方〉lose control of one's feelings: 别让他脸上～。Don't embarrass him.
【挂彩】guàcǎi〈动〉1（表庆贺）decorate for festive occasions 2（指负伤）be wounded in action: 连长～了。The company commander was wounded in action.
【挂车】guàchē〈名〉trailer
【挂齿】guàchǐ〈动〉〈书〉mention: 区区小事，何足～。Such a small thing is hardly worth mentioning.
【挂锄】guàchú〈动〉［农业］finish hoeing
【挂挡】guàdǎng〈动〉change gear: 挂倒挡 put into reverse ‖ 挂头/二挡 change to first/second gear
【挂斗】guàdǒu〈名〉trailer
【挂钩】guàgōu A〈动〉1（指车厢）couple 2〈喻〉（建立联系）link: 厂校～ establish a link-up between a school and a factory ‖ 养老金与消费品价格～。Pensions are linked to consumer prices. B〈名〉hook
【挂冠】guàguān〈动〉〈旧〉〈喻〉resign from office
【挂果】guàguǒ〈动〉bear fruit: 苹果树今年～早。The apple trees are producing fruit early this year.
【挂号】guàhào〈动〉1（指在医院）register: ～请排队。Please queue up to register. 2（指邮寄）send by registered post: 这封信要～吗？Do you want to have the letter sent registered?
【挂号信】guàhàoxìn〈名〉registered letter
【挂红】guàhóng〈动〉hang up red streamers for a celebration
【挂花】guàhuā〈动〉1（指树）blossom: 果树都已经～了。All the fruit trees have blossomed already. 2 = 挂彩 guàcǎi 2
【挂怀】guàhuái〈动〉〈书〉be concerned about: 区区小事，不必～。Don't worry yourself over such a little thing.
【挂幌子】guà huǎngzi〈动〉〈方〉1（指店铺）put up a shop sign 2〈喻〉（显露）reveal: 她假装没事，但其实很难堪，脸上都～了。She pretended to be calm, but her blushes told of her embarrassment.
【挂火】guàhuǒ〈动〉〈方〉be furious
【挂记】guàji〈动〉keep thinking about: 家里的事用不着他～。He has no worries about his family.
【挂甲】guàjiǎ〈动〉〈旧〉〈喻〉retire from the army: ～归田 leave the army and live in the countryside
【挂件】guàjiàn〈名〉pendant ornament
【挂靠】guàkào〈动〉be attached to a major department: ～单位 subsidiary unit ‖ 该协会～地方政府。The association is attached to the local government.
【挂累】guàlěi〈动〉〈书〉implicate: 没有任何～ not be implicated in any way ‖ 受此事件～的人很多。Many people are involved in the case.
【挂历】guàlì〈名〉wall calendar
【挂镰】guàlián〈动〉［农业］complete the year's harvesting
【挂零】guàlíng〈动〉be around: 年纪四十～ be 40 odd ‖ 到会人数四百～。There were 400 odd people at the meeting.
【挂漏】guàlòu〈动〉omit: ～之处，在所难免 cannot be free from errors
【挂虑】guàlǜ〈动〉〈书〉keep thinking about: 这里的事有我，你不必～。You don't have to worry yourself about things here. I will take care of them.
【挂面】guàmiàn〈名〉dried noodles
【挂名】guàmíng〈动〉1（列上姓名）put one's own name (to sb. else's work) 2（无实权）be nominal: 他只是个～主席，没有实权。He's a chairman in name only and no longer retains his post.
【挂名夫妻】guàmíng fūqī〈名〉nominal couple
【挂念】guàniàn〈动〉worry about: ～某人的安全 be concerned for sb.'s safety ‖ 你走后我们非常～。We have missed you badly since you were gone.
【挂拍】guàpāi〈动〉1（指退役）[of tennis, table tennis or badminton players] retire 2（指结束）[of a tennis, table tennis or badminton game] be over: 本次世界乒乓球锦标赛昨日～。The World Table Tennis Championships ended yesterday.
【挂牌】guàpái〈动〉1（指单位、机构）officially open an establishment: 外事办公室昨天～办公。The Foreign Affairs Office was officially opened yesterday. 2（指医生、律师等）start up: ～营业 set up business 3（指胸牌）wear a name plate 4（指公司）be listed on the stock market 5（指体育俱乐部）announce the transfer list
【挂牌公司】guàpái gōngsī〈名〉listed company
【挂牌股票】guàpái gǔpiào〈名〉listed stock
【挂屏】guàpíng〈名〉a set of hanging scrolls of painting or calligraphy
【挂牵】guàqiān = 牵挂 qiānguà
【挂欠】guàqiàn〈动〉buy sth. on credit
【挂失】guàshī〈动〉report a loss: 你丢了支票，向银行～了吗？Did you report the loss of your cheque to the bank?
【挂帅】guàshuài〈动〉be in command: 亲自～ take command in person ‖ 主任～ with the director taking command
【挂锁】guàsuǒ〈名〉padlock
【挂毯】guàtǎn〈名〉tapestry
【挂图】guàtú〈名〉1（指地图）wall map 2（指图表）hanging chart
【挂孝】guàxiào〈动〉wear mourning
【挂心】guàxīn〈动〉worry about
【挂靴】guàxuē〈动〉hang up one's boots: 她最终决定～。She has finally decided to hang up her boots.
【挂羊头，卖狗肉】guà yángtóu, mài gǒuròu〈俗〉〈喻〉offer chaff for grain
【挂一漏万】guàyī-lòuwàn〈成〉far from being complete
【挂衣钩】guàyīgōu〈名〉clothes-hook
【挂账】guàzhàng〈动〉run an account: 你是现在付款，还是～呢？Are you paying now or putting it on credit?
【挂职】guàzhí〈动〉1（指临时承担）hold a temporary leading post to gain experience 2（指保留原职）serve in a lower level unit for a short period of time while retaining one's position in the previous unit 3（指暂停职责）suspend duties
【挂钟】guàzhōng〈名〉wall clock
【挂轴】guàzhóu〈名〉hanging scroll

褂 guà〈名〉Chinese-style unlined jacket: 马～ mandarin jacket
【褂儿】guàr〈名〉Chinese-style unlined jacket: 短～ short gown ▸大～
【褂子】guàzi〈名〉Chinese-style unlined upper garment: 一件～ a short gown

guāi

乖[1] guāi〈形〉1（聪明）clever: 学～了 become wiser ‖ 他的女儿嘴挺～。His daughter is a real sweetie. ▸～巧 2（听话）obedient: ～孩子 obedient child

乖[2] guāi〈书〉
A〈动〉go against: 与原意相～ not in conformity with the original intention
B〈形〉abnormal: ▸～戾，～谬
【乖舛】guāichuǎn〈形〉〈书〉1（错误）false 2（不顺利）unlucky: 处境～ be badly circumstanced ‖ 命途～ be unlucky in life
【乖乖】guāiguāi A〈形〉well-behaved: 小男孩～地回家去了。The boy went home obediently. ‖ 小偷最后还是～地讲了真话。At last the thief cooperated and told the truth. B〈名〉[to a child] darling
【乖乖】guāiguai〈叹〉(good) gracious: ～，外面真冷！Oh God! It's really cold outside!
【乖蹇】guāijiǎn〈形〉〈书〉unlucky: 时运～ be unlucky
【乖觉】guāijué〈形〉quick: 松鼠对危险～得很。Squirrels are very alert to danger.
【乖戾】guāilì〈形〉（指行为）perverse;（指性格）disagreeable: 脾气～的老头 ill-tempered old man
【乖谬】guāimiù〈形〉absurd: ～难解 be too absurd to be understood
【乖僻】guāipì〈形〉eccentric: 性情～ be rather eccentric
【乖巧】guāiqiǎo〈形〉1（讨人喜欢）cute: ～的孩子 cute child 2（机灵）quick
【乖张】guāizhāng〈形〉1（怪僻）eccentric and unreasonable: 行为～ be rather eccentric in behaviour ‖ 脾气～的人 person of peevish temper 2〈书〉（不顺）unlucky: 命运～ be unlucky in life

g

掴（摑） guāi〈动〉slap: ～了他一巴掌 slap him on the face
▸guó

guǎi

拐¹（柺） guǎi〈名〉1（拐棍）walking stick: ▸～棍, ～杖 2（供患腿疾者使用）crutch: 架着双～走路 walk on crutches

拐² guǎi
A〈动〉1（跛）limp: 一瘸一～地走 walk with a limp 2（转弯）take a turn: ～进一条小巷 turn off into a narrow street ‖ 往右～ turn right
B ▸p. 691〈数〉seven [used for the numeral '7' when speaking of figures]: 幺～洞～ one seven zero seven

拐³ guǎi〈动〉1（指人）abduct: 孩子被人～走了。The child has been abducted. 2（指财物）swindle: ～款潜逃 swindle sb. out of his money and then take flight

【拐棒】guǎibàng〈名〉crooked stick
【拐脖儿】guǎibór〈名〉pipe elbow
【拐带】guǎidài〈动〉abduct: ～小孩勒索钱财 kidnap a child for ransom
【拐点】guǎidiǎn〈名〉break point
【拐棍】guǎigùn〈名〉1〈本〉walking stick: 拄着～走路 walk with a stick 2〈喻〉assistant: 汉语拼音是识字的～。Hanyu Pinyin helps with learning characters.
【拐角】guǎijiǎo ▸p. 781〈名〉corner: 过了～就是那家商店。The shop is just around the corner.
【拐卖】guǎimài〈动〉kidnap and sell: ～妇女 traffic in women
【拐骗】guǎipiàn〈动〉1（指钱财）swindle: ～钱财 cheat sb. out of his money 2（指人）abduct: ～儿童 abduct children
【拐弯】guǎiwān A〈动〉1 ▸p. 781（指方向）turn: 拐了一个大弯 make a great bend ‖ 在第一个路口右～ take the first right 2（指思想或说话）make an about turn: 思想还没有～。The thinking still hasn't changed. B〈名〉turning: 这条路有不少急～。The road makes many sudden turns.
【拐弯抹角】guǎiwān-mòjiǎo〈成〉1（指走路）proceed along a zigzag road: 我们在黑暗中～地往他家走。We zigzagged to his home in the dark. 2〈喻〉（指表达）talk in a roundabout way: ～地暗示 hint obliquely ‖ 她～地问了一个问题。She raised a question in a roundabout way.
【拐杖】guǎizhàng〈名〉walking stick: 拄～ support oneself with a stick
【拐子】guǎizi〈名〉1〈口〉（跛子）cripple 2（指工具）I-shaped reel 3（绑架者）abductor 4（骗子）swindler

guài

怪 guài
A〈形〉strange: ～念头 strange idea ‖ ～人 eccentric character ‖ ～石 unusual rock
B〈动〉1（感到奇怪）find strange: 那没什么可～的。There is nothing surprising here. 2（责怪）blame: 都～我不好。I should say that I am very much to blame. ‖ 你只能～自己。You have only yourself to blame.
C〈副〉unusually: 觉得～难堪的 feel rather embarrassed
D〈名〉monster: ▸鬼～, 妖～
【怪不得】guàibude A〈副〉no wonder: ～你没走，原来你妻子在这儿。So that's why you didn't go — your wife is here. B〈动〉be not to blame: 你考试不及格，这可～老师。Your teacher is not to blame for your failure in the exam.
【怪诞】guàidàn〈形〉weird: ～的故事 weird story ‖ ～的理论 whimsical theory
【怪诞不经】guàidàn-bùjīng〈成〉weird: 这种想法真是～。This idea is simply grotesque.
【怪话】guàihuà〈名〉1（怪诞的话）weird remark 2（指牢骚）unreasonable complaint
【怪谲】guàijué〈形〉〈书〉weird
【怪里怪气】guàili-guàiqì〈成〉〈贬〉peculiar: ～的年轻人 weird young man ‖ 她戴那顶帽子～的。In that hat she looks a perfect sight. ‖ 他讲话腔调～的。He speaks in a peculiar tone.
【怪模怪样】guàimú-guàiyàng〈成〉odd-looking: 那部电影中的人物都～的。All the people in the film were odd-looking.
【怪癖】guàipǐ〈名〉curious habit: 不少作家都有～。Many writers have their own peculiarities.
【怪僻】guàipì〈形〉eccentric: 这家伙行为～。This guy's behaviour is pretty odd.
【怪圈】guàiquān〈名〉vicious circle: 要打破这一～实属不易。It would be really difficult to break this vicious circle.
【怪声怪气】guàishēng-guàiqì〈成〉strange: 说话～ speak in a peculiar voice
【怪事】guàishì〈名〉oddity: 书店不卖小说，岂非～? Isn't it strange for a bookstore not to sell novels?
【怪胎】guàitāi〈名〉1［医学］congenital malformation or anomaly 2〈喻〉（怪人）crank
【怪味】guàiwèi〈名〉odd taste: ～豆 strange-tasting bean
【怪物】guàiwu〈名〉1（指妖魔）monster: 你穿着这些衣服看上去真像个～。You do look a freak in these clothes. 2（指人）eccentric
【怪象】guàixiàng〈名〉strange phenomenon
【怪异】guàiyì A〈形〉unusual: ～的声音 strange voice B〈名〉strange phenomenon
【怪怨】guàiyuàn〈动〉blame: 我只能～自己。I only have myself to blame.
【怪罪】guàizuì〈动〉blame: 这事不能～他。He is not to blame for it.

guān

关（關） guān
A〈动〉1（合拢）close: ～抽屉 shut a drawer ‖ 把门窗～好 secure the doors and windows 2（使不出来）shut away: 把某人～进监狱 put sb. behind bars ‖ 老虎被～在笼子里。The tiger is imprisoned in a cage. 3（倒闭）shut down: 由于缺乏资金，商店只好～了。The shop had to be shut down because of funds. 4（使停止工作）turn off: ～电视 switch off the television ‖ ～灯 turn off the light 5（牵涉）involve: 有～人员 people concerned ‖ 这不～你的事。It has nothing to do with you. ▸～心, ～照 6〈旧〉（发放）issue or receive payment: ▸～饷
B〈名〉1（关口）mountain pass:〈喻〉把好质量～ guarantee quality ▸～口, 过～ 2（山海关）Shanhaiguan Pass: ▸～东, ～内 3（关厢）area just outside a city gate: ▸城～ 4（海关）customs: 通～ go through customs ▸～税, 报～, 海～ 5（指环节）difficulty: 产量突破百万大～ boost production over the million mark ‖ 在国外求学，首先要过语言～。Language is the first barrier to be crossed when studying abroad. 6（指时间）critical juncture: ▸～键, ～节, ～头
【关爱】guān'ài〈动〉take good care of: ～弱势群体 attend to the needs of marginalized groups
【关隘】guān'ài〈名〉〈书〉mountain pass: 把守～ guard a pass
【关碍】guān'ài〈动〉〈书〉impede: 这一变化对工人个人收入大有～。The change will seriously affect the personal income of workers.
【关闭】guānbì〈动〉1（合上）shut: ～厂门 close a factory door ‖ 屋子的门窗～着。The house is shut up. 2（停止营业）shut down: 他～了两家高能耗工厂。He shut down two high energy consumption factories.
【关岛】Guāndǎo〈名〉Guam
【关帝庙】guāndìmiào〈名〉temple of Lord Guan

> **关帝庙**
> Lord Guan was a general in the kingdom of Shu Han in the Three Kingdoms period. He was later deified, and became known in folklore as the God of Wealth (▸财神). His birthday is on the 13th day of the 5th month of the lunar calendar. The temples at which offerings are made to Lord Guan are known as Guandi temples.

【关东】Guāndōng〈名〉north-east China: 闯～ go and seek a livelihood in northeast China
【关防】guānfáng〈名〉1（防守）measures to forestall leakage of secrets: ～严密。Strict measures were taken to forestall leakage of secrets. 2〈书〉（要塞）government/army seal
【关公门前耍大刀】Guāngōng ménqián shuǎ dàdāo〈俗〉teach one's grandmother how to suck eggs
【关顾】guāngù〈动〉care and concern: 谢谢～! Thanks for your care and concern.
【关乎】guānhū〈动〉concern: 这些计划～每个人的前途问题。These plans have a bearing on everyone's future.
【关怀】guānhuái〈动〉show loving care for: ～青年一代的成长 care for the growth of the younger generation ‖ 亲切～ kind considerations ‖ 无微不至的～ meticulous care
【关怀备至】guānhuái bèizhì〈成〉show the utmost solicitude
【关键】guānjiàn A〈名〉1（门闩）door bolt 2（指因素）key: 抓住～ possess the key to a problem ‖ 这个案子的～在于她的证词。This case stands on her testimony. B〈形〉crucial: ～人物 key person ‖ 到～时候 when it comes to the crunch ‖ 起～作用 play a pivotal role
【关键词】guānjiàncí〈名〉keyword: ～索引 keyword index ‖ 输入～ enter a keyword
【关键期】guānjiànqī〈名〉critical period: 企业转型的～ critical period for the transformation of the business ‖ 虫害繁殖～ critical stage in insect breeding
【关节】guānjié〈名〉1［解剖］joint: ～疼 ache in the joints ‖ 膝～ knee joint 2（关键环节）critical point: 这正是问

题的～所在。This is where the crux of the problem lies. 3▸（关键人物） someone who is of vital importance and who might block the progress of certain matter: 打～ bribe sb. into doing sth.

【关节炎】guānjiéyán ▸**p. 50** 〈名〉［医学］arthritis: 风湿性～ rheumatic arthritis

【关口】guānkǒu〈名〉 1▸（指地方） strategic pass: 把守～ guard a pass 2▸（关头） key point: 在紧要～ at a critical juncture

【关里】Guānlǐ = 关内 Guānnèi

【关连】guānlián = 关联 guānlián

【关联】guānlián〈动〉 be related: 没有～ have no connection with ‖ 各部门之间是相互～的。 Different sectors are interrelated.

【关联词】guānliáncí〈名〉［语言］connective

【关联方】guānliánfāng〈名〉 affiliated party: 彻查控股公司及其他～进行内幕交易的情况 thoroughly investigate the situation involving the holding company and other affiliated parties engaging in insider trading activities

【关贸总协定】Guānmào Zǒngxiédìng〈简称〉= 关税及贸易总协定

【关门】guānmén **A**〈动〉 1▸（暂停营业） close;（永久停业） close down: 杂货店下午5点～。 The grocery closes at 5 pm. 2▸〈喻〉（无回旋余地） close the door on: ～捉贼 close the door to catch the thief inside ‖ 和谈四方都不应～。 Any of the four sides should not close the door on further peace talks. **B**〈形〉 final: ～之作 one's last article ▸～弟子

【关门打狗】guānmén-dǎgǒu〈俗〉〈喻〉 block the enemy's retreat and then destroy them

【关门大吉】guānmén-dàjí〈成〉close down for good

【关门弟子】guānmén dìzǐ〈名〉 final student

【关内】Guānnèi〈名〉 area to the west of the Shanhaiguan Pass and to the east of the Jiayuguan Pass

【关卡】guānqiǎ〈名〉 1▸（为征税） tax office outpost 2▸（检查站） checkpoint: 设～ set up a checkpoint

【关切】guānqiè〈动〉 be deeply concerned: 表示极大的～ express the greatest concern ‖ 对他的不幸深表～ express deep concern at his misfortune

【关塞】guānsài〈名〉 fortress on a strategic pass

【关山】guānshān〈名〉forts and mountains

【关山迢递】guānshān-tiáodì〈成〉 a long journey

【关涉】guānshè〈动〉 concern: 这件事～到每个人的利益。 The matter directly concerns everyone's interests.

【关税】guānshuì〈名〉tariff: 降低～ reduce a tariff ‖ 征收～ levy a tariff (on)

【关税壁垒】guānshuì bìlěi〈名〉 customs barrier

【关税及贸易总协定】Guānshuì jí Màoyì Zǒngxiédìng〈名〉 General Agreement on Tariffs and Trade (GATT)

【关头】guāntóu〈名〉 critical moment: 紧要～ critical juncture ‖ 民族存亡的历史～ historic moment when the fate of the nation hangs in the balance ‖ 危急～ critical point

【关外】Guānwài〈名〉 area to the east of the Shanhaiguan Pass and to the west of the Jiayuguan Pass

【关系】guānxì **A**〈名〉 1▸（相互联系） relationship:（与某国）建立外交～ establish diplomatic relations (with another country) ‖ 跟某人发生～ have sexual relations with sb. ‖ 血缘～ blood relation ‖ 某些疾病与吸烟有直接～。 Certain diseases can be directly linked to cigarette smoking. ‖ 那件事与你一点～都没有。 That has nothing to do with you. ‖ 他和妻子～破裂了。 He and his wife broke up. 2▸（影响） importance: 对他～重大 be of no small concern to him ‖ 那些细节对主要问题～不大。 Those details have little bearing on the main issue. 3▸（原因） reason: 因年龄/健康～而辞职 resign on account of advanced age/poor health ‖ 由于天气～，比赛不得不延期进行。 The match has to be postponed on account of the weather. 4▸（与组织的联系） credentials: 工资～ salary credentials ‖ 组织～ Party membership credentials 5▸（私人交情） back-door connection: 拉～ try to form ties for personal gains 6▸（人际关系网络） *guanxi*: 培养/扩大～ develop/broaden one's *guanxi* ‖ ～网会影响一个人事业的成败。 *Guanxi* can affect a person's success in career. **B**〈动〉 concern: ～国计民生 involve the interests of the state and the people ‖ ～国民经济命脉 concern the life-blood of the national economy

【关系户】guānxihù〈名〉 connection: 她只是我生意上的～。 She is just a business connection of mine.

【关系学】guānxìxué〈名〉 art of cultivating good personal relations

【关饷】guānxiǎng〈动〉〈旧〉issue pay for soldiers

【关心】guānxīn〈动〉 care for: ～国家大事 be concerned about the major issues of one's country ‖ 双方共同～的问题 matter of mutual concern

【关押】guānyā〈动〉 lock up: 犯罪嫌疑人被～在警察局。 The suspect was held in custody in the police station.

【关于】guānyú〈介〉 about: ～孩子的教育问题 with regard to the children's education ‖ ～这个问题，请大家发表意见。 Please can everybody give their opinions on this issue.

【关张】guānzhāng〈动〉 shut down

【关照】guānzhào〈动〉 1▸（照顾） take care of: 母亲不在，谁来～孩子？ Who will look after the child in his mother's absence? ‖ 请多多～。 Please take very good care. 2▸（嘱咐） notify: 医生特别～他不要再抽烟。 The doctor told him specifically not to smoke any more.

【关中】Guānzhōng〈名〉 Central Shaanxi: ～平原 Central Shaanxi Plain

【关注】guānzhù〈动〉 pay close attention: ～亚洲的发展和繁荣 closely follow Asia's development and progress towards prosperity ‖ 引起广泛～ attract widespread attention

【关注度】guānzhùdù〈名〉 level of interest: 各国对上海世博会的～ the level of interest aroused in each country by the Shanghai World Expo

【关子】guānzi〈名〉 climax: ▸卖～

观（觀）guān

A〈动〉 watch: ～天象 observe movements of planets and stars ▸～察，～光，坐井～天
B〈名〉 1▸（外观） view: ▸改～，外～，壮～ 2▸（观点） outlook: 历史～ historical outlook ▸价值～，世界～
▸guàn

【观测】guāncè〈动〉 1▸（观察） survey: ～风力 gauge the intensity of wind ‖ 气象～站 meteorological observation station 2▸（侦察） keep a lookout for: ～敌情 keep a lookout for the enemy

【观测点】guāncèdiǎn〈名〉 observation point

【观测台】guāncètái〈名〉 observatory

【观测员】guāncèyuán ▸**p. 966**〈名〉 observer

【观察】guānchá〈动〉observe: ～蚂蚁的习性 observe the habits of ants ‖ 住院～ be hospitalized for observation ‖ 留心～ keep watch

【观察家】guāncháj iā ▸**p. 966**〈名〉 observer: 政治～ political observer

【观察哨】guāncháshào〈名〉 observation post

【观察所】guānchásuǒ〈名〉［军事］observation post

【观察员】guāncháyuán ▸**p. 966**〈名〉 observer: 军事～ military observer

【观潮派】guāncháopài〈名〉 person who takes a wait-and-see attitude

【观点】guāndiǎn〈名〉 1▸（看法） viewpoint: 坚持自己的～ stick to one's own point of view ‖ 同意某人的～ agree with sb.'s stand ‖ 群众～ mass viewpoint 2▸（立场） political position

【观风】guānfēng〈动〉 be on the lookout

【观感】guāngǎn〈名〉 impressions: 旅日～ impressions of Japan

【观光】guānguāng〈动〉 go sightseeing: 到各地旅游～ visit places and see things ‖ ～客 tourist

【观光农业】guānguāng nóngyè〈名〉 agricultural tourism

【观光厅】guānguāngtīng〈名〉 viewing hall

【观光团】guānguāngtuán〈名〉tour group

【观看】guānkàn〈动〉watch: ～演出 watch a performance ‖ 通过电视～比赛 watch a match on television

【观礼】guānlǐ〈动〉 attend a ceremony

【观礼台】guānlǐtái〈名〉 viewing stand: 登上～ ascend a viewing stand

【观摩】guānmó〈动〉 visit and draw on each other's experience: ～教学 demonstration lecture ‖ ～演出 demonstration for emulation and exchange of experience

【观念】guānniàn〈名〉 concept: 改变教育～ change the concept of education ‖ 家庭～很强 very family conscious ‖ 缺乏时间～ lack any concept of time

【观念形态】guānniàn xíngtài〈名〉 ideology

【观赏】guānshǎng〈动〉 enjoy: ～烟火 enjoy a fireworks display ‖ ～演出 attend a performance

【观赏艺术】guānshǎng yìshù〈名〉 visual arts

【观赏鱼】guānshǎngyú〈名〉 ornamental fish

【观赏植物】guānshǎng zhíwù〈名〉 decorative plant

【观世音】Guānshìyīn = 观音菩萨 Guānyīn Púsa

【观望】guānwàng〈动〉 1▸（旁观） wait and see: 持～态度 take a wait-and-see attitude ‖ 在一旁～ stand to one side and watch 2▸（看） look around: 四下～ look around

【观象台】guānxiàngtái〈名〉 observatory

【观音】Guānyīn = 观音菩萨 Guānyīn Púsa

【观音菩萨】Guānyīn Púsà ▸**p. 274**〈名〉 the Bodhisattva Guanyin

【观音粉】guānyīnfěn = 观音土 guānyīntǔ

【观音土】guānyīntǔ〈名〉 white clay eaten by victims of famine to appease their hunger

【观音竹】guānyīnzhú〈名〉 fern-leaf hedge bamboo

【观瞻】guānzhān **A**〈名〉 sight: 有碍～ be unsightly ‖ 以壮～ make a better sight **B**〈动〉 enjoy a sight: 寺庙重新开放后，

g

～者络绎不绝。 The temple has been drawing big crowds since it was reopened.

观音

Guan Yin is known as the *bodhisattva* of great mercy. In Chinese temples this *bodhisattva* often takes a female form. Chinese Buddhists traditionally see her as one of the four *bodhisattvas*. The place of ritual associated with her is Putuo Mountain in Zhejiang Province. Guan Yin is also popularly known as the goddess of childbirth, and she is usually represented as a standing figure with a female headdress, a cape, and a long shawl, holding a vase and a willow branch. The vase is filled with sweet dew, symbolizing the great mercy that she sprinkles over humankind. A boy and girl are often depicted on either side of her. The girl is the daughter of the dragon king, and the boy is the Buddhist disciple, Sudhana.

【观战】guānzhàn〈动〉 watch a battle

【观照】guānzhào〈动〉 scrutinize: ～传统文化 carefully observe traditional culture

【观止】guānzhǐ〈动〉 satisfy one's viewing needs: ▸叹为～

【观众】guānzhòng〈名〉 audience: 电视～ television viewers ‖ 电影～ film audience ‖ 这座体育场可容纳六万名～。 The stadium can hold 60,000 spectators.

【观众席】guānzhòngxí〈名〉 **1**（指剧院）auditorium **2**（指体育场） grandstand

纶（綸）guān

▸lún

【纶巾】guānjīn〈名〉〈方〉 scarf with a blue ribbon

g

官 guān

〈名〉 **1**（官员） government official: ～太太 wife of an official ‖ 外交～ diplomat **2**（官方） official: ▸～办, ～价, ～商 **3**（公共） public: ▸～话 **4**（器官） organ: ▸感～, 五～

【官办】guānbàn〈形〉 government-run: ～企业 state-owned enterprise

【官报私仇】guānbào-sīchóu ＝ 公报私仇 gōngbào-sīchóu

【官本位】guānběnwèi〈名〉 official rank standard

【官逼民反】guānbī-mínfǎn〈成〉 official exploitation drives the people to rebellion

【官兵】guānbīng〈名〉 officers and men: 处理～关系 handle the relationship between officers and the rank and file ‖ ～一致 unity between officers and men

【官差】guānchāi〈名〉〈旧〉 **1**（指出差） public business: 出～ go on a public errand **2**（指人） petty officer

【官场】guānchǎng〈名〉〈贬〉 official circles: ～丑闻 scandal in officialdom

【官倒】guāndǎo〈名〉 **1**（指行为）official profiteering **2**（指人） official speculator

【官邸】guāndǐ〈名〉 official residence: 首相～ prime minister's residence ‖ 总统～ president's residence

【官方】guānfāng〈名〉 government: 来自～的消息 information from an official source ‖ ～人士 government officials ‖ ～统计数据 official figures

【官方语言】guānfāng yǔyán ▸**p. 918**〈名〉 official language

【官费】guānfèi〈名〉〈旧〉 fund from the government: ～留学 study abroad on state funding

【官俸】guānfèng〈名〉〈旧〉 salaries of government officials

【官服】guānfú〈名〉〈旧〉 official robe

【官府】guānfǔ〈名〉〈旧〉 **1**（行政机关） local authorities **2**（官吏） administrative body

【官复原职】guānfùyuánzhí〈成〉 be restored to one's former post

【官官相护】guānguān-xiānghù〈成〉 officials protect each other

【官话】guānhuà〈名〉 **1**〈旧〉（普通话） Mandarin (Chinese) **2**（官腔） official jargon

【官宦】guānhuàn〈名〉〈旧〉 government official: ～人家 official's family

【官价】guānjià〈名〉 official price

【官架子】guānjiàzi〈名〉 bureaucratic airs

【官阶】guānjiē〈名〉 official rank

【官爵】guānjué〈名〉〈旧〉 official rank

【官军】guānjūn〈名〉〈旧〉 government troops

【官吏】guānlì〈名〉〈旧〉 government official

【官僚】guānliáo〈名〉 **1**（官吏） bureaucrats: ～作风 bureaucracy ‖ 这个人真～! This person is so bureaucratic! **2**（官僚作风） bureaucracy

【官僚主义】guānliáozhǔyì〈名〉 bureaucracy: 克服～ overcome bureaucracy

【官僚资本】guānliáo zīběn〈名〉 capital owned by the bureaucratic-capitalist class: ～主义 bureaucratic capitalism

【官僚资产阶级】guānliáo zīchǎnjiējí〈名〉 bureaucratic-capitalist class

【官迷】guānmí〈名〉 person who has a strong desire for power: 他是个～。 He is greedy for power.

【官名】guānmíng〈名〉〈旧〉 **1**（学名） formal name **2**（官衔） official title

【官能】guānnéng〈名〉 faculty

【官能性】guānnéngxìng〈形〉 functional

【官能症】guānnéngzhèng〈名〉 functional disease: 神经～ neurosis

【官气】guānqì〈名〉 bureaucratic airs: ～十足 put on excessive bureaucratic airs

【官腔】guānqiāng〈名〉 official jargon: 打～ speak in a bureaucratic tone

【官人】guānrén〈名〉〈旧〉 **1**（官员） government official **2**（指丈夫） my husband **3**（指男子） sir

【官商】guānshāng〈名〉 **1**（指商业） government-owned business **2**（指商人） bureaucrat-like personnel in a government-owned business **3**（官员与商人） officials and merchants

【官署】guānshǔ〈名〉 government office

【官司】guānsi〈名〉 **1**（诉讼） lawsuit: 打～ bring a lawsuit (against sb.) ▸吃～ **2**（争辩） battle of words: ▸笔墨～

【官厅】guāntīng〈名〉〈旧〉 government office

【官位】guānwèi〈名〉 official position

【官衔】guānxián〈名〉 official title

【官样文章】guānyàng-wénzhāng〈成〉 bureaucratic red tape

【官瘾】guānyǐn〈名〉 lust for power: ～很大 have a huge appetite for power

【官印】guānyìn〈名〉〈旧〉 official seal

【官员】guānyuán〈名〉 official: 高级～ high-level official ‖ 外交～ diplomatic official ‖ 政府～ government official

【官运】guānyùn〈名〉 luck in being promoted as an official

【官运亨通】guānyùn-hēngtōng〈成〉 have a successful official career

【官职】guānzhí〈名〉 official position

冠 guān

〈名〉 **1**（帽） hat: 衣～整齐 be neatly dressed ‖ 免～照片 bare-headed photograph ▸桂～, 怒发冲～, 王～ **2**（冠状物） hat-shaped thing: ▸花～, 鸡～, 树～ ▸guàn

【冠盖】guāngài〈名〉 **1**（指冠服和车盖） official hats and canopies **2**（指官吏） (high-ranking) officials: ～如云 a gathering of high officials

【冠冕】guānmiǎn **A**〈名〉 royal crown **B**〈形〉 stately

【冠冕堂皇】guānmiǎn-tánghuáng〈成〉 high-sounding: ～的话 high-sounding words

【冠心病】guānxīnbìng ▸**p. 50**〈名〉 coronary heart disease

【冠状动脉】guānzhuàng dòngmài〈名〉 coronary artery: ～硬化 coronary arteriosclerosis

【冠状动脉造影】guānzhuàng dòngmài zàoyǐng〈名〉 x-ray of the coronary arteries

【冠子】guānzi〈名〉 crown: 鸡～ crown

矜 guān

＝ 鳏 guān ▸jīn, qín

莞 guān

〈名〉 long-stem water grass ▸wǎn

倌 guān

〈名〉 **1**（侍候牲口者） herdsman: 马～儿 groom ‖ 羊～儿 shepherd **2**〈旧〉（干杂役者） hired hand: ▸堂～

棺 guān

〈名〉 coffin: 水晶～ crystal coffin ▸～材

【棺材】guāncai〈名〉 coffin; casket〈美〉: 楠木～ coffin made of nanmu wood

【棺床】guānchuáng〈名〉 coffin platform

【棺椁】guānguǒ〈名〉 **1**（棺和椁） inner and outer coffins **2**（棺材） coffin

【棺架】guānjià〈名〉 bier

【棺木】guānmù〈名〉 coffin

鳏（鰥）guān

A〈动〉 be widowed: ▸～夫

B〈名〉 widower

【鳏夫】guānfū〈名〉〈旧〉 widower: ～寡妇 widows and widowers

【鳏寡孤独】guān-guǎ-gū-dú〈成〉 incapacitated and helpless people

guǎn

馆（館、舘）guǎn

〈名〉 **1**（为提供食宿） accommodation for guests/tourists: ▸宾～, 旅～ **2**（住宅） mansion: ▸公～ **3**（指外交机构） embassy: ▸领事～, 使～ **4**（为陈列、开展活动） venue: 博物～, 体育～, 图书～ **5**〈旧〉（私塾） private school: 设～糊口 make a living by teaching privately ‖ 坐～ teach in a private school **6**（指店铺） service establishment: 印书～ publishing house ▸茶～, 照相～

【馆藏】guǎncáng **A**〈动〉 house: 那家图书馆～50万册图书。 The library houses 500,000 books. ‖ 这家博物馆～文物两万件。 This museum has a collection of 20,000 cultural relics. **B**〈名〉 collection: ～丰富 have a rich collection

【馆员】guǎnyuán〈名〉 librarian: 助理～ library assistant

【馆长】guǎnzhǎng〈名〉 curator: 博物馆/美术馆/图书馆～ curator of a museum/an art gallery/a library

【馆子】guǎnzi〈名〉〈口〉restaurant: 下～ go to a restaurant

管 guǎn

A〈名〉**1**（指乐器） wind instrument: ▸～弦乐, 单簧～ **2**（圆筒） tube: ▸钢～, 软～ **3**（管状物） valve: ▸电子～, 显像～ **4**［生理］ duct

B〈量〉[for tube-shaped objects]: 一～笛子 a flute ‖ 两～毛笔 two writing brushes

C〈动〉**1**（管理）administer: ～得宽 make everything one's own business ‖ 这一地区归陕西省～。 This district is under the jurisdiction of Shaanxi Province. **2**（负责） be in charge: ～家务 manage a household ‖ 主～一个分店 be in charge of a branch ‖ 这种事不属我～。 Such matters are beyond the scope of my charge. **3**（约束） subject sb. to discipline: ▸～教 **4**（过问） be concerned: ～闲事 concern oneself with other people's business ‖ 不要～别人的私事。 Don't interfere in others' personal affairs. ‖ 少～闲事! Mind your own business! **5**（提供） supply: ～吃～住 provide sb. with food and accommodation ‖ ～饱 guarantee adequate food

D〈连〉 despite: ～它天晴还是下雨，我都得回家。 Rain or shine, I must go home.

E〈介〉**1**（把） [used in the pattern 管…叫…] call: ～他叫"老板" call him 'boss' **2**〈方〉（向） to: 没钱～你爸要。 Go to your father if you need money.

【管保】guǎnbǎo〈动〉 guarantee: 我～这办法行。 I guarantee this method will work well.

【管不着】guǎnbuzháo〈动〉〈口〉have no right to interfere: 这事你～。 It's none of your business.

【管材】guǎncái〈名〉 tubing

【管道】guǎndào〈名〉**1**（管子） pipeline: ～公司 pipeline company ‖ ～破裂/泄漏 the pipe has burst/is leaking ‖ 煤气～ gas piping ‖ 污水～ sewage pipe **2**〈方〉（途径） channel: 对话～ dialogue channel

【管段】guǎnduàn〈名〉 beat

【管饭】guǎnfàn〈动〉 provide sb. with free meals

【管风琴】guǎnfēngqín ▸**p. 929**〈名〉 (pipe) organ

【管护】guǎnhù〈动〉 manage and protect: ～树林 manage and protect forests

【管家】guǎnjiā ▸**p. 966**〈名〉**1**（指家中） butler **2**（指单位里） manager

【管家婆】guǎnjiāpó〈名〉**1**（指女仆） chief female servant **2**（指主妇） female housekeeper

【管见】guǎnjiàn〈名〉〈谦〉 my humble opinion: 略陈～ briefly state my humble opinion ‖ ～所及 in my humble opinion

【管教】guǎnjiào〈动〉**1**（约束） discipline: ～孩子 discipline one's children ‖ 父亲对他们～很严。 The father is very strict with them. ‖ 这些孩子不听～。 These children were beyond control. **2**（劳动教养） reform through labour: ～干部 officer at a reformatory ‖ 解除～ relieved from surveillance and re-education through labour **3** = 管保 guǎnbǎo

【管教所】guǎnjiàosuǒ〈名〉 reformatory

【管界】guǎnjiè〈名〉**1**（指地区） jurisdiction zone **2**（指边界） boundary of an area under jurisdiction

【管井】guǎnjǐng〈名〉［水利］ tube well

【管控】guǎnkòng〈动〉manage and control

【管窥】guǎnkuī〈动〉〈书〉 have a limited understanding

【管窥蠡测】guǎnkuī-lícè〈成〉〈喻〉 be restricted in vision and shallow in understanding

【管理】guǎnlǐ **A**〈动〉**1**（料理） manage: ～国家大事 manage the overall situation of a country ‖ ～交通秩序 regulate the traffic ‖ ～不善 mismanage ‖ 精心～ manage with delicacy **2**（照看） look after: ～牲畜 tend the cattle ‖ 老师应当～好自己的学生。 Teachers ought to have good control over their classes. **B**〈名〉 management: 加强企业～ strengthen the administration of an enterprise ‖ ～人才 managerial talent ‖ ～条例 management regulations ‖ 城市～ city administration ‖ 物业～ property management

【管理处】guǎnlǐchù〈名〉 management office: 公园～ park office

【管理费】guǎnlǐfèi〈名〉 management fee

【管理局】guǎnlǐjú〈名〉 (bureau of) administration

【管理师】guǎnlǐshī ▸**p. 966**〈名〉 manager: 后勤/健康～ logistics/health manager

【管理委员会】guǎnlǐ wěiyuánhuì〈名〉 administration committee

【管理员】guǎnlǐyuán ▸**p. 966**〈名〉 attendant: 停车场～ parking attendant ‖ 养老院～ warden of a nursing home

【管路】guǎnlù〈名〉［机械］ pipeline

【管钳】guǎnqián〈名〉 pipe wrench

【管区】guǎnqū〈名〉district under jurisdiction

【管儿灯】guǎnrdēng〈名〉〈口〉 fluorescent lamp

【管事】guǎnshì **A**〈动〉 look after things: 这里谁～? Who's in charge here? **B**〈形〉 effective: 不～ be useless ‖ 这种药很～，一吃就见效。 This medicine has an immediate effect. **C**〈名〉〈旧〉 steward: 女～ stewardess

【管束】guǎnshù〈动〉 discipline: 严加～ keep under strict control

【管委会】guǎnwěihuì〈简称〉 = 管理委员会

【管辖】guǎnxiá〈动〉 have jurisdiction over: ～范围 limits of jurisdiction ‖ 该市～十个区县。 The city exercises control over ten districts and counties.

【管闲事】guǎn xiánshì〈动〉 meddle: 爱～的老太太 meddlesome old lady

【管弦乐】guǎnxiányuè〈名〉 orchestral music

【管弦乐队】guǎnxián yuèduì〈名〉 (symphony) orchestra

【管押】guǎnyā〈动〉 detain

【管涌】guǎnyǒng〈名〉 piping: 封堵～ stop up piping

【管用】guǎnyòng〈形〉 effective: 不～ be ineffective ‖ 只有父亲的话对这孩子～。 Only a word from his father has an effect on the child.

【管乐】guǎnyuè〈名〉 wind music: ～队 wind band

【管乐器】guǎnyuèqì〈名〉wind instrument

【管账】guǎnzhàng〈动〉 keep accounts

【管制】guǎnzhì〈动〉**1**（强制管理） control: ～灯火 enforce a blackout ‖ 交通～ traffic controls **2**（强制管束） put sb. under surveillance: ～劳动 labour under public surveillance ‖ 交群众～ put sb. under public surveillance

【管中窥豹】guǎnzhōng-kuībào〈成〉〈喻〉 have a limited knowledge

【管子】guǎnzi〈名〉 pipe: 水～ water pipe

【管子工】guǎnzigōng〈名〉 plumber

guàn

观（觀） guàn

〈名〉 Taoist temple: ▸道～

▸guān

贯（貫） guàn

A〈量〉〈旧〉 a string of 1,000 coins: ▸万～, 腰缠万～

B〈动〉**1**（贯通） pass through: ▸～穿, 如雷～耳 **2**（连通） link up: 一座山脉横～小岛南北。 A mountain chain connects the island from north to south. ▸～通 **3**（精通） be well versed in: 学～古今 be well versed in both ancient and modern learning **4**（衔接） file in/out: 鱼～而入/出 enter/leave in single file ▸连～

C〈名〉 one's native place: ▸籍～

【贯彻】guànchè〈动〉 carry out: 将计划～到底 carry a plan through to the end ‖ ～会议精神 act in the spirit of the conference

【贯穿】guànchuān〈动〉**1**（穿过） link up: 隧道～几座大山。 The tunnel runs through several mountains. **2** = 贯串 guànchuàn

【贯串】guànchuàn〈动〉**1**（穿过） penetrate: 她所有的小说都～着一种哀伤之情。 A feeling of sadness runs through all her novels. **2**（连贯） hang together: 前后意思～不起来。 The sum parts don't add up.

【贯通】guàntōng〈动〉**1**（精通） have a thorough knowledge: ～中西医学 be well versed in both traditional Chinese medicine and western medicine ‖ 豁然～ suddenly see everything clearly **2**（畅通） link up: 高速公路已全线～。 The expressway has been completely joined up.

【贯注】guànzhù〈动〉**1**（集中） concentrate: 全神～ be wholly absorbed **2**（连贯） be connected: 这些概念一气～，构成了一种理论。 These ideas are well connected to form a theory.

冠 guàn

A〈动〉**1**〈书〉（戴帽子） put on a hat **2**（出众） rank first: 勇～三军 distinguish oneself by being peerless in battle **3**（加上） precede with: 在名字前应～以头衔。 Names should be preceded with titles.

B〈名〉 champion: 三连～ three-time champion ‖ 在歌咏比赛中夺～ rank first in a singing contest

▸guān

【冠词】guàncí〈名〉 article: 定/不定～ definite/indefinite article

【冠军】guànjūn〈名〉 champion: 争夺～ vie for the championship ‖ 奥运～ Olympic title-holder ‖ 全能～ all-round champion ‖ 卫冕～ defending champion

【冠军杯】guànjūnbēi〈名〉 champions cup

【冠军赛】guànjūnsài〈名〉 championships

【冠名】guànmíng〈动〉 give a name to

【冠名权】guànmíngquán〈名〉 right to name: 获得～ obtain the right to name

掼（摜） guàn

〈动〉〈方〉**1**（扔） toss: ▸～纱帽 **2**（摔倒） fall: ～跟头 trip and fall

【掼纱帽】guàn shāmào〈动〉〈旧〉〈喻〉 quit a government post in anger

惯（慣） guàn

〈动〉**1**（习惯） be used to: 她一个人生活～了。 She was

used to the solitary life. ‖ 我吃不～米饭。 I'm not used to rice. 2 (溺爱) spoil: 别把孩子～坏了。 Don't spoil your child.
【惯常】guànchánɡ A〈形〉 customary: ～的做法 regular practice B〈副〉 most of the time: ～带孩子去公园玩 often take the children to play in the park C〈名〉 the usual: ～坐的椅子 one's usual chair
【惯犯】guànfàn〈名〉 habitual offender
【惯匪】guànfěi〈名〉 professional bandit
【惯技】guànjì〈名〉〈贬〉 old trick
【惯例】guànlì〈名〉 convention: 按照～ by convention ‖ 国际～ international practice
【惯骗】guànpiàn〈名〉 hardened swindler
【惯窃】guànqiè〈名〉 habitual thief
【惯偷】guàntōu〈名〉 habitual thief
【惯性】guànxìnɡ〈名〉［物理］ inertia: ～定律 law of inertia
【惯用】guànyònɡ〈动〉 habitually practise: ～的伎俩 customary tactic
【惯用法】guànyònɡfǎ〈名〉 usage
【惯用语】guànyònɡyǔ〈名〉 idiom
【惯于】guànyú〈动〉 be used to
【惯贼】guànzéi〈名〉 habitual thief
【惯纵】guànzònɡ〈动〉 indulge: ～孩子 pamper one's child

盥 guàn〈动〉〈书〉 wash: ▸～洗
【盥漱】guànshù〈动〉 wash one's hands and rinse one's mouth (out): ～室 washroom
【盥洗】guànxǐ〈动〉 wash one's hands and face
【盥洗间】guànxǐjiān〈名〉 washroom
【盥洗室】guànxǐshì〈名〉 washroom
【盥洗台】guànxǐtái〈名〉 washstand

g

灌 guàn〈动〉 1 (灌溉) irrigate: 引河水～田 irrigate a field with water from a river 2 (装) fill: 把瓶子～满 fill up a bottle ‖ 往暖水瓶～水 fill a Thermos with water 3 (录制) record: ～唱片 make a record
【灌肠】guànchánɡ A〈动〉 give an enema: 给病人～ administer an enema to a patient B〈名〉 sausage
【灌顶】guàndǐnɡ〈名〉［佛教］ abhiseca ritual [a Tibetan strength-giving ceremony]
【灌溉】guànɡài〈动〉 irrigate: ～农田 irrigate the fields ‖ ～渠 irrigation canal
【灌溉网】guànɡàiwǎnɡ〈名〉 irrigation network
【灌浆】guànjiānɡ〈动〉 1 ［建筑］ grout 2 (指植物) be in the milk 3 ［医学］ form a vesicle [during smallpox or after vaccination]
【灌流】guànliú〈动〉［医学］ perfuse
【灌录】guànlù〈动〉 record sth. to tape/disc
【灌迷魂汤】guàn míhúntānɡ = 灌米汤 guàn mǐtānɡ
【灌米汤】guàn mǐtānɡ〈俗〉 butter sb. up
【灌木】guànmù〈名〉 bush: ～林 shrubbery
【灌木丛】guànmùcónɡ〈名〉 shrubbery
【灌区】guànqū〈名〉 irrigated area
【灌渠】guànqú〈名〉 irrigation canal
【灌输】guànshū〈动〉 1 (指水) draw water 2〈喻〉(指思想) imbue with: 把一种思想～给某人 plant an idea in sb.'s mind
【灌洗】guànxǐ〈动〉［医学］ lavage
【灌音】guànyīn〈动〉 record one's voice
【灌制】guànzhì〈动〉 record sth. to tape/disc: ～唱片 make a disc ‖ ～教学磁带 record a teaching tape
【灌注】guànzhù〈动〉 pour into: 把全部心血～在孩子身上 pour all one's effort into a child

鹳 (鸛) guàn〈名〉［鸟类］ stork

罐 guàn
A〈名〉 1 (罐子) pot: 茶叶～ (tea) caddy ‖ 玻璃～ glass pot ‖ 水～ water pitcher ‖ 油～ oil can 2 (斗车) coal tub
B〈量〉 jar: 一～牛奶 a pitcher of milk ‖ 一～沙丁鱼 a tin of sardines ‖ 一～蜂蜜/油 a jar of honey/oil
【罐车】guànchē〈名〉 tanker
【罐笼】guànlónɡ〈名〉［矿业］ cage
【罐头】guàntou〈名〉 can; tin〈英〉: ～食品 canned food
【罐装】guànzhuānɡ〈动〉 can: ～啤酒 canned beer ‖ ～饮料 canned drink
【罐子】guànzi〈名〉 pot: 两～蜂蜜 two pots of honey ‖ 空～ empty jar ▸药～

guānɡ

光 guānɡ
A〈名〉 1 (光辉) light: 阳～ sunlight ‖ 月～ moonlight ‖ 别挡我的～。 Don't block my light. ▸～芒, 发～ 2 (荣誉) glory: 为国争～ bring glory to one's country ‖ 他偷人家东西，家人脸上也无～。 His stealing brought disgrace upon his family. 3 (好处) benefit: ▸借～, 沾～ 4 (时间) time: ▸～阴, 时～ 5 (风景) scene: ▸春～明媚, 风～
B〈形〉 1 (明亮) bright: ▸～辉 2 (光滑) glossy: 地面磨得很～。 The floor is polished to a shine. ‖ 这种纸不够～。 This paper is not smooth enough. 3 (不剩) used up: 把敌人消灭～ wipe out the enemy ‖ 把啤酒喝～ finish off the beer ‖ 一桶油漆用～了。 One tin of paint was used up.
C〈动〉 1 (使荣耀) bring glory to: ▸～宗耀祖 2 (露着) be naked: ～着膀子 be stripped to the waist ‖ ～着脚跑/走 run/walk barefoot ‖ 一年四季～着头 go bareheaded all year round
D〈副〉 1〈套〉(感到光荣) being honoured: ▸～顾, ～临 2 (只) merely: ～说没用。 Mere words won't help. ‖ 他不～听到了，也看到了。 He not only heard it, but also saw it. ‖ 他的工资～够吃饭。 His salary is just enough for food.
【光斑】guānɡbān〈名〉［天文］ facula
【光板儿】guānɡbǎnr〈名〉 1 (指毛皮) worn-out fur 2 (无图案) copper coin without a distinctive stamp
【光笔】guānɡbǐ〈名〉［计算机］ electronic pen: ～跟踪 light pen tracking
【光标】guānɡbiāo〈名〉［计算机］ cursor: 移动～ move the cursor ‖ ～位置 cursor position
【光波】guānɡbō〈名〉 optical wave: ～通信 light-wave communication
【光彩】guānɡcǎi A〈名〉 lustre: 宝石的～ splendour of jewels ‖ 新娘～照人。 The bride looked radiant. ‖ 她的眼里失去了往日的～。 Her eyes lost their previous lustre. B〈形〉 glorious: 儿子获得冠军，全家人都感到很～。 The son won the championship, and the whole family felt honoured. ‖ 你那样干很不～。 It is disgraceful of you to act in that way.
【光彩夺目】guānɡcǎi-duómù〈成〉 dazzlingly brilliant: ～的珠宝 dazzlingly splendid jewels
【光灿灿】guānɡcàncàn〈形〉 shining: ～的秋阳 bright autumn sun
【光赤】guānɡchì〈动〉 be bare: ～着上身 be naked to the waist
【光大】guānɡdà〈动〉〈书〉 glorify: ～门楣 bring glory to one's family ▸发扬～
【光导】guānɡdǎo〈名〉 light guide
【光导纤维】guānɡdǎo xiānwéi〈名〉 optical fibre
【光电】guānɡdiàn〈名〉 photoelectricity: ～材料 photoelectric material ‖ ～导体 photoconductor
【光电计】guānɡdiànjì〈名〉［电子］ photoelectrometer
【光电探测器】guānɡdiàn tàncèqì〈名〉［电子］ light sensor
【光电池】guānɡdiànchí〈名〉［电子］ photoelectric cell
【光电管】guānɡdiànɡuǎn〈名〉［电子］ phototube
【光电子】guānɡdiànzǐ〈名〉［电子］ photoelectron: ～扫描器 photoelectronic scanner
【光碟】guānɡdié〈名〉 compact disc (CD)
【光度】guānɡdù〈名〉 1 (指天体) luminosity: ～计 photometer 2 (光子) photon
【光风霁月】guānɡfēnɡ-jìyuè〈成〉〈喻〉 broad-minded and open-hearted
【光伏】guānɡfú〈名〉 photovoltaics (PVs): ～电池 photovoltaic cell
【光辐射】guānɡfúshè〈名〉 ray radiation: ～伤害 ray radiation injury
【光复】guānɡfù〈动〉 recover (lost territory): ～河山 recover lost land
【光杆儿】guānɡɡǎnr〈名〉 1 (指枝干) bare stalk: 冰雹把小树打成了～。 The hail storm stripped the young trees of all their leaves. 2 (指男子) man who has lost his family 3 (指领导) person without a following: ～司令 leader without a following
【光顾】guānɡɡù〈动〉 patronize: ～这家商店的人很多。 The shop enjoys a large patronage. ‖ 欢迎～。 We would very much like to have your custom.
【光怪陆离】guānɡɡuài-lùlí〈成〉 bizarre and motley
【光管】guānɡɡuǎn〈简称〉= 光电管
【光棍】guānɡɡùn〈名〉 hoodlum
【光棍不吃眼前亏】guānɡɡùn bù chī yǎnqián kuī〈俗〉 a wise man never fights against impossible odds
【光棍儿】guānɡɡùnr〈名〉 bachelor: 打～ live a bachelor's life
【光合作用】guānɡhé zuòyònɡ〈名〉 photosynthesis
【光华】guānɡhuá〈名〉 brilliance: 日月～ brilliance of the sun and the moon
【光滑】guānɡhuá〈形〉 smooth: ～度 smoothness ‖ 皮肤～细腻 satiny and delicate skin ‖ 表面～如镜。 The surface is as smooth as glass. ‖ 这种丝绒摸上去很～。 This velvet is smooth to the touch.
【光化学反应】guānɡhuàxué fǎnyìnɡ〈名〉［物理］［化学］ photochemical reaction
【光环】guānɡhuán〈名〉 1 (指行星) ring of light: 土星～ ring of Saturn 2 (发光的环子) luminous ring: 彩色灯泡构成了一个巨大的～。 Coloured light bulbs form a great big luminous ring. 3 ［宗教］ halo
【光辉】guānɡhuī A〈名〉 brilliance: 太阳的～ brilliance of the sun B〈形〉 glorious: ～的前程 glorious future ‖ ～榜样 shining example ‖ ～形象 lofty image
【光辉灿烂】guānɡhuī-cànlàn〈成〉 dazzling
【光火】guānɡhuǒ〈动〉〈方〉 fly into a rage: 别～。 Don't fly off the handle.
【光洁】guānɡjié〈形〉 bright and clean: ～

的皮肤 smooth skin
【光洁度】guāngjiédù〈名〉degree of finish: 表面～ surface smoothness
【光解作用】guāngjiě zuòyòng〈名〉photolysis
【光介子】guāngjièzǐ〈名〉［物理］photomeson
【光景】guāngjǐng〈名〉1（日子）days: 好～ good days 2（状况）circumstances: 他婚后的～还不错。He lived in fair comfort after his marriage. 3（左右）around: 离学校有二里地～。It's about two *li* from the school. ‖ 那女孩五六岁～。That girl was about five or six years old.
【光觉】guāngjué〈名〉light perception
【光控】guāngkòng〈形〉light control: ～开关 light switch
【光缆】guānglǎn〈名〉optical cable: 海底～ submarine optical cable
【光亮】guāngliàng A〈形〉shiny: ～的眸子 bright eyes ‖ 皮革～剂 leather polish B〈名〉light: 房间的～度 lightness of a room ‖ 山洞里几乎没有～。There's practically no light in the cave.
【光量子】guāngliàngzǐ〈名〉［物理］photon
【光疗】guāngliáo〈名〉phototherapy
【光临】guānglín〈动〉〈敬〉be present: 敬请～。We request the pleasure of your company. ‖ 欢迎专家～指导。Experts are welcome to come and give us guidance.
【光溜溜】guāngliūliū〈形〉1（光滑）slippery: ～的冰面 slippery ice 2（无遮盖）naked: 男孩们脱得～的下河去游泳。The boys stripped themselves to go swimming in the river.
【光溜】guāngliu〈形〉〈口〉smooth: 这种纸比油光纸还～。This kind of paper is even smoother than glossy paper.
【光芒】guāngmáng〈名〉radiance: 发出耀眼的～ shine with great brilliancy ‖ 爱国主义精神永放～。The patriotic spirit will shine on for ever.
【光芒万丈】guāngmáng-wànzhàng〈成〉gloriously radiant
【光面】guāngmiàn〈名〉plain noodles
【光敏】guāngmǐn〈形〉photosensitive
【光敏电阻】guāngmǐn diànzǔ〈名〉photoresistance
【光敏开关】guāngmǐn kāiguān〈名〉light-activated switch
【光明】guāngmíng A〈名〉light: 太阳给我们带来～。The sun gives us light. B〈形〉1（有希望）bright: 把中国引向～ lead China into the light ‖ 前途～ a bright future 2（坦白）open-hearted: ▸～磊落, ～正大
【光明磊落】guāngmíng-lěiluò〈成〉upright and honorable
【光明正大】guāngmíng-zhèngdà〈成〉just and honest: 做事～ play fair and square
【光能】guāngnéng〈名〉optical energy
【光年】guāngnián〈量〉［物理］light year: ～是天文学上的一个距离单位。A light year is a unit of distance in astronomy.
【光盘】guāngpán〈名〉compact disc (CD)
【光盘驱动器】guāngpán qūdòngqì〈名〉［计算机］CD-ROM drive
【光谱】guāngpǔ〈名〉spectrum
【光谱测定法】guāngpǔ cèdìngfǎ〈名〉spectrometry
【光谱分析】guāngpǔ fēnxī〈名〉spectrum analysis
【光谱仪】guāngpǔyí〈名〉spectrograph
【光漆】guāngqī〈名〉gloss paint: 亚～ matt paint
【光前裕后】guāngqián-yùhòu〈成〉glorify one's forefathers and enrich one's descendants
【光球】guāngqiú〈名〉［天文］photosphere
【光驱】guāngqū〈简称〉= 光盘驱动器
【光圈】guāngquān〈名〉［摄影］aperture: 调节～ adjust the aperture
【光荣】guāngróng A〈形〉glorious: ～称号 honourary title ‖ ～传统 glorious tradition ‖ ～地加入中国共产党 have the honour of being admitted into the Communist Party of China ‖ ～牺牲 die a glorious death B〈名〉glory: ～归于大家。The credit rests with us all. ‖ 总统莅临是我们的～。The President honoured us with his presence.
【光荣榜】guāngróngbǎng〈名〉roll of honour: 她儿子上了～。Her son is an honour roll student.
【光荣花】guāngrónghuā〈名〉rosette: 佩带～ wear a rosette
【光润】guāngrùn〈形〉smooth and delicate: 她两颊～透红。Her cheeks are rosy and smooth.
【光栅】guāngshān〈名〉［电子］grating
【光闪闪】guāngshǎnshǎn〈形〉brilliant: ～的金子 glittering gold
【光束】guāngshù〈名〉ray
【光速】guāngsù〈名〉［物理］speed of light
【光天化日】guāngtiān-huàrì〈成〉broad daylight: 他们在～之下抢劫了一位老太太。They robbed an old lady in broad daylight.
【光通量】guāngtōngliàng〈名〉［物理］luminous flux: ～的单位是流明。Luminous flux is measured in lumens.
【光通信】guāngtōngxìn〈名〉photocommunication
【光头】guāngtóu A〈动〉bare one's head: 一年四季总光着头 go bareheaded all year round B〈名〉shaven head: 剃～ have one's head shaved
【光秃秃】guāngtūtū〈形〉naked: ～的山坡 bare hillside
【光污染】guāngwūrǎn〈名〉light pollution
【光纤】guāngxiān〈名〉fibre optics: ～光缆 optical fibre and cable ‖ ～通信 optical fibre communication
【光鲜】guāngxiān〈形〉neat and clean: 衣着～ be neatly dressed
【光线】guāngxiàn〈名〉ray of light: 挡住～ shut out the light ‖ 这房子～不好。The lighting in the room isn't good.
【光学】guāngxué〈名〉optics
【光学玻璃】guāngxué bōli〈名〉optical glass
【光学仪器】guāngxué yíqì〈名〉［物理］optical instrument
【光艳】guāngyàn〈形〉bright and gorgeous
【光焰】guāngyàn〈名〉radiance: 烟花腾空而起，～四射。Fireworks shot into the sky, firing rays in all directions.
【光洋】guāngyáng〈名〉〈方〉silver dollar
【光耀】guāngyào A〈名〉brilliance: ～夺目 dazzlingly brilliant B〈形〉glorious C〈动〉glorify: ～祖宗 reflect glory on one's ancestors
【光阴】guāngyīn〈名〉time: 虚度～ loiter away one's time ‖ 一寸～一寸金。Time is money.
【光阴荏苒】guāngyīn-rěnrǎn〈成〉time passes very quickly
【光阴似箭】guāngyīnsìjiàn〈成〉time flies
【光源】guāngyuán〈名〉［物理］light source
【光泽】guāngzé〈名〉lustre: 失去～ lose the shine ‖ ～好的家具 furniture with a good gloss
【光泽度】guāngzédù〈名〉［物理］gloss
【光照】guāngzhào A〈名〉illumination: ～时间长/短 long/short period of light B〈动〉glorify: ～千秋 shine forever
【光柱】guāngzhù〈名〉beam of light: 探照灯的～ beam of a searchlight
【光子】guāngzǐ〈名〉［物理］photon: ～火箭 photon rocket
【光宗耀祖】guāngzōng-yàozǔ〈成〉bring glory to one's ancestors

咣 guāng〈拟〉bang: ～的一声关上了门 close the door with a bang

桄 guāng
▸guàng
【桄榔】guāngláng〈名〉［植物］gomuti palm

胱 guāng ▸膀胱 pángguāng
【胱氨酸】guāng'ānsuān〈名〉［化学］cystine

guǎng

广¹（廣） guǎng
A〈形〉1（宽广）wide: ～开财源 explore all possible sources of revenues ‖ 地～人稀 vast but sparsely populated ‖ 分布极～ be distributed far and wide ‖ 涉及面～ be far-ranging 2（众多）numerous: ▸大庭～众
B〈动〉expand: ▸推而～之

广²（廣） Guǎng〈名〉1（指省）Guangdong Province 2（指市）Guangzhou City
▸ān
【广播】guǎngbō A〈动〉broadcast: ～新闻 broadcast news ‖ 开始～ go on the air ‖ ～找人 broadcast announcement to find sb. B〈名〉broadcast: 收听外语～ listen to foreign language broadcast ‖ 新闻～ news broadcast ‖ 调频～ FM broadcast ▸有线～
【广播操】guǎngbōcāo〈简称〉= 广播体操
【广播电台】guǎngbō diàntái〈名〉radio station
【广播电影电视总局】Guǎngbō Diànyǐng Diànshì Zǒngjú〈名〉State Administration of Radio, Film and Television
【广播稿】guǎngbōgǎo〈名〉broadcast script
【广播公司】guǎngbō gōngsī〈名〉broadcast corporation: 英国～ British Broadcasting Corporation (BBC)
【广播节目】guǎngbō jiémù〈名〉radio programme
【广播剧】guǎngbōjù〈名〉radio play
【广播体操】guǎngbō tǐcāo〈名〉exercises to radio music: 做～ do exercises to radio music
【广播员】guǎngbōyuán ▸**p. 966**〈名〉radio announcer
【广播站】guǎngbōzhàn〈名〉broadcasting station
【广博】guǎngbó〈形〉extensive: 知识～ have extensive knowledge
【广场】guǎngchǎng〈名〉1（为公众活动之用）square: 天安门～ Tian'anmen Square 2（为商业活动之用）plaza: 购物～ shopping centre

【广大】guǎngdà〈形〉 1▸（指面积） vast: ～地区 vast regions ‖ 中国的～农村 vast countryside of China 2▸（指范围） large-scale 3▸（指人数） numerous: 教育～干部 educate the vast numbers of cadres ‖ 误导～消费者 misguide the purchaser
【广岛】Guǎngdǎo〈名〉 Hiroshima
【广电总局】Guǎngdiàn Zǒngjú〈简称〉= 广播电影电视总局
【广东】Guǎngdōng ▸p. 661〈名〉 Guangdong Province: ～话 Cantonese
【广东戏】guǎngdōngxì = 粤剧 yuèjù
【广东音乐】Guǎngdōng yīnyuè〈名〉 Cantonese music
【广度】guǎngdù〈名〉 scope: 知识的～和深度 width and depth of (sb.'s) knowledge
【广而告之】guǎng'érgàozhī〈成〉 spread far and wide
【广泛】guǎngfàn〈形〉 extensive: ～收集资料 gather materials on a wide scale ‖ ～宣传 publicize widely ‖ （与某人）进行～交流 make extensive contact (with sb.) ‖ 兴趣～ have a wide range of interests
【广柑】guǎnggān〈名〉 Guangdong orange
【广告】guǎnggào〈名〉 advertisement: 插播～ insert a commercial ‖ 登～ run an advertisement ‖ 室外～ outdoor advertising
【广告画】guǎnggàohuà〈名〉(pictorial) poster
【广告牌】guǎnggàopái〈名〉 billboard; hoarding〈英〉
【广告片】guǎnggàopiàn〈名〉 commercial
【广告衫】guǎnggàoshān〈名〉 advertising shirt
【广告条】guǎnggàotiáo〈名〉［计算机］ banner advertisement
【广寒宫】guǎnghánggōng〈名〉 Moon Palace
【广交会】Guǎngjiāohuì〈简称〉= 广州进出口商品交易会
【广角镜】guǎngjiǎojìng〈名〉 wide-angle lens
【广结良缘】guǎngjié-liángyuán〈成〉 do good deeds everywhere and win universal acclaim
【广开言路】guǎngkāi-yánlù〈成〉 advocate freedom of speech
【广阔】guǎngkuò〈形〉 vast: ～的草原 vast expanse of prairie ‖ ～的视野 wide field of vision ‖ 前景～。The future is bright.
【广袤】guǎngmào〈书〉 A〈名〉 length and breadth of land: ～千里 vast expanse B〈形〉 vast: ～的平原 broad plain
【广漠】guǎngmò〈形〉 wide and bare: ～的戈壁 bare expanse of Gobi
【广谱】guǎngpǔ〈形〉 broad-spectrum
【广厦】guǎngshà〈名〉〈书〉 large house
【广土众民】guǎngtǔ-zhòngmín〈成〉 vast land and large population
【广西】Guǎngxī ▸p. 661〈名〉 Guangxi: ～壮族自治区 Guangxi Zhuang Autonomous Region
【广义】guǎngyì〈名〉 broad sense: ～的文化 culture in a broad sense ‖ 从～上讲 in a broad sense
【广域网】guǎngyùwǎng〈名〉 wide area network (WAN)
【广征博引】guǎngzhēng-bóyǐn〈成〉 quote copiously
【广种薄收】guǎngzhòng-bóshōu〈成〉 extensive cultivation with low yield
【广州】Guǎngzhōu ▸p. 661〈名〉 Guangzhou [capital of Guangdong Province (广东)]
【广州进出口商品交易会】Guǎngzhōu Jìnchūkǒu Shāngpǐn Jiāoyìhuì〈名〉 Guangzhou Chinese Import/Export Commodities Fair

犷（獷） guǎng〈形〉 tough: ▸粗～
【犷悍】guǎnghàn〈形〉〈书〉 tough and intrepid

guàng

桄 guàng
A〈动〉 reel thread on a revolving frame
B〈名〉 reel: 线～儿 thread reel
C〈量〉 reel: 一～线 a reel of thread
▸guāng
【桄子】guàngzi〈名〉 reel: 线～ thread reel

逛 guàng〈动〉 stroll: ～公园 stroll around a park ‖ ～街 go window-shopping
【逛荡】guàngdang〈动〉 loiter: ～一上午 loaf about for a whole morning
【逛灯】guàngdēng〈动〉 [on the evening of the 15th of the first lunar month] walk around the streets or parks, enjoying the lanterns on display
【逛窑子】guàngyáozi〈动〉 visit a brothel
【逛游】guàngyou〈动〉 roam around

guī

归（歸） guī
A〈动〉 1▸（返回） go back: 从国外～来 return from abroad ‖ 无家可～ be homeless ▸～国，满载而～ 2▸（还给） give sth. back to: ▸～还，完璧～赵 3▸（聚拢） come together: 应～入另一类 belong in a different category ‖ 百川～海。All rivers flow into the sea. ▸～并，众望所～ 4▸（依附） depend on: ▸～顺，～依 5▸（属于） belong to: 房子～她，家具～你。The house will be hers and the furniture yours. ‖ 矿产资源～国家所有。Mineral resources are the property of the country. ▸～属 6▸（用于相同动词之间） [used between two identical verbs] be regardless of: 说～说，做～做。Talking is one thing, doing is another.
B〈介〉 to: 我不在时该部门～他负责。He will take charge of the department during my absence.
C〈名〉 division on the abacus with a one-digit divisor
【归案】guī'àn〈动〉 bring to justice: 罪犯终于被捉拿～。The offender was finally hunted down.
【归并】guībìng〈动〉 1▸（并入） merge into: 把一家公司～到另一家公司 merge one company into another 2▸（合计） amount to: 费用～起来是一万元。The costs added up to 10,000 *yuan*.
【归程】guīchéng〈名〉 homeward journey: 踏上～ set out on a journey home
【归除】guīchú〈名〉 division on the abacus with a divisor of two or more digits
【归档】guīdàng〈动〉 keep on file: ～备查 keep sth. on file for reference
【归队】guīduì〈动〉 1▸（指队伍） rejoin one's unit: 连长已病愈～。The company commander has already recovered and rejoined his unit. 2▸〈喻〉（指行业） return to one's former profession
【归附】guīfù〈动〉 come under
【归根】guīgēn〈动〉 finally return to one's native land: ▸落叶～
【归根到底】guīgēn-dàodǐ = 归根结底 guīgēn-jiédǐ
【归根结底】guīgēn-jiédǐ〈成〉 in the final analysis: 所有真正意义上的教育，～都是自我教育。When it comes down to it, all real education is self-education.
【归公】guīgōng〈动〉 turn in to the state: 一切缴获要～。Hand over everything captured.
【归功】guīgōng〈动〉 give credit to: 把成就～于团队的通力合作 owe the success to the team's concerted cooperative efforts
【归国】guīguó〈动〉 return to one's country: ～华侨 returned overseas Chinese
【归还】guīhuán〈动〉 return: ～贷款 pay back a loan ‖ 把书～图书馆 return a book to the library ‖ 将失物～失主 return lost property to its owner
【归回】guīhuí〈动〉 return: ～祖国 go back to one's motherland
【归结】guījié A〈动〉 sum up: 大家的意见～起来有三点。Everybody's opinions can be summed up in three points. B〈名〉 conclusion: 这件事总算有了个～。It finally came to an end.
【归咎】guījiù〈动〉 lay the blame: 把车祸～于驾驶员的疏忽大意 blame an accident on the driver's carelessness
【归口】guīkǒu〈动〉 1▸（划归） put under sb.'s administration: ～管理 put under administration 2▸ = 归队 guīduì 2
【归来】guīlái〈动〉 come back: 欢迎代表团～ welcome the return of a delegation ‖ 海外～ return from abroad
【归类】guīlèi〈动〉 classify: 按内容～ categorize according to content
【归零】guīlíng〈动〉［计算机］ return to zero
【归拢】guīlǒng〈动〉 collect: 把零碎东西～一下 get one's bits and pieces together
【归谬法】guīmiùfǎ〈名〉 reduction to absurdity
【归纳】guīnà A〈动〉 1▸（抽象得出） induce: 从事实中～出结论 come to a conclusion from facts 2▸（总结） sum up: 你们的建议～起来只有一条。Your suggestions boil down to one point only. B〈名〉 induction: ～和演绎 induction and deduction
【归纳法】guīnàfǎ〈名〉 induction method
【归宁】guīníng〈动〉〈旧〉 [of a married woman] visit one's parents
【归期】guīqī〈名〉 date of return: ～未定 have not decided on the date of one's return
【归侨】guīqiáo〈名〉 returned overseas national
【归入】guīrù〈动〉 classify: 鲸应～哺乳类动物。Whales fall under the class of mammals.
【归属】guīshǔ〈动〉 belong to: ～问题 the question of ownership ‖ 领土的～ ownership of a territory
【归属感】guīshǔgǎn〈名〉 sense of belonging
【归顺】guīshùn〈动〉 submit to an enemy force
【归宿】guīsù〈名〉 final settling place: 人生～ destination of one's life journey
【归天】guītiān ▸p. 772〈动〉〈婉〉 pass away
【归田】guītián〈动〉〈书〉 retire and return to one's homeland: ▸解甲～
【归途】guītú〈名〉 one's way home: 踏上～ begin one's journey home
【归西】guīxī ▸p. 772〈动〉〈婉〉 pass away
【归降】guīxiáng〈动〉 surrender: 向政府～

surrender to the government

【归向】guīxiàng〈动〉 incline towards: 人心～ trend of popular feeling

【归心】guīxīn **A**〈名〉 homesickness **B**〈动〉 offer one's submission: 四海～。People all over the country are tendering their submissions.

【归心似箭】guīxīn-sìjiàn〈成〉 anxious to return home

【归省】guīxǐng〈动〉〈书〉 return to one's homeland to visit one's family

【归一】guīyī〈动〉 unify: 天下～。 The country is unified. ▸九九～

【归依】guīyī〈动〉 **1** = 皈依 guīyī **2**（投靠） offer one's submission: 四海～。People all over the country are tendering their submissions.

【归隐】guīyǐn〈动〉〈旧〉 return to one's hometown and live in seclusion: 去官～ resign and live in seclusion

【归于】guīyú〈动〉 **1**（属于） belong to: 你不能把一切功劳～自己。 You can't claim all the credit for yourself. **2**（趋于） tend to: 意见～一致。 Be inclined towards the same opinions.

【归真】guīzhēn〈动〉 **1**［佛教］ pass away **2**［伊斯兰教］ return to Allah **3** = 归真返璞 guīzhēn-fǎnpú

【归真返璞】guīzhēn-fǎnpú〈成〉 return to nature

【归整】guīzhěng = 归置 guīzhi

【归置】guīzhi〈动〉〈口〉 put in order: 把书～整齐 put one's books in a tidy pile ‖ 把房间～一下。 Tidy up the room a bit.

【归总】guīzǒng〈动〉 put together: 把东西～一下 put the things together

【归罪】guīzuì〈动〉 lay the blame on: 他把一切都～于我。 He laid all blame on me.

圭[1] guī

〈名〉 **1**（指玉器） sceptre **2**（指圭表） ancient Chinese sundial: ▸～表

圭[2] guī

〈名〉 ancient measurement of volume [about ten microlitres]

【圭表】guībiǎo〈名〉〈古〉 sundial

【圭内斯郡】Guīnèisījùn〈名〉 Gwynedd

【圭臬】guīniè〈名〉〈书〉 criterion: 奉为～ look up to as the accepted criterion

【圭亚那】Guīyànà〈名〉 Guyana: ～合作共和国 Cooperative Republic of Guyana ‖ ～人 Guyanese

龟（龜） guī

〈名〉 tortoise: ▸乌～ ▸jūn, qiū

【龟板】guībǎn〈名〉［中药］ tortoiseshell

【龟背】guībèi〈名〉 tortoiseshell

【龟卜】guībǔ〈动〉 divine of tortoiseshell

【龟趺】guīfū〈名〉 tortoise-shaped base of a stone tablet

【龟甲】guījiǎ〈名〉 tortoiseshell

【龟鉴】guījiàn〈名〉〈喻〉 object lesson: 可为～ can be taken as an object lesson

【龟镜】guījìng = 龟鉴 guījiàn

【龟苓膏】guīlínggāo〈名〉［中药］ turtle shell gelatin

【龟纽】guīniǔ〈名〉 turtle-shaped knob of a seal

【龟缩】guīsuō〈动〉 withdraw into passive defence: 逃犯～在山洞里。 The escapee is holed up in a mountain cave.

【龟头】guītóu〈名〉［解剖］ glans penis

龟苓膏

A traditional medication made by boiling together turtle shells and the fungus *poria cocos*, honeysuckle flowers, and other traditional Chinese medicinal ingredients. It takes a jelly form that is black and slightly bitter to the taste. It is said to reduce internal heat and to be effective for the relief of mouth ulcers and constipation, and can be ingested hot or cold. Its use is prevalent primarily in southern China.

规（規） guī

A〈名〉 **1**（指工具） dividers: ▸两脚～, 圆～ **2**（规则） rule: 校～ school regulations ▸～则, 常～
B〈动〉 **1**（谋划） plan: ▸～避, ～划 **2**（劝告） advise: ▸～谏

【规避】guībì〈动〉 avoid: ～责任 evade one's responsibility ‖ ～战术 evasion tactics

【规程】guīchéng〈名〉 rules: 操作～ rules of operation

【规定】guīdìng **A**〈动〉 stipulate: 按～速度行驶 drive at a regulation speed ‖ 超过～的时间 run over the allotted time ‖ 工作时间由政府～。 It's up to the government to stipulate working hours. **B**〈名〉 specification: 按照公司的～ by rule of the company ‖ 实施新～ enforce a new regulation

【规定动作】guīdìng dòngzuò〈名〉［体育］ compulsory exercise

【规定数额】guīdìng shù'é〈名〉 quota

【规范】guīfàn **A**〈名〉 **1**（标准） standard: 合乎～ conform to the standard ‖ 道德～ moral standards ‖ 行为～ norms of conduct **2**［工程］ specification **B**〈形〉 standard: 不～ be below standard ‖ ～用法 standard usage ‖ ～管理 standardized administration **C**〈动〉 standardize: ～售后服务 standardize after-sales service

【规范化】guīfànhuà〈动〉 standardize: ～服务 standardized service

【规复】guīfù〈动〉〈书〉 resume: ～失地 recover lost land

【规格】guīgé〈名〉 **1**（标准） specifications: ～齐全 complete range of specifications ‖ 不合～ be below standard **2**（级别） rank: 那些来宾的～很高。 Those are high-ranking guests.

【规格化】guīgéhuà〈动〉 standardize

【规划】guīhuà **A**〈名〉 programme: 制订～ map out a plan ‖ 城市建设～ town planning ‖ 远景～ future plan **B**〈动〉 map out a plan: 现代城市要全面～才行。 A modern city requires an overall plan.

【规谏】guījiàn〈动〉〈书〉 expostulate

【规诫】guījiè〈动〉〈书〉 admonish

【规矩】guīju **A**〈名〉 **1**（标准） custom: 按～办事 do things according to conventional practice ‖ 教堂有教堂的～。 Churches have church rules. **2**（礼数） good manners: 不懂～ have no manners ‖ 没～ be free in manner **B**〈形〉 **1**（符合规范） well-behaved: 举止～谨慎 be prim and precise in manner ‖ 你的字写得很～。 Your handwriting shows disciplined practice. **2**（诚实） honest: 那个女人不～。 She is an indecent woman. ‖ 他看上去是个～人。 He looks like an honest man.

【规律】guīlǜ〈名〉 law: 自然～ law of nature ‖ 生活没有～ have no set norms in one's life

【规律性】guīlǜxìng〈名〉 regularity

【规模】guīmó **A**〈名〉 scale: 扩大～ enlarge the scale ‖ 经营～ scale of operation ‖ 市场～ market size **B**〈形〉 large-scale: ～生产 mass production ‖ ～经济 economy of scale

【规劝】guīquàn〈动〉 admonish: 好意～ give well-meaning advice ‖ ～某人不要赌博 admonish sb. against gambling

【规行矩步】guīxíng-jǔbù〈成〉〈喻〉 **1**（合乎规矩） behave cautiously and correctly **2**（墨守成规） follow the beaten track

【规约】guīyuē **A**〈名〉 agreed-upon regulation: 行业～ agreed trade regulations **B**〈动〉 restrain: 理智的人能～自己的感情。 Rational people restrain their passions.

【规则】guīzé **A**〈名〉 **1**（制度） rule: 游戏～ rules of the game ‖ 交通～ traffic regulations ‖ 比赛～ match rule **2**（法则） law: 自然～ law of nature **B**〈形〉 regular: ～动词 regular verb ‖ 海岸线很不～。 The coastline is very irregular.

【规章】guīzhāng〈名〉 regulation: 废除旧～，采用新～ abolish the old regulations and adopt new ones ‖ 违反～制度 violate rules and regulations

【规整】guīzhěng **A**〈形〉 regular: ～的汉字 standard Chinese character ‖ 不～的石板 random-sized slate **B**〈动〉 tidy and put in order: 把书架上的书好好～一下 put all the books on the shelves into proper order

【规制】guīzhì〈名〉 **1**（规则制度） rule **2**（规模形制） [of a building] size, shape and structure: 寺庙虽经多次修缮，但～未变。 The temple has been renovated several times but its size and structure has not changed.

皈 guī

〈动〉 be converted to

【皈依】guīyī〈动〉 be converted to: ～佛门/基督教 be converted to Buddhism/Christianity

闺（閨） guī

〈名〉 boudoir: ▸～房, 深～

【闺范】guīfàn〈名〉〈旧〉 female virtues

【闺房】guīfáng〈名〉〈旧〉 boudoir

【闺阁】guīgé = 闺房 guīfáng

【闺女】guīnü〈名〉 **1**（女孩） girl: ▸黄花～ **2**〈口〉（女儿） daughter

【闺秀】guīxiù〈名〉〈旧〉 girl from a rich and distinguished family: 大家～ girl from a rich and influential family

【闺怨】guīyuàn〈名〉〈书〉 boudoir repining

硅 guī

〈名〉 silicon (Si)

【硅肺】guīfèi ▸**p. 50**〈名〉［医学］ silicosis: ～是一种职业病。 Silicosis is an occupational disease.

【硅钢】guīgāng〈名〉［冶金］ silicon steel

【硅谷】guīgǔ〈名〉 Silicon Valley

【硅化木】guīhuàmù〈名〉［地质］ silicified wood

【硅胶】guījiāo〈名〉［化学］ silica gel: ～隆胸术 silicone breast implant

【硅片】guīpiàn〈名〉 silicon chip

【硅酸盐】guīsuānyán〈名〉［化学］ silicate: ～水泥 Portland cement

【硅酮】guītóng〈名〉［化学］ silicone

【硅藻】guīzǎo〈名〉［植物］ diatom

【硅砖】guīzhuān〈名〉 silica brick

瑰 guī

〈形〉 rare: ▸～宝, ～丽

【瑰宝】guībǎo〈名〉 treasure: 文化～ cultural treasure

【瑰丽】guīlì〈形〉 magnificent: 尼亚加拉大瀑布的景色雄伟～。 The view of the Niagara Falls is simply magnificent.

【瑰奇】guīqí〈形〉rare and precious
【瑰玮】guīwěi〈形〉〈书〉1（指品质）unusual 2（指文辞）ornate
【瑰异】guīyì〈形〉rare and precious

鲑（鮭） guī〈名〉salmon ▸xié

guǐ

轨（軌） guǐ〈名〉1（痕迹）path: ▸～迹 2（秩序）order: ▸常～，越～ 3（铁轨）rail: 铺～ lay tracks ‖ 单/双～ single/double track ‖ 火车出～了。The train was derailed. ▸脱～，无～电车
【轨道】guǐdào〈名〉1（铁轨）railway: 火车～ railway track ‖ 地铁～ underground railway track 2（天体运行路线）orbit: 同步～ synchronous orbit ‖ 卫星已经进入～。The space satellite has already reached orbit. 3（发展路线）track: 回到正确的～上来 get back onto the right path ‖ 使经济步入健康发展的～ put the economy on a healthy track
【轨道舱】guǐdàocāng〈名〉orbital pod
【轨道飞行器】guǐdào fēixíngqì〈名〉orbiter
【轨道空间站】guǐdào kōngjiānzhàn〈名〉orbital space station
【轨道运动】guǐdào yùndòng〈名〉orbital motion
【轨迹】guǐjì〈名〉1［数学］locus 2［电子］trace 3［天文］orbit:（人造）卫星的～ orbit of a satellite 4（发展路径）course: 改变历史发展的～ change the course of history 5［物理］trajectory
【轨距】guǐjù〈名〉［铁路］(track) gauge: 标准/宽～ standard/broad gauge
【轨辙】guǐzhé〈名〉1（痕迹）track 2（道路）beaten track
【轨枕】guǐzhěn〈名〉［铁路］sleeper〈英〉; railroad tie〈美〉: 纵向～ longitudinal sleeper

庋 guǐ
A〈书〉〈名〉shelf
B〈动〉1（保存）keep: ～藏 keep 2（搁置）shelve: ～置 shelve

诡（詭） guǐ〈形〉1（狡诈）crafty: ▸～辩，～计 2（怪异）unusual: ▸～怪，～异
【诡辩】guǐbiàn〈动〉1［逻辑］use sophistry 2（强词夺理）quibble
【诡辩术】guǐbiànshù〈名〉sophistry
【诡称】guǐchēng〈动〉pretend: 罪犯～自己不知情。The criminal pretended to know nothing about it.
【诡辞】guǐcí〈名〉artful word
【诡诞】guǐdàn〈形〉fabricated and weird
【诡怪】guǐguài〈形〉weird
【诡计】guǐjì〈名〉ruse: ▸阴谋～
【诡计多端】guǐjì-duōduān〈成〉be very crafty
【诡谲】guǐjué〈形〉〈书〉1（奇异多变）bizarre and changeable 2（怪诞）weird 3（狡黠）crafty
【诡秘】guǐmì〈形〉secretive: 行踪～ furtive in movement
【诡奇】guǐqí〈形〉bizarre: 情节～ bizarre plot
【诡异】guǐyì〈形〉unusual
【诡诈】guǐzhà〈形〉crafty: ～异常 extremely sly

鬼 guǐ
A〈名〉1（灵魂）ghost: 驱～ dispel a ghost ‖ 你信～吗? Do you believe in ghosts? ▸～魂，～神 2（对人的蔑称）demon: 捣蛋～ trouble-maker ▸胆小～，酒～，吝啬～ 3（打算）sinister plot: 心里有～ have an axe to grind 4（对人的昵称）devil: ▸机灵～，小～ 5（指星宿）one of the 28 constellations in ancient Chinese astronomy
B〈形〉1（不正大光明）dishonest: ▸～～祟祟，～话，～头～脑 2（糟糕）terrible: ～地方 damnable place ‖ ～天气! What horrible weather! 3（机灵）clever: 这家伙真～。He's a smart devil.
【鬼把戏】guǐbǎxì〈名〉1（指害人）wiles: 看穿～ see through an artifice 2（指捉弄人）tricks: 原来那是你的～。So that's your little game.
【鬼才】guǐcái〈名〉1（指才华）special skill 2（指人）wizard: 文坛～ literary wizard
【鬼点子】guǐdiǎnzi〈名〉wicked idea: 出～ make a wicked suggestion ‖ 他～真多。He's full of wicked ideas.
【鬼斧神工】guǐfǔ-shéngōng〈成〉superlative craftsmanship
【鬼怪】guǐguài〈名〉ghosts and monsters
【鬼鬼祟祟】guǐguǐ-suìsuì〈成〉furtive
【鬼画符】guǐhuàfú〈名〉〈喻〉1（指字迹）scrawl 2（指假话）hypocritical talk
【鬼话】guǐhuà〈名〉lie: 说～ tell lies ‖ ～连篇 a pack of lies ‖ 那些广告都是骗人的～。Those advertisements are all baloney.
【鬼魂】guǐhún〈名〉ghost
【鬼混】guǐhùn〈动〉fool around: 跟有夫之妇～ mess about with a married woman ‖ 和一帮坏人～ get mixed up with a bad gang
【鬼火】guǐhuǒ〈名〉〈口〉will-o'-the-wisp
【鬼节】Guǐjié〈名〉〈旧〉Spirit Festival [15th day of the 7th lunar month]
【鬼哭狼嚎】guǐkū-lángháo〈成〉wail like ghosts and howl like wolves
【鬼佬】guǐlǎo〈名〉〈方〉〈粗〉gweilo [derogatory Candonese term for Caucasians]
【鬼脸】guǐliǎn〈名〉1（指假面具）toy mask 2（指表情）funny face:（对某人）做～ make faces (at sb.)
【鬼魅】guǐmèi〈名〉〈书〉ghosts and monsters
【鬼门关】guǐménguān〈名〉1（地狱关口）gate of hell 2〈喻〉（凶险之地）danger spot
【鬼迷心窍】guǐmí-xīnqiào〈成〉be possessed: 你怎么能这样～? What possessed you?
【鬼神】guǐshén〈名〉ghosts and gods
【鬼使神差】guǐshǐ-shénchāi〈成〉unexpected occurrences
【鬼祟】guǐsuì A〈形〉sneaky: 行为～ be sneaky B = 鬼怪 guǐguài
【鬼胎】guǐtāi〈名〉ulterior motive: ▸心怀～
【鬼剃头】guǐtìtóu〈名〉〈口〉alopecia
【鬼头鬼脑】guǐtóu-guǐnǎo〈成〉sneaky: 三个人～地溜出商店。Three men sneaked out of the shop.
【鬼物】guǐwù〈名〉ghost
【鬼雄】guǐxióng〈名〉〈书〉person who dies a hero's death

ℹ "鬼"和"神"的概念

■ 由于文化的差异，汉语的"鬼"和"神"与英语的 devil 和 god 不同。英语里 god 和 devil 两个概念的意义一好一坏，泾渭分明。小写的 god（可数名词）象征一种控制自然和人类生活的神秘力量，常为人类崇拜作神灵。大写的 God 在基督教、天主教和犹太教等宗教里常指上帝，即宇宙的创造者。小写的 devil 指任何邪魔恶灵，大写的 Devil（the Devil）在基督教和犹太教里指上帝的敌人，即魔鬼"撒旦"。ghost 在英语里指人死后的灵魂。

■ "神"的字面翻译是 god。"鬼"的字面翻译是 devil 或 ghost。由于上述原因，"鬼"和"神"在英汉互译时并不能总按字面翻译，必须根据上下文来判断其确切含义，例如"鬼"是指邪恶的魔鬼，还是指死人的灵魂，或是用作中性的含义。

■ "鬼"和"神"在汉语里一起使用时，一般指好的事物或用作中性的含义，翻译成英语时一定要采用意译，而不能照字面来翻译：

鬼斧神工
= superb craftsmanship
而不是
devil's axe and god's work

鬼使神差
= unexpected happenings
而不是
doings of devils and gods

神不知鬼不觉
= without anybody knowing it
或 as if from nowhere
而不是
unknown to gods or devils

神出鬼没
= come and go mysteriously
而不是
gods appear and devils disappear

■ "鬼"和"神"单独使用时：

这孩子真是个机灵鬼
= This child is really clever
而不是
This child is really a clever devil

他说他在墓地里看到过鬼
= He said he had seen ghosts in the graveyard

我母亲信神（她是位天主教徒）
= My mother believes in God (she is a Catholic)

她信神又信鬼（各种神灵和鬼怪）
= She believes in gods and devils

■ "神"含贬义时：

请神容易送神难
= It is easier to call upon an evil spirit than to send it away
而不是
It is easier to call upon a god than to send it away

【鬼蜮】guǐyù〈名〉ghosts and monsters
【鬼蜮伎俩】guǐyù-jìliǎng〈成〉devilish tactics
【鬼主意】guǐzhǔyi〈名〉evil idea: 你又在打什么～? What evil tricks are you up to now?
【鬼子】guǐzi〈名〉devil [term of abuse for foreign invaders]

姽 guǐ〈形〉〈书〉graceful: ▸～婳
【姽婳】guǐhuà〈形〉[of a woman] graceful

癸 guǐ〈名〉last of the ten Heavenly Stems (天干)

晷 guǐ〈名〉1〈书〉(日影) shadows cast by the sun; (日光) sunlight: ▸焚膏继～ 2 (日晷) sundial 3〈书〉(时光) time: 余～ spare time

簋 guǐ〈名〉〈古〉*gui* [ancient food vessel]

guì

柜（櫃） guì〈名〉1 (器具) cabinet: 电视机～ TV cabinet ‖ 文件～ filing cabinet ▸～台, 保险～ 2 (钱柜) cash box: 现款都交～了。All the cash has been handed in to the cashier. ▸掌～
▸jǔ
【柜橱】guìchú〈名〉cupboard
【柜房】guìfáng〈名〉(指处所) cashier's office; (指人) shop cashier
【柜机】guìjī〈名〉cabinet air conditioner
【柜台】guìtái〈名〉counter
【柜员】guìyuán〈名〉counter clerk
【柜员机】guìyuánjī〈名〉automated teller machine (ATM)
【柜子】guìzi〈名〉cupboard

刽（劊） guì〈动〉〈书〉cut off
【刽子手】guìzishǒu〈名〉1〈旧〉(执行死刑的人) executioner 2〈喻〉(屠杀者) butcher

贵¹（貴） guì
A〈形〉1 (价格高) expensive: 太～了, 我买不起。It's too dear; I cannot afford it. ‖ 物以稀为～。It's always expensive to buy single items. 2 (尊贵) noble: ～妇人 noble lady ▸～宾, ～族 3 (值得珍视) highly valued: 和为～。Peace should be valued. ▸宝～, 珍～ 4〈套〉(你的) your: ～校/国 your school/country ‖ 请问～姓? May I ask your name?
B〈动〉be valuable: 人～有自知之明。A smart man knows how little he knows.

贵² Guì ▸**p. 661**〈名〉Gui [another name for Guizhou Province (贵州)]
【贵宾】guìbīn〈名〉distinguished guest: ～卡 VIP card ‖ ～席 distinguished guests' gallery
【贵妃】guìfēi〈名〉high-ranking imperial concubine: 杨～ Lady Yang
【贵妇人】guìfùrén〈名〉noble lady
【贵干】guìgàn〈名〉〈套〉your business: 请问有何～? What brings you here?
【贵庚】guìgēng〈名〉〈敬〉your age: 请问～? May I ask your age?
【贵贱】guìjiàn〈名〉1 (指价格) cost: 不管～, 只要喜欢我就买。Whatever the price, I'll take it if I really like it. 2 (指地位) high or low status: 无论～, 人人生来平等。Whether he is born high or low, all men are equal.
【贵金属】guìjīnshǔ〈名〉precious metal
【贵客】guìkè〈名〉distinguished guest: ～盈门。The house is full of distinguished guests.
【贵人】guìrén〈名〉1 (尊贵之人) distinguished person: 达官～ VIPs 2〈旧〉(指妃嫔) *guiren* [title of imperial concubine in a palace]
【贵人多忘事】guìrén duō wàng shì〈俗〉important people tend to have short memories
【贵姓】guìxìng〈名〉〈敬〉your surname: 请问～? May I know your surname?
【贵阳】Guìyáng ▸**p. 661**〈名〉Guiyang [capital of Guizhou Province (贵州)]
【贵重】guìzhòng〈形〉valuable: 把～东西锁起来 lock up one's valuables ‖ ～物品 valuables
【贵州】Guìzhōu ▸**p. 661**〈名〉Guizhou Province
【贵胄】guìzhòu〈名〉〈书〉descendants of an aristocratic family
【贵子】guìzǐ〈名〉〈敬〉your son: 喜得～! Congratulations on your new baby!
【贵族】guìzú〈名〉noble: ～家庭 noble family ‖ ～血统 noble blood ‖ 精神～ intellectual aristocrat ‖ ～学校 school for the nobility

桂¹ guì〈名〉1 (肉桂) cassia 2 (月桂) laurel 3 (桂花) sweet-scented osmanthus

桂² Guì ▸**p. 661**〈名〉Gui [another name for Guangxi Province (广西)]
【桂冠】guìguān〈名〉laurels: 夺取～ win one's laurels
【桂冠诗人】guìguān shīrén〈名〉(Poet) Laureate
【桂花】guìhuā〈名〉osmanthus flowers: ～酒 osmanthus wine
【桂剧】guìjù〈名〉Guangxi opera
【桂皮】guìpí〈名〉1 (指树) cassia-bark tree 2 (指树皮) cassia bark
【桂鱼】guìyú = 鳜鱼 guìyú
【桂圆】guìyuán〈名〉[植物] longan: ～肉 longan pulp

桧（檜） guì〈名〉Chinese juniper
▸huì

跪 guì〈动〉kneel: ～在佛像前 kneel before the image of Buddha ‖ 他腿～麻了。His legs were numb from kneeling.
【跪拜】guìbài〈动〉kowtow: 行～礼 perform a kowtow
【跪倒】guìdǎo〈动〉throw oneself on one's knees
【跪射】guìshè〈名〉[军事] kneeling fire
【跪姿】guìzī〈名〉[军事] kneeling position: ～射击 shoot from a kneeling position

鲋（鱖） guì〈名〉[鱼类] minnow
▸丁～

鳜（鱖） guì
【鳜鱼】guìyú〈名〉mandarin fish

gǔn

衮（袞） gǔn〈名〉〈古〉ceremonial robe of rulers
【衮衮】gǔngǔn〈形〉〈书〉endless
【衮衮诸公】gǔngǔn-zhūgōng〈成〉good-for-nothing high-ranking officials

绲（緄） gǔn
A〈名〉〈书〉braided band
B〈动〉trim: 给裙子～花边 trim a skirt with lace ‖ 穿一件～有金边的大衣 wear a coat hemmed with gold fringe
【绲边】gǔnbiān A〈动〉hem: 给连衣裙～ hem a dress B〈名〉border: 裙子的～ border of a skirt

辊（輥） gǔn〈名〉roller
【辊式】gǔnshì〈形〉roller-type: ～粉碎机 roller pulverizer ‖ ～输送机 roller path
【辊筒】gǔntǒng〈名〉roller
【辊轴】gǔnzhóu〈名〉roll shaft

滚（滾） gǔn
A〈动〉1 (滚动) roll: ～铁环 trundle a hoop ‖ 石块从山坡上～下来。Rocks rolled down the hillside. 2 (沸腾) boil: 壶里的水～了没有? Is the kettle boiling yet? 3〈粗〉(走开) get lost: ～出去! Get out of my face! 4 = 绲 gǔn B
B〈形〉round: ▸～圆
【滚边】gǔnbiān = 绲边 gǔnbiān
【滚槽机】gǔncáojī〈名〉[机械] channelling machine
【滚齿机】gǔnchǐjī〈名〉[机械] hobbing machine
【滚蛋】gǔndàn〈动〉〈粗〉get out
【滚刀肉】gǔndāoròu〈名〉〈方〉〈喻〉nuisance
【滚动】gǔndòng〈动〉1 (循环) roll: ～播出 rotating broadcast 2 (积累) gradually accumulate and expand: ～发展 develop at a progressive speed ‖ 资金～ capital turnover
【滚翻】gǔnfān〈名〉1 [体育] roll: 前/后/侧～ forward/backward/sideward roll 2 [航空] tumbling
【滚沸】gǔnfèi〈形〉scalding: ～的汤 scalding soup
【滚瓜烂熟】gǔnguālànshú〈成〉recite fluently
【滚瓜溜圆】gǔnguāliūyuán〈成〉roly-poly
【滚滚】gǔngǔn〈形〉rolling: 波涛～而来。The waves billowed in. ‖ 浓烟～涌进房里。Clouds of smoke surged into the room. ‖〈喻〉财源～。The money is rolling in.
【滚雷】gǔnléi〈名〉1 (指雷) roaring thunder 2 [军事] rolling mine
【滚轮】gǔnlún〈名〉[机械] trolley wheel
【滚木】gǔnmù〈名〉〈古〉battle log [as a weapon]: ～礌石 battle logs and rocks
【滚热】gǔnrè〈形〉burning hot
【滚水】gǔnshuǐ〈名〉boiling water
【滚水坝】gǔnshuǐbà〈名〉[建筑] overflow dam
【滚烫】gǔntàng〈形〉boiling hot: ～的咖啡 scalding coffee
【滚梯】gǔntī〈名〉escalator
【滚筒】gǔntǒng〈名〉rotary drum: ～式洗衣机 front-loading washing machine
【滚雪球】gǔn xuěqiú〈惯〉1〈本〉roll a snowball 2〈喻〉snowball: 产生～效应 produce a snowball effect

g

【滚圆】gǔnyuán〈形〉round as a ball: ～的胳膊 round arms
【滚轴】gǔnzhóu〈名〉roller
【滚珠轴承】gǔnzhū zhóuchéng〈名〉［机械］ball bearing
【滚柱轴承】gǔnzhù zhóuchéng〈名〉［机械］roller bearing

磙（磙） gǔn
A〈名〉roller: 石/铁～ stone/iron roller
B〈动〉level with a roller: 把路面～平 level the road surface with a roller
【磙子】gǔnzi〈名〉**1**（指石制农具）stone roller **2**（指碾压器具）roller

鲧（鯀） Gǔn〈名〉Gun [name of the father of King Yu (禹), legendary leader of remote antiquity]

gùn

棍 gùn〈名〉**1**（棍子）stick: 木/铁～ wood/iron rod ▸拐～, 警～ **2**（坏人）treacherous person: ▸赌～, 恶～
【棍棒】gùnbàng〈名〉**1**（棍和棒）cudgel: 防暴～ riot stick **2**［体育］staff
【棍术】gùnshù〈名〉［武术］cudgel play
【棍子】gùnzi〈名〉stick

guō

过（過） Guō〈名〉Guo [surname]
▸guò, guo

埚（堝） guō ▸坩埚 gānguō

郭 guō〈名〉**1**（指城墙）outer city wall: ▸城～ **2**（边框）frame: ▸耳～

聒 guō〈动〉〈书〉grate on one's ears: ▸～噪
【聒耳】guō'ěr〈动〉grate on one's ears: 蝉鸣～ stridulation of cicadas
【聒噪】guōzào〈形〉〈方〉noisy: ～声使我不能入睡。The noise kept me awake.

锅（鍋） guō〈名〉**1**（炊具）pot: 炒菜～ frying pan ‖ 铁～ iron pot **2**（加热器具）boiler: 蒸馏～ column boiler ▸～炉 **3**（锅状物）pot-shaped thing: 烟袋～ bowl of a pipe
【锅巴】guōbā〈名〉**1**（指烧焦）burnt rice crust **2**（指食品）crispy rice crust: ～肉片 crispy rice crust with pork slices
【锅饼】guōbing〈名〉large doughy cake
【锅铲】guōchǎn〈名〉spatula
【锅盖】guōgài〈名〉pot cover
【锅盔】guōkui〈名〉large round baked wheat pancake
【锅炉】guōlú〈名〉boiler: ～房 boiler-house ‖ ～工 boiler man
【锅台】guōtái〈名〉kitchen range surface
【锅贴】guōtiē〈名〉pot sticker [lightly fried dumpling]
【锅烟子】guōyānzi〈名〉soot on a pan
【锅庄】guōzhuāng〈名〉Tibetan folk dance
【锅子】guōzi〈名〉**1**〈方〉= 锅 guō **2**（锅状物）pot-shaped thing: 烟袋～ bowl of a pipe **3**（火锅）chafing dish

蝈（蟈） guō
【蝈蝈儿】guōguor〈名〉［昆虫］katydid

guó

国（國） guó〈名〉**1**（国家）country: 爱～ love one's country ‖ 建～ found a nation ‖ 世界各～ all the countries in the world ‖ 举～同庆。The whole nation joined in the celebrations. **2**（代表国家的）nation: ▸～难, ～情, ～事 **3**（中国的）China: ▸～产, ～画, ～货
【国宝】guóbǎo〈名〉national treasure: 大熊猫在中国被视为～。In China the giant panda is considered a national treasure. ‖〈喻〉这些老艺术家都是～。These old artists are national treasures.
【国本】guóběn〈名〉〈书〉fundamental principles for administering a country: 民为～。People form the basis of a country.
【国标】guóbiāo〈简称〉**1** = 国家标准 **2** = 国际标准舞
【国标码】guóbiāomǎ〈名〉GB code
【国别】guóbié〈名〉country name: ～研究 country study
【国宾】guóbīn〈名〉state guest: 设宴招待～ give a banquet in honour of state guests
【国宾馆】guóbīnguǎn〈名〉state guest house
【国策】guócè〈名〉national policy: 计划生育是中国的一项基本～。Family planning is a national policy in China.
【国产】guóchǎn〈形〉domestic: ～设备 domestically made equipment ‖ ～影片 domestically produced film
【国产化】guóchǎnhuà〈动〉localize: ～率 localization rate
【国产剧】guóchǎnjù〈名〉domestically-produced TV show
【国耻】guóchǐ〈名〉national disgrace: 不忘～ not forget the national humiliation
【国仇】guóchóu〈名〉national enmity: ～家恨 national enmity and family hatred
【国粹】guócuì〈名〉quintessence of Chinese culture: 京剧、中医和国画是中国的三大～。Beijing opera, Chinese medicine and traditional Chinese painting are three quintessential forms of Chinese culture.
【国道】guódào〈名〉national highway: 312～ National Route 312
【国都】guódū〈名〉national capital
【国度】guódù〈名〉nation: 他们来自不同的～。They are from different countries.
【国法】guófǎ〈名〉law of the land: 目无党纪～ disregard party discipline and state law
【国防】guófáng〈名〉national defence: 巩固～ strengthen the national defence
【国防部】Guófángbù〈名〉Ministry of Defence: 美国～ Department of Defence ‖ 美国～长 U.S. Defence Secretary
【国防科工委】Guófáng Kēgōngwěi〈简称〉= 国防科学技术工业委员会
【国防科学技术工业委员会】Guófáng Kēxué Jìshù Gōngyè Wěiyuánhuì〈名〉Commission of Science, Technology and Industry for National Defence
【国防绿】guófánglǜ〈名〉army green
【国防生】guófángshēng〈名〉college student sponsored by the armed forces
【国父】guófù〈名〉father of a nation
【国富民强】guófù-mínqiáng〈成〉the nation is prosperous and the people are powerful
【国歌】guógē〈名〉national anthem: 奏～ play the National Anthem
【国格】guógé〈名〉national honour: 有损～ undermine national prestige
【国共合作】GuóGòng Hézuò〈名〉［历史］Kuomintang-Communist cooperation
【国故】guógù〈名〉traditional Chinese culture and learning: 研究～ study our national cultural heritage
【国号】guóhào〈名〉title of a reigning dynasty: 改～为周 change the name of the dynasty to Zhou
【国花】guóhuā〈名〉national flower
【国画】guóhuà〈名〉traditional Chinese painting: 收藏～ collect traditional Chinese paintings ‖ ～大师 master of traditional Chinese painting

> **国画**
>
> Traditional Chinese painting employing the use of a writing brush, ink stone, ink, paper and strong, thin silk cloth (for backing). Styles of painting can be divided into ink and wash (水墨), meticulous brush technique (工笔), freehand brushwork (写意), and sketching (白描), among others. Subject matter includes portraits, landscapes, and flower and bird painting. Traditional Chinese painting adopts a shifting or moving perspective instead of the fixed perspective familiar in Western painting. More important than a realistic representation is the depiction of the aura of the object and the artist's subjective feelings. This reflects the theory in Chinese philosophy that human beings are an integral part of nature. Traditional Chinese painting and calligraphy have a common origin, focusing on the organic combination of poetry, calligraphy, drawing and the imprint of the seal.

【国徽】guóhuī〈名〉national emblem
【国会】guóhuì〈名〉（美国）congress;（英国）parliament: 解散～ dissolve parliament ‖ ～议员 member of parliament
【国会山】Guóhuìshān〈名〉Capitol Hill
【国魂】guóhún〈名〉national spirit
【国货】guóhuò〈名〉domestic goods: 提倡使用～ advocate using domestically-made products
【国籍】guójí ▸**p. 279**〈名〉**1**（指人）nationality: 双重～ dual nationality ‖ 美国～ American citizenship **2**（指交通工具）national identity: 不明～的船只 ship of unknown nationality
【国计民生】guójì-mínshēng〈成〉national economy and people's livelihood
【国际】guójì〈形〉international: ～长途电话 international call ‖ ～经济新秩序 new international economic order ‖ ～舞台 international arena ‖ ～形势 international situation
【国际奥林匹克委员会】Guójì Àolínpǐkè Wěiyuánhuì〈名〉International Olympic Committee (IOC)
【国际标准】guójì biāozhǔn〈名〉international standard: 制定ISO～ develop ISO standards
【国际标准化组织】Guójì Biāozhǔnhuà Zǔzhī〈名〉International Standards Organization (ISO)
【国际标准期刊编号】guójì biāozhǔn qīkān biānhào〈名〉International Standard Serial Number (ISSN)
【国际标准书号】guójì biāozhǔn shūhào〈名〉International Standard Book Number (ISBN)
【国际标准舞】guójì biāozhǔnwǔ〈名〉international standard dance
【国际博览会】guójì bólǎnhuì〈名〉international exposition

【国际裁判】guójì cáipàn〈名〉 international referee
【国际大家庭】guójì dàjiātíng〈名〉 family of nations
【国际单位制】guójì dānwèizhì〈名〉 international system of units
【国际地位】guójì dìwèi〈名〉 international status: 提高～ elevate the international status of the country
【国际电信联盟】Guójì Diànxìn Liánméng〈名〉 International Telecommunication Union (ITU)
【国际儿童节】Guójì Értóngjié〈名〉 International Children's Day
【国际法】guójìfǎ〈名〉 international law: 违反～ violate international law
【国际歌】Guójìgē〈名〉(the) Internationale: 大会在～声中结束。 The conference was concluded to the soundtrack of the Internationale.
【国际公约】guójì gōngyuē〈名〉 international convention
【国际公制】guójì gōngzhì〈名〉 metric system
【国际共管】guójì gòngguǎn〈名〉 international condominium
【国际惯例】guójì guànlì〈名〉 international practice: 公认的～ established international practice
【国际航班】guójì hángbān〈名〉 international flight
【国际航道】guójì hángdào〈名〉 international waterway
【国际航空运输协会】Guójì Hángkōng Yùnshū Xiéhuì〈名〉 International Air Transport Association (IATA)
【国际航线】guójì hángxiàn〈名〉 international airline
【国际和平年】Guójì Hépíngnián〈名〉 International Year of Peace
【国际红十字会】Guójì Hóngshízìhuì〈名〉 International Red Cross
【国际化】guójìhuà〈动〉 internationalize: ～大都市 international metropolis
【国际环境日】Guójì Huánjìngrì〈名〉 World Environment Day
【国际汇兑】guójì huìduì〈名〉 international exchange
【国际货币基金组织】Guójì Huòbì Jījīn Zǔzhī〈名〉 International Monetary Fund (IMF)
【国际金融】guójì jīnróng〈名〉 international finance
【国际金融组织】Guójì Jīnróng Zǔzhī〈名〉 International Finance Corporation (IFC)
【国际经济开发合作银行】Guójì Jīngjì Kāifā Hézuò Yínháng〈名〉 International Bank of Economic Cooperation (IBEC)
【国际空间站】guójì kōngjiānzhàn〈名〉 international space station
【国际劳动妇女节】Guójì Láodòng Fùnǚjié〈名〉 International Working Women's Day
【国际劳动节】Guójì Láodòngjié〈名〉 International Labour Day
【国际劳工组织】Guójì Láogōng Zǔzhī〈名〉 International Labour Organization (ILO)
【国际联盟】Guójì Liánméng〈名〉 League of Nations
【国际民航组织】Guójì Mínháng Zǔzhī〈名〉 International Civil Aviation Organization (ICAO)
【国际排球联合会】Guójì Páiqiú Liánhéhuì〈名〉 International Volleyball Federation
【国际乒联】Guójì Pīnglián〈简称〉= 国际乒乓球联合会
【国际乒乓球联合会】Guójì Pīngpāngqiú Liánhéhuì〈名〉 International Table Tennis Federation
【国际人权公约】Guójì Rénquán Gōngyuē〈名〉 International Human Rights Convention
【国际人权日】Guójì Rénquánrì〈名〉 International Human Rights Day
【国际日期变更线】guójì rìqī biàn gēng xiàn〈名〉 international date line
【国际扫盲年】Guójì Sǎomángnián〈名〉 International Literacy Year
【国际社会】guójì shèhuì〈名〉 international community
【国际市场】guójì shìchǎng〈名〉 international market
【国际事务】guójì shìwù〈名〉 international affairs: 处理～ deal with international affairs
【国际体操联合会】Guójì Tǐcāo Liánhéhuì〈名〉 International Gymnastic Federation (IGF)
【国际玩笑】guójì wánxiào〈名〉 big joke: 开～ tell a world-famous joke
【国际维和部队】Guójì Wéihé Bùduì〈名〉 International Peacekeeping Force
【国际象棋】guójì xiàngqí ▸p. 909〈名〉 chess: ～特级大师 International Grandmaster
【国际刑警组织】Guójì Xíngjǐng Zǔzhī〈名〉 International Criminal Police Organization (Interpol)
【国际性】guójìxìng〈名〉 internationalism: 有～ have international character
【国际音标】Guójì Yīnbiāo〈名〉 International Phonetic Alphabet (IPA)
【国际游资】guójì yóuzī〈名〉 hot money
【国际舆论】guójì yúlùn〈名〉 world opinion
【国际展览局】Guójì Zhǎnlǎnjú〈名〉 International Bureau of Expositions
【国际直拨电话】guójì zhíbō diànhuà〈名〉 international direct dialling (IDD)
【国际制裁】guójì zhìcái〈名〉 international sanction
【国际仲裁】guójì zhòngcái〈名〉 international arbitration
【国际主义】guójìzhǔyì〈名〉 internationalism: 发扬～精神 develop internationalism
【国际住房年】Guójì Zhùfángnián〈名〉 International Year of Shelter for the Homeless
【国际准则】guójì zhǔnzé〈名〉 international standard
【国际纵队】Guójì Zòngduì〈名〉 International Brigade
【国际足联】Guójì Zúlián〈简称〉= 国际足球协会联合会
【国际足球协会联合会】Guójì Zúqiú Xiéhuì Liánhéhuì〈名〉 Fédération Internationale de Football Association (FIFA)
【国家】guójiā〈名〉 country: 不结盟～ non-aligned nation ‖ 第一/三世界～ First/Third World country ‖ 欠发达/发展中/发达～ underdeveloped/developing/developed country
【国家安全部】Guójiā Ānquánbù〈名〉 Ministry of State Security
【国家版权局】Guójiā Bǎnquánjú〈名〉 State Copyright Bureau
【国家标准】guójiā biāozhǔn〈名〉 national standard
【国家标准化管理委员会】Guójiā Biāozhǔnhuà Guǎnlǐ Wěiyuánhuì〈名〉 State Administration for Standardization
【国家裁判】guójiā cáipàn〈名〉(指田径) national judge;(指排球、羽毛球、网球等) national umpire;(指篮球、足球等) national referee
【国家出入境检验检疫局】Guójiā Chūrùjìng Jiǎnyàn Jiǎnyìjú〈名〉 State Administration for Entry-Exit Inspection and Quarantine
【国家地震局】Guójiā Dìzhènjú〈名〉 State Seismological Bureau
【国家杜马】Guójiā Dùmǎ〈名〉State Duma [lower house of the Russian Parliament]
【国家队】guójiāduì〈名〉［体育］ national team
【国家发展计划委员会】Guójiā Fāzhǎn Jìhuà Wěiyuánhuì〈名〉 State Development Planning Commission
【国家工商行政管理局】Guójiā Gōngshāng Xíngzhèng Guǎnlǐjú〈名〉 State Administration of Industry and Commerce
【国家公园】guójiā gōngyuán〈名〉 national park
【国家广播电影电视总局】Guójiā Guǎngbō Diànyǐng Diànshì Zǒngjú〈名〉 State Administration of Radio, Film and Television
【国家航空航天局】Guójiā Hángkōng Hángtiānjú〈名〉 National Aeronautics and Space Administration (NASA)
【国家环境保护总局】Guójiā Huánjìng Bǎohù Zǒngjú〈名〉 State Environmental Protection Administration (SEPA)
【国家机关】guójiā jīguān〈名〉 state organ: ～工作人员 state personnel
【国家机器】guójiā jīqì〈名〉state apparatus
【国家级】guójiājí〈形〉 state-level: ～裁判 national referee
【国家计划生育委员会】Guójiā Jìhuà Shēngyù Wěiyuánhuì〈名〉 State Family Planning Commission
【国家纪录】guójiā jìlù〈名〉 national record: 打破～ break the national record
【国家民族事务委员会】Guójiā Mínzú Shìwù Wěiyuánhuì〈名〉 State Ethnic Affairs Commission
【国家年】guójiānián〈名〉 National Year [year promoting cooperation between two countries in a wide range of areas]
【国家赔偿】guójiā péicháng〈名〉 State compensation: 要求～ claim State compensation
【国家气象局】Guójiā Qìxiàngjú〈名〉 State Meteorological Bureau
【国家权力】guójiā quánlì〈名〉state power
【国家税务总局】Guójiā Shuìwù Zǒngjú〈名〉 State Taxation Administration
【国家体育总局】Guójiā Tǐyù Zǒngjú〈名〉 State Physical Culture Administration
【国家统计局】Guójiā Tǒngjìjú〈名〉 State Statistics Bureau
【国家图书馆】guójiā túshūguǎn〈名〉 national library
【国家外国专家局】Guójiā Wàiguó Zhuānjiājú〈名〉 State Bureau of Foreign Experts Affairs
【国家外汇管理局】Guójiā Wàihuì Guǎnlǐjú〈名〉 State Administration of Foreign Exchange
【国家文物局】Guójiā Wénwùjú〈名〉 State Cultural Relics Bureau
【国家兴亡，匹夫有责】guójiā xīngwáng, pǐfū yǒu zé〈成〉 every man shares responsibility for the fate of his country
【国家行为】guójiā xíngwéi〈名〉 state act
【国家烟草专卖局】Guójiā Yāncǎo Zhuānmàijú〈名〉State Tobacco Monopoly Bureau
【国家药品监督管理局】Guójiā Yàopǐn Jiāndū Guǎnlǐjú〈名〉 State Drug Administration
【国家银行】guójiā yínháng〈名〉 state bank
【国家语言文字工作委员会】Guójiā Yǔyán Wénzì Gōngzuò Wěiyuánhuì〈名〉 State Language Work Committee
【国家预算】guójiā yùsuàn〈名〉 national budget

【国家元首】guójiā yuánshǒu〈名〉head of state

【国家政权】guójiā zhèngquán〈名〉state power

【国家知识产权局】Guójiā Zhīshi Chǎnquánjú〈名〉State Intellectual Property Office

【国家主席】guójiā zhǔxí〈名〉president: 国家副主席 vice-president

【国脚】guójiǎo〈名〉national footballer

【国教】guójiào〈名〉state religion: 神道教是日本的～。Shintoism is the national religion of Japan.

【国界】guójiè〈名〉national boundary: 划定～ fix the borderline

【国境】guójìng〈名〉**1**（领土范围）national territory **2**（边境）national border: 出入～ leave and enter a country ‖ 偷越～ cross the border illegally ‖ ～线 boundary line of a country

【国舅】guójiù〈名〉〈旧〉emperor's brother-in-law

【国剧】guójù〈名〉**1**（指传统剧种）national opera **2**（京剧）Beijing opera

【国君】guójūn〈名〉monarch

【国库】guókù〈名〉national treasury: 充实～ replenish the national treasury ‖ ～收入 public revenue

【国库券】guókùquàn〈名〉state treasury bond: 发行～ issue state treasury bonds

【国力】guólì〈名〉national power: 增强～ strengthen national power ‖ ～雄厚 have a solid national strength

【国立】guólì〈形〉state-run: ～大学 national university

【国联】Guólián〈简称〉= 国际联盟

【国门】guómén〈名〉**1**〈书〉（城门）gate of a capital **2**〈喻〉（边境）border: 把入侵者赶出～ drive out the invaders

【国民】guómín〈名〉people of a nation: ～教育 national education

【国民待遇】guómín dàiyù〈名〉national treatment

【国民党】Guómíndǎng〈名〉**1**（泛指）nationalist party **2**（中国国民党）Kuomintang (KMT)

> **中国国民党**
>
> A political party of Taiwan. Known in its romanized form as the Kuomintang (KMT). The party was founded in 1912 by Sun Yat-sen (孙中山), following the overthrow of the Qing Dynasty. It became the ruling party of China with a provisional government based in Nanjing in 1927. Following the Communist victory in 1949, the Party, led by Chiang Kaishek (蒋介石), retreated to Taiwan. The KMT today forms part of the Pan-Blue coalition which supports reunification with the mainland. The KMT is guided by the 'Three People's Principles' (►三民主义). The party flag is a white sun against a blue sky.

【国民经济】guómín jīngjì〈名〉national economy: 发展～ develop the national economy ‖ ～持续、稳定、协调的发展 sustained, stable and coordinated growth of the national economy

【国民警卫队】Guómín Jǐngwèiduì〈名〉National Guard

【国民生产总值】guómín shēngchǎn zǒngzhí〈名〉gross national product (GNP)

【国民收入】guómín shōurù〈名〉national income: 提高～ increase the national income ‖ ～分配 distribution of national income

【国难】guónàn〈名〉national crisis: 共赴～ be united to save one's country ‖ ～当前 be faced with a national crisis

【国内】guónèi〈形〉domestic: ～市场 domestic market

【国内航线】guónèi hángxiàn〈名〉internal air route

【国内贸易】guónèi màoyì〈名〉internal trade

【国内生产总值】guónèi shēngchǎn zǒngzhí〈名〉gross domestic product (GDP)

【国内市场】guónèi shìchǎng〈名〉home market

【国内新闻】guónèi xīnwén〈名〉national news

【国内游】guónèiyóu〈名〉domestic tourism: ～市场 domestic tourism market

【国内战争】guónèi zhànzhēng〈名〉civil war

【国内直拨电话】guónèi zhíbō diànhuà〈名〉domestic direct dialling (DDD)

【国内总收入】guónèi zǒngshōurù〈名〉gross domestic income

【国破家亡】guópò-jiāwáng〈成〉country defeated and family ruined

【国戚】guóqī〈名〉〈旧〉relatives of an emperor: 皇亲～ relatives of the emperor

【国旗】guóqí〈名〉national flag: 升～ hoist the national flag

【国企】guóqǐ〈简称〉= 国有企业

【国情】guóqíng〈名〉national conditions: 从中国的～出发 proceed from China's actual conditions ‖ 合乎～ conform to the actual situations of a country

【国情咨文】guóqíng zīwén〈名〉State of the Union Message

【国庆】Guóqìng〈名〉National Day: 庆～ celebrate National Day

【国庆节】Guóqìngjié = 国庆 Guóqìng

> **国庆节**
>
> The 1st October, a national holiday commemorating the founding of the People's Republic of China on 1st October, 1949. The festival period lasts from 1st-7th October and forms part of Golden Week (►黄金周).

【国人】guórén〈名〉〈书〉compatriot

【国丧】guósāng〈名〉national mourning

【国色】guósè〈名〉〈旧〉national beauty: ►天姿～

【国色天香】guósè-tiānxiāng〈成〉be of peerless beauty

【国殇】guóshāng〈名〉〈书〉national martyr

【国史】guóshǐ〈名〉history of a country

【国事】guóshì〈名〉state affairs: 共商～ discuss state affairs together ‖ 关心～ concern oneself with affairs of state

【国事访问】guóshì fǎngwèn〈名〉state visit: 进行～ pay a state visit to a country

【国势】guóshì〈名〉**1**（国力）national strength **2**（国家形势）national situation

【国是】guóshì〈名〉〈书〉affairs of national interest: 共商～ confer with sb. upon major affairs of state

【国手】guóshǒu〈名〉player on a national team: 这支篮球队拥有两名～。Two players in this basketball team are from the national team.

【国书】guóshū〈名〉credentials: 递交～ present one's credentials

【国术】guóshù〈名〉*wushu* [traditional Chinese marshal arts]

【国税】guóshuì〈名〉state tax

【国台办】Guótáibàn〈简称〉= 国务院台湾事务办公室

【国泰民安】guótài-mín'ān〈成〉the country is prosperous and the people are living in peace

【国体】guótǐ〈名〉**1**（国家体制）state system **2**（国家尊严）national prestige: 有辱～ bring disgrace to national prestige

【国统区】guótǒngqū〈名〉area controlled by the Kuomintang

【国土】guótǔ〈名〉territory: 保卫我们神圣的～ defend our sacred territory

【国土安全】guótǔ ānquán〈名〉homeland security

【国土资源部】Guótǔ Zīyuánbù〈名〉Ministry of Land and Resources

【国外】guówài〈形〉overseas: 来自～ come from overseas ‖ 从～回来 return from abroad ‖ 在～旅行 travel abroad

【国外投资】guówài tóuzī〈名〉foreign investment

【国王】guówáng〈名〉king

【国威】guówēi〈名〉national prestige: 扬/振～ boost national prestige

【国文】guówén ►p. 918〈名〉**1**（本国语言）national language **2**〈旧〉（汉语）Chinese as the national language **3**（语文课）national Chinese language and literature

【国无宁日】guówúníngrì〈成〉there is no peace in the country

【国务】guówù〈名〉state affairs: 处理～ conduct state affairs

【国务会议】guówù huìyì〈名〉state conference

【国务卿】Guówùqīng〈名〉Secretary of State: 副～ Under-Secretary of State

【国务委员】guówù wěiyuán〈名〉member of the State Council

【国务院】guówùyuàn〈名〉**1**（指中国）State Council: ～秘书长 Secretary-General of the State Council ‖ ～总理 Premier of the State Council **2**（指美国）State Department: ～发言人 spokesman for the State Department

【国务院办公厅】Guówùyuàn Bàngōngtīng〈名〉General Office of the State Council

【国务院参事室】Guówùyuàn Cānshìshì〈名〉Councillor's Office of the State Council

【国务院法制办公室】Guówùyuàn Fǎzhì Bàngōngshì〈名〉Legislative Affairs Office of the State Council

【国务院港澳办公室】Guówùyuàn Gǎng-Ào Bàngōngshì〈名〉Hong Kong and Macao Affairs Office of the State Council

【国务院机关事务管理局】Guówùyuàn Jīguān Shìwù Guǎnlǐjú〈名〉Government Offices Administration of the State Council

【国务院台湾事务办公室】Guówùyuàn Táiwān Shìwù Bàngōngshì〈名〉Taiwan Affairs Office of the State Council

【国务院外事办公室】Guówùyuàn Wàishì Bàngōngshì〈名〉Foreign Affairs Office of the State Council

【国务院新闻办公室】Guówùyuàn Xīnwén Bàngōngshì〈名〉Information Office of the State Council

【国务院学位委员会】Guówùyuàn Xuéwèi Wěiyuánhuì〈名〉Academic Degrees Committee of the State Council

【国玺】guóxǐ〈名〉imperial seal

【国学】guóxué〈名〉Chinese cultural studies

【国宴】guóyàn〈名〉state banquet: 设～ serve a state banquet

【国药】guóyào〈名〉Chinese herbal medicine

【国音】guóyīn〈名〉〈旧〉standard Chinese pronunciation

【国营】guóyíng〈形〉state-operated: ～经济 state-run economy ‖ ～企业 state-run enterprise

【国优】guóyōu〈名〉national premium product

【国有】guóyǒu〈动〉be state-owned: 将铁路收归～ nationalize private railways ‖ ～财产 state-owned property ‖ 土地～。The land belongs to the state.
【国有股】guóyǒugǔ〈名〉state-owned shares: 持有～ keep the state-held shares ‖ 减持～ reduce the state's stake in listed companies
【国有股份制企业】guóyǒu gǔfènzhì qǐyè〈名〉state enterprise adopting the shareholding system
【国有化】guóyǒuhuà〈动〉nationalize: 实行～ nationalize
【国有民营】guóyǒu mínyíng〈名〉mechanism featuring the operation of state-owned enterprises on a non-state basis
【国有企业】guóyǒu qǐyè〈名〉state-owned enterprise (SOE): 搞活～ revitalize state-owned enterprises
【国有资产】guóyǒu zīchǎn〈名〉state-owned assets: ～流失 drain of state-owned assets
【国有国法，家有家规】guó yǒu guófǎ, jiā yǒu jiāguī〈俗〉a state has its laws and a family its rules
【国语】guóyǔ ►**p. 918**〈名〉**1**（本国语言）national language: 讲～ speak the national language **2**（汉语普通话）Chinese language
【国乐】guóyuè〈名〉traditional Chinese music
【国运】guóyùn〈名〉〈书〉destiny of a nation: ～昌盛 the nation has a flourishing future
【国葬】guózàng〈名〉state funeral: 举行～ hold a state funeral
【国贼】guózéi〈名〉national traitor
【国债】guózhài〈名〉national debt: 偿还～ pay back the national debts
【国子监】Guózǐjiàn〈名〉Imperial Academy [highest educational institute in feudal China]

掴（摑） guó = 掴 guāi

帼（幗） guó〈名〉〈旧〉women's headwear: ►巾～

虢 Guó〈名〉〈古〉Dukedom of Guo [a state in Zhou Dynasty]

guǒ

果[1] guǒ
A〈名〉**1**（果实）fruit: 干/鲜～ dried/fresh fruit ‖ 野～ wild fruit **2**（结果）result: ►前因后～
B〈副〉sure enough: ～如所料 just as expected ►～不其然, ～真

果[2] guǒ〈形〉determined: ►～断, ～敢
【果不其然】guǒbùqírán〈成〉just as expected: ～，天下雨了。It is raining just as was expected.
【果茶】guǒchá〈名〉fruit tea
【果丹皮】guǒdānpí〈名〉haw sheets
【果冻】guǒdòng〈名〉jelly〈英〉; jello〈美〉: 草莓～ strawberry jelly
【果断】guǒduàn〈形〉decisive: 做事～ act with decision ‖ 采取～措施 take decisive measures
【果饵】guǒ'ěr〈名〉sweets and snacks
【果脯】guǒfǔ〈名〉preserved fruit
【果腹】guǒfù〈动〉〈书〉satisfy one's hunger: 食不～ not have enough food to stay one's hunger
【果干儿】guǒgānr〈名〉dried fruit
【果敢】guǒgǎn〈形〉courageous and resolute: 采取～行动打击恐怖分子 take courageous and resolute action to fight terrorism
【果核】guǒhé〈名〉(fruit) stone〈英〉; pit〈美〉
【果酱】guǒjiàng〈名〉jam
【果胶】guǒjiāo〈名〉［生化］pectin
【果酒】guǒjiǔ〈名〉fruit wine
【果决】guǒjué〈形〉〈书〉firm and resolute: 办事～ act with decision and resolution
【果壳】guǒké〈名〉nutshell
【果篮】guǒlán〈名〉fruit basket
【果料】guǒliào〈名〉ingredients such as nuts, raisins, seeds, etc., used in making cakes
【果绿】guǒlǜ〈名〉light green
【果木】guǒmù〈名〉fruit tree
【果奶】guǒnǎi〈名〉fruit milk
【果农】guǒnóng〈名〉fruit grower
【果盘】guǒpán〈名〉fruit bowl
【果皮】guǒpí〈名〉rind
【果皮箱】guǒpíxiāng〈名〉litter bin
【果品】guǒpǐn〈名〉fruit: ～店 fruit shop ‖ 干鲜～ dried and fresh fruit
【果然】guǒrán〈副〉as expected: 我说情况会好转的，～如此。I said things would turn out well, and sure enough they did. ‖ 这种药～起了作用。As expected, this medicine has taken effect.
【果仁】guǒrén〈名〉kernel
【果肉】guǒròu〈名〉fruit flesh
【果实】guǒshí〈名〉**1**〈本〉fruit: ～累累 heaps of fruit **2**〈喻〉（结果）fruits: 劳动～ the fruits of one's labour ‖ 胜利～ fruits of victory
【果蔬】guǒshū〈名〉fruit and vegetable
【果树】guǒshù〈名〉fruit tree
【果穗】guǒsuì〈名〉（指玉米、高粱）ear;（指麦子等）spike
【果糖】guǒtáng〈名〉fructose
【果园】guǒyuán〈名〉orchard
【果真】guǒzhēn〈副〉as expected: 冠军～属于他。Sure enough, the championship went to him.
【果汁】guǒzhī〈名〉fruit juice: ～饮料 fruit drink ‖ 浓缩～ concentrated juice
【果子】guǒzi〈名〉fruit: ～熟了。The fruit is ripe.
【果子酱】guǒzijiàng = 果酱 guǒjiàng
【果子酒】guǒzijiǔ = 果酒 guǒjiǔ
【果子露】guǒzilù〈名〉fruit syrup
【果子狸】guǒzilí〈名〉［动物］masked civet

馃（餜） guǒ
【馃子】guǒzi〈名〉〈方〉deep-fried doughnut

i 国籍

■ 英语里有些表示国籍的词，可以做名词也可以做形容词。注意有些表示国籍的英语名词不能用作单数，这些名词通常以 -ese、-ish 或 -ch 结尾：

他是中国人
= He is Chinese
但不说
He is a Chinese

中国人以勤劳而著称
= The Chinese are renowned as hard workers

皮埃尔是法国人
= Pierre is French
或 Pierre is a Frenchman
但不说
Pierre is a French

法国人好客
= The French are hospitable

苏珊是英国人
= Susan is British
或 Susan is a British national
但不说
Susan is a British

英国人爱去酒吧
= The British like going to the pub

克洛艾是爱尔兰人
= Chloe is Irish
或 Chloe is an Irish girl
但不说
Chloe is an Irish

■ 英语里有时有专有名词表示某个国籍：

她是波兰人
= She is a Pole

亚当是冰岛人
= Adam is an Icelander

亚伯拉罕是丹麦人
= Abraham is a Dane

多莉是苏格兰人
= Dolly is a Scotswoman

■ 英语里还可用："表示国家的形容词 / 名词 + national/citizen/man/woman 等"。如表示国家的词没有形容词形式，可用名词代替（如 Thai）：

他是印度人
= He is an Indian man
或 He is an Indian national
或 He is an Indian citizen

她是西班牙人
= She is a Spanish woman

劳拉是泰国作家
= Laura is a Thai writer

谢里尔是美国歌手
= Cheryl is an American singer

■ 其他短语：

她是纯德国血统
= She is of German extraction

他们是意大利裔美国人
= They are Italian Americans

我是英籍华人
= I'm Chinese British

他出生在意大利
= He was born in Italy

他们来自墨西哥
= They come from Mexico

椁（槨） guǒ〈名〉outer coffin: ▸棺～

裹 guǒ〈动〉1（包裹）wrap: ～住伤口 bind a wound ‖ 用毯子～着小孩 wrap the child in a blanket ‖ 用绷带把受伤的腿～住 wrap the bandage round an injured leg ▸～腿, ～足不前 2（强行卷入）carry off: 匪徒们把一个年轻人～走了。The bandits took a young man and made away with him.

【裹脚】 guǒjiǎo〈名〉foot-binding: ～布 bandage for footbinding

【裹腿】 guǒtui〈名〉puttee

【裹胁】 guǒxié〈动〉coerce: 杀人犯逃跑时～了两个人质。The murderer ran away with two hostages.

【裹挟】 guǒxié〈动〉1（指风、流水）carry off: 河水～着小船滚滚而下。The river tossed the small boat about and carried it downstream. 2（指形势）sweep sb. along

【裹扎】 guǒzā〈动〉bind up: 用绷带～伤口 dress a wound with bandages

【裹足不前】 guǒzú-bùqián〈成〉drag one's heels

guò

过（過） guò

A〈动〉1（通过）pass: ～河 cross a river ‖ ～马路 cross a street ‖ 列车飞驰而～。The train whooshed past. 2（度过）spend time: ～一夜 stay overnight ‖ 你暑假在哪儿～? Where are you spending your summer holidays? ‖ 她日子～得不错。She is living a fairly comfortable life. 3（转移）transfer (ownership): ▸～继, ～门 4（看或回忆）go through: 您把这些钱～个数吧? Would you please count the money? 5（超过）surpass: 智慧～人 excel in wisdom ‖ ～了生育年龄 be past child-bearing age ‖ 年～六旬 be over sixty ‖ 她年龄～了，不能参加考试。She can't enter for the exam because she is over the age limit. 6（用在动词后）[used after another verb] a（表经过）[indicating passing by]: 翻～墙 get over a wall ‖ 她从他身边径直走～。She passed by him without stopping. ‖ 子弹在我们头顶飞～。Bullets were going over our heads. b（表调转方向）[indicating a change in direction]: 背～脸去 turn one's face away ‖ 她转～身，面对着我。She turned and faced me. c（表超过）[indicating an excess in degree or amount]: 错～机会 let a chance go by ‖ 坐～站 go past one's station ‖ 我看那位病人活不～今晚了。I don't think the patient will live through the night. d（表胜过）[indicating doing better (than)]: 他爱妻子胜～一切。His wife is everything to him. ‖ 我可比不～他。I'm no match for him. 7（用在形容词后，表超过）[used after an adjective to indicate an excess in degree]: 高～一头 be taller by a head ‖ 这座新楼将高～其他所有建筑物。The new building will be taller than all the others.

B〈副〉excessively: 吃得～饱 overeat ‖ 目标定得～高 aim too high

C〈名〉fault: 功大于～ merits outweighing faults ▸～错, 记～, 将功补～

▸Guō, guo

【过半】 guòbàn〈动〉be more than half: 时间～，任务～。More than half our job is done in over half the time.

【过磅】 guòbàng〈动〉weigh

【过不去】 guòbuqù〈动〉1（通不过）cannot go through: 入口处太窄，卡车～。The truck couldn't get through the narrow entrance. 2（为难）be hard on sb.: 跟自己～ be too hard on oneself ‖ 我并不是存心要跟你～。I didn't mean to be difficult with you. 3（抱歉）feel sorry for: 给你添了这么多麻烦，我心里真～。I'm really sorry for giving you so much trouble.

【过场】 guòchǎng A〈动〉walk through one's part: 走～ do sth. as a mere formality B〈名〉interlude

【过程】 guòchéng〈名〉process: 在谈判/生产～中 in the course of negotiation/manufacture ‖ 治疗顽症需要一个很长的～。It takes a long time to cure a deep-rooted disease.

【过秤】 guòchèng〈动〉weigh: 付钱之前先过一下称。Weigh it before you pay for it.

【过从】 guòcóng〈动〉〈书〉associate: 二人～甚密。They keep close contact with each other.

【过错】 guòcuò〈名〉fault: 不是他的～。It's not his fault. ‖ 是我的～吗? Am I at fault?

【过当】 guòdàng〈动〉be inappropriate: 言行～ inappropriate words and deeds

【过道】 guòdào〈名〉aisle; gangway〈英〉: 清理～ clean up the corridor ‖ 别站在～上。Don't stand in the aisle.

【过得去】 guòdequ〈动〉1（通得过）be able to get through: 门不窄，钢琴～。The door is not narrow so the piano can get through. 2（不困难）get by: 生活还勉强～ just manage to get by in life 3（说得过去）be passable: 她的英语马马虎虎还～。She speaks passable English. 4（无愧）feel at ease: 让你等了这么长时间，我心里怎能～。I feel terrible about keeping you waiting so long.

【过电】 guòdiàn〈动〉get an electric shock

【过电影】 guò diànyǐng〈动〉〈口〉〈喻〉go over past scenes in one's mind

【过冬】 guòdōng〈动〉pass the winter: 在南方～ winter in the south ‖ ～作物 winter crop

【过度】 guòdù〈形〉excessive: 操劳～ overstrain oneself ‖ ～开垦 excess reclamation ‖ ～捕捞 overfishing ‖ ～放牧 overgrazing ‖ 别～紧张。Don't overtax yourself.

【过渡】 guòdù〈动〉transit: 从计划经济向市场经济的平稳～ smooth transition from a planned economy to a market economy ‖ ～阶段 transition stage ‖ ～时期 transition period

【过渡期】 guòdùqī〈名〉transition period

【过渡政府】 guòdù zhèngfǔ〈名〉interim government

【过访】 guòfǎng〈动〉〈书〉pay a visit

【过分】 guòfèn〈形〉excessive: ～老实 be honest to a fault ‖ 玩笑开得太～ carry a joke too far

【过关】 guòguān〈动〉1〈本〉break through a pass 2〈喻〉be up to standard: 技术不～ the skills are below standard ‖ 考试～了 passed an exam

【过关斩将】 guòguān-zhǎnjiàng = 过五关，斩六将 guò wǔ guān, zhǎn liù jiàng

【过河拆桥】 guòhé-chāiqiáo〈成〉drop one's benefactors when they are no longer needed

【过后】 guòhòu〈副〉1（后来）later: ～怎么样了? What happened next? 2（之后）afterwards: 茶点～，会议继续进行。After tea, the meeting resumed.

【过户】 guòhù〈动〉transfer ownership: ～手续费 transfer charges ‖ 财产已～到他妻子的名下。The assets were transferred into his wife's name.

【过活】 guòhuó〈动〉make a living: 靠妻子的收入～ live off one's wife's earnings

【过火】 guòhuǒ〈形〉overdone: 电影里的爱情戏演得有点～。The love scenes in the film were a bit overdone. ‖ 你这样说也太～了。You're going too far in saying that.

【过激】 guòjī〈形〉extremist: ～行动 excessive action ‖ ～言论 radical opinions

【过继】 guòjì〈动〉1（收养）adopt a relative's son 2（给人收养）have one's son adopted by a relative

【过家家】 guòjiājia〈动〉〈方〉play house [children's game]

【过奖】 guòjiǎng〈动〉〈套〉praise excessively: 您～啦。You flatter me.

【过街老鼠】 guòjiē-lǎoshǔ〈成〉〈喻〉person hated by everyone

【过街楼】 guòjiēlóu〈名〉overhead projection spanning a lane

【过街天桥】 guòjiē tiānqiáo〈名〉overpass

【过节】 guòjié〈动〉celebrate a festival

【过节儿】 guòjier〈名〉grudge: 他们之间曾有～。They used to bear each other grudges.

【过劲儿】 guòjìnr〈动〉overdo

【过境】 guòjìng〈动〉cross the border: ～船只 ship in transit ‖ ～货物 transit goods ‖ ～贸易 transit trade

【过境签证】 guòjìng qiānzhèng〈名〉transit visa

【过客】 guòkè〈名〉passing visitor: 检查每位～ search everybody who passes by

【过来】 guòlái〈动〉come over: ～帮帮我。Come here and help me.

【过来】 guòlai〈动〉1（表充分）[indicating the sufficiency of time, quantity, etc.]: 一个人忙不～。It's all too much for one person. 2（表来到）[indicating motion towards the speaker]: 请把盐递～。Please pass me the salt. 3（表调转方向）[indicating turning in the direction of the speaker]: 把唱片翻～ turn over a gramophone record ‖ 把脸转～! Turn your face this way! 4（表状态）[indicating a return to the original/normal state]: 清醒～ regain consciousness ‖ 花又活～了。The flower came back to life.

【过来人】 guòlairén〈名〉person who has had a particular experience: 他是～，深知登山运动员的酸甜苦辣。He is a mountaineer so he knows all the joys and sorrows of people who climb mountains.

【过劳死】 guòláosǐ〈动〉karoshi [death by overwork]

【过梁】 guòliáng〈名〉［建筑］lintel

【过量】 guòliàng〈形〉excessive: 死于～服用海洛因 die from a heroin overdose ‖ 饮酒/吸烟～ drink/smoke too much

【过淋】 guòlín〈动〉filter: ～煎好的中药 filtrate the decocted medicinal herbs

【过磷酸钙】 guòlínsuāngài〈名〉［化学］calcium superphosphate

【过录】 guòlù〈动〉copy from one book to another: 把这几个句子～到笔记本上。Copy these sentences into your notebook.

【过路】 guòlù〈动〉pass by: ～费 road toll ‖ ～行人 passer-by

【过路财神】 guòlù-cáishén〈成〉person who temporarily handles a large sum of money but has no legal possession or standing

【过虑】 guòlǜ〈动〉worry unnecessarily: 不必～。Don't worry.

【过滤】guòlǜ〈动〉 filter: ～饮用水 filter the drinking water
【过滤嘴】guòlǜzuǐ〈名〉 filter tip: ～香烟 filter-tipped cigarette
【过门】guòmén〈动〉 [of a woman] get married: 刚～的新媳妇 newly-married wife
【过门儿】guòménr〈名〉［音乐］ prelude
【过敏】guòmǐn **A** ▸**p. 50**〈动〉［医学］ be anaphylactic: 对花粉～ be allergic to pollen ‖ 青霉素～ penicillin allergy ‖ 皮肤～ skin allergy **B**〈形〉 oversensitive: 不要太～，我只不过是在开玩笑。 Don't be so sensitive. I was only joking.
【过敏反应】guòmǐn fǎnyìng〈名〉 allergic reaction
【过敏试验】guòmǐn shìyàn〈名〉 allergic test
【过敏体质】guòmǐn tǐzhì〈名〉 allergic diathesis
【过敏性】guòmǐnxìng〈名〉 anaphylaxis: ～鼻炎 anaphylactic rhinitis ‖ ～皮炎 allergic dermatitis
【过目】guòmù〈动〉 look over: 有份文件请您～。 There's a document for you to run through.
【过目不忘】guòmù-bùwàng〈成〉 be able to learn sth. by heart after going over it once
【过目成诵】guòmù-chéngsòng〈成〉 be able to recite sth. after going over it once
【过年】guònián〈动〉 celebrate New Year: 回家～ go home for New Year
【过年】guònian〈名〉〈口〉 next year: 她～就十八岁了。 She will be eighteen next year.
【过期】guòqī〈动〉 be overdue: ～车票 expired ticket ‖ ～食品 food past its best before date ‖ 她的驾驶执照已～。 Her driving licence has expired.
【过谦】guòqiān〈形〉 too modest
【过去】guòqù〈名〉 former times: 回顾～ recall the past ‖ ～的事 thing of the past
【过去分词】guòqù fēncí〈名〉 past participle
【过去时】guòqùshí〈名〉 past tense
【过去式】guòqùshì〈名〉 past tense
【过去】guòqu〈动〉 **1**（表离开） pass: 你～帮她一把。 Go and help her. ‖ 事情已经～了，再别想它了。 The accident is behind you now, so forget about it. ‖ 一眨眼，三十年～了。 Thirty years passed in a flash. **2**（表经过） [indicating motion away from the speaker]: 警车从右边超了～。 The police car passed on the right. ‖ 我从她身旁径直走了～。 I passed by her without stopping. **3**（表调转方向） [indicating turning away from sb.]: 请转～，我看看你的背部。 Turn round and let me look at your back. ‖ 她把头转了～。 She turned her head away. **4**（表状态） [indicating loss of the original/normal state]: 当场吓得昏了～ faint from fright on the spot **5**（表通过） [indicating success of an action]: 不让任何拼写错误漏～ not allow any spelling mistakes to get through ‖ 没有你的帮助，我也能应付～。 I can get by without your help.
【过去了】guòqule ▸**p. 772**〈动〉〈婉〉 pass away: 他父亲昨天晚上～。 His father passed away last night.
【过热】guòrè〈形〉〈喻〉 overheated: ～的房地产市场 overheated property market
【过人】guòrén〈动〉 excel: 智慧～ excel in wisdom ‖ 记忆力～ have an exceptionally powerful memory
【过日子】guò rìzi〈动〉 **1**（生活） live one's life: 靠一点微薄的收入～ get by on a small income ‖ 一家六口靠他的稿费～。 The family of six depend solely on his income as a writer. **2**（节俭） live economically: 我妻子很会～。 My wife is an excellent manager.
【过筛子】guò shāizi〈动〉 **1**〈本〉 sift out: 把面粉～，筛出麸皮 sift the flour to remove the bran **2**〈喻〉 choose: 讨论之前先把这些问题～ go over the questions first so as to decide which one is to be discussed
【过山车】guòshānchē〈名〉 roller coaster; big dipper〈英〉
【过晌】guòshǎng〈方〉= 过午 guòwǔ
【过甚】guòshèn〈形〉〈书〉 exaggerated: 言之～ you're exaggerating
【过甚其词】guòshènqící〈成〉 stretch the truth
【过生日】guò shēngrì〈动〉 celebrate one's birthday
【过剩】guòshèng〈动〉 have an excess of: 精力～ be excessively energetic ‖ ～产品 surplus product
【过失】guòshī〈名〉 **1**（错误） fault: 承认～ acknowledge one's fault ‖ 隐瞒～ hide one's mistake ‖ 重大～ gross negligence **2**（疏忽犯罪） offence: ～犯罪 criminal negligence ‖ ～杀人 manslaughter
【过失行为】guòshī xíngwéi〈名〉 negligent act
【过失罪】guòshīzuì〈名〉 negligent crime
【过时】guòshí **A**〈动〉 pass the appointed time: ～不候 not wait after the appointed time **B**〈形〉 out-of-date: ～的款式 outdated design
【过世】guòshì ▸**p. 772**〈动〉〈婉〉 pass away: 他爷爷今早～了。 His grandfather passed away this morning.
【过手】guòshǒu〈动〉 handle
【过数】guòshù〈动〉 check the numbers: 这是你的钱，请过个数。 This is your money; please count it.
【过塑】guòsù〈动〉 have sth. plastic-coated: 给照片～ have the picture plastic-coated
【过堂】guòtáng〈动〉〈旧〉 stand trial in a court
【过堂风】guòtángfēng〈名〉 draught
【过头】guòtóu〈形〉 overdone: 她聪明～了。 She outsmarted herself. ‖ 这件事你做～了。 You overdid it.
【过屠门而大嚼】guò túmén ér dà jué〈成〉〈喻〉 feast oneself on illusions
【过往】guòwǎng〈动〉 **1**（来去） come and go: ～车辆 passing traffic ‖ ～行人 pedestrian **2**（交往） associate with: ～甚密 be closely associated with each other
【过问】guòwèn〈动〉 concern oneself with: 不～私事 not concern oneself with private affairs ‖ 亲自～（某事） take a personal interest (in sth.) ‖ 无人～ be left unattended
【过午】guòwǔ〈名〉 afternoon
【过五关，斩六将】guò wǔ guān, zhǎn liù jiàng〈惯〉〈喻〉 clear away all the obstacles in one's path
【过细】guòxì〈形〉 meticulous: 工作要～。 Meticulous care is required in the work.
【过眼】guòyǎn〈动〉 look over
【过眼烟云】guòyǎn-yānyún = 过眼云烟 guòyǎn-yúnyān
【过眼云烟】guòyǎn-yúnyān〈成〉 as transient as fleeting clouds
【过氧化氢】guòyǎnghuàqīng〈名〉［化学］ perhydrol
【过氧化锌】guòyǎnghuàxīn〈名〉［化学］ zinc peroxide
【过夜】guòyè〈动〉 **1**（留宿） spend a night: 留某人～ put sb. up ‖ 你是留下来～呢，还是回家? Are you spending the night, or are you going home? **2** = 隔夜 géyè
【过意不去】guòyìbùqù〈惯〉 feel sorry: 打扰了他，我心里真～。 I feel awful about having disturbed him.
【过瘾】guòyǐn〈动〉 enjoy oneself to the full: 今天玩得真～。 I had the time of my life today.
【过硬】guòyìng〈形〉 expert: 技术上～ be perfect at a skill ‖ ～本领 first-rate capability
【过犹不及】guòyóubùjí〈成〉 too much is as bad as too little
【过于】guòyú〈副〉 excessively: ～草率/自信 be overly hasty/confident ‖ 对某人的玩笑～认真 take sb.'s joke too much to heart
【过誉】guòyù〈动〉 overly praise: 你～啦。 You flatter me.
【过云雨】guòyúnyǔ〈名〉 passing shower
【过载】guòzài〈动〉 **1**（超载） overload: 电流～ overload of electric current **2**（指转移） trans-ship
【过载保护】guòzài bǎohù〈名〉 overcurrent protection
【过账】guòzhàng〈动〉 transfer items
【过招】guòzhāo〈动〉 compete to outwit
【过重】guòzhòng〈形〉 [of letters, luggage, etc.] overweight

guo

过（過） guo〈助〉 **1**（表结束） 会已经开～了。 The meeting's already been held. ‖ 她早上来～。 She was here this morning. ‖ 我没有去～加拿大。 I have never been to Canada. **2**（表过去） 老太太当姑娘时也漂亮～。 The old lady used to be very beautiful when she was a girl.
▸Guō, guò

g

Hh

hā

哈[1] hā〈动〉exhale with the mouth open: 往手上～气 blow on one's hands ▸～欠

哈[2] hā
A〈叹〉aha: ～～，我猜着了。Aha, I've got it.
B〈拟〉ha-ha: ～～大笑 laugh heartily

哈[3] hā〈动〉**1**（弯腰）bend: ▸～腰 **2**〈口〉（迷恋）be crazy for
▸hǎ, hà

【哈尔滨】Hā'ěrbīn ▸**p. 661**〈名〉Harbin [capital of Heilongjiang Province (黑龙江)]
【哈哈镜】hāhājìng〈名〉distorting mirror
【哈吉】hājí〈名〉［伊斯兰教］（指朝觐者）haji
【哈拉雷】Hālāléi〈名〉Harare
【哈喇子】hālázi〈名〉〈方〉dribble: 流～ drool
【哈喇】hāla **A**〈形〉〈口〉rancid: 这块猪油～了。This lump of lard has gone rancid. **B**〈动〉〈旧〉put sb. to death
【哈雷彗星】Hāléi Huìxīng〈名〉［天文］Halley's Comet
【哈里发】hālǐfā〈名〉［伊斯兰教］**1**（指领袖）caliph **2**（指学习者）Islamic caliph
【哈密瓜】hāmìguā〈名〉Hami melon
【哈尼族】Hānízú〈名〉Hani ethnic group
【哈欠】hāqian〈名〉yawn: 他又伸懒腰又打～。He stretched and yawned.
【哈萨克斯坦】Hāsàkèsītǎn〈名〉Kazakhstan: ～人 Kazakh ‖ ～语 Kazakh
【哈萨克族】Hāsàkèzú〈名〉Kazakh ethnic group, Kazak ethnic group, Qazaq ethnic group
【哈腰】hāyāo〈动〉**1**（弯腰）stoop: 他～拣起地上的几枚硬币。He bent over to pick a few coins up from the ground. **2**（表示恭敬）bow slightly: ▸点头～

铪（鉿） hā〈名〉［化学］hafnium (Hf)

há

虾（蝦） há
【虾蟆】háma = 蛤蟆 háma
▸xiā

蛤 há
▸gé
【蛤蟆】háma〈名〉**1**（青蛙）frog **2**（蟾蜍）toad
【蛤蟆镜】hámajìng〈名〉sunglasses with huge lenses

hǎ

哈 hǎ
▸hā, hà
【哈巴狗】hǎbagǒu〈名〉**1**（指狗）Pekinese **2**〈喻〉（指人）sycophant
【哈达】hǎdá〈名〉*khatag* [ceremonial length of silk used by Tibetans and Mongolians]: 献～ present a *khatag*

hà

哈 hà
▸hā, hǎ
【哈士蟆】hàshìmá〈名〉Chinese forest frog

hāi

咳 hāi〈叹〉**1**（用于引起注意）hey: ～，大家快来呀! Hey, come here! **2**（表惊异）oh: ～，别提啦! Oh, please don't say anything more about it. ‖ ～，我怎么这么糊涂! Damn it! How stupid I was!
▸ké

嗨 hāi
【嗨哟】hāiyō〈叹〉heave ho

hái

还（還） hái〈副〉**1**（仍然）still: 现在两点了，他～没有来。It's two o'clock now and he hasn't come yet. ‖ 夜深了，他～在工作。It was late at night and he was still working. **2**（尚且）even: 你～不知道，更不用说一个外国人。If you don't even know then a foreigner certainly won't. ‖ 你～害怕，何况一个小孩呢? If you're scared then what hope for a small child? **3**（也）also: 我们不但学英语，～学日语。We study Japanese as well as English. **4**（更加）even more: 今天比昨天～冷。It's even colder today than yesterday. ‖ 今年的产量比去年～要高。This year's output is even higher than last year's. **5**（勉强过得去）fairly: 教室不大，但～明亮。The classroom is not big, but it is fairly bright. **6**（表强调）[used for emphasis or to show sarcasm]: 这～了得! This is the limit! ‖ 这些～算他们的好作文呢。These are supposed to be their best compositions. **7**（表赞叹）[used to express unexpectedness]: 他～真有办法。He is really resourceful. **8**（早在）as early as: ～在初中时，她就通过了大学英语六级考试。She passed Band 6 of the College English Test when she was only a junior high school student.
▸huán
【还好】háihǎo〈形〉**1**（大体可以）not bad: 不吃饭～，一吃就肚子疼。I feel quite OK if I don't eat anything. It's when I try to eat that my stomach hurts. ‖ 你今天感觉如何? ——～。How are you feeling today? — Not so bad. **2**（还算幸运）fortunate: ～，当时有位医生在场。Fortunately enough, a doctor happened to be on the scene.
【还是】háishi **A**〈副〉**1**（仍然）nevertheless: 尽管如此，我～要感谢你。Thank you all the same. ‖ 他～赢了。He won after all. **2**（表劝说）had better: 你～带上手电筒吧。You'd better take a torch with you. ‖ 你～帮他个忙吧。You'd better lend him a hand. **B**〈连〉or: 你吃米饭，～吃面条? Do you want rice or noodles?

孩 hái〈名〉child: ▸男～儿, 女～儿
【孩提】háití〈名〉〈书〉infancy: ～时代的记忆 memories from early childhood
【孩童】háitóng〈名〉child
【孩子】háizi〈名〉child
【孩子气】háiziqì **A**〈形〉childish: 一脸的～ look childish **B**〈名〉childishness

骸 hái〈名〉**1**（骨头）skeleton: ▸～骨, 残～ **2**（身体）body: ▸形～, 遗～
【骸骨】háigǔ〈名〉skeleton

hǎi

胲 hǎi〈名〉［化学］hydroxylamine
▸gǎi

海 hǎi
A ▸**p. 164**〈名〉**1**（大海）sea: 在～里游泳 swim in the sea ▸～港, 内～ **2**〈旧〉（海外）overseas: ▸～棠 **3**（湖泊）big lake: ▸里～, 青～ **4**〈喻〉（大片）sea: 花～ sea of flowers ‖ 学～无涯 knowledge is infinite ▸火～, 林～, 人～
B〈形〉〈方〉profuse: 昨天展览会上的人可～了! What a lot of people visited the exhibition yesterday! ▸～报, ～量, ～碗
C〈副〉〈方〉without restraint: ～吃～喝 eat and drink to one's heart's content ‖ ～聊 chat randomly and aimlessly
【海岸】hǎi'àn〈名〉sea coast: 沿～ along the coast
【海岸警卫队】hǎi'àn jǐngwèiduì〈名〉coast guard
【海岸炮】hǎi'ànpào〈名〉coast gun: ～台 coast battery
【海岸线】hǎi'ànxiàn〈名〉coastline
【海拔】hǎibá〈名〉height above sea level:

～高度 altitude
【海白菜】hǎibáicài〈名〉sea lettuce
【海报】hǎibào〈名〉playbill: 张贴～ put up a poster ‖ 电影～ film programme
【海豹】hǎibào〈名〉［动物］seal: ～皮 sealskin
【海滨】hǎibīn〈名〉seaside: ～城市 seaside city ‖ ～浴场 bathing beach
【海波】hǎibō〈名〉［化学］hypo
【海菜】hǎicài〈名〉edible seaweed
【海草】hǎicǎo〈名〉seaweed
【海产】hǎichǎn **A**〈名〉marine product **B**〈形〉marine: ～植物 marine plant
【海昌蓝】hǎichānglán〈名〉［纺织］hydron blue
【海潮】hǎicháo〈名〉tide
【海程】hǎichéng〈名〉voyage
【海船】hǎichuán〈名〉seagoing vessel
【海床】hǎichuáng〈名〉seabed
【海带】hǎidài〈名〉［植物］kelp
【海胆】hǎidǎn〈名〉［动物］sea urchin
【海岛】hǎidǎo〈名〉island: ～居民 islander
【海盗】hǎidào〈名〉pirate: ～船 pirate ship
【海堤】hǎidī〈名〉coastal wall
【海底】hǎidǐ〈名〉seabed: ～电缆 submarine cable ‖ ～火山 submarine volcano
【海底捞月】hǎidǐ-lāoyuè〈成〉〈喻〉strive for the impossible: ～一场空 be as futile as trying to catch a shooting star
【海底捞针】hǎidǐ-lāozhēn〈成〉look for a needle in a haystack
【海地】Hǎidì〈名〉Haiti: ～共和国 Republic of Haiti ‖ ～人 Haitian
【海防】hǎifáng〈名〉coastal defence: ～部队 coastal defence force
【海风】hǎifēng〈名〉sea breeze
【海港】hǎigǎng〈名〉harbour
【海沟】hǎigōu〈名〉oceanic trench
【海狗】hǎigǒu〈名〉［动物］fur seal
【海关】hǎiguān〈名〉customs: 通过～ go through the customs ‖ ～报关 customs declaration ‖ ～官员 customs officer
【海关总署】hǎiguān zǒngshǔ〈名〉customs bureau
【海归】hǎiguī〈名〉student returned from overseas: 实验室里的～人员 laboratory staff who have returned from study overseas
【海龟】hǎiguī〈名〉［动物］sea turtle
【海涵】hǎihán ▸**p. 156**〈动〉〈敬〉be generous enough to forgive: 招待不周，还望～。I beg your forgiveness if I haven't looked after you well.
【海魂衫】hǎihúnshān〈名〉sailor's striped shirt
【海货】hǎihuò〈名〉marine product
【海基会】Hǎijīhuì〈简称〉= 海峡交流基金会
【海脊】hǎijǐ〈名〉［地质］sea ridge
【海疆】hǎijiāng〈名〉coastal areas and territorial seas: 万里～ a vast expanse of coastal areas and territorial seas
【海椒】hǎijiāo〈名〉〈方〉［植物］hot pepper
【海礁】hǎijiāo〈名〉reef
【海角天涯】hǎijiǎo-tiānyá = 天涯海角 tiānyá-hǎijiǎo
【海禁】hǎijìn〈名〉ban on foreign trade: ～大开 open to foreign trade
【海景】hǎijǐng〈名〉seascape
【海军】hǎijūn〈名〉navy: ～航空兵 naval air force ‖ ～基地 naval base
【海军蓝】hǎijūnlán〈形〉naval blue
【海军陆战队】hǎijūn lùzhànduì〈名〉marine corps
【海口】hǎikǒu〈名〉**1**（海港）sea port **2**（入海口）estuary **3**（大话）boast: 夸～ brag about **4** ▸**p. 661** Hǎikǒu（海口）Haikou [capital of Hainan Province (海南)]
【海枯石烂】hǎikū-shílàn〈成〉[in an oath expressing firm will or unchanging fidelity] no matter what happens: ～，此心不变。Seas may dry up and rocks turn to dust, but our hearts will always remain loyal.
【海葵】hǎikuí〈名〉［动物］sea anemone
【海阔凭鱼跃，天高任鸟飞】hǎi kuò píng yú yuè, tiān gāo rèn niǎo fēi〈俗〉the wide sea allows the fish to leap about freely and the vast sky the birds to fly at will
【海阔天空】hǎikuò-tiānkōng〈成〉**1**（广阔无边）as boundless as the sea and sky **2**（无拘无束）unrestrained and far-ranging: ～地聊 have a rambling chat
【海蓝】hǎilán ▸**p. 863**〈形〉sea blue
【海缆】hǎilǎn〈名〉submarine cable
【海浪】hǎilàng〈名〉sea wave
【海狸】hǎilí〈名〉［动物］beaver
【海狸鼠】hǎilíshǔ〈名〉［动物］nutria
【海里】hǎilǐ〈名〉nautical mile
【海蛎子】hǎilìzi〈名〉(sea) oyster
【海量】hǎiliàng〈名〉**1**〈敬〉（指度量）magnanimity: 怠慢之处，望～包涵。I hope you will be magnanimous enough to forgive any lack of attention on my part. **2**（指酒量）huge tolerance: 你是～，再来一杯没问题。You can hold your drink, so having one more glass isn't going to be a problem. **3**（指数量）huge amounts: ～信息 massive amounts of information
【海流】hǎiliú〈名〉ocean current: ～发电 current power generation
【海龙】hǎilóng〈名〉［鱼类］pipefish
【海龙卷】hǎilóngjuǎn〈名〉［气象］waterspout
【海鲈】hǎilú〈名〉［鱼类］sea bass
【海路】hǎilù〈名〉sea route: 走～ travel by sea
【海轮】hǎilún〈名〉ocean-going vessel
【海螺】hǎiluó〈名〉［动物］conch
【海洛因】hǎiluòyīn〈名〉heroin
【海马】hǎimǎ〈名〉［鱼类］sea horse
【海鳗】hǎimán〈名〉［鱼类］conger pike
【海米】hǎimǐ〈名〉dried shrimps
【海绵】hǎimián〈名〉**1**［动物］sponge: ～动物 spongia ‖ ～组织 spongy tissue **2**（指材料）sponge: ～垫 sponge cushion ‖ ～球拍 foam-rubber table tennis bat
【海面】hǎimiàn〈名〉sea surface
【海南】Hǎinán ▸**p. 661**〈名〉Hainan Province
【海难】hǎinàn〈名〉shipwreck
【海内】hǎinèi〈名〉throughout the country: ～存知己，天涯若比邻 a bosom friend afar brings a distant land near
【海内外】hǎinèiwài〈名〉home and abroad
【海鸟】hǎiniǎo〈名〉seabird
【海牛】hǎiniú〈名〉［动物］manatee
【海鸥】hǎi'ōu〈名〉seagull
【海派】hǎipài〈名〉**1**（指京剧流派）Shanghai style or school of Beijing opera **2**（指风格）Shanghai style: ～时装 Shanghai fashion ‖ ～文化 subculture of Shanghai
【海螵蛸】hǎipiāoxiāo〈名〉［中药］cuttlebone
【海平面】hǎipíngmiàn〈名〉sea level
【海鞘】hǎiqiào〈名〉［动物］sea squirt
【海侵】hǎiqīn〈名〉［地质］transgression
【海区】hǎiqū〈名〉［军事］sea area
【海鳃】hǎisāi〈名〉［动物］sea pen
【海山】hǎishān〈名〉［地质］seamount
【海鳝】hǎishàn〈名〉［鱼类］moray
【海商法】hǎishāngfǎ〈名〉maritime law: ～规 commercial maritime code
【海上】hǎishàng〈名〉sea: ～风暴 storm at sea ‖ ～交通 marine traffic ‖ ～平台 offshore platform ‖ ～作业 offshore operation ‖ ～补给 seaborne supply ‖ ～运输 marine transportation
【海蛇】hǎishé〈名〉［动物］sea snake
【海参】hǎishēn〈名〉［动物］sea cucumber
【海狮】hǎishī〈名〉［动物］sea lion
【海市蜃楼】hǎishì-shènlóu **A**〈名〉［气象］mirage **B**〈成〉〈喻〉（虚幻的事物）castles in the air
【海事】hǎishì〈名〉**1**（指事务）maritime affair: ～法 maritime law **2**（指事故）disaster at sea
【海誓山盟】hǎishì-shānméng〈成〉vow of eternal love: 他们已私下～，终身相爱。They have secretly exchanged vows and made pledges of eternal love.
【海兽】hǎishòu〈名〉marine animal
【海水】hǎishuǐ〈名〉sea water
【海水不可斗量】hǎishuǐ bùkě dǒu liáng〈俗〉great minds cannot be fathomed by common measure: 人不可貌相，～。People should not be judged by their appearance in the same way that great minds cannot be fathomed.
【海水淡化】hǎishuǐ dànhuà〈名〉desalination of seawater
【海水养殖】hǎishuǐ yǎngzhí〈名〉marine culture
【海水浴】hǎishuǐyù〈名〉sea bathing: 洗～ go bathing in the sea
【海损】hǎisǔn〈名〉［经济］average
【海獭】hǎitǎ〈名〉［动物］sea otter
【海苔】hǎitái〈名〉［植物］nori
【海滩】hǎitān〈名〉(sea) beach
【海棠】hǎitáng〈名〉［植物］Chinese flowering crab-apple
【海塘】hǎitáng〈名〉sea wall
【海图】hǎitú〈名〉nautical chart
【海涂】hǎitú〈名〉tidal flat: 围垦～ reclaim a tidal flat by building a sea wall
【海豚】hǎitún〈名〉［动物］dolphin: ～馆 dolphinarium
【海外】hǎiwài〈名〉abroad: ～归来 return from abroad ‖ ～版 overseas edition ‖ ～华侨 overseas Chinese
【海外奇谈】hǎiwài-qítán〈成〉traveller's tale
【海湾】hǎiwān〈名〉**1** ▸**p. 164**（指地形）bay **2** Hǎiwān（波斯湾）Persian Gulf: ～地区 Gulf area
【海湾战争】Hǎiwān Zhànzhēng〈名〉the Gulf War
【海碗】hǎiwǎn〈名〉extra-big bowl
【海王星】Hǎiwángxīng〈名〉［天文］Neptune
【海味】hǎiwèi〈名〉seafood: ▸山珍～
【海峡】hǎixiá ▸**p. 164**〈名〉channel: 台湾～ Taiwan Strait(s) ‖ 英吉利～ English Channel ‖ ～两岸 both sides of the Taiwan Strait(s)
【海峡交流基金会】Hǎixiá Jiāoliú Jījīnhuì〈名〉Strait Exchange Foundation (SEF)
【海峡两岸关系协会】Hǎixiá-liǎng'àn Guānxì Xiéhuì〈名〉Association for Relations Across the Taiwan Strait(s) (ARATS)
【海鲜】hǎixiān〈名〉seafood
【海鲜酱】hǎixiānjiàng〈名〉hoisin sauce
【海象】hǎixiàng〈名〉［动物］walrus
【海啸】hǎixiào〈名〉tsunami
【海协会】Hǎixiéhuì〈简称〉= 海峡两岸关系协会
【海蟹】hǎixiè〈名〉sea crab

h

【海星】hǎixīng〈名〉［动物］ starfish
【海熊】hǎixióng = 海狗 hǎigǒu
【海选】hǎixuǎn〈动〉 hold a mass election
【海牙】Hǎiyá〈名〉 the Hague
【海牙国际法庭】Hǎiyá Guójì Fǎtíng〈名〉 International Court of Justice at the Hague
【海盐】hǎiyán〈名〉 sea salt
【海蜒】hǎiyán〈名〉［动物］ anchovy
【海晏河清】 hǎiyàn-héqīng = 河清海晏 héqīng-hǎiyàn
【海燕】hǎiyàn〈名〉［鸟类］ (storm) petrel
【海洋】 hǎiyáng〈名〉 ocean: ～博物馆 maritime museum ‖ ～资源 marine resources
【海洋馆】hǎiyángguǎn〈名〉sea life centre: 参观香港～ visit the Hong Kong Aquarium
【海洋科学】hǎiyáng kēxué〈名〉 marine science
【海洋权】 hǎiyángquán〈名〉 maritime rights
【海洋生物】hǎiyáng shēngwù〈名〉marine life: ～资源 living marine resources
【海洋性气候】 hǎiyángxìng qìhòu〈名〉 maritime climate
【海涌】hǎiyǒng〈名〉 swell
【海鱼】hǎiyú〈名〉 sea fish
【海域】hǎiyù〈名〉 sea area: 南海～ South China Sea waters
【海员】hǎiyuán ▸**p. 966**〈名〉 seaman: ～俱乐部 seamen's club
【海运】hǎiyùn〈名〉 sea transportation
【海葬】hǎizàng〈名〉 sea-burial
【海藻】hǎizǎo〈名〉 seaweed
【海战】hǎizhàn〈名〉 naval battle
【海蜇】hǎizhé〈名〉［动物］ jellyfish
【海震】hǎizhèn〈名〉［地质］ seaquake
【海子】hǎizi〈名〉〈方〉 lake

hài

亥 hài〈名〉 last of the twelve Earthly Branches (地支)
【亥时】hàishí〈名〉〈旧〉 period of the day from 9 pm to 11 pm

骇（駭） hài〈动〉 frighten: ▸惊～, 惊涛～浪
【骇然】hàirán〈形〉〈书〉 dumbstruck: ～失色 turn pale with astonishment
【骇人听闻】hàirén-tīngwén〈成〉 shocking: ～的暴行 horrifying atrocities
【骇异】hàiyì〈形〉〈书〉 astonished: 消息传来，不胜～ be completely astonished at the news

氦 hài〈名〉［化学］ helium (He)
【氦气】hàiqì〈名〉 helium

害 hài
A〈动〉 **1**（损害） harm: ～人不浅 do people great harm ‖ ～人～已 do harm to oneself and others ▸～群之马, 伤～ **2**（杀死） kill: 遇～ be murdered ▸～命 **3**（患） suffer from: ～一场大病 have a serious attack of illness ▸～病, ～眼 **4**（感到） feel: ▸～怕, ～臊
B〈名〉 **1**（坏处） harm: 有益无～ be beneficial and harmless **2**（祸害） disaster: 为民除～ rid the people of the scourge ▸自然灾～
C〈形〉 harmful: ～鸟 harmful bird ▸～虫
【害病】hàibìng〈动〉 fall ill
【害虫】hàichóng〈名〉 pest
【害处】hàichu〈名〉 harm: 酗酒对身体有～。 Excessive alcohol intake damages one's health.
【害肚子】hài dùzi〈动〉〈方〉 have loose bowels
【害命】 hàimìng〈动〉 murder: 谋财～ murder for money
【害怕】hàipà〈动〉 fear: ～得发抖 tremble with fear ‖ 没有什么可～的。 There is nothing to be afraid of.
【害群之马】 hàiqúnzhīmǎ〈成〉〈喻〉 rotten apple in the barrel
【害人】hàirén〈动〉 do harm to people: 这种做法～不浅。 Such practice is tremendously harmful. ‖ ～之心不可有，防人之心不可无。 One should never intend to harm others, nor should one forget to guard against the harm others might inflict.
【害人虫】 hàirénchóng〈名〉〈喻〉 pest: 扫除一切～。 Away with all pests.
【害臊】hàisào〈形〉〈口〉 bashful: 这孩子见生人就～。 The child is shy with strangers.
【害羞】hàixiū〈形〉 shy: 她在生人面前显得～。 She feels shy in the presence of strangers.
【害眼】hàiyǎn〈动〉 suffer from eye trouble

hān

顸（頇） hān〈形〉〈方〉 thick: 这根擀面杖太～了。 This rolling pin is too thick.

蚶 hān
【蚶子】hānzi〈名〉［动物］ blood clam

酣 hān〈形〉 **1**（尽兴） to one's heart's content: ▸～饮, 酒～耳热 **2**（深沉） hearty: ～笑 laugh heartily ▸～畅, ～睡 **3**（指战斗） fierce: ▸～战
【酣畅】 hānchàng〈形〉 **1**（指喝酒） merry **2**（指睡觉） sound: ～尽兴 to one's heart's content ‖ 睡眠～ be fast asleep **3**（指文章表达） fluid: ～的笔墨 something written with ease and verve
【酣畅淋漓】hānchàng-línlí〈成〉 fluid: 这篇文章～地抒发了作者对祖国的无限热爱。 The article fully expressed the author's profound love for his motherland.
【酣梦】hānmèng〈名〉 sweet dream
【酣然】hānrán〈副〉〈书〉 merrily: ～大醉 be as drunk as a lord ‖ ～入梦 fall into a sound sleep
【酣睡】hānshuì〈动〉 be fast asleep: 都早上十点了，他还在～。 It's ten o'clock in the morning, but he's still fast asleep.
【酣饮】hānyǐn〈动〉〈书〉 drink to one's heart's content
【酣战】hānzhàn〈动〉 fight a fierce battle: 两军～ two armies locked in a fierce battle
【酣醉】hānzuì〈动〉 be dead drunk

憨 hān〈形〉 **1**（傻） foolish: ▸～痴, ～笑 **2**（朴实） naive: ▸～厚, ～直
【憨痴】hānchī〈形〉 idiotic
【憨厚】hānhòu〈形〉 simple and honest: 为人～ be kind and good-natured
【憨实】hānshí〈形〉 straightforward and honest
【憨态】hāntài〈名〉 air of charming naivety: 一脸～ look naive and innocent
【憨态可掬】hāntài-kějū〈成〉 charmingly naive: 那小男孩～，逗人喜爱。 With his air of charming naivety, the little boy is really adorable.
【憨笑】hānxiào〈动〉 simper: 你～什么? Why are you smiling in such a silly way?
【憨直】hānzhí〈形〉 simple and straightforward: 性格～ have a simple and straightforward disposition

鼾 hān〈名〉 snore: 打～ snore
【鼾声】hānshēng〈名〉 sound of snoring: ～大作 snore loudly ‖ ～如雷 snore thunderously
【鼾睡】hānshuì〈动〉 fall into a deep, snoring sleep

hán

汗 hán ▸可汗 kèhán
▸hàn

邯 hán
【邯郸学步】Hándān-xuébù〈成〉 copying others, one loses one's own way

含 hán〈动〉 **1**（放在嘴里） hold in the mouth: ～着润喉片 have a throat tablet in one's mouth ‖ 此药宜～服。 This pill should be sucked. ▸～英咀华 **2**（包括） contain: 蔬菜中～多种维生素。Vegetables contain many different vitamins. ▸～义, 包～ **3**（忍受） bear: ～泪告别 say goodbye with tears in one's eyes ▸～垢忍辱, ～辛茹苦 **4**（怀有） harbour: ▸～恨, ～羞, ～冤
【含苞】hánbāo〈动〉〈书〉 be in bud
【含苞待放】hánbāo-dàifàng〈成〉 **1**（指花） ready to burst **2**（指人） be in early puberty
【含碘食盐】 hándiǎn shíyán〈名〉 iodized salt
【含垢忍辱】 hángòu-rěnrǔ〈成〉 swallow shame and humiliation
【含恨】hánhèn〈动〉 nurse a grievance: ～在心 harbour a hatred ‖ ～终天 die with a deep regret
【含糊】hánhu〈形〉 **1**（不明确） ambiguous: 说话～ equivocate ‖ 他回答得含含糊糊。 He gave a very vague reply. **2**（马虎） careless: ～了事 finish a job carelessly ‖ 在原则问题上可～不得。 On a matter of principle, we must be meticulously careful. **3**（退缩） [usu in the negative] show weakness: 我说辞职就辞职，绝不～。 When I say I'm going to resign, I'm going to resign. I mean what I say.
【含糊其辞】hánhu-qící〈成〉 hum and haw
【含混】hánhùn〈形〉 unclear: 概念～不清 be unclear about a concept ‖ 言词～ ambiguous wording
【含金量】hánjīnliàng〈名〉 **1**〈本〉 gold content: 矿石的～ gold content of ore **2**〈喻〉 real worth: 学术～高 be of high academic value
【含量】hánliàng〈名〉content: 23% 的酒精～ 23% alcohol content
【含怒】hánnù〈动〉〈书〉 harbour resentment: ～不语 sulk
【含片】 hánpiàn〈名〉 lozenge: 止咳～ cough pastille
【含铅】hánqiān〈动〉 contain lead: ～汽油 leaded petrol
【含情脉脉】hánqíng-mòmò〈成〉 cherish a deep feeling: ～的目光 pretty eyes full of tenderness and love
【含权】hánquán〈名〉［金融］ have cum rights: ～股 cum rights stock

【含沙射影】 hánshā-shèyǐng〈成〉 make insinuating remarks: ～，恶语中伤 defame with vicious, insinuating remarks

【含税】 hánshuì〈动〉 include tax：～工资 wage including tax

【含漱剂】 hánshùjì〈名〉 gargle

【含水量】 hánshuǐliàng〈名〉 water content

【含笑】 hánxiào〈动〉 wear a smile: ～谢绝 decline politely with a smile ‖ ～九泉 die happy

【含辛茹苦】 hánxīn-rúkǔ〈成〉 suffer untold hardships: ～地拉扯孩子 suffer all sorts of hardships in raising one's child

【含羞】 hánxiū〈动〉 have a shy look: ～不语 feel too shy to speak

【含羞草】 hánxiūcǎo〈名〉［植物］mimosa

【含蓄】 hánxù A〈动〉 contain: ～着深刻的意义 contain a profound meaning B〈形〉 1（指思想、情感） implicit: ～的批评 implicit criticism 2（指表达） reserved: ～的性格 reserved character ‖ 他为人～。 He is a man of reserve.

【含血喷人】 hánxuè-pēnrén〈成〉 make slanderous accusations against sb.

【含饴弄孙】 hányí-nòngsūn〈成〉 lead a carefree life in one's old age

【含义】 hányì〈名〉 implication: 理解/弄清～ understand/figure out the implications ‖ 一个词可以有几种～。 One word can have several meanings.

【含意】 hányì〈名〉 implied meaning: 你说这话的～是什么？ What do you mean by saying this?

【含英咀华】 hányīng-jǔhuá〈成〉 study and relish the beauty and essence of sth.

【含油层】 hányóucéng〈名〉［地质］ oil-bearing stratum

【含冤】 hányuān〈动〉 suffer an injustice: ～死去 die without being vindicated

【含冤负屈】 hányuān-fùqū〈成〉 suffer an unjust grievance

【含怨】 hányuàn〈动〉 nurse a grievance: ～衔恨 bear a grudge

函 hán

〈名〉 1（书）（盒子） case: 剑～ case for a sword ‖ 石～ stone casket 2（信） letter: 致～ write a letter ▸～复, ～告

【函大】 hándà〈简称〉= 函授大学

【函电】 hándiàn〈名〉 correspondence

【函调】 hándiào〈动〉 conduct an investigation through correspondence

【函复】 hánfù〈动〉〈书〉 reply by letter

【函告】 hángào〈动〉〈书〉 inform by letter: 待行程确定后，当即～。 I'll write to inform you of my itinerary once it is set.

【函购】 hángòu〈动〉 order by mail: ～教材 purchase textbooks by mail

【函件】 hánjiàn〈名〉 correspondence: 收发～ receive and dispatch letters

【函售】 hánshòu〈动〉 sell by mail: ～书籍 sell books by mail order

【函授】 hánshòu〈动〉 teach by correspondence: ～部 correspondence department ‖ ～教育 correspondence education

【函授大学】 hánshòu dàxué〈名〉 correspondence college

【函数】 hánshù〈名〉［数学］ function: ～运算 functional operation ‖ 余弦/正弦～ sine/cosine function ‖ ～表 function table

【函索】 hánsuǒ〈动〉〈书〉 request by letter: ～即寄 send on request

琀 hán

〈名〉〈古〉 piece of jade or other jewel put in the mouth of the dead

晗 hán

〈动〉〈书〉 dawn

涵 hán

A〈动〉 contain: ▸～养, 包～, 海～

B〈名〉 culvert: ▸桥～

【涵洞】 hándòng〈名〉 culvert: ～闸门 clough

【涵盖】 hángài〈动〉 cover: ～面广 wide coverage ‖ 该书～了中国历史的各个时期。 This book covers every stage of Chinese history.

【涵管】 hánguǎn〈名〉 culvert pipe

【涵容】 hánróng〈动〉〈书〉 forgive: 招待不周，还望～。 Please excuse us for being poor hosts.

【涵养】 hányǎng A〈名〉 self-possession: 很有～ have good self-control B〈动〉 conserve: ～地力 conserve soil fertility

【涵义】 hányì = 含义 hányì

【涵闸】 hánzhá〈名〉 culvert and sluice

韩（韓） Hán

〈名〉 1（指国名） Han [state in the Zhou Dynasty] 2 = 韩国 Hánguó

【韩国】 Hánguó〈名〉 Republic of Korea: ～人 Korean

【韩剧】 hánjù〈名〉 South Korean TV drama

【韩流】 hánliú〈名〉 South Korean fashion and trends

寒 hán

A〈形〉 1（冷） cold: ▸～风, 春～, 天～地冻 2（贫困） poor: ～儒 needy scholar ▸～士, 贫～ 3〈谦〉（我的） my humble: ▸～门, ～舍

B〈名〉 1（指季节） cold season: ▸～假, ～来暑往 2［中医］ coldness: 外感风～ catch a cold

C〈动〉 tremble with fear: ▸胆～, 心～

【寒蝉】 hánchán〈名〉 cicada in cold weather: ～凄切 plaintive droning of a cicada in cold weather

【寒潮】 háncháo〈名〉［气象］ cold spell

【寒伧】 hánchen = 寒碜 hánchen

【寒碜】 hánchen A〈形〉 1（不好看） shabby: 穿得～ be shabbily dressed ‖ 长得～ plain-looking 2（不光彩） disgraceful: 哄骗一个小孩，你也不嫌～！ Don't you feel ashamed of yourself cheating a little child? B〈动〉 ridicule: 你知道我没有钱，请别～人。 Don't ridicule me. You know I'm not rich.

【寒窗】 hánchuāng〈名〉〈喻〉 harsh conditions for learning: 十年～ study under harsh conditions for ten years

【寒带】 hándài〈名〉［地理］ frigid zone

【寒冬】 hándōng〈名〉 cold winter

【寒冬腊月】 hándōng-làyuè〈成〉 the dead of winter

【寒风】 hánfēng〈名〉 cold wind: ～刺骨。 The cold wind cuts one to the bone. ‖ ～凛冽。 The wind is bitterly cold.

【寒光】 hánguāng〈名〉 chilly gleam: ～闪闪 glitter coldly ‖ 刺刀闪着～。 Bayonets gleamed with death.

【寒假】 hánjià〈名〉 winter vacation: 放～ have a winter vacation

【寒螀】 hánjiāng〈名〉〈古〉 a kind of cicada

【寒噤】 hánjìn〈名〉 cold shiver: 她打了个～。 A shiver ran down her back.

【寒苦】 hánkǔ〈形〉〈书〉 destitute: 出身～ be born of a poor family

【寒来暑往】 hánlái-shǔwǎng〈成〉 year in, year out

【寒冷】 hánlěng〈形〉 cold: ～的气候 cold climate

【寒冽】 hánliè〈形〉〈书〉 frigid

【寒流】 hánliú〈名〉 1（指水流） cold current 2［气象］ cold wave

【寒露】 Hánlù〈名〉 Cold Dew [beginning of the 17th of the 24th solar terms]

【寒毛】 hánmáo〈名〉 fine human body hair: 吓得～竖立 be scared stiff

【寒梅】 hánméi〈名〉 winter plum (tree)

【寒门】 hánmén〈名〉〈书〉 1（指家庭） humble and poor family: 出身～ be born to a poor family 2〈谦〉（我的家） my family

【寒气】 hánqì〈名〉 1（指空气） cold air 2（指感觉） chill

【寒峭】 hánqiào〈形〉〈书〉 icy

【寒秋】 hánqiū〈名〉 cold autumn

【寒热】 hánrè〈名〉 1［中医］ chill and fever 2〈方〉（发烧） fever: 发～ have a fever

【寒舍】 hánshè〈名〉〈谦〉 my humble abode: 请光临～小叙。 Please grant me the honour of inviting you to my humble house for a chat.

【寒食节】 Hánshíjié〈名〉 Cold Food Festival [period before Pure Brightness Festival during which only cold food was served]

【寒士】 hánshì〈名〉〈旧〉 poor scholar

【寒暑】 hánshǔ〈名〉 1（冷和热） cold and heat 2（指季节） summer and winter

【寒暑表】 hánshǔbiǎo〈名〉 thermometer

【寒酸】 hánsuān〈形〉 1（窘迫） miserable and shabby: ～相 miserable and shabby appearance 2（不体面） lowly: 如果要捐赠，就不能太～。 If you want to donate, you can't be too mean.

【寒腿】 hántuǐ〈名〉〈口〉 rheumatism in the legs

【寒微】 hánwēi〈形〉〈书〉 humble: 身世～ be of humble origin

【寒武纪】 Hánwǔjì〈名〉［地质］ Cambrian Period

【寒心】 hánxīn〈形〉 bitterly disappointed: 令人～ be bitterly disappointing

【寒暄】 hánxuān〈动〉 exchange greetings: 她同客人～了几句就上班走了。 She exchanged a few words of greeting with the guests before she left for work.

【寒鸦】 hányā〈名〉［鸟类］ jackdaw

【寒衣】 hányī〈名〉 winter clothing

【寒意】 hányì〈名〉 nip in the air: 这天已有几分～。 It's got a bit chilly.

【寒战】 hánzhàn〈名〉 tremble with cold: 我突然打了个～。 A sudden chill ran over me.

【寒症】 hánzhèng〈名〉［中医］ symptoms (eg chill, loose bowels, slow pulse, etc.) caused by cold factors

hǎn

罕 hǎn

〈形〉 rare: ～事 rare occurrence ▸～见, ～有, 人迹～至

【罕见】 hǎnjiàn〈形〉 seldom seen: ～的现象 rare sight

【罕有】 hǎnyǒu〈动〉 be rare: ～的机会 rare opportunity

喊 hǎn

〈动〉 1（大声呼叫） shout: ～口号 shout slogans ‖ 大～大叫 shout loudly ▸呼～, 叫～, 贼～捉贼 2（招呼） call for: ～他来帮个忙。 Send for him to help. ‖ 他把我～来征求意见。 He called me in to hear my opinion on the matter.

3〈方〉〈称呼〉 address: 孩子们都～他爷爷。 Children all call him Grandpa.
【喊话】hǎnhuà〈动〉 1（指在阵地前沿） shout messages to the enemy: 向敌兵～ shout at the enemy 2（指向远处的人） communicate by tele-equipment: 向机长～ communicate with the crew commander by radio
【喊叫】hǎnjiào〈动〉 cry out: 大声～ shout at the top of one's voice ‖ 疼得～起来 yell out in pain
【喊嗓子】 hǎn sǎngzi 〈动〉 1（喊叫） shout loudly 2（练声） train one's voice by shouting or singing exercises in the early morning
【喊冤】hǎnyuān〈动〉 cry out one's grievances: ～叫屈 complain loudly about an injustice ‖ 别～，你这是罪有应得。 Don't complain. You deserve it.

hàn

汉（漢） Hàn 〈名〉 1 hàn（银河） Milky Way: ▸河～, 银～ 2（汉朝） Han Dynasty 3（后汉） Later Han Dynasty 4（汉族） Han Chinese: ～人 Han people 5 hàn（男子） man: 大～ big fellow ▸～子, 老～ 6（汉语） Chinese language: 英～词典 English-Chinese dictionary ▸～字
【汉白玉】hànbáiyù〈名〉 white marble
【汉堡】hànbǎo〈名〉 Hamburg
【汉堡包】hànbǎobāo〈名〉 hamburger
【汉城】Hànchéng〈名〉〈旧〉 Seoul
【汉奸】hànjiān〈名〉 traitor (to China): ～卖国贼 traitor and collaborator
【汉民】Hànmín〈名〉 Han people
【汉普郡】Hànpǔjùn〈名〉 Hampshire
【汉人】 Hànrén 〈名〉 1（汉族） Han people 2（汉代的人） people of the Han Dynasty
【汉文】 Hànwén ▸**p. 918** 〈名〉〈旧〉 Chinese language: 请将下列英文译成～。 Please translate the following passage from English into Chinese.
【汉学】 Hànxué 〈名〉 1（指哲学流派） Han school of classical philology 2（有关中国） Sinology: ～家 Sinologist
【汉语】 Hànyǔ ▸**p. 918** 〈名〉 Chinese language
【汉语拼音】 Hànyǔ Pīnyīn 〈名〉 Hanyu Pinyin: ～方案 Hanyu Pinyin Phonetic Chinese Alphabet

> **汉语拼音**
>
> Phonetic system used for standard Chinese characters. Each syllable is made up of an initial consonant, a vowel and a tone mark. In standard Chinese there are 21 consonants, 35 vowels and 4 tones consisting of an upper even tone, a rising tone, a falling-rising tone, and a falling tone, which are marked above the vowel. Neutral tones are not marked. Hanyu Pinyin was officially adopted on the Chinese mainland in 1958 and assumed as the international standard for written Chinese in 1982. On January 1st 2009 it was adopted as the official system of Romanization in Taiwan.

【汉语水平考试】Hànyǔ Shuǐpíng Kǎoshì 〈名〉 Chinese Proficiency Test [HSK]
【汉藏语系】 Hàn-Zàng yǔxì 〈名〉 Sino-Tibetan family of languages
【汉字】Hànzì ▸**p. 999**〈名〉 Chinese character: 简化～ simplified Chinese characters
【汉字库】 Hànzìkù 〈名〉 Chinese character library
【汉子】 hànzi 〈名〉 1（男子） man 2〈方〉（丈夫） husband
【汉族】Hànzú〈名〉 Han nationality

汗 hàn
A〈名〉 sweat: 流～ sweat
B〈动〉〈口〉 be embarrassed
▸hán
【汗斑】hànbān〈名〉 1（指污渍） sweat stain 2 ▸**p. 50** ［医学］ tinea versicolour
【汗背心】 hànbèixīn 〈名〉 vest 〈英〉; sleeveless undershirt 〈美〉
【汗臭】hànchòu〈名〉 1（指臭味） stinking smell of sweat 2 ▸**p. 50** ［医学］ bromhidrosis
【汗碱】hànjiǎn〈名〉 sweat stain
【汗脚】hànjiǎo〈名〉 sweaty feet
【汗津津】hànjīnjīn〈形〉 sweaty
【汗孔】hànkǒng〈名〉［生理］ sweat pore
【汗淋淋】 hànlínlín 〈形〉 dripping with sweat
【汗流浃背】hànliú-jiābèi〈成〉 be dripping with sweat
【汗马功劳】hànmǎ-gōngláo〈成〉 distinctions won in battle: 立下了～ rendered great services
【汗毛】hànmáo = 寒毛 hánmáo
【汗牛充栋】 hànniú-chōngdòng 〈成〉 an immense number of books
【汗青】hànqīng〈名〉〈书〉 annals: 人生自古谁无死，留取丹心照～。 What man was ever immune from death? Let me but leave a loyal heart shining in the pages of history.
【汗衫】hànshān〈名〉 1（指T恤） T-shirt 2（指背心） vest 〈英〉; undershirt 〈美〉
【汗水】hànshuǐ〈名〉 sweat: ～湿透了衣衫 with one's shirt soaked in sweat
【汗腺】hànxiàn〈名〉［生理］ sweat gland
【汗颜】 hànyán 〈动〉〈书〉 blush with shame
【汗液】hànyè〈名〉 sweat: 分泌～ excrete sweat
【汗珠】hànzhū〈名〉 beads of sweat: 病人脸上的～直往下淌。 Beads of sweat rolled down the patient's face.
【汗渍】hànzì〈名〉 sweat stain: 他的衬衣～斑斑。 His shirt is sweat-stained.

旱 hàn
A〈形〉 1（干） dry: ▸～情, ～灾, 防～ 2（无水） [used in contrast with 水] dry: ▸～冰, ～船, ～稻
B〈名〉 dry land: ▸～路
【旱魃】 hànbá 〈名〉〈旧〉 drought: ～施虐。 There was a severe drought.
【旱冰】hànbīng〈名〉［体育］ roller skating: ～鞋 roller skates
【旱冰场】 hànbīngchǎng 〈名〉 roller-skating surface
【旱船】 hànchuán 〈名〉 land boat [model boat used as a stage prop in some folk dances]: 跑～ dance the 'land boat' dance
【旱道】hàndào〈名〉 overland route
【旱稻】hàndào〈名〉 dry rice
【旱地】hàndì〈名〉 1（指不蓄水） dry land: ～耕作 dry land farming ‖ ～作物 dry crops 2（指无灌溉） farmland that has not been irrigated
【旱季】hànjì〈名〉 dry season
【旱井】hànjǐng〈名〉 1（用于汲水） water-retention well 2（用于储水） dry well
【旱涝保收】 hànlào-bǎoshōu 〈成〉 1〈本〉 ensure stable yields despite drought or excessive rain: ～田 fields that yield good harvests regardless of drought or excessive rain 2〈喻〉 ensure a stable income: 这个行道赚钱不多，却可以～。 The trade doesn't pay very well, but it gives a guaranteed, stable income.
【旱路】hànlù〈名〉 overland route
【旱年】hànnián〈名〉 year of drought
【旱桥】hànqiáo〈名〉 viaduct
【旱情】hànqíng〈名〉 ravages of a drought: 北方地区～严重。 The drought was severe in the North.
【旱伞】hànsǎn〈名〉 parasol
【旱獭】hàntǎ〈名〉 marmot
【旱田】hàntián = 旱地 hàndì
【旱象】hànxiàng〈名〉 signs of drought
【旱鸭子】hànyāzi〈名〉〈诙〉 person who cannot swim
【旱烟】hànyān〈名〉 tobacco [usu smoked in a long-stemmed Chinese pipe]
【旱灾】hànzāi〈名〉 drought

捍 hàn〈动〉 1（保卫） defend 2（抵御） guard against: ～外侮 resist foreign aggression
【捍卫】hànwèi〈动〉 safeguard: ～国家主权 uphold state sovereignty ‖ ～民族利益 protect national interests
【捍御】 hànyù 〈动〉〈书〉 1（保卫） defend 2（抵御） guard against: ～外侮 resist foreign aggression

悍 hàn〈形〉 1（勇猛） brave: 一员～将 a brave warrior ▸短小精～, 剽～, 强～ 2（凶暴） fierce: ▸～然, 刁～, 凶～
【悍妇】hànfù〈名〉 shrew
【悍然】hànrán〈副〉 outrageously: ～入侵 invade brazenly ‖ ～撕毁协议 flagrantly tear up an agreement
【悍勇】hànyǒng〈形〉〈书〉 intrepid: ～好斗 intrepid and bellicose

焊（銲） hàn 〈动〉 weld: ▸～接, 点～
【焊工】hàngōng〈名〉 1（指工种） welding 2（指工人） welder
【焊机】hànjī〈名〉 welding machine
【焊剂】hànjì〈名〉 welding flux
【焊件】 hànjiàn 〈名〉 assembly of parts welded together
【焊接】hànjiē〈动〉 weld: ～车间 welding shop ‖ ～钢管 welded steel pipe
【焊料】hànliào〈名〉 solder
【焊枪】hànqiāng〈名〉 welding torch
【焊条】hàntiáo〈名〉 welding rod
【焊锡】hànxī〈名〉 soldering tin
【焊药】hànyào〈名〉 welding agent

颔（頷） hàn〈书〉
A〈名〉 chin
B〈动〉 nod
【颔联】hànlián〈名〉 third and fourth lines of a *lüshi* (律诗)
【颔首】hànshǒu〈动〉〈书〉 nod: ～赞许 nod one's approval ‖ ～之交 nodding acquaintance

撼 hàn〈动〉 shake: ▸蚍蜉～大树, 摇～, 震～
【撼动】hàndòng〈动〉 shake
【撼天动地】 hàntiān-dòngdì 〈成〉 cause a great sensation: ～的英雄气概 earth-shaking heroism

翰 hàn〈名〉〈书〉 1（毛笔） writing brush: ▸～墨 2（写作） writing: ▸华～

【翰林】hànlín〈名〉 member of the Imperial Academy: ～院 Imperial Academy

【翰墨】hànmò〈名〉 writing, painting, or calligraphy: 名家～ painting or calligraphy of a famous master

憾 hàn〈动〉 regret: 死而无～ die without regret ▸抱～, 缺～, 遗～

【憾事】hànshì〈名〉 regrettable matter: 一生中最大的～ the biggest regret of one's life

瀚 hàn〈形〉〈书〉 vast: ▸浩～

【瀚海】hànhǎi〈名〉〈书〉vast desert: ～无垠 endless desert

hāng

夯 hāng

A〈名〉 rammer: 石/铁～ stone/iron rammer ▸打～

B〈动〉 ram: ～地 ram the earth

▸bèn

【夯锤】hāngchuí〈名〉 rammer

【夯歌】hānggē〈名〉 rammers' chant

【夯路机】hānglùjī〈名〉 road-packer

【夯土机】hāngtǔjī〈名〉 ramming machine

háng

行 háng

A〈名〉 **1**（指排列） line: 另起一～ start a new line ‖ 排成两～ fall into two lines **2**（机构） business firm: ▸拍卖～, 商～, 银～ **3** ▸**p. 966**（职业） line of business: 干一～, 爱一～ love whatever job one does ▸～家, 懂～, 改～

B〈动〉 rank: 你～几? ——～二。 Where do you come among your brothers and sisters? — I'm the second.

C〈量〉 line: 两～树 two rows of trees ‖ 两～眼泪 two streams of tears ‖ 四～诗句 four lines of verse

▸hàng, héng, xíng

【行帮】hángbāng〈名〉〈旧〉 guild

【行辈】hángbèi〈名〉 position in the family hierarchy: 他的～比我大。 He ranks as my senior in terms of the family hierarchy.

【行播】hángbō〈名〉［农业］ row planting

【行车】hángchē〈名〉〈方〉 bridge crane

【行当】hángdang〈名〉 **1**（职业） trade: 喜欢教书这个～ like the teaching profession **2**［戏曲］ type of role: 她的～是花旦。 She plays *huadan*.

【行道】hángdao〈名〉〈方〉 trade

【行贩】hángfàn〈名〉 peddler

【行风】hángfēng〈名〉 tendencies in a particular social domain: ～不正 unhealthy tendencies in the profession

【行规】hángguī〈名〉 guild regulations

【行行出状元】hángháng chū zhuàngyuán〈俗〉 every trade has its master

【行话】hánghuà〈名〉 jargon: 法律～ legal jargon ‖ 黑道～ language of the underworld

【行会】hánghuì〈名〉〈旧〉 guild: ～制度 guild system

【行货】hánghuò〈名〉 **1**（指质量差） crudely-made goods **2**（指销售渠道正规） certified goods

【行家】hángjia〈名〉 expert: ～里手 expert and master hand

【行间】hángjiān〈名〉 between the lines: 从字里～体会隐含的意思 read between the lines

【行距】hángjù〈名〉 line width: 调整～ adjust the line width ‖ 单倍～ single space ‖ 玉米～ space between rows of maize

【行宽】hángkuān〈名〉 line width

【行列】hángliè〈名〉 ranks: 队伍～整齐 be drawn up in orderly ranks ‖ 进入先进～ enter the advanced ranks

【行列式】hánglièshì〈名〉［数学］ determinant

【行情】hángqíng〈名〉 market conditions: 外汇～ fluctuations of the foreign exchange market ‖ ～看涨。 The market is strong.

【行市】hángshi = 行情 hángqíng

【行伍】hángwǔ〈名〉〈旧〉 the ranks: ～出身 rise from the ranks

【行业】hángyè ▸**p. 966**〈名〉 industry: 服务～ service industry ‖ 建筑～ construction industry ‖ ～工会 trade union

【行业语】hángyèyǔ〈名〉 professional jargon

【行院】hángyuàn〈名〉〈旧〉 **1**（妓院） brothel **2**（妓女） prostitute

【行栈】hángzhàn〈名〉〈旧〉 broker's storehouse

【行长】hángzhǎng〈名〉 president of a bank

吭 háng〈名〉 throat: ▸引～高歌

▸kēng

杭 Háng〈名〉 Hangzhou: 上有天堂, 下有苏～。 There is Paradise above and Suzhou and Hangzhou below.

【杭纺】hángfǎng〈名〉 Hangzhou plain-weave silk

【杭育】hángyō〈拟〉 heave-ho

【杭州】Hángzhōu ▸**p. 661**〈名〉 Hangzhou [capital of Zhejiang Province (浙江)]: ～湾 Hangzhou Bay

绗（絎） háng〈动〉 sew with long stitches: ～被子 sew long stitches on the quilt

航 háng

A〈名〉 boat

B〈动〉 navigate: ▸～海, ～空, ～天, 出～

【航班】hángbān〈名〉 flight: 取消/增加～ cancel/add a flight ‖ 国际/国内～ international/domestic flight

【航标】hángbiāo〈名〉 navigation mark: ～灯 beacon

【航测】hángcè〈简称〉= 航空测量

【航程】hángchéng〈名〉 voyage

【航船】hángchuán〈名〉 **1**（航行的船只） regular boat **2**（短途船只） steamship

【航次】hángcì〈名〉 **1**（指顺序）（航空） flight number;（海运） voyage number **2**（指次数）（航空） number of flights;（海运） number of voyages

【航道】hángdào〈名〉（海运） course: 开辟新～ open up a route ‖ 偏离～ be off the course

【航海】hánghǎi〈名〉 navigation: ～家 navigator

【航海日志】hánghǎi rìzhì〈名〉 log book

【航海图】hánghǎitú〈名〉 nautical chart

【航空】hángkōng〈名〉aviation: ～班机 air liner ‖ 民用～ civil aviation ‖ ～保险 aviation insurance

【航空兵】hángkōngbīng〈名〉 **1**（指兵种） air force: ～部队 air unit **2**（指兵员） airman

【航空测量】hángkōng cèliáng〈名〉 aerial survey

【航空地图】hángkōng dìtú〈名〉 flight chart

【航空电子系统】hángkōng diànzǐ xìtǒng〈名〉 avionics

【航空港】hángkōnggǎng〈名〉 airport

【航空公司】hángkōng gōngsī〈名〉 airline company: 中国国际～ Air China

【航空和航天局】Hángkōng hé Hángtiānjú〈名〉 (US) National Aeronautics and Space Administration (NASA)

【航空模型】hángkōng móxíng〈名〉 model aeroplane

【航空母舰】hángkōng mǔjiàn〈名〉aircraft carrier

【航空拍摄】hángkōng pāishè〈动〉 take aerial photos

【航空器】hángkōngqì〈名〉 aircraft

【航空日志】hángkōng rìzhì〈名〉 aircraft logbook

【航空摄影】hángkōng shèyǐng〈名〉 aerial photography

【航空信】hángkōngxìn〈名〉 airmail

【航路】hánglù〈名〉（指航空） air route;（指海运） sea route: ～标志 route markings

【航模】hángmó〈简称〉= 航空模型

【航母】hángmǔ〈简称〉= 航空母舰

【航拍】hángpāi〈简称〉= 航空拍摄

【航速】hángsù〈名〉 carrier speed

【航天】hángtiān〈名〉 space flight: ～工程师 astro engineer

【航天飞机】hángtiān fēijī〈名〉 space shuttle

【航天服】hángtiānfú〈名〉 space suit

【航天器】hángtiānqì〈名〉 spacecraft: ～对接 spacecraft docking ‖ ～回收 spacecraft recovery

【航天食品】hángtiān shípǐn〈名〉 space food

【航天员】hángtiānyuán ▸**p. 966**〈名〉 astronaut

【航务】hángwù〈名〉 navigational matters: ～局 shipping administration bureau

【航线】hángxiàn〈名〉 air route: 国际～ international air line ‖ 内河～ inland navigation line

【航向】hángxiàng〈名〉 course: 改变～ change course ‖ 指引～ provide guidance

【航行】hángxíng〈动〉 **1**（指在水中） sail: 顺风～ sail downwind **2**（指在空中） fly

【航意险】hángyìxiǎn〈名〉 aviation personal accident insurance

【航运】hángyùn〈名〉 shipping

【航站楼】hángzhànlóu〈名〉 air terminal

hàng

行 hàng ▸树行子 shùhàngzi

▸háng, héng, xíng

沆 hàng〈形〉〈书〉 endless stretch of water

【沆瀣】hàngxiè〈名〉〈书〉 evening mist

【沆瀣一气】hàngxiè-yīqì〈成〉 act in collusion with

巷 hàng〈名〉［矿业］ tunnel

▸xiàng

【巷道】hàngdào〈名〉 tunnel

hāo

蒿 hāo〈名〉［植物］ wormwood

【蒿草】hāocǎo〈名〉 wormwood

【蒿子】hāozi〈名〉 wormwood

【蒿子秆儿】hāozigǎnr〈名〉leaves and stem of crown daisy

薅 hāo〈动〉**1**（拔去杂草） pull up: ～杂草 pull up weeds **2**（用手揪） seize tight: ～住头发不放 grab sb.'s hair and not let go

【薅草】hāocǎo〈动〉 weed

【薅锄】hāochú〈名〉 small hoe with a short handle

嚆 hāo

【嚆矢】hāoshǐ〈名〉〈书〉 **1**（指箭） whistling arrow **2**（开端） beginning **3**（先兆） harbinger

háo

号（號） háo〈动〉 **1**（呼啸） howl: 北风怒～。 A north wind is howling. ▸～叫, 呼～ **2**（大声哭） wail: ▸～哭, 哀～

▸hào

【号寒啼饥】háohán-tíjī = 啼饥号寒 tíjī-háohán

【号叫】háojiào〈动〉 wail: 疼得～ cry out with pain

【号哭】háokū〈动〉 howl: 为何～? Why are you wailing?

【号丧】háosāng〈动〉 cry at a funeral

【号啕】háotáo〈动〉 wail: ～大哭 cry one's eyes out

蚝（蠔） háo〈名〉 oyster

【蚝豉】háochǐ〈名〉 dried oyster meat

【蚝油】háoyóu〈名〉 oyster sauce

毫 háo

A〈名〉 **1**（动物的细毛） fine-tapering animal hair: 狼/羊～笔 writing brush made of weasel/goat hair ▸秋～ **2**（毛笔） writing brush: ▸挥～ **3**（提绳） loop handle of a steelyard: 二～ second loop handle (of a steelyard for *liang* measurement) ‖ 头～ first loop handle (of a steelyard for *jin* measurement)

B〈量〉 **1**（千分之一） milli-: ▸～米, ～升 **2**（计量单位） *hao* [units of length and weight, respectively equal to 0.0333 millimetre or 0.005 gram] **3**〈方〉（用于货币） *jiao* [equal to 0.1 *yuan*]

C〈副〉 [used in the negative only] in the least: ～无道理 for no reason whatsoever ‖ ～无顾忌 free from all inhibitions ‖ ～不动摇 unswervingly

【毫安】háo'ān〈量〉［电气］ milliampere (mA, ma): ～表 milliammeter

【毫巴】háobā〈量〉［气象］ millibar (mb)

【毫不】háobù〈副〉 not in the least: ～迟疑 without the slightest hesitation ‖ ～介意 not mind at all ‖ ～留情 without any consideration for others ‖ ～相干 have nothing to do with ‖ ～犹豫 without the slightest hesitation ‖ ～在乎 not care at all ‖ ～利己，专门利人 be utterly dedicated to serving others without any thought of oneself

【毫发不爽】háofà-bùshuǎng〈成〉without the slightest error

【毫克】háokè ▸**p. 978**〈量〉 milligram (mg)

【毫厘】háolí〈名〉 the least bit: ～不差 without the slightest error ▸失之～，谬以千里

【毫厘不爽】háolí-bùshuǎng = 毫发不爽 háofà-bùshuǎng

【毫毛】háomáo〈名〉 soft hair on the body: 谁敢动他一根～? Who dares to do him the slightest harm?

【毫米】háomǐ ▸**p. 82**〈量〉 millimetre (mm)

【毫米汞柱】háomǐ gǒngzhù〈名〉 millimetre of mercury (mmHG)

【毫秒】háomiǎo〈量〉 millisecond (msec)

【毫末】háomò〈名〉〈书〉 **1**（指末梢） tip of a fine hair **2**（形容极少） extremely small amount **3**（形容极细微） minutest detail

【毫升】háoshēng〈量〉 millilitre (ml)

【毫微米】háowēimǐ〈量〉 nanometre (nm)

【毫微秒】háowēimiǎo〈量〉 nanosecond (ns)

【毫无】háowú〈动〉 not have any at all: ～办法 be at a complete loss (as to what to do) ‖ ～道理 be utterly unjustifiable ‖ ～根据 be entirely groundless ‖ ～疑问 be out of question

【毫无二致】háowú-èrzhì〈成〉 without the slightest difference

【毫针】háozhēn〈名〉 acupuncture needle

【毫子】háozi〈名〉〈方〉 silver coin (of small denominations)

嗥（嘷） háo〈动〉 howl

【嗥叫】háojiào〈动〉 howl

貉 háo

▸hé

【貉绒】háoróng〈名〉 fine raccoon fur

【貉子】háozi〈名〉 raccoon dog

豪 háo

A〈名〉 **1**（指才华出众） person of extraordinary powers or endowments: ▸富～, 文～, 英～ **2**（指有财有势） despot: ▸土～

B〈形〉 **1**（有气魄） forthright: ▸～放, ～饮, ～雨 **2**（钱多势大） rich and powerful: ▸～富, ～门 **3**（强横） despotic: ▸巧取～夺 **4**（自豪） proud: ▸自～

【豪赌】háodǔ〈动〉 play for high stakes: 他在澳门～时被抓了。 He was caught while gambling for high stakes in Macao.

【豪放】háofàng〈形〉 bold and unconstrained: ～的性格 bold and uninhibited character ‖ 文笔～ bold style of writing

【豪放不羁】háofàng-bùjī〈成〉 unconventional and uninhibited

【豪富】háofù **A**〈形〉 powerful and wealthy **B**〈名〉 the rich and powerful

【豪横】háohèng〈形〉 despotic and bullying

【豪华】háohuá〈形〉 luxurious: 衣着～ be dressed in splendid clothes ‖ ～饭店 luxury hotel ‖ ～车 de luxe car

【豪杰】háojié〈名〉 hero

【豪举】háojǔ〈名〉 bold move

【豪迈】háomài〈形〉 heroic: ～的气概 heroic spirit ‖ ～的誓言 bold pledge

【豪门】háomén〈名〉 rich and powerful family: ～贵族 powerful family and honourable clan ‖ 出身～ be from a rich and influential family

【豪气】háoqì〈名〉 heroic spirit: 一身～ be every inch a hero

【豪强】háoqiáng **A**〈形〉 arrogant: 逞～ give free rein to one's arrogance **B**〈名〉 bully: 地方～ local despots and bullies

【豪情】háoqíng〈名〉 lofty sentiments: ～满怀 be full of heroic spirit and enthusiasm

【豪情壮志】háoqíng-zhuàngzhì〈成〉 lofty spirit and soaring determination

【豪绅】háoshēn〈名〉 despotic gentry

【豪爽】háoshuǎng〈形〉 straightforward and forthright

【豪侠】háoxiá **A**〈形〉 gallant **B**〈名〉 man of courage and chivalry

【豪兴】háoxìng〈名〉 high spirits: ～大发 be in exuberant spirit

【豪言壮语】háoyán-zhuàngyǔ〈成〉 brave and proud words

【豪饮】háoyǐn〈动〉 drink with wild abandon

【豪雨】háoyǔ〈名〉 heavy rain: ～成灾 disaster caused by torrential rain

【豪宅】háozhái〈名〉 luxury house

【豪猪】háozhū〈名〉 porcupine

【豪壮】háozhuàng〈形〉 grand and heroic: ～的事业 grand and heroic cause ‖ 气势～ with great force

【豪族】háozú〈名〉 wealthy and influential family

壕 háo〈名〉 **1**（护城河） moat: ▸城～ **2**（沟） trench: 掘～ dig trenches ▸防空～, 交通～, 战～

【壕沟】háogōu〈名〉 **1**［军事］ trench **2**（沟） ditch

【壕堑】háoqiàn〈名〉［军事］ trench: ～战 trench warfare

嚎 háo〈动〉 **1**（指动物） howl: 狼～ howl of a wolf ▸鬼哭狼～ **2** = 号 háo 2

【嚎春】háochūn〈动〉 be in heat: 这只猫在～。 The cat is in heat.

【嚎啕】háotáo = 号啕 háotáo

濠 háo〈名〉 moat: 城～ city moat

hǎo

好 hǎo

A〈形〉 **1**（令人满意） good: ～地方 nice place ‖ ～主意 good idea ‖ 脾气～ good-tempered ▸～人, 良～, 美～ **2**（指关系） kind: ～伙伴 friendly partner ‖ ～朋友 good friend ‖ 友～ be friendly ‖ 两个人又～了。 They were friends again. ▸和～, 友～ **3**（完成） done [used after verb to express readiness, completion, etc.]: 准备～了吗? Is everything ready? ‖ 我的信已经写～了。 I've finished writing the letter. **4**（健康） well: 爸爸身体很～。 Dad is in good health. ‖ 我的病～多了。 I'm better now. **5**（表语气） okay: ～了，不要再说了。 All right. Let's say no more about it. ‖ ～，咱们就这样定了。 OK, that's a deal. **6**（容易） easy: 这个病～治。 This disease can be cured easily. ‖ 这个问题～回答。 This question is easy to answer. **7**（令人满意） good: ～喝 good to drink ‖ 这把刀～用。 This knife cuts well. ▸～吃, ～看, ～听

B〈副〉 **1** **a**（强调程度） very: ～漂亮的衣服啊! What a beautiful dress that is! ‖ 今年夏天～热。 It's been quite hot this summer. ‖ 我～糊涂啊! How silly I was! **b**（强调数量） many: ～多人来应聘。 Many people have applied for the position. ‖ 他们提了～些建议。 They have come

up with quite a few suggestions. **C**（强调时间） long: 飞机～早就起飞了。 The plane took off ages ago. ‖ 她等了～久。 She has waited for a long time. **2**（询问数量） how: 来听课的有～多学生？ How many students turned up at the lecture? ‖ 你打算在美国住～久？ How long are you staying in the States?

C〈动〉 be in order to: 今晚早点睡，明早～赶火车。 Let's turn in early tonight, so as to get up early tomorrow for the train.

D〈名〉 **1**（赞扬） [used to express praise]: ▸叫～，讨～ **2**（问候） regards: 见着他别忘了替我捎个～儿。 Don't forget to give him my regards when you see him.

▸hào

【好办】hǎobàn〈形〉 easy to handle

【好比】hǎobǐ〈动〉 be just like: 时间～流水，有去无回。 Time flows like water, never to return.

【好不】hǎobù〈副〉 [used before disyllabic adjectives with exclamatory force] so: 大家～高兴! We are so glad! ‖ 人来人往，～热闹! What a busy place, with so many people coming and going!

【好不容易】hǎobù róngyì = 好容易 hǎoróngyì

【好吃】hǎochī〈形〉 good to eat

【好处】hǎochǔ〈形〉 easy-going: 新来的主任很～。 The new director is very easy to get along with.

【好处费】hǎochùfèi〈名〉 kickback: 不许给导游～。 It is forbidden to give kickbacks to tourist guides.

【好处】hǎochu〈名〉 **1**（益处） benefit: 读书～很多。 Reading can do us a lot of good. **2**（利益） profit: 他从中没有捞到任何～。 He has gained nothing out of it.

【好歹】hǎodǎi **A**〈名〉 **1**（好和坏） good and evil: ～不分 do not distinguish the good from the bad ‖ 不知～ be unable to tell what's good (or bad) for one **2**（不幸） mishap: 万一他有个～，我们可得承担责任呀! Should anything happen to him, we have to take the responsibility. **B**〈副〉 **1**（无论如何） in any case: 你不能丢下她不管。她～是你妈妈。 You cannot leave her alone. She is your mother after all. **2**（将就） somehow: 你～让我看一眼，好吗? Will you let me just have a look?

【好端端】hǎoduānduān〈形〉 in perfect condition: 他们俩～的一对，怎么就离婚了呢? Those two were such a perfect couple. How come they have got divorced?

【好多】hǎoduō〈形〉 many: 有～问题要问 have many questions to ask

【好感】hǎogǎn〈名〉 good opinion: 赢得～ win favour ‖ 对他有～ have a good opinion of him

【好钢用在刀刃上】hǎogāng yòng zài dāorènshang〈俗〉〈喻〉 use sth. where it is needed most

【好过】hǎoguò〈形〉 **1**（生活富裕） well-off: 现在我家的日子～多了。 My family is much better off now. ‖ 这家亏损企业日子不～。 The loss-making enterprise is having a tough time. **2**（感觉舒服） (feel) good: 他吃了药，觉得～一点了。 He felt a bit better after taking the medicine.

【好汉】hǎohàn〈名〉 true man: 不到长城非～。 He who does not make it to the Great Wall is no true man.

【好汉不吃眼前亏】hǎohàn bù chī yǎnqiánkuī〈俗〉 a wise man knows when to retreat

【好汉不提当年勇】hǎohàn bù tí dāngnián yǒng〈俗〉 a true hero does not mention his past glories

【好汉做事好汉当】hǎohàn zuòshì hǎohàn dāng〈俗〉 a true man has the courage to accept the consequences of his own actions

【好好儿】hǎohāor **A**〈形〉 all right: 电话刚才还～的，怎么就坏了? Why isn't the phone working now? It was all right just before. **B**〈副〉 to one's heart's content: ～想一想 think it over carefully ‖ 我得～谢谢你。 I really must thank you from the bottom of my heart.

【好好先生】hǎohǎo xiānsheng〈成〉 crowd-pleaser

【好好学习，天天向上】hǎohǎo xuéxí, tiāntiān xiàngshàng〈惯〉 study hard and make progress every day

【好话】hǎohuà〈名〉 **1**（劝告） well-meant advice: ～不听，迟早要吃亏。 If you don't follow my advice, you'll surely run into trouble some day. **2**（表扬） words of praise: 帮他说句～。 Put in a good word for him. **3**（好听的话） fine words: 他这个人只说～，从不行动。 This man talks the talk but cannot walk the walk. **4**（指道歉） plea: 去说句～，他或许会同意的。 He might approve it if we plead with him.

【好几】hǎojǐ ▸**p. 927**〈数〉 **1**（表示有零数） well over: 他父亲七十～了。 His father is well over seventy. **2**（表示多） a good few: ～次/回 quite a few times ‖ ～百/千人 several hundred/thousand people

【好家伙】hǎojiāhuo〈叹〉 good heavens: ～，你买了这么漂亮的一部车! Good Lord, you've bought such a fancy car! ‖ ～，谁让你们这样干的? My goodness, who let you do it like this?

【好借好还，再借不难】hǎojiè-hǎohuán, zàijiè-bùnán〈俗〉 return what you have borrowed promptly and you will have no difficulty borrowing again

【好景不长】hǎojǐng-bùcháng〈成〉 time flies when you're having fun

【好久】hǎojiǔ〈形〉 long: 他们已经来了～了。 They've been here a long time.

【好看】hǎokàn〈形〉 **1**（指外观） good-looking: 长得～ look pretty ‖ 她的照片比她本人～多了。 Her photo flatters her a great deal. **2**（指内容） interesting: 这出戏很～。 The play is very good. **3**（光彩） proud: 儿子有出息，父母脸上也～。 If they can see their son doing well, the parents will be very proud. **4**（难堪） embarrassed: 等着吧，有他～的。 You can be sure he'll soon find himself on the spot.

【好莱坞】Hǎoláiwū〈名〉 Hollywood

【好赖】hǎolài = 好歹 hǎodǎi A1, B

【好了疮疤忘了疼】hǎole chuāngbā wàngle téng〈俗〉 forget the pain once the wound is healed

【好脸】hǎoliǎn〈名〉 [usu used in the negative] happy expression: 他一见我就没～。 He pulled a long face as soon as he saw me.

【好马不吃回头草】hǎomǎ bù chī huítóucǎo〈俗〉 a true man never backtracks

【好男不跟女斗】hǎonán bù gēn nǚ dòu〈俗〉 a true man never fights with a woman

【好评】hǎopíng〈名〉 high opinion: 博得读者～ be well received by the readers ‖ ～如潮。 Good reviews flooded in.

【好气儿】hǎoqìr〈名〉〈口〉 [usu used in the negative] good humour: 我一见他就没～。 I get in a bad mood whenever I see him.

【好球】hǎoqiú〈名〉 good play

【好人】hǎorén〈名〉 **1**（好心人） good person: ～有好报 good things come to good people ▸～好事 **2**（健康的人） healthy person: 尽管有残疾，他比一般～还干得好。 Despite his disability, he does better than most able-bodied people. **3**（指不得罪人） person who tries to get along with everyone: 你做～，让我做恶人? So you want to be the good guy and have me look like the bad one?

【好人好事】hǎorén-hǎoshì〈成〉 good people and good deeds

【好人家】hǎorénjiā〈名〉 good family

【好日子】hǎorìzi〈名〉 **1**（吉日） auspicious day: 挑个～举行婚礼 choose an auspicious day for the wedding **2**（办喜事的日子） special day: 他俩把～订在星期天。 They've decided to have their wedding on a Sunday. **3**（美好生活） good times: ～还在后头呢。 Good times are ahead of us.

【好容易】hǎoróngyì〈形〉 difficult: 他～才找到这份工作。 He had a hard time getting the job.

【好生】hǎoshēng〈副〉〈书〉 **1**（非常） very: 没有见到他，我～失望。 I was quite disappointed not to see him. **2**〈方〉（好好儿地） properly: ～想一想 think it over carefully ‖ ～照料 take good care of

【好声好气】hǎoshēng-hǎoqì〈成〉 in a kindly manner: ～地道歉 gently apologize

【好使】hǎoshǐ〈动〉 work well: 人老了耳朵不～。 Our hearing goes when we get old.

【好事】hǎoshì〈名〉 **1**（有益的事） good deed: 做～ do a good turn ‖ 坏事可以变成～。 Bad things can be turned to good things. **2**（慈善的事） charitable deed: 多行～ do more good deeds **3**（喜庆事） happy event: ～从天降。 It's a godsend.

【好事不出门，坏事传千里】hǎoshì bù chūmén, huàishì chuán qiānlǐ〈俗〉 good news never travels far, while bad news spreads fast

【好事多磨】hǎoshì-duōmó〈成〉 **1**（指生活） the road to happiness is paved with setbacks **2**（指感情） the course of true love never runs smooth

【好手】hǎoshǒu〈名〉 expert: 做外科手术，他可是把～。 He is a master surgeon.

【好受】hǎoshòu〈动〉 feel good: 心里不～ feel awful

【好说】hǎoshuō〈套〉 **1**（不敢当） it's very good of you to say so: ～，～，您太夸奖了。 It's very good of you to say so, but I don't think I deserve such praise. **2**（好商量） no trouble: 你的住宿问题，～。 I can arrange for your accommodation. Don't let it worry you.

【好说歹说】hǎoshuō-dǎishuō〈成〉 try every possible way to persuade: 我～，他才同意去看病。 He agreed to see the doctor, but only after I had pleaded with him in every way I could.

【好说话】hǎoshuōhuà〈形〉 accommodating: 奶奶～，咱们去找她求情吧。 Grandma is open to persuasion. Let's go and ask her.

【好死不如赖活】hǎosǐ bùrú làihuó〈俗〉 it's better to live a wretched existence than to experience a good death

【好似】hǎosì〈动〉〈书〉 be like: 他坐在那儿纹丝不动，～一尊佛像。 He sat there motionless like a Buddha.

【好天】hǎotiān〈名〉 sunny day

【好听】hǎotīng〈形〉 **1**（指声音） easy on the ear: ～的故事 interesting story ‖ 这支歌很～。 This is a very good song. **2**（指话语） fine: 说那么多～的有什么用呢? What's the use of all these fine words?

【好玩儿】hǎowánr〈形〉〈口〉 fun: 找个～

的地方 find a fun place ‖ 太～了! What good fun!

【好望角】Hǎowàngjiǎo〈名〉Cape of Good Hope

【好戏】hǎoxì〈名〉1 (指戏剧) good play: ～不厌百回看。A really good drama is worth seeing a hundred times. 2〈喻〉(指局面) great fun: 这回可有他的～看了! Just wait and he is sure to make a fool of himself!

【好像】hǎoxiàng A〈动〉be like: ～要下雨了。It looks as if it's going to rain. B〈副〉seemingly: 她今天～有点心不在焉。She seems to be a bit absent-minded today. ‖ 我们～在哪儿见过。I think we have met before.

【好笑】hǎoxiào〈形〉funny: 又好气又～ be annoying and amusing at the same time ‖ 这有什么～? What's so funny then?

【好些】hǎoxiē ▸ p. 927〈数〉〈口〉lots of: 拖了～时间。It took quite a while. ‖ 我花了～钱。I spent quite a lot of money.

【好心】hǎoxīn〈名〉good intention: ～人 kind-hearted person ‖ 一片～ with the best of intentions

【好心没好报】hǎoxīn méi hǎobào〈俗〉get no thanks for one's good intentions

【好心当作驴肝肺】hǎoxīn dāngzuò lǘgān-fèi〈俗〉mistake sb.'s goodwill for ill intent

【好性儿】hǎoxìngr〈形〉〈方〉good-natured

【好言】hǎoyán〈名〉kind words: ～相劝 plead with sb. earnestly

【好样儿的】hǎoyàngrde〈名〉〈口〉great guy: 他真是个～。He's a good sort.

【好一个】hǎoyīge〈叹〉[used in an exclamation, often ironically] what a: ～慈善家! What a philanthropist (he is)!

【好意】hǎoyì〈名〉kindness: 你的～我心领了。I appreciate your kindness. ‖ 谢谢你的～。Thank you for your kindness.

【好意思】hǎoyìsi〈动〉have the nerve: 你怎么～又来要钱? How can you have the cheek to ask for more money? ‖ 我真不～讲给大家听。I can hardly bring myself to tell it to you.

【好运】hǎoyùn〈名〉good luck: 祝你～! Good luck!

【好在】hǎozài〈副〉luckily: ～系着安全带, 他才免受伤害。Thanks to the safety belt, he was not hurt.

【好转】hǎozhuǎn〈动〉take a turn for the better: 病情～。The patient is on the mend. ‖ 形势～。The situation took a favourable turn.

【好自为之】hǎozìwéizhī〈成〉do one's best: 现在有了一份好工作, 你当～。Now that you have a good job, you should do your best at it.

【好走】hǎozǒu〈动〉[words before parting] good-bye

hào

号(號) hào

A〈动〉1〈书〉(召唤) call: ▸～召 2 (做标记) mark: ～房子 earmark a room 3 [中医] feel (a pulse): ▸～脉

B〈名〉1 (命令) order: ▸发～施令 2 (指管乐器) brass wind instrument: 吹～ sound a trumpet ▸～兵, 军～, 小～ 3 (指军号) bugle call: 吹冲锋～ sound the call to charge ▸起床～, 熄灯～ 4 (名称) name: ▸～称, 绰～, 代～ 5〈旧〉(商店) firm: ▸分～, 商～, 银～ 6 (标记) sign: 举火为～ light a beacon as a signal ▸暗～, 符～, 记～ 7 (指大小) size: 四～字 No 4 type ▸大～, 小～, 型～ 8 (指人) person of a given type: ▸病～ 9 (别名) assumed name: 稼轩是辛弃疾的～。Xin Qiji is also known as Xin Jiaxuan.

C〈量〉1 (指排序) number: 第250～决议 Solution No 250 ‖ 门牌～ house number ▸～码, 编～, 挂～ 2 (指日期) date: 8月2～ August the second ‖ 今天几～? What date is it today? 3 (指人) 五百多～人 over five hundred people

▸háo

号
▸姓名

【号兵】hàobīng〈名〉trumpeter

【号称】hàochēng〈动〉1 (被称为) be known as: 秦兵马俑～世界第八奇迹。The terracotta Army excavated in the Qin Tomb is known as the world's eighth wonder. 2 (宣称) claim to be: ～百万大军 an army claiming to be a million strong

【号角】hàojiǎo〈名〉1 (号令用具) bugle 2 (指乐器) bugle call: 吹响～ sound the clarion call

【号令】hàolìng A〈名〉order: 发布～ issue (battle) orders B〈动〉give orders: ～三军 issue orders to the army

【号码】hàomǎ〈名〉number: 电话～ telephone number ‖ ～机 numbering machine

【号脉】hàomài〈动〉[中医] take sb.'s pulse: 大夫给我号了脉。The doctor felt my pulse.

【号手】hàoshǒu〈名〉bugler

【号外】hàowài〈名〉(指报纸) extra; (指内容) flash: 出版～ publish an extra

【号衣】hàoyī〈名〉〈旧〉livery or army uniform

【号召】hàozhào〈动〉call: 响应～ respond to a call ‖ 市政府～市民节约用水。The municipal government is appealing to citizens to conserve water.

【号志灯】hàozhìdēng〈名〉signal lamp

【号子】hàozi〈名〉1〈口〉(监狱) jail: 他们在～里交上了朋友。They became friends while they were in jail. 2 (指歌) labour chant: 船工～ boatman's song ‖ 打夯～ rammers' work chant

好 hào

〈动〉1 (喜欢) like: ～出风头 be fond of the limelight ‖ ～动 be active ‖ ～斗 be aggressive ‖ 虚心～学 be modest and keen to learn ▸～客, ～强, ～为人师 2 (容易) be apt to: ～流眼泪 cry easily ‖ 酒喝多了～惹事生非。Those who drink too much are likely to make trouble.

▸hǎo

【好吃懒做】hàochī-lǎnzuò〈成〉be gluttonous and lazy

【好大喜功】hàodà-xǐgōng〈成〉crave greatness and success

【好高骛远】hàogāo-wùyuǎn〈成〉aim too high

【好客】hàokè〈形〉hospitable: 以～而闻名 be known for one's hospitality

【好奇】hàoqí〈形〉be inquisitive: 出于～ out of curiosity ‖ ～心 curiosity ‖ 孩子们对什么都～。Children are curious about everything.

【好强】hàoqiáng〈形〉eager to do well in everything

【好色】hàosè〈形〉be lustful: ～之徒 womanizer

【好善嫉恶】hàoshàn-jí'è〈成〉love goodness and hate evil

【好善乐施】hàoshàn-lèshī〈成〉be philanthropic

【好尚】hàoshàng〈名〉one's preferences: 人各有～。Everyone has his own preferences.

【好胜】hàoshèng〈形〉striving to outdo others: 争强～ strive to outdo others in everything

【好事】hàoshì〈动〉be meddlesome: ～之徒 busybody

▸hǎoshì

【好为人师】hàowéirénshī〈成〉enjoy lecturing other people

【好恶】hàowù〈名〉likes and dislikes: 各人～不同。People's tastes vary.

【好逸恶劳】hàoyì-wùláo〈成〉love leisure and hate hard work

【好战】hàozhàn〈形〉bellicose

【好整以暇】hàozhěngyǐxiá〈成〉keep cool under pressure

昊 hào〈书〉

A〈形〉vast and boundless: ～天 vast sky

B〈名〉sky: 苍～ broad sky

耗 hào

A〈动〉1 (使用) consume: 壶里的水快要～干了。The kettle is boiling dry. ‖ 这种小汽车～油很厉害。Cars of this model are gas-guzzlers. ▸～资, 消～ 2〈方〉(浪费时间) waste time: 别～着了, 快走吧。Stop dawdling and get going.

B〈名〉bad news: ▸噩～

【耗材】hàocái A〈动〉consume materials B〈名〉consumable materials

【耗电量】hàodiànliàng〈名〉power consumption

【耗费】hàofèi〈动〉consume: ～人力物力 consume manpower and material resources ‖ ～时间 take time

【耗竭】hàojié〈动〉exhaust: 人力～ be drained of manpower ‖ 资源～ be depleted of natural resources

【耗尽】hàojìn〈动〉exhaust: ～体力 use up all one's strength ‖ 灯油～了。The lamp was running out of oil.

【耗能】hàonéng〈动〉consume energy: 高～企业 high energy consumption enterprise

【耗神】hàoshén〈动〉use up one's energy

【耗损】hàosǔn〈动〉consume: ～精力 wear sb. down ‖ 减少粮食在运输中的～ reduce the wastage of grain in transit

【耗油量】hàoyóuliàng〈名〉oil consumption

【耗资】hàozī〈动〉cost: ～800万元 at a cost of 8 million *yuan*

【耗子】hàozi〈名〉〈方〉rat

浩 hào

〈形〉1 (特别大) great 2 (众多) a great many: ▸～如烟海

【浩博】hàobó〈形〉abundant: 引证～ quote extensively

【浩大】hàodà〈形〉vast: ～的工程 huge project ‖ 声势～ powerful and dynamic

【浩荡】hàodàng〈形〉1 (指水势) expansive: ～的长江 the mighty Yangtze River 2 (指规模、场面等) mighty: ～的人群 huge crowds of people ‖ 军威～ mighty army

【浩繁】hàofán〈形〉vast and numerous: ～的工作任务 heavy work load ‖ ～的开支 heavy expenditure

【浩瀚】hàohàn〈形〉1 (无边无际) vast: ～的沙漠 vast expanse of desert ‖ ～无垠的海洋 boundless ocean 2 (繁多) numerous: 古代的典籍卷帙～。There are an immense number of ancient classical books.

h

【浩浩荡荡】hàohào-dàngdàng〈成〉vast and mighty: 游行队伍～地前进。The parade marched in mighty contingents.

【浩劫】hàojié〈名〉catastrophe: 空前～ unprecedented catastrophe ‖ 战争的～ scourge of war

【浩渺】hàomiǎo〈形〉vast: 湖上烟波～。On the lake, mists and waves stretch far into the distance.

【浩淼】hàomiǎo = 浩渺 hàomiǎo

【浩气】hàoqì〈名〉noble spirit: ～长存 imperishable noble spirit ‖ ～凛然 awe-inspiring noble spirit

【浩然】hàorán〈形〉〈书〉**1**（盛大广阔）expansive: 江流～ mighty rivers ‖ 洪波～ huge waves **2**（刚正豪迈）righteous: ～正气 awe-inspiring righteousness

【浩如烟海】hàorúyānhǎi〈成〉voluminous: 中国的古籍～。China has a vast collection of ancient books.

【浩叹】hàotàn〈动〉〈书〉heave a deep sigh

淏 hào〈形〉〈书〉[of water] clear

皓 hào〈形〉**1**（洁白）white: ～发 white hair ▸～齿, ～首 **2**（光亮）bright: ▸～月

【皓白】hàobái〈形〉white

【皓齿】hàochǐ〈名〉white teeth

【皓首】hàoshǒu〈名〉〈书〉old age: ～穷经 study the classics even though one is very old

【皓月】hàoyuè〈名〉〈书〉bright moon: ～当空 a bright moon hanging high in the sky

镐（鎬） Hào〈名〉Hao [early capital of the Zhou Dynasty]:
▸gǎo

颢（顥） hào〈形〉〈书〉white and shining

灏（灝） hào〈书〉**1** = 浩 hào **2** = 皓 hào

hē

诃（訶） hē

【诃子】hēzǐ〈名〉［植物］myrobalan

呵[1] hē〈动〉scold: ▸～斥, ～责

呵[2] hē〈动〉breathe out with the mouth open: ～一口气 give a puff ▸一气～成

呵[3] hē = 嗬 hē

【呵斥】hēchì〈动〉scold loudly

【呵呵】hēhē〈拟〉laugh loudly: ～大笑 roar with laughter

【呵护】hēhù〈动〉**1**（保佑）bless: 神灵～ God bless **2**（爱护）take good care of: ～备至 cherish most dearly

【呵责】hēzé〈动〉〈书〉berate

喝[1] hē〈动〉drink: ～茶/汤 drink tea/soup ‖ ～粥 eat porridge ‖ ～得酩酊大醉 get blind drunk ‖ 今天多～了几杯。I have had a few too many drinks today. ▸大吃大～

喝[2] hē = 嗬 hē
▸hè

【喝叱】hēchì = 呵斥 hēchì

【喝墨水】hē mòshuǐ〈惯〉〈喻〉study at a school: 喝过洋墨水 have studied abroad

【喝水不忘掘井人】hēshuǐ bù wàng juéjǐngrén〈俗〉when you drink the water, think of those who dug the well

【喝西北风】hē xīběifēng〈惯〉〈喻〉suffer from cold and hunger: 你不工作，难道让全家～去？If you don't work, what are the family going to eat?

嗬 hē〈叹〉[used to indicate astonishment] wow: ～，这小伙子真能干！Oh, what a capable young man! ‖ ～，新娘真漂亮！Wow, the bride is really beautiful!

hé

禾 hé〈名〉cereal seedlings: ▸～苗

【禾本植物】héběnzhíwù〈名〉［植物］grass

【禾场】hécháng〈名〉〈方〉threshing ground

【禾苗】hémiáo〈名〉grain seedlings

合[1] hé

A〈动〉**1**（闭上）close: ～上眼睛 close one's eyes ‖ 笑得～不拢嘴 grin from ear to ear ▸～抱 **2**（合并）join: 齐心～力 combine our efforts ▸～并, ～伙, ～唱 **3**（符合）conform with: ～胃口 be to one's taste ‖ 正～我意。It suits me fine. ▸不谋而～, 志同道～ **4**（相当于）be equal to: 一公顷～十五亩。A hectare is equal to 15 *mu*. ‖ 这张床连同两个床头柜～多少钱？How much is this bed, including the two bedside cupboards?

B〈形〉whole: ～家团聚 reunion of the whole family

C〈量〉round: 他们打了二十余～，不分胜负。Their fight ended in a draw after twenty-odd rounds.

合[2] hé〈名〉［音乐］note on the *gongche* (工尺) scale, corresponding to a low 5 in *jianpu* (简谱) numbered musical notation
▸gě

【合抱】hébào〈动〉get one's arms around: 五人～的松树 pine tree so thick that five people can put their arms around it

【合抱之木，生于毫末】hébào zhī mù, shēngyú háomò〈成〉great oaks from little acorns grow

【合璧】hébì〈动〉match well: 中西～ good combination of Chinese and Western elements

【合编】hébiān〈动〉co-edit

【合并】hébìng〈动〉**1**（合在一起）merge: 这两所大学已经～。These two universities have already merged. ‖ 这三项提议～讨论。The three proposals will be discussed together. **2**（指疾病）be complicated by another illness: ▸～症

【合并症】hébìngzhèng〈名〉complication

【合不来】hébulái〈动〉〈口〉be incompatible: 他跟谁都～。He could hardly get along with anybody.

【合不着】hébuzháo〈动〉〈方〉not worthwhile: 跑那么远路去看场电影太～了。It's not at all worthwhile going so far to see the film.

【合唱】héchàng〈动〉sing in chorus: 大～ cantata ‖ 男声/女声/童声～ male/female/children's chorus

【合唱团】héchàngtuán〈名〉chorus

【合成】héchéng〈动〉**1**（合在一起）be composed of: 由两部分～ be composed of two parts **2**（指化学反应）synthesize

【合成词】héchéngcí〈名〉［语言］compound word

【合成革】héchénggé〈名〉synthetic leather

【合成器】héchéngqì〈名〉synthesizer: 语音～ speech synthesizer ‖ 电子～ electronic synthesizer

【合成塔】héchéngtǎ〈名〉［化工］synthetic tower

【合成纤维】héchéng xiānwéi〈名〉synthetic fibre

【合成橡胶】héchéng xiàngjiāo〈名〉synthetic rubber

【合得来】hédelái〈动〉〈口〉get along well: 他脾气好，和谁都～。He is good-tempered and gets along well with everybody.

【合订本】hédìngběn〈名〉bound volume: 《人民日报》～ a *People's Daily* bound volume

【合度】hédù〈形〉appropriate

【合恩角】Hé'ēnjiǎo〈名〉Cape Horn

【合二而一】hé'èr'éryī〈成〉two combined into one

【合法】héfǎ〈形〉legal: ～婚姻 lawful marriage ‖ ～权利 legitimate right ‖ ～收入 lawful income ‖ ～途径 legal means

【合法化】héfǎhuà〈动〉legitimize

【合肥】Héféi ▸**p. 661**〈名〉Hefei [capital of Anhui Province (安徽)]

【合该】hégāi〈动〉should: ～如此。This is as it should be.

【合格】hégé〈形〉qualified: ～产品 quality assured product ‖ ～教师 qualified teacher ‖ ～证 certificate of quality

【合股】hégǔ〈动〉form a partnership: ～经营 run a business in partnership

【合乎】héhū〈动〉accord with: ～规格 be up to the specifications ‖ ～情理 be reasonable ‖ ～事实 tally with the facts

【合欢】héhuān **A**〈动〉make love **B**〈名〉［植物］silk tree

【合伙】héhuǒ〈动〉enter into partnership: ～打劫 collude in a robbery ‖ ～经营 run a business in partnership ‖ ～人 partner

【合击】héjī〈动〉make a concerted attack (on): 分进～ concerted attack by converging columns

【合计】héjì〈动〉amount to: 球队～18人。There are a total of 18 people in the team.

【合计】héji〈动〉**1**（考虑）mull over: 她心里老在～这件事。She kept thinking it over. **2**（商讨）consult: 大家～一下，看该怎么办。Let's put our heads together and see what's to be done.

【合剂】héjì〈名〉［药学］mixture: 复方甘草～ compound liquorice

【合家】héjiā〈名〉entire family: ～团圆 reunion of the whole family

【合家欢】héjiāhuān〈名〉family photo: 拍一张～ take a family photo

【合脚】héjiǎo〈形〉fit: 我的新鞋很～。My new shoes fit me perfectly.

【合金】héjīn〈名〉alloy: ～铸铁 alloy cast iron ‖ ～钢 alloy steel

【合卺】héjǐn〈动〉〈旧〉get married

【合刊】hékān〈名〉combined issue: 一、二月份～ combined periodical of the January and February issues

【合口】hékǒu〈动〉**1**（指伤口）heal up **2**（指食物）be to one's taste: 中国饭菜

h

更～。Chinese food is more suitable to one's taste.

【合理】hélǐ〈形〉 reasonable: 价格/收费～ reasonable price/charge ‖ ～安排 sensible arrangement ‖ 公平～ fair and equitable ▸合情～

【合理化】hélǐhuà〈动〉 rationalize: 使经济结构～ streamline the economic structure ‖ ～建议 rational proposal

【合力】hélì **A**〈动〉 work collaboratively: 同心～ unite and make a concerted effort **B**〈名〉［物理］ resultant force: 形成～ form a resultant force

【合流】héliú〈动〉 **1**（指江河） merge: 汉江在武汉与长江～。The Hanjiang River and the Yangtze River meet at Wuhan. **2**〈喻〉（指观点流派） collaborate: 中西文化～ the merging of cultures from the East and the West

【合龙】hélóng〈动〉 close up: 大桥～ the joining of two sections of a bridge

【合拢】hélǒng〈动〉 join together: 把大伙～起来 get everyone together ‖ 笑得合不拢嘴 laugh so much that one's jaws get stuck

【合霉素】héméisù〈名〉［药学］ syntomycin

【合谋】hémóu〈动〉 conspire: 售货员与门卫～盗窃商品。The shop assistant conspired with the doorkeeper to steal merchandise.

【合拍】hépāi **A**〈形〉 harmonious: 与时代潮流～ be in step with the trend of the times ‖ 舞步与音乐节奏不～。The dancing was not in time with the music. **B**〈动〉 **1**（指拍摄制作） co-produce a film **2**（指照相） take a group photo

【合情合理】héqíng-hélǐ〈成〉 stand to reason: 她的要求～。Her request is fair and reasonable.

【合群】héqún〈动〉 get on well with others: 这个小孩不～。This child is not very sociable.

【合身】héshēn〈形〉 suitable: 新衣服非常～。The new clothes are a really good fit.

【合十】héshí〈动〉 hold one's palms together: ～祷告/相迎 put one's palms together in prayer/greeting

【合时】héshí〈形〉 fashionable: 穿戴～ dress fashionably

【合适】héshì〈形〉 suitable: 你这样说不～。It's not appropriate for you to say so. ‖ 这个词用在这儿不～。This isn't the right word to use here. ‖ 这双鞋我穿正～。These shoes suit me beautifully.

【合数】héshù〈名〉［数学］ composite number

【合算】hésuàn **A**〈形〉 worthwhile: 很～ good value for money ‖ 不～ unprofitable **B**〈动〉 calculate: 仔细～一个月的开支 make a careful tally of monthly expenditure

【合体】hétǐ **A**〈形〉 fit: 她的晚礼服很～。Her evening dress fits her well. **B**〈名〉［语言］ compound character: ～字 Chinese character composed of two or more characters

【合同】hétong〈名〉 contract: 履行～ carry out a contract ‖ 签订～ sign a contract ‖ 修改～ alter a contract ‖ 终止～ terminate a contract ‖ 购货～ purchase contract

【合同工】hétonggōng〈名〉 contract worker

【合围】héwéi〈动〉 **1**［军事］ surround **2**〈书〉= 合抱 hébào

【合眼】héyǎn〈动〉 **1**（合上眼睛） close one's eyes;（睡着） sleep: 他昨晚一夜没～。He didn't get a wink of sleep last night. **2** ▸p. 772〈婉〉（去世） pass away

【合演】héyǎn〈动〉 co-star

【合叶】héyè〈名〉 hinge

【合页】héyè = 合叶 héyè

【合宜】héyí〈形〉 suitable: 穿牛仔服参加婚礼是不～的。It is not appropriate to wear jeans for a wedding.

【合议庭】héyìtíng〈名〉［法律］ full court

【合议制】héyìzhì〈名〉［法律］ collegiate system

【合意】héyì〈动〉 be to one's liking: 这样安排正合我意。This kind of arrangement is perfectly to my liking.

【合营】héyíng〈动〉 jointly operate: ～企业 joint venture

【合影】héyǐng **A**〈动〉 take a group photo: 师生们～留念。Teachers and students had a group photo taken to mark the occasion. **B**〈名〉 group photo: 师生～ group photo of teachers and students

【合用】héyòng **A**〈动〉 share: 我们三人～一间宿舍。Three of us share one dormitory. **B**〈形〉 suitable: 这件大衣太薄，在北方寒冷地区不～。The coat is too thin for the cold regions in the north.

【合约】héyuē〈名〉 contract: 签订～ sign a contract

【合葬】hézàng〈动〉 be buried in the same grave: ～墓 joint tomb

【合掌】hézhǎng = 合十 héshí

【合辙】hézhé〈动〉 **1**（押韵） be in rhyme: 快板儿～，所以容易记。Clapper talk is rhythmical, so it's easy to memorize. **2**（一致） agree: 两人一说就～。The moment they started talking they found themselves in complete agreement.

【合众国际社】Hézhòng Guójìshè〈名〉 United Press International (UPI)

【合资】hézī〈动〉 make a joint investment: ～企业 joint venture ‖ 他们～开了一家小饭馆。They have pooled their resources to open a small restaurant.

【合子】hézi〈名〉 fried pie with meat or vegetable filling

【合奏】hézòu〈动〉 play several musical instruments together: 民乐～ ensemble of folk instruments

【合作】hézuò〈动〉 cooperate: 进行～ enter into cooperation ‖ 经济/技术～ economic/technical cooperation ‖ ～伙伴 cooperating partner ‖ 亚太经济～论坛 Asia Pacific Economic Cooperation Forum

【合作化】hézuòhuà〈名〉 establishment of cooperatives: 农业～ cooperative transformation of agriculture

【合作企业】hézuò qǐyè〈名〉 cooperative venture

【合作社】hézuòshè〈名〉 cooperative: 生产～ production cooperative ‖ 信用～ credit cooperative

【合作医疗】hézuò yīliáo〈名〉 community-sponsored medical service: 发展农村～ develop rural cooperative medical services

纥（紇） hé ▸回纥 Huíhé

何 hé〈书〉〈代〉 **1**（什么） **a**（指人）（主语） who;（宾语） whom;（指事） what;（指物） which: ～人 who ‖ ～事 what ‖ 有～难处？What's up? **b**（哪里） where: ～处 where ‖ 从～而来？Where from? **2**（为什么） why: ～不求助于他？Why not go to him for help? ‖ 有～不可？Why not? ▸～足挂齿，谈～容易

【何必】hébì〈副〉why: ～小题大做？Why make such a fuss? ‖ 开个玩笑，～当真呢？I was only joking. Why did you take it seriously?

【何不】hébù〈副〉 why not: 你有困难，～早说？Why didn't you tell us your difficulties earlier? ‖ 既然来了，～多呆一会儿？Since you have come, why not stay a while longer?

【何曾】hécéng〈副〉 did ever: 我～给你说过此事。When did I ever say that to you?

【何尝】hécháng〈副〉 ever so: 我～不想去，只是囊中羞涩罢了。It's not that I don't want to go; I just haven't got the money.

【何啻】héchì〈副〉〈书〉 far more than: ～万千 way more than tens of thousands ‖ ～天壤之别! The difference is no less than that between heaven and earth!

【何等】héděng **A**〈代〉 what kind: 他受过～训练？What sort of training has he had? **B**〈副〉 [used in exclamations] how: 为国效劳是～的光荣! How glorious it is to serve our country! ‖ 买彩票中奖是～的幸运! What luck to win the lottery!

【何方】héfāng〈代〉〈书〉 where: ～人士？Where are you from?

【何妨】héfáng〈副〉〈书〉 why not: ～试一试？Why not have a go?

【何干】hégān〈动〉 have to do with: 此事与我～？What has that got to do with me?

【何故】hégù〈代〉〈书〉 why: 航班～取消？Why has the flight been cancelled?

【何苦】hékǔ〈副〉 why bother: ～自寻烦恼？Why worry yourself sick?

【何况】hékuàng〈连〉 **1**（不用说） let alone: 死都不怕，～困难呢。Not fearing death, naturally we fear no hardship. **2**（再说） what's more: 他高兴得不得了，因为他考上了大学，～又是所重点大学。He was very happy because he got into university, and what's more, it was a key university.

【何乐而不为】hé lè ér bù wéi〈成〉 what is the sense of not doing it: 这对大家都有好处，～呢？This will be good for everyone. Why not go ahead with it?

【何其】héqí〈副〉〈书〉 how: 用心～毒也! How malicious they are!

【何其相似乃尔】héqí xiāngsì nǎi'ěr〈成〉 What a striking likeness!

【何去何从】héqù-hécóng〈成〉 what course to follow: ～，速做抉择。You have to decide at once what course to follow.

【何日】hérì〈代〉〈书〉 what day: ～再相逢？When shall we meet again?

【何如】hérú **A**〈代〉〈书〉 how about: 请君一试，～? How about having a try? **B**〈连〉 [often used together with 与其 in rhetorical questions] wouldn't it be better: 与其强攻，～智取? Wouldn't it be better to use strategy than to attack by force?

【何时】héshí〈代〉〈书〉 when

【何首乌】héshǒuwū〈名〉［中药］ tuber of multiflower knotweed

【何谓】héwèi〈动〉〈书〉 **1**（什么是） what is: ～自由/民主？What is freedom/democracy? **2**（指什么） what is meant by: 此言～？What is the meaning of this word?

【何须】héxū〈副〉 there is no need: 打个电话就行了，～写信。You don't need to write a letter. Just give us a call.

【何许】héxǔ〈代〉〈书〉 what: 来者～人也？Who is there?

【何以】héyǐ〈副〉〈书〉 **1**（如何） how: ～自圆其说？How can you explain yourself? **2**（为什么） why: ～见得？What makes you think so? ‖ ～自食其言？Why have you gone back on your own promise?

h

【何在】hézài〈动〉〈书〉 where: 你居心～? What are you up to? ‖ 问题～? Wherein lies the problem?

【何止】hézhǐ〈动〉 [used in rhetorical questions to indicate a number or extent far greater than the one given] be far more than: 例子～这些。 There are far more instances than we have listed. ‖ 伤亡～五千。 There were way over five thousand casualties.

【何足挂齿】hézúguàchǐ〈惯〉 not be worth mentioning: 区区小事，～? That's nothing. Don't mention it.

【何足为怪】hézúwéiguài〈惯〉 nothing to wonder about

和[1] hé

A〈形〉 **1**（和睦） harmonious: ～为贵 peace is of paramount importance ‖ 兄弟不～ the brothers are not on good terms ▸～睦, ～谐, 失～ **2**（温和） gentle: ▸～蔼, ～善, 心平气～ **3**（温暖） warm: ▸～煦, 风～日丽

B〈动〉 **1**（和解） make peace: ▸～解, 讲～ **2**（平局） tie: 那盘棋～了。 That game of chess ended in a draw. ▸～局, ～棋

和[2] hé

A〈动〉 be with: ～衣而卧 sleep with one's clothes on ▸～盘托出

B〈介〉 with: 他～这件事没有关系。 It has nothing to do with him.

C ▸p. 448〈连〉 and: 一支钢笔～两支铅笔 one pen and two pencils

D〈名〉 sum: 两数之～ sum of two numbers ‖ 总～ (total) sum ▸～数

和[3] Hé

〈名〉 Japan: 汉～词典 Chinese-Japanese dictionary ▸～服
▸hè, hú, huó, huò

【和蔼】hé'ǎi〈形〉 affable: 态度～ be amiable (to sb.)

【和蔼可亲】hé'ǎi-kěqīn〈成〉 gentle and affable

【和畅】héchàng〈形〉 gentle and pleasant: 春风～。 The spring breeze is gentle and caressing.

【和风】héfēng〈名〉 gentle breeze

【和风细雨】héfēng-xìyǔ〈成〉〈喻〉 in a gentle and mild way

【和服】héfú〈名〉 kimono

【和好】héhǎo **A**〈形〉 harmonious: 关系～ be on good terms **B**〈动〉 become reconciled: ～如初 be on good terms again ‖ 他们吵过架，现在～了。 They had a quarrel, but have made it up now.

【和缓】héhuǎn **A**〈形〉 gentle: 水流～ gentle flow of a stream ‖ 用～的语气说话 speak in gentle tones **B**〈动〉 ease up: ～一下气氛 relieve the tension a little ‖ 紧张局势有所～。 The tension has eased off.

【和会】héhuì〈名〉 peace conference

【和解】héjiě〈动〉 become reconciled: 达成～ reach a compromise ‖ 使双方～ bring both sides together

【和局】héjú〈名〉 tie: 他俩这盘棋又下成了～。 They drew at chess once again.

【和乐】hélè〈形〉 harmonious and happy

【和美】héměi〈形〉 harmonious and happy: ～的家庭 happy family

【和睦】hémù〈形〉 harmonious: ～相处 live in harmony ‖ 家庭～ family harmony

【和暖】hénuǎn〈形〉 pleasantly warm: ～的阳光 warm sunshine ‖ 天气～ warm weather

【和盘托出】hépán-tuōchū〈成〉 lay all the cards on the table: 把事实真相～ disclose the whole truth

【和平】hépíng **A**〈名〉 peace: 热爱～ love peace ‖ ～环境 peacetime conditions ‖ ～集会 peace rally ‖ ～解放 peaceful liberation ‖ ～时期 peacetime ‖ ～统一祖国 peaceful unification of the motherland **B**〈形〉 mild: 药性～。 The medicine is mild.

【和平队】hépíngduì〈名〉 Peace Corps

【和平鸽】hépínggē〈名〉 dove of peace

【和平共处】hépíng gòngchǔ〈名〉 peaceful coexistence: ～五项原则 the Five Principles of Peaceful Coexistence

【和平过渡】hépíng guòdù〈名〉 peaceful transition

【和平谈判】hépíng tánpàn〈名〉 peace talks

【和平演变】hépíng yǎnbiàn〈名〉 peaceful evolution [usu referring to subverting a socialist state by peaceful means]

【和棋】héqí〈名〉 tie [in a board game]

【和气】héqi **A**〈形〉 **1**（温和） kind: 待人～ be friendly to people ‖ 说话～ speak kindly **2**（和睦） friendly: 他们彼此很～。 They are very friendly with each other. **B**〈名〉 friendship: 别为这事伤了～。 Don't let this hurt our friendship.

【和气生财】héqi-shēngcái〈成〉 good-naturedness is a source of wealth

【和洽】héqià〈形〉 harmonious: 关系～ harmonious relations

【和亲】héqīn〈名〉［历史］ attempt to pacify rulers of minority nationalities in the border areas by marrying daughters of the Han imperial family to them

【和善】héshàn〈形〉 kind and gentle: 心地～ kind-hearted ‖ ～的面容 benign face

【和尚】héshang〈名〉 Buddhist monk

【和尚打伞，无法无天】héshang dǎ sǎn, wúfǎwútiān〈歇后〉〈喻〉 be completely lawless

【和尚头】héshangtóu〈名〉〈口〉 shaven head: 她给儿子剃了个～。 She had her son's head shaved.

【和声】héshēng〈名〉［音乐］ harmony

【和事老】héshìlǎo〈名〉 unprincipled mediator: 你不能遇事总当～。 You can't act like a peacemaker every time there is a dispute.

【和数】héshù〈名〉［数学］ sum

【和顺】héshùn〈形〉 gentle, amiable and obliging: 他妻子性情很～。 His wife is gentle and obliging.

【和谈】hétán〈名〉 peace talks: 举行～ hold peace talks

【和为贵】hé wéi guì〈成〉 harmony above all

【和弦】héxián〈名〉［音乐］ chord: ～风琴 chord organ

【和祥】héxiáng〈形〉 kindly

【和谐】héxié〈形〉 harmonious: 音调～ melodious ‖ 色彩的～ consistency of colours ‖ 建设～社会 build a harmonious society

【和煦】héxù〈形〉 pleasantly warm: ～的阳光 pleasant sunshine ‖ 春风～。 The spring breeze is gentle and warm.

【和颜悦色】héyán-yuèsè〈成〉 with a kind and pleasant countenance: 老师～地回答了孩子们的问题。 The teacher answered the children's questions in a kind and pleasant way.

【和议】héyì〈名〉 peace talks: 签署～ sign a peace agreement

【和易】héyì〈形〉 amiable

【和约】héyuē〈名〉 peace treaty: 缔结～ conclude a peace treaty

【和悦】héyuè〈形〉 kindly

【和衷共济】hézhōng-gòngjì〈成〉 pull together for a common cause

郃 Hé

〈名〉 He [surname]

劾 hé

〈动〉 expose sb.'s crimes: ▸弹～

河 hé

〈名〉 **1** Hé（黄河） Yellow River: ▸～套, ～西走廊 **2** ▸p. 164（河流） river: 过～ cross a river ‖ ～对岸 across the river ▸～流, 护城～, 运～ **3**［天文］ Galaxy: ～外星云 extragalactic nebula ▸～汉, 天～

【河岸】hé'àn〈名〉 river bank

【河浜】hébāng〈名〉〈方〉 creek

【河北】Héběi ▸p. 661〈名〉 Hebei Province

【河北梆子】Héběi bāngzi〈名〉 Hebei clapper opera

【河边】hébiān〈名〉 river bank

【河滨】hébīn〈名〉 riverside: ～大道 riverside avenue

【河槽】hécáo〈名〉 riverbed

【河汊子】héchàzi〈名〉 tributary

【河川】héchuān〈名〉 rivers and creeks

【河床】héchuáng〈名〉 riverbed

【河道】hédào〈名〉 river course: 疏浚～ dredge a river

【河堤】hédī〈名〉 dyke: 加固～ reinforce the river embankment

【河东狮吼】Hédōng-shīhǒu〈成〉〈喻〉 the quick temper and sharp tongue of a fishwife

【河段】héduàn〈名〉 section of a river

【河防】héfáng〈名〉 **1**（防水患工作） flood-prevention work **2**（指军事防御） defence of a river

【河粉】héfěn〈名〉 rice noodles

【河港】hégǎng〈名〉 river port

【河工】hégōng〈名〉 **1**（指工程） river (conservancy) works **2**（指工人） river conservancy worker

【河沟】hégōu〈名〉 stream

【河谷】hégǔ ▸p. 164〈名〉 river valley

【河汉】héhàn〈名〉 Milky Way

【河口】hékǒu〈名〉 river mouth

【河狸】hélí〈名〉 beaver

【河流】héliú ▸p. 294〈名〉 river: ～改道 river diversion ‖ 不通航～ non-navigable river

【河马】hémǎ〈名〉 hippopotamus

【河鳗】hémán〈名〉 river eel

【河姆渡文化】Hémǔdù wénhuà〈名〉［考古］ Hemudu culture

【河南】Hénán ▸p. 661〈名〉 Henan Province

【河南梆子】Hénán bāngzi〈名〉 Henan clapper opera

【河南坠子】Hénán zhuìzi〈名〉 Henan Province ballad singing

【河内】Hénèi〈名〉 Hanoi

【河泥】hénì〈名〉 river mud

【河清海晏】héqīng-hǎiyàn〈成〉 there is peace and tranquillity throughout the land

【河曲】héqū〈名〉 bend

【河渠】héqú〈名〉 water ways: ～纵横 be crisscrossed by rivers and canals

【河山】héshān〈名〉 rivers and mountains: 大好～ beautiful rivers and mountains ‖ 锦绣～ land of enchanting beauty

【河身】héshēn = 河床 héchuáng

【河水】héshuǐ〈名〉 river water: ～漫过堤岸。 The river overflowed its banks. ‖ ～上涨。 The river swelled. ‖ ～退了。 The river receded.

h

【河滩】hétān〈名〉flood land
【河塘】hétáng〈名〉river embankment
【河套】hétào〈名〉**1** Hétào（特指黄河）Great Bend of the Yellow River **2**（河道圈围地）bend of a river
【河豚】hétún〈名〉globefish
【河外星系】héwài xīngxì〈名〉［天文］extragalactic nebula
【河网】héwǎng〈名〉network of waterways: ～化 build a network of waterways
【河西走廊】Héxī Zǒuláng〈名〉Hexi Corridor
【河鲜】héxiān〈名〉river fish
【河蟹】héxiè〈名〉freshwater crab
【河沿】héyán〈名〉river bank
【河鱼】héyú〈名〉river fish
【河岳】héyuè〈名〉〈书〉territory
【河运】héyùn〈名〉river transport

曷 hé〈代〉〈书〉**1**（为什么）why **2**（何时）when

饸（餄） hé
【饸饹】héle〈名〉*hele* noodles [made from buckwheat, sorghum flour, etc.]

阂（閡） hé〈动〉be cut off from: ▸隔～

盍 hé〈副〉〈书〉why not: ～尝问焉 why not ask

荷[1] hé〈名〉lotus: ▸～花, ～塘, ～叶

荷[2] Hé〈名〉Holland: ▸～兰
▸hè
【荷包】hébāo〈名〉pouch
【荷包蛋】hébāodàn〈名〉poached egg
【荷尔蒙】hé'ěrméng〈名〉［生理］hormone
【荷花】héhuā〈名〉lotus
【荷花坐姿】héhuā zuòzī〈名〉lotus posture
【荷兰】Hélán〈名〉Holland: ～共和国 Dutch Republic [1648-1795] ‖ ～人 Dutch person ‖ ～王国 Kingdom of the Netherlands ‖ ～语 Dutch
【荷兰豆】héländòu〈名〉mangetout
【荷塘】hétáng〈名〉lotus pond
【荷叶】héyè〈名〉lotus leaf

核[1] hé〈名〉**1**（果核）stone: 桃～ peach-stone ‖ 无～葡萄干 seedless raisins **2**［化学］nucleus: ▸细胞～, 原子～ **3**（原子核）atomic nucleus: ▸～能, ～燃料, ～武器

核[2] hé〈动〉examine: ▸～对, 考～
▸hú
【核安全】hé'ānquán〈名〉nuclear security
【核按钮】hé'ànniǔ〈名〉nuclear button
【核保护伞】hébǎohùsǎn〈名〉nuclear umbrella
【核不扩散条约】Hébùkuòsàn Tiáoyuē〈名〉Nuclear Non-proliferation Treaty
【核裁军】hécáijūn〈动〉disarm nuclear weapons
【核查】héchá **A**〈动〉examine: ～账目 audit the accounts **B**〈名〉nuclear inspection: 进行～ conduct a nuclear inspection
【核磁共振】hécí gòngzhèn〈名〉nuclear magnetic resonance
【核大国】hédàguó〈名〉nuclear power
【核弹】hédàn〈名〉nuclear bomb
【核弹头】hédàntóu〈名〉nuclear warhead: ～导弹 nuclear-tipped missile
【核蛋白】hédànbái〈名〉nucleoprotein
【核当量】hédāngliàng〈名〉nuclear equivalent
【核导弹】hédǎodàn〈名〉nuclear missile
【核电厂】hédiànchǎng〈名〉nuclear power plant
【核电站】hédiànzhàn〈名〉nuclear power plant
【核定】hédìng〈动〉check and ratify: ～地价 appraise and settle land prices ‖ ～预算 approved budget
【核冬天】hédōngtiān〈名〉nuclear winter
【核动力】hédònglì〈名〉nuclear power: ～航空母舰 nuclear-powered aircraft carrier ‖ ～潜艇 nuclear submarine
【核对】héduì〈动〉check: ～账目 verify the accounts ‖ ～事实 check the facts ‖ 把它与原文～一下 check it against the original
【核讹诈】hé'ézhà〈名〉nuclear blackmail
【核发】héfā〈动〉approve and issue: ～营业执照 approve and issue a business licence
【核反应】héfǎnyìng〈名〉nuclear reaction
【核反应堆】héfǎnyìngduī〈名〉nuclear reactor
【核辐射】héfúshè〈名〉nuclear radiation
【核果】héguǒ〈名〉［植物］drupe
【核黄素】héhuángsù〈名〉［药学］riboflavin
【核计】héjì〈动〉assess: ～成本 assess the cost
【核减】héjiǎn〈动〉trim: ～预算 cut a budget
【核聚变】héjùbiàn〈名〉nuclear fusion
【核扩散】hékuòsàn〈名〉nuclear proliferation: 防止～ prevent nuclear proliferation
【核裂变】hélièbiàn〈名〉nuclear fission
【核垄断】hélǒngduàn〈名〉nuclear monopoly
【核能】hénéng〈名〉nuclear power: 和平利用～ peaceful use of nuclear energy
【核潜艇】héqiántǐng〈名〉nuclear submarine
【核燃料】héránliào〈名〉nuclear fuel
【核仁】hérén〈名〉**1**［生物］nucleolus **2**（指果仁）kernel
【核审】héshěn〈动〉check and verify: ～代表资格 check and verify the credentials of the delegates
【核实】héshí〈动〉verify: ～的产量 verified output ‖ 请把这些数字～一下。Please check these figures.
【核试验】héshìyàn〈名〉nuclear test: 地下～ underground nuclear test
【核衰变】héshuāibiàn〈名〉nuclear disintegration
【核酸】hésuān〈名〉［生化］nucleic acid
【核算】hésuàn〈动〉examine and calculate: 成本～ cost accounting
【核糖】hétáng〈名〉［生化］ribose
【核糖核酸】hétáng hésuān〈名〉［生化］ribonucleic acid (RNA): 脱氧～ deoxyribonucleic acid (DNA)
【核桃】hétao〈名〉walnut: ～仁 walnut kernel
【核威慑】héwēishè〈名〉nuclear deterrence: ～力量 nuclear deterrent power
【核污染】héwūrǎn〈名〉nuclear pollution
【核武器】héwǔqì〈名〉nuclear weapon: 销毁～ destroy nuclear weapons
【核销】héxiāo〈动〉cancel after verification: ～流动资金 verify and write off the current assets
【核心】héxīn〈名〉nucleus: ～人物 key person ‖ 领导～ core of the leadership
【核心家庭】héxīn jiātíng〈名〉nuclear family

i 河流

■ 英语里表示河流的词是专有名词，第一个字母要大写，且河流名称的前面一定要加定冠词 the。英语里河流可用三种方式表达："the + River + 河流的名字"，"the + 河流的名字 + River"，或"the + 河流的名字"：

尼罗河
= the River Nile
或 the Nile River
或 the Nile

亚马孙河
= the River Amazon
或 the Amazon River
或 the Amazon

泰晤士河
= the River Thames
或 the Thames River
或 the Thames

■ 汉语里"河"可以说"河"、"江"或"水"，翻译成英语时都可用 river。河流从汉语翻译成英语时可全用汉语拼音，也可在河流的名字后加上 River：

淮河
= the Huai River
或 the Huai He

金沙江
= the Jinsha River
或 the Jinsha Jiang

溧水
= the Li River
或 the Li Shui

和其他名词的连用

莱茵河观光船游览
= River Rhine cruises

泰晤士河上的游艇
= Thames yachts

珠江上的灯塔
= a Pearl River lighthouse

塞纳河的一个支流
= a tributary of the River Seine

鸭绿江水源
= the source of the Yalu River

黄河河口
= the Yellow River estuary
或 the mouth of the Yellow River

长江的上游／中游／下游
= the upper/middle/lower reaches of the Changjiang

【核心期刊】héxīn qīkān〈名〉 key periodicals
【核验】héyàn〈动〉 examine
【核载】hézài〈动〉（指载重） authorized load;（指载客） authorized capacity: 该车～36人。The authorized seating capacity of the vehicle is 36. ‖ 该车～为10吨。The approved load capacity for this vehicle is 10 tons.
【核战争】hézhànzhēng〈名〉 nuclear warfare
【核装置】hézhuāngzhì〈名〉nuclear device
【核准】hézhǔn〈动〉 examine and approve: ～发行债券 authorized bonds ‖ 须经事先～ be subject to prior approval
【核资】hézī〈动〉 check up on funds and assets: 对破产企业进行～清产 conduct a general check-up on the assets of a bankrupt enterprise
【核子】hézǐ〈名〉［物理］ nucleon: ～武器 nuclear weapon

盒 hé

A〈名〉 box: 小铁～ small iron case ‖ 纸～ paper box ▸饭～, 铅笔～
B〈量〉 box: 一～火柴 a box of matches
【盒饭】héfàn〈名〉 boxed lunch
【盒式磁带】héshì cídài〈名〉 cassette tape
【盒式录像带】héshì lùxiàngdài〈名〉video cassette
【盒子】hézi〈名〉**1**（指容器）box **2**（指烟花） box-shaped fireworks
【盒子枪】héziqiāng〈名〉〈方〉 Mauser pistol

涸 hé〈形〉〈书〉 dry: ▸～辙之鲋, 干～, 枯～

【涸竭】héjié〈形〉 dried up
【涸泽而渔】hézé'éryú〈成〉 kill the goose that lays the golden eggs
【涸辙之鲋】hézhézhīfù〈成〉〈喻〉 person in a desperate situation

颌（頜） hé〈名〉 jaw: 上/下～ upper/lower jaw

貉 hé〈名〉［动物］ raccoon dog

▸háo

阖（闔） hé〈书〉

A〈动〉 shut: ～户 close the door
B〈形〉 whole: ～城 entire city ▸～家
【阖府】héfǔ〈名〉〈敬〉 your whole family
【阖家】héjiā〈名〉 whole family: ～团圆 family reunion

翮 hé〈名〉〈书〉 **1**（鸟羽） quill **2**（翅膀） wing: 振～高飞 flap the wings and soar high into the sky

鞨 hé ▸靺鞨 Mòhé

hè

吓（嚇） hè

A〈动〉 intimidate: ▸恫～, 恐～
B〈叹〉 tut-tut: ～, 两个人才弄来半桶水! Humph, the two of you and you brought only half a bucket of water!
▸xià

和 hè〈动〉 **1**（声音相应） join in the singing: ▸曲高～寡, 一唱百～ **2**（附和） echo what others say: ▸随声附～ **3**（指作诗、填词） compose a poem in reply: 奉～一首诗 write a poem in reply to sb. else's
▸hé, hú, huó, huò
【和诗】hèshī **A**〈动〉 compose a poem in reply **B**〈名〉 poems exchanged

贺（賀） hè〈动〉 congratulate: ▸～词, ～礼, 祝～

【贺词】hècí〈名〉 congratulatory speech: 致～ deliver a congratulatory speech ‖ 新年～ New Year greetings
【贺电】hèdiàn〈名〉 message of congratulations: 发～ telegraph one's congratulations (to sb.)
【贺函】hèhán = 贺信 hèxìn
【贺卡】hèkǎ〈名〉 greeting card: 生日～ birthday card ‖ 电子～ E-card
【贺礼】hèlǐ〈名〉 congratulatory gift: 结婚～ wedding present
【贺年】hènián〈动〉 extend New Year's greetings
【贺年卡】hèniánkǎ〈名〉 New Year' s card
【贺岁】hèsuì = 贺年 hènián
【贺岁档】hèsuìdàng〈名〉 new year's performance slot: 新片将在～上映。The new film will go out in the new year's slot.
【贺岁片】hèsuìpiàn〈名〉 New Year's film
【贺喜】hèxǐ〈动〉 congratulate sb.: 向获奖人员～ offer congratulations to the award-winners
【贺信】hèxìn〈名〉 letter of congratulations
【贺仪】hèyí〈书〉= 贺礼 hèlǐ
【贺幛】hèzhàng〈名〉〈旧〉 sheet of silk or cloth with congratulatory message written on it

荷 hè〈书〉

A〈动〉 **1**（背） carry on one's shoulder or back: ～锄 carry a hoe on one's shoulder **2**（承担） take on: ～天下之重任 assume responsibilities for one's country **3**（承受恩惠） be grateful: 无任感～ be very much obliged
B〈名〉 **1**（电荷） charge: ▸电～ **2**（压力） load;（责任） responsibility: 肩负重～ shoulder heavy responsibilities
▸hé
【荷负】hèfù〈动〉〈书〉 bear: ～重任 shoulder heavy responsibilities
【荷枪实弹】hèqiāng-shídàn〈成〉 carry loaded guns
【荷载】hèzài **A**〈动〉 carry a load **B**〈名〉 load: ～率 load rate
【荷重】hèzhòng〈名〉［建筑］ weight load: ～能力 loading capacity

喝 hè〈动〉 shout loudly: 大～一声 shout loudly ▸～彩, ～令, 吆～

▸hē
【喝彩】hècǎi〈动〉 cheer: 齐声～ cheer in chorus ‖ 观众大声～。The audience cheered loudly.
【喝倒彩】hè dàocǎi〈动〉 boo: 招致～ get booed
【喝道】hèdào〈动〉〈旧〉 shout out to make way for an approaching official
【喝令】hèlìng〈动〉 shout out an order
【喝问】hèwèn〈动〉 shout a question (to)

赫[1] hè〈形〉 distinguished: ▸～然

赫[2] hè = 赫兹 hèzī

【赫布里底群】Hèbùlǐdǐjùn〈名〉 Hebrides
【赫赫】hèhè〈形〉 illustrious: ～战功 outstanding military exploits
【赫赫有名】hèhè-yǒumíng〈成〉celebrated: ～的企业家 illustrious entrepreneur
【赫里福德郡】Hèlǐfúdéjùn〈名〉 Herefordshire
【赫然】hèrán〈形〉〈书〉 **1**（表惊讶） unexpected and shocking: ～在目 suddenly appear before one's eyes **2**（表盛怒） terribly angry: ～震怒 fly into a fury
【赫特福德郡】Hètèfúdéjùn〈名〉 Hertfordshire
【赫哲族】Hèzhézú〈名〉 Hezhen ethnic group
【赫兹】hèzī〈量〉［电气］ hertz

褐 hè

A〈名〉〈书〉coarse cloth: 短～ short jacket made of coarse cloth
B ▸**p. 863**〈形〉 brown: ～色外衣 brown overcoat
【褐斑】hèbān〈名〉 [on paper or fabrics] brown stain
【褐斑病】hèbānbìng〈名〉［植物］ brown rot
【褐红色】hèhóngsè ▸**p. 863**〈名〉maroon
【褐马鸡】hèmǎjī〈名〉［鸟类］ brown-eared pheasant
【褐煤】hèméi〈名〉 brown coal
【褐色】hèsè ▸**p. 863**〈名〉 brown
【褐铁矿】hètiěkuàng〈名〉 brown iron ore

鹤（鶴） hè〈名〉 crane: ▸丹顶～

【鹤发童颜】hèfà-tóngyán〈成〉 hale and hearty
【鹤立鸡群】hèlì-jīqún〈成〉 the best of the bunch
【鹤嘴镐】hèzuǐgǎo〈名〉 pickaxe

壑 hè〈名〉 gully: 丘～ hills and valleys ▸沟～, 以邻为～, 欲～难填

h

hēi

黑 hēi〈形〉 **1**（指颜色） black: ～发 black hair ▸～板 **2**（指天色） dark: 天～了。It's getting dark. ▸～夜, 漆～, 起早贪～ **3**（指人品） sinister: 心～手辣 be cruel and merciless ▸～心 **4**（不公开） shady: ▸～帮, ～社会, ～市

【黑暗】hēi'àn〈形〉**1**（无光亮）dark: ～的角落 dark corner ‖ 黎明前的～ pre-dawn darkness **2**（反动） evil: ～统治 reactionary rule ‖ ～势力 sinister forces
【黑白】hēibái〈名〉**1**〈本〉 black and white: ～胶片 black-and-white film ‖ ～电视机 black-and-white television set **2**〈喻〉（正和邪） right and wrong: ～不分 make no distinction between right and wrong ▸颠倒～
【黑白分明】hēibái fēnmíng〈成〉 with a clear distinction between black and white
【黑白片】hēibáipiàn〈名〉 black-and-white film
【黑斑病】hēibānbìng〈名〉［植物］ black rot
【黑板】hēibǎn〈名〉 blackboard〈英〉; chalkboard〈美〉: ～擦 blackboard eraser
【黑板报】hēibǎnbào〈名〉 blackboard bulletin
【黑帮】hēibāng〈名〉 underworld gang
【黑榜】hēibǎng〈名〉 blacklist of inferior quality products: 该厂有两种产品进入质检～。Two of this factory's products were put on the quality blacklist.

【黑豹】hēibào〈名〉black leopard
【黑不溜秋】hēibuliūqiū〈形〉〈方〉swarthy: 长得～ have a swarthy complexion
【黑车】hēichē〈名〉unlicensed vehicle
【黑沉沉】hēichénchén〈形〉very dark: ～的天 overcast sky
【黑吃黑】hēichīhēi〈惯〉engage in gangland in-fighting
【黑带】hēidài〈名〉black belt (in judo, karate)
【黑道】hēidào〈名〉1（指路）unlit road: 一个人别走～。You shouldn't walk down dark alleys on your own at night. 2（指途径）illegal activity: ～交易 shady deal 3（黑社会）underworld: ～人物 underworld figure
【黑灯瞎火】hēidēng-xiāhuǒ〈成〉dark: ～的，还能看什么书! How can we read in this darkness?
【黑店】hēidiàn〈名〉1（指谋财害命）inn run by outlaws 2（指非法经营）unlicensed inn
【黑洞】hēidòng〈名〉［天文］black hole: ～理论 theory of black holes
【黑洞洞】hēidòngdòng〈形〉pitch-dark: 井很深，～的。The well is deep and pitch-dark.
【黑豆】hēidòu〈名〉black soya bean
【黑更半夜】hēigēng-bànyè〈成〉in the middle of the night: ～还在工作 keep working into the middle of the night
【黑咕隆咚】hēigulōngdōng〈形〉〈口〉pitch-black: 屋里～的。The room was pitch-black.
【黑管】hēiguǎn ▸**p. 929**〈名〉［音乐］clarinet
【黑光】hēiguāng〈名〉ultraviolet rays: ～灯 black-light lamp ‖ ～诱虫灯 black-light trap
【黑锅】hēiguō〈名〉〈喻〉scapegoat: 背～ be made a scapegoat
【黑海】Hēihǎi〈名〉Black Sea
【黑乎乎】hēihūhū = 黑糊糊 hēihūhū
【黑糊糊】hēihūhū〈形〉1（颜色发黑）blackened: 墙熏得～的。The wall was blackened by smoke. 2（光线昏暗）dim: 屋子里～的。It's dark in the room. 3（模糊不清）blurry: 天上是一片～的乌云。A dark mass of clouds loomed in the sky.
【黑胡椒】hēihújiāo〈名〉black pepper
【黑户】hēihù〈名〉1（指住户）unregistered household 2（指经营户）unlicensed firm
【黑话】hēihuà〈名〉1（暗语）cant 2（反动言论）doublespeak
【黑货】hēihuò〈名〉1（指走私货）contraband 2（指赃物）ill-gotten goods: ～市场 dodgy goods market
【黑家鼠】hēijiāshǔ〈名〉black rat
【黑胶布】hēijiāobù〈名〉［电气］black tape
【黑金】hēijīn〈名〉〈方〉black money
【黑客】hēikè〈名〉hacker: 电脑～ computer hacker
【黑里俏】hēilǐqiào〈名〉a dark beauty
【黑亮】hēiliàng〈形〉jet-black
【黑溜溜】hēiliūliū〈形〉〈口〉shiny black
【黑龙江】Hēilóngjiāng ▸**p. 661**〈名〉Heilongjiang Province
【黑马】hēimǎ〈名〉〈喻〉dark horse: 他在百米赛中成为一匹～。He emerged as the dark horse in the 100-metre sprint.
【黑麦】hēimài〈名〉rye: ～威士忌酒 rye whisky
【黑茫茫】hēimángmáng〈形〉pitch-dark all around: 周围～一片。All around was pitch-black.
【黑莓】hēiméi〈名〉blackberry
【黑蒙蒙】hēiméngméng〈形〉dark and indistinct
【黑面包】hēimiànbāo〈名〉brown bread
【黑名单】hēimíngdān〈名〉blacklist: 上了～ be blacklisted
【黑木耳】hēimù'ěr〈名〉(edible) black fungus
【黑幕】hēimù〈名〉inside story of a plot: 揭穿～ expose a sinister scheme
【黑啤酒】hēipíjiǔ〈名〉dark beer
【黑钱】hēiqián〈名〉dirty money: 洗～ money laundering
【黑枪】hēiqiāng〈名〉1（指枪支）concealed firearms: 持～ possess illegal firearms 2（指枪弹）shoot from a hiding place:〈喻〉打～ stab sb. in the back
【黑黢黢】hēiqūqū〈形〉pitch-dark: 外面～的。It was pitch-dark outside.
【黑热病】hēirèbìng ▸**p. 50**〈名〉［医学］visceral leishmaniasis
【黑人】Hēirén〈名〉black people: 美国～ Afro-American ‖ ～英语 Black English
【黑人】hēirén〈名〉unregistered resident: ～黑户 unregistered household
【黑色】hēisè〈名〉black
【黑色火药】hēisè huǒyào〈名〉black powder
【黑色金属】hēisè jīnshǔ〈名〉ferrous metal
【黑色人种】hēisè rénzhǒng〈名〉black race
【黑色食品】hēisè shípǐn〈名〉black food
【黑色收入】hēisè shōurù〈名〉black income
【黑色素】hēisèsù〈名〉［生化］melanin
【黑色幽默】hēisè yōumò〈名〉black humour
【黑纱】hēishā〈名〉black armband: 戴～ wear a mourning band
【黑山】Hēishān〈名〉Montenegro
【黑哨】hēishào〈名〉corrupt refereeing
【黑社会】hēishèhuì〈名〉underworld: ～头目 gang leader ‖ ～性质的犯罪团伙 Mafia-like criminal group
【黑市】hēishì〈名〉black market: ～交易 trade on the black market
【黑势力】hēishìlì〈名〉criminal forces: 打击～，保障社会安宁。Fight criminal forces and maintain peace in society.
【黑手】hēishǒu〈名〉evil backstage manipulator: 有～在背后操纵。Somebody is pulling the strings from behind.
【黑手党】hēishǒudǎng〈名〉Mafia
【黑死病】hēisǐbìng ▸**p. 50**〈名〉［医学］Black Death
【黑穗病】hēisuìbìng〈名〉［农业］smut
【黑桃】hēitáo〈名〉[in cards] spade: ～K king of spades
【黑陶】hēitáo〈名〉［考古］black pottery
【黑体】hēitǐ〈名〉［印刷］bold: ～字 bold-face type
【黑天白日】hēitiān-báirì〈成〉day in, day out
【黑头】hēitóu〈名〉1（指花脸）*heitou* [male character in traditional Chinese opera with a black painted face] 2（指脸上）blackhead
【黑土】hēitǔ〈名〉black earth
【黑窝】hēiwō〈名〉nest of illegal activities: 警察在盗贼的～里找到了赃物。The police discovered the booty in the thieves' den.
【黑瞎子】hēixiāzi〈名〉〈方〉black bear
【黑匣子】hēixiázi〈名〉［航空］black box
【黑心】hēixīn〈名〉black heart: 看透他的～ see through his evil intention
【黑信】hēixìn〈名〉poison-pen letter
【黑猩猩】hēixīngxing〈名〉chimpanzee
【黑熊】hēixióng〈名〉black bear
【黑魆魆】hēixūxū〈形〉dark
【黑压压】hēiyāyā〈形〉dark and dense: 远处～的一片，看不清是些什么东西。We couldn't make out what the dark mass was from a distance.
【黑眼珠】hēiyǎnzhū〈名〉pupil
【黑夜】hēiyè〈名〉night
【黑影儿】hēiyǐngr〈名〉dark shadow
【黑油油】hēiyóuyóu〈形〉shiny black: 她的头发总是～的。Her hair is always shiny black.
【黑黝黝】hēiyǒuyǒu〈形〉1 = 黑油油 hēiyóuyóu 2（指光线）dim: 四周～的。It's dark all around.
【黑鱼】hēiyú〈名〉snake-headed fish
【黑枣】hēizǎo〈名〉date-plum persimmon
【黑芝麻】hēizhīma〈名〉black sesame
【黑种人】hēizhǒngrén〈名〉black people
【黑子】hēizǐ〈名〉1［天文］sunspot 2［体育］black chess piece

嘿 hēi〈叹〉hey: ～，当心点! Hey! Be careful! ‖ ～，快走吧! Hey! Hurry up! ‖ ～，这球扣得多棒啊! Wow! What a powerful smash! ‖ ～，下雪了! Why, it's snowing!
【嘿嘿】hēihēi〈拟〉ha ha: ～，这回我赢定了! Ha ha, I'll sure win this time!

𬭶（鐽） hēi［化学］Hassium (Hs)

hén

痕 hén〈名〉1（伤痕）scar: ▸瘢～，伤～ 2（痕迹）trace: ▸斑～，裂～
【痕迹】hénjì〈名〉trace: 留下～ leave traces ‖ 车轮碾压的～ tracks made by tyre marks
【痕量】hénliàng〈名〉［化学］trace: ～元素 trace element

hěn

很 hěn〈副〉very: ～好/坏 very good/bad ‖ ～满意 feel very satisfied ‖ ～有道理 contain a lot of truth ‖ 工作/学习～努力 work/study very hard

狠 hěn
A〈形〉1（凶狠）ruthless: 比豺狼还～ more savage than a wolf ▸～毒，心～手辣，凶～ 2（坚决）resolute: ～～打击歪风邪气 take vigorous measures against unhealthy tendencies ‖ ～下功夫 make a desperate effort
B〈动〉harden one's heart: 他～了～心，跟她分手了。He steeled his heart and said goodbye to her.
【狠毒】hěndú〈形〉venomous: 心肠～ be wicked at heart
【狠辣】hěnlà〈形〉vicious
【狠命】hěnmìng〈副〉desperately: 他～抓住小偷不放。He made a desperate effort to keep hold of the thief.
【狠心】hěnxīn A〈动〉harden one's heart: ～戒烟 resolve to stop smoking B〈形〉heartless: 你也太～了! You are so cruel!

hèn

恨 hèn
A〈动〉**1**（憎恨）hate: ～敌人 hate one's enemy ‖ ～得咬牙切齿 grind one's teeth with hatred ▸～之入骨，怨～ **2**（后悔）regret: ▸相见～晚，书到用时方～少
B〈名〉hatred: ▸抱～，怀～，遗～
【恨不得】hènbudé〈动〉be itching to: 我～现在就能听到她的消息。I'm dying to hear from her right now.
【恨事】hènshì〈名〉matter of regret: 当初没有学医，这是他终身～。It is his lifelong regret that he did not study medicine when he was young.
【恨铁不成钢】hèn tiě bù chéng gāng〈俗〉regret that sb. does not live up to one's expectations
【恨之入骨】hènzhī-rùgǔ〈成〉hate to the very marrow of one's bones: 对扒手～ hate the pickpocket with all one's heart

hēng

亨 hēng〈形〉prosperous ▸～通
【亨利】hēnglì〈量〉［电气］henry
【亨廷登郡】Hēngtíngdēngjùn〈名〉Huntingdonshire
【亨通】hēngtōng〈形〉smooth: ▸官运～，万事～

哼 hēng〈动〉**1**（发出鼻音）snort: 蔑视地～了一声 give a snort of contempt **2**（轻唱）hum: 他一边走，一边～着曲儿。He was humming a tune as he walked.
▸hèng, hng
【哼唱】hēngchàng〈动〉hum
【哼哧】hēngchī〈拟〉puff and blow: 他跑得～～直喘气。He was puffed out after the run.
【哼哈二将】Hēng-Hā èrjiàng〈成〉pair of accomplices serving one master or working hand in glove with each other
【哼哼】hēngheng〈拟〉groan: 痛得直～ groan and moan with pain
【哼哼唧唧】hēngheng-jījī〈动〉moan and groan
【哼唷】hēngyō〈叹〉heave ho, yo-heave-ho

脝 hēng ▸膨脝 pénghēng

héng

行 héng ▸道行 dàohéng
▸háng, hàng, xíng

恒（恆） héng
A〈形〉**1**（长久）lasting: ▸～心，～温，永～ **2**（经常）constant: ▸～量，～言
B〈名〉perseverance: ▸持之以～，有～
【恒产】héngchǎn〈名〉immovable property
【恒齿】héngchǐ〈名〉［生理］permanent tooth
【恒等】héngděng〈形〉［数学］identical: ～式 identical equation ‖ ～定理 identical theorem
【恒定】héngdìng〈形〉constant: ～电压 constant voltage
【恒河】Hénghé ▸**p. 294**〈名〉the Ganges
【恒河沙数】Hénghé-shāshù〈成〉countless
【恒久】héngjiǔ〈形〉long-lasting: ～不变的爱 everlasting love
【恒量】héngliàng〈名〉［物理］constant
【恒山】Héngshān〈名〉Hengshan Mountain
【恒生】Héngshēng〈名〉Hang Seng: ～银行 Hang Seng Bank ‖ ～指数 Hang Seng Index
【恒湿】héngshī〈名〉constant humidity: ～器 humidistat
【恒温】héngwēn〈名〉constant temperature: 保持～ keep the temperature constant ‖ ～室 thermostatic chamber
【恒心】héngxīn〈名〉perseverance: 他学习英语有～。He's got perseverance when it comes to learning English.
【恒星】héngxīng〈名〉［天文］star
【恒星年】héngxīngnián〈名〉［天文］sidereal year
【恒星系】héngxīngxì〈名〉［天文］stellar system
【恒性】héngxìng〈名〉perseverance: 有～ have perseverance (in doing sth.)
【恒牙】héngyá = 恒齿 héngchǐ
【恒言】héngyán〈名〉common saying

姮 héng
【姮娥】Héng'é〈名〉Heng'e [legendary goddess of the moon]

珩 héng〈名〉〈古〉top gem of a girdle-pendant [as worn by aristocrats and high officials]
【珩磨】héngmó〈名〉［机械］honing: ～机 honing machine

桁 héng〈名〉［建筑］purlin
【桁架】héngjià〈名〉［建筑］truss: ～跨度 truss span
【桁条】héngtiáo〈名〉［建筑］purlin

鸻（鴴） héng〈名〉［鸟类］plover

横 héng
A〈形〉**1**（水平方向）horizontal: ▸～幅，～梁，纵～ **2**（东西方向）east to west or west to east: 陇海铁路～穿中国中部。The Longhai railway runs from east to west across central China. **3**（左右方向）across: ～写 write across the page ‖ 人行～道 pedestrian crossing **4**（杂乱）unrestrained: ▸～溢，老泪纵～，妙趣～生 **5**（蛮不讲理）fierce: ▸～行霸道，～征暴敛
B〈名〉[in Chinese characters] horizontal stroke: "王"字是三～一竖。The character 王 consists of three horizontal strokes and one vertical one.
C〈动〉move crosswise: 把车～过来 put the car crosswise
▸hèng
【横匾】héngbiǎn〈名〉inscribed horizontal board
【横标】héngbiāo〈名〉horizontal banner
【横插一杠子】héng chā yī gàngzi〈俗〉stick one's nose into sb. else's business: 他俩都相爱了，你干吗～! They're very much in love. Why are you interfering?
【横冲直撞】héngchōng-zhízhuàng〈成〉jostle and elbow one's way
【横穿】héngchuān ▸**p. 781**〈动〉cross: 孩子们上学要～两条马路。The children have to cross two streets on their way to school.
【横档】héngdàng〈名〉crosspiece
【横倒竖歪】héngdǎo-shùwāi〈成〉in disorder: 战场上～地躺着敌军的尸体。Many dead enemy soldiers lay scattered on the battlefield.
【横笛】héngdí ▸**p. 929**〈名〉fife
【横渡】héngdù〈动〉sail across: ～长江 cross the Yangtze River
【横断面】héngduànmiàn = 横剖面 héngpōumiàn
【横队】héngduì〈名〉row: 排成三列～ line up three deep
【横幅】héngfú〈名〉**1**（指书画）horizontal scroll **2**（指标语）banner: 欢迎群众举着～标语。The welcoming crowd carried banners with slogans.
【横杆】hénggān〈名〉［体育］crossbar
【横格纸】hénggézhǐ〈名〉lined paper
【横膈膜】hénggémó〈名〉［生理］diaphragm
【横亘】hénggèn〈动〉span: 一座新桥～在大江上。A new bridge spans the river.
【横贯】héngguàn〈动〉traverse: 有两条铁路～欧亚大陆。There are two railways crossing Asia and Europe.
【横加】héngjiā〈动〉do sth. to sb. unreasonably, violently, flagrantly or forcibly: ～干涉 flagrantly interfere ‖ ～阻挠 wilfully obstruct
【横跨】héngkuà〈动〉stretch across: 一座新铁路桥～峡谷。A new railway bridge stretches over the canyon.
【横梁】héngliáng〈名〉**1**［建筑］crossbeam **2**（指汽车）cross member
【横流】héngliú〈动〉**1**（指眼泪）gush **2**（指水）flow in all directions
【横眉】héngméi〈动〉scowl
【横眉怒目】héngméi-nùmù〈成〉dart fierce looks
【横眉竖眼】héngméi-shùyǎn〈成〉glare with anger
【横拍握法】héngpāi wòfǎ〈名〉［体育］tennis grip
【横批】héngpī〈名〉[usu hung over a door] horizontal scroll
【横披】héngpī〈名〉horizontal scroll
【横剖面】héngpōumiàn〈名〉cross-section
【横七竖八】héngqī-shùbā〈成〉in a mess: 过道里～地放着各种东西。The passage was cluttered with all sorts of things.
【横切面】héngqiēmiàn = 横剖面 héngpōumiàn
【横肉】héngròu〈名〉fierce-looking face: 满脸～ look ugly and ferocious
【横扫】héngsǎo〈动〉**1**（扫荡）sweep away: ～千军如卷席 sweep off the enemy as one would do a mat **2**（扫视）glance quickly from side to side: 目光～教室 throw a glance across the classroom
【横生】héngshēng〈动〉**1**（指生长）grow wild: 蔓草～ be overgrown with weeds **2**（指出现）be full of: ▸妙趣～ **3**（指发生）happen unexpectedly: ～是非 a quarrel suddenly flared up ▸～枝节
【横生枝节】héngshēng-zhījié〈成〉**1**（突然出现）crop up unexpectedly **2**（故意制造问题）create obstacles
【横竖】héngshù〈副〉〈口〉anyhow: ～你是不能去。You can't go anyway.
【横挑鼻子竖挑眼】héng tiāo bízi shù tiāo yǎn〈俗〉nit-pick: 你别～的。Stop picking holes.
【横向】héngxiàng〈形〉crosswise: ～比较 parallel comparison ‖ ～交流 horizontal communication ‖ ～协作 parallel cooperation
【横向扫描】héngxiàng sǎomiáo〈名〉transverse scanning

h

【横心】héngxīn〈动〉 steel oneself: 他一～辞职不干了。 He made a firm resolve to quit the job.
【横行】héngxíng〈动〉 run wild: 四处～ run amok all over the place ‖ ～一时 run wild for a while
【横行霸道】héngxíng-bàdào〈成〉 ride roughshod over
【横溢】héngyì〈动〉1▸（指河流）overflow: 江河～ turbulent waters overflowing their banks 2▸（指人） brim: 才华～ be brimming with talent
【横征暴敛】héngzhēng-bàoliǎn〈成〉 levy exorbitant taxes
【横直】héngzhí = 横竖 héngshù
【横坐标】héngzuòbiāo〈名〉［数学］ horizontal ordinate: ～轴 abscissa axis

衡 héng
A〈名〉 graduated arm of a steelyard
B〈动〉 1▸（称重量） weighing apparatus: ▸～器 2▸（权衡） weigh: ▸权～利弊
C〈形〉〈书〉 balanced: ▸均～, 平～
【衡量】héngliáng〈动〉 weigh: ～得失 weigh up the gains and losses ‖ ～标准 standard by which to judge ‖ 他对农业的贡献是不能用金钱来～的。 His contributions to agriculture cannot be measured in monetary terms.
【衡平法】héngpíngfǎ〈名〉［法律］ law of equity
【衡器】héngqì〈名〉 weighing apparatus
【衡山】Héngshān〈名〉 Hengshan Mountain

蘅 héng ▸杜蘅 dùhéng

hèng

哼 hèng〈叹〉 damn: ～! 我非找他算账不可! Damn! I must get even with him!
▸hēng, hng

横 hèng〈形〉 1▸（粗暴） harsh and unreasonable: 发～ act in an unreasonable way ▸蛮～, 强～ 2▸（意外） unexpected: ▸～财, ～祸, ～死
▸héng
【横暴】hèngbào〈形〉 brutal and unreasonable
【横财】hèngcái〈名〉 ill-gotten gains: 发～ get rich by foul means
【横祸】hènghuò〈名〉 sudden misfortune: 飞来～ unforeseen disaster
【横蛮】hèngmán = 蛮横 mánhèng
【横事】hèngshi〈名〉〈书〉 unexpected misfortune: 连遭～ suffer a series of unexpected misfortunes
【横死】hèngsǐ〈动〉 die a violent death: 惨遭～ die a tragic and violent death

hm

噷 hm〈叹〉 humph: ～，你还没起床? Humph, why are you still in bed?

hng

哼 hng〈叹〉 humph: ～，谁还会指望你! Humph, I'll not count on you any more! ‖ ～，走着瞧吧! Humph, let's wait and see!
▸hēng, hèng

hōng

轰（轟）hōng
A〈拟〉 bang: ～的一声炮响 boom of a cannon
B〈动〉 1▸（爆炸） roar;（雷鸣） rumble;（炮击） boom: 万炮齐～ ten thousand cannons booming ‖ 雷～电闪。 Thunder rumbled and lightning flashed. 2▸（驱赶） shoo away: ～下台 drive sb. from power ‖ 把羊群～进棚子。 Drive the herd of sheep into the shed.
【轰动】hōngdòng〈动〉 cause a sensation: ～全国 create a great stir throughout the country ‖ 这部影片引起极大～，创造了票房最高记录。 The film made a huge splash and set a new box-office record.
【轰动效应】hōngdòng xiàoyìng〈名〉 sensational effect
【轰动一时】hōngdòng-yīshí〈成〉 cause a great sensation
【轰赶】hōnggǎn〈动〉 drive off: ～麻雀 shoo away the sparrows
【轰轰烈烈】hōnghōng-lièliè〈成〉 vigorous: ～的场面 spectacular scene
【轰击】hōngjī〈动〉 bombard: ～敌人阵地 shell enemy positions ‖ 中子～ neutron bombardment
【轰隆】hōnglōng〈拟〉 rumble: 远处雷声～作响。 Thunder rolled in the distance.
【轰鸣】hōngmíng〈动〉 roar: 引擎的～ roar of an engine ‖ 礼炮～。 Salvoes roared.
【轰然】hōngrán〈形〉 crashing: 屋顶～塌陷。 The roof caved in with a loud crash.
【轰响】hōngxiǎng〈动〉 roar: 大炮～。 The cannons roared.
【轰炸】hōngzhà〈动〉 bomb: ～目标 bomb a target ‖ 地毯式～ carpet bombing ‖ 轮番～ bomb in waves
【轰炸机】hōngzhàjī〈名〉 bomber

哄 hōng
A〈拟〉 whoop: 一～而散 disperse with a shriek
B〈动〉 roar: ▸～传, ～抬, ～堂大笑
▸hǒng, hòng
【哄传】hōngchuán〈动〉 spread: 这事很快就～开了。 This matter soon became widely known.
【哄闹】hōngnào〈动〉 make a racket: 一些足球迷在看台上～。 Some football fans raised a ruckus on the stand.
【哄抢】hōngqiǎng〈动〉 1▸（指购买） panic buy: ～紧俏商品 scramble to buy goods in short supply 2▸（指抢夺） openly loot: ～公共财物 loot public property
【哄然】hōngrán〈形〉 boisterous: ～大笑 burst into uproarious laughter
【哄抬】hōngtái〈动〉 drive up: ～物价 drive up prices
【哄堂大笑】hōngtáng-dàxiào〈成〉 the room filled with laughter: 引起～ make the whole room burst into laughter
【哄笑】hōngxiào〈动〉 roar with laughter

訇¹ hōng〈拟〉[used to describe loud noise]: ～然 with a loud crash

訇² hōng ▸阿訇 āhōng

烘 hōng〈动〉 1▸（烤） bake: ～蛋糕/面包 bake cakes/bread ▸～焙, ～烤 2▸（衬托） set off: ▸～衬, ～托
【烘焙】hōngbèi〈动〉 cure
【烘衬】hōngchèn = 烘托 hōngtuō
【烘干】hōnggān〈动〉 1▸（用火烤） dry beside or over fire 2▸［化学］ oven-dry
【烘干机】hōnggānjī〈名〉 dryer
【烘缸】hōnggāng〈名〉 dryer
【烘烘】hōnghōng〈拟〉 roar: 炉火～。 The flames in the stove were roaring.
【烘烤】hōngkǎo〈动〉 bake: ～面包 toast bread
【烘篮】hōnglán〈名〉 hand-held basketwork brazier
【烘染】hōngrǎn〈动〉 embroider
【烘托】hōngtuō〈动〉 1▸（指作画） set off by shading 2▸（陪衬） set off: 白色的山峰在蓝天的～下非常美丽。 The white peaks contrast beautifully with the blue sky. ‖ 文学作品中，反面人物常用来～正面人物。 In literature, negative characters often serve to set off the positive ones.
【烘箱】hōngxiāng〈名〉 oven
【烘云托月】hōngyún-tuōyuè〈成〉〈喻〉 provide a foil to set off a character or incident in a literary work: 收到～的艺术效果 achieve the artistic effect of prominence through contrast

薨 hōng〈动〉〈旧〉 die

hóng

弘 hóng
A = 宏 hóng
B〈动〉（发扬） expand: ▸～扬, 恢～
【弘扬】hóngyáng〈动〉develop and expand: ～民族文化 enhance the national cultural heritage ‖ ～正气，反对歪风 encourage healthy trends and discourage perverse practices

红（紅）hóng
A〈形〉 1▸（红色） red: ～墙 red wall ▸～旗, ～枣, 鲜～ 2▸（喜庆） happy: ▸～白喜事 3▸（成功） successful: ▸～运, 开门～, 走～ 4▸（革命） revolutionary: ▸～军, 又～又专
B〈名〉 1▸（红色物品） red cloth used on festive occasions: ▸挂～, 披～ 2▸（红利） bonus: ▸分～
▸gōng
【红案】hóng'àn〈名〉 meat or vegetable cooking
【红白喜事】hóng-bái xǐshì〈成〉 weddings and funerals
【红斑狼疮】hóngbān lángchuāng ▸**p. 50**〈名〉［医学］ lupus erythematosus
【红榜】hóngbǎng〈名〉 honour roll: 你上了～，我很高兴。 I'm glad to see your name in the honour roll.
【红包】hóngbāo〈名〉 1▸（礼金、压岁钱） red packet: 婚礼送～ give money as a wedding gift ‖ 给～ give money as a lunar New Year gift 2▸（奖金） bonus: 发～ give out money as a bonus 3▸（用于贿赂） bribe: 塞～ give sb. money as a bribe
【红宝石】hóngbǎoshí〈名〉 ruby: ～戒指 ruby ring
【红不棱登】hóngbulēngdēng〈形〉 (disagreeably) reddish in colour
【红茶】hóngchá〈名〉 black tea
【红场】Hóngchǎng〈名〉 Red Square
【红潮】hóngcháo〈名〉 1▸（脸红） blush 2▸（月经） menstruation 3▸（指潮水） red tide
【红尘】hóngchén〈名〉 mortal world: 看破～ be disillusioned with this human world

h

【红筹股】 hóngchóugǔ〈名〉［金融］ red chips

【红绸舞】 hóngchóuwǔ〈名〉 red silk dance

【红蛋】 hóngdàn〈名〉 red egg [celebrating the birth of a child]

【红得发紫】 hóngde-fāzǐ〈成〉 at the height of one's game

【红灯】 hóngdēng〈名〉 ❶（指灯笼） red lantern ❷（指信号灯） red light: 闯～ run a red light ‖〈喻〉亮～ run into trouble

【红灯区】 hóngdēngqū〈名〉 red-light district

【红点颏】 hóngdiǎnké〈名〉［鸟类］ Siberian rubythroat

【红豆】 hóngdòu〈名〉 ❶［植物］ red bean shrub ❷（相思豆） love pea: ～相思 red beans that inspire the memory of one's love

【红豆杉】 hóngdòushān〈名〉［植物］ Chinese yew

【红粉】 hóngfěn〈名〉〈旧〉 ❶（指粉） rouge and powder ❷（指人） the fair sex: ～知己 bosom lady friend who is young and beautiful

【红汞】 hónggǒng〈名〉［药学］ mercurochrome

【红股】 hónggǔ〈名〉［经济］ bonus stock

【红光满面】 hóngguāng-mǎnmiàn〈成〉 glowing with health

【红果】 hóngguǒ〈名〉〈方〉 haw

【红海】 Hónghǎi〈名〉 Red Sea

【红河】 Hónghé ▸p. 294〈名〉 Red River

【红红绿绿】 hónghóng-lǜlǜ〈形〉 colourful

【红狐】 hónghú〈名〉 red fox

【红花】 hónghuā〈名〉［中药］ safflower: 藏～ Tibetan safflower ‖ ～油 safflower oil

【红花虽好，也须绿叶扶持】 hónghuā suī hǎo, yě xū lǜyè fúchí〈俗〉 no matter how good you are, you still need the support of others

【红火蚁】 hónghuǒyǐ〈名〉［昆虫］ red imported fire ant (RIFA)

【红火】 hónghuo〈形〉 flourishing: 生意～ booming business

【红极一时】 hóngjí-yīshí〈成〉 be all the rage

【红教】 Hóngjiào〈名〉 Red Hat Sect of Tibetan Buddhism

【红巨星】 hóngjùxīng〈名〉［天文］ red giant

【红军】 Hóngjūn〈名〉 ❶（指中国） Chinese Workers' and Peasants' Red Army ❷（指前苏联） Red Army [army of the former Soviet Union before 1946]

【红利】 hónglì〈名〉 bonus, dividend

【红脸】 hóngliǎn〈动〉 ❶（脸红） blush: 每当提到他的名字她就会～。 She blushes every time his name is mentioned. ❷（发脾气） flush with anger: 他们夫妻俩从没红过脸。 The couple have never been angry with each other.

【红磷】 hónglín〈名〉［化学］ red phosphorus

【红领巾】 hónglǐngjīn〈名〉 ❶（指领巾） red scarf ❷（指人） Young Pioneer [member of the Young Pioneers of China, a youth organization run by the Communist Youth League]

【红楼梦】 hónglóumèng〈名〉 *A Dream of Red Mansions*

【红绿灯】 hónglǜdēng〈名〉 traffic lights

【红马甲】 hóngmǎjiǎ〈名〉 stock-broker's clerk [wearing a red waistcoat at a securities exchange]

【红毛丹】 hóngmáodān〈名〉［植物］ rambutan

> **《红楼梦》**
>
> A long work of fiction from the Qing Dynasty and one of the four famous classical Chinese novels. Its original name was *The Story of the Stone* (《石头记》) and the author is credited as Cao Xueqin (曹雪芹). However, only 80 of the work's 120 chapters are believed to have been written by Cao Xueqin, with the last 40 chapters added by Gao E (高鹗). The novel with its huge cast of characters tells the story of four big families named Jia, Wang, Shi and Xue and the tale of the rise and fall of the Jia household, the tragic love story of Jia Baoyu and Lin Daiyu and the unhappy lives of many young girls in feudal society.

【红帽子】 hóngmàozi〈名〉 ❶（指政治倾向） red cap ❷（搬运工） baggage porter

【红霉素】 hóngméisù〈名〉［药学］ erythromycin

【红焖】 hóngmèn〈动〉 stew in soy sauce: ～鸡 stewed chicken with soy sauce

【红米】 hóngmǐ〈名〉 red rice

【红棉】 hóngmián〈名〉［植物］ kapok

【红模子】 hóngmúzi〈名〉 sheet of paper with characters printed in red on it: 描～ trace in black ink over characters printed in red

【红木】 hóngmù〈名〉 mahogany

【红男绿女】 hóngnán-lǜnǚ〈成〉 young men and women in colourful clothes

【红娘】 hóngniáng〈名〉 matchmaker

【红牌】 hóngpái〈名〉［体育］ red card: 吃～ be shown the red card

【红盘】 hóngpán〈名〉［金融］ red listing

【红喷喷】 hóngpēnpēn〈形〉 reddish

【红皮书】 hóngpíshū〈名〉 red book

【红扑扑】 hóngpūpū〈形〉 rosy: ～的脸颊 ruddy cheeks

【红旗】 hóngqí〈名〉 red flag [of China]: 升起五星～ hoist the Five-Star Red Flag ‖ 在～下长大 be brought up under the red flag of New China ‖ 流动～ mobile red banner

【红旗手】 hóngqíshǒu〈名〉 pioneer: 三八～ female pacesetter

【红区】 hóngqū〈名〉 Red Area [base established by the Chinese Communist Party during the Second Revolutionary Civil War]

【红壤】 hóngrǎng〈名〉 red earth

【红热】 hóngrè〈名〉 red heat

【红人】 hóngrén〈名〉 favourite: 她是校长的～。 She is one of the headmaster's favourites.

【红润】 hóngrùn〈形〉 ruddy: 脸色～ rosy cheeks

【红色】 hóngsè **A**〈名〉 red **B**〈形〉 revolutionary: ～根据地 revolutionary base ‖ ～政权 red political power

【红色高棉】 Hóngsè Gāomián〈名〉 Khmer Rouge

【红杉】 hóngshān〈名〉 ❶（在中国） Chinese larch ❷（在北美） sequoia

【红衫军】 hóngshānjūn〈名〉 Red Shirts [National United Front of Democracy against Dictatorship, a major anti-government force in Thailand]

【红烧】 hóngshāo〈动〉 braise in soy sauce: ～肉 pork braised in brown sauce

【红苕】 hóngsháo〈名〉〈方〉 sweet potato

【红十字会】 Hóngshízìhuì〈名〉 Red Cross (Society): 中国～ Red Cross Society of China

【红薯】 hóngshǔ〈名〉 sweet potato

【红树】 hóngshù〈名〉［植物］ mangrove

【红丝带】 hóngsīdài〈名〉 red ribbon [symbol of solidarity for people with AIDS]

【红松】 hóngsōng〈名〉［植物］ Korean pine

【红糖】 hóngtáng〈名〉 brown sugar

【红桃】 hóngtáo〈名〉 [in cards] heart: ～Q the Queen of hearts

【红彤彤】 hóngtōngtōng〈形〉 bright red: ～的晚霞 evening glow ‖ 他的脸晒得～的。 His face has gone bright red in the sun.

【红通通】 hóngtōngtōng = 红彤彤 hóngtōngtōng

【红头文件】 hóngtóu wénjiàn〈名〉 official document [usu with the title printed in red]

【红土】 hóngtǔ〈名〉 ❶（指土壤） red soil ❷（指场地） clay: ～场地 clay court

【红外】 hóngwài = 红外线 hóngwàixiàn

【红外报警装置】 hóngwài bàojǐng zhuāngzhì〈名〉 infrared warning device

【红外探测】 hóngwài tàncè〈名〉 infrared detection

【红外线】 hóngwàixiàn〈名〉［物理］ infrared ray

【红卫兵】 Hóngwèibīng〈名〉 Red Guards [during the Cultural Revolution in China]

【红细胞】 hóngxìbāo〈名〉 red blood cell

【红线】 hóngxiàn〈名〉 main thread in literary works

【红小豆】 hóngxiǎodòu〈名〉 red bean

【红小鬼】 hóngxiǎoguǐ〈名〉 underage soldier [in Red Army]

【红心】 hóngxīn〈名〉〈喻〉 loyalty to the revolutionary cause: 一颗～为祖国 serve the motherland heart and soul

【红新月会】 hóngxīnyuèhuì〈名〉 Red Crescent

【红星】 hóngxīng〈名〉 red star: ～帽徽 red-star cap insignia

【红杏出墙】 hóngxìng-chūqiáng〈成〉 ❶（指春天） spring is very much in the air ❷（指女人） be unfaithful to one's husband

【红学】 Hóngxué〈名〉 studies of *A Dream of Red Mansions* (《红楼梦》): ～家 scholar engaging in the study of *A Dream of Red Mansions*

【红颜】 hóngyán〈名〉（指脸） rosy cheeks;（指人） beautiful woman: ～知己 female bosom friend

【红颜薄命】 hóngyán-bómìng〈成〉 beautiful women are often ill-fated

【红颜易老】 hóngyán-yìlǎo〈成〉 beauty is but transient

【红眼】 hóngyǎn **A**〈名〉 pinkeye **B**〈动〉 see red: 他一见对方得分超过了自己队就红了眼。 He began to see red when the opponents outscored his team.

【红眼病】 hóngyǎnbìng〈名〉 ❶ ▸p. 50［医学］ acute conjunctivitis ❷〈喻〉（忌妒） jealousy: 得了～ become jealous

【红眼航班】 hóngyǎn hángbān〈名〉 red-eye flight

【红艳艳】 hóngyànyàn〈形〉 bright red

【红样】 hóngyàng〈名〉［印刷］ corrected proof

【红药水】 hóngyàoshuǐ〈名〉 mercurochrome

【红叶】 hóngyè〈名〉 red autumn leaves

【红衣主教】 hóngyī zhǔjiào〈名〉［宗教］ cardinal

【红移】 hóngyí〈名〉［天文］ red shift

【红缨枪】 hóngyīngqiāng〈名〉 red-tasselled spear

【红油】 hóngyóu〈名〉 chilli oil: ～水饺 boiled *jiaozi* with chilli oil

【红鱼】 hóngyú〈名〉 (red) snapper

【红云】 hóngyún〈名〉 blush

【红运】 hóngyùn〈名〉 good luck: 走～ have good luck ‖ ～高照 have fortune on one's side

【红晕】 hóngyùn〈名〉 blush: 她脸上泛起了～。 A scarlet blush crept over her face.

【红枣】hóngzǎo〈名〉 red date
【红藻】hóngzǎo〈名〉 red alga
【红肿】hóngzhǒng〈形〉 red and swollen
【红妆】hóngzhuāng = 红装 hóngzhuāng
【红装】hóngzhuāng 〈名〉〈书〉 1（盛装） lady's Sunday best: 着～ be dressed in red 2（年轻女性） young woman

宏 hóng〈形〉 magnificent: ▸～大, ～伟
【宏病毒】hóngbìngdú 〈名〉［计算机］ macro virus
【宏博】hóngbó〈形〉 extensive
【宏大】hóngdà〈形〉 great: 规模～ on a grand scale ‖ ～的建筑 majestic building
【宏放】hóngfàng 〈形〉〈书〉 broad-minded
【宏富】hóngfù 〈形〉 abundant: 征引～ quote extensively ‖ 著述～ have written many books
【宏观】hóngguān A〈名〉 macroscopic view B〈形〉 macroscopic
【宏观经济】hóngguān jīngjì 〈名〉 macro-economy: ～学 macroeconomics
【宏观世界】hóngguān shìjiè 〈名〉 macro-cosm
【宏观调控】hóngguān tiáokòng 〈名〉 macro-control
【宏观政策】hóngguān zhèngcè 〈名〉 macro-policy
【宏丽】hónglì〈形〉 magnificent
【宏论】hónglùn〈名〉 informed opinion
【宏图】hóngtú〈名〉 ambitious plan: 立大志，展～ make great plans with lofty ambitions
【宏伟】hóngwěi〈形〉 magnificent: ～的目标 grand goal
【宏愿】hóngyuàn〈名〉 grand aspirations
【宏旨】hóngzhǐ〈名〉 main theme: 无关～ irrelevant to the topic

闳（閎） hóng〈书〉
A〈名〉 gate of a lane or alley
B〈形〉 grand

泓 hóng
A〈形〉〈书〉 deep and extensive
B〈量〉 stretch: 一～清泉 a clear spring ‖ 一～秋水 a stretch of limpid water

荭（葒） hóng
【荭草】hóngcǎo〈名〉［植物］ prince's feather

虹 hóng〈名〉 rainbow
▸jiàng
【虹膜】hóngmó 〈名〉［生理］ iris: ～炎 iritis
【虹吸管】hóngxīguǎn〈名〉 siphon
【虹吸现象】hóngxī xiànxiàng〈名〉 siphonage
【虹鳟】hóngzūn 〈名〉［鱼类］ rainbow trout

竑 hóng〈形〉〈书〉 broad

洪 hóng
A〈名〉 flood: ▸～水, 抗～
B〈形〉 vast: ▸～福, ～钟
【洪波】hóngbō〈名〉 great wave
【洪大】hóngdà 〈形〉 loud: ～的回声 resounding echoes
【洪都拉斯】Hóngdūlāsī 〈名〉 Honduras: ～共和国 Republic of Honduras ‖ ～人 Honduran
【洪泛区】hóngfànqū〈名〉 flood plain
【洪峰】hóngfēng〈名〉 flood peak
【洪福】hóngfú〈名〉 great blessing
【洪福齐天】hóngfú-qítiān 〈成〉 supreme bliss: 愿陛下～。 We wish Your Majesty supreme bliss.
【洪荒】hónghuāng 〈名〉 primeval chaos: ～时代 primeval times
【洪积平原】hóngjī píngyuán 〈名〉［地理］ diluvial plain
【洪亮】hóngliàng〈形〉 loud and clear: 嗓音～ sonorous voice
【洪量】hóngliàng〈名〉 1（指气量） magnanimity 2（指酒量） high alcohol tolerance
【洪流】hóngliú〈名〉 1（指水流） mighty torrent: 汹涌的～ surging torrents 2〈喻〉（指潮流） powerful trend: 时代的～ powerful trend of the times
【洪炉】hónglú〈名〉 great furnace: 在革命的～中经受锻炼 be tempered in the mighty furnace of revolution
【洪水】hóngshuǐ〈名〉 flood: ～泛滥。 The flood spread unchecked.
【洪水猛兽】hóngshuǐ-měngshòu 〈成〉〈喻〉 great misfortune and torment: 被视为～ be regarded as a great scourge
【洪灾】hóngzāi〈名〉 flood
【洪钟】hóngzhōng〈名〉〈书〉 large bell: 声如～ have a sonorous voice

翃 hóng〈动〉〈书〉 fly

魟（魟） hóng 〈名〉［鱼类］ stingray

鸿（鴻） hóng
A〈名〉 1（鸿雁） swan goose: ▸～毛, ～雁 2〈书〉（书信） letter: 远方来～ letter from afar
B〈形〉 great: ▸～篇巨制, ～儒, ～图
【鸿沟】hónggōu〈名〉 chasm: 弥合两代人之间的～ bridge the gulf between the two generations ‖ 不可逾越的～ unbridgeable gap
【鸿鹄】hónghú 〈名〉 1（天鹅） swan 2〈喻〉（指人） person of lofty aspirations: ～之志 lofty ambition
【鸿毛】hóngmáo〈名〉〈书〉〈喻〉 something very insignificant: 人固有一死，或重于泰山，或轻于～。 Though death befalls all men alike, it may be heavier than Mount Tai or lighter than a feather.
【鸿门宴】Hóngményàn 〈名〉 banquet set up as a trap for the invited
【鸿蒙】hóngméng〈名〉 primeval chaos
【鸿篇巨制】hóngpiān-jùzhì 〈成〉 masterpiece
【鸿儒】hóngrú 〈名〉〈旧〉 scholar with profound knowledge
【鸿图】hóngtú = 宏图 hóngtú
【鸿雁】hóngyàn 〈名〉 1（指鸟） swan goose 2〈书〉〈喻〉（指书信） letter: ～传书 letter from afar

渶 hóng = 荭 hóng

蕻 hóng ▸雪里蕻 xuělǐhóng
▸hòng

hǒng

哄 hǒng〈动〉 1（骗） fool: ～人 make a fool of sb. ‖ 不要～我。 Don't fool me. 2（逗弄） coax: ～孩子吃药 coax a child to take his medicine ‖ 他很会～孩子。 He is really good with children.
▸hōng, hòng
【哄逗】hǒngdòu〈动〉 coax: ～孩子笑 coax a smile from a child
【哄骗】hǒngpiàn〈动〉 hoodwink: 你～不了我。 You couldn't hoodwink me.
【哄劝】hǒngquàn〈动〉 coax

hòng

讧（訌） hòng〈动〉〈书〉 quarrel:
▸内～

哄（鬨） hòng 〈动〉 clamour:
▸起～
▸hōng, hǒng
【哄场】hòngchǎng〈动〉 make catcalls
【哄闹】hòngnào〈动〉 create an uproar

蕻 hòng〈形〉〈书〉 exuberant
▸hóng

hōu

齁[1] hōu〈名〉〈书〉 snore

齁[2] hōu
A〈动〉 (cause to) feel sick because of excessively salty or sweet food: 这道菜咸得～人。 This dish is so salty that it could make you feel ill.
B〈副〉〈方〉 awfully: ～咸 awfully salty ‖ 天气～冷。 It's terribly cold.
【齁声】hōushēng〈名〉 sound of snoring

hóu

侯 hóu 〈名〉 1（指爵位）（男） marquis;（女） marquess: ▸王～ 2（指贵族） nobleman: ～门 nobleman's mansion
▸诸～
【侯爵】hóujué〈名〉 marquis: ～夫人 marquise
【侯门似海】hóumén-sìhǎi 〈成〉 the mansions of the nobility are inaccessible to the common people

喉 hóu〈名〉［生理］ larynx
【喉癌】hóu'ái ▸p. 50〈名〉［医学］ throat cancer
【喉管】hóuguǎn〈名〉 windpipe
【喉结】hóujié〈名〉［生理］ larynx
【喉咙】hóulong〈名〉 throat
【喉舌】hóushé〈名〉〈喻〉 mouthpiece: 人民的～ mouthpiece of the people
【喉头】hóutóu〈名〉 throat
【喉炎】hóuyán ▸p. 50〈名〉［医学］ laryngitis: 慢性～ chronic laryngitis

猴 hóu
A〈名〉 monkey
B〈形〉〈方〉 clever
【猴急】hóují 〈形〉〈方〉 quick-tempered: 我没有说你不对，你别～。 I didn't say you were wrong. Don't get offended.
【猴年马月】hóunián-mǎyuè 〈成〉 God knows when: 不知～才能还清这笔债务。 God knows when we can pay off this debt.
【猴皮筋儿】hóupíjīnr〈名〉 rubber band: 跳

~ skip with rubber bands

【猴拳】 hóuquán 〈名〉［武术］ monkey boxing

【猴儿精】 hóurjīng〈形〉〈方〉 shrewd

【猴手猴脚】 hóushǒu-hóujiǎo〈俗〉 careless and rough

【猴头菇】 hóutóugū〈名〉［植物］ hedgehog fungus

【猴头猴脑】 hóutóu-hóunǎo〈形〉 funny-looking and foolish

【猴戏】 hóuxì〈名〉 1（耍猴） performing monkey show 2［戏曲］ performance with the Monkey King (孙悟空) as the hero

【猴子】 hóuzi〈名〉 monkey

瘊 hóu

【瘊子】 hóuzi〈名〉 wart

骺 hóu〈名〉［生理］ epiphysis

篌 hóu ▸箜篌 kōnghóu

hǒu

吼 hǒu〈动〉 1（指人） shout: 别对我大~大叫! Don't shout at me! ▸怒~ 2（指野兽） roar: 牛~。 A bull bellows. ‖ 狮~。 A lion roars. 3（指风、机器等） make great noise: 风在~。 The wind is blowing very hard. ‖ 飞机~叫着从上空飞过。 The planes roared by overhead.

【吼叫】 hǒujiào〈动〉 bellow: 愤怒地~ roar with anger

【吼声】 hǒushēng〈名〉 loud shout: ~从远处传来。 The shouts and calls came from afar.

hòu

后¹ hòu〈名〉 1（正宫） empress: ▸~妃，~宫，皇~ 2〈古〉（君主） monarch

后²（後） hòu〈名〉 1（指时间） afterwards: 不久以~ before long ‖ 课~ after class 2（后代） offspring: ▸绝~，无~ 3（指方位） rear: 敌~ enemy's rear ‖ 请往~站! Stand back, please! ▸~门，~院 4（指顺序） last: ~五名 last five (persons)

【后爸】 hòubà〈名〉〈口〉 stepfather

【后半辈子】 hòubànbèizi = 后半生 hòubànshēng

【后半晌】 hòubànshǎng〈名〉〈方〉 afternoon

【后半生】 hòubànshēng〈名〉 latter half of one's life

【后半天】 hòubàntiān〈名〉 afternoon

【后半夜】 hòubànyè〈名〉 second half of the night

【后备】 hòubèi A〈形〉 reserve: ~部队 reserve force ‖ ~基金 reserve fund B〈名〉 reserve: 留有~ keep sth. in reserve

【后备军】 hòubèijūn〈名〉 reserves: 编入~ place sb. on the reserves ‖ 产业~ industrial reserve force

ℹ 修饰语（二）：后置修饰语

英语中的后置修饰语主要包括：

■ 修饰不定代词如 everything、someone 等的形容词：

我们会采取一切必要措施来解决这件事
= We will do everything necessary to sort this out

我有些有趣的事告诉你
= I have something interesting to tell you

他没给我们讲什么新鲜事
= He didn't tell us anything new

她在找个可靠的人照顾孩子
= She's looking for someone reliable to look after the kids

■ 修饰不定副词如 somewhere、anywhere 等的形容词和副词：

我们能找个好地方吃饭吗?
= Can we find somewhere nice to eat?

这个地方和校园的其他地方一样好
= This place is as good as everywhere else on campus

■ 以 -ible 和 -able 结尾的形容词。这类词习惯放在所修饰的名词后面，但也可放在名词之前而意思不变：

你们有可住两晚的单人房吗?
= Do you have any single rooms available for two nights?

我会竭尽所能帮你
= I will help you out in every way possible
或 I will help you out in every possible way

这家商店的新鲜蔬菜应有尽有
= The shop sells fresh vegetables of every kind imaginable

■ 修饰名词的度量单位：

8 英尺深的沟
= a ditch eight feet deep

200 米宽的湖
= a lake 200 metres wide

■ 修饰表时间的名词词组的 ago 及 old：

5 个小时以前
= five hours ago

很久以前
= a long time ago

她 6 岁了
= She is six years old

■ 修饰不定代词、疑问代词的 else：

除了斯特拉之外，别的人都同意了
= Everybody else has agreed, apart from Stella

如果这不行，我试别的
= If this doesn't work, I will try something else

你还去别的地方了吗?
= Where else have you been?

你还见谁了?
= Who else have you seen?

■ 一些固定用法：

总督
= Governor General

秘书长
= Secretary General

桂冠诗人
= Poet Laureate

候任总统
= the president elect

■ 做定语的形容词短语：

没有那么多适合孩子的电影
= There are not so many films suitable for children

我找不到值得一提的话题
= I couldn't find any topics worthy of mention

■ 作定语的介词短语：

戴眼镜的男人
= a man with glasses

门钥匙
= the key to the door

关于摄影的书
= a book on photography

■ 作定语的不定式：

她总是第一个到办公室
= She is always the first to come to the office

我有作业要做
= I have homework to do

他需要找个人谈谈
= He needs someone to talk to

■ 做定语的现在分词或过去分词，用以强调分词本身的动作：

排队的人中大多数是女性
= Most of the people waiting in the queue are female

由母亲陪伴的那个女孩是我刚刚谈到的那个
= The girl accompanied by her mother is the one I was just talking about

■ 定语从句：

你喜欢的那只狗
= the dog you like

我住了 10 年的那个小镇
= the town where I lived (for) 10 years

正在读报的那些人
= those people who are reading newspapers

■ 英语中有些形容词既可前置又可后置，而意思不变：

附近的商店
= a shop nearby
或 a nearby shop

楼下的房间
= rooms downstairs
或 downstairs rooms

在过去的年代里
= in past years
或 in years past

■ 有些形容词在前置和后置时意思不同：

你现在的地址是什么?
= What is your present address?

所有在场的人都感动得流泪了
= All the people present were moved to tears

忧心忡忡的家长已向校方报告了此事
= Concerned parents have reported it to the school

我想对所有有关人员表示感谢
= I'd like to say thank you to all concerned

【后背】hòubèi〈名〉back

【后辈】hòubèi〈名〉**1**（后代）younger generation **2**（晚辈）descendants: ～要向老前辈学习。The younger generation should learn from their elders.

【后边】hòubian〈名〉rear: 屋子～是一片树林。There is a wood behind the house.

【后步】hòubù〈名〉leeway: 留～ leave room for manoeuvre

【后场】hòuchǎng〈名〉［体育］back-court

【后尘】hòuchén〈名〉〈书〉〈喻〉footstep: 步人～ follow in sb.'s footsteps

【后代】hòudài〈名〉**1**（指时代）later ages **2**（指人）descendants: 为～着想 for the sake of future generations **3**［生物］progeny: 一种杂交小麦的～ progeny of a wheat mix

【后挡板】hòudǎngbǎn〈名〉tailgate; tailboard〈英〉

【后灯】hòudēng〈名〉[of a car] tail light

【后爹】hòudiē〈名〉〈方〉stepfather

【后蝶】hòudié〈名〉queen butterfly

【后端】hòuduān〈名〉rear end: ～数据库 back-end database

【后盾】hòudùn〈名〉backing: 坚强的～ powerful backing

【后发制人】hòufāzhìrén〈成〉let one's opponent strike first and then get the better of him

【后方】hòufāng〈名〉**1**（指远离战场）rear: ～医院 rear hospital **2** = 后边 hòubian

【后妃】hòufēi〈名〉empress and imperial concubines

【后福】hòufú〈名〉future happiness: 大难不死，必有～。A disaster survived is a blessing in store.

【后父】hòufù〈名〉stepfather

【后付费】hòufùfèi〈动〉pay after use: ～用户 customer who pays after use

【后跟】hòugēn〈名〉heel

【后宫】hòugōng〈名〉**1**（指住处）living quarters for imperial concubines **2**（指人）concubines of a monarch

【后顾】hòugù〈动〉**1**（指顾及）turn back to take care of sth.: 无暇～ have no time to take care of things one has left behind ▸～之忧 **2**（回忆）look back

【后顾之忧】hòugùzhīyōu〈成〉trouble back at home: 有～ have family worries

【后滚翻】hòugǔnfān〈名〉［体育］backward roll

【后果】hòuguǒ〈名〉consequence: ～自负 take personal responsibility for the consequences ‖ 前因～ cause and effect ‖ ～不堪设想。The consequences would be too ghastly to contemplate.

【后汉】Hòu Hàn〈名〉**1**（东汉）Eastern Han Dynasty **2**（指五代之一）Later Han Dynasty

【后花园】hòuhuāyuán〈名〉back garden

【后话】hòuhuà〈名〉sth. to be taken up later: 此是～，暂且不提。More about this later.

【后患】hòuhuàn〈名〉future trouble: 消除～ remove the cause of future trouble

【后患无穷】hòuhuàn-wúqióng〈成〉endless trouble in store: 如果这个瘤子现在不摘除，恐怕～。If you don't have the tumour removed now, I'm afraid there will be all hell to pay.

【后悔】hòuhuǐ〈动〉regret: 对自己所作所为感到～ be repentant for what one has done ‖ ～不已 be overcome with regret

【后悔莫及】hòuhuǐ-mòjí〈成〉be too late to repent

【后悔药】hòuhuǐyào〈名〉〈喻〉medicine for remorse: 从来没有～可吃。There's no such thing as a medicine for regret.

【后会有期】hòuhuì-yǒuqī〈成〉we'll meet again some day

【后脊梁】hòujǐliang〈名〉〈方〉backbone:〈喻〉我没有做错事，不怕别人戳～。I did nothing wrong, and therefore I'm not afraid of people speaking ill of me behind my back.

【后记】hòujì〈名〉postscript

【后继】hòujì〈动〉succeed: ▸前仆～

【后继无人】hòujì-wúrén〈成〉have no qualified successors

【后继有人】hòujì-yǒurén〈成〉have qualified successors

【后脚】hòujiǎo **A**〈名〉back foot: 前脚一滑，～也站不稳。As the front foot slipped, the back foot became unsteady. **B**〈副〉[usu used together with 前脚] immediately after: 我前脚到车站，他～就赶到了。No sooner had I got to the station than he arrived.

【后街】hòujiē〈名〉back street

【后金】Hòu Jīn〈名〉Later Jin Dynasty

【后襟】hòujīn〈名〉back of a garment

【后进】hòujìn **A**〈形〉backward: 帮助～的学生 help slow students **B**〈名〉person or unit lagging behind: ～赶先进。The less advanced strive to catch up with the more advanced.

【后劲】hòujìn〈名〉**1**（指影响力）after-effect: 这酒～大。This wine has a strong after-effect. **2**（指持久力）staying power: 他干活有～。He has stamina in his work.

【后晋】Hòu Jìn〈名〉Later Jin Dynasty

【后颈】hòujǐng〈名〉back of the neck

【后景】hòujǐng〈名〉background

【后空翻】hòukōngfān〈名〉［体育］backward somersault

【后来】hòulái **A**〈名〉later: ～怎么样? What happened afterwards? ‖ 他找到一份工作，～就再没有消息了。He got a job and has not been heard of since. **B**〈形〉newly arrived: 给～的都留有座位。There are seats reserved for late comers.

【后来居上】hòulái-jūshàng〈成〉the new arrivals overtake those who have gone before

【后来人】hòuláirén〈名〉successor

【后浪推前浪】hòulàng tuī qiánlàng〈成〉making steady progress: 长江～，世上新人换旧人。As the Yangtze River surges on wave upon wave, so the new generation replaces the old.

【后梁】Hòu Liáng〈名〉Later Liang Dynasty

【后路】hòulù〈名〉**1**（指道路）escape route: 抄敌人的～ attack the enemy from the rear **2**（退路）room for manoeuvre: 留条～ leave oneself room for manoeuvre

【后掠翼】hòulüèyì〈名〉［航空］swept-back wing

【后轮】hòulún〈名〉rear wheel

【后妈】hòumā〈名〉〈口〉stepmother

【后门】hòumén〈名〉back door: 屋子的～ back door of a house ‖ 走～ get in by the back door ‖ 开～ give sb. a special advantage

【后面】hòumian〈名〉**1**（指方位）back: ～还有座位。There are vacant seats at the back. **2**（指时间）later: 这个问题～我还要讲。I'll come back to this point later on.

【后母】hòumǔ〈名〉stepmother

【后脑勺儿】hòunǎosháor〈名〉〈方〉back of the head

【后年】hòunián ▸**p. 618**〈名〉year after next

【后娘】hòuniáng〈名〉stepmother

【后怕】hòupà〈名〉fear after the event: 那次车祸我现在一想起来还～。The mere thought of the car crash scares me still.

【后排】hòupái〈名〉back row

【后期】hòuqī〈名〉later stage: ～管理 final-stage management ‖ ～制作 post-production ‖ 二十世纪九十年代～ late 1990s

【后起】hòuqǐ〈形〉up-and-coming: ～的青年作家 budding young writer

【后起之秀】hòuqǐzhīxiù〈成〉rising star

【后勤】hòuqín〈名〉logistics: 提供～支援 provide logistic support

【后勤部】hòuqínbù〈名〉logistics department

【后鞧】hòuqiū〈名〉harness

【后儿】hòur ▸**p. 618**〈名〉〈口〉day after tomorrow: 我～再来看你。I'll come to see you again the day after tomorrow.

【后儿个】hòurge = 后儿 hòur

【后人】hòurén〈名〉**1**（子孙后代）later generations: 如果我们今天不保护好生态环境，就会遭到～的唾骂。We will be reviled by future generations if we do not take good care of the ecological environment now. **2**（后世的人）descendants: 王家已没有～了。There are no more descendants of the Wang family.

【后任】hòurèn〈名〉successor

【后日】hòurì = 后天 hòutiān A

【后晌】hòushǎng〈名〉〈方〉afternoon: ～动身 start off in the afternoon

【后身】hòushēn〈名〉**1**（指人体）back: 我只看见个～，辨不清是谁。I couldn't make out who he was as I only saw his back. **2**（指衣服）back of a garment: 你大衣的～有个小口子。There's a small tear in the back of your coat. **3**（指房屋）back of a house, etc. **4**（转世之身）reincarnation **5**（指机构、团体）successor

【后生】hòushēng〈名〉〈方〉young man: 这～长得很英俊。The young man is good-looking.

【后生可畏】hòushēng-kěwèi〈成〉the younger generation will surpass the older

【后市】hòushì〈名〉afternoon market

【后世】hòushì〈名〉**1**（指时间）future generations **2**（指人）descendants: 华侨有许多～子孙都成为世界有名的科学家。Many overseas Chinese descendants have become world-famous scientists. **3**［宗教］next life

【后事】hòushì〈名〉**1**（后来发生的事）subsequent event: 欲知～如何，且听下回分解。If you want to know what happens afterwards, read the next chapter. **2**（丧事）funeral affairs: 料理～ make arrangements for a funeral

【后视镜】hòushìjìng〈名〉[of a car] rear-view mirror

【后手】hòushǒu〈名〉**1**（指下棋）defensive position **2**（退路）room for manoeuvre: 制定计划时，你得给自己留个～。When making plans, you must give yourself room for manoeuvre.

【后嗣】hòusì〈名〉〈书〉offspring

【后台】hòutái〈名〉**1**（指舞台）backstage **2**（支持）behind-the-scenes backer

【后台老板】hòutái lǎobǎn〈名〉backstage boss: 他能中标，是因为有很硬的～。He won the bid because he had strong backing.

【后唐】Hòu Táng〈名〉Later Tang Dynasty

【后天】hòutiān **A** ▸**p. 618**〈名〉day after tomorrow: 大～ three days from today **B**〈形〉acquired: 知识是～习得的。Knowledge is acquired.

【后头】hòutou = 后面 hòumian
【后腿】hòutuǐ〈名〉hind leg
【后退】hòutuì〈动〉retreat: 遇到困难决不～ never shrink from difficulties
【后卫】hòuwèi〈名〉**1**［军事］rearguard: ～战斗 rearguard action **2**［足球］full back: 右/左～ right/left back **3**［篮球］guard: 得分～ shooting guard
【后现代】hòuxiàndài〈名〉postmodern: ～主义 postmodernism
【后效】hòuxiào〈名〉after-effect: ▸以观～
【后行】hòuxíng〈副〉afterwards: 现在先行合并，～所有制转换 merge first and change the ownership afterwards
【后续】hòuxù〈形〉follow-up: ～部队 follow-up unit ‖ ～工作 follow-up work
【后学】hòuxué〈名〉〈谦〉junior scholar or student
【后腰】hòuyāo〈名〉small of the back
【后遗症】hòuyízhèng〈名〉**1** ▸**p. 50**［医学］sequelae: 小儿麻痹～ sequelae of infantile paralysis **2**（后续影响）after-effect: 经济萧条的～ after-effect of the economic depression
【后尾儿】hòuyǐr〈名〉〈口〉rear part: 车～ rear end of a vehicle
【后裔】hòuyì〈名〉descendants: 华侨～ descendants of overseas Chinese
【后影】hòuyǐng〈名〉shape of a person or thing as seen from the back: 我只看见他的～。I only caught sight of the back of him.
【后援】hòuyuán〈名〉reinforcements
【后援团】hòuyuántuán〈名〉backers: 决赛现场有声势浩大的～。There were huge numbers of supporters at the finals.
【后元音】hòuyuányīn〈名〉［语言］back vowel
【后院】hòuyuàn〈名〉**1**（院子）backyard **2**〈喻〉（内部）home: 总统因～起火中途结束海外访问。The president suspended his overseas visit because of trouble at home.
【后账】hòuzhàng〈名〉**1**（指账目）hidden accounts **2**（指责任）account to be settled later: 不怕别人算～ not be afraid of later investigation
【后者】hòuzhě〈代〉the latter
【后肢】hòuzhī〈名〉［动物］hind leg
【后置】hòuzhì ▸**p. 301**〈动〉postposition: ～定语 postpositive attributive
【后周】Hòu Zhōu〈名〉Later Zhou Dynasty
【后主】hòuzhǔ〈名〉〈古〉last king or emperor of a short-lived dynasty
【后缀】hòuzhuì〈名〉［语言］suffix
【后坐力】hòuzuòlì〈名〉［军事］backlash: 无～炮 recoilless gun

厚 hòu

A〈形〉**1**（不薄）thick: ～木板/嘴唇 thick plank/lips ‖ 被子太～了。The quilt is too thick. ▸～脸皮 **2**（多）large: 家底很～ have substantial resources ▸～礼，～利 **3**（深厚）deep: ▸～望，深情～谊 **4**（浓重）rich: 酒味很～。The wine tastes strong. ▸醇～ **5**（厚道）kind: ▸憨～，忠～
B〈名〉thickness: 雪下了一尺多～。Snow fell to a depth of over one foot. ‖ 这堵墙有多～？What's the thickness of the wall?
C〈动〉favour: ▸～此薄彼，～古薄今
【厚爱】hòu'ài〈名〉great kindness: 报答您的～ reciprocate the great favour you have shown me ‖ 承蒙～。Thanks to your care and support.
【厚薄】hòubó〈名〉**1**（厚度）thickness: 胶合板的质量比～更重要。The thickness of plywood matters less than its quality. **2**（亲疏）favour or disfavour: 女孩男孩都一样，不应分～。Boys and girls should be treated as equal.
【厚此薄彼】hòucǐ-bóbǐ〈成〉favour one and discriminate against the other
【厚待】hòudài〈动〉treat sb. kindly and generously: 老板这样～，我会好好干的。As the boss is so kind to me, I will certainly work hard.
【厚道】hòudao〈形〉honest and kind: 为人～ be honest and generous
【厚德载物】hòudé-zàiwù〈成〉a person of great virtue can shoulder great responsibilities
【厚度】hòudù〈名〉thickness
【厚墩墩】hòudūndūn〈形〉very thick: ～的大棉袄 heavy padded overcoat
【厚恩】hòu'ēn〈名〉great favour
【厚非】hòufēi〈名〉undue criticism: ▸无可～
【厚古薄今】hòugǔ-bójīn〈成〉value the past over the present
【厚积薄发】hòujī-bófā〈成〉be fully prepared and you will do a good job
【厚今薄古】hòujīn-bógǔ〈成〉value the present over the past
【厚金】hòujīn〈名〉high pay
【厚礼】hòulǐ〈名〉generous gift: 献上一份～ present a generous gift
【厚利】hòulì〈名〉substantial profit: 贪图～ hanker after fat profit
【厚脸皮】hòuliǎnpí〈惯〉cheeky: 厚着脸皮说 have the nerve to say ‖ 他是个～。He was an impudent fellow.
【厚禄】hòulù〈名〉handsome salary: 高官～ high position and good pay
【厚人薄己】hòurén-bójǐ〈成〉live simply but treat others generously
【厚势】hòushì〈名〉strong power: 中国乒乓球有领先世界的优势和～。China is the world's table-tennis leader in terms of dominance and power.
【厚实】hòushi〈形〉**1**（厚而密实）thick: 这布很～。This cloth is very thick. **2**（富足）abundant: 家底～ abundant family resources **3**（扎实）deep and solid: 打下～的英语基本功 lay a solid foundation for the mastery of English **4**（结实）thick and sturdy: ～的胸膛 thick and sturdy chest
【厚望】hòuwàng〈名〉high hopes: 不负～ not let sb. down ‖ 寄予～ pin high hopes on sb.
【厚颜无耻】hòuyán-wúchǐ〈成〉be shameless: 他竟然～地说他都是为了我好。He had the cheek to say that he had done all it for my sake.
【厚养薄葬】hòuyǎng-bózàng〈惯〉give substantial support to one's parents but hold simple funerals for them after their deaths
【厚谊】hòuyì〈名〉profound friendship: ▸深情～
【厚意】hòuyì〈名〉kindness: 多谢你的～。Thank you for your kindness.
【厚遇】hòuyù〈名〉excellent pay and conditions
【厚葬】hòuzàng〈名〉elaborate funeral
【厚重】hòuzhòng〈形〉**1**（指重量）thick and heavy: ～的棉大衣 heavy cotton-padded overcoat **2**（贵重）generous: ～的礼物 munificent gift **3**（稳重）kind and prudent: 为人～ be generous and discreet

逅 hòu ▸邂逅 xièhòu

候 hòu

A〈动〉**1**（问候）inquire after: 请代为致～ please give my regards (to) ▸问～ **2**（观测）observe: ▸～风地动仪，斥～ **3**（等候）wait: 请稍～。Please wait a moment. ▸～诊，等～，恭～
B〈名〉**1**（时节）time: ▸～鸟，季～，时～ **2**（气候）climate: ▸气～，天～ **3**（状态）state: ▸火～，征～，症～ **4**〈旧〉（五天）period of five days: ▸～温
【候补】hòubǔ〈动〉be a candidate: ～队员 substitute ‖ 政治局～委员 alternate member of the politburo
【候场】hòuchǎng〈动〉wait for one's turn to act on the stage
【候车】hòuchē〈动〉wait for a bus or train: 排队～ queue for a bus/train
【候车室】hòuchēshì〈名〉waiting room [in a railway or bus station]
【候虫】hòuchóng〈名〉seasonal insect
【候风地动仪】hòufēng dìdòngyí〈名〉ancient seismograph
【候机楼】hòujīlóu〈名〉air terminal
【候教】hòujiào〈动〉〈敬〉await instruction
【候鸟】hòuniǎo〈名〉migratory bird
【候审】hòushěn〈动〉［法律］await trial: 取保～ be on bail awaiting trial
【候温】hòuwēn〈名〉［气象］average temperature of a five-day period
【候选人】hòuxuǎnrén〈名〉candidate: ～名单 list of candidates
【候诊】hòuzhěn〈动〉wait to see the doctor: ～室 waiting room

堠 hòu〈名〉〈旧〉earthen watchtower: 烽～ beacon tower

hū

乎[1] hū〈助〉〈书〉used at the end of a question: 有朋自远方来，不亦乐～？Is it not delightful to have friends coming from afar? ‖ 成败之机，其在斯～？Does not success or failure hinge on this? ‖ 然～，否～？Yes or no?

乎[2] hū〈后缀〉**1**（于）[used after a verb, functioning as 于]: 出～意料 exceed one's expectations ‖ 合～客观规律 conform to an objective law **2**〈书〉（用于强调）[used after an adverb or adjective for emphasis]: 确～重要 be very important indeed ‖ 迥～不同 be entirely different

乎[3] hū〈叹〉〈书〉天～！Good Heavens!

呼[1] hū〈动〉**1**（排出）breathe out: ～出二氧化碳 exhale carbon dioxide ▸～吸 **2**（喊）shout: ～口号 shout slogans ▸～天抢地，高～，欢～ **3**（叫）call: 直～其名 address sb. disrespectfully by using name ‖ 有事你就～我。Don't hesitate to call me any time you need me. ▸千～万唤，招～

呼[2] hū〈拟〉howl: 北风～～地吹。A north wind is howling.
【呼哧】hūchī〈拟〉puff: ～～直喘 puff and blow
【呼风唤雨】hūfēng-huànyǔ〈成〉**1**（驱使

风雨） control the forces of nature 2（指力量强大） stir up trouble
【呼喊】hūhǎn〈动〉 call out: 大声～ raise a cry
【呼号】hūháo〈动〉〈书〉 cry out in distress: 奔走～ go around crying for help
【呼号】hūhào〈名〉 1［通信］ call sign: ～机 call signal apparatus 2（指口号） motto: 少先队的～是"时刻准备着"。The Young Pioneers' motto is: 'be prepared at all times.'
【呼和浩特】Hūhéhàotè ▸p. 661 〈名〉 Huhhot [capital of Inner Mongolia (内蒙古)]
【呼唤】hūhuàn〈动〉 1（召唤） call: 祖国在向你们青年人～。The motherland is calling on you young people. 2（呼叫） call out: 听，有人在远处～我们！ Listen! Someone is calling us in the distance.
【呼机】hūjī〈名〉 pager
【呼叫】hūjiào〈动〉 1（叫） call out: 有人听见他～，"着火了！" Somebody heard him calling out, 'Fire!' 2［通信］ call: ～信号 calling signal ‖ ～转移 call divert
【呼救】hūjiù〈动〉 call for help: ～信号 distress signal ‖ 有人在～! Someone is yelling for help.
【呼拉圈】hūlāquān〈名〉 hula hoop
【呼啦】hūlā〈拟〉 flap: 风卷红旗～～地响。The red flags are flapping in the wind.
【呼喇】hūlā = 呼啦 hūlā
【呼噜】hūlū〈拟〉 wheeze: 他喉咙里～～地直响。He's a bit wheezy.
【呼噜】hūlu〈名〉 snore: 打～ snore
【呼麦】hūmài〈名〉 Khoomei [throat singing]: ～原生态音乐会 Tuvan throat singing concert
【呼朋引类】hūpéng-yǐnlèi〈成〉〈贬〉 summon one's friends and followers: ～，合伙结帮 gather one's followers around and consolidate a set-up of one's own
【呼扇】hūshan〈动〉 1（颤动） flap: 风吹得帘子直～。The curtain keeps flapping in the wind. 2（扇风） fan: 他用扇子把蚊子～开。He fanned away the mosquitoes.
【呼哨】hūshào〈名〉 whistle: 打～ whistle
【呼声】hūshēng〈名〉 cry: 正义的～ cry of justice ‖ 要多听听下面的～。We must listen more to the voices of those at lower levels.
【呼天抢地】hūtiān-qiāngdì〈成〉 utter cries of anguish: 母亲去世，她哭得～。She cried her eyes out over the death of her mother.
【呼吸】hūxī〈动〉 breathe: ～新鲜空气 breathe in fresh air ‖ 进行人工～ practise artificial respiration ‖ 深～ breathe deeply
【呼吸道】hūxīdào〈名〉 respiratory tract
【呼吸机】hūxījī〈名〉 respirator
【呼吸器官】hūxī qìguān〈名〉［生理］ respiratory organ
【呼吸系统】hūxī xìtǒng〈名〉 respiratory system
【呼吸相通】hūxī-xiāngtōng〈成〉 be of the same mind
【呼啸】hūxiào〈动〉 whistle: 寒风～。A cold wind is whistling. ‖ 公路上汽车～而过。Cars are whizzing past on the highway.
【呼幺喝六】hūyāo-hèliù〈成〉 1（高声喊叫） shout for the winning number 2（形容傲慢） be domineering
【呼应】hūyìng〈动〉 1（呼喊与答应） echo: 遥相～ echo from afar 2（相互照应） coordinate: 前后～ be well-organized
【呼吁】hūyù〈动〉 call on: ～大家节约用水 appeal to the public to save water ‖ 发出紧急～ issue an urgent appeal ‖ ～书 letter of appeal
【呼之欲出】hūzhīyùchū〈成〉 be vividly portrayed

忽[1] hū〈动〉 neglect: ▸～略，～视

忽[2] hū〈副〉 1（突然） suddenly: ～发奇想 a strange idea comes to one's mind all of a sudden 2（一会儿） now ..., now ...: 灯光～明～暗。The lights keep flickering. ‖ 天气～冷～热。The weather is cold one minute and hot the next.

忽[3] hū〈量〉 1（指重量） *hu* [unit of weight, equalling to 0.00001 gram] 2（指长度） *hu* [unit of length, equalling to 0.00001 metre] 3（万分之一） one hundred thousandth of a unit
【忽地】hūdì〈副〉 abruptly: ～跳起来 jump to one's feet abruptly ‖ ～停下来 come to a sudden stop
【忽而】hū'ér〈副〉 now ..., now ...: ～哭，～笑 cry and laugh by turns ‖ ～谈笑风生，～郁郁寡欢 be now cheerful and now sad
【忽忽】hūhū〈形〉 quick: 三年～地过去了。Three years flew by.
【忽略】hūlüè〈动〉 overlook: ～不计 not take into account ‖ 不要～可能引起的副作用。Don't lose sight of the possible side effects.
【忽米】hūmǐ〈量〉 centimillimetre
【忽然】hūrán〈副〉 suddenly: ～，一辆警车在他面前停下。All of a sudden, a police car pulled up in front of him.
【忽闪】hūshǎn〈动〉 flash: 警车顶上的灯一直在～。The light on top of the police car kept flashing.
【忽闪】hūshan〈动〉 twinkle: 小姑娘～着眼睛。The little girl's eyes twinkled.
【忽视】hūshì〈动〉 ignore: 不可～的力量 force not to be overlooked ‖ 渐渐被～ fall into neglect
【忽悠】hūyou〈动〉〈方〉 1（晃动） flicker: 篝火在远处～。Campfires flickered in the distance. 2（糊弄） fool: ～消费者 deceive the consumers ‖ 你又～人了。You've been cheating people again. ‖ 别～人了！ Stop fooling around! ‖ 别听她～。Don't listen to her nonsense.

烀 hū〈动〉 stew in shallow water

唿 hū
【唿哨】hūshào = 呼哨 hūshào

惚 hū = 恍惚 huǎnghū

糊 hū〈动〉 plaster: ～墙 plaster a wall ‖ ～一层泥 spread a layer of mud
▸hú, hù

hú

囫 hú
【囫囵】húlún〈形〉 whole: ～吞下 swallow sth. whole
【囫囵觉】húlúnjiào〈名〉 sound sleep without interruption
【囫囵吞枣】húlún-tūnzǎo〈成〉 read without understanding

和 hú〈动〉 win (a mah-jong game): 我半天没开～了。I haven't won for a long time. ‖ 这一把我～了。I won this turn.
▸hé, hè, huó, huò

狐 hú〈名〉［动物］ fox
【狐步舞】húbùwǔ〈名〉 foxtrot
【狐臭】húchòu〈名〉 body odour
【狐猴】húhóu〈名〉［动物］ lemur
【狐假虎威】hújiǎ-hǔwēi〈成〉〈喻〉 bully people by flaunting one's powerful connections
【狐狸】húli〈名〉［动物］ fox
【狐狸精】húlijīng〈名〉〈贬〉〈喻〉 vixen
【狐狸尾巴】húli wěiba〈名〉〈贬〉〈喻〉 sth. that gives away a person's real character or evil intentions: ～总是要露出来的。A fox cannot hide its tail.
【狐媚】húmèi〈动〉 entice by flattery: ～淫态 attractive looks and seductive manners
【狐朋狗友】húpéng-gǒuyǒu〈成〉 disreputable company
【狐裘】húqiú〈名〉 fox-fur robe
【狐群狗党】húqún-gǒudǎng〈成〉 pack of scoundrels
【狐臊】húsāo〈名〉 body odour
【狐死首丘】húsǐ-shǒuqiū〈成〉 yearn for one's native place
【狐死兔悲】húsǐ-tùbēi = 兔死狐悲 tùsǐ-húbēi
【狐仙】húxiān〈名〉 fox fairy
【狐疑】húyí〈名〉 suspicion: 满腹～ be very suspicious

弧 hú〈名〉 1（弓） bow 2［数学］ arc
【弧度】húdù〈名〉［数学］ radian: ～测量 arc measurement
【弧光】húguāng〈名〉 arc light: ～灯 arc light
【弧圈球】húquānqiú〈名〉［体育］ loop drive
【弧线】húxiàn〈名〉 pitch arc
【弧形】húxíng〈名〉 arc: ～结构 arc structure

胡[1] hú
A Hú〈名〉 1（指民族） Hu ethnic groups: ▸～人 2（胡琴） *huqin* [a general term for two-stringed bowed instruments]: ▸板～，二～，京～
B〈形〉 introduced from the northern and western ethnic groups or from abroad: ～服 *hu* dress ▸～萝卜，～桃

胡[2] hú〈副〉 wantonly: ～吹 boast outrageously ▸～编乱造，～搞，～来

胡[3] hú〈代〉〈书〉 why: ～不归? Why not return?

胡[4]（鬍） hú〈名〉（在唇上） moustache;（在腮下） beard: ▸～须，八字～
【胡编乱造】húbiān-luànzào〈成〉 fabricate: 给别人～ fabricate stories about others
【胡扯】húchě〈动〉 talk nonsense: 别～，说正经的。Stop talking nonsense; let's get down to business.
【胡吹】húchuī〈动〉 boast: 你别～了。Stop boasting.
【胡豆】húdòu = 蚕豆 cándòu
【胡匪】húfěi〈名〉〈旧〉 bandit

【胡蜂】húfēng〈名〉wasp

【胡搞】húgǎo〈动〉1（胡乱做）mess up: 他能修什么钟表！纯属～一通。You really thought he was going to be able to fix the clock? All he did was mess things up! 2（指男女关系）be promiscuous: ～男女关系 be promiscuous

【胡话】húhuà〈名〉ravings: 病人又开始说～了。The patient began to rave again.

【胡笳】hújiā ▸**p. 929**〈名〉［音乐］reed pipe

【胡椒】hújiāo〈名〉pepper: 白/黑～ white/black pepper ‖ ～粉 ground pepper

【胡搅】hújiǎo〈动〉1（胡闹）be mischievous: 请别～了！Stop pestering, please! 2（狡辩）wrangle: 别以为你们这么～一下，我就会让步。Don't assume that I'll give in to your wrangling.

【胡搅蛮缠】hújiǎo-mánchán〈成〉pester sb. with unreasonable demands

【胡来】húlái〈动〉1（乱来）mess sth. up: 这机器很娇贵，你可不能～。The machine is expensive and delicate. You mustn't mess about with it. 2（捣乱）make trouble: 别打架，谁也不许～！Stop fighting! Nobody must make trouble here!

【胡狼】húláng〈名〉［动物］jackal

【胡噜】húlu〈动〉〈方〉1（擦）rub: 他用毛巾在脸上～了一把，就去上班了。He gave his face a quick rub with a towel and went off to work. 2（拂拭）sweep away: 把瓜子壳～到簸箕里 sweep the melon-seed husks into a dustpan

【胡乱】húluàn〈副〉1（马虎）casually: ～吃了点饭 eat a hasty meal 2（任意）at random: ～猜测 make wild guesses

【胡萝卜】húluóbo〈名〉carrot: ～素 carotene

【胡闹】húnào〈动〉make trouble: 不要在课堂上～！Don't play the fool in class.

【胡琴】húqin ▸**p. 929**〈名〉*huqin* [general term for two-stringed bowed instruments]

【胡人】húrén〈名〉〈古〉tribesmen inhabiting northern China

【胡说】húshuō A〈动〉talk nonsense: 别再～了！Stop talking nonsense! B〈名〉nonsense: 纯属～！Absolute nonsense!

【胡说八道】húshuō-bādào〈成〉1（瞎说）talk nonsense: 他这是在～。He is talking nonsense. 2（指话语）rubbish: 我看这纯属～。This looks like complete nonsense to me.

【胡思乱想】húsī-luànxiǎng〈成〉let one's imagination run wild: 喜欢～ be fond of daydreaming

【胡桃】hútáo〈名〉［植物］walnut

【胡同】hútòng〈名〉*hutong*

> **胡同**
>
> Beijing's lanes and alleys. In the past, Beijing was made up of neat rows of thousands of courtyard houses. For ease of entry and exit, there were passage ways, known as '*hutongs*', between the rows. The word *hutong* first appeared in the Yuan Dynasty during the construction of Dadu (大都, present-day Beijing). *Hutongs* and courtyard houses (▸四合院) are symbols of Beijing vernacular culture. Beijing people have a special affection for them. In the latter part of the 20th century and beginning of the 21st many *hutongs* disappeared to make way for new roads and modern buildings.

【胡图人】Hútúrén〈名〉Hutu ethnic group

【胡须】húxū〈名〉（指在腮下）beard;（在唇上）moustache

【胡言】húyán A〈动〉talk nonsense: 满口～ full of wild talk B = 胡说 húshuō B

【胡言乱语】húyán-luànyǔ〈成〉talk nonsense: 他在～，别信他。He is raving. Don't listen to what he says. ‖ 这篇社论全是～。This editorial is all rubbish.

【胡杨】húyáng〈名〉［植物］diversiform-leaved poplar

【胡诌】húzhōu〈动〉make up wild tales: ～一个理由 cook up an excuse ‖ 那只是我为逗她一笑而～的。That was just some nonsense that I made up to make her laugh.

【胡子】húzi = 胡须 húxū

【胡子工程】húzi gōngchéng〈名〉project that drags on for years

【胡子拉碴】húzilāchā〈形〉stubbly: 他好像总是～的。It seems he has permanent stubble.

【胡作非为】húzuò-fēiwéi〈成〉run amok: ～，肆无忌惮 give oneself up to evil without restraint

壶（壺）hú

〈名〉1（可加热的壶）kettle: 一～茶 a pot of tea ▸茶～, 水～ 2（指容器）flask〈英〉; canteen〈美〉: ▸油～, 暖～, 行军～

核 hú

▸hé

【核儿】húr〈名〉〈口〉1（果核）stone: 杏～ apricot stone 2（果核状物）sth. resembling a fruit stone: ▸煤～

斛 hú

A〈名〉dry measure used in former times
B〈量〉*hu* [originally equal to 10 *dou* (斗), later 5 *dou* (斗)]

葫 hú

【葫芦】húlu〈名〉calabash: 酒～ wine calabash ‖ 她～里到底装的是什么药？What has she got up her sleeve? ▸糖～

鹄（鵠）hú

〈名〉〈书〉［鸟类］swan
▸gǔ

【鹄立】húlì〈动〉〈书〉stand straight

【鹄望】húwàng〈动〉〈书〉eagerly look forward to

猢 hú

【猢狲】húsūn〈名〉monkey:〈喻〉树倒～散。When the boss falls from power, his lackeys disperse.

湖 hú

〈名〉1（湖泊）lake 2 Hú（指省份）Hu [another name for Hunan (湖南) or Hubei (湖北)]: 两～ Hunan and Hubei

【湖北】Húběi ▸**p. 661**〈名〉Hubei Province

【湖笔】húbǐ〈名〉Huzhou writing brush

h

ℹ 湖泊

■ 汉语里的“湖”、“池”、“泊”、“海”等都可指“湖”，大都用英语的 lake 来翻译。当然，像其他专有名词一样，也可将整个名称用汉语拼音来翻译：

鄱阳湖
= Lake Poyang
或 Poyang Hu

千岛湖
= Lake Qiandao
或 Qiandao Hu

长白山天池
= Lake Changbaishan Tianchi
或 Changbaishan Tianchi

罗布泊
= Lake Luobu Po
或 Luobu Po Lake
或 Luobu Po

净月潭
= Lake Jingyue
或 Jingyue Lake
或 Jingyuetan

洱海
= Lake Erhai
或 Erhai

■ lake 一词在英语中可置于湖泊名字的前面或后面，因此汉语的“湖泊”一般来说可有三种翻译方法：

巢湖
= Chao Lake
或 Lake Chao
或 Chao Hu

青海湖
= Lake Qinghai
或 Qinghai Lake
或 Qinghai Hu

纳木错
= Lake Nam Co
或 Nam Co Lake
或 Nam Co

■ 汉语里“湖”、“池”等都是出现在湖泊的名字后，而英语里 lake 一词通常出现在湖的名字前，但也有出现在后面的：

休伦湖
= Lake Huron

密歇根湖
= Lake Michigan

大熊湖
= Bear Lake

■ 英译汉时，英语中的湖泊名称都是用“湖”一词，但英语中有称 lake 的，也有称 water 的，在英国苏格兰还可称为 loch：

温德米尔湖
= Lake Windermere

贝加尔湖
= Lake Baikal

德文特湖
= Derwent Water
或 Derwentwater

恩纳代尔湖
= Ennerdale Water

尼斯湖
= Loch Ness

洛蒙德湖
= Loch Lomond

【湖滨】húbīn〈名〉lakeside
【湖吃海喝】húchī-hǎihē〈俗〉indulge in extravagant eating and drinking
【湖光山色】húguāng-shānsè〈成〉natural beauty of lakes and mountains
【湖广】Húguǎng〈名〉1（指元朝）province during the Yuan Dynasty [comprising present-day Hubei, Hunan, Guangdong and Guangxi] 2（指明朝）province in the Ming Dynasty [comprising present-day Hunan and Hubei]
【湖南】Húnán ▸**p. 661**〈名〉Hunan Province
【湖泊】húpō ▸**p. 305**〈名〉lake
【湖色】húsè〈名〉light green
【湖心亭】húxīntíng〈名〉mid-lake pavilion
【湖泽】húzé〈名〉lakes and marshes
【湖绉】húzhòu〈名〉［纺织］Huzhou crêpe silk

瑚 hú ▸珊瑚 shānhú

煳 hú〈形〉burnt: 饼子烤～了。The pancake is burnt.

鹕（鶘） hú ▸鹈鹕 tíhú

槲 hú〈名〉［植物］Mongolian oak
【槲寄生】hújìshēng〈名〉［植物］mistletoe
【槲栎】húlì〈名〉［植物］oriental white oak

蝴 hú
【蝴蝶】húdié〈名〉butterfly
【蝴蝶花】húdiéhuā〈名〉1［植物］fringed iris 2 = 蝴蝶结 húdiéjié
【蝴蝶结】húdiéjié〈名〉bow tie
【蝴蝶兰】húdiélán〈名〉［植物］iris

糊[1] hú
A〈名〉1（书）（粥）gruel 2（黏性物）paste: ▸糨～
B〈动〉1（以粥充饥）feed with gruel: ▸～口 2（粘）paste: ～窗户 paste a sheet of paper over a lattice window ▸裱～

糊[2] hú = 煳 hú
▸hū, hù
【糊糊】húhu〈名〉gruel
【糊精】hújīng〈名〉starch gum
【糊口】húkǒu〈动〉eke out a simple living: 养家～ provide for one's family
【糊里糊涂】húlihútū〈形〉muddle-headed: 她～地跟着那个男人离家出走了。She lost her head and went off with the man.
【糊墙纸】húqiángzhǐ〈名〉wallpaper
【糊涂】hútu〈形〉1（不明事理）confused: 装～ feign ignorance ‖ ～观念 muddled idea ‖ 聪明一世，～一时。No man can be free from occasional stupidities. 2（混乱）messy: 把事情搞得一塌～ make a mess of sth.
【糊涂虫】hútuchóng〈名〉blunderer
【糊涂账】hútuzhàng〈名〉chaotic accounts: 村上的财务全是一笔～。The village finances are in a total mess.

醐 hú ▸醍醐 tíhú

觳 hú
【觳觫】húsù〈动〉〈书〉tremble with fear

hǔ

虎 hǔ
A〈名〉tiger: 猛～ fierce tiger
B〈形〉vigorous: ▸～将
【虎斑草】hǔbāncǎo〈名〉［植物］tiger flower
【虎背熊腰】hǔbèi-xióngyāo〈成〉of powerful build
【虎贲】hǔbēn〈名〉〈古〉warrior
【虎步】hǔbù A〈名〉brisk and broad steps: 他几个～就追上了那个扒手，将其生擒。With a few brisk broad strides, he caught up with the pickpocket and got hold of him. B〈动〉exercise rule (over a region)
【虎胆】hǔdǎn A〈名〉tiger's gall bladder B〈形〉〈喻〉lion-hearted: ～英雄 fearless hero
【虎毒不食子】hǔ dú bù shí zǐ〈俗〉〈喻〉those who mistreat their children are worse than vicious beasts
【虎伏】hǔfú〈名〉［体育］hoop
【虎符】hǔfú〈名〉tiger tally
【虎父无犬子】hǔfù wú quǎnzǐ〈俗〉〈喻〉like father, like son
【虎虎有生气】hǔhǔ yǒu shēngqì〈俗〉full of vim and vigour
【虎将】hǔjiàng〈名〉brave general
【虎劲】hǔjìn〈名〉dash: 有一股子～ cut quite a dash
【虎鲸】hǔjīng〈名〉killer whale
【虎踞龙盘】hǔjù-lóngpán〈成〉forbidding strategic point
【虎口】hǔkǒu〈名〉1〈喻〉（险境）jaws of death: 落入～ fall into a dangerous situation 2（指部位）part of the hand between the thumb and the index finger
【虎口拔牙】hǔkǒu-báyá〈成〉〈喻〉dare to face the greatest danger
【虎口余生】hǔkǒu-yúshēng〈成〉〈喻〉have a narrow escape
【虎狼】hǔláng〈名〉person as ferocious or ruthless as a tiger and a wolf: ～之辈 cruel and ruthless person ‖ ～之心 voracious and wolfish heart
【虎落平阳被犬欺】hǔ luò píngyáng bèi quǎn qī〈俗〉〈喻〉a man who loses power or influence may be subjected to much indignity
【虎钳】hǔqián〈名〉vice: 万能～ universal vice
【虎生生】hǔshēngshēng〈形〉vigorous and forceful
【虎视】hǔshì〈动〉1（指贪婪）eye covetously 2（指威严）glare down
【虎视眈眈】hǔshì-dāndān〈成〉eye with hostility
【虎头虎脑】hǔtóu-hǔnǎo〈成〉sturdy and healthy: 这孩子长得～的。The child looks sturdy and healthy.
【虎头蛇尾】hǔtóu-shéwěi〈成〉fine start and poor finish: 做事情不能～。There's no point in getting things off to a good start and then letting them peter out.
【虎威】hǔwēi〈名〉power and prestige: 冒犯～ offend against sb.'s authority
【虎穴】hǔxué〈名〉tiger's den: ▸不入～，焉得虎子
【虎穴龙潭】hǔxué-lóngtán = 龙潭虎穴 lóngtán-hǔxué
【虎牙】hǔyá〈名〉〈口〉protruding canine tooth
【虎跃龙腾】hǔyuè-lóngténg = 龙腾虎跃 lóngténg-hǔyuè

浒（滸） hǔ〈名〉waterside:《水～传》*The Water Margin*

唬 hǔ〈动〉〈口〉bluff: 他在～人，别理他。He is bluffing. Don't take any notice of him. ▸吓～
▸xià

琥 hǔ
【琥珀】hǔpò〈名〉amber

hù

互 hù〈副〉mutually: ～帮～学 help each other and learn from each other ‖ ～不干涉内政 non-interference in each other's internal affairs ‖ ～通情报 keep each other informed ▸相～
【互补】hùbǔ〈动〉complement: 优势～ the virtues are mutually complementary ‖ 两国经济具有～性。The economies of the two countries are complementary to one another.
【互不通气】hùbùtōngqì〈动〉do not exchange information
【互动】hùdòng〈名〉interaction: 良性～ beneficial interaction ‖ 形成～效应 produce an interactive effect
【互访】hùfǎng〈动〉exchange visits: 两国体育代表团的～ exchange of sports delegations between the two countries
【互感】hùgǎn〈名〉［电气］mutual inductance
【互换】hùhuàn〈动〉exchange: ～备忘录 exchange memoranda ‖ ～座位 exchanged seats
【互惠】hùhuì〈动〉be mutually beneficial: ～关系 reciprocal relations ‖ ～待遇 reciprocal treatment ‖ ～关税 mutually preferential tariff ‖ 平等～ equality and mutual benefit
【互见】hùjiàn〈动〉1（参见）cross-refer 2（共存）coexist: ▸瑕瑜～
【互利】hùlì〈动〉be mutually beneficial: 平等～ equal and mutually beneficial
【互利共赢】húlì gòngyíng〈动〉reach a mutual benefit and win-win situation: 发展～的伙伴关系 develop a win-win parternship
【互联网】hùliánwǎng〈名〉Internet
【互让】hùràng〈动〉make concessions: 互谅～，解决争端 resolve disputes through mutual understanding and concessions
【互溶】hùróng〈名〉mutually dissolvable
【互生】hùshēng〈动〉［植物］alternate: ～叶 alternate leaves
【互通】hùtōng〈动〉exchange: ～情报 keep each other informed ‖ ～有无 help supply each other's needs
【互相】hùxiāng〈副〉mutually: ～爱慕 mutual love and admiration ‖ ～勾结 work in collusion ‖ ～配合 work in coordination ‖ ～依存 be interdependent
【互信】hùxìn〈动〉have mutual trust: 增进～ promote mutual trust
【互助】hùzhù〈动〉help each other
【互助会】hùzhùhuì〈名〉mutual help society
【互助组】hùzhùzǔ〈名〉mutual aid group

户 hù〈名〉1（门）door: 足不出～ never step out of one's house ‖ ～外活动 outdoor activities ▸门～，夜不闭～ 2（家）household: 挨～通知 notify

households door to door ‖ 困难～ family with financial or material difficulties ▸家家～～ 3（人） person engaged in certain business: ▸个体～, 猎～, 农～ 4（账户） bank account: ▸开～, 立～, 账～ 5（家境） family status: ▸门当～对

【户部】hùbù〈名〉〈旧〉 Ministry of Revenue in feudal China

【户籍】hùjí〈名〉 1（指册子） household register: ～警 policeman in charge of household registration ‖ ～科 household registration section 2（指身份） registered permanent residence: ～登记簿 census register

【户均】hùjūn〈名〉 per household average

【户口】hùkǒu〈名〉 1（指身份） registered permanent residence: 查～ check residence cards ‖ 迁～ report to the local authorities for change of domicile ‖ 长期～ permanent residence 2（住户和人口） number of households and total population

【户口簿】hùkǒubù〈名〉 permanent residence booklet

【户枢不蠹】hùshū-bùdù〈成〉 constant activities stave off decay

【户头】hùtóu〈名〉 (bank) account: 开～ open an account

【户限为穿】hùxiànwéichuān〈成〉 endless flow of guests

【户型】hùxíng〈名〉 type of layout of an apartment

【户长】hùzhǎng = 户主 hùzhǔ

【户政】hùzhèng〈名〉 household registration

【户主】hùzhǔ〈名〉 head of a household as registered on the residence card

护（護） hù〈动〉 1（保护） protect: ▸～墙板, ～林, 保～ 2（偏袒） be partial to: 遇事不要老～着自己的孩子。 In disputes, don't always take your child's side. ▸庇～, 袒～

【护岸】hù'àn〈名〉［水利］ bank revetment

【护壁】hùbì〈名〉［建筑］ wainscot

【护兵】hùbīng〈名〉 military guard

【护城河】hùchénghé〈名〉 city moat

【护持】hùchí〈动〉 1（维持） protect and maintain: 得有人～这个摊子。 We need someone to manage the business. 2（照看） look after: 她独自留在家～病母。 She was the only one left behind to take care of her sick mother.

【护从】hùcóng A〈动〉 follow and protect B〈名〉 follower and guard

【护犊子】hù dúzi〈动〉 protect one's own child

【护短】hùduǎn〈动〉 cover up one's mistakes: 想进步就不该给自己～。 If you want to improve, you shouldn't hide your shortcomings.

【护耳】hù'ěr〈名〉 earmuffs

【护法】hùfǎ〈动〉 1［宗教］ protect and maintain the Buddha dharma 2［历史］ uphold the constitution: ～运动 Campaign to Uphold the Provisional Constitution against the Northern Warlords

【护发】hùfà〈名〉 hair care: ～素 hair conditioner

【护封】hùfēng〈名〉 dust jacket

【护肤霜】hùfūshuāng〈名〉 body lotion

【护工】hùgōng〈名〉 nurse's aide

【护航】hùháng〈动〉 escort: 由军舰/战斗机～ be convoyed by warships/fighters

【护驾】hùjià〈动〉 escort the emperor

【护栏】hùlán〈名〉 railing

【护理】hùlǐ〈动〉 nurse: ～伤病员 tend to the sick and the wounded ‖ ～人员 nursing staff

【护理液】hùlǐyè〈名〉 contact lens solution

【护林】hùlín〈动〉 maintain and protect a forest: ～员 forest ranger

【护路】hùlù〈动〉 patrol and guard a road or railway: ～工 (railway) trackman

【护目镜】hùmùjìng〈名〉 goggles

【护盘】hùpán〈动〉［金融］ protect the stability of the market

【护坡】hùpō〈名〉［水利］［交通］ retaining wall: ～墙 slope wall

【护墙板】hùqiángbǎn〈名〉 wainscot

【护秋】hùqiū〈动〉 keep watch over autumn crops

【护身符】hùshēnfú〈名〉 1〈本〉 amulet 2〈喻〉 person or thing that protects one from punishment or censure

【护士】hùshi〈名〉 nurse: ～节 Nurses' Day ‖ 男～ male nurse

【护士长】hùshizhǎng〈名〉 head nurse

【护手霜】hùshǒushuāng〈名〉 hand cream

【护送】hùsòng〈动〉 escort: ～救灾物资车辆 convoy vehicles bringing relief to a disaster-stricken area ‖ ～伤员去医院 escort the wounded to a hospital

【护腿】hùtuǐ〈名〉［体育］ shin guard

【护腕】hùwàn〈名〉［体育］ wrist covering

【护卫】hùwèi A〈动〉 guard: ～大桥 guard the bridge B〈名〉 bodyguard

【护卫舰】hùwèijiàn〈名〉 corvette

【护卫艇】hùwèitǐng〈名〉 patrol gunboat

【护膝】hùxī〈名〉［体育］ kneecap

【护胸】hùxiōng〈名〉［体育］ chest protector

【护袖】hùxiù〈名〉〈方〉 oversleeve

【护养】hùyǎng〈动〉 1（护理培育） cultivate: ～秧苗 cultivate seedlings 2（保养维护） maintain: ～公路 maintain a highway

【护佑】hùyòu〈动〉〈书〉 safeguard: ～一方 safeguard a locality

【护照】hùzhào〈名〉 passport: 出示～ produce one's passport

沪（滬） Hù ▸p. 661〈名〉 Hu [another name for Shanghai（上海）]: ～宁铁路 Shanghai-Nanjing Railway

【沪剧】hùjù〈名〉 Shanghai opera

怙 hù〈书〉〈名〉 father: 失～ have lost one's father

【怙恶不悛】hù'è-bùquān〈成〉 be steeped in evil and refuse to repent

【怙恃】hùshì〈书〉 A〈名〉 parents: 少失～ become an orphan at a young age B〈动〉 depend on: ～权势 take advantage of one's power

戽 hù

A〈名〉 bailing bucket: ▸风～

B〈动〉 bail: ～水灌田 bail water to irrigate fields

【戽斗】hùdǒu〈名〉 bailing bucket

笏 hù〈名〉〈古〉 tablet held before the breast by officials when received in audience by the emperor

扈 hù〈动〉〈书〉 retinue

【扈从】hùcóng〈书〉 A〈名〉 retinue B〈动〉 escort

瓠 hù

【瓠子】hùzi〈名〉 1（指植物） calabash gourd 2（指果实） fruit of calabash gourd

鄠 Hù〈名〉 Hu [surname]

糊 hù〈名〉 paste: 辣椒～ chilli paste ‖ 芝麻～ sesame paste

▸hū, hú

【糊弄】hùnong〈动〉〈方〉 1（欺骗） fool: 你这是在～我们大家! You're making fools of us! 2（将就） go through the motions: 衣服是旧了些，先～着穿吧。 The clothes are a bit ragged but we'll just have to make do.

huā

花[1] huā

A〈名〉 1（花朵） flower: 采/摘～ pluck a flower ‖ 野～ wild flower ▸荷～, 开～, 茉莉～ 2（观赏植物） decorative plant: 浇～ water flowers ‖ 养～ raise flowers ▸～木, ～展 3（花状物） flower-like thing: ▸火～, 浪～, 雪～ 4（棉花） cotton: 纺～ spin cotton ‖ 废～ waste cotton ▸轧～ 5（烟花） fireworks: 放～ let off fireworks ▸～炮, 礼～ 6（滴珠） small drop; （颗粒状物） particle: ▸泪～, 盐～, 油～ 7（花纹） pattern: 白底蓝～ blue patterns on a white background ‖ 这块被面上的～儿很雅致。 The design on this quilt cover is quite elegant. 8（美女） pretty woman: ▸交际～, 校～ 9〈旧〉（妓女） courtesan: ▸～魁, 寻～问柳 10（外伤） wound: ▸挂～ 11（精华） cream: 文学之～ literary blossom ‖ 文艺之～ cream of literature and art 12（天花） smallpox: 出～儿 get smallpox ‖ 种～儿 vaccinate

B〈形〉 1（带有花饰） floral: ▸～灯, ～轿, ～篮 2（颜色斑驳） multicoloured: ～蝴蝶 multicoloured butterfly ‖ 小～狗 spotted puppy ▸～白, ～名册, ～哨 3（模糊） blurred: 看书看得眼～ read until the print becomes blurred ▸～镜, 老眼昏～ 4（不实在） florid: 你的字太～了。 Your handwriting is too fancy. ▸～架子, ～言巧语, ～招

花[2] huā〈动〉 spend: ～不少钱 spend a lot of money ‖ 很～时间 take a lot of time

【花把势】huābǎshi〈名〉 experienced florist

【花白】huābái〈形〉 grey: ～胡子 grey beard ‖ 头发～ grey-haired

【花瓣】huābàn〈名〉 petal

【花苞】huābāo〈名〉 bud

【花绷子】huābēngzi〈名〉 embroidery frame

【花边】huābiān〈名〉 1［印刷］ decorative border: 花瓶口上有一道～。 There is a floral border round the mouth of the vase. 2［纺织］ fancy lace: 镶～的衣服 dress trimmed with lace

【花边新闻】huābiān xīnwén〈名〉 1（轶闻趣事） titbit 2（绯闻） news of illicit love

【花布】huābù〈名〉 cotton print

【花不棱登】huābulēngdēng〈形〉〈口〉 loud: 她不喜欢穿～的衣服。 She doesn't like wearing loud clothes.

【花菜】huācài〈名〉［植物］ cauliflower

【花草】huācǎo〈名〉 flowers and plants

【花插】huāchā〈名〉 1（插花用的底座）

h

flower pad 2▸（花瓶） container for cut flowers

【花茶】huāchá〈名〉 scented tea: 茉莉～ jasmine tea

【花车】huāchē〈名〉 festooned vehicle

【花池】huāchí〈名〉 flower bed

【花丛】huācóng〈名〉 flowering shrubs

【花大姐】huādàjiě〈名〉〈口〉［昆虫］ ladybird

【花旦】huādàn〈名〉［戏曲］ *huadan* [one of the main female roles in Beijing opera]

【花道】huādào〈名〉 ikebana

【花灯】huādēng〈名〉 festive lantern: 看～ go to a festive lantern show

【花灯戏】huādēngxì〈名〉*Huadeng* opera

【花点子】huādiǎnzi〈名〉 1▸（怪主意） trick: 他又想耍～。 He's come out with his little tricks again. 2▸（指华而不实） fancy but impractical idea: 我要的不是这些～，而是可行性计划。 What I want is a workable plan, not any of these unrealistic ideas.

【花店】huādiàn〈名〉 florist's

【花凋叶落】huādiāo-yèluò〈成〉 flowers wither and leaves fall off

【花雕】huādiāo〈名〉 high-grade Shaoxing wine

【花缎】huāduàn〈名〉 figured satin

【花朵】huāduǒ〈名〉flower: 儿童是祖国的～。Children are the flowers of our motherland.

【花萼】huā'è〈名〉［植物］ calyx

【花儿】huā'er〈名〉*hua'er* [folk song]

【花房】huāfáng〈名〉 greenhouse

【花肥】huāféi〈名〉 fertilizer for potted plants

【花费】huāfèi A〈名〉 expense: 我觉得办公～太大。 I'm afraid the office expenses are too big. B〈动〉 spend: ～金钱 spend money ‖ ～精力 expend energy ‖ ～时间 spend time

【花粉】huāfěn〈名〉［植物］ pollen

【花岗岩】huāgāngyán A〈名〉 granite B〈形〉〈喻〉 incorrigibly obstinate: ～脑袋 obstinate thinking

【花格】huāgé〈名〉 lattice: ～呢 woollen check ‖ ～窗 lattice window ‖ 窗～ tracery

【花梗】huāgěng〈名〉 flower stalk

【花骨朵】huāgūduo〈名〉 bud

【花鼓】huāgǔ ▸**p. 929**〈名〉 flower-drum [folk dance]

【花鼓戏】huāgǔxì〈名〉 flower-drum opera

【花冠】huāguān〈名〉1▸（指花的一部分） corolla: 合瓣～ gamopetalous corolla 2▸（指帽子） wreath

【花好月圆】huāhǎo-yuèyuán〈成〉〈喻〉 perfect conjugal bliss: ～人长寿 perfect happiness and longevity

【花和尚】huāhéshang〈名〉 monks who violate religious discipline

【花红】huāhóng〈名〉 1▸［植物］ Chinese pear-leaved crab apple 2▸（指礼物） gift for a wedding or other happy events 3▸ = 红利 hónglì 4▸ = 赏钱 shǎngqián

【花红柳绿】huāhóng-liǔlǜ〈成〉 profusion of garden flowers

【花花公子】huāhuā-gōngzǐ〈成〉 playboy

【花花绿绿】huāhuā-lǜlǜ〈形〉 brightly coloured: 她都六十多了，还穿得～的。 Though over 60, she still dresses colourfully.

【花花世界】huāhuā-shìjiè〈成〉 this mortal world: 城市的～让她眼花缭乱。 She was dazzled by the gaiety and splendour of the city.

【花花肠子】huāhua-chángzi〈俗〉 cunning: 一肚子～ be full of cunning

【花环】huāhuán〈名〉 1▸（环状物） garland 2▸（指头戴装饰） wreath

【花卉】huāhuì〈名〉 1▸（花草）flowers and plants: ～展览 flower show ‖ 盆栽～ potted plants 2▸［美术］ painting of flowers and plants in traditional Chinese style: ～图 paintings of flowers and plants

【花会】huāhuì〈名〉 flower fair

【花季】huājì〈名〉〈喻〉 bloom of youth: ～少女 young girl

【花甲】huājiǎ〈名〉 cycle of sixty years: 年逾～ over sixty years old ‖ ～之年 sixty years of age

【花架】huājià〈名〉 shelf for holding potted flowers

【花架子】huājiàzi〈名〉 1▸（指武术架势） showy but useless martial arts movements: 他的剑术表演尽是些～。 His sword performance was full of showy movements. 2▸〈喻〉（指华而不实） mere form: 要练好基本功，不要学些～。 Spend time on basic training, not merely on outward form.

【花笺】huājiān〈名〉 fancy stationery paper

【花剑】huājiàn ▸**p. 909**〈名〉［体育］ foil

【花匠】huājiàng〈名〉 gardener

【花椒】huājiāo〈名〉［植物］ 1▸（指植物） Chinese prickly ash 2▸（指果实） seed of the Chinese prickly ash: ～粉 powder of Chinese prickly ash seed

【花轿】huājiào〈名〉〈旧〉 bridal sedan chair

【花街柳巷】huājiē-liǔxiàng〈成〉 red-light district

【花茎】huājīng = 花轴 huāzhóu

【花镜】huājìng〈名〉 presbyopic glasses

【花卷】huājuǎn〈名〉 steamed twisted roll

【花魁】huākuí〈名〉 1▸（指花） queen of flowers 2▸〈旧〉（指妓女） famous prostitute

【花篮】huālán〈名〉 1▸（装有花） flower basket 2▸（用花装饰） ornately decorated basket

【花蕾】huālěi〈名〉 bud: ～初绽 with first buds shooting out

【花里胡哨】huālihúshào〈形〉 1▸（指颜色） garish: 穿得～的 wearing garish clothes 2▸（指言辞） showy: 看他那～的样子，别指望他! Look how he's all show. You shouldn't count on him.

【花鲢】huālián〈名〉［鱼类］ variegated carp

【花脸】huāliǎn〈名〉［戏曲］ painted-face role [in traditional Chinese opera]

【花翎】huālíng〈名〉〈旧〉 peacock feather [as an adornment in Qing Dynasty times]

【花柳病】huāliǔbìng ▸**p. 50**〈名〉venereal disease (VD)

【花露水】huālùshuǐ〈名〉 toilet water

【花蜜】huāmì〈名〉 1▸（花露） nectar 2▸（蜂蜜） honey

【花面狸】huāmiànlí〈名〉［动物］ masked civet (cat)

【花名册】huāmíngcè〈名〉 register

【花木】huāmù〈名〉 flowers and trees: ～店 florist's

【花呢】huāní〈名〉 fancy suiting

【花鸟】huāniǎo〈名〉［美术］ traditional Chinese flower-and-bird painting: 从事～创作 do flower-and-bird paintings

【花农】huānóng〈名〉 flower grower

【花炮】huāpào〈名〉 fireworks and firecrackers

【花盆】huāpén〈名〉 flower pot

【花瓶】huāpíng〈名〉 1▸〈本〉 vase 2▸〈喻〉 woman employed for her beauty

【花圃】huāpǔ〈名〉 flower nursery

【花期】huāqī〈名〉［植物］ florescence: ～已过。 The flowering season is already past. ‖ ～将推迟。 The flowering season is going to be late.

【花旗】Huāqí〈名〉 Stars and Stripes: ～银行 First National City Bank of New York

【花旗参】huāqíshēn〈名〉 American ginseng

【花扦儿】huāqiānr〈名〉 1▸（指鲜花） fresh flowers picked with stems attached 2▸（指假花） artificial silk or paper flowers

【花前月下】huāqián-yuèxià〈成〉 setting for a couple in love

【花枪】huāqiāng〈名〉 1▸〈古〉（指兵器） short spear 2▸〈喻〉（花招） trickery: 耍～ play tricks

【花腔】huāqiāng〈名〉 1▸［音乐］ coloratura: ～女高音 coloratura soprano 2▸（指话语） guileful talk: 耍～ speak guilefully

【花墙】huāqiáng〈名〉 lattice wall

【花圈】huāquān〈名〉 (floral) wreath: 献～ place a wreath

【花拳绣腿】huāquán-xiùtuǐ〈成〉 boxing for show and without strength

【花容月貌】huāróng-yuèmào〈成〉 fair as a flower and beautiful as the moon

【花蕊】huāruǐ〈名〉［植物］ stamen

【花色】huāsè〈名〉 1▸（花纹和颜色） pattern and colour: ～好看 beautiful in design and colour 2▸（种类） variety: ～繁多 have a great variety of ‖ ～品种 range of goods

【花哨】huāshao〈形〉 1▸（指色彩） garish: 穿着～ garishly clad 2▸（指样式） ～的语言 flowery language

【花生】huāshēng〈名〉 peanut; groundnut〈英〉

【花生饼】huāshēngbǐng〈名〉 peanut cake

【花生酱】huāshēngjiàng〈名〉 peanut butter

【花生米】huāshēngmǐ〈名〉 shelled peanut

【花生糖】huāshēngtáng〈名〉 peanut brittle

【花生油】huāshēngyóu〈名〉 peanut oil

【花市】huāshì〈名〉 flower market

【花饰】huāshì〈名〉 1▸（花纹） decorative pattern: ～排版 ornament 2▸（花环） garland

【花束】huāshù〈名〉 bunch of flowers

【花丝】huāsī〈名〉 1▸［植物］ filament 2▸［美术］ filigree: ～工 filigree work ‖ ～镶嵌 filigree inlaying

【花坛】huātán〈名〉 raised flower bed

【花天酒地】huātiān-jiǔdì〈成〉 indulge in sensual pleasures

【花厅】huātīng〈名〉 drawing room in a large residence built in a garden or between courtyards

【花头】huātou〈名〉〈方〉 1▸（花招） ruse: 他的～真多。 He is full of fresh ideas. 2▸（奥妙）knack: 这种游戏的～真不少。 There are a lot of tricks involved in this kind of game. 3▸（花纹） decorative pattern

【花团锦簇】huātuán-jǐncù〈成〉highly decorative: 打扮得～ be splendidly dressed

【花托】huātuō〈名〉［植物］ receptacle

【花纹】huāwén〈名〉 decorative pattern: ～图案 floral design ‖ 这些瓷砖的～很别致。 These glazed bricks have very original designs on them.

【花坞】huāwù〈名〉 sunken flower bed

【花线】huāxiàn〈名〉 1▸（指线） coloured thread 2▸［电气］ wire; flex〈英〉

【花销】huāxiao〈口〉 A〈动〉 expend: 他每月挣的还不够自己～。 Every month he spends more than he makes. B〈名〉

expense: 这次旅游的～可不小。 The expenditure on this journey was quite large.

【花心】huāxīn〈形〉unfaithful: ～丈夫 unfaithful husband

【花序】huāxù〈名〉［植物］inflorescence: 伞形～ umbel ‖ 穗状～ spike

【花絮】huāxù〈名〉〈喻〉additional features: 运动会～ additional features on the sports meet

【花押】huāyā〈名〉〈旧〉signature: 在文件上画～ put one's signature on a document

【花芽】huāyá〈名〉［植物］flower bud

【花言巧语】huāyán-qiǎoyǔ〈成〉slick talk: 不管售货员怎样～，我太太还是没买那件衣裳。 My wife didn't buy the dress despite the salesperson's sweet-talk.

【花眼】huāyǎn **A** ▸**p. 50**〈名〉［医学］presbyopia **B**〈动〉be dazzled: 花色品种繁多，她都挑～了。 She was dazzled by the many varieties available.

【花样】huāyàng〈名〉**1**（花纹样式）variety: ～繁多 a great variety **2**（种类）kind **3**（花招）trick: 玩～ play tricks

【花样翻新】huāyàng-fānxīn〈成〉put old stuff in a new guise

【花样滑冰】huāyàng huábīng ▸**p. 909**〈名〉［体育］figure skating

【花样游泳】huāyàng yóuyǒng ▸**p. 909**〈名〉［体育］synchronized swimming

【花椰菜】huāyēcài〈名〉cauliflower

【花园】huāyuán〈名〉garden〈英〉; yard〈美〉: ～城市 garden city

【花展】huāzhǎn〈名〉flower show

【花账】huāzhàng〈名〉padded account: 开/造～ pad out one's accounts

【花招】huāzhāo〈名〉**1**（指武术招数）showy movement in *wushu* **2**（骗术）trick: 别耍～! None of your little tricks!

【花枝招展】huāzhī-zhāozhǎn〈成〉be gorgeously dressed: 打扮得～ gorgeously decked-out

【花钟】huāzhōng〈名〉flower clock

【花轴】huāzhóu〈名〉［植物］floral axis

【花烛】huāzhú〈名〉wedding candles: 洞房～夜 wedding night

【花柱】huāzhù〈名〉［植物］stylus

【花砖】huāzhuān〈名〉brick/tile with designs or holes: ～地 tile floor

【花子儿】huāzǐr〈名〉**1**（指花）flower seed **2**〈方〉（指棉花）cotton seed: ～油 cotton-seed oil

【花子】huāzi〈名〉beggar

哗（嘩）huā〈拟〉

clang: 大雨～～地下。 The rain poured down. ‖ 他～地一声拉上了铁门。 He pulled the iron-gate to with a clang.
▸huá

【哗啦】huālā〈拟〉crash: 碟子～一声掉了下去。The dishes fell with a crash. ‖ 风吹得树叶～～作响。The leaves rustled in the wind.

huá

划[1] huá〈动〉row: ▸～船, ～桨, ～水

划[2] huá〈动〉〈口〉pay: ▸～不来, ～得来, ～算

划[3]（劃）huá〈动〉scratch: ～火柴 strike a match ‖ 她的手～破了。 Her hands were scratched. ‖ 一道闪电～破长空。 A flash of lightning streaked across the sky.
▸huà

【划不来】huábulái〈形〉〈口〉not worthwhile: 现在有些农民认为种粮食作物～。 Some farmers now think that it is not worthwhile to grow grain crops.

【划船】huáchuán〈动〉row

【划船运动】huáchuán yùndòng〈名〉boating

【划得来】huádelái〈形〉〈口〉worthwhile: 接受良好的教育是～的。 It pays to get a good education.

【划桨】huájiǎng〈动〉paddle

【划拉】huála〈动〉〈方〉**1**（擦）brush away: 把大衣上的雪～掉 brush the snow off one's coat **2**（写）scribble: 小女孩用铅笔在纸上～。 The girl scribbled in pencil on the paper. **3**（捞取）procure

【划拳】huáquán〈动〉play a finger-guessing game

【划水】huáshuǐ〈动〉［体育］make strokes with one's arms

【划算】huásuàn **A**〈动〉calculate: ～来，～去，他决定不去旅行。 Having weighed up the pros and the cons, he decided not to make the journey. **B**〈形〉worthwhile: 很/不～ very/not worthwhile

【划艇】huátǐng ▸**p. 909**〈名〉［体育］Canadian canoe: 皮～ kayak

【划子】huázi〈名〉small rowboat

华[1]（華）huá

A〈古〉= 花 huā

B〈形〉**1**（繁荣）flourishing: ▸繁～, 荣～富贵 **2**（虚华）extravagant: ▸～而不实, 朴实无～, 奢～ **3**（光彩）magnificent: ～服 beautiful dress ‖ ～宅 magnificent house ▸～灯, ～丽 **4**〈敬〉（指对方）your: ▸～诞, ～章 **5**（指头发）grey: ▸～发

C〈名〉**1**［气象］corona: 日/月～ diffused sunlight/moonlight **2**（时光）time: ▸年～, 韶～ **3**（精华）cream: ▸才～, 精～

华[2]（華）Huá〈名〉

1（中国）China: 驻～大使 ambassador to China ▸～侨, ～人 **2**（汉语）Chinese: ～语广播 broadcast in Chinese ‖ 英～词典 English-Chinese dictionary
▸Huà

【华北】Huáběi〈名〉north China

【华表】huábiǎo〈名〉*huabiao* [ornamental column erected in front of palaces, tombs, etc.]

【华彩乐段】huácǎi yuèduàn〈名〉［音乐］cadenza

【华达呢】huádání〈名〉［纺织］gabardine

【华诞】huádàn〈名〉〈书〉〈敬〉your birthday

【华灯】huádēng〈名〉colourfully decorated lantern: ～初上 when the evening lights are lit

【华东】Huádōng〈名〉east China

【华而不实】huá'érbùshí〈成〉flashy and without substance: 我们应讲究实效，不搞～的东西。 We should be down-to-earth and strive for practical results in our work.

【华尔街】Huá'ěrjiē〈名〉Wall Street: 《～日报》*The Wall Street Journal*

【华尔兹】huá'ěrzī〈名〉waltz: 跳～ dance a waltz

【华发】huáfà〈名〉〈书〉grey hair: 早生～ have grey hair at an early age

【华服】huáfú〈名〉gorgeous clothes: 顶级名模展示了近50套～。 The top models modelled nearly fifty gorgeous outfits.

【华盖】huágài〈名〉〈书〉**1**（指伞盖）canopy **2**［天文］aureole **3**（恶运）bad luck: 交～运 have bad luck

【华工】huágōng〈名〉〈旧〉Chinese labourer working abroad

【华贵】huáguì〈形〉**1**（华美贵重）luxurious: ～的衣裳 luxurious clothes **2**（富有高贵）wealthy: ～之家 wealthy family

【华翰】huáhàn〈名〉〈书〉〈敬〉your esteemed letter

【华里】huálǐ〈名〉*li* [a Chinese unit of distance which equals to 1/2 kilometre]

【华丽】huálì〈形〉gorgeous: 服饰～ be gorgeously dressed and richly ornamented ‖ ～的辞藻 ornate language

【华美】huáměi = 华丽 huálì

【华南】Huánán〈名〉south China

【华侨】huáqiáo ▸**p. 279**〈名〉Chinese residing abroad: 归国～ returned overseas Chinese

【华人】huárén ▸**p. 279**〈名〉**1**（中国人）Chinese people **2**（有中国血统）foreign citizen of Chinese origin: 美籍～ Chinese American

【华沙】Huáshā〈名〉Warsaw

【华沙条约】Huáshā Tiáoyuē〈名〉Warsaw Treaty

【华盛顿州】Huáshèngdùnzhōu〈名〉Washington

【华盛顿哥伦比亚特区】Huáshèngdùn Gēlúnbǐyà Tèqū〈名〉Washington, DC

【华氏】Huáshì ▸**p. 776**〈名〉Fahrenheit: ～32度 thirty-two degrees Fahrenheit (32°F)

【华氏温标】Huáshì wēnbiāo〈名〉Fahrenheit temperature scale

【华文】Huáwén ▸**p. 918**〈名〉Chinese: ～报纸 Chinese language newspaper

【华西】Huáxī〈名〉west China

【华夏】Huáxià〈名〉〈古〉Cathay: ～子孙 descendants of Cathay

【华裔】huáyì ▸**p. 279**〈名〉foreign citizen of Chinese origin: ～社区 Chinese community overseas

【华语】Huáyǔ ▸**p. 918**〈名〉Chinese language: ～广播 Chinese broadcast

【华章】huázhāng〈名〉〈书〉〈敬〉your beautiful writing: 奉读～，受益匪浅。 I was greatly enlightened when I read your brilliant work.

【华中】Huázhōng〈名〉central China

【华胄】huázhòu〈名〉〈书〉**1**（指贵族）descendants of a noble family: 皇族～ descendants of an imperial family **2**〈旧〉（指华夏）people of Chinese ancestry

哗（嘩、譁）huá〈名〉

noise: ▸喧～
▸huā

【哗变】huábiàn〈动〉mutiny: 该国首都发生了军事～。 A mutiny took place in the country's capital.

【哗然】huárán〈形〉chaotic: 举座～。 The audience burst into an uproar. ‖ 舆论～。 Public opinion was turbulent.

【哗笑】huáxiào〈动〉laugh boisterously

【哗众取宠】huázhòng-qǔchǒng〈成〉play to the gallery: 无～之心 not have the intention of currying favour through twaddle

骅（驊）huá〈名〉〈书〉fine red steed

铧（鏵）huá〈名〉ploughshare: 双～犁 double-shared plough

猾 huá〈形〉sly: ▸奸～, 狡～

滑 huá

A〈形〉**1**（光溜） slippery: 雨后路～。The road becomes slippery after it's rained. ▸～腻, 光～ **2**（狡诈） cunning: ▸奸～, 油腔～调

B〈动〉**1**（快速移动） slip: ～了一跤 slip and fall ‖ 在冰上～行 glide on the ice ▸～冰, ～翔, ～行 **2**（蒙混） get away without punishment: 你别想能～过去。Don't think you can get away with it.

【滑板】huábǎn〈名〉［体育］skateboard

【滑板车】huábǎnchē〈名〉scooter

【滑冰】huábīng **A**〈名〉［体育］skating: 花样～ figure skating **B**〈动〉glide on ice: 在北方, 人们冬天常出外去～。In the north, people often go skating in winter.

【滑冰场】huábīngchǎng〈名〉skating rink

【滑草】huácǎo〈名〉［体育］grass skiing

【滑车】huáchē〈名〉［机械］pulley

【滑道】huádào〈名〉slide: 木材～ skid road

【滑动】huádòng〈动〉slide

【滑竿】huágān〈名〉litter made of bamboo poles

【滑旱冰】huá hànbīng〈动〉roller-skate

【滑稽】huájī **A**〈形〉comical: ～可笑 hilariously funny **B**〈名〉［戏曲］comic talk: ～剧团 farce troupe

【滑稽戏】huájīxì〈名〉farce

【滑精】huájīng〈名〉［中医］involuntary emission

【滑熘】huáliū〈动〉stir-fry with thick gravy: ～里脊 sautéed fillet with thick gravy

【滑溜】huáliu〈形〉〈口〉slippery: 这缎子摸起来很～。The satin feels smooth.

【滑轮】huálún〈名〉pulley: 定～ fixed pulley ‖ 动～ movable pulley

【滑腻】huánì〈形〉velvety: 皮肤～ creamy skin

【滑坡】huápō〈动〉**1**［地质］landslide: 因大雨造成山体～。There was a landslide because of the heavy rains. **2**〈喻〉slump: 经济～。The economy deteriorated.

【滑沙】huáshā〈名〉［体育］sand surfing

【滑石】huáshí〈名〉［矿业］talc

【滑石粉】huáshífěn〈名〉talcum powder

【滑爽】huáshuǎng〈形〉smooth and comfortable: 这件衬衫既挺括又～。The shirt looks firm and feels smooth.

【滑水】huáshuǐ〈名〉［体育］water skiing: ～板 hydro-ski

【滑膛枪】huátángqiāng〈名〉musket

【滑梯】huátī〈名〉slide

【滑天下之大稽】huá tiānxià zhī dàjī〈成〉be the biggest joke in the world

【滑头】huátóu **A**〈名〉slippery fellow: 他是个老～。He is a cunning old devil. **B**〈形〉slippery: 要～ act in a slick way

【滑头滑脑】huátóu-huánǎo〈成〉crafty

【滑翔】huáxiáng〈动〉glide

【滑翔机】huáxiángjī〈名〉glider

【滑行】huáxíng〈动〉**1**（滑动行进） coast: 冰上～ slide on the ice **2**（指飞机） taxi: 飞机在跑道上平稳地～。The plane taxied smoothly on the runway.

【滑雪】huáxuě ▸**p. 909**〈动〉ski: 高山～ alpine skiing ‖ 速度～ cross country ski racing

【滑雪板】huáxuěbǎn〈名〉skis

【滑雪衫】huāxuěshān〈名〉ski suit

【滑音】huáyīn〈名〉［音乐］portamento

豁 huá

▸huō, huò

【豁拳】huáquán = 划拳 huáquán

huà

化 huà

A〈动〉**1**（变化） change: ▸～合, ～石, 变～ **2**（使变为） turn: ～悲痛为力量 transform grief into strength ‖ ～敌为友 convert an enemy into a friend ▸～名, ～整为零 **3**（影响） influence: ▸感～, 教～, 潜移默～ **4**（募集） beg for alms: ▸～斋, 募～ **5**（融解） melt;（熔化） dissolve: 雪～了。The snow has melted. ‖ 塑料烤～了。The plastic was melted by heat. ▸溶～, 熔～ **6**（消化） digest: ～食 help digestion ‖ ～痰 reduce phlegm ▸消～ **7**（烧成灰烬） burn up: ▸焚～, 火～ **8**（死） die: ▸坐～

B〈名〉**1**（风气） customs and habits: 有伤风～ be a disgrace to the culture and the customs ▸文～ **2**（化学） chemistry: 数理～ mathematics, physics and chemistry ▸～肥, ～工, ～疗

C〈后缀〉-ify: ▸电气～, 工业～, 简～

【化除】huàchú〈动〉eliminate: ～隔阂 clear up misunderstandings ‖ ～偏见 dispel prejudice

【化冻】huàdòng〈动〉thaw

【化肥】huàféi〈名〉chemical fertilizer

【化粪池】huàfènchí〈名〉septic tank

【化腐朽为神奇】huà fǔxiǔ wéi shénqí〈成〉turn bad into good

【化干戈为玉帛】huà gāngē wéi yùbó〈成〉bury the hatchet

【化工】huàgōng〈简称〉= 化学工业

【化工厂】huàgōngchǎng〈名〉chemical plant

【化合】huàhé〈名〉［化学］chemical combination: ～反应 combination reaction ‖ ～物 chemical compound

【化合价】huàhéjià〈名〉valence

【化解】huàjiě〈动〉resolve: ～矛盾 settle a dispute

【化境】huàjìng〈名〉perfection: 这幅山水画已臻～。This landscape painting is a consummate work of art.

【化疗】huàliáo〈简称〉= 化学疗法

【化名】huàmíng **A**〈动〉use an assumed name **B**〈名〉alias: 嫌犯在犯罪期间用过许多～。The suspect went by several aliases in his criminal career.

【化募】huàmù = 募化 mùhuà

【化脓】huànóng〈动〉fester: 伤口～了。The wound is festering.

【化身】huàshēn〈名〉**1**（指形体） incarnation: 天使的～ incarnation of an angel **2**（指具体形象） embodiment: 智慧和勇敢的～ embodiment of wisdom and courage

【化石】huàshí〈名〉［考古］fossil: 活～ living fossil

【化痰】huàtán〈动〉［中医］reduce phlegm: ～止咳 reduce phlegm and stop coughing

【化外】huàwài〈名〉〈旧〉outside the pale of civilization

【化危为机】huà wēi wéi jī〈动〉turn a crisis into an opportunity: ～, 加快发展 turn crises into opportunities and accelerate development

【化为灰烬】huàwéi-huījìn〈成〉turn to dust and ashes

【化为泡影】huàwéi-pàoyǐng〈成〉vanish into thin air: 她的大学梦～。Her dream of going to college vanished into thin air.

【化为乌有】huàwéi-wūyǒu〈成〉come to nothing: 万贯家财一夜之间～。The immense wealth went up in smoke overnight.

【化纤】huàxiān〈简称〉= 化学纤维

【化险为夷】huàxiǎnwéiyí〈成〉head off a disaster

【化凶为吉】huàxiōngwéijí〈成〉change the portentous into the propitious

【化学】huàxué〈名〉chemistry: ▸无机～, 有机～

【化学变化】huàxué biànhuà〈名〉chemical change

【化学反应】huàxué fǎnyìng〈名〉chemical reaction

【化学方程式】huàxué fāngchéngshì〈名〉chemical equation

【化学分析】huàxué fēnxī〈名〉chemical analysis

【化学符号】huàxué fúhào〈名〉chemical symbol

【化学工业】huàxué gōngyè〈名〉chemical industry

【化学键】huàxuéjiàn〈名〉chemical bond

【化学疗法】huàxué liáofǎ〈名〉chemotherapy

【化学能】huàxuénéng〈名〉chemical energy

【化学式】huàxuéshì〈名〉chemical formula

【化学武器】huàxué wǔqì〈名〉chemical weapon

【化学纤维】huàxué xiānwéi〈名〉chemical fibre

【化学元素】huàxué yuánsù〈名〉chemical element

【化验】huàyàn〈动〉test: ～尿样/血型 test urine/sb.'s blood type ‖ ～结果 result of laboratory test

【化验单】huàyàndān〈名〉laboratory test report

【化验室】huàyànshì〈名〉laboratory

【化验员】huàyànyuán ▸**p. 966**〈名〉laboratory technician

【化油器】huàyóuqì〈名〉［机械］carburettor

【化淤】huàyū〈动〉［中医］eliminate stasis

【化育】huàyù〈动〉〈书〉bring up: ～万物 nourish all things on earth

【化缘】huàyuán〈动〉［宗教］beg for alms

【化斋】huàzhāi〈动〉[of a monk] beg for food

【化整为零】huàzhěngwéilíng〈成〉break the whole into parts

【化妆】huàzhuāng〈动〉put on make-up: ～师 make-up artist

【化妆品】huàzhuāngpǐn〈名〉cosmetics

【化装】huàzhuāng〈动〉**1**（为表演） make oneself up: 他在剧中～扮演一位教授。He made himself up for the part of a professor in the play. **2**（假扮） disguise oneself: 警察～成吸毒者接近毒枭。The policeman disguised himself as a drug user and approached the drug lord.

【化装舞会】huàzhuāng wǔhuì〈名〉fancy dress ball

划（劃）huà

A〈动〉**1**（分开） delimit: ～边界 delimit a boundary ‖ ～范围 delimit the sphere ▸～时代 **2**（计划） plan: ▸策～, 筹～, 出谋～策 **3**（指账目或钱财） assign: ▸～拨, ～款 **4** = 画 huà A4

B = 画 huà B3
▸huá
【划拨】huàbō〈动〉**1**（指账目或款项）transfer: 这笔款子将由中央银行～给你们。The sum of money will be transferred to you by the Central Bank. **2**（指财物）assign: ～物资 assign goods and materials
【划等号】huà děnghào〈动〉equate one thing with another
【划分】huàfēn〈动〉**1**（分成几部分）divide: ～行政区域 divide a country into administrative areas **2**（区别）differentiate: ～敌友 differentiate between enemies and friends
【划归】huàguī〈动〉put under sb.'s administration: 该企业已～地方管理。The enterprise has been put under the local administration.
【划价】huàjià〈动〉[of hospital] calculate medical expenses
【划款】huàkuǎn〈动〉transfer money
【划框框】huà kuàngkuang〈动〉〈喻〉set limits
【划清】huàqīng〈动〉draw a clear line of demarcation: （与某人）～界限 draw a clear line (with sb.)
【划时代】huàshídài〈形〉epoch-making: 具有～的意义 have epoch-making significance
【划一】huàyī〈形〉uniform: 整齐～ uniform
【划一不二】huàyī-bù'èr〈成〉**1**（不二价）fixed: 价钱～ fixed price **2**（无变化）cut and dried: ～的规定 hard and fast rule

华（華）Huà〈名〉Huashan Mountain
▸huá

画（畫）huà

A〈动〉**1**（指界限）delimit: ▸～地为牢 **2**（描绘）draw: ～水彩画 paint in watercolour ‖ ～油画 paint in oil ▸绘～ **3**（用文字描写）describe in words: ▸刻～，描～ **4**（做标记）draw: ～线 draw a line ▸～押 **5**（用手示意）gesture with one's hands: ▸比～，指手～脚
B〈名〉**1**（指美术作品类别）picture: 粉笔/蜡笔～ pastel ▸版～，壁～，风景～ **2**（装饰）sth. decorated with painting or pictures: ▸～舫，～廊，～屏 **3**（笔画）stroke of a Chinese character: "人"字有两～。The character 人 is made up of two strokes.
【画板】huàbǎn〈名〉［美术］drawing board
【画报】huàbào〈名〉pictorial
【画笔】huàbǐ〈名〉［美术］paintbrush
【画饼充饥】huàbǐng-chōngjī〈成〉feed on illusions: 望梅止渴，～ console oneself with false hopes
【画布】huàbù〈名〉canvas
【画册】huàcè〈名〉picture album
【画地为牢】huàdì-wéiláo〈成〉〈喻〉restrict activities to a designated area
【画舫】huàfǎng〈名〉gaily-painted pleasure boat
【画粉】huàfěn〈名〉tailor's chalk
【画符】huàfú〈动〉［道教］draw magic figures
【画幅】huàfú〈名〉**1**（图画）picture: 环湖风光是迷人的～。The scenery around the lake is a charming picture in itself. **2**（大小）size of a picture: ～虽小，所表现的景色却十分广阔。Small as the picture is, it expresses broad vistas.
【画稿】huàgǎo〈名〉rough sketch
【画工】huàgōng〈名〉**1**（指人）artisan painter **2**（指技艺）technique of painting: ～老道 expert painting technique
【画功】huàgōng = 画工 huàgōng 2
【画供】huàgòng〈动〉［法律］sign a written confession: 他们对他严刑拷打，逼迫～。They tortured him brutally and made him sign a written confession.
【画虎类犬】huàhǔ-lèiquǎn〈成〉〈喻〉aim high but achieve little
【画夹】huàjiā〈名〉portfolio
【画家】huàjiā ▸**p. 966**〈名〉artist
【画架】huàjià〈名〉easel
【画匠】huàjiàng〈名〉artisan painter
【画境】huàjìng〈名〉picturesque scene: 如入～ feel as though one were in a landscape painting
【画具】huàjù〈名〉［美术］painter's paraphernalia
【画句号】huà jùhào〈动〉〈喻〉finish
【画卷】huàjuàn〈名〉scroll painting
【画刊】huàkān〈名〉**1**（指报纸）pictorial section of a newspaper **2**（指杂志）pictorial
【画廊】huàláng〈名〉**1**（指走廊）painted corridor **2**（指展室）art gallery
【画龙点睛】huàlóng-diǎnjīng〈成〉〈喻〉add the finishing touch: 老师对我作文的几处改动，使主题跃然纸上，颇有～之效。The few modifications the teacher made to my composition helped to bring out the crucial point.
【画龙画虎难画骨，知人知面不知心】huà lóng huà hǔ nán huà gǔ, zhī rén zhī miàn bù zhī xīn〈俗〉in getting to know someone, you may know their face but not their heart
【画眉】huàméi〈名〉［鸟类］babbler
【画面】huàmiàn〈名〉**1**（指图画）tableau **2**［影视］frame
【画皮】huàpí〈名〉mask: 剥～ rip off a mask
【画片】huàpiàn〈名〉picture postcard: 电影明星～ picture of a film star ‖ 风景～ landscape postcard
【画屏】huàpíng〈名〉painted screen
【画谱】huàpǔ〈名〉**1**（指书）book on the art of drawing or painting **2** = 画帖 huàtiè
【画蛇添足】huàshé-tiānzú〈成〉〈喻〉ruin an effect by adding sth. superfluous
【画师】huàshī〈名〉**1**（指有造诣）master painter **2** ▸**p. 966**（指职业）artisan painter
【画十字】huà shízì〈动〉**1**［宗教］cross oneself: 在胸前～ cross oneself **2**（做标记）sign with an 'X': 在地契上画十字。mark a cross on the title deed
【画室】huàshì〈名〉studio
【画坛】huàtán〈名〉art world
【画帖】huàtiè〈名〉picture copybook
【画图】huàtú **A**〈动〉draw designs: ～员 designer **B** = 图画 túhuà
【画外音】huàwàiyīn〈名〉［影视］off-screen narration
【画像】huàxiàng **A**〈动〉draw a portrait: 他正在为一位老人～。He is drawing a portrait of an old man. **B**〈名〉portrait: 巨幅～ huge portrait ‖ 名人～ portrait of a celebrity
【画押】huàyā〈动〉make one's cross: 在合同上签字～ make one's cross on a contract
【画页】huàyè〈名〉plate
【画苑】huàyuàn〈名〉fine arts circles
【画院】huàyuàn〈名〉art academy
【画展】huàzhǎn〈名〉art exhibition
【画轴】huàzhóu〈名〉scroll painting: 山水～ landscape scroll painting
【画作】huàzuò〈名〉painting

话（話）huà

A〈名〉words: 让我把～说完。Let me finish. ‖ 她的～很有分量。Her words carry a lot of weight. ▸大～，说～，听～
B〈动〉talk about: ▸～别，～家常，～旧
【话白】huàbái〈名〉［戏曲］monologue
【话本】huàběn〈名〉script for storytelling
【话别】huàbié〈动〉say goodbye: 和朋友～ say goodbye to one's friend ‖ 与家人依依～ take a loving farewell of one's family
【话柄】huàbǐng〈名〉subject for ridicule: 给人以说长道短的～ give others a cause for gossip
【话不投机】huàbùtóujī〈成〉have a disagreeable conversation: ～半句多。When the conversation gets disagreeable, it's not worth wasting one's breath on another word.
【话茬儿】huàchár〈名〉**1**〈方〉（话题）thread of conversation: 接～ pick up the thread of a conversation ‖ 他没有接上～却又胡乱说了一通。He lost the thread of the conversation and went on talking nonsense for ages. **2**（语意）tone of one's speech: 听他的～，他知道一些内情。The way he talked suggested that he knew some inside story about the issue.
【话到嘴边留半句】huà dào zuǐbiān liú bànjù〈俗〉hold back what one wants or has to say even when it is on the tip of one's tongue
【话费】huàfèi〈名〉telephone bill: 缴纳～ pay a telephone bill
【话锋】huàfēng〈名〉topic of conversation: ～一转 switch the conversation to another subject
【话家常】huà jiācháng〈动〉chit-chat
【话旧】huàjiù〈动〉talk about the good old days: 故人相聚，难免～。When old friends meet, they can't help talking about the good old days.
【话剧】huàjù〈名〉stage play: ～团 theatrical troupe ‖ ～院 theatre
【话里有话】huàli-yǒuhuà〈成〉there is more to it than what is said: 他～，谁都听得出来。It was obvious to all that he meant something else.
【话篓子】huàlǒuzi〈名〉〈方〉chatterbox
【话梅】huàméi〈名〉preserved plum
【话说】huàshuō〈动〉[usu used to begin a story] the story says ...: ～三国时期… It is said that during the period of the Three Kingdoms ...
【话题】huàtí〈名〉subject of a talk: 热门～ hot topic ‖ 转换～ change the subject of a conversation
【话筒】huàtǒng〈名〉**1**（麦克风）microphone: ～噪声 microphone noise **2**（电话听筒）speaker: 放下/拿起～ put down/pick up the phone **3**（扩音器）megaphone
【话头】huàtóu〈名〉thread of discourse: 打断～ interrupt the flow of a conversation
【话务员】huàwùyuán ▸**p. 966**〈名〉(telephone) operator
【话匣子】huàxiázi〈名〉**1**〈方〉（留声机）gramophone **2**（收音机）radio receiving set **3**（指人）chatterbox: 他一打开～就说个没完没了。Once he starts talking, he never stops.
【话音】huàyīn〈名〉**1**（声音）sound of

one's voice: 第一个发言人的～刚落，第二个便站起来发言了。No sooner had the first speaker finished talking than the next stood up to speak. **2**〈口〉（语意）tone: 听他的～儿，准是另有打算。His tone implies that he has another axe to grind.

【话语】huàyǔ〈名〉remark: 他～不多，但切中要害。He said little, but what he said was very much to the point.

【话语权】huàyǔquán〈名〉right to speak: 发展中国家在国际事务中应有更多的～。Developing countries should have more right to express their views on international affairs.

【话中有话】huàzhōng-yǒuhuà = 话里有话 huàli-yǒuhuà

桦（樺）huà〈名〉［植物］birch

婳（嫿）huà ▸姽婳 guǐhuà

huái

怀（懷）huái

A〈名〉**1**（胸）bosom: 敞胸露～ bare one's chest ‖ 孩子在妈妈～里睡着了。The child fell asleep in his mother's arms. **2**（心意）mind: ▸耿耿于～, 情～
B〈动〉**1**（挂念）think of: ▸～旧, ～念, 缅～ **2**（怀有）cherish: ～有私心 harbour selfish motives ‖ 心～不满 nurse a grievance ▸～才不遇, ～恨, ～疑 **3**（怀孕）conceive: ～着他的孩子 conceive his child ▸～胎, ～孕

【怀抱】huáibào **A**〈名〉**1**（胸前）bosom: 回到祖国的～ return to the bosom of one's homeland ‖ 小女孩一下子扑到妈妈的～里。The girl threw herself into her mother's arms. **2**〈书〉（抱负）aspiration: 别有～ have other ambitions **B**〈动〉**1**（抱着）carry in one's arms: ～孩子 hold a baby in one's arms **2**（心中存有）cherish: ～远大的理想 cherish lofty ideals

【怀表】huáibiǎo〈名〉pocket watch

【怀才不遇】huáicái-bùyù〈成〉have unrecognized talents: 他常有～之感。He always felt like his talents went unrecognized.

【怀春】huáichūn〈动〉〈书〉become sexually awakened

【怀俄明州】Huái'émíngzhōu〈名〉Wyoming

【怀古】huáigǔ〈动〉be nostalgic for the past: 发～之幽情 express one's nostalgia for the past

【怀恨】huáihèn〈动〉bear a grudge against: ～在心 harbour a deep resentment

【怀旧】huáijiù〈动〉be nostalgic for the past: 人越老，越会～。The older we grow, the more we tend to get nostalgic for the past.

【怀恋】huáiliàn〈动〉look back nostalgically: ～童年生活 think fondly of one's childhood days

【怀念】huáiniàn〈动〉cherish the memory of: ～故乡 yearn for one's native land ‖ ～远方的友人 think of an absent friend who is far away

【怀柔】huáiróu〈动〉bring under control through conciliation: ～政策 policy of mollification

【怀胎】huáitāi〈动〉be pregnant: ～三月 be three months pregnant

【怀想】huáixiǎng〈动〉cherish the memory of: 我时常～我们在一起的愉快时光。I often think about the happy days we spent together.

【怀疑】huáiyí〈动〉**1**（不相信）doubt: 持～态度 take a sceptical attitude ‖ 我很～这个计划能否行得通。I very much doubt that this plan will work. **2**（推测）suspect: 我～这张百元钞票是假的。I suspect that this 100 *yuan* note is a counterfeit.

【怀有】huáiyǒu〈动〉harbour: ～敌意 harbour ill-intent ‖ ～野心 cherish wild ambitions

【怀孕】huáiyùn〈动〉be pregnant: 她～了。She is expecting.

徊 huái ▸徘徊 páihuái

淮 Huái〈名〉Huaihe River

【淮北】Huáiběi〈名〉northern part of Anhui Province

【淮海战役】Huáihǎi zhànyì〈名〉Huai-Hai Campaign

【淮河】Huáihé ▸**p. 294**〈名〉Huaihe River

【淮剧】huáijù〈名〉Huai opera

【淮南】Huáinán〈名〉southern part of Anhui Province

槐 huái〈名〉Chinese scholar tree: ▸刺～, 洋～

【槐花】huáihuā〈名〉flower of Chinese scholar tree

踝 huái〈名〉［生理］ankle

【踝骨】huáigǔ〈名〉ankle bone

耲 huái

【耲耙】huáibà〈名〉〈方〉north-east China harrow

huài

坏（壞）huài

A〈动〉**1**（变得无用）break down: 电视机～了。The TV set is out of order. **2**（破坏）destroy: ～某人的事 spoil sb.'s game ‖ 这孩子让父母给宠～了。The parents have spoiled the child.
B〈形〉**1**（不好）bad: ～消息 bad news ‖ ～影响 malign influence ‖ ～习惯 bad habit ▸～事 **2**（非常）very: 累～了 be exhausted ‖ 气～了 be beside oneself with rage ‖ 吓～了 be extremely scared
C〈名〉dirty trick: 使～ play a dirty trick

【坏处】huàichu〈名〉harm: 我看告诉她并没有什么～。I don't see any harm in telling her about it.

【坏蛋】huàidàn〈名〉scoundrel

【坏东西】huàidōngxi = 坏人 huàirén

【坏话】huàihuà〈名〉**1**（损害人的话）malicious remarks: 不要在背后讲别人的～。Don't say nasty things about people behind their backs. **2**（不顺耳的话）unpleasant words: 好话～都要听。We need to hear both nice and unpleasant words.

【坏疽】huàijū ▸**p. 50**〈名〉［医学］gangrene

【坏人】huàirén〈名〉bad person

【坏事】huàishì **A**〈名〉bad thing: 做～ do a bad thing ‖ ～可以变成好事。A bad thing can be turned into a good one. **B**〈动〉ruin sth.: 成事不足，～有余 unable to accomplish anything but liable to spoil everything ‖ 那样会～的。That will be the kiss of death.

【坏水】huàishuǐ〈名〉〈口〉evil trick: 满肚子的～ be full of deceit

【坏死】huàisǐ ▸**p. 50**〈动〉［医学］necrotize: 骨～ necrosis of bone

【坏血病】huàixuèbìng ▸**p. 50**〈名〉［医学］scurvy

【坏账】huàizhàng〈名〉［经济］bad debt or loan

huān

欢（歡）huān

A〈形〉**1**（高兴）happy: ▸～唱, ～庆, ～天喜地 **2**〈方〉（起劲）vigorous: 孩子们闹得正～。The kids are having a hell of a good time. ‖ 小伙子们干得可～了，都忘记了休息。The lads were so carried away with their work that they forgot to stop for a rest.
B〈名〉lover: 另有新～ carry on with another woman

【欢蹦乱跳】huānbèng-luàntiào〈成〉be healthy and vivacious: ～的年轻人 exuberant young people

【欢畅】huānchàng〈形〉〈书〉thoroughly delighted: 飞船发射成功，科学家们十分～。The scientists were elated by the successful launching of the spaceship.

【欢唱】huānchàng〈动〉sing merrily: 尽情～ sing to one's heart's content

【欢度】huāndù〈动〉pass a happy time: ～佳节 celebrate a festival with great joy ‖ ～晚年 spend one's remaining years in happiness

【欢歌】huāngē **A**〈动〉sing happily: ～曼舞 sing happily and dance gracefully **B**〈名〉happy singing: ～笑语 happy singing and cheerful talking

【欢呼】huānhū〈动〉hail: ～胜利 hail a victory ‖ 观众爆发出阵阵～声。Cheers broke out from among the spectators.

【欢呼雀跃】huānhū-quèyuè〈成〉shout and jump for joy: 当他们的领袖出现在主席台时，游行的人们～。When their leader appeared on the rostrum, the demonstrators started shouting and jumping for joy.

【欢聚】huānjù〈动〉have a happy reunion: 合家～ have a happy family reunion ‖ ～一堂 have a happy gathering

【欢快】huānkuài〈形〉lively: ～的气氛 cheerful atmosphere ‖ ～的音乐 merry music

【欢乐】huānlè〈形〉happy: ～的歌声 merry song ‖ ～的人群 happy crowd

【欢闹】huānnào **A**〈动〉play joyfully **B**〈名〉bustle

【欢洽】huānqià〈形〉friendly: 两情～ friendly relations between the two

【欢庆】huānqìng〈动〉celebrate joyously: 举行盛大游行～胜利 hold a great parade to celebrate the victory

【欢声】huānshēng〈名〉cheer

【欢声雷动】huānshēng-léidòng〈成〉cheers resound like rolls of thunder: 全场～。The audience broke into deafening cheers.

【欢声笑语】huānshēng-xiàoyǔ〈成〉cheers and laughter: 节日里处处洋溢着～。The day of the festival brimmed with cheers and laughter.

【欢送】huānsòng〈动〉see off: ～客人 cordially see the guests off ‖ ～仪式 farewell ceremony ‖ ～会 farewell party

【欢腾】huānténg〈动〉rejoice: 喜讯传来，举国～。The whole nation rejoiced at

h

the good news.

【欢天喜地】 huāntiān-xǐdì〈成〉 be overjoyed: ～庆丰收 celebrate the bumper harvest with great joy

【欢慰】 huānwèi〈动〉 be gratified

【欢喜】 huānxǐ **A**〈形〉 delighted: 满心～ be filled with joy ▸皆大～ **B**〈动〉 like: ～滑冰 like skating ‖ ～音乐 find delight in music

【欢笑】 huānxiào〈动〉 laugh heartily: 纵情～ laugh a hearty laugh

【欢心】 huānxīn〈名〉 liking: 讨人～ win people's favour ‖ 他竭尽所能想博取姑娘的～。 He did all he could to win the heart of the girl.

【欢欣鼓舞】 huānxīn-gǔwǔ〈成〉 be elated: 为成功而～ rejoice over one's success

【欢颜】 huānyán〈名〉 happy appearance: 强作～ force oneself to look happy

【欢宴】 huānyàn〈动〉 entertain sb. to dinner on some happy occasion

【欢迎】 huānyíng〈动〉 **1**（指迎接） welcome: ～惠顾 welcome to our shop ‖ 夹道～ line the street to welcome sb. **2**（指接受） receive favourably: 这首歌很受年轻人～。 The song is very popular with young people.

【欢迎词】 huānyíngcí〈名〉 welcoming speech

【欢悦】 huānyuè〈形〉 joyous: ～的笑声 merry laughter

【欢跃】 huānyuè〈动〉 be overjoyed

獾（貛） huān〈名〉［动物］ badger

【獾油】 huānyóu〈名〉［药学］ badger fat

huán

还（還） huán〈动〉 **1**（回） go back: ▸～家, ～俗, 生～ **2**（归还） give back: ～贷款 pay off one's loan ‖ ～东西 return borrowed articles ‖ 借你的钱下月～你。 I'll pay back the money I borrowed from you next month. ▸～债, 归～, 退～ **3**（回报） do sth. in return: ▸～击, ～礼, ～手

▸hái

【还报】 huánbào〈动〉 repay: 不图～ expect no return

【还本】 huánběn〈动〉 repay the capital: ～付息 repay capital with interest

【还魂】 huánhún〈动〉 return from the dead

【还击】 huánjī〈动〉 fight back: 自卫～ fight in self-defence

【还家】 huánjiā〈动〉 return home

【还价】 huánjià〈动〉 bargain: 明码标价，请勿～。 Prices as marked. No bargaining, please.

【还口】 huánkǒu〈动〉 answer back: 骂不～ give no comeback when sworn at

【还礼】 huánlǐ〈动〉 **1**（指敬礼） return a salute **2**（指礼物） give a gift in return

【还迁】 huánqiān〈动〉 move back

【还清】 huánqīng〈动〉 pay off

【还情】 huánqíng〈动〉 return a favour

【还请】 huánqǐng〈动〉 host a dinner in return

【还手】 huánshǒu〈动〉 hit back: 打不～ do not hit back when struck

【还俗】 huánsú〈动〉 return to secular life

【还席】 huánxí〈动〉 host a return dinner

【还乡】 huánxiāng〈动〉 return to one's native place: ▸告老～

【还乡团】 huánxiāngtuán〈名〉［历史］ landlords' restitution corps

【还阳】 huányáng〈动〉 come back to life

【还原】 huányuán **A**〈动〉 return to the original condition: ～颜色 return to the original colour **B**〈名〉［化学］ reduction: ～反应 reduction reaction ‖ ～剂 reductant

【还愿】 huányuàn〈动〉 **1**（指对神佛） redeem a vow **2**（指许诺） fulfil one's promise: 许愿就要～。 If you make a promise, you should keep it.

【还债】 huánzhài〈动〉 repay a debt: 借债容易～难。 It is much easier to run into debt than to get out of it.

【还账】 huánzhàng〈动〉 pay off one's debt

【还嘴】 huánzuǐ〈动〉〈口〉 answer back: 不许～! Don't give me any of your lip. ‖ 我没有立即～。 I didn't answer back at once.

环（環） huán

A〈名〉 **1**（圈） ring: ▸耳～ **2**（圈状物） hoop: ▸避孕～, 门～ **3**（环节） link: 关键的一～ key link ‖ 调查研究是解决问题的重要一～。 Investigation is an important part in solving a problem.

B〈动〉 surround: 四面～山 be surrounded by mountains ▸～城, ～球, ～行

C〈量〉［体育］ ring: 命中十～ hit the bull's eye ‖ 三枪打了29～ get 29-point rings with three hits

【环靶】 huánbǎ〈名〉［体育］ round target

【环保】 huánbǎo〈简称〉＝环境保护

【环抱】 huánbào〈动〉 encircle: 大海～的岛屿 island surrounded by sea ‖ 群山～的村庄 village nestling among hills

【环比】 huánbǐ〈动〉 link relative ratio: 房价～上涨10%，销量却～下降5%。 The link relative ratio of house prices has risen 10%, but the link relative ratio of sales volume has fallen 5%.

【环城】 huánchéng〈形〉 round the city: ～公路 ring road

【环城路】 huánchénglù〈名〉 ring road; beltway〈美〉

【环岛】 huándǎo〈名〉［交通］ roundabout〈英〉; traffic circle〈美〉

【环顾】 huángù〈动〉 look around: ～四周 look all around ‖ ～左右而言他 look around and start talking about other subjects

【环海】 huánhǎi〈动〉 surround the sea: 三面～ surrounded by sea on three sides

【环礁】 huánjiāo〈名〉［地理］ atoll

【环节】 huánjié〈名〉 **1**（一部分） link: 国民经济中最薄弱的～ weakest link in the national economy ‖ 中间～ intermediate link **2**［动物］ segment

【环节动物】 huánjié dòngwù〈名〉 annelid

【环境】 huánjìng〈名〉 **1**（自然环境） environment: 保护～ protect the environment ‖ 污染～ pollute the environment ‖ ～政策 environmental policy **2**（外在条件） surroundings: 适应新～ adjust to a new environment ‖ 投资～ investment climate

【环境保护】 huánjìng bǎohù〈名〉 environmental protection: ～标准 environmental protection standards

【环境壁垒】 huánjìng bìlěi〈名〉 green barrier or rampart

【环境标志】 huánjìng biāozhì〈名〉 eco-label

【环境监测】 huánjìng jiāncè〈名〉 environmental monitoring: ～系统 environmental monitoring system

【环境科学】 huánjìng kēxué〈名〉 environmental science

【环境卫生】 huánjìng wèishēng〈名〉 environmental sanitation

【环境污染】 huánjìng wūrǎn〈名〉 environmental pollution: 防止～ prevent environmental pollution

【环境要素】 huánjìng yàosù〈名〉 environmental element

【环境意识】 huánjìng yìshí〈名〉 environmental awareness: 增强～ enhance environmental awareness

【环境噪声】 huánjìng zàoshēng〈名〉 ambient noise

【环境质量】 huánjìng zhìliàng〈名〉 environmental quality: ～标准 environmental quality standards

【环流】 huánliú〈名〉［气象］ circulation: 大气～ atmospheric circulation

【环幕电影】 huánmù diànyǐng〈名〉 Circarama

【环球】 huánqiú **A**〈动〉 be around the world: ～旅行 round-the-world tour **B**＝寰球 huánqiú

【环绕】 huánrào〈动〉 encircle: 地球～太阳转。 The earth revolves round the sun. ‖ 小镇为群山～。 The little town nestles among hills.

【环山】 huánshān〈动〉 **1**（围绕着山） go round the mountain: ～公路 road going round a mountain **2**（被山围绕） be surrounded by hills: ～带水 surrounded by hills and girdled by water

【环生】 huánshēng〈动〉 occur in quick succession: ▸险象～

【环食】 huánshí〈名〉［天文］ annular eclipse

【环视】 huánshì〈动〉 look around

【环卫】 huánwèi〈简称〉＝环境卫生

【环线】 huánxiàn〈名〉 circular route: 地铁～ circular subway line

【环行】 huánxíng〈动〉 go in a circle: ～公共汽车 bus travelling a circular route ‖ ～公路 ring road

【环形】 huánxíng〈形〉 loop-like: ～公路 ring road

【环形山】 huánxíngshān〈名〉［天文］ lunar crater

【环氧树脂】 huányǎng shùzhī〈名〉［化学］ epoxy (resin)

【环游】 huányóu〈动〉 travel round: ～世界 make a round-the-world trip

【环宇】 huányǔ＝寰宇 huányǔ

【环子】 huánzi〈名〉 ring

桓 Huán〈名〉 Huan [surname]

圜 huán〈动〉〈书〉 encircle

▸yuán

阛（闤） huán

【阛阓】 huánhuì〈名〉〈书〉 business district

寰 huán〈名〉 extensive region: ▸尘～, 人～

【寰球】 huánqiú〈名〉〈旧〉 whole world

【寰宇】 huányǔ〈名〉〈书〉 whole world: 享誉～ be famous world-wide

缳（繯） huán〈书〉

A〈名〉 noose: 投～ hang oneself

B〈动〉 hang

【缳首】 huánshǒu〈动〉〈书〉 be hanged: ～之罪 crime punishable by hanging

鹮（鹮） huán〈名〉［鸟类］ ibis

鬟 huán〈名〉〈书〉coils of hair: ▸丫～, 云～

huǎn

缓（緩） huǎn
A〈形〉**1**（不紧张）relaxed: ▸～和, 弛～ **2**（慢）slow: ～步而行 walk slowly ‖ ～流 flow slowly ▸～慢, 迟～, 轻重～急
B〈动〉**1**（推迟）delay: ～办 put off doing sth. ‖ ～付 defer payment ▸～兵之计, ～期, ～限 **2**（恢复）recuperate: ～口气 have a respite ‖ 好半天才～过劲儿来。It took ages to recover the strength.

【缓兵之计】huǎnbīngzhījì〈成〉stalling tactics
【缓不济急】huǎnbùjìjí〈成〉be too slow to be of help
【缓步】huǎnbù〈动〉stroll: ～而来 advance slowly
【缓冲】huǎnchōng〈动〉buffer: ～余地 room for mitigation ‖ ～地带 buffer zone ‖ ～作用 cushioning effect
【缓冲器】huǎnchōngqì〈名〉buffer
【缓冲区】huǎnchōngqū〈名〉buffer
【缓和】huǎnhé **A**〈动〉ease off: ～紧张局势 relax the tension ‖ 形势有所～。Things have eased up a bit. **B**〈形〉mild: 口气～ mild tone ‖ 药性～。The medicine is quite mild.
【缓急】huǎnjí〈名〉**1**（指程度）degree of urgency: 处理问题要分别轻重～ handle matters in order of their importance and urgency **2**（指事）emergency: 今日储蓄以解来日之～。We deposit funds today to cover possible emergencies tomorrow.
【缓建】huǎnjiàn〈动〉delay construction
【缓解】huǎnjiě〈动〉alleviate: ～食品短缺状况 alleviate the food shortage ‖ ～痛苦 allay a pain
【缓慢】huǎnmàn〈形〉sluggish: 进展～ make slow progress
【缓坡】huǎnpō〈名〉gentle slope
【缓期】huǎnqī〈动〉put off: ～付款 defer payment ‖ 判处死刑，～二年执行 sentence to death with a two-year reprieve ‖ 会议因故～召开。For some reason, the conference has been postponed.
【缓气】huǎnqì〈动〉take a breather: 整天忙，一点～的时间也没有。We were busy all day and didn't have a moment's respite.
【缓限】huǎnxiàn〈动〉put off a deadline
【缓行】huǎnxíng〈动〉**1**（指行进）move slowly: 弯道～。Zigzag ahead. Drive slowly. **2**（指施行）put off: 工程～。The project has been postponed.
【缓刑】huǎnxíng〈动〉［法律］temporarily suspend the execution of a sentence: ～判决 probationary sentence
【缓役】huǎnyì〈动〉［军事］defer military service
【缓征】huǎnzhēng〈动〉postpone the imposition of a tax: ～税款 postpone tax payments

huàn

幻 huàn
A〈形〉imaginary: ▸～觉, ～听, ～想
B〈动〉be magical: ▸～术, 变～

【幻灯】huàndēng〈名〉slide show: 放～ show slides ‖ ～机 slide projector ‖ ～片 filmstrip
【幻化】huànhuà〈动〉change magically: 山间云雾～。Clouds and mist changed magically in the mountains.
【幻景】huànjǐng〈名〉illusion
【幻境】huànjìng〈名〉dreamland: 恍若置身～ feel as though one were in a fairyland
【幻觉】huànjué〈名〉［心理］hallucination
【幻梦】huànmèng〈名〉illusion
【幻灭】huànmiè〈动〉vanish into thin air: 他想暴富的美梦不久就～了。His dream of becoming rich overnight was soon dashed.
【幻视】huànshì ▸**p. 50**〈名〉［医学］photism
【幻术】huànshù〈名〉magic
【幻听】huàntīng ▸**p. 50**〈名〉［医学］auditory hallucination
【幻想】huànxiǎng **A**〈名〉illusion: 抱有～ entertain illusions ‖ 丢掉～ cast away illusions **B**〈动〉dream: 小女孩～自己有朝一日成为电影明星。The little girl fancies that she's going to be a film star some day.
【幻想曲】huànxiǎngqǔ〈名〉［音乐］fantasia
【幻象】huànxiàng〈名〉phantom
【幻影】huànyǐng〈名〉phantom
【幻影式战斗机】huànyǐngshì zhàndòujī〈名〉Mirage
【幻肢】huànzhī ▸**p. 50**〈名〉［医学］phantom limb

奂（奐） huàn〈形〉〈书〉**1**（众多）numerous **2**（鲜明）bright

宦 huàn
A〈动〉〈书〉hold public office: 仕～ have an official career
B〈名〉**1**（官吏）official: 官～ officialdom ▸～海, ～途, ～游 **2**（宦官）eunuch: 阉～ castrated official ▸～官

【宦场】huànchǎng〈名〉officialdom
【宦官】huànguān〈名〉eunuch
【宦海】huànhǎi〈名〉〈旧〉officialdom: ～沉浮 vicissitudes of official life
【宦门】huànmén〈名〉family of high officials
【宦途】huàntú〈名〉〈旧〉official career: ～坎坷 frustrated official career
【宦游】huànyóu〈动〉〈旧〉go seeking an official position: ～四方 go all over the place in pursuit of an official position

换（換） huàn〈动〉**1**（交换）exchange: 以物～物 barter one thing for another ‖ 用粮食～石油 trade grain for oil ▸互～, 交～ **2** ▸**p. 781**（改变）change: ～乘汽车 change buses ‖ ～衣服 change one's clothes ‖ ～个环境 change one's environment **3**（兑换）convert: 把人民币～成美元 convert *Renminbi* into US dollars

【换班】huànbān〈动〉change shifts
【换边】huànbiān〈动〉［体育］change sides
【换茬】huànchá〈名〉［农业］change of crops: ～轮作 change of crop in rotation
【换车】huànchē〈动〉change trains or buses: 在济南～ change (trains) at Jinan
【换乘站】huànchéngzhàn〈名〉interchange station: ～标志不清。Signs in the interchange station are not clear.
【换代】huàndài〈动〉**1**（指产品）replace: ～产品 new model ‖ 更新～ replace the old with the new **2**（指朝代、政权）change: ▸改朝～
【换挡】huàndǎng〈动〉［机械］shift gears: ～变速装置 power-shift gear box
【换发球】huànfāqiú〈名〉［体育］change of service
【换防】huànfáng〈动〉［军事］relieve a garrison
【换房】huànfáng〈动〉exchange housing
【换岗】huàngǎng〈动〉change the guard: 每两小时换一次岗。The guard changes every two hours.
【换个儿】huàngèr〈动〉〈口〉exchange positions: 试把床和沙发换个个儿，看怎么样。Let's see how it looks if we switch around the bed and the sofa.
【换工】huàngōng〈动〉exchange labour
【换货】huànhuò〈动〉exchange goods: ～贸易 barter trade
【换季】huànjì〈动〉change (clothes) with the season: 天热了，衣服该～了。It's getting hot. It's time we changed into summer clothes.
【换肩】huànjiān〈动〉shift the carrying pole from one shoulder onto the other
【换届】huànjiè〈动〉re-elect when a term of office expires: ～选举 re-election when the term of office expires
【换句话说】huànjùhuàshuō〈惯〉in other words
【换马】huànmǎ〈动〉〈喻〉have the person currently in charge replaced before his term is over: 即使球队连输两场，教练也不能中途～。We shouldn't change coaches halfway even if the team has suffered two straight losses.
【换毛】huànmáo〈动〉moult
【换脑筋】huàn nǎojīn〈动〉change one's way of thinking: 你得换换脑筋了，不然就落伍了。You've got to change your way of thinking, or you'll get behind the times.
【换气】huànqì〈动〉**1**（指游泳）come up for air **2**（指新鲜空气）change the air
【换气扇】huànqìshàn〈名〉ventilation fan
【换钱】huànqián〈动〉**1**（指零钱）change money **2**（指出售）sell
【换亲】huànqīn〈动〉[of two families] take each other's daughters as daughters-in-law
【换取】huànqǔ〈动〉get in return: ～外汇 get foreign exchange in return ‖ 以诚实～信任 earn the trust of others by one's honesty
【换人】huànrén〈动〉［体育］substitute one player for another: 客队～——13号下，7号上。Substitution for the visiting team: No 13 out; No 7 in.
【换算】huànsuàn〈动〉convert: 将英镑～成公斤 convert pounds into kilograms
【换汤不换药】huàn tāng bù huàn yào〈成〉same old stuff but with a different label: 他们的建议～，没有什么新东西。Their proposal has changed in form but not in content. There is nothing new here.
【换帖】huàntiě〈动〉〈旧〉exchange cards and become sworn brothers
【换位】huànwèi〈动〉change positions: ～思考 put oneself in sb. else's shoes
【换文】huànwén〈动〉exchange notes: 就建立外交关系～ exchange notes on the establishment of diplomatic relations
【换洗】huànxǐ〈动〉change and wash clothes: 带上～衣服 take a change of clothes ‖ 衣服要勤～。You should change and wash your clothes often.
【换血】huànxiě〈动〉〈喻〉reorganize by introducing fresh personnel: 球队要进行大～。The team is going to go through a radical shake-up.
【换牙】huànyá〈动〉[of a child] grow adult teeth

【换言之】huànyánzhī〈惯〉 in other words
【换样】huànyàng〈动〉 vary
【换药】huànyào〈动〉 redress (a wound): 我们必须给你的伤口按时～，三天一次。 We have to redress your wound on a three-day basis.

唤（喚） huàn〈动〉 call out: ▸呼～，叫～，召～
【唤起】huànqǐ〈动〉 **1**（使奋起） arouse: ～民众 spur on the masses **2**（引起） recall: ～对往事的回忆 evoke memories of the past ‖ ～公众的关注 arouse public attention to sth.
【唤醒】huànxǐng〈动〉 awaken: ～人民的良知 awaken people's conscience ‖ 把某人从梦中～ wake sb. out of a dream

涣（渙） huàn〈动〉 vanish
【涣然】huànrán〈形〉 vanishing: 晨雾～消散。 The morning mist has rapidly disappeared.
【涣然冰释】huànrán-bīngshì〈成〉 melt away: 听了他的解释，我们之间的误解～。 After his explanation, the misunderstanding between us cleared up.
【涣散】huànsàn **A**〈动〉 demoralize: ～斗志 lose morale **B**〈形〉 lax: 纪律～ be lax in discipline ‖ 精神～ be demoralized

浣 huàn〈动〉 wash: ～纱 rinse yarn ‖ ～衣 wash clothes
【浣熊】huànxióng〈名〉［动物］ raccoon

患 huàn
A〈动〉 **1**（担忧） worry: ▸～得～失，欲加之罪，何～无辞 **2**（得病） contract: ～肺炎/肝炎 contract pneumonia/hepatitis ‖ 身～重病 be seriously ill ▸～处，～者
B〈名〉 peril: ▸后～，水～，有备无～
【患病】huànbìng〈动〉 suffer from an illness
【患处】huànchù〈名〉 affected part of a patient's body
【患得患失】huàndé-huànshī〈成〉 worry about personal gains and losses
【患难】huànnàn〈名〉 trials and tribulations: 不经～不知福。 You cannot know the meaning of good fortune without experiencing bad. ▸同甘苦，共～
【患难夫妻】huànnàn fūqī〈名〉 husband and wife who have gone through thick and thin together
【患难见人心】huànnàn jiàn rénxīn〈俗〉 calamity is the touchstone of man
【患难见真情】huànnàn jiàn zhēnqíng〈俗〉 a friend in need is a friend indeed
【患难与共】huànnàn-yǔgòng〈成〉 go through thick and thin together
【患难之交】huànnànzhījiāo〈成〉 friend in need
【患者】huànzhě〈名〉 patient: 结核病～ TB patient

焕（煥） huàn〈形〉 shining: ▸～然一新
【焕发】huànfā〈动〉 **1**（光华四射） shine: ▸精神～，容光～ **2**（振奋） display vigour: ～精神 cheer up ‖ ～青春 radiate the vigour of youth
【焕然一新】huànrán-yīxīn〈成〉 take on an entirely new look: 经过翻修，我们的教学楼面貌～。 After renovation, our classroom building looks brand new.

痪（瘓） huàn ▸瘫痪 tānhuàn

豢 huàn
【豢养】huànyǎng〈动〉 keep: ～家禽 raise poultry ‖ 他不过是敌人～的一条走狗而已。 He was merely a cat's paw in the enemy's pay.

漶 huàn ▸漫漶 mànhuàn

鲩（鯇） huàn〈名〉 grass carp

huāng

肓 huāng ▸病入膏肓 bìngrùgāohuāng

荒 huāng
A〈形〉 **1**（荒芜） waste: 耕地～了。 The farmland lies in waste. ▸～芜 **2**（歉收） poor: ▸～年，～歉 **3**（荒凉） barren: ▸～岛，～郊 **4**（荒诞） absurd: ▸～诞，～谬 **5**（放纵） dissolute: ▸～淫
B〈名〉 **1**（荒地） wasteland: ▸开～，垦～ **2**（灾荒） famine: ▸救～，逃～ **3**（匮乏） shortage: ▸粮～，水～
C〈动〉 neglect: ～废学业 neglect one's studies ‖ 她的俄语有点儿～疏了。 Her Russian is a little rusty. ▸～废，～疏
【荒草】huāngcǎo〈名〉 weed: ～丛生 be overgrown with weeds
【荒村】huāngcūn〈名〉 deserted village
【荒村僻壤】huāngcūn-pìrǎng〈成〉 far-off village in a remote region
【荒诞】huāngdàn〈形〉 fantastic: ～离奇 absurd and incredible ‖ ～的想法 fantastic idea ‖ ～的行为 absurd behaviour
【荒诞不经】huāngdàn-bùjīng〈成〉 preposterous
【荒诞派】huāngdànpài〈名〉 the absurd: ～作家 absurdist
【荒诞无稽】huāngdàn-wújī〈成〉 fantastic and absurd: ～的故事 tall story
【荒岛】huāngdǎo〈名〉 uninhabited island
【荒地】huāngdì〈名〉 wasteland: 开垦～ reclaim wasteland ‖ ～造林 afforestation of wasteland
【荒废】huāngfèi〈动〉 **1**（无人耕种） leave uncultivated: 我们村没有～一亩土地。 Not a single *mu* of our land is left uncultivated. **2**（浪费） fall into disuse: ～的水渠又重新投入使用。 The irrigation canal that fell into disrepair is in use again. **3**（荒疏） neglect: ～学业 neglect one's studies ‖ 他的手艺曾经很高超，现在已经～了。 He used to be a good craftsman but now he's out of practice.
【荒古】huānggǔ〈名〉 remote antiquity
【荒火】huānghuǒ〈名〉 bush fire
【荒瘠】huāngjí〈形〉 bleak and barren: ～的土地 barren land in the wild
【荒寂】huāngjì〈形〉 wild and still: 四下空旷～。 It was bleak and quiet all round.
【荒郊】huāngjiāo〈名〉 wilderness: ～野外 desolate country
【荒凉】huāngliáng〈形〉 bleak and desolate: ～的景色 wild scenery ‖ 战乱使这个城市变得满目～。 The turmoil of war has desolated the city.
【荒乱】huāngluàn〈形〉 completely chaotic: 突然一阵枪响，人群陷入一片～。 The crowd fell into great disorder with the sudden roar of guns.
【荒谬】huāngmiù〈形〉 absurd: ～可笑 be ridiculous ‖ 他的建议太～。 His suggestion is completely absurd.
【荒谬绝伦】huāngmiù-juélún〈成〉 utterly absurd
【荒漠】huāngmò〈名〉 desert: ～变良田。 Desert turned into farmland.
【荒漠化】huāngmòhuà〈动〉 desertify
【荒年】huāngnián〈名〉 famine year
【荒僻】huāngpì〈形〉 desolate and out-of-the-way: 昔日～的草原如今变成了现代化的大油田。 The desolate grasslands of yesterday have now been turned into a modern oil field.
【荒弃】huāngqì〈动〉 lie waste
【荒歉】huāngqiàn〈形〉［of crops］ poor: 连年～ successive years of crop failure ‖ ～之年 lean year
【荒山】huāngshān〈名〉 barren mountain: ～秃岭 bare hills and mountains
【荒时暴月】huāngshí-bàoyuè〈成〉 lean year: 遇上～，最受煎熬的就是穷人。 It is the poor that suffer most in times of dearth.
【荒疏】huāngshū〈形〉 out of practice: 业务～了 become out of practice in one's work
【荒滩】huāngtān〈名〉 uncultivated beach
【荒唐】huāngtang〈形〉 **1**（古怪） absurd: ～可笑 ridiculous ‖ ～透顶 absolutely ridiculous **2**（放纵） dissipated: ～的生活 dissipated life
【荒无人烟】huāngwúrényān〈成〉 desolate and uninhabited: ～的地区 region with no sign of human habitation
【荒芜】huāngwú〈形〉 waste: 土地～。 The land lies desolate.
【荒墟】huāngxū〈名〉 waste land
【荒野】huāngyě〈名〉 wilderness
【荒淫】huāngyín〈形〉 dissolute: ～无度 indulge in sensual pleasures
【荒淫无耻】huāngyín-wúchǐ〈成〉 be openly given to debauchery: 过着～的生活 lead a loose and immoral life
【荒原】huāngyuán〈名〉 wasteland
【荒置】huāngzhì〈动〉 abandon: 设备长期～，造成极大浪费。 The equipment has lain unused for a long time, which is a terrible waste.
【荒冢】huāngzhǒng〈名〉〈书〉 abandoned grave

慌 huāng〈形〉 flustered: 一时～了手脚 be panicky for a time ‖ 沉住气，别～! Keep calm! Don't panic! ▸～乱，～张 ▸huang
【慌不择路】huāngbùzélù〈成〉 seize on any solution when hard pressed
【慌里慌张】huānglihuāngzhāng〈成〉 nervous and confused
【慌乱】huāngluàn〈形〉 flurried: 陷入～ be thrown into panic and confusion ‖ 枪击事件在学生中引起一阵～。 The shooting incident caused a fluster among the students.
【慌忙】huāngmáng〈形〉 greatly hurried: ～赶到现场 rush to the scene ‖ ～中走错路 take the wrong road in one's hurry
【慌神儿】huāngshénr〈动〉 be scared out of one's wits
【慌手慌脚】huāngshǒu-huāngjiǎo〈成〉 in a great flurry: 他办事总是～。 He always does things in a flustered way.
【慌张】huāngzhāng〈形〉 flustered: 神色～ look flustered ‖ 看他慌慌张张的样子，像是出了什么事。 From the frantic look about him, you could tell something had happened.

【慌作一团】 huāngzuòyītuán 〈成〉 be struck all of a heap

huáng

皇 huáng

A 〈形〉〈书〉 magnificent: ▸堂～

B 〈名〉 **1**（玉皇大帝） Jade Emperor: ▸玉～大帝 **2**（王帝） emperor: ▸～帝, 教～, 女～

【皇朝】 huángcháo 〈名〉 (imperial) dynasty

【皇城】 huángchéng 〈名〉 imperial city

【皇储】 huángchǔ 〈名〉 crown prince

【皇带鱼】 huángdàiyú 〈名〉 oarfish

【皇帝】 huángdì 〈名〉 emperor: ～的女儿不愁嫁。 Precious commodities never lack demand.

【皇恩】 huáng'ēn 〈名〉 imperial favour: ～浩荡。 The emperor's beneficence and magnanimity are vast and extensive.

【皇纲】 huánggāng 〈名〉 imperial law and order

【皇宫】 huánggōng 〈名〉 imperial palace

【皇冠】 huángguān 〈名〉 imperial crown

【皇后】 huánghòu 〈名〉 empress

【皇皇】 huánghuáng 〈形〉 magnificent: ～巨著 masterpiece

【皇家】 huángjiā 〈名〉 imperial family: ～卫士 imperial guard ‖ ～园林 imperial garden

【皇历】 huángli 〈名〉 almanac

【皇粮】 huángliáng 〈名〉 **1**〈旧〉（上交官府） grain tax to the government: 交～ pay grain tax **2**〈喻〉（由国家分发） funds, goods, etc. provided by the government: 吃～ be a government employee

【皇亲】 huángqīn 〈名〉 relative of the emperor

【皇亲国戚】 huángqīn-guóqì 〈名〉 member of the royal family

【皇权】 huángquán 〈名〉 imperial power

【皇上】 huángshang 〈名〉 **1**（指人） emperor **2**（用于称呼） Your Majesty

【皇室】 huángshì 〈名〉 **1**（指家族） imperial family **2**（指朝廷） imperial government: 背叛/忠于～ betray/be loyal to the imperial government

【皇太后】 huángtàihòu 〈名〉 empress dowager

【皇太子】 huángtàizǐ 〈名〉 crown prince

【皇天】 huángtiān 〈名〉 Heaven: ～在上 Heaven be my witness

【皇天不负苦心人】 huángtiān bù fù kǔxīnrén 〈俗〉 Heaven helps those who help themselves

【皇天后土】 huángtiān-hòutǔ 〈成〉 Heaven and Earth: ～, 可鉴吾心。 Heaven and Earth may witness my intention.

【皇位】 huángwèi 〈名〉 imperial throne

【皇子】 huángzǐ 〈名〉 emperor's son

【皇族】 huángzú 〈名〉 imperial kinsmen

黄 huáng ▸p. 863

A 〈形〉 yellow: 脸色发～ sallow face ▸面～肌瘦

B 〈名〉 **1** Huáng（黄河） Yellow River: 治～ harness the Yellow River ▸～泛区 **2**（黄色的东西） yellow-coloured animal product: ▸蛋～, 牛～, 蟹～ **3**（色情） pornography

C 〈动〉〈口〉 fizzle out: 昨天下大雨, 郊游～了。 Yesterday's excursion fell through because of the rain.

【黄斑】 huángbān 〈名〉 **1**［生理］ yellow spot **2**（指污渍） yellow stain

【黄包车】 huángbāochē 〈名〉〈方〉 rickshaw

【黄标车】 huángbiāochē 〈名〉 gas-guzzler: 加大～的更新力度 step up the replacement of gas-guzzling cars

【黄骠马】 huángbiāomǎ 〈名〉 horse with a yellow coat and white spots

【黄表纸】 huángbiǎozhǐ 〈名〉 yellow paper (for sacrificial use or worshipping gods)

【黄柏】 huángbò = 黄檗 huángbò

【黄檗】 huángbò 〈名〉 **1**［植物］ cork tree **2**［中药］ bark of the cork tree

【黄灿灿】 huángcàncàn 〈形〉 bright yellow: ～的麦子 golden wheat

【黄疸】 huángdǎn ▸p. 50 〈名〉［医学］ jaundice: 恶性～ malignant jaundice

【黄道】 huángdào 〈名〉［天文］ ecliptic

【黄道吉日】 huángdào-jírì 〈成〉 auspicious date

【黄澄澄】 huángdēngdēng ▸p. 863 〈形〉 golden: ～的金牌 glistening gold medal

【黄帝】 Huángdì 〈名〉 Yellow Emperor: ～陵 Mausoleum of the Yellow Emperor

> **黄帝**
>
> Huangdi (literally, 'Yellow Emperor'), the common ancestor of the peoples of the central China plain, according to tradition. Huangdi defeated the Yandi tribe, and formed an alliance to vanquish ignorant tribes. Huangdi and Yandi are regarded as the founders of China. Chinese people are therefore known as the descendants of Yan and Huang (炎黄子孙). Many things are believed to have been initiated during the time of Huangdi, such as Chinese medicine and the cultivation of silkworms.

【黄帝内经】 Huángdì Nèijīng 〈名〉 *Classic of Internal Medicine* [China's earliest classic work on medicine]

【黄豆】 huángdòu 〈名〉 soya bean: ～芽 soya bean sprout

【黄毒】 huángdú 〈名〉 pornographic material: 扫除～ eradicate pornography

【黄泛区】 huángfànqū 〈名〉 Yellow River Inundated Area

【黄蜂】 huángfēng 〈名〉 wasp: 大～ hornet

【黄姑鱼】 huánggūyú 〈名〉 spotted maigre

【黄瓜】 huángguā 〈名〉 cucumber

【黄海】 Huánghǎi 〈名〉 Yellow Sea

【黄河】 Huánghé ▸p. 294 〈名〉 Yellow River: ～故道 former course of the Yellow River

【黄褐斑】 huánghèbān ▸p. 50 〈名〉［医学］ chloasma

【黄褐色】 huánghèsè ▸p. 863 〈名〉 yellowish brown colour

【黄花】 huánghuā **A** 〈名〉 **1**（菊花） chrysanthemum **2**（金针菜） day lily **B** 〈形〉 virgin

【黄花菜】 huánghuācài 〈名〉 day lily

【黄花闺女】 huánghuā guīnü 〈名〉 virgin

【黄花鱼】 huánghuāyú = 黄鱼 huángyú 1

【黄昏】 huánghūn ▸p. 669 〈名〉 dusk: ～时分 twilight hours

【黄昏恋】 huánghūnliàn 〈名〉 twilight love

【黄酱】 huángjiàng 〈名〉 salted and fermented soya paste

【黄巾起义】 Huángjīn Qǐyì 〈名〉 Yellow Turban Uprising [peasant rebellion in 184 AD]

【黄金】 huángjīn **A** 〈名〉 gold: ～饰品 gold ornament ‖ ～储备 gold reserve **B** 〈形〉 golden: ～时段 golden time

【黄金搭档】 huángjīn dādàng 〈名〉 the best and most understanding partners

【黄金档】 huángjīndàng 〈名〉 prime time: 新电视剧将在～播出。 The new TV drama is going out on prime time.

【黄金地段】 huángjīn dìduàn 〈名〉 prime location

【黄金分割】 huángjīn fēngē 〈名〉［数学］ extreme and mean ratio

【黄金海岸】 Huángjīn Hǎi'àn 〈名〉 Gold Coast [former name of Ghana (加纳)]

【黄金时代】 huángjīn shídài 〈名〉 **1**（指时代） golden age **2**（指人生） prime of one's life

【黄金时间】 huángjīn shíjiān 〈名〉 prime time

【黄金周】 huángjīnzhōu ▸p. 836 〈名〉 golden week

> **黄金周**
>
> A seven-day public holiday, introduced in 1999. It takes place at National Day (1st to 7th October) and Spring Festival (Chinese New Year's Eve to the 6th of the first lunar month). Before 2008, it also included May Day. It is known as Golden Week because people spend money travelling and shopping at this time, and it is therefore a highly profitable period for business.

【黄精】 huángjīng 〈名〉［中药］ sealwort

【黄酒】 huángjiǔ 〈名〉 yellow rice wine

【黄口小儿】 huángkǒu-xiǎo'ér 〈成〉 baby

【黄蜡】 huánglà 〈名〉 beeswax

【黄鹂】 huánglí 〈名〉［鸟类］ oriole

【黄历】 huángli 〈旧〉 = 皇历 huángli

【黄连】 huánglián 〈名〉［中药］ rhizome of Chinese goldthread: 哑巴吃～ be a silent victim

【黄连木】 huángliánmù 〈名〉［植物］ Chinese Pistache

【黄连素】 huángliánsù 〈名〉［药学］ berberine

【黄粱美梦】 huángliáng-měimèng 〈成〉〈喻〉 pipe dream

【黄粱梦】 huángliángmèng = 黄粱美梦 huángliáng-měimèng

【黄磷】 huánglín 〈名〉 yellow phosphorus

【黄栌】 huánglú 〈名〉［植物］ smoke tree

【黄麻】 huángmá 〈名〉［植物］ jute: ～纸 jute paper

【黄毛丫头】 huángmáo yātou 〈名〉〈贬〉 saucy miss

【黄梅季】 huángméijì 〈名〉 rainy season

【黄梅天】 huángméitiān = 黄梅季 huángméijì

【黄梅戏】 huángméixì 〈名〉 Huangmei opera

【黄梅雨】 huángméiyǔ = 梅雨 méiyǔ

【黄米】 huángmǐ 〈名〉 glutinous millet

【黄鸟】 huángniǎo 〈名〉［鸟类］ canary

【黄牛】 huángniú 〈名〉 **1**（指动物） ox: 做人民的老～ be a willing horse for the people **2**〈方〉（倒票者） (ticket) tout 〈英〉; scalper 〈美〉

【黄牌】 huángpái 〈名〉 **1**［体育］ yellow card: 吃了一张～ get a yellow card ‖ 亮～ show a yellow card to sb. **2**（警告） serious warning

【黄袍】 huángpáo 〈名〉 imperial robe: ～加身 be acclaimed emperor

【黄皮书】 huángpíshū 〈名〉 **1**（指证明） International Certificate of Vaccination **2**（指文件） Yellow Paper

【黄浦江】 Huángpǔjiāng ▸p. 294 〈名〉 Huangpu River

【黄埔军校】 Huángpǔ Jūnxiào 〈名〉 Huangpu Military Academy

【黄芪】 huángqí 〈名〉［中药］ root of membranous milk vetch

【黄芩】 huángqín 〈名〉［中药］ root of large-flowered skullcap

【黄曲霉素】 huángqūméisù 〈名〉 aflatoxin

【黄泉】 huángquán 〈名〉 netherworld: 命

归～ die
【黄雀】huángquè〈名〉 siskin: ▸螳螂捕蝉，～在后
【黄壤】huángrǎng〈名〉 yellow earth
【黄热病】huángrèbìng ▸**p. 50**〈名〉［医学］ yellow fever
【黄色】huángsè ▸**p. 863** **A**〈名〉 yellow: ▸～人种 **B**〈形〉 obscene: ～电影 pornographic film ‖ ～书刊 pornographic books and periodicals
【黄色工会】huángsè gōnghuì〈名〉 blackleg union
【黄色领骑衫】huángsè lǐngqíshān〈名〉［体育］ yellow jersey
【黄色人种】 huángsè rénzhǒng 〈名〉 yellow race
【黄色炸药】huángsè zhàyào〈名〉trinitrotoluene (TNT)
【黄山】Huángshān〈名〉Huangshan mountain
【黄鳝】huángshàn〈名〉［鱼类］finless eel
【黄熟】 huángshú 〈名〉［农业］ yellow ripeness
【黄鼠狼】 huángshǔláng 〈名〉 yellow weasel
【黄鼠狼给鸡拜年，没安好心】huángshǔláng gěi jī bàinián, méi ānhǎoxīn〈歇后〉 harbouring no good intentions
【黄水仙】 huángshuǐxiān 〈名〉［植物］ daffodil
【黄汤】huángtāng〈名〉〈喻〉 wine
【黄糖】huángtáng〈名〉〈方〉brown sugar
【黄铁矿】huángtiěkuàng〈名〉 pyrite
【黄铜】huángtóng〈名〉 brass
【黄土】huángtǔ〈名〉［地质］ loess: ～高原 loess plateau
【黄萎病】 huángwěibìng 〈名〉［农业］ verticillium wilt: 棉花～ verticillium wilt of cotton
【黄癣】huángxuǎn ▸**p. 50**〈名〉［医学］ favus
【黄羊】huángyáng〈名〉 Mongolian gazelle
【黄杨】huángyáng〈名〉［植物］ Chinese little-leaf box: ～木 boxwood
【黄鼬】 huángyáo 〈名〉［动物］ yellow-throated marten
【黄页】huángyè〈名〉 yellow pages
【黄莺】huángyīng〈名〉 oriole
【黄油】 huángyóu 〈名〉 **1**（指食物） butter: 给面包上涂～ spread butter on bread **2**［化学］ grease: ～枪 grease gun
【黄鼬】huángyòu = 黄鼠狼 huángshǔláng
【黄鱼】huángyú〈名〉 **1**（指鱼） yellow croaker **2**〈方〉（金条） gold bar
【黄玉】huángyù〈名〉［矿业］ topaz
【黄种】huángzhǒng〈名〉 Mongoloid race: ～人 Mongoloid

凰 huáng ▸凤凰 fènghuáng

隍 huáng〈名〉 dry moat outside a city wall: ▸城～

喤 huáng
【喤喤】huánghuáng〈拟〉〈书〉 **1**（钟鼓声） sonorous and harmonious sound of bells and drums **2**（孩啼声） [of a baby] cry

遑 huáng〈名〉〈书〉 leisure: 不～ have no leisure time
【遑遑】huánghuáng〈形〉 hasty
【遑论】huánglùn〈动〉〈书〉 be out of the question: 衣食无着，～其他。 Without shelter and food, anything else is out of the question.

徨 huáng ▸彷徨 pánghuáng

惶 huáng〈名〉 anxiety
【惶惶】huánghuáng〈形〉 anxious: 人心～ in a state of anxiety
【惶惶不可终日】huánghuáng bùkě zhōngrì〈成〉 be in a constant state of anxiety
【惶惑】huánghuò〈形〉 perplexed and restless: ～不安 perplexed and uneasy
【惶惧】huángjù〈形〉〈书〉 terrified
【惶遽】huángjù〈形〉〈书〉 frightened: 神情～ look scared
【惶恐】 huángkǒng 〈形〉 terrified: ～不安 be seized with fear
【惶悚】huángsǒng〈形〉〈书〉 terrified

煌 huáng〈形〉 bright: ▸辉～
【煌煌】huánghuáng〈形〉 brilliant: 明星～。 The stars are sparkling.

潢[1] huáng〈名〉〈书〉 pool

潢[2] huáng〈动〉 dye or colour paper: ▸装～

璜 huáng〈名〉〈书〉 semi-annular jade pendant

蝗 huáng〈名〉 locust: 灭～ wipe out locusts
【蝗虫】huángchóng〈名〉 locust
【蝗蝻】huángnǎn〈名〉 nymph of a locust
【蝗灾】huángzāi〈名〉 plague of locusts

篁 huáng 〈名〉〈书〉 **1**（竹林） bamboo grove: 幽～ secluded and restful bamboo grove **2**（竹子） bamboo: 修～ tall bamboo

磺 huáng〈名〉 sulphur
【磺胺】huáng'àn〈名〉［药学］ sulphanilamide (SN)
【磺胺嘧啶】huáng'àn mìdìng〈名〉 sulphadiazine (SD)

癀 huáng
【癀病】huángbìng ▸**p. 50**〈名〉 anthrax

蟥 huáng ▸蚂蟥 mǎhuáng

簧 huáng〈名〉 **1** ▸**p. 929**［音乐］ reed: ▸巧舌如～ **2**（指部件） spring: 锁～ lock spring ▸弹～
【簧风琴】huángfēngqín ▸**p. 929**〈名〉［音乐］ reed organ
【簧片】huángpiàn〈名〉［音乐］ reed [in a musical instrument]

鳇（鰉） huáng〈名〉［鱼类］ kaluga

huǎng

恍 huǎng ▸惝恍 chǎnghuǎng

恍 huǎng
A〈形〉 not clear: ▸～惚
B〈副〉 seemingly: ▸～如梦境
【恍惚】 huǎnghū 〈形〉 **1**（神志不清） absent-minded: 精神～ be in a trance **2**（隐约） faint: ～记得 faintly remember ‖ 他～觉得有人在盯梢。 He was faintly aware that he was being followed.
【恍然】 huǎngrán 〈形〉 sudden: ～醒悟 suddenly wake up to reality
【恍然大悟】huǎngrán-dàwù〈成〉 suddenly see the light
【恍如隔世】huǎngrúgéshì〈成〉 feel as if one has been cut off from the outside world for a long time
【恍如梦境】huǎngrúmèngjìng〈成〉 as if in a dream
【恍若】huǎngruò〈连〉 as if
【恍悟】 huǎngwù 〈动〉〈书〉 suddenly wake up to reality

晃 huǎng
A〈形〉 shining: 明～～的刺刀 shining bayonet
B〈动〉 **1**（闪耀） dazzle: 汽车灯亮得～我的眼睛。 I was dazzled by the lights of a car. **2**（闪过） flash past: 大学四年一～就过去了。 Four years of college life passed in a flash.
▸huàng
【晃眼】huǎngyǎn **A**〈形〉 dazzling: 太阳光～，戴上墨镜吧。 Wear your sunglasses if you don't want to be dazzled by the blazing sun. **B**〈名〉 wink: 一～一个学期又过去了。 In the blink of an eye, another semester is over.

谎（謊） huǎng
A〈名〉 lie: ▸弥天大～，撒～
B〈形〉 false: ▸～话，～价
【谎报】huǎngbào〈动〉 lie about sth.: ～产量 lie about the output ‖ ～军情 make a false report about the (military) situation
【谎称】huǎngchēng〈动〉 falsely claim: 他～自己是大学毕业生。 He claimed he was a college graduate.
【谎话】huǎnghuà〈名〉 lie: 说～ tell a lie ‖ 她讲的全是～。 Her whole story was a tissue of lies.
【谎价】huǎngjià〈名〉 exorbitant price
【谎骗】huǎngpiàn〈动〉 cheat: 你讲的这一套～不了谁。 You can deceive no one with that story.
【谎信】huǎngxìn〈名〉〈方〉 rumour
【谎言】 huǎngyán 〈名〉 lie: 拆/戳穿～ expose a lie ‖ 捏造～ come up with a lie ‖ ～掩盖不了事实。 Lies cannot cover up facts.

幌 huǎng〈名〉 **1**〈书〉（幔帐） curtain: 窗～ window curtain **2**（店铺标志） shop sign: 酒～ signboard for a wine shop
【幌子】huǎngzi〈名〉 **1**（店铺标志） shop sign **2**（借口） cover: 他的话是骗人的～。 What he said was a facade.

huàng

晃 huàng〈动〉 shake: 他吓得两腿直～。 His legs were shaking with fear. ‖ 手别～，不然汤会撒出来。 Steady your hand, or the soup will spill over. ▸～动，摇～
▸huǎng
【晃荡】huàngdang〈动〉 **1**（摆动） rock: 来回～ swing to and fro ‖ 游艇在大浪中～。 The yacht pitched up and down on the waves. **2**（游荡） loaf around: 他整天在外面～。 He loafs around all day long.
【晃动】huàngdòng〈动〉 shake: 建筑物在

h

地震中剧烈地～。Buildings shook violently in the earthquake. ‖ 树枝在风中～。Branches sway in the wind.

【晃悠】huàngyou〈动〉 wobble: 梯子有点～。The ladder is wobbling. ‖ 他晃晃悠悠地往前走。He was staggering along.

huang

慌 huang〈形〉〈口〉[used after 得 as a complement] unbearable: 饿得～ be starving ‖ 心里闷得～ be bored to death ▸huāng

huī

灰 huī

A〈名〉**1**（燃烧后的粉末）ash: ▸～烬, 骨～, 火山～ **2**（粉状物）dust: 桌子上积了厚厚的一层～。There was a thick layer of dust on the desk. ▸～尘 **3**（石灰）lime: 抹～ apply mortar ▸～泥

B ▸**p. 863**〈形〉**1**（指颜色）grey〈英〉; gray〈美〉: ～制服 grey uniform ▸～色 **2**（沮丧）disheartened: ▸万念俱～, 心～意懒

【灰暗】huī'àn〈形〉 murky grey: ～的天空 gloomy sky

【灰白】huībái ▸**p. 863**〈形〉 pale: 脸色～ look pale

【灰不溜丢】huībuliūdiū ▸**p. 863**〈形〉〈方〉 greyish: ～的帽子 greyish cap

【灰不溜秋】huībùliūqiū = 灰不溜丢 huībuliūdiū

【灰尘】huīchén〈名〉 dust: 掸/拂去～ dust off ‖ 用吸尘器清除地毯上的～ do the carpets with a vacuum cleaner

【灰沉沉】huīchénchén〈形〉 gloomy: 天～的。The sky is overcast.

【灰度】huīdù〈名〉 shades of grey

【灰飞烟灭】huīfēi-yānmiè〈成〉 vanish like smoke

【灰肥】huīféi〈名〉［农业］ ash compost

【灰姑娘】Huīgūniang〈名〉 Cinderella

【灰光灯】huīguāngdēng〈名〉 limelight

【灰鹤】huīhè〈名〉［鸟类］ grey crane

【灰浆】huījiāng〈名〉［建筑］ mortar

【灰烬】huījìn〈名〉 ashes: 化为～ be reduced to ashes

【灰口铁】huīkǒutiě〈名〉［冶金］ grey iron

【灰领】huīlǐng〈名〉 grey collar

【灰溜溜】huīliūliū〈形〉 **1**（指颜色） dull grey: 墙上～的，该粉刷粉刷了。The wall is dingy and it needs whitewashing. **2**（指情绪、意志） dejected: 小伙子没有考上大学，感到～的。The young man felt crestfallen at his failure in the college entrance examinations.

【灰蒙蒙】huīméngméng ▸**p. 863**〈形〉 overcast: ～的夜色 dusky night scene ‖ 天色变得～的。The sky had become overcast.

【灰锰氧】huīměngyǎng〈名〉［化学］ potassium permanganate

【灰泥】huīní〈名〉［建筑］ plaster: 抹～ plaster

【灰雀】huīquè〈名〉［鸟类］ bullfinch

【灰色】huīsè **A**〈名〉 grey colour〈英〉; gray color〈美〉 **B**〈形〉 **1**（消极） gloomy: ～人生观 pessimistic outlook on life ‖ ～心情 gloomy mood **2**（不正当） ambiguous: ▸～收入

【灰色市场】huīsè shìchǎng〈名〉［金融］ grey market

【灰色收入】huīsè shōurù〈名〉 grey income

【灰沙】huīshā〈名〉 dust and sand

【灰鼠】huīshǔ〈名〉［动物］ squirrel

【灰头土脸】huītóu-tǔliǎn〈成〉 **1**（指外形） covered with dust **2**（指精神、心情） disheartened: 他受了挫折后就整天～的。He suffered a few setbacks and then felt miserable all day.

【灰土】huītǔ〈名〉 **1**（尘土） dust: 卡车开过，扬起一片～。The truck drove off in a cloud of dust. **2**［地质］ spodosol

【灰心】huīxīn〈动〉 lose heart: 别～! Don't lose heart! ‖ 虽连连失败，可他并不～。He's not discouraged despite repeated failures.

【灰心丧气】huīxīn-sàngqì〈成〉 be completely disheartened: 他的申请又被拒绝，他感到～。He felt totally depressed when his application was turned down again.

【灰熊】huīxióng〈名〉 grizzly (bear)

【灰指甲】huīzhǐjia ▸**p. 50**〈名〉［医学］ onychomycosis

【灰质】huīzhì〈名〉［生理］ grey matter: ▸脊髓～炎

诙（詼） huī〈书〉

A〈动〉 mock: ～谑 make fun of

B〈形〉 humorous: ▸～谐

【诙谐】huīxié〈形〉 humorous: 谈吐～ be witty in conversation

【诙谐曲】huīxiéqǔ〈名〉［音乐］ humoresque

挥（揮） huī〈动〉 **1**（挥动） wield: ～笔 wield a brush ‖ ～拳 wave one's fist ▸～动, ～戈, 一～而就 **2**（抹去） wipe off: ▸～汗如雨, ～泪 **3**（指挥） command: ▸～师 **4**（散发） scatter; （消耗） disperse: ▸～发, ～金如土

【挥动】huīdòng〈动〉 wield: ～警棍 wield a policeman's baton ‖ ～拳头 shake one's fist

【挥发】huīfā〈动〉 volatilize: ～性 volatility ‖ ～油 volatile oil ‖ 酒精～掉了。The alcohol evaporated.

【挥戈】huīgē〈动〉 lead troops to battle: ～东进 command one's army to march east

【挥汗如雨】huīhàn-rúyǔ〈成〉 be dripping with sweat

【挥毫】huīháo〈动〉〈书〉 wield one's brush: ～泼墨 take up a brush and paint ‖ ～作诗 take up a brush and write a poem

【挥霍】huīhuò〈动〉 spend lavishly: ～公款 squander public funds ‖ ～浪费 spend extravagantly ‖ 大肆～ recklessly squander

【挥霍无度】huīhuò-wúdù〈成〉 spend without restrain

【挥金如土】huījīn-rútǔ〈成〉 spend money like water: 他是个～的败家子。He is a wastrel who spends money like water.

【挥泪】huīlèi〈动〉 wipe away one's tears: ～告别 wipe away tears as one says farewell

【挥洒】huīsǎ〈动〉 **1**（指血、泪等） shed: 为祖国～热血 shed blood for one's country ‖ 将水～在马路上 sprinkle water over the street **2**（指作画、写作） paint or write with ease: ▸～自如

【挥洒自如】huīsǎ-zìrú〈成〉 write/paint with ease: 这位画家虽然年轻，却能～。Young as he is, the painter is able to wield his brush with facility and freedom.

【挥师】huīshī〈动〉〈书〉 command an army: ～南下 command an army to march south

【挥手】huīshǒu〈动〉 wave: ～告别 wave farewell ‖ 贵宾向欢迎人群～。The guest of honour waved to the welcoming crowds.

【挥舞】huīwǔ〈动〉 wield: ～花束表示欢迎 wave bouquets in welcome ‖ ～指挥棒 order people about

咴 huī

【咴儿咴儿】huīrhuīr〈拟〉 neigh

恢 huī〈形〉 vast: ▸～弘, 天网～～

【恢复】huīfù〈动〉 **1**（使还原） resume: ～邦交 resume diplomatic relations ‖ ～谈判 resume talks **2**（重新获得） regain: ～健康 recover one's health ‖ ～元气 recover one's strength ‖ ～知觉 regain consciousness ‖ ～自由 regain one's freedom **3**（重建） restore: ～名誉 rehabilitate a person's reputation ‖ ～原职 reinstate sb. in his old post ‖ ～原状 restore the original condition

【恢复期】huīfùqī〈名〉 convalescence

【恢弘】huīhóng〈书〉 **A**〈形〉 great: 气势～ with tremendous momentum **B**〈动〉 develop: ～士气 boost the morale

【恢宏】huīhóng = 恢弘 huīhóng

【恢恢】huīhuī〈形〉〈书〉 extensive: ▸天网～

晖（暉） huī〈名〉 sunlight: 落日余～ light of the setting sun ▸春～, 斜～, 朝～

辉（輝） huī

A〈名〉 radiance: ▸光～, 增～

B〈动〉 shine: ▸～映

【辉光灯】huīguāngdēng〈名〉 glow lamp

【辉煌】huīhuáng〈形〉 brilliant: ～成就 outstanding achievement ‖ 灯火～。The lights are spectacularly bright. ▸金碧～

【辉石】huīshí〈名〉［地质］ pyroxene

【辉映】huīyìng〈动〉〈书〉 reflect: ～成趣 cast beautiful reflections on each other ‖ 湖光山色，交相～。The lake and the hills lend each other radiance and beauty.

麾 huī

A〈名〉 standard of a commander

B〈动〉〈书〉 command: ～军前进 command an army to march forward

【麾下】huīxià〈名〉〈书〉 **1**〈套〉（将帅） commander **2**（部下） troops under one's command: 强将～无弱兵。There are no weak troops under an able general.

徽[1] huī

A〈名〉 emblem: ▸国～, 帽～

B〈形〉 excellent: ▸～号

徽[2] Huī〈名〉 Hui [another name for Anhui Province (安徽)]: ▸～剧

【徽标】huībiāo〈名〉 emblem: 设计～ design an insignia

【徽调】huīdiào〈名〉 tunes of Anhui opera

【徽号】huīhào〈名〉 **1**（指称号） title of honour **2**（指标识） insignia on a flag

【徽记】huījì〈名〉 sign

【徽剧】huījù〈名〉 Anhui opera

【徽墨】huīmò〈名〉 Huizhou ink stick

【徽章】huīzhāng〈名〉 badge: 戴～ wear a badge

huí

回[1] huí

A〈动〉 **1**（掉转） turn round: ～过身来 turn round ▸～顾, ～马枪, ～心转意

2（返回） return: ～到原处 return to where one came from ‖ 绝不能～到过去。 There must be no going back to the past. ▸～国, ～来 **3**（回答） reply: ▸～禀, ～复, ～信 **4**（谢绝） decline: ▸～绝 **5**（再处理） do again: ▸～锅, ～笼
B〈量〉 **1**（章节） chapter: 这部小说有35～。 This novel has 35 chapters. **2**（次） [used to indicate number of occurrences] time: 第一/二/三～ first/second/third time ‖ 来过一～ have been here once ‖ 头一～ first time **3**（件） [used for happenings or events]; piece: 我还弄不清是怎么一～事。 I can't make head or tail of it.

回[2]（**迴**） huí 〈动〉 **1**（旋绕） circle: ▸～旋, 峰～路转, 迂～ **2**（避开） avoid: ▸～避

回[3] Huí〈名〉 Hui ethnic group

【回拜】 huíbài〈动〉 pay a return visit: 改日～。 I'll return your visit some other day.
【回报】 huíbào 〈动〉 **1**（报告） report back: 我还没有向经理～出差情况。 I haven't yet reported back to the manager about the business trip. **2**（报答） repay: ～主人的盛情 repay the host for his kindness ‖ 施恩不图～。 We give without expecting anything in return. **3**（报复） get one's own back: 他干坏事定会遭～。 He will have to pay for his evil-doings.
【回避】 huíbì〈动〉 **1**（躲避） evade: ～矛盾 dodge contradictions ‖ ～要害问题 evade the crucial question **2**（不参与） withdraw: 你与案犯是亲属，应主动～。 As you are related to the defendant, you cannot be involved in the case.
【回禀】 huíbǐng〈动〉〈旧〉 report back
【回波】 huíbō〈名〉 ［电气］ echo
【回驳】 huíbó〈动〉 refute: ～原告的指控 refute the charge of an accuser ‖ 据理～ refute sb. on just grounds
【回采】 huícǎi〈名〉 ［矿业］ stoping: ～工作面 stope ‖ ～率 recovery rate
【回肠荡气】 huícháng-dàngqì 〈成〉 soul-stirring
【回肠九转】 huícháng-jiǔzhuǎn〈成〉 one's mind burning with anxiety and vexation
【回潮】 huícháo〈动〉 **1**（变潮） get damp: 草药要存放在干燥处，以免～。 The medicinal herbs must be kept in an arid place, or they will get damp. **2**〈喻〉（再现） resurge: 赌博之风有所～。 There has been a resurgence of gambling.
【回车】 huíchē〈动〉 **1**（指机动车） turn a vehicle back around **2**［计算机］ return: ～键 enter key
【回嗔作喜】 huíchēn-zuòxǐ 〈成〉 anger turns into joy
【回程】 huíchéng〈名〉 return trip: ～票 return ticket
【回抽】 huíchōu〈动〉 **1**［体育］ deliver a forehand strike: 快速发球，大力～ serve quickly with a powerful smash **2**［金融］ pull back: 股指迅速～ rapid pullback in the stock index
【回春】 huíchūn 〈动〉 **1**（指春天） [of spring] return: 大地～。 Spring has come around. **2**〈喻〉（指医术或药物） bring back to life: ～灵药 miraculous cure
【回答】 huídá〈动〉 respond: ～问题 answer a question ‖ 简要～ reply briefly ‖ 确切/明确的～ definite reply
【回单】 huídān〈名〉 receipt
【回荡】 huídàng〈动〉 resound: 牧羊人的歌声在山谷中～。 The shepherd's songs reverberated in the valleys. ‖ 体育馆里～着篮球迷们狂热的欢呼声。 The gymnasium reverberated with the wild cheers of the basketball fans.
【回电】 huídiàn **A**〈动〉 wire back: 请速～。 Wire back a reply immediately. **B**〈名〉 return cable: 这是经销部的～。 Here is the return cable of the sales department.
【回跌】 huídiē〈动〉 fall back: 股票大幅～。 Stocks dropped back sharply.
【回返】 huífǎn〈动〉 return
【回访】 huífǎng〈动〉 pay a return visit
【回放】 huífàng〈动〉 replay: ～磁带 replay the tape
【回复】 huífù〈动〉 **1**（回答） answer: 望速～。 We look forward to a speedy reply. **2**（复原） restore: ～到以前的水平 revert to the previous level
【回购】 huígòu〈名〉 buy back
【回顾】 huígù〈动〉 look back: ～过去，展望未来 look back at the past and look forward to the future
【回顾展】 huígùzhǎn 〈名〉 retrospective exhibition: 电影～ retrospective film show
【回光返照】 huíguāng-fǎnzhào 〈成〉〈喻〉 sudden spurt of activity prior to collapse
【回归】 huíguī **A**〈动〉 return: ～故里 return to one's homeland ‖ ～自然 return to nature **B**〈名〉［数学］ regression: ～方程 regression equation
【回归带】 huíguīdài〈名〉［地理］ tropics
【回归年】 huíguīnián〈名〉［天文］ solar year
【回归热】 huíguīrè ▸**p. 50**〈名〉［医学］ relapsing fever
【回归线】 huíguīxiàn〈名〉［地理］ tropic: 北～ Tropic of Cancer ‖ 南～ Tropic of Capricorn
【回锅】 huíguō〈动〉 cook again: 这菜回一下锅更好吃。 The dish tastes better when cooked twice.
【回锅肉】 huíguōròu 〈名〉 twice-cooked pork
【回国】 huíguó〈动〉 return to one's country
【回合】 huíhé〈名〉 round: 一场12～的比赛 a 12-round fighting
【回纥】 Huíhé〈名〉 *Huihe* [ancient name for the Chinese Uygur ethnic group]
【回护】 huíhù〈动〉 shield: ～孩子的错误是有害的。 It is harmful to shield the mistakes of your children.
【回话】 huíhuà **A**〈名〉 reply: 你能否接受我们的条件，请在一周内给个～。 Please confirm within a week whether you accept our offer. **B**〈动〉 reply: 事情成与不成，都请你尽快回个话。 Please reply as soon as possible as to whether you can do it or not.
【回还】 huíhuán〈动〉 return: 一去不～ leave and not come back
【回环】 huíhuán〈动〉 zigzag: 公路在山间蜿蜒～。 The highway winds along the mountain in zigzags and loops.
【回回】 Huíhui〈名〉〈旧〉 **1**（指民族） Hui ethnic group **2**（指人） *Hui* people
【回火】 huíhuǒ〈动〉 **1**［冶金］ temper **2**（逆火） backfire
【回击】 huíjī〈动〉 counter-attack: 给以有力的～ strike a powerful counter-blow
【回家】 huíjiā〈动〉 go home
【回见】 huíjiàn〈动〉 see you again
【回叫】 huíjiào〈名〉［通信］ callback
【回教】 Huíjiào〈名〉 Islam
【回敬】 huíjìng〈动〉 **1**（答谢） return a gift: ～一件更为珍贵的礼物 give a more precious gift in return **2**（报复） retaliate: ～一拳 return a blow
【回绝】 huíjué〈动〉 decline: 一口～ flatly refuse ‖ 我断然～了他的请求。 I vehemently rejected his request.
【回扣】 huíkòu〈名〉 kickback: 吃/拿～ take a kickback ‖ 他给中间人10%的～。 He offered the middleman a kickback of 10 per cent.
【回馈】 huíkuì〈动〉 **1**（回报） repay: ～社会 repay a debt to society **2**（反馈） feedback
【回来】 huílái〈动〉 return: 从外地～ return from other parts of the country ‖ 把他叫～! Get him back!
【回廊】 huíláng〈名〉 winding corridor
【回老家】 huí lǎojiā〈动〉 **1**（回故乡） return to one's hometown: ～探望年迈的双亲 go back to one's hometown to visit one's aged parents **2** ▸**p. 772**（死亡） [usu used mockingly or jocularly] die
【回礼】 huílǐ **A**〈动〉 **1**（指敬礼） return a salute: 来宾起立～。 The guests stood up in reply to a salute. **2**（指礼品） give a gift in return **B**〈名〉 return gift: 收到教授如此贵重的～，使我受宠若惊。 I felt flattered to get such a valuable return gift from my professor.
【回历】 Huílì〈名〉 Islamic calendar
【回流】 huíliú〈动〉 flow inversely: 人才～ the return of talents from abroad ‖ ～电路 return circuit ‖ 河水～。 The river flowed backwards.
【回笼】 huílóng〈动〉 **1**（指食品） steam again: 把凉馒头回回笼 heat up the cold steamed buns **2**（指货币） withdraw (currency) from circulation: ～货币 recover banknotes from circulation
【回笼觉】 huílóngjiào〈名〉〈口〉 another sleep (after waking up in the morning)
【回炉】 huílú〈动〉 **1**（指金属） melt down: 废铁～ melt down scrap iron **2**（指食品） bake again **3**（指学习） retrain by taking refresher courses: ～复读 retrain and restudy
【回路】 huílù〈名〉 **1**（指道路） retreat: 我们已经切断了敌人的～。 We have cut the enemy's retreat. **2**［电气］ return circuit: ～电流 loop current
【回落】 huíluò〈动〉 drop: 轿车价格一直在～。 The price of cars is steadily coming down.
【回马枪】 huímǎqiāng〈名〉 back thrust: 杀他个～ swing round and catch sb. off guard
【回门】 huímén〈动〉（指妻子） visit her own family with her newly-wed husband; （指丈夫） visit his in-laws with his newly-wed wife
【回民】 Huímín〈名〉 *Hui* people
【回眸】 huímóu〈动〉〈书〉 look back: ～一笑 [a young woman] show her charming expression
【回目】 huímù〈名〉 [of a traditional novel] chapter subtitle
【回念】 huíniàn〈动〉 recall: ～往事 think of past events
【回娘家】 huí niángjia〈动〉 **1**（指妻子） visit her parents **2**〈喻〉（回原处） return to his place of origin or former work unit
【回暖】 huínuǎn〈动〉 get warm again after a cold spell
【回聘】 huípìn = 返聘 fǎnpìn
【回棋】 huíqí = 悔棋 huǐqí
【回迁】 huíqiān〈动〉 move back: ～户 residents returning to new houses in their original place of residence
【回青】 huíqīng = 返青 fǎnqīng

【回请】huíqǐng〈动〉return hospitality
【回球】huíqiú〈动〉return: ～下网 the return went under the net ‖ 他的～质量不高。His returns are lousy.
【回去】huíqù〈动〉go back: 拿～ take sth. back ‖ 缩～ retract ‖ 明天～好吗? Will it be all right for you to go back home tomorrow?
【回绕】huírào〈形〉zigzagging
【回身】huíshēn〈动〉turn round
【回神】huíshén〈动〉〈口〉come to one's senses: 没等她回过神儿来，小偷已经逃之夭夭了。Before she realized what had happened, the pickpocket had disappeared.
【回升】huíshēng〈动〉pick up: 气温～。The temperature has gone up again. ‖ 指数～。The index is picking up.
【回生】huíshēng〈动〉1▸（重生）bring back to life: ～乏术 know no way of reviving the dead ▸起死～ 2▸（变生疏）be out of practice: 几十年不用，他的日语～了。He hasn't used his Japanese for decades and it has got rusty.
【回声】huíshēng〈名〉echo
【回师】huíshī〈动〉bring back the troops
【回收】huíshōu〈动〉recover: ～贷款 collect loans ‖ ～贵重金属 retrieve precious metals ‖ ～卫星 recover a satellite ‖ ～利用 recycle
【回收舱】huíshōucāng〈名〉［航天］recovery capsule
【回收箱】huíshōuxiāng〈名〉recycle bin: 垃圾～ rubbish recycle bin ‖ 废旧电池/过期药品～ used battery/expired drugs disposal bin
【回手】huíshǒu〈动〉1▸（指动作）turn round and stretch out one's hand: 他抱起孩子走下车，再～把门锁上。He held the baby in his arms, stepped out of the car and then turned round to lock the door. 2▸（还击）hit back: 她打了他，可他并没有～。She hit him, but he didn't hit her back.
【回首】huíshǒu〈动〉1▸（转回头）turn round: 她频频～，不忍离去。She kept looking back, not wanting to leave. 2▸〈书〉（回顾）look back: 往事不堪～ cannot bear to think of the past
【回书】huíshū〈动〉〈书〉write a letter in reply
【回赎】huíshú〈名〉redeem: ～首饰 redeem one's jewellery from a pawnshop
【回水】huíshuǐ〈名〉［水利］backwater: ～阀 water return valve
【回溯】huísù〈动〉look back upon: ～往事 recall past events
【回天】huítiān〈动〉save a desperate situation: ～乏术 be unable to save the situation ‖ ～之力 power capable of saving a desperate situation
【回填】huítián〈动〉［建筑］backfill: ～工程 stemming operation
【回条】huítiáo〈名〉receipt: 我给你写个～。I'll write you out a receipt.
【回头】huítóu A〈动〉1▸（扭回头）turn round: ～看看是谁在喊 turn round to see who is calling 2▸（返回来）go back: 我已经跟他分手，再也不会～了。We have split up and I would never go back to him. 3▸（悔改）repent: 你现在～还不晚。It's not too late for you to repent. B〈副〉〈口〉later: 咱们～再谈。Let's talk it over some other time.
【回头见】huítóujiàn〈动〉see you later
【回头客】huítóukè〈名〉regular: 这家餐馆能够兴旺，靠的是～。It's the regulars of this restaurant who make it flourish.
【回头路】huítóulù〈名〉road back to one's former position: 走～ backtrack
【回头率】huítóulǜ〈名〉rate of second glance
【回头是岸】huítóu-shì'àn〈成〉repent and be saved: 苦海无边，～。The sea of bitterness has no bounds; repent, and the shore is at hand.
【回味】huíwèi A〈名〉aftertaste: ～无穷。The aftertaste lingers on. B〈动〉ruminate over: 他的话耐人～。His words were thought provoking.
【回文】huíwén〈名〉palindrome: ～诗 palindromic poem
【回乡】huíxiāng〈动〉return to one's home village: ～务农 return to one's home and take up farming
【回翔】huíxiáng〈动〉circle: 直升机在飞机出事地点上空～。A helicopter kept circling over the area where the plane had crashed.
【回响】huíxiǎng〈动〉echo: 火车的轰鸣声在隧道中～。The roar of the train reverberated in the tunnel. ‖ 爸爸临终前的叮嘱一直在我耳际～。Father's final words on his deathbed keep ringing in my ears. ‖ 他们的主张在教师中并未引起～。What they advocated failed to make an impression on the teachers.
【回想】huíxiǎng〈动〉recollect: ～童年时代的生活 think back on one's childhood
【回销】huíxiāo = 返销 fǎnxiāo
【回心转意】huíxīn-zhuǎnyì〈成〉change one's mind: 如果她再不～，我俩的关系只好吹了。Should she still refuse to come round, our relationship would have to come to an end.
【回信】huíxìn A〈动〉write back: 望早日～。Looking forward to hearing from you soon. B〈名〉1▸（指信）sth. written in reply: 他立即写了～。He wrote an immediate reply. 2▸（指答复）sth. said in reply: 事情办妥后，我会给你个～。I'll let you know when I'm through with it.
【回形针】huíxíngzhēn〈名〉paper clip
【回旋】huíxuán〈动〉1▸（盘旋）circle: 成群的鸟在上空～。Flocks of birds are circling overhead. 2▸（变通）(room for) manoeuvre: 这件事还有～余地。There's still room for manoeuvre with this.
【回旋加速器】huíxuán jiāsùqì〈名〉［物理］cyclotron
【回旋曲】huíxuánqǔ〈名〉［音乐］rondo
【回旋余地】huíxuán yúdì〈名〉wiggle room
【回忆】huíyì〈动〉recollect: ～往事 recall the past ‖ ～对比 recall the past and contrast it with the present ‖ 美好/童年/幸福的～ lovely/childhood/happy memories
【回忆录】huíyìlù〈名〉recollections
【回音】huíyīn A〈动〉echo: 大厅空荡荡的，～很大。The hall is empty and it echoes loudly. B〈名〉response: 立候～ look forward to an immediate reply
【回音壁】huíyīnbì〈名〉Echo Wall [in the Temple of Heaven in Beijing]
【回应】huíyìng〈动〉respond: 电话铃响个不停，可是没有人～。The phone rang and rang but nobody answered it.
【回游】huíyóu = 洄游 huíyóu
【回赠】huízèng〈动〉give sb. a gift in return: ～一件纪念品 give (sb.) a souvenir in return
【回涨】huízhǎng〈动〉[of water or price] rise again after a fall
【回执】huízhí〈名〉receipt
【回注】huízhù〈动〉recycle
【回转】huízhuǎn〈动〉1▸（调转）turn round: 除非倒退一点，否则卡车～不开。The truck cannot turn round unless you back it up a bit. 2▸（循环往复）rotate
【回族】Huízú〈名〉Hui ethnic group
【回嘴】huízuǐ〈动〉〈口〉answer back: 受到长辈责备时最好别～ better not answer back when scolded by seniors

茴 huí

【茴香】huíxiāng〈名〉［植物］1▸（小茴香）fennel: ～油 fennel oil 2▸（八角）aniseed: ～豆 beans flavoured with aniseed

洄 huí〈动〉〈书〉whirl

【洄游】huíyóu〈动〉［鱼类］migrate: 产卵～ spawning migration

蛔 huí

【蛔虫】huíchóng〈名〉roundworm

huǐ

悔 huǐ〈动〉regret: ▸～过, 后～

【悔不当初】huǐbùdāngchū〈成〉regret having done sth.: 早知今日，～。If I'd known then what was going to happen, I wouldn't have done what I did.
【悔改】huǐgǎi〈动〉repent and mend one's ways: 不思～ be unwilling to repent ‖ 毫无～之心 have no intention of mending one's ways
【悔过】huǐguò〈动〉be repentant: ～前非 repent of former misdeeds
【悔过自新】huǐguò-zìxīn〈成〉repent and turn over a new leaf: 给某人一个～的机会 give sb. a chance to mend his ways
【悔恨】huǐhèn〈动〉be bitterly remorseful: ～交加 feel a mixture of remorse and shame ‖ ～终身 regret all one's life
【悔婚】huǐhūn〈动〉break an engagement
【悔棋】huǐqí〈动〉retract a false move in a chess game
【悔悟】huǐwù〈动〉acknowledge one's error and show repentance: 幡然～ quickly and completely repent one's ways
【悔约】huǐyuē〈动〉go back on one's word and request its cancellation
【悔之无及】huǐzhī-wújí〈成〉it is now too late to repent
【悔罪】huǐzuì〈动〉show repentance: 他丝毫没有～的意思。He had not a grain of true repentance for his crime.

毁[1] huǐ〈动〉destroy: ～了自己的前途 ruin one's future ‖ 战争中许多文物被～。Many cultural and historical artefacts were destroyed during the war. ▸～灭, 捣～, 撕～

毁[2]（燬）huǐ〈动〉burn up: ▸焚～, 销～

毁[3]（譭）huǐ〈动〉slander: ▸～谤, ～誉, 诋～

【毁谤】huǐbàng〈动〉defame: 背后～他人 slander sb. behind his back
【毁害】huǐhài〈动〉damage: ～桥梁 damage the bridge
【毁坏】huǐhuài〈动〉destroy: ～他人名誉 ruin sb.'s reputation ‖ ～文物古迹 destroy cultural and artefacts and sites
【毁家纾难】huǐjiā-shūnàn〈成〉offer all

one has to help in charity

【毁灭】huǐmiè〈动〉 exterminate: ～罪证 destroy criminal evidence ‖ 给以～性打击 deal a crushing blow ‖ ～性地震 ruinous earthquake

【毁弃】huǐqì〈动〉 annul: ～他人信件 destroy other people's papers

【毁容】huǐróng〈动〉 disfigure: 惨遭～ endure disfigurement

【毁伤】huǐshāng〈动〉 hurt: 请勿～花木。 Please do not damage the flowers and trees.

【毁尸灭迹】huǐshī-mièjì〈成〉burn a corpse to destroy the evidence

【毁损】huǐsǔn〈动〉 damage: 冰雹使即将成熟的小麦～严重。 The ripening wheat was severely damaged by the hailstorm.

【毁于一旦】huǐyú-yīdàn〈成〉be wiped out overnight: 垂成之功，岂可～。 How can we allow what is soon to be a success to be ruined overnight?

【毁誉】huǐyù **A**〈名〉 praise and blame **B**〈动〉 damage one's reputation

【毁誉参半】huǐyù cānbàn〈成〉 receive a mixed reception

【毁约】huǐyuē〈动〉 annul a treaty

huì

卉 huì〈名〉 grass: ▸花～

汇[1]（匯、滙）huì〈动〉 converge: ～成巨流 converge into a mighty torrent ‖ 千条江河～入大海。 All rivers flow to the sea.

汇[2]（匯、滙）huì
A〈动〉 remit: 给家里～钱 remit money to one's family ▸～兑，电～，信～
B〈名〉 foreign exchange: ▸创～

汇[3]（彙）huì
A〈动〉 collect: ～印成书 collect articles and publish in book form ▸～报，～总
B〈名〉 collection: ▸词～，语～，字～

【汇报】huìbào〈动〉 report: ～调查结果 report the findings of an investigation ‖ 听取～ listen to a report ‖ 口头～ verbal account

【汇编】huìbiān **A**〈动〉 compile: ～成册 compile into a book **B**〈名〉 collection: 文件～ collection of documents ‖ 资料～ corpus of data

【汇单】huìdān = 汇款单 huìkuǎndān

【汇兑】huìduì〈动〉 1（拨付） remit: 国内～ domestic remittance 2（兑换） exchange: ～银行 exchange bank

【汇费】huìfèi〈名〉 remittance fee

【汇改】huìgǎi〈名〉 exchange rate reform: 人民币对美元的汇率再创～以来新高。 Since the exchange rate reform, the *renminbi* has reached a new high against the dollar.

【汇合】huìhé〈动〉 converge: 工人和农民～成了一支大军。 The convergence of the workers and peasants formed a great army. ‖ 两条河流在此～。 The two rivers converge here.

【汇集】huìjí〈动〉 1（收集） collect: ～材料 collect all relevant data ‖ ～资金 collect funds 2（到一起） converge: 世界各国领导人～联合国总部。 World leaders converged at the headquarters of the United Nations.

【汇寄】huìjì〈动〉 remit

【汇价】huìjià〈名〉 exchange rate: ～上涨/下跌 exchange rate appreciation/depreciation

【汇聚】huìjù = 会聚 huìjù

【汇款】huìkuǎn **A**〈动〉 make a remittance **B**〈名〉 remittance: 收到一笔～ receive a remittance

【汇款单】huìkuǎndān〈名〉 remittance slip

【汇流】huìliú〈动〉 converge

【汇流点】huìliúdiǎn〈名〉［地理］ confluence: 天津是大运河和海河的～。 Tianjin is at the confluence of the Grand Canal and the Haihe River.

【汇拢】huìlǒng〈动〉 gather together: ～零散资金 assemble the fragmentary funds ‖ ～群众意见 gather together comments and suggestions from the masses

【汇率】huìlǜ ▸**p. 328**〈名〉 exchange rate: 浮动～ floating exchange rate

【汇票】huìpiào〈名〉 bill of exchange: 银行～ bank draft ‖ 邮政～ postal order

【汇市】huìshì〈名〉 1（指市场） foreign exchange market 2（指行情） foreign exchange quotations

【汇水】huìshuǐ = 汇费 huìfèi

【汇演】huìyǎn = 会演 huìyǎn

【汇映】huìyìng〈名〉 film festival: 法国电影～ French film festival

【汇展】huìzhǎn〈名〉 joint exhibition

【汇总】huìzǒng〈动〉 gather: ～各界人士的建议 gather together suggestions from people from all walks of life ‖ 导游把大家的行李～在一起。 The tourist guide collected together all of our luggage.

会[1]（會）huì
A〈动〉 1（会合） get together: ▸～餐，～师，～诊 2（见面） meet: 我们不期而～。 We met by accident. ▸～客，相～
B〈名〉 1（聚会） meeting: 欢送～ farewell gathering ▸茶话～，开～，座谈～ 2（庙会） temple fair: ▸庙～ 3（香会） religious festival: ▸香～ 4（指组织） association: ▸工～，教～，协～ 5（都市） capital city: ▸都～，省～ 6（机会） opportunity: ▸机～，适逢其～

会[2]（會）huì〈动〉 1（领悟） understand: ▸体～，误～，只可意～，不可言传 2（通晓） have knowledge of: ～几门外语 know several foreign languages 3（能够） be able to: ～弹钢琴 be able to play the piano ‖ ～游泳 be able to swim 4（擅长） be good at: ～木工 be skilled at carpentry ‖ ～修各种机器 be good at repairing various kinds of machines ‖ 很～学习 be good at studying ▸能说～道 5（可能出现） be likely to: 价格～有变动。 The prices are subject to change. ‖ 人人都～犯错误。 Every man makes mistakes. ‖ 天可能～下雨。 It is very likely to rain.

会[3]（會）huì〈动〉 foot a bill: 饭钱我～过了。 I have paid for the meal. ▸～钞，～账

会[4]（會）huì〈名〉 a moment: 我去一～儿就回来。 I'll be back in a moment.
▸kuài

【会标】huìbiāo〈名〉 logo: 奥运会～ Olympic Games logo

【会餐】huìcān〈动〉 have a dinner party: 节日～ festive dinner party

【会场】huìchǎng〈名〉 meeting place

【会钞】huìchāo〈动〉 foot the bill: 今天谁来～? Who'll pay the bill today?

【会车】huìchē〈动〉 cross: 有些司机～时不关大灯。 Some drivers do not turn off their headlights when they pass each other.

【会党】huìdǎng〈名〉〈旧〉 secret society [in the late Qing Dynasty]

【会道门】huì-dàomén〈名〉 superstitious sects and secret societies: 反动～ reactionary secret societies

【会典】huìdiǎn〈名〉 records of imperial laws and regulations

【会费】huìfèi〈名〉 membership fees: 交纳～ pay membership fees ‖ 联合国～ assessed contribution to the UN

【会风】huìfēng〈名〉 style of meeting: ～不正 unhealthy style of meeting

【会馆】huìguǎn〈名〉〈旧〉 guildhall

【会合】huìhé〈动〉 meet: 两批游客将在山麓下～。 Two groups of tourists will meet at the foot of the hill.

【会话】huìhuà **A**〈动〉 converse: 他们能用流利的英语～。 They can converse with each other fluently in English. **B**〈名〉 conversation

【会徽】huìhuī〈名〉 logo: 佩戴～ wear an emblem

【会集】huìjí〈动〉 gather together

【会籍】huìjí〈名〉 membership: 开除～ expel sb. from an association, etc.

【会见】huìjiàn〈动〉 have a meeting with: ～外国客人 meet with foreign guests

【会聚】huìjù〈动〉 assemble: 数以万计的黑人～在华盛顿。 Thousands upon thousands of black people converged on Washington.

【会刊】huìkān〈名〉 journal

【会考】huìkǎo〈名〉 general examination for students: 全市～ general examination for students in the city

【会客】huìkè〈动〉 receive a visitor: 因健康原因，暂不～ be unable to receive visitors for health reasons

【会客室】huìkèshì〈名〉 reception room

【会面】huìmiàn〈动〉meet: 近来我不常和他～。 I have not seen much of him lately.

【会期】huìqī〈名〉 1（指日期） date of a meeting: 确定～ fix a date for a meeting 2（指持续时间） duration of a meeting: ～为一个星期。 The meeting is scheduled to last for one week.

【会旗】huìqí〈名〉 standard of an association

【会签】huìqiān〈动〉 countersign: 此文件经各有关厅局～后方可生效。 This document is valid only when it is countersigned by the bureaus concerned.

【会儿】huìr〈量〉〈口〉 moment: 一～ a little while ‖ 请等～。 Wait a moment, please.

【会商】huìshāng〈动〉 have a consultation: ～解决办法 consult to find a solution ‖ 经过多次～ after repeated consultations

【会社】huìshè〈名〉 1（公司） commercial firm: 株式～ limited company 2（社团） society

【会审】huìshěn〈动〉 1（指审理） hold a joint hearing: 进行～ conduct a joint trial 2（指审查） make a joint check-up: ～施工方案 jointly check the construction plan

【会师】huìshī〈动〉 join forces: 与另一部队～ joint forces with another army

【会水】huìshuǐ〈动〉 be able to swim: 你～吗? Can you swim?

【会所】huìsuǒ〈名〉 office of an association, etc.

【会谈】huìtán〈动〉 talk: （与某人）举行～ hold talks (with sb.) ‖ ～纪要 minutes

of talks ‖ 双边～ bilateral talks ‖ 高峰～ summit talks
【会堂】huìtáng〈名〉 assembly hall: 人民大～ Great Hall of the People
【会同】huìtóng〈动〉 be in conjunction with: ～有关部门解决问题 solve a problem with the involvement of other relevant departments
【会务】huìwù〈名〉 routine affairs of a meeting: ～费 registration fee for a conference ‖ ～工作 routine conference work
【会悟】huìwù〈动〉〈书〉 come to understand
【会晤】huìwù〈动〉 meet: 两国外长定期～。 Foreign ministers of the two countries meet regularly.
【会心】huìxīn〈动〉 understand what is implied: ～的微笑 understanding smile
【会演】huìyǎn〈名〉 joint performance: 文艺～ art and literature festival
【会厌】huìyàn〈名〉［生理］ epiglottis
【会要】huìyào〈名〉 book of economic and political institutions and regulations of a dynasty
【会议】huìyì〈名〉 **1**（指集会） meeting: 出席～ attend a meeting ‖ 结束～ close a meeting ‖ 举行～ hold a meeting ‖ 宣布～开始/结束 declare a meeting open/closed ‖ 召开～ call a meeting ‖ ～记录 minutes ‖ ～日程 agenda of a meeting ‖ 紧急～ urgent meeting ‖ 全体～ plenary session ‖ 预备～ preparatory meeting **2**（指机构） council: 部长～ council of ministers ▶中国人民政治协商～
【会意】huìyì **A** = 会心 huìxīn **B**〈名〉 associative compound [Chinese character-formation method in which two characters are combined to form a new character, or two meanings are blended to create a new meaning]: ～字 associative compound
【会阴】huìyīn〈名〉［生理］ perineum
【会友】huìyǒu **A**〈名〉 fellow member **B**〈动〉〈书〉 make friends: 以文～ make friends through literary exchanges
【会员】huìyuán〈名〉 member: 正式～ full member ‖ 终身～ life member ‖ ～证 membership card
【会员国】huìyuánguó〈名〉 member state: 非～ non-member state
【会展】huìzhǎn〈名〉 exhibition: 北京国际～中心 Beijing International Exhibition Center
【会战】huìzhàn〈动〉 **1**〈本〉［军事］ meet for a decisive battle **2**〈喻〉 launch a mass campaign: 水利～ mass campaign for water conservancy
【会长】huìzhǎng〈名〉 president
【会账】huìzhàng〈动〉 pay a bill
【会诊】huìzhěn〈动〉［医学］ hold a group consultation: 病人家属要求进行内外科～。 The family of the patient requested that a consultation of physicians and surgeons be held.
【会址】huìzhǐ〈名〉 **1**（团体所在地） site of an association **2**（会议地址） site of a conference
【会众】huìzhòng〈名〉〈旧〉 members of a superstitious sect or secret society
【会子】huìzi〈量〉 period of time: 喝了～茶 drank tea for a while

讳（諱） huì
A〈动〉 avoid as taboo: ▶隐～, 直言不～
B〈名〉 **1**（指事物） taboo: 犯了老板的～。 It violated the boss's taboo. **2**〈旧〉（指名字） name of emperor, high-ranking official, etc. and the characters in their names
【讳疾忌医】huìjí-jìyī〈成〉 **1**（指疾病） avoid seeking medical advice for fear of facing an unpleasant reality **2**〈喻〉（指缺点） conceal one's shortcomings for fear of criticism: 有错就改，～，有害无益。 If there's a mistake then correct it. Trying to cover things up for fear of reproach will do no good but harm.
【讳忌】huìjì〈名〉 taboo: 不知～ know no taboo ‖ 毫不～ hold nothing back
【讳莫如深】huìmòrúshēn〈成〉 not breathe a word to a soul: 公司对外界的传闻～。 The company didn't utter a word about the external rumours.
【讳言】huìyán〈动〉 dare not speak up: 毫不～ make no attempt to conceal the truth ‖ 无可～，这不是一支好球队。 We needn't avoid mentioning the fact that this is not a strong team.

荟（薈） huì〈形〉〈书〉 luxuriant: 木～草蔚。 Trees and grasses grow luxuriantly.
【荟萃】huìcuì〈动〉〈书〉 assemble: 精品～ collection of fine works ‖ 人才～ galaxy of talents

哕（噦） huì〈拟〉〈书〉 chirp ▶yuě
【哕哕】huìhuì〈拟〉〈书〉 tinkling: 銮声～。 The bells of the imperial carriage tinkled rhythmically.

诲（誨） huì〈动〉 **1**（教导） instruct: ▶教～, 训～ **2**（诱使） seduce: ▶～淫～盗
【诲人不倦】huìrén-bùjuàn〈成〉 teach with tireless zeal: 学而不厌，～。 Never grow tired of learning, nor weary of teaching others.
【诲淫诲盗】huìyín-huìdào〈成〉 propagate sex and violence: ～的电影 film full of sex and violence

绘（繪） huì〈动〉 **1**（画） draw: ▶～画 **2**（描写） describe: ▶～声～色
【绘画】huìhuà〈动〉 draw: ～板 drawing board ‖ ～室 studio
【绘声绘色】huìshēng-huìsè〈成〉 true to life: ～的描述 vivid description
【绘图】huìtú〈动〉 map: ～员 draftsman ‖ ～纸 sketch paper
【绘影绘声】huìyǐng-huìshēng = 绘声绘色 huìshēng-huìsè
【绘制】huìzhì〈动〉 draw up: ～地图 draw up a map ‖ ～蓝图 map out a blueprint

恚 huì〈动〉〈书〉 resent: 既愧且～ be both ashamed and resentful
【恚恨】huìhèn〈动〉〈书〉 hate

桧（檜） huì used in the name of Qin Hui (秦桧) [treacherous court officail in the Southern Song Dynasty] ▶guì

贿（賄） huì
A〈名〉 **1**〈书〉（财物） valuables **2**（贿赂） property used to bribe: 受～ take bribes ‖ 行～ engage in bribery
B〈动〉 bribe: ▶～选
【贿金】huìjīn = 贿款 huìkuǎn
【贿款】huìkuǎn〈名〉 bribery money
【贿赂】huìlù **A**〈动〉 bribe: ～公务人员 bribe a government functionary ‖ ～证人 bribe a witness **B**〈名〉 bribery: 收受～ take bribes
【贿赂公行】huìlù-gōngxíng〈成〉 corruption is rife
【贿选】huìxuǎn〈动〉 get elected through bribery

烩（燴） huì〈动〉 **1**（指加水勾芡） braise: 白菜～豆腐 Chinese cabbage braised with bean curd **2**（指荤素一起炖） cook with meat, vegetables and water: ～饼 shredded pancakes cooked with vegetables and meat

彗 huì〈名〉〈书〉 broom
【彗尾】huìwěi〈名〉［天文］ tail of a comet
【彗星】huìxīng〈名〉［天文］ comet

晦 huì
A〈名〉 **1** ▶p. 618（农历最后一天） last day of a lunar month: ▶～朔 **2**（黑夜） night: ▶～明, 风雨如～
B〈形〉 **1**（昏暗） dark: ▶～暗, ～冥 **2**（不明显） not obvious: ▶～涩, 隐～
C〈动〉 conceal: ▶韬～, 韬光养～
【晦暗】huì'àn〈形〉 dark and gloomy: 天色～ murky skies ‖ 心情～ be gloomy
【晦迹】huìjì〈动〉 live in seclusion
【晦明】huìmíng〈书〉 **A**〈名〉 day and night **B**〈形〉 bright or dark
【晦冥】huìmíng〈形〉〈书〉 dim: 天地～。 It was dark all round.
【晦暝】huìmíng = 晦冥 huìmíng
【晦气】huìqì **A**〈形〉 unlucky: 自认～ be resigned to one's bad luck **B**〈名〉 pale and gloomy look: 满脸～ look sick
【晦涩】huìsè〈形〉 obscure: ～的语言 obscure language
【晦朔】huìshuò〈名〉〈书〉 time from dusk to dawn

秽（穢） huì〈形〉 **1**（脏） dirty: ▶～气, 污～ **2**（下流） obscene: ▶～行, ～语, 淫～ **3**（丑恶） abominable: ▶自惭形～
【秽迹】huìjì〈名〉〈书〉 unsavoury record: 他当学生时就有～。 He had an unsavoury record as a student.
【秽乱】huìluàn〈形〉 promiscuous
【秽气】huìqì〈名〉 foul stench
【秽土】huìtǔ〈名〉 dirt
【秽闻】huìwén〈名〉〈书〉 ill repute: ～广传 have a reputation for being immoral far and wide
【秽行】huìxíng〈名〉〈书〉 immoral conduct
【秽言】huìyán〈名〉 obscene language: 市井～ marketplace obscenities
【秽语】huìyǔ〈名〉 obscene language
【秽浊】huìzhuó〈形〉 filthy

惠 huì
A〈名〉 favour: ▶恩～, 施～, 优～
B〈动〉 grant a favour: 平等互～ equality and mutual benefit
C〈副〉〈套〉 [used as a form of compliment]: ～赐 your gift for me ▶～存, ～顾, ～临
D〈形〉 gentle: ▶～风
【惠存】huìcún〈动〉〈套〉 please keep: 刘轩谊教授～——王立新敬赠 To Professor Liu Xuanyi with compliments from Wang Lixin
【惠而不费】huì'érbùfèi〈成〉 give sb. a pleasure which would cost very little
【惠风】huìfēng〈名〉〈书〉 gentle breeze:

h

～和畅。A gentle breeze is blowing freely.

【惠顾】huìgù〈动〉〈套〉 your patronage: 欢迎～ welcome patronage ‖ 敬候～。We await your generous patronage.

【惠及】huìjí〈动〉〈书〉 be of benefit to: 你的好心将～子孙。Your kindness will bring benefits for generations to come.

【惠鉴】huìjiàn〈动〉〈书〉 be kind enough to read

【惠临】huìlín〈动〉〈套〉 your gracious presence: 敬请～。Your presence is requested. ‖ 如蒙～，不胜荣幸。We will be greatly honoured by your presence.

【惠灵顿】Huìlíngdùn〈名〉 Wellington

【惠农】huìnóng〈动〉 be of benefit to farmers: ～政策 policies that benefit farmers

【惠书】huìshū〈名〉〈敬〉 your kind letter

【惠允】huìyǔn〈动〉〈书〉 your generous consent: 承蒙～ with your kind consent

【惠泽】huìzé〈名〉〈书〉 kindness

【惠赠】huìzèng〈动〉〈套〉 gift: 承蒙～，不胜感激。Extreme thanks for your generous gift.

喙 huì

〈名〉〈书〉 **1**（指鸟）beak;（指兽）snout: 鸟～ beak of a bird **2**（指人）mouth: 百～莫辩 takes more than mere eloquence to make it clear ‖ 不容置～ not allow others to butt in

阓（闠） huì ▸阛阓 huánhuì

溃（潰） huì

〈动〉 fester: 如果伤口弄脏了，可能会～脓。If the cut gets dirty, it will probably fester.
▸kuì

慧 huì

〈形〉 intelligent: ▸聪～, 智～

【慧根】huìgēn〈名〉 root of wisdom that can lead one to truth

【慧黠】huìxiá〈形〉〈书〉 shrewd

【慧心】huìxīn〈名〉 wisdom

【慧眼】huìyǎn〈名〉 **1**［佛教］ mind which perceives both past and future **2**（指洞察力）acumen: ～独具 can see what others cannot ‖ ～识英雄 discerning eyes can tell greatness from mediocrity

【慧中秀外】huìzhōng-xiùwài〈成〉 be intelligent within and beautiful without

蕙 huì = 蕙兰 huìlán

【蕙兰】huìlán〈名〉［植物］ cymbidium orchid

【蕙心】huìxīn〈名〉〈书〉 [of a woman] pure heart

【蕙质】huìzhì〈名〉 goodness and purity (of a person)

蟪 huì

【蟪蛄】huìgū〈名〉［昆虫］a kind of cicada [platypleura kaempferi]

hūn

昏 hūn

A〈名〉 dusk: 晨～ at dawn and dusk ▸黄～
B〈形〉 **1**（指光线）dim: ▸～天黑地, 老眼～花, 天～地暗 **2**（头晕）confused: 感到头～ feel terribly dizzy ▸～庸, 发～
C〈动〉 lose consciousness: ～倒在地 faint ▸～厥, ～迷

【昏暗】hūn'àn〈形〉 dim: ～的灯光 dim light ‖ ～的天色 gloomy skies

【昏沉】hūnchén〈形〉 **1**（指天色）murky: 暮色～ murky twilight **2**（指头脑）befuddled: 我头脑昏昏沉沉的。I feel a bit out of it.

【昏黑】hūnhēi〈形〉 dark

【昏花】hūnhuā〈形〉 dim-sighted: 饿得两眼～ feel faint from hunger ▸老眼～

【昏话】hūnhuà〈名〉 absurd remarks

【昏黄】hūnhuáng〈形〉 faint: 月色～ faint moonlight

【昏昏欲睡】hūnhūn-yùshuì〈成〉 drowsy: 他的讲课枯燥乏味，许多学生在课堂上～。His lectures were boring and many of his students would feel sleepy in class.

【昏厥】hūnjué〈动〉 faint: ～过去 fall into a coma ‖ ～后恢复知觉 regain consciousness after fainting

【昏君】hūnjūn〈名〉 debauched monarch

【昏聩】hūnkuì〈形〉 decrepit and muddle-headed: ～无能 muddle-headed and incompetent

【昏聩龙钟】hūnkuì-lóngzhōng〈成〉 become dim-sighted and dull because of senility

【昏乱】hūnluàn〈形〉 **1**（指头脑、神智）dazed and confused **2**〈书〉（指政治、社会）chaotic: 世道～ social disorder

【昏迷】hūnmí〈动〉 be comatose: ～不醒 remain unconscious ‖ 深度～ heavy stupor

【昏睡】hūnshuì〈动〉 be in a lethargic state: 病人还在～。The patient is still in a lethargic state.

【昏死】hūnsǐ〈动〉 faint

【昏天黑地】hūntiān-hēidì〈成〉 **1**（指天色）pitch black: 这样～的夜里，我一个人可不敢去。In pitch-darkness like this, I dare not go all by myself. **2**（指神志）dizzy: 我突然觉得～，随即失去了知觉。All of a sudden I felt dizzy and fell unconscious. **3**（指社会）dark rule and social disorder: 那个地区让土匪一度搞得～。For a time, the area was in serious social turbulence because of the bandits. **4**（指生活方式）decadent: 过着～的生活 lead a dissipated life **5**（激烈）complete chaos: 他们为几块钱的事吵得～。They wrangled like crazy people over a few dollars.

【昏头昏脑】hūntóu-hūnnǎo〈成〉 **1**（思维混乱）muddle-headed: 那么多数学题累得我～。My head began to reel after working on so many mathematical problems. **2**（头脑糊涂）absent-minded: 他～的，连他们的结婚纪念日都忘了。He was so forgetful that he didn't even remember their wedding anniversary.

【昏星】hūnxīng〈名〉〈古〉 evening star

【昏眩】hūnxuàn〈形〉 dizzy: 突然一阵～，她几乎摔倒。She almost fell over in a sudden fit of giddiness.

【昏庸】hūnyōng〈形〉 fatuous: ～无能 fatuous and incompetent

荤（葷） hūn

A〈名〉 **1**［佛教］ fragrant vegetables: 不饮酒不茹～ do not drink and keep away from vegetables with special smells **2**（肉食）meat or fish dishes: 吃素不吃～ eat vegetables but not meat ▸开～
B〈形〉 obscene: ▸～话

【荤菜】hūncài〈名〉 meat dish

【荤话】hūnhuà〈名〉 obscene language

【荤口】hūnkǒu〈名〉 [in crosstalk and comic dialogues] coarse language

【荤腥】hūnxīng〈名〉 meat or fish: 不沾～ not eat meat at all

【荤油】hūnyóu〈名〉〈方〉 lard

阍（閽） hūn

〈名〉〈书〉 **1**（指人）doorkeeper: ～者 gatekeeper **2**（指门）palace gate: 叩～ knock at the palace door ‖ 掩～ close the door

婚 hūn

A〈动〉 marry: ▸未～, 新～, 已～
B〈名〉 wedding: ▸结～, 离～

【婚变】hūnbiàn〈动〉divorce: 她已经历了三次～。She has been divorced three times so far.

【婚典】hūndiǎn〈名〉 wedding ceremony: 传统～ traditional wedding

【婚假】hūnjià〈名〉 wedding leave

【婚嫁】hūnjià〈名〉 marriage

【婚检】hūnjiǎn〈动〉 have a physical check-up before marriage

【婚介】hūnjiè〈名〉 matchmaking: ～机构 matchmaking service

【婚礼】hūnlǐ〈名〉 wedding: 出席～ be present at a wedding ‖ 举行～ hold a wedding ‖ ～蛋糕 wedding cake

【婚恋】hūnliàn〈动〉 fall in love and get married

【婚龄】hūnlíng〈名〉 **1**［法律］ marriageable age: 达到法定～ reach the legal age of marriage **2**（指年数）years of marriage: 他们的～才三年。They have been married for only three years.

【婚内强奸】hūnnèi qiángjiān〈名〉［法律］ marital rape

【婚配】hūnpèi〈动〉 marry: 她女儿已年过三十，尚未～。Her daughter is over 30 but still not married.

【婚期】hūnqī〈名〉 wedding day: 推迟～ postpone one's wedding

【婚前协议】hūnqián xiéyì〈名〉 prenuptial agreement

【婚庆】hūnqìng〈名〉 wedding ceremony

【婚纱】hūnshā〈名〉 wedding dress: ～摄影 wedding photography

【婚生子女】hūnshēng zǐnǚ〈名〉［法律］ child born in wedlock: 非～ illegitimate child

【婚事】hūnshì〈名〉 **1**（婚姻）marriage **2**（婚礼）wedding: 办～ have one's wedding

【婚书】hūnshū〈名〉〈旧〉 marriage certificate

【婚俗】hūnsú〈名〉 marriage customs

【婚外恋】hūnwàiliàn = 婚外情 hūnwàiqíng

【婚外情】hūnwàiqíng〈名〉 extramarital affair

【婚筵】hūnyán〈名〉 wedding feast

【婚姻】hūnyīn〈名〉 marriage: ～登记 marriage registration ‖ 包办～ arranged marriage ‖ 美满～ successful marriage ‖ ～状况 marital status ‖ ～介绍所 dating agency

【婚姻法】hūnyīnfǎ〈名〉 marriage law

【婚育期】hūnyùqī〈名〉 marriageable and child-bearing age

【婚约】hūnyuē〈名〉 engagement: 订立～ get engaged ‖ 解除～ break off an engagement

hún

浑¹（渾） hún

〈形〉 muddy: 把水搅～ muddy up the water

浑²（渾） hún

A〈动〉 combine into one entity: ▸～然一体
B〈形〉 **1**（质朴）simple and natural:

▸～厚, ～朴 2▸（傻） foolish: ～人 idiot ▸～蛋 3▸（全） complete: ▸～身

【浑蛋】húndàn〈名〉〈粗〉 bastard〈粗〉: 滚开，你这个～! Get out of here, you bastard!

【浑厚】húnhòu〈形〉 1▸（朴实敦厚） simple and honest: 生性～ simple and honest by nature 2▸（指风格） simple but vigorous: 笔力～ bold and vigorous strokes 3▸（指声音） deep

【浑浑噩噩】húnhún-è'è〈成〉 simple-minded: ～地混日子 muddle away one's days

【浑家】húnjiā〈名〉〈旧〉 wife

【浑金璞玉】húnjīn-púyù = 璞玉浑金 púyù-húnjīn

【浑名】húnmíng〈名〉 nickname

【浑朴】húnpǔ〈形〉 simple and honest: 本文的语言与其作者本人一样～。 The language of the paper is as plain and simple as its writer.

【浑球儿】húnqiúr〈名〉〈方〉 scoundrel

【浑然】húnrán〈形〉 1▸（完全） complete: ～不觉 be totally unaware 2▸（不可分割） integral and indivisible: ～天成 integral whole

【浑然一体】húnrán-yītǐ〈成〉 integral whole: 文章结构严谨，～。 The article is very well constructed, with the facts coherently presented.

【浑如】húnrú = 浑似 húnsì

【浑身】húnshēn〈名〉 whole body: ～发抖 tremble all over ‖ ～是胆 full of courage ‖ ～是伤 be covered with wounds

【浑身解数】húnshēn-xièshù〈成〉 all that one can do: 使出～ exert oneself to the utmost

【浑水摸鱼】húnshuǐ-mōyú〈成〉 gain advantage in a confused situation: ～是他们惯用的伎俩。 Fishing in troubled waters is a trick they frequently employ.

【浑说】húnshuō〈动〉 talk nonsense: 信口～ shoot one's mouth off

【浑似】húnsì〈动〉 be exactly like: 那小家伙说起话来～个大人。The little guy spoke exactly like a grown-up.

【浑天仪】húntiānyí〈名〉 1▸［天文］ armillary sphere 2▸（天球仪） celestial globe

【浑象】húnxiàng〈名〉［天文］ celestial globe

【浑仪】húnyí〈名〉［天文］ armillary sphere

【浑圆】húnyuán〈形〉 perfectly round

【浑浊】húnzhuó〈形〉 muddy: 河水～ turbid river ‖ 空气～ foul air

珲（琿） hún〈名〉〈古〉 a kind of jade

馄（餛） hún

【馄饨】húntun〈名〉 wonton

> **馄饨**
>
> *Wonton*, dumplings made of a thin skin of dough, with a meat or vegetable filling, either boiled in a soup or steamed. *Wonton* are popular throughout China. In Guangdong they are known as *yuntun* (云吞) and in Sichuan, they are known as *chaoshou* (抄手).

混 hún = 浑¹ hún, 浑² hún B2

▸hùn

【混蛋】húndàn = 浑蛋 húndàn

【混球儿】húnqiúr = 浑球儿 húnqiúr

【混水摸鱼】húnshuǐ-mōyú = 浑水摸鱼 húnshuǐ-mōyú

魂 hún〈名〉 1▸（灵魂） soul: ▸借尸还～, 灵～ 2▸（情绪） mood: ▸神～颠倒, 失～落魄 3▸（高尚的精神） lofty spirit: 国～ national spirit 4▸（人格化的精神） the best part: 诗～ heart of a poem

【魂不附体】húnbùfùtǐ〈成〉 feel as if the soul had left the body: 吓得～ be scared out of one's wits

【魂不守舍】húnbùshǒushè〈成〉 have lost one's mind

【魂飞胆丧】húnfēi-dǎnsàng〈成〉 be panic-stricken

【魂飞魄散】húnfēi-pòsàn〈成〉 be frightened out of one's wits

【魂灵】húnlíng〈名〉 soul

【魂魄】húnpò〈名〉 soul

【魂牵梦萦】húnqiān-mèngyíng〈成〉 pine for

【魂兮归来】húnxīguīlái〈成〉 may the spirit of the deceased come back to us

【魂消魄散】húnxiāo-pòsàn〈成〉 be half dead with fright

hùn

诨（諢） hùn

A〈名〉 joke: ▸插科打～

B〈动〉 make fun of

【诨号】hùnhào = 诨名 hùnmíng

【诨名】hùnmíng〈名〉 nickname

图 hùn〈名〉〈书〉 1▸（猪圈） pigsty 2▸（厕所） toilet

混 hùn

A〈动〉 1▸（混合） mix: ～在一起 mix things up ‖ 这两个字容易搞～。 These two words are easily confused. ▸～为一谈, ～淆, ～杂 2▸（蒙混） pass off as: ▸鱼目～珠 3▸（指生活） muddle along: ～饭吃 do a job merely for the sake of making a living ‖ ～日子 drift along aimlessly 4▸（交往） get along with sb.: 同他们～得很熟 hit it off well with them

B〈形〉 aimless: ～猜 make a wild guess ‖ ～出主意 come up with a crazy idea

▸hún

【混充】hùnchōng〈动〉 pass oneself off as: ～内行 pass oneself off as an expert ‖ 把本地产品～进口货 palm off local products as imports

【混沌】hùndùn A〈名〉 primeval state of chaos: ～初开 at the dawn of civilization ‖ 原始的～状态 primal chaos B〈形〉 innocent: 他虽年轻，可一点也不～。 Young as he is, he's by no means simple-minded and ignorant.

【混饭】hùnfàn〈动〉 1▸（指糊口） earn one's pay without doing much work: 对有些人来说，工作仅仅是～罢了。 As far as some people are concerned, work is nothing more than a means of making money. 2▸〈方〉（蹭饭） eat at another's expense: 我老婆最近出差，我到岳母家～吃。 My wife has been on a business trip recently, so I've been having my meals at my mother-in-law's.

【混纺】hùnfǎng［纺织］ A〈动〉 blend: 棉毛～ blend cotton and wool B〈名〉 blend fabric

【混合】hùnhé〈动〉 mix: ～班 mixed class ‖ ～饲料 mixed feed

【混合编队】hùnhé biānduì〈名〉［军事］ composite formation

【混合阀】hùnhéfá〈名〉［工程］ mixing valve

【混合感染】hùnhé gǎnrǎn ▸p. 50〈名〉［医学］ mixed infection

【混合经济】hùnhé jīngjì〈名〉 mixed economy

【混合器】hùnhéqì〈名〉［化学］ mixer

【混合色】hùnhésè〈名〉 secondary colour

【混合双打】hùnhé shuāngdǎ〈名〉［体育］ mixed doubles

【混合所有制经济】hùnhé suǒyǒuzhì jīngjì〈名〉 mixed ownership economy

【混合物】hùnhéwù〈名〉 mixture

【混合泳】hùnhéyǒng〈名〉［体育］ individual medley

【混合语】hùnhéyǔ ▸p. 918〈名〉 mixed language

【混合运算】hùnhé yùnsuàn〈名〉［数学］ hybrid operation

【混混儿】hùnhunr〈名〉〈方〉 loafer

【混迹】hùnjì〈动〉〈书〉 unworthily mix with: ～江湖 unworthily associate with people from all over the country

【混交林】hùnjiāolín〈名〉 mixed forest

【混乱】hùnluàn〈形〉 chaotic: 交通～ chaotic traffic ‖ 思想～ muddled thinking ‖ ～不堪 utter disorder prevails ‖ 爆炸后发生～。 Pandemonium broke out after the blast.

【混凝土】hùnníngtǔ〈名〉 concrete: ～搅拌机 concrete mixer

【混日子】hùn rìzi〈动〉〈口〉 muddle along: 如果整天这样～，那你怎么能成功呢? How can you expect to be successful when you drift along like this all day?

【混声合唱】hùnshēng héchàng〈名〉 mixed chorus

【混世魔王】hùnshì mówáng〈成〉 devil incarnate

【混事】hùnshì〈动〉 muddle along: 我曾在政府部门～。 I once scraped a living in government office.

【混双】hùnshuāng〈简称〉= 混合双打

【混同】hùntóng〈动〉 confuse: 我们不能把二者～起来。 We shouldn't confuse the two things.

【混为一谈】hùnwéiyītán〈成〉 jumble together: 两者不能～。 The two things should not be mentioned in the same breath.

【混响】hùnxiǎng〈名〉［物理］ reverberation

【混淆】hùnxiáo〈动〉 mix up: ～敌友 confuse friend with foe ‖ 真假～ the false has been confused with the true ‖ ～是非 confuse right and wrong ‖ ～黑白 mix up black and white

【混淆视听】hùnxiáo-shìtīng〈成〉 mislead the public

【混血儿】hùnxuè'ér〈名〉 person of mixed race

【混业】hùnyè〈动〉 diversify: 银行业开始～经营。 Banks are beginning to diversify their businesses.

【混杂】hùnzá〈动〉 mix: 不要把不同的种子～在一起。 Don't mix up the different kinds of seeds. ▸鱼龙～

【混战】hùnzhàn〈名〉 scuffle: 军阀～ tangled fighting between warlords ‖ 两队～一场。 The two sides engaged in a bout of fierce fighting.

【混账】hùnzhàng〈形〉〈粗〉 unreasonable: ～话 impudent remark

【混浊】hùnzhuó〈形〉 turbid: ～的空气 foul

h

air
【混子】hùnzi〈名〉〈方〉 charlatan

溷 hùn〈名〉〈书〉 1（猪圈） pigsty 2（厕所） toilet

huō

耠 huō
A〈名〉 hoe
B〈动〉 hoe: ～地 hoe the earth
【耠子】huōzi〈名〉 hoe

劐 huō
A〈动〉〈口〉 slit with a knife: 把鱼肚子～开 slit open the fish ‖ 用刀子把面袋子～一个口子 cut open the flour bag with a knife
B = 耠 huō

嚄 huō〈叹〉 wow: ～，已经长成大人了! Wow, you're a grown-up already!
▸ǒ

豁 huō〈动〉 1（裂开） slit: 堤岸被敌机炸～了口。 The dykes were breached by the bombing of the enemy aircraft. ‖ 上衣～了一个口子。 There is a tear in the jacket. ▸～口, ～嘴 2（不惜代价） sacrifice: ～上这条老命 risk one's life to do sth. ‖ ～出三天时间，也要把它做好。 Even if it takes three days, we must get the job done.
▸huá, huò
【豁出去】huōchuqu〈动〉 go ahead at any price: ～了 be ready to risk everything
【豁口】huōkǒu〈名〉 opening: 城墙～ crack in the city wall ‖ 大堤上的～ break in the levee ‖ 碗边上的～ crack on a bowl
【豁命】huōmìng〈动〉 risk one's life
【豁子】huōzi〈名〉〈方〉 1 = 豁口 huōkǒu 2（指人） person with a harelip
【豁嘴】huōzuǐ〈名〉 1〈口〉（指唇） harelip 2〈方〉（指人） person with a harelip

攉 huō〈动〉 shovel from one place to another: ～土 shovel earth ‖ ～煤机 coal shovel

huó

和 huó〈动〉 mix with water: ～面 knead dough ‖ ～沙子灰 prepare some mortar
▸hé, hè, hú, huò

活 huó
A〈动〉 1（生存） live: ～到九十岁 live to ninety ‖ ～到老，学到老 never too old to learn ▸存～, 复～, 死去～来 2（使生存） save: ～人济世 save people's lives and benefit the society
B〈名〉 1（工作） work: 干～儿 work ‖ 体力～儿 manual work ‖ 针线～儿 needle work ▸农～ 2（产品） product: 不出～儿 not productive ‖ 这批～儿做得好。 This batch of products is well done.
C〈形〉 1（不固定） moving: ～水 flowing water ▸～期, ～塞 2（灵活） lively: 搞～经济 invigorate the economy ‖ 脑子很～ have a quick mind ‖ 这孩子心眼儿～。 The child has an active mind. ▸～泼, 灵～, 生龙～虎 3（有生命） alive, living, live: ～鱼 live fish
D〈副〉 exactly, simply: ▸～像
【活靶】huóbǎ〈名〉［军事］ manoeuvring target
【活靶子】huóbǎzi〈名〉 live target
【活扳手】huóbānshou〈名〉 adjustable spanner
【活版】huóbǎn〈名〉［印刷］ typography: ～印刷 typographic printing
【活宝】huóbǎo〈名〉 funny fellow: 他是个大～，常当众出洋相。 He is a bit of a clown, often making a fool of himself in public.
【活报剧】huóbàojù〈名〉 skit
【活蹦乱跳】huóbèng-luàntiào〈成〉 skip and jump about with joy: ～的孩子 children full of life
【活便】huóbian〈形〉〈口〉 1（灵活） nimble: 我上年纪啦，手脚不如以前～了。 I'm getting old and not as agile as I used to be. 2（方便） convenient: 用手机联系～多了。 Mobile phones make communication a lot more convenient.
【活地图】huódìtú〈名〉 walking map
【活地狱】huódìyù〈名〉 hell on earth
【活动】huódòng A〈动〉 1（运动） exercise: ～一下筋骨 limber up ‖ 站起来～～ stand up and stretch oneself a bit 2（松动） be unsteady: 这把椅子～了。 The chair is rickety. ‖ 这颗牙～了。 This tooth is loose. 3（打通关节） wangle: 替某人～ put in a word for sb. ‖ 为求晋升而四处～ jockey for promotion ‖ 他在为给儿子安排工作而～。 He is trying to use his influence to get a job for his son. B〈形〉 flexible: ～铅笔 mechanical pencil ‖ 经理的口气有点～了。 The manager began to relent a little. C〈名〉 activity: 非法～ illegal activities ‖ 户外～ outdoor activities
【活动房屋】huódòng fángwū〈名〉 movable house
【活动家】huódòngjiā〈名〉 activist: 政治～ political activist
【活动室】huódòngshì〈名〉 activity room: 老年～ activity room for elderly people
【活法】huófǎ〈名〉 one's approach to life: 各人有各人的～。 Everyone has their own approach to life.
【活泛】huófan〈形〉〈方〉 1（机敏） resourceful: 他脑子可真够～的。 He is very quick-minded. 2（有节余） have spare money: 我现在手头～得多。 I have enough money at my disposal now.
【活佛】huófó〈名〉 1［宗教］ Living Buddha: ～转世 reincarnation of a Living Buddha 2（指人） person who assists people in distress and saves people from danger: 济公～ Divine Monk Ji Gong
【活该】huógāi〈动〉〈口〉 serve sb. right: ～倒霉 get what one deserves ‖ 判他十年徒刑，～! He certainly deserves the ten-year sentence.
【活化】huóhuà〈名〉［化学］ activation: ～剂 activating agent
【活化石】huóhuàshí〈名〉 living fossil
【活话】huóhuà〈名〉 non-committal remark: 留下～ make a statement that is open to interpretation
【活活】huóhuó〈副〉 1（指状态） while still alive: ～烧死 be burnt alive 2（简直） simply: 这孩子要把我～气死! This child is simply driving me mad.
【活火山】huóhuǒshān〈名〉 active volcano
【活计】huóji〈名〉 1（劳动） manual work: 男人的～ man's work ‖ 针线～ needlework 2（手工制品） handiwork
【活见鬼】huójiànguǐ〈惯〉 it's sheer fantasy: 我怎么可能跟你讲这样的话? 简直是～! How could I have told you what you say I did? You are imagining things.
【活教材】huójiàocái〈名〉 vivid example for education
【活结】huójié〈名〉 slip knot: 打个～ make a slip knot
【活口】huókǒu A〈名〉 1（指受害人） living witness to a crime: 凶杀没有留下～，追捕凶手可就难了。 As no one survived the murder, it may be a challenge to track down the murderer. 2（指俘虏） criminal who can furnish information 3 = 活话 huóhuà B〈动〉 support oneself or one's family
【活扣】huókòu = 活结 huójié
【活力】huólì〈名〉 vigour: 充满青春～ be brimming with youthful vigour ‖ 恢复国家经济～ revive the nation's economy
【活灵活现】huólíng-huóxiàn〈成〉 lifelike: 描写得～ give a vivid description
【活龙活现】huólóng-huóxiàn = 活灵活现 huólíng-huóxiàn
【活路】huólù〈名〉 1（生计） means of subsistence: 这是我们唯一的～。 This is the only way out for us. 2（办法） workable method: 就在我们束手无策的时候，他的建议给了一条～。 When we were at a loss as to what to do, his proposal helped us out. 3（指道路） through road: 别向左拐，右边的路才是～。 Don't turn left. Only the road to the right is a through road. 4（指劳动） all kinds of physical labour
【活络】huóluò〈形〉〈方〉 1（松动） loose: 牙齿有点～。 The tooth has become a bit loose. 2（不肯定） indefinite: 他回答得很～，谁也说不清他下一步要干什么。 He was rather noncommittal in his answer, and nobody knew what he was about to do next.
【活埋】huómái〈动〉 bury alive
【活门】huómén〈名〉［机械］ valve
【活命】huómìng A〈动〉 1（为生） eke out an existence: 靠卖艺～ eke out an existence as a street entertainer 2（救命） save a life: ～之恩 indebtedness to sb. for saving one's life B〈名〉 life: ～的本能 instinct for survival ‖ 他从大火中逃出，拣了条～。 He escaped from the fire.
【活命哲学】huómìng zhéxué〈名〉 philosophy of survival
【活泼】huópo〈形〉 1（活跃） lively: 生动～的政治局面 vigorous lively political atmosphere ‖ 天真～的孩子 vivacious little kid 2［化学］ reactive: ～度 reactivity
【活菩萨】huópúsa〈名〉 Buddha incarnate
【活期】huóqī〈形〉 current: ～储蓄 current deposit ‖ ～存款 current deposit ‖ ～账户 current account
【活气】huóqì〈名〉 lively atmosphere: 车间里充满了～。 A lively atmosphere prevails in the workshop.
【活契】huóqì〈名〉 conditional real estate sales contract
【活钱儿】huóqiánr〈名〉〈口〉 ready money
【活塞】huósāi〈名〉［机械］ piston
【活神仙】huóshénxian〈名〉 clairvoyant
【活生生】huóshēngshēng A〈形〉 living: ～的例子 living example B = 活活 huóhuó
【活食】huóshí〈名〉 live prey
【活受罪】huóshòuzuì〈惯〉 suffer a living hell: 炎热的夏天忽然停电，那才叫～呢! You won't know what hell is like until you experience a power failure in the height of summer.

h

【活水】huóshuǐ〈名〉running water
【活死人】huósǐrén〈名〉〈方〉〈粗〉living corpse
【活似】huósì = 活像 huóxiàng
【活体】huótǐ〈名〉living body
【活体解剖】huótǐ jiěpōu〈名〉［医学］vivisection
【活头儿】huótour〈名〉〈口〉will to live: 仅仅因为被解雇了，他就觉得没多大～了。He lost interest in life simply because he was fired.
【活脱儿】huótuōr〈形〉〈口〉remarkably alike: 她长得～是她母亲。She is the very image of her mother.
【活现】huóxiàn〈动〉come alive: 他的英雄形象～在读者的眼前。His heroic image came alive before the readers' eyes. ▸活灵～, 神气～
【活像】huóxiàng〈动〉be the spitting image of: 这孩子～他父亲。The boy is the spitting image of his father.
【活性】huóxìng **A**〈形〉［化学］active **B**〈名〉activity: 抗氧～ antioxygenic activity
【活性染料】huóxìng rǎnliào〈名〉reactive dye
【活性炭】huóxìngtàn〈名〉［化学］active carbon
【活血】huóxuè〈动〉［中医］improve blood circulation
【活阎王】huóyánwang〈名〉demon king
【活页】huóyè〈名〉loose-leaf: ～夹 loose-leaf binder ‖ ～文选 loose-leaf selections
【活用】huóyòng〈动〉apply flexibly
【活跃】huóyuè **A**〈形〉dynamic: ～分子 activist ‖ 气氛～ lively atmosphere ‖ 思想～ active mind **B**〈动〉**1**（积极活动）be active: 他长期不懈地～在国际事务中。He has been very active in international affairs for a long time. ‖ 他是民族解放运动中的一位～人物。He was a dynamic figure in the national liberation movement. **2**（使活跃）invigorate: ～城乡物资交流 stimulate the interchange of urban and rural products ‖ 发展经济，～市场 develop the economy and invigorate the market
【活捉】huózhuō〈动〉capture alive: ～恐怖分子 capture the terrorist alive
【活字】huózì〈名〉［印刷］movable type: ～印刷 letter press
【活字版】huózìbǎn〈名〉original font
【活字典】huózìdiǎn〈名〉walking dictionary
【活组织检查】huózǔzhī jiǎnchá〈名〉［医学］biopsy
【活罪】huózuì〈名〉bitter suffering: 死罪可免，～难逃 exempt from the death penalty but not from punishment

huǒ

火 huǒ

A〈名〉**1**（指光和焰）fire: 严禁烟～! Keep away from fire! ‖ 大～在迅速蔓延。The fire was spreading quickly. ▸～海 **2**（指情绪）anger: 心头～起 burn with anger ▸发～, 窝～ **3**［中医］internal heat: ▸败～, 肝～ **4**（枪炮子弹）firearms: ▸～力, 交～, 军～
B〈副〉urgently: ▸～速, 风风～～, 十万～急
C〈动〉be angry: 被惹～了 be roused to anger ‖ 他可～儿了。He was furious. ▸恼～
D〈形〉**1** ▸**p. 863**（指颜色）fiery: ▸～红, ～鸡 **2**（兴旺）thriving: 生意很～。Business is brisk.

【火把】huǒbǎ〈名〉torch: 点燃～ light a torch
【火把节】Huǒbǎjié〈名〉Torchlight Festival
【火棒】huǒbàng〈名〉lighted torch in acrobatics : 要～ juggle lighted torches
【火暴】huǒbào〈形〉**1**（暴躁）fiery: ～性子 hot temper **2**（兴旺）vigorous: 数码相机的生意眼下很～。The market for digital cameras is currently very brisk. ‖ 小伙子干活很～。The young man is very enthusiastic about his work.
【火爆】huǒbào = 火暴 huǒbào
【火并】huǒbìng〈动〉engage in infighting: 流氓团伙头子在～中丧命。The ringleader was killed in a fight between two factions of his gang.
【火柴】huǒchái〈名〉match: 擦～ strike a match ‖ ～厂 match factory ‖ ～盒 matchbox
【火场】huǒchǎng〈名〉scene of a fire
【火车】huǒchē〈名〉train: ～车厢 railway coach ‖ ～票 train ticket ‖ ～时刻表 train timetable ‖ ～站 train station, railway station〈英〉‖ 高速～ bullet train
【火车头】huǒchētóu〈名〉**1**（指机车）locomotive; railway engine〈英〉**2**〈喻〉（指人或事）person or thing that plays a leading role: 他是车间的～。He has set a good example for his fellow workers in the workshop. ‖ 创新是发展的～。Creativity is the locomotive for development.
【火成岩】huǒchéngyán〈名〉［地质］igneous rock
【火炽】huǒchì〈形〉exuberant: 梅花开得正～。The plums are in full bloom. ‖ 那天战斗达到了最～的阶段。The fighting reached its greatest intensity that day.
【火电】huǒdiàn〈名〉thermal power
【火攻】huǒgōng〈动〉attack with fire
【火罐儿】huǒguànr〈名〉［中医］cupping jar: 拔～ cupping
【火光】huǒguāng〈名〉flame: ～耀眼 burn with a glaring light ‖ ～冲天 the flames lit up the sky
【火锅】huǒguō〈名〉hotpot: 涮～ have fondues
【火海】huǒhǎi〈名〉sea of flames: 敢闯～ dare to plunge into a sea of flames ‖ 葬身～ be buried in a sea of flames
【火红】huǒhóng ▸**p. 863**〈形〉**1**（指颜色）fiery: ～的朝霞 fiery morning glow ‖ ～的太阳 flaming sun **2**（兴旺）thriving: 生意～ brisk business
【火候】huǒhou〈名〉**1**（指火力）duration and degree of heating, cooking, smelting, etc.: 这鸭子烤得正到～。The roast duck is done to perfection. **2**（纯熟程度）level of attainment: 他的戏剧艺术到～了。His theatrical art has matured. **3**（关键时刻）crucial moment: 你来得正是～。You've arrived at a most opportune moment.
【火狐】huǒhú〈名〉red fox
【火花】huǒhuā〈名〉**1**（指火焰）spark: ～四溅 sparks flying off in all directions ‖ 生命的～ sparks of life ‖ 迸发出青春的～ beam with the vigour of youth **2**（指画纸）matchbox picture: ～收藏家 collector of matchbox pictures
【火花塞】huǒhuāsāi〈名〉［机械］spark plug
【火化】huǒhuà〈动〉cremate: ～场 crematorium
【火鸡】huǒjī〈名〉turkey
【火急】huǒjí〈形〉pressing: 十万～ most urgent ‖ 这是项～的任务。The task is pressing.
【火剪】huǒjiǎn〈名〉**1**（火钳）fire-tongs **2**（用于烫发）curling tongs
【火碱】huǒjiǎn〈名〉caustic soda
【火箭】huǒjiàn〈名〉rocket: 发射～ launch a rocket ‖ 捆绑式～ rocket with strap-on boosters ‖ ～发射场 rocket launching site
【火箭部队】huǒjiàn bùduì〈名〉rocket troops
【火箭弹】huǒjiàndàn〈名〉rocket shell
【火箭炮】huǒjiànpào〈名〉rocket gun
【火箭筒】huǒjiàntǒng〈名〉rocket launcher
【火警】huǒjǐng〈名〉fire alarm: ～自动报警器 automatic fire-alarm and extinguisher
【火炬】huǒjù〈名〉torch: ～接力 torch relay ‖ 奥运会～交接仪式 hand-over ceremony of the Olympic torch
【火炬跑】huǒjùpǎo〈名〉torch run: ～起跑仪式 a torch run opening ceremony
【火炕】huǒkàng〈名〉heated *kang* [brick or adobe bed common in North China]
【火坑】huǒkēng〈名〉abyss of suffering: 跳出～ escape a living hell ‖ 被拐骗的姑娘终于被救出了～。The abducted girl was finally rescued from her living hell.
【火筷子】huǒkuàizi〈名〉fire-tongs
【火辣辣】huǒlàlà〈形〉**1**（指疼痛感）scorching: ～的骄阳 scorching sun ‖ 觉得一阵～的疼痛 feel a searing pang **2**（指情绪）flushed: 她羞得脸上～的。Her face was hot with shame. **3**（指性格）bold and resolute;（指语言）sharp: ～的性格 bold and resolute character ‖ ～的批评 heated criticism
【火力】huǒlì〈名〉**1**（指燃烧）thermal power **2**［军事］firepower: 集中～ concentrate the fire (on) ‖ ～封锁 interdiction barrage ‖ ～侦察 reconnaissance by firing **3**（耐寒力）cold-resistance capacity of the human body: ～旺 full of vim and vigour
【火力发电】huǒlì fādiàn〈名〉thermal power generation: ～厂 thermal power plant
【火镰】huǒlián〈名〉steel (for flint): 用～取火 make fire by striking the steel on the flint
【火烈鸟】huǒlièniǎo〈名〉flamingo
【火流星】huǒliúxīng〈名〉［天文］bolide
【火龙】huǒlóng〈名〉procession of lanterns or torches
【火龙果】huǒlóngguǒ〈名〉［植物］pitaya
【火炉】huǒlú〈名〉**1**〈本〉stove **2**〈喻〉furnace: 武汉夏季天气酷热，向称中国三大～之一。Wuhan is known as one of China's three furnaces because it is so hot in summer.
【火轮】huǒlún〈名〉〈旧〉steamship
【火冒三丈】huǒmào-sānzhàng〈成〉fly into a rage: 流言蜚语使他～。The rumour made his blood boil.
【火苗】huǒmiáo〈名〉flame
【火捻】huǒniǎn〈名〉fuse: 鞭炮的～很短，点时可得小心。You should be very careful when you light the firecrackers as their fuses are rather short.
【火奴鲁鲁】Huǒnúlǔlǔ = 檀香山 Tánxiāngshān
【火炮】huǒpào〈名〉cannon
【火盆】huǒpén〈名〉brazier
【火拼】huǒpīn = 火并 huǒbìng
【火漆】huǒqī〈名〉sealing wax
【火气】huǒqì〈名〉**1**［中医］internal heat **2**（脾气）temper: ～很大 have a bad temper **3**（耐寒力）cold-resistant capacity: 年轻人～足，不怕冷。Young people

are full of energy. They don't mind the cold.
【火器】huǒqì〈名〉［军事］ firearm
【火钳】huǒqián〈名〉 fire-tongs
【火枪】huǒqiāng〈名〉 firelock
【火墙】huǒqiáng〈名〉1（指墙） hot-wall 2（指障碍） fire net
【火情】huǒqíng〈名〉 state of a fire
【火球】huǒqiú〈名〉 fire ball
【火热】huǒrè〈形〉1（极热） burning hot: ～的太阳 burning sun 2（热情） fiery: ～的心 fervent passion 3（亲密） intimate: 打得～ be as thick as thieves 4（激烈） intense: ～的斗争 fierce struggle
【火绒】huǒróng〈名〉 tinder: ～盒 tinder-box
【火绒草】huǒróngcǎo〈名〉 edelweiss
【火色】huǒsè〈名〉〈方〉 condition of fire [for cooking]
【火山】huǒshān ▸p. 164〈名〉 volcano: ～喷发 volcanic eruption ‖ ～熔岩 lava ‖ 活～ active volcano ‖ 死～ extinct volcano ‖ 休眠～ dormant volcano
【火山地震】huǒshān dìzhèn〈名〉 volcanic earthquake
【火山湖】huǒshānhú〈名〉 crater lake
【火山灰】huǒshānhuī〈名〉 volcanic ash
【火山口】huǒshānkǒu〈名〉 crater
【火上加油】huǒshàng-jiāyóu〈成〉pour oil on the fire
【火上浇油】huǒshàng-jiāoyóu = 火上加油 huǒshàng-jiāyóu
【火烧】huǒshāo〈动〉 burn
【火烧火燎】huǒshāo-huǒliǎo〈成〉1〈本〉 feeling terribly hot 2〈喻〉 restless with anxiety
【火烧眉毛】huǒshāo-méimao〈成〉 extremely urgent: 事情已经～了，我们不能再按常规办事！ Now that we've been plunged into an emergency, we mustn't cling to conventions any more.
【火烧云】huǒshāoyún〈名〉 morning/evening glow
【火烧】huǒshao〈名〉 baked wheaten cake
【火舌】huǒshé〈名〉 tongues of fire: 大火喷射出长长的～。 The fire shot up long tongues.
【火绳】huǒshéng〈名〉1（用于驱火） rope of plaited plants burnt as a mosquito repellent 2（用于取火） kindling rope
【火石】huǒshí〈名〉 flint
【火势】huǒshì〈名〉 intensity of fire: ～被控制住了。 The fire was brought under control.
【火树银花】huǒshù-yínhuā〈成〉 display of fireworks and a sea of lanterns on a festival night
【火速】huǒsù〈副〉 at full speed: ～增援 rush up reinforcements ‖ 大批医务人员～赶赴出事地点。 Large numbers of medical workers hurried to the spot of the accident.
【火损】huǒsǔn〈名〉 fire damage
【火炭】huǒtàn〈名〉 burning charcoal
【火塘】huǒtáng〈名〉〈方〉 fire pit
【火烫】huǒtàng A〈形〉 scalding B〈动〉 have one's hair permed with hot curling tongs
【火头】huǒtóu〈名〉1（火焰） flame 2（火候） duration and degree of heating, cooking, smelting, etc.: ～过了，饼子有点煳。 The heat was too strong and the cake was a little overdone. 3（怒气） fit of anger: 正在～上 be at the height of one's anger
【火头军】huǒtóujūn〈名〉〈诙〉 army cook
【火腿】huǒtuǐ〈名〉 ham: 金华～ Jinhua ham
【火网】huǒwǎng〈名〉［军事］ fire net
【火险】huǒxiǎn〈名〉1（指保险） fire insurance: 保～ buy fire insurance 2（指危险） fire danger: ～观察站 fire-danger station
【火线】huǒxiàn〈名〉1（一线战场） battle front: 上～ go to the front line ‖ ～立功 render meritorious service on the battlefield 2［电气］ live wire
【火星】huǒxīng〈名〉1（指火） spark: 从烟囱冒出的～引燃了屋顶木板。 Sparks from the chimney ignited the shingles. 2 Huǒxīng［天文］ Mars
【火星车】huǒxīngchē〈名〉 Mars rover
【火性】huǒxìng〈名〉〈口〉 hot temper: 他虽是个～子，心地却很善良。 Hot-tempered as he is, he has his heart in the right place.
【火眼】huǒyǎn ▸p. 50〈名〉［医学］ pinkeye: 害～ have pinkeye
【火眼金睛】huǒyǎn-jīnjīng〈成〉 piercing eye: 孙悟空～，妖魔鬼怪辨得清。 With his piercing eyes, Monkey King was able to tell monsters from ordinary human beings at a glance.
【火焰】huǒyàn〈名〉 flame: 扑不灭的～ unquenchable fire ‖ ～窜上来了。 Flames flared up. ‖ 他的来信又重新燃起了她心中爱情的～。 His reply rekindled the flames of love in her heart.
【火焰喷射器】huǒyàn pēnshèqì〈名〉 flame thrower
【火药】huǒyào〈名〉 gunpowder
【火药桶】huǒyàotǒng〈名〉 danger spot: 坐在～上 sit on a powder keg
【火药味】huǒyàowèi〈名〉 smell of gunpowder: 一篇充满～的声明 a statement smacking heavily of gunpowder
【火蚁】huǒyǐ〈名〉［昆虫］ fire ant
【火印】huǒyìn〈名〉 brand: 每件家具上都有～。 Every piece of furniture had a brand name.
【火油】huǒyóu〈名〉〈方〉 kerosene
【火源】huǒyuán〈名〉 source of fire
【火灾】huǒzāi〈名〉 inferno: ～损失 fire loss
【火葬】huǒzàng〈动〉cremate: ～场 crematorium
【火中取栗】huǒzhōng-qǔlì〈成〉help sb. to do sth. that puts them at risk
【火种】huǒzhǒng〈名〉 tinder: 革命的～ revolutionary tinder
【火烛】huǒzhú〈名〉 sth. that may cause a fire: 小心～! Caution against fire!
【火柱】huǒzhù〈名〉 column of fire
【火砖】huǒzhuān〈名〉 firebrick

伙[1] huǒ〈名〉1（伙食） meals: ▸～房, ～夫, 搭～ 2（同伴） partner: ▸～伴

伙[2]**（夥）** huǒ
A〈名〉1（集体） partnership: ▸拉帮结～, 散～ 2（伙计） shop salesman: 店～ salesman ▸～计
B〈量〉 group: 三个一群，五个一～ in small groups
C〈动〉 combine: ～着用 share in the use of sth. ‖ 他和同屋的同学～买了一台计算机。 He and his room-mates pooled their money and bought a computer. ▸～同, 合～
【伙伴】huǒbàn〈名〉 mate: ～关系 partnership ‖ 贸易～ trade partner
【伙房】huǒfáng〈名〉 kitchen: ～帮厨 help with food preparation in the kitchen
【伙夫】huǒfū〈名〉 mess cook
【伙计】huǒji〈名〉1（合伙人） partner 2〈口〉（朋友） mate: 让开，～! Excuse me, mate! 3〈旧〉（店内帮工） sales clerk: 他的店里只请了两个～。 He hired only two assistants in the store.
【伙食】huǒshi〈名〉 meals: ～自理 make one's own arrangement for food ‖ 你们这儿的～不错。 The food you have here is quite good.
【伙同】huǒtóng〈动〉 act in collusion with: 他～他的弟弟对付我。 He and his brother ganged up on me.
【伙子】huǒzi〈量〉〈口〉 gang: 他们是一～! They are in the same gang!

钬（鈥） huǒ〈名〉［化学］ holmium (Ho)

夥 huǒ〈形〉〈书〉 numerous: 获益甚～ have derived much benefit ‖ 游人甚～。 There were many tourists.

huò

或 huò
A〈代〉〈书〉 someone: 人固有一死，～重于泰山，～轻于鸿毛。 Man will die sooner or later. But some deaths are as heavy as Mount Tai, and some are as light as a feather.
B〈副〉1（可能） perhaps: 你去尝试，～能成功。 Go and try. You may be successful. 2（略微） slightly: ▸不可～缺
C〈连〉 either ... or ...: 她希望当个教师～医生。 She wants to be either a teacher or a doctor. ‖ 要找个好工作，去北京～上海都可以。 You could go either to Beijing or Shanghai to find a good job.
【或然】huòrán〈形〉 probable: ～性 probability
【或然率】huòránlǜ〈名〉 probability
【或许】huòxǔ〈副〉 maybe: 关上灯，～你能睡着。 Turn the light off, and you might fall asleep. ‖ ～明年我们还会在这里见面。 Maybe we'll see each other again here next year.
【或则】huòzé〈连〉 either ... or ...
【或者】huòzhě A〈副〉 perhaps: 这～是他们在表示感谢。 This may be their token of thanks. B〈连〉 either ... or ...: 你可以把钱存成活期～定期。 You can deposit your money either in a current account or a fixed account. ‖ ～反对，～赞成，你总得有个态度。 You must take a stand on the matter, either for or against.

和[1] huò〈动〉 mix: 搅～ stir in order to mix ▸～稀泥

和[2] huò〈量〉（指水） rinse;（指煎药） boiling: 衣服已经洗了三～。 The clothes have been rinsed three times. ‖ 每剂中药通常都煮两～。 Every dose of Chinese herbal medicine is normally boiled twice. ▸hé, hè, hú, huó
【和弄】huònong〈动〉〈方〉1（搅拌） mix: 要把鸡蛋和面粉～好。 Mix the egg and flour well together. 2（搀和） sow discord: 你可别在里边～。 You mustn't meddle in this.
【和稀泥】huò xīní〈动〉〈口〉〈喻〉 blur the line between right and wrong: 这是个原则问题，我们决不可～。 This is a matter of principle. There's no way we can paper it over.

h

货（貨） huò〈名〉 **1**〈书〉（钱财） property: ▸～币，通～ **2**（货物） goods: ～不对路 unwanted goods ▸交～，理～，盘～ **3**〈粗〉（指人） [used in reference to a person]: 他可不是个好～! He is not a decent person at all. ▸蠢～，贱～，骚～

【货比三家】huòbǐsānjiā〈成〉 compare different offers

【货币】huòbì〈名〉 currency

【货币单位】huòbì dānwèi〈名〉 monetary unit

【货币发行】huòbì fāxíng〈名〉 issue of banknotes

【货币回笼】huòbì huílóng〈名〉 withdrawal of currency from circulation

【货币流通量】huòbì liútōngliàng〈名〉 currency in circulation

【货币市场】huòbì shìchǎng〈名〉 money market: 国际～ international money market

【货币资本】huòbì zīběn〈名〉 money capital

【货仓】huòcāng〈名〉 warehouse

【货舱】huòcāng〈名〉 hold

【货场】huòchǎng〈名〉 freight yard

【货车】huòchē〈名〉 **1**（指火车） goods train〈英〉; freight train〈美〉 **2**（指马车） goods wagon **3**（指汽车） truck: 轻型～ pickup truck

【货船】huòchuán〈名〉 cargo ship: 定期～ cargo liner

【货单】huòdān〈名〉 shipping list: 按～发货 dispatch by shipping list

【货到付款】huòdào fùkuǎn〈动〉 cash on delivery (COD)

【货柜】huòguì〈名〉 **1**（柜台） counter: 廉价～ bargain counter **2**〈方〉（集装箱） container: ～码头 container terminal

【货机】huòjī〈名〉［航空］ cargo plane

【货架子】huòjiàzi〈名〉 **1**（用于摆放商品） goods shelf **2**（指自行车后座） bicycle luggage carrier

【货款】huòkuǎn〈名〉 payment for goods

【货郎】huòláng〈名〉 pedlar〈英〉; peddler〈美〉

【货郎担】huòlángdàn〈名〉 pedlar's load carried on a shoulder pole

【货郎鼓】huòlánggǔ〈名〉 pedlar's rattle-drum

【货轮】huòlún〈名〉 cargo ship

【货票】huòpiào〈名〉 delivery order

【货品】huòpǐn〈名〉 type of goods: ～充足 ample supply of goods

【货色】huòsè〈名〉 **1**（指东西） goods: 上等～ first-class goods ‖ ～齐全。 Goods of every description are available. **2**〈贬〉（指人） stuff: 他俩是半斤八两，一路～。 There's not much to choose between them. They're one of a kind.

【货损】huòsǔn〈名〉 cargo damage: ～折扣 allowance for damage

ℹ 货币与金钱

英国货币

■ 英国的货币为英镑（Pound Sterling 或 Great British Pound），其简写符号为 £，标准符号为 GBP。英镑符号要写在数字之前。1 英镑等于 100 便士，字母 p 代表便士，要写在数字之后：

写	读
1p	one p (或 penny)
5p	five p (或 pence)
£60	sixty pounds
£4.66	four pounds sixty-six p (或 pence) four pounds sixty-six four sixty-six
20 镑纸币	a twenty-pound note
1 镑硬币	a one-pound coin
2 便士硬币	a 2p piece/a 2p coin 或 a two-pence piece/ a two-pence coin

■ 英国人在日常生活中常用一些非正式的表达法来表示不同面值的钱，比如：

quid	£1
fiver	£5
tenner	£10
ton	£100
grand	£1,000

美国货币

■ 美国的货币为美元（U.S. Dollar），其简写符号为 U.S.$，标准符号为 USD。美元符号要写在数字之前。1 美元等于 100 美分，字母 c 代表美分，要写在数字之后：

写	读
1c	one cent
4c	four cents
U.S.$20	twenty dollars
U.S.$25.30	twenty-five dollars thirty cents
20 美元的纸币	a twenty-dollar bill
1 美元硬币	a one-dollar coin
5 美分硬币	a 5c piece/a 5c coin 或 a five-cent piece/ a five-cent coin

■ 美国人在日常生活中常用一些非正式的表达法来表示不同面值的钱，比如：

penny	1c
nickel	5c
dime	10c
quarter	25c
buck	U.S.$1
grand	U.S.$1,000

中国货币

■ 中国的法定货币为人民币（Renminbi Yuan），其简写符号为 RMB¥，标准符号为 CNY，都写在数字之前：

写	读
RMB¥0.05	five fen
RMB¥0.20	two jiao 或 two mao
RMB¥1.00	one yuan 或 one kuai
RMB¥3.65	three yuan six jiao five fen 或 three kuai six mao five fen
RMB¥200	two hundred yuan
RMB¥200.23	two hundred yuan and two jiao three fen
RMB¥1,000	one thousand yuan
RMB¥3,050.60	three thousand and fifty yuan six jiao
RMB¥10,000.00	ten thousand yuan
RMB¥100,000.00	a hundred thousand yuan
RMB¥1,000,000.00	one million yuan

问价钱

多少钱？—— 30 镑
= How much is it? — It's £30

这台电脑多少钱？—— 9,000 元
= How much does the computer cost?
— It costs RMB¥9,000

这张桌子价格是多少？
—— 500 元
或 超过 500 元
或 不到 500 元
或 500 元左右
= What is the price of this table?
— It is 500 yuan
或 It is over/more than 500 yuan
或 It is under/less than 500 yuan
或 It is about 500 yuan

其他短语

面值 29 便士的邮票
= a 29-pence stamp

10 镑 1 张的票
= a £10 ticket

1,000 镑支票
= a £1,000 cheque
或 a cheque for £1,000

5 镑零钱
= £5 in change

800 镑旅行支票
= £800 in traveller's cheques

两万人民币奖学金
= a twenty-thousand-yuan scholarship

一万元现金
= RMB¥10,000 in cash

两万元人民币支票
= a cheque for RMB¥20,000

你能把 100 元的纸币换成两张 50 的吗？
= Could you change a RMB¥100 note for two fifties, please?

你能把 10 镑纸币换成零钱吗？
= Could you change a £10 note for small change, please?

你能把英镑换成元吗？
= Can you change my pounds into yuan?

你想怎么付款？
—— 我想用支票 / 现金 / 银行卡付
= How would you like to pay?
— I'd like to pay by cheque/cash/card

你想用什么货币来付？—— 我想用英镑
= In what currency would you like to pay?
— I'd like to pay in pounds

人民币对英镑的兑换率是多少？
—— 100 元兑 8.9 镑
= What is the exchange rate from Renminbi Yuan into Pound Sterling?
— It is 100 yuan to 8.9 pounds

h

【货摊】huòtān〈动〉stall: ～执照 stall licence
【货位】huòwèi〈名〉1（储存位置）storage space 2［铁路］car load
【货物】huòwù〈名〉goods: 装卸～ handle cargo ‖ ～清单 bill of goods
【货箱】huòxiāng〈名〉packing box
【货样】huòyàng〈名〉sample (goods)
【货源】huòyuán〈名〉supply of goods: ～充足 ample supply of goods
【货运】huòyùn〈名〉freight transportation: ～码头 cargo terminal ‖ ～单 waybill
【货栈】huòzhàn〈名〉warehouse
【货真价实】huòzhēn-jiàshí〈成〉1（指货物质量）genuine goods at a fair price 2（完全彻底）out-and-out: 他是个～的骗子。He is an out-and-out swindler.
【货主】huòzhǔ〈名〉consignor of cargo

获[1]（獲）huò

〈动〉1（捉到）catch: ▸捕～, 俘～ 2（取得）win: ～冠军/金牌 win the championship/gold medal ‖ ～一等奖 win first prize ▸～奖, 不劳而～

获[2]（穫）huò

〈动〉reap: 喜～丰收 happily reap a bumper harvest ▸收～
【获得】huòdé〈动〉achieve: ～成功 attain success ‖ ～好评 win acclaim ‖ ～文学硕士学位 receive an MA ‖ ～自由 gain freedom
【获得性免疫缺陷综合征】huòdéxìng miǎnyì quēxiàn zōnghézhēng〈名〉acquired immune deficiency syndrome (AIDS)
【获奖】huòjiǎng〈动〉win an award: ～科学家 prize-winning scientist ‖ ～者 prize winner
【获救】huòjiù〈动〉be rescued: 人质～了。The hostage was rescued.
【获利】huòlì〈动〉make a profit
【获利盘】huòlìpán〈名〉［金融］profit-making shares: 面临～回吐的压力 face the pressure of selling out profit-making shares
【获取】huòqǔ〈动〉obtain: ～养分 obtain nourishment ‖ ～知识 acquire knowledge
【获胜】huòshèng〈动〉be victorious: 以微弱优势～ triumph by a slim margin ‖ 甲队以4:1～。Team A won the match four to one.
【获释】huòshì〈动〉be released: ～出狱 be released from prison ‖ 提前～ be released before one's prison term expires
【获悉】huòxī〈动〉〈书〉hear of: ～噩耗，他甚感悲痛。He was grieved to hear the sad news.
【获益匪浅】huòyì-fěiqiǎn〈成〉reap substantial benefits
【获知】huòzhī = 获悉 huòxī
【获准】huòzhǔn〈动〉secure approval: 你的留学申请业已～。Your application to study abroad has been approved.

祸（禍）huò

A〈名〉disaster: ～兮福所倚，福兮～所伏 good fortune lies within bad, bad fortune lurks within good ▸～首, 车～, 闯～
B〈动〉bring disaster upon: ▸～国殃民
【祸不单行】huòbùdānxíng〈成〉it never rains but it pours: ▸福无双至，～
【祸从口出】huòcóngkǒuchū〈成〉a loose tongue is a source of evil: 病从口入，～。Disease goes in by the mouth and disaster comes out of it.
【祸从天降】huòcóngtiānjiàng〈成〉unexpected adversity
【祸端】huòduān〈名〉〈书〉cause of ruin
【祸根】huògēn〈名〉root of trouble: ～不除，后患无穷。There will be endless trouble unless the source of the disaster is eradicated.
【祸国殃民】huòguó-yāngmín〈成〉damage the country and bring calamity to the people
【祸害】huòhai A〈名〉1（灾难）disaster 2（指源头）scourge: 法西斯主义是人类的～。Fascism is the scourge of the human race. B〈动〉wreck
【祸患】huòhuàn〈名〉calamity: 消除～ ward off disaster ‖ ～无穷 endless trouble
【祸乱】huòluàn〈名〉disaster and turmoil: 军阀连年混战，老百姓惨遭～。Over the years wars between the warlords plunged the people into calamity and chaos.
【祸起萧墙】huòqǐ-xiāoqiáng〈成〉trouble begins at home
【祸事】huòshì〈名〉disaster
【祸首】huòshǒu〈名〉chief offender: ▸罪魁～
【祸水】huòshuǐ〈名〉〈喻〉bane: 这个黑社会组织是当地的一股～。The underworld gang is the bane of this area.
【祸祟】huòsuì〈名〉ghost-afflicted disaster
【祸胎】huòtāi〈名〉root of trouble
【祸心】huòxīn〈名〉evil intent: 包藏～ harbour malicious intent
【祸殃】huòyāng〈名〉disaster: 招致～ court disaster
【祸种】huòzhǒng〈名〉cause of misfortune

惑 huò

〈动〉1（迷惑）be puzzled: ▸惶～, 困～, 疑～ 2（使迷惑）delude: ▸蛊～, 诱～
【惑乱】huòluàn〈动〉confuse: ～人心 confuse people
【惑众】huòzhòng〈动〉〈书〉confuse people: ▸造谣～

霍 huò

A〈副〉suddenly: ▸～地, ～然
B〈拟〉sound of grinding knives, etc.
【霍地】huòdì〈副〉suddenly: ～冲出房子 suddenly rush out of the room ‖ ～立起身来 spring to one's feet all of a sudden
【霍霍】huòhuò A〈拟〉sound of grinding knives, etc.: 磨刀～向猪羊 sharpen a knife to kill pigs and lambs B〈形〉shining: 电光～。Lightening flashed. ‖ 他两眼～闪光。His eyes sparkled.
【霍乱】huòluàn ▸**p. 50**〈名〉1［医学］cholera 2［中医］acute gastroenteritis
【霍然】huòrán A〈副〉suddenly: 手电筒～一亮。An electric torch suddenly flashed on. B〈形〉〈书〉be cured quickly: 数日之后，定当～。You will certainly recover in a matter of days.
【霍闪】huòshǎn A〈动〉flash: 小姑娘～着一双好奇的大眼睛。The little girl's eyes flashed with curiosity. B〈名〉〈方〉lightning: 紧跟着雷声就是一个～。The roar of thunder was followed by lightning.

豁 huò

A〈形〉1（阔）wide: ▸～亮 2（通达）open-minded: ▸～达
B〈动〉exempt: ▸～免
▸huá, huō
【豁达】huòdá〈形〉straightforward and open-minded: 心胸～ generous and open-minded
【豁达大度】huòdá-dàdù〈成〉open-minded and magnanimous
【豁朗】huòlǎng〈形〉cheerful
【豁亮】huòliàng〈形〉1（敞亮）roomy and bright: 这屋子又干净又～。The room is clean, bright and spacious. 2（洪亮）loud and clear: 嗓音～ have a sonorous voice
【豁免】huòmiǎn〈动〉exempt: ～某人捐税 exempt sb. from taxes ‖ ～权 immunity
【豁然】huòrán〈形〉broad and spacious
【豁然贯通】huòrán-guàntōng〈成〉suddenly see the whole thing in a clear light: 直读到最后一章，我才有～之感。It didn't dawn upon me until the very last chapter what the book was all about.
【豁然开朗】huòrán-kāilǎng〈成〉be fully enlightened: 他的一席话使我～。What he said enlightened me.

镬（鑊）huò

〈名〉1〈方〉（锅）pot 2〈旧〉（无足鼎）cauldron: 斧锯鼎～ hatchet, saw, tripod and cauldron [ancient instruments of torture]

藿 huò

〈名〉〈书〉leaves of pulse plants
【藿香】huòxiāng〈名〉［中药］wrinkled giant hyssop

嚯 huò

A〈叹〉wow: ～，这座楼可真高啊! Wow! This really is a tall building!
B〈拟〉chortle: ～～大笑 guffaw

蠖 huò

▸尺蠖 chǐhuò

h

Jj

jī

几[1] jī〈名〉small table: ▸茶～, 窗明～净, 条～

几[2]**（幾）** jī〈副〉〈书〉almost: ～可乱真 can almost pass for authentic ‖ 事故遇难者～20人。Nearly 20 people were killed in the accident.
▸jǐ

【几案】jī'àn〈名〉long narrow table

【几乎】jīhū〈副〉almost: ～丧命 be within an inch of one's life ‖ 天气～一日一变。The weather changes almost daily. ‖ 我们～误了火车。We nearly missed the train.

【几近】jījìn〈副〉〈书〉on the verge of: ～成功/灭绝/破产 be on the verge of success/extinction/bankruptcy ‖ 她兴奋得～歇斯底里。Her excitement bordered on hysteria. ‖ 这项工程～完工。The project is close to completion.

【几率】jīlǜ〈名〉probability

讥（譏） jī〈动〉mock: 冷言相～ make sarcastic comments ▸～讽, ～笑, 反唇相～

【讥嘲】jīcháo〈动〉mock: ～的笔调 satirical tone

【讥刺】jīcì〈动〉〈书〉ridicule: 冷语～ deride sb. with cutting remarks

【讥讽】jīfěng〈动〉satirize: 遭到～ meet with ridicule ‖ 用～的口吻讲话 speak in a satirical tone ‖ 他成了大家～的对象。He's become an object of ridicule.

【讥诮】jīqiào〈动〉〈书〉ridicule: ～这一想法 sneer at the idea

【讥笑】jīxiào〈动〉sneer at: ～某人胆小 mock sb.'s timidity ‖ 不理会别人的～ ignore sb.'s sneers ‖ 她常常被人～。She was often mocked by people.

击（擊） jī〈动〉**1**（敲）hit: ～成碎片 smash into pieces ‖ 他朝我的头上猛～了一下。He bashed me on the head. ▸～鼓, ～掌, 旁敲侧～ **2**（刺）stab: ▸～剑, 搏～, 反戈一～ **3**（攻击）attack: ▸攻～, 声东～西, 袭～ **4**（碰触）come into contact (with): ▸冲～, 目～, 撞～

【击败】jībài〈动〉beat: ～对手 defeat one's opponent ‖ 彻底～ totally thrash ‖ A队以悬殊的比分～B队。Team A beat Team B by a huge margin.

【击毙】jībì〈动〉〈贬〉shoot dead: 凶犯被当场～。The murderer was shot dead there and then.

【击沉】jīchén〈动〉attack and sink: 战舰被～了。The warship was attacked and sunk.

【击穿】jīchuān〈动〉puncture

【击打】jīdǎ〈动〉beat: 波浪～着岩石。The waves lashed the rocks.

【击倒】jīdǎo〈动〉knock down: ～对手 knock down one's opponent ‖ 技术性～ technical knockout ‖ 把他～在地 knock him to the floor

【击发】jīfā〈动〉pull the trigger

【击鼓】jīgǔ〈动〉beat a drum: ～助威 drum up morale ‖ ～升堂 sound the drum to show that the court is in session

【击鼓传花】jīgǔ chuánhuā〈名〉game involving the beating of a drum and the passing around a spray of blossom

【击鼓鸣冤】jīgǔ-míngyuān〈成〉beat the *yamen* drum to appeal for justice [in ancient China]

【击毁】jīhuǐ〈动〉smash: ～敌机一架 destroy an enemy plane

【击剑】jījiàn ▸**p. 909**〈名〉［体育］fencing: ～运动员 fencer

【击剑服】jījiànfú〈名〉fencing clothes

【击节】jījié〈动〉〈书〉beat time in appreciation: ～叹赏 clap one's hands in applause

【击溃】jīkuì〈动〉rout: ～敌军 crush the enemy

【击落】jīluò〈动〉shoot down: ～敌机 shoot down an enemy plane

【击破】jīpò〈动〉crush: ▸各个～

【击球】jīqiú〈动〉［体育］bat (a ball)

【击球手】jīqiúshǒu〈名〉（指板球）batsman；（指棒球）batter

【击伤】jīshāng〈动〉wound

【击水】jīshuǐ〈动〉**1**（拍打水面）strike water: 用桨～ strike water with oars **2**（游泳）swim: 在湖/江中～ swim in a lake/river

【击退】jītuì〈动〉beat off: ～侵略者 fight off invaders

【击以猛掌】jīyǐměngzhǎng〈成〉〈喻〉give a sharp warning

【击掌】jīzhǎng〈动〉**1**（拍手）clap one's hands: ～祝贺 clap one's hands in congratulation ‖ ～为号 signal by clapping hands **2**（相互拍手）give sb. a high-five: 运动员们相互～。The players high-fived each another.

【击中】jīzhòng〈动〉hit: ～目标 hit a target ‖ ～痛处 hit sb. where it hurts ‖ ～要害 hit home

叽（嘰） jī〈拟〉[used for sound of a bird or insect] chirp: 小鸟在树上～～地叫个不停。Little birds were chirping away in the trees.

【叽咕】jīgu〈动〉mutter: 别叽叽咕咕的! 我听不见。Don't mutter! I can't hear you. ‖ 那女人在～些什么? What was that woman whispering to herself?

【叽叽嘎嘎】jiji-gāgā〈拟〉**1**（指说笑声）[used for sound of chatting and laughing shrilly] cackle: 班上所有的学生都～地笑了起来。All the students in the classroom started cackling with laughter. **2**（指摩擦声）creak: 这门总是～地响。The door is always creaking.

【叽叽喳喳】jiji-zhāzhā ＝ 唧唧喳喳 jījizhāzhā

【叽里旮旯】jīligālá〈名〉〈方〉all nooks and crannies: 他的办公室里, ～都是书。Every corner of his office is full of books.

【叽里咕噜】jīligūlū〈拟〉**1**（指说话声）babble: ～地说着外国话 babble on in a foreign language ‖ 你～地说什么呢? What are you mumbling about? **2**（指滚动声）tumble: 水果～地滚下楼梯。The fruit tumbled down the stairs.

【叽哩呱啦】jīliguālā〈拟〉chatter: ～地说个没完 talk noisily and endlessly

饥[1]**（飢）** jī〈形〉hungry: ▸～饿, 充～, 如～似渴

饥[2]**（饑）** jī〈形〉famished: 连年大～ successive years of famine ▸～馑

【饥不择食】jībùzéshí〈成〉a hungry person is not choosy

【饥肠辘辘】jīcháng-lùlù〈成〉one's stomach rumbles with hunger

【饥饿】jī'è〈形〉starved: 缓解～ appease one's hunger ‖ 死于～ die of starvation ‖ ～难耐 feel unbearably hungry ‖ 因～而感到全身无力 feel weak all over with hunger

【饥饿疗法】jī'è liáofǎ〈名〉［医学］hunger cure

【饥寒交迫】jīhán-jiāopò〈成〉suffer from cold and hunger: 陷入～的困难境地 suffer the terrible hardships of cold and hunger

【饥荒】jīhuang〈名〉**1**（指灾荒）famine: 遭受～ suffer from famine ‖ 在～中饿死 die of starvation during a famine **2**〈喻〉（指经济困境）financial difficulties: 入不敷出, 月月闹～ live beyond one's means and run short of money month after month **3**〈喻〉（债务）debt: ▸拉～

【饥馑】jījǐn〈书〉＝饥荒 jīhuang 1

【饥渴】jīkě〈形〉hungry and thirsty: ～难耐 suffer from acute hunger and thirst

【饥民】jīmín〈名〉famine victim

【饥馁】jīněi〈形〉〈书〉starved

【饥色】jīsè〈名〉malnourished look: 面有～ look famished

玑（璣） jī〈名〉〈古〉**1**（指珠子）pearl that is not quite round **2**（指仪器）astronomical instrument

圾 jī ▸垃圾 lājī

芨 jī

【芨芨草】jījīcǎo〈名〉［植物］splendid Achnatherum

机（機）jī

A〈名〉**1**（射箭机关） trigger mechanism: ▸扳～ **2**（机器） machine: ▸～车，～器，计算～ **3**（生活机能） life force: ▸无～，有～体 **4**（飞机） aircraft: 敌～ enemy plane ▸～场，班～，战斗～ **5**（关键因素） crucial point: ▸契～，危～ **6**（时机） opportunity: ▸～会，乘～，随～应变 **7**（机密） important work: ▸～密，军～，日理万～ **8**（念头） idea: ▸动～，杀～，心～

B〈形〉quick-witted: ▸～动，～警

【机变】jībiàn〈动〉〈书〉 adapt oneself to circumstances: 善于～ be good at adapting oneself to changing circumstances

【机播】jībō〈动〉 sow by machine

【机不可失，时不再来】jībùkěshī, shíbùzàilái〈俗〉 seize the day

【机舱】jīcāng〈名〉**1**（用于放置机器） engine room **2**（用于载客装货） cabin

【机场】jīchǎng〈名〉 airport: 国际～ international airport ‖ 军用～ military airfield

【机场标塔】jīchǎng biāotǎ〈名〉 pylon

【机场灯标】jīchǎng dēngbiāo〈名〉airport beacon

【机场跑道】jīchǎng pǎodào〈名〉 airstrip

【机场税】jīchǎngshuì〈名〉 airport tax

【机场线】jīchǎngxiàn〈名〉 airport line: 地铁～已开通。 The underground line to the airport has been opened.

【机车】jīchē〈名〉 engine: 蒸汽～ steam engine

【机车车辆】jīchē chēliàng〈名〉 rolling stock: ～厂 rolling stock plant

【机车司机】jīchē sījī〈名〉 engine driver〈英〉; engineer〈美〉

【机船】jīchuán〈名〉 motor vessel

【机床】jīchuáng〈名〉 machine tool: 金属切削～ metal cutting machine tool

【机电】jīdiàn〈名〉electromechanical equipment: ～产品 mechanical and electrical products

【机顶盒】jīdǐnghé〈名〉 digital set-top box

【机动】jīdòng〈形〉**1**（装有发动机） motorized: ～化部队 motorized troops **2**（灵活） flexible: 灵活～的战略/战术 flexible strategy/tactics ‖ 有～的余地 have room for movement ▸～性 **3**（供灵活调用） standby: 留些～时间 leave some time to spare ‖ 留些钱作为～开支 set aside some money for extras ‖ ～力量 reserve force

【机动车】jīdòngchē〈名〉 motorized vehicle: ～禁止停靠。 No parking for motor vehicles.

【机动款】jīdòngkuǎn〈名〉 reserve funds

【机动性】jīdòngxìng〈名〉 flexibility: 有一定的～ be flexible within certain limits ‖ 游击战的～ mobility in guerrilla warfare

【机帆船】jīfānchuán〈名〉 motorized sailboat

【机房】jīfáng〈名〉 machine room: 计算机～ computer room

【机锋】jīfēng〈名〉［佛教］ sharp-witted and incisive remarks: 他语多～。 His remarks are often penetrating.

【机耕】jīgēng〈名〉［农业］tractor ploughing: ～面积 tractor-ploughed area

【机耕船】jīgēngchuán〈名〉 boat tractor

【机耕地】jīgēngdì〈名〉 tractor-ploughed land

【机工】jīgōng〈名〉 mechanic

【机构】jīgòu〈名〉**1**（指机械装置） mechanism: 变速/控制～ gear-shifting/control mechanism ‖ 传动/分离～ transmission/disengaging mechanism **2**（指机关团体） organization: 福利～ welfare agency ‖ 国家～ state organization ‖ 金融～ financial setup ‖ 科研～ scientific research institute ‖ 宣传～ publicity machine ▸政府～ **3**（组织结构） internal structure of an organization: 精简行政～ simplify an administrative structure ‖ ～重叠 overlapping institutions ‖ ～臃肿 overstaffed organization

【机构改革】jīgòu gǎigé〈名〉 structural reform

【机关】jīguān **A**〈名〉**1**［机械］ mechanism: 起动/锁定～ starting/locking gear **2**（单位、部门） body: 党政～ Party and government bodies ‖ 公安～ public security office ‖ 行政～ administrative organ ‖ 我在～工作。 I work in a government office. ▸国家～，政府～ **3**（计谋） scheme: 识破～ see through a trick ‖ ～算尽 use up all one's tricks **B**〈形〉 machine-operated: ～布景 machine-operated stage scenery ▸～炮，～枪

【机关报】jīguānbào〈名〉 official newspaper (of a political party, government, etc.): 政府～ government mouthpiece

【机关干部】jīguān gànbù〈名〉 government functionary

【机关炮】jīguānpào〈名〉 machine-cannon

【机关枪】jīguānqiāng〈名〉 machine-gun

【机灌】jīguàn〈名〉 motor-pumped irrigation: ～田 pump-irrigated field

【机徽】jīhuī〈名〉［航空］ plane emblem

【机会】jīhuì〈名〉 opportunity: 错过～ miss an opportunity ‖ 借此～（做某事） take the opportunity (to do sth.) ‖ 抓住～ seize an opportunity ‖ ～成本 opportunity cost ‖ 千载难逢的～ golden opportunity

【机会均等】jīhuì jūnděng〈成〉 equal opportunities

【机会球】jīhuìqiú〈名〉［体育］ set-up: 在～的把握上有待加强。 There is still scope for improvement in the conversion of set-ups.

【机会主义】jīhuìzhǔyì〈名〉 opportunism

【机架】jījià〈名〉 rack

【机件】jījiàn〈名〉［机械］ machine parts: 给～上油 oil the parts ‖ 精密～ precise mechanism

【机降】jījiàng〈形〉 air-landed: ～部队 air-landed forces

【机井】jījǐng〈名〉 power-operated well

【机警】jījǐng〈形〉 alert: ～的士兵 vigilant soldier ‖ 他可真～，一下子就注意到那个细节。 It was very sharp of him to have noticed that detail right away.

【机具】jījù〈名〉 machines and tools: 农业～ farm implements

【机考】jīkǎo〈动〉 test by computer

【机库】jīkù〈名〉［航空］ (aeroplane) hangar

【机理】jīlǐ = 机制 jīzhì B

【机灵】jīling〈形〉 clever: 做生意很～ be smart in business ‖ 这孩子特～。 This child is very clever.

【机灵鬼】jīlingguǐ〈名〉 smart fellow

【机米】jīmǐ = 籼米 xiānmǐ

【机密】jīmì **A**〈形〉 confidential: ～档案 secret archives ‖ ～情报 classified information ‖ ～文件 confidential document **B**〈名〉 secret: 泄露～ give away a secret ‖ 严守～ guard a secret closely ‖ 军事～ military secret

【机敏】jīmǐn〈形〉 dexterous: ～过人 extraordinarily resourceful ‖ 反应～ be quick-witted

【机谋】jīmóu〈名〉〈书〉 stratagem: 中了敌人的～ fall into an enemy trap

【机能】jīnéng〈名〉［生理］ function: 恢复大脑～ regain one's mental faculties ‖ 失去双手～ lose the use of one's hands ‖ 人体器官的正常～ proper functioning of the bodily organs

【机能亢进】jīnéng kàngjìn〈名〉 hyperfunction

【机能紊乱】jīnéng wěnluàn〈名〉 functional disorder

【机能障碍】jīnéng zhàng'ài〈名〉 malfunction

【机票】jīpiào〈名〉 air ticket: 预订～ make flight reservations

【机器】jīqì〈名〉 machine: 制造～ manufacture a machine ‖ ～运转正常。 The machine functions properly. ‖〈喻〉国家～ state machinery ‖〈喻〉宣传～ propaganda machine

【机器翻译】jīqì fānyì〈名〉［计算机］ machine translation

【机器零件】jīqì língjiàn〈名〉 machine part

【机器模型】jīqì móxíng〈名〉 machine mould

【机器人】jīqìrén〈名〉 robot: 设计/制造～ design/construct a robot

【机器语言】jīqì yǔyán〈名〉［计算机］ machine language

【机枪】jīqiāng〈名〉 machine-gun: 高射～ anti-aircraft machine-gun ‖ 轻/重～ light/heavy machine-gun

【机巧】jīqiǎo〈形〉 adroit: 应对～ be good at repartee ‖ ～地避开有争议的问题 skilfully avoid a controversial issue

【机群】jīqún〈名〉 aerial fleet

【机身】jīshēn〈名〉［航空］ fuselage

【机师】jīshī ▸**p. 966**〈名〉**1**（指操作机器） engineer **2**（飞行员） air pilot

【机首】jīshǒu = 机头 jītóu

【机体】jītǐ〈名〉［生理］ organism: 增强～免疫力 enhance the immunity of an organism ‖ 细菌侵入～，就会危害健康。 Bacteria harm an organism once they've entered it.

【机头】jītóu〈名〉 nose (of an aircraft)

【机尾】jīwěi〈名〉 tail (of an aircraft)

【机务】jīwù〈名〉 machine operation and maintenance: ～段 maintenance section ‖ ～人员 maintenance personnel

【机械】jīxiè **A**〈名〉 machinery: 纺织～ textile machinery ‖ 农业～ farm machinery ‖ 精密～ precision mechanism ‖ ～厂 machine works **B**〈形〉 mechanical: ～的动作 mechanical movement ‖ ～地搬用外国经验 mechanically copy foreign experience ‖ 你的工作方法太～了。 Your method of working is too inflexible.

【机械波】jīxièbō〈名〉 mechanical wave

【机械工】jīxiègōng〈名〉 mechanic

【机械故障】jīxiè gùzhàng〈名〉 mechanical failure

【机械化】jīxièhuà〈动〉 mechanize: 实现农业～ mechanize agriculture ‖ 组建～部队 form a mechanized force ‖ ～程度很低。 Mechanization is low.

【机械论】jīxièlùn = 机械唯物主义 jīxiè wéiwùzhǔyì

【机械能】jīxiènéng〈名〉［物理］ mechanical energy: ～守恒定律 law of conservation of mechanical energy

【机械师】jīxièshī ▸**p. 966**〈名〉 mechanic

【机械手】jīxièshǒu〈名〉［机械］ manipulator: 万能～ general-purpose manipulator

【机械唯物主义】jīxiè wéiwùzhǔyì〈名〉［哲学］ mechanical materialism

【机械原理】jīxiè yuánlǐ〈名〉 mechanical principle

【机械运动】jīxiè yùndòng〈名〉［物理］ mechanical movement

【机械制图】 jīxiè zhìtú 〈名〉 mechanical drawing
【机心】 jīxīn 〈名〉〈书〉 cunning idea: 他们各存~。They each had their own schemes.
【机芯】 jīxīn 〈名〉 parts
【机型】 jīxíng 〈名〉 type (of an aircraft)
【机修】 jīxiū 〈名〉 machine repair: ~工 maintenance man
【机绣】 jīxiù 〈名〉 machine embroidery
【机要】 jīyào 〈形〉 confidential: ~工作 confidential work ‖ ~文件 confidential document ‖ ~秘书 confidential secretary
【机要费】 jīyàofèi 〈名〉 confidential expenses: ~案 confidential expenses case
【机宜】 jīyí 〈名〉〈书〉 guidelines: ▸面授~
【机翼】 jīyì 〈名〉 [航空] wing
【机油】 jīyóu 〈名〉 machine oil
【机遇】 jīyù 〈名〉 opportunity: 等待~ bide one's time ‖ 抓住~ seize the opportunity ‖ ~与挑战并存。Opportunities exist alongside challenges.
【机遇期】 jīyùqī 〈名〉 window of opportunity: 战略~ period of strategic opportunity
【机缘】 jīyuán 〈名〉 lucky chance: ~凑巧 by chance ‖ ~让我们再次相遇。Chance has allowed us meet again.
【机运】 jīyùn 〈名〉 chance: ~不佳 not have much luck
【机载】 jīzài 〈形〉 airborne: ~导弹 aircraft missile
【机诈】 jīzhà 〈形〉〈书〉 crafty
【机长】 jīzhǎng 〈名〉 captain
【机制】 jīzhì **A** 〈形〉 machine-made: ~面粉/煤砖 machine-processed flour/briquette ‖ ~纸 machine-made paper **B** 〈名〉 mechanism: 大脑~ mechanism of the brain ‖ 竞争~ competition system ‖ 市场经济~ workings of market economy
【机智】 jīzhì 〈形〉 quick-witted: ~过人 be extremely intelligent ‖ ~灵活 be quick-witted and flexible ‖ ~勇敢 be brave and resourceful ‖ ~的回答 witty response
【机助翻译】 jīzhù fānyì 〈名〉 machine-aided translation
【机杼】 jīzhù 〈名〉〈书〉 **1**(织布机) loom **2**(指诗文) conception and composition: 自出~ be original in conception
【机子】 jīzi 〈名〉 **1**(指装置) small machine **2**(枪机) trigger
【机组】 jīzǔ 〈名〉 **1** [机械] unit: 发电~ generating unit **2** [航空] flight crew: ~人员 crew member ‖ 这架飞机有五名~成员。The plane has a crew of five.

j

乩 jī ▸扶乩 fújī

肌 jī 〈名〉 muscle: 腹/胸~ abdominal/pectoral muscle ▸~肤, ~肉, 面黄~瘦

【肌肤】 jīfū 〈名〉〈书〉 skin and muscle: ~之亲 intimate relations between man and woman
【肌苷】 jīgān 〈名〉 [生化] inosine: ~酸 inosinic acid
【肌腱】 jījiàn 〈名〉 [解剖] tendon: ~劳损 muscular strain ‖ ~炎 myotenositis
【肌理】 jīlǐ 〈名〉〈书〉 skin texture: ~粗糙/细腻 coarse-/fine-skinned texture
【肌肉】 jīròu 〈名〉 muscle: 放松~ relax one's muscles ‖ ~发达 be muscular ‖ ~萎缩 muscular atrophy ‖ 面部/手臂/腿部~ face/arm/leg muscles ‖ ~注射 intramuscular injection
【肌肉收缩】 jīròu shōusuō 〈名〉 contraction of muscle
【肌体】 jītǐ 〈名〉 organism: 病菌已侵入~。Bacteria have invaded the organisms.
【肌无力】 jīwúlì ▸**p. 50** 〈名〉 [医学] myasthenia

矶(磯) jī 〈名〉 rock projecting over the water: 钓~ projecting rock for angling

鸡(雞、鷄) jī 〈名〉 chicken: 养~ raise chickens ‖ 烤~ roast chicken ▸雏~, 公~, 烧~

【鸡巴】 jība 〈名〉〈口〉〈粗〉 cock 〈粗〉
【鸡雏】 jīchú 〈名〉 chick
【鸡蛋】 jīdàn 〈名〉 egg: 炒/煎/煮~ scramble/fry/boil eggs ‖ 煮得老/嫩的~ hard/soft-boiled eggs ‖ ~羹 steamed egg custard
【鸡蛋黄】 jīdànhuáng 〈名〉 yolk
【鸡蛋里挑骨头】 jīdànli tiāo gǔtou 〈俗〉〈喻〉 nit-pick
【鸡蛋碰石头】 jīdàn pèng shítou 〈俗〉〈喻〉 court destruction
【鸡飞蛋打】 jīfēi-dàndǎ 〈成〉〈喻〉 everything is lost: ~, 人财两空 lose everything
【鸡飞狗跳】 jīfēi-gǒutiào 〈成〉 utter confusion
【鸡冠】 jīguān 〈名〉 cockscomb
【鸡冠花】 jīguānhuā 〈名〉 [植物] cockscomb
【鸡奸】 jījiān 〈动〉 sodomize
【鸡精】 jījīng 〈名〉 chicken stock
【鸡口牛后】 jīkǒu-niúhòu 〈成〉 better reign in hell than serve in heaven
【鸡肋】 jīlèi 〈名〉〈书〉〈喻〉 things of little value that one still hesitates to discard
【鸡零狗碎】 jīlíng-gǒusuì 〈成〉 in bits and pieces: 这些~的材料, 没有多大价值。These fragmentary data are of little value.
【鸡笼】 jīlóng 〈名〉 chicken coop
【鸡毛掸子】 jīmáo dǎnzi 〈名〉 feather duster
【鸡毛飞上天】 jīmáo fēishàngtiān 〈俗〉〈喻〉 a miracle has occurred
【鸡毛蒜皮】 jīmáo-suànpí 〈成〉 trivial matters: 不要为~的事生气。Don't get angry about things that are not important.
【鸡毛信】 jīmáoxìn 〈名〉〈旧〉 urgent message
【鸡鸣狗盗】 jīmíng-gǒudào 〈成〉〈喻〉 get up to mean or petty tricks: ~之徒 mean people who resort to petty tricks
【鸡内金】 jīnèijīn 〈名〉 [中药] membrane of a chicken's gizzard
【鸡皮疙瘩】 jīpí gēda 〈名〉 goose pimples; goose bumps 〈美〉: 一提起蛇, 我就浑身起~。I get goose pimples all over at the mere mention of a snake.
【鸡犬不惊】 jīquǎn-bùjīng 〈成〉〈喻〉[even fowls and dogs are not alarmed] excellent army discipline
【鸡犬不留】 jīquǎn-bùliú 〈成〉〈喻〉 [even fowls and dogs are not spared] ruthless mass slaughter
【鸡犬不宁】 jīquǎn-bùníng 〈成〉 cause such confusion as to make everybody feel nervous: 闹得全城~ throw the whole city into chaos
【鸡犬升天】 jīquǎn-shēngtiān 〈成〉 relatives and followers of a high-ranking official get easy perks
【鸡肉】 jīròu 〈名〉 chicken (as food)
【鸡舍】 jīshè 〈名〉 chicken coop
【鸡食】 jīshí 〈名〉 chicken feed
【鸡尾酒】 jīwěijiǔ 〈名〉 cocktail: 调配~ mix cocktails ‖ ~会 cocktail party
【鸡瘟】 jīwēn 〈名〉 chicken pest
【鸡窝】 jīwō 〈名〉 chicken coop
【鸡窝里飞出金凤凰】 jīwōli fēichu jīnfènghuáng 〈俗〉 a person of humble origin makes it to the top
【鸡心领】 jīxīnlǐng 〈名〉 V-neck: ~羊绒衫 V-necked cashmere sweater
【鸡新城疫】 jīxīnchéngyì 〈名〉 [畜牧] Newcastle disease
【鸡胸】 jīxiōng ▸**p. 50** 〈名〉 [医学] pigeon breast: 她有些~。She is rather pigeon-breasted.
【鸡血石】 jīxuèshí 〈名〉 [矿业] bloodstone
【鸡血藤】 jīxuèténg 〈名〉 [植物] reticulate millettia
【鸡眼】 jīyǎn ▸**p. 50** 〈名〉 [医学] corn: ~膏 corn plaster
【鸡杂】 jīzá 〈名〉 chicken giblets: 炒~ fried chicken giblets
【鸡胗】 jīzhēn 〈名〉 chicken's gizzard
【鸡子儿】 jīzǐr 〈名〉〈方〉 egg

奇 jī

A 〈形〉 odd: ▸~偶, ~数
B 〈名〉〈书〉 remainder: 六十有~ sixty odd
▸qí

【奇零】 jīlíng 〈名〉〈书〉 fractional amount
【奇偶】 jī-ǒu 〈名〉 odd-even
【奇数】 jīshù ▸**p. 691** 〈名〉 [数学] odd number: ~页 odd-numbered pages

咭 jī = 叽 jī

唧 jī

A 〈动〉 spurt: 水~了我一身。The water squirted all over me. ▸~筒
B 〈拟〉 chirp: ▸~~喳喳

【唧咕】 jīgu = 叽咕 jīgu
【唧唧】 jījī 〈拟〉 chirp: 蟋蟀不停地~叫着。Crickets chirruped tirelessly.
【唧唧嘎嘎】 jīji-gāgā = 叽叽嘎嘎 jīji-gāgā
【唧唧喳喳】 jīji-zhāzhā 〈拟〉 twitter: 麻雀在树上~地叫着。The sparrows were twittering in the trees. ‖ 他~说什么呢? What is he jabbering on about?
【唧哝】 jīnong 〈动〉 mutter: 她在他耳边~了几句就走了。She whispered something in his ear and left.
【唧筒】 jītǒng 〈名〉 pump

积(積) jī

A 〈动〉 accumulate: 路上坑洼处~了雨水。The rain collected in depressions in the road. ‖ 云越~越厚。The clouds are gathering. ▸~累, 堆~, 日~月累
B 〈形〉 long-standing: ~垢 accumulated filth ▸~案, ~习, ~雪
C 〈名〉 **1** [中医] indigestion: 这孩子有~了。The child is suffering from indigestion. ▸食~ **2** [数学] product: 求~ find the product through multiplication ‖ 2乘3的~是6。The product of 3 multiplied by 2 is 6. ▸乘~

【积案】 jī'àn 〈名〉 long-pending case: 清理~ clear the docket
【积弊】 jībì 〈名〉 long-standing abuse: 根除~ strike deep-rooted evil at its source ‖ ~难除。It is very difficult to eradicate age-old evils.
【积存】 jīcún 〈动〉 stockpile: ~战略物资 stockpile strategic materials ‖ 库中~太多。There are too many goods in stock.
【积德】 jīdé 〈动〉 do good deeds whenever possible: ~从善 follow a virtuous path
【积淀】 jīdiàn **A** 〈动〉 accumulate: 多年来~的艺术功底 artistic skills accumulated over the years **B** 〈名〉 accumulation: 文化~ accumulation of culture

【积非成是】jīfēi-chéngshì〈成〉repeated lies become truths when repeated: 众口铄金，～。Public clamour can confound right and wrong, and incessant repetition can turn lies into truths.

【积肥】jīféi〈动〉collect compost

【积分】jīfēn〈名〉**1**（指比分）cumulative scoring: ～榜 standings ‖ 在这次联赛中，我们队～最高。Our team got the highest number of points in the tournament. **2**［数学］integral: ▸微～

【积分赛】jīfēnsài〈名〉tournament won according to the cumulative points scored

【积愤】jīfèn〈名〉pent-up anger: 发泄～ give vent to one's pent-up anger

【积谷防饥】jīgǔ-fángjī〈成〉store up grain against famine

【积极】jījí〈形〉**1**（正面）positive: 采取～的措施 take positive steps ‖ 起～作用 play a constructive role **2**（主动）active: ～努力 make active efforts ‖ ～的拥护者 vigorous supporter ‖ 他工作很～。He is very active in his work.

【积极分子】jījífènzǐ〈名〉activist: 体育运动～ sports enthusiast

【积极性】jījíxìng〈名〉enthusiasm: 挫伤～ dampen sb.'s enthusiasm ‖ 调动～ arouse sb.'s enthusiasm ‖ 工作/学习～ enthusiasm for work/study

【积久成习】jījiǔ-chéngxí〈成〉form a habit or custom over the years

【积聚】jījù〈动〉accumulate: ～财富 amass wealth ‖ ～力量 gather strength

【积劳成疾】jīláo-chéngjí〈成〉fall ill through overwork: 他～。His years of hard work took their toll on him.

【积累】jīlěi **A**〈动〉amass: ～知识 accumulate knowledge ‖ ～资料 accumulate information ‖ 长期～ amassed over a long period ‖ 资本的原始～ primitive accumulation of capital **B**〈名〉［经济］accumulation: 增加公共～ increase public accumulation

【积木】jīmù〈名〉building blocks: 堆～ pile up bricks

【积年】jīnián〈名〉〈书〉many years: ～旧案 cases that have been pending for years ‖ ～已久的隔阂/问题 long-standing estrangement/problem

【积年累月】jīnián-lěiyuè〈成〉year in, year out

【积欠】jīqiàn **A**〈动〉have one's debts piling up: ～房租 fail to pay rent for a long time ‖ ～的工资/税款 back pay/taxes ‖ ～的债务 outstanding debts **B**〈名〉outstanding debts: 清理～ clear up all outstanding debts

【积少成多】jīshǎo-chéngduō〈成〉accumulate little by little

【积食】jīshí〈动〉get indigestion: 饮食过量引起的～ indigestion induced by overeating

【积水】jīshuǐ〈名〉**1**（指水）collected water: 地下室里～了。Water collected in the basement. ‖ 雨后地上有～。There were pools of water on the ground after the rain. **2** ▸**p. 50**［医学］dropsy: ▸脑～

【积习】jīxí〈名〉old habit: ～已久的烟鬼 inveterate smoker ‖ ～难改 old habits die hard

【积蓄】jīxù **A**〈动〉accumulate:（为某事）～力量 store up strength (for sth.) ‖ ～钱财 put some money aside **B**〈名〉savings: 把～存入银行 keep one's savings in a bank ‖ 多年的～ years of savings

【积雪】jīxuě〈名〉accumulated snow: 铲除～ shovel the snow ‖ ～融化了。The snow melted away. ‖ 地上～很厚。The snow lay thick on the ground.

【积压】jīyā〈动〉overstock: ～商品 overstock commodities ‖ ～的案件/工作 backlog of cases/work ‖ ～在心头的郁闷 pent-up depression ‖ 盲目生产造成产品～。Unplanned production resulted in the overstocking of products.

【积余】jīyú〈动〉lay up: ～了一些钱 have saved some money

【积羽沉舟】jīyǔ-chénzhōu〈成〉tiny things may gather into a mighty force

【积雨云】jīyǔyún〈名〉［气象］cumulonimbus

【积郁】jīyù **A**〈动〉smoulder: 发泄～在心中的不平 pour out one's pent-up grievances **B** ▸**p. 50**〈名〉［医学］stasis: ～成疾 fall ill from stasis

【积怨】jīyuàn **A**〈动〉nurse a grudge: ～成仇 become enemies because of long-standing grievances ‖ ～多年 harbour grudges of many years' standing **B**〈名〉grudge: 消除～ get rid of long-standing grievances ‖ ～甚多 have many complaints

【积云】jīyún〈名〉［气象］cumulus

【积攒】jīzǎn〈动〉save: 经过多年～，他终于买下了这所房子。Over the years he saved enough money to buy the house.

【积重难返】jīzhòng-nánfǎn〈成〉ingrained habits are hard to break

【积铢累寸】jīzhū-lěicùn〈成〉accumulate bit by bit

笄 jī〈古〉〈名〉hairgrip

屐 jī〈名〉**1**（木底鞋）clogs: ▸木～ **2**〈书〉（鞋）shoes: 草～ straw sandals

姬 jī〈名〉**1**〈旧〉（妇女）beauty: 美～ beauty ‖ 仙～ goddess **2**〈书〉（妾）concubine: 爱/宠～ concubine in high favour ‖ ～妾 concubine **3**〈书〉（歌女）professional female singer: 歌～ female singer ‖ 舞～ professional female dancer

基 jī

A〈名〉**1**（基础）base: 坝～ foundation of a dam ‖ 柱～ base of a pillar ▸地～, 奠～ **2**［化学］base: 石蜡～ paraffin base ‖ 自由～ free radical ▸氨～, 羟～

B〈形〉basic: ▸～层, ～调, ～业

【基本】jīběn **A**〈名〉basis: 改革是企业充满活力的～。Reform is the basis upon which an enterprise can be energized. ‖ 稳定是国家兴旺发达的～。Stability is the foundation upon which a country can flourish and grow. **B**〈形〉**1**（根本）basic: ～纲领 basic programme ‖ ～观点 basic concept ‖ 这些都是～问题，应予以考虑。These are fundamental questions that call for careful consideration. **2**（主要）main: ～功能 key function ‖ ～形式 fundamental form ‖ 书的～内容 main contents of a book **C**〈副〉basically: ～属实 be basically true ‖ 我们的意见～相同。In general our opinions are the same.

【基本词汇】jīběn cíhuì〈名〉［语言］basic vocabulary: 英语的～ basic English vocabulary

【基本单位】jīběn dānwèi〈名〉［物理］basic unit

【基本法】jīběnfǎ〈名〉basic law: 香港特别行政区～ Basic Law of the Hong Kong Special Administrative Region

【基本工资】jīběn gōngzī〈名〉base pay

【基本功】jīběngōng〈名〉basic skill: 苦练～ practise hard in basic skills ‖ ～扎实 have a solid mastery of the basic skills

【基本规律】jīběn guīlǜ〈名〉fundamentals

【基本国策】jīběn guócè〈名〉basic state policy: 计划生育是中国的一项～。Birth control is a basic policy of China.

【基本技能】jīběn jìnéng〈名〉basic skills

【基本建设】jīběn jiànshè〈名〉capital construction: ～项目 capital construction project ‖ 控制～规模 control the scope of capital construction

【基本利率】jīběn lìlǜ〈名〉［经济］base rate

【基本粒子】jīběn lìzǐ〈名〉［物理］fundamental particle

【基本路线】jīběn lùxiàn〈名〉basic line: ～要长期不变。The basic line must be followed unswervingly for a very long time.

【基本矛盾】jīběn máodùn〈名〉［哲学］fundamental contradiction: 解决～ resolve fundamental contradictions

【基本上】jīběnshang〈副〉basically: 他对你的工作～是满意的。On the whole, he's satisfied with your work. ‖ 来听讲座的～是学生。Those who came to the lecture were mainly students.

【基本原理】jīběn yuánlǐ〈名〉basic principle

【基本原则】jīběn yuánzé〈名〉fundamental principles: 四项～ Four Cardinal Principles

【基本知识】jīběn zhīshi〈名〉elementary knowledge

【基层】jīcéng〈名〉grass roots: 深入～ go down to the grass-roots ‖ ～干部 cadre at the grass-roots level ‖ ～组织 grass-roots organization

【基础】jīchǔ〈名〉**1**（指建筑物）foundations: 为房子打～ lay the foundations of a house **2**〈喻〉（指根本起点）foundation: ～课程 basic curriculum ‖ 理论/社会～ theoretical/social basis ‖ 在原有的～上进一步提高 improve on what has been achieved ‖ 农业是国民经济的～。Agriculture is the basis of the national economy.

【基础代谢】jīchǔ dàixiè〈名〉［生理］basal metabolism

【基础工业】jīchǔ gōngyè〈名〉basic industry: 加强～投入 strengthen the investment of basic industry

【基础教育】jīchǔ jiàoyù〈名〉elementary education: 普及～ popularize elementary education

【基础科学】jīchǔ kēxué〈名〉basic science

【基础课】jīchǔkè〈名〉foundation course: 教授～ teach foundation courses

【基础理论】jīchǔ lǐlùn〈名〉basic theory

【基础设施】jīchǔ shèshī〈名〉infrastructure: 加强～的建设 intensify the construction of infrastructure

【基础知识】jīchǔ zhīshi〈名〉elementary knowledge: 缺乏物理～ lack rudimentary knowledge of physics ‖ 数学～ elementary knowledge of mathematics

【基地】jīdì〈名〉base: 空军～ air-force base ‖ 能源～ energy base ‖ 原料～ source of raw materials ▸军事～

【基地组织】Jīdì Zǔzhī〈名〉Al Qaeda

【基点】jīdiǎn〈名〉**1**（中心）centre: 建立科研～ set up a scientific research centre **2**（起点）basis: 分析问题是解决问题的～。The analysis of a problem is the starting point for its solution. ‖ 这将成为进一步研究的～。This will be the basis for further research. **3**［测绘］base point

【基调】jīdiào〈名〉**1**［音乐］main key: 定的～太低/高 set a keynote too low/high

2（基本精神） keynote: 定下本次活动的～ set the keynote for the activity ‖ 这部作品的～过于颓废。 The main message of this work is too dispiriting.
【基督】Jīdū〈名〉［宗教］ Christ: 信仰耶稣～ believe in Jesus Christ
【基督纪元】Jīdū jìyuán〈名〉 Christian era
【基督教】Jīdūjiào〈名〉 Christianity: 信奉～ believe in Christianity
【基督徒】jīdūtú〈名〉 Christian: 虔诚/热诚的～ devout Christian
【基多】Jīduō〈名〉 Quito
【基肥】jīféi〈名〉［农业］ base fertilizer
【基辅】Jīfǔ〈名〉 Kiev
【基干】jīgàn〈名〉 hard core: ～民兵 core members of the militia
【基加利】Jījiālì〈名〉 Kigali
【基价】jījià〈名〉 base price
【基建】jījiàn〈简称〉= 基本建设
【基金】jījīn〈名〉 fund: 设立～ set up a fund ‖ 慈善～ charitable foundation ‖ 教育～ education fund ‖ 退休/养老～ retirement/pension fund
【基金会】jījīnhuì〈名〉 foundation: 残疾人福利～ welfare foundation for the disabled
【基里巴斯】Jīlǐbāsī〈名〉 Kiribati
【基尼系数】Jīní xìshù〈名〉［统计］ Gini coefficient
【基诺族】Jīnuòzú〈名〉 Jino ethnic group, Jinuo ethnic group
【基期】jīqī〈名〉［统计］ base period
【基色】jīsè = 原色 yuánsè
【基石】jīshí〈名〉 cornerstone: 奠定～ lay a cornerstone ‖ 国家的～ cornerstone of the state ‖ 外交政策的～ cornerstone of foreign policy
【基数】jīshù〈名〉 **1** ▸**p. 691**［数学］ cardinal number **2**［统计］ base: 以100为～ take 100 as the base
【基态】jītài〈名〉［物理］ ground state: 原子的～ atomic ground state
【基围虾】jīwéixiā〈名〉 dam shrimp
【基线】jīxiàn〈名〉［测绘］ base line: ～基准 base line reference
【基岩】jīyán〈名〉［地质］ bedrock
【基业】jīyè〈名〉 foundation: 创立～ lay the foundations
【基因】jīyīn〈名〉 gene: ～分析 genetic analysis ‖ 遗传～ hereditary gene
【基因变异】jīyīn biànyì〈名〉 genovariation
【基因重组】jīyīn chóngzǔ〈名〉 gene recombination
【基因档案】jīyīn dàng'àn〈名〉 genetic profile
【基因复制】jīyīn fùzhì〈名〉 gene duplication
【基因改造】jīyīn gǎizào〈名〉 genetic modification: ～生物 genetically modified organism (GMO) ‖ ～食品 genetically modified food
【基因工程】jīyīn gōngchéng〈名〉 genetic engineering
【基因库】jīyīnkù〈名〉 gene bank
【基因疗法】jīyīn liáofǎ〈名〉 gene therapy
【基因突变】jīyīn tūbiàn〈名〉 genetic mutation
【基因芯片】jīyīn xīnpiàn〈名〉 biological chip
【基因组】jīyīnzǔ〈名〉 genome: 人类～ human genome
【基音】jīyīn〈名〉［音乐］ fundamental tone
【基于】jīyú〈介〉 on account of: ～国家安全原因 for national security reasons ‖ ～上述理由，我不同意。 For the above-mentioned reasons, I disagree.

j

【基质】jīzhì〈名〉［生物］ stroma
【基准】jīzhǔn〈名〉 **1**［测绘］ benchmark: ～点 reference point ‖ ～线 base line **2**（标准） standard: 工资的计算以周为～。 Rates of work are calculated on a weekly basis.
【基准兵】jīzhǔnbīng〈名〉［军事］ base marker
【基座】jīzuò〈名〉 pedestal: 塑像的～ base of a statue

期

jī〈名〉〈书〉 a whole year or month: ～年 a whole year ‖ ～月 a whole month ▸qī

赍（賫）

jī〈动〉〈书〉 **1**（心怀） nurse: ▸～恨, ～志而殁 **2**（给予） give: ▸～赏
【赍恨】jīhèn〈动〉〈书〉 have a gnawing regret: ～而亡 die with regret
【赍赏】jīshǎng〈动〉〈书〉 grant a reward
【赍志而殁】jīzhì'érmò〈成〉 die with one's ambitions unfulfilled

犄

jī
【犄角】jījiǎo〈名〉〈方〉 corner: 桌子/屋子/院子～ corner of a table/room/courtyard
【犄角】jījiao〈名〉〈方〉 horn: 鹿～ antler ‖ 牛/羊～ ox/sheep horn

嵇

Jī〈名〉 Ji [surname]

缉（緝）

jī〈动〉 seize: ▸～毒, 通～ ▸qī
【缉捕】jībǔ〈动〉 seize: ～凶手 hunt a murderer ‖ ～人员 arresting officer
【缉查】jīchá〈动〉 search: ～毒品 search for drugs ‖ 挨户～ make a door-to-door search
【缉毒】jīdú〈动〉 seize drugs or drug dealers
【缉获】jīhuò〈动〉 hunt down: ～违禁品/走私物品 seize illicit/smuggled goods ‖ ～在逃犯 track down an escaped criminal
【缉拿】jīná〈动〉 arrest: ～逃犯 capture an escaped criminal ‖ ～凶手 apprehend the murderer ‖ ～归案 apprehend and bring to justice ‖ 警方正在～此人。 The police are looking for the man.
【缉私】jīsī〈动〉 clamp down on smuggling: ～队 anti-smuggling squad

畸

jī
A〈形〉 **1**（不规则） irregular: ～胎 malformed foetus ▸～形 **2**（偏） unbalanced: ▸～轻～重
B〈名〉〈书〉 remainder: ▸～零
【畸变】jībiàn〈名〉 abnormal change
【畸恋】jīliàn〈名〉 abnormal love
【畸零】jīlíng **A** = 奇零 jīlíng **B**〈形〉 alone: ～无侣 all alone
【畸轻畸重】jīqīng-jīzhòng〈成〉 now too much, now too little
【畸形】jīxíng〈形〉 **1**（指生物体） abnormal: ～发育 grow in an abnormal way ‖ ～儿童 abnormal children **2**（指事物） lopsided: ～发展 develop in an unbalanced way ‖ ～增长 unbalanced increase

跻（躋）

jī〈动〉〈书〉 ascend: ▸～身
【跻身】jīshēn〈动〉 join the ranks of: ～发达国家之列 enter the ranks of the developed nations ‖ ～影坛 get into films ‖ 这次胜利使他～前十强。 This victory ranked him in the top ten.

箕

jī〈名〉 **1**（簸箕） dustpan: ▸簸～ **2**（指星宿） one of the 28 constellations in ancient Chinese astronomy **3**（指指纹） loop: ▸斗～
【箕斗】jīdǒu〈名〉〈古〉 **1**（指星宿） constellations **2**（虚名） false reputation **3**（指纹） fingerprint: 验明～ identify a fingerprint
【箕踞】jījù〈动〉〈书〉 sit with one's legs stretched out

稽[1]

jī〈动〉〈书〉 procrastinate: ▸～留, ～延

稽[2]

jī〈动〉 **1**（核查） investigate: ▸～查, 无～之谈, 有案可～ **2**（计较） dispute: 反唇相～ answer back ▸qǐ
【稽查】jīchá **A**〈动〉 check: ～走私活动 check on smuggling cases **B**〈名〉 customs officer: 铁路～ railway inspector
【稽核】jīhé〈动〉 check: ～账目 audit accounts
【稽考】jīkǎo〈动〉〈书〉 verify: 年深日久，此事无从～。 As it happened such a long time ago, the matter is hard to verify.
【稽留】jīliú〈动〉〈书〉 detain: 他因公在京～多日。 He was detained on business in Beijing for many days.
【稽延】jīyán〈动〉〈书〉 delay: 此案已～多日。 This case has been delayed for days.
【稽征】jīzhēng〈动〉 check and collect: ～税款 check and collect taxes

齑（齏）

jī〈书〉
A〈名〉 seasoning of finely chopped garlic, ginger, chives, etc.
B〈形〉 powdery: ▸～粉
【齑粉】jīfěn〈名〉〈书〉 fine powder: 化为～ be turned to dust

畿

jī〈名〉〈旧〉 vicinity of a capital: ▸～辅, 京～
【畿辅】jīfǔ〈名〉〈旧〉 vicinity of a capital

激

jī
A〈动〉 **1**（指液体） surge: ▸～荡 **2**（指情感） be stirred emotionally: ▸～于义愤 be stirred by righteous indignation ▸～昂, ～动, 感～ **3**（刺激） stimulate: 别拿话～他，不然他会揍你。 Stop needling him or he might hit you. ▸～发, ～怒, 刺～ **4**（指得病） catch a chill: 我被雨水～着了。 I caught a chill from getting wet in the rain. **5**〈方〉（使变冷） chill by putting in cold water, etc.: 把西瓜用冰水～一～ chill a watermelon in iced water
B〈形〉 fierce: ▸～烈, ～战, 偏～
【激昂】jī'áng〈形〉 roused: 情绪～地发表演说 deliver an impassioned speech ‖ 消息传来，群情～。 Everyone was roused at the news.
【激昂慷慨】jī'áng-kāngkǎi = 慷慨激昂 kāngkǎi-jī'áng
【激变】jībiàn〈动〉 change drastically: 形势～。 The situation has taken a radical turn.
【激波】jībō〈名〉［物理］ shock wave
【激荡】jīdàng〈动〉 agitate: 海水～。 The sea surged. ‖ 我心潮～。 Thoughts were whirling in my mind. ‖〈喻〉 歌声～人心。 The singing stirred people's hearts.
【激动】jīdòng **A**〈形〉 excited: ～得流下眼

泪 be moved to tears ‖ 情绪～ be hot with emotion ‖ 成功的喜悦使他非常～。He was overjoyed at the success. **B**〈动〉 excite: ～人心 be exciting

【激发】jīfā〈动〉**1**（引发） incite: ～灵感 stir sb.'s inspiration ‖ ～（对绘画的）兴趣 arouse sb.'s interest (in painting) ‖ ～学生的上进心 arouse the students' desire to do better **2**［物理］ excite: 热～ thermal excitation

【激奋】jīfèn **A**〈形〉 stimulating: 心情～ inspired mood **B**〈动〉 stir sb. to action: ～人心的场面 stirring scene

【激愤】jīfèn〈形〉 indignant: 心情～ be hot with rage

【激光】jīguāng〈名〉［物理］ laser: ～技术 laser technique ‖ 用～治病 cure diseases with a laser beam

【激光唱机】jīguāng chàngjī〈名〉 CD player

【激光唱片】jīguāng chàngpiàn〈名〉 compact disc (CD)

【激光打印机】jīguāng dǎyìnjī〈名〉 laser printer

【激光刀】jīguāngdāo〈名〉 laser scalpel

【激光器】jīguāngqì〈名〉 laser device

【激光视盘】jīguāng shìpán〈名〉 video compact disc (VCD): ～机 VCD player

【激光束】jīguāngshù〈名〉 laser beam

【激光武器】jīguāng wǔqì〈名〉 laser weapon

【激光照排】jīguāng zhàopái〈名〉［印刷］ laser phototypesetting

【激光制导】jīguāng zhìdǎo〈名〉［航空］ laser guidance: ～导弹 laser (guided) missile

【激化】jīhuà〈动〉 sharpen: ～对立情绪 sharpen one's antagonism ‖ ～矛盾 intensify contradictions ‖ 冲突～了。The conflict intensified. ‖ 斗争将进一步～。The struggle will become more acute.

【激活】jīhuó〈动〉**1**（使生效） activate: ～程序 activate a programme **2**〈喻〉（使活跃） stimulate: ～图书市场 stimulate the book market

【激将】jījiàng〈动〉 prod sb. into action: 请将不如～。Prodding sb. into action is better than imploring them.

【激将法】jījiàngfǎ〈名〉 prodding sb. into action

【激进】jījìn〈形〉 radical: ～情绪/思想 radical feeling/idea ‖ ～分子 radical ‖ ～派 radical party

【激剧】jījù〈形〉**1**（猛烈） intense: ～的斗争 violent struggle **2**（快速） rapid: 发展～ develop rapidly

【激浪】jīlàng〈名〉 turbulent waves: ～滔滔。The surf is very choppy.

【激励】jīlì〈动〉**1**（鼓励） encourage: 用英雄事迹～自己 draw inspiration from heroic deeds ‖ ～机制 incentive mechanism ‖ 将军～战士们勇敢作战。The general urged the soldiers to fight bravely. **2**［物理］ excite: ～器 driver

【激烈】jīliè〈形〉 violent: ～的斗争 violent struggle ‖ ～争吵 quarrel bitterly ‖ 辩论～ have a heated debate ‖ 竞争～ fierce competition ‖ 冲突会更加～。The conflict might intensify.

【激流】jīliú〈名〉 rapids: ～险滩 turbulent currents and dangerous shoals ‖ 小船在～中倾覆了。The boat overturned in the rapids.

【激怒】jīnù〈动〉 enrage: 她被这些话～了。She was enraged by these remarks. ‖ 他出言不逊，～了父亲。His impertinent remarks infuriated his father.

【激起公愤】jīqǐ gōngfèn〈成〉 arouse public indignation

【激切】jīqiè〈形〉〈书〉 impassioned: 言辞～ impassioned words

【激情】jīqíng〈名〉 passion: 充满～ full of fervour ‖ 创作～ ardour for creation ‖ 他满怀～地唱着这首歌。He sang the song with great passion.

【激素】jīsù〈名〉［生理］ hormone: 雌性/雄性～ female/male hormone

【激扬】jīyáng **A**〈动〉**1**（使振奋） urge: ～士气 boost the morale **2** = 激浊扬清 jīzhuó-yángqīng **B**〈形〉 excited: ～的欢呼声 excited cheers ‖ 大厅里响起了～的乐曲声。The sound of inspiring music was heard in the hall.

【激越】jīyuè〈形〉 intense: 感情～ intense emotion ‖ 校园里歌声～。Loud singing was heard on the campus.

【激增】jīzēng〈动〉 shoot up: 产量～ steep rise in output ‖ 今年房租～。Rents have shot up this year.

【激战】jīzhàn〈动〉 fight a pitched battle: 与敌人～ fiercely engage with the enemy

【激浊扬清】jīzhuó-yángqīng〈成〉〈喻〉 drive out evil and usher in good

羁（覊） jī〈书〉

A〈名〉 bridle: 无～之马 horse running wild **B**〈动〉**1**（约束） restrain: ▸～绊，～押，放荡不～ **2**（逗留） detain: ▸～留，～旅

【羁绊】jībàn〈动〉〈书〉 fetter: 摆脱旧观念的～ break the shackles of outdated conventional ideas ‖ 为家务所～ be bound by housework

【羁留】jīliú〈动〉〈书〉**1**（停留） stop over: 因大雾在机场～半天 be delayed at the airport for half a day due to the heavy fog ‖ 在北京～数日 stop over in Beijing for a couple of days **2**（拘押） keep in custody

【羁旅】jīlǚ〈动〉〈书〉 live away from one's native place: ～海外 live overseas ‖ ～异乡 live in a strange land

【羁束】jīshù〈动〉〈书〉 restrain

【羁押】jīyā〈动〉〈书〉 take into custody: ～候审 be committed for trial ‖ 被～并留作人质 be captured and detained as a hostage

jí

及 jí

A〈动〉**1**（赶上） catch up: 悔之不～ too late to repent ▸～时，～早，望尘莫～ **2**（到） reach: 目力所～ as far as the eye can see ‖ 由近～远 from near to far ▸～格，波～，触～，力所能～ **3**〈书〉（推广到） take into account: ▸爱屋～乌，推己～人，言不～义 **4**（比得上） be equal to: 什么也不～羊毛暖和。Nothing can compare with wool for warmth.

B ▸**p. 448**〈连〉 and: 工人、农民～知识分子 workers, farmers and intellectuals ‖ 图书、仪器、标本～其他 books, instruments, specimens and so on

【及第】jídì〈动〉〈古〉 pass an imperial examination

【及格】jígé〈动〉 pass: 考试～ pass an exam

【及冠】jíguàn〈动〉〈旧〉 [of a boy] come of age (at 20)

【及笄】jíjī〈动〉〈旧〉 [of a girl] come of age (at 15)

【及龄】jílíng〈动〉 reach a required age: ～儿童 children who reach the required age

【及时】jíshí **A**〈副〉**1**（适时） in time: ～播种 sow at the right time ‖ ～赶到 arrive in the nick of time **2**（马上） promptly: ～总结经验 summarize one's experiences without delay ‖ 有病要～治疗。Get prompt treatment when you are ill. **B**〈形〉 timely: ～的忠告 opportune advice ‖ 这场雪下得很～。This snow has come at the right time.

【及时行乐】jíshí-xínglè〈成〉 make merry while the sun shines

【及时雨】jíshíyǔ〈名〉**1**〈本〉 timely rain **2**〈喻〉 timely help

【及物动词】jíwù dòngcí〈名〉［语言］ transitive verb

【及早】jízǎo〈副〉 as soon as possible: ～回头 mend one's ways before it is too late ‖ ～做出安排 make timely arrangements

【及至】jízhì〈书〉**A**〈介〉 to: ～第二天，他们才找到她。They didn't find her until the next day. ‖ ～现在，我还没见过他。So far, I've never met him. **B**〈连〉 until: ～孩子出生，她才知道是个女儿。She didn't know it was going to be a girl until the baby was born.

吉¹ jí〈形〉 auspicious: ▸～利，～日，逢凶化～，万事大～

吉² Jí ▸**p. 661**〈名〉 Ji [another name for Jilin Province (吉林)]

【吉卜赛人】Jíbǔsàirén〈名〉 Gypsy

【吉布提】Jíbùtí〈名〉 Djibouti: ～人 Djiboutian

【吉达】Jídá〈名〉 Jidda(h)

【吉尔吉斯斯坦】Jí'ěrjísīsītǎn〈名〉 Kyrgyzstan: ～人 Kyrgyzstani

【吉光片羽】jíguāng-piànyǔ〈成〉〈喻〉 fragment of a highly treasured relic

【吉哈德】jíhādé〈名〉 jihad

【吉剧】jíjù〈名〉 Jilin opera

【吉利】jílì〈形〉 auspicious: 图～ do sth. for luck ‖ ～话 auspicious words ‖ 那数字不～。That number isn't lucky.

【吉林】Jílín ▸**p. 661**〈名〉 Jilin Province

【吉隆坡】Jílóngpō〈名〉 Kuala Lumpur

【吉尼斯】Jínísī〈名〉 Guinness: 打破～ break a Guinness World Record

【吉普车】jípǔchē〈名〉 jeep

【吉期】jíqī〈名〉 wedding day: ～一定，我就通知你们。I will tell you the happy day as soon as it is fixed. ‖ ～尚未确定。The date of the wedding is still up in the air.

【吉庆】jíqìng〈形〉 auspicious: ～日子喜事多。People prefer to get married on an auspicious date.

【吉庆有余】jíqìng-yǒuyú〈成〉 have an abundance of blessings

【吉人天相】jírén-tiānxiàng〈成〉 heaven assists the virtuous

【吉日】jírì〈名〉 auspicious day: 择～办喜事 choose an auspicious day for one's wedding

【吉日良辰】jírì-liángchén〈成〉 lucky day

【吉他】jítā ▸**p. 929**〈名〉［音乐］ guitar: 弹～ play the guitar ‖ 电～ electric guitar ‖ ～手 guitarist

【吉祥】jíxiáng〈形〉 auspicious: 说～话 make auspicious remarks ‖ 祝您～如意! Good luck and happiness to you!

【吉祥物】jíxiángwù〈名〉 mascot: 运动会的～ mascot of a sports meet

【吉星高照】jíxīng-gāozhào〈成〉 be blessed by a lucky star: 他工作以来，一直～。He has been blessed by a lucky star ever since he started work.

【吉凶】jíxiōng〈名〉 good or ill luck: ～未卜 one's fate is in the balance

j

【吉言】jíyán〈名〉 auspicious remarks: 借你的～ with your good wishes

【吉兆】jízhào〈名〉 auspicious omen: 视为～ regard sth. as an auspicious sign

岌 jí〈形〉〈书〉 lofty

【岌岌】jíjí〈形〉〈书〉 **1**（高耸） lofty **2**（危险） perilous

【岌岌可危】jíjí-kěwēi〈成〉 in imminent danger: 病人的生命～。The patient was in immediate danger.

汲 jí〈动〉 draw: ～水 draw water

【汲汲】jíjí〈形〉〈书〉 anxious: ～于富贵 crave riches and honours ‖ ～于名利 be eager for personal fame and gain

【汲取】jíqǔ〈动〉 draw: 从错误中～教训 draw a lesson from one's mistakes ‖ ～这次旅行的经验 draw on the experience of this trip ‖ ～营养 derive nourishment

级（級）jí

A〈名〉 **1**（级别） level: 部长～会议 ministerial-level conference ‖ 一～产品 grade A product ‖ 正教授～ rank of full professor ‖ 提升了一～ be promoted to the next level ▸～差，降～，越～ **2**（台阶） step: 拾～而上 follow the steps up ▸石～ **3**（年级） class: 同～不同班 be in the same grade but different classes ▸班～，升～

B〈量〉 [used for steps, towers, etc.]: 多～火箭 multistage rocket ‖ 七～浮屠 seven-storey tower ‖ 十二～台阶 a flight of a dozen steps

【级别】jíbié〈名〉 rank: ～高于某人 be above sb. in rank ‖ 干部/教授～ rank of cadre/professor ‖ 工资～ wage scale

【级差】jíchā〈名〉 differential: 工资～ wage differentials ‖ ～佣金 graded commission

【级任】jírèn〈名〉 form teacher: ～老师 teacher in charge of a primary or middle school class

【级数】jíshù〈名〉［数学］ series: 等比/等差～ geometric/arithmetic progression ‖ 按几何～减少 decrease in a geometrical series

极（極）jí

A〈名〉 **1**（极端） utmost point: 痛苦之～ be in extreme pain ‖ 贫富两～ extremes of poverty and wealth ▸登峰造～ **2**（地极） pole: 地球的两～略呈扁平形。The earth is slightly flattened at the poles. ▸～地，南～，阳～

B〈动〉 reach the limit: ～尽能事 spare no effort ‖ ～一时之盛 attain the utmost glory of the time ▸～力，乐～生悲，物～必反

C〈形〉 extreme: ～高的山 extremely high mountain ‖ 事业～盛期 height of one's career ▸～度，～端，～刑

D〈副〉 extremely: ～不满意 be not at all satisfied ‖ ～为重要 be of the utmost importance ‖ 状态～佳 be in perfectly good condition ‖ 痛苦～了 be in extreme agony ‖ 无聊～了 be bored to death ‖ ～少数 only a very few

【极大】jídà **A**〈形〉 immense: 取得～的成功 achieve a huge success **B**〈名〉［数学］ maximum

【极大化】jídàhuà〈动〉［数学］ maximize

【极大值】jídàzhí〈名〉［数学］ maximum value

【极地】jídì〈名〉 polar region: ～冰川 polar glacier ‖ 进行～科学考察 carry out scientific research in a polar region

【极地年】jídìnián〈名〉 polar year: 国际～ International Polar Year

【极地气候】jídì qìhòu〈名〉 polar climate

【极点】jídiǎn〈名〉 limit: 忍耐到了～ reach the limit of one's patience ‖ 他的运气坏到了～。His bad luck reached its peak.

【极顶】jídǐng **A**〈名〉 **1**（山顶） peak: 登上～ scale a peak ‖ 泰山～ summit of Mount Taishan **2**（极限） limit **B**〈副〉 extremely: ～狡猾/聪明 extremely tricky/clever

【极度】jídù **A**〈副〉 extremely: ～悲伤 be extremely sad ‖ ～疲劳 be exhausted ‖ ～兴奋 get extremely excited ‖ 自然资源～匮乏。There is a serious shortage of natural resources. **B**〈名〉 limit

【极端】jíduān **A**〈名〉 extreme: 从一个～走向另一个～ go from one extreme to the other ‖ 爱与恨是感情的两个～。Love and hate are extremes of passion. **B**〈副〉 extremely: ～仇视某人 show extreme hatred towards sb. ‖ ～贫困 be in dire poverty ‖ 他对工作～负责。He has the utmost sense of responsibility about his work.

【极端分子】jíduān fènzǐ〈名〉 extremist: 极端好战分子 ultra militant ‖ 极端激进分子 ultra radical

【极端民族主义】jíduān mínzúzhǔyì〈名〉 ultra nationalism

【极光】jíguāng〈名〉［天文］ aurora: ～弧 auroral arc

【极口】jíkǒu〈副〉 in extreme terms: ～抨击 attack with extreme violence ‖ ～赞扬 praise lavishly

【极乐鸟】jílèniǎo〈名〉 bird of paradise

【极乐世界】jílè shìjiè〈名〉［佛教］ Land of Ultimate Bliss

【极力】jílì〈副〉 extremely: ～帮助 do one's best to help ‖ ～鼓吹 vigorously advocate ‖ ～劝阻某人（不做某事） try very hard to dissuade sb. (from doing sth.) ‖ ～推荐某人/某事 highly recommend sb./sth.

【极量】jíliàng〈名〉 **1**［药学］ maximum dose **2**（最大量） maximum amount

【极目】jímù〈动〉〈书〉 look as far as the eye can see: ～远眺 gaze far into the distance ‖ ～望去，只见茫茫草原。As far as the eye could see all was boundless grasslands.

【极品】jípǐn〈名〉 **1**（指品质） highest grade: ～绿茶 best quality green tea ‖ 这是酒中～。This is the highest grade of spirit. **2**〈旧〉（指官阶） highest official rank: 官居～ hold the highest official rank

【极其】jíqí〈副〉 extremely: ～重视某事 attach great importance to sth. ‖ ～艰巨的任务 most arduous task ‖ ～深刻的教训 most profound lesson ‖ 那辆小汽车～豪华。The car is the ultimate in luxury.

【极圈】jíquān〈名〉［地理］ polar circle: ▸北～，南～

【极权】jíquán〈形〉 totalitarian: ～国家/政府 totalitarian state/government ‖ ～主义 totalitarianism

【极盛】jíshèng〈形〉 best: ～时期 golden age

【极为】jíwéi〈副〉 extremely: ～不满 be exceedingly dissatisfied ‖ 他表演得～出色。His performance is first-class. ‖ 学习～重要。Learning is of the utmost importance.

【极限】jíxiàn〈名〉 **1**（界限） maximum: 超过～ exceed the limit ‖ 达到～ reach the limit ‖ 挑战～ challenge one's limits **2**［数学］ limit: ～值 ultimate value

【极限运动】jíxiàn yùndòng〈名〉 extreme sports

【极小】jíxiǎo〈名〉［数学］ minimum

【极小化】jíxiǎohuà〈动〉 minimize

【极刑】jíxíng〈名〉 capital punishment: 处以～ sentence sb. to death ‖ 恢复/取消～ reinstate/abolish capital punishment

【极性】jíxìng〈名〉［物理］ polarity

【极夜】jíyè〈名〉 polar night

【极意】jíyì〈副〉〈书〉 trying one's best: ～奉承某人 flatter sb. lavishly ‖ ～模仿 try one's best to imitate

【极右】jíyòu〈形〉 ultra-Right: ～势力 ultra-Right forces

【极致】jízhì〈名〉〈书〉 ultimate achievement

【极昼】jízhòu〈名〉 polar day

【极左】jízuǒ〈形〉 ultra-Left: ～思潮 ultra-Left trend of thought

即 jí

A〈动〉 **1**（接近） approach: ▸可望而不可～，若～若离 **2**（到） assume: ▸～位

B〈介〉 prompted by the occasion: ▸～景，～席，～兴

C〈名〉 now: 成功在～。Success is in sight. ▸～期，～日，在～

D〈副〉 **1**（立刻） immediately: 黎明～起 get up at dawn ‖ 闻过～改 correct one's mistake as soon as it is pointed out ‖ 招之～来 be on call at any hour **2**（也就是） namely: 春节～农历新年。Spring Festival is the lunar New Year. ‖ 非此～彼。It must be either this or that.

E〈连〉〈书〉 even: ～无外援，我们也能克服目前的困难。We can overcome the difficulties even without outside assistance.

【即便】jíbiàn = 即使 jíshǐ

【即或】jíhuò〈书〉= 即使 jíshǐ

【即将】jíjiāng〈副〉 in no time: ～起程 be about to set off ‖ 暴风雨～来临。A storm is on its way. ‖ 这项工程～竣工。The project is nearing completion.

【即景】jíjǐng〈动〉〈书〉 be inspired by what one sees: ～赋诗 be inspired by the sight to write a poem

【即景生情】jíjǐng-shēngqíng〈成〉 the scene before one's eyes strikes a chord in one's heart

【即景诗】jíjǐngshī〈名〉 extempore poem

【即开型】jíkāixíng〈形〉 instant-win: ～体育彩票 instant-win sports lottery ticket

【即刻】jíkè〈副〉 immediately: ～采取行动 take immediate action ‖ ～开始工作 begin work immediately ‖ 我们～动身。We'll start at once.

【即令】jílìng〈书〉= 即使 jíshǐ

【即期】jíqī〈形〉［经济］ immediate: ～汇率 spot exchange rate

【即期交易】jíqī jiāoyì〈名〉 spot transaction

【即日】jírì〈名〉 **1**（当天） this very day: 本条例自～起施行。The regulations go into effect as of today. **2**（最近几天） the next few days: 本图书馆～对外开放。The library will open to the public in a few days.

【即如】jírú〈动〉〈书〉 be like

【即若】jíruò〈书〉= 即使 jíshǐ

【即时】jíshí〈副〉 immediately: ～答复 prompt reply ‖ ～获取信息 immediate access to information

【即食】jíshí〈形〉 instant: ～面 instant noodles ‖ 开袋～ ready to be served

【即使】jíshǐ〈连〉 even if/though: ～不成功，他们也会支持你的。They will stand by you even if you don't succeed. ‖ ～如此，我也会来的。I will be coming even so.

【即事】jíshì〈动〉 write out of inspiration: ～诗 extempore poem

【即位】jíwèi〈动〉〈书〉 1 (指就餐) take one's seat 2 (指登王位) ascend to the throne: 维多利亚女王于1837年～。Queen Victoria succeeded to the throne in 1837.

【即席】jíxí〈动〉〈书〉 1 (即兴) improvise: ～发表意见 deliver an off-the-cuff opinion ‖ ～赋诗一首 compose a poem impromptu 2 (入席) take one's seat

【即兴】jíxìng〈动〉 improvise: ～伴奏 improvise the accompaniment ‖ ～表演 improvised performance ‖ 这首歌是～之作。The song was composed extempore.

【即兴曲】jíxìngqǔ〈名〉［音乐］ impromptu

【即兴诗】jíxìngshī〈名〉 extempore verse

佶 jí〈形〉〈书〉 robust

【佶屈聱牙】jíqū-áoyá〈成〉 be awkward reading: 这个句子读着～。This sentence reads really awkwardly.

诘（詰）jí

▸jié

【诘屈聱牙】jíqū-áoyá = 佶屈聱牙 jíqū-áoyá

亟 jí〈副〉〈书〉 urgently: ～待解决 demand a prompt solution ‖ 教育状况～须改善。The teaching situation must be improved as a matter of urgency.

▸qì

【亟亟】jíjí〈形〉〈书〉 urgent: 不必～。There is no need to hurry.

革 jí〈形〉〈书〉 serious: 病～ be critically ill

▸gé

笈 jí〈名〉〈书〉 1 (箱子) satchel: ▸负～ 2 (书籍) book: 秘～ secret book collection

急 jí

A〈形〉 1 (快) rapid: 说话～ speak quickly ‖ ～转弯 sharp turn ‖ 水流很～。The current is strong. ▸～流勇退, ～刹车, ～症 2 (紧迫) urgent: ～事～办 handle urgent matters swiftly ‖ 不要～, 慢慢来。There is no hurry; take your time. ‖ 事情很～。The matter is pressing. ▸～件, ～救 3 (急躁) irascible: ～脾气 hot temper ▸～性子, 操之过～

B〈名〉 urgency: ▸当务之～, 救～, 应～

C〈动〉 1 (立即解决) be eager to help: ～群众之所急 be eager to meet the needs of the masses ▸～公好义, ～人之难 2 (着急) be anxious: ～出病来 become ill from anxiety ‖ ～得满头大汗 sweat profusely with anxiety ‖ ～得团团转 anxiously pace back and forth 3 (担忧) worry: ～死人了 be worried to death ‖ 什么事把你～成这个样子? What's worrying you so much? 4 (生气) become angry: 把某人惹～ irritate sb. ‖ 你要是再这样, 我就跟你～了。I'll become angry with you if you go on like this.

【急巴巴】jíbābā〈形〉〈口〉 impatient: ～地等待录取通知书 wait impatiently for the admission notice

【急板】jíbǎn〈名〉［音乐］ presto

【急暴】jíbào〈形〉 irascible: 脾气～ be short-tempered

【急变】jíbiàn〈名〉 abrupt change: 应付～ cope with sudden changes

【急病】jíbìng〈名〉 acute illness: 得～ contract an acute illness

【急不可待】jíbùkědài〈成〉 be too impatient to wait: 他～地想知道考试成绩。He was impatient to know the result of his examination.

【急不暇择】jíbù-xiázé〈成〉 no choice in an emergency

【急步】jíbù〈动〉 walk with quick steps

【急茬儿】jíchár〈名〉〈方〉 urgent matter

【急驰】jíchí〈动〉 go at high speed

【急匆匆】jícōngcōng〈形〉 hasty: 他一句话没说就～地走了。He hurried off without a word.

【急促】jícù〈形〉 1 (快) hurried: 呼吸～ be short of breath ‖ ～的脚步声 hurried footsteps 2 (紧急) pressing: 时间～, 我们必须立即行动。As time is running short, we must act immediately.

【急电】jídiàn A〈名〉 urgent cable: 收到～ receive an express telegram ‖ 有你一封～。There is an urgent telegram for you. B〈动〉 cable: ～前线指挥部 cable the headquarters at the front line

【急风暴雨】jífēng-bàoyǔ〈成〉 hurricane

【急腹症】jífùzhèng ▸p. 50〈名〉［医学］ acute abdominal disease

【急公好义】jígōng-hàoyì〈成〉 be public-spirited

【急功近利】jígōng-jìnlì〈成〉 seek instant success and quick profits: 治理环境不是～的事情。Improving the environment is not something that will bring quick returns and instant benefits.

【急活儿】jíhuór〈名〉〈口〉 urgent business

【急火】jíhuǒ〈名〉 1 (指火) high heat: ～煸炒 stir-fry on a high heat 2［中医］ internal heat as a cause of disease: ～攻心 become unconscious with a sudden attack of internal heat

【急急风】jíjífēng〈名〉 music with quick beat used in traditional opera

【急急巴巴】jíji-bābā〈形〉〈口〉 hasty: 你做事往往～的。You're always rushing things.

【急件】jíjiàn〈名〉 urgent document or dispatch

【急进】jíjìn〈动〉 move rapidly

【急惊风】jíjīngfēng〈名〉［中医］ acute infantile convulsions

【急惊风遇到了慢郎中】jíjīngfēng yùdàole màn lángzhōng〈俗〉〈喻〉 deferred action where prompt attention is needed

【急救】jíjiù〈动〉 give first aid: 进行～ give sb. first-aid ‖ ～站 first-aid station ‖ ～中心 emergency centre ‖ 这病需要～。The disease calls for emergency treatment.

【急救包】jíjiùbāo〈名〉 first-aid dressing

【急救车】jíjiùchē〈名〉 ambulance

【急救室】jíjiùshì〈名〉 emergency room

【急救药品】jíjiù yàopǐn〈名〉 first-aid medicine

【急就章】jíjiùzhāng〈名〉 hasty work

【急剧】jíjù〈形〉 drastic: 农业产量～减少。Agricultural production fell drastically. ‖ 气温～下降。There was a sudden drop in temperature. ‖ 形势～恶化。Things deteriorated fast.

【急遽】jíjù〈形〉〈书〉 rapid: ～恶化 go rapidly from bad to worse ‖ 石油价格～增长。There was a sharp increase in the price of oil.

【急流】jíliú〈名〉 rapids: 闯过～险滩 sweep over the rapids and shoals ‖ ～滚滚。The torrent surges ahead.

【急流勇进】jíliú-yǒngjìn〈成〉 forge ahead against a swift current

【急流勇退】jíliú-yǒngtuì〈成〉 make a quick retreat before crisis

【急忙】jímáng〈副〉 hastily: ～回家 hurry home ‖ 他～上前迎接她。He hurried forward to meet her. ‖ 她急急忙忙吃过早餐就出发了。She rushed her breakfast and set out.

【急难】jínàn A〈动〉〈书〉 be anxious to help: 扶危～ be eager to help those in need or in danger B〈名〉 misfortune: ～降临到他头上。Misfortunes befell him. ‖ ～之中见真情。True feelings are manifested in time of misfortune.

【急迫】jípò〈形〉 urgent: ～的任务 pressing task ‖ 情况～。The situation is urgent.

【急起直追】jíqǐ-zhízhuī〈成〉 strive to overtake: 我们要～, 攀登科学高峰。We must do our utmost to catch up and scale the heights of science.

【急切】jíqiè〈形〉 1 (迫切) impatient: ～地等待答复 wait impatiently for an answer ‖ 他的要求很～。He was impatient in his demands. 2 (仓促) hasty: ～间忘了锁门 forget to lock the door in one's haste

【急人之难】jírénzhīnán〈成〉 be eager to help those in need

【急如星火】jírúxīnghuǒ〈成〉 extremely pressing: ～的事情 matter of great urgency

【急刹车】jíshāchē〈动〉 brake sharply: 一个小孩跑过马路, 司机来了个～。The driver braked sharply when he saw a child running across the road.

【急事】jíshì〈名〉 urgent matter: 我有～, 得走了。I have something urgent to do and have to leave now.

【急速】jísù〈形〉 speedy: ～赶往出事地点 hurry to the place where an accident has occurred ‖ 部队～前进。The troops advanced rapidly.

【急湍】jítuān〈名〉〈书〉 rapids

【急弯】jíwān〈名〉 sharp turn: 向右/左拐了个～ make a sharp turn to the right/left ‖ 这条路前面有个～。There's a tight bend in the road ahead.

【急务】jíwù〈名〉〈书〉 urgent business: 他有～在身。He had some urgent task to deal with.

【急先锋】jíxiānfēng〈名〉 shock force: 充当技术革新的～ be in the vanguard of technological innovation

【急行军】jíxíngjūn〈动〉 forced march

【急性】jíxìng〈形〉 1［医学］ acute: ～传染病 acute infectious disease 2 = 急性子 jíxìngzi A

【急性病】jíxìngbìng〈名〉 1 ▸p. 50 (指疾病) acute disease 2 (指个性) impetuosity: 他爱犯～。He is liable to be too impetuous.

【急性子】jíxìngzi A〈形〉 impetuous: ～的人, 做事容易出差错。Impatient people tend to make a lot of mistakes. B〈名〉 hothead: 他是～, 爱为一些琐事生气。He is quick-tempered and often gets angry over trivial matters.

【急需】jíxū〈动〉 urgently need: ～帮助/救济 be in need of immediate help/relief ‖ 提供～的资金 provide urgently-needed funds

【急眼】jíyǎn〈动〉〈方〉 1 (生气) be angry: 她一听他的话就急了眼。She flew into a rage as soon as she heard him. 2 (着急) be anxious: 他一～就挠头。He scratches his head when he gets anxious.

【急用】jíyòng〈动〉 urgently need: 不～ be in no pressing need ‖ 留点钱, 以备～ put aside some money for a rainy day ‖ 请速汇款, 有～。Please remit the money as soon as possible. It is urgently needed.

j

【急于】jíyú〈动〉 be anxious: ～表态 be impatient to state one's position ‖ ～求胜 be eager to win ‖ 请不要～下结论。 Please don't jump to conclusions.
【急于求成】jíyú-qiúchéng〈成〉 be eager to succeed: 不要～。 Don't be in a hurry to succeed.
【急躁】jízào〈形〉 1（没耐性） irritable: 脾气～ be short-tempered ‖ 遇事要沉着，不要～。 When things crop up, it's important to keep a cool head and not to fly off the handle. 2（冲动） impetuous: 防止～情绪 guard against impetuousness ‖ ～冒进，中了埋伏 make a rash advance and fall into an ambush
【急诊】jízhěn〈名〉 emergency treatment: 挂～ register for emergency treatment ‖ ～室 emergency room ‖ ～病人 emergency case ‖ 马上去医院看～。 Go right to the hospital for emergency treatment.
【急症】jízhèng〈名〉 emergency case: ～病例 urgent case
【急智】jízhì〈名〉 quick-wittedness
【急中生智】jízhōng-shēngzhì〈成〉 show resourcefulness in an emergency
【急骤】jízhòu〈形〉 hurried: ～的脚步声 sound of hurried footsteps ‖ ～增加 drastic increase
【急转直下】jízhuǎn-zhíxià〈成〉 take a sudden unfavourable turn
【急转弯】jízhuǎnwān〈动〉 1〈本〉 curve sharply: 那条路上到处都是～。 That road is full of sharp curves. 2〈喻〉 make a radical change

姞

Jí〈名〉 Ji [surname]

疾 jí

A〈形〉 1（快） quick: ～走 walk quickly ‖ ～如闪电 as quick as lightning ▸～驰，眼～手快 2（迅猛） strong: ▸～风，～言厉色，大声～呼
B〈名〉 1（病） illness: 染～ catch an illness ‖ 耳～ ear trouble ▸～病，残～，积劳成～ 2（痛苦） pain: ▸～苦
C〈动〉 1（疼） ache: ▸痛心～首 2（憎恨） hate: ▸～恶如仇
【疾病】jíbìng〈名〉 disease: 预防～ guard against a disease ‖ 常见～ common illness ‖ 控制～的发生和蔓延 control the outbreak and spread of a disease ‖ 与～作斗争 combat a disease
【疾步】jíbù〈名〉〈书〉 quick step: ～向前 step forward quickly ‖ ～行走 walk with fast steps
【疾驰】jíchí〈动〉〈书〉 speed off: ～的火车 train running at great speed ‖ 他策马～而去。 He galloped off on his horse. ‖ 一辆小汽车～而过。 A car sped past.
【疾恶如仇】jí'è-rúchóu〈成〉 hate evil like an enemy
【疾风】jífēng〈名〉 1［气象］ moderate gale 2（强风） strong wind: ～暴雨 violent storm ‖ ～迅雷 strong wind and sudden clap of thunder
【疾风劲草】jífēng-jìngcǎo = 疾风知劲草 jífēng zhī jìngcǎo
【疾风知劲草】jífēng zhī jìngcǎo〈成〉〈喻〉 only strong characters can come through severe tests: ～，烈火见真金 the strength of character is tested in a crisis
【疾患】jíhuàn〈名〉〈书〉 ailment: 注意卫生，免生～ pay attention to hygiene to avoid disease
【疾控】jíkòng〈动〉 prevent and control diseases: ～人员 disease control personnel ‖ ～中心 centre for disease prevention and control
【疾苦】jíkǔ〈名〉 hardships: 关心群众～ be concerned about the sufferings of the people ‖ 把职工的～挂在心上 keep in mind the hardships of the workers
【疾驶】jíshǐ〈动〉〈书〉 speed: ～而去 speed past ‖ 小汽车～在高速公路上。 The car was speeding along the expressway.
【疾首蹙额】jíshǒu-cù'é〈成〉 frowning in disgust
【疾书】jíshū〈动〉〈书〉 write quickly: 挥笔～ put pen to paper and write swiftly
【疾言厉色】jíyán-lìsè〈成〉 harsh words and stern looks: 他待人和蔼，从不～。 He is always affable and never brusque with people.
【疾走】jízǒu〈动〉 walk quickly

棘 jí

A〈名〉 1（酸枣树） sour jujube 2（指草木） brambles: ▸荆～，披荆斩～
B〈动〉 prick, prickle: ▸～手
【棘齿轮】jíchǐlún〈名〉 ratchet gear wheel
【棘刺】jícì〈名〉 thorn
【棘轮】jílún〈名〉［机械］ ratchet wheel: ～传动 ratchet drive
【棘皮动物】jípí dòngwù〈名〉［动物］ echinoderm
【棘手】jíshǒu〈形〉 knotty: 感到～ feel one is in a tight fix ‖ ～的问题 thorny problem ‖ 这件工作很～。 This is tough work.
【棘爪】jízhuǎ〈名〉［机械］ pawl

戢

jí〈动〉〈书〉 conceal: ～怒 restrain one's anger

集 jí

A〈动〉 collect: ～各家之长 incorporate the strong points of various schools ▸～权，～中，调～
B〈名〉 1（指书） collection: 故事～ collection of stories ‖ 歌曲～ songbook ‖ 画～ collection of paintings ▸～锦，全～，文～ 2（集市） market: 赶～ go to a fair ▸～日，～市
C〈量〉 part: 第一～ part one ‖ 十二～电视连续剧 twelve-part TV serial ‖ 该书将分五～出版。 This book will be published in five volumes. ‖ 这部电影分上下两～。 The film is in two parts.
【集部】jíbù〈名〉 literary works [one of the four traditional divisions of a Chinese library]
【集材】jícái〈名〉［林业］ logging: 索道～ cable logging
【集藏】jícáng〈动〉 collect: ～品 collection
【集尘】jíchén〈名〉 dust-collecting: ～设备 dust-collecting equipment
【集尘器】jíchénqì〈名〉［机械］ dust collector
【集成】jíchéng〈动〉 1（汇集） collect 2［电子］ integrate: ▸～电路
【集成电路】jíchéng diànlù〈名〉 integrated circuit: ～晶体管 integrated circuit transistor ‖ ～卡/块 integrated circuit card/block
【集萃】jícuì〈名〉 fine collection: 新闻～ cache of popular news dispatches
【集大成】jí dàchéng〈动〉 synthesize: 集各流派之大成 be a comprehensive expression of various schools ‖ 这是一部～的鸿篇巨著。 This is a supreme masterpiece.
【集合】jíhé A〈动〉 1（聚集） assemble: ～队伍 rally forces ‖ ～地点 assembly point ‖ 紧急～ emergency gathering ‖ ～!［军事］ Fall in! 2（收集） collect: ～材料 collect material ‖ ～信息 compile information B〈名〉［数学］ set: ～函数 set function
【集合论】jíhélùn〈名〉［数学］ set theory
【集合名词】jíhé míngcí ▸p. 411〈名〉［语言］ collective noun
【集合体】jíhétǐ〈名〉 aggregate
【集会】jíhuì A〈动〉 assemble: 他们定期～。 They get together regularly. B〈名〉 assembly: 参加～ attend a gathering ‖ 举行～ hold a rally ‖ 隆重～ solemnly assemble ‖ 群众～ mass rally
【集结】jíjié〈动〉 concentrate: ～兵力 concentrate troops ‖ ～力量 build up strength ‖ ～待命 assemble and await orders ‖ 据悉敌军正在～。A build-up of enemy forces is reported.
【集结号】jíjiéhào〈名〉 assembly call: 一声～，数万战士迅速奔赴抗灾第一线。 As soon as the assembly call sounded, tens of thousands of recruits rushed to the disaster front line.
【集解】jíjiě〈名〉 collected commentaries
【集锦】jíjǐn〈名〉 outstanding collection: 名言～ collection of well-known sayings ‖ 邮票～ fine stamp collection
【集句】jíjù〈名〉 poem made up of lines from various poets
【集聚】jíjù〈动〉 gather: ～财富 amass a fortune ‖ 人们～在树下休息。 People gathered under the tree for a rest.
【集卡】jíkǎ A〈动〉 collect cards: ～爱好者 card collector B〈简称〉= 集装箱卡车
【集刊】jíkān〈名〉 collected papers: 英美文学研究～ collected papers on British and American literature
【集流环】jíliúhuán〈名〉［电气］ slip ring
【集拢】jílǒng〈动〉 assemble
【集录】jílù〈动〉 collect and compile: ～学术论文 collect and compile academic papers
【集贸市场】jímào shìchǎng〈名〉 fair trade market
【集权】jíquán〈动〉 centralize: ～统治 centralized rule
【集日】jírì〈名〉 market day
【集散地】jísàndì〈名〉 collection and distribution centre: 农产品～ distribution centre for agricultural produce ‖ 商品～ goods collection and distribution centre ‖ ～市场 terminal market
【集市】jíshì〈名〉 market: 到～上去买/卖（某物） go to the market to buy/sell (sth.) ‖ 镇上每三天有一次～。 The town has a market every three days.
【集市贸易】jíshì màoyì〈名〉 open market: 每星期日在广场进行～。Markets are held in the square every Sunday.
【集释】jíshì = 集解 jíjiě
【集束】jíshù〈动〉 bundle up: ～炸弹 cluster bomb unit
【集水】jíshuǐ〈名〉 catchment
【集思广益】jísī-guǎngyì〈成〉 draw on all useful opinions: 在这件事上我们一定要～。 We must solicit opinions extensively on this matter.
【集体】jítǐ〈名〉 collective: ～辞职 resign in a body ‖ 荣立～一等功 win a First Class Collective Award ‖ 团结/战斗的～ united/militant collective
【集体财产】jítǐ cáichǎn〈名〉 collective property
【集体化】jítǐhuà〈名〉 collectivization: 农业～ collectivization of agriculture
【集体婚礼】jítǐ hūnlǐ〈名〉 group wedding
【集体经济】jítǐ jīngjì〈名〉 collective economy: 引导～ guide the collective economy
【集体利益】jítǐ lìyì〈名〉 collective interests
【集体领导】jítǐ lǐngdǎo〈名〉 collective

leadership: 实行～ exercise collective leadership
【集体企业】jítǐ qǐyè〈名〉collective enterprise
【集体宿舍】jítǐ sùshè〈名〉dormitory: 住～ live in a dormitory
【集体所有制】jítǐ suǒyǒuzhì〈名〉collective ownership: 实行～ put collective ownership into practice
【集体舞】jítǐwǔ〈名〉group dancing: 跳～ perform group dancing
【集体照】jítǐzhào〈名〉group photo: 我们照张～吧。Let's have a group picture.
【集体主义】jítǐzhǔyì〈名〉collectivism: ～者 collectivist
【集团】jítuán〈名〉clique: 报业～ newspaper group ‖ 贩毒～ drug ring ‖ 间谍～ spy ring ‖ 军事～ military bloc ‖ 统治～ ruling clique
【集团犯罪】jítuán fànzuì〈名〉organized crime
【集团公司】jítuán gōngsī〈名〉conglomerate
【集团购买力】jítuán gòumǎilì〈名〉institutional purchasing power: 压缩～ cut the purchasing power of institutions
【集团军】jítuánjūn〈名〉group army
【集训】jíxùn〈动〉assemble for training: 参加～ take part in camp training ‖ 干部轮流～。Cadres receive training in turns.
【集训队】jíxùnduì〈名〉[体育] team of athletes in training
【集腋成裘】jíyè-chéngqiú〈成〉〈喻〉many little drops of water make a great ocean
【集邮】jíyóu〈名〉stamp-collecting: 爱好～ enjoy collecting stamps ‖ ～爱好者 stamp-collector
【集邮簿】jíyóubù = 集邮册 jíyóucè
【集邮册】jíyóucè〈名〉stamp-album
【集约】jíyuē〈形〉intensive: ～农业 intensive farming ‖ 劳动/技术～型企业 labour/technology-intensive enterprise
【集约化】jíyuēhuà〈名〉[农业] intensification: ～经营 intensive management ‖ 农业～ intensification of agriculture
【集约经营】jíyuē jīngyíng〈名〉intensive management: 由粗放经营向～转变 bring about a change from extensive to intensive management
【集运】jíyùn〈动〉gather together and transport: ～货物/粮食 transport goods/grain in large quantities
【集镇】jízhèn〈名〉market town
【集中】jízhōng **A**〈动〉concentrate: ～兵力 muster troops ‖ ～精力 focus one's energy ‖ ～群众的智慧 pool the wisdom of the masses ‖ ～思想 collect one's thoughts ‖ ～注意力 focus one's attention **B**〈形〉concentrated: 思想不～ scattered thinking ‖ 权力过于～ power is in the hands of too few
【集中处理】jízhōng chǔlǐ〈名〉centralized processing
【集中供热】jízhōng gōngrè〈名〉central heating
【集中营】jízhōngyíng〈名〉concentration camp: 被关在～ be kept in a concentration camp
【集中制】jízhōngzhì〈名〉centralism: 民主～ democratic centralism
【集注】jízhù **A**〈动〉focus: 人们的目光都～在他身上。All eyes were focused on him. **B**〈名〉variorum: 《莎士比亚～》*Shakespeare Variorum*
【集注本】jízhùběn〈名〉variorum edition
【集装箱】jízhuāngxiāng〈名〉container: ～船 container ship ‖ ～码头 container port
【集装箱卡车】jízhuāngxiāng kǎchē〈名〉container truck; container lorry〈英〉
【集资】jízī〈动〉raise money: ～建房 raise funds to build houses ‖ 非法～ illegal fund-raising
【集子】jízi〈名〉collected works: 这部～里收有三十首诗歌。There are thirty poems in the collection.

蒺 jí

【蒺藜】jílí〈名〉**1**[植物] puncture vine **2**（指有刺）barbed object: ▸铁～

楫 jí〈名〉〈书〉oar: ▸舟～

辑（輯）jí

A〈动〉compile: ▸～录, 编～
B〈量〉part: 新闻影片第一～ Newsreel No 1 ‖ 这套丛书分为十～。This set of books is in ten parts.
【辑录】jílù〈动〉compile: ～成册 be compiled into a book
【辑要】jíyào〈名〉summary: 会议记录～已在报上公布。An abstract of the proceedings of the conference has been published in the newspaper.
【辑佚】jíyì **A**〈动〉compile scattered writings **B**〈名〉collection of scattered writings

嫉 jí〈动〉**1**（嫉妒）envy: ▸～妒, ～贤妒能 **2**（愤恨）hate: ▸～恶如仇, 愤世～俗

【嫉妒】jídù〈动〉envy: ～某人年轻能干 envy sb. for their youth and capability
【嫉恶如仇】jí'è-rúchóu = 疾恶如仇 jí'è-rúchóu
【嫉恨】jíhèn〈动〉hate out of jealousy: 有人～他。Some people hate him out of sheer jealousy.
【嫉贤妒能】jíxián-dùnéng〈成〉envy the talented and the able

蕺 jí

【蕺菜】jícài〈名〉[植物] cordate houttuynia

瘠 jí〈形〉〈书〉**1**（指人）emaciated: ▸～瘦, 枯～ **2**（指土地）barren: ▸～薄, 贫～

【瘠薄】jíbó〈形〉barren: 岛上土地～, 人烟稀少。The island is barren and sparsely populated.
【瘠瘦】jíshòu〈形〉emaciated
【瘠田】jítián〈名〉infertile fields
【瘠土】jítǔ〈名〉infertile land

鹡（鶺）jí

【鹡鸰】jílíng〈名〉[鸟类] wagtail

藉 jí

A〈动〉〈书〉insult
B〈形〉muddled: ▸狼～
▸jiè
【藉藉】jíjí〈形〉disorderly

籍 jí ▸**p. 279**〈名〉**1**（书籍）record: 图～ map of a territory and census registers ▸古～, 户～ **2**（地方）hometown: ▸～贯, 原～ **3**（关系）membership: ▸国～, 党～, 外～

【籍贯】jíguàn〈名〉native place
【籍没】jímò〈动〉〈书〉register and confiscate (sb.'s property)

jǐ

几（幾）jǐ〈数〉**1**（用于询问）how many: ～点了? What time is it? ‖ 今天～号? What's the date today? ‖ 你～岁了? How old are you? **2** ▸**p. 927**（一些）a few: ～本书 a few books ‖ ～个问题 a few questions ‖ ～年前 a few years ago ‖ ～天之内 within a couple of days ‖ 所剩无～。There is hardly anything left.

▸jī
【几曾】jǐcéng〈副〉[used in a rhetorical question to indicate negation] when: 这事你～问过我? You never asked me about it, did you?
【几次三番】jǐcì-sānfān〈成〉time after time: 朋友们～地警告, 他都当成耳旁风。He turned a deaf ear to his friends' repeated warnings.
【几多】jǐduō〈方〉**A**〈代〉（表可数）how many;（表不可数）how much: ～人? How many people? ‖ 这袋米有～重? How much does this sack of rice weigh? **B**〈副〉[used in exclamations] to what an extent: 这孩子～聪明! What a clever kid!
【几分】jǐfēn〈数量〉a bit: 让他～ humour him a little ‖ 有～把握? How confident do you feel? ‖ 他说的有～道理。There is something in what he said.
【几何】jǐhé **A**〈代〉〈书〉（表可数）how many;（表不可数）how much: 价值～? How much is it worth? **B**〈名〉[数学] geometry
【几何级数】jǐhé jíshù〈名〉geometric series: 成～的人口增长 geometric population growth
【几何体】jǐhétǐ〈名〉solid
【几何图形】jǐhé túxíng〈名〉geometric figure: ～式建筑 geometrical architecture
【几何学】jǐhéxué〈名〉geometry
【几经】jǐjīng〈动〉be numerous: ～波折 after a lot of twists and turns ‖ 问题～交涉才得到解决。The problem was not solved until after repeated negotiations.
【几内亚】Jǐnèiyà〈名〉Guinea: ～人 Guinean
【几内亚法郎】Jǐnèiyà fǎláng〈名〉Guinean franc
【几内亚比绍】Jǐnèiyà-Bǐshào〈名〉Guinea-Bissau
【几起几落】jǐqǐ-jǐluò〈成〉repeated rises and falls
【几时】jǐshí〈代〉what time: 你～有空? When will you be free? ‖ 你们～走? What time are you leaving?
【几许】jǐxǔ〈代〉〈书〉how much/many: 不知～。No one can tell how much.

己[1] jǐ〈名〉sixth of the ten Heavenly Stems (天干)

己[2] jǐ〈代〉oneself: 舍～为公 make personal sacrifices for the public good ▸～见, 舍～为人, 身不由～

【己方】jǐfāng〈名〉one's own side
【己见】jǐjiàn〈名〉〈书〉one's own opinion: 坚持～ stick to one's own opinion
【己任】jǐrèn〈名〉〈书〉one's duty: 以经济建设为～ regard economic development as one's duty
【己所不欲, 勿施于人】jǐ suǒ bù yù, wù

shī yú rén〈成〉 do not impose on others what you yourself do not desire

纪（紀） Jǐ〈名〉 Ji [surname]
▸jì

虮（蟣） jǐ
【虮子】jǐzi〈名〉 nit

挤（擠） jǐ
A〈动〉 **1**（推挤） jostle: ～进商店 jostle into a department store ‖ 把某人～向一边 shove sb. aside ‖ 从大门～入 crowd in through the gate ‖ 别～我! Don't push me! ‖ 请排队，不要往里～。 Please queue up. Don't push in. **2**（排挤） crowd out: 被～出董事会 be excluded from the board of directors ‖ 卫冕冠军被～出比赛。 The defending champion was forced out the competition. **3**（用压力） squeeze: ～出几滴眼泪 squeeze out tears ‖ ～奶 milk ‖ ～牙膏 squeeze toothpaste out ‖〈喻〉 ～时间学习 find time to study **4**（紧挨） pack: ～在一起取暖 crowd against one another for warmth ‖ 入口处～得水泄不通。 The entrance was so packed that nothing could get through. ‖〈喻〉 几件事～在一起了。 Several things cropped up at the same time.
B〈形〉 packed: 车厢里特别～。 The carriage was totally packed.
【挤兑】jǐduì〈动〉 run on a bank: 储户向银行～。 Depositors are making a run on the bank.
【挤对】jǐdui〈动〉〈方〉 **1**（使屈从） force: 他不愿意，就别～他了。 He is unwilling, so don't push him. **2**（欺负） bully
【挤满】jǐmǎn〈动〉 be packed with: ～了人 be swarmed with people
【挤眉弄眼】jǐméi-nòngyǎn〈成〉 wink: 对某人～ make eyes at sb.
【挤奶】jǐnǎi〈动〉 milk (a cow, etc.)
【挤奶机】jǐnǎijī〈名〉 milking machine
【挤压】jǐyā〈动〉 press: 这种金属易于～成形。 This metal extracts easily.
【挤牙膏】jǐ yágāo〈惯〉〈喻〉 squeeze sth. out of sb.
【挤轧】jǐyà〈动〉 engage in internal strife or infighting
【挤眼】jǐyǎn〈动〉 wink: 向人～暗示 tip sb. the wink
【挤占】jǐzhàn〈动〉 encroach

济（濟） jǐ
▸jì
【济济】jǐjǐ〈形〉 numerous: ▸～一堂, 人才～
【济济一堂】jǐjǐ-yītáng〈成〉 numerous talented people congregate under the same roof
【济南】Jǐnán ▸p. 661〈名〉 Jinan [capital of Shandong Province (山东)]

给（給） jǐ
A〈动〉 provide: ▸～养, 补～, 自～自足
B〈形〉 abundant: ▸家～人足
▸gěi
【给付】jǐfù〈动〉 pay: 按保险条例～保险金 pay insurance money in accordance with insurance regulations
【给水】jǐshuǐ〈动〉 supply water: ～水质标准 water quality of tap water ‖ ～工程 water-supply engineering
【给水管】jǐshuǐguǎn〈名〉 feed pipe
【给水系统】jǐshuǐ xìtǒng〈名〉 water supply system
【给养】jǐyǎng〈名〉 provisions: 补充～ replenish the provisions ‖ ～充足 be abundantly supplied
【给油】jǐyóu〈名〉 oil feed
【给予】jǐyǔ〈动〉〈书〉 render: ～（某人）帮助 render assistance (to sb.) ‖ ～关怀/同情 show concern/sympathy ‖ ～很高的评价 appreciate highly ‖ ～纪律处分 take disciplinary measures ‖ ～人道主义援助 provide humanitarian assistance (to sb.) ‖ ～足够重视 attach great importance (to sth.)

脊 jǐ
〈名〉 **1**（背脊） spine: ▸～背, ～髓, ～椎 **2**（背脊状物） ridge: ▸山～, 书～, 屋～
【脊背】jǐbèi〈名〉 back
【脊梁】jǐliang〈名〉〈方〉 back: 光着～ be bare-backed ‖〈喻〉 国家经济的～ backbone of a country's economy
【脊梁骨】jǐlianggǔ〈名〉 spine: 断/扭了～ break/wrench one's spine ‖〈喻〉 做人不能没有～。 To be a real person one cannot be spineless. ▸戳～
【脊檩】jǐlǐn〈名〉［建筑］ ridge pole
【脊鳍】jǐqí〈名〉［鱼类］ dorsal fin
【脊髓】jǐsuǐ〈名〉 spinal cord: 抽/移植～ draw/graft spinal cord
【脊髓灰质炎】jǐsuǐ huīzhìyán ▸p. 50〈名〉［医学］ polio: ～疫苗 poliomyelitis vaccine
【脊髓炎】jǐsuǐyán ▸p. 50〈名〉［医学］ myelitis: 患～ infect myelitis
【脊索】jǐsuǒ〈名〉［动物］ notochord
【脊索动物】jǐsuǒ dòngwù〈名〉 chordate animal
【脊瓦】jǐwǎ〈名〉［建筑］ ridge tile
【脊柱】jǐzhù〈名〉［解剖］ spine
【脊柱炎】jǐzhùyán ▸p. 50〈名〉［医学］ rachitis
【脊椎】jǐzhuī〈名〉 **1**（脊柱） spinal column **2**（脊椎骨） vertebra
【脊椎动物】jǐzhuī dòngwù〈名〉 vertebrate: 进化成～ evolve into vertebrate
【脊椎骨】jǐzhuīgǔ〈名〉 vertebra
【脊椎炎】jǐzhuīyán ▸p. 50〈名〉［医学］ spondylitis

掎 jǐ
〈动〉〈书〉 **1**（拖） pull from behind **2**（牵制） pin down
【掎角之势】jǐjiǎozhīshì〈成〉 state of pinning down an enemy or attacking it from both sides: 对敌人形成～ attack the enemy from both sides

鲯（鮆） jǐ
〈名〉［鱼类］ girella punctata

戟 jǐ
〈名〉 **1**（指兵器） halberd **2**〈书〉（刺激） stimulate

麂 jǐ
〈名〉［动物］ muntjac
【麂皮】jǐpí〈名〉 chamois leather
【麂子】jǐzi〈名〉［动物］ muntjac

jì

计（計） jì
A〈动〉 **1**（计算） count: 不～成本 exclude the cost ‖ 数以千～ number in the thousands ▸～酬, ～量, 统～ **2**（总计） amount to: 损失～二十万元以上。 The losses totalled more than 200,000 *yuan*. **3**（计划） plan: ▸～议, 设～ **4**（计较） concern about: 不～报酬 not be bothered about pay ‖ 不～个人恩怨 not allow oneself to be swayed by personal feelings ▸～较
B〈名〉 **1**（计谋） idea: 定～ devise stratagems ‖ 施～ carry out a plot ▸～谋, 缓兵之～, 中～ **2**（指仪器） gauge: ▸温度～, 压力～
【计步器】jìbùqì〈名〉［体育］ pedometer
【计策】jìcè〈名〉 stratagem: 施用～ pursue a strategy ‖ 诱敌深入的～ plan to lure the enemy in
【计程表】jìchéngbiǎo〈名〉 mileometer〈英〉; odometer〈美〉
【计程车】jìchéngchē〈名〉〈方〉 taxi: 叫/雇/坐～ call/hire/take a taxi
【计程仪】jìchéngyí〈名〉［航海］ log apparatus: ～里程表 log indicator
【计酬】jìchóu〈动〉 calculate the payment: 按件/时～ pay by the piece/hour ‖ 按周/月～ pay by the week/month
【计出万全】jìchū-wànquán〈成〉 make a perfectly safe plan
【计费】jìfèi〈名〉 billing
【计划】jìhuà **A**〈名〉 plan: 打乱～ upset a plan ‖ 修改～ revise a plan ‖ 搁置～ shelf a plan ‖ 制定～ work out a plan/scheme ‖ 科研～ scientific research programme **B**〈动〉 plan: ～实行新政策 plan to put a new policy into practice ‖ 提前/周密～ plan sth. ahead/out
【计划单列市】jìhuà dānlièshì〈名〉 city specially designated in the state plan
【计划供应】jìhuà gōngyìng〈名〉 planned supply
【计划经济】jìhuà jīngjì〈名〉 planned economy: ～与市场调节相结合 combine a planned economy with market regulation
【计划生育】jìhuà shēngyù〈名〉 family planning: 实行～ practise birth control ‖ ～委员会 family planning commission
【计划外】jìhuàwài〈形〉 unplanned: ～项目 project outside the plan
【计划委员会】jìhuà wěiyuánhuì〈名〉 planning commission
【计价】jìjià〈动〉 calculate the price: 合理～ reasonable valuation
【计价器】jìjiàqì〈名〉 fee register
【计件】jìjiàn〈动〉 calculate by the piece: ～付酬 pay by the piece
【计件工】jìjiàngōng〈名〉 piece-worker
【计件工资】jìjiàn gōngzī〈名〉 piece-rate wage: ～制 piece work system
【计较】jìjiào〈动〉 **1**（计算比较） bother about: 不～个人得失 give no thought to personal gains or losses ‖ 小事上不必太～。 Don't fuss too much over small things. ▸斤斤～ **2**（争辩） argue: 我才不想同他～。 I don't want to argue with him. **3**（打算） think over: 这事我们以后再作～吧。 We'll talk it over some other time.
【计量】jìliàng〈动〉 **1**（测定） measure: ～单位 measuring unit ‖ ～技术 measurement technique **2**（求得） calculate: 其影响之大不可～。 Its influence is inestimable.
【计量经济学】jìliàng jīngjìxué〈名〉 econometrics
【计谋】jìmóu〈名〉 stratagem: 施用～ pursue a strategy ‖ 识破～ see through a stratagem ‖ 他的～落空了。 His scheme fell through.
【计票】jìpiào〈动〉 count the votes: 最后的～结果星期二才能出来。 The final count of the votes won't be announced until Tuesday.
【计日程功】jìrì-chénggōng〈成〉 have the completion of a project in sight
【计上心来】jìshàngxīnlái〈成〉 hit upon a stratagem

【计生委】jìshēngwěi〈名〉family planning commission

【计时】jìshí〈动〉calculate by time: ～存放 pay for storage according to the time stored ‖ ～收费 charge by the hour ‖ ～器 timer ▸倒～

【计时工】jìshígōng〈名〉time worker

【计时工资】jìshí gōngzī〈名〉payment by the hour

【计时赛】jìshísài〈名〉［体育］time trial

【计时员】jìshíyuán ▸**p. 966**〈名〉time-keeper

【计数】jìshǔ〈动〉count: 不可～ be countless ‖ 实际～为五百人。There were five hundred people by actual count.

【计数】jìshù〈动〉count the number

【计数器】jìshùqì〈名〉counter: 闪烁～ scintillation counter

【计算】jìsuàn〈动〉**1**（求得）calculate: ～成本 calculate the cost ‖ ～利润 count one's profits ‖ ～方法 computational method ‖ 粗略/仔细～ make a rough/careful calculation **2**（考虑）plan: 做事没个～可不行。We shouldn't do anything without a plan. **3**（算计）plot: 暗中～别人 secretly plot against others

【计算尺】jìsuànchǐ〈名〉slide rule

【计算机】jìsuànjī〈名〉computer: 打开/关闭～ turn on/off a computer ‖ 笔记本/便携式～ laptop/portable computer ‖ 个人～ personal computer (PC) ‖ 家用/商用～ home/business computer

【计算机病毒】jìsuànjī bìngdú〈名〉computer virus: 杀～ kill/disable a computer virus

【计算机程序】jìsuànjī chéngxù〈名〉computer programme: ～编制员 computer programmer

【计算机存储器】jìsuànjī cúnchǔqì〈名〉computer memory

【计算机断层扫描】jìsuànjī duàncéng sǎomiáo〈名〉［医学］computerized tomography (CT)

【计算机辅助教学】jìsuànjī fǔzhù jiàoxué〈名〉computer-assisted instruction

【计算机辅助设计】jìsuànjī fǔzhù shèjì〈名〉computer-aided design

【计算机技术】jìsuànjī jìshù〈名〉computer technology

【计算机监控系统】jìsuànjī jiānkòng xìtǒng〈名〉computer supervisory control system

【计算机科学】jìsuànjī kēxué〈名〉computer science

【计算机排版】jìsuànjī páibǎn〈名〉computer typesetting: ～系统 computer typesetting system

【计算机软件】jìsuànjī ruǎnjiàn〈名〉computer software

【计算机体层成像】jìsuànjī tǐcéng chéngxiàng = 计算机断层扫描 jìsuànjī duàncéng sǎomiáo

【计算机网络】jìsuànjī wǎngluò〈名〉computer network: ～部件/设备 computer network components/facilities ‖ 从～中获取信息 get information from the computer network

【计算机显示器】jìsuànjī xiǎnshìqì〈名〉computer display

【计算机芯片】jìsuànjī xīnpiàn〈名〉computer chip

【计算机硬件】jìsuànjī yìngjiàn〈名〉computer hardware

【计算机语言】jìsuànjī yǔyán〈名〉computer language

【计算机终端】jìsuànjī zhōngduān〈名〉computer terminal

【计算器】jìsuànqì〈名〉calculator: 电子/台式/袖珍～ electronic/desk/pocket calculator

【计算语言学】jìsuàn yǔyánxué〈名〉computational linguistics

【计算中心】jìsuàn zhōngxīn〈名〉computing centre

【计提】jìtí〈动〉［金融］accrue: ～呆坏账准备金 accrue for a bad debt ‖ ～费用 accrued charges

【计委】jìwěi〈简称〉= 计划委员会

【计议】jìyì〈动〉talk over: 二人～已定。The two of them settled on a scheme. ▸从长～

记（記）jì

A〈动〉**1**（写下）record: ～笔记 take notes ‖ ～日记 keep a diary ▸～事, ～载, 登～ **2**（记忆）remember: ～不清 remember only vaguely ‖ ～错了 remember wrongly ‖ 如果我没～错的话，你比我年长两岁。If my memory serves me right, you are two years my senior. ▸～仇, 惦～, 死～硬背

B〈名〉**1**（标记）mark: ▸～号, 标～, 印～ **2**（胎记）birthmark: 他背上有块～。There is a birthmark on his back. ▸胎～ **3**（记录）notes: ▸日～, 传～

C〈量〉[for a blow, etc.]: 一～耳光 a slap in the face ‖ 一～重扣 a powerful smash

【记仇】jìchóu〈动〉harbour bitter resentment: 从不～ never bear a grudge ‖ 记一辈子仇 harbour a hatred all one's life

【记得】jìde〈动〉remember: ～学生时代的往事 retain a memory of one's school days ‖ 清楚/清晰地～ remember clearly/vividly ‖ 我不～他说过那种话。I don't recall him saying that.

【记分】jìfēn〈动〉**1**（记录）keep score: 以出勤情况～ keep score by sb.'s attendance ‖ 以工作表现～ score sb.'s performance on their work **2**（指学生）register a student's marks: 不记分数 not register students' marks **3**（指工分）record work points: 出一天工记10分 score ten points for one day's work attendance

【记分册】jìfēncè〈名〉grade book

【记分牌】jìfēnpái〈名〉［体育］scoreboard: 电动～ electric scoreboard

【记工】jìgōng〈动〉record work points

【记功】jìgōng〈动〉award sb. a citation for a merit: 记一等功 award sb. a Citation of Merit ‖ 屡记战功 cite sb. time and again for meritorious military service

【记挂】jìguà〈动〉keep thinking about: ～年迈的父母 keep thinking about one's ageing parents ‖ 好好工作，不要～我。Do your work and don't worry about me.

【记过】jìguò〈动〉record a demerit: 给予～处分 give sb. a demerit ‖ 记大过一次 record a serious demerit

【记号】jìhao〈名〉sign: 在某物上标上～ put a sign on sth. ‖ 做～ make a sign

【记恨】jìhèn〈动〉harbour grudges: ～在心 nurse a grudge in one's heart ‖ 我并无恶意，别～我。I meant no harm. I hope you won't hold a grudge against me.

【记录】jìlù **A**〈动〉take notes: ～行动要点 make a record of the most important points of the action ‖ ～在案 document on record **B**〈名〉**1**（指文字）record: 察看～ view the records ‖ 犯罪～ crime record ‖ 会议～ minutes of a meeting ‖ 健康状况～ health record ‖ 他没有犯罪～。He has no record with the police. **2**（指人）note-taker **3** = 纪录 jìlù

【记录片】jìlùpiàn = 纪录片 jìlùpiàn

【记名】jìmíng〈动〉sign one's name: ～证券 registered securities ‖ ～支票 order cheque ‖ 无～投票 cast an anonymous vote

【记念】jìniàn = 纪念 jìniàn

【记念】jìnian〈动〉keep thinking about: 他心里老～着家里的老母亲。He kept thinking about his aged mother at home.

【记谱法】jìpǔfǎ〈名〉［音乐］musical notation

【记取】jìqǔ〈动〉bear in mind: （从某事中）～教训 learn a lesson (from sth.) ‖ ～正反两方面的经验 draw on both positive and negative experiences

【记认】jìrèn〈动〉identify: 她戴了顶红帽子，好～。She wore a bright red cap and was easy to recognize.

【记时器】jìshíqì〈名〉timer

【记时员】jìshíyuán ▸**p. 966**〈名〉［体育］time-keeper

【记事】jìshì〈动〉keep a record of events: 结绳～ record by tying knots ‖ ～本 notebook

【记事儿】jìshìr〈动〉begin to remember things: 三岁开始～ begin to remember things at the age of three

【记述】jìshù〈动〉recount: ～事件的经过 recount the whole course of the incident

【记诵】jìsòng〈动〉learn by heart: ～课文/诗歌 learn texts/poems by heart

【记协】jìxié〈简称〉= 记者协会

【记性】jìxing〈名〉memory: ～好/差 have a good/bad memory

【记叙】jìxù〈动〉recount: ～运动会的盛况 give an account of the grand sporting occasion ‖ ～简练 give a concise account

【记叙文】jìxùwén〈名〉narrative writing: 写一篇～ write an article narrating a series of events

【记要】jìyào = 纪要 jìyào

【记忆】jìyì **A**〈动〉remember: ～方法 memory method ‖ 如果我～无误 if I remember correctly **B**〈名〉memory: 唤起～ jog one's memory ‖ 失去～ lose one's memory ‖ 长时/短时～ long-term/short-term memory ‖ 父亲的话铭刻在我的～中。My father's words are inscribed in my memory.

【记忆合金】jìyì héjīn〈名〉shape memory alloy

【记忆力】jìyìlì〈名〉memory: 有惊人的～ have a remarkable memory ‖ 增强～ improve one's memory ‖ ～差 have a poor memory ‖ 我的～在减退。My memory is going.

【记忆犹新】jìyì-yóuxīn〈成〉remain fresh in one's memory: 这件事我～。I still remember it vividly.

【记载】jìzǎi **A**〈动〉record: ～所发生的一切 record everything that happens ‖ 有文字～的历史 recorded history **B**〈名〉record: 历史～ historical record ‖ 据～，该历史古迹毁于战争。It is recorded that this historical site was destroyed in war.

【记账】jìzhàng〈动〉**1**（记录收支）keep accounts: 记家庭收支账 keep household accounts **2**（赊账）charge to an account: ～购物 buy sth. on credit ‖ 你这双鞋是付现金还是～? Did you pay cash for the shoes or put them on credit?

【记账式国债】jìzhàngshì guózhài〈名〉registered treasury bond

【记者】jìzhě ▸**p. 966**〈名〉reporter: 当～ work as a journalist ‖ 新华社～ Xinhua correspondent ‖ 新闻～ newspaper reporter ‖ 答～问 news briefing ‖ 接受～采访 be interviewed by reporters ▸随军～, 战地～

【记者节】jìzhějié〈名〉Reporter's Day

【记者席】jìzhěxí〈名〉press gallery

【记者协会】jìzhě xiéhuì〈名〉journalists'

association: ～会员 be a member of the journalists' association
【记者招待会】jìzhě zhāodàihuì〈名〉 press conference: 举行～ hold a press conference
【记者证】jìzhězhèng〈名〉 press card
【记住】jìzhù〈动〉 memorize: ～教训 keep a lesson on one's mind ‖ ～亲人的嘱托 remember the entrustment made by one's loved ones ‖ 我们将永远～他。 He will always remain in our memory.

伎 jì〈名〉 **1**（本领） skill: ▸～俩 **2**（古）（指人） professional female performer: ▸歌～
【伎俩】jìliǎng〈名〉 trick: 惯用～ old trick ‖ 逃税～ tax dodge ‖ 卑鄙的～ mean trick

齐（齊） jì〈书〉
A〈动〉 mix
B〈名〉 seasoning
▸qí

纪（紀） jì〈名〉 **1**（纪律） discipline: 校～ school discipline ▸军～, 违法乱～, 遵～守法 **2**（一百年） age: ▸世～, 中世～ **3**［地质］ period: 侏罗～ Jurassic Period
▸Jǐ
【纪纲】jìgāng〈名〉〈书〉 **1**（法律） law **2**（道德标准） moral standard
【纪检】jìjiǎn〈动〉 inspect discipline: ～工作 discipline inspection work
【纪检委】jìjiǎnwěi〈简称〉= 纪律检查委员会
【纪录】jìlù〈名〉 record: 创造～ set a record ‖ 世界～保持者 world record holder
【纪录片】jìlùpiàn〈名〉 documentary: 电视～ televised documentary ‖ 大型～ full-length documentary
【纪律】jìlǜ〈名〉 discipline: 劳动～ labour discipline ‖ 违反～ violate discipline ‖ ～松懈 be lax in discipline ‖ ～严明 be highly disciplined ‖ ～处分 disciplinary punishment
【纪律检查委员会】jìlǜ jiǎnchá wěiyuánhuì〈名〉 discipline inspection commission
【纪年】jìnián **A**〈动〉 number the years: 中国过去用干支～。 China used to designate the years by the ten Heavenly Stems and the twelve Earthly Branches. **B**〈名〉 annals: ～体 chronological order
【纪念】jìniàn **A**〈动〉 commemorate: ～民族英雄 in memory of a national hero ‖ 举行～大会 hold a commemorative event ‖ 值得～的日子 memorable day **B**〈名〉 souvenir: 一起合影留作～ have a picture taken together as a memento
【纪念碑】jìniànbēi〈名〉 memorial: 烈士～ memorial to the martyrs ‖ 广场中心矗立着一座～。 At the centre of the square stands a monument. ▸人民英雄～
【纪念币】jìniànbì〈名〉 commemoration coin
【纪念册】jìniàncè〈名〉autograph book: 毕业～ yearbook
【纪念封】jìniànfēng〈名〉 commemorate envelope: 发行/收集～ issue/collect commemorative envelopes
【纪念馆】jìniànguǎn〈名〉 memorial hall: 鲁迅～ Lu Xun Museum
【纪念品】jìniànpǐn〈名〉 souvenir: 赠送某人～ present sb. with souvenirs as gifts ‖ 旅游～ souvenir for travellers
【纪念日】jìniànrì〈名〉commemoration day: 结婚～ wedding anniversary ‖ 50周年～ 50th anniversary
【纪念塔】jìniàntǎ〈名〉 memorial tower
【纪念堂】jìniàntáng〈名〉 memorial hall
【纪念邮票】jìniàn yóupiào〈名〉 commemorative stamp
【纪念章】jìniànzhāng〈名〉 souvenir badge
【纪实】jìshí **A**〈动〉 record events as they happen: ～文学 documentary writing ‖ ～小说 documentary novel **B**〈名〉 record of actual events: 奥运会开幕式/闭幕式～ on-the-spot report of the opening/closing ceremony of the Olympic Games
【纪实片】jìshípiàn〈名〉 documentary film
【纪事】jìshì **A**〈动〉 chronicle: ～诗/文 narrative poem/writing **B**〈名〉 chronicle
【纪事本末体】jìshì běnmòtǐ〈名〉［历史］ traditional historical accounts
【纪委】jìwěi〈简称〉= 纪律检查委员会
【纪行】jìxíng〈名〉 travel notes:《延安～》 *Notes on a Trip to Yan'an*
【纪要】jìyào〈名〉 summary: 会谈～ summary of the talks ‖ 新闻～ news summary
【纪元】jìyuán〈名〉 **1**（指起算年） beginning of an era **2**（指时代） era: 开创历史新～ usher in a new era in history
【纪传体】jìzhuàntǐ〈名〉 history presented in a series of biographies

技 jì〈名〉 skill: 献～ display one's feats ▸～巧, 绝～, 一～之长
【技法】jìfǎ〈名〉 skill and technique: 讲究～ pay special attention to technique
【技改】jìgǎi〈简称〉= 技术改造
【技工】jìgōng〈名〉 **1**（泛指工人） skilled worker **2**（特指修车人） mechanic: 熟练～ master mechanic
【技工学校】jìgōng xuéxiào〈名〉 technical school
【技击】jìjī〈名〉［武术］ art of attack and defence
【技能】jìnéng〈名〉 skill: 掌握（做某事的）～ master the skill (of doing sth.) ‖ ～训练 skills training
【技巧】jìqiǎo〈名〉 **1**（技能） skill: ～娴熟 display consummate skill ‖ 烹饪～ cooking skills ‖ 他的书法～令人惊叹。 His calligraphy is astonishing. **2**［体育］ acrobatic gymnastics
【技巧运动】jìqiǎo yùndòng〈名〉［体育］ acrobatic gymnastics
【技师】jìshī ▸**p. 966**〈名〉 technician
【技术】jìshù〈名〉 technique: 采用最新～ use the latest technology ‖ 改进～ improve a technique ‖ ～熟练 be skilful at ‖ ～转让 technology transfer ‖ 电子/通信～ electronic/communication technology
【技术壁垒】jìshù bìlěi〈名〉［经济］ technical barrier
【技术兵种】jìshù bīngzhǒng〈名〉 technical troops
【技术参数】jìshù cānshù〈名〉 technical parameter
【技术创新】jìshù chuàngxīn〈名〉 technology innovation
【技术等级】jìshù děngjí〈名〉 technical class
【技术犯规】jìshù fànguī〈名〉［体育］ technical foul
【技术改造】jìshù gǎizào〈名〉 technological transformation
【技术革命】jìshù gémìng〈名〉 technological revolution
【技术革新】jìshù géxīn〈名〉 technical innovation: 进行～ carry out technical innovation
【技术鉴定】jìshù jiàndìng〈名〉 technical appraisal
【技术交流】jìshù jiāoliú〈名〉 technical exchanges
【技术密集型产品】jìshù mìjíxíng chǎnpǐn〈名〉 technology-intensive product
【技术人员】jìshù rényuán〈名〉 technical staff
【技术手册】jìshù shǒucè〈名〉 technical manual
【技术术语】jìshù shùyǔ〈名〉 technical terminology
【技术突破】jìshù tūpò〈名〉 technological breakthrough
【技术推广站】jìshù tuīguǎngzhàn〈名〉 technical advice station
【技术性】jìshùxìng〈形〉 technical: 这工作～很强。 This job is highly technical.
【技术学校】jìshù xuéxiào〈名〉 technical school
【技术移民】jìshù yímín〈名〉 **1**（指迁入） skilled immigration; （指迁出） skilled migration **2**（指迁入者） skilled immigrant;（指迁出者） skilled migrant
【技术员】jìshùyuán ▸**p. 966**〈名〉 technician: 农业～ agronomist
【技术职称】jìshù zhíchēng〈名〉 technical title: 评定～ grade technical personnel and give them appropriate titles
【技术指导】jìshù zhǐdǎo〈名〉 technological guidance
【技术转让】jìshù zhuǎnràng〈名〉 technology transfer
【技术装备】jìshù zhuāngbèi〈名〉technical equipment
【技校】jìxiào〈简称〉= 技工学校, 技术学校
【技痒】jìyǎng〈动〉 itch to display one's skills: 他看见别人打乒乓球，不觉～。 Seeing other people playing table tennis, he itched to have a go.
【技艺】jìyì〈名〉 skill: 传授～ impart a skill ‖ 学到一门～ master a skill ‖ ～精湛 be highly skilled ‖ 传统手工～ traditional craft skill

系（繫） jì〈动〉 do up: ～安全带 fasten one's seat belt ‖ ～鞋带 do up one's shoe laces ‖ ～着红领巾 wear a Young Pioneer's red scarf
▸xì
【系泊】jìbó〈动〉 moor (a boat)
【系泊浮筒】jìbó fútǒng〈名〉mooring buoy
【系船索】jìchuánsuǒ〈名〉 mooring line/rope
【系留】jìliú〈动〉moor (a balloon/an airship)
【系留塔】jìliútǎ〈名〉 mooring tower

忌 jì〈动〉 **1**（忌妒） be jealous of: ～人之才 be jealous of people more capable than oneself ▸～恨, 猜～ **2**（畏惧） fear: ▸顾～, 肆无～惮 **3**（避免） avoid: ～荤腥 abstain from meat and fish ‖ ～食生冷 avoid cold and uncooked food ‖ 孕妇～服 not to be taken by pregnant women ▸～讳, ～口 **4**（戒除） give up: ～酒 give up alcohol ‖ ～烟 quit smoking
【忌辰】jìchén〈名〉 anniversary of a death: 在～送上鲜花 present flowers on the anniversary of sb.'s death
【忌惮】jìdàn〈动〉〈书〉 fear: 毫无～ be devoid of scruples ▸肆无～
【忌妒】jìdu〈动〉 be jealous of: ～某人的地位/名声 be jealous of sb.'s social position/fame ‖ 引起～ arouse sb.'s jealousy ‖ ～心 jealousy ‖ 他那样做是出于～。 He acted out of jealousy.
【忌恨】jìhèn = 嫉恨 jìhèn
【忌讳】jìhuì〈动〉 abstain from: 他～人家

叫他的绰号。 He doesn't like people calling him by his nickname. ‖ 学习最～有始无终。 Most to be avoided is to give up halfway through one's studies.

【忌讳】jìhuì〈名〉 taboo: 犯～ break a taboo

【忌刻】jìkè〈动〉〈书〉 be jealous and malicious

【忌口】jìkǒu〈动〉 avoid certain food: 她现在～，不吃油腻东西。 She is on a diet and is avoiding greasy food.

【忌日】jìrì〈名〉 **1** = 忌辰 jìchén **2**（指不宜做某事） date on which certain things should be avoided to ensure good luck

【忌食】jìshí〈动〉 avoid certain food: ～辛辣 avoid pungent food

【忌嘴】jìzuǐ = 忌口 jìkǒu

际（際）jì

A〈名〉 **1**（边界） boundary: 水～ edge of a body of water ▸边～，天～，一望无～ **2**（边缘） inside: ▸脑～ **3**（之间） between: 省～交流 exchange between provinces ▸国～，洲～ **4**（时候） moment: 临别之～ at the time of parting ‖ 危急之～ at a critical moment

B〈动〉 **1**（交往） associate: ▸交～ **2**〈书〉（恰逢） be on the occasion of: ～此佳节 on this festive occasion ‖ ～此盛会 on the occasion of this grand gathering **3**〈书〉（遭遇） be one's lot: ▸～遇，遭～

【际会】jìhuì〈动〉〈书〉 come across

【际涯】jìyá〈名〉〈书〉 boundary: 茫无～ be boundless

【际遇】jìyù〈书〉 **A**〈动〉 meet with **B**〈名〉 turns in life: ～不佳 be out of luck

妓 jì〈名〉 prostitute: ▸娼～，狎～

【妓女】jìnǚ〈名〉 prostitute

【妓院】jìyuàn〈名〉 brothel: 逛～ visit a brothel

季 jì〈名〉 **1**（季节） season: ▸～刊，春～，换～ **2**（时期） period of time: ▸淡～，雨～ **3**〈书〉（指月份） last month of a season: ▸～春，～冬 **4**〈书〉（指人） youngest among brothers: ～弟 youngest brother **5**（末期） last period: 唐～ end of the Tang Dynasty

【季报】jìbào〈名〉 quarterly bulletin

【季春】jìchūn〈名〉 last month of spring

【季冬】jìdōng〈名〉 last month of winter

【季度】jìdù〈名〉 quarter: ～报告 quarterly report ‖ 第一～ first quarter of the year

【季风】jìfēng〈名〉 monsoon: 冬季/夏季～ dry/wet monsoon

【季风期】jìfēngqī〈名〉 monsoon season

【季风气候】jìfēng qìhòu〈名〉 monsoon climate

【季候】jìhòu〈名〉〈方〉 season

【季节】jìjié ▸**p. 345**〈名〉 season: ～差价 seasonal price variations ‖ 农忙～ busy farming season ‖ 收获～ harvest season ‖ 在隆冬～ in the depths of winter

【季节工】jìjiégōng〈名〉 seasonal worker

【季节洄游】jìjié huíyóu〈名〉 seasonal migration

【季节迁徙】jìjié qiānxǐ〈名〉 seasonal migration: 鸟的～ seasonal migration of birds

【季节性】jìjiéxìng〈形〉 seasonal: ～风暴/气候/行业 seasonal storm/weather/trade ‖ ～降价/折扣 seasonal price-cut/discount

【季军】jìjūn〈名〉 third place

【季刊】jìkān〈名〉 quarterly

【季秋】jìqiū〈名〉 last month of autumn

【季世】jìshì〈名〉〈书〉 last phase

【季夏】jìxià〈名〉 last month of summer

剂（劑）jì

A〈动〉 make up: ▸调～

B〈名〉 **1**（指药） medication: ▸冲～，片～，针～ **2**［化工］ agent: 发酵～ raising agent ▸干燥～，试～ **3**（指面团） small piece of dough: ▸～子

C〈量〉 dose: 一～药 a dose of medicine ‖ 连服五～ take five doses in a row ▸～量

【剂量】jìliàng〈名〉［药学］ dose: 最大/最小～ maximum/minimum dose ‖ 孩子该服用多大的～? What's the correct dosage for children?

【剂型】jìxíng〈名〉［药学］ form of a drug

【剂子】jìzi〈名〉 dumpling dough

荠（薺）jì

▸qí

【荠菜】jìcài〈名〉［植物］ shepherd's purse

迹（跡、蹟）jì〈名〉 **1**（脚印） footprint: ▸人～罕至，足～ **2**（人为迹象） indication: ▸毁尸灭～，行～ **3**（行为） exploits: ▸奇～，事～ **4**（遗迹） remains: ▸古～，史～ **5**（痕迹） trace: 墨/油～ ink/grease mark ▸笔～，蛛丝马～

【迹象】jìxiàng〈名〉 indication: 没有好转的～ show no sign of improvement ‖ 火星上没有生命存在的～。 There is no sign of life on Mars. ‖ 种种～都表明天气要变。 There is every indication that the weather will change.

洎 jì〈动〉〈书〉 be up to: 自古～今 from ancient times to the present

济（濟）jì〈动〉 **1**〈书〉（过河） cross a river: ▸同舟共～ **2**（帮助） aid: ▸～世，接～ **3**（补益） benefit: ▸假公～私，无～于事

▸jǐ

【济急】jìjí〈动〉〈书〉 give urgent relief: 济燃眉之急 help meet an urgent need

【济贫】jìpín〈动〉 aid the poor: ～扶困 help those in need ▸劫富～

【济人之急】jìrénzhījí〈动〉 relieve one in need

【济世】jìshì〈动〉〈书〉 benefit mankind: 行医～ benefit society by practising medicine ‖ ～之才 person endowed with the talent to govern and to serve

【济世安民】jìshì-ānmín〈成〉 do good to society and bring peace to the people

【济事】jìshì〈动〉 [usu used in the negative] be of use: 光哭是不～的。 Crying won't help. ‖ 人少了不～。 Just a few people won't be much use.

既 jì

A〈动〉〈书〉 be over: 食～ have finished one's meal ‖ 言未～ before one finishes speaking

B〈副〉 already: ▸～成事实，～往不咎

C〈连〉 **1**（又） as well as: ～懂英语又懂法语 know French as well as English ‖ ～美观又实用 be both beautiful and practical ‖ ～能文，又能武 be able to wield both the pen and the sword **2**（既然） since: ～为夫妻，你们就应互敬互爱。 Now that you are husband and wife, you should respect and care for each other. ▸～来之，则安之

【既成事实】jìchéng shìshí〈成〉 fait accompli: 承认～ accept a fait accompli ‖ 造成～ create an established fact

【既得利益】jìdélìyì〈名〉 vested interest

【既定】jìdìng〈形〉 established: ～目标 set objective ‖ ～方针 established policy

【既而】jì'ér〈连〉〈书〉 then: 他开始时反对，～又表示同意。 He was opposed to it at first, but later he gave his consent.

【既来之，则安之】jì lái zhī, zé ān zhī〈成〉 since you are here, you may as well stay and make the best of it

【既然】jìrán〈连〉 since: ～大家都到了，咱们开会吧。 Now that everybody is here, let's begin our meeting. ‖ ～你知道错了，就该向他道个歉。 Since you know you are in the wrong, you should apologize to him.

【既是】jìshì〈连〉 as: ～你不愿意，那就以后再说吧。 As you are unwilling, let's talk about it later.

【既遂】jìsuì〈名〉［法律］ accomplished offence

【既往】jìwǎng〈名〉 **1**（过去） the past: ▸一如～ **2**（指错误） past mistakes: ▸～不咎

【既往不咎】jìwǎng-bùjiù〈成〉 forgive sb.'s past mistakes: ～，忘掉前嫌 let bygones be bygones ‖ ～，言归于好 wipe the slate clean and be friends again

【既望】jìwàng ▸**p. 618**〈名〉〈书〉 16th day of a lunar month

勣（勣）jì〈名〉〈书〉achievement

觊（覬）jì〈动〉〈书〉 covet

【觊觎】jìyú〈动〉〈书〉 covet: ～别国领土 covet another country's territory ‖ ～他人财产 cast greedy eyes over other people's property

继（繼）jì

A〈动〉 inherit: 子～父业。 The son inherited his father's business. ‖ 他～李教授之后当了校长。 He succeeded Professor Li as principal. ▸～任，～续，前赴后～

B〈连〉 then: ▸～而

【继承】jìchéng〈动〉 **1**（指获得） inherit: ～家产 inherit the family estate ‖ ～王位 succeed to the throne ‖ 财产由遗孀～。 The estate went to the widow. **2**（指接续） carry on: ～文化遗产 carry on the cultural heritage ‖ ～优良传统 carry forward fine traditions ‖ 这一理论是对先前思想的～和发展。 The theory is the continuation and development of previous thought.

【继承法】jìchéngfǎ〈名〉 inheritance law

【继承权】jìchéngquán〈名〉 right of succession/inheritance: 剥夺～ disinherit (sb.) ‖ 财产～ property inheritance right ‖ 他剥夺了子女的合法～。 He denied his children their rightful inheritance.

【继承人】jìchéngrén〈名〉 heir: 法定～ legal heir ‖ 合法～ lawful heir ‖ 女～ heiress ‖ 王位～ heir to the throne ‖ 指定～ heir by institution

【继电器】jìdiànqì〈名〉 relay

【继而】jì'ér〈连〉〈书〉 then: 他初感头晕，～昏倒。 He felt dizzy and then fainted. ‖ 先是鸦雀无声，～全场哗然。 There was dead silence first and then the audience burst into an uproar.

【继发性】jìfāxìng〈形〉 secondary: ～感染 secondary infection

【继父】jìfù〈名〉 stepfather

【继母】jìmǔ〈名〉 stepmother

【继女】jìnǚ〈名〉 stepdaughter

【继配】jìpèi〈名〉 second wife

【继任】jìrèn〈动〉 succeed to an office: ～人

j

successor ‖ 正职离职后，副职～。 After the resignation of the chief, his deputy succeeded him in his post.

【继室】jìshì = 继配 jìpèi

【继嗣】jìsì〈书〉 **A**〈动〉 adopt a son **B**〈名〉 adopted son

【继往开来】jìwǎng-kāilái〈成〉 carry a cause forward and forge ahead into the future

【继位】jìwèi〈动〉 succeed to the throne

【继续】jìxù〈动〉 continue: ～工作 proceed with one's work ‖ ～治疗 carry on with the treatment ‖ 请～收听。 Please stay tuned. ‖ 这项法律～有效。 The law remains valid.

【继续教育】jìxù jiàoyù〈名〉 further education: ～学院 institute of continuing education

【继子】jìzǐ〈名〉 **1**（养子） adopted son **2**（结婚对象带来的儿子） stepson

偈 jì〈名〉 libretto of Buddhist lyric ▸jié

祭 jì〈动〉 **1**（祭祀） offer sacrifices to: ～天 worship Heaven ‖ ～祖宗 offer sacrifices to one's ancestors **2**（祭奠） hold a memorial service: 公～死难烈士 hold a public memorial service for martyrs ▸～奠，～礼 **3**（指用咒语） wield

【祭典】jìdiǎn〈名〉 ceremony to offer sacrifices

【祭奠】jìdiàn〈动〉 hold a memorial service: ～先烈 hold a memorial ceremony for the martyrs

【祭礼】jìlǐ〈名〉 **1**（指礼仪） memorial ceremony: 举行～ hold memorial rites **2**（指物品） sacrificial offerings: 敬献～ formally present offerings

【祭品】jìpǐn〈名〉 sacrificial offering: 他们献上一只羔羊做～。 They offered a lamb as a sacrifice.

【祭器】jìqì〈名〉 sacrificial vessel

【祭扫】jìsǎo〈动〉 offer sacrifices and pay respects to a dead person at his tomb: ～烈士陵园 hold a memorial ceremony at the martyrs' cemetery

【祭司】jìsī〈名〉 high priest

【祭祀】jìsì〈动〉 offer sacrifices: ～祖先的仪式 ceremony honouring one's ancestors ‖ 以羊～众神 sacrifice a lamb to the gods

【祭坛】jìtán〈名〉 sacrificial altar: ～上摆着祭品。 There are oblations on the altar.

j

【祭文】jìwén〈名〉 funeral oration: 在墓前宣读～ deliver a funeral oration before a tomb

【祭灶】jìzào〈动〉 offer sacrifices to the kitchen god

悸 jì〈动〉〈书〉 throb: ▸心～ 1，心有余～

【悸动】jìdòng〈动〉 palpitate with fear

【悸栗】jìlì〈动〉〈书〉 tremble with fear

寄 jì

A〈动〉 **1**（托付） entrust: ～希望于青年 pin one's hope on the youth ‖ 把包～在寄存处 leave one's bag in the cloakroom ▸～存，～托 **2**（依附） depend on: ▸～居，～人篱下 **3**（邮寄） send: ～包裹 send a parcel by post ‖ ～钱 remit money ‖ ～信 post a letter ▸～卖，邮～

B〈形〉 adopted: ▸～父，～母

【寄存】jìcún〈动〉 deposit: ～行李 check one's luggage ‖ 把行李～在服务台 deposit one's packages at the service desk

【寄存器】jìcúnqì〈名〉［电子］ register

【寄放】jìfàng〈动〉 leave with: 她把几本书～在我这儿。 She left a number of books with me.

【寄费】jìfèi〈名〉 postage: 支付～ pay the postage

【寄父】jìfù〈名〉 foster father

【寄怀】jìhuái〈书〉= 寄情 jìqíng

【寄件人】jìjiànrén〈名〉 sender

【寄居】jìjū〈动〉 live away from home: ～他乡 live in an alien land ‖ 从小～在祖母家 live with one's grandmother from childhood

【寄居蟹】jìjūxiè〈名〉［动物］ hermit crab

【寄卖】jìmài〈动〉 consign for sale: ～业务 consignment business ‖ 把物品放到商店里～ consign one's goods in a shop for sale ‖ ～店 consignment shop ‖ ～人 consigner

【寄母】jìmǔ〈名〉 foster mother

【寄情】jìqíng〈动〉〈书〉 give expression to one's feelings: ～山水 abandon oneself to nature

【寄人篱下】jìrén-líxià〈成〉〈喻〉 depend on sb. for a living: 过着～的生活 live under subjugation

【寄身】jìshēn〈动〉〈书〉 stay in a place temporarily: ～异域 stay in an alien land for a time

【寄生】jìshēng〈动〉 **1**（指生物体） live off an organism of another species: ▸～蜂 **2**（指人） live by exploiting others: ～生活 parasitic life

【寄生虫】jìshēngchóng〈名〉 parasite: ～病 parasitic disease ‖ 社会的～ parasites on society ‖ 那懒汉是家里的～。 The lazy man was a parasite on his family.

【寄生动物】jìshēng dòngwù〈名〉parasitic animal

【寄生蜂】jìshēngfēng〈名〉 parasitic wasp

【寄生植物】jìshēng zhíwù〈名〉 parasitic plant

【寄食】jìshí〈动〉sponge off another person: 在朋友家～ sponge off one's friends

【寄售】jìshòu = 寄卖 jìmài

【寄宿】jìsù〈动〉 **1**（借住） lodge: ～在亲戚家 lodge with a relative **2**（住校） board: ～学校 boarding school

【寄宿生】jìsùshēng〈名〉 boarder

【寄托】jìtuō〈动〉 **1**（托付） entrust to sb.'s care: 把孩子～在邻居家 entrust one's child to the care of a neighbour **2**（倾注） pin (hope, etc.) on: ～哀思 give expression to one's grief ‖ 将所有希望～在下一代身上 place all one's hopes on the next generation ‖ 精神有所～ have spiritual sustenance

【寄望】jìwàng〈动〉 place one's hopes on: 不必对她～过高。 Don't expect too much of her.

【寄信】jìxìn〈动〉 send a letter

【寄养】jìyǎng〈动〉 entrust one's child or pet to sb.'s care: 母亲临终前把我～在叔叔家里。 Before her death, my mother left me in the care of my uncle.

【寄意】jìyì〈动〉〈书〉 send one's regards

【寄予】jìyǔ〈动〉 **1**（给予） place (hope, etc.) on: （对某人）～厚望 have high hopes (for sb.) ‖ 父母对我～很大的希望。 My parents put great hopes on me. **2**（寄托着） show: （对某人）～深切关怀 show heartfelt concern (for sb.) ‖ （对某人）～无限同情 show boundless sympathy (for sb.)

【寄语】jìyǔ **A**〈动〉 send word: ～青年朋友 send a message to young friends **B**〈名〉 message: 新春～ new year's good wishes

【寄寓】jìyù〈书〉 **1** = 寄居 jìjū **2** = 寄托 jìtuō 2

【寄主】jìzhǔ〈名〉［生物］ host

寂 jì〈形〉 **1**（安静） still: ▸～静，沉～，万籁俱～ **2**（孤独） lonely: ▸～寞，孤～

【寂静】jìjìng〈形〉 still: ～的夜晚 quiet night ‖ 死一般的～ deathly hush ‖ ～无声 silent as the grave ‖ 教室里一片～。 All was quiet in the classroom.

【寂苦】jìkǔ〈形〉 lonely and distressed

【寂寥】jìliáo〈形〉〈书〉 solitary: ～无人 be no one in sight

【寂寞】jìmò〈形〉 **1**（孤独） lonely: 感到～ feel lonely ‖ ～的旅途 lonesome journey **2**（安静） quiet: ～的草原 quiet prairie ‖ ～的原野 silent open country

【寂然】jìrán〈形〉〈书〉 still: 森林里～无声。 The forest was very still.

绩（績） jì

A〈动〉 twist hempen thread

B〈名〉 achievement: ▸成～，业～，政～

【绩差股】jìchàgǔ〈名〉［经济］ bad performance stock

【绩效】jìxiào〈名〉 achievement: ～显著 remarkable success ‖ ～工资 performance related pay

【绩优股】jìyōugǔ〈名〉［经济］ blue chip stock

蓟（薊） jì〈名〉［植物］setose thistle

霁（霽） jì〈动〉〈书〉 **1**（指雨、雪） clear up: 雨/雪～。 It has cleared up after the rain/snow. ▸光风～月 **2**（指人） calm down: ～颜 calm countenance after a fit of anger

【霁月光风】jìyuè-guāngfēng = 光风霁月 guāngfēng-jìyuè

鲚（鱭） jì〈名〉［鱼类］long-tailed anchovy

暨 jì

A〈动〉〈书〉 be up to: ～今 up till now

B〈连〉 and: 北大校庆～"五四运动"纪念活动 meeting in celebration of the founding of Peking University and the May Fourth Movement

稷 jì〈名〉 **1**〈古〉（指作物） millet **2**（指神） god of grains worshipped by ancient emperors: ▸社～

鲫（鯽） jì〈名〉［鱼类］ crucian carp

髻 jì〈名〉 hair worn in a bun: 蝴蝶～ butterfly-shaped hair bun ▸发～

冀[1] jì〈动〉〈书〉 look forward to: ～其成功 hope for success ‖ ～能有成。 We hope that it will turn out successful. ▸～求，希～

冀[2] Jì ▸p. 661〈名〉 Ji [another name for Hebei Province (河北)]

【冀求】jìqiú〈动〉〈书〉 hope to gain

【冀图】jìtú〈动〉〈书〉 long for

【冀望】jìwàng〈动〉〈书〉 hope for

【冀中平原】Jìzhōng Píngyuán〈名〉 Central Hebei Plain

鼙（鼙） jì ▸白鼙豚 báijìtún

骥（驥） jì〈名〉〈书〉 1（指马）steed: ▸按图索~, 老~伏枥 2〈喻〉（指人） outstanding talent: ~才 person of outstanding talent

jiā

加 jiā 〈动〉 1（放在上面）put one thing on top of another: ▸~冕 2（添加） add: ~标点 punctuate ‖ ~水 add water ‖ ~衣服 put on more clothes ‖ 食物需要~调味品。 The food needs seasoning. ▸添油~醋, 雪上~霜 3（增加） increase: ~把劲 make a push ‖ ~工资 raise sb.'s salary ‖ ~税 increase taxes ▸~大, ~强, 增~ 4（施加） impose: ▸~害, 施~ 5（给予） [used in the same way as 加以, but usu after a monosyllabic adverb]: 大~赞扬 praise profusely ‖ 稍~注意 be a little more careful ‖ 严~管束 keep sb. under strict control ‖ 多~小心! Be careful! 6［数学］ add: 二~三等于五。 Two plus three is five.

【加班】jiābān 〈动〉 work overtime: ~费 overtime ‖ 工人们在~。 The workers are on overtime. ‖ 他经常~。 It is quite common for him to work overtime.

【加班加点】jiābān-jiādiǎn〈成〉work extra hours

【加倍】jiābèi ▸**p. 31** **A**〈动〉 be twice as much: ~赔偿损失 compensate twice for the loss ‖ 产量~ the output doubles **B**〈副〉 doubly: ~努力 redouble one's efforts ‖ ~小心 be doubly careful

【加餐】jiācān〈动〉 have a snack: 课间~ have a snack in between classes

【加长】jiācháng〈动〉 lengthen: ~飞机跑道 lengthen the runway ‖ 把袖子~ lengthen the sleeves

【加车】jiāchē **A**〈动〉 put on extra buses or trains **B**〈名〉 extra bus/train: 我坐的是~。 I went on a special bus.

【加大】 jiādà 〈动〉 increase: ~改革力度 step up the pace of reform ‖ ~油门 step on the gas

【加德满都】Jiādémǎndū〈名〉Kathmandu

【加尔各答】 Jiā'ěrgèdá 〈名〉 Kolkata [formerly named Calcutta]

【加法】jiāfǎ〈名〉［数学］ addition

【加菲猫】jiāfēimāo〈名〉 Garfield

【加封】jiāfēng〈动〉 1（指封条） seal up: 给机密文件柜子~ seal up a confidential filing cabinet 2（指名位、土地等） confer additional titles or territories on nobles

【加工】jiāgōng〈动〉 1（制作） process: ~各类服装 make all kinds of clothes ‖ ~食品 process food ‖ 来料~ processing of investor's raw materials ‖ ~厂 processing plant ‖ ~费 processing charge ‖ ~工业 processing industry ▸粗~, 精~ 2（改善） polish: 他的论文需要~。 His thesis needs polishing.

【加工贸易】jiāgōng màoyì〈名〉 improvement trade: 促进~ promote improvement trade

【加固】 jiāgù 〈动〉 reinforce: ~工事 improve defence works ‖ ~堤坝 reinforce dykes and dams ‖ 这房子需要~。 The house needs some reinforcement work.

【加官进爵】 jiāguān-jìnjué 〈成〉 promote sb. to a higher office and rank

【加害】jiāhài〈动〉 injure: ~于人 do sb. harm ‖ 我无意~于你。 I don't mean any harm to you.

【加害方】jiāhàifāng〈名〉［法律］ injuring party

【加害人】jiāhàirén〈名〉［法律］ injurer

【加号】jiāhào〈名〉［数学］ plus sign (+)

【加厚】jiāhòu〈动〉 thicken: 把墙~ thicken a wall

【加急】 jiājí 〈形〉 urgent: ~信件 urgent mail ‖ ~订单 rush order

【加价】jiājià〈动〉 raise the price: 加量不~ increase the quantity without raising the price

【加紧】jiājǐn〈动〉 speed up: ~工作 speed up one's work ‖ ~训练/研究 intensify training/research

【加劲】jiājìn〈动〉〈口〉 put more energy into: ~工作 put more efforts with one's work ‖ 加把劲儿! Put your back into it!

【加剧】jiājù〈动〉 aggravate: 病情~ aggravate one's illness ‖ ~通货膨胀 increase inflation ‖ 两国间的紧张关系进一步~。 Tension between the two countries has risen to a new high. ‖ 矛盾在~。 The contradictions are sharpening.

【加快】jiākuài〈动〉 1（指速度）speed up: ~脚步 quicken one's pace ‖ ~农业/经济发展 accelerate agricultural/economic development ‖ ~速度 accelerate ‖ 他的心跳~。 His heartbeat quickened. 2（指火车票） exchange a slow train ticket for a fast one: 我想把这张票~。I'd like to exchange this ticket for an express train ticket.

【加快票】 jiākuàipiào 〈名〉 express-train ticket

【加宽】 jiākuān 〈动〉 broaden: ~路面 widen a road ‖ 河面从这儿~了。 The river broadens out at this point.

【加拉加斯】Jiālājiāsī〈名〉Caracas

【加勒比共同体】 Jiālèbǐ Gòngtóngtǐ 〈名〉 Caribbean Community

ℹ 季节

■ 汉语说某个季节时有不同的名称, 如春、春天、春季, 而英语里只有一个名称:

春天	spring
夏天	summer
秋天	autumn 或 fall〈美〉
冬天	winter

■ 其他与季节有关的表达法:

初春	early spring
仲春	the middle of spring
晚春	late spring
初夏	early summer
仲夏	midsummer
晚夏 / 夏末	late summer
初秋	early autumn
仲秋	the middle of autumn
晚秋	late autumn
初冬	early winter
仲冬	midwinter
晚冬	late winter

与介词的使用

■ 以下以“春天”为例加以说明, 其他季节用法均相同。

■ 下面的汉语例子中没有用介词或用了介词“在”, 但英语里一定要用适当的介词:

我喜欢春天旅游
= I like to travel in (the) spring

我们常在春天天气暖和的时候去北京
= We often go to Beijing in (the) spring when it is warm

她准备春季期间和父母待在一起
= She will stay with her parents during (the) spring

我整个春天都要准备英语考试
= I will prepare myself for the English exam throughout/all through (the) spring
或 I will prepare myself for the English exam for (the) whole spring

他 1995 年春天出生
= He was born in (the) spring of 1995

我弟弟将在初春毕业
= My brother will graduate in early spring

在春天的一个早晨我们结了婚
= We were married on a spring morning

不用介词的情况

■ 下面的短语在汉语和英语中都不需用介词:

每年夏天
= every summer

今年夏天
= this summer

那个冬天
= that winter

明年冬天
= next winter

去年秋天
= last autumn

每隔一个春天
= every other spring

一个春天的早上
= one morning in spring
或 one spring morning

修饰其他名词

春天的颜色
= spring colours

春天的鲜花
= spring flowers

夏令营
= summer camp

仲夏之夜
= midsummer nights

秋天的天气
= autumn weather

一个秋季的早晨
= one autumn morning

冬季大减价
= the winter sales

冬季运动
= winter sports

【加勒比海】Jiālèbǐhǎi〈名〉Caribbean Sea
【加利福尼亚州】Jiālìfúníyàzhōu〈名〉California
【加料】jiāliào **A**〈动〉feed in raw material: 自动～ feed in raw material automatically ‖ 改进～装置 improve the feeding apparatus **B**〈形〉reinforced: ～药酒 reinforced tonic wine
【加榴炮】jiāliúpào〈名〉gun-howitzer
【加仑】jiālún〈量〉gallon
【加码】jiāmǎ〈动〉**1**（指价格）raise the price of goods: 商品价格不断～。Commodity prices keep rising. **2**（指指标）raise the quota: 层层～ raise the quota at each level
【加盟】jiāméng〈动〉become a member: 外籍球员～，有利于提高球队的整体水平。The inclusion of foreign players helps to raise the skills level of the whole team. ‖ 该国于去年～北大西洋公约组织。The country joined NATO last year.
【加密】jiāmì〈动〉［通信］encrypt
【加冕】jiāmiǎn〈动〉crown: 为国王～ crown a king ‖ ～典礼 coronation
【加拿大】Jiānádà〈名〉Canada: ～人 Canadian ‖ ～元 Canadian dollar
【加纳】Jiānà〈名〉Ghana: ～人 Ghanaian
【加农炮】jiānóngpào〈名〉cannon
【加蓬】Jiāpéng〈名〉Gabon: ～人 Gabonese
【加强】jiāqiáng〈动〉strengthen: ～管理 energize the management ‖ ～纪律/团结 strengthen the discipline/unity ‖ ～经贸合作 strengthen economic and trade cooperation ‖ ～军事力量 reinforce military power ‖ ～排/连/营 reinforced platoon/company/battalion
【加权】jiāquán〈动〉［统计］weight: ～指数 weighted index (number)
【加热】jiārè〈动〉heat: ～消毒 sterilize by heating ‖ 蒸汽～ steam heating ‖ ～器 heater
【加入】jiārù〈动〉**1**（放入）add: 给食盐里～碘 add iodine to salt **2**（参加）join: ～工会 join the labour union ‖ ～国籍 acquire citizenship ‖ ～世贸组织 accede to the WTO ‖ 我可以～你们的活动吗? May I join you?
【加塞儿】jiāsāir〈动〉〈口〉queue-jump
【加赛】jiāsài〈名〉［体育］additional tie-breaker
【加沙地区】Jiāshā Dìqū〈名〉Gaza Strip
【加上】jiāshàng **A**〈动〉add **B**〈连〉moreover: 渴～饿，搞得他精疲力竭。Thirst and hunger wore him out.
【加深】jiāshēn〈动〉deepen: ～分歧 sharpen the difference ‖ ～理解 deepen one's understanding ‖ ～印象 deepen one's impression (of sth.)
【加湿器】jiāshīqì〈名〉humidifier
【加时赛】jiāshísài〈名〉［体育］extra time: 进入～ go into extra time
【加试】jiāshì〈名〉add more items to an examination: ～科目 additional subjects for examination
【加数】jiāshù〈名〉［数学］addend
【加速】jiāsù〈动〉speed up: ～经济改革步伐 accelerate the pace of economic reforms ‖ ～行驶 speed up ‖ ～资本周转 expedite capital turnover ‖ 汽车突然～。The car suddenly accelerated.
【加速度】jiāsùdù〈名〉acceleration
【加速剂】jiāsùjì〈名〉accelerator
【加速器】jiāsùqì〈名〉accelerator: 回旋～ cyclotron ‖ 同步～ synchrotron
【加速运动】jiāsù yùndòng〈名〉［物理］accelerated motion
【加温】jiāwēn〈动〉heat up
【加薪】jiāxīn〈动〉raise the pay: 获得～ get a pay rise ‖ 要求～ ask for a pay raise
【加刑】jiāxíng〈动〉increase a penalty
【加压】jiāyā〈动〉pressurize: ～处理设备 pressure treater ‖ ～密封 pressure seal
【加以】jiāyǐ **A**〈动〉[used before a disyllabic verb to indicate that the action is directed towards sth. or sb. mentioned above]: ～限制 lay down restrictions ‖ 对文物～保护 give protection to cultural relics ‖ 有问题要及时～解决。Problems should be resolved in good time. **B**〈连〉moreover: 他工作态度好，～特别谦虚，所以人缘儿很好。He holds a positive attitude towards work and, moreover, he is very modest; so he is on good terms with everyone.
【加意】jiāyì〈动〉take special care: ～保护文化遗产 take special care to protect cultural relics
【加油】jiāyóu〈动〉**1**（使润滑）lubricate: 给轴承～ lubricate the bearing **2**（加燃料）fill up: 给汽车～ fill up a car **3**（加把劲儿）step up efforts: ～! ～! Come on! Come on! ‖ 大家都为我们队～。Everyone cheered our team.
【加油泵】jiāyóubèng〈名〉petrol pump
【加油机】jiāyóujī〈名〉tanker aircraft
【加油添醋】jiāyóu-tiāncù = 添油加醋 tiānyóu-jiācù
【加油站】jiāyóuzhàn〈名〉petrol station〈英〉; gas station〈美〉
【加之】jiāzhī〈连〉moreover: 这房子价钱太高，～位置不好，所以我不想要。I don't want to buy the house because the price is too high and, moreover, the location isn't good.
【加重】jiāzhòng〈动〉**1**（指分量）make heavier: ～学生负担 increase the burdens on students ‖ ～语气 in an emphatic tone **2**（指程度）become more serious: 他的病情这几天～了。His condition has deteriorated in the past few days.
【加重自行车】jiāzhòng zìxíngchē〈名〉heavy-weight-bearing bicycle

夹（夾）jiā

A〈动〉**1**（固定）press from both sides: 胳膊下～着一只公文包 carry a briefcase under one's arm ‖ 用筷子～饭菜 pick up food with chopsticks ‖ 他的手指～在门缝里了。He got his finger caught in the door. **2**（使在中间）be in between: 孩子～在父母中间。The child was sandwiched between his parents. ‖ 两山之间～着一条小河。A stream runs between the two mountains. ▸～道, ～缝, ～角 **3**（掺杂）mix: ～在人群里 mingle with the crowd ‖ 普通话～粤语 Mandarin mixed with Cantonese ▸～生, ～杂
B〈名〉clip: 报～ newspaper stand ‖ 活页～ loose-leaf binder ▸发～, 文件～
▸gā, jiá
【夹板】jiābǎn〈名〉**1**（用于物体）board for holding things together **2**（用于肢体）splint: 给受伤的胳膊上～ put the injured arm in splints
【夹板气】jiābǎnqì〈名〉state of being caught in the crossfire: 婆媳不和，儿子在中间受～。When the mother quarrelled with her daughter-in-law, the son got caught in the crossfire.
【夹层】jiācéng〈名〉［建筑］mezzanine: ～玻璃/结构 sandwich glass/structure
【夹带】jiādài **A**〈动〉**1**（指携带）smuggle: 行李中不许～危险品。No dangerous articles are allowed in passengers' luggage. **2**（夹杂）mix: ～私心 with some selfish interest **B**〈名〉notes smuggled into an examination hall: 严禁带～进入考场。It is strictly forbidden to smuggle notes into the examination room.
【夹道】jiādào **A**〈名〉passageway **B**〈动〉line both sides of a road: ～欢迎英雄归来 line the street to welcome home a hero
【夹缝】jiāfèng〈名〉crack
【夹攻】jiāgōng〈动〉attack from both sides: 受到～ be caught in a two-way squeeze ‖ 两面～ attack from both sides ‖ 内外～ attack from both within and without
【夹棍】jiāgùn〈名〉〈旧〉clamping rod
【夹击】jiājī〈动〉attack from both sides: 受到两面～ be caught in a crossfire
【夹剪】jiājiǎn〈名〉tweezers
【夹角】jiājiǎo〈名〉［数学］intersection angle: 三角形两边的～ angle contained by two sides of a triangle
【夹具】jiājù〈名〉［机械］holder
【夹克】jiākè〈名〉jacket: 皮～ leather jacket
【夹批】jiāpī〈名〉annotations and comments written between lines of writing
【夹七夹八】jiāqī-jiābā〈成〉incoherent: 他～地说个不停。He rambled on incoherently.
【夹生】jiāshēng〈形〉**1**（指食物）half-cooked **2**（指工作）not thoroughly done **3**（指问题）not completely solved
【夹生饭】jiāshēngfàn〈名〉**1**（指米饭）half-cooked rice **2**〈喻〉（指工作）half-finished job
【夹丝玻璃】jiāsī bōli〈名〉wired glass
【夹尾巴】jiā wěiba〈动〉**1**（指动物）hold its tail between its legs **2**〈喻〉（失败）be depressed/crestfallen: 敌人夹着尾巴逃跑了。The enemy fled with their tails between their legs. **3**〈喻〉（不张狂）be prudent and modest: 从今以后你必须夹起尾巴做人。You must be prudent and modest from now on.
【夹馅】jiāxiàn〈名〉stuffing: ～烧饼 stuffed pancake
【夹心】jiāxīn〈形〉filled: 巧克力～糖 sweets with chocolate centres ‖ ～饼干 sandwich biscuit
【夹叙夹议】jiāxù-jiāyì〈成〉narration interspersed with comments
【夹杂】jiāzá〈动〉be mixed with: 说话～着口音 speak with an accent ‖ 在讲话中～着外国词 intersperse one's speech with foreign words
【夹竹桃】jiāzhútáo〈名〉［植物］oleander
【夹注】jiāzhù〈名〉interlinear notes
【夹子】jiāzi〈名〉**1**（用于固定）clip;（用于拿东西）tongs: 点心～ cake tongs ‖ 头发～ hairpin **2**（文件夹）folder: 讲义～ folder for teaching-materials ‖ 文件～ binder

伽 jiā

[used in transliteration of foreign or special terms]
▸gā, qié
【伽倻琴】jiāyēqín ▸**p. 929**〈名〉plucked stringed instrument used by the Korean ethnic group

茄 jiā

▸茄克 jiākè, 雪茄 xuějiā
▸qié
【茄克】jiākè = 夹克 jiākè

佳 jiā

〈形〉excellent: 身体欠～ not be in very good health ‖ 成绩甚～。The results

j

are very good. ▸～话, ～作
【佳宾】jiābīn = 嘉宾 jiābīn
【佳话】jiāhuà〈名〉 much-told story: 传为～ become a favourite topic
【佳绩】jiājì〈名〉 outstanding achievement: 再创～ make another outstanding achievement
【佳节】jiājié〈名〉 festival: 新春～ happy Spring Festival ‖ 每逢～倍思亲。 On festive occasions, people think even more of estranged loved-ones.
【佳境】jiājìng〈名〉 **1**（指地方） scenic spot: 西山～ scenic Western Hills **2**（指状态） consummate state: ▸渐入～
【佳句】jiājù〈名〉 beautiful line of verse: 广为流传的～ widely-quoted beautiful lines of verse
【佳丽】jiālì〈书〉 **A**〈形〉 beautiful: 容颜～ look beautiful **B**〈名〉 beautiful woman: ～云集 crowds of beauties
【佳酿】jiāniàng〈名〉〈书〉 good wine: 陈年～ wine aged to perfection
【佳偶】jiā'ǒu〈名〉〈书〉 **1**（指夫妻） well-matched couple: 他俩郎才女貌，是天生～。 A talented scholar and a beautiful lady, they are a match made in heaven. **2**（理想的配偶） ideal spouse: 夫妻好找，～难得。 A husband or wife is easy to find, but an ideal spouse is hard to come by.
【佳品】jiāpǐn〈名〉 choice product: 滋补～ excellent tonic ‖ 荔枝是果中～。 Lychees are one of the best fruits.
【佳期】jiāqī〈名〉 **1**（指结婚） wedding day: ～渐近，芳心大乱。 As the wedding approached, the young woman became nervous and excited. **2**（指约会） dating
【佳人】jiārén〈名〉 beautiful woman: 绝代～ woman of incomparable beauty ▸才子～
【佳肴】jiāyáo〈名〉 delicacies: 美酒～ vintage wine and delicious food ‖ 美味～ delicious food
【佳音】jiāyīn〈名〉〈书〉 good news: 静候～。 I am awaiting the good news of your success.
【佳作】jiāzuò〈名〉 excellent work: 文学～ literary gem

迦 jiā [used in transliteration of foreign or special terms]
【迦太基】Jiātàijī〈名〉 Carthage: ～人 Carthaginian

珈 jiā〈名〉〈古〉 jade ornament worn by noble women

枷 jiā〈名〉〈旧〉 cangue
【枷锁】jiāsuǒ〈名〉 yoke: 摆脱～ cast off the yoke ‖ 精神～ mental shackles

浃（浹） jiā〈动〉〈书〉 be soaked: ▸汗流～背

痂 jiā〈名〉 scab: ▸疮～, 结～

家¹ jiā
A〈名〉 **1**（住所） home: 呆在～里 stay at home ‖〈喻〉 老年之～ old people's home ▸搬～, 四海为～, 想～ **2**（家庭） family: 名门世～ ancient and highly respectable family ‖ 三口之～ family of three ‖ 他是个顾～的人。 He is a family man. ▸成～, 持～, 养～糊口 **3**（指从事某种行业） family engaged in a certain trade: ▸船～, 东～, 农～ **4**（专家） specialist in a certain field: ▸科学～, 专～ **5**（指具有某种特质） person of certain characteristics: ▸冒险～, 野心～ **6**（指与自己有某种关系） person related to oneself: ▸仇～, 亲～, 冤～ **7**〈谦〉（我的） my: ▸～父, ～兄 **8**（民族） ethnic group: 傣～姑娘 girl of the Dai ethnic group ‖ 苗～儿女 sons and daughters of the Miao ethnic group **9**（流派） school (of thought): ▸百～争鸣, 儒～ **10**（一方） side: 两～最后打成平手。 The two sides tied in the end. ▸对～, 上～, 庄～
B〈形〉 domestic: ▸～畜, ～禽
C〈量〉 [used for families or enterprises]: 两～公司 two companies ‖ 三～商店 three stores ‖ 五～工厂 five factories

家²（傢） jiā ▸家伙 jiāhuo, 家具 jiājù, 家什 jiāshi
▸jia
【家财】jiācái = 家产 jiāchǎn
【家蚕】jiācán〈名〉 silkworm
【家产】jiāchǎn〈名〉 family fortune: 变卖～ liquidate one's family property
【家长里短】jiācháng-lǐduǎn〈成〉 domestic trivialities: 谈谈～ make chit-chat
【家常】jiācháng〈名〉 daily life of a family: ～菜 home cooking ‖ ～便服 leisure wear ‖ 说说～ make chit-chat ▸拉～
【家常便饭】jiācháng-biànfàn〈成〉 **1**（指饭菜） simple meal: 到我家去吃顿～吧。 Come and eat some simple fare at our house. **2**〈喻〉（平常事） common occurrence: 现在坐飞机是～。 Air travel is routine nowadays.
【家常饭】jiāchángfàn = 家常便饭 jiācháng-biànfàn
【家仇】jiāchóu〈名〉 family feud: 国难～ national calamity and family hatred
【家丑】jiāchǒu〈名〉 family scandal
【家丑不可外扬】jiāchǒu bùkě wàiyáng〈成〉 don't wash your dirty linen in public
【家畜】jiāchù〈名〉 domestic animal
【家传】jiāchuán〈动〉 hand down in a family: ～秘方/手艺 secret recipe/trade handed down in the family
【家慈】jiācí〈名〉〈书〉〈谦〉 my mother
【家当】jiādàng〈名〉 family assets: 我没什么值钱的～。 I have no valuable property to speak of. ‖ 这就是你的全部～? Is this all you have?
【家道】jiādào〈名〉 family circumstances: ～中落 suffer a fall in one's family fortune
【家底】jiādǐ〈名〉 family property accumulated over a long time: ～厚/薄 with/without substantial resources
【家电】jiādiàn〈简称〉= 家用电器
【家电产品】jiādiàn chǎnpǐn〈名〉 household appliance product
【家丁】jiādīng〈名〉〈旧〉 retainer of a big family
【家法】jiāfǎ〈名〉 **1**〈旧〉（指学派内部） theories and research methods handed down from a master to his pupils **2**（指家族内部） domestic discipline exercised by the head of a feudal household **3**（指用具） tool for punishing children or servants in a feudal household
【家访】jiāfǎng〈名〉 visit to the parents of schoolchildren
【家纺】jiāfǎng〈名〉 home textiles: ～企业/市场 home textiles company/market
【家风】jiāfēng〈名〉 family tradition
【家父】jiāfù〈名〉〈谦〉 my father
【家鸽】jiāgē〈名〉 pigeon
【家规】jiāguī〈名〉 family discipline: 国有国法，家有～。 As each country has its laws, so does each family have its rules.
【家和万事兴】jiā hé wànshì xīng〈俗〉 harmony in the family leads to prosperity in all undertakings
【家伙】jiāhuo〈名〉〈口〉 **1**（工具） tool: 好使的～ handy tool ‖ 他们夜间出门时，身上都带着～。 They are usually armed when they go out at night. **2**（人） fellow: 他是个精明的～。 He is a smart guy. ‖ 你这个～真幸运! You lucky devil! **3**（指动物） [used to refer to domestic animals]: 这～见了主人就摇尾巴。 The dog wags its tail when it sees its master.
【家给人足】jiājǐ-rénzú〈成〉 all live in plenty
【家计】jiājì〈名〉〈书〉 family livelihood: ～艰难 straitened family circumstances ‖ 靠微薄的收入维持～ bring up a family on a low income
【家家】jiājiā〈名〉 every household: 村里～都有电视机。 Every family in this village has a TV set.
【家家都有一本难念的经】jiājiā dōu yǒu yīběn nánniànde jīng〈俗〉 every family has its problems
【家家户户】jiājiā-hùhù〈名〉 every household: 现在～有存款。 Every family has bank savings nowadays.
【家教】jiājiào〈名〉 **1**（指教养） domestic upbringing: 没有～ be not properly brought up ‖ ～很严 be strict with one's child **2**（指教师） private teacher
【家景】jiājǐng = 家境 jiājìng
【家境】jiājìng〈名〉 family circumstances: ～富裕/清寒 wealthy/poor family
【家居】jiājū **A**〈动〉 stay at home without a job: 他～五年，学到的东西都忘掉了。 After hanging around at home for five years, he couldn't remember anything he had studied. **B**〈名〉 home: ～陈设 home furnishings
【家具】jiājù ▸**p. 411**〈名〉 furniture: 一套～ a set of furniture ‖ 古式/新式～ antique/modern furniture
【家眷】jiājuàn〈名〉 **1**（家人） wife and children: 携～回国 return to one's native land with one's family **2**（妻子） wife: 尚无～ remain single
【家口】jiākǒu〈名〉 number of people in a family: ～不多 have a small family
【家累】jiālěi〈名〉〈书〉 family burden: ～不轻 have a heavy family burden
【家里】jiālǐ〈名〉 **1**（家人） family: ～都好，你不要操心。 Don't worry: everyone in the family is safe and sound. **2**（家） home: 在～ be at home
【家里的】jiālǐde〈名〉〈口〉 my wife
【家门】jiāmén〈名〉 **1**（指门） gate of one's house: 他三过～而不入。 He passed his house three times without entering it. **2**〈书〉（家族） one's own family: 辱没～ bring disgrace to one's family **3**（家庭背景） family background
【家母】jiāmǔ〈名〉〈谦〉 my mother
【家奴】jiānú〈名〉〈旧〉 bond servant
【家贫如洗】jiāpín-rúxǐ〈成〉 be completely destitute: 他现在～。 He is now as poor as a church mouse.
【家破人亡】jiāpò-rénwáng〈成〉 with the family broken up and decimated
【家谱】jiāpǔ〈名〉 family tree: 修～ compile a genealogy
【家雀儿】jiāqiǎor〈名〉〈方〉 sparrow
【家禽】jiāqín〈名〉 domestic fowl
【家人】jiārén〈名〉 family member: ～团聚 family reunion ‖ ～不接受她的婚姻。 Her marriage was not welcomed by the family.

【家史】jiāshǐ〈名〉 family history: 血泪～ family history of blood and tears
【家世】jiāshì〈名〉〈书〉 social standing of one's family: ～寒微 be of humble origin ‖ ～显赫 be of outstanding family background
【家事】jiāshì〈名〉 domestic affairs: 处理～ handle family affairs
【家室】jiāshì〈名〉 **1**（家庭） family: 无/有～之累 have no/a family to provide for **2**（妻子） wife: 已有～ have a wife **3**〈书〉（住宅） residence
【家什】jiāshi〈名〉 utensils, furniture, etc.: 锣鼓～ drums and gongs ‖ 厨房～都已清洗干净。 All the kitchen utensils have been cleaned.
【家书】jiāshū〈名〉 letter home: 写～ write a letter home
【家书抵万金】jiāshū dǐ wànjīn〈成〉 a letter from home is worthy of ten thousand pieces of gold
【家塾】jiāshú〈名〉〈旧〉 family school
【家属】jiāshǔ〈名〉 family members: 干部～ cadre's family
【家属院】jiāshǔyuàn〈名〉 residential quarters [of a school, factory, institution, etc.]
【家鼠】jiāshǔ〈名〉 house mouse
【家私】jiāsī〈名〉 family wealth
【家庭】jiātíng〈名〉 family: 建立～ start a family ‖ 大～ large family ‖ 单亲～ single-parent family ‖ 高收入/低收入～ upper-income/lower-income family ‖ 核心～ nuclear family
【家庭暴力】jiātíng bàolì〈名〉 domestic violence: 防止并根除～ prevent and eradicate domestic violence
【家庭背景】jiātíng bèijǐng〈名〉 family background
【家庭病床】jiātíng bìngchuáng〈名〉 hospital bed set up at home
【家庭成员】jiātíng chéngyuán〈名〉 family member
【家庭出身】jiātíng chūshēn〈名〉 family origin
【家庭负担】jiātíng fùdān〈名〉 family burden
【家庭妇女】jiātíng fùnǚ〈名〉 housewife
【家庭副业】jiātíng fùyè〈名〉 household sideline production
【家庭工厂】jiātíng gōngchǎng〈名〉 household factory
【家庭观念】jiātíng guānniàn〈名〉 attachment to one's family
【家庭教师】jiātíng jiàoshī ▸**p. 966**〈名〉 private teacher: 聘请～ engage a private tutor
【家庭教育】jiātíng jiàoyù〈名〉 family education
【家庭联产承包责任制】jiātíng liánchǎn chéngbāo zérènzhì〈名〉 household contract responsibility system with remuneration linked to output
【家庭旅馆】jiātíng lǚguǎn〈名〉 family hotel
【家庭收入】jiātíng shōurù〈名〉 family income
【家庭医生】jiātíng yīshēng〈名〉 family doctor
【家庭影院】jiātíng yǐngyuàn〈名〉 home cinema
【家庭主妇】jiātíng zhǔfù〈名〉 housewife
【家庭住址】jiātíng zhùzhǐ〈名〉 home address
【家庭作业】jiātíng zuòyè〈名〉 homework: 布置～ assign homework
【家童】jiātóng〈名〉〈旧〉 boy servant

【家徒壁立】jiātúbìlì = 家徒四壁 jiātúsìbì
【家徒四壁】jiātúsìbì〈成〉 be completely destitute
【家兔】jiātù〈名〉 rabbit
【家务】jiāwù〈名〉 household chores: 料理～ keep house ‖ ～劳动 housework
【家务活儿】jiāwùhuór〈名〉 housework
【家务事】jiāwùshì〈名〉 family affairs
【家乡】jiāxiāng〈名〉 hometown: 思念～ feel homesick ‖ ～话 native dialect
【家小】jiāxiǎo〈名〉 **1**（妻子和子女） wife and children: 丢下～无人照料 leave one's wife and children in the lurch **2**〈旧〉（妻子） wife: 未娶～ not have a wife yet
【家信】jiāxìn〈名〉 letter to or from one's family
【家兄】jiāxiōng〈名〉〈谦〉 my elder brother
【家学】jiāxué〈名〉〈书〉 learning handed down in a family: 他有～渊源。 His family has a long tradition of learning.
【家训】jiāxùn〈名〉〈书〉 family motto
【家严】jiāyán〈名〉〈书〉〈谦〉 my father
【家宴】jiāyàn〈名〉 family feast: 设～ hold a family dinner party
【家燕】jiāyàn〈名〉 barn swallow
【家养】jiāyǎng〈形〉 domesticated
【家业】jiāyè〈名〉 **1**（指家产） family property: 继承～ inherit family property ‖ 他父亲把～败光了。His father squandered the family inheritance. **2**〈书〉（指事业） family business handed down from one's ancestors: ～兴旺 thriving family business
【家蝇】jiāyíng〈名〉 housefly
【家用】jiāyòng **A**〈名〉 household expenses: 贴补～ supplement housekeeping money **B**〈形〉 domestic: ～冰箱 domestic refrigerator ‖ ～电脑 home computer
【家用电器】jiāyòng diànqì〈名〉 domestic appliances: ～市场 domestic appliance market
【家有千口，主事一人】jiā yǒu qiān kǒu, zhǔshì yī rén〈俗〉 a house can't have more than one master
【家喻户晓】jiāyù-hùxiǎo〈成〉 be known to all: ～的格言 familiar precept ‖ ～的名字 household name
【家园】jiāyuán〈名〉 homeland: 重返～ return to one's homeland ‖ 重建～ rebuild one's homeland
【家贼】jiāzéi〈名〉〈喻〉 traitor in the midst: ～难防 it's difficult to guard against a thief within the house
【家宅】jiāzhái〈名〉 **1**（住宅） residence **2**（家庭） family: 闹得～鸡犬不宁 give the family no peace
【家长】jiāzhǎng〈名〉 **1**（一家之长） head of a household: ～作风 patriarchal behaviour **2**（父母） parent: ～会议 parents' meeting
【家长制】jiāzhǎngzhì〈名〉 patriarchy: 不许搞～ not allow to follow the patriarchal system
【家政】jiāzhèng〈名〉 housekeeping: 主持～ run a household ‖ ～服务 domestic service
【家政学】jiāzhèngxué〈名〉 home economics
【家装】jiāzhuāng〈名〉 home decoration
【家子】jiāzi〈名〉〈口〉 family: 一大～ a big family
【家族】jiāzú〈名〉 clan: 这个～有精神病史。 There was a history of mental illness in the family.

笳 jiā ▸胡笳 hújiā

袈 jiā

【袈裟】jiāshā〈名〉 kasaya [patchwork outer vestment worn by a Buddhist monk]

葭 jiā〈名〉〈书〉 young shoot of a reed

筴（筴） jiā〈名〉〈古〉 chopsticks

嘉 jiā

A〈形〉 good: ▸～宾, ～言懿行
B〈动〉 praise: 精神可～ praiseworthy spirit ▸～奖, ～勉, ～许
【嘉宾】jiābīn〈名〉 distinguished guest: 特邀～ special guest
【嘉奖】jiājiǎng **A**〈动〉 commend: 受到中央军委～ receive a citation from the Central Military Commission ‖ ～令 citation **B**〈名〉 commendation: 最高～ the highest acclaim
【嘉靖】Jiājìng〈名〉 Jiajing [title of the reign of Zhu Houcong (朱厚熜), Ming Dynasty emperor]
【嘉勉】jiāmiǎn〈动〉〈书〉 praise and encourage: 热情～ warmly encourage sb.
【嘉年华】jiāniánhuá〈名〉 carnival: 环球～ global carnival
【嘉庆】Jiāqìng〈名〉 Jiaqing [title of the reign of Aisin Gioro Yongyan (爱新觉罗·颙琰), Qing Dynasty emperor]
【嘉许】jiāxǔ〈动〉〈书〉 praise: 深得上司～ receive a lot of praise from one's superiors
【嘉言懿行】jiāyán-yìxíng〈成〉 wise words and noble deeds: 他的～被广为传颂。 His wise words and admirable conduct were spoken of far and wide.

镓（鎵） jiā〈名〉［化学］ gallium (Ga)

jiá

夹（夾） jiá〈形〉 double-layered: ～袄 lined jacket
▸gā, jiā

荚（莢） jiá〈名〉 pod: 结～ produce pods ▸豆～, 皂～
【荚果】jiáguǒ〈名〉 pod

恝 jiá〈形〉〈书〉 indifferent

【恝然】jiárán〈形〉〈书〉 indifferent: ～置之 be indifferent to sth.

戛 jiá〈动〉〈书〉 tap

【戛然】jiárán〈形〉〈书〉 **1**（指鸟鸣声） squawking: ～长鸣 cry long and loud **2**（形容声音骤止） stopping suddenly: ～而止 stop abruptly ‖ 音乐～。 The music stopped abruptly.

铗（鋏） jiá〈名〉〈书〉 **1**（钳子） tongs: 火～ fire tongs ‖ 铁～ iron pincers **2**（剑） sword: 长～ long sword **3**（剑柄） hilt of a sword

颊（頰） jiá〈名〉 cheek: 两～红润 with rosy cheeks ‖ 双～凹陷/丰满 with hollow/plump cheeks ▸脸～, 面～
【颊骨】jiágǔ〈名〉［解剖］ cheekbone
【颊囊】jiánáng〈名〉［动物］ cheek pouch

蛱（蛺）jiá

【蛱蝶】jiádié〈名〉［昆虫］ vanessa [brush-footed butterfly]

jiǎ

甲[1] jiǎ

A〈名〉**1**（指天干） first of the ten Heavenly Stems (天干): ～班 Class A ‖ ～等 first class **2**（第一） first

B〈动〉〈书〉 be in first place: 桂林山水～天下。 The mountains and rivers of Guilin are the finest under heaven.

甲[2] jiǎ

〈名〉**1**（壳） shell: ▸～壳, ～鱼, 龟～ **2**（指甲） nail: ▸指～ **3**（盔甲） armour: ▸盔～, 装～车 **4**〈旧〉（指户口编制单位） unit of civil administration consisting of ten households: ▸保～制度

【甲板】jiǎbǎn〈名〉 deck: 上层/下层～ upper/lower deck ‖ 他在～上。 He is on deck.

【甲苯】jiǎběn〈名〉［化工］ toluene

【甲兵】jiǎbīng〈名〉〈旧〉**1**（武器） military equipment **2**（指士兵） soldier in armour

【甲虫】jiǎchóng〈名〉 beetle

【甲醇】jiǎchún〈名〉［化工］ methanol: ～中毒 methanol poisoning

【甲肝】jiǎgān〈简称〉= 甲型肝炎

【甲骨文】jiǎgǔwén ▸**p. 918**〈名〉 inscriptions on bones or tortoise shells

> **甲骨文**
>
> Ancient Chinese writing inscribed on animal bones and turtle shells to record divinations. The earliest oracle bones, dating from the Shang Dynasty, were discovered in Anyang, Henan Province, in the 19th century. Many more were excavated in the 20th century. The Zhou Dynasty oracle bones found in Shaanxi Province are of particular significance. To date, more than 100,000 bones have been discovered, containing 4,500 characters, of which 1,700 have been deciphered. Their basic lexis, grammar, and character structure are similar to Chinese writing of later periods. Oracle bone script is a direct ancestor of present-day Chinese characters.

【甲级】jiǎjí〈名〉 first-rate: ～队 first division team ‖ ～战犯 top war criminal

【甲流】jiǎliú ▸**p. 50**〈名〉 influenza A: ～病例 a case of type A influenza virus ‖ 加大防控～的力度 step up prevention and control of influenza A

【甲壳】jiǎqiào〈名〉 shell

【甲壳动物】jiǎqiào dòngwù〈名〉 crustacean

【甲醛】jiǎquán〈名〉［化学］formaldehyde: ～溶液 formalin

【甲酸】jiǎsuān〈名〉［化学］ methanoic acid

【甲烷】jiǎwán〈名〉［化学］ methane: ～细菌 methane bacteria

【甲午战争】Jiǎwǔ Zhànzhēng〈名〉 Sino-Japanese War of 1894-1895

【甲型肝炎】jiǎxíng gānyán ▸**p. 50**〈名〉 hepatitis A

【甲癣】jiǎxuǎn ▸**p. 50**〈名〉［医学］ ringworm of the nails

【甲鱼】jiǎyú = 鳖 biē

【甲胄】jiǎzhòu〈名〉〈书〉 armour

【甲状腺】jiǎzhuàngxiàn〈名〉［生理］ thyroid gland: ～肥大 hypertrophy of the thyroid gland ‖ ～机能亢进 hyperthyroidism

【甲状腺炎】jiǎzhuàngxiànyán ▸**p. 50**〈名〉［医学］ thyroiditis

【甲状腺肿】jiǎzhuàngxiànzhǒng ▸**p. 50**〈名〉［医学］ goitre

【甲子】jiǎzǐ〈名〉 cycle of sixty years in traditional Chinese chronology

岬 jiǎ

〈名〉**1**（指陆地） cape: 成山～ Cape of Chengshan **2**（指通道） narrow passage between mountains

【岬角】jiǎjiǎo〈名〉 cape

胛 jiǎ

【胛骨】jiǎgǔ〈名〉 shoulder blade

贾（賈）Jiǎ

▸gǔ

【贾宪三角】Jiǎ Xiàn sānjiǎo = 杨辉三角 Yáng Huī sānjiǎo

钾（鉀）jiǎ

〈名〉［化学］ potassium (K): ▸氯化～

【钾肥】jiǎféi〈名〉 potash fertilizer

【钾盐】jiǎyán〈名〉［矿业］ sylvite: ～矿床 potash salt deposit

假 jiǎ

A〈动〉**1**〈书〉（借） borrow: 久～不归 put off indefinitely the return of sth. one has borrowed ▸～道, ～借 **2**（利用） make use of: ▸～公济私, 狐～虎威 **3**（设想） suppose: ▸～定, ～设, ～说 **4**（假装） pretend to be: ▸～冒, ～托

B〈连〉 if: ▸～若, ～使

C〈形〉 false: ～慈悲 crocodile tears ‖ ～积极 in the guise of an activist ‖ ～地址 fictitious address ‖ ～护照 fake passport ‖ ～酒 adulterated wine ‖ ～珠宝 sham jewellery ‖ 以～乱真 mix the spurious with the genuine

▸jià

【假扮】jiǎbàn〈动〉 disguise oneself as: 他～记者混进了大楼。 He posed as a reporter to get into the building.

【假币】jiǎbì〈名〉 counterfeit money

【假唱】jiǎchàng〈动〉lip-sync: 为演出时的～行为向公众道歉 apologize to the public for lip-syncing on the show

【假钞】jiǎchāo〈名〉 counterfeit banknote

【假充】jiǎchōng〈动〉 pretend to be: ～内行 pose as an expert ‖ ～正经 pretend to be a respectable person

【假传圣旨】jiǎchuán-shèngzhǐ〈成〉〈喻〉 deliver a false order

【假大空】jiǎ-dà-kōng〈名〉〈俗〉 false, boastful and empty talk

【假道】jiǎdào〈介〉via: 她～日本去美国。 She went to the United States via Japan.

【假道学】jiǎdàoxué〈名〉 hypocrite

【假定】jiǎdìng **A**〈动〉 suppose: ～这消息是真的，我们该怎么办？ Suppose the news is true, what should we do then? **B**〈名〉 hypothesis

【假动作】jiǎdòngzuò〈名〉［体育］ trick move: 他做了一个～，把球传给了队友。 He faked a pass and then handed the ball over to his fellow player.

【假发】jiǎfà〈名〉 wig: 戴～ wear a wig

【假分数】jiǎfēnshù ▸**p. 691**〈名〉［数学］ improper fraction

【假公济私】jiǎgōng-jìsī〈成〉exploit public office for private gain

【假果】jiǎguǒ〈名〉［植物］ spurious fruit

【假花】jiǎhuā〈名〉 artificial flower

【假话】jiǎhuà〈名〉 lie: 说～ tell lies

【假货】jiǎhuò〈名〉 fake products

【假借】jiǎjiè **A**〈动〉 make use of: ～他人名义 in another person's name ‖ ～外力 make use of outside forces **B**〈名〉［语言］ phonetic loan characters

【假令】jiǎlìng〈连〉 in case

【假冒】jiǎmào〈动〉 pose as: ～警察 pass oneself off as a policeman ‖ 谨防～。 Beware of bogus imitations.

【假冒伪劣产品】jiǎmào wěiliè chǎnpǐn〈名〉 fake and shoddy goods

【假寐】jiǎmèi〈动〉〈书〉 doze: ～片刻 doze for a while

【假面具】jiǎmiànjù〈名〉 mask: 戴着～ wear masks ‖ 撕下伪君子的～ unmask a hypocrite

【假面舞会】jiǎmiàn wǔhuì〈名〉 masked ball: 参加～ join in a masquerade

【假名】jiǎmíng〈名〉[Japanese syllabic script] kana: 片～ katakana ‖ 平～ hiragana

【假模假式】jiǎmo-jiǎshì〈成〉 insincere: 他没有必要这样～。 He does not need to go through all this play-acting.

【假模假样】jiǎmo-jiǎyàng = 假模假式 jiǎmo-jiǎshì

【假情报】jiǎqíngbào〈名〉 disinformation: 提供～ misinform (sb.) about (sth.)

【假情假意】jiǎqíng-jiǎyì〈成〉 pretence of affection and goodness: 他那副～的样子让她感到讨厌。 His unctuous manner bothered her.

【假球】jiǎqiú〈名〉 rigged match: 打～ rig a match

【假仁假义】jiǎrén-jiǎyì〈成〉 hypocrisy

【假如】jiǎrú〈连〉 if: ～她不在，就留个口信。 Please leave a message if she isn't in. ‖ ～我忘了，请提醒一下。 In case I forget, please remind me of it.

【假若】jiǎruò = 假如 jiǎrú

【假嗓子】jiǎsǎngzi〈名〉 falsetto: 用～唱 sing falsetto

【假山】jiǎshān〈名〉 rockery

【假设】jiǎshè ▸**p. 350** **A**〈动〉**1**（假定）presume: 我们～这种说法是正确的。 We assume the statement to be correct. **2**（虚构）make up: 故事的情节是～的。 The plot of the story is fictitious. **B**〈名〉 hypothesis: 提出/证实～ suggest/verify a hypothesis ‖ 合理/科学～ reasonable/scientific hypothesis

【假声】jiǎshēng〈名〉［音乐］ falsetto: 用～唱 sing falsetto

【假使】jiǎshǐ = 假如 jiǎrú

【假释】jiǎshì〈动〉［法律］ release on parole: 准予～ release sb. on parole ‖ 他希望获得～。 He is hoping to get parole.

【假手】jiǎshǒu **A**〈动〉 make use of sb.: ～杀人 kill sb. using a hitman **B**〈名〉 artificial hand

【假手于人】jiǎshǒuyúrén〈成〉 achieve one's end through sb. else: 他～击败了竞争对手。 He beat his rival through someone else.

【假摔】jiǎshuāi〈动〉［足球］ do a fake dive: 他被判～吃了一张黄牌。 His fake dive got him a yellow card.

【假说】jiǎshuō = 假设 jiǎshè B

【假死】jiǎsǐ **A**〈名〉［医学］ false death **B**〈动〉［动物］ play dead

【假腿】jiǎtuǐ〈名〉 artificial leg

【假托】jiǎtuō〈动〉**1**（借故推托） feign: 她～有急事先走了。 She left before others on the pretext of some emergency. **2**（假冒） do sth. under sb. else's name: 他～经理的名义签了合同。 He signed the contract under the manager's name. **3**（凭

j

借) rely on: ～古事以喻今 use ancient events to comment on present affairs by innuendo ‖ 寓言～故事以说明道理。A fable conveys a moral in stories.
【假戏真做】jiǎxì-zhēnzuò〈成〉 what was make-believe turns out to be reality
【假想】jiǎxiǎng〈动〉 imagine: ～防卫 imaginative defence
【假想敌】jiǎxiǎngdí〈名〉[军事] imaginary enemy
【假象】jiǎxiàng〈名〉 false impression: 识破～ see through false appearances ‖ 制造～ put up a false front
【假小子】jiǎxiǎozi〈名〉 tomboy
【假惺惺】jiǎxīngxīng〈形〉 unctuous: ～的承诺/赞扬 unctuous assurance/praise
【假性】jiǎxìng〈形〉 false, pseudo: ～近视 pseudomyopia
【假牙】jiǎyá〈名〉 false teeth
【假洋鬼子】jiǎyángguǐzi〈名〉〈贬〉 fake foreign devil
【假以辞色】jiǎyǐcísè〈成〉 speak to sb. encouragingly
【假意】jiǎyì〈书〉 **A**〈名〉 insincerity: ▸虚情～ **B**〈副〉 intentionally: ～称赞 be insincere in one's praise
【假造】jiǎzào〈动〉 **1**（伪造）fake: ～公章 forge an official seal ‖ ～签名 fake sb.'s signature ‖ ～文凭/证件 forge a diploma/certificate **2**（捏造）invent: ～理由/事实 invent an excuse/a story ‖ ～罪名 cook up a false charge
【假账】jiǎzhàng〈名〉 false accounts: 查～ audit false accounts ‖ 做～ cook the books
【假正经】jiǎzhèngjing〈动〉 pretend to be a saint
【假肢】jiǎzhī〈名〉 artificial limb: 截肢之后安上了～。A prosthesis was fitted after the amputation.
【假装】jiǎzhuāng〈动〉 pretend: ～读书 make a show of reading ‖ ～虔诚 feign piousness ‖ 他没有病，是～的。He is not ill; he is just pretending.

jià

价（價） jià〈名〉 **1**（价格）price: 高/低～出售 sell at a high/low price ▸定～, 降～ **2**（价值） value: ▸～值, 等～ **3**［化学］ valence: 氢是一～元素。Hydrogen is a one-valence element.
▸jie
【价差】jiàchā〈名〉 price difference
【价格】jiàgé〈名〉 price: 调整～ readjust prices ‖ ～公道 be reasonable in price ‖ 出厂～ factory price ‖ 优惠～ favourable price ‖ ～飞涨。Prices soar.
【价格标签】jiàgé biāoqiān〈名〉 price tag
【价格波动】jiàgé bōdòng〈名〉 price fluctuation
【价格补贴】jiàgé bǔtiē〈名〉 price subsidy
【价格浮动】jiàgé fúdòng〈名〉 price variation
【价格管制】jiàgé guǎnzhì〈名〉 price control
【价格监督】jiàgé jiāndū〈名〉 price supervision
【价格战】jiàgézhàn〈名〉 price war
【价格指数】jiàgé zhǐshù〈名〉［经济］ price index
【价款】jiàkuǎn〈名〉 cost
【价廉物美】jiàlián-wùměi〈成〉 attractive in price and quality
【价码】jiàmǎ〈名〉 marked price
【价目】jiàmù〈名〉 marked price: ～表 price list
【价钱】jiàqian〈名〉 price: 讲～ bargain ‖ ～公道 fair price
【价位】jiàwèi〈名〉 price: 低～ low price
【价值】jiàzhí〈名〉 **1**［经济］ value: 票面～ face value ▸剩余～ **2**（用途、作用） worth: 毫无～ be completely worthless ‖ ～取向 value orientation ‖ 艺术～ artistic value ‖ 营养～ nutritional value
【价值观】jiàzhíguān〈名〉 values: 年轻人和我们的～不同。Young people have values different from ours.
【价值规律】jiàzhí guīlǜ〈名〉 law of value
【价值连城】jiàzhí-liánchéng〈成〉 priceless: ～的钻石 diamond of great value
【价值量】jiàzhíliàng〈名〉 magnitude of value
【价值形态】jiàzhí xíngtài〈名〉［经济］ form of value

驾（駕） jià
A〈动〉 **1**（用牲口拉） harness: ～上牲口犁地 harness cattle to plough the fields ‖ 两匹马～着车。Two horses are drawing a cart. **2**（骑、乘） ride: ～鹤升天 ride a crane to ascend to heaven ▸腾云～雾 **3**（操纵）（指汽车）drive;（指飞机）fly;（指船）sail: 酒后～驶 drunk driving ‖ 他们～车沿海岸兜风。They went for a drive along the coast. ▸～轻就熟, ～驶 **4**（控制） control: ▸～驭
B〈名〉 **1**〈敬〉（您） you: ▸～临, 大～, 劳～ **2**（帝王的车） emperor's carriage **3**（帝王） emperor: ▸～崩, 起～
【驾崩】jiàbēng〈动〉 [of an emperor] pass away
【驾到】jiàdào〈动〉〈敬〉 arrive

ℹ 假设情况

■“如果”、“假如”、“假使”、“倘若”等表示假设的关联词，用在偏正复句的偏句中（前面分句），偏句必须置于主句前。汉语的偏句相当于英语的 if 从句，但英语的 if 从句可置于主句前也可以置于主句后。所有表示假设的汉语关联词，不管是用于口语中的“如果”、“要是”等，还是用于书面语中的“倘若”、“如”等，都可用 if 来翻译：

如果开车去，你会按时到那儿的
= If you drive, you will get there on time
或 You will get there on time if you drive

你倘若遇到麻烦，我们定当尽力相助
= We will try our utmost to assist if you are in trouble
或 If you are in trouble, we will try our utmost to assist

如发现不妥，请务必向我汇报
= If anything wrong is discovered, please report it to me
或 Should anything wrong be discovered, please report it to me

■ 汉语中，“如果”、“假如”、“假使”和“倘若”可以省去，用主句中的“就”来表示假设和结果的关系。英语中，if 一般不能省去（含有 should、were、助动词 had 等的从句例外）：

明天天好，我们就去野餐
= If it is fine tomorrow, let's go for a picnic

火车票太贵，我们就租个车
= If the train tickets are too expensive, we can rent a car instead
或 We can rent a car if the train tickets are too expensive

■ 在英语里有三种不同的条件句，都是通过动词时态的变化来表达的。第一种是表示可能会发生的条件句：if 从句用一般现在时，主句用一般将来时。第二种是表示与已知事实相反或对将来不希望发生的状况的一种假设，称虚拟语气：if 从句用一般过去时，主句动词是“would/might/could 等 + 动词原形”。第三种是表示与过去事实相反的假设，也称虚拟语气：if 从句采用过去完成时，主句动词形式是“would/could/might + have + 动词的过去分词”。注意这些条件句中的动词时态变化。

■ 在正式英语中，含有“if + 主语 + 助动词／were”的从句可用倒装语序，把 if 省去，即采用“助动词／were + 主语”的结构：

如果你用特快专递，他明天就能收到
= If you send it by special delivery, it will reach him tomorrow

如果想减肥，你必须坚持锻炼
= If you want to lose weight, you must keep exercising

如果我处于你的状况，我会和老板谈谈的
= If I were in your shoes, I would speak to the boss
或 Were I in your shoes, I would speak to the boss

假如车祸身亡，我愿意捐献我的心脏
= If I were to die in a car accident, I would donate my heart
或 Were I to die in a car accident, I would donate my heart
或 If I died in a car accident, I would donate my heart

假如我知道你今天到，我会去机场接你的
= I would have met you at the airport if I had known you were arriving today
或 Had I known you were arriving today, I would have met you at the airport

倘若救护车早一点到，我父亲的命就能够保住了
= If the ambulance had come earlier, my father's life would have been saved
或 Had the ambulance come earlier, my father's life would have been saved

■ 从句用“should + 主语 + 动词原形”而主句用祈使句时，可以用作书面指令，表示某事如果发生的话，应该怎样做（尽管不太可能）：

若需更多帮助，请拨打此号
= Should you require more assistance, please ring this number

如产品送到时有破损，请退往此地址
= Should the product arrive in a damaged condition, please return it to this address

j

【驾临】jiàlín〈动〉〈敬〉arrive: 恭候～。Your presence is cordially requested. ‖ 女王～使我们不胜荣幸。The Queen is gracing us with her presence.

【驾凌】jiàlíng = 凌驾 língjià

【驾龄】jiàlíng〈名〉length of service as a driver: 二十年的～ a driver of twenty years' standing

【驾轻就熟】jiàqīng-jiùshú〈成〉〈喻〉handle a job with ease because of previous experience

【驾驶】jiàshǐ〈动〉（指汽车） drive;（指飞机、船） pilot: ～飞机/轮船 pilot a plane/ship ‖ ～汽车/坦克 drive a car/tank ‖ 谨慎/小心～ drive with caution/care

【驾驶舱】jiàshǐcāng〈名〉［航空］cockpit

【驾驶盘】jiàshǐpán〈名〉steering wheel

【驾驶室】jiàshǐshì〈名〉（指汽车） driver's cab;（指飞机） cockpit;（指船） bridge

【驾驶台】jiàshǐtái〈名〉［航海］bridge (of a ship)

【驾驶学校】jiàshǐ xuéxiào〈名〉training school for drivers

【驾驶员】jiàshǐyuán ▸**p. 966**〈名〉（指汽车） driver;（指飞机或船） pilot: 公共汽车/卡车～ bus/truck driver ‖ 喷气机/战斗机～ jet/fighter pilot ‖ 实习～ learner driver ‖ 特级/一级～ command/senior pilot

【驾驶执照】jiàshǐ zhízhào〈名〉driving licence〈英〉; driver's licence〈美〉: 出示～ show one's driver's licence ‖ 吊销～ suspend a driver's licence

【驾校】jiàxiào〈简称〉= 驾驶学校

【驾驭】jiàyù〈动〉**1**（驱使） drive: 这匹马难以～。This horse is hard to control. **2**（控制） control: 有智慧、有能力～复杂局面 have the wisdom and capability to cope with complicated situations

【驾辕】jiàyuán〈动〉pull a cart from between the shafts

【驾照】jiàzhào〈简称〉= 驾驶执照

架 jià

A〈名〉**1**（指用具） shelf: 葡萄～ grape trellis ‖ 商品陈列～ store shelf ▸笔～, 书～, 行李～ **2**（指组织、结构） frame: ▸骨～, 框～ **3**（指殴打或争吵事件） fight: ▸吵～, 打～, 劝～

B〈动〉**1**（搭起） erect: ～电话线 put up telephone lines ‖ ～起机枪 set up a machine-gun ‖〈喻〉～起通往未来的桥梁 build a bridge to the future **2**（搀扶） support: ～着伤员慢慢走 help the wounded soldier to walk slowly **3**（劫持） kidnap: 她被几个匪徒～走了。She was kidnapped by some bandits. **4**（抵挡） ward off: ～住砍来的刀 fend off a sword thrust

C〈量〉[used for sth. with a stand or mechanism]: 一～飞机/钢琴 a plane/piano

【架不住】jiàbuzhù〈动〉〈口〉**1**（禁不住） cannot withstand: ～诱惑 cannot resist the temptation ‖ 树枝几乎～果实的重量。The branches could hardly sustain the weight of the fruits. **2**（比不上） be no match for: 客队技术娴熟，我们还是～。The guest team were very skilful and we could not compete with them.

【架次】jiàcì〈量〉sortie: 出动飞机五十～ fly fifty sorties

【架得住】jiàdezhù〈动〉〈口〉be able to bear: 这么重的工作，你～吗？ Can you cope with such a heavy load of work?

【架构】jiàgòu **A**〈动〉construct **B**〈名〉**1**（支架） scaffold **2**〈喻〉（格局、结构） structure

【架空】jiàkōng〈动〉**1**（指架设） be built on stilts: ～电车线 aerial contact line ‖ ～索道 cable way ‖ 那个竹楼是～的。The bamboo hut is built on stilts. **2**〈喻〉（指根基） be impractical: 这个计划不过是～的构想。The plan is no more than an impractical idea. **3**〈喻〉（指权力） take away one's power by subtle means: 企图～董事长 try to strip away the power of the director of the board

【架设】jiàshè〈动〉erect: ～电线 erect power lines ‖ ～桥梁 erect a bridge across a river

【架式】jiàshi = 架势 jiàshi

【架势】jiàshi〈名〉**1**（姿态） posture: 摆出一副～ assume a posture ‖ 拉开打架的～ get ready for a fight **2**（势头） situation: 看～这雨一下子还停不了。There is no sign that the rain will stop soon.

【架子】jiàzi〈名〉**1**（指用具） rack: 花瓶～ vase stand ‖ 脸盆～ washstand **2**〈喻〉（指结构） framework: 写论文先得搭好～。You should come up with an outline before you write your thesis. **3**〈喻〉（指作风） airs: 摆官/臭～ put on bureaucratic/nauseating airs ‖ 放下～ get down from one's high horse ‖ 没有～ be modest and unassuming **4**〈喻〉（姿态） posture

【架子车】jiàzichē〈名〉handcart

【架子工】jiàzigōng〈名〉［建筑］**1**（指工种） scaffolding **2**（指工人） scaffolder

【架子鼓】jiàzigǔ ▸**p. 929**〈名〉［音乐］traps

【架子猪】jiàzizhū〈名〉［畜牧］feeder pig

假 jià

〈名〉**1**（放假） holiday〈英〉; vacation〈美〉: ▸～期, 度～, 暑～ **2**（离开） leave of absence: 准～ grant sb. leave of absence ‖ 他续了一个月的～。He had his leave extended for another month. ▸病～, 事～

▸jiǎ

【假期】jiàqī〈名〉holiday〈英〉; vacation〈美〉: 带薪～ paid holiday ‖ 我有两周的～。I have a fortnight's holiday.

【假日】jiàrì〈名〉day off: ～旅游 holiday outing ‖ 法定/公共～ legal/public holiday

【假日经济】jiàrì jīngjì〈名〉holiday economy

【假条】jiàtiáo〈名〉**1**（指申请） application for leave: 交/写～ hand in/write an application for leave **2**（指证明） leave permit: 医生给她开了一周的～。She has got a doctor's certificate for a week's sick leave.

嫁 jià

〈动〉**1**（指女性） marry: ～不出去 be left on the shelf ‖ 皇帝女儿不愁～。A scarce item has no lack of demand. ‖ 她～了个大学老师。She married a college teacher. ▸出～, 改～ **2**（转移） transfer: ▸～祸于人, 转～

【嫁祸于人】jiàhuòyúrén〈成〉put the blame on sb. else

【嫁鸡随鸡，嫁狗随狗】jià jī suí jī, jià gǒu suí gǒu〈俗〉a woman follows her husband no matter how good or bad his lot

【嫁接】jiàjiē〈动〉［植物］graft: ～法 grafting

【嫁奁】jiàlián〈名〉dowry

【嫁娶】jiàqǔ〈动〉marry: ～风俗 marriage customs

【嫁人】jiàrén〈动〉〈口〉[of a woman] get married

【嫁妆】jiàzhuang〈名〉dowry: 为女儿准备～ provide a dowry for one's daughter ‖ 新娘的～ bridal trousseau

稼 jià

A〈动〉〈书〉sow: ▸～穑

B〈名〉crops: ▸庄～

【稼穑】jiàsè〈名〉〈书〉farm work

jia

家 jia

〈后缀〉[used after certain nouns to indicate a specified group of people]: 小孩子～ children ‖ 女人～ women ‖ 姑娘～ girls ‖ 一个男人～ a man

▸jiā

jiān

戋（戔）jiān

【戋戋】jiānjiān〈形〉〈书〉tiny: ～之数 very small amount

尖 jiān

A〈形〉**1**（末端细小） pointed;（锐利） sharp: ～下巴 pointed chin ‖ ～头的铅笔 sharp pencil **2**（在前） leading: ▸～兵, ～端 **3**（声音细高） piercing: ～声～气 in a shrill voice **4**（敏锐） acute: 耳朵～ have sharp ears ‖ 眼睛～ be sharp-eyed **5**（刻薄） caustic: 她嘴～。She has a sharp tongue. ▸～刻, ～酸, ～嘴薄舌

B〈名〉**1**（细端） tip: 鼻～儿 tip of one's nose ‖ 舌～儿 tip of one's tongue ‖ 塔～ top of a pagoda ▸笔～ **2**（出众者） pick of the bunch: ▸～子, 拔～儿, 冒～

C〈动〉raise one's voice to a high pitch: ～着嗓子喊 cry in a shrill voice

【尖兵】jiānbīng〈名〉**1**［军事］point: ～连 point company **2**〈喻〉（先锋模范） trailblazer: 他们是地质战线上的～。They were pioneers of the geological field.

【尖刀】jiāndāo〈名〉dagger: 像一把插入敌人心脏的～ like a dagger stuck into the enemy's heart

【尖顶】jiāndǐng〈名〉spire: ～塔 fleche

【尖端】jiānduān **A**〈名〉point: 标枪的～ javelin point ‖ 这把匕首的～很锐利。The dagger is very sharp at its point. **B**〈形〉most advanced: ～产品 highly sophisticated products

【尖端技术】jiānduān jìshù〈名〉cutting-edge technology

【尖端科学】jiānduān kēxué〈名〉frontier science

【尖端武器】jiānduān wǔqì〈名〉sophisticated weapon

【尖叫】jiānjiào〈动〉scream: 刺耳/歇斯底里的～声 shrill/hysterical scream ‖ ～声刺破长空。Screams pierced the air.

【尖刻】jiānkè〈形〉caustic: 说话～ speak with biting sarcasm ‖ 他的那些～的话刺伤了她。His sharp words hurt her.

【尖括号】jiānkuòhào〈名〉angle bracket (〈 〉)

【尖厉】jiānlì〈形〉[of voice] piercing: ～的叫声 piercing scream

【尖利】jiānlì〈形〉**1**（锋利） sharp: ～的刀锋 knife with a thin blade **2**（敏锐） sharp: 目光～ be sharp-eyed **3** = 尖厉 jiānlì

【尖脐】jiānqí〈名〉**1**（指甲壳） triangular abdomen of a male crab **2**（公蟹） male crab

【尖锐】jiānruì〈形〉**1**（锋利） pointy: 这种植物长着～的刺。The plant has pointy thorns. **2**（敏锐） keen: 眼光～ keen

sight ‖ 她看问题很～。 She sees things with a keen eye. **3**（尖利） shrill: ～的汽笛声 shrill whistle ‖ ～的声音 shrill voice **4**（激烈） sharp: ～的矛盾 sharp contradictions ‖ ～的批评 sharp criticism

【尖锐化】jiānruìhuà〈动〉 intensify: 矛盾～了。 The contradictions became all the more acute.

【尖酸】 jiānsuān 〈形〉 acrid: ～的话 tart remarks ‖ ～刻薄 bitterly sarcastic

【尖细】jiānxì〈形〉 [of a voice] small and shrill

【尖音】 jiānyīn 〈名〉［语言］ *jianyin* [the combination of z, c and s with i, ü or compound vowels beginning with i, ü]

【尖子】jiānzi〈名〉**1**（指物体）tip **2**（指人） pick of the bunch: ～队员 best of a team ‖ 她是班上的～。 She is the top student in her class.

【尖嘴薄舌】jiānzuǐ-bóshé〈成〉〈贬〉have a sharp tongue

【尖嘴猴腮】jiānzuǐ-hóusāi〈成〉〈贬〉thin angular face

奸¹ jiān

A〈形〉**1**（狡诈） evil: ▸～计, ～商, ～诈 **2**（不忠） treacherous: ▸～臣, ～细 **3**〈口〉（虚伪） self-seeking and wily: 藏～耍滑 try to shirk one's work or responsibility

B〈名〉 traitor: ▸汉～, 内～

奸²（姦） jiān

〈动〉 commit adultery: ▸～污, 通～

【奸臣】 jiānchén 〈名〉 treacherous court official: ～逆子 disloyal ministers and unfilial sons

【奸党】jiāndǎng〈名〉 cabal

【奸刁】jiāndiāo〈形〉 treacherous and sly

【奸夫】jiānfū〈名〉 adulterer

【奸妇】jiānfù〈名〉 adulteress

【奸滑】jiānhuá = 奸猾 jiānhuá

【奸猾】jiānhuá〈形〉 treacherous: ～的对手 treacherous adversary

【奸计】jiānjì〈名〉 evil plot: 中～ fall into sb.'s trap

【奸佞】jiānnìng **A**〈书〉〈形〉 crafty and fawning **B**〈名〉 crafty sycophant

【奸情】jiānqíng〈名〉 adultery: 与某人有～ have an adulterous affair with sb.

【奸商】jiānshāng〈名〉 profiteer: 严惩～ punish unscrupulous merchants severely

【奸污】jiānwū〈动〉 rape: ～妇女 rape a woman

【奸细】 jiānxì 〈名〉 spy: 被～盯梢 be watched by spies

【奸险】jiānxiǎn〈形〉 malicious: 他为人～狠毒。 He is sinister and ruthless.

【奸笑】jiānxiào〈名〉 sinister smile: 面带～ have a sinister smile on one's face

【奸邪】jiānxié **A**〈形〉 crafty and evil **B**〈名〉 crafty and evil person

【奸雄】jiānxióng〈名〉 person who achieves high position through unscrupulous scheming: 乱世之～ treacherous pretender in times of turmoil

【奸淫】jiānyín〈动〉 rape or seduce: ～幼女 seduce an underage girl

【奸淫掳掠】jiānyín-lǔlüè〈成〉rape and loot

【奸贼】jiānzéi〈名〉 conspirator: 铲除～ get rid of traitors

【奸诈】 jiānzhà 〈形〉 crafty: 为人～ be treacherous

歼（殲） jiān

〈动〉 annihilate: ～敌三千人 annihilate 3,000 enemy troops ‖ 全～来犯之敌 wipe out the invading enemy ▸～灭, 围～

【歼击】jiānjī〈动〉 attack and wipe out

【歼击机】jiānjījī〈名〉［军事］fighter plane

【歼灭】jiānmiè〈动〉 wipe out: 给予～性的打击 strike a crushing blow ‖ 集中优势兵力, ～敌人有生力量 concentrate superior forces to wipe out the enemy's effective strength

【歼灭战】jiānmièzhàn〈名〉 battle of annihilation: 打～ fight a battle of annihilation

坚（堅） jiān

A〈形〉**1**（硬） hard: ～冰 hard ice ‖ ～石 solid rock ‖ ～质陶器 ironstone china ▸～不可摧, ～固, ～硬 **2**（坚强） staunch: ～拒 flatly refuse ‖ 身残志～ disabled in body but resolute in spirit ▸～持, ～守, ～毅

B〈名〉 stronghold: ▸攻～, 披～执锐, 无～不摧

【坚壁】jiānbì〈动〉〈书〉 hide supplies to prevent the enemy from seizing them

【坚壁清野】jiānbì-qīngyě〈成〉 strengthen defence works, evacuate the civilian population, and hide provisions and livestock

【坚不可摧】 jiānbùkěcuī 〈成〉 indestructible: ～的要塞 impregnable fortress

【坚持】jiānchí〈动〉 persist in: ～改革开放 persevere in reform and opening-up ‖ ～己见 hold on to one's own views ‖ ～实事求是 persist in seeking truth from facts ‖ ～原则 uphold one's principles ‖ ～真理 keep to the truth ‖ ～到底 hold out to the last ‖ 带病～工作 not stop working despite one's poor health

【坚持不懈】 jiānchí-bùxiè 〈成〉 persistent: ～地工作 persevere with a task

【坚定】jiāndìng **A**〈形〉 firm: 立场～ be firm in one's stand ‖ 意志～ be strong-willed ‖ ～的信念 strong belief **B**〈动〉 strengthen: ～立场/信心 strengthen one's stand/confidence ‖ ～信仰 corroborate a belief

【坚定不移】jiāndìng-bùyí〈成〉be firm and unshakeable: ～的决心 unswerving determination ‖ 中国对这一问题的立场是～的。 China maintains a firm stance on the matter.

【坚固】 jiāngù 〈形〉 sturdy: ～耐用 be sturdy and durable ‖ ～的堡垒 well-protected fortress

【坚果】jiānguǒ〈名〉［植物］ nut

【坚甲利兵】jiānjiǎ-lìbīng〈成〉 be equipped with strong armour and sharp weapons

【坚决】jiānjué〈形〉 firm: 态度～ maintain a firm attitude ‖ ～执行计划 carry out the plan with determination ‖ ～的斗争 inexorable struggle

【坚苦】jiānkǔ〈形〉 steadfast and assiduous: ～的任务 arduous task

【坚苦卓绝】 jiānkǔ-zhuōjué〈成〉 showing the utmost fortitude: ～的精神 indomitable and tireless spirit

【坚强】jiānqiáng〈形〉 staunch: 意志～ be strong-willed ‖ ～的后盾 powerful backing ‖ 她是个性格～的人。 She is a person of strong character.

【坚忍】jiānrěn〈形〉 steadfast and persevering: ～不拔的意志 a strong, persevering determination

【坚韧】jiānrèn〈形〉 firm and tenacious

【坚韧不拔】jiānrèn-bùbá〈成〉staunch and unyielding: ～的毅力 inflexible will

【坚如磐石】jiānrúpánshí 〈成〉 solid as a rock

【坚实】jiānshí〈形〉**1**（坚固） solid: 打下～的基础 lay a solid foundation ‖ 迈出～的步子 make steady progress **2**（强壮） robust: 身体～ be of solid build

【坚守】jiānshǒu〈动〉 stick to: ～岗位/诺言 stick to one's post/word ‖ ～阵地 hold one's ground

【坚挺】jiāntǐng〈形〉 strong: ～的货币 strong currency ‖ 英镑对美元的汇价～。 The pound held firm against the dollar.

【坚信】jiānxìn〈动〉 firmly believe: ～自己的能力 have a strong belief in one's own capability ‖ 我们～会成功。 We are fully confident of success.

【坚信不疑】jiānxìn-bùyí〈成〉 have infinite faith in

【坚毅】jiānyì〈形〉 firm and persistent: ～的性格 strong character ‖ ～顽强 be firm and indomitable

【坚硬】jiānyìng〈形〉 hard: ～的岩石 solid rock ‖ 乌龟长有～的甲壳。 Tortoises have very hard shells.

【坚贞】jiānzhēn〈形〉 faithful: 对丈夫～不二 feel undivided loyalty to one's husband

【坚贞不屈】jiānzhēn-bùqū〈成〉stand firm and unyielding: 虽然受尽严刑, 他仍～。 He remained faithful and unyielding even under severe torture.

【坚贞不渝】jiānzhēn-bùyú〈成〉 be faithful through thick and thin: 对爱情～ be constant in love

间（間） jiān

A〈名〉**1**（指空间） space between: 夫妻之～ between husband and wife ‖ 两山之～有条小溪。 There is a small stream between the two mountains. ▸字里行～ **2**（指时间） (within) a definite time: 假期～ during the vacation ▸工～, 课～, 夜～ **3**（房间） room: ▸车～, 套～, 衣帽～

B〈量〉 [used of smallest units of housing]: 两～门面 two shopfronts ‖ 一～卧室 a bedroom

▸jiàn

【间冰期】jiānbīngqī〈名〉［地质］interglacial (stage)

【间不容发】jiānbùróngfà 〈成〉 **1**（指间距）extremely close **2**（指情势） extremely critical

【间架】 jiānjià 〈名〉 **1**（指房屋） framework [of a house] **2**（指汉字） structure [of a Chinese character, essay or painting]

【间距】jiānjù〈名〉 spacing: ～调整 spacing adjustment

【间质】jiānzhì〈名〉［生理］ mesenchyme: ～性角膜炎 interstitial keratitis

【间奏曲】 jiānzòuqǔ 〈名〉［音乐］ intermezzo

浅（淺） jiān

▸qiǎn

【浅浅】jiānjiān〈拟〉〈书〉 gurgle: ～流水 babble of running water

肩 jiān

A ▸**p. 614**〈名〉 shoulder: 并～而立 stand shoulder to shoulder ‖ 擦～而过 brush past sb. ‖ 耸～ shrug one's shoulders ‖ 这项任务全部落在我们～上。 The task rested squarely on our shoulders. ▸垫～, 披～

B〈动〉 shoulder: 身～重任 shoulder heavy responsibilities ▸～负

【肩膀】jiānbǎng〈名〉 shoulder: 拍拍某人的～ tap sb. on the shoulder

【肩负】jiānfù〈动〉 take on: ～历史/神圣的使命 assume a historical/sacred mission ‖ ～重任 shoulder heavy responsibilities

【肩关节】jiānguānjié〈名〉shoulder joint

【肩胛骨】jiānjiǎgǔ〈名〉[生理] scapula: ～脱臼 dislocate one's shoulder

【肩头】jiāntóu〈名〉shoulder: 男孩骑在父亲的～。The boy rode on his father's shoulders.

【肩窝】jiānwō〈名〉shallow part of the shoulder

【肩舆】jiānyú〈名〉〈书〉sedan chair

【肩章】jiānzhāng〈名〉**1**（行业、级别标志）shoulder strap **2**（佩饰）epaulette

【肩周炎】jiānzhōuyán ▸**p. 50**〈名〉[医学] periarthritis

艰（艱） jiān〈形〉difficult

【艰巨】jiānjù〈形〉arduous: ～的任务 arduous task ‖ 这项工程很～。This is a formidable project.

【艰苦】jiānkǔ〈形〉arduous: 备尝～ have endured great hardships ‖ ～的工作 painstaking job ‖ ～的生活 tough life ‖ ～的岁月 hard times ‖ 在～的环境中磨炼自己 temper oneself in difficult circumstances

【艰苦创业】jiānkǔ-chuàngyè〈成〉build an enterprise through hard work

【艰苦奋斗】jiānkǔ-fèndòu〈成〉work hard and perseveringly: 保持～的作风 keep to the style of hard struggle and plain living

【艰苦朴素】jiānkǔ-pǔsù〈成〉work hard and live simply: 保持～的优良传统 keep up the fine tradition of hard work and plain living

【艰苦卓绝】jiānkǔ-zhuōjué〈成〉extremely hard and bitter: ～的斗争 most arduous struggle

【艰难】jiānnán〈形〉hard: ～度日 eke out a difficult existence ‖ 步履～ walk with difficulty ‖ 会谈将很～。The talks will be tough.

【艰难曲折】jiānnán-qūzhé〈成〉difficulties and setbacks

【艰难险阻】jiānnán-xiǎnzǔ〈成〉difficulties and dangers

【艰涩】jiānsè〈形〉intricate and obscure: 文词～ involved, incomprehensible writing

【艰深】jiānshēn〈形〉abstruse: 文字～ abstruse writing ‖ ～的理论 abstruse theory

【艰危】jiānwēi〈形〉〈书〉difficult and dangerous: 形势日益～。The situation is getting increasingly difficult and dangerous.

【艰险】jiānxiǎn〈名〉hardships and dangers: 不畏～ brave hardships and dangers ‖ 历尽～ experience all hardships and perils

【艰辛】jiānxīn〈形〉hard: 不辞～ despite hardships ‖ 历尽～ have experienced all kinds of hardships

鹣（鶼） jiān〈名〉[鸟类] bittern

监（監） jiān

A〈动〉**1**（督察）supervise: ▸～察，～督，～视 **2**（关押）put in prison: ▸～禁

B〈名〉prison: ▸～牢，收～，探～

▸jiàn

【监测】jiāncè〈动〉monitor: ～病人的脉搏 monitor a patient's pulse ‖ ～全球环境变化 monitor global environmental changes ‖ ～器 monitor

【监察】jiānchá〈动〉supervise: ～部 Ministry of Supervision ‖ ～委员会 control commission

【监督】jiāndū **A**〈动〉supervise: 加强/进行～ tighten/exercise supervision ‖ 接受～ subject oneself to supervision **B**〈名〉supervisor: 安全～ safety supervisor ‖ 选举～ election monitor

【监督电话】jiāndū diànhuà〈名〉supervision telephone (number)

【监督权】jiāndūquán〈名〉right of supervision: 行使～ exercise authority to supervise

【监房】jiānfáng〈名〉prison cell

【监工】jiāngōng **A**〈动〉oversee: ～员 watch master **B**〈名〉supervisor

【监管】jiānguǎn〈动〉keep watch on: ～犯人 supervise and control prisoners

【监规】jiānguī〈名〉prison regulations

【监护】jiānhù〈动〉**1**[法律] act as a guardian: 父母对年幼的子女有～权。Parents have the guardianship of their young children. **2**（看护）observe and nurse: ～病人 nurse a patient ‖ 重症～室 intensive care unit (ICU)

【监护权】jiānhùquán〈名〉[法律] guardianship: 剥夺～ deprive sb. of his guardianship (over)

【监护人】jiānhùrén〈名〉guardian: 当然～ natural guardian ‖ 孩子的～ guardian to a child ‖ 诉讼～ guardian ad litem ‖ 指定～ legal guardian

【监禁】jiānjìn〈动〉put in prison: 被判十年～ receive a ten-year jail sentence ‖ 终生～ life imprisonment

【监考】jiānkǎo **A**〈动〉invigilate: 她今天下午要～。She'll be invigilating an examination this afternoon. **B**〈名〉invigilator

【监控】jiānkòng〈动〉**1**（指监测）monitor and control: ～器 monitor unit ‖ 安全～系统 security monitoring system **2**（指监督）supervise and control: 物价～ supervision over prices

【监牢】jiānláo〈名〉prison: 被关入～ be put in prison

【监理】jiānlǐ **A**〈动〉inspect and control: 交通～部门 traffic control department **B**〈名〉supervisor

【监票】jiānpiào〈动〉monitor balloting: ～人 ballot examiner

【监舍】jiānshè〈名〉prison house

【监事】jiānshì〈名〉supervisor: 首席～ chief supervisor

【监事会】jiānshìhuì〈名〉board of supervisors

【监视】jiānshì〈动〉keep watch on: ～病情 monitor the disease ‖ 暗中～ keep watch in secret ‖ 对嫌疑犯昼夜～ keep the suspects under round-the-clock surveillance ‖ 他受到警方严密～。He was kept under observation by the police.

【监视器】jiānshìqì〈名〉monitor: 图像～ picture monitor

【监守】jiānshǒu〈动〉have custody of

【监守自盗】jiānshǒu-zìdào〈成〉embezzle

【监听】jiāntīng〈动〉monitor: ～器 audio monitor ‖ 警察～了嫌疑犯的所有电话。The police monitored all of the suspect's phone calls.

【监外】jiānwài〈形〉outside prison: ～就医 undergo medical treatment outside a prison under surveillance ‖ ～执行 serve a sentence outside prison under surveillance

【监押】jiānyā〈动〉**1**（拘押）keep in custody: ～犯人 take criminals into custody **2**（押送）send away under escort: 罪犯被～到当地监狱。The convicted criminals were taken under escort to the local jail.

【监狱】jiānyù〈名〉prison: 被关进～ be put in prison ‖ ～长 prison governor ‖ 他蹲过～。He is a former prison inmate.

【监制】jiānzhì〈动〉**1**（指商品）supervise the manufacture of: 本饮品由可口可乐公司～。The drink is produced under the supervision of the Coca Cola Company. **2**（指影片、电视片）supervise the production of

兼 jiān

A〈动〉hold two or more posts concurrently: 身～数职 wear several hats ‖ ～管教学和科研 be concurrently in charge of teaching and scientific research ‖ 他是副厂长～总工程师。He is the vice-director and chief engineer concurrently. ▸～课，～职

B〈形〉double: ▸～程

【兼备】jiānbèi〈动〉have both at the same time: ▸德才～

【兼并】jiānbìng〈动〉**1**（侵占）annex: ～邻国 annex a neighbouring country **2**（并购）amalgamate: 企业的～ amalgamation of enterprises

【兼差】jiānchāi〈旧〉= 兼职 jiānzhí

【兼程】jiānchéng〈动〉travel at double speed: 风雨～ travel regardless of wind or rain ‖ 日夜～ travel day and night

【兼而有之】jiān'éryǒuzhī〈成〉have both at the same time

【兼顾】jiāngù〈动〉give consideration to two or more things: ～长远利益和眼前利益 take into account both long-term and immediate interests ‖ 公私～ give consideration to both public and private interests

【兼课】jiānkè〈动〉teach part-time: ～教师 part-time teacher ‖ 王教授在我们学校～。Professor Wang offers a part-time course at our school.

【兼任】jiānrèn **A**〈动〉hold a concurrent post: 我们学院总务主任～工会主席。The chief of the General Affairs Section of our college is concurrently the chairman of the college's Labour Union. **B**〈形〉part-time: ～教师 part-time teacher

【兼容】jiānróng〈动〉be compatible: ～机 compatible computer ‖ ～性 compatibility ‖ 善恶不能～。Virtues are not compatible with vices.

【兼容并包】jiānróng-bìngbāo〈成〉be all-embracing

【兼容并蓄】jiānróng-bìngxù = 兼收并蓄 jiānshōu-bìngxù

【兼收并蓄】jiānshōu-bìngxù〈成〉absorb anything and everything

【兼听则明，偏信则暗】jiān tīng zé míng, piān xìn zé àn〈成〉broad consultation makes one wise; one-sided consideration makes one blind

【兼修】jiānxiū〈动〉study two or more courses concurrently: 专攻法律，～英语 specialize in law and take an extra course in English

【兼营】jiānyíng〈动〉sideline in

【兼之】jiānzhī〈连〉〈书〉furthermore

【兼职】jiānzhí ▸**p. 966** **A**〈动〉hold a concurrent post: ～过多 hold too many posts at the same time ‖ ～教师 part-time teacher **B**〈名〉concurrent post: 辞去～ resign from one's part-time job ‖ 减少～ reduce the number of posts one holds concurrently

菅 jiān〈名〉[植物] villous themeda: ▸草～人命

笺¹（箋） jiān〈名〉commentary: ▸～注

笺²（牋） jiān〈名〉**1**（信）letter: ▸～札 **2**（纸）writing paper: ▸便～，信～

【笺札】jiānzhá〈名〉correspondence

【笺注】jiānzhù〈名〉〈书〉notes and commentary on ancient texts

渐（漸） jiān〈动〉〈书〉**1**（流入）flow into: 东～入海 flow east and empty into the sea **2**（浸渍）soak: ～润 be saturated with water ▸～染 ▸jiàn

【渐染】jiānrǎn〈动〉〈书〉be imperceptibly influenced: ～恶习 gradually develop a bad habit

犍 jiān〈名〉bullock

【犍牛】jiānniú〈名〉bullock

湔 jiān〈动〉〈书〉wash: ▸～洗, ～雪

【湔洗】jiānxǐ〈动〉〈书〉**1**（洗涤）wash **2**（洗掉）purge

【湔雪】jiānxuě〈动〉〈书〉redress: ～沉冤 redress a long-standing injustice

缄（緘） jiān〈动〉**1**（关闭）close: ▸～口, ～默 **2**（特指信）seal: 李～ from Li

【缄口】jiānkǒu〈动〉〈书〉keep one's mouth shut: ～不答 make no response

【缄默】jiānmò〈动〉keep silent: 保持～ keep silent ‖（对某事）～不语 keep silent (about sth.)

蒹 jiān〈名〉〈书〉〈古〉earless reed

搛 jiān〈动〉pick up with chopsticks

煎 jiān

A〈动〉**1**（指用油）fry: ～鸡蛋/香肠 fry eggs/sausages **2**（用水熬煮）simmer in water: ～药 decoct medical herbs

B〈量〉decoction: 头/二～ first/second decoction

【煎熬】jiān'áo〈动〉〈喻〉suffer: 受尽～ endure all kinds of sufferings ‖ 他饱受悔恨的～。He was consumed with remorse.

【煎饼】jiānbing〈名〉thin pancake made of millet flour, etc.

【煎蛋卷】jiāndànjuǎn〈名〉omelette

【煎锅】jiānguō〈名〉frying-pan

【煎剂】jiānjì〈名〉[中药] decoction

jiǎn

j

拣（揀） jiǎn〈动〉**1**（挑）select: ～重活干 choose to do the heavy work ‖ 请～要紧的说。Please concentrate on what is most important. ▸挑肥～瘦 **2** = 捡 jiǎn

【拣便宜】jiǎn piányi〈动〉**1**（指价钱）get a bargain: 拣了个便宜 get a good bargain **2**（指好处）gain a small advantage: 别想拣我的便宜。Don't try to take advantage of me.

【拣选】jiǎnxuǎn〈动〉select: ～上等药材 select high-quality medicinal herbs

【拣择】jiǎnzé〈动〉choose

枧（梘） jiǎn〈名〉〈方〉soap: 香～ scented soap

茧（繭） jiǎn〈名〉**1**（指蚕）cocoon: 剥～抽丝 reel silk from cocoons ▸蚕～, 作～自缚 **2** = 趼 jiǎn

【茧绸】jiǎnchóu〈名〉pongee

【茧子】jiǎnzi〈名〉**1**〈方〉（蚕茧）silkworm cocoon **2** = 趼子 jiǎnzi

柬 jiǎn〈名〉note: ▸～帖, 请～

【柬埔寨】Jiǎnpǔzhài〈名〉Cambodia: ～人 Cambodian

【柬帖】jiǎntiě〈名〉note

俭（儉） jiǎn〈形〉economical: ～以防匮 waste not, want not ‖ ～以养廉。Frugality makes honesty. ▸～朴, 勤～, 省吃～用

【俭朴】jiǎnpǔ〈形〉thrifty and simple: 生活～ lead a thrifty and simple life ‖ 衣着～ dress simply

【俭省】jiǎnshěng〈形〉thrifty: 吃饭～ have economical meals ‖ 过日子～ live a frugal life

【俭约】jiǎnyuē〈形〉〈书〉economical

捡（撿） jiǎn〈动〉gather: ～麦穗 gather wheat ears ‖ 我昨天～了一个钱夹。I picked up a wallet yesterday. ‖〈喻〉他～了一条命。He came back from the dead.

【捡了芝麻，丢了西瓜】jiǎnle zhīma, diūle xīguā〈俗〉〈喻〉concentrate on minor matters to the neglect of major ones

【捡漏】jiǎnlòu〈动〉repair a leaky roof

【捡漏儿】jiǎnlòur〈动〉〈方〉nit-pick

【捡破烂儿】jiǎn pòlànr〈动〉pick odds and ends from refuse heaps: ～的 rag and bone man

【捡拾】jiǎnshí〈动〉gather: ～田间的麦穗 gather up wheat ends ‖ 在海滩～贝壳 collect seashells on the beach

笕（筧） jiǎn〈名〉bamboo water pipe

检（檢） jiǎn〈动〉**1**（约束）keep oneself in check: 行为不～ behave improperly ‖ 言行失～ be indiscreet in the way one speaks and behaves **2**（查）inspect: ▸～查, ～阅, 体～ **3** = 捡 jiǎn

【检波】jiǎnbō〈名〉[通信] detection: ～器 detector

【检测】jiǎncè〈动〉examine: 进行～ carry out a test ‖ ～仪器 detecting instrument ‖ 初步～ preliminary test

【检查】jiǎnchá〈动〉**1**（细心查看）examine: ～产品质量 check the quality of products ‖ ～工作 check up on work ‖ ～身体 have a physical check-up ‖ ～视力 test sb.'s eyesight ‖ ～卫生 inspect sanitary conditions ‖ ～账目 audit the accounts ‖ 安全～ security check ‖ 常规～ routine examination ‖ 抽样/健康～ spot/health check **2**（翻阅查考）refer to: 把这些文件放在桌上，以便随时～。Keep these documents on your desk for easy reference. **3**（检讨）make a self-criticism: 写～ write a self-criticism

【检查团】jiǎnchátuán〈名〉inspection party

【检查员】jiǎncháyuán ▸p. 966〈名〉inspector: 健康～ health inspector

【检查站】jiǎncházhàn〈名〉checkpoint: 边境～ border checkpoint

【检察】jiǎnchá〈名〉procuratorial work

【检察官】jiǎncháguān〈名〉public prosecutor〈英〉; district attorney〈美〉

【检察机关】jiǎnchá jīguān〈名〉procuratorial organ

【检察院】jiǎncháyuàn〈名〉procuratorate

【检察长】jiǎncházhǎng〈名〉chief procurator

【检出率】jiǎnchūlǜ〈名〉detection rate: 女性乳腺癌～持续上升。Detection rates of female breast cancer continue to rise.

【检点】jiǎndiǎn〈动〉**1**（查点）check carefully: ～货物 inspect merchandise ‖ ～随身物品 check one's personal articles **2**（约束）be cautious: 品行不～ be of easy morals ‖ 言行有失～ be indiscreet in one's speech and conduct

【检定】jiǎndìng〈动〉examine and determine: ～药品 test drugs

【检获】jiǎnhuò〈动〉discover and seize: ～走私货物 root out smuggled goods

【检举】jiǎnjǔ〈动〉report (an offence) to the authorities: ～不法分子 inform against wrongdoers ‖ ～人 informer ‖ ～信 accusation letter

【检控】jiǎnkòng〈动〉**1**（检举控告）prosecute: ～不法商贩 prosecute illegal pedlers **2**（检查控制）investigate and control

【检控方】jiǎnkòngfāng〈名〉the prosecution: ～的最后陈述 the closing remarks of the prosecution ‖ ～撤消了对他们的指控。The prosecution withdrew the charges against them.

【检录】jiǎnlù〈动〉call a roll of contestants in athletic events: 运动员请到检录处～。Contestants please come to the assembly area for roll-call.

【检票】jiǎnpiào〈动〉check a ticket: 在～口出示火车票 show one's train ticket at the barrier

【检审】jiǎnshěn〈动〉test and examine

【检视】jiǎnshì〈动〉inspect: ～现场 inspect the scene of a crime or an accident

【检束】jiǎnshù〈动〉restrain

【检索】jiǎnsuǒ〈动〉retrieve: ～储存在磁盘中的资料 retrieve data from a disc ‖ 按音序～ search by order of pronunciation

【检讨】jiǎntǎo〈动〉**1**（自我批评）make a self-criticism: ～自己的错误 examine one's mistakes ‖ 口头/书面～ oral/written self-criticism **2**〈书〉（分析研究）study: ～前人的学术成果 study the academic achievements of one's predecessors

【检修】jiǎnxiū〈动〉overhaul: ～机器/汽车 overhaul a machine/car

【检验】jiǎnyàn〈动〉test: ～产品质量 examine the quality of the products ‖ ～员 inspector ‖ 实践是～真理的唯一标准。Practice is the sole criterion for testing truth.

【检疫】jiǎnyì〈动〉quarantine:（对进口商品）进行～ impose a quarantine (on imported goods) ‖ ～站 quarantine station ‖ 该船正在接受严格～。The ship has been put under strict quarantine.

【检阅】jiǎnyuè〈动〉**1**（视察）inspect: ～部队 inspect the troops ‖ ～仪仗队 inspect a guard of honour ‖ 接受～ undergo inspection **2**（翻阅）leaf through: ～报纸 browse through a newspaper

【检阅台】jiǎnyuètái〈名〉reviewing stand

【检字表】jiǎnzìbiǎo〈名〉[语言] word index [in a dictionary]

【检字法】jiǎnzìfǎ〈名〉[语言] indexing system for Chinese characters: 音序～ indexing by pronunciation ‖ 部首～ indexing by radical ‖ 笔画～ indexing by stroke count

趼 jiǎn〈名〉callus

【趼子】jiǎnzi〈名〉callus

减（減） jiǎn〈动〉**1**（去掉）subtract: 五～二等于三。Five minus two is three. **2**（降低）reduce: ～薪 reduce a

salary ‖ ～半 reduce by half ▸～轻, ～弱, ～速

【减磅】jiǎnbàng〈动〉［金融］reduce one's holding: 逢高～, 逢低吸纳 reduce one's holdings when share prices are high, and buy more when prices are low

【减仓】jiǎncāng〈动〉sell shares: 逢高～, 注意风险。Sell shares when their price is high as a precaution against risk.

【减产】jiǎnchǎn〈动〉reduce output: 粮食～5%。Grain output dropped by five per cent. ‖ 由于产品滞销, 工厂不得不～。The factory had to cut production owing to sluggish sales of the products.

【减低】jiǎndī〈动〉lower: ～成本 cut the cost ‖ ～城市噪声 bring down the noise in the city ‖ ～速度 reduce speed

【减法】jiǎnfǎ〈名〉［数学］subtraction

【减肥】jiǎnféi〈动〉lose weight: ～食品 diet food ‖ ～茶 fat-reducing tea ‖ ～药 slimming pill ‖ 她在节食～。She is dieting in order to lose weight.

【减幅】jiǎnfú〈名〉amount of reduction

【减负】jiǎnfù〈动〉ease a burden: 给学生～ lighten students' load

【减号】jiǎnhào〈名〉［数学］minus sign (–)

【减缓】jiǎnhuǎn〈动〉slow down: ～经济增长速度 slow the economic growth ‖ 日照不足会～植物的生长。Lack of sunlight can slow plant growth.

【减价】jiǎnjià〈动〉mark down: ～20% mark down 20% ‖ 该店的服装全部～出售。The store slashed prices on all clothes.

【减亏】jiǎnkuī〈动〉reduce losses: ～增盈 reduce losses and increase profits

【减免】jiǎnmiǎn〈动〉**1**（指刑罚）go lightly on: ～刑罚 reduce a punishment **2**（指负担）exempt and reduce: ～房租/税收/学费 reduce the rents/taxes/tuition fees

【减贫】jiǎnpín〈动〉reduce poverty: 拉美国家～成效显著。Latin American countries have achieved remarkable results in poverty reduction.

【减轻】jiǎnqīng〈动〉lighten: ～处分 lessen a punishment ‖ ～农民负担 relieve farmers of their burdens ‖ ～（某人的）压力 ease the pressure (on sb.) ‖ 病痛～了。The pain ebbed.

【减弱】jiǎnruò〈动〉weaken: 视力～ one's eyesight is failing ‖ 火势～了。The fire has died down. ‖ 我的兴趣逐渐～, 最后完全消失了。My interest waned to extinction.

【减色】jiǎnsè〈动〉lose shine: 照明不好使晚会大为～。Poor lighting greatly spoilt the evening party.

【减少】jiǎnshǎo〈动〉reduce: ～赤字 narrow the deficit ‖ ～污染 cut down pollution ‖ 出口量有所～。Export volumes have decreased. ‖ 各种非生产性开支不断～。Nonproductive expenditures keep falling. ‖ 耕地面积在～。The amount of arable land is dwindling.

【减声器】jiǎnshēngqì〈名〉［机械］muffler

【减数】jiǎnshù〈名〉［数学］subtrahend

【减税】jiǎnshuì〈动〉reduce taxation: ～百分之20% reduce taxes by 20% ‖ ～让利 reduce tax on enterprises, allowing them to retain more profits

【减速】jiǎnsù〈动〉slow down: ～器 reduction gear ‖ 汽车～后停了下来。The car slowed down and stopped.

【减速带】jiǎnsùdài〈名〉［交通］speed bump

【减缩】jiǎnsuō〈动〉cut down: ～军费 cut back on military expenditure ‖ ～开支 reduce expenditure

【减退】jiǎntuì〈动〉abate: 热度～ the fever has gone down ‖ 这孩子的视力在～。The child's eyesight is failing.

【减薪】jiǎnxīn〈动〉reduce sb.'s salary

【减刑】jiǎnxíng〈动〉give a reduced sentence: ～判决 commuted sentence

【减压】jiǎnyā〈动〉reduce pressure

【减压阀】jiǎnyāfá〈名〉compression release valve

【减员】jiǎnyuán〈动〉downsize: ～增效 cut down on staff numbers to improve efficiency ‖ 战斗～ combat depletion of strength

【减灾】jiǎnzāi〈动〉reduce natural disasters: ～措施 measure for disaster reduction

【减震】jiǎnzhèn〈名〉damping: ～材料 vibration-absorptive material ‖ ～器 shock absorber

【减征】jiǎnzhēng〈动〉reduce (taxes): ～土地使用税 reduce land tax ‖ ～车船税 reduce taxes on travel

剪 jiǎn

A〈动〉**1**（割断）cut off: ▸～草除根 **2**（除掉）exterminate: ▸～除, ～灭 **3**（铰）trim: ～去枯枝 prune the dead branches ‖ ～羊毛 shear sheep ‖ ～指甲 trim one's nails ▸～彩, ～贴, 修～
B〈名〉**1**（剪刀）scissors: 理发～ hair clippers ‖ 手术～ surgery scissors ▸～刀, 子¹ **2**（剪刀状工具）instrument/implement shaped like scissors: ▸火～, 夹～

【剪报】jiǎnbào **A**〈动〉clip out **B**〈名〉clipping; cutting〈英〉: ～集 collection of press cuttings

【剪裁】jiǎncái〈动〉**1**（指衣料）tailor: ～衣服 tailored clothes ‖ 这套衣服～得体, 做工也好。The suit is well cut and well made. **2**（指写作素材）prune: 对文章进行～ prune an article of superfluities

【剪彩】jiǎncǎi〈动〉cut the ribbon at an opening ceremony etc.: 市长为展览会开幕～。The mayor cut the ribbon to open the exhibition.

【剪草除根】jiǎncǎo-chúgēn = 斩草除根 zhǎncǎo-chúgēn

【剪草机】jiǎncǎojī〈名〉lawn mower

【剪除】jiǎnchú〈动〉exterminate: ～恶势力 root out vicious powers

【剪刀】jiǎndāo〈名〉scissors

【剪刀差】jiǎndāochā〈名〉［经济］scissors differential: 扩大/缩小～ widen/narrow the price scissors

【剪辑】jiǎnjí **A**〈动〉edit and rearrange: ～资料 cut out materials for a montage ‖ 电影录音～ highlights of a live recording of a film **B**〈名〉［影视］film editing: ～导演 director of editing

【剪辑机】jiǎnjíjī〈名〉editing machine: 电影～ motion-picture editing machine

【剪接】jiǎnjiē = 剪辑 jiǎnjí A

【剪径】jiǎnjìng〈动〉waylay and rob

【剪毛】jiǎnmáo〈动〉［畜牧］shear

【剪毛机】jiǎnmáojī〈名〉shearing machine

【剪灭】jiǎnmiè〈动〉〈书〉wipe out: ～残敌 wipe out what remains of the enemy

【剪票】jiǎnpiào〈动〉punch a ticket: ～口 ticket-punching entrance ‖ ～员 puncher

【剪切】jiǎnqiē〈动〉［机械］shear

【剪贴】jiǎntiē **A**〈动〉cut and paste: 写文章并非是剪剪贴贴的拼凑。Writing an article is not a scissors-and-paste affair. **B**〈名〉cutting out

【剪贴簿】jiǎntiēbù〈名〉scrapbook

【剪影】jiǎnyǐng〈名〉**1**（指剪纸）paper-cut silhouette: 他的～惟妙惟肖。His paper-cut silhouette is a vivid image of him. **2**〈喻〉（指描写）outline: 社会～ sketches of society

【剪枝】jiǎnzhī〈动〉prune

【剪纸】jiǎnzhǐ〈名〉paper-cut: 一张/幅～ a paper-cut

> **剪纸**
> Traditional Chinese handicraft in which decorative flowers, animals and story-book characters are cut out of sheets of paper using scissors or a small knife. Yu County in Hebei Province, Yangzhou in Jiangsu Province, and Foshan in Guangdong Province are all famed for their paper-cuts.

【剪纸片】jiǎnzhǐpiàn〈名〉［影视］cartoon film with paper-cut figures

【剪子】jiǎnzi〈名〉scissors

硷（鹼）jiǎn = 碱 jiǎn

睑（瞼）jiǎn〈名〉eyelid: ▸眼～

【睑结膜】jiǎnjiémó〈名〉［解剖］palpebral conjunctiva

【睑腺炎】jiǎnxiànyán ▸**p. 50**〈名〉［医学］sty

锏（鐧）jiǎn〈名〉mace ▸jiàn

裥（襉）jiǎn〈名〉pleat: 打～ make folds

简¹（簡）jiǎn〈名〉**1**（竹片）bamboo slip: ▸竹～ **2**〈书〉（信）letter: 一封短～ a short letter ▸书～

简²（簡）jiǎn

A〈形〉simple: ▸～便, ～体, 言～意赅
B〈动〉**1**（使减少）simplify: ▸精兵～政, 精～ **2**（慢待）slight: ▸～慢

简³（簡）jiǎn〈动〉〈书〉select: ▸～拔

【简拔】jiǎnbá〈动〉〈书〉select and promote

【简报】jiǎnbào〈名〉bulletin: 工作～ brief report on work ‖ 会议/新闻～ conference/news bulletin

【简本】jiǎnběn〈名〉concise edition

【简笔画】jiǎnbǐhuà〈名〉sketch

【简编】jiǎnbiān〈名〉[usu used in book titles] abridged edition: 《美国文学～》*American Literature Abridged*

【简便】jiǎnbiàn〈形〉handy: 操作～ easy to operate ‖ ～的方法 handy method

【简册】jiǎncè〈名〉〈古〉bamboo slips strung together

【简称】jiǎnchēng **A**〈名〉abbreviation **B**〈动〉be abbreviated to: 外交部长可～外长。The Minister of Foreign Affairs may be called the Foreign Minister for short.

【简单】jiǎndān〈形〉**1**（不复杂）simple: 构造～ be simple in structure ‖ 头脑～ be simple-minded ‖ ～的装置 simple device ‖ 手续～。The procedure is straightforward. **2**（平凡）[usu used in the negative] ordinary: 她精通四门外语, 真不～。She's a marvel to have mastered four foreign languages. **3**（马虎）oversimplified: ～从事 do things in a casual way ‖ 这种想法太～。The idea is too simplistic.

【简单化】jiǎndānhuà〈动〉oversimplify:

看问题～ take an over-simplified view of a matter ‖ 思想工作不能～。 Ideological work cannot be done in a crude way.

【简单句】jiǎndānjù〈名〉［语法］ simple sentence

【简单劳动】jiǎndān láodòng〈名〉［经济］simple labour

【简单明了】jiǎndān-míngliǎo〈成〉 simple and clear

【简单商品生产】jiǎndān shāngpǐn shēngchǎn〈名〉［经济］simple commodity production

【简单再生产】 jiǎndān zàishēngchǎn〈名〉［经济］simple reproduction

【简短】jiǎnduǎn〈形〉 brief: ～的报道 brief report ‖ 做～陈述 make a brief statement

【简而言之】 jiǎn'éryánzhī〈成〉 briefly speaking: ～，我不同意你的看法。 In short, I don't agree with you.

【简化】jiǎnhuà〈动〉 simplify: ～手续 simplify the procedures ‖ 力求～ strive for simplification

【简化汉字】jiǎnhuà Hànzì A〈动〉 simplify Chinese characters B〈名〉 simplified Chinese character

【简化字】jiǎnhuàzì = 简化汉字 jiǎnhuà Hànzì B

【简洁】jiǎnjié〈形〉 concise: 文笔～ write concisely ‖ 他的话～而犀利。 His remarks are always succinct and pointed.

【简捷】jiǎnjié〈形〉 1（直截了当） simple and direct: ～了当 straightforward 2（简便快捷） simple and convenient: 做事的～方法 neat way of doing a job

【简介】jiǎnjiè A〈动〉 introduce briefly B〈名〉 brief introduction: 剧情～ synopsis of a play ‖ 作者生平～ biographical note of the author

【简况】jiǎnkuàng〈名〉 short introduction: 候选人～ brief introduction to the candidates

【简括】jiǎnkuò〈形〉 succinct: ～的说明 brief but comprehensive explanation ‖ ～的总结 succinct summary

【简历】jiǎnlì〈名〉 curriculum vitae (CV)〈英〉; résumé〈美〉: 个人～ personal résumé

【简练】jiǎnliàn〈形〉 succinct: 文字～ succinct in style

【简陋】jiǎnlòu〈形〉 simple and crude: ～的校舍 simple school building ‖ 设备极其～。 The facilities are extremely basic.

【简略】jiǎnlüè〈形〉 brief: ～报告计划要点 sketch out the main points of the report

【简慢】jiǎnmàn〈动〉 be negligent: 他对我～无礼。 He was short with me.

【简明】jiǎnmíng〈形〉 simple and clear: ～扼要 brief and to the point ‖ 《～汉英词典》*A Concise Chinese-English Dictionary*

【简明新闻】jiǎnmíng xīnwén〈名〉 news in brief

【简朴】jiǎnpǔ〈形〉 plain: 生活～ lead/live a simple and frugal life ‖ 衣着～ be simply dressed

【简谱】jiǎnpǔ〈名〉numbered musical notation

【简省】jiǎnshěng〈动〉 economize: ～用电 economize on electricity

【简史】jiǎnshǐ〈名〉 concise history: 人类文化发展～ a short outline of the development of human culture

【简缩】jiǎnsuō〈动〉 condense: 将长篇报告～为摘要 condense a long report into a brief summary

【简体】jiǎntǐ〈名〉 1（指形式） simplified style of Chinese characters 2 = 简体字 jiǎntǐzì

【简体字】jiǎntǐzì〈名〉 simplified Chinese character

【简图】jiǎntú〈名〉 sketch

【简写】jiǎnxiě〈动〉 1（指汉字） write a Chinese character in simplified form 2（指书） simplify a book for beginners

【简写本】jiǎnxiěběn〈名〉 simplified edition

【简讯】jiǎnxùn〈名〉 news in brief

【简言之】jiǎnyánzhi〈惯〉 briefly

【简要】jiǎnyào〈形〉 concise: ～概括（文章内容） give a neat summary (of an article) ‖ ～介绍（某事） give a brief introduction (to sth.)

【简易】 jiǎnyì〈形〉 1（简单而容易） simple and easy: ～办法 simple and easy method 2（设施简陋） unsophisticated: ～门诊 walk-in clinic ‖ ～公路 simply-built highway ‖ ～机场 airstrip

【简易读物】jiǎnyì dúwù〈名〉 easy reader

【简约】jiǎnyuē〈形〉 1（简要） concise: 文字～ concise writing style 2（节俭） frugal: 生活～ live a frugal life

【简则】jiǎnzé〈名〉 brief rules

【简札】jiǎnzhá〈名〉〈书〉 correspondence

【简章】jiǎnzhāng〈名〉 general regulations: 招生～ enrolment regulations

【简政放权】 jiǎnzhèng-fàngquán〈成〉 streamline administration and decentralize

【简直】jiǎnzhí〈副〉 simply: ～不可思议 be virtually unimaginable ‖ ～是浪费时间。 It's a sheer waste of time. ‖ 那～是胡说八道。 That's sheer nonsense.

【简装】jiǎnzhuāng〈形〉 simply packed: ～本 paperback

谫（謭） jiǎn〈形〉〈书〉 shallow

【谫陋】jiǎnlòu〈形〉〈书〉 shallow and ignorant: 学识～ be possessed of meagre knowledge

碱 jiǎn

A〈名〉 1（指氢氧化物）alkali 2（苏打） soda: 洗涤～ washing soda

B〈动〉 be eroded by alkali: 墙根～了。 The foot of the wall has been eroded by alkali.

【碱地】jiǎndì〈名〉 alkaline land

【碱化】 jiǎnhuà〈动〉 alkalize: ～作用 alkalinization

【碱荒】jiǎnhuāng〈名〉 alkaline land that lies in waste

【碱土】jiǎntǔ〈名〉 alkali soil

【碱性】 jiǎnxìng〈名〉 alkalinity: ～反应 alkaline reaction

翦 Jiǎn〈名〉 Jian [surname]

蹇 Jiǎn〈名〉 Jian [surname]

jiàn

见¹（見） jiàn

A〈动〉 1（看到） see: 从未～过 have never seen (sb./sth.) ‖ 亲眼所～ see with one's own eyes ▸～多识广，喜闻乐～ 2（见面） meet: 去～主任 go to see the director ‖ 我明天去～律师。 I'm meeting with my solicitor tomorrow. ▸拜～，会～，接～ 3（碰上） meet with: 冰～热就化。 Ice melts with heat. ‖ 胶卷不能～光。 Film should not be exposed to daylight. 4（显露） show evidence of: ▸～效，日久～人心 5（参看） refer to: ～第四课。 See Lesson 4. ‖ 详～60页。 For further information, please see page 60. ▸参～ 6（感觉到） [used after some verbs to indicate the result]: ▸看～，梦～，听～

B〈名〉 opinion: ▸成～，固执己～，真知灼～

见²（見） jiàn〈助〉〈书〉 1（表被动） [used before a verb to indicate the passive]: ▸～笑 2（表示对我如何） [used before a verb in a polite request]: ▸～教，～谅 ▸xiàn

【见爱】jiàn'ài〈动〉〈书〉 be liked

【见报】jiànbào〈动〉 appear in the newspapers: 那篇报道已经～。 The report has hit the papers.

【见背】jiànbèi ▸p. 772〈动〉〈书〉〈婉〉 [of a senior] pass away

【见不得】jiànbudé〈动〉 1（不能接触） not expose to: 病人～阳光。 The patient cannot stand sunlight. 2（不能被人知道） be not fit to be seen: ～人的勾当 under-the-table deal ‖ 不要做～人的事。 Don't do anything that'll bring shame on yourself. 3〈方〉（不能容忍） cannot bear the sight of: 她～儿子留长发。 She frowned upon her son's wearing his hair long.

【见财起意】 jiàncái-qǐyì〈成〉 have evil thoughts at the sight of riches

【见长】jiàncháng〈动〉〈书〉 be good at: 他是著名翻译家，尤以译诗～。 He is a well-known translator, and is especially good at translating poems. ▸jiànzhǎng

【见称】jiànchēng〈动〉〈书〉 be noted

【见得】jiànde〈动〉 [used only in the negative or questions] seem: 何以～? How so? ‖ 你不～比他差。 It doesn't seem to me that you are in any way inferior to him.

【见地】jiàndì〈名〉 insight: 很有～ display sound judgement

【见多识广】jiànduō-shíguǎng〈成〉 experienced and knowledgeable: 记者～。 Journalists are experienced and knowledgeable.

【见方】jiànfāng〈名〉 square: 这间屋子20米～。 This room is 20 metres square.

【见风使舵】 jiànfēng-shǐduò〈成〉〈喻〉 act as a weathercock

【见风就是雨】jiàn fēng jiù shì yǔ〈俗〉〈喻〉 jump to conclusions

【见风转舵】jiànfēng-zhuǎnduò = 见风使舵 jiànfēng-shǐduò

【见缝插针】jiànfèng-chāzhēn〈成〉〈喻〉 make use of every little bit

【见告】 jiàngào〈动〉〈套〉 keep me informed

【见怪】jiànguài〈动〉 take offence: 要是我的话说得不合适，请不要～。 I hope you won't find my remarks inappropriate.

【见怪不怪】jiànguài-bùguài〈成〉 not be surprised by anything unusual: 对腐败～，腐败就难以根除。 If we become inured to corruption, we won't be able to wipe it out.

【见鬼】jiànguǐ〈动〉 1（奇怪） be absurd: 真～，我一转身她就不见了。 It's funny. She disappeared as soon as I turned my back. 2（消亡） go to hell: 让旧制度～去吧! To hell with the old system!

【见好】jiànhǎo〈动〉 get better: 他的病明显～了。 He is plainly on the mend.

【见好就收】 jiànhǎo-jiùshōu〈成〉 leave while the going is still good

【见机行事】 jiànjī-xíngshì〈成〉 use one's discretion

【见教】jiànjiào〈动〉〈套〉 favour me with your advice: 承蒙～ many thanks for your kind instruction ‖ 你找我不知有何～? Is there anything you want to see me about?

【见解】 jiànjiě〈名〉 view: 提出不同～ advance a different view ‖ ～独到/新颖 have original/novel views
【见景生情】jiànjǐng-shēngqíng = 触景生情 chùjǐng-shēngqíng
【见老】jiànlǎo〈动〉 look older: 你一点也不～。You don't look older at all.
【见利忘义】 jiànlì-wàngyì 〈成〉 forsake good for the sake of gold
【见谅】jiànliàng〈动〉〈套〉 excuse me: 字迹潦草，请～。Please forgive me if you find my writing a little scribbled.
【见猎心喜】 jiànliè-xīnxǐ 〈成〉〈喻〉 be inclined to do what one is used to doing
【见面】jiànmiàn〈动〉 meet: 使产销直接～ establish direct links between the producer and the seller ‖ 他的新作将于下个月与读者～。His new work will be out next month.
【见面会】jiànmiànhuì〈名〉 meet-and-greet event: 用人单位和毕业生～ meet-and-greet event for recruiting employers and college graduates
【见面礼】jiànmiànlǐ〈名〉 present given to sb. on meeting them for the first time
【见票即付】jiànpiào-jífù〈动〉［经济］ be payable on demand
【见钱眼开】 jiànqián-yǎnkāi 〈成〉 be hungry for money
【见轻】 jiànqīng 〈动〉〈书〉 get better: 病势～。The patient's condition has improved.
【见人说人话，见鬼说鬼话】jiàn rén shuō rénhuà, jiàn guǐ shuō guǐhuà〈俗〉〈贬〉 be all things to all people
【见仁见智】 jiànrén-jiànzhì 〈成〉 different people, different views: 代表们～。The delegates all had different opinions.
【见世面】jiàn shìmiàn〈动〉 see the world: 你该出去见见世面了。It's high time you saw something of the world.
【见势不妙】jiànshì-bùmiào〈成〉 see that the tide has turned against oneself: 歹徒～，拔腿就跑。The bandits sensed trouble and immediately took to their heels.
【见识】jiànshi **A**〈动〉 enrich one's experience: 让他～～。Let him live a little. **B**〈名〉 experience: 长～ broaden one's horizons ‖ ～广 have rich experience
【见树不见林】jiàn shù bù jiàn lín〈俗〉 not see the wood for the trees
【见死不救】 jiànsǐ-bùjiù 〈成〉 **1**〈本〉 make no efforts to save sb. whose life is endangered **2**〈喻〉 be indifferent to others' misfortunes
【见所未见】jiànsuǒwèijiàn〈成〉 see what one has never seen before
【见天】jiàntiān〈副〉〈口〉 every day: 她～做早操。She does morning exercises every day.
【见外】jiànwài〈形〉 overly polite: 到我这儿可别～。Just make yourself at home.
【见危授命】 jiànwēi-shòumìng 〈成〉 be ready to die for one's country when it is in danger
【见微知著】jiànwēi-zhīzhù〈成〉 from one small clue one can see what is coming
【见闻】jiànwén〈名〉 information: 增长～ broaden one's knowledge ‖ 香港～ sights and sounds of Hong Kong
【见物不见人】jiàn wù bù jiàn rén〈俗〉 see things but not people
【见习】jiànxí〈动〉 learn on the job: ～护士/技术员 probationary nurse/technician ‖ ～医生 student doctor ‖ ～期 probation
【见习生】jiànxíshēng〈名〉 probationer
【见贤思齐】jiànxián-sīqí〈成〉〈喻〉 emulate those better than oneself
【见效】jiànxiào〈动〉 be effective: ～快 obtain quick results ‖ 这药一吃就～。This medicine produces an instant effect.
【见笑】 jiànxiào 〈动〉 **1**〈谦〉（被人笑话） incur ridicule: 唱得不好，～了。Excuse my poor singing. **2**（笑话我） laugh at: 我刚开始学，请别～。Don't laugh at me. I am just learning.
【见阎王】jiàn Yánwang〈惯〉〈喻〉 kick the bucket: 他去年就～了。He died last year.
【见义勇为】jiànyì-yǒngwéi〈成〉 act bravely for a just cause
【见异思迁】jiànyì-sīqiān〈成〉 be fickle
【见责】jiànzé〈动〉〈书〉 be reproached
【见长】jiànzhǎng〈动〉 grow perceptibly: 麦苗～了。The wheat sprouts seem to have grown quite a bit. ‖ 这孩子怎么不～? How come the child doesn't seem to be growing?
▸jiàncháng
【见证】jiànzhèng **A**〈动〉 bear witness: ～人 eyewitness **B**〈名〉 witness: 历史是最有力的～。History is the most telling witness.
【见罪】 jiànzuì 〈动〉〈书〉〈套〉 take offence: 招待不周，请勿～。Forgive me for my poor hospitality.

件 jiàn

A〈名〉 **1**（指事物） item: ▸案～，零～，条～ **2**（指文件） document: ▸附～，急～，密～
B〈量〉 piece: 两～衬衫 two shirts ‖ 三～行李 three pieces of luggage ‖ 一～事 a matter

间（間） jiàn

A〈名〉 opening: ▸～隙，亲密无～
B〈动〉 **1**（隔开） separate: 黑白相～ be checked with black and white ‖ 晴～多云。It is fine with occasional clouds. ▸～断，～隔，～作 **2**（挑拨） sow discord: ▸反～计，离～ **3**（除去） thin out: ▸～苗
▸jiān
【间壁】jiànbì〈名〉 next door
【间谍】jiàndié〈名〉 spy: ～活动 espionage ‖ 军事/商业～ military/commercial spy
【间断】jiànduàn〈动〉 be interrupted: 他不～地讲了两个小时。He kept talking for two hours without pause. ‖ 他天天跑步，从不～。He runs every day without fail.
【间伐】 jiànfá 〈名〉［林业］ intermediate cutting
【间隔】jiàngé **A**〈名〉 interval: 以10米的～排列 be arranged at intervals of ten metres ‖ 菜苗～匀整。The vegetable seedlings are evenly spaced. **B**〈动〉 cut off: 两节课之间～十分钟。There is a ten-minute break between the two classes.
【间隔号】jiàngéhào〈名〉 separation dot (·)
【间或】jiànhuò〈副〉〈书〉 now and then: 会场里很肃静，～有一两下咳嗽声。There was complete silence in the meeting hall, with occasional coughs here and there.
【间接】jiànjiē〈形〉 indirect: 他只～提到这件事。He only made indirect reference to it. ‖ 这事我是～听到的。I heard about it second-hand.
【间接宾语】 jiànjiē bīnyǔ 〈名〉［语言］ indirect object
【间接经验】 jiànjiē jīngyàn 〈名〉 indirect experience
【间接贸易】 jiànjiē màoyì 〈名〉 indirect trade
【间接税】jiànjiēshuì〈名〉 indirect tax
【间接损失】jiànjiē sǔnshī〈名〉 consequential loss
【间接选举】 jiànjiē xuǎnjǔ 〈名〉 indirect election
【间接引语】 jiànjiē yǐnyǔ 〈名〉［语言］ indirect speech
【间接证据】 jiànjiē zhèngjù 〈名〉 circumstantial evidence
【间苗】jiànmiáo〈动〉 thin out seedlings
【间日】jiànrì〈名〉〈书〉 every other day
【间隙】 jiànxì 〈名〉 gap: 利用工作～读书 read during one's breaks ‖ 电视和墙壁之间应留有～。You should leave a space between the television and the wall.
【间歇】 jiànxiē 〈动〉 intermit: ～性发作 intermittent attack ‖ ～性疼痛 intermittent ache ‖ ～喷泉 geyser
【间杂】jiànzá〈动〉 be mixed: 黑白～ mixture of black and white ‖ 歌声中～着笑声。Singing intermingled with laughing.
【间作】jiànzuò〈动〉［农业］ intercrop: 实行～套种 adopt intercropping and interplanting

饯[1]（餞） jiàn〈动〉 give a farewell dinner: ▸～别，～行

饯[2]（餞） jiàn〈动〉 preserved fruit: ▸蜜～

【饯别】jiànbié = 饯行 jiànxíng
【饯行】jiànxíng〈动〉 give a farewell dinner: 为代表团～ hold a farewell dinner in honour of the delegation

建 jiàn

〈动〉 **1**（修筑） build: ～桥 construct a bridge ‖ ～一座纪念碑 erect a monument ▸～造，～筑，扩～，修～ **2**（成立） establish: ～一家公司 establish a company ▸～国，～交，创～ **3**（提出） propose: ▸～议
【建安】jiàn'ān〈名〉 Jian'an [title of the reign of Liu Xie (刘协), last emperor of the Eastern Han Dynasty]
【建材】jiàncái〈简称〉= 建筑材料
【建仓】jiàncāng〈动〉 buy stocks
【建党】jiàndǎng〈动〉 **1**（指成立） found a political party **2**（指建设） build up the Party
【建档】jiàndàng〈动〉 place sth. on file
【建都】jiàndū〈动〉 establish a capital: ～北京 make Beijing the capital
【建功立业】jiàngōng-lìyè〈成〉 make great contributions and accomplish great tasks
【建构】jiàngòu = 构建 gòujiàn
【建国】jiànguó〈动〉 **1**（指成立） establish a state: 庆祝中华人民共和国～60周年 celebrate the sixtieth anniversary of the founding of the People's Republic of China **2**（指建设） build up a country: ～大计 important matters relating to national construction
【建交】 jiànjiāo 〈动〉 establish diplomatic relations: 两国于1983年～。The two countries established diplomatic relations in 1983.
【建军】jiànjūn〈动〉 **1**（指组建） found an army: ～节 Army Day **2**（指建设） build up the army: ～准则 principles of building an army
【建兰】jiànlán〈名〉［植物］ sword-leaved cymbidium
【建立】jiànlì〈动〉 **1**（指实体） set up: ～办事处 establish an office ‖ ～家庭 build up a family ‖ ～实验室 set up a laboratory **2**（指关系） establish: ～功勋 perform meritorious deeds ‖ ～合作关系 establish

j

cooperative ties ‖ ～联盟 forge an alliance ‖ ～联系 establish ties (with) ‖ ～新的经济体制 establish a new economic structure ‖ ～在牢固的基础上 be built on a solid foundation

【建设】jiànshè〈动〉build: ～国防/家乡 build up national defence/one's hometown ‖ ～有中国特色的社会主义国家 build a socialist country with Chinese characteristics ‖ 城市/经济～ urban/economic development

【建设性】jiànshèxìng〈形〉constructive: 提出～意见 come up with a constructive idea

【建设银行】jiànshè yínháng〈名〉Construction Bank

【建树】jiànshù **A**〈动〉make a contribution: 有所～ make something of a contribution **B**〈名〉contribution: 毫无～ accomplish nothing ‖ 颇有～ have many attainments to one's credit

【建言】jiànyán〈动〉offer a suggestion

【建议】jiànyì **A**〈动〉propose: 他～乘飞机去。He suggested travelling by plane. ‖ 医生～他戒烟。The doctor advised him to give up smoking. **B**〈名〉proposal: 提出～ put forward suggestions ‖ 按照某人的～行事 act on sb.'s suggestion ‖ 合理/可行的～ reasonable/workable suggestion

【建造】jiànzào〈动〉build: ～办公大楼 erect an office block ‖ ～房屋 build houses ‖ 新的摩天大楼正在～中。A new skyscraper is under construction.

【建制】jiànzhì〈名〉organizational system: 军队～ organizational system of the army

【建筑】jiànzhù **A**〈动〉construct: ～公路/桥梁 build a highway/bridge ‖ ～承包商/工程师 construction contractor/engineer ‖ ～造型艺术 the art of architectural modelling ‖ 住宅～ residential construction ‖〈喻〉不要把自己的幸福～在别人的痛苦之上。Don't build your happiness on the suffering of other people. **B**〈名〉building: 高层/低层～ high-rise/low-rise building ‖ 古～ ancient buildings ‖ 临时～ temporary structures ►上层～

【建筑材料】jiànzhù cáiliào〈名〉building materials: 轻型～ light-weight building material

【建筑采光】jiànzhù cǎiguāng〈名〉[建筑] architectural lighting

【建筑队】jiànzhùduì〈名〉construction team

【建筑工地】jiànzhù gōngdì〈名〉construction site

【建筑面积】jiànzhù miànjī〈名〉floor space: 总～ total floor area

【建筑群】jiànzhùqún〈名〉groups of buildings

【建筑师】jiànzhùshī ►p. 966〈名〉architect

【建筑物】jiànzhùwù〈名〉building

【建筑学】jiànzhùxué〈名〉architecture

【建筑业】jiànzhùyè〈名〉building industry

荐¹（薦）jiàn〈名〉〈书〉1（草席）straw mat: ►草～ 2（草料）straw

荐²（薦）jiàn〈动〉1（推举）recommend: ►～举，推～，毛遂自～ 2〈书〉（祭）sacrifice: 我以我血～轩辕。I am determined to give my life to my motherland.

【荐举】jiànjǔ〈动〉recommend: 他们～他当主席。They recommended him for the chair.

【荐贤举能】jiànxián-jǔnéng〈成〉recommend virtuous and talented people

【荐引】jiànyǐn〈动〉〈书〉recommend: 经他～，我进了银行工作。With his recommendation, I got into banking work.

贱（賤）jiàn〈形〉1（价格低）inexpensive: ～买贵卖 buy cheap and sell high ‖ 菜价～了。Vegetable prices went down. 2（地位低）lowly: ►～民，贫～，微～ 3（品格低）base: ►～骨头，～货，下～ 4〈谦〉（我的）my: ►～内

【贱骨头】jiàngǔtou〈名〉1〈粗〉（指不自重）miserable wretch 2〈诙〉（指自甘受苦）trouble seeker: 这个～宁可走路也不愿坐车。The poor wretch would rather walk than take a bus.

【贱货】jiànhuò〈名〉1（指物）shoddy goods 2〈粗〉（指人）miserable wretch

【贱卖】jiànmài〈动〉sell cheap: 大～ sell sth. at a crazy price

【贱民】jiànmín〈名〉〈旧〉person of the lowest social status: 他们被视若～。They were treated as social pariahs.

【贱内】jiànnèi〈名〉〈旧〉〈谦〉my humble wife

【贱人】jiànrén〈名〉〈旧〉〈粗〉[usu used in novels] slut〈粗〉

氼 jiàn〈动〉1（支撑）support at an oblique angle: 打～拨正 support and right sth. 2（用土石挡水）keep water off with earth and rocks

剑（劍）jiàn〈名〉sword: 佩～ carry a sword ►～客，击～，刻舟求～

【剑拔弩张】jiànbá-nǔzhāng〈成〉at daggers drawn: 两国处于～、势不两立的状态。The two countries were bitterly hostile and irreconcilable.

【剑齿虎】jiànchǐhǔ〈名〉[考古] sabre-toothed tiger

【剑齿象】jiànchǐxiàng〈名〉[考古] stegodon

【剑道】jiàndào〈名〉[体育] kendo

【剑客】jiànkè〈名〉〈旧〉chivalrous swordsman: 女～ swordswoman

【剑兰】jiànlán〈名〉[植物] gladiolus

【剑麻】jiànmá〈名〉[植物] sisal

【剑眉】jiànméi〈名〉dashing eyebrows: ～倒竖 flare one's eyebrows

【剑桥】Jiànqiáo〈名〉Cambridge

【剑桥郡】Jiànqiáojùn〈名〉Cambridgeshire

【剑鞘】jiànqiào〈名〉scabbard

【剑术】jiànshù〈名〉swordsmanship: 练习～ practise swordsmanship

【剑坛】jiàntán〈名〉swordplay circles: ～高手 swordplay master ‖ ～新秀 rising star fencer

【剑舞】jiànwǔ〈名〉sword dance

【剑侠】jiànxiá〈名〉〈旧〉chivalrous swordsman: 女～ swordswoman

涧（澗）jiàn〈名〉ravine: ►山～，溪～

监（監）jiàn〈名〉imperial office: 钦天～ Board of Astronomy ►～生，国子～ ►jiān

【监生】jiànshēng〈名〉〈古〉student of the Imperial College in the Ming and Qing dynasties

健 jiàn

A〈形〉healthy: 体～貌美 be healthy and handsome ►～康，～美，强～
B〈动〉1（使强壮）strengthen: ～脑/脾/胃 invigorate the brain/spleen/stomach ►～身，保～ 2（善于）be good at: ►～谈，～忘

【健步】jiànbù〈动〉walk with vigorous strides: ～走上讲台 mount the platform with vigorous steps ‖ ～如飞 walk fast and vigorously

【健存】jiàncún = 健在 jiànzài

【健儿】jiàn'ér〈名〉top athlete: 体操～ skilful gymnasts ‖ 中国奥运～ Chinese Olympians

【健将】jiànjiàng〈名〉1（指运动员）top sportsman: 乒乓球～ ace ping-pong player ‖ 游泳～ top-notch swimmer 2（指称号）master sportsman: 国家男篮有六个～。There are six top sportsmen in the Men's National Basketball Team. 3（能手）master: 文坛～ man of letters

【健康】jiànkāng〈形〉healthy: 恢复～ be restored to health ‖ 有害/有益～ do harm/good to sb.'s health ‖ 身体～ physical health ‖ 祝您～长寿! I wish you health and longevity! ‖ 身心～ be sound in mind and body ‖ 工业在～发展。The industry is doing fairly well.

【健康状况】jiànkāng zhuàngkuàng〈名〉health conditions: ～不佳 out of shape ‖ ～良好 in good health

【健美】jiànměi **A**〈形〉strong and handsome: 体形～ have a healthy and graceful body **B**〈名〉body-building: ～比赛 body-building contest

【健美操】jiànměicāo〈名〉aerobic exercise

【健美运动】jiànměi yùndòng〈名〉body-building

【健全】jiànquán **A**〈形〉sound: 四肢～ be physically sound ‖ 头脑～ be of sound mind ‖ ～人 able-bodied person ‖ 组织很～。The organization is sound. **B**〈动〉strengthen: ～必要的规章制度 strengthen necessary rules and regulations ‖ ～领导班子 strengthen the leadership ‖ ～社会保障制度 refine the social security system

【健身】jiànshēn〈动〉keep fit: ～场 health farm ‖ ～中心 fitness centre

【健身操】jiànshēncāo〈名〉callisthenics

【健身车】jiànshēnchē〈名〉stationary bike

【健身房】jiànshēnfáng〈名〉gym

【健身俱乐部】jiànshēn jùlèbù〈名〉health club

【健身器】jiànshēnqì〈名〉exercise equipment

【健身球】jiànshēnqiú〈名〉medicine ball

【健身运动】jiànshēn yùndòng〈名〉body-building: 全民～ Nationwide Bodybuilding campaign

【健谈】jiàntán〈形〉talkative: 她很～。She is a good talker.

【健忘】jiànwàng〈形〉forgetful: 他越来越～。His memory is getting worse and worse.

【健忘症】jiànwàngzhèng ►p. 50〈名〉[医学] amnesia

【健旺】jiànwàng〈形〉〈书〉healthy and vigorous: 祖父年近八旬，精神还很～。My grandfather is almost eighty, and he is still healthy and vigorous.

【健在】jiànzài〈动〉[of a person of advanced age] be still living and in good health: 父母都还～。The parents are both still alive and in good health.

【健壮】jiànzhuàng〈形〉healthy and strong: ～的体魄 strong body

j

舰（艦） jiàn〈名〉naval vessel: ▸～队，航空母～，战～
【舰船】jiànchuán〈名〉ships
【舰队】jiànduì〈名〉fleet: 第七～ Seventh Fleet [US] ‖ 海军～ naval fleet ‖ 特混～ task fleet ‖ ～司令 admiral
【舰首】jiànshǒu〈名〉bow
【舰艇】jiàntǐng〈名〉naval vessel: 作战～ combat ship
【舰尾】jiànwěi〈名〉stern
【舰载】jiànzài〈形〉ship-based: ～导弹 ship-based missile ‖ ～雷达 ship-borne radar
【舰长】jiànzhǎng〈名〉captain
【舰只】jiànzhī〈名〉naval vessel: 海军～ naval vessels

渐（漸） jiàn〈副〉gradually: 天气～热。The weather is getting hot. ‖ 夜色～浓。Darkness is gathering.
▸jiān
【渐变】jiànbiàn〈动〉change gradually: 由～到突变 from a gradual change to a sudden change
【渐次】jiàncì〈副〉〈书〉gradually: 脚步声～停息。The footsteps gradually stopped.
【渐渐】jiànjiàn〈副〉gradually: 雪～融化了。Little by little the snow melted. ‖ 战斗～平息。The fighting died down.
【渐进】jiànjìn〈动〉advance gradually: ▸循序～
【渐入佳境】jiànrù-jiājìng〈成〉getting better
【渐悟】jiànwù〈动〉1 [佛教] gradually awaken to the truth 2（指领悟）come to realize

谏（諫） jiàn〈动〉〈书〉admonish: 拒～ reject sb.'s criticisms ‖ 直言敢～ be outspoken and dare to make remonstrances ▸兵～，进～
【谏诤】jiànzhèng〈动〉〈书〉point out sb.'s faults frankly and urge him to correct them
【谏阻】jiànzǔ〈动〉admonish sb. not to do sth.

楗 jiàn〈名〉〈书〉1（门闩）door bolt 2（桩柱）materials used to stop the breaching of a dyke

践（踐） jiàn〈动〉1（踏）tread: ▸～踏 2（履行）carry out: ▸～约，实～
【践诺】jiànnuò〈动〉〈书〉keep one's promise
【践踏】jiàntà〈动〉1（踩）tread on: 请勿～草地! Keep off the grass! 2（摧残）trample on: ～民主与法制 show no consideration for democracy or law ‖ ～别国主权 infringe on the sovereignty of another country
【践约】jiànyuē〈动〉keep a promise: 他如时～，来到我们学院。He kept his promise and came to our university at the scheduled time.

锏（鐧） jiàn〈名〉iron protection for a wheel axle
▸jiǎn

毽 jiàn〈名〉shuttlecock
【毽子】jiànzi〈名〉shuttlecock: 踢～ play shuttlecock

> **踢毽子**
>
> A traditional Chinese shuttlecock sport. A base is made from copper coins or pieces of metal bound together with cloth. A bunch of chicken feathers or strips of paper are stuck on top. The sport involves kicking the shuttlecock in the air as many times as possible without letting it fall to the ground. There are four basic movements: '*pan*' (盘), which is kicking in turn with the insides of one's feet; '*ke*' (磕), which is knocking the shuttlecock with one's knee; '*guai*' (拐), which is hitting the shuttlecock with the outside of one's foot; and '*beng*' (蹦), which is kicking the shuttlecock with the tip of one's toes.

腱 jiàn〈名〉[解剖] tendon: ～组织 tendinous tissue ▸肌～
【腱鞘】jiànqiào〈名〉tendon sheath: ～炎 tenosynovitis
【腱子】jiànzi〈名〉shank: 烤牛～ roast beef shank

溅（濺） jiàn〈动〉splatter: 火花四～ sparks flying in all directions ‖ 汽车～了我们一身泥水。A passing car splashed us with mud and water from head to foot.
【溅落】jiànluò〈动〉1（指液体）spatter down: 雨水～下来。The rain spattered down. 2 [航天] splash down: ～点 splash point ‖ 宇宙飞船成功～在预定海域。The spaceship made a successful landing in the designated marine area.

鉴（鑒、鑑） jiàn
A〈名〉1（铜镜）ancient bronze mirror 2（借鉴）warning: 以史为～ take warning from history ▸～戒，借～
B〈动〉1（照）mirror: 光可～人 so shining and bright that it can serve as a mirror ‖ 水清可～。The water is so clear that you can see your reflection in it. 2（观察）scrutinize: ▸～别，～定，～赏
C〈套〉[usu used in the opening phrase in an old-fashioned letter]: ▸钧～，台～
【鉴别】jiànbié〈动〉distinguish: ～古董 appraise antiques ‖ ～真伪 discern the false from the genuine ‖ 没有比较就没有～。There can be no differentiation without contrast.
【鉴定】jiàndìng **A**〈动〉determine: ～笔迹/指纹 identify handwriting/a fingerprint ‖ ～产品/工程质量 appraise the quality of a product/project ‖ ～文物年代 determine the date of a cultural relic ‖ 自我～ self-evaluation **B**〈名〉appraisal: 给学生写～ write an appraisal of a student ‖ 毕业～ graduation appraisal
【鉴定会】jiàndìnghuì〈名〉appraising meeting
【鉴定人】jiàndìngrén〈名〉surveyor
【鉴定书】jiàndìngshū〈名〉written appraisal
【鉴戒】jiànjiè〈名〉〈书〉warning: 引为～ heed a warning
【鉴谅】jiànliàng〈动〉〈书〉〈套〉excuse me
【鉴赏】jiànshǎng〈动〉discriminate and appreciate: ～古典音乐 appreciate classical music ‖ ～家 connoisseur ‖ ～力 connoisseurship
【鉴往知来】jiànwǎng-zhīlái〈成〉predict the future by reviewing the past
【鉴于】jiànyú **A**〈介〉in view of: ～过去的经验教训，我们决定改变方法。Bearing in mind the lessons of the past, we decided to change our approach. **B**〈连〉considering: ～他已改正错误，你就原谅他吧。Considering he has already corrected his mistake, you really should forgive him.

键（鍵） jiàn〈名〉1〈书〉（金属棍）metal bolt [of a door] 2（部件）key: 功能～ function key ‖ 快捷～ shortcut key ▸～盘，琴～ 3 [机械] key: 轴～ shaft key 4 [化学] bond: ▸共价～
【键盘】jiànpán〈名〉keyboard: 钢琴～ piano keyboard ‖ 计算机～ computer keyboard
【键盘记录】jiànpán jìlù〈名〉keylogging
【键盘乐器】jiànpán yuèqì〈名〉keyboard instrument
【键入】jiànrù〈动〉key in: ～网址 key in a website address

槛（檻） jiàn〈名〉1（栅栏）cage: 兽～ animal cage 2（囚笼）cell: ～车 prison van 3（栏杆）balustrade
▸kǎn

僭 jiàn〈动〉〈书〉overstep one's authority: ～号 usurp the title of an emperor
【僭位】jiànwèi〈动〉〈书〉usurp the throne
【僭越】jiànyuè〈动〉〈书〉overstep one's authority

踺 jiàn
【踺子】jiànzi〈名〉[体育] somersault: ～前空翻/后空翻 do forward/backward somersault in the air

箭 jiàn〈名〉1（指兵器）arrow: 射～ shoot an arrow ▸～靶子，一～双雕 2（指距离）distance covered by a flying arrow: 一～之遥 a stone's throw 3（箭状物）arrow-like thing: ▸火～
【箭靶子】jiànbǎzi〈名〉archery target: 瞄准～ aim at the archery target
【箭步】jiànbù〈名〉sudden big stride forward: 他一个～上前抓住了小偷。He made a big stride forward and caught the thief.
【箭垛子】jiànduǒzi〈名〉1（箭靶）parapet 2（指目标）archery target
【箭杆】jiàngǎn〈名〉arrow shaft
【箭楼】jiànlóu〈名〉embrasured watchtower over a city gate
【箭筒】jiàntǒng〈名〉arrow quiver
【箭头】jiàntóu〈名〉1（箭的尖头）arrowhead: 带毒药的～ poisoned arrowhead 2（指符号）arrow: ～方向 direction of an arrow ‖ 交通～标志 traffic arrow
【箭在弦上，不得不发】jiàn zài xián shàng, bùdébù fā〈歇后〉〈喻〉everything is ready and there can be no turning back: 如今已是～。We have already reached a point of no return.
【箭猪】jiànzhū〈名〉porcupine
【箭竹】jiànzhú〈名〉arrow bamboo
【箭镞】jiànzú〈名〉metal arrowhead

jiāng

江 jiāng〈名〉1 Jiāng（长江）the Yangtze River: ～汉 Yangtze-Hanshui Valley ‖ ～淮 Yangtze-Huaihe Valley ▸～北，～南 2 ▸**p. 164**（大河）river: 渡～ cross a

j

river ‖ 湘～ the Xiangjiang River ▸长～, 大～

【江北】Jiāngběi〈名〉1（长江下游北岸）areas north of the lower reaches of the Yangtze River 2（长江以北）north of the Yangtze River

【江东】Jiāngdōng〈名〉〈旧〉lower reaches of the Yangtze River

【江东父老】Jiāngdōng fùlǎo〈成〉elders of one's native place

【江防】jiāngfáng〈名〉1（水患防护）preventive flooding measures along a river 2（指军事防御）defence works along the Yangtze River: ～工事 defensive works along the Yangtze River

【江河日下】jiānghé-rìxià〈成〉go from bad to worse: 这家企业如今已～。The enterprise has gone from bad to worse.

【江湖】jiānghú〈名〉1（江河湖海）rivers and lakes 2（各地）all corners of the country: 流落～ lead a drifter's life ▸闯～, 走～ 3（指人）itinerant entertainers: ～郎中 quack

【江湖好汉】jiānghú hǎohàn〈名〉good fellow of the wide world

【江湖骗子】jiānghú piànzi〈名〉charlatan

【江湖医生】jiānghú yīshēng〈名〉quack

【江湖义气】jiānghú yìqi〈名〉loyalty to a brotherhood

【江湖艺人】jiānghú yìrén〈名〉wandering performer

【江郎才尽】Jiāngláng-cáijìn〈成〉have exhausted one's literary creative powers: 这位名作家晚年～，没有好作品问世。The renowned writer did not publish any quality works in his later years as his creative powers had dried up.

【江轮】jiānglún〈名〉river steamer

【江米】jiāngmǐ〈名〉polished glutinous rice: ～酒 fermented glutinous rice wine

【江米纸】jiāngmǐzhǐ〈名〉paper made of glutinous rice

【江南】Jiāngnán〈名〉1（长江下游以南）areas south of the lower reaches of the Yangtze River 2（长江以南）south of the Yangtze River: 春风又绿～岸。Spring breezes bring greenness to the southern Yangtze region again.

【江畔】jiāngpàn〈名〉river bank

【江山】jiāngshān〈名〉1（自然风光）landscape: ～如画 beautiful scenery ‖ ～如此多娇。The land is so rich in beauty. 2（国家）country: 人民的～ the people's country ‖ 不爱～爱美人 love beauty rather than the throne

【江山易改，秉性难移】jiāngshān yì gǎi, bǐngxìng nán yí〈俗〉a leopard cannot change its spots

【江苏】Jiāngsū ▸**p. 661**〈名〉Jiangsu Province

【江天】jiāngtiān〈名〉vast sky over the river: ～一色。The river and the sky are of the same hue.

【江豚】jiāngtún〈名〉［动物］finless porpoise

【江西】Jiāngxī ▸**p. 661**〈名〉Jiangxi Province

【江心】jiāngxīn〈名〉middle of a river

【江心补漏】jiāngxīn-bǔlòu〈成〉〈喻〉too late to mend

【江洋大盗】jiāngyáng-dàdào〈名〉infamous pirate

将（將）jiāng

A〈动〉1〈书〉（带着）bring: 挈妇～雏 bring one's wife and children along 2（保养）take care of one's health: ▸～息, ～养 3〈书〉（拿）fetch: ～宝剑来。Bring me the sword. 4（指下象棋）check: 他没走几步棋就把我～死了。He checkmated my king in under several moves. 5（激将）incite sb. to action: 你再～他也没用。It's no use egging him on. 6〈书〉（处理）handle: 慎重～事 handle a matter with care **B**〈介〉1（用）with: ～鸡蛋碰石头 hit the stone with an egg ▸～错就错, ～功折罪, 恩～仇报 2（把）[used in the same way as 把]: ～医生请来 send for a doctor ‖ ～灯打开。Turn on the light. **C**〈副〉will: 我～尽力而为。I will try my best to do it well. **D**〈助〉〈方〉[used between a verb and its complement of direction]: 唱～起来 start to sing ‖ 走～出来 walk out

▸jiàng, qiāng

【将错就错】jiāngcuò-jiùcuò〈成〉accept a mistake and make the best of it: 人要知错就改，岂能～? If you've made a mistake then you should correct it. How could you just live with it?

【将功补过】jiānggōng-bǔguò〈成〉make up for one's mistakes with good deeds

【将功赎罪】jiānggōng-shúzuì〈成〉redeem one's sins by doing good deeds

【将功折罪】jiānggōng-zhézuì = 将功赎罪 jiānggōng-shúzuì

【将计就计】jiāngjì-jiùjì〈成〉beat sb. at his own game

【将将】jiāngjiāng〈副〉〈口〉barely: 他的工资～够过日子。His salary is barely enough to make a living.

【将近】jiāngjìn〈动〉be close to: ～半年 almost half a year ‖ ～完工 be almost completed

【将就】jiāngjiu〈动〉make do with: 我们没有空调，只能～点了。We haven't got an air conditioner, so we'll have to make do without.

【将军】jiāngjūn **A**〈动〉1（指下象棋）check 2（难为）put sb. on the spot: 他们将了我一军，要我给大家唱京剧。They put me on the spot by asking me to sing them Beijing opera. **B**〈名〉1（将级军官）general: 他是一位～。He is a general. 2（高级将领）high-ranking military officer

【将军肚】jiāngjūndù〈名〉〈诙〉pot-belly: 挺着～ stick out one's big belly

【将来】jiānglái〈名〉future: 在不久的～ in the near future ‖ ～会发生什么事呢? What will happen in the future?

【将息】jiāngxī〈动〉rest: 她出院以后一直在家～。She's been recuperating at home after being discharged from hospital.

【将心比心】jiāngxīn-bǐxīn〈成〉〈喻〉put oneself in another person's shoes

【将信将疑】jiāngxìn-jiāngyí〈成〉half believing, half doubting: 我对她的话～。I only half believe what she said.

【将养】jiāngyǎng〈动〉convalesce: 你还要～几个月才能痊愈。You have to rest for several months before you fully recover.

【将要】jiāngyào〈副〉going to: ～下雨了。It's going to rain. ‖ 我孩子～上大学。My child is going to university.

姜（薑）jiāng〈名〉ginger: ～粉 ground ginger ‖ ～片 ginger slice

【姜还是老的辣】jiāng háishi lǎode là〈俗〉veterans are better than newcomers

【姜黄】jiānghuáng **A**〈名〉［植物］turmeric **B**〈形〉ginger-coloured: 他的头发略带～色。His hair was a bright shade of ginger.

【姜太公钓鱼，愿者上钩】Jiāng Tàigōng diàoyú, yuànzhě shànggōu〈歇后〉willingly play into sb.'s hands

【姜汤】jiāngtāng〈名〉ginger tea

【姜糖】jiāngtáng〈名〉ginger candy

【姜汁】jiāngzhī〈名〉ginger juice: ～汽水 ginger ale

豇 jiāng

【豇豆】jiāngdòu〈名〉cowpea

浆（漿）jiāng

A〈名〉thick liquid: ▸泥～, 糖～, 纸～ **B**〈动〉starch: 把衣服～挺 stiffen clothes with starch ‖ ～过的制服 starched uniforms

▸jiàng

【浆果】jiāngguǒ〈名〉berry: ～类果树 berry-bearing tree

【浆洗】jiāngxǐ〈动〉wash and starch: ～衣服 wash and starch clothes

【浆液】jiāngyè〈名〉serous fluid: ～浸润 serous infiltration

僵 jiāng〈形〉1（僵硬）stiff: 冻～ numb with cold ‖ 发～ get stiff ▸～化, ～硬, ～直 2（僵持）deadlocked: 把事情弄～ bring things to a deadlock ‖ 他俩闹～了。Those two are difficult with each other. ▸～持, ～局

【僵持】jiāngchí〈动〉be locked in a stalemate: 形成～局面 a stalemate situation is developing ‖ 双方～不下。The two parties are caught in a deadlock.

【僵化】jiānghuà〈动〉become rigid: 思想～ have a rigid way of thinking ‖ ～的经济体制 rigid economic structures

【僵局】jiāngjú〈名〉deadlock: 打破～ break a deadlock ‖ 陷入～ reach an impasse ‖ 谈判中的～ deadlock in negotiations ‖ 谈判陷入～。The negotiations have reached a deadlock.

【僵尸】jiāngshī〈名〉1（指尸体）stiffened corpse: 发现一具～ find a corpse 2〈喻〉walking dead

【僵死】jiāngsǐ〈动〉die: ～的教条 dead dogma

【僵硬】jiāngyìng〈形〉1（指肢体）stiff: 脖子～ have a stiff neck ‖ 肢体～ stiff limbs 2（呆板）rigid: ～的方法/态度 inflexible approach/attitude

【僵直】jiāngzhí〈形〉stiff and rigid: 两腿～ feel stiff in both legs

螀 jiāng ▸寒螀 hánjiāng

缰（韁、繮）jiāng〈名〉reins: 马脱～了。The horse slipped its reins. ▸～绳

【缰绳】jiāngshéng〈名〉reins: 勒紧～ pull on the reins

鳉（鱂）jiāng

【鳉鱼】jiāngyú〈名〉killifish

疆 jiāng〈名〉1（边界）border: ▸～界, ～土, 边～ 2 Jiāng（新疆）Jiang [another name for Xinjiang Uygur Autonomous Region（新疆）]: 南～ southern part of the Xinjiang Uygur Autonomous Region

【疆场】jiāngchǎng〈名〉battlefield: 驰骋～ gallop across the battlefield ‖ 战死～ die on the battlefield

【疆界】jiāngjiè〈名〉border: 划定～ designate a border

j

【疆土】jiāngtǔ〈名〉territory: 保卫国家的～ defend one's country territory ‖ ～辽阔 have a vast territory

【疆域】jiāngyù〈名〉territory: ～辽阔 have a vast territory

jiǎng

讲（講） jiǎng〈动〉**1**（说）tell: ～故事 tell a story ‖ 她日语～得很流利。She speaks Japanese fluently. ‖ 这件事你对他～了吗？ Have you told him about it? **2**（就…而言）be regarding: ～口语，他不如你；～写作，他比你强。His spoken English is not as good as yours, but when it comes to writing, he is better than you. ‖ ～容貌，她比两个妹妹都漂亮。As far as appearance goes, she is more beautiful than her two younger sisters. **3**（商议）discuss: ～条件 negotiate the terms ‖ 我们已经～定：他上街买东西，我做饭。We've made a pact that he will do the shopping and I'll cook. **4**（解说）explain: 摆事实，～道理 present the facts and reason things out ‖ 这本书是～语法的。This is a book about grammar. **5**（注重）stress: ～礼貌 stress courtesy ‖ ～卫生 pay attention to hygiene ‖ 首先要～质量，不能只～数量。We should put quality above everything else, not just emphasize quantity.

【讲法】jiǎngfǎ〈名〉**1**（措词）wording: 换一种～ in other words **2**（看法）explanation: 他的～很牵强。His explanation was far-fetched.

【讲稿】jiǎnggǎo〈名〉**1**（为讲演）draft or text of a speech: 发言不用～ speak without notes **2**（为授课）lecture notes: 念～ read out the lecture notes

【讲和】jiǎnghé〈动〉make peace: 她拒绝同丈夫～。She refused to settle things with her husband. ‖ 他们已经～了。They have made peace with each other.

【讲话】jiǎnghuà **A**〈动〉**1**（说话）talk: 会上大家都讲了话。Everybody spoke at the meeting. ‖ 她很会～。She is a very good speaker. **2**（批评）criticize: 你搞特殊，人家当然要～。You seek personal privileges and naturally others will take you to task for it. **B**〈名〉**1**（讲演）speech: 发表电视～ make a televised address ‖ 精彩/振奋人心的～ excellent/inspiring speech ‖ 劳模的～使听众深受感动。The model worker's speech moved his audience deeply. **2**（解释）[often used in book titles] guide: 《现代汉语语法～》*A Handbook of Modern Chinese Grammar*

【讲价】jiǎngjià〈动〉bargain: 拒绝～ refuse to bargain over the price

【讲价钱】jiǎng jiàqian〈动〉**1**（指价格）bargain **2**〈喻〉（指条件）negotiate the terms: 她在执行任务时从不～。Whatever task she takes on she makes sure to do the job thoroughly.

【讲解】jiǎngjiě〈动〉explain: ～课文 explain a text ‖ ～新法律 interpret the new law

【讲解员】jiǎngjiěyuán ▸**p. 966**〈名〉**1**（指展览）stand-attendant **2**（指博物馆）guide

【讲究】jiǎngjiu **A**〈动〉be particular about: ～吃喝/穿戴 be particular about one's food/clothes ‖ ～实事求是 strive to seek truth from facts ‖ ～卫生 pay attention to hygiene **B**〈名〉careful study: 插花大有～。Flower arranging is quite an art. **C**〈形〉tasteful: 做工～的上衣 coat of exquisite workmanship ‖ 屋子布置得很～。The house was tastefully furnished.

【讲课】jiǎngkè〈动〉teach: 讲历史/地理课 give lessons in history/geography ‖ 给学生～ lecture to students

【讲阔气】jiǎng kuòqi〈动〉go in for extravagance

【讲理】jiǎnglǐ〈动〉**1**（辩明是非）argue: 跟他没什么道理可讲。There is no reasoning with him. ‖ 咱们跟他～去。Let's reason things out with him. **2**（通情理）be reasonable: 蛮不～ be impervious to reason

【讲面子】jiǎng miànzi〈动〉care about sb.'s sensibilities

【讲明】jiǎngmíng〈动〉explain

【讲排场】jiǎng páichang〈动〉go in for ostentation and extravagance: 爱虚荣，～ be very vain and ostentatious

【讲评】jiǎngpíng〈动〉comment on: ～时事 comment on current affairs ‖ ～学生作文 appraise student compositions

【讲情】jiǎngqíng〈动〉plead: 替某人向法官～ plead with a judge for sb.

【讲求】jiǎngqiú〈动〉strive for: ～实效 strive for practical results ‖ 教学要～方法。We should pay attention to our teaching methods.

【讲师】jiǎngshī〈名〉lecturer: 被聘为～ be offered a lectureship ‖ ～资格 lectureship ‖ 高级～ senior lecturer

【讲授】jiǎngshòu〈动〉teach: ～历史/汉语 teach history/Chinese ‖ 她～美国文学。She lectures on American literature.

【讲述】jiǎngshù〈动〉relate: ～个人经历 give an account of one's personal history ‖ 受害人向警方～了这起事件。The victim related his version of the incident to the police.

【讲台】jiǎngtái〈名〉platform: 登上～ mount a platform

【讲坛】jiǎngtán〈名〉**1**（指台子）platform **2**（指场合）forum: 为学术交流提供～ provide a forum for academic exchange

【讲堂】jiǎngtáng〈名〉lecture room

【讲习】jiǎngxí〈动〉**1**（讲课和学习）lecture and study: ～班 study group **2**（研究）research

【讲学】jiǎngxué〈动〉give lectures: 应邀出国～ be invited to give lectures abroad

【讲演】jiǎngyǎn **A**〈动〉give a lecture: ～比赛 speech contest ‖ 他将在附近高校巡回～。He will tour the nearby universities to give lectures. **B**〈名〉lecture, speech: 听～ attend a lecture ‖ 专题～ lecture on a special topic

【讲演者】jiǎngyǎnzhě〈名〉lecturer

【讲义】jiǎngyì〈名〉lecture notes: 编写～ compile teaching materials ‖ ～夹 lecture portfolio

【讲义气】jiǎng yìqi〈动〉be loyal to friends

【讲桌】jiǎngzhuō〈名〉lectern

【讲座】jiǎngzuò〈名〉course of lectures: 举办英语～ give lectures on English ‖ 系列～ series of lectures

奖（奬） jiǎng

A〈动〉**1**（表扬）commend: ▸～励，褒～，夸～ **2**（奖赏）reward: 有功者～。Those who have gained merit will be rewarded. **B**〈名〉**1**（指荣誉）prize: 得～ win a prize ‖ 诺贝尔～ Nobel Prize ‖ 最佳男/女演员～ award for the best actor/actress ▸颁～，获～，评～ **2**（奖金）prize money: ▸中～

【奖杯】jiǎngbēi〈名〉trophy: 颁发～ present the cup ‖ 世界杯～ World Cup Trophy

【奖惩】jiǎngchéng〈动〉reward and punish: ～分明 be fair in meting out rewards and punishments ‖ ～条例 regulations concerning rewards and disciplinary sanctions

【奖级】jiǎngjí〈名〉grade of prizes or awards

【奖金】jiǎngjīn〈名〉bonus: （给某人）发～ award bonuses (to sb.) ‖ 本公司～上不封顶，下不保底。Our company imposes no upper or lower limits on bonuses.

【奖励】jiǎnglì〈动〉reward: ～发明创造 encourage inventions by giving awards ‖ ～贡献突出者 reward those who have made outstanding contributions ‖ 受到～ be awarded ‖ 物质～ material reward

【奖牌】jiǎngpái〈名〉medal: 囊括所有～ bag all the medals ‖ ～榜 medal tally ‖ 奥运～得主 Olympic medallist

【奖品】jiǎngpǐn〈名〉prize: 颁发～ present an award

【奖旗】jiǎngqí〈名〉(silk) banner: 墙上挂着几面～。Several silk banners hung on the wall.

【奖勤罚懒】jiǎngqín-fálǎn〈成〉reward the diligent and punish the lazy

【奖券】jiǎngquàn〈名〉lottery ticket: 发行～ institute a lottery ‖ 福利/体育～ welfare/sports lottery

【奖赏】jiǎngshǎng〈动〉reward: ～有功人员 award those who have performed meritorious deeds ‖ 受到～ receive a reward

【奖售】jiǎngshòu〈动〉**1**（指鼓励出售）encourage sales (to the state by giving incentives): ～化肥 state-subsidized fertilizer ‖ ～政策 policy of premiums for sale **2**（指作为奖励）sell (sth. that is hard to get or at a reduced price) as a reward: 这些房子将～给劳模。These flats will be sold to the model workers at a reduced price as a reward.

【奖项】jiǎngxiàng〈名〉prize: 获得两个～ win two prizes ‖ 最高～ highest prize

【奖许】jiǎngxǔ〈动〉give encouragement (to)

【奖学金】jiǎngxuéjīn〈名〉scholarship: 获得～ receive a scholarship ‖ 设立～ found a scholarship ‖ 申请～ apply for a scholarship ‖ 享受～ hold a scholarship

【奖掖】jiǎngyè〈动〉〈书〉reward and promote: ～后进 encourage and promote one's juniors

【奖章】jiǎngzhāng〈名〉medal: 获得～ get a medal ‖ 授予～ award a medal ‖ 金/银/铜质～ gold/silver/bronze medal

【奖状】jiǎngzhuàng〈名〉certificate of merit: （给某人）颁发～ award a certificate of merit (to sb.)

桨（槳） jiǎng〈名〉oar: 划～ feather oars

蒋（蔣） Jiǎng〈名〉Jiang [surname]

耩 jiǎng〈动〉sow with a drill

膙 jiǎng

【膙子】jiǎngzi〈名〉〈方〉callus: 双手长满～ have calluses on one's hands

jiàng

匠 jiàng〈名〉 1（工匠）craftsman: 皮～ artisan in leatherwork ▸工～, 木～, 能工巧～ 2（专家）master: ▸巨～

【匠气】jiàngqì〈名〉 unimaginative craftsmanship: ～十足的印章 a rather mediocre seal

【匠人】jiàngrén〈名〉 craftsman

【匠心】jiàngxīn〈名〉〈书〉 craftsmanship: 颇具～ show great originality ▸独具～

【匠心独运】jiàngxīn-dúyùn〈成〉 have great originality

降 jiàng〈动〉 1（落下）fall: 从天而～ fall from the sky ‖ 温度大幅下～。The temperature has dropped considerably. ▸～落 2（使降低）reduce: ～下帷幕 bring down a curtain ‖ ～薪 cut sb.'s salary ▸～级, ～旗, ～压 3（出生）be born: ▸～生
▸xiáng

【降班】jiàngbān〈动〉 1（降级）send to a lower grade 2（留级）repeat a year

【降半旗】jiàng bànqí = 下半旗 xià bànqí

【降尘】jiàngchén〈名〉 fallen dust

【降低】jiàngdī〈动〉 reduce: ～价格 lower prices ‖ ～生产成本 lower the production cost ‖ ～要求 moderate one's demands ‖ 把损失～到最低限度 reduce damage to the minimum

【降调】jiàngdiào〈名〉［语言］falling tone/tune

【降幅】jiàngfú〈名〉 extent of decrease: 汽车价格～达20%。Car prices have fallen at a rate of up to 20%.

【降格】jiànggé〈动〉 lower one's standard: ～录取 admit sb. by lowering standards ‖ 两国关系～ lower the level of diplomatic relations between the two countries

【降格以求】jiànggéyǐqiú〈成〉 settle for second best

【降号】jiànghào〈名〉［音乐］flat

【降耗】jiànghào〈动〉 reduce consumption: 节能～ save energy and reduce consumption

【降级】jiàngjí〈动〉 1（指级别）demote: 因受贿被～ be demoted for taking bribes 2（指年级）send to a lower grade: 他因考试不及格被～。He was sent down a grade for his failure in the examination.

【降价】jiàngjià〈动〉 bring down the price: ～处理 sell sth. at a reduced price ‖ 大幅度～ sweeping reductions in price

【降解】jiàngjiě〈名〉［化学］degradation: 可～塑料 degradable plastics

【降临】jiànglín〈动〉〈书〉befall: 夜幕～。Dusk descended. ‖ 一场大难～到他的头上。A great misfortune befell him.

【降落】jiàngluò〈动〉 land: 安全～ make a safe landing ‖ 在机场～ touch down at the airport

【降落伞】jiàngluòsǎn〈名〉 parachute: 打开～ open a parachute

【降幂】jiàngmì〈名〉［数学］descending power: ～级数 series of descending powers

【降旗】jiàngqí〈动〉 lower a flag

【降生】jiàngshēng〈动〉 be born: 一个小生命～了。A baby was born.

【降水】jiàngshuǐ〈动〉［气象］fall: 人工～ artificial precipitation ‖ 未来两天将有强～。There will be heavy precipitation in the next two days.

【降水概率】jiàngshuǐ gàilǜ〈名〉 precipitation probability

【降水量】jiàngshuǐliàng〈名〉 precipitation: 年～ annual precipitation

【降温】jiàngwēn〈动〉 1（指体温）lower the temperature: 防暑～ lower the temperature to prevent heatstroke 2（指气温）fall: 受寒流影响，本市今夜开始～。Due to a cold current, the temperature in our city will start falling tonight. 3〈喻〉（指势头）cool down: 房地产热开始～。The property market craze is beginning to cool down.

【降息】jiàngxī〈动〉 lower the interest rate

【降心相从】jiàngxīn-xiāngcóng〈成〉 submit to others against one's will

【降薪】jiàngxīn〈动〉 reduce a salary: 国企高管主动～。Executives of state-owned enterprises are volunteering to take a salary cut.

【降雪】jiàngxuě〈动〉 snow

【降雪量】jiàngxuěliàng〈名〉 snowfall

【降压】jiàngyā〈动〉 1［电气］reduce voltage: ～变压器 step-down transformer 2（指血压）bring down blood pressure: ～药 hypertensive medicine

【降雨】jiàngyǔ〈动〉rain: 人工～ make rain

【降雨量】jiàngyǔliàng〈名〉 rainfall: 年～ annual rainfall

【降噪】jiàngzào〈动〉 reduce the noise

【降职】jiàngzhí〈动〉 demote: ～处分 punish by demoting

【降旨】jiàngzhǐ〈动〉〈旧〉 issue an imperial edict

虹 jiàng〈名〉 rainbow
▸hóng

将（將） jiàng

A〈动〉〈书〉 command: ～兵出征 lead troops to battle

B〈名〉 1（将领）high-ranking officer: ▸～士, 损兵折～ 2（将军）general: ▸～官, 少～, 中～ 3〈喻〉（中坚力量）backbone: ▸干～, 老～
▸jiāng, qiāng

【将才】jiàngcái〈名〉 1（指能力）ability to lead or command troops 2（指人）person with military talent: 难得的～ rare person with the ability to command troops

【将官】jiàngguān〈名〉 general

【将官】jiàngguan〈名〉 high-ranking military officer

【将领】jiànglǐng〈名〉 high-ranking military officer: 高级～ high-ranking officer

【将门】jiàngmén〈名〉 family of a general: 出身～ come from a general's family ‖ ～之子 descendant of a general

【将门虎子】jiàngmén-hǔzǐ〈成〉〈喻〉 capable young man of distinguished parentage

【将门无犬子】jiàngmén wú quǎnzǐ〈俗〉〈喻〉 a good tree cannot produce rotten fruit

【将士】jiàngshì〈名〉〈书〉 officers and men: 全军～ all the officers and soldiers

【将帅】jiàngshuài〈名〉 high-ranking commander: 他有～之才。He is a man with the talent to be a good general.

【将校】jiàngxiào〈名〉 1（指将官和校官）generals and field officers 2（指高级军官）high-ranking military officers

【将遇良材】jiàngyùliángcái〈成〉find one's own match: 棋逢对手，～。As an ace chess player meets his peer, so a general finds his own match in military talent.

【将在外，君命有所不受】jiàng zài wài, jūn mìng yǒusuǒ bù shòu〈成〉 a general at the front is not bound by orders from his sovereign

【将指】jiàngzhǐ〈名〉〈书〉 1（中指）middle finger 2（大脚趾）big toe

【将佐】jiàngzuǒ〈名〉〈书〉 high-ranking military officer

洚 jiàng〈动〉〈书〉overflow: ～水 flood

绛（絳） jiàng〈形〉 crimson

【绛紫】jiàngzǐ〈形〉 dark reddish purple: ～色的布料 cloth in dark reddish purple

浆（漿） jiàng = 糨 jiàng
▸jiāng

弶 jiàng

A〈名〉 trap

B〈动〉 trap

强 jiàng〈形〉 stubborn: ▸～嘴, 倔～
▸qiáng, qiǎng

【强嘴】jiàngzuǐ = 犟嘴 jiàngzuǐ

酱（醬） jiàng

A〈名〉 1（调味品）thick sauce made from soybeans, flour, etc. by fermenting: 豆瓣～ broad bean sauce ▸甜面～, 炸～面 2（糊状食品）sauce: 番茄～ tomato ketchup ‖ 果子～ fruit jam ‖ 辣椒～ chilli sauce ‖ 芝麻～ sesame paste

B〈动〉cook sth. in soy sauce: 把萝卜～一下 cook the radish in soy sauce

【酱爆】jiàngbào〈动〉 stir-fry with soy sauce: ～鸡丁 stir-fried diced chicken with soybean paste

【酱菜】jiàngcài〈名〉 vegetables in soy sauce

【酱豆腐】jiàngdòufu = 豆腐乳 dòufurǔ

【酱坊】jiàngfáng = 酱园 jiàngyuán

【酱缸】jiànggāng〈名〉jar for making thick soybean sauce, pickled vegetables, etc.

【酱肉】jiàngròu〈名〉 meat cooked in soy sauce

【酱色】jiàngsè ▸**p. 863**〈名〉 dark reddish brown

【酱油】jiàngyóu〈名〉 soy sauce

【酱园】jiàngyuán〈名〉 sauce and pickle shop

【酱紫】jiàngzǐ = 绛紫 jiàngzǐ

犟 jiàng〈形〉 stubborn: ～得像头牛 as stubborn as a mule ‖ 他脾气很～。He is very obstinate.

【犟劲】jiàngjìn〈名〉 indomitable will

【犟嘴】jiàngzuǐ〈动〉 answer back: 别和你母亲～。Don't talk back to your mother.

糨 jiàng〈形〉 thick: 小米粥熬得太～了。The millet porridge is cooked too thick.

【糨糊】jiànghu〈名〉 paste

【糨子】jiàngzi〈名〉〈口〉 paste: 打～ make paste

jiāo

艽 jiāo ▸秦艽 qínjiāo

交 jiāo

A〈动〉 1（交叉）cross: 那条路同铁道相～。That road crosses the railway tracks. ‖ 平行线永远不相～。Parallel lines never

intersect. **2**（交替） meet: 春夏之～ when spring meets summer ‖ 世纪之～ turn of the century **3**（到达） reach: 明天就～冬至了。 Tomorrow will be the Winter Solstice. ▸～九 **4**（碰到） meet: ～好运 meet with good fortune **5**（结交） associate with: ～朋友 make friends ▸～际, 建～, 外～ **6**（接触） exchange: ▸～兵, ～手, ～头接耳 **7**（性交） have sexual intercourse: ▸～媾, 性～ **8**（交配） mate: ▸～配, ～尾, 杂～ **9**（缴纳） hand over: ～稿 hand in one's manuscripts ‖ ～会费 pay one's membership fee ‖ 把任务～给某人 assign a task to sb. ‖ 一手～钱，一手～货 cash on delivery

B〈名〉 acquaintance: 点头之～ nodding acquaintance ‖ 一面之～ casual acquaintance ▸绝～, 忘年～

C〈副〉 **1**（互相） mutually: ▸～换, ～谈, ～易 **2**（一齐） simultaneously: 风雪～加。 A snowstorm is raging. ▸百感～集, 内外～困

【交白卷】jiāo báijuàn〈惯〉 **1**（指试卷） hand in a blank examination paper **2**〈喻〉（指任务） completely fail to accomplish a task: 我们这次没有完成任务，只好～了。 We didn't finish the task this time so we had no option but to hand in a blank sheet.

【交班】jiāobān〈动〉 **1**（指工作） hand over to the next shift: 你们几点钟～? What time do you hand over to the next shift? **2**〈喻〉（指权力） leave one's post and hand over to a successor: 即将～的政府 outgoing government

【交办】jiāobàn〈动〉 assign a task to: 上级～的工作 task assigned by higher authorities

【交保】jiāobǎo〈动〉 release on bail: ～释放 release on bail

【交杯酒】jiāobēijiǔ〈名〉 a toast in which one links one's arm with a partner to drink from one's cup of wine: 喝～ drink wine by linking arms to drink from one's cup

【交兵】jiāobīng〈动〉〈书〉 be at war: 两国～，不斩来使。 Two states at war will not kill each other's envoys.

【交叉】jiāochā〈动〉 **1**（互相穿过） cross: 两臂～在胸前 cross one's arms on one's chest ‖ 在两条街的～处 at the crossroads **2**（重叠） overlap: 两种理论明显互有～。 The two theories obviously overlap. **3**（间隔穿插） alternate: ～作业 operate alternately

【交叉点】jiāochādiǎn〈名〉 intersection

【交叉感染】jiāochā gǎnrǎn ▸**p. 50**〈名〉［医学］ cross infection

【交叉学科】jiāochā xuékē〈名〉 interdisciplinary course

【交差】jiāochāi〈动〉 report to the leadership after accomplishing a task: 任务完成，我可以～了。 The task is finished so I can now hand it in.

【交存】jiāocún〈动〉 deposit: 把钱～银行 make a deposit in a bank

【交错】jiāocuò〈动〉 criss-cross: 光影～ interplay of light and shadow ‖ 沟渠～。 Ditches criss-cross with canals. ▸犬牙～, 纵横～

【交代】jiāodài〈动〉 **1**（移交） hand over: 他已将工作～好。 He has handed over his work to his successor. **2**（告诉） tell: 厂长一再～我们要注意安全生产。 The factory director repeatedly told us to ensure safety in production. **3**（解释） brief: ～任务 brief sb. on his task ‖ ～政策 explain a policy ‖ 我们得把出差时所花的每一分钱～清楚。 We must account for every penny we spent during the business trip. **4**（坦白） confess: ～罪行 confess one's crime ‖ 坦白～ make a frank confession

【交待】jiāodài〈动〉 **1** = 交代 jiāodài 3, 4 **2**〈诙〉（死） end: 我这条命差点～了。 I was almost killed.

【交道】jiāodào〈名〉 dealings: 和某人打过～ have some dealings with sb. ‖ 他知道如何与人打～。 He knows how to handle people.

【交底】jiāodǐ〈动〉 show one's hand: 你向大家交个底吧。 You'd better put everybody in the picture.

【交点】jiāodiǎn〈名〉［数学］ intersection point

【交锋】jiāofēng〈动〉 cross swords: 思想～ confrontation of ideas ‖ 与敌人～ cross swords with the enemy ‖ 两支篮球队将在明天～。 The two basketball teams will meet tomorrow.

【交付】jiāofù〈动〉 **1**（支付） pay: ～订金 put down a down payment ‖ ～学费 pay school fees ‖ 现金～ pay in cash **2**（交给） hand over: ～表决 put to the vote ‖ ～审判 submit to trial ‖ 大楼将于年底～使用。 The building will be ready for occupancy by the end of the year.

【交感神经】jiāogǎn shénjīng〈名〉［生理］ sympathetic nerve

【交割】jiāogē〈动〉 **1**（结清） complete a business transaction: 那笔货款还未～。 The money for the consignment has not yet been paid. **2**（移交） hand over: ～工作 hand over one's work (to)

【交工】jiāogōng〈动〉 hand over a completed project: 那条高速公路将于明年～。 The expressway will be completed and handed over next year.

【交公】jiāogōng〈动〉 hand over to the collective or the state

【交媾】jiāogòu〈动〉 have sexual intercourse

【交关】jiāoguān **A**〈动〉 have to do with: ▸性命～ **B**〈副〉〈方〉 extremely: 这里夏天～热。 It gets very hot here in summer. **C**〈形〉〈方〉 numerous: 车站里乘客～。 There are a lot of passengers at the station.

【交好】jiāohǎo〈动〉 be on friendly terms: 两国～。 The two countries have friendly relations. ‖ 他们～有年。 They have been friends for years.

【交合】jiāohé〈动〉 **1**（相连） link together **2**（性交） have sexual intercourse

【交互】jiāohù〈副〉 **1**（互相） mutually: 学生们～纠正语法错误。 The students corrected each other's grammatical mistakes. **2**（交替） alternately: 两本字典可以～使用。 The two dictionaries can be used alternately.

【交欢】jiāohuān〈动〉〈书〉 **1**（交好） make friends: 握手～ shake hands and be friends **2**（性交） have sexual intercourse

【交还】jiāohuán〈动〉 hand back: ～房间钥匙 hand back a room key ‖ 借阅的图书必须按时～。 Borrowed books must be returned on time.

【交换】jiāohuàn〈动〉 exchange: ～场地 change ends ‖ ～名片 exchange visiting cards ‖ ～意见 exchange views ‖ ～战俘 exchange prisoners of war ‖ 信息～ message exchanges

【交换机】jiāohuànjī〈名〉 switchboard: 程控～ program-controlled switchboard

【交换价值】jiāohuàn jiàzhí〈名〉 exchange value

【交换台】jiāohuàntái〈名〉［通信］ exchange

【交汇】jiāohuì〈动〉 meet: 两条河在这里～。 The two rivers meet here.

【交会】jiāohuì〈动〉 meet: 朋友们在两条路的～点见面。 The friends met where the two roads crossed.

【交火】jiāohuǒ〈动〉 open fire: 与敌人～ exchange fire with the enemy

【交货】jiāohuò〈动〉 deliver goods

【交货单】jiāohuòdān〈名〉 delivery order

【交集】jiāojí **A**〈动〉（指感情） be mixed: 惊喜～ surprise mixed with joy ▸百感～, 悲喜～ **B**〈名〉［数学］ intersection

【交际】jiāojì **A**〈动〉 associate: 不喜欢～ not like to have contact with other people ‖ 善于～ be sociable ‖ ～很广 have a large circle of acquaintances **B**〈名〉 social intercourse

【交际费】jiāojìfèi〈名〉 expense account

【交际花】jiāojìhuā〈名〉〈贬〉 society beauty

【交际舞】jiāojìwǔ〈名〉 ballroom dancing

【交加】jiāojiā〈动〉〈书〉 occur simultaneously: 贫病～ be plagued by both poverty and illness ‖ 风雨～。 It's raining and windy. ‖ 雷电～。 The lightning was accompanied by thunder.

【交接】jiāojiē〈动〉 **1**（交替） meet: 夏秋～之季 time when summer meets autumn **2**（移交） hand over and take over: ～工作 hand over work to one's successor ‖ ～手续 hand-over procedure ‖ 政权的平稳～ steady transition of power **3**（结交） associate with: 俱乐部是个～朋友的好地方。 The club is a good place to make friends.

【交结】jiāojié〈动〉 associate with: 她在电影界～很广。 She has a large number of friends in film circles.

【交界】jiāojiè〈动〉 have a common border: 三省～之地 juncture of three provinces

【交颈】jiāojǐng〈动〉 fondle and kiss

【交警】jiāojǐng〈名〉 traffic police

【交九】jiāojiǔ〈动〉 enter the nine periods (of nine days each) following the Winter Solstice

【交卷】jiāojuàn〈动〉 **1**（指试卷） hand in an examination paper: 提前/准时～ hand in an examination paper ahead of time/on time **2**〈喻〉（指任务） fulfil one's task: 交一份满意的答卷 complete an assignment satisfactorily ‖ 这项任务我们一定争取提前～。 We'll try our best to fulfil the task ahead of time.

【交口】jiāokǒu〈副〉 with one voice: ～称誉 receive unanimous acclaim

【交困】jiāokùn〈动〉 be in difficulty: 内外～ in dire straits both at home and abroad

【交流】jiāoliú〈动〉 **1**（同时流淌） flow simultaneously: 涕泪～ shed tears and have a runny nose **2**（相互交换） exchange: ～经验 exchange experience ‖ 城乡物资～ interflow of goods and materials between town and country ‖ 人才～ exchange of qualified personnel ‖ 文化～ cultural exchange

【交流电】jiāoliúdiàn〈名〉 alternating current

【交流发电机】jiāoliú fādiànjī〈名〉 alternator

【交流年】jiāoliúnián〈名〉 exchange year: 中韩～ China-Korea Exchange Year

【交纳】jiāonà〈动〉 pay: ～会费 pay membership fees ‖ ～税款/租金 pay taxes/rent

【交配】jiāopèi〈动〉 mate: 使鸽子～繁殖 mate pigeons ‖ ～期 mating season ‖ 蜂王可能会与两三只雄蜂～。 The queen bee is likely to mate with two or three drones.

【交迫】jiāopò〈动〉〈书〉be hard pressed on both sides: ▸饥寒～

【交强险】jiāoqiángxiǎn〈名〉compulsory vehicle liability insurance

【交情】jiāoqing〈名〉friendship: 与某人～好 be on friendly terms with sb. ‖ 老～ long-standing friendship ‖ 私人～ personal friendship ‖ 他们之间很有～。They are on very friendly terms.

【交融】jiāoróng〈动〉blend: 相互～ blend with each other ▸情景～, 水乳～

【交涉】jiāoshè〈动〉negotiate: （就某事与某人）进行～ conduct negotiations (with sb. about sth.) ‖ （向某人）提出严正～ lodge serious representations (with sb.)

【交手】jiāoshǒu〈动〉exchange blows: 敌对双方终于～了。At last the two enemies came to blows. ‖ 两名选手曾多次～。The two players have met many times.

【交售】jiāoshòu〈动〉sell: 向国家～粮食/棉花 sell grain/cotton to the state

【交税】jiāoshuì〈动〉pay taxes

【交谈】jiāotán〈动〉converse: 流利地用英语～ converse in fluent English ‖ 亲切友好的～ cordial and friendly talks

【交替】jiāotì〈动〉**1**（接替）replace: 新旧～。The new replaces the old. **2**（轮流）alternate: 季节～ succession of the seasons ‖ 比分～上升。The score seesawed. ‖ 这两种工具可～使用。The two tools can be used alternately.

【交通】jiāotōng **A**〈动〉〈书〉be linked: 阡陌～。Linking paths lead everywhere. **B**〈名〉**1**（指运输）traffic: ～便利 be accessible ‖ 公路/铁路～ road/railway traffic ‖ ～陷于瘫痪。Traffic has come to a standstill. **2**（指联络）liaison: 跑～ do liaison work **3**（指人）liaison person

【交通安全】jiāotōng ānquán〈名〉traffic safety

【交通标线】jiāotōng biāoxiàn〈名〉traffic marking

【交通标志】jiāotōng biāozhì〈名〉traffic sign

【交通部】jiāotōngbù〈名〉Ministry of Communications

【交通岛】jiāotōngdǎo〈名〉traffic island

【交通干线】jiāotōng gànxiàn〈名〉main communication artery

【交通工具】jiāotōng gōngjù〈名〉means of transportation: 提供～ provide transport

【交通规则】jiāotōng guīzé〈名〉traffic regulations: 违反～ violate traffic regulations ‖ 遵守～ obey traffic rules

【交通壕】jiāotōngháo〈名〉［军事］communication trench

【交通量】jiāotōngliàng〈名〉volume of traffic

【交通事故】jiāotōng shìgù〈名〉road accident: 一起～ a road accident ‖ ～多发地段 black spot

【交通枢纽】jiāotōng shūniǔ〈名〉hub of communication

【交通线】jiāotōngxiàn〈名〉communication line: 重要的～ vital communication line

【交通信号】jiāotōng xìnhào〈名〉traffic signal: ～灯 traffic lights

【交通银行】Jiāotōng Yínháng〈名〉Bank of Communications

【交通拥堵费】jiāotōng yōngdǔfèi〈名〉congestion charge

【交通员】jiāotōngyuán〈名〉liaison person

【交通运输】jiāotōng yùnshū〈名〉communications and transport

【交通阻塞】jiāotōng zǔsè〈名〉traffic jam

【交头接耳】jiāotóu-jiē'ěr〈成〉whisper to each other: 考试中严禁～。Whispering is forbidden during exams.

【交投】jiāotóu〈名〉［金融］trade: ～活跃 trade is brisk

【交往】jiāowǎng〈动〉contact: （与某人）～密切 have a close association (with sb.) ‖ 友好～ friendly contact ‖ 她不太和人们～。She does not mingle much with people.

【交尾】jiāowěi〈动〉mate

【交恶】jiāowù〈动〉fall foul of one other: 两国～ The two countries became hostile towards each other.

【交相辉映】jiāoxiāng-huīyìng〈成〉enhance one another's beauty: 湖光山色，～。The lake and the hills lend radiance and beauty to one another.

【交响曲】jiāoxiǎngqǔ〈名〉symphony: 演奏～ perform a symphony ‖ 《第六～》*Sixth Symphony*

【交响诗】jiāoxiǎngshī〈名〉［音乐］symphonic poem

【交响乐】jiāoxiǎngyuè〈名〉symphony

【交响乐团】jiāoxiǎng yuètuán〈名〉philharmonic orchestra

【交心】jiāoxīn〈动〉lay one's heart bare: 领导要经常与群众～。Leaders should often open up to the masses.

【交学费】jiāo xuéfèi〈动〉**1**〈本〉pay a tuition fee **2**〈喻〉pay a price

【交椅】jiāoyǐ〈名〉**1**（指椅子）ancient folding chair **2**（指地位）post: 坐头把～ be in command

【交易】jiāoyì〈动〉trade: 房地产～ real property transactions ‖ 公平～ fair deal ‖ 黑市～ black market transaction ‖ 现金～ cash transaction ‖ 证券～ stock market dealings ‖ 拿原则做～ trade away one's principles ‖ 权钱～ deal between power and money

【交易额】jiāoyì'é〈名〉trading volume

【交易会】jiāoyìhuì〈名〉trade fair: 商品～ commodities fair ‖ 食品/图书～ food/book fair

【交易所】jiāoyìsuǒ〈名〉exchange: 伦敦证券～ London Stock Exchange

【交谊】jiāoyì〈名〉〈书〉friendship

【交谊舞】jiāoyìwǔ = 交际舞 jiāojìwǔ

【交游】jiāoyóu〈动〉〈书〉make friends: 喜欢～ enjoy making friends ‖ 他～甚广。He has a large circle of friends.

【交友】jiāoyǒu〈动〉make friends: ～之道 art of making friends

【交运】jiāoyùn〈动〉be in luck, have good luck: 交好运 a golden shower comes in one's way, good fortune befalls sb. ‖ 交桃花运 be lucky in love

【交战】jiāozhàn〈动〉be at war: ～双方 two warring parties ‖ 两军～。The two armies clashed.

【交战国】jiāozhànguó〈名〉warring state

【交账】jiāozhàng〈动〉**1**（指账务）hand over the accounts **2**（指任务）account for: 如果完不成任务，我们怎么向老板～? If we can't finish the work, what are we going to say to our boss?

【交织】jiāozhī〈动〉**1**（指编织）interweave: 棉毛～ interweave wool and cotton **2**（错杂）intertwine: 笑声、赞美声和音乐声～在一起。The music was accompanied by laughter and appreciative comments.

【交嘴雀】jiāozuǐquè〈名〉crossbill

郊 jiāo〈名〉suburbs: 城镇南～ southern outskirts of a town ▸～区, 四～, 远～

【郊区】jiāoqū〈名〉suburbs: 延伸至～ stretch to the outskirts ‖ 他住在～。He lives in the suburbs.

【郊县】jiāoxiàn〈名〉suburban county

【郊外】jiāowài〈名〉suburbs

【郊野】jiāoyě〈名〉countryside: 空旷的～ open country

【郊游】jiāoyóu〈动〉go on an excursion: 骑车～ bicycle outing ‖ 学校组织的～ school outing

茭 jiāo〈名〉hay

【茭白】jiāobái〈名〉［植物］edible expanded stem of wild rice

浇（澆） jiāo〈动〉**1**（灌溉）irrigate: ～地 irrigate the fields ‖ ～花/树 water flowers/trees **2**（淋）sprinkle water on: 我被雨～透了! The rain has drenched me to the skin. ▸火上～油 **3**（浇铸）cast: ▸～铸

【浇薄】jiāobó〈形〉〈书〉unkind: 人情～。Human relationships are tenuous. ‖ 世风～。Morals and manners have degenerated.

【浇灌】jiāoguàn〈动〉**1**（浇铸）pour into a mould: ～混凝土 pour concrete **2**（灌溉）irrigate: 用河水～庄稼 irrigate the crops with river water

【浇冷水】jiāo lěngshuǐ = 泼冷水 pō lěngshuǐ

【浇注】jiāozhù〈动〉pour: ～钢水/混凝土 pour molten steel/concrete into a mould

【浇铸】jiāozhù〈动〉［冶金］cast: ～铜像 mould a bronze statue

娇（嬌） jiāo

A〈形〉**1**（指人）lovely: ▸～憨, ～小玲珑 **2**（指颜色）tender: 嫩红～绿 tender blossoms and delicate green ▸～艳 **3**（娇气）fragile: 这女孩太～了。The girl was too frail. ▸～贵, ～气 **B**〈名〉beauty: ▸金屋藏～ **C**〈动〉spoil: 小女孩被奶奶～坏了。The little girl has been spoilt rotten by her grandmother. ▸～惯, ～纵

【娇嗔】jiāochēn〈动〉grumble in a flirtatious manner

【娇宠】jiāochǒng〈动〉indulge: 不要过分～孩子。Don't indulge your children too much.

【娇滴滴】jiāodīdī〈形〉affectedly sweet: ～的声音 sweet and charming voice ‖ 她说起话来～的。She speaks in an affectedly sweet voice.

【娇儿】jiāo'ér〈名〉**1**（指儿子）darling son **2**（指儿女）lovely young son or daughter

【娇惯】jiāoguàn〈动〉spoil: 他把儿子～坏了。He spoiled his son.

【娇贵】jiāoguì〈形〉**1**（过分爱护）pampered: 身子骨～ be enervated **2**（易坏）fragile: 这台仪器很～，要小心轻放。This instrument is very fragile and should be handled with care.

【娇憨】jiāohān〈形〉lovely and innocent: 这孩子脸上的～气 the child's beautiful, innocent expression

【娇美】jiāoměi〈形〉tender and beautiful: ～动人 charming and touching

【娇媚】jiāomèi〈形〉**1**（撒娇献媚）coquettish **2**（妩媚）sweet and charming: 舞姿～ dance gracefully ‖ ～的容颜 beautiful face

【娇嫩】jiāonen〈形〉delicate: ～的幼芽 tender shoots ‖ 她身体～，容易得病。She is fragile and gets ill easily.

【娇娘】jiāoniáng〈名〉beautiful young lady

【娇女】jiāonǚ〈名〉beloved daughter
【娇妻】jiāoqī〈名〉pretty young wife: 他娶了一位～。He married a beautiful young woman.
【娇气】jiāoqì〈形〉**1**（指人）delicate: 她太～了，这么近的路都走不了。She is too delicate to walk such a short distance. **2**（指物品、花草）fragile: 这花太～，在这儿养不活。The flower is too delicate to grow here.
【娇娆】jiāoráo〈形〉〈书〉enchantingly beautiful: 体态～ charming and beautiful carriage
【娇柔】jiāoróu〈形〉charming and gentle
【娇生惯养】jiāoshēng-guànyǎng〈成〉grow up pampered and spoiled: ～的孩子吃不得苦。Mollycoddled children can't handle things when they go wrong.
【娇声娇气】jiāoshēng-jiāoqì〈成〉tender and sweet voice: 说话～ speak in a seductive voice
【娇小】jiāoxiǎo〈形〉dainty: ～的女孩子 petite girl ‖ ～的野花 delicate wild flowers
【娇小玲珑】jiāoxiǎo-línglóng〈成〉petite and dainty: 她的身材～。She is small, slim and very graceful.
【娇羞】jiāoxiū〈形〉bashful: ～的新娘 coy bride ‖ 少女的～ maidenly shyness
【娇艳】jiāoyàn〈形〉delicate and charming: ～的红玫瑰 dazzling red rose
【娇养】jiāoyǎng〈动〉spoil: 不要～孩子。Don't spoil your child.
【娇纵】jiāozòng〈动〉indulge: ～孩子就是害孩子。To indulge children is to put them in harm's way.

姣 jiāo〈形〉〈书〉handsome

【姣好】jiāohǎo〈形〉beautiful and charming: 体态～ beautiful and charming carriage
【姣美】jiāoměi〈形〉beautiful: ～的少女 beautiful girl

骄（驕）jiāo〈形〉**1**（强烈）fierce: ►～阳 **2**（傲慢）arrogant: ►～傲, ～横, 戒～戒躁 **3**（受宠爱）spoiled: ►～子

【骄傲】jiāo'ào **A**〈形〉proud: 虚心使人进步，～使人落后。Modesty will help one to progress while conceit makes one lag behind. **B**〈动〉be proud of: 为祖国的强盛而～ be proud of the prosperity of one's country **C**〈名〉pride: 他是父母的快乐和～。He is the pride and joy of his parents.
【骄傲自大】jiāo'ào-zìdà〈成〉be conceited and arrogant
【骄傲自满】jiāo'ào-zìmǎn〈成〉be conceited and self-satisfied
【骄兵必败】jiāobīng-bìbài〈成〉pride comes before a fall
【骄横】jiāohèng〈形〉domineering
【骄横跋扈】jiāohèng-báhù〈成〉be arrogant and overbearing
【骄矜】jiāojīn〈形〉〈书〉self-important: ～自负 be proud and conceited
【骄慢】jiāomàn〈形〉high and mighty: 态度～ have an arrogant manner
【骄气】jiāoqì〈名〉arrogance: ～十足 be full of overbearing airs
【骄人】jiāorén〈形〉praiseworthy: 取得～的成绩 make satisfying achievements
【骄奢淫逸】jiāoshē-yínyì〈成〉loose-living and idle: 过着～的生活 lead a luxurious and dissipated life
【骄阳】jiāoyáng〈名〉〈书〉scorching sun: ～似火。The scorching sun is beating down.
【骄躁】jiāozào〈形〉arrogant and impetuous: 情绪～ feel arrogant and impulsive
【骄子】jiāozǐ〈名〉〈喻〉favourite: 时代的～ favourite of one's times
【骄纵】jiāozòng〈形〉arrogant and wilful: ～任性 arrogant and headstrong

胶（膠）jiāo

A〈名〉**1**（黏性物质）glue: 强力～ strong adhesive ►如～似漆 **2**（橡胶）rubber: ►～布, ～靴
B〈动〉glue
C〈形〉sticky: ►～泥

【胶版】jiāobǎn〈名〉offset plate: ～印刷 offset printing
【胶布】jiāobù〈名〉**1**（指布）tape: 绝缘～ insulating tape **2**（橡皮膏）adhesive tape: 用～固定 stabilize with an adhesive plaster
【胶带】jiāodài〈名〉Sellotape〈英〉; Scotch tape〈美〉: 一卷～ a roll of Sellotape ‖ 用～把通知贴在墙上 Sellotape a notice to the wall
【胶合】jiāohé〈动〉glue together: ～剂 glue bond ‖ 把木板～在一起。Glue the boards together.
【胶合板】jiāohébǎn〈名〉plywood
【胶结】jiāojié〈动〉glue: 把两块玻璃～起来 cement two pieces of glass together
【胶卷】jiāojuǎn〈名〉film: 彩色～ colour film
【胶木】jiāomù〈名〉bakelite
【胶囊】jiāonáng〈名〉capsule
【胶泥】jiāoní〈名〉daub
【胶凝作用】jiāoníng zuòyòng〈名〉gelation
【胶皮】jiāopí〈名〉rubber: ～手套 rubber gloves ‖ ～管 rubber tube
【胶片】jiāopiàn〈名〉film: 彩色～ colour film ‖ 电影～ cine film
【胶水】jiāoshuǐ〈名〉glue
【胶态】jiāotài〈名〉［物理］colloidal state
【胶体】jiāotǐ〈名〉［化学］colloid
【胶体化学】jiāotǐ huàxué〈名〉colloid chemistry
【胶体溶液】jiāotǐ róngyè〈名〉colloid solution
【胶鞋】jiāoxié〈名〉**1**（橡胶制成的鞋）rubber shoes **2**（胶底鞋）rubber-soled shoes
【胶靴】jiāoxuē〈名〉rubber boots; wellington boots〈英〉
【胶印】jiāoyìn〈名〉offset printing: ～机 offset printer
【胶质】jiāozhì〈名〉gel
【胶柱鼓瑟】jiāozhù-gǔsè〈成〉〈喻〉stubbornly stick to old ways in the face of changed circumstances
【胶着】jiāozhuó〈动〉reach a deadlock: 战斗处于～状态。The war has reached a stalemate.

教 jiāo〈动〉teach: ～人游泳 teach sb. (how) to swim ►～书, ～学 ►jiào

【教书】jiāoshū〈动〉teach: 在中学～ teach in a middle school ‖ 他以～为生。He teaches for a living.
【教书匠】jiāoshūjiàng〈名〉〈贬〉pedagogue
【教书先生】jiāoshū xiānsheng〈名〉〈口〉school teacher
【教书育人】jiāoshū-yùrén〈成〉impart knowledge and educate people
【教学】jiāoxué = 教书 jiāoshū ►jiàoxué

椒 jiāo〈名〉hot spice plant: ►花～, 胡～, 辣～

【椒盐】jiāoyán〈名〉spiced salt: ～排骨 spareribs with spiced salt

蛟 jiāo

【蛟龙】jiāolóng〈名〉flood dragon [a mythical creature capable of invoking storms and floods]
【蛟龙得水】jiāolóng-déshuǐ〈成〉〈喻〉get a good opportunity to display one's talent

焦¹ jiāo

A〈形〉**1**（糊）burnt: 面包烤～了。The bread is burnt. ‖ 树被烧～了。The trees are charred. ►～头烂额 **2**（干）dry: 舌枯唇～ talk oneself hoarse ►～渴 **3**（脆）crispy: 麻花炸得真～。The fried dough twist is very crispy. **4**（焦急）anxious: 他为考试成绩心～。He was worried about the result of his examination. ►～急, ～虑
B〈名〉**1**（炭渣）agglomerated coal cinder **2**（焦炭）coke: ►～煤, 炼～

焦² jiāo = 焦耳 jiāo'ěr

【焦比】jiāobǐ〈名〉［冶金］coke ratio
【焦点】jiāodiǎn〈名〉**1**［物理］［数学］focus **2**（关键）crux: 矛盾的～ focal points of contradictions ‖ 争论的～ point at issue
【焦耳】jiāo'ěr〈量〉［物理］joule
【焦黑】jiāohēi〈形〉burnt black: 被烧得～的门窗 doors and windows blackened with fire
【焦化】jiāohuà〈名〉［化学］coking: ～厂 coking plant
【焦黄】jiāohuáng〈形〉sallow: 脸色～ have a sallow complexion ‖ 把饼子烤得～ toast a cake until it's brown
【焦急】jiāojí〈形〉anxious: 万分～ be desperately anxious ‖ ～地等待 anxiously await
【焦距】jiāojù〈名〉［物理］focal distance: 调节～ adjust the focus
【焦渴】jiāokě〈形〉〈书〉parched: 热得～万分 be parched with the heat
【焦枯】jiāokū〈形〉dried up: 秧苗在骄阳下～了。The rice seedlings withered in the hot sun.
【焦炉】jiāolú〈名〉coke oven
【焦虑】jiāolǜ〈形〉worried: ～不安 anxious and unsettled ‖ 神色～ worried expression
【焦煤】jiāoméi〈名〉coking coal
【焦圈儿】jiāoquānr〈名〉crisply fried ring of dough
【焦炭】jiāotàn〈名〉coke
【焦糖】jiāotáng〈名〉［化学］caramel
【焦头烂额】jiāotóu-làn'é〈成〉be in a terrible state: 最近工作很忙，弄得我～。I have been terribly busy with work lately, and it's totally knocked me out.
【焦土】jiāotǔ〈名〉**1**（指土地）scorched earth **2**（指景象）scene of devastation: 宫殿被烧成了一片～。The palace was burned down.
【焦心】jiāoxīn〈形〉very anxious: 越等越～ wait in growing anxiety
【焦油】jiāoyóu〈名〉［化学］tar: 煤～ coal tar
【焦枣】jiāozǎo〈名〉fire-dried stoned jujube
【焦躁】jiāozào〈形〉anxious and impatient: ～不安 feel restless and ill-tempered
【焦灼】jiāozhì〈形〉terribly worried

【焦灼】jiāozhuó〈形〉〈书〉 very anxious: ～不安 be fretful and worried

跤 jiāo〈名〉 fall: 摔了一～ have a fall ▸跌～, 摔～

鲛（鮫） jiāo〈名〉［鱼类］ shark

蕉 jiāo〈名〉 broadleaf plant: ▸美人～, 香～

【蕉农】jiāonóng〈名〉 banana grower

【蕉扇】jiāoshàn〈名〉 palm-leaf fan: 一把～ a palm-leaf fan

礁 jiāo ▸**p. 164**〈名〉 reef: 触～ hit a reef ▸暗～, 珊瑚～

【礁石】jiāoshí〈名〉 reef: 水下～ underwater reef

鹪（鷦） jiāo

【鹪鹩】jiāoliáo〈名〉［鸟类］ wren

jiáo

矫（矯） jiáo
▸jiǎo

【矫情】jiáoqing〈形〉〈方〉 unreasonable: 他太～。 He is simply unreasonable.
▸jiǎoqíng

嚼 jiáo〈动〉 chew: ～花生米 crunch peanuts ‖ ～口香糖 chew gum ▸细～慢咽, 咬文～字
▸jiào, jué

【嚼舌】jiáoshé〈动〉 **1**（挑拨是非） gossip: 不要在别人背后～。 Don't talk behind other people's backs. **2**（费口舌） squabble: 我没工夫跟你～。 I have no time to squabble with you.

【嚼舌头】jiáoshétou = 嚼舌 jiáoshé

【嚼烟】jiáoyān〈名〉 chewing tobacco

【嚼子】jiáozi〈名〉 bit (of a bridle)

jiǎo

角[1] jiǎo

A〈名〉 **1**（指坚硬骨状物） horn: ▸凤毛麟～, 牛～ **2**（触角） antenna: ▸触～ **3**（指星宿） one of the 28 constellations in ancient Chinese astronomy **4**（指乐器） bugle: ▸号～ **5**（角状物） horn-shaped thing: ▸菱～, 皂～ **6**（角落） corner: 右上～ upper right-hand corner ‖ 桌子～儿 corner of a table ‖〈喻〉英语～ English corner **7**［数学］ angle: 成15°～倾斜 incline at angle of 15 degrees ▸钝～, 夹～, 直～ **8**（岬角） cape: ▸好望～

B〈量〉 quarter: 一～儿饼 a quarter of a pancake

角[2] jiǎo ▸**p. 328**〈量〉 *jiao* [fractional unit of Chinese currency equal to 1/10 of a *yuan*]: 七元八～ seven *yuan* and eight *jiao*
▸jué

【角尺】jiǎochǐ〈名〉 angle square

【角度】jiǎodù〈名〉 **1**（指大小） angle: 测量～ measure an angle ‖ 调整灯光/相机的～ angle a spotlight/camera **2**（出发点） point of view: 换个～思考 think in different ways

【角度计】jiǎodùjì〈名〉 angle gauge

【角阀】jiǎofá〈名〉［机械］ corner valve

【角钢】jiǎogāng〈名〉 angle iron

【角规】jiǎoguī〈名〉 angle gauge

【角柜】jiǎoguì〈名〉 corner cabinet

【角楼】jiǎolóu〈名〉 corner tower

【角落】jiǎoluò〈名〉 **1**（指凹角） corner: 找遍每一个～ search every nook and cranny **2**（指地方） remote place: 黑暗的～ murky corners ‖ 偏僻的～ out-of-the-way place

【角马】jiǎomǎ〈名〉［动物］ gnu

【角门】jiǎomén〈名〉 side gate

【角膜】jiǎomó〈名〉［解剖］ cornea: ～炎 keratitis ‖ ～移植 corneal transplant

【角票】jiǎopiào〈名〉 banknotes with a face value of under one *yuan*

【角球】jiǎoqiú〈名〉 **1**［足球］ corner kick: 发～ take a corner ‖ 获得一个～ be awarded a corner kick **2**（指曲棍球） corner hit

【角速度】jiǎosùdù〈名〉［物理］ angular velocity

【角铁】jiǎotiě = 角钢 jiǎogāng

【角岩】jiǎoyán〈名〉［矿业］ hornstone

【角质】jiǎozhì〈名〉［生物］ cutin: ～层 cuticle

【角柱体】jiǎozhùtǐ〈名〉 prism

【角锥体】jiǎozhuītǐ〈名〉 pyramid

侥（僥） jiǎo

【侥幸】jiǎoxìng〈形〉 lucky: ～取胜 win by a fluke ‖ 抱有～心理 trust in luck ‖ 我～通过了考试。 By sheer luck I was able to pass the examination.

佼 jiǎo〈形〉 **1**（出众） outstanding: ▸～～ **2**（美好） handsome: 面目～好 be good-looking

【佼佼】jiǎojiǎo〈形〉 outstanding: ～者 one of the best

狡 jiǎo〈形〉 crafty: ▸～辩, ～猾, ～兔三窟

【狡辩】jiǎobiàn〈动〉 argue in an unreasonable manner: 无理～ quibble groundlessly

【狡猾】jiǎohuá〈形〉 sly: 为人～ be crafty ‖ 像狐狸一样～ as cunning as a fox

【狡计】jiǎojì〈名〉 cunning trick: 他的～落空了。 His ruse failed.

【狡谲】jiǎojué〈形〉〈书〉 sly and treacherous

【狡狯】jiǎokuài〈形〉〈书〉 cunning

【狡赖】jiǎolài〈动〉 deny by resorting to sophistry: 他在事实面前无法～。 He was unable to deny it before the facts.

【狡兔三窟】jiǎotùsānkū〈成〉 a crafty person has more than one hideout

【狡黠】jiǎoxiá〈形〉〈书〉 cunning: ～的微笑 sly smile

【狡诈】jiǎozhà〈形〉 cunning: ～多疑 be crafty and suspicious ‖ 为人～ be of deceitful temperament

饺（餃） jiǎo〈名〉 *jiaozi* [Chinese dumpling]: 水～ boiled *jiaozi* ‖ 蒸～ steamed *jiaozi*

【饺子】jiǎozi〈名〉 *jiaozi* [Chinese dumpling]: 包～ make *jiaozi* ‖ ～馅儿 stuffing for *jiaozi*

> **饺子**
>
> A traditional Chinese food popular throughout China. In North China, the whole family come together on Chinese New Year's Eve to make *jiaozi*. This symbolizes family unity. *Jiaozi* dough, made of flour and cold water, is rolled into small discs, with the centre slightly thicker than the edges. The filling, either of meat and vegetables, or just vegetables, is placed in the middle of the disc. This is then folded in half and the edges pressed together, forming a crescent shape. *Jiaozi* are boiled in water, steamed or fried.

绞（絞） jiǎo

A〈动〉 **1**（扭在一起） twist: 把铜丝的两端～在一起。 Twist the two ends of the copper wire together. **2**（拧） wring: 把衣服～干 wring out the clothes ▸～尽脑汁 **3**（勒死） hang: 被～死 be hanged ▸～杀, ～刑 **4**（转动） wind: ～着辘轳打水 draw water by winding a windlass **5**（混杂） mix up: 许多问题～在一起。 A lot of issues mixed together.

B〈量〉 skein: 一～毛线 a skein of woollen yarn

【绞肠痧】jiǎochángshā ▸**p. 50**〈名〉［中医］ dry cholera

【绞车】jiǎochē〈名〉 winch

【绞刀】jiǎodāo〈名〉［机械］ reamer

【绞架】jiǎojià = 绞刑架 jiǎoxíngjià

【绞尽脑汁】jiǎojìn-nǎozhī〈成〉 rack one's brains: ～想办法 rack one's brains to figure out a solution

【绞脸】jiǎoliǎn〈动〉 [of a woman] have the fine hair on one's face removed by twisting and untwisting thin threads alternately to pull it out

【绞盘】jiǎopán〈名〉 capstan: ～棒 capstan bar

【绞肉机】jiǎoròujī〈名〉 mincer〈英〉; meat grinder〈美〉

【绞杀】jiǎoshā〈动〉 strangle: ～新生事物 strangle new things ‖〈喻〉～在摇篮里 nip in the bud

【绞索】jiǎosuǒ〈名〉 noose

【绞痛】jiǎotòng ▸**p. 50**〈动〉 have angina: 胸部一阵～ have an attack of acute chest pain

【绞刑】jiǎoxíng〈名〉 death by hanging: 处以～ condemn sb. to death by hanging

【绞刑架】jiǎoxíngjià〈名〉 gallows: 送上～ send sb. to the gallows

铰（鉸） jiǎo

A〈动〉 **1**（用剪刀） cut with scissors: ～成碎片 cut into pieces ‖ ～个窗花 cut a paper-cut for window decoration **2**（用铰刀） ream: ～孔 ream a hole

B〈名〉 hinge: ▸～接, ～链

【铰车】jiǎochē〈名〉［机械］ lift

【铰刀】jiǎodāo〈名〉［机械］ reamer

【铰接】jiǎojiē〈动〉 join with a hinge: ～式无轨电车 articulated trolley bus

【铰链】jiǎoliàn〈名〉 hinge

矫[1]（矯） jiǎo〈动〉 **1**（矫正） rectify: ▸～形, ～正, ～治 **2**（假托） pretend: ▸～命, ～情, ～揉造作

矫[2]（矯） jiǎo〈形〉 strong: ▸～健, ～捷
▸jiáo

【矫健】jiǎojiàn〈形〉 strong and vigorous: ～的步伐 vigorous strides

j

【矫捷】jiǎojié〈形〉 brisk: 动作～ quick in movement
【矫命】jiǎomìng〈动〉〈书〉 issue a false order
【矫情】jiǎoqíng〈动〉〈书〉 be affectedly unconventional
▸jiáoqing
【矫揉造作】jiǎoróu-zàozuò〈成〉behave in an affected way: 摆出一副～的姿态 make an affected pose
【矫饰】jiǎoshì〈动〉 dissemble: 摒除一切～ keep clear of all affectations
【矫枉过正】jiǎowǎng-guòzhèng〈成〉 overstep the mark
【矫形】jiǎoxíng〈动〉 conduct an orthopaedic operation: 为畸形腿～ cure a deformed leg ‖ ～手术 orthopaedic operation
【矫正】jiǎozhèng〈动〉 correct: ～发音 correct a mistake in pronunciation ‖ ～偏差 rectify a deviation ‖ ～视力 correct defects of vision
【矫治】jiǎozhì〈动〉 correct and cure: ～口吃 correct and cure a stammer ‖ ～斜视 correct a strabismus

皎 jiǎo〈形〉 clear and bright: ～月 bright moon ▸～洁
【皎皎】jiǎojiǎo〈形〉 very clear and bright: 明月～。The moon shone clear and bright.
【皎洁】jiǎojié〈形〉 luminous: ～晶莹的玉石 sparkling and crystal-clear jade ‖ 月光～。The moon was shining brightly.

脚（腳） jiǎo〈名〉 1 ▸p. 614（指肢体） foot: 双～ two feet ‖ 光着～在草坪上跑 run barefoot on the grass ▸～板, ～背 2（指物体） base: 这张课桌少了一只～。This desk has one leg missing. ▸裤～, 墙～, 山～ 3（指废料） waste material: ▸下～料 4（指人） football player: 国～ national football player 5（指文字） footnote: ▸韵～, 注～ 6（与体力有关） transportation of people or goods by cart for a fee: 拉～ transport by cart at a charge ‖ 捎～ give sb. a lift ▸～夫
▸jué
【脚板】jiǎobǎn〈名〉 sole of the foot: 有一副铁～ have a pair of toughened feet
【脚背】jiǎobèi〈名〉 instep
【脚本】jiǎoběn〈名〉 script: 电影～ film script
【脚脖子】jiǎobózi〈名〉〈口〉 ankle: 扭了～ sprain one's ankle
【脚步】jiǎobù〈名〉 1（指距离） step: ～大 stride 2（指动作） footstep: 放慢～ slow one's pace ‖ 沉重的～ heavy step
【脚踩两只船】jiǎo cǎi liǎng zhī chuán〈俗〉〈喻〉 have a foot in both camps
【脚灯】jiǎodēng〈名〉 footlights
【脚蹬子】jiǎodēngzi〈名〉〈口〉 pedal
【脚凳】jiǎodèng〈名〉 footstool
【脚底】jiǎodǐ〈名〉 sole of the foot
【脚底板】jiǎodǐbǎn = 脚底 jiǎodǐ
【脚法】jiǎofǎ〈名〉 footwork: ～细腻 have nimble footwork
【脚夫】jiǎofū〈名〉〈旧〉 1（搬运工） porter 2（赶牲口的人） one who drives a donkey, mule or horse for hire
【脚跟】jiǎogēn〈名〉 1〈本〉 heel: 用～传球 pass the ball with one's heel 2〈喻〉（立场） position: 站稳～ keep one's footing
【脚行】jiǎoháng〈名〉〈旧〉 1（指机构） porterage firm 2（指人） porter
【脚后跟】jiǎohòugen〈名〉 heel
【脚踝】jiǎohuái〈名〉 ankle
【脚迹】jiǎojì〈名〉 footprint
【脚尖】jiǎojiān〈名〉 tiptoe: 踮着～走路 walk on tiptoe
【脚劲】jiǎojìn〈名〉〈方〉 strength of one's legs: 母亲虽然视力不行了，但～还不错。Mother has got strong legs but her eyesight is failing.
【脚扣】jiǎokòu〈名〉 climbing iron
【脚力】jiǎolì〈名〉 1（指力量） strength of one's legs 2〈旧〉（指人） porter 3〈旧〉（指脚钱） payment to a porter 4〈旧〉（指赏钱） tip
【脚镣】jiǎoliào〈名〉 shackles: 戴着～ be kept in shackles
【脚炉】jiǎolú〈名〉 foot warmer
【脚轮】jiǎolún〈名〉 castor
【脚面】jiǎomiàn〈名〉 instep
【脚盆】jiǎopén〈名〉 foot basin
【脚蹼】jiǎopǔ〈名〉 flippers
【脚气】jiǎoqì ▸p. 50〈名〉［医学］ 1（脚癣） athlete's foot 2（因缺乏维生素B） beriberi
【脚刹车】jiǎoshāchē〈名〉 pedal brake: 踩～ apply the foot brake
【脚手架】jiǎoshǒujià〈名〉［建筑］scaffold: 搭～ put up a scaffold
【脚踏板】jiǎotàbǎn〈名〉 treadle
【脚踏车】jiǎotàchē〈名〉〈方〉 bicycle
【脚踏两只船】jiǎo tà liǎng zhī chuán = 脚踩两只船 jiǎo cǎi liǎng zhī chuán
【脚踏实地】jiǎotà-shídì〈成〉 have one's feet on the ground
【脚腕】jiǎowàn = 脚腕子 jiǎowànzi
【脚腕子】jiǎowànzi〈名〉 ankle
【脚下】jiǎoxià〈名〉 underfoot: 当心～，别摔倒。Mind your step. ‖ ～的雪又软又厚。The snow underfoot was soft and deep.
【脚心】jiǎoxīn〈名〉 underside of the arch of the foot
【脚癣】jiǎoxuǎn ▸p. 50〈名〉 athlete's foot
【脚丫子】jiǎoyāzi〈名〉〈方〉 foot: 光着～ go barefoot
【脚印】jiǎoyìn〈名〉 footprint: 雪地里留下一行行～ leave lines of footprints in the snow
【脚闸】jiǎozhá〈名〉 [of a bicycle] back-pedalling brake
【脚掌】jiǎozhǎng〈名〉 sole of the foot
【脚爪】jiǎozhǎo〈名〉〈方〉 claw
【脚正不怕鞋歪】jiǎo zhèng bùpà xié wāi〈俗〉 an honest man fears no gossip
【脚指甲】jiǎozhǐjia〈名〉 toenail
【脚指头】jiǎozhǐtou = 脚趾 jiǎozhǐ
【脚趾】jiǎozhǐ〈名〉 toe: 新皮鞋夹痛了他的～。His new leather shoes pinched his toes.
【脚注】jiǎozhù〈名〉 footnote: 加～ add footnotes
【脚镯】jiǎozhuó〈名〉 anklet

搅（攪） jiǎo〈动〉 1（扰乱） annoy: 事情给他～黄了。He spoiled everything. ▸打～, 胡～蛮缠 2（搅拌） stir: 把配料～匀 mix the ingredients well ‖ 隔一会儿把汤～一下。Give the soup an occasional stir. ▸～拌, ～浑
【搅拌】jiǎobàn〈动〉 mix: ～混凝土 mix the concrete ‖ 把配料～在一起 mix the ingredients together
【搅拌车】jiǎobànchē〈名〉 truck mixer
【搅拌机】jiǎobànjī〈名〉 mixer: 混凝土～ concrete mixer
【搅动】jiǎodòng〈动〉 1（搅拌） stir: 他用勺子～咖啡。He stirred his coffee with a spoon. 2（搅乱） annoy: 他被汽车的噪声～得心神不安。He was really disturbed by the noise of cars.
【搅浑】jiǎohún〈动〉 stir up and muddy: 把水～ muddy the water
【搅和】jiǎohuo〈动〉 1（混合） mix: 把两件不同的事情～在一起 mix up two different matters 2（扰乱） mess up: 事情全让他给～糟了。He's spoiled the whole thing.
【搅局】jiǎojú〈动〉 upset a plan
【搅乱】jiǎoluàn〈动〉 throw into disorder: ～人心 create confusion among people ‖ 大雨将飞机的班次～了。Flight timetables are all messed up because of the heavy rain.
【搅扰】jiǎorǎo〈动〉 disturb: 请勿～。Please do not disturb.

剿 jiǎo〈动〉 put down: ～匪 suppress bandits ▸～灭, 围～
▸chāo
【剿除】jiǎochú = 剿灭 jiǎomiè
【剿灭】jiǎomiè〈动〉 wipe out: ～残敌 wipe out the enemy remnants

缴（繳） jiǎo〈动〉 1（指钱款） pay: ～电费 pay an electricity bill ‖ ～税 pay taxes ▸～纳, 上～ 2（指武器） capture: 他们～了许多枪炮。They captured many guns and cannons. ▸～获, ～械
▸zhuó
【缴获】jiǎohuò〈动〉 seize: ～毒品 seize illegal drugs ‖ 一切～要归公。Everything that has been seized must be turned in.
【缴纳】jiǎonà〈动〉 pay: 向工会～会费 pay one's union membership fee
【缴枪】jiǎoqiāng〈动〉 lay down one's arms: ～不杀 put down your arms, or we'll shoot
【缴销】jiǎoxiāo〈动〉 hand in for cancellation: ～驾驶执照 hand in a driver's licence for cancellation
【缴械】jiǎoxiè〈动〉 1（使人交出） disarm: 警察缴了暴徒的械。The police disarmed the hoodlum. 2（交出） lay down one's arms: 向当局～ surrender one's weapons to the authorities

皦 jiǎo〈形〉〈书〉 1（纯白） pure white 2（清白） clear

jiào

叫 jiào
A〈动〉 1（呼喊） shout: 大～一声 give a loud cry ▸～好, ～卖, ～嚣 2（鸣叫） cry: 狗～ bark ‖ 驴～ bray ‖ 羊～ bleat ‖ 猫～声 the mew of a cat ‖ 青蛙/乌鸦呱呱～。Frogs/Ravens are croaking. ‖ 喜鹊在树上喳喳～。A magpie chattered in the tree. 3（说出） be called: 孩子会～爸爸妈妈了吗? Can the child say Daddy and Mummy? ‖ 你～什么名字? What's your name? 4（招呼） call: ～警察/医生 call the police/a doctor ‖ 把他～回来 call him back 5（通知） send for: ～出租车 call a taxi ‖ 再～两个菜 order some more dishes 6（要求） ask: 老师～他注意拼写。The teacher told him to watch his spelling. ‖ 她～我送送她。She asked me to see her off. 7（允许） allow: 是谁～他们早走的? Who let them leave early?
B〈介〉 [used in a passive sentence to introduce the doer of the action]: 别～人笑话! Don't make a fool of yourself. ‖ 他的钱包～人偷了。He had his wallet stolen.

j

C〈形〉〈方〉[of animal] male: ▸～驴
【叫板】jiàobǎn〈动〉**1**［戏曲］rhyme the last sentence of a spoken part to introduce a vocal passage **2**〈口〉(挑战) challenge: 向世界冠军～ challenge world champions
【叫菜】jiàocài〈动〉〈口〉order from the menu
【叫春】jiàochūn〈动〉miaow when in heat
【叫喊】jiàohǎn〈动〉shout: 大声～ yell out ‖ 疼得～起来 howl with pain
【叫好】jiàohǎo〈动〉applaud: 拍手～ clap and cheer
【叫号】jiàohào〈动〉**1**(指序号) call out numbers: 她坐在诊室外，等着医生～。She sat outside the treatment room, waiting for her number to be called. **2**〈方〉(指号子) chant a work song
【叫花子】jiàohuāzi〈名〉〈方〉beggar
【叫唤】jiàohuan〈动〉**1**(指人) call out: 疼得直～ cry out with pain **2**(指动物) call: 猴子遇到危险时会尖声～。Monkeys cry shrilly when they see danger.
【叫魂】jiàohún〈动〉call back the spirit of the sick
【叫价】jiàojià〈动〉quote: ～竞买 competitive quote
【叫劲】jiàojìn = 较劲 jiàojìn
【叫绝】jiàojué〈动〉applaud: ▸拍案～
【叫苦】jiàokǔ〈动〉complain of hardship or suffering: ～叫累 complain of hardships and fatigue
【叫苦不迭】jiàokǔ-bùdié〈成〉complain incessantly
【叫苦连天】jiàokǔ-liántiān〈成〉complain to high heaven
【叫驴】jiàolǘ〈名〉〈方〉jackass
【叫骂】jiàomà〈动〉shout curses: ～声 shouts of cursing
【叫卖】jiàomài〈动〉peddle: 沿街～ hawk ‖ 大声～的小贩 bawling hawker
【叫门】jiàomén〈动〉call at the door to be let in: 有人～。There is someone calling at the door.
【叫牌】jiàopái〈动〉bid: 该你～了。It's your bid now.
【叫屈】jiàoqū〈动〉protest against an injustice: 她为自己～。She complained of the wrongs she had suffered. ▸鸣冤～
【叫嚷】jiàorǎng〈动〉shout: 不要对我大声～。Don't yell at me. ‖ 孩子们～着要吃糖。The children were clamouring for sweets.
【叫停】jiàotíng〈动〉call an end to sth.
【叫嚣】jiàoxiāo〈动〉demand: 发出战争～ clamour for war ‖ 一些人～着要修改法律。Some people are clamouring for changes in the law.
【叫啸】jiàoxiào〈动〉howl: 风在林间～。The wind was roaring in the forest.
【叫醒】jiàoxǐng〈动〉wake up: 请在六点～我。Please wake me (up) at six (o'clock).
【叫早】jiàozǎo〈动〉wake sb. up in the morning: ～服务 morning call
【叫阵】jiàozhèn〈动〉〈旧〉challenge the enemy to battle
【叫子】jiàozi〈名〉〈方〉whistle
【叫座】jiàozuò〈动〉be a hit with the audience: 最～的电影 hottest movie ‖ 这部新片很～。The new film is drawing the crowds.
【叫做】jiàozuò〈动〉be known as: 你这～白日做梦! You are simply daydreaming! ‖ 这东西～三角板。This is called a set square.

j

峤（嶠）jiào〈名〉〈书〉mountain path
▸qiáo

觉（覺）jiào〈名〉sleep: 好好睡一～ have a good sleep ▸睡～, 午～
▸jué

校 jiào〈动〉**1**(比较) compare **2**(校对) check: 四～ fourth proof ▸～订, ～对, ～样
▸xiào

【校本】jiàoběn〈名〉collated edition
【校场】jiàochǎng〈名〉〈旧〉drill ground
【校雠】jiàochóu〈动〉〈旧〉collate
【校点】jiàodiǎn〈动〉check and punctuate: ～古籍 check and punctuate ancient books
【校订】jiàodìng〈动〉check against the authoritative text: 对照原文～译稿 check the translation against the original
【校对】jiàoduì **A**〈动〉**1**(根据原稿) proofread: 再～一遍 read it through once again ‖ ～符号 proofreader's mark **2**(根据标准) calibrate: ～水表/电表 calibrate water/the electric meter **B**〈名〉proofreader
【校对员】jiàoduìyuán ▸**p. 966**〈名〉proofreader
【校改】jiàogǎi〈动〉read and correct proofs
【校核】jiàohé〈动〉proofread
【校勘】jiàokān〈动〉collate
【校验】jiàoyàn〈动〉calibrate: ～仪表 check the meter
【校样】jiàoyàng〈名〉proof: 审阅书稿～ read the proofs of a book ‖ 付印～ final proof
【校阅】jiàoyuè〈动〉read and revise: ～清样 read and revise the final proof
【校正】jiàozhèng〈动〉proofread and correct: ～拼写错误 correct misspellings
【校正液】jiàozhèngyè〈名〉correcting fluid
【校注】jiàozhù〈动〉check against the authoritative text and annotate
【校准】jiàozhǔn〈动〉［机械］calibrate: ～仪器 calibrate an instrument

轿（轎）jiào〈名〉sedan (chair): 抬～ carry sb. in a sedan chair ‖ 坐～ sit in a sedan chair ▸～夫, 花～

【轿车】jiàochē〈名〉(saloon) car〈英〉; sedan〈美〉: 大～ bus ‖ 小～ car
【轿夫】jiàofū〈名〉sedan-chair bearer
【轿子】jiàozi〈名〉sedan chair

较（較）jiào

A〈动〉**1**(比较) compare: ▸～量, ～劲, 比～ **2**(计较) haggle: ▸锱铢必～
B〈副〉comparatively: ～好 relatively good ‖ ～满意 fairly satisfactory ‖ ～便宜 quite cheap
C〈介〉[used to introduce the object of comparison]: ～前大有进步 make greater progress than before ‖ 滑雪～滑冰更加刺激。Skiing is more exciting than skating.
D〈形〉〈书〉obvious: 二者～然不同。There is a clear difference between the two.
【较比】jiàobǐ〈副〉〈方〉= 比较 bǐjiào
【较劲】jiàojìn〈动〉〈口〉**1**(作对) set oneself against: 别和我～了! Don't oppose me. ‖ 你越说，她越～。The more you talked to her, the more defiant she became. **2**(努力) call for great efforts: 考试即将来临，正是～的时候。As the examination approaches, we must redouble our efforts.
【较量】jiàoliàng〈动〉have a contest: ～一下高低 contest and see who is better ‖ 百米赛跑是速度的激烈～。The 100-metre dash is a bitter contest of speed.
【较为】jiàowéi〈副〉〈书〉comparatively: 生活～舒适 live in comparative comfort ‖ 这本词典～实用。This dictionary is fairly functional.
【较真】jiàozhēn〈形〉earnest: 他做事挺～。He is a conscientious worker.

教[1] jiào

A〈动〉teach: ▸～养, 管～, 言传身～
B〈名〉religion: ▸传～, 佛～, 宗～

教[2] jiào = 叫 jiào A6, A7, B
▸jiāo

【教案】jiào'àn〈名〉lesson plan: 写～ prepare one's teaching plan
【教本】jiàoběn〈名〉textbook
【教鞭】jiàobiān〈名〉(teacher's) pointer
【教材】jiàocái〈名〉teaching material: 编写～ compile and write a textbook ‖ 辅导～ guidance material
【教参】jiàocān〈名〉reference material for teaching
【教程】jiàochéng〈名〉course of study: 初级英语～ course in basic English
【教导】jiàodǎo〈动〉instruct: 牢记老师的～ keep in mind the teacher's instructions
【教导团】jiàodǎotuán ▸**p. 966**〈名〉officer-training corps
【教导员】jiàodǎoyuán〈名〉political instructor
【教范】jiàofàn〈名〉［军事］manual: 兵器～ manual of arms
【教辅】jiàofǔ〈形〉support: ～人员 support staff ‖ ～读物 supplementary teaching materials
【教父】jiàofù〈名〉godfather
【教改】jiàogǎi〈简称〉= 教育改革
【教工】jiàogōng〈名〉teaching and administrative staff: 全体～ faculty
【教官】jiàoguān〈名〉instructor
【教规】jiàoguī〈名〉canon
【教化】jiàohuà〈动〉cultivate
【教皇】jiàohuáng〈名〉pope
【教会】jiàohuì〈名〉Christian church: ～学校 missionary school
【教诲】jiàohuì〈名〉〈书〉teachings: 遵照老师的～ follow the instruction of one's teacher ‖ 谆谆～ earnest teachings
【教具】jiàojù〈名〉teaching aid: 视听～ audio-visual aids
【教科书】jiàokēshū〈名〉textbook: 历史～ history textbook ‖ 语法～ grammar textbook
【教练】jiàoliàn **A**〈动〉train: 他～得法。He trained the team very well. **B**〈名〉coach: 排球/足球～ volleyball/football coach ‖ 主～ head coach
【教练车】jiàoliànchē〈名〉vehicle driven by learners
【教练弹】jiàoliàndàn〈名〉practice projectile
【教练机】jiàoliànjī〈名〉trainer aircraft
【教练员】jiàoliànyuán ▸**p. 966**〈名〉coach
【教龄】jiàolíng〈名〉length of service as a teacher: 他已有30年的～。He has been teaching for 30 years.
【教令】jiàolìng〈名〉［军事］instruction manual
【教门】jiàomén〈名〉**1**(伊斯兰教) Islam **2** = 教派 jiàopài
【教母】jiàomǔ〈名〉godmother
【教派】jiàopài〈名〉religious sect

【教区】jiàoqū〈名〉parish: ～牧师 rector
【教师】jiàoshī ▸**p. 966**〈名〉teacher: 大学/中学/小学/幼儿～ university/secondary school/primary school/kindergarten teacher ‖ 兼职/专职～ part-time/full-time teacher ‖ 外籍～ foreign teacher ▸家庭～
【教师节】Jiàoshījié〈名〉Teachers' Day
【教师用书】jiàoshī yòngshū〈名〉teacher's book
【教师资格证书】jiàoshī zīgé zhèngshū〈名〉teacher's certificate
【教士】jiàoshì〈名〉priest
【教室】jiàoshì〈名〉classroom: 走进～ enter a classroom ‖ 阶梯～ lecture theatre
【教授】jiàoshòu **A**〈名〉professor: 副/正～ associate/full professor ‖ 客座～ visiting professor ‖ 名誉～ honorary professor **B**〈动〉teach: ～地理/历史/文学 teach geography/history/literature ‖ ～有方 be good at teaching
【教唆】jiàosuō〈动〉incite: ～青少年犯罪 abet youngsters to commit crimes ‖ 受人～ at the instigation of sb.
【教唆犯】jiàosuōfàn〈名〉instigator
【教堂】jiàotáng〈名〉church: 在～举行婚礼 hold a wedding ceremony at a church
【教条】jiàotiáo **A**〈名〉**1**（原则）doctrine **2**（教条主义）dogmatism **B**〈形〉doctrinal
【教条主义】jiàotiáo zhǔyì〈名〉dogmatism
【教廷】jiàotíng〈名〉the Vatican
【教头】jiàotóu〈名〉**1**〈旧〉（指教练武艺）chief military instructor **2**〈诙〉（教练员）coach
【教徒】jiàotú〈名〉believer of a religion: 佛～ Buddhist ‖ 基督～ Christian
【教委】jiàowěi〈简称〉= 教育委员会
【教务】jiàowù〈名〉educational administration: ～处 Dean's Office ‖ ～长 Dean of Studies
【教习】jiàoxí〈动〉〈书〉teach: ～书法 teach calligraphy
【教学】jiàoxué〈名〉teaching: ～计划/经验 teaching plan/experience ‖ ～大纲 syllabus ‖ ～人员 teaching staff ‖ 课堂～ classroom teaching ‖ 示范～ demonstration teaching
▸jiāoxué
【教学法】jiàoxuéfǎ〈名〉teaching method: 采用新的～ adopt a new teaching method
【教学相长】jiàoxué-xiāngzhǎng〈成〉teaching benefits teachers as well as students
【教训】jiàoxun **A**〈名〉lesson: 吸取～ learn one's lessons ‖ 深刻的～ profound lesson **B**〈动〉teach sb. a lesson: 被～一顿 receive a talking-to
【教研室】jiàoyánshì〈名〉teaching and research section
【教研组】jiàoyánzǔ〈名〉teaching and research group
【教养】jiàoyǎng **A**〈动〉bring up: ～子女 bring up one's children **B**〈名〉**1**（修养）upbringing: 没有～ be ill-bred ‖ 有～ be well-bred **2**［法律］reform: 进行劳动～ undergo reform through labour
【教养所】jiàoyǎngsuǒ〈名〉reformatory
【教义】jiàoyì〈名〉religious teachings
【教益】jiàoyì〈名〉enlightenment: 从谈话中得到～ benefit from a talk
【教友】jiàoyǒu〈名〉fellow believer
【教友会】Jiàoyǒuhuì〈名〉Religious Society of Friends
【教育】jiàoyù **A**〈名〉education: 受～ receive education ‖ 爱国主义～ patriotic education ‖ 成人～ adult education ‖ 初等/中等/高等～ elementary/secondary/higher education ‖ 家庭～ home schooling ‖ 素质～ education for all-round development ‖ 义务～ compulsory education ‖ 职业～ vocational education **B**〈动〉teach: ～孩子懂礼貌 educate a child to behave well ‖ 事实～了我。Facts have taught me a lesson.
【教育背景】jiàoyù bèijǐng〈名〉educational background
【教育部】jiàoyùbù〈名〉Ministry of Education
【教育方针】jiàoyù fāngzhēn〈名〉educational policy
【教育改革】jiàoyù gǎigé〈名〉educational reform
【教育机构】jiàoyù jīgòu〈名〉educational institution
【教育家】jiàoyùjiā ▸**p. 966**〈名〉educator
【教育界】jiàoyùjiè〈名〉educational circles
【教育局】jiàoyùjú〈名〉bureau of education
【教育厅】jiàoyùtīng〈名〉department of education
【教育投入】jiàoyù tóurù〈名〉investment in education: 加大～ increase investment in education
【教育委员会】jiàoyù wěiyuánhuì〈名〉commission of education
【教育学】jiàoyùxué〈名〉pedagogy
【教育学院】jiàoyù xuéyuàn〈名〉college of education
【教育制度】jiàoyù zhìdù〈名〉system of education
【教员】jiàoyuán〈名〉teacher: ～休息室 faculty room
【教正】jiàozhèng〈动〉〈套〉give comments and criticism
【教职员】jiàozhíyuán〈名〉teaching and administrative staff
【教主】jiàozhǔ〈名〉founder of a religion

窖 jiào
A〈名〉cellar: 白菜～ Chinese cabbage cellar ‖ 酒～ wine cellar ▸冰～, 地～
B〈动〉store in a cellar: 这些马铃薯应该～起来。These potatoes should be kept in a cellar.
【窖藏】jiàocáng〈动〉store sth. in a cellar: ～佳酿 excellent wine stored in a cellar

斠 jiào〈动〉〈书〉collate

酵 jiào〈动〉ferment
【酵母】jiàomǔ〈名〉yeast: ～菌 saccharomycete

噍 jiào〈动〉〈书〉masticate
【噍类】jiàolèi〈名〉〈古〉human beings

徼 jiào〈名〉〈书〉frontier

藠 jiào
【藠头】jiàotou〈名〉［植物］Chinese onion

醮 jiào〈动〉**1**（嫁人）marry: ▸再～ **2**（设坛祈祷）Taoist or Buddhist sacrificial ceremony: ▸打～

嚼 jiào ▸倒嚼 dǎojiào
▸jiáo, jué

jiē

节（節）jiē
▸jié
【节骨眼】jiēguyǎn〈名〉critical juncture: 在这个～上 at this critical moment
【节子】jiēzi〈名〉knot [in wood]

阶（階）jiē〈名〉**1**（台阶）steps: ▸～梯, ～下囚 **2**（级别）rank: ▸官～, 军～, 音～
【阶层】jiēcéng〈名〉social stratum: 低/高收入～ low/high income group ‖ 工薪～ wage earners ‖ 社会各～人士 people of all walks of life
【阶地】jiēdì〈名〉［地理］terrace
【阶段】jiēduàn〈名〉stage: 进入新的历史～ enter a new historical period ‖ 取得～性胜利 achieve success for the first phase ‖ 社会主义初级～ primary stage of socialism ‖ 分～ in stages
【阶级】jiējí〈名〉**1**〈书〉（台阶）steps **2**（社会等级）social class: 剥削/被剥削～ exploiting/exploited class ‖ 工人～ working class ‖ 统治～ ruling class ▸无产～, 资产～
【阶级本能】jiējí běnnéng〈名〉class instinct
【阶级成分】jiējí chéngfèn〈名〉class status
【阶级斗争】jiējí dòuzhēng〈名〉class struggle
【阶级分化】jiējí fēnhuà〈名〉class differentiation
【阶级立场】jiējí lìchǎng〈名〉class stand
【阶级矛盾】jiējí máodùn〈名〉class contradiction
【阶级社会】jiējí shèhuì〈名〉class society
【阶级性】jiējíxìng〈名〉class character
【阶梯】jiētī〈名〉ladder: ～教室 lecture theatre ‖ 发奋工作是通向成功的～。Hard work is a ladder to success.
【阶下囚】jiēxiàqiú〈名〉prisoner: 沦为～ be reduced to a prisoner

疖（癤）jiē〈名〉boil
【疖子】jiēzi〈名〉boil

皆 jiē〈副〉〈书〉all: 人人～知。It is public knowledge. ▸比比～是, 啼笑～非
【皆大欢喜】jiēdàhuānxǐ〈成〉to the satisfaction of all

结（結）jiē〈动〉（指果实）bear;（指种子）form: 这棵树～了许多苹果。This tree produces many apples.
▸jié
【结巴】jiēba **A**〈动〉stammer: 说话～ speak with a stammer **B**〈名〉stammerer
【结果】jiēguǒ〈动〉bear fruit: 结满果实的树 trees covered in fruit ‖ 那棵树不～。That tree doesn't yield fruit.
▸jiéguǒ
【结实】jiēshi〈形〉**1**（坚固耐用）sturdy: ～的家具 durable furniture ‖ 那梯子～吗? Is that ladder safe? **2**（强壮）strong: 他的身体很～。He is very strong.

接 jiē〈动〉**1**（触碰）come into contact with: ▸～近, 交头～耳, 摩肩～踵 **2**（连接）connect: ～电线 connect wires ‖ ～好断臂 set a broken arm ▸焊～, 嫁～, 衔～ **3**（继续）continue: ～下页 continued on the next page ‖ 请你～着说。Please go on. ▸上气不～下气 **4**（接替）take over: ～校长的职务 take over as president ▸～班,

～力 5 (抓住) catch: ▸～球 6 (收到) receive: ～到命令 receive orders ‖ ～到一份请帖 receive an invitation ‖ ～到一封信 receive a letter ‖ 请他来～电话。Please call him to the phone. ▸～待, ～纳 7 (会面) meet: 到汽车站～人 meet sb. at the bus station

【接班】jiēbān〈动〉1 (指工作任务) take one's turn on duty: 白班八点～。The day shift begins at 8 am. 2 (指职务) succeed: 我们系谁来接主任的班? Who will succeed as chair of our department? ▸～人

【接班人】jiēbānrén〈名〉successor: 培养～ train a successor ‖ 理想的～ ideal successor

【接棒】jiēbàng〈名〉[体育] takeover

【接茬儿】jiēchár〈动〉〈口〉chime in

【接车】jiēchē〈动〉get ready for the arrival of a bus/train

【接触】jiēchù〈动〉1 (交往) come into contact with: 保持～ maintain contact ‖ 有机会～普通老百姓 have the opportunity to make contact with ordinary people ‖ 这孩子与猩红热患者～过。The child has been exposed to scarlet fever. 2 (交火) engage: 与敌人～ engage the enemy 3 [电气] contact: ～不良 poor contact

【接触传染】jiēchù chuánrǎn〈名〉contagion: ～病 contagious disease

【接待】jiēdài〈动〉receive: ～外宾 play host to a foreign guest ‖ 受到热情～ be warmly received

【接待处】jiēdàichù〈名〉reception desk: 在～签到 sign in at reception

【接待日】jiēdàirì〈名〉reception day

【接待站】jiēdàizhàn〈名〉reception centre

【接地】jiēdì〈名〉[电气] ground connection

【接二连三】jiē'èr-liánsān〈成〉one after another: 不要～地提问了。Please stop your continual questions.

【接发球】jiēfāqiú〈动〉[体育] return the service

【接防】jiēfáng〈动〉relieve a garrison

【接风】jiēfēng〈动〉host a welcome dinner: 设宴～ give a welcome dinner ‖ ～洗尘 give a welcome dinner

【接缝】jiēfèng〈名〉joint

【接羔】jiēgāo〈动〉deliver lambs

【接骨】jiēgǔ〈动〉set a bone: ～术 osteopathy

【接骨木】jiēgǔmù〈名〉[植物] elder

【接管】jiēguǎn〈动〉take over: ～权力 take over power ‖ 该公司已被一家企业集团～。The firm has been taken over by a conglomerate.

【接轨】jiēguǐ〈动〉1 (指轨道) join up the track: 这两条地方铁路～了。The two regional railway systems were integrated. 2〈喻〉(指制度办法等) integrate: 加快与世界经济～ hasten integration with the global economy ‖ 加入世贸组织标志着中国与国际社会全面～。China's WTO accession marks the full integration of China with the international community.

【接合】jiēhé〈动〉[机械] connect: ～件 fastener

【接合处】jiēhéchù〈名〉junction

【接合点】jiēhédiǎn〈名〉[军事] junction point

【接火】jiēhuǒ〈动〉1 [军事] start to exchange fire 2 [电气] energize

【接济】jiējì〈动〉provide financial assistance to: 他经常～穷人。He often gives to the poor.

【接见】jiējiàn〈动〉receive: ～外宾 receive foreign guests

【接界】jiējiè = 交界 jiāojiè

【接近】jiējìn〈动〉draw near: ～冰点 be close on freezing ‖ ～尾声 near the end ‖ ～完美 approach perfection ‖ 比分很～。It was a very close match.

【接警】jiējǐng〈动〉receive a crime report

【接境】jiējìng〈动〉border on: 朝鲜与中国和俄国～。Korea borders on China and Russia.

【接客】jiēkè〈动〉1 (指主人) receive guest 2 (指妓女) receive a client

【接口】jiēkǒu〈名〉port

【接力】jiēlì〈动〉relay: 一站站～传送讯息 relay a message

【接力棒】jiēlìbàng〈名〉relay baton

【接力区】jiēlìqū〈名〉takeover zone

【接力赛】jiēlìsài〈名〉relay (race): 女子4×100米～ women's 4×100m relay

【接连】jiēlián〈动〉happen in succession: ～不断 continuously ‖ ～四次获得胜利 win four victories in succession

【接龙】jiēlóng〈动〉[in cards/dominoes] build a sequence

【接纳】jiēnà〈动〉1 (接收) admit: ～新党员 admit new members into the party ‖ 她被～为该学会成员。She was granted membership of the Society. 2 (采纳) accept: ～建议 take advice

【接洽】jiēqià〈动〉take up a matter with: 与有关单位～ consult with the departments concerned ‖ 他来～业务。He was here on business.

【接腔】jiēqiāng〈动〉respond: 他讲得声嘶力竭, 但没有人～。He talked himself hoarse, but there wasn't any reaction.

【接亲】jiēqīn = 迎亲 yíngqīn

【接球】jiēqiú〈动〉[体育] catch a ball

【接壤】jiērǎng〈动〉share a border: 美国与加拿大～。The US borders Canada.

【接任】jiērèn〈动〉succeed: ～总经理 take over as general manager

【接入】jiērù〈动〉[计算机] access

【接生】jiēshēng〈动〉deliver a child: ～员 midwife

【接生婆】jiēshēngpó〈名〉〈旧〉midwife

【接收】jiēshōu〈动〉1 (收到) receive: ～订单 receive orders ‖ 新收音机～效果良好。The new radio has good reception. 2 (接管) take over: ～一家工厂 take over a factory 3 (接纳) admit: ～新成员 recruit new members

【接收机】jiēshōujī〈名〉radio set

【接收天线】jiēshōu tiānxiàn〈名〉receiving antenna

【接手】jiēshǒu A〈动〉take over: ～一起案子 take over a case B〈名〉[体育] catcher

【接受】jiēshòu〈动〉accept: ～群众监督 subject oneself to supervision by the masses ‖ ～教训 learn a lesson ‖ ～礼物 accept a gift ‖ ～邀请 accept an invitation ‖ 虚心～ accept with an open heart

【接受国】jiēshòuguó〈名〉recipient country

【接榫】jiēsǔn〈动〉1 (连接榫头) connect tenons 2〈喻〉(前后衔接) be coherent

【接替】jiētì〈动〉replace: ～某人的工作 take over sb.'s job ‖ ～王教授任副校长 replace Professor Wang as vice-president

【接听】jiētīng〈动〉receive: ～电话 receive a call

【接通】jiētōng〈动〉get a connection: 电话～了。The call has been put through.

【接头】jiētóu〈动〉1 (指物体) connect 2 (联系) get in touch with: ～地点 meeting place ‖ 咱们在哪儿～? Where shall we meet? 3 (熟悉) have knowledge of: 这事他不～。He knows nothing about it.

【接吻】jiēwěn〈动〉kiss

【接线】jiēxiàn〈动〉connect with a lead: ～板 terminal block

【接线员】jiēxiànyuán ▸p. 966〈名〉telephone operator

【接续】jiēxù〈动〉continue: ～前页 continued from the previous page ‖ ～香火 continue the family line

【接应】jiēyìng〈动〉1 (配合) coordinate with: ～先遣部队 reinforce the advance troops 2 (供应) supply: 钢材一时～不上。Steel was in short supply for a time.

【接援】jiēyuán〈动〉reinforce

【接站】jiēzhàn〈动〉meet sb. at the station: 我母亲乘坐的火车马上就到, 我得去～了。My mother is coming. I must go to the railway station to pick her up.

【接着】jiēzhe〈动〉carry on: ～干吧。Carry on with your work. ‖ 她迟疑了一下,然后～往下说。She hesitated for a moment, and then went on with her talk. ‖ 这本书你看完了我～看。I'll read the book after you.

【接诊】jiēzhěn〈动〉receive a patient

【接枝】jiēzhī〈名〉branch grafting

【接踵】jiēzhǒng〈动〉〈书〉follow on sb.'s heels: 不幸事件～而至。One misfortune followed hard on another. ▸摩肩～

【接种】jiēzhòng〈动〉be vaccinated: ～天花疫苗 be inoculated against smallpox

秸 (稭) jiē〈名〉stalks remaining left after threshing: ▸豆～, 麦～

【秸秆】jiēgǎn〈名〉stalks remaining after threshing

揭 jiē〈动〉1 (举) raise: ▸～竿而起 2 (掀开) uncover: ～锅盖 lift the pot lid off ‖ ～去面纱 unveil ‖ 盖子～不开。The lid won't come off. 3 (揭露) expose: ～人短处 expose sb.'s weaknesses ‖ ～人隐私 reveal sb.'s secrets ▸～穿, ～发, ～老底 4 (撕下) take off: ～开封条 tear off the paper strip seal ‖ ～下信封上的邮票 take a stamp off an envelope

【揭榜】jiēbǎng = 发榜 fābǎng

【揭标】jiēbiāo = 开标 kāibiāo

【揭不开锅】jiēbukāiguō〈惯〉run out of food: 他家～了。His household has run out of food.

【揭穿】jiēchuān〈动〉expose: ～阴谋 unmask a conspiracy ‖ 他的谎言被～了。His lie was exposed.

【揭疮疤】jiēchuāngbā〈惯〉〈喻〉touch sb.'s sore spot: 不要总是揭人的疮疤。Don't always be prodding other people's sore points.

【揭底】jiēdǐ〈动〉reveal the truth: 怕人～ be worried about people digging up the past

【揭短】jiēduǎn〈动〉expose sb.'s shortcomings: 别人当众～ dish the dirt in public

【揭发】jiēfā〈动〉expose: ～罪行 expose a crime ‖ ～检举 expose and denounce sb. ‖ 有人～他服用兴奋剂。It was brought to light that he was using performance-enhancing drugs.

【揭盖子】jiē gàizi〈惯〉〈喻〉bring sth. out into the open

【揭竿而起】jiēgān'érqǐ〈成〉rise in rebellion

【揭开】jiēkāi〈动〉uncover: ～历史新的一页 uncover a new historical page ‖ ～序幕 raise the curtain

【揭老底】jiē lǎodǐ〈惯〉dig up the past: 不

要～。Don't dig up the past.

【揭露】jiēlù〈动〉expose: ～丑闻 expose a scandal ‖ ～阴谋 uncover a plot ‖ ～真相 reveal the truth

【揭秘】jiēmì〈动〉reveal a secret

【揭幕】jiēmù〈动〉**1**（指落成典礼）unveil: 为雕像/纪念碑～ unveil a statue/monument **2**（指重大活动）inaugurate: ～式 unveiling ceremony ‖ 展览会于昨天～。The exhibition was opened yesterday.

【揭牌】jiēpái〈动〉be set up: 公司举行～仪式。The company held an opening ceremony.

【揭示】jiēshì〈动〉**1**（公布）announce: ～牌 bulletin board **2**（指出）reveal: ～客观规律 bring to light the objective laws ‖ 这部小说没有～出生活的真谛。The novel failed to reveal any life truths.

【揭晓】jiēxiǎo〈动〉publish: 候选人名单刚刚～。The list for the candidates has just been published. ‖ 联赛结果已经～。The result of the tournament has already been announced.

喈 jiē

【喈喈】jiējiē〈拟〉〈书〉**1**（指敲击声）harmonious sound: 钟鼓～。Bells and drums resounded. **2**（指鸟鸣声）chirp: 鸡鸣～。A rooster was crowing.

嗟 jiē〈动〉〈书〉sigh: ▸～叹

【嗟悔无及】jiēhuǐ-wújí〈成〉too late to regret

【嗟来之食】jiēláizhīshí〈成〉handout offered contemptuously

【嗟叹】jiētàn〈动〉〈书〉sigh with regret

街 jiē〈名〉street: 临～ overlook the street ‖ 华尔～ Wall Street ▸步行～

【街道】jiēdào〈名〉**1**（道路）street: ～清扫工 street cleaner ‖ 这条～禁止车辆通行。The street is closed to cars. **2**（与居民相关）residential neighbourhood: ～工厂 neighbourhood factory

【街道办事处】jiēdào bànshìchù〈名〉neighbourhood office

【街道居委会】jiēdào jūwěihuì〈名〉neighbourhood committee

【街灯】jiēdēng〈名〉street lamp

【街坊】jiēfang〈名〉〈口〉neighbour

【街坊四邻】jiēfang-sìlín〈成〉neighbours

【街景】jiējǐng〈名〉streetscape: 观～ enjoy wandering the streets

【街垒】jiēlěi〈名〉street barricade: 设～ set up barricades across the street

【街面儿上】jiēmiànrshang〈名〉〈口〉**1**（道路）street conditions: 一到假日，～特别热闹。On holidays, the street is extremely busy. **2**（附近街巷）neighbourhood: 他是这里的老住户，～没有人不知道他。He is an old resident here and everyone in the neighbourhood knows him.

【街区】jiēqū〈名〉block

【街市】jiēshì〈名〉shopping street

【街谈巷议】jiētán-xiàngyì〈成〉talk of the town: 这件事成了～的话题。This matter has become the talk of the town.

【街头】jiētóu〈名〉street: 流落～ wander homeless in the streets ‖ ～艺人 street artist ‖ 成千上万的人涌上～。Thousands of people filled the streets.

【街头巷尾】jiētóu-xiàngwěi〈成〉streets and lanes

【街舞】jiēwǔ〈名〉street dancing

【街心】jiēxīn〈名〉central part of a street: ～花园 street garden

湝 jiē

【湝湝】jiējiē〈形〉〈书〉flowing: 水流～。The water is flowing.

楷 jiē〈名〉［植物］Chinese Pistache ▸kǎi

jié

孑 jié〈形〉lonely: ▸～然, 茕茕～立

【孑孓】jiéjué〈名〉［昆虫］mosquito larva

【孑然】jiérán〈形〉alone: ～一身 all alone in the world

【孑遗】jiéyí〈名〉〈书〉few survivors

【孑遗生物】jiéyí shēngwù〈名〉living fossil

节¹（節）jié

A〈名〉**1**（指植物）node: 竹～ bamboo joint ▸盘根错～ **2**（指动物）joint: ▸骨～, 关～ **3**（节气）solar term: ▸～令, 季～ **4**（节日）holiday: 电影/音乐～ film/music festival ▸春～, 过～ **5**（部分）part: 第四章第五～ Section Five, Chapter Four ▸～目, 环～, 脱～ **6**（事项）item: ▸细～ **7**（礼节）formality: ▸繁文缛～ **8**（节操）moral integrity: ▸～操, 变～, 贞～ **9**（节奏）rhythm: ▸～律, ～拍

B〈动〉**1**（节略）abridge: ▸～本, ～录, 删～ **2**（限制）restrict: ▸～哀, ～制, 调～ **3**（节约）economize: ～电/煤/气 save (on) electricity/coal/gas ▸～俭, ～衣缩食, 开源～流

C〈量〉length: 两～火车 two railway coaches ‖ 三～课 three classes ‖ 一～电池 a battery

节²（節）jié〈量〉［航海］knot: 船速20～的船每小时能航行20海里。A ship with 20-knot speed can go at 20 nautical miles an hour.

▸jiē

【节哀】jié'āi〈动〉〈书〉restrain one's grief

【节哀顺变】jié'āi-shùnbiàn〈成〉restrain one's grief and accord with inevitable changes

【节疤】jiébā〈名〉node

【节本】jiéběn〈名〉abridged version

【节操】jiécāo〈名〉〈书〉moral integrity

【节点】jiédiǎn〈名〉node: 时间～ time node

【节电】jiédiàn〈动〉save electricity

【节妇】jiéfù〈名〉〈旧〉chaste widow

【节假日】jiéjiàrì〈名〉festival and holiday

【节俭】jiéjiǎn〈形〉frugal: 生活～ live economically ‖ ～是美德。Thrift is a virtue.

【节减】jiéjiǎn〈动〉economize: ～开支 cut down expenditure

【节节】jiéjié〈副〉steadily: ～败退 steadily lose ground ‖ 产量～上升。Production rose steadily. ▸芝麻开花～高

【节礼】jiélǐ〈名〉present sent at a festival

【节令】jiélìng〈名〉climate and other natural seasonal phenomena: 正是草莓上市的～。Strawberries are in season.

【节流】jiéliú〈动〉reduce expenditure: 该国正面临～的压力。The country is now under pressure to reduce expenditure. ▸开源～

【节录】jiélù **A**〈动〉extract: 把讲话～几段 extract several passages from the speech **B**〈名〉excerpt: 小说～ extracts from a novel

【节律】jiélǜ〈名〉rhythm: 脉搏/心动～ rhythm of one's pulse/heart

【节略】jiélüè **A**〈名〉outline: 演讲稿的～ excerpt from a speech **B**〈动〉leave out: 文章的最后一段～了。The last paragraph of the article has been omitted.

【节略本】jiélüèběn〈名〉abridged edition

【节目】jiémù〈名〉programme: 主持～ present a programme ‖ 电视/广播～ television/radio programme ‖ 广告～ commercial programme

【节目单】jiémùdān〈名〉programme: 音乐会～ programme of the concert

【节目主持人】jiémù zhǔchírén〈名〉programme host

【节能】jiénéng〈动〉conserve energy: ～措施 energy-saving measures ‖ ～灯 energy-saving light

【节能减排】jiénéng jiǎnpái〈动〉save energy and reduce emissions: 出台多项～政策措施 put into effect many energy-saving and emissions-reducing policies and measures

【节拍】jiépāi〈名〉metre

【节拍器】jiépāiqì〈名〉metronome

【节气阀】jiéqìfá〈名〉air throttle

【节气】jiéqi〈名〉point marking one of the 24 divisions of the solar year in the traditional Chinese calendar

【节庆】jiéqìng〈名〉holiday and festival: ～活动 festival activities

【节日】jiérì〈名〉holiday: 欢度～ celebrate a holiday ‖ 沉浸在～气氛中 be in festive mood ‖ 传统～ traditional holiday ‖ 盛大～ magnificent festival

【节省】jiéshěng〈动〉save: ～费用/篇幅/时间 save on expenses/space/time ‖ ～体力/资源 save one's strength/resources ‖ 能～就～。Cut down on whatever you can.

【节食】jiéshí〈动〉be on a diet: ～减肥 diet to lose weight

【节外生枝】jiéwài-shēngzhī〈成〉〈喻〉muddy an issue: 请不要～。Please don't complicate the problem.

【节下】jiéxia〈名〉days around a major festival

【节选】jiéxuǎn〈动〉extract: 小说～ excerpts from a novel

【节衣缩食】jiéyī-suōshí〈成〉scrimp and save: 为把孩子拉扯大，他们不得不～。They had to scrimp and save to bring up their children.

【节译】jiéyì〈动〉abridge and translate

【节油器】jiéyóuqì〈名〉(petrol) economizer

【节余】jiéyú **A**〈动〉save: ～足够的钱 save enough money **B**〈名〉surplus: 大量的～ huge surplus

【节育】jiéyù〈动〉practise birth control: ～手术 birth control surgery

【节育环】jiéyùhuán〈名〉intrauterine device (IUD)

【节约】jiéyuē〈动〉economize: ～时间 save time ‖ ～用电 economize on electricity ‖ 厉行～ exercise strict economy

【节肢动物】jiézhī dòngwù〈名〉arthropod

【节制】jiézhì〈动〉**1**（管辖）command and manage: 这三个团全归你～。All three regiments are under your command. **2**（限制）restrict: ～饮食 restrict what one eats and drinks

【节奏】jiézòu〈名〉**1**（指音乐）rhythm: 用不同的～演奏同一曲子 play the same tune in a different rhythm ‖ ～鲜明的乐曲 music with a swing **2**（指进程）tempo: 快～的生活 fast-paced lifestyle ‖ 这部影片的～太慢。This film is too slow.

【节奏感】jiézòugǎn〈名〉sense of rhythm

讦（訐） jié 〈动〉〈书〉 **1**（斥责）chide sb. for their mistakes **2**（揭发）expose sb.'s unmentionable past: ▸攻～

劫[1] jié〈动〉 **1**（抢） rob: ～车 hijack a car ‖ 钱包被歹徒～走了。 The wallet was pinched by some ruffians. ▸～机，趁火打～，洗～ **2**（威逼） coerce: ▸～持

劫[2] jié〈名〉 disaster: ▸～后余生，～数，在～难逃

【劫持】jiéchí〈动〉 hold under duress: ～飞机 hijack an aeroplane ‖ ～人质 kidnap a hostage ‖ 两名乘客被恐怖分子～。 Two passengers have been abducted by terrorists. ‖ ～者被当场击毙。 The hijacker was shot dead on the spot.

【劫材】jiécái〈名〉 captured stones [in the game 'go']

【劫夺】jiéduó〈动〉 seize by force: ～贵重物品/珍宝 plunder valuables/treasures

【劫匪】 jiéfěi 〈名〉 robber: 带面具的～ masked robber

【劫富济贫】jiéfù-jìpín〈成〉 rob the rich to help the poor: ～的办法 Robin Hood solution

【劫后余生】jiéhòu-yúshēng〈成〉 survive a disaster

【劫机】jiéjī〈动〉 hijack an aeroplane: ～犯 hijacker

【劫掠】jiélüè〈动〉 plunder: ～一空 make a clean sweep

【劫难】jiénàn〈名〉 calamity: 历经～ have experienced successive disasters

【劫数】 jiéshù 〈名〉［佛教］ inexorable doom: ～难逃。 There's no escaping fate.

【劫狱】jiéyù〈动〉 break into a jail and rescue a prisoner

劼 jié〈形〉〈书〉 **1**（谨慎） prudent **2**（努力） diligent

杰（傑） jié

A〈形〉 outstanding: ▸～出，～作

B〈名〉 hero: ▸豪～，俊～

【杰出】 jiéchū 〈形〉 outstanding: ～贡献 outstanding contributions ‖ ～人物 prominent figure

【杰作】 jiézuò 〈名〉 masterpiece: 《名利场》是英国文学的～之一。 *Vanity Fair* is one of the masterpieces of British literature.

j

诘（詰） jié 〈动〉 interrogate: ▸～问，～责，反～，盘～

▸jí

【诘难】jiénàn〈动〉〈书〉 censure

【诘问】jiéwèn〈动〉 interrogate: 证人受到辩护律师的～。 The witness was cross-examined by the defending counsel.

【诘责】jiézé〈动〉〈书〉 rebuke

拮 jié

【拮据】jiéjū〈形〉 hard up: 生活～ live from hand to mouth ‖ 手头～ be hard up

洁（潔） jié〈形〉 **1**（干净） clean: ▸～净，皎～，整～ **2**（纯洁） pure: ▸廉～，贞～

【洁白】jiébái〈形〉 pure white: ～的床单 spotlessly white sheet ‖ ～的雪 pure white snow

【洁白无瑕】jiébái-wúxiá〈成〉 spotless and flawless

【洁齿】jiéchǐ〈动〉 clean the teeth

【洁净】jiéjìng〈形〉 spotless: ～的教室 spotless classroom

【洁净煤】jiéjìngméi〈名〉 clean coal: ～技术 clean coal technology

【洁具】jiéjù〈名〉 bathroom equipment

【洁面乳】jiémiànrǔ〈名〉 cleansing cream

【洁癖】jiépǐ〈名〉 mysophobia

【洁身自好】jiéshēn-zìhào〈成〉 **1**（不同流合污） keep one's integrity **2**（只关心自己） keep oneself to oneself

【洁牙】jiéyá〈动〉 clean one's teeth

结（結） jié

A〈动〉 **1**（打结） tie: ▸～彩，～绳 **2**（形成） form: ～疤 become scarred ‖ 湖面上～了一层冰。 A layer of ice formed on the surface of the lake. ▸～冰，～痂，凝～ **3**（指关系） unite: ～下深厚的友谊 forge a profound friendship ▸～仇，～交，～盟 **4**（了结） conclude: ▸～局，～账，归根～底

B〈名〉 **1**（疙瘩） knot: 在绳子上打～ tie a knot in a rope ▸活～，领～，死～ **2**［解剖］ node: ▸喉～，淋巴～

▸jiē

【结案】 jié'àn 〈动〉 conclude a case: 已经～。 The case is already closed.

【结拜】jiébài〈动〉 become sworn brothers /sisters: ～姐妹/兄弟 sworn sisters/brothers

【结伴】jiébàn〈动〉 go with: 与某人～同行 travel with sb.

【结冰】jiébīng ▸**p. 776**〈动〉 freeze

【结彩】jiécǎi〈动〉 festoon: ▸张灯～

【结草衔环】 jiécǎo-xiánhuán 〈成〉〈喻〉 repay a debt of gratitude

【结肠】jiécháng〈名〉［解剖］ colon: ～癌 carcinoma of the colon ‖ ～炎 colitis

【结成】 jiéchéng 〈动〉 form: ～夫妻 be made man and wife ‖ ～同盟 form an alliance ‖ ～最广泛的统一战线 form the broadest united front

【结仇】jiéchóu〈动〉 become enemies: 这两个家族世代～。 The two families have been feuding with each other for generations.

【结存】jiécún **A**〈动〉 be in credit: 银行里有～ have cash in the bank **B**〈名〉 goods on hand

【结党营私】jiédǎng-yíngsī〈成〉 band together for selfish purposes

【结缔组织】jiédì zǔzhī〈名〉［生理］ connective tissue

【结点】jiédiǎn〈名〉 intersection: 交通～ traffic intersections

【结发夫妻】jiéfà fūqī〈名〉 husband and wife by the first marriage

【结构】jiégòu **A**〈名〉 **1**（比例） organization: ～合理 be properly organized ‖ ～严谨 be compact and well-organized ‖ ～调整 structural adjustment ‖ 产业～ industrial structure ‖ 文章～ structure of an article ‖ 知识～ knowledge composition **2**［建筑］ structure: 钢筋混凝土～ reinforced concrete structure ‖ 砖木～ brick and wood structure **B**〈动〉 plot: 根据主线来～故事 plot a story around the main theme

【结构钢】jiégòugāng〈名〉 structural steel

【结构工资制】jiégòu gōngzīzhì〈名〉 composite wage system

【结构力学】jiégòu lìxué〈名〉 structural mechanics

【结构式】jiégòushì〈名〉［化学］ constitutional formula

【结构主义】jiégòu zhǔyì〈名〉 structuralism

【结关】jiéguān〈动〉 clear customs: ～手续 customs clearance procedures

【结果】jiéguǒ **A**〈名〉 result: 毫无～ without result ‖ 初步/最后～ preliminary/final result ‖ 实验/统计～ experimental/statistical result ‖ 面试/选举～ outcome of an interview/election ‖ 你这样下去不会有好～的。 You will come to no good end if you go on like that. **B**〈动〉 kill: 他一枪～了那个歹徒。 He finished that ruffian off with one shot.

▸jiēguǒ

【结合】jiéhé〈动〉 **1**（发生联系） unite: 理论～实践 combine theory with practice ‖ 实现经济效益与社会效益的最佳～ achieve an optimal combination of social and economic benefits ‖ 教育必须与实践相～。 Education must be combined with practice. **2**（结婚） get married: 他们的～从一开始就是个错误。 Their marriage was a mistake from the very beginning.

【结合部】jiéhébù〈名〉 part connecting two or more things: 城乡～ meeting point of town and country

【结核】jiéhé **A**〈形〉 tubercle: ～性皮肤病 tuberculoderma ‖ ～性心包炎 tuberculous pericarditis **B**〈名〉 **1**（指病） tuberculosis: ▸肺～ **2**［矿业］ nodule: 铜～ copper nodule

【结核病】jiéhébìng ▸**p. 50**〈名〉 tuberculosis (TB): ～杆菌 tubercle bacillus ‖ ～防治中心 TB prevention and treatment centre

【结汇】jiéhuì〈名〉 settlement of exchange

【结婚】jiéhūn〈动〉 get married: 登记～ register for marriage ‖ 旅行～ destination wedding ‖ 他去年结的婚。 He got married last year. ‖ 我们～25年了。 We have been married for 25 years.

【结婚登记】jiéhūn dēngjì〈名〉 marriage registration

【结婚典礼】jiéhūn diǎnlǐ〈名〉 wedding ceremony

【结婚戒指】jiéhūn jièzhi〈名〉wedding ring

【结婚证书】jiéhūn zhèngshū〈名〉 marriage certificate

【结伙】jiéhuǒ〈动〉 gang up: ～闹事 band together to make trouble ‖ ～抢劫 commit a gang robbery

【结集】jiéjí〈动〉 **1**（指军队） concentrate: ～兵力 concentrate troops **2**（指文章） anthologize: ～成册 compile into a book

【结痂】jiéjiā〈动〉 scab over: 伤口已经～。 The wound has scabbed over.

【结交】jiéjiāo〈动〉 make friends with: ～新朋友 make new friends

【结晶】jiéjīng **A**〈动〉 crystallize: 盐会～。 Salt forms crystals. **B**〈名〉 **1**（晶体） crystal: ～硅太阳能电池 crystalline silicon solar cell **2**（成果） crystallization: 爱情/劳动的～ fruits of one's love/labour ‖ 智慧的～ crystallization of wisdom

【结晶体】jiéjīngtǐ〈名〉 crystal

【结局】jiéjú〈名〉 final result: 悲惨的～ tragic ending ‖ 故事的～很圆满。 The story has a happy ending.

【结论】jiélùn〈名〉 **1**［逻辑］ conclusion **2**（论断） verdict: 匆忙下～ jump to a conclusion ‖ 相反/最后的～ opposite/final verdict

【结盟】jiéméng〈动〉 form an alliance: 与另一国～ be in league with another country ‖ 不～国家/运动 non-aligned nations/movement

【结膜】jiémó〈名〉［解剖］ conjunctiva: ～炎 conjunctivitis

【结欠】jiéqiàn〈动〉 have a balance due

【结亲】jiéqīn〈动〉 **1**（结婚） marry: 三

十岁还未～ still unmarried at the age of 30 **2**（联姻） become relatives by marriage: 两家已经～。The two families have joined in marriage.

【结清】jiéqīng〈动〉 settle up: ～餐费 settle up a restaurant bill ‖ ～账目 settle accounts (with sb.) ‖ 账～了。The account was closed.

【结球甘蓝】jiéqiú gānlán〈名〉[植物] cabbage

【结舌】jiéshé〈动〉 be at a loss for words: ～缄口 tongue-tied ▸瞠目～, 张口～

【结社】jiéshè〈动〉 form an association: ～自由 freedom of association

【结绳】jiéshéng〈动〉 tie knots: ～记事 keep records by tying knots

【结石】jiéshí〈名〉 stone: 胆～ gall stone ‖ 膀胱/肾～ bladder/kidney stone

【结识】jiéshí〈动〉 make sb.'s acquaintance: ～新朋友 make new friends ‖ 他们～不久就结婚了。They married after just a brief acquaintance.

【结束】jiéshù〈动〉 end: ～罢工 bring an end to the strike ‖ ～比赛 close a match ‖ 宣布会议～ declare a meeting closed ‖ 工作已告～。The work is finished. ‖ 演出到此～。That's the end of our performance.

【结束语】jiéshùyǔ〈名〉 concluding remarks

【结算】jiésuàn〈动〉 settle an account: ～余额 strike a balance ‖ 用美元～ use US dollars for settling accounts

【结算价】jiésuànjià〈名〉 settlement price: 黄金的～略有下跌。The settlement price of gold fell slightly.

【结算日】jiésuànrì〈名〉 settlement day

【结尾】jiéwěi〈名〉 ending: ～部分 epilogue ‖ ～工程 the final stages of a project ‖ 故事/小说～ end of a story/novel

【结业】jiéyè〈动〉 complete a course: ～典礼 graduation ceremony ‖ ～证书 certificate for courses completed

【结义】jiéyì = 结拜 jiébài

【结余】jiéyú **A**〈动〉 have a surplus after a settlement **B**〈名〉 surplus: 现金～ cash surplus

【结语】jiéyǔ = 结束语 jiéshùyǔ

【结冤】jiéyuān〈动〉 start a feud

【结缘】jiéyuán〈动〉 form ties: 与书法～ start enjoying calligraphy

【结怨】jiéyuàn〈动〉 incur hatred: （与某人）～甚深 have deep enmity (with sb.)

【结扎】jiézā〈动〉[医学] ligate: ～出血的动脉 ligate a bleeding artery ‖ 输卵管/输精管～ ligation of oviducts/spermaduct

【结账】jiézhàng〈动〉 settle accounts: 请用现金～。Please settle your bill in cash.

【结转】jiézhuǎn〈动〉 carry down

【结子】jiézi〈名〉〈口〉 knot: 打个～ tie a knot

桔 jié

▸jú

【桔槔】jiégāo〈名〉 pole with bucket and counterpoise for raising water

【桔梗】jiégěng〈名〉[中药] root of balloon flower

桀 jié〈形〉 cruel: ▸～骜不驯

【桀骜不驯】jié'ào-bùxùn〈成〉 wild and intractable

【桀犬吠尧】Jiéquǎn-fèiYáo〈成〉〈喻〉 a lackey is servile to his master

【桀纣】Jié-Zhòu〈名〉〈喻〉 tyrants

捷[1] jié〈动〉 triumph: 首战告～ win the first battle ▸～报, 大～, 告～

捷[2] jié〈形〉 **1**（快） quick: ～运公司 express delivery company ▸～足先登, 矫～, 敏～ **2**（方便） close and convenient: ▸～径, 便～

【捷报】jiébào〈名〉 news of victory: ～频传 good news keeps pouring in

【捷径】jiéjìng〈名〉 shortcut: 走～ take shortcut

【捷克】Jiékè〈名〉 Czech: ～共和国 the Czech Republic ‖ ～人 Czech ‖ ～语 Czech

【捷足先登】jiézú-xiāndēng〈成〉 the early bird catches the worm

蛣（蠞） jié〈名〉[动物] stick insect

偈 jié〈形〉〈书〉 valiant

▸jì

婕 jié

【婕妤】jiéyú〈名〉〈古〉 title of a female official

睫 jié〈名〉 eyelash: ▸～毛, 目不交～, 迫在眉～

【睫毛】jiémáo〈名〉 eyelash

【睫毛膏】jiémáogāo〈名〉 mascara: 涂～ apply mascara

截 jié

A〈动〉 **1**（割断） cut: ～成两段 cut in two ▸～长补短, ～取, ～肢 **2**（阻拦） check: 他被～住了。He was intercepted. ▸～获, ～击, 拦～ **3**（截止） close by a particular time: ▸～止, ～至

B〈量〉 section: 一～儿木头 a log ‖〈喻〉他话说了半～儿又缩回去了。He broke off halfway and didn't say any more.

【截长补短】jiécháng-bǔduǎn〈成〉 draw on the strength of each to offset the weakness of the other

【截除】jiéchú〈名〉[医学] amputation

【截道】jiédào〈动〉 rob people on highways

【截断】jiéduàn〈动〉 **1**（切断） block: ～敌人的退路 cut off an enemy retreat ‖ ～河流 dam a river **2**（打断） cut short: 电话铃声～了他的话。He was interrupted by the ringing of the telephone.

【截稿】jiégǎo〈动〉 stop accepting contributions: ～日期 deadline for contributions

【截获】jiéhuò〈动〉 intercept: ～敌军的作战计划 intercept the enemy's battle plan ‖ ～情报 intercept information

【截击】jiéjī〈动〉 intercept: ～导弹 intercept a missile ‖ ～敌机 intercept enemy planes

【截孔】jiékǒng〈名〉 cut-out hole

【截口】jiékǒu〈名〉 section

【截流】jiéliú〈动〉 dam a river: ～坝 cut-off dam

【截流井】jiéliújǐng〈名〉[建筑] catch basin

【截留】jiéliú〈动〉 hold back: ～国家财政收入 hold back state revenue ‖ ～税款 withhold a tax payment

【截门】jiémén〈名〉 pipe valve

【截面】jiémiàn〈名〉 section: ～图 sectional drawing ‖ 横～ cross section

【截取】jiéqǔ〈动〉 cut off: ～文中的部分内容 extract a chunk of text

【截然】jiérán〈副〉〈书〉 completely: ～不同 as different as chalk and cheese ‖ ～相反 poles apart

【截瘫】jiétān ▸**p. 50**〈名〉[医学] paraplegia: 高位～ high paraplegia

【截污】jiéwū〈动〉 block the release of sewage

【截肢】jiézhī〈名〉[医学] amputation: 高位～ high amputation

【截止】jiézhǐ〈动〉 end: ～日期 closing date ‖ 报名已经～。Registration has already closed.

【截趾适履】jiézhǐ-shìlǚ〈成〉 cut the toes to fit the shoes

【截至】jiézhì〈动〉 be no later than: ～目前 up to now ‖ ～上月底 by the end of last month

【截子】jiézi = 截 jié B

碣 jié〈名〉 stone tablet: 墓～ tombstone

竭 jié

A〈动〉 **1**（耗尽） run out: ▸精疲力～, 声嘶力～, 衰～ **2**（用尽） use up: ▸～诚, ～尽全力, ～力

B〈形〉 dried-up: ▸枯～

【竭诚】jiéchéng〈副〉 wholeheartedly: ～为读者服务 serve the readers wholeheartedly ‖ ～拥护 give wholehearted support

【竭尽】jiéjìn〈动〉 use up: ～财力 expend one's resources

【竭尽全力】jiéjìn-quánlì〈成〉 do one's utmost

【竭力】jiélì〈动〉 do one's utmost: ～反对 strongly oppose ‖ ～支持 give all-out support ‖ ～抢救伤员 spare no effort to save wounded soldiers

【竭泽而渔】jiézé'éryú〈成〉〈喻〉 make a thorough but unwise exploitation

羯[1] jié〈名〉 wether

羯[2] jié〈名〉 Jie [ancient ethnic group in China]

【羯羊】jiéyáng〈名〉 castrated ram

jiě

姐 jiě〈名〉 **1**（指同父母） elder sister: 大～ eldest sister ‖ 二～ second elder sister **2**（指同辈） elder female relative of the same generation: ▸表～ **3**（年轻女子） general term for young women: 李～ Sister Li **4**（小姐） miss: 空～ air hostess

【姐夫】jiěfu ▸**p. 588**〈名〉 brother-in-law [elder sister's husband]

【姐姐】jiějie ▸**p. 588**〈名〉 elder sister

【姐妹】jiěmèi〈名〉 **1**（姐姐和妹妹） sisters: 孪生～ twin sisters ‖ 同胞～ full sisters **2**（同胞） siblings: ～情 sisterly affection

【姐妹城市】jiěmèi chéngshì〈名〉 sister city: 西安和奈良是～。Xi'an is twinned with Nara.

【姐妹篇】jiěmèipiān〈名〉 sister piece

【姐儿们】jiěrmen〈名〉〈方〉 sisters

【姐丈】jiězhàng〈方〉= 姐夫 jiěfu

解 jiě

A〈动〉 **1**（分开） dissect: ▸～剖 **2**（使分散） separate: ▸～散, 瓦～ **3**（去除） dismiss: ～油腻 get rid of the grease ▸～除, ～闷, ～围 **4**（上厕所） relieve oneself: ▸大～, 小～ **5**（打开） untie: ～鞋带

j

undo a shoelace ‖ ～纽扣 unbutton ▸～铃系铃 **6**（解释） explain: ▸～释, 讲～ **7**（理解） understand: 令人不～ puzzling ▸费～, 了～ **8**（解答） solve: ～出一道数学题 solve a mathematical problem ‖ ～方程式 solve an equation

B〈名〉［数学］ solution: 近似/精确/数值～ approximate/exact/numerical solution ▸求～

▸jiè, xiè

【解表】jiěbiǎo〈动〉［中医］ induce sweat

【解馋】jiěchán〈动〉 satisfy a food craving

【解嘲】jiěcháo〈动〉 try to get out of a scrape when ridiculed: 他经常自我～。 He often finds excuses to console himself.

【解愁】jiěchóu〈动〉 relieve one's worries: ～释闷 put an end to one's worries

【解除】jiěchú〈动〉 get rid of: ～顾虑 free one's mind of apprehensions ‖ ～婚约 call off an engagement ‖ 旱情已经～。 The dry spell is over.

【解答】 jiědá 〈动〉 answer: ～疑难问题 answer difficult questions ‖ 习题～ key to an exercise

【解冻】jiědòng〈动〉 **1**（融化） thaw: 冷冻食品烹煮前必须先～。 Frozen food must be thawed before cooking. ‖ 今年河流～早。 The river thawed early this year. ‖〈喻〉 两国关系逐渐～。 The relations between the two countries gradually thawed. **2**〈喻〉（解除冻结） unfreeze: 被冻结的资产～了。 The frozen assets were thawed out.

【解毒】 jiědú 〈动〉 **1**［医学］ detoxify **2**［中医］ relieve internal heat: 清热～ relieve internal heat

【解读】 jiědú 〈动〉 decode: ～历史文化 analyse and understand history and culture ‖ 对此事件人们有不同的～。 People have different interpretations of this matter.

【解饿】jiě'è〈动〉 satisfy one's hunger: 用马铃薯～ satisfy one's appetite with potatoes

【解乏】jiěfá〈动〉 refresh oneself: 洗个澡解～。 Take a bath and you won't feel so tired.

【解放】jiěfàng **A**〈动〉 liberate: ～生产力 emancipate the productive forces ‖ ～思想，大胆创新 liberate your thinking and boldly create ‖ 妇女～ women's liberation ‖ 民族～运动 national liberation movement **B**〈名〉 Liberation [especially referring to the overthrow of the Kuomintang rule in China in 1949]: ～前 before liberation

【解放军】jiěfàngjūn〈简称〉= 中国人民解放军

【解放区】jiěfàngqū〈名〉 liberated area

【解放战争】 jiěfàng zhànzhēng 〈名〉 **1**（指为解放） war of liberation **2**（特指中国） China's War of Liberation

【解构】jiěgòu〈动〉 deconstruct: ～主义 deconstructionism ‖ ～传统文化 deconstruct traditional culture

【解雇】jiěgù〈动〉 dismiss: ～工人 sack a worker ‖ 你被～了。 You are fired.

【解恨】jiěhèn〈动〉 vent one's hatred: 杀了这个恶棍为民～ kill the ruffian to assuage people's hatred

【解惑】jiěhuò〈动〉 dispel a doubt: 答疑～ answer questions and remove doubts

【解甲归田】jiějiǎ-guītián〈成〉 be demobilized: ～的士兵 demobbed soldier

【解禁】jiějìn〈动〉 lift a ban

【解救】jiějiù〈动〉 rescue: ～人质 free a hostage ‖ 把孩子从人贩子手中～出来 rescue a child from human traffickers

【解决】jiějué〈动〉 **1**（处理） solve: ～国际争端 settle international disputes ‖ ～粮食短缺问题 resolve grain shortages ‖ ～问题 resolve a problem ‖ 切实可行的～办法 workable solution **2**（消灭） finish off: 这一仗他们～了敌人一个营。 In the battle they wiped out an enemy battalion.

【解开】jiěkāi〈动〉 untie: ～领带 loosen one's tie ‖ ～鞋带 undo one's shoelaces ‖〈喻〉 ～一个谜 unravel a mystery

【解渴】jiěkě〈动〉 **1**（指感觉） quench one's thirst: 吃西瓜～ assuage one's thirst with a watermelon ‖ 矿泉水真～。 Mineral water really quenches your thirst. **2**〈喻〉（指问题） be satisfying and beneficial: 这堂辅导课真～。 This tutorial has been really useful.

【解困】jiěkùn〈动〉 resolve difficulties: 扶贫～ help the needy and resolve difficulties

【解铃还须系铃人】jiě líng hái xū xì líng rén = 解铃系铃 jiělíng-xìlíng

【解铃系铃】jiělíng-xìlíng〈成〉 let he who created the problem resolve it

【解码】jiěmǎ〈动〉 decode: ～器 decoder

【解闷】jiěmèn〈动〉 relieve boredom: 打乒乓球～ kill time by playing table tennis ‖ 今晚没什么～的。 Tonight, there is nothing to break the monotony.

【解密】jiěmì〈动〉 **1**（指秘密） declassify: ～文件 declassified document **2**（指密码） decode

【解民倒悬】jiěmín-dàoxuán〈成〉 relieve people of their sufferings

【解难】jiěnán〈动〉 overcome a difficulty: 释疑～ clear up doubts and overcome difficulties ‖ 为民～ help people overcome difficulties

【解难】jiěnàn〈动〉 resolve a disaster: 消灾～ dispel calamities and remove dangers ▸排忧～

【解囊】 jiěnáng 〈动〉 be generous with money: ▸慷慨～

【解囊相助】jiěnáng xiāngzhù〈成〉 give generous financial assistance

【解聘】jiěpìn〈动〉 dismiss an employee: ～员工 lay off staff

【解剖】jiěpōu〈动〉 dissect: 尸体～ autopsy ‖〈喻〉 严于～自己 severely examine oneself

【解剖麻雀】 jiěpōu-máquè 〈惯〉〈喻〉 analyse a typical case

【解剖学】jiěpōuxué〈名〉 anatomy

【解气】jiěqì〈动〉 vent one's spleen: 他用咒骂来～。 His anger vented itself in curses.

【解劝】jiěquàn〈动〉 soothe: 她不听我的～。 She didn't allow herself to be comforted by my words.

【解热】jiěrè 〈动〉［中医］ allay a fever: ～剂 antipyretic ‖ ～镇痛药 analgesic-antipyretic

【解散】jiěsàn〈动〉 **1**（使离去） dismiss: 让学生～ dismiss the students ‖ ～! Dismiss! **2**（取缔） dissolve: ～非法组织 disband an illegal organization ‖ ～议会 dissolve parliament

【解释】jiěshì〈动〉 explain: ～词义 explain the meaning of a word ‖ ～法律 interpret the law ‖ 这无须～。 This needs no explanation.

【解释权】jiěshìquán〈名〉 right to interpret

【解手】jiěshǒu〈动〉 relieve oneself: 解大手 defecate ‖ 解小手 urinate

【解说】jiěshuō〈动〉 commentate: 为足球比赛做～ commentate on a football match ‖ ～词 commentary ‖ ～员 commentator

【解溲】jiěsōu〈动〉〈书〉 relieve oneself

【解套】jiětào〈动〉［金融］ unlock

【解题】jiětí〈动〉 solve a (mathematical, etc.) problem

【解体】jiětǐ 〈动〉 disintegrate: 社会的～ social disintegration ‖ 家庭～了。 The family dissolved.

【解痛】jiětòng〈动〉 have relief from pain

【解脱】jiětuō〈动〉 **1**［佛教］ moksha **2**（摆脱） free oneself: ～精神负担 free oneself from a mental burden ‖ 从家务中～出来 relieve sb. of the housework **3**（开脱） exonerate: 为某人～罪责 exonerate sb. from a crime

【解围】jiěwéi〈动〉 **1**（指包围） raise a siege **2**（指困境） get sb. out of a fix: 快去给他～ get to his help quickly

【解悟】 jiěwù 〈动〉〈书〉 come to understand

【解析】jiěxī〈名〉 analysis: 精辟的～ incisive analysis

【解析几何】jiěxī jǐhé〈名〉 analytic geometry

【解严】jiěyán〈动〉 lift a curfew: ～令 order for lifting a curfew

【解衣】jiěyī〈动〉〈书〉 undress

【解衣推食】jiěyī-tuīshí〈成〉〈喻〉 treat sb. with great kindness

【解颐】jiěyí〈动〉〈书〉 smile

【解疑】jiěyí〈动〉 get rid of doubts and misgivings

【解忧】jiěyōu〈动〉 alleviate sorrow: 借酒～ drink one's sorrows away

【解约】jiěyuē〈动〉 break off an agreement: 他与这家公司～了。 He broke his contract with the firm.

【解约金】jiěyuējīn〈名〉cancellation money

【解约书】jiěyuēshū〈名〉 letter of cancellation

【解职】jiězhí〈动〉 dismiss: 他因贪污而被～。 He was discharged for embezzlement.

jiè

介[1] jiè〈动〉 **1**（位于其间） lie between: ～于两者之间 be situated between the two ▸～音, 媒～ **2**（介绍） give a brief introduction: ▸简～ **3**（放在心里） mind: ▸～怀, ～意

介[2] jiè〈名〉 **1**〈书〉（铠甲） armour **2**（甲壳） shell: ▸～壳

介[3] jiè

A〈量〉 [used with words denoting persons] a, an: 一～书生 an intellectual ‖ 一～武夫 a warrior

B〈形〉〈书〉 upright: ▸耿～

介[4] jiè〈名〉［戏曲］ word indicating motion or action: 饮酒～ action of drinking

【介词】jiècí〈名〉 preposition: ～短语 prepositional phrase

【介怀】jièhuái〈动〉〈书〉 take offence: 他对她的话毫不～。 He was not at all offended by her remarks.

【介壳】jièqiào〈名〉 shell: ～虫 scale insect

【介入】jièrù〈动〉 get involved: ～争论 get involved in a dispute ‖ 不要～别人的私生活。 Don't interfere in others' private lives.

【介入疗法】jièrù liáofǎ〈名〉［医学］interventional therapy

【介绍】jièshào〈动〉 **1**（引见） introduce: ～对象 introduce sb. to a potential partner ‖ 自我～ introduce oneself ‖ 历史背景～

historical introduction [2]（推荐） recommend: 为某人~工作 recommend sb. for a job ‖ ~某人入党 recommend sb. for Party membership [3]（推广） let known: ~经验 pass on experience ‖ ~先进事迹 let sb.'s good deeds be known ‖ ~新产品 introduce a new product

【介绍人】jièshàorén〈名〉[1]（引见人） sponsor [2]（媒人） go-between

【介绍所】jièshàosuǒ〈名〉 agency: 婚姻~ matrimonial agency ‖ 职业~ employment agency

【介绍信】jièshàoxìn〈名〉 letter of introduction

【介意】jièyì〈动〉 mind: 一点也不~ not mind at all ‖ 我在这儿吸烟你不~吧? Do you mind my smoking here?

【介音】jièyīn〈名〉［语言］ semivowel [any of the three vowels i, u and ü used in compound vowels]

【介于】jièyú〈动〉 lie between: 这条河~两省之间。 The river is situated between the two provinces.

【介质】jièzhì〈名〉[1]［物理］ medium [2]［电气］ insulating substance

【介胄】jièzhòu〈名〉〈书〉 armour

【介子】jièzǐ〈名〉［物理］ meson

戒 jiè

A〈动〉[1]（防备） take precautions against: ►~备, ~心 [2]（放弃） give up: ~掉烟瘾 give up smoking ‖ ~赌 abstain from gambling ►~除, ~酒

B〈名〉[1]（禁令） Buddhist monastic discipline: ►~律, 杀~, 受~ [2]（戒指） ring: 婚/金/钻~ wedding/gold/diamond ring

【戒备】jièbèi〈动〉[1]（警戒） be on the alert: ~森严 be heavily guarded ‖ 毫无~ be caught completely off guard ‖ 处于高度~状态 be on high alert [2]（防备） take precautions against: 我想让你有所~。 I wanted to put you on your guard.

【戒尺】jièchǐ〈名〉〈旧〉 teacher's ruler used for punishing pupils

【戒除】jièchú〈动〉 give up: ~恶习 break a bad habit ‖ ~嗜好 kick the habit

【戒刀】jièdāo〈名〉〈旧〉 Buddhist monk's knife

【戒毒】jièdú〈动〉 give up drugs: 强制性~ compulsory narcotics detoxification ‖ ~所 drug rehabilitation centre

【戒忌】jièjì〈书〉 **A**〈名〉 taboo **B**〈动〉 guard against violating a taboo

【戒骄戒躁】jièjiāo-jièzào〈成〉 guard against arrogance and rashness

【戒酒】jièjiǔ〈动〉 give up drinking

【戒惧】jièjù〈动〉〈书〉 be frightened and watchful

【戒律】jièlǜ〈名〉 commandment: 宗教~ religious precepts ►清规~

【戒条】jiètiáo = 戒律 jièlǜ

【戒心】jièxīn〈名〉 wariness: 怀有~ harbour suspicions

【戒烟】jièyān〈动〉 quit smoking

【戒严】jièyán〈动〉 enforce martial law: 实行~ impose martial law ‖ ~令 martial law

【戒指】jièzhi〈名〉 ring: 金/钻石~ gold/diamond ring

芥 jiè

〈名〉[1]（芥菜） mustard [2]〈书〉（小草） small grass [3]〈书〉（指事物） triviality

►gài

【芥菜】jiècài〈名〉 leaf mustard

►gàicài

【芥菜疙瘩】jiècài gēda〈名〉 swede〈英〉; rutabaga〈美〉

【芥蒂】jièdì〈名〉 grudge: 消除~ settle a grudge ‖ 心存~ harbour a grudge

【芥末】jièmo〈名〉 mustard

【芥子】jièzǐ〈名〉 mustard seed

【芥子气】jièzǐqì〈名〉［化学］ mustard gas

【芥子油】jièzǐyóu〈名〉 mustard oil

届（屆） jiè

A〈动〉 expire: ►~期, ~时

B〈量〉 session: 第二~全国人民代表大会 second National People's Congress ‖ 08~毕业生 graduates from 2008 ►历~

【届满】jièmǎn〈动〉[of a term] expire: 他的任期即将~。 His term of office is going to expire very soon.

【届期】jièqī〈副〉〈书〉 when the time comes: ~恭请莅临指导。 Please come and give instructions at the appointed time.

【届时】jièshí〈副〉〈书〉 when the time comes: ~务请光临。 Your presence is requested for the occasion.

界 jiè

〈名〉[1]（边界） boundary: 省~ provincial boundaries ‖ 以某物为~ be fringed by sth. ►~碑, ~面, 边~ [2]（范围） scope, extent: ►境~, 外~, 眼~ [3]（领域） circles: 经济~ economic circles ‖ 文化~ cultural circles ‖ 宗教~ religious circles ►教育~, 政~ [4]（指生物系统） kingdom: 动物/植物/昆虫~ animal/vegetable/insect kingdom ►自然~ [5]［地质］ era: 古生~ Palaeozoic era

【界碑】jièbēi〈名〉 boundary monument

【界标】jièbiāo〈名〉 boundary mark

【界尺】jièchǐ〈名〉 ungraduated ruler

【界定】jièdìng〈动〉 delimit

【界河】jièhé〈名〉 boundary river

【界面】jièmiàn〈名〉[1]（接触面） interface: ~面积 boundary area ‖ ~阻力 interfacial resistance [2]［计算机］ user interface

【界内球】jiènèiqiú〈名〉［体育］ in bounds

【界墙】jièqiáng〈名〉 partition wall

【界山】jièshān〈名〉 boundary mountain

【界石】jièshí〈名〉 boundary stone

【界说】jièshuō〈名〉〈旧〉 definition

【界外球】jièwàiqiú〈名〉［体育］ out-of-bounds

【界限】jièxiàn〈名〉[1]（分界） demarcation line: 划清~ draw a clear line of demarcation ‖ 爱情与友情的~ dividing line between love and friendship [2]（限度） limit: 他的野心没有~。 His ambition knows no bounds.

【界线】jièxiàn〈名〉[1]（指分界线） boundary line: 超越~ get across the boundary line ►分~ [2] = 界限 jièxiàn 1 [3]（边缘） edge

【界桩】jièzhuāng〈名〉 boundary marker

疥 jiè

〈名〉 scabies

【疥虫】jièchóng〈名〉［医学］ sarcoptic mite

【疥疮】jièchuāng ►**p. 50**〈名〉［医学］ scabies

【疥蛤蟆】jièháma〈名〉 toad

诫（誡） jiè

〈动〉 admonish: ►告~, 规~, 训~

蚧 jiè

►蛤蚧 géjiè

借[1] jiè

〈动〉[1]（借入） borrow: 向朋友~钱 borrow money from a friend ‖ 有~有还，再~不难。 Return whatever you borrow so that you can borrow more easily next time. [2]（借出） lend, loan: 他从不~钱给别人。 He never lends money.

借[2]（藉） jiè

〈动〉[1]（利用） make use of: ~此机会感谢你 take the opportunity to thank you ►~助 [2]（假托） make a pretext of: ►~端, ~故, ~口

【借词】jiècí〈名〉［语言］ loanword

【借代】jièdài〈名〉［语言］ rhetorical devices such as metonymy, antonomasia and synecdoche

【借贷】jièdài **A**〈动〉（借入） borrow money;（借出） lend money: ~无门 have no means of borrowing ‖ ~业务 borrowing and lending business **B**〈名〉 debit and credit sides

【借刀杀人】jièdāo-shārén〈成〉〈喻〉 get sb. else to kill on one's behalf

【借调】jièdiào〈动〉 loan: 他被~到我院编写词典。 He is on loan to our university to compile a dictionary.

【借读】jièdú〈动〉 study at a school beyond the area of one's registered permanent residence: ~生 transient student

【借端】jièduān〈动〉 find an excuse: ~滋事 make trouble under some pretext ‖ ~寻衅 find an excuse to look for a fight

【借方】jièfāng〈名〉［会计］ debit side

【借风使船】jièfēng-shǐchuán〈成〉〈喻〉 achieve one's goal with the help of sb. else

【借古讽今】jiègǔ-fěngjīn〈成〉 use the past to satirize the present

【借故】jiègù〈动〉 find an excuse: ~拖延 find an excuse to delay ‖ 他~事情急，就离开了。 He left on the pretext of urgent matters.

【借光】jièguāng〈动〉〈套〉 excuse me: ~，请让让路! Out of the way, please.

【借花献佛】jièhuā-xiànfó〈成〉〈喻〉 offer gifts given by sb. else

【借火】jièhuǒ〈动〉 ask for a light: 对不起，能借个火吗? Excuse me, have you got a light?

【借记卡】jièjìkǎ〈名〉 debit card

【借鉴】jièjiàn〈动〉 draw lessons from: ~外国经验 use the experience of other countries for reference ‖ 相互~ learn from each other

【借景】jièjǐng〈动〉 use a scene to harmonize with other scenes in designing a garden

【借景抒情】jièjǐng-shūqíng〈成〉 take advantage of a scene to express one's emotions

【借酒浇愁】jièjiǔ-jiāochóu〈成〉 drown one's sorrows in drink

【借据】jièjù〈名〉 IOU: 索要~ ask for a receipt for a loan

【借壳上市】jièké shàngshì〈动〉［金融］ engage in back-door listing

【借口】jièkǒu **A**〈动〉 use as an excuse: 她~胃疼，没参加考试。 She pleaded a stomach-ache and so didn't take the examination. ‖ 他~太忙，谢绝了邀请。 He refused the invitation on the pretext of being too busy. **B**〈名〉 excuse: 寻找~不去 find an excuse for not going ‖ 我找了个~走了。 I made an excuse and left.

【借款】jièkuǎn **A**〈动〉（借入） borrow money;（借出） lend money **B**〈名〉 loan: 偿还~ redeem a loan ‖ 拖欠银行~ default on one's bank loan

【借尸还魂】jièshī-huánhún〈成〉[1]〈本〉 find reincarnation in another's corpse [2]〈喻〉（指思想、行为等） revive in a new guise

【借书证】jièshūzhèng〈名〉 library card
【借水行舟】jièshuǐ-xíngzhōu〈成〉〈喻〉 achieve one's purpose through the agency of sb. else
【借宿】jièsù〈动〉 sleep over: 在朋友家～ stay overnight at a friend's house
【借题发挥】jiètí-fāhuī〈成〉 seize upon an incident to exaggerate matters
【借条】jiètiáo〈名〉 IOU
【借位】jièwèi〈动〉［数学］ borrow
【借问】jièwèn〈动〉〈套〉 may I ask: ～这儿离火车站还有多远? Will you please tell me how far it is to the railway station from here?
【借以】jièyǐ〈连〉〈书〉 so as to: 我在此略举几例，～说明这项工程的重要性。 I'll give you a few examples to illustrate the importance of the project.
【借用】jièyòng〈动〉 **1**（指物品） borrow: ～一下你的伞，好吗? May I use your umbrella? **2**（指事物） use sth. for another purpose: ～一首诗表白爱情 declare one's love with a poem
【借喻】jièyù〈名〉［语言］ metonymy
【借阅】jièyuè〈动〉 borrow for reading: ～图书要如期归还。 Borrowed books must be returned on time.
【借债】jièzhài〈动〉 borrow money: ～度日 live off loans
【借账】jièzhàng = 借债 jièzhài
【借支】jièzhī〈动〉 get an advance on one's pay: 他想～下个月的薪水。 He wants to get next month's salary in advance.
【借重】jièzhòng〈动〉〈敬〉 rely on for support
【借住】jièzhù〈动〉 stay at sb. else's place: 在姑母家～几周 stay at one's aunt's home for several weeks
【借助】jièzhù〈动〉 have the aid of: ～词典学习英语 study English with the help of dictionaries ‖ 他们～地图和指南针走出了丛林。 They got out of the jungle with the help of a map and a compass.
【借箸代筹】jièzhù-dàichóu〈成〉 plan for others

骱 jiè〈名〉〈方〉 joint: 脱～ dislocation

解 jiè〈动〉 escort: ▸～送, 押～
▸jiě, xiè
【解款】jièkuǎn〈动〉 transfer funds: ～单 cash remittance note
【解送】jièsòng〈动〉 send under guard: ～犯人 send criminals under guard
【解元】jièyuán〈名〉 [in the Ming and Qing dynasties in China] scholar winning first place in provincial imperial examinations

藉 jiè
A〈名〉〈书〉 mat
B〈动〉 place sth. underneath: ▸枕～
▸jí

jie

价（價） jie〈助〉 **1**〈口〉（用于状语后） [used after adverbials]: 震天～响 make a thunderous noise ‖ 整天～忙 be busy all day long **2**〈方〉（用于强调） [used to form an emphatic statement]: 别/不～。 Don't/No!
▸jià

jīn

巾 jīn〈名〉 piece of cloth: 汗～ sweat-band ▸毛～, 头～, 围～
【巾帼】jīnguó〈名〉〈喻〉 woman: ～英雄 heroine ‖ ～不让须眉。 Women refuse to be outdone by men.

斤[1] jīn〈名〉〈古〉 axe

斤[2] jīn ▸**p. 978**〈量〉 *jin* [unit of weight, equal to 0.5 kilogram]: 五～米 five catties of rice ▸公～, 市～
【斤斤计较】jīnjīn-jìjiào〈成〉 square accounts down to the smallest detail: 不必～。 There is no need to quibble over every detail.
【斤两】jīnliǎng〈名〉 weight: ～不足 under weight ‖〈喻〉 他的话很有～。 What he says carries much weight.

今 jīn
A〈名〉 **1**（现在） now: 从～以后 from now on **2**（现代） modern: ▸至～, 古为～用, 厚～薄古
B〈代〉 this: ～冬/夏 this winter/summer
【今不如昔】jīnbùrúxī〈成〉 be worse than before
【今晨】jīnchén〈名〉 this morning
【今非昔比】jīnfēixībǐ〈成〉 times change
【今后】jīnhòu〈名〉 days to come: 在～很长一段时间里 for a long time to come ‖ ～我们要更加努力。 We should work even harder in future.
【今年】jīnnián ▸**p. 618**〈名〉 this year: ～将是一个丰收年。 This year we will have a bumper harvest.
【今儿】jīnr ▸**p. 618**〈名〉〈方〉 today: ～是星期六。 It's Saturday today.
【今人】jīnrén〈名〉 modern people
【今日】jīnrì ▸**p. 618**〈名〉 today: ～事，～毕。 Never put off till tomorrow what can be done today.
【今生】jīnshēng ▸**p. 618**〈名〉 this life: ～今世 this very life
【今世】jīnshì ▸**p. 618**〈名〉 **1**（今生） this life **2**（当代） this age
【今天】jīntiān ▸**p. 618**〈名〉 **1**（指日子） today: ～的报纸 today's newspaper ‖ ～是我的生日。 Today is my birthday. **2**（现在） present: ～的中国已跻身于世界强国之列。 Present-day China ranks among the powerful nations of the world.
【今晚】jīnwǎn〈名〉 this evening: ～的电视节目 tonight's TV programme
【今夕】jīnxī〈名〉〈书〉 tonight
【今昔】jīn-xī〈名〉 present and past: ～对比 contrast the past with the present
【今宵】jīnxiāo〈名〉〈书〉 tonight: ～月圆。 It's a full moon tonight.
【今夜】jīnyè〈名〉 tonight: ～星光灿烂。 The stars are shining bright tonight.
【今译】jīnyì〈名〉 modern translation: 古籍～ ancient books rendered into the modern vernacular
【今音】jīnyīn〈名〉 modern pronunciation
【今朝】jīnzhāo〈名〉 **1**〈方〉= 今天 jīntiān 1 **2** = 今天 jīntiān 2

金[1] jīn
A〈名〉 **1**（金属） metals: ▸五～, 冶～ **2**（钱） money: ▸～额, 现～ **3**（指乐器） ancient metal percussion instruments: ▸～鼓齐鸣, 鸣～收兵 **4**（金子） gold: 镀～ gild gold ‖ 纯～ solid gold
B〈形〉 **1**（指价值） precious: ▸～婚, ～科玉律, ～口玉言 **2** ▸**p. 863**（指颜色） golden: ～发女郎 blondes

金[2] jīn〈名〉 Jin Dynasty
【金榜】jīnbǎng〈名〉〈旧〉 billboard announcing the names of successful candidates in the imperial examinations
【金榜题名】jīnbǎng-tímíng〈成〉 succeed in an examination
【金镑】jīnbàng〈名〉 sterling
【金杯】jīnbēi〈名〉 gold cup: 获得～ win a gold cup
【金本位】jīnběnwèi〈名〉［金融］ gold standard: 放弃～ abandon the gold standard ‖ ～国/制 gold standard country/system ‖ ～货币 gold currency ‖ ～集团 gold bloc ‖ ～条例 gold standard act
【金笔】jīnbǐ〈名〉 fountain pen with a gold nib
【金币】jīnbì〈名〉 gold coin: 一枚～ a gold coin
【金碧辉煌】jīnbì-huīhuáng〈成〉 magnificent and glittering: 这～的宫殿 this resplendent palace
【金边】Jīnbiān〈名〉 Phnom Penh
【金边债券】Jīnbiān zhàiquàn〈名〉 gilt-edged bonds
【金箔】jīnbó〈名〉 gold leaf
【金不换】jīnbuhuàn〈形〉 invaluable:〈喻〉浪子回头～。 A wastrel's repentance for his actions is more precious than gold.
【金灿灿】jīncàncàn ▸**p. 863**〈形〉 golden: ～的奖杯 gold trophy ‖ ～的阳光 golden sunlight
【金蝉脱壳】jīnchán-tuōqiào〈成〉〈喻〉 escape a predicament through cunning manoeuvring
【金城汤池】jīnchéng-tāngchí〈成〉 strongly fortified city
【金翅雀】jīnchìquè〈名〉［鸟类］ greenfinch
【金疮】jīnchuāng〈名〉［中医］ incised wound
【金额】jīn'é〈名〉 sum of money: 合同外资～ volume of contracted foreign investment
【金饭碗】jīnfànwǎn〈名〉 **1**〈本〉 golden rice-bowl **2**〈喻〉（指工作） well-paid job
【金刚】jīngāng〈名〉 Buddha's warrior attendant: 四大～ four guardian warriors
【金刚怒目】jīngāng-nùmù〈成〉〈喻〉 appear to be very fierce
【金刚砂】jīngāngshā〈名〉［机械］ emery: ～布 emery cloth ‖ ～合金钻头 adamantine drill ‖ ～磨床 emery grinder ‖ ～抛光 diamond polishing ‖ ～纸 emery paper
【金刚石】jīngāngshí〈名〉 diamond: ～砂轮 diamond wheel ‖ ～矿床 diamond deposit
【金刚钻】jīngāngzuàn〈名〉 diamond drill: 没有～，别揽瓷器活。 If you are not competent for the job, don't take it.
【金糕】jīngāo〈名〉 haw jelly
【金戈铁马】jīngē-tiěmǎ〈成〉 mighty and powerful army
【金工】jīngōng〈名〉 metalworking: ～车间 metalworking workshop
【金箍棒】jīngūbàng〈名〉 golden cudgel [weapon used by the Monkey King in the novel *Pilgrimage to the West*]
【金鼓齐鸣】jīngǔ-qímíng〈成〉 with all the gongs and drums beating
【金光大道】jīnguāng dàdào〈成〉 golden road
【金龟】jīnguī〈名〉［动物］ tortoise

【金龟子】jīnguīzǐ〈名〉［昆虫］scarab
【金贵】jīnguì〈形〉valuable: 这里水比油还～。Water is more precious than oil here.
【金衡】jīnhéng〈名〉troy (weight)
【金黄】jīnhuáng ▸p. 863〈形〉golden: ～色的头发 blonde hair ‖ 麦田里一片～ vast stretch of golden wheat in the field
【金婚】jīnhūn〈名〉golden wedding anniversary
【金鸡独立】jīnjī-dúlì〈成〉standing on one leg like a rooster
【金鸡奖】Jīnjījiǎng〈名〉［影视］Golden Rooster Award
【金鸡纳霜】jīnjīnàshuāng〈名〉［药学］quinine
【金奖】jīnjiǎng〈名〉gold prize: 获得～ win the gold prize ‖ ～得主 gold prize winner
【金橘】jīnjú〈名〉［植物］kumquat
【金卡】jīnkǎ〈名〉gold card
【金卡丁郡】Jīnkǎdīngjùn〈名〉Kincardineshire
【金科玉律】jīnkē-yùlǜ〈成〉laws and regulations that cannot be bent
【金口玉言】jīnkǒu-yùyán〈成〉valuable advice
【金库】jīnkù〈名〉1（国库）state coffers: ～空虚。The nation's coffers are empty. 2（保险箱）vault: 存放在银行的～里 keep in a bank's vault
【金块】jīnkuài〈名〉gold bullion
【金矿】jīnkuàng〈名〉gold mine
【金兰】jīnlán〈名〉intimate relationship
【金兰之交】jīnlánzhījiāo〈成〉close friendship
【金莲】jīnlián〈名〉〈旧〉lily feet [formerly, a laudatory term for women's bound feet]
【金莲花】jīnliánhuā〈名〉［植物］nasturtium
【金领】jīnlǐng〈名〉gold collar: ～阶层 gold collar class
【金缕玉衣】jīnlǚ-yùyī〈名〉［考古］jade suit sewn with gold thread
【金銮殿】jīnluándiàn〈名〉emperor's audience hall
【金罗斯郡】Jīnluósījùn〈名〉Kinross-shire
【金马奖】Jīnmǎjiǎng〈名〉［影视］Golden Horse Awards
【金霉素】jīnméisù〈名〉［药学］aureomycin
【金门】Jīnmén〈名〉Jinmen [in Fujian Province]
【金牛座】Jīnniúzuò〈名〉［天文］Taurus: ～流星群 Taurid meteor
【金瓯】jīn'ōu〈名〉1（指器皿）metal goblet 2〈喻〉（国土）national territory: ～无缺 unimpaired territorial integrity
【金牌】jīnpái〈名〉［体育］gold medal: 获得～ win a gold medal ‖ ～得主 gold medallist
【金牌榜】jīnpáibǎng〈名〉gold medals table: 位列～榜首 rank first in the gold medals table
【金盘玉食】jīnpán-yùshí〈成〉〈喻〉luxurious food
【金器】jīnqì〈名〉gold utensil
【金钱】jīnqián ▸p. 328〈名〉money: 浪费～ waste money
【金钱豹】jīnqiánbào〈名〉［动物］leopard
【金钱松】jīnqiánsōng〈名〉［植物］golden larch
【金枪鱼】jīnqiāngyú〈名〉tuna
【金秋】jīnqiū〈名〉autumn; fall〈美〉
【金球】jīnqiú〈名〉［足球］gold goal
【金球奖】Jīnqiújiǎng〈名〉［影视］Golden Globes Awards
【金曲】jīnqǔ〈名〉hit song
【金融】jīnróng〈名〉finance: ～服务业 financial service industry ‖ 国际～ international finance ‖ ～寡头 financial oligarch
【金融风暴】jīnróng fēngbào〈名〉financial crisis
【金融杠杆】jīnróng gànggǎn〈名〉financial lever
【金融工具】jīnróng gōngjù〈名〉financial instrument
【金融机构】jīnróng jīgòu〈名〉financial institution
【金融家】jīnróngjiā ▸p. 966〈名〉financier
【金融监管】jīnróng jiānguǎn〈名〉financial supervision
【金融巨头】jīnróng jùtóu〈名〉financial magnate
【金融全球化】jīnróng quánqiúhuà〈名〉financial globalization
【金融市场】jīnróng shìchǎng〈名〉financial market: 扰乱～ upset the money market
【金融体制】jīnróng tǐzhì〈名〉monetary system
【金融危机】jīnróng wēijī〈名〉financial crisis
【金融中心】jīnróng zhōngxīn〈名〉financial centre
【金三角】jīnsānjiǎo〈名〉golden triangle
【金嗓子】jīnsǎngzi〈名〉golden voice: 她有一副～。She has a voice of gold.
【金色】jīnsè ▸p. 863〈名〉gold colour: ～的晚霞 golden sunset ‖〈喻〉～年华 golden years ‖〈喻〉～童年 golden childhood
【金沙萨】Jīnshāsà〈名〉Kinshasa
【金闪闪】jīnshǎnshǎn〈形〉glittering: ～的奖杯/项链 glittering cup/necklace
【金石】jīnshí〈名〉1（强调坚硬）symbol of hardness and strength: ～同盟 alliance of perpetuity ▸精诚所至，～为开 2（指史料）inscriptions on ancient bronzes and stone tablets
【金石为开】jīnshí-wéikāi〈成〉〈喻〉sincerity works wonders
【金石之交】jīnshízhījiāo〈成〉firm and intimate friendship
【金属】jīnshǔ〈名〉metal: 稀有～ rare metal ‖ 有色～ non-ferrous metal
【金斯敦】Jīnsīdūn〈名〉Kingston
【金丝猴】jīnsīhóu〈名〉golden monkey
【金丝雀】jīnsīquè〈名〉canary
【金丝燕】jīnsīyàn〈名〉［鸟类］esculent swift
【金丝枣】jīnsīzǎo〈名〉golden thread date
【金条】jīntiáo〈名〉gold bar
【金童】jīntóng〈名〉golden boy
【金童玉女】jīntóng-yùnǚ〈成〉innocent young people
【金文】jīnwén ▸p. 918〈名〉inscriptions on ancient bronze objects
【金窝银窝，不如自家草窝】jīnwō yínwō, bùrú zìjiā cǎowō〈俗〉there is no place like home
【金乌】jīnwū〈名〉〈书〉sun: ～玉兔 the sun and the moon ‖ ～西坠。The sun is sinking in the west.
【金屋藏娇】jīnwū-cángjiāo〈成〉keep a mistress in a love nest
【金无足赤，人无完人】jīn wú zúchì, rén wú wánrén〈成〉to err is human
【金相学】jīnxiàngxué〈名〉metallography
【金星】jīnxīng〈名〉1［天文］Venus 2（指五角星）golden star: ～勋章 golden star medal 3（指视觉）flashes of light [as from dizziness or a blow on the head]: 眼冒～ see stars
【金熊奖】Jīnxióngjiǎng〈名〉［影视］Golden Bear Award
【金靴】jīnxuē〈名〉Golden Boot [an award and acknowledgment given to the player who scores the most goals in a football tournament]: ～奖 Golden Shoe Award ‖ ～射手 Golden Boot striker
【金钥匙】jīnyàoshi〈名〉1〈本〉golden key 2〈喻〉（指方法）best solution to a problem: 一本好的英语词典是学好英语的～。A good English dictionary is the key to an impressive command of English.
【金银财宝】jīnyín-cáibǎo〈名〉treasures
【金银花】jīnyínhuā〈名〉［植物］honeysuckle
【金鱼】jīnyú〈名〉goldfish
【金鱼缸】jīnyúgāng〈名〉goldfish basin
【金玉良言】jīnyù-liángyán〈成〉invaluable advice
【金玉满堂】jīnyù-mǎntáng〈成〉〈喻〉wealthy and erudite
【金玉其外，败絮其中】jīnyù qí wài, bàixù qí zhōng〈成〉〈喻〉shining on the outside but rotten on the inside
【金元】jīnyuán〈名〉gold dollar: ～外交 dollar diplomacy
【金针】jīnzhēn〈名〉1〈书〉（指金属针）pins used in sewing and embroidery 2［中医］acupuncture needle: ～治疗 treat sb. with acupuncture 3（指植物）dried day-lily flower
【金针菜】jīnzhēncài〈名〉1［植物］day lily 2（指花）day-lily flower
【金枝玉叶】jīnzhī-yùyè〈成〉〈喻〉descendants of aristocracy
【金砖四国】jīnzhuān sì guó〈名〉the BRIC countries [Brazil, Russian, India, and China]
【金紫荆奖】Jīnzǐjīngjiǎng〈名〉［影视］Golden Bauhinia Award [Hong Kong Film Critics Association award]
【金字塔】jīnzìtǎ〈名〉pyramid
【金字招牌】jīnzì zhāopái〈成〉vain glorious title
【金子】jīnzi〈名〉gold: 提炼～ extract gold ‖〈喻〉他有一颗～般的心。He has a heart of gold.
【金棕榈奖】Jīnzōnglǘjiǎng〈名〉［影视］Golden Palm Award

津[1] jīn〈名〉〈书〉1（渡口）ford: ▸无人问～ 2 ▸p. 661 Jīn（天津）Jin [another name for Tianjin (天津)]: ▸天～

津[2] jīn
A〈名〉1（体液）body fluids: ▸～液 2（唾液）saliva 3（汗）sweat: 遍体生～ perspire all over
B〈动〉dampen: ▸～贴
【津巴布韦】Jīnbābùwéi〈名〉Zimbabwe: ～人 Zimbabwean
【津渡】jīndù〈名〉〈书〉ferry crossing
【津津乐道】jīnjīn-lèdào〈成〉talk with great relish: 成为～的话题 become sb.'s favourite topic
【津津有味】jīnjīn-yǒuwèi〈成〉with great gusto: 吃得～ eat with great relish ‖ 读得～ read with great interest
【津贴】jīntiē A〈名〉allowance: 岗位～ subsidies appropriate to particular jobs ‖ 生活～ living allowance ‖ 政府～ government allowance B〈动〉pay an allowance: 每月～他一些钱。He was granted an allowance every month.
【津要】jīnyào〈名〉〈书〉1（指地方）

key place **2**〈喻〉（指职位） key post: 身居～ hold a key post

【津液】jīnyè〈名〉 **1**［中医］ body fluid **2**（唾液） saliva

衿 jīn〈名〉 **1** = 襟 jīn **2**（衣带） belt

矜 jīn〈书〉

A〈动〉 **1**（怜悯）sympathize with: ▸～恤 **2**（自大） be self-important: 骄～之气 arrogant airs ▸～夸，自～

B〈形〉 restrained: ▸～持

▸guān, qín

【矜持】jīnchí〈形〉 reserved: 举止～ conduct oneself with circumspection ‖ 态度～ have a reserved manner

【矜功自负】jīngōng-zìfù〈成〉 be conceited about one's merits

【矜夸】jīnkuā〈动〉 be conceited and boastful: 力戒～ guard against conceit and boasting

【矜悯】jīnmǐn〈动〉 have pity on

【矜恤】jīnxù〈动〉 sympathize with

【矜重】jīnzhòng〈形〉 reserved and dignified

筋 jīn〈名〉 **1**（韧带） sinew: ▸抽～，伤～动骨 **2**（肌肉） muscle: ▸～骨，～疲力尽 **3**（静脉） veins that stand out under the skin: ▸青～ **4**（筋状物） anything resembling a tendon or vein: ▸钢～，橡皮～

【筋道】jīndao〈形〉〈口〉 chewy: ～的面条 chewy noodles

【筋斗】jīndǒu〈名〉〈口〉 somersault: 翻～ turn a somersault

【筋骨】jīngǔ〈名〉 bones and muscles: 活动～ stretch oneself ‖ ～强健 enjoy excellent health

【筋节】jīnjié〈名〉 **1**（肌肉和关节） muscles and joints **2**〈喻〉（指转折承接处） vital links in a speech or piece of writing

【筋疲力尽】jīnpí-lìjìn〈成〉 worn out: 干得～ be worn out with work ‖ 他已经～了。 He is exhausted.

禁 jīn〈动〉 **1**（耐受） bear: ～得起考验 endure a trial ‖ 这件衣服不～穿。 These clothes are not going to last. ▸～受，弱不～风 **2**（忍住） contain oneself: 不～伤心落泪 unable to contain tears of sadness ▸情不自～，忍俊不～

▸jìn

【禁不起】jīnbuqǐ〈动〉 be unable to stand: ～推敲 cannot bear close scrutiny ‖ ～诱惑 fail to withstand the temptation

【禁不住】jīnbuzhù〈动〉 **1**（承受不住） be unable to bear: ～批评 cannot stand criticism ‖ 冰层太薄了，～你身体的重量。 The ice is too thin to bear your weight. **2**（抑制不住） cannot help: 他～笑出声来。 He could scarcely suppress a laugh.

【禁得起】jīndeqǐ〈动〉 be able to stand: ～高热 can endure heat ‖ ～考验 withstand testing

【禁得住】jīndezhù〈动〉 be able to bear: ～高温 stand up well to high temperatures ‖ ～各种诱惑 be able to resist all temptations

【禁受】jīnshòu〈动〉 endure: ～不住打击 be unable to endure a blow ‖ 他们的爱情～了艰苦生活的考验。 Their love has stood the test of a hard life.

襟 jīn〈名〉 **1**（指衣服） front of a garment: ▸对～，衣～ **2**（抱负） (breadth of) mind: ▸～怀，胸～ **3**（指人） brothers-in-law whose wives are sisters: ～兄/弟 husband of one's wife's elder/younger sister

【襟怀】jīnhuái〈名〉 mind: 博大的～ breadth of mind

【襟怀坦白】jīnhuái-tǎnbái〈成〉 open-hearted

jǐn

仅（僅） jǐn〈副〉 only: ～次于 rank only second to ‖ ～供参考 for reference only

▸jìn

【仅见】jǐnjiàn〈动〉 be rarely seen: 这在奥运会历史上是～的。 It was unprecedented in the history of the Olympic Games.

【仅仅】jǐnjǐn〈副〉 merely: 我～是开个玩笑而已。 I was just kidding. ‖ 这～是个开始。 This is just the beginning.

尽（儘） jǐn

A〈动〉 try to reach the greatest extent: ▸～快，～先

B〈介〉 **1**（指限度） within the limits of: ～着这些钱把事情办好。 Get the job done within the budget. **2**（指顺序） first: 先～孩子们喝。 Let the children drink first. ‖ 先～旧衣服穿。 Wear the old clothes first.

C〈副〉 **1**（同"最"） [used before a noun of locality] extremely: ～里头 innermost part ‖ ～西边 westernmost end **2**〈方〉（总是） always: 这些天～碰上倒霉的事。 I've been having continuous bad luck these last few days.

▸jìn

【尽管】jǐnguǎn **A**〈副〉 unhesitatingly: 你～放心好了。 Don't worry in the slightest. ‖ 有什么意见～提。 If you have any thoughts, just come right out with them. **B**〈连〉 despite: ～病得很重，他仍然去上班了。 He went to work in spite of his serious illness. ‖ ～在下雨，他还是出去了。 He went out even though it was raining.

【尽可能】jǐnkěnéng〈副〉 as ... as possible: ～早点来。 Come here as early as possible.

【尽快】jǐnkuài〈副〉 as soon as possible: 要求～解决 press for a speedy resolution ‖ 我会～回来。 I'll come back as quickly as possible.

【尽量】jǐnliàng〈副〉 to the best of one's ability: ～多学些东西 learn as much as possible ‖ 我会～做好这项工作。 I'll do the work as best as I can.

▸jìnliàng

【尽先】jǐnxiān〈副〉 firstly: ～照顾老人 look after the aged first

【尽早】jǐnzǎo〈副〉 as soon as possible: ～交货 deliver the goods the first chance one has ‖ 希望～回复 hope for an immediate reply

【尽自】jǐnzi〈副〉〈方〉 always: 他头也不抬地～看书。 He kept on reading without raising his head.

紧（緊） jǐn

A〈形〉 **1**（绷紧） tight: 把绳子拉～ pull the rope taut ‖ 鼓面绷得～～的。 The drum face is very stretched. **2**（牢固） firm: 拧～螺母 screw the nut tight ‖ 她～～抓住我的胳膊。 She held me tightly by the arm. **3**（靠近） close: ～挨着 be close to ‖ 这双鞋我穿着太～。 These shoes are too tight for me. ‖ 这抽屉太～，我打不开。 The drawer is so tight that I can't open it. **4**（紧接着） quick: 事情一件～接着一件发生。 One incident follows close on another. **5**（严格） strict: 老师对我们的学习抓得很～。 Our teacher works us very hard. **6**（紧张） tense: 任务很～。 The task is urgent. ‖ 我们时间很～。 We are pressed for time. ‖ 风声很～。 The situation is getting tense. **7**（不宽裕） short of money: 他手头～。 He's hard up. ‖ 眼下银根正～。 Money is short at the moment. **8**（紧迫） urgent: 日程很～ have a tight schedule ‖ 功课很～。 The schoolwork is pressing.

B〈动〉 tighten: ～裤带/鞋带 tighten one's belt/shoelace ‖ ～一～弦 tighten the strings

【紧巴巴】jǐnbābā〈形〉 **1**（指外观） tight: 那件外套看着～的。 That coat looks tight. **2**（指钱财） hard up: 日子过得～的 be in straitened circumstances

【紧绷绷】jǐnbēngbēng〈形〉 **1**（绷得紧） tight: 皮带系得～的 with a belt fastened tight **2**（指表情） taut: 脸～的 look strained

【紧逼】jǐnbī〈动〉 press hard: 步步～ press on at every stage

【紧凑】jǐncòu〈形〉 tight-knit: 情节～ have a well-knit plot ‖ 学校布局显得很～。 The school is laid out compactly.

【紧跟】jǐngēn〈动〉 follow closely: ～时代步伐 keep in step with the times ‖ ～形势 keep abreast of the situation ‖ 她妈妈走到哪里，她就～到哪里。 Wherever her mother goes, she is always close at heel.

【紧箍咒】jǐngūzhòu〈名〉〈喻〉 sth. used as a device of inhibition

【紧固】jǐngù〈动〉 fasten securely: ～件 fastener

【紧急】jǐnjí〈形〉 urgent: ～出口 emergency exit ‖ ～措施 emergency measures ‖ ～会议/集合 emergency meeting/gathering ‖ ～救援 emergency aid ‖ 情况～。 The situation is critical.

【紧急状态】jǐnjí zhuàngtài〈名〉 state of emergency: 宣布该地区处于～ declare a state of emergency in the area

【紧紧】jǐnjǐn〈副〉 closely: ～盯住 fasten/fix one's eyes on (sb. or sth.)

【紧邻】jǐnlín〈名〉 next-door neighbour: 他们是～。 They are next-door neighbours.

【紧锣密鼓】jǐnluó-mìgǔ〈成〉〈喻〉intense publicity drive

【紧密】jǐnmì〈形〉 **1**（不可分） close together: ～结合 close cooperation ‖ ～团结 close unity ‖ ～的联系 inseparable ties **2**（密集） rapid and intense: ～的防守 tight defence ‖ ～的枪声/雨点 rapid and intense firings/raindrops

【紧迫】jǐnpò〈形〉 pressing: 时间～。 Time is running short. ‖ 这件事非常～。 The matter is extremely urgent.

【紧迫感】jǐnpògǎn〈名〉 sense of urgency: 他没有～。 He has no sense of urgency.

【紧俏】jǐnqiào〈形〉 in great demand but short supply: ～商品 merchandise in high demand

【紧缺】jǐnquē〈形〉 in short supply: ～商品 goods in short supply ‖ ～人才 badly needed qualified personnel ‖ 钢材～。 Steel is in short supply.

【紧身儿】jǐnshēnr〈形〉 close-fitting: ～连衣裙 figure-hugging dress ‖ ～裤 tights ‖ ～衣 shape suit

【紧缩】jǐnsuō〈动〉 tighten: ～编制 cut back on staff ‖ ～开支 cut down one's expenses ‖ ～银根 curtail bank facility ‖ ～货币投放和信贷 tighten the money

j

supply and credit

【紧要】jǐnyào〈形〉crucial: 无关～ a matter of no importance ‖ ～关头 critical juncture

【紧张】jǐnzhāng〈形〉**1**（不安） nervous: 克服～情绪 overcome one's nervousness ‖ 神情～ look uneasy ‖ 别～! Don't be nervous! **2**（紧迫） tense: ～的学习 intense study ‖ 缓和～局势 ease the tension ‖ 气氛越来越～。 Tensions are mounting. **3**（不充裕） in short supply: 时间～ be pressed for time ‖ 供应～。 Supplies are short. ‖ 资金周转～。 There is a strain on capital liquidity.

【紧着】jǐnzhe〈动〉 speed up: 这活我们得～干。 We have to press on with the work.

【紧追不舍】jǐnzhuī-bùshě〈成〉 in hot pursuit

堇 jǐn

【堇菜】jǐncài〈名〉［植物］ violet

锦（錦）jǐn

A〈名〉 brocade: 蜀～ Sichuan brocade ▸～旗, ～上添花, 织～

B〈形〉 bright and beautiful: ▸～缎, ～鸡, ～绣

【锦标】jǐnbiāo〈名〉 trophy

【锦标赛】jǐnbiāosài〈名〉championship: 篮球～ basketball tournament ‖ 世界田径～ World Track and Field Championship

【锦缎】jǐnduàn〈名〉 brocade

【锦鸡】jǐnjī〈名〉［鸟类］ golden pheasant

【锦葵】jǐnkuí〈名〉［植物］ high mallow

【锦纶】jǐnlún〈名〉 polyamide fibre

【锦囊妙计】 jǐnnáng-miàojì 〈成〉 plan up one's sleeve

【锦旗】jǐnqí〈名〉 silk banner

【锦上添花】jǐnshàng-tiānhuā〈成〉〈喻〉 embellish what is already beautiful: 他们的演出使晚会～。 Their performance provided the crowning touch to the evening's entertainments.

【锦绣】jǐnxiù〈形〉 as beautiful as brocade: ～前程 glorious future

【锦绣河山】 jǐnxiù héshān 〈成〉 land of charm and beauty

【锦衣玉食】jǐnyī-yùshí〈成〉 live a luxurious life

谨（謹）jǐn

〈形〉**1**（慎重） cautious: ～守规则 strictly adhere to the rules ▸～防, ～慎, 拘～ **2**〈套〉（表恭敬） sincere: ～致节日的祝贺 with season's greetings ▸～启

【谨饬】jǐnchì〈形〉〈书〉 prudent

【谨防】jǐnfáng〈动〉 guard against: ～假冒 beware of imitations ‖ ～扒手 beware of pickpockets

【谨启】jǐnqǐ〈动〉〈套〉 [used after the signature in a formal letter] yours sincerely

【谨慎】jǐnshèn〈形〉 prudent: ～行事 act with caution ‖ ～驾驶! Drive carefully! ‖ 你说话要～小心。 You must be careful with your language.

【谨小慎微】jǐnxiǎo-shènwēi〈成〉 overcautious: 你怎么变得这样～? How come you've become so cautious?

【谨严】jǐnyán〈形〉 careful and precise: 治学～ be rigorous and precise in academic pursuits ‖ 文章结构～。 The article is rigorous and precise.

【谨言慎行】jǐnyán-shènxíng〈成〉 watch your step and mind what you are saying

馑（饉）jǐn ▸ 饥馑 jījǐn

槿 jǐn ▸ 木槿 mùjǐn

jìn

仅（僅）jìn

〈副〉〈书〉 nearly: 士卒～万人。 The soldiers numbered close to 10,000.

▸ jǐn

尽（盡）jìn

A〈动〉**1**（完） finish: 想～办法 leave no stone unturned ‖ 用～全身力气 exhaust all one's strength ▸竭～全力, 取之不～, 用之不竭 **2**（达到极限） reach the limit: ▸～善～美, ～头, 山穷水～ **3**（死） die: ▸同归于～, 自～ **4**（全部使出） exhaust: ～全力 with all one's might ‖ ～其所能 to the utmost of one's capability ▸～力, ～心 **5**（竭力做到） try one's best: ▸～责, ～职, ～忠

B〈形〉 exhaustive: 钥匙已～数交回。 All the keys have been handed back. ▸～人皆知

C〈副〉 entirely: 店里～是中国货。 The store is filled with Chinese goods.

▸ jǐn

【尽欢】jìnhuān〈动〉 enjoy oneself to the full

【尽力】jìnlì〈动〉 do one's utmost: ～帮忙 try one's best to help ‖ ～做好（某事） do (sth.) to the best of one's ability

【尽力而为】jìnlì'érwéi〈成〉 do everything in one's power: 我们将～。 We'll try our best.

【尽量】jìnliàng〈动〉 reach the limit: 喝酒尚未～ not yet drink to one's full

▸ jǐnliàng

【尽其所有】jìnqísuǒyǒu〈成〉 give all one has

【尽情】jìnqíng〈副〉 to one's heart's content: ～唱歌 sing to one's heart's content ‖ ～欢呼 cheer heartily ‖ ～享乐 enjoy oneself to the utmost

【尽然】jìnrán〈动〉 [usu used in the negative] be entirely so: 也不～ not be exactly the case

【尽人皆知】jìnrénjiēzhī〈成〉 be common knowledge: 那是～的事。 That is common knowledge.

【尽人事】jìn rénshì〈动〉 do all that is humanly possible: ～而听天命 do one's level best and leave the rest to God's will

【尽如人意】jìnrú-rényì〈成〉 be just as one wishes: 事实并非～。 The truth is not always very palatable.

【尽善尽美】jìnshàn-jìnměi〈成〉leave nothing to be desired: 凡事要求～ not tolerate imperfection

【尽释前嫌】jìnshì-qiánxián〈成〉 forget old grudges entirely

【尽数】jìnshù〈副〉 total number: 欠款～归还。 All the debts have been paid off.

【尽态极妍】jìntài-jíyán〈成〉 beauty shown to the best advantage

【尽头】jìntóu〈名〉 end: 走到路的～ walk to the end of the road ‖ 她已走到了生命的～。 She's nearing her end.

【尽孝】jìnxiào〈动〉 do one's filial duty: 对自己的父母～ do one's duty by one's parents

【尽心】jìnxīn〈动〉 do with all one's heart: ～照看孩子 do one's utmost to look after a child ‖ 她～照顾父母。 She did all she could to take care of her parents.

【尽心竭力】jìnxīn-jiélì〈成〉do one's utmost: 我们应当～做好本职工作。We should try our best to do our job well.

【尽兴】jìnxìng〈动〉 enjoy oneself to the full: ～而归 come back after thoroughly enjoying oneself ‖ 我玩得很～。 I enjoyed myself to my heart's content.

【尽责】jìnzé〈动〉 do one's duty: 没有～ fail to honour one's duty ‖ 对学生～ fulfil one's responsibilities towards one's students

【尽职】jìnzhí〈动〉 fulfil one's duty: 他工作一向～。 He has always been a conscientious worker.

【尽忠】jìnzhōng〈动〉 **1**（竭尽忠诚） be utterly loyal to: ～报国 dedicate one's life to one's country **2**（献出生命） lay down one's life: 为国～ sacrifice one's life for one's motherland

进（進）jìn

A〈动〉**1**（前进） advance: ▸～步, ～取, 不～则退, 前～ **2**（呈上） submit: ▸～献, ～言 **3**（进入） enter: 请～! Come in, please! ‖ 我们～屋吧。 Let's go into the house. ▸～城, ～站 **4**（聘用） recruit: 今年我们单位不～人。 We will not recruit the staff this year. ‖ 我们系～了一名博士。 Our department has taken on a new faculty member with a doctoral degree. ▸～货, ～款, ～项 **5**（表趋向） [used after a verb] get into: 掉～水里 fall into the water ‖ 走～办公室 walk into an office

B〈量〉 any of the several rows of houses within an old-style residential compound

【进逼】jìnbī〈动〉 advance on: 步步～ press forward steadily

【进兵】 jìnbīng 〈动〉 dispatch troops to attack

【进补】jìnbǔ〈动〉 take a supplement: 冬令～ take extra supplements in winter

【进步】jìnbù **A**〈动〉 progress: ～快/慢 make rapid/slow progress ‖ 学习～ make progress in one's studies ‖ 没有～ make no progress ‖ 取得明显～ make marked progress **B**〈形〉 progressive: ～团体 progressive organizations

【进餐】jìncān〈动〉 have a meal: 按时～ take meals on time ‖ 与某人一起～ dine together with sb.

【进场】jìnchǎng〈动〉 **1**（入场） march into an arena **2**［航空］ approach

【进场费】jìnchǎngfèi〈名〉entrance fee: 本市场免收～、摊位费。 There is no charge for entrance to either the market or the stalls.

【进城】jìnchéng〈动〉 go to town

【进程】jìnchéng〈名〉 course: 历史～ process of history ‖ ～加快 accelerate a process ‖ 民主～ democratic process

【进尺】jìnchǐ〈名〉［矿业］ footage

【进出】jìn-chū **A**〈动〉 go in and out: 他经常～酒吧和夜总会。 He often goes to bars and nightclubs. ‖ 楼里的住户都从这个门～。 The residents of this building get in and out through this door. **B**〈名〉 turnover: 我们每周都有一千元的～。 We have a turnover of ¥1,000 a week.

【进出口】 jìn-chūkǒu 〈名〉 import and export: 经营～业务 engage in import and export ‖ ～公司 import and export corporation

【进出口贸易】 jìn-chūkǒu màoyì 〈名〉 import and export trade: 扩大～ increase foreign trade

【进抵】jìndǐ〈动〉 reach a place

【进度】jìndù〈名〉 rate of progress: 加快

～ quicken the pace ‖ 生产～ pace of production ‖ ～表 progress chart

【进而】jìn'ér〈连〉 and then: 先订计划，～实施 work out a plan and then carry it out

【进发】jìnfā〈动〉 set out: 列车向上海～。 The train set off for Shanghai. ‖ 部队向目标～。 The troops set off for their targets.

【进犯】jìnfàn〈动〉 invade: 打败～之敌 beat back the invading enemy

【进风口】jìnfēngkǒu〈名〉 air intake

【进攻】jìngōng〈动〉 attack: 打退～ repel the attack ‖ 发动～ launch an attack ‖ 粉碎～ crush an attack ‖ 猛烈的～ fierce attack

【进贡】jìngòng〈动〉 **1**（进献财物） pay tribute to a sovereign **2**（送礼） grease sb.'s palm: 我得向他～。 I have to grease his palm with silver.

【进化】jìnhuà〈动〉 evolve: 哺乳动物是从爬行动物～而来的。 Mammals evolved from reptiles.

【进化论】jìnhuàlùn〈名〉 theory of evolution

【进货】jìnhuò〈动〉 replenish one's stock: ～渠道 channel to replenish one's goods ‖ ～价格 prime cost

【进击】jìnjī〈动〉 advance: 向敌人～ advance on the enemy

【进见】jìnjiàn〈动〉 have an audience with: 来京～总理 come to Beijing to have an audience with the Premier

【进谏】jìnjiàn〈动〉〈书〉remonstrate with a monarch

【进军】jìnjūn〈动〉 advance: 吹响～的号角 sound the advance ‖〈喻〉 向科学～ make scientific advances ‖ ～号 bugle call to advance

【进口】jìnkǒu **A**〈名〉 entrance: 公园的～ entrance to the park **B**〈动〉 **1**（指港口） enter a port: 我们的船尚未～。 Our ship still hasn't entered the port. **2**（指海关） import: ～钢材 import steel ‖ ～壁垒 import barrier ‖ ～货 imported goods

【进口关税】jìnkǒu guānshuì〈名〉 import tariff

【进口检疫】jìnkǒu jiǎnyì〈名〉 import quarantine

【进口税】jìnkǒushuì〈名〉 import duty: ～率 rate of import duty

【进款】jìnkuǎn〈名〉 income: 两万元的～ income of 20,000 *yuan*

【进来】jìnlai〈动〉 **1**（指动作） enter: 让来访者～ show the visitor in ‖ 请敲门后再～。 Please knock before entering. **2**（表趋向） [used after a verb] get in: 他匆匆忙忙走了～。 He walked in hurriedly. ‖ 女孩从院子里跑～。 The girl came running in from the yard.

【进球】jìnqiú〈动〉 score a goal

【进球荒】jìnqiúhuāng〈名〉 goal drought: 激战95分钟，未能打破～。 After 95 minutes of playing, they still couldn't break their goal drought.

【进取】jìnqǔ〈动〉 be enterprising: ～精神 enterprising spirit

【进取心】jìnqǔxīn〈名〉 gumption: 缺乏～ lack drive ‖ ～很强的人 person with real gumption

【进去】jìnqu〈动〉 **1**（指动作） enter: 从后门～ enter by the back door **2**（表趋向） [used after a verb] get in: 把行李搬～ get the luggage in ‖ 卡车开不～。 The truck can't get in.

【进入】jìnrù〈动〉 enter: ～角色 get inside a character ‖ ～阵地 get into position ‖ 比赛已～高潮。 The match has reached its climax.

【进身之阶】jìnshēnzhījiē〈成〉 stepping-stone

【进深】jìnshēn〈名〉 length of a room

【进食】jìnshí〈动〉 take food: 病人还不能～。 The patient can't take food.

【进士】jìnshì〈名〉〈古〉 candidate in the highest imperial examination

【进退】jìntuì **A**〈动〉 advance and retreat: ～自如 have room for manoeuvre ►～两难，～维谷 **B**〈名〉 sense of propriety: 年轻人经常不知～。 Young people often have no sense of propriety.

【进退两难】jìntuì-liǎngnán〈成〉 be caught in a fix: 使某人～ hold sb. at bay

【进退失据】jìntuì-shījù〈成〉 in a hopeless position

【进退维谷】jìntuì-wéigǔ〈成〉 be caught between the devil and the deep blue sea

【进位】jìnwèi〈动〉［数学］ carry

【进献】jìnxiàn〈动〉 offer as a tribute: ～花篮 present a basket of flowers

【进香】jìnxiāng〈动〉 worship in a temple: ～朝拜 worship in a temple

【进项】jìnxiàng〈名〉 income: 公司的～增加了。 The company's income has increased.

【进行】jìnxíng〈动〉 proceed: ～调查 conduct a survey ‖ ～核试验 conduct a nuclear test ‖ ～教育改革 carry out reforms in education ‖ ～访问 make a visit ‖ 按计划～ go forward as planned ‖ 战斗仍在～。 The fight is still in progress. ‖ 手术～得很顺利。 The operation went smoothly.

【进行曲】jìnxíngqǔ〈名〉 march: 军队～ military march

【进修】jìnxiū〈动〉 pursue further studies: ～课程 refresher course ‖ ～学院 college of continuing education ‖ 脱产～ full time training

【进修生】jìnxiūshēng〈名〉 student in further education

【进言】jìnyán〈动〉 offer a piece of advice: 我可以冒昧～吗？ May I take the liberty of so offering an opinion?

【进谒】jìnyè〈动〉〈书〉 call on (a superior)

【进一步】jìnyībù〈副〉 further: ～提高产量 raise the yields still further ‖ 两国关系将得到～发展。 Ties between the two countries will continue to develop.

【进益】jìnyì〈名〉 **1**〈书〉（提高） progress **2**（收入） income

【进展】jìnzhǎn〈动〉 make progress: ～顺利 go smoothly ‖ 取得～ gain ground ‖ 工作有～。 There has been some progress with the work.

【进占】jìnzhàn〈动〉 march on and occupy

【进站】jìnzhàn〈动〉 pull into a station

【进账】jìnzhàng **A**〈名〉 income: 他每月有两千元的～。 He has an income of 2,000 *yuan* a month. **B**〈动〉 enter in an account

【进驻】jìnzhù〈动〉 enter and garrison: 士兵～该城。 The soldiers garrisoned the town.

近 jìn

A〈形〉 **1**（指时间） recent: ～照 recent photo **2**（指距离） close: 住得很～ live very near ‖ ～距离射击 fire at close quarters ►～代，～郊，附～ **3**（指关系） intimate: ►～亲，亲～

B〈动〉 approach: 年～八旬 be getting on for 80 ‖ 与会者～千人。 Almost 1,000 people attended the meeting. ►～朱者赤，～墨者黑，平易～人

【近便】jìnbian〈形〉 close and convenient: 他们找了家～的旅馆住下来。 They stopped at the nearest hotel.

【近程】jìnchéng〈形〉 short-range: ～导弹 short-range missile

【近处】jìnchù〈名〉 vicinity

【近代】jìndài〈名〉 **1**（指历史时期） modern times: ～史 modern history **2**（资本主义时代） capitalist times

【近道】jìndào〈名〉 shortcut: 走～回家 take a shortcut home

【近地点】jìndìdiǎn〈名〉［天文］ perigee

【近东】Jìndōng〈名〉 Near East

【近古】jìngǔ〈名〉 age of recent antiquity [in Chinese history, the period from 9th to mid-19th centuries]

【近海】jìnhǎi〈名〉 coastal waters: ～捕鱼 offshore fishing ‖ ～油田 inshore oil field

【近乎】jìnhū〈动〉 be close to: ～粗鲁/疯狂 border on rudeness/madness ‖ 一种～爱的感情 feeling akin to love

【近乎】jìnhu〈形〉〈方〉 intimate: 他们越说越～。 The more they talked, the more intimate they became. ►拉～，套～

【近郊】jìnjiāo〈名〉 suburbs: 城市～ immediate vicinity of a city

【近景】jìnjǐng〈名〉 **1**（指景观） scenery close by **2**［摄影］ close shot: ～摄影 close-up shot ‖ ～摄影机 close-range camera **3**（指景况） immediate prospect: ～规划 plan for the immediate future

【近况】jìnkuàng〈名〉 recent developments: 你～如何？ How are you getting along?

【近来】jìnlái〈名〉 recent times: 你～在干些什么？ What have you been doing lately?

【近邻】jìnlín〈名〉 next-door neighbour: 我们是～。 We are next-door neighbours. ‖ 远亲不如～。 A next-door neighbour is better than a far-away brother.

【近路】jìnlù〈名〉 shortcut: 抄～ take a shortcut

【近年】jìnnián〈名〉 recent years

【近旁】jìnpáng〈名〉 nearby place: 田地的～有条河。 There is a river near the field.

【近期】jìnqī〈名〉near future: ～目标 short-term objective ‖ ～预报 short-term forecast

【近前】jìnqián〈名〉 place close to one: 他走到～我才认出来。 I didn't recognize him until he came close.

【近亲】jìnqīn〈名〉 close relative: ～婚姻 consanguineous marriage ‖ 她是我的～。 She is my kin.

【近亲繁殖】jìnqīn fánzhí〈名〉 nepotism: 〈喻〉 学术界的～ exclusive practices in academic circles

【近情】jìnqíng〈形〉 reasonable: ～近理 fair and reasonable

【近人】jìnrén〈名〉 people today

【近日】jìnrì〈名〉 **1**（指过去） recent days: 我～没有收到他的信。 I haven't heard from him recently. **2**（指未来） next few days: 他～就来。 He will come within the next few days.

【近日点】jìnrìdiǎn〈名〉［天文］ perihelion

【近世】jìnshì〈名〉 modern times

【近视】jìnshì〈形〉 short-sighted〈英〉; near-sighted〈美〉: 他高度～。 He is very short-sighted. ‖〈喻〉～政策 short-sighted policy

【近视眼】jìnshìyǎn〈名〉 myopia

【近水楼台】jìnshuǐ-lóutái〈成〉〈喻〉 favourable position: ～先得月 enjoy the benefits of a favourable position

【近似】jìnsì〈动〉 be similar: 黄金和黄铜的颜色～。 Gold is similar in colour to brass. ‖ 你和他的长相极为～。 You really look a lot like him.

【近似值】jìnsìzhí〈名〉 approximate value

【近岁】jìnsuì〈名〉〈书〉 recent years
【近体诗】 jìntǐshī 〈名〉 'modern style' poetry [referring to the innovations in classical poetry during the Tang Dynasty, marked by strict tonal patterns and rhyming schemes]
【近卫军】jìnwèijūn〈名〉 guards [in European countries]: 青年～ Youth Guards [in the former Soviet Union]
【近义词】jìnyìcí〈名〉 near synonym
【近因】jìnyīn〈名〉 immediate cause
【近于】jìnyú〈动〉border on: ～愚蠢 border on foolishness
【近月点】jìnyuèdiǎn〈名〉［航天］perilune
【近在咫尺】jìnzàizhǐchǐ〈成〉 be close at hand: 我们的营地～。 Our camp is only a short haul from here.
【近战】jìnzhàn〈动〉 fight at close quarters
【近照】jìnzhào〈名〉 recent photo
【近朱者赤，近墨者黑】jìn zhūzhě chì, jìn mòzhě hēi〈成〉〈喻〉 who keeps company with the wolf will learn to howl
【近作】jìnzuò〈名〉 recent work

妗 jìn
【妗子】jìnzi〈名〉 ①（舅母） wife of one's mother's brother ②（妻兄、妻弟之妻） wife of one's wife's brother

劲（勁） jìn〈名〉 ①（力气） energy: 感到浑身没～儿 feel weak all over ‖ 他有使不完的～儿。 He has inexhaustible energy. ▸手～儿，用～ ②（效力） potency: 这酒很有～儿。 This drink is very strong. ③（精神） vigour: 埋头苦干的～儿 hard-working spirit ▸～头，干～ ④（神情） manner: 瞧他们那股子高兴～儿。 See how happy they look. ⑤（兴致） interest: 这部影片太没～了。 There's nothing interesting about this film.
▸jìng
【劲头】jìntóu〈名〉 ①（力量） strength: 鼓起～ gather one's strength ②（热情） zeal: 工作没～ show no drive for one's work ‖ ～十足 do with great vigour

晋[1]（晉） jìn〈动〉 ①（前移） advance: ▸～见，～谒 ②（提升） promote: ▸～级，～升

晋[2]（晉） Jìn〈名〉 ①（指国名） Jin [state in the Zhou Dynasty] ②（晋朝） Jin Dynasty: ▸东～，西～ ③ ▸**p. 661**（山西） Jin [another name for Shanxi Province (山西)]
【晋级】jìnjí〈动〉〈书〉 promote: 他由上尉～为少校。 He was promoted from captain to major.
【晋见】jìnjiàn〈动〉 have an audience with: 他要～主席。 He will have an audience with the chairman.
【晋剧】jìnjù〈名〉 Shanxi opera
【晋升】jìnshēng〈动〉〈书〉 promote: ～为上尉/教授 be promoted to captain/professor
【晋谒】jìnyè〈动〉〈旧〉 call on (sb. holding higher office)

烬（燼） jìn〈名〉 cinder: ▸灰～，余～

浸 jìn〈动〉 ①（泡） soak: 把衣服在水里～一～ soak the clothes in water ▸～渍，～泡，～种 ②（渗透） saturate: 被汗水/雨水～湿 wet with perspiration/rain ▸～润，～透
【浸沉】jìnchén〈动〉 soak
【浸膏】jìngāo〈名〉［药学］ extract
【浸礼】jìnlǐ〈名〉［基督教］ baptism
【浸没】jìnmò〈动〉 ①（淹没） submerge: 河水泛滥，～了农田。 The river overflowed and flooded the farmland. ②（沉浸） be immersed in: ～在快乐之中 be filled with happiness
【浸泡】jìnpào〈动〉 soak: 把菠萝～在盐水里 soak pineapples in brine ‖ 把豆子～后再煮 soak the beans before cooking
【浸染】jìnrǎn〈动〉 ①（污染） contaminate: 泄漏的石油～了河流。 The oil spill contaminated the river. ②（浸泡） soak: 墨水～了纸张。 The ink went through the paper. ③（指染色） dip-dye: ～衣服 dip-dye a garment ④（指受影响） subtly influence
【浸润】jìnrùn **A**〈动〉 soak: 被雨水～的田野 rain-soaked field **B**〈名〉［医学］ infiltration: ～型肺结核 infiltrative pulmonary tuberculosis
【浸透】jìntòu〈动〉 ①（指浸泡） soak: 她浑身都让雨水～了。 Rain soaked her to the skin. ‖ 汗水～了衬衫。 The shirt was sodden with sweat. ②〈喻〉（饱含） be imbued with: 他的著作～着进化论精神。 His work is imbued with the evolutionary spirit.
【浸种】jìnzhǒng〈动〉 soak seeds: ～催芽 soak seeds to hasten germination
【浸渍】 jìnzì 〈动〉 soak: 在水中～亚麻 macerate flax in water

祲 jìn〈名〉 evil atmosphere

靳 jìn〈动〉〈书〉 be stingy

禁 jìn
A〈动〉 ①（禁止） prohibit: ～售黄色书刊 ban the sale of pornographic books and periodicals ‖ 严～入内 strictly no entrance ▸～毒，～赌 ②（监禁） imprison: ▸～闭，囚～
B〈名〉 ①（指物） banned item: ▸～忌，解～，入国问～ ②（指地方） restricted area: ▸紫～城 ③〈书〉（监狱） prison
▸jīn
【禁闭】jìnbì〈动〉 lock up: 被～三天 be placed in confinement for three days ‖ ～室 guard room
【禁地】jìndì〈名〉 restricted area
【禁毒】jìndú〈动〉 fight drugs: 开展～统一行动 implement a unified drugs ban
【禁赌】jìndǔ〈动〉 prohibit gambling
【禁宫】jìngōng〈名〉 sacred precincts
【禁锢】 jìngù 〈动〉 ①〈旧〉（指做官） debar from office [in feudal times] ②（监禁） imprison: ～犯人 put a criminal in custody ③（限制） confine: 被世俗观念所～ be imprisoned by secular thoughts
【禁果】jìnguǒ〈名〉［宗教］forbidden fruit: 偷吃～ engage in clandestine sexual activity
【禁忌】jìnjì **A**〈名〉 taboo: 触犯～ violate a taboo ‖ 部落的～ tribal taboo **B**〈动〉 abstain from: ～烟酒 abstain from smoking and drinking ‖ ～语 taboo terms
【禁酒】jìnjiǔ〈动〉 prohibit alcoholic drinks
【禁绝】jìnjué〈动〉 completely prohibit: ～卖淫 impose a strict ban on prostitution
【禁军】jìnjūn〈名〉〈旧〉 imperial guards
【禁例】jìnlì〈名〉 prohibitions: 触犯～ violate prohibitions
【禁猎】jìnliè〈动〉 prohibit hunting: ～国家保护动物 prohibit the hunting of nationally protected wild life
【禁猎区】jìnlièqū〈名〉 preserve area
【禁令】jìnlìng〈名〉 ban: 解除～ lift a ban ‖ 宣布～ announce a prohibition (on sth.)
【禁脔】jìnluán〈名〉〈喻〉 one's exclusive domain
【禁牧】jìnmù〈动〉 prohibit grazing: ～期 period during which grazing is prohibited
【禁区】jìnqū〈名〉 ①（指领域） forbidden area: 过去把性的问题视为～。 Sex used to be considered a taboo subject. ②（保护区） [of wild life or plant] preserve ③［医学］ parts of the body which are considered to be dangerous for operations or acupuncture: 针灸～ forbidden acupuncture zone ④［体育］ penalty area
【禁赛】jìnsài〈动〉 suspend sb. from competition: 给予（某人）～两场的处罚 impose a two-match ban (against sb.) ‖ 因服用违禁药品被终身～ be banned for life for taking drugs
【禁食】jìnshí〈动〉 fast: ～三日 three-day fast
【禁书】jìnshū〈名〉 banned book
【禁卫军】 jìnwèijūn 〈名〉〈旧〉 imperial guards
【禁烟】jìnyān〈动〉 prohibit opium
【禁药】jìnyào〈名〉 illegal drugs: 运动员一旦被检测出服用～，将面对严重后果。 An athlete caught doping may face serious consequences.
【禁渔】jìnyú〈动〉 prohibit fishing: ～期 closed fishing season
【禁欲】jìnyù〈动〉 be ascetic
【禁苑】jìnyuàn〈名〉〈旧〉 imperial garden
【禁运】jìnyùn〈动〉 embargo: 石油/武器～ oil/arms embargo
【禁止】jìnzhǐ〈动〉 prohibit: ～使用化学武器 ban (the use of) chemical weapons ‖ ～吸烟。 Smoking is prohibited. ‖ ～车辆通行。 No entry to traffic.

缙（縉） jìn〈名〉〈书〉 red silk: ▸～绅
【缙绅】jìnshēn〈名〉〈旧〉 ①（指在职） government official ②（指退休） retired official

觐（覲） jìn〈动〉 ①（朝见） present oneself before a monarch: ▸～见 ②（朝拜） go on a pilgrimage
【觐见】jìnjiàn〈动〉 present oneself before a monarch: 他要求～教皇。 He requested an audience with the Pope.

殣 jìn〈动〉〈书〉 starve to death

噤 jìn〈动〉 ①〈书〉（不出声） keep silent: ～口 shut one's mouth ②（发抖） shiver: ▸寒～，冷～
【噤若寒蝉】jìnruòhánchán〈成〉keep quiet out of fear

jīng

茎（莖） jīng
A〈名〉 ①（指植物） stalk: 地下～ subterranean stem ▸根～，块～，球～ ②（茎状物） stalk-like thing: ▸阴～
B〈量〉〈书〉 [used for long and narrow things]: 数～韭菜 some Chinese chives

京[1] jīng ▸**p. 661**〈名〉 ①（首都） capital of a country: ▸～城，～华，～师 ②（北京） Jing [another name for Beijing (北京)]: ▸～腔，～戏，～味儿

京² Jīng = 京族 Jīngzú

【京白】jīngbái〈名〉spoken dialect in Beijing opera
【京城】jīngchéng〈名〉capital of a country
【京都】jīngdū〈名〉**1**〈旧〉(首都) capital of a country **2** Jīngdū (日本地名) Kyoto
【京官】jīngguān〈名〉officials in the capital
【京胡】jīnghú ▸**p. 929**〈名〉*jinghu* [Peking opera fiddle]
【京华】jīnghuá〈名〉〈书〉capital of a country: 誉满～。His fame resounded throughout the capital.
【京畿】jīngjī〈名〉〈旧〉capital city and its environs
【京剧】jīngjù〈名〉Peking opera: ～团 Peking opera troupe

> **京剧**
>
> Peking Opera, a traditional Chinese opera form established in Beijing in the Qing Dynasty. Musical instruments used are the *erhu* (two-stringed fiddle), the *jinghu* (Peking Opera fiddle), and the *sanxian* (three-stringed plucked instrument). Percussion instruments are the drum, gong and cymbals. The acting involves a combination of singing, recitation, and movement, as well as many invented and formulaic movements. Characters are divided into *sheng* (male), *dan* (female), *jing* (aggressive and fierce male, also known as *hualian*), and *chou* (male and female clowns). Performers paint their faces using fixed designs and colours. This is particularly the case for the *jing*. Known as *lianpu* (脸谱), this type of make-up reflects the personality and moral stature of the character. For example, red always indicates bravery and loyalty, while white indicates treachery.

【京派】jīngpài〈名〉Beijing school of Beijing opera
【京腔】jīngqiāng〈名〉Beijing accent
【京师】jīngshī〈名〉〈旧〉capital of a country
【京味儿】jīngwèir〈名〉Beijing flavour: ～小吃 snacks with a Beijing flavour ‖ ～十足 full of the special flavours of Beijing
【京戏】jīngxì〈名〉〈口〉Beijing opera
【京油子】jīngyóuzi〈名〉〈贬〉sly old Beijing hand
【京韵大鼓】jīngyùn dàgǔ〈名〉[曲艺] story-telling in Beijing dialect with drum accompaniment
【京族】Jīngzú〈名〉Kinh ethnic group, Gin ethnic group

泾 (涇) jīng

【泾渭分明】Jīng-Wèi fēnmíng〈成〉〈喻〉be chalk and cheese: 两人的态度～。The two of them had entirely different attitudes.

经 (經) jīng

A〈名〉**1** [纺织] warp: ▸～纱，～线 **2** (法则) unchanged law: ▸天～地义 **3** (经文) scripture: 取～ go on a pilgrimage for Buddhist scriptures ▸～典，佛～，四书五～ **4** (月经) menstruation: ▸～期，调～，痛～ **5** [中医] channels: ▸～络，～脉 **6** [地理] longitude: ▸～度，东～ **B**〈形〉constant: ▸～常，不～之谈，荒诞不～ **C**〈动〉**1** (管理) manage: ▸～理，～商，～营 **2** (经过) pass through: ～互联网发送 send via the Internet ‖ ～检查，该产品合格。The inspection proved that the product was qualified. ‖ ～你一解释，我就全明白了。With the help of your explanation, I understood it completely. ▸～历，～手，饱～风霜，身～百战 **3** (承受) bear: 那种布不～穿。That kind of material doesn't stand much wear. ‖ 这种布～洗。This cloth can take washing. ▸jìng
【经办】jīngbàn〈动〉deal with: 这件事由他～。The matter is being handled by him.
【经部】jīngbù〈名〉category of classics [ancient writings including *The Four Books* and *The Five Classics* and other books concerning character, phonological and exegetical studies]
【经常】jīngcháng **A**〈形〉daily: 加班对他来说是～的事。It is quite common for him to work overtime. **B**〈副〉frequently: ～喝酒 drink regularly ‖ ～加班 often work overtime ‖ 他们～吵架。They are constantly quarrelling.
【经常性】jīngchángxìng〈形〉daily: ～工作 routine work ‖ ～开支 running expenses ‖ ～业务 current operation
【经典】jīngdiǎn **A**〈名〉**1** (指著作) classic: 博览～ be well-read in the classics **2** (指宗教典籍) scripture: 佛教～ Buddhist Scripture **B**〈形〉classic: ～作品 classical works ‖ ～理论 classical theory
【经度】jīngdù〈名〉longitude
【经费】jīngfèi〈名〉outlay: ～不足 be short of funds ‖ 筹措～ raise funds ‖ 行政～ administrative expenditure
【经风雨，见世面】jīng fēngyǔ, jiàn shìmiàn〈俗〉see life and stand its tests
【经管】jīngguǎn〈动〉be in charge of: ～信托基金 administer a trust fund ‖ 此事由他～。He is in charge of this matter.
【经过】jīngguò **A**〈动〉**1** (通过某处) pass by: 从桥上/下～ pass through/under a bridge ‖ 游行队伍正好～我家门口。The procession passed right by my door. **2** (经历) experience: ～初步分析 after preliminary analysis ‖ ～检验/认真考虑 as a result of the examination/careful consideration ‖ ～协商，双方达成协议。The two sides reached an agreement through negotiations. **B**〈名〉course: 调查事情的～ investigate the ins and outs of a matter ‖ 请新娘新郎谈谈恋爱的～。Ask a bride and bridegroom to relate the story of their love.
【经籍】jīngjí〈名〉〈书〉**1** (经典书籍) classic books **2** (图书) books
【经纪】jīngjì **A**〈动〉manage a business: 不善～ be bad at management ‖ 善于～ be experienced in management **B**〈名〉manager: 当～ be a broker
【经纪人】jīngjìrén〈名〉broker: 房地产～ estate agent〈英〉, realtor〈美〉‖ 保险业/证券～ insurance/stock broker
【经济】jīngjì **A**〈名〉**1** (指宏观) economy: 发展～ develop the economy ‖ 振兴～ revitalize the economy ‖ ～繁荣 booming economy ‖ 以～建设为中心 keep economic development as the central focus ‖ ～不景气。The economy is slack. ▸计划～，商品～，市场～ **2** (个人收支) income: ～宽裕 be well-off ‖ 减轻～负担 ease the financial burden ‖ 遇到～困难 be in financial difficulties **B**〈形〉**1** (与经济相关) of industrial or economic value: ▸～林，～作物 **2** (实惠) economical: ～实惠 economical but practical ‖ 与石油相比，用煤并不～。Using coal is uneconomical compared to using oil.
【经济舱】jīngjìcāng〈名〉economy class
【经济舱综合征】jīngjìcāng zōnghézhēng ▸**p. 50**〈名〉economy-class syndrome
【经济法】jīngjìfǎ〈名〉economic law
【经济法规】jīngjì fǎguī〈名〉economic legislation
【经济法庭】jīngjì fǎtíng〈名〉economic court
【经济犯罪】jīngjì fànzuì〈名〉economic crime: 打击～活动 crack down on economic crimes
【经济封锁】jīngjì fēngsuǒ〈名〉economic blockade: (对某国) 实行～ impose an economic blockade (on another country)
【经济复苏】jīngjì fùsū〈名〉economic resurgence
【经济改革】jīngjì gǎigé〈名〉economic reform: 加快～ accelerate economic reform
【经济杠杆】jīngjì gànggǎn〈名〉economic lever: 利用～ use economic levers
【经济共同体】jīngjì gòngtóngtǐ〈名〉economic community
【经济管理】jīngjì guǎnlǐ〈名〉business administration: ～硕士 Master of Business Administration (MBA)
【经济规律】jīngjì guīlǜ〈名〉economic law
【经济过热】jīngjì guòrè〈名〉economic overheating
【经济核算】jīngjì hésuàn〈名〉business accounting: ～单位 business accounting unit
【经济基础】jīngjì jīchǔ〈名〉economic base: ～和上层建筑 the economic base and the superstructure
【经济技术开发区】jīngjì jìshù kāifāqū〈名〉economic and technological development zone
【经济建设】jīngjì jiànshè〈名〉economic construction: 以～为中心 focus on economic development
【经济林】jīngjìlín〈名〉cash tree
【经济贸易委员会】jīngjì màoyì wěiyuánhuì〈名〉economic and trade commission
【经济命脉】jīngjì mìngmài〈名〉key branches of the economy
【经济模式】jīngjì móshì〈名〉economic mould
【经济难民】jīngjì nànmín〈名〉economic refugee
【经济全球化】jīngjì quánqiúhuà〈名〉economic globalization
【经济师】jīngjìshī ▸**p. 966**〈名〉economic administrator
【经济实体】jīngjì shítǐ〈名〉economic entity
【经济适用房】jīngjì shìyòngfáng〈名〉economy housing: 为低收入家庭提供～ provide economy housing for low-income families
【经济手段】jīngjì shǒuduàn〈名〉economic means
【经济特区】jīngjì tèqū〈名〉special economic zone: 设立～ establish a special economic zone
【经济体制】jīngjì tǐzhì〈名〉economic structure: 加快～改革 speed up the restructuring of economic systems
【经济危机】jīngjì wēijī〈名〉economic crisis
【经济萧条】jīngjì xiāotiáo〈名〉economic depression
【经济效益】jīngjì xiàoyì〈名〉economic returns: ～显著提高。There has been a marked improvement in economic efficiency.
【经济学】jīngjìxué〈名〉economics: ～家 economist ‖ 宏观～ macro-economics
【经济一体化】jīngjì yītǐhuà〈名〉economic integration
【经济制裁】jīngjì zhìcái〈名〉economic

sanction: （对某国）实行～ impose economic sanctions (on another country)

【经济制度】jīngjì zhìdù〈名〉economic system

【经济周期】jīngjì zhōuqī〈名〉economic cycle

【经济状况】jīngjì zhuàngkuàng〈名〉economic conditions

【经济作物】jīngjì zuòwù〈名〉cash crop

【经久】jīngjiǔ **A**〈动〉last long: ～不息的掌声 prolonged applause **B**〈形〉durable: ～耐用 durable

【经久不衰】jīngjiǔ-bùshuāi〈成〉enduring

【经理】jīnglǐ **A**〈动〉manage: ～一家小厂 run a small factory **B**〈名〉manager: 部门～ department manager ‖ 销售～ sales manager ‖ 总～ general manager

【经历】jīnglì **A**〈动〉experience: ～千难万险 go through hazards and hardships ‖ 亲身～ experience first hand **B**〈名〉experience: 工作/生活～ work/life experience ‖ 一段不平凡的～ an extraordinary experience

【经纶】jīnglún〈书〉〈喻〉**A**〈动〉manage state affairs: ～天下 run the country **B**〈名〉statesmanship: 大展～ put one's statesmanship to full use ►满腹～

【经略】jīnglüè〈动〉〈书〉plan and control

【经络】jīngluò〈名〉［中医］main and collateral channels in the human body: ～分布 channel distribution

【经脉】jīngmài〈名〉［中医］passages through which vital energy circulates, regulating bodily functions

【经贸】jīngmào〈名〉economy and trade: ～合作/关系 economic and trade cooperation/relation

【经年累月】jīngnián-lěiyuè〈成〉year in, year out

【经期】jīngqī〈名〉(menstrual) period

【经纱】jīngshā〈名〉［纺织］warp: ～和纬纱 warp and weft

【经商】jīngshāng ►**p. 966**〈动〉be in business: 开始～ take to business

【经史子集】jīng-shǐ-zǐ-jí〈名〉classical works, historical works, philosophical works, and belles-lettres [the four traditional divisions of a Chinese library]

【经手】jīngshǒu〈动〉handle: 该律师～承办这宗案件。The lawyer undertook the case. ‖ 这些文件是由他～的。He is the man who dealt with these documents.

【经手人】jīngshǒurén〈名〉person handling a particular job

【经受】jīngshòu〈动〉undergo: ～暴风雨的袭击 weather a storm ‖ ～严峻的考验 withstand severe trials

【经售】jīngshòu〈动〉deal in: 此店～各种日用必需品。This shop sells a wide variety of daily necessities.

【经书】jīngshū〈名〉Confucian classics

【经天纬地】jīngtiān-wěidì〈成〉having exceptional ability: ～之才 person of exceptional ability

【经纬】jīngwěi〈名〉**1**（重要事件）highlights: 时事～ news line **2**（经线和纬线）meridian and parallel (lines)

【经纬度】jīngwěidù〈名〉latitude and longitude

【经纬仪】jīngwěiyí〈名〉theodolite

【经文】jīngwén〈名〉text from the Confucian classics or religious scriptures

【经线】jīngxiàn〈名〉**1**［纺织］warp **2**［地理］meridian (line)

【经销】jīngxiāo〈动〉deal in: ～店 outlet ‖ ～商 dealer

【经心】jīngxīn〈动〉be careful: ～点，别出差错。Be careful not to make any mistakes. ►漫不～

【经学】jīngxué〈名〉study of Confucian classics: ～大师 great master of Confucian studies

【经血】jīngxuè〈名〉［中医］menses

【经验】jīngyàn **A**〈名〉experience: 积累～ accumulate experience ‖ 交流～ exchange experience ‖ 总结～ sum up one's experience ‖ 工作～ work experience **B**〈动〉go through: 这样的事，我从来没有～过。I have never experienced a situation like this.

【经验之谈】jīngyànzhītán〈名〉observation based on personal experience

【经验主义】jīngyàn zhǔyì〈名〉empiricism: ～者 empiricist

【经一事，长一智】jīng yī shì, zhǎng yī zhì〈俗〉what does not kill you makes you stronger

【经意】jīngyì〈动〉care: 我不～踩了他的脚。I inadvertently stepped on his toe.

【经营】jīngyíng ►**p. 966**〈动〉**1**（从事）engage in: ～零售/批发生意 carry on retail/wholesale business ‖ 独立～ operate independently ‖ 非法～ illegal operations ‖ 公司因～不善而倒闭。The company went bankrupt due to poor operation. **2**（计划和安排）plan and organize: 这个展览会煞费～。Great efforts have been made to plan and organize this exhibition. ►惨淡～, 苦心～

【经营范围】jīngyíng fànwéi〈名〉scope of business

【经营管理】jīngyíng guǎnlǐ〈名〉business management

【经由】jīngyóu〈介〉via: ～日本去美国 be bound for USA via Japan

【经院哲学】jīngyuàn zhéxué〈名〉［哲学］scholasticism

【经传】jīngzhuàn〈名〉**1**（儒家典籍）Confucian canon **2**（古书）classical works: 名不见～ not well-known

【经子】jīngzi〈名〉〈方〉flax: 捻～ twist flaxen thread

荆 jīng

〈名〉vitex: ►～棘, ～条

【荆钗布裙】jīngchāi-bùqún〈成〉plain simple dress of a poor woman

【荆棘】jīngjí〈名〉brambles:〈喻〉～丛生 beset with difficulties

【荆棘载途】jīngjí-zàitú〈成〉path beset with difficulties

【荆条】jīngtiáo〈名〉twigs of the vitex

菁 jīng

【菁华】jīnghuá〈名〉quintessence

【菁菁】jīngjīng〈形〉〈书〉luxuriant

旌 jīng

A〈名〉**1**（古旗）ancient type of banner [consisting of ox tails and multicolour plumes, hoisted on a mast] **2**（旗帜）flags and banners: ►～旗

B〈动〉〈书〉praise: ►～表

【旌表】jīngbiǎo〈动〉[of an emperor] confer honours on the virtuous and the worthy

【旌旗】jīngqí〈名〉flags and banners: ～迎风招展。Flags are fluttering in the wind.

惊（驚）jīng

〈动〉**1**（指骡、马）shy: 马～了。The horse shied. **2**（受惊）start: 吃了一～ take fright ‖ 这婴孩很容易受～。The baby gets frightened easily. ►～慌, ～恐, 胆战心～ **3**（惊动）startle: ►～天动地, 打草～蛇

【惊诧】jīngchà〈形〉amazed: 他没有来，我很～。I'm astonished that he didn't come.

【惊呆】jīngdāi〈形〉stupefied: 陪审团判决他有罪，他～了。He was completely stunned by the jury's guilty verdict.

【惊动】jīngdòng〈动〉startle: 别～孩子，他睡着了。Don't disturb the baby; he is asleep. ‖ 消息～了全城。The whole city was startled by the news.

【惊愕】jīng'è〈形〉〈书〉stupefied: 你的无礼使我非常～。I was completely dumbfounded by your rudeness.

【惊风】jīngfēng〈名〉［中医］infantile convulsions

【惊弓之鸟】jīnggōngzhīniǎo〈成〉〈喻〉badly frightened person

【惊骇】jīnghài〈形〉〈书〉panic-stricken

【惊鸿一瞥】jīnghóng yīpiē〈成〉have a fleeting glimpse of a beauty

【惊呼】jīnghū〈动〉cry out in alarm: ～救命 cry for help suddenly

【惊慌】jīnghuāng〈形〉alarmed: ～不安 be panic-stricken ‖ 神色～ look alarmed ‖ 不必～。There's no cause for alarm.

【惊慌失措】jīnghuāng-shīcuò〈成〉be panic-stricken: 出了事故，他～。He was completely panic-stricken by the accident.

【惊惶】jīnghuáng〈形〉panic-stricken: ～不安 be panic-stricken

【惊魂】jīnghún〈名〉state of being frightened: ～未定 still badly shaken

【惊悸】jīngjì〈动〉〈书〉palpitate with fear

【惊叫】jīngjiào〈动〉cry in fear

【惊惧】jīngjù〈形〉alarmed and frightened

【惊厥】jīngjué **A**〈动〉faint from fear **B** ►**p. 50**〈名〉［医学］convulsions: 癫痫性～ epileptic convulsions

【惊恐】jīngkǒng〈形〉panic-stricken: ～极了 be completely panic-stricken ‖ ～失色 pale with fear

【惊恐万状】jīngkǒng-wànzhuàng〈成〉be in complete panic: 洪水到来时，人们～。When the flood hit, the people were completely panic-stricken.

【惊雷】jīngléi〈名〉sudden clap of thunder: 一声～ a sudden clap of thunder

【惊怕】jīngpà〈形〉scared

【惊奇】jīngqí〈形〉amazed: 毫不～ show no sign of surprise ‖ 对他的行为感到极为～ be completely astounded by his behaviour ‖ 对这个消息感到极为～ be very shocked at the news ‖ 使某人～的是 to sb.'s surprise

【惊扰】jīngrǎo〈动〉disturb: 不要～他。Do not bother him.

【惊人】jīngrén〈形〉astonishing: ～的毅力 amazing willpower ‖ ～的消息 startling news ‖ 数字大得～。The figures are staggeringly large.

【惊人之举】jīngrénzhījǔ〈成〉stunning feat

【惊师动众】jīngshī-dòngzhòng〈成〉make a tremendous fuss

【惊世骇俗】jīngshì-hàisú〈成〉earth-shattering: 此举真可谓～。This move is really earth-shattering.

【惊悚片】jīngsǒngpiàn〈名〉thriller

【惊叹】jīngtàn〈动〉marvel: 看到雄伟的宫殿，人们～不已。People are filled with wonder at the sight of the magnificent palace. ‖ 山中的自然美景使游客大为～。Visitors marvel at the natural beauty of the mountain.

【惊叹不已】jīngtànbùyǐ〈成〉marvel at (sth.) greatly

【惊叹号】jīngtànhào〈名〉exclamation mark; exclamation point〈美〉

【惊涛骇浪】jīngtāo-hàilàng〈成〉 1（指波涛） stormy seas 2（指境遇） hazards in life: 船在～中前进。 The boat is braving the stormy sea. ‖〈喻〉 他的一生充满了～。 His life was full of hazards.

【惊天动地】jīngtiān-dòngdì〈成〉 earth-shattering: 创造～的奇迹 work incredible wonders

【惊悉】jīngxī〈动〉〈书〉 be shocked to learn: ～某人不幸逝世 be distressed to learn of sb.'s passing

【惊喜】jīngxǐ A〈形〉 pleasantly surprised: 令我们～的是 to our pleasant surprise B〈名〉 pleasant surprise: 给你一个～。 Here's a pleasant surprise for you.

【惊吓】jīngxià〈动〉 frighten: 小女孩受了～，不肯讲话。 The little girl was scared and wouldn't speak.

【惊险】jīngxiǎn〈形〉 breathtaking: ～动作 astounding feat ‖ ～片 thriller ‖ ～小说 thriller

【惊羡】jīngxiàn〈动〉 marvel: 他的成就令人～。 His success is staggering.

【惊心动魄】jīngxīn-dòngpò〈成〉 be soul-stirring: ～的场面 soul-stirring scene

【惊醒】jīngxǐng〈动〉 1（突然醒来） wake up with a start: 他从睡梦中～。 He awoke with a start. 2（使人突然醒来） awake: 别把孩子～了。 Don't wake the child.

【惊醒】jīngxing〈形〉 sleeping lightly: 他睡觉很～。 He is a very light sleeper.

【惊讶】jīngyà〈形〉 surprised: 令人～的是 to sb.'s amazement ‖ 这个裁决让大家感到～。 The ruling came as a surprise to everyone.

【惊疑】jīngyí〈形〉 surprised and bewildered: ～的神色 surprised and bewildered expression

【惊异】jīngyì〈形〉 astonished: ～的目光 astounded look

【惊蛰】Jīngzhé〈名〉 Awakening of Insects [beginning of the 3rd of the 24 solar terms]

晶 jīng

A〈形〉 brilliant: ▸～莹，亮～～

B〈名〉 1（水晶） quartz: ▸茶～，墨～ 2（晶体） any crystalline substance: ▸结～

【晶粒】jīnglì〈名〉［物理］ crystalline grain

【晶体】jīngtǐ〈名〉 crystal: 单～ monocrystal ‖ 多～ polycrystal

【晶体管】jīngtǐguǎn〈名〉 transistor: ～收音机 transistor radio

【晶莹】jīngyíng〈形〉 sparkling and crystal-clear: ～的露珠 sparkling dewdrops ‖ ～剔透 glittering and translucent

【晶圆】jīngyuán〈名〉［材料］ wafer

【晶状体】jīngzhuàngtǐ〈名〉［生理］ crystalline lens

腈 jīng〈名〉［化学］ nitrile

【腈纶】jīnglún〈名〉 acrylic fibres: ～毛线 knitting wool made of acrylic fibres

睛 jīng〈名〉 eyeball: ▸画龙点～，火眼金～，目不转～

粳 jīng

【粳稻】jīngdào〈名〉 round-grained non-glutinous rice

【粳米】jīngmǐ〈名〉 polished round-grained rice

兢 jīng

【兢兢业业】jīngjīng-yèyè〈成〉 cautious and conscientious: ～地工作 work conscientiously

精 jīng

A〈名〉 1（提炼物） concentrate: 薄荷～ essence of peppermint ‖ 樟脑～ spirit of camphor ▸酒～，糖～，味～ 2（精力） energy: ▸～疲力竭，聚～会神，养～蓄锐 3（精子） sperm: ▸～子，受～ 4（某类人） spirit: 害人～ poltergeist ▸狐狸～

B〈形〉 1（经提纯或挑选） refined: ▸～兵，～盐 2（完美） perfect: ▸～彩，～良，～美，～益求～ 3（精通） skilled: ～于此道 be great on the subject ‖ ～于绘画 be skilled at painting ▸～通，博大～深，业～于勤 4（细致） exquisite: 这手镯工艺很～。 The bracelet was made with exquisite craftsmanship. ▸～密，～巧，～确，～选 5（机敏） smart: 他太～了，我们斗不过他。 He was too clever for us. ‖ 他做生意挺～的。 He is a shrewd businessman. ▸～干，～明

C〈副〉〈口〉 extremely: ▸～光

【精白】jīngbái〈形〉 pure white

【精兵】jīngbīng〈名〉 crack troops: ～强将 crack team

【精兵简政】jīngbīng-jiǎnzhèng〈成〉 streamlined administration

【精彩】jīngcǎi〈形〉 wonderful: ～的表演 fabulous performance ‖ 晚会节目～纷呈。 The evening's entertainment was consistently excellent.

【精巢】jīngcháo〈名〉 1（指动物） gonads 2（指人） testicle

【精诚】jīngchéng〈形〉〈书〉 absolutely sincere: ～团结 unite in all sincerity and dedication

【精诚所至，金石为开】jīngchéng suǒ zhì, jīnshí wéi kāi〈成〉 sincerity smooths the way to success

【精赤】jīngchì〈形〉 naked: ～条条 stark naked

【精虫】jīngchóng〈名〉〈口〉［生理］ spermatozoon

【精粹】jīngcuì A〈形〉 succinct: 文章必须短小而～。 The article must be short and succinct. B〈名〉 succinctness: 学术思想的～ the succinctness of academic thought

【精打细算】jīngdǎ-xìsuàn〈成〉 careful and meticulous calculations: ～过日子 live to a careful budget

【精当】jīngdàng〈形〉 precise and appropriate: 用词～ be precise and appropriate in wording

【精到】jīngdào〈形〉 keen and cautious: 分析十分～ precise and insightful analysis

【精雕细刻】jīngdiāo-xìkè〈成〉 1〈本〉 sculpt with exquisite craftsmanship 2〈喻〉 work painstakingly at sth.: ～的作品 exquisite piece of work

【精读】jīngdú A〈动〉 read carefully and thoroughly: 这些名篇要～。 These famous articles must be read thoroughly and with care. B〈名〉 intensive reading

【精度】jīngdù〈名〉 precision: 高～ high precision ‖ 这台仪器的～符合国家标准。 The precision of this instrument meets national standards.

【精干】jīnggàn〈形〉 keen-witted and capable: 他看起来挺～的。 He looks quite capable.

【精耕细作】jīnggēng-xìzuò〈成〉 intensive cultivation

【精工】jīnggōng〈形〉 refined: ～制作 fine workmanship

【精怪】jīngguài〈名〉 demon

【精光】jīngguāng〈形〉 1（全无） used up: 忘得～ have clean forgotten ‖ 票已卖个～。 The tickets are already sold out. 2（闪亮） bright and clean: 把鞋擦得～锃亮 polish one's shoes to a nice shine

【精悍】jīnghàn〈形〉 1（指人） smart and efficient 2（指文笔） pithy and poignant: 文笔～ be succinct and penetrating in one's writing ▸短小～

【精华】jīnghuá〈名〉 1（指最好部分） essence: 去其糟粕，取其～ weed out the dross and select the best ‖ 汲取传统文化的～ absorb the essence of traditional culture ‖ 他们是这一代人中的～。 They are the pick of this generation. 2〈书〉（光华） brilliance: 日月之～ radiance of the sun and moon

【精加工】jīngjiāgōng〈名〉［机械］ finish machining

【精简】jīngjiǎn〈动〉 streamline: ～手续 simplify the formalities ‖ ～会议 cut the number of meetings ‖ ～行政机构 streamline the administration

【精矿】jīngkuàng〈名〉［矿业］ concentrate

【精力】jīnglì〈名〉 energy: 集中～ concentrate one's energy ‖ ～充沛 be full of vitality ‖ ～旺盛 be full of energy

【精练】jīngliàn〈形〉 succinct: 语言～ succinct language

【精炼】jīngliàn A〈动〉［冶金］ refine: ～生铁 refined pig iron B = 精练 jīngliàn

【精良】jīngliáng〈形〉 superior: 武器～ highly sophisticated weapons ‖ 制作～ be of excellent workmanship

【精灵】jīnglíng〈名〉 spirit: 小～ elf

【精馏】jīngliú〈动〉［化学］ rectify

【精馏器】jīngliúqì〈名〉 finestilling machine

【精美】jīngměi〈形〉 exquisite: 制作～ be exquisitely made ‖ ～的礼品 exquisite gift

【精密】jīngmì〈形〉 precise: ～仪器 precision instrument

【精密度】jīngmìdù〈名〉 precision

【精妙】jīngmiào〈形〉 exquisite and ingenious: ～的手工艺品 exquisite handicrafts

【精明】jīngmíng〈形〉 astute: 为人～ be shrewd about people ‖ ～之举 smart move ‖ ～能干 know one's business

【精明强干】jīngmíng-qiánggàn〈成〉 be capable and efficient: 一位～的经理 a clever and capable manager

【精囊】jīngnáng〈名〉［生理］ seminal vesicle

【精疲力竭】jīngpí-lìjié〈成〉 be worn out: 累得～ be deadbeat

【精辟】jīngpì〈形〉 sharp: ～的见解 incisive view

【精品】jīngpǐn〈名〉 1（指作品） fine works: 艺术～ artistic treasures 2（指物品） quality goods: ～货 choice goods ‖ ～屋 choice quality store

【精气】jīngqì〈名〉［中医］ vital substance which maintains the functioning of the body

【精气神儿】jīngqìshénr〈名〉〈口〉 vigour: 他休息了一会儿，～又来了。 He became refreshed and energetic after a short nap.

【精巧】jīngqiǎo〈形〉 exquisite: 手工～ be of fine workmanship ‖ ～的工艺品 exquisite handicraft

【精确】jīngquè〈形〉 accurate: 计算～ be accurate in one's calculation ‖ ～无误 with unerring precision ‖ 提供～数据 offer precise data

【精确度】jīngquèdù〈名〉 (measure of) precision

【精肉】jīngròu〈名〉 lean meat

【精锐】jīngruì〈形〉 selected: ～部队 crack

troops

【精深】jīngshēn〈形〉 profound: 博大～ erudite ‖ 文学造诣～ of high literacy attainments

【精神】jīngshén〈名〉 1（指心理状态）spirit: 时代～ the spirit of the times ‖ ～振奋 be in fine mettle 2（宗旨）essence: 传达会议～ pass on the substance of the meeting ‖ 领会文件～ understand the gist of a document

【精神病】jīngshénbìng ▸p. 50〈名〉psychosis: 患～ be mentally ill ‖ ～患者 psychiatric patient

【精神财富】jīngshén cáifù〈名〉 intellectual wealth

【精神产品】jīngshén chǎnpǐn〈名〉 intellectual product

【精神错乱】jīngshén cuòluàn〈名〉 amentia

【精神抖擞】jīngshén dǒusǒu〈成〉 in high spirits

【精神分裂症】jīngshén fēnlièzhèng〈名〉schizophrenia: ～患者 schizophrenic

【精神分析】jīngshén fēnxī〈名〉 psychoanalysis

【精神鼓励】jīngshén gǔlì〈名〉 moral support: 给予～ give moral encouragement

【精神焕发】jīngshén huànfā〈成〉 in high spirits

【精神枷锁】jīngshén jiāsuǒ〈名〉ideological fetters

【精神境界】jīngshén jìngjiè〈名〉 mental outlook

【精神恋爱】jīngshén liàn'ài〈名〉 platonic love

【精神疗法】jīngshén liáofǎ〈名〉 psychotherapy

【精神面貌】 jīngshén miànmào 〈名〉 mental outlook

【精神赔偿】 jīngshén péicháng 〈名〉 mental reparation

【精神生活】jīngshén shēnghuó 〈名〉 intellectual life

【精神胜利】jīngshén shènglì〈名〉 moral victory

【精神失常】jīngshén shīcháng〈动〉 be deranged

【精神食粮】jīngshén shíliáng〈名〉 nourishment for the mind

【精神世界】 jīngshén shìjiè〈名〉 inner world

【精神衰弱】 jīngshén shuāiruò ▸p. 50〈名〉［医学］psychasthenia

【精神损失】jīngshén sǔnshī〈名〉 emotional damage

【精神文明】jīngshén wénmíng〈名〉 cultural and ideological progress: 物质文明和～一起抓 attend to both spiritual and material civilization

【精神压力】jīngshén yālì〈名〉mental pressure

【精神支柱】jīngshén zhīzhù〈名〉 moral support: 强大的～ powerful ideological pillar

【精神状态】 jīngshén zhuàngtài 〈名〉 mental condition

【精神准备】jīngshén zhǔnbèi〈名〉 mental preparation

【精审】jīngshěn〈形〉〈书〉 well-thought-out: 释义～ define accurately and comprehensively

【精神】jīngshen **A**〈名〉 energy: 没有～ be listless ‖ 振作～ cheer up ‖ ～矍铄 be as fit as a fiddle **B**〈形〉 1（有活力）spirited: ～点! Show your mettle. 2（英俊）smart: 看上去特别～ look especially smart

【精梳】jīngshū〈名〉［纺织］ combing

【精饲料】jīngsìliào〈名〉 concentrate

【精算】jīngsuàn **A**〈动〉 accurate calculation **B**〈名〉 actuarial evaluation

【精算师】jīngsuànshī ▸p. 966〈名〉 actuary

【精髓】jīngsuǐ〈名〉 essence: 古典文学～ quintessence of classical literature ‖ 马克思主义～ essence of Marxism

【精通】jīngtōng〈动〉 be proficient in: ～业务 be expert at one's trade ‖ ～一门外语 perfect a foreign language

【精微】jīngwēi **A**〈形〉 deep and profound **B**〈名〉 mystery: 探索宇宙的～ explore the mysteries of the universe

【精卫填海】Jīngwèi-tiánhǎi〈成〉〈喻〉 dogged determination

【精细】jīngxì〈形〉 1（细致） meticulous: 虑事～ think matters over carefully ‖ 做工～ be of fine workmanship 2（精明） shrewd

【精细化】jīngxìhuà〈动〉 fine-tune: 社会管理的～ the fine-tuning of social management ‖ 数值预报～ numerical prediction refinement

【精心】jīngxīn〈形〉 meticulous: ～安排 arrange carefully ‖ ～护理某人 nurse sb. with painstaking care ‖ ～照料 take good care (of) ‖ ～挑选的礼物 hand-picked gift

【精选】jīngxuǎn〈动〉 be carefully chosen: 十八世纪英国诗歌～ choice selection of 18th century English poetry

【精盐】jīngyán〈名〉 table salt

【精液】jīngyè〈名〉 semen

【精益求精】 jīngyìqiújīng 〈成〉 keep on improving: 业务上～ constantly improve and perfect one's professional skill

【精英】jīngyīng〈名〉 1（精华） quintessence: 国画是中国的艺术～。 Traditional Chinese painting is the quintessence of Chinese art. 2（杰出人物） elite: 选拔社会～ choose the cream of society ‖ 体坛～ outstanding sportsperson

【精英政治】jīngyīng zhèngzhì〈名〉 elitism

【精油】jīngyóu〈名〉 essential oil: 柠檬/玫瑰～ lemon/rose essential oil

【精于】jīngyú〈动〉 be good at: ～此道 be skilled in this field

【精湛】jīngzhàn〈形〉 superb: 工艺～ be of exquisite craftsmanship ‖ 技艺～ consummate skill

【精制】jīngzhì〈动〉 refine: ～品 highly finished product ‖ ～面粉 fine flour ‖ ～糖 refined sugar ‖ ～盐 purified salt

【精致】jīngzhì〈形〉 exquisite: 做工～ be delicately made ‖ ～的雕刻品 exquisite carving

【精忠报国】jīngzhōng-bàoguó〈成〉serve one's country with utmost loyalty

【精装】jīngzhuāng〈形〉 1（指书） hardback: ～本 hardback edition 2（指商品） elaborately-packed: ～茶叶 elaborately-packed tea

【精壮】jīngzhuàng〈形〉 strong: ～的小伙子 sturdy lad

【精准】 jīngzhǔn 〈形〉 accurate: 预算～ accurate budget ‖ 投篮～ shoot a perfect basket

【精子】jīngzǐ〈名〉 sperm: ～库 sperm bank

鲸（鯨）jīng〈名〉 whale: 雌/雄～ cow/bull whale ‖ 幼～ whale calf

【鲸鲨】jīngshā〈名〉 whale shark

【鲸吞】jīngtūn〈动〉 swallow

【鲸鱼】jīngyú〈名〉 whale

【鲸鱼座】Jīngyúzuò〈名〉［天文］ Cetus

腈 jīng ▸ 鼩腈 qújīng

jǐng

井 jǐng

A〈名〉 1（水井） well: 打～ sink a well ‖ 钻～ drill a well ▸枯～, 水～, 落～下石, 坐～观天 2（井状物） well-shaped thing: ▸矿～, 油～ 3（家乡） hometown: ▸背～离乡, 市～ 4（指星宿） one of the 28 constellations in ancient Chinese astronomy **B**〈形〉 orderly: ▸～～有条, ～然有序

【井底之蛙】jǐngdǐzhīwā〈成〉〈喻〉person with a very limited outlook

【井冈山】 Jǐnggāngshān 〈名〉 Jinggang Mountains

【井架】jǐngjià〈名〉［石油］ derrick

【井井有条】 jǐngjǐng-yǒutiáo 〈成〉 shipshape: 把房子收拾得～ get the house in order ‖ 他办事～。 He is a very methodical person.

【井喷】jǐngpēn **A**〈名〉［石油］ blowout **B**〈动〉 spurt: ～式的消费增长 consumption growth spurt

【井然】jǐngrán〈形〉〈书〉 orderly: 秩序～ be in good order

【井然有序】 jǐngrán-yǒuxù 〈成〉 in good order

【井绳】jǐngshéng〈名〉 rope used for drawing water from a well

【井水不犯河水】jǐngshuǐ bù fàn héshuǐ〈俗〉〈喻〉 each one minds their own business

【井台】jǐngtái〈名〉 well head

【井田制】 jǐngtiánzhì 〈名〉［历史］ nine-square farming system

【井盐】jǐngyán〈名〉 well salt

阱 jǐng〈名〉 trap: ▸陷～

刭（剄） jǐng〈动〉〈书〉 cut the throat: ▸自～

颈（頸） jǐng 〈名〉 1（脖子） neck: ▸～项, ～椎, 长～鹿 2（颈状物） neck-shaped thing: 瓶～ bottle neck ▸gěng

【颈动脉】jǐngdòngmài〈名〉 carotid artery

【颈静脉】jǐngjìngmài〈名〉 jugular vein

【颈饰】jǐngshì〈名〉 neckwear

【颈项】jǐngxiàng〈名〉 neck

【颈椎】jǐngzhuī〈名〉 cervical vertebra

【颈椎病】jǐngzhuībìng ▸p. 50〈名〉 cervical spondylosis

景 jǐng

A〈名〉 1（情况） situation: 好～不长。 Good times do not last long. ▸～象, 背～, 年～, 前～ 2（景观） scene: 夜～ night view ‖ 雪～ snowscape ▸～色, ～物, 取～ 3（布景） setting: 换～ change of scenery ▸布～, 内～, 外～ 4（指剧本段落） scene: 第二幕第一～ Act II, scene I **B**〈动〉 admire: ▸～慕, ～仰

【景德镇】Jǐngdézhèn〈名〉 Jingdezhen: ～瓷器 porcelain of Jingdezhen

【景点】jǐngdiǎn〈名〉 scenic spot: 保护/开发～ protect/develop scenic spots ‖ 旅游～ tourist attraction

【景观】jǐngguān〈名〉 landscape: 人文～ sight of human interest ‖ 自然～ natural scenery

【景观带】jǐngguāndài〈名〉 scenic area: 滨

江/绿色～ a riverside/green scenic area
【景况】jǐngkuàng〈名〉 circumstances: ～极佳 be in top condition
【景慕】jǐngmù〈动〉〈书〉 revere: 受人～ be held in respect
【景颇族】Jǐngpōzú〈名〉 Jingpo ethnic group
【景气】jǐngqì **A**〈形〉 booming: 经济不～ economic slump **B**〈名〉 scene
【景气指数】jǐngqì zhǐshù〈名〉[经济] climate index: ～持续走高。The business economic climate index continues to rise.
【景区】jǐngqū〈名〉 scenic spot: 开辟新～ open up new scenic spots
【景色】jǐngsè〈名〉 scene: 眺望周围的～ survey the surrounding landscape ‖ ～如画 picturesque scenery ‖ 自然～ natural scenery
【景深】jǐngshēn〈名〉[摄影] depth of field
【景泰蓝】jǐngtàilán〈名〉 cloisonné: ～花瓶 cloisonné vase

> **景泰蓝**
>
> A Chinese handicraft. Cloisonné technology originated in the Middle East, and began to be produced on a large scale in Beijing during the reign of Emperor Jingtai (1450-1457) of the Ming Dynasty, from which it derived its Chinese name. The technique involves using copper as a base to form an object such as a vase or a piece of jewellery. A filigree of copper wire is then glued onto the base, and the spaces in the filigree are filled with enamel. The object is then fired. These two steps are repeated until the spaces are completely filled. After the final firing, the object is polished until the enamel and the copper wire are smooth and level. In the final stage, the object is gilded to add lustre.

【景物】jǐngwù〈名〉 scene: ～宜人 delightful scene ‖ ～依旧。The scenery is just as it was before.
【景象】jǐngxiàng〈名〉 scene: 一片繁忙～ a busy scene
【景仰】jǐngyǎng〈动〉 respect and admire: ～某人知识渊博 admire sb. for their profound knowledge ‖ 令人～ admirable
【景遇】jǐngyù〈名〉〈书〉 circumstances: ～不佳 in unfavourable circumstances
【景致】jǐngzhì〈名〉 scene: 别有一番～ be a unique scene ‖ 引人入胜的～ alluring scenery

j

儆 jǐng〈动〉〈书〉 admonish: ▸杀一儆百, 以～效尤
【儆戒】jǐngjiè〈动〉 guard against

憬 jǐng〈动〉〈书〉 wake up to reality
【憬悟】jǐngwù〈动〉〈书〉 wake up to reality

警 jǐng
A〈动〉 **1**（告诫） warn: 鸣枪示～ fire a warning shot ▸～报, ～告, ～钟 **2**（防备） guard: ▸～戒, ～卫
B〈形〉 alert: ▸～觉, ～惕, 机～
C〈名〉 **1**（警察） police: ▸～官, 交～, 民～, 武～ **2**（危急状况） alarm: ▸报～, 火～
【警报】jǐngbào〈名〉 alarm: 发出～ sound the alarm ‖ 台风～ typhoon alert ‖ 紧急～ red alert ‖ 空袭～ air-raid siren
【警报器】jǐngbàoqì〈名〉 alarm: 防盗～ burglar alarm
【警备】jǐngbèi〈动〉 guard: ～森严 be tightly garrisoned ‖ ～司令部 garrison headquarters
【警察】jǐngchá〈名〉 police: 女～ policewoman ‖ 武装～ armed police ‖ 森林～ forest police ‖ 特种～ special police ‖ 治安～ security police
【警察局】jǐngchájú〈名〉 police station
【警车】jǐngchē〈名〉 police car
【警灯】jǐngdēng〈名〉 warning lamp
【警笛】jǐngdí〈名〉 **1**（指哨子） police siren **2**（指汽笛） alarm: 鸣～ sound an alarm
【警方】jǐngfāng〈名〉 police: 向～报案 report a crime to the police ‖ ～正在缉拿此人。The police are searching for the man.
【警匪片】jǐngfěipiàn〈名〉 cops-and-robbers film
【警风】jǐngfēng〈名〉 police conduct: 端正～ rectify police conduct
【警服】jǐngfú〈名〉 police uniform
【警告】jǐnggào **A**〈动〉 warn: ～顾客提防扒手 warn customers against pickpockets **B**〈名〉 **1**（指告诫） caution: 发出～ issue a warning ‖ 书面～ written warning **2**（指处分） warning: ～处分 disciplinary warning
【警官】jǐngguān〈名〉 police officer
【警官学校】jǐngguān xuéxiào〈名〉 police academy
【警棍】jǐnggùn〈名〉 truncheon; nightstick〈美〉
【警号】jǐnghào〈名〉 **1**（指信号） alarm **2**（指徽章） policeman's number-badge
【警花】jǐnghuā〈名〉 policewoman
【警徽】jǐnghuī〈名〉 police badge
【警籍】jǐngjí〈名〉 police status: 保留～ retain one's status as a policeman
【警戒】jǐngjiè〈动〉 be on one's guard: 加强～ intensify one's vigilance ‖ 执行～任务 carry out guard duties
【警戒色】jǐngjièsè〈名〉[生物] aposematic coloration
【警戒水位】jǐngjiè shuǐwèi〈名〉 warning water level: 高于～ above the dangerous water line ‖ 尚未达到～。The water mark has not been reached.
【警戒线】jǐngjièxiàn〈名〉 cordon: 超过～ pass the danger mark ‖ 设置～ cordon off
【警戒状态】jǐngjiè zhuàngtài〈名〉 state of alert: 处于全面～ be on full alert ‖ 进入～ go on (the) alert
【警诫】jǐngjiè〈动〉 warn
【警句】jǐngjù〈名〉 aphorism: 名人～ epigrams by famous persons
【警觉】jǐngjué **A**〈名〉 vigilance: 提高～ sharpen one's vigilance ‖ 他～性很高。He is highly vigilant. **B**〈动〉 alert: 他对此已有所～。He is already alert to this.
【警力】jǐnglì〈名〉 police force: 投入～展开侦查 send the police in to investigate ‖ ～不足。There is a shortage of police.
【警铃】jǐnglíng〈名〉 alarm bell
【警龄】jǐnglíng〈名〉 length of police service: 他有15年的～。He has 15 years of police service.
【警犬】jǐngquǎn〈名〉 police dog
【警容】jǐngróng〈名〉 policeman's discipline, appearance and bearing
【警嫂】jǐngsǎo〈名〉 policeman's wife
【警绳】jǐngshéng〈名〉 police rope
【警示】jǐngshì〈名〉 caution: ～后人 warning to younger generations
【警示灯】jǐngshìdēng〈名〉 warning light
【警世】jǐngshì〈动〉 warn the world: ～良言 wise counsel that acts as a warning to the world
【警惕】jǐngtì〈动〉 be on the alert: ～犯同样的错误 guard against repeating the mistake ‖ 保持～ remain vigilant ‖ 放松～ lower one's guard ‖ 提高～ sharpen one's vigilance
【警惕性】jǐngtìxìng〈名〉 vigilance: 提高～ sharpen one's vigilance
【警亭】jǐngtíng〈名〉 police box
【警卫】jǐngwèi **A**〈名〉 (security) guard: 门口有～站岗。There are guards at the gate. **B**〈动〉 guard with the armed forces: ～森严 under heavy police guard ‖ ～连 guards company
【警卫员】jǐngwèiyuán ▸**p. 966**〈名〉 bodyguard
【警务】jǐngwù〈名〉 police affairs: ～繁忙 be busy with police affairs
【警衔】jǐngxián〈名〉 police rank
【警校】jǐngxiào〈简称〉= 警官学校
【警械】jǐngxiè〈名〉 police instruments
【警醒】jǐngxǐng **A**〈形〉 light: 我睡觉很～。I'm a very light sleeper. **B**〈动〉 warn: 这次事故使我们～起来。The accident sounded an alarm bell for us.
【警员】jǐngyuán ▸**p. 966**〈名〉 police
【警长】jǐngzhǎng〈名〉 sergeant
【警钟】jǐngzhōng〈名〉 alarm bell: 这次失败给我们敲起了～。This failure sounded the alarm for us.
【警钟长鸣】jǐngzhōng-chángmíng〈成〉〈喻〉 be constantly on one's guard

jìng

劲（勁） jìng〈形〉 strong: ▸～敌, 刚～, 强～
▸jìn
【劲拔】jìngbá〈形〉〈书〉 tall and erect: ～的苍松 tall and sturdy pine tree
【劲爆】jìngbào **A**〈形〉 exciting: 场面十分～。The scene was extremely exciting. **B**〈动〉 crop up
【劲吹】jìngchuī〈动〉 blow hard: 北风～。The north wind is blowing hard.
【劲敌】jìngdí〈名〉 formidable opponent: 战胜～ beat one's nearest rival
【劲风】jìngfēng〈名〉 strong wind
【劲歌】jìnggē〈名〉 pop song characterized by a strong beat
【劲旅】jìnglǚ〈名〉〈书〉 crack force:〈喻〉足球～ strong football team
【劲射】jìngshè〈名〉 powerful shot: ～破门 score a goal with a powerful shot
【劲升】jìngshēng〈动〉 rise sharply: 股市行情～。Stock prices are soaring.
【劲松】jìngsōng〈名〉〈书〉 sturdy pine
【劲舞】jìngwǔ〈名〉 modern dance characterized by a strong beat
【劲秀】jìngxiù〈形〉 vigorous and graceful: 字迹～ vigorous and graceful handwriting

径[1]（徑） jìng
A〈名〉 **1**（路） path: 山～ mountain path ▸路～, 田～, 曲～ **2**（方法） way: ▸独辟蹊～, 捷～, 门～, 途～
B〈副〉 directly: ～飞北京 fly direct to Beijing ‖ ～行处理 handle sth. straight away ▸～直

径[2]（徑） jìng〈名〉 diameter: ▸半～, 口～, 直～
【径迹】jìngjì〈名〉[物理] track
【径流】jìngliú〈名〉[水利] run-off
【径情直遂】jìngqíng-zhísuì〈成〉 achieve

one's goal as smoothly as one would wish

【径赛】jìngsài〈名〉［体育］track: ～项目 track event ‖ ～选手 track athlete

【径庭】jìngtíng〈形〉〈书〉quite different: ▸大相～

【径向】jìngxiàng〈形〉［物理］radial: ～传送/分布 radial transfer/distribution

【径直】jìngzhí〈副〉**1**（直接前往）straight: ～回家 go straight home **2**（直接做）directly: 别绕弯子，～说吧。Stop beating about the bush and talk straight.

【径自】jìngzì〈副〉without consulting anyone: ～离岗 resign without consulting anyone

净（淨）jìng

A〈形〉**1**（干净）clean: 把脸洗～ wash one's face ▸纯～, 洁～ **2**（用完）used up: 吃/喝/用～ eat/drink/use up **3**（纯）net: ～利润 net profit ▸～利, ～收入, ～重

B〈动〉clean: ～～桌面 clean the top of the table

C〈副〉only: ～说废话 talk nothing but nonsense ‖ 街上～是水。Water filled the streets. ‖ 这些天～下雨。It's been raining constantly the last few days.

D〈名〉［戏曲］*jing* [the painted face role, one of the four main roles in traditional Chinese opera]

【净白】jìngbái〈形〉pure white

【净菜】jìngcài〈名〉clean vegetable

【净产值】jìngchǎnzhí〈名〉net output value

【净出口国】jìngchūkǒuguó〈名〉net exporter

【净额】jìng'é〈名〉net amount

【净高】jìnggāo〈名〉［建筑］clear height

【净化】jìnghuà〈动〉purify: ～城市空气 purify city air ‖〈喻〉～灵魂 cleanse one's soul

【净化器】jìnghuàqì〈名〉purifier: 空气～ air purifier

【净价】jìngjià〈名〉net price

【净尽】jìngjìn〈形〉complete: 消灭～ completely annihilate

【净空】jìngkōng〈名〉［建筑］clearance

【净口】jìngkǒu〈动〉purify the language in folk art performances

【净跨】jìngkuà〈名〉［建筑］clear span

【净宽】jìngkuān〈名〉clear width

【净亏】jìngkuī〈名〉net loss

【净利】jìnglì〈名〉net profit: 获得25%的～ clear a profit of 25 per cent

【净面】jìngmiàn〈动〉〈方〉wash one's face

【净身】jìngshēn〈动〉〈旧〉[of a man] be castrated

【净收入】jìngshōurù〈名〉net income

【净收益】jìngshōuyì〈名〉［经济］net profit

【净手】jìngshǒu〈动〉**1**〈方〉（洗手）clean one's hands **2** ▸**p. 772**〈婉〉（大小便）relieve oneself

【净桶】jìngtǒng ▸**p. 772**〈名〉〈婉〉chamber pot

【净土】jìngtǔ〈名〉**1**［佛教］Paradise of the West **2**（指地方）clean and unpolluted place

【净心修身】jìngxīn-xiūshēn〈成〉cleanse one's heart and order one's behaviour

【净余】jìngyú〈动〉remain: 除去所有花费，我还～500元。After paying all the expenses, I still have ¥500.

【净增】jìngzēng〈动〉have a net growth (of)

【净值】jìngzhí〈名〉net value

【净重】jìngzhòng〈名〉net weight: 箱子～50公斤。The box weighs 50 kilograms net.

【净赚】jìngzhuàn〈动〉make a net profit of

经（經）jìng

〈动〉［纺织］warp: ～纱 warp yarn

▸jīng

胫（脛）jìng

〈名〉shin: ▸～骨，不～而走

【胫骨】jìnggǔ〈名〉［生理］tibia

痉（痙）jìng

【痉挛】jìngluán〈动〉go into convulsions: 全身～ have convulsions all over

竞（競）jìng

A〈动〉compete: ▸～赛, ～选, ～争, ～走

B〈副〉〈书〉eagerly: ▸～相

【竞标】jìngbiāo〈动〉compete for a bid: 参加工程～ bid on a project

【竞猜】jìngcāi〈动〉compete to solve: 有奖～活动 guessing game with prizes

【竞答】jìngdá〈动〉compete to solve

【竞渡】jìngdù〈动〉**1**（指划船）have a boat race: 龙舟～ dragon-boat race **2**（指游泳）have a swimming race: ～长江 have a swimming race across the Yangtze River

【竞岗】jìnggǎng〈动〉compete for a post: 参加～ compete for a post

【竞购】jìnggòu〈动〉compete to buy: 吸引顾客～的原因 the reason why customers rush to buy

【竞技】jìngjì〈动〉do athletics: 同场～ compete in the same arena ‖ ～场 sports arena

【竞技体操】jìngjì tǐcāo〈名〉gymnastics

【竞技状态】jìngjì zhuàngtài〈名〉form: 保持最佳～ maintain top form

【竞价】jìngjià〈动〉bid against each other: ～拍卖 compete in bidding at an auction

【竞买】jìngmǎi〈动〉compete to buy: ～失败 failure in competitive buying

【竞卖】jìngmài〈动〉compete to sell: ～交易 competitive sale

【竞拍】jìngpāi〈动〉**1**（指拍卖）auction: ～活动 auctioning activity **2**（指报价）make bids at an auction

【竞聘】jìngpìn〈动〉compete for a post: ～执教 compete for a teaching post

【竞赛】jìngsài〈动〉compete: 获得数学～一等奖 win first prize in a mathematics contest ‖ 军备～ arms race ‖ 体育～ athletics competition ‖ ～规则 rules of a competition

【竞速】jìngsù〈动〉race: 轮椅～比赛 wheelchair race

【竞投】jìngtóu〈动〉bid competitively: 无底价～ competitive bid with no bottom line

【竞相】jìngxiāng〈副〉competitively: ～购买 compete to buy ‖ ～压价 compete in a price war

【竞销】jìngxiāo〈动〉compete for the market: 提高产品～能力 make one's product more marketable ‖ ～活动 sales promotion

【竞选】jìngxuǎn〈动〉run for: ～连任 campaign for re-election ‖ ～总统 run for the presidency ‖ 退出～ drop out of the race ‖ ～活动 election campaign ‖ ～伙伴 running mate

【竞业】jìngyè〈动〉act in competition: ～限制 non-competition restrictions

【竞争】jìngzhēng〈动〉compete: 参与国际～ enter world competition ‖ 价格～ compete in price ‖ 与某人～ compete with sb. ‖ ～日趋激烈。The competition is heating up.

【竞争机制】jìngzhēng jīzhì〈名〉competitive mechanism: 引进～ introduce competitive mechanisms

【竞争力】jìngzhēnglì〈名〉competitiveness: 提高/增强～ sharpen one's competitive edge

【竞走】jìngzǒu ▸**p. 909**〈动〉［体育］race-walk: ～运动员 (race) walker

竟 jìng

A〈动〉finish: 未～之业 unfulfilled task

B〈副〉**1**〈书〉（最终）eventually: 有志者事～成 **2**（竟然）unexpectedly: 他～厚着脸皮向我要钱。He had the nerve to ask me for money. ▸～敢, ～然

C〈形〉whole: ▸～日

【竟敢】jìnggǎn〈动〉have the audacity: 你～做这种事! How dare you do such a thing!

【竟然】jìngrán〈副〉unexpectedly: ～不顾事实 go so far as to disregard the facts ‖ ～大打出手 go so far as to get into a fist fight

【竟日】jìngrì〈副〉〈书〉all day (long): ～伏案写作 sit at one's desk writing all day

【竟至】jìngzhì〈动〉〈书〉go so far as to: 为达目的，他～以武力相威胁。To achieve his objective, he went so far as to threaten to use force.

婧 jìng

〈形〉〈书〉slender

靓（靚）jìng

〈动〉〈书〉dress up

▸liàng

【靓妆】jìngzhuāng〈名〉〈书〉beautiful adornments

敬 jìng

A〈动〉**1**（尊敬）respect: ～老 respect one's elders ▸～爱, ～而远之, 尊～ **2**（献上）offer politely: ～茶 serve tea ‖ ～烟 offer a cigarette ‖ ～新娘一杯。Here's to the bride. ▸～酒, 回～ **3**（专注）be dedicated to: ▸～业

B〈形〉respectful: ～请光临 respectfully invite ▸～告, ～候, ～赠

【敬爱】jìng'ài〈动〉respect and love: ～父母 love and respect one's parents ‖ ～的老师/领袖 beloved teacher/leader

【敬称】jìngchēng〈名〉honorific

【敬辞】jìngcí〈名〉term of respect

【敬而远之】jìng'éryuǎnzhī〈成〉stay at a respectful distance

【敬奉】jìngfèng〈动〉**1**（指供奉）worship piously: ～上帝/神明 worship God/gods **2**（指敬献）offer respectfully: ～薄礼 respectfully present a small gift

【敬服】jìngfú〈动〉esteem and admire: 受人～ be held in esteem

【敬告】jìnggào〈动〉〈敬〉notify: ～读者 notice to readers

【敬贺】jìnghè〈动〉〈敬〉respectfully congratulate: ～八十华诞 congratulations on your 80th birthday

【敬候】jìnghòu〈动〉**1**〈敬〉（等候）respectfully await: ～回复 look forward to your reply ‖ ～光临。We are respectfully waiting for your presence. **2**（指问候）greet respectfully

【敬酒】jìngjiǔ〈动〉propose a toast: 相互～ exchange toasts

【敬酒不吃吃罚酒】jìngjiǔ bù chī chī fájiǔ〈俗〉〈喻〉submit to sb.'s pressure after first turning down their request

【敬老爱幼】jìnglǎo-àiyòu〈成〉respect the aged and cherish the young

【敬老院】jìnglǎoyuàn = 养老院 yǎnglǎoyuàn

【敬礼】jìnglǐ〈动〉1（指动作）salute: 举手～ raise one's hand in salute ‖ 向国旗～ salute the national flag 2〈敬〉（指问候语）[used at the end of a letter]: 此致～ with best regards

【敬慕】jìngmù〈动〉revere: ～某人的品德 admire sb. for their moral character

【敬佩】jìngpèi〈动〉admire: 对他渊博的知识深感～ feel great respect for his profound knowledge

【敬启者】jìngqǐzhě〈套〉to whom it may concern

【敬上】jìngshàng〈动〉[used after the signature in a letter to one's senior or superior] yours truly

【敬挽】jìngwǎn〈动〉[used on funeral scrolls] present with deep condolences from sb.

【敬畏】jìngwèi〈动〉revere: 对老师心存～ stand in awe of the teachers

【敬贤礼士】jìngxián-lǐshì〈成〉respect wisdom and revere scholarship

【敬献】jìngxiàn〈动〉respectfully offer: 向烈士墓～花圈 offer a wreath at the tomb of a revolutionary martyr

【敬谢不敏】jìngxiè-bùmǐn〈成〉〈套〉I beg to be excused

【敬仰】jìngyǎng〈动〉venerate: 总理深受人民的爱戴和～。The premier commands deep love and reverence among the people.

【敬业】jìngyè〈动〉be devoted to one's career: ～精神 professional dedication

【敬意】jìngyì〈名〉respect: 向某人致以崇高的～ pay high tribute to sb. ‖ 区区薄礼，不成～。This small gift is just a token of my respect.

【敬语】jìngyǔ〈名〉respectful remarks

【敬赠】jìngzèng〈动〉〈敬〉present respectfully: ～花篮 present a basket of flowers respectfully

【敬重】jìngzhòng〈动〉deeply respect: 受人～ be deeply respected

【敬祝】jìngzhù〈动〉〈敬〉sincerely wish: ～身体健康! I wish you good health!

靖 jìng

A〈书〉〈形〉peaceful: ▸宁～
B〈动〉pacify: ～乱 quell a rebellion ▸绥～

静（靜）jìng

A〈形〉1（不动）calm: ～中有动。There is movement in the stillness. ‖ 她～～地坐着。She sat motionless. ▸～物，～止，安～，风平浪～ 2（不出声）silent: 夜深人～ in the depths of night ▸寂～，清～，肃～
B〈动〉calm down: ～下来好好想想 calm down and think it over carefully ‖ 你先～一～。Just calm down a bit.

【静场】jìngchǎng〈动〉vacate a theatre [after a performance]

【静电】jìngdiàn〈名〉［物理］static electricity

【静电场】jìngdiànchǎng〈名〉electrostatic field

【静电复印机】jìngdiàn fùyìnjī〈名〉xerographic printer

【静电感应】jìngdiàn gǎnyìng〈名〉electrostatic induction

【静电荷】jìngdiànhè〈名〉electrostatic charge

【静观】jìngguān〈动〉observe quietly: ～时局的发展 quietly observe the development of a situation

【静候】jìnghòu〈动〉quietly await: ～佳音 quietly await the good news

【静寂】jìngjì〈形〉still: ～的森林 still forest

【静脉】jìngmài〈名〉vein: ～注射 intravenous injection

【静脉曲张】jìngmài qūzhāng〈名〉varicose veins

【静谧】jìngmì〈形〉〈书〉tranquil: ～的夜晚 still night

【静默】jìngmò〈动〉1（寂静）be silent: 课堂上又是一阵～。Another spell of silence fell upon the classroom. 2（肃立）observe a silence: 全场起立，～致哀。All rose in silent tribute.

【静穆】jìngmù〈形〉solemn and quiet

【静悄悄】jìngqiāoqiāo〈形〉very quiet: 屋里～的。The room was very still.

【静水流深】jìngshuǐ-liúshēn〈成〉still waters run deep

【静态】jìngtài A〈名〉［物理］static state: ～电流 quiescent current ‖ ～平衡 static equilibrium B〈形〉static: ～分析 static analysis

【静物】jìngwù〈名〉still life: ～写生 paint a still life ‖ ～摄影 still life photography

【静物画】jìngwùhuà〈名〉still life

【静心】jìngxīn〈动〉have peace of mind: ～读书 be engrossed in study

【静养】jìngyǎng〈动〉recuperate in quiet surroundings: 安心～ put aside one's worries and have a good rest

【静音】jìngyīn〈动〉be silent: 生活家电的～设计 silent domestic appliances ‖ 超～效果 super-silent effect

【静园】jìngyuán〈动〉close a park

【静止】jìngzhǐ〈动〉be static: 不要～地、孤立地看待事物。Don't view things as static and isolated.

【静坐】jìngzuò〈动〉1（指疗法）sit still: 他凝思～。He sat in brooding silence. 2（指抗议）sit in: 参加～ take part in a sit-in

境 jìng

〈名〉1（边境）border: 大兵压～。A massive enemy force was bearing down on the border. ▸～外，出～，国～ 2（地方）place: ▸身临其～，学无止～ 3（处境）condition: ▸～遇，处～，事过～迁，意～

【境地】jìngdì〈名〉1（情况）condition: 处于尴尬～ be in embarrassing circumstances ‖ 陷入完全孤立的～ fall into complete isolation 2 = 境界 jìngjiè 2

【境界】jìngjiè〈名〉1（界限）boundary: ～线 boundary line 2（程度）state: 思想～ realm of thought ‖ 他的演技已经达到出神入化的～。His performance has reached the acme of perfection.

【境况】jìngkuàng〈名〉circumstances: ～不佳 be in straitened circumstances ‖ 家庭～已有改善。The family's financial situation has already improved.

【境内】jìngnèi〈名〉area inside a border: ～机构 domestic institution

【境外】jìngwài〈名〉area outside a border: ～办事处 overseas office

【境遇】jìngyù〈名〉circumstances: 悲惨的～ hard lot ‖ ～不同，感受各异。People in different circumstances feel differently.

镜（鏡）jìng

〈名〉1（镜子）mirror: 穿衣～ full-length mirror ‖ 后视～ rear-view mirror ▸哈哈～，明～ 2（透镜）glass: ▸放大～，望远～，眼～

【镜花水月】jìnghuā-shuǐyuè〈成〉〈喻〉mirage

【镜框】jìngkuàng〈名〉1（指画）picture frame 2（指眼镜）glasses frame: 树脂～ resin spectacles frame

【镜片】jìngpiàn〈名〉lens: 隐形～ contact lenses

【镜台】jìngtái〈名〉dressing table

【镜头】jìngtóu〈名〉［摄影］1（指装置）camera lens: 广角～ wide-angle lens ‖ 长焦距～ telephoto lens 2（指画面）scene: 电影～ cinema scene ‖ 全景～ pan shot ‖ 影片开始的几个～ the first few scenes of the film ▸慢～

【镜头盖】jìngtóugài〈名〉[of a camera] lens cap

【镜匣】jìngxiá〈名〉dressing case

【镜像】jìngxiàng〈名〉mirror image

【镜子】jìngzi〈名〉1（用于成像）mirror: 照～ look in the mirror ‖〈喻〉报刊是舆论的一面～。The press is a mirror of public opinion. 2〈口〉（眼镜）glasses: 戴上～ put on one's glasses ‖ 摘下～ take off one's spectacles

jiōng

扃 jiōng

A〈书〉〈名〉1（门闩）bolt 2（门）door
B〈动〉close a door

jiǒng

囧 jiǒng

〈形〉dumbfounded

迥 jiǒng

〈形〉1（远）remote 2（差别大）highly different: ～若两人 not look like the same person

【迥然】jiǒngrán〈形〉widely different: ～不同 poles apart

【迥异】jiǒngyì〈形〉poles apart: 性格～ be poles apart in character

炯 jiǒng

〈形〉bright

【炯炯】jiǒngjiǒng〈形〉bright: 目光～ sparkling eyes ‖ 两眼～有神 two bright, sparkling eyes

窘 jiǒng

A〈形〉1（穷困）impoverished: 日子过得很～ live a very hard life ‖ 他家家境很～。His family lives in straitened circumstances. ▸～困，～迫 2（为难）embarrassed: ～得脸红了 be flushed with embarrassment ‖ 感到有些～ feel a bit embarrassed ▸～境，～况，～态
B〈动〉embarrass: 他故意～我。He embarrassed me on purpose.

【窘促】jiǒngcù〈形〉〈书〉1（穷困）poverty-stricken 2（处境困难）in a predicament

【窘境】jiǒngjìng〈名〉awkward situation: 摆脱～ get out of a predicament ‖ 陷入～ be landed in an awkward predicament

【窘况】jiǒngkuàng〈名〉awkward situation: 摆脱～ get out of a predicament

【窘困】jiǒngkùn〈形〉awkward: 处境～ be in a predicament

【窘迫】jiǒngpò〈形〉1（穷困）poverty-stricken: 生活～ live in poverty 2（为难）embarrassed: 令人～的境遇 embarrassing circumstances ‖ 她满脸通红，显得十分～。Blushes showed her embarrassment.

【窘态】jiǒngtài〈名〉embarrassed look: 露出～ show signs of embarrassment ‖ 掩盖～ hide one's embarrassment

【窘相】jiǒngxiàng〈名〉 embarrassed look: 一脸～ look ill at ease

jiū

纠（糾） jiū 〈动〉 **1**（集合） gather together: ▸～合, ～集 **2**（缠） entangle: ▸～缠, ～纷, ～结 **3**（纠正） correct: ▸～错, ～正 **4**（督察） supervise: ▸～察

【纠察】jiūchá **A**〈动〉 picket **B**〈名〉 picket: 担任～ be on the picket line

【纠察队】jiūcháduì〈名〉 pickets: 组成～ form a picket squad

【纠缠】jiūchán〈动〉 **1**（缠绕） get in a tangle: 钓鱼线跟水草～在一起了。 The fishing line got entangled in some water weeds. **2**（搅扰） trouble: 常被债主～ be pestered by creditors ‖ 疾病～着他。 He was dogged by ill health. ‖ 别～他。 Stop bothering him.

【纠缠不清】 jiūchánbùqīng〈成〉 become too tangled up to unravel

【纠错】jiūcuò〈动〉 correct a mistake: ～程序 error correcting program

【纠纷】jiūfēn〈名〉 dispute: 调解～ mediate a dispute ‖ 法律～ legal dispute ‖ 家庭～ domestic conflict

【纠风】jiūfēng〈动〉 rectify unhealthy tendencies: ～办 State Council Office for Rectifying

【纠葛】jiūgé〈名〉 entanglement: 感情～ emotional entanglement ‖ 我们之间没有什么～。 There is no dispute between us.

【纠合】jiūhé〈动〉〈贬〉 band together: ～无业游民，扰乱社会治安 band together a bunch of jobless vagrants to disrupt social order

【纠集】jiūjí〈动〉〈贬〉 band together: ～流氓团伙 mass a gang of hooligans

【纠结】jiūjié〈动〉 **1**（缠绕） entangle: 别把我的毛线～在一起。 Don't tangle up my wool. **2** = 纠合 jiūhé

【纠偏】jiūpiān〈动〉 correct an error

【纠正】jiūzhèng〈动〉 correct: ～不正之风 rectify unhealthy tendencies ‖ ～错误 right a wrong ‖ ～冤、假、错案 redress cases in which people have been wronged, misjudged or framed

鸠（鳩） jiū 〈名〉 turtle dove: ▸～占鹊巢

【鸠占鹊巢】jiūzhàn-quècháo = 鹊巢鸠占 quècháo-jiūzhàn

究 jiū

A〈动〉 **1**（学） study intensively: ▸探～, 研～ **2**（查） investigate: ～其根源 probe to the roots of sth. ‖ 此事要一～到底。 We will get to the bottom of the matter. ▸追～

B〈副〉〈书〉 actually: 责任～属何方? Who on earth is responsible for this?

【究办】jiūbàn〈动〉 investigate and deal with: 依法～ investigate and deal with according to law

【究诘】jiūjié〈动〉〈书〉 try to get to the heart of a matter: 犯罪嫌疑人受到警方～。 The suspect was interrogated by the police.

【究竟】jiūjìng **A**〈名〉 outcome: 爱问个～ like to get to the heart of a matter ‖ 我们都想知道个～。 We all want to know what actually happened. **B**〈副〉 **1**（表追问） exactly: 他～把你怎么了? What on earth did he do to you? ‖ 你～想说什么? What exactly do you want to say? **2**（毕竟） after all: 他～是个生手。 He is a rookie after all. ‖ 他～是个孩子， 原谅他吧。 Please forgive him; after all, he is still a child.

【究问】jiūwèn〈动〉 investigate thoroughly

赳 jiū〈形〉 spirited

【赳赳】jiūjiū〈形〉 valiant

阄（鬮） jiū〈名〉 lot: ▸抓～儿

揪 jiū〈动〉 hold tight and pull: ～耳朵/头发 pull sb.'s ear/hair ‖ 把某人从床上～起来 drag sb. from his bed

【揪辫子】jiū biànzi〈惯〉〈喻〉 seize upon sb.'s mistakes or shortcomings

【揪出】jiūchū〈动〉 uncover

【揪心】jiūxīn〈动〉 **1**（担心） be anxious: 这孩子真叫人～。 This kid is a real worry to me. **2**（痛苦） be agonizing: 伤口痛得～。 There was a gnawing pain from the wound.

啾 jiū

【啾唧】jiūjī〈拟〉 chirp

【啾啾】jiūjiū〈拟〉 chirp: 秋虫～。 Autumn insects chirped.

鬏 jiū〈名〉 [of hair] bun: 头上梳盘着一个～ have one's hair coiled into a bun

jiǔ

九 jiǔ

A ▸**p. 691**〈数〉 **1**（表数目） nine: ～折酬宾 be sold at a 10% discount ‖ 五加四得～。 Five plus four is nine. ▸十有八～ **2**（多） many: ▸～牛一毛, ～死一生

B〈名〉 each of the nine nine-day periods [beginning from the day after the Winter Solstice]: 三～ the coldest days of winter ▸数～

【九边形】 jiǔbiānxíng 〈名〉 ［数学］ enneagon

【九重霄】jiǔchóngxiāo〈名〉 heaven

【九鼎】jiǔdǐng〈名〉 **1**（指物） nine big tripods cast by King Yu (夏禹) and handed down as state treasure **2**（指分量） great weight: ▸一言～

【九段】 jiǔduàn 〈名〉 ninth-dan [highest grade in go or *weiqi*]

【九宫】jiǔgōng〈名〉 nine modes of ancient Chinese music

【九宫格】jiǔgōnggé〈名〉squared paper for practising Chinese calligraphy

【九九表】 jiǔjiǔbiǎo 〈名〉 multiplication table

【九九歌】jiǔjiǔgē = 小九九 xiǎojiǔjiǔ 1

【九九归一】jiǔjiǔguīyī〈成〉 when all is said and done: ～，我们还是去的好。 All things considered, it is better for us to go.

【九流三教】 jiǔliú-sānjiào = 三教九流 sānjiào-jiǔliú

【九牛二虎之力】jiǔ niú èr hǔ zhī lì〈成〉〈喻〉 tremendous effort: 费尽～ use all one's might

【九牛一毛】jiǔniú-yīmáo〈成〉〈喻〉a drop in the ocean

【九泉】jiǔquán〈名〉〈书〉 nether world: 含笑于～ rest in peace

【九三学社】Jiǔ-Sān Xuéshè〈名〉 September 3rd Society [one of China's 8 political parties]

【九死一生】jiǔsǐ-yīshēng〈成〉 hairbreadth escape: 身经百战，～ escape from the jaws of death after fighting a hundred battles

【九天】jiǔtiān〈名〉 highest of heavens

【九头鸟】jiǔtóuniǎo〈名〉 nine-headed bird [a legendary ominous bird]

【九尾狐】 jiǔwěihú 〈名〉〈喻〉 crafty villainous person

【九五之尊】 jiǔwǔzhīzūn 〈名〉 imperial throne

【九霄】jiǔxiāo〈名〉 highest heavens

【九霄云外】jiǔxiāoyúnwài〈成〉〈喻〉 far, far away: 把个人安危抛到～ cast personal safety to the winds

【九一八事变】Jiǔ-Yībā Shìbiàn〈名〉［历史］ September 18th Incident

【九月】jiǔyuè ▸**p. 928**〈名〉 **1**（阳历） September **2**（阴历） ninth month of the lunar year

【九州】 jiǔzhōu 〈名〉 **1**（指行政区划） nine administrative divisions of China in remote antiquity **2**（中国） China

【九族】jiǔzú〈名〉 nine degrees of kinship: 诛～ put to death all one's family members

久 jiǔ

A〈形〉 long: ～旱无雨 suffer from a long drought ‖ 蓄谋已～ long premeditated ‖ 这首歌～唱不衰。 The song has stood the test of time. ▸～别, 天长日～

B〈名〉 length: 四年之～ for as long as four years ‖ 你来多～了? How long have you been here?

【久别】jiǔbié〈动〉 be separated for a long time: ～重逢 be reunited after a long separation

【久病成医】 jiǔbìng-chéngyī 〈成〉 prolonged illness makes a doctor of a patient

【久病床前无孝子】jiǔbìng chuángqián wú xiàozǐ〈俗〉 a parent with a prolonged illness finds no filial children at the bedside

【久等】jiǔděng〈动〉 wait for a long time

【久而久之】jiǔ'érjiǔzhī〈成〉 in the course of time: 机器要不好好养护，～就会生锈。 If not properly maintained, machinery will get rusty over time.

【久负盛名】 jiǔfù-shèngmíng 〈成〉 have long enjoyed a good reputation

【久旱逢甘雨】jiǔ hàn féng gānyǔ〈成〉 **1**〈本〉 welcome rain after a long drought **2**〈喻〉 satisfy a long-held desire: ～， 他乡遇故知。 To meet an old friend in a distant land is like experiencing rain after a long drought.

【久经考验】jiǔjīngkǎoyàn〈成〉 seasoned

【久久】jiǔjiǔ〈副〉 for a long time: ～不愿离去 unable to tear oneself away for a long time ‖ 心情～不能平静 feel out of sorts for a long time

【久居人下】jiǔjūrénxià〈惯〉 remain in a subordinate position for a long period

【久留】jiǔliú〈动〉 stay long: 此地不宜～。 This is not a place where you can stay long.

【久违】jiǔwéi〈动〉〈套〉 not to have met for a long time: ～了! Long time no see.

【久闻大名】jiǔwén-dàmíng〈惯〉 I've long heard about your great name

【久仰】jiǔyǎng〈动〉〈套〉 have long been looking forward to meeting sb.: ～了。 I've been looking forward to meeting you for a long time.

【久已】jiǔyǐ〈副〉 for a long time: ～不在人世 long since dead

【久远】jiǔyuǎn〈形〉remote: 年代～ be age-old

玖 jiǔ ▸p. 691〈名〉 nine [used for the numeral 九 on cheques, etc. to avoid alterations or mistakes]

灸 jiǔ〈名〉[中医] moxibustion: ▸针～

韭（韮） jiǔ〈名〉[植物] Chinese chives

【韭菜】jiǔcài〈名〉Chinese chives

【韭黄】jiǔhuáng〈名〉hotbed chives

酒 jiǔ〈名〉alcoholic drink: 喝～ drink alcohol ‖ 敬～ raise a toast ▸白～, 葡萄～, 花天～地, 酗～

> **酒**
>
> Wines and spirits. *Baijiu* (白酒) is a high-alcohol content spirit made from grain. Types of *baijiu* include *gaoliang* (高粱), which is made from sorghum. The most famous *gaoliang* liquor is *maotai* (茅台), a vintage Chinese spirit produced in the town of Maotai in Guizhou Province, and often served at high-level banquets. *Erguotou* (二锅头) is an inexpensive *baijiu* popular in north China. *Huangjiu* (黄酒) is made from polished glutinous rice or millet, and has a low alcohol content. Rice wine (米酒) is a type of *huangjiu* with a pure aroma and a clean taste. *Huangjiu* may be yellowish in colour, hence the name. The most famous *huangjiu* is Shaoxing wine (绍兴酒).

【酒吧】jiǔbā〈名〉bar; pub〈英〉

【酒保】jiǔbǎo〈名〉〈旧〉barman〈英〉; bartender〈美〉

【酒杯】jiǔbēi〈名〉wine glass

【酒菜】jiǔcài〈名〉1（食物、饮料）food and drink: 准备～, 招待客人 prepare food and drink for the guests 2（下酒菜）food to go with wine

【酒池肉林】jiǔchí-ròulín〈成〉〈喻〉extravagant orgy

【酒店】jiǔdiàn〈名〉1（酒吧）pub 2（饭店）hotel: 五星级～ five-star hotel

【酒饭】jiǔfàn〈名〉food and drink: ～招待 entertain sb. with food and wine

【酒疯】jiǔfēng〈名〉drunken fit: 发～ have a drunken fit

【酒逢知己千杯少】jiǔ féng zhījǐ qiān bēi shǎo〈俗〉for a congenial friend a thousand toasts are too few

【酒馆】jiǔguǎn〈名〉bar; pub〈英〉: 去～喝酒 go to a pub for a drink

【酒鬼】jiǔguǐ〈名〉〈粗〉drunkard

【酒酣耳热】jiǔhān-ěrrè〈成〉mellow with drink

【酒后吐真言】jiǔhòu tǔ zhēnyán〈俗〉in vino veritas

【酒壶】jiǔhú〈名〉wine pot

【酒会】jiǔhuì〈名〉cocktail party: 鸡尾～ cocktail party

【酒家】jiǔjiā〈名〉1（餐馆）restaurant 2（指人）bartender

【酒浆】jiǔjiāng〈名〉〈书〉alcohol

【酒窖】jiǔjiào〈名〉wine cellar

【酒精】jiǔjīng〈名〉alcohol: 工业用～ industrial alcohol ‖ ～中毒 alcoholism

【酒精灯】jiǔjīngdēng〈名〉alcohol burner

【酒精炉】jiǔjīnglú〈名〉alcohol heater

【酒精饮料】jiǔjīng yǐnliào〈名〉alcoholic drink

【酒具】jiǔjù〈名〉drinking set

【酒阑人散】jiǔlán-rénsàn〈成〉the party is coming to its end

【酒力】jiǔlì〈名〉effect of alcohol: 不胜～ cannot hold one's liquor

【酒帘】jiǔlián = 酒望 jiǔwàng

【酒量】jiǔliàng〈名〉alcohol tolerance: ～大 be able to take one's drink

【酒令】jiǔlìng〈名〉drinking game: 行～ play a drinking game

【酒楼】jiǔlóu〈名〉restaurant

【酒囊饭袋】jiǔnáng-fàndài〈成〉〈喻〉good-for-nothing

【酒酿】jiǔniàng〈名〉fermented glutinous rice

【酒气熏天】jiǔqì xūntiān〈动〉have a strong smell of alcohol

【酒器】jiǔqì〈名〉drinking vessel

【酒曲】jiǔqū〈名〉distiller's yeast

【酒肉朋友】jiǔròu-péngyǒu〈成〉fair-weather friend

【酒色】jiǔsè〈名〉wine and women: 沉湎于～ abandon oneself to wine and women ‖ ～财气 wine, women, wealth, and temper [generally considered to be the four arch evils of life] ‖ ～之徒 libertine

【酒水】jiǔshuǐ〈名〉wine and other beverages: 自带～ BYO

【酒肆】jiǔsì〈名〉〈书〉public house

【酒提】jiǔtí〈名〉wine dipper

【酒徒】jiǔtú〈名〉drunkard

【酒望】jiǔwàng〈名〉〈旧〉streamer hanging in front of a wine shop

【酒窝】jiǔwō〈名〉dimple: 她脸上有个～。She's got dimples.

【酒席】jiǔxí〈名〉banquet: 大摆～ entertain sb. to a sumptuous banquet

【酒香不怕巷子深】jiǔxiāng bùpà xiàngzi shēn〈俗〉good wine sells well even deep in an outlying lane

【酒兴】jiǔxìng〈名〉euphoria from drinking: ～正浓 be in a euphoric drunken state

【酒性】jiǔxìng〈名〉alcoholic strength

【酒宴】jiǔyàn〈名〉feast: 设～ give a banquet ‖ 丰盛的～ sumptuous banquet

【酒药】jiǔyào〈名〉yeast for brewing rice wine

【酒靥】jiǔyè〈名〉dimple

【酒意】jiǔyì〈名〉tipsy feeling: 有了几分～ become slightly tipsy

【酒瘾】jiǔyǐn〈名〉alcohol dependence

【酒糟】jiǔzāo〈名〉distillers' grains: ～可以喂猪。Distillers' grains can be used as pig feed.

【酒糟鼻】jiǔzāobí〈名〉acne rosacea

【酒盅】jiǔzhōng〈名〉small handleless wine cup

【酒足饭饱】jiǔzú-fànbǎo〈成〉be replete with food and drink

jiù

旧（舊） jiù

A〈形〉1（用过的）used: ～家具 second-hand furniture ‖ ～衣服 used clothing ▸喜新厌～ 2（过时的）antiquated: ～观念 outdated ideas ‖ ～社会 old society ‖ ～思想 antiquated ideas 3（以往的）former: ▸～交, ～居, ～事

B〈名〉1（往事）things in the past: ▸怀～, 守～, 叙～ 2（老交情）old friendship; （老朋友）old friend: 访～ visit an old friend ▸故～, 念～

【旧案】jiù'àn〈名〉1（指案件）case of long standing: 清理～ clear long-standing court cases 2〈旧〉（指条例等）former practice: 按～办理 handle all cases according to former regulations

【旧病】jiùbìng〈名〉chronic illness

【旧病复发】jiùbìng-fùfā〈成〉1〈本〉have a recurrence of an old illness 2〈喻〉slip back into old ways

【旧部】jiùbù〈名〉former subordinate

【旧称】jiùchēng〈动〉be formerly known as

【旧的不去，新的不来】jiùde bùqù, xīnde bùlái〈俗〉the new should replace the old

【旧地】jiùdì〈名〉once familiar place: ～重游 revisit a once familiar place

【旧调重弹】jiùdiào-chóngtán〈成〉〈喻〉play the same old tune

【旧都】jiùdū〈名〉former capital

【旧恶】jiù'è〈名〉〈书〉old grievance: 重提～ rip up old grievances

【旧故】jiùgù〈名〉old friend

【旧观】jiùguān〈名〉former appearance: 恢复～ be restored to the original form ‖ 一改～ take on a completely new look

【旧国】jiùguó〈名〉old capital

【旧好】jiùhǎo〈名〉〈书〉1（指友情）old friendship: ▸重修～ 2（指好友）old friend

【旧恨新仇】jiùhèn-xīnchóu〈成〉new hatred piled on old

【旧货】jiùhuò〈名〉second-hand goods: ～市场 flea market

【旧货摊】jiùhuòtān〈名〉second-hand stall

【旧迹】jiùjì〈名〉historic site

【旧交】jiùjiāo〈名〉old friend

【旧教】jiùjiào〈名〉Catholicism

【旧金山】Jiùjīnshān〈名〉San Francisco

【旧居】jiùjū〈名〉former residence

【旧历】jiùlì〈名〉traditional Chinese calendar: 沿用～ follow the lunar calendar ‖ ～年 lunar New Year

【旧例】jiùlì〈名〉outdated rules and regulations

【旧梦重温】jiùmèng-chóngwēn〈成〉renew a sweet experience of bygone days

【旧瓶装新酒】jiùpíng zhuāng xīnjiǔ〈惯〉〈喻〉new content in an old form

【旧情】jiùqíng〈名〉1（指友情）old friendship: 不忘～ not forget old friendship 2（指恋情）past love: ～复燃 revive a past love

【旧日】jiùrì〈名〉old days: 失去～的威严 lose one's former authority ‖ 想念～的朋友 miss one's former friends

【旧社会】jiùshèhuì〈名〉old society [usually referring to China before 1949]

【旧诗】jiùshī〈名〉classical Chinese poetry

【旧石器时代】Jiùshíqì Shídài〈名〉Paleolithic Age

【旧时】jiùshí〈名〉old times: ～这儿有块麦田。There was a wheat field here in the past.

【旧识】jiùshí〈名〉old acquaintance

【旧式】jiùshì〈形〉old-fashioned: ～家具 old-fashioned furniture ‖ ～婚礼 traditional wedding

【旧事】jiùshì〈名〉past event: ～重提 rake up something from the past

【旧书】jiùshū〈名〉1（用过的书）second-hand book: ～店 secondhand bookstore 2（古书）ancient text

【旧俗】jiùsú〈名〉old custom: 破～, 立新风 do away with old customs and introduce new ones

【旧体】jiùtǐ〈名〉old style: ～诗词 classical poetry

【旧闻】jiùwén〈名〉old news

【旧物】jiùwù〈名〉1（指物品）old relics 2（指领土）lost territory: 光复～ recover lost territories

【旧习】jiùxí〈名〉old habit and custom: ～难改。It's difficult to change old habits and customs.

【旧学】jiùxué〈名〉old Chinese learning [as

distinct from the new or Western learning]
【旧业】jiùyè〈名〉old trade: ▸重操～
【旧友】jiùyǒu〈名〉old friend
【旧约】Jiùyuē〈名〉［宗教］*Old Testament*
【旧宅】jiùzhái〈名〉former residence
【旧账】jiùzhàng〈名〉old feud: 翻～ rake up the past
【旧知】jiùzhī〈名〉〈书〉old acquaintance
【旧址】jiùzhǐ〈名〉former site: 古堡～ site of an old castle ‖ 学校～ former site of a school
【旧制】jiùzhì〈名〉**1**（指制度）old system **2**（指计量制）old system of weights and measures in China

臼

jiù〈名〉**1**（用于舂米）mortar: 石/蒜～ stone/garlic mortar **2**（臼状物）mortar-shaped thing: ▸～齿, 脱～
【臼齿】jiùchǐ〈名〉molar: 拔掉两颗～ have two molars taken out

咎

jiù
A〈名〉blame: ▸～由自取, 归～, 引～
B〈动〉blame: ▸既往不～
【咎由自取】jiùyóuzìqǔ〈成〉have only oneself to blame: 如果他考试不及格，那是～。If he fails his exams, he'll only have himself to blame.
【咎有应得】jiùyǒuyīngdé〈成〉deserve the blame

疚

jiù〈动〉〈书〉be filled with remorse: ▸负～, 愧～, 内～

柩

jiù〈名〉coffin with a corpse in it: ▸灵～
【柩车】jiùchē〈名〉hearse

柏

jiù ▸乌桕 wūjiù

救

jiù〈动〉**1**（援助）help: ▸～火, ～急, ～灾, 自～ **2**（拯救）rescue: ～溺水儿童 save a drowning child ‖ 守门员～了六个球。The goalkeeper saved six goals. ‖ 全体船员得～了。The entire crew were rescued. ▸～命, 营～, 拯～
【救兵】jiùbīng〈名〉reinforcements: 搬/派～ call in/dispatch reinforcements
【救场】jiùchǎng〈动〉save the show
【救国】jiùguó〈动〉save the nation: ～救民 save the country and the people from impending danger
【救护】jiùhù〈动〉give emergency assistance: ～伤员 rescue the wounded ‖ 战地～工作 rescue work on the battlefield
【救护车】jiùhùchē〈名〉ambulance
【救荒】jiùhuāng〈动〉provide famine relief: 生产～ tide over a crop failure through production
【救火】jiùhuǒ〈动〉fight a fire: 许多人参加了～。Many people joined in the fire-fighting.
【救火车】jiùhuǒchē〈名〉fire engine
【救火队员】jiùhuǒ duìyuán ▸**p. 966**〈名〉firefighter
【救急】jiùjí〈动〉provide help in an emergency: ～款 emergency funds ‖ 你给我的钱正好～。You gave me the money just in time for my emergency.
【救济】jiùjì〈动〉relieve: ～穷人 provide relief to the poor ‖ 失业～ unemployment relief ‖ ～粮 relief grain
【救济金】jiùjìjīn〈名〉relief funds: 失业～ unemployment relief
【救济物资】jiùjì wùzī〈名〉relief supply
【救驾】jiùjià〈动〉〈诙〉save sb. from an awkward situation
【救苦救难】jiùkǔ-jiùnàn〈成〉help the needy and relieve the distressed
【救困扶危】jiùkùn-fúwēi〈成〉relieve and help people in danger
【救命】jiùmìng〈动〉save sb.'s life: 大声呼叫～ scream for help ‖ ～恩人 saviour ‖ ～之恩终身难忘。You saved my life and I shall never forget it.
【救命稻草】jiùmìng-dàocǎo〈名〉straw to clutch at
【救人一命，胜造七级浮屠】jiùrén yī mìng, shèng zào qī jí fútú〈俗〉it is better to save one life than to build a seven-storeyed pagoda
【救生】jiùshēng〈动〉save a life
【救生筏】jiùshēngfá〈名〉life raft
【救生圈】jiùshēngquān〈名〉life ring
【救生艇】jiùshēngtǐng〈名〉lifeboat: 放下～ launch a lifeboat
【救生衣】jiùshēngyī〈名〉life jacket
【救生员】jiùshēngyuán ▸**p. 966**〈名〉lifeguard
【救世军】Jiùshìjūn〈名〉［基督教］Salvation Army
【救世主】Jiùshìzhǔ〈名〉［基督教］Saviour
【救死扶伤】jiùsǐ-fúshāng〈成〉heal the wounded and rescue the dying
【救亡】jiùwáng〈动〉strive for national salvation
【救亡图存】jiùwáng-túcún〈成〉save the nation from doom and strive for its survival
【救险】jiùxiǎn〈动〉rescue and deliver from danger
【救险车】jiùxiǎnchē〈名〉breakdown truck〈英〉; tow truck〈美〉
【救星】jiùxīng〈名〉liberator: 人民的～ liberator of the people
【救援】jiùyuán〈动〉rescue: 参加～工作 join the relief efforts ‖ 紧急～ emergency relief
【救援车】jiùyuánchē〈名〉rescue vehicle: ～全天候待命 rescue vehicles on 24-hour standby
【救援人员】jiùyuán rényuán〈名〉relief worker
【救援物资】jiùyuán wùzī〈名〉relief supply
【救灾】jiùzāi〈动〉**1**（救济）provide disaster relief: 参加～ join in disaster relief efforts ‖ ～物资 disaster relief materials **2**（解除灾害）ward off disaster: 防洪～ control flood and ward off disaster
【救治】jiùzhì〈动〉bring (sb.) out of danger: ～伤员 give treatment to the wounded
【救助】jiùzhù〈动〉render assistance in time of distress: ～失学儿童 provide assistance to children deprived of education ‖ ～难民 help refugees ‖ 司法～ court relief
【救助点】jiùzhùdiǎn〈名〉relief distribution point: 把流浪人员送到～ bring homeless people to relief distribution points ‖ 捐赠物资按各～的实际需要分发 allocate donations according to the actual needs of each relief distribution point

厩（廐）

jiù〈名〉enclosure: ▸～肥, 马～
【厩肥】jiùféi〈名〉barnyard manure

就

jiù
A〈动〉**1**（靠近）approach: 删繁～简 take the simple, less complicated way ‖ ～近入学 go to school locally ▸避重～轻, 驾轻～熟 **2**（到达）reach: ▸～席, ～座, 各～各位 **3**（从事）engage in: ▸～寝, ～学, ～业, ～医 **4**（顺从）comply with: ▸半推半～, 迁～ **5**（完成）accomplish: ▸～绪, 功成名～, 一蹴而～ **6**（搭配）go with: ～着咸菜吃馒头 have buns with pickles
B〈介〉**1**（趁）by: ～此机会谈谈 avail oneself of the opportunity to have a talk **2**（根据）with regard to: ～目前情况看来 in the light of the present situation ‖ ～职工教育问题展开讨论 talk over the problem of staff education **3**（被）[used to form a set phrase with a passive meaning]: ▸～擒
C〈副〉**1**（立刻）at once: 我～来。I'm coming in a minute. ‖ 马上～走 leave immediately **2**（强调早）already: 他昨天八点～睡了。He went to bed as early as 8 o'clock last night. ‖ 她十四岁～上了大学。She went to college when she was only fourteen. **3**（便会）then [used after 只要, 要是 to introduce a natural development of the previous statement]: 要是你没来，我～尴尬了。If you hadn't come, I would have been embarrassed. ‖ 只要努力，～有可能成功。If you work hard, you can be successful. **4**（强调数量）as many/much as: 他光买书～花了500元。He spent as much as 500 *yuan* on books alone. ‖ 一天～来三次 come as much as three times a day **5**（只）only: ～等你一个了。You're the only one we're waiting for. ‖ 他～住在附近。He just lives somewhere nearby. **6**（强调准确）exactly: 我～知道他会等我们的。I knew he would be waiting for us. ‖ 我要的～是这个。This is exactly what I want. **7**（表示容忍）[used between two identical elements to indicate resignation]: 五块～五块，我买了。I'll take it for five *yuan* anyhow.
D〈连〉even if: 你～再等他也不会来。He won't come even if you wait even longer.
【就伴】jiùbàn〈动〉accompany sb.
【就便】jiùbiàn〈动〉be at sb.'s convenience: ～给我买点香蕉吧。While you're at it, buy me some bananas.
【就餐】jiùcān〈动〉have a meal: 外出～ eat out ‖ 在食堂～ have one's meal at the canteen ‖ ～券 meal-ticket
【就此】jiùcǐ〈副〉at this point: 会议～结束。The meeting is over now.
【就地】jiùdì〈副〉on the spot: ～解决 settle on the spot ‖ ～免职 make a dismissal then and there ‖ ～正法 execute on the spot
【就地取材】jiùdì-qǔcái〈成〉draw on local resources
【就读】jiùdú〈动〉take a course: ～于北京大学 study at Beijing University
【就范】jiùfàn〈动〉submit: 逼其～ force sb. to submit ‖ 使敌人～ subdue an enemy
【就歼】jiùjiān〈动〉be wiped out: 敌人全部～。The enemy were totally wiped out.
【就教】jiùjiào〈动〉ask for advice: ～于专家 consult an expert
【就近】jiùjìn〈副〉nearby: ～找个住处 find accommodation in the neighbourhood
【就里】jiùlǐ〈名〉inside information: 不知～ have no inside information
【就擒】jiùqín〈动〉be captured: 当场～ be caught red-handed ▸束手～
【就寝】jiùqǐn〈动〉turn in: ～时间 bedtime
【就任】jiùrèn〈动〉take office: ～市长 fill the office of mayor ‖ ～新职 take up a new post
【就势】jiùshì〈副〉[making use of the momentum of a previous action]: 他把铺盖放在地上，～坐在上面。He put his bedding roll on the ground and sat right down on it.

【就事论事】jiùshì-lùnshì〈成〉judge a case as it stands
【就是】jiùshì **A**〈助〉[usu used with 了 at the end of a sentence to give force to the statement]: 别害怕，只管说～了。 Don't be afraid. Just say it. **B**〈副〉**1**（表同意）[used alone to express agreement] exactly: 我～这个意思。 That's exactly what I mean. **2**（表强调）[used for emphasis]: 不懂～不懂，不要装懂。 If you don't understand, you don't understand. Don't pretend otherwise. **C**〈连〉**1**（即使）[used correlatively with 也] even: ～在日常生活中，也需要有一定的科学知识。 We need some scientific knowledge even in our daily life. ‖ 你～不说，我也知道是怎么回事。 Even if you don't tell me, I know what it is. **2**（只是） only: 他这个人很聪明，～有些懒惰。 He is quite intelligent but a little lazy.
【就是说】jiùshìshuō〈惯〉that is to say
【就手】jiùshǒu〈副〉while you're at it: 请～把门关上。 Close the door behind you, please.
【就算】jiùsuàn〈连〉even if: ～她错了，你也不能那样对待她。 Even if she was wrong, you shouldn't have treated her like that.
【就位】jiùwèi〈动〉take a seat: 主席团已经～。 The members of the presidium have already taken their places.
【就席】jiùxí〈动〉take a seat [at a banquet]
【就绪】jiùxù〈动〉be in order: 一切都已～。 Everything is all set.
【就学】jiùxué〈动〉go to school: ～于该校 study at this school
【就要】jiùyào〈副〉about to: 飞机～起飞了。 The plane is about to take off.
【就业】jiùyè〈动〉find a job: 打开～门路 open up new avenues of employment ‖ 减轻～压力 ease the pressure of employment ‖ 解决～问题 solve the employment problem
【就业机会】jiùyè jīhuì〈名〉job opportunity: 创造～ create new jobs
【就业率】jiùyèlǜ〈名〉rate of employment
【就业培训】jiùyè péixùn〈名〉job training
【就业市场】jiùyè shìchǎng〈名〉job market
【就业指导】jiùyè zhǐdǎo〈名〉career guidance
【就医】jiùyī〈动〉see a doctor
【就义】jiùyì〈动〉die a martyr: 英勇～ die a hero's death ▸从容～
【就诊】jiùzhěn = 就医 jiùyī
【就正】jiùzhèng〈动〉〈书〉〈敬〉 solicit criticism: ～于读者 invite criticism from the readers
【就职】jiùzhí〈动〉take office: 宣誓～ be sworn into office ‖ ～典礼 inauguration
【就中】jiùzhōng **A**〈副〉in between: ～调停 mediate a dispute **B**〈名〉among: 这件事他们几个都知道，～他知道得最多。 They all know about it and of all of them he knows most.
【就座】jiùzuò〈动〉take a seat: 在主席台～ be seated on the rostrum ‖ 请～! Please be seated.

舅

舅 jiù〈名〉**1**（指长辈） uncle: ▸～～，～父 **2**（指同辈） brother-in-law: ▸～子
【舅父】jiùfù ▸**p. 588**〈名〉uncle
【舅舅】jiùjiu〈口〉= 舅父 jiùfù
【舅妈】jiùmā〈口〉= 舅母 jiùmu
【舅母】jiùmu ▸**p. 588**〈名〉aunt
【舅子】jiùzi ▸**p. 588**〈名〉brother-in-law: ▸大～，小～

僦

僦 jiù〈动〉〈书〉lease: ～屋而居 rent a room to live in

鹫（鷲）

鹫（鷲） jiù〈名〉［鸟类］ vulture

jū

车（車）

车（車） jū〈名〉**1**（指中国象棋） chariot **2**（指国际象棋） castle ▸chē

且

且 jū〈助〉〈书〉oh ▸qiě

沮

沮 jū ▸jǔ
【沮水】jūshuǐ〈名〉a river in Hubei Province

拘

拘 jū〈动〉**1**（扣留） detain: ▸～留，～押 **2**（拘束） restrain: ～于礼节 observe politeness ▸～谨，无～无束 **3**（限制） restrict: 长短不～ with no limit on the length ‖ 大小不～ regardless of size ▸不～一格 **4**（不变通） be inflexible: ▸～礼，～泥，～执
【拘捕】jūbǔ〈动〉arrest: ～归案 arrest and bring to justice ‖ 他被依法～。 He was arrested in the name of the law.
【拘传】jūchuán〈动〉summon for detention
【拘管】jūguǎn〈动〉restrain: 严加～ keep under strict control
【拘谨】jūjǐn〈形〉reserved: 为人～ be rather reserved
【拘禁】jūjìn〈动〉take into custody: 受到～ be taken into custody
【拘礼】jūlǐ〈动〉be punctilious: 朋友之间不必～。 There is no need for ceremony between friends.
【拘留】jūliú〈动〉detain: ～审查 detain sb. for questioning ‖ ～处罚 punishment of detention ‖ 行政～ disciplinary detention
【拘留所】jūliúsuǒ〈名〉lock-up: 军人～ detention barracks
【拘留证】jūliúzhèng〈名〉detention warrant
【拘挛】jūluán〈动〉get cramps
【拘泥】jūnì **A**〈动〉rigidly adhere to: ～于成说 rigidly adhere to accepted theories ‖ ～于形式 cling to form **B**〈形〉ill at ease: 在熟人面前，不必太～。 There's no need to be nervous with people you know.
【拘束】jūshù **A**〈动〉restrict: 学生们都受校规的～。 The students are tied down by school regulations. **B**〈形〉constrained: 不要～ make yourself at home ‖ 感到～ feel ill at ease ‖ 和这么多陌生人在一起，我感到有点～。 I feel a bit awkward with so many strangers here.
【拘押】jūyā〈动〉detain: ～恐怖分子 detain a terrorist
【拘役】jūyì〈名〉［法律］ criminal detention
【拘囿】jūyòu〈动〉〈书〉rigidly adhere to: 为陈规陋习所～ confine oneself to bad customs and habits
【拘执】jūzhí〈动〉be inflexible: 办事～ be inflexible in handling things

苴

苴 jū
【苴麻】jūmá〈名〉female hemp plant

狙

狙 jū〈动〉〈书〉watch for: ▸～击
【狙击】jūjī〈动〉snipe: ～敌人 ambush the enemy ‖ ～战 sniping action
【狙击手】jūjīshǒu〈名〉sniper

居

居 jū
A〈动〉**1**（住） live: ▸～民，～住，分～，侨～，同～ **2**（在） occupy (a position): ～全国首位 rank first in the country ‖ 身～要职 hold an important post ▸～中，后来～上 **3**（当） claim: ▸～功，自～ **4**（存） store up: ▸奇货可～，囤积～奇 **5**〈书〉（停留） stay put: 变动不～ keep changing **6**（属于） belong to a certain category: ▸～多
B〈名〉**1**（居所） house: ▸安～乐业，新～，迁～ **2**（用于店铺名称） restaurant: 京味～ Beijing Speciality Restaurant
【居安思危】jū'ān-sīwēi〈成〉maintain vigilance in peace time
【居多】jūduō〈动〉be in the majority: 他的作品中写农村生活的～。 Most of his literary works are about country life.
【居高不下】jūgāobùxià〈成〉stay high: 物价/气温～。 Prices/Temperatures remain high.
【居高临下】jūgāo-línxià〈成〉be in a commanding position
【居功】jūgōng〈动〉claim credit for oneself
【居功自傲】jūgōng-zì'ào〈成〉pride oneself on one's achievements: 不要～。 Don't be smug about your achievements.
【居家】jūjiā〈动〉stay at home: ～不出 stay at home
【居间】jūjiān〈副〉〈书〉between two parties: ～促和 mediate a peace ‖ ～调停 act as a mediator between two parties
【居里】jūlǐ〈量〉［物理］ curie (Ci)
【居留】jūliú〈动〉reside: 申请临时/永久～ apply for temporary/permanent residence
【居留权】jūliúquán〈名〉right of residence
【居留证】jūliúzhèng〈名〉residence permit
【居民】jūmín〈名〉resident: 常住～ permanent resident ‖ 城镇～ urban resident
【居民点】jūmíndiǎn〈名〉residential area
【居民楼】jūmínlóu〈名〉residential building
【居民区】jūmínqū〈名〉residential area
【居民身份证】jūmín shēnfènzhèng〈名〉resident identification card
【居民委员会】jūmín wěiyuánhuì〈名〉residents' committee
【居民小区】jūmín xiǎoqū〈名〉residential quarters
【居然】jūrán〈副〉unexpectedly: ～有这种事! Who would have thought of such a thing! ‖ 她～干出这种事来。 No one expected that she would do such a thing.
【居丧】jūsāng〈动〉〈书〉be in mourning for one's dead parent
【居士】jūshì〈名〉**1**（在家修行者） lay Buddhist **2**〈书〉（隐居者） retired scholar
【居室】jūshì〈名〉room: 两～公寓 two-bedroom apartment ‖ ～装潢 interior decoration
【居所】jūsuǒ〈名〉dwelling: 建立永久性～ establish a permanent abode
【居委会】jūwěihuì〈简称〉= 居民委员会
【居心】jūxīn〈动〉harbour an (evil) intention: ～不良 harbour an evil intention ‖ 你～何在? What are you cooking up?
【居心叵测】jūxīn-pǒcè〈成〉be up to no good
【居于】jūyú〈动〉occupy: ～领导地位 be

in a leading position
【居中】jūzhōng **A**〈副〉 between two parties: ～斡旋 mediate between disputants **B**〈动〉 centre: 标题～。 The title is centred.
【居住】 jūzhù 〈动〉 live: ～海外 reside abroad ‖ 这儿无人～。 No one lives here.
【居住地】jūzhùdì〈名〉 place of residence
【居住面积】jūzhù miànjī〈名〉 floor space
【居住证】 jūzhùzhèng 〈名〉 residence permit

驹（駒） jū 〈名〉 **1**（少壮的马） colt **2**（驹子） foal: 驴～儿 foal
【驹子】jūzi〈名〉 foal: ▸马～

疽 jū〈名〉［中医］ subcutaneous ulcer: ▸炭～

掬 jū〈动〉〈书〉 hold with both hands: ～水 scoop up water with both hands ▸憨态可～, 笑容可～

据 jū ▸拮据 jiéjū
▸jù

趄 jū ▸趑趄 zījū
▸qiè

锔（鋦） jū 〈动〉 mend (crockery) with clamps: ～缸/碗 mend a jar/bowl with clamps
▸jú
【锔子】 jūzi 〈名〉 clamp used in mending crockery

雎 jū
【雎鸠】jūjiū〈名〉〈古〉 turtle dove

鮈（鮈） jū〈名〉［鱼类］ gudgeon

裾 jū〈名〉〈书〉 full front/back of a Chinese gown

鞠 jū〈动〉 **1**〈书〉（养育） rear: ▸～养 **2**（弯曲） bow: ▸～躬
【鞠躬】jūgōng **A**〈动〉 bow: ～道谢 bow one's thanks ‖ 深深地～ make a deep bow **B**〈形〉〈书〉 discreet and scrupulous: ▸～尽瘁
【鞠躬尽瘁】jūgōng-jìncuì〈成〉 work with utter devotion: ～, 死而后已 give one's all until one's heart ceases to beat
【鞠养】jūyǎng〈动〉〈书〉 raise: ～之恩 gratitude for sb.'s loving care in bringing oneself up

jú

局¹（侷、跼） jú〈形〉confined: ▸～促, ～限

局² jú 〈名〉 **1**（部分） part: ▸～部 **2**（机关单位） department: ～级干部 bureau-level official ▸公安～, 税务～ **3**（业务机构） functional office: ▸电信～, 邮～ **4**（指商店名称） store: ▸书～

局³ jú
A〈名〉 **1**〈书〉（棋盘） chessboard: ▸棋～ **2**（局面） situation: ▸～势, 大～, 僵～, 结～ **3**（圈套） trick: ▸骗～ **4**（聚会） gathering: ▸赌～, 饭～, 牌～
B〈量〉 game: 输（给某人）一～ lose a set (to sb.) ‖ 下一～棋 play a game of chess ‖ 平～ draw
【局部】júbù〈名〉 part: ～地区 some areas ‖ ～利益 partial and local interests ‖ ～麻醉 local anaesthesia ‖ ～战争 local war
【局促】júcù〈形〉 **1**（狭小） poky: ～的房间 cramped room **2**（拘谨） constrained: ～不安 feel ill at ease
【局点】júdiǎn〈名〉［体育］ game point
【局面】júmiàn〈名〉 situation: 打开～ make a breakthrough ‖ 控制～ bring the situation under control
【局内人】júnèirén〈名〉 insider
【局骗】júpiàn〈动〉〈书〉 swindle: ～钱财 swindle money (out of sb.)
【局势】júshì〈名〉 situation: 稳定/整顿～ stabilize the situation ‖ 制造紧张～ create tensions ‖ ～正在恶化。 The situation is deteriorating.
【局外人】júwàirén〈名〉 outsider
【局限】júxiàn〈动〉 limit: 克服自身的～ overcome one's limitations ‖ ～于学术问题 be confined to academics
【局限性】júxiànxìng〈名〉 limitations: 每个人都有自己的～。 Everyone has their own limitations.
【局域网】 júyùwǎng 〈名〉 local area network (LAN)
【局子】júzi〈名〉〈旧〉 police station

桔 jú〈名〉 tangerine
▸jié

菊 jú〈名〉 chrysanthemum: 赏～ enjoy beautiful chrysanthemums
【菊花】júhuā〈名〉 chrysanthemum
【菊石】júshí〈名〉［地质］ ammonite
【菊坛】jútán〈名〉 theatrical circles

焗 jú〈动〉〈方〉 steam: 盐～鸡 salted and steamed chicken
【焗油】júyóu〈动〉 put treatment cream on one's hair: ～膏 hair treatment cream

锔（鋦） jú〈名〉［化学］ curium (Cm)
▸jū

橘 jú〈名〉 tangerine
【橘红】júhóng **A**〈形〉 reddish orange **B**〈名〉［中药］ dried tangerine peel
【橘黄】júhuáng〈形〉 orange
【橘络】júluò〈名〉［中药］ tangerine pith
【橘汁】júzhī〈名〉 orange juice
【橘子】júzi〈名〉 tangerine

jǔ

柜 jǔ
▸guì
【柜柳】jǔliǔ〈名〉［植物］ acer truncatum

咀 jǔ〈动〉 chew: ▸～嚼, 含英～华
▸zuǐ
【咀嚼】jǔjué〈动〉 **1**〈本〉 chew: 食物要仔细～后再吞咽。 Chew your food well before swallowing it. **2**〈喻〉 mull over: ～文义 mull over the meaning of the phrase

沮 jǔ〈动〉〈书〉 **1**（阻止） prevent: ▸～遏 **2**（颓丧） turn gloomy: ▸～丧
▸jū
【沮遏】jǔ'è〈动〉〈书〉 hold back
【沮丧】jǔsàng **A**〈形〉 depressed: 神情～ look dejected **B**〈动〉 dishearten: ～敌人的士气 sap the enemy's morale

枸 jǔ
▸gōu, gǒu
【枸橼】jǔyuán〈名〉［植物］ citron
【枸橼酸】jǔyuánsuān〈名〉［化学］ citric acid
【枸橼酸钠】jǔyuánsuānnà〈名〉［化学］ sodium citrate

矩 jǔ〈名〉 **1**（曲尺） (carpenter's) square: ▸～尺 **2**（方形） rectangle: ▸～形 **3**（规则） rules: ▸规～, 循规蹈～
【矩臂】jǔbì〈名〉［物理］ moment arm
【矩尺】jǔchǐ = 曲尺 qūchǐ
【矩形】jǔxíng〈名〉 rectangle
【矩阵】jǔzhèn〈名〉［数学］ matrix: ～式 matrix type

举（舉） jǔ
A〈动〉 **1**（往上托） raise: ～起双手 raise one's hands ‖ ～杯畅饮 raise a glass and drink to one's heart's content ‖ ～杯祝酒 raise one's glass in a toast ▸～案齐眉, 纲～目张 **2**（发动） start: ▸～办, ～兵, ～行 **3**（选举） elect: ▸～荐, 推～, 选～ **4**（列举） cite: ～个具体的例子 cite a concrete example ▸～例, ～一反三, 不胜枚～
B〈名〉 **1**（行为） act: ▸～止, 多此一～, 善～ **2** = 举人 jǔrén
C〈形〉〈书〉 entire: ～家出游 the whole family go on a tour ▸～国
【举哀】jǔ'āi〈动〉〈书〉 go into mourning: 为死者～ go into mourning for the deceased
【举案齐眉】jǔ'àn-qíméi〈成〉 live in conjugal harmony
【举办】jǔbàn〈动〉hold: ～奥运会 hold the Olympic Games ‖ 他下月将～个人画展。 He is staging an exhibition of his paintings.
【举报】jǔbào〈动〉 report an offence: ～不法行为 report illegal activities ‖ ～电话 tip-off (phone) call ‖ ～人 informer ‖ ～信 written accusation
【举兵】jǔbīng〈动〉〈书〉 raise an army: ～起义 raise an army to revolt
【举不胜举】jǔbùshèngjǔ〈成〉 the list is endless: 这样的例子～。 There are too many examples like this to count.
【举步维艰】jǔbù-wéijiān〈成〉 have difficulty moving forward: 公司刚刚成立, ～。 The company has just set up and is having trouble making progress.
【举措】jǔcuò〈名〉〈书〉 measure: 重大～ important measures ‖ 改革的新～ new moves toward reform ‖ ～失当 make a bad move
【举动】jǔdòng〈名〉 movement: 报告敌人的～ report on enemy activity ‖ ～灵活 be nimble in movement ‖ 轻率的～ rash act
【举发】jǔfā〈动〉〈书〉 report to the authorities: 向公安机关～腐败现象 report corrupt dealings to the public security bureau
【举凡】jǔfán〈副〉〈书〉 ranging from ... to ...
【举国】jǔguó〈名〉 whole nation: ～上下 the whole nation from top to bottom ‖ ～欢腾 the whole nation is jubilant
【举家】jǔjiā〈名〉〈书〉 whole family: ～南迁。 The whole family moved to the south.

【举荐】jǔjiàn〈动〉 recommend: ～人才 recommend talents ‖ 大力～ highly recommend

【举借】jǔjiè〈动〉〈书〉 borrow money: ～无门 can borrow money from nobody

【举例】jǔlì〈动〉 give an example: ～说明 illustrate with examples ‖ ～说 for example

【举目】jǔmù〈动〉〈书〉 raise one's eyes: ～远眺 look into the distance

【举目无亲】jǔmù-wúqīn〈成〉 be a stranger in a new place

【举棋不定】jǔqí-bùdìng〈成〉 be unable to make up one's mind: 在两种选择之间～ vacillate between two options

【举人】jǔrén〈名〉〈旧〉 successful candidate in the imperial examinations at the provincial level [in Ming and Qing dynasties]

【举世】jǔshì〈名〉 whole world: ～公认 universally acknowledged

【举世闻名】jǔshì-wénmíng〈成〉 world-famous: 中国的长城～。 The Great Wall of China is world-famous.

【举世无双】jǔshì-wúshuāng〈成〉 be unrivalled: ～的发明 unrivalled invention

【举世瞩目】jǔshì-zhǔmù〈成〉 draw worldwide attention: ～的成就 achievements of world interest

【举事】jǔshì〈动〉〈书〉 stage an uprising

【举手】jǔshǒu〈动〉 raise one's hand

【举手投足】jǔshǒu-tóuzú〈成〉 any move

【举手之劳】jǔshǒuzhīláo〈成〉 not at all difficult: ～，何足挂齿! That's nothing. Don't mention it.

【举贤荐能】jǔxián-jiànnéng〈成〉 recommend the virtuous and the able

【举行】jǔxíng〈动〉 hold: ～闭幕式/开幕式 hold the concluding/opening ceremony ‖ ～会谈 hold a talk ‖ ～记者招待会 give a press conference ‖ 婚礼什么时候～? When does the wedding take place?

【举一反三】jǔyī-fǎnsān〈成〉 make inferences by analogy: 在学习上要～，触类旁通 learn by analogy and judge the whole from the part

【举债】jǔzhài〈动〉〈书〉 raise a loan: ～筹资 debt financing ‖ ～度日 live on borrowed money

【举证】jǔzhèng〈动〉 show evidence

【举止】jǔzhǐ〈名〉 carriage: ～沉稳 have a calm and steady manner ‖ ～大方 have an easy manner ‖ ～得体 behave properly ‖ ～高雅 be refined in manner

【举重】jǔzhòng ▸**p. 909**〈名〉 weightlifting: ～运动员 weightlifter

【举重若轻】jǔzhòng-ruòqīng〈成〉 handle complicated matters with great ease

【举足轻重】jǔzú-qīngzhòng〈成〉 play a decisive role: ～的角色 big part ‖ 他的意见～。 His opinion counts for a lot.

【举坐】jǔzuò〈名〉 all those present

榉（櫸）jǔ〈名〉［植物］ beech

龃（齟）jǔ

【龃龉】jǔyǔ〈动〉〈书〉 be in disagreement: 他和妻子总是发生～。 He and his wife are always at loggerheads.

踽 jǔ

【踽踽】jǔjǔ〈形〉〈书〉 alone: ～独行 walk alone

jù

巨（鉅）jù〈形〉 huge: ～幅标语/画像 huge poster/portrait ‖ 一声～响 a loud bang ▸～变，～大，～款，～人，艰～

【巨变】jùbiàn〈动〉 change enormously: 山村～ dramatic changes in a mountain village ‖ 面貌发生～ make big changes in appearance

【巨波】jùbō〈名〉［海洋］ high sea

【巨擘】jùbò〈名〉〈书〉 **1**〈本〉 thumb **2**〈喻〉 foremost authority: 商界～ business magnate ‖ 诗坛～ prince of poets

【巨大】jùdà〈形〉 huge: 影响～ have a large impact (on sb./sth.) ‖ ～的工程 mammoth project ‖ ～的胜利 crowning victory

【巨额】jù'é〈名〉 fat sum: ～赤字 huge financial deficits ‖ ～利润 enormous profit ‖ ～债务 huge debt ‖ ～资金 immense capital

【巨富】jùfù〈名〉〈书〉 **1**（指财富） immense wealth: ～之家 family of immense wealth **2**（指人） multimillionaire

【巨祸】jùhuò〈名〉 great calamity

【巨奸】jùjiān〈名〉〈书〉 very treacherous person

【巨奖】jùjiǎng〈名〉 huge prize

【巨匠】jùjiàng〈名〉〈书〉 great master: 画坛～ master painter

【巨款】jùkuǎn〈名〉 huge sum of money: 携～逃跑 flee with a huge amount of money

【巨浪】jùlàng〈名〉 billow: ～打翻了帆船。 The huge wave overwhelmed the sailing boat.

【巨流】jùliú〈名〉 mighty current: 滚滚～ surging current

【巨轮】jùlún〈名〉 **1**（指车轮） largewheel:〈喻〉 历史的～不可逆转。 The wheel of history cannot be turned back. **2**（指船） large ship: 万吨～ ocean liner of ten thousand tons

【巨人】jùrén〈名〉 giant: 篮坛～ giant on the basketball court ‖〈喻〉 民族/时代的～ colossus of the nation/age ‖〈喻〉 文坛～ literary giant

【巨人症】jùrénzhèng〈名〉［医学］ gigantism

【巨贪】jùtān〈名〉 massive bribe-taker

【巨头】jùtóu〈名〉 tycoon: 航运～ shipping magnate ‖ 银行界～ banking prince

【巨无霸】jùwúbà〈名〉 giant

【巨细】jù-xì〈名〉 all matters, big and small: 事无～ all matters, big and small

【巨蟹座】Jùxièzuò〈名〉［天文］ Cancer

【巨星】jùxīng〈名〉 **1**［天文］ giant star **2**〈喻〉（杰出的人） superstar: 体坛/影视～ sporting/movie giant

【巨型】jùxíng〈形〉 giant: ～客机 giant airliner

【巨制】jùzhì〈名〉〈书〉 massive work: ▸鸿篇～

【巨著】jùzhù〈名〉 monumental work: 科学～ scientific masterpiece

【巨子】jùzǐ〈名〉 giant: 报界～ press magnate ‖ 船运业～ shipping tycoon ‖ 电影界～ movie giant ‖ 商业～ business tycoon ‖ 文坛～ literary giant

【巨作】jùzuò〈名〉 great masterpiece

句 jù

A〈名〉 sentence: 主题～ topic sentence ▸～子，陈述～，警～，例～，造～

B〈量〉 sentence: 两～诗 two lines of verse ‖ 聊几～ exchange a few words ▸三～话不离本行

【句点】jùdiǎn〈名〉 period; full stop（。）〈英〉

【句读】jùdòu〈名〉 **1**（停顿） pause **2**（句和词组） sentences and phrases

【句法】jùfǎ〈名〉［语言］ syntax: ～分析 syntactic analysis ‖ ～结构 syntactic construction

【句号】jùhào〈名〉 **1**〈本〉 period; full stop（。）〈英〉 **2**〈喻〉 conclusion: 这次研讨会划上了～。 The symposium has come to an end.

【句型】jùxíng〈名〉 sentence pattern

【句子】jùzi〈名〉 sentence: ～成分 part of a sentence ‖ 划分～成分 differentiate the sentence elements ‖ ～结构 sentence structure

讵（詎）jù〈副〉〈书〉 [used to introduce a rhetorical question]: ～料事与愿违。 Who expected that things would turn out any other way?

拒 jù〈动〉 **1**（抵抗） resist: ～腐蚀 resist corruption ‖ ～敌 resist the enemy ▸～捕，抗～ **2**（拒绝） refuse: ～不回答 refuse to answer ‖ ～不交代罪行 refuse to confess a crime ▸～绝，来者不～

【拒捕】jùbǔ〈动〉 resist arrest

【拒付】jùfù〈动〉［经济］ refuse payment: 全部～ refuse payment in full

【拒谏饰非】jùjiàn-shìfēi〈成〉 reject criticisms and gloss over one's mistakes

【拒绝】jùjué〈动〉 refuse: ～承担责任 refuse to accept responsibility ‖ ～签证 refuse sb. a visa ‖ ～延长签证 decline a visa extension ‖ 断然～ reject outright

【拒聘】jùpìn〈动〉 turn down an appointment

【拒签】jùqiān〈动〉 **1**（指签证） refuse a visa: ～理由 grounds for visa refusal ‖ 他已是第三次被～。 It's the third time that his application for a visa has been declined. **2**（指签字） refuse to sign one's name

【拒人于千里之外】jù rén yú qiānlǐ zhī wài〈俗〉 keep sb. at arm's length

【拒收】jùshōu〈动〉 reject

【拒载】jùzài〈动〉 [of a taxi driver, etc.] refuse to take a passenger

【拒之门外】jùzhī-ménwài〈成〉〈喻〉 refuse sb. entry

苣 jù ▸莴苣 wōjù

▸qǔ

具 jù

A〈动〉 **1**〈书〉（备办） provide: 谨～薄礼 allow me to present you with this small gift **2**（具有） possess: 独～慧眼 have exceptional insight ‖ 颇～特色 have some special features ▸～有，别～一格 **3**（写） write out: ▸～保，～结，～名

B〈名〉 **1**（用具） tool: ▸工～，家～，玩～ **2**〈书〉（才干） capability: ▸才～

C〈量〉 [for coffins, dead bodies, certain instruments]: 一～尸体 a corpse

【具保】jùbǎo〈动〉 sign a guarantee: ～释放 be released on bail

【具备】jùbèi〈动〉 have: ～当教师的素质 be qualified as a teacher ‖ ～条件 meet the requirements

【具结】jùjié〈动〉〈旧〉 sign an undertaking: ～领回失物 sign a receipt for restored lost property

【具名】jùmíng〈动〉 put one's name (to a

document, etc.): 在申请书上～ sign an application ‖ ～支票 stamped cheque

【具体】jùtǐ **A**〈形〉**1**（不抽象）concrete: 提出～建议 come up with concrete proposals ‖ ～问题～分析 make a concrete analysis of a concrete problem **2**（特定）particular: 解决～问题 solve a particular problem ‖ 根据～情况 according to specific situations **B**〈动〉[used with 到] apply to: 改革必须～到每个行业。Reform must be implemented in every field.

【具体而微】jùtǐ'érwēi〈成〉miniature

【具体名词】jùtǐ míngcí〈名〉［语法］concrete noun

【具有】jùyǒu〈动〉possess: ～法人资格 possess legal qualifications ‖ ～强大的生命力 have great vitality ‖ ～深远的历史意义 be of profound historical significance

炬 jù〈名〉flame: ▶火～

俱 jù〈副〉〈书〉all: ▶百废～兴, 面面～到, 声泪～下, 万事～备, 只欠东风

【俱乐部】jùlèbù〈名〉club: 篮球/足球～ basketball/football club

【俱全】jùquán〈形〉complete: 这道菜色香味～。This dish looks good, smells good and tastes good. ▶一应～

倨 jù〈形〉〈书〉haughty: ▶前～后恭

【倨傲】jù'ào〈形〉〈书〉arrogant: ～不逊 be arrogant and rude

剧[1]（劇）jù〈形〉acute: ▶～痛, 急～

剧[2]（劇）jù〈名〉drama: 音乐～ musical ‖ 该～久演不衰。The play has a long run. ▶～本, 悲～, 编～, 京～

【剧本】jùběn〈名〉play: ～创作 script ‖ 电影～ screenplay

【剧变】jùbiàn〈动〉change drastically: 局势～。The situation has changed drastically.

【剧场】jùchǎng〈名〉theatre: 露天～ open-air theatre

【剧跌】jùdiē〈动〉drop sharply

【剧毒】jùdú〈名〉rank poison: 有～ be highly poisonous

【剧烈】jùliè〈形〉acute: ～疼痛 acute pain ‖ ～运动 strenuous exercises ‖ 疼痛越来越～。The pain increased in intensity.

【剧目】jùmù〈名〉programme: 传统～ traditional plays ▶保留～

【剧评】jùpíng〈名〉review of a play/opera

【剧情】jùqíng〈名〉plot of a play/opera: ～复杂/简单 intricate/simple plot ‖ ～简介 synopsis

【剧坛】jùtán〈名〉theatrical circles

【剧痛】jùtòng〈动〉feel severe pain: 耳部～ acute earache

【剧团】jùtuán〈名〉theatrical troupe: 芭蕾舞～ ballet troupe ‖ 业余/专业～ amateur/professional troupe

【剧务】jùwù〈名〉**1**（指事务）stage management: ～组 stage crew **2**（指人）stage manager

【剧院】jùyuàn〈名〉**1**（剧场）theatre: 去～看戏 go to the theatre to see a play **2**（剧团）theatrical troupe

【剧增】jùzēng〈动〉increase sharply: 人口～。The population has increased sharply.

【剧照】jùzhào〈名〉still: 电影～ film still

【剧中人】jùzhōngrén〈名〉characters in a play

【剧终】jùzhōng〈动〉[of a play, a film etc.] end

【剧种】jùzhǒng〈名〉**1**（指戏曲）type of traditional opera **2**（指戏剧）genre of dramatic art

【剧组】jùzǔ〈名〉（指戏剧）stage crew; （指影视）film crew

【剧作】jùzuò〈名〉drama: ～家 playwright

据（據）jù

A〈动〉**1**（凭借）depend on: ▶～点 **2**（占据）occupy: ▶～为己有, 割～, 占～
B〈介〉according to: ～报道 according to the reports ‖ ～同名小说改编 adapted from a novel of the same name ‖ ～我看来 in my opinion ▶～理力争
C〈名〉evidence: 言之无～。There is no evidence to say so. ▶单～, 凭～, 言之有～ ▶jū

【据称】jùchēng〈动〉it is said (that)

【据传】jùchuán〈动〉rumour has it (that)

【据此】jùcǐ〈动〉judge on these grounds

【据点】jùdiǎn〈名〉stronghold

【据理力争】jùlǐ-lìzhēng〈成〉argue strongly on just grounds

【据实】jùshí〈动〉be based on the fact: ～上报 report facts to one's superiors

【据守】jùshǒu〈动〉defend: ～阵地 hold a position

【据说】jùshuō〈动〉it is said (that): ～明天有雨。It is said that it will rain tomorrow. ‖ ～情况是这样的。This is allegedly the case.

【据为己有】jùwéijǐyǒu〈成〉appropriate: 不能将别人的东西～。You shouldn't appropriate others' belongings.

【据闻】jùwén = 据说 jùshuō

【据悉】jùxī〈动〉it is reported (that): ～, 中国不久将发射探月卫星。It is reported that China will soon be launching a lunar exploration satellite.

距[1] jù

A〈动〉be away from: ～此不远 not far from here ‖ 这事～今已有多年。It happened many years ago.
B〈名〉distance: ▶焦～, 行～

距[2] jù〈名〉spur (of a cock, pheasant, etc.)

【距离】jùlí **A**〈名〉distance: 保持～ keep some distance ‖ 学校离这儿有一段～。The school is some distance away. **B**〈动〉be away from: ～首都五十里 50 *li* from the capital

惧（懼）jù〈动〉fear: 无所～ be fearless ‖ ～某人三分 be a little afraid of sb. ▶～怕, 恐～, 临危不～

【惧内】jùnèi〈动〉be henpecked: ～的丈夫 henpecked husband

【惧怕】jùpà〈动〉fear: 毫不～ know no fear ‖ 不要～批评。Don't be afraid of criticism.

【惧色】jùsè〈名〉look of fear: 面对敌人, 毫无～ remain undaunted in the face of the enemy

飓（颶）jù

【飓风】jùfēng〈名〉hurricane

锯（鋸）jù

A〈名〉saw: ▶～齿, 电～, 钢～
B〈动〉saw: ～木头 saw wood ‖ 把圆木～成两段 saw a log in two

【锯齿】jùchǐ〈名〉sawtooth

【锯床】jùchuáng〈名〉sawing machine

【锯末】jùmò〈名〉sawdust

【锯条】jùtiáo〈名〉saw blade

【锯屑】jùxiè〈名〉sawdust

【锯子】jùzi〈名〉saw: 一把～ a saw

聚 jù〈动〉assemble: 大家～在一起商量一下。Let's get together and talk it over. ▶～餐, 欢～, 凝～, 物以类～, 人以群分

【聚氨酯】jù'ānzhǐ〈名〉［化学］polyurethane

【聚宝盆】jùbǎopén〈名〉〈喻〉place rich in natural resources: 此地矿产资源丰富, 真是个～。This place abounds in mineral resources and is indeed a natural treasure.

【聚苯乙烯】jùběnyǐxī〈名〉［化学］polystyrene

【聚变】jùbiàn = 热核反应 rèhé fǎnyìng

【聚变反应】jùbiàn fǎnyìng〈名〉［物理］fusion reaction: ～堆 fusion reactor

【聚丙烯】jùbǐngxī〈名〉［化学］polypropylene

【聚餐】jùcān〈动〉have a dinner party

【聚赌】jùdǔ〈动〉get together to gamble

【聚光灯】jùguāngdēng〈名〉spotlight

【聚光镜】jùguāngjìng〈名〉condensing lens

【聚合】jùhé〈动〉**1**（聚集）get together **2**［化学］polymerize

【聚合物】jùhéwù〈名〉polymer: 高分子～ high polymer

【聚会】jùhuì **A**〈动〉get together: 老同学～一次不容易。It is not easy for all the old classmates to get together. **B**〈名〉get-together: 参加～ go to a party ‖ 节日/家庭～ festive/family gathering

【聚积】jùjī〈动〉accumulate: ～财富 amass wealth ‖ ～力量 build up strength

【聚集】jùjí〈动〉gather: ～兵力 assemble forces ‖ 学生们～在大厅里。The students were assembled in the hall.

【聚歼】jùjiān〈动〉round up and wipe out: ～残敌 round up and eliminate the enemy remnants

【聚焦】jùjiāo〈动〉focus: 定向～ directional focusing ‖ 新闻报道～于一个共同的话题。The news reports focus on a common topic.

【聚精会神】jùjīng-huìshén〈成〉be all eyes and ears: ～地听 listen attentively

【聚居】jùjū〈动〉inhabit a region: 少数民族～地区 regions inhabited by ethnic groups in compact communities

【聚居点】jùjūdiǎn〈名〉settlement

【聚敛】jùliǎn〈动〉accumulate wealth illegally: ～钱财 amass wealth and property illegally

【聚拢】jùlǒng〈动〉gather together: 孩子们～在他周围。The children gathered round him.

【聚氯乙烯】jùlǜyǐxī〈名〉［化学］polyvinyl chloride (PVC)

【聚落】jùluò〈名〉settlement: 原始～ primitive settlement

【聚齐】jùqí〈动〉assemble: 在校门口～ assemble at the school gate

【聚散】jùsàn〈动〉meet and part

【聚沙成塔】jùshā-chéngtǎ〈成〉〈喻〉many a little makes a mickle

【聚生】jùshēng〈动〉cluster

【聚首】jùshǒu〈动〉〈书〉gather: 各国领导人～巴黎。World leaders assembled in Paris.

【聚乙烯】jùyǐxī〈名〉［化学］polythene: ～绝缘电缆 polyethylene insulated cable

【聚酯】jùzhǐ〈名〉［化学］ polyester: ～纤维 polyester fibre
【聚众】jùzhòng〈动〉 assemble a crowd: ～斗殴 incite a crowd to a brawl ‖ ～滋事 gather a crowd to make trouble

踞 jù〈动〉 1（蹲坐） crouch: ▸虎～龙盘 2（占据） occupy: ▸盘～

屦（屨） jù〈名〉 hemp sandals

遽 jù
A〈副〉 hurriedly: ～下结论 jump to a hasty conclusion
B〈形〉 frightened: ▸惶～
【遽然】jùrán〈副〉〈书〉 abruptly: ～离去 make an abrupt departure

juān

捐 juān
A〈动〉 1（舍弃） abandon: ～弃 relinquish 2（献出） contribute: ～钱 donate money ▸～献, ～赠
B〈名〉 tax: ▸～税, 苛～杂税
【捐款】juānkuǎn A〈动〉 make a donation: 为慈善事业～ contribute to a charity collection B〈名〉 donation: 得到企业～ get donations from an enterprise
【捐款人】juānkuǎnrén〈名〉 donator
【捐弃前嫌】juānqì-qiánxián〈成〉 bury old grudges
【捐躯】juānqū〈动〉 lay down one's life: 为国～ sacrifice one's life for one's country
【捐税】juānshuì〈名〉 taxes and levies: 交纳～ pay taxes and levies
【捐献】juānxiàn〈动〉 contribute: ～骨髓/器官 donate marrow/organs ‖ 慷慨～ donate generously
【捐赠】juānzèng〈动〉 donate: 音乐会的收入将～给慈善事业。 The proceeds from the concert will go to charity.
【捐赠者】juānzèngzhě〈名〉 donor
【捐助】juānzhù〈动〉 donate: ～灾区人民 make donations to disaster victims
【捐资】juānzī〈动〉 donate money: ～建校 donate money to build a school

涓 juān〈名〉〈书〉 tiny stream
【涓埃】juān'āi〈名〉〈书〉〈喻〉 insignificant bit: 略尽～之力 do one's bit
【涓滴】juāndī〈名〉〈书〉〈喻〉 tiny amount: ～归公 turn in every penny of public money
【涓涓】juānjuān〈形〉〈书〉 trickling sluggishly: ～细流 small brook

娟 juān〈形〉〈书〉 beautiful
【娟秀】juānxiù〈形〉 beautiful: 容貌～ be good-looking ‖ 字迹～ beautiful handwriting

圈 juān〈动〉 1（指禽畜） pen in: 把鸡～起来 put the chicken in a coop 2（指人） lock up: 我不喜欢天天～在家里。 I hate being cooped up in the house every day.
▸juàn, quān

鹃（鵑） juān ▸杜鹃 dùjuān

镌（鎸、鐫） juān〈动〉〈书〉 engrave
【镌刻】juānkè〈动〉 engrave: ～印章 engrave a seal ‖〈喻〉老师的一番话深深～在我心里。 I have kept the teacher's words firmly in mind.
【镌心铭骨】juānxīn-mínggǔ〈成〉 be engraved on one's memory

蠲 juān〈动〉〈书〉 exempt
【蠲除】juānchú〈动〉〈书〉 exempt
【蠲免】juānmiǎn〈动〉〈书〉（指租税） remit;（指劳役、惩罚等） mitigate

juǎn

卷（捲） juǎn
A〈动〉 1（使成筒形） roll up: ～起地毯 roll up a carpet ‖ ～起袖子 roll up one's sleeves 2（掀起） sweep up: 急驰的汽车～起一阵尘土。 The speeding car swept up a cloud of dust. ‖ 她被潮水～到海里去了。 She was swept out to sea by the tide. 3（涉及） embroil: ～进纠纷 get involved in a dispute ▸～入
B〈名〉 1（指物） roll: ▸胶～, 铺盖～ル 2（指食品） roll: ▸蛋～
C〈量〉 roll: 两～铅丝 two reels of galvanized wire ‖ 一～胶片 a roll of film ‖ 一～纸 a roll of paper
▸juàn
【卷笔刀】juǎnbǐdāo〈名〉 pencil sharpener
【卷材】juǎncái〈名〉 coiled material
【卷层云】juǎncéngyún〈名〉［气象］cirrostratus
【卷尺】juǎnchǐ〈名〉 tape measure
【卷发】juǎnfà〈名〉 curly hair: 一头～ be curly-headed ‖ ～器 curler
【卷积云】juǎnjīyún〈名〉［气象］ cirrocumulus
【卷帘门】juǎnliánmén〈名〉 folding door
【卷毛狗】juǎnmáogǒu〈名〉［动物］ poodle
【卷铺盖】juǎn pūgai〈惯〉 1（离开） pack up and leave: 我受够了! 马上～走人。 I've had enough. I'm packing my things and leaving right now. 2（被解雇） be sent packing: 干了没几天，老板就叫他～走人。 The boss sent him packing after only a few days.
【卷曲】juǎnqū〈形〉 curly: ～的头发 curly hair
【卷入】juǎnrù〈动〉 get mixed up with: ～纠纷 become involved in a dispute
【卷舌音】juǎnshéyīn〈名〉［语言］ retroflex
【卷逃】juǎntáo〈动〉 abscond with money, etc.
【卷筒】juǎntǒng〈名〉 reel: ～纸 web
【卷土重来】juǎntǔ-chónglái〈成〉 make a comeback: 结核病等旧病又～。 Old diseases like tuberculosis have returned.
【卷尾猴】juǎnwěihóu〈名〉［动物］(weeping) capuchin
【卷心菜】juǎnxīncài〈名〉〈方〉 cabbage
【卷须】juǎnxū〈名〉［植物］ tendril
【卷烟】juǎnyān〈名〉 1（香烟） cigarette 2（雪茄） cigar: 嘴上叼着一支～ with a cigar in one's mouth
【卷烟厂】juǎnyānchǎng〈名〉cigarette factory
【卷扬机】juǎnyángjī〈名〉 hoist
【卷叶病】juǎnyèbìng〈名〉［植物］ leaf roll
【卷轴】juǎnzhóu〈名〉 reel

锩（錈） juǎn〈动〉 [of the blade of a knife, etc.] be turned: 刀～刃了。 The edge of the knife has turned.

juàn

卷 juàn
A〈量〉 volume: 第一～ Volume I ‖ 家有藏书一万～ have a 10,000 volume collection in one's house
B〈名〉 1（书） book;（画） scroll: ▸画～, 开～有益 2（文件） file: 查～ look through the files ▸～宗, 案～, 调～ 3（试卷） examination paper: ▸答～, 试～, 阅～
▸juǎn
【卷标】juànbiāo〈名〉 volume label
【卷次】juàncì〈名〉 volume number
【卷帙】juànzhì〈名〉〈书〉 book: ～浩繁 numerous books
【卷轴】juànzhóu〈名〉〈书〉 scroll
▸juǎnzhóu
【卷子】juànzi〈名〉 1（试卷） examination paper: 出～ set a test paper ‖ 发/批～ hand out/mark the examination papers 2（古抄本） hand-copied scroll
【卷宗】juànzōng〈名〉 1（文件） file: 信件～ file of correspondence 2（文件夹） folder

隽（雋） juàn〈形〉〈书〉 meaningful:
▸jùn
【隽永】juànyǒng〈形〉〈书〉 meaningful: 文辞～ the language is meaningful
【隽语】juànyǔ〈名〉 pithy remark

倦 juàn〈形〉 1（劳累） tired: ～得要命 be dead tired ▸困～, 疲～ 2（厌烦） bored: ▸诲人不～, 厌～
【倦怠】juàndài〈形〉 sluggish: 神色～ look languid
【倦容】juànróng〈名〉 tired look: 面带～ look tired
【倦色】juànsè〈名〉 languid look: 满脸～ look extremely tired
【倦意】juànyì〈名〉 weariness: 毫无～ not feel in the least bit tired

狷 juàn〈形〉〈书〉 1（急躁） impetuous: ▸～急 2（刚正） upright: ▸～介
【狷急】juànjí〈形〉〈书〉 impetuous
【狷介】juànjiè〈形〉〈书〉 upright and incorruptible: ～之士 incorruptible person

绢（絹） juàn〈名〉thin strong silk
【绢本】juànběn〈名〉 silk scroll
【绢花】juànhuā〈名〉 silk flower
【绢画】juànhuà〈名〉 painting on silk
【绢丝】juànsī〈名〉 spun silk

圈 juàn〈名〉 pen [for livestock]: ▸猪～
▸juān, quān
【圈肥】juànféi = 厩肥 jiùféi
【圈养】juànyǎng〈动〉 raise in a pen

眷 juàn
A〈名〉 family dependant: ▸～属, 家～
B〈动〉〈书〉 care for: ▸～顾, ～恋, ～念
【眷爱】juàn'ài〈动〉 have deep affection for
【眷顾】juàngù〈动〉〈书〉 be concerned about: ～百姓 care for the common people
【眷眷】juànjuàn〈形〉〈书〉 yearning: ～

之情 loving care

【眷恋】 juànliàn〈动〉〈书〉 have deep affection for: 对祖国怀有深深的～之情 have a strong attachment to one's motherland

【眷念】 juànniàn〈动〉〈书〉 think affectionately of: ～亲人 miss one's family members

【眷属】 juànshǔ〈名〉 1（家人） family member: 照顾烈士的～ look after the families of the martyrs 2（夫妻） husband and wife: 愿天下有情人终成～。 May all those who are in love get married.

juē

撅¹ juē〈动〉 pout: ～嘴 pout one's lips ‖ ～着两根小辫儿 with two pigtails sticking up

撅² juē〈动〉〈口〉 snap: 树枝咔嚓一声～断了。 The branch snapped.

噘 juē〈动〉 pout

【噘嘴】 juēzuǐ〈动〉 purse one's lips

jué

孓 jué ▸孑孓 jiéjué

决¹（決） jué

A〈动〉 1（决定） decide: 议而不～ discuss sth. without reaching a decision ‖ 我意已～。 I've made up my mind. ▸～定, 表～, 判～ 2（执行死刑） execute: ▸处～, 枪～ 3（分出胜负） decide the outcome: 今天的比赛要～出前三名。 The first three places will be decided in the matches today. ▸～赛, ～战

B〈副〉 [used before a negative] definitely: ～非偶然 by no means accidental

决²（決） jué〈动〉 1（决口） burst: ～堤 burst a dyke ▸～口, 溃～ 2（破裂） break: ▸～裂

【决策】 juécè A〈动〉 make a strategic decision: 参与～ be involved in decision-making ‖ ～失误 make a wrong strategic decision B〈名〉 policy decision: 英明～ wise decision ‖ 重大～ major policy decision ‖ ～机构 policy-making body

【决策权】 juécèquán〈名〉 policy-making power

【决策人】 juécèrén〈名〉 policy-maker

【决雌雄】 jué cíxióng = 决一雌雄 juéyīcíxióng

【决定】 juédìng A〈动〉 1（做出主张） decide: 以投票的方式～ decide by a vote ‖ 我～不参加比赛。 I resolved against participating in the contest. 2（主导） determine: 存在～意识。 Man's social being determines his consciousness. ‖ 供求规律～商品价格。 The law of supply and demand governs the prices of goods. B〈名〉 decision: 通过一项～ pass a resolution ‖ 做出～ make a decision

【决定性】 juédìngxìng〈名〉 decisiveness: ～胜利 decisive victory ‖ 在谈判中起～作用 play a decisive role in the negotiations

【决斗】 juédòu〈名〉 1（指格斗） duel: （与某人）进行～ have a duel (with sb.) 2（指斗争） decisive struggle: 生死存亡的～ life-and-death struggle

【决断】 juéduàn A〈动〉 make a decision: 请你最后～。 Please can you make the final decision. B〈名〉 decisiveness: 做事很有～ be very decisive about one's business

【决计】 juéjì A〈动〉 come to a decision: 他～辞职。 He was determined to resign. B〈副〉 definitely: 这样办～没错。 We definitely won't go wrong the way we do it.

【决绝】 juéjué A〈动〉 sever: ～一切往来 sever all relations ‖ 和不良嗜好～ break with bad habits B〈形〉 firm: 态度～ resolute attitude

【决口】 juékǒu〈动〉 burst: 大雨使河堤～。 Heavy rains caused the river to burst its banks.

【决裂】 juéliè〈动〉 break with: 与传统观念～ break with traditional ideas ‖ 双方关系彻底～。 Relations between the two sides completely broke down.

【决明子】 juémíngzǐ〈名〉［中药］ cassia seed

【决然】 juérán〈副〉〈书〉 1（坚决） resolutely: ～拒绝作出让步 resolutely refuse to make any concession ▸毅然～ 2（必然） definitely: 这种人～没有好下场。 Such people are bound to come to no good end.

【决赛】 juésài〈名〉 finals: 进入～ reach the finals ‖ ～选手 finalist ▸半～, 四分之一～

【决胜】 juéshèng〈动〉 determine the outcome: ～局 decider

【决胜盘】 juéshèngpán〈名〉 decider: 比赛进入～。 The competition has reached the decider stage.

【决死】 juésǐ〈形〉 concerning life-and-death: ～的斗争 life-and-death struggle

【决算】 juésuàn〈名〉 final accounts

【决心】 juéxīn A〈动〉 be determined: ～改正错误 be determined to correct one's mistakes ‖ ～抵抗到底 resolve to resist to the end B〈名〉 determination: 表～ express firm determination ‖ 下定～ come to a resolution

【决心书】 juéxīnshū〈名〉 written pledge: 写～ write a pledge

【决一雌雄】 juéyīcíxióng〈成〉 fight it out: 在商场上～ fight it out in the business world

【决一死战】 juéyīsǐzhàn〈成〉 fight to the death: 与敌人～ fight the enemy to the death

【决议】 juéyì〈名〉 resolution: 通过～ carry a resolution ‖ ～草案 draft resolution

【决意】 juéyì〈动〉 be determined: 她～要离婚。 She made up her mind to get a divorce.

【决战】 juézhàn〈动〉 fight a decisive battle

诀¹（訣） jué〈名〉 1（指词句） rhymed instruction: ▸歌～, 口～ 2（诀窍） knack: ▸～窍, 秘～

诀²（訣） jué〈动〉 bid farewell: ▸～别, 永～

【诀别】 juébié〈动〉 bid farewell: 做最后的～ bid an eternal farewell

【诀窍】 juéqiào〈名〉 knack: 成功的～ secret of success ‖ 这里头有～。 There is a knack to it.

【诀要】 juéyào〈书〉= 诀窍 juéqiào

抉 jué〈动〉〈书〉 single out: ▸～择

【抉择】 juézé〈动〉〈书〉 choose: 面临～ stand at the crossroads ‖ 是去是留，请速～。 Stay or leave, you have to make a quick decision.

【抉摘】 juézhāi〈动〉〈书〉 1（抉择） choose 2（揭发指摘） expose and condemn: ～弊端 expose and censure malpractices

角¹ jué〈名〉〈古〉 three-legged wine cup

角² jué〈名〉 1（角色） role: 你扮演什么～儿? What role do you play? ▸配～, 主～, 丑～, 旦～ 2（演员）（男） actor; （女） actress: 名～ famous actor

角³ jué〈动〉 contend: ▸～斗, ～逐, 口～

角⁴ jué〈名〉［音乐］ note on the ancient Chinese pentatonic (五音) scale, corresponding to 3 in *jianpu* (简谱) numbered musical notation
▸jiǎo

【角斗】 juédòu〈动〉 wrestle: ～场 wrestling ring

【角力】 juélì〈动〉 wrestle

【角色】 juésè〈名〉 1〈本〉 role: 在剧中担任主要～ have the major part in the play ‖ 反面/正面～ negative/positive character 2〈喻〉 type of character: 在这件事上她扮演了极不光彩的～。 She played a completely contemptible part in it.

【角逐】 juézhú〈动〉 contend: 群雄～ tussle among separatist warlords ‖ 明天我们将与对手展开～。 We will carry on the contest against our opponents tomorrow.

珏 jué〈名〉〈古〉 two pieces of jade joined together

觉（覺） jué

A〈动〉 1〈书〉（睡醒） wake up: 大梦初～ wake up from a dream 2（觉悟） become aware: ▸～悟, 自～ 3（感到） feel: ～得饿 feel hungry ‖ ～着有些发烧 feel one has a temperature ▸～得, 不知不～

B〈名〉 sense: ▸触～, 错～, 幻～
▸jiào

【觉察】 juéchá〈动〉 detect: ～到危险 sense a danger ‖ 我很快就～出他在骗我。 I soon sensed that he was fooling me.

【觉得】 juéde〈动〉 1（感觉到） feel: ～身体不舒服 not feel (like) oneself ‖ ～有点累 feel a bit tired 2（认为） think: 你～这本书怎么样? What do you think of the book? ‖ 我～不会有问题。 My feeling is that there would be no problem.

【觉悟】 juéwù A〈动〉 1（清醒） come to realize: 他终于～了。 He finally came to understand. 2［佛教］ attain enlightenment B〈名〉 consciousness: 政治～高 high political awareness

【觉醒】 juéxǐng〈动〉〈喻〉 wake up (to reality): 是该～的时候了。 It's time to wake up.

绝（絕） jué

A〈动〉 1（断绝） cut off: ▸～交, 拒～, 滔滔不～ 2（穷尽） exhaust: 别把话说～了。 Don't say anything uncompromising. ‖ 手段都用～了。 We've tried every possible means. ▸弹尽粮～, 斩尽杀～ 3（死亡） die: ▸悲痛欲～, 气～

B〈形〉 1（独一无二） matchless: ～好的机会 golden opportunity ‖ 他的书法真叫～。 His calligraphy is simply superb. ▸～唱, ～活 2（无出路） desperate: ▸～境, ～路, ～症

C〈副〉 1（最） extremely: ～大部分 the lion's share ‖ ～大多数 vast majority

▶～密，深恶痛～ 2 (绝对) [used before a negative] in the least: ～不答应 not in the least agree ‖ ～不可能 be absolutely impossible ‖ ～非偶然 be by no means an accident
D 〈名〉 quatrain: ▶五～，七～
【绝版】juébǎn〈动〉 be out of print: 这本书已经～。This book has already gone out of print.
【绝笔】juébǐ〈名〉 1 (指最后的) final work 2 〈书〉 (指绝妙的) masterpiece: 堪称～ may be called a masterpiece
【绝壁】juébì〈名〉 precipice: 攀缘～ climb a precipice
【绝产】juéchǎn = 绝收 juéshōu
【绝唱】juéchàng〈名〉 1 (指诗文) peak of perfection: 千古～ ancient poetic masterpiece 2 (指唱曲) swansong: 想不到这竟成了她的～。I didn't expect it to be her swansong.
【绝处逢生】juéchù-féngshēng〈成〉 escape by the skin of one's teeth
【绝代】juédài〈动〉〈书〉 be unique among one's contemporaries: 才华～ unrivalled talent
【绝代佳人】juédài-jiārén〈成〉 beauty of beauties
【绝倒】juédǎo〈动〉〈书〉 rock with laughter: 令人～ be side-splitting
【绝地】juédì〈名〉 1 (险恶之地) extremely dangerous place 2 = 绝境 juéjìng 2
【绝顶】juédǐng A 〈副〉 extremely: ～聪明 extremely clever B 〈名〉〈书〉 peak
【绝对】juéduì A 〈形〉 absolute: ～服从 absolute obedience ‖ ～高度 absolute altitude ‖ ～零度 absolute zero ▶～真理 B 〈副〉 absolutely: ～安全 perfectly safe ‖ ～可靠 completely reliable ‖ 答案～正确。The answer is definitely true.
【绝对贫困】juéduì pínkùn〈名〉 absolute impoverishment
【绝对权力】juéduì quánlì〈名〉 absolute power
【绝对温度】juéduì wēndù〈名〉 [物理] absolute temperature
【绝对优势】juéduì yōushì〈名〉 absolute superiority
【绝对真理】juéduì zhēnlǐ〈名〉 [哲学] absolute truth
【绝对值】juéduìzhí〈名〉 [数学] absolute value
【绝后】juéhòu〈动〉 1 (没有后代) have no offspring 2 (不会重现) never be repeated: ▶空前～
【绝户】juéhù A = 绝后 juéhòu 1 B 〈名〉 (指家庭) childless family; (指人) childless person
【绝活】juéhuó〈名〉 unrivalled skill: 有一手～ have a unique skill
【绝技】juéjì〈名〉 consummate skill: 身怀～ have unique skill
【绝迹】juéjì〈动〉 vanish: 濒临～ be on the verge of extinction ‖ 天花在这个地区早已～。Smallpox was stamped out in this area long ago.
【绝交】juéjiāo〈动〉 sever ties: 她跟他～了。She severed ties with him.
【绝经】juéjīng〈动〉 [生理] stop menstruating
【绝经期】juéjīngqī〈名〉 [生理] menopause
【绝境】juéjìng〈名〉〈书〉 1 (指隔绝) remote and out-of-the-way place 2 (指无出路) hopeless situation: 濒临～ be on the edge of a precipice ‖ 陷入～ fall into an impasse

j

【绝句】juéjù〈名〉 quatrain: 五言～ pentasyllabic quatrain ‖ 七言～ heptasyllabic quatrain
【绝口】juékǒu〈动〉 1 (停止说话) stop talking: 骂不～ pour out unceasing abuse ▶赞不～ 2 (闭口) keep one's mouth shut: ～不提此事 make no mention of this matter
【绝路】juélù〈名〉 road to ruin: 走上～ come to a dead end ‖ 他被逼上～。He was driven into a corner.
【绝伦】juélún〈动〉〈书〉 be matchless: 聪明～ incomparably intelligent ‖ 精美～ exquisite beyond compare
【绝门】juémén〈名〉 family without offspring: ～绝户 household without offspring
【绝门儿】juéménr A 〈名〉 1 (指行业) extinct trade: 这个行当已成了～。The trade has already become extinct. 2 (指技艺) unique skill B 〈形〉 greatly surprising: 他这件事做得也太～了。He's gone too far on the matter!
【绝密】juémì〈形〉 top-secret: ～文件 top-secret papers
【绝妙】juémiào〈形〉 ingenious: ～的讽刺 superb irony ‖ ～的主意 marvellous idea
【绝命书】juémìngshū〈名〉 note written on the eve of one's execution
【绝情】juéqíng〈形〉 heartless: 你这话太～。It's cruel of you to say so.
【绝然】juérán〈副〉 completely: ～不同 be entirely different
【绝色】juésè〈名〉〈书〉 [of woman] unrivalled beauty: ～佳人 great beauty
【绝食】juéshí〈动〉 fast: ～斗争 hunger strike
【绝世】juéshì〈动〉 be unique: ～佳作 enduring masterpiece ‖ ～珍品 unique treasure
【绝世无双】juéshì-wúshuāng〈成〉 be incomparable
【绝收】juéshōu〈动〉 have a total failure of the harvest: 庄稼因干旱而～。The drought led to total crop failure.
【绝嗣】juésì〈动〉〈书〉 have no offspring
【绝望】juéwàng〈动〉 despair: 感到～ feel desperate ‖ 在极度～中自杀 commit suicide in the depths of despair
【绝无仅有】juéwú-jǐnyǒu〈成〉 only one of its kind: 大熊猫是世界上～的珍奇动物。The giant panda is the only one of its kind in the world.
【绝响】juéxiǎng〈名〉 1 (指音乐) extinct music 2 (指艺术) extinct art: 几近～ almost become a lost art
【绝学】juéxué〈名〉 1 (失传的学问) lost body of knowledge 2 (高深的学问) profound learning
【绝艺】juéyì〈名〉 consummate skill
【绝育】juéyù〈动〉 [医学] sterilize: ～手术 sterilization operation
【绝缘】juéyuán〈动〉 1 (隔绝) cut all ties with: 与外界～ be cut off from the outside world ‖ 与烟酒～ have stopped smoking and drinking 2 [电气] insulate: ～材料 insulating material ‖ 橡胶具有良好的～性能。Rubber provides good insulation.
【绝缘胶带】juéyuán jiāodài〈名〉 insulating tape
【绝缘体】juéyuántǐ〈名〉 insulator: 热～ thermal insulator
【绝缘子】juéyuánzǐ〈名〉 insulator
【绝招】juézhāo〈名〉 1 (指技艺) unique skill: 杂技～ acrobatic stunt 2 (指手段) master stroke: 想出了一个～ come up with a master stroke
【绝症】juézhèng〈名〉 terminal illness: 身患～ be terminally ill
【绝种】juézhǒng〈动〉 die out: ～动物 extinct animal ‖ 恐龙～已久。Dinosaurs have been extinct for a long time.

倔 jué
▶juè
【倔强】juéjiàng〈形〉 stubborn: 性格非常～ be as stubborn as a mule
【倔犟】juéjiàng = 倔强 juéjiàng

掘 jué
〈动〉 dig: ～一眼井 dig a well ‖ ～墓 dig a grave ▶采～，发～，挖～
【掘进】juéjìn〈动〉 [矿业] drill: 平巷～ drilling ‖ ～机 tunneller
【掘墓人】juémùrén〈名〉 gravedigger
【掘土机】juétǔjī〈名〉 excavator

桷 jué
〈名〉 square rafter

崛 jué
〈动〉〈书〉 rise abruptly
【崛起】juéqǐ〈动〉 1 (突起) suddenly appear: 高楼大厦平地～。Tall sky-scrapers are rising from the ground. 2 (兴起) rise to prominence: 为人才～创造条件 create conditions for the emergence of talents ‖ 为中华之～而奋斗 struggle for the rise of China

脚（腳） jué
= 角² jué
▶jiǎo

厥¹ jué
〈动〉 lose consciousness

厥² jué
〈书〉
A 〈代〉 (他的) his; (她的) her; (它的) its; (他们的) their: ▶大放～词
B 〈副〉 then

谲（譎） jué
〈形〉〈书〉 1 (欺诈) crafty: ▶～诈 2 (奇特) odd: ▶诡～
【谲诈】juézhà〈形〉〈书〉 cunning

蕨 jué
〈名〉 [植物] bracken
【蕨菜】juécài〈名〉 edible tender leaves of bracken
【蕨类植物】juélèi zhíwù〈名〉 pteridophyte

獗 jué
▶猖獗 chāngjué

橛 jué
〈名〉 peg: 小木～儿 short wooden stake
【橛子】juézi〈名〉 peg

噱 jué
〈动〉〈书〉 laugh loudly: 她的行动令人发～。Her behaviour was laughable.
▶xué

爵¹ jué
〈名〉〈古〉 wine vessel with three legs and a loop handle

爵² jué
〈名〉 rank of nobility: 封～ confer a title upon sb. ▶伯～，公～
【爵士】juéshì〈名〉 1 (指封号) knight: 授予～封号 confer the title of knight upon sb. 2 (指称谓) sir: 约翰·史密斯～ Sir John Smith
【爵士乐】juéshìyuè〈名〉 jazz
【爵位】juéwèi〈名〉 rank of nobility

蹶 jué〈动〉 **1**〈本〉 fall **2**〈喻〉 suffer a setback: ▸一～不振
▸juě

矍 jué〈形〉 alarmed-looking

【矍铄】juéshuò〈形〉〈书〉hale and hearty: 精神～ be hale and hearty

嚼 jué ▸咀嚼 jǔjué
▸jiáo, jiào

攫 jué〈动〉〈书〉seize: ～为己有 appropriate

【攫取】juéqǔ〈动〉 seize: ～暴利 rake in exorbitant profits ‖ ～自然资源 grab natural resources

镢（钁） jué〈名〉〈方〉pickaxe

【镢头】juétou〈名〉〈方〉pickaxe

juě

蹶 juě
▸jué

【蹶子】juězi〈名〉 [of horses, donkeys, etc.] kick with the hind leg: ▸尥～

juè

倔 juè〈形〉 surly: 脾气～ be rather surly
▸jué

【倔头倔脑】juètóu-juènǎo〈成〉be blunt of speech and gruff of manner

jūn

军（軍） jūn〈名〉 **1**（军队） armed forces: 海～ naval forces ▸～队, 参～, 陆～, 驻～ **2**（指编制单位） army [military unit]: 第二十二～ 22nd army ‖ ～以上干部 officers of army level and above ▸～长

【军备】jūnbèi〈名〉 arms: 裁减～ reduce armaments ‖ ～竞赛 arms race

【军部】jūnbù〈名〉 army headquarters

【军车】jūnchē〈名〉 army vehicle

【军大衣】jūndàyī〈名〉 army overcoat

【军刀】jūndāo〈名〉 sabre

【军地两用人才】 jūn-dì liǎngyòng réncái〈名〉 personnel competent for both military and civilian services

【军队】jūnduì〈名〉 armed forces: 部署～ assemble troops ‖ 从前线撤回～ withdraw troops from the front line ‖ 集结～ mass troops ‖ ～转业干部 military officer transferred to civilian work

【军阀】jūnfá〈名〉 warlord: ～割据 separatist warlord regime ▸北洋～

【军法】jūnfǎ〈名〉 military law: 触犯～ violate military law

【军方】jūnfāng〈名〉 the military: ～代表 representative from the military

【军费】jūnfèi〈名〉 military expenditure: 削减～开支 cut down on military expenditure

【军服】jūnfú〈名〉 military uniform

【军港】jūngǎng〈名〉 naval port

【军歌】jūngē〈名〉 army song

【军工】jūngōng〈名〉 **1**（指工业） war industry: ～产品 military product ‖ ～企业 military enterprise **2**（指工程） military project

【军工厂】 jūngōngchǎng〈名〉 munitions factory

【军功】jūngōng〈名〉 military exploit: 立～ render meritorious military service

【军功章】 jūngōngzhāng〈名〉 medal for military merits

【军官】jūnguān〈名〉 officer: 海军～ navy officer ‖ ～学校 military academy

【军规】jūnguī〈名〉 military discipline: 遵守～ observe military discipline

【军国主义】 jūnguózhǔyì〈名〉 militarism: ～者 militarist

【军号】jūnhào〈名〉 bugle: ～手 bugler

【军徽】jūnhuī〈名〉 army emblem

【军婚】jūnhūn〈名〉 marriage of sb. in military service

【军火】 jūnhuǒ〈名〉 munitions: ～贸易 arms trade ‖ ～库 arsenal ‖ ～商 arms dealer

【军机】jūnjī〈名〉 **1**（军事机宜） military plan: 贻误～ delay the realization of a military plan **2**（军事机密） military secret: 泄露～ leak a military secret

【军籍】jūnjí〈名〉 military status: 开除～ discharge sb. from the army

【军纪】jūnjì〈名〉 military discipline: ～严明 strict military discipline

【军舰】jūnjiàn〈名〉 warship

【军阶】jūnjiē〈名〉 military rank

【军界】jūnjiè〈名〉 the military: 服务～ serve in the military

【军垦】jūnkěn〈名〉 reclamation of wasteland by army units: ～农场 army reclamation farm

【军礼】jūnlǐ〈名〉 military salute: 行～ give a military salute

【军力】jūnlì〈名〉 military strength: 展示～ display military might

【军粮】jūnliáng〈名〉 army provisions: 发放～ release military rations

【军烈属】jūnlièshǔ〈名〉 family members of active servicemen or of martyrs

【军龄】jūnlíng〈名〉 length of military service

【军令】jūnlìng〈名〉 military order: 执行～ carry out a military order ‖ ～如山 military orders must be obeyed

【军令状】 jūnlìngzhuàng〈名〉 military pledge written by an officer indicating acceptance of severe punishment in the case of an unsuccessful mission: 立下～ write a pledge

【军旅】 jūnlǚ〈名〉〈书〉 army: ～生涯 army life

【军马】jūnmǎ〈名〉 **1**（指马） army horse: ～场 army horse ranch **2**（军队） troops: 各路～ all units

【军帽】jūnmào〈名〉 army cap

【军民】jūnmín〈名〉 soldiers and civilians: ～团结 unity of the army and the people ‖ ～联防 army-civilian joint defence ‖ ～鱼水情。 The army and the people are like peas in a pod.

【军棋】jūnqí〈名〉 military chess

【军旗】jūnqí〈名〉 army flag

【军情】jūnqíng〈名〉 military situation: 刺探～ spy out military secrets

【军区】jūnqū〈名〉 military region: 省～ provincial military command ‖ ～司令员 commander of a military area

【军权】jūnquán〈名〉 military power: 掌握～ hold military power

【军犬】jūnquǎn〈名〉 military dog

【军人】jūnrén ▸**p. 966**〈名〉 soldier: 复员～ demobilized serviceman ‖ ～家属 soldier's dependants

【军容】jūnróng〈名〉 soldiers' appearance, discipline and bearing: ～严整。 The troops are in gallant array.

【军嫂】jūnsǎo〈名〉 serviceman's wife

【军师】jūnshī〈名〉〈旧〉 military adviser

【军史】jūnshǐ〈名〉 history of an army

【军士】jūnshì〈名〉 non-commissioned officer (NCO)

【军事】jūnshì〈名〉 military affairs: 进行～干预 intervene militarily ‖ ～策略 military policy ‖ ～冲突 military conflict ‖ ～打击 military strike ‖ ～设施 military installation

【军事法庭】jūnshì fǎtíng〈名〉 military tribunal

【军事分界线】jūnshì fēnjièxiàn〈名〉 military demarcation line

【军事观察员】 jūnshì guāncháyuán ▸**p. 966**〈名〉 military observer

【军事管制】jūnshì guǎnzhì〈名〉 military control: 实行～ impose martial law

【军事基地】jūnshì jīdì〈名〉 military base: 扩大～ enlarge a military base

【军事科学】jūnshì kēxué〈名〉 military science

【军事情报】jūnshì qíngbào〈名〉 military intelligence

【军事体育】jūnshì tǐyù〈名〉 military sports: 发展～ promote military sports

【军事委员会】 jūnshì wěiyuánhuì〈名〉 military commission: 中国共产党中央～ Central Military Commission of the CPC

【军事文学】 jūnshì wénxué〈名〉 military literature

【军事行动】 jūnshì xíngdòng〈名〉 military operation

【军事学院】 jūnshì xuéyuàn〈名〉 military academy

【军事训练】 jūnshì xùnliàn〈名〉 military training

【军事演习】 jūnshì yǎnxí〈名〉 military exercise: 进行～ conduct military exercises

【军事院校】jūnshì yuànxiào〈名〉 military academy

【军事政变】 jūnshì zhèngbiàn〈名〉 military coup

【军售】jūnshòu〈名〉 arms sale

【军属】jūnshǔ〈名〉 soldier's dependants

【军团】jūntuán〈名〉 legion: 第一～ First Legion

【军威】jūnwēi〈名〉 military might: ～大振。 The might of the army was made felt.

【军委】jūnwěi〈简称〉= 军事委员会

【军务】jūnwù〈名〉 military affairs: ～繁忙 be busy with military affairs ‖ ～在身 be tied up with military duties

【军衔】jūnxián〈名〉 military rank

【军饷】jūnxiǎng〈名〉〈旧〉 soldier's pay and provisions: 发放/克扣～ distribute/embezzle soldier's pay and provisions

【军械】jūnxiè〈名〉 ordnance

【军械库】jūnxièkù〈名〉 arms depot

【军心】jūnxīn〈名〉 troop morale: 动摇～ shake the army's morale ‖ 振奋～ boost the morale of the troops

【军需】jūnxū〈名〉 military supplies: ～品 military supplies

【军训】jūnxùn〈名〉 military training

【军演】jūnyǎn〈简称〉= 军事演习

【军医】jūnyī〈名〉 medical officer

【军医大学】jūnyī dàxué〈名〉military medical university

【军营】jūnyíng〈名〉 barracks: ～生活 life in the barracks

j

【军用】jūnyòng〈形〉 military: ～地图 military map ‖ ～物资 military supplies

【军乐】jūnyuè〈名〉 military music: ～队 military band

【军长】jūnzhǎng〈名〉 army commander

【军政】jūnzhèng〈名〉 1（军事和政治） military affairs and politics: ～大学 military and political university 2（指行政工作） military administration 3（军队和政府） army and government: ～团结 unity of the army and the government

【军政府】jūnzhèngfǔ〈名〉 military government

【军职】jūnzhí〈名〉 military appointment: ～人员 army personnel

【军制】jūnzhì〈名〉 military system

【军中无戏言】jūnzhōng wú xìyán〈成〉 there is no room for frivolity in the army

【军种】jūnzhǒng〈名〉 armed services

【军转民】jūnzhuǎnmín〈动〉 [of a factory] switch from manufacturing military products to goods for civilian use

【军装】jūnzhuāng〈名〉 army uniform

均 jūn

A〈形〉 equal: 分配不～ uneven distribution ‖ 贫富不～ unequal distribution of wealth ▸～衡, 平～, 势～力敌

B〈副〉 all: 诸事～已办妥。 Everything has been properly arranged. ‖ 所有代表～已到达。 All the delegates have arrived.

【均等】jūnděng〈形〉 equal: 机会～ equal opportunity

【均等化】jūnděnghuà〈动〉 equalize: 促进基本公共医疗服务～ expedite equalization of basic public health services

【均分】jūnfēn〈动〉 share out equally: 那笔钱将～给大家。 The money will be divided equally among everybody.

【均衡】jūnhéng〈形〉 balanced: 供求～ equilibrium of supply and demand ‖ 国民经济～发展 harmonious development of the national economy

【均价】jūnjià〈名〉 average price

【均势】jūnshì〈名〉 balance of power: 保持～ maintain the balance ‖ 打破～ break the balance

【均摊】jūntān〈动〉 share equally: ～费用 go fifty-fifty on expenses

【均线】jūnxiàn〈名〉 average line

【均一】jūnyī〈形〉 even

【均匀】jūnyún〈形〉 even: 间隔～ even spacing ‖ 今年的降水很～。 Rainfall has been fairly well distributed this year.

【均沾】jūnzhān〈动〉 share equally: 利润～ equal share of profits

【均值】jūnzhí〈名〉 mean value

龟（龜）jūn

▸guī, qiū

【龟裂】jūnliè〈动〉 1 = 皲裂 jūnliè 2（裂开） be full of cracks: 地面～。 The ground was completely cracked.

君 jūn

〈名〉 1（君主） monarch: ▸～主, 暴～, 国～ 2〈书〉（用于称呼） [polite form of address] Mr: 诸～ gentlemen ‖ 祝～一路平安! I wish you a good journey!

【君临】jūnlín〈动〉〈旧〉 govern: ～天下 rule the country

【君权】jūnquán〈名〉 monarchical power: ～神授论 theory of the divine right of kings

【君王】jūnwáng〈名〉 monarch

【君主】jūnzhǔ〈名〉 monarch: 为～加冕 crown a monarch ‖ 世袭～ hereditary sovereign

【君主国】jūnzhǔguó〈名〉 monarchy: 建立～ establish a monarchy ‖ 专制～ despotic monarchy

【君主立宪】jūnzhǔ lìxiàn〈名〉 constitutional monarchy: 英国是一个～制国家。 Britain is a constitutional monarchy.

【君主制】jūnzhǔzhì〈名〉 monarchy: 废除～ abolish the monarchy

【君子】jūnzǐ〈名〉 gentleman: ～成人之美 a gentleman is always ready to help others attain their goals ‖ 他不是个～。 He is no gentleman. ▸梁上～, 正人～

【君子动口不动手】jūnzǐ dòng kǒu bú dòng shǒu〈俗〉 a gentleman uses his tongue, not his fists

【君子国】jūnzǐguó〈名〉 legendary land of the virtuous

【君子协定】jūnzǐ xiédìng〈名〉gentlemen's agreement

【君子一言，驷马难追】jūnzǐ yī yán, sìmǎ nán zhuī〈成〉 what is said can never be taken back

【君子之交淡如水】jūnzǐ zhī jiāo dàn rú shuǐ〈成〉 the friendship between gentlemen is as pure as water

【君子兰】jūnzǐlán〈名〉［植物］ kaffir lily

钧（鈞）jūn

A〈量〉 *jun* [ancient unit of weight, equal to 30 *jin*]: ▸千～一发

B〈名〉 potter's wheel

C〈代〉〈书〉〈敬〉 you: ▸～鉴, ～启

【钧鉴】jūnjiàn〈名〉〈书〉〈敬〉 your attention

【钧启】jūnqǐ〈名〉〈书〉〈敬〉 to be opened by [written on envelope]

莙 jūn

【莙荙菜】jūndácài〈名〉［植物］ spinach beet

菌 jūn

〈名〉 1（真菌） fungus: ▸真～ 2（细菌） bacterium: ▸病～, 抗～素, 细～

▸jùn

【菌落】jūnluò〈名〉［生物］ colony

【菌苗】jūnmiáo〈名〉［药学］ (bacterial) vaccine

皲（皸）jūn

【皲裂】jūnliè〈动〉 chap: 手足～ chapped hands and feet

鲪（鮶）jūn

〈名〉［鱼类］ sebastodes [extinct genus of prehistoric bony fish]

jùn

俊 jùn

〈形〉 1（漂亮） handsome: 她模样很～。 She has a pretty face. ‖ 小伙子长得挺～的。 The lad is very handsome. ▸～秀, ～美, 英～ 2（有才华） unusually talented: ▸～杰

【俊杰】jùnjié〈名〉 hero

【俊美】jùnměi〈形〉 pretty

【俊男倩女】jùnnán-qiànnǚ〈成〉handsome boys and pretty girls

【俊俏】jùnqiào〈形〉 pretty and charming: ～的姑娘 pretty and charming girl

【俊秀】jùnxiù〈形〉 pretty

【俊雅】jùnyǎ〈形〉〈书〉pretty and tasteful

郡 jùn

〈名〉〈旧〉 prefecture

【郡县制】jùnxiànzhì〈名〉 prefecture and county system

峻 jùn

〈形〉 1（高大） towering: ▸～峭, 崇山～岭, 险～ 2（严厉） harsh: ▸冷～, 严～

【峻拔】jùnbá〈形〉 high and steep: 山势～ high and steep mountains

【峻拒】jùnjù〈动〉〈书〉 refuse sternly

【峻峭】jùnqiào〈形〉 high and steep: ～的山岭 high and steep mountains

隽（雋）jùn

= 俊 jùn 2

▸juàn

浚（濬）jùn

〈动〉 dredge: ～渠 dredge a canal ▸疏～

骏（駿）jùn

〈名〉 steed

【骏马】jùnmǎ〈名〉 steed: 飞奔的～ galloping steed

菌 jùn

〈名〉 mushroom

▸jūn

竣 jùn

〈动〉 complete: ▸～工

【竣工】jùngōng〈动〉 be completed: 提前～ be completed ahead of schedule ‖ ～仪式 completion ceremony ‖ 工程将于年底～。 The project is due for completion by the end of the year.

j

Kk

kā

咔 kā〈拟〉 click: ～的一声断了 break with a clack
▸kǎ

【咔吧】kābā〈拟〉 crack: 树枝～一声断了。The branch broke with a snap.

【咔嚓】kāchā〈拟〉 crack: ～一声按下快门 click a camera

【咔嗒】kādā〈拟〉 clatter: 门～一声关上了。The door clicked shut.

咖 kā
▸gā

【咖啡】kāfēi〈名〉 coffee: 种植～ grow coffee ‖ 速溶～ instant coffee ‖ 请来两杯～。Two coffees, please.

【咖啡豆】kāfēidòu〈名〉 coffee bean: ～研磨机 coffee grinder

【咖啡馆】kāfēiguǎn〈名〉 café

【咖啡色】kāfēisè ▸**p. 863**〈名〉 coffee colour

【咖啡厅】kāfēitīng〈名〉 café

【咖啡因】kāfēiyīn〈名〉［药学］ caffeine

喀 kā〈拟〉 sound made in coughing or vomiting

【喀吧】kābā = 咔吧 kābā

【喀布尔】Kābù'ěr〈名〉 Kabul

【喀嚓】kāchā = 咔嚓 kāchā

【喀麦隆】Kāmàilóng〈名〉 Cameroon: ～人 Cameroonian

【喀秋莎】kāqiūshā〈名〉 Katyusha [rocket launcher]

【喀什】Kāshí〈名〉 Kashgar

【喀斯特】kāsītè〈名〉［地质］ karst: ～地貌 karst topography

【喀土穆】Kātǔmù〈名〉 Khartoum

揢 kā〈动〉〈方〉 scrape with a blade: ～猪毛 scrape hair off pork ‖ ～鱼鳞 scale a fish

kǎ

卡 kǎ

A〈量〉［物理］ calorie: 大～ kilocalorie ‖ 一盎司糖约能产生100～的热量。An ounce of sugar produces about 100 calories. ▸～路里

B〈名〉 **1**（卡片）card: 电话～ phone card ‖ 声～ sound card ‖ 钥匙～ key card ‖ 智能～ smart card ▸打～ **2**（卡车） truck: 十轮～ ten-wheel truck ▸～车 **3**（指装置） cassette: ～式录音机 audio cassette recorder
▸qiǎ

【卡巴迪】kǎbādí〈名〉［体育］ kabaddi

【卡宾枪】kǎbīnqiāng〈名〉 carbine

【卡车】kǎchē〈名〉 truck; lorry〈英〉: 一～水泥 a truckload of cement ‖ 装～ load a truck ‖ ～荷载 truck load ‖ ～司机 truck driver

【卡尺】kǎchǐ = 游标卡尺 yóubiāo kǎchǐ

【卡带】kǎdài〈名〉 cassette tape

【卡迪根郡】Kǎdígēnjùn〈名〉 Cardiganshire

【卡丁车】kǎdīngchē〈名〉 go-kart: ～比赛 go-karting

【卡介苗】kǎjièmiáo〈名〉［药学］ Bacille Calmette-Guérin vaccine (BCG): 打～ have a BCG vaccine ‖ ～接种 BCG vaccination

【卡拉OK】kǎlā'ōukèi〈名〉 karaoke: 唱～ sing karaoke

【卡拉奇】Kǎlāqí〈名〉 Karachi

【卡路里】kǎlùlǐ〈量〉［物理］ calorie

【卡马森郡】Kǎmǎsēnjùn〈名〉 Carmarthenshire

【卡那封郡】Kǎnàfēngjùn〈名〉 Caernarvonshire

【卡那霉素】kǎnàméisù〈名〉［药学］ kanamycin

【卡能】kǎnéng〈名〉 caloric energy

【卡片】kǎpiàn〈名〉 card: 填写～ fill in a card ‖ 制作～ make a card ‖ 资料～ reference card

【卡其】kǎqí = 咔叽 kǎjī

【卡钳】kǎqián〈名〉［机械］ calipers

【卡斯特里】Kǎsītèlǐ〈名〉 Castries

【卡塔尔】Kǎtǎ'ěr〈名〉 Qatar: ～人 Qatari

【卡特尔】kǎtè'ěr〈名〉［经济］ cartel: 钢铁/石油～ steel/oil cartel

【卡通】kǎtōng〈名〉 cartoon: ～人物 cartoon character

【卡通片】kǎtōngpiàn〈名〉 animated cartoon

咔 kǎ
▸kā

【咔叽】kǎjī〈名〉［纺织］khaki: ～布 khaki cloth

咯 kǎ〈动〉 cough up: ～痰 cough up phlegm
▸gē, lo, luò

【咯痰】kǎtán〈动〉 cough up phlegm

【咯血】kǎxiě〈动〉 cough up blood

kāi

开¹（開） kāi

A〈动〉 **1**（打开） open: ～窗户 open a window ‖ 在墙上～个洞 make a hole in the wall ‖ 门～着。The door is open. ‖ 锁打不～。The lock won't open. ▸～幕, 公～, 网～一面 **2**（使开始工作） turn on: ～电视/空调 turn on the TV/air conditioner ‖ 电视机～着。The TV is on. **3**（操作） operate: ～船 sail a ship ‖ ～汽车 drive a car **4**（指交通工具） move: 班车什么时候～? When does the bus leave? ‖ 火车～进站了。The train pulled into the station. **5**（舒展） open out: 花～了。The flower bloomed. ▸～屏, 盛～ **6**（散开） come loose: 鞋带～了。The shoe lace came undone. **7**（融化） thaw out: 河～了。The river has cleared. ▸～冻 **8**（开辟） open up: ～50亩水稻田 open up 50 *mu* of paddy fields ‖ ～运河 dig a canal ▸～荒, ～垦 **9**（解除） lift: ▸～荤, ～戒, ～禁 **10**（出发） set out: ～往前线 set out for the front line ▸～拔 **11**（创立） start: ～餐馆 start a restaurant ‖ ～工厂 open a factory ▸～业 **12**（举行） hold: ～辩论会 hold a debate ‖ ～欢送会 hold a farewell party ▸～会, 召～ **13**（写出） write out: ～发票 make out an invoice ‖ ～处方 write a prescription **14**（开始） start: 会什么时候～? When will the meeting begin? ▸～工, ～拍, ～始 **15**（支付） pay: ～工资 pay (out) wages **16**（沸腾） boil: 把汤烧～。Bring the soup to the boil. ▸～水 **17**〈口〉（开除） fire: 他被～了。He was sacked. ▸～除 **18**〈口〉（吃） eat up: 他把蛋糕都～了。He polished off the whole cake. **19**（按比例分开） divide into: 四六～ in the proportion of four to six

B〈量〉［印刷］ division of standard size printing paper: 32～ 32mo ▸～本

开²（開） kāi〈量〉 carat: 24～金 24-carat gold

开³（開） kāi〈动〉 **1**（表分开或离开） [indicating separation or departure]: 分～ separate ‖ 铺～ spread out ‖ 闪～! Get out of the way! **2**（表动作开始） [indicating the beginning and continuation of an action]: 唱～了 begin to sing ‖ 哭～了 start crying **3**（表扩展） [indicating spreading]: 流感蔓延～了。The flu spread. ‖ 喜讯传～了。The good news spread. **4**（表容纳） [indicating capacity]: 这屋太小，我们坐不～。The room is not big enough to seat all of us. **5**（表放开） [indicating resignation]: ▸看～, 想～ **6**（表受欢迎程度） [indicating popularity]: ▸吃得～

【开拔】kāibá〈动〉 set out: 部队将于拂晓～。The troops will set out at dawn.

【开班】kāibān〈动〉 start a class

【开办】kāibàn〈动〉 open: ～工厂 open a factory ‖ ～培训班 hold a training course ‖ ～牙科诊所 set up a dental practice

【开本】kāiběn〈名〉［印刷］ format: 十六～ 16mo

【开标】kāibiāo〈动〉 open bids: ～价格 price for the selected tenders

【开播】kāibō〈动〉 **1**（指播种） begin sowing **2**（指播放） start broadcasting: 庆

祝电视台～25周年 celebrate the 25th anniversary of a TV station ‖ 新闻联播每晚7点～。 The news hook-up begins at 19:00 every evening.

【开博】kāibó〈动〉 start a blog

【开采】kāicǎi〈动〉 extract: ～石油 mine petroleum ‖ ～天然气 extract natural gas

【开仓济贫】kāicāng-jìpín〈成〉〈旧〉 open the granaries to relieve poverty

【开衩】kāichà **A**〈动〉 make a slit at the sides or back of a garment: 旁边/中间～ make an opening at the side/centre ‖ 你的上衣开不开衩? Do you want a vent made in your coat? **B**〈名〉 slit: 她的旗袍两边有～。 Her cheongsam has slits on both sides.

【开场】kāichǎng〈动〉 begin: 戏已～。 The play has already started.

【开场白】kāichǎngbái〈名〉 **1**（指戏曲） prologue to a play **2**（指讲演） opening words

【开场戏】kāichǎngxì〈名〉 first item of a performance

【开车】kāichē〈动〉 **1**（指驾驶） drive: 学～ learn to drive ‖ 我爸是～的。 My father is a driver. **2**（指开动） depart: ～时间 time of departure

【开诚布公】kāichéng-bùgōng〈成〉 frank and sincere: ～地谈一谈 talk frankly and sincerely

【开诚相见】kāichéng-xiāngjiàn〈成〉 be frank and open with sb.: 双方能～。 Both parties can be frank and open.

【开秤】kāichèng〈动〉 start purchasing

【开初】kāichū〈名〉 beginning: ～我不同意，但最终还是让步了。 At first I disagreed, but I compromised in the end.

【开除】kāichú〈动〉 dismiss: ～党籍 expel sb. from the Party ‖ ～公职 discharge sb. from public employment ‖ 被学校～ be expelled from school

【开锄】kāichú〈动〉［农业］start the year's hoeing

【开船】kāichuán〈动〉 set sail

【开创】kāichuàng〈动〉 found: ～新纪元 usher in a new era ‖ ～新局面 open up a new prospect

【开春】kāichūn〈动〉 be the start of spring: 一开春天气就会暖和起来。 It will warm up when spring arrives.

【开打】kāidǎ〈动〉 **1**（指戏剧） [of Chinese traditional opera] perform acrobatic fighting **2**（动武） start a fight **3**（开赛） start a match

【开裆裤】kāidāngkù〈名〉 open-split pants (for young children)

【开刀】kāidāo〈动〉 **1**〈旧〉（处死） decapitate: ～问斩 execute by decapitation **2**〈口〉（动手术） perform an operation: 给病人～ operate on a patient **3**〈喻〉（整治） make sb. the first target of an attack: 拿某人～ make an example of sb.

【开导】kāidǎo〈动〉 bring sb. to reason: 他一时想不通，我去～～他。 He hasn't come round yet. Let me try and put things in the right perspective for him.

【开倒车】kāi dàochē〈动〉〈喻〉 turn the clock back: 开历史倒车 try to turn back the wheel of history

【开道】kāidào〈动〉 clear the way: 由警车～ be let through by a police car ▸鸣锣～

【开动】kāidòng〈动〉 set in motion: ～机器 start a machine ‖〈喻〉 ～脑筋 get one's brain in gear

【开冻】kāidòng〈动〉 thaw: 河面～。 The river surface has thawed.

【开端】kāiduān〈名〉 beginning: 成功的～ successful start ‖ 良好的～是成功的一半。 A good beginning is half the battle.

【开多边形】kāiduōbiānxíng〈名〉［数学］ open polygon

【开恩】kāi'ēn〈动〉 show mercy: 希望老板～ hope that the boss will have mercy

【开发】kāifā〈动〉 develop: ～土地/软件/新产品 develop land/software/new products ‖ ～人力资源 develop human resources

【开发区】kāifāqū〈名〉 development zone: 经济技术～ economic and technological development zone

【开发商】kāifāshāng〈名〉 developer: 软件～ software developer

【开饭】kāifàn〈动〉 serve a meal: ～时间 service hours ‖ ～了。 The meal is ready. ‖ 她摆好桌子，准备～。 She's set the table for dinner.

【开方】kāifāng〈动〉 **1**［数学］ extract a root **2**（开处方） write (out) a prescription

【开方子】kāi fāngzi = 开方 kāifāng 2

【开房】kāifáng〈动〉 book a room: 在一家豪华酒店～度蜜月 book a room for a honeymoon in a luxury hotel

【开放】kāifàng **A**〈动〉 **1**（指花） come into bloom: 百花～。 All the flowers are in bloom. **2**（解除禁令） open: ～港口 open a port ‖ ～市场 open markets **3**（开张） be open: 图书馆从上午9点～到下午6点。 The library is open from 9 am to 6 pm. ‖ 新公园将于下月向游客～。 The new park will be open to visitors next month. **4**（对外开放） open up: ～边界 open the borders ‖ 改革～ reform and open up ‖ 沿海～城市 open coastal cities **B**〈形〉 optimistic: 性格～ have a cheerful disposition

【开放大学】kāifàng dàxué〈名〉 open university

【开封】kāifēng **A**〈动〉 break a seal **B** Kāifēng〈名〉 Kaifeng

【开缝】kāifèng〈名〉 crack: 杯子上开了一道缝儿。 There was a crack in the cup.

【开赴】kāifù〈动〉 head for: ～前线 march to the front

【开杆】kāigān〈动〉（指台球） open a game of snooker;（指高尔夫球） open a golf tournament

【开工】kāigōng〈动〉 **1**（指工厂） go into production: 工厂～了。 The factory has gone into operation. **2**（指工程） start construction: 破土～ break ground for construction ‖ 大桥工程已～。 Construction has already started on the bridge.

【开关】kāiguān〈名〉 **1**（电门） switch: 电灯～ light switch **2**（用于控制流量） button: 煤气～ gas-tap ‖ 油门～ oil button

【开棺验尸】kāiguān yànshī〈成〉 open the coffin and perform an autopsy on the corpse

【开馆】kāiguǎn〈动〉 open to the public: 图书馆八点～。 The library opens at eight o'clock.

【开罐器】kāiguànqì〈名〉 can-opener

【开光】kāiguāng〈动〉 consecrate: ～仪式 consecration ceremony

【开锅】kāiguō〈动〉〈口〉 **1**〈本〉 [of something cooking in a pot] boil: 水～了。 The water is boiling. **2**〈喻〉 run wild: 老师刚离开教室，原本肃静的教室里登时闹开了锅。 The discipline of the class collapsed immediately after the teacher left the classroom.

【开国】kāiguó〈动〉 found a state: ～大典 inauguration ‖ ～元勋 founding father

【开航】kāiháng〈动〉 **1**（指空运） become open for navigation: 新航线～了。 A new air route has opened. **2**（指水运） be open and navigable: 大河开冻后又重新～了。 The river is clear again since the thaw. **3**（起航） set sail: 乘客上船之后，船就～了。 Once the passengers were on board, the boat set sail.

【开合桥】kāihéqiáo〈名〉 folding bridge

【开河】kāihé〈动〉 **1**（解冻） thaw: 这条河刚～。 The river has just thawed. **2**（指挖掘） dig a canal

【开后门】kāi hòumén〈惯〉〈喻〉 give sb. an unfair secret advantage

【开户】kāihù〈动〉 open an account: ～银行 bank of deposit

【开户费】kāihùfèi〈名〉 activation fee: 不收～ no activation fee

【开花】kāihuā〈动〉 **1**（指植物） blossom: ～结果 bloom and bear fruit ▸芝麻～节节高 **2**（崩裂） burst: 他一拳打得刺客脑袋～。 He brained the assassin with one blow. **3**（形容高兴） bloom: 心里乐开了花 burst with joy **4**（指经验） spread over;（指事业） spring up: 先进技术遍地～。 Advanced technologies have spread far and wide.

【开花弹】kāihuādàn〈名〉［军事］ expanding bullet

【开花馒头】kāihuā mántou〈名〉 split-top steamed bun

【开化】kāihuà **A**〈动〉 **1**（进入文明时期） become civilized: 中国是世界上～最早的文明古国之一。 China is one of the oldest civilizations in the world. **2**（解冻） thaw: 冻土～了。 The frozen earth is thawing. **B**〈形〉 open-minded: 脑子不～ closed mentality

【开怀】kāihuái〈形〉〈书〉 light-hearted: ～大笑 laugh heartily ‖ ～畅饮 drink to one's heart's content

【开荒】kāihuāng〈动〉 open up cultivate wasteland: ～种地 cultivate wasteland for farming

【开会】kāihuì〈动〉 have a meeting: 宣布～ call a meeting

【开荤】kānhūn〈动〉 break a vegetarian diet

【开火】kāihuǒ〈动〉 **1**（指枪炮） open fire on: 两支舰队相互猛烈～。 The two fleets pounded away at each other. **2**〈喻〉（抨击） attack: 会上几个人同时向他～。 Several people attacked him at the meeting.

【开伙】kāihuǒ〈动〉 **1**（办伙食） run a cafeteria **2**（供应伙食） provide food

【开机】kāijī〈动〉 **1**（指机器） start: ～印刷 start printing **2**（指拍摄） start shooting: 该片最近在北京～。 The film recently started shooting in Beijing.

【开价】kāijià〈动〉 make a quote: 开天价 ask for an absurd price ‖ ～高/低 charge a high/low price

【开架】kāijià〈动〉 provide direct access to shelves: ～借阅 open the shelves to readers ‖ ～销售 open-shelf selling

【开间】kāijiān **A**〈量〉 standard width of a room in an old-style house: 单/双～ one-room house about 10/20 *chi* wide **B**〈名〉 **1**（宽度） width of a room: 这房子～很大。 The room is very wide. **2**［建筑］ bay

【开讲】kāijiǎng〈动〉 begin lecturing or telling a story

【开奖】kāijiǎng〈动〉 draw a lottery and announce the winner: 摇号～ roll out lottery numbers

【开胶】kāijiāo〈动〉 come unstuck: 鞋～了。 These shoes have come unstuck.

【开解】kāijiě〈动〉 console

【开戒】kāijiè〈动〉 **1**（指生活禁忌） break an abstinence **2**（指宗教戒律） be freed from religious restrictions

k

【开金】kāijīn〈名〉gold alloy
【开襟】kāijīn〈动〉button down: ～羊毛衫 cardigan
【开禁】kāijìn〈动〉lift a ban
【开镜】kāijìng〈动〉start shooting a film: 该片于2002年12月～。The film started shooting in December, 2002.
【开局】kāijú **A**〈名〉opening: 打好～ make a good start in a match **B**〈动〉make a start: 工业生产～很好。Industrial production is off to a very good start.
【开具】kāijù〈动〉〈书〉write out: ～证明 issue a certificate
【开卷】kāijuàn **A**〈动〉〈书〉open a book: ▸～有益 **B**〈名〉open-book exam: ～考试 open-book examination
【开卷有益】kāijuàn-yǒuyì〈成〉reading enriches the mind
【开掘】kāijué〈动〉dig: ～矿井 open up a mine ‖ ～水井/运河 dig a well/canal ‖ 从墓中～出很多珍贵的文物 dig up many precious cultural and historical artefacts from ancient mausoleums
【开科】kāikē〈动〉〈书〉hold an imperial examination: ～取士 select officials through imperial examinations
【开课】kāikè〈动〉**1**（开始上课）begin classes: 学校什么时候～? When is school starting? **2**（开设课程）teach a course: 给研究生～ teach a course for graduate students
【开垦】kāikěn〈动〉bring under cultivation: ～荒地 reclaim wasteland
【开口】kāikǒu〈动〉**1**（指说话）open one's mouth: ～说话 open one's mouth to talk **2** = 开刃儿 kāirènr
【开口闭口】kāikǒu-bìkǒu〈俗〉whenever one speaks
【开口饭】kāikǒufàn〈名〉〈旧〉professional street performance
【开口子】kāi kǒuzi〈惯〉**1**（指堤岸）burst **2**〈喻〉（指破例）break a rule: 你这个口子我不能开。I can't make an exception in your case.
【开快车】kāi kuàichē〈惯〉**1**（指开车）drive at a high speed **2**〈喻〉（指工作学习）hurry through one's work
【开矿】kāikuàng〈动〉open up a mine
【开阔】kāikuò **A**〈形〉**1**（指空间或范围）wide: 视野～ wide vision ‖ 河面在入海处变得～起来。The river grows broader where it enters the sea. **2**（指思想或心胸）broad-minded: 胸襟～ be broad-minded ‖ 思路～ have a broad outlook **B**〈动〉broaden: ～眼界 expand one's outlook
【开阔地】kāikuòdì〈名〉open terrain: 走出森林，我们来到一片～。We came out of the forest into open terrain.
【开朗】kāilǎng〈形〉**1**（指天气）open and clear: 阴了几天之后，天突然～起来。It suddenly cleared up after several days of overcast weather. ▸豁然～ **2**（指人）optimistic: 她性格～。She has a sunny personality.
【开犁】kāilí〈动〉start the year's ploughing
【开立】kāilì〈动〉open: ～账户 open an account
【开例】kāilì〈动〉set a precedent: 如果从他这里～，以后的事情就不好办了。If we make an exception for him, it will make things difficult for us in the future.
【开镰】kāilián〈动〉start harvesting with sickles
【开脸】kāiliǎn〈动〉〈旧〉[of a girl on the eve of marriage] remove the fine hairs on the face and neck and tidy up the hairline at the temples
【开列】kāiliè〈动〉draw up a list: ～参考书目 make a list of reference books ‖ ～名单 draw up a list of names
【开裂】kāiliè〈动〉crack: 木板～了。The board was cracked. ‖ 碗底～了。The bowl was cracked across the bottom.
【开领】kāilǐng〈形〉open-necked: ～短袖衬衫 polo shirt ‖ ～衫 open-necked shirt
【开溜】kāiliū〈动〉slink off: 中途～ sneak off halfway
【开颅术】kāilúshù〈名〉[医学] craniotomy
【开路】kāilù〈动〉**1**（开辟道路）blaze a trail: 逢山～，遇水搭桥 cut paths through mountains and build bridges across rivers **2**（在前引路）lead the way: ～先锋 trailblazer ‖ 仪仗队在前头～。The guard of honour led the way.
【开绿灯】kāi lùdēng〈惯〉〈喻〉give the green light: 不能给劣质产品～。You can't give the green light to inferior products.
【开罗】Kāiluó〈名〉Cairo
【开锣】kāiluó〈动〉[of traditional Chinese opera] start: 戏马上就要～了。The performance is about to start.
【开曼群岛】Kāimànqúndǎo〈名〉Cayman Islands
【开门】kāimén〈动〉**1**（敞开门）open the door **2**〈喻〉（指公开）do sth. in an open-door fashion: ～办学 run a school in an open-door fashion **3**（指营业）open for business: 上午9点起～营业。The store is open from 9 am to 6 pm.
【开门红】kāiménhóng〈惯〉get off to a good start: "十五"计划头一年就来了个～。The first year of the Tenth Five-Year Plan has got off to a good start.
【开门见山】kāimén-jiànshān〈成〉get straight to the point: 他～地说明了来意。He made clear what he had come for from the very start.
【开门七件事】kāimén qījiànshì〈俗〉seven necessities of life [ie firewood, rice, cooking oil, salt, soy sauce, vinegar, and tea]
【开门揖盗】kāimén-yīdào〈成〉invite trouble by letting in evil-doers
【开蒙】kāiméng〈动〉**1**〈旧〉（指孩子）start schooling: 他五岁～，七岁就会写诗。He started schooling at five and began to write poems at seven. **2**〈书〉（指老师）teach a beginner: 王老师是我的～老师。Mr Wang was my first teacher.
【开明】kāimíng〈形〉open-minded: 思想～ be open-minded ‖ ～人士 enlightened person
【开幕】kāimù〈动〉**1**（打开幕布）raise the curtain: ～时间 curtain time **2**（开始）open: 主席宣布大会～。The chairman declared the conference open.
【开幕词】kāimùcí〈名〉opening address: 致～ deliver an opening address
【开幕典礼】kāimù diǎnlǐ〈名〉opening ceremony
【开幕式】kāimùshì〈名〉opening ceremony: 举行～ hold an opening ceremony
【开拍】kāipāi〈动〉**1**（指拍摄）start filming: ～! Action! **2**（指竞拍）start: ～价格 upset price
【开盘】kāipán〈动〉[金融] give the opening quotation: ～价 opening price ‖ 一～便一路起高。As soon as the market opened the price went up.
【开炮】kāipào〈动〉**1**（指炮火）open fire: 向敌人～ open fire on the enemy **2**〈喻〉（指批评）fire criticism (at)
【开辟】kāipì〈动〉**1**（开通）open up: ～新航线 open a new route ‖ ～新路 open a new road **2**（创建）set up: ～财源 tap financial sources ‖ ～革命根据地 set up a revolutionary base ‖ ～新市场 open up new markets ‖ ～新天地 break new ground ‖ ～专栏 launch a special column
【开篇】kāipiān〈名〉**1**[曲艺] introductory song: 弹词～ introductory song of *tanci* opera **2**（指文章）opening: 文章～很精彩。The essay has got a brilliant opening.
【开瓢儿】kāipiáor〈动〉〈方〉make a cut in sb.'s head
【开票】kāipiào〈动〉**1**（指发票）make out an invoice: ～处 receipt counter ‖ 请给我开个票。Please write out an invoice for me. **2**（指选票）open the ballot box and count the ballots: ～监督人 count witness
【开枰】kāipíng〈动〉open a 'go' tournament: 围棋名人战今日～。The 'go' contest featuring all the top players kicked off today.
【开屏】kāipíng〈动〉fan a tail: 孔雀～了。The peacock is fanning its tail.
【开瓶费】kāipíngfèi〈名〉corkage: 收取～ charge corkage
【开瓶器】kāipíngqì〈名〉bottle opener
【开普敦】Kāipǔdūn〈名〉Cape Town
【开启】kāiqǐ〈动〉**1**（打开）open: ～闸门 open the watergate **2**（开创）inaugurate: ～一代新风 start an era of new trends
【开枪】kāiqiāng〈动〉fire a gun
【开腔】kāiqiāng〈动〉open one's mouth: 会上他一直没有～。He kept silent throughout the meeting.
【开窍】kāiqiào〈动〉**1**（得到启发）begin to understand: 老师的一番话使我开了窍。The teacher's words enlightened me. **2**（开始明事理）begin to know things: 这孩子～早。This child started to know things at a very early age.
【开球】kāiqiú〈动〉[体育]（指足球）kick off;（指排球、网球等）serve
【开刃儿】kāirènr〈动〉sharpen before first use
【开赛】kāisài〈动〉begin a game
【开山】kāishān〈动〉**1**（指开凿）cut into a mountain: ～劈岭 open up a mountain ‖ ～修路 build a road by blasting mountains **2**（指开发利用）develop a closed mountain for use **3**[佛教] build the first temple on a famous mountain
【开山祖师】kāishān-zǔshī〈成〉forefather
【开衫】kāishān〈名〉cardigan
【开墒】kāishāng = 开犁 kāilí
【开设】kāishè〈动〉**1**（开办）open: ～办事处 open an office ‖ ～店铺/诊所 set up a store/clinic **2**（设立）establish: ～选修课/专业课 establish a selective/specialized course
【开审】kāishěn〈动〉[法律] hold a court hearing: ～日期 hearing time ‖ ～通知 notice of trial
【开始】kāishǐ **A**〈动〉**1**（从头起）begin: ～调查 start an investigation (into) ‖ ～工作 start work ‖ 从头～ start from the very beginning ‖ 新的一年～了。A new year has begun. **2**（着手做）set about doing sth.: ～一项新的工作 set about a new task **B**〈名〉beginning: 良好的～ a good start
【开市】kāishì〈动〉**1**（指营业）reopen after a cessation of business **2**（指成交）make the first transaction of the day: ～行情 opening quotation
【开释】kāishì〈动〉release: 无罪～ be released on account of one's innocence
【开涮】kāishuàn〈动〉〈方〉〈喻〉tease: 他老拿我～。He always made fun of me.

【开水】kāishuǐ〈名〉 boiling water
【开司米】kāisīmǐ〈名〉［纺织］ cashmere: ～羊毛衫 cashmere sweater
【开台】kāitái〈动〉 begin a theatrical performance: 戏已～。 The performance has started.
【开台锣鼓】kāitái luógǔ〈名〉 flourish of gongs and drums introducing a theatrical performance
【开膛】kāitáng〈动〉 disembowel: ～剖肚 cut open the stomach
【开天窗】kāi tiānchuāng〈动〉〈喻〉 leave a blank space in a newspaper to indicate that sth. has been censored
【开天辟地】kāitiān-pìdì〈成〉 1〈本〉the dawn of heaven 2〈喻〉 heroic: 人类历史上～的壮举 most heroic event in human history
【开庭】kāitíng〈动〉 call a court to order: ～审理 hold a hearing
【开通】kāitōng〈动〉 be open to traffic: ～热线 establish a hotline ‖ 该铁路已全线～。 The railway is already fully opened to traffic.
【开通】kāitong〈形〉 open-minded: 思想～ be open-minded ‖ 思想～的人 man with an open mind
【开头】kāitóu A〈动〉 begin: 以大写字母～ begin with a capital letter ‖ 这本书以一段引言～。 The book opens with a quotation. B〈名〉 beginning: 万事～难。 Everything's hard at the start.
【开脱】kāituō〈动〉 exonerate: 为某人～责任 exonerate sb. from responsibility ‖ 别老替他～。 Don't always make excuses for him.
【开拓】kāituò A〈动〉 open up: ～市场 open up a market ‖ ～新领域 develop new frontiers ‖ ～者 pioneer B〈名〉［矿业］ opening: ～进尺 tunnelling footage
【开拓进取】kāituòjìnqǔ〈动〉 break new paths: 竞争意识和～精神 competitive awareness and pioneering spirit
【开外】kāiwài〈名〉over: 他只有三十岁，但看起来却有四十～了。 He is only thirty but he looks over forty. ‖ 三百米～是一所学校。There's a school just over 300 metres away.
【开玩笑】kāi wánxiào〈动〉 joke: 你可真会～! You can really tell a good joke! ‖ 我可不是～。 I'm serious.
【开胃】kāiwèi〈动〉 stimulate the appetite: ～酒 aperitif ‖ ～菜 starter〈英〉, appetizer〈美〉 ‖ 这药吃了能～。 This medicine will improve your appetite.
【开先例】kāi xiānlì〈动〉 set a precedent: 你这样做可是开了个不好的先例。 You have set a bad example by doing this.
【开销】kāixiāo A〈动〉 pay expenses: 你带的钱够～吗? Have you brought enough money to cover the expenses? B〈名〉 expense: 削减不必要的～ cut down on unnecessary expenses
【开小差】kāi xiǎochāi〈惯〉 1（指士兵） desert: 有些士兵在战争中～。 Some soldiers deserted in the combat. 2〈喻〉（精力分散） be absent-minded: 刚上课他就开始～了。 His mind wandered soon after the class began.
【开小会】kāi xiǎohuì〈动〉 chatter in a whisper (at a meeting)
【开小灶】kāi xiǎozào〈动〉 1〈本〉 cook better food for sb. (as a privilege) 2〈喻〉 bestow special favours on sb.: 教练给他～。 The coach gave him special training.
【开心】kāixīn A〈形〉 happy: 玩得很～ have a great time ‖ ～的日子 happy days B〈动〉 make fun of: ▸寻～
【开心果】kāixīnguǒ〈名〉 1〈本〉 pistachio 2〈喻〉 someone who makes other people laugh
【开行】kāixíng〈动〉 set off
【开学】kāixué〈动〉（指学校）open;（指学期） begin: 学校什么时候～? When does school start?
【开颜】kāiyán〈动〉 smile: 她～一笑。 A happy smile spread across her face.
【开眼】kāiyǎn〈动〉 broaden sb.'s mind: 这场演出真叫人～。 The performance is a real eye-opener.
【开演】kāiyǎn〈动〉 [of a play, film, etc.] begin: 戏八点～。 The opera starts at 8:00.
【开洋荤】kāi yánghūn〈惯〉〈喻〉 experience sth. new: 他想出国转转，开开洋荤。 He wants to go abroad for some new experiences.
【开业】kāiyè〈动〉 1（指商店等） open for business: 重新～ resume business ‖ 这家医院已经～了。 The hospital is now accepting patients. 2（指律师、医生等） open a private practice
【开业律师】kāiyè lǜshī〈名〉 legal practitioner
【开业医师】kāiyè yīshī〈名〉 private practitioner
【开夜车】kāi yèchē〈惯〉〈喻〉 burn the midnight oil: 考前他开了几天夜车。 He worked late into the night for a few days before the examination.
【开音节】kāiyīnjié〈名〉［语言］ open syllable
【开印】kāiyìn〈动〉 go to press: 报纸半夜～。 The newspaper goes to press at midnight.
【开映】kāiyìng〈动〉 begin screening: 电影马上～。 The film will begin in a minute.
【开元】Kāiyuán〈名〉 Kaiyuan [title of the reign of Tang Dynasty emperor Li Longji (李隆基)]
【开元音】kāiyuányīn〈名〉［语言］ open vowel
【开园】kāiyuán〈动〉 start picking fruit at an orchard or melon field
【开源节流】kāiyuán-jiéliú〈成〉 increase income and reduce expenditure
【开云见日】kāiyún-jiànrì〈成〉〈喻〉dispel misunderstanding
【开凿】kāizáo〈动〉 cut: ～隧道 cut a tunnel ‖ ～运河 dig a canal
【开斋】kāizhāi〈动〉 1（开荤） resume a meat diet 2［伊斯兰教］ come to the end of Ramadan
【开斋节】Kāizhāijié〈名〉［伊斯兰教］ Eid ul-Fitr
【开展】kāizhǎn A〈动〉1（从事）launch: ～多种经营 promote a diversified economy ‖ ～国际交流 develop international exchanges ‖ ～体育活动 develop an athletics programme 2（指展览） open: 画展在美术馆～。 A painting exhibition is opening at the art gallery. B〈形〉 open-minded: 思想～ be open-minded ‖ 政治上不～ be behind in political understanding
【开战】kāizhàn〈动〉 1（指战争） wage war on/upon/against: 向敌人～ wage war on the enemy 2〈喻〉（指斗争） battle: 向腐败现象～ battle corruption
【开绽】kāizhàn〈动〉 come unsewn: 鞋跟～了。 The shoe has split at the heel.
【开张】kāizhāng〈动〉 1（开始营业） open for business: 择吉日～ choose an auspicious day to open a business ‖ 这家新店是昨天～的。 The new shop opened yesterday. 2（指成交） conduct the first transaction of the working day: 今天还没～。 We haven't had any business yet today. 3（开始） begin: ▸重打锣鼓另～
【开仗】kāizhàng〈动〉 make war
【开征】kāizhēng〈动〉 start to collect taxes: ～个人所得税 start collecting individual income taxes
【开支】kāizhī A〈动〉 1（花费） pay: 这个月我～了800元。 I spent 800 *yuan* this month. ‖ 这笔钱不够～。 This will not cover the costs. 2〈方〉（发工资） pay wages: 每月十二号～。 We get paid on the 12th of every month. B〈名〉 expenses: 节省～ reduce spending ‖ 额外～ additional outlay ‖ 国防～ national defence spending
【开宗明义】kāizōng-míngyì〈成〉[in speech or writing] make one's purpose clear right at the outset
【开足马力】kāizú-mǎlì〈成〉 go full steam ahead
【开钻】kāizuàn〈动〉［石油］ spud
【开罪】kāizuì〈动〉 offend: ～不起 cannot afford to offend

揩 kāi
〈动〉 wipe: ～干净 wipe clean ‖ 用抹布～桌子 wipe a cloth over a table
【揩拭】kāishì〈动〉 wipe: 把杯子～干净 wipe the glasses clean
【揩油】kāiyóu〈动〉〈喻〉 scrounge off sb.

锎（鐦） kāi
〈名〉［化学］ californium (Cf): ～化合物 californium compound

kǎi

剀（剴） kǎi
【剀切】kǎiqiè〈形〉〈书〉 1（完全属实） true and pertinent: ～详明 be true and clear in every detail 2（切实） earnest and sincere: ～教导 teach earnestly

凯（凱） kǎi
〈名〉 victory: ▸～旋, 奏～
【凯歌】kǎigē〈名〉 victory song: 高唱～而归 return to songs of triumph
【凯斯内斯郡】Kǎisīnèisījùn〈名〉Caithness
【凯旋】kǎixuán〈动〉 return in triumph: 欢迎体育健儿～ give the sportsmen a triumphant welcome
【凯旋门】Kǎixuánmén〈名〉 Arc de Triomphe

恺（愷） kǎi
〈形〉〈书〉 joyful: ▸～悌
【恺悌】kǎitì〈形〉〈书〉 amiable

铠（鎧） kǎi
〈名〉 armour
【铠甲】kǎijiǎ〈名〉 armour

慨 kǎi
A〈形〉 1（愤激） indignant: ▸愤～ 2（慷慨） generous: ▸～然, ～允, 慷～
B〈动〉 sigh with emotion: ▸～叹, 感～
【慨诺】kǎinuò〈动〉〈书〉 readily consent
【慨然】kǎirán〈副〉〈书〉1（感慨） with deep feeling: ～长叹 heave a sigh of regret 2（慷慨） generously: ～允诺 kindly promise
【慨叹】kǎitàn〈动〉〈书〉 sigh with regret
【慨允】kǎiyǔn〈动〉〈书〉 generously permit

楷 kǎi〈名〉1（模范） model: ▸~模 2（指字体） standard script: ▸~体, 大~ ▸jiē

【楷模】kǎimó〈名〉 model: 堪称~ can be regarded as a model for others

【楷书】kǎishū〈名〉［书法］ regular script, model script

【楷体】kǎitǐ〈名〉1 = 楷书 kǎishū 2（印刷体） block letter

锴（鍇） kǎi〈名〉〈古〉 quality iron

kài

忾（愾） kài〈动〉〈书〉hate: ▸同仇敌~

kān

刊 kān

A〈动〉1（印刷） print: ▸~行, 停~ 2（订正） correct: ▸~误

B〈名〉 publication: 党~ party journal ‖ 副~ supplement ▸半月~, 报~

【刊本】kānběn〈名〉〈书〉 block-printed edition: 宋~ Song Dynasty block-printed edition

【刊布】kānbù〈动〉〈书〉 publish

【刊登】kāndēng〈动〉 publish: ~广告 carry an advertisement ‖ 全文~ publish the full text

【刊号】kānhào〈名〉 issue number

【刊谬补缺】kānmiù-bǔquē〈成〉errata and supplements

【刊授】kānshòu〈动〉 give courses through periodicals: ~大学 school offering courses through periodicals

【刊头】kāntóu〈名〉 masthead: 设计~ design a masthead ‖ ~题字 masthead inscription

【刊物】kānwù〈名〉 publication: 定期/不定期~ regular/irregular publication ‖ 内部~ restricted publication ‖ 文学~ literary journal

【刊误】kānwù〈动〉 correct errors in printing: ~表 errata

【刊行】kānxíng〈动〉 print and publish

【刊载】kānzǎi〈动〉 publish: 分期~ publish in serialized form

看 kān〈动〉1（照看） look after: ~孩子 look after a child ‖ ~机器 tend a machine ‖ ~铺子 mind a store 2（监管） keep an eye on: ~犯人 guard prisoners ▸~管, ~护, ~押 ▸kàn

【看场】kānchǎng〈动〉guard the threshing floor (during the harvest season)

【看管】kānguǎn〈动〉1（照看） look after: ~好随身物品 take good care of one's belongings ‖ 他不在的时候, 母亲替他~房子。 His mother looks after the house while he's away. 2（监管） guard: ~犯人 guard prisoners ‖ 严加~ keep a close guard on

【看护】kānhù A〈动〉 look after: ~病人 attend to a patient B〈名〉〈旧〉 nurse

【看家】kānjiā A〈动〉 look after the house: 狗为主人~。 The dog watched over its master's house. ▸~狗 B〈形〉 outstanding: ~本领 special skill

【看家狗】kānjiāgǒu〈名〉〈旧〉〈贬〉 person who takes care of the affairs and property of a rich and powerful person

【看家戏】kānjiāxì〈名〉 most successful repertoire (of an actor or actress)

【看门】kānmén〈动〉 look after the house

【看门人】kānménrén〈名〉 doorkeeper

【看守】kānshǒu A〈名〉〈旧〉 warder〈英〉; guard〈美〉: 女~ female guard B〈动〉1（看护） guard: ~仓库 guard a storehouse ‖ ~门户 mind the door 2（监管） guard: ~犯人 guard prisoners ‖ ~俘虏 keep watch over a prisoner

【看守所】kānshǒusuǒ〈名〉 lock-up: ~所长 prison chief

【看守内阁】kānshǒu nèigé〈名〉 caretaker cabinet

【看守政府】kānshǒu zhèngfǔ〈名〉 caretaker government

【看押】kānyā〈动〉 detain: ~俘虏 detain prisoners ‖ 他被~了一夜。 He was detained for one night.

勘 kān〈动〉1（校订） proofread: ▸~误, 校~ 2（探测） investigate: ▸~测, 踏~

【勘测】kāncè〈动〉 survey: ~地形 survey the terrain ‖ 地质~ geological survey

【勘查】kānchá = 勘察 kānchá

【勘察】kānchá A〈动〉 reconnoitre: ~现场 inspect the scene of a crime or an accident ‖ 实地~ on-the-spot investigation B〈名〉［地质］ prospecting

【勘界】kānjiè〈名〉 boundary settlement

【勘探】kāntàn〈动〉 prospect: ~石油 prospect for oil ‖ 地质~ geological prospecting

【勘探队】kāntànduì〈名〉prospecting team

【勘误】kānwù〈动〉 correct errors in printing: ~表 list of errata

【勘验】kānyàn〈动〉 examine on the spot: ~尸体 perform an autopsy ‖ ~犯罪现场 investigate the scene of a crime

【勘正】kānzhèng〈动〉 proofread and correct: ~错误 proofread and correct errors

龛（龕） kān〈名〉 shrine: 石~ stone shrine ▸佛~, 神~

堪 kān〈动〉1（能） may: ~称佳作 may be rated as a fine piece of work ‖ ~当重任 be capable of shouldering important tasks 2（指承受） bear: ▸不~一击, 狼狈不~

【堪布】kānbù〈名〉 lama priest

【堪萨斯】Kānsàsī〈名〉 Kansas

戡 kān〈动〉 suppress

【戡乱】kānluàn〈动〉〈书〉 suppress a rebellion

kǎn

坎 kǎn〈名〉1〈书〉（坑） pit: ▸~坷, 心~ 2（指八卦） one of the Eight Trigrams, symbolizing 'water' 3（台阶状物） bank: 田~ raised ridge through fields ▸门~

【坎伯兰郡】Kǎnbólánjùn〈名〉 Cumberland

【坎布里亚郡】Kǎnbùlǐyàjùn〈名〉 Cumbria

【坎肩】kǎnjiān〈名〉 sleeveless jacket: 皮~ leather waistcoat

【坎坷】kǎnkě〈形〉1（指道路） bumpy: ~的道路 rough road 2〈喻〉（不得志） unsuccessful: ~的经历 chequered past ‖ 他的一生充满了~。 His life is full of frustrations.

【坎儿】kǎnr〈名〉〈口〉 critical juncture: 过了这个~你就顺了。 You just need to get through this important time and then everything will be fine.

【坎儿井】kǎnrjǐng〈名〉 karez [irrigating system of wells connected by underground channels common in Xinjiang]

【坎土曼】kǎntǔmàn〈名〉 Uygur mattock

【坎子】kǎnzi〈名〉〈方〉 mound

侃 kǎn

A〈形〉 upright and outspoken: ▸~~而谈

B〈动〉1〈口〉（聊） gossip: 我俩~了一宿。 The two of us chatted all night. ▸~大山, ~爷 2（调笑） tease: ▸调~

【侃大山】kǎn dàshān〈动〉〈方〉chat idly

【侃侃而谈】kǎnkǎn'értán〈成〉 talk with ease and fluency

【侃爷】kǎnyé〈名〉〈方〉 big talker

砍 kǎn〈动〉1（指用刀斧） chop: ~柴 chop firewood ‖ ~树 fell a tree ‖ ~头 be beheaded ▸~伐 2（削减） cut (down/off): 把预算~掉一半 chop a budget in half ‖ ~掉冗词 cut superfluous remarks out of an article ‖ 有两段被~掉了。 Two paragraphs were cut out. ‖ 我们有几项计划被~掉了。 Several of our plans got the axe. 3〈方〉（扔） throw sth. at: 拿石头~狗 throw a stone at a dog

【砍大山】kǎn dàshān = 侃大山 kǎn dàshān

【砍刀】kǎndāo〈名〉 chopper

【砍伐】kǎnfá〈动〉 cut down: ~林木 fell trees

【砍价】kǎnjià〈动〉 bargain: 他很会~。 He drives a hard bargain.

槛（檻） kǎn〈名〉 threshold: ▸门~ ▸jiàn

kàn

看 kàn

A〈动〉1（指用眼） look at: ~报/书 read a newspaper/book ‖ ~电视 watch TV ‖ ~电影 watch a movie ‖ ~照片 look at a photo ▸~热闹, 观~, 雾里~花 2（照顾） look after: ▸照~ 3（判断） consider: ~清形势 size up the situation ‖ 孤立地~问题 look at things in isolation ‖ 你对形势怎么~? How do you view the situation? 4（对待） look upon: 把人民的利益~得高于一切 put the interests of the people above all else ▸~待, 刮目相~ 5（诊疗）（指病人） see a doctor;（指医生） treat a patient: ~中医 go to hospital for traditional Chinese medical treatment ‖ ~牙 see the dentist ‖ 他一上午~了10个病人。 He treated 10 patients in the morning. 6（拜访） call on: ~朋友 call on a friend ‖ 谢谢你顺道来~我。 Thank you for looking in on me. ▸~望 7（取决） depend on: 能否夺魁就~这局比赛了。 Winning the championship hinges on this set. ‖ 这件事就全~你了。 It all depends on you. 8（当心） watch out: 过马路时~着点! Take care while crossing the street!

B〈助〉 [used after a reduplicated verb or a verb phrase] try and see: 等等~ wait and see ‖ 试试~ have a try ▸kān

【看扁】kànbiǎn〈动〉 underestimate: 别把他~了。Don't underestimate him.
【看病】kànbìng〈动〉 1▸(指医生) treat a patient: 李大夫~很仔细。Dr Li handles his patients with great care. 2▸(指病人) see a doctor: 带孩子~ take one's child to the doctor's
【看不惯】kànbuguàn〈动〉 cannot bear the sight of: 我~他这副奴才相。I can't bear his servile manners.
【看不过去】kànbuguòqù〈俗〉 cannot bear (to see) any more of: 我实在~了，便说了他一顿。I couldn't put up with it any more, so I gave him a scolding.
【看不起】kànbuqǐ〈动〉 look down upon: 自己~自己 despise oneself ‖ 她~别人。She holds others in contempt.
【看菜吃饭，量体裁衣】kàn cài chīfàn, liàng tǐ cáiyī〈俗〉〈喻〉 act according to specific conditions
【看茶】kànchá〈动〉〈旧〉 [said to a servant] serve tea
【看成】kànchéng〈动〉 regard as: 你把我~什么人了？What do you take me for? ‖ 他们把我~自己家里人。They treated me as one of their family.
【看承】kànchéng〈动〉〈书〉 look after
【看出】kànchū〈动〉 make out: ~苗头 smell a rat ‖ ~问题所在 see where the trouble is ‖ 看不出他还能写一手好字。I never expected that he could write such a beautiful hand.
【看穿】kànchuān〈动〉 see through: ~敌人的阴谋 see through the enemy's plot
【看待】kàndài〈动〉 treat: 同等~ treat equally ‖ 他把我当朋友~。He regards me as a friend.
【看淡】kàndàn〈动〉 1▸(指价格、市场等) show a slack trend: 近来股市行情~。The stock market has gone bearish recently. 2▸(指预见) foresee a slack trend
【看得过去】kàndeguòqù〈形〉 passable
【看得起】kàndeqǐ〈动〉 think highly of: 领导~他。The leadership had a very high opinion of him.
【看低】kàndī〈动〉 belittle
【看点】kàndiǎn〈名〉 highlight: 这场比赛的~出现在最后一节。The highlight of the match happened in the last quarter.
【看跌】kàndiē〈动〉 be inclined to fall: 股票行情~。Stock market quotations are expected to fall soon.
【看法】kànfa〈名〉 1▸(观点) view: 发表~ express one's point of view ‖ 改变~ change one's mind ‖ ~一致 take the same view 2▸(否定意见) critical view: 我对这种做法有~。I'm critical of such practice.
【看风色】kàn fēngsè〈动〉 see which way the wind blows
【看风使舵】kànfēng-shǐduò〈成〉〈贬〉 bend with the wind
【看顾】kàngù〈动〉 look after: ~病人 take care of the sick ‖ 请帮助~我母亲。Please look after my mother.
【看官】kànguān〈名〉〈旧〉 [used in old novels to address the readers and in storytelling to address the audience] dear readers
【看惯】kànguàn〈动〉 be accustomed to the sight of: 这种事他~了。He's got used to such things.
【看好】kànhǎo〈动〉 1▸(指观点) have good prospects: 这次比赛大家普遍~主队。Most people expect that the home team will win in this match. 2▸(指势头) look good: 经济前景~。The economic outlook is good.
【看见】kànjian〈动〉 see: 他四处张望，但什么也没~。He looked around but saw nothing. ‖ 有人~他离开房间。He was seen leaving the room.
【看开】kànkāi〈动〉 be philosophical: 看不开 take sth. too much to heart ‖ 看得开 get through sth. with composure ‖ ~些，不要过分悲伤。Just try to accept it. Don't take it too hard.
【看空】kànkōng〈动〉［金融］ be in bearish mood: 股民大多~短期市场。Most of the investors are bearish in short-term markets.
【看来】kànlái〈动〉〈口〉 it seems: ~他全都知道了。It seems that he has learned everything. ‖ ~抢劫案是内部人干的。The robbery appears to have been an inside job.
【看破】kànpò〈动〉 see through: 我~了他那套把戏。I've seen through his trick.
【看破红尘】kànpò-hóngchén〈成〉 be disillusioned with the world
【看齐】kànqí〈动〉 1▸(指列队) dress: 向左~! Dress left! 2▸(学习) emulate: 向先进工作者~ follow the example of leading workers
【看起来】kànqilai = 看来 kànlái
【看俏】kànqiào〈动〉 be in demand: 宽屏液晶彩电~。Wide screen LCD TVs are in great demand.
【看轻】kànqīng〈动〉 belittle: 不要~管理工作。Don't underestimate the importance of management.
【看清】kànqīng〈动〉 see clearly: ~形势 judge the situation correctly ‖ ~真相 see sth. in its true colours
【看热闹】kàn rènao〈动〉 enjoy the excitement
【看人下菜碟儿】kànrén-xiàcàidiér〈俗〉〈贬〉〈喻〉 treat a person according to his social standing
【看上】kànshang〈动〉 take a fancy to: 她~了一个帅小伙子。She's taken a fancy to a handsome young man. ‖ 她这个人谁都看不上。She turns her nose up at everyone.
【看死】kànsǐ〈动〉 form an unchangeable opinion of: 别把他~了。Don't be so stubborn about him.
【看台】kàntái〈名〉 stand: 露天~ bleachers ‖ ~突然坍塌。The stand gave way all of a sudden.
【看透】kàntòu〈动〉 see through: 敌人的这一招我没~。I hadn't grasped that the enemy would make this move. ‖ 我把一切世事都~了。I've seen through the world.
【看头】kàntou〈名〉〈方〉 that which is worth looking at: 这本书有~。This book is worth reading. ‖ 这部电影没有什么~。This film isn't worth seeing.
【看图识字】kàntú shízì〈动〉 learn to read with the aid of pictures
【看望】kànwang〈动〉 call on: ~老同学 call on an old classmate ‖ ~病人 visit a patient
【看相】kànxiàng〈动〉 practise physiognomy
【看笑话】kàn xiàohua〈动〉 amuse oneself by watching other people make fools of themselves: 我们不能让别人~。We mustn't let others make laughing stocks of us.
【看眼色】kàn yǎnsè〈动〉 take one's cue (from sb.): ~行事 act upon a hint
【看样子】kàn yàngzi〈动〉〈口〉 it seems: ~要下雨了。It looks as if it's going to rain.
【看涨】kànzhǎng〈动〉 [of market prices] be inclined to rise: 行情~。The market looks strong. ‖ 价格~。The price is on the rise.
【看着办】kànzhebàn〈动〉 do as one sees fit: 这件事你~吧。Do it the way you see fit.
【看中】kànzhòng〈动〉 take a fancy to: 她~了一件黑色的皮衣。She had her eye on a black fur coat.
【看重】kànzhòng〈动〉 set store by: ~人才/知识 value talent/knowledge ‖ 领导很~她。The leadership thinks highly of her.
【看座】kànzuò〈动〉〈旧〉 [said to a servant, waiter, etc.] find a seat for the guest
【看做】kànzuò〈动〉 regard as: 不要把忍让~软弱可欺。Don't take tolerance for weakness. ‖ 我把她~最好的朋友。I regard her as one of my best friends.

阚（闞） Kàn〈名〉 Kan [surname]

瞰 kàn〈动〉 1▸(从高处看) overlook: ▸俯~, 鸟~ 2▸〈书〉(窥视) spy

kāng

康 kāng〈形〉 1▸(安乐) peaceful and happy: ▸~乐 2▸(富裕) bountiful: ▸小~ 3▸(健康) healthy: ▸~复, ~泰, 健~ 4▸(宽阔) broad: ▸~庄大道

【康拜因】kāngbàiyīn〈名〉〈旧〉 combine harvester
【康采恩】kāngcǎi'ēn〈名〉［经济］ conglomerate
【康复】kāngfù〈动〉 recover: 病体~ recover from illness ‖ 祝你早日~。I wish you a speedy recovery.
【康复期】kāngfùqī〈名〉 convalescence
【康健】kāngjiàn〈书〉= 健康 jiànkāng
【康乐】kānglè〈形〉〈书〉 happy and peaceful
【康乐球】kānglèqiú〈名〉［体育］ carom
【康乃馨】kāngnǎixīn〈名〉［植物］ carnation
【康涅狄格】Kāngnièdígé〈名〉 Connecticut
【康宁】kāngníng〈形〉〈书〉 healthy and free from worry
【康泰】kāngtài〈形〉〈书〉 healthy and well: 全家~ all of the family are healthy and well ‖ 身体~ be in good health
【康沃尔郡】Kāngwò'ěrjùn〈名〉 Cornwall
【康庄大道】kāngzhuāng-dàdào〈成〉 1▸〈本〉 broad road 2▸〈喻〉(指前途) bright prospect

慷 kāng

【慷慨】kāngkǎi〈形〉 1▸(不吝啬) generous: ~助人 help sb. in a magnanimous way ‖ 他~捐款。He made a generous donation. ▸~解囊 2▸(充满正气) fervent: ~就义 die a martyr's death ▸~激昂
【慷慨悲歌】kāngkǎi-bēigē〈成〉 sing with passionate sorrow
【慷慨陈词】kāngkǎi-chéncí〈成〉 speak with fervour: 这位将领~。The general spoke with righteous indignation.
【慷慨激昂】kāngkǎi-jī'áng〈成〉 impassioned: ~的演说 impassioned speech
【慷慨解囊】kāngkǎi-jiěnáng〈成〉 be generous with one's money: 为了支援灾区，当地居民纷纷~。The local residents donated generously to help the disaster-stricken area.

【慷他人之慨】kāng tārén zhī kǎi〈成〉〈贬〉 be generous with other people's money or possessions

糠 kāng
A〈名〉 chaff: 米～ rice bran ▸～秕, 糟～
B〈形〉 [usu of a radish] spongy: 这萝卜～了。 This radish has gone spongy.
【糠秕】kāngbǐ = 秕糠 bǐkāng
【糠里榨油】kānglǐzhàyóu〈俗〉〈喻〉 squeeze water out of stone
【糠油】kāngyóu〈名〉 oil extracted from rice husks
【糠疹】kāngzhěn ▸**p. 50**〈名〉［医学］ pityriasis

鱇（鱇） kāng ▸鮟鱇 ānkāng

káng

扛 káng〈动〉 shoulder: ～枪 shoulder a gun ‖ ～行李 carry baggage ‖ ～起重任 shoulder heavy responsibilities ▸gāng
【扛长工】káng chánggōng〈动〉〈旧〉 work as a farm labourer on a yearly basis
【扛长活】káng chánghuó = 扛长工 káng chánggōng
【扛大个儿】káng dàgèr〈动〉〈方〉 work as a porter
【扛活】kánghuó〈动〉〈旧〉 work as a farm labourer: 给地主～ work as a farm labourer for a landlord

kàng

亢 kàng
A〈形〉 **1**（高） high: ▸高～ **2**（傲慢） haughty: ▸不卑不～ **3**〈书〉（过度） excessive: ▸～奋, ～进
B〈名〉 one of the 28 constellations in ancient Chinese astronomy
【亢奋】kàngfèn〈形〉 extremely excited: 精神～ run an adrenalin high
【亢旱】kànghàn〈形〉〈书〉 severe drought: ～之年 year of severe drought
【亢进】kàngjìn〈名〉［医学］ hyperfunction: 甲状腺机能～ hyperthyroidism
【亢直】kàngzhí〈形〉〈书〉 upright and unyielding

伉 kàng〈书〉
A〈动〉 [of a married couple] be well-matched: ▸～俪
B〈形〉 strong: ～健 be strong and healthy
【伉俪】kànglì〈名〉〈书〉 married couple: 结为～ become man and wife
【伉俪情深】kànglì-qíngshēn〈成〉 married couple very much in love

抗 kàng〈动〉 **1**（抵御） resist: 喝杯酒～～风寒。 Have a drink to warm you up. ▸～癌, ～旱, 抵～ **2**（不接受） defy: ▸～命, ～议, 违～ **3**（对等） contend with: ▸～衡, 对～, 分庭～礼
【抗癌】kàng'ái〈动〉 be anti-cancerous: ～药 anticarcinogen
【抗暴】kàngbào〈动〉 fight against violent repression: ～斗争 struggle against violent repression
【抗爆】kàngbào〈形〉［化学］ anti-detonation
【抗辩】kàngbiàn **A**〈动〉 contradict: 当场～ contradict there and then **B**〈名〉［法律］ plea: 提出～ raise a plea
【抗病】kàngbìng〈动〉 be disease-resistant
【抗病毒】kàngbìngdú〈动〉 be antiviral
【抗虫害】kàngchónghài〈动〉［农业］ be pest-resistant
【抗跌】kàngdiē〈动〉［金融］ be resilient: 基金的～能力很強。 The fund has a lot of resilience.
【抗跌性】kàngdiēxìng〈名〉［金融］ ability to maintain a stable price: 该基金具有较强的～。 This fund should be quite capable of maintaining a steady price.
【抗毒素】kàngdúsù〈名〉［生物］ antitoxin: ～疗法 antitoxin therapy
【抗辐射】kàngfúshè〈动〉 be radio-resistant
【抗干扰】kànggānrǎo〈动〉 be anti-interference
【抗感染药】kànggǎnrǎnyào〈名〉［药学］ anti-infective
【抗寒】kànghán〈动〉 be cold-resistant
【抗旱】kànghàn〈动〉 **1**（指措施） combat drought: 参加～斗争 take part in a battle against drought **2**（指特性） be drought resistant: ～作物 drought-resistant crop
【抗衡】kànghéng〈动〉 contend with: 无人能与他～。 There is no one can match him.
【抗洪】kànghóng〈动〉 fight a flood: ～抢险 combat a flood and rush to deal with an emergency
【抗洪救灾】kànghóng jiùzāi〈动〉 fight floods and provide disaster relief: 奔赴～第一线 rush to help with flood relief
【抗坏血酸】kànghuàixuèsuān〈名〉 ascorbic acid
【抗婚】kànghūn〈动〉 resist a forced marriage
【抗击】kàngjī〈动〉 resist: ～侵略 resist aggressors
【抗静电】kàngjìngdiàn〈动〉 be anti-static: ～处理 anti-static treatment
【抗拒】kàngjù〈动〉 defy: ～命令 defy orders ‖ 无法～的诱惑 irresistible temptation ‖ 历史的潮流不可～。 The tide of history is irresistible.
【抗捐】kàngjuān〈动〉〈旧〉 refuse to pay levies and taxes
【抗菌素】kàngjūnsù = 抗生素 kàngshēngsù
【抗老剂】kànglǎojì〈名〉［化学］ anti-ager
【抗涝】kànglào〈动〉 prevent waterlogging
【抗粮】kàngliáng〈动〉〈旧〉 resist the grain levy
【抗美援朝战争】 Kàng-Měi Yuán-Cháo Zhànzhēng〈名〉 War to Resist US Aggression and Aid Korea [1950-1953]
【抗命】kàngmìng〈动〉〈书〉 defy an order: ～不遵 refuse to follow an order
【抗日】Kàng-Rì〈动〉 resist Japanese aggression: ～救国 resist Japanese aggression and save the nation
【抗日战争】Kàng-Rì Zhànzhēng〈名〉 War of Resistance Against Japan [1937-1945]
【抗生素】kàngshēngsù〈名〉［药学］ antibiotic: 服用～ be on antibiotics
【抗水性】kàngshuǐxìng〈名〉 water-resistance
【抗税】kàngshuì〈动〉 refuse to pay taxes
【抗诉】kàngsù〈动〉［法律］ protest
【抗体】kàngtǐ〈名〉［医学］ antibody: 艾滋病～ AIDS antibodies
【抗性】kàngxìng〈名〉 resistance
【抗炎】kàngyán〈动〉 be anti-inflammatory: 该药具有～功效。 This medicine has an anti-inflammatory effect.
【抗药性】kàngyàoxìng〈名〉［药学］ drug resistance: 产生～ develop resistance to a drug
【抗议】kàngyì〈动〉 protest: 提出～ lodge a protest ‖ 强烈～ vigorous protest
【抗议书】kàngyìshū〈名〉 protest letter
【抗御】kàngyù〈动〉 resist and guard against: ～外侮 resist foreign aggression
【抗原】kàngyuán〈名〉［医学］ antigen: ～抗体反应 antigen-antibody reaction
【抗灾】kàngzāi〈动〉 combat natural calamities
【抗战】kàngzhàn **A**〈动〉〈书〉 resist: 与恶势力～ oppose evil forces **B**〈简称〉= 抗日战争
【抗震】kàngzhèn〈动〉 **1**（指性能） be quake-proof: ～能力 shock resistance ‖ ～性能 earthquake-resistant behaviour **2**（指措施） take precautions against an earthquake: ～救灾 engage in earthquake relief work
【抗争】kàngzhēng〈动〉 take a stand against: 以理～ fight sb. with argument and reasoning ‖ 与命运～ resist one's fate

炕 kàng
A〈名〉 *kang* [heatable brick or adobe bed, common in North China]: 热～ hot *kang* ▸～头
B〈动〉〈方〉 dry by the heat of a fire: ～红薯 bake sweet potatoes ‖ 把湿衣服～干 dry wet clothes

> **炕**
>
> A platform with an adobe or brick base containing an interior cavity that can be heated up using the fire from a cooking stove. A *kang* normally consists of three connected parts: the stove, the platform itself, and the flue. The stove is used for cooking, and the platform, kept warm by the heat from the stove, is used for sitting or sleeping on. The saying 'having a wife, children and a warm *kang*' (老婆孩子热炕头) is used to refer to someone who has no ambition or ideals and is satisfied with very little. *Kang* were already widely used in the Sui and Tang dynasties.

【炕梢】kàngshāo〈名〉 colder end of a *kang*
【炕头】kàngtóu〈名〉 warmer end of a *kang*
【炕席】kàngxí〈名〉 *kang* mat
【炕桌】kàngzhuō〈名〉 *kang* table

钪（鈧） kàng〈名〉［化学］ scandium (Sc)

kāo

尻 kāo〈名〉〈古〉 buttocks

kǎo

考[1] kǎo〈动〉 **1**（考查对方） set an examination;（参加考试） take a test: ～驾照 take a driving test ‖ ～上重点大学 pass the entrance examination to a key university ‖ ～第一 come out first in an examination ▸报～, 监～ **2**（调查） inspect: ▸～核, ～勤 **3**（考证） study: ▸～古, ～证 **4**（考虑） consider: ▸～虑, 思～

考[2] kǎo〈名〉〈书〉 one's deceased father: ▸～妣, 先～

k

【考妣】kǎobǐ〈名〉〈书〉one's deceased parents: ▸如丧～

【考博】kǎobó〈动〉take examinations to enter a doctorate programme

【考查】kǎochá〈动〉examine: ～学生成绩 check students' work

【考察】kǎochá〈动〉**1**（实地调查）inspect: ～水利工程 inspect a water conservancy project ‖ 出国～ go abroad on a study tour ‖ 科学～ scientific investigation ▸～团 **2**（深入了解）observe and study: ～和识别干部 test and judge cadres

【考察团】kǎochátuán〈名〉inspection team

【考场】kǎochǎng〈名〉examination site: ～纪律 examination rules

【考点】kǎodiǎn〈名〉test centre: 设立～ set up a test site

【考订】kǎodìng〈动〉do textual research: ～经史 do textual research into classical and historical works

【考分】kǎofēn〈名〉test score: 公布～ publish exam scores

【考古】kǎogǔ **A**〈动〉engage in archaeological studies **B**〈名〉archaeology: ～发掘 archaeological excavation ‖ ～工作 archaeological work

【考古学】kǎogǔxué〈名〉archaeology

【考官】kǎoguān〈名〉examiner: 主～ chief examiner

【考核】kǎohé〈动〉assess: ～干部 check on cadres ‖ ～标准 assessment criteria

【考级】kǎojí〈动〉sit for a graded examination: 钢琴～ graded piano examination

【考绩】kǎojì〈动〉evaluate an employee

【考究】kǎojiu **A**〈动〉**1**（考查研究）investigate: ～一下问题究竟出在哪里。Dig a little into the root of a problem. **2**（刻意讲求）be particular about: 过分～衣着 be fastidious about one's clothes **B**〈形〉exquisite: 用料～ use choice materials ‖ 做工～ fine workmanship

【考据】kǎojù〈动〉do textual research

【考据学】kǎojùxué〈名〉textual criticism

【考卷】kǎojuàn〈名〉examination paper

【考量】kǎoliáng〈动〉mull over

【考虑】kǎolǜ〈动〉consider: ～各方面的意见 take all kinds of opinions into consideration ‖ ～个人得失 be concerned with one's own personal gains and losses ‖ 进一步～ give further thought to ‖ ～不周 ill-considered ‖ 这个问题没有～到。This issue has not been considered.

【考评】kǎopíng〈动〉test and assess: ～干部 test and assess cadres

【考期】kǎoqī〈名〉test date: ～临近。The examination is approaching.

【考勤】kǎoqín〈动〉keep attendance records: ～情况很好。Attendance records are excellent.

【考求】kǎoqiú〈动〉〈书〉examine and enquire: ～真谛 seek truth

【考区】kǎoqū〈名〉examination district

【考取】kǎoqǔ〈动〉pass an entrance examination: 她去年～了北京大学。She passed the entrance examination to Beijing University last year.

【考生】kǎoshēng〈名〉candidate: ～须知 notice to examinees

【考试】kǎoshì〈动〉take an examination: 报名参加～ sign up for an examination ‖ 公务员～ civil service examination ‖ 入学～ entrance examination ▸自学～

【考释】kǎoshì〈动〉make philological studies of ancient texts: ～古籍 make philological studies of ancient books

【考题】kǎotí〈名〉examination question: 出～ set an exam ‖ 解答～ answer exam questions

【考问】kǎowèn〈动〉examine orally: 我被他～住了。His question got me stumped.

【考研】kǎoyán〈动〉take examinations for a graduate programme

【考验】kǎoyàn〈动〉test: 战争～了他。He was tested by wars. ‖ 马拉松～我们的体力和耐力。A marathon tests our physical strength and perseverance.

【考证】kǎozhèng〈动〉do textual research: 这个问题有待～。This issue is still to be put to textual research.

【考中】kǎozhòng〈动〉pass an examination

拷

kǎo〈动〉**1**（棒打）flog: ▸～问 **2**（复制）copy: 把程序～在移动硬盘里 copy a program onto an external hard drive ▸～贝

【拷贝】kǎobèi **A**〈名〉［影视］［计算机］copy: 发行～ issue copies ‖ 电影～ copies of a film ‖ 带一份软件～来 bring over a copy of the software **B**〈动〉copy

【拷边】kǎobiān〈动〉overlock [in sewing]

【拷绸】kǎochóu〈名〉rust-coloured summer silk

【拷打】kǎodǎ〈动〉torture: 严刑～ cruelly torture

【拷问】kǎowèn〈动〉torture sb. during interrogation: ～逼供 use torture to extort a confession

栲

kǎo〈名〉［植物］evergreen chinquapin

【栲胶】kǎojiāo〈名〉tannin extract

【栲栳】kǎolǎo〈名〉round-bottomed wicker basket

烤

kǎo〈动〉**1**（使变熟）bake: ～鸡 roast a chicken ‖ ～面包 toast bread ▸烧～ **2**（使温暖）warm oneself up: ▸～火

【烤电】kǎodiàn〈名〉［医学］diathermy

【烤麸】kǎofū〈名〉［食品］steamed gluten

【烤火】kǎohuǒ〈动〉warm oneself by the fire: ～取暖 take warmth by fire

【烤鸡】kǎojī〈名〉roast chicken

【烤炉】kǎolú〈名〉oven

【烤面包】kǎomiànbāo〈名〉toast: 两片～ two slices of toast ‖ ～炉 toaster

【烤漆】kǎoqī〈名〉stove varnish

【烤肉】kǎoròu〈名〉barbecue

【烤箱】kǎoxiāng〈名〉oven: 电～ electric oven

【烤鸭】kǎoyā〈名〉roast duck: 北京～ roast Beijing duck

【烤烟】kǎoyān〈名〉flue-cured tobacco

【烤羊肉串】kǎoyángròuchuàn〈名〉mutton shish kebab

kào

铐（銬）

kào

A〈名〉handcuffs: ▸镣～, 手～

B〈动〉handcuff: 把犯人～起来 handcuff a prisoner

犒

kào〈动〉reward with food and drink: ▸～劳, ～赏

【犒军】kàojūn〈动〉provide a congratulatory feast for officers and men

【犒劳】kàoláo **A**〈动〉reward with food and drink: ～全军将士 reward the whole army, officers and men alike, with food and drink **B**〈名〉food and drink as reward: 吃～ enjoy food and drink rewards ‖ 送～ reward sb. by sending them food and drink

【犒赏】kàoshǎng〈动〉〈旧〉reward a victorious army unit with bounties: ～三军 feast and offer bounties to officers and men

靠[1]

kào〈动〉**1**（倚靠）（指人）lean against;（指物）stand sth. against sth. else: 把头～在某人的肩上 lean one's head on sb.'s shoulder ‖ 背～背坐着 sit back to back ‖ 把自行车～在树上 lean one's bike against a tree ‖ ～墙放着一台洗衣机。A washing machine stood against the wall. ▸～垫, 倚～ **2**（挨近）get close to: ～窗的座位 window seat ‖ 船～码头了。The ship has docked. ‖ 车辆一律～右行驶。Cars drive on the right. ▸～边, 停～ **3**（依靠）depend on: ～教书为生 earn a livelihood through teaching ‖ ～养老金生活 live off one's pension ‖ 农业发展一～政策，二～科技。Agricultural development hinges first on policy and then on science and technology. ▸投～, 依～ A **4**（信赖）trust: ▸可～

靠[2]

kào〈名〉[in traditional opera] stage armour: 扎～ wear stage armour

【靠岸】kào'àn〈动〉pull in to shore

【靠背】kàobèi〈名〉back: ～椅 chair ‖ 沙发～ back of a sofa

【靠边】kàobiān〈动〉**1**（靠近边缘）keep to the side: 行人～走。Pedestrians should keep to the side of the road. **2**〈口〉〈喻〉（合乎情理）reasonable: 这事一点也不～儿。It's totally pointless.

【靠边儿站】kàobiānrzhàn〈惯〉**1**〈本〉step aside **2**〈喻〉（指失势）be forced out

【靠不住】kàobuzhù〈动〉be unreliable: 他这个人～。He is untrustworthy. ‖ 这消息～。This news can not be relied upon.

【靠得住】kàodezhù〈动〉be reliable: 你的朋友～吗？Is your friend reliable?

【靠垫】kàodiàn〈名〉cushion: 沙发～ sofa cushion

【靠近】kàojìn〈动〉**1**（距离近）be close: ～那家酒店有一个超级市场。There's a supermarket near the hotel. ‖ 他的房间～厕所。His room is close to the toilet. **2**（缩小距离）approach: 船向岸边～。The boat is drawing close to the shore. ‖ 侦察员偷偷地向敌人～。The scouts gradually moved in on the enemy.

【靠拢】kàolǒng〈动〉draw close: 向群众～ get close to the masses ‖ 请大家～点站。Everyone stand closer, please!

【靠谱】kàopǔ〈动〉〈口〉reasonable: 说话不～ speak unreasonably

【靠旗】kàoqí〈名〉［戏曲］triangular armour flags

【靠山】kàoshān〈名〉〈喻〉backer: 有～ have the backing of sb.

【靠山吃山，靠水吃水】kào shān chī shān, kào shuǐ chī shuǐ〈俗〉make use of what is near at hand

【靠手】kàoshǒu〈名〉armrest

【靠天吃饭】kàotiān-chīfàn〈俗〉live at the mercy of the weather: 这个地方严重缺水，农民只能～。There is a severe shortage of water in this area, and farmers must live at the mercy of the weather.

【靠枕】kàozhěn〈名〉back cushion

kē

坷 kē
▸kě
【坷垃】kēlā〈名〉〈方〉clod: 土～ clod of earth

苛 kē〈形〉1（苛刻）harsh: 你的要求太～了。Your demands are excessive. ▸～求, ～政 2（繁琐）excessively detailed: ▸～细, ～捐杂税
【苛待】kēdài〈动〉treat harshly: ～下级 be hard on one's subordinates
【苛法】kēfǎ〈名〉harsh law
【苛捐杂税】kējuān-záshuì〈成〉exorbitant and multifarious taxes and levies
【苛刻】kēkè〈形〉harsh: ～的条件 exacting terms ‖ 他对自己很～。He is very hard on himself.
【苛求】kēqiú〈动〉make excessive demands: 不要～于人。Don't make excessive demands on others.
【苛细】kēxì〈形〉〈书〉severe and exacting: ～的规则 over-elaborate and exacting rules
【苛责】kēzé〈动〉castigate: 因犯了错误而受～ be criticized severely for one's mistakes
【苛政】kēzhèng〈名〉tyrannical government: 反抗～ revolt against tyranny
【苛政猛于虎】kēzhèng měngyú hǔ〈成〉an oppressive government is more fearful than a ferocious tiger

珂 kē〈名〉〈书〉jade-like stone
【珂罗版】kēluóbǎn〈名〉［印刷］collotype

柯 kē〈名〉〈书〉1（枝茎）branch: 交～错叶 interlacing branches and leaves 2（柄）axe-handle
【柯尔克孜族】Kē'ěrkèzīzú〈名〉Kirgiz ethnic group
【柯库布里郡】Kēkùbùlǐjùn〈名〉Kirkcudbrightshire

轲（軻） kē〈名〉[used in personal names]: 孟～ Mencius

科[1] kē〈名〉1（指分类）subject: 理/文～硕士 Master of Science/Arts ‖ 学习偏～ [of a student] favour one subject over another ▸内～, 学～ 2（指部门）department: 财务～ finance section ‖ 人事～ personnel department ▸～员, ～长 3［生物］family: 猫～动物 animals of the cat family ‖ 蔷薇～植物 plants of the rose family 4（科举考试）（指考试）imperial civil examination;（指科目）subjects of the imperial civil examination: 开～取士 hold imperial examinations to select talented people for government service ▸～场, ～举, 登～

科[2] kē
A〈名〉1〈书〉（法律条文）article: ▸金～玉律 2（刑罚）punishment: ▸前～
B〈动〉〈书〉impose a punishment: ～以罚金 impose a fine ▸～处

科[3] kē〈名〉［戏曲］stage directions in classical Chinese opera: 笑～ laughs ▸插～打诨
【科白】kēbái〈名〉[in classical Chinese opera] actions and spoken parts
【科班】kēbān〈名〉1（戏曲训练班）old-type opera school 2（正规教育）regular professional training: ～出身 be a professional by training
【科场】kēchǎng〈名〉［历史］imperial civil examination hall: ～失利 fail in the imperial civil examination
【科处】kēchǔ〈动〉pass a sentence: ～罚金 impose a fine on sb. ‖ ～徒刑 sentence sb. to imprisonment
【科第】kēdì〈名〉［历史］grading of the candidates in the imperial civil examinations
【科幻】kēhuàn〈名〉science fiction: ～片 science fiction film ‖ ～小说 science fiction (novel)
【科技】kējì〈名〉science and technology: ～攻关 tackle key problems in science and technology ‖ ～合作 scientific and technical cooperation ‖ ～园 technology park
【科技成果】kējì chéngguǒ〈名〉scientific and technological achievements
【科技协会】kējì xiéhuì〈名〉association of science and technology
【科教】kējiào〈名〉science and education: ～兴国 revitalize a country through science and education
【科教片】kējiàopiàn〈简称〉= 科学教育片
【科举】kējǔ〈名〉imperial civil examination

> **科举**
> Examinations held at county, provincial and central levels, and used as the basis for selecting officials for appointment into the imperial bureaucracy. Founded in the Sui Dynasty, the system lasted until its abolition in 1905 at the end of the Qing Dynasty. During the Ming and Qing dynasties, the Eight-Part Essay (▸八股文) formed an important part of the examination.

【科考】kēkǎo A〈简称〉= 科学考察 B = 科举 kējǔ
【科伦坡】Kēlúnpō〈名〉Colombo
【科罗拉多州】Kēluólāduōzhōu〈名〉Colorado
【科盲】kēmáng〈名〉person with little or no knowledge of science: 扫除～ eliminate ignorance of science
【科摩罗】Kēmóluó〈名〉Comoros: ～人 Comorian ‖ ～语 Comorian
【科目】kēmù〈名〉subject: 考试～ examination subject ‖ 选修～ optional subject
【科纳克里】Kēnàkèlǐ〈名〉Conakry
【科普】kēpǔ〈简称〉= 科学普及
【科普读物】kēpǔ dúwù〈名〉popular science reader
【科室】kēshì〈名〉departments and offices: ～人员 office personnel
【科特迪瓦】Kētèdíwǎ〈名〉Côte d'Ivoire
【科威特】Kēwēitè〈名〉Kuwait: ～人 Kuwaiti
【科协】kēxié〈简称〉= 科技协会
【科学】kēxué A〈名〉science: 军事～ military science ‖ 生命～ life science ▸边缘～, 尖端～ B〈形〉scientific: ～分析 scientific analysis ‖ 这样做很不～。It's not at all scientific to do it this way.
【科学发展观】kēxué fāzhǎnguān〈名〉concept of scientific development
【科学家】kēxuéjiā ▸p. 966〈名〉scientist: 核～ nuclear scientist
【科学教育片】kēxué jiàoyùpiàn〈名〉science and education film
【科学考察】kēxué kǎochá〈名〉scientific investigation: ～队 scientific investigation team
【科学普及】kēxué pǔjí〈名〉science popularization
【科学社会主义】kēxué shèhuìzhǔyì〈名〉scientific socialism
【科学性】kēxuéxìng〈名〉the state or quality of being scientific
【科学学】kēxuéxué〈名〉science studies
【科学院】kēxuéyuàn〈名〉academy of sciences: 中国～ Chinese Academy of Sciences ‖ 中国社会～ Chinese Academy of Social Sciences
【科学知识】kēxué zhīshi〈名〉scientific knowledge
【科研】kēyán〈名〉scientific research: ～人员 scientific research personnel ‖ ～成果 achievements in scientific research
【科研经费】kēyán jīngfèi〈名〉research fund
【科研项目】kēyán xiàngmù〈名〉(scientific) research project
【科员】kēyuán〈名〉section member
【科长】kēzhǎng〈名〉section chief

疴 kē〈名〉〈书〉illness: 染～ contract an illness ▸沉～

棵 kē〈量〉[usu for plants]: 两～梨树 two pear trees ‖ 一～大白菜 a head of Chinese cabbage
【棵儿】kēr〈名〉size of a plant: 这棵白菜～不小。This cabbage is quite big.

颏（頦） kē〈名〉chin: 下巴～儿 chin
▸ké

嗑 kē〈方〉〈名〉word: 唠～ have a chat
▸kè

稞 kē〈名〉highland barley

窠 kē〈名〉nest: 马蜂～ hornets' nest ‖ 鸟～ bird's nest ‖ 筑～ build a nest
【窠臼】kējiù〈名〉〈书〉[usu of writing or artistic creation] set pattern: 摆脱前人的～ break free of old conventions ▸不落～

颗（顆） kē〈量〉[usu for things small and roundish]: 两～牙齿 two teeth ‖ 一～种子 a seed ‖ 一～子弹 a bullet
【颗粒】kēlì〈名〉1（大小）size of a grain, pellet, etc.: 小麦的～很饱满。The ears of wheat are plump. ‖ 珍珠的～大小不一。The pearls are irregular in size. 2（指粮食）each grain: ～归仓 harvest every single grain ‖ ～无收 suffer a total crop failure
【颗粒肥料】kēlì féiliào〈名〉granulated fertilizer
【颗粒物】kēlìwù〈名〉particulate matter

磕 kē〈动〉1（撞）knock: 跌了一跤，～破了膝盖 fall and graze one's knee ‖ 脑门上～了一个包 get a bump on one's forehead ‖ 他～掉了两颗牙。He knocked two teeth out. 2（磕打）knock sth. out of sth.: ～掉鞋上的泥 beat the mud off one's shoes ‖ ～掉烟斗里的灰 empty out one's pipe
【磕巴】kēba〈方〉A〈动〉stammer: 他说话一向有点～。He's always had a slight stammer. B〈名〉stammerer
【磕打】kēda〈动〉knock sth. out of sth.: 抽屉里面尘土太多，拿出去～～。Take the drawer out and knock the dust out of it.
【磕磕绊绊】kēke-bànbàn〈成〉1（不平坦）rough: 这条路～的，实在难走。The road is very bumpy and hard to negotiate.

2 (不灵便) jerky: 他患了关节炎，走路～的。He suffers from arthritis and walks jerkily. 3 (不顺利) bumpy: 工作上总是～的。Work is always up and down.

【磕磕撞撞】kēke-zhuàngzhuàng 〈成〉 unsteady: 一个酒鬼～地从我们身旁走过。A drunk stumbled past us.

【磕碰】kēpèng 〈动〉 1 (碰撞) bump into: 禁得起～ can withstand a bit of jostling 2 (发生矛盾) squabble: 就是一家人，也难免会有磕磕碰碰。Squabbles are inevitable even among members of the same family.

【磕头】kētóu 〈动〉 kowtow: ～作揖 kowtow with a bow and one's hands folded

【磕头虫】kētóuchóng 〈名〉 click beetle

【磕头碰脑】kētóu-pèngnǎo 〈动〉 1 (相互挤碰) push and bump against each other: 一大群人～。A large crowd of people pushed and jostled against each other. 2 (发生冲突) be at odds with one another: 街坊四邻有个～的事，他都出面调停。When the neighbours are at odds with one another, he will try and smooth it over. 3 (经常碰见) rub shoulders with one another: 我们几个都住这个院子，整天～的。Living in the same courtyard, we bump into each other all the time.

瞌 kē

【瞌睡】kēshuì 〈动〉 doze: 打～ doze off ‖ 吃完饭犯～ feel sleepy after a meal

【瞌睡虫】kēshuìchóng 〈名〉〈喻〉 sleepyhead: 起来吧，你这个～。Come on, sleepyhead, wake up!

蝌 kē

【蝌蚪】kēdǒu 〈名〉 tadpole

髁 kē 〈名〉 [生理] condyle

ké

壳（殻） ké 〈名〉〈口〉 shell: 鸡蛋～儿 egg shell ‖ 子弹～儿 spent cartridge ▸贝～

▸qiào

【壳郎猪】kélangzhū 〈名〉〈方〉 feeder pig

【壳资源】kézīyuán 〈名〉 [金融] back-door listing resource

咳 ké 〈动〉 cough: ～血 cough up blood ‖ ～得很厉害 have a bad cough ‖ 干～ dry cough ‖ 止～药 cough medicine ▸～嗽，百日～

▸hāi

【咳嗽】késou ▸p. 50 〈动〉 cough: ～糖浆 cough syrup

颏（頦） ké ▸蓝点颏 lándiǎnké

▸kē

搭 ké 〈动〉〈方〉 1 (卡住) get stuck: 抽屉～住了。The drawer is stuck. ‖ 鞋太小，～脚。This pair of shoes is too small. They pinch my feet. 2 (刁难) create difficulties: ～人 make things difficult for sb.

kě

可¹ kě

A 〈动〉 1 (表许可) approve: 不置～否 decline to comment ▸认～，许～ 2 (表可能) can: 她的话不～尽信。You cannot believe everything she says. ‖ 你～去～不去。You can either go or stay. ▸～望，由此～见 3 (表值得) be worth: 图书馆～看的书真不少。There are quite a lot of books worth reading in the library. ▸～爱，～靠

B 〈副〉〈书〉 about: 年～三十 be about 30

可² kě

A 〈连〉 but: 别看他年龄小，志气～不小。Young as he is, he is quite ambitious. ‖ 她嘴上不说，～心里偷着乐。She said nothing, but felt happy at heart.

B 〈副〉 1 (用于陈述句，表强调) [used in a declarative sentence for emphasis]: 她的脾气～好了。She has such a good disposition. ‖ 昨晚的风～大了。The wind was really strong last night. 2 (用于感叹句，表强调) [used in an exclamatory sentence for emphasis]: 你～别忘了! Mind you don't forget it! ‖ 要是让老板发现了，～够你受的! God help you if the boss finds out! 3 (用于反问句，表强调) [used in a rhetorical question for emphasis]: 这～叫我怎么办呢? What can I do about it? 4 (用于疑问句) [used in a question for emphasis]: 近来～好? How have you been doing? 5 (用于祈使句，表劝导) [used in an imperative sentence for emphasis or persuasion]: 你～要给我来信啊! Remember to write to me! ‖ 下楼梯的时候～得小心呵! Take care going downstairs!

可³ kě 〈动〉 suit: ▸～口，～心

▸kè

【可爱】kě'ài 〈形〉 lovely: 活泼～ lively and adorable ‖ ～的小狗 a sweet little dog ‖ 他女儿多～啊! What a lovely young lady his daughter is!

【可悲】kěbēi 〈形〉 sad: ～的结局 tragic outcome ‖ 落得一个～的下场 come to a sorry end

【可比】kěbǐ 〈动〉 be comparable: 这两组数字是不～的。These two sets of figures are not comparable.

【可比价格】kěbǐ jiàgé 〈名〉 comparable price

【可比性】kěbǐxìng 〈名〉 comparability: 这两件事没有～。The two things cannot be compared.

【可鄙】kěbǐ 〈形〉 contemptible: ～的手段 dirty tricks ‖ 他的行为实在～。His behaviour is completely despicable.

【可变】kěbiàn 〈形〉 variable: ～电容器 variable capacitor

【可变性】kěbiànxìng 〈名〉 variability

【可变翼】kěbiànyì 〈名〉 [航空] adjustable wing

【可不】kěbù 〈副〉〈口〉 exactly: 今天真热! ——～，你看我的衣服都湿透了。It's really hot today. — It certainly is! Look, my shirt is soaking.

【可怖】kěbù 〈形〉 horrible

【可不是】kěbushì = 可不 kěbù

【可操左券】kěcāozuǒquàn 〈成〉 be sure to succeed

【可乘之机】kěchéngzhījī 〈成〉 opportunity that can be exploited to one's advantage: 给某人以～ give sb. an opportunity

【可持续发展】kěchíxù fāzhǎn 〈名〉 sustainable development: 推动国民经济的～ promote the sustainable development of the national economy

【可持续性】kěchíxùxìng 〈名〉 sustainability

【可耻】kěchǐ 〈形〉 shameful: ～的下场 ignominious end ‖ 这样的行为真～! What a disgraceful way to behave!

【可的松】kědìsōng 〈名〉 [药学] cortisone

【可读】kědú 〈形〉 1 (值得读) worth reading 2 (易懂) readable

【可读写光盘】kědúxiě guāngpán 〈名〉 recordable compact disc

【可读性】kědúxìng 〈名〉 readability: 这本书～很强。This book is very readable.

【可歌可泣】kěgē-kěqì 〈成〉 move one to song and to tears: ～的英雄事迹 heroic and moving deeds

【可耕地】kěgēngdì 〈名〉 arable land

【可观】kěguān 〈形〉 1 (表程度高) considerable: ～的收入 sizeable income ‖ 这笔数目相当～。The amount is pretty high. 2 〈书〉 (值得观看) worth seeing: 这部影片大有～之处。This film is well worth seeing.

【可贵】kěguì 〈形〉 valuable: ～的品质 fine quality ‖ 自由比生命更～。Freedom is more precious than life. ▸难能～

【可好】kěhǎo 〈副〉 as luck would have it: 我正想去找他，～他自个儿来了。I was just about to look for him when he showed up.

【可恨】kěhèn 〈形〉 hateful: ～之至 be most hateful

【可回收】kěhuíshōu 〈形〉 retrievable: ～卫星 retrievable satellite ‖ ～废弃物 waste

【可回收运载火箭】kěhuíshōu yùnzài huǒjiàn 〈名〉 recoverable launching vehicle

【可嘉】kějiā 〈动〉 be commendable: 精神～ commendable spirit

【可见】kějiàn 〈连〉 so you can see that: 她是被抬进医院的，～病得很重。She was carried to the hospital on a stretcher, so she must be seriously ill.

【可见度】kějiàndù = 能见度 néngjiàndù

【可见光】kějiànguāng 〈名〉 [物理] visible light

【可脚】kějiǎo 〈形〉 [of shoes, socks] well-fitting

【可敬】kějìng 〈形〉 respectable: 一位～的教授 respected professor

【可卡因】kěkǎyīn 〈名〉 cocaine

【可靠】kěkào 〈形〉 1 (可信赖) reliable: ～的朋友 unfailing friend ‖ 诚实～ be honest and trustworthy 2 (真实可信) authentic and reliable: ～的消息来源 reliable sources ‖ 这条信息～不～? Is the information trustworthy?

【可靠性】kěkàoxìng 〈名〉 reliability

【可可】kěkě [生物] cocoa

【可可脂】kěkězhī 〈名〉 cocoa butter

【可控性】kěkòngxìng 〈名〉 controllability: 输出～ output controllability

【可口】kěkǒu 〈形〉 tasty: ～的饭菜 tasty food

【可口可乐】Kěkǒu Kělè 〈名〉 Coca-Cola

【可兰经】Kělánjīng 〈名〉 [宗教] Koran: 《～》是伊斯兰教的经典。The Koran is the holy book of Islam.

【可乐】kělè 〈名〉 Coke: 百事～ Pepsi Cola ‖ 请来一大瓶～! A large Coke, please. ▸可口～

【可怜】kělián A 〈形〉 1 (值得怜悯) pitiful: 装出一副～相 put on a pitiful look ‖ 她的情况一天天坏下去，真～。It was awful the way her condition deteriorated day by day. 2 (数量极少) meagre: 少得～ be pathetically meagre ‖ 报酬低得～ miserably paid B 〈动〉 pity: ～某人 feel pity for sb. ‖ 没有人～他。Nobody feels sorry for him.

【可怜巴巴】kěliánbābā 〈形〉〈口〉 pathetic: ～的一点薪水 pitifully small salary

【可怜虫】 kěliánchóng 〈名〉 miserable wretch
【可怜见】 kěliánjiàn 〈形〉〈方〉 pathetic: 这孩子小小年纪就没了爹娘，怪～的。 Poor little thing! He has lost both his parents at such a young age.
【可怜天下父母心】 kělián tiānxià fùmǔxīn 〈俗〉 all parents go soft when it comes to their children
【可恼】 kěnǎo 〈形〉 annoying
【可能】 kěnéng **A** 〈形〉 possible: 唯一～的解决方法 the only possible solution ‖ 三天完成任务是不～的。 It will be impossible to finish the task within three days. **B** 〈副〉 perhaps: 他～会晚到一会儿。 He is likely to arrive a bit late. ‖ 这～有几个原因。 This may be attributed to several causes. **C** 〈名〉 possibility: 有～获胜 have a chance of winning ‖ 我们不能排除这种～。 We cannot exclude this possibility.
【可能性】 kěnéngxìng 〈名〉 possibility: 该队没有获胜的～。This team has no chance of winning. ‖ 这种～是有的，但是不大。 That's possible, but hardly probable.
【可怕】 kěpà 〈形〉 terrifying: 没什么～的。 There is nothing to be afraid of. ‖ 形势令人感到～。 The situation is really scary.
【可欺】 kěqī 〈形〉 gullible: 软弱～ be weak and easily bullied
【可气】 kěqì 〈形〉 exasperating: 令人～的事 annoying things
【可巧】 kěqiǎo 〈副〉 as luck would have it: 突然下起雨来，～我带着伞。 It suddenly started to rain. Fortunately, I had an umbrella with me.
【可亲】 kěqīn 〈形〉 amiable: 他是一个和蔼～的人。 He is an amiable man.
【可取】 kěqǔ 〈形〉 desirable: 该计划有～之处。 The plan has its merits.
【可圈可点】 kěquān-kědiǎn 〈成〉 praiseworthy
【可燃】 kěrán 〈形〉［化学］combustible: ～物 flammable matter
【可人】 kěrén 〈书〉 **A** 〈名〉 person with admirable qualities **B** 〈形〉 likeable: 楚楚～ be delicate and charming ‖ 气候～。 The climate is very agreeable.
【可身】 kěshēn 〈形〉〈方〉 nicely fitting: 这件外套穿着很～。 This coat is a good fit.
【可视电话】 kěshì diànhuà 〈名〉 videophone
【可是】 kěshì **A** 〈连〉 but: 这篇文章不错，～仍有改进的余地。 The essay is all right. However, there is still room for improvement. **B** 〈副〉 [used for emphasis]: 任务～够艰巨的。 The task is by no means easy. ‖ 她～个了不起的人物。 She is simply fantastic.
【可塑性】 kěsùxìng 〈名〉 **1**（指人） malleability: 小孩子有很强的～。 A child is very malleable. **2**（指物） plasticity: ～物质 plastic material
【可体】 kětǐ = 可身 kěshēn
【可望】 kěwàng 〈形〉 hopeful: 夏季粮油～获得丰收。 Bumper crops of grain and oil seed are expected this summer. ‖ 母亲～周末出院。 We are hopeful that Mother will be discharged from hospital this weekend.
【可望而不可即】 kě wàng ér bùkě jí 〈成〉 within sight but beyond reach: 这个目标决非～。 This goal is by no means unattainable.

❶ 可数与不可数名词

■ 英语里除了专有名词外，其他的名词一般来说都有可数与不可数之分，也有单复数形式的区别。

英语的可数名词

■ 英语的可数名词，是指能以数目来计算，并且可以分成个体的人或事物，比如 calculators、lamps、tables、pens、books、TVs 等。可数名词可以是单数，也可以是复数。英语词如 a、an、one、this、that 等可以和单数名词一起使用；two、some、any、many、these、those 等可以和复数名词一起使用。英语里由于没有量词的存在，这些词后面直接跟名词：

一部小说
= one novel

三部小说
= three novels

一个孩子
= a child

一些孩子
= some children

这家酒店
= this hotel

这些酒店
= these hotels

那个男人
= that man

那些男人
= those men

我的橡皮在哪？
= Where is my rubber?

你家里有报纸吗？
= Do you have any newspapers in the house?

他糖果吃得太多
= He eats too many sweets

■ 英语里有些词总是复数形式，如 glasses、shoes、trousers、clothes 等。这些词做主语时要接复数动词：

她的眼镜很漂亮
= Her glasses are beautiful

睡衣是我的
= The pyjamas are mine

不可数名词

■ 英语的不可数名词，是指不能以数目来计算、或被看成是一个整体的事物或概念，比如 bread、water、love、air、information 等。这类名词只有单数形式，而且做主语时要带单数动词。注意有些名词如 news、darts 等，用的是复数形式，但实际上是不可数的单数名词，做主语时也要带单数动词：

你的帮助对我意义很大
= Your help means lots to me

他给了我一些建议
= He gave me some advice

这信息很有用
= This information is useful

英国一些酒吧里通常会玩掷镖游戏
= Darts is often played in some British pubs

■ 英语里有些词如 furniture、luggage、baggage 等被看作不可数名词：

他们买了一些家具
= They bought some furniture
而不是
They bought some furnitures

我们有 3 件行李
= We have three pieces of luggage
而不是
We have three luggages

■ 不定冠词 a/an 不能和不可数名词连用，但可用"a ... of + 不可数名词"的形式来代替：

一条消息
= a piece of news

一粒米
= a grain of rice

一杯水
= a glass of water

一品托啤酒
= a pint of beer

■ 英语词如 much、some、any、little、a little、little、no 等可以和不可数名词连用：

我想要点橙汁
= I'd like to have some orange juice

你买牛奶了吗？
= Did you buy any milk?

她的饮食中脂肪吃得太多
= She eats too much fat in her diet

我还有一点儿工作要做
= I still have a little work to do

我身上没带钱
= I have no money on me

既可数又不可数的名词

■ 英语里有些名词有可数和不可数两种形式，但意义有所不同。可数时是指较具体的事物或活动，而不可数时是泛指：

我喜欢运动
= I like sport

网球是一项运动
= Tennis is a sport

他头上没头发了
= He has no hair on his head

你大衣上有两根头发
= There are two hairs on your coat

■ 表示饮品的词在英语里常常是不可数的，但在饭馆或酒吧里要饮品或请别人喝点什么的时候，可以用可数：

我喜欢葡萄酒
= I like wine

你想来杯葡萄酒还是啤酒？（让酒时）
= Would you like a wine or a beer?

我不喝咖啡或茶
= I don't drink coffee or tea

请来两杯咖啡和三杯茶（在饭店里）
= Two coffees and three teas, please

【可谓】kěwèi〈动〉〈书〉may be said: 这机会真～千载难逢。This could be described as the chance of a lifetime.
【可恶】kěwù〈形〉hateful: 说那样的话真是太～了。That's a horrid thing to say.
【可吸入颗粒物】kěxīrù kēlìwù〈名〉inhalable particle (IP)
【可惜】kěxī〈形〉regrettable: 这件事你半途而废，实在太～了。It was really a shame that you gave it up halfway.
【可喜】kěxǐ〈形〉heartening: ～的进步 gratifying progress ‖ ～可贺 it's really heartening that ...
【可想而知】kěxiǎng'érzhī〈成〉one may well imagine: 他对自己的父母都这么粗鲁，对其他人就～了。If he's that rude to his parents, just imagine what he's like with other people.
【可笑】kěxiào〈形〉**1**（有趣）funny: 样子～ look funny **2**（令人耻笑）ridiculous: 幼稚得～ ridiculously naive ‖ 愚蠢得～ laughably foolish
【可心】kěxīn〈形〉〈书〉satisfactory: 新买的家具不～。The new furniture is not to my liking.
【可信】kěxìn〈动〉be believable: 证人的供述～/不～。The witness's statement was credible/lacked credibility.
【可信度】kěxìndù〈名〉credibility
【可行】kěxíng〈形〉workable: 切实～的计划 realistic plan ‖ 事实证明这个办法不～。The facts prove that this method is not workable.
【可行性】kěxíngxìng〈名〉feasibility: 项目的～ the feasibility of a project ‖ ～报告 feasibility report
【可疑】kěyí〈形〉suspicious: 形迹～ look suspicious ‖ 这事有点～。There's something fishy about this.
【可以】kěyǐ **A**〈动〉**1**（值得）be worth: 这部影片～一看。This film is worth seeing. **2**（能够）be able to: ～理解 be understandable ‖ 你完全～这样说。You may well say so. ‖ 星星之火，～燎原。A single spark can start a prairie fire. **3**（表选择）may: 你～走了。You may go. ‖ 你不～去。Not allowed you are to go. **B**〈形〉**1**（不错）pretty good: 开始一段时间情况还～。It went on well for a while. ‖ 他的英语怎么样？——还～。How's his English? — Not bad. **2**（程度深）terrible: 天气实在热得～。It's terribly hot.
【可意】kěyì〈形〉satisfactory: 他终于找到了～的女朋友。He finally got a girlfriend after his own heart. ‖ 这房子还～吧？Are you satisfied with the house?
【可有可无】kěyǒu-kěwú〈成〉be as well without it as with it
【可遇而不可求】kě yù ér bùkě qiú〈成〉can be found only by accident, and not through seeking
【可再生】kězàishēng〈形〉renewable: ～能源 renewable energy ‖ 不～资源 non-renewable resources
【可造之才】kězàozhīcái〈名〉promising young man
【可憎】kězēng〈形〉abominable: 面目～ look repulsive
【可支配收入】kězhīpèi shōurù〈名〉［经济］disposable income: 个人～ personal disposable income
【可知性】kězhīxìng〈名〉［哲学］knowability

坷 kě ▸坎坷 kǎnkě
▸kē

渴 kě

A〈形〉thirsty: 感到口～ feel a thirst ‖ 又饥又～ be both hungry and thirsty ▸干～, 解～, 止～
B〈副〉eagerly: ▸～求, ～望
【渴慕】kěmù〈动〉admire deeply: ～已久 admire sb. for a long time ‖ 我们怀着～的心情拜访了那位老教授。Filled with respect we visited the old professor.
【渴念】kěniàn〈动〉〈书〉long for: ～故乡 pine for one's native land ‖ ～家人 miss one's family
【渴盼】kěpàn〈动〉look forward to sth. eagerly: ～早日团圆 long for an early reunion ‖ ～速复。I am looking forward with eagerness to your early reply.
【渴求】kěqiú〈动〉yearn for: ～真理 yearn for the truth ‖ ～知识 hanker after knowledge
【渴望】kěwàng〈动〉long for: ～成功 be eager for success ‖ ～自由 yearn for freedom
【渴想】kěxiǎng〈动〉miss sb. very much
【渴仰】kěyǎng〈动〉〈书〉admire

kè

可 kè
▸kě
【可汗】kèhán〈名〉khan

克[1] kè〈动〉〈书〉be able to: 不～分身 can't get away ▸～勤～俭

克[2] kè〈动〉**1**（攻克）conquer: 连～数城 conquer one city after another ▸～敌制胜, ～复 **2**（消化）digest: ▸～食 **3**（制服）restrain: ▸～服, ～己奉公, ～制 **4**（减少）decrease: ▸～扣

克[3]（剋）kè〈动〉〈书〉set a time limit: ▸～期, ～日

克[4] kè ▸**p. 978**〈量〉gram: 一公斤等于一千～。One kilogram is equivalent to one thousand grams.
【克当量】kèdāngliàng〈名〉gram equivalent
【克敌制胜】kèdí-zhìshèng〈成〉defeat the enemy and win victory: ～的法宝 the magic formula for seeing off one's enemy
【克服】kèfú〈动〉**1**（战胜）overcome: ～困难 overcome a difficulty ‖ ～语言障碍 overcome a language barrier **2**〈口〉（忍耐）put up with: 这儿条件不太好，请大家～一下。The conditions here are not very good. Please bear with them for a while.
【克复】kèfù〈动〉〈书〉recover: ～失地 recover lost territory
【克格勃】Kègébó〈名〉**1**（指组织）KGB **2**（指人）member of the KGB
【克己】kèjǐ〈动〉**1**（克制私欲）restrain oneself: ～待人 exercise self-control in the service of others **2**（节俭）be frugal: 过日子～ live a thrifty life
【克己奉公】kèjǐ-fènggōng〈成〉work selflessly in the public interest: ～的工作作风 style of work characterized by complete selflessness and devotion to one's duty
【克尽职守】kèjìn-zhíshǒu〈成〉devote oneself to one's duties
【克扣】kèkòu〈动〉embezzle part of what should be issued: ～分量 give short measure ‖ ～工钱 underpay
【克拉】kèlā ▸**p. 978**〈量〉carat: 一～等于200毫克。One carat is equivalent to 200 milligrams.
【克拉克曼南郡】Kèlākèmànnánjùn〈名〉Clackmannanshire
【克郎球】kèlángqiú = 康乐球 kānglèqiú
【克朗】kèlǎng ▸**p. 328**〈名〉**1**（捷克货币）koruna **2**（丹麦等国货币）crown
【克厘米】kèlímǐ〈名〉［物理］gram-centimetre
【克里奥尔语】Kèlǐ'ào'ěryǔ ▸**p. 918**〈名〉Creole
【克里姆林宫】Kèlǐmǔlíngōng〈名〉Kremlin
【克隆】kèlóng〈动〉clone: ～羊 cloned sheep
【克卢伊德郡】Kèlúyīdéjùn〈名〉Clwyd
【克罗地亚】Kèluódìyà〈名〉Croatia: ～共和国 Republic of Croatia ‖ ～人 Croatian ‖ ～语 Croatian
【克罗马努人】Kèluómǎnǔrén〈名〉［考古］Cro-Magnon man
【克罗默蒂郡】Kèluómòdìjùn〈名〉Cromartyshire
【克期】kèqī〈副〉〈书〉set a date: ～完工 set a date for completing the work
【克勤克俭】kèqín-kèjiǎn〈成〉be both hard-working and thrifty: ～是中国人民的优良传统。Diligence and thriftiness are the great virtues of the Chinese people.
【克日】kèrì〈副〉〈书〉set a date: ～竣工 set a date for completion
【克山病】kèshānbìng ▸**p. 50**〈名〉［医学］*keshan* disease
【克什米尔】Kèshímǐ'ěr〈名〉Kashmir: ～人 Kashmiri ‖ ～语 Kashmiri
【克食】kèshí〈动〉aid digestion: 山楂能～。Hawthorn aids digestion.
【克星】kèxīng〈名〉natural enemy:〈喻〉猫是老鼠的～。The cat is a natural enemy of the mouse.
【克制】kèzhì〈动〉restrain: 保持～ exercise self-control ‖ ～的态度 attitude of restraint ‖ 她无法～自己。She couldn't control herself.

刻 kè

A〈动〉carve: ～图章 engrave a seal ‖ 把大理石～成石像 carve a block of marble into a statue ▸～字, 雕～, 篆～
B〈量〉quarter: 八点一～ a quarter past eight ‖ 这路公共汽车一～钟发一趟。The buses come every fifteen minutes.
C〈名〉**1**（时间）moment: ▸～不容缓, 此～, 即～ **2**（雕刻品）carved things: ▸木～, 石～
D〈形〉**1**（刻薄）harsh: ▸～薄, ～毒 **2**（程度深）profound: ▸～苦, 深～
【刻板】kèbǎn **A**〈动〉cut blocks for printing: ～印刷 block printing **B**〈形〉stiff: ～地照抄照搬 copy mechanically ‖ 他待人处事十分～。He is very formal in all his dealings.
【刻版】kèbǎn = 刻板 kèbǎn A
【刻本】kèběn〈名〉block-printed edition
【刻薄】kèbó〈形〉harsh: 尖酸～ be biting and harsh ‖ 说话～ have a sharp tongue
【刻不容缓】kèbùrónghuǎn〈成〉be of great urgency: 此事～。The matter is of great urgency.
【刻刀】kèdāo〈名〉burin
【刻毒】kèdú〈形〉venomous: ～的语言 vicious remarks ‖ 用心～ with spiteful intention

【刻度】kèdù〈名〉scale
【刻工】kègōng〈名〉1（指人）engraver 2（指工艺）engraving: ～精细 fine engraving
【刻骨】kègǔ〈形〉deep-rooted: ～仇恨 deep-seated hatred
【刻骨铭心】kègǔ-míngxīn〈成〉be engraved in one's memory: ～之言 words which make an indelible impression
【刻花】kèhuā〈动〉engrave designs
【刻花玻璃】kèhuā bōli〈名〉cut-glass
【刻画】kèhuà〈动〉1（描绘）depict: 人物～ characterization ‖ 这本小说～了一个英雄形象。This novel portrays a hero. 2（涂画）draw: 不要随意～! No graffiti!
【刻苦】kèkǔ〈形〉1（用功）hard-working: ～攻读 plug away at one's lessons ‖ ～钻研 study assiduously 2（俭朴）simple and frugal: 过着～的生活 lead a simple and frugal life
【刻录机】kèlùjī〈名〉CD writer
【刻期】kèqī = 克期 kèqī
【刻日】kèrì = 克日 kèrì
【刻石】kèshí A〈动〉carve a stone B〈名〉stone engraved with characters or designs
【刻下】kèxià〈副〉〈书〉at present: ～最大的问题是失业问题。The biggest problem at present is unemployment. ‖ 经理～很忙。The manager is busy at the moment.
【刻写】kèxiě〈动〉1（指用铁笔）cut 2（指用刻刀）carve
【刻意】kèyì〈副〉painstakingly: ～打扮 be very meticulous about one's clothes or make-up ‖ ～模仿 take great pains to imitate
【刻意求工】kèyì-qiúgōng〈成〉sedulously seek perfection
【刻舟求剑】kèzhōu-qiújiàn〈成〉〈喻〉take measures without regard to changes in circumstances
【刻字】kèzì〈动〉engrave characters

恪

恪 kè〈形〉〈书〉scrupulous and respectful: ～尽职守 perform one's duty scrupulously
【恪守】kèshǒu〈动〉〈书〉faithfully observe: ～诺言 honour one's promise ‖ ～立场 maintain a firm stance
【恪守不渝】kèshǒu-bùyú〈成〉firmly and faithfully abide by

客 kè

A〈名〉1（来客）visitor: 今晚有～来访。I have a visitor tonight. ▸常～, 请～, 稀～ 2（乘客）passenger: ▸～舱, ～车, ～运 3（客商）travelling merchant: 珠宝～ jewellers 4（顾客）customer: ▸顾～ 5（特指某种人）person engaged in a particular pursuit: ▸刺～, 说～, 政～ 6（指外来的）non-native: ▸～串, ～队, ～座
B〈动〉live in a strange land: ～死他乡 die abroad ‖ 作～他乡 live in a strange land ▸～籍, ～居
C〈形〉objective: ▸～观, ～体
D〈量〉〈方〉portion: 两～冰淇淋 two ice creams ‖ 两～馅饼 two pies
【客舱】kècāng〈名〉passenger cabin: 头等～ first-class cabin
【客场】kèchǎng〈名〉［体育］opponent's ground: 我队～失利。We lost our away matches.
【客车】kèchē〈名〉1（指火车）passenger car: ～车厢 carriage 2（指汽车）bus: ～票 bus ticket ‖ 小～ minibus
【客船】kèchuán〈名〉passenger ship: 定期～ liner
【客串】kèchuàn〈动〉give a guest performance: 歌星～演京剧。The singer guested an operatic performance.
【客串演员】kèchuàn yǎnyuán〈名〉guest (actor or actress)
【客地】kèdì〈名〉place far away from home
【客店】kèdiàn〈名〉inn
【客队】kèduì〈名〉［体育］visiting team: 比赛结果～获胜。The match was won by the visitors.
【客饭】kèfàn〈名〉1（为来客做的饭）special menu 2（套餐）set meal
【客房】kèfáng〈名〉1（供来客住）guest room 2（供旅客住）room (in a hotel)
【客服】kèfú〈名〉customer service: ～中心 customer service centre
【客观】kèguān〈形〉objective: ～条件 objective conditions ‖ ～原因 objective cause ‖ ～的报道 objective report ‖ 他的评价比较～。His appraisal is quite objective.
【客观规律】kèguān guīlǜ〈名〉objective law: 按照～办事 work according to objective laws
【客观世界】kèguān shìjiè〈名〉objective world: 改造～ transform the objective world
【客观唯心主义】kèguān wéixīnzhǔyì〈名〉objective idealism
【客官】kèguān〈名〉〈旧〉[a form of address to a customer at a shop or to a guest at a hotel]（男性）sir;（女性）madam
【客滚船】kègǔnchuán〈名〉passenger ship
【客户】kèhù〈名〉customer: 接待～ serve a client ‖ 老～ regular customer
【客户端】kèhùduān〈名〉client
【客货】kè-huò〈名〉freight and passenger
【客机】kèjī〈名〉passenger plane: 北京到纽约的～ plane from Beijing to New York
【客籍】kèjí〈名〉1（外地人）settler from another province: 我是这里的～。I am a settler here. 2〈书〉（寄居的籍贯）province into which settlers move: 我原籍河南，～陕西。My native place is Henan and Shaanxi is my second home.
【客家】Kèjiā〈名〉Hakka
【客家话】Kèjiāhuà ▸p. 918〈名〉Hakka
【客居】kèjū〈动〉〈书〉live in a place other than one's hometown: ～他乡 live in a strange place
【客流】kèliú〈名〉flow of passengers: ～量 volume of passenger traffic
【客轮】kèlún〈名〉passenger ship
【客满】kèmǎn〈动〉[of a theatre, cinema, etc.] have a full house
【客票】kèpiào〈名〉passenger ticket
【客气】kèqi A〈形〉polite: ～话 polite remarks ‖ 他待我们很～。He treated us politely. B〈动〉be polite: 他～了一番就收下了礼物。After a few words of courtesy, he accepted the present.
【客人】kèrén〈名〉1（来访者）visitor: 款待～ entertain a guest ‖ 宴请～ fête a guest 2（旅客）guest: 旅馆对常住～的住宿费实行优惠。The hotel charges less rent to permanent guests. 3（客商）travelling merchant
【客商】kèshāng〈名〉travelling merchant: ～云集展销会。Business people from various places flocked to the exhibition.
【客死】kèsǐ〈动〉〈书〉die in a strange land: ～他乡 die in a foreign land
【客随主便】kèsuízhǔbiàn〈成〉the guest should comply with the wishes of the host
【客堂】kètáng〈名〉〈方〉drawing room
【客套】kètào A〈名〉civilities: 不讲～ do away with formalities B〈动〉exchange courtesies: 生人见面免不了要～几句。When people first meet, they usually exchange greetings.
【客套话】kètàohuà〈名〉polite remarks
【客体】kètǐ〈名〉［哲学］［法律］object: 犯罪～ object of a crime
【客厅】kètīng〈名〉living room; sitting room〈英〉
【客土】kètǔ〈名〉1（指土壤）soil brought in to improve the original 2〈书〉（指地方）foreign land: 侨居～ live abroad
【客位】kèwèi〈名〉seats reserved for guests or passengers
【客星】kèxīng〈名〉〈旧〉［天文］nova and comet
【客姓】kèxìng〈名〉non-native person among a village clan
【客源】kèyuán〈名〉source of tourists
【客运】kèyùn〈名〉passenger transport: ～高峰期 peak time for passenger transport ‖ ～能力 number of passengers able to be transported ‖ ～量 volume of passenger transport ‖ ～站 passenger station
【客栈】kèzhàn〈名〉〈旧〉inn: ～老板 inn keeper
【客座】kèzuò A〈形〉visiting: ～教授 visiting professor B〈名〉guest seat

课（課）kè

A〈名〉1（指课堂）class: 上/下～ start/finish class ‖ 英语～ English class ‖ 四节～ four classes ‖ 这节～不上了。The class has been cancelled. ▸备～, 旷～ 2（科目）course: 开新～ offer a new course ‖ 这学期我有三门选修～。This term I have three elective courses. ▸～程, 必修～ 3（指教材）lesson: 第五～ lesson five ‖ 今天我们上第十～。Let's take the tenth lesson today. 4〈旧〉（指部门）section: 会计/秘书～ accounting/secretarial section 5（指占卜）session at divination: ▸卜～, 起～
B〈动〉〈书〉impose: ～以罚金 impose a fine on sb. ‖ ～以重税 levy a heavy tax on sb. ‖ ～税 levy taxes
【课本】kèběn〈名〉textbook: 编写～ compile a textbook ‖ 语文～ language textbook
【课表】kèbiǎo〈名〉school timetable: 排～ make up a school timetable
【课程】kèchéng〈名〉course: 安排～ arrange a curriculum ‖ ～设置 curriculum ‖ 本科生/研究生～ undergraduate/graduate course
【课程标准】kèchéng biāozhǔn〈名〉syllabus
【课程表】kèchéngbiǎo = 课表 kèbiǎo
【课程软件】kèchéng ruǎnjiàn〈名〉courseware
【课代表】kèdàibiǎo〈名〉class prefect
【课间】kèjiān〈名〉break: ～休息 break
【课间操】kèjiāncāo〈名〉exercise during break
【课件】kèjiàn〈名〉［计算机］courseware
【课目】kèmù〈名〉course
【课时】kèshí〈名〉period
【课室】kèshì〈名〉〈方〉classroom
【课堂】kètáng〈名〉classroom: ～讨论 classroom discussion
【课题】kètí〈名〉1（指项目）topic for discussion: 研究～ research topic ‖ ～负责人 project leader 2（指问题）problem: 提出新～ pose a new problem ‖ 摆在我们面前的重大～ a major task before us

【课题组】kètízǔ〈名〉 research group (for an assigned subject or topic)
【课外】kèwài〈名〉 after-class time: ～活动 extracurricular activities ‖ ～作业 homework
【课文】kèwén〈名〉 text: 背诵～ recite a text
【课业】kèyè〈名〉 schoolwork: 荒废～ neglect one's schoolwork ‖ 减轻～负担 reduce the burden of schoolwork
【课余】kèyú〈名〉 after-school time: ～文体活动 after-school recreational and sports activities ‖ ～时间 after-school time

氪 kè〈名〉［化学］ krypton (Kr)
【氪灯】kèdēng〈名〉［电气］krypton lamp

骒（騍） kè〈形〉 [of horse, mule, etc.] female
【骒马】kèmǎ〈名〉 mare

缂（緙） kè
【缂丝】kèsī **A**〈动〉［美术］ weave with fine silks and gold thread **B**〈名〉 *kesi* product

嗑 kè〈动〉 crack sth. between the teeth: ～瓜子 crack sunflower seeds
▸kē

锞（錁） kè〈名〉 small ingot of gold or silver: 金～ gold ingot ‖ 银～ silver ingot
【锞子】kèzi〈名〉〈旧〉 small ingot of gold or silver

溘 kè〈副〉〈书〉 suddenly
【溘然】kèrán〈副〉〈书〉 suddenly: ～长逝 pass away suddenly

kěn

肯¹ kěn
A〈动〉 agree: 他为什么不～来？ Why won't he come? ‖ 我再三请求，他才～去。 He agreed to go only after I'd asked him several times. ▸～定，首～
B〈助〉 be willing to: ～干 be willing to work hard ‖ 我邀请了她，可她不～来。 I have invited her, but she is not willing to come.

肯² kěn〈名〉〈书〉 flesh attached to bone: ▸～綮，中～
【肯定】kěndìng **A**〈动〉 confirm: 他的方案得到了领导的～。 His plan was approved by the leaders. ‖ 应该充分～成绩。 The achievements should all be affirmed. **B**〈形〉 **1**（正面） positive: ～的评价 positive assessment ‖ 多数人做了～的回答。 The majority replied in the affirmative. **2**（明确） definite: ～的答复 reply in the affirmative **C**〈副〉 definitely: 目前的形势～对我们有利。 The current situation is definitely favourable to us. ‖ 他～会来。 He's sure to come.
【肯定句】kěndìngjù〈名〉［语法］ affirmative sentence
【肯尼亚】Kěnníyà〈名〉 Kenya: ～人 Kenyan
【肯綮】kěnqǐng〈名〉〈书〉〈喻〉 key point: 深中～ get to the heart of the matter
【肯塔基】Kěntǎjī〈名〉 Kentucky
【肯特郡】Kěntèjùn〈名〉 Kent

垦（墾） kěn〈动〉 **1**（翻土） cultivate: ～地 plough the soil **2**（开发） reclaim: ▸～荒，开～
【垦荒】kěnhuāng〈动〉 reclaim wasteland: 该农场今年～100亩。 The farm has reclaimed 100 *mu* of wasteland this year.
【垦区】kěnqū〈名〉 reclamation area
【垦殖】kěnzhí〈动〉 reclaim and cultivate wasteland
【垦种】kěnzhòng〈动〉 reclaim wasteland and plant crops in it

恳（懇） kěn
A〈形〉 sincere: ～劝 earnestly try to persuade ‖ ～谢 thank sincerely ▸～辞，～求，诚～
B〈动〉〈书〉 entreat: 敬～慨允 respectfully request your kind consent
【恳辞】kěncí〈动〉〈书〉 sincerely decline
【恳切】kěnqiè〈形〉 earnest: ～希望 earnestly hope ‖ 言词～ speak in an earnest tone
【恳请】kěnqǐng〈动〉 earnestly request: ～原谅 make an earnest request for forgiveness ‖ ～光临。 Your presence is earnestly requested.
【恳求】kěnqiú〈动〉 entreat: ～原谅 implore pardon (from sb.) ‖ 他～再给他一次机会。 He pleaded that he should be given one more chance.
【恳谈】kěntán〈动〉 talk earnestly: ～会 gathering for free and cordial conversation
【恳托】kěntuō〈动〉 make a sincere request: ～朋友照顾自己年迈的父母 earnestly ask one's friends to take care of one's aged parents
【恳挚】kěnzhì〈形〉〈书〉 sincere: 情意～ show sincere feeling ‖ ～的期望 sincere expectation

啃 kěn〈动〉 **1**（用牙咬） nibble: ～骨头 gnaw at a bone ‖ 老鼠将一些木器～坏了。 The rats had gnawed away some of the woodwork. **2**（费力做） take great pains with one's studies: 这篇文章我～了两个小时才弄懂。 I wrestled with this article for two hours before I got a grip on it.
【啃老】kěnlǎo〈动〉 live off one's parents: ～族 adults living off their parents ‖ 他失业后也加入了～的行列。 After he lost his job, he joined the ranks of those who live off their parents.
【啃硬骨头】kěnyìnggǔtou〈惯〉〈喻〉 tackle an arduous task: 困难再大，也要啃下这块硬骨头。 No matter how difficult it is, we must keep working on it until it is done.
【啃书本儿】kěnshūběnr〈惯〉 read slowly, taking everything in: 不能死～，要联系实际。 There's no use just plodding through a book. You should consider its practical uses.

kèn

裉 kèn〈名〉 seam between the body and the sleeve: 煞～ sew a sleeve on to the body of a jacket ‖ 抬～ measurement from the shoulder to the armpit

kēng

坑 kēng
A〈名〉 **1**（凹陷处） pit: 填～ fill in a hole ‖ 挖～ dig a hole ‖ 路面上的一个～ a hollow in the road ▸泥～，沙～，水～ **2**（地道） pit: ～木 mine timber ▸～道，～井，矿～
B〈动〉 **1**〈书〉（挖坑活埋） bury alive: ▸焚书～儒 **2**（陷害） entrap: ～人 cheat ‖ 她被人～了。 She was hoodwinked. ▸～蒙拐骗
【坑道】kēngdào〈名〉 **1**［矿业］ pit **2**［军事］ tunnel: ～工事 underground fortifications
【坑害】kēnghài〈动〉 lead into a trap: ～顾客 swindle customers ‖ ～青少年 harm youngsters
【坑井】kēngjǐng〈名〉 mine pit
【坑坑洼洼】kēngkeng-wāwā〈形〉 full of bumps and hollows: 这条路～的。 This road is very bumpy.
【坑蒙】kēngmēng〈动〉 swindle: ～顾客 swindle customers
【坑蒙拐骗】kēngmēng-guǎipiàn〈成〉 cheat
【坑骗】kēngpiàn〈动〉 entrap and deceive: ～消费者 cheat consumers
【坑人】kēngrén〈动〉 entrap
【坑洼】kēngwā〈名〉 hole

吭 kēng〈动〉 utter: 她紧闭嘴唇，一声不～。 She pursed her lips and kept silent. ‖ 有什么事需要帮忙，你就～一声。 If you need help, just let me know. ▸～气，～声
▸háng
【吭哧】kēngchi **A**〈拟〉 puff and blow: 累得～～直喘气 puffing and blowing with fatigue to the point of gasping **B**〈动〉 **1**（指做事） toil: 她～了半天才把照相机修好。 She spent ages tinkering with her camera before she fixed it. **2**（指说话） hum and haw: 他～了好久也没把意思说清楚。 He hemmed and hawed for ages and still didn't make himself clear.
【吭气】kēngqì = 吭声 kēngshēng
【吭声】kēngshēng〈动〉 utter a sound: 你到底要不要，快吭一声啊。 Well, do you want it or not? Out with it. ‖ 他正在气头上，谁也不敢～。 He was in a fit of anger and nobody dared to utter a word.

硁（硜） kēng〈拟〉〈书〉 [of stones] clang

铿（鏗） kēng〈拟〉 clang: 坦克在路上～～作响。 Tanks clattered along the road.
【铿锵】kēngqiāng〈形〉 rhythmic and sonorous: ～悦耳 sonorous and pleasant to the ear
【铿然】kēngrán〈形〉〈书〉 loud and clear: 铃声～。 The bell jingles loud and clear.

kōng

空 kōng
A〈形〉 **1**（没东西） empty: 两手～～ be empty-handed ‖ ～盒子 empty box ‖ 那棵老树中间是～的。 The old tree is hollow inside. ▸～腹，囊～如洗 **2**（空洞） lacking substance: ▸～洞，～泛，～想

B〈名〉 sky: 碧～ clear blue sky ‖ 晴～ clear sky ▸～中楼阁, 领～
C〈副〉 in vain: ～忙 make fruitless efforts ‖ ～跑一趟 make a journey for nothing
D〈动〉 be without: ▸～前绝后, 目～一切 ▸kòng

【空靶】kōngbǎ〈名〉 aerial target: ～实弹射击 aerial target live firing

【空包弹】kōngbāodàn〈名〉［军事］ dummy cartridge

【空仓】kōngcāng［金融］**A**〈动〉[of investors] sell all securities **B**〈名〉 short position: ～股民 investors with short positions

【空巢家庭】kōngcháo jiātíng〈名〉 empty-nest family

【空乘】kōngchéng〈名〉 **1**（指服务） on-board service: ～人员 airline attendants **2**（乘务员）（男性） airline steward;（女性） airline stewardess

【空城计】kōngchéngjì〈名〉 **1**〈本〉 presenting a bold front to conceal a weak defence **2**〈喻〉（空腹） empty stomach: 我的肚子在唱～。 I'm so hungry that my stomach keeps rumbling.

【空挡】kōngdǎng〈名〉［机械］neutral: 挂～ put into neutral

【空荡荡】kōngdàngdàng〈形〉 deserted: ～的街道 empty street ‖ 屋子里～的，没有一件摆设。 The room was completely bare.

【空洞】kōngdòng **A**〈名〉 cavity: 肺～ pulmonary cavity **B**〈形〉 empty: ～的说教 empty preaching ‖ 内容～ devoid of content

【空洞无物】kōngdòng-wúwù〈成〉 devoid of content

【空洞洞】kōngdòngdòng〈形〉 deserted: 村子里面～的。 The village was completely deserted.

【空对地】kōngduìdì〈形〉［军事］ air-to-surface: ～导弹 air-to-surface missile (ASM)

【空对空】kōngduìkōng〈形〉 **1**［军事］ air-to-air: ～导弹 air-to-air missile (AAM) **2**（空话） impractical: 这些空话有什么用处，完全是～嘛。 What's the point of such empty talk? It's completely useless.

【空乏】kōngfá〈形〉 empty and dull: 此文辞藻华丽，但内容～。 The article is ornate but devoid of content.

【空翻】kōngfān〈名〉［体育］ somersault: 后/前～ backward/forward somersault

【空泛】kōngfàn〈形〉 vague and general: 发表～的议论 talk generalities ‖ 内容～ be devoid of content

【空防】kōngfáng〈名〉 air defence

【空房】kōngfáng〈名〉 empty room: 独守～ be abandoned at home

【空腹】kōngfù〈动〉 be on an empty stomach: ～抽血化验 take a blood test on an empty stomach

【空港】kōnggǎng〈简称〉= 航空港

【空谷足音】kōnggǔ-zúyīn〈成〉〈喻〉 unexpected good news

【空喊】kōnghǎn〈动〉 clamour but not take action: 光是～不行，应该采取行动了。 Mere talk is not going to get us anywhere. It's high time we took action.

【空号】kōnghào〈名〉 out-of-service number: 对不起，您拨的是～。 Sorry, the number you dialled is not in service.

【空耗】kōnghào〈动〉 waste: ～金钱/精力/时间 waste money/energy/time

【空话】kōnghuà〈名〉 empty talk: ～连篇，言之无物 long-winded and devoid of substance ‖ 他光讲～，没有实际行动。 He is all talk but no action.

【空欢喜】kōnghuānxǐ〈动〉 rejoice too soon

【空幻】kōnghuàn〈形〉 illusory: 情节～ imaginary plot

【空际】kōngjì〈名〉〈书〉 sky: 电视塔高入～。 The television tower rises high into the air.

【空寂】kōngjì〈形〉〈书〉 quiet and deserted: 街道上～无人。 There's not a single soul in the street.

【空架子】kōngjiàzi〈名〉 skeleton: 那家公司既无人员，又无资金，完全是个～。 That company is a mere skeleton, with neither staff nor funds.

【空间】kōngjiān〈名〉 room: 留出～ leave space ‖ 生存～ living space ‖ 没有活动的～。 There is no room to move around in.

【空间技术】kōngjiān jìshù〈名〉 space technology

【空间科学】kōngjiān kēxué〈名〉 space science

【空间站】kōngjiānzhàn〈名〉 space station

【空降】kōngjiàng〈动〉 be airborne: ～地点 landing area ‖ ～师 airborne division ‖ ～部队 airborne unit

【空降兵】kōngjiàngbīng〈名〉 airborne troops

【空姐】kōngjiě〈简称〉= 空中小姐

【空警】kōngjǐng〈名〉 air police

【空军】kōngjūn〈名〉 air force: ～司令 commander of the air force

【空空】kōngkōng〈形〉 empty: 两手～ be empty-handed

【空空如也】kōngkōngrúyě〈成〉 absolutely empty: 有些人巧舌如簧，可是肚子里却～。 Some people have the gift of the gab but turn out to be totally empty at heart.

【空口】kōngkǒu **A**〈副〉 on its own: ～吃饭 eat rice without dishes to go with it **B**〈名〉 prattle: 光～说不行，我们得采取实际行动。 Hollow promises alone are of no use. We must adopt real measures.

【空口说白话】kōngkǒu shuō báihuà〈惯〉 all talk and no action: 不能～ must not merely pay lip service

【空口无凭】kōngkǒu-wúpíng〈成〉 the spoken word cannot be taken as proof: ～，立字为证。 Word of mouth being no guarantee, a written statement is hereby given.

【空旷】kōngkuàng〈形〉 spacious: ～的原野 expanse of open country ‖ 家具搬出去后，屋子显得～了些。 When the furniture was removed, the house looked a bit more spacious.

【空阔】kōngkuò〈形〉 open and vast: 一片～的草原 a vast expanse of grassland

【空廓】kōngkuò〈形〉 vast: ～的蓝天 vast blue sky

【空灵】kōnglíng〈形〉 free and natural: 笔触～ free and natural style of writing

【空论】kōnglùn〈名〉 idle talk: 发～ make empty remarks

【空落落】kōngluòluò〈形〉 empty and desolate: 院子里～的，一个人也没有。 The courtyard was empty and desolate with not a soul around. ‖ 丈夫离家后，她心里感到～的。 After her husband left home, she felt a void in her heart.

【空门】kōngmén〈名〉 **1**［佛教］ Buddhism: 遁入～ become a Buddhist monk or nun **2**［体育］ free goal

【空濛】kōngméng〈形〉〈书〉 hazy: 山色～。 The hills were shrouded in mist.

【空名】kōngmíng〈名〉 empty title: 他的主席头衔只是～而已。 He is chairman only in name.

【空难】kōngnàn〈名〉 plane crash: 死于～ die in a plane crash

【空炮】kōngpào〈名〉 empty talk: 放～ make empty talk

【空气】kōngqì〈名〉 **1**（大气） air: 污染～ pollute the air ‖ ～清新。 The air is crisp. **2**（气氛） atmosphere: 制造紧张～ create a tense atmosphere ‖ 学习～很浓。 It's a very concentrated environment for study.

【空气动力学】kōngqì dònglìxué〈名〉 aerodynamics

【空气过滤器】kōngqì guòlǜqì〈名〉 air filter

【空气加湿器】kōngqì jiāshīqì〈名〉 humidifier

【空气力学】kōngqì lìxué〈名〉 aeromechanics

【空气流通】kōngqì liútōng〈名〉 ventilation

【空气污染】kōngqì wūrǎn〈名〉 air pollution: ～指数 air pollution index

【空气质量】kōngqì zhìliàng〈名〉 air quality: ～优 very good air quality

【空前】kōngqián〈动〉 be unprecedented: ～高涨 reach an all-time high ‖ 文艺界出现了～的繁荣。 Literature and art have never flourished so much.

【空前绝后】kōngqián-juéhòu〈成〉 be unprecedented and unrepeatable: 在历史上～ be historically unique

【空勤】kōngqín〈名〉 air duty: ～人员 flight crew

【空嫂】kōngsǎo〈名〉 married female flight attendant

【空身】kōngshēn〈动〉 carry no luggage: 我看见她～儿出去了。 I saw her leaving empty-handed.

【空驶】kōngshǐ〈动〉 run without carrying passengers or freight: ～的出租车 empty cab

【空手】kōngshǒu〈动〉 be empty-handed: ～搏斗 wrestle bare-handed ‖ ～而归 return empty-handed

【空手道】kōngshǒudào ▸p. 909〈名〉［体育］ karate: ～运动员 karateka

【空手套白狼】kōngshǒu tào báiláng〈俗〉 get something for nothing

【空疏】kōngshū〈形〉〈书〉 lacking in substance: 才学～ have little learning

【空谈】kōngtán **A**〈名〉 idle talk: ～家 prattler ‖ 要实干，不要～ less talk, more action ‖ 行动胜于～。 Actions speak louder than words. **B**〈动〉 indulge in empty talk

【空调】kōngtiáo〈名〉 air conditioning: 中央～ central air conditioning

【空头】kōngtóu **A**〈名〉［经济］ bear: 做～ short-sell **B**〈形〉 nominal: ～政治家 armchair politician ‖ ～人情 nominal friendship

【空头支票】kōngtóu zhīpiào〈名〉 **1**〈本〉 bad cheque **2**〈喻〉 empty promise

【空投】kōngtóu〈动〉 airdrop: ～救灾物资 airdrop relief supplies ‖ ～伞兵 drop paratroops from the air

【空文】kōngwén〈名〉 ineffective law: 一纸～ a mere scrap of paper

【空袭】kōngxí〈动〉 air raid: 进行～ make an air raid ‖ 在～中丧生 be killed in an air raid ‖ ～警报 air-raid alarm

【空想】kōngxiǎng **A**〈动〉 daydream: 闭门～ indulge in fantasy behind closed doors **B**〈名〉 daydream: 这并不是～。 This is not an idle dream.

【空想社会主义】kōngxiǎng shèhuìzhǔyì〈名〉 utopian socialism

【空心】kōngxīn **A**〈动〉 become hollow: 那

k

棵树～了。The tree has become hollow inside. **B** 〈形〉 hollow: ～管子 hollow pipe ▸kòngxīn
【空心菜】kōngxīncài〈名〉 water spinach
【空心萝卜】kōngxīn luóbo 〈名〉〈喻〉 unlettered, incompetent or useless person
【空心面】kōngxīnmiàn = 通心粉 tōngxīnfěn
【空心砖】kōngxīnzhuān〈名〉 block
【空虚】kōngxū 〈形〉 hollow: 后方～ weakly defended rear ‖ 精神～ be spiritually empty
【空穴来风】kōngxué-láifēng〈成〉〈喻〉 weakness lends wings to rumours
【空言无补】kōngyán-wúbǔ 〈成〉 empty talk is of no use
【空域】kōngyù〈名〉 airspace: ～划分 airspace division
【空运】kōngyùn〈动〉 transport by air: ～救灾物资 airlift relief supplies
【空载】kōngzài〈名〉 idle load
【空战】kōngzhàn〈名〉 aerial combat
【空置】kōngzhì〈形〉 unoccupied: 客房～率 rate of vacant rooms in a hotel
【空中】kōngzhōng 〈名〉 air: ～打击 air strike ‖ 鸟儿在～飞翔。Birds are flying in the air.
【空中飞人】kōngzhōng fēirén 〈名〉［杂技］ trapeze acrobat
【空中加油】kōngzhōng jiāyóu 〈名〉 air refuelling
【空中客车】Kōngzhōng Kèchē 〈名〉 Airbus
【空中楼阁】kōngzhōng-lóugé〈成〉〈喻〉 castle in the air
【空中小姐】kōngzhōng xiǎojiě 〈名〉 air hostess
【空竹】kōngzhú 〈名〉 diabolo: 抖～ play diabolo
【空转】kōngzhuàn〈动〉 **1**（指机器） idle: 机器～着。The machine is running idle. **2**（指轮子） spin

倥 kōng

▸kǒng
【倥侗】kōngtóng 〈形〉〈书〉 unenlightened

箜 kōng

【箜篌】kōnghóu〈名〉 *konghou* [ancient Chinese stringed instrument]

kǒng

孔 kǒng

A 〈名〉 hole: 钻～ bore a hole ‖ 钥匙～ keyhole ‖ 四～桥 bridge of four spans ▸鼻～, 穿～, 无～不入
B 〈量〉 [for cave-dwellings, oil wells, etc.]: 三～窑洞 three cave-dwellings
【孔道】kǒngdào〈名〉 pass: 交通～ traffic junction
【孔洞】kǒngdòng〈名〉 opening
【孔方兄】kǒngfāngxiōng 〈名〉〈诙〉 money
【孔夫子】Kǒngfūzǐ〈名〉〈敬〉 Confucius
【孔教】Kǒngjiào〈名〉 Confucianism
【孔径】kǒngjìng〈名〉 **1**［物理］ aperture **2**［机械］ bore diameter
【孔孟之道】Kǒng-Mèng zhī dào〈名〉 doctrines of Confucius and Mencius
【孔庙】Kǒngmiào〈名〉 Confucian temple
【孔明灯】Kǒngmíngdēng〈名〉 Kongming lantern [a paper lantern that ascends into the sky when lit]
【孔丘】Kǒngqiū〈名〉 Confucius
【孔雀】kǒngquè〈名〉［鸟类］ peacock: ～开屏 peacock fanning its tail
【孔雀蓝】kǒngquèlán〈名〉 peacock blue
【孔雀绿】kǒngquèlǜ〈名〉 peacock green
【孔雀石】kǒngquèshí〈名〉 malachite
【孔雀石绿】kǒngquèshílǜ〈名〉 malachite green
【孔武有力】kǒngwǔ-yǒulì〈成〉 have great physical strength and courage
【孔隙】kǒngxì〈名〉 pore
【孔穴】kǒngxué〈名〉 cavity
【孔眼】kǒngyǎn〈名〉 eyelet
【孔子】Kǒngzǐ〈名〉 Confucius

> **孔子**
>
> Confucius (551-479 BC), philosopher, politician, moral teacher, and founder of the Confucian School. Confucius was born in Zouyi in the Kingdom of Lu (today's Qufu in Shandong Province). His teaching emphasizes morality in personal and governmental affairs, justice, and correct observance of social relationships. The Confucian school of thought has had a profound social and cultural influence on Chinese, Japanese, Korean and Vietnamese culture. *The Analects of Confucius* (《论语》) records the sage's conversations with his disciples. *The Spring and Autumn Annals* (《春秋》), which he revised based on the records of Kingdom of Lu historians, became China's first historical work founded on annalistic principles.

恐 kǒng

A 〈动〉 **1**（害怕） fear: ▸～惧, 惊～, 有恃无～ **2**（使害怕） terrify: ▸～吓
B 〈副〉 perhaps: 传闻～不真实。The rumour may not be true.
【恐怖】kǒngbù〈形〉 terrifying: 从事～活动 engage in terror ‖ ～分子 terrorist ‖ 极其～的场面 horrific scenes
【恐怖症】kǒngbùzhèng ▸**p. 50**〈名〉［医学］ phobia
【恐怖主义】kǒngbùzhǔyì〈名〉 terrorism
【恐怖组织】kǒngbù zǔzhī 〈名〉 terrorist organization
【恐高症】kǒnggāozhèng 〈名〉［心理］ acrophobia
【恐吓】kǒnghè 〈动〉 intimidate: ～信 threatening letter ‖ 小偷用刀子～她。The thief threatened her with a knife.
【恐慌】kǒnghuāng〈形〉 frightened: 感到～ feel scared ‖ 引起～ cause panic
【恐惧】kǒngjù〈形〉 frightened: ～不安 be frightened and restless ‖ 无所～ feel no fear
【恐龙】kǒnglóng〈名〉 dinosaur: ～蛋化石 fossilized dinosaur egg
【恐怕】kǒngpà **A**〈动〉 fear: 他～迟到，老早就起来了。He got up very early for fear of being late. **B**〈副〉 maybe: 天～要下雨了。It looks like it's going to rain. ‖ 他的英语～是说得最好的了。He probably speaks the best English.

倥 kǒng

▸kōng
【倥偬】kǒngzǒng 〈形〉〈书〉 pressing: ▸戎马～

kòng

空 kòng

A〈动〉 leave empty: ～出前三排座位来。Leave the first three rows of seats vacant. ‖ 每个段落开头～两格。Leave two spaces at the start of each paragraph.
B〈形〉 vacant: ～位子 vacant seat ‖ 该职位仍然～着。The post is still vacant. ▸～白, ～地, ～额
C〈名〉 **1**（指空间） empty space: 车里挤满了人，没～儿了。The bus is already packed with people; there is no more room. ‖ 屋里堆得连下脚的～儿都没有。The house was so crammed that it was hard to get in. ▸填～ **2**（指时间） free time: 你明天有～吗? Are you free tomorrow? ‖ 他没～看书。He had no time for reading. ▸抽～
▸kōng
【空白】kòngbái〈名〉 blank space: 填补～ fill in a gap ‖ 记忆中的～ a blank in one's memory ‖ 我的脑子突然间一片～。Suddenly my mind went blank.
【空白点】kòngbáidiǎn 〈名〉 blank: 过去该地区的高等教育是个～。Higher education used to be non-existent in this area.
【空当】kòngdāng 〈名〉 **1**（指空间） space: 抽屉满了，没有～放这本书。The drawer is full; there's no space for this book. **2**（指时间） break: 趁这～，我去寄封信。I'll go and post a letter during the break.
【空地】kòngdì〈名〉 **1**（指土地） vacant lot: 利用～种菜 grow vegetables on vacant lots **2**（指空间） available space: 屋里还有～儿加张床吗? Is there still room for another bed in the house?
【空额】kòng'é〈名〉 vacancy: 吃～ pocket wages from vacant positions ‖ 该部门有六个～。This department has six vacancies.
【空格】kònggé〈名〉 **1**（指文档） blank space **2**［计算机］ space: ～键 space bar
【空缺】kòngquē 〈名〉 **1**（空职位） vacancy: 造成～ create a vacancy ‖ 英语系有个～。There's a vacancy in the English Department. **2**（不足之处） gap: 填补～ fill a gap
【空位】kòngwèi〈名〉 **1**（指座位） vacant seat: 还有一个～。There's still one vacant seat left. **2**（指职位） vacancy: 他退休后公司里留出一个～。His retirement created a vacancy in the company. **3**（指空间） free space: 停车场内还有～吗? Are there still spaces in the car park?
【空隙】kòngxì〈名〉 **1**（指空间） gap: 桌子挨得很紧，没有一点～。The desks are very close to each other, with no space in between. **2**（指时间） interval: 战斗～ intervals between battles **3** = 空子 kòngzi 1
【空暇】kòngxiá〈名〉 free time: 工作太忙，没有一点～。Work is too busy. There's no free time.
【空闲】kòngxián **A**〈形〉 free: ～时间 leisure time **B**〈名〉 free time: 他很忙，很少有～。He is very busy and has little leisure time. ‖ 他一有～就看书。He reads whenever he has some spare time.
【空心】kòngxīn〈动〉 take on an empty stomach: ～喝酒 drink on an empty stomach
▸kōngxīn
【空余】kòngyú〈形〉 vacant: ～房间 vacant room ‖ ～时间 free time ‖ ～座位 unoccupied seats
【空子】kòngzi〈名〉 **1**（可乘之机） opportunity: 钻～ exploit an opportunity **2**〈口〉（指空间） unoccupied place: 行李架满了，一点儿～都没有。The rack is full; there's absolutely no more room.

3（指时间） free time: 抽～来西安看看。Find time to come to Xi'an for a visit.

控[1] kòng〈动〉accuse: 他被～杀人。He was accused of murder. ▸～告, ～诉

控[2] kòng〈动〉control: ～盘 manipulate stock quotations ▸～制, 遥～

控[3] kòng〈动〉**1**（指身体） fail to be sufficiently supported: 别让他～着头睡。Don't let him sleep with his head unsupported. ‖ 你整天这样坐着，腿会～肿的。Your legs will swell up if you sit all day long in that position. **2**（指容器） turn a container upside down to empty the contents: 把瓶子～干净。Turn the bottle upside down to empty it.

【控方】kòngfāng〈名〉［法律］prosecuting party: ～律师 prosecuting counsel

【控告】kònggào〈动〉accuse: ～某人 bring in an indictment against sb. ‖ 有人～他犯有叛国罪。He was charged with treason.

【控购】kònggòu〈动〉control purchase: ～商品 merchandise subject to controlled purchases ‖ ～指标 quota for controlled purchases

【控股】kònggǔ〈动〉［金融］hold a controlling number of the shares: ～公司 holding company

【控诉】kòngsù〈动〉accuse: 提出～ file an appeal ‖ ～书 written accusation

【控制】kòngzhì〈动〉control: ～火势蔓延 keep a fire under control ‖ 失去～ lose control ‖ 实行严格～ impose strict controls (over) ‖ 局势已得到～。The situation has been brought under control.

【控制论】kòngzhìlùn〈名〉［数学］cybernetics

【控制面板】kòngzhì miànbǎn〈名〉control panel

【控制台】kòngzhìtái〈名〉［计算机］console

kōu

抠（摳） kōu

A〈动〉**1**（挖） pick at: ～鼻孔/耳屎 pick one's nose/ear **2**（刻） carve: 在椅子上～花 carve a design on the chair **3**（细究） study meticulously: 死～书本 pore over books ‖ 一字一句地～ puzzle over every single word ▸～字眼儿

B〈形〉〈口〉stingy: 她这人可真～! She's really stingy! ▸～门儿

【抠门儿】kōuménr〈形〉〈口〉〈贬〉stingy

【抠搜】kōusou **A**〈动〉pick at: 别老～脚丫子! Stop picking at your feet! **B**〈形〉stingy

【抠唆】kōusuo = 抠搜 kōusou

【抠字眼儿】kōu zìyǎnr〈动〉be particular about words: 他爱～。He's very particular about wording.

眍（瞘） kōu〈动〉become sunken: 手术后他的眼睛都～进去了。His eyes became quite sunken after the operation.

【眍䁖】kōulou = 眍 kōu

kǒu

口 kǒu

A〈名〉**1** ▸p. 614（嘴） mouth: 开～说话 open one's mouth to speak ‖ 病从～入 disease enters through the mouth ▸～技, ～试, 祸从～出 **2**（出口） opening: 胡同～ mouth of an alley ‖ 火山～ mouth of a volcano ‖ 瓶～ mouth of a bottle ▸出～, 封～, 枪～ **3**（关口） gateway of the Great Wall: 张家～ Zhangjiakou **4**（口子） hole: 报纸上撕了一个～。There's a tear in the paper. ‖ 墙上裂了道～儿。There is a crack in the wall. ▸豁～, 决～, 伤～ **5**（刃） blade: 刀卷～了。The edge of the knife is blunted. ‖ 这把剪刀还没开～。The scissors have not been sharpened. ▸刀～ **6**（指动物年龄） age of an animal: 五岁～ five years of age ‖ 这牛～还轻。The ox is still young. **7**（指管理系统） departments of a certain type: 文教～ departments of education and culture ▸归～ **8**（口味） one's taste: 香甜可～ delicious ▸～轻, ～重 **9**（话语） talk: ▸～才, ～吃, ～语 **10**（人口） people: ▸户～, 拖家带～ **11**（港口） port: ▸出～, 进～, 转～

B〈量〉[family members, population, mouthfuls, wells, etc.]: 吸～气 take a breath ‖ 咬一～蛋糕 take a bite of a cake ‖ 两～棺材/井 two coffins/wells ‖ 三～之家 a family of three ‖ 一～好牙齿 a mouthful of good teeth ‖ 我被蚊子叮了一～。I was bitten by a mosquito.

【口岸】kǒu'àn〈名〉port: 开放～ open a port ‖ 入境～ port of entry ‖ 通商～ commercial port

【口杯】kǒubēi〈名〉cup

【口碑】kǒubēi〈名〉reputation: ～不好 have a bad name ‖ ～很好 have a good reputation

【口碑载道】kǒubēi-zàidào〈成〉be praised everywhere by the people

【口才】kǒucái〈名〉eloquence: 有～ be articulate ‖ ～好 be a good talker

【口彩】kǒucǎi〈名〉auspicious remarks

【口吃】kǒuchī〈动〉stammer: 有点儿～ have a slight stutter ‖ 讲话～ have a speech impediment

【口齿】kǒuchǐ〈名〉**1**（发音） enunciation: ～不清 be inarticulate **2**（口头表达能力） ability to speak: 她～伶俐。She has a quick tongue. **3**（指动物年龄） age of a draught animal: 看一下～，就知道这头牛的年岁。You can tell the age of a cow from its teeth.

【口臭】kǒuchòu〈名〉bad breath: 有～ have bad breath

【口传】kǒuchuán〈动〉instruct orally: ～心授 oral teaching inspires true understanding ‖ 这部史诗是～下来的。The story has been handed down orally.

【口疮】kǒuchuāng ▸p. 50〈名〉［医学］aphtha: 生～ have aphtha

【口袋】kǒudai〈名〉**1**（衣兜） pocket: 把钥匙装进～ put the key in one's pocket ‖ 外衣/裤子～ coat/trouser pocket **2**（用于装物） bag: 面～ flour sack ‖ 一～苹果 a bag of apples

【口淡】kǒudàn〈形〉〈方〉**1**（指食物） not too salty **2**（指人） fond of food that is not too salty

【口耳相传】kǒu-ěr xiāngchuán〈成〉be passed down orally: 有些风俗习惯是～保存下来的。Some customs have been passed down orally.

【口耳之学】kǒu-ěrzhīxué〈成〉fragmentary knowledge from hearsay

【口风】kǒufeng〈名〉one's intention or view as revealed in what one says: ～紧 be tight-lipped ‖ 听他的～，好像不赞成这件事。From the way he talks about it, he doesn't seem to approve of this. ‖ 先探探她的～。Sound her out first.

【口服】kǒufú〈动〉take orally: ～液 oral liquid ‖ 此药不可～。This medicine is not to be taken orally.

【口福】kǒufú〈名〉gourmet's luck: ～不浅 be lucky to enjoy good food ‖ 一饱～ satisfy one's appetite for good food

【口腹】kǒufù〈名〉food: 不贪～ not indulge one's appetite

【口干舌燥】kǒugān-shézào〈成〉be parched: 他讲得～。His mouth was dry with talking.

【口感】kǒugǎn〈名〉food texture: ～不错 have a nice texture

【口供】kǒugòng〈名〉verbal confession: 录～ record a confession

【口号】kǒuhào〈名〉slogan: 喊～ chant slogans ‖ 宣传～ propaganda slogan

【口红】kǒuhóng〈名〉lipstick: 涂～ put on lipstick

【口惠而实不至】kǒuhuì ér shí bù zhì〈成〉pay lip service

【口技】kǒujì〈名〉mimicry: ～演员 mimic

【口交】kǒujiāo〈名〉oral sex

【口角】kǒujiǎo〈名〉corner of the mouth: ～挂笑 have a faint smile playing about the corners of one's mouth
▸kǒujué

【口角春风】kǒujiǎo-chūnfēng〈成〉put in a good word for sb.

【口角生风】kǒujiǎo-shēngfēng〈成〉speak fluently

【口紧】kǒujǐn〈形〉tight-lipped

【口径】kǒujìng〈名〉**1**（指直径） calibre: 大～炮 heavy-calibre gun ‖ 小～手枪 small-calibre pistol **2**（指规格） specifications: 不合～ not meet the requirements ‖ 螺钉与螺母～不合。The diameters of the screw and the nut are not the same. **3**（指看法、原则） account of an event: 统一～ agree on a uniform version ‖ ～一致 speak along the same lines

【口诀】kǒujué〈名〉mnemonic rhyme: 背～ memorize a formula ‖ 乘法～ multiplication formula ‖ 珠算～ abacus rhymes

【口角】kǒujué〈动〉quarrel: 不要为小事和人～。Don't quarrel with people about small things.
▸kǒujiǎo

【口渴】kǒukě〈形〉thirsty: 感到～ feel thirsty

【口口声声】kǒukou-shēngshēng〈成〉keep on saying: 他～说自己是冤枉的。He kept on saying that he had been wronged.

【口快】kǒukuài〈形〉outspoken

【口粮】kǒuliáng〈名〉grain ration: 准备一周的～ prepare a week's provisions

【口令】kǒulìng〈名〉**1**（指命令） word of command: 听我的～! Hear my order! **2**（指密码） codeword: 今晚的～是什么? What's tonight's watchword?

【口蜜腹剑】kǒumì-fùjiàn〈成〉〈喻〉play a double game: ～的人 treacherous person

【口蘑】kǒumó〈名〉Saint George's mushroom

【口器】kǒuqì〈名〉［昆虫］mouthparts

【口气】kǒuqi〈名〉**1**（语气） tone: 命令的～ commanding tone of voice ‖ ～强硬的声明 strongly worded statement ‖ 别用那种～跟我说话。Don't speak to me in that tone. **2**（说话的气势） way of speaking: 说话～很硬 speak in an unyielding tone ‖ 好大的～! What high-flown sentiments! **3**（口风） implication: 听他的～，这事可能希望不大。From the way he spoke, there seems to be little hope for this.

k

【口腔】kǒuqiāng〈名〉［生理］ oral cavity: ～疾病 disease of the mouth ‖ ～医院 stomatological hospital ‖ ～科 department of stomatology

【口琴】kǒuqín ▸**p. 929**〈名〉 harmonica

【口轻】kǒuqīng〈形〉 **1**（指食物） not too salty: 这菜太～了，再加点盐。 This dish is too bland. Put some more salt in it. **2**（指人） fond of food that is not too salty: 我～，别把菜做咸了。 I don't like salty food. Please don't make my food too salty. **3**（指马、骡等） young: ～的马 young horse

【口若悬河】kǒuruò-xuánhé〈成〉 speak torrents, and with eloquence: 演讲者～地说了一大通。 The speaker gushed forth in streams of wondrous eloquence.

【口哨】kǒushào〈名〉 whistling sound made through rounded lips: 吹～ whistle

【口舌】kǒushé〈名〉 **1**（纠纷） dispute or misunderstanding caused by gossip: 与人发生～ quarrel with sb. **2**（话语） talking: 不要白费～ save one's breath

【口实】kǒushí〈名〉〈书〉 cause for gossip: 说话时要小心，免得落下～。 Be careful about what you say. You don't want to give anyone anything they could use against you.

【口试】kǒushì〈动〉 take an oral examination: 通过～ pass one's oral ‖ 英语～ English oral

【口是心非】kǒushì-xīnfēi〈成〉 be two-faced: ～的人是靠不住的。 You can't trust people who say one thing but mean another.

【口授】kǒushòu〈动〉 **1**（讲授） instruct orally: ～弟子 teach one's pupils orally **2**（口述） dictate: 记录～内容 take fast dictation

【口述】kǒushù〈动〉 give an oral account: ～自己的冒险经历 give an oral account of one's adventure

【口述历史】kǒushù lìshǐ〈名〉 oral history

【口水】kǒushuǐ〈名〉 saliva: 流～ drool

【口水战】kǒushuǐzhàn〈名〉 war of words: 两国的～愈演愈烈。 The war of words between the two countries intensified.

【口说无凭】kǒushuō-wúpíng〈成〉 verbal statements are no guarantee

【口算】kǒusuàn〈动〉 calculate orally

【口蹄疫】kǒutíyì〈名〉 foot-and-mouth disease

【口条】kǒutiáo〈名〉 tongue (as food)

【口头】kǒutóu **A**〈名〉 words: 心里愿意，～上却不说 be willing in one's heart, but not express it in words **B**〈形〉 oral: ～汇报 make a verbal statement ‖ ～通知 notify orally ‖ ～翻译 oral interpretation

【口头禅】kǒutóuchán〈名〉 one's favourite saying: "我才不在乎呢"成了她的～。 'I don't care' has become her pet phrase.

k

【口头文学】kǒutóu wénxué〈名〉 oral literature

【口头语】kǒutóuyǔ〈名〉 pet phrase

【口吐莲花】kǒutǔ-liánhuā〈成〉 have the gift of the gab

【口味】kǒuwèi〈名〉 **1**（偏好） one's taste: 合～ be to one's taste ‖ 爵士乐不怎么对我的～。 Jazz isn't really my scene. **2**（味道） flavour: 这菜～不错。 The dish is tasty. ‖ 这些菜都是四川～。 These are all Sichuan-style dishes.

【口吻】kǒuwěn〈名〉 **1**［动物］ snout **2**（语气） tone: 责备的～ note of reproach ‖ 他说话时略带嘲弄的～。 His voice carried a note of mockery.

【口误】kǒuwù **A**〈动〉 make a slip of the tongue **B**〈名〉 slip of the tongue

【口涎】kǒuxián〈名〉 saliva

【口香糖】kǒuxiāngtáng〈名〉 chewing gum

【口信】kǒuxìn〈名〉 oral message: 给人带～ pass on a message to sb. ‖ 给人留～ leave a message for sb.

【口形】kǒuxíng〈名〉 degree of lip-rounding

【口型】kǒuxíng〈名〉 shape of the mouth as one speaks or produces a sound: 对～ lip-sync

【口眼歪斜】kǒu-yǎn wāixié〈名〉［中医］ facial paralysis

【口译】kǒuyì〈动〉 interpret: 为某人做～ interpret for sb.

【口音】kǒuyīn〈名〉 **1**（声音） voice: 她一下就听出了儿子的～。 She recognized her son's voice immediately. **2** ▸**p. 918**（乡音） accent: 说话带有浓重的地方～ speak with a strong accent ‖ 听他的～就知道他是河南人。 You can tell from the way he speaks that he comes from Henan Province.

【口语】kǒuyǔ〈名〉 spoken language: ～考试 oral examination ‖ 英语～ spoken English

【口谕】kǒuyù〈名〉〈旧〉 verbal instruction

【口燥唇干】kǒuzào-chúngān ＝ 口干舌燥 kǒugān-shézào

【口占】kǒuzhàn〈动〉 improvise: ～一绝 improvise a quatrain

【口罩】kǒuzhào〈名〉 surgical mask

【口重】kǒuzhòng〈形〉 **1**（指食物） salty: 他不爱吃～的，少放点儿盐。 Just a little salt, please. He doesn't like salty food. **2**（指人） fond of salty food: 我这位朋友～。 This friend of mine is fond of salty food.

【口诛笔伐】kǒuzhū-bǐfá〈成〉 condemn in both speech and writing: 对腐败现象应该～。 Corruption should be condemned both by word of mouth and in writing.

【口髭】kǒuzī〈名〉 moustache

【口子】kǒuzi **A**〈量〉 person: 我家有五～。 There are five people in my family. **B**〈名〉 **1**〈口〉（夫妻） my husband or wife: 两～生活很幸福。 The husband and wife lived a very blessed life. **2**（缺口） opening: 洪水将堤防冲了一个～。 The floods found a vent through the dykes. **3**（裂缝） crack: 玻璃杯裂了一道～。 There is a crack in the cup. ‖ 衬衣上给撕了一个～。 There's a tear in the shirt. **4**（破例） precedent: 我们可不能开这个～啊！ We cannot afford to set such a precedent!

kòu

叩 kòu

〈动〉 **1**（敲） knock: ～门 knock at the door ▸～诊 **2**（磕头） kowtow: ▸～首, ～头, ～谢 **3**〈书〉（问） enquire: ～其姓名 ask sb.'s name

【叩拜】kòubài〈动〉〈旧〉 kowtow: ～祖先 kowtow to one's ancestors

【叩齿】kòuchǐ〈动〉 click the teeth

【叩打】kòudǎ〈动〉 tap: 老师用手指～着办公桌。 The teacher tapped the desk with her fingers.

【叩见】kòujiàn〈动〉〈旧〉 pay a visit to

【叩首】kòushǒu〈动〉 kowtow: 三跪九～ kneel down three times and kowtow nine times

【叩头】kòutóu〈动〉 kowtow

【叩头虫】kòutóuchóng〈名〉 click beetle

【叩头求饶】kòutóu-qiúráo〈成〉 kowtow begging for mercy

【叩问】kòuwèn〈动〉〈书〉 make enquiries

【叩谢】kòuxiè〈动〉 kowtow in thanks: 登门～ call on sb. to express one's earnest thanks

【叩诊】kòuzhěn〈动〉［医学］ percuss

扣[1] kòu

A〈动〉 **1**（套住） button up: ～纽扣 do up the buttons ‖ 把门窗～上 bolt up the doors and windows **2**（罩住） place a cup, bowl, etc. upside down: 用碗把菜～上 cover the dish with a bowl **3**〈喻〉（安上） label: ～上叛国的罪名 label sb. as a traitor ▸～帽子 **4**（扣押） detain: ～了两名人质 take two hostages ‖ 警察～了他的车。 The police took away his car. ▸～留, ～押 **5**（扣除） deduct: ～工资 dock sb.'s pay ‖ ～奖金 withhold sb.'s bonus ▸～除, ～发, 折～ **6**（向下猛击） smash: ～球 smash (a ball) **7**（扳动） press: ～动扳机 pull the trigger

B〈名〉 **1**（绳结） knot: 系个～儿 tie a knot ‖ 绳～儿 knot ▸活～, 死～儿 **2**（螺纹） turn: ▸螺丝～ **3** ＝ 筘 kòu

扣[2]（釦） kòu

〈名〉 button: 双排～ double-breasted ▸～子, 风纪～

【扣除】kòuchú〈动〉 deduct: 从工资中～房租 deduct rent from one's wages

【扣发】kòufā〈动〉 withhold: ～全年奖金 hold sb.'s bonus for a whole year

【扣减】kòujiǎn〈动〉 deduct: ～奖金 cut a bonus

【扣缴】kòujiǎo〈动〉 withhold: 所得税每月从个人工资中～。 Income tax is deducted from your pay every month.

【扣篮】kòulán〈动〉［体育］ dunk

【扣留】kòuliú〈动〉 detain: ～嫌疑犯 detain a suspect ‖ 该船被～在港口进行检疫。 The vessel is being held in quarantine.

【扣帽子】kòu màozi〈惯〉 pin a label on sb.: 别乱给人～。 Don't just go about pinning labels on people.

【扣人心弦】kòurén-xīnxián〈成〉 thrilling: ～的比赛 exciting match

【扣肉】kòuròu〈名〉 steamed pork

【扣杀】kòushā〈动〉［体育］ smash (a ball): 网前～ smash the ball from the net

【扣题】kòutí〈动〉 stick to the point: 作文一定要～。 Compositions must be kept to the point.

【扣压】kòuyā〈动〉 shelve: ～稿件 withhold a manuscript from publication ‖ ～申请 pigeonhole a request

【扣押】kòuyā〈动〉［法律］ detain: ～人质 hold sb. hostage ‖ 他被～在警察局里。 He was detained at a police station.

【扣眼】kòuyǎn〈名〉 buttonhole

【扣子】kòuzi〈名〉 **1**（绳结） knot: 解开～ untie a knot **2**（纽扣） button: 钉～ sew on a button ‖ 解开～ undo a button **3**（悬念） point of high suspense

寇 kòu

A〈名〉 bandit: 敌～ invader ‖ 海～ pirate ▸外～, 贼～

B〈动〉 invade: ～边 invade the border areas ▸入～

【寇仇】kòuchóu〈名〉〈旧〉 enemy: 视若～ regard as one's enemy

筘 kòu〈名〉［纺织］ reed

蔻 kòu

【蔻丹】kòudān〈名〉 nail polish

【蔻蔻】kòukòu ＝ 可可 kěkě

kū

矻 kū

【矻矻】kūkū〈形〉〈书〉 assiduous: 终日～ work diligently all day long ‖ 孜孜～ diligent

刳 kū〈动〉〈书〉 hollow out: ～木为舟 make a canoe out of a tree trunk

枯 kū

A〈形〉 ❶（枯萎） withered: ～草 withered grass ‖ ～叶 dead leaves ►～木逢春, ～萎 ❷（干涸） dried up: ►～井, 海～石烂 ❸（干瘪） skinny: ►～瘦 ❹（枯燥） dull: ►～燥

B〈名〉〈方〉 dregs of sesame, soybean, etc.: 菜～ rapeseed residue

【枯肠】kūcháng〈名〉〈书〉〈喻〉 impoverished mind: 搜索～ rack one's brains

【枯干】kūgān〈形〉 dried-up: 那条河几乎～了。 The river is almost dry. ‖ 由于久旱无雨，庄稼都～了。 The crops shrivelled up after a long drought.

【枯槁】kūgǎo〈形〉 ❶（干枯） withered: 草木～。 Trees and grass were all withered. ❷（憔悴） haggard: 容颜～ look haggard

【枯骨】kūgǔ〈名〉 dry bones (of a person long dead)

【枯涸】kūhé〈形〉 dried-up

【枯黄】kūhuáng〈形〉 withered and yellow: 树叶逐渐～。 The tree leaves are gradually turning yellow.

【枯瘠】kūjí〈形〉 emaciated

【枯寂】kūjì〈形〉〈书〉 bored and lonely: 妻子离开他后，他感到极其～。 He has been desperately bored and lonely since his wife left him.

【枯焦】kūjiāo〈形〉 dried-up: 久旱不雨，禾苗～。 The seedlings became withered after the long drought.

【枯竭】kūjié〈形〉 ❶（干涸） dried-up: 水源～。 The water source has dried up. ❷（用尽） exhausted: 精力～。 One's energy is drained. ‖ 自然资源～。 The natural resources were exhausted.

【枯井】kūjǐng〈名〉 dry well

【枯木逢春】kūmù-féngchūn〈成〉〈喻〉 get a new lease of life

【枯木朽株】kūmù-xiǔzhū〈成〉〈喻〉 declining power

【枯涩】kūsè〈形〉 ❶（不流畅） dull and heavy: 文字～ plodding writing style ❷（不润滑） rough: ～的眼睛 dry eyes

【枯瘦】kūshòu〈形〉 skinny: ～如柴 be all skin and bones ‖ 形容～ look emaciated

【枯水期】kūshuǐqī〈名〉 low-water season

【枯萎】kūwěi〈形〉 withered: 庄稼～了。 The crops have withered.

【枯朽】kūxiǔ〈形〉 dry and decayed

【枯燥】kūzào〈形〉 dry and dull: ～乏味的工作 dull work ‖ 这堂课～无味。 The lesson was as dull as ditch water.

【枯枝败叶】kūzhī-bàiyè〈成〉 dead twigs and withered leaves

【枯坐】kūzuò〈动〉 sit idly: 他常常独自～在屋里。 He often sat idle in the room, all alone.

哭 kū〈动〉 cry: ～个不停 keep crying ‖ 放声大～ weep noisily ►～泣, 痛～

【哭鼻子】kū bízi〈动〉〈口〉 weep: 她经常因为想家～。 She often snivelled about being homesick.

【哭哭啼啼】kūku-títí〈成〉 weepy: 她近来经常～的。 She has been very weepy lately.

【哭灵】kūlíng〈动〉 wail bitterly before a tomb

【哭泣】kūqì〈动〉 sob: 为自己的不幸而～ weep over one's misfortunes

【哭腔】kūqiāng〈名〉 ❶（指声音） tearful voice: 她带着～打电话报了案。 She tearfully reported the crime. ❷（指行腔） [in traditional opera] sobbing tune

【哭穷】kūqióng〈动〉 complain about being hard up: 别在我这儿～。 Don't complain to me about being hard up!

【哭丧】kūsāng〈动〉 wail for the dead: ～着脸 wear a long face

【哭丧棒】kūsāngbàng〈名〉〈旧〉 a staff wrapped with white paper, carried by the relatives of the deceased in a funeral procession

【哭诉】kūsù〈动〉 complain tearfully

【哭天抹泪】kūtiān-mǒlèi〈成〉〈贬〉 weep and wail

【哭笑不得】kūxiào-bùdé〈成〉 not know whether to laugh or cry: 看到他那副狼狈相，真叫我～。 His sorry state both amused and saddened me.

窟 kū〈名〉 ❶（洞穴） cave: 山～ mountain cave ►狡兔三～, 石～ ❷（场所） den: ►赌～, 魔～, 贫民～

【窟窿】kūlong〈名〉 ❶（洞穴） hole: 冰～ ice hole ‖ 船触礁时撞了个大～。 The ship was badly holed when it hit the rock. ❷〈喻〉（亏空） deficit: 这给公司造成了两万美元的～。 This caused a deficit of over $20,000 to the company.

【窟窿眼儿】kūlongyǎnr〈名〉 small hole: 这张桌子上有些虫蛀的～。 There are a few woodworm holes on this desk.

【窟穴】kūxué〈名〉 den: 破获一个走私毒品的～ uncover a drug den

骷 kū

【骷髅】kūlóu〈名〉 ❶（指头骨） human skeleton ❷（指骨骼） human skull

kǔ

苦 kǔ

A〈形〉 ❶（指味道） bitter: 这个果子很～。 The fruit tastes very bitter. ►～胆, ～瓜, 良药～口 ❷（痛苦） painful: ～日子 hard life ►～恼, 愁眉～脸 ❸〈方〉（过分） excessive: 树枝修得太～了。 The trees are over-pruned.

B〈动〉 ❶（使受苦） cause sb. suffering: 这可真～了他。 This really gave him a hard time. ❷（苦于） suffer from: ～于不识字 be handicapped by illiteracy ‖ 为风湿病所～ suffer from rheumatism

C〈副〉 painstakingly: ～读 study hard ‖ ～练 practise hard ►～功, ～思

【苦熬】kǔ'áo〈动〉 endure: ～岁月 endure years of suffering

【苦不堪言】kǔbùkānyán〈成〉（指人） suffer untold misery and hardship;（指事） be indescribably painful: 大病一场，～ the illness is indescribably miserable

【苦差】kǔchāi〈名〉 thankless job

【苦楚】kǔchǔ〈名〉 suffering: 诉说～ voice one's misery

【苦处】kǔchu〈名〉 hardship: 你怎么就不了解我的～呢! If only you knew the difficulties I have got into!

【苦大仇深】kǔdà-chóushēn〈成〉 have suffered bitterly and harbour deep hatred

【苦胆】kǔdǎn = 胆囊 dǎnnáng

【苦丁茶】kǔdīngchá〈名〉 colyx tea

【苦干】kǔgàn〈动〉 work hard

【苦工】kǔgōng〈名〉 ❶（指工作） hard labour: 做～ do hard manual work ❷（指人） person doing hard manual work: 当～ work as a coolie

【苦功】kǔgōng〈名〉 hard work: 下～学习 study hard

【苦瓜】kǔguā〈名〉［植物］ bitter gourd: 一副～脸 miserable look

【苦果】kǔguǒ〈名〉〈喻〉 bitter pill: 自食～ reap what one has sown

【苦海】kǔhǎi〈名〉 sea of bitterness: 脱离～ escape from the abyss of misery

【苦海无边，回头是岸】kǔhǎi wúbiān, huítóu shì àn〈俗〉 it is never too late to mend one's ways

【苦寒】kǔhán〈形〉 ❶（严寒） bitter cold ❷（贫寒） poverty-stricken: 生活极度～ live in dire poverty

【苦活儿】kǔhuór〈名〉 hard and unprofitable job: 干～ do a hard and low-paying job

【苦尽甘来】kǔjìn-gānlái〈成〉 there is always light at the end of the tunnel

【苦境】kǔjìng〈名〉 hard and difficult circumstances: 身陷～ land on tough times

【苦酒】kǔjiǔ〈名〉 ❶〈本〉 wine with tart flavour ❷〈喻〉 awful result

【苦口】kǔkǒu〈动〉 ❶（指言语） admonish in earnest: ～相劝 earnestly advise ❷（指味道） taste bitter: 良药～。 Good medicine tastes bitter.

【苦口婆心】kǔkǒu-póxīn〈成〉 admonish with patience and sincerity

【苦苦】kǔkǔ〈副〉 strenuously: ～哀求 implore urgently ‖ ～思索 rack one's brains ‖ ～追求 try hard to get

【苦力】kǔlì〈名〉 coolie

【苦闷】kǔmèn〈形〉 sick at heart: 陷入抑郁～之中 become depressed ‖ 因失败而～ be depressed at one's failure

【苦命】kǔmìng〈名〉 cruel fate: ～人 person born under an unlucky star

【苦难】kǔnàn〈名〉 suffering: 经受很多～ undergo much suffering ‖ ～的年代 era of suffering ‖ 深重的～ deep adversity

【苦恼】kǔnǎo〈形〉 vexed: 感到非常～ be deeply distressed ‖ 因失败而～ be vexed at one's failure

【苦肉计】kǔròujì〈名〉 feigning of injury in order to win confidence: 中了敌人的～ be taken in by an enemy's trick of self-torture

【苦涩】kǔsè〈形〉 ❶（指味道） bitter and astringent: ～的柿子 sharp-tasting persimmon ❷（指内心感受） pained: 表情～ anguished look

【苦水】kǔshuǐ〈名〉 ❶（苦涩的水） hard, bitter water: ～湖 bitter lake ‖ ～井 bitter water well ❷（指胃液） gastric secretion ❸〈喻〉（指痛苦） bitterness: 吐～ pour out one's grievances ‖ 他是在～里泡大的。 He grew up in deep misery.

【苦思】kǔsī〈动〉〈书〉 rack one's brains: ～终日 ponder over sth. all day long

【苦思冥想】kǔsī-míngxiǎng〈成〉 think long and hard: 他～，还是不得其解。 He racked his brains but still failed to find an answer.

【苦痛】kǔtòng = 痛苦 tòngkǔ

【苦头】kǔtou〈名〉〈口〉 suffering: 早晚要吃～ must suffer sooner or later

【苦夏】kǔxià〈动〉 lose appetite and weight in summer

【苦相】kǔxiàng〈名〉 agonized look

【苦笑】kǔxiào〈动〉 force a smile

【苦心】kǔxīn **A**〈名〉 pains: 煞费～ take great pains (to do/with sth.) ‖ 别辜负了她的一片～。 Don't let her down. **B**〈副〉 with great effort: ～钻研 do painstaking research ▸～孤诣
【苦心孤诣】kǔxīn-gūyì〈成〉 make extraordinarily painstaking efforts: 他～地制定了周密的计划。 He took great pains to draw up a careful plan.
【苦心经营】kǔxīn-jīngyíng〈成〉 take great pains to do sth.: 由于她的苦心～，企业终于扭亏为盈了。 Thanks to her painstaking efforts, the business is back in the black.
【苦刑】kǔxíng〈名〉 torture: 受～ be subjected to torture
【苦行】kǔxíng〈名〉［宗教］ ascetic practices: ～主义 asceticism
【苦行僧】kǔxíngsēng〈名〉 **1**（指信徒） ascetic monk **2**〈喻〉（禁欲者） puritan
【苦役】kǔyì〈名〉〈旧〉［法律］ hard labour: 被判三年～ be sentenced to three years' penal servitude
【苦于】kǔyú〈动〉 **1**（感到苦恼） suffer from: ～人手不够 suffer from a shortage of manpower ‖ ～资金短缺 be hard pressed for funds **2**（更加艰苦） be worse off than: 乡下一些人的生活～我们。 Some people in the countryside were worse off than us.
【苦雨】kǔyǔ〈名〉 incessant rain: 凄风～ bitterly cold rain and wind
【苦战】kǔzhàn〈动〉 **1**（指战斗）fight bitterly: 他们～两天，终于得以脱险。 After a hard battle that lasted two days, they finally fought their way out. **2**（指工作或劳动） struggle hard: 他为考大学通宵～。 He worked through the night in order to pass the college entrance examination.
【苦中作乐】kǔzhōng-zuòlè〈成〉 seek joy amidst sorrow
【苦衷】kǔzhōng〈名〉 suffering: 体谅别人的～ make allowances for others' difficulties ‖ 难言的～ sth. that is too painful to talk about
【苦主】kǔzhǔ〈名〉〈旧〉［法律］ family of the victim in a murder case

kù

库[1]（庫） kù〈名〉 **1**（指处所） storehouse: 粮～ grain store ‖ 书～ book warehouse ▸水～, 血～ **2**（指文件） library: ▸数据～, 题～

库[2]（庫） kù = 库仑 kùlún
【库藏】kùcáng〈动〉 have in storage: 我校图书馆～图书近一百万册。 There are nearly 1 million books in our school library. ▸kùzàng
【库存】kùcún〈名〉 stock: 减少～ reduce one's stock ‖ 清点～ do a stock check ‖ 这种商品没有～。 This item is not in stock.
【库房】kùfáng〈名〉 storehouse
【库克群岛】Kùkèqúndǎo〈名〉 the Cook Islands
【库仑】kùlún〈量〉［电气］ coulomb
【库容】kùróng〈名〉 storage capacity: 这个水库～约为3,000万立方米。 The reservoir has a storage capacity of about 30 million cubic metres.
【库藏】kùzàng〈名〉〈书〉 depository ▸kùcáng

绔（絝） kù ▸纨绔 wánkù

裤（褲、袴） kù〈名〉 trousers〈英〉; pants〈美〉: 一条长～ a pair of trousers ‖ 毛～ woollen tights ‖ 棉～ cotton-padded trousers ‖ 游泳～ swimming trunks ▸短～, 喇叭～, 裙～
【裤衩】kùchǎ〈名〉 underpants: 三角～ briefs
【裤带】kùdài〈名〉 waist belt
【裤裆】kùdāng〈名〉 (trouser) crotch
【裤兜】kùdōu〈名〉 trouser pocket
【裤缝】kùfèng〈名〉 seam of a trouser leg
【裤脚】kùjiǎo〈名〉 trouser bottom
【裤裙】kùqún〈名〉 culottes
【裤头】kùtóu〈名〉〈方〉 underpants
【裤腿】kùtuǐ〈名〉 trouser leg
【裤线】kùxiàn〈名〉 (trouser) creases: 笔直的～ sharp creases
【裤腰】kùyāo〈名〉 trouser waist
【裤腰带】kùyāodài〈名〉 girdle
【裤子】kùzi〈名〉 trousers〈英〉; pants〈美〉: 一条～ a pair of trousers ‖ 宽松的～ baggy trousers ‖ 条纹～ striped pants

酷[1] kù
A〈形〉 cruel: ▸～吏, 冷～, 严～
B〈副〉 extremely: ▸～爱, ～热, ～似

酷[2] kù〈形〉〈口〉 cool: 她的打扮真～。 Her get-up is really cool.
【酷爱】kù'ài〈动〉 be very fond of: ～钓鱼 love fishing
【酷毙】kùbì〈形〉〈口〉 fucking cool
【酷哥】kùgē〈名〉〈口〉 hot guy: ～靓女 cool guys and pretty girls
【酷寒】kùhán〈形〉 bitterly cold
【酷吏】kùlì〈名〉〈旧〉 cruel official
【酷烈】kùliè〈形〉〈书〉 **1**（残酷） cruel: ～的苦难 severe sufferings **2**（浓郁） strong: 异香～ strong fragrance **3**（强烈） fierce: ～的阳光 scorching sun
【酷虐】kùnüè〈形〉 savage: ～的暴政 savage tyranny
【酷热】kùrè〈形〉 scorching hot: ～的天气 sweltering hot weather
【酷暑】kùshǔ〈名〉 sweltering summer heat: ～难当 suffocating heat
【酷似】kùsì〈动〉 bear a striking resemblance to: 她长得～她的母亲。 She is the spitting image of her mother.
【酷肖】kùxiào = 酷似 kùsì
【酷刑】kùxíng〈名〉 torture: ～逼供 extort a confession (from sb.) by torture

kuā

夸[1]（誇） kuā〈动〉 **1**（夸大） exaggerate: 这事实被～大了。 The fact has been completely exaggerated. ▸～口, ～张 **2**（夸奖） praise: 大家都～他老实。 He is praised for his honesty. ▸～奖, ～耀

夸[2] kuā ▸夸克 kuākè, 夸父追日 Kuāfù-zhuīrì
【夸大】kuādà〈动〉 exaggerate: ～事实 stretch the facts ‖ 过分～个人的作用 completely exaggerate the role of the individual
【夸大其词】kuādà-qící〈成〉 exaggerate beyond the bounds of truth: 这篇报告有些～。 This is an exaggerated report.
【夸大其辞】kuādà-qící = 夸大其词 kuādà-qící
【夸诞】kuādàn〈形〉〈书〉 exaggerated: ～之词，不足为据。 Exaggeration can not be taken as evidence.
【夸父追日】Kuāfù-zhuīrì〈成〉〈喻〉 be ignorant of one's own limits and do sth. beyond one's ability
【夸海口】kuā hǎikǒu〈惯〉 boast wildly: 你先别～ Stop bragging, will you?
【夸奖】kuājiǎng〈动〉 compliment: 外教～她英语熟练。 The foreign teacher complimented her on her English.
【夸克】kuākè〈名〉［物理］ quark
【夸口】kuākǒu〈动〉 boast: 她～说比我跑得快。 She boasted that she could run faster than me.
【夸夸其谈】kuākuā-qítán〈成〉 be full of hot air: 他老是～，我们不能相信他。 We cannot believe him because he is inclined to stretch the truth.
【夸示】kuāshì〈动〉〈书〉 show off: ～自己的成绩 flaunt one's achievements
【夸饰】kuāshì〈动〉 give an exaggerated account
【夸脱】kuātuō〈量〉 quart
【夸耀】kuāyào〈动〉〈贬〉 brag about: ～自己的财富 flaunt one's riches ‖ 不值得～ not worth bragging about
【夸赞】kuāzàn〈动〉 speak highly of: 她因勇敢而受到～。 She was commended for bravery.
【夸张】kuāzhāng **A**〈动〉 exaggerate: 大肆～ grossly exaggerate ‖ 艺术～ artistic exaggeration ‖ 我认为电视的威力怎么说也不～。 I don't think you can exaggerate the power of television. **B**〈形〉 exaggerated: 这种说法太～了。 This kind of talk is completely exaggerated. **C**〈名〉［语言］ hyperbole
【夸嘴】kuāzuǐ = 夸口 kuākǒu

kuǎ

侉 kuǎ〈形〉〈口〉 **1**（指口音） non-local: 他说话有点～。 He speaks with a slight accent. **2**（指体积） unwieldy: ～大个儿 big clumsy fellow ‖ 这个箱子太～了，携带不方便。 The suitcase is too unwieldy to carry.
【侉子】kuǎzi〈名〉〈方〉 person who speaks with a non-local accent

垮 kuǎ〈动〉 collapse: 洪水冲～了堤坝。 The floodwaters burst the dyke. ‖ 他的身体彻底～了。 His health has completely collapsed.
【垮塌】kuǎtā〈动〉 collapse: 大桥突然～。 The bridge suddenly collapsed.
【垮台】kuǎtái〈动〉〈喻〉 collapse: 政府一夜之间就～了。 The government fell overnight.

kuà

挎 kuà〈动〉 **1**（用胳膊） carry on one's arm: 她胳膊上～着一只篮子。 She carried a basket on her arm. ‖ 他和女友～着胳膊在散步。 He and his girlfriend walked arm in arm. **2**（用肩） carry sth. over one's shoulder: ～着书包 have a schoolbag slung over one's shoulder
【挎包】kuàbāo〈名〉 satchel
【挎兜】kuàdōu〈名〉 satchel
【挎斗】kuàdǒu〈名〉 sidecar: 带～的摩托车 motorcycle with a sidecar

胯 kuà〈名〉hip: ～下 between one's legs
【胯裆】kuàdāng〈名〉trouser crotch
【胯骨】kuàgǔ〈名〉hip bone
【胯下之辱】kuàxià-zhīrǔ〈成〉〈喻〉cup of humiliation: 忍受～ drain the cup of humiliation

跨 kuà
A〈动〉**1**（迈步越过）step: ～进大门 step into a doorway ‖ 向前～一步 take a step forward **2**（骑上）straddle: ～上车子 straddle a bike ‖ ～在栅栏上 straddle a fence **3**（越过界限）cut across: ～地区 inter-regional ‖ ～行业 trans-sectoral
B〈形〉attached: ～间 attached room ▸～院儿
【跨度】kuàdù〈名〉span: ～距离 span length ‖ 时间～ time span
【跨国】kuàguó〈动〉be multinational: ～犯罪 transnational crime ‖ ～经营 transnational management
【跨国公司】kuàguó gōngsī〈名〉multinational
【跨栏】kuàlán ▸**p. 909**〈名〉［体育］hurdles: 110米～ 110m hurdles
【跨年度】kuà niándù〈动〉straddle a year: ～预算 budget to be carried over to the next year
【跨世纪】kuà shìjì〈动〉cross-century: 培养～人才 foster cross-century talents
【跨文化】kuà wénhuà〈动〉be cross-cultural: ～交际 cross-cultural communication
【跨学科】kuà xuékē〈动〉be interdisciplinary
【跨院儿】kuàyuànr〈名〉side courtyard
【跨越】kuàyuè〈动〉span: ～国界 go beyond the national boundary ‖ ～时空 cut across space and time ‖ ～障碍 surmount an obstacle

kuǎi

𢫬[1]（擓） kuǎi〈动〉〈方〉scratch: ～痒痒 have a scratch ‖ ～掉一点皮 get a scratch

𢫬[2]（擓） kuǎi〈动〉〈方〉**1**（挎着）carry on the arm **2**（舀）spoon out: 从锅里～出点汤 ladle out some soup from the pot

蒯 kuǎi〈名〉［植物］wool grass
【蒯草】kuǎicǎo〈名〉wool grass

kuài

会（會） kuài〈动〉compute ▸huì
【会计】kuàijì〈名〉**1**（指工作）accountancy: 财务～ financial accounting ‖ 成本～ cost accounting **2**（指人）accountant
【会计年度】kuàijì niándù〈名〉fiscal year
【会计师】kuàijìshī ▸**p. 966**〈名〉certified public accountant (CPA): 注册～ certified public accountant
【会计事务所】kuàijì shìwùsuǒ〈名〉accounting firm

块（塊） kuài
A〈名〉lump: 把肉切成～ cut the meat into cubes ‖ 木～ wood block ‖ 糖～儿 lump of sugar ▸冰～儿, 血～, 肿～
B〈量〉**1**（用于物品）piece: 三～肥皂 three cakes of soap ‖ 一～蛋糕 a slice of cake ‖ 一～手表 a wrist watch ‖ 一～衣料 a dress length **2** ▸**p. 328**〈口〉（用于货币）*yuan*: 三～银洋 three silver dollars ‖ 一～钱 one *yuan* ‖ ～儿八毛 one *yuan* or slightly less
【块根】kuàigēn〈名〉［植物］root tuber
【块茎】kuàijīng〈名〉［植物］tuber
【块垒】kuàilěi〈名〉〈书〉depression: 借他人的酒杯，浇自己的～ drown one's sorrows in sb. else's cup
【块儿】kuàir〈名〉size: 大～煤 big lumps of coal ‖ 他儿子～大。His son is big.
【块头】kuàitóu〈名〉〈口〉physical build: 他～很大。He is a big burly man.

快 kuài
A〈形〉**1**（快速）fast: 跑得～ run fast ‖ 学业进步很～ make rapid progress in one's studies ‖ 车子越开越～了。The car is gaining speed. ▸～马加鞭 **2**（敏捷）quick-witted: 反应～ be quick in response ‖ 她脑子～。She is quick-witted. ▸眼明手～ **3**（锋利）sharp: 这把斧子很～。The axe is very sharp. **4**（直爽）straightforward: ▸～人～语, 爽～, 心直口～ **5**（快乐）happy: 拍手称～ clap and cheer ‖ 不～ feel unhappy ▸大～人心, 亲痛仇～, 先睹为～
B〈名〉speed: 开～车 drive fast ‖ 你的摩托车能跑多～? How fast can your motorcycle go?
C〈副〉**1**（赶快）quickly: ～请大夫来。Go and fetch a doctor, and be quick about it. ‖ ～回去干活! Hurry back to your work! **2**（即将）soon: 春节～到了。Spring Festival is drawing near. ‖ 天～亮了。Soon it will be dawn. ‖ 那位老人～90岁了。The old man is nearly 90.
【快板】kuàibǎn〈名〉**1**［音乐］allegro **2**［戏曲］quick tempo
【快板儿】kuàibǎnr〈名〉［曲艺］clapper talk: 说～ perform a clapper talk
【快板儿书】kuàibǎnrshū〈名〉story recited to the rhythm of bamboo clappers
【快报】kuàibào〈名〉bulletin
【快步流星】kuàibù-liúxīng = 大步流星 dàbù-liúxīng
【快餐】kuàicān〈名〉fast food: 吃～ have a quick meal ‖ ～店 fast-food restaurant
【快车】kuàichē〈名〉**1**（指汽车）express bus **2**（指火车）fast train: 直达～ non-stop express train
【快车道】kuàichēdào〈名〉fast lane
【快当】kuàidang〈形〉prompt: 他办事～。He does everything promptly.
【快刀斩乱麻】kuàidāo zhǎn luànmá〈俗〉〈喻〉take resolute and effective measures to solve a complicated problem
【快递】kuàidì〈动〉express delivery: ～业务 express delivery service ‖ ～邮件 express post
【快感】kuàigǎn〈名〉pleasure: 感到一阵～ experience a pleasant sensation
【快攻】kuàigōng〈名〉**1**［体育］（指快速进攻）quick attack: 打～ use the strategy of quick attack **2**（指快速突破）fast break
【快活】kuàihuo〈形〉happy: 心里～ feel happy ‖ 非常～ extremely jolly
【快件】kuàijiàn〈名〉express post: 发～ send by express ‖ 寄～ send an express post
【快捷】kuàijié〈形〉nimble: 动作～ quick in one's movements
【快捷键】kuàijiéjiàn〈名〉［计算机］accelerator key
【快镜头】kuàijìngtóu〈名〉fast motion
【快乐】kuàilè〈形〉happy: ～的童年 happy childhood ‖ 生日～! Happy birthday to you! ‖ 祝你～! I wish you joy!
【快马加鞭】kuàimǎ-jiābiān〈成〉〈喻〉pick up speed: 要赶上世界水平，我们还得～。In order to catch up with world levels, we'll have to pick up speed.
【快慢】kuàimàn〈名〉speed: 那个按钮是管～的。That button controls the speed.
【快门】kuàimén〈名〉［摄影］shutter: 按～ click the shutter
【快人快语】kuàirén-kuàiyǔ〈成〉straight-forward talk from a straightforward person
【快闪族】kuàishǎnzú〈名〉flash mob
【快事】kuàishì〈名〉pleasure: 读书是我生活中的一大～。Reading is a great pleasure in my life.
【快手】kuàishǒu〈名〉fast worker: 她是个打毛衣的～。She is quick at knitting.
【快书】kuàishū〈名〉［曲艺］quick-patter [a folk vocal art form]: 山东～ Shandong clapper ballad
【快速】kuàisù〈形〉fast: ～起动 quick start ‖ ～扫描 fast scan ‖ ～反应能力 quick-reaction ability
【快速阅读】kuàisù yuèdú〈名〉speed-reading
【快艇】kuàitǐng = 汽艇 qìtǐng
【快慰】kuàiwèi〈形〉〈书〉delighted and pleased: 母亲听了他的话感到十分～。His mother felt really pleased at what he said.
【快信】kuàixìn〈名〉express post: 我会寄～给你。I'll send you the letter by express post.
【快讯】kuàixùn〈名〉newsflash
【快要】kuàiyào〈副〉〈口〉soon: ～下雨了。It's about to rain. ‖ 这家公司～破产了。The company is on the verge of bankruptcy.
【快意】kuàiyì〈形〉pleased
【快运】kuàiyùn〈动〉ship express: ～公司 express company
【快照】kuàizhào〈名〉［摄影］snapshot: 拍～ take a snapshot
【快嘴】kuàizuǐ〈名〉**1**（表直爽）one who is quick to voice his ideas **2**（指不谨慎）blabbermouth

侩（儈） kuài〈名〉〈旧〉middleman: ▸市～

哙（噲） kuài〈动〉〈书〉swallow

狯（獪） kuài〈形〉〈书〉sly: ▸狡～

脍（膾） kuài〈名〉〈古〉minced meat
【脍炙人口】kuàizhì-rénkǒu〈成〉〈喻〉enjoy great popularity: ～的诗篇 oft-quoted poems

筷 kuài〈名〉chopsticks: 竹～ bamboo chopsticks
【筷子】kuàizi〈名〉chopsticks: 一双～ a pair of chopsticks

鲙（鱠） kuài
【鲙鱼】kuàiyú〈名〉Chinese herring

k

kuān

宽（寬） kuān ▸p. 82
A〈形〉1（指宽度） wide: ～边眼镜 broad-rimmed glasses ‖ ～肩膀 broad shoulders ‖ 马路很～。The road is very wide. ‖ 他管得太～了。He is taking too much on. ▸～敞, ～广 2（不严厉） generous: ～严相济 temper justice with mercy ‖ 严以律己，～以待人 be strict with oneself and lenient with others ▸～厚, ～容 3（富余） comfortably off: 手头～多了 be comfortably off ▸～绰, ～裕
B〈名〉 width: 这间房子～20米。The room measures 20 metres across. ‖ 这儿河面有一英里～。The river is one mile wide here.
C〈动〉 relax: 放～政策 relax a policy ‖ ～期限 extend a deadline ‖ 得知他们安然无恙，我的心就～多了。I was relieved to learn that they were safe. ▸～心, ～限

【宽畅】kuānchàng〈形〉 happy: 胸怀～ cheerful in one's mind
【宽敞】kuānchang〈形〉 spacious: ～的大厅 roomy hall ‖ 新居～而舒适。The new flat is spacious and comfortable.
【宽绰】kuānchuo〈形〉 1（宽敞） spacious: 这间客厅既～又舒适。This living room is spacious and comfortable. 2（舒畅） relieved: 孩子病好了，妈妈心里感到～多了。The mother was relieved to see her child cured of illness. 3（充裕） well-off: 手头比以前～多了 much better off than before
【宽打窄用】kuāndǎ-zhǎiyòng〈成〉 budget liberally and spend sparingly
【宽大】kuāndà〈形〉 1（宽敞） spacious: ～的客厅 spacious sitting room 2（不苛刻） lenient: 待人～仁慈 be lenient in one's treatment of people ‖ ～政策 policy of leniency ‖ 请求法庭～处理 ask the court for leniency
【宽大为怀】kuāndà-wéihuái〈成〉 be magnanimous with sb.
【宽带】kuāndài〈名〉 broadband: ～传输 broadband transmission ‖ ～网 broadband network
【宽贷】kuāndài〈动〉〈书〉 pardon: 对毒犯决不～ show no leniency to criminals involved in drugs
【宽待】kuāndài〈动〉 treat with leniency: ～俘虏 treat prisoners of war with leniency
【宽度】kuāndù ▸p. 82〈名〉 width: 长度和～ length and width ‖ 有各种～的地毯出售。Carpets are available in various widths.
【宽泛】kuānfàn〈形〉 broad: 内容～。The content is wide-ranging.
【宽幅】kuānfú〈名〉 broad width: ～布 broad cloth
【宽广】kuānguǎng〈形〉 broad: 胸怀～ be broad-minded ‖ ～的水域 a broad expanse of water
【宽和】kuānhé〈形〉 generous and kind: 待人～ be generous and kind to people
【宽宏大量】kuānhóng-dàliàng〈成〉 magnanimous: 他是个～的人。He has a large heart.
【宽洪】kuānhóng〈形〉〈书〉 resonant: ～的歌声 broad and resonant singing
【宽厚】kuānhòu〈形〉 1（宽而厚） thick and broad: ～的胸膛 broad and strong chest 2（宽容） kind: 待人～ be generous to people 3（嗓音浑厚） deep and rich: 他的嗓音～嘹亮。His voice is rich and loud.
【宽怀】kuānhuái〈动〉 set one's mind at rest
【宽假】kuānjiǎ〈动〉〈书〉 pardon
【宽解】kuānjiě〈动〉 ease sb.'s anxiety
【宽旷】kuānkuàng〈形〉 extensive: ～的草原 extensive grasslands
【宽阔】kuānkuò〈形〉 1（宽敞开阔） broad: ～的道路 wide road ‖ ～的水域 vast expanse of waters 2（心胸开朗） open-minded: 心怀～ be broad-minded
【宽谅】kuānliàng〈动〉 forgive
【宽猛相济】kuānměng-xiāngjì〈成〉 alternate leniency with severity
【宽免】kuānmiǎn〈动〉 exempt (from taxation, punishment, etc.)
【宽屏】kuānpíng〈形〉 widescreen: ～笔记本电脑 widescreen notebook computer
【宽让】kuānràng〈动〉 be lenient
【宽饶】kuānráo〈动〉 pardon: 依法惩治，决不～。Punish according to law, without leniency.
【宽容】kuānróng〈动〉 lenient: ～待人 be lenient with people ‖ ～大度 tolerant and generous
【宽赦】kuānshè〈动〉 show mercy: ～坦白的犯人 accord lenient treatment to criminals who confess their crimes
【宽舒】kuānshū〈形〉 1（愉悦） free from worry: 心境～ have ease of mind 2（宽敞舒适） spacious
【宽恕】kuānshù ▸p. 156〈动〉 forgive: 请求～ ask for forgiveness ‖ 他乞求上苍～他的罪恶。He begged Heaven to pardon his sin.
【宽松】kuānsōng〈形〉 1（指空间） spacious 2（指氛围、心情） relaxed: ～的环境 relaxed environment ‖ ～的气氛 free and unrestrained atmosphere 3（指钱财） well-to-do: 手头～多了 be very well-off 4（指衣服） loose-fitting: ～的衣服 loose-fitting garment
【宽慰】kuānwèi A〈动〉 comfort: 自我～ console oneself ‖ 你去～他几句。Go and give him a few words of comfort. B〈形〉 relieved: 听到这个消息我很～。I was greatly relieved at the news.
【宽限】kuānxiàn〈动〉 extend a time limit: ～期 grace period ‖ ～几天 give a few days' grace
【宽心】kuānxīn〈动〉 put sb.'s mind at rest: 说几句～话 say a few reassuring words
【宽心丸】kuānxīnwán〈名〉〈喻〉 words of comfort: 给某人吃～ say comforting words to sb.
【宽衣】kuānyī〈动〉〈敬〉 take off your coat: 屋里热，请～。It's hot in here; do take your coat off.
【宽衣解带】kuānyī-jiědài〈动〉 undress
【宽银幕电影】kuānyínmù diànyǐng〈名〉 wide-screen film
【宽宥】kuānyòu ▸p. 156〈动〉〈书〉 pardon
【宽余】kuānyú〈形〉 1（安适） free and comfortable: 今日得～。I have some leisure time today. 2 = 宽裕 kuānyù
【宽裕】kuānyù〈形〉 comfortably off: 经济～ be well-off ‖ 时间～。There is plenty of time to spare.
【宽窄】kuānzhǎi〈名〉 width: 这条路～不一。The width of this road is not consistent.
【宽纵】kuānzòng〈动〉 indulge: 过分～子女 be over-indulgent with one's children

髋（髖） kuān
【髋骨】kuāngǔ〈名〉［解剖］ hip bone
【髋关节】kuānguānjié〈名〉［解剖］ hip joint

kuǎn

款[1] kuǎn〈形〉1（恳切） sincere: ▸～待, ～留 2〈书〉（缓慢） leisurely: ▸～步

款[2] kuǎn
A〈名〉1（指条文） section: 第二条第三～ Article 2, Section 3 2（指钱） sum of money: 一大笔～ a large sum of money ▸～项, 贷～, 付～, 借～, 赃～ 3（名字） name of the sender or recipient inscribed on a painting or a piece of calligraphy presented as a gift: ▸～识, 落～, 上～, 下～ 4（款式） style: 新～风衣 new-style windbreaker
B〈量〉 kind: 一～新装 a new style suit ‖ 一～西式糕点 a kind of Western-style pastry

【款步】kuǎnbù〈动〉 take slow steps: ～湖滨 walk leisurely along the lakeside
【款诚】kuǎnchéng〈形〉〈书〉 hearty: ～相待 treat sb. with sincerity
【款待】kuǎndài〈动〉 entertain with courtesy and warmth: 设宴～某人 give a banquet to sb. ‖ 盛情～ entertain hospitably
【款额】kuǎn'é〈名〉 sum of money: ～巨大 large sum of money
【款姐】kuǎnjiě〈名〉〈方〉 female moneybags
【款款】kuǎnkuǎn A〈形〉 sincere: 情意～ with deep affection ‖ ～深情 sincere feelings B〈副〉 slowly: ～而行 walk leisurely
【款留】kuǎnliú〈动〉 cordially urge (a guest or friend) to stay
【款洽】kuǎnqià〈形〉〈书〉 cordial and harmonious: 情意～ cordial and harmonious feelings
【款式】kuǎnshì〈名〉 style: ～新颖 novel design ‖ 流行～ popular style
【款项】kuǎnxiàng〈名〉1（指钱） sum of money: 一大笔～ a huge sum of money 2（指条文） sections and items
【款型】kuǎnxíng〈名〉 style: 时髦的～ latest fashion
【款爷】kuǎnyé〈名〉〈方〉 moneybags
【款识】kuǎnzhì〈名〉1（指刻痕） inscriptions 2（指题名） signature
【款子】kuǎnzi〈名〉〈口〉 sum of money: 一大笔～ a large sum of money

kuāng

匡 kuāng〈动〉1〈书〉（纠正） rectify: ▸～谬, ～正 2〈书〉（帮助） assist: ～乏困，救灾难 aid the poor and save disaster victims 3（估算） roughly estimate: ～一～ give a rough estimate ▸～计, ～算

【匡扶】kuāngfú〈动〉〈书〉 assist: ～社稷 help to run the state
【匡计】kuāngjì = 匡算 kuāngsuàn
【匡救】kuāngjiù〈动〉〈书〉 rescue
【匡谬】kuāngmiù〈动〉〈书〉 correct mistakes: ～正俗 correct mistakes and establish good customs
【匡算】kuāngsuàn〈动〉 estimate: 初步～ make a preliminary estimate
【匡正】kuāngzhèng〈动〉 rectify: 寄上拙译，敬请～。I am sending you a translation of mine for correction.
【匡助】kuāngzhù〈动〉〈书〉 assist

诓（誆） kuāng〈动〉 deceive: ～人 cheat sb. ‖ 你别想～我! Don't you try to deceive me!

【诓骗】kuāngpiàn〈动〉 deceive: 设圈套～客户 set traps for clients

哐 kuāng〈拟〉 bang: ～的一声，脸盆掉在地上。 The basin fell to the ground with a crash.

【哐当】kuāngdāng〈拟〉 bang: 她～一声把电话挂了。She banged the phone down.

【哐啷】kuānglāng〈拟〉 bang: ～一声窗户关上了。 The window banged shut.

筐 kuāng〈名〉 basket: 购物～ shopping basket ▸粪～

【筐子】kuāngzi〈名〉 small basket: 菜～ vegetable basket

kuáng

狂 kuáng

A〈形〉 **1**（疯） mad: ▸发～, 丧心病～ **2**（猛烈） violent: 股价～跌。 The share price tumbled. ▸～奔, ～风, 力挽～澜 **3**（狂妄） arrogant: 未免太～了。 It's sheer arrogance. ▸～言

B〈副〉 wildly: ～笑 laugh wildly ‖ ～饮 drink heavily ▸～欢, ～怒, ～喜

【狂傲】kuáng'ào〈形〉 wildly arrogant: ～不羁 arrogant and unrestrained

【狂暴】kuángbào〈形〉 violent: 脾气～ have a violent temper ‖ ～的山洪 furious mountain torrents

【狂悖】kuángbèi〈形〉〈书〉 arrogant and unreasonable

【狂奔】kuángbēn〈动〉 run like mad: ～的野马 bolting wild horse

【狂飙】kuángbiāo〈名〉 **1**（暴风） hurricane **2**〈喻〉（指力量或潮流） vigorous force

【狂草】kuángcǎo〈名〉［书法］ wild cursive script

【狂潮】kuángcháo〈名〉〈喻〉 raging tide: 革命的～势不可挡。 The turbulent tide of revolution is unstoppable.

【狂放】kuángfàng〈形〉 unruly: ～不羁 be extravagant and unrestrained

【狂吠】kuángfèi〈动〉 howl

【狂风】kuángfēng〈名〉 **1**［气象］ gale **2**（大风） fierce wind: ～巨浪 violent storm and roaring waves ‖ ～大作。 It is blowing a gale.

【狂风暴雨】kuángfēng-bàoyǔ〈成〉 furious storm

【狂轰滥炸】kuánghōng-lànzhà〈成〉 bomb savagely

【狂欢】kuánghuān〈动〉 be wild with joy: ～之夜 night of revelry

【狂欢节】kuánghuānjié〈名〉 carnival

【狂澜】kuánglán〈名〉 roaring waves: ▸力挽～

【狂怒】kuángnù〈动〉 be in a wild fury: ～之下 in a towering rage

【狂气】kuángqi〈名〉 conceit: 一脸～ look arrogant

【狂犬病】kuángquǎnbìng ▸**p. 50**〈名〉 rabies: ～患者 rabies carrier

【狂犬吠日】kuángquǎn-fèirì〈成〉〈喻〉 an evil person slandering a good person

【狂热】kuángrè〈形〉 rabid: ～追求 go crazy for ‖ ～的举动 madcap activity

【狂人】kuángrén〈名〉 **1**（精神失常者） lunatic: 《～日记》 *Diary of a Madman* ‖ 战争～ war maniac **2**（狂妄自大者） extremely arrogant person

【狂人呓语】kuángrén-yìyǔ〈成〉 ravings of a madman

【狂胜】kuángshèng〈动〉 win an overwhelming victory

【狂涛】kuángtāo〈名〉 **1**〈本〉 raging waves: ～怒浪 roaring waves **2**〈喻〉（指声势） great momentum

【狂妄】kuángwàng〈形〉 wildly arrogant: ～的野心 wild ambition ‖ ～自大 be arrogant and conceited

【狂喜】kuángxǐ〈形〉 wild with joy: 心中一阵～ feel a surge of wild joy

【狂想】kuángxiǎng〈名〉 **1**（幻想） fantasy: 突发～ be struck with a fancy **2**（妄想） wishful thinking

【狂笑】kuángxiào〈动〉 laugh wildly: ～不止 laugh hysterically and incessantly

【狂言】kuángyán〈名〉 crazy talk: 口出～ rant wildly

【狂躁】kuángzào ▸**p. 50**〈名〉［医学］ mania: ～不安 manic agitation

【狂恣】kuángzì〈形〉〈书〉 unrestrained

诳（誑） kuáng〈动〉 deceive: 别～我。 Don't cheat me.

【诳话】kuánghuà = 诳语 kuángyǔ

【诳骗】kuángpiàn〈动〉 cheat

【诳语】kuángyǔ〈名〉 lie: 出家人不打～。 Monks and nuns are not supposed to tell lies.

鵟（鵟） kuáng〈名〉［鸟类］ buzzard

kuǎng

夼 kuǎng〈名〉〈方〉 low-lying land [often used in place names]

kuàng

邝（鄺） Kuàng〈名〉 Kuang [surname]

圹（壙） kuàng〈名〉 **1**（墓穴） open grave **2**〈书〉（原野） open country

【圹埌】kuànglàng〈形〉〈书〉 boundless

【圹穴】kuàngxué〈名〉 open grave

旷（曠） kuàng

A〈形〉 **1**（空旷） vast: 地～人稀 vast territory with a sparse population ▸～野, 空～ **2**（心胸开朗） free from worries and petty ideas: ▸～达, 心～神怡 **3**（松动） loose-fitting: 螺丝～了。 The screw has come loose. ‖ 这条裙子我穿着太～了。 The dress is too loose for me.

B〈动〉 waste: ～日费时 waste time ▸～工, ～课, ～日持久

【旷达】kuàngdá〈形〉〈书〉 broad-minded: ～之士 scholar with an open mind

【旷代】kuàngdài〈形〉〈书〉 unequalled by one's contemporaries: ～佳作 best work of an age ‖ ～文豪 unrivalled literary giant

【旷荡】kuàngdàng〈形〉 **1**（空旷） boundless: ～的沙漠 vast desert **2**（开朗） optimistic: 心怀～ be open-minded

【旷废】kuàngfèi〈动〉 neglect: ～学业 neglect one's studies

【旷费】kuàngfèi〈动〉 waste: ～钱财 waste money ‖ ～时间 squander one's time

【旷夫怨女】kuàngfū-yuànnǚ〈成〉 bachelors and spinsters

【旷工】kuànggōng〈动〉 be absent from work without leave: 无故～ be absent from work without reason

【旷古】kuànggǔ **A**〈形〉 everlasting: ～奇闻 unheard-of story ▸～未闻 **B**〈名〉 ancient times: ～绝伦 unprecedented and unrivalled

【旷古未闻】kuànggǔ-wèiwén〈成〉 unheard-of

【旷课】kuàngkè〈动〉 play truant

【旷日持久】kuàngrì-chíjiǔ〈成〉 long-drawn-out: ～的谈判 long-drawn-out negotiations

【旷世】kuàngshì〈形〉〈书〉 unequalled in one's time: ～功勋 unique deeds ‖ ～奇才 person of brilliance unequalled in their time

【旷世无双】kuàngshì-wúshuāng〈成〉 stand without peer in one's generation

【旷野】kuàngyě〈名〉 wilderness: ～荒郊 uninhabited wilderness

【旷远】kuàngyuǎn〈形〉〈书〉 **1**（辽远） vast and extending far into the distance: 秋空～ vast autumn sky stretching far away into the distance **2**（久远） remote: 年代～ age-old

【旷职】kuàngzhí〈动〉 be absent from duty without leave

况¹（況） kuàng

A〈名〉 situation: ▸概～, 近～, 盛～, 状～

B〈动〉 compare: 比～ draw an analogy ‖ 以古～今 draw parallels from history

况²（況） kuàng〈连〉〈书〉 moreover: 十人尚不能为，～一人乎? How can one person do what even ten cannot do?

【况且】kuàngqiě〈连〉 moreover: 这套房子不够大，～离市区又太远。 This flat isn't big enough; moreover, it's too far away from town.

【况味】kuàngwèi〈名〉〈书〉 circumstances and sentiment

矿（礦） kuàng〈名〉 **1**（矿床） mineral deposit: 找～ try to discover mineral deposits ▸采～, 探～ **2**（矿石） ore: 金～ gold ore **3**（指场所） mine: 在～上工作 work at a mine ▸露天～

【矿藏】kuàngcáng〈名〉 mineral reserves: ～丰富 be rich in mineral resources ‖ 未开采的～ untouched mineral deposits

【矿层】kuàngcéng〈名〉 seam: ～厚度 seam thickness

【矿产】kuàngchǎn〈名〉 mineral deposits: ～资源 mineral resources

【矿车】kuàngchē〈名〉 pit car

【矿床】kuàngchuáng〈名〉 mineral deposit: 海底～ submarine deposit

【矿灯】kuàngdēng〈名〉 miner's lamp

【矿工】kuànggōng〈名〉 miner

【矿化】kuànghuà〈动〉［地质］ mineralize: ～水 mineralized water

【矿井】kuàngjǐng〈名〉 pit

【矿警】kuàngjǐng〈名〉 mine police

【矿坑】kuàngkēng〈名〉 pit: ～下陷 mining subsidence

【矿脉】kuàngmài〈名〉 mineral vein

【矿苗】kuàngmiáo〈名〉［矿业］ outcropping

【矿难】kuàngnàn〈名〉 mine disaster

【矿区】kuàngqū〈名〉 mining area

【矿泉】kuàngquán〈名〉 mineral spring: ～浴 mineral water bath

【矿泉水】kuàngquánshuǐ〈名〉mineral water
【矿砂】kuàngshā〈名〉ore in sand form
【矿山】kuàngshān〈名〉mine: ～机械 mining machinery
【矿石】kuàngshí〈名〉ore
【矿体】kuàngtǐ = 矿床 kuàngchuáng
【矿物】kuàngwù〈名〉mineral: ～资源 mineral resources
【矿物油】kuàngwùyóu〈名〉mineral oil
【矿务局】kuàngwùjú〈名〉bureau of mines
【矿物质】kuàngwùzhì〈名〉mineral: ～水 mineral water ‖ 含有丰富的～ rich in minerals
【矿业】kuàngyè〈名〉mining industry: ～投资 mining industry capital investment
【矿源】kuàngyuán〈名〉mineral resources: 勘察～ prospect for mineral resources
【矿渣】kuàngzhā〈名〉slag: ～混凝土 slag concrete ‖ ～砖 slag brick
【矿柱】kuàngzhù〈名〉ore pillar

框 kuàng
A〈名〉frame: 黑～眼镜 glasses with black frames ▸窗～, 镜～, 门～
B〈动〉**1**（加边框） draw a frame around: 用红线把标题～起来 frame the heading in red **2**（限制） restrict: 对私营企业～得太死不利于其发展。 Rigid restrictions on private enterprises hinder their development.
【框定】kuàngdìng〈动〉pinpoint: ～作案人的范围 isolate the possible culprits
【框格】kuànggé〈名〉window lattice
【框架】kuàngjià〈名〉**1**（支撑结构） frame **2**（总体结构） framework: 一部小说的～ framework for a novel
【框架协议】kuàngjià xiéyì〈名〉framework agreement
【框框】kuàngkuang〈名〉**1**（边线） frame **2**（原有限制） convention: 废除老～ abolish the old rules ‖ 条条～束缚了我们的手脚。 Our hands were tied with all the rules and regulations.
【框子】kuàngzi〈名〉frame: 门～ door frame ‖ 眼镜～ glasses rim

眶 kuàng〈名〉eye socket: ▸热泪盈～, 眼～

kuī

亏（虧） kuī〈动〉**1**（损失） have a deficit: ～了100元 lose 100 *yuan* ‖ 把老本～光了 have lost all one's capital ▸～本, ～损, 吃～, 扭～为盈, 盈～ **2**（缺少） lack: 气血两～ dual depletion of *qi* and blood ‖ 我～你20元。 I owe you 20 *yuan*. ▸功～一篑, 理～ **3**（亏待） treat unfairly: 放心，～不了你。 Don't worry. We will not be unfair to you. ‖ 人不～地，地不～人。 The land won't fail people as long as people don't fail the land. **4**（幸亏） fortunately: ～我妻子有钥匙，要不我进不了门。 Luckily my wife had the key; otherwise I couldn't have got in. **5**（表斥责） [used to show irony]: ～你还是个大学生，连这个都不知道。 For a college student, you ought to know better than that!
【亏本】kuīběn〈动〉lose one's capital: 买卖～ lose money in a deal ‖ ～生意 loss-making business
【亏产】kuīchǎn〈动〉fall short of a production quota: 变～为超产 make up the shortfall (in output) and exceed the production quota
【亏秤】kuīchèng〈动〉**1**（缺斤短两） give short weight **2**（分量减少） lose weight: 青菜水分大，一放就会～。 As the vegetable has a high water content, it will certainly lose weight when stored.
【亏待】kuīdài〈动〉treat shabbily: 好好干，我不会～你的。 Work hard, and I will give you your due.
【亏得】kuīde〈动〉**1**（幸亏） thanks to: ～你帮忙，我才渡过了难关。 Thanks to your help, I overcame the difficulties. **2**（说反话） [used to show irony]: ～他还是你的老朋友，你有困难他都不帮忙。 Fancy an old friend of yours not lending you a hand when you are in difficulty.
【亏短】kuīduǎn〈动〉be deficient: ～分量 give short measure
【亏负】kuīfù〈动〉**1**（对不住） let down: 我没有任何～你的地方。 I didn't let you down in any way. **2**（使吃亏） lose money
【亏耗】kuīhào **A**〈动〉lose: ～体力 lose one's strength **B**〈名〉loss by a natural process: 运输中的～ losses incurred in the course of transportation
【亏空】kuīkong **A**〈动〉be in debt: 这家工厂～五万元。 The factory had a deficit of 50,000 *yuan*. **B**〈名〉deficit: 巨额～ huge deficit
【亏累】kuīlěi〈动〉sustain repeated losses: 账面～100万元。 The cumulative deficit in the account stands at one million *yuan*.
【亏欠】kuīqiàn〈动〉**1**（指钱财） be in debt **2**（指情分） owe: 我～家人很多。 I owe a lot to my family.
【亏弱】kuīruò〈形〉weak
【亏折】kuīshé〈动〉lose money in business: ～殆尽 lose all one's capital
【亏蚀】kuīshí〈动〉**1**（日食或月食） eclipse **2**（亏损） lose money in business: 连年～ lose money year upon year
【亏损】kuīsǔn〈动〉**1**（折本） lose money: 长期～ run at a loss for years ‖ 这个厂已经连续几年严重～。 This factory has been running at a heavy loss for years on end. **2**（变虚弱） become weak: 久病而元气～ be flagging after a long illness
【亏损额】kuīsǔn'é〈名〉amount of loss
【亏损企业】kuīsǔn qǐyè〈名〉loss-making enterprise
【亏心】kuīxīn〈形〉against one's conscience: 不做～事 not do things that give one a guilty conscience ‖ 你做这种事不～吗? Doesn't your conscience trouble you for doing that?

岿（巋） kuī
【岿然】kuīrán〈形〉〈书〉lofty: ～高耸 soar high
【岿然不动】kuīrán-bùdòng〈成〉〈喻〉stand one's ground
【岿巍】kuīwēi〈形〉〈书〉lofty: 山峰～。 The peaks towered aloft.

盔 kuī〈名〉helmet: ▸～甲, 钢～, 头～
【盔甲】kuījiǎ〈名〉suit of armour
【盔头】kuītou〈名〉headpiece worn by opera singers

窥（窺） kuī〈动〉peep
【窥豹一斑】kuībào-yībān〈成〉〈喻〉have only a limited understanding of sth.
【窥测】kuīcè〈动〉spy out: ～时机 await an opportunity ‖ ～方向 see which way the wind blows in order to achieve one's evil ends
【窥察】kuīchá〈动〉spy upon
【窥度】kuīduó〈动〉surmise in secret
【窥见】kuījiàn〈动〉glimpse: ～一斑 see a segment of a whole ‖ ～一个人影一闪而过 catch a glimpse of a figure dodging by
【窥视】kuīshì〈动〉spy on: ～敌情 spy on enemy activities ‖ 往屋内～ peep into a room
【窥视镜】kuīshìjìng〈名〉spyhole
【窥伺】kuīsì〈动〉〈贬〉lie in wait for: ～良机 lie in wait for a good opportunity
【窥探】kuītàn〈动〉pry into: ～敌情 spy on the enemy situation ‖ ～隐私 poke one's nose into sth. private
【窥望】kuīwàng〈动〉peep at

kuí

奎 kuí〈名〉one of the 28 constellations in ancient Chinese astronomy
【奎宁】kuíníng〈名〉［药学］quinine

逵 kuí〈名〉〈书〉thoroughfare

馗 kuí = 逵 kuí

隗 Kuí〈名〉Kui [surname]
▸Wěi

葵 kuí〈名〉certain herbaceous plants with big flowers: ▸锦～, 蒲～, 向日～
【葵花】kuíhuā〈名〉sunflower
【葵花油】kuíhuāyóu〈名〉sunflower oil
【葵花子】kuíhuāzǐ〈名〉sunflower seeds
【葵扇】kuíshàn〈名〉palm-leaf fan

揆 kuí〈动〉〈书〉conjecture: ～其本意，或非如此。 Presumably that was not his original intention.
【揆度】kuíduó〈动〉〈书〉estimate: ～得失 estimate gains and losses

喹 kuí
【喹啉】kuílín〈名〉［化学］quinoline

骙（騤） kuí
【骙骙】kuíkuí〈形〉〈书〉[of a horse] strong

睽 kuí〈动〉〈书〉part
【睽别】kuíbié〈动〉〈书〉be apart: ～经年 haven't seen each other for years
【睽隔】kuígé〈动〉〈书〉be apart: ～故乡已有十载 have been away from one's hometown for ten years
【睽违】kuíwéi〈动〉〈书〉[used in letters] part: ～数载。 It's been years since we parted.

魁 kuí
A〈名〉chief: ▸～首, 花～, 罪～祸首
B〈形〉**1**（高大） of sturdy build: ▸～伟, ～梧 **2** = 魁星 kuíxīng 1
【魁岸】kuí'àn〈形〉〈书〉tall and burly: 身材～ be tall and sturdy
【魁首】kuíshǒu〈名〉**1**（最强者） person who is head and shoulders above others: 女中～ most outstanding woman **2**（首领） chief: 强盗～ bandit chief
【魁伟】kuíwěi〈形〉big and tall: 体态～ be of strong build
【魁梧】kuíwú〈形〉big and tall: 身量～ be tall and sturdy

k

【魁星】 kuíxīng 〈名〉 [1]（指天体） four stars in the bowl of the Big Dipper (北斗), or the one at the tip of the bowl [2] Kuíxīng（指神仙） god of literature and writing

睽 kuí〈动〉〈书〉 go against
【睽睽】 kuíkuí〈形〉 gazing: ▸众目～
【睽异】 kuíyì〈动〉〈书〉 disagree: 委员们对此意见尚有～。 The committee members still differ about this.

蝰 kuí
【蝰蛇】 kuíshé〈名〉 viper

夔 kuí〈名〉 one-legged monster in ancient legends

kuǐ

傀 kuǐ
【傀儡】 kuǐlěi〈名〉 puppet:〈喻〉 ～政权 puppet regime ▸～戏
【傀儡戏】 kuǐlěixì = 木偶戏 mù'ǒuxì

跬 kuǐ〈名〉〈古〉 small step
【跬步千里】 kuǐbù-qiānlǐ〈成〉 continued efforts may lead to great success

kuì

匮（匱） kuì〈形〉〈书〉 deficient
【匮乏】 kuìfá〈动〉〈书〉 be deficient in: 劳动力～ have a labour shortage ‖ 资源～ lack natural resources
【匮竭】 kuìjié〈动〉〈书〉 be in short supply: 森林资源～。 The forest reserves are exhausted.
【匮缺】 kuìquē = 匮乏 kuìfá

喟 kuì〈动〉〈书〉 sigh: ▸感～
【喟然】 kuìrán〈动〉〈书〉 sigh deeply: ～长叹 heave a deep sigh
【喟叹】 kuìtàn〈动〉〈书〉 sigh with deep feeling

馈（饋、餽） kuì〈动〉 [1]（赠送） present (a gift) [2]（传输） transmit
【馈电】 kuìdiàn〈动〉［电气］ feed
【馈送】 kuìsòng〈动〉 present a gift
【馈线】 kuìxiàn〈名〉［电气］ feeder
【馈献】 kuìxiàn〈动〉〈书〉 present (a gift to one's seniors)
【馈赠】 kuìzèng〈动〉 present a gift: ～礼品 present gifts

溃（潰） kuì〈动〉 [1]（指堤岸） burst: ～口 break ▸～决 [2]〈书〉（突破） break through: ▸～围 [3]（溃败） be defeated: 不战而～ collapse without a battle ‖ 一触即～ be defeated at the first encounter ▸～不成军 [4]（指肌肉） ulcerate: ▸～烂, ～疡
▸huì
【溃败】 kuìbài〈动〉 be defeated
【溃兵】 kuìbīng〈名〉 routed troops
【溃不成军】 kuìbùchéngjūn〈成〉 be defeated and flee in great disorder: 我们把敌人打得～。 We demolished the enemy.
【溃决】 kuìjué〈动〉 burst: 堤坝～。 The dam burst.
【溃军】 kuìjūn = 溃兵 kuìbīng
【溃烂】 kuìlàn〈动〉 ulcerate: 伤口～了。 The wound has become infected.
【溃乱】 kuìluàn〈动〉 be defeated and thrown into disarray
【溃灭】 kuìmiè〈动〉 crumble and fall: 旧的社会制度终于～了。 The old social system finally crumbled.
【溃散】 kuìsàn〈动〉 be defeated and dispersed: 仓皇～ flee helter-skelter after being defeated
【溃逃】 kuìtáo〈动〉 be defeated and flee in disorder: 四处～ flee in all directions
【溃退】 kuìtuì〈动〉 retreat after a defeat: 败兵～，争相逃命。 The defeated soldiers fled for their lives.
【溃围】 kuìwéi〈动〉〈书〉 break through an encirclement: 乘势～ take advantage of a situation to break through an encirclement
【溃疡】 kuìyáng ▸**p. 50**〈名〉［医学］ ulcer: 口腔～ oral ulcer ‖ 胃～ gastric ulcer ‖ ～面 ulcerous side

愦（憒） kuì〈形〉〈书〉 befuddled: 昏～ be muddle-headed
【愦乱】 kuìluàn〈形〉〈书〉 dazed and confused

愧 kuì〈形〉 ashamed: 于心有～ have a guilty conscience ▸～色, 羞～, 问心无～
【愧恨】 kuìhèn〈动〉 be ashamed and remorseful: ～交集 be overcome with shame and remorse
【愧悔】 kuìhuǐ〈形〉 ashamed and regretful: ～不及 be extremely ashamed and sorry
【愧疚】 kuìjiù〈形〉 conscience-stricken: 深感～ feel extremely guilty ‖ ～的心情 feeling of shame and remorse
【愧领】 kuìlǐng〈动〉〈套〉 [used when one accepts others' regards, presents, etc.]: 您的心意，我们～了。 We very much appreciate your kindness.
【愧色】 kuìsè〈名〉 ashamed look: 面带～ look ashamed
【愧痛】 kuìtòng〈形〉 agonized and shameful: 万分～ extremely agonized and shameful
【愧怍】 kuìzuò〈形〉〈书〉 ashamed: ～万分 be extremely ashamed

聩（聵） kuì〈形〉〈书〉 deaf: 昏～ be decrepit and befuddled ▸发聋振～

篑（簣） kuì〈名〉〈古〉 basket for holding earth: ▸功亏一～

kūn

坤 kūn〈名〉 [1]（指八卦） one of the Eight Trigrams, symbolizing 'earth': ▸乾～ [2]（女性） female: ～包 lady's handbag
【坤表】 kūnbiǎo〈名〉 women's wristwatch
【坤角儿】 kūnjuér〈名〉〈旧〉 [in Chinese traditional opera] actress
【坤宅】 kūnzhái〈名〉〈旧〉 bride's/wife's family

昆 kūn〈名〉〈书〉 elder brother
【昆布】 kūnbù〈名〉［中药］ kelp
【昆虫】 kūnchóng〈名〉 insect: ～标本 insect specimen
【昆弟】 kūndì〈名〉〈书〉 brother: ～俱已成人。 All the brothers have grown to manhood.
【昆剧】 kūnjù = 昆曲 kūnqǔ 1
【昆仑】 Kūnlún〈名〉 Kunlun Mountains
【昆明】 Kūnmíng ▸**p. 661**〈名〉 Kunming [capital of Yunnan Province (云南)]
【昆腔】 kūnqiāng〈名〉 melodies for *Kunqu* opera
【昆曲】 kūnqǔ〈名〉 [1]（指戏曲） Kunqu opera [2] = 昆腔 kūnqiāng

> **昆曲**
>
> One of the most ancient forms of Chinese traditional opera, also known as *kunju* (昆剧). The music originated in the Yuan Dynasty in Kunshan in Jiangsu Province, gaining popularity by the Ming and the first part of the Qing dynasties. The melodies and the songs are mainly based on legend. One of the most famous *Kunqu* operas is *The Peony Pavilion* (《牡丹亭》). Musical instruments used include flutes and other wind instruments, lutes (琵琶), drums, clappers, and gongs, amongst others. *Kunqu* is divided into northern and southern forms. The former is popular in Beijing and Hebei Province, and the latter is popular in southern Jiangsu. *Kunqu* has had a significant influence on Peking Opera (▸京剧) and other Chinese operatic forms.

【昆士兰】 Kūnshìlán〈名〉 Queensland
【昆仲】 kūnzhòng〈名〉〈书〉 other people's brothers

堃 kūn = 坤 kūn

鲲（鯤） kūn〈名〉 enormous legendary fish which could change into a roc
【鲲鹏】 kūnpéng〈名〉 roc: ～展翅 taking off with tremendous power and momentum

kǔn

捆（綑） kǔn
A〈动〉 tie: ～行李 tie up the baggage ‖ 把柳条～在一起 tie willow twigs together ‖ 稻草～儿 straw bundle
B〈量〉 bundle: 两～干草 two bales of hay ‖ 一～葱 a bunch of spring onions
【捆绑】 kǔnbǎng〈动〉 tie up: ～式火箭 E-strap rocket ‖ ～销售 bundling ‖ 他被～起来。 He was tied up.
【捆扎】 kǔnzā〈动〉 tie up: 这些书已～好了。 The books have already been bundled up.
【捆子】 kǔnzi = 捆 kǔn B

阃（閫） kǔn〈名〉〈书〉 [1]（门槛） threshold [2]（闺门） women's quarters [3]（妇女） women: ～范 model of women's moral character

悃 kǔn〈形〉〈书〉 sincere

kùn

困[1] kùn
A〈动〉 [1]（围困） be stranded: ～在车上 be stranded in a car ‖ 为病所～ be afflicted with illness ▸内外交～ [2]（包围） encircle: 把敌人～死在据点里 surround the enemy in their stronghold ‖ 我们要被～在这儿多久? How long are we going to stay cooped up in here? ▸～守, 围～
B〈形〉 [1]（艰难） difficult: ▸～苦 [2]（疲乏） tired: ▸～乏, 人～马乏

k

困²（睏） kùn〈形〉 sleepy: 我～得连眼睛都睁不开了。 I am so sleepy that I can hardly keep my eyes open.
【困惫】kùnbèi〈形〉〈书〉 exhausted: ～不堪 be in a state of utter exhaustion
【困顿】kùndùn〈形〉 1（疲乏） exhausted: ～不堪 be utterly exhausted 2（穷困） poverty-stricken: ～潦倒 be frustrated and in dire financial straits
【困厄】kùn'è〈名〉 dire straits: 从～中奋起 pull oneself out of dire straits ‖ 在～中挣扎 struggle for existence in distress
【困乏】kùnfá〈形〉 1（疲乏） weary: 她看上去～极了。 She looks exhausted. 2〈书〉（穷困） impoverished: 他家生活～。 His family is in dire financial straits.
【困惑】kùnhuò A〈形〉 puzzled: 我对目前的情况感到～。 I feel puzzled about the current situation. B〈动〉 confuse: 这个问题一直～着我。 This problem has always had me tied up in knots.
【困惑不解】kùnhuò-bùjiě〈成〉 be at a loss: 对某事感到～ feel confused about sth.
【困觉】kùnjiào〈动〉〈方〉 sleep: 困中觉 take a nap after lunch
【困境】kùnjìng〈名〉 predicament: 摆脱～ extricate oneself from a difficult position ‖ 陷入～ be in a fix
【困窘】kùnjiǒng〈形〉 1（为难） embarrassed: 大为～ be extremely embarrassed 2（穷困） destitute: ～的生活 poverty-stricken life ‖ 他家境～。 His family is in a dire financial situation.
【困居】kùnjū〈动〉 be stranded
【困倦】kùnjuàn〈形〉 feel sleepy: 大家都十分～。 Everybody felt terribly sleepy.
【困苦】kùnkǔ〈形〉 poverty-stricken: 生活很～ live in dire poverty
【困苦劳顿】kùnkǔ-láodùn〈成〉 in great distress and weariness
【困难】kùnnan A〈名〉 difficulty: 克服～ overcome difficulties ‖ 呼吸～ have difficulty breathing ‖ 财政～ financial difficulties B〈形〉 financially strained: 生活～ live in straitened circumstances ‖ 经济～的学生 students in financial straits
【困难重重】kùnnan-chóngchóng〈成〉 be beset with difficulties
【困难户】kùnnanhù〈名〉 families with financial difficulties
【困扰】kùnrǎo〈动〉 perplex: 为沉重的负担所～ be plagued by heavy burdens ‖ 萧条～着市场。 The slump is plaguing the market.
【困守】kùnshǒu〈动〉defend against a siege: ～孤城 defend a besieged city
【困兽犹斗】kùnshòu-yóudòu〈成〉in a desperate situation people will put up a desperate fight

kuò

扩（擴） kuò〈动〉 expand: ▸～编，～充，～张
【扩版】kuòbǎn〈动〉 increase the number of pages
【扩编】kuòbiān〈动〉 increase the size of a force: ～部队 enlarge an army
【扩充】kuòchōng〈动〉 expand and strengthen: ～编辑人员 augment the editorial staff ‖ ～军备 engage in arms expansion ‖ ～内容 add to the contents
【扩大】kuòdà〈动〉 expand: ～对外开放 open up wider to the outside world ‖ ～经营范围 expand the scope of business ‖ ～内需 expand domestic demand ‖ ～再生产 expanded reproduction ‖ ～影响 extend one's influence ‖ ～战果 exploit a victory
【扩大化】kuòdàhuà〈动〉 extend unreasonably: 不要使事态～。 Don't let the incident get out of hand.
【扩大会议】kuòdà huìyì〈名〉 enlarged session: 中央全会～ enlarged plenary session of the central committee
【扩建】kuòjiàn〈动〉extend: ～工厂 enlarge a factory ‖ ～工程 extension project
【扩军】kuòjūn〈动〉 engage in arms expansion: ～备战 intensify arms expansion and war preparations
【扩容】kuòróng〈动〉 1（指通讯设备） expand tele communication capacity: 电信～工程 telecommunication capacity expansion project 2（指规模、范围） expand in scale: 最近这几年股市～很快。 The stock market has expanded rapidly in the past few years.
【扩散】kuòsàn〈动〉 spread: 癌细胞已经～。 The cancer cells have already spread.
【扩胸】kuòxiōng〈动〉 expand one's chest: ～运动 chest-expanding exercises
【扩胸器】kuòxiōngqì〈名〉 chest expander
【扩音机】kuòyīnjī〈名〉 audio amplifier
【扩音器】kuòyīnqì〈名〉 1（喇叭） loudspeaker; bullhorn〈美〉 2（指仪器） acoustic amplifier
【扩印】kuòyìn〈动〉 enlarge a photo: ～彩色照片 enlarge colour photos
【扩展】kuòzhǎn〈动〉 expand: ～市场 expand the market ‖ ～公司业务 develop company business
【扩展名】kuòzhǎnmíng〈名〉［计算机］ filename extension
【扩展坞】kuòzhǎnwū〈名〉［计算机］ docking station
【扩张】kuòzhāng〈动〉 1（向外伸展） expand: ～领土 expand one's territory ‖ 向海外～ expand overseas 2［医学］ dilate: 血管～ blood vessel dilatation
【扩张主义】kuòzhāng zhǔyì〈名〉 expansionism
【扩招】kuòzhāo〈动〉extend the enrolment: 我校将～300名新生。 Our school is taking on an additional 300 new students.

括 kuò〈动〉 1（束） contract: ▸～约肌 2（包括） include: ▸包～，总～ 3（加括号） enclose with brackets: 把解释性的话～起来。 Put the explanatory words in brackets.
▸guā
【括号】kuòhào〈名〉 brackets
【括弧】kuòhú〈名〉 brackets
【括约肌】kuòyuējī〈名〉［解剖］(sphincter) muscle
【括注】kuòzhù〈名〉 explanatory note in brackets

蛞 kuò
【蛞蝓】kuòyú〈名〉［动物］ slug

阔（闊） kuò〈形〉 1（宽广） wide: ▸广～，海～天空 2（距离大） long: ▸～步，～别 3（空泛） empty: ▸高谈～论，迂～ 4（阔绰） wealthy: ～起来 get rich ▸～少，摆～
【阔别】kuòbié〈动〉 be separated for a long time: ～多年的老同学 classmates who have not seen each other for a long time
【阔步】kuòbù〈动〉 take big strides: ～前进 advance with great strides
【阔绰】kuòchuò〈形〉 extravagant: 生活～ lead an extravagant life
【阔佬】kuòlǎo〈名〉 wealthy person
【阔气】kuòqi〈形〉 luxurious: 摆～ parade one's wealth
【阔少】kuòshào〈名〉 son of a rich family
【阔叶林】kuòyèlín〈名〉 broad-leaved forest
【阔叶树】kuòyèshù〈名〉 broadleaf tree

廓 kuò
A〈形〉 wide: ▸寥～
B〈名〉 outline: ▸耳～，轮～
【廓清】kuòqīng〈动〉 1（使清明） clear up: ～天下 bring peace and unity to the country 2（清除） clear away: ～积弊 sweep away outstanding abuses ‖ ～障碍 remove obstacles

Ll

lā

垃 lā

【垃圾】 lājī 〈名〉 rubbish 〈英〉; garbage 〈美〉: 处理～ dispose of rubbish ‖ 倒～ dump rubbish ‖ 清除～ remove rubbish ‖ 建筑～ demolition debris ‖ 生活～ household refuse ‖ ～回收箱 recycling bin ‖ ～箱 dustbin 〈英〉, garbage can 〈美〉 ‖ 〈喻〉 她的建议只是一堆～。 Her advice turned out to be nothing but rubbish.

【垃圾场】 lājīchǎng 〈名〉 tip 〈英〉; dump 〈美〉

【垃圾车】 lājīchē 〈名〉 dustcart 〈英〉; garbage truck 〈美〉

【垃圾袋】 lājīdài 〈名〉 rubbish bag 〈英〉; garbage bag 〈美〉

【垃圾堆】 lājīduī 〈名〉 dustheap 〈英〉; garbage heap 〈美〉: 你的房间像个～。 Your room looks like a real dump.

【垃圾分类】 lājī fēnlèi 〈名〉 refuse classification

【垃圾焚化炉】 lājī fénhuàlú 〈名〉 incinerator

【垃圾股】 lājīgǔ 〈名〉 [经济] junk stock

【垃圾食品】 lājī shípǐn 〈名〉 junk food

【垃圾桶】 lājītǒng 〈名〉 dustbin 〈英〉; trash can 〈美〉: 大～ dumpster

【垃圾填埋场】 lājī tiánmáichǎng 〈名〉 landfill site

【垃圾邮件】 lājī yóujiàn 〈名〉 junk mail: 发～ send spam

拉[1] lā 〈动〉 ①〈牵引〉 pull: ～窗帘 draw the curtains ‖ ～绳子 tug at a rope ‖ 手～手 hand in hand ‖ 把绳子再～紧点儿! Tighten the rope a bit more, please! ►～锯, ～纤, ～下水 ②〈载运〉 transport by vehicle: ～客人去机场 take a customer to the airport ‖ 用货车～东西 haul sth. by lorry ③〈鸣响〉 sound: ～警笛 sound the alarm ‖ ～二胡/手风琴/小提琴 play the *erhu* /accordion/violin ④〈组织〉 organize: ～一帮人 gather a band of people ‖ ～起一支队伍 raise a contingent of troops ⑤〈拖长〉 draw out: 把文章～长到十页 stretch the essay to ten pages ‖ 说话拖腔～调 speak with a drawl ⑥〈拖欠〉 owe: ～下债 fall into debt ►～饥荒, ～亏空, ～账 ⑦〈方〉〈抚养〉 bring up: 父母把我们～大实在不容易。 It was not at all easy for our parents to bring us up. ⑧〈帮助〉 lend a helping hand: ～他一把 give him a helping hand ⑨〈牵累〉 involve: 不要～上别人。 Don't drag others into it. ⑩〈联络〉 solicit: ～广告 winning advertisement ‖ ～选票 canvass for votes ►～关系, ～交情, ～买卖 ⑪〈口〉〈闲谈〉 chat: ►～家常 ⑫〈排泄〉 empty one's bowels: ～不出来 have difficulty in moving one's bowels ►～肚子, ～稀

拉[2] Lā ►拉祜族 Lāhùzú ►lá, lǎ, là

【拉巴斯】 Lābāsī 〈名〉 La Paz

【拉巴特】 Lābātè 〈名〉 Rabat

【拉帮结伙】 lābāng-jiéhuǒ 〈成〉 gang up: 他们～反对我。 They are ganging up on me.

【拉帮结派】 lābāng-jiépài = 拉帮结伙 lābāng-jiéhuǒ

【拉比】 lābǐ 〈名〉 [宗教] rabbi

【拉场子】 lā chǎngzi 〈动〉 ①〈指表演〉 give an outdoor performance ②〈撑场面〉 make a big show: 请客～ entertain people and throw a big show

【拉扯】 lāche 〈动〉 ①〈拖曳〉 drag: 他要想走，谁也～不住他。 If he wants to go, no one can hold him back. ②〈抚养〉 take pains to raise: 把孩子～大 bring up one's children with great difficulty ③〈帮助〉 support: 他的上司有心～他一把。 His boss had a mind to help him on his way. ④〈勾结〉 gang up with: 他是个很会～和找门道的人。 He knows how to strike up an acquaintance and take advantage of it. ⑤〈牵扯〉 implicate: 你们吵架，别把我～进去。 Don't drag me into your quarrels. ⑥〈闲谈〉 chat: 我没工夫跟你～。 I'm too busy to chat with you.

【拉床】 lāchuáng 〈名〉 [机械] broaching machine

【拉大旗，作虎皮】 lā dàqí, zuò hǔpí 〈成〉〈喻〉 deck oneself out to intimidate people

【拉倒】 lādǎo 〈动〉〈口〉 drop it: 你不要就～。 If you don't like it, let's forget about it.

【拉德诺郡】 Lādénuòjùn 〈名〉 Radnorshire

【拉丁】 Lādīng 〈名〉 Latin: ～舞 Latin dance ►～美洲

【拉丁美洲】 Lādīng Měizhōu 〈名〉 Latin America: ～共同市场 Latin American Common Market

【拉丁文】 Lādīngwén ►p. 918 〈名〉 Latin

【拉丁语】 Lādīngyǔ ►p. 918 〈名〉 Latin

【拉丁字母】 Lādīng zìmǔ 〈名〉 Roman alphabet

【拉动】 lādòng 〈动〉 drive: ～经济增长 fuel economic growth

【拉肚子】 lā dùzi ►p. 50 〈动〉〈口〉 have diarrhoea

【拉杆】 lāgān 〈名〉 ①[机械] pull rod ②〈可伸缩〉 extendable telescopic rod: ～天线 extendable telescopic aerial

【拉杆箱】 lāgānxiāng 〈名〉 draw-bar box

【拉各斯】 Lāgèsī 〈名〉 Lagos

【拉钩】 lāgōu 〈动〉 [of two people] hook up the little fingers of each other's right hands and pull them as a token of good faith

【拉关系】 lā guānxi 〈惯〉〈贬〉 cosy up to: ～, 走后门 establish underhand connections and exploit them for personal gain

【拉管】 lāguǎn ►p. 929 〈名〉 [音乐] trombone

【拉呱儿】 lāguǎr 〈动〉〈方〉 chit-chat

【拉后腿】 lā hòutuǐ 〈惯〉 hold sb. back: 拉企业的后腿 be a hindrance to an enterprise

【拉祜族】 Lāhùzú 〈名〉 Lahu ethnic group

【拉花儿】 lāhuār 〈名〉 garland

【拉饥荒】 lā jīhuang 〈惯〉〈口〉 fall into debt: 因生病住院～ run into debts because of illness and hospitalization

【拉家常】 lā jiācháng 〈动〉 engage in chit-chat: 边喝茶边～ have a chat over a cup of tea

【拉家带口】 lājiā-dàikǒu 〈成〉 be tied down by one's family

【拉架】 lājià 〈动〉 try to stop two people in a fist fight: 他们打起来了，快去拉拉架吧。 They've started fighting. Quick, go and separate them!

【拉交情】 lā jiāoqing 〈动〉〈贬〉 cosy up to: 他们试图和我们～。 They attempted to cosy up to us.

【拉脚】 lājiǎo 〈动〉 transport by cart

【拉近乎】 lā jìnhu 〈动〉〈贬〉 try to get in with

【拉锯】 lājù 〈动〉 ①〈本〉 work a two-handed saw ②〈喻〉〈指局面〉 be locked in an up-and-down struggle: ～战 seesaw (battle) ‖ 战事呈～状态。 The battle seesawed back and forth.

【拉开】 lākāi 〈动〉 ①〈摆出〉 pull open: ～架势 assume a fighting posture ②〈使扩大〉 space out: ～档次 widen the gap between different grades ‖ 把比分～至101 比 90 pull away to 101 to 90

【拉客】 lākè 〈动〉 ①〈指饭店、旅馆等〉 tout for custom: 强行～ forcibly solicit customers ②〈指运输工具〉 take passengers: 卡车是不允许～的。 Lorries are not permitted to take passengers. ③〈指妓女〉 solicit

【拉亏空】 lā kuīkong 〈动〉 fall into debt: 他家人口多，拉下了亏空。 He has a big family and has fallen into debt.

【拉拉扯扯】 lālā-chěchě 〈动〉 ①〈拖曳〉 pull sb. about: 别～的，把我的衣服都快撕破了。 Don't pull at my clothes. You are going to tear them. ‖ 放自重点，别～! Take your hands off me and behave yourself! ②〈表亲昵〉 be hand in glove ③〈不正当交往〉 strike up an acquaintance with sb. for personal gains: 他们背地里～。 They are very tight behind the scenes.

【拉拉队】 lālāduì 〈名〉 cheering squad: ～员 cheerleader

【拉力】 lālì 〈名〉 pulling force

【拉力器】 lālìqì 〈名〉 chest expander

【拉力赛】 lālìsài ►p. 909 〈名〉 [体育] rally: 汽车～ auto rally

【拉练】lāliàn〈名〉camp and field training

【拉链】lāliàn〈名〉zip〈英〉; zipper〈美〉: 把裤子的～拉上 zip up one's trousers

【拉拢】lālǒng〈动〉〈贬〉rope in: ～腐蚀干部 woo and corrupt cadres

【拉买卖】lā mǎimai〈动〉drum up trade: 商家充分利用广告～。Businesses make full use of advertising to drum up trade.

【拉美】Lāměi〈简称〉= 拉丁美洲

【拉面】lāmiàn〈名〉hand-pulled noodles

【拉纳克郡】Lānàkèjùn〈名〉Lanarkshire

【拉尼娜现象】Lānínà xiànxiàng〈名〉[气象] La Niña

【拉皮】lāpí〈动〉lift: 面部～美容术 face-lift

【拉皮条】lā pítiáo〈动〉procure

【拉平】lāpíng〈动〉even up: 渐渐把比分～ gradually even up the score

【拉纤】lāqiàn〈动〉**1**（指船）tow **2**（指说媒）act as a go-between: 说媒～ act as a matchmaker

【拉萨】Lāsà ►**p. 661**〈名〉Lhasa [capital of Tibet (西藏)]

【拉山头】lā shāntóu〈惯〉form a clique

【拉生意】lā shēngyi = 拉买卖 lā mǎimai

【拉屎】lāshǐ〈动〉〈口〉empty one's bowels

【拉手】lāshǒu〈动〉**1**〈口〉（握手）shake hands **2**（牵手）be hand in hand: 手拉着手跳舞 dance hand in hand

【拉手】lāshou〈名〉handle: 抽屉～ drawer pull ‖ 门～ door handle

【拉斯维加斯】Lāsīwéijiāsī〈名〉Las Vegas

【拉锁】lāsuǒ = 拉链 lāliàn

【拉抬】lātái〈动〉boost: ～房价/股价 boost housing/stock prices

【拉特兰郡】Lātèlánjùn〈名〉Rutland

【拉条】lātiáo〈名〉hand-pulled noodles

【拉脱维亚】Lātuōwéiyà〈名〉Latvia: ～共和国 Republic of Latvia ‖ ～人 Latvian ‖ ～语 Latvian

【拉网】lāwǎng〈动〉draw in the net

【拉稀】lāxī〈动〉〈口〉have diarrhoea

【拉下脸】lāxià liǎn〈惯〉**1**（不顾情面）not spare sb.'s sensibilities: 拉不下脸 be unable to do sth. for fear of offending sb. **2**（面露不快）pull a long face: 他听了这句话很不高兴，立刻～来。Displeased at the remark, he immediately pulled a long face.

【拉下马】lāxià mǎ〈惯〉〈喻〉topple

【拉下水】lāxià shuǐ〈惯〉〈喻〉drag sb. into the mire

【拉线开关】lāxiàn kāiguān〈名〉[电气] pull switch

【拉秧】lāyāng〈动〉[农业] uproot plants after harvest time

【拉洋片】lā yángpiān〈动〉give a peep-show

【拉杂】lāzá〈形〉jumbled: 这篇文章写得有点～。This essay is a bit rambling. ‖ 我就拉拉杂杂谈这些。I'll stop rambling now.

【拉闸】lāzhá〈动〉switch off the power

【拉账】lāzhàng〈动〉fall into debt: 拉了一屁股账 owe a mountain of debts

啦 lā ►哗啦 huālā
►la

喇 lā ►呼喇 hūlā
►lá, lǎ

邋 lā

【邋遢】lāta〈形〉〈口〉slovenly: 这屋子太～了。This room is a complete mess.

lá

旯 lá ►旮旯儿 gālár

拉 lá〈动〉slash: ～个双眼皮 have a slit made in one's eyelids to make double-fold ‖ 我的手背上～了个长口子。I gashed the back of my hand.
►lā, lǎ, là

剌 lá = 拉 lá
►là

砬 lá〈名〉big rock on a mountain [usu used in place names]

喇 lá ►哈喇子 hālázi
►lā, lǎ

lǎ

拉 lǎ ►半拉 bànlǎ
►lā, lá, là

喇 lǎ
►lā, lá

【喇叭】lǎba〈名〉**1** ►**p. 929** [音乐] trumpet: 吹～ blow a trumpet **2**（扩音器）loudspeaker: 鸣汽车～ sound the car horn

【喇叭花】lǎbahuā〈名〉[植物] white-edged morning glory

【喇叭裤】lǎbakù〈名〉bell-bottoms

【喇嘛】lǎma〈名〉〈尊〉[宗教] lama

> **喇嘛**
>
> An honorific title originally applied to a spiritual leader in Tibetan Buddhism, specifically a reincarnate lama, or one who had earned the title. Today, the term is used as a respectful general form of address for a Tibetan or Mongolian Buddhist monk.

【喇嘛教】Lǎmajiào〈名〉Tibetan Buddhism: ～徒 Lamaist

【喇嘛庙】lǎmamiào〈名〉lamasery

là

拉[1] là = 落 là

拉[2] là
►lā, lá, lǎ

【拉拉蛄】làlàgǔ = 蝲蝲蛄 làlàgǔ

剌 là〈形〉〈书〉perverse
►lá

落 là〈动〉**1**（落后）fall behind: 远远～在后面 lag far behind ‖ 他～了整整一个星期的课。He is a whole week behind with his lessons. **2**（遗漏）leave out: 名册上把他的名字给～了。His name was missing from the list. **3**（忘带）leave behind: 把书～在家里 leave a book at home ►丢三～四
►lào, luò

腊（臘） là〈名〉**1**（指祭祀）ancient sacrificial rite conducted shortly after the winter solstice each (lunar) year **2**（农历十二月）twelfth lunar month: ►～八，～月 **3**（指食物）cured fish, meat, etc. (prepared in the twelfth lunar month): ►～肠，～肉，～味
►xī

【腊八】làbā〈名〉eighth day of the twelfth lunar month

【腊八粥】làbāzhōu〈名〉*laba* porridge

> **腊八粥**
>
> The 12th month of the lunar year is known as *layue* (腊月), and *laba* (腊八) is the 8th day of this month. In ancient times, offerings were made to the gods on this day. Buddhist temples would make a porridge called *laba* porridge, and the tradition has become a folk custom. Porridge ingredients include rice, glutinous rice, red beans, peanuts, raisins, chestnuts, jujubes, lotus seeds, and dried longan.

【腊肠】làcháng〈名〉sausage

【腊梅】làméi = 蜡梅 làméi

【腊日】làrì〈名〉day of winter sacrifice [usu the eighth day of the twelfth lunar month]

【腊肉】làròu〈名〉cured meat

【腊味】làwèi〈名〉cured meat, fish, etc.

【腊鱼】làyú〈名〉cured fish

【腊月】làyuè ►**p. 928**〈名〉twelfth month of the lunar year: 寒冬～ severe winter

蜡（蠟） là〈名〉**1**（指油质）wax: 给地板打～ wax the floor ‖ 白～ white wax ►蜂～，味同嚼～ **2**（蜡烛）candle: 把～吹灭 blow out a candle ‖ 点一支～ light a candle ►～烛，瞎子点灯白费～
►zhà

【蜡白】làbái〈形〉pallid: 脸色～ look pasty

【蜡板】làbǎn〈名〉tool for making white wax

【蜡笔】làbǐ〈名〉(wax) crayon: 彩色～ colour crayon ‖ ～画 crayon drawing

【蜡封】làfēng〈动〉be sealed with wax

【蜡光纸】làguāngzhǐ〈名〉glazed paper

【蜡果】làguǒ〈名〉[美术] wax fruit

【蜡花】làhuā〈名〉snuff of a candle wick

【蜡黄】làhuáng〈形〉waxen: 脸色～ have a sallow complexion

【蜡炬】làjù〈名〉〈书〉wax candle

【蜡泪】làlèi〈名〉drips from a burning candle

【蜡梅】làméi〈名〉**1** [植物] wintersweet **2**（指花）flower of wintersweet

【蜡扦】làqiān〈名〉candlestick

【蜡染】làrǎn〈动〉[纺织] do wax printing: ～布 batik cloth

【蜡人】làrén〈名〉wax figure

【蜡台】làtái〈名〉candlestick

【蜡丸】làwán〈名〉**1**（指空心球）wax coating **2**（指药丸）wax-coated pill

【蜡像】làxiàng〈名〉waxwork: ～馆 waxworks

【蜡印】làyìn〈名〉wax seal

【蜡纸】làzhǐ〈名〉**1**（用于防潮）waxed paper **2**（指油质底板）stencil: 刻～ cut a stencil

【蜡烛】làzhú〈名〉(wax) candle: 点～ light a candle

【蜡烛台】làzhútái〈名〉candlestick

【蜡嘴雀】làzuǐquè〈名〉[鸟类] hawfinch

瘌 là

【瘌痢头】làlìtóu〈名〉〈方〉1（指脑袋）favus of the head 2（指人）person with favus of the scalp

辣 là

A〈形〉1（指味道）spicy: ～味 peppery taste ‖ 这道菜太～了。This dish is too hot. ▸辛～ 2（狠毒）vicious: ▸毒～, 心狠手～
B〈动〉burn: ～得我满头是汗。It was so spicy that it made me sweat all over.

【辣肠】làcháng〈名〉saveloy

【辣根】làgēn〈名〉［植物］horse-radish

【辣乎乎】làhūhū〈形〉spicy: 这菜～的。This dish is hot.

【辣酱】làjiàng〈名〉chilli paste

【辣酱油】làjiàngyóu〈名〉piquant sauce

【辣椒】làjiāo〈名〉chilli pepper: 红～ cayenne (pepper) ‖ ～粉 chilli powder ‖ ～酱 chilli sauce ‖ ～油 chilli oil

【辣妹】làmèi〈名〉〈口〉hot chick: ～与帅哥同台表演。Sexy chicks and hot guys shared the stage.

【辣妹子】làmèizi〈名〉virago

【辣手】làshǒu A〈名〉ruthless method B〈形〉1〈方〉（狠毒）ruthless: 这一招真够～的。What a malicious move! 2〈口〉（棘手）thorny: 这事很～。This is a sticky business.

【辣丝丝】làsīsī〈形〉slightly hot

【辣子】làzi〈名〉〈口〉chilli: ～鸡丁 diced chicken with chilli

蝲 là

【蝲蛄】làgǔ〈名〉［动物］crayfish

【蝲蝲蛄】làlàgǔ〈名〉［昆虫］mole cricket

鯻（鯻）là〈名〉［鱼类］tiger-fish

癞（癩）là = 瘌 là

▸lài

镴（鑞）là〈名〉alloy of tin and lead

la

啦 la〈助〉[fusion of 了 and 啊]: 他走～! He's gone. ‖ 我们已经干完～。We've finished it!

▸lā

lái

来¹（來）lái

A〈动〉1（过来）come: 新～的 newcomer ‖ 到这儿～! Come here! ‖ 公共汽车～了。Here comes the bus. ‖ 邮件～了吗? Has the post arrived yet? ‖ 有空～玩。Drop round when you have time. ▸～往 2（出现）arise: 今年雨季～得晚。The rainy season came late this year. ‖ 问题～了也不要怕。Stay cool when a problem arises. 3 a（表示来的目的）[used after a verb or verbal expression] come in order to do sth.: 老师看望大家～了。Our teacher has come to visit us. b（表示要做某事）[used before a verb or a verbal expression] will do sth.: 让他先～说两句。Let him say a few words first. ‖ 我～讲个故事。Let me tell you a story. 4（用于代表具体动词）[used as a substitute for a verb so as to avoid repetition]: 不要跟我～这一套。Don't play that trick on me! ‖ 唱得真好，再～一个! Bravo! 5（表动作朝向）[used after another verb or verbal phrase to indicate the movement toward the speaker]: 拿榔头～。Bring me a hammer. ‖ 对面开～一辆警车。A police car is driving towards us. 6（表结果）[used after a verb to indicate the result or estimation]: 一觉醒～ after a good sleep ‖ 说～话长。It is a long story. 7（表目的）[used between a verbal or prepositional phrase and a verb or its equivalent with the former indicating the manner or attitude and the latter the purpose]: 扒着门缝～偷看 take a peep through the slit ‖ 我们一定尽最大努力～完成任务。We will do our best to fulfil the task. 8（表能力）[used with 得 or 不, indicating capability or incapability]: 我和他还合得～。I get along with him pretty well. ‖ 这道题我做不～。I can't work this problem out.
B〈形〉future: ▸～年, ～日, 继往开～
C〈名〉[used after a time expression, indicating a period of time that extends from the past to this moment]: 多年～ for many years ‖ 几天～ for the last few days ‖ 这两年～ over the past two years ▸别～无恙, 近～, 向～

来²（來）lái〈助〉[used as a syllable filler in ballads]: 二月里～呀好春光。What a gorgeous spring in February!

来³（來）lái〈助〉1（来着）[used at the end of a sentence indicating a completed action]: 你昨天干什么～? What did you get up to yesterday? ‖ 这话我什么时候说～? When did I ever say that? 2 ▸p. 927（大概）[used after a round number or after a numeral plus a unit of measurement] approximately: 十～个人 about 10 people ‖ 四十～岁 about 40 years old 3（表列举）[used after the numerals 一, 二 and 三 to list the points in an explanation or argument]: 我这次到西安，一～是办点事，二～是看看朋友。I've come to Xi'an this time, first, to attend some business, and second, to see some friends.

【来宾】láibīn〈名〉guest: 接待～ receive guests ‖ 设宴招待～ give a dinner in honour of one's guests

【来不得】láibude〈动〉〈口〉be impermissible: ～半点马虎。Half measures will not do.

【来不及】láibují〈动〉not have enough time to do sth.: ～多想。It's too late to think twice. ‖ 快点儿! 时间～了。Hurry up! Time is short!

【来潮】láicháo〈动〉1（涨潮）rise: 一来了潮，沙滩就全淹没了。When the tide rises, the beach will be flooded. 2〈喻〉（指思绪）surge: ▸心血～ 3（指月经）menstruate

【来得】láide〈动〉〈口〉1（胜任）be capable: 唱歌、跳舞她都～。She is not only good at singing but she can dance as well. ‖ 办公室的事他样样～。He can do everything in the office. 2（显得）come out as: 他的脑瓜儿比我的脑瓜儿～快! He is more quick-witted than I am.

【来得及】láidejí〈动〉have enough time to do sth.: 如果抓紧时间，我们还～。We can make it if we hurry up. ‖ 这件事我还没～告诉他呢。I still haven't had the time to tell him about this yet.

【来电】láidiàn A〈名〉incoming telegram: 五月一日～收悉。Your telegram of May 1st has been received. B〈动〉send us a telegram: 请～告知。Please notify us by telegram. ‖ 她～告诉我她的行期。She telegraphed me the date of her departure.

【来电显示】láidiàn xiǎnshì〈名〉call display: ～电话机 caller ID telephone

【来而不往非礼也】lái ér bù wǎng fēi lǐ yě〈成〉one should give as good as one gets

【来犯】láifàn〈动〉come to attack: 消灭一切～之敌 wipe out all invading enemies

【来访】láifǎng〈动〉come to visit: ～贵宾在机场受到热烈欢迎。Visiting guests are warmly welcomed at the airport.

【来复枪】láifùqiāng〈名〉〈旧〉rifle

【来复线】láifùxiàn = 膛线 tángxiàn

【来稿】láigǎo A〈动〉contribute (to a newspaper or magazine) B〈名〉contribution: ～概不退还。No unused contribution will be returned.

【来函】láihán〈书〉A〈名〉incoming letter: ～敬悉，迟复为歉。I'm honoured to have received your letter and am sorry for not having been able to reply earlier. B〈动〉send a letter here: 请～告知准确日期。Please inform us of the exact date by letter.

【来鸿】láihóng〈名〉〈旧〉incoming letter: 海外～ letter from abroad

【来回】láihuí A〈动〉1（往返）make a return journey: ～飞行 make a round-trip flight ‖ ～来去 again and again ‖ ～来去地说些车轱辘话 keep on repeating the same old story 2（来回）move back and forth: 在房间里～走动 pace up and down the room ‖ ～票 return ticket〈英〉, round-trip ticket〈美〉B〈名〉round trip: 打个～儿得一天。A round trip takes a day.

【来火】láihuǒ〈动〉〈口〉fly into a rage: 我一听他说这事就～。I flew into a temper as soon as I heard what he had to say.

【来件】láijiàn〈名〉1（指文件）package received: ～妥收无误。Your documents have been duly received. 2（指配件）supplied parts: ～组装 assemble end products with supplied parts

【来劲】láijìn〈动〉〈方〉1（起劲）be in high spirits: 越干越～ work with increasing energy ‖ 一听说去旅游就～儿了。Spirits lifted at the mention of travel. 2（令人振奋）be inspiring: 这首歌真～。This song is so energizing.

【来客】láikè〈名〉visitor: 远方～ visitor from afar

【来历】láilì〈名〉source: ～不明 of questionable origin ‖ 查明～ trace past history ‖ 一笔～不明的钱 a sum of money from a dubious source

【来料加工】láiliào jiāgōng〈动〉accept customers' materials for processing

【来临】láilín〈动〉approach: 春节即将～。Spring Festival is drawing near. ‖ 汛期～。The flood season is approaching.

【来龙去脉】láilóng-qùmài〈成〉ins and outs: 搞清事情的～ uncover the ins and outs of an affair

【来路】láilù〈名〉1（指道路）incoming way 2 = 来源 láiyuán A

【来路】láilu = 来历 láilì

【来年】láinián〈名〉next year: ～的收成一定不错。There surely will be a bumper harvest next year.

【来去】láiqù〈动〉1（往返）make a round trip 2（到来和离去）come and go: ～自由 come and go of one's own will ‖ 他总是～匆匆。He is always here today and gone tomorrow.

【来人】láirén〈名〉messenger: 东西已由～拿走。Everything has already been taken away by the bearer.
【来日】láirì〈名〉days to come
【来日方长】láirì-fāngcháng〈成〉there will be plenty of time
【来神】láishén〈动〉〈口〉full of enthusiasm
【来生】láishēng〈名〉next life: 你相信有～吗? Do you believe in the afterlife?
【来使】láishǐ〈名〉envoy from another country or state: 两国交战，不斩～。When two countries are at war, their envoys are exempt from execution.
【来世】láishì = 来生 láishēng
【来事】láishì〈动〉〈方〉know how to cope with people
【来势】láishì〈名〉oncoming force: ～汹汹 bear down menacingly ‖ 暴风雨～很猛。The momentum of the storm is fierce.
【来书】láishū〈书〉= 来信 láixìn
【来苏】láisū〈名〉［药学］lysol
【来头】láitou〈名〉〈口〉1（背景）backing: 这家伙很有～。This guy has strong backing. 2（来由）cause: 她这样说不是没有～的。She said this with good reason. 3（来势）gathering momentum: 他一见～不对，转身就跑。Seeing things taking an ominous turn, he made off at once.
【来往】láiwǎng〈动〉1（往返）come and go: ～车辆 traffic ‖ 他们一直保持着书信～。They continued to shuttle letters back and forth. 2（交往）have dealings with sb.: 两人～密切。The two of them are on intimate terms. ‖ 两家已断绝～。Relations between the two families have already broken down.
【来无影，去无踪】lái wú yǐng, qù wú zōng〈俗〉come and go without leaving any trace
【来项】láixiàng〈名〉income
【来信】láixìn A〈动〉send a letter here: 爸爸～了。Dad sent us a letter. B〈名〉incoming letter: 收到～ receive a letter ‖ 读者～ letters to the editor
【来意】láiyì〈名〉purpose in coming: 我猜不透他的～。I'm not clear what he is here for.
【来由】láiyóu〈名〉reason: 她说这些话不是没有～的。Her remarks were not groundless.
【来源】láiyuán A〈名〉source: 消息～ source of information ‖ 经济～ source of income B〈动〉originate: 知识～于实践。Knowledge stems from experience.
【来账】láizhàng〈名〉vostro account [the account a correspondent bank holds on behalf of a foreign bank]
【来者】láizhě〈名〉1（指将来）things to come: 前无古人，后无～ be unprecedented 2（指到来）person or thing that comes or has come: ～何人? Who is it?
【来者不拒】láizhě-bùjù〈成〉keep an open house
【来着】láizhe〈助〉〈口〉[used at the end of a sentence indicating a completed action]: 你刚才说什么～? What were you saying just now? ‖ 你昨天让我买什么～? What did you ask me to buy yesterday?
【来之不易】láizhī-bùyì〈成〉not easily come by: 胜利～。Victory did not come easily. ‖ 一粥一饭，当思～。Think about how hard it is to get each meal on the table.

莱（萊） lái〈名〉〈书〉［植物］lamb's-quarters
【莱比锡】Láibǐxī〈名〉Leipzig
【莱斯特郡】Láisītèjùn〈名〉Leicestershire
【莱索托】Láisuǒtuō〈名〉Lesotho: ～人 Mosotho ‖ ～王国 Kingdom of Lesotho
【莱茵河】Láiyīnhé ▸p. 294〈名〉The Rhine

徕（徠） lái ▸招徕 zhāolái

梾（棶） lái
【梾木】láimù〈名〉large-leaved dogwood

铼（錸） lái〈名〉［化学］rhenium (Re)

lài

赉（賚） lài〈动〉〈书〉bestow: ～银二百两 grant a reward of two hundred taels of silver ▸赏～

睐（睞） lài〈动〉〈书〉squint at: ▸青～

赖（賴） lài
A〈动〉1（依靠）depend on: ～以生存的环境 the environment on which we rely ‖ 取胜有～于大家共同的努力。Progress depends on our concerted efforts. ▸百无聊～，信～，依～ 2（撒泼）drag out one's stay in a place: 孩子们眼馋路边地摊上的玩具，～着不肯走。Covetously eyeing the toys at the vendor's roadside stand, the children couldn't tear themselves away. 3（抵赖）shirk one's responsibility: 事实确凿，～是～不掉的。Facts speak for themselves. It's no use trying to deny them. ▸～账，抵～ 4（诬赖）shift the blame onto sb. else: 她一有错就～别人。She always shifts the blame onto others. 5（怪罪）blame: 这次输球不能～他一个人。We should not blame the loss of the game on him alone.
B〈形〉1（无赖）shameless: ▸～皮，耍～ 2〈口〉（差）bad: 不分好～ make no distinction between good and bad ‖ 今年收成不～。This year's harvest is quite good.
【赖氨酸】lài'ānsuān〈名〉［生化］lysine
【赖床】làichuáng〈动〉feel too lazy to get out of bed: 他养成了～的坏毛病。He has developed a lazy habit of staying in bed after waking up.
【赖婚】làihūn〈动〉breach a marriage contract
【赖皮】làipí A〈动〉be shameless: 你真～，说话不算数。Shame on you! You always go back on your word. B〈名〉shameless person: 跟一个～讲道理是白费口舌。To reason with a person without shame is a complete waste of breath.
【赖学】làixué〈动〉〈口〉bunk off class: 孩子们经常装病～。Children often skip class by pretending to be ill.
【赖账】làizhàng〈动〉1〈口〉（指账）repudiate a debt: 欠账要还，～是不行的。A debt must be paid, and there is no way to disown it. 2〈喻〉（指话语）go back on one's word: 想～? 没门! Thinking of breaking a promise? No way!
【赖子】làizi〈名〉rascal

濑（瀨） lài〈名〉〈书〉torrent

癞（癩） lài〈名〉〈方〉favus of the scalp
▸là
【癞蛤蟆】làiháma〈名〉toad
【癞蛤蟆想吃天鹅肉】làiháma xiǎng chī tiān'é ròu〈俗〉aspire after sth. one is not worthy of: 他想娶时装模特作老婆，真是～。Marrying a fashion model is truly wishful thinking for him.
【癞皮狗】làipígǒu〈名〉1（指狗）mangy dog 2〈喻〉（指人）loathsome creature: 他不过是一条～罢了。He is just a nuisance.
【癞子】làizi〈名〉〈方〉1（指癣）favus: 他头上长了～。His head was affected with favus. 2（指人）person affected with favus

籁（籟） lài〈名〉1〈古〉（指乐器）musical pipe 2〈书〉（声音）sound: ▸天～，万～俱寂

lán

兰（蘭） lán〈名〉orchid: ▸～花
【兰草】láncǎo = 兰花 lánhuā
【兰摧玉折】láncuī-yùzhé〈成〉premature death of gifted people
【兰花】lánhuā〈名〉orchid
【兰花指】lánhuāzhǐ〈名〉orchid fingers [woman's hand gesture to show grace]
【兰开斯特】Lánkāisītè〈名〉Lancaster
【兰开夏郡】Lánkāixiàjùn〈名〉Lancashire
【兰圃】lánpǔ〈名〉orchid garden
【兰因絮果】lányīn-xùguǒ〈成〉a happy marriage ends in a divorce
【兰章】lánzhāng〈名〉〈书〉〈敬〉(your) beautiful writing
【兰州】Lánzhōu ▸p. 661〈名〉Lanzhou [capital of Gansu Province (甘肃)]

岚（嵐） lán〈名〉〈书〉mountain haze: 晓～ morning mists ▸山～
【岚烟】lányān〈名〉mountain mist

拦（攔） lán〈动〉1（阻拦）block: ～住行人 block the pedestrian way ‖ 大坝～住了洪水。The dam held the floods back. ‖ 一条河～住了我们的去路。A river blocked our way. 2（正对着）be directed right at: ～头一棒 give sb. a head-on blow ▸～腰
【拦挡】lándǎng〈动〉block: ～去路 block sb.'s way
【拦道木】lándàomù〈名〉roadblock
【拦河坝】lánhébà〈名〉dam
【拦洪坝】lánhóngbà〈名〉flood control dam
【拦击】lánjī〈动〉1（拦截并打击）intercept and attack: ～来犯的敌机 intercept and fire at the invading enemy planes 2［体育］volley
【拦劫】lánjié〈动〉intercept and rob: ～货船/商船 intercept and rob merchant/cargo ships ‖ 歹徒～行人。The ruffians mugged passers-by.
【拦截】lánjié〈动〉intercept: ～过往车辆 stop passing vehicles ‖ 空中～ air interception
【拦路】lánlù〈动〉block the way: ～抢劫 mug
【拦路虎】lánlùhǔ〈名〉〈喻〉stumbling block: 语法是英语学习的～。Grammar

presents a difficulty in the study of English.
【拦网】lánwǎng〈动〉[体育] block: ～得分 win a block point ‖ 双人～ two-man block
【拦蓄】lánxù〈动〉impound: ～洪水 impound floodwater
【拦腰】lányāo〈动〉cut across the middle: ～抱住 seize sb. round the middle ‖ 大树被龙卷风～吹断。The force of the tornado snapped the big tree in half.
【拦阻】lánzǔ〈动〉block: 她一心要走，谁也～不住。She was bent on leaving and nobody could stop her.

栏（欄） lán〈名〉**1**（栏杆）railing: 木/石～ wooden/stone railing ▸栅～ **2**（围栏）pen: ▸存～, 牛～ **3**（表格）column: 如实填写申请表中的每一～。Fill in each column of the form accurately. **4**（指版面）column: 广告～ classified ads ‖ 通～标题 banner headline ▸专～ **5**（用于张贴信息）notice board: ▸布告～ **6** [体育] hurdle: 高/低～ high/low hurdle ‖ 110米～ the 110m hurdles ▸跨～
【栏杆】lángān〈名〉railing: 翻越～ jump over the rails ‖ 桥～ railing of a bridge
【栏目】lánmù〈名〉title of a column: 体育～ sports column ‖ ～主编 chief editor of a column

婪 lán ▸贪婪 tānlán

阑（闌） lán
A = 栏 lán 1
B〈形〉〈书〉drawing to an end: 岁～ the end of the year ▸夜～人静
C〈副〉〈书〉without authorization: ▸～入
【阑干】lángān **A**〈形〉〈书〉criss-crossing: 泪～。Tears streamed down. **B** = 栏杆 lángān
【阑入】lánrù〈动〉〈书〉**1**（进入）enter a forbidden place without permission: ～宫门 enter the imperial palace without permission **2**（加入）interlace: ～一段文字 interpolate a passage
【阑珊】lánshān〈形〉〈书〉waning: 春意～。Spring is on the wane. ‖ 意兴～。Interest is flagging.
【阑尾】lánwěi〈名〉[生理] appendix: 切除～ have one's appendix removed
【阑尾炎】lánwěiyán ▸**p. 50**〈名〉[医学] appendicitis

蓝（藍） lán ▸**p. 863**
A = 蓼蓝 liǎolán
B〈形〉blue: ～眼睛 blue eyes ‖ 深/浅～ dark/pale blue ▸蔚～, 湛～
【蓝宝石】lánbǎoshí〈名〉sapphire: ～胸针 sapphire brooch
【蓝本】lánběn〈名〉source: 这部电影是以同名小说为～改编的。The film is adapted from a novel of the same title.
【蓝筹股】lánchóugǔ〈名〉[金融] blue chips
【蓝点颏】lándiǎnké〈名〉[鸟类] bluethroat
【蓝靛】lándiàn ▸**p. 863**〈名〉indigo
【蓝调】lándiào〈名〉blues: ～爵士乐 blues jazz
【蓝矾】lánfán〈名〉[化学] blue vitriol
【蓝黑】lánhēi〈名〉blue-black
【蓝晶晶】lánjīngjīng ▸**p. 863**〈形〉bright blue: ～的宝石 shiny blue precious stones
【蓝鲸】lánjīng〈名〉blue whale
【蓝军】lánjūn〈名〉Blue Army [opponent in a military manoeuvre]: "红军"对"～"实施分割包围。The 'Red Army' broke apart and encircled the 'Blue Army'.
【蓝领】lánlǐng〈名〉blue-collar (worker)
【蓝莓】lánméi〈名〉[植物] blueberry
【蓝皮书】lánpíshū〈名〉blue book
【蓝色】lánsè ▸**p. 863**〈名〉blue: ～的天空 blue sky
【蓝色农业】lánsè nóngyè〈名〉oceanic cultivation, plantation and fishing industries
【蓝田猿人】Lántián yuánrén〈名〉[考古] Lantian Man
【蓝图】lántú〈名〉blueprint: 工程～ blueprint for a project ‖〈喻〉经济建设～ blueprint for economic construction
【蓝牙】lányá〈名〉[通信] blue tooth: ～技术 blue-tooth technology
【蓝盈盈】lányīngyīng〈形〉bright blue
【蓝莹莹】lányíngyíng = 蓝盈盈 lányīngyīng
【蓝藻】lánzǎo〈名〉[植物] blue-green algae

谰（讕） lán〈动〉〈书〉**1**（诬赖）falsely incriminate **2**（抵赖）disavow
【谰言】lányán〈名〉slander: 无耻～ shameless slander

澜（瀾） lán〈名〉waves: ▸波～壮阔, 力挽狂～
【澜沧江】Láncāngjiāng ▸**p. 294**〈名〉Lancang River

褴（襤） lán
【褴褛】lánlǚ〈形〉ragged: 衣衫～ be in rags

篮（籃） lán〈名〉**1**（篮子）basket: 菜～ shopping basket ‖ 竹～ bamboo basket ‖ 一～鸡蛋 a basket of eggs ▸花～ **2** [篮球] basket: ▸扣～, 投～ **3**（指球队）basketball team: 男/女～ men's/women's basketball team ▸～坛
【篮板】lánbǎn〈名〉[篮球] backboard
【篮板球】lánbǎnqiú〈名〉[篮球] rebound: 争夺～ seize the rebound
【篮框】lánkuàng〈名〉[篮球] basket
【篮联】lánlián〈简称〉= 篮球联合会
【篮球】lánqiú〈名〉**1** ▸**p. 909**（指运动）basketball: 打～ play basketball ‖ ～运动员 basketball player **2**（指球）basketball
【篮球场】lánqiúchǎng〈名〉basketball court
【篮球队】lánqiúduì〈名〉basketball team
【篮球架】lánqiújià〈名〉basketball stand
【篮球联合会】lánqiú liánhéhuì〈名〉Federation of Basketball Associations
【篮球赛】lánqiúsài〈名〉basketball game: 打一场～ play a basketball match
【篮圈】lánquān〈名〉[篮球] ring
【篮坛】lántán〈名〉basketball circles: ～新秀 rising star in the basketball world
【篮子】lánzi〈名〉basket: 购物～ shopping ‖ 一～桃子 a basket of peaches ▸菜～工程

斓（斕） lán ▸斑斓 bānlán

镧（鑭） lán〈名〉[化学] lanthanum (La)

lǎn

览（覽） lǎn〈动〉view: ▸博～, 展～, 浏～, 阅～
【览胜】lǎnshèng〈动〉〈书〉visit places of beauty: 到泰山～ go on a tour of Mount Tai

揽（攬） lǎn〈动〉**1**（把持）grasp: ▸～总, 独～ **2**（吸引）attract: 延～人才 recruit talents **3**（承担）take on: 把责任都～到自己身上 take all the responsibility upon oneself ‖ 这种闲事～起来没完。If you're going to concern yourself with such little things, there will be no end to it. ▸～活, 招～ **4**（搂）hold in one's arms: ～在怀里 hold sb./sth. to one's bosom ‖ 把孩子～到怀里 clasp a child to one's bosom **5**（捆）fasten with a rope: 用绳子～住柴禾 tie a rope around the firewood
【揽承】lǎnchéng〈动〉undertake: ～工程项目 contract an engineering project
【揽储】lǎnchǔ〈动〉solicit for savings: 高息～ solicit for savings with high interest rates
【揽活】lǎnhuó〈动〉take on work: 他每天出外～。Everyday he went out to look for work.
【揽客】lǎnkè〈动〉solicit customers
【揽权】lǎnquán〈动〉seize power: 四处～ take every opportunity to seize power
【揽总】lǎnzǒng〈动〉assume overall responsibility: 那一摊工作应由一人～。One person should be given sole charge of the whole work.

缆（纜） lǎn
A〈名〉**1**（缆绳）(mooring) rope: 解～ set sail ▸～绳 **2**（粗绳状物）thick rope: ▸电～, 光～
B〈动〉fasten with a rope: ～舟 moor a boat with the hawser
【缆车】lǎnchē〈名〉**1**（指交通工具）cable car **2**（指绞车）winch
【缆道】lǎndào〈名〉cableway
【缆绳】lǎnshéng〈名〉thick rope: ～快要绷断了。The cable is about to break.
【缆索】lǎnsuǒ〈名〉hawser

榄（欖） lǎn ▸橄榄 gǎnlǎn

罱 lǎn〈动〉dredge up: ～河泥 dredge (up) sludge from a river
【罱泥船】lǎnníchuán〈名〉dredger

漤 lǎn〈动〉**1**（指调味）mix with salt or other seasonings: 把萝卜抹上盐～一下。Soak the radish in some salt. **2**（指去涩）soak fruits in hot water or limewater: ～柿子 soak persimmons in hot water

懒（懶） lǎn〈形〉**1**（懒惰）lazy: ～猫 indolent cat ▸～惰, 偷～ **2**（疲乏）sluggish: 身上发～ feel listless ‖ 伸了伸～腰 stretch oneself ▸～洋洋, 心灰意～
【懒虫】lǎnchóng〈名〉〈口〉lazybones: ～，快起床吧! Get up, lazybones!
【懒怠】lǎndai **A**〈形〉lazy **B**〈动〉not feel like doing: 我～听你们说笑话。I'm in no mood for your jokes.
【懒蛋】lǎndàn〈名〉〈口〉lazybones
【懒得】lǎnde〈动〉be in no mood to do sth.: ～跟他辩论 be in no mood to argue

with him ‖ 她生病了，饭都～吃。 She was ill and did not feel like eating.
【懒惰】lǎnduò〈形〉 lazy
【懒骨头】lǎngǔtou〈名〉〈口〉 lazybones
【懒鬼】lǎnguǐ〈名〉〈口〉 lazybones
【懒汉】lǎnhàn〈名〉 loafer: 克服～思想 conquer sluggish mentality
【懒汉鞋】lǎnhànxié〈名〉 loafers [Chinese cloth shoe with elasticated sides]
【懒猴】lǎnhóu〈名〉［动物］ sloth monkey
【懒散】lǎnsǎn〈形〉 indolent: 他～惯了，不适应快节奏的工作。 Habitually indolent, he can't keep up with the pace of the work.
【懒婆娘的裹脚，又臭又长】lǎnpóniáng de guǒjiǎo, yòu chòu yòu cháng〈歇后〉 interminably tedious
【懒洋洋】lǎnyángyáng〈形〉 listless: 炎热的天气使人～的。 Heat makes one listless.

làn

烂（爛） làn
A〈形〉 **1**（软） soft: 把蒜捣～ mash the garlic ‖ 用文火把牛肉焖～ use a slow fire to stew the beef thoroughly **2**（腐烂） rotten: ～苹果/梨 rotten apples/pears ‖ 地下的木桩子～了。 The wooden piles left in the ground have decayed. **3**（残破） worn-out: 鞋穿～了。 The shoes are worn out. ▸破～, 海枯石～ **4**（混乱） jumbled: ▸～摊子, ～账
B〈副〉 completely: 睡得～熟 be sound asleep ‖ 喝得～醉 be drunk out of one's mind
【烂糊】lànhu〈形〉〈口〉 mashed: 奶奶喜欢吃～的东西。 My grandma likes to have her food cooked to a pulp.
【烂漫】lànmàn〈形〉 **1**（颜色鲜艳） bright-coloured: 山花～。 Brilliant mountain flowers are in full bloom. **2**（天真自然） natural: ▸天真～
【烂泥】lànní〈名〉 mud: 车轮陷进～里。 The wheels sank into the mud.
【烂熟】lànshú〈形〉 **1**（指食物） thoroughly cooked: ～的牛肉 thoroughly cooked beef **2**（指熟练程度） thoroughly familiar: 这首诗他背得～。 He had the poem off pat.
【烂摊子】làntānzi〈名〉〈喻〉 shambles: 收拾～ clear up the mess ‖ 前任留下一个～。 The predecessor had left things in a complete shambles.
【烂尾】lànwěi〈形〉 unfinished: ～工程 unfinished project
【烂尾楼】lànwěilóu〈名〉 unfinished building project: 开发商一夜蒸发，20层的办公楼成了～。 The developers disappeared overnight, leaving a 20-storey office building project incomplete.
【烂账】lànzhàng〈名〉 **1**（指账目） messy account **2**（指欠账） bad debt
【烂醉】lànzuì〈动〉 be dead drunk: ～如泥 be as drunk as a lord

l

滥（濫） làn
A〈动〉 overflow: ▸泛～
B〈形〉 **1**（过度） excessive: ～砍～伐 wantonly fell trees ▸狂轰～炸, 宁缺毋～ **2**（不切实际） trite: ▸～调
【滥调】làndiào〈名〉 cliché: ▸陈词～
【滥杀无辜】lànshā-wúgū〈成〉 wanton slaughter of innocent people
【滥觞】lànshāng〈书〉 **A**〈名〉 **1**（指河流） source of a river **2**〈喻〉（起源） origin **B**〈动〉〈喻〉 originate
【滥套子】làntàozi〈名〉 cliché
【滥用】lànyòng〈动〉 abuse: ～成语典故 misuse idioms and allusions ‖ ～职权 abuse one's power
【滥竽充数】lànyú-chōngshù〈成〉〈喻〉 fill a post without real qualifications

láng

郎[1] láng〈名〉〈古〉 an official title: 兵部侍～ vice minister of the national defence

郎[2] láng〈名〉 **1**（指男子） [used by a woman in addressing her husband or lover] darling: ▸情～ **2**（指儿子） someone else's son: ▸令～ **3**（指某类人） [form of address to a particular category of people]: ▸货～, 女～
▸làng
【郎才女貌】lángcái-nǚmào〈成〉 well-matched couple
【郎当】lángdāng〈形〉 **1**（不合身） baggy: 衣裤～ be slovenly dressed **2**（颓唐） dispirited **3**（不成器） useless: ▸吊儿～
【郎舅】lángjiù〈名〉 a man and his wife's brother
【郎君】lángjūn〈名〉〈旧〉 [used by a woman in addressing her husband] you
【郎中】lángzhōng〈名〉 **1**〈古〉（指官职） director (of a section or bureau) **2**〈方〉（指医生） doctor of Chinese herbal medicine: 江湖～ quack doctor

狼 láng〈名〉 wolf: ▸豺～, 黄鼠～
【狼狈】lángbèi〈形〉 awkward: ～逃窜 flee helter-skelter ‖ 处境～ be in a fix
【狼狈不堪】lángbèi-bùkān〈成〉 be in an embarrassing predicament
【狼狈为奸】lángbèi-wéijiān〈成〉 collude: 他们～，干尽了坏事。 They were hand in glove in doing all kinds of foul and evil things.
【狼奔豕突】lángbēn-shǐtū〈成〉〈贬〉〈喻〉 tear about like wild beasts
【狼疮】lángchuāng ▸p. 50〈名〉［医学］ lupus: 红斑～ lupus erythematosus
【狼狗】lánggǒu〈名〉 wolf dog
【狼孩】lánghái〈名〉 wolf child
【狼毫】lángháo〈名〉 writing brush made of weasel's hair
【狼藉】lángjí〈形〉〈书〉 **1**（凌乱） disorderly: ▸杯盘～ **2**（名声极坏） hopelessly discredited: ▸声名～
【狼吞虎咽】lángtūn-hǔyàn〈成〉 eat voraciously: 他～地把饭吃光了。 He gobbled down all the food.
【狼尾草】lángwěicǎo〈名〉［植物］ Chinese pennisetum
【狼心狗肺】lángxīn-gǒufèi〈成〉〈喻〉 **1**（狠毒） brutal and cold-blooded **2**（忘恩负义） heartless and ungrateful
【狼牙棒】lángyábàng〈名〉 mace
【狼烟】lángyān〈名〉〈古〉〈喻〉 war: ▸～四起
【狼烟四起】lángyān-sìqǐ〈成〉 with war alarms raised everywhere
【狼子野心】lángzǐ-yěxīn〈成〉〈喻〉 be full of wild ambitions: 他的～尽人皆知。 His wolfish intent is no secret to anyone.

琅 láng〈书〉
A〈名〉 a kind of jade
B〈形〉 pure white
【琅玕】lánggān〈名〉〈书〉 pearl-like stone
【琅琅】lángláng〈拟〉 **1**（指碰撞声） jingle **2**（指人声） loud and clear: 笑声～ the chatter of laughter

廊 láng〈名〉 **1**（廊子） corridor: ▸长～, 走～ **2**（指场所） salon: ▸发～, 画～
【廊檐】lángyán〈名〉 eaves of a veranda or porch
【廊子】lángzi〈名〉 veranda〈英〉; porch〈美〉

榔 láng
【榔头】lángtou〈名〉 hammer

锒（鋃） láng
【锒铛】lángdāng **A**〈名〉〈书〉 iron chains: ～入狱 be chained and put in prison **B**〈拟〉 clang: 铁索～ iron chains clanking

稂 láng〈名〉〈古〉［植物］ Chinese pennisetum
【稂莠】lángyǒu〈名〉〈喻〉 evildoers

螂 láng ▸螳螂 tángláng, 蟑螂 zhāngláng

lǎng

朗 lǎng〈形〉 **1**（明亮） light: ▸开～, 晴～ **2**（响亮） loud and clear: ▸～读, ～诵
【朗读】lǎngdú〈动〉 read aloud: ～课文 read a text aloud
【朗朗】lǎnglǎng **A**〈拟〉 loud and clear: 书声～ read aloud with clear, carrying tones ‖ ～上口 be catchy **B**〈形〉 bright and clear: ～星光 shiny stars
【朗姆酒】lǎngmǔjiǔ〈名〉 rum
【朗声】lǎngshēng〈形〉 loud and clear: ～大笑 laugh a hearty laugh
【朗诵】lǎngsòng〈动〉 recite: ～诗歌 recite poetry ‖ 诗歌～ poetry reading/recitation ‖ ～者 reciter

làng

郎 làng ▸屎壳郎 shǐkelàng
▸láng

埌 làng ▸圹埌 kuànglàng

莨 làng
▸liáng
【莨菪】làngdàng〈名〉［植物］ black henbane

阆（閬） làng
【阆苑】làngyuàn〈名〉〈书〉 **1**（神仙居住处） legendary place where immortals live **2**（宫苑） [in classic poetry] imperial garden

浪 làng
A〈名〉 **1**（波浪） wave: 巨～ huge waves ▸风平～静, 惊涛骇～ **2**（波浪状物） something resembling waves: ▸麦～, 热～, 声～
B〈动〉 indulge: ▸～费, ～迹, 放～
C〈形〉 dissolute: ▸～荡 B

【浪潮】làngcháo〈名〉1〈指波浪〉wave: ～汹涌。The waves are surging high. 2〈喻〉〈指社会运动〉wave: 罢工～ wave of strikes ‖ 革命～ tide of revolution

【浪船】làngchuán〈名〉swingboat

【浪荡】làngdàng A〈动〉dawdle: 整日～不务正业 idle along day after day doing nothing useful ‖ 他～惯了。He has become used to loafing around. B〈形〉dissipated: ～公子 playboy

【浪费】làngfèi〈动〉waste: ～电/水 waste electricity/water ‖ ～时间 waste time ‖ ～自然资源 squander natural resources ‖ 反对～，提倡节约。Curtail waste and encourage frugality.

【浪花】lànghuā〈名〉1〈本〉spindrift: ～四溅。Spray is flying in all directions. 2〈喻〉〈指生活片断〉episode: 生活的～ episodes in one's life

【浪迹】làngjì〈动〉wander about: ～江湖 live a nomadic existence ‖ ～天涯 roam all over the world

【浪漫】làngmàn〈形〉1〈富有幻想〉romantic: ～故事 romantic story 2〈放荡〉loose, lax: 生活～ lead a loose life

【浪漫史】làngmànshǐ〈名〉romance: 他俩的～始于两年前。Their romance began two years ago.

【浪漫主义】làngmànzhǔyì〈名〉romanticism: ～诗人/作家 romantic poet/writer ‖ 一首富于～色彩的诗歌 a highly romantic poem

【浪木】làngmù〈名〉swing log [used for physical exercise]

【浪桥】làngqiáo = 浪木 làngmù

【浪人】làngrén〈名〉1〈流浪的人〉vagabond 2〈日本武士〉ronin

【浪涛】làngtāo〈名〉huge waves: ～汹涌。The waves are surging.

【浪头】làngtou〈名〉〈口〉1〈指波浪〉wave 2〈喻〉〈指潮流〉trend: 赶～ follow the trend

【浪游】làngyóu〈动〉roam aimlessly: ～四方 wander from place to place

【浪子】làngzǐ〈名〉loafer

【浪子回头金不换】làngzǐ huítóu jīnbùhuàn〈俗〉a repentant libertine is worth more than gold

lāo

捞（撈） lāo〈动〉1〈指从水中〉dredge up: ～起沉在水里的箱子 fish for a sunken chest ‖ ～鱼 net fish ▸捕～，打～，水中～月 2〈获取〉get by improper means: 趁机～一把 grab the chance to make a buck ▸～外快 3〈方〉〈顺手拿〉take up: ～起铁锨 grab a shovel

【捞本】lāoběn〈动〉〈贬〉recoup one's losses: 一心要捞回老本的赌徒 a gambler hell-bent on recovering lost wagers

【捞稻草】lāo dàocǎo〈惯〉〈喻〉clutch at straws

【捞面】lāomiàn〈名〉boiled noodles

【捞钱】lāoqián〈动〉make money by questionable means: 捞一笔钱 wangle a sum of money

【捞取】lāoqǔ〈动〉1〈指从水里〉dredge up: 桶掉进井里，不好～。The bucket has fallen into the well, and it's difficult to get it out. 2〈贬〉〈指手段不当〉fish for: ～政治资本 seek political advantage

【捞外快】lāo wàikuài〈惯〉make extra income: 他下了班就忙着～。He has been busy making extra money after work.

【捞一把】lāo yībǎ〈惯〉take undue advantages to seek personal profits

【捞油水】lāo yóushui〈惯〉try to line one's pockets: 滥用权力大～ abuse one's power to line one's pockets

【捞着】lāozháo〈动〉〈口〉get an opportunity: 上周的音乐会，我没～听。I missed last week's concert.

láo

劳（勞） láo

A〈形〉hard-working: ▸～瘁，疲～，辛～

B〈动〉1〈使劳苦〉make sb. toil: ▸～民伤财 2〈套〉〈烦劳〉trouble: ～您帮个忙。Would you please give me a hand? ▸～驾，～神，有～ 3〈慰劳〉express one's appreciation: ▸～军，酬～，慰～ 4〈劳动〉labour: ▸不～而获，多～多得

C〈名〉1〈功劳〉meritorious deed: 立下汗马之～ win glory in battle ▸功～，犬马之～ 2〈劳动者〉labourer: ▸～方，～资

【劳保】láobǎo〈名〉1〈指保险〉labour insurance: 吃～ depend on labour insurance for support ‖ ～福利 labour insurance and welfare 2〈指保护〉labour protection: ～用品 labour protection necessities

【劳唇费舌】láochún-fèishé〈成〉waste one's breath: 跟他这种人～没有用。It's no use talking to such a man as him.

【劳瘁】láocuì〈动〉〈书〉be exhausted from hard work: 不辞～ spare no pains ‖ ～一生 drudge for one's whole life

【劳动】láodòng A〈名〉1〈指活动〉work: 家务～ household chores ‖ 脑力～ brain work ‖ ～创造一切。Hard work creates everything. 2〈体力劳动〉manual labour: ～锻炼 temper oneself through physical labour ‖ 义务～ volunteer work B〈动〉do physical labour: 他正在地里～。He is working in the fields now.

【劳动保护】láodòng bǎohù〈名〉labour protection

【劳动保险】láodòng bǎoxiǎn〈名〉labour insurance

【劳动报酬】láodòng bàochóu〈名〉payment for labour

【劳动布】láodòngbù〈名〉denim

【劳动法】láodòngfǎ〈名〉labour law

【劳动分工】láodòng fēngōng〈名〉division of labour

【劳动服】láodòngfú〈名〉work clothes

【劳动服务公司】láodòng fúwù gōngsī〈名〉(labour) service company

【劳动改造】láodòng gǎizào〈动〉reform through labour

【劳动合同】láodòng hétong〈名〉labour contract: 签署～ sign a labour contract

【劳动和社会保障部】Láodòng Hé Shèhuì Bǎozhàng Bù〈名〉(Chinese) Ministry of Labour and Social Security

【劳动教养】láodòng jiàoyǎng〈动〉re-educate through labour

【劳动节】láodòngjié〈简称〉= 五一国际劳动节

【劳动力】láodònglì〈名〉1〈劳动能力〉capacity for physical labour: 丧失～ be unable to work 2〈体力劳动者〉able-bodied labourer: ▸半～，强～，全～ 3〈指人工〉manpower: ～不足 be short of manpower ‖ 廉价～ cheap labour

【劳动密集型】láodòng mìjíxíng〈形〉labour-intensive: ～产业 labour-intensive industry

【劳动模范】láodòng mófàn〈名〉model worker: 荣获"～"称号 win the title of 'Model Worker'

【劳动人民】láodòng rénmín〈名〉working people

【劳动日】láodòngrì〈名〉working day

【劳动生产率】láodòng shēngchǎnlǜ〈名〉labour productivity: 提高～ raise productivity

【劳动者】láodòngzhě〈名〉labourer: 体力～ manual worker ‖ 普通～ common labourer

【劳动】láodong〈动〉〈敬〉trouble: 不敢～各位 do not dare to trouble everybody

【劳顿】láodùn〈形〉〈书〉weary: 旅途～ be travel-worn

【劳而无功】láo'érwúgōng〈成〉work hard but to no avail

【劳乏】láofá〈形〉〈书〉weary: ～过度，不能入睡 too exhausted to go to sleep

【劳烦】láofán〈动〉〈方〉trouble: ～您把书递给我。Can I trouble you to pass me the book?

【劳方】láofāng〈名〉labour: ～与资方 labour and capital

【劳改】láogǎi〈简称〉= 劳动改造

【劳改队】láogǎiduì〈名〉reform-through-labour brigade

【劳改犯】láogǎifàn〈名〉prisoner serving a sentence of reform through labour

【劳改农场】láogǎi nóngchǎng〈名〉reformatory

【劳工】láogōng〈名〉labour: ～介绍所 labour exchange ‖ ～运动 labour movement ‖ 调解～纠纷 mediate a labour dispute

【劳工组织】láogōng zǔzhī〈名〉labour organization: 国际～ International Labour Organization (ILO)

【劳绩】láojì〈名〉merits and accomplishments: ～卓著 have remarkable merits and accomplishments

【劳驾】láojià ▸p. 236〈动〉〈套〉may I trouble you: ～，帮我寄封信。May I trouble you to post a letter for me? ‖ ～，请让我过一下。Excuse me, please let me pass.

【劳教】láojiào〈简称〉= 劳动教养

【劳教人员】láojiào rényuán〈名〉person subjected to re-education in a reform school

【劳教所】láojiàosuǒ〈名〉reform centre

【劳倦】láojuàn〈形〉exhausted

【劳军】láojūn〈动〉reward troops: 上前线进行～演出 go to the front to entertain the soldiers

【劳苦】láokǔ〈形〉hard-working: 不辞～ spare no pains

【劳苦大众】láokǔ dàzhòng〈名〉toiling masses

【劳苦功高】láokǔ-gōnggāo〈成〉have laboured hard and achieved much

【劳累】láolèi A〈形〉overworked: 感到十分～ feel totally run-down B〈动〉〈敬〉trouble: ～您了。Sorry to have troubled you.

【劳力】láolì A〈名〉1〈指力气〉physical strength 2〈指人〉labour: 雇用～ hire labour ‖ ～不足 be short of manpower B〈动〉〈书〉do manual labour: ～费心 tax one's mind and strength

【劳碌】láolù〈形〉overworked: ～一生 toil all one's life ‖ 她是个～命。She is doomed to a life of toil.

【劳民伤财】láomín-shāngcái〈成〉waste both labour and money: 这是个～的工程。This project is draining in terms of both manpower and cash.

【劳模】láomó〈简称〉= 劳动模范

【劳神】láoshén〈动〉1〈操心〉be taxing:

别为这事～了。 Don't bother yourself about this. 2 〈套〉（麻烦） trouble: ～, 帮我照看一下行李。 Would you mind keeping an eye on some luggage for me?

【劳师】láoshī〈动〉〈书〉 reward troops

【劳师动众】láoshī-dòngzhòng〈成〉 drag in lots of people (to do sth.): 区区小事, 不必～。 This is a trivial matter. There's no need for so many people to be involved.

【劳什子】láoshízi〈名〉〈方〉 pest: 要这个～做甚! What's the use in keeping such a nuisance!

【劳损】láosǔn ▸p. 50〈动〉［医学］ strain: 腰肌～ psoatic strain

【劳务】láowù〈名〉 labour services: ～人员 contract workers ‖ ～市场 job market ‖ ～输出 export of labour services

【劳务费】láowùfèi〈名〉 service charge

【劳心】láoxīn〈动〉 1（操心） take pains: 不为小事～。 Don't worry yourself over small things. 2〈书〉（从事脑力劳动） work one's mind

【劳燕分飞】láoyàn-fēnfēi〈成〉〈喻〉 [of a couple] separate from each other

【劳役】láoyì A〈名〉 forced labour: 服～ do forced labour B〈动〉 use (as a draught animal)

【劳逸结合】láo-yì jiéhé〈成〉 strike a balance between work and rest

【劳资】láo-zī〈名〉 labour and capital: ～关系 relations between labour and capital ‖ ～纠纷 dispute between employer and employee

【劳作】láozuò A〈名〉 handicraft (as a school subject) B〈动〉〈书〉 do manual labour: 在田间～ work in the fields

牢 láo

A〈名〉 1（用于圈牲口） pen: ▸亡羊补～ 2（监牢） prison: 坐了5年～ be in prison for five years ▸监～, 水～, 坐～

B〈形〉 1（牢固） firm: ～～地抓住绳子 take a firm hold on the rope ‖ 这种线比那种～多了。 This kind of thread is more durable than that kind. ▸～记 2（稳妥） dependable: ▸～靠 2

【牢不可破】láobùkěpò〈成〉 unbreakable: ～的友谊 unbreakable friendship ‖ 我们的边疆防御是～的铜墙铁壁。 Our border defences are a truly indestructible bastion of iron.

【牢房】láofáng〈名〉 prison: 他被关进了～。 He has been put in prison.

【牢固】láogù〈形〉 firm: 打下～的基础 lay a solid foundation ‖ 桥墩很～。 The pier is very secure.

【牢记】láojì〈动〉 always remember: ～导师的教导 bear in mind the teacher's instructions ‖ 您的话我会～在心。 Your words will be engraved on my heart.

【牢靠】láokao〈形〉 1（牢固） sturdy: 这书架不够～。 The bookshelf is not strong enough. 2（稳妥） dependable: 办事～ reliable in handling matters

【牢笼】láolóng〈名〉〈喻〉 1（禁锢） prison: 冲破旧思想的～ break the bonds of old ideas ‖ 走出封建家庭的～ shake off the bonds of feudal families 2（陷阱） trap: 陷入～ fall into a trap

【牢骚】láosao A〈名〉 grumble: 发～ voice a complaint ‖ 满腹～ be full of complaints B〈动〉 complain: 对低工资大发～ keep on complaining about the low pay

【牢什子】láoshízi = 劳什子 láoshízi

【牢实】láoshi〈形〉 firm and solid: 基础～ have a solid and secure foundation

【牢头】láotóu〈名〉〈旧〉 jailer

【牢稳】láowěn〈形〉 safe: 最好有银行担保, 这才～。 It's only safe and reliable when you have a bank guarantee.

【牢稳】láowen〈形〉 steady: 这凳子够～, 可以站上去。 The stool is steady enough to stand on.

【牢狱】láoyù〈名〉 prison: 身陷～ be imprisoned ‖ ～之苦 sufferings behind bars

唠（嘮） láo

▸lào

【唠叨】láodao〈动〉 chatter: ～个不停 go on and on ‖ 您别再～了。 Stop nagging!

铹（鐒） láo

〈名〉［化学］ Lawrencium (Lw)

痨（癆） láo

▸p. 50〈名〉［医学］ tuberculosis (TB): ▸肺～

【痨病】láobìng ▸p. 50〈名〉［中医］ tuberculosis (TB)

醪 láo

〈名〉〈书〉 1（浊酒） wine that has not been decanted 2（醇酒） mellow wine

【醪糟】láozāo〈名〉 fermented glutinous rice

lǎo

老 lǎo

A〈形〉 1（年龄大） old: 妈妈～多了。 Mum has aged considerably. ‖ 他看上去比实际年龄要～。 He looks old for his age. ▸～大哥, ～奶奶, ～人 2（有经验） experienced: ～战士 war veteran ‖ ～作家 veteran writer ▸～兵, ～干部, ～手 3（时间久） long-standing: ～关系 long-standing connections ‖ ～朋友 old friend ‖ ～习惯 old habit ▸～字号 4（陈旧） old-fashioned: ～思想 old-fashioned ideas ▸～规矩, ～脑筋 5（先前） former: ～地方 same old place ‖ 他还是～样子。 He is still his former self. ‖ 他还是那个～脾气。 He's still got the same old temperament. ▸～毛病 6 ▸p. 863（指颜色） dark: ～红/绿/蓝 dark red/green/blue 7（指蔬菜） overgrown: 芹菜长～了。 The celery is overgrown. 8（指食物） overdone: 煮～了的鸡蛋 hard-boiled eggs ‖ 牛排要嫩的还是～的? Do you like your steak rare or well-done? 9［化学］ ageing: ▸～化 10〈口〉（最年幼） youngest: ～闺女 youngest daughter

B〈名〉 1（老年人） old people: 敬～ show respect for the aged ‖ 尊～爱幼 respect the old and care for the young 2（用于称呼） [used to address a venerable old man]: 李～ our revered Mr Li

C〈副〉 1（长时间） for a long time: 那屋～没人住。 The room has been left vacant for a long time. ‖ 他最近～害头痛。 He has been suffering from headaches lately. 2（经常） often: 她～迟到。 She is always late. ‖ 小时候我～去那儿。 When I was small, I often went there. 3（非常） very: ～早就来了 came very early ‖ 嘴撅得～高 give an exaggerated pout

D〈前缀〉 1（用于动植物前） [used before some names of animals and plants]: ▸～虎, ～鼠, ～玉米 2（用于姓氏前） [used before a person's surname indicating seniority]: ～高 Lao Gao 3（用于排行） [used before 大 and 二, 三, 四 and other numerals indicating order of birth or rank]: 吴家～二 second son/daughter of the Wu's ▸～大

E ▸p. 772〈动〉〈口〉〈婉〉 pass away: 他家～了人了。 The old man of that family passed away.

【老媪】lǎo'ǎo〈名〉〈书〉 old woman

【老八辈子】lǎobābèizi〈形〉 old-fashioned: 这是～的话了, 没人听了。 No one listens to this kind of old-fashioned stuff any more.

【老爸】lǎobà〈名〉〈口〉 guv'nor

【老白干儿】lǎobáigānr〈名〉〈方〉 strong liquor

【老百姓】lǎobǎixìng〈名〉〈口〉 common people: 关心～的切身利益 care for the vital interests of the common people

【老板】lǎobǎn〈名〉 1（上司） boss: 她是公司的～。 She is the president of a company. 2〈尊〉（用于称呼） master: 梅～ Master Mei

【老板娘】lǎobǎnniáng〈名〉 1（女老板） proprietress 2（老板的妻子） wife of one's boss

【老半天】lǎobàntiān〈数量〉〈口〉 a long while: 他过了～才接电话。 He took ages to answer the phone.

【老伴儿】lǎobànr〈名〉〈口〉〈诙〉 [of an old couple] husband or wife: 我的～ my old man/woman

【老鸨】lǎobǎo〈名〉 procuress

【老辈】lǎobèi〈名〉 1（年长者） one's elders 2（前代） forefathers: 他家～是做官的。 His forefathers were government officials.

【老本】lǎoběn〈名〉 1（指本钱） capital: 赔光～ sustain the loss of every cent of one's capital ‖ 把～输光 lose one's last stakes 2〈喻〉（指基础） assets 3〈喻〉（指成绩） one's past merits: ▸吃～

【老鼻子】lǎobízi〈形〉〈方〉 an awful lot: 这质量差～了。 The quality is far inferior.

【老表】lǎobiǎo〈名〉 1（表兄弟） male cousin (on the maternal side or on the paternal aunt's side) 2〈方〉〈敬〉（用于称呼） a polite form of address to a male stranger who is of similar age with oneself

【老兵】lǎobīng〈名〉 veteran: 身历百战的～ a veteran of many battles

【老病】lǎobìng A〈名〉 chronic illness B〈形〉 old and sick

【老伯】lǎobó〈名〉〈敬〉 1（指父辈男子） uncle 2（指老年男子） old man

【老伯伯】lǎobóbo〈名〉〈敬〉 grandad

【老布】lǎobù〈名〉 homespun cloth

【老财】lǎocái〈名〉〈旧〉 moneybags: 地主～ wealthy land owner

【老巢】lǎocháo〈名〉 nest: 捣毁敌人的～ destroy an enemy nest

【老成】lǎochéng〈形〉 experienced and steady: 为人～ be experienced and mature

【老成持重】lǎochéng-chízhòng〈成〉 experienced and prudent: 他们～, 不会轻举妄动。 They are experienced and prudent and will not do anything rash.

【老诚】lǎochéng〈形〉 honest and sincere

【老痴瞬间】lǎochī shùnjiān〈名〉 senior moment

【老处女】lǎochǔnǚ〈名〉 spinster

【老粗】lǎocū〈名〉〈谦〉 uneducated person: 我是个～, 文化水平不高。 I'm a bit rough and ready and I'm not very well educated.

【老搭档】lǎodādàng〈名〉 old partner

【老大】lǎodà A〈形〉〈书〉 old: 少小离家～回 leave home young and return old B〈名〉 1（长子、长女） eldest child in a family: ～当兵, 老二经商。 The eldest child is an army man and the second eldest child is a businessman. 2〈方〉（指船夫）

chief crewman of a boat: ▸船～ [3]（指帮会） chief [4]（第一名） number one: 本行业的龙头～ the number one in the industry **C**〈副〉 very: ～不愿意 be extremely unwilling (to do sth.) ‖ 心里～不痛快 feel very annoyed

【老大不小】lǎodà-bùxiǎo〈成〉 grown up: 你也～，该懂事了。 You are no longer a child and should have some sense.

【老大哥】lǎodàgē〈名〉〈尊〉 elder brother

【老大姐】lādàjiě〈名〉〈尊〉 elder sister

【老大难】lǎodànán〈形〉 complicated and unsettled: ～案件 difficult and pending case ‖ ～问题 knotty and long-pending problem

【老大娘】lǎodàniang〈名〉〈口〉〈尊〉 [a form of address to an old woman, esp a stranger] auntie

【老大爷】lǎodàye〈名〉〈口〉〈尊〉 [a form of address to an old man, esp a stranger] uncle

【老旦】lǎodàn〈名〉 *laodan* [an old female role in traditional Chinese opera]

【老当益壮】lǎodāng-yìzhuàng〈成〉 be old in age, but young in spirit: 有风华正茂的后生，也有～的前辈。 There are promising young members as well as vigorous veteran members.

【老道】lǎodào〈名〉〈口〉 Taoist priest

【老到】lǎodào〈形〉 experienced and thoughtful: 做事～ be experienced, careful and reliable in business

【老底】lǎodǐ〈名〉 [1]（底细） sb.'s past: 把～抖搂出来 disclose sb.'s unsavoury past ‖ 揭～ drag the skeleton out of sb.'s closet [2]（祖产） ancestral estate: 把～全败光 squander what one inherited

【老弟】lǎodì〈名〉 [a form of address to a man younger than oneself] my boy: ～，你要听劝。 Young man, you'd better listen to my advice.

【老调】lǎodiào〈名〉 [1]（指话语） platitude [2]（指剧种） *laodiao* [local opera of Hebei Province]

【老调重弹】lǎodiào-chóngtán〈成〉 play the same old tune

【老掉牙】lǎodiàoyá〈形〉 out-of-date: ～的交通工具 obsolete means of transportation

【老爹】lǎodiē〈名〉 [1]（爸爸） father [2]〈方〉〈敬〉（指老年男子） [a form of address to an old man] grandad

【老东西】lǎodōngxi〈名〉〈粗〉 old fool

【老豆腐】lǎodòufu〈名〉 processed bean curd

【老而弥坚】lǎo'érmíjiān〈成〉 become even firmer in one's conviction as one grows old

【老佛爷】lǎofóye〈名〉 [1]（指佛） old Buddha [2]〈尊〉（指人） empress dowager or emperor's father in the Qing Dynasty [3]（特指慈禧） Empress Dowager *Cixi*

【老夫】lǎofū〈名〉 [1]（指丈夫） old husband [2]〈旧〉（用于自称） [a form of self-address used by an old man]（作主语） I;（作宾语） me

【老夫老妻】lǎofū-lǎoqī〈成〉 old married couple

【老夫少妻】lǎofū-shàoqī〈成〉 old man with a young wife

【老夫子】lǎofūzǐ〈名〉 [1]〈旧〉〈尊〉（指私塾老师） tutor in an old-style private school [2]（指读书人） pedant

【老赶】lǎogǎn〈方〉 **A**〈形〉 inexperienced **B**〈名〉 greenhorn

【老干部】lǎogànbù〈名〉 veteran cadre

【老疙瘩】lǎogēda〈名〉〈方〉 youngest child

【老哥】lǎogē〈名〉 [a form of address used among friends] my elder brother

【老革命】lǎogémìng〈名〉 veteran revolutionary

【老公】lǎogōng〈名〉〈口〉 husband

【老公公】lǎogōnggong〈名〉〈方〉 [1]〈尊〉（老年男子） grandpa [2]（公公） father-in-law

【老姑娘】lǎogūniang〈名〉 [1]（超龄未婚女子） spinster [2]（小女儿） youngest daughter

【老古董】lǎogǔdǒng〈名〉 [1]（古董） antique, curio [2]（过时之物） sth. old-fashioned: 当年时髦的东西现在变成了～。 The things that were in fashion in those days are all out of fashion now. [3]（迂腐之人） fuddy-duddy: ～换上新脑筋。 The old fogeys are equipped with the new ways of thinking.

【老鸹】lǎoguā〈方〉= 乌鸦 wūyā

【老规矩】lǎoguīju〈名〉 old rules and regulations

【老憨】lǎohān〈名〉〈方〉 simpleton

【老汉】lǎohàn〈名〉 [1]（老年男子） old man [2]（用于自称） old fellow like me;（作主语） I;（作宾语） me: ～我今年七十五。 I'm 75 years old this year.

【老好人】lǎohǎorén〈名〉 crowd-pleaser

【老狐狸】lǎohúli〈名〉〈喻〉 sly old fox

【老虎】lǎohǔ〈名〉 [1]（虎） tiger [2]〈喻〉（指物） energy-consuming unit: ▸电～ [3]〈喻〉（指人） person who works against the interests of the people by large scale embezzlement, stealing or tax evasion

【老虎屁股摸不得】lǎohǔ pìgu mōbude〈俗〉〈喻〉 not to be provoked

【老虎头上拍苍蝇】lǎohǔ tóu shang pāi cāngying〈俗〉〈喻〉 foolish and dangerous action

【老虎嘴里拔牙】lǎohǔ zuǐli báyá〈俗〉〈喻〉 step into the lion's den

【老虎窗】lǎohǔchuāng〈名〉 dormer window

【老虎凳】lǎohǔdèng〈名〉〈旧〉 torture-rack

【老虎机】lǎohǔjī〈名〉 slot machine; fruit machine〈英〉

【老虎钳】lǎohǔqián〈名〉 [1]（指手工工具） vice [2]（台钳） pincer

【老虎灶】lǎohǔzào〈名〉〈方〉 [1]（用于烧水） kitchen range for boiling water [2]（用于供水） place that provides boiling water

【老花】lǎohuā〈形〉 presbyopic: ～镜 presbyopic glasses

【老花眼】lǎohuāyǎn〈名〉 [1]（远视） presbyopia [2]（远视的人） presbyope

【老化】lǎohuà〈动〉 [1]［化学］ [of macromolecular compound] age: 塑料盆已经～。 The plastic tub has already aged. [2]（指机能） degenerate: 动脉血管～变硬。 Arterial blood vessels become degenerated and hardened. [3]（指年龄） grow old: 教师队伍～。 The teaching corps is ageing. [4]（指知识、技术） become outdated: 设备～ obsolete equipment ‖ 知识～。 The knowledge becomes outdated.

【老话】lǎohuà〈名〉 [1]（指流传已久） old saying: 有句～说，"无巧不成书"。 An old saying has it that accidental happenings make good stories. [2]（指关于过去） remarks about the old days: ～重提 bring up the old days once again

【老皇历】lǎohuángli〈名〉〈喻〉 obsolete practice: 不能按～来解决问题。 You can't rely on outdated practices to solve your problems.

【老黄牛】lǎohuángniú〈名〉〈喻〉 diligent and conscientious person: 甘做人民的～ be willing to serve the people heart and soul

【老几】lǎojǐ〈名〉 [1]（指排行） order of seniority among brothers or sisters: 你排行～? Where do you come in the family? [2]（指地位） [used in rhetorical questions to express disparagement]: 你算～? Who do you think you are? ‖ 我算～，去参加那样重要的会议? Who would I think I were to attend that important meeting?

【老骥伏枥】lǎojì-fúlì〈成〉〈喻〉 an old hero still cherishes high aspirations

【老家】lǎojiā〈名〉 [1]（指故乡） place of origin: 西安是我的～。 Xi'an is my hometown. [2]〈讳〉（指阴间） nether world: ▸回～

【老奸巨滑】lǎojiān-jùhuá〈成〉 sly old fox: ～的政客 crafty and duplicitous politicians

【老茧】lǎojiǎn = 老趼 lǎojiǎn

【老趼】lǎojiǎn〈名〉 callus: 手上磨出了～ have calloused hands

【老江湖】lǎojiānghú〈名〉 worldly-wise person

【老将】lǎojiàng〈名〉 veteran: 派～上场 dispatch a veteran to the stage

【老将出马，一个顶俩】lǎojiàng chū mǎ, yīgè dǐng liǎ〈俗〉 one veteran is worth two novices

【老交情】lǎojiāoqing〈名〉 long-standing friendship

【老景】lǎojǐng〈名〉 life in old age: ～凄凉 live a pathetic existence in one's old age

【老境】lǎojìng〈名〉 [1]（老年） old age: 渐入～ be getting on in years [2] = 老景 lǎojǐng

【老酒】lǎojiǔ〈名〉〈方〉 wine [esp Shaoxing rice wine]

【老框框】lǎokuàngkuang〈名〉〈喻〉 old way of doing things

【老辣】lǎolà〈形〉 [1]（老练毒辣） shrewd and ruthless [2]（纯熟泼辣） smooth and vigorous

【老来俏】lǎoláiqiào〈形〉〈口〉 [of an elderly woman] like mutton dressed as lamb

【老来少】lǎoláishào〈形〉 [of an old person] having a young heart

【老赖】lǎolài〈名〉〈口〉 loan repudiator: 用强制执行的办法对付"～" use tough enforcement measures to deal with loan defaulters

【老老实实】lǎolao-shíshí〈成〉 honestly

【老泪纵横】lǎolèi-zònghéng〈成〉 [of an old person] burst into floods of tears

【老例】lǎolì〈名〉 old practice: 按～办理 follow an old practice

【老脸】lǎoliǎn〈名〉〈谦〉 [used by an old person in speaking of his dignity or self-respect] face: 你叫我这张～往哪儿搁? How could I ever face people again?

【老两口】lǎoliǎngkǒu〈名〉 old couple

【老脸皮】lǎoliǎnpí〈形〉 thick-skinned

【老练】lǎoliàn〈形〉 experienced: 她办事很～。 She handles things with a seasoned hand.

【老林】lǎolín〈名〉 virgin forest: 深山～ the depths of mountains and forests

【老龄】lǎolíng〈名〉 [1]（老年） old age: ～保险 old-age insurance ‖ ～化 ageing process [2]（老年人） the elderly: ～问题 ageing problem

【老路】lǎolù〈名〉 [1]（走过的路） beaten track: 走～返回 return on a well-worn path [2]〈喻〉（旧办法） old method: 我们要创新，不要走～。 We should innovate, not follow the beaten track.

【老妈子】lǎomāzi〈名〉〈旧〉 maidservant

【老马识途】lǎomǎ-shítú〈成〉〈喻〉an old hand is a good guide
【老迈】lǎomài〈形〉aged: ～昏庸 senile and muddle-headed
【老毛病】lǎomáobìng〈名〉1（指病痛）chronic disease 2（指弱点）old weakness
【老谋深算】lǎomóu-shēnsuàn〈成〉experienced and astute
【老衲】lǎonà〈名〉1〈书〉（指僧侣）old Buddhist monk 2〈旧〉（用于自称）[a form of self-address used by an old monk]（主格）I;（宾格）me
【老奶奶】lǎonǎinai〈名〉1（曾祖母）paternal great-grandmother 2〈尊〉（老年女子）[used by children in addressing an old woman] granny
【老脑筋】lǎonǎojīn〈名〉old way of thinking
【老年】lǎonián ▸p. 526〈名〉old age: ～疾病 disease of old age
【老年斑】lǎoniánbān〈名〉age pigment
【老年大学】lǎonián dàxué〈名〉university for the elderly
【老年公寓】lǎonián gōngyù〈名〉sheltered accommodation for the elderly
【老年人】lǎoniánrén〈名〉senior citizen: ～活动中心 club for the elderly
【老年型社会】lǎoniánxíng shèhuì〈名〉aged society
【老年性痴呆】lǎoniánxìng chīdāi ▸p. 50〈名〉［医学］senile dementia
【老娘】lǎoniáng〈名〉1（老母）old mother 2（用于自称）[a form of self-address used by a married woman of middle or old age to refer to herself proudly]（主格）I;（宾格）me
【老娘们儿】lǎoniángmenr〈名〉〈方〉1（已婚女子）married woman 2〈贬〉（成年妇女）woman
【老牛破车】lǎoniú-pòchē〈成〉〈喻〉making slow progress
【老牛舐犊】lǎoniú-shìdú〈成〉〈喻〉doting parent
【老农】lǎonóng〈名〉1（强调有经验）old and experienced farmer 2（泛指农民）farmer
【老牌】lǎopái A〈名〉old and well-established brand: "飞鸽"牌自行车是个～。The brand name of the bicycle 'Flying Pigeon' is old and well-established. B〈形〉veteran: ～特务 experienced special agent ‖ ～足球劲旅 veteran footballing force
【老派】lǎopài A〈形〉old-fashioned: ～作风 obsolete working style B〈名〉old fogey
【老婆婆】lǎopópo〈名〉〈方〉1（老年女子）granny [used by children in addressing an old woman] 2（婆婆）mother-in-law
【老婆子】lǎopózi〈名〉1（老年女子）old biddy 2（老妻）my old woman [used by husband for his aged wife]
【老婆】lǎopo〈名〉〈口〉wife
【老气】lǎoqì〈形〉1（老练）seasoned: 虽然他刚参加工作，但办事很～。Though he's just started work, he has a sure hand. 2（陈旧）dark and old-fashioned: 客厅里的家具显得太～。The furniture in the sitting room is dark and old-fashioned.
【老气横秋】lǎoqì-héngqiū〈成〉1（自负）flaunt one's seniority 2（缺乏活力）lacking in youthful vigour: 他年纪轻轻的，说起话来却～。He is young in age but beyond his years in speech.
【老前辈】lǎoqiánbèi〈名〉〈尊〉one's elder: 革命～ veteran of the revolution ‖ 体育界的～ doyen of sportsmen
【老亲】lǎoqīn〈名〉1（指父母）old parents 2（指亲戚）old relative: ～旧邻 old relatives and neighbours
【老区】lǎoqū〈名〉old revolutionary base
【老拳】lǎoquán〈名〉powerful fist
【老人】lǎorén〈名〉1（老年人）old people: 给～让座 give up one's seat to the elderly ‖ 尊敬～ respect the elderly 2（长辈）one's parents or grandparents: 赡养～ provide for one's parents/grandparents ‖ 孝敬～ do one's filial duty to one's elderly parents
【老人斑】lǎorénbān = 老年斑 lǎoniánbān
【老人家】lǎorenjia〈名〉〈尊〉1（老年人）venerable old person: 你～一向可好？How are things with you? ‖ 祝您～福如东海，寿比南山。I wish you happiness and a long life. 2（父母）parent: ～都好吗？How are your parents?
【老弱】lǎo-ruò〈名〉1（老人和年轻人）the old and the young 2（老人和体弱的人）the old and the weak: ～妇幼 the old and the weak, women and children ‖ ～病残 old, weak, sick and disabled
【老弱病残】lǎoruò-bìngcán〈成〉the old, weak, sick and disabled
【老弱残兵】lǎoruò-cánbīng〈成〉〈喻〉people who are no longer active or efficient in work on account of old age, illness, etc.
【老三届】lǎosānjiè〈名〉junior and senior high school graduates of 1966-1968 in China
【老少边穷地区】lǎo-shǎo-biān-qióng dìqū〈名〉old revolutionary base areas, minority-inhabited areas, frontier areas and poverty-stricken areas
【老少咸宜】lǎoshào-xiányí〈成〉be good for both the old and the young
【老生】lǎoshēng〈名〉*laosheng* [aged male role in traditional Chinese opera]
【老生常谈】lǎoshēng-chángtán〈成〉cliché
【老师】lǎoshī〈名〉〈尊〉teacher
【老师傅】lǎoshīfu〈名〉〈尊〉master craftsman
【老式】lǎoshì〈形〉old-fashioned: ～家具/汽车 old-fashioned furniture/car
【老视】lǎoshì = 老花 lǎohuā
【老实】lǎoshi〈形〉1（坦白）honest: ～人 honest person ‖ ～说 to be frank ‖ ～交代！Tell the truth and nothing but the truth! ‖ 做～人，说～话，办～事。Be a person of principle, don't tell lies and do decent work. 2（听话）well-behaved: 放～点！Behave yourself! ‖ 这孩子很～。The child is very good. 3（单纯）naive: 他太～了。He is too gullible.
【老实巴交】lǎoshibājiāo〈成〉well-behaved and cautious: ～的庄稼人 an honest and simple farmer
【老手】lǎoshǒu〈名〉old hand: 谈判～ veteran negotiator ‖ 处理这类事情，他是～。He is an old hand in dealing with such things.
【老寿星】lǎoshòuxing〈名〉1〈尊〉（高寿的人）[used as a respectful form of address for old people] venerable old person 2（被庆寿的人）elderly person whose birthday is being celebrated
【老鼠】lǎoshǔ〈名〉（小鼠）mouse;（大鼠）rat
【老鼠仓】lǎoshǔcāng〈名〉rat trading: 痛打基金经理～ come down hard on rat trading by fund managers
【老鼠过街，人人喊打】lǎoshǔ guò jiē, rénrén hǎn dǎ〈歇后〉object of public condemnation
【老鼠药】lǎoshǔyào〈名〉rat poison
【老帅】lǎoshuài〈名〉veteran marshal
【老死】lǎosǐ〈动〉die of natural causes
【老死不相往来】lǎosǐ bù xiāng wǎnglái〈成〉never be in contact with one another
【老太婆】lǎotàipó〈名〉old woman
【老太太】lǎotàitai〈名〉〈尊〉1（老年女子）old lady 2（用于称呼）（指母亲）my mother;（指婆婆）my mother-in-law
【老太爷】lǎotàiyé〈名〉〈尊〉1（老年男子）elderly gentleman 2（用于称呼）（指父亲）my father;（指公公）my father-in-law
【老态龙钟】lǎotài-lóngzhōng〈成〉senile and doddering: 昔日风华正茂的小伙子，如今已～。The youths of the old days are now doddering old men.
【老汤】lǎotāng〈名〉1（卤汁）leftover sauce 2〈方〉（腌菜的汤）residual salt water from previous salting or pickling
【老饕】lǎotāo〈名〉〈书〉glutton
【老套】lǎotào = 老一套 lǎoyītào
【老套子】lǎotàozi = 老一套 lǎoyītào
【老天爷】lǎotiānyé〈名〉1（上天）god 2（表惊叹）[used in exclamations] good heavens: 我的～！My God!
【老头儿】lǎotóur〈名〉1（老年男子）old man: 白胡子～ white-bearded old man 2（家父）my father: 我家～就要退休了。My old father is to retire.
【老头子】lǎotóuzi〈名〉1〈贬〉（老年男子）old codger 2（指丈夫）my old man [used by an old woman] 3（指首领）chief of a gang or a secret society
【老外】lǎowài〈名〉〈口〉1（外行）layman: 修汽车你是～。You're a complete novice when it comes to fixing cars. 2（外国人）foreigner
【老顽固】lǎowángù〈名〉old fogey: 这家伙是个～，不容易说服。This fellow is a real stick-in-the-mud. It's hard to win him over.
【老王卖瓜，自卖自夸】Lǎo Wáng mài guā, zì mài zì kuā〈歇后〉praise one's own work or wares
【老翁】lǎowēng〈名〉〈书〉old man
【老挝】Lǎowō〈名〉Laos: ～人 Laotian ‖ ～人民民主共和国 Lao People's Democratic Republic ‖ ～语 Laotian
【老倭瓜】lǎowōguā〈名〉〈方〉pumpkin
【老窝】lǎowō〈名〉den: 端掉造假酒的～ shut down hideaways where fake alcohol is made
【老乡】lǎoxiāng〈名〉1（同乡人）person from one's fellow town or village 2（用于称呼）[friendly form of address to a countryman]: ～，这是去车站的路吗？Hi there! Is this the right road to the station?
【老相】lǎoxiang〈形〉old-looking: 他长得～。He looks old for his age.
【老小】lǎoxiǎo〈名〉1（老人和小孩）the whole family: 一家～ the whole family 2（所有人）all the people: 全村～ the whole village, old and young
【老兄】lǎoxiōng〈名〉〈尊〉[a form of address among friends] brother: 你～真行！Man, you're great!
【老羞成怒】lǎoxiū-chéngnù = 恼羞成怒 nǎoxiū-chéngnù
【老朽】lǎoxiǔ A〈形〉decrepit and behind the times: ～无能 old and useless B〈名〉〈旧〉〈谦〉[a form of self-address used by an old man] I
【老鸦】lǎoyā〈名〉〈方〉crow
【老眼光】lǎoyǎnguāng〈名〉old way of judging things
【老眼昏花】lǎoyǎn-hūnhuā〈成〉be dim-sighted from old age
【老爷爷】lǎoyéye〈名〉1（曾祖父）great

grandfather **2**〈尊〉（用于称呼） [a form of address to an old man used by children] grandpa

【老爷子】 lǎoyézi〈名〉〈方〉 **1**〈尊〉（老年男子） old man **2**（指父亲） my/your old father: 你家～身体可好? How is your father?

【老爷】 lǎoye **A**〈名〉 **1**〈旧〉（有权势的人） bureaucrat: 做官当～ [of officials] act like a bureaucrat **2**〈旧〉（指主人） [used by a domestic servant] master **B**〈形〉 old/old-fashioned thing: ～车 vintage car

【老一辈】 lǎoyībèi〈名〉 older generation: ～革命家 veteran revolutionaries

【老一套】 lǎoyītào〈名〉 same old story: 研究来研究去，你还是～。 After repeated consideration you are still stuck in the old ways.

【老鹰】 lǎoyīng〈名〉 hawk

【老油条】 lǎoyóutiáo = 老油子 lǎoyóuzi

【老油子】 lǎoyóuzi〈名〉 wily old fox

【老有所为】 lǎoyǒusuǒwéi〈成〉 have sth. to do when one gets old

【老有所养】 lǎoyǒusuǒyǎng〈成〉 the old will be provided for

【老于世故】 lǎoyú-shìgù〈成〉〈贬〉 be a know-it-all

【老玉米】 lǎoyùmi〈名〉〈方〉 maize

【老妪】 lǎoyù〈名〉〈书〉 old woman

【老丈人】 lǎozhàngren〈名〉 father-in-law

【老账】 lǎozhàng〈名〉 **1**（指债务） long-standing debts: 他～未还，又欠新债。 Without repaying old debts, he is accumulating new ones. **2**（指事情） old scores: 翻～ bring up old scores

【老者】 lǎozhě〈名〉〈书〉 old gentleman: 受人尊敬的～ revered old man

【老中青】 lǎo-zhōng-qīng〈名〉 the old, the middle-aged and the young

【老主顾】 lǎozhǔgù〈名〉 regular customer

【老庄股】 lǎozhuāngǔ〈名〉［金融］ stock manipulated long-term by the banks

【老资格】 lǎozīgé〈名〉 seniority: 摆～ flaunt one's seniority

【老子】 lǎozi〈名〉〈口〉 **1**（父亲） father **2**（我） [a form of self-address used by an arrogant person]（主格） I;（宾格） me: ～怕谁? 谁都不怕! Whom am I scared of? Nobody!

【老子天下第一】 lǎozi tiānxià dìyī〈俗〉 regard oneself as number one under heaven

【老字号】 lǎozìhào〈名〉 old name in business: 百年～ century-old shop ‖ 中华～ China's time-honoured brand

【老总】 lǎozǒng〈名〉 **1**〈旧〉（指军人） [form of address] soldier **2**〈尊〉（指将领） general or commander-in-chief (of the PLA) **3**〈尊〉 [form of address]（总工） chief engineer;（总经理） general manager;（总编） editor in chief

【老祖宗】 lǎozǔzong〈名〉 ancestor

佬 lǎo〈名〉〈贬〉 fellow: ▸阔～, 乡巴～

姥 lǎo

▸mǔ

【姥姥】 lǎolao〈名〉〈口〉 (maternal) grandmother

【姥爷】 lǎoye〈名〉〈口〉 (maternal) grandfather

栳 lǎo ▸栲栳 kǎolǎo

铑（銠） lǎo〈名〉［化学］ rhodium (Rh)

潦 lǎo〈书〉

A〈形〉 [of rain] heavy

B〈名〉 heavy rainfall

▸liáo

lào

络（絡） lào

▸luò

【络子】 làozi〈名〉 **1**（指网袋） thread-woven bag **2**（指器具） spindle

唠（嘮） lào〈动〉〈方〉 chat: 有空儿咱俩再好好～一～。 Let's have another good chat next time.

▸láo

【唠嗑】 làokē〈动〉〈方〉 chat: 我们好长时间没在一起～了。 We haven't had a chat together for a long time.

烙 lào〈动〉 **1**（熨烫） iron: ～衬衫 iron a shirt ‖ 在木器上～个印记 brand a seal into the wooden furniture **2**（烤熟） bake in a pan: ～两张饼 bake a couple of cakes

▸luò

【烙饼】 làobǐng〈名〉 pancake

【烙花】 làohuā〈名〉［美术］ pyrograph

【烙铁】 làotie〈名〉 **1**（用于熨烫） iron: 电～ electric iron **2**（用于焊接） soldering iron

【烙印】 làoyìn〈名〉 **1**（指火印） brand: 打上～ put a brand (on sth.) **2**〈喻〉（指痕迹） indelible mark: 抹不去的时代～ marks of time that can't be removed

涝（澇） lào

A〈动〉 be waterlogged: 庄稼～了。 The crops were waterlogged. ▸旱～保收

B〈名〉 water logging: 排～ drain a waterlogged area

【涝害】 làohài〈名〉 water logging

【涝洼地】 làowādì〈名〉 waterlogged lowland

【涝灾】 làozāi〈名〉 damage or crop failure caused by waterlogging

落 lào = 落 luò A1, A2, A7, A8, A9

▸là, luò

【落不是】 lào bùshi〈动〉 get the blame: 他怕～，处处谨小慎微。 He did everything with the utmost care in order to escape blame.

【落汗】 làohàn〈动〉〈口〉 stop sweating: 歇一会儿，落～。 Let's take a short rest to cool off the sweat.

【落价】 làojià〈动〉 drop in price: 蔬菜落价了。 Vegetables have gone down in price.

【落忍】 làorěn〈动〉〈方〉 [often used in the negative] have the heart to do sth.: 他累成那样儿，我们心里怪不～的。 We felt sympathetic about how tired his work had made him.

【落色】 làoshǎi〈动〉〈方〉 fade: 这种布料容易～。 This kind of cloth fades easily.

【落枕】 làozhěn〈动〉 get a stiff neck

【落子】 làozi〈名〉 **1**〈方〉（莲花落） [a form of folk art] popular ballad sung to the accompaniment of bamboo clappers with every stanza ending in 'lianhualao, laolianhua' (莲花落, 落莲花) **2**〈旧〉 = 评剧 píngjù

耢（耮） lào

A〈名〉 leveller [a kind of farm implement used to level land]

B〈动〉 level land with a leveller

酪 lào〈名〉 **1**（用乳汁做成） junket: ▸奶～ **2**（用果子做成） paste: 杏仁～ almond cream

lē

肋 lē

▸lèi

【肋脦】 lēde〈形〉〈方〉 [of clothes] slovenly: 瞧你那～样! What a slovenly person you are!

嘞 lē

▸lei

【嘞嘞】 lēle〈动〉〈方〉 chatter: 你少～两句行不行? Stop chattering, won't you?

lè

仂 lè〈名〉〈书〉 remainder

【仂语】 lèyǔ〈名〉［语言］ phrase

乐（樂） lè

A〈形〉 happy: 以…为～ take joy in sth. ‖ 她心里～开了花。 Her heart was filled with joy. ▸～极生悲, 欢～

B〈动〉 **1**（乐于） enjoy: ▸～此不疲, 津津～道, 幸灾～祸 **2**〈口〉（笑） laugh: ～得合不上嘴 laugh broadly ▸傻～

▸yuè

【乐不可支】 lèbùkězhī〈成〉 be overwhelmed with joy: 大家听到这个消息都～。 We were all beside ourselves with joy at the news.

【乐不思蜀】 lèbùsīShǔ〈成〉 be so happy as to forget home and duty

【乐此不疲】 lècǐ-bùpí〈成〉 never get tired of it: 他每天养鱼，～。 He never tires of looking after his fish every day.

【乐得】 lèdé〈动〉 be only too glad: 他们不让我帮忙，我～清闲。 They didn't need my help, so I was only too happy to have the chance to take things easy.

【乐而忘返】 lè'érwàngfǎn〈成〉 enjoy oneself so much that one doesn't want to return

【乐观】 lèguān〈形〉 optimistic: 前景～ have bright prospects ‖ 过分/盲目～ be unduly/blindly optimistic

【乐观主义】 lèguānzhǔyì〈名〉 optimism: ～者 optimist

【乐果】 lèguǒ〈名〉［农业］ Cygon [insecticide]

【乐呵呵】 lèhēhē〈形〉 buoyant: 他整天～的。 He is happy all day long.

【乐和】 lèhe〈形〉〈方〉 happy: 日子过得挺～ lead a happy life

【乐活】 lèhuó〈名〉 lifestyles of health and sustainability (LOHAS): ～的理念已逐渐深入人心。 The concept of healthy lifestyles has gradually taken root.

【乐极生悲】 lèjí-shēngbēi〈成〉 extreme joy is tinged with sorrow

【乐趣】 lèqù〈名〉 delight: 生活～ joys of life ‖ 他们从中得到了很多～。 They got a lot of pleasure out of it.

【乐融融】 lèróngróng〈形〉 happy and

L

harmonious: 家家户户～。 Each and every family lives a happy and harmonious life.

【乐善好施】lèshàn-hàoshī〈成〉 love to do philanthropic work

【乐事】 lèshì 〈名〉 pleasure: 以助人为～ find pleasure in helping others ‖ 人生～ joy of life

【乐陶陶】lètáotáo〈形〉 happy

【乐天】lètiān〈动〉 be carefree: ～派 optimist

【乐天知命】 lètiān-zhīmìng 〈成〉 accept whatever comes one's way and be content with one's fate

【乐土】lètǔ〈名〉 paradise: 这里是远离城市喧嚣的一方～。 This is a paradise far removed from the hubbub of city life.

【乐意】lèyì **A**〈动〉 be ready: ～帮忙 be ready to assist ‖ 我们～出资赞助。 We are willing to provide the financial support. **B**〈形〉 pleased: 听了我的批评，她似乎有点儿不～。 When she heard my criticisms, she seemed somewhat displeased.

【乐于】 lèyú 〈动〉 be happy to: ～接受 accept with pleasure ‖ ～助人 love to help others

【乐园】 lèyuán 〈名〉 **1**（游乐场） playground: 迪斯尼～ Disneyland ‖ 儿童～ children's playground **2**［宗教］ paradise

【乐在其中】lèzàiqízhōng〈成〉 find pleasure in: 别人都觉得编词典是个苦活，但她却～。 Other people believe that the making of dictionaries is drudgery, but she finds it a source of pleasure.

【乐滋滋】lèzīzī〈形〉〈口〉 pleased: 心里～的 feel delighted

【乐子】lèzi〈名〉〈方〉 fun: 找～ go looking for some fun

勒[1] lè

A〈名〉〈书〉 head collar

B〈动〉 **1**（拉紧缰绳） rein in: ▸悬崖～马 **2**（逼迫） force: ▸～令，～索 **3**〈书〉（统率） command: 亲～三军 take command of the army

勒[2] lè〈动〉〈书〉 carve: ～碑 engrave inscriptions on a stone tablet ▸勾～

勒[3] lè = 勒克斯 lèkèsī
▸lēi

【勒克斯】lèkèsī〈量〉［物理］ lux

【勒令】lèlìng〈动〉 order: ～退学 expel a student from school ‖ 被～停业整顿 be forced to close for consolidation

【勒石】lèshí〈动〉〈书〉 carve on a stone tablet: ～墓旁 erect a stone tablet by the tomb

【勒索】lèsuǒ〈动〉 extort: ～钱财 extort money (from sb.)

le

了 le〈助〉 **1**（表完成） [used after a verb or an adjective to indicate the completion of an action, at a point in the past or before the beginning of another action]: 车站上挤满～人。 People crowded the railway station. ‖ 等雨停～再走。 Wait till the rain stops. **2**（表状态改变） [used at the end of a sentence to indicate a change of situation or state]: 天快亮～。 The day will break soon. ‖ 我明白他的意思～。 I see what he meant now. **3**（表劝诫或要求） [used at the end or in the middle of a sentence to indicate a persuasion or request]: 该走～。 It's time to go. ‖ 可别再大意～。 Don't be careless any more. **4**（表感叹） [used at the end or in the middle of a sentence to express an exclamation]: 太好～! Wonderful!
▸liǎo

饹（餎） le ▸饸饹 héle
▸gē

lēi

勒 lēi〈动〉 tie sth. tight: ～紧裤带 tighten a belt
▸lè

【勒紧裤腰带】lēijǐn kùyāodài〈俗〉〈喻〉 tighten one's belt

léi

累（纍） léi
▸lěi, lèi

【累累】léiléi〈形〉〈书〉 **1**（颓丧） haggard and dejected: ～若丧家之犬 wretched as a stray dog **2**（强调多） numerous: 硕果～ numerous significant achievements
▸lěilěi

【累赘】léizhui **A**〈形〉 cumbersome: 带两个孩子去旅行太～。 It's inconvenient to travel with two children. **B**〈名〉 burden: 旅游带着孩子是个～。 Travelling with children is a real nuisance.

雷 léi

A〈名〉 **1**（指自然现象） thunder: 一声炸～ a clap of thunder ▸～霆，春～，打～ **2**（指武器） mine: 触～ hit a mine ‖ 扫～ sweep mines ▸地～，水～，鱼～

B〈动〉〈口〉 astonish: 她的衣服真～人。 Her dress is truly astonishing.

【雷暴】léibào〈名〉［气象］ thunderstorm

【雷场】léichǎng〈名〉 minefield

【雷达】 léidá 〈名〉 radar: ～跟踪 radar tracking ‖ ～兵 radar operator

【雷打不动】 léidǎ-bùdòng 〈成〉 unshakeable: 他每天坚持晨练，～。 He has never for a single day stopped doing morning exercises.

【雷电】léidiàn〈名〉 thunder and lightning: ～交加 lightning accompanied by claps of thunder

【雷动】léidòng〈动〉**1**（指天气）thunder **2**（指反应） be thunderous: 欢声/掌声～ thunderous cheers/applause

【雷公】Léigōng〈名〉 Thunder God

【雷管】léiguǎn〈名〉 detonator

【雷击】léijī〈动〉 [of lightning] strike: 遭～ be struck by a thunderbolt

【雷克雅未克】Léikèyǎwèikè 〈名〉 Reykjavik

【雷厉风行】léilì-fēngxíng〈成〉 act immediately and resolutely

【雷鸣】léimíng〈动〉**1**（指天气） thunder: 电闪～ lightening flashed and thunder rumbled **2**（指反应） be thunderous: 爆发出～般的掌声。 Thunderous applause burst out.

【雷鸟】 léiniǎo 〈名〉 ［鸟类］ white partridge

【雷区】léiqū〈名〉 minefield

【雷人】 léirén 〈动〉 be startling: ～新闻 startling news

【雷声大，雨点小】léishēng dà, yǔdiǎn xiǎo〈俗〉〈喻〉 all talk and no action

【雷霆】léitíng〈名〉 **1**（指天气） thunderclap **2**〈喻〉（指威力） thundering;（指怒气） rage: ▸大发～

【雷霆万钧】léitíng-wànjūn〈成〉 as powerful as a thunderbolt: 我军以～之势横扫残敌。 Our army routed the enemy remnants with overwhelming power.

【雷同】léitóng〈动〉 be identical: 答案～的两份试卷 two exam papers with identical answers

【雷雨】léiyǔ〈名〉 thunderstorm

【雷雨云】léiyǔyún〈名〉［气象］ thundercloud

【雷阵雨】léizhènyǔ〈名〉 thunder shower

嫘 léi

【嫘祖】Léizǔ〈名〉 Leizu [wife of the legendary Yellow Emperor (黄帝), and the reputed founder of sericulture]

缧（縲） léi

【缧绁】 léixiè 〈名〉〈书〉 **1**（指绳索） thick rope for binding prisoners **2**（指狱牢） prison: 身陷～ be in prison

擂 léi〈动〉 **1**（打） hit: ～鼓 beat the drum ‖ 有人在我背上狠狠～了一拳。 Someone thumped me on the back. **2**（研磨） grind: ～药 pestle medicine ‖ ～钵 mortar
▸lèi

檑 léi〈动〉 push huge logs from a great height to crush enemies

【檑木】léimù〈名〉 huge log pushed down from a great height to crush enemies

礌 léi〈动〉 roll down huge stones from a great height to crush enemies

【礌石】léishí〈名〉 huge stone rolled down from a great height to crush enemies

镭（鐳） léi〈名〉［化学］ radium (Ra)

羸 léi〈形〉〈书〉 emaciated: ▸～弱

【羸惫】léibèi〈形〉〈书〉 exhausted

【羸顿】 léidùn 〈形〉〈书〉 feeble and wasted

【羸弱】léiruò〈形〉〈书〉 feeble: 身体～ be physically weak

罍 léi〈名〉〈古〉 urn-shaped wine container in ancient times

lěi

耒 lěi〈名〉 **1**（指柄） handle of a plough-like farm implement **2**（指农具） ancient fork-like farm implement

【耒耜】 lěisì 〈名〉〈古〉 **1**（犁状农具） plough-like farm implement **2**（农具） farm implements in general

诔（誄） lěi〈古〉

A〈动〉 eulogize the dead to express one's condolences

B〈名〉 dirge: ～辞 dirge

垒（壘） lěi

A〈名〉 **1**［军事］ rampart: ▸堡～，对～ **2**［体育］ base: 一～ first base

B 〈动〉 build up: ～一堵墙 build a wall ‖ ～灶 build a stove ‖ 把锅台再～高点儿。 Make the kitchen range a little higher.
【垒球】lěiqiú ▸**p. 909**〈名〉 softball: 打～ play softball ‖ ～棒 softball bat ‖ ～场 softball field ‖ ～手套 mitt

累[1] lěi

A 〈动〉 accumulate: ▸～卵, 积～, 长年～月
B 〈副〉 repeatedly: ～建功勋 perform good deeds repeatedly ▸～次, 连篇～牍

累[2] lěi 〈动〉 involve: ▸连～, 拖～

▸léi, lèi
【累次】lěicì〈副〉 again and again: ～三番 time after time
【累犯】lěifàn〈名〉 **1**（指行为）recidivism **2**（指人） reoffender
【累积】lěijī〈动〉 accumulate: ～资料 amass information ‖ ～红利 cumulative bonus
【累及】lěijí〈动〉 implicate: ～无辜 involve the innocent
【累计】lěijì〈动〉 add up to: ～利润 accumulated profit
【累教不改】lěijiào-bùgǎi = 屡教不改 lǚjiào-bùgǎi
【累进】lěijìn〈动〉［经济］ graduate: ～制 progressive system
【累进税】lěijìnshuì〈名〉 progressive tax: ～制 progressive taxation
【累累】lěilěi **A**〈副〉 repeatedly: 失误～ make repeated errors **B**〈形〉 countless: 罪行～ commit countless crimes
▸léiléi
【累卵】lěiluǎn〈名〉〈书〉〈喻〉 delicate balancing act: ▸危如～
【累年】lěinián〈名〉 year after year: ～亏损 have deficits year after year
【累世】lěishì〈名〉 many generations: ～侨居海外 have lived overseas for generations

磊 lěi

【磊磊】lěilěi〈形〉〈书〉 heaped: 山石～ piles of stones
【磊落】lěiluò〈形〉 **1**（光明正大） open and upright: 胸怀～ open-hearted and upright ▸光明～ **2**〈书〉（堆积很多） many and jumbled

蕾 lěi〈名〉 (flower) bud: ▸蓓～

【蕾铃】lěilíng〈名〉［植物］ cotton buds and bolls
【蕾丝】lěisī〈名〉 lace: ～婚纱 lacy wedding dress ‖ ～透明装 lacy transparent clothing

儡 lěi ▸傀儡 kuǐlěi

lèi

肋 lèi〈名〉 rib: 两～ both sides of the chest ▸～骨, ～条

▸lē
【肋骨】lèigǔ〈名〉 rib
【肋膜】lèimó〈名〉［生理］ pleura: ～炎 pleurisy
【肋条】lèitiáo〈名〉〈方〉 animal rib [as food]
【肋窝】lèiwō〈名〉 armpit

泪（淚） lèi〈名〉 tear: 流～ shed tears ‖ 伤心～ bitter tears ‖ 挥～告别 have a tearful farewell ▸～如雨下, 眼～

【泪痕】lèihén〈名〉 tear stain: 他脸上带着～。 His face bore signs of tears.
【泪花】lèihuā〈名〉 tears in one's eyes: 她眼里闪烁着喜悦的～。 Her eyes glistened with tears of joy.
【泪涟涟】lèiliánlián〈形〉 tearful
【泪流满面】lèiliú-mǎnmiàn〈成〉 be all tears
【泪流如注】lèiliú-rúzhù〈成〉 tears streaming down one's cheeks
【泪人儿】lèirénr〈名〉 tearful person: 哭成～ be all tears
【泪如泉涌】lèirúquányǒng〈成〉 tears streaming down one's face
【泪如雨下】lèirúyǔxià〈成〉 shed floods of tears
【泪水】lèishuǐ〈名〉 tear: 流下感激/喜悦的～ shed tears of gratitude/joy ‖ 她眼里噙着～。 Tears welled in her eyes.
【泪汪汪】lèiwāngwāng〈形〉 tearful: ～的眼睛 eyes filled with tears
【泪腺】lèixiàn〈名〉［生理］ tear gland
【泪眼】lèiyǎn〈名〉 tearful eyes: ～模糊 eyes blurred by tears
【泪盈盈】lèiyíngyíng〈形〉 tearful
【泪珠】lèizhū〈名〉 teardrop: ～簌簌滑过她的面颊。 Tears ran down her cheeks like pearls.

类（類） lèi

A〈名〉 type: 同～ of the same kind ‖ 分～ divide into categories ▸～别, 归～, 种～
B〈量〉 kind: 我对这～事不感兴趣。 I'm not interested in that sort of thing.
C〈动〉 be similar to: ▸～人猿, ～似, ～同
【类比】lèibǐ **A**〈动〉 make an analogy: 把两件事情进行～ make an analogy between the two events **B**〈名〉 analogy
【类别】lèibié〈名〉 classification: 分成不同的～ classify into different categories ‖ 商品～ commodity classification
【类风湿】lèifēngshī ▸**p. 50**〈形〉［医学］ rheumatoid: ～性关节炎 rheumatoid arthritis
【类固醇】lèigùchún〈名〉［生化］ steroid: 他因服用～被取消参赛资格。 He was disqualified because of his abuse of steroids.
【类乎】lèihu〈动〉〈书〉 look like: 这个故事很离奇, ～神话。 This fantastic story sounds like a fairy tale.
【类金属】lèijīnshǔ〈名〉［化学］ metalloid
【类人猿】lèirényuán〈名〉［考古］ anthropoid
【类书】lèishū〈名〉 work combining the characteristics of encyclopedias and concordances and methodically arranged according to subjects
【类似】lèisì〈形〉 similar: ～的例子 similar cases ‖ 保证不再发生～事件 guarantee against the occurrence of similar incidents
【类同】lèitóng〈形〉 similar: 样式～ similar in style
【类推】lèituī〈动〉 reason by analogy: 其余～ reason out the rest by analogy ‖ 依此～ on the analogy of this
【类星体】lèixīngtǐ〈名〉［天文］ quasi-stellar object (QSO)
【类型】lèixíng〈名〉 type: 分成几种～ classify into several categories ‖ 同一～ be of the same kind
【类型学】lèixíngxué〈名〉 typology

累 lèi

A〈形〉 tired: 走～了 be weary with walking ‖ 今天～坏了。 I'm exhausted today.
B〈动〉 **1**（使疲乏） tire: 看小字～眼睛。 Reading small print strains the eyes. ‖ 他操劳过度, ～垮了身体。 His health broke down from overwork. **2**（操劳） toil: ～了一天, 真想躺下休息一会儿。 I've been working hard all day and would really like to lie down and rest a little.
▸léi, lěi
【累活】lèihuó〈名〉 tiring labour: 脏活～ filthy and strenuous work
【累死累活】lèisǐ-lèihuó〈成〉 work oneself to death

酹 lèi〈动〉〈书〉 pour a libation

擂 lèi〈名〉 ring: ▸～主

▸léi
【擂台】lèitái〈名〉 ring: ▸摆～, 打～
【擂台赛】lèitáisài〈名〉 **1**（指比武） martial arts contest **2**（竞赛） contest: 中日围棋～ China-Japan 'go' contest
【擂主】lèizhǔ〈名〉 **1**（指比武） ring master **2**（指胜者） winner of a contest

lei

嘞 lei〈助〉 [used the way 了 is used, with positive connotation]: 好～, 就这么办吧! Great, let's do it like this then! ‖ 走～! Let's go.

▸lē

lēng

棱 lēng ▸扑棱 pūlēng

▸léng

嘞 lēng〈拟〉 [of reel] creak

léng

崚 léng

【崚嶒】léngcéng〈形〉〈书〉 precipitous

塄 léng〈名〉〈方〉 sloping bank along a field

【塄坎】léngkǎn〈名〉〈方〉 sloping bank and ridge of a field

棱（稜） léng〈名〉 **1**（指连接处） edge: 桌子～儿 edges of a table ‖ 三～镜 triangular prism **2**（指凸起处） corrugation: 这块搓板都没～了。 The corrugations of the washboard have worn off.

▸lēng
【棱角】léngjiǎo〈名〉 **1**〈本〉 edges and corners: 晶体～分明。 Crystal has defined edges. **2**〈喻〉（指锋芒） edge: 他很有心计, 但表面却不露～。 He is a man of shrewdness but he keeps a low profile.
【棱镜】léngjìng〈名〉［物理］ prism
【棱台】léngtái〈名〉［数学］ frustum of a pyramid
【棱柱】léngzhù〈名〉 prism: 三～ triangular prism
【棱锥】léngzhuī〈名〉［数学］ pyramid
【棱锥体】léngzhuītǐ〈名〉［数学］ pyramid

楞 léng = 棱 léng

薐 léng ▸菠薐菜 bōléngcài

lěng

冷 lěng〈形〉**1**（温度低）cold: ～得发抖 shiver from cold ‖ ～空气 cold air ‖ 天渐渐～了。 It's getting colder. ▸～风, 寒～ **2**（不热情） frosty: ～面孔 frosty looks ‖ 他～～地看了我一眼。 He gave me an icy stare. ▸～淡, ～言～语 **3**（不热闹） out-of-the-way: ▸～寂, ～清 **4**（偏僻） unusual: ▸～僻, ～字 **5**（突然） sudden: ▸～不丁, ～枪 **6**（不受欢迎） unpopular: ▸～货, ～门 **7**〈喻〉（失望） disappointed: 心灰意～ be disappointed and frustrated at the lack of hope

【冷傲】lěng'ào〈形〉 cold and arrogant

【冷冰冰】lěngbīngbīng〈形〉**1**（指人） icy: ～的态度 icy manner ‖ 他对人老是～的。 He is always cold towards people. **2**（指物） cold: 他把脸贴在～的窗户上。 He pressed his face against the cold window.

【冷兵器】lěngbīngqì〈名〉［军事］ cold steel

【冷不丁】lěngbudīng〈副〉〈方〉 unexpectedly: ～吓了我一跳。 I got a sudden fright.

【冷不防】lěngbufáng〈副〉 suddenly: ～从山上滚下一块石头来。 Without warning, a stone suddenly hurtled down from the top of the mountain.

【冷菜】lěngcài〈名〉 cold dish

【冷餐】lěngcān〈名〉 buffet: ～会 buffet party

【冷藏】lěngcáng〈动〉 refrigerate: 把肉～起来 refrigerate the meat ‖ ～箱 refrigerator ‖ ～车 refrigerator van

【冷藏室】lěngcángshì〈名〉 refrigerating compartment [in a refrigerator]

【冷场】lěngchǎng〈名〉**1**（指演出时） awkward silence on the stage when an actor enters late or forgets his lines **2**（指开会时） awkward silence at a meeting or discussion when nobody speaks: 大家都积极发言, 就不会～。 If everyone voices their opinion actively, the discussion won't drag.

【冷嘲热讽】lěngcháo-rèfěng〈成〉 biting sarcasm: 他的杂文极尽～之能事。 He was at his best in his scathing prose.

【冷处理】lěngchǔlǐ〈动〉**1**［机械］ give sth. a cold treatment **2**〈喻〉（暂缓处理） give sth. a cooling-off period before dealing with it

【冷待】lěngdài〈动〉 treat sb. coldly

【冷淡】lěngdàn **A**〈形〉**1**（冷清） sluggish: 生意～。 Business is slack. **2**（不热情） cold: 态度～ indifferent attitude ‖ 她对丈夫的朋友很～。 She is cool towards her husband's friends. **B**〈动〉 give sb. the cold-shoulder: 他不经意～了一位重要客人。 Without realizing it, he slighted a very important guest.

【冷冻】lěngdòng〈动〉 freeze: 把牛奶～起来 freeze milk ‖ ～食品 frozen food

【冷冻室】lěngdòngshì〈名〉 freezer compartment [in a refrigerator]

【冷风】lěngfēng〈名〉**1**〈本〉 cold air **2**〈喻〉（指言论） rumour: ▸吹～

【冷锋】lěngfēng〈名〉［气象］ cold front

【冷敷】lěngfū〈动〉［医学］ cold compress

【冷宫】lěnggōng〈名〉〈喻〉 place for people that are out of favour: ▸打入～

【冷光】lěngguāng〈名〉**1**［物理］ cold light: 月亮发着～。 The moon shone with a cold light. **2**（指目光） cold expression

【冷光灯】lěngguāngdēng〈名〉 cold light lamp

【冷柜】lěngguì〈名〉 ice box

【冷害】lěnghài〈名〉［农业］ damage to plants caused by a cold spell

【冷汗】lěnghàn〈名〉 cold sweat: 吓出了一身～ so scared that the whole body came out in a cold sweat

【冷荤】lěnghūn〈名〉 cold meat dish

【冷货】lěnghuò〈名〉**1**（指滞销） unmarketable goods **2**（指冷冻） frozen product

【冷寂】lěngjì〈形〉 cold and still: ～的秋夜 cold and quiet autumn night

【冷加工】lěngjiāgōng〈动〉［冶金］ treat at room temperature

【冷箭】lěngjiàn〈名〉 sniper's shot: 散布谣言, ～伤人 take a shot at sb. by spreading rumours ▸放～

【冷噤】lěngjìn〈名〉 shiver: 吓得打～ tremble with fear

【冷静】lěngjìng〈形〉**1**（冷清） still and quiet: 咱们找个～的地方说话。 Let's find a quiet place to talk. **2**（沉稳） calm: 头脑～ have a cool head ‖ 遇事要～。 When anything crops up, you must keep calm.

【冷峻】lěngjùn〈形〉 sober and grave: 面色～ look stony-faced

【冷库】lěngkù〈名〉 cold store

【冷酷】lěngkù〈形〉 unfeeling: 他是个～无情的人。 He is a man with a heart of stone.

【冷链】lěngliàn〈名〉［食品］ cold chain

【冷落】lěngluò **A**〈形〉 deserted: 这家店铺门前～。 That store has few customers. **B**〈动〉 give sb. the cold shoulder: ～客人 slight a guest ‖ 受到～ get the cold shoulder

【冷门】lěngmén〈名〉**1**（指不引人注目） unpopular trade, subject, etc.: ～专业 less popular field of study **2**（指出乎意料） dark horse: 那次运动会爆了好几个～。 The sports meet brought forth several unexpected winners. ▸爆～

【冷门货】lěngménhuò = 冷货 lěnghuò 1

【冷面】lěngmiàn〈名〉**1**（指面条） cold noodles: 朝鲜～ Korean-style cold noodles **2**（指表情） stern look: ～杀手 poker-faced assassin **3**（指态度） impartiality and incorruptibility: ～法官 stony-faced judge

【冷面孔】lěngmiànkǒng〈名〉 poker face: 板着～ pull a poker face

【冷漠】lěngmò〈形〉 indifferent: 态度～ indifferent attitude

【冷凝】lěngníng〈名〉［物理］ condensation

【冷暖】lěngnuǎn〈名〉**1**（温度变化） change in temperature: 注意～变化 watch out for changes in temperature ‖〈喻〉把百姓的～挂在心上 concern oneself with the well-being of the common people **2**（世态炎凉） ways of the world: 人情～ ways of the world

【冷盘】lěngpán〈名〉 cold dish: 什锦～ assorted hors d'oeuvres

【冷僻】lěngpì〈形〉**1**（偏远） desolate: ～的山区 isolated mountain area **2**（不常用） unfamiliar: ～字 rarely used word

【冷气】lěngqì〈名〉**1**（指空气） cold air: ▸～团 **2**〈方〉（指空调） air-conditioner: 打开/关上～ turn on/off the air-conditioner ‖ ～机 air conditioner

【冷气团】lěngqìtuán〈名〉［气象］ cold air mass

【冷枪】lěngqiāng〈名〉 sniper's shot: ▸打～

【冷峭】lěngqiào〈形〉**1**（指寒气） icy: 北风～ piercing north wind **2**（指言语） sharp: 言语～ scathing remark

【冷清清】lěngqīngqīng〈形〉 deserted: ～的小巷 deserted lane ‖ 他独自一人过着～的日子。 He lived a lonely life.

【冷清】lěngqing〈形〉 cold and cheerless: ～的月光洒满河谷。 Dreary moonlight flooded the valley. ‖ 景区游人稀少, 显得很～。 There were few visitors in the scenic area, making it look really desolate.

【冷泉】lěngquán〈名〉 cold spring

【冷却】lěngquè〈动〉 cool: 发动机要等半小时后才能～下来。 The engine will take half an hour to cool down.

【冷却泵】lěngquèbèng〈名〉 cooling pump

【冷却塔】lěngquètǎ〈名〉 cooling tower

【冷热病】lěngrèbìng〈名〉**1** ▸**p. 50**〈方〉（指疟疾病） malaria **2**〈喻〉（指情绪） mood changes: 他的～又犯了。 He's in one of his moods again.

【冷若冰霜】lěngruòbīngshuāng〈成〉 be as cold as ice: 她那～的样子让人很难接近。 Her icy manner keeps people at a distance.

【冷色】lěngsè ▸**p. 863**〈名〉 cool colour: ～调 cool colour-tone ‖ 白色、蓝色、绿色都是～。 White, blue and green are cool colours.

【冷森森】lěngsēnsēn〈形〉 chilly: 山洞里～的。 It's chilly inside the cave.

【冷杉】lěngshān〈名〉［植物］ fir

【冷射】lěngshè〈动〉 make an unexpected shot at goal

【冷食】lěngshí〈名〉 cold food: 忌～ avoid cold food

【冷水】lěngshuǐ〈名〉**1**（凉水） cold water: 洗～澡 take a cold shower ▸泼～ **2**（生水） water that has not been boiled

【冷丝丝】lěngsīsī〈形〉 cool

【冷飕飕】lěngsōusōu〈形〉 chilly: 这里～的, 还是回去吧。 It's chilly here. Let's go back.

【冷烫】lěngtàng〈动〉 cold perm

【冷天】lěngtiān〈名〉 cold weather

【冷笑】lěngxiào〈动〉 sneer: 他脸上露出一丝～。 A slight sneer crept over his face.

【冷血动物】lěngxuè dòngwù〈名〉**1**〈本〉 cold-blooded animal **2**〈喻〉（指心狠） cold-hearted person

【冷言冷语】lěngyán-lěngyǔ〈成〉 sarcastic remarks: 不要介意别人的～。 Don't mind the sarcastic comments from others.

【冷眼】lěngyǎn〈名〉**1**（指冷静客观） icy look: ～观察市场的变化 coolly observe market changes **2**（指冷淡轻蔑） cold shoulder: 遭人～ get the cold shoulder

【冷眼旁观】lěngyǎn-pángguān〈成〉 look on coldly

【冷艳】lěngyàn〈形〉 coldly elegant

【冷饮】lěngyǐn〈名〉 cold drink

【冷遇】lěngyù〈名〉 cold reception: 遭到～ get the cold shoulder

【冷轧】lěngzhá〈名〉［冶金］ cold rolling: ～车间 cold rolling workshop

【冷战】lěngzhàn〈名〉 cold war: ～思维 cold-war thinking

【冷战】lěngzhan〈名〉 shiver: 冻得打～ shiver with cold ‖ 吓得打～ tremble with fear

【冷颤】lěngzhan = 冷战 lěngzhan

【冷字】lěngzì〈名〉 rarely used word

lèng

愣 lèng

A〈动〉 be dumbfounded: 听到消息后, 他～住了。 He was stupefied at the news. ▸发～

B〈形〉 reckless: ～小子 rash young fellow ▸～头～脑

C〈副〉〈口〉 wilfully: 这么简单的道理，他～不懂。He won't even follow reasoning as simple as this! ‖ 叫他别说，他～要说。Even when I order him to stop talking, he insists on speaking.

【愣干】lènggàn〈动〉〈口〉do things recklessly

【愣劲儿】lèngjìnr〈名〉〈方〉dash

【愣神儿】lèngshénr〈动〉〈方〉 be in a daze: 别站在那儿～，该吃晚饭了。Don't just stand there staring! Supper is ready.

【愣说】lèngshuō〈动〉〈口〉 insist on saying

【愣头愣脑】lèngtóu-lèngnǎo〈成〉 hot-headed: ～的小子 rash young fellow

【愣头青】lèngtóuqīng〈名〉〈方〉hothead

【愣怔】lèngzheng = 睖睁 lèngzheng

睖 lèng〈动〉〈方〉 stare in dissatisfaction

【睖睁】lèngzheng〈动〉**1**（发呆直视）stare blankly **2**（发愣）be in a daze: 吓得他一～。He was struck dumb with terror.

lī

哩 lī
►lǐ, li

【哩哩啦啦】līli-lālā〈形〉〈口〉on and off: 这雨～下了一个月，真烦人。It's been raining on and off for a month now. It's so annoying!

【哩哩啰啰】līli-luōluō〈形〉〈口〉rambling and indistinct: 他说话老是～的，谁也听不懂。He always mumbles when he talks and no one can follow him.

lí

丽（麗） lí ►高丽 Gāolí
►lì

厘（釐） lí

A〈动〉〈书〉rectify: ►～定，～正

B〈量〉**1**（计量单位）*li* [units of length, weight and area, respectively equal to 0.333 millimetre, 0.05 grams and 0.666 square metre] **2**〈旧〉（货币单位）*li* [a unit of Chinese currency, equal to 0.1 *fen* or 0.001 *yuan*]: 四元六角三分五～ 4.635 *yuan* **3**（市制利率）*li* [a unit of interest rate, equal to 0.1% monthly interest; or 1% annual interest]: 月利率五～七 0.57% monthly interest

【厘定】lídìng〈动〉〈书〉collate and stipulate (rules and regulations, etc.)

【厘米】límǐ ►**p. 82**〈量〉centimetre (cm)

【厘正】lízhèng〈动〉〈书〉correct

狸（貍） lí

【狸猫】límāo = 豹猫 bàomāo

离[1]（離） lí〈动〉**1**（离开）leave: ～京赴沪 leave Beijing for Shanghai ‖ ～家出走 leave home ‖ 水手们获准～船上岸。The sailors were given shore leave. ►～别，妻～子散 **2**（距离）be away from: ～考试还有两个星期。The examination is still two weeks away. ‖ 体育馆～我们学校很远。The gymnasium is far away from our school. **3**（缺少）be without: 所有生物都～不开空气和水。All living things would die without air and water. ‖ 这件事～了你不行。It won't do without you.

离[2]（離） lí〈名〉 one of the Eight Trigrams, symbolizing 'fire'

【离岸价格】lí'àn jiàgé〈名〉［经济］free on board (FOB)

【离别】líbié〈动〉part: ～亲人 bid farewell to one's beloved ‖ 痛苦的～ painful farewell

【离愁】líchóu〈名〉〈书〉sorrow of parting: ～别绪 sorrows of parting

【离岛】lídǎo〈名〉islet off a big island

【离队】líduì〈动〉leave one's post: 两名足球运动员～了。Two footballers left the team.

【离岗】lígǎng〈动〉leave one's post: 擅自～ go AWOL

【离格儿】lígér = 离谱 lípǔ

【离宫】lígōng〈名〉imperial abode built outside the capital for an emperor on an inspection tour

【离合】líhé〈动〉**1**（指人）be separated and reunited: ►悲欢～ **2**（指物）be separated and recombined: ►～器

【离合器】líhéqì〈名〉［机械］clutch

【离婚】líhūn〈动〉divorce: 提出～诉讼 initiate divorce proceedings ‖ ～率 divorce rate ‖ ～协议书 divorce agreement

【离婚证】líhūnzhèng〈名〉divorce certificate

【离间】líjiàn〈动〉 set one party against another: ～师生关系 drive a wedge between teachers and students ►挑拨～

【离间计】líjiànjì〈名〉 scheme of sowing discord: 识破对方的～ see through the opponent's scheme to disunite us

【离经叛道】líjīng-pàndào〈成〉 depart from the classics and rebel against orthodoxy: 他的行为被视为～。His conduct was regarded as heresy.

【离境】líjìng〈动〉leave a country: 限24小时内～ order sb. to leave the country within 24 hours

【离开】líkāi〈动〉leave: ～房间 leave the room ‖ ～家人 be away from one's family members ‖ 离不开身 be fully occupied ‖ 别～，等我回来。Stay here till I return.

【离乱】líluàn〈动〉be separated by war: 八年～使他痛苦不堪。He was tormented after eight years of estrangement through war.

【离谱】lípǔ〈动〉go too far: 你的玩笑开得太～了。You've carried this joke too far. ‖ 这价格太～了。The price is completely exorbitant.

【离奇】líqí〈形〉bizarre: ～的故事 bizarre story ‖ 这事儿很～。This is weird.

【离弃】líqì〈动〉abandon: ～家人 desert one's family

【离情】líqíng〈名〉pain of separation

【离情别绪】líqíng-biéxù〈成〉 sorrows of parting

【离群索居】líqún-suǒjū〈成〉live in seclusion: ～二十多年 live as a recluse for over 20 years

【离任】lírèn〈动〉leave one's official post: ～回国 leave one's post for home ‖ 即将～的部长 outgoing minister

【离散】lísàn **A**〈动〉 be separated from one another: 战争期间他与家人～了。He was separated from other members of the family during the war. **B**〈形〉［数学］discrete: ～值 discrete value

【离世】líshì〈动〉**1** ►**p. 772**〈婉〉（死亡）pass away **2**（与世隔绝）detach oneself from this mortal world

【离题】lítí〈动〉digress: 下笔千言，～万里 long-winded and irrelevant ‖ 他的话～太远。His remarks have nothing to do with the subject.

【离退休人员】lí-tuìxiū rényuán〈名〉 the retired

【离析】líxī〈动〉〈书〉**1**（离散）disintegrate: ►分崩～ **2**（分析）analyse: ～同义词义 analyse the subtle differences between synonyms

【离弦走板】líxián-zǒubǎn〈成〉deviate from generally acknowledged norms of conduct

【离乡背井】líxiāng-bèijǐng = 背井离乡 bèijǐng-líxiāng

【离心】líxīn〈动〉**1**（不同心）be at odds with the community or the leadership: ►～离德 **2**［物理］be centrifugal: ～作用 centrifugation

【离心泵】líxīnbèng〈名〉［机械］centrifugal pump

【离心机】líxīnjī〈名〉［机械］centrifugal machine

【离心离德】líxīn-lídé〈成〉 be different in thinking and faith

【离心力】líxīnlì〈名〉［物理］centrifugal force

【离休】líxiū〈动〉[of veteran cadres] retire: ～干部 retired veteran cadre

【离异】líyì〈动〉〈书〉 divorce: 父母～ divorced parents ‖ ～家庭 broken family

【离辙】lízhé〈动〉〈口〉be off the track

【离职】lízhí〈动〉**1**（指短时离岗） leave one's job temporarily: ～学习 leave one's job temporarily and study full time **2**（指辞职）resign

【离子】lízǐ〈名〉［物理］ion: 正/负～ positive/negative ion

【离子键】lízǐjiàn〈名〉［化学］ionic bond

【离子束】lízǐshù〈名〉ion beam

骊（驪） lí〈名〉〈书〉 pure black horse

梨（棃） lí〈名〉**1**（指树） pear tree **2**（指果实） pear: 京白～ white pear ‖ 雪花～ snow pear

【梨膏】lígāo〈名〉 pear syrup [for cough relief]: ～糖 pear drop

【梨园】líyuán〈名〉 the theatre: ～世家 well-known theatrical family ‖ ～子弟 theatrical performer

【梨园戏】líyuánxì〈名〉*liyuan* opera [popular in Fujian Province]

【梨子】lízi = 梨 lí 2

犁（犂） lí

A〈名〉plough〈英〉; plow〈美〉: 木/铁～ wooden/iron plough ►～铧

B〈动〉plough〈英〉; plow〈美〉: ～地/田 plough fields

【犁铧】líhuá〈名〉ploughshare

鹂（鸝） lí ►黄鹂 huánglí

喱 lí ►咖喱 gālí

蜊 lí ►蛤蜊 gélí

漓[1] lí ►淋漓 línlí

漓[2]（灕） lí

【漓江】Líjiāng ►**p. 294**〈名〉Lijiang River

缡（縭） lí〈名〉〈古〉silk veil: 结～ [of a woman] get married

璃 lí ▸玻璃 bōli, 琉璃 liúlí

嫠 lí〈名〉〈书〉widow
【嫠妇】lífù〈名〉〈书〉widow

犛 lí〈名〉yak
【犛牛】líniú〈名〉yak

黎 lí〈形〉〈书〉**1**（众多）numerous: ▸～民, ～庶 **2**（黑）black: ▸～黑
【黎巴嫩】Líbānèn〈名〉Lebanon: ～共和国 Republic of Lebanon ‖ ～人 Lebanese
【黎黑】líhēi = 黧黑 líhēi
【黎锦】líjǐn〈名〉brocade made by the Li ethnic group
【黎民】límín〈名〉〈书〉the populace: ～百姓 common people
【黎明】límíng〈名〉daybreak: ～即起 rise at dawn ‖ ～前的黑暗 darkest hours before the dawn
【黎庶】líshù = 黎民 límín
【黎族】Lízú〈名〉Li ethnic group

鲡（鱺） lí ▸鳗鲡 mánlí

罹 lí〈动〉〈书〉suffer from: ～病 suffer from a disease
【罹难】línàn〈动〉〈书〉**1**（遇难）die in a disaster: 二十名乘客～。Twenty passengers died. **2**（被害）be murdered

篱[1]（籬） lí ▸笊篱 zhàoli

篱[2]（籬） lí〈名〉hedge: 竹～ bamboo fence
【篱笆】líba〈名〉fence: ～墙 wattled wall
【篱落】líluò〈名〉〈书〉bamboo fence
【篱栅】lízhà〈名〉fence

醨 lí〈名〉〈书〉weak wine

藜 lí〈名〉[植物] lamb's-quarters

黧 lí〈形〉〈书〉[of complexion] dark and sallow
【黧黑】líhēi〈形〉〈书〉dark: 面目～ dark complexion

蠡 lí〈名〉〈书〉**1**（瓢）gourd ladle **2**（贝壳）seashell
【蠡测】lícè〈动〉〈书〉make an appraisal in the light of limited knowledge

lǐ

礼（禮） lǐ
A〈名〉**1**（仪式）rite: ▸～仪, 婚～ **2**（准则）ethics: ▸～教, ～义廉耻 **3**（指言语、动作）etiquette: ▸～节, 敬～, 军～ **4**（礼物）gift: 一份大～ a generous present ‖ 不收～ refuse a gift ▸厚～, 送～
B〈动〉〈书〉respect: ▸～贤下士
【礼拜】lǐbài **A**〈动〉[宗教] attend a religious service: 做～ go to church **B** ▸**p. 836**〈名〉〈口〉**1**（星期）week **2**（指某一天）day of the week: ～一/二/三/四/五/六/日 Monday/Tuesday/Wednesday/Thursday/Friday/Saturday/Sunday ‖ 今天～几? What day is it today? **3**（周日）Sunday: 明天是～。It's Sunday tomorrow.
【礼拜寺】lǐbàisì = 清真寺 qīngzhēnsì
【礼拜堂】lǐbàitáng〈名〉[基督教] church
【礼拜天】lǐbàitiān ▸**p. 836**〈名〉〈口〉Sunday
【礼宾】lǐbīn〈动〉receive guests according to protocol: ～司 department of protocol
【礼部】Lǐbù〈名〉[历史] Board of Rites
【礼成】lǐchéng〈动〉[said by the master of ceremonies] the ceremony is over
【礼单】lǐdān〈名〉present list
【礼多人不怪】lǐ duō rén bù guài〈俗〉one can never be too polite
【礼法】lǐfǎ〈名〉rule of etiquette: 崇尚～ respect the proprieties
【礼服】lǐfú〈名〉formal attire: 结婚～ wedding outfit
【礼花】lǐhuā〈名〉fireworks: 燃放～ set off fireworks
【礼教】lǐjiào〈名〉Confucian or feudal ethic code: 封建～ feudal ethics
【礼节】lǐjié〈名〉courtesy: 合乎～ be in accord with the etiquette ‖ 讲究～ attach importance to proprieties ‖ ～性拜访 courtesy call ‖ 外交～ diplomatic etiquette
【礼金】lǐjīn〈名〉gift of money
【礼帽】lǐmào〈名〉hat to accompany formal dress
【礼貌】lǐmào **A**〈名〉politeness: 没～ have no manners ‖ 有～ be courteous **B**〈形〉polite: ～待客 be polite to one's guests ‖ 他的举动太不～了。What he did was so rude.
【礼炮】lǐpào〈名〉gun salute: 鸣～二十一响 sound a 21-gun salute
【礼品】lǐpǐn〈名〉present: 赠送～ present a gift ‖ 结婚/生日～ wedding/birthday present
【礼品券】lǐpǐnquàn〈名〉gift voucher
【礼聘】lǐpìn〈动〉invite sb. cordially: 高薪～ engage sb. on a high salary
【礼器】lǐqì〈名〉sacrificial vessel
【礼轻情意重】lǐ qīng qíngyì zhòng〈惯〉the gift is trifling, but the feeling is profound
【礼券】lǐquàn〈名〉gift voucher
【礼让】lǐràng〈动〉give precedence to sb. out of courtesy: 中速行驶，安全～。Drive at a moderate speed and give way in the name of safety.
【礼尚往来】lǐshàng-wǎnglái〈成〉**1**（指礼节）courtesy demands reciprocation **2**（指相处）give as good as one gets
【礼数】lǐshù〈名〉courtesy: 不懂～ have no manners
【礼俗】lǐsú〈名〉etiquette and customs
【礼堂】lǐtáng〈名〉auditorium
【礼物】lǐwù〈名〉present: 赠送～ present gifts ‖ 订婚/结婚～ betrothal/wedding gift ‖ 生日～ birthday gift ‖ 圣诞～ Christmas present
【礼贤下士】lǐxián-xiàshì〈成〉[of a ruler] treat worthy men and men of virtue with courtesy
【礼仪】lǐyí〈名〉etiquette: 外交～ diplomatic proprieties ‖ ～小姐 young lady serving at a ceremony ‖ ～之邦 land of courtesy and propriety
【礼仪电报】lǐyí diànbào〈名〉courtesy telegram
【礼仪先生】lǐyí xiānsheng〈名〉young man performing services at ceremonies
【礼义廉耻】lǐ-yì-lián-chǐ〈成〉propriety, righteousness, honesty, and a sense of shame [formerly upheld as the 'four social bonds' (四维) in China]
【礼遇】lǐyù〈名〉courteous reception: 受到～ receive a courteous reception
【礼乐】lǐyuè〈名〉〈古〉rites and music
【礼赞】lǐzàn〈动〉sing the praises of: 英雄～ ode to the heroes

李 lǐ〈名〉**1**（指树）plum tree **2**（指果实）plum: ▸桃～
【李代桃僵】lǐdàitáojiāng〈成〉**1**（以此代彼）substitute one thing for another **2**（代人受过）take the blame for another person's mistake
【李子】lǐzi〈名〉**1**（指树）plum tree **2**（指果实）plum

里[1] lǐ
A〈名〉**1**（街坊）neighbourhood: ▸邻～ **2**（家乡）native place: ▸故～, 乡～
B〈量〉*li* [unit of length, equal to 500 metres or a half kilometre]: 地球直径是四万公里，合八万～。The diameter of the earth is 40,000 kilometres, equivalent to 80,000 Chinese *li*.

里[2]（裏、裡） lǐ〈名〉**1**（指反面）lining: 衣服～儿 lining of a garment ‖ 这面是～儿，那面是面儿。This is the inside, and that is the outside. ▸被～ **2**（指内部）inside: 他住在城～。He lives in the town. ▸～间, ～应外合, 表～如一
▸li
【里昂】Lǐ'áng〈名〉Lyon
【里边】lǐbian〈名〉inside: 从～把门锁上 lock the door from the inside ‖ ～请! Come in, please! ‖ 屋子～挤满了人。The room was packed with people.
【里程】lǐchéng〈名〉**1**（路程）mileage: 总～ total mileage **2**（过程）course: 人生的～ the course of life
【里程碑】lǐchéngbēi〈名〉milestone:〈喻〉历史的～ milestone in history
【里程标】lǐchéngbiāo〈名〉milestone: 高速公路沿线的～ milestones along the highway
【里程表】lǐchéngbiǎo〈名〉mileometer〈英〉; odometer〈美〉
【里带】lǐdài〈名〉inner tube (of a tyre)
【里勾外联】lǐgōu-wàilián〈成〉collude with people on both the inside and the outside
【里海】Lǐhǎi〈名〉Caspian Sea
【里急后重】lǐjí-hòuzhòng〈名〉[中医] tenesmus
【里脊】lǐji〈名〉fillet: ～肉 tenderloin meat
【里加】Lǐjiā〈名〉Riga
【里间】lǐjiān〈名〉inner room
【里拉】lǐlā ▸**p. 328**〈名〉lira [former Italian monetary unit]
【里里外外】lǐli-wàiwài〈成〉inside and outside: ～一把手 be competent in handling things both inside and outside the house
【里弄】lǐlòng〈名〉〈方〉**1**（小巷）lanes and alleys **2**（邻里）neighbourhood
【里面】lǐmiàn〈名〉inside: 衣服放在柜子～。The clothes are inside the chest.
【里圈】lǐquān〈名〉[体育] inside lane
【里三层，外三层】lǐ sān céng, wài sān céng〈惯〉crowds of people
【里士满】Lǐshìmǎn〈名〉Richmond
【里氏震级】Lǐshì zhènjí〈名〉Richter scale: 那次地震为7.25～。That earthquake registered 7.25 on the Richter scale.
【里手】lǐshǒu〈名〉**1**（左边）left-hand side: 把车往～靠一靠 move the car nearer

to the left 2 〈专家〉 expert: 行家～ old hand
【里斯本】Lǐsīběn〈名〉Lisbon
【里通外国】lǐtōngwàiguó〈成〉 serve as a spy for a hostile foreign country
【里头】lǐtou〈口〉= 里边 lǐbian
【里外不是人】lǐwài bùshìrén〈惯〉be blamed either way
【里外里】lǐwàilǐ〈副〉〈方〉 1 〈总共〉 taken all together: ～有二百五十块钱。 Altogether I have two hundred and fifty *yuan*. 2 〈无论怎么计算〉 either way: 三个人干五天跟五个人干三天，～是一样的。 Three people working five days or five people working three days — either way it's all the same.
【里屋】lǐwū〈名〉inner room
【里巷】lǐxiàng〈名〉lane
【里应外合】lǐyìng-wàihé〈成〉 collaborate from within with forces from without
【里约热内卢】Lǐyuērènèilú〈名〉Rio de Janeiro
【里子】lǐzi〈名〉lining: 大衣～ lining of an overcoat

俚

lǐ〈形〉 1 〈书〉〈粗俗〉 vulgar 2 〈通俗〉 popular
【俚歌】lǐgē〈名〉rustic song
【俚曲】lǐqǔ〈名〉pop song
【俚俗】lǐsú〈形〉vulgar
【俚语】lǐyǔ〈名〉slang

逦（邐）

lǐ ►迤逦 yǐlǐ

哩

lǐ〈量〉〈旧〉= 英里 yīnglǐ ►lī, li

浬

lǐ〈量〉〈旧〉= 海里 hǎilǐ

娌

lǐ ►妯娌 zhóuli

理

lǐ
A 〈动〉 1 〈料理〉 manage: ►～财, 护～, 日～万机 2 〈理睬〉 heed: 不爱～人 be stand-offish ‖ 别～他。 Don't take any notice of him. ►～睬, 搭～ 3 〈修整〉 put in order: ～不出头绪 be unable to get things into good order ►～发, 清～, 整～
B 〈名〉 1 〈纹路〉 grain: 木～ wood texture ►肌～, 纹～ 2 〈道理〉 reason: ►～论, 道～, 据～力争 3 〈自然科学〉 natural science 4 〈物理学〉 physics: ～学院 college of science ►～工, ～科
【理财】lǐcái〈动〉manage financial matters: 不善～ lack skills in financial affairs ‖ ～顾问 financial consultant ‖ ～之道 way to manage money matters
【理财师】lǐcáishī ►p. 966〈名〉 Certified Financial Planner (CFP): 向～咨询 consult a Certified Financial Planner
【理睬】lǐcǎi〈动〉[usu used in the negative] pay attention: 没人～这事。 Nobody shows interest in this matter. ‖ 我向她打招呼，但她没～我。 I said hello to her, but she ignored me completely.
【理当】lǐdāng〈动〉 ought to: ～（向某人）道歉 owe an apology (to sb.) ‖ ～如此。 That's just as it should be.
【理短】lǐduǎn〈形〉be in the wrong
【理发】lǐfà〈动〉 have one's hair cut: 我去～。 I'm going to have my hair cut.
【理发店】lǐfàdiàn〈名〉barber's shop〈英〉; barbershop〈美〉
【理发馆】lǐfàguǎn = 理发店 lǐfàdiàn
【理发师】lǐfàshī ►p. 966〈名〉hairdresser
【理该】lǐgāi = 理当 lǐdāng
【理工】lǐgōng〈名〉 science and engineering: ～大学 college of science and engineering
【理化】lǐhuà〈名〉physics and chemistry
【理会】lǐhuì〈动〉 1 〈理解〉 understand: 我～你的意思。 I understand what you mean. 2 〈注意〉 [usu used in the negative] pay attention: 不要～那件事。 Just ignore it. ‖ 他没～我的警告。 He paid no heed to my warning. 3 〈争论〉 [often used in the early vernacular] debate: 休与他～是非曲直。 Don't try and reason the rights and wrongs with him.
【理货】lǐhuò〈名〉［经济］ freight forwarding
【理解】lǐjiě〈动〉 understand: 难以～ be difficult to understand ‖ 你的意思我完全～。 I understand you completely.
【理解力】lǐjiělì〈名〉 comprehension: ～强/差 have good/poor comprehension
【理据】lǐjù〈名〉argument
【理科】lǐkē〈名〉 science: 学～ study science ‖ ～学校 science school
【理亏】lǐkuī〈形〉 be in the wrong: 自知～ know that one is in the wrong
【理疗】lǐliáo A〈名〉 physiotherapy B〈动〉undergo physiotherapy
【理路】lǐlù〈名〉 line of reasoning: 他的论文～不清。 His paper lacks coherence.
【理论】lǐlùn A〈名〉 theory: ～和实践相结合 integrate theory with practice ‖ ～联系实际 unite theory with practice ‖ 具有很高的～水平 be of a high theoretical level B〈动〉 debate: 他不讲道理，别跟他多～了。 He's not talking any sense, so there's no use in continuing to argue with him.
【理论家】lǐlùnjiā ►p. 966〈名〉theorist
【理念】lǐniàn〈名〉 1 〈思想〉 concept: 经营～ management idea 2 〈信仰〉 belief: 人生～ belief about life
【理赔】lǐpéi〈动〉 settle claims: 保险公司不予～。 The insurance company is refusing to settle claims.
【理清】lǐqīng〈动〉 sort out: ～思路 get one's thoughts straight
【理屈】lǐqū〈形〉 be in the wrong: 自知～ know that one is in the wrong
【理屈词穷】lǐqū-cíqióng〈成〉 find oneself tongue-tied when one realizes that justice is not on one's side
【理事】lǐshì A〈动〉 handle matters: 当家～ manage household affairs B〈名〉 member of an executive council or of a board of directors: 常务～ managing director
【理事国】lǐshìguó〈名〉 member of the UN Security Council: 联合国常任～ permanent member of the United Nations Security Council
【理事会】lǐshìhuì〈名〉executive council
【理事长】lǐshìzhǎng〈名〉 chairman of an executive council
【理数】lǐshù〈名〉 reason: 懂～ be reasonable
【理顺】lǐshùn〈动〉 straighten out: ～产权关系 straighten out property relations
【理所当然】lǐsuǒdāngrán〈成〉 naturally: 欠债还钱，～。 It is only right and proper to repay one's debts.
【理想】lǐxiǎng A〈名〉 ideal: 实现～ fulfil an ideal ‖ 树立崇高～ establish lofty ideals ‖ ～破灭 become disillusioned B〈形〉 ideal: ～的工作 ideal job ‖ 成绩很不～。 The outcome was definitely not ideal. ‖ 他考得不够～。 He didn't do well as in the exam as he had expected.
【理性】lǐxìng A〈形〉 rational: ～认识 rational knowledge B〈名〉 reason: 失去～ become irrational
【理性主义】lǐxìng zhǔyì〈名〉rationalism
【理学】lǐxué〈名〉 1 〈儒家哲学〉 rationalistic Confucian philosophical school [developed during the Song and Ming dynasties, known to the West as Neo-Confucianism] 2 〈自然科学〉 natural science: ～士 Bachelor of Science ‖ ～硕士 Master of Science ‖ ～博士 Doctor of Science
【理应】lǐyīng〈动〉 ought to be: 对他的建议～认真考虑。 His proposal deserves serious consideration.
【理由】lǐyóu〈名〉 reason: 陈述～ state one's reasons ‖ 找～ find an excuse ‖ ～充分 adequate reason ‖ 他们没有～这样做。 They have no excuse to do this.
【理喻】lǐyù〈动〉reason with: ►不可～
【理直气壮】lǐzhí-qìzhuàng〈成〉speak with confidence because justice is on one's side: ～地回答 reply with perfect assurance
【理智】lǐzhì A〈名〉 reason: 恢复～ regain one's senses ‖ 丧失～ be out of one's mind B〈形〉 rational: 当时我很～。 I was very rational then.
【理中】lǐzhōng〈动〉［中医］ regulate the functions of the stomach and spleen

锂（鋰）

lǐ〈名〉［化学］ lithium (Li): ～电池 lithium battery
【锂离子】lǐlízǐ〈名〉 lithium-ion: ～电池 Li-ion battery

鲤（鯉）

lǐ
【鲤鱼】lǐyú〈名〉carp

醴

lǐ〈名〉〈书〉 1 〈指酒〉 sweet wine: ～酒 sweet wine 2 〈指水〉 sweet spring water

鳢（鱧）

lǐ〈名〉 snakehead: ►乌～

lì

力

lì
A 〈名〉 1 〈力气〉 physical strength: 大～士 man of unusual strength ►～气, 体～ 2 〈能力〉 power: ►创造～, 脑～, 药～ 3 ［物理］ force: ►～学, 磁～, 重～
B 〈副〉 with all one's might: ～保经济增长 do all in one's power to promote economic growth ‖ ～邀 make efforts to invite ►～排众议, ～争
【力避】lìbì〈动〉〈书〉 try hard to avoid: ～事故发生 do all one can to avoid accidents
【力臂】lìbì〈名〉［物理］ arm of force
【力不从心】lìbùcóngxīn〈成〉 one's ability is not equal to one's ambition: 老王年事已高，工作有些～。 As Lao Wang is advanced in years, he is not able to work as he would have liked to do.
【力不能支】lìbùnéngzhī〈成〉 be unable to stand the strain any longer
【力不胜任】lìbùshèngrèn〈成〉 be beyond one's ability
【力持】lìchí〈动〉 uphold: ～正义 uphold justice
【力畜】lìchù〈名〉draught animal
【力促】lìcù〈动〉 try one's best to urge: ～和解 try one's best to effect a reconciliation
【力挫】lìcuò〈动〉 do everything one can to defeat: ～对手 do all one can to beat one's opponent

【力度】lìdù〈名〉1（指力量、强度等）strength: 加大改革～ strengthen reforms 2［音乐］dynamics 3（指功力、内涵等）intensity
【力疾从公】lìjí-cónggōng〈成〉attend to one's duties in spite of illness
【力荐】lìjiàn〈动〉highly recommend: ～他出任校长 highly recommend him to the post of headmaster
【力竭声嘶】lìjié-shēngsī = 声嘶力竭 shēngsī-lìjié
【力戒】lìjiè〈动〉do everything possible to avoid: ～骄傲 be sure to guard against conceit
【力矩】lìjǔ〈名〉［物理］moment of force: 俯仰～ pitching moment ‖ 合～ resultant moment
【力克】lìkè〈动〉try one's best to defeat: ～强手 do all one can to beat a formidable opponent
【力量】lìliàng〈名〉1（体力）physical strength: 人多～大。Many hands make light work. 2（能力）power: 动员社会～办学 mobilize social resources to run schools ‖ 团结就是～。Unity is strength. 3（效能）efficacy: 充分发挥科技～振兴农业 invigorate agriculture by applying science and technology ‖ 这种农药的～很大。This pesticide is very effective. 4（指人）force: ～对比 balance of forces
【力排众议】lìpái-zhòngyì〈成〉override all objections: 他～，坚持继续试验。Bravely brushing aside all objections, he insisted on continuing with the experiment.
【力捧】lìpěng〈动〉lionize: ～艺坛新人 rave about new talents on the art scene
【力拼】lìpīn〈动〉struggle with all one's might: ～对手，争取获胜 struggle with all one's might against one's opponent, and secure victory
【力气】lìqi〈名〉〈口〉physical strength: 我的～没他大。I'm no match for him in strength. ‖ 学什么都要舍得花～。Whatever one is studying, one should spare no effort.
【力气活】lìqihuó〈名〉manual labour
【力求】lìqiú〈动〉do one's best to do sth.: ～完美 aim at perfection ‖ 法官应～公正。A judge should strive for impartiality.
【力士】lìshì〈名〉man of great strength
【力所能及】lìsuǒnéngjí〈成〉to the best of one's ability: 提供～的帮助 offer all the help within one's power
【力透纸背】lìtòuzhǐbèi〈成〉1（指书法）powerful 2（指作品）penetrating
【力图】lìtú〈动〉try hard to do sth.: ～摆脱困境 do everything possible to get out of a difficult situation
【力挽狂澜】lìwǎn-kuánglán〈成〉〈喻〉do one's utmost to save a desperate situation
【力行】lìxíng〈动〉〈书〉practise in complete earnest: ▸身体～
【力学】lìxué〈名〉mechanics: 材料～ material mechanics ‖ 天体～ celestial mechanics ‖ 工程～ engineering mechanics ‖ 流体～ fluid mechanics
【力战】lìzhàn〈动〉fight with all one's might
【力争】lìzhēng〈动〉1（指争取）do all one can to do sth.: ～有所突破 strive for a breakthrough ‖ ～主动 do one's best to gain the initiative 2（指争辩）argue strongly: ▸据理～
【力争上游】lìzhēng-shàngyóu〈成〉aim high: 我们要～，保证今年生产上一个新台阶。We should aim high to ensure a marked advance in production.
【力证】lìzhèng〈名〉strong evidence
【力主】lìzhǔ〈动〉vigorously advocate: ～和谈 be a strong advocate of peace talks
【力作】lìzuò〈名〉masterpiece: 这是他近几年的一部～。The work is his tour de force of recent years.

历[1]（歷）lì

A〈动〉experience: ▸～险
B〈名〉experience: ▸～程，简～，阅～
C〈形〉previous: ▸～次，～代，～年
D〈副〉one by one: ～游名山大川 visit the famous mountains and great rivers one after another ▸～～在目，～数

历[2]（曆）lì〈名〉1（指历法）calendar: 回～ Islamic calendar ▸～法，阳～，阴～ 2（指书、表等）calendar: ▸挂～，日～

【历本】lìběn〈名〉〈方〉almanac
【历朝】lìcháo〈名〉1（指不同朝代）past dynasties: ～典章制度各不相同。Different dynasties have different historical institutions. 2（指同一朝代）successive reigns of a dynasty
【历陈】lìchén〈动〉〈书〉enumerate
【历程】lìchéng〈名〉course: 光辉～ glorious past ‖ 战斗～ course of struggle
【历次】lìcì〈形〉previous: ～谈判都很艰难。All previous negotiations were very difficult.
【历代】lìdài〈名〉1（指朝代）past dynasties: ～文人墨客 literary men of past dynasties 2（指世代）previous generations: 他家～务农。He comes from a long line of farmers.
【历法】lìfǎ〈名〉calendric system
【历届】lìjiè〈形〉previous: ～毕业生 graduates of all previous years ‖ ～全国人民代表大会 all the previous National People's Congresses
【历尽】lìjìn〈动〉go through: ～沧桑 experience the ups and downs of life ‖ ～千辛万苦 suffer countless hardships
【历经】lìjīng〈动〉experience: ～磨难 suffer all kinds of trials and tribulations
【历久】lìjiǔ〈动〉last for a long time: ～不衰 long-lasting
【历来】lìlái〈副〉always: ～如此 have always been the case
【历历】lìlì〈形〉clear: 往事～在心头。Past events are still clear in my memory.
【历历在目】lìlì-zàimù〈成〉come clearly into view: 往事～。Past events are still fresh in my mind.
【历练】lìliàn A〈动〉temper oneself: 让他到部队～～。Let him sign up for the army and have him see the world. B〈形〉experienced: ～老成 experienced and prudent
【历年】lìnián〈名〉past years: ～的积蓄花光了。Years of savings have all been spent.
【历任】lìrèn A〈动〉serve successively as: 他～县长、市长、省长等职。He has successively held the posts of county magistrate, mayor and provincial governor. B〈形〉successive: ～学院院长都是博士。The successive college presidents all have doctorates.
【历时】lìshí〈动〉take (a period of time): 双边会谈～两个小时。The bilateral conference lasted two hours.
【历史】lìshǐ〈名〉1（指发展过程）history: 歪曲～ distort history ‖ ～悠久 have a long history ‖ ～背景 historical background ‖ ～事件 historical event ‖ 从～的角度看 from a historical perspective 2（指事实）past event: ～清白 have a clean personal record ‖ 这件事早已成为～。That's past history already. 3（指记录）historical record: 查阅～资料 refer to historical materials 4（指学科）history
【历史博物馆】lìshǐ bówùguǎn〈名〉historical museum: 陕西～ Shaanxi History Museum
【历史潮流】lìshǐ cháoliú〈名〉historical trend: 顺应～ follow the historical trend
【历史观】lìshǐguān〈名〉view of history
【历史剧】lìshǐjù〈名〉historical drama
【历史人物】lìshǐ rénwù〈名〉historical figure
【历史唯物主义】lìshǐ wéiwùzhǔyì〈名〉historical materialism
【历史唯心主义】lìshǐ wéixīnzhǔyì〈名〉historical idealism
【历史学】lìshǐxué〈名〉history: ～家 historian
【历史遗产】lìshǐ yíchǎn〈名〉legacy of history
【历世】lìshì〈名〉= 历代 lìdài
【历书】lìshū〈名〉almanac
【历数】lìshǔ〈动〉enumerate: ～侵略者的种种暴行 enumerate the invaders' many different atrocities
【历险】lìxiǎn〈动〉have a narrow escape: ～记 adventures

厉（厲）lì〈形〉1（严肃）stern; （猛烈）violent: ▸雷～风行，凌～，色～内荏 2（严格）strict: ▸～行

【厉兵秣马】lìbīng-mòmǎ = 秣马厉兵 mòmǎ-lìbīng
【厉鬼】lìguǐ〈名〉evil spirit
【厉害】lìhai〈形〉1（凶猛）fierce: 老虎和狮子哪个～？Which is more fierce, the tiger or the lion? ‖ 他这张嘴真～。He's got a sharp tongue. 2（严厉）strict: 样子很～ wear a stern look ‖ 给他点～看看。Teach him a lesson. 3（剧烈）severe: 他头疼得～。He's got a terrible headache. ‖ 我的心跳得～。My heart is beating loudly.
【厉禁】lìjìn〈动〉enforce a strict ban on: ～赌博 strictly prohibit gambling
【厉色】lìsè〈名〉stern expression: ▸正言～
【厉声】lìshēng〈名〉stern voice: ～责问 ask reprovingly in a stern voice
【厉行】lìxíng〈动〉make great efforts to carry out: ～节约 practise strict frugality

立 lì

A〈动〉1（站）stand: 门口～着一根旗杆。Outside the gate stands a banner staff. ▸～定，鹤～鸡群，站～ 2（竖起）erect: ～碑 erect a monument ‖ 把伞～在门后 stand the umbrella behind the door ▸～竿见影，～锥之地 3（建立）establish: ▸～案，～业，私～ 4（订立）formulate: ～遗嘱 make a will ‖ ～章程 draw up rules and regulations ‖ 这是谁～的规矩？Whose rule is this? 5（存在）exist: ▸独～，势不两～ 6〈旧〉（继位）ascend the throne: ～君 enthrone a monarch 7（确立）appoint: ～太子 designate a crown prince
B〈形〉upright: ▸～柜
C〈副〉immediately: ～等答复 wait for a prompt reply ‖ ～见功效 feel the effect immediately ▸～即，～马，当机～断
【立案】lì'àn〈动〉1（备案登记）register: 申请～ apply for registration 2［法律］place a case on file for investigation and prosecution: ～调查 place on file for investigation

【立场】lìchǎng〈名〉 standpoint: 表明～ make clear one's position ‖ 坚持～ maintain one's standpoint ‖ 丧失～ lose one's position ‖ ～坚定 take a firm stand ‖ 政治～ political stand

【立春】lìchūn **A**〈动〉 [of spring] begin: 今天～。 Spring begins today. **B** Lìchūn〈名〉 Beginning of Spring [beginning of the first of the 24 solar terms]

【立此存照】lìcǐ-cúnzhào〈成〉 an agreement is hereby concluded and filed for future reference

【立等可取】lìděngkěqǔ〈惯〉 ready while you wait

【立地】lìdì **A**〈动〉 stand: ▶顶天～ **B**〈副〉 immediately

【立地成佛】lìdì-chéngfó〈成〉 become a Buddha as soon as one repents

【立定】lìdìng〈动〉 **1**（指口令） halt: ～! Halt! **2**（站稳） stand firm: ～脚跟 gain a foothold **3**（确定） firmly determine: ～目标 firmly determine one's objective

【立冬】lìdōng **A**〈动〉 [of winter] begin: 立了冬，天气就开始变冷了。 Once winter sets in, it will get colder and colder. **B** Lìdōng〈名〉 Beginning of Winter [beginning of the 19th of the 24 solar terms]

【立法】lìfǎ〈动〉 legislate: ～机关 legislature ‖ 行政～ administrative legislation ‖ ～委员会 legislation council

【立法权】lìfǎquán〈名〉 legislative power

【立方】lìfāng〈名〉 **1**［数学］ cube: 3的～是27。 The cube of 3 is 27. **2**（立方米） cubic metre: 十～土 ten cubic metres of earth

【立方根】lìfānggēn〈名〉［数学］cube root

【立方米】lìfāngmǐ〈名〉 cubic metre

【立方体】lìfāngtǐ〈名〉 cube

【立竿见影】lìgān-jiànyǐng〈成〉〈喻〉 produce an immediate effect

【立功】lìgōng〈动〉 render meritorious service: 立一等功 win a first class merit citation ‖ ～受奖 be awarded for the merits one has performed

【立功赎罪】lìgōng-shúzuì〈成〉 do good deeds to atone for one's crimes

【立柜】lìguì〈名〉 wardrobe

【立国】lìguó〈动〉 establish a nation: ～之本 the basis for establishing a nation

【立候】lìhòu〈动〉 **1**（指站着） stand waiting: ～多时 have stood waiting for a long time **2**（强调迅速） wait for sth. to be done immediately: ～回音 wait for an immediate reply

【立户】lìhù〈动〉 **1**（指户口） register for permanent residence **2**（指账户） open an account: 在银行～ open an account at a bank

【立即】lìjí〈副〉 immediately: 一有结果我们～通知你。 We shall inform you of the results at once.

【立交】lìjiāo〈简称〉= 立体交叉

【立交桥】lìjiāoqiáo〈名〉 **1**（为行人） footbridge; pedestrian overpass〈美〉 **2**（为行车） flyover〈英〉; overpass〈美〉

【立脚】lìjiǎo〈动〉 have a foothold: 无处～ cannot gain a foothold ‖ 在社会上～ establish oneself in society

【立脚点】lìjiǎodiǎn〈名〉 standpoint: 为人民服务是我们工作的～。 Serving the people is the starting point of our work.

【立决】lìjué〈动〉〈书〉 carry out a summary execution

【立刻】lìkè〈副〉 at once: 我～就去。 I'll go right away. ‖ 他～做了回答。 He came up with a prompt answer.

【立领】lìlǐng〈名〉 stand-up collar: ～衬衫 shirt with a stand-up collar

【立论】lìlùn〈动〉 set forth one's argument: ～新颖 put forward an original view

【立马】lìmǎ〈副〉〈方〉 immediately: 我～就来。 I'll be there in a second.

【立眉瞪眼】lìméi-dèngyǎn〈成〉 get angry

【立面图】lìmiàntú〈名〉［建筑］ elevation drawing

【立秋】lìqiū **A**〈动〉 [of autumn] begin **B** Lìqiū〈名〉 Beginning of Autumn [beginning of the 13th of the 24 solar terms]

【立射】lìshè〈动〉［军事］ fire from a standing position

【立身处世】lìshēn-chǔshì〈成〉 way to get on in the world

【立时】lìshí〈副〉 at once: ～见效 see immediate effects

【立时三刻】lìshí-sānkè〈成〉 right away

【立式】lìshì〈形〉 vertical: ～空调 vertical chamber air-conditioner

【立誓】lìshì〈动〉 take an oath: 他～戒烟。 He pledged that he would give up smoking.

【立说】lìshuō〈动〉 establish a theory: 著书～ write books to expound a theory

【立嗣】lìsì〈动〉〈书〉 adopt an heir

【立陶宛】Lìtáowǎn〈名〉 Lithuania: ～共和国 Republic of Lithuania ‖ ～人 Lithuanian ‖ ～语 Lithuanian

【立体】lìtǐ **A**〈形〉 **1**（指图形） three-dimensional **2**（多层面） multi-level: ▶～交叉, ～战争 **3**（指效果） stereoscopic: ▶～电影 **B**〈名〉［数学］ solid: 六个面的～ solid with six faces

【立体电影】lìtǐ diànyǐng〈名〉 three-dimensional film , 3-D film

【立体几何】lìtǐ jǐhé〈名〉 solid geometry

【立体交叉】lìtǐ jiāochā〈名〉 grade separation

【立体声】lìtǐshēng〈名〉 stereo

【立体战争】lìtǐ zhànzhēng〈名〉 three-dimensional warfare

【立夏】lìxià **A**〈动〉 [of summer] begin **B** Lìxià〈名〉 Beginning of Summer [beginning of the 7th of the 24 solar terms]

【立宪】lìxiàn〈动〉 formulate a constitution: 君主～ constitutional monarchy

【立项】lìxiàng〈动〉 have a project registered and authorized: ～同意 agree to set up the proposed project

【立像】lìxiàng〈名〉 standing statue

【立言】lìyán〈动〉 expound one's theory in writing

【立业】lìyè〈动〉 **1**（指事业） build a career: 建功～ perform meritorious service and build a career **2**（指家业） purchase an estate: 成家～ get married and start a career

【立意】lìyì〈动〉 **1**（指决定） be determined (to do sth.): 他～留在农村从事教育工作。 He was resolved to stay in the countryside and to pursue a career in teaching. **2**（指创意） determine an approach: 一幅～新颖的画 a painting of original conception

【立于不败之地】lìyú bù bài zhī dì〈成〉 be invincible

【立约】lìyuē〈动〉 sign a contract: 签字～ sign a treaty ‖ ～人 contractor

【立账】lìzhàng〈动〉 open an account

【立正】lìzhèng〈动〉 stand to attention: ～! Attention!

【立志】lìzhì〈动〉 set one's mind on: 她～做一名教师。 She has set her mind on becoming a teacher.

【立轴】lìzhóu〈名〉 wall scroll

【立柱】lìzhù〈名〉［建筑］ upright column

【立传】lìzhuàn〈动〉 write a biography: ▶树碑～

【立锥之地】lìzhuīzhīdì〈成〉 tiny bit of land: 天下之大，而我却无～。 There was no place for me in the whole wide world.

【立字】lìzì〈动〉〈旧〉 write and sign an agreement: ～为据 sign an agreement as proof

【立足】lìzú〈动〉 **1**（指生存） gain a foothold: 在社会上～ gain a foothold in society ‖ 在公司没有他的～之地。 There is no place for him to establish himself at the company. **2**（指立场） base oneself upon: ～本职工作 give priority to one's own work ‖ ～现实，展望未来 be based on present realities whilst looking to the future

【立足点】lìzúdiǎn = 立脚点 lìjiǎodiǎn

吏

吏 lì〈名〉〈旧〉 **1**（官员） government official: ▶官～ **2**（差役） petty official

【吏部】Lìbù〈名〉［历史］ Board of Civil Office

【吏治】lìzhì〈名〉〈旧〉 administration of local officials

丽¹（麗）

丽¹（麗） lì〈形〉 beautiful: ▶风和日～, 美～

丽²（麗）

丽²（麗） lì〈动〉〈书〉 attach oneself to: ▶附～

▶lí

【丽人】lìrén〈名〉〈书〉 beautiful woman

【丽日】lìrì〈名〉〈书〉 bright sun: ～蓝天 bright sun and blue sky

【丽姝】lìshū〈名〉〈书〉 beauty

【丽质】lìzhì〈名〉 beauty (of a woman): 天生～ be born beautiful

励（勵）

励（勵） lì〈动〉 encourage: ▶鼓～, 奖～

【励精图治】lìjīng-túzhì〈成〉 strive for the prosperity of one's country

【励志】lìzhì〈动〉〈书〉 be determined to fulfil one's aspirations: ～报国 be determined to serve one's country

呖（嚦）

呖（嚦） lì

【呖呖】lìlì〈拟〉〈书〉 warble: 莺声～。 The orioles are warbling.

利

利 lì

A〈形〉 **1**（锋利） sharp: ～剑 sharp sword ‖ ～爪 sharp claw ▶～刃, 锋～ **2**（顺利） favourable: ▶吉～, 顺～

B〈名〉 **1**（利益） advantage: ▶～益, 名～, 兴～除弊 **2**（利润） profit: 薄～多销 small profits and quick returns ▶～润, 一本万～ **3**（利息） interest: ▶～率, ～息

C〈动〉 benefit: ～国～民 benefit the people and the country as a whole

【利比里亚】Lìbǐlǐyà〈名〉 Liberia: ～共和国 Republic of Liberia ‖ ～人 Liberian

【利比亚】Lìbǐyà〈名〉 Libya: ～人 Libyan

【利弊】lìbì〈名〉 advantages and disadvantages: 权衡～ weigh up the pros and cons ‖ 各有～ have both advantages and disadvantages ‖ 利大于弊。 The advantages outweigh the disadvantages.

【利得】lìdé〈动〉［经济］ gain: 资本～ capital gain

【利得税】lìdéshuì〈名〉capital gains tax: 开征资本～ introduction of a capital gains tax

【利钝】lìdùn〈名〉 **1**（指锋利程度） sharpness or bluntness: 刀剑有～。 There are

sharp as well as blunt weapons. 2（指顺利程度） smoothness or roughness: 成败～ success or failure
【利多】lìduō〈名〉 favourable information for the market
【利福平】lìfúpíng〈名〉［药学］ Rifampin (RFP)
【利改税】lìgǎishuì〈名〉 substitution of tax payment for profit
【利滚利】lìgǔnlì〈名〉 compound interest
【利害】lì-hài〈名〉 advantages and disadvantages: ～冲突 conflict of interests ‖ 企业盈亏与职工有直接的～关系。The gains and losses of an enterprise directly affect the interests of its employees.
【利害攸关】lìhài-yōuguān〈成〉 share a stake in
【利害】lìhai = 厉害 lìhai
【利好】lìhǎo〈名〉［金融］favourable news: ～消息 favourable news
【利己】lìjǐ〈动〉 be selfish: 毫不～，专门利人 be devoted to the interests of others without any concern for oneself ▸损人～
【利己主义】lìjǐ zhǔyì〈名〉 egoism: ～者 egoist
【利空】lìkōng〈名〉［金融］ unfavourable information for the market
【利口】lìkǒu〈名〉 glib tongue
【利令智昏】lìlìngzhìhūn〈成〉 be blinded by material gains
【利禄】lìlù〈名〉〈书〉 rank and wealth: 贪图～ hanker after money and position
【利率】lìlǜ〈名〉［经济］ interest rate: 存款～ interest rate on deposits ‖ 调整～ adjust interest rates
【利落】lìluo〈形〉 1（敏捷） nimble: 动作～ be quick in one's movements ‖ 手脚～ be dexterous 2（整齐） orderly: 把房间收拾～ tidy up a room ‖ 他做每件事都干净～。He approaches everything in an efficient and orderly manner. 3（完结） done: 活干～了吗？ Have you finished your work? ‖ 她的病好～了。 She has completely recovered from the illness.
【利马】Lìmǎ〈名〉 Lima
【利尿剂】lìniàojì〈名〉［药学］ diuretic
【利器】lìqì〈名〉 1（指兵器） sharp weapon: 精兵～ picked troops and sophisticated weapons 2（指工具） efficient instrument: 良工～ skilled workers and good tools
【利钱】lìqian〈名〉 interest: 付～ pay interest
【利权】lìquán〈名〉〈书〉 economic rights: ～外溢 lose economic rights to foreigners
【利刃】lìrèn〈名〉 1（指刀刃） sharp edge 2（指刀） sharp knife 3（指剑） sharp sword
【利润】lìrùn〈名〉 profit: 创造～ create profits ‖ 上缴～ turn over profits to higher authorities ‖ 高额～ high returns
【利市】lìshì〈形〉〈方〉 lucky: 讨个～ for good luck
【利税】lìshuì〈名〉 profit and tax: 上缴～ turn over profits and taxes to the state
【利索】lìsuo = 利落 lìluo
【利他主义】lìtā zhǔyì〈名〉 altruism
【利息】lìxī〈名〉 interest: 付贷款～ pay interest on a loan ‖ 存款～ interest on a deposit
【利息税】lìxīshuì〈名〉 interest tax
【利雅得】Lìyǎdé〈名〉 Riyadh
【利益】lìyì〈名〉 interest: 为人民谋～ work for the benefit of the people ‖ 个人～服从国家～ subordinate private interest to national interest ‖ 既得～ vested interest
【利用】lìyòng〈动〉 1（使用） utilize: ～外资 utilize foreign capital ‖ 废物～ make use of waste material 2（为己所用） exploit: ～职权 take advantage of one's position and power ‖ 受人～ be taken advantage of
【利诱】lìyòu〈动〉 lure by promise of gain: 经不起～ cannot resist the temptation of personal gain ▸威逼～
【利于】lìyú〈动〉 be beneficial to: 忠言逆耳～行。 Candid advice may grate on the ear but is beneficial to conduct.
【利欲熏心】lìyù-xūnxīn〈成〉 be blinded by greed
【利嘴】lìzuǐ〈名〉 glib tongue

沥（瀝）lì
A〈动〉 drip: ▸呕心～血
B〈名〉 drop: ▸余～
【沥沥】lìlì〈拟〉〈书〉 1（指风） whistle: 风声～。 The wind was rustling. 2（指流水） babble: 溪水～而下。 The stream was babbling down.
【沥青】lìqīng〈名〉 asphalt: ～路面 bituminous pavement
【沥青矿】lìqīngkuàng〈名〉 asphaltite
【沥青纸】lìqīngzhǐ〈名〉 asphalt paper
【沥水】lìshuǐ〈名〉 waterlogging caused by excessive rainfall

枥（櫪）lì
〈名〉〈古〉 manger: ▸老骥伏～

例 lì
A〈名〉 1（例子） example: 举～ give an example 2（成规） convention: 先～ precedent ▸成～, 破～, 史无前～ 3（事例） case: 病～ medical case 4（规则） rule: ▸凡～, 体～, 条～
B〈形〉 regular: ▸～会, ～假
【例规】lìguī〈名〉 1（惯例） usual practice 2（条例、规章） rules and regulations
【例会】lìhuì〈名〉 regular meeting
【例假】lìjià〈名〉 1（指假期） official holiday 2 ▸p. 772〈婉〉［生理］(menstrual) period: 每月初来～ menstruate at the beginning of each month
【例禁】lìjìn〈名〉〈书〉decreed prohibitions
【例句】lìjù〈名〉 illustrative sentence: 给出～ give a sentence as an example ‖ 用～加以说明 illustrate with sample sentences
【例如】lìrú〈动〉 take for example: 绘画技法有多种，～油画、水彩画、炭笔画等。 There are many painting techniques such as oil painting, watercolour, charcoal, etc.
【例题】lìtí〈名〉 example
【例外】lìwài A〈动〉 be an exception: 大家都得遵守规定，谁也不能～。 Everyone must abide by the regulations; there can be no exceptions. B〈名〉 exception: 凡事都有～。 There is an exception to everything.
【例行】lìxíng〈动〉 do as a routine: ～检查 routine inspection ‖ ～手续 business routine
【例行公事】lìxíng-gōngshì〈成〉 1（指常规事务） do one's routine (business): 我们只是～。 We are just doing our job. 2（指徒有形式） do as a mere formality: 面试只不过是～而已。 The interview was a mere formality.
【例言】lìyán〈名〉 introductory remarks
【例证】lìzhèng〈名〉 illustration: 典型～ case in point ‖ 该词典～丰富。 This dictionary is full of illustrative examples.
【例子】lìzi〈名〉〈口〉 example: 补充几个～ give some more examples ‖ 举个～ give an example

疠（癘）lì
〈名〉〈书〉 1（瘟疫） plague 2（恶疮） malignant sore: 疥～ scabies
【疠疫】lìyì〈名〉〈书〉 pestilence

戾 lì
〈书〉
A〈形〉 perverse: ▸暴～, 乖～
B〈名〉 offence: ▸罪～

隶（隸）lì
A〈名〉 1〈旧〉（被奴役者） person in servitude: 仆～ servant ▸奴～ 2〈旧〉（衙役） runner: ▸～卒, 皂～ 3 = 隶书 lìshū
B〈动〉 be subordinate to: ▸～属
【隶书】lìshū〈名〉［书法］ official script
【隶属】lìshǔ〈动〉 be affiliated to: ～关系 affiliation ‖ 这支部队～市警备区。 This unit is under the command of the municipal garrison.
【隶字】lìzì = 隶书 lìshū
【隶卒】lìzú〈名〉〈旧〉 *yamen* runner

荔 lì
【荔枝】lìzhī〈名〉 lychee

栎（櫟）lì
〈名〉 oak: ▸麻～

郦（酈）Lì
〈名〉 Li [surname]

轹（轢）lì
〈动〉〈书〉 1（碾轧） run over 2（欺压） ride roughshod over: 以富～贫 use one's wealth to oppress the poor

俪（儷）lì
A〈形〉 parallel: ▸～句, 骈～
B〈名〉 married couple: ▸～影, 伉～
【俪辞】lìcí〈名〉〈书〉 form of literary writing marked by antitheses
【俪句】lìjù〈名〉〈书〉 parallel sentences
【俪影】lìyǐng〈名〉〈书〉 photograph of a couple

俐 lì
▸伶俐 línglì

疬（癧）lì
▸瘰疬 luǒlì

莉 lì
▸茉莉 mòlì

莅（蒞）lì
〈动〉〈书〉 be present: ～场 be present on the occasion
【莅会】lìhuì〈动〉〈书〉 attend a meeting: ～致辞 come and address a conference
【莅临】lìlín〈动〉〈书〉 be present in person: 敬请～指导。 Your presence and instructions are appreciated.
【莅任】lìrèn〈动〉〈书〉 take office

鬲 lì
〈名〉〈古〉 cooking tripod with hollow legs: 青铜～ bronze cooking tripod ‖ 陶～ pottery cooking tripod

栗[1] lì
〈名〉 chestnut: ▸～子, 板～

栗[2]（慄）lì
〈动〉 shiver with fear or cold: ▸不寒而～, 战～
【栗暴】lìbào〈名〉 knock on the head with the knuckles: 打～ rap sb. on the head with

one's knuckles
【栗钙土】lìgàitǔ〈名〉 chestnut soil
【栗然】lìrán〈形〉〈书〉 trembling: 令人～ terrifying
【栗色】lìsè〈名〉 maroon: ～头发 chestnut-coloured hair
【栗子】lìzi〈名〉 chestnut: 糖炒～ sugar-roasted chestnuts
【栗子树】lìzishù〈名〉 chestnut tree

砺（礪） lì〈书〉
A〈名〉 whetstone: ▸～石
B〈动〉 sharpen: ～剑 sharpen a sword
【砺石】lìshí〈名〉〈书〉 1（磨刀石）whetstone 2（粗石） rough stone

砾（礫） lì〈名〉gravel: ▸沙～, 瓦～
【砾石】lìshí〈名〉 gravel: ～混凝土 gravel concrete

猁 lì ▸猞猁 shēlì

莨 lì
【莨草】lìcǎo〈名〉 Chinese pennisetum

蛎（蠣） lì = 牡蛎 mǔlì

唳 lì〈动〉〈书〉 [of a crane or wild goose] cry: ▸风声鹤～

笠 lì〈名〉 large bamboo hat with a conical crown and broad brim: ▸斗～

粝（糲） lì〈名〉〈书〉 coarse rice
【粝米】lìmǐ〈名〉〈书〉 coarse rice

粒 lì
A〈名〉 grain: 豆～儿 beans ‖ 谷～儿 grains of millet ‖ 盐～儿 grains of salt ▸颗～, 米～
B〈量〉 [for grain-like things]: 两～珍珠 two pearls ‖ 三～子弹 three bullets ‖ 一～沙子 a grain of sand
【粒度】lìdù〈名〉 grain size
【粒雪】lìxuě〈名〉［水文］ granular snow
【粒状】lìzhuàng〈形〉 granular
【粒子】lìzǐ〈名〉［物理］ particle: 高能～ high energy particle
【粒子加速器】lìzǐ jiāsùqì〈名〉［物理］ particle accelerator
【粒子束】lìzǐshù〈名〉［物理］ particle beam: ～武器 particle beam weapon
【粒子物理学】lìzǐ wùlǐxué〈名〉 particle physics
【粒子】lìzi〈名〉 grain: 豆～ beans ‖ 盐～ grains of salt

雳 lì ▸霹雳 pīlì

跞 lì〈动〉〈书〉 leap: 跨～古今 transcend time and space ‖ 骐骥一～, 不能千里。 A strong fast horse cannot cover a thousand *li* in one leap.

詈 lì〈动〉〈书〉 scold: ▸～辞
【詈辞】lìcí〈名〉〈书〉 curse
【詈骂】lìmà〈动〉〈书〉 scold: 互相～ hurl insults at each other

傈 lì
【傈僳族】Lìsùzú〈名〉 Lisu ethnic group

溧 lì〈形〉〈书〉 cold
【溧冽】lìliè〈形〉〈书〉 bitterly cold

痢 lì〈名〉 dysentery
【痢疾】lìji〈名〉dysentery: 阿米巴～ amoebic dysentery

li

里（裏、裡） li
A〈名〉 [used after nouns and some monosyllabic adjectives to indicate place, time, limit, direction, etc.]: 房间～ in a room ‖ 假期～ during the holidays ‖ 心～有数 know what one wants ‖ 脑子～一片空白 one's mind is completely blank
B〈后缀〉 [used after some demonstrative pronouns indicating place]: 哪～ where ‖ 那～ there ‖ 这～ here
▸lǐ

哩 li〈助〉〈方〉 1（呢） [equivalent to 呢, used only in non-interrogative sentence]: 他还在吃早饭～。 He is still having breakfast. 2（啦） [equivalent to 啦, used to list things]
▸lī, lǐ

liǎ

俩（倆） liǎ ▸p. 691〈数〉〈口〉
1（两个） [a fusion of 两 and 个] two: 姐妹～ the two sisters ‖ 兄弟～ the two brothers ‖ 买～冰棍 buy two ice-lollies 2（几个）a few: 挣～辛苦钱 make some honest money ‖ 一共就这么～人儿,恐怕不够。 I'm afraid it's not enough to have so few people.
▸liǎng

lián

奁（奩） lián〈名〉 toilet kit used by women in ancient China: ▸妆～

连（連） lián
A〈动〉 connect: 根～着根 roots joining roots ‖ 两村由一条小路相～。 A path connects the two villages. ▸～接, 藕断丝～, 心～心
B〈副〉 one after another: ～进三球 score three goals in a row ‖ 六～胜 have six straight wins ‖ 好运～～ have a streak of good luck ▸～任
C〈介〉 1（包括） including: ～你一共三个人。 There are three people, including you. ▸～本带利 2（甚至） [used correlatively with 也 or 都] even: 他～自己的名字都不会写。 He can't even write his own name. ‖ 她激动得～话都说不出来了。 She was too excited to say a word.
D〈名〉［军事］ company: ▸～队, ～长
【连本带利】liánběn-dàilì〈成〉 both principal and interest
【连笔】liánbǐ〈动〉 write without lifting the pen from the paper
【连鬓胡子】liánbìn húzi〈名〉 sideburns
【连播】liánbō〈动〉 serialize: 小说～ serialized novel
【连词】liáncí ▸p. 448〈名〉［语法］ conjunction
【连带】liándài〈动〉 1（相关） be related to: 人的观念与其所处的文化环境是有～关系的。 One's ideology has a lot to do with the culture one inhabits. 2（牵连）involve: 这事都怪我，不要～别人。 This is all my fault. Don't blame anybody else. 3（顺便） do sth. in passing: 修房顶时，～把门窗也修一下。 When you repair the roof of the house, you may repair the door and the windows as well.
【连带责任】liándài zérèn〈名〉 joint liability
【连裆裤】liándāngkù〈名〉 child's pants without a slit in the seat
【连队】liánduì〈名〉［军事］ company: 下～锻炼 temper oneself in a company
【连发】liánfā〈动〉［军事］ make a running fire
【连番】liánfān〈副〉 repeatedly
【连根拔】liángēnbá〈动〉 1〈本〉 eradicate 2〈喻〉（指铲除） root out
【连亘】liángèn〈动〉〈书〉 [of mountain ranges] extend: 群山～ range upon range of mountains
【连贯】liánguàn〈动〉 1（连接贯通） link up: 这条铁路～中国西北五省区的交通。 This railway links up the transportation systems of the five provinces and autonomous regions of north-west China. 2（连续） be coherent: 她讲话不～。 She spoke incoherently.
【连贯性】liánguànxìng〈名〉 coherence: 缺乏～ lack coherence
【连滚带爬】liángǔn-dàipá〈成〉 roll and crawl: 我～地到达了泰山山顶。 I crawled my way to the top of Mount Tai.
【连锅端】liánguōduān〈惯〉〈喻〉 wipe out completely: 警方把那个贩毒窝点给～了。 The police busted the drug traffickers' den.
【连环】liánhuán〈名〉 chain of rings: ～链 hoop-linked chain
【连环画】liánhuánhuà〈名〉 illustrated story/storybook
【连环计】liánhuánjì〈名〉 set of interlocking plots: 设/施～ devise/employ a series of stratagems
【连环杀手】liánhuán shāshǒu〈名〉 serial killer
【连环套】liánhuántào〈名〉 interlocking traps
【连击】liánjī〈名〉［体育］（指乒乓球） double hit;（指排球） double contact
【连枷】liánjiā〈名〉［农业］ flail
【连脚裤】liánjiǎokù〈名〉 trousers with bootees attached
【连接】liánjiē〈动〉 join: 这两部分～得不好。 The two parts do not connect properly.
【连接线】liánjiēxiàn〈名〉［音乐］ tie
【连结】liánjié = 联结 liánjié
【连襟】liánjīn〈名〉 brothers-in-law: 他们是～。 Their wives are sisters.
【连裤袜】liánkùwà〈名〉 tights〈英〉; pantyhose〈美〉
【连累】liánlěi〈动〉 implicate: 她因贪污～了全家人。 Her embezzlement brought her whole family into trouble.
【连理】liánlǐ〈书〉 A〈动〉 [branches of trees/plants] interlock B〈名〉〈喻〉 loving couple: 喜结～ become husband and wife
【连理枝】liánlǐzhī〈名〉〈喻〉loving couple: 在天愿作比翼鸟，在地愿为～。 May we be together until death do us part.
【连连】liánlián〈副〉 over and over again: ～称好 keep praising ‖ ～得手 make it again and again
【连忙】liánmáng〈副〉 promptly: ～改口 immediately correct oneself ‖ 见一位老太

l

太上车，他～让座。Seeing an old lady get on the bus, he promptly gave up his seat.

【连绵】liánmián〈形〉 continuous: 阴雨～ unbroken spell of wet weather ‖ ～起伏的群山 rolling hills

【连绵不绝】liánmián-bùjué〈成〉 incessant: ～的思绪 unbroken train of thought

【连年】liánnián〈名〉 several years running: ～丰收 have bumper harvests for many consecutive years ‖ 工厂～亏损。The factory has been in the red for several years in a row.

【连皮】liánpí〈名〉 gross (weight)

【连篇】liánpiān〈动〉 1（一篇接一篇）one article follows another 2（满篇都是）appear throughout a piece of writing: 空话～ pages and pages of empty verbiage ‖ 这篇文章错字～。The article is full of wrong characters.

【连篇累牍】liánpiān-lěidú〈成〉 at great length: ～的报道 lengthy coverage

【连谱号】liánpǔhào〈名〉［音乐］ brace

【连翘】liánqiào〈名〉［中药］ forsythia

【连任】liánrèn〈动〉 hold office for two or more consecutive terms: ～总统 be re-elected president ‖ 竞选～ run for re-election

【连日】liánrì〈名〉 several days running: ～奔波，疲惫不堪 be exhausted after rushing about for several days in a row ‖ ～感冒 be ill with a cold for days on end

【连射】liánshè〈动〉［军事］ spray bullets

【连声】liánshēng〈副〉 repeatedly: ～称赞 keep praising ‖ ～叫好 shout 'Bravo!' again and again

【连锁】liánsuǒ〈形〉 linked together

【连锁店】liánsuǒdiàn〈名〉 chain store

【连锁反应】liánsuǒ fǎnyìng〈名〉 chain reaction: 引起～ have a ripple effect on

【连台】liántái〈动〉 give performance after performance: 好戏～。One good performance came after another.

【连台本戏】liántái běnxì〈名〉［戏曲］ drama serial

【连体婴儿】liántǐyīng'ér〈名〉［医学］ conjoined twins

【连天】liántiān〈动〉 1（好几天）be for days in a row: ～作战 battle for days and nights on end 2（不间断）be incessant: 叫苦～ make endless complaints ‖ 炮声～ gunshots keeping rumbling 3（与天空相接）reach the sky: 芳草碧～。Sweet green grass extends to the horizon in the distance.

【连通】liántōng〈动〉 connect: 大洋和大海相～。Oceans and seas are connected.

【连同】liántóng〈连〉 together with: 将样品～报价单一并送去。Send the samples along with the quotation list.

【连谓式】liánwèishì〈名〉［语言］ sentence with consecutive predicates

【连写】liánxiě〈动〉 1（无空格）[in Chinese phonetic transcription] write the two or more syllables of a word together [eg Zhōnghuá 中华, kāfēiguǎn 咖啡馆] 2 = 连笔 liánbǐ

【连心】liánxīn〈动〉 be closely related: ～锁 lovers' lock

【连续】liánxù〈动〉 go on uninterruptedly: ～工作几小时 work several hours at a stretch ‖ ～报道 serial coverage ‖ ～下了三天雪。It snowed for three days straight.

【连续剧】liánxùjù〈名〉 serial: 电视～ TV serial

【连续性】liánxùxìng〈名〉 continuance: 保持政策的～ maintain the continuity of a policy

【连夜】liányè〈副〉 1（当天夜里）through the night: ～出发赴灾区 set out that very night to attend to the disaster area 2（接连几夜）for several nights running: 连天～地干 work day and night

【连衣裤】liányīkù〈名〉 catsuit

【连衣裙】liányīqún〈名〉 dress

【连阴天】liányīntiān〈名〉 spell of cloudy weather

【连阴雨】liányīnyǔ〈名〉 spell of rainy days

【连用】liányòng〈动〉 1（指一起）use together: 这两个词不能～。The two words cannot be used together. 2（指连续）use consecutively: 这把牙刷～几次就掉毛了。After it had been used a few times bristles started to come off the toothbrush.

【连载】liánzǎi〈动〉 publish in instalments: 小说～ serialization of a novel

【连长】liánzhǎng〈名〉 company commander

【连指手套】liánzhǐ shǒutào〈名〉 mitten

【连中三元】liánzhòng-sānyuán〈成〉 1〈旧〉（指科举考试）rank first in the imperial civil examinations at the provincial capital, the national capital and the palace in succession 2（指考试）succeed in three examinations 3（指三次比赛）have three straight wins;（指单次比赛）score a hat-trick

【连轴转】liánzhóuzhuàn〈惯〉〈喻〉 work round the clock

【连珠】liánzhū〈名〉 1〈本〉 string of pearls 2〈喻〉（指声音、话语）rapid succession: 妙语～ witticism upon witticism

【连珠炮】liánzhūpào〈名〉 shooting in rapid succession: ～似地说话 barrage with talk ‖ 说话像～ talk like one is firing a machine gun

【连属】liánzhǔ〈动〉〈书〉 join, link

【连缀】liánzhuì A〈动〉 join together: 把碎布～成被面 piece together small pieces of cloth to make a quilt cover B〈名〉［语言］ cluster: 辅音～ consonant cluster

【连字符】liánzìfú = 连字号 liánzìhào

【连字号】liánzìhào〈名〉 hyphen (-)

【连作】liánzuò〈动〉［农业］ continuous cropping on the same plot of land

【连坐】liánzuò〈动〉〈旧〉 [of kinsfolk, neighbours, etc.] be punished together with the criminal

怜（憐） lián〈动〉 1（怜悯）pity: ▸～悯, 同病相～, 摇尾乞～ 2（爱）love tenderly: ▸～香惜玉, 爱～

【怜爱】lián'ài〈动〉 love tenderly

【怜悯】liánmǐn〈动〉 pity: 不需要别人的～ do not need to be taken pity on ‖ 我帮助他是出于～。I helped him out of pity.

【怜贫惜老】liánpín-xīlǎo〈成〉 feel compassion for the aged and the poor

连词:“和、跟、同、与、及、以及”

■“和”、“跟”、“同”、“与”用作介词时可表示不同的意义，翻译成英语时应根据语境选择适当的词，不能千篇一律地翻译成英语介词 with，很多情况下更要用英语短语来翻译。

■“和”、“跟”、“同”、“与”用作连词时一般翻译成 and。

■“及”或“以及”是连词，一般翻译成 and。

■“和”可用于口语又可用于书面语，“跟”一般用于口语，“同”、“与”、“及”、“以及”主要用于书面语。英语的 with 和 and 既可用于口语，又可用于书面语。

“和”、“跟”、“同”、“与”用作介词

■ 表示对象与关联时:

她和那件事有牵连
= She was involved in that business

他跟我去了杭州
= He went to Hangzhou with me

我想跟你聊聊
= I want to have a chat with you

我跟她相处不好
= I can't get on well with her

我想同你一起去看电影
= I would like to go to the cinema with you

经理与诈骗有关
= The manager is connected with the fraud

战士们在与洪水斗争
= Soldiers are battling against the flood

我与他没有共同语言
= I have nothing in common with him

他跟我借了一些钱
= He borrowed some money from me

■ 表示比较的对象时:

和上学期相比，他进步了很多
= He has made a lot of progress compared with last term

这支笔同你的完全一样
= This pen is exactly the same as yours

我的意见与他的不同
= My opinions are different from his

“和”、“跟”、“同”、“与”用作连词

我去过北京、上海和广州
= I have been to Beijing, Shanghai and Guangzhou

我跟丈夫是北方人
= My husband and I are northerners

我同邻居共用一个花园
= My neighbours and I use the same garden 或 I share a garden with my neighbours

《战争与和平》
= *War and Peace*

“及”、“以及”

阳光、空气及水是生物赖以生存的基本条件
= Sunlight, air and water are essentials for life

这家杂货店卖新鲜水果、蔬菜以及其他食品
= This grocery sells fresh fruit, vegetables and other foods

【怜惜】liánxī〈动〉 take pity on: 决不能～恶人。 You should never pity a villain.
【怜香惜玉】liánxiāng-xīyù〈成〉 show compassion and care for women
【怜恤】liánxù〈动〉〈书〉 be sympathetic towards: ～孤寡 have compassion for orphans and widows

帘¹ lián〈名〉 shop banner: 酒～ wine banner

帘²（簾） lián〈名〉 hanging screen: 珠～ bead curtain ‖ 竹～ bamboo screen ▸窗～, 门～
【帘布】liánbù〈名〉 cord fabric (in tyres)
【帘幕】liánmù〈名〉 heavy curtain
【帘子】liánzi〈名〉〈口〉 curtain: 窗～ window curtain ‖ 门～ door curtain ‖ 竹～ bamboo screen

莲（蓮） lián〈名〉 1（指植物） lotus: 采～ pick lotus ▸并蒂～, 睡～, 雪～ 2（指莲子） lotus seed: ▸湘～
【莲步】liánbù〈名〉〈旧〉 beautiful woman's light and graceful way of walking: ～轻移 walk in a gliding and graceful manner
【莲房】liánfáng〈名〉 1（莲蓬） lotus pod 2（指居室） monk's bedroom
【莲花】liánhuā〈名〉 1（指花） lotus flower 2（指莲） lotus: 一池～ a pool of lotus
【莲花落】liánhuālào〈名〉 popular ballad sung to the accompaniment of the castanets and each stanza ending with 莲花落, 落莲花 (and so fall the lotus flowers)
【莲藕】lián'ǒu〈名〉（指莲和藕） lotus plant; （指藕） lotus root
【莲蓬】liánpeng〈名〉 lotus pod
【莲蓬头】liánpengtóu〈方〉= 喷头 pēntóu
【莲蓉】liánróng〈名〉 lotus seed paste
【莲台】liántái = 莲座 liánzuò 2
【莲心】liánxīn〈名〉 heart of lotus seed
【莲子】liánzǐ〈名〉 lotus seed: ～羹 lotus seed soup
【莲座】liánzuò〈名〉 1（莲花的底部） bottom of the lotus flower 2（佛像的底座） (Buddha's) lotus seat

涟（漣） lián
A〈名〉〈书〉 ripple: ▸～漪
B〈形〉 streaming: 泪水～～ teardrops kept falling
【涟洏】lián'ér〈形〉〈书〉 [of tears] streaming
【涟涟】liánlián〈形〉〈书〉 [of tears] flowing continuously
【涟漪】liányī〈名〉〈书〉 ripple: 微风吹过，湖面上泛起层层～。 The breeze rippled the surface of the lake.

梿（槤） lián
【梿枷】liánjiā = 连枷 liánjiā

联（聯） lián
A〈动〉 1（不间断） extend: ▸～运, 蝉～ 2（联合） unite: ▸～合, ～盟 3（联络） contact: ▸～络, ～系
B〈名〉 antithesis: ▸春～, 对～, 下～
【联办】liánbàn〈动〉 1（指举办） co-sponsor: ～展览 co-sponsor an exhibition 2（指经营） jointly manage: ～学校 jointly run a school
【联邦】liánbāng〈名〉 federation: ～制 federal system ▸英～
【联邦储备银行】Liánbāng Chǔbèi Yínháng〈名〉 Federal Reserve Bank (FRB)
【联邦调查局】Liánbāng Diàochájú〈名〉 Federal Bureau of Investigation (FBI)
【联邦政府】liánbāng zhèngfǔ〈名〉 federal government
【联播】liánbō〈动〉 broadcast: 新闻～ network news
【联产承包责任制】liánchǎn chéngbāo zérènzhì〈名〉 contract system with remuneration linked to output
【联唱】liánchàng〈动〉 1（指多人） sing songs of the same sort or theme in succession 2（指多支歌曲） sing more than two songs, etc.: 民歌/戏曲大～ serial singing of folk songs/operas
【联大】liándà〈简称〉 1 = 联合大学 2 = 联合国大会
【联单】liándān〈名〉 receipt or other document in duplicate
【联动】liándòng〈动〉 create a chain reaction: ～效应 chain reaction
【联队】liánduì〈名〉［体育］ joint team: 明星～ star team
【联防】liánfáng〈名〉 joint defence: 军民～ army-civilian defence
【联合】liánhé A〈动〉 unite: 加强～ strengthen a union ‖ 实现～ effect a union ‖ 他们～起来对付我。 They all ganged up on me. B〈形〉 joint: ～举办 jointly organize ‖ ～演习 joint exercise ‖ ～签署 joint signature ‖ ～投资 joint investment
【联合大学】liánhé dàxué〈名〉 associated university
【联合担保】liánhé dānbǎo〈名〉［经济］ joint mortgage
【联合公报】liánhé gōngbào〈名〉 joint communiqué: 中美建交～ Joint Communiqué on the Establishment of Diplomatic Relations between the United States and the People's Republic of China
【联合国】Liánhéguó〈名〉 United Nations (UN): ～总部 headquarters of the United Nations
【联合国安全理事会】Liánhéguó Ānquán Lǐshìhuì〈名〉 United Nations Security Council (UNSC)
【联合国大会】Liánhéguó Dàhuì〈名〉 United Nations General Assembly (UNGA)
【联合国儿童基金会】Liánhéguó Értóng Jījīnhuì〈名〉 United Nations Children's Fund (UNICEF)
【联合国环境规划署】Liánhéguó Huánjìng Guīhuàshǔ〈名〉 United Nations Environment Programme (UNEP)
【联合国教科文组织】Liánhéguó Jiào Kē Wén Zǔzhī〈简称〉= 联合国教育、科学及文化组织
【联合国教育、科学及文化组织】Liánhéguó Jiàoyù Kēxué Jí Wénhuà Zǔzhī〈名〉 United Nations Educational, Scientific and Cultural Organization (UNESCO)
【联合国粮农组织】Liánhéguó Liángnóng Zǔzhī〈名〉 Food and Agriculture Organization of the United Nations (FAO)
【联合国秘书长】Liánhéguó Mìshūzhǎng〈名〉 United Nations Secretary General
【联合国宪章】Liánhéguó Xiànzhāng〈名〉 United Nations Charter
【联合声明】liánhé shēngmíng〈名〉 joint statement: 发表～ issue a joint statement
【联合收割机】liánhé shōugējī〈名〉 combine harvester
【联合王国】Liánhé Wángguó〈名〉 United Kingdom (UK): ～国旗 Union Jack
【联合宣言】liánhé xuānyán〈名〉 joint declaration
【联合战线】liánhé zhànxiàn〈名〉 united front: 结成～ form a united front
【联合政府】liánhé zhèngfǔ〈名〉 coalition government: 创建～ form a coalition government
【联欢】liánhuān〈动〉 have a get-together: 军民～ get-together of soldiers and civilians ‖ 春节～晚会 Spring Festival party
【联欢会】liánhuānhuì〈名〉 get-together
【联机】liánjī〈形〉［计算机］ on-line: ～操作 on-line operation
【联接】liánjiē = 连接 liánjiē
【联结】liánjié〈动〉 connect: ～欧亚大陆的桥梁 bridge that links Europe and Asia ‖ 共同的兴趣爱好把他们～在一起。 Common interests and hobbies bring them together.
【联句】liánjù〈动〉 compose linking verse: 即景～ [of several people] be inspired by a sight and improvise a poem together
【联军】liánjūn〈名〉 allied forces: ▸八国～
【联络】liánluò〈动〉 have contact: ～感情 keep up a friendship ‖ （与某人）保持～ keep in contact with sb. ‖ 取得～ get in touch (with) ‖ 失去～ lose contact (with sb.) ‖ ～不上 unable to make contact
【联络处】liánluòchù〈名〉 liaison office
【联络员】liánluòyuán ▸p. 966〈名〉 contact person
【联袂】liánmèi〈副〉〈书〉 jointly: ～演出 act in collaboration
【联盟】liánméng〈名〉 alliance: 结成～ form an alliance (with sb.) ‖ 工农～ worker-peasant alliance ‖ 欧洲自由贸易～ European Free Trade Association (EFTA)
【联绵字】liánmiánzì〈名〉 compound word consisting of two characters, often alliterated or rhymed
【联名】liánmíng〈动〉 sign jointly: ～发起 jointly sponsor ‖ ～上书 submit a joint petition
【联翩】liánpiān〈形〉 1（鸟飞的样子） flying like a bird 2（不间断） continuous: ～起舞 dance continuously ‖ 浮想～ have a busy mind
【联赛】liánsài〈名〉［体育］ league matches: 篮球～ league basketball matches ‖ 网球～ tennis circuit
【联手】liánshǒu〈动〉 team up: ～举办 co-sponsor ‖ ～打击犯罪活动 join forces to crack down on crime
【联署】liánshǔ〈动〉 sign jointly
【联网】liánwǎng〈动〉 network: ～发电 networked electric power generating ‖ 计算机～ computer networking
【联席会议】liánxí huìyì〈名〉 joint meeting: 党政～ joint meeting of the Party and administration leadership
【联系】liánxì〈动〉 1（接触） contact: ～工作 look for a job ‖ 业务～ business contact ‖ 你跟他还有～吗? Are you still in contact with him? 2（结合） connect: 理论～实际 unite theory with practice ‖ 密切～群众 keep close ties with the masses
【联想】liánxiǎng〈动〉 associate with: 产生～ form an association ‖ 蓝色能使你～起什么? What association do you make with the blue colour?
【联谊】liányì〈动〉 keep up a friendship: ～会 sodality
【联姻】liányīn〈动〉〈书〉 1〈本〉 be united through marriage: 两家～成了亲家。 The two families are united through marriage. 2〈喻〉（指合作） form a partnership
【联营】liányíng〈动〉 jointly manage
【联运】liányùn〈名〉［交通］ through

l

transport: 火车汽车～ train-and-bus coordinated transport ‖ 水陆～ through transport by land and water
【联展】liánzhǎn〈动〉jointly hold an exhibition
【联宗】liánzōng〈动〉 accept one another as belonging to the same clan

裢（褳） lián ▸褡裢 dālian

廉 lián〈形〉 **1**（廉洁） honest and clean: ▸～洁, 寡～鲜耻, 清～ **2**（低廉） inexpensive: ▸～价, 低～, 价～物美
【廉耻】liánchǐ〈名〉 sense of honour: 不知～ be shameless ‖ 毫无～之心 be past shame
【廉价】liánjià〈形〉 cheap: ～出售 sell cheap ‖ ～商品 cheap goods
【廉洁】liánjié〈形〉 incorruptible: 刚正～ upright and honest ‖ ～奉公 be honest in performing one's official duties ‖ ～自律 be honest and self-disciplined
【廉明】liánmíng〈形〉 [of officials] upright and incorruptible: 为官～ a clean and honest official ‖ 公正～ be fair and incorruptible
【廉正】liánzhèng〈形〉 upright and honest
【廉政】liánzhèng〈动〉 make a government honest and transparent: ～措施 anti-corruption measures ‖ ～建设 building up a righteous and honest government
【廉政公署】Liánzhèng Gōngshǔ〈名〉 Independent Commission Against Corruption (ICAC) [HK]
【廉直】liánzhí〈形〉 upright and honest: ～之士 person of integrity
【廉租】liánzū〈动〉 rent cheaply
【廉租房】liánzūfáng〈名〉low-rent housing: 建设～ build low-rent housing

鲢（鰱） lián〈名〉 silver carp
【鲢鱼】liányú〈名〉 silver carp

镰（鐮） lián〈名〉 sickle: ▸挂～, 开～
【镰刀】liándāo〈名〉 sickle

liǎn

琏（璉） liǎn〈名〉 grain vessel for the imperial sacrifice in an ancestral temple

敛（斂、歛） liǎn〈动〉 **1**〈书〉（收回） check: ▸～容, ～足 **2**〈书〉（约束） restrain: ▸～迹, 收～ **3**（征收） gather: 把工具～起来 collect together the tools ▸～财, 横征暴～
【敛步】liǎnbù〈动〉〈书〉 halt
【敛财】liǎncái〈动〉 extort money
【敛迹】liǎnjì〈动〉〈书〉 **1**（指行迹） lie low: ～潜踪 go into hiding ‖ 销声～ disappear from the scene **2**（指人） retire from public life ‖ ～山林 retire deep into the mountains
【敛钱】liǎnqián〈动〉 raise money: ～办学 raise money to run a school
【敛容】liǎnróng〈动〉〈书〉 assume a serious expression
【敛声屏气】liǎnshēng-bǐngqì〈成〉 keep silent and hold one's breath
【敛足】liǎnzú = 敛步 liǎnbù

脸（臉） liǎn〈名〉 **1** ▸p. 614（面部） face: 洗～ wash one's face ‖ 圆～ round face ‖ 转过～去 turn one's face away **2**（面子） honour: 没～见人 be too ashamed to face anyone ▸～面 2, 丢～, 赏～ **3**（神情） facial expression: ～不变色心不跳 without one's face turning pale or one's heart skipping a beat ▸愁眉苦～, 翻～, 笑～ **4**（表面） front part of sth.: 鞋～儿 instep ▸门～儿
【脸蛋儿】liǎndànr〈名〉 cheek: 抚摸孩子的～ stroke a child's cheeks ‖ 红润的～ rosy cheeks
【脸红】liǎnhóng〈动〉 blush: 你说这话也不～? Aren't you ashamed of yourself for saying this? ‖ 一想到自己干的蠢事, 她就～。 She blushed at the thought of her stupid mistake.
【脸红脖子粗】liǎnhóng bózicū〈俗〉 flush with agitation: 争得～ argue until one is red in the face
【脸红耳赤】liǎnhóng-ěrchì〈成〉 flush up to the temples
【脸颊】liǎnjiá〈名〉 cheek: ～红润 rosy cheeks
【脸孔】liǎnkǒng〈名〉 face: 板起～ pull a long face
【脸面】liǎnmiàn〈名〉 **1**（面部） face: ～消瘦 sunken cheeks **2**（面子） self-respect: 挽回～ save one's face ‖ 看在我的～上, 原谅他吧。 For my sake, please forgive him.
【脸嫩】liǎnnèn〈形〉 bashful
【脸盘儿】liǎnpánr〈名〉〈口〉 shape of one's face: 方～ square face ‖ 鸭蛋形～ oval face
【脸庞】liǎnpáng〈书〉= 脸盘儿 liǎnpánr
【脸盆】liǎnpén〈名〉 washbasin
【脸皮】liǎnpí〈名〉 **1**（面部皮肤） skin of the face: ～白净 have a fair complexion **2**（情面） feelings: 撕破～ put aside all considerations of face **3**（羞耻感） sense of shame: ～薄 thin-skinned ‖ ～厚 thick-skinned
【脸谱】liǎnpǔ〈名〉［戏曲］ type of facial make-up in traditional Chinese operas [indicating various personalities of characters]
【脸谱化】liǎnpǔhuà〈动〉 create a stereotype: 英雄人物描写～。 The heroes were described stereotypically.
【脸热】liǎnrè〈形〉 flushed: 一想到自己的婚事, 她就～。 The mere thought of her wedding brought a blush into her cheeks.
【脸软】liǎnruǎn〈形〉 good-natured and sensitive towards others
【脸色】liǎnsè〈名〉 **1**（面色） complexion: ～苍白 pasty complexion ‖ ～红润 ruddy complexion **2**（气色） [indicating sb.'s physical condition] look: ～很好 look healthy ‖ 她这几天～不好。 She hasn't been looking well these last few days. **3**（表情） facial expression: ～阴沉 wear a sullen look ‖ 看人的～行事, 真不好受。 It is really hard to enjoy doing things according to someone else's likes and dislikes.
【脸上无光】liǎnshang-wúguāng〈俗〉 lose face
【脸膛儿】liǎntángr〈方〉= 脸盘儿 liǎnpánr
【脸相】liǎnxiàng〈名〉 facial feature
【脸形】liǎnxíng〈名〉 facial features: ～瘦长 have a long, thin face ‖ 长方～ long, squarish face
【脸型】liǎnxíng = 脸形 liǎnxíng

蔹（蘞） liǎn ▸白蔹 báiliǎn

liàn

练（練） liàn
A〈动〉 **1**〈书〉（煮熟） boil and scour raw silk: ～丝 boil and scour silk **2**（练习） practise: ～打字 practise typing ‖ ～气功 practise *qigong* ‖ ～枪法 practise marksmanship ▸～兵, 操～, 勤学苦～
B〈名〉〈书〉 white silk: 澄江静如～。 The crystal river is as still as silk. ▸彩～
C〈形〉 experienced: ▸～达, 干～, 熟～
【练笔】liànbǐ〈动〉 **1**（指写作） practise writing **2**（指书法） practise calligraphy **3**（指绘画） practise drawing
【练兵】liànbīng〈动〉 **1**（指军队） train troops, drill soldiers: 在练兵场上～ drill troops on a parade ground **2**（泛指训练） train: 赛前～ train before a game
【练达】liàndá〈形〉〈书〉 experienced and worldly-wise: ～老成 be experienced and worldly-wise
【练队】liànduì〈动〉 drill in formation
【练功】liàngōng〈动〉 practise one's skill: ～房 gym ‖ 舞蹈演员必须坚持～。 Dancers must consistently practise their skills.
【练球】liànqiú〈动〉 practise a ball game
【练声】liànshēng〈动〉 do voice exercises: 歌手们在赛前～。 The singers are warming up before the contest.
【练手】liànshǒu〈动〉 practise one's skill: 先让他跟着你练练手。 Let him practise his skills first with you.
【练摊儿】liàntānr〈动〉〈口〉 set up a vendor's stall
【练武】liànwǔ〈动〉 **1**（指武艺） practise *wushu*: ～强身 practise martial arts to improve one's health **2**（指军事技术） practise military skills: 民兵利用农闲时间～。 Militiamen practised military skills during the slack farming season. **3**（指本领） practise a skill: 进行技术～ practise technical skills
【练习】liànxí **A**〈动〉 practise: ～讲英语 practise speaking English ‖ ～射击 practise firing ‖ 刻苦～ practise hard **B**〈名〉 exercise: 做～ do exercises ‖ 翻译～ translation exercise ‖ 课堂～ class exercise ‖ ～题 exercise
【练习簿】liànxíbù〈名〉 exercise book
【练习册】liànxícè〈名〉 workbook
【练习曲】liànxíqǔ〈名〉［音乐］ étude

炼（煉、鍊） liàn〈动〉 **1**（指提纯） smelt: ～铁/钢 smelt iron/steel ▸～油, 提～ **2**（指推敲） strive to find the exact word: ▸～句, ～字 **3**（指磨炼） temper: ▸真金不怕火～
【炼丹】liàndān〈动〉［道教］ make pills of immortality
【炼钢】liàngāng〈动〉 make steel
【炼钢厂】liàngāngchǎng〈名〉 steel mill
【炼钢工人】liàngāng gōngrén〈名〉 steelworker
【炼焦】liànjiāo〈动〉 make coke
【炼金术】liànjīnshù〈名〉 alchemy
【炼句】liànjù〈动〉 try to find the best turn of phrase: 要写好一篇文章, 必须炼字～。 It is polishing that makes an essay good.
【炼乳】liànrǔ〈名〉 condensed milk
【炼铁】liàntiě〈动〉 smelt iron
【炼油】liànyóu〈动〉 **1**（指石油） refine oil **2**（指食用油） extract oil by heat: 炼猪油 render pork fat **3**（加热食用油） heat edible oil

【炼狱】liànyù〈名〉 **1** ［宗教］ purgatory **2**〈喻〉（指环境） abyss of misery

【炼制】liànzhì〈动〉［化工］ refine: ～原油 refine crude oil

【炼字】liànzì〈动〉 polish one's wording

恋（戀） liàn

〈动〉 **1**（依恋） long for: ▸～家，怀～ **2**（恋爱） love: 热～ be passionately in love ▸～爱，初～

【恋爱】liàn'ài **A**〈动〉 be in love: 他们～不久就结婚了。 They married after a brief courtship. ‖ 他们俩在～呢！ They are in love! **B**〈名〉 love: （与某人）谈～ be going out (with sb.) ▸三角～，自由～

【恋父情结】liànfù qíngjié〈名〉［心理］ Electra complex

【恋歌】liàngē〈名〉 love song

【恋家】liànjiā〈动〉 be attached to one's home: 这孩子～，不愿意去外地工作。 The child is too attached to his home to leave for work.

【恋旧】liànjiù〈动〉 be nostalgic: 老年人容易～。 Old people are inclined to be nostalgic.

【恋恋不舍】liànliàn-bùshě〈成〉 be reluctant to bid farewell: 她～地看着儿子从视野中消失。 Reluctantly, she watched her son disappear from view.

【恋母情结】liànmǔ qíngjié〈名〉［心理］ Oedipus complex

【恋慕】liànmù〈动〉 admire: （向某人）表达～之情 express one's admiration (for sb.)

【恋念】liànniàn〈动〉 be nostalgic: ～祖国 miss one's home country

【恋情】liànqíng〈名〉 **1**（指依恋） affection: 对故乡的～ attachment towards one's hometown **2**（指爱情） love: 表白～ declare one's love ‖ 两人的～已到了神魂颠倒的地步。 They are head over heels in love.

【恋群】liànqún〈动〉 **1**（指人） be attached to one's own group of people **2**（指动物） be gregarious

【恋人】liànrén〈名〉 sweetheart: 他和以前的～结婚了。 He married his former love.

【恋物癖】liànwùpǐ〈名〉［心理］ fetishism

【恋栈】liànzhàn〈动〉〈贬〉 **1**（指马） feel reluctant to leave its stable **2**〈喻〉（指人） feel reluctant to leave office

【恋战】liànzhàn〈动〉 [usu used in the negative] be reluctant to withdraw from action: 无心～ have no desire to continue fighting

殓（殮） liàn

〈动〉 put a dead body into a coffin: ▸入～

链（鏈） liàn

〈名〉 chain: 手～ wrist-chain ▸～条，锁～，项～

【链轨】liànguǐ = 履带 lǚdài

【链接】liànjiē〈名〉 interlinkage

【链锯】liànjù〈名〉［机械］ chain saw

【链霉素】liànméisù〈名〉［药学］ streptomycin

【链球】liànqiú〈名〉［体育］ **1** ▸**p. 909**（指运动） hammer event **2**（指球） hammer: 掷～ hammer throw

【链球菌】liànqiújūn〈名〉［医学］ streptococcus

【链式】liànshì〈形〉 chain-type: ～传动 chain gearing

【链式反应】liànshì fǎnyìng〈名〉［化学］ chain reaction

【链条】liàntiáo〈名〉［机械］ chain

【链子】liànzi〈名〉 **1**（指金属条状物） chain: 铁～ iron chain ‖ 一条金～ a gold chain **2**〈口〉（车链条） bicycle chain

【链子锁】liànzisuǒ〈名〉 chain lock

楝 liàn

【楝树】liànshù〈名〉 chinaberry

潋（瀲） liàn

【潋滟】liànyàn〈形〉〈书〉 rippling and glistening: 月色下，波光～。 The waves sparkled in the moonlight.

liáng

良 liáng

A〈形〉 good: ▸～策，善～，优～
B〈名〉 good people: ▸～莠不齐，除暴安～
C〈副〉〈书〉 very: 获益～多 benefit a great deal (from sth.) ▸～久，用心～苦

【良材】liángcái〈名〉 talented person

【良策】liángcè〈名〉 sound plan: 别无～ have no other good plans

【良辰】liángchén〈名〉 **1**（指日子） auspicious day: ～吉日 auspicious day **2**（指时光） pleasant time

【良辰美景】liángchén-měijǐng〈名〉 fine moment and beautiful scene

【良导体】liángdǎotǐ〈名〉［物理］ good conductor

【良方】liángfāng〈名〉 **1**（指药方） effective prescription: 寻找治病～ seek effective prescriptions to cure a disease **2**（指办法） effective measure: 治国～ sound strategy for running a country

【良港】liánggǎng〈名〉 good harbour: 天然～ fine natural harbour

【良好】liánghǎo〈形〉 fine: 自我感觉～ feel pleased with oneself ‖ （向某人）表达～的祝愿 express one's good wishes (to sb.) ‖ 养成～的习惯 form good habits ‖ 小麦长势～。 The wheat is growing well.

【良机】liángjī〈名〉〈书〉 golden opportunity: 错失～ let slip a golden opportunity ‖ 抓住～ seize a good chance

【良家】liángjiā〈名〉〈旧〉 respectable family: ～妇女 respectable woman ‖ ～子弟 child from a good family

【良姜】liángjiāng〈名〉［植物］ galangal

【良将】liángjiàng〈名〉 good general

【良久】liángjiǔ〈形〉〈书〉 for a long time: 沉思～ ponder for a long time

【良民】liángmín〈名〉〈旧〉 **1**（普通人） common people **2**（守法公民） law-abiding citizen

【良禽择木】liángqín-zémù〈成〉〈旧〉 a fine bird chooses a solid tree to perch in

【良人】liángrén〈名〉〈古〉 **1**（指丈夫） my good old man **2**（指普通人） common people

【良师益友】liángshī-yìyǒu〈成〉 good teacher and worthy friend: 他是我们大家的～。 He is our good teacher and helpful friend.

【良田】liángtián〈名〉 fertile land: 荒漠变～。 Deserts are turned into fertile farmland.

【良宵】liángxiāo〈名〉〈书〉 pleasant evening: 共度～ spend a happy evening together

【良心】liángxīn〈名〉 conscience: 没～ have no conscience ‖ ～发现 stir one's conscience ‖ ～不安 have a guilty conscience ‖ 凭～办事 act as one's conscience dictates ‖ 说句～话 in all fairness

【良性】liángxìng〈形〉 **1**（指效果好） good: ～循环 beneficial cycle **2**［医学］ benign: ～肿瘤 benign tumour

【良言】liángyán〈名〉〈书〉 good advice: ～相劝 give good advice ▸金玉～

【良药】liángyào〈名〉 effective medicine: 对症～ correct remedy

【良药苦口】liángyào-kǔkǒu〈成〉 good medicine tastes bitter: ～利于病，忠言逆耳利于行。 Just as bitter medicine cures sickness, unpalatable advice benefits conduct.

【良医】liángyī〈名〉 skilful doctor

【良友】liángyǒu〈名〉 good friend: ～来做伴，路遥不觉远。 Good company helps to make the journey go faster.

【良莠不齐】liángyǒu-bùqí〈成〉〈喻〉 the good is mixed up with the bad: 鱼龙混杂，～ good and bad people jumbled together

【良缘】liángyuán〈名〉 good match: 喜结～ be happily married ‖ 天赐～ heaven-sent pairing

【良知】liángzhī〈名〉 conscience: 唤醒某人的～ rouse sb.'s conscience

【良种】liángzhǒng〈名〉 **1**（指植物） improved strain: 培育小麦～ cultivate improved strains of wheat ‖ 水稻～ improved varieties of rice **2**（指动物） fine breed: ～马/牛 fine breed horses/cows

【良种场】liángzhǒngchǎng〈名〉 seed multiplication farm

莨 liáng ▸薯莨 shǔliáng

▸làng

【莨绸】liángchóu〈名〉 gambiered Guangdong gauze

凉（涼） liáng

〈形〉 **1**（温度低） cool: 秋～天气 cool autumn weather ‖ 水还不够～，不能喝。 The water is not cool enough to drink. ▸～菜，～爽 **2**（悲伤） discouraged: 他的话让他父母心～。 His words made his parents' hearts sink. ▸悲～ **3**（冷落） forlorn: ▸荒～，凄～ **4**（用于避热） heat-preventing: ▸～棚，～鞋

▸liàng

【凉白开】liángbáikāi〈名〉〈口〉 cold boiled water

【凉拌】liángbàn〈动〉 dress cold food with sauce: ～面 cold noodles in sauce ‖ 黄瓜可以～着吃。 Cucumbers can be eaten cold with a sauce.

【凉冰冰】liángbīngbīng〈形〉 chilly: 她的手摸上去～的。 Her hands were cold to the touch.

【凉菜】liángcài〈名〉 cold dish: 上～ serve a cold dish

【凉床】liángchuáng〈名〉 bamboo couch

【凉粉】liángfěn〈名〉 bean-starch noodles

【凉风】liángfēng〈名〉 cool breeze

【凉糕】liánggāo〈名〉 glutinous rice cake [served cold]

【凉快】liángkuai **A**〈形〉 pleasantly cool: 屋子里面很～。 It is delightfully cool inside the house. ‖ 一场大雨过后，天气～下来了。 It cooled off after the downpour. **B**〈动〉 cool off: 咱们开车出去兜兜风，～～。 Let's have a little drive and cool ourselves off.

【凉帽】liángmào〈名〉 sun hat

【凉面】liángmiàn〈名〉 cold noodles with sauce

【凉棚】liángpéng〈名〉 bower: ▸手搭～

【凉气】liángqì〈名〉 cold air: 吓得倒吸一口～ gasp in horror

【凉伞】liángsǎn〈名〉 parasol

【凉森森】liángsēnsēn〈形〉 chilly

【凉薯】liángshǔ〈名〉〈方〉［植物］ yam bean

【凉爽】liángshuǎng〈形〉 pleasantly cool: 天气～宜人。 It is delightfully cool.
【凉水】liángshuǐ〈名〉 1▸（冷水） cold water: 冲～澡 have a cold bath 2▸（生水） water that has not been boiled: 喝～ drink tap water
【凉丝丝】liángsīsī〈形〉 coolish: 清晨的空气～的。 The early morning air is rather cool.
【凉飕飕】liángsōusōu〈形〉 chilly: 今早有点～的。 There was a chill in the air this morning.
【凉台】liángtái〈名〉 veranda〈英〉; porch〈美〉
【凉亭】liángtíng〈名〉 summer house
【凉席】liángxí〈名〉 summer sleeping mat
【凉鞋】liángxié〈名〉 sandals: 塑料～ plastic sandals
【凉药】liángyào〈名〉［中医］ medicine of a cold nature
【凉意】liángyì〈名〉 slight chill in the air: 她感到有点～。 A little chill ran over her.

梁¹（樑）liáng
〈名〉 1▸（桥） bridge: ▸桥～ 2▸（横木） roof beam: 架～ set a roof beam in place ▸～上君子, 栋～, 横～, 正～ 3▸（隆起部分） ridge: ▸鼻～, 脊～

梁² Liáng
〈名〉 1▸（指国名） Liang [state in the Zhou Dynasty] 2▸（南朝之一） Liang Dynasty 3▸（后梁） Later Liang Dynasty
【梁上君子】liángshàng-jūnzǐ〈成〉〈诙〉 burglar

椋 liáng
【椋鸟】liángniǎo〈名〉 starling

量 liáng
〈动〉 1▸（测定） measure: ～长度 measure the length (of sth.) ‖ ～距离 measure a distance ‖ ～血压 take sb.'s blood pressure ‖ ～腰围 take sb.'s waist measurement ▸～具, 测～, 车载斗～ 2▸（估计） estimate: ▸估～, 衡～ ▸liàng
【量杯】liángbēi〈名〉 measuring glass
【量程】liángchéng〈名〉 measuring range (of measuring instruments): 仪表～ range of an instrument
【量度】liángdù〈名〉 measurement: ～单位 unit of measurement
【量规】liángguī〈名〉 gauge
【量角器】liángjiǎoqì〈名〉 angle gauge
【量具】liángjù〈名〉 measuring tool
【量器】liángqì〈名〉 measure
【量身打造】liángshēn dǎzào〈动〉 tailor: 为她～的一部电视剧/一首歌 a TV show/song tailor-written for her
【量筒】liángtǒng〈名〉 measuring cylinder
【量油尺】liángyóuchǐ〈名〉［机械］ dipstick
【量雨筒】liángyǔtǒng〈名〉［气象］ precipitation gauge

粮（糧）liáng
〈名〉 1▸（粮食） grain: 种～大户 large-scale grain-growing farmer ‖ 产～大省 major grain-producing province ▸～仓, 细～, 杂～ 2▸（税粮） grain tax paid in kind: ▸公～
【粮仓】liángcāng〈名〉 granary: 东北是中国的～。 The north-east is China's granary.
【粮草】liángcǎo〈名〉〈旧〉 army provisions: ▸兵马未动, ～先行
【粮店】liángdiàn〈名〉 grain shop
【粮荒】liánghuāng〈名〉 food shortage: 闹～ be hit by a famine
【粮库】liángkù〈名〉 grain depot
【粮秣】liángmò〈名〉〈旧〉 army provisions: ～被服 grain, fodder, bedding and clothing
【粮农】liángnóng〈名〉 grain farmer
【粮票】liángpiào〈名〉〈旧〉 food coupon
【粮食】liángshi〈名〉 grain: ～产量 grain yield ‖ ～储备 grain reserves
【粮食定量】liángshi dìngliàng〈名〉 grain ration
【粮食供应】liángshi gōngyìng〈名〉 staple food supply
【粮食加工】liángshi jiāgōng〈名〉 grain processing
【粮食作物】liángshi zuòwù〈名〉 cereal crops
【粮饷】liángxiǎng〈名〉〈旧〉 troop provisions and pay
【粮油】liángyóu〈名〉 grain and oil: ～补贴 grain and oil subsidy
【粮栈】liángzhàn〈名〉 grain depot
【粮站】liángzhàn〈名〉 grain supply centre

粱 liáng
〈名〉〈书〉 1▸（指谷子） fine strain of millet: ▸高～ 2▸（指饭食） fine grain: ▸～肉, 膏～
【粱肉】liángròu〈名〉〈书〉 delicacies

liǎng

两¹（兩）liǎng
〈数〉 1▸ ▸p. 691（二） two: ～百/千 two hundred/thousand ‖ ～间房 two rooms ‖ ～位数 double figures ‖ ～张纸 two pieces of paper ▸～半儿, ～小无猜 2▸（双方） both parties: ～利 be beneficial to both sides ‖ ～不吃亏。 Neither side suffers any loss. ▸～便, ～可, ～全其美 3▸ ▸p. 927（几） a few: 我想讲～句。 I'd like to say a few words. ‖ 这事过～天再说。 Let's put it aside for a couple of days. ▸～下子

两²（兩）liǎng
〈量〉 1▸ ▸p. 978（指重量） *liang* [unit of weight, equal to 50 grams]: 二～茶叶 two *liang* of tea 2▸〈旧〉（指金、银） tael: 十～银子 10 taels of silver
【两岸】liǎng'àn〈名〉 1▸（指堤岸） both sides (of a river, strait, etc.): ～柳树成行。 Willows lined the banks. ‖ 河～挤满了人。 Both sides of the river were crowded with people. 2▸（指海峡两边） both sides of the Taiwan Strait(s): ～同胞 people on both sides of the Taiwan Strait(s)
【两岸三地】liǎng'àn sāndì〈名〉[three parts of China on both sides of the Taiwan Strait(s)] China's mainland, Hong Kong and Taiwan
【两败俱伤】liǎngbài-jùshāng〈成〉 neither side gains: 还是讲和为好, 免得～。 It would be better for both sides to make peace than to wear each other out.
【两半儿】liǎngbànr〈名〉 two halves: 把蛋糕切成～。 Cut the cake in half.
【两边】liǎngbiān〈名〉 1▸（指边缘） both sides: 路的～长着白杨树。 Poplars grow on both sides of the road. 2▸（指方向） both directions: 这间屋子～有窗户, 光线很好。 With windows on both sides, the house gets lots of light. 3▸（指双方） both sides: ～都同意货到付款。 Both sides agreed on cash on delivery.
【两边倒】liǎngbiāndǎo〈动〉 lean now to one side, now to the other
【两便】liǎngbiàn〈形〉 1▸（指方便） convenient for both: 定活～ flexible deposit ‖ 主客～。 It's convenient for both the host and the guest. 2▸（指有好处） beneficial to both: 公私～ benefit both public and individual interests
【两鬓斑白】liǎngbìn-bānbái〈成〉 greying at the temples
【两不找】liǎngbùzhǎo〈动〉 goods and payments match
【两重】liǎngchóng〈形〉 double: ～目的 dual purpose ‖ 新旧社会～天。 The new society is very distinct from the old.
【两重性】liǎngchóngxìng = 二重性 èrchóngxìng
【两次三番】liǎngcì-sānfān〈成〉 again and again
【两次运球】liǎngcì yùnqiú〈名〉［篮球］ double dribbling
【两党制】liǎngdǎngzhì〈名〉 two-party system
【两抵】liǎngdǐ〈动〉 balance each other out: 收支～。 The account balances out.
【两地】liǎngdì〈名〉 two places: ～分居 [of husband and wife] live apart
【两点】liǎngdiǎn〈名〉 [in gambling] snake eyes
【两耳不闻窗外事】liǎng ěr bù wén chuāngwài shì〈俗〉 turn a deaf ear to what is going on outside the window
【两分法】liǎngfēnfǎ = 二分法 èrfēnfǎ
【两个文明】liǎnggè wénmíng〈名〉 material and spiritual civilization: ～一起抓 place equal emphasis on both material and cultural and ideological development
【两广】Liǎng Guǎng〈名〉 Guangdong and Guangxi
【两汉】Liǎng Hàn〈名〉 Western and Eastern Han dynasties
【两湖】Liǎng Hú〈名〉 Hubei and Hunan
【两虎相斗，必有一伤】liǎng hǔ xiāng dòu, bì yǒu yī shāng〈俗〉 when two tigers fight, one is sure to get hurt
【两回事】liǎnghuíshì〈名〉 two entirely different matters: 参考和剽窃是截然不同的～。 Citing for reference is completely different from plagiarism.
【两极】liǎngjí〈名〉 1▸（指地极） North Pole and South Pole 2▸［物理］ cathode and anode 3▸（指极端） two opposing extremes: 贫富～分化 polarity between rich and poor
【两江】Liǎng Jiāng〈名〉〈旧〉 Jiangnan and Jiangxi provinces in the early Qing Dynasty
【两脚规】liǎngjiǎoguī〈名〉 compasses
【两晋】Liǎng Jìn〈名〉 Western Jin and Eastern Jin dynasties
【两可】liǎngkě〈动〉 1▸（表可以） either will do: 这次会议你参加不参加～。 Whether or not you attend this meeting, either way is fine. ▸模棱～ 2▸（表未定） be uncertain yet: 成与不成还在～之间。 Success still hangs in the balance.
【两口儿】liǎngkǒur〈名〉 couple: 老～ old couple
【两口子】liǎngkǒuzi〈名〉〈口〉 husband and wife: 他们～感情很好。 The couple are completely devoted to each other.
【两肋插刀】liǎnglèi-chādāo〈成〉 risk one's life: 为朋友～ risk one's life to help a friend
【两利】liǎnglì〈动〉 be mutually beneficial: 劳资～ benefit both the labour and the management
【两码事】liǎngmǎshì = 两回事 liǎnghuíshì
【两面】liǎngmiàn〈名〉 1▸（正面和反面）

both sides: 纸的～都可以写字。 You may write on both sides of the paper. **2**（两旁）both directions: 公路～都是山。There are mountains on both sides of the highway. **3**（两方面） opposite sides: ～讨好 curry favour with two opposing parties ‖ ～手法 double-dealing ▸～性

【两面光】 liǎngmiànguāng 〈惯〉〈贬〉 please both sides: 他做事向来～，谁都不得罪。 He is always ingratiating himself with both sides, so he offends no one.

【两面派】 liǎngmiànpài 〈名〉 **1**（指人） double-dealer: 他是个～。 He is a double-crosser. **2**（指行为） double-dealing: 要～ be two-faced

【两面三刀】 liǎngmiàn-sāndāo 〈成〉 double-dealing: ～的人 two-faced person

【两面性】 liǎngmiànxìng〈名〉 duplicity

【两难】 liǎngnán〈形〉 being in a dilemma: 陷入～境地 be caught in a dilemma ‖ 进退～ be in a dilemma

【两旁】 liǎngpáng〈名〉 both sides: 街道～都是高楼大厦。 High-rise buildings line both sides of the street.

【两栖】 liǎngqī〈动〉 **1**［生物］［军事］ be amphibious: ～车辆 amphibious vehicles **2**（指人） be engaged in two distinct fields: ～明星 bi-media star

【两栖动物】 liǎngqī dòngwù〈名〉 amphibian: 青蛙是～。 Frogs are amphibious.

【两栖植物】 liǎngqī zhíwù〈名〉 amphibious plant

【两歧】 liǎngqí〈动〉〈书〉 [of opinions, judgements, decisions, etc.] diverge: 双方意见～，因此很难达成共识。 The two sides cannot agree with each other and a consensus is therefore hard to reach.

【两讫】 liǎngqì〈动〉［经济］ have goods delivered and paid for: 货款～。 The goods have been delivered and the bill has been paid.

【两清】 liǎngqīng〈动〉 [of the seller and the buyer] square up the accounts

【两全】 liǎngquán〈动〉 be satisfactory to both sides: ～之策 solution satisfactory to both parties ‖ 忠孝难以～。 It's hard to be a loyal subject and a filial son at the same time.

【两全其美】 liǎngquánqíměi 〈成〉 satisfy both sides: ～的办法 method that satisfies both parties

【两世为人】 liǎngshì-wéirén〈成〉 be lucky to have escaped death

【两手】 liǎngshǒu〈名〉 **1**（指技艺） a few tricks: 露～ show a few tricks of the trade ‖ 有～儿 be skilful **2**（指两方面） both aspects: 做～准备 prepare oneself for both possibilities

【两条腿走路】 liǎngtiáotuǐ zǒulù 〈俗〉〈喻〉 adopt a two-way strategy

【两头】 liǎngtóu〈名〉 **1**（指两端） both ends: ～小，中间大 small at both ends and big in the middle **2**（指双方） both sides: ～受气 be bullied by both sides ‖ ～讨好 please both parties ‖ ～为难 find it hard to please both parties **3**（指地方） two places: ～儿跑 go back and forth between two places

【两下里】 liǎngxiàli〈名〉 both sides

【两下子】 liǎngxiàzi〈口〉 **A**〈数量〉 a few times: 我～就把钉子砸进去了。 I drove in the nail with a few strokes of the hammer. **B**〈名〉 a few tricks: 你真有～! You're cool!

【两相情愿】 liǎngxiāng-qíngyuàn〈成〉 by mutual consent: ～的离婚 divorce by mutual consent ‖ 婚姻须～，不能强求。 Marriage should be by mutual consent. It cannot be arranged.

【两厢】 liǎngxiāng〈名〉 **1**（指房间） wing-rooms on either side of a one-storey house **2**（两边） both sides: 站立～ stand on either side

【两厢情愿】 liǎngxiāng-qíngyuàn = 两相情愿 liǎngxiāng-qíngyuàn

【两小无猜】 liǎngxiǎowúcāi〈成〉 [of a boy and a girl] be innocent playmates

【两新】 liǎngxīn〈名〉 'Two New' organizations [new social circles of economic professionals from economic and social organizations]: 加强～组织的党建工作 strengthen the party-building work of the 'Two New' organizations

【两性】 liǎngxìng〈名〉 **1**（指性别） both sexes: ～关系 sexual relations ▸～人 **2**［化学］ amphoteric quality: ～化合物 amphoteric compound

【两性人】 liǎngxìngrén 〈名〉［医学］ hermaphrodite

【两袖清风】 liǎngxiù-qīngfēng〈成〉remain uncorrupted: ～，一身正气 be upright and uncorrupted

【两眼一摸黑】 liǎngyǎn yīmōhēi 〈俗〉〈喻〉 be completely ignorant of sth.

【两样】 liǎngyàng〈形〉 different: 没什么～ there's no difference ‖ 待遇～ be treated differently

【两翼】 liǎngyì 〈名〉 **1**（指翅膀） both wings: 展开～ spread out both wings ‖ 飞机的～ both wings of an aeroplane **2**［军事］ both flanks: ～包抄 make a pincer attack

【两用】 liǎngyòng〈形〉 dual-purpose: ～产品 dual-use product

【两院制】 liǎngyuànzhì〈名〉 bicameral system

【两造】 liǎngzào〈名〉〈旧〉［法律］ both parties in a lawsuit

俩 liǎng ▸伎俩 jìliǎng ▸liǎ

魉（魎） liǎng ▸魍魉 wǎngliǎng

liàng

亮 liàng

A〈形〉 **1**（光亮） bright: 灯很～ bright light ‖ 他把皮鞋擦得闪闪发～。 He polished his shoes till they shone. ‖ 这屋子真～。 The room is very bright. ▸～光, ～晶晶, 明～ **2**（响亮） loud and clear: 他的嗓音很～。 He has a resonant voice. ▸洪～, 嘹～, 响～ **3**（清楚） clear: 你这么一说，我心里头～了。 What you said made complete sense to me. ▸打开天窗说～话, 心明眼～

B〈动〉 **1**（发光） shine: 房间还～着灯。 A light was still burning in the room. ‖ 天～了。 The day is dawning. **2**（使响亮） make one's voice loud and clear: ～嗓子 raise one's voice **3**（显示） reveal: ～观点 voice one's position ‖ ～身份 reveal one's identity ▸～分, ～牌, ～相

【亮敞】 liàngchǎng〈形〉 bright and roomy

【亮底】 liàngdǐ〈动〉 **1**（指内情） tell the whole story: 你就～吧。 Show your real intention. **2**（指结果） reveal the result: 比赛还没～呢。 The outcome of the game is still undecided.

【亮底牌】 liàng dǐpái〈动〉 **1**〈本〉 play one's trump card **2**〈喻〉 reveal one's real intention

【亮点】 liàngdiǎn〈名〉 **1**（发光点） bright spot **2**〈喻〉（焦点） focus of attention: 拍卖会上的～ the main focus of attention at the auction **3**〈喻〉（优点） merit

【亮度】 liàngdù〈名〉［物理］ brightness: ～调节 brightness control ‖ 荧光屏～ screen brilliance

【亮分】 liàngfēn〈动〉 present one's marks: 请评委～。 Will the judges please show their marks.

【亮光】 liàngguāng 〈名〉 **1**（指光亮） light: 黑暗中突然出现一道～。 A light gleamed in the darkness. **2**（指光泽） shine: 这种布料有～。 This kind of cloth is shiny.

【亮光光】 liàngguāngguāng〈形〉 dazzling: 菜刀磨得～的。 The kitchen knife has been polished to a shine.

【亮光漆】 liàngguāngqī〈名〉polish lacquer

【亮红牌】 liàng hóngpái 〈动〉 **1**（指比赛） show a red card **2**〈喻〉（指许可） order (a factory, etc.) to suspend production, etc.

【亮话】 liànghuà〈名〉 blunt words: 说～吧，我不能帮你这个忙。 To put it bluntly, I can't help you. ▸打开天窗说～

【亮黄牌】 liàng huángpái〈动〉 **1**（指比赛） show a yellow card **2**〈喻〉（警告） give a warning

【亮晃晃】 liànghuǎnghuǎng〈形〉 dazzling: ～的金币 shiny gold coins

【亮晶晶】 liàngjīngjīng〈形〉 glistening: ～的露珠 glistening dew drops ‖ ～的星星 glittering stars

【亮菌甲素】 liàngjūnjiǎsù 〈名〉［药学］ Armillarisin A

【亮丽】 liànglì 〈形〉 **1**（明亮而美丽） bright and beautiful: 色彩～ bright and beautiful colours ‖ 一道～的风景线 a splendid scene **2**（优美） graceful: 她的诗歌很有韵味，散文也写得～。 She writes lyrical poems and elegant prose.

【亮牌】 liàngpái = 亮底牌 liàng dǐpái

【亮牌子】 liàng páizi〈动〉 reveal one's identity

【亮儿】 liàngr〈名〉〈口〉 light: 快拿个～来! Get a light, quick! ‖ 别挡～。 Don't block the light.

【亮色】 liàngsè ▸**p. 863** 〈名〉 bright colour: ～衣料 brightly-coloured cloth

【亮闪闪】 liàngshǎnshǎn〈形〉 glistening: ～的星星 glittering stars ‖ ～的眼睛 sparkling eyes

【亮堂堂】 liàngtángtáng〈形〉 brightly lit: ～的教室 well-lit classroom ‖ 灯火通明，把广场照得～的。 The square was ablaze with lights.

【亮堂】 liàngtang〈形〉 **1**（豁亮） bright: 新建的办公楼既宽敞又～。 The newly built office buildings are bright and spacious. **2**（明白） clear: 经过学习，心里更～了。 Through study we became more enlightened.

【亮相】 liàngxiàng〈动〉 **1**［戏曲］ strike a pose on the stage: 登台～ strike a pose on the stage **2**〈喻〉（出现） perform in public: 首次～ make one's debut ‖ 他最近常在电视上～。 He has been on television a lot lately. **3**〈喻〉（表明观点） make one's position known to the public: 事情还没完，先别急着～。 Don't make your position known before the matter is completely finished.

【亮锃锃】 liàngzèngzèng〈形〉 shiny

【亮铮铮】 liàngzhēngzhēng〈形〉 shiny: 一副～的手铐 a shiny pair of handcuffs

凉（涼） liàng〈动〉 let sth. cool (off/down): 汤太烫，～一会儿再喝。 The soup is too hot. Let it cool down a bit before you drink it.
▸liáng

谅（諒） liàng〈动〉 **1**（理解） understand: 互～互让 mutual understanding and accommodation ▸～解，体～，原～ **2**（估计） suppose: ～他不敢。 I don't suppose he dares. ‖ 前函～已收到。 I presume you have received my last letter.

【谅察】liàngchá〈动〉〈书〉 [used in correspondence] ask for understanding and forgiveness: 不当之处，尚希～。 If anything is improper, I ask for your understanding and forgiveness.

【谅解】liàngjiě〈动〉 understand: 相互～ mutual understanding ‖ 达成～ come to an understanding ‖ ～备忘录 memorandum of understanding ‖ 我～你的苦衷。 I understand your plight.

辆（輛） liàng〈量〉 [for vehicles]: 两～坦克 two tanks ‖ 一～汽车 a car

靓（靚） liàng〈形〉〈方〉 good-looking: ～妹 pretty girl ‖ ～女 pretty girl ‖ ～仔 handsome young man
▸jìng

【靓丽】liànglì〈形〉 beautiful: 扮相～ prettily costumed and made up ‖ ～的容颜 beautiful facial features

量 liàng

A〈名〉 **1**〈书〉（指器物） measure [such as *dou* (斗) and *sheng* (升), used as a standard unit for measuring the volume in ancient times]: ▸度～衡 **2**（指限度） capacity: ▸胆～，力～，气～ **3**（指数量） volume: 出口/进口～ volume of exports/imports ▸～变，产～，总～

B〈动〉 estimate: ～才录用 employ sb. according to his abilities ▸～体裁衣，不自～力，估～
▸liáng

【量变】liàngbiàn〈名〉［哲学］ quantitative change: 从～到质变 from quantitative change to qualitative change

【量产】liàngchǎn〈动〉 mass-produce: 具备～条件 be equipped with all the requirements for mass production

【量词】liàngcí〈名〉［语法］ measure word

【量贩店】liàngfàndiàn〈名〉 wholesale store: 大型～ hypermarket

【量化】liànghuà〈动〉 quantify: ～考核 quantitative examination

【量化宽松】liànghuà kuānsōng〈名〉［经济］ quantitative easing: ～的货币政策 quantitative easing monetary policy

【量价】liàngjià〈名〉 transaction volume and pricing: 农产品批发市场出现～齐跌的局面。 Agricultural wholesale markets are showing a fall in volume and pricing.

【量力】liànglì〈动〉 estimate one's ability: 你太不～了。 You're completely overreaching yourself. ▸不自～

【量力而行】liànglì'érxíng〈成〉 act according to one's capability

【量能】liàngnéng〈名〉［金融］ trading volume and money flow: 股市冲高需要～配合。 When the stock market shoots up, trading volume and money flow have to match the new conditions.

【量入为出】liàngrù-wéichū〈成〉 budget one's expenses according to one's income: 过日子应该～。 One should live within one's means.

【量体裁衣】liàngtǐ-cáiyī〈成〉〈喻〉 act according to actual circumstances

【量小力微】liàngxiǎo-lìwēi〈成〉 few in number and weak in strength

【量刑】liàngxíng〈动〉［法律］ mete out punishment according to the crime committed: ～适当 impose appropriate punishment

【量子】liàngzǐ〈名〉［物理］ quantum

【量子力学】liàngzǐ lìxué〈名〉［物理］ quantum mechanics

【量子论】liàngzǐlùn〈名〉［物理］ quantum theory

【量子物理学】liàngzǐ wùlǐxué〈名〉 quantum physics

晾 liàng〈动〉 **1**（风干） air-dry: ～鱼干 air fish slices **2**（晒干） dry in the sun: ～衣服 put the washing out to dry ▸～晒 **3**（冷落） cold-shoulder: 他们又说又笑，把我～在一边儿了。 Chatting and laughing together, they left me out in the cold.

【晾干】liànggān〈动〉 dry by airing

【晾晒】liàngshài〈动〉 air-dry: ～被褥/衣服 air the bedding/clothes in the sun ‖ ～粮食 dry grain in the sun

【晾台】liàngtái〈名〉 sun terrace

【晾衣架】liàngyījià〈名〉 clothes horse

【晾衣绳】liàngyīshéng〈名〉 clothesline; washing line〈英〉

踉 liàng

【踉跄】liàngqiàng〈动〉 totter: 他～了几步，跌倒在地。 He staggered and fell.

liāo

撩 liāo〈动〉 **1**（掀起） prop up: ～开面纱 lift up a veil ‖ ～起裙子 lift the hem of a skirt **2**（洒） sprinkle with one's hand: 给花儿～些水。 Sprinkle some water on the flowers.
▸liáo

蹽 liāo〈动〉〈方〉 **1**（跑） run: 一口气～出十几里地 run over ten *li* in one breath **2**（蹓走） sneak off: 他一看形势不妙就～了。 As soon as he saw that all was not well, he slipped away.

liáo

辽[1]（遼） liáo〈形〉 distant: ▸～阔

辽[2]（遼） Liáo〈名〉 **1**（指朝代） Liao Dynasty **2** ▸**p. 661**（辽宁） Liao [another name for Liaoning Province (辽宁)]

【辽东半岛】Liáodōng Bàndǎo〈名〉 Liaodong Peninsula

【辽阔】liáokuò〈形〉 extensive: 幅员～ have a vast territory ‖ ～的水域 vast expanse of water

【辽宁】Liáoníng ▸**p. 661**〈名〉 Liaoning Province

【辽远】liáoyuǎn〈形〉 distant: ～的边疆 remote frontiers ‖ ～的未来 distant future

疗（療） liáo〈动〉 cure: ▸～伤，～养，医～

【疗程】liáochéng〈名〉 course of treatment: ～短，见效快 quick recovery after just a short course of treatment ‖ 服两个～的药 take two courses of medicine

【疗法】liáofǎ〈名〉 treatment: 保守～ conservative treatment ‖ 放射～ radiation therapy ‖ 药物～ drug treatment ‖ 饮食～ diet cure

【疗伤】liáoshāng〈动〉 treat and dress a wound

【疗效】liáoxiào〈名〉 therapeutic effect: ～显著 with a marked curative effect

【疗养】liáoyǎng〈动〉 take remedial rest: 去海滨～ go to the seaside for a period of repose

【疗养院】liáoyǎngyuàn〈名〉 sanatorium

聊[1] liáo〈副〉〈书〉 **1**（暂且） tentatively: ▸～备一格，～以自慰 **2**（稍微） slightly: ～表谢意 just to show my gratitude/appreciation ‖ ～胜一筹 be a little better ▸～胜于无

聊[2] liáo〈动〉〈书〉 rely on: ▸百无～赖，民不～生

聊[3] liáo〈动〉〈口〉 chat: 吃完晚饭后过来～～。 Come over to my place after supper for a chat. ▸～天儿，闲～

【聊备一格】liáobèi-yīgé〈成〉 may serve as a stopgap

【聊赖】liáolài〈名〉 [usu used in the negative] something to depend on: ▸百无～

【聊胜于无】liáoshèngyúwú〈成〉 better than nothing: 这点钱帮不了你多大忙，但总归～。 Although this small sum of money won't be of much help to you, it's better than nothing.

【聊天儿】liáotiānr〈动〉 chat: 网上～ chat on-line ‖ 边喝茶边～ chat over a cup of tea

【聊天室】liáotiānshì〈名〉 chat room

【聊以解嘲】liáoyǐjiěcháo〈成〉 do sth. to extricate oneself from embarrassment

【聊以塞责】liáoyǐsèzé〈成〉 barely meet the requirements so as to avoid blame

【聊以自慰】liáoyǐzìwèi〈成〉 just to console oneself: 令他～的是，儿子考上了大学。 He consoled himself with the thought that his son had got into college.

【聊以卒岁】liáoyǐzúsuì〈成〉〈书〉 barely make ends meet at the end of the year

【聊斋志异】liáozhāizhìyì〈名〉 *Strange Tales from a Scholar's Studio*

> **《聊斋志异》**
>
> A collection of supernatural tales from the Qing Dynasty written by Pu Songling (蒲松龄). The *liaozhai* (聊斋) of the title refers to the author's study. *Zhi* (志) means 'record' and *yi* (异) means 'something extraordinary'. The stories are often allegories reflecting social realities, and extolling high morality and pure love. Many of them are romantic love stories between men and foxes and ghosts posing as women.

僚 liáo〈名〉 **1**（官员） official: ▸官～ **2**〈旧〉（同事） associate in office: ▸同～

【僚机】liáojī〈名〉［军事］ companion plane

【僚舰】liáojiàn〈名〉［军事］ consort

【僚属】liáoshǔ〈名〉〈旧〉 subordinate

寥 liáo〈形〉 **1**〈书〉（空旷高远） open and spacious: ▸～廓 **2**（寂静） quiet:

▸寂～ 3（稀少） sparse: ▸～落，～若晨星
【寥廓】liáokuò〈形〉〈书〉 boundless: ～的天空 vast sky
【寥寥】liáoliáo〈形〉 very few: ～数语 few words ‖ 与会者～可数。 A small number of people attended the meeting.
【寥寥无几】liáoliáo-wújǐ〈成〉 very few: 听众～。 The audience was very sparse.
【寥落】liáoluò〈形〉 1（稀少零落） few and far between: 疏星～ only a few solitary stars in the sky 2（孤寂） deserted: ～的小巷 deserted lane
【寥若晨星】liáoruòchénxīng〈成〉 as rare as stars at dawn: 像爱因斯坦那样的天才可谓～。 There are very few people who could be said to be as clever as Einstein.

撩 liáo〈动〉 tease: 春色～人。 The beauty of spring is intoxicating.
▸liāo
【撩拨】liáobō〈动〉 tease: 任你百般～，他就是不动声色。 Despite all your provocation, he remains calm and unmoved.
【撩动】liáodòng〈动〉 stir: ～心弦 tug at sb.'s heartstrings ‖ 微风～她的头发。 A gentle breeze ruffled her hair.
【撩逗】liáodòu〈动〉 tease: 不要～他。 Don't tease him.
【撩惹】liáorě〈动〉 provoke: 没事别去～他。 Don't provoke him without good reason.

嘹 liáo
【嘹亮】liáoliàng〈形〉 loud and clear: 军号～ loud and clear bugle call ‖ 歌声～。 The singing is loud and clear.

獠 liáo〈形〉〈书〉 fierce-looking
【獠牙】liáoyá〈名〉 bucktooth: ▸青面～

潦 liáo
▸lǎo
【潦草】liáocǎo〈形〉 1（指字迹） illegible: 字迹～ illegible handwriting 2（指做事） sloppy: 敷衍～ work without due care ‖ 做事～ work in a perfunctory way
【潦倒】liáodǎo〈形〉 down on one's luck: 一生～ be down on one's luck all one's life ▸穷困～

寮 liáo〈名〉〈方〉 hut: 竹～ bamboo shack ‖ 茶～ tea house
【寮房】liáofáng〈名〉 1（指僧舍） monk's cell 2〈方〉（指住房） hut
【寮棚】liáopéng〈名〉 shed

缭（繚） liáo〈动〉 1（绕） entwine: ▸～乱，～绕 2（缝） sew with slanting stitches: ～（衣服）边儿 hem ‖ 随便～上几针 just sew a few stitches
【缭乱】liáoluàn〈形〉〈书〉 confused: 心绪～ in a confused state of mind ▸眼花～
【缭绕】liáorào〈动〉 spiral upwards: 炊烟～ smoke curling up from kitchen chimneys ‖ 歌声～。 The singing reverberated in the air.

燎 liáo〈动〉 1（燃烧） ignite: ～荒 burn dry weeds ▸～原 2（烫） burn: ～了个泡 get burned and blistered
▸liǎo
【燎泡】liáopào〈名〉 blister caused by a burn
【燎原】liáoyuán〈动〉 set a prairie ablaze:〈喻〉～烈火 large-scale mass movement

鹩（鷯） liáo
【鹩哥】liáogē〈名〉［鸟类］ hill myna

髎 liáo〈名〉［中医］ space between two joints

liǎo

了¹ liǎo
A〈动〉 1（了结） finish: ～了一桩心愿 have fulfilled a wish ‖ 案子～了没有? Has the case concluded yet? ▸～结，没完没～，私～ 2（表可能性） [used with 得 or 不 after a verb, indicating possibility] be able/unable to do sth.: 去不～ be unable to go ‖ 受不～ be unable to bear it ‖ 你来得～还是来不～? Will you be able to come or not?
B〈副〉〈书〉 [used in the negative] completely: ～不相干 be totally irrelevant ▸～无

了²（瞭） liǎo〈动〉 know clearly: ▸～解，明～，一目～然
▸le
【了不得】liǎobudé〈形〉 1〈口〉（不寻常） extraordinary: 多得～ be in great abundance ‖ 自以为～ think oneself terrific ‖ ～的大事 matter of utmost importance 2（表情况严重） terrible: 只是擦破了一点皮，没有什么～的。 It's just a scratch, nothing serious.
【了不起】liǎobuqǐ〈形〉 1（不平凡） amazing: ～的科学家 extraordinary scientist ‖ 你真～! You're really terrific. 2（严重） serious: 没什么～的困难。 There is nothing so difficult about it. ‖ 只是淤伤，没什么～的。 It's just a bruise, nothing serious.
【了当】liǎodàng〈形〉 1（直爽） frank: 他说话～。 He does not mince his words. ▸直截～ 2（完结） settled: 安排～ be properly arranged ‖ 收拾～ have put everything in order
【了得】liǎodé〈形〉 1（表情况严重） [used at the end of a sentence after 还 in an exclamation] terrible: 你竟敢骂老师，这还～! How dare you abuse your teacher? ‖ 你这样混下去，怎么～? What will become of you if you continue to muddle along like this? 2〈旧〉（不平常） extraordinary: 他武艺十分～。 He is amazingly good at martial arts.
【了断】liǎoduàn〈动〉 finish: 事情已经～。 The matter has been settled.
【了结】liǎojié〈动〉 settle: ～一桩心事 take a load off one's mind ‖ 案子已经～。 The case is already concluded.
【了解】liǎojiě〈动〉 1（知道） understand: ～实际情况 understand the facts ‖ 增进～ promote understanding ‖ 我～你的心情。 I understand how you feel. 2（调查） inquire about: 我想跟您～一件事。 I'd like to ask you about something. ‖ 咱们去～一下股市情况。 Let's try and find out what's happening on the stock market.
【了局】liǎojú A〈动〉 conclude: 你猜这件事是怎样～的? Can you guess how it ended? B〈名〉 permanent solution: 分居终归不是～。 Separation is no permanent solution.
【了了】liǎoliǎo〈形〉〈书〉 clear: 我对真实情况也不甚～。 I don't have a clear picture of the real situation either.
【了却】liǎoquè〈动〉 settle: ～心愿 fulfil a wish ‖ ～一桩心事 take a load off one's mind
【了然】liǎorán〈形〉〈书〉 clear: ～于心 be clear ‖ 事情的始末我也不甚～。 I'm not very clear about the whole matter. ▸一目～
【了如指掌】liǎorúzhǐzhǎng〈成〉 know sb./sth. like the palm of one's hand: 她对当地的情况～。 She knows the place very well.
【了事】liǎoshì〈动〉 settle a matter: 草草～ finish sth. quickly and carelessly ‖ 应付～ do sth. perfunctorily
【了无】liǎowú〈动〉 be not in the least: ～长进 make no progress at all ‖ ～音信 have absolutely no word ‖ ～惧色 show no trace of fear
【了悟】liǎowù〈动〉〈书〉 understand: 书中奥妙，尚未～。 I still fail to grasp the profundity of the book.
【了愿】liǎoyuàn〈动〉 fulfil a wish
【了账】liǎozhàng〈动〉 settle a matter: 咱们之间就此～。 It's all settled between us.

钌（釕） liǎo〈名〉［化学］ ruthenium (Ru)
▸liào

蓼 liǎo〈名〉［植物］ knotweed
▸lù
【蓼蓝】liǎolán〈名〉［植物］ indigo plant

燎 liǎo〈动〉 burn: 他的头发让火苗～了一大片。 The flame singed a big patch of his hair.
▸liáo

liào

尥 liào
【尥蹶子】liào juězi〈动〉 1（指牲口） give a backward kick 2〈喻〉（指人） get angry

钌 liào
▸liǎo
【钌铞儿】liàodiàor〈名〉〈口〉 hasp and staple: 挂上～，锁上门。 Fasten the hasp and lock the door.

料 liào
A〈动〉 1（预料） expect: 我～他会来。 I expect he should come. ▸～想，始～不及，预～ 2（处理） deal with: ▸～理，照～
B〈名〉 1（原料） material: 盖新房子的～都备齐了。 The material is all ready for building the new house. ▸废～，木～，偷工减～ 2（食料） fodder: 多给牲口加点～。 Put more in the fodder. ▸草～，饲～ 3（资料） data 4（肥料） substance that makes the soil fertile
C〈量〉 [for pills of Chinese medicine] prescription: 配一～药 make up one prescription of pills
【料场】liàochǎng〈名〉 stock yard
【料车】liàochē〈名〉 skip car
【料到】liàodào〈动〉 expect: 没～的困难 unforeseen difficulties ‖ 谁能～事情会这样发展呢? Who could have expected that things would develop in such a way?
【料定】liàodìng〈动〉 anticipate: 我～会在这里见到他。 I fully expect to see him here.

l

【料斗】liàodǒu〈名〉 feed container
【料豆儿】liàodòur〈名〉 soybeans or black beans used as livestock feed
【料度】liàoduó〈动〉〈书〉 surmise
【料货】liàohuò = 料器 liàoqì
【料及】liàojí〈动〉〈书〉 anticipate: 形势变化之快，原未～。 We did not expect that things would develop so quickly.
【料酒】liàojiǔ〈名〉 cooking wine
【料理】liàolǐ **A**〈动〉 **1**（处理） manage: ～后事 make arrangements for a funeral ‖ ～家务 do household chores ‖ 事情还没～好。 The matter has still not been dealt with. **2**（烹调） cook: 名厨～ dishes prepared by famous chefs **B**〈名〉 cuisine: 日本～ Japanese cuisine
【料器】liàoqì〈名〉 glassware
【料峭】liàoqiào〈形〉〈书〉 chilly: 春寒～ The spring chill is piercing.
【料事如神】liàoshì-rúshén〈成〉 predict like a prophet
【料想】liàoxiǎng〈动〉 suppose: ～不会有问题。 I presume things will be fine. ‖ 我真没有～到。 It is beyond my expectations.
【料子】liàozi〈名〉 **1**（衣料） dressmaking material: 买几块～做衣服 buy some fabric to make clothes **2**〈喻〉〈口〉（指人） material: 她是做律师的好～。 She is good lawyer material.

撂

liào〈动〉 **1**（搁下） place carelessly: 把报纸～在一边 throw the newspapers to one side ‖ 这件事～几天再说。 Put the matter aside for a couple of days. **2**（抛弃） abandon: ～下妻儿不管 abandon one's wife and children **3**（摔倒） knock down: 把对方～翻在地 bring down an opponent
【撂倒】liàodǎo〈动〉 knock down
【撂荒】liàohuāng〈动〉〈方〉 let a piece of farmland go to waste
【撂手】liàoshǒu〈动〉 leave undone: ～不管 wash one's hands of a matter ‖ 事情没有做完，不能～。 We can't leave it unfinished.
【撂挑子】liào tiāozi〈惯〉〈喻〉 quit one's job: 他动不动就～。 He has threatened to resign at every turn.

廖

Liào〈名〉 Liao [surname]

瞭

liào〈动〉 watch from a height or distance: 在阳台上～着点。 Keep watch from the balcony.
【瞭哨】liàoshào〈动〉 be on patrol: 巡营～ go on patrol
【瞭望】liàowàng〈动〉 **1**（望远） look far into the distance: 极目～ look as far as the eye can see **2**（放哨） keep a lookout
【瞭望哨】liàowàngshào〈名〉 lookout post
【瞭望台】liàowàngtái〈名〉 observation tower

镣（鐐）

liào〈名〉 fetters: ▸脚～
【镣铐】liàokào〈名〉 shackles: 戴着～ be in chains

liē

咧

liē
▸liě, lie
【咧咧】liēliē ▸大大咧咧 dàda-liēliē

liě

咧

liě〈动〉 draw back one's lips: ▸～嘴
▸liē, lie
【咧嘴】liězuǐ〈动〉 draw back one's lips: ～傻笑 grin a silly grin ▸龇牙～

裂

liě〈动〉〈方〉 split open: 敞胸～怀 bare one's chest ‖ 麻袋缝儿～开了。 The sack burst at the seam.
▸liè

liè

列

liè
A〈动〉 **1**（排列） arrange: ～出理由 set out one's reasons ‖ 把你想买的东西～出来。 Make a list of the things you want to buy. ▸～队, 陈～, 罗～ **2**（安排） rank: ～入议程 put on the agenda ‖ 把发展经济～为首要任务 give priority to economic development ▸名～前茅
B〈名〉 **1**（行列） queue〈英〉; line〈美〉: ▸出～, 队～, 序～ **2**（类） kind: 不在讨论之～ not among the subjects under discussion ▸系～
C〈代〉 all: ▸～岛, ～国, ～位
D〈量〉 [used of a line/row of things]: 一～火车 a train
【列兵】lièbīng〈名〉 private
【列车】lièchē〈名〉 train: 磁悬浮～ Maglev train ‖ 高速～ bullet train ‖ 客运～ passenger train
【列车时刻表】lièchē shíkèbiǎo〈名〉 train schedule
【列车员】lièchēyuán ▸**p. 966**〈名〉 train attendant
【列车长】lièchēzhǎng〈名〉 conductor; guard〈英〉
【列岛】lièdǎo〈名〉 archipelago: ▸澎湖～
【列队】lièduì〈动〉 line up: ～欢迎 queue up to welcome sb. ‖ ～游行 line up for a parade
【列国】lièguó〈名〉 various countries: 周游～ tour various countries
【列举】lièjǔ〈动〉 list: ～事实 cite facts ‖ 报告里～了大量统计数字。 Numerous statistics were given in the report.
【列宁主义】Lièníng zhǔyì〈名〉 Leninism: 马克思～ Marxism-Leninism
【列强】lièqiáng〈名〉〈旧〉 great powers: 打倒帝国主义～! Down with the imperialist powers!
【列位】lièwèi〈代〉〈书〉 all of you: ～来宾 distinguished guests ‖ ～请坐。 Ladies and gentlemen, please be seated.
【列席】lièxí〈动〉 observe a meeting: ～会议 observe a meeting ‖ ～代表 non-voting delegate
【列支敦士登】Lièzhīdūnshìdēng〈名〉 Liechtenstein: ～人 Liechtensteiner
【列传】lièzhuàn〈名〉 biography (of a historical figure)
【列祖列宗】lièzǔ-lièzōng〈成〉 successive generations of ancestors: 对得起～ live up to the expectations of one's ancestors

劣

liè〈形〉 inferior: ▸～等, ～迹, 恶～
【劣币】lièbì〈名〉［金融］ bad money: ～驱逐良币的现象 the phenomenon of bad money driving out good money
【劣等】lièděng〈形〉 low-grade: ～品 inferior goods
【劣根性】liègēnxìng〈名〉 inherent weaknesses: 民族～ innate weaknesses of a nation
【劣弧】lièhú〈名〉［数学］ minor arc
【劣货】lièhuò〈名〉 poor-quality goods
【劣迹】lièjì〈名〉 wrongdoing: ～昭著 be notorious
【劣绅】lièshēn〈名〉〈旧〉 evil gentry: ▸土豪～
【劣势】lièshì〈名〉 disadvantage: 处于～ be at a disadvantage ‖ 扭转～ turn the tables
【劣质】lièzhì〈形〉 inferior: ～产品 substandard product
【劣种】lièzhǒng〈名〉 inferior breed

冽

liè〈形〉〈书〉 cold: ▸凛～

洌

liè〈形〉〈书〉 clear: 泉香而酒～。 Sweet spring water helps make the wine clear and smooth to the palate.

埒

liè
A〈动〉〈书〉 be sb.'s equal: 才力相～ be equally talented and skilled
B〈名〉 embankment: 河～ river embankment

烈

liè
A〈形〉 **1**（指火势） intense: ▸～火, ～焰 **2**（指程度） strong: ▸～酒, 剧～, 兴高采～ **3**（指性情） staunch: ▸刚～
B〈名〉 **1**（指人） person who dies for a just cause: ▸～属, 先～, 英～ **2**〈书〉（功绩） exploits: 功～ merits and achievements
【烈度】lièdù〈名〉 earthquake intensity
【烈风】lièfēng〈名〉 **1**［气象］ force 9 wind **2**（强风） strong wind
【烈火】lièhuǒ〈名〉 raging fire: 熊熊～ roaring fire ‖ ～熊熊燃烧。 The fire raged. ‖〈喻〉 革命～ revolutionary fire
【烈火见真金】lièhuǒ jiàn zhēnjīn〈俗〉〈喻〉 people of worth show their mettle in difficult situations
【烈酒】lièjiǔ〈名〉 stiff drink
【烈马】lièmǎ〈名〉 untamed horse
【烈女】lièn ǚ〈名〉〈旧〉 **1**（指刚正守节） upright and principled woman **2**（指以死守节） woman who dies in defence of her chastity
【烈日】lièrì〈名〉 scorching sun: ～当头。 The hot sun is shining directly over our heads.
【烈士】lièshì〈名〉 **1**（指死者） martyr: 革命～永垂不朽! Eternal life to the revolutionary martyrs! **2**〈书〉（有志之士） hero: ～暮年，壮心不已 a noble-hearted man retains his high aspirations even in old age
【烈士陵园】lièshì língyuán〈名〉 revolutionary martyrs' cemetery
【烈属】lièshǔ〈名〉 member of a revolutionary martyr's family
【烈性】lièxìng〈形〉 **1**（指人） upright and unyielding: ～男儿 upright and unyielding man ‖ ～女子 woman of fiery character **2**（指物） strong: ～酒 strong drink ‖ ～炸药 powerful explosive
【烈焰】lièyàn〈名〉 raging flames: ～腾空。 Raging flames shot into the sky.

捩

liè〈动〉〈书〉 turn: ▸转～点
【捩转】lièzhuǎn〈动〉 turn around: 形势发展不可～。 The course of events cannot be reversed.

鴷（鴷） liè〈名〉〈书〉［鸟类］ woodpecker

猎（獵） liè〈动〉[1]（打猎） hunt: ▸～枪, ～手, 狩～ [2]（寻求） hunt for: ▸～奇

【猎豹】lièbào〈名〉 cheetah
【猎捕】lièbǔ〈动〉 hunt
【猎场】lièchǎng〈名〉 hunting ground
【猎刀】lièdāo〈名〉 hunting knife
【猎狗】liègǒu〈名〉 hound
【猎户】lièhù〈名〉[1]（指人家） household specializing in hunting [2]（指人） hunter
【猎户座】Lièhùzuò〈名〉［天文］ Orion
【猎获物】lièhuòwù〈名〉 game
【猎具】lièjù〈名〉 hunting equipment
【猎猎】lièliè〈拟〉〈书〉 flutter: 北风～ howling north wind ‖ 红旗～。 The red flag was fluttering in the wind.
【猎奇】lièqí〈动〉〈贬〉 seek novelty
【猎潜艇】lièqiántǐng〈名〉 submarine chaser
【猎枪】lièqiāng〈名〉 shotgun: 双管～ double-barrelled shotgun
【猎区】lièqū〈名〉 hunting zone
【猎取】lièqǔ〈动〉[1]（捕猎） hunt: ～食物 hunt for food ‖ ～野兽 hunt wild animals [2]（取得） seek: ～高额利润 seek big profits ‖ ～名利 pursue fame and gain
【猎犬】lièquǎn = 猎狗 liègǒu
【猎人】lièrén〈名〉 hunter
【猎杀】lièshā〈动〉 hunt and kill
【猎手】lièshǒu〈名〉 hunter
【猎头】liètóu〈名〉 headhunter: ～公司 headhunting firm
【猎物】lièwù〈名〉 prey: 寻找～ look for one's prey
【猎艳】lièyàn〈动〉[1]〈贬〉（搜寻词句） strive for ornate diction: ～搜奇 seek flowery and exotic expressions [2]（追逐女色） womanize
【猎鹰】lièyīng〈名〉 falcon
【猎装】lièzhuāng〈名〉 hunting jacket

裂 liè〈动〉[1]（破开） split open: 镜子掉在地上，～成碎片。 The mirror dropped onto the floor and cracked into small pieces. ‖ 她的手冻～了。 Her hands were chapped in the cold. ▸分～, 决～, 身败名～ [2]（有裂缝） crack: 杯子～了。 The cup is cracked. ▸～痕, ～纹
▸liě

【裂变】lièbiàn〈动〉[1]［物理］ fission: 核～ nuclear fission [2]（分裂改变） split: 一个大家庭～为几个小家庭 an extended family split into several nuclear families
【裂唇】lièchún ▸p. 50〈名〉［医学］ harelip
【裂缝】lièfèng [A]〈动〉 crack: 墙～了。 The wall is cracked. [B]〈名〉 crack: 墙上有一道～。 There is a crack in the wall.
【裂谷】liègǔ ▸p. 164〈名〉［地质］ rift valley
【裂果】lièguǒ〈名〉［植物］ dehiscent fruit
【裂痕】lièhén〈名〉 crack: 玻璃杯上有一道～。 There is a crack in the glass. ‖〈喻〉 夫妻间的～很快弥合了。 The marital rift was quickly resolved.
【裂化】lièhuà〈动〉［化工］ crack: 催化～ catalytic cracking ‖ ～炉 cracking furnace
【裂解】lièjiě〈动〉［化工］ split: 加碱～ alkaline splitting
【裂开】lièkāi〈动〉 crack: 核桃～了。 The walnut cracked open.
【裂口】lièkǒu [A]〈动〉 crack: 裙子接缝处～了。 The dress has split at the seams. ‖ 手冻得～了。 My hands are chapped by the cold. [B]〈名〉[1]（裂缝） crack: 堵住堤坝上的～ stop up the breach in the dyke ‖ 他裤子上的～缝上了。 The slit in his trousers was sewn up. [2]（指火山） vent
【裂片】lièpiàn〈名〉［植物］ lobe (of a leaf)
【裂伤】lièshāng ▸p. 50〈名〉［医学］ laceration
【裂纹】lièwén〈名〉[1]（裂缝） crack: 杯子上有一条～。 The cup has a crack in it. [2]（指花纹） crackle
【裂隙】lièxì〈名〉crack: 桌面上有一道～。 There is a crack on the surface of the desk. ‖〈喻〉 弥合夫妻感情上的～ mend the rift between husband and wife

趔 liè

【趔趄】lièqie〈形〉 stumbling: 打～ stumble ‖ 他～着走过来。 He staggered over.

躐 liè〈动〉〈书〉[1]（超过） surpass: ▸～等 [2]（践踏） tread

【躐等】lièděng〈动〉〈书〉 ignore normal procedure

鱲（鱲） liè〈名〉［鱼类］ minnow

鬣 liè〈名〉 mane: 马/狮～ mane of a horse/lion

【鬣狗】liègǒu〈名〉 striped hyena

lie

咧 lie〈助〉〈方〉 [used in the same way as 了, 啦 and 哩]: 车来～。 Here comes the bus.
▸liē, liě

līn

拎 līn〈动〉〈方〉 carry in one's hand: 把箱子～上楼去。 Take the suitcase upstairs. ‖ 太沉，～不动。 It is too heavy to carry.

【拎包】līnbāo〈名〉〈方〉 handbag

lín

邻（鄰） lín
[A]〈名〉 neighbour: 紧～ immediate neighbour ▸～里, 近～, 四～
[B]〈动〉 be adjacent: ～县/省 neighbouring county/province ‖ ～座 adjacent seat ▸～国, ～近, 毗～

【邻邦】línbāng〈名〉 neighbouring country
【邻国】línguó〈名〉 neighbouring country
【邻角】línjiǎo〈名〉［数学］ adjacent angle
【邻接】línjiē〈动〉 be adjacent to: 中国北面与蒙古国相～。 China borders Mongolia to the north.
【邻近】línjìn [A]〈动〉 be near: 疗养院～西湖。 The sanatorium is close to the West Lake. [B]〈名〉 neighbourhood: ～没有学校。 There is no school in the neighbourhood. ‖ 住宅区～有个邮局。 There is a post office in the vicinity of the residential area.
【邻居】línjū〈名〉 neighbour: 隔壁～ next-door neighbour
【邻里】línlǐ〈名〉[1]（指乡里或街道） neighbourhood: ～服务站 neighbourhood service centre [2]（指人家或人） neighbours: ～都来道贺。 The neighbours all came to extend their congratulations.
【邻人】línrén〈名〉 neighbour
【邻舍】línshè〈名〉〈方〉 neighbour: 街坊～ neighbours

林 lín〈名〉[1]（森林） forest: 植树造～ plant a forest of trees ‖ 退耕还～ convert cultivated land back into forest ‖ 竹～ bamboo forest ‖ 自然～ natural forests ▸～海, 防护～ [2]（林业） forestry: ▸～业 [3]〈喻〉（指同类） circles: ▸碑～, 枪～弹雨, 武～

【林产】línchǎn〈名〉 forest products
【林场】línchǎng〈名〉 forestry centre
【林丛】líncóng〈名〉 forest
【林带】líndài〈名〉 forest belt: 防风/防沙～ windbreak/sandbreak forest belt ‖ 防护～ shelterbelt
【林地】líndì〈名〉 woodland: 原始～ virgin forest
【林改】língǎi〈名〉 forest property rights reform
【林冠】línguān〈名〉［林业］ crown cover
【林海】línhǎi〈名〉 vast forest: 茫茫～ vast expanse of forest
【林肯郡】Línkěnjùn〈名〉 Lincolnshire
【林垦】línkěn〈动〉 afforest uncultivated land
【林立】línlì〈动〉 stand like trees in a forest: 高楼～ forest of high-rises ‖ 只见港湾里帆樯～ see nothing but a forest of masts in the harbour
【林林总总】línlín-zǒngzǒng〈成〉 numerous: ～的商品摆满了货架。 The shelves are filled with all kinds of goods.
【林莽】línmǎng〈名〉 jungle
【林木】línmù〈名〉[1]（树林） forest: ～葱郁 lush forest [2]（树木） forest tree
【林檎】línqín = 花红 huāhóng
【林区】línqū〈名〉 forest area
【林泉】línquán〈名〉〈书〉[1]（森林和山泉） forests and streams [2]（指住处） mountain retreat: 终老～ spend one's remaining years among the forest and streams
【林涛】líntāo〈名〉 roaring of the wind in a forest
【林网】línwǎng〈名〉 criss-cross forest belts
【林业】línyè〈名〉 forestry: ～工人 forester
【林荫道】línyīndào〈名〉 boulevard
【林苑】línyuàn〈名〉 imperial hunting park
【林政】línzhèng〈名〉 forestry administration
【林子】línzi〈名〉〈口〉 forest: 茂密的～ thick forest

临（臨） lín
[A]〈动〉[1]（向下看） overlook: ▸居高～下 [2]（到下面） come down: ▸光～, 降～, 亲～ [3]（来到） arrive: ▸大难～头, 身～其境 [4]（面对） face: 东～大海 border on the sea in the east ‖ ～河的房子 house overlooking a river ‖ 疗养院～湖。 The sanatorium faces a lake. ▸～街, 如～大敌 [5]（描摹） copy: ～画 copy a painting ▸～摹, ～帖
[B]〈介〉 just before: ～睡前 just before going to bed ‖ ～上飞机前 just before boarding the plane ▸～别, ～行, ～终

【临本】línběn〈名〉 copy
【临别】línbié〈动〉 be just before parting: ～纪念 parting souvenir ‖ ～赠言 parting advice
【临产】línchǎn〈动〉 be about to give birth

l

【临场】línchǎng〈动〉 **1**（指考试） sit an exam;（指竞赛） enter a contest: ～发挥 on-site performance ‖ 缺乏～经验 lack exam experience **2**（在现场） be on the spot: ～指导 give on-the-spot guidance

【临床】línchuáng〈动〉 attend a sickbed to provide medical services: ～经验 clinical experience ‖ ～应用 clinical application/practice

【临床医生】 línchuáng yīshēng〈名〉 clinician

【临床医学】 línchuáng yīxué〈名〉 clinical medicine

【临到】líndào〈动〉 **1**（接近） be about to: ～上飞机，我才想起没带机票。 I didn't realize that I had forgotten my ticket until I was about to board the plane. **2**（落到） happen to: 如果～你头上，你会如何? What would you do if it happened to you?

【临风】línfēng〈动〉〈书〉 face the wind: ～而立 stand against the wind

【临机】línjī〈动〉 seize the opportunity: ～立断 decide quickly

【临街】línjiē〈动〉 overlook a street: ～的窗户 window overlooking the street

【临界】línjiè〈形〉［物理］ critical: ～温度 critical temperature ‖ ～状态 critical state

【临近】línjìn〈动〉 be near: ～黎明 close on daybreak ‖ 国庆节～了。 National Day is approaching.

【临渴掘井】línkě-juéjǐng〈成〉〈喻〉 make no preparation until the last moment

【临客】 línkè〈名〉 temporary passenger train [used to relieve traffic pressure during peak holiday periods]

【临了】línliǎo〈副〉〈口〉 eventually: ～他才说了实话。 Finally, he told the truth.

【临门】línmén〈动〉 **1**（到门口） come to the house: 贵客～。 Distinguished guests are coming to visit us. ▶双喜～ **2**［足球］ be close to the goal: ～一脚功夫不够 be unable to score when close to goal

【临摹】línmó〈动〉 copy: ～一幅油画 make an imitation copy of an oil painting

【临盆】línpén = 临产 línchǎn

【临深履薄】línshēn-lǚbó〈成〉〈喻〉acting with extreme caution

【临时】línshí **A**〈副〉 at the last moment: ～变卦 change one's mind at the last moment ‖ ～调整 last-minute adjustments ‖ ～抱佛脚 make a last-ditch attempt **B**〈形〉 temporary: ～建筑物 temporary building ▶～工，～户口，～政府

【临时代办】 línshí dàibàn〈名〉［外交］ chargé d'affaires ad interim

【临时工】línshígōng ▶**p. 966**〈名〉 temp: 雇几个～当餐馆服务员 hire a few casual workers as waiters and waitresses

【临时户口】línshí hùkǒu〈名〉 temporary residence permit

【临时委员会】 línshí wěiyuánhuì〈名〉 interim commission

【临时协议】línshí xiéyì〈名〉 interim agreement

【临时政府】 línshí zhèngfǔ〈名〉 interim government: 建立～ form a transitional government

【临死】línsǐ〈动〉 be on one's deathbed

【临眺】 líntiào〈动〉〈书〉 ascend to a height and have a distant view

【临帖】líntiè〈动〉 practise calligraphy from a copybook

【临头】líntóu〈动〉 happen to: 大难～ be faced with imminent disaster ‖ 死到～ be at death's door

【临危】 línwēi〈动〉 **1**（临终） be approaching one's end **2**（面临危险） face death or great danger: ～退缩 shrink in the face of great peril

【临危不惧】línwēi-bùjù〈成〉 be fearless in the face of danger

【临危受命】línwēi-shòumìng〈成〉 accept a mission at a critical moment

【临刑】línxíng〈动〉 be shortly before an execution

【临行】línxíng〈动〉 be before departure: ～前，他向在场的人一一告别。 He said goodbye to everyone present before his departure.

【临幸】línxìng〈动〉〈旧〉 [of an emperor] make a personal visit

【临渊羡鱼】línyuān-xiànyú〈成〉 fantasize about something good but take no action to obtain it: ～，不如退而结网。 It is best to take practical steps to achieve one's aims.

【临月】línyuè〈动〉 be about to give birth

【临战】línzhàn〈动〉 face a battle: 进入～状态 be ready to fight

【临阵】línzhèn〈动〉 **1**（战斗前） be just about to enter a battle: 做好～准备 be ready to fight **2**（到战场） be at the front line: ～指挥 direct military operations at the front line

【临阵磨枪】línzhèn-móqiāng〈成〉〈喻〉 make preparations only at the last moment

【临阵脱逃】línzhèn-tuōtáo〈成〉 turn tail in the face of danger: ～无异于叛国。 Fleeing the battlefield is nothing but treason.

【临终】línzhōng〈动〉 breathe one's last: ～遗言 last words

【临终关怀】 línzhōng guānhuái〈名〉 hospice care

啉 lín ▶喹啉 kuílín

淋 lín〈动〉 **1**（下雨） drench: 日晒雨～ be weather-beaten **2**（洒落） sprinkle: 在花上～点儿水。 Sprinkle some water on the flowers.
▶lìn

【淋巴】línbā〈名〉［生理］ lymph: ～癌 lymphoma

【淋巴结】 línbājié〈名〉［生理］ lymph node

【淋巴结核】línbā jiéhé ▶**p. 50**〈名〉［医学］ scrofula

【淋巴瘤】línbāliú ▶**p. 50**〈名〉［医学］ lymphoma

【淋巴细胞】 línbā xìbāo〈名〉［生理］ lymphocyte

【淋漓】línlí〈形〉**1**（指液体）dripping wet: 大汗～ be drenched with sweat ‖ 鲜血～ be dripping with blood **2**（指感觉） free from inhibition: 酣畅～ with great ease and verve ‖ 痛快～ hearty and unreserved

【淋漓尽致】línlí-jìnzhì〈成〉 thoroughly: 把人物刻画得～ portray characters vividly ‖ 文章将其丑恶嘴脸揭露得～。 This article revealed their ugly features very thoroughly.

【淋淋】línlín〈形〉 dripping wet: 汗/血～ be dripping with sweat/blood ‖ 湿～的毛巾 dripping towel

【淋雨】línyǔ〈动〉 be caught in the rain

【淋浴】línyù〈名〉 shower: 洗～ take a shower

琳 lín〈名〉〈书〉 fine jade

【琳琅满目】línláng-mǎnmù〈成〉a feast for the eyes: 展览会上的工艺品～，美不胜收。 There was an endless array of beautiful handicrafts at the exhibition.

粼 lín

【粼粼】línlín〈形〉（指水）clear;（指石头）crystalline: 波光～ clear ripples

嶙 lín

【嶙峋】 línxún〈形〉〈书〉 **1**（指山石） craggy: 怪石～ strange-shaped jagged rocks **2**（瘦削） skinny: ▶瘦骨～ **3**（刚正） upright: 傲骨～ be of unyielding character

遴 lín〈动〉〈书〉 select carefully: ～才 select talented people ‖ ～聘教师 carefully select and engage teachers

【遴派】línpài〈动〉 select and dispatch: ～代表出国考察 select and dispatch representatives abroad on a tour of investigation

【遴选】línxuǎn〈动〉 **1**（选拔） select sb. for a post: ～德才兼备者担任领导工作 appoint people with both ability and integrity to leading positions **2**（挑选） select carefully: ～参展作品 carefully select works for the exhibition

霖 lín〈名〉〈书〉 continuous heavy rain: ▶甘～

【霖雨】línyǔ〈名〉 continuous heavy rain

辚（轔） lín

【辚辚】línlín〈拟〉〈书〉 rumble: 车～，马萧萧。The chariots rumbled and the horses neighed.

磷（燐） lín〈名〉［化学］ phosphorus (P): 白/红～ white/red phosphorus

【磷肥】línféi〈名〉［农业］ phosphate fertilizer

【磷光】 línguāng〈名〉［物理］ phosphorescence

【磷火】línhuǒ〈名〉 will-o'-the-wisp

【磷酸】 línsuān〈名〉［化学］ phosphoric acid

【磷酸钙】línsuāngài〈名〉 calcium phosphate

【磷酸钾】línsuānjiǎ〈名〉 potassium phosphate

【磷酸钠】línsuānnà〈名〉 sodium phosphate

【磷虾】línxiā〈名〉［动物］ krill

【磷脂】línzhī〈名〉［生化］ phosphatide

瞵 lín〈动〉〈书〉 look attentively at: 鹰～ [of an eagle] watch with sharp eyes

鳞（鱗） lín

A〈名〉 scale: 把鱼洗一下，再用刀把～刮掉。 Wash the fish and scrape the scales off it with a knife. ▶～甲，～片，鱼～ **B**〈形〉 scaly: ▶～波，遍体～伤

【鳞比】línbǐ〈形〉 [of buildings, etc.] arranged like fish scales

【鳞波】 línbō〈名〉 scaly ripples: ～闪闪 glistening ripples

【鳞翅目】línchìmù〈名〉［昆虫］ lepidoptera

【鳞次栉比】líncì-zhìbǐ〈成〉 tightly-packed: 高层建筑～ row upon row of high-rises

【鳞甲】línjiǎ〈名〉 scales and shell (of reptiles and arthropods)

【鳞茎】línjīng〈名〉［植物］ bulb

【鳞片】línpiàn〈名〉 **1**（指鱼） fish scale: 做鱼前要刮掉～。 Fish should be scaled before cooking. **2**（指昆虫） insect scale **3**［植物］ bud scale

【鳞伤】línshāng〈名〉 cuts and bruises all

over the body: ▸遍体～
【鳞屑】línxiè〈名〉(skin) scale
【鳞爪】línzhǎo〈名〉〈书〉〈喻〉odd scraps

麟 lín〈名〉〈书〉unicorn: ▸麒～
【麟角凤嘴】línjiǎo-fèngzuǐ〈成〉〈喻〉rare treasure

lǐn

凛（凜） lǐn〈形〉**1**（冷）cold: ▸～冽 **2**〈书〉（怕）afraid: ～畏 feel scared **3**（威严）stern: ▸～然
【凛冽】lǐnliè〈形〉bitingly cold: 寒气～。There is a chill in the air.
【凛凛】lǐnlǐn〈形〉**1**（冷）chilly: 寒风～ biting wind **2**（严肃）stern: ～正气 awe-inspiring righteousness ▸威风～
【凛然】lǐnrán〈形〉stern: 态度～ be stern in manner ‖ 一副～不可侵犯的样子 stern and forbidding airs ▸大义～
【凛若冰霜】lǐnruò-bīngshuāng〈成〉cold as ice and frost

廪（廩） lǐn〈名〉〈书〉**1**（粮仓）granary: ▸仓～ **2**（粮食）grain

檩（檁） lǐn〈名〉［建筑］purlin
【檩条】lǐntiáo = 檩 lǐn

lìn

吝 lìn〈形〉stingy: ▸悭～
【吝色】lìnsè〈名〉〈书〉look of reluctance: 他全力相助，毫无～。He went all out to help him without showing the slightest reluctance.
【吝啬】lìnsè〈形〉stingy: ～的老头 mean old man
【吝啬鬼】lìnsèguǐ〈名〉miser
【吝惜】lìnxī〈动〉begrudge: 毫不～气力 spare no efforts ‖ 只要是我们真正需要的东西，爸爸不会～。Father will not begrudge us what we really need.

赁（賃） lìn〈动〉lease: 我们公司～了一幢办公大楼。Our company rented an office building. ▸租～
【赁金】lìnjīn〈名〉rent

淋 lìn
A〈动〉（过滤）filter: ～咖啡/茶 strain coffee/tea
B ▸淋病 lìnbìng
▸lín
【淋病】lìnbìng ▸**p. 50**〈名〉［医学］gonorrhoea

蔺（藺） lìn ▸马蔺 mǎlìn

膦 lìn〈名〉［化学］phosphine

躏（躪） lìn ▸蹂躏 róulìn

líng

〇 líng ▸**p. 691**〈数〉zero; nought〈英〉: 二〇〇八年 year 2008

伶 líng〈名〉〈旧〉actor: 坤～ actress ▸名～, 优～
【伶仃】língdīng〈形〉**1**（孤独）lonesome: ▸孤苦～ **2**（瘦弱）emaciated: 瘦骨～ be all skin and bones
【伶俐】línglì〈形〉bright: 聪明～ bright and quick-witted ‖ 口齿～ be clever and eloquent
【伶俜】língpīng〈形〉〈书〉solitary: ～独居 live in solitude
【伶人】língrén〈名〉〈旧〉actor or actress
【伶牙俐齿】língyá-lìchǐ〈成〉be endowed with the gift of the gab

灵（靈） líng
A〈名〉**1**（神）god: ▸精～, 神～, 显～ **2**（灵魂）spirit;（精神）soul: ～与肉 soul and body ▸心～, 英～, 在天之～ **3**（灵柩）coffin: 他的～前摆着花圈。Wreaths were laid in front of his coffin. ▸～车, ～位, 守～
B〈形〉**1**（灵验）extraordinarily effective: 你的办法根本不～。What you suggested didn't work at all. ‖ 这药真～。This medicine is very effective. ▸～丹妙药, ～验 **2**（灵敏）bright: 耳朵～ have keen hearing ‖ 他脑子～。He is quick-witted. ▸机～, 心～手巧 **3**（灵活）nimble
【灵便】língbiàn〈形〉**1**（敏捷）nimble **2**（敏锐）sharp: 手脚～ be nimble about one's hands and feet ‖ 老人的耳朵已不～。The old man is hard of hearing. **3**（好用）handy: 这把电钻使着真～。The electric drill is really handy.
【灵车】língchē〈名〉hearse
【灵床】língchuáng〈名〉**1**（用于停放尸体）bier **2**（为死人虚设）bed kept as if it was when the dead person was still alive
【灵丹妙药】língdān-miàoyào〈成〉miracle cure: 要摆脱目前的困境，你有什么～? What miracle cure have you got for the current set of problems?
【灵动】língdòng〈形〉clever: ～的大眼睛 intelligent eyes ‖ 色彩～。Many colours were interwoven to a startling effect.
【灵幡】língfān〈名〉〈旧〉funeral banner
【灵符】língfú〈名〉magic figures [drawn to lay a ghost or bring good luck to people]
【灵感】línggǎn〈名〉inspiration: 获得～ derive inspiration (from sb./sth.) ‖ 缺乏～ lack inspiration ‖ 创作～ creative inspiration
【灵怪】língguài〈名〉gods and spirits: ～故事 legend
【灵光】língguāng **A**〈名〉**1**〈旧〉（神异的光辉）divine light **2**（指神灵头部光环）halo **B**〈形〉〈方〉good
【灵慧】línghuì〈形〉bright: 天资～ naturally intelligent
【灵魂】línghún〈名〉soul: 将～托付给上帝 commend one's soul to God ‖ ～深处 in one's soul of souls ‖ 为金钱出卖～ sell one's soul for money ‖ 愿他的～安息吧! May his soul rest in peace! ‖ 教师是人类～的工程师。Teachers are the architects of the human spirit. ‖ 创新是改革的～。Creativity is the soul of reform.
【灵活】línghuó〈形〉**1**（敏捷）quick: 脑筋～ be quick-witted ‖ 手指～ be deft with one's fingers **2**（善于变通）flexible: ～机动的战略战术 flexible strategy and tactics ‖ ～多样的方法 flexible and diverse methods
【灵活性】línghuóxìng〈名〉flexibility: 表现出～ demonstrate one's flexibility
【灵机】língjī〈名〉brainwave: 我～一动，计上心来。I had a sudden inspiration and hit upon an idea.
【灵柩】língjiù〈名〉bier
【灵快】língkuài〈形〉nimble
【灵猫】língmāo〈名〉［动物］civet cat: 大～ zibet
【灵敏】língmǐn〈形〉keen: 动作～ be quick in one's movements ‖ 嗅觉～ have a keen sense of smell ‖ ～的反应 sensitive reaction
【灵敏度】língmǐndù〈名〉sensitivity: 高～的照相机 highly sensitive camera
【灵牌】língpái = 灵位 língwèi
【灵气】língqì〈名〉intelligence: 两眼透着～ one's eyes reveal one's intelligence ‖ 这孩子有～，学啥都快。He is an intelligent child, quick to learn things.
【灵巧】língqiǎo〈形〉dexterous: 双手～ be quick with one's hands ‖ 这个机器人造得好～啊! What an ingenious robot!
【灵寝】língqǐn〈名〉seat of a coffin
【灵塔】língtǎ〈名〉tower containing the body or bones of a dead Buddhist
【灵台】língtái〈名〉**1**（指台子）platform for a coffin or funerary urn **2**〈书〉（心灵）heart
【灵堂】língtáng〈名〉mourning hall
【灵猩】língtí〈名〉grey hound
【灵通】língtōng〈形〉well-informed: 消息～人士 well-informed person
【灵童】língtóng〈名〉［宗教］soul boy [regarded as the transmigrated living Buddha]: 十世班禅转世～ reincarnated soul boy for the 10th Panchen Lama
【灵位】língwèi〈名〉spirit tablet [with the name, birthday, etc., of the dead inscribed]
【灵犀】língxī〈名〉〈喻〉power of comprehension: ▸心有～一点通
【灵性】língxìng〈名〉**1**（指人）wit: 他具有当领导的～。He has wisdom enough to be a leader. **2**（指动物）intelligence: 这狗很有～，能领会主人的意图。The dog is intelligent and capable of sensing what its master wants.
【灵秀】língxiù〈形〉delicately beautiful: 模样～ of fine delicate features
【灵验】língyàn〈形〉**1**（有效）effective: 药物～ effective remedy **2**（准确）accurate: 天气预报果然很～。The weather forecast turned out to be accurate.
【灵异】língyì **A**〈名〉gods and spirits **B**〈形〉mystical
【灵长目】língzhǎngmù〈名〉［动物］primate
【灵芝】língzhī〈名〉glossy ganoderma [symbol of longevity or good luck]

苓 líng ▸茯苓 fúlíng

囹 líng
【囹圄】língyǔ〈名〉〈古〉prison: 身陷～ be thrown into jail

泠 líng〈形〉〈书〉cool: ～风 cool breeze
【泠泠】línglíng〈形〉〈书〉**1**（清凉）cool **2**（清越）clear and far-reaching
【泠然】língrán〈形〉〈书〉clear and far-reaching

玲 líng
【玲玲】línglíng〈拟〉〈书〉jingle
【玲珑】línglóng〈形〉**1**（指物）exquisite: ▸小巧～ **2**（指人）clever and nimble: ▸八面～, 娇小～
【玲珑剔透】línglóng-tītòu〈成〉**1**（指物）be ingeniously and exquisitely carved: ～的

玉雕 exquisite jade carvings **2**（指人） be quick-witted

柃 líng
【柃木】língmù〈名〉［植物］Eurya japonica

瓴 líng〈名〉 water jar: ▶高屋建～

铃（鈴） líng〈名〉 **1**（指响器） bell: 门～ doorbell ‖ 电话～ telephone ring bell ‖ ～声 ring ▶～铛 **2**（铃状物） bell-shaped object: ▶杠～, 哑～ **3**（蕾铃） cotton bud: ▶棉～
【铃钹】língbó〈名〉 bell cymbals
【铃铛】língdang〈名〉 small bell
【铃铎】língduó〈名〉 bell hung under eaves of palaces or towers
【铃鼓】línggǔ ▶**p. 929**〈名〉 tambourine
【铃兰】línglán〈名〉［植物］ lily of the valley

鸰（鴒） líng ▶鹡鸰 jílíng

凌[1] líng〈名〉 ice: ▶～汛, 冰～

凌[2]（淩） líng〈动〉 **1**（升高） rise high: ▶～驾, ～霄, 壮志～云 **2**（欺负） bully and humiliate: ▶欺～, 盛气～人, 恃强～弱 **3**（逼近） approach: ▶～晨
【凌波】língbō〈书〉**A**〈名〉 dashing waves **B**〈形〉 [of a woman's graceful way of walking] like treading the waves
【凌晨】língchén ▶**p. 669**〈名〉early morning: ～两点 two o'clock in the morning
【凌迟】língchí〈动〉〈古〉 execute by dismembering: ～处死 execute by dismemberment and let the convicted die a slow painful death
【凌驾】língjià〈动〉 **1**（超越） place oneself above: ～于法律之上 place oneself above the law ‖ 个人利益绝不能～于人民的利益之上。 No one is allowed to place their own interests above that of the people. **2**（控制） control
【凌空】língkōng〈动〉 be high up in the air: ～射门 make a volley shot ‖ 飞机～而过。 The plane streaked across the sky. ‖ 红旗～飘扬。 The red flag is fluttering in the air.
【凌厉】línglì〈形〉 swift and fierce: 发起～的攻势 launch a swift and fierce attack ‖ 朔风～ fierce north wind
【凌轹】línglì〈动〉〈书〉 **1**（欺压） ride roughshod over: ～百姓 ride roughshod over the people **2**（排挤） squeeze out: ～同仁 squeeze out one's colleagues
【凌乱】língluàn〈形〉 disorderly: 一阵～的脚步声 a flurry of footsteps ‖ 屋子里～不堪。 The room is in an impossible mess.
【凌虐】língnüè〈动〉〈书〉 tyrannize over: ～百姓 oppress the people
【凌日】língrì〈名〉［天文］ transit: 金星～ transit of Venus
【凌辱】língrǔ〈动〉 bully and humiliate: 备受～ suffer all kinds of insults
【凌侮】língwǔ = 凌辱 língrǔ
【凌霄】língxiāo〈动〉〈书〉 rise high in the sky: 浩气～ a noble spirit reaching up to heaven
【凌霄花】língxiāohuā〈名〉［植物］ Chinese trumpet creeper
【凌汛】língxùn〈名〉 spring flood caused by melting ice from the upper reaches of a river
【凌云】língyún〈动〉〈书〉reach the clouds: 高耸～ tower into the clouds ▶壮志～
【凌杂】língzá〈形〉 disorderly

陵 líng〈名〉 **1**（土山） mound: ▶丘～ **2**（陵墓） mausoleum: 掘/扫～ open/visit a mausoleum ‖ 谒～ pay homage at sb.'s mausoleum ‖ 黄帝～ Yellow Emperor's Mausoleum ▶～墓
【陵迟】língchí〈动〉 **1**〈书〉（衰败） ebb **2** = 凌迟 língchí
【陵谷变迁】línggǔ-biànqiān〈成〉〈喻〉 ups and downs
【陵轹】línglì = 凌轹 línglì
【陵墓】língmù〈名〉 mausoleum: 帝王～ imperial mausoleum
【陵寝】língqǐn〈名〉〈书〉 emperor's final resting place
【陵替】língtì〈动〉〈书〉 **1**（废弛） break down **2**（衰败） decline: 家道～。 The family fortunes were at a low ebb.
【陵园】língyuán〈名〉 graveyard: ▶烈士～

聆 líng〈动〉〈书〉 listen attentively
【聆教】língjiào〈动〉〈套〉 [used in correspondence] hear your words of wisdom
【聆听】língtīng〈动〉〈书〉 listen respectfully: ～教诲 listen respectfully to sb.'s instructions

菱 líng〈名〉［植物］ water chestnut: ▶～角
【菱角】língjiao〈名〉 water chestnut
【菱铁矿】língtiěkuàng〈名〉 siderite
【菱形】língxíng〈名〉 diamond

棂（欞） líng〈名〉(window) lattice: ▶窗～

蛉 líng ▶螟蛉 mínglíng

翎 líng〈名〉 **1**（羽毛） plume: 孔雀～ peacock feathers ‖ 雁～ goose quill ‖ 野鸡～ pheasant quill **2** ▶翎子 língzi 1
【翎毛】língmáo〈名〉 **1**（羽毛） plume **2**（指中国画） a type of classical Chinese painting featuring birds and animals: 长于～ be good at painting birds and animals
【翎子】língzi〈名〉 **1**（指在官服上） peacock feathers worn at the back of an official's hat [as an indication of his rank in the Qing Dynasty] **2**（指在戏服上） pheasant quill worn on warriors' helmets

羚 líng〈名〉 **1**（羚羊） antelope **2**（羚羊角） antelope's horn
【羚牛】língniú〈名〉 takin
【羚羊】língyáng〈名〉 antelope: 藏～ Tibetan antelope

绫（綾） líng〈名〉 damask silk
【绫罗绸缎】língluó-chóuduàn〈成〉 silks and satins
【绫子】língzi = 绫 líng

零[1] líng〈动〉 **1**（落下） drop: ▶涕～ **2**〈书〉（凋落） wither: ▶～落, 凋～, 飘～

零[2] líng
A〈形〉 fragmentary: ▶～件, ～售, ～碎
B〈名〉 fragment: 他四十有～。 He is forty odd. ▶～数, ～头
C ▶**p. 691**〈数〉 **1**（表单位附属关系） [used in expressions of time, age, weight, etc. between two different denominations]: 十块～五毛 ten *yuan* and five *jiao* ‖ 一岁～两个月大 one year and two months old **2**（表没有） zero; nought〈英〉: 二减二等于～。 Two minus two equals zero. ‖〈喻〉将风险降到～ reduce the risks to zero ‖〈喻〉效果等于～。 There was zero effect. **3**（表空位） [used in a number to indicate the absence of a unit, representing a final or medial zero and often appearing as ○ in written language]: 二～～八年 2008 ‖ 四～五号房间 Room 405 **4**（表计算起点） zero [on the thermometer, etc.]: ～上二十八度 twenty-eight degrees above zero ‖ 摄氏～下十度 minus ten degrees centigrade
【零部件】língbùjiàn〈名〉parts: 机器～ machine parts
【零存整取】língcún-zhěngqǔ〈动〉 deposit small sums of money every month and draw out both the principal and the interest when the specified time comes up
【零打碎敲】língdǎ-suìqiāo = 零敲碎打 língqiāo-suìdǎ
【零担】língdàn〈名〉 less-than-carload (LCL): ～托运 less-than-carload freight
【零蛋】língdàn〈名〉〈诙〉〈喻〉 zero: 得～ score a duck
【零点】língdiǎn ▶**p. 669**〈名〉 midnight: ～三十分 half past midnight
【零点方案】língdiǎn fāng'àn〈名〉 zero option
【零丁】língdīng = 伶仃 língdīng
【零度】língdù ▶**p. 776**〈名〉 zero: 气温降到～。 The temperature has fallen to zero.
【零风险】língfēngxiǎn〈名〉 zero risk: ～投资 zero-risk investment
【零工】línggōng〈名〉 **1**（指活计） casual labour: 靠打～过活 make a living by doing odd jobs **2**（指人） casual labourer: 雇几个～ hire a couple of odd-job men
【零和】línghé〈名〉 zero sum: ～游戏 zero-sum game
【零花】línghuā **A**〈动〉 spend money on small things: 这钱你拿着～。 Keep it as pocket money. **B**〈名〉 pocket money
【零花钱】línghuāqián〈名〉 pocket money
【零活儿】línghuór〈名〉 odd job: 做～ do odd jobs
【零件】língjiàn〈名〉 part: 更换～ change a part
【零就业】língjiùyè〈名〉 unemployment: ～家庭 zero-employment family
【零距离】língjùlí〈名〉 zero distance: ～接触 zero-distance contact
【零口供】língkǒugōng〈名〉zero confession
【零库存】língkùcún〈名〉 zero stock
【零利率】línglìlǜ〈名〉 zero rate
【零料】língliào〈名〉 remnant: 一块～ a remnant
【零落】língluò **A**〈动〉 **1**（凋谢） wither: 草木～ bare trees and withered grass **2**（衰败） be in desperate circumstances: 凄凉～的景象 scene of desolation ‖ 家业～。 The family property is in decline. **B**〈形〉 scattered: ～的枪声 sporadic gunfire
【零卖】língmài〈动〉 retail
【零排放】língpáifàng〈名〉 zero emissions: 污水～ zero output of raw sewage ‖ 工厂实现了二氧化碳～。 The plant achieved zero carbon dioxide emission.
【零配件】língpèijiàn〈名〉 parts and accessories
【零七八碎】língqī-bāsuì〈成〉 **1**（指零乱） scattered and disorderly: 阁楼用来放置一些～的家具。The attic is used to store odds and ends of furniture. **2**（指数量小）

odds and ends: 只剩下一些～儿。 There are just a few odds and ends left.

【零钱】língqián ▸**p. 328**〈名〉**1**（指面值小） change: ～不用找了。 Keep the change. ‖ 他要换十块钱的～。 He wanted change for a ten-*yuan* note. **2**（零花钱） pocket money: 给孩子一些～ give one's children some pocket money **3**（指收入） additional income: 业余时间挣～ work for extra money in one's spare time

【零敲碎打】língqiāo-suìdǎ〈成〉 do sth. in bits and pieces: 这本书他～地写了一年才完成。 He worked on and off for a year before he finished it on the book.

【零容忍】língróngrěn〈名〉 zero tolerance: 采取毫不留情的"～"政策 adopt a dispassionate zero-tolerance policy

【零散】língsǎn〈形〉 scattered: 人口分布～ sparsely populated ‖ 演说结束后，掌声零零散散。 The speech met with only sporadic applause.

【零声母】língshēngmǔ〈名〉［语言］ zero initial

【零时】língshí〈名〉 zero hour

【零食】língshí〈名〉 snack: 吃～ eat snacks

【零首付】língshǒufù〈名〉 zero down payment: 以～方式贷款买了一辆汽车 buy a car with a zero down payment loan

【零售】língshòu〈动〉 retail: ～兼批发 retail and wholesale ‖ ～店 retail shop ‖ ～价 retail price

【零售商】língshòushāng〈名〉 retailer

【零售物价指数】 língshòu wùjià zhǐshù〈名〉 retail price index (RPI)

【零售业】língshòuyè〈名〉 retailing

【零数】língshù〈名〉 remainder

【零碎】língsuì **A**〈形〉 fragmentary: ～布料 scraps of cloth ‖ ～活儿 odd jobs **B**〈名〉 bits and pieces: 他把口袋里的～儿都掏了出来。 He fished out all the odds and ends from his pocket.

【零头】língtóu〈名〉**1** ▸**p. 328**（指钱） remainder: 有～要找我吗？ Is there any change coming my way? **2**（剩余物） remnant: 这块～布足够做个围裙了。 The leftover bits of cloth will be enough to make an apron.

【零投诉】líng tóusù〈名〉 no complaints: 服务～ no complaints about the service

【零星】língxīng〈形〉**1**（零碎） fragmentary: ～材料 fragmentary material ‖ ～支出 minor expenditures ‖ ～土地 odd pieces of land **2**（稀疏） sporadic: ～小雨 scattered showers ‖ ～的枪声 occasional gunshots

【零讯】língxùn〈名〉 scraps of news [usu used as the title of a newspaper column]: 房地产～ Real Estate News

【零用】língyòng **A**〈动〉 spend money on minor purchases: 这一百元钱你留着～吧。 Keep this 100-*yuan* note for small and incidental purchases. **B**〈名〉 pocket money: 我身边一点儿～都没有了。 I don't have any spending money on me.

【零用钱】língyòngqián〈名〉 pocket money

【零增长】língzēngzhǎng〈名〉 zero growth: 经济～ zero economic growth ‖ 人口～ zero population growth

【零嘴】língzuǐ〈方〉= 零食 língshí

龄（齡）líng

〈名〉**1**（年纪） age: ▸年～, 适～ **2**（年限） length of time: 舰～ ship's length of service ▸党～, 工～ **3**［生物］ instar: 幼虫～ larval instar

鲮（鯪）líng

【鲮鲤】línglǐ〈名〉 pangolin

【鲮鱼】língyú〈名〉 dace

lǐng

令 lǐng

〈量〉 ream: 两～新闻纸 two reams of newsprint ‖ 一～牛皮纸 a ream of brown paper

▸lìng

岭（嶺）lǐng

〈名〉**1**（山） mountain: ▸崇山峻～, 分水～, 山～ **2**（山脉） mountain range: 大/小兴安～ Greater/Lesser Xing'an Mountains ▸秦～ **3**（指五岭） Five Ridges [across the borders between Hunan and Jiangxi and Guangdong and Guangxi]: ▸～南

【岭南】Lǐngnán〈名〉 regions south of the Five Ridges [covering Guangdong and Guangxi provinces]

领（領）lǐng

A〈名〉**1**（脖） neck: ▸～带, ～巾 **2**（衣领） collar: 衬衫～儿 shirt collar ‖ 软/硬～ soft/hard collar ▸～扣, 衣～ **3**（要点） main point: ▸纲～, 提纲挈～, 要～ **4**（领口） neckline: 方/圆～ square/round neck ‖ 鸡心～ heart-shaped neck ‖ 中式立～ mandarin collar ‖ 圆～衫 round-necked shirt ▸～口, 翻～

B〈动〉**1**（拥有） possess: ▸～海, ～事, 占～ **2**（带领） lead: ～客人入座 usher guests to their seats ‖ ～来宾参观校园 show the visitors round the campus ‖ ～盲人过马路 guide a blind man across a road ▸～航, ～路, 带～, 率～ **3**（接受） accept: ▸～情, ～受 **4**（领取） receive: ～工资 receive a salary ‖ ～退休金 draw one's pension ▸～奖, 冒～, 认～ **5**（了解） understand: ▸～会, ～悟, 心～神会

C〈量〉 [for robes, mats, etc.]: 三～席 three mats ‖ 一～道袍 a Taoist gown

【领班】lǐngbān **A**〈动〉 lead a team of workers: 下星期该她～。 It's her turn to lead the work team next week. **B**〈名〉 foreman: 由服务员提升为～ be promoted from waiting staff to head waiter

【领唱】lǐngchàng **A**〈动〉 lead a chorus **B**〈名〉 lead singer: 担任～ be a lead singer

【领带】lǐngdài〈名〉 tie: 系～ tie one's tie ‖ 真丝～ silk tie

【领导】lǐngdǎo **A**〈动〉 lead: ～大家奔小康 lead people to a wealthy life ‖ ～有方 exercise good leadership ‖ 集体～ collective leadership **B**〈名〉 leader: ～要深入群众。 Leaders should go among the masses. ‖ 他是我校的老～。 He is the former leader of our school.

【领导班子】lǐngdǎo bānzi〈名〉 leadership: 调整～ reshuffle the leadership

【领导地位】lǐngdǎo dìwèi〈名〉 leadership: 处于～ be in leading position

【领导干部】lǐngdǎo gànbù〈名〉 leading cadre: ～要以身作则。 All government officials must lead by example.

【领导骨干】lǐngdǎo gǔgàn〈名〉 key members of the leadership

【领导核心】lǐngdǎo héxīn〈名〉 core of leadership

【领导水平】lǐngdǎo shuǐpíng〈名〉 level of leadership

【领导艺术】lǐngdǎo yìshù〈名〉 art of leadership

【领道】lǐngdào〈动〉〈方〉 lead the way: 你熟悉这地方，就在前面～吧。 As you know this place well, you lead the way.

【领地】lǐngdì〈名〉**1**（指私人） manor **2**（指国家） domain: 中国的～ Chinese territory

【领跌】lǐngdiē〈动〉［金融］ fall in price first: 在银行股～后，地产股也随之下跌。 After the bank shares fell, property shares fell as well.

【领读】lǐngdú〈动〉 lead in reading aloud

【领队】lǐngduì **A**〈动〉 lead a group: ～参加比赛 lead a group to take part in a competition **B**〈名〉 group leader: 乒乓球～ captain of a table tennis team

【领港】lǐnggǎng **A**〈动〉 pilot a ship **B**〈名〉 pilot

【领钩】lǐnggōu〈名〉 collar hook

【领海】lǐnghǎi〈名〉 territorial waters: ～范围 extent of territorial waters

【领航】lǐngháng **A**〈动〉 navigate **B** ▸**p. 966**〈名〉 navigator

【领航员】lǐnghángyuán = 领航 lǐngháng B

【领花】lǐnghuā〈名〉**1**（领结） bow tie **2**（军、警服标志） collar insignia

【领会】lǐnghuì〈动〉 grasp: ～文件精神 grasp the essence of a document ‖ 我当时没有～你的意思。 I didn't see your point at the time.

【领江】lǐngjiāng **A**〈动〉 navigate a ship on a river **B**〈名〉 river pilot

【领奖】lǐngjiǎng〈动〉 receive a prize: ～台 winner's podium

【领教】lǐngjiào〈动〉**1**〈套〉（接受） [used to express thanks for sb.'s advice, etc.] receive your instructions: 你说得很对，～～。 You are quite right. Thanks for your advice. **2**（请教） seek advice: 有件私事想～。 I'd like to consult you about a private matter. **3**（感受） [used ironically] experience: 我今天总算～了她的厉害。 Today I finally found myself on the receiving end of her sharp tongue.

【领结】lǐngjié〈名〉 bow tie: 打/扎～ tie a bow tie

【领巾】lǐngjīn〈名〉 scarf: ▸红～

【领军】lǐngjūn〈动〉**1**（率领军队） command an army: ～打仗 lead an army to war **2**〈喻〉（领队） play a leading role

【领军人】lǐngjūnrén〈名〉〈喻〉 leader: 国家体操队的～ the star of the national gymnastic team

【领空】lǐngkōng〈名〉 territorial airspace: 侵犯～ intrude into territorial airspace

【领空权】lǐngkōngquán〈名〉 sovereign right over territorial sky

【领口】lǐngkǒu〈名〉**1**（脖颈处空当） neck: 衬衫的～小了点。 The collar of the shirt is a bit too small. **2**（领子接合处） place where the two ends of a collar meet: ～没扣紧。 The collar of the shirt is not properly buttoned up.

【领扣】lǐngkòu〈名〉 collar button

【领路】lǐnglù〈动〉 show the way: ～人 guide ‖ 找个人～吧。 Find a guide to show the way.

【领略】lǐnglüè〈动〉 appreciate: ～大自然的美 enjoy the beauty of nature

【领命】lǐngmìng〈动〉 take an order

【领情】lǐngqíng〈动〉 appreciate sb.'s kindness: 我们给了他面子，他却不～。 We did show him respect, but he did not appreciate the gesture.

【领取】lǐngqǔ〈动〉 receive: ～薪水 get one's salary ‖ ～养老金 receive one's old-age pension ‖ 包裹只能在邮局～。

l

You can get your parcel only at the post office.

【领事】lǐngshì〈名〉consul: ～豁免权 consular immunity ‖ 总～ consul general

【领事裁判权】lǐngshì cáipànquán〈名〉consular jurisdiction

【领事处】lǐngshìchù〈名〉consular office

【领事馆】lǐngshìguǎn〈名〉consulate: 中国驻纽约总～ Consulate General of the People's Republic of China in New York

【领受】lǐngshòu〈动〉receive: 虚心～老师的教诲 listen with an open mind to the teacher's instructions ‖ 这份礼物我不能～。I cannot accept this gift.

【领属】lǐngshǔ〈动〉possess and control: ～关系 relationship of control and being controlled

【领水】lǐngshuǐ〈名〉**1**（内陆水系）inland waters **2**（领海）territorial waters

【领水员】lǐngshuǐyuán ▸**p. 966**〈名〉navigator

【领头】lǐngtóu〈动〉〈口〉take the lead: 你～，我们跟着。You lead and we'll follow.

【领头羊】lǐngtóuyáng〈名〉bellwether: 股票市场的～ market bellwether

【领土】lǐngtǔ〈名〉territory: 保卫国家的神圣～ defend the sacred territory of one's country ‖ 扩张～ expand one's territory

【领土扩张】lǐngtǔ kuòzhāng〈名〉territorial expansion

【领土完整】lǐngtǔ wánzhěng〈名〉territorial integrity

【领土要求】lǐngtǔ yāoqiú〈名〉territorial claim

【领舞】lǐngwǔ **A**〈动〉lead a dance **B**〈名〉leading dancer

【领悟】lǐngwù〈动〉understand: ～个中奥妙 grasp the subtlety (of sth.) ‖ ～某人真实意图 come to know sb.'s real intention

【领洗】lǐngxǐ〈动〉［宗教］be baptized

【领先】lǐngxiān〈动〉be in the lead: 处于～地位 be in the lead ‖ 遥遥～ hold a safe lead ‖ 该校在许多方面～于其他学校。This school is ahead of the others in many ways.

【领衔】lǐngxián〈动〉**1**（指署名）head a list **2**（指表演）lead a cast: ～主演 play the leading role

【领袖】lǐngxiù〈名〉**1**（指衣服）collar and sleeves **2**（指人）leader: 革命～ revolutionary leader ‖ 工会～ union leader ‖ 文坛～ leader of the literary world

【领养】lǐngyǎng〈动〉adopt: ～孩子 adopt a child ‖ ～人 adopter ‖ 被～人 adoptee

【领有】lǐngyǒu〈动〉possess

【领域】lǐngyù〈名〉**1**（指主权范围）territory **2**（指范畴）field: 扩大知识～ widen the field of knowledge ‖ 意识形态～ ideological field ‖ 政治/经济～ political/economic realm

【领章】lǐngzhāng〈名〉collar badge

【领涨】lǐngzhǎng〈动〉［金融］rise in price first: 科技股扮演～角色。Technology stocks play a role in leading price rises.

【领主】lǐngzhǔ〈名〉feudal lord

【领子】lǐngzi〈名〉collar: 把～翻起来 turn the collar up ‖ 衬衫～ neck of a shirt

【领奏】lǐngzòu **A**〈动〉lead an instrument ensemble **B**〈名〉leading player

【领罪】lǐngzuì〈动〉admit one's guilt: 甘愿～ readily confess one's crime

【领座】lǐngzuò〈动〉usher sb. to their seat

【领座员】lǐngzuòyuán ▸**p. 966**〈名〉usher

lìng

另 lìng

A〈代〉other: ～一只手 the other hand ‖ 走～一条路 take another route ‖ 那是～一码事。That's a different kettle of fish. ▸～案, ～册

B〈副〉in addition: ～搞一套 do otherwise ‖ ～谋出路 try to find another way out ‖ ～想办法 find some other ways ‖ ～有打算 have some other plans ‖ ～有企图 have other intentions ‖ ～有所爱 have another love ▸～起炉灶, ～请高明

【另案】lìng'àn〈名〉separate case: ～办理/侦察 be handled/investigated as a separate case

【另册】lìngcè〈名〉other register [a Qing Dynasty census book for listing disreputable people]: 入～ register sb. as undesirable

【另当别论】lìngdāng-biélùn〈成〉should be treated differently: 如果他是因病缺席，那就～。If he were absent because of illness, that would be a different matter.

【另类】lìnglèi **A**〈形〉alternative: ～服装 alternative clothing **B**〈名〉nonconformist

【另立门户】lìnglì-ménhù〈成〉〈喻〉become independent

【另立山头】lìnglì-shāntóu〈成〉form a faction of one's own

【另辟蹊径】lìngpì-xījìng〈成〉blaze a trail

【另起炉灶】lìngqǐ-lúzào〈成〉〈喻〉**1**（重新开始）make a fresh start: 咱们～吧。Let's start all over again then. **2**（独立做）do sth. on one's own: 公司有人打算～，成立新公司。Some people in the company are planning to set up a new company of their own.

【另请高明】lìngqǐng-gāomíng〈成〉find a better qualified replacement for a job: 恐怕你们得～了。I'm afraid you'll have to find someone more competent.

【另外】lìngwài **A**〈代〉other: 现在讨论～一个问题。Now let's talk about another issue. **B**〈副〉separately: 这件事～处理。This will be dealt with separately. **C**〈连〉besides: 请把这份报告送交校长，～告诉他有位外国专家想约见他。Take this report to the president and also tell him that a foreign expert wants to make an appointment with him.

【另行】lìngxíng〈动〉do separately: ～安排 make separate arrangements ‖ ～通知 issue a separate notice

【另眼相看】lìngyǎn-xiāngkàn〈成〉see sb. in a new light: 成功后人们对他就～了。People began to see him in a new light after his success.

【另议】lìngyì〈动〉discuss separately: 那个问题需要～。That needs another discussion.

令[1] lìng

A〈动〉**1**（命令）order: ～部队停止前进 order the troops to halt their advance ▸三～五申, 通～ **2**（使得）make: ～人费解 beyond comprehension ‖ ～人鼓舞 be encouraging ▸利～智昏

B〈名〉**1**（命令）command: 大赦～ order of general amnesty ‖ 停火～ cease-fire order ▸法～, 禁～, 下～, 指～ **2**（时节）season: ▸当～, 时～, 夏～ **3**（酒令）drinking game: 猜拳行～ drink and play finger-guessing ▸酒～ **4**（指官名）ancient official title: ▸县～ **5**（小令）ditty:《叨叨～》*Chattering Song* ‖《如梦～》*Dream Ditty*

令[2] lìng

〈形〉**1**〈书〉（美好）excellent: ▸～名 **2**〈敬〉（用于称呼）your: ～妹/兄 your sister/brother ▸～爱, ～郎, ～堂 ▸lǐng

【令爱】lìng'ài〈名〉〈敬〉your daughter

【令嫒】lìng'ài = 令爱 lìng'ài

【令出法随】lìngchū-fǎsuí〈成〉an issued order must be observed strictly

【令出如山】lìngchū-rúshān〈成〉〈喻〉every order must be obeyed

【令德】lìngdé〈名〉〈书〉excellent virtue

【令箭】lìngjiàn〈名〉arrow used as symbol of military orders in ancient China: ▸拿着鸡毛当～

【令箭荷花】lìngjiàn héhuā〈名〉［植物］nopalxochia ackermannii

【令阃】lìngkǔn〈名〉〈旧〉〈敬〉your wife

【令郎】lìngláng〈名〉〈敬〉your son

【令名】lìngmíng〈名〉〈书〉good name

【令旗】lìngqí〈名〉flag of command

【令亲】lìngqīn〈名〉〈敬〉your relative

【令人齿冷】lìngrénchǐlěng〈成〉arouse scorn

【令人发指】lìngrénfàzhǐ〈成〉make one's blood boil

【令人喷饭】lìngrénpēnfàn〈成〉be screamingly funny

【令人捧腹】lìngrénpěngfù〈成〉make people burst out laughing

【令人起敬】lìngrénqǐjìng〈成〉fill one with respect

【令人神往】lìngrénshénwǎng〈成〉have a strong appeal

【令人作呕】lìngrénzuò'ǒu〈成〉make one sick

【令堂】lìngtáng〈名〉〈敬〉your mother

【令行禁止】lìngxíng-jìnzhǐ〈成〉strict enforcement of law

【令尊】lìngzūn〈名〉〈敬〉your father

liū

溜 liū

A〈动〉**1**（滑行）slide: 从滑梯上～下来 slide down the chute ▸～冰 **2**（溜走）sneak off: 他悄悄地～了过去，没被人发现。He slipped past without being seen. ‖ 小偷从后门～出去了。The thief slipped out by the back door. ▸～之大吉 **3**（顺着）go along: ～着墙根儿走 walk along the wall **4** = 熘 liū

B〈形〉slippery: ▸～光, 滑～ ▸liù

【溜边】liūbiān〈动〉〈口〉**1**（靠着边）keep to the edge **2**〈喻〉（不介入）stay detached: 他一向怕事，见到矛盾就～。He is timid and always keeps himself out of disputes.

【溜冰】liūbīng〈动〉go skating: ～场 skating rink ‖ ～鞋 skates

【溜达】liūda〈动〉〈方〉stroll: 来回～ stroll up and down ‖ 你想去～～吗? Would you like to go for a stroll?

【溜工】liūgōng〈动〉〈口〉sneak away during work hours

【溜光】liūguāng〈形〉〈口〉**1**（光滑）very smooth: ～的鹅卵石 smooth cobbles ‖ 他的头发梳得～。His hair is combed sleek. **2**（精光）totally bare: 山上的树砍得～。The mountain was totally deforested.

【溜旱冰】liū hànbīng〈动〉roller-skate

【溜号】liūhào〈动〉〈口〉sneak off: 会没开完他就～了。He slipped away before

the end of the meeting.

【溜滑】liūhuá〈形〉〈口〉① (光滑) slippery: 雨后路上～。The road is quite slippery after the rain. ②〈喻〉(狡猾) sly

【溜肩膀】liūjiānbǎng〈名〉 sloping shoulders: ～的人 people with sloping shoulders

【溜溜球】liūliūqiú〈名〉 yo-yo

【溜溜转】liūliūzhuàn〈动〉 spin round and round: 小男孩把陀螺抽得～。The little boy spun the top so that it kept turning round and round. ‖〈喻〉他被她的甜言蜜语哄得～。He was whirled around by her sweet-talk.

【溜门撬锁】liūmén-qiàosuǒ〈动〉〈俗〉 burglary

【溜须拍马】liūxū-pāimǎ〈成〉〈喻〉 toady to

【溜圆】liūyuán〈形〉〈方〉 perfectly round: 双眼瞪得～ pop open one's eyes

【溜之大吉】liūzhīdàjí〈成〉〈诙〉 sneak off: 他见势不妙，便～。Aware of the unfavourable situation, he made himself scarce.

【溜走】liūzǒu〈动〉 sneak away

熘 liū〈动〉 sauté with thick gravy: ～鱼片 sautéed fish slices ‖ 醋～白菜 sautéed cabbage
▸liù

蹓 liū〈动〉 slip off
▸liù

【蹓跶】liūda = 溜达 liūda

liú

刘（劉） liú

【刘海儿】liúhǎir〈名〉 fringe〈英〉; bangs〈美〉: 一排整齐的～ a tidy fringe of hair

浏（瀏） liú

【浏览】liúlǎn〈动〉 skim through: ～报纸 browse a newspaper ‖ ～市容 go sightseeing round the city

【浏览器】liúlǎnqì〈名〉［计算机］ browser

留 liú〈动〉① (停留) stay: ～下来照看病人 stay to take care of the patients ‖ 独自～在家里 stay at home alone ▸～级, ～任, 停～ ② (使不离去) ask sb. to stay: ～客人吃饭 ask the guests to stay for dinner ‖ 那我就不～你了。In that case, I won't keep you any longer. ▸扣～, 收～, 挽～ ③ (保留) save: ～底稿 keep the draft ‖ ～出一些钱备用 have some money saved ‖ 这些座位是～给老人和残疾人的。These seats are reserved for the elderly and the disabled. ▸～后路, 保～, 自～地 ④ (遗留) leave behind: ～下大笔遗产 bequeath a legacy ‖ 把财产～给孩子 leave one's property to one's children ‖ 给听众～下深刻的印象 make a strong impression on an audience ▸～言, 残～ ⑤ (收下) accept: 我给他送去四本书，他只～了一本。He only accepted one of the four books I sent to him. ⑥ (留意) concentrate on: ▸～神, ～心, ～意 ⑦ (留学) study abroad: ～法/美 study in France/America ▸～学, ～洋 ⑧ (蓄) grow: ～长发 wear one's hair long ‖ ～胡子 grow a beard

【留白】liúbái〈动〉［美术］ leave a blank space [as an artistic technique]: ～是中国画的一种技法。Leaving blank space is one of the techniques of Chinese painting.

【留班】liúbān〈动〉〈口〉= 留级 liújí

【留别】liúbié〈动〉〈书〉 give sb. a parting gift or write a poem for him when taking leave of him

【留别纪念】liúbié jìniàn〈名〉 souvenir

【留步】liúbù〈动〉〈套〉 [said by a departing guest to a host] don't bother to see me out: 请～! Please don't worry about seeing me out!

【留成】liúchéng〈动〉 retain a percentage: 利润/外汇～ retain a percentage of profits/foreign exchange

【留传】liúchuán〈动〉 preserve and pass down: ～下来的秘方 secret recipe handed down through generations

【留存】liúcún〈动〉① (保留) keep: 必须～一些资金以备急用。Some money must be put aside for emergencies. ‖ 这份文件～备查。This document should be kept on file for future reference. ② (存在) exist: 二十年来～下来的一些老照片 some old photos collected over the past twenty years ‖ 他将永远～在我们的记忆中。His memory will always remain with us.

【留待】liúdài〈动〉 wait till later: 这个问题～以后再讨论。Let's discuss the matter later.

【留党察看】liúdǎng chákàn〈动〉 be placed on probation within the Party [as an inner-Party disciplinary measure]

【留得青山在，不怕没柴烧】liúdé qīngshān zài, bùpà méi chái shāo〈俗〉〈喻〉 while there is life, there is hope

【留底】liúdǐ〈动〉 keep a copy as a record

【留饭】liúfàn〈动〉 keep food for sb.

【留后路】liú hòulù〈惯〉 leave oneself options: 给自己～ leave oneself a way out

【留后手】liú hòushǒu〈惯〉 leave room for manoeuvre

【留话】liúhuà〈动〉 leave a message

【留级】liújí〈动〉 be kept back a year: ～生 pupil resitting a year

【留局待领】liújú dàilǐng〈名〉 Poste Restante

【留空】liúkòng〈动〉 leave a blank

【留兰香】liúlánxiāng〈名〉［植物］ spearmint

【留连】liúlián = 流连 liúlián

【留恋】liúliàn〈动〉 be reluctant to leave: ～故土 yearn for one's native land ‖ ～家乡 be reluctant to leave one's native land

【留门】liúmén〈动〉 leave the door unlocked in expectation of sb.: 他交代妻子晚上给他～。He told his wife to leave the door unlocked for him at night.

【留面子】liú miànzi〈动〉 let sb. keep some self-respect

【留难】liúnàn〈动〉 make things difficult for sb.: 他在故意～我们。He is deliberately making things difficult for us.

【留尼汪岛】Liúníwāngdǎo〈名〉 Réunion

【留念】liúniàn〈动〉 do as a souvenir: 合影～ have a group photo taken to mark an occasion ‖ 互赠礼物～ exchange gifts as souvenirs

【留鸟】liúniǎo〈名〉 non-migratory bird: 树多了，～也多了。More trees mean that there are more resident birds.

【留情】liúqíng〈动〉 show mercy: 毫不～ show no mercy ▸手下～

【留任】liúrèn〈动〉 retain a post: ～厂长 continue as the director of a factory

【留神】liúshén〈动〉 take care: 过马路要～。Look out when crossing the street. ‖ 下雨路滑，脚下要多～。Watch your step. The road is slippery after the rain.

【留声机】liúshēngjī〈名〉 record player

【留守】liúshǒu〈动〉① (指留在原处) stay behind to keep guard: 我们需要一些人～后方。We need some people to stay behind to take care of things at the rear. ② (指留在家) be left at home while one's spouse is abroad: ～男士/女士 man/woman left at home while his/her spouse is abroad ‖ 丈夫出国了，她～在家。With her husband abroad, she stayed behind at home.

【留守处】liúshǒuchù〈名〉 rear office

【留守人员】liúshǒu rényuán〈名〉 rear personnel

【留宿】liúsù〈动〉① (留人住宿) put up a guest for the night: 集体宿舍，不得～。Having guests overnight in the dormitory is not allowed. ② (留下来住宿) stay overnight: 在一家小旅馆～ put up for the night in an inn

【留头】liútóu〈动〉 let one's hair grow long

【留退步】liú tuìbù〈动〉 keep a way open for retreat

【留尾巴】liú wěiba〈惯〉 leave sth. unfinished: 赶天黑前把活干完，别再～了。Try to finish the work before it gets dark. Don't leave any of it unfinished.

【留校】liúxiào〈动〉 remain at one's alma mater as a faculty member after graduation

【留校察看】liúxiào chákàn〈动〉 be allowed to remain in school on probation

【留心】liúxīn〈动〉 be careful: ～股市行情 watch the stock market very closely ‖ ～别上当。Take care not to be taken in.

【留学】liúxué〈动〉 study abroad: 出国～ go abroad to study ‖ 在英国～ study in Britain

【留学生】liúxuéshēng〈名〉 overseas student

【留言】liúyán A〈动〉 leave a message: ～簿 visitors' book ‖ 他不在，你想～吗？He is not in. May I take a message? B〈名〉 message: 有我的～吗？Is there a message for me?

【留洋】liúyáng〈动〉〈旧〉 study abroad

【留医】liúyī〈动〉 be hospitalized: 大夫建议病人～治疗。The doctor advised that the patient be hospitalized for further treatment.

【留一手】liú yīshǒu〈惯〉 hold back a trick or two: 那位老师傅总是把自己的技艺倾囊相授，从不～。The old master always taught his apprentices his craftsmanship without holding anything back.

【留意】liúyì〈动〉 keep an eye out: 请～看看书店有没有这本书。Keep your eyes open to see if the book is available in the bookshop.

【留影】liúyǐng A〈动〉 have one's picture taken as a memento: 在天安门前～ have one's photo taken in front of the Gate of Tian An Men B〈名〉 photo taken as a keepsake: 这是我中学毕业时的～。This is a photo taken when I left middle school.

【留用】liúyòng〈动〉 continue to employ: 降职～ be demoted

【留余地】liú yúdì〈动〉 leave some leeway: 说话、办事时一定要给自己～。We must leave ourselves some leeway when we talk about or do something.

【留针】liúzhēn〈动〉［中医］ keep the acupuncture needle in a certain point for a designated period of time

【留职】liúzhí〈动〉 retain one's post: ～停薪 be on leave with suspension of pay

【留滞】liúzhì〈动〉 be detained

【留种】liúzhǒng〈动〉［农业］make a stock of seeds

【留种地】liúzhǒngdì〈名〉 seedbed

【留驻】liúzhù〈动〉 remain stationed: 部队

～县城待命。 The army was stationed in the county town awaiting the order for the next manoeuvre.

流 liú

A〈动〉**1**（指液体） flow: ～汗 sweat ‖ ～口水 slaver ‖〈喻〉资金外～。 Capital flowed out of the country. ▸～淌，细水长～ **2**（移动） drift: ▸～动，～通，漂～ **3**（传播） pass on: ▸～传，～芳百世，～行 **4**（趋向） degenerate: ～于庸俗 become vulgar ‖ ～于形式 become a mere formality **5**（指刑罚） banish: ▸～放，～刑

B〈名〉**1**（流水） flowing water: 顺～而行 sail with the current ▸河～，激～，逆～，湍～ **2**（类水流事物） flow: ▸电～，寒～，人～ **3**（等级） grade: 二～歌手 second-rate singer ‖ 三～旅馆 third-rate hotel ‖ 一～作家 first-class writer ▸～派，名～，三教九～ **4**〈贬〉（指人） people of a certain sort: ▸女～

C〈形〉 flowing: ▸～畅，～利

【流弊】liúbì〈名〉 corrupt practice: 干部终身制的～ the abuses of a lifetime in official office

【流变】liúbiàn〈动〉〈书〉 evolve

【流标】liúbiāo〈动〉 fail to be sold at auction because of no bids

【流别】liúbié〈名〉〈书〉 **1**（指江河） tributary **2**（指文章或学术） school

【流播】liúbō〈动〉〈书〉 diffuse: ～甚广 be widespread

【流布】liúbù〈动〉〈书〉 spread: 广为～ be widespread

【流产】liúchǎn〈动〉 **1**（指女子） have a miscarriage: 人工～ induced abortion **2**〈喻〉（失败） abort: 那次行动～了。 The mission was aborted.

【流畅】liúchàng〈形〉 smooth: 动作协调～ smooth movement ‖ 文笔～ write with ease and grace ‖ 线条～ graceful lines

【流程】liúchéng〈名〉 **1**（指水流） distance travelled over water: ～很长的河 river of great length **2**（指工序） technological process: ～图 flow chart

【流传】liúchuán〈动〉 spread: 广为～ circulate widely ‖ 消息很快～开了。 The news spread quickly.

【流窜】liúcuàn〈动〉 be on the run: ～作案 run amok committing offences ‖ 追歼～的残匪 hunt down the remaining bandits and wipe them out

【流窜犯】liúcuànfàn〈名〉 serial offender at large

【流弹】liúdàn〈名〉 stray bullet: 为～所伤 be wounded by a stray bullet

【流荡】liúdàng〈动〉 **1**（飘荡） float: 天空中～着朵朵白云。 White clouds were floating in the sky. **2**（流浪） wander: ～街头 roam the streets

【流动】liúdòng〈动〉 **1**（指液体或气体） flow: 空气～。 The air is circulating. ‖ 水向低处～。 Water gathers in low places. **2**（移动） be on the move: 促进人才合理～ facilitate a rational flow of talented personnel ‖ ～摊贩 mobile stall vendor ‖ ～货车 shop-on-wheels

【流动基金】liúdòng jījīn〈名〉 circulating fund

【流动人口】liúdòng rénkǒu〈名〉 transient population

【流动哨】liúdòngshào〈名〉 patrol

【流动图书馆】liúdòng túshūguǎn〈名〉 bookmobile

【流动性】liúdòngxìng〈名〉［经济］ liquidity: ～危机 liquidity crisis

【流动资产】liúdòng zīchǎn〈名〉 liquid assets

【流动资金】liúdòng zījīn〈名〉 circulating funds

【流毒】liúdú **A**〈动〉 exert an evil influence: ～无穷 exert an endless evil influence **B**〈名〉 harmful effect: 肃清～ liquidate the harmful effects

【流芳百世】liúfāng-bǎishì〈成〉 one's name will go down in history

【流放】liúfàng〈动〉 **1**（指人） send into exile: 终身～ be exiled for life ‖ 她被～到西伯利亚。 She was banished to Siberia. **2**（指物） float downstream: ～木材 float logs downstream

【流风余韵】liúfēng-yúyùn〈成〉 surviving influence (of poets, etc.)

【流感】liúgǎn ▸**p. 50**〈名〉 flu

【流光】liúguāng〈名〉〈书〉 **1**（指时光） time: ～易逝。 Time flies. **2**（指光亮） flowing light

【流光溢彩】liúguāng-yìcǎi〈成〉 rich display of lights and colours

【流金铄石】liújīn-shuòshí〈成〉 sweltering

【流浸膏】liújìngāo〈名〉［药学］ liquid extract [prepared from medicinal herbs]

【流寇】liúkòu〈名〉 roving bandits

【流浪】liúlàng〈动〉 drift about: ～街头 roam the streets ‖ 到处～ wander from place to place

【流浪汉】liúlànghàn〈名〉 vagrant

【流泪】liúlèi〈动〉 shed tears

【流离】liúlí〈动〉〈书〉 wander the streets: ▸颠沛～

【流离失所】liúlí-shīsuǒ〈成〉 live a life of vagrancy: 战争使那个地区的居民～。 The war forced the residents of that area into a life of vagrancy.

【流利】liúlì〈形〉 fluent: 文笔～ write smoothly ‖ 说话～的人 fluent speaker ‖ 她说一口～的英语。 She speaks fluent English. ‖ 这支笔写起来很～。 This pen writes smoothly.

【流里流气】liúli-liúqì〈成〉 rascally: 行为～ behave like a rascal

【流连】liúlián〈动〉 linger: 她在湖边～了很久。 She lingered long at the lake.

【流连忘返】liúlián-wàngfǎn〈成〉 be unable to tear oneself away: 那里风景如画，令游人～。 Tourists are unable to tear themselves away from the picture-postcard view.

【流量】liúliàng〈名〉 **1**（指流体） volume of flow: ～调节 flow regulation **2**（指交通流量） flow of traffic: 交通～ traffic flow ‖ 旅客～ flow of passengers

【流露】liúlù〈动〉 betray involuntarily: ～出不满 reveal one's dissatisfaction ‖ 真情～ one's true feelings are revealed

【流落】liúluò〈动〉 wander about destitute: ～街头 become a beggar ‖ ～他乡 be stranded in a strange land

【流氓】liúmáng〈名〉 **1**（指人） rascal: 足球～ football hooligan **2**（指行为） hooliganism: ▸耍～

【流氓兔】liúmángtù〈名〉 Mashimaro [Korean cartoon character]

【流氓无产者】liúmáng wúchǎnzhě〈名〉〈旧〉 lumpenproletarian

【流氓习气】liúmáng xíqì〈名〉 hooliganism

【流氓行为】liúmáng xíngwéi〈名〉 indecent behaviour

【流媒体】liúméitǐ〈名〉［通信］ streaming media

【流民】liúmín〈名〉〈旧〉 refugee

【流明】liúmíng〈量〉［物理］ lumen

【流脑】liúnǎo〈简称〉＝流行性脑膜炎

【流年】liúnián〈名〉〈书〉 **1**（指岁月） fleeting time: ▸似水～ **2**（指运气） [in fortune-telling or palm-reading] prediction of a person's luck in a given year: ～不利 unlucky year

【流拍】liúpāi＝流标 liúbiāo

【流派】liúpài〈名〉 **1**（指支流） river branch, tributary **2**（指派别） school: 戏剧～ school of drama ‖ 学术～ school of thought

【流盼】liúpàn〈动〉〈书〉 cast a sidelong glance

【流配】liúpèi〈动〉〈旧〉 banish

【流品】liúpǐn〈名〉〈书〉 family status: 不入～ be of no standing in society

【流气】liúqì **A**〈形〉 rascally: 他这个人很～。 He is a regular rascal. **B**〈名〉 hooliganism

【流散】liúsàn〈动〉 scatter: ～人口 drifting population ‖ 他的字画大都～于民间。 Most of his calligraphy and paintings are scattered in folk collections.

【流沙】liúshā〈名〉 quicksand

【流失】liúshī〈动〉 **1**（指物质） be washed away: 防止水土～ prevent loss of water and soil erosion **2**（指人、财） drain: 人才～ brain drain ‖ 国有资产～ loss of state assets **3**（指学生） drop out: ～生 school dropout

【流食】liúshí〈名〉 liquid diet: 吃～ take fluids

【流矢】liúshǐ〈名〉 stray arrow: 为～所伤 be injured by a stray arrow

【流势】liúshì〈名〉 force and velocity of a current

【流逝】liúshì〈动〉 elapse: 随着时间的～ with the passage of time ‖ 光阴～。 Time passes.

【流水】liúshuǐ〈名〉 **1**（指水） current: 潺潺～ the babbling of flowing water **2**（指营业额） turnover: 他们本周做了25万元的～。 They have had a turnover of 250,000 *yuan* this week.

【流水不腐，户枢不蠹】liúshuǐ bù fǔ, hùshū bù dù〈成〉〈喻〉 keeping things in use keeps them working

【流水号】liúshuǐhào〈名〉 serial number

【流水席】liúshuǐxí〈名〉 open banquet

【流水线】liúshuǐxiàn〈名〉 assembly line

【流水账】liúshuǐzhàng〈名〉 day-to-day account: 记～ keep a day-to-day account

【流水作业】liúshuǐ zuòyè〈名〉 assembly line method

【流苏】liúsū〈名〉 tassels, fringe

【流俗】liúsú〈名〉〈贬〉 current fashion: 不为～所囿 not be confined by conventions

【流速】liúsù〈名〉 flow rate

【流淌】liútǎng〈动〉 flow: 河水缓缓～。 The river flowed along slowly.

【流体】liútǐ〈名〉 fluid: ～力学 fluid mechanics

【流通】liútōng〈动〉 flow: 空气～ circulation of air ‖ 加速商品～ increase the flow of goods ‖ 货币～ currency circulation

【流通股】liútōnggǔ〈名〉［金融］ tradable stock

【流通环节】liútōng huánjié〈名〉［经济］ intermediate link

【流通货币】liútōng huòbì〈名〉 currency

【流通领域】liútōng lǐngyù〈名〉 field of circulation

【流通盘】liútōngpán〈名〉［金融］ quantity of shares in circulation: 该股的～较大。 There are quite a lot of these shares in circulation.

【流通市场】liútōng shìchǎng〈名〉 circulation market

【流通性】liútōngxìng〈名〉 **1**（指气体）circulation: 飞机客舱的空气～ the air circulation in the air aircraft cabin **2**（指资产）flow: 大盘蓝筹股的～较好。The flow of blue chips on the stock market is pretty consistent.
【流通资产】liútōng zīchǎn〈名〉circulating asset
【流亡】liúwáng〈动〉 go into exile: ～国外 be exiled from one's own country ‖ ～生涯 a life in exile ‖ ～政府 government-in-exile
【流徙】liúxǐ〈动〉 **1**（指迁徙） wander about **2**〈旧〉（指刑罚） send into exile: ～边远 be banished to a remote place
【流线型】liúxiànxíng〈形〉 streamlined: ～设计 streamlined design
【流向】liúxiàng〈名〉 **1**（指水流） direction of a current: 河水的～ flow direction of a current **2**（指人、财） flow direction: 旅客的～ the direction passengers are flowing in ‖ 资金的～ flow direction of capital ‖ 人才的合理～ the rational flow of talented people
【流泻】liúxiè〈动〉〈书〉 gush out: 我打开窗户，月光～进来。Moonlight poured in as I opened the window.
【流星】liúxīng〈名〉 **1**［天文］ meteor: ～划过天空。A meteor shot across the sky. **2**［杂技］ meteors: 火～ fire-meteors ‖ 水～ water-meteors
【流星赶月】liúxīng-gǎnyuè〈成〉 at top speed: 她～般地赶往医院。She travelled post-haste to the hospital.
【流星体】liúxīngtǐ〈名〉 meteoroid
【流星雨】liúxīngyǔ〈名〉 meteor shower
【流刑】liúxíng〈名〉〈旧〉 forced labour in a remote region: 被判～ be sentenced to forced labour in a remote region
【流行】liúxíng〈动〉 be popular: 最新～时尚 latest fad ‖ 这种发型现在很～。This hairstyle is in fashion. ‖ 瘟疫～。The plague was widespread.
【流行病】liúxíngbìng〈名〉 **1**〈本〉 epidemic: 预防～的蔓延 prevent the spread of an epidemic **2**〈喻〉 prevalent social evil
【流行歌曲】liúxíng gēqǔ〈名〉 pop song: ～排行榜 pop charts
【流行歌手】liúxíng gēshǒu〈名〉pop singer
【流行色】liúxíngsè〈名〉 colour in fashion
【流行音乐】liúxíng yīnyuè〈名〉 pop music
【流行性】liúxíngxìng〈形〉 epidemic
【流行性感冒】liúxíngxìng gǎnmào ▸**p. 50**〈名〉 influenza
【流行性脑膜炎】liúxíngxìng nǎomóyán ▸**p. 50**〈名〉 epidemic meningitis
【流血】liúxuè〈动〉 **1**（指血液） bleed: ～冲突 bloody conflict ‖ 为祖国～牺牲 shed blood and lay down one's life for one's country ‖ 伤口在～。The wound is bleeding. **2**（指伤亡） be injured or die
【流言】liúyán〈名〉 rumour
【流言飞语】liúyán-fēiyǔ = 流言蜚语 liúyán-fēiyǔ
【流言蜚语】liúyán-fēiyǔ〈成〉 unfounded rumours and malicious gossip: 散布～ spread rumours
【流溢】liúyì〈动〉 overflow
【流萤】liúyíng〈名〉 flying firework
【流于形式】liúyú-xíngshì〈成〉 become a mere formality
【流域】liúyù〈名〉 river basin: 长江～ Yangtze River basin
【流贼】liúzéi〈名〉 roving bandit
【流质】liúzhì **A**〈形〉 liquid: 半～饮食 semi-liquid diet **B**〈名〉 liquid diet: 这个病人只能吃～。The patient can only consume liquids.
【流转】liúzhuǎn〈动〉 **1**（转移） wander about: ～四方 wander all over the country ‖ 岁月～。Time passes. **2**（周转） circulate: ～环节 intermediate links ‖ 资金～ cash flow **3**〈书〉（流畅） [of poetry, etc.] be smooth and natural

琉 liú
【琉璃】liúlí〈名〉 coloured glaze
【琉璃塔】liúlítǎ〈名〉 glazed pagoda
【琉璃瓦】liúliwǎ〈名〉 glazed tile
【琉球群岛】Liúqiú Qúndǎo〈名〉 Ryukyu Islands

硫 liú〈名〉［化学］ sulphur (S): ▸～磺
【硫化】liúhuà〈动〉［化学］vulcanize: ～氢 hydrogen sulphide
【硫化橡胶】liúhuà xiàngjiāo〈名〉 vulcanized rubber
【硫磺】liúhuáng〈名〉 sulphur: ～泉 sulphur spring
【硫酸】liúsuān〈名〉［化学］sulphuric acid: ～盐 sulphate
【硫酸铵】liúsuān'ǎn〈名〉 ammonium sulphate
【硫酸钡】liúsuānbèi〈名〉 barium sulphate
【硫酸钠】liúsuānnà〈名〉 sodium sulphate
【硫酸铜】liúsuāntóng〈名〉copper sulphate

馏（餾） liú〈动〉 distil: ▸蒸～ ▸liù

榴 liú〈名〉 pomegranate: ▸石～
【榴弹】liúdàn〈名〉 **1**（指炮弹） high explosive shell: ▸～炮 **2**（指武器） grenade, fragmentation shell and shells fired by cannon: ▸手～
【榴弹炮】liúdànpào〈名〉 howitzer
【榴莲】liúlián〈名〉 durian
【榴霰弹】liúxiàndàn〈名〉 canister shot

飗（飀） liú
【飗飗】liúliú〈形〉〈书〉 gently blowing

镏（鎦） liú ▸镏金 liújīn ▸liù
【镏金】liújīn〈动〉 gild: ～器皿 gilded utensils

鹠（鶹） liú ▸鸺鹠 xiūliú

瘤 liú〈名〉 tumour: ▸毒～, 肉～, 肿～
【瘤胃】liúwèi〈名〉［动物］ rumen
【瘤子】liúzi〈名〉〈口〉 tumour

鎏 liú
A〈名〉〈书〉（指黄金） fine gold
B = 镏 liú

liǔ

柳 liǔ〈名〉 **1**（柳树） willow: ▸垂～ **2**（指星宿） one of the 28 constellations in ancient Chinese astronomy
【柳暗花明】liǔ'àn-huāmíng〈成〉〈喻〉 see light at the end of the tunnel
【柳编】liǔbiān〈名〉 wickerwork
【柳笛】liǔdí ▸**p. 929**〈名〉 willow whistle
【柳眉】liǔméi〈名〉 long and slender eyebrows of a woman
【柳腔】liǔqiāng〈名〉 a kind of opera popular in Shandong Province
【柳琴】liǔqín ▸**p. 929**〈名〉 *liuqin* [stringed instrument]
【柳树】liǔshù〈名〉 willow (tree)
【柳丝】liǔsī〈名〉 thin willow twig
【柳体】Liǔtǐ〈名〉［书法］ Liu style [calligraphy of Liu Gongquan (柳公权) of the Tang Dynasty]
【柳条】liǔtiáo〈名〉 wicker: ～帽 wicker safety helmet
【柳条箱】liǔtiáoxiāng〈名〉 wicker suitcase
【柳絮】liǔxù〈名〉willow catkins: ～纷飞。Willow catkins are dancing in the air.
【柳腰】liǔyāo〈名〉 slender waist of a woman
【柳叶眉】liǔyèméi = 柳眉 liǔméi
【柳荫】liǔyīn〈名〉 shade of a willow tree
【柳莺】liǔyīng〈名〉 willow warbler: 黄腰～ yellow-rumped willow warbler
【柳子戏】liǔzixì〈名〉 Liuzi opera

绺（綹） liǔ〈量〉 strand: 三～毛线 three strands of wool ‖ 一～头发 a strand of hair
【绺子】liǔzi〈量〉 strand: 一～头发 a strand of hair

liù

六[1] liù ▸**p. 691**〈数〉 six: ～元钱 six *yuan* ‖ 一加五等于～。One plus five is six.

六[2] liù〈名〉［音乐］ note on the *gongche* (工尺) scale, corresponding to 5 in *jianpu* (简谱) numbered musical notation
【六边形】liùbiānxíng〈名〉 hexagon
【六朝】Liùcháo〈名〉Six Dynasties [Wu (吴), Eastern Jin (东晋), Song (宋), Qi (齐), Liang (梁), and Chen (陈), 220-589]
【六重唱】liùchóngchàng〈名〉(vocal) sestet
【六重奏】liùchóngzòu〈名〉 (instrumental) sestet
【六畜】liùchù〈名〉 six domestic animals — pig, ox, horse, goat, chicken, and dog: ～兴旺 prosperous country life
【六分仪】liùfēnyí〈名〉［天文］ sextant
【六腑】liùfǔ〈名〉［中医］ six hollow organs [the stomach, gall bladder, large intestine, small intestine, bladder, and *sanjiao* (三焦)]: ▸五脏～
【六根】liùgēn〈名〉［佛教］ the six roots of sensation — eyes, ears, nose, tongue, body and mind [believed to be the roots of sin]: ～清净 be free of human weaknesses
【六宫】liùgōng〈名〉 empress and imperial concubines or their residence
【六合】liùhé〈名〉〈古〉 **1**（指方位） six directions — north, south, east, west, up and down **2**（天下） whole country: 秦王扫～。The king of Qin conquered the whole country.
【六甲】liùjiǎ〈名〉 **1**（指天干地支） six of the sixty combinations of the ten Heavenly Stems and twelve Earthly Branches: 学～ learn to write Chinese characters **2**〈旧〉（怀孕） pregnancy: ▸身怀～
【六角形】liùjiǎoxíng = 六边形 liùbiānxíng
【六六大顺】liùliùdàshùn〈惯〉 two sixes together foretelling good luck [such as 66, June 6, etc.]
【六六六】liùliùliù〈名〉〈口〉［化学］ benzene hexachloride (BHC)
【六路】liùlù〈名〉 six directions [above, below, front, back, left and right]: 眼观～，耳听八方 have sharp eyes and keen ears

l

【六面体】liùmiàntǐ〈名〉 hexahedron: 正～ regular hexahedron

【六亲不认】liùqīn-bùrèn〈成〉 1（指无情无义） ruthless: 想不到他竟～。 I didn't expect him to be so heartless. 2（指公正） be committed to the public interest with no attempt to seek personal gains: 法官应严格执法，～。 Judges should be strict in the practice of law and never do favours for their relatives and friends.

【六亲无靠】liùqīn-wúkào〈成〉 have neither relatives nor friends to turn to (for help)

【六神】liùshén〈名〉［道教］ god that controls the six vital organs of human beings — heart, lungs, liver, gall bladder, kidneys and spleen

【六神不安】liùshén-bù'ān ＝ 六神无主 liùshén-wúzhǔ

【六神无主】liùshén-wúzhǔ〈成〉be at a loss: 可怕的消息吓得他～。 The terrible news completely shattered him.

【六书】liùshū〈名〉 six categories of Chinese characters [namely 指事zhǐshì、象形xiàngxíng、形声xíngshēng、会意huìyì、转注zhuǎnzhù and 假借jiǎjiè]

【六弦琴】liùxiánqín ▸**p. 929**〈名〉 guitar

【六一国际儿童节】Liù-Yī Guójì Értóngjié〈名〉 International Children's Day [June 1]

【六欲】liùyù〈名〉［佛教］ human desires: 七情～ human emotions and desires

【六月】liùyuè ▸**p. 928**〈名〉 1（阳历） June 2（阴历） sixth month of the lunar year

【六指儿】liùzhǐr〈名〉person with six fingers on one hand

陆（陸） liù ▸**p. 691**〈数〉 six [used for the numeral 六 on cheques, etc. to avoid alterations or mistakes]
▸lù

碌（磟） liù
▸lù

【碌碡】liùzhou〈名〉 stone roller

遛 liù〈动〉 1（指人） stroll: ～大街 take a stroll in the streets ‖ 咱们去～一圈吧。 Let's go for a stroll. 2（指牲口或鸟） walk (an animal): ～狗 walk a dog ‖ ～马 walk a horse ‖ ～鸟 walk in a quiet place with caged birds

【遛食】liùshí〈动〉〈方〉go for a walk after a meal

【遛弯儿】liùwānr〈动〉〈方〉 take a walk: 他带着狗～去了。 He took his dog for a walk.

馏（餾） liù〈动〉〈口〉 heat up in a steamer: ～馒头 heat up steamed bread
▸liú

溜[1] liù

A〈名〉 1（水流） swift current: 大～ torrent ‖ 河里～很大。 The river has a strong current. 2（雨水） rainwater from the roof 3（排水沟） eaves gutter: 水～ rainwater pipe 4（方）（附近） neighbourhood: 我们这一～儿很安静。 Ours is a quiet neighbourhood.

B〈量〉 line: 三～课桌 three rows of desks ‖ 靠墙是一～书架。 Bookshelves line the wall.

溜[2] liù〈动〉〈方〉 seal: 用灰浆～墙缝 seal the cracks in a wall with mortar
▸liū

熘 liù ＝ 馏 liù
▸liū

镏（鎦） liù
▸liú

【镏子】liùzi〈名〉〈方〉 ring: 钻石/金～ diamond/gold ring

鹨（鷚） liù〈名〉［鸟类］ pipit: 树～ tree pipit

蹓 liù ＝ 遛 liù
▸liū

lo

咯 lo〈助〉 [used in the same way as 了 (le), but slightly stronger]: 当然～! Of course!
▸gē, kǎ, luò

lōng

隆 lōng ▸轰隆 hōnglōng
▸lóng

lóng

龙（龍） lóng〈名〉 1（指传说中的动物） (Chinese) dragon: ▸～飞凤舞，画～点睛，蛟～ 2（象征帝王） emperor: ～袍 imperial robe ‖〈喻〉 ～的传人 the Chinese nation 3（指图案） dragon-like thing: ▸～灯，～舟 4（指爬行动物） huge extinct reptile: ▸恐～

> **龙**
>
> (Chinese) dragon, a mythical creature with a huge snake-like body covered in fish scales, and adorned with horns, a beard, claws, and feet. The dragon is able to fly. In ancient times, the dragon was a totem for the Han Chinese, and even today Chinese people often refer to themselves as descendants of the dragon (龙的传人). In ancient times almost all places had a dragon king temple where the dragon king was worshipped. It was believed that the dragon king controlled the forces of nature. A feudal ruler regarded the dragon as a symbol of power, and would refer to himself as 'the true dragon son of heaven' (真龙天子). Imperial possessions such as the emperor's robes and bed were decorated with dragons. Today, dragon dances take place at the Lantern Festival (▸元宵节), and dragon boat races are held during the Dragon Boat Festival (▸端午节).

【龙船】lóngchuán〈名〉 dragon boat [dragon-shaped racing boat]: 划～ row a dragon boat

【龙胆】lóngdǎn〈名〉［植物］ rough gentian

【龙胆紫】lóngdǎnzǐ〈名〉［药学］ gentian violet

【龙灯】lóngdēng〈名〉 dragon lantern: 舞～ dance with a dragon lantern

【龙飞凤舞】lóngfēi-fèngwǔ〈成〉1（形容书法） lively and vigorous: 他的字写得～。 His calligraphy assumes a vigorous but graceful style. 2（形容山势） majestic and zigzagging

【龙凤】lóngfèng〈名〉 1〈喻〉（杰出的人） virtuous and talented person 2（男女） a man and a woman: ～胎 boy and girl twins

【龙凤呈祥】lóngfèng-chéngxiáng〈成〉 symbol of harmony and good fortune

【龙肝凤髓】lónggān-fèngsuǐ〈成〉〈喻〉 rare delicacies

【龙宫】lónggōng〈名〉palace of the Dragon King: ～探宝 hunt for underwater treasures in the Palace of the Dragon King

【龙骨】lónggǔ〈名〉 1（指骨骼） breastbone of a bird 2［中药］ fossils of ancient mammals 3（指构件） keel (of a boat, plane, etc.)

【龙骨车】lónggǔchē〈名〉 chain pump

【龙井】lóngjǐng〈名〉 Dragon Well tea

【龙驹凤雏】lóngjū-fèngchú〈成〉〈喻〉 young, talented scholar

【龙卷风】lóngjuǎnfēng〈名〉 tornado

【龙口夺粮】lóngkǒu-duóliáng〈成〉 speed up the summer harvest before the storms break

【龙马精神】lóngmǎ jīngshén〈成〉 vigorous spirit

【龙门刨】lóngménbào〈名〉［机械］ double housing planer

【龙门吊】lóngméndiào〈名〉［机械］ gantry crane

【龙门石窟】Lóngmén Shíkū〈名〉Longmen Grottoes [in Luoyang, Henan Province]

【龙门阵】lóngménzhèn ＝ 摆龙门阵 bǎi lóngménzhèn

【龙脑】lóngnǎo〈名〉［化学］ borneol

【龙盘虎踞】lóngpán-hǔjù ＝ 虎踞龙盘 hǔjù-lóngpán

【龙袍】lóngpáo〈名〉 imperial robe

【龙山文化】Lóngshān wénhuà〈名〉 Longshan Culture [late Neolithic culture characterized by burnished black pottery]

【龙蛇混杂】lóngshé-hùnzá〈成〉 the good and the bad mixed together

【龙舌兰】lóngshélán〈名〉［植物］ agave

【龙生龙，凤生凤】lóng shēng lóng, fèng shēng fèng〈俗〉〈喻〉 like begets like

【龙潭虎穴】lóngtán-hǔxué〈成〉〈喻〉 danger spot

【龙套】lóngtào〈名〉 1（指戏服） costumes with dragon designs worn by soldiers or attendants 2（指人） actor playing a walk-on part in traditional opera: ▸跑～

【龙腾虎跃】lóngténg-hǔyuè〈成〉 hustle and bustle about: 全厂～搞生产。 The whole factory is engaged heart and soul in the production process.

【龙头】lóngtóu〈名〉 1（指开关） tap〈英〉; spigot〈美〉: 打开/关上～ turn a tap on/off ▸水～ 2〈方〉（指车把手） handlebar 3（指龙灯） head of a dragon lantern 4（领头者） leader: ～企业 leading enterprise ‖ 行业的～老大 flagship of the industry

【龙头凤尾】lóngtóu-fèngwěi〈成〉〈喻〉 be good from beginning to end

【龙王】Lóngwáng〈名〉 Dragon King [sea and rain god]

【龙虾】lóngxiā〈名〉 lobster

【龙涎香】lóngxiánxiāng〈名〉 ambergris

【龙骧虎步】lóngxiāng-hǔbù〈成〉〈喻〉 walk with majestic steps

【龙须菜】lóngxūcài〈名〉〈方〉 asparagus

【龙须草】lóngxūcǎo〈名〉 Chinese alpine rush

【龙须面】lóngxūmiàn〈名〉 dragon whiskers noodles [a kind of long thin noodle]

【龙牙草】lóngyácǎo〈名〉［植物］

hairyvein agrimony

【龙颜】lóngyán〈名〉〈书〉 1 (指容颜) countenance of an emperor 2 (指帝王) emperor: ～大怒。 The emperor flew into rage.

【龙眼】lóngyǎn〈名〉［植物］ longan

【龙爪槐】lóngzhǎohuái〈名〉 Chinese pagoda tree

【龙争虎斗】lóngzhēng-hǔdòu〈成〉 fierce struggle between well-matched opponents

【龙钟】lóngzhōng〈形〉〈书〉 senile: ▸老态～

【龙舟】lóngzhōu〈名〉 dragon boat [dragon-shaped racing boat]: ～竞渡 dragon-boat race

茏（蘢）lóng

【茏葱】lóngcōng〈形〉 luxuriant: 草木～ luxuriant vegetation

咙（嚨）lóng ▸喉咙 hóulong

珑（瓏）lóng〈名〉 jade with dragon-design carvings [used by ancient Chinese in supplicating the rain god]

【珑璁】lóngcōng〈书〉 A〈拟〉 jingle B = 茏葱 lóngcōng

栊（櫳）lóng〈名〉〈书〉 1 (栅栏) pen 2 (窗户) window: 帘～ curtained window

眬（矓）lóng ▸曚眬 ménglóng

胧（朧）lóng ▸朦胧 ménglóng

砻（礱）lóng

A〈名〉 huller

B〈动〉 hull

【砻糠】lóngkāng〈名〉 rice chaff

昽（曨）lóng ▸蒙昽 ménglóng

聋（聾）lóng〈形〉 deaf: 耳朵有点～ be slightly hard of hearing ▸～哑，震耳欲～

【聋聩】lóngkuì〈形〉〈书〉 1 (耳聋) deaf 2 (愚昧无知) ignorant

【聋哑】lóngyǎ〈形〉 deaf and dumb: ～人 someone who cannot hear or speak

【聋哑学校】lóngyǎ xuéxiào〈名〉 school for people who cannot hear or speak

【聋子】lóngzi〈名〉 deaf person

【聋子的耳朵】lóngzide ěrduo〈歇后〉 impractical object

笼（籠）lóng

A〈名〉 1 (笼子) cage: 鸡～ chicken coop ‖ 鸟～ bird cage 2〈旧〉(囚笼) cell: ▸囚～ 3 (笼屉) steamer: 刚出～的馒头 buns fresh from the steamer ▸蒸～

B〈动〉 ignite: ▸～火

▸lǒng

【笼火】lónghuǒ〈动〉 make a fire

【笼屉】lóngtì〈名〉 bamboo steamer: ～盖儿 steamer cover

【笼头】lóngtou〈名〉 harness

【笼养】lóngyǎng〈动〉 raise (poultry) in cages

【笼中鸟】lóngzhōngniǎo〈成〉 caged bird

【笼子】lóngzi〈名〉 cage

【笼嘴】lóngzuǐ〈名〉 muzzle

隆 lóng〈形〉 1 (盛大) magnificent: ▸～重 2 (兴旺) thriving: ▸～盛，兴～ 3 (凸起) bulging: ▸～准 4 (程度深) deep: ～恩 great favours ▸～冬

▸lōng

【隆背】lóngbèi〈名〉 hunchback

【隆鼻】lóngbí〈动〉 elevate the bridge of sb.'s nose through plastic surgery: ～手术 operation to raise the bridge of a nose

【隆冬】lóngdōng ▸**p. 345**〈名〉 depths of winter: ～季节 in the dead of winter

【隆隆】lónglóng〈拟〉 rumble: ～的炮声 thunder of guns ‖ 雷声～。 The thunder rumbled.

【隆起】lóngqǐ〈动〉 swell: 青筋～。 Blue veins stood out.

【隆情】lóngqíng〈名〉〈书〉 profound feelings

【隆乳】lóngrǔ = 隆胸 lóngxiōng

【隆盛】lóngshèng〈形〉〈书〉 1 (兴盛) thriving: 国势～。 The country is prosperous. 2 (隆重) magnificent: ～的仪式 grand ceremony

【隆头鱼】lóngtóuyú〈名〉 wrasse

【隆胸】lóngxiōng〈动〉 enhance sb.'s breasts through plastic surgery: ～手术 breast enhancement surgery

【隆重】lóngzhòng〈形〉 grand: ～欢迎 welcome with great ceremony ‖ ～开幕 be solemnly opened

【隆准】lóngzhǔn〈名〉〈书〉 prominent nose

癃 lóng

A〈形〉〈书〉(病弱) infirm: ～病 weak and sickly ‖ 疲～ bent with age

B = 癃闭 lóngbì

【癃闭】lóngbì〈名〉［中医］ difficulty in urination

窿 lóng ▸窟窿 kūlong

lǒng

陇（隴）Lǒng ▸**p. 661**〈名〉 Long [another name for Gansu Province (甘肃)]: ～东/西 Eastern/Western Gansu ‖ ～海铁路 *Longhai* railway line ▸得～望蜀

【陇剧】lǒngjù〈名〉 Gansu opera

拢（攏）lǒng〈动〉 1 (聚合) bring together: 笑得合不～嘴 smile from ear to ear ‖ 他们怎么谈也谈不～。 No matter how much they talked, they could never bridge the gap between them. ▸聚～，拉～，收～ 2 (靠近) approach: ▸～岸，靠～ 3 (总计) add up: 把账～一～ tot up the accounts ▸～共，归～ 4 (梳理) comb: ～一～头发 comb one's hair

【拢岸】lǒng'àn〈动〉 pull a ship up alongside the shore

【拢共】lǒnggòng〈副〉 altogether: 出席会议的～只有五人。 There were only five people at the meeting, all told.

【拢音】lǒngyīn〈动〉 carry sound well: 这家音乐厅很～。 This music hall has excellent acoustics.

【拢子】lǒngzi〈名〉 fine-toothed comb

【拢总】lǒngzǒng = 拢共 lǒnggòng

垄（壟）lǒng〈名〉 1 (田间小路) raised path between fields 2 (土埂) ridge: 田～ field ridge ‖ 一～地 a strip of land ▸～沟，～作 3 (垄状物) ridge-shaped object: ▸瓦～

【垄断】lǒngduàn〈动〉 monopolize: ～市场 corner the market ‖ 保持/失去～地位 maintain/lose the monopoly (of) ‖ ～行业 monopoly industry

【垄断价格】lǒngduàn jiàgé〈名〉 monopoly price

【垄断利润】lǒngduàn lìrùn〈名〉 monopolist profit

【垄断企业】lǒngduàn qǐyè〈名〉 monopoly enterprise

【垄沟】lǒnggōu〈名〉 furrow

【垄作】lǒngzuò〈名〉［农业］ ridge culture

笼（籠）lǒng

A〈动〉 envelop: 烟～雾罩 be veiled in smoke and fog ‖ 薄雾～着山顶。 Mist enveloped the hilltops. ▸～罩

B〈名〉 trunk: ▸箱～

▸lóng

【笼络】lǒngluò〈动〉〈贬〉 rope in: ～人心 buy people's support ‖ 他很会～人。 He's very good at winning people over.

【笼统】lǒngtǒng〈形〉 general: 说得很～ speak in very general terms ‖ ～地说 generally speaking

【笼罩】lǒngzhào〈动〉 envelop: 群山～在薄雾之中。 The hills were shrouded in mist. ‖〈喻〉紧张的气氛～着整个会场。 An atmosphere of tension suffused the conference hall.

lòng

弄 lòng〈名〉〈方〉 alley: ▸里～

▸nòng

【弄堂】lòngtáng〈名〉〈方〉 lane: 一条～ a lane

lōu

搂（摟）lōu〈动〉 1 (聚集) gather up: ～树叶 rake up fallen leaves 2 (搜刮) extort: ～了不少 eke out a small fortune ‖ 大把大把地～钱 extort great amounts of money 3 (挽起) tuck up: ～起袖子 tuck up one's sleeves ‖ ～起裙子上楼 hold up the lower part of one's skirt and go upstairs 4〈方〉(核算) calculate with an abacus: 拿算盘一～，就知道赚了多少钱。 Tot it up on the abacus, and you'll know how much we have earned.

▸lǒu

【搂草机】lōucǎojī〈名〉 rake

【搂头盖脸】lōutóu-gàiliǎn〈成〉 right in the face: ～一巴掌 slap sb. across the face

瞜（瞜）lōu〈动〉〈方〉 look: 让我～一眼。 Let me take a look.

lóu

娄（婁）lóu〈形〉〈口〉 1 (过熟而变质) overripe and unfit to eat: 西瓜～了。 The watermelon is overripe. 2 (衰弱) weak: 他这几年身子骨可～了。 He has been in poor health in recent years. 3 (指星宿) one of the 28 constellations in ancient Chinese astronomy

【娄子】lóuzi〈名〉〈口〉 trouble: 惹～ stir up trouble ‖ 捅～ make a blunder

偻（僂） lóu ▸佝偻 gōulóu
▸lǚ
【偻㑩】lóuluó = 喽啰 lóuluó

蒌（蔞） lóu
【蒌蒿】lóuhāo〈名〉［植物］ beach wormwood
【蒌叶】lóuyè〈名〉［植物］ betel

喽（嘍） lóu
▸lou
【喽啰】lóuluó〈名〉**1**（旧）（指强盗）rank and file of a band of outlaws **2**（指追随者） underling: 贩毒集团的小～ an underling in a drugs racket

楼（樓） lóu〈名〉**1**（楼房）building with more than one storey: 高～ tall building ‖ 办公～ office building ‖ 教学～ classroom building ▸～房，摩天大～ **2**（加盖的房子） superstructure: ▸城～，箭～，角～ **3**（用于名称） [used in shop names, etc.]: ▸茶～，酒～ **4**（楼层） floor: 一～ ground floor〈英〉, first floor〈美〉 ‖ 二～ first floor〈英〉, second floor〈美〉
【楼板】lóubǎn〈名〉floor slab
【楼板价】lóubǎnjià〈名〉floor price
【楼层】lóucéng〈名〉 floor: 每个～都应有消火栓。 Every floor should be equipped with a fire hydrant.
【楼船】lóuchuán〈名〉towered ship
【楼道】lóudào〈名〉 corridor: ～内禁止堆放杂物。 Keep the corridor clear.
【楼房】lóufáng〈名〉 building of two or more storeys
【楼阁】lóugé〈名〉**1**（楼和阁） tower: 亭台～ imposing buildings **2**（建筑物） building
【楼花】lóuhuā〈名〉 building that is put up for sale before construction is completed: 出售～ sell unfinished buildings
【楼盘】lóupán〈名〉 commercial building being built or sold: 开发新～ develop new commercial buildings ‖ 推销～ market commercial buildings
【楼群】lóuqún〈名〉building complex
【楼上】lóushàng〈名〉 upstairs: 住～ live upstairs
【楼市】lóushì〈名〉 property market: ～过热 overheated property market
【楼台】lóutái〈名〉**1**〈方〉（凉台） balcony: 在～上养花 grow flowers on the balcony **2**〈书〉（楼房） high building: ▸近水～
【楼堂馆所】lóutáng-guǎnsuǒ〈名〉 office buildings, large halls and guest houses
【楼梯】lóutī〈名〉 staircase: 爬～ climb the stairs
【楼体】lóutǐ〈名〉 body of a building: ～坍塌事件 collapse of the building framework
【楼下】lóuxià〈名〉 downstairs: ～的房间 downstairs room
【楼宇】lóuyǔ〈名〉 building
【楼主】lóuzhǔ〈名〉 original poster [on a BBS forum]

耧（耬） lóu〈名〉drill (barrow): 摇～ shake the drill
【耧播】lóubō〈动〉sow with a drill

蝼（螻） lóu〈名〉［昆虫］ mole cricket
【蝼蛄】lóugū〈名〉mole cricket
【蝼蚁】lóuyǐ〈名〉 nonentity
【蝼蚁贪生】lóuyǐ-tānshēng〈成〉 even an ant clings to life
【蝼蛞】lóuzhì〈名〉〈古〉mole cricket

髅（髏） lóu ▸髑髅 dúlóu，骷髅 kūlóu

lǒu

搂（摟） lǒu
A〈动〉 embrace: ～住脖子/腰 hug around the neck/waist ‖ 把孩子～在怀里 hold a child in one's arms
B〈量〉 [measurement of thickness] perimeter of the rough circle formed by the two arms in a hugging position: 门前的杨树有两～粗。 The poplar tree at the front gate is already as thick as two pairs of arms encircling it.
▸lōu
【搂抱】lǒubào〈动〉 hug: 紧紧～在一起 hug each other tight

篓（簍） lǒu〈名〉 basket: 背～ basket to be carried on the back ‖ 废纸～ waste-paper basket
【篓子】lǒuzi〈名〉 basket

lòu

陋 lòu〈形〉**1**（简陋） humble: ▸～室，～巷 **2**（浅薄） shallow: ▸鄙～，孤～寡闻，浅～ **3**（不好） vulgar: ▸～规，～俗，～习 **4**（丑） unsightly: ▸丑～ **5**（粗劣） rough: ▸粗～，简～，因～就简
【陋规】lòuguī〈名〉objectionable practice
【陋见】lòujiàn〈名〉〈书〉shallow view
【陋识】lòushí = 陋见 lòujiàn
【陋室】lòushì〈名〉 humble abode: 身居～ live in a small simple room
【陋俗】lòusú〈名〉undesirable custom
【陋习】lòuxí〈名〉bad habit: ▸陈规～
【陋巷】lòuxiàng〈名〉 narrow and dreary alley

镂（鏤） lòu〈动〉carve: ▸～刻
【镂骨铭心】lòugǔ-míngxīn = 刻骨铭心 kègǔ-míngxīn
【镂花】lòuhuā〈动〉engrave designs
【镂刻】lòukè〈动〉**1**（雕刻） engrave: 在瓶子上～花形图案 engrave flowers on a bottle **2**（记住） etch: 老师的教诲～在心中。 The teacher's instructions are engraved in one's mind.
【镂空】lòukōng〈动〉 hollow out: ～花瓶 bottle with carved flowers on it ‖ ～的象牙球 work-ivory ball

瘘（瘻） lòu〈名〉［医学］ fistula
【瘘管】lòuguǎn〈名〉［医学］ fistula

漏 lòu
A〈动〉**1**（泄漏） leak: ～气/油 leak gas/oil ‖ 屋顶～水。 The roof is leaking. **2**（透露） leak: 这件事从来没～过半个字。 Not a word leaked out about the affair. ▸透～，泄～ **3**（落掉） leave out: ～读一个字 miss a word when reading ‖ ～印一行 miss out a line in printing ▸挂一～万
B〈名〉 hourglass: ▸～壶
【漏报】lòubào〈动〉 fail to declare: ～收入 fail to declare one's income
【漏窗】lòuchuāng〈名〉［建筑］ unglazed or unpapered window
【漏底】lòudǐ〈动〉 leak out a secret: 这件事我不妨先给你漏个底。 I may as well tell you about the matter in advance.
【漏电】lòudiàn = 跑电 pǎodiàn
【漏洞】lòudòng〈名〉**1**（小窟窿） leak: 查找～ look for the leak ‖ 堵住～ stop a leak **2**（破绽） flaw: 管理上的～ loopholes in management ‖ 文章里～百出。 The article is full of flaws.
【漏斗】lòudǒu〈名〉 funnel
【漏风】lòufēng〈动〉**1**（挡不住风） not be airtight: 密不～ be airtight **2**（说话不清） speak indistinctly [because one or more of one's front teeth are missing]: 他两颗门牙没了，讲话～。 He speaks indistinctly because he is missing two front teeth. **3**〈喻〉（走漏风声） leak confidential information: 这件事绝不能～。 Not a single word should be leaked out about it.
【漏缝】lòufèng〈名〉 crack
【漏光】lòuguāng〈动〉 leak light: 照相机～。 The camera leaks light.
【漏壶】lòuhú〈名〉 hourglass
【漏勺】lòusháo〈名〉 scoop strainer
【漏失】lòushī **A**〈动〉 lose: ～水分 lose moisture **B**〈名〉 oversight: 这工作不能有半点～。 No mistakes can be permitted in the work.
【漏税】lòushuì〈动〉 evade taxation: 偷税～ evade taxes
【漏网】lòuwǎng〈动〉〈喻〉 slip through the net: 不让一个罪犯～。 No criminal will be left unpunished. ‖ 贩毒分子无一～。 None of the drug traffickers have slipped through the net.
【漏网之鱼】lòuwǎngzhīyú〈成〉〈喻〉fugitive
【漏泄】lòuxiè〈动〉 leak out: 几束阳光～进洞里。 A few rays of sunshine filtered into the cave. ‖ 汽缸～了。 The cylinder is leaking. ‖ ～秘密 leak a secret ‖ ～试题 leak out exam questions
【漏泄春光】lòuxiè-chūnguāng〈成〉 [of a woman] expose a private part of one's body by accident
【漏夜】lòuyè〈名〉〈书〉 dead of night: ～加班 work overtime in the dead of night
【漏诊】lòuzhěn〈动〉 fail to diagnose a disease
【漏子】lòuzi〈名〉**1**〈口〉（漏斗） funnel **2**（破绽） loophole: 发现～ find a loophole
【漏嘴】lòuzuǐ〈动〉 let slip a remark: 说～ make a slip of the tongue

露 lòu〈动〉〈口〉 reveal: ～背 backless
▸lù
【露白】lòubái〈动〉 unintentionally expose one's wealth to others: 财不～。 One should not reveal one's wealth to others.
【露丑】lòuchǒu〈动〉 make a fool of oneself: 当众～ make a spectacle of oneself in public
【露底】lòudǐ〈动〉 let out a secret: 这事暂时还不能～。 This should be kept secret for the time being.
【露风】lòufēng〈动〉 divulge a secret
【露富】lòufù〈动〉 flaunt one's wealth: 她好虚荣，爱～。 She is vain and likes to make a show of her money.
【露脸】lòuliǎn〈动〉**1**（出彩） cut a dashing figure: 她在今天的比赛中真露了脸。 She really shone in today's contest. **2**〈方〉（出现） make an appearance: 那

人有好几天没～。 That person had not appeared for several days.

【露马脚】lòu mǎjiǎo〈惯〉 let the cat out of the bag: 我一说谎就～。 Whenever I try to tell a lie, I give myself away.

【露面】lòumiàn〈动〉 make an appearance: 公开～ make a public appearance ‖ 不敢～ not dare to show one's face ►抛头～

【露苗】lòumiáo〈动〉 sprout

【露脐装】lòuqízhuāng〈名〉 crop top

【露怯】lòuqiè〈动〉 display one's ignorance

【露头】lòutóu〈动〉 [1]（露出头） show one's head: 罪犯从洞里爬出来，刚一～就被我们发现了。 We saw the criminal the moment he showed his head as he crawled out from the cave. [2]〈喻〉（刚出现） begin to emerge: 腐败又～了。 Corruption has raised its head again.
►lùtóu

【露馅儿】lòuxiànr〈惯〉〈喻〉 let the cat out of the bag: 他一张口就～。 He gave the game away as soon as he began to speak.

【露相】lòuxiàng〈动〉 show one's true colours: 真人不～。 A truly talented person does not show off.

【露一手】lòu yīshǒu〈惯〉 show off: 给大家～吧。 Please show us your unique skills.

lou

喽（嘍） lou〈助〉〈口〉 [1]（用于提醒） [in exclamation to call attention]: 客人来～! Here come the guests! ‖ 起床～。 It's time to get up. ‖ 水开～。 The water is boiling. [2]（表示肯定） [used to indicate a certainty]: 那当然是可以的～。 That will be OK. ‖ 那样就更好～。 That will be better.
►lóu

lū

撸（擼） lū〈动〉〈方〉 [1]（捋） rub one's palm along: ～袖子 roll up one's sleeves [2]（撤去） dismiss a person from his post: 他的厂长职位给～了。 He was dismissed as factory director. [3]（训斥） scold: 我因为迟到被老师～了一通。 I was reprimanded by the teacher for being late.

噜（嚕） lū

【噜苏】lūsū〈方〉= 啰唆 luōsuo

lú

卢（盧） lú

【卢比】lúbǐ ►p. 328〈名〉 [1]（印度、巴基斯坦等国货币） rupee [2]（印尼货币） rupiah (Rp)

【卢布】lúbù ►p. 328〈名〉 rouble

【卢浮宫】Lúfúgōng〈名〉 Louvre

【卢沟桥】Lúgōuqiáo〈名〉 Lugou Bridge

【卢萨卡】Lúsàkǎ〈名〉 Lusaka

【卢森堡】Lúsēnbǎo〈名〉 Luxembourg: ～人 Luxembourger

【卢旺达】Lúwàngdá〈名〉 Rwanda: ～共和国 Republic of Rwanda ‖ ～人 Rwandan

> **卢沟桥**
>
> Also known in English as the Marco Polo Bridge, it is located in the south-west of Beijing on the banks of the Yongding River. It was built in 1192, and is 265 metres long. The sides of the bridge are carved with 400-500 stone lions, each one different and, according to tradition, uncountable. In the past, 'the moon at dawn over the Lugou Bridge' (卢沟晓月) was held to be one of the eight wondrous sights of Beijing, and these words, written by Emperor Qianlong, can still be seen on the bridge today. On July 7th 1937, Japanese troops engaged with Chinese troops in what is known as the Incident at Marco Polo Bridge. This marked the start of China's eight-year war of resistance against Japan.

芦（蘆） lú〈名〉［植物］ reed: ►～根, ～花, ～席
►lǔ

【芦柴】lúchái〈名〉 reed stems

【芦荡】lúdàng〈名〉 reed marshes

【芦丁】lúdīng〈名〉［药学］ rutin

【芦根】lúgēn〈名〉［中药］ reed rhizome

【芦花】lúhuā〈名〉 reed catkins

【芦花鸡】lúhuājī〈名〉 Plymouth Rock chicken

【芦荟】lúhuì〈名〉［植物］ aloe

【芦笙】lúshēng〈名〉 *lusheng* [reed-pipe wind instrument]: ～舞 *lusheng* dance

【芦笋】lúsǔn〈名〉［植物］ asparagus

【芦苇】lúwěi〈名〉 reed: ～荡 reed marshes

【芦席】lúxí〈名〉 reed mat

庐（廬） lú〈名〉 hut: 草～ thatched cottage ►～舍, 茅～

【庐剧】lújù〈名〉 Lu opera [local opera in Anhui Province]

【庐山】Lúshān〈名〉 Lushan Mountain [in Jiangxi Province]

【庐山真面目】Lúshān zhēnmiànmù〈成〉〈喻〉 truth about a person or matter: 终于看清了他的～ finally see his true colours

【庐舍】lúshè〈名〉〈书〉 [1]（房屋） hut [2]（田舍） farmhouse

垆[1]（壚） lú〈名〉 black earth

垆[2]（壚） lú〈名〉〈旧〉 wine shop: 当～ sell wine ‖ 酒～ wine shop

炉（爐） lú〈名〉 stove: 煤～ coal stove ‖ 刚出～的饼子 cake fresh from the oven ►壁～, 电～, 锅～, 微波～, 香～

【炉箅子】lúbìzi〈名〉 fire grate

【炉灰】lúhuī〈名〉 stove ashes

【炉火纯青】lúhuǒ-chúnqīng〈成〉〈喻〉 reach the acme of perfection: 达到～的地步 reach high excellence

【炉具】lújù〈名〉 cooker

【炉龄】lúlíng〈名〉［冶金］ furnace life

【炉前工】lúqiángōng〈名〉 furnace worker

【炉台】lútái〈名〉 stove top

【炉膛】lútáng〈名〉 stove chamber

【炉条】lútiáo〈名〉 grate

【炉瓦】lúwǎ〈名〉 stove files

【炉灶】lúzào〈名〉 kitchen range: 修理～ repair a kitchen range ►另起～

【炉渣】lúzhā〈名〉 [1]［冶金］ slag [2]（焦渣） cinder

【炉子】lúzi〈名〉 stove

泸（瀘） lú

【泸州大曲】Lúzhōu dàqū〈名〉 Luzhou Daqu Liquor

𬘘（纑） lú〈名〉〈书〉 hemp thread

栌（櫨） lú ►黄栌 huánglú

轳（轤） lú ►辘轳 lùlu

胪（臚） lú〈动〉〈书〉 exhibit: ►～陈, ～列

【胪陈】lúchén〈动〉〈书〉 present item by item: ～实情 give a detailed account of what has happened

【胪列】lúliè〈动〉〈书〉 enumerate: ～三种方案 list three plans

鸬（鸕） lú

【鸬鹚】lúcí〈名〉［鸟类］ cormorant: 用～捕鱼 cormorant fishing

矑（矑） lú〈名〉〈书〉 pupil

𬬻（鑪） lú〈名〉［化学］ rutherfordium (Rf)

颅（顱） lú〈名〉 [1]（头盖骨） cranium: 开～手术 brain surgery ►～骨, 头～ [2]（头） head

【颅盖】lúgài〈名〉 skullcap

【颅骨】lúgǔ = 头骨 tóugǔ

【颅内压】lúnèiyā〈名〉［医学］ intracranial pressure

【颅腔】lúqiāng〈名〉 cranial cavity

【颅相学】lúxiàngxué〈名〉 phrenology

舻（艫） lú〈名〉〈书〉 [1]（船头） bow [2]（船） ship

鲈（鱸） lú

【鲈鱼】lúyú〈名〉 perch

lǔ

芦（蘆） lǔ ►油葫芦 yóuhulǔ
►lú

卤[1]（鹵） lǔ〈名〉 [1]（盐卤） bittern: ►盐～ [2]［化学］ halogen: ►～素

卤[2]（滷） lǔ
A〈动〉 stew with spices in salty water or soy sauce: ～鸡 pot-stewed chicken ►～味
B〈名〉 [1]（浓汁） thick salted sauce: 打～ make gravy ►～面 [2]（指饮料） thick infusion: ►茶～

【卤菜】lǔcài〈名〉 pot-stewed meat dish

【卤化】lǔhuà〈动〉［化学］ halogenate

【卤面】lǔmiàn〈名〉 noodles with meat and gravy

【卤莽】lǔmǎng = 鲁莽 lǔmǎng

【卤肉饭】lǔròufàn〈名〉 stewed minced pork with rice

【卤水】lǔshuǐ〈名〉 [1] = 卤[1] lǔ 1 [2]（指地下水） brine

【卤水点豆腐】lǔshuǐ diǎn dòufu〈歇后〉 everything has its superior

【卤素】lǔsù〈简称〉= 卤族元素

【卤味】lǔwèi〈名〉pot-stewed meat served cold
【卤虾油】lǔxiāyóu〈名〉shrimp sauce
【卤汁】lǔzhī〈名〉salty sauce with spices for stewing
【卤制】lǔzhì〈动〉stew with spices in salty water or soy sauce
【卤族元素】lǔzú yuánsù〈名〉halogen

虏（虜）lǔ
A〈动〉capture: ▸～获, 俘～
B〈名〉**1**（俘虏）captive **2**〈书〉〈贬〉（敌人）enemy
【虏获】lǔhuò〈动〉capture

掳（擄）lǔ〈动〉loot: ▸～掠
【掳掠】lǔlüè〈动〉loot: ～财物 plunder for loot

鲁[1]（魯）lǔ〈形〉**1**〈书〉（蠢笨）dull-witted: ▸～钝, 愚～ **2**（冒失）imprudent: ▸～莽, 粗～

鲁[2]（魯）Lǔ〈名〉**1**（指国名）Lu [state in the Zhou Dynasty] **2** ▸**p. 661**（山东）Lu [another name for Shandong Province]
【鲁班尺】lǔbānchǐ〈名〉carpenter's square
【鲁班门前弄大斧】Lǔbān ménqián nòng dàfǔ〈俗〉〈喻〉display one's skill before a master
【鲁菜】lǔcài〈名〉Shandong cuisine
【鲁钝】lǔdùn〈形〉〈书〉dull-witted
【鲁莽】lǔmǎng〈形〉rash: 行事～ act rashly ‖ 你这样做太～了。It was reckless of you to do such a thing.
【鲁莽灭裂】lǔmǎng-mièliè〈成〉be rash and careless: ～的举动 rash and careless move
【鲁鱼亥豕】lǔyú-hàishǐ〈成〉typographical errors made by confusing similar characters
【鲁直】lǔzhí〈形〉〈书〉rash and blunt: 为人～ be a rash and blunt person

橹（櫓）lǔ〈名〉oar: 摇～ row the boat ‖ ～声 sound of the rowing of a boat

镥（鑥）lǔ〈名〉［化学］lutecium (Lu)

lù

陆（陸）lù〈名〉dry land: ▸～地, ～军, 大～, 登～, 着～
▸liù
【陆标】lùbiāo〈名〉［航空］landmark
【陆沉】lùchén〈动〉**1**（指陆地）submerge **2**〈书〉（指国土）be seized by invaders **3**〈书〉（指官员）retire from public life
【陆稻】lùdào = 旱稻 hàndào
【陆地】lùdì〈名〉dry land: ～边界 land frontier ‖ ～资源 land resources
【陆龟】lùguī〈名〉(land) tortoise
【陆海空】lù-hǎi-kōng〈名〉land, sea, and air: ～三军 army, navy, and air force
【陆基导弹】lùjī dǎodàn〈名〉land-based missile
【陆界】lùjiè〈名〉land boundary
【陆军】lùjūn〈名〉［军事］ground force: ～医院 army hospital
【陆离】lùlí〈形〉motley: ▸光怪～
【陆龙卷】lùlóngjuǎn〈名〉［气象］tornado
【陆路】lùlù〈名〉land route: ～交通 overland communication
【陆棚】lùpéng = 大陆架 dàlùjià
【陆桥】lùqiáo〈名〉［地理］land bridge: 欧亚大～ Eurasian land bridge
【陆禽】lùqín〈名〉birds that can only fly a short distance
【陆相】lùxiàng〈名〉［地质］land facies
【陆续】lùxù〈副〉in succession: 代表们～到达。The delegates arrived one after another. ‖ 花园里的花陆陆续续地都开了。The flowers in the garden came into bloom one after the other.
【陆运】lùyùn〈动〉land transport
【陆战】lùzhàn〈名〉land warfare
【陆战队】lùzhànduì〈名〉［军事］marine corps: 美国海军～ US Marine Corps
【陆战棋】lùzhànqí〈名〉land-battle chess

录（錄）lù
A〈动〉**1**（记载）record: 笔～ record in writing ▸抄～, 记～, 摘～ **2**（任用）employ: ▸～取, ～用 **3**（录制）record: ～电视节目 video a TV programme ‖ ～歌曲 record songs ‖ ～下声音 record sb.'s voice ▸～像, ～音
B〈名〉record: ▸目～, 通讯～, 语～
【录播】lùbō〈动〉broadcast a taped programme: 所谓"直播"其实是～。The so-called 'live' broadcast was actually taped.
【录放】lùfàng〈动〉record and play back
【录供】lùgòng〈动〉［法律］take down a confession or testimony during an interrogation
【录取】lùqǔ〈动〉admit: 择优～ admit on the basis of competitive selection ‖ ～名单 list of enrollees ‖ ～名额 admission quota ‖ ～通知书 admission notice ‖ ～分数线 passing marks for admission ‖ 该校今年秋季～了1,500名学生。The school had an enrolment of 1,500 students this autumn.
【录取线】lùqǔxiàn〈名〉admission pass mark: 上了重点大学的～ achieve the score required for admission to key universities
【录入】lùrù〈动〉key in: ～员 data inputter
【录像】lùxiàng **A**〈动〉video: 现场～ record live ‖ 家用～设备 home video equipment **B**〈名〉video: 放～ play a video ‖ 看～ watch a video
【录像带】lùxiàngdài〈名〉video: 空白～ blank video ‖ 这部电影有～。The film is on video.
【录像机】lùxiàngjī〈名〉video cassette recorder (VCR)
【录像片】lùxiàngpiàn〈名〉video show
【录音】lùyīn **A**〈动〉tape: ～采访 recorded interview ‖ 实况～ live recording **B**〈名〉sound-recording: 放～ play a recording ‖ 听～ listen to a recording
【录音笔】lùyīnbǐ〈名〉recording pen
【录音带】lùyīndài〈名〉magnetic recording tape
【录音电话】lùyīn diànhuà〈名〉answerphone
【录音机】lùyīnjī〈名〉cassette recorder
【录音室】lùyīnshì〈名〉recording room
【录用】lùyòng〈动〉employ: 量才～ assign jobs to people according to their abilities ‖ 择优～ admit on the basis of competitive selection
【录制】lùzhì〈动〉record: ～唱片 make a record ‖ ～电视节目 video a TV programme ‖ 现场～ record live

辂（輅）lù〈名〉〈古〉**1**（指横木）horizontal beam on an ancient chariot **2**（指大车）chariot: 龙～ imperial chariot

赂（賂）lù
A〈动〉**1**〈古〉（送礼）send a gift **2**（贿赂）buy off: ▸贿～
B〈名〉〈书〉bribe

鹿 lù〈名〉deer: 公/雄～ buck ‖ 母/雌～ doe ‖ 小～ fawn ▸～角, ～茸
【鹿角】lùjiǎo〈名〉antler
【鹿角菜】lùjiǎocài〈名〉［植物］siliquose pelvetia
【鹿皮】lùpí〈名〉deerskin
【鹿茸】lùróng〈名〉［中药］pilose antler of a young stag
【鹿肉】lùròu〈名〉venison
【鹿死谁手】lùsǐshuíshǒu〈成〉who will emerge victorious: ～，尚难逆料。It is still hard to tell who will emerge the victor.
【鹿特丹】Lùtèdān〈名〉Rotterdam
【鹿苑】lùyuàn〈名〉deer park
【鹿砦】lùzhài〈名〉［军事］abatis
【鹿寨】lùzhài = 鹿砦 lùzhài

逯 Lù〈名〉Lu [surname]

绿（綠）lù = 绿 lǜ
▸lǜ
【绿林】lùlín〈名〉outlaws: ～好汉 outlaws of the forest

禄（祿）lù〈名〉emolument: 福～寿 happiness, wealth and longevity ‖ 高官厚～ high position and a handsome salary ▸俸～
【禄蠹】lùdù〈名〉〈书〉〈贬〉person who runs after position and wealth
【禄位】lùwèi〈名〉〈旧〉official position and emolument

碌（碌）lù〈形〉**1**（平庸）commonplace: ▸庸～ **2**（繁忙）busy: ▸劳～, 忙～
▸liù
【碌碌】lùlù〈形〉**1**（平庸）mediocre: 庸庸～ be mediocre and unambitious **2**（繁忙）busy with miscellaneous work: ～一生 toil through life
【碌碌无为】lùlù-wúwéi〈成〉plodding hard but accomplishing little of significance: 这么多年来～，想起来非常后悔。I regret that I attempted so much and accomplished so little all these years.

路 lù
A〈名〉**1**（道路）road: 问～ ask sb. the way ‖ 修～ mend a road ‖ 养～ maintain a road/railway ‖ 指～ give directions ‖ 筑～ build a road ‖ 乡间小～ country road ‖ 此～不通。No through road. ▸道～, 公～ **2**（路程）journey: ～不远，开车去只要十五分钟。It's not far; it's only a fifteen minute drive. ‖ 他们走了五公里～。They covered a distance of five kilometres. **3**（途径）way: 无～可走 have no way out ▸～子, 财～, 门～, 生～ **4**（轨迹）line: ▸思～, 纹～ **5**（线路）route: 6～公共汽车 No 6 bus ‖ 三～进军 advance along three routes **6**（区域）region: 各～人马 people from all walks of life ‖ 南～货 products from the south ▸外～

B〈量〉**1**（类） kind: 这～人 this type of person ▸大～货，一～货色 **2**（行列） line: 排成一～ form a line ‖ 士兵们按四～纵队前进。 The soldiers marched in fours.

【路霸】lùbà〈名〉 overlord of a section of a highway: 严厉打击车匪～ crack down on illegal road tolls and highway and railroad banditry

【路边】lùbiān〈名〉 roadside

【路标】lùbiāo〈名〉**1**（交通标识） road sign **2**［军事］route marker

【路不拾遗】lùbùshíyí〈成〉honesty prevails throughout society

【路程】lùchéng〈名〉**1**（指总长度） total distance from start to finish **2**（指远近） journey: ～遥远 be far away ‖ 两天的～ two-day journey

【路德教】Lùdéjiào〈名〉［宗教］ Lutheranism: ～徒 Lutheran

【路灯】lùdēng〈名〉 street lamp: ～亮了。 The street lamps came on.

【路段】lùduàn〈名〉 section of a highway or railway

【路费】lùfèi〈名〉 travelling expenses: 凑足～ scrape together enough money for a trip

【路风】lùfēng〈名〉 railway service quality

【路规】lùguī〈名〉 railway rules and regulations

【路轨】lùguǐ〈名〉**1**（钢轨） rail **2**（轨道） track: 铺设～ lay tracks

【路过】lùguò〈动〉 pass by: 每天回家的路上我都～这家书店。 I pass this bookstore every day on my way home.

【路徽】lùhuī〈名〉 railway emblem

【路基】lùjī〈名〉 roadbed

【路祭】lùjì〈动〉〈旧〉 offer sacrifices by the roadside as a funeral procession passes

【路见不平，拔刀相助】lù jiàn bùpíng, bá dāo xiāngzhù〈成〉 take up one's sword to protect those in need

【路劫】lùjié〈动〉 commit highway robbery

【路警】lùjǐng〈名〉 railway police

【路径】lùjìng〈名〉**1**（道路） way: 迷失～ lose one's way ‖ ～不熟 not know one's way around **2**（门道） means: 成功的～ road to success **3**［计算机］ path

【路局】lùjú〈名〉 railway administration

【路考】lùkǎo〈动〉 road-test: 参加～ take a driving test

【路口】lùkǒu〈名〉 junction: 丁字～ T-junction ‖ 三岔～ road fork ▸十字～

【路况】lùkuàng〈名〉 road conditions: ～很差 conditions on the road are very bad

【路面】lùmiàn〈名〉 road surface〈英〉; pavement〈美〉: 加宽～ widen the pavement ‖ 柏油～ asphalt road

【路牌】lùpái〈名〉 street sign

【路卡】lùqiǎ〈名〉 toll gate

【路签】lùqiān〈名〉［交通］ transport staff

【路堑】lùqiàn〈名〉［交通］ cutting

【路桥】lùqiáo〈名〉 roads and bridges: ～工程 highway and bridge project

【路权】lùquán〈名〉 right of way: 拥有～ have right of way ‖ 公交～优先原则 principle of giving priority right of way to public transport vehicles

【路人】lùrén〈名〉**1**〈本〉 passer-by **2**〈喻〉 stranger: 形同～ be as indifferent as a stranger

【路上】lùshang〈名〉**1**（道路上） road: 昨天～有很多车辆。 There was a lot of traffic on the road yesterday. **2**（旅途中） way: 上学～不慎丢了钱包。 The student carelessly lost his wallet en route.

【路试】lùshì〈动〉 road-test: 接受～ (of a vehicle) undergo a road test

【路数】lùshù〈名〉**1** = 路子 lùzi **2**（招数） movement in *wushu* **3**（底细） inside story: 摸不清某人的～ cannot get inside information on sb.

【路条】lùtiáo〈名〉〈旧〉 travel permit

【路透社】Lùtòushè〈名〉 Reuter's News Agency

【路途】lùtú〈名〉**1**（道路） way: 熟识～ know the way around **2**（旅途） journey: ～遥远 be far away

【路线】lùxiàn〈名〉**1**（道路） route: 参观～ visitor's itinerary ‖ 飞行～ flight course ‖ 行军～ route of the march **2**（原则） line: 走群众～ follow the mass line ‖ 基本～ basic line ‖ 思想～ ideological line ‖ 政治～ political line

【路线图】lùxiàntú〈名〉 route chart

【路向】lùxiàng〈名〉 direction: 青少年成长的～ direction of juvenile growth

【路演】lùyǎn〈名〉 road show

【路遥知马力，日久见人心】lù yáo zhī mǎlì, rì jiǔ jiàn rénxīn〈俗〉 as distance tests a horse's strength, so time reveals a person's heart

【路椅】lùyǐ〈名〉 roadside bench

【路易斯安那州】Lùyìsī'ānnàzhōu〈名〉 Louisiana

【路由器】lùyóuqì〈名〉［计算机］ router

【路障】lùzhàng〈名〉 roadblock: 拆除～ tear down a barricade ‖ 清除～ clear an obstacle on the road ‖ 设置～ erect a barricade

【路政】lùzhèng〈名〉（指公路） road administration;（指铁路） railway administration

【路子】lùzi〈名〉**1**（途径） way: 他办事的～有时不太正。 His dealings are not always completely straight. **2**（门路） connections: 找～ try to secure help from potential backer

蓼

蓼 lù〈形〉〈书〉[of plants] tall ▸liǎo

箓（籙）

箓（籙） lù ▸符箓 fúlù

漉

漉 lù〈动〉 strain: ～酒 filter rice wine

【漉网】lùwǎng〈名〉［化工］ vat-net

辘（轆）

辘（轆） lù

【辘轳】lùlu〈名〉 winch

【辘辘】lùlù〈拟〉 rumble: 牛车～沿街而去。 The ox cart rumbled down the road. ▸饥肠～

戮¹

戮¹ lù〈动〉 kill: ▸杀～, 屠～

戮²（勠）

戮²（勠） lù〈动〉〈书〉 unite

【戮力】lùlì〈动〉〈书〉 join forces

【戮力同心】lùlì-tóngxīn〈成〉 make concerted efforts

鹭（鷺）

鹭（鷺） lù〈名〉［鸟类］ heron: ▸白～, 苍～

【鹭鸶】lùsī = 白鹭 báilù

麓

麓 lù〈名〉 foot of a hill: 天山北～ the northern foot of Tianshan Mountain ▸山～

露

露 lù

A〈名〉**1**（露水） dew: ▸～珠, 甘～, 雨～ **2**（指饮料） fruity beverage: 草莓～ strawberry syrup ‖ 杏仁～ almond juice ▸果子～ **3**（化妆品） cosmetics made by distilling flowers, fruit or leaves: 沐浴～ body wash ▸花～水

B〈动〉**1**（无遮盖） be in the open: ▸～宿, ～天, ～营 **2**（显出） expose: ～出原形 reveal one's true colours ‖ 他的脸上～出笑容。 A smile crept over his face. ▸暴～, 流～, 原形毕～

▸lòu

【露布】lùbù〈名〉**1**〈书〉（檄文） war proclamation **2**〈书〉（捷报） announcement of victory **3**（文书） unsealed imperial edict or memorial to the throne **4**〈方〉（通告） notice

【露点】lùdiǎn〈名〉［气象］ dew point

【露骨】lùgǔ〈形〉〈贬〉 barefaced: 说得十分～ speak in unequivocal terms

【露酒】lùjiǔ〈名〉 alcoholic drink mixed with fruit juice

【露水】lùshui〈名〉**1**〈本〉 dew: ～很大，树叶上湿漉漉的。 The heavy dew made the leaves quite wet. **2**〈喻〉 transitory things

【露水夫妻】lùshui-fūqī〈名〉 one-night stand

【露宿】lùsù〈动〉 sleep in the open: ～街头 sleep out in the street ▸风餐～

【露台】lùtái〈名〉 balcony

【露天】lùtiān **A**〈名〉 the open: ～放映 show a film outdoors **B**〈形〉 open-air: ～影院/剧场 open-air cinema/theatre

【露天看台】lùtiān kàntái〈名〉 bleacher

【露天矿】lùtiānkuàng〈名〉［矿业］ open-hit

【露天煤矿】lùtiān méikuàng〈名〉opencast coal mine

【露天游泳池】lùtiān yóuyǒngchí〈名〉 open-air swimming pool

【露头】lùtóu〈名〉［矿业］ outcropping ▸lòutóu

【露头角】lù tóujiǎo〈惯〉 be budding: ▸崭～

【露尾巴】lù wěiba〈动〉〈喻〉 show one's true colours

【露营】lùyíng〈动〉 camp: 士兵们在城外～。 The soldiers were encamped outside the town. ‖ 周末我们打算去～。 We are going camping this weekend.

【露珠】lùzhū〈名〉 dewdrop

lu

氇 lu ▸氆氇 pǔlu

lǘ

驴（驢）

驴（驢） lǘ〈名〉 donkey: 骑～ ride a donkey ‖ ～叫 donkey's bray ▸蠢～

【驴唇不对马嘴】lǘchún bù duì mǎzuǐ〈俗〉〈喻〉 be beside the point: 他的回答～。 His answer is irrelevant.

【驴打滚】lǘdǎgǔn〈名〉**1**（指高利贷） usurious loan **2**（指食品） steamed glutinous millet flour coated with soybean powder

【驴肝肺】lǘgānfèi〈名〉〈喻〉 ill intent: 好心当作～ take someone's good will for ill intent

【驴脸】lǘliǎn〈名〉〈贬〉〈喻〉 long face

【驴骡】lǘluó〈名〉 hinny

【驴年马月】lǘnián-mǎyuè = 猴年马月 hóunián-mǎyuè

【驴皮胶】lǘpíjiāo = 阿胶 ējiāo

【驴皮影】lǘpíyǐng〈方〉= 皮影戏 píyǐngxì

【驴头不对马嘴】lǘtóu bù duì mǎzuǐ = 驴唇不对马嘴 lǘchún bù duì mǎzuǐ
【驴友】lǘyǒu〈名〉〈诙〉travelling companion
【驴子】lǘzi〈名〉donkey

闾（閭） lǘ〈名〉**1**〈书〉（大门）gate to an alley: 依～而望 wait at the entrance to the alley **2**（户籍编制单位）neighbourhood of 25 families in ancient China **3**〈书〉（里巷）neighbourhood: 村～ village ‖ 穷～隘巷 poor district of a town
【闾里】lǘlǐ〈名〉〈书〉hometown
【闾巷】lǘxiàng〈名〉〈书〉alleyway

榈（櫚） lǘ ▸棕榈 zōnglǘ

lǚ

吕（呂） lǚ〈名〉〈旧〉six even-numbered note in the ancient Chinese musical temperament: ▸律～
【吕剧】lǚjù〈名〉Lü opera
【吕宋】Lǚsòng〈名〉Luzon: ～烟 Luzon cigar

侣（侶） lǚ〈名〉companion: ▸伴～, 情～
【侣伴】lǚbàn = 伴侣 bànlǚ

捋 lǚ〈动〉smooth out with the fingers: ～胡子 stroke one's beard ‖ ～平头发 smooth down one's hair
▸luō

旅[1] lǚ
A〈名〉**1**［军事］brigade: ▸～长 **2**（军队）troops: ▸劲～, 军～
B〈副〉〈书〉together: ▸～进～退

旅[2] lǚ〈动〉travel: 沙漠/文化之～ desert/cultural tour ▸～客, ～居, ～游
【旅伴】lǚbàn〈名〉travelling companion: 她和她的～在一起很快乐。She enjoyed being with her travelling companions.
【旅差费】lǚchāifèi〈名〉= 差旅费 chāilǚfèi
【旅程】lǚchéng〈名〉journey: 踏上～ step out on a journey
【旅次】lǚcì〈名〉〈书〉stopover
【旅店】lǚdiàn〈名〉inn: 乡村～ country inn
【旅费】lǚfèi〈名〉travelling expenses: 报销～ reimburse travelling expenses
【旅馆】lǚguǎn〈名〉hotel: 登记入住～ check in at a hotel ‖ 住～ stay at a hotel ‖ 五星级～ five-star hotel ▸汽车～
【旅进旅退】lǚjìn-lǚtuì〈成〉follow the crowd
【旅居】lǚjū〈动〉live abroad: ～海外 live in a foreign country
【旅客】lǚkè〈名〉traveller: 运送～ transport passengers ‖ 出境/入境～ outgoing/incoming passenger
【旅客列车】lǚkè lièchē〈名〉passenger train
【旅客运输】lǚkè yùnshū〈名〉passenger transport
【旅社】lǚshè〈名〉hotel: 在～过夜 put up at a hotel
【旅舍】lǚshè〈名〉〈书〉hotel
【旅途】lǚtú〈名〉journey: ～劳顿 be travel-worn ‖ 祝您～愉快! Bon voyage.
【旅行】lǚxíng〈动〉travel: 计划～ plan a tour ‖ 组织～ organize a tour ‖ 长途～ long journey ‖ 假日～ holiday travel ‖ 去国外～ travel abroad ‖ 商务～ business tour ‖ 徒步～ hiking ‖ 团体～ group travel ‖ ～结婚 have a honeymoon trip
【旅行包】lǚxíngbāo〈名〉travelling bag
【旅行袋】lǚxíngdài〈名〉travelling bag
【旅行社】lǚxíngshè〈名〉travel agency: 国际～ international travel service
【旅行团】lǚxíngtuán〈名〉tour group
【旅行箱】lǚxíngxiāng〈名〉travelling case
【旅行者】lǚxíngzhě〈名〉traveller
【旅行证件】lǚxíng zhèngjiàn〈名〉travel documents
【旅行支票】lǚxíng zhīpiào〈名〉traveller's cheque
【旅行装】lǚxíngzhuāng〈名〉travelling outfit
【旅游】lǚyóu〈动〉tour: ～城市 tourist city ‖ ～胜地 tourist attraction ‖ ～旺季 peak tourist season ‖ ～英语 tourist English ‖ 包价～ package tour ‖ 观光～ sightseeing tour ‖ 国内～ domestic travel ‖ 假期～ vacation trip ‖ 境外～ travel abroad
【旅游产品】lǚyóu chǎnpǐn〈名〉tourist product
【旅游车】lǚyóuchē〈名〉sightseeing bus
【旅游点】lǚyóudiǎn〈名〉tourist spot
【旅游纪念品】lǚyóu jìniànpǐn〈名〉tourist souvenirs
【旅游结婚】lǚyóu jiéhūn〈名〉destination wedding
【旅游局】lǚyóujú〈名〉tourism administrative bureau: 国家～ National Tourism Administration
【旅游年】lǚyóunián〈名〉tourist year: 国际～ international tourist year
【旅游农业】lǚyóu nóngyè〈名〉agritourism
【旅游签证】lǚyóu qiānzhèng〈名〉tourist visa
【旅游团】lǚyóutuán〈名〉tour group
【旅游鞋】lǚyóuxié〈名〉walking shoes
【旅游业】lǚyóuyè〈名〉tourist industry
【旅游者】lǚyóuzhě〈名〉tourist
【旅游指南】lǚyóu zhǐnán〈名〉tourist guide
【旅游资源】lǚyóu zīyuán〈名〉tourism resources: 开发～ open up tourism resources
【旅栈】lǚzhàn〈名〉inn
【旅长】lǚzhǎng〈名〉brigade commander
【旅资】lǚzī〈名〉travelling expenses

铝（鋁） lǚ〈名〉［化学］aluminium (Al)〈英〉; aluminum〈美〉: 电解～ electrolytic aluminium ‖ 氧化～ aluminium oxide
【铝箔】lǚbó〈名〉［材料］aluminium foil
【铝锭】lǚdìng〈名〉aluminium ingot
【铝矾土】lǚfántǔ〈名〉［矿业］bauxite
【铝粉】lǚfěn〈名〉［材料］powdered aluminium
【铝合金】lǚhéjīn〈名〉aluminium alloy: ～门窗 aluminium alloy door and window frames
【铝化物】lǚhuàwù〈名〉［化学］aluminide
【铝矿】lǚkuàng〈名〉aluminium ore
【铝土矿】lǚtǔkuàng〈名〉［矿业］bauxite

稆（穭） lǚ〈动〉be self-sown

偻（僂） lǚ〈书〉
A〈形〉hunchbacked: ▸伛～
B〈副〉instantly: 不能～答 be unable to reply right now
▸lóu

屡（屢） lǚ〈副〉repeatedly: ～战～胜 have fought many battles and won every one of them ‖ ～遭挫折 suffer repeated setbacks
【屡次】lǚcì〈副〉repeatedly: ～受到表扬 be praised again and again
【屡次三番】lǚcì-sānfān〈成〉over and over again: 我～警告他不要那样做。I've warned him over and over again not to do that.
【屡见不鲜】lǚjiàn-bùxiān〈成〉very common
【屡建奇功】lǚjiàn qígōng〈成〉perform repeatedly outstanding service
【屡教不改】lǚjiào-bùgǎi〈成〉be incorrigible
【屡屡】lǚlǚ〈副〉again and again: ～出错 make mistakes over and over again ‖ ～请求 make repeated requests
【屡试不爽】lǚshì-bùshuǎng〈成〉pass many tests: ～的办法 time-tested method

缕（縷） lǚ
A〈名〉thread: ▸千丝万～
B〈形〉detailed: ▸～陈, ～析
C〈量〉wisp: 一～麻 a strand of hemp ‖ 一～轻烟 a curl of smoke ‖ 一～头发 a tuft of hair
【缕陈】lǚchén〈动〉〈书〉give a detailed account
【缕缕】lǚlǚ〈形〉continuous: 天空布满了～薄雾。The sky was full of mist.
【缕析】lǚxī〈动〉〈书〉make a detailed analysis: ▸条分～

膂 lǚ〈名〉〈书〉backbone
【膂力】lǚlì〈名〉physical strength: ～过人 possess extraordinary physical strength

褛（褸） lǚ ▸褴褛 lánlǚ

履 lǚ
A〈动〉**1**（踩）tread on: 如～薄冰 as dangerous as treading on thin ice ▸～险如夷 **2**（实践）carry out: ▸～行, ～约
B〈名〉**1**（鞋）shoe: 草～ straw sandals ▸革～, 削足适～ **2**（脚步）footstep: ▸步～
【履带】lǚdài〈名〉［机械］caterpillar track: ～起重机/拖拉机 caterpillar crane/tractor
【履历】lǚlì〈名〉**1**（指经历）personal history **2**（指文字材料）curriculum vitae (CV)〈英〉; résumé〈美〉: ～表 curriculum vitae ‖ 递交～ submit a curriculum vitae
【履险如夷】lǚxiǎn-rúyí〈成〉cope with a crisis without difficulty
【履行】lǚxíng〈动〉carry out: ～承诺/诺言 carry out one's promise ‖ ～合同 fulfil a contract ‖ ～义务 fulfil obligations
【履约】lǚyuē〈动〉honour an agreement: 如期～ keep to a scheduled appointment
【履职】lǚzhí〈动〉perform one's duties: 兢兢业业～ carry out one's duties conscientiously

lǜ

律 lǜ
A〈名〉**1**［音乐］ancient Chinese standards for setting the pitch for singing or

tuning: ▸音～, 乐～ 2 (法律) law; (规章) rule: ▸～师, 定～, 规～, 纪～ 3 = 律诗 lǜshī
B 〈动〉 keep under control: ～己甚严 exercise strict self-discipline ▸严以～己, 宽以待人
【律动】lǜdòng〈名〉1〈本〉regular movements: 心脏～ regular heartbeats 2〈喻〉rhythm: 社会的～ rhythm of society
【律己】lǜjǐ〈动〉 restrain oneself: 严于～ be strict with oneself
【律令】lǜlìng〈名〉 laws and decrees
【律吕】lǜlǚ〈名〉［音乐］ 1 (指器具) a series of 12 bamboo pitch-pipes adopted in ancient Chinese music [with the six odd-numbered ones being called 律 and the six even-numbered ones 吕] 2 (乐律) temperament
【律师】lǜshī ▸p. 966〈名〉barrister〈英〉; lawyer〈美〉: 聘请～ engage a lawyer ‖ ～事务所 law firm
【律师费】lǜshīfèi〈名〉 counsel fee
【律师界】lǜshījiè〈名〉 the bar
【律师袍】lǜshīpáo〈名〉 attorney's robe
【律诗】lǜshī〈名〉 *lushi* [poem of eight lines]: 七言～ heptasyllabic regulated verse ‖ 五言～ pentasyllabic regulated verse
【律条】lǜtiáo〈名〉 1 (法律条文) legal article: 触犯～ violate a legal clause 2 (法则) norm: 做人的～ code of conduct
【律宗】lǜzōng〈名〉［佛教］ Lu Sect [sect of Buddhism]

虑 (慮) lǜ〈动〉 1 (思考) consider: ▸考～, 深思熟～, 思～ 2 (担忧) be anxious: 不足为～ give no cause for concern ▸过～, 焦～, 忧～

率 lǜ〈名〉 rate: ▸概～, 功～, 利～ ▸shuài

绿 (綠) lǜ ▸p. 863〈形〉 green: 深～ dark green ‖ 树都～了。 The trees are turning green. ▸～草如茵, 碧～, 橄榄～, 墨～ ▸lù
【绿宝石】lǜbǎoshí〈名〉 emerald
【绿菜花】lǜcàihuā〈名〉 broccoli
【绿草如茵】lǜcǎo-rúyīn〈成〉carpet of lush green grass
【绿茶】lǜchá〈名〉 green tea
【绿葱葱】lǜcōngcōng〈形〉 verdant and luxuriant
【绿灯】lǜdēng〈名〉 green light
【绿地】lǜdì〈名〉 green
【绿豆】lǜdòu〈名〉 mung bean: ～糕 mung bean cake
【绿豆芽】lǜdòuyá〈名〉 mung bean sprouts
【绿肥】lǜféi〈名〉 green manure
【绿化】lǜhuà〈动〉 afforest: ～城市 make a city green by planting trees in and around the city ‖ ～荒山 afforest barren hills ‖ ～工程 landscape engineering ‖ ～面积 green area ‖ 庭院～ courtyard greening
【绿卡】lǜkǎ〈名〉 green card
【绿篱】lǜlí〈名〉 hedgerow
【绿帽子】lǜmàozi〈名〉〈喻〉 cuckold: 戴～ be a cuckold
【绿内障】lǜnèizhàng = 青光眼 qīngguāngyǎn
【绿盘】lǜpán〈名〉［金融］ green listing
【绿皮书】lǜpíshū〈名〉 Green Paper
【绿茸茸】lǜróngróng ▸p. 863〈形〉 luxuriantly green: ～的草地 lush green meadows
【绿色】lǜsè ▸p. 863 A〈名〉 green (colour): ～的田野 green fields B〈形〉 green: ～奥运 Green Olympics ‖ ～产品 green product
【绿色壁垒】lǜsè bìlěi〈名〉 green barrier
【绿色标志】lǜsè biāozhì〈名〉 eco-label
【绿色革命】lǜsè gémìng〈名〉 green revolution
【绿色和平组织】Lǜsè Hépíng Zǔzhī〈名〉 Greenpeace
【绿色食品】lǜsè shípǐn〈名〉 eco-food
【绿色通道】lǜsè tōngdào〈名〉green channel [duty-free]
【绿色植物】lǜsè zhíwù〈名〉 green plants
【绿生生】lǜshēngshēng〈形〉 fresh and green: ～的菠菜 fresh green spinach
【绿松石】lǜsōngshí〈名〉［矿业］ turquoise
【绿头巾】lǜtóujīn = 绿帽子 lǜmàozi
【绿头鸭】lǜtóuyā〈名〉 mallard
【绿叶菜】lǜyècài〈名〉 greens
【绿叶成阴】lǜyè-chéngyīn〈成〉 green leaves make a shade
【绿茵】lǜyīn〈名〉 1 (草地) lawn 2 (足球场) football field 3 (足球) football: ～健儿 skilful footballers ‖ ～场 football field
【绿茵茵】lǜyīnyīn ▸p. 863〈形〉 green: ～的草坪 verdant lawn
【绿荫】lǜyìn〈名〉 shade: 那边有片～。 There is some shade over there.
【绿莹莹】lǜyíngyíng ▸p. 863〈形〉 glittering green: 麦苗在雨中显得～的。 In the rain the wheat seedlings were a glistening green.
【绿油油】lǜyóuyóu ▸p. 863〈形〉 lush green: ～的农田 green fields
【绿藻】lǜzǎo〈名〉［植物］ green algae
【绿洲】lǜzhōu〈名〉 oasis: 变沙漠为～ turn deserts into oases
【绿柱石】lǜzhùshí〈名〉［矿业］ beryl

葎 lǜ
【葎草】lǜcǎo〈名〉 scandent hop

氯 (氯) lǜ〈名〉［化学］ chlorine (Cl): ▸～气
【氯胺酮】lǜàntóng〈名〉［药学］ ketamine
【氯化钾】lǜhuàjiǎ〈名〉［化学］ potassium chloride
【氯化钠】lǜhuànà〈名〉［化学］ sodium chloride
【氯碱】lǜjiǎn = 烧碱 shāojiǎn
【氯纶】lǜlún〈名〉［纺织］ polyvinyl chloride fibre
【氯霉素】lǜméisù〈名〉［药学］ chloromycetin
【氯气】lǜqì〈名〉［化学］ chlorine
【氯酸钾】lǜsuānjiǎ〈名〉［化学］ potassium chlorate
【氯酸钠】lǜsuānnà〈名〉［化学］ sodium chlorate
【氯乙烯】lǜyǐxī〈名〉［化学］ vinyl chloride: ～塑料 Koroseal® ‖ 聚～ polyvinyl chloride
【氯中毒】lǜzhòngdú〈名〉 chlorine poisoning

滤 (濾) lǜ〈动〉 strain: 把水～干 strain the water ‖ 中药煎好后用纱布～一下再喝。 Herbal medicine must be boiled and filtered with a piece of gauze before it is taken. ▸～器, ～纸, 过～
【滤波】lǜbō〈动〉 filter waves: ～器 (wave) filter
【滤布】lǜbù〈名〉 filter cloth
【滤尘】lǜchén〈动〉 filter out dust
【滤器】lǜqì〈名〉 filter: 用～净化水 use a filter to purify water
【滤色镜】lǜsèjìng〈名〉［摄影］ (colour) filter
【滤网】lǜwǎng〈名〉 filter screen
【滤液】lǜyè〈名〉 filtrate
【滤渣】lǜzhā〈名〉 filter residue
【滤纸】lǜzhǐ〈名〉 filter paper

镳 (鑢) lǜ〈书〉
A〈动〉 file
B〈名〉 file

luán

峦 (巒) luán〈名〉 peak: ▸层～叠嶂, 峰～, 山～
【峦嶂】luánzhàng〈名〉〈书〉 screen-shaped mountain peaks

孪 (孿) luán〈动〉 be born a twin
【孪生】luánshēng〈形〉 twin: ～姐妹/兄弟 twin sisters/brothers ‖ ～子 twins

娈 (孌) luán〈形〉〈书〉 handsome

栾 (欒) luán
【栾树】luánshù〈名〉 golden rain tree

挛 (攣) luán〈动〉 contract and become rigid: ▸痉～
【挛缩】luánsuō ▸p. 50〈动〉［医学］ suffer from contracture

鸾 (鸞) luán〈名〉 legendary phoenix-type bird in Chinese folklore
【鸾俦】luánchóu〈名〉〈书〉 married couple
【鸾凤】luánfèng〈名〉 1 (夫妻) husband and wife: ～分飞 separated couple 2 (贤哲) distinguished talents
【鸾凤和鸣】luánfèng-hémíng〈成〉 be a happy couple

脔 (臠) luán〈书〉
A〈动〉 cut meat into pieces
B〈名〉 pieces of meat: ▸尝鼎一～
【脔割】luángē〈动〉〈书〉 1 (分割) slice up 2 (瓜分) carve up: ～弱国领土 carve up the territory of a weak nation

圞 (圝) luán ▸团圞 tuánluán

銮 (鑾) luán〈名〉 1 (指铃铛) small tinkling bell on an imperial carriage 2〈书〉(指车驾) imperial carriage
【銮驾】luánjià〈名〉 1 (指车驾) imperial carriage 2 (指皇帝) emperor
【銮铃】luánlíng〈名〉 tinkling bell on a carriage
【銮舆】luányú〈名〉 1 (指车架) imperial carriage 2 (指皇帝) emperor

luǎn

卵 luǎn〈名〉 1 (卵子) ovum; (鸟蛋) egg: 产～ lay eggs 2［昆虫］ fertilized egg 3〈方〉(睾丸) testicles
【卵巢】luǎncháo〈名〉［解剖］ ovary

【卵巢癌】luǎncháo'ái ▸p. 50〈名〉［医学］ovarian cancer
【卵黄】luǎnhuáng = 蛋黄 dànhuáng
【卵磷脂】luǎnlínzhī〈名〉［化学］lecithin
【卵生】luǎnshēng〈形〉［动物］oviparous
【卵石】luǎnshí〈名〉pebble: ▸鹅～
【卵胎生】luǎntāishēng〈形〉［动物］ovoviviparous
【卵胎生动物】luǎntāishēng dòngwù〈名〉ovoviviparous animal
【卵细胞】luǎnxìbāo〈名〉［生物］ovum
【卵翼】luǎnyì〈动〉〈贬〉〈喻〉shield: 在～下 be shielded by sb.
【卵子】luǎnzǐ〈名〉ovum: ～捐献者 egg donor

luàn

乱（亂）luàn

A〈形〉**1**（无秩序）disorderly: 一团～麻 a knot of entangled hemp ‖ 他把我整理好的文件搞～了。He messed up the papers that I had put in order. ▸～七八糟, 打～, 杂～ **2**（动荡不安）turbulent: ▸～世, 天下大～ **3**（烦乱）confused: 我心里很～。My mind is in a turmoil. ▸心烦意～ **4**（不正当）promiscuous: ▸淫～
B〈动〉throw into disorder: ～了敌人的阵脚 throw the enemy into confusion ‖ 以假～真 pass off a fake as the real thing ▸～伦
C〈副〉arbitrarily: ～罚款 impose arbitrary fines ‖ ～花钱 spend money like water ‖ ～扣帽子 label people indiscriminately ▸～说, 胡言～语
【乱兵】luànbīng〈名〉**1**（指叛变）mutinous soldiers **2**（指纪律差）undisciplined troops
【乱臣贼子】luànchén-zéizǐ〈成〉traitors and usurpers: ～, 人人得而诛之 kill the traitors and usurpers no matter who captures them
【乱点鸳鸯谱】luàndiǎn yuānyangpǔ〈成〉〈喻〉**1**（指夫妻）mistake two people for a couple **2**（指人力）arrange personnel mistakenly
【乱纷纷】luànfēnfēn〈形〉chaotic: ～的人群 uproarious crowd ‖ 他心里～的。His mind is in turmoil.
【乱坟岗】luànféngǎng = 乱葬岗子 luànzàng gǎngzi
【乱哄哄】luànhōnghōng〈形〉**1**（指嘈杂）uproarious: 市场里～的一片。There was a hubbub in the market. **2**（指混乱）chaotic: 城里～的。The city is in turmoil.
【乱来】luànlái〈动〉act indiscreetly: 别～, 孩子们。Behave yourselves, children.
【乱伦】luànlún〈动〉commit incest
【乱码】luànmǎ〈名〉error codes
【乱蓬蓬】luànpéngpéng〈形〉dishevelled: ～的干草 jumbled mass of hay
【乱七八糟】luànqībāzāo〈成〉in an awful mess: 房间里～。The room is a complete mess.
【乱世】luànshì〈名〉troubled times: 生于～ be born in troubled times ‖ ～英雄 heroes in times of disorder
【乱说】luànshuō〈动〉speak indiscreetly
【乱弹琴】luàntánqín〈惯〉act like a fool: 这简直是～。It is downright nonsense.
【乱套】luàntào〈动〉〈口〉muddle things up: 各行其是, 非～不可。If everyone acts as he pleases, everything will be complete chaos.
【乱腾腾】luànténgténg〈形〉restless: 门外～地挤满了人。There is a noisy crowd outside.
【乱营】luànyíng〈动〉be thrown into confusion: 炮火下, 敌人乱了营。The gunfire threw the enemy into complete disarray.
【乱葬岗子】luànzàng gǎngzi〈名〉unmarked graves
【乱糟糟】luànzāozāo〈形〉**1**（杂乱）chaotic: 把厨房搞得～的 make a mess in the kitchen ‖ 到处都是～的。Everywhere was in chaos. **2**（烦乱）confused: 心里～的 feel perturbed
【乱真】luànzhēn〈动〉look genuine: 这仿制品, 几可～。This imitation looks genuine. ▸以假～
【乱子】luànzi〈名〉trouble: 出～ go wrong ‖ 别再添～了。Don't add further to the confusion.
【乱作一团】luànzuòyītuán〈成〉be in great disorder

lüè

掠 lüè

〈动〉**1**（抢夺）rob: ▸～夺, 掳～, 抢～ **2**（拂过）brush past: 探照灯～过夜空。The searchlights swept the night sky. ‖ 一群野鸭～过水面。A flock of wild ducks skimmed over the water.
【掠夺】lüèduó〈动〉plunder: ～财富 plunder wealth ‖ ～资源 plunder resources ‖ ～艺术珍品 loot art ‖ ～成性 be plunderous by nature
【掠美】lüèměi〈动〉claim (the) credit for sth.: 这是她的高见, 我可不敢～。It was her idea. I can't claim credit for it.
【掠取】lüèqǔ〈动〉plunder: ～资源 plunder resources
【掠视】lüèshì〈动〉〈书〉[of one's eyes or glance] sweep: 他向室内～一周。His eyes swept the room.
【掠影】lüèyǐng〈名〉glimpses: 北京～ glimpses of Beijing ▸浮光～

略[1] lüè

A〈名〉outline: ▸概～, 要～
B〈形〉brief: ▸～图, 简～
C〈动〉omit: ～去不提 make no mention of ‖ ～去细节 leave out the details ▸从～, 忽～, 省～
D〈副〉slightly: ～表寸心 as a small token of good will ‖ ～加修改 make slight changes ‖ ～有所闻 have heard a little about it ‖ 请～等片刻。Please wait a moment. ▸～微

略[2] lüè

〈名〉strategy: ▸策～, 胆～

略[3] lüè

〈动〉plunder: ▸攻城～地, 侵～
【略称】lüèchēng〈名〉abbreviation: 陕西省～为陕。Shaanxi Province is called Shaan for short.
【略见一斑】lüèjiàn-yībān〈成〉get a rough idea of
【略略】lüèlüè〈副〉a little: 你能把收音机～关小一点吗? Could you turn the radio down a bit, please?
【略胜一筹】lüèshèng-yīchóu〈成〉be a notch above
【略识之无】lüèshí-zhīwú〈成〉〈谦〉know only a few simple characters
【略图】lüètú〈名〉sketch (map)
【略微】lüèwēi〈副〉slightly: ～有点感冒 have a slight cold ‖ 计划～有些变化。There's been a slight change of plan.
【略为】lüèwéi〈副〉slightly: ～增加 increase slightly ‖ 他感觉～好了些。He felt a bit better.
【略逊一筹】lüèxùn-yīchóu〈成〉be slightly inferior
【略语】lüèyǔ〈名〉abbreviation
【略知一二】lüèzhī-yī'èr〈成〉have only a smattering knowledge of: 他对德语～。He knows a little German.

lūn

抡（掄）lūn

〈动〉brandish: ～大锤 swing a sledgehammer ‖ ～起拳头就打 swing one's fist and hit ▸lún

lún

仑[1]（侖）lún ▸加仑 jiālún

仑[2]（崙）lún ▸昆仑 Kūnlún

伦（倫）lún

〈名〉**1**（同类）match: ▸不～不类, 绝～ **2**（人伦）ethics: ▸～常, 人～, 天～ **3**（条理）order: ▸～次
【伦巴】lúnbā〈名〉rumba
【伦比】lúnbǐ〈动〉〈书〉equal: 史无～ be unrivalled in history ▸无与～
【伦常】lúncháng〈名〉feudal order of seniority in human relationships
【伦次】lúncì〈名〉〈书〉logical sequence: ▸语无～
【伦敦】Lúndūn〈名〉London
【伦敦德里郡】Lúndūndélǐjùn〈名〉Londonderry
【伦弗鲁希尔郡】Lúnfúlǔxī'ěrjùn〈名〉Renfrewshire
【伦理】lúnlǐ〈名〉ethics: ～观念 concept of ethics
【伦理学】lúnlǐxué〈名〉ethics
【伦琴】lúnqín〈名〉［物理］roentgen: ～射线 roentgen rays

论（論）Lún

▸lùn
【论语】Lúnyǔ〈名〉*The Analects of Confucius*

抡（掄）lún

〈动〉〈书〉select: ～才 select men of ability ▸lūn

囵（圇）lún ▸囫囵 húlún

沦（淪）lún

〈动〉**1**（沉没）sink: ～于海底 sink to the bottom of the sea ▸沉～ **2**（陷入）be reduced to: ～为殖民地 be reduced to the status of a colony ‖ ～为乞丐 be reduced to begging ▸～落, ～陷 **3**（丧亡）be ruined: ▸～丧, ～亡
【沦落】lúnluò〈动〉**1**（流落）lead a wandering life in poverty: ～异乡 lead a wretched life in a strange land **2**〈书〉（衰落）come down in the world: 道德～ moral depravity ‖ 家境～。The family fortunes declined. **3**（陷入）sink: 国土～敌手。The territory fell into enemy hands. ▸～风尘
【沦落风尘】lúnluò-fēngchén〈成〉be driven to prostitution
【沦落街头】lúnluò-jiētóu〈成〉become a tramp

【沦灭】lúnmiè〈动〉be ruined

【沦没】lúnmò〈动〉〈书〉**1**（沉没）submerge **2**（死亡）die

【沦丧】lúnsàng〈动〉be ruined: 道德～ moral decay ‖ 国土～ lost territory

【沦亡】lúnwáng〈动〉**1**（灭亡）be subjugated **2**（丧失）decay: 道德～ moral decay

【沦陷】lúnxiàn〈动〉fall into enemy hands: ～区 enemy-occupied area ‖ 守军撤退，城市～。After the defending troops retreated, the city fell into enemy hands.

纶（綸）lún

〈名〉**1**〈书〉（指丝带）black silk ribbon **2**〈书〉（指丝线）silk fishing line: 垂～ go fishing **3**（指纤维）synthetic fibre: ▸涤～
▸guān

轮（輪）lún

A〈名〉**1**（车轮）wheel: 十～大卡车 ten-wheel truck ‖ 四～马车 four-wheeled carriage ▸～胎, 车～, 齿～, 滑～ **2**（轮状物）ring: ▸耳～, 年～ **3**（轮船）steamer: ▸～船, 渡～, 货～ **4**（12年）a cycle of twelve years: 我比他大一～。I am twelve years older than him.
B〈动〉take turns: ～到她了。Her turn came. ‖ 清扫工作，一人～一天。Every day a different person will do the cleaning. ▸～班, ～流, ～休
C〈量〉**1**（用于日、月）[for the sun, the moon, etc.]: 一～红日 a red sun ‖ 一～明月 a bright moon **2**（回合）round: 新一～谈判 a new round of talks ‖ 比赛第一～他就把对手打倒了。He knocked down his opponent in the first round of the match.

【轮班】lúnbān〈动〉take turns: ～看护病人 take turns tending the sick ‖ 二十四小时～工作 work in shifts around the clock

【轮班制】lúnbānzhì〈名〉rotation system

【轮拨儿】lúnbōr〈动〉〈口〉take turns

【轮唱】lúnchàng〈名〉［音乐］round

【轮船】lúnchuán〈名〉steamer

【轮次】lúncì **A**〈副〉alternately: ～入内 enter in turn ‖ 学生们～回答老师的问题。The students answered the teacher's questions in turns. **B**〈名〉number of turns or rounds

【轮带】lúndài〈名〉tyre

【轮渡】lúndù **A**〈名〉ferry: 乘～ travel by ferry **B**〈动〉ferry: 把货物～过江 ferry goods across the river

【轮番】lúnfān〈副〉alternately: ～轰炸 bomb in waves

【轮辐】lúnfú〈名〉spoke

【轮岗】lúngǎng〈动〉rotate jobs

【轮箍】lúngū〈名〉tyre

【轮毂】lúngǔ〈名〉(wheel) hub

【轮换】lúnhuàn〈动〉take turns: ～休假 stagger holidays ‖ 定期～ take turns with fixed intervals

【轮回】lúnhuí **A**〈名〉［佛教］transmigration **B**〈动〉rotate: 四季～。The seasons rotate.

【轮机】lúnjī〈名〉engine

【轮机长】lúnjīzhǎng〈名〉chief engineer

【轮奸】lúnjiān〈动〉gang-rape

【轮距】lúnjù〈名〉tread

【轮空】lúnkōng〈动〉［体育］draw a bye: 他第一轮～。He drew a bye in the first round.

【轮廓】lúnkuò〈名〉**1**（指线条）outline: 面部～ shape of a face ‖ 先勾勒出～，再画上细节 sketch an outline before filling in the details **2**（指概况）rough idea: 这件事我只知道大致的～。I only had a rough idea about the matter.

【轮流】lúnliú〈动〉be alternate: ～值班 take turns to be on duty ‖ ～坐庄 take turns to be the banker ‖ 她和妹妹～做家务。She and her sister do household chores in rotation.

【轮牧】lúnmù〈名〉rotation grazing

【轮盘赌】lúnpándǔ〈名〉roulette

【轮批】lúnpī〈动〉do in batches

【轮生】lúnshēng〈形〉［植物］verticillate: ～花/叶 verticillate flowers/leaves

【轮式】lúnshì〈形〉wheeled: ～拖拉机 wheeled tractor

【轮胎】lúntāi〈名〉tyre〈英〉; tire〈美〉: 给～充气 pump up a tyre ‖ ～瘪了 have a flat tyre ‖ 备用～ spare tyre

【轮替】lúntì〈动〉rotate: 四季～。The seasons rotate.

【轮辋】lúnwǎng〈名〉wheel rim

【轮休】lúnxiū〈动〉**1**（指耕种）lie fallow in rotation **2**（指休假）stagger holidays

【轮训】lúnxùn〈动〉train by turns: 干部～ the cadres receive training in turn

【轮椅】lúnyǐ〈名〉wheelchair: 坐～ sit in a wheelchair

【轮值】lúnzhí〈动〉take turns to be on duty: 每人必须～一天。Each person must take it in turns to be on duty for a day.

【轮值主席】lúnzhí zhǔxí〈名〉rotating chairperson

【轮轴】lúnzhóu〈名〉**1**［物理］wheel and axle **2**（指机械）wheel axle

【轮转】lúnzhuàn〈动〉rotate: 四季～。The seasons follow each other in rotation.

【轮子】lúnzi〈名〉wheel

【轮作】lúnzuò〈动〉rotate crops: 粮棉～ alternate cereal crops and cotton

lùn

论（論）lùn

A〈动〉**1**（讨论）discuss: ▸～文, 辩～, 议～ **2**（决定）determine: 按质～价 determine the price according to the quality ‖ 迟到15分钟以上按旷课～。Being late by 15 minutes or more is regarded as absence. ▸～处, ～功行赏, ～罪 **3**（看待）regard: 相提并～ mention in the same breath ▸一概而～
B〈介〉according to: ～斤卖 sell by the *jin* ‖ ～小时/日给钱 pay by the hour/day
C〈名〉**1**（言论）view: ▸公～, 谬～, 社～, 绪～ **2**（学说）theory: 唯物～ materialism ▸进化～, 相对～
▸Lún

【论辩】lùnbiàn〈动〉argue: ～有力 strong argument ‖ 他～得头头是道。He argued convincingly.

【论处】lùnchǔ〈动〉punish: 按违反纪律～ be punished for a breach of discipline ‖ 依法～ deal with in accordance with the law

【论丛】lùncóng〈名〉collected essays

【论敌】lùndí〈名〉adversary

【论点】lùndiǎn〈名〉argument: 驳斥～ refute an argument ‖ 提出～ put forward an argument ‖ 证明～ prove an argument ‖ 中心～ central argument ‖ 文章的～站不住脚。The argument of the article does not stand up.

【论调】lùndiào〈名〉〈贬〉view: 悲观的～ pessimistic view ‖ 这种～是荒谬的。Such arguments are absurd.

【论断】lùnduàn **A**〈动〉infer: 大胆～ daringly infer **B**〈名〉inference: 科学的～ scientific thesis

【论功行赏】lùngōng-xíngshǎng〈成〉reward according to merit

【论据】lùnjù〈名〉grounds: ～不足 insufficient grounds ‖ 有力的～ strong argument

【论理】lùnlǐ **A**〈动〉reason with: 跟这种人～能有什么结果? What could possibly be gained by trying to reason with this man? **B**〈副〉normally: ～他早该退休了。He should have retired long ago.

【论难】lùnnàn〈动〉〈书〉argue

【论述】lùnshù〈动〉expound: ～精辟 brilliant exposition

【论说】lùnshuō **A**〈名〉exposition and argumentation: ～不充分 not well demonstrated ▸～文 **B**〈副〉normally: ～他该来了，不知怎么到现在还没见人。He should be here. I wonder why he hasn't turned up yet.

【论说文】lùnshuōwén〈名〉argumentative writing

【论坛】lùntán〈名〉forum: 学术～ academic forum

【论题】lùntí〈名〉**1**［逻辑］proposition **2**（指题目）topic for discussion: ～选得好 well-chosen subject for discussion

【论文】lùnwén〈名〉thesis: 发表～ publish a paper ‖ 写～ write a thesis ‖ 宣读～ read one's paper ‖ 准备～ prepare a paper ‖ 毕业～ graduation thesis ‖ 博士～ doctoral thesis ‖ 学期～ term paper ‖ 学术～ academic paper ‖ 研究～ research paper ‖ ～答辩 viva

【论战】lùnzhàn〈动〉have a debate: 结束～ conclude a debate ‖ 画家与评论家之间的～ disputation between painters and critics

【论争】lùnzhēng〈动〉debate: ～的焦点 point at issue

【论证】lùnzhèng **A**〈名〉**1**［逻辑］demonstration **2**（依据）argument: 有力的～ forcible/strong argument **B**〈动〉expound and prove: ～方案的可行性 discuss the feasibility of a proposal ‖ ～会 feasibility seminar

【论著】lùnzhù〈名〉treatise: 出版一部～ publish a treatise

【论资排辈】lùnzī-páibèi〈成〉arrange in order of seniority

【论罪】lùnzuì〈动〉decide on the nature of the crime: 以过失杀人～ be found guilty of manslaughter

luō

捋 luō

〈动〉rub one's palm along sth. long: ～起袖子 roll up one's sleeves ‖ ～树叶 strip a tree of its leaves
▸lǚ

【捋虎须】luō hǔxū〈俗〉〈喻〉run a great risk

啰（囉）luō

▸啰唆 luōsuo
▸luó, luo

【啰唆】luōsuo〈形〉**1**（絮叨）long-winded: 说话～的人 long-winded speaker ‖ 他～了半天，也没说明白。He prattled on for hours without explaining it. **2**（琐碎）troublesome: 这手续太～。The procedure is too demanding.

【啰嗦】luōsuo = 啰唆 luōsuo

luó

罗¹（羅） luó
A〈名〉**1**（指网） net for catching birds: ►～网，天～地网 **2**（指丝织品） silk gauze: ►绫～绸缎 **3**（指筛子） sieve: 细～ close-meshed sieve ‖ 再过一次～，粉就更细了。 The flour will be finer if sifted once more.
B〈动〉**1**（捉） catch birds with a net: ►门可～雀 **2**（搜集） gather together: ►～致，包～万象，网～ **3**（筛） sift: 面磨好后至少要～一遍。 After the flour has been ground it must be sieved at least once. **4**（排列） spread out: ►～列，星～棋布

罗²（羅） luó〈量〉twelve dozen

【罗安达】Luó'āndá〈名〉Luanda
【罗布】luóbù〈动〉〈书〉scatter
【罗布泊】Luóbùpō ►**p. 305**〈名〉Lop Nor
【罗刹】luóchà ►**p. 274**〈名〉［佛教］rakshas
【罗得岛州】Luódédǎozhōu〈名〉Rhode Island
【罗得西亚】Luódéxīyà〈名〉Rhodesia [now the Republic of Zimbabwe]
【罗锅】luóguō **A**〈动〉be hunchbacked: 这两个人都有点～儿。 The two men were both a bit hunchbacked. ‖ 他痛得～着腰站在那里。 He stood there hunched with pain. **B**〈名〉hunchback: 他是个～儿。 He is a hunchback. **C**〈形〉arched: ～桥 humpback bridge
【罗汉】luóhàn〈名〉［佛教］arhat

> **罗汉**
>
> A disciple of the Buddha. In Buddhism, the term refers to a Buddhist monk who has relinquished all sensual desire and released himself from all worldly troubles. In Hinayana Buddhism, it means someone who has achieved the highest level of accomplishment. In Mahayana Buddhism, it means a lower rank than the Buddha and bodhisattvas. Images of arhats are often seen in Chinese paintings and sculptures. Rows of either 18 arhats or 500 arhats are usually enshrined in Chinese Buddhist temples.

【罗汉豆】luóhàndòu〈名〉〈方〉broad bean
【罗汉果】luóhànguǒ〈名〉［植物］mangosteen
【罗汉松】luóhànsōng〈名〉［植物］yew podocarpus
【罗经】luójīng = 罗盘 luópán
【罗克斯堡郡】Luókèsībǎojùn〈名〉Roxburgh
【罗口】luókǒu〈名〉（纺织） rib top
【罗勒】luólè〈名〉［植物］sweet basil
【罗列】luóliè〈动〉**1**（排列） display: 手工艺品～在展厅的中央。 The handicrafts are set out in the centre of the exhibition hall. **2**（列举） enumerate: ～理由 list reasons ‖ ～现象 list phenomena
【罗马】Luómǎ〈名〉Rome: ～人 Roman ‖ ～非一日建成。 Rome was not built in a day. ‖ 条条大路通～。 All roads lead to Rome.
【罗马帝国】Luómǎ Dìguó〈名〉［历史］Roman Empire
【罗马公教】Luómǎ Gōngjiào = 天主教 Tiānzhǔjiào
【罗马教廷】Luómǎ Jiàotíng〈名〉Roman Curia: ～敕令 Vatican edict
【罗马数字】Luómǎ shùzì〈名〉Roman numerals
【罗马天主教】Luómǎ Tiānzhǔjiào〈名〉Roman Catholic Church
【罗马语族】Luómǎ yǔzú〈名〉［语言］Romance languages
【罗马尼亚】Luómǎníyà〈名〉Romania: ～人 Romanian ‖ ～语 Romanian
【罗曼蒂克】luómàndìkè〈形〉romantic: ～的爱情故事 romantic love story
【罗曼史】luómànshǐ〈名〉romance
【罗盘】luópán〈名〉compass
【罗圈】luóquān〈名〉frame of a sieve
【罗圈腿】luóquāntuǐ〈名〉bow legs
【罗圈椅】luóquānyǐ〈名〉easy chair
【罗裙】luóqún〈名〉silk skirt
【罗斯郡】Luósījùn〈名〉Ross-shire
【罗宋汤】luósòngtāng〈名〉borscht
【罗网】luówǎng〈名〉snare: 布下/设下～ set a trap ►自投～
【罗织】luózhī〈动〉〈书〉frame up: ～罪名 cook up charges against
【罗致】luózhì〈动〉〈书〉enlist the services of: ～人才 enlist the services of talented people

㑩（儸） luó ►偻㑩 lóuluó

萝（蘿） luó〈名〉trailing plants: ►藤～
【萝卜】luóbo〈名〉radish: 胡～ carrot ‖ 白～ white radish ‖ 红～ red radish ‖ ～干儿 dried radish slices
【萝芙木】luófúmù〈名〉［植物］devil pepper

啰（囉） luó ►喽啰 lóuluó ►luō, luo
【啰唣】luózào〈动〉〈旧〉kick up a racket: 休要～。 Stop making such a racket!

逻¹（邏） luó〈动〉patrol: ►巡～

逻²（邏） luó ►逻辑 luójí
【逻辑】luójí〈名〉**1**（规律） logic: 不合～ be illogical ‖ 合乎～ be logical **2**（逻辑学） logic: 辩证～ dialectical logic ‖ 形式～ formal logic
【逻辑电路】luójí diànlù〈名〉［计算机］logic circuit
【逻辑思维】luójí sīwéi〈名〉logical thinking
【逻辑主语】luójí zhǔyǔ〈名〉［语法］logical subject

脶（腡） luó〈名〉〈书〉fingerprint

猡（玀） luó ►猪猡 zhūluó

锣（鑼） luó ►**p. 929**〈名〉gong: 敲～ beat a gong
【锣鼓】luógǔ ►**p. 929**〈名〉**1**（锣和鼓） gong and drum **2**（指打击乐器） traditional percussion instruments
【锣鼓喧天】luógǔ-xuāntiān〈成〉loud music of drums and gongs

箩（籮） luó〈名〉square-bottomed bamboo basket: 竹～ bamboo basket ‖ 柳条～ wicker basket
【箩筐】luókuāng〈名〉large wicker basket

骡（騾） luó〈名〉mule
【骡马店】luómǎdiàn〈名〉inn with sheds for carts and animals
【骡子】luózi〈名〉mule

螺 luó〈名〉**1**（指动物） conch: ►海～，田～ **2**（指物体） whorl: ►～钉，～丝，～纹
【螺钿】luódiàn〈名〉［美术］mother-of-pearl inlay: ～家具/漆器 furniture/lacquerware inlaid with mother-of-pearl
【螺钉】luódīng〈名〉screw: 卸～ remove a screw ‖ 钢/木～ steel/wood screw ‖ 紧固～ attachment screw ‖ 平头～ flat-head screw ‖ 十字槽～ cross-head screw ‖ 把～上紧 tighten a screw
【螺号】luóhào〈名〉conch: 吹～ blow a conch
【螺距】luójù〈名〉［机械］screw pitch
【螺口】luókǒu〈名〉screw (socket): ～灯泡 screw-socket bulb
【螺帽】luómào = 螺母 luómǔ
【螺母】luómǔ〈名〉(screw) nut
【螺栓】luóshuān〈名〉［机械］(screw) bolt: 地脚～ foundation bolt
【螺丝】luósī = 螺钉 luódīng
【螺丝刀】luósīdāo〈名〉screwdriver: 十字型～ cross-head screwdriver ‖ 一字型～ flat blade screwdriver
【螺丝钉】luósīdīng = 螺钉 luódīng
【螺丝扣】luósīkòu = 螺纹 luówén
【螺丝帽】luósīmào = 螺母 luómǔ
【螺丝母】luósīmǔ = 螺母 luómǔ
【螺丝起子】luósī qǐzi = 改锥 gǎizhuī
【螺蛳】luósī〈名〉snail
【螺纹】luówén〈名〉**1**（指纹） whorl **2**［机械］screw thread
【螺旋】luóxuán〈名〉**1**（指曲线） spiral: ～天线 helix antenna **2**［机械］screw: 阳～ external screw ‖ 阴～ internal screw ‖ 右/左～ right-handed/left-handed screw
【螺旋桨】luóxuánjiǎng〈名〉(screw) propeller
【螺旋式】luóxuánshì〈形〉spiral: ～上升 rise spirally ‖ ～楼梯 spiral stairs
【螺旋体】luóxuántǐ〈名〉［医学］spirochaeta
【螺旋线】luóxuánxiàn〈名〉helix
【螺旋钻】luóxuánzuàn〈名〉［机械］spiral drill

luǒ

裸 luǒ〈动〉be bare: ～导体 bare conductor ‖ 他～着上身。 He was stripped to his waist. ►～露，～体，赤～
【裸奔】luǒbēn〈动〉streak: ～者 streaker
【裸机】luǒjī〈名〉**1**（指手机） mobile phone sold without subscription or service **2**（指计算机） computer sold without an operating system or other software
【裸捐】luǒjuān〈动〉donate all one's wealth: 慷慨～ a generous donation of the entire estate
【裸聊】luǒliáo〈动〉engage in nude online chat
【裸露】luǒlù〈动〉be uncovered: ～身体 bare one's body ‖ 岩石～ exposed rocks ‖ ～的电线 exposed electric wire
【裸露癖】luǒlùpǐ〈名〉exhibitionism
【裸视】luǒshì **A**〈动〉see with the naked eye: ～视力 unaided eyesight **B**〈名〉unaided eyesight
【裸体】luǒtǐ〈动〉be nude: ～画 nude (painting) ►赤身～
【裸替】luǒtì〈名〉nude body double
【裸线】luǒxiàn〈名〉bare wire

【裸眼】luǒyǎn〈名〉naked eye: ～看不到细菌。Bacteria can't be seen with the naked eye.
【裸泳】luǒyǒng〈动〉swim naked
【裸照】luǒzhào〈名〉nude photo
【裸子植物】luǒzǐ zhíwù〈名〉［植物］gymnosperm

瘰 luǒ
【瘰疬】luǒlì ▸**p. 50**〈名〉［医学］scrofula

luò

荦（犖）luò〈形〉〈书〉outstanding: ▸卓～
【荦荦】luòluò〈形〉〈书〉obvious: ～大端 salient points

咯 luò ▸吡咯 bǐluò
▸gē, kǎ, lo

洛 Luò ▸**p. 294**〈名〉Luohe River [name of rivers in Shaanxi and Henan provinces]
【洛美】Luòměi〈名〉Lome
【洛桑】Luòsāng〈名〉Lausanne
【洛杉矶】Luòshānjī〈名〉Los Angeles (LA)
【洛阳纸贵】Luòyáng-zhǐguì〈成〉[of works] be all the rage for a time

骆（駱）luò
【骆驼】luòtuo〈名〉camel: 单峰～ dromedary ‖ 双峰～ Bactrian camel
【骆驼刺】luòtuocì〈名〉［植物］alhagi
【骆驼绒】luòtuoróng〈名〉［纺织］camel-hair cloth

络（絡）luò
A〈名〉**1**（网状物）net-like object: ▸橘～, 网～ **2**［中医］subsidiary channels in the human body through which vital energy, blood and nutriments circulate: ▸经～
B〈动〉**1**（兜住）hold sth. in place with a net: 用发网～住头发 use a net to hold one's hair in place ▸笼～ **2**（缠绕）wind: ～丝 wind the silk ▸～纱
▸lào
【络合物】luòhéwù〈名〉complex compound
【络离子】luòlízǐ〈名〉［化学］complex ion
【络脉】luòmài〈名〉［中医］branches of channels
【络腮胡子】luòsāi húzi〈名〉sideburns
【络纱】luòshā〈动〉［纺织］doff: ～工 doffer
【络筒机】luòtǒngjī〈名〉［纺织］cone winder
【络绎不绝】luòyì-bùjué〈成〉in an endless stream: 参观者～。Visitors came in an endless stream.

珞[1] luò ▸赛璐珞 sàilùluò

珞[2] luò
【珞巴族】Luòbāzú〈名〉Lhoba ethnic group

烙 luò ▸炮烙 páoluò
▸lào

硌 luò〈名〉〈书〉huge rock
▸gè

落 luò
A〈动〉**1**（掉下）fall: ～泪 shed tears ‖ 树叶～了。The leaves have fallen. ▸叶～归根 **2**（下降）go down: 飞机平稳降～。The plane landed smoothly. ‖ 太阳～山了。The sun set behind the hills. ▸～日, 降～ **3**（使降下）lower: ～帆 lower the sails ‖ 把窗帘～下来。Lower the curtain. ▸～幕 **4**（跌入）fall into: ～入法网 be caught in the net of justice ‖ ～入圈套 fall into a trap ▸～水, ～网 **5**（落后）fall behind: ▸～榜, ～伍 **6**（衰败）decline: ▸零～, 沦～, 没～, 衰～ **7**（归属）fall onto: 任务～在我们的肩上。The task fell on our shoulders. ▸大权旁～ **8**（得到）get: ～个清闲 live a life of leisure ‖ ～下好名声 get a good reputation ▸～空 **9**（停留）stop: 话音未～ when one has hardly finished speaking ▸～脚 **10**（留下）leave: 不～痕迹 leave no trace ▸～款, ～账
B〈名〉**1**（停留处）place where one/sth. stops: ▸段～, 下～, 着～ **2**（聚居处）settlement: ▸部～, 村～, 院～
▸là, lào
【落败】luòbài〈动〉meet with failure: 选举～ fail in the election
【落榜】luòbǎng〈动〉fail an examination: 高考～ fail a university entrance examination ‖ ～生 candidate failing in an examination
【落笔】luòbǐ〈动〉put pen to paper: ～前好好想一想。Think before you write.
【落标】luòbiāo〈动〉**1**（指竞标）lose a bid **2**（指比赛）fail in a competition
【落膘】luòbiāo〈动〉［畜牧］[of livestock] become thin
【落泊】luòbó〈形〉〈书〉frustrated: 一生～ be down on one's luck all one's life
【落魄】luòbó = 落泊 luòbó
▸luòpò
【落槽】luòcáo〈动〉**1**（指水位）recede into its normal course **2**（指榫头）fall into a mortise **3**〈方〉（安心）have peace of mind: 工程未完，我的心不～。The project is still not finished, so I can't yet feel at ease.
【落草】luòcǎo〈动〉become an outlaw: ～为寇 become an outlaw
【落差】luòchā〈名〉**1**〈本〉drop in elevation: 瀑布的～ waterfall drop ‖ 50米的垂直～ a vertical drop of fifty metres **2**〈喻〉discrepancy
【落潮】luòcháo = 退潮 tuìcháo
【落成】luòchéng〈动〉be completed: 新图书馆已经～。The new library has been completed. ‖ ～典礼 inauguration ceremony
【落槌】luòchuí〈动〉**1**（指成交）wind up a deal: ～价 closing bid **2**（指结束）wrap up: 拍卖会已于昨日～。The auction wound up yesterday.
【落单】luòdān〈动〉〈方〉be alone
【落得】luòde〈动〉end up: ～个身败名裂 end up losing one's power and reputation ‖ 他～个自杀的下场。He wound up killing himself.
【落地】luòdì〈动〉**1**（落到地上）fall to the ground: 人头～ be beheaded ‖〈喻〉问题顺利地解决了，我们心里的石头落了地。The problem was settled smoothly, and our minds were set to rest. **2**（出生）be born: 呱呱～ come into the world with a loud cry
【落地窗】luòdìchuāng〈名〉French windows; French doors〈美〉: 一扇～ a French window
【落地灯】luòdìdēng〈名〉standard lamp〈英〉; floor lamp〈美〉: 一盏～ a standard lamp
【落地签证】luòdìqiānzhèng〈名〉landing visa
【落地生根】luòdì shēnggēn〈成〉〈喻〉settle down: 在农村～ settle down in the countryside
【落地扇】luòdìshàn〈名〉standard fan
【落第】luòdì〈动〉**1**〈古〉（指科举考试）fail in an imperial examination at and above township level **2**（指考试）fail an exam: 高考～ fail the entrance examination to college
【落点】luòdiǎn〈名〉［体育］placement
【落发】luòfà〈动〉（指女性）become a Buddhist nun;（指男性）become a monk: ～为尼/僧 take the tonsure and become a nun/monk
【落黑】luòhēi〈动〉〈口〉get dark
【落后】luòhòu **A**〈动〉lag behind: ～于时代 fall behind the times ‖ ～第一名有30米。Be 30 metres behind the lead. **B**〈形〉backward: 技术～ be backward in skill ‖ 改变山区的～面貌 bring development to mountainous areas
【落后分子】luòhòufènzǐ〈名〉backward element
【落户】luòhù〈动〉**1**（安家）settle (down): 在农村～ settle in the countryside ‖ 三只海豚～北京动物园。Three dolphins have begun their new life in the Beijing Zoo. **2**（取得户籍）register for permanent residence: 新生婴儿应及时～。Newborn babies should be registered promptly.
【落花流水】luòhuā-liúshuǐ〈成〉**1**（春景衰败）sorry sight of late spring **2**〈喻〉（大败）suffer a crushing defeat: 主队将客队打得～。The home team gave the guest team a good drubbing.
【落花生】luòhuāshēng〈名〉peanut
【落荒】luòhuāng〈动〉flee into the wilds: ～而逃 flee in panic
【落籍】luòjí〈动〉take up permanent residence in a new place
【落脚】luòjiǎo〈动〉put up: 我们得找个～的地方才行。We should find a place to stop over. ‖ 昨晚我们在镇上的一家旅馆～。We put up at an inn in the town last night.
【落脚点】luòjiǎodiǎn〈名〉footing: 政府工作的出发点和～ the basis and starting point for government work
【落脚处】luòjiǎochù〈名〉temporary lodging
【落井下石】luòjǐng-xiàshí〈成〉〈喻〉hit a person when they are down
【落空】luòkōng〈动〉come to nothing: 希望～ hopes are shattered ‖ 我们的计划～了。Our plan came to nothing.
【落款】luòkuǎn **A**〈名〉names of the sender and the recipient **B**〈动〉sign one's name: 这幅画刚完成，还没～。He has just finished the painting and hasn't yet signed his name.
【落泪】luòlèi〈动〉shed tears
【落落】luòluò〈形〉**1**（潇洒自然）natural and poised: ～大方 be natural and at ease **2**（指难相处）stand-offish: ～寡合 stand-offish
【落马】luòmǎ〈动〉**1**〈本〉fall off a horse **2**〈喻〉be defeated: 头号种子选手在半决赛中～。The top seed was beaten in the semi-final.
【落寞】luòmò〈形〉desolate
【落墨】luòmò〈动〉put pen to paper

【落幕】luòmù〈动〉 come to a close: 电影节～。The curtain came down on the film festival.

【落难】luònàn〈动〉 fall into dire straits

【落聘】luòpìn〈动〉 fail as a candidate for a job

【落魄】luòpò〈形〉〈书〉 dejected: 一生～ be down on one's luck all one's life
▸luòbó

【落日】luòrì〈名〉 setting sun: ～余辉 last rays of the setting sun

【落腮胡子】luòsāi húzi = 络腮胡子 luòsāi húzi

【落实】luòshí **A**〈动〉 **1**（可实现） fix in advance : 计划还未最后～。The plan hasn't been implemented yet. **2**（使落实） implement: ～人选 decide on the candidates ‖ ～任务 fulfil a task ‖ ～政策 implement a policy **B**〈形〉〈方〉 relaxed: 任务没完成，我心里总是不～。I'll not feel at ease until I finish the task.

【落市】luòshì〈动〉〈方〉 be out of season

【落水】luòshuǐ〈动〉 **1**〈本〉 fall into water: 搭救～儿童 save a drowning child **2**〈喻〉 fall into evil ways

【落水狗】luòshuǐgǒu〈名〉〈喻〉 bad person out of favour

【落俗】luòsú〈动〉 show poor taste

【落汤鸡】luòtāngjī〈名〉〈喻〉be drenched and bedraggled

【落套】luòtào〈动〉 conform to a conventional pattern: 他的作品不～。His is a work of real originality.

【落体】luòtǐ〈名〉［物理］ falling body: ～加速度 acceleration of a falling body

【落拓】luòtuò〈形〉〈书〉 **1**（潦倒） frustrated **2**（豪迈） unconventional: ～不羁 unconventional and uninhibited

【落网】luòwǎng〈动〉 get caught: 主犯及同谋纷纷～。The main suspects and their accomplices were tracked down and caught one after another.

【落伍】luòwǔ〈动〉 **1**（掉队） fall behind **2**（过时） be behind the times: 你的思想～了。Your thoughts are behind the times. ‖ 这种款式的衣服已～。This style of dress is out-of-date already.

【落选】luòxuǎn〈动〉 lose an election

【落叶归根】luòyè-guīgēn = 叶落归根 yèluò-guīgēn

【落叶林】luòyèlín〈名〉 deciduous forest

【落叶树】luòyèshù〈名〉 deciduous tree

【落音】luòyīn〈动〉 [of speaking or singing] just stop: 话未～ before one stops speaking

【落英】luòyīng〈名〉〈书〉 **1**（落下的花） fallen flowers: ～缤纷 petals falling in riotous profusion **2**（初开的花） newly-bloomed flowers

【落葬】luòzàng〈动〉 bury

【落账】luòzhàng〈动〉 enter sth. in an account

【落照】luòzhào〈名〉〈书〉 glow of the setting sun

【落座】luòzuò〈动〉take a seat: 请大家～。Please be seated, everybody.

摞 luò

A〈动〉 pile up: ～盘子 stack the dishes ‖ ～砖头 stack bricks
B〈量〉 pile: 一～碟子/碗 a pile of dishes/bowls ‖ 一～文件 a pile of documents ‖ 一～书 a stack of books

luo

啰（囉）luo

〈助〉 [used at the end of a sentence to show an affirmative tone]: 放心好～，我会处理的。Please be assured; I'll take care of it. ‖ 你这样说当然也是对的～! You are certainly right to say so.
▸luō, luó

l

Mm

m̄

姆 m̄
▸mǔ

【姆妈】 m̄ma 〈名〉〈方〉 1（妈妈） mummy 2（阿姨） auntie [a respectful way of addressing an elderly married woman]: 李家～ Auntie Li

ḿ

呣 ḿ 〈叹〉〈口〉 [used interrogatively] eh: ～，什么? Eh? What? ‖ ～，是那样的吗? Eh? Is that so?
▸m̀

m̀

呣 m̀ 〈叹〉〈口〉 [expressing response] mm: ～，对。 Mm, that's right. ‖ ～，我知道了。 Uh-huh, I see.
▸ḿ

mā

妈（媽） mā 〈名〉 1〈口〉（妈妈） mum: 爹～ mum and dad ▸干～，后～ 2（亲属） auntie [a way of addressing an elderly female relative]: ▸姑～，舅～，姨～ 3（非亲属） aunt [a respectful way of addressing an aged married woman]: 张大～ Auntie Zhang 4〈旧〉（女佣） nanny: 张～ Nanny Zhang ▸老～子，奶～

【妈妈】 māma ▸**p. 588**〈名〉 mum〈英〉; mom〈美〉

【妈咪】 māmi 〈名〉 1（妈妈） mummy〈英〉; mommy〈美〉 2（老鸨） procuress

【妈祖】 Māzǔ〈名〉 Mazu [goddess of the sea]: ～庙 Mazu Temple

抹 mā〈动〉 1（擦） wipe: ～桌子 wipe a table clean ‖ ～掉桌子上的灰尘 wipe the dust off the table 2（去除） slip sth. off: ～掉帽子/手套 slip one's cap/gloves off
▸mǒ, mò

【抹布】 mābù〈名〉 cloth (for cleaning)

【抹脸】 māliǎn〈动〉〈口〉 suddenly turn angry: 抹不下脸来 find it difficult to hurt sb.'s feelings

【抹澡】 māzǎo〈动〉 take a sponge bath

麻 mā
▸má

【麻麻黑】 māmahēi〈形〉〈方〉 dusky: 天～路灯就亮了。 The street lights go on at dusk.

【麻麻亮】 māmaliàng〈形〉〈方〉 break-of-dawn: 天刚～她就起床了。 She got up at the crack of dawn.

摩 mā
▸mó

【摩挲】 māsā〈动〉 smooth sth. out: ～衣裳 smooth the wrinkles out of one's clothes ‖ 向后～头发 smooth one's hair back
▸mósuō

má

吗（嗎） má〈代〉〈方〉 what: 要～有～ have whatever one wants ‖ ～事? What's the matter?
▸mǎ, ma

麻[1] má
A〈名〉 1（指植物） general name for hemp, flax, jute, etc.: ▸剑～，亚～ 2（指植物纤维） fibre of hemp, flax, etc. for textile materials: 一缕～ a skein of hemp ‖ ～织品 linen fabrics ▸～布，～袋，～绳 3（芝麻） sesame: ▸～酱，～油 4（雀斑） pockmarks: ▸～脸
B〈形〉 1（不光滑） coarse: 这种布料一面光，一面～。 This cloth is smooth on one side and rough on the other. 2（有斑点） spotted: ▸～雀

麻[2] má〈形〉 1（麻木） numb: 舌头有点～ have a tingling tongue ‖ 腿脚～了 have pins and needles in one's legs and feet ‖ 她的脚都冻～了。 Her feet were numb with cold. ▸～木，肉～ 2（麻辣） burning: 这道菜又～又辣。 This dish is hot and spicy.
▸mā

【麻包】 mábāo〈名〉 sack: 一个/条～ a sack

【麻痹】 mábì A ▸**p. 50**〈名〉［医学］ paralysis: 面部神经～ facial paralysis ▸小儿～症 B〈形〉 slack: 思想～ slackening of vigilance ‖ ～大意 drop one's guard C〈动〉 benumb: ～对方 lower the other party's vigilance

【麻布】 mábù〈名〉 1（粗麻布） sackcloth: 织～ weave gunny cloth 2（指衣料） linen: ～衣服 linen clothes

【麻袋】 mádài〈名〉 sack

【麻豆腐】 mádòufu〈名〉 cooking starch residue

【麻烦】 máfan A〈形〉 troublesome: 办手续很～。 Going through the formalities is troublesome. ‖ 解决这个问题挺～。 Solving this problem is tricky. B〈名〉 bother, trouble: 省了某人许多～ save sb. a lot of trouble ‖ 自找～ invite trouble ‖ 我们遇到的～没完没了。 There was no end to our troubles. C〈动〉 trouble sb.: ～您给我再来一杯。 I will have another cup, please. ‖ 自己能做的事，决不～别人。 Don't bother other people with work you can do by yourself.

【麻纺】 máfǎng〈形〉 bast fibre spinning: ～机械 bast fibre spinning machinery ‖ ～厂 flax mill

【麻风】 máfēng ▸**p. 50**〈名〉［医学］ leprosy: ～病 lepriasis

【麻风树】 máfēngshù〈名〉［植物］ jatropha curcas

【麻花】 máhuā〈名〉［食品］ fried dough twist: 脆～ crisp fried dough twist

【麻花钻】 máhuāzuàn〈名〉［机械］ double worm screw

【麻黄】 máhuáng〈名〉［植物］ Chinese ephedra: ～碱 ephedrine ‖ ～素 ephedrine

【麻将】 májiàng〈名〉 mah-jong: 打～ play mah-jong ‖ ～牌/桌 mah-jong tiles/table

> **麻将**
>
> A game invented in China and played using 144 rectangular bamboo bone or plastic tiles. The 144 tiles are divided as follows: *wanzi* (万子), *suozi* (索子) (also known as *tiao* 条) and *tongzi* (筒子) (also known as *bing* 饼). There are 36 tiles in each set: 16 wind tiles (north, south, east and west winds, 4 in each set); 12 tiles called *hongzhong* (红中), *facai* (发财), and *baiban* (白板) (also 4 in each set); four flower tiles for spring, summer, autumn and winter; and four wild tiles (百搭牌). The game is usually played by 4 people, each with 13 tiles. The aim is to create four sets of tiles, each containing three matching tiles or three in sequence. The remaining single tile must match one from the central pool of tiles in order to win.

【麻酱】 májiàng〈名〉 sesame paste

【麻辣】 málà〈形〉 hot and spicy: ～豆腐 hot and spicy bean curd

【麻栎】 málì = 栎 lì

【麻利】 máli〈形〉 dexterous: 手脚～ be keen and quick in one's work ‖ 他干活很～。 He is smart at his work.

【麻脸】 máliǎn〈名〉 pockmarked face

【麻乱】 máluàn〈形〉 confused

【麻木】 mámù〈形〉 1（指感觉） numb: 她被冻得手脚～。 Both her hands and feet went numb with cold. ‖ 她牙痛得下巴都～了。 Her teeth were aching and her jaw numb. 2〈喻〉（指反应） apathetic: ～地生活 lead an inert life ‖ 思想～ lifeless mind

【麻木不仁】 mámù-bùrén〈成〉 insensitive: 对他人的痛苦～ show indifference towards the sufferings of others

【麻婆豆腐】 mápó dòufu〈名〉 stir-fried bean curd in hot sauce [the recipe is attributed to a certain pockmarked old woman]

【麻雀】máquè〈名〉sparrow
【麻雀虽小，五脏俱全】máquè suī xiǎo, wǔzàng jù quán〈成〉small but perfectly formed
【麻纱】máshā〈名〉**1**（指纱）yarn of ramie, flax, etc. **2**（指布）cambric
【麻绳】máshéng〈名〉hemp rope
【麻省理工学院】Máshěng Lǐgōng Xuéyuàn〈名〉Massachusetts Institute of Technology (MIT)
【麻石】máshí〈名〉［建筑］cut-stone [used in construction or paved walkways]: ～板 chiselled slate
【麻酥酥】másūsū〈形〉tingling: 冬天手放在冷水里会冻得～的。In winter cold water makes your hands tingle.
【麻糖】mátáng〈名〉sesame candy
【麻团】mátuán〈名〉deep-fried sesame seed ball
【麻线】máxiàn〈名〉linen thread
【麻药】máyào〈名〉anaesthetic: 你得打～。You need to have an anaesthetic.
【麻衣】máyī〈名〉**1**〈旧〉（指丧服）gunny mourning garment **2**（麻布衣服）hemp clothes
【麻油】máyóu〈名〉sesame oil
【麻疹】mázhěn ▸**p. 50**〈名〉［医学］measles: 患～ contract measles ‖ ～疫苗 measles virus vaccine
【麻织品】mázhīpǐn〈名〉linen fabrics
【麻子】mázi〈名〉**1**（天花疤痕）pockmarks: 他满脸～。His face was covered with pockmarks. **2**（指人）pockmarked person
【麻醉】mázuì〈动〉**1**（指身体）anaesthetize: 药物～ drug anaesthesia ‖ 局部～ local anaesthesia **2**〈喻〉（毒害）poison: ～年轻人的思想 poison young people's minds
【麻醉剂】mázuìjì〈名〉anaesthetic: 给某人注射～ inject sb. with an anaesthetic
【麻醉品】mázuìpǐn〈名〉drug: 国际～管制局 International Drug Control Board
【麻醉师】mázuìshī〈名〉anaesthetist

痳 má

【痳风】máfēng = 麻风 máfēng
【痳疹】mázhěn = 麻疹 mázhěn

蟆 má ▸蛤蟆 háma

mǎ

马（馬）mǎ

A〈名〉horse: 赛～ race horse
B〈形〉big: ▸～蜂, ～勺
【马鞍】mǎ'ān〈名〉saddle
【马鞍形】mǎ'ānxíng〈名〉falling-off between two peak periods: 旅游业一度出现了～。There was a temporary drop in tourism.
【马帮】mǎbāng〈名〉〈旧〉caravan
【马背】mǎbèi〈名〉horseback
【马鞭】mǎbiān〈名〉horsewhip
【马弁】mǎbiàn〈名〉〈旧〉(officer's) bodyguard
【马表】mǎbiǎo〈名〉stopwatch
【马不停蹄】mǎbùtíngtí〈成〉〈喻〉non-stop: 部队～地赶到了地震灾区。The troops rushed non-stop to the earthquake-stricken area.
【马步】mǎbù〈名〉［武术］horse-riding step
【马槽】mǎcáo〈名〉manger
【马场】mǎchǎng〈名〉stud farm
【马车】mǎchē〈名〉carriage: 敞篷～ open horse-drawn carriage
【马车夫】mǎchēfū〈名〉cart driver
【马齿徒增】mǎchǐ-túzēng〈成〉fritter away one's time and accomplish nothing
【马齿苋】mǎchǐxiàn〈名〉［植物］purslane
【马刺】mǎcì〈名〉spur: 用～策马前进 apply the spurs to a horse
【马达】mǎdá〈名〉motor
【马达加斯加】Mǎdájiāsījiā〈名〉Madagascar: ～共和国 Democratic Republic of Madagascar ‖ ～人 Madagascan ‖ ～语 Malagasy
【马大哈】mǎdàhā〈口〉**A**〈名〉scatterbrain: 他是个～。He is a complete scatterbrain. **B**〈形〉scatterbrained: 你太～了。You're too all over the place.
【马刀】mǎdāo〈名〉sabre
【马到成功】mǎdào-chénggōng〈成〉win instant success: 旗开得胜，～。Win victory as soon as one's banner is unfurled. ‖ 祝你～! I wish you instant success!
【马德里】Mǎdélǐ〈名〉Madrid
【马灯】mǎdēng〈名〉barn lantern
【马镫】mǎdèng〈名〉stirrup
【马店】mǎdiàn〈名〉〈旧〉caravanserai
【马丁尼酒】mǎdīngníjiǔ〈名〉martini
【马队】mǎduì〈名〉**1**（运货队伍）caravan **2**（骑兵队）cavalry
【马尔代夫】Mǎ'ěrdàifū〈名〉Maldives: ～共和国 Republic of Maldives ‖ ～人 Maldivian ‖ ～语 Maldivian
【马尔加什语】Mǎ'ěrjiāshíyǔ ▸**p. 918**〈名〉Malagasy
【马尔萨斯人口论】Mǎ'ěrsàsī rénkǒulùn〈名〉Malthusian theory of population
【马尔维纳斯群岛】Mǎ'ěrwéinàsī Qúndǎo〈名〉Falkland Islands
【马耳他】Mǎ'ěrtā〈名〉Malta: ～共和国 Republic of Malta ‖ ～人 Maltese ‖ ～语 Maltese
【马贩子】mǎfànzi〈名〉horse dealer
【马粪纸】mǎfènzhǐ〈名〉cardboard
【马蜂】mǎfēng〈名〉hornet, wasp
【马蜂窝】mǎfēngwō〈名〉hornet's nest: 别去捅这个～。Don't go stirring up this hornet's nest. ▸捅～
【马夫】mǎfū〈名〉〈旧〉groom
【马竿】mǎgān〈名〉white stick [used by a blind person]
【马革裹尸】mǎgé-guǒshī〈成〉die on the battlefield: 男儿若战死边野，当以～还葬。A man who has died in defence of his country's border should be buried wrapped in horse hide.
【马格里布】Mǎgélǐbù〈名〉Maghrib
【马褂】mǎguà〈名〉mandarin jacket
【马关条约】Mǎguān Tiáoyuē〈名〉Treaty of Shimonoseki
【马倌】mǎguān〈名〉stableman
【马海毛】mǎhǎimáo〈名〉mohair: 马海羔羊毛 kid mohair
【马号】mǎhào〈名〉**1**（马圈）stable **2**（军号）cavalry bugle: 吹～ sound a cavalry bugle
【马赫】mǎhè〈名〉［物理］Mach: 以两～速度飞行 fly at Mach 2
【马后炮】mǎhòupào〈名〉〈喻〉belated effort: 他这人就爱放～。He is always slow off the mark.
【马虎】mǎhu〈形〉sloppy: 他这个人做事太～。This guy does things in a very slapdash way.
【马甲】mǎjiǎ〈名〉〈方〉waistcoat〈英〉; vest〈美〉
【马鲛鱼】mǎjiāoyú〈名〉Spanish mackerel
【马脚】mǎjiǎo〈名〉〈喻〉giveaway: 露出～ give oneself away
【马厩】mǎjiù〈名〉stable
【马驹子】mǎjūzi〈名〉〈口〉（小公马）colt;（小母马）filly
【马具】mǎjù〈名〉harness
【马可福音】Mǎkě Fúyīn〈名〉［基督教］*Gospel According to Mark*
【马克】mǎkè ▸**p. 328**〈名〉**1**（德国原货币）mark: 德国～ Deutsche Mark (DM) **2**（芬兰原货币）markka: 芬兰～ Finnish Markka (FIM)
【马克思列宁主义】Mǎkèsī-Lièníngzhǔyì〈名〉Marxism-Leninism: ～者 Marxist-Leninist
【马克思主义】Mǎkèsīzhǔyì〈名〉Marxism: ～者 Marxist
【马口铁】mǎkǒutiě〈名〉tinplate: ～壶 tinpot ‖ ～皮 sheet tin ‖ ～器皿 tinware
【马裤】mǎkù〈名〉jodhpurs
【马裤呢】mǎkùní〈名〉［纺织］whipcord
【马拉博】Mǎlābó〈名〉Malabo
【马拉犁】mǎlālí〈名〉［农业］horse-drawn plough
【马拉松】mǎlāsōng〈名〉**1** ▸**p. 909**［体育］marathon: 半程～ half marathon **2**〈喻〉marathon: ～式会议/谈判 marathon meeting/negotiation
【马拉维】Mǎlāwéi〈名〉Malawi: ～共和国 Republic of Malawi ‖ ～人 Malawian
【马来半岛】Mǎlái Bàndǎo〈名〉Malay Peninsula
【马来群岛】Mǎlái Qúndǎo〈名〉Malay Archipelago
【马来西亚】Mǎláixīyà〈名〉Malaysia: ～人 Malaysian
【马来亚】Mǎláiyà〈名〉Malaya
【马来语】Mǎláiyǔ ▸**p. 918**〈名〉Malay
【马兰】mǎlán〈名〉［植物］Kalimeris indica
【马蓝】mǎlán〈名〉［植物］acanthaceous indigo
【马勒】mǎlè〈名〉bridle
【马累】Mǎlěi〈名〉Malé
【马里】Mǎlǐ〈名〉Mali: ～共和国 Republic of Mali ‖ ～人 Malian
【马里郡】Mǎlǐjùn〈名〉Moray
【马里兰州】Mǎlǐlánzhōu〈名〉Maryland
【马里亚纳海沟】Mǎlǐyànà Hǎigōu〈名〉Mariana Trench
【马里亚纳群岛】Mǎlǐyànà Qúndǎo〈名〉Mariana Islands
【马力】mǎlì〈名〉horsepower (hp): 三十五～的发动机 thirty-five horsepower engine ▸开足～
【马立克派】Mǎlìkèpài〈名〉［伊斯兰教］Malikite school [school of law now prevalent in western North Africa]
【马利亚】mǎlìyà〈名〉Virgin Mary: 圣母～ Holy Mary
【马列主义】Mǎ-Lièzhǔyì〈简称〉= 马克思列宁主义
【马蔺】mǎlìn〈名〉［植物］Chinese small iris
【马铃薯】mǎlíngshǔ〈名〉potato: ～片 potato chips
【马六甲海峡】Mǎliùjiǎ Hǎixiá〈名〉Strait of Malacca
【马笼头】mǎlóngtou〈名〉head harness: 套上～ put a halter on a horse
【马陆】mǎlù〈名〉［动物］diplopod
【马鹿】mǎlù〈名〉［动物］red deer
【马路】mǎlù〈名〉road: 过～ cross a road ‖ 柏油～ asphalt road ‖ 水泥～ cement road
【马路新闻】mǎlù xīnwén〈名〉hearsay: 不

要轻信～。 Don't take what you hear at face value.

【马骡】mǎluó〈名〉［动物］mule

【马马虎虎】mǎmǎ-hūhū〈成〉1（草率）careless: 终身大事岂能～? How can you be careless about your marriage? 2（凑合）passable: 西瓜怎么样? ——～。How's the watermelon? — OK.

【马面鲀】mǎmiàntún〈名〉［鱼类］black scraper

【马那瓜】Mǎnàguā〈名〉Managua

【马奶】mǎnǎi〈名〉mare's milk

【马奶酒】mǎnǎijiǔ〈名〉kumiss [mare's or camel's milk fermented and used as a drink by Tatar nomads]

【马尼拉】Mǎnílā〈名〉Manila

【马尿】mǎniào〈名〉1〈本〉horse urine 2〈喻〉〈贬〉（指酒）alcohol

【马趴】mǎpā〈名〉a fall that lands one flat on one's face: 摔了个大～ fall flat on one's face

【马棚】mǎpéng〈名〉stable

【马匹】mǎpǐ〈名〉horses

【马屁】mǎpì〈名〉〈喻〉flattery: 拍～ lick sb.'s boots

【马屁精】mǎpìjīng〈名〉〈贬〉bootlicker

【马票】mǎpiào〈名〉pari-mutuel ticket

【马普托】Mǎpǔtuō〈名〉Maputo

【马其顿】Mǎqídùn〈名〉Macedonia: ～共和国 Republic of Macedonia ‖ ～人 Macedonian ‖ ～语 Macedonian

【马其诺防线】Mǎqínuò Fángxiàn〈名〉Maginot Line

【马前卒】mǎqiánzú〈名〉1〈本〉〈旧〉foot soldier: 革命军中～ foot soldier in the revolutionary army 2〈喻〉〈贬〉（效力者）pawn: 充当反动派的～ act as a pawn for the reactionaries

【马钱子】mǎqiánzǐ〈名〉［植物］vomiting nut

【马枪】mǎqiāng〈名〉carbine

【马球】mǎqiú ►**p. 909**〈名〉［体育］polo: 打～ play polo

【马萨诸塞州】Mǎsàzhūsàizhōu〈名〉Massachusetts

【马塞卢】Mǎsàilú〈名〉Maseru

【马赛】Mǎsài〈名〉Marseilles

【马赛曲】Mǎsàiqǔ〈名〉La Marseillaise [national anthem of France]

【马赛克】mǎsàikè〈名〉［建筑］1（指瓷砖）mosaic: ～铺面 mosaic pavement 2（指图案）pattern or picture in mosaic: ～图案 mosaic pattern

【马上】mǎshàng〈副〉immediately: ～出发 set off right away ‖ 电影～就要开演了。The film will begin in a minute. ‖ 我～就回来。I'll be right back.

【马勺】mǎsháo〈名〉ladle

【马绍尔群岛】Mǎshào'ěr Qúndǎo〈名〉Marshall Islands: ～共和国 Republic of the Marshall Islands

【马失前蹄】mǎshīqiántí〈成〉〈喻〉make a mistake by accident: 有～的时候 have occasional slip-ups

【马首是瞻】mǎshǒu-shìzhān〈成〉〈喻〉follow sb.'s lead

【马术】mǎshù〈名〉1（骑术）horsemanship 2 ►**p. 909**［体育］equestrianism

【马术比赛项目】mǎshù bǐsài xiàngmù〈名〉equestrian events

【马斯喀特】Mǎsīkātè〈名〉Muscat

【马太福音】Mǎtài Fúyīn〈名〉［基督教］*The Gospel According to Matthew*

【马蹄】mǎtí〈名〉1（指蹄子）horse's hoof: ～声 clatter of a horse's hoofs 2〈方〉［植物］water chestnut

【马蹄表】mǎtíbiǎo〈名〉(round or hoof-shaped) desk clock

【马蹄莲】mǎtílián〈名〉［植物］calla lily

【马蹄铁】mǎtítiě〈名〉1（马掌）horseshoe: 锻造～ forge a horseshoe 2（磁铁）U-shaped magnet

【马蹄形】mǎtíxíng〈名〉U-shape: ～磁铁 horseshoe magnet ‖ ～弯道 horseshoe bend, oxbow

【马铁】mǎtiě〈名〉malleable (cast) iron

【马桶】mǎtǒng〈名〉1（木制）toilet: ～刷子 toilet brush 2（瓷制）toilet bowl: ►抽水～

【马头琴】mǎtóuqín ►**p. 929**〈名〉*matouqin* [Mongolian stringed instrument]

【马王堆汉墓】Mǎwángduī Hànmù〈名〉Western Han Tombs at Mawangdui (马王堆)

【马尾辫】mǎwěibiàn〈名〉ponytail

【马尾松】mǎwěisōng〈名〉masson pine

【马戏】mǎxì〈名〉circus: ～团 circus troupe ‖ ～团小丑 clown

【马熊】mǎxióng = 棕熊 zōngxióng

【马靴】mǎxuē〈名〉riding boots

【马眼罩】mǎyǎnzhào〈名〉blinkers

【马仰人翻】mǎyǎng-rénfān = 人仰马翻 rényǎng-mǎfān

【马缨花】mǎyīnghuā = 合欢 héhuān B

【马蝇】mǎyíng〈名〉horsefly

【马仔】mǎzǎi〈名〉〈方〉follower

【马贼】mǎzéi〈名〉〈旧〉mounted gangsters

【马扎】mǎzhá〈名〉folding stool

【马掌】mǎzhǎng〈名〉1（指角质皮）cutin skin of a horse's hoof 2（马蹄铁）horseshoe: 钉～ shoe a horse

【马桩】mǎzhuāng〈名〉hitching post

【马子】mǎzi〈名〉〈方〉〈粗〉girl: 泡～ fool around with a girl

【马鬃】mǎzōng〈名〉horsehair

【马祖岛】Mǎzǔdǎo〈名〉Matsu Island

吗（嗎）mǎ

►má, ma

【吗啡】mǎfēi〈名〉morphine

犸（獁）mǎ ►猛犸 měngmǎ

玛（瑪）mǎ

【玛瑙】mǎnǎo〈名〉agate: 血点～ blood agate

【玛雅人】Mǎyǎrén〈名〉Mayan

【玛雅文化】Mǎyǎ wénhuà〈名〉Mayan Civilization

【玛雅语】Mǎyǎyǔ ►**p. 918**〈名〉Mayan

【玛祖卡舞】mǎzǔkǎwǔ〈名〉［音乐］mazurka

码[1]（碼）mǎ

A〈名〉1（表数字）sign or thing indicating number: ►号～，价～，页～ 2（指用具）instrument indicating number: ►尺～，砝～ 3（代码）code: ►电～，密～，明～ 4［计算机］method of inputting: 五笔型～ WBX input method

B〈量〉[indicating the same thing or the same kind]: 这完全是两～事。These are two entirely different matters.

码[2]（碼）mǎ〈动〉〈口〉pile up: ～积木 stack the toy bricks ‖ 把这些书～齐。Put these books in a neat pile.

码[3]（碼）mǎ ►**p. 82**〈量〉yard (yd): 五～棉布 five yards of cotton cloth ‖ 以～为单位买布 buy cloth by the yard

【码放】mǎfàng〈动〉pile up

【码分多址】mǎfēn duōzhǐ〈名〉［通信］code division multiple access (CDMA)

【码头】mǎtou〈名〉1（指建筑物）dock: 集装箱～ container berth ‖ 客运～ passenger wharf ‖ ～工人 docker ►深水～ 2〈方〉（指城市）port city: 跑～ travel from port to port as a trader ‖ 上海是一座水陆～。Shanghai is a port city with both land and water transport.

【码头搬运工】mǎtou bānyùngōng〈名〉docker

【码头泊位】mǎtou bówèi〈名〉quay berth

【码洋】mǎyáng〈名〉total list price: 本词典印刷五万册，～一千万元。This dictionary has an impression of 50,000 copies and the total price is 10 million *yuan*.

【码子】mǎzi〈名〉1（指符号）numeral: 苏州～ Suzhou numerals 2（指筹码）chip

蚂（螞）mǎ

►mà

【蚂蜂】mǎfēng = 马蜂 mǎfēng

【蚂蟥】mǎhuáng〈名〉［动物］leech

【蚂蚁】mǎyǐ〈名〉ant: 像热锅上的～ like a cat on a hot tin roof

【蚂蚁啃骨头】mǎyǐ kěn gǔtou〈成〉attack a big job bit by bit

mà

杩（榪）mà

【杩头】màtou〈名〉crossbar

蚂（螞）mà

►mǎ

【蚂蚱】màzha〈名〉〈口〉locust: ►秋后的～

骂（駡、罵）mà〈动〉1（侮辱人）curse: ～人 swear at sb. ‖ ～不还口 do not return a curse with a curse ‖ 有人～他是疯子。Some people called him a madman. ►～街，挨～ 2（斥责）chide: ～他不长进 blame him for not striving to make progress ‖ 爸爸～他不争气。Father scolded him for letting himself down. ►责～

【骂大街】mà dàjiē = 骂街 màjiē

【骂架】màjià〈动〉quarrel: ～后言归于好 patch up a quarrel

【骂街】màjiē〈动〉swear in public: ～是不对的。It is improper to shout abuse in public.

【骂骂咧咧】màma-liēliē〈形〉foul-mouthed: 那个家伙的嘴特别不干净，整天满口脏话～的。That guy has a foul mouth. He's constantly swearing like a trooper.

【骂名】màmíng〈名〉bad name: 留下千古～ earn oneself eternal infamy

【骂娘】màniáng〈动〉curse

【骂人】màrén〈动〉abuse

【骂阵】màzhèn〈动〉provoke the enemy to battle with a stream of abuse

ma

吗（嗎）ma〈助〉1（表疑问）[used at the end of an interrogative sentence]: 晚上有讲座～? Is there a lecture tonight? ‖ 你找我～? Are you looking for me?

2（表停顿）[used within a sentence to mark a pause before introducing the theme of what one is going to say]: 这本书～，其实还不错。 As for this book, it's actually not bad. ‖ 钱～，能省点就省点。 Money, of course, should be saved as much as possible. **3**（表反问）[used at the end of a rhetorical question]: 你不跟我们去了～? Aren't you coming with us? ‖ 你难道不明白我这是为你好～? Don't you see I am doing this for your good?
▸má, mǎ

嘛 ma〈助〉**1**（表理所当然）[indicating that something is obvious]: 领导也是人～，怎么能不犯错误? Leaders are human too: they make mistakes. ‖ 有话就说～。 If you have something to say, just come out with it. ‖ 这也不能怪他，他还是个孩子～。 He's not to blame. After all, he is still a child. **2**（表劝阻）[used at the end of an imperative sentence to express a hope or give advice]: 既然没邀请你，就别去～。 If you're not invited, then don't go. ‖ 别走得那么快～! Don't walk so fast! **3**（表停顿）[used within a sentence to indicate a pause to draw listener's attention]: 你～，就不必亲自去了。 As for you, I don't think you have to be there in person. ‖ 好～，让我们一起去吧。 OK, let's go together.

mái

埋 mái〈动〉**1**（盖住）bury: ～电缆/地雷 lay a cable/mines ‖ 把胡萝卜～在土里保存 store carrots by burying them in the earth ▸～藏, ～没, 活～, 掩～ **2**〈喻〉（隐藏）hide: ▸～伏, 隐姓～名
▸mán

【埋藏】máicáng〈动〉**1**（掩埋）bury: 地下～着丰富的矿产。 The ground is rich in mineral deposits. **2**（隐藏）hide: 把秘密～在心底 bury a secret deep in one's heart ‖ 倾诉～在心底的感情 reveal one's innermost feelings **3**（指在皮下）implant some preparation in the subcutaneous tissue of a person or animal

【埋单】máidān = 买单 mǎidān B

【埋伏】máifu〈动〉lie in ambush: ～一个团的兵力 have a regiment of troops wait in ambush ‖ 设～ lay an ambush ▸打～

【埋名】máimíng〈动〉conceal one's identity: ▸隐姓～

【埋没】máimò〈动〉**1**（掩埋）bury: 沙尘～了整个工厂。 The dust submerged the whole factory. **2**（使无法显露）stifle: ～人才 suppress real talents ‖ 他的绘画天赋被～了。 His talent for painting was neglected.

【埋设】máishè〈动〉fit sth. underground: ～管道 lay a pipeline ‖ ～光缆 lay an optical cable

【埋设线路】máishè xiànlù〈名〉buried line

【埋汰】máitai〈方〉**A**〈形〉dirty: 这件大衣太～了。 This overcoat is too dirty. **B**〈动〉ridicule: 别再～他了。 Stop making fun of him.

【埋头】máitóu〈动〉bury oneself in: ～工作 lose oneself in one's work ‖ ～写作 engross oneself in writing ‖ ～苦干 bury oneself in hard work

【埋葬】máizàng〈动〉**1**〈本〉inter: 按当地习俗～（某人）bury (sb.) according to local customs ‖ 他已被～在公墓里。 He has been laid to rest at the cemetery. **2**〈喻〉abolish: ～旧世界，建立新世界。 Bury the old world and build a new one.

霾 mái〈名〉thick haze: ▸阴～

mǎi

买（買） mǎi〈动〉**1**（购买）buy: ～东西 go shopping ‖ ～房子 buy a house ‖ ～一辆新车 purchase a new car **2**（拉拢）bribe: ▸～通

【买办】mǎibàn〈名〉comprador: ～资产阶级 comprador bourgeoisie

> **买办**
> At the beginning of the Qing Dynasty, *maiban* originally referred to someone hired by a foreign merchant trading in China, who was responsible for purchasing and managing affairs. Later it was used to apply to the Chinese managers hired by foreign capitalists who set up businesses, companies and banks, etc. in pre-revolutionary China.

【买办资本】mǎibàn zīběn〈名〉comprador's capital: ～家 comprador capitalist ‖ ～主义 comprador capitalism

【买单】mǎidān **A**〈名〉［金融］voucher of purchase **B**〈动〉〈方〉pay the bill: 小姐，～。 Waitress, bring me the bill.

【买点】mǎidiǎn〈名〉**1**（指商品优势）buying point **2**（指价位）buy point

【买椟还珠】mǎidú-huánzhū〈成〉〈喻〉show a lack of sound judgment

【买断】mǎiduàn〈动〉buy sth. outright: ～版权 buy the copyright

【买方】mǎifāng〈名〉buyer: 根据～的要求定做 have sth. made according to the buyer's request

【买方市场】mǎifāng shìchǎng〈名〉buyer's market

【买关节】mǎi guānjié〈惯〉bribe one's way out: ～钻进议会 bribe oneself into parliament

【买好】mǎihǎo〈动〉ingratiate oneself with: 千方百计向某人～ do whatever one can to win sb.'s favour

【买价】mǎijià〈名〉purchase price

【买进】mǎijìn〈动〉buy in: ～债券 buy in bonds ‖ 整批～ buy at wholesale

【买壳上市】mǎiké shàngshì〈动〉go public by acquiring control of a listed company

【买空】mǎikōng〈动〉be long on

【买空卖空】mǎikōng-màikōng〈成〉**1**〈本〉speculate **2**〈喻〉engage in profiteering

【买空者】mǎikōngzhě〈名〉bull

【买路钱】mǎilùqián〈名〉**1**〈旧〉（针对行人）toll money demanded by highwayman for passage **2**（针对车辆）toll

【买卖】mǎimài〈动〉buy and sell: ～公平 buy and sell at reasonable prices ‖ ～婚姻 mercenary marriage

【买卖】mǎimai〈名〉**1**（生意）business: 做～ do business (with sb.) ‖ 做成一笔～ close a deal ‖ ～兴隆。 Business is booming. **2**（商店）shop: 她在西安开了一家～。 She opened a shop in Xi'an.

【买卖不成仁义在】mǎimai bùchéng rényì zài〈俗〉benevolence and uprightness should exist between professionals even if the two parties fail to clinch a deal

【买卖人】mǎimairén〈名〉businessman

【买面子】mǎi miànzi〈惯〉defer to sb.: 她一定会买我的面子接受邀请。 She is sure to accept the invitation for my sake.

【买入】mǎirù〈动〉buy in

【买手】mǎishǒu ▸**p. 966**〈名〉buyer: 专业/国际～ professional/international buyer

【买通】mǎitōng〈动〉buy off: ～法官/陪审团 bribe a judge/jury

【买凶】mǎixiōng〈动〉contract a killer: ～杀人 contract killing

【买一送一】mǎiyī-sòngyī〈动〉buy one, get one free

【买账】mǎizhàng〈动〉[usu used in negative construction] acknowledge sb.'s seniority and show respect for him: 没人买他的账。 No one cares what he says. ‖ 不提工资，工人们决不～。 The workforce won't listen unless they get a pay rise.

【买主】mǎizhǔ〈名〉buyer: 寻找～ look for customers ‖ 有偿付能力的～ solvent purchaser

【买醉】mǎizuì〈动〉buy alcohol and drink oneself drunk

mài

迈¹（邁） mài〈动〉stride: ～大步 take huge strides ‖ ～过门槛 step over the threshold ‖ ～着整齐的步伐 march in step

迈²（邁） mài〈形〉advanced in years: 一位年～的老人 a man much advanced in years ▸老～, 年～

迈³（邁） mài〈名〉mile: 时速一百八十～ 180 miles an hour

【迈步】màibù〈动〉take a step: ～走向讲台 move towards the platform ‖ 迈着方步走上舞台 walk slowly onto the stage

【迈进】màijìn〈动〉forge ahead: ～新世纪 forge ahead into the new century ‖ 以巨人的步伐向前～ advance with giant steps

麦（麥） mài〈名〉**1**（泛指麦类）general term for wheat, barley, oats, rye, etc. **2**（小麦）wheat: 割/收～ reap/harvest wheat ▸～茬, ～子, 大～, 小～

【麦草】màicǎo〈名〉〈方〉wheat straw

【麦茬】màichá〈名〉wheat stubble: ～白薯 sweet potatoes grown after the wheat harvest ‖ ～地 a field of wheat stubble

【麦当劳】Màidāngláo〈名〉McDonald's [US fast food chain]: 吃～ eat McDonald's

【麦地那】Màidìnà〈名〉Medina

【麦冬】màidōng〈名〉［中药］lilyturf root

【麦垛】màiduò〈名〉wheat stack

【麦尔登呢】mài'ěrdēngní〈名〉［纺织］melton

【麦饭石】màifànshí〈名〉medical stone

【麦麸】màifū〈名〉wheat bran

【麦秆】màigǎn〈名〉wheat straw

【麦秆画】màigǎnhuà〈名〉straw patchwork picture

【麦季】màijì〈名〉wheat harvest season

【麦加】Màijiā〈名〉Mecca: 去～朝圣 make a pilgrimage to Mecca

【麦秸】màijiē〈名〉wheat straw

【麦精】màijīng〈名〉malt extract: ～鱼肝油 cod-liver oil with malt extract

【麦酒】màijiǔ〈名〉beer

【麦卡锡主义】Màikǎxīzhǔyì〈名〉McCarthyism

【麦糠】màikāng〈名〉wheat husk

【麦克风】màikèfēng〈名〉microphone: 对着～讲话 speak into a microphone

【麦克马洪线】Màikèmǎhóngxiàn〈名〉McMahon line

【麦浪】 màilàng 〈名〉 billowing wheat fields: 金黄色的～ golden waves of wheat ‖ ～滚滚。 The wheat is billowing in the wind.
【麦粒】 màilì 〈名〉 grain of wheat
【麦粒肿】 màilìzhǒng ▸p. 50 〈名〉 [医学] sty
【麦芒】 màimáng 〈名〉 beard of wheat: ▸针尖对～
【麦门冬】 màiméndōng = 麦冬 màidōng
【麦苗】 màimiáo 〈名〉 wheat seedling: 绿油油的～ fresh green wheat seedlings
【麦纳麦】 Mànàmài 〈名〉 Manama
【麦片】 màipiàn 〈名〉 oatmeal: 速溶～ instant oatmeal ‖ ～粥 porridge 〈英〉, oatmeal 〈美〉
【麦淇淋】 màiqílín 〈名〉 margarine
【麦秋】 màiqiū 〈名〉 wheat harvest season
【麦乳精】 màirǔjīng 〈名〉 malted milk
【麦收】 màishōu 〈名〉 wheat harvest: ～季节 wheat harvest season
【麦穗】 màisuì 〈名〉 ear of wheat: 沉甸甸的～ dropping ears of wheat
【麦田】 màitián 〈名〉 wheatland
【麦芽】 màiyá 〈名〉 malt
【麦芽糖】 màiyátáng 〈名〉 maltose
【麦蚜虫】 màiyáchóng 〈名〉 [昆虫] wheat aphid
【麦哲伦海峡】 Màizhélún Hǎixiá 〈名〉 Strait of Magellan
【麦种】 màizhǒng 〈名〉 wheat seeds
【麦子】 màizi 〈名〉 wheat

卖（賣） mài

A 〈动〉 1 （出售） sell: ～菜/余粮 sell vegetables/surplus grain ‖ ～花女 flower girl ‖ 这件古董能～高价。 This antique can sell for a high price. ▸拍～, 甩～, 专～ 2 （出卖技艺） make a living by one's labour, skill, etc.: ▸～唱, ～艺 3 （背叛） betray: ▸～国, 出～ 4 （不吝惜） spare no effort: ▸～劲儿, ～力气 5 （炫耀） parade: ▸～弄, ～俏, 倚老～老
B 〈量〉 〈旧〉 one dish: 一～炒鸡蛋 a dish of scrambled eggs
【卖场】 màichǎng 〈名〉 big marketplace
【卖唱】 màichàng 〈动〉 sing for a living: 靠～过活 earn one's livelihood by singing
【卖出】 màichū 〈动〉 sell
【卖出价】 màichūjià 〈名〉 selling prices
【卖春】 màichūn = 卖淫 màiyín
【卖呆】 màidāi 〈动〉 〈方〉 pretend to be naive or stupid
【卖单】 màidān 〈名〉 vouchers of sale at a financial market
【卖点】 màidiǎn 〈名〉 1 （指商品优点） selling point: 价廉和便携是这款电脑的两大～。 The computer's two main selling points are that it's cheap and that it's portable. 2 （指价格） sell point
【卖方】 màifāng 〈名〉 seller
【卖方市场】 màifāng shìchǎng 〈名〉 seller's market
【卖功】 màigōng 〈动〉 parade one's merits: ～邀赏 take credit and seek rewards for one's own achievements
【卖狗皮膏药】 mài gǒupí gāoyao 〈俗〉 sell quack remedies
【卖乖】 màiguāi 〈动〉 show off one's cleverness: 得了便宜还～ swagger and brag after having gained an advantage
【卖关节】 mài guānjié 〈惯〉 take bribes in secret and offer favours in return
【卖关子】 mài guānzi 〈惯〉 1 （制造悬念） stop a story at a climax to keep the listeners in suspense 2 〈喻〉 （故弄玄虚） win acceptance by deliberately mystifying something at a crucial point: 别～了，快告诉我们那场足球赛的结果。 Spare us the suspense and just tell us who won the football game.
【卖官鬻爵】 màiguān-yùjué 〈成〉 sell ranks and titles
【卖国】 màiguó 〈动〉 betray one's country: ～投降 capitulate and engage in national betrayal
【卖国求荣】 màiguó-qiúróng 〈成〉 turn traitor for personal gain
【卖国贼】 màiguózéi 〈名〉 traitor to one's country
【卖好】 màihǎo 〈动〉 curry favour with: 向顶头上司～ curry favour with one's immediate superior
【卖价】 màijià 〈名〉 selling price
【卖劲儿】 màijìnr 〈动〉 〈口〉 go all out: 干活很～ spare no effort in one's work
【卖空】 màikōng 〈动〉 sell short (of stocks)
【卖老】 màilǎo 〈动〉 assume the airs of an elderly person: 我不敢在您面前～。 I dare not assume an air of seniority before you. ▸倚老～
【卖力】 màilì = 卖力气 mài lìqi 1
【卖力气】 mài lìqi 〈动〉 〈口〉 1 （尽力） do one's very best: 他学习法语很～。 He works hard at studying French. 2 （出卖体力） do manual labour for a living: ～养家糊口 support one's family by doing manual labour
【卖命】 màimìng 〈动〉 work one's fingers to the bone for: 雇主迫使雇员们为他～。 The employer forced the employees to sweat blood for him.
【卖弄】 màinong 〈动〉 parade: ～口舌 show one's glibness in speech or wit ‖ ～小聪明 make a show of one's smartness
【卖弄风骚】 màinong-fēngsāo 〈成〉 flirt
【卖破绽】 mài pòzhàn 〈动〉 feign weakness in order to hoodwink an opponent
【卖钱】 màiqián 〈动〉 sell for money: 这块地能卖一大笔钱。 You can get a large sum of money for this piece of land if you sell it.
【卖俏】 màiqiào 〈动〉 flirt
【卖人情】 mài rénqíng 〈惯〉 win gratitude by doing favours
【卖身】 màishēn 〈动〉 1 〈旧〉 （出卖自身） sell oneself or a member of one's family 2 〈口〉 （卖淫） sell one's body: 卖艺不～ sell one's art and not one's body
【卖身契】 màishēnqì 〈名〉 indenture for sale of oneself or one's family member
【卖身投靠】 màishēn-tóukào 〈成〉 sell oneself to the enemy: 他以出卖国家绝密～敌人。 He sold out to the enemy by giving away his country's top secrets.
【卖相】 màixiàng 〈名〉 〈方〉 appearance
【卖笑】 màixiào 〈动〉 make a living as a good-time girl: ～生涯 live as a good-time girl
【卖艺】 màiyì 〈动〉 make a living as a performer: 街头～ be a street-performer ‖ ～者 performer
【卖淫】 màiyín 〈动〉 sell sex: 严厉打击～嫖娼活动 come down very hard on activities involving the sale of sex ‖ ～业 sex trade
【卖淫女】 màiyínnǚ 〈名〉 prostitute
【卖友】 màiyǒu 〈动〉 betray one's friend: ～求荣 betray one's friend for personal gains
【卖主】 màizhǔ 〈名〉 seller: 与～当面议价 negotiate the price face to face with a seller
【卖嘴】 màizuǐ 〈动〉 indulge in clever talk: 他只会～，没有行动。 He is all talk and no action.
【卖座】 màizuò A 〈名〉 crowd-puller: ～率高/低 have a high/low rate of drawing audiences B 〈形〉 crowd-pleasing: 不～ cannot attract large audiences ‖ ～的电影 box-office hit ‖ 这部电影很～。 The film was a great draw.

脉（脈） mài

〈名〉 1 [生理] arteries and veins: ▸动～, 静～ 2 （脉搏） pulse: 把～ take sb.'s pulse ▸～搏, ～象 3 （脉络） vein: ▸叶～ 4 （血管状物） sth. linking up to form a blood-vessel-like network: ▸山～, 来龙去～, 一～相承
▸mò
【脉案】 mài'àn 〈名〉 [中医] diagnosis
【脉搏】 màibó 〈名〉 pulse: ～微弱/有力 have a weak/strong pulse ‖ 她的～跳得很快。 Her pulse raced. ‖ 〈喻〉 时代的～ the pulse of our times
【脉冲】 màichōng 〈名〉 [物理] pulse: 光～ pulse of light ‖ 声～ pulse of sound ‖ ～发射 pulse emission
【脉冲信号】 màichōng xìnhào 〈名〉 pulse signal
【脉冲星】 màichōngxīng 〈名〉 [天文] pulsar
【脉动】 màidòng 〈名〉 [物理] pulsation
【脉动星】 màidòngxīng 〈名〉 [天文] pulsating star
【脉管炎】 màiguǎnyán ▸p. 50 〈名〉 [医学] vasculitis
【脉金】 màijīn 〈名〉 [中医] consultation fee
【脉理】 màilǐ 〈名〉 1 〈书〉 （脉络条理） mountain range 2 [中医] principles of Chinese medicine: 他精通～。 He is an expert in Chinese medicine.
【脉络】 màiluò 〈名〉 1 [中医] general term for arteries and veins 2 〈喻〉 （条理） train of thought: ～分明 present ideas clearly and logically
【脉络图】 màiluòtú 〈名〉 chart of arteries and veins
【脉石】 màishí 〈名〉 [矿业] gangue
【脉息】 màixī 〈名〉 pulse: ～微弱 have a weak pulse
【脉象】 màixiàng 〈名〉 [中医] type of pulse
【脉压】 màiyā 〈名〉 pulse pressure
【脉泽】 màizé 〈名〉 [物理] maser
【脉诊】 màizhěn 〈名〉 [中医] pulse diagnosis
【脉枕】 màizhěn 〈名〉 wrist cushion

唛（嘜） mài 〈名〉 〈方〉 trademark

mān

嫚 mān 〈名〉 〈方〉 girl
▸màn

颟（顢） mān

【颟顸】 mānhān 〈形〉 1 （糊涂） foolish 2 （马虎） muddle-headed and careless: 他这人太～，什么事都做不好。 This guy is completely all over the place and can't do anything right.

m

mán

埋 mán
▸mái

【埋怨】mányuàn〈动〉blame: ～自己记性不好 complain of one's bad memory ‖ 相互～ blame one another ‖ 她～我粗心大意。She blamed me for being careless.

蛮（蠻）mán

A〈形〉**1**（粗野）rough: ▸～不讲理, ～横, 野～ **2**（鲁莽）rash: ▸～干, ～劲
B〈名〉ancient ethnic groups in the south of China
C〈副〉〈方〉quite: 威信～高 enjoy high prestige ‖ ～有趣 pretty interesting ‖ 小姑娘～漂亮。The little girl is very pretty.

【蛮不讲理】mánbùjiǎnglǐ〈成〉not listen to reason: 说话～ not listen to reason
【蛮干】mángàn〈动〉act rashly: 不能～ must not rush headlong into things ‖ 提倡苦干加巧干，避免～ advocate hard work and intelligence, and not rushing into things
【蛮横】mánhèng〈形〉rude and unreasonable: 态度～ take an unreasonable attitude ‖ 他们的要求～无理。Their demands are beyond all reason.
【蛮荒】mánhuāng **A**〈形〉savage and wild: ～时代 barbarous age **B**〈名〉uncivilized region: ～之地 wild, uncivilized region
【蛮劲】mánjìn〈名〉sheer muscle: 小伙子有股～。The young fellow has got sheer masculine strength.
【蛮勇】mányǒng〈名〉daredevil gallantry
【蛮子】mánzi〈名〉〈旧〉〈贬〉barbarian [contemptuous term applied by northerners to southerners]: 南～ barbarian from the south

谩（謾）mán

〈动〉〈书〉hoodwink
▸màn

【谩语】mányǔ〈名〉deceitful words

蔓 mán

▸màn, wàn

【蔓菁】mánjing = 芜菁 wújīng

馒（饅）mán

【馒头】mántou〈名〉**1**（无馅儿）*mantou* [steamed bun]: 蒸～ steam *mantou* ‖ 热气腾腾的～ steaming hot *mantou* **2**〈方〉（有馅儿）steamed stuffed bun: 肉～ a steamed bun with meat stuffing

> **馒头**
> A traditional Chinese steamed bun made from a dough of flour, water, and yeast, either round or long in shape, and usually with no filling. Buns containing a filling are known as *baozi* (包子). In some parts of south China *mantou* refers to buns with or without filling. *Mantou* are a staple food of north China.

瞒（瞞）mán

〈动〉conceal sth. from: 什么事也～不过你。Nothing can escape your attention. ‖ 他似乎有事～着我。He seems to be keeping something from me. ▸欺上～下, 隐～

【瞒报】mánbào〈动〉give a false report
【瞒得了一时，瞒不了一世】mán déliǎo yīshí, mán bùliǎo yīshì〈俗〉you can cheat people for some of the time, but not for all of the time
【瞒哄】mánhǒng〈动〉deceive: ～父母 hide the truth from one's parents
【瞒上欺下】mánshàng-qīxià〈成〉deceive those above and bully those below
【瞒天过海】mántiān-guòhǎi〈成〉〈喻〉engage in underhand activity: 识破了～的手段 see through deceptive tactics

鞔 mán

〈动〉**1**（指鼓）cover a drum: 牛皮可以～鼓。Oxhide can be used to cover a drum. **2**（指鞋）cover the upper of a shoe with cloth: ～鞋 cover the upper of a shoe with cloth

鳗（鰻）mán

〈名〉eel: ～鱼苗 eel fry

【鳗鲡】mánlí〈名〉common eel

mǎn

满[1]（滿）mǎn

A〈形〉**1**（充满）full: 杯子里倒～了啤酒。The glass is full of beer. ‖ 礼堂里坐～了人。The auditorium was packed with people. **2**（骄傲）conceited: ▸自～ **3**（全部）entire: ～腿是泥 have muddy legs ‖ ～园鲜花。The garden was full of flowers. ▸～身
B〈动〉**1**（满足）feel satisfied: ▸～意, ～足, 踌躇～志 **2**（达到）expire: 合同到今年年底期～。The contract expires by the end of this year. ‖ 他已年～二十岁。He is already 20. **3**（装满）fill: 请给我再～上一杯酒。Please pour me out another glass of wine.
C〈副〉entirely: ～以为 firmly believe ▸～不在乎

满[2]（滿）Mǎn

〈名〉Man ethnic group

【满不在乎】mǎnbùzàihu〈成〉not worry at all: 对地位/名利～ not care in the least about one's position/fame ‖ 对警告～ pay no heed to sb.'s warning ‖ 装作～ pretend not to give a damn ‖ 装出～的样子 put on a brave face ‖ 你没瞧见她那～的样子，连问也不问就把我的收音机拿走了。You should have seen her casual manner; she took my radio without even asking. ‖ 他英语考试不及格，却还～。He wasn't bothered at all after failing the English exam.
【满不在意】mǎnbùzàiyì = 满不在乎 mǎnbùzàihu
【满仓】mǎncāng〈动〉[经济] turn all one's capital into securities
【满城风雨】mǎnchéng-fēngyǔ〈成〉become the talk of the town: 这件事已闹得～。This affair has already created quite a stir.
【满打满算】mǎndǎ-mǎnsuàn〈成〉at the very most: 修建这座桥～300人就够了。It will need a maximum of 300 people to build this bridge.
【满当当】mǎndāngdāng〈形〉full to the brim: 会议室里人坐得～的。The meeting room was packed with people.
【满登登】mǎndēngdēng〈形〉full: 粮囤里麦子都装得～的。The grain bins were stuffed full with wheat.
【满点】mǎndiǎn〈名〉required hours of work: 这家商店坚持～营业。This store maintains full working hours.
【满舵】mǎnduò〈名〉full rudder
【满额】mǎn'é〈动〉fulfil a quota: 今年招收的新学员已经～了。The quota for new trainees for this year has already been filled.
【满分】mǎnfēn〈名〉perfect score: 英语考试得～ get full marks in the English exam ‖ 老师给这位学生数学打了个～。The teacher gave the student full marks in mathematics.
【满服】mǎnfú〈动〉〈旧〉complete a mourning period for one's deceased parent
【满负荷】mǎnfùhè〈名〉full capacity: ～工作 work at full capacity ‖ ～运转 operate at full capacity
【满腹】mǎnfù〈动〉be full of: ～心事 be laden with anxiety ‖ 牢骚～ be full of grievances
【满腹狐疑】mǎnfù-húyí〈成〉be extremely suspicious
【满腹经纶】mǎnfù-jīnglún〈成〉be profoundly learned and talented: 他～。He is profoundly learned and talented.
【满贯】mǎnguàn〈名〉perfect score: 大～ grand slam
【满怀】mǎnhuái **A**〈动〉be full of: ～信心 be full of confidence ‖ ～喜悦 be brimming with joy ‖ 他～感激之情。He is burning with gratitude. **B**〈名〉chest: 撞了个～ bump right into sb.
【满口】mǎnkǒu **A**〈名〉**1**（指口腔）whole mouth: ～假牙 a mouthful of dentures **2**（指话语）standard accent: ～脏话 pour out dirty words ‖ 他～陕西话。He speaks with a pure Shaanxi accent. **B**〈副〉readily: ～应承 readily agree ‖ ～称赞 praise profusely
【满脸】mǎnliǎn〈名〉entire face: ～愁容 look glum ‖ ～杀气 wear a murderous look ‖ ～笑容 be all smiles ‖ ～皱纹 have a wrinkly face ‖ 被打得～花 badly battered
【满满当当】mǎnmǎn-dāngdāng〈形〉full to the brim: ～一卡车蔬菜 a whole truck load of vegetables
【满满登登】mǎnmǎn-dēngdēng〈形〉full: 他的日程总是排得～的。He is always on a tight schedule.
【满门】mǎnmén〈名〉〈旧〉whole family: 祸及～ bring disaster on the whole family ‖ ～抄斩 [in feudal China] execute the whole family
【满面】mǎnmiàn〈动〉cover one's whole face: ～笑容 be all smiles ‖ 她泪流～。She was streaming with tears. ▸～春风
【满面春风】mǎnmiàn-chūnfēng〈成〉beam with joy: ～地站在大门口 stand at the door radiant with happiness
【满面红光】mǎnmiàn-hóngguāng〈成〉be glowing with health
【满目】mǎnmù〈动〉fill one's gaze: ～荒凉 desolation as far as the eye can see ▸琳琅～
【满目疮痍】mǎnmù-chuāngyí = 疮痍满目 chuāngyí-mǎnmù
【满脑子】mǎnnǎozi〈名〉one's whole mind: ～名利思想 have one's head filled with thoughts of personal fame and gain ‖ ～封建思想 be steeped in feudal ideology ‖ 那家伙～坏主意。The guy's head is full of bad thoughts.
【满拧】mǎnnǐng〈动〉〈方〉contradict
【满七】mǎnqī〈动〉come to the end of the seventh 7-day period of mourning
【满期】mǎnqī〈动〉fall due
【满腔】mǎnqiāng〈动〉have one's heart filled with: ～怒火 be burning with rage ‖ ～热情 be full of enthusiasm
【满腔热忱】mǎnqiāng-rèchén〈成〉in the fullness of one's heart: ～地为顾客服务 serve customers enthusiastically
【满勤】mǎnqín〈动〉regularly attend: 出～ have a perfect attendance record ‖ 获得～奖 earn a full attendance bonus
【满人】Mǎnrén〈名〉Manchu
【满山遍野】mǎnshān-biànyě = 漫山遍野

mànshān-biànyě

【满身】mǎnshēn〈名〉one's entire body: ～大汗 sweat all over

【满师】mǎnshī〈动〉serve out one's apprenticeship: 她学画还没有～。She has not yet served out her apprenticeship as a painter.

【满世界】mǎnshìjie〈副〉〈方〉from place to place: 为了找份好工作，她不得不～跑。She had to run all over the place to find a good job.

【满速】mǎnsù〈名〉full gear

【满堂】mǎntáng **A**〈名〉all those present: ～喝彩。A round of applause burst out. **B**〈动〉fill a hall with: 金玉～ house replete with wealth

【满堂彩】mǎntángcǎi〈名〉universal applause: 他的歌声博得了～。His singing elicited unanimous applause.

【满堂灌】mǎntángguàn〈动〉spoon-feed students: 反对～ oppose the cramming style of teaching

【满堂红】mǎntánghóng〈名〉all-round victory: 中国乒乓球队在43届世乒赛中得了个～。The Chinese national table tennis team had an all-round victory in the 43rd World Table Tennis Championships.

【满天】mǎntiān〈名〉whole sky: ～繁星。The sky was studded with numerous stars.

【满天飞】mǎntiānfēi〈动〉〈喻〉**1**（指人）rush everywhere: 这人～，让我到哪儿去找？That man goes all over the place. Where am I supposed to find him? **2**（指谣言）spread far and wide: 谣言～。Rumours were flying everywhere.

【满头大汗】mǎntóu-dàhàn〈成〉one's face streaming with sweat

【满孝】mǎnxiào = 满服 mǎnfú

【满心】mǎnxīn〈副〉with one's whole heart: ～欢喜 be filled with joy ‖ ～想当歌星 long to be a singing star

【满眼】mǎnyǎn〈名〉**1**（指眼睛）whole eyes: ～泪水 eyes full of tears ‖ ～血丝 bloodshot eyes **2**（指视野）all one can see: ～山花 mountain flowers as far as the eye can see

【满意】mǎnyì〈动〉be satisfied: 感到～ be gratified ‖ 对这一结果非常～ be pleased with the result ‖ 双方对两国关系的发展表示～。The two sides expressed satisfaction with the development of the relations between the two countries.

【满员】mǎnyuán〈动〉**1**（指军队）be at full strength **2**（指人员）be fully staffed: 我们系已经～。Our department is already fully staffed. **3**（指乘客）be full: 2537号航班已经～。Flight No 2537 is full.

【满月】mǎnyuè **A**〈动〉be one month old: 我的孩子今天～了。My child is one month old today. **B**〈名〉full moon

【满载】mǎnzài **A**〈动〉be loaded to capacity: 一辆～木炭的卡车 a truck fully loaded with charcoal ‖ 一艘～中国丝绸的货轮 a freighter loaded with Chinese silk **B**〈名〉full load: ～运行 full-load run

【满载而归】mǎnzài'érguī〈成〉return from a fruitful journey: 热烈欢迎～的中国奥运代表团。We warmly welcome the return of the successful Chinese Olympic Delegation.

【满招损，谦受益】mǎn zhāo sǔn, qiān shòu yì〈成〉conceit leads to losses while modesty brings gain

【满洲】Mǎnzhōu〈名〉**1**（指民族）Manchu **2**（指地方）Manchuria

【满足】mǎnzú〈动〉**1**（满意）be content (with): 不～现状 be dissatisfied with things as they are ‖ 学习的敌人是自己的～。Complacency is the enemy of study. **2**（使满足）satisfy: ～求知欲 gratify one's thirst for knowledge ‖ ～好奇心 indulge one's curiosity ‖ ～虚荣心 minister to a person's vanity ‖ ～对方的要求 meet the other party's demands ‖ 不能～合理的生活需求 fall short of reasonable living demands

【满族】Mǎnzú〈名〉Manchu ethnic group

【满嘴】mǎnzuǐ = 满口 mǎnkǒu A1

【满座】mǎnzuò〈动〉have a full house: 引起～哄堂大笑 set the whole table laughing ‖ 场场～ have a capacity audience for every show ▸高朋～

螨（蟎） mǎn〈名〉［昆虫］mite

【螨虫】mǎnchóng〈名〉mite

màn

曼 màn〈形〉**1**（柔美）graceful: ～舞 graceful dances **2**（长）long-drawn-out: ▸～声, ～延

【曼彻斯特】Mànchèsītè〈名〉Manchester

【曼德琳】màndélín ▸**p. 929**〈名〉［音乐］mandolin

【曼丁哥人】Màndīnggērén〈名〉Mandingo

【曼丁哥语】Màndīnggēyǔ ▸**p. 918**〈名〉Mandingo

【曼谷】Màngǔ〈名〉Bangkok

【曼哈顿】mànhādùn〈名〉Manhattan

【曼妙】mànmiào〈形〉〈书〉lithe and graceful: 姿态～ have a graceful carriage ‖ 舞姿～。The dancer's posture and movements are very graceful.

【曼声】mànshēng〈动〉drawl: ～而歌 drawl out a song ‖ ～吟诵 recite in slow, measured tones

【曼陀罗】màntuóluó〈名〉［植物］datura

【曼延】mànyán〈动〉stretch: 大海一直～到遥远的天边。The ocean stretches to the distant horizon.

谩（謾） màn〈动〉be disrespectful: ▸～骂

▸mán

【谩骂】mànmà〈动〉hurl abuse at: 相互～ have a slanging match

墁 màn〈动〉pave: 客厅用瓷砖～地 lay the floor of the drawing room with ceramic tiles ‖ 大厅是大理石～地。The lobby is paved with marble slabs.

蔓 màn

A〈名〉trailing plant's stems and branches: ▸～草, 枝～

B〈动〉grow: ▸～延, 滋～

▸mán, wàn

【蔓草】màncǎo〈名〉creeping weed

【蔓生】mànshēng〈动〉overgrow: ～植物 trailing plant

【蔓延】mànyán〈动〉（指火、疾病）spread;（指植物）trail: 防止疾病～ stop the disease from spreading ‖ 控制火势～ check the spread of the flames ‖ 腐败现象仍在一些地区～。Corruption is still spreading in some areas.

幔 màn〈名〉curtain: 布～ cotton curtain ‖ 窗～ window curtain

【幔帐】mànzhàng〈名〉curtain

漫 màn

A〈动〉**1**（溢出）overflow: 杯子里的水～出来了。The cup is brimming over. ‖ 河水～出了堤岸。The river overflowed its banks. **2**（遍布）be everywhere: ▸～山遍野, ～天, 弥～

B〈形〉**1**（长）endless: 长夜～～。The night seemed to have no end. ▸～长 **2**（随意）free: ～无目的 be aimless ‖ ～无限制 be without restrictions ▸～谈, 散～

C〈副〉not: ～说是你，连她都解决不了这个问题。Even she can't solve the problem, let alone you. ▸～道

【漫笔】mànbǐ〈名〉[usu used as the title of an essay] literary notes: 灯下～ random thoughts by lamplight

【漫不经心】mànbùjīngxīn〈成〉be careless: ～地说 speak in a careless way

【漫步】mànbù〈动〉roam: ～街头 roam the streets ‖ ～在校园的林荫道上 stroll along the campus boulevard

【漫长】màncháng〈形〉endless: 熬过～的冬季 endure a long winter ‖ ～的夜晚 endless night ‖ 中国有～的海岸线。China has a long coastline.

【漫道】màndào〈连〉let alone: ～群众有意见，连我们自己也感到不满。Even we are not satisfied with it, to say nothing of the masses.

【漫反射】mànfǎnshè〈名〉［物理］diffuse reflection

【漫灌】mànguàn〈动〉**1**［农业］irrigate: ～特别浪费水。Flood irrigation wastes a lot of water. **2**（指洪水）overflow: 洪水～了村子，淹没了所有街道。The flood overflowed into the village and submerged all the streets.

【漫画】mànhuà〈名〉cartoon: 画～ draw a cartoon ‖ 政治～ political cartoon ‖ ～家 cartoonist

【漫话】mànhuà〈动〉have an informal chat

【漫漶】mànhuàn〈形〉indistinct: 碑文已字迹～。The inscription on the tablet has become illegible.

【漫卷】mànjuǎn〈动〉[of banners] flutter freely: 彩旗随风～。The coloured flags wave freely in the wind.

【漫骂】mànmà〈动〉fling abuse

【漫漫】mànmàn〈形〉boundless: ～长夜 endless night ‖ 四野是一望无际的～牧场。A boundless expanse of pastureland extended as far as the eye could see.

【漫山遍野】mànshān-biànyě〈成〉over hill and dale: 山花～。Wild flowers blanketed hill and dale.

【漫射】mànshè〈名〉［物理］diffusion: ～光 diffused light

【漫说】mànshuō = 慢说 mànshuō

【漫谈】màntán〈动〉chat about: ～当前形势 talk freely about the current situation ‖ 分组～ divide into groups for an informal discussion

【漫天】màntiān **A**〈动〉fill the whole sky: ～大雪。The snow fell in a whirl. ‖ 沙尘～。Sand and dust filled the sky. **B**〈形〉boundless: 撒个～大谎 tell a monstrous lie ‖ ～要价 demand an exorbitant price

【漫无边际】mànwúbiānjì〈成〉**1**（无边无际）boundless: ～的草原 boundless prairie ‖ ～的海洋 vast sea **2**（离题太远）discursive: 谈话～ be rambling in one's speech ‖ 这篇文章写得～。The article strays far from the subject.

【漫无止境】mànwúzhǐjìng〈成〉know no bounds

【漫延】mànyán = 曼延 mànyán
【漫野】mànyě〈动〉 be all over the plains
【漫溢】mànyì〈动〉 brim over: 洪水～。The floodwaters were overflowing.
【漫游】mànyóu〈动〉 1▸（指游览） go on a pleasure trip: ～世界 wander all over the world ‖ 骑自行车～ go on a spin on one's bike 2▸（指网络） browse: ～因特网 surf the Internet ‖ 网上～ net surf 3▸（指在水中） float 4▸（指通信） roam: ▸～费
【漫游费】mànyóufèi〈名〉 roaming fee
【漫游生物】mànyóu shēngwù〈名〉 nomadic aquatic animal
【漫语】mànyǔ〈书〉 A〈形〉 irrelevant: ～空言 irrelevant remarks B〈名〉 random remarks

慢 màn

A〈形〉 1▸（没礼貌） rude: ▸傲～, 怠～ 2▸（速度低） slow: 反应～ slow to react ‖ 前方道路施工，请～行! Roadworks ahead, please drive slowly! ‖ 我的表～15分钟。My watch is 15 minutes slow.
B〈动〉 postpone: 这事～点儿告诉她，等她父亲回来再说。 Don't tell her the news yet, not until her father comes back. ▸且～
C〈副〉 not: ▸～道, ～说
【慢班】mànbān〈名〉 slow class: 班级分快班和～。 The class is split into a fast class and a slow class.
【慢板】mànbǎn〈名〉［音乐］ lento
【慢车】mànchē〈名〉 slow train: 乘～ take the slow train
【慢车道】mànchēdào〈名〉 inside lane; nearside lane 〈英〉: 不要在～超车。Don't overtake on the inside.
【慢待】màndài〈动〉 1▸（怠慢） treat coldly: 千万不能～了朋友。 You should never be discourteous or dishonest with friends. 2▸〈套〉（招待不周） not be attentive enough to: 今天～了诸位，请多包涵。 Apologies for not having taken enough care of you today.
【慢道】màndào = 漫道 màndào
【慢动作】màndòngzuò〈名〉［影视］ slow motion
【慢工出细活】màngōng chū xìhuó〈俗〉 slow work yields fine results
【慢火】mànhuǒ〈名〉 gentle fire
【慢件】mànjiàn〈名〉 ordinary mail
【慢镜头】mànjìngtóu〈名〉［影视］ slow motion: ～枪战 slo-mo shoot-out ‖ 让我们用～把那个进球再放一遍。 Let's show that goal again in slow motion.
【慢慢腾腾】mànman-tēngtēng〈形〉 sluggish: 这样～地走，什么时候才能到车站呢? When will we ever get to the station if we walk so slowly?
【慢慢吞吞】mànman-tūntūn = 慢慢腾腾 mànman-tēngtēng
【慢慢悠悠】mànman-yōuyōu = 慢悠悠 mànyōuyōu
【慢跑】mànpǎo〈名〉 jogging: 去～ go jogging ‖ ～运动鞋 jogging shoes
【慢坡】mànpō〈名〉 gentle slope
【慢热】mànrè〈动〉 be slow to warm up: ～型球员 a player who tends to be slow to warm up
【慢说】mànshuō〈连〉 let alone: 这部动画片，～孩子，连大人都爱看。 Even adults like to watch this cartoon, to say nothing of children. ‖ 我连自行车都买不起，～是汽车。 I can't even afford a bicycle, let alone a car.
【慢速】mànsù〈名〉 low speed
【慢腾腾】màntēngtēng〈形〉 sluggish: 你这么～的，几时能把这部小说看完? When will you ever finish reading this novel if you continue at such a leisurely pace?
【慢条斯理】màntiáosīlǐ〈成〉 leisurely: 说话办事～ speak slowly and act unhurriedly
【慢吞吞】màntūntūn = 慢腾腾 màntēngtēng
【慢性】mànxìng A〈形〉 1▸（发作慢） chronic: ～病毒 slow virus ▸～病, ～支气管炎 2▸（时间久） slow B = 慢性子 mànxìngzi 2
【慢性病】mànxìngbìng ▸p. 50〈名〉 chronic disease: ～患者 person with a chronic disease
【慢性胃炎】mànxìng wèiyán ▸p. 50〈名〉 chronic gastritis
【慢性支气管炎】mànxìng zhīqìguǎnyán ▸p. 50〈名〉 chronic bronchitis
【慢性中毒】mànxìng zhòngdú ▸p. 50〈名〉 chronic poisoning
【慢性子】mànxìngzi〈名〉 1▸（指个性） phlegmatic temperament 2▸（指人） slowcoach〈英〉; slowpoke〈美〉: 他是个～，家里失了火也不会着急。 He is such a slowcoach that he wouldn't feel the urgency even if his house caught fire.
【慢悠悠】mànyōuyōu〈形〉 unhurried: 他～地走过来。 He is walking leisurely toward us.
【慢走】mànzǒu〈动〉〈口〉 1▸（留步） wait a minute: ～，我有话要跟你说。Wait a minute, please. I have got something to tell you. 2▸〈套〉（保重） take care, good-bye: 您～。 Take care.

嫚 màn〈动〉〈书〉 despise

▸mān
【嫚骂】mànmà〈书〉= 谩骂 mànmà

缦（縵） màn〈名〉〈书〉 plain silk fabric

镘（鏝） màn〈名〉〈书〉 trowel: ～刀 trowel

māng

牤 māng

【牤牛】māngniú〈名〉〈方〉 bull

máng

芒 máng〈名〉 1▸［植物］ Chinese silver grass 2▸（指细刺） awn: ▸～刺在背, 麦～ 3▸（刺状物） needle-like things: ▸锋～, 光～

【芒草】mángcǎo〈名〉［植物］ Chinese silvergrass
【芒刺在背】mángcì-zàibèi〈成〉 feel prickles down one's back
【芒果】mángguǒ = 杧果 mángguǒ
【芒硝】mángxiāo〈名〉［化学］ Glauber's salt
【芒种】Mángzhòng〈名〉 Grain in Ear [beginning of the 9th of the 24 solar terms]

忙 máng

A〈形〉 busy: ～得团团转 be as busy as a bee ‖ ～得脱不开身 be too busy to get away ‖ 我现在正～着呢。 I'm in a rush now. ▸繁～, 农～
B〈动〉 hurry: ～于下结论 jump to conclusions ‖ 最近在～什么? What have you been up to lately?
【忙不迭】mángbùdié〈副〉 in a hurry: ～地赔不是 make a hurried apology
【忙叨】mángdao〈动〉〈方〉 be busy: 你～啥呢? What are you busy with?
【忙乎】mánghu〈动〉〈口〉 be busy: 他～了一下午。 He has been busy the whole afternoon.
【忙活】mánghuó A〈名〉 urgent work: 这是件～，要马上做。 This is an urgent piece of work. It must be done at once. B〈动〉〈口〉 be busy doing sth.: 你在忙什么活? What are you busy with?
【忙活】mánghuo〈动〉〈口〉 be busy: 你东奔西跑～什么呢? What are you busy with? ‖ 他们已经～了一个星期了。 They have been busy the whole week.
【忙里忙外】mánglǐ-mángwài〈成〉 bustle around
【忙里偷闲】mánglǐ-tōuxián〈成〉 snatch a little free time out of a busy life
【忙碌】mánglù〈形〉 busy: 成天～个不停 be busy all day long ‖ 为了谋生，他一天到晚～着。 Making his living keeps him busy all day long.
【忙乱】mángluàn〈形〉 hasty and disorderly: 工作～。 The work is in a muddle.
【忙忙碌碌】mángmáng-lùlù〈成〉 busy: 整天～的 bustle about all day
【忙人】mángrén〈名〉 busy person: 他是个大～。 He is a very busy person.
【忙音】mángyīn〈名〉［通信］ busy tone
【忙于】mángyú〈动〉 be busy with: ～工作 be busy with one's work ‖ 母亲整天～家务。 Mother was busy about the house all day.
【忙中出错】mángzhōng-chūcuò〈成〉 haste makes waste

杧 máng

【杧果】mángguǒ〈名〉 1▸（指树） mango tree 2▸（指果实） mango

尨 máng〈书〉

A〈名〉 hairydog
B〈形〉 particoloured

盲 máng

A〈形〉 blind: ▸～人, 夜～症
B〈名〉〈喻〉 illiterate: 扫～ wipe out illiteracy ‖ 科～ someone who is scientifically illiterate ▸法～, 色～, 文～
C〈副〉 blindly: ▸～动, ～从
【盲肠】mángcháng〈名〉［生理］ caecum
【盲肠炎】mángchángyán ▸p. 50〈名〉 1▸（指盲肠） typhlitis 2▸ = 阑尾炎 lánwěiyán
【盲椿象】mángchūnxiàng〈名〉［昆虫］ plant bug
【盲从】mángcóng〈动〉 follow blindly: 不要～。 Don't be led away.
【盲打】mángdǎ〈动〉 touch-type: 他能～。He can touch-type.
【盲道】mángdào〈名〉 tactile paving [for the blind]
【盲点】mángdiǎn〈名〉 blind spot: 卡车正处在我的～上。 The truck was right in my blind spot.
【盲动】mángdòng〈动〉 act blindly
【盲干】mánggàn〈动〉 act rashly: 只凭热情～是解决不了问题的。 Rash enthusiasm cannot solve the problem.
【盲降】mángjiàng〈名〉［航空］ blind landing
【盲井】mángjǐng = 暗井 ànjǐng
【盲流】mángliú〈名〉〈旧〉 1▸（指现象） blind influx [referring to labourers aimlessly

flowing from the countryside to the cities] **2**（指人员） wandering migrants: ～收容站 tramp collecting post

【盲目】mángmù〈形〉 blind: ～崇拜 worship blindly ‖ ～乐观 unfounded optimism ‖ ～引进 make a blind introduction ‖ ～追随 follow blindly

【盲目性】mángmùxìng〈名〉 blindness: 克服～ refrain from blind action

【盲棋】mángqí〈名〉 blind chess: （与某人）下～ play blind chess (with sb.)

【盲区】mángqū〈名〉 **1**［通信］ blind zone **2**（被忽视之处） neglected areas

【盲人】mángrén〈名〉 blind person: ～学校 blind school

【盲人摸象】mángrén-mōxiàng〈成〉〈喻〉 mistake a part for the whole

【盲人瞎马】mángrén-xiāmǎ〈成〉〈喻〉 the blind leading the blind

【盲蛇】mángshé〈名〉 blind snake

【盲鼠】mángshǔ〈名〉［动物］ zokor

【盲文】mángwén ▸**p. 918**〈名〉 **1**（指文字） Braille: ～书籍 books printed in Braille **2**（指文章） Braille publication: ～读物 book in Braille

【盲信】mángxìn = 死信 sǐxìn

【盲杖】mángzhàng〈名〉 white cane [used by the blind]

【盲字】mángzì = 盲文 mángwén

氓 máng ▸流氓 liúmáng ▸méng

茫 máng

〈形〉 **1**（无边际） boundless and indistinct: ▸渺～, 迷～ **2**（无所知） ignorant: ▸～然

【茫茫】mángmáng〈形〉 **1**（无边际） vast: ～戈壁 boundless Gobi desert ‖ ～云海 immense sea of clouds **2**（不清晰） indistinct: 前途～ bleak prospects

【茫然】mángrán〈形〉 **1**（不了解） ignorant: ～不知所措 be at a loss as to what to do ‖ 大家对她的解释～不解。 Her explanations were met with blank incomprehension. **2**（失意） frustrated: ～若失 feel lost ‖ ～的眼神 vacant-looking eyes

【茫无头绪】mángwútóuxù〈成〉 not know where to begin: 案子～。 The case is in a complete muddle.

硭 máng

【硭硝】mángxiāo = 芒硝 mángxiāo

铓（鋩） máng

【铓锣】mángluó〈名〉 *mangluo* [percussion instrument popular with ethnic groups in Yunnan Province]

mǎng

莽[1] mǎng

A〈名〉 rank grass: ▸草～

B〈形〉 **1**（茂盛） thick: ▸～原 **2**〈书〉（广阔） huge: ▸苍～

莽[2] mǎng

〈形〉 rash: ▸～汉, ～撞, 鲁～

【莽苍】mǎngcāng **A**〈形〉 misty: 烟雨～ a vast blur of mist and rain **B**〈名〉 wilderness

【莽汉】mǎnghàn〈名〉 boor: 他是个十足的～。 He is a regular boor.

【莽莽】mǎngmǎng〈形〉 **1**（草木茂盛） luxuriant: 杂草～的土地 a field rank with weeds **2**（无边际） boundless: ～草原 boundless grasslands ‖ ～大地 vast expanse of land

【莽原】mǎngyuán〈名〉 wilderness overgrown with grass

【莽撞】mǎngzhuàng〈形〉 reckless: ～无礼 rash and discourteous ‖ 做事～ act rashly ‖ 恕我～。 Forgive me for my bluntness.

漭 mǎng

【漭漭】mǎngmǎng〈形〉〈书〉 [of water] boundless: ～沧沧 vast and blue

蟒 mǎng

〈名〉 **1**（蟒蛇） python **2** = 蟒袍 mǎngpáo

【蟒袍】mǎngpáo〈名〉 boa-design robe [ceremonial robe worn by ministers during the Ming and Qing dynasties]

【蟒蛇】mǎngshé〈名〉 python

māo

猫（貓） māo

A〈名〉 cat: 雄～ tomcat ▸照～画虎

B〈动〉〈方〉 hide oneself: 整天～在屋里 hole oneself up in one's room all day

▸máo

【猫步】māobù〈名〉 cat-like gait

【猫耳洞】māo'ěrdòng〈名〉 bunker

【猫哭耗子】māokūhàozi = 猫哭老鼠 māokūlǎoshǔ

【猫哭老鼠】māokūlǎoshǔ〈歇后〉〈喻〉 shedding crocodile tears

【猫儿不在老鼠猖狂】māor bùzài lǎoshǔ chāngkuáng〈俗〉 when the cat's away the mice will play

【猫腻】māoni〈名〉〈方〉 cunning plot: 玩～ play tricks ‖ 我们看穿了他们的～。 We have seen through their little game. ‖ 他竞选成功，这里头准有～。 There is something very fishy about his success in the election.

【猫头鹰】māotóuyīng〈名〉 owl

【猫熊】māoxióng〈名〉 giant panda

【猫眼】māoyǎn〈名〉 **1**（指宝石） cat's eye **2**（指门镜） spyhole

【猫鱼】māoyú〈名〉 small fish for cats

máo

毛[1] máo

A〈名〉 **1**（兽毛） hair;（羽毛） feather;（短绒毛） down: 给羊剪～ shear a sheep ‖ 桃子上的～ peach hair ‖ 鸡～ chicken feather ▸脱～ **2**（须发） hair: 多～的双腿/胸脯 hairy legs/chest ▸～发 **3** ▸▸**p. 328**〈口〉（指钱） *mao* [fractional unit of money in China, = 1/10 *yuan* or 10 *fen*]: 五～钱 five *mao* **4**（霉） mould: 面包长～了。 The bread has gone mouldy.

B〈形〉 **1**（细小） fine: ～贼 petty thief ▸～细血管 **2**（指贬值） depreciated: 钱～了。 The money has gone down in value.

毛[2] máo

A〈形〉 **1**（粗略） rough: ▸～估 **2**（不纯净） gross: ▸～利, ～重 **3**（粗糙） rough: ▸～布, ～坯, ～样 **4**（粗率） rash: 他是个～头～脑的家伙。 He is an impetuous fellow. ▸～糙, ～手～脚 **5**（惊慌） scared: 心里直发～ be panic-stricken ‖ 他一见女的就发～。 He's scared stiff of women.

B〈动〉〈方〉 be angry: 我把她惹～了。 I made her angry.

【毛白杨】máobáiyáng〈名〉［植物］ Chinese white poplar

【毛笔】máobǐ〈名〉 Chinese writing brush: ～字 characters written with a writing brush

【毛边】máobiān〈名〉 **1**（指衣服） rough selvedge;（指书） deckle edge: ～书 uncut book **2** = 毛边纸 máobiānzhǐ

【毛边纸】máobiānzhǐ〈名〉 *maobian* paper [Chinese writing paper made from bamboo]

【毛病】máobìng〈名〉 **1**（故障） trouble: 电梯出～了。 The lift is out of order. ‖ 这台电脑有点～。 There is something wrong with this computer. **2**（恶习） fault: 克服主观主义的～ overcome the mistake of subjectivity ‖ 他有个嗜酒贪杯的～。 He is too fond of drinking. That's the trouble with him. **3**（疾病） disease: 腿有～ have leg trouble ‖ 她的心脏有～。 She has a heart condition.

【毛玻璃】máobōlí〈名〉 frosted glass: 一块～ a piece of frosted glass

【毛布】máobù〈名〉 coarse cotton cloth

【毛糙】máocao〈形〉 careless: 作业写得～ be careless in one's homework ‖ 这活儿干得太～了。 That's rather crude work.

【毛茶】máochá〈名〉 raw tea leaves

【毛虫】máochóng〈名〉 caterpillar

【毛刺】máocì〈名〉［机械］ burr

【毛涤】máodí〈名〉 polyester wool

【毛地黄】máodìhuáng〈名〉［中药］ digitalis

【毛豆】máodòu〈名〉 young soya bean

【毛发】máofà〈名〉 hair: ～再生剂 hair-restorer

【毛纺】máofǎng〈名〉 wool spinning: ～织品 woollen textiles ‖ ～厂 woollen mill

【毛葛】máogé〈名〉［纺织］ poplin: ～大衣 poplin coat

【毛茛】máogèn〈名〉［植物］ buttercup

【毛估】máogū〈动〉 make a rough estimate: ～一下，他家今年的收入约为100,000元。 A rough estimate puts his family income at 100,000 *yuan*.

【毛骨悚然】máogǔ-sǒngrán〈成〉 be absolutely terrified: 令人～的故事 blood-curdling story

【毛孩】máohái〈名〉 hairy baby

【毛孩子】máoháizi〈名〉 mere child: 你是一个不懂事的～。 You were a mere innocent child.

【毛蚶】máohān〈名〉〈方〉［动物］ blood clam

【毛烘烘】máohōnghōng〈形〉 hairy: ～的胸膛 hairy chest

【毛乎乎】máohūhū〈形〉 hairy

【毛活】máohuó〈名〉 knitting work: 打～ make woollen knitwear ‖ 钩～ crochet a sweater

【毛尖】máojiān〈名〉 *maojian* tea [green tea made of the young sprouts of superior tea plants]

【毛校样】máojiàoyàng〈名〉［印刷］ foul proof

【毛巾】máojīn〈名〉 towel: 拧～ wring a towel ‖ 洗脸～ hand towel

【毛巾被】máojīnbèi〈名〉 towelling coverlet

【毛巾架】máojīnjià〈名〉 towel rail

【毛举细故】máojǔ-xìgù〈成〉 bring up trifling affairs

【毛孔】máokǒng〈名〉 pore

【毛口】máokǒu〈名〉［机械］ burr: 去～ burring

【毛拉】máolā〈名〉［伊斯兰教］ **1**（指学者） mullah **2**（指阿訇） *maula* [respectful

address of an imam by Muslims in Xinjiang Uygur Autonomous Region]
【毛蓝】máolán〈名〉 darkish blue: ～土布 blue nankeen
【毛里求斯】Máolǐqiúsī〈名〉 Mauritius: ～共和国 Republic of Mauritius ‖ ～人 Mauritian
【毛里塔尼亚】Máolǐtǎníyà〈名〉 Mauritania: ～人 Mauritanian ‖ ～伊斯兰共和国 Islamic Republic of Mauritania
【毛利】máolì〈名〉 gross profit: 获～五百万元 make a gross profit of five million *yuan*
【毛利人】Máolìrén〈名〉 Maori
【毛料】máoliào〈名〉 **1**（指衣料） woollen cloth: ～大衣 woollen coat **2**（指木料） rough lumber
【毛驴】máolǘ〈名〉 donkey
【毛毛虫】máomaochóng = 毛虫 máochóng
【毛毛雨】máomaoyǔ〈名〉 **1**（指雨） drizzle: 下着～。 It is drizzling. **2**（指消息） tip-off: 你能否在开会前给我们先下点～? Can you tip us off before the meeting?
【毛南族】Máonánzú〈名〉 Maonan ethnic group
【毛囊】máonáng〈名〉 hair follicle
【毛囊腺】máonángxiàn〈名〉 hair follicle gland
【毛呢】máoní〈名〉 heavy woollen cloth
【毛坯】máopī〈名〉 **1**（指产品） semi-finished product: ～房 completed but undecorated house **2**［冶金］ rough cast: ～贮存 rough storage **3**［机械］ blank
【毛皮】máopí〈名〉 fur: ～大衣 fur coat
【毛片】máopiàn〈名〉 **1**（影视样片） rushes: 看前一天拍摄的～ watch the rushes of the previous day's shoot **2**（黄色影片） pornographic film
【毛票】máopiào ▸**p. 328**〈名〉〈口〉 banknotes of one, two or five *jiao* denominations
【毛钱儿】máoqiánr ▸**p. 328**〈名〉〈口〉 coins of one, two or five *jiao* denominations
【毛茸茸】máoróngróng〈形〉 hairy: ～的小兔子 downy little rabbit
【毛瑟枪】máosèqiāng〈名〉 Mauser rifle
【毛石】máoshí〈名〉［建筑］ rubble: ～混凝土 rubble concrete
【毛收入】máoshōurù〈名〉 gross income
【毛手毛脚】máoshǒu-máojiǎo〈成〉 be careless
【毛刷】máoshuā〈名〉 brush
【毛遂自荐】Máosuì-zìjiàn〈成〉〈喻〉 volunteer one's services: 我可以～给你当导游。 I volunteer to be your (tour) guide.
【毛笋】máosǔn〈名〉 shoot of *mao* bamboo
【毛毯】máotǎn〈名〉 woollen blanket
【毛桃】máotáo〈名〉 **1**（指树） wild peach tree **2**（指果实） wild peach
【毛条样】máotiáoyàng〈名〉［印刷］ galley proof
【毛细管】máoxìguǎn〈名〉 **1**［生理］ capillary **2**［物理］ capillary tube
【毛细现象】máoxì xiànxiàng〈名〉［物理］ capillarity
【毛细血管】máoxì xuèguǎn〈名〉［生理］ capillary
【毛虾】máoxiā〈名〉 cocktail shrimp
【毛线】máoxiàn〈名〉 knitting wool: 打～ do knitting work ‖ ～袜子 woollen socks
【毛线衫】máoxiànshān〈名〉 sweater: 冬天穿的～ winter woollies ‖ 紧身/宽松～ tight/loose sweater
【毛线衣】máoxiànyī = 毛线衫 máoxiànshān
【毛丫头】máoyātou〈名〉 slip of a girl: 她只是个～。 She is a mere slip of girl.
【毛样】máoyàng〈名〉［印刷］ galley proof
【毛衣】máoyī〈名〉 sweater; jumper〈英〉: 打/织～ knit a sweater
【毛躁】máozao〈形〉 **1**（急躁） short-tempered: 脾气～ have a quick temper **2**（不沉着） rash and careless: 我们做事情决不能毛毛躁躁。 We must not do things in a careless way.
【毛泽东】Máo Zédōng〈名〉 Mao Zedong [1893-1976]: 《～选集》 *Selected Works of Mao Zedong*
【毛泽东思想】Máo Zédōng Sīxiǎng〈名〉 Mao Zedong Thought

> **毛泽东思想**
>
> Maoism, also known as Mao Zedong Thought. An ideology, developed in the 1920s and '30s, and adopted by the Chinese constitution in 1975, that unites Marxist-Leninist theory and the ideas and teachings of Mao Zedong. Although the main architect of Maoism was Mao Zedong himself, it also embodies the collective wisdom of other Chinese Communist leaders including Liu Shaoqi, Zhou Enlai, etc. Maoism stresses the ideological transformation of the masses, and emphasizes the role of agriculture and that played by the rural population in building socialism.

【毛毡】máozhān〈名〉 felt
【毛织品】máozhīpǐn〈名〉 **1**（指料子） woollens **2**（指衣物） woollen knitwear: ～制造商 woollen manufacturer
【毛重】máozhòng〈名〉 gross weight
【毛猪】máozhū〈名〉［经济］ live pig
【毛竹】máozhú〈名〉 Moso bamboo
【毛装】máozhuāng〈形〉 bound but untrimmed
【毛子】máozi〈名〉〈旧〉 **1**（贬）（西洋人） westerner **2**〈方〉（土匪） bandit

矛 máo〈名〉 spear: 长～ lance ▸～盾

【矛盾】máodùn **A**〈名〉 **1**（矛和盾） spear and shield: 以子之矛攻子之盾 turn sb.'s weapons against him **2**［哲学］ contradiction: ～的转化 transformation of a contradiction ‖ 对抗性/非对抗性～ antagonistic/non-antagonistic contradiction **3**（指相互排斥） conflict: 解决～ solve a problem ‖ 属于人民内部～ be part of the problem between the people ‖ ～百出 be full of holes and contradictions **B**〈形〉 contradictory: 心情很～ be in two minds (about sth.) **C**〈动〉 be contradictory: 与国际惯例相～ contradict international practice ‖ 自相～ paradox
【矛盾律】máodùnlǜ〈名〉 law of contradiction
【矛头】máotóu〈名〉 spearhead: 把讽刺的～指向坏人坏事 direct one's satire at evildoers and evil deeds ‖ ～所向 target of attack

茅 máo〈名〉 cogongrass

【茅草】máocǎo〈名〉［植物］ cogongrass: ～棚 thatched shed
【茅厕】máocè〈名〉〈口〉〈方〉 latrine
【茅房】máofáng〈名〉〈口〉 latrine
【茅膏菜】máogāocài〈名〉［植物］ sundew
【茅坑】máokēng〈名〉 cesspit: ▸占着～不拉屎
【茅庐】máolú〈名〉 thatched cottage: ▸三顾～
【茅塞顿开】máosè-dùnkāi〈成〉 suddenly see the light: 你的一番话使我～。 Your words made me all of a sudden see the light.
【茅舍】máoshè〈名〉〈书〉 thatched cottage
【茅台酒】máotáijiǔ〈名〉 *Moutai* [famous Chinese spirit]
【茅屋】máowū〈名〉 thatched cottage

牦（犛、氂） máo

【牦牛】máoniú〈名〉 yak

旄 máo〈名〉〈古〉 flag with yak's tail

猫（貓） máo

▸māo
【猫腰】máoyāo〈动〉 arch one's back

锚（錨） máo〈名〉 anchor: 抛～ cast anchor ‖ 起～ raise anchor

【锚泊】máobó〈动〉 anchor: 这艘船在上海港～。 The ship is anchored in Shanghai.
【锚地】máodì〈名〉 anchorage (ground)
【锚缆】máolǎn〈名〉 anchor cable
【锚雷】máoléi〈名〉［军事］ mooring mine
【锚位】máowèi〈名〉 anchorage

髦 máo〈名〉〈旧〉 fringe

蝥 máo ▸斑蝥 bānmáo

蟊 máo〈名〉 plant pest

【蟊贼】máozéi〈名〉 social vermin: 铲除一切～ eradicate all pests

mǎo

冇 mǎo〈动〉〈方〉 be without

卯[1] mǎo〈名〉 **1**（指地支） fourth of the twelve Earthly Branches: ▸寅吃～粮 **2**〈旧〉（点名、签到） alternative name for roll call or signing in one's arrival in an office: 画～ sign in one's arrival in an office

卯[2] mǎo〈名〉 mortise: 凿个～ chisel a mortise

【卯时】mǎoshí〈名〉〈旧〉 period of the day from 5 am to 7 am
【卯榫】mǎosǔn〈名〉 mortise and tenon
【卯眼】mǎoyǎn〈名〉 mortise: 凿～ chisel a mortise

昴 mǎo〈名〉 one of the 28 constellations in ancient Chinese astronomy

铆（鉚） mǎo〈动〉 **1**（铆接） rivet: 把钢板～接在一起 rivet the steel sheets together **2**〈口〉（集中力量） make a sudden all-out effort: ～足了劲儿 summon all one's strength

【铆钉】mǎodīng〈名〉 rivet: 盘头～ pan head rivet ‖ ～枪 rivet gun
【铆工】mǎogōng〈名〉 **1**（指工作） riveting **2**（指工人） riveter
【铆接】mǎojiē〈动〉 fasten with rivets
【铆劲儿】mǎojìnr〈动〉 make a sudden all-out effort: 他一～就把沉甸甸的箱子举过了头顶。 With a sudden effort, he lifted the heavy box over his head.

mào

芼 mào〈动〉〈书〉（摘） pick (flower); （拔） pull (vegetables or weeds)

茂 mào〈形〉**1**（茂盛） luxuriant: 根深叶～ deep roots and luxuriant foliage ▸～密 **2**（丰富精美） excellent: 图文并～ contain splendid pictures and fine text ▸声情并～

【茂林修竹】 màolín-xiūzhú 〈成〉 thick forest and tall bamboos

【茂密】 màomì〈形〉 dense: ～的竹林 dense bamboo grove ‖ 树上枝叶～。 The trees have thick branches and leaves.

【茂盛】 màoshèng〈形〉**1**（指植物） luxuriant: 园里花木～。 The flowers in the garden are growing luxuriantly. **2**〈喻〉（指经济） flourishing: 财源～ rich in financial resources

冒 mào

A〈动〉**1**（向外透） emit: ～黑烟 emit black smoke ‖ ～泡 be bubbling ‖ ～气 give off steam ‖ ～汗 sweat ‖ 罪犯～出一批抓一批 arrest criminals as soon as they surface **2**（不顾） risk: ～着生命危险 risk one's life ‖ 改革是要～风险的。 Reform involves risks. ‖ 人们～着大雨上街游行。 People braved the heavy rain to take to the streets. **3**（冒犯） affront: ▸～犯, ～天下之大不韪 **4**（冒充） assume a false identity: ～领救济金 claim relief under false pretences ‖ 谨防假～。 Guard against imitations.

B〈形〉 rash: ▸～进, ～昧, ～失
▸mò

【冒充】 màochōng〈动〉 pretend to be: ～记者 pass oneself off as a journalist ‖ ～警察 pose as a policeman ‖ 拿假宝石～真宝石骗人 palm sb. off with a stone instead of a gem

【冒顶】 màodǐng〈动〉［矿业］ cave a roof

【冒渎】 màodú〈动〉〈书〉 blaspheme: ～神灵 blaspheme (against) the gods

【冒犯】 màofàn〈动〉 affront: ～尊严 offend sb.'s dignity ‖ 我宁愿～他，也不愿～公众。 I would rather offend him than the public.

【冒功】 màogōng〈动〉 claim the credit due to others: ～请赏 take credit and seek rewards for someone else's achievements

【冒汗】 màohàn〈动〉 perspire

【冒号】 màohào〈名〉 colon (:)

【冒坏】 màohuài〈动〉 be up to mischief

【冒火】 màohuǒ〈动〉 fly into a rage: 他气得两眼直～。 His eyes were blazing with anger.

【冒尖】 màojiān〈动〉**1**（指容量） be piled high: 筐里的柿子装得～了。 The basket is heaped with persimmons. **2**（指数量） be a little over: 他父亲六十岁刚～。 His father is just over 60 years old. **3**（突出） stand out: ～人物 conspicuous figure ‖ 她在班上学习～。 She stands out from the rest of her class. **4**（出现） begin to pop up: 问题一～，就要及时解决。 Proper measures should be taken as soon as the problem crops up.

【冒进】 màojìn〈动〉 advance prematurely

【冒领】 màolǐng〈动〉 lodge a bogus claim: ～失物 claim lost items under false pretences

【冒昧】 màomèi〈形〉〈谦〉 presumptuous: 不揣～ may I take the liberty of doing sth. ‖ ～陈辞 venture an opinion ‖ ～地问一下 pardon my asking ‖ 这么晚了还给您打电话，真是太～了。 Is it too presumptuous of me to call you at this late hour?

【冒名】 màomíng〈动〉 go under sb. else's name: ～替考 take an examination under a false name

【冒名顶替】 màomíng dǐngtì〈成〉 take someone else's place by assuming their name

【冒牌】 màopái〈形〉 imitation: ～货 imitation ‖ ～警察 bogus policeman ［冒泡］ mào pào〈动〉 bubble

【冒泡】 mào pào〈动〉 bubble

【冒傻气】 mào shǎqì〈动〉〈口〉 speak or act like a fool

【冒失】 màoshi〈形〉 rash: ～行事 handle things thoughtlessly ‖ 说话做事不能冒冒失失。 One should neither speak nor act without due consideration.

【冒失鬼】 màoshiguǐ〈名〉 daredevil

【冒死】 màosǐ〈副〉 with life threatened: ～救人 risk one's life to help sb. ‖ ～直言 frank talk without considering one's own safety

【冒天下之大不韪】 mào tiānxià zhī dà bùwěi〈成〉 disregard universal opinion

【冒头】 màotóu〈动〉**1**（出现） begin to crop up: 自满情绪开始～。 Self-conceit has started to raise its head. **2**（超过） be a little over: 二十～ be in one's early twenties

【冒险】 màoxiǎn〈动〉 take a risk: ～办公司 take a risk with one's money in opening up a business ‖ ～套汇 venture arbitrage

【冒险家】 màoxiǎnjiā ▸**p. 966**〈名〉 adventurer

【冒烟】 màoyān〈动〉［of smoke］ belch: 烟囱里冒着黑烟。 Black smoke is rising from the chimney.

【冒雨】 màoyǔ〈动〉 brave the rain: 冒着倾盆大雨，他们开赴前线。 Braving the pouring rain, they marched to the front.

贸（貿） mào

A〈动〉 deal: ▸～易, 内～, 外～

B〈形〉 hasty: ▸～然

【贸促会】 màocùhuì〈简称〉= 贸易促进会

【贸然】 màorán〈副〉 hastily: ～下结论 draw a hasty conclusion ‖ ～行事 act thoughtlessly

【贸易】 màoyì〈名〉 trade: 促进两国间的～ promote trade between the two countries ‖ ～不平衡 trade imbalance ‖ 农产品～ farm trade ▸边境～, 补偿～

【贸易保护主义】 màoyì bǎohùzhǔyì〈名〉 trade protectionism

【贸易壁垒】 màoyì bìlěi〈名〉 trade barriers: 设置～ build trade barriers

【贸易赤字】 màoyì chìzì〈名〉 trade deficit: 减少～ reduce a trade deficit

【贸易促进会】 màoyì cùjìnhuì〈名〉 trade promotion council

【贸易额】 màoyì'é〈名〉 turnover

【贸易公司】 màoyì gōngsī〈名〉 trading company

【贸易会谈】 màoyì huìtán〈名〉 trade talks

【贸易伙伴】 màoyì huǒbàn〈名〉 trade partner

【贸易集团】 màoyì jítuán〈名〉 trade group

【贸易禁令】 màoyì jìnlìng〈名〉 trade ban

【贸易纠纷】 màoyì jiūfēn〈名〉 trade dispute

【贸易口岸】 màoyì kǒu'àn〈名〉 trading post: 开辟～ open a trade pass

【贸易逆差】 màoyì nìchā〈名〉 trade deficit

【贸易平衡】 màoyì pínghéng〈名〉 balance of trade

【贸易商】 màoyìshāng ▸**p. 966**〈名〉 trader: 钢材/牛肉～ steel/beef trader

【贸易顺差】 màoyì shùnchā〈名〉 trade surplus

【贸易谈判】 màoyì tánpàn〈名〉 trade talks

【贸易往来】 màoyì wǎnglái〈名〉 trade contacts

【贸易自由】 màoyì zìyóu〈名〉 freedom of trade

耄 mào〈名〉〈书〉**1**（八旬） octogenarian **2**（高龄） very old person

【耄耋】 màodié〈名〉〈书〉 octogenarian old age: 活到～之年 live to a very old age

袤 mào〈名〉〈书〉 length from north to south: ▸广～

帽 mào〈名〉**1**（帽子） hat: 脱～致敬 take off one's hat in salute ‖ 滑雪～ ski mask ‖ 学位～ mortar board ▸贝雷～, 草～, 军～ **2**（帽状物） cap: ▸笔～, 螺丝～

【帽翅】 màochì〈名〉〈古〉 cap wings

【帽店】 màodiàn〈名〉 hat shop

【帽耳】 mào'ěr〈名〉 ear flaps [of a cap]

【帽花】 màohuā = 帽徽 màohuī

【帽徽】 màohuī〈名〉 insignia on a cap: 别/戴～ pin/wear a badge on one's cap

【帽架】 màojià〈名〉 hat stand

【帽盔】 màokuī〈名〉 helmet

【帽舌】 màoshé〈名〉 visor

【帽檐】 màoyán〈名〉**1**（指帽子四周） brim of a hat **2**（指帽子前部） peak

【帽子】 màozi〈名〉**1**〈本〉 hat: 戴上～ put on a hat ‖ 摘下～ take off a hat **2**〈喻〉（坏名义） label: 摘掉贫穷落后的～ remove the label of backwardness and poverty ‖ 乱扣～ apply a random label to sth.

【帽子戏法】 màozi xìfǎ〈名〉［足球］ hat trick

瑁 mào ▸玳瑁 dàimào

貌 mào〈名〉**1**（相貌） face: ▸美～, 容～, 相～ **2**（外表） appearance: ～丑 ugly in appearance ‖ ～美 have an attractive appearance ▸其～不扬, 外～ **3**（样子） look: 呈现新～ take on a new look ▸概～, 全～

【貌不惊人】 màobùjīngrén〈成〉 be of undistinguished appearance

【貌合神离】 màohé-shénlí〈成〉 be seemingly in agreement, but actually at odds

【貌似】 màosì〈动〉 appear to be: ～诚实 appear to be honest ‖ ～公允 appear to be impartial

【貌相】 màoxiàng **A**〈名〉 appearance **B**〈动〉 judge by appearances: 人不可～，海水不可斗量。 You can't judge a book by its cover.

瞀 mào〈形〉〈书〉**1**（目眩） dizzy: 眼～ have indistinct vision **2**（心绪纷乱） confused: ▸～乱 **3**（愚昧） ignorant: ～儒 ignorant scholar

【瞀乱】 màoluàn〈形〉〈书〉**1**（不明） muddled **2**（混乱） chaotic

懋 mào〈书〉

A〈动〉 encourage

B〈形〉**1**（勤勉） diligent **2**（盛大） grand: ～典 grand occasion ‖ ～勋 great contributions

m

me

么（麽） me〈后缀〉 1（用在某些汉字后） [used after some Chinese characters]: ▸多～，什～，怎～ 2（用作衬字） [used as a syllable inserted in a line of a song for balance]: 幸福的歌儿唱呀～唱起来。 Let's sing a song of happiness.

嚜 me〈口〉= 嘛 ma

méi

没（沒） méi ▸**p. 221**
A〈动〉 1（没有） not have: ～见过世面 be inexperienced ‖ ～钱了 have no more money ‖ 今天～雨。 There is no rain today. ‖ 她～孩子。 She has no children. 2（不到） be less than: 那房子的面积～20平方米。 That house covers a floor space of less than 20 square metres. 3（不如） [used in comparison] be not so ... as: 父亲～儿子高。 The father is not as tall as his son.
B〈副〉 not: 他的病还～全好。 He has not yet fully recovered. ‖ 我们老师还～来。 Our teacher hasn't come yet.
▸mò

【没边儿】 méibiānr〈动〉〈方〉 1（无根据）be groundless: 他的话～。 His remarks were groundless. 2（无边际） have no limit: 这男孩淘气淘得～。 The boy is extremely mischievous.

【没出息】 méi chūxi〈动〉 [of persons] show no promise: 他埋怨儿子～。 He complained that his son was good for nothing.

【没词儿】 méicír〈动〉〈口〉 be at a loss for words: 他没说几句就～了。 After just a few sentences, he was at a loss for words.

【没错儿】 méicuòr〈动〉〈口〉 1（的确如此） be sure: ～，我是不同意。 That's right. I am against it. 2（不出错） can't go wrong: 听我的建议，保你～。 If you follow my advice, you can't go wrong.

【没大没小】 méidà-méixiǎo〈俗〉 show no respect for one's elders: 他真是～，怎能那样对他父亲说话呢？ He has no manners. How could he speak to his father like that?

【没的说】 méideshuō = 没说的 méishuōde

【没骨头】 méi gǔtou〈动〉 be weak-kneed

【没关系】 méi guānxi ▸**p. 156**〈惯〉 it doesn't matter: 你晚到一会儿～。It doesn't matter if you're a bit late. ‖ 很抱歉给您添这么多麻烦。——～。 I'm sorry to have brought you so much trouble. — That's all right.

【没劲】 méijìn **A**〈动〉 be exhausted: 她病后浑身～。 She was listless after an illness. **B**〈形〉 boring: 今晚的讲座真～。 Tonight's lecture was completely uninteresting.

【没精打采】 méijīng-dǎcǎi〈成〉 be out of sorts: 手术后他一直～。 He remained in low spirits after the operation. ‖ 早上他总是～。 He is always out of it in the morning.

【没救】 méijiù〈动〉 be incurable

【没空儿】 méikòngr〈动〉 have no time (for sth./sb.)

【没来由】 méi láiyóu〈惯〉 for no reason: ～地挨了一顿揍 get a beating for no reason

【没脸】 méiliǎn〈动〉 feel ashamed: ～见人 be too embarrassed to face anybody

【没门儿】 méiménr〈动〉〈方〉 1（没办法） have no means of doing sth.: 我可～。 There's nothing I can do about it. 2（不可能） be a no-go: 他想贿赂我。——～! He wants to bribe me. — It's no-go. 3（不同意） be not a chance: 可以借你车吗？——～。 Can I borrow your car? — No way.

【没命】 méimìng〈动〉 1（丧命） die: 要不是医生及时抢救，他早就～了。 He would have died if the doctor hadn't given him emergency treatment. 2（拼命） be desperate: ～地挣钱 earn money for all one's worth ‖ 他～地逃跑。 He ran off as fast as his legs could carry him. 3（没福气） be out of luck: 看来他没有中大奖的命。 It seems as if he was not destined to hit the jackpot.

【没皮没脸】 méipí-méiliǎn〈俗〉 have no sense of shame

【没谱儿】 méipǔr〈动〉〈口〉 have no idea: 怎样处理这个问题，我们心里还～呢。 We have no idea yet as to how to tackle this problem.

【没轻没重】 méiqīng-méizhòng〈俗〉 1（指行为） without manners 2（指言语） rash and rude

【没趣】 méiqù〈形〉 1（无聊）dull 2（难堪）awkward: 他们觉得～。 They felt very much put out. ▸自讨～

【没商量】 méi shāngliang〈惯〉 irrevocable: 这是最后决定，～。 The decision is final and irrevocable.

【没什么】 méi shénme〈惯〉 it doesn't matter: 只是碰破了点皮，～。 It's only a scratch. It's nothing.

【没事】 méishì〈动〉 1（空闲） have nothing to do: 本周他一直～。 He is free all this week. 2（没关系） be all right: 对不起，给你添了很多麻烦。——～。 Sorry to have brought you so much trouble. — That's all right. 3（没危险） be free from danger: 经过抢救，他～了。 He is out of danger after the emergency treatment. 4（没责任） have no responsibility: 你只要把问题讲清楚就～了。 You will not be held responsible for it if you state the matter clearly.

【没事人】 méishìrén〈名〉 unconcerned person: 捅了那么大的娄子，他却像个～似的。 Even though he has made an awful blunder, he still looks very unconcerned.

【没事找事】 méishì-zhǎoshì〈惯〉 1（找麻烦） ask for trouble 2（找茬儿） try hard to find fault (with)

【没说的】 méishuōde〈惯〉 1（无可挑剔） above criticism: 他的工作～。 His work is above criticism. 2（没商量） be indisputable: 今天该我了，～。 Today it's my turn. No arguments. 3（没问题） it goes without saying: 他是一个好老师，～。 It goes without saying that he is a good teacher.

【没挑儿】 méitiāor〈动〉 be faultless: 今晚的演出那是～了。 The performance tonight is perfect. ‖ 他的新小说真是～。 His new novel is faultless.

【没头没脑】 méitóu-méinǎo〈成〉 without rhyme or reason: ～的话 pointless remark ‖ 老师把约翰～地训斥了一顿。 The teacher gave John a good dressing down.

【没完】 méiwán〈动〉〈口〉 have not finished with sb.: 这次我和你～。 I will not let you off this time.

【没完没了】 méiwán-méiliǎo〈成〉 be endless: 讲个～ talk on and on ‖ ～的琐事 endless petty concerns

【没戏】 méixì〈动〉〈方〉 be hopeless: 他今年出国留学的事～了。 There's no longer any hope for him to study abroad this year.

【没心没肺】 méixīn-méifèi〈成〉 1（单纯） be simple-minded 2（没良心） be heartless

【没羞】 méixiū〈动〉 have no sense of shame

【没样儿】 méiyàngr〈动〉〈口〉 have no manners: 这孩子给宠得～了。 The spoiled child has no manners.

【没意思】 méi yìsi〈形〉 1（感到无聊） bored: 一个人整天呆在家里实在～。 I'm bored stiff staying at home all day long. 2（没有趣味） boring: 这部新电影～极了。 This new film is extremely boring.

【没影儿】 méi yǐngr〈动〉 1（无踪迹） disappear without a trace: 没几分钟他就跑得～了。 He ran out of sight in just a few minutes. 2（无根据） be unfounded: 他说的都是～的事。 What he said is utter nonsense.

【没有】 méiyǒu **A**〈动〉 not have: ～把握 not sure ‖ ～结果 come to nothing ‖ ～任何附加条件 with no conditions attached **B**〈副〉 1（表否定） not: ～明白 fail to understand ‖ ～达到要求 fall short 2（表比较） not so ... as: 这部电影～那部电影有趣。 This film is not as interesting as that one. 3（不足） less than: 她在西安呆了～两天。 She stayed in Xi'an for less than two days. 4（尚未） not yet: 她～去过北京。 She has not been to Beijing yet.

【没有不透风的墙】 méiyǒu bù tòufēng de qiáng〈俗〉 walls have ears

【没有功劳有苦劳】 méiyǒu gōngláo yǒu kǔláo〈俗〉 one should be given some credit for hard work if not for merit

【没缘】 méiyuán〈动〉 have no opportunity

【没辙】 méizhé〈动〉〈口〉 be at the end of one's tether: 他这人太难缠，我拿他～。 How unreasonable he is! I haven't the faintest idea of how to deal with him.

【没治】 méizhì〈口〉 **A**〈动〉 cannot do anything with sb.: 这孩子太淘气了，他爸拿他～。 The boy is so mischievous that his father can't do anything with him. **B**〈形〉 superb: 这场表演真～了。 The show is really terrific.

【没种】 méizhǒng〈动〉 be gutless

【没准儿】 méizhǔnr〈动〉〈口〉 have no idea: 他什么时候回来～。 There is no telling when he will be back. ‖ 这问题怎么解决，他自己没个准儿。 He has no idea how to solve the problem.

玫 méi〈名〉〈书〉 a kind of jade

【玫瑰】 méigui〈名〉 rose: ～丛 rose bushes ‖ 白/红/黄～ white/red/yellow roses

【玫瑰红】 méiguihóng〈名〉 rose-red

【玫瑰油】 méiguiyóu〈名〉 rose oil

【玫瑰紫】 méiguizǐ = 玫瑰红 méiguihóng

枚 méi〈量〉 [used in connection with coins, stamps, bombs, etc.]: 两～奖章 two medals ‖ 三～纪念邮票 three commemorative stamps ‖ 一～五毛钱硬币 a five-*mao* coin

【枚举】 méijǔ〈动〉〈书〉 enumerate: ▸不胜～

眉 méi〈名〉 1（眉毛） eyebrow: 浓～ bushy eyebrows ‖ 秀～ shapely eyebrows ▸挤～弄眼，须～ 2（指空白处） top margin: ▸～批，书～

【眉笔】 méibǐ〈名〉 eyebrow pencil

【眉端】 méiduān〈名〉 1（指面部） space between the eyebrows: 愁上～ have a worried look 2（指空白处） top margin

【眉飞色舞】 méifēi-sèwǔ〈成〉 beam with

joy: ～的表情 animated expression ‖ 她不禁～。She couldn't stop beaming.
【眉峰】méifēng〈名〉〈书〉 brows: ～紧皱 with knitted brows
【眉高眼低】méigāo-yǎndī〈成〉 take one's cue from the expression on sb.'s face: 他不愿看别人的～来行事。He is not willing to take his cue from others.
【眉尖】méijiān〈名〉 brows: ～一皱 knit one's brows
【眉睫】méijié〈名〉〈喻〉 imminent: 战争迫在～。War was imminent.
【眉开眼笑】méikāi-yǎnxiào〈成〉 beam with joy: 孩子们收到礼物时，个个～。The children beamed with delight when they received their presents.
【眉来眼去】méilái-yǎnqù〈成〉 make eyes at each other: 他俩～的。The two of them exchanged amorous glances.
【眉毛】méimao〈名〉 eyebrow: 一道～ an eyebrow ‖ 一对～ a pair of eyebrows ‖ 一根～ an eyebrow hair ‖ 修～ pluck one's eyebrows ▸火烧～
【眉毛胡子一把抓】méimao húzi yībǎzhuā〈俗〉〈喻〉 try to do everything at once
【眉目】méimù〈名〉 **1**（面目） features: ～清秀 have delicate features **2**（安排） sequence of ideas: 这篇作文～很清楚。The composition is clear and well-organized.
【眉目传情】méimù-chuánqíng〈成〉 make eyes at sb.
【眉目】méimu〈名〉 prospect of a positive outcome: 案子有点～了。There are already prospects of a solution in the case.
【眉批】méipī〈名〉 comments at the top of a page: 加～ make notes at the top of a page
【眉清目秀】méiqīng-mùxiù〈成〉 have delicate features: ～的女子 woman with finely chiselled features
【眉梢】méishāo〈名〉 tip of the brow: ～间流露出忧郁的神色 melancholy cast between the brows ‖ 喜上～ be radiant with joy
【眉题】méití〈名〉 strapline
【眉头】méitóu〈名〉 brows: 皱～ knit one's brows ‖ ～紧锁 with knitted brows
【眉头一皱，计上心来】méitóu yī zhòu, jì shàng xīn lái〈成〉 do some thinking and hit upon an idea
【眉心】méixīn〈名〉 space between the eyebrows
【眉眼】méiyǎn〈名〉 appearance: 他的小妹～长得很俊。His little sister is very pretty.
【眉眼高低】méiyǎn-gāodī = 眉高眼低 méigāo-yǎndī
【眉宇】méiyǔ〈名〉〈书〉 appearance: ～不凡 an imposing appearance

莓 méi〈名〉 certain kinds of berries: ▸草～

梅 méi〈名〉 **1**（梅花） Chinese plum **2**（蜡梅） wintersweet
【梅毒】méidú ▸**p. 50**〈名〉［医学］ syphilis: ～患者 syphilitic
【梅花】méihuā〈名〉 **1**（梅花） plum blossom **2**〈方〉（蜡梅） wintersweet **3**（指纸牌） [in cards] club: ～A the ace of clubs
【梅花鹿】méihuālù〈名〉 spotted deer
【梅花桩】méihuāzhuāng〈名〉［武术］ plum blossom stake [set in the ground in front of positions or barracks to impede enemy movement]: 练～ do plum blossom stake exercises
【梅花针】méihuāzhēn〈名〉［中医］ plum blossom needle: ～疗法 plum blossom needle therapy
【梅里奥尼斯郡】Méilǐ'àonísījùn〈名〉 Merionethshire
【梅天】méitiān = 黄梅季 huángméijì
【梅雨】méiyǔ〈名〉 intermittent drizzle (in the middle and lower reaches of the Yangtze River): ～季节 rainy season
【梅子】méizi〈名〉 plum

嵋 méi ▸峨嵋山 Éméishān

猸 méi
【猸子】méizi〈名〉［动物］ crab-eating mongoose

湄 méi〈名〉〈书〉 river bank
【湄公河】Méigōnghé ▸**p. 294**〈名〉 Mekong River: ～三角洲 Mekong Delta

媒 méi〈名〉 **1**（媒人） matchmaker: 做～ be a matchmaker **2**（媒介） intermediary: ▸～介, 传～
【媒介】méijiè〈名〉 intermediary: 新闻～ news media ‖ 蚊蝇是传播疾病的～。Flies and mosquitoes are carriers of diseases.
【媒婆】méipó〈名〉〈旧〉 female matchmaker
【媒人】méiren〈名〉 matchmaker
【媒妁】méishuò〈名〉〈书〉 matchmaker: ～之言 matchmaker's remarks
【媒体】méitǐ〈名〉 medium: ～报道 medium report ‖ 大众～ mass media
【媒体人】méitǐrén ▸**p. 966**〈名〉 media worker: 资深～ media veteran
【媒质】méizhì〈名〉［物理］ medium

楣 méi〈名〉 lintel: ▸门～

煤 méi〈名〉 coal: 采～ mine coal
【煤饼】méibǐng〈名〉 briquette
【煤仓】méicāng〈名〉 coal bunker
【煤层】méicéng〈名〉 coal bed: ～厚度 coal seam thickness
【煤铲】méichǎn〈名〉 coal shovel
【煤场】méichǎng〈名〉 coal yard
【煤尘】méichén〈名〉 coal dust: ～爆炸 coal-dust explosion
【煤斗】méidǒu〈名〉 (coal) scuttle
【煤矸石】méigānshí〈名〉 coal gangue
【煤耗】méihào〈名〉 coal consumption: 减少～ reduce coal consumption
【煤黑子】méihēizi〈名〉〈旧〉〈贬〉 coal miner
【煤核儿】méihúr〈名〉 partly-burnt briquette
【煤化】méihuà〈动〉 carbonize
【煤焦油】méijiāoyóu〈名〉 coal tar
【煤精】méijīng〈名〉 black amber
【煤矿】méikuàng〈名〉 coal mine: ～工人 coal miner ‖ 露天～ open-cut coal mine
【煤泥】méiní〈名〉 silt coal
【煤气】méiqì〈名〉 gas: 烧～ burn gas ‖ ～中毒 gas poisoning ‖ ～表 gas meter
【煤气阀】méiqìfá〈名〉 gas tap
【煤气工】méiqìgōng〈名〉 gasman
【煤气公司】méiqì gōngsī〈名〉 gas company
【煤气管道】méiqì guǎndào〈名〉 gas pipe
【煤气罐】méiqìguàn〈名〉 gas tank
【煤气机】méiqìjī〈名〉 gas engine
【煤气灶】méiqìzào〈名〉 gas cooker〈英〉; gas range〈美〉
【煤气中毒】méiqì zhòngdú〈名〉 carbon monoxide poisoning
【煤球】méiqiú〈名〉 briquette: ～炉 briquette stove
【煤炭】méitàn〈名〉 coal: ～码头 coal wharf ‖ ～资源 coal resources
【煤田】méitián〈名〉 coalfield
【煤矽肺】méixīfèi〈名〉 anthracosilicosis
【煤屑】méixiè〈名〉 coal dust
【煤窑】méiyáo〈名〉 coal pit: 关闭小～ shut down small coal pits
【煤油】méiyóu〈名〉 paraffin〈英〉; kerosene〈美〉
【煤渣】méizhā〈名〉 coal cinder: ～砖 cinder block
【煤砟子】méizhǎzi〈名〉 small piece of coal
【煤砖】méizhuān〈名〉 briquette

酶 méi〈名〉［生化］ enzyme: ▸蛋白～, 转氨～

镅（鎇） méi〈名〉［化学］ americium (Am)

鹛（鶥） méi〈名〉［鸟类］ babbler: 钩嘴～ scimitar babbler ‖ 红顶～ red-crowned babbler

霉[1] méi〈动〉 go mouldy: ～味 mouldy smell ‖ 面包～了。This bread's gone mouldy. ▸～烂, 倒～, 发～

霉[2]（黴） méi〈名〉 mould: ▸青～素
【霉变】méibiàn〈动〉 go mouldy: 防止食品～ prevent food from going mouldy
【霉病】méibìng〈名〉［农业］ mildew
【霉干菜】méigāncài〈名〉 dry-cured vegetable
【霉菌】méijūn〈名〉 mould
【霉烂】méilàn〈动〉 mildew and rot: ～食品 mouldy and rotten food
【霉雨】méiyǔ = 梅雨 méiyǔ

糜 méi
▸mí
【糜子】méizi〈名〉 broom corn millet

měi

每 měi
A〈代〉 every: ～个角落 every nook and cranny ‖ ～天 every day ‖ ～月开一次例会 hold a regular meeting every month ‖ 以～小时八百公里的速度飞行 fly at the speed of 800 kilometres per hour
B〈副〉 **1**（每次） each time: ～当我看见他的时候 each time I saw him ‖ 我们～逢生日必开派对。We have parties every time someone has a birthday. ▸～逢佳节倍思亲 **2**〈书〉（总是） often: 她～～不在家。She is often away from home.
【每当】měidāng〈副〉 whenever
【每逢】měiféng〈副〉 whenever: ～星期日，我们一定回家看父母。Every Sunday we have to go home to see our parents.
【每逢佳节倍思亲】měiféng jiājié bèi sī qīn〈俗〉 it is on festival occasions that one misses those dearest to one the most
【每况愈下】měikuàngyùxià〈成〉 go from bad to worse: 身体～ be in declining health
【每每】měiměi〈副〉 often: 他～借酒浇愁。He often drowns his sorrows in alcohol.
【每时每刻】měishí-měikè〈成〉 all the time:

m

我～都想着远方的亲人。I think of my dear ones far away all the time.

【每下愈况】měixiàyùkuàng = 每况愈下 měikuàngyùxià

美[1] měi

A〈形〉**1**（美丽）beautiful: ～如画 be as pretty as a picture ‖ 这里的风景真～。The scenery here is very beautiful. ►～丽，秀～ **2**（令人满足）very satisfactory: 日子过得挺～ lead a happy life ►～德，～酒，～名

B〈动〉**1**（使美丽）beautify: ►～发，～化，～容 **2**〈方〉（得意）be pleased with oneself: 他～得不知怎么好。He was so pleased he didn't know what to do with himself.

C〈名〉beautiful things: 审～ appreciate beauty ‖ 曲线～ curvaceous beauty ►成人之～，两全其～

美[2] Měi

〈名〉**1**（美洲）America: ►北～ **2**（美国）United States of America (USA): 中～关系 Sino-US relations ►～利坚合众国

【美不胜收】měibùshèngshōu〈成〉more beauty than one can take in: 这里风景如画，～。The scenery is so picturesque that it's hard to take it all in.

【美餐】měicān **A**〈名〉tasty food: 一顿～ a big tasty meal **B**〈动〉eat and drink to one's fill: ～一顿 have a big meal

【美差】měichāi〈名〉**1**（指职位）cushy job: 她弄到了一份～。She's got herself a cushy little number. **2**（指差事）enviable task: 去国外开会可是趟～! What an enviable task you've got going abroad for the conference!

【美钞】měichāo〈名〉US banknote

【美称】měichēng〈名〉good name: 四川有天府之国的～。Sichuan enjoys the reputation of being a land of plenty.

【美传】měichuán〈名〉appreciative story about a person or an event: 他舍身救人的事迹已成为当地的～。His story of saving a life at the risk of his own was told with approval in the locality.

【美德】měidé〈名〉virtue: 传统～ traditional virtue ‖ 谦虚是一种～。Modesty is a virtue.

【美吨】měidūn〈名〉short ton

【美发】měifà〈动〉have one's hair done: ～厅 hairdresser's

【美发店】měifàdiàn〈名〉hair salon

【美发师】měifàshī ►**p. 966**〈名〉hairdresser

【美感】měigǎn〈名〉sense of beauty: 给人以～ give sb. a sense of beauty

【美工】měigōng〈名〉［影视］**1**（指工作）art design: ～人员 art designer **2**（指人）art designer

【美观】měiguān〈形〉artistic: ～大方 elegant and in good taste ‖ 布置得很～ be artistically decorated

【美国】Měiguó〈名〉United States of America (USA)

【美国广播公司】Měiguó Guǎngbō Gōngsī〈名〉American Broadcasting Company Inc. (ABC)

【美国国务院】Měiguó Guówùyuàn〈名〉US State Department

【美国联邦储备委员会】Měiguó Liánbāng Chǔbèi Wěiyuánhuì〈名〉US Federal Reserve Board (FRB)

【美国联邦调查局】Měiguó Liánbāng Diàochájú〈名〉Federal Bureau of Investigation (FBI): ～特工 FBI agent

【美国联合通讯社】Měiguó Liánhé Tōngxùnshè〈名〉Associated Press (AP)

【美国学】Měiguóxué〈名〉American studies

【美国英语】Měiguó Yīngyǔ〈名〉American English

【美国之音】Měiguó Zhī Yīn〈名〉Voice of America (VOA)

【美好】měihǎo〈形〉good: 生活～ lead a happy life ‖ ～的回忆 happy memories ‖ ～的前程 bright future

【美化】měihuà〈动〉beautify: ～环境/市容/校园 beautify the environment/city/campus ‖ ～自己 glorify oneself

【美籍华人】Měijí Huárén ►**p. 279**〈名〉Chinese American: ～作家 American writer of Chinese descent

【美甲】měijiǎ〈动〉get a manicure: ～沙龙 a nail salon

【美金】měijīn = 美元 měiyuán

【美景】měijǐng〈名〉beautiful scenery: 桂林～ enchanting scenery of Guilin ►良辰～

【美酒】měijiǔ〈名〉good wine: ～佳肴 good wine and delicious food

【美拉尼西亚】Měilāníxīyà〈名〉Melanesia: ～人 Melanesian ‖ ～语 the Melanesian language

【美利坚合众国】Měilìjiān Hézhòngguó〈名〉United States of America (USA)

【美利奴羊】měilìnúyáng〈名〉merino sheep

【美丽】měilì〈形〉beautiful: ～的花朵 beautiful flower ‖ ～富饶的海岛 beautiful and richly-endowed island ‖ ～如画的风景 picturesque scenery

【美联储】Měiliánchǔ〈简称〉= 美国联邦储备委员会

【美联社】Měiliánshè〈简称〉= 美国联合通讯社

【美轮美奂】měilún-měihuàn〈成〉magnificent

【美满】měimǎn〈形〉perfectly satisfactory: 家庭～ have a happy family ‖ ～的婚姻 happy marriage

【美貌】měimào **A**〈名〉good looks: 她的～迷住了他。Her beauty captivated him. **B**〈形〉beautiful: 年轻～的女演员 beautiful young actress

【美眉】měiméi〈名〉beautiful girl

【美美】měiměi〈副〉to one's heart's content: ～地吃一顿 have a good meal ‖ ～地睡一觉 have a sound sleep

【美梦】měimèng〈名〉beautiful dream: 她终于～成真。Her dream finally came true. ‖ ～破灭了。The beautiful dream was shattered.

【美妙】měimiào〈形〉wonderful: ～的歌喉 sweet voice ‖ ～的诗句 beautiful verse ‖ ～的音乐 splendid music

【美名】měimíng〈名〉good reputation: 留下～ leave a good name ‖ ～远扬。A good reputation spreads far and wide.

【美男子】měinánzǐ〈名〉very good-looking man

【美女】měinǚ〈名〉beauty: 绝代～ woman of unparalleled beauty ‖ 她出落成了一个～。She is blossoming into a beautiful woman.

【美其名曰】měiqímíngyuē〈成〉call it by the fine-sounding name of

【美人】měirén〈名〉beautiful woman, beauty: 公认的大～ acknowledged great beauty ‖ 睡～ Sleeping Beauty

【美人斑】měirénbān〈名〉beauty spot

【美人迟暮】měirén-chímù〈成〉〈喻〉regret over the passing of sb.'s adolescence

【美人计】měirénjì〈名〉honey trap:（对某人）施～ lay a sex trap (for sb.) ‖ 中～ be caught in a honey trap

【美人蕉】měirénjiāo〈名〉［植物］Indian canna

【美人鱼】měirényú〈名〉mermaid

【美人痣】měirénzhì = 美人斑 měirénbān

【美容】měiróng〈动〉have a beauty treatment: 去做～ go for a facial ‖ ～院 beauty salon

【美容师】měiróngshī ►**p. 966**〈名〉beautician

【美若天仙】měiruòtiānxiān〈成〉[of a woman] be as pretty as a fairy

【美色】měisè〈名〉beauty: 禁不起～的诱惑 be unable to resist temptation of beauty

【美沙酮】měishātóng〈名〉［药学］methadone

【美声唱法】měishēng chàngfǎ〈名〉［音乐］bel canto

【美食】měishí〈名〉choice food: 品尝中国～ sample the delights of Chinese food

【美食家】měishíjiā ►**p. 966**〈名〉epicure

【美食节】měishíjié〈名〉food festival

【美食文化】měishí wénhuà〈名〉food culture

【美式】měishì〈形〉American-style

【美式足球】měishì zúqiú ►**p. 909**〈名〉American football: ～运动员 American football player

【美事】měishì〈名〉**1**（指行为）worthy deed **2**（指运气）good fortune

【美术】měishù〈名〉**1**（造型艺术）fine arts: ～工作者 artist ‖ 应用～ applied art ‖ 工艺～ arts and crafts **2**（绘画）painting

【美术馆】měishùguǎn〈名〉art gallery: ～馆长 curator

【美术家】měishùjiā ►**p. 966**〈名〉artist

【美术片】měishùpiàn〈名〉animated film [using puppets, paper-cuts, etc.]

【美术设计】měishù shèjì〈名〉artistic design

【美术陶瓷】měishù táocí〈名〉artistic ceramics

【美术字】měishùzì〈名〉artistic calligraphy

【美术作品】měishù zuòpǐn〈名〉works of fine art

【美索不达米亚】Měisuǒbùdámǐyà〈名〉Mesopotamia

【美谈】měitán〈名〉salutary tale: 传为～ become a salutary tale

【美体】měitǐ〈动〉make the body beautiful: ～健身 make the body beautiful and healthy

【美味】měiwèi〈名〉delicious food: ～佳肴 delicious delicacies ‖ ～小吃 dainty snacks

【美学】měixué〈名〉aesthetics: ～价值 aesthetic values ‖ ～原理 principles of aesthetics

【美言】měiyán **A**〈动〉make complimentary remarks: 请你在总经理面前为我～几句。Please put in a few good words for me when you are with the manager. **B**〈名〉〈书〉fine saying

【美艳】měiyàn〈形〉gorgeous

【美意】měiyì〈名〉kindness: 谢谢您的～。Thanks for your kindness. ‖ 你的～我心领了。I appreciate your kindness.

【美育】měiyù〈名〉aesthetic education

【美誉】měiyù〈名〉good reputation: 教师享有人类灵魂工程师的～。Teachers enjoy a good reputation as engineers of the human soul.

【美誉度】měiyùdù〈名〉reputation: 企业的知名度和～ corporate visibility and reputation

【美元】měiyuán ▸**p. 328**〈名〉US dollar: ～危机 dollar crisis
【美圆】měiyuán＝美元 měiyuán
【美院】měiyuàn〈名〉art college
【美展】měizhǎn〈名〉art exhibition
【美制】měizhì〈名〉American system
【美中不足】měizhōng-bùzú〈成〉fly in the ointment: 她受聘当秘书，～的是薪水不太高。She's got a job as a secretary. The only fly in the ointment is that the pay is not too good.
【美洲】Měizhōu〈名〉America: ▸拉丁～，南～
【美洲豹】měizhōubào〈名〉panther
【美洲国家组织】Měizhōu Guójiā Zǔzhī〈名〉Organization of American States (OAS)
【美洲虎】měizhōuhǔ〈名〉jaguar
【美洲狮】měizhōushī〈名〉puma
【美滋滋】měizīzī〈形〉very pleased with oneself: 听说考试通过了，她心里～的。She was very pleased on hearing that she had passed the examination.

镁（鎂） měi〈名〉［化学］magnesium (Mg)
【镁光】měiguāng〈名〉magnesium light: ～灯 magnesium lamp

mèi

妹 mèi〈名〉**1**（妹妹）younger sister: 小～ youngest sister ‖ 兄～ brother and sister ▸～夫，表～ **2**（指同辈女子）address to a woman who is younger than the speaker and of the same generation: ▸师～ **3**〈方〉（年轻女子）address to a young woman or girl: 农家～ country girl ‖ 外来～ young female migrant
【妹夫】mèifu ▸**p. 588**〈名〉brother-in-law
【妹妹】mèimei ▸**p. 588**〈名〉**1**（指直系）younger sister **2**（指非直系）cousin: 叔伯～ cousin ‖ 远房～ distant cousin
【妹婿】mèixù〈名〉〈书〉brother-in-law
【妹子】mèizi〈名〉〈方〉**1**（妹妹）(younger) sister **2**（年轻女子）young girl: 川～ girl from Sichuan Province

昧 mèi
A〈形〉**1**〈书〉（昏暗）dim: 幽～ dim and gloomy **2**（糊涂）ignorant: ▸暧～，素～平生，愚～
B〈动〉**1**（隐藏）conceal: ▸～良心，拾金不～ **2**〈书〉（冒犯）offend: ▸～死，冒～
【昧良心】mèi liángxīn〈动〉go against one's conscience: ～赚黑钱 make ill-gotten gains against one's conscience ‖ 不做～的事 not do evil against one's conscience
【昧死】mèisǐ〈动〉〈书〉risk one's life
【昧心】mèixīn〈动〉go against one's conscience: 不说～话 not say anything against one's conscience ‖ 挣～钱 earn money by dishonest means

袂 mèi〈名〉〈书〉sleeve: ▸分～，联～

谜（謎） mèi
▸mí
【谜儿】mèir〈名〉〈方〉riddle: 猜～ guess a riddle ‖ 破～ solve a riddle

寐 mèi〈动〉〈书〉sleep: 夜不能～ unable to sleep at night ▸假～，梦～以求

媚 mèi
A〈动〉curry favour with: ▸～外，谄～
B〈形〉**1**（讨好）ingratiating: ▸～态，奴颜～骨 **2**（美好）charming: ～人的西湖美景 the enchanting scenery of the West Lake ▸娇～，明～，妩～
【媚敌】mèidí〈动〉curry favour with the enemy
【媚骨】mèigǔ〈名〉obsequiousness: 没有丝毫的奴颜与～ be free from all sycophancy or obsequiousness
【媚惑】mèihuò〈动〉seduce
【媚上欺下】mèishàng-qīxià〈成〉fawn upon one's superiors and bully one's inferiors
【媚世】mèishì〈动〉play to the gallery: ～之作 works catering to the reader's poor taste
【媚俗】mèisú＝媚世 mèishì
【媚态】mèitài〈名〉**1**（指讨好他人）obsequiousness **2**（指妩媚）feminine charms: ～娇容 coquettish
【媚外】mèiwài〈动〉toady to foreign powers: 崇洋～ worship foreign things and toady to foreign powers
【媚眼】mèiyǎn〈名〉seductive eyes
【媚悦】mèiyuè〈动〉curry favour with: ～流俗 cater to the prevalent custom

魅 mèi〈名〉〈书〉demon: ▸魑～，鬼～
【魅惑】mèihuò〈动〉captivate: ～力 charm
【魅力】mèilì〈名〉charm: 艺术～ artistic charm ‖ 大自然的～ charms of nature ‖ 富有～的影星 glamorous film star ‖ 足球的～ charm of football
【魅人】mèirén〈形〉enchanting: 景色～。The scenery is enchanting.

mēn

闷（悶） mēn
A〈形〉**1**（指感觉）stuffy: 今天又～又热。It is very hot and oppressive today. ‖ 这里太～了。It's too stuffy in here. **2**〈方〉（指声音）muffled: 他父亲说话～声～气的。His father spoke in a muffled voice.
B〈动〉**1**（使不透气）cover tightly: 把茶～三分钟后再喝。Let the tea brew for three minutes before drinking it. ‖ 饭～在锅里。The meal is covered up in the pot. **2**（呆在屋里）shut indoors: 别整天～在家里看电视。Don't shut yourself indoors watching TV all day. **3**（不吭声）say nothing: ～～不乐地想问题 brood over one's problems ▸～声不响
▸mèn
【闷沉沉】mēnchénchén〈形〉**1**（指感觉）close: ～的房间 stuffy room **2**（指声音）muffled: 我们听见远处有～的雷声。We heard muffled thunder in the distance.
▸mènchénchén
【闷气】mēnqì〈形〉close: 又～又潮湿的地方 close and wet place
▸mènqì
【闷热】mēnrè〈形〉muggy: ～的天气 sultry weather ‖ 空气又～又潮湿。The air is muggy.
【闷声不响】mēnshēng-bùxiǎng〈成〉remain silent: 他～地听着老师讲话。He listened to the teacher in silence.
【闷声闷气】mēnshēng-mēnqì〈成〉muffled: 他感冒了，说话有些～的。He spoke in a muffled voice because of a cold.
【闷头儿】mēntóur〈副〉with one's head down: ～备考 get one's head down and work for one's exam ‖ ～干活儿 plod away silently at a task
【闷战】mēnzhàn〈动〉compete in an uninspiring contest: 经过一场～以0：0互交白卷。Both sides kept clean sheets in an uninspiring 0-0 draw.

mén

门（門） mén
A〈名〉**1**（指出入口）door: 关～ shut the door ‖ 锁～ lock a door ‖ 旋转/推拉～ revolving/sliding door ‖ 送货上～。We deliver your order to your door. ▸防盗～，太平～ **2**（指可开、关部分）door: 冰箱～ fridge door ‖ 柜～ cupboard door ‖ 炉～ stove door ▸球～ **3**（指开关）switch: ▸电～，气～，油～ **4**（指人体）opening in the human body: ▸贲～，肛～，幽～ **5**（家族）family: 赵～李氏 Mrs Zhao, née Li ▸～风，寒～，满～ **6**（指思想派别）school;（指宗教派系）sect: 佛～弟子 Buddhist follower ▸会道～ **7**（指师门）a teacher's or master's entrance hall: 同～弟子 pupils of the same master ▸～生，～徒 **8**（指分类）category: ▸分～别类，五花八～ **9**［生物］phylum: 脊椎动物～ Vertebrata ‖ 软体动物～ mollusc phylum **10**（窍门）knack: 我对计算机总算摸着点儿～了。I finally gained an understanding of how computers work. ▸～路，窍～
B〈量〉**1**（指学科）[for subjects of study or branches of science]: 两～技术 two skills ‖ 一～必修课 a compulsory course **2**（指亲戚、婚事）[for a marriage or for relatives]: 一～亲事 a marriage ‖ 一～亲戚 a set of relatives **3**（指火炮）[for artillery]: 一～大炮 a cannon **4**（指话机）[for telephone]: 万～程控电话交换机 ten thousand-line programme-controlled telephone switchboard
【门巴】ménbā〈名〉doctor [in Tibetan language]
【门巴族】Ménbāzú〈名〉Monba ethnic group
【门把】ménbà〈名〉door knob
【门板】ménbǎn〈名〉**1**（指门）door plank **2**（指木板）shutters: 这家店铺已上了～。The shop has already put up the shutters.
【门鼻儿】ménbír〈名〉bolt staple
【门匾】ménbiǎn〈名〉board with inscriptions of praise [fixed to a door]
【门钹】ménbó〈名〉door knocker
【门插关儿】ménchāguanr〈名〉door bolt
【门齿】ménchǐ〈名〉incisor: 人的上下颌各有四颗～。Humans have four incisors in each jaw.
【门刺】ménci〈名〉〈旧〉calling card
【门当户对】méndāng-hùduì〈成〉family of similar backgrounds
【门道】méndào〈名〉doorway
【门道】méndao〈名〉knack: 外行看热闹，内行看～。A layman just watches but a professional understands. ‖ 在挣钱方面，王先生可有～了。Mr Wang has always had ways of making money.
【门第】méndì〈名〉family status: 出身于书香～ be from a scholarly family
【门钉】méndīng〈名〉doornail
【门洞】méndòng〈名〉**1**（指过道）doorway **2**（指大门）gate: 东起第三～ third gate from the east

【门墩】méndūn〈名〉gate pier: 一对～ a pair of gate piers
【门阀】ménfá〈名〉influential family
【门房】ménfáng〈名〉1（指房）porter's lodge 2（指人）gatekeeper
【门扉】ménfēi〈名〉door leaf: 半掩着～ leave the door half-closed ‖〈喻〉打开心灵的～ open one's heart (to sb.)
【门风】ménfēng〈名〉moral standing of a family: 败坏～ discredit one's family's moral standing
【门缝里看人】ménfèng li kànrén〈歇后〉have a low opinion of sb.
【门岗】méngǎng〈名〉gate sentry
【门户】ménhù〈名〉1（门）door: ～紧闭。The doors are all shut tight. ‖ ～虚掩。The door is off the latch. 2〈喻〉（要地）gateway: 欧洲的～ gateway to Europe 3（家）family: 兄弟俩已经自立～。The two brothers have set up their own homes. 4（派别）faction: ▸～之见 5（门第）family status: ～相当的两家 two families well-matched in social status
【门户网站】ménhù wǎngzhàn〈名〉［计算机］portal
【门户之见】ménhùzhījiàn〈成〉sectarianism
【门环】ménhuán〈名〉door knocker: 一对/副～ a pair of knockers
【门将】ménjiàng〈名〉［体育］goalkeeper in ball games
【门阶】ménjiē〈名〉doorstep: ～石 door stone
【门捷列夫周期表】Ménjiélièfū zhōuqībiǎo〈名〉Mendeleev's periodic table of the elements
【门禁】ménjìn〈名〉entrance guard: 此处～森严。The gate here is heavily guarded.
【门警】ménjǐng〈名〉police guard at an entrance
【门径】ménjìng〈名〉way: 反复练习是通往成功的～。Repeated practice is the key to success.
【门静脉】ménjìngmài〈名〉［生理］portal vein
【门镜】ménjìng〈名〉spyhole
【门坎】ménkǎn = 门槛 ménkǎn
【门槛】ménkǎn〈名〉threshold
【门可罗雀】ménkěluóquè〈成〉〈喻〉1（指宾客）visitors are few and far between 2（指店铺）have few customers
【门客】ménkè〈名〉〈旧〉parasitic guest
【门口】ménkǒu〈名〉entrance: 送客人到～ see/walk a guest to the door ‖ 在公园～ at the entrance to the park
【门框】ménkuàng〈名〉doorf rame
【门拉手】ménlāshǒu〈名〉door pull
【门廊】ménláng〈名〉porch
【门类】ménlèi〈名〉category: ～齐全的工业体系 a complete range of industrial systems
【门帘】ménlián〈名〉door curtain
【门联】ménlián〈名〉couplets pasted on doorposts
【门脸儿】ménliǎnr〈名〉〈方〉1（指城市）vicinity of a city gate: 西安南城门～有一个广场。There is a square outside the Southern Gate of Xi'an. 2（指店铺）facade of a shop: 两间～的铺子 shop with a two-bay front
【门链】ménliàn〈名〉door chain
【门铃】ménlíng〈名〉doorbell
【门楼】ménlóu〈名〉［建筑］gate-tower
【门路】ménlu〈名〉1（诀窍）knack: 摸到～ know the ropes ‖ 广开就业～ create job opportunities on an extensive scale 2（途径）connections: 找～ solicit connections ‖ 钻～ jockey for favours
【门楣】ménméi〈名〉1（指横木）lintel 2（指门第）family status: 光耀～ bring honour to one's family
【门面】ménmian〈名〉1（指店门）shop front: ～房 house with a street frontage ‖ 装修～ fit a shop front ‖ 五开间～ five-bay shop front 2〈喻〉（指外表）facade: 装～ maintain a facade
【门面话】ménmianhuà〈名〉lip service
【门牌】ménpái〈名〉house number: 你家～几号? What's your house number? ‖ 我家的～是长安路8号。My house number is No 8, Chang'an Road.
【门票】ménpiào〈名〉entrance ticket: ～收入 door money ‖ ～已售完。The (admission) tickets are sold out.
【门球】ménqiú〈名〉［体育］croquet: 打～ play croquet
【门儿清】ménrqīng〈动〉〈方〉be clear (about)
【门人】ménrén〈名〉1 = 门生 ménshēng 1 2（门客）parasitic guest
【门扇】ménshàn〈名〉door leaf
【门神】ménshén ▸**p. 274**〈名〉door-god: 贴～ paste a picture of door-gods on the front door

> **门神**
>
> A deity that guards a doorway. The earliest depictions of door gods were of the immortals. In the Tang Dynasty, the Emperor Taizong was said to have created images of two of his military ministers, Qin Qiong (秦琼) and Yuchi Gong (尉迟恭), to keep evil spirits at bay. The mythological figure Zhong Kui (钟馗) also appears as a door god. On Chinese New Year's Eve, images of the gods were traditionally pasted on either side of the door to ward off evil spirits.

【门生】ménshēng〈名〉1（学生）disciple: 得意～ favourite pupil 2（我）I [term used by successful imperial examination candidates in front of their examiners]
【门市】ménshì〈名〉retail sales: 兼营批发和～ sideline in wholesale and retail ‖ 今天是星期天，～不错。It is Sunday today, so business is brisk.
【门市部】ménshìbù〈名〉sales department ‖ ～部 outpatient department
【门闩】ménshuān〈名〉door bolt
【门厅】méntīng〈名〉lobby: ～镜 hall mirror
【门庭】méntíng〈名〉1（门口和庭院）front yard: 洒扫～ sweep a courtyard 2（门第）family status: 改换～ change one's family status ‖ 光耀～ bring honour to one's family
【门庭若市】méntíng-ruòshì〈成〉a much visited establishment
【门徒】méntú〈名〉follower
【门外汉】ménwàihàn〈名〉layman: 对于法律，我是个～。I am a layman in law.
【门卫】ménwèi〈名〉entrance guard: 学校～ school caretaker
【门下】ménxià〈名〉1（门客）hanger-on of an aristocrat 2（学生）pupil 3（跟前）under the instruction of a teacher: 我想投在您的～学习书法。I want to learn Chinese calligraphy from you. ‖ 许多年轻画家都出自他的～。Many young artists have studied under him.
【门牙】ményá〈名〉front tooth
【门迎】ményíng〈名〉greeter [at a shop, restaurant, etc.]: ～小姐 female greeter
【门诊】ménzhěn〈动〉provide an outpatient service: ～时间 consulting hours ‖ 专家～ specialist for outpatient consultation
【门子】ménzi **A**〈名〉connections: 找～ solicit help from one's connections **B**〈量〉〈方〉[for marriage]: 这～亲事他的父母很满意。His parents are very pleased with this marriage.

扪（捫）mén〈动〉〈书〉touch

【扪心】ménxīn〈动〉〈书〉search one's heart: ～无愧 have a clear conscience
【扪心自问】ménxīn-zìwèn〈成〉examine one's conscience: ～，我不敢说这是对的。With my hand on my heart, I can't say it is right.

钔（鍆）mén〈名〉［化学］mendelevium (Md)

mèn

闷（悶）mèn〈形〉1（心烦）depressed: ～出病来 be depressed into illness ‖ 她一个人整天呆在家里～得发慌。She felt terribly bored staying at home alone all day. ▸～～不乐，愁～，烦～ 2（密闭）tightly closed: 窒～ stuffy ▸mēn

【闷沉沉】mènchénchén〈形〉depressed: 独自在家，他心里～的。He felt very depressed staying at home all alone. ▸mēnchénchén
【闷罐车】mènguànchē〈方〉= 闷子车 mènzichē
【闷棍】mèngùn〈名〉heavy blow: 头上挨了一～ take a sudden blow on the head ‖ 吃了一～ suffer a heavy blow
【闷葫芦】mènhúlu〈名〉〈喻〉1（不解的事）puzzle: 他的话对我来说真是个～。His words were really a puzzle to me. 2（话少的人）man of few words
【闷酒】mènjiǔ〈名〉drink taken alone to drown one's sorrows: 喝～ drink one's sorrows from a bottle
【闷倦】mènjuàn〈动〉be in low spirits
【闷雷】mènléi〈名〉1〈本〉muffled thunder 2〈喻〉（指打击）shock
【闷闷不乐】mènmèn-bùlè〈成〉in low spirits: 他几天来一直～。He's been feeling depressed for several days.
【闷气】mènqì〈名〉sulk: 生～ have the sulks ▸mēnqì
【闷子车】mènzichē〈名〉boxcar

焖（燜）mèn〈动〉stew: ～饭/肉 cook rice/meat over a slow fire ‖ ～羊肉 stewed mutton ▸红～

【焖烧锅】mènshāoguō〈名〉stew-pot

懑（懣）mèn〈形〉〈书〉1（烦闷）unhappy 2（愤慨）indignant: ▸愤～

men

们（們）men〈后缀〉[used after a personal pronoun or a noun to show plural number]: 女士～、先生～ ladies and gentlemen ‖ 朋友～ friends ‖ 兄弟姐妹～ brothers and sisters ▸你～，他～，我～

mēng

蒙¹（矇） mēng〈动〉1（欺骗）cheat: 她上周结婚了。——你没~我吧? She got married last week. — You're not kidding me, are you? ▸~骗, ~事 2（胡乱猜测）make a wild guess: 他~对/错了。He has made a lucky/wrong guess.

蒙² mēng〈动〉lose consciousness: 头发~ feel one's head swimming ‖ 男孩给打~了。The boy was knocked senseless. ▸méng, Měng

【蒙蒙黑】mēngmēnghēi〈形〉dusky

【蒙蒙亮】mēngmēngliàng〈形〉dawn-like: 天刚~, 我们就开始干活。As soon as a faint light appeared in the sky, we started to work.

【蒙骗】mēngpiàn〈动〉deceive: ~顾客 cheat customers ‖ 用花言巧语~ deceive sb. with sweet-talk

【蒙事】mēngshi〈动〉〈方〉deceive

【蒙头转向】mēngtóu-zhuànxiàng〈成〉be completely confused: 使某人~ send sb. into tailspins of confusion

méng

氓 méng〈名〉〈书〉people migrating from other places: ▸愚~ ▸máng

虻 méng〈名〉gadfly: ▸牛~

萌 méng〈动〉1（发芽）bud: ▸~发, ~芽 2（开始）begin: ▸~动, 故态复~

【萌动】méngdòng〈动〉1（发芽）bud: 早春草木~。Trees and flowers sprout in early spring. 2（开始）initiate: 春意~。Spring is in the air.

【萌发】méngfā〈动〉1（生芽）bud: ~新枝 sprout new buds ‖ 雨后杂草~。Weeds begin to sprout after a rain. 2〈喻〉（发生）come about: ~强烈的求知欲望 develop a strong desire for knowledge

【萌生】méngshēng〈动〉conceive: ~强烈的愿望 be seized with a strong desire ‖ ~邪念 a wicked idea enters sb.'s head ‖ ~一线希望 a ray of hope arises in one's heart

【萌芽】méngyá〈动〉1〈本〉bud: ~生根 sprout and grow roots 2〈喻〉germinate: 新型生产关系的~ rudimentary stage of new production relations ‖ 这门学科还处于~状态。This science is still in (its) embryonic stage.

蒙 méng

A〈动〉1（遮盖）cover: ~上眼睛 blindfold sb.'s eyes ‖ ~上一层灰 be covered with a layer of dust ‖ 用手~住脸 hide one's face in one's hands 2（遭受）suffer from: ~羞而死 die an ignominious death ▸~难, ~冤 3（受）meet with: ~你照料, 非常感谢。Thank you very much for your care and attention. ▸承~ 4（欺骗）deceive: ▸~哄, ~混

B〈形〉ignorant: ▸~昧, 开~, 启~ ▸mēng, Měng

【蒙蔽】méngbì〈动〉deceive: ~群众 deceive the masses ‖ 被花言巧语所~ be fooled by sweet-talk

【蒙大拿州】Méngdànázhōu〈名〉Montana

【蒙得维的亚】Méngdéwéidìyà〈名〉Montevideo

【蒙哥马利郡】Ménggēmǎlìjùn〈名〉Montgomeryshire

【蒙垢】ménggòu〈动〉〈书〉be humiliated

【蒙馆】méngguǎn〈名〉〈旧〉private elementary school

【蒙汗药】ménghànyào〈名〉narcotic

【蒙哄】ménghǒng〈动〉cheat

【蒙混】ménghùn〈动〉deceive people: ~过关 get by under false pretences

【蒙眬】ménglóng = 曚昽 ménglóng

【蒙罗维亚】Méngluówéiyà〈名〉Monrovia

【蒙茅斯郡】Méngmáosījùn〈名〉Monmouthshire

【蒙昧】méngmèi〈形〉1（未开化）barbaric: ~时代 age of barbarism 2（不懂事理）benighted: ~无知 be unenlightened

【蒙蒙】méngméng〈形〉1 = 濛濛 méngméng 2（模糊）misty: 雾~的天空 hazy sky ‖ 烟雾~的早晨 misty morning

【蒙面】méngmiàn〈动〉cover one's face with sth.

【蒙面大盗】méngmiàndàdào〈名〉masked bandit/burglar

【蒙面人】méngmiànrén〈名〉masked person

【蒙难】méngnàn〈动〉〈书〉[of a well-known person or a person of high position] suffer a catastrophe

【蒙师】méngshī〈名〉〈旧〉first teacher

【蒙受】méngshòu〈动〉suffer: ~不白之冤 be grievously wronged ‖ ~巨大损失 suffer a tremendous loss

【蒙太奇】méngtàiqí〈名〉［影视］montage

【蒙特利尔】Měngtèlì'ěr〈名〉Montreal

【蒙童】méngtóng〈名〉〈旧〉pupil (in a private school)

【蒙头】méngtóu〈动〉cover one's head: ~大睡 tuck oneself in and sleep like a log

【蒙学】méngxué = 蒙馆 méngguǎn

【蒙药】méngyào〈名〉anaesthetic

【蒙冤】méngyuān〈动〉suffer an injustice: ~而死 die suffering an injustice

【蒙在鼓里】méngzàigǔlǐ〈惯〉be kept in the dark: 全村都知道了, 他却还~。The whole village knew about it, but he was still in the dark.

【蒙子】méngzi〈名〉watch glass

盟 méng

A〈名〉1（缔约）alliance: ▸~国, 加~, 同~ 2（指蒙古民族）league [administrative division of the Inner Mongolian Autonomous Region]: 呼伦贝尔~ Hulun Buir League

B〈动〉1（发誓）pledge: ▸~誓 2（结拜）become sworn brothers or sisters: ▸~兄弟

【盟邦】méngbāng〈名〉ally

【盟国】méngguó〈名〉allied state, ally: 欧洲~ European allies

【盟军】méngjūn〈名〉allied forces

【盟誓】méngshì **A**〈名〉〈书〉oath of alliance **B**〈动〉take an oath: 对天~ swear by Heaven

【盟兄弟】méngxiōngdì〈名〉sworn brothers: 拜~ become sworn brothers

【盟友】méngyǒu〈名〉1（指人）ally 2（指国家）allied state

【盟员】méngyuán〈名〉member of an alliance or a league

【盟约】méngyuē〈名〉oath of alliance: 订立~ sign the treaty of alliance

【盟主】méngzhǔ〈名〉〈旧〉leader of an alliance

濛 méng〈形〉drizzly: ▸~~

【濛濛】méngméng〈形〉drizzly: ~细雨 fine drizzle

檬 méng ▸柠檬 níngméng

曚 méng

【曚昽】ménglóng〈形〉〈书〉[of sunlight] dim

朦 méng

【朦胧】ménglóng〈形〉1（指月光）hazy: ~的月光 hazy moonlight 2（模糊）dim: ~的景色 hazy view ‖ 烟雾~。It is misty. ‖〈喻〉~的回忆 hazy memories

【朦胧诗】ménglóngshī〈名〉obscure poem: ~人 obscure poet

矇 méng〈形〉〈书〉blind

【矇眬】ménglóng〈形〉sleepy: 睡眼~ be bleary-eyed

艨 méng

【艨艟】méngchōng〈名〉〈旧〉war vessel protected with cowhide

měng

勐¹ měng〈形〉〈书〉valiant

勐² měng〈名〉*meng* [old administrative division in the *Dai* ethnic group area, Xishuangbanna, Yunnan Province]

猛 měng

A〈形〉1（猛烈）fierce 2（凶猛）violent: ▸~虎, ~禽, 凶~ 3（力量大）vigorous: 用力过~ use too much strength ‖ 昨晚炮火很~。There was heavy gunfire last night. ▸~将, 勇~

B〈副〉abruptly: ~地站起来 jump to one's feet ‖ 钢产量~增 steep rise in steel output ‖ 价格~涨/跌 sharp rise/fall in prices ▸~然, ~醒

C〈动〉be vigorous: ~着劲儿干 work energetically

【猛不防】měngbufáng〈副〉unexpectedly: 有人~从黑地里窜出来, 吓了我一跳。Someone came out of the dark unexpectedly and gave me quite a start.

【猛冲猛打】měngchōng-měngdǎ〈成〉go full steam ahead

【猛攻】měnggōng〈动〉attack violently

【猛虎】měnghǔ〈名〉fierce tiger

【猛虎扑食】měnghǔ-pūshí〈成〉〈喻〉come with a devastating force

【猛虎下山】měnghǔ-xiàshān〈成〉with overwhelming momentum

【猛击】měngjī〈动〉smash: ~头部 hit sb. on the head with a sudden force

【猛将】měngjiàng〈名〉valiant general: ~如云 a great number of brave warriors

【猛进】měngjìn〈动〉push ahead vigorously: ▸突飞~

【猛劲儿】měngjìnr **A**〈动〉show a spurt of energy, dash: 一~, 他把那块巨石举了起来。He lifted up the huge stone with a sudden burst of strength. **B**〈名〉great vigour: 干活有股子~ work energetically

【猛料】měngliào〈名〉sensational news: 影星婚外恋的~ sensational stories of extra-marital affairs among film stars

【猛烈】měngliè〈形〉 1 (凶猛) fierce: ～的炮火 heavy gunfire ‖ 向敌人发动～的进攻 launch a fierce attack against the enemy 2 (急剧) rapid: 我的心脏～地跳动着。 My heart was beating furiously.
【猛犸】měngmǎ〈名〉 mammoth
【猛男】měngnán〈名〉 hard man: NBA的～们 NBA hard men
【猛禽】měngqín〈名〉 bird of prey
【猛然】měngrán〈副〉 suddenly: ～回头 turn one's head sharply ‖ ～停住 jerk to a halt ‖ ～醒悟 suddenly wake up
【猛士】měngshì〈名〉〈旧〉 brave man
【猛兽】měngshòu〈名〉 predator
【猛省】měngxǐng = 猛醒 měngxǐng
【猛醒】měngxǐng〈动〉 suddenly wake up to the truth
【猛涨】měngzhǎng〈动〉 increase drastically: 物价～。 The prices soared.
【猛鸷】měngzhì〈名〉〈书〉 hawk
【猛子】měngzi〈名〉 dive: 他一个～便消失在水中。 With one dive he disappeared into the water. ▸扎～

蒙 Měng〈名〉 Mongol ethnic group ▸mēng, méng
【蒙古】Měnggǔ〈名〉 Mongolia: ～人 Mongol ‖ ～语 Mongolian ▸内～
【蒙古包】měnggǔbāo〈名〉 (Mongolian) yurt

> **蒙古包**
> A domed tent (yurt) with a circular frame, and walls made of a lattice of wood, used by Mongolian and other nomadic peoples. The roof and walls are covered with felt made of wool, and fastened down with rope. At the crown of the roof is a round skylight that lets in light and provides ventilation. There are two types of yurt: fixed or mobile. The word *menggubao* is Manchu in origin. Yurts are known as *ger* (格儿) in Mongolian, and in ancient times were called *qionglu* (穹庐).

【蒙古国】Měnggǔguó〈名〉 State of Mongolia
【蒙古族】Měnggǔzú〈名〉 1 (指中国) Mongol ethnic group 2 (指蒙古) Mongols
【蒙文】Měngwén ▸**p. 918**〈名〉 Mongolian language
【蒙医】Měngyī〈名〉 traditional Mongolian medicine
【蒙族】Měngzú〈简称〉= 蒙古族

锰（錳） měng〈名〉［化学］ manganese (Mn)
【锰钢】měnggāng〈名〉 manganese steel

蜢 měng ▸蚱蜢 zhàměng

艋 měng ▸舴艋 zéměng

獴 měng〈名〉［动物］ mongoose

蠓 měng〈名〉［昆虫］ midge
【蠓虫儿】měngchóngr〈名〉［昆虫］ midge

懵 měng〈形〉 ignorant: ～然无知 be totally ignorant
【懵懂】měngdǒng〈形〉 ignorant: 聪明一世，～一时 smart as a rule, but this time a fool

mèng

孟 mèng〈名〉〈书〉 1 (指人) eldest brother or sister: ～仲叔季 [of brothers] the eldest, second eldest, third eldest and the youngest 2 (指时间) first month of a season: ▸～春, ～冬
【孟春】mèngchūn ▸**p. 345**〈名〉〈书〉 first month of spring
【孟冬】mèngdōng ▸**p. 345**〈名〉〈书〉 first month of winter
【孟加拉】Mèngjiālā〈名〉 Bengal: ～国 Bangladesh ‖ ～人 Bengali ‖ ～人民共和国 People's Republic of Bangladesh ‖ ～语 Bengali
【孟轲】Mèngkē = 孟子 Mèngzǐ
【孟浪】mènglàng〈形〉〈书〉 rash: 话语/行为～ speak/act rashly
【孟买】Mèngmǎi〈名〉 Mumbai
【孟秋】mèngqiū ▸**p. 345**〈名〉〈书〉 first month of autumn
【孟什维克】Mèngshíwéikè〈名〉 Menshevik
【孟夏】mèngxià ▸**p. 345**〈名〉〈书〉 first month of summer
【孟子】Mèngzǐ〈名〉 Mencius

梦（夢） mèng
A〈名〉 dream: 做～ have a dream ‖ 入～ drift off into dreamland ▸～境, 美～
B〈动〉 dream: ▸～见
【梦笔生花】mèngbǐ-shēnghuā〈成〉〈喻〉 begin to show one's literary brilliance
【梦话】mènghuà〈名〉 1〈本〉 sleep-talking: 说～ talk in one's sleep 2〈喻〉 daydream: 三个月掌握一门外语? 简直是在说～。 To master a foreign language within three months? That's pure delusion!
【梦幻】mènghuàn〈名〉 dream: 生活在～中 live in a dream ‖ 从～中醒来 awaken from a dream
【梦幻泡影】mènghuàn-pàoyǐng〈成〉 pipe dream
【梦见】mèngjiàn〈动〉 have a dream about: 昨晚我～了母亲。 I saw my mother in my dream last night.
【梦境】mèngjìng〈名〉 dreamland: 如入～ feel as if one were in a dreamland
【梦寐】mèngmèi〈名〉 dream: ～难忘 be unable to forget sth. even in one's dream
【梦寐以求】mèngmèiyǐqiú〈成〉 long for sth. so much that one even dreams about it: ～的房子 dream house
【梦乡】mèngxiāng〈名〉 dreamland: 进入～ go off to dreamland
【梦想】mèngxiǎng A〈动〉 1 (幻想) indulge in wishful thinking: 别～一夜成巨富。 Don't dream of getting rich overnight. 2 (渴望) dream: 她～有朝一日成为电影明星。 She dreamed that one day she would be a movie star. B〈名〉 cherished desire: ～成真。 It is a dream come true. ‖ 她的～终于实现了。 Her dream has finally come true.
【梦魇】mèngyǎn〈动〉 have a nightmare
【梦遗】mèngyí〈名〉［医学］ wet dream
【梦呓】mèngyì = 梦话 mènghuà
【梦游症】mèngyóuzhèng ▸**p. 50**〈名〉［医学］ somnambulism
【梦之队】mèngzhīduì〈名〉［体育］ dream team

mī

咪 mī
【咪表】mībiǎo〈名〉 parking meter
【咪咪】mīmī〈拟〉 miaow: 小猫～叫。 A kitten mews.

眯（瞇） mī〈动〉 1 (眯缝) narrow one's eyes: ～着眼看 squint at (sb./sth.) ‖ ～着眼笑 narrow one's eyes into a smile 2〈方〉(小睡) doze off: 他想～一会儿。 He wants to take a short nap. ▸mí
【眯瞪】mīdeng〈动〉〈方〉 doze off: 你困了就～一会儿。 Take a nap if you are tired.
【眯缝】mīfeng〈动〉 narrow one's eyes: ～着眼睛笑 narrow one's eyes into a smile

mí

弥¹（瀰） mí〈形〉 full: 大雾～天。 Thick fog filled the sky. ▸～漫, ～天大谎, ～月

弥²（彌） mí
A〈动〉 fill: ▸～补, ～缝, ～合
B〈副〉 more: 意志～坚 become more strong-willed ▸欲盖～彰
【弥补】míbǔ〈动〉 make up: ～不足 make up the deficiency ‖ ～损失 make good a loss ‖ 今年的利润将～去年的亏损。 This year's profits will make up for last year's losses.
【弥封】mífēng〈动〉 seal the examinee's name on an exam paper so as to prevent fraudulence
【弥缝】míféng〈动〉〈喻〉 cover up mistakes
【弥合】míhé〈动〉 bridge: ～伤口 close up a wound ‖ ～夫妻感情的裂痕 heal a rift between husband and wife
【弥勒】Mílè〈名〉［佛教］ Maitreya: ～佛 Laughing Buddha
【弥留】míliú〈动〉〈书〉 be dying: ～之际立下遗嘱 make a will on one's deathbed
【弥漫】mímàn〈动〉 permeate: 烟雾～ heavy with smoke ‖ 空气中～着浓烈的泥土气息。 The strong odour of dirt filled the air. ‖ 乌云～了天空。 The sky is overcast with black clouds.
【弥蒙】míméng〈形〉 suffused: 硝烟～。 The fumes of gunpowder filled the air.
【弥撒】mísa〈名〉［宗教］ Mass: 做～ say Mass
【弥散】mísàn〈动〉 spread in all directions: 公园里～着一股花香。 The park was filled with the scent of flowers.
【弥天】mítiān〈动〉 be huge
【弥天大谎】mítiān-dàhuǎng〈成〉 monstrous lie: 撒个～ tell a real whopper
【弥天大罪】mítiān-dàzuì〈成〉 heinous crime
【弥陀佛】Mítuófó〈名〉 Amida
【弥月】míyuè〈动〉〈书〉 1 (满月) complete the first month of life: ～之喜 celebration of a one-month-old baby 2 (满一个月) complete a full month

迷 mí
A〈动〉 1 (分辨不清) be confused: ～路 lost one's way ▸～失, ～途 2 (使沉醉) be crazy about: ～上了足球 be mad about football ‖ 她的精彩演说～住了听众。 Her

m

wonderful speech captivated the audience. ▸~恋, ~信, 痴~ **3**（使迷惑） confuse: ▸~魂阵, ~惑

B〈名〉 enthusiast: 电影~ film freak ‖ 篮球~ basketball fan ‖ 戏~ opera fiend

【迷彩】mícǎi〈名〉 camouflage colour: ~服 battle fatigues

【迷迭香】mídiéxiāng〈名〉［植物］ rosemary

【迷宫】mígōng〈名〉 labyrinth: 如入~ like entering a labyrinth ‖ ~般的隧道 maze of tunnels

【迷航】míháng〈动〉 drift off course

【迷糊】míhu〈形〉 confused: 喝酒喝~了 get tipsy ‖ 有点~ feel a bit muddled ‖ 病人有时清醒，有时~。 The patient was sometimes clear-headed, sometimes completely muddled.

【迷幻药】míhuànyào〈名〉 hallucinogen

【迷魂汤】míhúntāng〈名〉 **1**（指汤药） magic potion **2**〈喻〉（指言行） flattery: 灌~ try to ensnare sb. with sweet-talk

【迷魂药】míhúnyào = 迷魂汤 míhúntāng

【迷魂阵】míhúnzhèn〈名〉 decoy: 摆~ set a trap ‖ 落入~ fall into a trap

【迷惑】míhuò **A**〈形〉 confused: ~不解 feel puzzled (about) **B**〈动〉 confuse: ~敌人 confuse the enemy ‖ 他被假象所~。 He was misled by false appearances.

【迷津】míjīn〈书〉〈名〉 labyrinth: 指点~ show sb. how to get on the right path

【迷离】mílí〈形〉 blurred: ~恍惚 be in a stupor ‖ 睡眼~ eyes dim with sleep

【迷离惝恍】mílí-tǎnghuǎng〈成〉 misted

【迷恋】míliàn〈动〉 be infatuated with: ~酒色 be obsessed with wine and women ‖ 她~上了他。 She was infatuated with him.

【迷路】mílù〈动〉 **1**〈本〉 get lost: 森林里容易~。 It's easy to lose your way in the forest. **2**〈喻〉 go astray

【迷乱】míluàn〈形〉 befuddled

【迷漫】mímàn〈动〉 fill the air: 烟雾~ be enveloped in mist

【迷茫】mímáng〈形〉 **1**（广阔而模糊） vast and hazy: 远处一片~。 It is hazy in the distance. **2**（迷惑） confused: 她脸上露出~的神情。 There was a confused look on her face.

【迷蒙】míméng〈形〉 **1** = 迷茫 mímáng 1 **2**（恍惚） confused: 从~中醒来 become clear-headed

【迷梦】mímèng〈名〉 pipe dream

【迷迷怔怔】mími-zhēngzhēng〈形〉 dazed

【迷你】mínǐ〈形〉 mini: ~计算机 minicomputer ‖ ~裙 miniskirt

【迷人】mírén〈形〉 charming: ~的故事 fascinating story ‖ ~的景色 entrancing views

【迷失】míshī〈动〉 lose (one's way, etc.): ~方向 lose one's bearings

【迷途】mítú **A**〈动〉 lose one's way: ~羔羊 stray lamb **B**〈名〉 wrong path: 误入~ go astray

【迷途知返】mítú-zhīfǎn〈成〉 realize one's errors and mend one's ways

【迷惘】míwǎng〈形〉 perplexed: 精神~ be at a loss

【迷雾】míwù〈名〉 **1**〈本〉 dense fog **2**〈喻〉 misguiding force: 驱散愚昧的~ dispel the mists of ignorance

【迷信】míxìn〈动〉 **1**（指超自然事物） hold superstitious beliefs: 破除~ abolish superstition ‖ ~活动 superstitious activities ‖ ~鬼神 have a superstitious belief in ghosts and spirits **2**（盲目信仰） have blind faith in: ~名人 worship celebrities

【迷走神经】mízǒu shénjīng〈名〉［解剖］ vagus (nerve)

【迷醉】mízuì〈动〉 be fascinated by

眯（瞇） mí〈动〉 get into one's eye: 灰尘~了我的眼睛。 The dust has got into my eye.
▸mī

猕（獼） mí

【猕猴】míhóu〈名〉［动物］ macaque

【猕猴桃】míhóutáo〈名〉［植物］ **1**（指植物） kiwi **2**（指果实） kiwi (fruit)

谜（謎） mí〈名〉 **1**（谜语） riddle: 猜~ guess a riddle ▸~语, 灯~ **2**〈喻〉（疑团） puzzle: 解开宇宙起源之~ solve the riddle of how the universe originated ‖ 他的死仍是未解之~。 His death remains an unsolved mystery.
▸mèi

【谜底】mídǐ〈名〉 **1**（答案） solution to a riddle: 猜出~ work out a riddle **2**〈喻〉（真相） truth: 揭开~ solve a mystery

【谜面】mímiàn〈名〉 clue to a riddle

【谜团】mítuán〈名〉〈喻〉 doubts and suspicions: 解开~ clear up a mystery

【谜语】míyǔ〈名〉 riddle

弥（镾） mí〈名〉 thin bamboo strip

醚 mí〈名〉［化学］ ether: ▸乙~

糜 mí

A〈名〉 gruel: ▸肉~

B〈动〉 **1**（烂） rot: ▸~烂 **2**（浪费） waste: ▸~费
▸méi

【糜费】mífèi = 靡费 mífèi

【糜烂】mílàn **A**〈动〉 fester: 伤口~。 The wound is festering. **B**〈形〉 debauched: 生活~ live a dissipated life

縻 mí〈动〉〈书〉 tie

麋 mí〈名〉 elk

【麋鹿】mílù〈名〉 elk

靡 mí〈动〉 spend extravagantly: ▸奢~
▸mǐ

【靡费】mífèi〈动〉〈书〉 spend extravagantly: ~钱财 waste money ‖ ~人力物力 waste manpower and material resources

蘼 mí ▸荼蘼 túmí

醾 mí ▸酴醾 túmí

mǐ

米¹ mǐ〈名〉 **1**（指种子） husked seed: ▸花生~ **2**（大米） (husked) rice: ▸大~, 糯~ **3**（米粒状物） grain-like things: ▸海~, 虾~

米² mǐ ▸**p. 82**〈名〉 metre: 一公里等于一千~。 One kilometre equals 1,000 metres.

【米波】mǐbō〈名〉［通信］ metric wave

【米尺】mǐchǐ〈名〉 metre rule

【米醋】mǐcù〈名〉 rice vinegar

【米袋子】mǐdàizi〈名〉〈喻〉 provision of basic foodstuffs, like grain, oil, etc.

【米德尔塞克斯郡】 Mǐdé'ěrsàikèsījùn〈名〉 Middlesex

【米店】mǐdiàn〈名〉 rice store

【米豆腐】mǐdòufu〈名〉 rice curd

【米饭】mǐfàn〈名〉 (cooked) rice: 煮~ cook rice ‖ 炒~ fried rice

【米粉】mǐfěn〈名〉 **1**（指粉） rice flour **2**（指面食） rice noodles: 炒~ stir-fried rice noodles

【米粉肉】mǐfěnròu〈名〉 pork steamed with seasoned rice flour

【米泔水】mǐgānshuǐ〈名〉 water in which rice has been washed

【米格】mǐgé〈名〉 MiG: ~战斗机 MiG fighter jet

【米花】mǐhuā〈名〉 puffed rice: ~糖 puffed rice cake ▸爆~

【米黄】mǐhuáng ▸**p. 863**〈名〉 cream (colour): ~色 off-white

【米酒】mǐjiǔ〈名〉 rice wine

【米糠】mǐkāng〈名〉 rice bran

【米粒】mǐlì〈名〉 rice grain

【米粮川】mǐliángchuān〈名〉 rich rice-producing area: 荒滩变成了~。 Large tracts of wasteland have become a granary.

【米面】mǐmiàn〈名〉 **1**（米和面） rice and wheat flour **2**（米粉） rice flour

【米色】mǐsè ▸**p. 863**〈名〉 cream (colour)

【米汤】mǐtāng〈名〉 **1**（指汤） water in which rice has been cooked **2**（指粥） millet gruel **3**（指话） flattering words: ▸灌~

【米线】mǐxiàn〈名〉〈方〉 rice noodles: 过桥~ cross-bridge rice noodles

【米象】mǐxiàng〈名〉［昆虫］ rice weevil

【米制】mǐzhì〈名〉 metric system

【米珠薪桂】mǐzhū-xīnguì〈成〉 exorbitantly high cost of living

【米猪肉】mǐzhūròu〈名〉 pork infected with cysticercus

芈 mǐ〈拟〉 baa

弭 mǐ〈动〉〈书〉 stop: 风停雨~。 The wind has died down and the rain has stopped. ▸消~

【弭谤】mǐbàng〈动〉〈书〉 stop slanders

【弭兵】mǐbīng〈动〉〈书〉 have a truce

【弭除】mǐchú〈动〉〈书〉 eliminate: ~患 eliminate trouble

【弭乱】mǐluàn〈动〉〈书〉 put down a rebellion

敉 mǐ〈动〉〈书〉 pacify

【敉平】mǐpíng〈动〉〈书〉 put down: ~叛乱 quell a rebellion

靡¹ mǐ〈书〉

A〈动〉 collapse: ▸所向披~, 望风披~

B〈形〉 gorgeous: ▸~丽

靡² mǐ〈动〉〈书〉 not have: ~日不思 not a day passes without thinking of sb./sth.
▸mí

【靡不有初】mǐbùyǒuchū〈成〉 good in the beginning but usually bad in the end

【靡丽】mǐlì〈形〉〈书〉 extravagant

【靡靡】mǐmǐ〈形〉 lewd

【靡靡之音】mǐmǐzhīyīn〈成〉 decadent music

【靡然】mǐrán〈形〉〈书〉 leaning to one side: ~从之 go with the fashion

mì

汨 mì
【汨罗江】Miluójiāng ▸p. 294〈名〉Miluo River

觅（覓） mì〈动〉hunt for: ～知音 seek an understanding friend ‖ ～食 hunt for food ▸寻～
【觅求】mìqiú〈动〉seek: ～真理 seek truth
【觅取】mìqǔ〈动〉hunt for: ～宝藏/食物 hunt for treasure/food

泌 mì〈动〉secrete: ▸～尿, 分～
【泌尿】mìniào〈动〉［医学］urinate: ～科 urological department ‖ ～系统 urinary system
【泌尿生殖系统】mìniào shēngzhí xìtǒng〈名〉urogenital system

宓 mì〈形〉〈书〉tranquil

秘（祕） mì
A〈形〉**1**（神秘）mysterious: ▸～密, 奥～, 神～ **2**（罕见）rare: ▸～本, ～籍
B〈动〉**1**（保密）keep sth. secret (from): ▸～而不宣 **2**（阻塞）block: ▸便～
C〈名〉secretary: ▸文～
▸bì
【秘奥】mì'ào〈名〉profound mystery
【秘宝】mìbǎo〈名〉rare treasure
【秘本】mìběn〈名〉treasured private copy of a rare book
【秘传】mìchuán〈动〉hand down (a recipe, formula, etc.) from generation to generation exclusively inside the family
【秘而不宣】mì'érbùxuān〈成〉hush sth. up: 对自己的意图～ keep one's intentions to oneself
【秘方】mìfāng〈名〉secret recipe: 宫廷～ secret recipe from the court ▸祖传～
【秘府】mìfǔ〈名〉secret repository (in the imperial court)
【秘笈】mìjí = 秘籍 mìjí
【秘籍】mìjí〈名〉rare book: 孤本～ only existing copy of a rare book
【秘结】mìjié〈形〉constipated
【秘诀】mìjué〈名〉secret: 成功的～ secret of success
【秘密】mìmì **A**〈形〉secret: ～结婚 marry in secret ‖ ～会谈/外交 secret talks/diplomacy ‖ 会议～举行。The meeting was conducted in secrecy. **B**〈名〉secret: 保守～ keep a secret ‖ 国家/军事～ state/military secrets ‖ 提供～ offer secrets (to sb.) ‖ 向某人透露～ let sb. in on the secret ‖ 泄漏～ give away a secret
【秘密会议】mìmì huìyì〈名〉secret meeting
【秘密警察】mìmì jǐngchá〈名〉secret police
【秘密文件】mìmì wénjiàn〈名〉classified document
【秘史】mìshǐ〈名〉secret history
【秘书】mìshū〈名〉secretary: 大使馆一/二/三等～ first/second/third secretary of the embassy ‖ 私人～ private secretary ‖ ～处 secretariat ‖ ～长 secretary-general
【秘术】mìshù〈名〉occult arts
【秘闻】mìwén〈名〉secret news: ～轶事 secrets and anecdotes ‖ 宫闱～ palace secrets

m

密[1] mì
A〈形〉secret: ▸～件, ～码, ～谈
B〈名〉secret: 与谈判有关的文件是保密的，20年内不会解～。The papers about the negotiations are classified and will not be declassified for 20 years. ▸保～, 告～, 泄～

密[2] mì〈形〉**1**（密集）close: 果树栽得太～。The fruit trees have been planted too close together. ‖ 雨点越来越～。The rain is falling harder and harder. ▸～布, ～度, ～集 **2**（亲密）close: ▸～切, ～友, 亲～ **3**（细致）fine: ▸精～, 细～, 周～
【密报】mìbào **A**〈动〉inform against/on sb. **B**〈名〉secret report
【密闭】mìbì〈动〉close tightly: ～容器 airtight container ‖ 门窗～。The doors and windows are tightly sealed.
【密布】mìbù〈动〉cover densely: 阴云～。Dark clouds cover the sky. ‖ 该地区河湖～。This area is thick with rivers and lakes.
【密电】mìdiàn **A**〈名〉coded telegram: 收到一封～ receive a coded telegram **B**〈动〉secretly wire sb.: ～前线指挥部 secretly wire headquarters at the front line
【密电码】mìdiànmǎ〈名〉cipher, code
【密度】mìdù〈名〉density: 人口～ population density ‖ 水的～比空气大得多。Water has a much greater density than air.
【密访】mìfǎng〈动〉pay a secret visit
【密封】mìfēng〈动〉seal: ～试卷 seal up test papers ‖ ～舱 airtight cabin ‖ ～保存 preserve sth. by sealing it airtight ‖ 用白蜡～瓶口 seal up a bottle with white wax
【密封胶】mìfēngjiāo〈名〉fluid sealant
【密封圈】mìfēngquān〈名〉seal ring
【密封容器】mìfēng róngqì〈名〉airtight container
【密告】mìgào = 密报 mìbào
【密会】mìhuì **A**〈动〉meet with sb. secretly **B**〈名〉secret meeting
【密级】mìjí〈名〉classification of government confidential documents: 标明文件的～ mark the classification of a document
【密集】mìjí **A**〈动〉crowd together: 人口～的地区 densely populated area ‖ ～队形 close formation **B**〈形〉crowded: ～的炮火 heavy artillery fire
【密集型】mìjíxíng〈形〉intensive: 劳动～ labour-intensive ‖ 资本～ capital-intensive
【密件】mìjiàn〈名〉classified material: 一份～ a confidential paper ‖ 发/写～ send out/write a confidential paper
【密克罗尼西亚】Mìkèluóníxīyà〈名〉Micronesia
【密林】mìlín〈名〉thick forest: 在～深处 in the depths of the forest
【密令】mìlìng **A**〈动〉give a secret order **B**〈名〉secret order
【密码】mìmǎ〈名〉secret code: 破译～ crack a code ‖ 输入～ enter a password ‖ ～箱 code box
【密密层层】mìmi-céngcéng〈形〉dense: ～的人群 dense crowd
【密密丛丛】mìmi-cóngcóng〈形〉[of trees or grass] dense: ～的橡树林 dense oak forest
【密密麻麻】mìmi-mámá〈形〉thickly dotted: 天上的星星～。The sky is filled with stars.
【密谋】mìmóu〈动〉plot: ～暗杀 plot to murder (sb.) ‖ ～抢劫银行 conspire to rob a bank
【密切】mìqiè **A**〈形〉**1**（关系亲近）close: 关系～ be on intimate terms with sb. ‖ 这两件事有～的联系。The two events are closely connected. **2**（严密周到）careful: 与同事～配合 act in close coordination with one's colleagues ‖ ～注意 watch closely **B**〈动〉establish close ties with: ～党群关系 build closer relations between the party and the people
【密商】mìshāng〈动〉hold secret talks: ～对策 discuss countermeasures secretly
【密使】mìshǐ〈名〉secret envoy: 派出～ send out a secret envoy
【密室】mìshì〈名〉back room: 会议在～里进行。The meeting was held behind closed doors.
【密实】mìshi〈形〉dense: 针脚真～。The stitching is very close.
【密苏里河】Mìsūlǐhé ▸p. 294〈名〉Missouri River
【密苏里州】Mìsūlǐzhōu〈名〉Missouri: ～人 Missourian
【密谈】mìtán〈动〉have a private talk
【密探】mìtàn〈名〉secret agent: 发现一名～ detect a spy
【密纹唱片】mìwén chàngpiàn〈名〉long-playing record (LP)
【密西西比河】Mìxīxībǐhé ▸p. 294〈名〉Mississippi River
【密西西比州】Mìxīxībǐzhōu〈名〉Mississippi: ～人 Mississippian
【密歇根州】Mìxiēgēnzhōu〈名〉Michigan
【密写】mìxiě〈动〉write in invisible ink: ～情报 intelligence written in invisible ink
【密信】mìxìn〈名〉confidential letter
【密友】mìyǒu〈名〉bosom friend: 至亲～ close relatives and bosom friends
【密语】mìyǔ **A**〈名〉cipher **B**〈动〉talk secretly
【密约】mìyuē **A**〈动〉make a secret appointment **B**〈名〉secret agreement: 签订～ sign a secret treaty
【密云不雨】mìyún-bùyǔ〈成〉〈喻〉trouble is brewing
【密召】mìzhào〈动〉summon in secret: ～回京 be secretly summoned back to the capital
【密诏】mìzhào〈名〉secret imperial edict
【密植】mìzhí〈名〉［农业］close planting: 合理～ rational close planting
【密旨】mìzhǐ〈名〉secret imperial edict
【密致】mìzhì〈形〉fine and close: ～材料 dense material
【密宗】mìzōng〈名〉［佛教］Tantrism

幂（冪） mì
A〈名〉**1**〈书〉（指覆盖物）cloth cover **2**［数学］power: 2的三次～ third power of 2
B〈动〉〈书〉cover with cloth

谧（謐） mì〈形〉〈书〉tranquil: ▸安～, 静～
【谧静】mìjìng〈形〉〈书〉tranquil

嘧 mì
【嘧啶】mìdìng〈名〉［化学］pyrimidine

蜜 mì
A〈名〉honey: 采～ [of bees] collect nectar ‖ 酿～ make honey
B〈形〉**1**（味甜）honey-sweet: ▸～柑, ～橘 **2**〈喻〉（甜美）sweet: ▸柔情～意, 甜～
【蜜蜂】mìfēng〈名〉bee: ～养殖 bee-keeping ‖ ～嗡嗡叫。Bees buzz.
【蜜蜂窝】mìfēngwō〈名〉beehive
【蜜柑】mìgān〈名〉mandarin orange
【蜜饯】mìjiàn **A**〈动〉preserve fruits in syrup: ～海棠 sweetened crab apples

B 〈名〉 preserved fruit
【蜜橘】mìjú〈名〉 tangerine
【蜜色】mìsè ▸**p. 863**〈名〉 light yellow: ～的头发 honey-coloured hair
【蜜丸子】mìwánzi 〈名〉［中药］ bolus made from powdered Chinese medicines and honey
【蜜腺】mìxiàn〈名〉［植物］ nectary
【蜜源】mìyuán〈名〉 nectar source: ～植物 nectariferous plant
【蜜月】mìyuè〈名〉 honeymoon: 度～ go on honeymoon ‖ ～旅行 honeymoon trip
【蜜月期】mìyuèqī〈名〉 honeymoon period: 美俄关系在"9.11"时间之后进入"～"。 After 9/11, relations between the United States and Russia entered a honeymoon period.
【蜜枣】mìzǎo〈名〉 candied date

mián

眠 mián〈动〉 **1**（睡） sleep: ▸安～, 催～, 睡～ **2**（冬眠） hibernate: 蚕～ silkworm's dormancy ▸冬～, 休～

绵（綿） mián
A〈动〉 be continuous: ▸～亘, ～延, 连～
B〈名〉 silk floss
C〈形〉 soft: ▸～薄, ～软, 缠～
【绵白糖】miánbáitáng〈名〉 fine white sugar
【绵薄】miánbó〈名〉〈谦〉 humble effort: 愿尽～之力。 I'll do what little I can to help.
【绵长】miáncháng〈形〉〈书〉 very long: 岁月～ long period of time ‖ 福寿～。 I wish you a happy and long life.
【绵绸】miánchóu 〈名〉［纺织］ fabric made from waste silk
【绵亘】miángèn 〈动〉 stretch in an unbroken chain: 这座山脉～几百公里。 The mountain range stretches for several hundred kilometres.
【绵里藏针】miánlǐ-cángzhēn〈成〉〈喻〉 an iron fist in a velvet glove
【绵力】miánlì〈名〉〈书〉 humble effort
【绵连】miánlián〈形〉 unbroken
【绵密】miánmì〈形〉 [of speech, thinking, etc.] meticulous: 文思～ meticulously logical writings
【绵绵】miánmián〈形〉 continuous: 春雨～ continuous spring rains ‖ 情思～。 The tender affection and loving thoughts are endless.
【绵软】miánruǎn〈形〉 **1**（柔软） soft: ～的羊毛 soft wool **2**（无力） feeble: 觉得浑身～ feel weak all over
【绵甜】miántián〈形〉 [of spirits] mild and sweet
【绵延】miányán〈动〉be continuous: ～数百公里的沙漠 desert stretching for hundreds of kilometres ‖ 长城从东向西～万里。 The Great Wall stretches ten thousand *li* from east to west.
【绵羊】miányáng〈名〉 sheep
【绵纸】miánzhǐ〈名〉 tissue paper

棉 mián〈名〉 **1**（指植物） cotton and kapok **2**（棉花） cotton: 采～ pick cotton ‖ 纯～ pure cotton ‖ 全～衬衣 shirt made of pure cotton ▸～布, ～纺, 皮～ **3**（絮状物） things like cotton-wool: ▸石～
【棉袄】mián'ǎo〈名〉 cotton-padded jacket
【棉背心】miánbèixīn〈名〉 cotton-padded waistcoat
【棉被】miánbèi〈名〉 cotton-wadded quilt
【棉饼】miánbǐng〈名〉 cottonseed cake
【棉布】miánbù〈名〉 cotton (cloth): 印花～ cotton print
【棉大衣】miándàyī〈名〉 cotton-padded overcoat
【棉纺】miánfǎng〈名〉 cotton spinning: ～厂 cotton mill
【棉猴儿】miánhóur〈名〉〈方〉 cotton-padded anorak
【棉花】miánhua〈名〉 **1**（指植物）cotton: 种～ grow cotton **2**（指纤维） cotton: 摘～ pick cotton
【棉花胎】miánhuatāi〈名〉〈方〉 cotton wadding (for a quilt, winter jacket, etc.)
【棉花糖】miánhuatáng〈名〉 candyfloss〈英〉; cotton candy〈美〉
【棉兰】Miánlán〈名〉 Medan
【棉兰老】Miánlánlǎo〈名〉 Mindanao
【棉铃】miánlíng〈名〉 cotton boll
【棉铃虫】miánlíngchóng〈名〉 bollworm
【棉毛】miánmáo〈名〉 cotton interlock: ～织物 fabrics made of cotton and wool
【棉毛裤】miánmáokù〈名〉 cotton long johns
【棉毛衫】miánmáoshān〈名〉 cotton jersey
【棉帽】miánmào〈名〉 cotton-padded cap
【棉农】miánnóng〈名〉 cotton grower
【棉皮鞋】miánpíxié〈名〉 warmly-lined leather shoes
【棉签】miánqiān〈名〉 **1**［医学］ cotton applicator **2**（指日用品） cotton bud: 用～掏耳朵 use a cotton bud to clear the ears
【棉球】miánqiú〈名〉 cotton ball
【棉绒】miánróng〈名〉 cotton velvet
【棉纱】miánshā〈名〉 cotton yarn
【棉桃】miántáo〈名〉 cotton boll
【棉线】miánxiàn〈名〉 cotton thread: 一卷/轴缝纫～ a reel of sewing cotton
【棉鞋】miánxié〈名〉 cotton-padded shoes
【棉絮】miánxù〈名〉 **1**（指纤维） cotton fibre: ～状的白云 fluffy white cloud **2**（指内胎） cotton wadding
【棉蚜虫】miányáchóng〈名〉 cotton aphid
【棉衣】miányī〈名〉 cotton-padded clothes
【棉织品】miánzhīpǐn〈名〉 cotton fabrics
【棉子】miánzǐ〈名〉 cottonseed: ～油 cottonseed oil
【棉籽】miánzǐ = 棉子 miánzǐ

miǎn

丏 miǎn〈动〉〈书〉 cover

免 miǎn〈动〉 **1**（免除） exempt: ～服兵役 be exempt from military service ‖ ～签证 exempt from a visa ‖ ～受惩罚 be immune from punishment ‖ ～收一切费用 be excused from paying the total amount ▸～礼, ～试, ～税 **2**（除掉） dismiss from a post: ▸～疫, 在所难～ **3**（不要） be not allowed: 闲人～进 staff only ▸～开尊口
【免不得】miǎnbude = 免不了 miǎnbuliǎo
【免不了】miǎnbuliǎo〈动〉 be unavoidable: 工作中～要得罪人。 You are bound to offend people in the course of your work. ‖ 一生中～会有失败和挫折。 Failures and setbacks are inevitable in life.
【免除】miǎnchú〈动〉 **1**（避免） avoid: ～隐患 remove a hidden peril ‖ 兴修水利可有效～水旱灾害。 Building irrigation works can effectively prevent droughts and floods. **2**（除掉） exempt: ～罚款/债务 forgive a fine/debt ‖ ～烦恼 relieve sb. of their worries
【免得】miǎnde〈连〉 so as to avoid: 带上雨衣，～淋雨。 Take a raincoat so you don't get drenched. ‖ 早点起来，～饿着肚子上课。 Get up early so that you will not have to go to the lecture on an empty stomach.
【免费】miǎnfèi〈动〉 be free of charge: ～参观展览 be admitted to the exhibition free of charge ‖ ～入学 be enrolled with one's tuition waived ‖ ～送货 free delivery ‖ ～医疗 free medical care ‖ ～安装。 There will be no charge for installation.
【免耕农业】miǎngēng nóngyè〈名〉 till-less agriculture
【免官】miǎnguān〈动〉 remove from official position
【免冠】miǎnguān **A**〈动〉 take one's hat off in salutation **B**〈形〉 bare-headed: 半身～正面相片 half-length, bare-headed, full-faced photo
【免检】miǎnjiǎn〈动〉 be exempt from inspection: ～物品 goods exempt from inspection
【免开尊口】miǎnkāizūnkǒu〈成〉 keep one's mouth shut
【免考】miǎnkǎo = 免试 miǎnshì
【免礼】miǎnlǐ〈动〉〈套〉 dispense with politenesses
【免赔额】miǎnpéi'é〈名〉 excess〈英〉; deductable〈美〉: 车损～ car damage excess
【免票】miǎnpiào **A**〈名〉 free ticket **B**〈动〉 be free of charge: 身高不满1.1米的儿童坐火车～。 Children under 1.1 metres take the train free of charge.
【免试】miǎnshì〈动〉 be exempt from an examination: ～入学 be admitted to a school without sitting the entrance examination ‖ ～外语 be exempt from the foreign language examination
【免税】miǎnshuì〈动〉 exempt from taxation: ～放行 release without payment of duty ‖ ～商店 duty-free shop
【免税额】miǎnshuì'é〈名〉 tax allowance: 1,000美元的～ exemption of $1,000
【免税区】miǎnshuìqū〈名〉 free zone
【免俗】miǎnsú〈动〉 act contrary to prevailing practice: 不能～ be unable to depart from convention
【免烫】miǎntàng〈动〉[of clothes] be unable to be ironed: ～衬衣 drip-dry shirt
【免提电话】miǎntí diànhuà〈名〉 hands-free phone
【免提键】miǎntíjiàn〈名〉hands-free button
【免刑】miǎnxíng〈动〉［法律］ be exempt from punishment
【免修】miǎnxiū〈动〉 be excused from a required course: ～英语 be exempt from required English courses
【免验】miǎnyàn〈动〉 be exempt from examination: ～产品 products exempt from examination ‖ ～放行 pass without examination
【免役】miǎnyì〈动〉 be exempt from military service
【免疫】miǎnyì〈动〉［医学］ immunize
【免疫力】miǎnyìlì〈名〉 immunity: 增强～ improve one's immunity
【免疫缺陷】miǎnyì quēxiàn〈名〉 immunodeficiency
【免疫系统】miǎnyì xìtǒng〈名〉 immune system
【免疫学】miǎnyìxué〈名〉 immunology: ～家 immunologist
【免予】miǎnyǔ〈动〉 exempt: ～处分 be

exempt from punishment ‖ ～起诉 be exempt from prosecution

【免责】miǎnzé〈动〉 exonerate: 不存在～的可能。 There's no chance of exemption.

【免战牌】miǎnzhànpái〈名〉tablet of truce: 挂～ beg off from a battle

【免征】miǎnzhēng〈动〉 be exempt from taxation: ～农业税 be exempted from agricultural tax

【免职】miǎnzhí〈动〉 relieve sb. of his post: 他因玩忽职守被～。 He has been dismissed from office because of dereliction of duty.

【免罪】miǎnzuì〈动〉 exempt from punishment: ～释放 be exempt from punishment and released

眄

miǎn variant pronunciation for 眄 miàn

勉

miǎn〈动〉 1（努力） exert oneself: ▸奋～, 勤～ 2（勉励） encourage: 互～ encourage one another ‖ 自～ spur oneself on ▸～励, 共～ 3（勉强） strive to do what seems beyond one's power: ▸～强, ～为其难

【勉力】miǎnlì〈动〉 exert oneself: ～而为 do one's best

【勉励】miǎnlì〈动〉 encourage: ～某人努力工作 urge sb. to work hard ‖ 在同事的～下，他参加了竞选。 Urged on by his colleagues, he stood for election.

【勉强】miǎnqiǎng A〈动〉 1（指能力不够） do with difficulty: ～凑足了钱上大学 scrape together enough money for a college education ‖ 他～把那个沉重的箱子搬了起来。 With some difficulty he lifted up the heavy trunk. 2（强迫） force: 他决不～别人接纳自己。 He'd never think of imposing himself on others. B〈形〉 1（不情愿） reluctant: ～同意赔款协议 reluctantly agree to the indemnity clause ‖ 他很～地道了歉。 He apologized grudgingly. 2（牵强） unconvincing: 他的证据很～。 His evidence is rather unconvincing. C〈副〉 barely: ～维持生计 eke out a living ‖ 他考试～及格。 He only just scraped through the examination.

【勉为其难】miǎnwéiqínán〈成〉 undertake to do a difficult job as best as one can

娩

miǎn〈动〉 give birth to a child: ▸分～

冕

miǎn〈名〉 1（皇冠） royal crown; （礼帽） official hat: ▸冠～堂皇, 加～ 2〈喻〉（第一） first place: ▸卫～

湎

miǎn〈动〉〈书〉 be given to: ～于酒色 indulge in sensual pleasures ▸沉～

缅（緬）

miǎn〈形〉 remote: ▸～怀, ～想

【缅甸】Miǎndiàn〈名〉 Burma: ～联邦 Union of Myanmar ‖ ～人 Burmese ‖ ～语 Burmese

【缅因州】Miǎnyīnzhōu〈名〉 Maine

【缅怀】miǎnhuái〈动〉 cherish the memory of: ～烈士们的英雄事迹 recall the heroic deeds of the martyrs ‖ ～先父 cherish the memory of one's dead father

【缅想】miǎnxiǎng = 缅怀 miǎnhuái

腼

miǎn

【腼腆】miǎntiǎn〈形〉 shy: ～的孩子 bashful child ‖ 第一次见公婆，她有些～。 She was bashful in the presence of her parents-in-law for the first time.

miàn

面[1] miàn

A〈名〉 1（脸） face: ～带喜色 have a happy look on one's face ‖ 汗流满～ perspiration all over one's face ▸～孔, 见～ 2（表面） surface: 大理石～桌子 marble-topped table ‖ 湖～ surface of a lake 3（前部） front: 店～ shop front ▸门～ 4（外侧） outside: ▸背～, 封～, 鞋～ 5［数学］ surface: 点、线、～ points, lines and surfaces 6（方面） side: 硬币的正反～ obverse and reverse sides of a coin ▸～～俱到, 片～, 正～ 7（范围） extent: 知识～宽 have a wide range of knowledge

B〈动〉 1（朝着） face: 背山～水 fronting a river and backing onto a hill ‖ 寺庙坐北～南。 The temple faces the south. 2（见面） meet: ▸～世, 谋～

C〈副〉 personally: ～交（某人） present personally (to sb.) ▸～试, ～谈

D〈后缀〉 [used to form a noun of locality]: ▸前～, 上～, 右～

E〈量〉 1（指扁平物） [used for flags, mirrors, etc.]: 两～国旗/镜子 two national flags/mirrors ‖ 一～鼓 a drum 2（指次数） [used for times to meet sb.]: 见过两～ have met sb. twice

面[2]（麵、麪） miàn

A〈名〉 1（面粉） (wheat) flour: 和/揉～ knead/make dough ‖ 玉米～ cornmeal ▸～茶, ～条, 米～ 2（面条） noodles: ▸拌～, 方便～, 挂～ 3（粉状物） powder: 胡椒～ ground pepper

B〈形〉〈方〉 soft and mealy: 这个瓜很～。 This melon is very soft and mealy.

【面案】miàn'àn〈名〉 1（案板） table on which flour is mixed and kneaded 2（白案） work involved in Chinese cooking

【面包】miànbāo〈名〉 bread: 烤～ toast bread

【面包车】miànbāochē〈名〉 minivan

【面包店】miànbāodiàn〈名〉 bakery

【面包房】miànbāofáng〈名〉 bakery

【面包干】miànbāogān〈名〉 rusk

【面包果】miànbāoguǒ〈名〉［植物］ breadfruit (tree)

【面包圈】miànbāoquān〈名〉 doughnut

【面包师】miànbāoshī ▸**p. 966**〈名〉 baker

【面包屑】miànbāoxiè〈名〉 breadcrumb

【面壁】miànbì〈动〉 1［佛教］ face the wall and meditate;〈喻〉 study with undivided attention 2（脸对墙） stand facing the wall

【面不改色】miànbùgǎisè〈成〉 not turn a hair: ～心不跳 remain absolutely calm

【面部】miànbù〈名〉 face: ～表情 facial expression ‖ ～按摩 facial massage

【面茶】miànchá〈名〉［食品］ seasoned flour mush: 沏一碗～ make a bowl of seasoned flour mush

【面陈】miànchén〈动〉 tell personally

【面呈】miànchéng〈动〉 submit in person

【面的】miàndī〈名〉〈口〉minivan [used as a cheap taxi]: 打～ take a minivan taxi

【面点】miàndiǎn〈名〉 pastry made from wheat flour: 西式～ western-style pastry

【面对】miànduì〈动〉 face: ～现实 face reality ‖ ～新的挑战 face new challenges

【面对面】miànduìmiàn〈副〉 face-to-face: ～坐着 sit face-to-face ‖ 举行～的谈判 have a face-to-face bargaining session

【面额】miàn'é〈名〉 face value: 大/小～纸币 notes of small/large denominations ‖ ～20元的人民币 *Renminbi* in 20-*yuan* notes

【面坊】miànfáng〈名〉 flour mill

【面肥】miànféi〈名〉 leavening dough

【面粉】miànfěn〈名〉 (wheat) flour: 精白～ white flour ‖ 普通～ plain flour

【面疙瘩】miàngēda〈名〉 balls of dough: ～汤 dough ball soup

【面馆】miànguǎn〈名〉 noodle restaurant

【面和心不和】miàn hé xīn bùhé〈俗〉 remain friendly in appearance but estranged at heart

【面红耳赤】miànhóng-ěrchì〈成〉be red in the face: 羞得～ blush with shame

【面糊】miànhù〈名〉 flour paste

【面糊】miànhu〈形〉 soft and floury

【面黄肌瘦】miànhuáng-jīshòu〈成〉 sallow and emaciated

【面积】miànjī〈名〉 area: 建筑～ built-up area ‖ 小麦种植～ area under wheat cultivation

【面颊】miànjiá〈名〉 cheek: ～红润 have rosy cheeks

【面交】miànjiāo〈动〉 hand-deliver

【面巾】miànjīn〈名〉〈方〉 facecloth

【面巾纸】miànjīnzhǐ〈名〉 tissue

【面筋】miànjin〈名〉［食品］ gluten

【面具】miànjù〈名〉 mask: 防毒～ gas mask ‖ 撕下伪善的～ unmask hypocrisy

【面孔】miànkǒng〈名〉 face: 板起～ keep a straight face ‖ 熟悉/陌生的～ familiar/strange face

【面料】miànliào〈名〉 1（布料） fabric for making clothing: 大衣～ material for making overcoats 2（材料） veneer: 家具～ material for furniture veneer

【面临】miànlín〈动〉 be faced with: ～激烈竞争 be up against fierce competition ‖ ～重大选择 be confronted with an important choice

【面貌】miànmào〈名〉 1（相貌） features: ～清秀 have delicate features ‖ 兄弟俩～相似。 The two brothers look alike. 2（状态） appearance: ～一新 take on an entirely new look ‖ 精神～ mental outlook ‖ 改变一穷二白的～ overhaul a state of poverty and blankness

【面面观】miànmiànguān〈名〉[often used in the title of an essay] comprehensive survey: 《婚姻问题～》 *An Overview of Marriage*

【面面俱到】miànmiàn-jùdào〈成〉 try to cover every aspect: 写文章切忌～。 In your writing you should guard against attempts to cover every aspect of the topic.

【面面相觑】miànmiàn-xiāngqù〈成〉 look at each other in surprise

【面膜】miànmó〈名〉 face pack

【面目】miànmù〈名〉 1（相貌） appearance: ～清秀 be of fine and delicate features ‖ ～可憎 have ugly facial features 2（状态） aspect: 恢复历史的本来～ restore the historical truth ‖ 露出本来～ show one's true colours ▸庐山真～ 3（颜面） face: 有何～去见江东父老 feel ashamed to face the people in one's hometown

【面目全非】miànmù-quánfēi〈成〉〈贬〉 be changed beyond recognition: 那堵墙被涂画得～。 The wall has been defaced with graffiti.

【面目一新】miànmù-yīxīn〈成〉 take on an entirely new look

【面目狰狞】miànmù-zhēngníng〈成〉 ferocious features

【面嫩】miànnèn〈形〉1（不显老）younger than one's age: 他看上去～。He looks younger than his age. 2（脸皮薄）shy

【面庞】miànpáng〈名〉face: 圆圆的～round face

【面盆】miànpén〈名〉〈方〉washbasin

【面皮】miànpí〈名〉〈方〉1（脸皮）cheek: ～薄 sensitive ‖ ～厚 cheeky 2（指面食）wrapper (of *jiaozi*, *baozi* or *wonton*)

【面片儿】miànpiànr〈名〉dough strips

【面洽】miànqià〈动〉〈书〉take up a matter with sb. personally: ～事宜 discuss matters with sb. face to face

【面前】miànqián〈名〉presence: 在困难～不低头 not yield to difficulties ‖ 法律～人人平等。All men are equal before the law.

【面人儿】miànrénr〈名〉dough figurine: 捏～ sculpt dough figurines

【面容】miànróng〈名〉countenance: 毁坏～ disfigure ‖ 慈祥的～ kindly face

【面如死灰】miànrúsǐhuī〈成〉be deathly pale

【面如土色】miànrútǔsè〈成〉look pale: 她吓得～。She went deathly pale with fright.

【面软】miànruǎn〈形〉shy

【面色】miànsè〈名〉complexion: ～苍白 look pale ‖ ～红润 have rosy cheeks

【面纱】miànshā〈名〉1（指纱）thin veil: 戴～ wear a veil ‖ 新娘的～ bridal veil 2〈喻〉veil: 揭开所谓慈善家的神秘～ lift the veil on so-called philanthropists

【面善】miànshàn〈形〉1（面熟）familiar: 她看着很～。She looks familiar. 2（面容和蔼）affable: ～心慈 affable and kind-hearted ‖ ～心险 be a wolf in sheep's clothing

【面商】miànshāng〈动〉discuss with sb. face to face

【面神经】miànshénjīng〈名〉［生理］facial nerve

【面生】miànshēng〈形〉unfamiliar: 我觉得她很～。Her face was unfamiliar to me.

【面食】miànshí〈名〉wheaten food: 他喜欢～，不爱吃米饭。He prefers wheaten food to rice.

【面世】miànshì〈动〉come out: 他的新小说下月～。His new novel will be published next month.

【面市】miànshì〈动〉be put on sale: 一款新车下月～。A new model of the car goes on sale next month.

【面试】miànshì〈动〉interview: ～小组 interview panel ‖ 通过～后，公司破格录用了他。After the interview, the corporation broke a rule and took him on.

【面首】miànshǒu〈名〉〈书〉gigolo

【面授】miànshòu〈动〉1（指传授）instruct personally: ▸～机宜 2（指讲课）conduct classroom teaching

【面授机宜】miànshòu-jīyí〈成〉brief sb. on how to act

【面熟】miànshú〈形〉familiar: 他看着～，可我想不起他的名字。He looks familiar, but I can't recall his name.

【面塑】miànsù〈名〉［美术］dough modelling

【面谈】miàntán〈动〉talk with sb. face to face: 与经理～ have an interview with the manager

【面汤】miàntāng〈名〉1〈方〉（洗脸水）hot water for washing face 2（面条汤）water in which noodles have been boiled

【面条】miàntiáo〈名〉noodles

【面团】miàntuán〈名〉paste

【面无惧色】miànwújùsè〈成〉show no sign of fear

【面无人色】miànwúrénsè〈成〉be (as) pale as death: 吓得～ so frightened that one's face has gone ashen

【面晤】miànwù〈动〉〈书〉meet in person

【面向】miànxiàng〈动〉1（面对）face: 我卧室的窗户～花园。My bedroom window faces the garden. 2（针对）be geared to the needs of: ～市场 be market-oriented

【面相】miànxiàng〈名〉facial features: 看～，他是个老师。He had the look of a teacher.

【面谢】miànxiè〈动〉thank sb. in person

【面叙】miànxù〈动〉talk face to face

【面议】miànyì〈动〉negotiate face to face: 工资待遇～。We'll discuss your salary and benefits face to face.

【面有菜色】miànyǒu-càisè〈成〉look famished

【面有难色】miànyǒu-nánsè〈成〉appear to be reluctant

【面谕】miànyù〈动〉[of a superior] instruct sb. in person

【面誉背毁】miànyù-bèihuǐ〈成〉praise sb. to their face and abuse them behind their back

【面源】miànyuán〈名〉area source: 防治农业～污染 control agricultural area source pollution

【面罩】miànzhào〈名〉mask: 电焊～ welding mask ‖ 氧气～ oxygen mask

【面值】miànzhí〈名〉1（指有价证券）face value 2（指钱币）denomination

【面砖】miànzhuān〈名〉［建筑］face brick

【面子】miànzi〈名〉1（表面）outer part: 被～ outside (fabric) of a quilt 2（虚荣）reputation: 爱～ like to keep up appearances 3（情面）feelings: 失～ lose face ‖ 给～ show respect for sb.'s feelings ‖ 不顾～ show no consideration for sb.'s feelings ‖ 留～ spare sb.'s feelings

眄 miàn〈动〉〈书〉cast sidelong glances at sb.

【眄视】miànshì〈动〉〈书〉give a sidelong glance

miāo

喵 miāo〈拟〉miaow: 猫～～叫。A cat mews.

miáo

苗[1] miáo〈名〉1（指植物）seedling: 补～ fill the gaps with seedlings ‖ 间～ thin out young shoots ▸～圃，麦～，育～，蒜～ 2（后代）descendant: 他是这家的独～儿。He is the only son and heir of this family. ▸～裔 3（迹象）symptom of a trend: 祸～ root cause of a disaster ▸～头，矿～ 4（指动物）young: ▸鱼～ 5（疫苗）vaccine: ▸卡介～，牛痘～ 6（苗状物）sth. resembling a young plant: ▸火～

苗[2] Miáo〈名〉Miao ethnic group: ～绣 Miao embroidery ‖ ～语 Miao language

【苗床】miáochuáng〈名〉nursery bed: ～播种机 nursery bed planter

【苗而不秀】miáo'érbùxiù〈成〉〈喻〉show great potential but fail to produce any result

【苗剧】miáojù〈名〉Miao opera

【苗木】miáomù〈名〉［林业］nursery stock

【苗圃】miáopǔ〈名〉nursery garden

【苗期】miáoqī〈名〉［农业］seedling stage: ～管理 seedling management

【苗情】miáoqíng〈名〉growth of seedlings

【苗条】miáotiao〈形〉slim: 身材～ have a slender figure

【苗头】miáotou〈名〉symptom of a trend: 好/坏～ symptom of a good/bad trend ‖ 我们要注意不良倾向的～。We should watch out for symptoms of unhealthy tendencies.

【苗裔】miáoyì〈名〉〈书〉descendants: 炎黄～ descendants of Yandi and Huangdi [two legendary founders of the Chinese nation]

【苗子】miáozi〈名〉1〈本〉〈方〉seedling: 麦～ wheat seedlings ‖ 树～ tree seedlings 2〈喻〉young successor: 这男孩是踢球的好～。The boy is showing great promise at football.

【苗族】Miáozú〈名〉Miao ethnic group

描 miáo〈动〉1（画）copy: ～图样 trace designs ‖ ～一幅画 copy a painting ▸～红，～画，～绘 2（涂抹）touch up: 写毛笔字不要来回～。When writing Chinese characters with a brush, don't go over the strokes again and again.

【描红】miáohóng A〈动〉trace in black ink over the strokes of model Chinese characters printed in red [in learning to write with a brush]: 练毛笔字，先～，后临帖。While practising Chinese calligraphy, one should first trace the model characters before going on to imitate a calligraphy copybook. B〈名〉sheet printed with red characters, to be traced over, usu by children learning calligraphy

【描红本】miáohóngběn〈名〉calligraphy exercise book

【描画】miáohuà〈动〉draw: ～美好前景 paint a bright future ‖ ～蓝图 draw a blueprint

【描绘】miáohuì〈动〉depict: 把人物～得栩栩如生 portray the characters in a lifelike way ‖ ～场景/景色 paint a scene/landscape

【描金】miáojīn〈动〉［美术］trace a design in gold

【描摹】miáomó〈动〉1（用笔）trace: 练毛笔字，～临帖不可少。In practising Chinese calligraphy, one should trace and imitate characters written by famous calligraphers. 2（用文字）depict

【描述】miáoshù〈动〉describe: ～所见所闻 describe what one has seen and heard ‖ 非笔墨所能～ be beyond description

【描图】miáotú〈动〉trace (an engineering drawing)

【描写】miáoxiě〈动〉depict: ～景色/人物 describe a landscape/a character ‖ 栩栩如生的～ vivid picture

【描写语言学】miáoxiě yǔyánxué〈名〉descriptive linguistics

【描眼笔】miáoyǎnbǐ〈名〉eyeliner

鹋（鶓） miáo ▸鸸鹋 érmiáo

瞄 miáo〈动〉take aim at: ～靶子 take aim at the target ‖ 偷偷地～一眼答案 steal a glance at the answer ▸～准

【瞄准】miáozhǔn〈动〉1（指射击）aim at: ～靶心 aim at the bull's-eye ‖ 用大炮～敌人的阵地 train artillery on the enemy's positions 2（对准）cater to: ～欧洲市场 cater to the European market

miǎo

杪 miǎo〈名〉〈书〉**1**（树梢） tip of a twig on a tree: 树～ tree top **2**（末期） end (of a year, month or season): 秋～ end of autumn ‖ 岁～ end of the year

眇 miǎo〈形〉〈书〉**1**（瞎） blind: 目～耳聋 be both blind and deaf **2**（小） tiny: ～小 tiny

秒 miǎo〈量〉**1**（指时间） second: 一分零九～ one minute nine seconds ▸争分夺～ **2**（指弧度） second **3**（指经纬度） second

【秒表】miǎobiǎo〈名〉 stopwatch

【秒针】miǎozhēn〈名〉 second hand

淼 miǎo〈形〉〈书〉 [of an expanse of water] vast: ▸浩～

【淼茫】miǎománg〈形〉 [of an expanse of water] vast

渺 miǎo〈形〉**1**（水大） vast: ▸烟波浩～ **2**（渺茫） vague: ～无人烟 uninhabited ‖ 他走后一直～无音信。 After he left he was never heard of again. **3**（渺小） tiny: ～不足道 insignificant ▸～小

【渺茫】miǎománg〈形〉 **1**（模糊不清） vague: 她出国后音信～。 We haven't heard from her since she went abroad. **2**（不确定） uncertain: 前途～ have an uncertain future ‖ 希望～ have a slim hope ‖ 他获胜的希望相当～。 The odds against him winning are rather long.

【渺小】miǎoxiǎo〈形〉 insignificant: 个人的力量是～的。 The strength of an individual is insignificant.

缈（緲） miǎo ▸缥缈 piāomiǎo

藐 miǎo〈形〉 small: ▸～视

【藐视】miǎoshì〈动〉 look down upon: ～法庭罪 contempt of court ‖ 战略上要～敌人，战术上要重视敌人。 Strategically we should condemn our enemies, but tactically we should take them seriously.

【藐小】miǎoxiǎo〈形〉 tiny: 这件事很～，不足挂齿。 It's a trivial thing, not worth mentioning.

邈 miǎo〈形〉〈书〉 remote: ～然 distant

【邈远】miǎoyuǎn〈形〉 distant: ～的古代 remote ages ‖ ～的天际 distant horizon

miào

妙 miào〈形〉**1**（好） fine and subtle: 深得其中之～ have got the trick of it ▸奥～, 精～, 莫名其～, 灵丹～药 **2**（神奇） excellent: ～极了 wonderful ‖ 情况不～。 The situation is not very encouraging. ▸～不可言, ～龄, ～语如珠

【妙笔】miàobǐ〈名〉 ingenious or exquisite writing

【妙笔生花】miàobǐ-shēnghuā〈成〉 ingenious writing with exquisite description

【妙不可言】miàobùkěyán〈成〉 too wonderful for words: 那里的景色～。 The scenery there is beautiful beyond words.

【妙计】miàojì〈名〉 ingenious plot: 顿生～ hit upon a smart idea ▸锦囊～

【妙境】miàojìng〈名〉 wonderland

【妙句】miàojù〈名〉 beautiful sentence

【妙诀】miàojué〈名〉 knack: 得到～ acquire an ingenious method

【妙龄】miàolíng〈名〉 youth: ～女郎 woman in the flower of her youth ‖ ～少女 young charming girl

【妙论】miàolùn〈名〉 clever remarks

【妙棋】miàoqí〈名〉 clever (chess) move

【妙趣】miàoqù〈名〉 charming wit: ～天成 natural wit and humour

【妙趣横生】miàoqù-héngshēng〈成〉 full of wit and humour: 言谈～ have a witty turn of phrase

【妙手】miàoshǒu〈名〉 highly skilled person: ～偶得 get sth. by chance with rare skill

【妙手回春】miàoshǒu-huíchūn〈成〉 [of a doctor] effect a miraculous cure and bring the dying back to life

【妙算】miàosuàn〈名〉 ingenious plan: ▸神机～

【妙药】miàoyào〈名〉 wonder drug: ▸灵丹～

【妙用】miàoyòng〈名〉 magical effect: 计算机大有～。 Computers can work wonders.

【妙语】miàoyǔ〈名〉 witty remark: ～惊人 surprisingly witty remarks

【妙语解颐】miàoyǔ-jiěyí〈成〉 witty remarks that make people laugh

【妙语如珠】miàoyǔ-rúzhū〈成〉 a stream of witticisms

【妙招】miàozhāo〈名〉 clever move

【妙着】miàozhāo = 妙招 miàozhāo

庙（廟） miào〈名〉**1**（用于供奉） temple: 山神～ mountain god temple ▸孔～, 寺～, 宗～ **2**〈书〉（朝廷） imperial court: ▸～堂 **3**（庙号） posthumous title of an emperor: ▸～号 **4**（庙会） temple fair: ▸～会

【庙号】miàohào〈名〉 posthumous title of an emperor

【庙会】miàohuì〈名〉 temple fair: 赶～ go to a temple fair ‖ 逛～ stroll around a temple fair

【庙堂】miàotáng〈名〉**1**（用于供奉） temple **2**〈书〉（朝廷） imperial court

【庙宇】miàoyǔ〈名〉 temple

【庙主】miàozhǔ〈名〉**1**（指人） head Buddhist monk or Taoist priest in charge of a temple **2**〈书〉（指牌位） memorial tablet

【庙祝】miàozhù〈名〉 temple attendant

缪（繆） Miào〈名〉 Miao [surname] ▸miù, móu

miē

乜 miē ▸Niè

【乜斜】miēxie〈动〉**1**〈方〉（指斜视） squint (at): ～着眼睛看 take a squint (at sb./sth.) **2**（指眯眼） be half-closed: ～的睡眼 half-closed eyes heavy with sleep

咩 miē〈拟〉 baa: 小羊～～叫。 The lamb bleated.

miè

灭（滅） miè〈动〉**1**（熄灭） go out: 灯～了。 The light went out. ‖ 炉子～了。 The stove has gone out. **2**（使熄灭） extinguish: 把灯～了 turn off the light ▸～火器 **3**（淹没） drown: ▸～顶 **4**（消亡） disappear: ▸自生自～ **5**（除去） exterminate: ～草/虫/鼠 kill off weeds/insects/rats ‖ ～敌人的威风 deflate the arrogance of the enemy

【灭此朝食】mièců-zhāoshí〈成〉 be anxious to finish off the enemy at the earliest opportunity

【灭顶】mièdǐng〈动〉 be completely overwhelmed: 遭受～之灾 be completely annihilated

【灭火】mièhuǒ〈动〉 extinguish a fire

【灭火器】mièhuǒqì〈名〉 fire extinguisher

【灭迹】mièjì〈动〉 destroy the evidence: 焚尸～ burn the corpse so as to destroy the evidence ‖ 销赃～ destroy the evidence by disposing of the stolen goods

【灭绝】mièjué〈动〉**1**（指消灭） wipe out: 濒于～ be on the verge of extinction ‖ ～的物种 extinct species **2**（指丧失） lose completely: ～人性 brutal

【灭口】mièkǒu〈动〉 do away with a witness to prevent leakage of information: 杀人～ silence a witness by killing him

【灭门】mièmén〈动〉 kill off the entire family: 遭～之祸 suffer the calamity of one's family being exterminated

【灭亡】mièwáng〈动〉 be destroyed: 濒于～ be on the brink of extinction ‖ 注定要～ be doomed to extinction ▸自取～

【灭种】mièzhǒng〈动〉**1**（指人） commit genocide: 亡国～ national doom and racial extinction **2**（指动植物） become extinct: 秃鹰是一种面临～的鸟类。 The bald eagle is an endangered species.

【灭族】mièzú〈动〉〈古〉 exterminate a clan (as punishment)

蔑[1] miè〈形〉〈书〉 small: ▸～视, 轻～

蔑[2]**（衊）** miè〈动〉 smear: ▸诬～

【蔑称】mièchēng **A**〈动〉 address sb. scornfully **B**〈名〉 contemptuous name

【蔑视】mièshì〈动〉 scorn: ～困难 scorn difficulties ‖ ～世俗 show contempt for social norms

篾 miè〈名〉**1**（竹片） thin bamboo strip: ▸～席, 竹～ **2**（指苇子或高粱秆） outer skin of reeds or sorghum stalks

【篾刀】mièdāo〈名〉 bamboo splitter

【篾黄】mièhuáng〈名〉 inner skin of a bamboo stem

【篾匠】mièjiàng〈名〉 bamboo craftsman

【篾片】mièpiàn〈名〉 thin bamboo strip

【篾青】mièqīng〈名〉 outer skin of a bamboo stem

【篾条】miètiáo〈名〉 bamboo strip for weaving

【篾席】mièxí〈名〉 mat made of thin bamboo strips

mín

民 mín〈名〉**1**（人民） the people: ▸～众, 人～ **2**（民间） folk: ▸～风, ～歌, ～谣 **3**（民族） member of an ethnic

group: 藏～ Tibetan ▸汉～, 回～ 4（从事者） person of a certain occupation: 股～ stock investor ‖ 烟～ smoker ▸牧～, 农～, 渔～ 5（非军方） civilian: 军转～ [of a factory or firm] change from military production to civilian production ▸～航

【民办】mínbàn A〈动〉 be run by the local people: ～公助 run by the private sector and subsidized by the state B〈形〉 privately-run: ～企业 community-run enterprise ‖ ～学校 community-run school

【民兵】mínbīng〈名〉 militia: 女～ female militia member

【民不聊生】mínbùliáoshēng〈成〉 the masses live in dire poverty: 横征暴敛, ～。 Exorbitant taxes and levies made life impossible for the common people.

【民法】mínfǎ〈名〉 civil law: ～大全 corpus of the civil law

【民法通则】mínfǎ tōngzé〈名〉 general principles of civil law

【民法总则】mínfǎ zǒngzé〈名〉 general provisions of civil law

【民防】mínfáng〈名〉 civil defence

【民房】mínfáng〈名〉 private house: 侵占～ seize a private house

【民愤】mínfèn〈名〉 public indignation: 激起～ arouse public anger ‖ 不杀不足以平～ have to execute a criminal to assuage public wrath

【民风】mínfēng〈名〉 local ways: ～淳朴。 The people are simple, honest and unspoiled.

【民夫】mínfū〈名〉〈旧〉 corvée labourer

【民富国强】mínfù-guóqiáng〈成〉 the people are wealthy and the nation is strong

【民歌】míngē〈名〉 folk song: ～手 folk singer ‖ ～节 folk song festival

【民革】Míngé〈简称〉= 中国国民党革命委员会

【民工】míngōng〈名〉 1（建筑工）labourer working on a public project 2（打工者） farmer labourer: ～潮 massive influx of rural labourers into towns

【民工荒】míngōnghuāng〈名〉 migrant worker shortage: 东莞、深圳又出现～。 There's another shortage of migrant labour in Dongguan and Shenzhen.

【民国】Mínguó〈名〉 Republic of China [1912-1949]: ～初年 in the early years of the Chinese Republic

【民航】mínháng〈名〉 civil aviation: ～班机 civil airliner ‖ 中国～总局 CAAC (Civil Aviation Administration of China)

【民间】mínjiān〈形〉 1（民众中间） popular: ～疾苦 hardships of the people ‖ 在～广为流传 spread far and wide among the people 2（非官方） non-governmental: ～往来 non-governmental exchange ‖ ～组织 non-governmental organization (NGO)

【民间传说】mínjiān chuánshuō〈名〉 folk tale

【民间故事】mínjiān gùshi〈名〉 folk tale

【民间贸易】mínjiān màoyì〈名〉 non-governmental trade

【民间团体】mínjiān tuántǐ〈名〉 non-governmental organization (NGO)

【民间文学】mínjiān wénxué〈名〉 folk literature

【民间艺术】mínjiān yìshù〈名〉 folk art

【民间资本】mínjiān zīběn〈名〉 private capital

【民建】Mínjiàn〈简称〉= 中国民主建国会

【民进】Mínjìn〈简称〉= 中国民主促进会

【民警】mínjǐng〈名〉 police: 女～ policewoman

【民居】mínjū〈名〉 civilian residence

【民康物阜】mínkāng-wùfù〈成〉 the people live in peace and products abound

【民力】mínlì〈名〉〈书〉 financial resources of the people: 珍惜～ treasure the financial resources of the people

【民盟】Mínméng〈简称〉= 中国民主同盟

【民女】mínnǚ〈名〉〈旧〉 girl from an ordinary family

【民品】mínpǐn〈名〉 products for civilian use: 许多军工企业转产～。 Many military enterprises are shifting to production of goods for civilian use.

【民气】mínqì〈名〉〈书〉 popular morale: ～激昂。 Public feeling is high.

【民情】mínqíng〈名〉 1（指情况） situation of the people: 了解～ learn about the people's situation ‖ 熟悉当地的风土～ be familiar with local conditions, customs and the people 2（指感受） public feeling: 体恤～ show concern for public feeling

【民权】mínquán〈名〉 civil rights: 侵犯～ violate democratic rights ‖ 享有～ enjoy civil rights ‖ ～运动 civil rights movement

【民权法案】mínquán fǎ'àn〈名〉civil rights bill

【民生】mínshēng〈名〉 people's livelihood: ～凋敝 the people live in destitution ▸国计～

【民声】mínshēng〈名〉 voice of the people: 倾听～ hear the voice of the people ‖ 讨论民生问题, 不能忽视～。 When discussing people's livelihood, the voice of the people cannot be ignored.

【民事】mínshì〈形〉［法律］ civil: ～案件 civil case ‖ ～纠纷 civil dispute

【民事法庭】mínshì fǎtíng〈名〉 civil court

【民事管辖权】mínshì guǎnxiáquán〈名〉 civil jurisdiction

【民事豁免】mínshì huòmiǎn〈名〉 civil immunity

【民事能力】mínshì nénglì〈名〉 civil capacity

【民事判决】mínshì pànjué〈名〉civil judgement: ～书 paper of civil judgement

【民事权利】mínshì quánlì〈名〉 civil rights: 依法享有～, 承担民事义务 enjoy civil rights and bear civil obligations in accordance with the law

【民事诉讼】mínshì sùsòng〈名〉 civil action: ～法 civil procedure law

【民事调解】mínshì tiáojiě〈名〉 civil mediation

【民事义务】mínshì yìwù〈名〉 civil obligation

【民事责任】mínshì zérèn〈名〉 civil liability: 承担～ bear civil liabilities

【民俗】mínsú〈名〉 folkways: 尊重当地～ respect local customs

【民俗学】mínsúxué〈名〉 folklore: ～家 folklorist

【民庭】míntíng〈简称〉= 民事法庭

【民团】míntuán〈名〉〈旧〉 civil corps

【民望】mínwàng〈名〉〈书〉 popular expectation: ～所归 enjoy popular trust

【民委】Mínwěi〈简称〉= 民族事务委员会

【民校】mínxiào〈名〉 1（指供成人业余学习） after-hours school for adults 2（指民间开办） school run by the local people

【民心】mínxīn〈名〉 will of the people: 深得～ enjoy great popularity ‖ ～所向 where the popular will inclines ‖ ～向背 the will of the people

【民选】mínxuǎn〈动〉 be elected by the people: ～代表 representative elected by the people

【民谚】mínyàn〈名〉 popular proverb or saying

【民谣】mínyáo〈名〉 folk song

【民以食为天】mín yǐ shí wéi tiān〈成〉 food is the first necessity of the people

【民意】mínyì〈名〉 popular will: 顺从～ obey the will of the people ‖ ～测验 poll

【民营】mínyíng〈形〉 privately-run: ～企业 privately-run enterprise

【民营经济】mínyíng jīngjì〈名〉 non-state sector

【民用】mínyòng〈形〉 civil: ～产品 products for civilian use ‖ ～航空 civil aviation ‖ ～机场 civil airport

【民怨】mínyuàn〈名〉 popular discontent: ～沸腾 popular grievances run high

【民乐】mínyuè〈名〉 folk music: ～合奏 ensemble of traditional instruments ‖ ～队 band with traditional instruments

【民运】mínyùn〈名〉 1（指民用物资） civil transport 2〈旧〉（指民营运输） private transport service 3（指民众运动） mass movement: ～工作 mass movement work

【民贼】mínzéi〈名〉 traitor to the people: 铲除～ expel traitors ▸独夫～

【民宅】mínzhái〈名〉 private residence: 闯入～ break into a civilian residence

【民政】mínzhèng〈名〉 civil administration: ～部门 civil affairs department ‖ ～事务 civil affairs

【民政部】Mínzhèngbù〈名〉 Ministry of Civil Affairs: ～部长 Minister of Civil Affairs

【民脂民膏】mínzhī-míngāo〈成〉 fruits of the people's toil: 搜刮～ amass great wealth by fleecing the people

【民众】mínzhòng〈名〉 the masses: 唤起～ arouse the masses ‖ 为～服务 serve the general populace

【民主】mínzhǔ A〈名〉 democracy: 加强～政治建设 strengthen democracy and encourage democratic participation ‖ 建立～ establish democracy ‖ 压制～ suppress democracy ‖ 增强～法制观念 enhance people's concept of democracy and the rule of law B〈形〉 democratic: ～管理 democratic management ‖ 作风～ democratic work-style

【民主党】Mínzhǔdǎng〈名〉 Democratic Party [US]: ～党员 Democrat

【民主党派】mínzhǔ dǎngpài〈名〉 democratic parties

【民主革命】mínzhǔ gémìng〈名〉 democratic revolution

【民主集中制】mínzhǔ jízhōngzhì〈名〉 democratic centralism [the organizational principle of the Chinese Communist Party]

【民主监督】mínzhǔ jiāndū〈名〉 democratic supervision

【民主进程】mínzhǔ jìnchéng〈名〉 democratic process

【民主权利】mínzhǔ quánlì〈名〉 democratic rights: 行使～ exercise one's democratic rights

【民主人士】mínzhǔ rénshì〈名〉 democratic personage: 党外～ non-Party democrats

【民主生活】mínzhǔ shēnghuó〈名〉 democratic life (within the Communist Party of China): ～会 democratic life meeting

【民主协商】mínzhǔ xiéshāng〈名〉 democratic consultation: ～制度 democratic consultation system

【民主选举】mínzhǔ xuǎnjǔ〈名〉 democratic election

【民资】mínzī〈名〉 private capital: 杭州湾跨海大桥有～参与建造。 Private capital was used in the construction of Hangzhou Bay Bridge.

【民族】mínzú〈名〉 1（指各种人的共同

体）nation: ～败类 scum of a nation ‖ ～服装 national costume ‖ ～感情 national sentiments ‖ ～工业 national industry ‖ ～团结 national unity ‖ ～遗产 national heritage ‖ ～自尊心 national pride 2（指同文化者的共同体）ethnic group: 中国的56个～ the 56 ethnic groups of China

【民族共同语】mínzú gòngtóngyǔ〈名〉common national language

【民族区域自治】mínzú qūyù zìzhì〈名〉regional autonomy of ethnic groups: 实行～ exercise regional national autonomy

【民族事务委员会】Mínzú Shìwù Wěiyuánhuì〈名〉Ethnic Affairs Commission

【民族文化】mínzú wénhuà〈名〉national culture

【民族学】mínzúxué〈名〉ethnology

【民族音乐】mínzú yīnyuè〈名〉ethnic music

【民族英雄】mínzú yīngxióng〈名〉national hero

【民族运动】mínzú yùndòng〈名〉nationalist movement

【民族政策】mínzú zhèngcè〈名〉policy towards ethnic minorities

【民族主义】mínzúzhǔyì〈名〉nationalism

【民族资本】mínzú zīběn〈名〉national capital: ～家 national capitalist

【民族资产阶级】mínzú zīchǎnjiējí〈名〉national bourgeoisie

旻 mín〈名〉〈书〉1（秋天）autumn 2（天空）sky: 苍～ blue sky ▸～天

【旻天】míntiān〈名〉〈书〉1（秋天）autumn 2（天空）sky

缗（緡） mín

A〈名〉〈书〉cord used to string holed coins together in ancient times: ～钱 stringed coins

B〈量〉string of 1,000 coins: 一～钱 a string of 1,000 coins

mǐn

皿 mǐn ▸器皿 qìmǐn

闵（閔） mǐn = 悯 mǐn

抿¹ mǐn〈动〉smooth with a brush that has been dipped in water/oil: ～头发 smooth one's hair with a wet brush

抿² mǐn〈动〉1（微合）tuck: ～着嘴笑 compress one's lips in a smile ‖ 鸟儿一～翅膀落在树枝上。The bird tucked back its wings and landed on a tree branch. 2（小口喝）sip: ～几口酒 take a few sips of wine

【抿子】mǐnzi〈名〉small hair brush

泯 mǐn〈动〉die out: 良心未～ maintain one's conscience

【泯灭】mǐnmiè〈动〉vanish: 良心～ have no conscience ‖ 留下难以～的印象 leave/make a lasting impression (on sb.)

【泯没】mǐnmò〈动〉sink into oblivion: 英雄们的功绩永远不会～。The contributions of the heroes will never be forgotten.

闽（閩） Mǐn ▸p. 661〈名〉Min [another name for Fujian Province (福建)]: ～南话 Southern Fujian dialect

【闽菜】mǐncài〈名〉Fujian cuisine

【闽剧】mǐnjù〈名〉Fujian opera

【闽语】mǐnyǔ ▸p. 918〈名〉Fujian dialect

悯（憫） mǐn〈动〉feel for: ～其不幸 show sympathy for sb.'s misfortune ▸怜～

【悯惜】mǐnxī〈动〉take pity on: 最可～的是那些无家可归的孩子们。The most pitiable were those homeless children.

【悯恤】mǐnxù〈动〉pity: ～穷人 show compassion for the poor

筤 mǐn〈名〉thin bamboo strip

敏 mǐn〈形〉1（快）quick: ▸～感, ～捷, 灵～ 2（机灵）smart: ▸～慧, 聪～, 机～

【敏感】mǐngǎn〈形〉sensitive: 对天气变化很～ be very susceptible to changes in weather ‖ ～话题 touchy subject

【敏感度】mǐngǎndù〈名〉sensibility

【敏慧】mǐnhuì〈形〉clever: ～的孩子 intelligent child

【敏捷】mǐnjié〈形〉quick: 才思～ be quick in thought ‖ 反应～ be quick in response

【敏锐】mǐnruì〈形〉sharp: 目光～ be sharp-eyed ‖ 思想～ have a discerning mind ‖ 具有～的政治目光 have sharp political vision

湣 mǐn〈名〉Chinese character used in the posthumous titles of emperor and distinguished minister, such as the late Duke Min of Lu (鲁湣公)

míng

名 míng

A〈名〉1（名字）name: ▸～单, 报～, 签～ 2（借口）excuse: ～为考察, 实为旅游 enjoy a holiday in the name of a business trip ▸～正言顺, 师出无～ 3（名誉）fame: 他很快就出了～。He quickly rose to fame. ▸～利, 成～, 著～

B〈动〉1（表述）describe: ▸不可～状, 莫～其妙 2（名叫）be called: 她～叫李凡。Her name is Li Fan. 3〈书〉（拥有）have sth. to one's name: ▸不～一文

C〈形〉famous: ～车/店 famous car/shop ‖ ～演员 famous actors and actresses ‖ 世界～画 world-famous paintings

D〈量〉1（用于名次）place: 获第一～ get/take/win first/top place ‖ 降到第五～ fall to fifth place 2（用于人）[used for people]: 十～士兵 ten soldiers

【名不副实】míngbùfùshí〈成〉be unworthy of the name: ～的投资公司 investment company more in name than in reality

【名不见经传】míng bù jiàn jīngzhuàn〈成〉be a nobody: ～的年轻人 a young unknown man

【名不虚传】míngbùxūchuán〈成〉be true to one's name: 杭州织锦～。The brocade of Hangzhou lives up to its reputation.

【名册】míngcè〈名〉register: 学生～ students' register ▸花～

【名刹】míngchà〈名〉famous Buddhist temple

【名产】míngchǎn〈名〉famous product: 石榴是此地的～。The pomegranate is a famous product of this place.

【名称】míngchēng〈名〉name: 商标～ brand name

【名城】míngchéng〈名〉famous city: 历史～ famous historical city

【名垂千古】míngchuíqiāngǔ〈成〉be crowned with eternal glory: 这篇传记使他～。The biographical sketch has immortalized his name.

【名垂青史】míngchuíqīngshǐ〈成〉earn one's place in history: ～的民族英雄 a national hero who will go down in history

【名词】míngcí ▸p. 411〈名〉1［语法］noun 2（词语）term: 专业～ technical term ‖ 新～ new terms

【名次】míngcì〈名〉（指比赛）place in a competition;（指顺序）position in a name list: 以净胜球来决定～ determine the ranking by calculating goal difference ‖ ～靠前/后 place near the front/back

【名刺】míngcì〈名〉〈旧〉visiting card

【名存实亡】míngcún-shíwáng〈成〉exist in name only

【名单】míngdān〈名〉name list: 公布～ publish a name list ▸黑～

【名额】míng'é〈名〉quota of people: 招生～ admission quota ‖ 招聘～ recruitment quota ‖ ～已满。The quota has been filled.

【名分】míngfèn〈名〉person's social status: 争～ win status

【名副其实】míngfùqíshí〈成〉live up to one's reputation: ～的强国 powerful nation that lives up to its name

【名古屋】Mínggǔwū〈名〉Nagoya

【名贵】míngguì〈形〉famous and precious: ～药材 rare medicinal herbs ‖ ～字画 priceless scrolls of calligraphy and painting

【名号】mínghào〈名〉official name and alias

【名花有主】mínghuā-yǒuzhǔ〈成〉[of a girl] be spoken for

【名讳】mínghuì〈名〉〈旧〉name of a respected person, not to be written or spoken casually

【名家】míngjiā〈名〉1 Míngjiā（指学派）School of Logicians [in the Spring and Autumn and Warring States periods] 2（指专家）master: 受～指点 have been instructed by a master ‖ ～手笔 calligraphy or paintings by famous artists

【名缰利锁】míngjiāng-lìsuǒ〈成〉chains of fame and wealth

【名将】míngjiàng〈名〉1（指将军）famous general: 一代～ famous general of his time 2（指运动员）star player: 足球～ football star

【名教】míngjiào〈名〉Confucian ethical code

【名节】míngjié〈名〉reputation and moral integrity: 保全～ preserve one's good name and integrity

【名句】míngjù〈名〉well-known phrase: 千古～ saying that will go down in history

【名角】míngjué〈名〉famous actor: 由～主演 played by a famous actor

【名款】míngkuǎn〈名〉signature of a painter/calligrapher on his work: 这幅画没有～。There is no signature on this painting.

【名利】mínglì〈名〉fame and fortune: 不逐～ not seek fame and gain ‖ 追求～ seek fame and fortune ‖ ～双收 win both fame and fortune

【名列前茅】mínglièqiánmáo〈成〉come out on top: 考试～ come top in an examination

【名伶】mínglíng〈名〉〈旧〉renowned actor in Chinese opera

【名流】míngliú〈名〉big name: 各界～ prominent figures from all walks of life ‖ 社会～ noted public figures

m

【名录】mínglù〈名〉 name list: 毕业生～ roster of graduates
【名落孙山】míngluòsūnshān〈成〉 fail in a competitive examination
【名满天下】míngmǎntiānxià〈成〉 be world-famous
【名门】míngmén〈名〉 distinguished family: 出身～ come from an illustrious family ‖ ～闺秀 virtuous daughter of an eminent family ‖ ～世家 highly respectable family with a long history
【名门望族】míngmén-wàngzú〈成〉 distinguished ancestry: 他出身～。 He is of good stock.
【名模】míngmó〈名〉 famous model
【名目】míngmù〈名〉 items: 以各种～乱收费 wantonly levy fees under all kinds of names ▸巧立～
【名目繁多】míngmù-fánduō〈成〉 multitude of names/items: 各种摊派～。 There are various apportionments of expenses, too numerous to be named.
【名牌】míngpái〈名〉 **1**（指品牌） famous brand: 创～ establish a famous brand ‖ ～产品 brand product ‖ ～大学 big-name university **2**（指牌子） name tag: 佩带～ wear a name tag ‖ 展品都附有～。 All exhibits are shown with name plates.
【名篇】míngpiān〈名〉 famous literary piece
【名片】míngpiàn〈名〉 visiting card: 交换～ exchange cards (with sb.)
【名票】míngpiào〈名〉 popular amateur opera performing artist
【名品】míngpǐn〈名〉 valuable object
【名企】míngqǐ〈名〉 renowned business
【名气】míngqi〈名〉 fame: 小有～ have something of a reputation ‖ 很有～的作曲家 composer of great repute
【名人】míngrén〈名〉 famous person: 历史～ great name in history ‖ 文化界～ eminent figure in cultural circles ‖ ～访谈 talk show
【名人录】míngrénlù〈名〉 *Who's Who* [reference publications containing biographical information on noted people]
【名人效应】míngrén xiàoyìng〈名〉 celebrity effect
【名山大川】míngshān-dàchuān〈成〉 famous mountains and great rivers
【名声】míngshēng〈名〉 fame: 获得好～ win a favourable reputation ‖ ～远扬 gain a reputation far and wide ‖ ～不好的人 person with a bad reputation ‖ 他～大振。 His fame sky-rocketed.
【名胜】míngshèng〈名〉 well-known scenic spot: 游览～ tour historical sights ～古迹 scenic spots and historical sites
【名师】míngshī〈名〉 famous teacher: 经～指点 have had the benefit of guidance by a master
【名师出高徒】míngshī chū gāotú〈俗〉 a great teacher produces brilliant students
【名士】míngshì〈名〉 literary celebrity
【名氏】míngshi〈名〉 surname
【名手】míngshǒu〈名〉 **1**（指画家） famous artist: 国画～ master of traditional Chinese painting **2**（指棋手） famous player: 围棋～ *weiqi* master
【名宿】míngsù〈名〉 well-known veteran in a certain field of achievement: 教育界～ well-known veteran teacher ‖ 武林～ renowned *wushu* veteran
【名堂】míngtang〈名〉 **1**（花样） variety: 他们的婚礼～不少。 They have made a big do of their wedding. ‖ 他在搞什么～? What is he up to? **2**（结果） outcome: 他肯定搞不出什么～来。 He will certainly accomplish nothing. **3**（原因） reason: 他突然辞职，这里面一定有～。 There must be something behind his sudden resignation.
【名帖】míngtiě〈名〉〈旧〉 full-size visiting card: 递上～ present one's visiting card
【名望】míngwàng〈名〉 good reputation: ～很高的律师 lawyer of high standing ‖ 有～的科学家 famous scientist
【名位】míngwèi〈名〉 fame and position: 不计～ not care about one's position or fame
【名物】míngwù〈名〉 thing and its name
【名下】míngxià〈名〉 sth. under sb.'s name: 这些账怎能记在我的～? How can these expenses be charged to my account?
【名下无虚】míngxià-wúxū〈成〉 deserve the reputation one enjoys
【名校】míngxiào〈名〉 elite school
【名姓】míngxìng〈名〉 name and surname
【名言】míngyán〈名〉 well-known saying: 名人～ famous sayings of prominent figures ▸至理～
【名扬四海】míngyángsìhǎi〈成〉 become famous all over the world
【名医】míngyī〈名〉 famous doctor
【名义】míngyì〈名〉 **1**（名分） name: 以董事长的～讲话 speak in one's capacity as chairman ‖ 以革命的～ in the name of revolution **2**（表面上） form: ～上裁军，实际上扩军 disarmament in name, arms expansion in reality
【名义工资】míngyì gōngzī〈名〉 nominal wage
【名义关税】míngyì guānshuì〈名〉 nominal tariff
【名优】míngyōu **A**〈名〉〈旧〉 famous actor: 一代～ famous actor of one's time **B**〈形〉 famous: ～产品 famous, high-quality product
【名誉】míngyù **A**〈名〉 good name: 爱惜～ cherish one's reputation ‖ 恢复～ rehabilitate sb.'s reputation ‖ 使某人～扫地 drag sb.'s reputation through the mud ‖ 以～担保 give one's word ‖ 对于这一点，我用～担保。 To this I pledge my honour. **B**〈形〉 honorary: ～教授 emeritus professor ‖ ～主席 honorary chairman
【名媛】míngyuàn〈名〉〈书〉 famous woman
【名噪一时】míngzào-yīshí〈成〉 have one's brief moment of fame: 使某人～ bring sb. into temporary prominence
【名正言顺】míngzhèng-yánshùn〈成〉 fitting and proper: ～地继承财产 inherit a fortune by right and title
【名著】míngzhù〈名〉 masterpiece: 文学～ literary classic
【名状】míngzhuàng〈动〉 [usu used in the negative] describe: 景色之美难以～。 Words cannot describe the beauty of the scene.
【名字】míngzi〈名〉 name: 以发明者的～命名 be named after its inventor ‖ 你叫什么～? What's your name? ‖ 电影的～ title of a film ‖ 公司的～ name of a company
【名嘴】míngzuǐ〈名〉 popular anchorperson: 央视～ famous host on CCTV
【名作】míngzuò〈名〉 masterpiece

明[1] míng

A〈形〉 **1**（明亮） bright: ～月 bright moon ▸～亮, 鲜～, 照～, 黎～ **2**（天亮） light: 天就要～了。 Day is about to dawn. **3**（指下一个） next: ～晨 tomorrow morning ‖ ～春 next spring ‖ ～晚 tomorrow evening ▸～年, ～天 **4**（清楚） clear: 去向不～ whereabouts unknown ‖ 你应问～他的来意。 You should have asked what he had come for. ▸～快, ～晰, 爱憎分～ **5**（公开） open: 有话～说 air one's views openly ▸～争暗斗 **6**（视力好） sharp-eyed: ▸耳聪目～, 眼～手快
B〈动〉 **1**（知道） know: ～是非 know right from wrong ▸深～大义 **2**〈书〉（使明确） make known: ▸开宗～义
C〈副〉 evidently: ▸～知故犯
D〈名〉 sight: ▸复～, 失～

明[2] Míng〈名〉 Ming Dynasty

【明白】míngbai **A**〈形〉 **1**（易懂） clear: 让我把话说～ let me be clear **2**（公开） open: 他父亲～表示支持他。 His father stated unequivocally that he would back him. **3**（通情达理） sensible: ▸～人 **B**〈动〉 realize: ～事理 know what's what ‖ 我～你的意思。 I understand what you mean.
【明白人】míngbairén〈名〉 sensible person
【明辨是非】míngbiàn-shìfēi〈成〉 make a clear distinction between right and wrong
【明察】míngchá〈动〉 observe clearly
【明察暗访】míngchá-ànfǎng〈成〉 conduct a thorough investigation
【明察秋毫】míngchá-qiūháo〈成〉 be perceptive of the minutest detail
【明畅】míngchàng〈形〉 clear and lucid: 文笔～ write in a clear and lucid style
【明澈】míngchè〈形〉 crystalline: ～的眼睛 bright and shining eyes ‖ 湖水～如镜。 The lake is like a mirror.
【明处】míngchù〈名〉 **1**（亮处） where there is light: 把东西摆在～ put sth. in the light **2**（指公开） public place: 让我们把话说在～。 Let's talk openly.
【明达】míngdá〈书〉 **A**〈动〉 know: ～事理 have good sense **B**〈形〉 sensible: ～公正 sensible and fair-minded
【明灯】míngdēng〈名〉 **1**〈本〉 bright lamp **2**〈喻〉 beacon: 指路～ beacon light
【明兜】míngdōu〈名〉 patch pocket
【明断】míngduàn〈动〉〈书〉 pass fair judgement
【明矾】míngfán〈名〉 alum: ～石 alunite
【明沟】mínggōu〈名〉 open drain: ～排水 open-ditch drainage
【明后天】míng-hòutiān ▸**p. 618**〈名〉〈口〉 tomorrow or the day after tomorrow
【明晃晃】mínghuǎnghuǎng〈形〉 gleaming: ～的刺刀 gleaming bayonet ‖ ～的奖章 shining medal
【明黄】mínghuáng〈名〉 bright yellow
【明慧】mínghuì〈形〉〈书〉 intelligent
【明火】mínghuǒ〈名〉 flame: ～已全部扑灭。 The flames have completely died out.
【明火执仗】mínghuǒ-zhízhàng〈成〉 do evil things openly
【明间儿】míngjiānr〈名〉 outer room opening on to a yard
【明鉴】míngjiàn **A**〈名〉〈古〉 clear mirror **B**〈动〉〈书〉〈敬〉 judge judiciously
【明胶】míngjiāo〈名〉 gelatin
【明净】míngjìng〈形〉 bright and clean: 今天的天空格外～。 Today's sky is especially clear and bright.
【明镜】míngjìng〈名〉 clear mirror: 湖水清澈，犹如～。 The lake is bright and clear like a mirror.
【明镜高悬】míngjìng-gāoxuán〈成〉〈喻〉 impartial and perspicacious in judgement
【明快】míngkuài〈形〉 **1**（明白流畅） lucid and lively: 笔调～ write in a lucid and

lively style ‖ 节奏～ have sprightly rhythm 2（开朗爽快） straightforward: 他作风～。 He has a straightforward working style.

【明来暗往】mínglái-ànwǎng〈成〉〈贬〉have overt and covert contact (with sb.)

【明朗】mínglǎng〈形〉1（明亮） bright and clear: ～的天空 clear sky ‖ ～的月色 bright moonlight 2（清楚） unequivocal: 态度～ adopt an unequivocal attitude ‖ 局势逐渐～。 The situation is becoming clear. 3（爽朗） forthright: 他性格～。 He has an open and forthright character.

【明理】mínglǐ A〈动〉 be reasonable B〈名〉 obvious fact

【明丽】mínglì〈形〉〈书〉 bright and beautiful: 风光～。 The scenes are bright and beautiful.

【明亮】míngliàng〈形〉1（亮堂） bright: 灯光～ be brightly lit ‖ 宽敞～的书房 bright and spacious study 2（闪亮） shining: ～的星星 shining stars ‖ ～的眼睛 bright eyes 3（明白） clear: 老师的话使他心里～了。 His teacher's words helped him straighten out his thinking.

【明了】míngliǎo A〈动〉 understand: 你的话我不～。 I don't understand what you mean. B〈形〉 clear: 他的解释简单～。 His explanation is clear and concise.

【明令】mínglìng〈名〉 formal decree: ～嘉奖 issue a commendation ‖ ～禁止 prohibit by official order

【明楼】mínglóu〈名〉 watchtower

【明码】míngmǎ〈名〉1（指电码） plain code: ～电报 plain-code telegram 2（指价码） clearly marked price

【明码标价】míngmǎ biāojià〈成〉 affix price tags

【明媒正娶】míngméi-zhèngqǔ〈成〉 legal marriage

【明媚】míngmèi〈形〉1（指风景） bright and beautiful: ～的河山 land of magnificent beauty ‖ 阳光～。 The sun is shining brightly. 2（指眼睛） bright: ～的大眼睛 big bright eyes

【明灭】míngmiè〈动〉〈书〉 appear one moment and vanish the next: 星光～。 The stars twinkled in the sky. ‖ 远处灯光～。 Lights blinking in the distance.

【明明】míngmíng〈副〉 obviously: 那～是错的。 That is plainly wrong. ‖ 他～是在撒谎。 Clearly, he was lying.

【明明白白】míngmíng-báibái〈成〉 obviously

【明眸】míngmóu〈名〉〈书〉 bright eyes

【明眸皓齿】míngmóu-hàochǐ〈成〉 [of a woman] have clear bright eyes and gleaming white teeth

【明目】míngmù〈动〉 improve eyesight: 这药可以～。 This medicine can improve the sight.

【明目张胆】míngmù-zhāngdǎn〈成〉 brazenly: ～地干涉别国内政 flagrantly intervene in the internal affairs of other countries

【明尼苏达州】Míngnísūdázhōu〈名〉 Minnesota: ～人 Minnesotan

【明年】míngnián ▸**p. 618**〈名〉 next year

【明盘】míngpán〈名〉［经济］ negotiated price

【明器】míngqì〈名〉〈古〉 burial objects

【明前】míngqián〈名〉 green tea picked before Pure Brightness (清明)

【明枪暗箭】míngqiāng-ànjiàn〈成〉〈喻〉 both overt and covert attacks

【明枪易躲，暗箭难防】míngqiāng yì duǒ, ànjiàn nán fáng〈俗〉〈喻〉 false friends are worse than known enemies

【明渠】míngqú〈名〉 open ditch: ～灌溉/排水 irrigation by open canal

【明确】míngquè A〈形〉 clear-cut: 分工～ clear division of labour ‖ 目标～ have a clear objective B〈动〉 clarify: 这次会议～了当前的任务。 This conference clarified our present tasks.

【明儿】míngr ▸**p. 618**〈名〉〈口〉1（明天） tomorrow: 他～来。 He will come tomorrow. 2（某一天） some day: ～你长大了，当个足球运动员怎样? How about being a football player when you grow up?

【明人】míngrén〈名〉 honest person

【明人不做暗事】míngrén bù zuò ànshì〈俗〉 an honest person doesn't engage in dodgy deals

【明日】míngrì ▸**p. 618**〈名〉 tomorrow

【明日黄花】míngrì-huánghuā〈成〉〈喻〉 things that are stale and no longer of interest: 这种款式已成～。 This style is out of fashion.

【明锐】míngruì〈形〉 bright and sharp: 目光～ have sharp eyes ‖ ～的刀锋 bright and sharp blade

【明闪闪】míngshǎnshǎn〈形〉 sparkling: 一双～的大眼睛 two big shining eyes

【明升暗降】míngshēng-ànjiàng〈成〉 a promotion in name but a demotion in fact: 他被授予贵族头衔，～到上议院。 He was given a peerage and kicked upstairs to the House of Lords.

【明十三陵】Míngshísānlíng〈名〉 the Ming Tombs

> **明十三陵**
>
> The tombs of thirteen Ming Dynasty emperors located in Changping district, Beijing, in the foothills of Mount Tianshou. The tombs cover an area of more than 40 square kilometres. The heart of the Ming Tombs is Changling, the tomb of the Yongle Emperor, Zhu Di (朱棣). This was the first to be built. The other twelve tombs are arranged around it. The tombs are approached through an imposing marble arch. Beyond this is the Great Red Gate (大红门) and a Sacred Way (神路), flanked by stone animals and guardian figures, that leads to Changling.

【明示】míngshì〈动〉 clearly indicate: 敬请～。 Please give me your honest advice.

【明誓】míngshì = 盟誓 méngshì A

【明说】míngshuō〈动〉 speak openly: 不便～ had better not state explicitly ‖ 有意见就～。 If anyone disagrees, please air your views openly.

【明斯克】Míngsīkè〈名〉 Minsk

【明太鱼】míngtàiyú〈名〉［鱼类］ walleye pollack

【明堂】míngtáng〈名〉 courtyard

【明天】míngtiān ▸**p. 618**〈名〉1〈本〉 tomorrow 2〈喻〉（未来） near future: 展望美好的～ look towards a bright future

【明文】míngwén〈名〉 [of laws, regulations, etc.] existing writing: ～规定 be clearly defined in explicit terms

【明晰】míngxī〈形〉 clear: 思路～ clear thinking

【明细】míngxì〈形〉 definite and detailed: ～账 itemized account

【明虾】míngxiā = 对虾 duìxiā

【明显】míngxiǎn〈形〉 obvious: 优势～ have a distinct advantage ‖ 病情～好转。 The illness took a clear turn for the better.

【明线】míngxiàn〈名〉1（指作品线索） apparent plot line 2［电气］ open-wire line

【明晓】míngxiǎo〈动〉 thoroughly understand: ～地理 have a good knowledge of geography

【明效】míngxiào〈名〉 obvious results

【明效大验】míngxiào-dàyàn〈成〉 marked effects

【明信片】míngxìnpiàn〈名〉 postcard: 寄～ send sb. a postcard ‖ 风景～ scenic postcard

【明星】míngxīng〈名〉 star: ～气质 star quality ‖ ～企业 star enterprise ‖ 超级～ superstar ‖ 电影/篮球～ movie/basketball star ‖ 体育～ sporting hero

【明星赛】míngxīngsài〈名〉 all-star game: NBA全～ NBA All-Star Game

【明修栈道，暗度陈仓】míng xiū zhàndào, àn dù Chéncāng〈成〉〈喻〉 do one thing under cover of another

【明言】míngyán〈动〉 speak up

【明眼人】míngyǎnrén〈名〉 person with a discerning eye: ～一看便知 anyone with any sense can see it easily

【明艳】míngyàn〈形〉 bright and beautiful

【明一套，暗一套】míng yī tào, àn yī tào〈俗〉 act one way in the open and another way in secret

【明油】míngyóu〈名〉 clear oil sprinkled on a cooked dish: 淋点～ sprinkle some clear oil on a cooked dish

【明喻】míngyù〈名〉 simile: 使用～ use a simile

【明月】míngyuè〈名〉 bright moon

【明早】míngzǎo〈名〉 tomorrow morning

【明杖】míngzhàng〈名〉 white cane [used by a blind person]

【明朝】míngzhāo〈名〉〈方〉 tomorrow

【明哲保身】míngzhé-bǎoshēn〈成〉 be worldly-wise and play safe

【明争暗斗】míngzhēng-àndòu〈成〉 both open strife and veiled struggle: 政治上的～ political infighting

【明正典刑】míngzhèng-diǎnxíng〈成〉 carry out a death sentence according to law

【明证】míngzhèng〈名〉 clear proof: 出示～ produce clear proof ‖ 提供～ supply clear proof

【明知】míngzhī〈动〉 be fully aware: ～故问 ask while knowing the answer

【明知故犯】míngzhī-gùfàn〈成〉 knowingly violate

【明知山有虎，偏向虎山行】míngzhī shān yǒu hǔ, piān xiàng hǔshān xíng〈俗〉 press on undeterred by the dangers ahead

【明志】míngzhì〈动〉〈书〉 state one's own views: 蓄须～ grow a beard as an expression of one's ideals ‖ 赋诗以～ write a poem as an expression of one's high ideals

【明治维新】Míngzhì Wéixīn〈名〉 Meiji Reform [in Japan, 1868-1912]

【明智】míngzhì〈形〉 sensible: ～的决策 wise decision ‖ 不～的举动 ill-considered act

【明珠】míngzhū〈名〉1〈本〉 bright pearl 2〈喻〉 jewel: 东方～ pearl of the orient ‖ 掌上～ the apple of one's eye

【明珠暗投】míngzhū-àntóu〈成〉〈喻〉1（指物） cast pearls before swine 2（指人） a good person fallen among bad company

【明柱】míngzhù〈名〉［建筑］ outside pillar

鸣（鳴）

míng〈动〉1（叫） call: 鸟～ chirping of birds ‖ 蛙～ croaking of frogs 2（发出响声） make a sound: ～礼炮二十一响 fire a 21-gun salute ‖ 电闪雷～。 Lightning flashed and thunder rolled. ▸自～钟 3（公开表达） express: ▸～谢,

百家争～
【鸣不平】 míngbùpíng〈动〉 complain of unfairness
【鸣笛】 míngdí〈动〉 sound a siren: 禁止～。 Honking is forbidden.
【鸣镝】 míngdí〈名〉 whistling arrow
【鸣鼓而攻之】 míng gǔ ér gōng zhī〈成〉 make a scathing indictment
【鸣叫】 míngjiào〈动〉 [of birds, animals or insects] call: 蟋蟀～ chirping of crickets ‖ 这只鸟的～声很特别。 This bird has a very distinctive call.
【鸣金收兵】 míngjīn-shōubīng〈成〉 1（指战争） call off a battle 2〈喻〉（指比赛） come to a close
【鸣锣开道】 míngluó-kāidào〈成〉〈喻〉 pave the way for sth.
【鸣枪】 míngqiāng〈动〉 fire a shot: ～示警 fire a warning shot ‖ ～致意 fire a salute
【鸣禽】 míngqín〈名〉 songbird
【鸣哨】 míngshào〈动〉 blow a whistle: 裁判～，比赛结束。 The referee whistled and the match ended.
【鸣谢】 míngxiè〈动〉 express one's thanks formally: 登报～ put a letter of thanks in the newspaper
【鸣冤】 míngyuān〈动〉 voice grievances: 击鼓～ strike the drum to demand a hearing on how one has been wronged
【鸣冤叫屈】 míngyuān-jiàoqū〈成〉 make bitter complaints
【鸣啭】 míngzhuàn〈动〉〈书〉 [of birds] sing: 麻雀在林中～。 Sparrows are chirping in the woods.

茗 míng〈名〉 good quality tea: 品～ sip tea

冥 míng
A〈形〉 1〈书〉（昏暗） murky: ▸晦～，幽～ 2〈书〉（愚昧） stupid: ▸～顽 3（深刻） deep: ▸～思苦想，～想
B〈名〉 the nether world: ▸～府
【冥暗】 míng'àn〈形〉 dim
【冥钞】 míngchāo〈名〉 ceremonial paper money burned for the deceased
【冥府】 míngfǔ〈名〉 the nether world
【冥茫】 míngmáng〈形〉〈书〉 boundless
【冥器】 míngqì = 明器 míngqì
【冥寿】 míngshòu〈名〉 birthday anniversary of the dead
【冥思苦想】 míngsī-kǔxiǎng〈成〉 rack one's brains
【冥顽】 míngwán〈形〉〈书〉 thickheaded
【冥顽不灵】 míngwán-bùlíng〈成〉 stupid and obstinate
【冥王星】 Míngwángxīng〈名〉［天文］ Pluto
【冥想】 míngxiǎng〈动〉 think seriously and deeply: 歌声把我带入～。 On hearing the song, I fell into a reverie.
【冥衣】 míngyī〈名〉 burial clothes

铭（銘） míng
A〈名〉 1（指文字） inscription: ▸～文 2（指文体） epigraph: ▸墓志～，座右～
B〈动〉 engrave: ▸～记，刻骨～心
【铭感】 mínggǎn ▸p. 236〈动〉〈书〉 be deeply grateful: ～终身 remain deeply grateful for the rest of one's life
【铭记】 míngjì〈动〉 always remember: ～教诲 remember sb.'s instructions ‖ ～在心 be engraved on one's mind
【铭旌】 míngjīng〈名〉〈旧〉 funeral streamer bearing the titles of the deceased
【铭刻】 míngkè A〈名〉 inscription: 青铜器～ inscriptions on bronze wares B〈动〉 be engraved on one's mind: ～在心中 be engraved in one's heart
【铭牌】 míngpái〈名〉 nameplate
【铭文】 míngwén〈名〉 inscription: 刻有～ bear an inscription ‖ 铜器的～ inscriptions on bronze ware
【铭心】 míngxīn〈动〉 be engraved on one's heart: ▸刻骨～
【铭诸肺腑】 míngzhū-fèifǔ〈成〉 be borne firmly in mind

溟 míng〈名〉〈书〉 sea: 南～ south sea
【溟茫】 míngmáng = 冥茫 míngmáng
【溟濛】 míngméng〈形〉〈书〉 hazy

暝 míng〈书〉
A〈形〉 gloomy
B〈动〉（指太阳） set;（指天空） get dark: 日已～。 The sun has set.
C〈名〉 dusk

瞑 míng〈动〉 close one's eyes: ▸～目
【瞑目】 míngmù〈动〉 1（闭眼） close one's eyes 2（指无牵挂） die content: ▸死不～
【瞑眩】 míngxuàn〈名〉 dizziness

螟 míng〈名〉 larva of the snout moth
【螟虫】 míngchóng〈名〉 larva of the snout moth
【螟蛾】 míng'é〈名〉 snout moth
【螟蛉】 mínglíng〈名〉 1（指虫） corn earworm 2〈书〉（指人） adopted son
【螟蛉之子】 mínglíngzhīzǐ〈成〉 foster son

mǐng

酩 mǐng
【酩酊】 mǐngdǐng〈形〉 blind drunk: 喝得～大醉 completely intoxicated

mìng

命 mìng
A〈动〉 1（命令） order: ～舰队立即返航 order the fleet to return to base immediately ‖ ～士兵出击 command the soldiers to attack 2（确定） assign (a name, title, etc.): ▸～名，～题
B〈名〉 1（命令） order: 奉～转移部队 transfer troops under orders ‖ 遵～ obey orders 2（命运） fate: ～好 be born under a lucky star ‖ 苦～ cruel fate ▸认～，听天由～ 3（生命） life: 丧～ lose one's life ‖ 这可差点要了他的～。 This nearly cost him his life. ▸长～百岁，救～
【命案】 mìng'àn〈名〉 homicide case: 他有～在身。 He has committed a murder.
【命笔】 mìngbǐ〈动〉〈书〉 put pen to paper: ～抒怀 set pen to paper to express one's sentiments ‖ 欣然～ be happy to start writing
【命不该绝】 mìngbùgāijué〈成〉 not be destined to die
【命大】 mìngdà〈形〉 1（幸运） lucky: ～福大 have both luck and fortune 2（大难不死） death-defying: 她真～，撞车后竟然安然无恙。 She was lucky to survive the crash all in one piece.
【命定】 mìngdìng〈动〉 be predestined
【命根】 mìnggēn〈名〉 lifeblood: 她是家里的～。 She is the lifeblood of the family. ‖ 这件古董是他的～。 This antique is his very lifeblood.
【命根子】 mìnggēnzi = 命根 mìnggēn
【命官】 mìngguān〈名〉〈旧〉 official appointed by the imperial court
【命驾】 mìngjià〈动〉〈书〉 set out in a carriage
【命苦】 mìngkǔ〈形〉 doomed to a life of misfortune: ～的孩子 wretched child
【命令】 mìnglìng A〈动〉 command: ～士兵挺进 command the troops to advance B〈名〉 order: 服从～ obey orders ‖ 接受～ take orders ‖ 执行～ carry out an order ‖ 行政～ executive order
【命脉】 mìngmài〈名〉 lifeblood: 经济～ economic lifeblood ‖ 水利是农业的～。 Irrigation is the lifeline of agriculture.
【命名】 mìngmíng〈动〉 name: 哈雷彗星是以其发现者埃得蒙·哈雷的名字～的。 Halley's Comet was named after its discoverer, Edmond Halley.
【命名法】 mìngmíngfǎ〈名〉 nomenclature
【命若游丝】 mìngruòyóusī〈成〉 one's life hangs by a thread
【命数】 mìngshù〈名〉 fate: ～已尽 one's hour has come
【命题】 mìngtí〈动〉 set a question: ～作文 writing on an assigned subject ‖ 全国统一～ nationally unified examinations
【命途】 mìngtú〈名〉〈书〉 course of one's life as determined by fate: ～坎坷 rough path through life
【命途多舛】 mìngtú-duōchuǎn〈成〉 suffer many setbacks during one's life
【命相】 mìngxiàng〈名〉〈旧〉 [of a person's birthday] eight characters and any one of the twelve animals
【命运】 mìngyùn〈名〉 fate: 共～ throw in one's lot (with sb.) ‖ 不幸的～ hapless fate ‖ 关心国家的前途和～ be concerned about the future and destiny of the country
【命在旦夕】 mìngzàidànxī〈成〉 death may come any minute: 她～。 She is going to die at any time.
【命中注定】 mìngzhōngzhùdìng〈成〉 be predestined: ～当演员 be destined to be an actress ‖ 如～的那样 as fate would have it
【命中】 mìngzhòng〈动〉 hit the target: ～目标 find the target ‖ ～率 percentage of hits

miù

谬（謬） miù〈形〉 wrong: ▸～论
【谬爱】 miù'ài〈动〉〈书〉〈谦〉 show undeserved kindness
【谬传】 miùchuán〈动〉 falsely report
【谬奖】 miùjiǎng〈动〉〈书〉〈谦〉 win undeserved praise
【谬论】 miùlùn〈名〉 fallacy: 驳斥～ refute a fallacy ‖ 散布～ spread absurd theories
【谬说】 miùshuō = 谬论 miùlùn
【谬误】 miùwù〈名〉 error: 纠正～ correct errors ‖ 明显的～ transparent fallacy
【谬种】 miùzhǒng〈名〉 1（指言论观点） fallacy: ～流传 dissemination of errors 2〈粗〉（指人或物） blighter

缪 miù ▸纰缪 pīmiù
▸Miào, móu

mō

摸 mō〈动〉**1**（轻抚） feel: ～孩子的脸 stroke a child's face ‖ 大理石～起来很光滑。 Marble is smooth to the touch. **2**（探取） fish for: 从口袋里～出一个硬币 fish out a coin from one's pocket ▸浑水～鱼 **3**（探求） sound out: ～出一套记新词的方法 test out a number of methods for memorizing new words ‖ ～～他对这一问题的看法 sound him out on this matter **4**（摸索） grope for in the dark: 在黑暗中～找开关 feel about in the dark for the light switch

【摸不透】 mōbutòu〈动〉 be unable to fathom

【摸不着头脑】 mōbuzháo tóunǎo〈惯〉 be unable to make head or tail of sth.: 这件事我～。 I cannot make head or tail of this matter.

【摸彩】 mōcǎi〈动〉 draw lots

【摸查】 mōchá〈动〉 fully investigate: ～水灾死亡人数 work to come up with the number of people who died in the flood ‖ ～资金流向 make a thorough investigation into the whereabouts of the funds

【摸底】 mōdǐ〈动〉 try to know the real situation: 举行～测验 conduct an assessment test ‖ 对领导的意图不～ know little about the intentions of the leadership

【摸高】 mōgāo〈动〉 **1**［体育］ jump up to reach: 主攻身高2米，～超过3.60米。 The forward is 2 metres tall and can jump to a reach of 3.6m. **2**［经济］ reach a high: 铜价一度～至每吨85,000元。 The price of copper reached a high of 85,000 yuan per tonne.

【摸黑儿】 mōhēir〈动〉 grope in the dark: ～赶路 press on with a journey at night

【摸奖】 mōjiǎng〈动〉 draw lots

【摸门儿】 mōménr〈动〉〈口〉〈喻〉 get the hang of sth.: 对业务还不～ still haven't got the hang of the work

【摸排】 mōpái〈动〉 investigate a range of people in a criminal case

【摸哨】 mōshào〈动〉 attack enemy sentinels in the dark

【摸索】 mōsuǒ〈动〉 **1**（试探） fumble: 在黑暗中～前进 feel one's way in the dark **2**（寻求） try to find out: 通过～掌握饲养家禽的方法 learn how to raise poultry through trial and error

【摸头】 mōtóu〈动〉〈口〉 [often used in negative construction] begin to understand: 我对网球赛记分方法不～。 I am at a loss as to how the scoring system works in tennis.

【摸透】 mōtòu〈动〉 get to know sb. or sth. very well: ～脾气 get to know sb. inside out

【摸营】 mōyíng〈动〉 attack an enemy encampment under cover of night

【摸着石头过河】 mōzhe shítou guò hé〈俗〉 learn how to do something through trial and error

mó

无（無） mó ▸南无 nāmó
▸wú

谟（謨） mó〈名〉〈书〉 plan: 远～ long-range plan

馍（饃） mó〈名〉〈方〉 *mantou* [steamed bun made of wheat flour]: 白面～ steamed bun of wheat flour ‖ 羊肉泡～ shredded pancakes cooked in mutton broth

【馍馍】 mómo〈名〉〈方〉 *mantou* [steamed bun made of wheat flour]

嫫 mó〈名〉 a character used in a lady's name

【嫫母】 Mómǔ〈名〉 *Momu* [ugly-looking lady in a Chinese legend]

摹 mó〈动〉 copy: ▸临～, 描～

【摹本】 móběn〈名〉 copy

【摹绘】 móhuì〈动〉〈书〉 reproduce

【摹刻】 mókè **A**〈动〉 carve a reproduction of an inscription or painting **B**〈名〉 carved reproduction of an inscription or painting

【摹写】 móxiě〈动〉 **1**（临摹） copy **2**（描写） depict: 这位作家擅长～人物情状。 The writer is accomplished in depicting characters in various situations.

【摹印】 móyìn **A**〈动〉 copy and print **B**〈名〉 distinctive style of characters on ancient imperial seals

【摹状】 mózhuàng〈动〉 depict

模 mó
A〈名〉 **1**（指物） pattern: ▸～型, 楷～ **2**（指人） model: ▸劳～, 英～
B〈动〉 copy: ▸～仿, ～拟
▸mú

【模本】 móběn〈名〉（指书法） calligraphy model;（指绘画） painting model

【模范】 mófàn〈名〉 model: 劳动～ labour hero ‖ 起～作用 play an exemplary role ‖ ～教师 model teacher ‖ ～事迹 exemplary deeds ‖ 他是我们的～。 He is an example for us.

【模仿】 mófǎng〈动〉 copy: ～某人的口音 copy sb.'s accent ‖ ～鸟叫 imitate a bird call ‖ ～得惟妙惟肖 do a good imitation

【模仿秀】 mófǎngxiù〈名〉 imitation show

【模仿者】 mófǎngzhě〈名〉 imitator

【模糊】 móhu **A**〈形〉 blurred: ～的记忆 dim memory ‖ ～的印象 vague impression ‖ 病人神志有点～。 The patient's mind is a bit fuzzy. ‖ 字迹～。 The writing is faint. **B**〈动〉 mix up: ～是非界限 confuse right and wrong

【模糊理论】 móhu lǐlùn〈名〉［数学］ fuzzy theory

【模糊逻辑】 móhu luójí〈名〉 fuzzy logic

【模糊数学】 móhu shùxué〈名〉［数学］ fuzzy mathematics

【模块】 mókuài〈名〉 module

【模棱两可】 móléng-liǎngkě〈成〉 ambivalent: ～的话 ambiguous remarks ‖ ～的回答 evasive reply

【模拟】 mónǐ〈动〉 imitate: ～考试 mock exams ‖ ～战 mock battle

【模拟法庭】 mónǐ fǎtíng〈名〉 moot court

【模拟人】 mónǐrén〈名〉 human test dummy: 采用～代替宇航员进行试验 carry out experiments with test dummies in place of astronauts

【模拟人像】 mónǐ rénxiàng〈名〉 effigy

【模拟通信】 mónǐ tōngxìn〈名〉 analogue communication

【模拟信号】 mónǐ xìnhào〈名〉 analogue signal

【模拟装置】 mónǐ zhuāngzhì〈名〉 simulator

【模式】 móshì〈名〉 model: 管理～ management model ‖ 经济增长～ economic growth model

【模数】 móshù〈名〉［物理］ modulus

【模特儿】 mótèr〈名〉 model: 当画家的～ model for a painter ‖ 真人～ living model ‖ 时装～ fashion model

【模型】 móxíng〈名〉 **1**（指仿制物） model: 飞机～ model aeroplane ‖ 人体～ model of the human body **2**（指模子） matrix

【模压】 móyā〈名〉 mould pressing: ～机 moulding press

膜 mó〈名〉 **1**（指生物体组织） membrane: ▸耳～, 细胞～ **2**（膜状物） film: 塑料薄～ plastic film ‖ 橡皮～ rubber film

【膜拜】 móbài〈动〉 prostrate oneself in worship: ▸顶礼～

麽 mó ▸幺麽 yāomó

摩[1] mó〈动〉 **1**（摩擦） rub: ▸～擦 **2**（轻抚） stroke: 抚～着孩子的脸 stroke a child's face ▸～挲, 按～ **3**（接触） approach: ▸～肩接踵, ～天大楼 **4**（研究） study: ▸揣～, 观～

摩[2] mó = 摩尔 mó'ěr
▸mā

【摩擦】 mócā **A**〈动〉 rub: ～双手 rub one's hands together **B**〈名〉 **1**［物理］ friction: 减少～ reduce friction ‖ ～的痕迹 abrasion marks **2**（冲突） clash: 与某人发生～ have a brush with sb. ‖ 制造～ create friction ‖ 两国边境的～日益加剧。 Friction is increasing on the border between the two countries.

【摩擦力】 mócālì〈名〉［物理］ friction: 空气～造成阻力。 Air friction causes drag.

【摩擦系数】 mócā xìshù〈名〉［物理］ friction factor

【摩擦音】 mócāyīn〈名〉［语言］ fricative

【摩登】 módēng〈形〉 modern: ～女郎 fashionable girl

【摩的】 módī〈名〉 motorcycle used to carry passengers

【摩电灯】 módiàndēng〈名〉 dynamo-powered lamp

【摩尔】 mó'ěr〈量〉［物理］ mole

【摩尔多瓦】 Mó'ěrduōwǎ〈名〉 Moldova: ～共和国 Republic of Moldova ‖ ～人 Moldovan ‖ ～语 Moldavian

【摩肩接踵】 mójiān-jiēzhǒng〈成〉 be jam-packed with people: 广场上行人～。 The square was jammed with people.

【摩羯座】 Mójiézuò〈名〉［天文］ Capricorn

【摩洛哥】 Móluògē〈名〉 Morocco: ～人 Moroccan ‖ ～王国 Kingdom of Morocco

【摩门教徒】 Mómén jiàotú〈名〉 Mormon

【摩纳哥】 Mónàgē〈名〉 Monaco: ～公国 Principality of Monaco ‖ ～人 Monacan

【摩拳擦掌】 móquán-cāzhǎng〈成〉 be itching to have a go: 战士们个个～。 The soldiers were itching to go into battle.

【摩丝】 mósī〈名〉 (styling) mousse: 打～ put mousse in one's hair ‖ 用～定发型 style the hair with mousse

【摩挲】 mósuō〈动〉〈书〉 stroke
▸māsā

【摩天】 mótiān〈形〉 towering: ～岭 towering mountain ridge

【摩天大楼】 mótiān dàlóu〈名〉 skyscraper

【摩天轮】 mótiānlún〈名〉 big wheel〈英〉; Ferris wheel〈美〉

【摩托】 mótuō〈名〉 **1**（指内燃机） motor **2**（指车辆） motorcycle

【摩托车】mótuōchē〈名〉〈口〉motorcycle: ～越野赛 cross-country motorcycle race
【摩托化部队】mótuōhuàbùduì〈名〉motorized troop
【摩托艇】mótuōtǐng〈名〉motor boat: ～比赛 motor boat racing
【摩托自行车】mótuō zìxíngchē〈名〉moped
【摩托罗拉】Mótuōluólā〈名〉Motorola Inc: ～手机 Motorola mobile phone
【摩崖】móyá〈名〉cliff carving: ～石刻 inscriptions on cliffs

磨 mó〈动〉**1**（用磨具加工）grind: ～剪子 sharpen a pair of scissors ‖ ～镜片 grind a lens ▸打～, 研～, 琢～ **2**（摩擦）rub: 手上～出了泡 get blisters on one's hands from rubbing ‖ 我的鞋后跟～脚。The heels of my shoes are pinching. ‖ 鞋底～破了。Holes have worn into the soles. **3**（消失）obliterate: 百世不～ will endure for centuries ▸～灭 **4**（拖延）dawdle: ～时间 waste time ▸～洋工 **5**（折磨）wear out: 这病把她～得都脱形了。The illness has worn her into a mere shadow of her former self. ▸～难, 好事多～ **6**（纠缠）pester: 软～硬泡 tiresomely pursue sb. (for sth.) ‖ 他跟我～个没完。He kept plaguing me.
▸mò
【磨蹭】móceng〈动〉**1**（磨擦）rub: 别用脚～地板。Don't scrape your feet on the floor. **2**（拖延）dawdle: 别～了。Stop dawdling. **3**（纠缠）pester: 小姑娘～了半天，妈妈才答应给她买那个娃娃。The little girl kept on at her mother until she promised to buy her the doll.
【磨杵成针】móchǔ-chéngzhēn〈成〉〈喻〉any difficult task can be accomplished as long as one persists to the end
【磨穿铁砚】móchuān-tiěyàn〈成〉study long and hard: 发扬～的精神 display a persevering spirit
【磨床】móchuáng〈名〉［机械］grinder: 一台～ a grinding machine
【磨刀不误砍柴工】módāo bù wù kǎnchái gōng〈俗〉〈喻〉good preparation saves work time
【磨刀霍霍】módāo-huòhuò〈成〉sharpen one's sword
【磨刀石】módāoshí〈名〉whetstone
【磨光】móguāng〈动〉polish
【磨耗】móhào〈动〉wear and tear
【磨合】móhé〈动〉break in: 我的新车还在～。I am still breaking in my new car. ‖〈喻〉这支球队需要～。The team needs time to gel.
【磨合期】móhéqī〈名〉break-in period: 新汽车发动机的～ break-in period for the engine of a new car
【磨砺】mólì〈动〉〈喻〉harden oneself: ～心志 steel one's will ‖ 宝剑锋从～出。Work efficiency comes out of hard practice.
【磨炼】móliàn〈动〉steel oneself: ～才干 cultivate one's ability ‖ 在实际工作中～自己 steel oneself in practical work
【磨练】móliàn = 磨炼 móliàn
【磨料】móliào〈名〉abrasive
【磨轮】mólún〈名〉［机械］abrasive wheel
【磨灭】mómiè〈动〉wear away: 留下难以～的印象 leave a lasting impression (on sb.) ‖ 做出不可～的贡献 make an indelible contribution
【磨难】mónàn〈名〉hardship: 历经各种～ undergo all kinds of hardships
【磨砂玻璃】móshā bōli〈名〉frosted glass
【磨砂灯泡】móshā dēngpào〈名〉frosted light bulb
【磨舌头】mó shétou〈动〉〈方〉indulge in idle talk
【磨石】móshí〈名〉grinding stone
【磨蚀】móshí **A**〈名〉［地质］abrasion **B**〈动〉wear sth. down: ～锐气 wear down one's spirit
【磨损】mósǔn〈动〉wear and tear: 滚柱轴承～严重。The roller bearing shows serious signs of wear and tear.
【磨洗】móxǐ〈动〉corrode: 这些壁画经受了时间的～。These frescoes had been worn away over the years.
【磨牙】móyá〈动〉**1**（指牙齿）grind one's teeth (in one's sleep): 有些人睡觉时～。Some people grind their teeth while they sleep. **2**〈方〉（争辩）argue pointlessly: 跟他～没用。It's no use arguing with him.
【磨洋工】mó yánggōng〈惯〉dawdle over one's work: 他不能容忍雇员～。He cannot tolerate employees dawdling over their work.
【磨嘴皮子】mó zuǐpízi〈惯〉**1**（劝说）do a lot of talking: 我磨破了嘴皮子，终于把他说服了。I talked till my jaws ached before I eventually brought him round. **2**（争辩）argue pointlessly: 就那件事跟他～没用。It's no use arguing with him about that matter.

嬷 mó
【嬷嬷】mómo〈名〉**1**〈方〉（指老年妇女）granny **2**〈方〉（奶妈）wet nurse **3**（指修女）nun

蘑 mó〈名〉mushroom: 白～ white mushroom ‖ 鲜～ fresh mushroom ▸口～
【蘑菇】mógu **A**〈名〉mushroom: 采～ pick mushrooms ‖ ～中毒 mushroom poisoning **B**〈动〉〈口〉**1**（纠缠）pester: 你别跟我～了。Stop pestering me. **2**（拖拉）dawdle: 你再这么～下去，非误了班机不可。If you go on dilly-dallying like this, you'll miss your flight.
【蘑菇云】móguyún〈名〉mushroom cloud

魔 mó
A〈名〉**1**（魔鬼）demon: ▸～鬼, 妖～ **2**〈喻〉（害人的）fiend: ▸～爪, 病～
B〈形〉magic: ▸～力, ～术
【魔法】mófǎ〈名〉sorcery: 施～ work magic
【魔方】mófāng〈名〉Rubik's cube: 玩～ play Rubik's cube
【魔怪】móguài ▸**p. 274**〈名〉**1**（鬼怪）demons and monsters **2**〈喻〉evil force
【魔鬼】móguǐ ▸**p. 274**〈名〉**1**（鬼怪）demon: 驱除～ lay a ghost **2**〈喻〉monster: 她丈夫是个混世～。Her husband is the devil incarnate.
【魔幻】móhuàn〈形〉unpredictable: ～手法 magic trick ‖ ～小说 fantasy novel
【魔窟】mókū〈名〉den of monsters
【魔力】mólì〈名〉magical power
【魔女】mónǚ〈名〉bewitching woman
【魔术】móshù〈名〉magic: 变～ perform magic ‖ ～师 magician
【魔王】mówáng ▸**p. 274**〈名〉**1**（魔鬼）the Devil **2**〈喻〉fiend: 杀人～ mass murderer ▸混世～
【魔影】móyǐng〈名〉phantom
【魔芋】móyù〈名〉［植物］konjack
【魔掌】mózhǎng〈名〉devil's clutches: 落入敌人的～ fall into the clutches of the enemy
【魔杖】mózhàng〈名〉magic wand
【魔障】mózhàng ▸**p. 274**〈名〉demon
【魔爪】mózhǎo〈名〉claws: 斩断侵略者的～ cut off the claws of the aggressors
【魔怔】mózheng〈名〉〈口〉abnormal behaviour

mǒ

抹 mǒ
A〈动〉**1**（涂抹）apply: ～粉 put on powder ‖ ～口红 apply lipstick ‖ 给她的伤口～点药膏。Smear some ointment over her wound. ‖ 给面包上～点黄油。Spread some butter on the bread. **2**（消除）erase: 仇恨不易从人们心中～去。Hatred is not easily erased from people's hearts. ‖ 她把他的形象从记忆中～去。She wiped his image from her memory. ▸～零, ～杀 **3**（擦去）wipe: ～去额头上的汗水 wipe the sweat off one's forehead ‖ ～眼泪 wipe away one's tears
B〈量〉ray: 一～斜阳 a ray of the setting sun ‖ 一～月光 a moon beam
▸mā, mò
【抹鼻子】mǒ bízi〈动〉〈方〉cry
【抹脖子】mǒ bózi〈惯〉slit one's own throat
【抹刀】mǒdāo = 抹子 mǒzi
【抹掉】mǒdiào〈动〉erase: ～磁盘上的文件 erase a file from a disc ‖ 从名单上～名字 delete one's name from a list
【抹黑】mǒhēi〈动〉〈喻〉discredit: 因考试作弊给班级～ bring shame to one's class by cheating in an examination
【抹零】mǒlíng〈动〉drop the remainder and make a round sum
【抹杀】mǒshā〈动〉erase: ～成绩 obliterate one's achievements ‖ 一笔～ write off at one stroke
【抹煞】mǒshā = 抹杀 mǒshā
【抹稀泥】mǒ xīní = 和稀泥 huò xīní
【抹香鲸】mǒxiāngjīng〈名〉［动物］sperm whale
【抹一鼻子灰】mǒ yī bízi huī = 碰一鼻子灰 pèng yī bízi huī
【抹子】mǒzi〈名〉trowel

mò

末[1] mò
A〈名〉**1**（指部位）end: ▸～梢 **2**（指时间）last stage: 秋～ the end of autumn ‖ 在二十世纪～ in the late twentieth century ▸～尾, 周～ **3**（次要事物）minor details: ▸本～倒置, 舍本逐～ **4**（碎屑）dust: 茶叶～ tea dust ‖ 粉笔～ chalk powder ‖ 肉～ minced meat ▸锯～
B〈形〉last: 最～一个 last one ▸～日, 穷途～路

末[2] mò〈名〉［戏曲］*mo* [type of character in traditional Chinese opera, often a middle-aged man]
【末班车】mòbānchē〈名〉**1**（指公共汽车）last bus;（指火车）last train: 赶上～ catch the last bus **2**〈喻〉（指机会）last chance
【末代】mòdài〈名〉last dynastic reign: ～皇帝 last emperor
【末端】mòduān〈名〉terminal
【末伏】mòfú〈名〉**1**（指时期）third *fu* [last of the three ten-day periods of the hot season] **2**（指日子）first day of the third

fu [first day of the last period of the hot season]

【末后】mòhòu〈名〉end: 排在队的～ stand at the end of a line

【末节】mòjié〈名〉minor details: ▸细枝～

【末了】mòliǎo〈名〉end: ～她还是辞了职。In the end she resigned from office.

【末流】mòliú **A**〈名〉later stage of a school of thought, literature, etc. **B**〈形〉inferior: ～演员 minor actor ‖ ～足球队 third-rate football team

【末路】mòlù〈名〉dead end: ▸穷途～

【末年】mònián〈名〉last years of a person or a dynasty: 唐朝～ last years of the Tang Dynasty

【末期】mòqī ▸**p. 618**〈名〉final stage: 八十年代～ in the late eighties

【末日】mòrì〈名〉**1**［基督教］Judgement Day **2**（指灭亡）doom: ～将至 the end is near ‖ 世界～ end of the world

【末梢】mòshāo〈名〉end: 辫子的～ tip of a plait ‖ 神经～ nerve ending

【末世】mòshì〈名〉last phase of an age: 封建～ last years of feudalism

【末尾】mòwěi〈名〉end: 站在～ stand at the end of a queue ‖ 小说的～ end of a novel

【末席】mòxí〈名〉end seat

【末叶】mòyè〈名〉last years of a century or dynasty: 二十世纪～ late twentieth century ‖ 明朝～ last years of the Ming Dynasty

【末子】mòzi〈名〉dust: 煤～ coal dust

【末座】mòzuò〈名〉lowliest seat at the table

没（沒）mò〈动〉**1**（沉没）sink: ～入水中 submerge into water ‖ ～水而亡 be drowned ▸沉～ **2**〈书〉（终结）come to an end: ▸～齿不忘，～世 **3**（消失）disappear: ▸出～无常，神出鬼～ **4**（没收）confiscate: 抄～ search and confiscate ▸～收 **5**（漫过）rise beyond: 草高～腰。The grass is waist-high. ‖ 洪水～过了河堤。The flood ran over the riverbank. ▸méi

【没齿不忘】mòchǐ-bùwàng〈成〉remember for the rest of one's life

【没顶】mòdǐng〈动〉[of water] come over one's head: 水深～。The water comes up above a person's head.

【没落】mòluò〈动〉decline: ～地主/贵族 declining landlord/aristocrat ‖ 腐朽～的制度 rotten and degenerate system ‖ 劳工实力日趋～。Labour power is on the decline.

【没奈何】mònàihé〈动〉have no way out: 我错过了晚班车，～只好第二天一大早再走。I missed the night train, so I had no alternative but to go early the next morning.

【没世】mòshì〈名〉one's whole life: ～难忘 be unforgettable for the rest of one's life

【没收】mòshōu〈动〉confiscate: ～非法所得 confiscate illegal income ‖ ～违禁品 confiscate the contraband

【没药】mòyào〈名〉［中药］myrrh

抹 mò〈动〉**1**（涂抹）plaster: ～墙 plaster a wall ‖ ～水泥地 seal a cement floor **2**（绕过）bypass: ▸拐弯～角 ▸mā, mǒ

【抹不开】mòbukāi = 磨不开 mòbukāi

【抹得开】mòdekāi = 磨得开 mòdekāi

【抹灰】mòhuī〈动〉［建筑］plaster (a wall): ～工 plasterer

茉 mò

【茉莉】mòli〈名〉［植物］jasmine

【茉莉花】mòlìhuā〈名〉jasmine: ～茶 jasmine tea

殁 mò〈动〉〈书〉die: 病～ die of illness

沫 mò〈名〉**1**（泡沫）foam: 肥皂～儿 soapsuds ‖ 啤酒～ beer froth ‖ 口吐白～ form bubbles at the mouth ▸泡～ **2**（唾液）saliva: ▸唾～，相濡以～

【沫子】mòzi〈名〉foam

陌 mò〈名〉**1**（田间小路）footpath between fields: ▸阡～ **2**（道路）roads: ▸～路，巷～

【陌路】mòlù〈名〉**1**（指路）streets and paths **2**（指人）stranger (whom one passes in the street): 视同～ treat sb. like a stranger

【陌路人】mòlùrén = 陌路 mòlù 2

【陌生】mòshēng〈形〉strange: ～面孔 unfamiliar face ‖ 在～的环境里 in an alien environment ‖ ～人 stranger

冒 mò

▸mào

【冒顿】Mòdú〈名〉name of a Xiongnu chieftain in the early Han Dynasty

脉（脈）mò

▸mài

【脉脉】mòmò〈形〉affectionate: ～含情地看着某人 watch over sb. tenderly and silently ‖ 温情～ full of tender affection

莫 mò

A〈代〉〈书〉none: 最雄辩的～过于事实。Facts are more eloquent than words. ▸～不，哀～大于心死

B〈副〉**1**（不）not: ～为儿孙做牛马。Do not slave for your children. ▸～衷一是，望尘～及 **2**（表禁止）don't: 非公/非请～入。No admittance except on business by invitation. **3**（表猜测）[indicating a guess or a rhetorical question]: 他没来，～不是生气了？He didn't come. Do you think it's because he is angry?

【莫不】mòbù〈副〉without exception: 全家人～欢欣鼓舞。The whole family were completely elated.

【莫不是】mòbùshì = 莫非 mòfēi

【莫测高深】mòcè-gāoshēn〈成〉mystifying: ～的表情 enigmatic expression

【莫此为甚】mòcǐwéishèn〈成〉there is nothing worse than this

【莫大】mòdà〈形〉greatest: ～的光荣/幸福 greatest honour/happiness ‖ 能同你认识是我～的荣幸。It is a great honour for me to meet you.

【莫非】mòfēi〈副〉can it be that: ～他撒谎了？Could it be that he told a lie?

【莫过于】mòguòyú〈动〉nothing is more ... than: 我国古代的思想家，名气大的恐怕～孔子。Of all the ancient Chinese thinkers, perhaps no one is more famous than Confucius.

【莫可指数】mòkě-zhǐshǔ〈成〉〈喻〉countless

【莫名】mòmíng〈动〉be impossible to explain: ～的恐怖 nameless horror

【莫名其妙】mòmíng-qímiào〈成〉**1**（不可猜测）be unable to make head or tail of sth.: 他变幻莫测的情绪，总是令我们～。We could never make head or tail of his changing moods. **2**（奇怪）without rhyme or reason: 他今天～地缺席。He is unaccountably absent today.

【莫明其妙】mòmíng-qímiào = 莫名其妙 mòmíng-qímiào

【莫逆之交】mònìzhījiāo〈成〉close friends

【莫如】mòrú〈连〉〈书〉might as well: 与其呆在家里，～出去走走。It would be better to go out for a walk than to stay at home.

【莫若】mòruò = 莫如 mòrú

【莫桑比克】Mòsāngbǐkè〈名〉Mozambique: ～共和国 Republic of Mozambique ‖ ～人 Mozambican

【莫斯科】Mòsīkē〈名〉Moscow

【莫须有】mòxūyǒu〈成〉trumped-up: ～的罪名 trumped-up charge

【莫衷一是】mòzhōngyīshì〈成〉be at variance: 议论纷纷，～。There were all sorts of comments but no consensus.

秣 mò

A〈名〉fodder: ▸粮～

B〈动〉feed animals: ▸～马厉兵

【秣马厉兵】mòmǎ-lìbīng〈成〉make preparations for war: 两个国家都忙着～。Both countries were busy preparing for war.

蓦（驀）mò〈副〉〈书〉suddenly: ▸～地，～然

【蓦地】mòdì〈副〉〈书〉all of a sudden: ～一跃而起 jump to one's feet all of a sudden

【蓦然】mòrán〈副〉〈书〉all of a sudden: ～狂风大作，大雨倾盆。Suddenly a high wind sprang up and the rain started pouring down.

貊（貉）Mò〈名〉〈古〉Mo [ethnic group living in north-east China]

漠 mò

A〈名〉desert: 大～ vast desert ▸沙～

B〈形〉indifferent: ▸～视，冷～

【漠不关心】mòbùguānxīn〈成〉indifferent: 对群众的疾苦～ be indifferent to the sufferings of the people

【漠漠】mòmò〈形〉**1**（指云雾）misty: 村子笼罩在一层～的烟雾中。A thick mist spread over the village. **2**（广漠而沉寂）vast and lonely: 远处有～的草原。A vast stretch of grassland could be seen in the distance.

【漠然】mòrán〈形〉indifferent: ～处之 be unconcerned

【漠然置之】mòrán-zhìzhī〈成〉remain indifferent: 对名利～ be indifferent to worldly gains

【漠视】mòshì〈动〉overlook: ～群众的根本利益 show no regard for the fundamental interests of the masses

寞 mò〈形〉deserted: ▸寂～

靺 mò

【靺鞨】Mòhé〈名〉〈古〉Mohe [ethnic group living in northeast China in ancient times]

墨 mò

A〈名〉**1**（墨汁）Chinese ink: 磨/研～ rub an ink stick (against an ink stone) ‖ ～太浓/稀了。The ink is too thick/thin. ▸～斗，～汁 **2**（颜料）ink: ▸～水，油～ **3**（指字画）a substitute word for sb.'s poetry, essays, handwriting or painting:

▸～宝, 文～, 遗～ **4**〈喻〉(学问) learning: 胸无点～的人 unlearned man **5** Mò (墨家) Mohism: ▸～守成规

B〈形〉black: ▸～镜

C〈动〉**1**(指刑罚) tattoo the face (as a punishment in ancient China): ▸～刑 **2**〈书〉(贪污) embezzle: ▸～吏, 贪～

【墨宝】mòbǎo〈名〉**1**(指字画) treasured scrolls of calligraphy/painting: 搜求～ seek out calligraphic treasures **2**〈尊〉(代指对方的作品) your beautiful hand-writing/painting

【墨斗】mòdǒu〈名〉carpenter's ink marker

【墨斗鱼】mòdǒuyú〈名〉cuttlefish

【墨尔本】Mò'ěrběn〈名〉Melbourne

【墨粉】mòfěn〈名〉toner

【墨海】mòhǎi〈名〉big basin-like ink dish

【墨盒】mòhé〈名〉ink cartridge: 更换打印机～ change a printer cartridge

【墨黑】mòhēi〈形〉pitch-black: 在一个～的夜晚 on a pitch-black night ‖〈喻〉他对那件事两眼～。He is completely in the dark about that.

【墨迹】mòjì〈名〉**1**(指污迹) ink stains: 衣服上的～ ink stains on one's clothes **2**(指字画) sb.'s writing/painting: 于右任的～ Yu Youren's calligraphy

【墨迹未干】mòjì-wèigān〈成〉before the ink is dry: 停火协议～, 他们就把它撕毁了。They tore up the cease-fire agreement before the ink was dry.

【墨家】Mòjiā〈名〉Mohist school [school of thought based on the teachings of Mo Di (墨翟, c. 468-376BC)]: ～学说 Mohism

【墨晶】mòjīng〈名〉smoky quartz

【墨镜】mòjìng〈名〉sunglasses: 戴～ wear sunglasses

【墨菊】mòjú〈名〉dark chrysanthemum

【墨客】mòkè〈名〉〈书〉men of letters: ▸骚人～

【墨累河】Mòlěihé ▸**p. 294**〈名〉Murray River

【墨吏】mòlì〈名〉〈书〉〈旧〉corrupt officials

【墨绿】mòlǜ〈形〉dark green: ～色 blackish green

【墨守陈规】mòshǒu-chénguī = 墨守成规 mòshǒu-chéngguī

【墨守成规】mòshǒu-chéngguī〈成〉stick to convention: ～的人 slave to convention ‖ 我们要敢于创新, 不要～。We should dare to be creative instead of getting stuck in a rut.

【墨水】mòshuǐ〈名〉**1**(墨汁) writing ink **2**(用于钢笔) ink: 红/蓝～ red/blue ink **3**〈喻〉(学问) book learning: 他肚子里还有点～。He is something of a scholar.

【墨西哥】Mòxīgē〈名〉Mexico: ～合众国 United Mexican States ‖ ～人 Mexican

【墨西哥城】Mòxīgēchéng〈名〉Mexico City

【墨线】mòxiàn〈名〉**1**(墨斗上的线) line in a carpenter's ink marker **2**(用墨斗打出的直线) line made by a carpenter's ink marker

【墨刑】mòxíng〈名〉〈古〉tattooing of the face (as punishment)

【墨鱼】mòyú = 乌贼 wūzéi

【墨汁】mòzhī〈名〉prepared Chinese ink

【墨子】Mòzǐ〈名〉**1**(指人) Mozi [a reverent name for Mo Di (墨翟), a thinker of the pre-Qin period and founder of Mohism] **2**(指著作) *The Book of Mozi* [complete works of the Mohist school of thought]

【墨渍】mòzì〈名〉ink blot

瘼 mò〈名〉〈书〉hardships: 民～ sufferings of the people

默 mò〈动〉**1**(沉默) be silent: ～不作声 keep silent ▸～读, ～许, 沉～ **2**(默写) write from memory: ～课文 write out the text from memory ▸～写

【默哀】mò'āi〈动〉stand in silent tribute: 为死者～ stand in silent tribute to the dead

【默察】mòchá〈动〉watch quietly

【默祷】mòdǎo〈动〉say a silent prayer

【默读】mòdú〈动〉read silently: 请～课文。Please read the text silently.

【默记】mòjì〈动〉make a mental note

【默剧】mòjù〈名〉silent show

【默默】mòmò〈形〉quiet, silent: ～无言 without uttering a word

【默默无闻】mòmò-wúwén〈成〉unknown to the public: ～地工作 work in anonymity

【默念】mòniàn〈动〉**1**(默读) read silently: ～一首诗 read a poem silently **2**(暗想) recall: ～儿时情景 recall one's childhood

【默契】mòqì **A**〈形〉well-coordinated: 配合～ be well-coordinated **B**〈名〉secret agreement: 达成～ reach a tacit understanding

【默然】mòrán〈形〉silent: ～无语 be speechless

【默认】mòrèn〈动〉**1**(指承认) tacitly approve: ～既成事实 tacitly acknowledge a fait accompli **2**［计算机］default: ～打印机 default printer

【默书】mòshū〈动〉write out a text from memory

【默诵】mòsòng〈动〉read silently to oneself from memory

【默算】mòsuàn〈动〉do mental arithmetic

【默西塞德郡】Mòxīsàidéjùn〈名〉Merseyside

【默想】mòxiǎng〈动〉ponder over

【默写】mòxiě〈动〉write from memory: ～生词 write out new words from memory

【默许】mòxǔ〈动〉tacitly consent to: 得到～ win tacit consent ‖ 她不说话, 就是～了。Her silence implies consent.

磨 mò

A〈名〉mill: 电/石～ electric/stone mill ▸～盘

B〈动〉**1**(弄碎) grind: ～麦子 mill wheat ‖ ～豆腐 grind soya beans to make bean curd ▸～房 **2**(掉转) turn round: 这地方太小, 汽车～不过来。This place is too narrow to turn the car round.

▸mó

【磨不开】mòbukāi〈动〉〈口〉**1**(没面子) feel miffed: 没有被邀请参加婚礼他脸上有点～。He was a little put out at not being invited to the wedding. **2**(不好意思) hesitate for fear of impairing personal relations: 对他有意见就提, 有什么～的? If you have complaints about him, you should make them without fear of offending him. **3**〈方〉(想不通) not be convinced: 一有～的事, 我就找他商量。Whenever I cannot figure something out, I talk it over with him.

【磨叨】mòdao〈动〉**1**(唠叨) nag: 说两句就行了, 别再～啦。That's enough. Don't keep going on and on about it. **2**〈方〉(谈论) talk: 你们在～啥呢? What are you chatting about?

【磨得开】mòdekāi〈动〉〈口〉**1**(有面子) not take offence: 你当面挖苦他, 脸上～吗? Don't you think making sarcastic remarks to his face would embarrass him? **2**(好意思) be able to act impartially: 你拒绝她请你吃饭, 你～吗? Don't you find it difficult to refuse her invitation to dinner? **3**〈方〉(想得通) be convinced: 这件事我～, 您就放心吧。You can rest assured that I will come round to it.

【磨烦】mòfan〈动〉**1**(纠缠) pester: ～母亲 pester one's mother **2**(拖延) hesitate: 别～了,我们开始吧。Stop dawdling. Let's get started.

【磨坊】mòfáng〈名〉mill

【磨房】mòfáng = 磨坊 mòfáng

【磨面机】mòmiànjī〈名〉flour-milling machine

【磨盘】mòpán〈名〉lower millstone

【磨盘柿】mòpánshì〈名〉lid persimmon

【磨棚】mòpéng〈名〉mill shed

【磨扇】mòshàn〈名〉millstone

【磨子】mòzi〈名〉mill

貘 mò〈名〉［动物］tapir

耱 mò

A = 耢 lào A

B〈动〉level land with this kind of tool

mōu

哞 mōu〈拟〉(指母牛) moo; (指群羊) low; (指公牛) bellow: 母牛～～叫了。The cow mooed.

móu

牟 móu〈动〉seek: ▸～利, ～取

【牟利】móulì〈动〉seek profit: 非法～ seek illicit profits

【牟取】móuqǔ〈动〉seek: ～暴利 strive after fat profits

侔 móu〈动〉〈书〉match: 两者各不相～。The two don't match.

眸 móu〈名〉〈书〉pupil (of eye): ▸明～皓齿, 凝～

【眸子】móuzi〈名〉pupil (of eye)

谋 (謀) móu

A〈动〉**1**(图谋) plan: ▸～划, 预～ **2**(谋取) seek: ～私利 seek private gains ‖ 另～出路 look for another way out ‖ 为人民～幸福 work for the happiness of the people **3**(商议) consult: ▸不～而合, 与虎～皮

B〈名〉plan: ▸～略, 智～

【谋财害命】móucái-hàimìng〈成〉conspire to kill and rob

【谋臣】móuchén〈名〉emperor's councillor

【谋反】móufǎn〈动〉conspire against the state: 蓄意～ plot treason

【谋害】móuhài〈动〉**1**(指杀害) conspire to murder: ～亲夫 plot against one's husband's life **2**(指陷害) plot a frame-up against: 遭到～ be framed

【谋和】móuhé〈动〉strive for peace

【谋划】móuhuà〈动〉plot: ～赈灾义演 plan a benefit performance for disaster relief ‖ 精心～ plan meticulously

【谋利】móulì〈动〉strive for profit

【谋虑】móulǜ〈动〉contemplate: ～深远 be circumspect and far-sighted
【谋略】móulüè〈名〉tactics: 他是个颇有～的人。He is a man of great resource.
【谋面】móumiàn〈动〉〈书〉meet each other: 素未～ have never met before
【谋篇】móupiān〈动〉〈书〉plan a composition
【谋求】móuqiú〈动〉seek: ～解决办法 try to find a solution ‖ ～两国关系正常化 seek normalization of relations between the two countries
【谋取】móuqǔ〈动〉seek: ～私利 seek personal gain ‖ ～职位 try to gain a position
【谋杀】móushā〈动〉murder: 惨遭～ be brutally murdered ‖ ～案 murder case ‖ ～罪 murder charge
【谋生】móushēng ▸**p. 966**〈动〉make a living: 出外～ leave home and seek a living elsewhere ‖ 靠写作～ earn a living as a writer
【谋士】móushì〈名〉〈旧〉adviser
【谋事】móushì〈动〉**1**（作计划）plan matters: ～在人，成事在天。The planning lies with Man, the outcome with Heaven. **2**（找工作）look for a job: 设法～ try to find a job
【谋私】móusī〈动〉seek personal gains: ▸以权～
【谋算】móusuàn〈动〉scheme
【谋陷】móuxiàn〈动〉plot a frame-up against: ～忠良 frame loyal officials and honest persons ‖ 遭人～ be framed
【谋职】móuzhí〈动〉try to find employment: 四处～ look for a job everywhere

缪（繆） móu ▸绸缪 chóumóu
▸Miào, miù

mǒu

某 mǒu〈代〉**1**（指代特定对象）[referring to a specific person or thing] certain: 赵～ a certain Zhao ‖ 海军～部 a certain unit of the Navy **2**（指代不定对象）[referring to an unspecified person or thing] certain: 在～种条件下 under certain conditions ‖ ～年～月～日 on a certain day in a certain month in a certain year **3**（用于自称）[referring to oneself or one's surname]: 我周～可不是好欺负的。I, Zhou, am not easily bullied. **4**（用于称呼他人）[referring to someone else's surname, often impolitely]: 请告诉王～，我的忍耐是有限度的。Please tell Wang that my patience has its limits.
【某某】mǒumǒu〈代〉so-and-so: ～人 someone ‖ ～医院 a certain hospital
【某人】mǒurén〈名〉certain person
【某些】mǒuxiē〈代〉some: ～人 certain people

mú

毪 mú
【毪子】múzi〈名〉Tibetan woollen fabric

模 mú〈名〉**1**（模子）mould: 钢～ steel mould ‖ 铜～ copper mould ▸～板, ～子 **2**（外表）appearance: ▸～样
▸mó
【模板】múbǎn〈名〉**1**［建筑］formwork **2**［计算机］template
【模具】mújù〈名〉mould: ～钢 die steel
【模块】múkuài〈名〉mould block
【模压】múyā〈名〉mould pressing: ～胶底皮鞋 leather shoes with moulded-on rubber soles
【模样】múyàng〈名〉**1**（外表）appearance: 学生～ appearance of a student ‖ 她的～很像她姐姐。She looks very much like her sister. ‖ 他～非常英俊。He looks very handsome. **2**（表约略）around [usu used after a numeral-classifier compound and expressing a rough time]: 半小时～ about half an hour ‖ 那姑娘有二十岁～。The girl was around twenty. **3**（形势）situation: 看～，这家饭馆要关门了。It appears that the restaurant is about to close.
【模子】múzi〈名〉mould: 糕点～ pastry mould ‖ 一个～铸出来的 like two peas in a pod

mǔ

母 mǔ
A〈名〉**1**（母亲）mother: ～女 mother and daughter ‖ 生～ biological mother ▸～爱, ～亲 **2**（女性长辈）one's female elders: ▸伯～, 岳～, 祖～ **3**（指零件）nut: ▸螺～ **4**（指源头）origin: 失败乃成功之～。Failure is the mother of success. ▸～本
B〈形〉female: ～牛 cow ‖ ～猪 sow
【母爱】mǔ'ài〈名〉motherly love: 得到～ receive motherly love ‖ 无私的～ selfless motherly love
【母本】mǔběn〈名〉［植物］female parent: ～植株 maternal plant
【母畜】mǔchù〈名〉female animal
【母带】mǔdài〈名〉master tape
【母公司】mǔgōngsī〈名〉parent company: ～及其子公司 mother company and its affiliates
【母机】mǔjī〈名〉machine tool
【母鸡】mǔjī〈名〉hen
【母老虎】mǔlǎohǔ〈名〉**1**〈本〉tigress **2**〈喻〉（指人）shrew: 她姐姐真是个～。Her sister is a veritable man-eater.
【母马】mǔmǎ〈名〉mare
【母牛】mǔniú〈名〉cow
【母亲】mǔqīn ▸**p. 588**〈名〉mother: 慈爱的～ loving mother ‖ 代孕～ surrogate mother ‖ 生身～ biological mother
【母亲河】mǔqīnhé〈名〉mother river: 黄河和长江是中国人的～。The Chinese nation has been nurtured by the Yellow River and the Yangtze River.
【母亲节】Mǔqīnjié〈名〉Mother's Day
【母权制】mǔquánzhì〈名〉matriarchy
【母乳】mǔrǔ〈名〉breast milk: ～喂养 breast-feed (a baby)
【母树】mǔshù〈名〉mother tree: ～林 seed forest
【母体】mǔtǐ〈名〉female parent: ～免疫 maternal immunity
【母系】mǔxì〈形〉**1**（指血统归属）maternal: ～亲属 maternal relatives **2**（母女相承）matriarchal: ～社会 matriarchal society
【母校】mǔxiào〈名〉alma mater: 返回～ return to one's alma mater ‖ 献给～ dedicate sth. to one's alma mater
【母性】mǔxìng〈名〉motherhood: ～本能 maternal instinct
【母夜叉】mǔyèchā〈名〉**1**〈本〉female devil **2**〈喻〉〈粗〉tartar: 那妇人真是个～。That woman is a real dragon.
【母仪】mǔyí〈名〉paragon of motherhood
【母以子贵】mǔyǐzǐguì〈成〉the mother's honour increases as her son's position rises
【母音】mǔyīn〈名〉〈旧〉［语言］vowel
【母语】mǔyǔ ▸**p. 918**〈名〉**1**（第一语言）mother tongue: 用～写作 write in one's mother tongue **2**［语言］parent language
【母质】mǔzhì〈名〉matrix
【母株】mǔzhū〈名〉［植物］mother plant
【母子】mǔzǐ〈名〉mother and son: ～候车室 waiting room for mothers with babies ‖ ～平安。Both mother and baby are doing well.

牡 mǔ〈形〉male: ～牛 bull
【牡丹】mǔdan〈名〉peony
【牡丹虽好，也要绿叶扶持】mǔdan suī hǎo, yě yào lǜyè fúchí〈俗〉though the peony is lovely, it needs the support of green leaves to set it off
【牡丹江】Mǔdanjiāng ▸**p. 294**〈名〉Mudanjiang [river and city in Heilongjiang Province]
【牡蛎】mǔlì〈名〉oyster: ～养殖场 oyster farm
【牡马】mǔmǎ〈名〉stallion

亩（畝） mǔ〈量〉*mu* [unit of area, equal to 0.0667 hectare]
【亩产】mǔchǎn〈名〉yield per *mu*

拇 mǔ
【拇指】mǔzhǐ〈名〉**1**（手指）thumb: 竖起大～ give (sb./sth.) the thumbs up **2**（脚趾）big toe

姆 mǔ ▸保姆 bǎomǔ
▸m̄

姥 mǔ〈名〉〈书〉old woman
▸lǎo

鉧（鉧） mǔ ▸钴鉧 gǔmǔ

mù

木 mù
A〈名〉**1**（树木）tree: 伐～ cut down trees ▸林～, 果～ **2**（木材）wood: ～箱 wooden box ▸～头, 楠～ **3**（棺材）coffin: ▸棺～, 行将就～
B〈形〉**1**（麻木）numb: 我双手冻～了。My hands were numb with cold. **2**（质朴）plain: ▸～讷 **3**（反应慢）wooden: ▸～头～脑
【木板】mùbǎn〈名〉plank: ～床 plank bed
【木版】mùbǎn〈名〉［印刷］printing block: ～印刷 block printing
【木版画】mùbǎnhuà = 木刻 mùkè
【木本】mùběn〈名〉woody plant: ～经济作物 tree crop
【木本水源】mùběn-shuǐyuán〈成〉〈喻〉root of a matter
【木本植物】mùběn zhíwù〈名〉woody plant
【木菠萝】mùbōluó〈名〉［植物］jackfruit
【木材】mùcái〈名〉timber〈英〉; lumber〈美〉: ～加工 timber processing ‖ 名贵～ choice wood
【木材厂】mùcáichǎng〈名〉sawmill
【木柴】mùchái〈名〉firewood: 劈～ chop wood ‖ 把～烧成木炭 burn wood into

charcoal
【木醇】mùchún〈名〉［化学］ methyl alcohol
【木锉】mùcuò〈名〉 wood file
【木呆呆】mùdāidāi〈形〉 dazed: ～地站着 stand in a daze
【木地板】mùdìbǎn〈名〉 floorboard
【木雕】mùdiāo〈名〉 woodcarving: ～艺人 woodcarver
【木雕泥塑】mùdiāo-nísù〈成〉 as motionless and useless as a statue
【木牍】mùdú〈名〉［考古］ inscribed wooden tablet
【木耳】mù'ěr〈名〉 edible tree fungus
【木筏】mùfá〈名〉 raft: 乘～过河 cross a stream on a raft
【木芙蓉】mùfúróng〈名〉［植物］ cotton rose
【木工】mùgōng〈名〉 1（指工种） carpentry: 做～活儿 do woodwork 2（指人） carpenter
【木瓜】mùguā〈名〉［植物］ Chinese quince
【木管乐器】mùguǎn yuèqì〈名〉woodwind instrument
【木化石】mùhuàshí〈名〉 petrified wood
【木屐】mùjī〈名〉 clogs
【木简】mùjiǎn〈名〉［考古］ inscribed wooden slip
【木浆】mùjiāng〈名〉 wood pulp
【木匠】mùjiang〈名〉 carpenter
【木结构】mùjiégòu〈名〉 timber structure
【木槿】mùjǐn〈名〉［植物］ hibiscus
【木刻】mùkè〈名〉 woodcut: ～水印 watercolour block printing
【木兰】mùlán〈名〉［植物］ magnolia
【木立】mùlì〈动〉 stand motionless
【木料】mùliào〈名〉 timber〈英〉; lumber〈美〉
【木马】mùmǎ〈名〉 1（木制马） wooden horse 2［体育］ pommel horse 3（指游戏器械） hobby horse: ▸旋转～
【木马计】mùmǎjì〈名〉 stratagem of the Trojan Horse
【木棉】mùmián〈名〉［植物］ 1（指乔木） bombax 2（指纤维） kapok
【木模】mùmú〈名〉 wooden mould
【木乃伊】mùnǎiyī〈名〉 1〈本〉 mummy [embalmed body] 2〈喻〉 something rigid
【木讷】mùnè〈形〉〈书〉 inarticulate: 他总是～寡言。 He is always inarticulate and hesitant to speak.
【木偶】mù'ǒu〈名〉 1〈本〉 puppet: 牵线～ marionette ‖ 手套式～ glove puppet 2〈喻〉 wooden person: 像～一样毫无表情 be as expressionless as a carved figure
【木偶片】mù'ǒupiān〈名〉 puppet cartoon film
【木偶戏】mù'ǒuxì〈名〉 puppet show
【木排】mùpái〈名〉 raft: 放～ raft logs
【木片】mùpiàn〈名〉 wood chip
【木器】mùqì〈名〉 wooden furniture: ～厂 wood factory
【木琴】mùqín ▸**p. 929**〈名〉［音乐］ xylophone
【木然】mùrán〈形〉 dumbfounded: 神情～ look stupefied
【木人石心】mùrén-shíxīn〈成〉〈喻〉 insusceptible
【木石】mùshí〈名〉 1〈本〉 wood and stone: ～结构 structure of wood and stone 2〈喻〉 lifeless thing: 人非～，孰能无情？ A man is neither wood nor stone, how can one be apathetic?
【木梳】mùshū〈名〉 wooden comb
【木薯】mùshǔ〈名〉［植物］ cassava
【木丝】mùsī〈名〉 excelsior
【木丝板】mùsībǎn〈名〉［建筑］ wood wool board
【木髓】mùsuǐ〈名〉 pith
【木炭】mùtàn〈名〉 charcoal
【木炭画】mùtànhuà〈名〉charcoal drawing
【木糖醇】mùtángchún〈名〉［化学］ xylitol
【木头木脑】mùtóu-mùnǎo〈形〉dull-witted
【木头】mùtou〈名〉 wood
【木头人】mùtourén〈名〉 blockhead
【木纹】mùwén〈名〉 wood grain
【木樨】mùxi〈名〉 1［植物］ sweet-scented osmanthus 2（指鸡蛋） eggs beaten and then cooked: ～汤 egg drop soup
【木屑】mùxiè〈名〉 saw dust: ～板 xylolite slab
【木星】Mùxīng〈名〉 Jupiter
【木须肉】mùxūròu〈名〉 stir-fried shredded pork and beaten eggs with black fungus
【木已成舟】mùyǐchéngzhōu〈成〉〈喻〉 what is done cannot be undone
【木俑】mùyǒng〈名〉［考古］ wooden figurine
【木鱼】mùyú〈名〉 wooden fish [percussion instrument made of a hollow wooden block]: 敲～ beat a wooden fish
【木贼】mùzéi〈名〉［植物］ scouring rush
【木质部】mùzhìbù〈名〉［植物］ xylem
【木制】mùzhì〈形〉 wooden: ～玩具 wooden toys ‖ ～品 wood products

目 mù

A〈名〉 1（眼睛） eye: ▸～光，耳闻～睹 2（网孔） mesh: ▸纲举～张 3（项目） item: ▸细～，要～ 4（目录） list: ▸节～，剧～，账～ 5［生物］ order: 亚～ suborder ▸灵长～ 6（名称） title: ▸名～，题～
B〈动〉〈书〉 look: ～为奇迹 regard as miracle ▸一～了然
C〈量〉（指围棋） eye: 以一～半获胜/告负 win/lose by an eye and a half
【目标】mùbiāo〈名〉 1（指对象） target: 暴露～ give away one's position ‖ 发现～ find the target ‖ 他是警察追捕的～之一。 He was one of those targeted by the police. 2（指境地） goal: 实现经济增长～ meet economic growth targets ‖ 宏伟～ grand goal ‖ 我的～是当冠军。 I've set my sights on winning the championship.
【目标管理】mùbiāo guǎnlǐ〈名〉 management by objectives
【目不见睫】mùbùjiànjié〈成〉〈喻〉 lack self-knowledge
【目不交睫】mùbùjiāojié〈成〉 not sleep a wink
【目不窥园】mùbùkuīyuán〈成〉 bury oneself in one's studies
【目不忍睹】mùbùrěndǔ〈成〉 cannot bear to look at
【目不忍视】mùbùrěnshì = 目不忍睹 mùbùrěndǔ
【目不识丁】mùbùshídīng〈成〉 be completely illiterate
【目不暇给】mùbùxiájǐ = 目不暇接 mùbùxiájiē
【目不暇接】mùbùxiájiē〈成〉 there are too many things for the eye to take in
【目不斜视】mùbùxiéshì〈成〉 refuse to be distracted
【目不转睛】mùbùzhuǎnjīng〈成〉 gaze steadily: ～地看着 never take one's eyes off sb./sth.
【目测】mùcè〈动〉 estimate the distance with one's eyes: ～距离 estimate the distance with one's eyes
【目次】mùcì〈名〉 table of contents
【目瞪口呆】mùdèng-kǒudāi〈成〉 be flabbergasted: 吓得～ be struck dumb with fear
【目的】mùdì〈名〉 aim: 达到～ accomplish one's objective ‖ 预期的～ intended purpose ‖ 他那样做的～何在？ What's the point of his doing that?
【目的地】mùdìdì〈名〉 destination
【目的港】mùdìgǎng〈名〉 port of destination
【目的论】mùdìlùn〈名〉［哲学］ teleology
【目睹】mùdǔ〈动〉 witness: ▸耳闻～
【目光】mùguāng〈名〉 1（视线） view: 人们的～都投向发言者。 All eyes were on the speaker. 2（眼神） gaze: 期待的～ look of expectation ‖ ～炯炯 flashing eyes 3（眼光） sight: ～远大 be far-sighted
【目光短浅】mùguāng-duǎnqiǎn〈成〉 be short-sighted
【目光如豆】mùguāng-rúdòu〈成〉 have a narrow vision
【目光如炬】mùguāng-rújù〈成〉 1（指发怒） with eyes blazing 2（有远见） be bright-eyed
【目击】mùjī〈动〉 see with one's own eyes: ～证据 ocular proof ‖ ～者 eyewitness
【目见】mùjiàn〈动〉 see for oneself: 耳闻不如～。 Seeing is believing.
【目镜】mùjìng〈名〉［物理］ eyepiece
【目空一切】mùkōngyīqiè〈成〉be extremely arrogant: 他是个～的人。 He is a snooty sort of person.
【目力】mùlì〈名〉〈书〉vision: ～不济 have poor eyesight
【目录】mùlù〈名〉 1（指事物名目） catalogue: 分类～ classified catalogue ‖ 图书～ library catalogue 2（指篇章名目） table of contents: 给书编出～ make up the table of contents of a book 3［计算机］ directory: 创建～ create a directory
【目迷五色】mùmíwǔsè〈成〉〈喻〉 be dazzled by a complicated situation
【目前】mùqián〈名〉 present moment: 到～为止 so far ‖ ～的国际形势 present international situation
【目视飞行】mùshì fēixíng〈名〉［航空］ visual flight
【目送】mùsòng〈动〉 follow sb. with one's eyes: ～帆船远航 watch the boat sail into the distance
【目无法纪】mùwúfǎjì〈成〉 show contempt for the law
【目无全牛】mùwúquánniú〈成〉 have a very analytical mind
【目无余子】mùwúyúzǐ〈成〉be supercilious
【目无尊长】mùwú-zūnzhǎng〈成〉show no respect to one's elders and superiors
【目下】mùxià〈名〉 the present time: ～我忙着准备履历表。 At the moment I am busy preparing my curriculum vitae.
【目眩】mùxuàn〈动〉 feel dizzy: 感到头晕～ feel dizzy and faint ‖ 正午的阳光令人～。 The noon sunlight is dazzling.
【目指气使】mùzhǐ-qìshǐ〈成〉 order people about with glares
【目中无人】mùzhōng-wúrén〈成〉 be supercilious: 你看他的神气，简直是～。 Just look at the airs he's giving himself, looking down his nose at everybody.

仫 mù

【仫佬族】Mùlǎozú〈名〉 Mulam ethnic group

沐 mù〈动〉 wash one's hair: ►～浴, 栉风～雨

【沐猴而冠】 mùhóu'érguàn〈成〉〈喻〉 a worthless person in imposing attire

【沐浴】 mùyù〈动〉 1 (洗澡) take a bath: ～更衣 take a bath and change into clean clothes 2 〈喻〉(沉浸) bathe: ～在节日的气氛里 revel in a festive atmosphere ‖ ～在阳光里 be bathed in sunshine

苜 mù

【苜蓿】 mùxu〈名〉［植物］ alfalfa

牧 mù〈动〉 herd: ～马 herd horses ►～场, 放～

【牧草】 mùcǎo〈名〉 herbage: ～肥美。 The herbage is rich.

【牧场】 mùchǎng〈名〉 1 (指草场) pastureland: 天然～ natural grazing ground 2 (指企业单位) livestock farm

【牧放】 mùfàng〈动〉 herd

【牧歌】 mùgē〈名〉 1 (指歌) pastoral song 2［音乐］ madrigal

【牧工】 mùgōng〈名〉 hired herdsman

【牧民】 mùmín〈名〉 herdsman: 女～ herdswoman

【牧区】 mùqū〈名〉 1 (牧场) pastureland 2 (指以畜牧为主) pastoral area

【牧犬】 mùquǎn〈名〉 sheep dog

【牧人】 mùrén〈名〉 herdsman

【牧师】 mùshī ►**p. 966**〈名〉［基督教］ pastor

【牧童】 mùtóng〈名〉 shepherd boy

【牧畜】 mùxù = 畜牧 xùmù

【牧羊犬】 mùyángquǎn〈名〉 sheep dog

【牧业】 mùyè〈名〉 livestock farming: ～兴旺。 Animal husbandry is flourishing.

【牧主】 mùzhǔ〈名〉 herd owner

钼(鉬) mù〈名〉［化学］ molybdenum (Mo)

募 mù〈动〉 1 (指钱财) collect: 你们～到了多少款子? How much have you raised? ►～化, ～捐 2 (指人) enlist: ～兵 recruit soldiers

【募兵制】 mùbīngzhì〈名〉 mercenary system

【募股】 mùgǔ〈动〉 raise capital by floating shares

【募化】 mùhuà〈动〉 [of monks, Taoists] beg for alms

【募集】 mùjí〈动〉 collect: ～慈善基金 raise funds for charity

【募捐】 mùjuān〈动〉 collect donations: ～选举资金 solicit campaign contributions ‖ 为白血病学生～ collect money for a student with leukaemia

墓 mù〈名〉 grave: 盗～ rob a grave ‖ 掘～ dig a grave ‖ 扫～ visit sb.'s grave ‖ 烈士～ tombs of revolutionary martyrs ►～地, 陵～

【墓碑】 mùbēi〈名〉 gravestone

【墓表】 mùbiǎo〈名〉 1 (墓碑) gravestone 2 (指文体) inscriptions on a tombstone

【墓场】 mùchǎng〈名〉 graveyard

【墓道】 mùdào〈名〉 1 (指坟墓前) path leading to a grave 2 (指墓室前) aisle leading to the coffin chamber of an ancient tomb

【墓地】 mùdì〈名〉 cemetery

【墓祭】 mùjì〈名〉 memorial ceremony at a tomb

【墓室】 mùshì〈名〉 coffin chamber

【墓穴】 mùxué〈名〉 coffin pit

【墓园】 mùyuán = 陵园 língyuán

【墓葬】 mùzàng〈名〉［考古］ grave: ～群 group of graves

【墓志】 mùzhì〈名〉 inscription on a memorial tablet within a tomb

【墓志铭】 mùzhìmíng〈名〉 epitaph

幕 mù〈名〉 1 (帐篷) tent: ►帷～ 2 〈古〉(府署) office of a commanding general in ancient China: ►～府, ～僚 3 (幕布) curtain: ～启。 The curtain goes up. ‖ ～落。 The curtain comes down. ►～布, 银～ 4 (场次) act: 一出三～话剧 a play in three acts ‖ 一～～壮丽的景色 one splendid view followed by another ►独～剧, 序～

【幕布】 mùbù = 幕 mù 3

【幕府】 mùfǔ〈名〉 1 〈古〉(指中国) office of a commanding general in ancient China 2 (指日本) shogun: ～制度 shogunate

【幕后】 mùhòu〈名〉〈喻〉〈贬〉 behind closed doors: ～操纵 pull strings behind the scenes ‖ ～策划 plot behind closed doors ‖ ～交易 backstage deal ‖ ～人物 wire-puller ‖ 退居～ retire behind closed doors

【幕间休息】 mùjiān xiūxi〈名〉 intermission; interval〈英〉

【幕僚】 mùliáo〈名〉 1 〈旧〉(指属官) assistant to a high official in ancient China 2 (助理) aides and staff

【幕墙】 mùqiáng〈名〉 curtain wall: 玻璃～ glass curtain wall

【幕天席地】 mùtiān-xídì〈成〉〈喻〉 1 (指心胸开阔) have great breadth of view 2 (指环境艰苦) in the open

睦 mù〈形〉 harmonious: ►和～

【睦邻】 mùlín〈动〉 get along well with one's neighbours: 发展～友好关系 cultivate good neighbourly relations ‖ ～政策 good-neighbour policy

慕 mù〈动〉 1 (敬仰) admire: ～虚荣 be given to vanity ►羡～, 仰～ 2 (思念) yearn for: ►爱～, 思～

【慕名】 mùmíng〈动〉 admire a famous person: ～求见 have admiration for sb. and ask for an interview

【慕尼黑】 Mùníhēi〈名〉 Munich

暮 mù

A〈名〉 dusk: ►～霭, ～色

B〈形〉 late: ►～年, 岁～

【暮霭】 mù'ǎi〈名〉 evening haze

【暮齿】 mùchǐ〈名〉〈书〉 old age

【暮春】 mùchūn ►**p. 345**〈名〉 late spring

【暮鼓晨钟】 mùgǔ-chénzhōng〈成〉〈喻〉 sounds to inspire feelings of the passage of time and the vanity of fame and fortune

【暮景】 mùjǐng〈名〉 1 (指傍晚) scene at dusk 2 (指老年) life in old age: 桑榆～ evening of one's life

【暮年】 mùnián〈名〉 twilight of one's life: 烈士～，壮心不已。 In old age, bold heroes still aspire to great deeds.

【暮气】 mùqì〈名〉 apathy, lethargy: ～沉沉 listless

【暮秋】 mùqiū ►**p. 345**〈名〉 late autumn

【暮色】 mùsè〈名〉 twilight: ～苍茫 deepening dusk ‖ 在渐暗的～中 in the falling evening gloom

【暮岁】 mùsuì〈名〉 1 (一年将尽) last days of the year 2 (晚年) one's later years

穆 mù〈形〉 reverent: ►静～, 肃～

【穆罕默德】 Mùhǎnmòdé〈名〉 Mohammed

【穆斯林】 mùsīlín〈名〉 Muslim: ～国家 Muslim country ‖ 什叶派～ Shiite Muslims ‖ 逊尼派～ Sunni Muslims

Nn

nā

那 Nā〈名〉Na [surname]
▸nà

南 nā
▸nán

【南无】nāmó〈名〉［佛教］ Namah: ～阿弥陀佛 Namo Amitabha [homage to Amitabha Buddha]

ná

拿 ná

A〈动〉**1**（用手抓） hold: 你手里～着什么？ What's in your hand? ‖ 谁把我的钢笔～走了？Who's taken my pen? **2**（捉） catch: 猫～耗子。 Cats catch mice. ‖ 逃犯终于被～住了。 The escaped prisoner was finally captured. ▸～获，缉～，捉～ **3**〈口〉（刁难）corner: 不帮忙就算了，别想～住我。 If you don't want to help me, that's OK. Don't think you can force me into a corner. **4**（装出） act: 你要～出当哥哥的样子来。 As an elder brother, you should act like one. ▸～架子 **5**（领取） get: ～工资 receive one's pay ‖ 一共～了16块金牌 win a total of 16 gold medals **6**（掌握） be in charge: ▸～权，～事
B〈介〉**1**（用） by means of: ～斧子砍 hack with an axe ‖ ～美元支付 pay in US dollars ‖ 幸福是不能～钱买的。 Happiness cannot be bought. **2**（用以引出对象） [used to introduce the object of a following verbal phrase]: ～孩子出气 vent one's anger on a child ‖ ～我当傻瓜 treat me as a fool ‖ ～原则做交易 barter away one's principles ‖ 我真～他没办法。 I simply don't know what to do with him.

【拿班作势】nábān-zuòshì〈成〉 act affectively

【拿办】nábàn〈动〉 arrest and bring to justice

【拿不出手】nábuchūshǒu〈动〉〈俗〉 be unpresentable

【拿不准】nábuzhǔn〈动〉〈口〉 be unsure: 这件事我～。 I am not sure about it.

【拿大】nádà〈动〉〈方〉 give oneself airs

【拿大顶】ná dàdǐng〈动〉［体育］ do handstand

【拿大头】ná dàtóu〈动〉 take the lion's share

【拿得起，放得下】nádeqǐ, fàngdexià〈俗〉 can afford to accept whatever happens to one

【拿顶】nádǐng = 拿大顶 ná dàdǐng

【拿获】náhuò〈动〉 capture: 罪犯被当场～。 The criminal was caught red-handed.

【拿架子】ná jiàzi〈惯〉 assume airs: 不要～。 Don't give yourself airs.

【拿来主义】náláizhǔyì〈名〉 take it and use it

【拿捏】nánie〈动〉〈方〉 **1**（扭捏） be affectedly bashful **2**（刁难） put pressure on (sb.)

【拿腔拿调】náqiāng-nádiào〈成〉 speak with an affected tone

【拿腔作势】náqiāng-zuòshì = 装腔作势 zhuāngqiāng-zuòshì

【拿权】náquán〈动〉 hold the reins: 他退居二线不～了。 He is no longer at the helm after stepping down from active service.

【拿事】náshì〈动〉〈口〉 be in a position to make decisions: 他在家里不～， 一切都得听夫人的。 His wife wears the trousers, leaving him with little say.

【拿手】náshǒu〈形〉 good at: 他开车很～。 He is a very good driver.

【拿手菜】náshǒucài〈名〉 signature dish

【拿手好戏】náshǒu-hǎoxì〈成〉 **1**（指表演） showpiece **2**（指本领） one's forte: 他们喜欢谈论自己的～。 They enjoy talking about their own strengths.

【拿问】náwèn〈动〉〈旧〉 detain for interrogation

【拿一把】náyībǎ〈动〉〈口〉 put on airs

【拿印把儿】ná yìnbàr〈动〉 hold power

【拿着鸡毛当令箭】názhe jīmáo dàng lìngjiàn〈俗〉〈喻〉 treat one's superior's casual remarks as an order and make a big fuss about them

【拿主意】ná zhǔyi〈动〉 make up one's mind: 究竟怎么办，你～吧。 You just tell me what to do.

镎（鎿） ná〈名〉［化学］ neptunium (Np)

nǎ

哪 nǎ〈代〉**1**（表选择或疑问）（指物） which;（指人） who;（指事物） what: 分不清～是对，～是错 be unable to tell right from wrong ‖ ～位是西安来的？ Which of you is from Xi'an? **2**（表不定选择） whichever: ～个最好就选～个。 Choose whichever is the best. ‖ ～天有空过来坐坐。 Come for a visit when you have a moment. **3**（表否定） how is it possible: ～有这回事！Nothing of the sort! ‖ 我～能忘记呢？ How can I forget? ‖ 他～会来？ Who would thought that he would come?
▸na, né, něi

【哪个】nǎge〈代〉**1**（哪一个） which: 想要～拿～。 Take whichever you want. **2**（谁） who: ～要来？ Who is coming?

【哪壶不开提哪壶】nǎhú bùkāi tí nǎhú〈俗〉〈喻〉 air sb.'s dirty laundry

【哪会儿】nǎhuìr〈副〉**1**（表疑问） when: 他是～来的？ When did he come? ‖ 你～有时间？ When will you be free? **2**（表泛指） whenever: 你们～都可以来。 You can come whenever you like.

【哪里】nǎli〈代〉**1**（表疑问） where: 你刚才去～了？ Where have you been? **2**（表泛指） everywhere: ～都有我们的朋友。 Our friends are everywhere. ‖ ～需要我，我就去～。 I will go wherever I am needed. **3**（表反问） [used in rhetorical questions to express negation]: 他～像个学生？ He is nothing like a student! ‖ 他又瘦又小，～是你的对手。 He is short and thin and is no match for you. **4**〈谦〉 [used as a polite response to a compliment]: 你的舞跳得真好！——～～。 You're an excellent dancer. — You're flattering me.

【哪门子】nǎménzi〈代〉〈方〉 [used in rhetorical questions to express unreasonableness] why: 你生～气呀？ What are you so upset for?

【哪能】nǎnéng〈副〉 [used in rhetorical questions] how can: 我～干那种事。 How could I have done that kind of thing.

【哪怕】nǎpà〈连〉 no matter how: ～困难再大，也要按时完成任务。 We have to finish the task on time no matter how difficult it is.

【哪儿】nǎr〈代〉**1**（表疑问） where: 你在～看见他了？ Where did you see him? ‖ 你到底上～去了？ Where on earth have you been? **2**（表泛指） wherever: 他无论走到～都受到热烈欢迎。 He is always enthusiastically received wherever he goes. **3**（表反问） how can: 我～知道？ How could I know?

【哪儿的话】nǎrdehuà〈惯〉〈谦〉 you shouldn't say that

【哪些】nǎxiē〈代〉 which: ～学生考试不及格？ Which students failed the examination?

【哪样】nǎyàng〈代〉**1**（表疑问） what kind: 你喜欢～的书包？ What kind of bag do you like? **2**（表泛指） whatever kind: 世上～的人都有。 It takes all sorts to make a world.

nà

那[1] nà ▸**p. 968**〈代〉 that: ～本书 that book ‖ ～个人 that person ‖ ～时候 in those days ‖ ～是很久以前的事了。 That was a long time ago. ‖ ～是谁的孩子？ Whose child is that?

那[2] nà〈连〉 in that case: 既然来了，～你就呆会儿吧。 Since you are here, stay for a while. ‖ ～你说我该怎么办呢？ Then what do you think I should do next?
▸Nā

n

【那般】nàbān〈代〉 that way
【那不勒斯】Nàbùlèsī〈名〉 Naples
【那程子】nàchéngzi〈代〉〈方〉 in those days: ～只要有吃有穿就不错了。 In those days, if we had something to eat and wear, we would be very satisfied.
【那达慕】Nàdámù〈名〉 Nadam Fair [Mongolian traditional sports fair]
【那当儿】nàdāngr〈副〉〈口〉 at that time
【那个】nàge ▸**p. 968**〈代〉 **1**（那一个） that [as opposed to this]: ～比这个好。 That one is better than this one. **2**（那事） that thing: 再提～就是多余的了。 It's unnecessary to mention that again. **3**〈口〉（表夸张） [used before a verb or adjective for emphasis]: 他～高兴劲儿就甭提了。 His joy is beyond description. **4**〈口〉（指不便直说的话） [used as a euphemism or humorously to replace sth. funny or embarrassing]: 对妻子发脾气，你也太～了。 It's not the done thing to get angry with your wife.
【那会儿】nàhuìr〈代〉 that time: ～还没有我呢。 I was not even born at that time. ‖ 到～你就会后悔的。 You will feel regretful in time.
【那里】nàli ▸**p. 968**〈代〉 there: ～是我的家。 My home is there. ‖ 你的座位在～。 Your seat is over there.
【那么】nàme **A**〈代〉 **1**（指程度、方式等）like that: 别～干。Don't do it that way. **2**（指数量） [used before numerals] around: 教室里只有～七八个学生。There are only about seven or eight students in the classroom. **B**〈连〉 then: 你不想听，～我就不说了。 If you don't want to listen, then I have nothing more to say. ‖ 既然志向不同，～咱们分道扬镳吧。 Since we're going in different directions, let's part company.
【那么点儿】nàmediǎnr〈代〉 so little: ～面包够谁吃? That much bread is hardly enough.
【那么些】nàmexiē〈代〉 so much: 一下子来了～人，叫我怎么安排! How am I going to be able to cope with so many people arriving all at once?
【那么着】nàmezhe〈代〉 that way: 你再～，我可就不客气了。 If you go on like that, I won't be easy on you.
【那末】nàme = 那么 nàme
【那儿】nàr〈代〉 **1** = 那里 nàli **2**（那时） [used after 打，从，由] that (time): 打～起，我就喜欢上英语了。 I started to like English after that.
【那些】nàxiē ▸**p. 968**〈代〉 those: ～人在干什么? What are those people doing?
【那样】nàyàng〈代〉 like that: 你怎么能～做呢? How can you act like that? ‖ 我不是～的人。 I'm not that kind of person.
【那阵儿】nàzhènr〈代〉 at that time: ～我正在睡觉。 I was sleeping at that time. ‖ ～日子真苦啊! Life was so hard in those days.
【那阵子】nàzhènzi = 那阵儿 nàzhènr

呐 nà

▸nè
【呐喊】nàhǎn〈动〉 cry out: ～助威 shout encouragement ▸摇旗～

纳（納） nà

〈动〉 **1**（放进）admit: 闭门不～ refuse to receive visitors ▸出～ **2**（接受） accept: ▸～降，采～，容～ **3**（享受） enjoy: ▸～福，～凉 **4**（交纳） pay: ▸～贿，～税，缴～ **5**（收入） bring into: ▸～入 **6**（缝） sew close stitches: ～鞋底 stitch soles (of cloth shoes)
【纳彩】nàcǎi〈动〉〈旧〉 send betrothal gifts to the girl's family
【纳粹】Nàcuì〈名〉 Nazi: ～军官 Nazi officer
【纳粹主义】Nàcuìzhǔyì〈名〉 Nazism: 新～ neo-Nazism
【纳福】nàfú〈动〉〈书〉 [usu of elderly people] enjoy an easy and comfortable life
【纳贡】nàgòng〈动〉〈旧〉 present tribute
【纳罕】nàhǎn〈形〉〈书〉 surprised: 他突然离去的消息使我们感到～。 We were surprised at the news of his sudden departure.
【纳贿】nàhuì〈动〉 **1**（行贿） give bribes **2**（受贿） take bribes
【纳谏】nàjiàn〈动〉〈书〉 **1**（指接受） take advice **2**（指给予） offer advice to an emperor
【纳凉】nàliáng〈动〉 enjoy the cool: 在树荫下～ enjoy the cool shade of a tree
【纳粮】nàliáng〈动〉〈旧〉 pay grain tax
【纳闷儿】nàmènr〈动〉 feel perplexed: 老不见他人影，真叫人～。 I am really puzzled as to why he hasn't turned up yet.
【纳米】nàmǐ〈量〉 nanometre (nm)
【纳米比亚】Nàmǐbǐyà〈名〉 Namibia: ～人 Namibian
【纳米材料】nàmǐ cáiliào〈名〉 nanometre materials
【纳米技术】nàmǐ jìshù〈名〉 nanotechnology: ～专家 nanotechnologist
【纳米科学】nàmǐ kēxué〈名〉 nanoscience
【纳妾】nàqiè〈动〉〈旧〉 take a concubine
【纳入】nàrù〈动〉 bring into: ～国家计划 bring into line with the state plan ‖ ～议事日程 put on the agenda ‖ ～正轨 put sth. on the right track
【纳税】nàshuì〈动〉 pay taxes: 照章～ pay taxes according to the regulations ‖ 申报收入并～ declare one's income and pay taxes
【纳税年度】nàshuì niándù〈名〉 tax year
【纳税凭证】nàshuì píngzhèng〈名〉 tax payment receipt
【纳税人】nàshuìrén〈名〉 taxpayer
【纳税申报】nàshuì shēnbào〈名〉 declaration for payment of tax: ～表格 tax form ‖ ～单 tax return ‖ ～制度 tax declaration system
【纳税证明】nàshuì zhèngmíng〈名〉 certificate of tax payment
【纳斯达克指数】Nàsīdákè zhǐshù〈名〉［经济］ NASDAQ index
【纳西族】Nàxīzú〈名〉 Naxi ethnic group
【纳降】nàxiáng〈动〉〈旧〉 accept the enemy's surrender
【纳新】nàxīn〈动〉 take in the fresh: ▸吐故～

肭 nà ▸腽肭 wànà

钠（鈉） nà

〈名〉［化学］ sodium (Na): ▸氯化～，碳酸～
【钠灯】nàdēng〈名〉 sodium (vapour) lamp
【钠盐】nàyán〈名〉 sodium salt

衲 nà

A〈动〉 patch up: ▸百～衣
B〈名〉 **1**（指衣服） Buddhist monk's robe: 破～芒鞋 monk's worn-out patchwork robe and straw sandals **2**（指人） Buddhist monk: ▸老～

娜 nà

〈名〉 used in feminine names
▸nuó

捺 nà

A〈动〉 **1**（按） press down heavily: ～手印 leave a thumbprint **2**（抑制） restrain: 强～心头的怒火 try to suppress one's anger ▸按～
B〈名〉 [in Chinese characters] right falling stroke

na

哪 na

〈助〉 [used in the same way as 啊, but only after words ending with consonant 'n']: 我还没看完～! I haven't finished reading it yet! ‖ 他是什么人～? Who is he?
▸nǎ, né, něi

nǎi

乃 nǎi

〈书〉
A〈动〉 be: 真～怪事。 It's really strange. ‖ 失败～成功之母。 Failure is the mother of success.
B〈副〉 **1**（表顺承） therefore: 他因不满当朝，～隐居山中。 Discontented with the authorities, he lived in seclusion in a mountain. **2**（表结果） then: 服药后病～缓解。 Only after taking the medicine did his condition improve.
C〈代〉 your: ～翁 your father ‖ ～兄 your brother
【乃尔】nǎi'ěr〈助〉〈书〉 to such an extent: 何其相似～! How similar they are!
【乃至】nǎizhì〈连〉〈书〉 even: 为了人民的利益，他不惜付出一切，～献出生命。 In the interests of the people, he didn't hesitate to sacrifice everything, even his life.

艿 nǎi ▸芋艿 yùnǎi

奶 nǎi

A〈名〉 **1**（乳房） breast: ▸～头，～罩 **2**（乳汁） milk: 产～ produce milk ‖ 吃～ drink milk ‖ 全脂～ whole milk ‖ 脱脂～ skimmed milk ▸～茶，～粉，豆～
B〈动〉 breast-feed: ～孩子 breast-feed a baby
【奶白】nǎibái〈名〉 milky white
【奶茶】nǎichá〈名〉 tea with milk
【奶疮】nǎichuāng〈口〉= 乳腺炎 rǔxiànyán
【奶粉】nǎifěn〈名〉 milk powder
【奶糕】nǎigāo〈名〉 rice-flour cake [as substitute for milk in feeding babies]
【奶酒】nǎijiǔ〈名〉 fermented milk
【奶酪】nǎilào〈名〉 cheese
【奶妈】nǎimā〈名〉 wet nurse
【奶毛】nǎimáo〈名〉 foetal hair
【奶名】nǎimíng〈名〉 childhood nickname
【奶奶】nǎinai〈名〉 **1** ▸**p. 588**（祖母） grandma **2**（指老年妇女） granny **3**〈口〉（指年轻女子） young mistress of the house
【奶娘】nǎiniáng〈名〉〈方〉 wet nurse
【奶牛】nǎiniú〈名〉 milking cow
【奶牛场】nǎiniúchǎng〈名〉 dairy farm
【奶皮】nǎipí〈名〉 skin formed on boiled milk
【奶瓶】nǎipíng〈名〉 feeding bottle: 用～给婴儿喂奶 give the baby its bottle
【奶声奶气】nǎishēng nǎiqì〈名〉 child-like voice
【奶水】nǎishuǐ〈名〉 milk

【奶糖】nǎitáng〈名〉 toffee
【奶头】nǎitóu〈名〉〈口〉 nipple
【奶昔】nǎixī〈名〉 milk shake
【奶牙】nǎiyá = 乳齿 rǔchǐ
【奶羊】nǎiyáng〈名〉 dairy goat
【奶油】nǎiyóu〈名〉 cream: ～巧克力 milk chocolate ‖ ～蛋糕 cream cake
【奶油小生】nǎiyóu xiǎoshēng〈名〉〈贬〉 handsome but effeminate young man
【奶罩】nǎizhào〈名〉〈口〉 bra
【奶汁】nǎizhī〈名〉 milk
【奶制品】nǎizhìpǐn〈名〉 dairy product
【奶子】nǎizi〈名〉〈方〉 breast
【奶嘴】nǎizuǐ〈名〉 teat (on feeding bottle)〈英〉; nipple〈美〉

氖 nǎi〈名〉［化学］ neon (Ne)
【氖灯】nǎidēng〈名〉 neon light

nài

奈 nài〈动〉〈书〉 1 (处置) deal with: ～他不得 can do nothing with him ‖ ～之何 what to do with it 2 = 奈何 nàihé
【奈恩郡】Nài'ēnjùn〈名〉 Nairnshire
【奈何】nàihé A〈动〉 1 (怎么办) have no alternative: 无可～ have no alternative 2 (怎样对待) deal with: 我们能奈他何? What can we do with him? B〈代〉〈书〉 [used in rhetorical questions] why: 她既然不肯吐露真情，你又～苦苦相逼? Since she refused to tell the truth, why did you pressure her so much?

柰 nài〈名〉［植物］ Chinese pear-leaved crab-apple

耐 nài〈动〉 withstand: ～不住寂寞 cannot bear loneliness ‖ ～磨 wear-resistant ‖ ～腐蚀 rot-proof ‖ ～高温 withstand high temperatures ▸吃苦～劳
【耐潮湿】nàicháoshī〈形〉 damp-proof
【耐尘】nàichén〈形〉 dust-fast
【耐穿】nàichuān〈动〉 wear well: ～的衣服 clothing that can withstand hard wear ‖ 这双鞋不～。 These shoes wear out quickly.
【耐烦】nàifán〈形〉 [usu in the negative] patient: 等得不～ be weary of waiting
【耐高温】nàigāowēn〈形〉 high-temperature resistant
【耐寒】nàihán〈形〉 cold-resistant: ～品种 hardy variety
【耐旱】nàihàn〈形〉 drought-tolerant
【耐火材料】nàihuǒ cáiliào〈名〉 fire-proof material
【耐久】nàijiǔ〈形〉 durable: ～性 endurance
【耐看】nàikàn〈动〉 have lasting appeal
【耐苦】nàikǔ〈形〉 able to endure hardships
【耐劳】nàiláo〈形〉 able to endure hard work: ▸吃苦～
【耐力】nàilì〈名〉 endurance: 考验～ test sb.'s endurance
【耐磨】nàimó〈形〉 wear-resistant
【耐燃】nàirán〈形〉 flame-resistant
【耐热】nàirè〈形〉 heat-resistant
【耐热性】nàirèxìng〈名〉 heat resistance
【耐人寻味】nàirénxúnwèi〈成〉 provide food for thought: 他的讲话～。 His speech gives much food for thought.
【耐水】nàishuǐ〈形〉 water-fast
【耐酸】nàisuān〈形〉 acid-resistant
【耐缩】nàisuō〈形〉 anti-shrink
【耐洗】nàixǐ〈形〉 wash-resistant
【耐心】nàixīn A〈形〉 patient: ～等待 wait patiently ‖ ～说服教育 patient persuasion and education B〈名〉 patience: 缺乏～ lack patience ‖ 有～ have patience
【耐性】nàixìng〈名〉 perseverance: 学外语要有～。 Learning a foreign language requires perseverance.
【耐用】nàiyòng〈形〉 durable: 经久～ prolong durability ‖ ～品 consumer durables

能 Nài〈名〉 Nai [surname] ▸néng

萘 nài〈名〉［化学］ naphthalene

鼐 nài〈名〉〈古〉 big tripod

nān

囡 nān〈名〉〈方〉 1 (小孩) child: 小～ small child 2 (女儿) daughter: 他们家只有一个～。 They have only one daughter in the family.
【囡囡】nānnān〈名〉〈方〉 kid

nán

男[1] nán〈名〉 1 (男子) man: ～大学生 college boy ‖ ～主持人 host ▸～厕所, ～声 2 (儿子) son: 长～ eldest son

男[2] nán〈名〉 baron: ▸～爵
【男扮女装】nánbàn-nǚzhuāng〈成〉 [of a man] disguise oneself as a woman
【男傧相】nánbīnxiàng〈名〉 best man
【男才女貌】náncái-nǚmào〈成〉 talented man and beautiful woman
【男厕所】náncèsuǒ〈名〉 Gents〈英〉; men's room〈美〉
【男大当婚，女大当嫁】nán dà dāng hūn, nǚ dà dāng jià〈俗〉 when men and women come of age, they must marry
【男单】nándān〈名〉［体育］ men's singles
【男盗女娼】nándào-nǚchāng〈成〉 out-and-out scoundrels: 满嘴仁义道德，一肚子～ keep talking of humanity, justice and morality while thinking of nothing but greed and lust
【男低音】nándīyīn〈名〉 1 (指声调) bass 2 (指歌手) bass
【男儿】nán'ér〈名〉 man: 好～ true man
【男儿有泪不轻弹】nán'ér yǒu lèi bù qīng tán〈俗〉 men do not easily shed tears
【男方】nánfāng〈名〉 husband's side
【男高音】nángāoyīn〈名〉 tenor
【男耕女织】nángēng-nǚzhī〈成〉 men plough and women weave [an agricultural society's ideal of peace and order]
【男孩儿】nánháir〈名〉 boy
【男欢女爱】nánhuān-nǚ'ài〈成〉 love between a man and a woman
【男婚女嫁】nánhūn-nǚjià〈成〉 get married: ～是终身大事，应慎重对待。 Marriage is a lifetime business and must be treated seriously.
【男家】nánjiā〈名〉 bridegroom's or husband's family
【男爵】nánjué〈名〉 baron: ～夫人 baroness
【男科】nánkē〈名〉 andrology department
【男篮】nánlán〈名〉 1 (指球队) men's basketball team 2 (指运动) men's basketball game
【男模】nánmó ▸p. 966〈名〉 male model
【男男女女】nánnán-nǚnǚ〈成〉 men and women
【男女】nán-nǚ〈名〉 men and women: ～比例 ratio of the male to the female ‖ ～不限。 Either a man or a woman will do.
【男女关系】nán-nǚ guānxì〈名〉 relations between men and women: 乱搞～ have illicit sexual relations
【男女混合双打】nán-nǚ hùnhé shuāngdǎ〈名〉［体育］ mixed doubles
【男女老少】nán-nǚ-lǎo-shào〈成〉 men and women, old and young
【男女平等】nán-nǚ píngděng〈名〉 equality between the sexes
【男排】nánpái〈名〉 men's volleyball
【男配角】nánpèijué〈名〉 male supporting role: 最佳～ the best supporting actor
【男朋友】nánpéngyou〈名〉 boyfriend
【男人】nánrén〈名〉 man
【男人】nánren〈名〉〈方〉 husband: 她～不在家。 Her husband is out.
【男生】nánshēng〈名〉 1 (男学生) male student: 我们班有二十个～，二十三个女生。 There are twenty boys and twenty-three girls in our class. 2〈方〉(男人) male
【男声】nánshēng〈名〉 male voice: ～合唱 male chorus
【男士】nánshì〈名〉 man: ～聚会 stag party ‖ ～用品 products for men
【男式】nánshì〈形〉 men's: ～衬衣 shirt
【男双】nánshuāng〈名〉 men's doubles
【男童】nántóng〈名〉 boy
【男性】nánxìng〈名〉 the male sex: ～公民 male citizen
【男演员】nányǎnyuán ▸p. 966〈名〉 actor
【男一号】nányīhào〈名〉 1 (男主力) top-ranking male: 王皓是中国乒乓球队的～。 Wang Hao is China's top-ranking men's table-tennis player. 2 (男主角) male lead: 影片中的～ the male lead in the film
【男婴】nányīng〈名〉 baby boy
【男中音】nánzhōngyīn〈名〉 baritone
【男主角】nánzhǔjué〈名〉 hero
【男装】nánzhuāng〈名〉 men's clothing
【男子】nánzǐ〈名〉 man: 中年～ middle-aged man
【男子单打】nánzǐ dāndǎ〈名〉［体育］ men's singles
【男子汉】nánzǐhàn〈名〉 man: ～大丈夫 real man ‖ 他们表现出～的气概。 They acquitted themselves like men.
【男子双打】nánzǐ shuāngdǎ〈名〉［体育］ men's doubles
【男足】nánzú〈名〉 1 (指运动) man's football 2 (指运动队) man's football team
【男尊女卑】nánzūn-nǚbēi〈成〉 treatment of females as inferior to males

南 nán〈名〉 1 ▸p. 205 (指方向) south: 朝～ face south ‖ ～去的列车 southbound trains ‖ 学校的门朝～开。 The school gate faces south. 2 (指地区) southern region: ～巡 make an inspection trip to the south ‖ ～菜北运 transport vegetables from the south to the north ▸～货, ～水北调, ～味 ▸nā
【南半球】nánbànqiú〈名〉 Southern Hemisphere
【南北】nánběi ▸p. 205〈名〉 1 (南方和北方) north and south: 大江～ north and south of the Yangtze River ‖ ～走向的山

脉 mountains running from south to north **2**（从南到北） distance from north to south: 这片草原~有上百公里。 It is over a hundred kilometres to these grasslands.

【南北朝】Nán-Běicháo〈名〉Northern and Southern Dynasties

【南北对话】Nán-Běi duìhuà〈名〉North-South dialogue

【南边】nánbian ▸**p. 205**〈名〉**1**（指方位） south: 越南在中国的~。 Vietnam is to the south of China. **2** = 南 nán 2

【南部】nánbù ▸**p. 205**〈名〉southern part: 陕西~ southern part of Shaanxi ‖ 广州是中国~的一座城市。 Guangzhou is a city in southern China.

【南昌】Nánchāng ▸**p. 661**〈名〉Nanchang [capital of Jiangxi Province (江西)]

【南昌起义】Nánchāng Qǐyì = 八一南昌起义 Bā-Yī Nánchāng Qǐyì

【南朝】Náncháo〈名〉Southern Dynasties

【南达科他州】Nándákētāzhōu〈名〉South Dakota

【南斗】Nándǒu〈名〉［天文］Southern Dipper

【南豆腐】nándòufu〈名〉southern-style tofu

【南方】nánfāng〈名〉**1** ▸**p. 205**（指方向） south **2**（指地区） southern region: ~人 southerner ‖ 去~旅行 travel south

【南非】Nánfēi〈名〉South Africa: ~共和国 Republic of South Africa

【南风】nánfēng〈名〉southerly wind

【南格拉摩根郡】Nángélāmógēnjùn〈名〉South Glamorgan

【南瓜】nánguā〈名〉pumpkin: ~子 pumpkin seed

【南国】nánguó〈名〉〈书〉the South: ~风光 southern scenery

【南海】Nánhǎi〈名〉South China Sea

【南韩】Nán Hán〈名〉South Korea

【南寒带】nánhándài〈名〉South Frigid Zone

【南胡】nánhú = 二胡 èrhú

【南回归线】nánhuíguīxiàn〈名〉Tropic of Capricorn

【南货】nánhuò〈名〉delicacies from south China

【南箕北斗】nánjī-běidǒu〈成〉something which is well-known but useless

【南极】nánjí〈名〉**1**（指地轴） South Pole **2**（指磁场） south magnetic pole

【南极圈】nánjíquān〈名〉Antarctic Circle

【南极洲】Nánjízhōu〈名〉Antarctica

【南疆】nánjiāng〈名〉**1**（指新疆） southern part of Xinjiang **2**（指边疆） southern part of China

【南京】Nánjīng ▸**p. 661**〈名〉Nanjing [capital of Jiangsu Province (江苏)]

【南京大屠杀】Nánjīng Dàtúshā〈名〉Nanjing Massacre

【南卡罗来纳州】Nánkǎluóláinàzhōu〈名〉South Carolina

【南柯一梦】Nánkē-yīmèng〈成〉pipe dream

【南来北往】nánlái-běiwǎng〈成〉[of heavy traffic or crowds] going south and north

【南美洲】Nánměizhōu〈名〉South America

【南面】nánmiàn **A** ▸**p. 205**〈名〉the south: 非洲位于欧洲的~。 Africa is to the south of Europe. **B**〈动〉proclaim oneself emperor

【南南合作】Nán-Nán hézuò〈名〉South-South cooperation

【南宁】Nánníng ▸**p. 661**〈名〉Nanning [capital of Guangxi (广西)]

【南欧】Nán Ōu〈名〉Southern Europe

【南腔北调】nánqiāng-běidiào〈成〉with mixed accents: 说话~ speak with a mixture of accents

【南拳】nánquán〈名〉［武术］*nanquan* [southern style boxing]

【南沙群岛】Nánshā Qúndǎo〈名〉Spratly Islands [called 'Nansha Islands' in China]

【南十字座】Nánshízìzuò〈名〉［天文］Crux

【南水北调】nánshuǐ-běidiào〈名〉South-to-North water diversion: ~工程 projects to divert water from the south to the north

【南斯拉夫】Nánsīlāfū〈名〉Yugoslavia: ~联盟共和国 Federal Republic of Yugoslavia ‖ ~人 Yugoslav

【南宋】Nán Sòng〈名〉Southern Song Dynasty

【南太平洋】Nántàipíngyáng〈名〉South Pacific

【南糖】nántáng〈名〉southern-style sweets

【南天竹】nántiānzhú〈名〉［植物］nandina

【南纬】nánwěi〈名〉southern latitude: 这个地区位于~二十度。 The area is 20 degrees south in latitude.

【南味】nánwèi〈名〉of southern taste and flavour: ~小吃 southern style snack

【南温带】nánwēndài〈名〉South Temperate Zone

【南下】nánxià〈动〉go south: 从北京~广州 go down to Guangzhou from Beijing

【南巡】nánxún〈动〉inspection tour of the south: 邓小平1992年~讲话 Deng Xiaoping's talks on his 1992 inspection tour to the south

【南亚】Nán Yà〈名〉South Asia: ~区域合作联盟 South Asian Association for Regional Cooperation (SAARC)

【南亚次大陆】Nányà Cìdàlù〈名〉South Asian Subcontinent

【南洋】Nányáng〈名〉old name for south-east-Asia including the Malay Archipelago, the Malay Peninsula and Indonesia

【南音】nányīn〈名〉southern music

【南辕北辙】nányuán-běizhé〈成〉〈喻〉act in a way that defeats one's purpose

【南约克郡】Nányuēkèjùn〈名〉South Yorkshire

【南岳】Nányuè〈名〉Southern Sacred Mountain [Hengshan Mountain (衡山) in Hunan Province]

【南征北战】nánzhēng-běizhàn〈成〉fight up and down the country

【南竹】nánzhú = 毛竹 máozhú

难（難）nán

A〈形〉**1**（不容易） difficult: ~对付 be difficult to tackle ‖ 比登天还~ like getting blood from stone ‖ ~就~在这里。 Therein lies the problem. ‖ 万事开头~。 All things are difficult at the beginning. **2**（不好） bad: ▸~看，~听，~闻

B〈动〉put sb. in a difficult position: 你可~住我了。 You've got me there.

▸nàn

【难熬】nán'áo〈形〉difficult to bear: ~的冬天 harsh winter

【难办】nánbàn〈形〉difficult to handle

【难保】nánbǎo〈动〉**1**（指保证） can't guarantee: ~他们说的就是真话。 There is no guarantee that they are telling the truth. **2**（指保全） hard to keep: 他性命~。 His life is in danger now.

【难缠】nánchán〈形〉unreasonable: 她这个人很~。 She is very unreasonable.

【难产】nánchǎn〈动〉**1**［医学］ have a difficult labour: 她死于~。 She had a difficult delivery and died. **2**〈喻〉（难以实现） be difficult to realize: 成立公司的事要~。 It will be difficult to set up the company.

【难吃】nánchī〈形〉tasteless

【难处】nánchǔ〈动〉hard to get along with: 时间长了你会发现她并不~。 As time goes by you'll find that she's easy to get on with.

【难处】nánchù〈名〉difficulty: 你有什么~尽管跟我说。 Let me know if you have any difficulties. ‖ 她也有她的~。 She has her own troubles.

【难辞其咎】náncí-qíjiù〈成〉hard to absolve oneself from the blame: 公司出了事，经理~。 The manager will surely be blamed if something goes wrong with the company.

【难当】nándāng〈动〉**1**（不易担当） be hard to cope with: 我~此项任务。 I'm not up to the task. **2**（不易承受） be hard to endure: 羞愧~ be mortified with shame

【难倒】nándǎo〈动〉daunt

【难道】nándào〈副〉[used to reinforce a rhetorical question]: ~他病了不成? Is it possible that he is ill? ‖ ~真是我错了? Do you really mean to say that it is my fault?

【难得】nándé〈形〉**1**（难以得到） hard to come by: 机会~ a once-in-a-life chance ‖ 人才~。 People of talent are hard to come by. **2**（不常） rare: 我们~见面。 We seldom see each other. ‖ 这地区~下雪。 Snow is rare in this region.

【难点】nándiǎn〈名〉difficulty: 突破~ crack a nut ‖ 向学生讲解课文中的~ explain the difficult points of the text to students

【难度】nándù〈名〉degree of difficulty: ~大 be extremely difficult ‖ 这道题有一定的~。 The question is quite difficult.

【难度系数】nándù xìshù〈名〉degree of difficulty

【难分难解】nánfēn-nánjiě〈成〉**1**（相持不下） be locked **2**（难以分离） be attached (to)

【难分难舍】nánfēn-nánshě = 难舍难分 nánshě-nánfēn

【难怪】nánguài **A**〈副〉no wonder: ~他有点不高兴。 No wonder he was a bit upset. **B**〈动〉be understandable: 他很害怕，这也~。 It's understandable that he was frightened.

【难关】nánguān〈名〉barrier: 渡过~ weather a hard time ‖ 攻克技术~ surmount technical difficulties

【难过】nánguò〈形〉**1**（指生活） difficult: 我知道他们的日子很~。 I know they are having a rough time. **2**（指感受） sorry: 听到不幸的消息大家都很~。 Everyone was grieved to hear the sad news.

【难解难分】nánjiě-nánfēn = 难分难解 nánfēn-nánjiě

【难堪】nánkān **A**〈动〉be intolerable: ~重负 bear an intolerably heavy burden ‖ 痛苦~。 The pain is unbearable. **B**〈形〉embarrassed: 使对手~ embarrass one's opponent ‖ 她感到~，脸上发烧。 Her cheeks were burning with embarrassment.

【难看】nánkàn〈形〉**1**（不好看） ugly: 这衣服真~。 What an ugly garment! **2**（不光彩） awkward: 你这不是给我~嘛。 You are embarrassing me. **3**（气色差） out of sorts: 你的脸色很~，是不是

病了? You look awful. Are you sick? **4** (不和悦) icy: 脸～ unfriendly-looking

【难免】nánmiǎn〈形〉unavoidable: 人～要犯错误。To err is human. ‖ 有分歧是～的。Differences are inevitable.

【难耐】nánnài〈动〉be unbearable: 寂寞～ unbearable loneliness ‖ 疼痛/炎热～ unbearable pain/heat

【难能可贵】nánnéng-kěguì〈成〉be rare and commendable

【难人】nánrén **A**〈动〉be difficult: 这事真～。This is really hard. ‖ 你这不是在～吗? You are making things difficult for me. **B**〈名〉person handling a difficult matter: 别担心，我不会让你做～的。Don't worry. I won't leave the trouble to you.

【难色】nánsè〈名〉expression of reluctance: 面有～ show signs of reluctance or embarrassment

【难上加难】nánshàng-jiānán〈成〉be extremely difficult

【难舍难分】nánshě-nánfēn〈成〉cannot bear to part (with)

【难事】nánshì〈名〉difficulty: 世上无～，只怕有心人。Nothing is impossible to a willing heart.

【难受】nánshòu〈形〉**1** (不舒服) uncomfortable: 我的胃很～。My stomach hurts. **2** (伤心) sad: 他考试没及格，心里很～。He felt very bad because he had failed the examination.

【难说】nánshuō〈动〉**1** (说不准) be hard to say: 天下不下雨很～。It's hard to predict whether it will rain or not. **2** (不便说出) be embarrassing to say: 这没什么～的。There's nothing embarrassing about saying this.

【难题】nántí〈名〉thorny issue: 出～ create a difficult situation ‖ 失业问题在全世界都是个令人头痛的～。Unemployment is a real problem all over the world.

【难听】nántīng〈形〉**1** (不悦耳) unpleasant to the ear: ～的嗓音 voice that is unpleasant to the ear **2** (粗俗) coarse: ～的话 vulgar remarks **3** (不光彩) scandalous: 这事要传出去多～。It would be embarrassing if it leaked out.

【难忘】nánwàng〈形〉unforgettable: ～的经历 memorable experience

【难为情】nánwéiqíng〈形〉**1** (不好意思) embarrassed: 老板批评了她，她感到有些～。Her boss's criticism left her feeling rather embarrassed. **2** (指情面) afraid of hurting others' feelings: 让我给她讲这件事，挺～的。I'm afraid of hurting her feelings by breaking the news to her.

【难为】nánwei〈动〉**1** (使难堪) embarrass: 她不愿意就别～她。Don't make it hard on her if she's unwilling. **2** (为难) be a difficult job: 让你三天拿出一篇稿子来，也真～你了。Giving you three days to come up with an article is pretty tough on you. **3**〈套〉(表感谢) it is kind of sb. to do sth.: 这件事～你了。Thanks for the trouble you have taken.

【难闻】nánwén〈形〉smelling unpleasant

【难兄难弟】nánxiōng-nándì〈成〉〈贬〉two of a kind
►nànxiōng-nàndì

【难言之隐】nányánzhīyǐn〈成〉painful secret

【难以】nányǐ〈动〉be difficult to (do): ～接受 hard to accept ‖ ～置信 beyond belief ‖ ～预料 still in doubt

【难以启齿】nányǐqǐchǐ〈成〉be too shy to speak out

【难以为继】nányǐwéijì〈成〉hard to continue

【难于】nányú〈动〉**1** (难以) be hard to do sth.: ～启齿 too embarrassed to mention **2** (更难) be harder than: ～上青天 sky-high difficulty ‖ 第一题～第二题。The first question is more difficult than the second.

【难字】nánzì〈名〉rarely used word

喃 nán

【喃喃】nánnán〈拟〉mumble: ～自语 mutter to oneself

楠 nán

【楠木】nánmù〈名〉*nanmu* [name of wood and tree]

nǎn

赧 nǎn〈动〉blush: ►～颜

【赧愧】nǎnkuì〈形〉ashamed

【赧然】nǎnrán〈形〉〈书〉blushing

【赧颜】nǎnyán〈形〉〈书〉blush

腩 nǎn ►牛腩 niúnǎn

蝻 nǎn

【蝻子】nǎnzi〈名〉nymph of a locust

nàn

难(難) nàn

A〈名〉disaster: 逃～ escape disaster ‖ 遇～ be killed ►～民, 空～

B〈动〉reprimand: ►刁～, 责～
►nán

【难胞】nànbāo〈名〉fellow countrymen suffering persecution

【难船】nànchuán〈名〉ship in distress: 将～拖离主航道 tug the distressed ship off the main channel

【难民】nànmín〈名〉refugee: 安置～ relocate refugees ‖ ～潮 flood of refugees ‖ ～营 refugee camp

【难侨】nànqiáo〈名〉distressed overseas compatriot

【难兄难弟】nànxiōng-nàndì〈成〉fellow sufferers: 我们是～。We are in the same boat.
►nánxiōng-nándì

【难友】nànyǒu〈名〉fellow sufferer

nāng

囊 nāng
►náng

【囊揣】nāngchuài = 囊膪 nāngchuài

【囊膪】nāngchuài〈名〉fat meat from a pig's belly and breast

囔 nāng

【囔囔】nāngnang〈动〉murmur

náng

囊 náng

A〈名〉**1** (口袋) bag: 药～ medicine bag ►酒～饭袋, 皮～ **2** (袋状物) other bag-shaped objects: ►胆～

B〈动〉put in a bag: ►～括
►nāng

【囊虫】nángchóng〈名〉cysticercus

【囊空如洗】nángkōng-rúxǐ〈成〉be penniless: 他～。He doesn't have a penny to his name.

【囊括】nángkuò〈动〉be all-inclusive: 中国队～了全部金牌。The Chinese team bagged all the gold medals.

【囊中取物】nángzhōng-qǔwù〈成〉〈喻〉as easy as taking sth. out of one's pocket

【囊中物】nángzhōngwù〈成〉sth. in the bag:〈喻〉这场比赛已如囊中之物了。The game is already in the bag.

【囊中羞涩】nángzhōng-xiūsè〈成〉be low on cash: 我本想为你开个生日晚会，可～，只好算了。I wanted to hold a birthday party for you, but I have to give up the idea because I couldn't afford it.

【囊肿】nángzhǒng〈名〉cyst: 卵巢～ ovarian cyst

馕(饢) náng〈名〉*nang* flatbread [staple food of the Uygur and Kazak ethnic groups]
►nǎng

nǎng

曩 nǎng〈名〉〈书〉former: ～日 bygone days ‖ ～昔 in former times

攮 nǎng〈动〉stab

【攮子】nǎngzi〈名〉〈方〉dagger

馕(饢) nǎng〈动〉cram food into one's mouth
►náng

nàng

齉 nàng〈形〉blocked: 我感冒了，鼻子发～。I've got a cold and my nose is blocked.

【齉鼻儿】nàngbír **A**〈形〉snuffling **B**〈名〉person who speaks with a strong nasal twang

nāo

孬 nāo〈形〉〈方〉**1** (坏) bad **2** (怯懦) cowardly

【孬种】nāozhǒng〈名〉〈方〉**1**〈粗〉(坏人) bastard〈粗〉: 别和这个～计较。Don't bother yourself with this rascal. **2** (懦夫) coward

náo

呶 náo〈动〉〈书〉clamour: 喧～ talk boisterously

【呶呶不休】náonáo-bùxiū〈成〉talk endlessly

挠(撓) náo〈动〉**1** (搔) scratch: ～痒痒 have a scratch ►～头 **2** (阻挠) hinder: ►阻～ **3** (屈服) bend: ►百折不～, 不屈不～

【挠钩】náogōu〈名〉long-handled hook

【挠曲】náoqū **A**〈名〉［物理］ flexure **B**〈形〉 curved
【挠头】náotóu〈动〉 be tricky: 这事儿真让人~。 This is a really tricky issue.
【挠秧】náoyāng〈动〉［农业］ weed rice fields and loosen the soil

侬（憹） náo ▸懊侬 àonáo

硇 náo
【硇砂】náoshā〈名〉［化学］sal ammoniac

铙（鐃） náo〈名〉**1**（指打击乐器）cymbal **2**（指军用乐器）ancient musical instrument used in the army, resembling a small tongueless bell
【铙钹】náobó〈名〉 big cymbals

蛲（蟯） náo
【蛲虫】náochóng〈名〉 pinworm

nǎo

恼（惱） nǎo
A〈动〉 be annoyed: 主任~了，现在不想见人。 The dean is angry and doesn't want to see anyone now. ‖ 你别~我! Stop annoying me!
B〈形〉 unhappy: ▸懊~, 烦~
【恼恨】nǎohèn〈动〉 resent: 她嘴上不说，心里却十分~。 She didn't say anything but in her heart she resented it dreadfully.
【恼火】nǎohuǒ〈形〉 irritated: 她对受到冷落大为~。 She was really annoyed at being left out in the cold.
【恼怒】nǎonù **A**〈动〉 be annoyed: 我又~了他。 I've annoyed him again. **B**〈形〉 annoyed: 他的做法让人很~。 His ways really annoy people.
【恼人】nǎorén〈形〉 annoying: ~的噪声 irritating noise
【恼羞成怒】nǎoxiū-chéngnù〈成〉 become angry out of embarrassment

脑（腦） nǎo〈名〉**1**（大脑）brain: 大~ cerebrum ‖ ~神经 cranial nerve **2**（头部）head: ▸~袋, 摇头晃~ **3**（脑筋）mind: 用~过度 excessively taxing **4**（精华）essence: ▸豆腐~儿, 樟~ **5**（零碎）odds and ends: 田头地~ bits and pieces of land ▸针头线~
【脑出血】nǎochūxuè ▸**p. 50**〈名〉 cerebral haemorrhage
【脑垂体】nǎochuítǐ〈名〉 pituitary gland
【脑袋】nǎodai〈名〉〈口〉**1**（头部）head: 耷拉着~ hang one's head ‖ 拿~担保 stake one's life on **2**（脑筋）brains: ~好使 have a good brain
【脑袋瓜儿】nǎodaiguār〈口〉= 脑袋 nǎodai
【脑电波】nǎodiànbō〈名〉 brain wave
【脑电图】nǎodiàntú〈名〉 electroencephalogram (EEG)
【脑干】nǎogàn〈名〉［解剖］brainstem
【脑瓜儿】nǎoguār = 脑袋 nǎodai
【脑海】nǎohǎi〈名〉 mind: 这件事深深地印在了我的~中。 The experience was imprinted on my memory.
【脑积水】nǎojīshuǐ ▸**p. 50**〈名〉 hydrocephalus
【脑际】nǎojì〈名〉 mind: 当年的情景又浮现在她的~。 Memories of that time flashed through her mind again.
【脑浆】nǎojiāng〈名〉 brains: ~迸裂 have one's brains dashed out
【脑筋】nǎojīn〈名〉**1**（脑力）brains: 动~ use one's head ‖ ~简单 be simple-minded ‖ 这可是个伤~的问题。 This is really a vexing problem. **2**（观念）way of thinking: 换~ change one's way of thinking ‖ 死~ be inflexible
【脑筋急转弯】nǎojīn jízhuǎnwān〈名〉 brain-twister
【脑壳】nǎoké〈名〉〈方〉 head
【脑库】nǎokù〈名〉 think tank: 企业有难处，不妨找~。 If the business finds itself in difficulty then there's no harm in seeking out a think tank.
【脑力】nǎolì〈名〉 brainpower: ~工作 intellectual work
【脑力劳动】nǎolì-láodòng〈名〉brainwork: ~者 brain worker
【脑瘤】nǎoliú ▸**p. 50**〈名〉 brain tumour
【脑满肠肥】nǎomǎn-chángféi〈成〉［of the idle rich］with heavy jowls and a pot belly
【脑门儿】nǎoménr〈名〉 forehead
【脑门子】nǎoménzi〈名〉〈口〉 forehead
【脑膜】nǎomó〈名〉 meninges
【脑膜炎】nǎomóyán ▸**p. 50**〈名〉 meningitis
【脑儿】nǎor〈名〉 animal brains (for food): 猪~ pig's brains ▸豆腐~
【脑勺】nǎosháo〈名〉〈口〉 back of the head
【脑神经】nǎoshénjīng〈名〉 cranial nerve
【脑室】nǎoshì〈名〉［生理］ventricle of the brain
【脑死亡】nǎosǐwáng ▸**p. 50**〈名〉 brain death
【脑髓】nǎosuǐ = 脑浆 nǎojiāng
【脑瘫】nǎotān ▸**p. 50**〈名〉 brain failure
【脑体倒挂】nǎotǐ-dàoguà〈成〉 irrational income differential between mental and manual workers in favour of the latter
【脑外科】nǎowàikē〈名〉 brain surgery: ~医生 brain surgeon
【脑外伤】nǎowàishāng ▸**p. 50**〈名〉［医学］brain trauma
【脑萎缩】nǎowěisuō ▸**p. 50**〈名〉［医学］brain atrophy
【脑细胞】nǎoxìbāo〈名〉 brain cell
【脑血管】nǎoxuèguǎn〈名〉 cerebral blood vessel
【脑血管硬化症】nǎoxuèguǎn yìnghuàzhèng ▸**p. 50**〈名〉 cerebral arteriosclerosis
【脑血栓】nǎoxuèshuān ▸**p. 50**〈名〉 cerebral thrombus
【脑炎】nǎoyán ▸**p. 50**〈名〉 encephalitis: 流行性乙型~ epidemic encephalitis B
【脑溢血】nǎoyìxuè ▸**p. 50**〈名〉 cerebral haemorrhage
【脑震荡】nǎozhèndàng ▸**p. 50**〈名〉 concussion: 轻微~ mild concussion
【脑汁】nǎozhī〈名〉 brains: 绞尽~ rack one's brains
【脑中风】nǎozhòngfēng ▸**p. 50**〈名〉 cerebral apoplexy
【脑子】nǎozi〈名〉**1**（大脑）brain **2**（脑筋）brains: ~活 have a supple mind ‖ 他~好使。 He's got a good brain.

瑙 nǎo ▸玛瑙 mǎnǎo
【瑙鲁】Nǎolǔ〈名〉 Nauru: ~人 Nauruan

nào

闹（鬧） nào
A〈形〉 noisy: 教室里~得无法学习。 The classroom is too noisy to study in. ▸喧~
B〈动〉**1**（吵闹）make a noise: 别胡~，我在想问题。 Don't pester me, I am thinking over a problem. **2**（扰乱）create confusion: ~公堂 raise havoc in the law court ▸~事 **3**（发泄）give vent to: ▸~情绪 **4**（发生）be affected by: ~地震 be affected by the earthquake ‖ ~水灾 be hit by floods ▸~肚子, ~鬼, ~饥荒 **5**（从事）do: ~学潮 make a student movement ‖（与某人）~矛盾 be at loggerheads (with sb.) **6**（戏耍）tease: ▸~洞房
【闹别扭】nào bièniu〈动〉 be at odds with: 她在跟丈夫~。 She is at odds with her husband.
【闹病】nàobìng〈动〉〈口〉 be taken ill: 这孩子爱~，得让医生看看。 This child often falls ill, we must let the doctor have a look at him.
【闹洞房】nào dòngfáng〈动〉 tease newly-weds on their wedding night
【闹肚子】nào dùzi〈动〉〈口〉 have diarrhoea
【闹翻】nàofān〈动〉 fall out: 他和女朋友~了。 He fell out with his girlfriend.
【闹房】nàofáng = 闹洞房 nào dòngfáng
【闹革命】nào gémìng〈动〉〈口〉 make revolution
【闹鬼】nàoguǐ〈动〉**1**（指鬼怪）be haunted: 据说这所旧屋常常~。 It is said that ghosts often haunt this old house. **2**〈喻〉（搞阴谋）play tricks behind sb.'s back: 肯定有人在背后~。 There must be someone playing tricks from behind the scenes.
【闹哄哄】nàohōnghōng〈形〉 uproarious: 街上~的。 It was very noisy in the street.
【闹哄】nàohong〈动〉〈口〉**1**（吵闹）make a noise **2**（共同做）bustle about doing sth.: 他们~着搬家具。 They bustled about moving the furniture.
【闹饥荒】nào jīhuang〈动〉**1**（指粮荒）suffer from famine: 去年这个地区~。 There was a famine in this area last year. **2**〈喻〉〈方〉（经济困难）be hard up
【闹架】nàojià〈动〉〈方〉 quarrel and fight
【闹僵】nàojiāng〈动〉 be deadlocked
【闹剧】nàojù〈名〉 farce:〈喻〉 这次审判成了一场~。 The trial is becoming a farce.
【闹离婚】nào líhūn〈动〉 seek a divorce
【闹铃】nàolíng〈名〉 alarm bell
【闹乱子】nào luànzi〈动〉 make trouble
【闹脾气】nào píqi〈动〉 lose one's temper: 她爱~。 She is short-tempered.
【闹情绪】nào qíngxù〈动〉 be disgruntled: 几天来他一直在为这事~。 He has been in low spirits for a few days now because of this.
【闹嚷嚷】nàorāngrāng〈形〉 noisy: 礼堂里~的，什么也听不清。 I couldn't really hear anything because of the noise in the auditorium.
【闹市】nàoshì〈名〉 downtown (area): ~区 downtown area
【闹事】nàoshì〈动〉 create a disturbance: 聚众~ gather a crowd to stir up trouble
【闹腾】nàoteng〈动〉〈口〉**1**（吵闹）wrangle: 两口子~着要离婚。 The couple wrangled their way towards a divorce. **2**（逗趣打闹）laugh and joke noisily: 你们到底在~什么呢? What on earth are you up to here? **3**（搞）make: 他把事情

～得一团糟。 He made a mess of it.

【闹笑话】 nào xiàohua〈动〉 make a fool of oneself: 不懂装懂，容易～。 You'll make a fool of yourself by pretending to understand.

【闹心】 nàoxīn〈动〉〈方〉 ❶（烦心） be worried: 这孩子真让我～。 The child really disturbed me. ❷（胃不适） feel sick/queasy

【闹新房】 nào xīnfáng = 闹洞房 nào dòngfáng

【闹意见】 nào yìjiàn〈动〉 be at odds: 为一点小事和某人～ be at odds with sb. over a small thing

【闹意气】 nào yìqì〈动〉 sulk

【闹灾】 nàozāi〈动〉 be struck by disaster: 这儿去年闹水灾，死了好多人。 Last year this area was hit by a flood and many people lost their lives.

【闹贼】 nàozéi〈动〉〈口〉 burgle

【闹着玩儿】 nàozhe wánr〈动〉 ❶（玩耍） have fun: 孩子们在那儿～呢。 The children are playing over there. ❷（开玩笑） joke: 别担心，我是～的。 Don't worry. I was just kidding. ❸（轻率地对待） be a joke: 做手术可不是～的。 Performing an operation is no joke.

【闹中取静】 nàozhōng-qǔjìng〈成〉 seek peace and quiet in noisy surroundings

【闹钟】 nàozhōng〈名〉 alarm clock: 把～调在六点 set the alarm clock for 6:00

淖 nào〈名〉〈书〉 mire: ►泥～

né

哪 né
►nǎ, na, něi

【哪吒】 Nézhā〈名〉 *Nezha* [god in Chinese mythology]

nè

讷（訥） nè〈形〉〈书〉 slow (of speech): ～于言而敏于行 deliberate in speech but swift in action ►木～

【讷讷】 nènè〈形〉〈书〉 slow of speech

呐 nè = 讷 nè
►nà

ne

呢 ne〈助〉 ❶（表疑问） [marker of a special, alternative or rhetorical question]: 妈妈～? Where is Mum? ‖ 你想吃面条～，还是想吃米饭? What do you want, noodles or rice? ❷（表强调） [marker of a declarative sentence]: 天还早着～。 It's still early. ‖ 我在问你～! I was asking you! ❸（表状态） [used at the end of a declarative sentence to indicate the continuation of an action or a state]: 我听着～。 I am listening. ‖ 他还在睡～。 He is still sleeping. ❹（表停顿） [used to mark a pause in a sentence]: 想来～，就来; 不想来～，就拉倒。 Come if you want to, if you don't, then forget it.
►ní

něi

哪 něi = 哪 nǎ 1, 2
►nǎ, na, né

馁（餒） něi〈形〉 ❶〈书〉（饿） hungry: ►冻～ ❷（灰心丧气） disheartened: ►气～, 胜不骄，败不～

【馁怯】 něiqiè〈动〉〈书〉 lose heart

nèi

内 nèi〈名〉 ❶（范围内） interior: 几天之～ in a few days ‖ 室～ indoors ‖ 一公里之～ within a kilometre ‖ 请勿入～。 No admittance. ►～外，～衣，国～ ❷〈谦〉（指妻子） one's wife;（指亲戚） one's wife's relatives: ►～人，～侄 ❸（内脏） internal organs: ►～伤，五～如焚 ❹（心里） heart: ►～疚，～省 ❺〈书〉（皇宫） the imperial palace: 大～高手 *kung fu* master in the imperial palace

【内白】 nèibái〈名〉［戏曲］ offstage words by an actor

【内宾】 nèibīn〈名〉 ❶（本国客人） domestic visitor ❷（女宾） female guest

【内部】 nèibù〈名〉 inside: ～事务 internal affairs ‖ ～装修 interior decoration ‖ 人民～矛盾 contradictions among the people

【内布拉斯加州】 Nèibùlāsījiāzhōu〈名〉 Nebraska

【内参】 nèicān〈名〉 internal reference

【内侧】 nèicè〈名〉 inside: 窗/墙的～ the inside of a window/wall

【内查外调】 nèichá-wàidiào〈成〉 investigate internally and externally

【内臣】 nèichén〈名〉 ❶（近臣） chamberlain ❷（宦官） eunuch

【内衬】 nèichèn〈名〉 ❶（衬里） lining: 给大衣加～ interline a coat ❷［机械］ inner liner

【内城】 nèichéng〈名〉 inner city

【内出血】 nèichūxuè〈名〉 internal bleeding

【内存】 nèicún〈名〉［计算机］ ❶（指存储器） internal storage ❷（存储量） RAM

【内存储器】 nèicúnchǔqì〈名〉［计算机］ internal storage

【内当家】 nèidāngjiā〈名〉〈诙〉 wife

【内地】 nèidì〈名〉 ❶（内陆地区） inland: 销往～ be sold inland ‖ ～工业 inland industry ❷（中国大陆） mainland: 最近他去过～。 He has been to the mainland recently.

【内弟】 nèidì〈名〉 wife's younger brother

【内定】 nèidìng〈动〉 be decided internally but not yet announced: 他被～为驻日本大使。 He is slated to be the ambassador to Japan.

【内斗】 nèidòu〈名〉 internal conflict

【内耳】 nèi'ěr〈名〉 inner ear

【内分泌】 nèifēnmì〈名〉［生理］ internal secretion: ～失调 endocrine imbalance

【内分泌紊乱】 nèifēnmì wěnluàn〈名〉 endocrine disorder

【内分泌系统】 nèifēnmì xìtǒng〈名〉 endocrine system

【内封】 nèifēng〈名〉［印刷］ title page

【内服】 nèifú〈动〉 be taken orally: ～药 oral medicine

【内附】 nèifù〈动〉 be enclosed

【内刚外柔】 nèigāng-wàiróu〈成〉 iron hand in a velvet glove

【内阁】 nèigé〈名〉 cabinet: 改组～ reshuffle the cabinet ‖ 解散～ break up the cabinet ‖ ～成员 cabinet member ►影子～

【内阁大臣】 nèigé dàchén〈名〉 cabinet minister

【内阁总理】 nèigé zǒnglǐ〈名〉 prime minister

【内功】 nèigōng〈名〉 ❶（指武术或气功） internal exercises ❷（指人） quality and capability ❸（指企业） capability of managing internal affairs well

【内顾之忧】 nèigùzhīyōu〈成〉 domestic worries

【内海】 nèihǎi〈名〉 ❶（内陆海） inland sea: ～水域 internal sea waters ❷（指领海） continental waters

【内涵】 nèihán〈名〉 ❶（指概念） intention: ～定义 intention definition ‖ ～意义 connotative meaning ❷（指语言） implication ❸（指人） hidden depths: 他～深厚。 He has profound knowledge and moral integrity.

【内寒】 nèihán〈名〉［中医］ internal cold

【内行】 nèiháng **A**〈形〉 expert: 在破译军事信号方面很～ be expert at deciphering military signals **B**〈名〉 expert: 充～ pose as an expert

【内行看门道，外行看热闹】 nèiháng kàn méndao, wàiháng kàn rènao〈俗〉 laymen just watch while professionals understand

【内耗】 nèihào〈名〉 ❶（指机器、装置） internal consumption ❷〈喻〉（指部门、机构） internal waste

【内河】 nèihé〈名〉 inland waters: ～航行 internal navigation

【内讧】 nèihòng〈动〉 have internal conflict: 引发～ foment internal dissension

【内华达州】 Nèihuádázhōu〈名〉 Nevada

【内画】 nèihuà〈名〉 pictures painted on the inside (of a vessel)

【内踝】 nèihuái〈名〉［生理］ malleolus medialis

【内环】 nèihuán〈简称〉= 内环线

【内环线】 nèihuánxiàn〈名〉 inner-ring road

【内患外侮】 nèihuàn-wàiwǔ〈成〉 be plagued by internal trouble and foreign aggression

【内火】 nèihuǒ〈名〉［中医］ internal heat

【内急】 nèijí ►**p. 772**〈动〉〈婉〉 be dying for the toilet

【内奸】 nèijiān〈名〉 enemy agent

【内角】 nèijiǎo〈名〉［数学］ interior angle

【内景】 nèijǐng〈名〉 indoor scene: ～拍摄 indoor shot

【内径】 nèijìng〈名〉 inside diameter: ～规 internal gauge

【内镜】 nèijìng = 内窥镜 nèikuījìng

【内疚】 nèijiù ►**p. 156**〈形〉 conscience-stricken: 深感～ have a terribly guilty conscience

【内聚力】 nèijùlì〈名〉 ❶［物理］ cohesive force ❷〈喻〉（凝聚力） cohesion: 增强公司员工的～ strengthen cohesion amongst the company's employees

【内眷】 nèijuàn〈名〉 female family members

【内卡钳】 nèikǎqián〈名〉［机械］ inside calipers

【内科】 nèikē〈名〉 general medicine: ～病房 medical ward ‖ ～学 internal medicine ‖ ～医生 physician

【内控】 nèikòng〈动〉 control from within: ～对象 target of internal control

【内库】 nèikù〈名〉〈旧〉 imperial treasury

【内裤】 nèikù〈名〉 underwear: 男～

n

underpants, underwear〈美〉‖ 女～ panties, knickers〈英〉

【内窥镜】nèikuījìng〈名〉［医学］endoscope

【内涝】nèilào〈名〉waterlogging

【内里】nèilǐ〈名〉inside: 这事～有一些原因你还不知道呢。You don't know some of the details involved.

【内力】nèilì〈名〉［物理］internal force

【内敛】nèiliǎn〈形〉introverted: 性格～ be introverted by nature

【内流河】nèiliúhé〈名〉inland river

【内陆】nèilù〈名〉interior: ～城市 inland city ‖ ～性气候 inland climate

【内陆国】nèilùguó〈名〉landlocked country

【内陆河】nèilùhé〈名〉continental river

【内陆湖】nèilùhú〈名〉inland lake

【内乱】nèiluàn〈名〉domestic turmoil: 平息～ appease internal strife ‖ 引起～ beget civil strife

【内罗毕】Nèiluóbì〈名〉Nairobi

【内贸】nèimào〈名〉domestic trade: 扩大～ expand domestic trade

【内蒙】Nèiměng〈简称〉= 内蒙古

【内蒙古】Nèiměnggǔ ►p. 661〈名〉Inner Mongolia: ～自治区 Inner Mongolian Autonomous Region

【内幕】nèimù〈名〉inside story: 揭开～ reveal the inside story ‖ ～新闻 keyhole report

【内聘】nèipìn〈动〉be appointed within one's place of work

【内企】nèiqǐ〈简称〉= 内资企业

【内切圆】nèiqiēyuán〈名〉inscribed circle (of a triangle)

【内亲】nèiqīn〈名〉relatives of one's wife

【内勤】nèiqín〈名〉1（指工作）office work 2（指人）office staff

【内情】nèiqíng〈名〉inside story: 不了解～ be ignorant of the inside story ‖ 熟悉～ be in the know

【内燃机】nèiránjī〈名〉internal combustion engine: ～机车 diesel locomotive

【内热】nèirè〈名〉［中医］internal heat

【内人】nèirén〈名〉my wife

【内容】nèiróng〈名〉content: ～不详 content unknown ‖ ～丰富 be rich in content ‖ ～贫乏 be poor in content ‖ ～提要 synopsis

【内伤】nèishāng ►p. 50〈名〉1（指身体损伤）internal injury 2（指身体不调）internal disorder 3〈喻〉（指损坏）internal damage

【内设】nèishè〈动〉install inside: 大型商场～卫生间要提高标准。Toilets inside large shopping centres should be upgraded.

【内室】nèishì〈名〉inner room

【内侍】nèishì〈名〉〈旧〉eunuch

【内水】nèishuǐ〈名〉inland waters

【内胎】nèitāi〈名〉inner tube

【内廷】nèitíng〈名〉inner chambers in an imperial palace

【内退】nèituì〈名〉early retirement: 给一些职工安排～ arrange early retirement for some staff members

【内外】nèiwài A〈名〉inside and outside: ～勾结 collaborate from within and without ‖ ～夹攻 attack from both inside and outside ‖ 国～ home and abroad B〈副〉approximately: 二十天～ about twenty days

【内外交困】nèiwài jiāokùn〈成〉be beset with difficulties both at home and abroad

【内外有别】nèiwài yǒubié〈成〉differentiate between insiders and the outsiders

【内务】nèiwù〈名〉1（国内事务）internal affairs: ～部 ministry of internal affairs 2（日常事务）daily tasks: 整理～ deal with one's personal matters

【内线】nèixiàn〈名〉1（指人）mole 2（指战线）interior lines: ～作战 fight on interior lines 3（指电话线）internal telephone connection: ～电话 house phone 4（指关系）inside connections: 走～ make use of connections on the inside ‖ 工资抢劫案是有～的。The payroll theft was an inside job.

【内详】nèixiáng〈动〉[written on an envelope] name and address of the sender enclosed

【内向】nèixiàng〈形〉1（针对国内）domestic-oriented: ～型企业 domestic-oriented enterprise 2（指性格）introverted: 她性格～。She is introverted by nature.

【内销】nèixiāo〈动〉sell domestically: ～商品 commodities for domestic sale ‖ 出口转～ export goods sold on the domestic market

【内斜视】nèixiéshì ►p. 50〈名〉［医学］esotropia

【内心】nèixīn〈名〉heart: 发自～ come from one's heart ‖ ～的秘密 innermost secret ‖ ～世界 inner world

【内心独白】nèixīn dúbái〈名〉interior monologue

【内省】nèixǐng〈动〉introspect

【内兄】nèixiōng〈名〉wife's elder brother

【内秀】nèixiù〈形〉intelligent but unassuming

【内需】nèixū〈名〉domestic demand: 扩大～ increase domestic demand

【内延】nèiyán〈名〉interior extent

【内衣】nèiyī〈名〉underwear

【内因】nèiyīn〈名〉［哲学］internal cause: 外因通过～起作用。External causes become operative through internal causes.

【内应】nèiyìng A〈动〉work from within in coordination with outside forces：有～ have someone on the inside B〈名〉planted agent

【内忧外患】nèiyōu-wàihuàn〈成〉domestic trouble and foreign invasion

【内援】nèiyuán〈名〉sportsperson on the national team: 招来几名外援和～组成一支新的球队 call up a few national and international sportspeople to form a new team

【内在】nèizài〈形〉1（本身固有）inherent: ～规律 internal law ‖ ～缺陷 inherent defect 2（不外露）closely-guarded: 感情～ feelings are closely guarded

【内在价值】nèizài jiàzhí〈名〉intrinsic value

【内在美】nèizàiměi〈名〉internal beauty

【内脏】nèizàng〈名〉internal organs: ～器官移植 viscera transplantation

【内贼】nèizéi〈名〉internal thief

【内宅】nèizhái〈名〉〈书〉inner chambers

【内债】nèizhài〈名〉internal debt

【内战】nèizhàn〈名〉civil war: 引起～ cause a civil war

【内掌柜】nèizhǎngguì〈名〉〈口〉wife of a shopkeeper

【内争】nèizhēng〈名〉internal strife

【内政】nèizhèng〈名〉domestic affairs: 不干涉别国～ do not interfere in other's internal affairs ‖ ～部 ministry of the interior

【内侄】nèizhí〈名〉nephew

【内侄女】nèizhínǚ〈名〉niece

【内痔】nèizhì〈名〉internal haemorrhoids

【内中】nèizhōng〈名〉the inside: ～的事无人知晓。No one knows the inside information.

【内助】nèizhù〈名〉〈书〉wife: 贤～ one's better half

【内传】nèizhuàn〈名〉intimate biography

【内资】nèizī〈名〉domestic capital

【内资企业】nèizī qǐyè〈名〉domestically-funded enterprise

【内子】nèizǐ〈名〉〈书〉my wife

nèn

恁 nèn〈代〉〈方〉1（那样）so: 天气～热! What a hot day! ‖ 来了～多的人。So many people have arrived. 2（那）that: ～时 at that time ‖ 别走～快。Don't walk so fast.
►nín

【恁地】nèndì〈代〉〈方〉1（如此）such: 让他别～麻烦人家! Don't let him trouble people like that! 2（如何）how come: 我的确把书放在这儿了，～找不到? I did put my book here, how come I can't find it?

嫩 nèn〈形〉1（娇嫩）delicate: ～姜 new ginger ‖ ～肉 tender meat ‖ ～芽 tender sprout 2►p. 863（色浅）light: ►～黄, ～绿 3（不老练）inexperienced: 你还～了点。You are still green. ‖ 他干这活恐怕～了点。I am afraid he is a bit inexperienced for such a job. 4（指食物）tender: ～牛排 rare beef steak, tenderloin steak

【嫩白】nènbái〈形〉fair and delicate

【嫩豆腐】nèndòufu〈名〉soft tofu

【嫩红】nènhóng ►p. 863〈形〉pale-red

【嫩黄】nènhuáng ►p. 863〈形〉light yellow

【嫩绿】nènlǜ ►p. 863〈形〉light green

【嫩气】nènqi〈名〉delicate looks

【嫩手】nènshǒu〈名〉green hand

【嫩枝】nènzhī〈名〉shoot

néng

能 néng
A〈名〉1（能力）ability: ►逞～, 才～, 技～, 无～ 2（能量）energy: ►电～, 热～, 势～, 原子～
B〈形〉able: ►～人, ～者多劳
C〈动〉1（有能力）be able to：～读会写 can read and write ►～歌善舞, ～说会道 2（可能）[expressing possibility] can: 他～答应吗? Would he agree? ‖ 我相信～找到一种解决办法。I am confident that a solution can be found. 3（表请求）[used in questions as a polite way of asking someone to do sth.] could: 你～帮我个忙吗? Could you do me a favour? ‖ 你～告诉我几点了吗? Can you tell me the time? 4（表允许）[expressing permission] may: 这里～抽烟吗? Can I smoke here?
►Nài

【能吹会拍】néngchuī-huìpāi〈成〉be good at bragging and toadying

【能动】néngdòng〈形〉active: ～作用 dynamic role

【能动性】néngdòngxìng〈名〉initiative: 调动大家的主观～ rouse everybody's spirits

【能干】nénggàn〈形〉capable: 他是个非常～的经理。He is a highly competent manager.

【能歌善舞】nénggē-shànwǔ〈成〉be good at singing and dancing

【能工巧匠】nénggōng-qiǎojiàng〈成〉skilled craftsman

【能够】nénggòu〈动〉**1**（表能力）be able to do: 她～独当一面了。She can work independently now. ‖ 中国人口多，但～养活自己。China has a large population, but its people are able to feed themselves. **2**（表可能）can: 这个目标是～实现的。The target is achievable.

【能官能民】néngguān-néngmín〈成〉be ready to serve as an official or to be one of the common people

【能耗】nénghào〈名〉energy consumption: 把～降到最低程度 reduce energy consumption to the minimum

【能级】néngjí〈名〉**1**［物理］energy level: 基态～ ground state level **2**（能力级别）level of competence: 技术～ technical proficiency

【能见度】néngjiàndù〈名〉visibility: ～很差。Visibility is very poor.

【能力】nénglì〈名〉ability: 管理～ administrative ability ‖ 生产～ productive capacity ‖ 写作～ the ability to write ‖ 业务～ professional competence

【能量】néngliàng〈名〉energy: ～消耗 energy consumption ‖ ～守恒定律 law of conservation of energy ‖〈喻〉人小～大 young but very capable

【能耐】néngnai **A**〈名〉skill, resourcefulness: 他的～确实不小。He is exceptionally skilled. **B**〈形〉capable: 他真～，一个人管这么大一个厂子。He is really capable, running this big factory all by himself.

【能掐会算】néngqiā-huìsuàn〈成〉**1**（指掐诀算卦）be able to calculate on one's fingers and tell people's fortunes **2**（指预测未来）be capable of prediction and foreknowledge

【能屈能伸】néngqū-néngshēn〈成〉be adaptable to circumstances: 大丈夫～。A true man knows when to keep a low profile and when to hold his head high.

【能人】néngrén〈名〉capable person: ～背后有～ for every able person there is always one still abler ‖ 这儿的～可真多! There are so many capable people here!

【能上能下】néngshàng-néngxià〈成〉be ready to work either at higher or at lower levels: 干部要～。A cadre should be ready to take a lower as well as a higher post.

【能诗善画】néngshī-shànhuà〈成〉have superior abilities to write poetry and paint

【能事】néngshì〈名〉sth. one is particularly good at: 极尽造谣中伤之～ stop at nothing to spread slanderous rumours

【能手】néngshǒu〈名〉dab hand (at sth.): 技术革新～ a dab hand at technical innovation ‖ 植棉～ expert cotton grower

【能说会道】néngshuō-huìdào〈成〉have the gift of the gab: ～的小贩 pedlar with the gift of the gab

【能文能武】néngwén-néngwǔ〈成〉be able to wield both the pen and the sword

【能效比】néngxiàobǐ〈名〉energy efficiency ratio (EER): 季节性～ seasonal energy efficiency ratio (SEER)

【能言快语】néngyán-kuàiyǔ〈成〉eloquent and frank in speech

【能言善辩】néngyán-shànbiàn〈成〉be skilled in debate

【能源】néngyuán〈名〉sources of energy: 开发新～ tap new energy sources ‖ 可再生～ renewable sources of energy ‖ ～短缺 energy shortage

【能者多劳】néngzhě-duōláo〈成〉an able man is always busy

【能者为师】néngzhě-wéishī〈成〉let those who know teach

ńg

嗯 ńg〈叹〉[expressing question]: ～? 这人是谁? Eh, who is that man?
▸ňg, ǹg

ňg

嗯 ňg〈叹〉[expressing surprise or disapproval]: ～! 我的书怎么不见了? What! My book is gone!
▸ńg, ǹg

ǹg

嗯 ǹg〈叹〉[expressing agreement]: 别忘了吃药。——～。Don't forget to take your medicine. — Uh-huh.
▸ńg, ňg

nī

妮 nī

【妮子】nīzi〈名〉〈方〉lass

ní

尼 ní〈名〉Buddhist nun: ▸～姑, 僧～

【尼泊尔】Níbó'ěr〈名〉Nepal: ～人 Nepalese ‖ ～语 Nepali

【尼格罗－澳大利亚人种】Nígéluó-Àodàlìyà rénzhǒng〈名〉Negroid-Australian race

【尼姑】nígū〈名〉Buddhist nun: ～庵 Buddhist nunnery

【尼古丁】nígǔdīng〈名〉nicotine: ～中毒 nicotine intoxication ‖ ～贴片 nicotine patch

【尼加拉瓜】Níjiālāguā〈名〉Nicaragua: ～共和国 Republic of Nicaragua ‖ ～人 Nicaraguan

【尼龙】nílóng〈名〉nylon: ～丝袜 nylon hose

【尼龙绳】nílóngshéng〈名〉nylon cord

【尼罗河】Níluóhé ▸**p. 294**〈名〉Nile

【尼日尔】Nírì'ěr〈名〉Niger: ～共和国 Republic of Niger ‖ ～人 Nigerois

【尼日利亚】Nírìlìyà〈名〉Nigeria: ～联邦共和国 Federal Republic of Nigeria ‖ ～人 Nigerian

【尼亚加拉瀑布】Níyàjiālā Pùbù〈名〉Niagara Falls

【尼亚美】Níyàměi〈名〉Niamey

呢 ní〈名〉woollen cloth: ～大衣 woollen coat ‖ 海军～ navy cloth
▸ne

【呢料】níliào〈名〉woollen cloth material

【呢喃】nínán〈拟〉**1**（指燕子）twitter **2**〈书〉（指小声说话）murmur: ～细语 whisper

【呢绒】níróng〈名〉woollen goods

【呢子】nízi〈名〉heavy woollen cloth

泥 ní〈名〉**1**（泥土）mud: 鞋上全是～。The shoes were covered with mud. ▸～巴, 淤～ **2**（泥状物）mash: 土豆～ mashed potato ▸蒜～, 印～, 枣～
▸nì

【泥巴】níbā〈名〉mud: 刮掉鞋子上的～ scrape the mud off one's shoes

【泥刀】nídāo = 瓦刀 wǎdāo

【泥饭碗】nífànwǎn〈名〉〈喻〉insecure job

【泥肥】níféi〈名〉sludge

【泥封】nífēng〈名〉lute

【泥工】nígōng = 泥水匠 níshuǐjiàng

【泥垢】nígòu〈名〉dirt: 他满身～。He is covered in mud.

【泥浆】níjiāng〈名〉mud: 雨后路上全是～。After the rain, the roads were covered with mud.

【泥金】níjīn〈名〉coating material made of powdered metals

【泥坑】níkēng〈名〉mire: 陷入～ sink into the mire

【泥疗】níliáo〈名〉mud therapy

【泥煤】níméi = 泥炭 nítàn

【泥淖】nínào〈名〉bog

【泥泞】nínìng **A**〈形〉muddy: ～的道路 muddy road ‖ ～的田地 muddy field **B**〈名〉mud

【泥牛入海】níniú-rùhǎi〈成〉〈喻〉gone forever

【泥盆纪】Nípénjì〈名〉［地质］Devonian Period

【泥盆系】Nípénxì〈名〉［地质］Devonian (System)

【泥坯】nípī〈名〉moulded pottery to be baked in a kiln

【泥菩萨过河，自身难保】nípúsà guòhé, zìshēn nánbǎo〈歇后〉hardly able to save oneself, let alone anyone else: 现在他已是～。Now he is looking out for himself.

【泥鳅】níqiū〈名〉loach

【泥人】nírén〈名〉clay figurine: 彩塑～ painted clay figurine

【泥沙】níshā〈名〉silt

【泥沙俱下】níshā-jùxià〈成〉〈喻〉the good is carried with the bad

【泥石流】níshíliú〈名〉mudslide

【泥水匠】níshuǐjiàng〈名〉plasterer

【泥塑】nísù〈名〉clay sculpture: ～展览 exhibition of clay sculptures

【泥塑木雕】nísù-mùdiāo = 木雕泥塑 mùdiāo-nísù

【泥胎】nítāi〈名〉unpainted clay idol

【泥胎】nítāi〈名〉unbaked and unfired pottery: 师傅正在做一个瓷瓶的～。The master is making a roughcast of a porcelain vase.

【泥潭】nítán〈名〉mire: 陷入～ sink into the mud ‖〈喻〉该国正滑入内战～。That country is slipping into the mire of civil war.

【泥炭】nítàn〈名〉peat: ～开采 peat digging ‖ ～气化 peat gasification

【泥塘】nítáng〈名〉bog

【泥土】nítǔ〈名〉**1**（土壤）soil: 家乡的～ soil of one's native place ‖ 雨后的空气有股～的芳香。After the rain there is an earthy smell in the air. **2**（黏土）clay

【泥腿子】nítuǐzi〈名〉〈旧〉〈贬〉bumpkin

【泥瓦匠】níwǎjiàng = 泥水匠 níshuǐjiàng

【泥俑】níyǒng〈名〉funerary clay figure

【泥沼】nízhǎo〈名〉**1**（烂泥坑）swamp: 一片广阔的～ a vast mire **2**〈喻〉（指境地）mire: 陷入～ sink into the mire

【泥足巨人】nízú-jùrén〈成〉〈喻〉paper tiger

【泥醉】nízuì〈形〉dead drunk

怩 ní ▸忸怩 niǔní

铌（鈮） ní〈名〉［化学］ niobium (Nb)

倪 ní〈名〉〈书〉 beginning: ►端～

霓 ní〈名〉 secondary rainbow

【霓虹灯】 níhóngdēng〈名〉 neon lamp

鲵（鯢） ní〈名〉［动物］ salamander

nǐ

拟（擬） nǐ〈动〉 **1**（比较） compare: ►比～ **2**（模仿） imitate: ►～古, 模～ **3**（计划） plan: ～于周五赴京 plan to go to Beijing on Friday **4**（设计） devise: ～方案 draw up a plan/programme ►～订, ～稿, 草～ **5**（假设） suppose: ►虚～

【拟订】 nǐdìng〈动〉 draft: ～计划 draw up a plan ‖ ～实施办法 work out implementation measures

【拟定】 nǐdìng〈动〉 draft: ～计划 draw up a plan

【拟稿】 nǐgǎo〈动〉 prepare a draft: 你先拟个稿子供大家讨论。 Will you please prepare a draft for discussion?

【拟古】 nǐgǔ〈动〉 model after ancient artistic forms: ～之作 work modelled after ancient styles

【拟人】 nǐrén〈名〉［语言］ personification

【拟声词】 nǐshēngcí〈名〉 onomatopoetic word

【拟态】 nǐtài〈名〉［动物］ mimicry

【拟物】 nǐwù〈名〉［语言］ objectification

【拟议】 nǐyì **A**〈名〉 proposal: 她的～被接受了。 Her recommendations were accepted. **B**〈动〉 draft: 你还是先～个初步方案吧。 You'd better draw up a tentative programme first.

【拟音】 nǐyīn〈名〉［影视］ sound effect

【拟作】 nǐzuò〈名〉 imitation works

你 nǐ〈代〉 **1** ►**p. 780**（指对方） you: ～好! Hello! ‖ ～昨天怎么没有来? Why didn't you come yesterday? **2**（泛指任何人） one: 对陌生人～得当心。 You have to be careful with people you don't know. ‖ 这种人～不能相信。 You can't trust a person like that. **3**（表示人多） [used co-ordinately with 我 or 他 in parallel structures to]: ～一言, 我一语 everyone joins in the conversation ‖ 大家～看看我, 我看看～, 谁也不说话。 We kept looking at one another without saying a word. **4**（你们） you: ～厂/队/校 your factory/team/school ►～方

【你方】 nǐfāng〈名〉 your side: ～代表 your representatives

【你们】 nǐmen〈代〉 you: ～谁来试试? Who would like to have a go?

【你死我活】 nǐsǐ-wǒhuó〈成〉 life-and-death: 拼个～ fight to the bitter end

【你争我夺】 nǐzhēng-wǒduó〈成〉 vie with each other

【你中有我, 我中有你】 nǐzhōngyǒuwǒ, wǒzhōngyǒunǐ〈俗〉 there is something of each in the other

【你追我赶】 nǐzhuī-wǒgǎn〈成〉 try to catch up and overtake one another

【你走你的阳关道, 我过我的独木桥】 nǐ zǒu nǐde yángguāndào, wǒ guò wǒde dúmùqiáo〈俗〉 you go your way, and I'll go mine

旎 nǐ ►旖旎 yǐnǐ

nì

泥 nì
A〈动〉 plaster: ～缝儿 cover the cracks with plaster ‖ ～墙 plaster a wall ►～子
B〈形〉 obstinate: ►～古不化, 拘～
►ní

【泥古】 nìgǔ〈动〉 obstinately follow ancient ways

【泥古不化】 nìgǔ-bùhuà〈成〉 be a slave to all things ancient

【泥子】 nìzi〈名〉 putty

昵（暱） nì〈形〉 close: ►亲～

【昵称】 nìchēng〈名〉 term of endearment

【昵友】 nìyǒu〈名〉 intimate friend

逆 nì
A〈动〉 **1**〈书〉（迎接） welcome: ～旅 hotel **2**（指方向相反） go against: ～流而上 go upstream ►～行, ～运算, 倒行～施, ～时针 **3**（不顺从） disobey: ►～子, 忤～, 忠言～耳
B〈形〉 adverse: ►～境
C〈名〉 traitor: ►～贼, 叛～
D〈副〉 in advance: ►～料

【逆差】 nìchā〈名〉 unfavourable balance: 国际收支～ unfavourable balance of international payments ►贸易～

【逆产】 nìchǎn〈名〉 **1**（指财产） traitor's estate: 没收～ confiscate a traitor's property **2**［医学］ breech birth

【逆潮】 nìcháo〈名〉 reversed tide

【逆定理】 nìdìnglǐ〈名〉［数学］ inverse theorem

【逆耳】 nì'ěr〈动〉 be unpleasant to the ear: ～之言 unwelcome advice or statement ►忠言～

【逆反心理】 nìfǎn xīnlǐ〈名〉 mind to rebel: 父母管教过严, 孩子可能产生～。 Children may develop a rebellious mind if their parents are too strict with them.

【逆反应】 nìfǎnyìng〈名〉［化学］ reverse reaction

【逆风】 nìfēng **A**〈名〉 head wind **B**〈动〉 be against the wind: ～而行 go against the wind ‖ ～飞行 make a headwind flight

【逆光】 nìguāng〈名〉［摄影］ backlight

【逆境】 nìjìng〈名〉 adverse conditions: 身处～ be in a tight fix ‖ ～能锻炼人。 Adversity is a great teacher.

【逆来顺受】 nìlái-shùnshòu〈成〉 take hardships or insults lying down

【逆料】 nìliào〈动〉〈书〉 foresee: 胜负难以～ success or failure are hard to predict

【逆流】 nìliú **A**〈动〉 go against the current: ～而上 go upstream **B**〈名〉 countercurrent: 顶住～ resist the countercurrent

【逆旅】 nìlǚ〈名〉〈书〉 inn

【逆时针】 nìshízhēn〈名〉 anticlockwise〈英〉; counterclockwise〈美〉: 按～方向移动 move anticlockwise

【逆市】 nìshì〈动〉［金融］ buck the market: 在金融危机中, 我国装备制造业～而上, 产值大幅提高。 In the midst of the financial crisis, Chinese equipment manufacturers bucked the market by increasing output substantially.

【逆势】 nìshì〈动〉［金融］ bcuk the trend: 在商品房销售量严重萎缩的情况下, 一些高档楼盘却～上扬。 During the severe decline in commercial housing sales, some high-end real estate bucked the trend and rose in price.

【逆水】 nìshuǐ〈动〉 go against the current: ～而上 go upstream

【逆水行舟】 nìshuǐ-xíngzhōu〈成〉 sail against the current: 学如～, 不进则退。 Learning is like sailing against the current — you must press ahead or you will be driven back.

【逆温层】 nìwēncéng〈名〉［气象］ inversion layer

【逆向】 nìxiàng〈动〉 go in the opposite direction: ～行驶 drive in the wrong direction

【逆行】 nìxíng〈动〉 go against the traffic

【逆序】 nìxù〈名〉 inverse order: ～词典 reverse dictionary

【逆运算】 nìyùnsuàn〈名〉［数学］ inverse operation

【逆贼】 nìzéi〈名〉 rebel

【逆证】 nìzhèng〈名〉［中医］ severe case with unfavourable prognosis

【逆转】 nìzhuǎn〈动〉 take a turn for better or worse: 历史潮流, 不可～。 The trend of history is irreversible.

【逆子】 nìzǐ〈名〉 unfilial son

匿 nì〈动〉 hide: ►～名, 藏～

【匿报】 nìbào〈动〉 withhold information

【匿藏】 nìcáng〈动〉 conceal

【匿迹】 nìjì〈动〉 go into hiding: ～海外 go into hiding abroad ►销声～

【匿名】 nìmíng〈动〉 be anonymous: ～举报 inform against sb. anonymously

【匿名信】 nìmíngxìn〈名〉 anonymous letter

【匿影藏形】 nìyǐng-cángxíng〈成〉 lie low

【匿影潜形】 nìyǐng-qiánxíng = 匿影藏形 nìyǐng-cángxíng

睨 nì〈动〉〈书〉 look askance: ►～视, 睥～

【睨视】 nìshì〈动〉〈书〉 cast a sidelong look

腻（膩） nì
A〈形〉 **1**（油脂多） fatty: 这块肉又肥又～。 This piece of meat is fatty and greasy. ►油～ **2**（细致） meticulous: ►细～ 2 **3**（又黏又滑） greasy: 油～的抹布 oily rags
B〈动〉 **1**（不想吃） disgust sb.: 奶油太多～人。 Eating too much cream will make you feel sick. **2**（厌烦） be tired of: 他电视广告看～了。 He's fed up with watching TV commercials. ‖ 他吃鱼吃～了。 He is tired of eating fish. ►～烦
C〈名〉〈书〉 dirt: 垢～ dirty stain

【腻虫】 nìchóng〈名〉 aphid

【腻烦】 nìfan〈口〉 **A**〈形〉 fed up: 这话我都听～了。 I'm sick of listening to this talk. ‖ 她对他～了。 She is tired of him. **B**〈动〉 loathe: 冗长的讲座真让人～。 I hate going to lengthy lectures.

【腻人】 nìrén〈形〉 tedious

【腻味】 nìwei = 腻烦 nìfan

【腻友】 nìyǒu〈名〉〈书〉 bosom friend

【腻子】 nìzi = 泥子 nìzi

溺 nì〈动〉 **1**（淹没） drown: ～水而死 drown **2**（沉迷于） abandon oneself (to): ～于酒色 be given to wine and women ►～爱, 沉～
►niào

【溺爱】 nì'ài〈动〉 dote on: ～子女 pamper one's children

【溺水】nìshuǐ〈动〉 drown: 抢救～儿童 rescue a drowning child
【溺婴】nìyīng〈动〉drown an infant
【溺于酒色】nìyújiǔsè〈成〉 be given over to wine and women
【溺职】nìzhí〈动〉neglect one's duty

niān

拈 niān〈动〉 pick up: ～起一张报纸 pick up a newspaper ▸～阄儿, 信手～来, ～轻怕重
【拈花惹草】niānhuā-rěcǎo 〈成〉 fool around with women
【拈阄儿】niānjiūr〈动〉draw lots
【拈轻怕重】niānqīng-pàzhòng〈成〉prefer easy work to hard work
【拈香】niānxiāng〈动〉burn incense

蔫 niān〈形〉 1（枯萎）drooping: 花儿～了。The flowers have wilted. ‖ 秧苗被烈日晒～了。The seedlings had shrivelled up in the hot sun. 2（无精打采）listless: 这孩子～～的，是不是生病了？The child seems listless. Is he ill? 3（不活泼）sluggish: ～性子 sluggish nature
【蔫巴】niānba〈形〉〈口〉 drooping: 天气炎热，叶子都～了。The leaves shrivelled up in the heat.
【蔫不唧】niānbujī〈形〉〈方〉 1（情绪低落）sluggish: 他变得～的，原来是被女朋友甩了。He has become despondent ever since his girlfriend dumped him. 2（悄无声息）on the quiet: 他～地进来，把我吓了一跳。He came in quietly and gave me quite a start.
【蔫呼呼】niānhūhū〈形〉sluggish
【蔫儿坏】niānrhuài〈形〉 behaving in an underhanded manner
【蔫头耷脑】niāntóu-dānǎo〈成〉 listless: 打输了没关系，别～的。It doesn't matter that you have lost the game. Don't be so despondent.
【蔫萎】niānwěi〈动〉shrivel up

nián

年 nián
A〈名〉 1 ▸p. 618（指时间）year: 进入/迎接新的一～ enter/usher in a new year ▸今～, 学～ 2（指收成）harvest: ▸～成, 丰～, 荒～ 3（每年）annual: ～产量 annual yield ‖ ～发电量 annual power generation ▸～会, ～鉴 4（岁数）age: ～近半百 be getting on for fifty ‖ ～满二十 be 20 years old ▸～纪, 延～益寿 5（指年龄段）one of the periods of life: ▸青～, 童～ 6（指历史时期）period in history: 清朝末～ last years of the Qing Dynasty ▸～间, 早～ 7（年节）New Year: ▸～关, 拜～, 过～, 新～ 8（指用品）things for the New Year: ▸～糕, ～画, ～货
B〈量〉 year: 奥运会每四～举办一次。The Olympics is held once every four years. ▸三～五载
【年报】niánbào〈名〉annual report
【年表】niánbiǎo〈名〉chronological table
【年产】niánchǎn〈名〉annual yield
【年成】niáncheng〈名〉 year's harvest: ～好 bumper year ‖ ～不好 lean year
【年齿】niánchǐ〈名〉〈书〉 age: ～日增 grow older with each passing day
【年初】niánchū ▸p. 618〈名〉 beginning of the year: 明年～ at the beginning of next year
【年代】niándài ▸p. 618〈名〉 1（时代）age: ～久远 be age-old ‖ 在战争～ during the war years ‖ 展出的文物都标明了～。The antiques displayed are all marked with dates. 2（十年）decade of a century: 二十世纪三十～ the 1930s
【年代测定】niándài cèdìng〈名〉［考古］dating
【年代学】niándàixué〈名〉 chronology: ～家 chronologist
【年底】niándǐ ▸p. 618〈名〉 year-end: 去年～ the end of last year
【年度】niándù〈名〉 year: ～财务报表 annual financial statement ‖ ～计划 annual plan ‖ ～审计 annual audit ‖ ～风云人物 man of the year ▸财政～
【年饭】niánfàn = 年夜饭 niányèfàn
【年份】niánfèn ▸p. 618〈名〉 1（某一年）a particular year: 出生～ the year one was born ‖ 小麦收成最好～ banner year for wheat 2（时间）age: 这件古董～一定很久了。This antique must be very old.
【年富力强】niánfù-lìqiáng〈成〉 in one's prime: 提拔～的干部 promote young and energetic cadres
【年复一年】niánfù-yīnián〈成〉 year in, year out
【年高德劭】niángāo-déshào〈成〉 be of venerable age and eminent virtue
【年糕】niángāo〈名〉 rice cake: 炒～ stir-fry rice cakes
【年根】niángēn ▸p. 618〈名〉〈方〉year's end: 快到～了。The end of the year drew near.
【年庚】niángēng〈名〉〈书〉 time of a person's birth [the hour, day, month and year]
【年关】niánguān ▸p. 618〈名〉 end of the year: ～荏苒 the quick passing of time
【年光】niánguāng〈名〉 1（时光）time: ～易逝。Time passes easily. 2（年成）year's harvest: ～不好 lean year ‖ ～好 bumper year 3〈方〉（年头儿）times: 那～生活很苦。Life was very tough in those days.
【年号】niánhào〈名〉〈古〉reign title
【年华】niánhuá〈名〉 time: 青春～ the period of youth ▸虚度～
【年画】niánhuà〈名〉New Year picture
【年会】niánhuì〈名〉annual meeting
【年货】niánhuò〈名〉 New Year purchases: 置办～ do Spring Festival shopping
【年级】niánjí〈名〉grade: 二～学生 second-year student
【年纪】niánji〈名〉 age: ～轻 be young ‖ 上了～ be advanced in years ‖ 他小小～，懂得还挺多。Young as he is, he knows quite a lot.
【年假】niánjià〈名〉1（寒假）winter vacation 2（春节假期）Spring Festival holidays
【年间】niánjiān ▸p. 618〈名〉 certain period of time: 康熙～ during the reign of Emperor Kangxi
【年检】niánjiǎn〈名〉annual inspection: 进行～ conduct an annual inspection
【年鉴】niánjiàn〈名〉 yearbook: 科学～ science almanac
【年节】niánjié〈名〉Spring Festival
【年金】niánjīn〈名〉 annuity: 退休～ pension annuities
【年景】niánjǐng〈名〉1（年成）year's harvest: 好～ good harvest ‖ 丰收～ bumper harvest 2（过年的景象）Spring Festival holiday atmosphere
【年久失修】niánjiǔshīxiū〈成〉 worn down by the years without repair
【年均】niánjūn〈名〉 annual average: ～收入 average annual income ‖ ～增产 average annual increase in production
【年来】niánlái ▸p. 618〈名〉 in recent years: ～她的学业大有进步。She has made great progress in her studies over the past year.
【年老昏聩】niánlǎo-hūnkuì〈成〉 lose one's wits with age
【年老体衰】niánlǎo-tǐshuāi〈成〉 be decrepit with old age
【年历】niánlì〈名〉one-page calendar
【年利】niánlì〈名〉annual interest
【年龄】niánlíng ▸p. 526〈名〉 age: 入学～ school age ‖ 退休～ retirement age ‖ ～段 age group ‖ ～性别组成 age-sex structure
【年率】niánlǜ〈名〉annual rate
【年轮】niánlún〈名〉［植物］growth ring
【年迈】niánmài〈形〉〈书〉 aged: ～力衰 old and infirm
【年末】niánmò ▸p. 618〈名〉year's end
【年年】niánnián〈名〉every year
【年年岁岁】niánnián-suìsuì〈成〉year after year
【年谱】niánpǔ〈名〉chronicle of one's life
【年前】niánqián〈副〉 before the turn of the year
【年青】niánqīng〈形〉 young: ～的一代 young generation ‖ 她～的时候 when she was young
【年轻】niánqīng〈形〉 young: 他显得很～。He looks very young for his age. ‖ ～力壮 young and vigorous ‖ ～有为 be young and promising
【年轻气盛】niánqīng-qìshèng〈成〉 be young and aggressive
【年轻人】niánqīngrén〈名〉 young person: 这对～相识一个月就结婚了。The young couple met a month before they got married.
【年三十】niánsānshí ▸p. 618〈名〉 Chinese New Year's Eve
【年少】niánshào A〈形〉 young: ～气盛 young and impetuous B〈名〉youngster
【年深日久】niánshēn-rìjiǔ〈成〉 with the passage of time
【年事】niánshì〈名〉〈书〉 age: ～已高 be at an advanced age
【年岁】niánsuì〈名〉1（年纪）age: 上了～ be advanced in years ‖ 你～不小了，该结婚了。You are old enough to get married. 2（年代）time: ～久远 long time ago
【年同比】niántóngbǐ〈副〉on annual basis
【年头儿】niántóur〈名〉1（年份）year: 我学英语已有三个～了。I have been learning English for three years. 2（时间）years: 他教书有些～了。He has been teaching for many years. 3（时代）times: 好～ good times ‖ 谁说这～没有好心人？Who said there aren't any good people these days? 4（年成）harvest: 今年的～真不错。This year's harvest has been pretty good.
【年尾】niánwěi ▸p. 618〈名〉 end of a year
【年息】niánxī〈名〉annual interest
【年下】niánxià〈名〉〈口〉 lunar New Year holidays
【年限】niánxiàn〈名〉 fixed number of years: 工作～ working years ‖ 学习～ required years of study
【年薪】niánxīn〈名〉annual salary: ～多少？What's the annual salary?
【年夜】niányè ▸p. 618〈名〉 lunar New Year's Eve

【年夜饭】niányèfàn〈名〉 family reunion dinner on lunar New Year's Eve

年夜饭

The meal eaten on the eve of the Chinese Lunar New Year. On this day family members reunite, couplets are pasted on the door (▸对联), firecrackers are let off, and in many places people make offerings to the ancestors. The food eaten at the meal will have propitious associations. For example, 鱼 (fish) and 余 (surplus) have the same pronunciation in Chinese (yu). By eating fish at this time diners are observing the idiom '*nian nian you yu*' (年年有余, '*year after year* there is a surplus'). The idea is that not all of the fish should be eaten, so that there is some left over. After the meal the older generation give children money (▸压岁钱), and many people stay up all night.

【年幼】niányòu〈形〉 young: 他还得抚养～的子女。 He still has young children to support.
【年幼无知】niányòu-wúzhī〈成〉 be young and inexperienced
【年逾古稀】niányú-gǔxī〈成〉 be over seventy years old
【年月】niányuè〈名〉 1▸（年代） years: 饥荒～ famine years 2▸〈口〉（岁月） times
【年长】niánzhǎng〈形〉 senior: 他比我～三岁。 He is three years my senior.
【年中】niánzhōng ▸**p. 618**〈名〉 middle of the year: ～报告 mid-year report
【年终】niánzhōng ▸**p. 618**〈名〉 end of the year: ～结算 year-end settlement of accounts ‖ ～分红 year-end dividend ‖ ～奖 year-end bonus
【年资】niánzī〈名〉 seniority
【年尊】niánzūn〈形〉〈书〉 advanced in age

鲇（鮎、鯰） nián〈名〉 catfish
【鲇鱼】niányú〈名〉 catfish

黏 nián〈形〉 sticky: 这胶水不太～。 This glue isn't very sticky. ▸～附, ～液
【黏巴】niánba〈形〉〈口〉 sticky
【黏虫】niánchóng〈名〉 armyworm
【黏稠】niánchóu〈形〉 stringy
【黏度】niándù〈名〉［物理］ viscosity
【黏附】niánfù〈动〉 stick to: ～力 adhesion
【黏合】niánhé〈动〉 adhere: ～剂 adhesive
【黏合力】niánhélì〈名〉 adhesion
【黏糊糊】niánhūhū〈形〉 sticky: 他的手上都是～的糖果汁。 His fingers were sticky from the sweets.
【黏糊】niánhu〈形〉 1▸（指物） sticky: ～的米饭 glutinous rice 2▸（指人） slow-moving
【黏胶】niánjiāo〈名〉［化学］ viscose: ～纤维 viscose fibre
【黏结】niánjié〈动〉 cement: ～材料 binding material
【黏结剂】niánjiéjì〈名〉 glue
【黏米】niánmǐ〈名〉 1▸〈方〉（黍米） broomcorn millet 2▸（糯米） glutinous rice
【黏膜】niánmó〈名〉 mucous membrane: 口腔～ oral mucosa
【黏土】niántǔ〈名〉 clay
【黏性】niánxìng〈名〉 stickiness: ～不够 not be sticky enough
【黏液】niányè〈名〉［生理］ mucus
【黏着】niánzhuó〈动〉 stick together: ～力 adhesive force
【黏着语】niánzhuóyǔ〈名〉［语言］ agglutinative language

niǎn

捻 niǎn
A〈动〉 twist with one's fingers: ～线 twist thread
B〈名〉 wick: ▸灯～, ～子
【捻军】Niǎnjūn〈名〉 Nian Army [peasant army that rose up against the Qing Dynasty]: ～起义 Nian Uprising
【捻捻转儿】niǎnnianzhuànr〈名〉 teetotum
【捻线机】niǎnxiànjī〈名〉［纺织］ twisting machine
【捻针】niǎnzhēn〈名〉［中医］ twisting of an acupuncture needle
【捻子】niǎnzi〈名〉 wick: 灯～ lamp wick

ℹ 年龄

询问年龄

■ 英语里，向不同年龄的人询问年龄，可以用同样的表达法:

你几岁了?
或 你多大岁数了?
或 你多大了?
= How old are you?
或 What age are you?

你能告诉我你的年龄吗?
= Could you tell me your age, please?（正式）
或 Could you tell me how old you are, please?

表达准确年龄

■ 英语里常用 x year(s)/month(s), etc. old 来表达年龄。在表示某人多大时，谓语动词经常用系动词 be（是），be 不能省去。注意 old 的用法及用英语表达年龄的多样化:

她 37
= She is 37
或 She is 37 years old
或 She is 37 years of age（正式）

宝宝 10 天了
= The baby is 10 days old

玛丽 11 个月
= Mary is 11 months old

■ 注意事物年龄的英语表达法:

这所教堂有 100 年了
= The church is a hundred years old
而不是
The church is a hundred

■ 表示年龄的短语做定语时，英语里常用的表达方式有 3 种:

50 岁的男人
= a man of 50
或 a man aged 50
或 a 50-year-old man
但

用了 5 年的车
= a five-year-old car

10 年陈酒
= a ten-year-old wine

■ 注意英语里表示年龄的复合名词:

16 岁青年聚会
= a party for sixteen-year-olds

一个 20 岁的人
= a twenty-year-old

表达近似年龄

■ 注意英语与汉语的不同表达方式:

这对夫妻三十几岁
= The couple are in their thirties

我 40 出头
= I am in my early forties

他二十五六岁
= He is in his mid-twenties

她四十八九岁
= She is in her late forties

她大约 20
= She is about 20
或 She is 20 or so

我差不多 50 了
= I am almost 50
或 I am nearly 50

我母亲五十多了
= My mother is over 50

我弟弟不到 15
= My brother is under 15
或 My brother is not yet 15

这猫大概 9 岁了
= The cat is about 9 years old

这件外罩至少穿 5 年了
= The coat is at least 5 years old

适合 5 岁以下儿童的玩具
= toys for under-fives
或 toys for children under 5

60 岁以上老人俱乐部
= clubs for the over-sixties
或 clubs for people over 60

■ 注意用英语如何表示"与…同龄":

像简一样大的孩子
= children of Jane's age

同她父母一样大的人
= people of her parents' age

她和你同岁
= She is the same age as you
或 She is as old as you

他们同岁
= They are the same age

■ 注意英语里 than（比）及 older、younger（形容词比较级）的用法:

她比你大
= She is older than you

她比你小
= She is younger than you

她比你大 5 岁
= She is five years older than you

他比你小 3 岁
= He is 3 years younger than you

辇（輦） niǎn〈名〉〈古〉 **1**（用人拉的车） man-drawn carriage **2**（指皇后、皇帝的车） imperial carriage

辗（輾） niǎn = 碾 niǎn B ▸zhǎn

撵（攆） niǎn〈动〉 **1**（驱逐） oust: ～（某人）下台 oust (sb.) from power ‖ ～走 drive out **2**〈方〉（追赶） catch up with: 你走得太快，我～不上。 You are walking so fast, I can't catch up with you.

碾 niǎn
A〈名〉 (stone) roller
B〈动〉 crush: ～得粉碎 pulverize ‖ ～米 husk rice
【碾场】niǎnchǎng〈动〉〈方〉 thresh grain
【碾槌】niǎnchuí〈名〉 pestle
【碾坊】niǎnfáng〈名〉 grain mill
【碾房】niǎnfáng = 碾坊 niǎnfáng
【碾磙子】niǎngǔnzi〈名〉 stone roller
【碾盘】niǎnpán〈名〉 millstone
【碾砣】niǎntuó = 碾磙子 niǎngǔnzi
【碾子】niǎnzi〈名〉 **1**（用于处理谷物） roller and millstone **2**（用于碾压东西） roller

niàn

廿 niàn ▸**p. 691**〈数〉 twenty

念[1] niàn
A〈动〉 **1**（想念） miss: 不～旧恶 forgive and forget ▸～旧, 挂～, 怀～ **2**（考虑） consider: ～你年幼无知，原谅这一次。 Considering your youth and your ignorance, I'll forgive you this time.
B〈名〉 idea: ▸～头, 私心杂～, 一～之差

念[2]（唸） niàn〈动〉 **1**（读） read out: ～一篇文章 read out a passage ‖ 给母亲～信 read a letter to one's mother ▸～经 **2**（上学） study: ～大学/高中 attend college/senior high school

念[3] niàn ▸**p. 691**〈数〉 twenty
【念白】niànbái〈名〉 spoken parts (of a Chinese opera)
【念叨】niàndao〈动〉 **1**（提到） talkabout: 我们经常～你。 We often talk about you. **2**〈口〉（说） talk over: 我想跟您～个事儿。 I have something to talk over with you.
【念道】niàndao = 念叨 niàndao
【念佛】niànfó〈动〉 pray to Buddha: 吃斋～ be a vegetarian and a devout Buddhist
【念经】niànjīng〈动〉 recite Buddhist scriptures
【念旧】niànjiù〈动〉 remember old friends and acquaintances
【念念不忘】niànniàn-bùwàng〈成〉 always keep in mind: 他～的只有工作。 He has nothing but work on the brain.
【念念有词】niànniàn-yǒucí〈成〉 mumble to oneself
【念书】niànshū〈动〉 **1**（读书） read: 学生们正在教室里～。 The students are reading in the classroom. **2**（上学） attend school: 他从没念过书。 He has never been to school.
【念颂】niànsòng〈动〉 read aloud
【念头】niàntou〈名〉 idea: 打消～ dismiss an idea ‖ 荒唐的～ absurd idea ‖ 邪恶的～ wicked intention ‖ 她放弃了出国的～。 She dropped the idea of going abroad.
【念咒】niànzhòu〈动〉 utter a spell
【念珠】niànzhū〈名〉 bead: 拨～ finger one's beads

埝 niàn〈名〉 low bank between fields or shallow waters: 打～ build low banks between fields

niáng

娘（孃） niáng〈名〉 **1** ▸**p. 588**（妈） mum: 亲～ biological mother ‖ 爹～ mum and dad **2**（指已婚女子） aunt: ▸姨～, 婶～ **3**（年轻女子） girl: ▸姑～, 新～
【娘家】niángjia〈名〉 married woman's parents' home: 回～ [of a married woman] return to one's parents' home (for a visit) ‖ 在～住些日子 stay in one's parents' home for a few days
【娘舅】niángjiù〈名〉〈方〉 brother of one's mother
【娘娘】niángniang〈名〉 **1**（指人） empress: 正宫～ emperor's wife **2**（指神） goddess: ～庙 temple of goddess of fertility
【娘娘腔】niángniangqiāng **A**〈形〉 sissy **B**〈名〉 camp person
【娘亲】niángqīn〈名〉 mother [in Peking Opera]
【娘儿】niángr〈名〉 mother and her children: ～仨痛哭了一场。 The mother and her two children had a good cry.
【娘儿们】niángrmen〈名〉 **1**〈口〉（指长辈和晚辈） mother and son/daughter **2**〈方〉〈贬〉（女人） women **3**〈方〉（妻子） wife
【娘胎】niángtāi〈名〉 mother's womb
【娘姨】niángyí〈名〉〈方〉 maidservant
【娘子】niángzǐ〈名〉 **1**〈方〉（妻子） [a form of address for one's wife] my wife **2**〈旧〉（指妇女） [a polite address for a young woman] ma'am
【娘子军】niángzǐjūn〈名〉 detachment of women

niàng

酿 niàng
A〈动〉 **1**（酿造） brew: 家～ home-brewed wine ‖ ～酒 make wine **2**（形成） lead to: ～成大祸 result in calamity **3**（指蜜蜂） make honey: 蜜蜂～蜜。 Bees make honey. **4**（指烹调方法） cook by frying or steaming
B〈名〉 wine: 陈年佳～ vintage wine
【酿成大祸】niàngchéng dàhuò〈动〉 lead to disaster
【酿酒】niàngjiǔ〈动〉 brew wine
【酿酒厂】niàngjiǔchǎng〈名〉 brewery
【酿造】niàngzào〈动〉 brew: ～业 brewery industry
【酿制】niàngzhì = 酿造 niàngzào

niǎo

鸟（鳥） niǎo〈名〉 bird: 养～ breed birds ▸比翼～, 雏～, 鸵～, 水～ ▸diǎo
【鸟巢】niǎocháo〈名〉 bird's-nest
【鸟铳】niǎochòng〈名〉 fowling piece
【鸟粪】niǎofèn〈名〉 bird droppings
【鸟尽弓藏】niǎojìn-gōngcáng〈成〉〈喻〉 cast sb. aside when he has served his purpose
【鸟瞰】niǎokàn **A**〈动〉 have a bird's-eye view of sth.: 从塔上可以～整个城市。 You can get a bird's-eye view of the whole city from this tower. **B**〈名〉 bird's-eye view: 化学～ general survey of chemistry
【鸟类】niǎolèi〈名〉 birds
【鸟类学】niǎolèixué〈名〉 ornithology: ～家 ornithologist
【鸟笼】niǎolóng〈名〉 bird cage
【鸟鸣】niǎomíng〈名〉 chirp (of bird)
【鸟枪】niǎoqiāng〈名〉 **1**（用于打鸟） fowling piece **2**（气枪） air gun: ～子弹 bird shot
【鸟枪换炮】niǎoqiāng-huànpào〈成〉〈喻〉 have been drastically improved
【鸟儿】niǎor〈名〉 bird: 养～ keep birds ‖ 热带～ tropical birds
【鸟舍】niǎoshè〈名〉 aviary
【鸟兽散】niǎoshòusàn〈成〉 scatter like birds and animals
【鸟为食亡，人为财死】niǎo wèi shí wáng, rén wèi cái sǐ〈俗〉 birds die in pursuit of food, human beings in pursuit of wealth
【鸟窝】niǎowō = 鸟巢 niǎocháo
【鸟语花香】niǎoyǔ-huāxiāng〈成〉 birds sing and flowers emit their fragrance
【鸟篆】niǎozhuàn〈名〉［书法］ bird script

袅（嫋） niǎo〈形〉 slender and delicate
【袅袅】niǎoniǎo〈形〉 **1**（指烟气） curling upwards: 炊烟～。 The smoke is spiralling upwards from the kitchen chimneys. **2**（指细长物） waving in the wind: 柳枝～。 The willow branches are dancing gracefully. **3**（指声音） lingering: 余音～。 The voice is still lingering in the air.
【袅袅婷婷】niǎoniǎo-tíngtíng〈成〉〈书〉 [of a lady's gait] lissom
【袅娜】niǎonuó〈形〉〈书〉 **1**（指草木） soft and slender: ～的柳丝 slender willow twigs **2**（形容女子） willowy
【袅绕】niǎorào〈动〉〈书〉 linger in the air: 歌声～。 The song is lingering in the air.

嬲 niǎo〈动〉〈书〉 **1**（戏弄） tease **2**（纠缠） pester

niào

尿 niào
A〈名〉 urine: 导～ draw off urine through a catheter ‖ 撒～ urinate
B〈动〉 urinate: ▸～床
▸suī
【尿闭】niàobì ▸**p. 50**〈名〉［医学］ anuresis
【尿不湿】niàobùshī〈名〉 disposable nappy
【尿布】niàobù〈名〉 nappy〈英〉; diaper〈美〉: 换～ change a baby's nappy ‖ 一次性～ disposable nappy ‖ 纸～ disposable nappy
【尿池】niàochí〈名〉 urinal
【尿床】niàochuáng〈动〉 wet the bed
【尿道】niàodào〈名〉 urethra: ～感染 urinary tract infection

【尿毒症】niàodúzhèng ▸**p. 50**〈名〉［医学］urinaemia
【尿壶】niàohú〈名〉chamber pot
【尿急】niàojí ▸**p. 50**〈名〉［医学］urgency of micturition
【尿检】niàojiǎn〈名〉uroscopy
【尿炕】niàokàng〈动〉〈方〉wet the bed
【尿路结石】niàolù jiéshí ▸**p. 50**〈名〉［医学］lithangiuria
【尿盆】niàopén〈名〉chamber pot
【尿频】niàopín ▸**p. 50**〈名〉sychnuria
【尿失禁】niàoshījìn ▸**p. 50**〈名〉［医学］urinary incontinence
【尿素】niàosù〈名〉［化学］urea
【尿素氮】niàosùdàn〈名〉urea nitrogen
【尿酸】niàosuān〈名〉［化学］uric acid
【尿血】niàoxiě **A**〈动〉piss blood **B** ▸**p. 50**〈名〉［医学］haematuria
【尿样】niàoyàng〈名〉urine sample
【尿潴留】niàozhūliú ▸**p. 50**〈名〉［医学］uroschesis

脲 niào = 尿素 niàosù

溺 niào = 尿 niào
▸nì

niē

捏（揑） niē〈动〉**1**（用手指夹）pinch: 他～了一下她的脸蛋。He pinched her cheek. ‖〈喻〉孩子的生命～在她的手中。The baby's life was in her hands. **2**（捻成形）knead: ～面团儿 knead dough ‖ ～泥人 mould a figure out of clay **3**（撮合）bring together: ▸～合 **4**（编造）concoct: ▸～造 **5**（握）clench: ～闸 apply the handbrake ‖ ～紧拳头 clench one's fist ‖ 把信～在手里 clench the letter in one's hand
【捏把汗】niēbǎhàn = 捏一把汗 niē yībǎhàn
【捏合】niēhé〈动〉bring together: 他俩性格不和，～不到一起。They can't be brought together because of the differences of their character.
【捏积】niējī〈动〉［中医］massage the muscles along the spine
【捏弄】niēnong〈动〉**1**（指用手）fiddle with: 他坐在那里，不安地～着一支钢笔。He sat there nervously fiddling with a pen. **2**（耍弄）order around: 他常常无理地把我～来～去的。He always ordered me around in a way that was offensive. **3**（指商量）discuss in private: 这事是他们早就～好的。They have already decided the matter after discussing it in private. **4** = 捏造 niēzào
【捏一把汗】niē yībǎhàn〈惯〉be keyed up: 参赛者捏着一把汗，在等待结果。The contestants were on edge as they waited for the results.
【捏造】niēzào〈动〉concoct: ～事实 make up a story ‖ ～证据 fabricate evidence ‖ ～罪名 trump up charges ‖ 那些指控纯属～。Those charges are sheer fabrications.

nié

苶 nié〈形〉〈方〉listless: 他今天怎么～～的？Why is he so lethargic today?

niè

乜 Niè〈名〉Nie [surname]
▸miē

聂（聶） Niè〈名〉Nie [surname]

臬 niè〈名〉**1**〈古〉（箭靶）arrow target **2**〈古〉（用于测量日影）gnomon **3**〈书〉（准则）criterion: ▸奉为圭～

涅（湼） niè〈书〉
A〈名〉alunite
B〈动〉blacken
【涅槃】nièpán［佛教］**A**〈名〉nirvana **B**〈动〉reach the state of nirvana

啮（嚙、齧） niè〈动〉〈书〉gnaw: 虫咬鼠～ be eaten by worms and gnawed by mice
【啮齿动物】nièchǐ dòngwù〈名〉rodent
【啮合】nièhé〈动〉**1**（指牙齿）clench one's teeth **2**（指齿轮）mesh: 这些轮齿～不严。These cogs don't quite connect.
【啮噬】nièshì〈动〉torment: 悲痛～着她的心。Grief gnaws at her heart.
【啮咬】nièyǎo〈动〉nibble

嗫（囁） niè
【嗫嚅】nièrú〈形〉〈书〉speak haltingly

镊（鑷） niè
A〈名〉tweezers
B〈动〉pick up sth. with tweezers
【镊子】nièzi〈名〉tweezers: 一把～ a pair of tweezers

镍（鎳） niè〈名〉［化学］nickel (Ni)
【镍币】nièbì〈名〉nickel (coin)
【镍钢】niègāng〈名〉［冶金］nickel steel
【镍镉电池】niègé diànchí〈名〉nickel-cadmium battery
【镍铬合金】niègè héjīn〈名〉［冶金］nickel-chrome
【镍合金】nièhéjīn〈名〉［冶金］nickel alloy
【镍氢电池】nièqīng diànchí〈名〉nickel-hydrogen battery

颞（顳） niè
【颞骨】niègǔ〈名〉［生理］temporal bone
【颞颥】nièrú〈名〉［生理］temple

蹑（躡） niè〈动〉**1**（放轻脚步）tiptoe **2**（追随）follow: ▸～踪 **3**〈书〉（踩）tread: ▸～足
【蹑手蹑脚】nièshǒu-nièjiǎo〈成〉tiptoe: 她～地走出屋子。She tiptoed out of the room.
【蹑踪】nièzōng〈动〉〈书〉trail
【蹑足】nièzú〈动〉**1**（放轻脚步）tiptoe: ～不前 not move a step forward **2**〈书〉（参与）join: ～其间 participate in
【蹑足潜踪】nièzú-qiánzōng〈成〉walk on tiptoe so as not to be discovered

孽 niè
A〈名〉**1**（邪恶）monster: ▸妖～ **2**（罪恶）evil: ▸造～, 作～
B〈形〉〈书〉treacherous: ～臣 traitorous vassal ▸～子
【孽根】niègēn〈名〉source of evils: ～未除。The root of evil remains to be eradicated.
【孽海】nièhǎi〈名〉［佛教］ocean of bad karma
【孽债】nièzhài〈名〉sin for which one has not yet paid the penalty
【孽障】nièzhàng = 业障 yèzhàng
【孽种】nièzhǒng〈名〉**1**（祸根）root of evil **2**〈粗〉（指人）unworthy descendent
【孽子】nièzǐ〈名〉〈旧〉**1**（指庶出）son of a concubine **2**（指不孝顺）unfilial son

蘖 niè〈名〉［植物］tiller: ▸分～

nín

恁 nín〈旧〉= 您 nín
▸nèn

您 nín ▸**p. 780**〈代〉〈敬〉you: ～好！How do you do!

níng

宁（寧） níng
A〈形〉peaceful: ▸～静, 安～
B〈动〉〈书〉**1**（使安定）pacify: ▸息事～人 **2**（指已婚女子）visit (with one's parents, relatives, etc.): ▸～亲, 归～
C ▸**p. 661**〈名〉Níng [another name for Nanjing (南京)]: 沪～线 Shanghai-Nanjing railway
▸nìng
【宁波】Níngbō〈名〉Ningbo
【宁靖】níngjìng〈形〉〈书〉tranquil
【宁静】níngjìng〈形〉peaceful: ～的生活/夜晚 tranquil life/night
【宁静以致远】níngjìng yǐ zhìyuǎn〈成〉accomplish something lasting by leading a quiet life
【宁亲】níngqīn = 省亲 xǐngqīn
【宁日】níngrì〈名〉peaceful days: 国无～ there is no peace in the country for a single day
【宁夏】Níngxià ▸**p. 661**〈名〉Ningxia: ～回族自治区 Ningxia Hui Autonomous Region
【宁馨儿】níngxīn'ér〈名〉〈书〉lovely child

拧（擰） níng〈动〉**1**（用双手）twist: ～干毛巾 wring out a towel ‖ ～湿衣服 wring wet clothes ‖ 丝绸衣服千万不能～。Never twist or wring silk cloth. **2**（用手指）pinch: ～胳膊 pinch sb.'s arm ‖ ～耳朵 tweak sb.'s ear
▸nǐng, nìng
【拧成一股绳】níngchéng yī gǔ shéng〈惯〉〈喻〉make joint efforts: 只要我们～，就一定能克服困难。So long as we are united, we can surely overcome difficulties.

苧（薴） níng〈名〉［化学］limonene

咛（嚀） níng ▸叮咛 dīngníng

狞（獰） níng〈形〉ferocious: ▸狰～

【狞视】níngshì〈动〉stare fiercely at
【狞笑】níngxiào〈动〉laugh malignantly

柠（檸）níng

【柠檬】níngméng〈名〉1（指树）lemon tree 2（指果实）lemon: ～茶 lemon tea
【柠檬酸】níngméngsuān〈名〉citric acid
【柠檬汁】níngméngzhī〈名〉lemon juice

聍（聹）níng ▸耵聍 dīngníng

凝 níng〈动〉1（凝结）congeal: 鲜血～成的战斗友谊 militant friendship cemented with blood ▸～结 2（集中）concentrate: ▸～思, ～视

【凝点】níngdiǎn〈名〉［物理］condensation point
【凝冻】níngdòng〈动〉freeze: 湖水～了。The lake has frozen over. ‖ 水～了。The water has frozen solid.
【凝固】nínggù〈动〉1（指状态变化）solidify: 血液～ blood coagulation ‖ 水泥需要两到三天才能～。It takes two or three days for the cement to set. 2（停滞）be static: 思想～ have set ways of thinking
【凝固点】nínggùdiǎn〈名〉freezing point
【凝固剂】nínggùjì〈名〉coagulant
【凝固汽油】nínggù qìyóu〈名〉napalm: ～弹 napalm bomb
【凝积】níngjī〈动〉congeal
【凝集】níngjí〈动〉gather: 这些诗篇～着诗人对人民深深的爱。These poems are concentrated expressions of the poet's deep love for his people.
【凝胶】níngjiāo〈名〉［化学］gel
【凝结】níngjié〈动〉（指液体）solidify;（指气体）condense: 寒风使雾气～成雨。The cold wind condenses vapour into rain. ‖〈喻〉我所取得的每一点成绩都～着恩师的谆谆教诲。Every bit of the progress I have made in my studies reflects my teachers' patient guidance.
【凝聚】níngjù〈动〉1（指气体）condense: 大气中的水汽在夜间～成露珠。Moisture in the atmosphere condensed into dew during the night. 2（积聚）crystallize: 该书～着她多年的心血。The book embodies her years of painstaking effort.
【凝聚力】níngjùlì〈名〉1［物理］cohesive force 2〈喻〉（指团结）cohesion: 增强集体～ strengthen the cohesiveness of the group ‖ 爱国主义是一种～。Patriotism can bind people together.
【凝练】níngliàn〈形〉concise: 他文笔～。He has a concise writing style.
【凝炼】níngliàn = 凝练 níngliàn
【凝眸】níngmóu〈动〉〈书〉gaze: ～远望 gaze into the distance
【凝目】níngmù〈动〉fix one's eyes on: 她～注视着丈夫。She fixed her eyes on her husband.
【凝神】níngshén〈动〉focus one's attention on: ～聆听 listen with rapt attention ‖ ～思索 be in deep thought
【凝视】níngshì〈动〉gaze at: ～着窗外 gaze out of the window
【凝思】níngsī〈动〉be buried in thought: ～默想 muse
【凝听】níngtīng〈动〉listen attentively
【凝望】níngwàng〈动〉stare at: 孩子们惊奇地～着圣诞树。The children gazed in wonderment at the Christmas tree.
【凝想】níngxiǎng = 凝思 níngsī
【凝血酶】níngxuèméi〈名〉［药学］thrombin
【凝脂】níngzhī〈名〉〈书〉1（指油脂）congealed fat 2〈喻〉（指皮肤）creamy skin: 肤如～ smooth, soft and glossy skin
【凝滞】níngzhì〈动〉stagnate: 他吓得似乎浑身的血液都～了。He was so scared that his blood seemed to stop flowing.
【凝重】níngzhòng〈形〉1（沉重）solemn: 他的面容变得～起来。His face grew grave. ‖ 她神态～地走了进来。She walked in a dignified manner. 2（浑厚）deep and rich: 他那～的歌声打动了听众。His deep, rich voice touched the audience. 3（浓重）dense: ～的乌云 thick dark clouds

nǐng

拧（擰）nǐng〈动〉1（使旋转）screw: ～紧螺丝钉 tighten a screw ‖ ～开瓶盖 unscrew a bottle cap 2（颠倒）get wrong: 他把话说～了。He got his words the wrong way round. 3（别扭）disagree: 双方越谈越～。The more the two sides talked, the more they differed.
▸níng, nìng

【拧眉瞪眼】nǐngméi-dèngyǎn〈成〉raise one's eyebrows and stare in anger

nìng

宁（寧）nìng〈副〉1（宁可）rather: ▸～死不屈 2〈书〉（岂）how: 山之险峻，～有逾此? Could there be a mountain more precipitous than this?
▸níng

【宁可】nìngkě〈副〉would rather: ～信其有，不可信其无 we would rather believe that it is true than not
【宁肯】nìngkěn = 宁可 nìngkě
【宁缺毋滥】nìngquē-wúlàn〈成〉place quality above quantity
【宁死不屈】nìngsǐ-bùqū〈成〉would rather die than submit
【宁为鸡口，不为牛后】nìng wéi jīkǒu, bù wéi niúhòu〈成〉〈喻〉better to reign in hell than serve in heaven
【宁为玉碎，不为瓦全】nìng wéi yù suì, bù wéi wǎ quán〈成〉〈喻〉better to die proud than to live in disgrace
【宁愿】nìngyuàn〈副〉rather: 我～呆在家里，也不愿去逛街。I'd rather stay at home than go shopping.

佞 nìng〈形〉1（好奉承）given to flattery: ～人 sycophant ▸～臣, 奸～ 2〈书〉（有才智）wise: ▸不～

【佞臣】nìngchén〈名〉sycophantic official
【佞笑】nìngxiào〈动〉1（奸笑）smile sinisterly 2（谄笑）smile ingratiatingly

拧（擰）nìng〈形〉〈方〉obstinate: 这人很～。The guy is rather headstrong.
▸níng, nǐng

泞（濘）nìng〈名〉〈书〉mud: ▸泥～

【泞滑】nìnghuá〈形〉muddy and slippery

niū

妞 niū〈名〉girl: 小～ little girl ‖ 她有三个～。She has three daughters.

【妞妞】niūniu〈名〉〈方〉little girl

niú

牛[1] niú

A〈名〉1（指动物）ox: ▸公～, 母～ 2（指星宿）one of the 28 constellations in ancient Chinese astronomy
B〈形〉1（固执）obstinate: 他是个～脾气。He is very stubborn. ▸～劲, ～脾气 2（傲慢）arrogant: ▸～气 3〈口〉（极好）awesome

牛[2] niú〈量〉［物理］newton [unit of force]

【牛百叶】niúbǎiyè〈名〉［食品］stomach of cow or ox
【牛蒡】niúbàng〈名〉［植物］great burdock
【牛逼】niúbī〈形〉〈粗〉fucking great
【牛鼻子】niúbízi〈名〉1〈本〉muzzle of an ox: 牵着～走 lead an ox by its halter 2〈喻〉（关键）crucial point
【牛不喝水强按头】niú bù hēshuǐ qiáng àn tóu〈俗〉try to impose one's will on sb.
【牛车】niúchē〈名〉bullock cart
【牛刀小试】niúdāo-xiǎoshì〈成〉〈喻〉display only a small part of one's talent
【牛痘】niúdòu〈名〉1（指传染病）cowpox 2（指疫苗）smallpox vaccine: 种～ get/give a vaccination against smallpox
【牛痘苗】niúdòumiáo〈名〉(smallpox) vaccine
【牛犊】niúdú〈名〉calf
【牛肚】niúdǔ〈名〉［食品］tripe
【牛顿】niúdùn〈量〉［物理］newton [unit of force]
【牛轭】niú'è〈名〉oxbow
【牛股】niúgǔ〈名〉［金融］rising stock
【牛倌】niúguān〈名〉cowherd
【牛鬼蛇神】niúguǐ-shéshén〈成〉〈喻〉evil people of all descriptions: ～纷纷出笼。Monsters come out in large numbers.
【牛黄】niúhuáng〈名〉［中药］bezoar
【牛角】niújiǎo〈名〉ox horn
【牛角尖】niújiǎojiān〈名〉〈喻〉insignificant problem: ▸钻～
【牛津】Niújīn〈名〉Oxford
【牛津大学】Niújīn Dàxué〈名〉Oxford University: ～出版社 Oxford University Press
【牛津郡】Niújīnjùn〈名〉Oxfordshire
【牛劲】niújìn〈名〉1（指力气）tremendous effort: 这件事可让我费了～了。I spent a lot of time and efforts on this. 2（指脾气）stubbornness: 他又犯～了。He was obstinate again.
【牛圈】niújuàn〈名〉lair
【牛栏】niúlán〈名〉cattle pen
【牛郎星】Niúlángxīng〈名〉［天文］Altair
【牛郎织女】niúláng-zhīnǚ〈名〉〈喻〉husband and wife who have to live in two different places: 过着～的生活 [of a couple] live in two different places
【牛马】niúmǎ〈名〉〈喻〉beasts of burden: 过着～不如的生活 live a dog's life
【牛毛】niúmáo〈名〉〈喻〉be numerous, thick and fine: ～细雨 drizzle
【牛虻】niúméng〈名〉［昆虫］gadfly
【牛奶】niúnǎi〈名〉milk: 挤～ milk a cow ‖ 酸～ yogurt ‖ 消毒～ pasteurized milk
【牛腩】niúnǎn〈名〉〈方〉sirloin
【牛年马月】niúnián-mǎyuè = 猴年马月 hóunián-mǎyuè
【牛排】niúpái〈名〉beefsteak
【牛棚】niúpéng〈名〉cowshed
【牛皮】niúpí A〈名〉1〈本〉cattle hide

n

2（大话） big talk: 吹～ brag **B**〈形〉 tough: ▸～糖, ～纸

> **牛郎和织女**
>
> The Cowherd and the Weaving Girl is a popular Chinese legend dating from the Han Dynasty. It is associated with the seventh evening of the seventh month of the lunar year, when the two stars, Altair and Vega, appear closest together in the sky. The Cowherd (Altair) and the Weaver Girl (Vega), doomed by the Emperor of Heaven to live apart on either side of the Milky Way, meet just once a year when a flock of magpies builds a bridge enabling the lovers to cross.

【牛皮糖】niúpítáng〈名〉 sticky candy
【牛皮癣】niúpíxuǎn ▸**p. 50**〈名〉［医学］ psoriasis
【牛皮纸】niúpízhǐ〈名〉 kraft paper: ～袋 paper bag
【牛脾气】niúpíqi〈名〉 stubbornness: 最让我担心的是他的～。 What worries me most is his stubbornness.
【牛气】niúqi〈形〉〈方〉 arrogant: 他可真～! How arrogant he is! ‖〈喻〉 纽约股市～冲天。 The New York stock market is extremely bullish.
【牛肉】niúròu〈名〉 beef: ～干 beef jerky
【牛屎】niúshǐ〈名〉 cow dung
【牛市】niúshì〈名〉［金融］ bull market
【牛溲马勃】niúsōu-mǎbó〈成〉 cheap but useful things
【牛头不对马嘴】niútóu bù duì mǎzuǐ〈成〉 be incongruous: 她的话～，叫人听了莫名其妙。 Her irrelevant remarks baffled everyone.
【牛头马面】niútóu-mǎmiàn〈成〉〈喻〉 evil people of all kinds
【牛蛙】niúwā〈名〉 bullfrog
【牛瘟】niúwēn〈名〉 cattle plague
【牛性】niúxìng = 牛脾气 niúpíqi
【牛鞅】niúyàng〈名〉 wooden yoke for a draught ox
【牛饮】niúyǐn〈动〉 drink like a fish
【牛油果】niúyóuguǒ〈名〉［植物］ avocado
【牛仔】niúzǎi〈名〉 cowboy
【牛仔裤】niúzǎikù〈名〉 jeans
【牛崽】niúzai〈名〉 calf

niǔ

扭 niǔ

A〈动〉 **1**（转动） turn round: ～过头去 turn one's head ▸～转 **2**（拧伤） sprain: 我的膝盖～伤了。 I twisted my knee. **3**（拧） twist: ～断一根树枝 twist a twig off a tree ‖ 把门～开 wrench the door open **4**（摇动） wriggle: 要是你～来～去，我可没法给你梳头。 I can't brush your hair if you keep wriggling all the time. **5**（揪住） grapple with: 和某人扭作一团 grapple with sb. ‖ 他～住小偷不放。 He tussled with the thief and did not let go. ▸～打, ～送
B〈形〉 crooked: 她的字写得歪歪～～的。 Her handwriting is all over the place.
【扭摆】niǔbǎi〈动〉 sway: 舞蹈家随着音乐～着身躯。 The dancer swayed to the music.
【扭打】niǔdǎ〈动〉 grapple with: 他们与警察～起来。They scuffled with the police.
【扭动】niǔdòng〈动〉 wriggle: ～屁股 wiggle one's hips ‖ ～尾巴 wag the tail ‖ 随着音乐～身体 sway to the music
【扭角羚】niǔjiǎolíng〈名〉［动物］ takin
【扭结】niǔjié〈动〉 tangle: 电线～在一起。 The wires got all tangled. ‖ 几件事～在一起。 Several things have got tangled up.
【扭亏为盈】niǔkuī-wéiyíng〈成〉 turn loss into gain: 公司终于～。 The company finally is in the black.
【扭力】niǔlì〈名〉［物理］ twisting force
【扭捏】niǔnie **A**〈动〉 walk affectedly **B**〈形〉〈贬〉 coy
【扭扭捏捏】niǔniǔ-niēniē〈成〉〈贬〉 coy
【扭曲】niǔqū〈动〉 **1**（使变形） contort: ～变形 be twisted out of shape **2**〈喻〉（歪曲） distort: ～事实 distort the facts ‖ ～的心态 twisted mentality
【扭伤】niǔshāng ▸**p. 50**〈动〉 sprain
【扭送】niǔsòng〈动〉 seize and turn over to: ～公安机关 seize and turn over to the public security organ
【扭头】niǔtóu〈动〉 **1**（转动头）turn one's head: 他～就跑。 He turned his head and ran. **2**（转身） turn (around/round): 她～哭了起来。 She turned away and wept.
【扭秧歌】niǔ yāngge〈动〉 do the *yangge* dance
【扭转】niǔzhuǎn〈动〉 **1**（掉转） turn around: ～身子 turn round **2**（改变） reverse: ～局面 turn a situation around ‖ ～下降趋势 reverse a declining trend
【扭转乾坤】niǔzhuǎn-qiánkūn〈成〉 reverse the course of events

忸 niǔ

【忸怩】niǔní〈形〉 bashful: ～作态 behave affectedly

纽（紐） niǔ

〈名〉 **1**（指器物上） handle: ▸秤～ **2**（纽扣） button: ▸～扣, ～襻 **3**（联结） bond: ▸～带 **4**（关键） pivot: ▸枢～
【纽埃】Niǔ'āi〈名〉 Niue
【纽带】niǔdài〈名〉bond: 两国间的～ bond between two countries ‖ 孩子是家庭的～。 A child binds a family together.
【纽芬兰岛】Niǔfēnlándǎo〈名〉 Newfoundland
【纽扣】niǔkòu〈名〉 button
【纽襻】niǔpàn〈名〉 button loop
【纽约】Niǔyuē〈名〉 New York: ～人 New Yorker
【纽约时报】Niǔyuē Shíbào〈名〉 New York Times
【纽约证券交易所】 Niǔyuē Zhèngquàn Jiāoyìsuǒ〈名〉 New York Stock Exchange
【纽约州】Niǔyuēzhōu〈名〉 State of New York
【纽子】niǔzi〈名〉 button

钮（鈕） niǔ

〈名〉 **1** = 纽 niǔ **2**（指部件） knob: ▸按～, 电～, 旋～

niù

拗 niù

〈形〉 obstinate: 脾气～ be difficult ▸执～
▸ ǎo, ào
【拗不过】niùbuguò〈动〉 fail to talk sb. out of doing sth.: 他非要去，我～他。 He was determined to go and I couldn't make him change his mind.
【拗劲】niùjìn〈名〉 obstinacy

nóng

农（農） nóng

〈名〉 **1**（农事） land cultivation: 务～ do farming ▸～时, ～田, ～具 **2**（农业） farming **3**（农民） farmer: 菜～ vegetable grower ‖ 老～ old farmer ‖ 棉～ cotton grower ▸果～
【农残】nóngcán〈名〉 pesticide residue: ～检验 pesticide residue inspection
【农产品】nóngchǎnpǐn〈名〉 farm produce: ～加工 farm product processing ‖ ～贸易 farm trade
【农场】nóngchǎng〈名〉farm: 国营～ state farm ‖ ～工人 farmhand ‖ ～主 farm owner
【农村】nóngcūn〈名〉 countryside: ～城镇化 urbanization of the countryside ‖ ～生活 country life ‖ ～户口 registered rural residence
【农村工作】nóngcūn gōngzuò〈名〉 rural work: ～会议 conference on rural work
【农村经济】 nóngcūn jīngjì〈名〉 rural economy: ～改革 rural economic reform ‖ ～体制 rural economic system
【农村信用合作社】nóngcūn xìnyòng hézuòshè〈名〉 rural credit association
【农夫】nóngfū〈名〉〈旧〉 farmer
【农妇】nóngfù〈名〉 peasant woman
【农副产品】nóngfù chǎnpǐn〈名〉 subsidiary agricultural products
【农耕】nónggēng〈名〉 farming
【农工】nónggōng〈名〉 **1**（指人） peasants and workers: 扶助～ help the peasants and workers **2**（指产业） agriculture and industry: ～联合企业 agro-industrial complex
【农工商联合企业】nónggōngshāng liánhé qǐyè〈名〉 agriculture-processing-marketing allied enterprise
【农户】nónghù〈名〉 farming household
【农活】nónghuó〈名〉 farm work: 干～ do farm work
【农机】nóngjī〈名〉 agricultural machinery: ～站 agricultural machinery station
【农技站】 nóngjìzhàn〈名〉 agro-technical station
【农家】nóngjiā〈名〉 **1**（指家庭） farming family: ～肥料 farmyard manure ‖ ～子弟 farmers' children ‖ ～生活 farming life **2**Nóngjiā（指学术派别） School of Agriculturalists [school of thought in the Spring and Autumn and Warring States periods]
【农家乐】nóngjiālè〈名〉 agritourism
【农具】nóngjù〈名〉 farm tool
【农科院】Nóngkēyuàn〈名〉 Academy of Agricultural Sciences
【农垦】nóngkěn〈名〉 land reclamation and cultivation
【农历】nónglì ▸**p. 618**〈名〉 lunar calendar
【农林牧副渔】nóng-lín-mù-fù-yú〈名〉 farming, forestry, animal husbandry, sideline production and fishery: ～全面发展 all-round development of farming, forestry, animal husbandry, sideline production and fishery
【农林院校】nónglín yuànxiào〈名〉 agricultural and forestry colleges and universities
【农忙】nóngmáng〈名〉［农业］busy farming season: ～季节 busy farming season
【农贸市场】nóngmào shìchǎng〈名〉 farmers' market
【农民】nóngmín〈名〉 farmer: ～阶级 the peasantry

【农民工】 nóngmíngōng 〈名〉 migrant worker
【农民起义】 nóngmín qǐyì 〈名〉 peasant uprising
【农民运动会】 nóngmín yùndònghuì 〈名〉 rural sports meet
【农民运动讲习所】 Nóngmín Yùndòng Jiǎngxísuǒ 〈名〉 Peasant Movement Institute
【农民战争】 nóngmín zhànzhēng 〈名〉 peasant war
【农膜】 nóngmó 〈名〉 plastic film for agricultural use
【农牧区】 nóngmùqū 〈名〉 agricultural and pastoral areas
【农牧业】 nóngmùyè 〈名〉 agricultural and livestock breeding
【农奴】 nóngnú 〈名〉 serf
【农奴制】 nóngnúzhì 〈名〉 serfdom
【农奴主】 nóngnúzhǔ 〈名〉 serf owner
【农人】 nóngrén 〈名〉 farmer
【农舍】 nóngshè 〈名〉 farmhouse
【农时】 nóngshí 〈名〉 farming season: 不误～ do the farm work in the right season
【农事】 nóngshì 〈名〉 farming: ～繁忙 be busy with farm work
【农田】 nóngtián 〈名〉 farmland: ～灌溉 field irrigation ‖ ～水利 irrigation and water conservancy
【农闲】 nóngxián 〈名〉 farmers' slack season
【农学】 nóngxué 〈名〉 agronomy: ～家 agronomist
【农学院】 nóngxuéyuàn 〈名〉 agricultural college
【农谚】 nóngyàn 〈名〉 farmer's saying
【农药】 nóngyào 〈名〉 pesticide: 喷洒～ spray pesticide ‖ ～残留物 pesticide residue
【农业】 nóngyè 〈名〉 agriculture: ～、农村、农民问题 issues concerning agriculture, countryside and farmers ‖ 发展～ develop agriculture ‖ 以～为基础 take agriculture as the foundation (of) ‖ ～投入 agricultural input ‖ 生态～ ecological agriculture
【农业部】 Nóngyèbù 〈名〉 Ministry of Agriculture: ～部长 minister of agriculture
【农业工人】 nóngyè gōngrén 〈名〉 farm worker
【农业国】 nóngyèguó 〈名〉 agricultural country
【农业合作化】 nóngyè hézuòhuà 〈名〉 agricultural cooperative movement
【农业机械】 nóngyè jīxiè 〈名〉 farm machinery: ～化 agricultural mechanization
【农业技术】 nóngyè jìshù 〈名〉 agricultural techniques
【农业局】 nóngyèjú 〈名〉 bureau of agriculture
【农业人口】 nóngyè rénkǒu 〈名〉 farm population: 非～ non-farm population
【农业生产合作社】 nóngyè shēngchǎn hézuòshè 〈名〉 agricultural producers' cooperative
【农业税】 nóngyèshuì 〈名〉 agricultural tax: 取消～ abolish the agricultural tax
【农业银行】 nóngyè yínháng 〈名〉 agricultural bank
【农艺师】 nóngyìshī ▸**p. 966** 〈名〉 agronomist
【农用】 nóngyòng 〈形〉 agricultural: ～机械 machinery for agricultural use ‖ ～物资 agricultural goods
【农用车】 nóngyòngchē 〈名〉 farm truck
【农用地】 nóngyòngdì 〈名〉 farmland
【农用喷雾器】 nóngyòng pēnwùqì 〈名〉 agro sprayer
【农用塑料薄膜】 nóngyòng sùliào bómó = 农膜 nóngmó
【农运会】 nóngyùnhuì 〈简称〉 = 农民运动会
【农转非】 nóngzhuǎnfēi 〈名〉 rural-urban migration
【农庄】 nóngzhuāng 〈名〉 farm
【农资】 nóngzī 〈名〉 means of agricultural production
【农作物】 nóngzuòwù 〈名〉 crops: ～歉收 crop failure ‖ ～病虫害 plant diseases and insect pests

侬（儂） nóng 〈代〉 **1**〈方〉（你） you **2**（我）（主语） I;（宾语） me

哝（噥） nóng
【哝哝】 nóngnong 〈动〉 whisper: 他们～了半天。 They talked in whispers for quite a while.

浓（濃） nóng 〈形〉 **1**（稠） concentrated: ～茶/咖啡 strong tea/coffee ‖ ～～的香味 strong fragrance ‖ ～汤 thick soup ‖ ～雾 heavy mist ‖ ～烟 dense smoke ‖ ～烟滚滚。 Thick smoke is billowing. ‖ 血～于水。 Blood is thicker than water. **2** ▸**p. 863**（颜色重） deep: ～绿 deep green ▸～艳 **3**（程度深） great: ▸～厚
【浓淡】 nóngdàn 〈名〉（指颜色） shade;（指味道） strength;（指化妆） density;（指液体） consistency: ～适宜 be just right
【浓度】 nóngdù 〈名〉 concentration: 高/低～ high/low density
【浓厚】 nónghòu 〈形〉 **1**（多而密） thick: ～的烟雾 dense smog **2**（厚重） strong: ～的节日气氛 strong festive atmosphere ‖ ～的民族色彩 marked national characteristic **3**（强烈） strong: 兴趣～ take a keen interest (in sth.) ‖ 有～的兴趣 have a strong interest
【浓烈】 nóngliè 〈形〉 strong: ～的香味 strong fragrance
【浓眉】 nóngméi 〈名〉 bushy eyebrows: ～大眼 have big eyes and bushy eyebrows
【浓密】 nóngmì 〈形〉 thick: 头发～ have thick hair ‖ ～的枝叶 dense foliage
【浓墨重彩】 nóngmò-zhòngcǎi 〈成〉〈喻〉 describe at length
【浓缩】 nóngsuō 〈动〉 **1**（指溶液） condense: ～果汁 fruit juice concentrate ‖ ～维生素 vitamin concentrate **2**［化学］ concentrate: ～核燃料 concentrated nuclear fuel ‖ ～铀 enriched uranium
【浓艳】 nóngyàn 〈形〉 garish: ～的色彩 rich colours ‖ 着色～ be garishly coloured
【浓荫】 nóngyīn 〈名〉 dense leafy shade
【浓郁】 nóngyù 〈形〉 **1**（浓重） rich: 花香～。 The fragrance of the flowers is strong. **2**（茂密） thick: ～的森林 dense forest **3**（强烈） strong: 乡土气息～ have a strong rural flavour ‖ ～的感情 strong affection **4**（程度深） intense: ～的兴趣 keen interest
【浓重】 nóngzhòng 〈形〉 strong: ～的色彩 rich colours ‖ ～的香气 strong fragrance ‖ 他说话带着～的四川口音。 He speaks with a thick Sichuan accent.
【浓妆】 nóngzhuāng **A**〈动〉 be heavily made up ▸～艳抹 **B**〈名〉 heavy make-up
【浓妆艳抹】 nóngzhuāng-yànmǒ 〈成〉 be richly attired and heavily made-up

脓（膿） nóng 〈名〉 pus: 流～ discharge pus ▸～包, ～肿, 化～
【脓包】 nóngbāo 〈名〉 **1** ▸**p. 50**［医学］ pustule **2**〈喻〉（指人） good-for-nothing
【脓疮】 nóngchuāng ▸**p. 50** 〈名〉 running sore
【脓血症】 nóngxuèzhèng ▸**p. 50** 〈名〉［医学］ pyaemia
【脓肿】 nóngzhǒng ▸**p. 50** 〈名〉［医学］ abscess: 齿龈～ abscesses on the gums

秾（穠） nóng 〈形〉〈书〉 luxuriant

nòng

弄 nòng 〈动〉 **1**（摆弄） play with: 别乱～那支枪! Don't play with that gun! ‖ 小孩一般都喜欢～水。 Most children like to play around with water. **2**（做） do: 那个问题你～懂了没有? Have you understood that question? ‖ ～不好就会前功尽弃。 All the work will be wasted if you don't do it right. **3**（取得） get: 你～到电影票了吗? Did you manage to get tickets for the film? ‖ 请给病人～点水来。 Will you please fetch some water for the patient? **4**（耍弄） play: ～手段 play tricks ▸装神～鬼, ～虚作假
▸lòng
【弄潮】 nòngcháo 〈动〉〈书〉 ride the sea
【弄潮儿】 nòngcháo'ér 〈名〉 **1**（指在水中） young person playing in the waves **2**〈喻〉（指在风险中） risk-taker
【弄臣】 nòngchén 〈名〉 favourite courtier
【弄鬼】 nòngguǐ 〈动〉 create mischief: ▸装神～
【弄假成真】 nòngjiǎ-chéngzhēn 〈成〉 make fiction become reality
【弄僵】 nòngjiāng 〈动〉 bring to a deadlock: 把会谈～了 brought the talks to a deadlock
【弄巧成拙】 nòngqiǎo-chéngzhuō 〈成〉 make a fool of oneself in trying to be clever: 这一次他可是～了。 This time, he outsmarted himself.
【弄权】 nòngquán 〈动〉 abuse power
【弄瓦】 nòngwǎ 〈动〉〈书〉 give birth to a girl: ～之喜 joy of bearing a daughter
【弄虚作假】 nòngxū-zuòjiǎ 〈成〉 resort to deception
【弄璋】 nòngzhāng 〈动〉〈书〉 give birth to a son: ～之喜 joy of bearing a boy

nòu

耨 nòu 〈书〉
A〈名〉 weeding hoe
B〈动〉 weed

nú

奴 nú
A〈名〉 **1**（奴隶） slave: ▸～隶, ～仆, 农～ **2**〈喻〉〈贬〉（指受控制的） flunkey: ▸守财～, 洋～
B〈代〉〈旧〉（女子自称）（用作主语） I;（用作宾语） me: ▸～家
C〈动〉 enslave: ▸～役
【奴婢】 núbì 〈名〉〈旧〉 **1**（男女仆役） slave **2**（太监自称） [self-reference of

n

eunuchs when speaking to an emperor or empress] I

【奴才】núcai **A**〈名〉 **1**（奴仆） slave **2**（帮凶） lackey **B**〈代〉 [self-reference of an official when addressing the emperor esp in Ming and Qing dynasties] I

【奴才相】núcaixiàng〈名〉 servile manner

【奴化】núhuà 〈动〉 enslave: ～教育 enslavement education ‖ ～政策 policy of enslavement

【奴家】nújiā〈名〉〈旧〉 [self-address of a young woman]（用作主语） I;（用作宾语） me

【奴隶】núlì〈名〉 slave: 解放～ free slaves ‖〈喻〉 金钱的～ slave to money

【奴隶起义】núlì qǐyì〈名〉 slave uprising

【奴隶社会】núlì shèhuì〈名〉 slave society

【奴隶制】núlìzhì〈名〉 slavery

【奴隶主】núlìzhǔ〈名〉 slave owner

【奴仆】núpú〈名〉 servant

【奴使】núshǐ〈动〉 enslave

【奴性】núxìng〈名〉 servility: ～十足 sheer subservience

【奴颜婢膝】núyán-bìxī〈成〉 fawn on: 她对老板～，极力讨好。 She was obsequious with her boss, trying every possible means to please him.

【奴颜媚骨】núyán-mèigǔ〈成〉sycophancy and obsequiousness

【奴役】núyì〈动〉enslave: 不堪～ be unable to bear the misery of slavery

孥 nú〈名〉〈书〉 **1**（儿女） children **2**（妻儿） wife and children

驽（駑） nú〈书〉

A〈名〉 inferior horse

B〈形〉〈喻〉 incompetent

【驽钝】núdùn〈形〉〈书〉 dumb

【驽马】númǎ〈名〉〈书〉 inferior horse

nǔ

努 nǔ〈动〉 **1**（使出） exert oneself: 再～一把力 make another effort ▸～力 **2**（凸出） bulge: ～着眼睛 with bulging eyes ‖ 他不满地～～嘴。 He pursed his lips in distaste.

【努力】nǔlì **A**〈动〉 make an effort: ～赚钱 make an effort to make money ‖ 加倍～ redouble one's efforts ‖ 共同～ make joint efforts ‖ ～工作/学习 work/study hard **B**〈形〉 conscientious: ～地学习 study hard ‖ 学习很～ study very diligently

【努目】nǔmù〈动〉 stare with bulging eyes

【努嘴】nǔzuǐ〈动〉 pout one's lips as a signal: 她努努嘴，示意他走开。 She pouted her lips to show she wanted him to go away.

弩 nǔ〈名〉 crossbow: 万～齐发。 The crossbows shot all at once. ▸剑拔～张, 强～之末

【弩弓】nǔgōng〈名〉 crossbow

【弩炮】nǔpào〈名〉 catapult

【弩手】nǔshǒu〈名〉 crossbowman

胬 nǔ

【胬肉】nǔròu〈名〉［中医］triangular mass of mucous membrane growing from the inner corner of the eye

nù

怒[1] nù

A〈动〉 get angry: 大～ fly into fury ‖ 一～之下 in a rage ▸～气, 发～

B〈形〉 raging: ▸～潮, ～放

怒[2] Nù ▸怒族 Nùzú

【怒不可遏】nùbùkě'è〈成〉 be beside oneself with anger: 他～，把照片撕得粉碎。 In a burst of uncontrollable anger he tore the picture into pieces.

【怒潮】nùcháo〈名〉 **1**（指潮水） surging tide: 钱塘江的～ the surging tide in the Qiantang River **2**〈喻〉（指反抗运动） raging tide: 革命～ the revolutionary tide

【怒叱】nùchì〈动〉 angrily rebuke

【怒斥】nùchì〈动〉 angrily denounce

【怒冲冲】nùchōngchōng〈形〉 furious: 他～地走出了房间。 He left the room in a rage.

【怒发冲冠】nùfà-chōngguān〈成〉 bristle with anger

【怒放】nùfàng〈动〉 be in full bloom: 春季里鲜花～。 In spring, flowers burst into bloom. ▸心花～

【怒海扁舟】nùhǎi-piānzhōu〈成〉 small boat on an angry sea

【怒号】nùháo〈动〉 roar: 风在～。 The wind is howling.

【怒喝】nùhè〈动〉 shout angrily

【怒吼】nùhǒu〈动〉 roar: 狂风～。 A gale raged. ‖ 群众～着表示不满。 The crowd shouted its displeasure.

【怒火】nùhuǒ〈名〉 fury: 强压～ swallow one's anger ‖ 他满腔～。 He was simmering with rage.

【怒火中烧】nùhuǒ-zhōngshāo〈成〉 be simmering with rage: 他～。 He burned with anger.

【怒目】nùmù **A**〈动〉 glare with rage: ～而视 glower at **B**〈名〉 glaring eyes: ▸横眉～

【怒目切齿】nùmù-qièchǐ〈成〉 darting fierce looks and gnashing one's teeth

【怒气】nùqì〈名〉 anger: ～冲冲 be in a great rage ‖ 他的～很快就消了。 His anger soon abated.

【怒容】nùróng〈名〉 scowl: ～满面 wear a scowl

【怒色】nùsè〈名〉 angry look: 面带～ wear an angry look

【怒视】nùshì〈动〉 glare at

【怒涛】nùtāo〈名〉 turbulent waters: ～澎湃 billows raging with great fury

【怒形于色】nùxíngyúsè〈成〉show signs of anger

【怒族】Nùzú〈名〉 Nu ethnic group

nǚ

女 nǚ〈名〉 **1**（指人） woman;（指性别） female: ～代表 woman delegate ‖ ～医生 lady doctor ‖ ～作家 woman of letters ▸～工, 妇～, 少～ **2**（女儿） daughter: ▸独生～, 儿～ **3**（指星宿） one of the 28 constellations in ancient Chinese astronomy

【女扮男装】nǚbàn-nánzhuāng〈成〉 disguise oneself as a man

【女傧相】nǚbīnxiàng〈名〉 bridesmaid

【女兵】nǚbīng〈名〉 service woman

【女厕所】nǚcèsuǒ〈名〉 Ladies〈英〉; ladies' room〈美〉

【女超】nǚchāo〈名〉 Women's Football Super League

【女大当嫁】nǚdà-dāngjià〈成〉 girl of age should be married

【女大十八变】nǚ dà shíbā biàn〈俗〉 as girls mature, so their beauty becomes more alluring

【女单】nǚdān〈名〉［体育］ women's singles

【女低音】nǚdīyīn〈名〉 contralto

【女儿】nǚ'ér〈名〉 daughter: 大～ the eldest daughter ‖ 她有两个～。 She has two girls.

【女儿墙】nǚ'érqiáng = 女墙 nǚqiáng

【女犯人】nǚfànrén〈名〉 female inmate

【女方】nǚfāng〈名〉 wife's side

【女服务员】nǚfúwùyuán ▸p. 966〈名〉 waitress

【女高音】nǚgāoyīn〈名〉 soprano

【女工】nǚgōng〈名〉 **1**（指工人） female worker **2**（女红） needlework done by women

【女公子】nǚgōngzǐ〈名〉〈旧〉 [address to sb. else's daughter] daughter

【女红】nǚgōng〈名〉〈书〉 needlework

【女孩儿】nǚháir〈名〉 girl

【女皇】nǚhuáng〈名〉 empress

【女家】nǚjiā〈名〉 wife's family

【女监】nǚjiān〈名〉 prison for female criminals

【女将】nǚjiàng〈名〉 **1**（指将领） woman general **2**（指能干的人） female expert

【女杰】nǚjié〈名〉 distinguished woman

【女眷】nǚjuàn〈名〉 women of a family

【女篮】nǚlán〈名〉 women's basketball

【女郎】nǚláng〈名〉 girl: 摩登～ modern girl ‖ 妙龄～ lady in her prime

【女垒】nǚlěi〈名〉 women's softball

【女伶】nǚlíng〈名〉〈旧〉 actress

【女流】nǚliú〈名〉〈贬〉 weaker sex: ～之辈 the weaker sex

【女排】nǚpái〈名〉 women's volleyball

【女朋友】nǚpéngyou〈名〉 **1**（指恋爱对象） girl friend: 他有～。 He has a girl friend. **2**（女性朋友） female friend

【女气】nǚqì〈形〉 effeminate

【女强人】nǚqiángrén〈名〉 superwoman

【女墙】nǚqiáng〈名〉［建筑］ parapet

【女曲】nǚqū〈名〉 **1**（指球队） women's hockey team **2**（指运动） women's hockey

【女权】nǚquán〈名〉 women's rights: ～主义者 feminist

【女人】nǚrén〈名〉 woman: 温柔的～ gentle woman ‖ 缺少～味 be unfeminine

【女人】nǚren〈名〉〈口〉 wife: 她是我的～。 She's my wife.

【女色】nǚsè〈名〉 feminine charm: 贪恋～ lust after women

【女神】nǚshén〈名〉 goddess

【女生】nǚshēng〈名〉 **1**（指学生） schoolgirl: ～公寓 girl's dormitory **2**〈口〉（指女人） female

【女声】nǚshēng〈名〉 female voice: ～独唱 female solo

【女士】nǚshì〈名〉 lady: ～优先。 Ladies first.

【女式】nǚshì〈形〉 woman's: ～手提包 woman's handbag ‖ ～自行车 woman's bicycle

【女双】nǚshuāng〈名〉［体育］ women's doubles

【女体盛】nǚtǐchéng〈名〉 nyotaimori [Japanese practice of serving sushi on the body of a woman]

【女同性恋者】nǚtóngxìngliànzhě〈名〉lesbian

【女童】nǚtóng〈名〉little girl

【女娲】Nǚwā ▸**p. 274**〈名〉Nüwa [goddess who patched the holes in the sky with stone blocks]

> **女娲**
>
> In Chinese mythology, Nüwa is a goddess who created people out of the yellow earth. First she made officials and aristocrats. Later, swinging a mud-covered rope, she created ordinary people from the scattered mud spots. She also melted five precious stones to patch up the sky when the heavens collapsed and the earth caved in, and birds of prey and fierce beasts appeared to destroy mankind. To this day, the Miao and Dong people in Yunnan Province still honour Nüwa as their people's earliest ancestor.

【女王】nǚwáng〈名〉queen

【女为悦己者容】nǚ wèi yuèjǐzhě róng〈成〉A woman makes herself beautiful only for the man who loves her

【女巫】nǚwū〈名〉witch

【女校友】nǚxiàoyǒu〈名〉alumna

【女性】nǚxìng〈名〉**1**（指性别）female sex **2**（指人）woman: 新～ modern woman ‖ 知识～ educated woman

【女性化】nǚxìnghuà **A**〈动〉feminize **B**〈名〉feminization

【女性生殖器】nǚxìng shēngzhíqì〈名〉female genital organs

【女修道院】nǚxiūdàoyuàn〈名〉convent

【女秀才】nǚxiùcai〈名〉〈旧〉woman scholar

【女婿】nǚxu〈名〉**1**（女儿的丈夫）son-in-law **2**〈口〉（丈夫）husband: 找～ hunt for a husband

【女演员】nǚyǎnyuán ▸**p. 966**〈名〉actress

【女一号】nǚyīhào〈名〉**1**（女主角）top-ranking female: 张怡宁是中国乒乓球队的～。Zhang Yining is China's top female table tennis player. **2**（女主角）female lead: 她出演该话剧的～。She is the female lead in the play.

【女英雄】nǚyīngxióng〈名〉heroine

【女婴】nǚyīng〈名〉baby girl

【女佣】nǚyōng〈名〉maidservant

【女优】nǚyōu〈名〉〈旧〉actress

【女友】nǚyǒu = 女朋友 nǚpéngyou

【女运动员】nǚyùndòngyuán ▸**p. 966**〈名〉sportswoman

【女贞】nǚzhēn〈名〉［植物］glossy privet

【女真】Nǚzhēn〈名〉Nüzhen [pre-17th century name of the Manchu ethnic group]

【女中豪杰】nǚzhōng-háojié〈成〉woman of great ability

【女中音】nǚzhōngyīn〈名〉mezzo-soprano

【女主角】nǚzhǔjué〈名〉heroine

【女主人公】nǚzhǔréngōng〈名〉heroine

【女主人】nǚzhǔren〈名〉**1**（指主办聚会）hostess **2**（指一家之主）lady of the house

【女装】nǚzhuāng〈名〉ladies' wear

【女子】nǚzǐ〈名〉woman: ～组项目 women's division events ‖ 已婚～ married woman

【女子学校】nǚzǐ xuéxiào〈名〉girls' school

【女足】nǚzú〈名〉women's football

钕（釹） nǚ〈名〉［化学］neodymium (Nd)

nǜ

衄 nǜ〈动〉〈书〉**1**（流鼻血）have a nosebleed **2**（流血）bleed: 齿～ bleed from the gums ‖ 耳～ bleed from the ear **3**（战败）be defeated in battle

nuǎn

暖 nuǎn

A〈形〉warm: 冬～夏凉 warm in winter and cool in summer ‖ 天～了。It's getting warm. ▸～烘烘, 温～

B〈动〉warm: ～酒/手 warm the wine/one's hands ‖ 过来在火前～～身子吧。Come and warm yourself in front of the fire.

【暖冬】nuǎndōng〈名〉warm winter

【暖房】nuǎnfáng **A**〈动〉〈旧〉（指新房）visit the bridal chamber on the eve of sb.'s wedding **B**〈口〉= 温室 wēnshì

【暖风机】nuǎnfēngjī〈名〉convection heater

【暖锋】nuǎnfēng〈名〉［气象］warm front

【暖阁】nuǎngé〈名〉〈旧〉small heating room with a stove partitioned off in a large house

【暖烘烘】nuǎnhōnghōng〈形〉snug

【暖呼呼】nuǎnhūhū〈形〉nice and warm: 看到家她心里～的。The sight of home warmed her heart.

【暖壶】nuǎnhú〈名〉**1**（暖水瓶）Thermos **2**（用于取暖）water pot with a cosy **3**（汤壶）hot-water bottle

【暖和】nuǎnhuo **A**〈形〉snug: 我们家有暖气，冬天很～。With central heating, our home is very warm in winter. **B**〈动〉warm (up): 快进来烤烤火，～一下身子。Come quick and warm yourself up by the fire.

【暖帘】nuǎnlián〈名〉quilted door curtain

【暖流】nuǎnliú〈名〉**1**［气象］warm current **2**（指感觉）warm feeling: 一股～涌上心头 feel a glow in one's heart

【暖瓶】nuǎnpíng = 暖水瓶 nuǎnshuǐpíng

【暖气】nuǎnqì〈名〉**1**（指供暖）central heating **2**（指设备）central heating equipment: ～片 radiator **3**（指气体）warm air

【暖气团】nuǎnqìtuán〈名〉［气象］warm air mass

【暖融融】nuǎnróngróng〈形〉warm, cosy and comfortable

【暖色】nuǎnsè〈名〉warm colour: 红、黄、橙称为～。Red, yellow and orange are called warm colours.

【暖手炉】nuǎnshǒulú〈名〉hand-warmer

【暖水瓶】nuǎnshuǐpíng〈名〉Thermos; (vacuum) flask〈英〉

【暖洋洋】nuǎnyángyáng〈形〉warm: ～的春风 warm spring breeze ‖〈喻〉他的话说得我心里～的。His words warmed my heart.

nüè

疟（瘧） nüè〈名〉malaria ▸yào

【疟疾】nüèji ▸**p. 50**〈名〉［医学］malaria

【疟蚊】nüèwén〈名〉malarial mosquito

【疟原虫】nüèyuánchóng〈名〉［医学］plasmodium

虐 nüè〈形〉savage: ▸～待, 肆～

【虐待】nüèdài〈动〉abuse: ～战俘 maltreat prisoners of war ‖ 精神～ emotional abuse

【虐待狂】nüèdàikuáng〈名〉sadist

【虐俘】nüèfú〈动〉mistreat prisoners: ～丑闻 prisoner abuse scandal

【虐囚】nüèqiú〈动〉abuse a prisoner: 美军～丑闻 US military prisoner abuse scandal

【虐童】nüètóng〈动〉abuse a child: ～现象 the phenomenon of child abuse

【虐杀】nüèshā〈动〉kill with maltreatment

【虐政】nüèzhèng〈名〉tyranny

nuó

挪 nuó〈动〉**1**（指位置、时间）shift: 把比赛日期～到星期五 move the date of the game to Friday ‖ 把椅子向床跟前～一～ shift the chair closer to the bed **2**（指用途）divert: ▸～用

【挪东补西】nuódōng-bǔxī〈成〉make up a loss in one area by drawing upon the surpluses in another

【挪动】nuódòng〈动〉move: 请向前～几步。Please move a few steps forward. ‖ 不要～我桌子上的东西。Don't move the things on my desk.

【挪借】nuójiè〈动〉get a short-term loan

【挪威】Nuówēi〈名〉Norway: ～人 Norwegian ‖ ～王国 Kingdom of Norway ‖ ～语 Norwegian

【挪窝儿】nuówōr〈动〉〈方〉**1**（离开原地）move to another place: 我年纪大了，不想～了。I am old and don't want to move to a new place. **2**（搬家）move house

【挪用】nuóyòng〈动〉**1**（移用）divert: 教育资金不能～。The educational fund cannot be diverted to any other purpose. **2**（私自动用）misappropriate: ～公款罪 misappropriation of public funds

娜 nuó ▸婀娜 ēnuó, 袅娜 niǎonuó ▸nà

傩（儺） nuó〈动〉〈旧〉exorcize

【傩神】nuóshén〈名〉god that drives away pestilence

【傩舞】nuówǔ〈名〉exorcizing dance

nuò

诺（諾） nuò

A〈叹〉yeah: ▸～～连声, 唯唯～～

B〈动〉promise: ▸～言, 许～

【诺贝尔奖】Nuòbèi'ěrjiǎng〈名〉Nobel Prize: ～获得者 Nobel Prize winner

【诺丁汉】Nuòdīnghàn〈名〉Nottingham

【诺丁汉郡】Nuòdīnghànjùn〈名〉Nottinghamshire

【诺福克郡】Nuòfúkèjùn〈名〉Norfolk

【诺奖】Nuòjiǎng〈简称〉= 诺贝尔奖

【诺曼底登陆】Nuòmàndǐ Dēnglù〈名〉Normandy landing

【诺诺连声】nuònuò-liánshēng〈成〉keep on saying 'yes'

【诺森伯兰郡】Nuòsēnbólánjùn〈名〉Northumberland

【诺亚方舟】Nuòyàfāngzhōu〈名〉Noah's Ark

【诺言】nuòyán〈名〉 promise: 违背～ go back on one's word ‖ 信守～ keep one's promise

喏 nuò〈叹〉〈方〉 [used to call attention to what one refers to]: ～，这不就是你那本书吗？ There! Isn't that your book?
►rě

搦 nuò〈动〉〈书〉 1 （握）hold: ►～管 2 （挑动） challenge: ►～战

【搦笔疾书】 nuòbǐ-jíshū 〈成〉 (hold the brush and) write swiftly

【搦管】nuòguǎn〈动〉〈书〉 hold a writing brush: ～疾书 write swiftly with a pen

【搦战】nuòzhàn〈动〉〈书〉 challenge to a fight

锘（鍩） nuò〈名〉［化学］ nobelium (No)

懦 nuò〈形〉 cowardly: ►怯～

【懦夫】nuòfū〈名〉 coward: 他是个～。 He is a coward.

【懦弱】nuòruò〈形〉 weak: ～无能 be weak and useless

糯 nuò〈形〉 glutinous

【糯稻】nuòdào〈名〉 sticky rice

【糯米】nuòmǐ〈名〉 polished glutinous rice: ～酒 glutinous rice wine

【糯米纸】 nuòmǐzhǐ 〈名〉 glutinous rice paper

Oo

ō

噢 ō〈叹〉[expressing realization] oh: ～，原来是你! Oh, it's you!

ó

哦 ó〈叹〉[expressing doubt] oh: ～，是这么回事吗? Oh, is that so?
▸é, ò

ǒ

嚄 ǒ〈叹〉[expressing surprise]: ～，他有两米零四高? What! He's two point four metres tall?
▸huō

ò

哦 ò〈叹〉[expressing realization, understanding, etc.] oh: ～，我懂了。 Oh, I've got it.
▸é, ó

ōu

区（區） Ōu〈名〉Ou [surname]
▸qū

讴（謳） ōu
A〈动〉sing: ▸～歌
B〈名〉ballad
【讴歌】ōugē〈动〉〈书〉sing the praises of: ～人民英雄 eulogize the people's heroes ‖ ～伟大的祖国 sing the praises of the great motherland

沤（漚） ōu〈名〉froth: 浮～ forth
▸òu

瓯[1]（甌） ōu〈名〉〈方〉bowl: 茶～ tea cup ‖ 酒～ wine bowl

瓯[2]（甌） Ōu〈名〉Ou [another name for Wenzhou (温州)]
【瓯绣】ōuxiù〈名〉Wenzhou embroidery

欧[1]（歐） Ōu〈名〉Europe: ▸～化, ～元, 西～

欧[2]（歐） ōu = 欧姆 ōumǔ
【欧安会】Ōu'ānhuì〈简称〉= 欧洲安全理事会
【欧分】ōufēn ▸**p. 328**〈名〉Euro cent
【欧共体】Ōugòngtǐ〈简称〉= 欧洲共同体
【欧化】ōuhuà〈动〉be assimilated into European ways
【欧几里得几何】Ōujǐlǐdé jǐhé〈名〉Euclidean geometry
【欧罗巴人种】Ōuluóbā rénzhǒng〈名〉Caucasian race
【欧罗巴洲】Ōuluóbāzhōu = 欧洲 Ōuzhōu
【欧美】Ōu-Měi〈名〉Europe and America
【欧盟】Ōuméng〈名〉EU (European Union): ～轮值主席 rotating president of the EU
【欧姆】ōumǔ〈名〉[物理] ohm: ～定律 Ohm's Law
【欧佩克】Ōupèikè〈名〉OPEC (Organization of Petroleum Exporting Countries): ～成员国 OPEC countries
【欧芹】ōuqín〈名〉[植物] parsley
【欧鸲】ōuqú〈名〉[鸟类] robin
【欧体】Ōutǐ〈名〉[书法] Ouyang style [calligraphy of Ouyang Xun (欧阳洵) of the Tang Dynasty]
【欧亚大陆】Ōu-Yà Dàlù〈名〉Eurasia: ～桥 Eurasia Land Bridge
【欧元】ōuyuán ▸**p. 328**〈名〉euro: ～区 Euroland
【欧洲】Ōuzhōu〈名〉Europe
【欧洲安全理事会】Ōuzhōu Ānquán Lǐshìhuì〈名〉European Security Council
【欧洲共同体】Ōuzhōu Gòngtóngtǐ〈名〉European Community
【欧洲货币一体化】Ōuzhōu huòbì yītǐhuà〈名〉European monetary integration
【欧洲联盟】Ōuzhōu Liánméng = 欧盟 Ōuméng
【欧洲市场】Ōuzhōu Shìchǎng〈名〉Euromarket

殴（毆） ōu〈动〉beat up: ▸～打, 斗～
【殴打】ōudǎ〈动〉beat up: 互相～ exchange blows
【殴斗】ōudòu〈动〉brawl

鸥（鷗） ōu〈名〉gull: ▸海～
【鸥鸟】ōuniǎo〈名〉hagdon

噢（噢） ōu
A〈叹〉[expressing realization, surprise etc.] oh: ～，你们俩倒挺对脾气。Aha, you two are of a kind. ‖ 你这样蛮干可不行～! Hey! You can't act in such a rash way!
B〈拟〉急得～～直哭。 She was so anxious that she was sobbing.
▸óu, ǒu, òu

óu

噢（噢） óu〈叹〉[expressing surprise] aha: ～，原来是他捣的鬼。 So! He was behind all this!
▸ōu, ǒu, òu

ǒu

呕（嘔） ǒu〈动〉vomit: ▸～血, 作～
【呕吐】ǒutù〈动〉vomit: 她酒喝得太多，回家的路上就～了。 She drank too much and threw up on the way home.
【呕心】ǒuxīn〈动〉exert one's utmost effort: ～之作 work embodying one's utmost efforts
【呕心沥血】ǒuxīn-lìxuè〈成〉work one's heart out: 她～写了这本书。 She sweated blood writing the book.
【呕血】ǒuxuè〈动〉vomit blood

炽（熰） ǒu〈动〉**1**（冒烟）give off a lot of smoke as a result of poor burning: ～了一屋子的烟。 The room was full of smoke. **2**（闷燃）smoulder: 那儿～着一堆火。 A fire smouldered there. **3**（用烟驱）smoke out: ～蚊子 smoke out mosquitoes

噢（噢） ǒu〈叹〉[expressing great surprise] oh: ～，这里竟变得认不出来了! Wow, this place has changed beyond all recognition!
▸ōu, óu, òu

偶[1] ǒu〈名〉idol: ▸～像, 木～, 玩～

偶[2] ǒu
A〈形〉even: ▸～数
B〈名〉mate: ▸对～, 佳～, 配～

偶[3] ǒu〈副〉occasionally: ▸～尔, ～然
【偶尔】ǒu'ěr〈副〉once in a while: 我们～见面。 We saw each other once in a while. ‖ ～会有客人来这儿。 We had occasional visitors here.
【偶发】ǒufā〈形〉chance: ～事件 chance occurrence
【偶感】ǒugǎn **A**〈名〉random thoughts **B**〈动〉suddenly feel: ～不适 feel out of sorts occasionally
【偶合】ǒuhé〈动〉coincide: 我妹妹跟我同坐一趟车，完全是～。 It was a complete coincidence that my sister was on the same train.
【偶或】ǒuhuò = 偶尔 ǒu'ěr

O

【偶然】ǒurán **A**〈形〉 accidental: ～事故 accident ‖ ～因素 occasional factors **B**〈副〉 once in a while: 我只是～去一次舞厅。 I visited the ballroom only occasionally.
【偶然性】ǒuránxìng〈名〉 chance
【偶数】ǒushù ►**p. 691**〈名〉 even number
【偶数页】ǒushùyè〈名〉［印刷］even page
【偶蹄动物】ǒutí dòngwù〈名〉 even-toed mammal
【偶蹄目】ǒutímù〈名〉［生物］Artiodactyla
【偶像】ǒuxiàng〈名〉 idol: 崇拜～ worship an image ‖ ～明星 famous idol
【偶像崇拜】ǒuxiàng chóngbài〈名〉 idolatry
【偶像化】ǒuxiànghuà〈动〉 idolize
【偶像剧】ǒuxiàngjù〈名〉 idol drama [TV drama starring pop idols]
【偶像派】ǒuxiàngpài〈名〉 idol : 导演要找的是实力派而非～。 The director is looking for real talent and not just an idol.
【偶一为之】ǒuyīwéizhī〈成〉 do sth. once in a while

耦 ǒu
A〈动〉〈书〉 plough side by side
B = 偶² ǒu
【耦合】ǒuhé〈名〉［物理］ coupling: ～电路 coupling circuit

藕 ǒu〈名〉 lotus root: ►莲～
【藕断丝连】ǒuduàn-sīlián〈成〉〈喻〉 separated but still in each other's thoughts
【藕粉】ǒufěn〈名〉 lotus root starch: 冲～ prepare some lotus root paste
【藕荷】ǒuhé〈名〉 pale pinkish purple
【藕灰】ǒuhuī = 藕色 ǒusè
【藕色】ǒusè ►**p. 863**〈名〉 pale pinkish grey

òu

沤（漚）òu〈动〉 soak: 长时间浸泡，衣服会～烂的。 If soaked for a long time, clothes will rot.
►ōu
【沤肥】òuféi **A**〈动〉 make compost **B**〈名〉 wet compost

怄（慪）òu〈动〉〈方〉 **1**（怄气） be irritated: ►～气 **2**（使生气） annoy: 别～我了! Stop annoying me!
【怄气】òuqì〈动〉 sulk: 别为这点小事～了。 Don't go getting into a sulk about this small thing.

嘔（噢）òu〈叹〉 [expressing gradual realization] oh: ～，你这是在说我呀。 So, you have been talking about me all this while.
►ōu, óu, ǒu

Pp

pā

趴 pā〈动〉**1**（俯卧）lie on one's front: ～在床上 lie face down on the bed ‖ ～下 lie on one's stomach ‖ 狗～在主人的脚下。 The dog lay at his master's feet. **2**（依靠） lean on: ～在桌子上睡着了 bent over the desk, asleep ‖ 她～在窗台上向外看。 She leaned on the window sill, looking out.

【趴伏】 pāfú〈动〉 lie prone

【趴窝】 pāwō〈动〉〈方〉**1**（指母鸡） be brooding: 那只母鸡在～。 The hen is sitting on her eggs. **2**〈喻〉（指人） be broken in health: 他累得～了。 He broke down from overwork.

啪 pā〈拟〉 bang: ～的一声，杯子掉在地上摔碎了。 The cup dropped to the ground and broke with a crash. ‖ 他～～地甩着鞭子。 He cracked his whip.

【啪嚓】 pāchā〈拟〉 crash: 碟子～一声掉在地上碎了。 The saucer fell to the floor and broke with a crash.

【啪嗒】 pādā〈拟〉 patter: 雨点～～打在窗子上。 Raindrops were pattering against the window.

葩 pā〈名〉〈书〉 flower: 艺术新～ new work of art ▸奇～

pá

扒 pá〈动〉**1**（使聚拢） gather up: ～干草/柴 rake up hay/firewood **2**（偷窃） pinch: 他的钱包让小偷～走了。 His purse was stolen by a pickpocket. ▸～窃，～手 **3**（指烹饪） braise: ～芹菜 braised celery ‖ ～鸡/羊肉 stewed chicken/mutton
▸bā

【扒分】 páfēn〈动〉〈方〉 make money

【扒糕】 págāo〈名〉 buckwheat cake served cold with sweet sauce

【扒灰】 páhuī = 爬灰 páhuī

【扒拉】 pála〈动〉〈方〉 push rice into one's mouth with one's chopsticks: ～几口饭 whisk a few mouthfuls of rice into one's mouth
▸bāla

【扒犁】 páli〈方〉= 爬犁 páli

【扒窃】 páqiè〈动〉 pick sb.'s pockets: 有人在公共汽车上～了他的皮夹子。 Someone lifted his wallet on the bus.

【扒手】 páshǒu〈名〉 pickpocket: 谨防～! Beware of pickpockets! ‖ ～偷了我的包。 I had my pocket picked.

杷 pá ▸枇杷 pípa

爬 pá〈动〉**1**（指向前） crawl: ～出洞 crawl out of a hole ‖ 她的孩子现在可以到处～了。 Her baby is crawling now. ▸～行 **2**（指向上） climb: ～竿 climb a pole ‖ ～树 climb a tree ‖ 常春藤沿着墙往上～。 Ivy creeps up the wall. ‖〈喻〉 他一心向上～。 He is an eager social climber. **3**（坐起或站起） get up: 从床上～起来 get out of bed ‖〈喻〉 从哪儿跌倒，就从哪儿～起来。 Pick yourself up from where you fall.

【爬虫】 páchóng〈名〉［动物］ reptile

【爬得高，跌得重】 pá de gāo, diē de zhòng〈俗〉 the higher the climb, the harder the fall

【爬竿】 págān〈名〉［体育］ pole-climbing

【爬格子】 pá gézi〈惯〉〈口〉 engage in writing: 以～为生 live by one's pen

【爬灰】 páhuī〈动〉〈俗〉 have sex with one's daughter-in-law

【爬犁】 páli〈名〉〈方〉 sledge

【爬坡】 pápō〈动〉**1**〈本〉 climb a slope **2**〈喻〉（指困难） strive towards a higher goal

【爬山虎】 páshānhǔ〈名〉［植物］ ivy

【爬升】 páshēng〈动〉**1**（指高度） ascend: 飞机～到1万米高度。 The plane climbed to 10,000 metres. **2**〈喻〉（指数额、地位等） climb: 商品销售额开始～。 The sales began to climb. ‖ 他～得很快。 He moved up quickly through the ranks.

【爬绳】 páshéng〈名〉［体育］ rope-climbing

【爬梯】 pátī〈名〉**1**（指楼梯） staircase **2**（指梯状设施） rope ladder

【爬行】 páxíng〈动〉**1**（爬） crawl **2**〈喻〉（行动迟缓） drop behind: 跟在别人后面～ trail behind others at a snail's pace

【爬行动物】 páxíng dòngwù〈名〉 reptile

【爬泳】 páyǒng **A**〈名〉［体育］ crawl: ～运动员 crawl swimmer **B**〈动〉 do the crawl

耙 pá
A〈名〉 rake: 竹～ bamboo rake ▸～子，钉～
B〈动〉 level with a rake: ～松土地 harrow a field ‖ 把枯叶～成一堆 rake dead leaves together into a heap ‖ 把炉灰～出来 rake the ashes out of a stove
▸bà

【耙地】 pádì〈动〉 level the ground with a rake

【耙子】 pázi〈名〉 rake

琶 pá ▸琵琶 pípa

筢 pá〈名〉 bamboo rake

【筢子】 pázi〈名〉 bamboo rake

pà

帕[1] pà〈名〉 handkerchief

帕[2] pà = 帕斯卡 pàsīkǎ

【帕金森病】 Pàjīnsēnbìng ▸p. 50〈名〉［医学］ Parkinson's disease: ～患者 parkinsonian

【帕劳】 Pàláo〈名〉 Palau

【帕米尔高原】 Pàmǐ'ěr Gāoyuán〈名〉 Pamirs

【帕斯卡】 pàsīkǎ〈量〉［物理］ pascal

怕 pà
A〈动〉**1**（害怕） fear: ～苦 fear hardships ‖ ～挨骂 be afraid of getting a scolding ‖ ～老婆 be henpecked ‖ 不要～，我们很安全。 Don't be frightened. We are quite safe. **2**（担心） worry: 他～我忘了。 He was worried I would forget. ‖ 我～他太累。 I was afraid of his getting too tired. **3**（经不住） cannot withstand: 这种材料不～火。 This kind of material is fireproof. ‖ 玻璃器皿～摔。 Glass breaks easily when dropped.
B〈副〉 perhaps: ～要下雨了。 I am afraid it's going to rain. ‖ 这孩子～有一岁了吧。 This child is one year old, I suppose.

【怕人】 pàrén **A**〈动〉 be timid: 动物园里的动物不～。 Zoo animals are not afraid of people. **B**〈形〉 frightening: 洞里黑得～。 The cave was terrifyingly dark. ‖ 失业率高得～。 Unemployment is frighteningly high.

【怕三怕四】 pàsān-pàsì〈成〉 have too many worries: 你要想干大事就不要总是～，畏缩不前。 If you want to achieve something big, you must not be apprehensive and hesitant all the time.

【怕生】 pàshēng〈形〉 be shy with strangers: 这小孩～。 The small child is timid with strangers.

【怕事】 pàshì〈形〉 afraid of getting into trouble: 胆小～ be timid and overcautious

【怕是】 pàshì〈副〉 maybe: 他脸色苍白，～病了。 He's probably ill, judging by his pale colour.

【怕死】 pàsǐ〈动〉 be afraid of death: 他不～。 He did not fear to die. ▸贪生～

【怕死鬼】 pàsǐguǐ〈名〉 coward

【怕羞】 pàxiū〈动〉 be shy: 她～。 She is bashful.

【怕字当头】 pàzì-dāngtóu〈成〉 put fear before everything else: ～是办不成事的。 Endless fear won't get you anywhere.

P

pāi

拍 pāi

A〈动〉**1**（拍打） pat: ～掉身上的土 pat the dust off one's clothes ‖ ～球 bounce a ball ‖ ～桌子 slap the table ‖ 海浪～岸。The waves beat at the shore. ▸～手 **2**（摄影） take (a picture): ～电影 shoot a film ‖ ～照片 take a photo ‖ ～外景 shoot on location **3**（发出） wire: ～电报 send a telegram **4**（吹捧） flatter: ▸能吹会～ **B**〈名〉**1**（指球拍） bat: 网球～ tennis racket ‖ 羽毛球～ badminton racket **2**［音乐］ beat: 不合/合～ off/on beat ‖ 四分之四～ four-four time ▸～子

【拍案】pāi'àn〈动〉strike the table: ～称奇 pound the table and exclaim with admiration

【拍案而起】pāi'àn'érqǐ〈成〉pound the table and stand up in anger

【拍案叫绝】pāi'àn-jiàojué〈成〉bang one's fist on the table and shout with pleasure

【拍巴掌】pāi bāzhang〈动〉clap one's hands

【拍板】pāibǎn **A**〈动〉**1**（指用手） beat time **2**［经济］ rap the gavel: 拍卖～ knocked down ‖ ～成交 clinch a deal **3**〈喻〉（做决定） have the final say: 这件事由谁来～? Who has the final say in the matter? **B**〈名〉［音乐］ clappers

【拍打】pāida〈动〉**1**（击打） beat: ～衣服上的尘土 beat the dust off one's clothes ‖ 海浪轻轻～着海岸。Waves are gently lapping against the shore. **2**（扇动） flap: ～双翅 flap the wings

【拍档】pāidàng〈名〉〈方〉**1**（指关系） cooperation: 两位名演员在影片中～饰演主角。The two famous actors co-starred in the film. **2**（指人） partner: 最佳～ best partner

【拍发】pāifā〈动〉send: ～电报 send a telegram

【拍号】pāihào〈名〉［音乐］ time signature

【拍击】pāijī〈动〉[of waves] beat against: 浪花～着堤岸。The waves lapped on the bank.

【拍价】pāijià〈名〉auction price

【拍节器】pāijiéqì〈名〉［音乐］ metronome

【拍马】pāimǎ〈动〉flatter:（向某人）奉迎～ toady up to sb. ▸溜须～

【拍马屁】pāi mǎpì〈惯〉suck up (to sb.): 他擅长～。He is good at sucking up.

【拍卖】pāimài〈动〉**1**（指竞价） auction: 公开～ public auction **2**（指减价） sell off goods at reduced prices: 清仓～ clearance sale ‖ 削价～ Dutch auction

【拍卖槌】pāimàichuí〈名〉gavel

【拍卖行】pāimàiháng〈名〉auction house

【拍卖师】pāimàishī ▸**p. 966**〈名〉auctioneer

【拍品】pāipǐn〈名〉lot [goods at auction]

【拍摄】pāishè〈动〉take (a picture): ～电影 shoot a film ‖ ～照片 take a picture ‖ ～场地 set ‖ 到达～场地 arrive on set

【拍手】pāishǒu〈动〉clap: ～叫好 clap and shout 'bravo' ‖ ～赞成 clap one's hands in approval

【拍手称快】pāishǒu-chēngkuài〈成〉clap with joy

【拍拖】pāituō〈动〉〈方〉date: 他俩～已经几年了。They've been dating for several years.

【拍戏】pāixì〈动〉shoot a film

【拍胸脯】pāi xiōngpú〈惯〉〈口〉hand on heart: 你敢～，我就放心了。I'll not worry if you can vouch for it.

【拍照】pāizhào〈动〉take a picture: ～留念 take a photo to remember the occasion by

【拍纸簿】pāizhǐbù〈名〉note pad

【拍子】pāizi〈名〉**1**（指球拍） bat: 网球/羽毛球～ tennis/badminton racket ‖ 乒乓球～ table-tennis bat **2**［音乐］ beat: 打～ beat time

pái

俳 pái

A〈名〉〈旧〉farce **B**〈形〉〈书〉humorous: ▸～谐

【俳句】páijù〈名〉［语言］ haiku

【俳谐】páixié〈形〉〈书〉farcical: ～文 satire in ancient China

排¹ pái

A〈动〉**1**（按序放） put in order: ～名次 arrange the rankings ‖ ～座次 arrange the seating order ‖ ～成一行 form a line ▸～版, ～队, 论资～辈 **2**（排练） rehearse: ～节目 rehearse a show ▸彩～ **B**〈名〉**1**（行列） row: 站成一～ stand in a row ‖ 坐在前/后～座位上 take a seat in the front/back row **2**（指交通工具） raft: ▸木～, 竹～ **3**［军事］ platoon: ▸～长 **4**（排球） volleyball team: 女/男～ women's/men's volleyball team **C**〈量〉line: 一～房子 a row of houses ‖ 两～椅子 two lines of chairs

排² pái

〈动〉**1**（除去） eject: ～脓 secrete pus ‖ 下水道的污水～入海里。The sewers discharge out to sea. ▸～除, ～放, ～泄 **2**（推） push: 他生气地～门而出。He pushed the door open angrily and left. ▸～山倒海

▸pǎi

【排班】páibān〈动〉arrange the order of classes or shifts

【排版】páibǎn〈动〉［印刷］ typeset: 照相～ phototypesetting ‖ 自动～ automatic typesetting

【排比】páibǐ〈名〉［语言］ parallelism

【排笔】páibǐ〈名〉broad brush

【排便】páibiàn〈动〉［医学］ defecate

【排查】páichá〈动〉investigate people one by one within a given scope in order to crack a case

【排叉儿】páichàr〈名〉［食品］ crispy thin deep-fried biscuit

【排场】páichang **A**〈名〉ostentation and extravagance: 讲～ go in for ostentation and extravagance **B**〈形〉**1**（铺张） showy **2**（体面） dignified: 这个仪式既～，又省钱。The ceremony is both magnificent and economical.

【排斥】páichì〈动〉repel: ～异体器官 reject an alien organ ‖ 被～在外 be ostracized as an outsider

【排斥异己】páichì-yìjǐ〈成〉exclude those who hold different views

【排出】páichū〈动〉**1**（放出） discharge: ～废气 emit waste gas **2**（排列） arrange: 按比赛成绩～名次 organize the rankings according to the contestants' performance

【排除】páichú〈动〉get rid of: ～故障 fix a breakdown ‖ ～险情 defuse a potential danger ‖ ～障碍 smooth away obstacles ‖ ～万难 overcome all the difficulties ‖ 不～使用武力 not forswear the use of force

【排挡】páidǎng〈名〉gear: 前进/倒车～ forward/reverse gear ‖ 手动～ manual gear lever

【排档】páidàng〈名〉〈方〉stalls: 服装～ clothing stands ▸大～

【排灯】páidēng〈名〉bank light

【排毒】páidú〈动〉［医学］ eliminate toxicant

【排队】páiduì〈动〉queue (up): ～登机 queue up to check in ‖ ～买票 queue for tickets

【排筏】páifá〈名〉raft

【排放】páifàng〈动〉**1**（排出） discharge: ～污水 discharge waste water ‖ ～量 discharge amount ‖ ～标准 effluent standard **2**（指母兽） ovulate;（指公兽） ejaculate **3**（陈列） arrange in order: 货架上整齐地～着各种商品。A variety of commodities are displayed tidily on the shelf.

【排放权】páifàngquán〈名〉emission rights: 二氧化碳～额度分配 allocation of carbon dioxide emission quotas

【排风扇】páifēngshàn〈名〉ventilating fan

【排骨】páigǔ〈名〉spare ribs: ～汤 pork rib soup ‖ 红烧～ pork ribs braised in soy sauce ‖ 瘦得像～一样 be a bag of bones

【排灌】páiguàn〈动〉drain and irrigate: ～设备 irrigation and drainage equipment ‖ ～站 irrigation and drainage pumping station

【排汗】páihàn〈动〉perspire

【排行】páiháng〈名〉seniority among siblings: 他～第二。He is the second child of the family.

【排行榜】páihángbǎng〈名〉charts: 流行歌曲～ pop charts ‖ 最佳唱片～ top albums chart

【排号】páihào〈动〉**1**（按号排列） arrange in numerical order **2**〈方〉（排队） queue up

【排洪】páihóng〈动〉drain off floodwater: ～渠 drainage channel

【排华】páihuá〈动〉discriminate against the Chinese: ～势力 anti-Chinese force

【排挤】páijǐ〈动〉elbow out: 受到～ be excluded from ‖ 该公司已被～出数码相机市场。The company has been squeezed out of the digital camera market.

【排检】páijiǎn〈动〉categorize: 资料～ data indexing

【排解】páijiě〈动〉**1**（调解） mediate: ～纠纷 mediate a dispute **2**（排遣） distract one's mind from: ～愁闷 get rid of worries

【排涝】páilào〈动〉waterlogged fields: ～桥 relief bridge

【排雷】páiléi〈动〉［军事］ sweep mines

【排立】páilì〈动〉stand in line: 人群～在马路两边。The crowds lined the streets.

【排练】páiliàn〈动〉rehearse: ～节目 rehearse a show ‖ ～芭蕾舞剧 rehearse a ballet

【排列】páiliè〈动〉arrange: ～成纵队 form columns ‖ 按字母顺序～ arrange in alphabetical order

【排律】páilǜ〈名〉long regulated verse

【排卵】páiluǎn〈动〉［生理］ ovulate

【排名】páimíng〈动〉rank: ～第一 rank first ‖ ～从第五位降至第十位 drop from No 5 to No 10 in the standings

【排难解纷】páinàn-jiěfēn〈成〉settle a dispute

【排尿】páiniào〈动〉［医学］ urinate

【排偶】pái'ǒu〈名〉［语言］ parallelism and antithesis

【排炮】páipào〈名〉**1**（指炮火） (artillery) salvo **2**（指爆破） simultaneous

vollies

【排气】páiqì〈动〉［机械］ exhaust: ～管 exhaust pipe ‖ ～孔 vent ‖ ～扇 exhaust fan

【排遣】páiqiǎn〈动〉 find diversion from loneliness or boredom: ～思乡的郁闷 distract one's mind from homesickness

【排枪】páiqiāng〈名〉 fusillade

【排球】páiqiú ►**p. 909**〈名〉 volleyball: ～赛 volleyball match ‖ ～运动员 volleyball player ‖ 沙滩～ beach volleyball

【排山倒海】páishān-dǎohǎi〈成〉 with great power and influence: 以～之势 overwhelmingly

【排射】páishè〈名〉 volley of guns

【排笙】páishēng ►**p. 929**〈名〉［音乐］ wind instrument with a row of reed pipes and a keyboard

【排水】páishuǐ〈动〉 drain water: 开沟～ dig trenches to drain off water ‖ ～工程 drainage works

【排水沟】páishuǐgōu〈名〉 gutter

【排水管】páishuǐguǎn〈名〉 drainpipe: 疏通～ unblock a drain

【排水量】páishuǐliàng〈名〉 **1**（指船舶） displacement (tonnage): ～吨位 displacement tonnage ‖ 一艘～为两万吨的船 a ship with a displacement of 20,000 tons **2**（指河道、水渠） discharge capacity

【排他】páitā〈动〉 exclude others: ～性 exclusiveness

【排坛】páitán〈名〉 volleyball arena: ～健将 ace volleyball player

【排头】páitóu〈名〉 person at the head of a row: 站在～ stand at the head of the row ‖ 向～看齐。 Keep level with the leader.

【排头兵】páitóubīng〈名〉 **1**（指士兵） file leader **2**〈喻〉（带头人） pacesetter: 争当新时代的～。 Strive to be the pacesetter of the new age.

【排外】páiwài〈动〉 discriminate against foreign things: 盲目～ blindly oppose everything foreign ‖ ～心理 xenophobia ‖ ～政策 exclusion policy

【排外主义】páiwài zhǔyì〈名〉 exclusivism

【排尾】páiwěi〈名〉 last person in a row: 站在～ stand at the end of the row

【排污】páiwū〈动〉 dispose of pollutants: ～量 discharge capacity

【排污权】páiwūquán〈名〉 dumping right

【排戏】páixì〈动〉 rehearse a play

【排险】páixiǎn〈动〉 defuse a dangerous situation: ～抢修 eliminate dangers and do rush repairs

【排箫】páixiāo ►**p. 929**〈名〉［音乐］pan pipes

【排泄】páixiè〈动〉 **1**（指水） drain: ～不畅 drainage difficulty **2**（指代谢废物） excrete: ～粪便 excrete faeces and urine ‖ ～汗液 excrete sweat ‖ ～器官 excretory organ ‖ ～物 excrement

【排序】páixù〈动〉 sequence

【排揎】páixuan〈动〉〈方〉 scold: 别再～他了。 Stop telling him off.

【排烟】páiyān〈动〉 discharge fumes

【排演】páiyǎn〈动〉 rehearse: ～节目 rehearse a performance

【排椅】páiyǐ〈名〉 rows of seats

【排印】páiyìn〈动〉 typeset and print: 文稿已交付～。 The article is in the typesetting and printing stage.

【排忧解难】páiyōu-jiěnàn〈成〉 get rid of worries and help to overcome difficulties: 为人民群众～ relieve the populace of worries and help solve their problems

【排运】páiyùn〈名〉 rafting

【排长】páizhǎng〈名〉 platoon leader

【排阵】páizhèn〈动〉 arrange troops: ～布兵 strategically arrange troops

【排中律】páizhōnglǜ〈名〉［逻辑］ law of excluded middle

【排钟】páizhōng ►**p. 929**〈名〉［音乐］ chimes

【排字】páizì〈动〉 typeset: 计算机～ computer typesetting ‖ ～工人 typesetter

徘 pái

【徘徊】páihuái〈动〉 **1**（指走动） wander around: 他独自在江边～。 He wandered alone by the river. **2**〈喻〉（犹豫不决） hesitate: ～歧路 hesitate at the crossroads ‖ ～不前 hesitate to go forward ‖ ～观望 wait and see **3**〈喻〉（浮动） fluctuate: 产值在三百万元左右～。 The production value fluctuates at around 3 million *yuan*.

牌 pái〈名〉

1（板状物） board: 标语～ bulletin board ‖ 广告～ billboard ‖ 自行车～ number plate of a bike ►门～, 招～ **2**（品牌） make: 老～ time-honoured brand ‖ 这是什么～的电视机? What make of TV is it? ►冒～, 名～ **3**（娱乐品） cards, dominoes, mah-jong, etc.: 打～ play cards ‖ 扑克～ playing cards ►骨～, 王～, 洗～ **4**（盾牌） shield: ►挡箭～, 盾～ **5**（指词曲调子） score: ►词～, 曲～

【牌匾】páibiǎn〈名〉 plaque

【牌额】pái'é〈名〉 horizontal inscribed board

【牌坊】páifāng〈名〉［建筑］ memorial gateway: 功德～ arch of benevolent rule ‖ 贞节～ archway of chastity

【牌号】páihào〈名〉 **1**（店名） name of a shop: 这个商店换了～。 The shop has changed its name. **2**（品牌） brand: 货架上陈列着各种～的摄像机。 Video cameras of various different brands are displayed on the shelves.

【牌价】páijià〈名〉 **1**（指价格） list price: 零售～ listed retail price ‖ 批发～ set price for wholesale **2**（指兑换率） (market) quotation: 开盘～ opening quotations ‖ 外汇～ foreign exchange quotations

【牌九】páijiǔ〈名〉 *paijiu* [a kind of Chinese dominoes]: 推～ play *paijiu*

【牌局】páijú〈名〉 game of cards (dominoes, mah-jong): ～散了。 The game is over.

【牌楼】páilou〈名〉［建筑］ **1**（用于装饰） *pailou* [decorative archway] **2**（用于庆祝） temporary ceremonial gateway: 为庆祝新年，他们搭了座～。 They set up a gateway in celebration of New Year's Day.

【牌手】páishǒu〈名〉 poker player

【牌位】páiwèi〈名〉 memorial tablet: 祖宗～ ancestral memorial tablet

【牌照】páizhào〈名〉 licence plate: 吊销～ revoke a licence ‖ 汽车～ number plate of a car ‖ 营业～ business licence

【牌子】páizi〈名〉 **1**（板状物） plate;（标识） sign: 存车～ parking sign ‖ 广告～ advertising billboards **2**（品牌） brand: 努力打造～ work hard to publicize a new brand ‖ 老～产品 products of time-honoured reputation **3**（曲调） tune of *ci*（词）and *qu*（曲）

【牌子曲】páiziqǔ〈名〉［曲艺］ a kind of folk art form, involving singing of lyrics set to titled tunes, accompanied by simple instruments

pǎi

迫 pǎi

►pò

【迫击炮】pǎijīpào〈名〉 mortar: ～弹 trench mortar shell

排 pǎi〈动〉〈方〉

shape a shoe with a last: 这鞋穿着有点ル紧，得～一～。 The shoes are a little bit tight and need to be enlarged with lasts.

►pái

【排子车】pǎizichē〈名〉〈方〉 handcart

P

pài

哌 pài

【哌嗪】pàiqín〈名〉［化学］ piperazine

派 pài

A〈名〉 **1**（流派） school of thought;（派别） faction: 乐观～ optimists ‖ 反对～ the opposition ‖ 两～意见不合。 The two factions hold differing views. ►党～, 流～ **2**（作风） style: ►～头, 气～, 正～ **3**〈书〉（支流） tributary: 长江九～ nine tributaries of the Yangtze River **4**（指糕点） pie: 巧克力～ chocolate pie ‖ 苹果/草莓～ apple/strawberry pie

B〈量〉 **a**（用于景象、言语等） [used with the numeral to describe a scene, an atmosphere, a speech, a sound, etc.]: 一～胡言 sheer nonsense ‖ 好一～北国风光。 What beautiful northern scenery! **b**（用于派别） [used for political group, school of thought, art, etc.]: 各～政治力量 different political groups

C〈动〉 **1**（分配） send: ～工作 set sb. a task ‖ ～人送去。 Send someone to deliver it. ►分～ **2**（安排） apportion: ～款 impose levies **3**（指责） censure: 别～她的不是。 Don't put the blame on her. ►编～

【派别】pàibié〈名〉 sect: ～斗争 factional strife ‖ 政治～ political factions

【派差】pàichāi〈动〉 send sb. on a task or an errand

【派出所】pàichūsuǒ〈名〉 local police station

【派对】pàiduì〈名〉 party: 生日～ birthday party

【派发】pàifā〈动〉 distribute: ～商品广告 hand out promotional advertising material

【派饭】pàifàn **A**〈动〉 assign officials, teachers, etc. to board with village households **B**〈名〉 arranged meals in peasants' households for visiting officials, local teachers, etc.

【派购】pàigòu〈动〉 purchase by state quota

【派活儿】pàihuór〈动〉 assign work

【派立司】pàilìsī〈名〉［纺织］ palace

【派遣】pàiqiǎn〈动〉 dispatch: ～代表团 send a delegation ‖ ～两个连去前线 dispatch two companies to the front

【派遣国】pàiqiǎnguó〈名〉 accrediting state

【派生】pàishēng〈动〉 derive: 由此～的一系列问题 a series of problems derived therefrom ‖ 法语是由拉丁语～出来的。 French is a derivative of Latin.

【派生词】pàishēngcí〈名〉［语言］ derivative

【派送】pàisòng〈动〉 distribute: 向顾客～小礼品 hand out small gifts to customers
【派头】pàitóu〈名〉 style: 讲～ have a penchant for style ‖ ～不小 put on quite a show ‖ 他很有教授的～。He has the air of a professor.
【派位】pàiwèi〈动〉 allocate seats: 电脑～ random allocation of (school) places by computer
【派系】pàixì〈名〉 factions: ～斗争 factional strife ‖ 学术～ academic clique
【派销】pàixiāo〈动〉 promote the sale by mandatory or compulsory means
【派性】pàixìng〈名〉 factionalism: 闹～ engage in factionalist activities ‖ 消除～ eliminate factionalism
【派用场】pài yòngchǎng〈动〉〈口〉 put to use: 留下它，说不定将来会派上用场。Don't throw it away. It might come in handy some day.
【派驻】pàizhù〈动〉 post: ～军队 station troops ‖ ～巴黎的路透社记者 Reuters correspondent in Paris

湃 pài ▸澎湃 péngpài

pān

潘 Pān〈名〉 Pan [surname]

攀 pān〈动〉 1（往上爬） climb: ～树 climb a tree ‖ ～着窗台往上爬 climb up by holding on to the window sill ▸～登, ～缘, 高不可～ 2（攀附） seek connections in high places: 人家有钱有势，我怎么能～得上! He is both rich and influential. How can I hope to befriend him! ▸～龙附凤, ～亲 3（牵扯） involve: 这是你自己的事，别总是～着我。This is your business. Stop trying to rope me in. ▸～扯, ～谈
【攀比】pānbǐ〈动〉 try to keep up with the Joneses: 互相～ strive to keep up with each other ‖ 盲目～ blindly vie with those who are better off than oneself
【攀扯】pānchě〈动〉 involve: 这件事和他没关系，你别～他。This has nothing to do with him, so do not try to bring him into it.
【攀登】pāndēng〈动〉 climb: ～悬崖 ascend a cliff ‖〈喻〉～科学高峰 scale new heights in science
【攀附】pānfù〈动〉 1（指位置） climb against: ～树木的藤蔓 vines climbing trees 2（指关系） play up to influential people: ～权贵 seek connections with the rich and powerful
【攀高】pāngāo〈动〉 1（攀升） climb up to a higher place 2〈方〉（高攀） befriend sb. with a higher social position 3（攀比） try to keep up with the Joneses: ～心理 a keeping up with the Joneses mentality
【攀高枝儿】pān gāozhīr〈惯〉= 攀高 pāngāo 2
【攀龙附凤】pānlóng-fùfèng〈成〉 play up to people of power and influence
【攀爬】pānpá〈动〉 hold onto sth. and climb
【攀亲】pānqīn〈动〉 1（指拉关系） claim kinship: ～道故 claim to be sb.'s relative or friend 2（订婚） arrange a match: 给儿子攀了一门亲 arrange a match for one's son
【攀禽】pānqín〈名〉［鸟类］ bird adapted for climbing
【攀绕】pānrào〈动〉 spiral upwards
【攀升】pānshēng〈动〉climb: 汽车销量逐年～。Car sales are increasing year by year.
【攀谈】pāntán〈动〉 engage in small talk: 他俩～起来，十分投机。They struck up a very agreeable conversation.
【攀诬】pānwū〈动〉frame a case against sb.: ～好人 frame a case against an innocent man
【攀岩】pānyán〈名〉［体育］rock climbing
【攀援】pānyuán = 攀缘 pānyuán
【攀缘】pānyuán〈动〉 1（指动植物） climb: 常春藤沿墙～生长。Ivy climbs the wall. ‖ 猴子善于～。Monkeys climb well. 2〈喻〉（指人） climb the social ladder through one's connections: 找不到工作，也没有人可以～ find neither a job nor someone to lend a hand
【攀越】pānyuè〈动〉 climb over: ～隔离墙 scale a dividing wall
【攀折】pānzhé〈动〉 pull down and break off: 请勿～。Please don't pick the flowers or break off the branches.
【攀枝花】pānzhīhuā〈名〉［植物］Bombax

pán

爿 pán〈方〉
A〈名〉 strip of split bamboo or chopped wood: 竹～ split bamboo
B〈量〉 1（指田地） [used for land, equal to 片]: 一～地 a plot 2（指店、厂房） [used for shops, factories, etc., equal to 家]: 一～店 a shop ‖ 一～厂 a factory

胖 pán〈形〉〈书〉 easy and comfortable: ▸心广体～
▸pàng

盘（盤） pán
A〈名〉 1（盘子） plate: 瓷/木/塑料～ china/wooden/plastic dishes ▸茶～, 托～ 2（盘状物） sth. in the shape of a plate: ▸磨～, 棋～ 3（指行情） market price: ▸开～, 收～ 4（领地） domain: ▸地～
B〈量〉 1（用于回旋地绕的东西） reel: 两～电影拷贝 two reels of film ‖ 一～蚊香 a mosquito coil 2（用于盘状物） [used for dishes, millstones, etc.]: 两～磁带 two spools of tape ‖ 一～石磨 a pair of millstones 3［体育］ game: 下～棋 play a game of chess ‖ 以8比6赢了第三～ win the third set 8-6
C〈动〉 1（绕） twist: ～头发 coil up one's hair ‖ 把发辫～在头上 twist braids of hair on top of the head ▸～腿, ～绕, ～山 2（垒） build: ～炕/灶 build a *kang* / cooking stove 3（盘点） check: 一年应～一次账。The accounts should be checked annually. ▸～点, ～问 4（转让） transfer the ownership of: 把铺子～给人家 transfer the ownership of the store to another person ‖ 他把店～给了我。He has transferred the shop to me. 5（运送） transport: 由仓库向外～货 carry things out of the warehouse
【盘剥】pánbō〈动〉 exploit: 重利～ exploit by practising usury
【盘查】pánchá〈动〉 interrogate and examine: ～过路人 interrogate passers-by ‖ 受到～ be interrogated
【盘缠】pánchan〈名〉〈旧〉 travelling expenses: 出门要多带～。Make sure that you take enough money with you when you go travelling.
【盘秤】pánchèng〈名〉steelyard with a pan
【盘存】páncún〈动〉 take stock (of): ～国有资产 take an inventory of state assets ‖ 商品～ merchandise inventory
【盘错】páncuò〈动〉〈书〉 intertwine: 枝桠～ intertwined twigs and branches ‖〈喻〉问题～难解。The problem is complicated and difficult to solve.
【盘道】pándào〈名〉 winding path
【盘点】pándiǎn〈动〉 take stock (of): ～库存 take stock in the warehouse ‖ 今日～，明日照常营业。Stocktaking today. Business as usual tomorrow.
【盘店】pándiàn〈动〉 transfer a business
【盘跌】pándiē〈动〉［金融］fall slowly: 股价大幅～。Stock prices are falling sharply.
【盘费】pánfei〈名〉〈旧〉 money needed on a journey
【盘杠子】pán gàngzi〈动〉〈口〉 perform on a horizontal bar
【盘根错节】pángēn-cuòjié〈成〉 1（指树） interwoven roots and stems: 那棵老树～。The old tree has twisted roots and gnarled branches. 2〈喻〉（表复杂） intricate: 这个案子～。This case is complex.
【盘根问底】pángēn-wèndǐ〈成〉 get to the bottom of things: 凡事她总要～。She wants to know all the whys and wherefores of everything.
【盘亘】pángèn〈动〉〈书〉 [of mountains] link up with one another: 峰峦～。The mountain ridges and peaks link up with one another.
【盘古】Pángǔ ▸**p. 274**〈名〉 *Pan Gu* [creator of universe in Chinese mythology]: 自从～开天地 since the beginning of time

> **盘古**
> In Chinese mythology, Pan Gu was the god who created the world. Heaven and earth were originally formless and indistinct, like an egg, with Pan Gu living in the middle. After 18,000 years, heaven and earth split (another version has it that Pan Gu split them with a huge axe). The light part, resembling egg white, rose up and became heaven. The heavy part, resembling egg yolk, sank down and became the earth. Each day heaven increased in height, and so did Pan Gu. After his death, the parts of his body became the sun, moon and stars, rivers and mountains, minerals and stone, and grass and forests.

【盘桓】pánhuán〈动〉〈书〉 1（逗留） linger: 在校门口～ linger around the school gate ‖ 他在北海道～了几天，游览了各处名胜。He stayed at Hokkaido for a few days and visited the famous places of interest there. 2（旋绕） wind round and round: 在耳际/脑际～ linger in one's mind
【盘簧】pánhuáng〈名〉［机械］ coil spring
【盘活】pánhuó〈动〉 adopt measures to revitalize assets or capital funds to bring economic returns: ～资金 revitalize capital funds
【盘货】pánhuò〈动〉 take stock: 今日～，暂停营业。Closed for stocktaking today.
【盘诘】pánjié〈动〉 cross-examine: 戒严期间，进城的人都被严加～。During the curfew, all those coming to the city were cross-examined closely.
【盘结】pánjié〈动〉 coil and twine: 葛藤～ twining vines
【盘究】pánjiū〈动〉 cross-examine and investigate
【盘踞】pánjù〈动〉 forcibly occupy: 一股海盗～小岛。A gang of pirates were

entrenched on the small island.

【盘口】pánkǒu〈名〉**1**［金融］trading tendency on the stock exchange: 从～看，成交量在不断萎缩。Looking at the fluctuations in price, the volume of trade is continually shrinking. **2**（指博彩）active odds

【盘库】pánkù〈动〉make an inventory of goods in stock

【盘轮】pánlún〈名〉disk wheel

【盘马弯弓】pánmǎ-wāngōng〈成〉〈喻〉assume a militant posture but take no immediate action

【盘面】pánmiàn〈名〉［金融］market situation of stock, futures, etc. at a given point or during a given period of time

【盘尼西林】pánníxīlín〈名〉［药学］penicillin

【盘弄】pánnòng〈动〉fondle

【盘曲】pánqū〈形〉〈书〉winding: 山路～ zigzagging path up the hill ‖ ～的溪流 winding brook

【盘儿菜】pánrcài〈名〉ready-to-cook dishes

【盘绕】pánrào〈动〉coil: 长长的藤葛～在树干上。The long vines coil around the tree.

【盘山】pánshān〈动〉wind up a mountain: ～公路 winding road up the mountain ‖ 汽车～而上。The car wound its way up the mountain.

【盘升】pánshēng〈动〉［金融］rise slowly: 近期股市呈～走势。Recently the stock market has been picking up.

【盘式】pánshì〈形〉disc-type: ～磁带录像机 reel videotape recorder

【盘算】pánsuan〈动〉calculate: 他～着怎样搞到这笔钱。He was deliberating on how to procure the money.

【盘梯】pántī〈名〉spiral staircase

【盘条】pántiáo〈名〉［冶金］wire rod

【盘头】pántóu〈名〉hair worn in a bun: 留着～ wear one's hair in a bun

【盘腿】pántuǐ〈动〉cross one's legs: ～而坐 sit cross-legged

【盘陀】pántuó〈形〉〈书〉**1**（指不平）uneven: ～石 rough stone **2**（指曲折）zigzag: ～路 zigzag road

【盘问】pánwèn〈动〉cross-examine: ～犯人 interrogate a criminal ‖ 经再三～，他才说出实情。He told the truth only after repeated close questioning.

【盘膝】pánxī〈动〉cross one's legs at the ankles: ～而坐 sit cross-legged

【盘香】pánxiāng〈名〉incense coil

【盘旋】pánxuán〈动〉**1**（环绕）circle: 飞机在天空～。The plane circled in the air. ‖ 山路曲折，游人～而上。The tourists went up the winding mountain road. **2**（逗留）linger: 他在花房里～了半天才离开。He lingered in the greenhouse for quite some time before he left.

【盘羊】pányáng〈名〉［动物］argali

【盘运】pányùn〈动〉carry

【盘账】pánzhàng〈动〉audit accounts

【盘整】pánzhěng〈动〉**1**［金融］make slow, small adjustments in a given scope **2**（整顿）consolidate

【盘子】pánzi〈名〉**1**（指器具）plate: 塑料～ plastic plate **2**（指行情）market rate **3**〈喻〉（指规模、范围）overall size: 年度消费～过大。Annual consumption has been excessive.

槃 pán〈书〉= 盘 pán A1

磐 pán〈名〉〈书〉monolith

【磐石】pánshí〈名〉huge rock: 坚如～ as solid as a rock

蹒 pán

【蹒跚】pánshān〈形〉staggering: 步履～ stagger ‖ 老人拄着拐棍～而行。The old man hobbled along with the aid of a stick.

蟠 pán〈动〉curl

【蟠桃】pántáo〈名〉**1**（指水果）flat peach **2**（指仙桃）legendary peach of immortality

pàn

判 pàn

A〈动〉**1**（区别）distinguish: ▸～别，～断，～明 **2**（判断）judge: ～卷子 mark examination papers ▸裁～，评～ **3**（判决）sentence: 法庭～我们胜诉。The court has decided in our favour. ‖ 他因抢劫罪被～5年。He was sentenced to five years for robbery. ▸～案，审～

B〈形〉obvious: ▸～若两人

【判案】pàn'àn〈动〉decide a case: 秉公～ decide a case impartially

【判别】pànbié〈动〉distinguish: ～真伪 distinguish truth from falsehood ‖ 提高～能力 improve one's powers of discrimination

【判处】pànchǔ〈动〉sentence: ～死刑 sentence sb. to death ‖ 被～终身监禁 be sentenced to life imprisonment

【判词】pàncí〈名〉**1**〈旧〉［法律］verdict: 司法～ judicial dictum **2**（结论）conclusion: 模棱两可的～ equivocal conclusion

【判定】pàndìng〈动〉decide: ～谁是谁非 decide which of them is in the wrong ‖ 我们无法～他是否有罪。We cannot judge whether he is guilty.

【判读】pàndú〈动〉interpret: ～卫星照片 interpret satellite photographs

【判断】pànduàn **A**〈名〉［逻辑］judgement **B**〈动〉judge: 做出～ pass judgement on ‖ 你～得正确。You made the right judgement. ‖ 根据这些线索～，案犯是晚上作的案。Judging from these clues, the criminal must have committed the crime at night.

【判断力】pànduànlì〈名〉judgement

【判罚】pànfá〈动〉penalize: 运动员在禁区犯规，～点球。Violation in the penalty area will result in a penalty kick.

【判分】pànfēn〈动〉mark: 给试卷～ grade the papers

【判官】pànguān〈名〉**1**［历史］assistant to the chief local magistrate [in the Tang and Song dynasties] **2** ▸**p. 274**（指神话）judge in hell

【判决】pànjué **A**〈动〉［法律］pronounce (judgement): ～有罪/无罪 pronounce sb. guilty/innocent ‖ 不服～ refuse to accept the verdict ‖ 终审～ final judgement ▸～书 **B**〈名〉［体育］decision: 运动员要服从裁判的～。Sportsmen should respect the decision of the referee.

【判决书】pànjuéshū〈名〉［法律］court verdict: 宣读～ announce the verdict

【判例】pànlì〈名〉［法律］legal precedent: 国际法～ cases in international law

【判明】pànmíng〈动〉clearly distinguish: ～是非 distinguish between right and wrong ‖ ～真伪 ascertain whether sth. is genuine

【判若鸿沟】pànruòhónggōu〈成〉be worlds apart: 两党的界限～。The difference between the two parties is irreconcilable.

【判若两人】pànruòliǎngrén〈成〉be no longer one's former self: 他前后～。He is different from how he used to be.

【判若云泥】pànruòyúnní〈成〉be poles apart

【判刑】pànxíng〈动〉sentence: 量罪～ sentence in accordance with the crime committed

【判罪】pànzuì〈动〉declare sb. guilty: 量刑～ pass judgement and mete out punishment compatible with the crime

拚 pàn〈动〉give up: ～命 risk one's life

泮 pàn

【泮宫】pàngōng〈名〉〈古〉government school

盼 pàn〈动〉**1**（期待）look forward to: 孩子～过年。Children always look forward to the New Year. ‖ ～尽早函复。I am looking forward to a reply at your earliest convenience. ▸～望，期～ **2**（看）look: ▸左顾右～

【盼念】pànniàn〈动〉look forward to seeing: 妻子日夜～着远在非洲工作的丈夫。The wife longed day and night to see her husband who worked far away in Africa.

【盼头】pàntou〈名〉〈口〉hope: 这事情现在有～了。There is hope in this matter now.

【盼望】pànwàng〈动〉look forward to: ～与亲人团聚 long for a reunion with one's relatives ‖ ～已久的来信 long-awaited letter

【盼星星盼月亮】pànxīngxing-pànyuèliang〈俗〉long for sth. day and night

叛 pàn〈动〉betray: ～贼 traitor ▸背～，众～亲离

【叛变】pànbiàn〈动〉betray: ～投敌 defect to the enemy

【叛党】pàndǎng〈动〉turn traitor to one's party: ～分子 traitor to one's party

【叛匪】pànfěi〈名〉bandit rebels

【叛国】pànguó〈动〉betray one's country: ～投敌 betray one's country and defect to the enemy ‖ ～罪 high treason

【叛军】pànjūn〈名〉rebel forces

【叛离】pànlí〈动〉betray: ～祖国 turn traitor to and desert one's country

【叛乱】pànluàn〈名〉revolt: 发动～ stage a rebellion ‖ 武装～ armed rebellion ‖ ～分子 rebel

【叛卖】pànmài〈动〉betray: ～革命/民族利益 betray the revolution/national interests

【叛逆】pànnì **A**〈动〉rebel against: ～行为/性格 rebellious behaviour/character **B**〈名〉rebel: 封建礼教的～ rebel against feudal ethics

【叛逃】pàntáo〈动〉defect: 集体～ wholesale defection

【叛徒】pàntú〈名〉traitor: 革命事业的～ traitor to the revolutionary cause

畔 pàn〈名〉**1**（旁边）side: 河～ river bank ‖ 湖～ shore of a lake ‖ 路～ roadside ‖ 他的话仍然萦绕在我耳～。His words still rang in my ears. **2**（边界）border of a field: 田～ border of a field

袢 pàn ▸袷袢 qiāpàn

P

襻 pàn

A〈名〉**1**（用于扣纽扣）button loop: ▸纽～ **2**（襻状物）loop-like thing: 车～ strap of a handcart ‖ 鞋～儿 shoe strap
B〈动〉fasten with a rope: ～上几针 sew it up a bit

pāng

乓 pāng

〈拟〉bang: ～的一声关上窗子 bang the window shut ‖ 热水瓶～的一声炸了。'Bang!' the Thermos burst. ‖ 他～的一声打开了香槟瓶盖。He opened the bottle of champagne with a loud pop.

滂 pāng

〈形〉〈书〉**1**（水势浩大）great **2**（喷涌而出）gushing

【滂湃】pāngpài〈形〉roaring and rushing
【滂沛】pāngpèi〈形〉〈书〉pouring
【滂沱】pāngtuó〈形〉pouring: 大雨～ torrential rain

膀 pāng

〈形〉〈方〉swollen: 他的肾病不轻，腿都～了。He had serious kidney trouble and his legs were swollen.
▸bǎng, bàng, páng

páng

彷 páng

【彷徨】pánghuáng〈动〉pace up and down: ～不定 be wavering ‖ 他在门口～。He paced up and down at the entrance.
【彷徨歧途】pánghuáng-qítú〈成〉hesitate at the crossroads

庞[1]（龎）páng

〈形〉**1**（大）colossal: ▸～然大物 **2**（多而杂乱）numerous and disorderly: ▸～杂

庞[2]（龎）páng

〈名〉face: ▸脸～, 面～

【庞大】pángdà〈形〉colossal: ～的工程 mammoth project ‖ 机构～ unwieldy organization ‖ ～的开支 enormous expenditure
【庞然大物】pángrán-dàwù〈成〉giant: 敌人看上去是个～，其实不堪一击。The enemy looks like a huge monster but in fact it will collapse at a single blow.
【庞杂】pángzá〈形〉enormous and disorderly: 机构～ cumbersome administrative structure ‖ 内容～ multifarious and disorderly contents

逄 Páng

〈名〉Pang [surname]

旁 páng

A〈名〉**1**（旁边）side: 路～ roadside ‖ 小河～ riverside ‖ 街道两～栽满了树。The street is lined with trees on both sides. ▸～边, ～门, ～听 **2**（偏旁）lateral radical (of a Chinese character): ▸偏～
B〈代〉other: 教室里除了几个学生再没有～的人了。There's nobody in the classroom aside from a few students. ‖ 他有～的事先走了。He left because he had some other business to attend to. ▸～人, ～证
C〈形〉extensive: ▸～征博引

【旁白】pángbái〈名〉aside: ～人物 chorus member ‖ 剧中的～很精彩。The play's asides were superb.
【旁边】pángbiān〈名〉side: 坐在某人～ sit at sb.'s side
【旁出】pángchū〈动〉branch off: 其枝～。Its twigs branch out.
【旁道】pángdào〈名〉bypass
【旁顾】pánggù〈动〉attend to other things: 无暇～ have no time to attend to other things
【旁观】pángguān〈动〉look on: 冷眼～ look on coldly
【旁观者清】pángguānzhěqīng〈成〉the spectator sees most of the game
【旁及】pángjí〈动〉〈书〉take up: 主攻历史，～文学 major in history but have a sideline interest in literature
【旁路】pánglù〈名〉bypass
【旁落】pángluò〈动〉lose: 大权～ lose one's powers to others
【旁门】pángmén〈名〉side door: 他是从～进去的。He entered from the side door.
【旁门左道】pángmén-zuǒdào = 左道旁门 zuǒdào-pángmén
【旁敲侧击】pángqiāo-cèjī〈成〉attack by innuendo: 有话直说，不必～。If you have something to say, then tell it straight. Don't beat about the bush.
【旁人】pángrén〈名〉other people: 这件事最好不要叫～知道。Better keep it among ourselves.
【旁若无人】pángruòwúrén〈成〉have no regard for the presence of other people: 他高谈阔论，～。He talked volubly and loudly without due respect for people around.
【旁听】pángtīng〈动〉**1**（指参加会议）act as observer: 法庭～者 visitor attending a court trial **2**（指听课）audit: ～生 auditor student ‖ 他在北京大学～过课。He once audited classes at Peking University.
【旁通】pángtōng〈动〉〈书〉gain an understanding of the subject through mastery of other relevant subjects: ▸触类～
【旁骛】pángwù〈形〉〈书〉inattentive: 他潜心钻研，从不～。He devotes himself to his research and is never distracted.
【旁系亲属】pángxì qīnshǔ〈名〉［法律］collateral relative
【旁征博引】pángzhēng-bóyǐn〈成〉quote extensively
【旁证】pángzhèng〈名〉［法律］circumstantial evidence
【旁支】pángzhī〈名〉offset

膀 páng

▸bǎng, bàng, pāng

【膀胱】pángguāng〈名〉bladder: ～结石 bladder calculi

磅 páng

▸bàng

【磅礴】pángbó **A**〈形〉boundless: 气势～ be of great momentum **B**〈动〉permeate: ～宇内。Tremendous momentum fills the universe.

螃 páng

【螃蟹】pángxiè〈名〉crab

鳑（鰟）páng

【鳑鲏】pángpí〈名〉［鱼类］bitterling

pǎng

耪 pǎng

〈动〉hoe: ～地 hoe the field ‖ ～玉米 hoe maize

pàng

胖 pàng

〈形〉fat: ～小子 chubby baby boy ‖ 他越来越～了。He is putting on weight. ▸～子, 发～
▸pán

【胖大海】pàngdàhǎi〈名〉［中药］sterculia seed
【胖墩墩】pàngdūndūn〈形〉〈口〉pudgy
【胖墩儿】pàngdūnr〈名〉〈口〉chubby child
【胖鼓鼓】pànggǔgǔ〈形〉plump
【胖乎乎】pànghūhū〈形〉plump: ～的脸蛋 chubby cheeks
【胖头鱼】pàngtóuyú〈名〉bighead carp
【胖子】pàngzi〈名〉fatty

pāo

抛 pāo

〈动〉**1**（向上扔）cast: ～球/硬币 toss a ball/coin ‖ 把忧虑～到脑后 cast one's cares away ‖ 不许乱～杂物! No littering! ▸～锚, ～物线, ～砖引玉 **2**（离弃）abandon: ～妻别子 desert one's wife and children ‖ 把别人远远～在后面 leave others far behind ‖ ～到九霄云外 put entirely out of one's mind ▸～弃 **3**（暴露）show: ▸～头露面 **4**（抛售）sell in large quantities and/or at low prices: ～出股票 sell stocks in large quantities and/or at low prices ▸～售

【抛费】pāofèi〈动〉waste
【抛光】pāoguāng〈动〉polish: 这枚戒指需要～一下。The ring needs polishing.
【抛荒】pāohuāng〈动〉**1**（指耕地）lie waste: 这块地～了。The plot lay waste. **2**（指学业）be neglected;（指技艺）get rusty: 我的打字技术～了。My typing has got rusty.
【抛货】pāohuò〈动〉dump goods on the market
【抛锚】pāomáo〈动〉**1**（指船）drop anchor: ～停泊 lie at anchor **2**（指车辆）break down: 警车在十字路口～了。The police car broke down at the crossroads. **3**〈喻〉（因故中止）be suspended: 搜寻工作中途～了。The search was abandoned midway.
【抛盘】pāopán〈动〉［金融］sell out stocks, futures, etc.
【抛弃】pāoqì〈动〉abandon: ～家园 abandon one's home ‖ 被社会所～ be cast aside by society ‖ 就在她最需要朋友的时候，他们却～了她。Her friends failed her when she most needed them.
【抛却】pāoquè〈动〉abandon: ～幻想 discard fanciful ideas
【抛洒】pāosǎ〈动〉**1**（指液体）shed: ～热血 shed one's blood **2**（指固体）scatter: 把沙石～在路面上。Scatter the road with gravel.
【抛撒】pāosǎ〈动〉scatter: ～传单 distribute leaflets
【抛舍】pāoshě〈动〉abandon: ～妻儿 abandon one's wife and children
【抛射】pāoshè〈动〉project
【抛售】pāoshòu〈动〉dump: ～劣质货物 dump shoddy goods

【抛售风】pāoshòufēng〈名〉 heavy selling
【抛头颅，洒热血】pāo tóulú, sǎ rèxuè〈成〉 shed one's blood and lay down one's life for: 为祖国的利益～ sacrifice oneself for the interests of the country
【抛头露面】pāotóu-lùmiàn〈成〉**1**（指女子） come out in public **2**（公开露面） parade oneself in public: 从不～ never make public appearances
【抛物面】pāowùmiàn〈名〉［数学］ paraboloid: 旋转～ paraboloid of revolution
【抛物线】pāowùxiàn〈名〉［数学］ parabola: ～轨迹 parabolic trajectory
【抛压】pāoyā〈名〉［金融］ share sale pressure: 出现～后股指迅速下挫。 Facing to the pressure to sell shares, the stock index dropped fast.
【抛掷】pāozhì〈动〉 cast: ～雪球 throw snow-balls ‖ 莫把年华轻～。 Do not squander away your youth.
【抛砖引玉】pāozhuān-yǐnyù〈成〉〈谦〉〈喻〉 make some introductory remarks to set the ball rolling: 我来说几句，算是～吧。 Let me say a few words, just to set the ball rolling.

泡[1] pāo〈名〉 puffy and soft thing: 豆～儿 puffy beans ‖ 肿眼～儿 puffy eyelids

泡[2] pāo〈名〉〈方〉 small lake: 月亮～ Moon Lake ‖ 莲花～ Lotus Lake

泡[3] pāo〈量〉〈口〉 [used for the number of excretions, slightly vulgar]: 拉一～屎 have a shit ‖ 撒一～尿 piss
▸pào
【泡桐】pāotóng〈名〉［植物］ paulownia
【泡子】pāozi〈名〉〈方〉 small lake

脬 pāo
A〈名〉（膀胱） bladder
B = 泡[3] pāo

páo

刨 páo〈动〉**1**（挖） dig: ～坑 dig a hole ‖ ～马铃薯 dig (up) potatoes ‖ ～土 dig earth **2**（除去） exclude: ～去个人所得税，你月收入是4,250元。 With personal income tax deducted, your monthly income is 4,250 *yuan*.
▸bào
【刨除】páochú〈动〉 deduct
【刨分】páofēn〈名〉 deduct marks: 这道题刨了他10分。 Ten marks were deducted for his wrong answer to this question.
【刨根儿】páogēnr〈动〉〈喻〉 get to the bottom of a matter
【刨根问底】páogēn-wèndǐ〈成〉 get to the bottom of a matter: 他这个人就爱～。 He's never satisfied until he gets to the bottom of things.

咆 páo〈动〉 roar: ▸～哮
【咆哮】páoxiào〈动〉**1**（指动物） roar: 狮子在～。 The lion was roaring. **2**（指人） bellow: ～着警告 growl out a warning **3**（指风、水） roar on: ～的黄河 roaring Yellow River

狍（麅） páo
【狍子】páozi〈名〉［动物］ roe deer

庖 páo〈名〉〈书〉**1**（厨房） kitchen: ▸～厨 **2**（厨师） cook: 名～ famous chef ▸越俎代～
【庖厨】páochú〈名〉〈旧〉**1**（厨房） kitchen **2**（厨师） chef
【庖代】páodài〈动〉〈书〉 interfere with others' affairs
【庖丁解牛】páodīng-jiěniú〈成〉〈喻〉 do sth. with great ease

炮 páo〈动〉［中医］ prepare herbal Chinese medicine by roasting or parching it in a pan: ～姜 roasted ginger ▸～炼
▸bāo, pào
【炮炼】páoliàn〈动〉［中医］ parch and refine medical herbs
【炮烙】páoluò〈名〉 hot bronze pillar torture
【炮制】páozhì〈动〉**1**［中医］ prepare medical herbs by parching, roasting, baking, steaming, soaking, simmering, etc. **2**〈贬〉（编造） cook up: ～反动纲领 concoct a reactionary programme ▸如法～

袍 páo〈名〉 robe: 棉～ cotton gown ‖ 皮～ fur-lined robe ▸旗～
【袍泽】páozé〈名〉〈书〉 fellow officers: ～之谊 friendship among fellow officers
【袍子】páozi〈名〉 robe

匏 páo
【匏瓜】páoguā〈名〉［植物］ gourd

跑 páo〈动〉 paw: ～地 paw at the ground
▸pǎo

pǎo

跑 pǎo〈动〉**1**（快速行进） run: ～得快 run fast ‖ ～三圈儿 run three laps around the track ‖ ～完全程 finish the whole distance ▸～步，赛～ **2**（逃） run away: 别让兔子～了。 Don't let the rabbit run away. ‖ 他趁着夜色～了。 He fled by night. ▸逃～ **3**〈方〉（去往） go to: ～遍全国 travel all over the country ‖ 一天～了几个地方 have been to several places within the space of one day ‖ 我～了几条街道才找到这个商店。 I walked about several blocks before I found that shop. **4**（为某事奔走） run errands: ～材料 rush about collecting data ‖ 他现在给一家小报～新闻。 He is running around snooping out stories for a tabloid. ▸～单帮，～买卖 **5**（泄漏、移位） leak: ～电/气/油 electricity/gas/oil leakage ‖ 信纸叫风刮～了。 The writing paper was blown away by the wind. **6**（挥发） evaporate, give off: 瓶子没盖严，汽油都～了。 The bottle was not tightly sealed so the gas all escaped.
▸páo
【跑表】pǎobiǎo〈名〉［体育］ stopwatch
【跑步】pǎobù〈动〉**1**（快速行进） march at the double: ～前进! Double time! ‖ ～走! At the double, quick march! **2**（慢跑） jog: ～机 jogging machine ‖ 我每天早晨在公园里～。 I go jogging in the park every morning.
【跑车】pǎochē **A**〈名〉**1**（赛车）（指汽车） racing car;（指自行车） bicycle **2**（用于运木材） timber-transporting vehicle in forest zones **B**〈动〉〈口〉（随车工作） work on public transport
【跑单帮】pǎo dānbāng〈动〉〈旧〉 travel long distances on one's own doing retail business: ～的 travelling trader
【跑刀】pǎodāo〈名〉［体育］ racing skates
【跑道】pǎodào〈名〉**1**［航空］ runway: ～指示灯 runway light ‖ 飞机～ landing strip **2**［体育］ track: 塑胶～ plastic track ‖ 他跑第三～。 He is running in lane three. **3**（赛车道） raceway **4**（赛狗或赛马） race track: 赛马～ race course
【跑电】pǎodiàn〈动〉〈口〉 [of electricity] leak
【跑调儿】pǎodiàor〈动〉 be out of tune: 她有些地方唱得明显～了。 She sang distinctly out of tune in places.
【跑肚】pǎodù〈动〉〈口〉 have diarrhoea
【跑官要官】pǎoguān-yàoguān〈动〉 seek to obtain office by gaining influence from officials: 严肃查处～的不正之风 seriously investigate the bad practice of using one's influence to obtain office
【跑光】pǎoguāng〈动〉［摄影］ get accidentally exposed to light: 这卷胶卷～了。 This roll of film has been exposed to light.
【跑旱船】pǎo hànchuán〈名〉 boat dance
【跑江湖】pǎo jiānghú〈惯〉 roam the country making one's living as one goes
【跑街】pǎojiē〈方〉**A**〈动〉 go around in a city working as a business agent for a firm **B**〈名〉 roving business agent or salesman
【跑了和尚跑不了庙】pǎole héshang pǎobuliǎo miào〈俗〉〈喻〉 you can run away but the home you leave behind is never going anywhere
【跑垒】pǎolěi〈名〉［体育］ base-running
【跑龙套】pǎo lóngtào〈动〉**1**［戏曲］ have a walk-on part: 刚开始我跑跑龙套，后来我演上了主角。 I started as a walk-on, and later played principal roles. **2**〈喻〉（做杂事） play a minor role: 我只是个～的，不拿事儿。 My job is to run errands, not to make decisions.
【跑马】pǎomǎ〈动〉**1**（指骑马） ride a horse **2**〈旧〉（指赛马） horse racing: ～场 race course
【跑码头】pǎo mǎtou〈动〉 be a travelling merchant
【跑买卖】pǎo mǎimai〈动〉 travel around doing business
【跑跑颠颠】pǎopǎo-diāndiān〈动〉 bustle about: 他一天到晚～，为社区服务。 He bustles about day and night, performing services for the community.
【跑坡】pǎopō〈动〉 slip down a (mountain) slope
【跑生意】pǎo shēngyi = 跑买卖 pǎo mǎimai
【跑堂】pǎotáng **A**〈动〉〈旧〉 work as a waiter **B** = 跑堂儿的 pǎotángrde
【跑堂儿的】pǎotángrde〈名〉〈旧〉 waiter
【跑题】pǎotí〈动〉 wander off the point: 这段话～了，应该删去。 This paragraph is a digression from the subject and should be deleted.
【跑跳】pǎotiào〈名〉［体育］ running jump
【跑腿儿】pǎotuǐr〈动〉 run errands: 替某人～ run errands for sb.
【跑外】pǎowài〈动〉 work as a travelling salesman for a firm: ～的 travelling salesman
【跑位】pǎowèi〈动〉［体育］ run off the ball: 球员～不积极。 The players were not doing a lot of running off the ball.
【跑鞋】pǎoxié〈名〉 running shoes
【跑圆场】pǎo yuánchǎng〈动〉［戏曲］ [of actors in traditional opera] walk in circles

on the stage to signify travelling a long distance

【跑账】pǎozhàng〈动〉 run around collecting bills

【跑猪靶】pǎozhūbǎ〈名〉［体育］running boar target

pào

泡 pào

A〈名〉**1**（指液体） bubble: 冒～ rise in bubbles ‖ 肥皂～儿 soap bubbles ▸～沫，气～ **2**（泡状物） bubble-shaped thing: 手上起～了 get blisters on one's palm ‖ 新鞋把我的脚磨起了～。 The new shoes have given me blisters. ▸灯～，燎～

B〈动〉**1**（浸泡） soak: 用沸水～茶 infuse tea in boiling water ‖ 把床单好好～一～再洗。 Give the sheet a good soak before washing it. ▸浸～ **2**（消磨时光） kill time: 他在茶馆里～了两个钟头。 He lingered two hours in the tea house.

▸pāo

【泡吧】pàobā〈动〉 hang out in a bar

【泡病号】pào bìnghào〈动〉〈口〉 take leave on the pretext of sickness

【泡菜】pàocài〈名〉 pickled vegetables: 朝鲜～ *kimchi* ‖ 四川～ Sichuan pickles

【泡茶】pàochá〈动〉 make tea

【泡饭】pàofàn〈名〉 cooked rice simmered in soup or water

【泡蘑菇】pào mógu〈惯〉**1**（拖延） dawdle: 别～了，快点干活儿吧。 Stop dawdling and get down to work. **2**（纠缠） importune: 别跟我～了，我不会答应的。 Don't pester me. I'm not going to agree.

【泡沫】pàomò〈名〉 froth: 口吐～ foam at the mouth ‖ 肥皂～ soap bubbles ‖ 这种啤酒～很多。 This beer has a good head.

【泡沫玻璃】pàomò bōli〈名〉 foamed glass

【泡沫混凝土】pàomò hùnníngtǔ〈名〉 foamed concrete

【泡沫经济】pàomò jīngjì〈名〉bubble economy

【泡沫灭火器】pàomò mièhuǒqì〈名〉foam extinguisher

【泡沫塑料】pàomò sùliào〈名〉 foamed plastics

【泡沫橡胶】pàomò xiàngjiāo〈名〉 foam rubber

【泡妞儿】pào niūr〈动〉〈口〉 dawdle away one's time with a young girl

【泡泡纱】pàopaoshā〈名〉［纺织］ seersucker

【泡泡糖】pàopaotáng〈名〉 bubble gum

【泡汤】pàotāng〈动〉〈口〉 fall through: 这笔买卖～了。 The transaction has failed.

【泡影】pàoyǐng〈名〉 visionary hope: 成为～ fall through ‖ 她的希望已化作～。 Her hopes came to nothing.

【泡澡】pàozǎo〈动〉 soak in a bath

炮（砲） pào

〈名〉**1**（指武器） cannon: 开～ fire a gun ‖ 火箭～ rocket launcher ▸高射～，火～，迫击～ **2**（爆竹） firecracker: ▸～仗，鞭～，花～ **3**（爆破物） blast hole filled with dynamite: ▸哑～

▸bāo, páo

【炮兵】pàobīng〈名〉**1**（指兵种） artillery: ～阵地 artillery position **2**（指人） artilleryman

【炮舱】pàocāng〈名〉 gun bay

【炮车】pàochē〈名〉 gun carriage

【炮铳】pàochong〈名〉〈旧〉 ceremonial device for letting off bangs

【炮弹】pàodàn〈名〉 (artillery) shell: 发射～ lob shells ‖ ～击中了目标。 The shell found its mark.

【炮管】pàoguǎn〈名〉 gun barrel

【炮轰】pàohōng〈动〉 shell: ～敌方补给线 shell the enemy supply lines

【炮灰】pàohuī〈名〉 cannon fodder:〈喻〉充当～ serve as cannon fodder

【炮火】pàohuǒ〈名〉 gunfire: ～连天 continuous gunfire ‖ ～掩护 artillery fire cover

【炮击】pàojī〈动〉 shell: 停止～ stop the bombardment ‖ 遭到～ be under fire

【炮舰】pàojiàn〈名〉 gunboat

【炮舰外交】pàojiàn wàijiāo〈名〉 gunboat diplomacy

【炮口】pàokǒu〈名〉 gun muzzle

【炮楼】pàolóu〈名〉［军事］ blockhouse: 炸毁～ blow up a blockhouse

【炮钎】pàoqiān〈名〉［矿业］ rock drill

【炮手】pàoshǒu〈名〉 artilleryman

【炮栓】pàoshuān〈名〉 breechblock

【炮塔】pàotǎ〈名〉 (gun) turret: 旋转～ revolving turret

【炮台】pàotái〈名〉 barbette: ～甲板 gun deck

【炮膛】pàotáng〈名〉 bore (of a big gun): ～壁 bore surface

【炮艇】pàotǐng〈名〉 gunboat

【炮筒子】pàotǒngzi〈名〉**1**（指物） gun barrel **2**〈喻〉（指人） motormouth: 他是个～，有时难免得罪人。 He is blunt and often offends people.

【炮位】pàowèi〈名〉 emplacement

【炮眼】pàoyǎn〈名〉**1**［军事］ gun port **2**［矿业］ blast hole

【炮衣】pàoyī〈名〉 gun cover

【炮仗】pàozhang〈名〉 firecracker

【炮子儿】pàozǐr〈名〉〈方〉 bullet

【炮座】pàozuò〈名〉 gun platform

疱 pào

〈名〉 blister

【疱疹】pàozhěn ▸p. 50〈名〉［医学］**1**（指水泡） bleb **2**（指皮肤感染） herpes: 带状～ herpes zoster

pēi

呸 pēi

〈叹〉 pah: ～! 你怎么干那种损人利己的事! Bah! How could you do such a selfish thing!

胚 pēi

〈名〉［生物］ embryo

【胚根】pēigēn〈名〉［植物］ radicle

【胚胎】pēitāi〈名〉**1**［生物］ embryo: ～发育 embryonic development **2**〈喻〉（萌芽） embryonic stage

【胚芽】pēiyá〈名〉**1**［植物］ plumule: ～生殖 germiparity **2**〈喻〉（萌芽） bud: 矛盾的～ the origins of a contradiction

【胚珠】pēizhū〈名〉［植物］ ovule

péi

陪 péi

〈动〉**1**（陪伴） accompany: ～某人逛公园 stroll around the park with sb. ‖ 我～你到车站。 I'll go with you as far as the station. ‖ 住院期间，母亲一直～着他。 When he was in hospital, his mother was constantly at his bedside. **2**（协助） assist: ▸～审

【陪伴】péibàn〈动〉 accompany: ～某人参观 show sb. around ‖ 人们感到寂寞时，需要人～。 When people feel lonely, they want company.

【陪绑】péibǎng〈动〉**1**（指犯人） be taken to the execution ground together with those about to be executed and be shot at with blank cartridges as a form of intimidation **2**〈喻〉（一同受罚） be criticized or punished together with the guilty

【陪衬】péichèn **A**〈动〉 set off: 红花还需绿叶来～。 Red flowers need green leaves to set them off. ‖ 在黑色衣服的～下，她的皮肤显得更白皙了。 The black dress showed off her fair skin to great advantage. **B**〈名〉 foil: 给女主角做～ play foil to the leading actress

【陪床】péichuáng〈动〉 stay in a ward to look after a patient: 病人晚上需要～。 Someone needs to stay in the ward to look after the patient.

【陪都】péidū〈名〉〈旧〉 secondary capital of a country

【陪读】péidú〈动〉**1**（指与子女） help one's children with their study **2**（指与配偶） accompany a spouse studying abroad

【陪房】péifang〈名〉〈旧〉 maid servant brought by the bride from her parents' home

【陪护】péihù〈动〉 accompany and attend to: ～病人 accompany and take care of a patient

【陪嫁】péijià〈名〉 dowry

【陪酒】péijiǔ〈动〉 accompany (a guest) in drinking: ～女郎 bar girl

【陪客】péikè〈动〉 accompany a guest: 他很忙，没有时间～。 He is very busy and has no time to accompany the guests.

【陪客】péike〈名〉 person invited to be company for the guests at a dinner

【陪奁】péilián〈名〉 dowry

【陪练】péiliàn **A**〈动〉［体育］accompany sb. in training **B**〈名〉 training partner

【陪审】péishěn〈动〉**1**（指非专业人员） serve as an assessor in a court trial **2**（指专业人员） serve on a jury

【陪审团】péishěntuán〈名〉 jury: 大～ grand jury ‖ 小～ petit jury

【陪审员】péishěnyuán ▸p. 966〈名〉juror: 人民～ people's assessor

【陪侍】péishì〈动〉 attend to: 母亲病重期间，我们一直轮流～。 When Mother was seriously ill, we took turns to look after her.

【陪送】péisong〈名〉〈口〉 dowry

【陪同】péitóng〈动〉 accompany: ～前往参观 accompany sb. on a visit ‖ ～人员 escort

【陪舞】péiwǔ〈动〉 be a dancing partner

【陪夜】péiyè〈动〉 look after an inpatient at night

【陪葬】péizàng〈动〉〈旧〉**1**（指人） be buried alive with the dead **2**（指物品） be buried together with

【陪葬品】péizàngpǐn〈名〉 burial object

培 péi

〈动〉**1**（指土） bank up with earth: ～堤 bank up the dam with earth **2**（指人） train: ▸～训，代～

【培土】péitǔ〈动〉［农业］ bank up with earth: 给小树～ earth up small trees ‖ 给玉米～ ridge the corn

【培修】péixiū〈动〉 repair and reinforce (earthwork): ～堤坝 reinforce the dykes and dams

【培训】péixùn〈动〉 train: 在职～ on-the-job training ‖ 职业～ professional training

【培训班】péixùnbān〈名〉 training course: 短期～ short-term training course ‖ 暑期～ summer training school

【培训中心】péixùn zhōngxīn〈名〉training centre

【培养】péiyǎng〈动〉1（使繁殖）cultivate: ～细菌 incubate germs ‖ 人工～的病毒 cultured virus 2（使成长）train: ～接班人 train successors ‖ ～良好习惯 cultivate good habits ‖ ～学生自学能力 foster the students' ability to study on their own

【培养基】péiyǎngjī〈名〉［生物］culture medium

【培壅】péiyōng〈动〉〈书〉earth up (flowers, crops, etc.)

【培育】péiyù〈动〉1（使发育）cultivate: ～小麦新品种 develop a new strain of wheat ‖ 他们～出一种良种牛。They bred an improved breed of cattle. 2（教育）bring up: ～一代新人 raise a new generation

【培植】péizhí〈动〉1（指植物）cultivate: ～防护林带 plant a shelter belt ‖ 许多野生草药已开始人工～。A lot of medicinal herbs are being artificially cultivated. 2（指人）train: ～亲信 train one's own cohorts ‖ ～新生力量 foster new forces

【培智】péizhì〈动〉educate children with learning disabilities

【培种】péizhòng〈动〉cultivate (plants): ～蔬菜 cultivate vegetables

赔（賠） péi〈动〉1（赔偿）compensate: 足球是我丢的，我来～。I lost the football, so I'll pay for it. ▸～偿，退～ 2（道歉）ask for forgiveness: ▸～不是，～礼，～罪 3（亏损）lose money in business: 不赚不～ break even ‖ 做生意～了 suffer a loss in business ▸～本，～钱

【赔本】péiběn〈动〉lose money in business: ～买卖 bad deal ‖ ～生意 losing business

【赔不是】péi bùshi〈动〉apologize: 这事是你的错，你应该给她赔个不是。It's your fault and you should apologize to her.

【赔偿】péicháng〈动〉compensate: ～损失 make good a loss ‖ 如数～ pay back the exact amount ‖ 照价～ compensate according to the loss

【赔偿额】péicháng'é〈名〉amount of compensation

【赔偿费】péichángfèi〈名〉solatium

【赔偿金】péichángjīn〈名〉compensation money

【赔偿责任】péicháng zérèn〈名〉liability for compensation

【赔错】péicuò〈动〉apologize for one's wrongdoing

【赔付】péifù〈动〉pay as compensation: 保险公司正在处理～事宜。The insurance company is dealing with matters concerning indemnity.

【赔付金】péifùjīn〈名〉compensation

【赔话】péihuà〈动〉say a word in apology: 你得罪了他，总得赔个话才是。If you have offended him, you owe him an apology.

【赔款】péikuǎn **A**〈动〉pay an indemnity: 割地～ cede territories and pay reparations **B**〈名〉indemnity: 战争～ war reparations

【赔了夫人又折兵】péile fūrén yòu zhé bīng〈俗〉〈喻〉suffer a double loss

【赔礼】péilǐ〈动〉apologize: ～道歉 make an apology ‖ 我错怪了你，特来向你～。I blamed you wrongly, so I have come especially to apologize to you.

【赔钱】péiqián〈动〉1（指损失）lose money in business: ～买卖 losing business 2（指补偿）compensate: 损坏公物要～。If you damage public property, you have to pay for it.

【赔钱货】péiqiánhuò〈名〉〈贬〉girl

【赔小心】péi xiǎoxīn〈动〉1 = 赔不是 péi bùshi 2（言行谨慎）act with great caution

【赔笑】péixiào〈动〉smile placatingly or apologetically

【赔笑脸】péi xiàoliǎn = 赔笑 péixiào

【赔账】péizhàng〈动〉1（补偿损失）pay for the loss of cash or goods entrusted to one: 仓库丢了东西，保管员是要～的。If anything in the warehouse is missing, the keeper will have to pay for the loss. 2〈方〉（赔本）lose money in business: 他的时装精品屋不仅没赢利，反而～了。Instead of making a profit, his boutique is running in the red.

【赔罪】péizuì〈动〉ask forgiveness for one's wrongdoing: 都是我不对，我向你～。It's all my fault. I apologize to you.

锫（錇） péi〈名〉［化学］berkelium (Bk)

裴 Péi〈名〉Pei [surname]

pèi

沛 pèi〈形〉〈书〉abundant: ▸充～，丰～

帔 pèi〈名〉〈旧〉short embroidered cape (worn over a woman's shoulders): ▸霞～

佩[1] pèi〈动〉1（佩带）wear: 腰～一把手枪 wear a pistol in one's belt ‖ 胸前～着一枚胸针 wear a brooch on one's breast ▸～戴，～刀 2（佩服）revere: 这种献身精神可敬可～。The spirit of selfless devotion is honourable and admirable. ▸～服，敬～

佩[2]（珮） pèi〈名〉ornament worn as a pendant at the waist in ancient times: 玉～ jade pendant

【佩带】pèidài〈动〉bear: ～武器 carry a weapon

【佩戴】pèidài〈动〉wear: ～肩章 wear epaulettes ‖ ～校徽 wear badges

【佩刀】pèidāo **A**〈动〉wear a sword at one's side **B**〈名〉sword worn at the waist

【佩服】pèifu〈动〉admire: ～得五体投地 prostrate oneself before sb. in admiration ‖ 令人～ command admiration ‖ 我～他事业有成。I admire him for his success in his career.

【佩剑】pèijiàn〈名〉sabre: ～运动员 sabre fencer

【佩兰】pèilán〈名〉［植物］fragrant thoroughwort

配 pèi

A〈动〉1（两性结合）join in marriage: 才子～佳人。A fine scholar and a beautiful girl make a good match. ▸～偶，婚～ 2（使交配）mate: ～马/猪 mate horses/pigs ▸～种，交～ 3（调配）mix: ～鸡尾酒 mix cocktails ‖ ～颜色 match up colours ‖ ～药 make up a prescription ▸搭～，调～ 4（分派）apportion: ～一名秘书 designate a secretary (to sb.) ‖ 给办公室～台打印机 provide a printer for the office ▸～备，分～ 5（补足）find sth. to fit or replace sth. else: ～零件 replace parts ‖ ～钥匙 have a duplicate key cut 6（陪衬）be in harmony with: ～乐诗朗诵 recite a poem to the accompaniment of music ‖ 红花～绿叶 green leaves setting off red flowers ‖ 窗帘的颜色与家具的颜色很相～。The curtain goes perfectly with the furniture. ▸～殿，～角 7（有资格）deserve: 他不～当老师。He is not qualified to be a teacher. ‖ 她的穿着和她的年龄很不相～。She doesn't dress right for her age. ▸般～ 8（充军）exile: ▸发～ **B**〈名〉mate: 择～ choose one's mate ▸原～

【配备】pèibèi **A**〈动〉1（分配）equip: ～骨干力量 provide key members ‖ 给办公室～碎纸机 equip the office with a shredder ‖ 每个宿舍都～了电话。A telephone is installed in each dormitory room. 2（布置）deploy: 按地形～火力 deploy gun power according to the terrain **B**〈名〉equipment: 现代化的～ modern equipment

【配比】pèibǐ〈名〉proportion of different elements in the composition of sth.

【配菜】pèicài〈动〉garnish food

【配餐】pèicān **A**〈动〉decide on menus and prepare foods for a meal: 根据病人的需要～ prepare foods according to the needs of the patients **B**〈名〉assorted food: 方便～ convenient assorted food

【配餐室】pèicānshì〈名〉pantry

【配搭】pèidā〈动〉1（做陪衬）supplement: 这出戏配角～得不错。The minor roles of the play have been well chosen. 2（搭配）arrange in pairs or groups

【配电盘】pèidiànpán〈名〉distributor

【配电室】pèidiànshì〈名〉switch room

【配电箱】pèidiànxiāng〈名〉switch/distribution box

【配殿】pèidiàn〈名〉［建筑］side hall

【配对】pèiduì〈动〉1（成双）match: 两只鞋不～。The two shoes don't match. ‖ 这两名选手～参加双打比赛。The two athletes are paired up in the doubles. 2（交配）mate: 使驴与母马～ mate a donkey with a mare

【配额】pèi'é〈名〉quota: 超过～ exceed the quota ‖ 进口～ import quota ‖ ～管理 quota administration

【配发】pèifā〈动〉1（发给）distribute: 给每个工人～一套工作服 allocate each worker a set of work clothes 2（指报刊）publish: ～的评论 commentary published together with a news report

【配方】pèifāng **A**〈动〉1［数学］make an incomplete square form a complete one 2（指药品）make up a prescription **B**〈名〉formula: 新药的～ formula for a new drug

【配房】pèifáng〈名〉wing (of a house): 房子的两边有～。The house has a wing on each side.

【配购】pèigòu〈动〉buy according to rationed quota

【配股】pèigǔ〈名〉［金融］scrip issue

【配合】pèihé〈动〉1（指合作）cooperate: （与某人）～默契 cooperate tacitly and harmoniously (with sb.) ‖ 给予积极～ give active cooperation (to) 2（相协调）keep time with: 舞步要跟乐曲节奏～。Dance steps must be in time with the music.

【配合饲料】pèihé sìliào〈名〉［畜牧］compound feed

【配合】pèihe〈形〉suitable: 颜色很～。The colours go well together.

【配给】pèijǐ〈动〉ration: 战时实行食物～供应。Food was rationed during the war.

【配给制】pèijǐzhì〈名〉ration system

P

【配件】pèijiàn〈名〉1（用于装配）accessory part: 机器～ machine parts 2（用于替换）replacement: 汽车～ car spare parts
【配角】pèijué A〈动〉co-star: 他俩常在一起～。They often perform together. B〈名〉1（指角色）minor role: 当～ play a supporting role ‖ 最佳男/女～ best supporting actor/actress 2（喻）（指作用）subordinate role: 在项目中他起～作用。He is playing a supporting role in the project.
【配军】pèijūn〈名〉〈旧〉exile
【配克】pèikè〈量〉peck
【配料】pèiliào A〈动〉mix materials in the right proportion: ～车间 compounding workshop ‖ ～员 compounder B〈名〉components
【配偶】pèi'ǒu〈名〉spouse: 选择～ choose one's mate
【配器】pèiqì〈名〉［音乐］orchestration
【配曲】pèiqǔ〈动〉set to music: 为歌词～ set a song to music
【配色】pèisè〈动〉harmonize colours
【配售】pèishòu〈动〉ration (at set price)
【配水】pèishuǐ〈动〉［农业］distribute water: ～管 distributing pipe
【配送】pèisòng〈名〉distribution: 水产品～中心 aquatic products distribution centre
【配套】pèitào〈动〉coordinate: ～设施 supporting facilities ‖ ～工程 auxiliary/supporting project
【配套成龙】pèitào-chénglóng = 成龙配套 chénglóng-pèitào
【配套资金】pèitào zījīn〈名〉counterpart funds
【配伍】pèiwǔ〈名〉［药学］compatibility of medicines: ～禁忌 incompatibility of medicines
【配戏】pèixì〈动〉play a supporting role: 为某人～ play a supporting role for sb.
【配系】pèixì〈名〉system of military disposition
【配线板】pèixiànbǎn〈名〉plugboard
【配药】pèiyào〈动〉make up a prescription: 按处方～ make up a prescription
【配音】pèiyīn〈动〉dub: 用英语给一部中国电影～ dub a Chinese film into English
【配乐】pèiyuè〈动〉provide background music: 为影片～ do a film score ‖ ～诗朗诵 poem recital with background music
【配乐广播】pèiyuè guǎngbō〈名〉dubbed-in radio broadcast
【配制】pèizhì〈动〉concoct: ～调味汁 confect a sauce ‖ ～药剂 put together a medicine ‖ 为字典～了插图 come up with some illustrations for a dictionary
【配置】pèizhì〈动〉deploy: ～兵力 deploy troops ‖ 资源～ resource allocation
【配种】pèizhǒng〈动〉［畜牧］breed: 这头母牛是上个星期～的。This cow was mated last week.
【配子】pèizǐ〈名〉［生物］gamete: ～生殖 gametogony
【配租】pèizū〈动〉allocate low-rent housing: 把廉租房～给困难群体 allocate low-cost housing to disadvantaged groups

旆 pèi〈名〉〈古〉1（燕尾旗）swallow-tailed pennant 2（旌旗）banner

辔（轡） pèi〈名〉bridle: 鞍～ saddle and bridle
【辔头】pèitóu〈名〉bridle

霈 pèi〈书〉
A〈名〉heavy rain: 甘～ welcome rain
B〈形〉profuse: 雨～ profuse rain

pēn

喷（噴） pēn〈动〉1（喷溅）spurt: ～出火焰 jet out flames ‖ 溪水从岩石缝中～涌而出。The stream spews forth from the crevasses among the rocks. ‖ 油井～油。The well gushed oil. ▸～泉 2（撒）spray: 给庄稼～农药 spray a crop with insecticide ‖ ～香水 spray perfume ▸～洒
▸pèn
【喷薄】pēnbó〈形〉〈书〉spurting: ～欲出的一轮红日 an emerging sun in all its splendour
【喷灯】pēndēng〈名〉blowtorch; blowlamp〈英〉
【喷发】pēnfā〈动〉erupt: 火山～。The volcano erupted.
【喷发胶】pēnfàjiāo〈名〉hair spray
【喷饭】pēnfàn〈动〉split one's sides with laughter: 令人～ side-splitting
【喷放】pēnfàng〈动〉spout: ～着火花 sending out sparks
【喷粉器】pēnfěnqì〈名〉duster: 手摇～ dust gun
【喷粪】pēnfèn〈动〉〈粗〉〈喻〉talk shit〈粗〉: 满嘴～ use abusive language
【喷灌】pēnguàn〈名〉sprinkler irrigation: 机械化～ mechanized spray irrigation
【喷壶】pēnhú〈名〉watering can
【喷火器】pēnhuǒqì〈名〉flame-thrower
【喷剂】pēnjì〈名〉spray: 杀虫～ insect spray
【喷溅】pēnjiàn〈动〉splash: 泥水～了她一身。She was spattered all over with the mud.
【喷井】pēnjǐng〈名〉gusher well
【喷口】pēnkǒu〈名〉exhaust nozzle
【喷淋】pēnlín〈动〉spray: ～塔 spray tower
【喷墨打印机】pēnmò dǎyìnjī〈名〉［印刷］ink-jet printer
【喷漆】pēnqī A〈动〉spray paint B〈名〉spray paint: 速干～ quick-drying spray paint
【喷气发动机】pēnqì fādòngjī〈名〉jet engine
【喷气式】pēnqìshì〈形〉jet-propelled: ～飞机 jet plane ‖ ～客机 jet airliner
【喷气织机】pēnqì zhījī〈名〉［纺织］air-jet loom
【喷枪】pēnqiāng〈名〉spray gun
【喷泉】pēnquán〈名〉fountain: 间歇～ geyser
【喷洒】pēnsǎ〈动〉spray: 给庄稼～农药 spray crops with insecticide ‖ ～灌溉法 spray irrigation
【喷射】pēnshè〈动〉spray: 火焰～器 flame injector ‖ 水从消防栓中～出来。Water spewed from the hydrant.
【喷水池】pēnshuǐchí〈名〉fountain
【喷腾】pēnténg〈动〉spurt up
【喷嚏】pēntì〈名〉sneeze: 打～ sneeze
【喷桶】pēntǒng = 喷壶 pēnhú
【喷头】pēntóu〈名〉1（莲蓬状）sprinkler head 2（管状）shower nozzle
【喷涂】pēntú〈动〉spray
【喷吐】pēntǔ〈动〉spurt forth: 炉口～着火苗。The stove shoots out flames.
【喷雾器】pēnwùqì〈名〉sprayer: 农作物～ crop sprayer ‖ 油漆～ paint sprayer
【喷泻】pēnxiè〈动〉gush forth: 岩浆从火山口～而出。Lava gushed out of the volcano.
【喷涌】pēnyǒng〈动〉gush forth: 黑色的原油从油井～出来。Black oil is spurting out of the well. ‖ 鲜血从伤口～而出。Blood gushed out of the wound.
【喷云吐雾】pēnyún-tǔwù〈成〉1（指吸烟）puff away 2（指烟囱）belch out smoke: 工厂的烟囱正在～。Factory chimneys are belching out smoke.
【喷子】pēnzi〈名〉sprayer
【喷嘴】pēnzuǐ〈名〉spray nozzle: ～调节阀 nozzle regulator ‖ 煤气灶～ gas jet

pén

盆 pén〈名〉1（用于盛物）basin: 锅碗瓢～ pots and pans ‖ 洗衣～ washing tub ‖ 把花栽到～里 pot a flower ▸～景, 花～, 聚宝～ 2（盆状物）basin-shaped thing: ▸～地, ～腔, 骨～
【盆菜】péncài〈名〉ready-to-cook dish
【盆地】péndì ▸**p. 164**〈名〉basin: 四川～ Sichuan Basin ‖ 柴达木～ Qaidam Basin
【盆花】pénhuā〈名〉potted plant: ～培植 cultivation of potted plants
【盆景】pénjǐng〈名〉bonsai

> **盆景**
>
> An artistic miniature landscape in a pot, using trees, flowers, grass, stones, water and earth. The art of *penjing* originated in China, and later spread to Japan (where it is known as *bonsai*). There are two types of *penjing*: tree stump and landscape. Skilfully pruned miniature trees are the main element used in the former; stones, water and earth are used in the latter. The main schools of *penjing* are the Lingnan school of Guangdong and Guangxi, the Chuan school of Chengdu and Chongqing, and the Hai school of Shanghai.

【盆满钵满】pénmǎn-bōmǎn〈成〉brimming: 房产开发商个个赚得～。The real estate developers made so much cash that it was falling out of their pockets.
【盆腔】pénqiāng〈名〉［解剖］pelvic cavity: ～炎 pelvic inflammation
【盆汤】péntāng〈名〉tub bath in a bath-house
【盆浴】pényù〈名〉tub bath: 洗～ have a bath
【盆栽】pénzāi A〈动〉pot: ～花卉 potted flowers B〈名〉potted plants: 案头摆着常绿的～。On the desk are some evergreen pot plants.
【盆子】pénzi〈名〉basin

pèn

喷（噴） pèn〈形〉〈方〉strong: ▸～香
▸pēn
【喷红】pènhóng〈形〉crimson: ～的苹果 crimson apples
【喷香】pènxiāng〈形〉delicious-smelling: 大米饭～扑鼻。The smell of cooked rice is very inviting.

pēng

抨 pēng〈动〉〈书〉censure

【抨击】pēngjī〈动〉lash out at: ～时弊 attack current malpractice ‖ 遭到猛烈～ come under severe attack

怦 pēng〈拟〉thump: ～然心动 one's heart is pounding ‖ 她兴奋得心～～直跳。Her heart fluttered with excitement.

砰 pēng〈拟〉bang: 屋门～地一声关上了。The door banged shut.

烹 pēng〈动〉**1**（煮）boil: ▸～饪, ～调 **2**（炒）fry quickly in hot oil and stir in sauce: ～对虾 quick-fried prawns in brown sauce

【烹茶】pēngchá〈动〉make tea

【烹饪】pēngrèn〈动〉cook: 学习～ learn to cook ‖ ～比赛 cooking competition

【烹调】pēngtiáo〈动〉cook (dishes): ～技术 cooking skills ‖ 他～手艺不错。He is quite a cook.

嘭 pēng〈拟〉bang: ～～～的敲门声 the banging of knocking at the door ‖ ～的一声，气球爆炸了。The balloon burst with a bang.

péng

朋 péng

A〈名〉friend: 亲～好友 one's relatives and friends ‖ 有～自远方来 have friends coming from afar ▸宾～, 狐～狗友

B〈动〉〈书〉**1**（结党）gang up with: ▸～比为奸 **2**（伦比）rival: ▸硕大无～

【朋辈】péngbèi〈名〉〈书〉friends

【朋比为奸】péngbǐ-wéijiān〈成〉band together for evil purposes

【朋党】péngdǎng〈名〉clique: ～之争 factional strife

【朋克】péngkè〈名〉punk

【朋僚】péngliáo〈名〉〈书〉**1**（朋友）friend **2**（同事）colleague

【朋友】péngyou〈名〉**1**（指友情关系）friend: 老/新～ old/new friend ‖ 知心～ bosom friend ▸酒肉～ **2**（指恋爱关系）partner: 他～是他的同班同学。His girlfriend is his classmate.

彭 Péng〈名〉Peng [surname]

【彭布罗克郡】Péngbùluókèjùn〈名〉Pembrokeshire

棚 péng〈名〉**1**（遮蔽物）canopy of reed mats, etc.: 在园子里搭一个～ set up an awning in the garden ▸凉～, 天～ **2**（指小屋）shed: 瓜～ melon hut ‖ 茅草～ thatched hut ▸工～, 牛～, 牲口～ **3**（天花板）ceiling: 糊～ paper the ceiling ▸顶～

【棚车】péngchē = 篷车 péngchē

【棚户】pénghù〈名〉slum-dwellers: ～区 shanty town

【棚圈】péngjuàn〈名〉covered pen

【棚寮】péngliáo〈名〉shack

【棚屋】péngwū〈名〉shed

【棚子】péngzi〈名〉shed: 草～ straw mat shed ‖ 马～ horse shed

蓬 péng

A〈名〉［植物］fleabane

B〈动〉be unkempt: ～着头 with dishevelled hair ▸～松, ～头垢面

C〈量〉[of luxuriant plants] clump: 一～～野花 clusters of wild flowers ‖ 一～竹子 a clump of bamboo

【蓬荜生辉】péngbì-shēnghuī〈成〉〈谦〉[said in thanks for a visit or a gift such as a scroll] you bring radiance to my humble house: 您的到来使我们的出版社～。We are greatly honoured to have you as a visitor to our press.

【蓬勃】péngbó〈形〉flourishing: ～发展 develop vigorously ‖ ～兴起 spring up vigorously ▸朝气～

【蓬蒿】pénghāo〈名〉**1**〈方〉［植物］crown daisy chrysanthemum **2**〈旧〉〈指人〉common people: ～人 commoner

【蓬户瓮牖】pénghù-wèngyǒu〈成〉humble abode

【蓬莱】Pénglái〈名〉〈喻〉fabled abode of the immortals [in Chinese mythology]: ～仙境 fairyland

【蓬乱】péngluàn〈形〉unkempt: ～的头发 dishevelled hair

【蓬门荜户】péngmén-bìhù〈成〉humble abode

【蓬茸】péngróng〈形〉〈书〉[of grasses] luxuriant: 绿草～ exuberant grass

【蓬松】péngsōng〈形〉fluffy: ～的被子/头发/枕头 fluffy quilt/hair/pillow

【蓬头垢面】péngtóu-gòumiàn〈成〉with an unkempt and unwashed appearance

【蓬头历齿】péngtóu-lìchǐ〈成〉be old and feeble

硼 péng〈名〉［化学］boron (B)

【硼砂】péngshā〈名〉borax: ～玻璃 borax glass

【硼酸】péngsuān〈名〉boric acid: ～钙 calcium borate ‖ ～盐 borate

鹏（鵬） péng〈名〉roc

【鹏程万里】péngchéng-wànlǐ〈成〉〈喻〉have a bright future

澎 péng

【澎湖列岛】Pénghú Lièdǎo〈名〉Penghu Islands

【澎湃】péngpài〈形〉〈书〉**1**（形容波浪）surging: 波涛汹涌～。The waves surged high. **2**〈喻〉（声势浩大）powerful: 激情～的诗歌 poetry charged with emotion ‖ 革命浪潮汹涌～。The tide of revolution is raging with great momentum. ▸心潮～

篷 péng〈名〉**1**（遮蔽物）awning: 敞～马车 open-top buggy ‖ 遮阳～ sunshade ▸车～, 斗～, 帐～ **2**（船帆）sail: 扯～ hoist the sails ‖ 落～ drop the sail

【篷布】péngbù〈名〉tarpaulin

【篷车】péngchē〈名〉**1**［铁路］boxcar: 轻型帆布～ canvassed light van **2**（指货车）covered truck **3**〈旧〉（指马车）horse-drawn carriage with a covering

【篷船】péngchuán〈名〉houseboat: 乌～ covered boat

【篷帐】péngzhàng〈名〉tent

【篷子】péngzi〈名〉awning: 搭～ put up an awning

膨 péng〈动〉balloon: ▸～大, ～胀

【膨大】péngdà〈动〉swell

【膨脝】pénghēng〈形〉〈书〉ventricular: ～大腹 be potbellied

【膨化】pénghuà〈动〉[of rice, corn, etc.] be puffed: ～剂 swelling agent ‖ ～食品 inflated food

【膨松剂】péngsōngjì〈名〉bulking agent

【膨体纱】péngtǐshā〈名〉［纺织］bulky yarn

【膨胀】péngzhàng〈动〉**1**（指具体物体）expand: 体积～ volume expansion ‖ 金属受热会～。When a metal is heated, it will expand. **2**（指抽象事物）swell: 人口～ swell in population ‖〈喻〉他的个人主义日益～。His individualism is growing with each passing day. ▸通货～

【膨胀剂】péngzhàngjì〈名〉swelling agent

【膨胀力】péngzhànglì〈名〉［物理］expansive force: 冰/热～ expansive force of ice/heat

【膨胀率】péngzhànglǜ〈名〉［物理］rate of expansion

【膨胀系数】péngzhàng xìshù〈名〉［物理］expansion coefficient: 热～ coefficient of thermal expansion

【膨胀性】péngzhàngxìng〈名〉expansibility

鬅 péng〈形〉〈书〉[of hair] fluffy

【鬅松】péngsōng〈形〉[of hair] fluffy

【鬅头散发】péngtóu-sànfà〈成〉with dishevelled hair

蟛 péng

【蟛蜞】péngqí〈名〉［动物］amphibious crab

pěng

捧 pěng

A〈动〉**1**（双手托起）hold sth. in both hands: ～着奖杯 hold a cup in both hands ‖ 手～一束鲜花 hold a bouquet of flowers in one's hands ▸～腹, 众星～月 **2**（吹捧）compliment: 把某人～上天 laud/praise sb. to the skies ▸～场, 吹～

B〈量〉double handful: 两～米 two double handfuls of rice ‖ 一～枣儿 a double handful of jujubes

【捧杯】pěngbēi〈动〉**1**（指奖杯）win the cup: 20名歌手在本届青年大奖赛中～。Twenty singers won prizes at this year's Grand Prix for young singers. **2**（夺冠）win first place

【捧场】pěngchǎng〈动〉**1**（到场声援）boost sb. in a show: 谢谢你～，来参加我的宴会。You do me a great honour by attending my banquet. **2**（赞扬）lavish praise on: 评论家们极力为这个歌星～。The reviewers were lavish in the singer's praise.

【捧臭脚】pěng chòujiǎo〈动〉〈口〉bootlick

【捧腹】pěngfù〈动〉split one's sides (with laughter): 他的滑稽动作引得大家～大笑。His antics had the people convulsed in laughter.

【捧哏】pěnggén **A**〈动〉［曲艺］[of the supporting role of a comic dialogue] play the fool to help to make people laugh **B**〈名〉the straight man (in a comic dialogue)

【捧角】pěngjué〈动〉lavish praise on a particular actor or actress

P

P

【捧杀】pěngshā〈动〉destroy sb. by heaping excessive praises on him

pèng

椪 pèng
【椪柑】pènggān〈名〉a kind of mandarin orange

碰 pèng〈动〉1 (撞) knock (against): ～倒 knock sb. down ‖ 他的头～到门上了。He banged his head on the door. ‖ 别～我！ Don't touch me! ▸～撞，磕～ 2 (遇上) bump into: ～到麻烦事儿 run into trouble ‖ ～到熟人 bump into an acquaintance ▸～面，～头 3 (试探) try one's luck: ～机会 take a chance ‖ ～运气 try one's luck
【碰杯】pèngbēi〈动〉clink glasses: 为成功～ clink glasses to success
【碰壁】pèngbì〈动〉〈喻〉bash one's head against a wall: 四处～ be buffeted from pillar to post
【碰钉子】pèng dīngzi〈惯〉suffer setbacks: 假如你不想～，就别去求他帮忙。If you don't want to be brushed off, forget about asking him to give you a hand. ‖ 碰软钉子 be tactfully rebuked
【碰见】pèngjiàn〈动〉bump into sb.: 他在电影院～了前妻。He ran into his ex-wife at the cinema.
【碰面】pèngmiàn〈动〉meet: 在咖啡馆～ meet in a café
【碰碰车】pèngpèngchē〈名〉bumper car; dodgem car〈英〉
【碰碰船】pèngpèngchuán〈名〉bumper boat
【碰巧】pèngqiǎo〈副〉coincidentally: 我正要找你，～你来了。I was going to look for you when as luck would have it you came to find me.
【碰锁】pèngsuǒ〈名〉latch
【碰头】pèngtóu〈动〉meet: 他们天天都～。They see each other every day. ‖ 我们8点钟在电影院～。We'll meet at the cinema at 8 o'clock.
【碰头会】pèngtóuhuì〈名〉brief meeting: 开～ hold a brief meeting
【碰一鼻子灰】pèng yī bízi huī〈惯〉be unceremoniously snubbed
【碰硬】pèngyìng〈动〉confront difficult problems: 他在反腐斗争中敢于～。He dares to challenge the influential in combating corruption.
【碰撞】pèngzhuàng〈动〉1 (撞击) run into: 离港时轮船发生了～。The boat ran aground on leaving harbour. ‖ 汽车和卡车～在一起。The car collided with the truck. 2 (冒犯) offend: 他正在气头上，别去～他。He is in a fury right now. Don't offend him.

pī

丕 pī〈形〉〈书〉great: ～业 great deeds

批¹ pī〈动〉slap: ～耳光子 slap sb.'s face

批² pī
A〈动〉1 (批改) write comments on (a report from a subordinate, etc.): ～作业 correct homework ‖ ～假 grant leave ‖ 报告还没有～下来。The report has not been approved. ▸～准，审～ 2 (批评) criticize: 挨～ be criticized ‖ 揭～ expose and criticize ▸～判，～评
B〈名〉comment: ▸横～，眉～

批³ pī
A〈形〉wholesale: ▸～发，～量
B〈动〉buy wholesale: ～了一些货 buy some goods wholesale
C〈量〉batch: 一～货物/客人 a batch of goods/visitors ‖ 第一～录取的考生 first batch of examinees to be enrolled

批⁴ pī〈名〉〈口〉untwisted fibres of cotton, flax, etc. in thin strips ready to be drawn and twisted: 线～ thin strip of cotton fibre
【批驳】pībó〈动〉criticize: ～错误论点 refute wrong views
【批捕】pībǔ〈动〉[法律] approve an arrest: ～案犯 approve the arrest of a criminal
【批处理】pīchǔlǐ〈名〉[计算机] batch processing
【批次】pīcì〈量〉batch
【批次号】pīcìhào = 批号 pīhào
【批点】pīdiǎn〈动〉punctuate and annotate
【批斗】pīdòu〈动〉〈旧〉criticize and denounce: ～会 criticism and denunciation meeting
【批发】pīfā〈动〉buy wholesale: ～兼零售 wholesale and retail distribution ‖ 这种钢笔～价每打60元。These pens wholesale at 60 *yuan* per dozen.
【批发价】pīfājià〈名〉wholesale price
【批发商】pīfāshāng〈名〉wholesaler
【批复】pīfù〈动〉give an official written reply to a subordinate body
【批改】pīgǎi〈动〉correct: ～作文 correct compositions
【批号】pīhào〈名〉batch number: 产品～ product batch number
【批件】pījiàn〈名〉official written reply to a subordinate body
【批量】pīliàng A〈副〉in batches: ～购买折扣 quantity buying discount ‖ 大～生产 mass production B〈名〉batch: 大～ big batches ‖ 小～ small batches
【批零】pīlíng〈名〉wholesale and retail: ～差价 wholesale and retail differential
【批判】pīpàn〈动〉1 (否定) criticize: ～错误观点 criticize an erroneous view ‖ ～个人主义 criticize individualism 2 (分析判别) critique: ～地继承文学遗产 critically inherit a literary legacy ‖ ～地吸收 assimilate with discrimination
【批判现实主义】pīpàn xiànshízhǔyì〈名〉[语言] critical realism
【批评】pīpíng A〈动〉criticize: ～与自我～ criticism and self-criticism ‖ 老师～学生迟到。The teacher reproved his pupils for coming late to school. ‖ 经理～她对顾客粗暴无礼。The manager criticized her for her rudeness to customers. B〈名〉criticism: 文艺～ literary criticism
【批评家】pīpíngjiā ▸p. 966〈名〉critic: 文学/戏剧～ literary/theatre critic ‖ 文艺～ critics of art and literature
【批示】pīshì A〈动〉write comments or instructions (on a report, memorandum, etc. submitted by a subordinate body): 请领导～ ask one's superior for instructions B〈名〉written comments or instructions (on a report, memorandum, etc. submitted by a subordinate): 认真执行领导的～ strictly carry out a leader's instructions on the memo
【批售】pīshòu〈动〉sell wholesale
【批条】pītiáo〈名〉note with comments or instructions from a superior
【批文】pīwén〈名〉written instructions (on a report, memorandum, etc. submitted by a subordinate body)
【批语】pīyǔ〈名〉1 (评语) comments or remarks (on schoolwork, or a piece of writing): 作文后面有老师的～。There are some comments from the teacher at the end of the composition. 2 = 批示 pīshì B
【批阅】pīyuè〈动〉read over and comment on: ～文件 read over and comment on documents or official papers
【批注】pīzhù A〈动〉annotate and comment on B〈名〉annotations and commentaries: 书眉上的小字～ commentaries in small characters in the top margin
【批转】pīzhuǎn〈动〉endorse
【批准】pīzhǔn〈动〉ratify: 正式～ give formal approval ‖ 公约需经各方政府～后才生效。The convention requires the ratification of the respective governments before it can go into effect.
【批准书】pīzhǔnshū〈名〉instrument of ratification
【批租】pīzū〈动〉approve the lease of

纰（紕） pī〈动〉[of cloth, thread, etc.] come apart: 线～了。The thread has come untwisted.
【纰漏】pīlòu〈名〉careless mistake: 出～ slip up
【纰缪】pīmiù〈名〉〈书〉error: ～百出 be full of errors

坯 pī〈名〉1 (指砖瓦、陶器等) base: 铜～ copper base ‖ 砖～ unbaked brick ▸～子 2 (土坯) adobe: 打～ make adobe ‖ 脱～ mould adobe blocks 3〈方〉(半成品) semi-finished product: 钢～ steel billet ▸～布
【坯布】pībù〈名〉[纺织] unbleached and undyed cloth
【坯革】pīgé〈名〉crust leather
【坯件】pījiàn〈名〉[机械] blank
【坯料】pīliào〈名〉semi-finished product
【坯胎】pītāi〈名〉mould: 搪瓷的金属～ metal mould of enamelware
【坯子】pīzi〈名〉1 = 坯 pī 1 2 (指人) makings: 她是个当芭蕾舞演员的好～。She has the makings of a good ballerina.

披 pī〈动〉1 (盖或搭) drape over one's shoulder: ～上节日的盛装 be colourfully kitted out for a festival ‖ ～着大衣 have an overcoat draped over one's shoulders ‖ ～着合法的外衣 under the cloak of legitimacy ‖ ～着羊皮的狼 a wolf in sheep's clothing ▸～肩 2 (打开) unroll: ▸～露，～阅 3 (裂开) split (open): 竹筒～了。The bamboo tube has split. 4 (散开) hang loose: ▸～散，～头散发
【披风】pīfēng〈名〉cloak: 脱下～ remove a cloak
【披拂】pīfú〈动〉〈书〉1 (飘动) sway: 树木枝叶～。The branches and leaves of the trees are swaying. 2 (吹动) blow gently: 春风～。A spring breeze was blowing gently.
【披肝沥胆】pīgān-lìdǎn〈成〉be extremely open and sincere
【披挂】pīguà A〈动〉1 (指盔甲) put on a suit of armour: ～上阵 buckle on one's armour and go into action 2 (指衣装) get accoutred: 猎人们～整齐，准备上路。

The hunters are attired and ready to leave. **B**〈名〉 a suit of armour

【披红】pīhóng〈动〉 drape a length of red cloth over the shoulders [as a token of honour or on a festive occasion]

【披红戴绿】pīhóng-dàilǜ〈成〉be in bright-coloured clothes

【披坚执锐】pījiān-zhíruì〈成〉 be armed to the teeth

【披肩】pījiān **A**〈名〉 **1**（指外衣） shawl **2**（用于披在肩上） cape: 毛～ fur stole **B**〈动〉 [of hair] be shoulder-length: 她长发～。 Her hair is shoulder-length.

【披肩发】pījiānfà〈名〉shoulder-length hair

【披荆斩棘】pījīng-zhǎnjí〈成〉〈喻〉 break through difficulties: 在丛林中～ hack one's way through the jungle ‖〈喻〉 我们～，终于取得了胜利。 We hacked our way through before we finally succeeded.

【披览】pīlǎn〈动〉〈书〉 leaf through: ～群书 read extensively

【披沥】pīlì〈形〉〈书〉 be open and sincere in communicating to others: ～陈词 sincerely state one's views

【披露】pīlù〈动〉 **1**（公布） announce: ～谈话内容 make a talk public ‖ 这条新闻是由一位不愿～姓名的人提供的。 This news was provided by a person who asked not to be identified. ‖ 这种丑闻应通过媒体予以～。 Such scandals should be exposed by the media. **2**（表露） reveal: ～心曲 disclose one's innermost thoughts

【披麻戴孝】pīmá-dàixiào〈成〉 be in mourning dress

【披靡】pīmǐ〈动〉〈书〉 **1**（指草） be windswept: 草儿随风～。 The grass was swept by the wind. **2**（指军队） be defeated and dispersed: 敌军望风～。 The enemy troops fled in disorder. ▸所向～

【披散】pīsan〈动〉 hang loosely: 她的头发～着。 Her hair was down.

【披沙拣金】pīshā-jiǎnjīn〈成〉〈喻〉 separate the wheat from the chaff

【披头散发】pītóu-sànfà〈成〉 with one's hair in disarray: 她～地冲出了失火的房子。 She rushed out of the burning house with her hair in disarray.

【披头士】pītóushì〈名〉 Beatles: ～乐队 the Beatles

【披屋】pīwū〈名〉 lean-to

【披星戴月】pīxīng-dàiyuè〈成〉 work from dawn till dusk

【披阅】pīyuè〈动〉 open and read: ～文稿 read a manuscript

砒 pī

〈名〉［化学］ **1**〈旧〉（砷） arsenic (As) **2**（砒霜） arsenic trioxide

【砒霜】pīshuāng〈名〉［化学］ arsenic trioxide

铍（鈹） pī

〈名〉〈书〉 **1**（长矛） lance **2**（长针） long acupuncture needle ▸pí

劈 pī

A〈动〉 **1**（使破开） chop: ～柴 chop (fire) wood ‖ ～成两半 chop in two ▸～波斩浪 **2**（裂开） be split: 板子～了。 The board was split. ‖ 钢笔尖摔～了。 When the pen fell to the ground, the tip split apart. **3**（指雷电） strike: 老树让雷～了。 The old tree was struck by lightning.

B〈名〉［物理］ wedge ▸pǐ

【劈波斩浪】pībō-zhǎnlàng〈成〉 slash through the waves:〈喻〉 ～，乘胜前进 cleave through obstacles and advance upon a victory

【劈刺】pīcì〈名〉［军事］ bayonet fighting

【劈刀】pīdāo〈名〉 **1**（用于劈东西） cleaver **2**［军事］ sabre fighting

【劈风斩浪】pīfēng-zhǎnlàng〈成〉〈喻〉 slash one's way through difficulties

【劈里啪啦】pīlipālā = 噼里啪啦 pīlipālā

【劈脸】pīliǎn〈副〉 right in the face: 他～打了对手一个耳光。 He hit his opponent square in the face.

【劈面】pīmiàn = 劈脸 pīliǎn

【劈啪】pīpā = 噼啪 pīpā

【劈杀】pīshā〈动〉 [usu of a man on horseback] slash at and kill

【劈山】pīshān〈动〉 blast cliffs: ～引水 tunnel through mountains to conduct water ‖ ～筑路 level mountains to make roads

【劈手】pīshǒu〈副〉 in a snatching: ～夺过球拍 snatch a racket from sb. ‖ ～一巴掌 give sb. a sudden slap

【劈头】pītóu〈副〉 **1**（迎头） straight on the head: 走到门口，我～碰见他从里边出来。 As I reached the door, I bumped straight into him. **2**（一开头） at the very beginning: 他进了屋，～第一句话就问试验成功了没有。 The first thing he asked as he entered the room was whether the experiment had been successful.

【劈头盖脸】pītóu-gàiliǎn〈成〉 right in the face: 瓢泼大雨～地浇下来。The rain came pelting down on our heads.

【劈腿】pītuǐ〈名〉［体育］ axe kick

【劈胸】pīxiōng〈副〉 right in the chest: ～一把抓住 grasp sb. by the lapels

噼 pī

【噼里啪啦】pīlipālā〈拟〉 crackle: 鞭炮～地响着。 The firecrackers were crackling.

【噼啪】pīpā〈拟〉 crack: ～的鞭子声 snap of a whip ‖ 鞭炮～作响。 The firecrackers cracked.

霹 pī

【霹雷】pīléi〈口〉= 霹雳 pīlì

【霹雳】pīlì〈名〉 thunderbolt: 一个～打下来，劈死了一头牛。 A bull was struck dead by a bolt of thunder. ▸晴天～

【霹雳舞】pīlìwǔ〈名〉 break dancing: 表演/跳～ perform/do break dancing

pí

皮 pí

A〈名〉 **1**（表层）（指人或动物） skin;（指果蔬） peel;（指谷物、坚果） shell: 剥～ skin ‖ 削～ peel ‖ 香蕉～ banana skin ‖ 西瓜～ watermelon rind ▸～肤，表～，植～ **2**（皮制） hide: ～凉鞋 leather sandals ‖ ～袄 fur-lined jacket ‖ 狐～ pelt of fox ▸～货，～鞋 **3**（外皮） wrapper: 饺子～ dumpling wrapper ‖ 书～儿 book jacket ▸封～ **4**（表面） surface: 蜻蜓擦着水～儿飞过。 The dragonfly skimmed the surface of the water. ▸地～ **5**（橡胶） rubber: ▸～筋儿，橡～ **6**（薄片状物） thin sheet: 白铁～ tinplate ‖ 豆腐～ bean curd sheet ‖ 铅～ lead sheet ▸粉～，奶～，铁～

B〈形〉 **1**（粘） sticky: ▸～糖 **2**（受潮变韧） soggy: 炒花生放久了会～。 Roasted peanuts lose their crispness over time. **3**（淘气） naughty: 这孩子真～，一刻也不安生。 The kid is so naughty. He won't keep still for a single moment. ▸调～，顽～ **4**（无所谓） thick-skinned: 他天天挨批，已经～了。 He gets scolded every day and as a result he no longer cares.

【皮包】píbāo〈名〉 leather case

【皮包公司】píbāo gōngsī〈名〉fly-by-night company

【皮包骨头】pí bāo gǔtou〈成〉 be skin and bone(s): 他瘦得～。 He was all skin and bones.

【皮鞭】píbiān〈名〉 leather crop

【皮布尔斯郡】Píbù'ěrsījùn〈名〉 Peeblesshire

【皮草】pícǎo〈名〉 fur garments and leather wear: ～时装 fur fashions ‖ ～行 [in southern China] shop selling fur and leather garments in the cold months and straw mats in the warm months

【皮层】pícéng〈名〉［解剖］［植物］ cortex: ～顶叶 parietal lobe of cortex ‖ 肾～ renal cortex

【皮尺】píchǐ〈名〉 tape measure

【皮带】pídài〈名〉 **1**（指腰带） leather belt **2**［机械］ (driving) belt: ～传动 belt drive ‖ 三角～ triangle belt

【皮蛋】pídàn〈方〉= 松花蛋 sōnghuādàn

> **皮蛋**
>
> Preserved eggs, usually duck eggs, covered with a paste of salt, quicklime, tea and ash, then rolled in rice husks and sealed in an earthenware jar for 15-20 days. After the process is completed, the egg white has set to a dark-brown jelly-like consistency, and the egg yolk has become dark-green and creamy in texture. Preserved eggs can be eaten with chopped ginger and chives, soy sauce and vinegar.

【皮筏】pífá〈名〉 skin raft

【皮肤】pífū **A**〈名〉 skin: 保养/呵护～ take good care of one's skin ‖ ～白/黑/嫩 be fair-/dark-/tender-skinned ‖ ～过敏 cutaneous allergy **B**〈形〉〈书〉 skin-deep: ～之见 shallow views

【皮肤病】pífūbìng〈名〉 skin disease: ～学 dermatology

【皮肤护理】pífū hùlǐ〈名〉 skincare

【皮肤科】pífūkē〈名〉［医学］ dermatological department: ～医生 dermatologist

【皮肤移植】pífū yízhí〈名〉［医学］ skin graft

【皮傅】pífù〈动〉〈书〉 draw far-fetched conclusions based on superficial knowledge: ～之论 superficial remarks

【皮革】pígé〈名〉 leather: ～制品 leatherware

【皮猴儿】píhóur〈名〉〈方〉 hooded fur overcoat

【皮划艇】píhuátǐng〈名〉［体育］ kayak: 单人～ single kayak ‖ 双人～ two-seater kayak

【皮黄】píhuáng〈名〉 **1**（指声腔） short for *xipi* (西皮) and *erhuang* (二黄) [two chief groups of basic vocal motifs in traditional opera] **2**（指京剧） Beijing opera

【皮货】píhuò〈名〉 leather goods

【皮夹子】píjiāzi〈名〉 wallet

【皮匠】píjiang〈名〉 **1**（修鞋人） cobbler: ▸三个臭～，顶个诸葛亮 **2**（皮革加工者） tanner

【皮胶】píjiāo〈名〉［材料］ hide glue

【皮筋儿】píjīnr〈名〉〈口〉 rubber band: ▸跳～

【皮具】píjù〈名〉 leatherware

【皮开肉绽】píkāi-ròuzhàn〈成〉 serious physical injuries: 他被打得～。 He was beaten to a pulp.

【皮里阳秋】pílǐ YángQiū〈成〉 veil one's genuine views on sth. or sb.: ～的笔法 making implicit remarks

【皮毛】pímáo〈名〉〈喻〉superficial knowledge: 略知～ have only a superficial knowledge of ‖ 他们只学到该语言的一点～。They have only picked up a smattering of the language.
【皮棉】pímián〈名〉ginned cotton
【皮囊】pínáng〈名〉**1**〈本〉leather bag **2**〈喻〉〈贬〉human body: 空有一副好～ be outwardly attractive but hollow at heart
【皮球】píqiú〈名〉rubber ball: 拍～ bounce a rubber ball
【皮肉】píròu〈名〉skin and flesh: ～之苦 physical pain ‖ 我不过伤了点～,没什么关系。I was slightly hurt but it's not serious.
【皮试】píshì〈名〉[医学] skin test: 做～ do a skin test on sb.
【皮实】píshi〈形〉**1**（不易得病）sturdy: 这孩子真～，从不闹病。He is a tough child and never gets ill. **2**（耐用）durable: 这种产品很～。This type of product is very durable.
【皮糖】pítáng = 牛皮糖 niúpítáng
【皮艇】pítǐng〈名〉**1**（指艇）kayak **2**（指比赛）canoe racing
【皮桶子】pítǒngzi〈名〉semi-finished fur lining
【皮下】píxià〈形〉subcutaneous
【皮下注射】píxià zhùshè〈动〉[医学] inject subcutaneously: ～器 hypodermic syringe ‖ ～海洛因 skin-pop heroin
【皮下组织】píxià zǔzhī〈名〉[解剖] subcutaneous tissue
【皮箱】píxiāng〈名〉leather suitcase
【皮相】píxiàng〈形〉〈书〉superficial: ～之见 superficial opinion
【皮硝】píxiāo〈名〉[矿业] mirabilite
【皮笑肉不笑】pí xiào ròu bù xiào〈成〉smile hypocritically
【皮鞋】píxié〈名〉leather shoes
【皮鞋油】píxiéyóu〈名〉shoe polish
【皮屑】píxiè〈名〉scurf: ▸头～
【皮靴】píxuē〈名〉leather boots
【皮炎】píyán ▸**p. 50**〈名〉[医学] dermatitis: 神经性～ neurodermatitis ‖ 湿疹性～ eczematous dermatitis
【皮衣】píyī〈名〉leather coat
【皮影戏】píyǐngxì〈名〉shadow puppet show
【皮张】pízhāng〈名〉pelt
【皮疹】pízhěn ▸**p. 50**〈名〉[医学] (skin) rash: 出～ develop rashes
【皮之不存，毛将焉附】pí zhī bù cún, máo jiāng yān fù〈成〉〈喻〉a thing cannot exist without its basis
【皮脂】pízhī〈名〉(cutaneous) sebum: ～分泌过多 hypersteatosis
【皮脂腺】pízhīxiàn〈名〉[生理] sebaceous gland: ～囊肿 sebaceous cyst
【皮质】pízhì〈名〉**1**[解剖] cortex: 肾上腺～ adrenal cortex **2**（大脑皮层）cerebral cortex
【皮重】pízhòng〈名〉tare: 扣除～ tare allowance
【皮子】pízi〈名〉**1**（皮革）hide: 一块～ a piece of hide **2**（毛皮）fur

枇 pí

【枇杷】pípa〈名〉loquat
【枇杷膏】pípagāo〈名〉condensed loquat extract

毗 pí〈动〉〈书〉be adjacent to: ▸～连, ～邻

【毗连】pílián〈动〉be adjacent to: 陕西与甘肃～。Shaanxi Province borders on Gansu Province.
【毗邻】pílín〈动〉border on: 中国与蒙古～。China borders on Mongolia.

蚍 pí

【蚍蜉】pífú〈名〉〈书〉ant
【蚍蜉撼大树】pífú hàn dàshù〈成〉〈喻〉ridiculously overrate one's own ability or strength

铍（鈹）pí〈名〉[化学] beryllium (Be) ▸pī

疲 pí〈形〉**1**（累）exhausted: ▸～倦, 筋～力尽 **2**（软）slack: ▸～软, ～沓

【疲惫】píbèi〈形〉weary: 感到～ feel worn out ‖ 精神～ be mentally exhausted
【疲敝】píbì〈动〉〈书〉[of manpower, resources, etc.] become inadequate: 连年的战争使人民异常～。The people were completely drained of their resources after years of war.
【疲顿】pídùn〈形〉〈书〉exhausted: ～不堪 be dog-tired
【疲乏】pífá〈形〉tired: 她看了一天书，眼睛～极了。Her eyes were strained after a whole day's reading.
【疲倦】píjuàn〈形〉weary: 他因熬夜而感到～。He felt tired after staying up all night.
【疲困】píkùn〈形〉**1**（疲乏）fatigued: 他日夜操劳，不知～。He works tirelessly day and night. **2**（疲软）slack: ～不振的经济 sluggish economy
【疲劳】píláo **A**〈形〉tired: ～过度 be completely exhausted ‖ 身心～ be mentally and physically exhausted **B**〈名〉**1**（劳累）fatigue: 肌肉～ muscular fatigue ‖ 精神～ mental fatigue **2**[物理] fatigue: 磁性～ magnetic fatigue ‖ 金属～ metal fatigue
【疲劳极限】píláo jíxiàn〈名〉endurance limit
【疲劳战术】píláo zhànshù〈名〉gruelling tactic
【疲累】pílèi〈形〉worn out
【疲软】píruǎn〈形〉**1**（乏力）tired and weak: 两腿～ be weak in the legs ‖ 身体～ be tired and weak **2**[经济] sluggish: 市场～ weak market ‖ 美元仍然～。The dollar is still weak.
【疲弱】píruò〈形〉tired and weak: 他拖着～的双腿继续前进。He plodded on with tired legs.
【疲沓】píta〈形〉slack: 工作～ be slack in one's work ‖ 他这个人很～。He is a slacker.
【疲于奔命】píyú-bēnmìng〈成〉be run off one's feet: 为生计～ be rushed off one's feet all day long trying to make ends meet

啤 pí

【啤酒】píjiǔ〈名〉beer: 冰镇～ iced beer ‖ 罐装/瓶装/桶装～ canned/bottled/barrelled beer ‖ 散装～ beer on tap
【啤酒肚】píjiǔdù〈名〉〈口〉beer belly
【啤酒花】píjiǔhuā〈名〉[生物] hop(s)
【啤酒节】píjiǔjié〈名〉beer festival

琵 pí

【琵琶】pípa ▸**p. 929**〈名〉*pipa* [Chinese stringed musical instrument with a fretted fingerboard]: 弹～ pluck the *pipa*

脾 pí〈名〉[解剖] spleen

【脾气】píqi〈名〉**1**（性情）temperament: ～古怪 have a strange disposition ‖ 各人有各人的～。Every person has their own temperament. **2**（指易怒急躁）bad temper: 发～ lose one's temper ‖ ～暴躁 have an explosive temper ‖ 火爆～ volcanic temper
【脾胃】píwèi〈名〉**1**（指内脏）spleen and stomach **2**〈喻〉（兴趣）taste: 这不合他的～。It is not his style. ‖ 两人～相投。They have similar likes and dislikes.
【脾性】píxìng〈名〉disposition: 各人有各人的～。Everybody's disposition is different.
【脾脏】pízàng〈名〉spleen: ～切除 splenectomy

鲏（鮍）pí ▸鳑鲏pángpí

裨 pí〈形〉〈书〉subordinate: ▸～将 ▸bì

【裨将】píjiàng〈名〉〈古〉lower-ranking general [esp one under a commander-in-chief]

蜱 pí〈名〉[昆虫] tick

罴（羆）pí〈名〉[动物] brown bear

貔 pí〈名〉mythical bear-like wild animal

【貔虎】píhǔ〈名〉〈书〉〈喻〉fierce warriors
【貔貅】píxiū〈名〉〈书〉**1**（指动物）a type of mythical wild animal **2**〈喻〉（指人）fierce warriors

鼙 pí〈名〉〈古〉small drum used in the army

【鼙鼓】pígǔ〈名〉〈喻〉warfare

pǐ

匹[1] pǐ

A〈动〉be a match for: 难与为～ cannot compete with ‖ 举世无～ be unrivalled ▸～敌, ～配
B〈形〉single: ▸单枪～马, ～夫
C〈量〉[for mules, horses, etc.]: 两～骡子 two mules ‖ 三～马 three horses

匹[2]（疋）pǐ〈量〉[for rolls of cloth or silk]: 两～布 two bolts of cloth ‖ 一～绸子 a bolt of silk

【匹敌】pǐdí〈动〉can compare with: 无可～ be without parallel ‖ 双方实力～。The two sides are equally matched.
【匹夫】pǐfū〈名〉**1**（普通人）ordinary man: ▸国家兴亡，～有责 **2**（无知者）ignoramus
【匹夫之勇】pǐfūzhīyǒng〈成〉bravado
【匹马单枪】pǐmǎ-dānqiāng = 单枪匹马 dānqiāng-pǐmǎ
【匹配】pǐpèi〈动〉**1**（婚配）marry: ～良缘 be happily married ‖ 他俩十分～。They make a good match. **2**[电气] be matching: 功率～ power matching ‖ 阻抗～ impedance matching
【匹染】pǐrǎn〈名〉[纺织] piece dyeing

圮 pǐ〈动〉〈书〉collapse: ▸倾～

仳 pǐ
【仳离】pǐlí〈动〉〈书〉**1**（指夫妻） be separated **2**（指丈夫） divorce one's spouse

否 pǐ〈书〉
A〈形〉 wicked: ▸～极泰来
B〈动〉 censure: ▸臧～
▸fǒu
【否极泰来】pǐjí-tàilái〈成〉 extreme adversity marks the beginning of fortune

吡 pǐ〈动〉 slander
▸bǐ

痞 pǐ〈名〉**1**（指硬块） lump in the abdomen: ▸～块 **2**（指人） scoundrel: ▸兵～, 地～, 文～
【痞块】pǐkuài〈名〉［中医］ lump in the abdomen
【痞子】pǐzi〈名〉 lout: 小～ ruffian

劈 pǐ〈动〉**1**（分） divide: ～成三股 split sth. into three strands ▸～柴 **2**（使分开） break off: ～莴苣叶 strip off the outer leaves of a head of lettuce **3**（指腿） spread one's legs as widely as one can;（指手指） spread one's fingers as widely apart as possible: ▸～叉
▸pī
【劈叉】pǐchà〈动〉［体育］ do the splits: ～跳 splits jump
【劈柴】pǐchái〈名〉 firewood: 一捆～ a bundle of firewood
【劈账】pǐzhàng〈动〉 share out according to a certain rate: 四六～ share out sixty-forty

擗 pǐ〈动〉**1**（使分开） break off: ～玉米棒子 pick corn ‖ ～菜叶子 strip off vegetable leaves **2**〈书〉（用手捶胸） beat one's breast: ▸～踊
【擗踊】pǐyǒng〈动〉〈书〉 be grief-stricken

癖 pǐ〈名〉 addiction: 吸毒成～ be addicted to drugs ‖ 书～ partiality to books and reading ▸～好, 怪～, 洁～
【癖好】pǐhào〈名〉 favourite hobby: 形成～ develop a predilection ‖ 不良～ undesirable habit
【癖习】pǐxí〈名〉 old habit
【癖性】pǐxìng〈名〉 natural inclination: 害羞的～ natural inclination to shyness ‖ ～难改 deep-seated biases are hard to change

pì

屁 pì
A〈名〉**1**（指臭气） fart: ▸～滚尿流, 放～ **2**〈口〉〈粗〉（指无价值） rubbish: 用不着为这点～事大动干戈。 Don't make a fuss about such a tiny thing. ▸～话, 狗～
B〈代〉〈粗〉 [usu used negatively] what: 你懂个～! You don't know a damn thing! ‖ 我把包翻遍了，但包里～都没有。 I've turned the bag inside out but found absolutely nothing.
【屁股】pìgu〈名〉**1**〈口〉（指人体） bottom: 护士在我～上打了一针。 The nurse gave me a shot in the bum. ▸擦～, 打～ **2**（指动物） hindquarters: 胡蜂的～上有刺。 A wasp has a sting on its rump. **3**〈口〉（末尾处） butt: 香烟/雪茄～ cigarette butt ‖ 汽车～冒烟了。 Petrol poured from the tail of the car.
【屁股帘儿】pìguliánr〈名〉 piece of cloth tied to the waist of a child with slit pants to cover his behind
【屁滚尿流】pìgǔn-niàoliú〈成〉 piss oneself (with fear): 吓得～ be scared shitless
【屁话】pìhuà〈名〉 nonsense

睥 pì
【睥睨】pìnì〈动〉〈书〉 look at sb./sth. disdainfully out of the corner of one's eye: ～一切 treat everything with disdain

辟[1]（闢） pì
A〈动〉**1**（开拓） open up: ～地垦荒 open up a field and reclaim wasteland ‖ 另～蹊径 find another way out ‖ 另～专栏 launch a new column ▸开～, 开天～地 **2**（批驳） refute: ～邪说 refute heresy
B〈形〉 incisive: ▸精～, 透～

辟[2] pì〈名〉〈古〉 law
▸bì
【辟谣】pìyáo〈动〉 deny a rumour

媲 pì〈动〉 be a match for
【媲美】pìměi〈动〉 compare favourably with: 该产品可与世界名牌～。 This product compares favourably with world-famous brands.

僻 pì〈形〉**1**（偏远） out-of-the-way: ～巷 back lane ▸～静, ～陋, 荒～ **2**（指性情） eccentric: ▸乖～, 怪～, 孤～ **3**（不常见） rare: ～字 rare words ▸冷～, 生～
【僻径】pìjìng〈名〉 out-of-the-way path
【僻静】pìjìng〈形〉 secluded: ～的山间小路 secluded mountain road ‖ ～之处 quiet, secluded place
【僻陋】pìlòu〈形〉 remote and desolate
【僻壤】pìrǎng〈名〉outlying place: ▸穷乡～
【僻野】pìyě〈名〉 remote wilderness
【僻远】pìyuǎn〈形〉 remote and outlying: ～的山村 remote mountain village

甓 pì〈名〉〈古〉 brick

鸊（鷿） pì
【鸊鷉】pìtī〈名〉［鸟类］ grebe

譬 pì〈动〉 make an analogy: ▸～如, ～喻
【譬方】pìfāng〈名〉 analogy: ～说 for instance
【譬如】pìrú〈动〉 take for example: ～他，就是个说话太直的人。 Take him for example, he is much too straightforward.
【譬喻】pìyù〈动〉 use analogy: 煤被～为黑色的金子。 Black gold is a metaphor for coal.

piān

片 piān
▸piàn
【片儿】piānr = 片 piàn A1, A2
【片子】piānzi〈名〉**1**（胶片） roll of film: 洗～ develop an exposed film **2**（影片） film: 拍～ shoot a film **3**（唱片） disc: 灌～ cut a disc **4**［医学］ X-ray: 拍～ take an X-ray
▸piànzi

扁 piān
▸biǎn
【扁舟】piānzhōu〈名〉〈书〉 small boat: 一叶～ a small boat

偏 piān
A〈形〉**1**（歪斜） slanting: ～北/西风 northerly/westerly wind ‖ 画挂～了。 The picture has been hung askew. ‖ 球踢～了。 The ball went wide. ▸～头痛 **2**（注重一方） partial: ～于基础理论的研究 show partiality for the study of basic theories ▸～爱, ～食, ～听～信 **3**（不常见） uncommon: ▸～僻, ～题, ～远 **4**（辅助） subordinate: ～将 assistant general ▸～方, ～房, ～师
B〈动〉**1**（指方向） deviate from the correct course **2**（偏离标准） deviate from the normal standard: 试题～难。 The test was a little bit on the difficult side. ‖ 体温～高。 The body temperature was slightly higher than normal. **3**〈套〉〈方〉（用茶饭） [used to indicate one has already had one's tea, meal, etc. and will not join one's hosts at theirs]: 我～过了。 I've eaten already.
C〈副〉 wilfully: 他～不去。 He insists on not going. ‖ 他～要跟我一块走。 He insisted on going with me. ▸明知山有虎，～向虎山行
【偏爱】piān'ài〈动〉 show a preference for: 英国诗人中，他～拜伦的诗歌。 Of the English poets, he has a preference for Byron.
【偏安】piān'ān〈动〉 [of a feudal regime] be content to retain sovereignty over a part of the country: ～一隅 be content to exercise sovereignty over only a lesser part of the country
【偏差】piānchā〈名〉 deviation: 纠正工作中的～ correct an error in one's work ‖ 20度的～ declination of 20 degrees
【偏殿】piāndiàn〈名〉 side hall
【偏饭】piānfàn〈名〉preferential treatment: ▸吃～
【偏方】piānfāng〈名〉［中医］ special formula: 治疗牙痛的～ home-made remedy for toothache
【偏房】piānfáng〈名〉**1**（指房） wing **2**〈旧〉（指人） concubine
【偏废】piānfèi〈动〉 emphasize one thing at the expense of another: 学生要德智体全面发展，任何一个方面都不可～。 Students are expected to develop in an all-round way — morally, intellectually and physically. None of the three is to be neglected.
【偏光】piānguāng〈名〉 polarized light
【偏光镜】piānguāngjìng〈名〉［物理］ polariscope
【偏航】piānháng〈动〉 go off course
【偏好】piānhào〈动〉 have a special fondness for sth.: 球类运动中，他～足球。 Of all the ball games, he is partial to football.
【偏护】piānhù〈动〉 be partial to and side with: 不～任何一方 be completely impartial
【偏激】piānjī〈形〉 extreme: 采取～的行动 go to extremes ‖ 言辞～ be extreme in one's wording
【偏见】piānjiàn〈名〉 bias: 抱有～ display a bias ‖ 抛弃～ throw aside one's prejudices ‖ 种族～ racial bias
【偏科】piānkē〈动〉 favour one subject over another: 学生不该～。 Students shouldn't

prioritize some subjects at the expense of others.
【偏口鱼】piānkǒuyú〈名〉flatfish
【偏枯】piānkū〈名〉［中医］hemiplegia
【偏劳】piānláo〈动〉〈套〉[used when asking sb. for help or thanking sb. for help rendered]: 谢谢你，多～了。Thank you for all the trouble you have gone to.
【偏离】piānlí〈动〉deviate: ～航道/线 stray off course ‖ ～跑道 veer off the runway ‖ ～正题 digress from the main subject
【偏旁】piānpáng〈名〉radical
【偏僻】piānpì〈形〉remote: ～的地区 remote areas ‖ 这个村子很～。This village is very much out of the way.
【偏偏】piānpiān〈副〉1（指故意）wilfully: 我急着要出门，可他～一点也没有告辞的意思。I was in a hurry to go out, but he didn't have the least intention of leaving. 2（指碰巧）as luck would have it: 他来找我，～我不在家。I happened to be out when he came to see me. 3（只）only: 为什么我～喜欢你而不是别的姑娘? Why is it that I love you and not some other girl?
【偏颇】piānpō〈形〉〈书〉biased: 这种议论未免～。Such comments are unfair.
【偏巧】piānqiǎo〈副〉1（碰巧）it so happened that: 人们正在找替罪羊，～他来了。They were just looking for a scapegoat when he came along. 2 = 偏偏 piānpiān 2
【偏衫】piānshān〈名〉Buddhist vestment draped over the left shoulder
【偏生】piānshēng〈方〉= 偏偏 piānpiān 1, 2
【偏师】piānshī〈名〉〈书〉auxiliary force
【偏食】piānshí A〈名〉［天文］partial eclipse: 日～ partial solar eclipse ‖ 月～ partial lunar eclipse B〈动〉have a preference for a certain type of food: ～会造成孩子营养不良。Children's partiality for particular kinds of food may cause malnourishment.
【偏蚀】piānshí = 偏食 piānshí A
【偏嗜】piānshì〈名〉food preference
【偏私】piānsī〈动〉show bias: 秉公办案，决不～。Handle a legal case justly and impartially.
【偏瘫】piāntān ▸p. 50〈名〉［医学］hemiplegia: 面臂～ faciobrachial hemiplegia ‖ 脑性～ cerebral hemiplegia
【偏袒】piāntǎn〈动〉be biased towards: 你不要～任何一方。You mustn't take sides.
【偏疼】piānténg〈动〉〈口〉favour one (child, etc.) over others: 她～最小的孩子。The youngest child is her favourite.
【偏题】piāntí〈名〉tricky questions (in an examination): 出～ set tricky questions
【偏听偏信】piāntīng-piānxìn〈成〉listen only to one side: 不可～。One must not be partisan.
【偏头痛】piāntóutòng ▸p. 50〈名〉［医学］migraine
【偏狭】piānxiá〈形〉biased and narrow-minded
【偏向】piānxiàng A〈名〉deviation: 纠正～ correct a deviation ‖ 单纯追求效益的～ the tendency to pursue profit B〈动〉1（偏袒）be partial to: 他总是～男孩子。He always shows a preference for boys. 2（偏于赞成）prefer: 我～于留在学校。I prefer to stay at school.
【偏斜】piānxié〈形〉slanted: 古塔已出现～。The ancient tower has started to lean.
【偏心】piānxīn〈形〉1（不公正）biased: 学生们都不喜欢这个老师，因为他很～。The teacher is unpopular with the students because he has favourites. 2［机械］eccentric: ～轮 eccentric wheel ‖ ～圆 eccentric circle
【偏心眼儿】piānxīnyǎnr A〈名〉bias: 他妈～，特别喜欢小儿子。His mother was biased in favour of her youngest son. B〈形〉biased
【偏远】piānyuǎn〈形〉remote: ～地区 remote areas
【偏振】piānzhèn〈名〉［物理］polarization: 光的～ polarization of light
【偏正词组】piānzhèng cízǔ〈名〉［语法］word group consisting of a modifier and the word it modifies
【偏执】piānzhí〈形〉stubbornly biased: ～的见解 extreme and stubborn opinions ‖ ～狂 paranoia
【偏重】piānzhòng〈动〉stress one aspect to the neglect of another: 科学研究不应只～理论而忽视实践。In scientific research, we shouldn't stress theory at the expense of experiment. ‖ 他的杂文～于说理。His essays focuses mainly on reasoning and argument.
【偏转】piānzhuǎn〈动〉［物理］deflect

犏 piān

【犏牛】piānniú〈名〉*pien niu* [offspring of a bull and a female yak]

篇 piān

A〈名〉1（指语言作品）piece of writing: 姐妹～ companion to a piece of work ‖ 名～ famous piece of writing ▸～幅, ～目, 续～, 开～ 2（指单张纸）sheet: 单～儿讲义 unbound sheets of teaching material ‖ 歌～儿 song sheet
B〈量〉[for paper, book leaves, articles, etc.] piece: 一～杰作 a brilliant piece of work ‖ 一～社论 an editorial ‖ 这本书缺了两～儿。Two leaves are missing from this book.
【篇幅】piānfú〈名〉1（指长短）length: 增加～ fill out ‖ 这篇文章～不长。This article is not long. 2（指数量）space: 整版～ whole page ‖ 该报用很大～刊登国际新闻。The newspaper devotes a good deal of space to international reports.
【篇目】piānmù〈名〉1（指标题）title of chapters or articles 2（指目录）table of contents
【篇章】piānzhāng〈名〉sections and chapters: ～结构 structure of an article ‖ 谱写新的～ write a new chapter ‖ 历史～ historical chapter

翩 piān〈动〉〈书〉fly swiftly and lightly: ▸～然

【翩翩】piānpiān〈形〉1（形容轻快）light: 孩子们随着音乐～起舞。The children are dancing lightly to the music. 2〈书〉（形容洒脱）genteel: ～少年 a genteel young man ‖ 他风度～。He has elegant and smart deportment.
【翩然】piānrán〈形〉〈书〉light: ～而至 come lightly ‖ 蝴蝶在花丛中～飞舞。Butterflies are flitting from flower to flower.
【翩若惊鸿】piānruòjīnghóng〈成〉tripping gracefully as a startled swan
【翩跹】piānxiān〈形〉〈书〉light: ～起舞 dance with quick, light steps

pián

便 pián

▸biàn
【便便】piánpián〈形〉〈书〉bulging: ▸大腹～
【便宜】piányi A〈形〉cheap: 二手车很～。Second-hand cars are very inexpensive. ‖ ～没好货。Cheap goods soon wear out. B〈名〉unearned gains: 不要贪～。Don't be tempted to buy things just because they are cheap. ▸占～ C〈动〉let sb. off lightly: 小偷只被判坐牢20天，实在太～了他。The thief got twenty days' imprisonment, and he got off easily at that.
▸biànyí

骈（駢）pián〈形〉〈书〉parallel: ～句 parallel sentences ▸～俪, ～体, ～文

【骈比】piánbǐ〈动〉〈书〉be next to each other
【骈肩】piánjiān〈形〉〈书〉[of people] crowded together shoulder to shoulder
【骈俪】piánlì〈名〉ornate writing style of parallel, antithetical sentences
【骈拇枝指】piánmǔ-zhīzhǐ〈成〉〈喻〉redundant things
【骈体】piántǐ〈名〉［语言］parallel style [ornate prose style, prevalent during the Six Dynasties]
【骈阗】piántián〈动〉〈书〉gather: 车马～。Carts and horses are crowded together.
【骈文】piánwén〈名〉parallel prose

胼 pián

【胼手胝足】piánshǒu-zhīzú〈成〉a life of toil
【胼胝】piánzhī〈名〉callus
【胼胝体】piánzhītǐ〈名〉［生理］corpus callosum

缏 pián〈动〉〈方〉sew

▸biàn

跰 pián

【跰跹】piánzhī = 胼胝 piánzhī

蹁 pián〈形〉〈书〉limping

【蹁跹】piánxiān〈形〉〈书〉light and agile

piǎn

谝（諞）piǎn〈动〉〈方〉show off: ～能 show off one's skills

piàn

片 piàn

A〈名〉1（薄片）flat, thin piece: 玻璃～儿 sheets of glass ‖ 土豆～ potato chips ‖ 羊肉～ lamb slices ▸胶～, 名～, 照～ 2（影片）film: 功夫～ *kung fu* film ‖ 广告～ advertisement ‖ 教育～ educational film ▸～酬, ～约, 科教～ 3（区域）part of a place: 他分管这一～儿的治安。He is in charge of the security of this area. ▸～儿警
B〈动〉slice: ～肉片儿 slice meat ‖ ～鱼片儿 flake a fish
C〈形〉1（不全）one-sided: ～面之词 a partisan view 2（简短）brief: ▸～段, ～

刻, ～时

D〈量〉 **1**（指片状物） slice: 两～药 two tablets ‖ 一～面包 a slice of bread **2**（指地面、水面等） [of land, field, waters, etc.]: 一～草地 a stretch of grassland ‖ 一～汪洋 a wide expanse of water **3**（指声音、情景等） [of voice, scene, etc.]: 一～欢腾 a scene of great rejoicing ‖ 一～抗议声 a chorus of protests ‖ 一～真心 with complete sincerity

▸piān

【片酬】piànchóu〈名〉 actor's pay: ～最高的演员 the most highly-paid actor

【片段】piànduàn〈名〉 part: 生活～ a slice of one's life ‖ 他只听到谈话的一些～。 He only heard some fragments of the conversation.

【片断】piànduàn **A**〈形〉 incomplete: ～经验 scattered experience ‖ ～回忆 fragments of one's memory **B** = 片段 piànduàn

【片盒】piànhé〈名〉［摄影］ film magazine

【片花】piànhuā〈名〉 film clips: 剪辑～ edit film clips

【片剂】piànjì〈名〉［药学］ tablet

【片甲不存】piànjiǎ-bùcún〈成〉 the army is completely wiped out: 我们把敌人杀得～。 We annihilated the enemy until there was not one person left.

【片甲不留】 piànjiǎ-bùliú = 片甲不存 piànjiǎ-bùcún

【片假名】piànjiǎmíng〈名〉［语言］ katakana

【片刻】piànkè〈名〉 an instant: ～不离 be with sb. all the time ‖ 稍等～。 Please wait for a moment.

【片麻岩】piànmáyán〈名〉［地质］ gneiss

【片面】piànmiàn〈形〉 **1**（单方面） unilateral **2**（不公正） uneven: ～发展 lopsided development ‖ ～地看问题 take a one-sided approach to problems ▸～性

【片面性】 piànmiànxìng〈名〉 one-sidedness

【片儿警】piànrjǐng〈名〉 community police

【片儿汤】 piànrtāng〈名〉 soup with flat pieces of dough cooked in it

【片时】piànshí〈名〉〈书〉 moment: 迟疑～ hesitate for a moment

【片头】piàntóu〈名〉 opening credits (for film or TV programme)

【片头曲】piàntóuqǔ〈名〉［影视］opening theme music

【片瓦无存】piànwǎ-wúcún〈成〉 be razed to the ground: 丛林火灾之后，整个村庄～。 The bush fire left the whole village completely destroyed.

【片尾】piànwěi〈名〉 closing credits (for film or TV programme)

【片尾曲】 piànwěiqǔ〈名〉 end credits music

【片言只字】 piànyán-zhīzì = 片纸只字 piànzhǐ-zhīzì

【片约】piànyuē〈名〉 actor's contract: 他跟电影制片厂签了新～。 He signed a new contract with the film studio.

【片纸只字】piànzhǐ-zhīzì〈成〉 just a few words

【片子】piànzi〈名〉 **1** = 片 piàn A1 **2**〈口〉（名片） visiting card

▸piānzi

骗¹（騙）

piàn〈动〉 **1**（使上当） cheat: 受～ be taken in ‖ 你～不了我。 You can't fool me! ▸～子, 哄～ **2**（骗取） cheat sb. of sth.: ～钱 cheat sb. out of his money

骗²

piàn〈动〉〈口〉 leap into the saddle: ～马 mount a horse

【骗婚】piànhūn〈动〉 trick sb. into marriage

【骗奸】piànjiān〈动〉 defraud and rape

【骗局】piànjú〈名〉 fraud: 设下～ devise a trick ‖ 识破～ see through a deception

【骗取】piànqǔ〈动〉 defraud: ～钱财 get money by fraud ‖ ～同情 obtain sympathy from sb. by misrepresentation ‖ ～上级的信任 gain the trust of one's superior by fraudulent means

【骗人】piànrén〈动〉 **1**（指调侃） pull sb.'s leg **2**（指欺骗） deceive people

【骗术】piànshù〈名〉 art of trickery: 高明的～ high-level chicanery ‖ 江湖～ quack methods

【骗税】piànshuì〈动〉 cheat on tax

【骗腿儿】piàntuǐr〈动〉〈口〉 swing one's leg sideways: 他一～跳过了栅栏。 He swung himself sideways over the picket fence.

【骗子】piànzi〈名〉 con man: 江湖～ quack ‖ 政治～ political swindler

【骗子手】piànzishǒu = 骗子 piànzi

piāo

剽

piāo

A〈动〉 **1**〈书〉（抢） rob: ▸～掠 **2**（窃取） copy: ▸～窃, ～袭

B〈形〉〈书〉 nimble: ▸～悍

【剽悍】piāohàn〈形〉 quick and fierce: ～的牧民 brave and agile herders

【剽掠】piāolüè〈动〉 plunder: 土匪～村庄。 The villages were looted by bandits.

【剽窃】piāoqiè〈动〉 plagiarize: ～别人的观点/发明成果 steal others' ideas/inventions ‖ ～行为 act of plagiarism

【剽取】piāoqǔ = 剽窃 piāoqiè

【剽袭】piāoxí〈动〉 plagiarize: 该文纯属～之作。 This article is full of plagiarisms.

漂

piāo〈动〉 float: ～向大海 drift seaward ‖ 小船～在水面上。 A small boat was floating on the water. ▸～流, ～移

▸piǎo, piào

【漂泊】piāobó〈动〉 **1**（指在水面） float: 一艘游艇～在海面上。 A yacht is floating in the sea. **2**（指生活） drift aimlessly: ～异乡 roam in a foreign land ‖ 过着～不定的生活 lead a wandering life

【漂浮】piāofú〈动〉 float: ～植物 floating plant ‖ 几只小船～在水面上。 Several small boats were drifting on the water. ‖ 天空中～着一朵白云。 A white cloud was floating in the sky.

【漂流】piāoliú〈动〉 **1**［体育］ go white-water rafting **2**（指随水流动） drift about: ～长江 float on the Yangtze River ‖ 船顺水～而下。 The boat drifted down the stream. **3** = 漂泊 piāobó 2

【漂流瓶】piāoliúpíng〈名〉 bottle with a message in it

【漂萍】piāopíng〈名〉 floating duckweed: 此生如～。 I wandered about all my life like floating duckweed.

【漂洋过海】 piāoyáng-guòhǎi〈成〉 sail across an ocean

【漂移】piāoyí〈动〉 drift about: 冰块随着海流～。 The ice drifted about with the sea currents.

【漂游】piāoyóu〈动〉 lead a wandering life: 四处～ drift aimlessly

缥（縹）

piāo

▸piǎo

【缥缈】piāomiǎo〈形〉 dimly discernible: 云雾～ gauzy mist and cloud ▸虚无～

飘（飄）

piāo

A〈动〉 flutter: 白云从我们头上～过。 White clouds hovered over us. ‖ 兰花的清香随风～来。 The scent of orchids wafted in the breeze. ‖ 天空开始～雪花。 Snow flakes began to flutter down. ▸～尘, ～扬, ～舞

B〈形〉 **1**（不稳）unsteady: 两腿发～ walk unsteadily **2**（轻浮） self-satisfied: ▸～～然 2

【飘泊】piāobó = 漂泊 piāobó

【飘尘】piāochén〈名〉 floating dust: ～污染 floating dust pollution

【飘带】piāodài〈名〉 streamer

【飘荡】piāodàng〈动〉 **1**（指物） flutter: 红旗迎风～。 Red flags are swaying in the wind. ‖ 小船随风～。 The boat drifted about at the mercy of the wind. **2**（指人） = 漂泊 piāobó 2

【飘动】piāodòng〈动〉 flutter: 窗帘随风～。 The curtain flapped in the breeze.

【飘拂】piāofú〈动〉 flutter: 落花随风～人面。 The fallen petals fluttered in front of us.

【飘浮】piāofú = 漂浮 piāofú

【飘红】piāohóng〈名〉 rise in stock prices: 股价全线～。 All stock prices are rising.

【飘忽】piāohū〈动〉 **1**（轻快移动） flutter to and fro: 山雾～ fleeting mountain mist **2**（摇摆） move in an unsteady manner: ～不定 be unsteady in motion

【飘零】piāolíng〈动〉 **1**（指物） fade and fall: 残叶～。 Withered leaves are whirling and scattering. ‖ 雪花～。 Snowflakes were dancing in the air. **2**（指人） wander: ～半世 be adrift half of one's life ‖ ～异乡 roam on a foreign land

【飘落】piāoluò〈动〉 drift and fall slowly

【飘绿】piāolǜ〈名〉 fall in stock prices

【飘飘然】piāopiāorán〈形〉 **1**（指感觉） light-headed: 他喝了些酒，不觉有些～。 After a few glasses, he felt light-headed. **2**（指心态） smug: 听了几句奉承话，他便～起来。 The flattery went to his head.

【飘飘欲仙】piāopiāo-yùxiān〈成〉feel that one is flying up towards heaven like an immortal

【飘球】piāoqiú〈名〉［排球］ floater: 钩手～ hook-float (service)

【飘然】piāorán〈形〉 **1**（飘摇状） floating: 团团白烟从急驰的火车上空～而过。 Clouds of white smoke floated past over the speeding train. **2**（轻捷状） speedy: 他骑上马～而去。 He rode away swiftly. **3**（惬意状） relaxed and happy: ～自在 be happy and comfortable

【飘洒】piāosǎ **A**〈动〉 drift with the wind: 天空～着雪花。 Snowflakes are swirling in the air. ‖ 细雨～。 A fine rain is drifting down. **B**〈形〉 natural and unstrained: 风度～ carry oneself with ease and natural poise ‖ 他的字写得十分～。 His handwriting is very elegant.

【飘散】piāosàn〈动〉 drift away: 花香在空气中～。The fragrance of flowers wafted in the air. ‖ 雨停了，云也～了。 The rain ceased and the clouds sailed away.

【飘逝】piāoshì〈动〉 **1**（飘动流散） float away and vanish: 白云～。 White clouds are floating past. **2**（消逝） pass: 岁月～。 The years are slipping away.

P

【飘舞】piāowǔ〈动〉 dance in the wind: 柳条迎风～。 The willow branches are dancing in the wind.
【飘扬】piāoyáng〈动〉 flutter: 彩旗迎风～。 The bunting fluttered in the wind.
【飘摇】piāoyáo〈动〉 1 (随风飘摆) sway in the wind: 炊烟袅袅，～上升。 Smoke was curling upward from kitchen chimneys. 2 (动荡不安) be turbulent: ▸风雨～
【飘曳】piāoyè〈动〉 sway: 柳枝在晨风中～。 The willow was swaying in the morning breeze.
【飘移】piāoyí〈动〉 drift: 大陆～ continental drift
【飘逸】piāoyì A〈形〉〈书〉 natural and unrestrained: 神采～ have an elegant bearing B〈动〉 waft away: 花香～。 The scent of the flowers wafted away.
【飘溢】piāoyì〈动〉 float and brim with: 花房里花香～。 Fragrance emanated from the flowers in the greenhouse.
【飘游】piāoyóu〈动〉 drift
【飘族】piāozú〈名〉 drifters: 校～ university floaters

螵 piāo

【螵蛸】piāoxiāo〈名〉［昆虫］ egg capsule of a mantis

piáo

朴 Piáo〈名〉 Piao [surname]
▸pō, pò, pǔ

嫖 piáo〈动〉 visit prostitutes: ▸～娼, ～客
【嫖娼】piáochāng〈动〉 visit prostitutes
【嫖妓】piáojì = 嫖娼 piáochāng
【嫖客】piáokè〈名〉 client at a brothel
【嫖宿】piáosù〈动〉 sleep with a prostitute

瓢 piáo〈名〉 gourd ladle: 舀一～水 scoop up a gourd of water
【瓢虫】piáochóng〈名〉［昆虫］ ladybird; ladybug〈美〉
【瓢瓜】piáoguā〈名〉［植物］ bottle gourd
【瓢泼】piáopō〈动〉 [of rain] pour down
【瓢泼大雨】piáopō-dàyǔ〈成〉 torrential rain

piǎo

莩 piǎo = 殍 piǎo
▸fú

殍 piǎo〈名〉〈书〉 bodies of the starved: ▸饿～遍野

漂 piǎo〈动〉 1 (用化学药剂) bleach: ～过的布特别白。 Bleached cloth is very white. 2 (用水) rinse: ～净衣服 give the clothes a good rinse
▸piāo, piào
【漂白】piǎobái〈动〉 bleach
【漂白粉】piǎobáifěn〈名〉 bleaching powder
【漂白剂】piǎobáijì〈名〉 bleach: 强力家用～ strong household bleach
【漂染】piǎorǎn〈动〉 bleach and dye
【漂洗】piǎoxǐ〈动〉 rinse: 把衣服上的肥皂水～干净 rinse the soap out of one's washing

缥（縹） piǎo〈书〉
A〈形〉 pale-green: ～玉 pale-green jade
B〈名〉 light-blue silk
▸piāo

瞟 piǎo〈动〉 cast a sidelong glance at: 营业员～了他一眼。 The salesman flashed his eyes at him.

piào

票 piào〈名〉 1 (指凭证) ticket: 检～ check a ticket ‖ 电影～ cinema ticket ‖ 火车～ train ticket ‖ 凭～入场。 Admission by ticket only. ▸彩～, 发～, 邮～ 2 (纸币) banknote: 大～ large denomination note ‖ 零～儿 notes of small denominations ▸钞～ 3 (人质) hostage: ▸绑～, 撕～ 4 (指业余) amateur performance: ▸～友
【票额】piào'é〈名〉 face value: 10张～百元的人民币 ten 100 *yuan* RMB notes
【票贩子】piàofànzi〈名〉 (ticket) tout〈英〉; scalper〈美〉
【票房】piàofáng〈名〉 1 (售票处) booking office 2 (指影剧收入) box office: ▸～收入 3〈旧〉(指组织) club for amateur performers of Beijing opera, etc.
【票房收入】piàofáng shōurù〈名〉 box-office income: 该剧～再创新高。 The play has taken a new box office high once again.
【票匪】piàofěi〈名〉〈旧〉 kidnapper
【票根】piàogēn〈名〉 ticket stub
【票汇】piàohuì〈动〉 send bank draft
【票价】piàojià〈名〉 ticket price: ～下调 fare reductions ‖ 优惠～ get a discount
【票据】piàojù〈名〉 1 (与货币相关) bill: 兑现～ cash a note ‖ ～交易所 clearing house ‖ 外汇～ foreign exchange note ‖ 银行～ bank note 2 (与货物相关) receipt: 凭～提货。 Take delivery of goods upon receipt.
【票面】piàomiàn〈名〉 face value: 大～的钞票 big bills ‖ ～利率 contract rate of interest
【票箱】piàoxiāng〈名〉 ballot box: 打开～ open the ballot box
【票选】piàoxuǎn〈动〉 cast a ballot: 采用记名～ vote by registered ballot
【票友】piàoyǒu〈名〉 amateur performer
【票证】piàozhèng〈名〉 coupons: 发放～ issue coupons
【票庄】piàozhuāng〈名〉〈旧〉 draft bank
【票子】piàozi〈名〉 (bank)note: 一大沓～ a thick wad of banknotes

嘌 piào

【嘌呤】piàolìng〈名〉［生化］ purine

漂 piào
▸piāo, piǎo
【漂亮】piàoliang〈形〉 1 (美) beautiful: 外表/衣着～ be smart in appearance/dress ‖ 她打扮得漂漂亮亮去参加舞会。 She dressed herself up for the dance. ‖ 她长得很～。 She is very pretty. 2 (出色) remarkable: 打了一个～仗 win a brilliant victory ‖ 干得～ well done ‖ 她的英语说得很～。 She speaks beautiful English.
【漂亮话】piàolianghuà〈名〉 fine words: 光说～没用，做出来才算数。 Actions speak louder than words.

骠（驃） piào〈形〉〈书〉 1 (指马) fast 2 (指人) valiant: ▸～悍, ～勇
▸biāo
【骠悍】piàohàn〈形〉 intrepid: ～的骑兵 intrepid cavalry
【骠勇】piàoyǒng〈形〉 valiant: ～的斗士 gallant fighter

piē

氕 piē〈名〉［化学］ protium (^{1}H)

撇 piē〈动〉 1 (抛弃) cast aside: 把坏习惯都～了 cast aside all bad habits ‖ 丈夫一年前去世了，～下她一个人。 Her husband died a year ago, leaving her all alone in this world. ▸～开, ～弃 2 (舀去) skim off: ～去泡沫 skim off the scum
▸piě
【撇开】piēkāi〈动〉 cast aside: 我们先～这个问题不谈。 We will bypass this issue for the moment.
【撇弃】piēqì〈动〉 abandon: ～原配 abandon one's first wife
【撇清】piēqīng〈动〉 plead ignorance

瞥 piē〈动〉 shoot a glance at: 匆匆一～ a fleeting glance ‖ 哥哥不满地～了弟弟一眼。 The elder brother shot the younger brother a disapproving look.
【瞥见】piējiàn〈动〉 catch sight of: 在公共汽车上，他无意间～一个小偷在扒窃。 On the bus, he caught sight of a thief picking a passenger's pocket.
【瞥视】piēshì〈动〉 cast a quick glance at: 他～了一下听众，便开始发言。 He cast a quick look at the audience before he spoke.

piě

苤 piě

【苤蓝】piělan〈名〉［植物］ kohlrabi

撇 piě
A〈动〉 1 (扔) fling: ～石头 throw a stone ‖ ～手榴弹 throw hand grenades 2 (指嘴) curl one's lips: 她嘴一～就哭起来了。 Her mouth twitched and she began to cry. 3〈口〉(指姿势) turn one's feet out when walking: 他走路时两脚老向外～。 His feet turn out when he walks.
B〈名〉 [in Chinese characters] left-falling wedge-shaped stroke: ▸八字没一～
C〈量〉 [for things resembling the left-falling stroke]: 他留着两～小胡子。 He has two wisps of a moustache.
▸piē
【撇嘴】piězuǐ〈动〉 curl one's lips: 他不以为然地撇撇嘴。 He curled his lips with disapproval. ‖ 她鄙夷地～一笑。 Her lips curled in a contemptuous smile.

pīn

拼[1] pīn〈动〉 1 (连接) piece together to form a bigger whole: 把两张桌子～起来 join two desks together ‖ 把破碎的花瓶～在一起 piece together shards of a broken vase ▸～版, ～凑 2 (拼写) spell: 这个词～错了。 This word is spelled wrongly. ‖

你的名字怎么～? How do you spell your name?

拼²（拚） pīn〈动〉go all out: ～个你死我活 fight to the bitter end ‖ 敢打敢～ dare to stand up to strong opponents ▸～搏, ～刺, ～命

【拼版】pīnbǎn〈动〉［印刷］impose

【拼板玩具】pīnbǎn wánjù〈名〉jigsaw puzzle

【拼搏】pīnbó〈动〉exert oneself to the utmost: 顽强～ struggle tenaciously ‖ ～精神 spirit of fighting relentlessly

【拼车】pīnchē〈动〉car pool: 出行时尽量～，费用由大家分摊。You should do your best to car pool – that way everybody can split the expense of the ride.

【拼刺】pīncì〈动〉1（指练习）do drill with bayonet 2（指格斗）charge with bayonets: 冲锋～ mount a bayonet charge

【拼刺刀】pīn cìdāo = 拼刺 pīncì

【拼凑】pīncòu〈动〉piece together: ～钱款 scrape together a sum of money ‖ ～人马 put together a force

【拼攒】pīncuán〈动〉assemble (spare parts): ～一辆摩托 assemble parts into a motorbike

【拼法】pīnfǎ〈名〉spelling: 一个词的不同～ variant spellings of a word

【拼合】pīnhé〈动〉piece together: 把七巧板重新～成正方形。Form the tangram into a square again.

【拼接】pīnjiē〈动〉piece together: 他把几块木板～在一起。He pieced together several planks.

【拼劲儿】pīnjìnr〈名〉energy and determination: 他～十足。He has a real fighting spirit.

【拼老本】pīn lǎoběn〈动〉exert all one's might and main

【拼老命】pīn lǎomìng〈动〉display a death-defying spirit in spite of one's age

【拼力】pīnlì〈动〉do one's utmost: ～夺冠 go all out for the championship ‖ ～死战 fight fiercely and desperately

【拼拢】pīnlǒng〈动〉put together

【拼命】pīnmìng A〈动〉risk one's life: 跟歹徒～ risk one's life with the ruffians B〈副〉as hard as possible: ～工作 go all out in one's work ‖ ～挣扎 struggle desperately

【拼盘】pīnpán〈名〉assorted hors d'oeuvre: 水果～ fruit hors d'oeuvres

【拼抢】pīnqiǎng〈动〉wrestle for a ball

【拼杀】pīnshā〈动〉1（指厮杀）fight fiercely: 战士们在浴血～。The soldiers were fighting a bloody battle. 2〈喻〉（指争胜）do one's utmost to win: 经过激烈～，他终于取得了胜利。He went all out and finally gained victory.

【拼死】pīnsǐ = 拼命 pīnmìng B

【拼死拼活】pīnsǐ-pīnhuó〈成〉1（指争斗）put up a life-and-death fight 2（指努力）for all one is worth: 她～地非离婚不可。She fought desperately to divorce her husband.

【拼贴画】pīntiēhuà〈名〉collage

【拼图游戏】pīntú yóuxì〈名〉jigsaw puzzle: ～块 jigsaw puzzle piece

【拼写】pīnxiě〈动〉spell: ～错误 spelling mistakes ‖ ～规则 rules of spelling

【拼音】pīnyīn〈动〉combine sounds into syllables

【拼音文字】pīnyīn wénzì〈名〉phonetic writing

【拼音字母】pīnyīn zìmǔ〈名〉1（指拼音文字）phonetic letter(s) 2（指汉语拼音）Chinese phonetic letter(s)

【拼争】pīnzhēng〈动〉compete with all one's might: 不畏强手，奋力～ not fear a strong opponent and contend with all one's strength

【拼装】pīnzhuāng〈动〉assemble: ～自行车 assemble a bicycle

【拼缀】pīnzhuì〈动〉piece together: 她把碎花布～起来做了个靠垫。She quilted together some small bits of coloured cloth to make a cushion.

【拼字游戏】pīnzì yóuxì〈名〉scrabble

姘 pīn〈动〉have illicit sexual relations with: ▸～夫, ～妇

【姘夫】pīnfū〈名〉illicit male lover

【姘妇】pīnfù〈名〉mistress

【姘居】pīnjū〈动〉[of a man and a woman] live illicitly together

【姘头】pīntou〈名〉paramour

pín

贫¹（貧） pín

A〈形〉poor: ▸～寒, ～困, 安～乐道, 扶～, 清～, 脱～

B〈动〉lack: ▸～乏, ～矿, ～血

C〈名〉〈谦〉a term of humble self-address for a monk, nun. etc.: ▸～道

贫²（貧） pín〈形〉〈方〉〈贬〉talkative: 你这个人嘴真～。You've really got a mouth on you. ▸～嘴薄舌

【贫病交迫】pínbìng jiāopò〈成〉be worn down by poverty and illness

【贫道】píndào〈名〉〈谦〉[term of humble self-reference used by a Taoist priest] I

【贫乏】pínfá〈形〉1（穷）poor: 家境～ a poor family 2（缺乏）wretchedly lacking: 内容～ be insufficient in content ‖ 知识～ be lacking in knowledge ‖ 资源～ be short of natural resources

【贫富】pín-fù〈名〉the rich and the poor: ～差距 gap between the rich and the poor ‖ ～分化 polarization of the rich and the poor

【贫寒】pínhán〈形〉poor and lowly-born: 他出身～。He came from a poor family.

【贫瘠】pínjí〈形〉poor: ～的土壤 infertile soil

【贫贱】pínjiàn〈形〉poor and lowly: ～之交不可忘。A man should not forget the friends he made when he was poor.

【贫窭】pínjù〈形〉〈书〉poverty-stricken

【贫苦】pínkǔ〈形〉poor: 出生～ be born into poverty ‖ 他～一生。He lived in poverty all his life.

【贫矿】pínkuàng〈名〉low-grade ore

【贫困】pínkùn〈形〉impoverished: ～的家庭 destitute family ‖ ～学生 needy students ‖ 消除～ eradicate poverty

【贫困线】pínkùnxiàn〈名〉poverty line: 生活在～以下 live below the poverty line

【贫民】pínmín〈名〉poor people: 城市～ the urban poor

【贫民窟】pínmínkū〈名〉slum: 城市～ urban slums

【贫农】pínnóng〈名〉〈旧〉poor farmer: ～出身 be born into a poor farming family

【贫气】pínqi〈形〉1（小气）mean: 他太～了，女孩都不愿跟他一起出去。None of the girls want to go out with him because he is such a cheapskate. 2（絮叨）tediously jocular: 这事儿你抱怨起来没完，真～。How tedious you are to keep complaining about this.

【贫穷】pínqióng〈形〉poor: 过着～的生活 live in poverty ‖ ～落后 be poor and backward

【贫弱】pínruò〈形〉poor and weak

【贫僧】pínsēng〈名〉〈谦〉[term of humble self-reference used by a Buddhist monk] I

【贫无立锥之地】pín wú lì zhuī zhī dì〈成〉extremely impoverished

【贫下中农】pín-xiàzhōngnóng〈名〉〈旧〉poor and lower-middle farmers

【贫血】pínxuè ▸p. 50〈名〉［医学］anaemia: 缺铁性～ iron deficiency anaemia ‖ 营养性～ nutritional anaemia

【贫油】pínyóu〈动〉be poor in oil deposits: ～地区/国家 oil-poor region/country

【贫铀】pínyóu〈名〉depleted uranium

【贫铀弹】pínyóudàn〈名〉depleted uranium bomb

【贫嘴】pínzuǐ〈形〉〈口〉talkative: 要～ banter tediously

【贫嘴薄舌】pínzuǐ-bóshé〈成〉go on and on sarcastically

频（頻） pín

A〈副〉〈书〉repeatedly: ～～点头 nod one's head repeatedly ▸～繁, 尿～

B〈名〉［电子］frequency: 超高～ ultrahigh frequency ‖ 低/高/中～ low/high/intermediate frequency ▸声～, 视～, 音～

【频传】pínchuán〈动〉keep pouring in: 捷讯～。News of victory kept pouring in. ‖ 喜讯～。Good news kept pouring in.

【频次】píncì〈名〉rate of recurrence

【频带】píndài〈名〉［物理］frequency range: ～宽度 bandwidth

【频道】píndào〈名〉channel: ～搜索 channel search ‖ 电视/电影/音乐～ television/film/music channel ‖ 这台电视机能收到100个～。This is a hundred-channel TV set. ‖ 中央电视台过去只有9个～。CCTV used to have only nine channels.

【频段】pínduàn〈名〉［通信］frequency band

【频繁】pínfán〈形〉frequent: 交往～ have frequent exchanges ‖ 下半场教练～换人。The coach made countless substitutions in the second half.

【频率】pínlǜ〈名〉frequency: 振动～ vibration frequency ‖ 词的出现～ word frequency ‖ 使用～ frequency of use

【频密】pínmì〈形〉frequent: 赛事～。There are regular competitions.

【频年】pínnián〈副〉for years running

【频频】pínpín〈副〉again and again: ～催促 urge repeatedly

【频谱】pínpǔ〈名〉［物理］frequency spectrum: ～仪 frequency spectrograph

【频仍】pínréng〈形〉〈书〉frequent: 灾害～ frequent outbreak of disasters ‖ 战事～ be subject to repeated wars

【频数】pínshuò〈形〉〈书〉frequent and successive: 病人腹泻～。The patient suffered from frequent, successive bowel movements.

嫔（嬪） pín〈名〉〈书〉1（指妾）concubine of an emperor: ▸～妃 2（指女官）court attendant: ▸～嫱

【嫔妃】pínfēi〈名〉concubine of an emperor

【嫔嫱】pínqiáng〈名〉〈古〉female court official

P

颦（顰） pín〈动〉〈书〉 frown: ～眉 knit one's brows ▸～蹙

【颦蹙】píncù〈动〉 be gloomy

pǐn

品 pǐn

A〈名〉 **1**（物品） article: 畅销～ best seller ‖ 易燃～ inflammable items ▸～牌, 产～, 展～, 织～ **2**（等级） grade: ▸～位, 精～, 极～, 上～, 下～ **3**（德行） character: ▸～德, 人～ **4**（种类） variety: ▸～种, ～类

B〈动〉 **1**（品尝） savour: ～茶 sip tea and assess its flavour and quality ‖ 你慢慢就会～出他的为人了。 You will gradually find out what sort of person he is. ▸～尝, ～茗 **2**（评论） appraise: ▸～鉴, ～评, ～头论足 **3**（吹奏） play: ～箫 play the flute

【品尝】pǐncháng〈动〉 taste: ～海鲜 taste fresh sea food ‖ 他～到了初为人父的滋味。 He got his first taste of being a father.

【品德】pǐndé〈名〉 integrity: ～高尚 be of lofty character ‖ ～教育 character education

【品第】pǐndì〈书〉 **A**〈动〉 appraise **B**〈名〉 grade

【品读】pǐndú〈动〉 read carefully: 这本书值得～。 The book is worth reading carefully.

【品格】pǐngé〈名〉 **1**（指人） moral character: ～优秀 be of noble character **2**（指作品） quality and style: 诗人近期和早期的作品～迥异。 The style of the poet's recent works is very different to that of his early works.

【品红】pǐnhóng ▸**p. 863**〈形〉 fuchsin red

【品级】pǐnjí〈名〉 **1**（指人） official rank **2**（指物品） grade: 橄榄油是高～的食用油。 Olive oil is a high-grade edible oil.

【品鉴】pǐnjiàn〈动〉 appraise: ～古籍 appraise ancient books

【品节】pǐnjié〈名〉〈书〉 moral character: ～卓异 outstanding moral character

【品酒】pǐnjiǔ〈动〉 taste wine: ～师 wine taster

【品蓝】pǐnlán ▸**p. 863**〈形〉 reddish blue

【品类】pǐnlèi〈名〉 class: ～繁多 a wide variety (of)

【品绿】pǐnlǜ ▸**p. 863**〈形〉 malachite green

【品貌】pǐnmào〈名〉 **1**（外表） appearance: ～俊俏 be handsome and charming **2**（品格和外貌） character and looks: ～兼优 pretty and of good character

【品名】pǐnmíng〈名〉 classification

【品茗】pǐnmíng〈动〉〈书〉 sample tea

【品目】pǐnmù〈名〉 names of goods: ～繁多 wide variety of goods

【品牌】pǐnpái〈名〉 brand name: ～效应 brand effect ‖ 国际～ global brand ‖ 特许～ licensed brand ‖ 知名～ famous brand ‖ 自有～ private brand ‖ ～机 brand-name computer

【品牌盗用】pǐnpái dàoyòng〈名〉 brand piracy

【品牌店】pǐnpáidiàn〈名〉 brand store: 时装～ fashion brand store

【品牌意识】pǐnpái yìshí〈名〉 brand-awareness

【品评】pǐnpíng〈动〉 judge: ～产品质量 appraise the quality of a product

【品色】pǐnsè〈名〉 **1**（种类） variety: ～多样的茶叶 a variety of tea **2**（颜色） colours **3**（等级） classification according to quality

【品头论足】pǐntóu-lùnzú = 评头论足 píngtóu-lùnzú

【品脱】pǐntuō〈量〉 pint: 两～啤酒/水 two pints of beer/water

【品位】pǐnwèi〈名〉 **1**〈旧〉（指官阶） official rank **2**［矿业］ grade: 高/低～矿 high-/low-grade ore **3**（指品质、价值） taste and quality: 文化～ cultural taste

【品味】pǐnwèi **A**〈动〉 **1**（品尝） taste: 他～了这种酒，认为质量优良。 He sampled the wine and found it excellent. **2**（体会） consider: 他经过仔细～，明白了那句话的含义。 After careful consideration, he understood what the sentence really meant. **B**〈名〉 taste: ～低下的笑话 jokes of questionable taste ‖ 橱窗的陈列很有～。 The window displays are in good taste.

【品系】pǐnxì〈名〉［生物］ strain

【品行】pǐnxíng〈名〉 behaviour: ～不良的人 person of bad conduct ‖ ～端正 be upright in character

【品行不端】pǐnxíng bùduān〈成〉 be badly behaved

【品性】pǐnxìng〈名〉 one's nature and moral character: ～敦厚 be of a kind and generous nature

【品学兼优】pǐnxué-jiānyōu〈成〉 be excellent not only morally but also academically: 他是一位～的学生。 He is a good student of good character.

【品议】pǐnyì〈动〉 appraise

【品藻】pǐnzǎo〈动〉〈书〉 evaluate

【品质】pǐnzhì〈名〉 **1**（指人） character: 道德～ moral character ‖ 高贵的～ fine character ‖ 磨难能考验一个人的～。 Hardships test a person's true character. ‖ 小说的主人翁具有许多优秀～。 The hero of the novel has many good qualities. **2**（指产品） quality: ～低劣 be of poor quality ‖ ～优良 be of excellent quality ‖ 高～的葡萄酒 quality wine

【品种】pǐnzhǒng〈名〉 variety: 改良～ improve variety ‖ 培育水稻新～ breed a new strain of grain ‖ 产品～繁多。 The many different products come in many different forms. ‖ 该购物中心商品～齐全。 The shopping centre has a good assortment of goods.

pìn

牝 pìn〈形〉 [of some birds and animals] female: ～鸡 hen ‖ ～马 mare ‖ ～牛 cow ‖ ～猪 sow

【牝鸡司晨】pìnjī-sīchén〈成〉〈旧〉〈贬〉〈喻〉 the woman wears the trousers

聘 pìn〈动〉 **1**（聘用） employ: ～为顾问 engage sb. as a consultant ‖ ～为教授 appoint sb. to a professorship ▸～用, 延～, 应～ **2**〈书〉（出使） visit a state as an envoy: ～使往来 exchange state visits **3**（订婚） betroth: 定～ formally betroth ▸～金, ～礼 **4**〈口〉（出嫁） get married: ～姑娘/闺女 marry a daughter off ▸出～

【聘金】pìnjīn〈名〉〈旧〉 **1**（指彩礼） betrothal money for the bride's family **2**（指酬金） commission

【聘礼】pìnlǐ〈名〉〈旧〉 **1**（指彩礼） betrothal gifts: 下～ deliver betrothal gifts **2**（指谢礼） gifts for inviting service

【聘期】pìnqī〈名〉 term of employment

【聘请】pìnqǐng〈动〉 engage: ～律师 engage sb. as a lawyer ‖ 高薪～ employ sb. with a high salary

【聘任】pìnrèn〈动〉 employ: ～制 appointment system ‖ ～她为项目总工程师。 She was appointed chief engineer of the project.

【聘书】pìnshū〈名〉 letter of appointment: 他已接到～。 He has received the appointment letter.

【聘贤任能】pìnxián-rènnéng〈成〉 engage worthies and men of ability for service

【聘用】pìnyòng〈动〉 employ: 该厂～了一千工人。 The factory employed one thousand workers. ‖ 我们～他当顾问。 We employed him as an adviser.

【聘约】pìnyuē〈名〉 employment contract: 解除～ terminate an employment contract (with sb.) ‖ 签订～ sign an employment contract (with sb.)

pīng

乒 pīng

A〈拟〉 ping: ～的一声枪响 the crack of a gun ‖ 大风吹得窗户～～作响。 The windows rattled in the wind.

B〈名〉 ping-pong: ▸～乓, ～赛, ～坛

【乒联】pīnglián〈简称〉= 乒乓球联合会

【乒乓】pīngpāng **A**〈拟〉 rattle: 雹子打在屋顶上～乱响。 Hailstones were rattling against the roofs. **B**〈名〉〈口〉 ping-pong: 打～ play ping-pong ‖ ～比赛 table tennis match

【乒乓球】pīngpāngqiú〈名〉 **1** ▸**p. 909**（指运动） table tennis: 打～ play table tennis ‖ ～运动员 table tennis player **2**（指球） ping-pong ball

【乒乓球联合会】pīngpāngqiú liánhéhuì〈名〉 table tennis federation: 国际～ International Table Tennis Federation

【乒乓球拍】pīngpāngqiúpāi〈名〉 table tennis bat

【乒乓球台】pīngpāngqiútái〈名〉 table tennis table

【乒乒乓乓】pīngpīng-pāngpāng〈拟〉 rattle: 那一叠碟子～跌到地上都砸碎了。 The pile of plates fell with a great clatter and smashed to pieces.

【乒赛】pīngsài〈名〉 table tennis match: 世～ World Table Tennis Championships

【乒坛】pīngtán〈名〉 table tennis world: ～新星 rising star in table tennis

俜 pīng ▸伶俜 língpīng

娉 pīng

【娉娉袅袅】pīngpīng-niǎoniǎo〈成〉 [of a woman] slender and beautiful

【娉婷】pīngtíng〈形〉〈书〉 slender and elegant: 举止～ have a graceful manner ‖ 体态～ have a graceful carriage

píng

平 píng

A〈形〉 **1**（平坦） level: 把地图～铺在桌上 spread the map on the table ‖ 让病人躺～ help the patient to lie flat ‖ 马路不～。 The road is not even. ▸～川, ～坦 **2**（不相上下） equal: ～世界记录 equal a world record ‖ 双方打成七～。 The two teams tied at 7-7. ▸～辈, ～等, ～局, ～摊 **3**（公正） fair: 不～则鸣。 Complaint comes when there is injustice. ▸公～

4（安定） calm: ▸～安, ～静, 心～气和 **5**（普通） ordinary: 考试成绩～～ have average test results ▸～常, ～淡, ～凡

B〈动〉 **1**（使平整） level: ～地 level the ground ‖ 把沟～了种庄稼 fill in the gully to grow crops **2**（改正） set right: ▸～反 **3**（征服） suppress: 治国～天下 manage state affairs and put the country in order ▸～乱, ～叛 **4**（平息） calm: ～民愤 assuage popular indignation ‖ 你先～～气! Just calm down a bit!

C = 平声 píngshēng

【平安】 píng'ān〈形〉 safe and sound: ～到达 arrive safe and sound ‖ 一路～! Have a good trip! ‖ 祝你旅途～! Have a safe journey!

【平安无事】 píng'ān-wúshì〈成〉 all is well

【平白】 píngbái **A**〈副〉 for no reason: ～挨了一顿打 get a thrashing for no reason at all ▸～无故 **B**〈形〉 plain and simple: ～易懂 simple and easy to understand

【平白无故】 píngbái-wúgù〈成〉 for no apparent reason: 她不可能～离开他。 It is impossible for her to have left him without reason.

【平板】 píngbǎn **A**〈形〉 boring: 文章写得太～。 The article is written in a very lifeless manner. **B**〈名〉 flat sheet: ～玻璃 sheet glass ‖ ～彩电 flat-screen colour TV

【平板车】 píngbǎnchē〈名〉 flatbed tricycle

【平版】 píngbǎn〈名〉［印刷］ lithographic plate: ～印刷机 offset press

【平辈】 píngbèi〈名〉 peers: 他不大与～人交往。 He doesn't spend much time with his peers.

【平步青云】 píngbù-qīngyún〈成〉〈喻〉 have a meteoric rise

【平仓】 píngcāng〈动〉［金融］ close a position

【平产】 píngchǎn〈动〉 show no increase in output: 今年全县粮食，～的乡占5%。 This year five per cent of the townships in the county have shown no increase in grain production.

【平常】 píngcháng **A**〈形〉 ordinary: 手艺不～ of different craftsmanship ‖ 话虽～，意义却很深刻。 The words sound commonplace, but they carry important meanings. **B**〈副〉 usually: ～我们是七点吃早餐。 Usually we have our breakfast at seven. ‖ 我～起得很早。 I generally get up early.

【平车】 píngchē〈名〉 **1**（铁路货运车） flatcar **2**（用于运送病人） flatbed cart

【平畴】 píngchóu〈名〉〈书〉 level farmland: ～沃野 fertile level farmland ‖ 千里～ large stretch of flat farmland

【平川】 píngchuān〈名〉 open country: ～广野 vast plain ▸一马～

【平传】 píngchuán〈名〉［体育］ parallel toss

【平喘】 píngchuǎn〈动〉［中医］ relieve asthma

【平旦】 píngdàn〈名〉〈书〉 dawn: ～即起 get up soon after daybreak

【平淡】 píngdàn〈形〉 pedestrian: ～无味的谈话 dull conversation ‖ 对他来说生活似乎～无味。 Life seemed very flat to him.

【平淡无奇】 píngdàn-wúqí〈成〉 commonplace

【平等】 píngděng〈形〉 equal: ～待人 treat sb. as one's equal ‖ ～待遇 equal treatment ‖ 消除不～ abolish all inequalities ‖ 男女～ equality between the sexes ‖ 法律面前，人人～。 All people are equal in the eyes of the law.

【平等互利】 píngděng-hùlì〈名〉 equality and mutual benefit [one of the Five Principles of Peaceful Coexistence]

【平籴】 píngdí〈动〉〈旧〉 [of local authorities] buy in grain at a normal price in good years so as to sell it in famine years at the same price

【平底】 píngdǐ〈名〉 flat bottom: ～便鞋 loafers ‖ ～拖鞋 scuff slippers

【平底锅】 píngdǐguō〈名〉 frying pan; skillet〈美〉

【平地】 píngdì **A**〈动〉 level the ground: 播种前要翻地和～。 We must plough and level the ground before sowing. **B**〈名〉 level ground

【平地风波】 píngdì-fēngbō〈成〉〈喻〉 bolt from the blue

【平地起风波】 píngdì qǐ fēngbō = 平地风波 píngdì-fēngbō

【平地一声雷】 píngdì yī shēng léi〈惯〉〈喻〉 sudden rise to fame or position

【平顶房】 píngdǐngfáng〈名〉 flat-roofed house

【平定】 píngdìng **A**〈动〉 **1**（使稳定） calm down: ～政局 stabilize the political situation **2**（武力平息） put down: ～叛乱 suppress a rebellion **B**〈形〉 calm: 时局～。 The political situation is stable. ‖ 情绪已～下来。 The agitation has already subsided.

【平动】 píngdòng〈名〉［物理］ translatory motion, translation

【平凡】 píngfán〈形〉 ordinary: ～的岗位 ordinary post ‖ ～的人 ordinary person ‖ 他们在～的工作中做出了不～的成绩。 They have made extraordinary achievements in run-of-the-mill work.

【平反】 píngfǎn〈动〉 redress: ～冤案 redress a grievance ‖ 宣布给某人～ announce sb.'s rehabilitation

【平方】 píngfāng〈名〉 **1**［数学］ square: 四是二的～。 Four is two squared. **2**（平方米） square metre: 这套房有120个～。 This flat has a floor space of 120 square metres.

【平方根】 píngfānggēn〈名〉［数学］ square root: 求X的～ find the square root of X

【平方公里】 píngfāng gōnglǐ〈量〉 square kilometre

【平方米】 píngfāngmǐ〈量〉 square metre

【平房】 píngfáng〈名〉 single-storey house

【平分】 píngfēn〈动〉 share out equally: ～利润 divide the profits fifty-fifty

【平分秋色】 píngfēn-qiūsè〈成〉 share equally: 这次比赛中，两队～，各得两枚金牌。 In this contest, both teams had an equal share of the honours, with two gold medals each.

【平分线】 píngfēnxiàn〈名〉［数学］ bisector

【平伏】 píngfú〈动〉 calm down

【平服】 píngfú〈动〉 **1**（心情安定） calm down: 他心情难以～。 He couldn't calm down. **2**（服气） be convinced: 你只有拿出真本事，才能叫人～。 Your real abilities are what count.

【平复】 píngfù〈动〉 **1**（恢复平静） return to normal: 等他情绪～后再告诉他。 Tell him after he calms down. ‖ 局势已经～。 The situation has returned to normal. **2**（康复） recover: 病体日渐～。 The patient is recovering.

【平跟】 pínggēn〈名〉 flat heel: ～鞋 flat shoes

【平光】 píngguāng〈名〉 plain glass: ～眼镜 plain glass spectacles

【平和】 pínghé〈形〉 **1**（温和） gentle: 性情～ even-tempered ‖ 语气～ in a mild tone **2**（指药性） mild: 这种药药性～，无副作用。 This medicine is quite mild and has no side effects. **3**（和谐） peaceful: 气氛～ peaceful atmosphere

【平衡】 pínghéng **A**〈形〉 balanced: 失去～ lose one's balance ‖ 发展不～ uneven development ‖ 收支～。 Income and expenditure are balanced. **B**〈动〉 balance: ～工业布局 balance out the distribution of industry ‖ ～预算 balance a budget

【平衡木】 pínghéngmù〈名〉［体育］ **1**（指器械） balance beam **2**（指项目） balance beam exercises

【平滑】 pínghuá〈形〉 even and smooth: 手感～ smooth to the touch ‖ 冰面～如镜。 The surface of the ice is as smooth as a mirror.

【平滑肌】 pínghuájī〈名〉［生理］ smooth muscle

【平话】 pínghuà〈名〉 *pinghua* [a kind of story-telling as an entertainment popular in the Song Dynasty]

【平缓】 pínghuǎn〈形〉 **1**（平坦） even: 地势～ smooth terrain ‖ 水流～。 The currents flow gently. **2**（平静和缓） gentle: 语调～ be mild in tone

【平假名】 píngjiǎmíng〈名〉［语言］ hiragana [cursive forms of the Japanese kana (written letters) as opposed to katakana (片假名)]

【平价】 píngjià **A**〈动〉 stabilize prices **B**〈名〉 **1**（指货物） fixed prices: ～收购 buy in at a fair price ‖ ～米 rice sold or bought at a fixed-price **2**（指货币） par: ～兑换 exchange at par ‖ ～发行 par issue ‖ 这两种货币现已达到～。 The two currencies have now reached parity.

【平价商店】 píngjià shāngdiàn〈名〉 fair-price shop

【平交】 píngjiāo〈动〉 deal with one another on an equal footing

【平角】 píngjiǎo〈名〉 straight angle: ～为180°。 A straight angle is 180°.

【平脚裤】 píngjiǎokù〈名〉 boxer shorts

【平靖】 píngjìng **A**〈动〉〈旧〉 pacify: ～动乱 suppress a turmoil **B**〈形〉〈书〉 tranquil: 时局～ peaceful political situation

【平静】 píngjìng〈形〉 calm: 恢复～ regain one's composure ‖ ～的生活/夜晚 quiet life/night ‖ 他心情激动，久久不能～。 He was so excited that it took a long time for him to calm down.

【平局】 píngjú〈名〉 tie: 扳成～ equalize the score ‖ 与客队打成～ tie with the visiting team

【平均】 píngjūn **A**〈动〉 average: 这些孩子～六岁。 These children have an average age of six years. ‖ 年～降水量为700毫米。 The mean yearly precipitation is 700 mm. **B**〈形〉 equal: ～分摊 share out equally ‖ ～主义 egalitarianism

【平均期望寿命】 píngjūn qīwàng shòumìng〈名〉 average life expectancy

【平均数】 píngjūnshù〈名〉 mean

【平均值】 píngjūnzhí〈名〉 mean value: 求～ obtain the mean value

【平旷】 píngkuàng〈形〉〈书〉 flat and open: ～的原野 level and broad plains

【平列】 píngliè〈动〉 place side by side: 我们不能把这两种情况～起来分析。 We should not put these two sets of circumstances on a par when analysing them.

【平流层】 píngliúcéng〈名〉［气象］ stratosphere

【平炉】 pínglú〈名〉［冶金］ open hearth: ～炼钢法 open-hearth process

【平乱】 píngluàn〈动〉 put down a rebellion

【平落】pínglùo〈动〉[of prices] drop to normal
【平米】píngmǐ〈名〉square metre
【平面】píngmiàn〈名〉[数学] plane: 垂直～ vertical plane ‖ 水～ horizontal plane
【平面几何】píngmiàn jǐhé〈名〉[数学] plane geometry: ～学 plane geometry
【平面角】píngmiànjiǎo〈名〉[数学] plain angle
【平面镜】píngmiànjìng〈名〉[物理] plane mirror
【平面三角】píngmiàn sānjiǎo〈名〉plane trigonometry
【平面图】píngmiàntú〈名〉1（指正射投影地图）plan 2（指物体垂直投影图）plane: 铁路～ rail alignment 3 [数学] planar graph
【平民】píngmín〈名〉commoner: ～百姓 common people ‖ ～生活 civilian life
【平明】píngmíng〈名〉〈书〉dawn
【平年】píngnián〈名〉1（指非闰年）non-leap year 2（指收成一般）year of average harvest
【平叛】píngpàn = 平乱 píngluàn
【平平】píngpíng〈形〉average: 相貌～ average looks ‖ 成绩～。The results are average.
【平平当当】píngpíng-dāngdāng〈成〉done smoothly
【平铺直叙】píngpū-zhíxù〈成〉speak or write in a simple, straightforward style
【平棋】píngqí〈名〉draw (in chess or other board games)
【平起平坐】píngqǐ-píngzuò〈成〉〈喻〉be on an equal footing: 那些孩子要和大人们～。Those children want to be treated as equals by the adults.
【平权】píngquán〈名〉equal rights: 男女～ equal rights for men and women
【平壤】Píngrǎng〈名〉Pyongyang
【平日】píngrì〈名〉normal days: 今天城里的人比～多。There are more people in town than usual.
【平绒】píngróng〈名〉[纺织] velveteen: ～地毯 velveteen rug
【平上去入】píng-shàng-qù-rù〈名〉[语言] the level, rising, falling and entering tones [the four tones in classical Chinese pronunciation]
【平射炮】píngshèpào〈名〉[军事] flat fire gun
【平身】píngshēn〈动〉〈旧〉stand up after kowtowing
【平生】píngshēng〈名〉1（一生）one's whole life;（有生以来）ever in one's life: 那是他～第一次看到大海。That was the first time in his life that he saw the sea. 2（平时）normal times: 他～艰苦朴素。He usually lives a simple life.
【平声】píngshēng〈名〉[语言] level tone [one of the four tones in classical Chinese pronunciation]
【平时】píngshí〈名〉1（通常的时候）normal times: 像～一样，他第一个到达。As usual, he arrived first. 2（平常时期）peacetime: ～体制 peacetime system ‖ ～多流汗，战时少流血。Sweat more in peacetime, bleed less in war.
【平时不烧香，急来抱佛脚】píngshí bù shāoxiāng, jí lái bào fójiǎo〈俗〉〈喻〉do nothing till one is driven to desperation
【平实】píngshí〈形〉simple and honest: 文笔～ natural writing style
【平视】píngshì〈动〉look straight ahead: 立正时两眼要～前方。Look straight ahead when you stand to attention.
【平手】píngshǒu〈名〉draw: 甲乙两队打成～。Team A drew with team B.
【平水期】píngshuǐqī〈名〉period when a river is at its normal level
【平顺】píngshùn〈形〉plain sailing: 生活～如常 live a smooth and orderly life ‖ 病人呼吸～。The patient is breathing normally.
【平素】píngsù〈名〉normal times: 他～不爱说话。He is a man of few words.
【平塌】píngtā〈形〉flat: ～鼻 flat nose
【平台】píngtái〈名〉1（晒台）terrace 2（工作台）movable platform: 装货～ loading platform 3（指计算机系统）platform: IBM～ IBM platform 4〈喻〉（指条件）platform: 交易～ trade platform
【平摊】píngtān = 均摊 jūntān
【平坦】píngtǎn〈形〉level: 宽阔～的马路 wide and flat road ‖ 他的人生道路并不～。His path in life was not at all smooth.
【平添】píngtiān〈动〉add naturally: 新建的公园给周围的居民～了许多乐趣。The newly-built park has given a lot of joy to the residents.
【平粜】píngtiào〈动〉〈旧〉[of local authorities] sell the grain stored in public granaries at fair prices in famine years
【平头】píngtóu〈名〉crop: 理～ have a crew cut ‖ 眼下又兴～了。The crop has become trendy again.
【平头百姓】píngtóu bǎixìng〈名〉common people
【平头钉】píngtóudīng〈名〉tack [small nail]
【平妥】píngtuǒ〈形〉simple and proper: 文章措辞～。The wording of the article is accessible and appropriate.
【平纹】píngwén〈名〉[纺织] plain weave: ～布 plain cloth
【平稳】píngwěn〈形〉1（无波动）smooth and steady: 经济增长～ steady economic growth ‖ 病人病情已经～。The patient's condition has now stabilized. ‖ 物价～。Prices are stable. 2（不晃动）stable: 飞行～ have a smooth flight ‖ 把桌子放～ make the table steady
【平西】píngxī〈动〉[of the sun] set: 太阳～了。The sun is setting.
【平昔】píngxī〈名〉〈书〉the past: 我～对烹饪3天兴趣。I never used to be interested in cooking.
【平息】píngxī〈动〉1（停息）calm down: 这场风波～了。The dispute has blown over. ‖ 暴风雨已经～了。The storm has subsided. 2（使停息）put down: ～暴乱 suppress a riot ‖ ～叛乱 put down a rebellion
【平销】píngxiāo〈名〉sale at low prices
【平心而论】píngxīn'érlùn〈成〉discuss sth. fairly: ～，他并不想从中获利。To give him his due, he had no desire to make any personal profit.
【平心静气】píngxīn-jìngqì〈成〉dispassionately: ～谈一谈 talk with sb. calmly
【平信】píngxìn〈名〉ordinary mail
【平行】píngxíng A〈形〉1（同等级）equal: 这两个机构是～的。The two units are of equal rank. 2（同时）simultaneous: ～发展 concurrent development ‖ 就各个问题进行～讨论 hold simultaneous discussions on different subjects B〈动〉[数学] be parallel: 这条公路与铁路～。The road runs parallel to the railway.
【平行四边形】píngxíng sìbiānxíng〈名〉[数学] parallelogram
【平行线】píngxíngxiàn〈名〉[数学] parallel lines: ～永不相交。Parallel lines never join.
【平行作业】píngxíng zuòyè〈名〉parallel operations
【平野】píngyě〈名〉flat open country: 一望无际的～ vast plain
【平移】píngyí〈名〉[物理] translation: ～运动 translational motion
【平抑】píngyì〈动〉stabilize: ～物价 keep prices down ‖ 他尽力使自己的怒火～下来。He tried his best to restrain his anger.
【平易】píngyì〈形〉1（易于相处）amiable: ～可亲 be amiable ▸～近人 2（浅显易懂）simple: 他行文简洁～。He writes in a simple and approachable style.
【平易近人】píngyì-jìnrén〈成〉1（指人）unassuming and approachable: 他学识渊博而又～。He is a man of great learning but approachable. 2（指文字）simple
【平庸】píngyōng〈形〉middle-of-the-road: 才能～ of mediocre ability ‖ ～之辈 men of ordinary talents
【平鱼】píngyú〈名〉butterfish
【平原】píngyuán ▸**p. 164**〈名〉plain: ～地区 flat country ‖ 冲积～ alluvial plain
【平月】píngyuè〈名〉February of a non-leap year
【平允】píngyǔn〈形〉〈书〉fair and just: 他话说得很～，令人心服。His words were very fair and so won people over.
【平仄】píngzè〈名〉1（指声调）level and oblique tones 2（指韵律）tonal patterns in classical Chinese poetry: 中国古诗要求～相谐。Classical Chinese poetry requires harmony in tonal patterns.
【平展】píngzhǎn〈形〉1（指地势）open and flat: ～的场院 open courtyard ‖ ～的地势 flat land 2（指衣着）unruffled: 他穿一身～合体的军装。He wears a pressed, well-fitting army uniform.
【平针】píngzhēn〈名〉plain stitch: ～织物 jersey
【平整】píngzhěng A〈动〉level: ～土地 level the ground B〈形〉smooth: 马路又宽又～。The streets are wide and flat. ‖ 地砖铺得很～。The tiles of the floor are all flush.
【平正】píngzheng〈形〉straight and even: 被子叠得很～。The quilt was neatly folded. ‖ 他墁的砖又～又密合。The bricks he laid are fitted evenly and closely together.
【平直】píngzhí〈形〉1（指形状）level and straight 2（指文章）simple and straightforward: ～浅露 simple and shallow
【平治】píngzhì〈动〉〈书〉put in order: ～水土 harness rivers and conserve soil
【平装】píngzhuāng〈形〉paperback: ～本 paperback (book) ‖ ～书 paperback book
【平准基金】píngzhǔn jījīn〈名〉buffer fund
【平足】píngzú〈名〉flat foot

冯（馮）

píng〈动〉〈书〉cross (a stream, etc.) on foot: ～河 wade across a river
▸Féng
【冯妇】píngfù〈名〉〈贬〉person who resumes their (lowly) old trade after having given it up for many years

评（評）

píng〈动〉1（讨论）comment on: ▸～介，～论，批～，书～ 2（评判）appraise: 我们找他～个理。Let's reason things out with him. ‖ 他再次被～为劳模。He was elected as a model worker for a second time. ▸～估，～选
【评比】píngbǐ〈动〉appraise through comparison: ～产品质量 compare and appraise the quality of different products ‖ 年终～

year-end appraisal
【评标】píngbiāo〈动〉evaluate a bid
【评产】píngchǎn〈动〉evaluate output
【评点】píngdiǎn〈动〉annotate and comment on
【评定】píngdìng〈动〉assess: ～职称 determine staff titles ‖ 成绩～ evaluation of achievements
【评断】píngduàn〈动〉decide: ～得失 weigh up the pros and cons ‖ ～是非 determine right and wrong
【评分】píngfēn **A**〈动〉mark: 给试卷～ grade papers ‖ ～标准 marking criterion **B**〈名〉mark
【评改】pínggǎi〈动〉read and correct: ～作文 correct and grade essays
【评功】pínggōng〈动〉evaluate achievements: ～授奖 give rewards on the basis of assessed merits
【评功摆好】pínggōng-bǎihǎo〈成〉sing sb.'s praises
【评估】pínggū〈动〉evaluate: 资产～ evaluation of assets ‖ 对教学质量进行～ conduct an assessment of teaching quality
【评估团】pínggūtuán〈名〉evaluation commission
【评话】pínghuà〈名〉**1** = 平话 pínghuà **2**［曲艺］pinghua [form of storytelling in certain dialect]
【评级】píngjí〈动〉grade: 给产品～ grade products
【评价】píngjià **A**〈动〉judge: ～文学作品 evaluate literary works ‖ 正确地～历史人物 correctly appraise historical figures **B**〈名〉evaluation: 给予高度～ speak highly of sth. ‖ 公正/客观的～ fair/objective evaluation
【评奖】píngjiǎng〈动〉determine awards on the basis of discussions with staff: 年终～ decide on awards through discussion at the end of the year
【评教】píngjiào〈动〉evaluate a teacher's work
【评介】píngjiè〈动〉review and introduce: ～新书 review of new books
【评剧】píngjù〈名〉Pingju opera
【评卷】píngjuàn〈动〉mark examination papers
【评理】pínglǐ〈动〉reason things out: 我们找个人～去。Let's find someone who can reason this out.
【评论】pínglùn **A**〈动〉comment on: ～好坏 decide on the strength and weakness of ‖ ～时事 comment on current events **B**〈名〉comment: 发表～ publish a review ‖ 文艺～ art and literary criticism ‖ 新闻～ news review
【评论家】pínglùnjiā〈名〉critic
【评论员】pínglùnyuán ▸**p. 966**〈名〉commentator: 足球～ football commentator
【评判】píngpàn〈动〉judge: ～得失 judge the advantages and disadvantages ‖ 留待后人～ await the verdict of time
【评聘】píngpìn〈动〉evaluate sb.'s qualifications and appoint them to a position
【评审】píngshěn〈动〉examine and appraise: ～国家重大发明奖 judge and determine the national awards for important inventions ‖ ～文艺作品 make a critical examination and appraisal of a literary work
【评书】píngshū〈名〉［曲艺］*pingshu* [folk art form in which the performer tells a long story using a folding fan, a handkerchief, and a gavel as props]: ～艺人 *pingshu* storyteller
【评述】píngshù〈动〉comment on and describe: 对局势做全面～ give a running commentary on the situation
【评说】píngshuō〈动〉comment on: 任人～ be open to comments ‖ 功过自有～。A person's merits and demerits, contributions and blunders will be duly evaluated.
【评弹】píngtán〈名〉［曲艺］*pingtan* [form of storytelling and ballad singing in Suzhou dialect]

> **评弹**
>
> A term that combines *pinghua* (评话, storytelling) and *tanci* (弹词, storytelling accompanied by stringed instruments) in local Suzhou dialect. In *pinghua* a performer holding a folding fan and a storyteller's gavel tells a long story. The *pinghua* repertoire of more than 50 pieces includes *The Romance of the Three Kingdoms* (▸《三国演义》) and *The Water Margin* (▸《水浒传》). In *tanci*, while speaking is the most important feature, there is also singing. The musical instruments used for *tanci* include the *sanxian* (三弦, a three-stringed plucked instrument) and the *pipa* (琵琶, an instrument similar to a lute). The libretto mostly consists of seven words in a line. *Tanci* is usually performed by two people, though occasionally there may be one or three. *Pingtan* can also refer to a performance which is a mixture of the two forms.

【评头论足】píngtóu-lùnzú〈成〉make personal remarks: 批评家对他的书～。The critic sat in judgement on his book. ‖ 不要对同事～。Don't make critical remarks about your colleagues.
【评头品足】píngtóu-pǐnzú = 评头论足 píngtóu-lùnzú
【评委】píngwěi〈名〉member of a review committee
【评委会】píngwěihuì〈名〉review committee
【评析】píngxī〈动〉comment on and analyse: ～古文名篇 make a comment on a famous classical piece of writing
【评薪】píngxīn〈动〉discuss and determine a person's wage grade on his qualifications and performance
【评选】píngxuǎn〈动〉choose through public appraisal: ～先进工作者 select advanced workers through a public appraisal ‖ ～优秀文学作品 select fine literary works through consultation with a panel
【评议】píngyì〈动〉comment on and appraise: ～干部 make an appraisal of an official ‖ 群众～ popular appraisal ‖ ～小组 appraisal group
【评语】píngyǔ〈名〉comment: 操行～ comments on sb.'s behaviour ‖ 老师给学生的作文写了～。The teacher commented on the student's essay.
【评阅】píngyuè〈动〉read and appraise: ～作文 read and appraise sb.'s essay ‖ 考卷已经～完毕。The examination papers have already been gone over and graded.
【评骘】píngzhì〈动〉〈书〉pass judgement on
【评注】píngzhù〈动〉annotate: ～一本书 annotate a book
【评传】píngzhuàn〈名〉critical biography: 《杜甫～》*A Critical Biography of Du Fu*

坪 píng〈名〉terrace: ▸草～, 停机～
【坪坝】píngbà〈名〉〈方〉open and flat space

苹（蘋）píng
【苹果】píngguǒ〈名〉apple
【苹果酱】píngguǒjiàng〈名〉apple jam
【苹果绿】píngguǒlǜ〈形〉apple-green

凭（憑）píng
A〈动〉**1**（倚靠）lean on: ～窗远眺 stand at a window gazing into the distance ▸～栏 **2**（依赖）depend on: 与别人竞争不能靠运气，要～本事。One can only compete with others by virtue of one's ability and not through luck.
B〈介〉**1**（凭着）on the basis of: ～单据报销 refund through invoices ‖ ～票入场。Admission by ticket only. ‖ 你～什么这么说？What do you base your statement on? **2**（根据）according to: ～常识判断 judge according to common sense ‖ ～经验办事 act by rule of thumb ‖ ～良心说 in all conscience
C〈连〉no matter (how, what, where, when, etc.): ～你跑多快，我也赶得上。No matter how fast you run, I can catch up with you. ‖ ～你怎么说，我也不动心。No matter what you say, I won't be perturbed. ▸任～
D〈名〉proof: 真～实据 substantial evidence ‖ 口说无～。Verbal statements are no guarantee. ▸～据, 文～
【凭单】píngdān〈名〉voucher: 旅馆～ hotel voucher
【凭吊】píngdiào〈动〉visit (a historical site, tomb, etc.) to remember a dead person or past event: ～烈士墓 pay a visit to martyrs' tombs ‖ ～死者 pay homage to the dead
【凭借】píngjiè〈动〉rely on: ～个人努力 rely on one's own efforts ‖ ～众人的帮助，他终于还清了债务。With the help of others, he finally managed to pay off his debts.
【凭据】píngjù〈名〉evidence: 出示～ produce evidence ‖ 说话没有～ make groundless allegations
【凭靠】píngkào〈动〉depend on
【凭空】píngkōng〈副〉groundlessly: ～捏造 make up a story ‖ ～想象 sheer imagination
【凭栏】pínglán〈动〉〈书〉lean on a railing: ～远眺 lean on a railing and gaze into the distance
【凭恃】píngshì〈动〉〈书〉rely on: ～天险 rely on natural barriers for defence
【凭眺】píngtiào〈动〉〈书〉gaze into the distance from a height: ～大海 gaze into the distant sea
【凭险】píngxiǎn〈动〉rely on natural barriers: ～抵抗 defend by taking advantage of favourable terrain ‖ ～据守 hold fast to natural barriers for defence
【凭信】píngxìn **A**〈动〉trust: 他的话不足～。His remarks are not to be trusted. **B**〈名〉proof: 立字据作为～ write down evidence as proof
【凭依】píngyī〈动〉depend on: 无所～ have nothing to fall back on
【凭倚】píngyǐ〈动〉lean against
【凭仗】píngzhàng〈动〉depend upon: 他今天的成绩～的是平日工作的积累。His present achievements are the result of daily, hard work.
【凭照】píngzhào〈名〉licence: 领取～ receive a licence
【凭证】píngzhèng〈名〉proof: 报销～ invoice for payment ‖ 完税～ tax payment receipt

枰 píng〈名〉〈书〉chessboard: 棋～ chessboard

P

屏 píng

A〈名〉**1**（屏风）screen: ▸画～ **2**（屏条）set of vertical scrolls: 四扇～儿 a set of four scrolls ▸挂～, 条～
B〈动〉shield: ▸～蔽, ～障
▸bǐng

【屏蔽】píngbì **A**〈动〉screen: ～一方 provide a protective screen for the area ‖ 这些树林能挡住旱风，～农田。These trees will shield off arid winds and protect the fields. **B**〈名〉**1**（屏障）protective screen: 该岛是渤海湾的～。This island serves as a protective screen for Bohai Bay. **2**［物理］screen: ～天线 screened/shielded antenna

【屏蔽门】píngbìmén〈名〉platform screen door: 地铁站台都安装了～。Subway platforms have all been equipped with platform screen doors.

【屏蔽器】píngbìqì = 屏蔽仪 píngbìyí

【屏蔽仪】píngbìyí〈名〉blocking device: 手机～ mobile phone signal blocker

【屏藩】píngfān〈名〉〈书〉**1**〈本〉screen and fence **2**〈旧〉〈喻〉（指疆土）surrounding territories

【屏风】píngfēng〈名〉screen: 竖起～ put up a screen

> **屏风**
>
> A screen placed in a room to block draughts, provide concealment, divide a room, or for decoration. Screens already existed in the Zhou Dynasty. After the Eastern Jin period, screens began to be decorated with paintings and calligraphy. There are two types of screen. The free-standing screen (座屏风) is made up of one or more decorated screens on a pedestal. The folding screen (围屏) is made up of an even number of panels and is placed on the floor in a zigzag to provide stability. Smaller folding screens, placed on a *kang* (▸炕) for decoration, are known as *kang* screens.

【屏极】píngjí〈名〉［电子］plate: ～电池 plate battery ‖ ～电路 plate circuit ‖ ～电源 plate (power) supply

【屏幕】píngmù〈名〉［电子］screen: 大～ big screen ‖ ～保护程序 screen saver ▸电视～

【屏条】píngtiáo〈名〉set of hanging scrolls [usu four in a row]

【屏障】píngzhàng **A**〈名〉protective screen: 后山是我们镇的天然～。The mountains behind our town provide us with a natural defence. **B**〈动〉〈书〉protect: ～中原 protect the Central Plains

瓶 píng

〈名〉bottle: 玻璃～ glass jar ‖ 酱油～ bottle of soy sauce ‖ 酒～ wine bottle ▸～胆, 保温～

【瓶胆】píngdǎn〈名〉glass liner of a Thermos

【瓶盖】pínggài〈名〉cap

【瓶颈】píngjǐng〈名〉bottleneck: 交通～ traffic bottleneck

【瓶塞】píngsāi〈名〉bottle stopper

【瓶装】píngzhuāng〈形〉bottled: ～啤酒 bottled beer ‖ ～饮料 bottled drink

【瓶子】píngzi〈名〉bottle: 可回收的～ returnable bottle

萍 píng

〈名〉［植物］duckweed: ▸浮～

【萍水相逢】píngshuǐ-xiāngféng〈成〉〈喻〉meet by chance: 他们～成知己。They became friends through a chance meeting.

【萍水之交】píngshuǐzhījiāo〈成〉brief acquaintance

【萍踪】píngzōng〈名〉〈书〉uncertain whereabouts: ～不定 drift about with great uncertainty

【萍踪浪迹】píngzōng-làngjì〈成〉wander from place to place

pō

朴 pō

▸Piáo, pò, pǔ

【朴刀】pōdāo〈名〉sword with a long blade and a short hilt, to be wielded with both hands

钋（釙）pō

〈名〉［化学］polonium (Po)

陂 pō

▸bēi

【陂陀】pōtuó〈形〉〈书〉uneven: ～不平 be slanting and uneven

坡 pō

A〈名〉slope: 爬～ climb a slope ‖ 上/下～ go up/down a slope ▸陡～, 滑～, 斜～
B〈形〉sloping: 板子～着放 put the board at a slant ▸～度

【坡岸】pō'àn〈名〉sloping bank

【坡道】pōdào〈名〉sloping path: 顺～而下 go down a sloping path

【坡地】pōdì〈名〉hillside fields: ～梯田化 terracing of the land on the slopes

【坡度】pōdù〈名〉gradient: 这条弯道越往上～越大。The slope increases as you go up the curve.

【坡跟鞋】pōgēnxié〈名〉wedge heels

【坡田】pōtián = 坡地 pōdì

泊 pō

〈名〉lake: ▸湖～, 血～
▸bó

泼¹（潑）pō

〈动〉splash: 她不小心把墨水～到了书上。She accidentally spilled some ink on her book. ▸瓢～大雨

泼²（潑）pō

〈形〉**1**（凶悍）uncouth: ▸～妇, 撒～ **2**〈方〉（有魄力）bold and vigorous: 他做事很～。He is bold and resolute in action. ▸活～

【泼妇】pōfù〈名〉virago

【泼妇骂街】pōfù-màjiē〈成〉like a shrewish woman shouting abuse in the street

【泼辣】pōla〈形〉**1**（凶悍）fierce and tough **2**（有魄力）daring and resolute: 她干活很～。She is bold and vigorous in her work.

【泼冷水】pō lěngshuǐ〈惯〉pour cold water on: 别再给他们～了。Stop discouraging them.

【泼墨】pōmò **A**〈名〉splash-ink: ～山水 splash-ink landscape **B**〈动〉paint in splash-ink: 挥毫～ wield one's brush in splash-ink style

【泼皮】pōpí〈名〉rogue: ～无赖 rascals and scoundrels

【泼洒】pōsǎ〈动〉splash: 牛奶～了一桌子。The milk spilt over the table. ‖ 月光～在原野上。The moon shone over the fields.

【泼水节】Pōshuǐjié〈名〉Water Sprinkling Festival

> **泼水节**
>
> A festival to welcome the New Year, celebrated by the Dai people of Yunnan Province. The festival takes place in the middle of April and usually lasts for three to five days. People sprinkle each other with water, make offerings at Buddhist temples, and take part in dragon-boat races.

【泼野】pōyě〈形〉uncivilized in behaviour and fiery in temper

【泼脏水】pō zāngshuǐ〈惯〉〈喻〉slander

颇（頗）pō〈书〉

A〈形〉oblique: ▸偏～
B〈副〉rather: ～不以为然 quite disagree with ‖ ～感兴趣 have considerable interest in ‖ ～有名气 quite famous

【颇为】pōwéi〈副〉rather

pó

婆 pó

〈名〉**1**（年长女性）old woman: ▸老太～ **2**（旧指从事某种职业的女性）woman in a certain occupation: ▸产～, 管家～ **3**（丈夫的母亲）husband's mother: ▸～媳, 公～ **4**（祖母辈妇女）woman from one's grandmother's generation: ▸姑～, 外～

【婆家】pójia〈名〉husband's family: 给她找个～ find a husband for her

【婆罗门】Póluómén〈名〉Brahman: ～教 Brahmanism

【婆母】pómǔ〈名〉husband's mother

【婆娘】póniáng〈名〉〈方〉**1**（已婚女性）married woman **2**（妻子）wife

【婆婆】pópo〈名〉**1**（丈夫的母亲）husband's mother **2**〈方〉（奶奶或姥姥）granny **3**〈喻〉（上级）higher authorities: ～太多事难办。It's hard to get anything done when you have too many people to report to.

【婆婆妈妈】pópo-māmā〈成〉**1**（不干脆）old-womanish: 别～的了。我们已经晚了。Don't dawdle. We're late already. **2**（脆弱）sentimental: 他就是这么～的，动不动就掉眼泪。He is so sentimental that he will cry for the slightest reason.

【婆婆嘴】pópozuǐ〈名〉**1**（指嘴）nagging tongue of an old woman **2**（指人）nagging person

【婆娑】pósuō〈形〉〈书〉whirling: 微风徐徐，树影～。The shadows of the trees are dancing in the breeze.

【婆媳】pó-xí〈名〉mother-in-law and daughter-in-law: ～关系 relationship between mother-in-law and daughter-in-law

【婆姨】póyí〈名〉〈方〉**1**（已婚女性）married woman **2**（妻子）wife

鄱 pó

【鄱阳湖】Póyánghú ▸**p. 305**〈名〉Poyang Lake [in Jiangxi Province]

繁 Pó

〈名〉Po [surname]
▸fán

皤 pó

〈形〉〈书〉white: 须发～然 white-haired

pǒ

叵 pǒ〈副〉〈书〉 impossibly: ▸～测

【叵测】pǒcè〈动〉〈书〉〈贬〉 be unpredictable: 心怀～ harbour evil intentions ▸居心～

【叵耐】pǒnài〈动〉 cannot bear

钷（鉕） pǒ〈名〉［化学］ promethium (Pm): ～化合物 promethium compound

笸 pǒ

【笸箩】pǒluo〈名〉 shallow basket: 针线～ sewing basket

pò

朴 pò〈名〉［植物］ Chinese hackberry ▸Piáo, pō, pǔ

【朴硝】pòxiāo〈名〉 mirabilite

迫 pò

A〈动〉 1（压制） force: ～于压力（做某事） under pressure (to do sth.) ‖ 为饥饿所～，他不得不沿街乞讨。 Hard pressed by hunger, he resorted to begging from door to door. ▸～害，压～ 2（接近） approach: ▸～近

B〈形〉 urgent: ▸～不及待，急～

▸pǎi

【迫不得已】pòbùdéyǐ〈成〉 have no alternative (but to): 他那样做完全是～。 He had no alternative but to do that.

【迫不及待】pòbùjídài〈成〉 be unable to hold oneself back: 她～地要告诉大家这个好消息。 She couldn't wait to tell them the good news.

【迫害】pòhài〈动〉 persecute: 屡遭～ undergo numerous persecutions ‖ 政治～ political persecution

【迫降】pòjiàng〈名〉 forced landing ▸pòxiáng

【迫近】pòjìn〈动〉 approach: ～胜利 be nearing victory ‖ 考期～。 The examination is approaching.

【迫临】pòlín〈动〉 be around the corner: 寒冬～。 Winter is coming.

【迫令】pòlìng〈动〉 force sb. to (do sth.): ～前进 order an advance ‖ 地方法院～关闭这家医院。 The local court ordered that the hospital be closed.

【迫切】pòqiè〈形〉 pressing: ～需要 have an urgent need ‖ ～的愿望 fervent wish

【迫使】pòshǐ〈动〉 force: ～囚犯认罪 coerce a prisoner into confessing their crimes ‖ 时间～我们不得不改变计划。 Time forced us to make some changes to our plan.

【迫视】pòshì〈动〉 look at from close-up

【迫降】pòxiáng〈动〉 force sb. to surrender ▸pòjiàng

【迫在眉睫】pòzàiméijié〈成〉 extremely urgent: 战争～。 War was imminent.

珀 pò ▸琥珀 hǔpò

【珀斯郡】Pòsījùn〈名〉 Perthshire

破 pò

A〈动〉 1（受损） break: 没关系，就～了一点皮。 It's nothing serious, just a graze. ‖ 我徒步旅行穿～了两双靴子。 I wore out two pairs of boots on the walking tour. 2（毁坏） destroy: ▸～釜沉舟，～坏 3（劈开） cut: ～开西瓜 cut open a melon ‖ 一～两半 split into two ▸乘风～浪，势如～竹 4（兑成零钱） break a banknote into small change: 你能替我～开100元钱吗？ Can you break a hundred *yuan* note for me? 5（突破） break with: ～记录 break a record ‖ ～旧俗，立新风 break with outmoded customs and establish new ones ▸～格，～戒，突～ 6（打败） defeat: 大～敌军 rout the enemy ▸攻～ 7（花费） spend (money, time, etc.): 请你～点工夫看看我的论文，行吗？ Will you please take some time out to read my essay? ▸～费 8（揭穿） crack: 那起杀人案至今未～。 The murder case remains unsolved. ▸～案，～译

B〈形〉 1（受损） broken: ～草帽 shabby straw hat ‖ ～房子 dilapidated house ‖ ～衣服 tattered clothes ▸～烂 2〈口〉（差劲） poor: 谁看那～戏。 Nobody wants to see that lousy play. ‖ 处理这点～事用不了多长时间。 This is a petty matter that won't take too long to resolve.

【破案】pò'àn〈动〉 crack a case: 限期～ set a deadline for solving the case

【破败】pòbài〈形〉 ruined: 那城堡已～不堪。 The castle is now in a terrible state of dilapidation.

【破冰船】pòbīngchuán〈名〉 ice-breaker

【破冰之旅】 pòbīng zhī lǚ〈名〉 ice-breaking diplomatic visit: 1972年美国总统尼克松的～ U.S. President Nixon's 1972 ice-breaking diplomatic tour

【破财】pòcái〈动〉 lose money: ～免灾 pay money to avoid misfortune

【破产】pòchǎn A〈名〉 bankruptcy: 濒临～ be on the verge of bankruptcy ‖ 宣告～ declare bankruptcy B〈动〉 1（丧失全部财产） go bankrupt: 企业因负债而告～。 The enterprise went bankrupt because of its debts. ‖ 该公司因产品滞销而～。 The company went bankrupt because it couldn't sell its products. 2〈喻〉〈贬〉（失败） come to nothing: 他的计划～了。 His plan came to nothing. ‖ 敌人的阴谋～了。 The enemy's scheme fell through.

【破产保护】 pòchǎn bǎohù〈名〉 bankruptcy protection: 寻求～ seek bankruptcy protection

【破产法】pòchǎnfǎ〈名〉 bankruptcy law: 企业～ enterprise bankruptcy law

【破产公告】pòchǎn gōnggào〈名〉 bankruptcy notice

【破钞】pòchāo〈动〉〈套〉 [often used in showing one's thanks] go to some expense

【破除】pòchú〈动〉 abolish: ～迷信 banish all blind faith ‖ ～旧习 break with old habits

【破读】pòdú〈名〉［语言］ split pronunciation [due to alternative meaning or function]

【破读字】pòdúzì〈名〉 character not pronounced in the usual way because of a different meaning or function

【破发】pòfā〈动〉 1［体育］ win a service break: 获得一个～点 win a break point 2［金融］ fall below the issue price

【破费】pòfèi〈动〉 spend money or time: 吃顿便饭就行了，不用多～。 A light meal will do; you needn't go to any big expense. ‖ 要完成这项工作，得～些工夫。 It will take some time to finish this work.

【破釜沉舟】 pòfǔ-chénzhōu〈成〉〈喻〉 cut off all means of retreat to show one's determination to press ahead

【破格】pògé〈动〉 break a rule: ～录用 break a rule to employ sb.

【破瓜】pòguā〈动〉〈旧〉 1（满十六岁） [of a girl] reach 16 years of age 2（失身） [of a girl] lose one's virginity

【破罐破摔】pòguàn-pòshuāi〈成〉〈喻〉 write oneself off as hopeless and act recklessly

【破坏】pòhuài〈动〉 1（损坏） destroy: ～桥梁 destroy a bridge ‖ 遭到～ meet destruction 2（损害） harm: ～环境 damage the environment ‖ ～生产 sabotage production ‖ 他～了我的幸福家庭。 He ruined my happy family. 3（改变） overhaul: ～旧世界，建设新世界 destroy the old world and build a new one 4（不遵守） violate: ～纪律 breach a discipline ‖ ～协定 break an agreement 5（改变结构） destroy the composition of a substance: 维生素C受热过度会被～。 Vitamin C is destroyed when overheated.

【破坏分子】pòhuàifènzǐ〈名〉 saboteur

【破坏力】pòhuàilì〈名〉 destructive power

【破获】pòhuò〈动〉 unearth: ～一起凶杀案/重大刑事案件 crack a murder case/a major criminal case ‖ 警方～了一个走私集团。 The police uncovered a gang of smugglers.

【破解】pòjiě〈动〉 1（揭示） unlock: ～生命之谜 unravel the mystery of life 2（解决） resolve: 终于～了这道难题 finally resolve this difficult problem 3（解除） avert (misfortune, calamity, etc.) by magic: ～之术 tricks for averting calamity

【破戒】pòjiè〈动〉 1（指戒律） break a commandment 2（指戒掉的事） make an exception: 他昨天又～抽烟了。 He broke his vow and smoked again yesterday.

【破镜重圆】pòjìng-chóngyuán〈成〉〈喻〉 reunion of a couple after separation: 他们离婚后不久又～了。 Not long after their divorce they remarried.

【破旧】pòjiù〈形〉 worn out: ～的家具 old and shabby furniture ‖ 院墙和屋子都很～。 The wall and the room are both in a dilapidated condition.

【破旧立新】pòjiù-lìxīn〈成〉 destroy the old and establish the new

【破句】pòjù〈动〉 break a sentence in the wrong place

【破口大骂】 pòkǒu-dàmà〈成〉 shower abuse on sb.

【破烂】pòlàn A〈形〉 ragged: 衣衫～ tattered clothes B〈名〉 scrap: 一堆～儿 a heap of junk ‖ 在垃圾堆里捡～儿 search a garbage heap for odds and ends ‖ 收～儿 collect scrap

【破烂不堪】 pòlàn-bùkān〈成〉 be completely worn-out: 穿得～ be dressed in rags

【破浪】pòlàng〈动〉 brave the waves: 在急流中～前进 ride the waves on a swift current ▸乘风～

【破例】pòlì〈动〉 make an exception: 公司制度要严格遵守，不能～。 The company rules must be strictly observed. No exceptions can be made.

【破脸】pòliǎn〈动〉 fall out: 她不愿和男朋友～。 She didn't want to fall out with her boyfriend.

【破裂】pòliè〈动〉 1（指实体） burst: 病人的一根血管～了。 One of the patient's blood vessels burst. ‖ 锅炉管道已经～。 The boiler tube has burst. 2（指关系） break down: 他们的婚姻～了。 Their marriage broke down. ‖ 谈判～。 The negotiations have broken through.

【破陋】pòlòu〈形〉 old and crude: ～的房屋 old shabby house

P

【破落】pòluò〈动〉fall into reduced circumstances: 家境～ with one's family in decline ▸～户
【破落户】pòluòhù〈名〉family that has gone down in the world
【破门】pòmén〈动〉1（指房门）force a door open: ～而入 break into a house 2（指球门）score a goal: 头球～ head the ball into the goal ‖ 我队防守失误，对方～得分。We failed to keep the ball out of the goal and the other team scored.
【破灭】pòmiè〈动〉go up in smoke: 他的希望～了。His hopes went up in smoke.
【破伤风】pòshāngfēng ▸**p. 50**〈名〉［医学］tetanus
【破身】pòshēn〈动〉〈旧〉[of a girl] lose one's virginity
【破私立公】pòsī-lìgōng〈成〉get rid of selfishness and foster public spirit
【破碎】pòsuì〈动〉1（碎裂）come to pieces: 山河～。The country went to rack and ruin. ‖ 这纸年代太久，一翻就～了。The paper fell apart as soon as it was turned because it was so old. 2（使碎裂）crush: ～矿石 crush ore ‖ ～机 crusher
【破损】pòsǔn〈形〉damaged: ～货物 damaged goods ‖ 瓷器容易～。Porcelain damages easily.
【破题】pòtí A〈名〉first two sentences giving the theme in an eight-legged essay B〈动〉provide the theme in one or two sentences
【破题儿第一遭】pòtír dì yī zāo〈惯〉for the first time: 登台演戏我还是～。It was the first time that I had performed on the stage.
【破涕】pòtì〈动〉stop crying
【破涕为笑】pòtì-wéixiào〈成〉tears give way to smiles
【破天荒】pòtiānhuāng〈成〉occur for the first time: 村里出了个大学生，这可是～的事情。For the first time in its history, this village had someone admitted to college.
【破土】pòtǔ〈动〉1（指施工）begin a construction project: ～动工 begin construction ‖ ～兴建 break ground for the building of 2（指耕种）start spring ploughing: ～春耕 start spring ploughing 3（指生长）break through the soil: 春笋～而出。Bamboo shoots break through in spring.
【破网】pòwǎng〈动〉［体育］score a goal
【破五】pòwǔ〈名〉the fifth of the first lunar month
【破相】pòxiàng〈动〉be disfigured: 严重的烧伤使他破了相。His face was disfigured by a serious burn.
【破晓】pòxiǎo〈动〉dawn: ～时分 at daybreak ‖ 天色～。Day is breaking.
【破鞋】pòxié〈名〉1（指鞋）worn-out shoe 2（指人）loose woman
【破颜】pòyán〈动〉〈书〉break into a smile: 她～一笑。She broke into a smile.
【破衣烂衫】pòyī-lànshān〈成〉ragged clothes
【破译】pòyì〈动〉decipher: ～密码 crack a code
【破绽】pòzhàn〈名〉flaw: 看出～ spot a weak point ‖ 露出～ betray one's weakness
【破折号】pòzhéhào〈名〉dash

粕 pò〈名〉〈书〉dregs of grain after distillation: 豆～ bean dregs ▸糟～

魄 pò〈名〉1（灵魂）soul: ▸魂～, 失魂落～ 2（胆识）vigour: ▸～力, 气～ ▸tuò, bó
【魄力】pòlì〈名〉boldness: 工作有～ be bold and resolute in one's work

po

桲 po ▸榅桲 wēnpo

pōu

剖 pōu〈动〉1（切开）cut open: ～开鱼肚 cut open a fish ▸～腹, ～面, 解～ 2（分析）dissect: ▸～白, ～析
【剖白】pōubái〈动〉explain oneself: ～心迹 lay one's heart bare ‖ 你找个机会向他～几句也好。It would be good if you could find an opportunity to explain yourself to him.
【剖腹】pōufù〈动〉disembowel: ～自杀 commit hara-kiri
【剖腹藏珠】pōufù-cángzhū〈成〉〈喻〉sacrifice one's life for gain
【剖肝泣血】pōugān-qìxuè〈成〉be heartbroken
【剖宫产】pōugōngchǎn〈名〉［医学］Caesarean section
【剖解】pōujiě〈动〉analyse: ～细密 make a careful analysis
【剖面】pōumiàn〈名〉1［植物］section 2［测绘］profile 3［数学］cut plane
【剖视】pōushì〈动〉analyse and observe: ～人物的内心世界 make an analytical observation of the inner world of a character
【剖视图】pōushìtú〈名〉sectional view
【剖析】pōuxī〈动〉analyse: ～当前国际形势 analyse the present international situation ‖ 这篇文章～事理十分透彻。This article makes a very close analysis of the issue.

póu

抔 póu〈书〉
A〈动〉hold with cupped hands: ～饮 scoop up with cupped hands and drink
B〈量〉double handful: 一～土 a double handful of earth

掊 póu〈动〉〈书〉1（搜刮）amass wealth by heavy taxation: ～敛 amass wealth by unfair means 2（挖掘）dig ▸pǒu

裒 póu〈动〉〈书〉1（聚集）gather: ～然成集 be collected into a volume ▸～辑 2（取出）draw out: ～多益寡 take from the fat to pad the lean
【裒辑】póují〈动〉〈书〉collect and edit: 此书系由类书～而成。This book is a collection of selections from various reference books.

pǒu

掊 pǒu〈动〉〈书〉1（击）hit: ～击权贵 lash out at people of means 2（击碎）split ▸póu

pū

仆 pū〈动〉fall forward: ▸前～后继 ▸pú

扑（撲） pū〈动〉1（指身体）throw oneself at: ～出一球 fend off a shot ‖ 向敌人～过去 pounce on the enemy ‖ 孩子高兴地～到了我的怀里。The child threw himself into my arms with joy. ▸饿虎～食, 飞蛾～火 2（指精力）devote oneself fully: 他一心～在教育事业上。He devotes himself heart and soul to the cause of education. 3（抓）rush at: ～苍蝇 swat a fly ‖ ～蝶 catch butterflies 4（拍打）flap: 海鸥～着翅膀，冲向天空。The seagull flapped its wings and rose into the sky. 5（涂抹）dab: 孩子身上～了爽身粉。The child was dabbed all over with talcum powder. 6（趴）bend over: ～在桌上看地图 bend over a map on the desk
【扑鼻】pūbí〈动〉assail the nostrils: 香气～。A fragrant smell greeted us. ‖ 玫瑰发出～的芳香。The roses are sending forth wafts of sweet fragrance.
【扑哧】pūchī〈拟〉titter: ～一笑 chuckle ‖ ～一声，皮球泄了气。With a fizz, the ball lost all its air.
【扑打】pūdǎ〈动〉swat: ～苍蝇/蝗虫 swat flies/locusts
【扑打】pūda〈动〉pat: ～身上的灰尘 dust oneself down ‖ ～衣服上的雪花 beat the snow off one's clothes
【扑跌】pūdiē A〈名〉wrestling B〈动〉fall forward: 老人脚下一绊，～在地上。The old man stumbled and fell on the ground.
【扑尔敏】pū'ěrmǐn〈名〉［药学］chlorpheniramine
【扑粉】pūfěn A〈名〉1（用于脸上）face powder 2（用于身上）talcum powder B〈动〉apply powder: 往脸上～ powder the face
【扑击】pūjī〈动〉pounce on
【扑救】pūjiù〈动〉1（指火灾）put out a fire to prevent disaster: 幸亏～及时，这场火灾才没造成重大损失。Thanks to prompt fighting, the fire didn't cause any great loss. 2（指球）dive for the ball
【扑克】pūkè〈名〉poker: 打～ play cards
【扑空】pūkōng〈动〉come away empty-handed: 由于有人走漏消息，警察扑了个空。Due to a leakage of information, the police came away with nothing.
【扑拉】pūla〈动〉1（指翅膀）flap or spread (wings): 母鸡～着翅膀咕咕叫。The hen cackled, flapping its wings. 2（指衣物）slap: ～～身上的雪 whisk the snow off one's clothes
【扑棱】pūlēng〈拟〉flutter: 随着一阵～声，树丛中飞起一群鸟。There was a flutter of wings and a flock of birds flew away from the trees.
【扑棱】pūleng〈动〉flap: 小燕子～着翅膀学飞了。Flapping their wings, the young swallows learned to fly.
【扑满】pūmǎn〈名〉piggy bank
【扑面】pūmiàn〈动〉blow against one's face: 清风～。The fresh and cool breeze caressed our faces. ‖ 细雨～而来。A fine drizzle was brushing our faces.
【扑灭】pūmiè〈动〉1（熄灭）extinguish: ～大火 put out a big fire 2（消灭）exterminate: ～蚊蝇 wipe out mosquitoes and flies
【扑闪】pūshan〈动〉blink: 她～着一双大

眼睛。She blinked her big eyes.
【扑朔迷离】pūshuò-mílí〈成〉complicated and confusing: ～的故事情节 complicated plot of a story ‖ 案情变得愈发～。The case has become more intricate.
【扑簌】pūsù〈拟〉trickle: 她～～掉着眼泪。The tears trickled down her cheeks.
【扑腾】pūtēng〈拟〉thump: 字典～一声掉到了地上。The dictionary fell to the floor with a thud.
【扑腾】pūteng〈动〉1（打水）move one's legs up and down in the water: 他刚学游泳，只能在水里瞎～。He was just learning to swim and could only flop about in the water. 2（跳动）palpitate: 他吓得心里直～。His heart was throbbing with fear. 3（浪费）waste: 钱都让他～光了。He squandered all his money.
【扑通】pūtōng〈拟〉thump: 他～一声掉进了水里。He fell into the water with a splash. ‖ 她的心～～地跳。Her heart went pit-a-pat.

铺（鋪）pū

A〈动〉1（摊平）spread: ～被子 spread a quilt ‖ ～桌布 spread a tablecloth ►～床 2（铺设）lay: ～地板 lay down a floor ‖ ～地毯 lay a carpet on the floor ‖ 用柏油～马路 pave a street with asphalt ►～轨，平～直叙
B〈量〉〈方〉[for 炕 *kang*]: 一～土炕 a heatable adobe bed
►pù
【铺摆】pūbai〈动〉put (goods, etc.) on display
【铺陈】pūchén〈动〉〈书〉1（布置）arrange: 室内～得很雅致。The room was tastefully furnished. 2（铺叙）elaborate: ～经过 give a detailed account of what happened
【铺床】pūchuáng〈动〉make the bed
【铺地砖】pūdìzhuān〈名〉floor tile
【铺垫】pūdiàn A〈动〉1（铺放）spread: 床上～了厚厚的褥子。The bed is spread with thick bedding. 2（衬托）foreshadow: 故事情节的早期发展为最后的悲剧结局做了～。Early events in the development of the story foreshadowed the tragic ending of the novel. B〈名〉bedding
【铺盖】pūgài〈动〉cover with sth.
【铺盖】pūgai〈名〉bedding
【铺盖卷儿】pūgaijuǎnr〈名〉bedroll
【铺轨】pūguǐ〈动〉lay a railway track
【铺路】pūlù〈动〉1（铺设道路）pave a road: ～修桥 construct roads and bridges ‖ 用混凝土～ pave a road with concrete 2〈喻〉（创造条件）pave the way: 为日后升迁～ pave the way for future promotion
【铺路石】pūlùshí〈名〉1（指石头）paving stone 2〈喻〉（指人）stepping-stone
【铺排】pūpái〈动〉put in order: 一切都已～停当。Everything has been put in order.
【铺平】pūpíng〈动〉smooth out: ～道路 pave the way for
【铺砌】pūqì〈动〉[建筑] pave: 广场用方砖～。The square was paved with square bricks.
【铺设】pūshè〈动〉lay: ～电缆 lay a cable ‖ ～双轨 lay a double-track ‖ ～铁路 construct a railway
【铺天盖地】pūtiān-gàidì〈成〉flood in: ～的蝗虫吞噬着庄稼。Swarms of locusts were destroying the crops. ‖ 电视里的广告～，令人眼花缭乱。TV commercials flooded in and dazzled their audience.
【铺叙】pūxù〈动〉give a detailed account: ～家史 give a detailed account of one's family history ‖ ～事实 elaborate on the facts
【铺展】pūzhǎn〈动〉spread out: 把地图～在桌上 lay out a map on the table ‖ 一片碧绿的田野在眼前～开来。A great expanse of green fields greeted the eye.
【铺张】pūzhāng〈形〉1（过于奢华）extravagant: 宴会极其～。The banquet was a lavish affair. ‖ 反对～浪费 oppose extravagance and waste 2（夸张）exaggerated: 汇报工作应该实事求是，不可～。Work reports should be factual and free from exaggeration.
【铺植】pūzhí〈动〉plant: ～草坪 lay out a lawn

噗 pū

〈拟〉puff: ～地一口气吹灭了灯 blow out an oil lamp with one puff ‖ 泉水～～地往上冒。Water kept gushing from the fountain.
【噗噜噜】pūlūlū〈拟〉trickle: 她的眼泪～地往下掉。Tears trickled down her cheeks.

潽 pū

〈动〉〈口〉boil over: 稀粥～出来了。The rice gruel is boiling over.

pú

仆（僕）pú

〈名〉servant: 男～ man servant ‖ 女～ maid servant ►～人，奴～
►pū
【仆从】púcóng〈名〉footman
【仆从国】púcóngguó〈名〉vassal country
【仆仆】púpú〈形〉〈书〉travel-worn: ►风尘～
【仆人】púrén〈名〉(domestic) servant: 当～ work as a servant
【仆役】púyì〈名〉〈旧〉(domestic) servant

匍 pú

【匍匐】púfú〈动〉1（爬行）crawl: ～前进 crawl forward 2（趴着）lie prostrate: 狗～在主人脚下。The dog lay prostrate before its owner. 3（指植物）trail: 红薯蔓～在地面上。Sweet potato vines are growing along the ground.
【匍匐植物】púfú zhíwù〈名〉[植物] creeper

菩 pú

【菩萨】púsà〈名〉1（指地位仅次于佛的人）Bodhisattva: ►观音～ 2（泛指神佛）Buddha 3〈喻〉（指人）kind-hearted person
【菩萨心肠】púsà-xīncháng〈成〉kind-heartedness: 他有一副～。He has a kind heart.
【菩提】pútí〈名〉bodhi [supreme wisdom or enlightenment, necessary to the attainment of Buddhahood]
【菩提树】pútíshù〈名〉bodhi tree

脯 pú

〈名〉breast: ►胸～
►fǔ
【脯子】púzi〈名〉breast meat: 鸡～ chicken breast

葡 pú

【葡萄】pútáo〈名〉grape
【葡萄干】pútáogān〈名〉raisin
【葡萄酒】pútáojiǔ〈名〉wine: 白/红～ white/red wine
【葡萄球菌】pútáo qiújūn〈名〉[医学] staphylococcus
【葡萄糖】pútáotáng〈名〉glucose
【葡萄园】pútáoyuán〈名〉vineyard
【葡萄紫】pútáozǐ〈名〉dark greyish purple
【葡萄牙】Pútáoyá〈名〉Portugal: ～人 Portuguese person ‖ ～语 Portuguese

蒲 pú

〈名〉[植物] 1（香蒲）cattail: ►香～ 2（菖蒲）plant of genus calamus: ～剑 calamus leaf
【蒲棒】púbàng〈名〉〈口〉club-like flower spike of cattail
【蒲包】púbāo〈名〉1（指袋子）cattail bag 2〈旧〉（指礼品）gift of fruit or pastries packed in a cattail bag
【蒲草】púcǎo〈名〉1（指茎叶）cattail leaf 2〈方〉（指植物）dwarf lilyturf
【蒲墩】púdūn〈名〉thick firm rush cushion
【蒲公英】púgōngyīng〈名〉[植物] dandelion
【蒲剧】pújù〈名〉*Pu* opera [local opera popular in southern parts of Shanxi Province]
【蒲葵】púkuí〈名〉[植物] Chinese fan palm
【蒲柳】púliǔ〈名〉[植物] big catkin willow:〈喻〉～之姿 be frail
【蒲绒】púróng〈名〉cattail wool
【蒲扇】púshàn〈名〉cattail leaf fan
【蒲式耳】púshì'ěr〈量〉bushel: 1～等于8加仑。A bushel contains eight gallons.
【蒲团】pútuán〈名〉cattail hassock
【蒲苇】púwěi〈名〉[植物] pampas grass
【蒲席】púxí〈名〉cattail mat

璞 pú

〈名〉uncut jade
【璞玉浑金】púyù-húnjīn〈成〉〈喻〉simple and pure character

镤（鏷）pú

[化学] protactinium (Pa)

濮 Pú

〈名〉Pu [surname]

pǔ

朴（樸）pǔ

〈形〉simple: ►～素，诚～，俭～
►Piáo, pō, pò
【朴厚】pǔhòu〈形〉simple and honest: 心地～ be simple-minded and kind-hearted ‖ 此地民风～。People here are simple and sincere.
【朴实】pǔshí〈形〉1（朴素）simple: 他穿着～。He is plainly dressed. ‖ 客厅布置得～而雅致。The sitting room is arranged simply but elegantly. 2（淳朴）sincere and honest: ～的工作作风 down-to-earth style of work ‖ 他为人～。He is a sincere person. 3（不做作）solid and unpretentious: 她的写作风格～而优美。Her writing style is simple yet graceful.
【朴实无华】pǔshí-wúhuá〈成〉simple and unadorned
【朴素】pǔsù〈形〉1（不艳丽）simple: ～大方 simple and in good taste ‖ 衣着～ be simply dressed 2（节俭）plain and modest: 生活～ live frugally ►艰苦～
【朴学】pǔxué〈名〉textual study of the Chinese classics during the Qing Dynasty

【朴直】pǔzhí〈形〉 honest and straightforward: 文笔～ simple and straightforward writing ‖ 性格～ be honest and straightforward

【朴质】pǔzhì〈形〉 simple and unadorned: ～的性格 be unaffected ‖ ～的言辞 plain words

圃 pǔ〈名〉 garden: ▸花～, 苗～

浦 pǔ〈名〉 1（水边） riverside 2（入海处） river mouth: ～东新区 Pudong New Area

普 pǔ〈形〉 general: ～天下 all over the world ▸～查, ～选, ～照

【普遍】pǔbiàn〈形〉 widespread: 有～意义 be of universal significance ‖ ～感兴趣的问题 issue of universal interest ‖ ～现象 widespread phenomenon ▸～性

【普遍性】pǔbiànxìng〈名〉 generality: 这种现象具有～。 This kind of phenomenon is universal.

【普查】pǔchá〈动〉 conduct a general survey: 常见病～ general survey of common diseases ‖ 人口～ census

【普跌】pǔdiē〈动〉 fall into a general slump: 个股出现～。 The shares suffered a general slump.

【普度众生】pǔdù-zhòngshēng〈成〉［佛教］ deliver all living creatures from torment: 佛教的宗旨是～。 The purpose of Buddhism is to deliver all beings.

【普洱茶】pǔ'ěrchá〈名〉 Pu'er tea

【普法】pǔfǎ〈动〉 popularize law: ～工作 law-popularizing work ‖ ～教育 law-popularizing education

【普工】pǔgōng〈名〉 unskilled worker

【普及】pǔjí〈动〉 1（广泛接受） be popular among: 电脑在中国现在很～。 Computers are now used extensively throughout China. 2（推广） popularize: ～法律知识 popularize legal knowledge ‖ ～与提高相结合 combine popularization with the raising of standards

【普及本】pǔjíběn〈名〉 popular edition

【普及教育】pǔjí jiàoyù A〈名〉 universal education: ～法 law of universal education B〈动〉 popularize education

【普降】pǔjiàng〈动〉［of rain or snow］ fall over a large area: 昨天华南～甘雨。 A timely rain fell all over south China yesterday.

【普快】pǔkuài〈名〉［交通］ standard express train

【普教】pǔjiào = 普通教育 pǔtōng jiàoyù

【普鲁卡因】pǔlǔkǎyīn〈名〉［药学］ procaine

【普利策奖】Pǔlìcèjiǎng〈名〉 Pulitzer prize

【普米族】Pǔmǐzú〈名〉 Primi ethnic group, Pumi ethnic group

【普氏原羚】pǔshì yuánlíng〈名〉［动物］ Przewalski's Gazelle

【普世】pǔshì〈形〉 universal: ～价值 universal value

【普天同庆】pǔtiān-tóngqìng〈成〉 everybody joins in the celebration

【普天之下】pǔtiānzhīxià〈成〉 all over the world

【普通】pǔtōng〈形〉 ordinary: ～读者 common reader ‖ ～劳动者 ordinary labourer ‖ ～老百姓 the common people

【普通话】pǔtōnghuà ▸**p. 918**〈名〉 standard Chinese

【普通教育】pǔtōng jiàoyù〈名〉 general education

【普通名词】pǔtōng míngcí〈名〉［语法］ common noun

【普通邮票】pǔtōng yóupiào〈名〉 postage stamp

【普选】pǔxuǎn〈名〉 general election

【普照】pǔzhào〈动〉 illuminate all things: 阳光～大地。 The sun shines on every corner of the land.

溥 pǔ〈形〉〈书〉 1（广大） vast: ～原 immense plain 2（普遍） universal: ～天之下 all over the world

谱（譜） pǔ

A〈名〉 1（用于参考） record for easy reference: ▸家～, 年～ 2（用于指导练习） manual: ▸画～, 脸～, 棋～ 3（乐谱） score: 钢琴～ piano score ▸简～, 五线～, 乐～ 4〈口〉（把握） grasp: 心里有～儿 have a basic grasp ‖ 心里没个～儿 have nothing definite in mind ▸离～ 5〈口〉（派头） airs: 如今他的～儿可真不小。 He's putting on a lot of airs and graces these days. ▸摆～儿

B〈动〉 set to music: 为这首诗～曲 set the poem to music ▸～写

【谱表】pǔbiǎo〈名〉［音乐］ stave: 大～ great stave

【谱号】pǔhào〈名〉［音乐］ clef: 低音～ bass clef ‖ 高音～ treble clef

【谱架】pǔjià〈名〉 music stand

【谱曲】pǔqǔ〈动〉 put to music: 这首诗后来被谱上了曲子。 This poem was later set to music.

【谱系】pǔxì〈名〉 1［生物］ pedigree 2（指家谱） system of a family tree 3（指事物变化） system of development (of a thing): 语言～分类 classification of language families

【谱写】pǔxiě〈动〉 compose: ～乐曲 compose music ‖〈喻〉～历史新篇章 write a new page in history

【谱制】pǔzhì〈动〉 compose: ～乐曲 compose music

【谱子】pǔzi〈名〉 musical score

氆 pǔ

【氆氇】pǔlu〈名〉 woollen fabric produced in Tibet

镨（鐠） pǔ〈名〉［化学］ praseodymium (Pr)

蹼 pǔ〈名〉 web [that connects the digits of ducks, frogs, etc.]

【蹼趾】pǔzhǐ〈名〉 webbed toe

【蹼足】pǔzú〈名〉 web foot

【蹼泳】pǔyǒng〈名〉 swimming with fins

pù

铺[1]（鋪、舖） pù〈名〉 shop: 肉～ butcher's shop ‖ 铁匠～ blacksmith shop ▸当～, 店～, 药～

铺[2]（鋪、舖） pù〈名〉 plank bed: ▸床～, 卧～

铺[3]（鋪、舖） pù〈名〉 courier station in old times, now often used in place names: 十里～ Shilipu

▸pū

【铺板】pùbǎn〈名〉 bed board

【铺保】pùbǎo〈名〉 shop guarantee

【铺底】pùdǐ〈名〉〈旧〉 shop furniture

【铺户】pùhù〈名〉 shop

【铺面】pùmiàn〈名〉 1（店面） shop front: ～装修 shop front renovations 2（营业面积） sales area: 这家新店～很大。 The new shop is very spacious.

【铺位】pùwèi〈名〉 berth

【铺子】pùzi〈名〉 shop: 杂货～ grocery store

堡 pù = 铺[3] pù

▸bǎo, bǔ

瀑 pù〈名〉 waterfall: 飞～ falling waterfall ▸～布

【瀑布】pùbù ▸**p. 164**〈名〉 waterfall: 黄果树～ Huangguoshu Falls ‖ 尼亚加拉大～ Niagara Falls

曝 pù〈动〉〈书〉 expose to the sun: ～露于荒野 be exposed in the wilderness ▸一～十寒

▸bào

【曝气池】pùqìchí〈名〉［化工］ aeration tank

【曝晒】pùshài〈动〉 expose to the sun: 夏日应防～。 You should avoid exposure to the sun during summer.

Qq

qī

七 qī

A ▸p. 691 〈数〉 seven: ～点钟 seven o'clock ‖ 第～ seventh ‖ ～～四十九。Seven times seven is forty-nine.
B 〈名〉〈旧〉 each of the seven seventh-day memorial ceremonies after sb.'s death: 头～ first seventh-day memorial ceremony

【七边形】qībiānxíng〈名〉［数学］ heptagon

【七步之才】qībùzhīcái〈成〉 talent for spontaneous literary creation

【七尺之躯】qīchǐzhīqū〈名〉 adult male

【七重奏】qīchóngzòu〈名〉［音乐］ septet

【七搭八搭】qīdā-bādā〈成〉 talk in an off-hand way

【七大姑八大姨】qīdàgū-bādàyí〈俗〉 very distant relatives

【七颠八倒】qīdiān-bādǎo〈成〉 be at sixes and sevens

【七分裤】qīfēnkù〈名〉 trousers that are seven-tenths of full length

【七高八低】qīgāo-bādī〈成〉 bumpy and rough

【七古】qīgǔ = 七言诗 qīyánshī

【七级浮屠】qījí-fútú〈成〉 seven-tiered pagoda: ▸救人一命，胜造～

【七绝】qījué〈简称〉= 七言绝句

【七老八十】qīlǎo-bāshí〈成〉 in one's late seventies or early eighties: 虽说～了，我的饭量还可以。Even though I am well over 70 years old, my appetite is still quite good.

【七零八落】qīlíng-bāluò〈成〉 in total disarray: 敌人的王牌军被打得～。The enemy's crack division was badly battered and thrown into confusion.

【七律】qīlǜ〈简称〉= 七言律诗

【七拼八凑】qīpīn-bācòu〈成〉 scrape together: ～好不容易搞来几个钱。It was no easy thing scraping together the small sum of money.

【七品芝麻官】qīpǐn zhīmaguān〈名〉 minor official [usu referring to a county magistrate]

【七七】qīqī〈名〉 last seventh-day memorial ceremony [held on the 49th day after sb.'s death]

【七七事变】Qī-Qī Shìbiàn〈名〉 July 7 Incident of 1937 [marking the beginning of the War of Resistance Against Japan by China]

【七巧板】qīqiǎobǎn〈名〉 tangram

【七窍】qīqiào〈名〉 the seven apertures of the human head: ～流血 bleed from one's mouth, nostrils, eyes and ears

【七窍生烟】qīqiào-shēngyān〈成〉 fume with rage

【七情】qīqíng〈名〉 the seven human emotions [joy, anger, sorrow, fear, desire, hate and love]

> **七巧板**
> A traditional Chinese intelligence game consisting of seven geometrical shapes that can be placed together to form a square or other patterns and shapes. The tangram has its origins in the '*yanjitu*' (燕几图), a Song Dynasty set of tables that could be arranged into a square. The modern tangram emerged as a game in the early Qing Dynasty, its popularity spreading to America and Europe during the 19th century.

【七情六欲】qīqíng-liùyù〈成〉 various human emotions and desires

【七色板】qīsèbǎn〈名〉 spectrum board

【七上八下】qīshàng-bāxià〈成〉 be in an unsettled state of mind: 她心里～，不知如何是好。She was so agitated that she did not know what to do.

【七十二行】qīshí'èrháng〈成〉 all sorts of occupations: ～，行行出状元。Of all professions, each one produces its own leading authority.

【七手八脚】qīshǒu-bājiǎo〈成〉 with many people lending a hand: 大伙儿～制服了罪犯。With everybody's help the criminal was subdued.

【七夕】qīxī〈名〉 seventh evening of the seventh month of the lunar calendar

【七弦琴】qīxiánqín = 古琴 gǔqín

【七项全能】qīxiàng quánnéng〈名〉［体育］ heptathlon

【七言绝句】qīyán juéjù〈名〉 seven-character quatrain [four-line poem with seven characters to each line and a strict tonal pattern and rhyme scheme]

【七言律诗】qīyán lǜshī〈名〉 eight-line poem with seven characters to each line

【七言诗】qīyánshī〈名〉 poem with seven characters to each line

【七一】Qī-Yī〈名〉 July 1 [anniversary of the founding of the Communist Party of China]

【七月】qīyuè ▸p. 928〈名〉 **1**（阳历）July **2**（阴历） seventh month of the lunar year

【七折八扣】qīzhé-bākòu〈成〉 various deductions

【七嘴八舌】qīzuǐ-bāshé〈成〉 all talking at the same time: 大家～议论纷纷。Everyone was trying to get their bit in at the same time.

沏 qī〈动〉 infuse: ～茶 brew tea

妻 qī〈名〉 wife: 娶某人为～ take sb. as one's wife ‖ 爱～ beloved wife ▸夫～, 前～, 未婚～

【妻弟】qīdì〈名〉 brother-in-law

【妻儿老小】qī'ér-lǎoxiǎo〈成〉 entire family of a married man: 他有～要抚养。He has a family to support.

【妻管严】qīguǎnyán〈惯〉〈诙〉 henpecked husband: 他是～。He is henpecked.

【妻舅】qījiù〈名〉 brother-in-law

【妻离子散】qīlí-zǐsàn〈成〉 breaking up of one's family: 战争使许多人～，家破人亡。The war caused the break-up of many families and the deaths of many people.

【妻孥】qīnú〈名〉〈旧〉 wife and children

【妻妾】qīqiè〈名〉〈旧〉 wife and concubine

【妻室】qīshì〈名〉〈书〉 wife: 尚无～ [of a man] not yet married

【妻小】qīxiǎo〈名〉〈书〉 wife and children: 使～过上优裕的生活 provide handsomely for one's wife and children

【妻子】qīzǐ〈名〉 wife and children

【妻子】qīzi〈名〉 wife: 虐待～ abuse one's wife ‖ 模范～ model wife

柒 qī ▸p. 691〈数〉 seven [used for the numeral 七 on cheques, etc. to avoid alterations or mistakes]

栖（棲） qī〈动〉 **1**（指鸟） perch: ▸～息 **2**（指人） stay: ▸～身, 两～ ▸xī

【栖居】qījū〈动〉 inhabit: 大熊猫～在中国西南部的高山上。Giant pandas inhabit some of the high mountains of south-west China.

【栖身】qīshēn〈动〉 stay: ～之所 place to stay ‖ 他在岩洞里～。He took shelter in a cave.

【栖息】qīxī〈动〉 perch, rest: 鸟儿在树上～。Birds perch on trees.

【栖息地】qīxīdì〈名〉 habitat

【栖止】qīzhǐ〈动〉〈书〉 reside

桤（榿） qī

【桤木】qīmù〈名〉 alder

凄[1]（淒） qī〈形〉 **1**（寒冷） chilly: 风～月冷。The wind was chilly and the moon shone coldly. ‖ 风雨～～。Cold, cold are the wind and the rain. **2**（冷清） bleak and desolate: ▸～凉, ～清

凄[2]（悽） qī〈形〉 sad: ▸～楚, ～切

【凄惨】qīcǎn〈形〉 miserable: 生活～ lead a wretched existence ‖ 叫声～ plaintive cries

【凄恻】qīcè〈形〉〈书〉 sorrowful: 备感～ be filled with sad feelings

【凄楚】qīchǔ〈形〉〈书〉 wretched: 这本书写得～动人。The book is full of pathos.

【凄怆】qīchuàng〈形〉〈书〉 wretched

【凄风苦雨】qīfēng-kǔyǔ〈成〉 wretched circumstances: ～，夜不能眠。With the wailing wind and the driving rain, I lay awake all night.

【凄寒】qīhán〈形〉 desolate and cold: 荒凉～之地 bleak and cold place

【凄寂】qījì〈形〉 1（荒凉） desolate and still: ～的原野 desolate open country 2（寂寞） dreary and lonely
【凄苦】qīkǔ〈形〉 sad and miserable: 生活～ lead a wretched existence
【凄冷】qīlěng〈形〉 1（凄凉） desolate 2（寒冷） chilly: 北风～ chilly north wind
【凄厉】qīlì〈形〉 sad and shrill: ～的叫声 sad and shrill cries ‖ 风声～。 The wind was howling.
【凄凉】qīliáng〈形〉 1（寂寞冷落） bleak: ～的景象 sad sight ‖ 孤独～ be forlorn 2（凄惨） miserable: 生活～ lead a wretched existence ‖ ～的岁月 years of misery and drudgery
【凄迷】qīmí〈形〉〈书〉 1（荒凉模糊） desolate and indistinct: 夜色～。 It was a dreary and hazy night. 2（悲伤） melancholy: 神情～ look melancholy
【凄凄】qīqī〈形〉 frigid
【凄切】qīqiè〈形〉〈书〉 mournful
【凄清】qīqīng〈形〉〈书〉 1（清冷） sombre: ～的月光 cheerless moonlight 2（凄凉） sad: 琴声～ plaintive tune of a zither
【凄然】qīrán〈形〉〈书〉 mournful: ～泪下 shed tears of sorrow
【凄伤】qīshāng〈形〉 desolate: 神色～ look grieved
【凄酸】qīsuān〈形〉 grieved
【凄婉】qīwǎn〈形〉〈书〉 1（哀伤） sad: 神情～ wear a sad look 2（悲哀而婉转） sad but moving: 笛声～ plaintive tone of a flute
【凄惘】qīwǎng〈形〉〈书〉 listless: ～之情 feeling of frustration and sadness
【凄怨】qīyuàn〈形〉 plaintive: 歌声～ sad singing
【凄壮】qīzhuàng〈形〉 sad and stirring

萋 qī

【萋萋】qīqī〈形〉〈书〉 lush: 芳草～ luxuriant growth of fragrant grass

戚¹（鏚） qī〈名〉 axe-like ancient weapon

戚²（慼） qī〈形〉〈书〉 sorrowful: ～然动容 see distress in the change of expression ▸悲～, 休～相关

戚³ qī〈名〉 relative: ▸亲～

【戚戚】qīqī〈形〉〈书〉 anxious: 君子坦荡荡，小人长～。 A gentleman's mind is at peace all the time, while the petty man is always full of anxiety.

期 qī

A〈动〉 1（约定） make an appointment: ▸不～而遇 2（期盼） expect: 指日可～ the day is not far off ▸～待, ～求, 预～
B〈名〉 1（日期） scheduled time: 约～会晤 schedule a date for an interview ▸～货, 到～, 延～ 2（一段时间） period: 一年～国库券 one-year treasury bonds ‖ 过渡～ interim period ‖ 哺乳～ lactation ▸假～, 任～
C〈量〉 [for things scheduled by periods] issue: 最新一～《北京周报》 current issue of *Beijing Review* ‖ 训练班先后办了三～。 The training class has been running for three sessions. ‖ 这本杂志两周出一～。 The magazine appears fortnightly.
▸jī
【期待】qīdài〈动〉 look forward to: ～好收成 expect a good harvest ‖ 母亲向他投去～的目光。 Mother looked at him with expectant eyes.
【期房】qīfáng〈名〉 forward house (on the property market)
【期汇】qīhuì〈名〉 forward exchange
【期货】qīhuò〈名〉［金融］ futures: ～交割 futures delivery ‖ 做～生意 deal in futures ‖ ～行市 futures quotation
【期货交易】qīhuò jiāoyì〈名〉 futures trading
【期货市场】qīhuò shìchǎng〈名〉 futures market
【期冀】qījì〈动〉〈书〉 ardently hope
【期价】qījià〈名〉［金融］ futures price
【期间】qījiān〈名〉 time: 会议～ in the course of the conference ‖ 节日～ during the holidays ‖ 农忙～ during the busy farming season ‖ 任职～ during one's time in office
【期刊】qīkān〈名〉 periodical: 查阅～ consult a journal ‖ 订阅～ subscribe to a periodical ‖ 学术～ academic journals
【期刊号】qīkānhào〈名〉 serial number: 国际标准～ International Standard Serial Number (ISSN)
【期考】qīkǎo〈名〉 final examination
【期满】qīmǎn〈动〉 come to an end: 服刑～ serve out one's sentence ‖ 任职～ serve out one's term of office
【期末】qīmò〈名〉 end of a term: 临近～ be nearing the end of the term
【期盼】qīpàn〈动〉 look forward to: ～您早日到来。 I am looking forward to seeing you soon.
【期票】qīpiào〈名〉 promissory note
【期期艾艾】qīqī-àiài〈成〉 stutter: 那人～的，说不上一句完整的话。 The man stuttered and stammered and could not utter a single coherent sentence.
【期求】qīqiú〈动〉 long for: 无所～ have nothing to long for
【期权】qīquán〈名〉［金融］ option
【期市】qīshì〈名〉 1（指市场） futures market 2（指价格） futures prices
【期望】qīwàng〈动〉 expect: ～和家人团聚 look forward to joining one's family ‖ ～过高 set one's expectations too high ‖ 家人对他寄予了很大～。 His family have high hopes for him.
【期望值】qīwàngzhí〈名〉 expectations
【期限】qīxiàn〈名〉 time limit: 超过～ exceed the deadline ‖ 以三个月为～ allot three months as the limit ‖ ～快到了。 The deadline is drawing near.
【期许】qīxǔ〈动〉 expect: 有负师长～ fall short of one's teachers' expectations
【期指】qīzhǐ〈名〉［金融］ futures index
【期中】qīzhōng〈名〉midterm: ～考试 midterm examination
【期终】qīzhōng〈名〉 end of a term

欺 qī〈动〉 1（欺骗） cheat: ▸～瞒, ～世盗名, ～诈 2（欺负） bully: 软弱可～ be weak and so open to exploitation

【欺负】qīfu〈动〉 bully: ～人 play the bully ‖ 受人～ be bullied
【欺行霸市】qīháng-bàshì〈成〉 bully fellow traders and dominate the market: 打击～的不法商人 crack down on business people who bully fellow traders and dominate the market
【欺哄】qīhǒng〈动〉 deceive: 这话只能～三岁小孩。 This talk would only fool a three-year old.
【欺凌】qīlíng〈动〉 bully and humiliate: ～百姓 bully and humiliate the common people ‖ 受尽～ suffer endless bullying and humiliation
【欺瞒】qīmán〈动〉 hoodwink: 这件事我没有～任何人。 I did not deceive anybody in this matter.
【欺蒙】qīméng〈动〉 dupe: ～群众 deceive the masses
【欺弄】qīnòng〈动〉 dupe
【欺骗】qīpiàn〈动〉 cheat: ～消费者 deceive consumers ‖ 采用～手段 use tricks
【欺骗性】qīpiànxìng〈名〉 duplicity: 外表具有～。 Looks can be deceptive.
【欺人太甚】qīrén-tàishèn〈成〉 push people too hard: 你不要～。 Don't you dare push me too hard!
【欺人之谈】qīrénzhītán〈成〉deceptive talk: 纯属～。 It's a pack of lies.
【欺辱】qīrǔ〈动〉 bully and humiliate
【欺软怕硬】qīruǎn-pàyìng〈成〉 bully the weak and fear the strong
【欺上瞒下】qīshàng-mánxià〈成〉 conceal the true state of affairs from both above and below
【欺生】qīshēng〈动〉 1（指人） bully strangers: 那儿的人～。 People there mess strangers around. 2（指动物） be ungovernable by strangers: 这马～。 The horse refuses to obey strangers.
【欺世盗名】qīshì-dàomíng〈成〉 win fame by deceiving the public: ～之徒 those who seek fame by deceiving the public
【欺罔】qīwǎng〈动〉〈书〉 deceive
【欺侮】qīwǔ〈动〉 treat sb. high-handedly: 受人～ be bullied
【欺压】qīyā〈动〉 ride roughshod over: ～百姓 tyrannize the people ‖ 受尽～ suffer endless bullying and oppression
【欺诈】qīzhà〈动〉 cheat: ～消费者 cheat consumers ‖ ～行为 fraudulent conduct ‖ 因犯～罪入狱 be sent to prison for fraud

攲 qī〈形〉〈书〉 inclined

【攲侧】qīcè〈形〉〈书〉 inclined

缉（緝） qī〈动〉 sew stitches close and joined together: ～边儿 sew a hem with close stitches

▸jī

嘁 qī〈拟〉 whisper

【嘁哩喀喳】qīlikāchā〈形〉 quick and efficient
【嘁嘁喳喳】qīqī-chāchā〈拟〉 babble: 我听见许多妇女在～地说话。 I heard the jabber of women's voices.

漆 qī

A〈名〉 1（油漆） paint: 快干～ quick-drying paint ‖ 生～ raw lacquer ▸磁～, 清～, 油～ 2（漆树） lacquer tree
B〈动〉 paint: ～成红色 paint sth. red ‖ 箱子里里外外都～过了。 The case has been painted both inside and out.
【漆包线】qībāoxiàn〈名〉 enamel-insulated wire
【漆布】qībù〈名〉 varnished cloth
【漆雕】qīdiāo〈名〉 lacquerware
【漆工】qīgōng〈名〉 1（指工作） painting: ～精细 fine lacquering 2（指人） painter: 这活儿得要熟练～来干。 We need a skilled painter to do this work.
【漆黑】qīhēi〈形〉 pitch-black: 在一片～中 in pitch darkness ‖ 四周～一片。 It is pitch-dark all around.
【漆黑一团】qīhēi-yītuán〈成〉 1〈本〉 pitch-dark: 洞内～。 It was pitch-dark

inside the cave. **2**〈喻〉(毫无希望) utterly hopeless: 他们把那儿的情况说成～。They painted a very dark picture of the situation there. **3**〈喻〉(一无所知) be in the dark: 这个问题在我的心中还是～。I am still completely in the dark about the matter.

【漆画】qīhuà〈名〉lacquer painting

【漆匠】qījiang〈名〉lacquerware worker

【漆皮】qīpí〈名〉coat of paint

【漆片】qīpiàn〈名〉shellac

【漆器】qīqì〈名〉lacquerware: 上等～ choice works in lacquer

【漆树】qīshù〈名〉lacquer tree

蹊 qī

▸xī

【蹊跷】qīqiāo〈形〉fishy: 这件事有点～。There is something funny about it.

㬤 qī

〈动〉**1**(用沙土吸水分) absorb water with sand, etc. **2**(将要变干) become dry

qí

亓 Qí

〈名〉Qi [surname]

齐¹(齊) qí

A〈形〉**1**(整齐) neat: 靠左边对～ be flush on the left ‖ 队伍排得很～。The procession lined up in a neat line. ▸参差不～ **2**(一致) identical: 只要心～，就没有办不成的事。When we act with one mind, there is nothing we cannot do. **3**(完备) ready: 客人都来～了。All the guests have arrived. ‖ 钱都凑～了。We have pooled enough money. ▸～备，～全

B〈动〉be level with: ～膝深的水 knee-deep water ‖ 向日葵都～房檐了。The sunflowers have reached the height of the eaves.

C〈副〉simultaneously: 百鸟～鸣 all birds sing in chorus ‖ 男女老幼～动手。Men and women, old and young, all pitched in. ▸百花～放，并驾～驱

D〈介〉along a line: ～根剪断 cut right down to the roots ‖ ～着边儿划一条线 draw a line along the edge

齐²(齊) Qí

〈名〉**1**(指国名) Qi [state in the Zhou Dynasty] **2**(南朝之一) Qi Dynasty **3**(北朝齐) Northern Qi Dynasty **4**(指国号) Qi [title of a regime established towards the end of the Tang Dynasty]

▸jì

【齐备】qíbèi〈形〉complete: 工具～ have complete set of tools ‖ 货色～ goods of every conceivable variety available

【齐步走】qíbùzǒu〈动〉[军事] quick march: ～! Quick, march!

【齐唱】qíchàng **A**〈名〉singing in unison **B**〈动〉sing in unison: ～一首歌 sing a song in unison

【齐楚】qíchǔ〈形〉〈书〉**1**(整齐) neat and smart: 衣冠～ be smartly dressed **2**(齐全) complete: 准备～ get everything ready

【齐东野语】Qídōng-yěyǔ〈成〉just talk: ～，不足为信。It is only hearsay and not to be taken seriously.

【齐集】qíjí〈动〉assemble: ～一堂 assemble under the same roof ‖ 各国朋友～北京。Friends from all nations gathered in Beijing.

【齐民】qímín〈名〉〈书〉common people

【齐名】qímíng〈动〉be equally famous: 他可与一流作家～。He ranks among the best class of writers.

【齐全】qíquán〈形〉complete: 功能～ have complete functionality ‖ 设备～ have all the necessary equipment ‖ 装备～ be fully equipped

【齐声】qíshēng〈副〉in chorus: ～欢呼 cheer in unison ‖ ～朗读 read in chorus

【齐刷刷】qíshuāshuā〈形〉uniform: 十个姑娘～一般高。The ten girls are of the same height.

【齐头并进】qítóu-bìngjìn〈成〉keep in step: 几项工作～ do several jobs all at once

【齐心】qíxīn〈形〉be of one mind: 只要大家～，事情就好办。So long as we are of one mind, we are sure to accomplish what we are out to do.

【齐心协力】qíxīn-xiélì〈成〉make concerted efforts: 只要～，就没有办不成的事。When we act with one mind, there is nothing we can't do.

【齐整】qízhěng〈形〉neat: 公路两旁的白杨树长得很～。The road is flanked with neat rows of poplars.

【齐奏】qízòu〈动〉play in unison

祁 Qí

【祁红】qíhóng〈名〉*keemun* [a kind of black tea]

圻 qí

〈名〉〈书〉boundary

芪 qí

▸黄芪 huángqí

岐 qí

【岐黄】qíhuáng〈名〉traditional Chinese medicine: ～之术 traditional Chinese medical science

其 qí

A〈代〉**1**(那个) that: 正当～时 just the right time ‖ 查无～事。Investigation shows that nothing of the kind has happened. ▸不厌～烦 **2**(他的) his;(她的) her;(它的) its;(他们的) their: ～父/母 his father/mother ▸物尽～用，自圆～说 **3**(他) he;(她) she;(它) it;(他们) they: 不能任～自流 cannot let things slide ‖ 劝～尽早戒烟 advise him to give up smoking as early as possible ▸察～言，观～行，出～不意 **4**(虚指) [rhetorical word referring to nothing in particular] it: 忘～所以 forget all else

B〈后缀〉[used after an adverb]: ▸极～，尤～

【其次】qícì〈代〉**1**(第二) next: 他第一个发言，～就轮到我。He spoke first, and then it was my turn. **2**(次要) secondary: 内容是主要的，形式还在～。Content comes first; what form it takes is secondary.

【其后】qíhòu〈副〉later

【其间】qíjiān〈名〉**1**(那中间) among them: 厕身～ occupy a place among them ‖ ～定有缘故。There must be some reason for it. **2**(指时间) time: 他出国三年，～到过纽约和巴黎。During his three years abroad, he visited New York and Paris.

【其乐无穷】qílè-wúqióng〈成〉find it an infinite delight/a boundless joy (to do sth.): 与众同乐，～。Joys shared with others are more enjoyed.

【其貌不扬】qímào-bùyáng〈成〉of undistinguished appearance: 别以为他～就小看他。Don't slight him just because he is unimposing in appearance.

【其实】qíshí〈副〉actually: ～没这个必要。As a matter of fact, it isn't necessary at all.

【其它】qítā = 其他 qítā

【其他】qítā〈代〉[referring to either people or things] other: 我们去了动物园，～什么地方也没去。We went to the zoo and nowhere else.

【其余】qíyú〈代〉the rest: 这个包是我的随身行李，～的是托运行李。This is my carry-on bag; all the rest is to be checked in.

【其中】qízhōng〈名〉among: 不知～底细 not know the ins and outs of the matter ‖ 果园里一共有五千棵果树，～苹果树占80%。There are altogether 5,000 trees in the orchard, of which 80% are apple trees.

奇 qí

A〈形〉**1**(罕见) unusual: ～男子/女子 remarkable man/woman ‖ ～松怪石 unique pine trees and strangely-shaped rocks ▸～耻大辱，～迹，～妙 **2**(出人意料) unexpected: ▸～兵，～袭，～遇，出～制胜

B〈动〉surprise: ▸不足为～，惊～

C〈副〉extremely: ～丑 very ugly ‖ ～痒 be terribly itchy ▸～缺

▸jī

【奇案】qí'àn〈名〉quirky case: 侦破一桩～ solve a strange case

【奇拔】qíbá〈形〉〈书〉unique and outstanding: 山峰～ towering mountain peaks

【奇兵】qíbīng〈名〉ingenious military move: 出～ launch a surprise attack

【奇才】qícái〈名〉**1**(指才能) rare talent: 在数学方面有～ be exceptionally gifted at maths **2**(指人才) genius: 数学～ maths prodigy ‖ 他是语言～。He is a linguistic wonder.

【奇彩】qícǎi〈名〉extraordinary splendour

【奇耻大辱】qíchǐ-dàrǔ〈成〉burning shame: 蒙受～ be deeply disgraced

【奇峰】qífēng〈名〉strangely-shaped peak: ～突起 peaks towering magnificently

【奇功】qígōng〈名〉outstanding service: 屡建～ repeatedly perform outstanding service

【奇怪】qíguài **A**〈形〉strange: ～的念头 weird idea ‖ ～的现象 unusual phenomena **B**〈动〉be surprising: 我们都～经理为什么要辞职。We all feel surprised at the manager's resignation.

【奇观】qíguān〈名〉wonder: 自然～ natural wonders ‖ 钱塘潮是一大～。The tidal bore on the Qiantang River is indeed a spectacle.

【奇瑰】qíguī〈形〉singular and beautiful: ～的海景 unsurpassably magnificent seascape

【奇诡】qíguǐ〈形〉odd

【奇花异草】qíhuā-yìcǎo〈成〉exotic flowers and rare herbs

【奇幻】qíhuàn〈形〉**1**(指虚幻) fantastic: ～莫测 be too mysterious to predict **2**(指变幻) kaleidoscopic: 景色～ kaleidoscopic scenes

【奇货可居】qíhuò-kějū〈成〉〈喻〉sth. that can be capitalized on

【奇技淫巧】qíjì-yínqiǎo〈成〉diabolic tricks and wicked craft

【奇迹】qíjì〈名〉miracle: 创造～ work wonders ‖ 她～般地好起来了。She is making a miraculous recovery.

【奇景】qíjǐng〈名〉marvel: 雪山～ wonderful view of snow-capped mountains
【奇境】qíjìng〈名〉fairyland
【奇绝】qíjué〈形〉unsurpassably wonderful: 山势～ bewitchingly magnificent mountains
【奇崛】qíjué〈形〉〈书〉outstanding: 文笔～ unusual style of writing
【奇丽】qílì〈形〉gorgeous: 景色～ beautiful scenery
【奇妙】qímiào〈形〉wonderful: 构思～ intriguing conception ‖ ～的世界 wonderful world
【奇谋】qímóu〈名〉very clever strategy
【奇葩】qípā〈名〉exotic flower:〈喻〉艺坛～ exquisite works of art
【奇僻】qípì〈形〉rare
【奇巧】qíqiǎo〈形〉exquisite: 园内假山造型～。The rockery in the garden was ingeniously formed.
【奇趣】qíqù〈名〉unusual charm
【奇缺】qíquē〈动〉be extremely short of: 管理人才～。There is a critical shortage of management personnel.
【奇人】qírén〈名〉**1**（怪人）eccentric person **2**（奇才）rare talent
【奇思妙想】qísī-miàoxiǎng〈成〉marvellous idea
【奇谈】qítán〈名〉strange tale: 海外～ strange tales from overseas
【奇谈怪论】qítán-guàilùn〈成〉ridiculous argument
【奇特】qítè〈形〉singular: 设计～ be unusual in design ‖ 在沙漠地区常常可以看到～的景象。In desert areas one often sees strange mirages.
【奇突】qítū〈形〉**1**（意外）unexpected: 事情发生得太～。It happened all of a sudden. **2**（奇特）peculiar
【奇伟】qíwěi〈形〉peculiar and magnificent: 建筑～ peculiar and magnificent architecture
【奇文】qíwén〈名〉**1**（指新奇）remarkable piece of writing **2**（指荒诞）absurd writing
【奇文共赏】qíwén-gòngshǎng〈成〉share the pleasure of reading a remarkable piece of writing
【奇闻】qíwén〈名〉fantastic story: ～趣事 strange news and amusing incidents ‖ 天下～ incredible story
【奇袭】qíxí〈动〉make a surprise attack
【奇想】qíxiǎng〈名〉strange idea: 突发～ come up with a strange idea
【奇效】qíxiào〈名〉miraculous effect: 这种新药有～。The new drug works miracles.
【奇形怪状】qíxíng-guàizhuàng〈成〉of queer shapes and forms: ～的钟乳石 unusually-shaped stalactites
【奇勋】qíxūn〈名〉〈书〉outstanding service: 屡建～ make repeated outstanding contributions
【奇异】qíyì〈形〉**1**（奇特）strange: 形状～ be grotesque in shape ‖ 海底是一个～的世界。The ocean floor is a wonderland. **2**（惊异）surprised: 用～眼光看着来自远方的客人 look at the guests in astonishment
【奇遇】qíyù〈名〉chance encounter: 与故友在海外的～ fortuitous meeting with an old friend abroad
【奇珍异宝】qízhēn-yìbǎo〈成〉rare treasures: 寻找～ seek rare treasures
【奇装异服】qízhuāng-yìfú〈成〉outlandish clothes: 穿着～ be bizarrely dressed

歧 qí〈形〉**1**（分岔）forked: ▸～路, ～途 **2**（不相同）divergent: ▸～视, ～义, ～异
【歧出】qíchū〈动〉〈书〉be inconsistent
【歧见】qíjiàn〈名〉difference: 消除～ eliminate differences
【歧路】qílù〈名〉fork: ～徘徊 hesitate at a crossroads
【歧路亡羊】qílù-wángyáng〈成〉〈喻〉go astray in a complex situation
【歧视】qíshì〈动〉discriminate: ～妇女 discrimination against women ‖ 种族～ racial discrimination
【歧途】qítú〈名〉wrong path: 误入～ go astray ‖ 引入～ lead sb. astray
【歧义】qíyì〈名〉ambiguity: 产生～ create ambiguity ‖ 消除～ clear up an ambiguity
【歧异】qíyì〈名〉difference

祈 qí〈动〉**1**（祈祷）pray: ～雨 pray for rain ‖ ～福 pray for blessings **2**（请求）beg: 敬～指导。We respectfully request your guidance. ▸～望
【祈祷】qídǎo〈动〉pray: 向上帝～ pray to God
【祈年殿】Qíniándiàn〈名〉Hall of Prayer for Good Harvests [in Beijing]
【祈盼】qípàn〈动〉look forward to: ～回复 look forward to a reply ‖ 这是我们的～。This is our wish.
【祈求】qíqiú〈动〉pray for: ～保佑 pray for a blessing ‖ ～宽恕 plead (with sb.) for mercy
【祈使句】qíshǐjù〈名〉［语法］imperative sentence
【祈望】qíwàng〈动〉wish: ～丰收 wish for a bumper harvest
【祈雨】qíyǔ〈动〉pray for rain

祇 qí〈名〉〈书〉god of the earth: ▸神～

荠（薺） qí ▸荸荠 bíqí
▸jì

耆 qí〈形〉〈书〉over sixty years old
【耆老】qílǎo〈名〉〈书〉**1**（指年纪）aged person **2**（指德行）venerable old person
【耆年】qínián〈名〉venerable age
【耆宿】qísù〈名〉〈书〉venerable old person of a community: ～大贤 venerable sage

颀（頎） qí〈形〉〈书〉tall
【颀长】qícháng〈形〉〈书〉tall: 身材～ tall in build
【颀伟】qíwěi〈形〉〈书〉tall and strong in build

脐（臍） qí〈名〉**1**（指人）navel **2**（指蟹）abdomen: ▸尖～, 团～
【脐橙】qíchéng〈名〉navel orange
【脐带】qídài〈名〉umbilical cord: ～血 umbilical cord blood
【脐风】qífēng〈名〉［中医］umbilical convulsion

萁 qí〈名〉beanstalk: ▸豆～

畦 qí〈名〉ridge-bordered plot of land in a field: 种了三～大蒜 grow three beds of garlic
【畦灌】qíguàn〈名〉［农业］check irrigation
【畦田】qítián〈名〉ridge-bordered plot

跂 qí〈名〉〈书〉extra toe

崎 qí〈形〉〈书〉sloping
【崎岖】qíqū〈形〉bumpy: 山路～ rugged mountain path ‖ ～坎坷的人生道路 rough and rugged paths of life
【崎岖不平】qíqū-bùpíng〈成〉uneven: ～的路 rugged road ‖ 人生的道路是～的。The road of life is not smooth.

淇 qí ▸冰淇淋 bīngqílín

骐（騏） qí〈名〉〈书〉black horse: ～骥 steed

骑（騎） qí
A〈动〉**1**（跨坐）ride: ～马 ride a horse ‖ ～摩托车/自行车 ride a motorcycle/bicycle ‖〈喻〉～在百姓头上作威作福 ride roughshod over the people **2**（兼跨）straddle: ▸～缝
B〈名〉**1**（指动物）horse or other animal that is ridden: ▸坐～ **2**（指人）cavalry: ▸轻～, 铁～
【骑兵】qíbīng〈名〉cavalry: ～部队 cavalry
【骑缝】qífèng〈名〉perforation: ～章 seal on the perforation
【骑虎难下】qíhǔ-nánxià〈成〉〈喻〉be unable to extricate oneself from a difficult situation
【骑虎之势】qíhǔzhīshì〈成〉〈喻〉dilemma
【骑警】qíjǐng〈名〉mounted police: ～冲散了示威集会。Police on horseback broke up the demonstration.
【骑楼】qílóu〈名〉〈方〉covered passageway
【骑驴找驴】qílǘ-zhǎolǘ = 骑马找马 qímǎ-zhǎomǎ
【骑马找马】qímǎ-zhǎomǎ〈成〉〈喻〉**1**（指物品）look for sth. that is right under one's nose **2**（指工作）hold on to one's job while seeking another
【骑墙】qíqiáng〈动〉sit on the fence: 采取～态度 sit on the fence ‖ ～派 hedger
【骑射】qíshè〈名〉horsemanship and archery
【骑师】qíshī〈名〉jockey
【骑士】qíshì〈名〉knight: ～的美德 knightly virtues
【骑手】qíshǒu〈名〉horseback rider: 马戏团的～ circuit rider ‖ 男～ equestrian ‖ 女～ equestrienne
【骑术】qíshù〈名〉horsemanship: 精通～ excel in horsemanship

琪 qí〈名〉〈书〉fine jade

琦 qí〈书〉
A〈名〉fine jade
B〈形〉outstanding: ～行 admirable conduct

棋 qí〈名〉**1**（指项目）chess: ～类比赛 chess competitions ▸跳～, 象～ **2**（指棋子）chess piece: 落～无悔 no retraction of a chess move
【棋布】qíbù〈形〉as many as pieces scattered over a chessboard: ▸星罗～
【棋道】qídào〈名〉chess expertise
【棋逢敌手】qíféng-díshǒu = 棋逢对手

qíféng-duìshǒu

【棋逢对手】qíféng-duìshǒu〈成〉**1**〈本〉meet one's match in a game of chess **2**〈喻〉be well-matched: ～难相胜。When players of equal skill are pitted against each other, victory hangs in the balance.

【棋高一着】qígāoyīzhāo〈成〉〈喻〉be superior to one's opponent in stratagem

【棋局】qíjú〈名〉arrangement of chess pieces on the chessboard

【棋力】qílì〈名〉chess skill

【棋路】qílù〈名〉chess tactics: 他的～很高明。He has superior tactics in chess.

【棋迷】qímí〈名〉chess fan

【棋盘】qípán〈名〉chessboard: 他取出～摆好棋子。He got out the chessboard and arranged the pieces.

【棋谱】qípǔ〈名〉chess manual

【棋圣】qíshèng〈名〉grand master of chess

【棋士】qíshì〈名〉chess player: 三级～ level 3 chess player

【棋手】qíshǒu〈名〉chess player: 不高明的～ poor hand at chess

【棋坛】qítán〈名〉chess circles: ～老将 veteran in chess circles

【棋艺】qíyì〈名〉chess skill: ～精湛 be a chess expert

【棋友】qíyǒu〈名〉chess friend

【棋苑】qíyuàn〈名〉chess circles

【棋子】qízǐ〈名〉chess piece: 吃掉对手～ capture one's opponent's chess piece ‖ 移动一个～ move a man at chess

蛴（蠐）qí

【蛴螬】qícáo〈名〉［昆虫］grub

祺 qí〈形〉〈书〉lucky: 顺颂近～ [used at the end of a letter] wishing you the best of luck

綦 qí〈副〉〈书〉very: 家境～寒 with one's family in very bad circumstances ‖ 言之～详 extremely detailed description

蜞 qí ►蟛蜞 péngqí

旗 qí〈名〉**1**（旗子）flag: 升～ raise a flag ‖ 校～ school banner ►彩～, 党～, 国～ **2**（八旗）'Eight Banners' [military-administrative organizations of the Manchu nationality before and during the Qing Dynasty] **3**（与八旗相关）[referring to the the 'Eight Banners', esp of the Manchus]: ►～人, ～袍 **4**（指地方）garrisons of the 'Eight Banners', which have become place names **5**（指行政区划）banner [administrative division of the county level in the Inner Mongolia Autonomous Region]

【旗杆】qígān〈名〉flagpole

【旗鼓相当】qígǔ-xiāngdāng〈成〉be well-matched: ～, 胜负难分。The two sides were so well-matched that neither could gain the upper hand.

【旗号】qíhào〈名〉**1**〈本〉banner **2**〈喻〉pretext: 打着人权的～干涉别国内政 interfere in the internal affairs of other countries under the pretext of human rights

【旗舰】qíjiàn〈名〉flagship: ～店 flagship store

【旗开得胜】qíkāi-déshèng〈成〉achieve immediate success: 祝君～, 马到成功。I wish you a speedy success.

【旗袍】qípáo〈名〉cheongsam

> **旗袍**
>
> A woman's garment dating from the Qing Dynasty. Manchus were known as *qiren* (旗人), which forms the origin of the word. The dress became popular among women after the 1911 Revolution, and was fashionable in the 1930s and '40s. The *qipao* is tightly fitting and has a high collar, buttons on the right, and slits up either side. The front of the garment may be edged and embroidered. The height of the collar and the length of the sleeves and the dress have varied greatly throughout different periods.

【旗袍裙】qípáoqún〈名〉wrap-over skirt

【旗人】qírén〈名〉〈旧〉**1**（八旗的人）banner people [member of any one of the 'Eight Banners' during the Qing Dynasty] **2**（满族人）Manchu

【旗手】qíshǒu〈名〉**1**（打旗者）banner bearer **2**〈喻〉（领路者）standard-bearer: 鲁迅是新文化运动的～。Lu Xun was a great standard-bearer of the New Culture Movement.

【旗桅杆】qíwéigān〈名〉flag mast

【旗语】qíyǔ〈名〉semaphore: 打～ semaphore

【旗帜】qízhì〈名〉**1**（旗子）banner: 挥舞～ wave a flag ‖ 聚集/团结在…的～下 gather under the banner of ‖ 十月一日, 首都到处飘扬着五彩缤纷的～。On October 1, colourful flags were fluttering everywhere in the nation's capital. **2**（典范）model: 培养典型, 树立～ cultivate a model and set a good example **3**（立场）stand: ～鲜明地反对一切不正之风 take a clear stand against all malpractices

【旗子】qízi〈名〉flag

蕲（蘄）qí〈动〉〈书〉beg: ～求 earnestly hope

鲯（鯕）qí

【鲯鳅】qíqiū〈名〉［鱼类］dolphin

鳍（鰭）qí〈名〉fin: 背～ dorsal fin ‖ 尾～ tail fin

麒 qí

【麒麟】qílín〈名〉kylin [mythical chimerical creature]

> **麒麟**
>
> A mythological beast with the shape of a deer, the tail of an ox, a single horn, and scales all over its body. The kylin is regarded as a propitious symbol, and together with the dragon, phoenix and turtle, is one of the four spirits (四灵) of ancient times. It was traditionally believed that the kylin would bring offspring, and a common depiction in Chinese folklore is of the kylin bringing a child to a woman.

qǐ

乞 qǐ〈动〉beg: ►行～

【乞哀告怜】qǐ'āi-gàolián〈成〉beg for mercy

【乞丐】qǐgài〈名〉beggar: 沦为～ be reduced to begging

【乞力马扎罗山】Qǐlìmǎzhāluóshān〈名〉Kilimanjaro

【乞怜】qǐlián〈动〉beg for mercy: ►摇尾～

【乞灵】qǐlíng〈动〉**1**〈本〉invoke help from deities **2**〈喻〉seek help that cannot be counted on: ～于骗术 resort to fraud

【乞求】qǐqiú〈动〉beg for: ～宽恕 beg for mercy ‖ ～某人原谅 implore sb.'s pardon

【乞饶】qǐráo〈动〉plead for pardon

【乞食】qǐshí〈动〉〈书〉beg for food

【乞讨】qǐtǎo〈动〉beg: 沿街～ go begging from door to door

【乞降】qǐxiáng〈动〉beg to surrender

【乞援】qǐyuán〈动〉beg for aid

岂（豈）qǐ〈副〉〈书〉[used to ask a rhetorical question]: 你～能这样胡说八道? How can you talk such nonsense? ►～有此理

【岂不】qǐbù〈副〉[used to give emphasis to the tone of a rhetorical question, to make the sentence affirmative in meaning] isn't that: 这～成了笑话? Isn't it ridiculous?

【岂但】qǐdàn〈连〉〈书〉not only: ～你不知道, 连我自己也不清楚呢。It's not just you who don't know. Even I am unclear myself.

【岂非】qǐfēi〈副〉[used to ask a rhetorical question] isn't it: ～咄咄怪事? Isn't that absurd?

【岂敢】qǐgǎn〈动〉**1**（怎么敢）how dare: 我～单独行动? How dare I act alone? **2**〈谦〉（担当不起）you flatter me: 你帮了我大忙, 我可得好好谢谢你。——～, ～。些许小事, 何足挂齿? You have done me a great favour. How can I thank you enough? — It's nothing, hardly worth mentioning.

【岂可】qǐkě = 岂能 qǐnéng

【岂肯】qǐkěn〈动〉how could: 你如此无礼, 她～善罢甘休? You have been so rude to her. How could you expect her to take it lying down?

【岂能】qǐnéng〈动〉[used to ask a rhetorical question] how could: 你～言而无信? How could you go back on your word? ‖ 我～对此置之不理? How is it possible that I could take no notice of it?

【岂有此理】qǐyǒucǐlǐ〈成〉outrageous: 你做错了事, 还要怪别人, 真是～! It's outrageous for you to put the blame on others when it was all your own fault.

【岂止】qǐzhǐ〈副〉[used to ask a rhetorical question] more than: 他做的好事多得很, ～这些? He's done a lot more good stuff than just this.

企 qǐ〈动〉**1**（踮脚）stand on tiptoe: ►～盼, ～足而待 **2**（盼望）anxiously expect: ►～及, ～求, ～图

【企待】qǐdài〈动〉expect: ～你的回音。I am looking forward to your reply.

【企鹅】qǐ'é〈名〉penguin

【企管】qǐguǎn〈简称〉= 企业管理

【企划】qǐhuà〈动〉plan and arrange: 公司～部 planning department of a company

【企及】qǐjí〈动〉hope to reach: 难以～ hard to attain

【企口】qǐkǒu〈名〉［建筑］tongue-and-groove: ～板 tongue-and-groove board

【企慕】qǐmù〈动〉〈书〉admire: ～人品 admire sb. for his excellent character ‖ 我对他～已久。I have looked up to him for a long time.

【企盼】qǐpàn〈动〉long for: ～合家欢聚 look forward to a happy reunion of the family ‖ ～自由 yearn for freedom

【企求】qǐqiú〈动〉seek: 别无～ have nothing to hanker after ‖ 他一心只想把工作搞好, 从不～什么。All he wanted was to do his job well; he desired nothing else.

【企事业】qǐ-shìyè〈名〉enterprises and institutions: ～单位 enterprises and institutions

【企图】qǐtú A〈动〉try: ～谋害性命 make an attempt on sb.'s life ‖ ～掩盖事实 seek to conceal the facts B〈名〉attempt: 别有/另有～ have an ulterior motive ‖ 他的～失败了。His attempt was a failure.

【企望】qǐwàng〈动〉yearn for: 翘首～ eagerly look forward to ‖ 国富民强是我们所～的。It is our hope that our country will become strong and the people prosperous.

【企羡】qǐxiàn〈动〉admire

【企业】qǐyè〈名〉enterprise: 创办～ build up a business ‖ 国有～ state-owned enterprises ‖ 工矿～ factories, mines and other enterprises

【企业管理】qǐyè guǎnlǐ〈名〉business management

【企业化】qǐyèhuà〈动〉1（指商业机构）run an enterprise on a commercial basis 2（指事业机构）apply business methods to institutions

【企业集团】qǐyè jítuán〈名〉enterprise group

【企业家】qǐyèjiā ▸**p. 966**〈名〉entrepreneur

【企业界】qǐyèjiè〈名〉business communities

【企业文化】qǐyè wénhuà〈名〉corporate culture

【企业形象】qǐyè xíngxiàng〈名〉corporate image

【企业债券】qǐyè zhàiquàn〈名〉corporate bonds

【企业主】qǐyèzhǔ〈名〉business proprietor

【企足而待】qǐzú'érdài〈成〉expect sth. to come true in the near future

杞 Qǐ〈名〉Qi [state in the Zhou Dynasty]

【杞柳】qǐliǔ〈名〉purple willow

【杞人忧天】Qǐrén-yōutiān〈成〉〈喻〉entertain imaginary fears: 不要～。Don't cross the bridge until you come to it.

启（啓、啟）qǐ

A〈动〉1（打开）open: ～口 open one's mouth ‖ ～幕 raise the curtain ‖ 某某～ To so-and-so [written on the envelope after the name of the person to whom the letter is sent] ▸～齿, ～封 2（开导）awaken: ▸～迪, ～发, ～蒙 3（开始）start: ▸～动, ～用 4（陈述）state: 谨～ respectfully yours ‖ 某某～ by so-and-so [closing words of a letter] ‖ 敬～者 I wish to inform you ▸～事

B〈名〉〈旧〉note: 谢～ thank-you letter ‖ 小～ note

【启禀】qǐbǐng〈动〉〈旧〉report (to one's superior)

【启程】qǐchéng = 起程 qǐchéng

【启齿】qǐchǐ〈动〉open one's mouth: 羞于～ feel ashamed to bring it up

【启迪】qǐdí〈动〉enlighten: ～后人 inspire and enlighten future generations ‖ 给人以～ give enlightenment

【启碇】qǐdìng〈动〉set sail

【启动】qǐdòng〈动〉1（指仪器设备等）start (up): ～发动机/汽车 start (up) a generator/car ‖ ～装置 starting equipment ‖ ～器 starter 2（指项目等）set in motion: 新工程已经～。The new project is already under way. 3（开展）open up: ～新一轮多边贸易谈判 launch a new round of multilateral trade negotiations

【启动资金】qǐdòng zījīn〈名〉start-up fund

【启发】qǐfā〈动〉inspire: ～诱导 enlighten and persuade ‖ ～式教学 heuristic education ‖ 他的话给了我们很多～。His remarks greatly inspired us.

【启封】qǐfēng〈动〉1（指封条）break a seal: 当众～ remove the seal in public 2（指信件）open a package: 此函未经允许不得～。This letter is not to be opened without authorization.

【启航】qǐháng = 起航 qǐháng

【启蒙】qǐméng〈动〉1（指初学）impart rudimentary knowledge to beginners: ～读物 children's primer ‖ ～老师 first teacher 2（指普及）enlighten: ▸～运动

【启蒙运动】qǐméng yùndòng〈名〉1（欧洲民主文化运动）The Enlightenment 2（普及运动）enlightenment movement

【启明星】Qǐmíngxīng〈名〉［天文］morning star [Venus]

【启示】qǐshì〈动〉enlighten: 这本书～我们应该怎样度过一生。This book enlightens us as to how we should live.

【启示录】Qǐshìlù〈名〉［宗教］*The Book of Revelation*

【启事】qǐshì〈名〉notice: 寻人～ missing person's notice ‖ 招领～ lost-and-found notice ‖ 征婚～ marriage notice

【启衅】qǐxìn〈动〉〈书〉provoke discord: 两次世界大战都是德国军国主义者首先～。Both World Wars were instigated by German militarists.

【启用】qǐyòng〈动〉start using: 大胆～年轻人 boldly put young people in important positions ‖ 铁路已建成～。The railway is completed and opened to traffic.

【启运】qǐyùn〈动〉start shipment: 货已～。The goods are on their way.

【启奏】qǐzòu〈动〉present a memorial to the emperor

起[1] qǐ

A〈动〉1（起身）rise: 早～ get up early ‖ 黎明即～ rise at dawn ▸～床, ～来, ～立 2（上升）move up: 这球不～了。There is no spring left in this ball. ▸～伏, 大～大落 3（长出）break out: ～鸡皮疙瘩 get goose pimples ‖ 小孩背上～痱子了。Prickly heat broke out on the baby's back. 4（发生）start: ～疑心 become suspicious ‖ ～作用 take effect ‖ ～风暴了。A storm is coming. ▸～飞, ～火, ～跑 5（建立）establish: 平地～高楼 high buildings rise from previously empty ground ▸白手～家 6（拟写）draw up: ～草稿 prepare a draft ‖ ～名字 come up with a name ▸～草, ～稿 7（开始）[used before a noun of time or place preceded by 从 or 由] begin: 从今天～ starting from today ‖ 从现在～ from now on ‖ 从二号算～ start from No 2 ‖ 从头做～ start from the very beginning ▸～讫, ～止 8（拔出）extract: ～钉子 pull out a nail ‖ ～瓶塞 remove the cork from a bottle ▸～子 9（领取）draw: ～护照 get one's passport 10（发动）initiate: ▸～兵, ～事, ～义

B〈量〉1（件）case: 一～谋杀 a murder case ‖ 防止了一～事故 forestall an accident 2（批次）batch: 他们分六～往地里送肥料。Six groups of men delivered fertilizer to the fields.

起[2] qǐ〈动〉1（表向上）[used after a verb] move sth. upwards: 他提～箱子走出门。He lifted up the case and went out. 2（表开始）[used after a verb or action] begin to: 会场响～热烈的掌声。A warm applause broke out at the meeting. ‖ 乐队奏～迎宾曲。The orchestra struck up a welcoming tune. 3（表足够）[used after a verb preceded by 得 or 不] be up to a certain standard: 经得～考验 can stand the test ‖ 太贵了，买不～。It's too expensive; I can't afford it. ▸看不～, 看得～ 4（表涉及）[used after a verb to indicate the result of an action]: 她多次问～你。She asked about you many times. ‖ 我现在记～来了。Now I remember.

【起岸】qǐ'àn〈动〉unload a ship: ～时间 unloading time

【起爆】qǐbào〈动〉detonate: ～雷管 primer detonator ‖ ～装置 priming device

【起笔】qǐbǐ〈名〉1（指书法）start of each stroke in Chinese calligraphy: 写汉字～很重要。To write a Chinese character well, it is important to start each stroke properly. 2（指检字法）first stroke of a Chinese character in a radical index 3（指文章）the beginning: 这篇文章～不凡。The beginning of the article is superb.

【起兵】qǐbīng〈动〉dispatch troops: ～发难 rise in rebellion ‖ ～抗敌 dispatch troops against enemy invasion

【起搏器】qǐbóqì〈名〉［医学］pacemaker

【起步】qǐbù〈动〉1（启动）start to move: ～价 starting price ‖ 这车～快。The car has fast acceleration. 2〈喻〉（开始）start doing sth.: 刚～的业务 business in its initial stage ‖ 他～比别人晚，但进步快。He started later than others but made rapid progress.

【起草】qǐcǎo〈动〉draft: ～文件 draft a document ‖ ～新章程 draw up a new set of regulations

【起草人】qǐcǎorén〈名〉drafter

【起场】qǐcháng〈动〉［农业］gather in threshed grain on a threshing ground

【起承转合】qǐ-chéng-zhuǎn-hé〈成〉the four-step formula for writing Chinese classic essays

【起程】qǐchéng〈动〉set out: ～去法国 leave for France ‖ 我们定于明晨6时～。Our departure is scheduled for 6 am tomorrow.

【起初】qǐchū〈名〉in the beginning: ～她很紧张，但很快就镇定下来。She was nervous at the start, but she soon got over it. ‖ 这所大学～是一所中专。The university was originally a polytechnic.

【起床】qǐchuáng〈动〉get up: 他每天总是天刚亮就～。He gets up at first light every day.

【起床号】qǐchuánghào〈名〉reveille

【起点】qǐdiǎn〈名〉1（指开始）starting point: ～价格 threshold price ‖ ～站 starting station ‖ 任何伟大的成就都只是继续前进的新～。All great achievements should only serve as starting points for further progress. 2［体育］starting line: 赛跑的～ starting line of a race

【起点运费】qǐdiǎn yùnfèi〈名〉minimum freight

【起吊】qǐdiào〈动〉lift with a crane: ～高度 sling height

【起钉钳】qǐdīngqián〈名〉nail nippers

【起碇】qǐdìng〈动〉weigh anchor

【起端】qǐduān〈名〉beginning or origin (of an event, etc.)

【起飞】qǐfēi〈动〉take off: 班机正点～。The airliner took off on time. ‖〈喻〉经济～ economic take-off ‖ 这个厂所以能～，主要靠科学管理。The main reason that the factory has taken off is because of its scientific management.

q

【起伏】qǐfú〈动〉**1**（一起一落）rise and fall: 波涛～ heaving billows ‖ ～的山峦 rolling hills **2**〈喻〉（变化）fluctuate: 病人病情又有～。The patient has yet had another relapse. ‖ 他们的关系～不定。There have been ups and downs in their relations.

【起稿】qǐgǎo〈动〉draft: 市长的讲话，从来都是自己～。The mayor has always drafted his own speeches.

【起更】qǐgēng〈动〉〈旧〉sound the first night watch

【起旱】qǐhàn〈动〉〈旧〉take an overland route: ～去洛阳 trek to Luoyang

【起航】qǐháng〈动〉（指船）set sail;（指飞机）take off: 他们的船什么时候～? When does their steamer set sail? ‖ 我们的轮船五点～。Our ship leaves at 5.

【起哄】qǐhòng〈动〉**1**（胡闹）get together to stir up trouble: 不得聚众～。No one should assemble a crowd to make trouble. **2**（嘲笑）jeer: 人家拿我开心，你干吗也跟着～? They are making fun of me. Why do you have to join them with your jeers?

【起火】qǐhuǒ〈动〉**1**（做饭）prepare meals: 在食堂吃饭比自己～方便。It's more convenient to dine in the cafeteria than to cook for oneself. **2**（着火）catch fire: 仓库～啦! The warehouse is on fire! **3**（生气）get angry: 你别～，听我慢慢儿对你说。Don't get angry. Let me give you the whole story.

【起货】qǐhuò〈动〉**1**（发货）take goods (from a warehouse) **2**（提货）unload (from a ship, etc.): ～机 winch

【起获】qǐhuò〈动〉track down and seize: ～一批黄色书刊 track and seize a hoard of pornographic books and periodicals

【起火】qǐhuo〈名〉a kind of firecracker

【起急】qǐjí〈动〉〈方〉**1**（焦急）get worried: 问题解决不了，他心里～。He became anxious when he couldn't resolve the problem. **2**（发急）lose one's patience: 你先别～，好好听我说。Don't lose your temper. Be patient and listen to me.

【起家】qǐjiā〈动〉build up: 勤俭～ make one's fortune through thrift and hard work ▸白手～

【起价】qǐjià **A**〈动〉go up in price **B**〈名〉starting price: ～二百美元。The price starts at $200.

【起驾】qǐjià〈动〉〈旧〉[of emperors, kings, etc.] set out

【起见】qǐjiàn〈动〉[used in the phrase 为…起见] be for the sake of: 为安全～ for safety's sake ‖ 为慎重～ for caution's sake

【起降】qǐjiàng〈动〉take off and land: 这个机场每天有上百架飞机～。Up to a hundred airplanes take off from and land on this airfield every day.

【起解】qǐjiè〈动〉〈旧〉[of a criminal or prisoner] be escorted somewhere

【起劲】qǐjìn〈形〉vigorous: 大家干得很～。Everyone works enthusiastically. ‖ 他愈讲愈～。The more he talked the more enthusiastic he became.

【起敬】qǐjìng〈动〉〈书〉show respect: 令人～ command respect from others ▸肃然～

【起居】qǐjū〈名〉daily life: 我饮食～都很有规律。I keep a strict regimen in all aspects of my daily life.

【起居室】qǐjūshì〈名〉living room; sitting room〈英〉

【起句】qǐjù〈名〉first line of a poem

【起圈】qǐjuàn〈动〉remove manure from a pigsty, sheepfold, cattle pen, etc.

【起课】qǐkè〈动〉divine by tossing coins or counting the Heavenly Stems and Earthly Branches on one's fingers

【起来】qǐlái〈动〉**1**（起立）stand up: 快～吃药吧。Sit up and take your medicine. ‖ 小伙子～把座位让给一位老太太。The young man stood up and offered his seat to an old lady. **2**（起床）get up: 他刚～就忙着下地干活儿去了。He went to work in the fields as soon as he got up. **3**（奋起）rise (up): ～反抗压迫 rise up against oppression

【起来】qilai〈动〉**1**（表向上）[used after a verb to indicate an upward movement]: 拣～ pick up ‖ 坐～ sit up ‖ 中国人民站～了。The Chinese people have arisen. **2**（表开始并持续）[used after a verb or an adjective to indicate the beginning and continuation of an action]: 天气渐渐暖和～。It's getting warm. ‖ 一句话把屋里的人都逗得笑了～。The remark set everyone in the room roaring with laughter. ‖ 雨下～了。It has started raining. **3**（表完成）[used after a verb to indicate completeness or effectiveness]: 把钱存～ save up money ‖ 他的名字我记不～了。I can't recall his name. ‖ 想～了，这是鲁迅的话。I remember now! It's a quotation from Lu Xun. **4**（表估计）[used after a verb to indicate an impression or judgement]: 看～要下雨。It looks like rain. ‖ 听～这是件好事。It sounds like this is a good thing.

【起立】qǐlì〈动〉stand up: 全场～为演员喝彩。The whole house rose to its feet to applaud the actors. ‖ 全体～! Everybody, stand up!

【起灵】qǐlíng〈动〉move sb.'s coffin or ashes to a burial place

【起垄】qǐlǒng〈动〉［农业］ridge

【起落】qǐluò〈动〉**1**（起飞和降落）take off and land: 垂直～ vertical take-off and landing ‖ 飞机～ take-off and landing of an aircraft **2**（波动）rise and fall: 价格～ price fluctuations ‖〈喻〉心潮～ fluctuations of emotions

【起落架】qǐluòjià〈名〉［航空］landing gear: 放下～ gear down ‖ 收起～ gear up ‖ ～轮胎 undercarriage wheel

【起码】qǐmǎ〈形〉basic: ～的常识 elementary common sense ‖ ～的条件 basic condition ‖ 我这次出差，～要一个月。The business trip will take me one month at least.

【起毛】qǐmáo〈动〉fluff

【起锚】qǐmáo〈动〉raise anchor: 水手们各就各位，准备～。The sailors are all set for weighing anchor.

【起名儿】qǐmíngr〈动〉name: 给书～ give a title to a book ‖ 请给孩子起个名儿吧。Please choose a name for the baby.

【起腻】qǐnì〈动〉〈口〉**1**（厌恶）feel sick **2**（纠缠）pester

【起拍】qǐpāi〈动〉[of a bid] start (at the price of): ～价 starting price ‖ 从两万元～ start at 20,000 *yuan*

【起跑】qǐpǎo〈动〉［体育］start a race: ～速度 runaway speed ‖ 在～点上排开 line up at the start

【起跑器】qǐpǎoqì〈名〉［体育］starting block

【起跑线】qǐpǎoxiàn〈名〉starting line: 〈喻〉在同一～上展开平等竞争 race from the same starting line

【起泡】qǐpào〈动〉**1**（指水泡）get blisters: 新鞋易把脚磨起泡。New shoes give one's feet blisters. **2**（指泡沫）foam

【起讫】qǐ-qì〈名〉beginning and end: 写明～日期 mark the beginning and end dates

【起色】qǐsè〈名〉improvement: 他的工作有很大～。He has made great progress in his work. ‖ 病人的病情大有～。The patient's condition has greatly improved.

【起身】qǐshēn〈动〉**1**（出发）set off: 我们明天～去上海。We'll leave for Shanghai tomorrow. **2**（起床）get up: 她还没～呢。She isn't up yet. **3**（起立）stand up: ～告辞 rise and take one's leave ‖ ～让座 stand up and offer one's seat to sb.

【起事】qǐshì〈动〉rise in revolt

【起誓】qǐshì〈动〉take an oath: 对天～ swear to God ‖ 你～不再抽烟! Swear that you'll never smoke again!

【起首】qǐshǒu〈副〉〈书〉originally: ～我并不会下棋，是他教我的。I didn't know how to play chess at first. It was he who taught me.

【起死回生】qǐsǐ-huíshēng〈成〉bring the dying back to life: ～之术 the skill to save a patient from the brink of death

【起诉】qǐsù〈动〉prosecute: 撤回～ drop a case ‖ 免于～ be immune from prosecution

【起诉人】qǐsùrén〈名〉prosecutor

【起诉书】qǐsùshū〈名〉indictment: 宣读～ read out an indictment

【起诉状】qǐsùzhuàng〈名〉petition for appeal

【起跳】qǐtiào〈动〉［体育］take off

【起跳板】qǐtiàobǎn〈名〉take-off board

【起头】qǐtóu **A**〈动〉start: 先从我这儿～。I'll be first. ‖ 这事情是谁起的头儿? Who started all this? **B**〈名〉beginning: ～他答应过来，后来又改变了主意。At first he promised to come but later he changed his mind. ‖ 万事～难。Everything is difficult at the start. ‖ 小说的～写得不错。The opening of the novel is good.

【起网】qǐwǎng〈动〉haul a net

【起先】qǐxiān〈名〉beginning: ～我们对此一无所知。I knew nothing about it in the beginning.

【起小儿】qǐxiǎor〈副〉since childhood: 他～身体就很结实。He has been strong and healthy since childhood.

【起薪】qǐxīn〈名〉starting salary

【起衅】qǐxìn = 启衅 qǐxìn

【起行】qǐxíng〈动〉set out: 他今天下午三点～。He is leaving at three o'clock this afternoon.

【起眼】qǐyǎn〈形〉[usu used in the negative] attractive: 别看这些东西不怎么～，日常生活却离不开它们。These things may not be nice to look at, but they are necessities for daily life.

【起夜】qǐyè〈动〉get up in the night to urinate

【起疑】qǐyí〈动〉become suspicious: 他的举动反常，让人～。His abnormal activities aroused suspicion.

【起义】qǐyì〈动〉rise in revolt: 发动～ launch a revolt ‖ 农民～。The peasants revolted. ‖ 敌军纷纷～投诚。Many enemy soldiers revolted and crossed over to the other side.

【起意】qǐyì〈动〉〈贬〉come up with an evil design: 见财～ entertain evil thoughts at the sight of money

【起因】qǐyīn〈名〉origin: 事故的～正在调查之中。The cause of the accident is under investigation. ‖ 这场火灾～可疑。The fire is of suspicious origin.

【起用】qǐyòng〈动〉**1**（重新任用）

q

reinstate: 卸任的部长又被～了。 The retired minister was reinstated in his former job. **2**（提拔使用） appoint sb. to an important position: 大胆～年轻干部 boldly place young cadres in important positions

【起源】qǐyuán **A**〈动〉 originate: 知识无不～于实践。 All knowledge originates in practice. ‖ 这一习俗～于国外。 The custom has its origin in another country. **B**〈名〉 origin: 生命的～ origin of life ‖《物种～》*The Origin of Species*

【起运】qǐyùn〈动〉 start shipment: 办理～手续 go through shipping formalities ‖ 货已～。 The goods are on their way.

【起赃】qǐzāng〈动〉track down and recover stolen goods

【起早摸黑】qǐzǎo-mōhēi = 起早贪黑 qǐzǎo-tānhēi

【起早贪黑】qǐzǎo-tānhēi〈成〉 work from dawn to dusk: ～地苦干 toil from dawn to dusk

【起征点】qǐzhēngdiǎn〈名〉［经济］ tax threshold: 提高个人所得税～ raise the personal income tax threshold

【起止】qǐ-zhǐ〈名〉 beginning and end: ～日期 starting and finishing dates

【起重船】qǐzhòngchuán = 浮吊 fúdiào

【起重机】qǐzhòngjī〈名〉 crane: 固定式悬臂～ fixed cantilever crane ‖ 移动式转臂～ mobile jib crane

【起皱】qǐzhòu〈动〉 crinkle: 脸上～ get wrinkles on one's face

【起子】qǐzi〈名〉 **1**（开瓶器） bottle opener: 瓶～ bottle opener **2**〈方〉（螺丝刀） screwdriver **3**〈方〉（焙粉） baking powder

q

绮（綺）qǐ

A〈名〉〈书〉 damask: 罗～ thin silk gauze

B〈形〉 excellent: ▸～丽

【绮丽】qǐlì〈形〉 beautiful: 风光～ beautiful scenery

【绮思】qǐsī〈名〉〈书〉 beautiful thoughts (in literature)

稽 qǐ

▸jī

【稽首】qǐshǒu〈动〉〈书〉 kowtow

qì

气（氣）qì

A〈名〉 **1**（气体） gas: 管道漏～。 The gas pipe is leaking. ▸毒～, 煤～, 氧～ **2**（空气） air: 打开窗子透透～ open the window to let in some fresh air ‖ 轮胎打足了～。 The tyre is fully inflated. ▸～流, ～压, 大～层 **3**（天气） weather: ▸～候, ～象, 天～ **4**（呼吸） breath: 没～儿了 stop breathing ‖ 停下来歇口～ stop to catch one's breath ▸喘～, 吐～, 吸～ **5**（生气） anger: 她的～消了。 Her anger melted. ▸赌～, 怄～, 生～ **6**（气息） smell: 泥土～ smell of the earth ‖ 他满嘴酒～。 His breath smells strongly of wine. ▸臭～, 臊～, 香～ **7**（气势） spirit: ▸～概, ～吞山河, 垂头丧～ **8**（习气） airs: 书生～十足 bookish in the extreme ▸官～, 娇～, 锐～ **9**［中医］ **a**（原动力） vital energy: ▸～虚, 血～, 元～ **b**（症状） symptoms of disease: ▸肝～, 湿～, 痰～ **10**（欺压） bullying: 挨打受～ be bullied and beaten ‖ 我再也无法忍受他的～了。 I can no longer bear his bullying. ▸忍～吞声

B〈动〉 **1**（生气） get angry: ～得发抖 tremble with anger ‖ ～得说不出话来 choke with anger ▸～愤, ～恼 **2**（使生气） enrage: 故意～人 deliberately rub sb. up the wrong way ‖ 你别～我了! Stop annoying me!

【气昂昂】qì'áng'áng〈形〉 full of dash

【气包子】qìbāozi〈名〉〈口〉 person who is easy to take offence

【气泵】qìbèng〈名〉 air pump

【气不打一处来】qì bù dǎ yīchù lái〈惯〉 be seized with fury: 一看见她我就～。 I was filled with anger at the sight of her.

【气不过】qìbùguò〈动〉 be beside oneself with rage

【气不平】qìbùpíng〈动〉 be indignant over an injustice

【气冲冲】qìchōngchōng〈形〉 furious: ～地走进/出房间 storm into/out of the room ‖ 他～地走了。 He left angrily.

【气冲牛斗】qìchōng-niúdǒu〈成〉 be in a towering rage

【气冲霄汉】qìchōng-xiāohàn〈成〉be completely fearless

【气喘】qìchuǎn **A** ▸**p. 50**〈名〉［医学］ asthma: ～病人 asthmatic patient **B**〈动〉 pant

【气喘吁吁】qìchuǎnxūxū〈成〉 puff and pant: 她跑得～。 The run left her breathless.

【气窗】qìchuāng〈名〉［建筑］ fanlight

【气锤】qìchuí〈名〉 air hammer

【气粗】qìcū〈形〉 **1**（暴躁） hot-tempered: 我有点儿～, 希望你不要介意。 I hope you won't mind if you find me a little quick-tempered. **2**（傲慢） overbearing: 财大～ he who is wealthy has the loudest voice

【气促】qìcù〈形〉 short of breath

【气垫】qìdiàn〈名〉 **1**（指垫子） air cushion: ～床 hover bed **2**（指空气） high-pressure air from the bottom of a hovercraft

【气垫船】qìdiànchuán〈名〉 hovercraft

【气动】qìdòng〈形〉 pneumatic: ～工具 pneumatic tool ‖ ～锤 pneumatic hammer

【气度】qìdù〈名〉 **1**（度量） tolerance: ～不凡 be impressive in appearance **2**（气概） manner

【气短】qìduǎn **A**〈形〉 short of breath: 爬到半山, 我们感到有点～。 By the time we had climbed half way up the hill, we were all out of breath. **B**〈动〉 lose heart: 实验失败并没有使他～。 He was not discouraged by the failure of the experiment.

【气氛】qìfēn〈名〉 atmosphere: 沉浸在节日～中 be immersed in a festival atmosphere ‖ 会谈在亲切友好的～中进行。 The talks were held in a cordial and friendly atmosphere.

【气愤】qìfèn〈形〉 furious: 得知他贪污公司的资金, 我非常～。 I was enraged to learn that he had embezzled company funds.

【气概】qìgài〈名〉 mettle: 大无畏的～ dauntless mettle ‖ 英雄～ heroic spirit

【气缸】qìgāng〈名〉［机械］ (air) cylinder

【气根】qìgēn〈名〉［植物］ aerial root

【气功】qìgōng〈名〉 *qigong*, breathing exercise: ～师 *qigong* master

【气鼓鼓】qìgǔgǔ〈形〉 furious

【气管】qìguǎn〈名〉［生理］ windpipe

【气管炎】qìguǎnyán **A** ▸**p. 50**〈名〉［医学］ tracheitis **B**〈惯〉〈诙〉 henpecked husband

【气贯长虹】qìguàn-chánghóng〈成〉 be full of noble aspiration and daring

> **气功**
>
> A distinctive Chinese technique for promoting physical and spiritual well-being, and involving breathing exercises, self-massage, and movement of the limbs. *Qi* means 'air' and, by extension, life breath or energy. *Gong* means skill. There are five main schools of *qigong*: the Medical, which concentrates on prevention and cure of illness; the Confucian, which is concerned with the cultivation of one's moral character; the Taoist, which focuses on both body and spirit; the Buddhist, which works on freeing the heart and mind, and the *Wushu*, which practices physical exercise and self-defence.

【气锅】qìguō〈名〉 Yunnan steaming pot: ～鸡 Yunnan style steamed chicken

【气焊】qìhàn〈名〉［冶金］ gas welding: ～机 gas welding machine

【气候】qìhòu〈名〉 **1**（气象概况） climate: ～干燥 dry climate ‖ 大陆性/海洋性～ continental/maritime climate **2**〈喻〉（情势） situation: 政治～ political climate ‖ 大～决定小～。 Macroclimates determine microclimates. **3**（成果） success: ～变化框架公约 Framework Convention of Climate Change ‖ 几个人瞎闹腾, 成不了～。 A few people are going at it blind. They will get nowhere.

【气候变化】qìhòu biànhuà〈名〉 climate change: 《～框架公约》*Framework Convention of Climate Change*

【气呼呼】qìhūhū〈形〉 panting with rage: ～地走了 go off in a huff

【气化】qìhuà〈动〉［化工］ gasify

【气话】qìhuà〈名〉 remarks made in a fit of rage: 她说的只是～, 千万别在意。 You mustn't take it too seriously. She just said it to vent her anger.

【气急】qìjí〈形〉 out of breath

【气急败坏】qìjí-bàihuài〈成〉 be flustered and exasperated: ～, 暴跳如雷 be exasperated and furious

【气节】qìjié〈名〉 moral integrity: 坚贞不屈的～ unyielding integrity ‖ 民族～ national integrity

【气井】qìjǐng〈名〉［石油］ gas well

【气绝】qìjué〈动〉 stop breathing: ～身亡 breathe one's last

【气可鼓而不可泄】qì kě gǔ ér bùkě xiè〈成〉 morale should be boosted, not dampened

【气孔】qìkǒng〈名〉 **1**［植物］ stoma **2** = 气门 qìmén 1 **3**［冶金］ gas cavity: 任何焊缝上都没有发现裂缝或～。 No cracking or porosity was noted in any of the welds. **4**［建筑］ air hole

【气浪】qìlàng〈名〉 blast: 爆炸引起的一股～ a blast caused by an explosion

【气力】qìlì〈名〉 effort: 花～ make an effort ‖ 用尽～ exhaust one's strength

【气量】qìliàng〈名〉 tolerance: ～大 broad-minded ‖ 这个人很有～, 从不计较别人说他什么。 He is a man of great tolerance and he never cares what others say about him.

【气流】qìliú〈名〉 **1**（指空气） air current: 暖湿～ currents of warm, humid air **2**［语言］ breath

【气楼】qìlóu〈名〉 small ventilation tower on the top of a roof

【气脉】qìmài〈名〉 **1**（血气和脉息） sap and pulse: ～调和 be harmonious in blood and pulse **2**（诗文脉络） line of thought

【气门】qìmén〈名〉 **1**［动物］ spiracle **2**（指活门） air valve: ▸～芯 **3**［机械］ air drain

【气门芯】qìménxīn〈名〉〈口〉 **1**（指活

门） valve inside 2)（指橡皮管） valve rubber tube

【气闷】qìmèn〈形〉1)（心情烦闷） vexed: 心中～ feel vexed 2)（憋闷） close: 打开一扇窗户吧，这儿太～。 Shall we open a window? It's very stuffy here.

【气密】qìmì〈形〉［机械］ airtight

【气囊】qìnáng〈名〉 1)（指鸟、昆虫等） air sac;（指水生植物） air vesicle 2)（指航空器） gasbag 3)（指汽车等） air bag

【气恼】qìnǎo〈动〉 get angry: 他的话真叫我们～。 What he said really offended us.

【气馁】qìněi〈动〉 be discouraged: 胜利了不要骄傲，失败了不要～。 Never let success go to your head or failure bring you down.

【气派】qìpài〈名〉 imposing manner: 好～的大楼啊! What an imposing building! ‖ 他有政治家的～吗? Does he have the air of a statesman?

【气泡】qìpào〈名〉 bubble: 冒～ bubble up

【气魄】qìpò〈名〉 1)（魄力） boldness of vision: 他办事很有～。 He is very bold and decisive in doing things. 2)（气势） imposing manner: 天安门城楼～雄伟。 The gate tower of Tiananmen is a structure of imposing grandeur.

【气枪】qìqiāng〈名〉 air rifle

【气球】qìqiú〈名〉 balloon: 氢/热～ hydrogen/hot-air balloon

【气色】qìsè〈名〉 complexion: 近来他的～很好，满面红光。 Recently he's been looking fine, glowing with health. ‖ 她这几天～不好。 She hasn't been looking well these past few days.

【气生根】qìshēnggēn = 气根 qìgēn

【气盛】qìshèng〈形〉 overbearing: 年轻～ be young and impetuous

【气势】qìshì〈名〉 imposing manner: ～雄伟的人民大会堂 imposing grandeur of the Great Hall of the People

【气势磅礴】qìshì-pángbó〈成〉 be of great momentum: ～的乐章 movements of great power

【气势汹汹】qìshì-xiōngxiōng〈成〉 overbearing: 他～，不可一世。 He is overbearing and insufferably arrogant.

【气数】qìshu〈名〉 fate: ～已尽 be nearing its fated end

【气态】qìtài〈名〉［物理］ gaseous state

【气体】qìtǐ〈名〉 gas: 易燃～ inflammable gas

【气体常数】qìtǐ chángshù〈名〉［物理］ gas constant

【气体动力学】qìtǐ dònglìxué〈名〉［物理］ aerodynamics

【气体燃料】qìtǐ ránliào〈名〉 gaseous fuel

【气体压缩机】qìtǐ yāsuōjī〈名〉［机械］ gas compressor

【气田】qìtián〈名〉 gas field: ～开发 gas field development

【气筒】qìtǒng〈名〉 pump

【气头上】qìtóushang〈名〉〈口〉 foul temper: 他正在～，别人的话听不进去。 He is in temper right now, and won't listen to anyone.

【气团】qìtuán〈名〉［气象］ air mass

【气吞山河】qìtūn-shānhé〈成〉 be full of daring

【气味】qìwèi〈名〉 1)（指味儿） smell: 刺鼻的～ pungent smell ‖ 茉莉花散发出宜人的芬芳～。 Jasmine flowers emit a pleasant aroma. 2)〈贬〉（指品性） smack: 霸权主义的～ smack of hegemonism

【气味相投】qìwèi-xiāngtóu〈成〉 be two of a kind

【气温】qìwēn〈名〉 temperature: 平均～ average temperature ‖ ～降到了零度。 The temperature has fallen to zero.

【气息】qìxī〈名〉 1)（呼吸） breath: 屏住～ hold one's breath 2)（气味） smell: 散发出春天的～ emit a scent of spring ‖〈喻〉 生活～ flavour of life ‖〈喻〉 时代～ spirit of the times

【气息奄奄】qìxī-yǎnyǎn〈成〉 breathe one's last: 他已～了。 He is nearing the end. ‖〈喻〉这种手工艺已～，后继无人。 This kind of handicraft is on its way out. There is no one to carry on the tradition.

【气象】qìxiàng〈名〉 1)（指大气） meteorological phenomena: ～报告 weather report ‖ ～卫星 meteorological satellite 2)（指学科） meteorology 3)（情景） atmosphere: 一片新～ a new atmosphere 4)（气派） imposing manner: ～宏伟 imposing and magnificent

【气象局】qìxiàngjú〈名〉 weather bureau

【气象台】qìxiàngtái〈名〉 meteorological observatory

【气象图】qìxiàngtú〈名〉 meteorological chart

【气象万千】qìxiàng-wànqiān〈成〉 spectacular and kaleidoscopic: 远望群山，～。 Far in the distance mountains rise up range after range in all their majesty.

【气象学】qìxiàngxué〈名〉 meteorology: ～家 meteorologist

【气象预报】qìxiàng yùbào〈名〉 weather forecast

【气象站】qìxiàngzhàn〈名〉 weather station

【气性】qìxing〈名〉 1)（脾气） temperament: ～温顺 have a docile disposition 2)（指性格） bad temper: 这孩子～大。 The child is prone to throwing tantrums.

【气汹汹】qìxiōngxiōng〈形〉 furious: 他～地冲进屋子。 He stormed into the room.

【气胸】qìxiōng ▸p. 50〈名〉［医学］ pneumothorax

【气咻咻】qìxiūxiū = 气吁吁 qìxūxū

【气吁吁】qìxūxū〈形〉 out of breath: 他跑得～的。 He was huffing and puffing after the run.

【气虚】qìxū〈名〉［中医］ deficiency of vital energy

【气旋】qìxuán〈名〉［气象］ cyclone

【气血】qì-xuè〈名〉［中医］ vital energy and state of blood: ～两虚 deficiency of both vital energy and blood

【气压】qìyā〈名〉 atmospheric pressure: 低/高～ low/high pressure

【气压计】qìyājì〈名〉 barometer

【气眼】qìyǎn = 气孔 qìkǒng 3, 4

【气焰】qìyàn〈名〉〈贬〉 arrogance: ～嚣张 be swollen with arrogance

【气宇】qìyǔ〈名〉〈书〉 manner: ～不凡 no common-looking man

【气宇轩昂】qìyǔ-xuān'áng〈成〉 be dignified in appearance: ～的男子 man of remarkable presence

【气运】qìyùn〈名〉〈书〉 fate: ～不佳 be down on one's luck

【气韵】qìyùn〈名〉〈书〉 spirit, character, tone, or style of a work of art/literature: 画面简洁，～无穷。 The painting looks simple but there is something immortal in its style.

【气闸】qìzhá〈名〉 air brake

【气质】qìzhì〈名〉 1)（指个性） temperament: 诗人～ poetical temperament ‖ 我看到她身上有她父亲的某些～。 I can see her father in her. 2)（指风格） qualities: 缺乏军人～ lack soldierly qualities ‖ 表现出革命者的～ exhibit revolutionary qualities

【气滞】qìzhì〈名〉［中医］ stagnation of the circulation of vital energy

【气壮如牛】qìzhuàng-rúniú〈成〉 be as sturdy as a bull

【气壮山河】qìzhuàngshānhé〈成〉 be full of power and grandeur: 红军二万五千里长征是一部～的史诗。 The Red Army's 25,000 *li* Long March is a sublime and heroic epic in Chinese history.

【气钻】qìzuàn〈名〉［机械］ air drill

讫（訖） qì〈动〉1)〈书〉（截止） end: ▸起～ 2)（完结） settle: 银货两～。 The goods have been received and paid for.

迄 qì

A 〈介〉 till: ▸～今

B 〈副〉〈书〉 [used before 未 or 无] so far: ～未见效。 So far there haven't been any results. ‖ ～无音信。 We have received no information so far.

【迄今】qìjīn〈副〉 so far: ～为止，这种病找不到任何治疗方法。 The disease has so far defied all attempts at a cure.

弃（棄） qì〈动〉 abandon: ～恶从善 shun evil and do good ‖ ～卒保帅 sacrifice one's pawn to save the queen ▸～权, 放～, 遗～

【弃暗投明】qì'àn-tóumíng〈成〉〈喻〉 leave the reactionary camp and cross over to the side of progress

【弃儿】qì'ér〈名〉 abandoned child

【弃妇】qìfù〈名〉〈书〉 abandoned wife

【弃甲曳兵】qìjiǎ-yèbīng〈成〉 flee helter-skelter

【弃旧图新】qìjiù-túxīn〈成〉 turn over a new leaf: 你唯一的选择是～，此外别无出路。 The only choice left for you is to turn things around. There is no alternative.

【弃权】qìquán〈动〉 1)（指投票） abstain: 五票赞成，三票反对，二票～。 Five votes for, three against, and two abstentions. 2)［体育］ default: 他在四分之一决赛中～。 He defaulted in the quarter-finals.

【弃舍】qìshě〈动〉 abandon

【弃世】qìshì〈动〉〈书〉 pass away

【弃学】qìxué〈动〉 quit school

【弃养】qìyǎng〈动〉〈旧〉 [of one's parents] pass away

【弃婴】qìyīng〈名〉 abandoned baby

【弃置】qìzhì〈动〉 discard: ～不顾 leave out in the cold ‖ 许多机器被～不用。 Many machines were cast aside and lay idle.

汽 qì〈名〉 vapour: ▸～船, ～锤, 蒸～

【汽车】qìchē〈名〉 car: ～发动机 car engine ‖ ～废气排放 motor vehicle exhaust emission ‖ 双座～ two-seater ‖ 微型～ mini-car

【汽车厂】qìchēchǎng〈名〉 car factory

【汽车吊】qìchēdiào〈名〉 truck crane

【汽车工业】qìchē gōngyè〈名〉 motor industry

【汽车旅馆】qìchē lǚguǎn〈名〉 motel

【汽车展】qìchēzhǎn〈名〉 motor show

【汽车站】qìchēzhàn〈名〉 bus stop

【汽船】qìchuán〈名〉 1)（指船）steamship 2)（指汽艇） motor boat

【汽锤】qìchuí〈名〉 steam hammer

【汽灯】qìdēng〈名〉 gas lamp: ～罩 gas mantle

【汽笛】qìdí〈名〉 siren: ～长鸣。 The siren is sounding.

【汽缸】qìgāng〈名〉［机械］ (steam) cylinder

【汽化】qìhuà〈动〉［物理］ vaporize: 水受热就会～。 Water will change to vapour when heated.

【汽酒】qìjiǔ〈名〉light sparkling wine

【汽轮发电机】qìlún fādiànjī〈名〉turbo-generator

【汽轮机】qìlúnjī〈名〉steam turbine

【汽暖】qìnuǎn〈名〉steam heating

【汽配厂】qìpèichǎng〈名〉motor repair shop

【汽水】qìshuǐ〈名〉soft drink: 桔子～ fizzy orange ‖ 柠檬～ lemonade

【汽艇】qìtǐng〈名〉motor boat

【汽修厂】qìxiūchǎng〈名〉garage

【汽油】qìyóu〈名〉petrol〈英〉; gasoline〈美〉: 含铅/无铅～ leaded/unleaded gasoline ‖ 凝固～ napalm

【汽油弹】qìyóudàn〈名〉［军事］petrol bomb: 凝固～ napalm bomb

【汽油机】qìyóujī〈名〉［机械］petrol engine

泣 qì

A〈动〉weep: 暗～ sob in secret ▸抽～, 可歌可～

B〈名〉tears: ▸饮～

【泣不成声】qìbùchéngshēng〈成〉choke with sobs: 说到伤心处，她～。When she got to the saddest part of the story, she sobbed so much that she couldn't get the words out.

【泣诉】qìsù〈动〉accuse while weeping, accuse amid tears

【泣下如雨】qìxià-rúyǔ〈成〉shed copious tears

亟 qì

〈副〉〈书〉repeatedly: ～经磋商 after repeated consultations ‖ ～来问讯 come repeatedly to ask for information

▸jí

契 qì

A〈动〉**1**▸〈书〉（雕刻）carve: ▸～文 **2**▸（投合）agree: ▸～友, 默～

B〈名〉**1**▸〈书〉（指文字）carved characters: 殷～ inscriptions found on bones and tortoise shells **2**▸（指文书）contract: 租～ lease ▸地～, 房～, 卖身～

【契丹】Qìdān〈名〉［历史］Khitan [Mongol people who ruled Manchuria and part of north China from the 10th to the early 12th century under the Liao Dynasty]

【契合】qìhé〈动〉**1**▸（符合）tally with: 她的衣着不～她的身份。Her attire does not tally with her status. **2**▸（合得来）be compatible: 他俩说话投机，感情～。The two had an agreeable chat and found that they enjoyed each other's company.

【契机】qìjī〈名〉**1**▸［哲学］moment **2**▸（关键）turning point: 以此为～ with this as a turning point ‖ 抓住～，夺回主动权。Seize the opportunity and regain the initiative.

【契据】qìjù〈名〉contract: 信托～ deed of trust

【契文】qìwén ▸**p. 918**〈名〉inscriptions on bones or tortoise shells

【契友】qìyǒu〈名〉close friend: 成为～ become close friends

【契约】qìyuē〈名〉deed: 抵押～ mortgage a deed ‖ 产权转让～ quitclaim deed

砌 qì

A〈名〉step: 石～ stone steps ▸雕栏玉～

B〈动〉build by laying bricks/stones: ～墙 build a wall ‖ ～灶 build a kitchen range ‖ ～砖 lay bricks ▸堆～

葺 qì

〈动〉**1**▸〈书〉（指房顶）thatch a roof **2**▸（指房屋）repair: ▸修～

碛（磧）qì

〈名〉**1**▸〈书〉（指浅滩）gravel shoal: 冰～ glacial drift **2**▸（指沙漠）desert

碶 qì

〈名〉〈方〉stone sluice: ～闸 stone sluice

槭 qì

〈名〉maple

【槭树】qìshù〈名〉［植物］maple

【槭糖】qìtáng〈名〉maple: ～浆 maple syrup

器 qì

A〈名〉**1**▸（器具）utensil: ▸～物, 电～, 仪～, 乐～ **2**▸（度量）tolerance: ▸～量, ～宇轩昂 **3**▸（才能）talent: ▸大～晚成 **4**▸（器官）organ: ▸～官

B〈动〉think highly of: ▸～重

【器材】qìcái〈名〉equipment: 防火～ fire protection equipment ‖ 通讯～ communication equipment ‖ 照相～ photographic equipment

【器官】qìguān〈名〉organ: 发音～ speech organs ‖ 呼吸～ respiratory organs ‖ ～移植 organ transplant ‖ 听觉～ auditory organs ‖ 消化～ digestive organs

【器件】qìjiàn〈名〉components: 电子～ electronic device

【器具】qìjù〈名〉utensil: 厨房～ kitchen utensils ‖ 灭火～ fire extinguisher

【器量】qìliàng〈名〉tolerance: ～大 broad-minded ‖ ～小 narrow-minded

【器皿】qìmǐn〈名〉utensils: 玻璃～ glassware ‖ 家用～ household utensils

【器识】qìshí〈名〉〈书〉capability and judgement

【器物】qìwù〈名〉implement

【器械】qìxiè〈名〉**1**▸（器具）apparatus: 体育～ sports apparatus ‖ 医疗～ medical appliance **2**▸（武器）weapon

【器械体操】qìxiè tǐcāo〈名〉gymnastics on apparatus

【器宇轩昂】qìyǔ-xuān'áng = 气宇轩昂 qìyǔ-xuān'áng

【器乐】qìyuè〈名〉［音乐］instrumental music: ～作品 instrumental work

【器质】qìzhì〈名〉**1**▸（指器官结构）structure of the human organs: ～性心脏病 organic heart disease **2**▸ = 气质 qìzhì

【器质性】qìzhìxìng〈形〉organic: ～疾病 organic disease

【器重】qìzhòng〈动〉regard highly: 他的工作能力强，领导很～他。He is very capable and his superiors think highly of him.

憩（憇）qì

〈动〉〈书〉have a rest: 同作同～ work and rest together ▸小～, 休～, 游～

【憩室】qìshì〈名〉［解剖］diverticulum

【憩息】qìxī〈动〉〈书〉rest

qiā

掐 qiā

A〈动〉**1**▸（用指甲）pinch: ～嫩芽 nip buds ‖ 把豆芽菜的须子～一～ pinch back the fibrous roots of bean sprouts ‖ 请把烟～灭。Stub out your cigarette, please. ▸～头去尾 **2**▸（用手）grip: ～住脖子 seize sb. by the throat ‖ 一把～住 seize hold of

B〈量〉〈方〉bunch: 一～儿葱 a handful of green onions

【掐断】qiāduàn〈动〉nip off: 电话被～了。The telephone has been cut off.

【掐尖儿】qiājiānr〈动〉pinch off young shoots: 给棉花～ top the cotton plants

【掐诀】qiājué〈动〉pinch one's fingers with the thumb while chanting incantations: ～念咒 calculate on one's fingers while chanting incantations

【掐丝】qiāsī〈名〉［美术］wire inlay

【掐算】qiāsuàn〈动〉count sth. on one's fingers: 母亲～女儿的归期。The mother was counting down to her daughter's return.

【掐头去尾】qiātóu-qùwěi〈成〉leave out the beginning and the end: 引用别人的话不能～。When quoting others you can't leave bits out.

【掐钟点儿】qiā zhōngdiǎnr〈动〉〈口〉do sth. as scheduled

袷 qiā

【袷袢】qiāpàn〈名〉Uyghur or Tajik robe buttoning down the front

qiá

拤 qiá

〈动〉〈口〉clutch with both hands

qiǎ

卡 qiǎ

A〈动〉**1**▸（夹住）get stuck: 抽屉被～住了，打不开。The drawer got stuck and would not open. ‖ 钥匙～在锁里了。The key has stuck in the lock. ‖ 鱼刺～在我嗓子里。A fish bone stuck in my throat. **2**▸（约束）have a tight control of: ～住敌人的退路 block the enemy's retreat ‖ 会计对不必要的开支～得很紧。The accountant has a very tight control of unnecessary expenses. **3**▸（按住）clutch: 他差点儿把她～死了。He put his hands round her neck and nearly choked her to death. ▸～脖子

B〈名〉**1**▸（指器具）clip, fastener: ▸发～ **2**▸（指岗哨）checkpoint: ▸关～, 哨～, 税～

▸kǎ

【卡脖子】qiǎ bózi〈动〉**1**▸〈本〉seize sb. by the throat **2**▸〈喻〉have in a stranglehold: ～工程 bottleneck project ‖ 用经济制裁来卡别国的脖子 apply economic sanctions against another country in an attempt to force it into submission

【卡具】qiǎjù〈名〉［机械］clamping apparatus

【卡壳】qiǎké〈动〉**1**▸（指物）jam: 子弹～了。The cartridge got jammed in the magazine. **2**▸〈喻〉（指办事）be held up: 会谈～了。The negotiations came to a halt. **3**▸〈喻〉（指说话）have a temporary stoppage: 他说着说着就～了。He got stuck for words.

【卡口】qiǎkǒu〈名〉bayonet: ～灯泡 bayonet-socket bulb

【卡位】qiǎwèi〈动〉［篮球］screen

【卡子】qiǎzi〈名〉**1**▸（用于固定）clip: 头发～ hairpin **2**▸（用于阻拦）checkpoint:

禁止在公路上设～乱收费。It is forbidden to set up check posts collecting illegal tolls.

qià

洽¹ qià〈形〉extensive: ▸博识～闻

洽² qià
A〈形〉harmonious: 意见不～ not see eye to eye ▸融～
B〈动〉consult: ～借 borrow sth. through consultation ▸～商, 接～, 面～

【洽购】qiàgòu〈动〉negotiate a purchase: ～粮油 arrange a purchase of grain and oil ‖ 函电～ negotiate the purchase of sth. by mail or telephone

【洽商】qiàshāng〈动〉talk over with: ～有关事宜 hold talks with sb. over the matters concerned ‖ 欢迎当面～。Personal consultation is welcome.

【洽谈】qiàtán〈动〉hold talks: ～生意 hold trade talks ‖ ～投资事宜 hold talks on investment ‖ 贸易～会 trade talks

恰 qià
A〈形〉appropriate: 措词不～ be inappropriately worded ▸～当
B〈副〉just: ～逢其时 at exactly that time ▸～～, ～巧, ～如其分

【恰当】qiàdàng〈形〉proper: 找不到～的字眼 be unable to come up with suitable wording ‖ 你认为怎么～就怎么做。Do as you see fit. ‖ 事情处理得很～。The matter was properly handled.

【恰到好处】qiàdào-hǎochù〈成〉just right: 小说的结尾～。The ending of the novel was just right. ‖ 这事处理得～。The matter was handled just fine.

【恰好】qiàhǎo〈副〉**1**（碰巧）as luck would have it: 她要看的那本书～我这里有。It so happened that I had just the book she wanted. **2**（正好）just right: 尺寸大小～合适。It is just the right size. ‖ 事实～相反。The reverse is exactly the case.

【恰恰】qiàqià〈副〉just: ～相反 quite the contrary ‖ ～在那个时候 at that very moment

【恰恰舞】qiàqiàwǔ〈名〉cha-cha: 跳～ dance the cha-cha

【恰巧】qiàqiǎo〈副〉by chance: 朋友来访时，我～外出。It so happened that I was out when a friend of mine called. ‖ 他正愁没人帮他卸车，～这时老张来了。He was worrying about having nobody help him unload the truck, when Lao Zhang arrived.

【恰切】qiàqiè〈形〉apt and accurate

【恰如】qiàrú〈动〉be just like: 晚霞～一幅图画。The evening glow is just like a picture.

【恰如其分】qiàrú-qífèn〈成〉just right: 措词～ appropriate wording ‖ ～的评价 apt appraisal

【恰似】qiàsì〈动〉be just like: 这消息～晴天霹雳，令人万分震惊。The shocking news came as a bolt from the blue.

髂 qià
【髂骨】qiàgǔ〈名〉［解剖］ilium

qiān

千¹ qiān ▸**p. 691**〈数〉**1**（一千）thousand: ～分之一 one thousandth ‖ 数以～计 count by the thousand ‖ 小麦亩产突破～斤。Wheat output topped a thousand *jin* per mu. **2**（许多）a great amount/number of: ▸～锤百炼, ～方百计

千²（韆） qiān ▸秋千 qiūqiān

【千变万化】qiānbiàn-wànhuà〈成〉be ever changing: ～的国际局势 volatile international situation

【千不该，万不该】qiān bùgāi, wàn bùgāi〈惯〉deeply regret: ～，我不该让孩子一个人夜里出去。I should never have let the child go out alone at night.

【千层饼】qiāncéngbǐng〈名〉layered cake

【千层底】qiāncéngdǐ〈名〉shoe sole made of many layers of cloth stitched together

【千差万别】qiānchā-wànbié〈成〉be multifarious: 各地情况～。Conditions vary greatly from place to place.

【千疮百孔】qiānchuāng-bǎikǒng = 百孔千疮 bǎikǒng-qiānchuāng

【千锤百炼】qiānchuí-bǎiliàn〈成〉〈喻〉**1**（指人）be well-seasoned: 这些老干部都曾经过～。These veteran cadres have gone through many trials. **2**（指作品）be revised and rewritten many times

【千刀万剐】qiāndāo-wànguǎ〈成〉tear sb. to pieces: 他杀了那么多人，真该～。Guilty of so many murders, he deserves nothing less than dismemberment.

【千岛群岛】qiāndǎoqúndǎo〈名〉Kuril Islands

【千叮咛，万嘱咐】qiān dīngníng, wàn zhǔfù〈惯〉give repeated exhortations

【千吨】qiāndūn〈名〉［物理］kiloton (kt): ～能量 kiloton energy

【千恩万谢】qiān'ēn-wànxiè〈成〉express a thousand thanks

【千方百计】qiānfāng-bǎijì〈成〉by every conceivable means: ～提高单位面积产量 do everything possible to raise the per unit yield

【千分表】qiānfēnbiǎo〈名〉dial gauge

【千分尺】qiānfēnchǐ〈名〉micrometer

【千分点】qiānfēndiǎn〈名〉one-tenth of a percentage point: 上升/下降一个～ be one permillage point higher/lower (than)

【千分号】qiānfēnhào ▸**p. 691**〈名〉per mil

【千分数】qiānfēnshù = 千分号 qiānfēnhào

【千佛洞】Qiānfódòng〈名〉Thousand-Buddha Cave

【千夫所指】qiānfūsuǒzhǐ〈成〉be universally condemned: ～，无病而死。It is dangerous to incur public hostility.

【千伏】qiānfú〈量〉［电气］kilovolt

【千古】qiāngǔ **A**〈名〉ages: ～绝唱 poetic masterpiece known throughout the ages ‖ ～奇闻 fantastic story ‖ ～罪人 criminal who has been condemned through the ages **B** ▸**p. 772**〈动〉〈婉〉（表永别）eternity [used in an elegiac couplet or on wreaths dedicated to the dead]: 某某先生～! Eternal peace to Mr so-and-so!

【千赫】qiānhè〈量〉kilohertz

【千呼万唤】qiānhū-wànhuàn〈成〉invite sb. time and again: ～始出来。She came out only after being urged repeatedly.

【千回百转】qiānhuí-bǎizhuǎn〈成〉be full of twists and turns

【千家万户】qiānjiā-wànhù〈成〉every family: 这件事关系到～，必须妥善处理。This issue affects the livelihood of every family and must be handled properly.

【千娇百媚】qiānjiāo-bǎimèi〈成〉[of a woman] be the pinnacle of beauty

【千斤】qiānjīn〈数量〉very heavy:〈喻〉～重担勇承担 have the courage to shoulder heavy loads

【千斤顶】qiānjīndǐng〈名〉jack: 液压/油压～ hydraulic/oil jack

【千金】qiānjīn **A**〈名〉**1**（指金钱）huge amount of money: ～难买 be priceless **2**〈敬〉（指女儿）daughter (other than one's own): 这是你的～吧? Is that your daughter? **B**〈形〉〈喻〉extremely valuable: 一字～ extremely valuable character ▸一诺～

【千金难买老来瘦】qiānjīn nán mǎi lǎo lái shòu〈俗〉it is invaluable to remain slim in one's old age

【千金一刻】qiānjīn-yīkè〈成〉〈喻〉time is precious

【千军万马】qiānjūn-wànmǎ〈成〉a powerful army: 指挥～ hold command of thousands upon thousands of horses and soldiers

【千军易得，一将难求】qiānjūn yì dé, yī jiàng nán qiú〈成〉able people are hard to come by

【千钧一发】qiānjūn-yīfà〈俗〉be in an extremely precarious situation: ～之际 at the extremely critical moment

【千卡】qiānkǎ = 大卡 dàkǎ

【千克】qiānkè ▸**p. 978**〈量〉kilogram (kg): 一～等于2.2磅。One kilogram equals 2.2 pounds.

【千里马】qiānlǐmǎ〈名〉〈喻〉person of great talent

【千里送鹅毛】qiānlǐ sòng émáo〈俗〉a small gift sent from afar testifies to deep affection: ～，礼轻情意重。The gift is small but the feeling is profound.

【千里迢迢】qiānlǐ-tiáotiáo〈成〉from afar: 欢迎各位～来参加这次商品交易会。Welcome to all who have travelled great distances to make it to this trade fair.

【千里眼】qiānlǐyǎn〈名〉**1**（指人）far-seeing/far-sighted person **2**〈旧〉（指物）telescope, field glasses

【千里姻缘一线牵】qiānlǐ yīnyuán yī xiàn qiān〈俗〉two people destined to marry each other, though a thousand *li* apart, are tied together as if by a thread

【千里之堤，溃于蚁穴】qiānlǐ zhī dī, kuì yú yǐxué〈成〉slight negligence may lead to great disaster

【千里之行，始于足下】qiānlǐ zhī xíng, shǐ yú zú xià〈成〉a journey of a thousand *li* starts with a single step

【千里光】qiānlǐguāng〈名〉［植物］climbing groundsel

【千里挑一】qiānlǐ-tiāoyī〈成〉one in a million: 新厨师真是～，做得一手好菜。The new cook is indeed one in a thousand. He prepares excellent dishes.

【千虑一得】qiānlǜ-yīdé〈成〉even the slow-witted may sometimes hit upon a good idea

【千虑一失】qiānlǜ-yīshī〈成〉even the wisest man occasionally slips up

【千米】qiānmǐ ▸**p. 82**〈量〉kilometre (km)

【千难万险】qiānnán-wànxiǎn〈成〉numerous difficulties and dangers: 红军经过～，终于到达陕北。The Red Army experienced numerous hardships before they got to Northern Shaanxi.

【千年虫】qiānniánchóng〈名〉［计算机］millennium bug: ～问题 Y2K problem

q

【千篇一律】qiānpiān-yīlǜ〈成〉follow the same pattern: ～的论调 stereotyped views ‖ 这里的老房子外观～。The old houses here have a uniform appearance.
【千奇百怪】qiānqí-bǎiguài〈成〉all kinds of strange things
【千千万万】qiānqiān-wànwàn〈成〉1（表数量多）thousands upon thousands 2（务必）be sure to, must: 此事～不可掉以轻心。Under no circumstances should we take this lightly.
【千秋】qiānqiū〈名〉1（千年）ages 2〈敬〉（寿辰）birthday (other than one's own): 为所有老人做～之祝 extend one's congratulations to all elderly people on the occasion of their birthdays
【千秋大业】qiānqiū-dàyè〈成〉great undertaking of lasting importance
【千秋万代】qiānqiū-wàndài〈成〉generation after generation
【千儿八百】qiānrbābǎi〈数量〉〈口〉about a thousand: ～块钱 about a thousand *yuan* ‖ 这东西没个～是买不来的。You can't buy this for less than about a thousand.
【千人一面】qiānrén-yīmiàn〈成〉[of literary writings] stereotyped
【千日红】qiānrìhóng〈名〉［植物］globe amaranth
【千山万壑】qiānshān-wànhè〈成〉numerous mountains and gullies
【千山万水】qiānshān-wànshuǐ〈成〉long and arduous journey
【千手观音】Qiānshǒu Guānyīn〈名〉Goddess of Mercy with a thousand hands
【千丝万缕】qiānsī-wànlǚ〈成〉countless ties: 两者之间有着～的联系。There are countless ties between the two.
【千岁】qiānsuì〈名〉〈尊〉Your/His/Her Royal Highness [used esp in traditional operas]
【千头万绪】qiāntóu-wànxù〈成〉a multitude of things: 要做的事～，我真不知从哪儿下手。There are so many things to do that I just don't know where to start.
【千瓦】qiānwǎ〈量〉kilowatt (kw)
【千瓦时】qiānwǎshí〈量〉kilowatt-hour (kwh)
【千万】qiānwàn **A** ►**p. 691**〈数〉ten million: 这家乡镇企业固定资产达～。The fixed assets of this township enterprise now stand at a value of 10 million *yuan*. **B**〈副〉[used in entreating, exhortation, etc.] be sure to: ～不可大意。You must be very careful! ‖ 我们～不能那样。We absolutely can't do that.
【千禧年】qiānxǐnián〈名〉millennium
【千辛万苦】qiānxīn-wànkǔ〈成〉untold hardships: 历尽～ go through untold hardships
【千言万语】qiānyán-wànyǔ〈成〉innumerable words: ～难以表达我们的感激之情。Our gratitude is beyond words.
【千依百顺】qiānyī-bǎishùn〈成〉obey sb. in everything
【千载难逢】qiānzǎi-nánféng〈成〉once in a blue moon: ～的机会 chance of a lifetime
【千载一时】qiānzǎi-yīshí〈成〉a million-to-one opportunity: ～的好机会 a golden opportunity
【千张】qiānzhang〈名〉［食品］sheets of dried bean curd
【千真万确】qiānzhēn-wànquè〈成〉incontrovertibly true: ～的事 God's own truth
【千姿百态】qiānzī-bǎitài〈成〉of all kinds of shapes and postures: 这里的山峰～，美不胜收。The mountain peaks here, of every shape imaginable, are fantastically beautiful.
【千字节】qiānzìjié〈名〉［计算机］kilobyte
【千足虫】qiānzúchóng〈名〉［昆虫］millipede

仟

qiān ►**p. 691**〈数〉thousand [used for the numeral 千 on cheques, etc. to avoid mistakes or alterations]

阡

qiān〈名〉〈书〉footpath between fields, running north and south: ►～陌
【阡陌】qiānmò〈名〉〈书〉criss-crossing footpaths between fields: ～纵横 paths criss-crossing in the fields

扦

qiān
A〈动〉〈方〉1（插）insert: 把花～在瓶里 put flowers in a vase 2（修脚）have a pedicure;（削）peel with a knife
B〈名〉1（针状物）short slender pointed piece of metal, bamboo, etc.: ►蜡～ 2（用于取样）sharp-pointed metal tube used to extract samples of grain, etc. from sacks
【扦插】qiānchā〈名〉［农业］cuttage
【扦脚】qiānjiǎo〈动〉〈方〉have a pedicure
【扦子】qiānzi〈名〉1（针状物）a slender pointed piece of metal, bamboo, etc.: 铁～ iron rod ‖ 竹～ bamboo spike 2（用于取样）sharp-pointed metal tube used to extract samples of grain, etc. from sacks

芊

qiān
【芊绵】qiānmián〈形〉〈书〉[of grass or trees] dense: 春草～ lush grass in spring
【芊芊】qiānqiān〈形〉〈书〉luxuriant: 郁郁～ dense and luxuriant

迁（遷）

qiān〈动〉1（迁移）move: ～户口 change one's residence registration ‖ ～入新居 move into one's new home ‖ ～往外地 move to another place ►～居, ～移 2（改变）change: ►变～, 事过境～ 3〈书〉（升级）change one's official post: ►升～, 左～
【迁都】qiāndū〈动〉move the capital to another place
【迁飞】qiānfēi〈动〉[of birds] migrate
【迁就】qiānjiù〈动〉yield to: 姑息～ be excessively accommodating ‖ 坚持原则，不能～。We must stick to the principle and not compromise.
【迁居】qiānjū〈动〉move house: ～外地 move to another place
【迁离】qiānlí〈动〉move to another place: ～故土 leave one's native land
【迁怒】qiānnù〈动〉vent one's anger: ～于人 take it out on sb.
【迁徙】qiānxǐ〈动〉move: 人口～ population migration ‖ 有些鸟随季节～。Some birds migrate as the season changes.
【迁徙流离】qiānxǐ-liúlí〈成〉wander from place to place
【迁延】qiānyán〈动〉〈书〉delay: 此事应立即办理，不得～。This issue calls for prompt attention and brooks no delay.
【迁移】qiānyí〈动〉move: 从农村向城市～ move from the country to the city ‖〈喻〉随着时间的～，这件事逐渐被淡忘了。The matter faded from our memories as time flew by.
【迁葬】qiānzàng〈动〉move a grave to another site

瓩

qiān〈旧〉= 千瓦 qiānwǎ

佥（僉）

qiān〈副〉〈书〉all

钎（釬）

qiān〈名〉drill rod: 钢～ steel drill
【钎子】qiānzi〈名〉hammer drill

牵（牽）

qiān〈动〉1（拉）pull: ～着一头牛往地里走 lead an ox to the fields ‖ 他们手～着手走过来。They came over hand in hand. ►～动, ～引 2（连带）implicate: ►～扯, ～连 3（挂念）be concerned about: ►～肠挂肚 4（制约）hold up: ►～制
【牵缠】qiānchán〈动〉involve: 家事～ get entangled in domestic affairs ‖ 这件事～了许多人。Many people have become involved in the matter.
【牵肠挂肚】qiāncháng-guàdù〈成〉be deeply concerned: 孩子身在异乡，母亲总是～。The mother always felt very worried about her children when they were away from home.
【牵扯】qiānchě〈动〉drag in: 这事与我无关，不要把我～进去。It's nothing to do with me, so don't try to drag me in.
【牵掣】qiānchè〈动〉〈书〉1（影响）hinder: 互相～ get in each other's way ‖ 抓住主要问题，不要被枝节问题～。Let's focus our attention on the main problem and not get bogged down in minor issues. 2（牵制）contain
【牵动】qiāndòng〈动〉〈喻〉affect: ～全局 affect the situation as a whole ‖ 申奥～着每个中国人的心。The bid to host the Olympic Games excited every Chinese citizen.
【牵挂】qiānguà〈动〉worry: 爸爸妈妈嘱咐她在外边要好好工作，家里的事不用～。Her parents told her to work well and not to worry about family affairs.
【牵合】qiānhé〈动〉make a match
【牵记】qiānji〈动〉be anxious about: 时刻～远方的母亲 keep thinking about one's mother who lives far away
【牵累】qiānlěi〈动〉1（使受累）tie down: 无儿女～ without the burden of children 2（连累）involve (in trouble): 他自己闯了祸，还～别人。He got into trouble himself and dragged others along with him.
【牵连】qiānlián〈动〉1（牵涉）involve: 否认与此案有任何～ deny any involvement in the case 2（关联）tie up with: 这两件事互相～，要妥善处理。The two matters are inextricably linked and must be handled with the utmost discretion.
【牵念】qiānniàn〈动〉think constantly of: ～远方的亲人 worry about distant loved ones
【牵牛花】qiānniúhuā〈名〉［植物］morning glory
【牵牛星】Qiānniúxīng〈名〉［天文］Altair
【牵强】qiānqiǎng〈形〉far-fetched: ～的解释 far-fetched explanation ‖ 这些理由听起来有些～。These reasons sound far-fetched.
【牵强附会】qiānqiǎng-fùhuì〈成〉make a far-fetched comparison: 你这样解释这句话太～了。Your interpretation of this sentence is much too forced.
【牵涉】qiānshè〈动〉involve: ～许多部门 concern many departments ‖ 这起案件～到很多人。A lot of people were dragged into this case.
【牵手】qiānshǒu〈动〉1（手拉手）be hand-in-hand 2〈喻〉（联手）cooperate:

q

两大公司～，研发新产品。The two companies cooperated on the research and development of new products.

【牵头】qiāntóu〈动〉 1▸（领头） take the lead: 这件事你来～吧。 Would you please take the lead in this? 2▸（撮合） act as go-between

【牵系】qiānxì〈动〉 link: 美好的回忆始终～着他们的心。 Fond memories always link their hearts together.

【牵线】qiānxiàn〈动〉 1▸（背后操纵） manipulate from behind the scenes: 幕后～ pull strings from behind the scenes 2▸（撮合） act as go-between

【牵线搭桥】qiānxiàn-dāqiáo〈成〉 act as middleman: 电视广告为买主和商家～。 TV commercials serve as a link between businesses and their clients.

【牵线木偶】qiānxiàn-mù'ǒu〈名〉 1▸〈本〉 marionette 2▸〈喻〉 puppet

【牵一发而动全身】qiān yī fà ér dòng quánshēn〈成〉〈喻〉 a slight move in one part may affect the overall situation

【牵引】qiānyǐn A〈动〉 drag: ～轮船入港 tow a ship into a harbour ‖ 机车～着列车前进。 The train is drawn forward by the engine. B〈名〉［医学］ traction: 我的左腿在做～治疗。 My left leg is in traction.

【牵引车】qiānyǐnchē〈名〉 tractor

【牵着鼻子走】qiānzhe bízi zǒu〈惯〉 lead by the nose: 我不愿被人～。 I don't want to be led by the nose.

【牵制】qiānzhì〈动〉 check: ～敌军 check the enemy forces ‖ 互相～ hold each other up

铅（鉛）qiān

〈名〉 1▸［化学］ lead (Pb): ～中毒 lead poisoning ‖ 无～汽油 unleaded petrol 2▸（铅笔芯） lead

【铅板】qiānbǎn〈名〉 lead plate

【铅版】qiānbǎn〈名〉［印刷］ stereotype: 用～印刷 print with stereotypes

【铅笔】qiānbǐ〈名〉 lead pencil: ～芯 black lead ‖ 绘图～ drawing pencil

【铅笔刀】qiānbǐdāo〈名〉 pen-knife

【铅笔盒】qiānbǐhé〈名〉 pencil case

【铅笔画】qiānbǐhuà〈名〉 pencil drawing

【铅玻璃】qiānbōli〈名〉 lead glass

【铅垂线】qiānchuíxiàn〈名〉［建筑］ plumb line

【铅锤】qiānchuí〈名〉［建筑］ plummet

【铅封】qiānfēng〈名〉 lead sealing

【铅华】qiānhuá〈名〉 1▸（化妆品） face-powder: 不施～ wear no cosmetics 2▸（容颜） beauty

【铅灰】qiānhuī〈形〉 lead grey: ～的天空飘着雪花。 Snowflakes are falling from the leaden sky.

【铅球】qiānqiú〈名〉［体育］ 1▸ ▸p. 909（指运动项目） shot: 推～ shot put ‖ ～运动员 shot-putter 2▸（指运动器械） ball of lead

【铅丝】qiānsī〈名〉 1▸（指镀锌） galvanized wire 2▸［电气］ lead wire

【铅印】qiānyìn〈名〉［印刷］ stereotype

【铅字】qiānzì〈名〉［印刷］ type: ～排版 typesetting

悭（慳）qiān

A〈形〉 miserly: ▸～吝

B〈动〉 lack: 缘～一面 not have had the luck of meeting sb.

【悭吝】qiānlìn〈形〉〈书〉 miserly: ～鬼 miser

谦（謙）qiān

〈形〉 modest: ▸～恭, ～虚, 自～

【谦卑】qiānbēi〈形〉 humble: 他因～而受人爱戴。 He was loved for his self-effacing modesty.

【谦称】qiānchēng A〈动〉 refer to oneself modestly: 他～自己是门外汉。 He modestly referred to himself as a layman. B〈名〉 modest form of address

【谦诚】qiānchéng〈形〉 modest and sincere: ～待人 treat people with modesty and sincerity

【谦辞】qiāncí A〈名〉 self-depreciatory expression B〈动〉 modestly decline: 我们诚意推荐你，你就别～了。 Don't decline our sincere recommendation.

【谦恭】qiāngōng〈形〉 modest and courteous: ～好学 be modest and willing to learn ‖ ～有礼 be respectful and polite

【谦和】qiānhé〈形〉 modest and amiable: 态度～ take modest and amiable stance

【谦谦君子】qiānqiān-jūnzǐ〈成〉 modest and scrupulous gentleman

【谦让】qiānràng〈动〉 modestly decline: 不必～了。 Don't decline out of modesty. ‖ 客人互相～了一番，然后落了座。 The guests politely asked each other to be seated first before finally settling down in their seats.

【谦受益，满招损】qiān shòu yì, mǎn zhāo sǔn〈成〉 modesty is beneficial while conceit detrimental

【谦顺】qiānshùn〈形〉 modest and deferential: 态度～ deferential attitude

【谦虚】qiānxū A〈形〉 modest: ～是一种美德。 Modesty is a virtue. ‖ ～使人进步，骄傲使人落后。 Modesty helps one to go forward, whereas conceit makes one lag behind. B〈动〉 speak modestly: 他～了一番，终于答应了我的邀请。 After making a few modest remarks he finally accepted my request.

【谦虚谨慎】qiānxū-jǐnshèn〈成〉 modest and prudent

【谦逊】qiānxùn〈形〉 modest and unassuming: ～的态度 modest attitude

签¹（簽）qiān

〈动〉 1▸（签字） sign: ～文件 sign one's name on a document ▸～约, ～字 2▸（写批注） make brief comments on a document: ～写意见 write down one's comments on a document

签²（籤）qiān

A〈名〉 1▸（指竹片） bamboo slips used for divination or drawing lots: ▸抽～, 求～ 2▸（指小细棍） slender pointed piece of wood/bamboo: ▸牙～ 3▸（指小条儿） sticker: 航空邮～ airmail sticker ▸标～, 书～

B〈动〉 tack: ～花边 tack on a piece of lace

【签呈】qiānchéng〈名〉memorial [submitted to a superior]

【签单】qiāndān〈动〉 sign for sth.

【签到】qiāndào〈动〉 sign in: ～簿 attendance book

【签订】qiāndìng〈动〉 conclude and sign: ～合同 formalize a contract ‖ ～条约 sign a treaty

【签发】qiānfā〈动〉 sign and issue: ～护照 issue a passport ‖ ～许可证 issue a permit

【签名】qiānmíng〈动〉 sign: ～盖章 sign and seal ‖ 亲笔～ sign one's autograph ‖ ～售书 sell a book carrying one's autograph

【签名簿】qiānmíngbù〈名〉 visitors' book

【签收】qiānshōu〈动〉 sign for sth.: ～挂号信 sign for a registered letter ‖ 我能替他～这些文件吗？ Can I sign for these documents on his behalf?

【签售】qiānshòu〈动〉 sign autographs on a product for sale: 在书店举办～活动 organize a book signing at a book shop

【签售会】qiānshòuhuì〈名〉 signing and sales event

【签署】qiānshǔ〈动〉 sign: ～联合公报 sign a joint communiqué ‖ ～命令 sign a decree ‖ ～意见 write comments and sign one's name (on a document)

【签筒】qiāntǒng〈名〉 container for lots or clips

【签押】qiānyā〈动〉〈旧〉 sign

【签约】qiānyuē〈动〉 sign an agreement: ～双方 two parties to the contract ‖ 他已和该俱乐部～当教练。 He has signed a contract to be club coach.

【签证】qiānzhèng A〈动〉 grant a visa: 给护照～ put a visa on a passport ‖ ～处 visa office B〈名〉 visa: 发给/发放～ grant/issue a visa ‖ 持旅游～入境 enter a country on a tourist visa ‖ 他们的～已期满。 Their visas have run out.

【签证官】qiānzhèngguān ▸p. 966〈名〉 visa officer

【签注】qiānzhù〈动〉 1▸（在文稿中） attach a slip of paper to a document with comments on it 2▸（在证件表册上） write comments or points for attention on a certificate, book or tables, etc.

【签字】qiānzì〈动〉 sign: ～盖章 sign and seal ‖ ～仪式 signing ceremony ‖ ～后立即生效 come into force upon signature

【签子】qiānzi〈口〉= 签² qiān A1

愆 qiān〈书〉

A〈动〉 delay

B〈名〉 fault: ～尤 fault

【愆期】qiānqī〈动〉〈书〉 delay

鸽（鴿）qiān〈动〉

peck: 别让鸡～了地里的麦穗。 Don't let the chickens peck at the wheat heads in the field.

骞（騫）qiān〈动〉〈书〉

hold high up

搴 qiān〈动〉〈书〉

pull out: 斩将～旗 behead the enemy generals and pull out enemy flags on the battle fields

qián

荨（蕁）qián

▸xún

【荨麻】qiánmá〈名〉［植物］ nettle

钤（鈐）qián

A〈名〉 official seal: ▸～记

B〈动〉 affix a seal to

【钤记】qiánjì〈名〉〈旧〉 seal of a low-ranking official

前 qián

A〈动〉 move forward: ▸停滞不～, 勇往直～

B〈名〉 1▸（正面） front: ～花园 front garden ‖ 大楼～有个喷水池。 There is a fountain in front of the building. 2▸（过去） past: ～几年 past few years ‖ 战～ pre-war period ▸～所未有, ～天, 从～, 日～ 3▸（前任） former: ～市长 ex-mayor ‖ ～苏联 former Soviet Union ‖ ～总统

former president ▸～夫，～人 **4**（产生之前） preceding: ～科学观点 pre-scientific view **5**（未来） future: 向～看 look towards the future ▸～程，～景 **6**（指次序） first: ～三名 first three places ‖ ～十名选手 top ten players ▸～排，～座 **7**（前线） battlefront: 支～ support the front

【前半晌】qiánbànshǎng〈名〉〈方〉morning

【前半生】qiánbànshēng〈名〉 first half of one's life

【前半天】qiánbàntiān〈名〉 morning

【前半夜】qiánbànyè〈名〉 first half of the night (from nightfall to midnight)

【前辈】qiánbèi〈名〉 senior: 革命～ revolutionary predecessor ‖ 同行中的老～ senior of a profession

【前臂】qiánbì〈名〉 forearm

【前边】qiánbian = 前面 qiánmian

【前不着村，后不着店】qián bù zháo cūn, hòu bù zháo diàn〈惯〉 be stranded in a desolate place

【前叉】qiánchā〈名〉 front fork (of a bicycle)

【前场】qiánchǎng〈名〉［体育］forecourt

【前车之鉴】qiánchēzhījiàn〈成〉〈喻〉 lesson drawn from others' mistakes: 前车之覆，后车之鉴。 The overturned cart ahead is a warning to those behind. ‖ 你应该把他作为～。 You should take heed from his example.

【前尘】qiánchén〈名〉〈书〉 past: 回首～ look back at the past

【前程】qiánchéng〈名〉 **1**（未来） future: 锦绣～ have a glorious future ‖ ～远大。 The prospects are far-reaching. **2**〈旧〉（前途） desired career: 毁掉～ mar sb.'s career

【前程似锦】qiánchéng-sìjǐn〈成〉 have a glorious future

【前程万里】qiánchéng-wànlǐ〈成〉 have a brilliant prospect

【前导】qiándǎo **A**〈动〉 lead the way **B**〈名〉 leader: 以仪仗队为～ with the guards of honour marching at the head

【前灯】qiándēng〈名〉 [of a car] headlight

【前敌】qiándí〈名〉front line: 身临～ come personally to the front ‖ ～总指挥 front-line commander-in-chief

【前额】qián'é〈名〉forehead: ～突出 prominent forehead

【前番】qiánfān〈名〉 last time

【前方】qiánfāng〈名〉 **1**（前面） front: 正～ straight ahead ‖ 左/右～ ahead to the left/right **2**（前线） front line: 开赴～ be dispatched to the front ‖ 支援～ support the front

【前房】qiánfáng〈名〉 deceased wife

【前锋】qiánfēng〈名〉 **1**（先头部队） vanguard: 红军的～渡过了湘江。 The vanguard units of the Red Army had crossed the Xiangjiang River. **2**［体育］ forward: ～线 forward line ‖ 他打～。 He plays forward. **3**［气象］ front: 冷空气的～ cold front

【前夫】qiánfū〈名〉 ex-husband

【前赴后继】qiánfù-hòujì〈成〉 advance wave upon wave

【前功尽弃】qiángōng-jìnqì〈成〉 all the previous efforts are wasted: 大坝一定要在雨季到来前合拢，否则就会～。 The dam must be closed before the rainy season sets in or all our labour will be lost.

【前滚翻】qiángǔnfān〈名〉［体育］ forward roll

【前后】qiánhòu〈名〉 **1** ▸**p. 927**（左右） period around: 元旦～ around New Year's Day **2**（从头至尾） period from beginning to end: 这项工程从动工到完成～仅用了半年。 The entire project, from beginning to end, took only half a year. **3**（前面和后面） front and rear: ～夹击 attack sb. both in front and from the rear ‖ 村子～都有路。 There are roads both in front and at the back of the village. **4**（先后） people /things of the same kind in succession: ～两任经理 two successive managers ‖ ～三种版本 three consecutive editions

【前后脚】qiánhòujiǎo〈副〉〈口〉 almost simultaneously: 我俩～到家。 We got back home almost at the same time.

【前呼后拥】qiánhū-hòuyōng〈成〉 be accompanied by a large retinue: 他们每次出行都～，戒备森严。 Whenever they went out there was a great fanfare, with people waiting on them and guards swarming round.

【前记】qiánjì = 前言 qiányán 1

【前脚】qiánjiǎo **A**〈名〉 front foot: ～一滑，后脚也站不稳。 As the front foot slipped, the rear foot became unsteady. **B**〈副〉 [used together with 后脚] no sooner ... than: 真不巧，你～走，他后脚就到了。 Too bad, no sooner had you left than he arrived.

【前襟】qiánjīn〈名〉 front part of a Chinese garment

【前进】qiánjìn〈动〉 advance: 加快～的步伐 quicken one's forward pace ‖ 士兵们趁着夜色匍匐～。 The soldiers crept forward under the cover of darkness.

【前景】qiánjǐng〈名〉 **1**（指景物） foreground: 这幅画的～是一个男子的形象。 In the foreground of the picture is the figure of a man. **2**（指前途） prospect: 市场～堪忧/乐观。 The outlook for the market is grim/promising. ‖ 中国经济～美好。 Prospects for the Chinese economy are bright.

【前倨后恭】qiánjù-hòugōng〈成〉 switch from arrogance to humility

【前科】qiánkē〈名〉 criminal record: 有～ have a criminal record

【前空翻】qiánkōngfān〈名〉［体育］ forward somersault in the air

【前来】qiánlái〈动〉 come: 我～向您请教。 I've come to seek your instruction.

【前例】qiánlì〈名〉 precedent: 无～可援 have no precedent to go by ▸史无～

【前列】qiánliè〈名〉 forefront: 居世界～ rank among the first in the world ‖ 走在时代最～ be at the vanguard of one's epoch

【前列腺】qiánlièxiàn〈名〉［解剖］ prostate gland: ～增生 prostatic hyperplasia

【前列腺肥大】qiánlièxiàn féidà〈名〉 hypertrophy of the prostate

【前掠翼】qiánlüèyì〈名〉［航空］ buzzard-type wing

【前门拒虎，后门进狼】qiánmén jù hǔ, hòumén jìn láng〈俗〉〈喻〉 fend off one danger only to fall a prey to another

【前面】qiánmian〈名〉 **1**（指方位） front: 走在～ march at the head ‖ 亭子～有一棵松树。 There is a pine tree in front of the pavilion. **2**（指次序） preceding part: ～两章 two preceding chapters ‖ 这个道理，～已经讲得很清楚了。 I already clarified my argument earlier in my speech.

【前年】qiánnián ▸**p. 618**〈名〉 the year before last

【前怕狼，后怕虎】qián pà láng, hòu pà hǔ〈成〉 be full of fear: 要大胆尝试，不要～。 We must make a bold attempt and not allow ourselves to be engulfed in fear.

【前排】qiánpái〈名〉 front row: ～座位 front-row seats

【前仆后继】qiánpū-hòujì〈成〉 as those in front fall, those behind take up their positions

【前妻】qiánqī〈名〉 ex-wife

【前期】qiánqī〈名〉 earlier stage: ～准备工作 first-phase preparations ‖ 十九世纪～ in the early 19th century

【前前后后】qiánqián-hòuhòu〈成〉 **1**（全部） whole story: 事情的～ ins and outs of a matter ‖ 她给我讲了事情的～。 She told me the whole story. **2**（从头至尾） period from beginning to end: 他的案子～拖了五年才结案。 It took five long years to get his case settled.

【前驱】qiánqū〈名〉 forerunner: 革命～ revolutionary pioneer

【前去】qiánqù〈动〉 go to: ～问他。 Go and ask him.

【前人】qiánrén〈名〉 forefathers: 超过～ surpass one's predecessors

【前人栽树，后人乘凉】qiánrén zāi shù, hòurén chéng liáng〈成〉 profit from the labour of one's ancestors

【前任】qiánrèn〈名〉 predecessor: ～总统 former president

【前日】qiánrì = 前天 qiántiān

【前晌】qiánshǎng〈名〉〈方〉 morning

【前哨】qiánshào〈名〉outpost: 与敌～接火 skirmish with the enemy's advance guards

【前身】qiánshēn〈名〉 **1**（指组织、名称） predecessor: 这所学院的～是师范学校。 This college grew out of a normal school. **2**（指衣服） front part of a Chinese garment

【前生】qiánshēng〈名〉 previous incarnation: 这是她～修来的福分。 Her good fortune now was built up in her previous life.

【前世】qiánshì = 前生 qiánshēng

【前事不忘，后事之师】qiánshì bù wàng, hòushì zhī shī〈成〉 lessons one has learned from the past can guide one in the future

【前思后想】qiánsī-hòuxiǎng〈成〉 turn over in one's mind

【前所未闻】qiánsuǒwèiwén〈成〉 hitherto unknown: 此事～。 This matter was hitherto unknown.

【前所未有】qiánsuǒwèiyǒu〈成〉 unprecedented: ～的机遇 unprecedented opportunity ‖ 遇到～的巨大困难 encounter unparalleled difficulties

【前台】qiántái〈名〉 **1**（指舞台） stage **2**〈贬〉（指公开场合） public place: 他在～表演，背后有人操纵。 He appears on the stage, while somebody else pulls strings behind the scenes. **3**（指接待处） front desk **4**［计算机］ foreground: ～程序 foreground program

【前提】qiántí〈名〉 **1**［逻辑］ premise: 大/小～ major/minor premise **2**（先决条件） prerequisite: 成功的～ prerequisite for success

【前蹄】qiántí〈名〉 [of a horse, etc.] front hoof

【前天】qiántiān〈名〉 the day before yesterday: ～上午 the morning before last

【前庭】qiántíng〈名〉［解剖］ vestibule

【前头】qiántou = 前面 qiánmian

【前途】qiántú〈名〉 future: 没有～ have no future ‖ ～暗淡 have a dark future before sb. ‖ ～光明 have a bright future ‖ 这工作很有～。 The job offers good prospects.

【前途渺茫】qiántú-miǎománg〈成〉 have a bleak future

【前途无量】qiántú-wúliàng〈成〉 have boundless prospects

【前腿】qiántuǐ〈名〉 foreleg

【前往】qiánwǎng〈动〉 go to: ～机场接人 go to the airport to meet sb. ‖ 经上海～纽约 go to New York via Shanghai
【前桅】qiánwéi〈名〉 foremast
【前卫】qiánwèi **A**〈名〉 **1**［军事］ vanguard: ～部队 vanguard troops **2**［体育］ halfback: 左～ left half **B**〈形〉 avant-garde: 思想～ be very forward-thinking
【前无古人】qiánwúgǔrén〈成〉 without parallel in history: ～，后无来者 be unprecedented
【前夕】qiánxī〈名〉 eve: 国庆～ on the eve of National Day ‖ 激战～ on the eve of a fierce battle
【前贤】qiánxián〈名〉〈书〉 sage
【前嫌】qiánxián〈名〉 old grudge: ▸捐弃～
【前线】qiánxiàn〈名〉 battlefront: 开赴～ be dispatched to the front line ‖ 支援～ support the front
【前项】qiánxiàng〈名〉［数学］antecedent
【前言】qiányán〈名〉 **1**（指文字） foreword: 每章都有一段简短的～。 Each chapter is prefaced by a short introduction. **2**（指言语） earlier remarks: ～不搭后语 babble incoherently
【前沿】qiányán〈名〉 forward position: ～阵地 forward position ‖ ～科学 frontier science
【前仰后合】qiányǎng-hòuhé〈成〉 rock back and forth: 笑得～ shake with laughter
【前夜】qiányè = 前夕 qiánxī
【前因后果】qiányīn-hòuguǒ〈成〉 cause and effect: 每件事情都有～。 Everything has its cause and effect.
【前元音】qiányuányīn〈名〉［语言］ front vowel
【前缘】qiányuán〈名〉 predestined ties: ～未了。 The predestined ties are not yet severed.
【前院】qiányuàn〈名〉 forecourt
【前约】qiányuē〈名〉 previous engagement
【前瞻性】qiánzhānxìng〈名〉 foresightness
【前站】qiánzhàn〈名〉 next stop: ▸打～
【前爪】qiánzhǎo〈名〉 forepaw
【前兆】qiánzhào〈名〉 forewarning: 地震的～ warning signs of an earthquake
【前者】qiánzhě〈名〉 former: 两者之间，我选择～。 Of the two I choose the former.
【前震】qiánzhèn〈名〉 foreshock
【前肢】qiánzhī〈名〉［动物］ forelimb
【前置词】qiánzhìcí〈名〉 preposition
【前缀】qiánzhuì〈名〉［语言］ prefix
【前奏】qiánzòu〈名〉 prelude:〈喻〉 革命的～ prelude to a revolution
【前奏曲】qiánzòuqǔ〈名〉［音乐］prelude
【前座】qiánzuò〈名〉 front seat: 坐在～ be seated in a front seat

虔 qián

〈形〉 sincere: ▸～诚, ～心
【虔诚】qiánchéng〈形〉 pious: ～的信徒 devout believer
【虔敬】qiánjìng〈形〉 pious: ～地听布道 give reverent attention to the sermon
【虔心】qiánxīn **A**〈名〉 piety **B**〈形〉 pious: ～忏悔 repent sincerely

钱（錢）qián

A ▸**p. 328**〈名〉 **1**（铜钱） coin: 古～ ancient coins ▸～串子 **2**（铜钱状物） coin-shaped thing: ▸榆～ **3**（钱款） money: 借～给我 lend me money ‖ 乱花～ squander one's money ‖ 从银行取～ withdraw money from a bank ▸凑～, 存～, 见～眼开, 零～ **4**（财富） money: 他为了～而不顾廉耻。 He has sold his honour for money. ‖ 有～能使鬼推磨。 Money makes the mare go. **5**（资金） sum: 一大笔～ a large fortune ‖ 这笔费用由政府出～偿还。 The cost is being repaid out of government funds. ▸车～, 工～
B ▸**p. 978**〈量〉〈旧〉 *qian* [unit of weight, equal to 5 grams]
【钱包】qiánbāo〈名〉 purse: 鼓鼓（囊囊）的～ fat wallet ‖ 他的～被偷了。 His wallet has been stolen.
【钱币】qiánbì〈名〉 coin: 收藏～ collect coins
【钱币学】qiánbìxué〈名〉 numismatics
【钱财】qiáncái〈名〉 money: 聚敛～ accumulate money ‖ 诈骗～ swindle some cash out of sb.
【钱串子】qiánchuànzi〈名〉 **1**〈本〉 cash

q

ℹ 修饰语（一）：前置修饰语

■ 汉语中的名词修饰语要置于名词之前，而英语中的名词修饰语既有前置修饰语又有后置修饰语。英语的多层前置修饰语和汉语多层修饰语的排列顺序既有相似也有相异。下面提供的例句可以说明这一点，请对这些句子和其英语翻译加以比较。

■ 英语前置修饰语与汉语修饰语最主要的不同，是多层修饰语做名词定语时修饰语的排列顺序。英语中前置修饰语的排列顺序比较固定，一般来说：

放在第一位的是限定词。包括冠词、指示代词、名词所有格和形容词性物主代词。

其次是数词，包括基数词、序数词及 next 和 last。如果基数词和序数词放在一起，则序数词或 next/last 在前，基数词在后。

接下来是描绘性形容词。这类形容词的排列顺序是：

大小（small、long、thick 等，但不包括 little，见例句）
→ 一般描述性的词语（如 beautiful、famous 等）
→ 新旧、年龄（old、new 等）
→ 形状 （round、tall、fat 等）
→ 颜色（如 red、black 等）
→ 材料（velvet、fluffy 等，也包括名词，如 leather、suede 等）
→ 来源（French、Chinese 等）
→ 用途（一般是现在分词用在名词短语中，如 walking stick、building material）

一本好书
= a good book

最好的办法
= the best method

小刘的好朋友
= Xiao Liu's good friend

这座漂亮的大厦
= this beautiful mansion

我的蓝色天鹅绒大衣
= my blue velvet coat

他三个英俊的儿子
= his three handsome boys

那两个勤奋的学生
= those two diligent students

头三张长方形桌子
= the first three rectangular tables

最后 10 本红色封面的书
= the last ten red-covered books

小方茶几
或 **方形小茶几**
= a small square tea-table

一个方便的小吸尘器
= a small handy vacuum cleaner

一张漂亮的圆形白色大木桌
或 **一张漂亮的白色大圆木桌**
= a big, beautiful, round, white, wooden table

一件崭新又漂亮的皮制大衣
或 **一件漂亮的皮制新大衣**
= a beautiful brand new leather overcoat

我母亲又长又旧的拐杖
或 **我母亲又旧又长的拐杖**
= my mother's long, old walking stick

■ little 常用来表达说话人的意见，含有可爱的意思，常放在中心名词之前：

我好心的小姑娘
= my kind-hearted little girl

一家可爱的小旅馆
= a lovely little hotel

一个漂亮的小毛绒玩具
= a beautiful fluffy little toy

一个漂亮的小花园
= a beautiful little garden

■ little 也可置于其他描绘性形容词前，表示强调：

一只白色小卷毛狗
= a little white poodle

■ 英语中 fine、lovely、nice、beautiful 也可置于表示大小的词前面，表示一种赞同的语气：

好看的短裙子
= a nice short skirt

漂亮的大花园
= a lovely big garden
或 a beautiful big garden

上等的厚牛排
= fine thick steaks

■ 英语里要强调某一个形容词，可将该形容词提前：

一位雄心勃勃的年轻科学家
= an ambitious young scientist

一位年轻的、雄心勃勃的科学家
= a young, ambitious scientist

■ 两个或两个以上同类的形容词修饰同一个名词时，英语里一般用逗号隔开，其词序像汉语一样比较灵活，但一般是短的在前，长的在后，而汉语是多音节在前，单音节在后：

一套典雅、做工考究、舒适的沙发
= an elegant, well-made, comfortable set of sofas

一个心地善良、漂亮又能干的女人
= a pretty, capable, kind-hearted woman
或 a capable, beautiful, kind-hearted woman

string 2〈喻〉money-grubber 3［昆虫］millipede
【钱袋】qiándài〈名〉money bag
【钱柜】qiánguì〈名〉till
【钱夹】qiánjiā〈名〉wallet
【钱款】qiánkuǎn〈名〉money
【钱可通神】qiánkètōngshén〈成〉money makes the mare go
【钱粮】qiánliáng〈名〉〈旧〉land tax
【钱迷心窍】qiánmí-xīnqiào〈成〉be blinded by lust for money
【钱塘潮】Qiántángcháo〈名〉Qiantang tidal bore
【钱塘江】Qiántángjiāng ▸p. 294〈名〉Qiantang River
【钱眼】qiányǎn〈名〉hole in the centre of a coin:〈喻〉钻～儿 be money-grubbing
【钱庄】qiánzhuāng〈名〉〈旧〉private bank

q

钳（鉗）qián

A〈名〉pliers: 尖嘴～ sharp-nose pliers ‖ 老虎～ vice
B〈动〉1（夹）clamp: 把铁丝～紧。Make a nip in the wire to clamp it. 2（限制）restrain: ▸～口结舌, ～制
【钳工】qiángōng〈名〉1（指工种）benchwork 2（指人）fitter
【钳击】qiánjī〈动〉make a pincer attack
【钳口结舌】qiánkǒu-jiéshé〈成〉keep one's mouth shut
【钳制】qiánzhì〈动〉clamp down on: ～敌人的兵力 pin down the enemy forces
【钳子】qiánzi〈名〉pliers

乾 qián

〈名〉1（指八卦）one of the Eight Trigrams, symbolizing 'heaven' 2〈旧〉（指人）male: ～宅 husband's family
【乾坤】qiánkūn〈名〉cosmos: 扭转～ bring about a radical change in the situation

掮 qián

〈动〉〈方〉carry on the shoulder: ～着行李 carry one's luggage on one's shoulder
【掮客】qiánkè〈名〉broker: 房地产～ property broker ‖〈喻〉政治～ political broker

潜（濳）qián

A〈动〉1（沉入水下）go underwater: ～向海底 dive toward the bottom of the sea ▸～水, ～泳 2（隐藏）hide: ▸～伏, ～在
B〈副〉secretly: ▸～逃
C〈名〉potential: 革新挖～ carry out reforms and tap potentials ▸～力
【潜藏】qiáncáng〈动〉hide: ～海底 hide at the bottom of the sea ‖ ～在心里的痛苦 pain hidden in one's heart
【潜遁】qiándùn〈动〉abscond
【潜伏】qiánfú〈动〉hide: ～敌特 hidden enemy agent ‖ 一条蛇～在草丛中。A snake was lurking in the grass.
【潜伏期】qiánfúqī〈名〉［医学］incubation period: 疾病～ incubation period of a disease
【潜规则】qiánguīzé〈名〉latent rule: 医药分开打破了医院"以药养医"的～。The separation of prescribing and dispensing of medicine has broken the latent rule of 'medicine as nourishment for hospitals'.
【潜航】qiánháng〈动〉[of a submarine] submerge: ～深度 submerged depth
【潜居】qiánjū〈动〉live in seclusion: ～乡间 live in seclusion in the countryside
【潜科学】qiánkēxué〈名〉potential science
【潜亏】qiánkuī〈名〉potential loss
【潜力】qiánlì〈名〉potential: 挖掘～ tap potential ‖ 有成为管理人才的～ have executive potential
【潜力股】qiánlìgǔ〈名〉［金融］stocks with high potential: 高科技～ high-potential high-tech stocks
【潜流】qiánliú〈名〉undercurrent
【潜能】qiánnéng〈名〉1［物理］latent energy 2（指能力）potential: 发挥～ realize one's potential ‖ 挖掘～ draw out sb.'s potential
【潜匿】qiánnì〈动〉〈书〉hide
【潜鸟】qiánniǎo〈名〉diving bird
【潜热】qiánrè〈名〉［物理］latent heat: ～释放 latent heat release
【潜入】qiánrù〈动〉1（指水中）dive into: ～海底 submerge to the bottom of the sea ‖ ～水中 dive into the water 2（指地方）sneak into: ～国境 sneak into a country ‖ ～室内 slip into a room
【潜水】qiánshuǐ A〈动〉dive: ～采珠 dive for pearls ‖ ～作业 diving operation B〈名〉［地质］phreatic water
【潜水镜】qiánshuǐjìng〈名〉diving goggles
【潜水器】qiánshuǐqì〈名〉scuba
【潜水艇】qiánshuǐtǐng = 潜艇 qiántǐng
【潜水员】qiánshuǐyuán ▸p. 966〈名〉diver
【潜水钟】qiánshuǐzhōng〈名〉［工程］diving bell
【潜台词】qiántáicí〈名〉1［戏剧］unspoken words (left to the audience to understand) 2〈喻〉subtext
【潜逃】qiántáo〈动〉abscond: 携公款～ abscond with public funds ‖ 畏罪～ abscond to avoid punishment
【潜艇】qiántǐng〈名〉submarine: 核～ nuclear submarine
【潜望镜】qiánwàngjìng〈名〉periscope
【潜心】qiánxīn〈动〉concentrate hard: ～写作 devote oneself to writing ‖ ～研究 concentrate on one's research
【潜行】qiánxíng〈动〉1（指在水下）move under water: 潜水艇可以在海底～。Submarines can move under water. 2（指行走）move stealthily
【潜血】qiánxuè = 隐血 yǐnxuè
【潜移默化】qiányí-mòhuà〈成〉influence imperceptibly: 教师每日每时都对学生起着～的作用。Teachers are exerting an invisible, formative influence on pupils every hour of every day.
【潜意识】qiányìshí〈名〉the subconscious
【潜隐】qiányǐn〈动〉conceal
【潜泳】qiányǒng〈名〉［体育］underwater swimming
【潜在】qiánzài〈形〉potential: ～力量 latent force ‖ ～威胁 hidden threat ‖ ～影响 potential impact
【潜质】qiánzhì〈名〉potential qualities
【潜滋暗长】qiánzī-àn zhǎng〈成〉grow and develop imperceptibly
【潜踪】qiánzōng〈动〉〈贬〉go into hiding: ～匿迹 go into hiding

黔¹ qián

〈形〉〈书〉black

黔² Qián

▸p. 661〈名〉Qian [another name for Guizhou Province (贵州)]
【黔剧】qiánjù〈名〉Guizhou opera
【黔驴技穷】qiánlǘ-jìqióng〈成〉〈喻〉be at the end of one's tether
【黔驴之技】qiánlǘzhījì〈成〉〈喻〉cheap tricks
【黔首】qiánshǒu〈名〉〈古〉commoner

qiǎn

浅（淺）qiǎn

〈形〉1 ▸p. 82（指深度）shallow: ～水 shallow water ‖ ～湖 shallow lake ‖ 屋子的进深～。The room is not deep. ▸～滩 2（指经历、能力）superficial: 功夫～ have superficial mastery of a skill ‖ 阅历～ know little of the world ▸～薄, 浮～ 3（指难度）simple: 这些读物内容～，容易懂。These reading materials are simple in content and easy to understand. ▸～显, 深入～出 4 ▸p. 863（指颜色）light: ～红 light red ‖ ～蓝 pale blue ‖ ～色 light colour 5（指时间）short: 相处的日子还～ have not been together long ‖ 资历很～ be new in a business 6（指关系）not intimate: 交情～ not on familiar terms 7（指程度）slight: 她睡觉很～。She is a light sleeper. ▸～尝辄止
▸jiān
【浅薄】qiǎnbó〈形〉1（指学识、修养）shallow: 思想～ have a shallow mind ‖ 学识～ have superficial knowledge 2（指感情）not deep: 交情～ shallow acquaintance relationship 3（指言行）frivolous: 举止～ behave frivolously
【浅尝辄止】qiǎncháng-zhézhǐ〈成〉be satisfied with superficial knowledge
【浅淡】qiǎndàn ▸p. 863〈形〉pale
【浅浮雕】qiǎnfúdiāo〈名〉bas-relief
【浅耕】qiǎngēng〈名〉shallow ploughing
【浅海】qiǎnhǎi〈名〉shallow sea: ～养殖 fish-farming in shallow marine water
【浅见】qiǎnjiàn〈名〉1（肤浅之见）superficial view 2〈谦〉（用于自称）humble opinion: 依我～ in my humble opinion
【浅近】qiǎnjìn〈形〉simple: ～易懂 be simple and easy to understand ‖ 文字～ simple language
【浅口鞋】qiǎnkǒuxié〈名〉shoes with low-cut uppers
【浅陋】qiǎnlòu〈形〉shallow: 学识～ have meagre knowledge
【浅露】qiǎnlù〈形〉〈书〉blunt: 词意～ blunt words
【浅明】qiǎnmíng〈形〉simple: ～的道理 plain truth
【浅色】qiǎnsè ▸p. 863〈名〉light colour
【浅水池】qiǎnshuǐchí〈名〉1（指池子）shallow pool 2 = 浅水区 qiǎnshuǐqū
【浅水区】qiǎnshuǐqū〈名〉shallow end
【浅说】qiǎnshuō〈名〉basic introduction [usu used in titles of books and articles]
【浅滩】qiǎntān〈名〉shoal: 在～上搁浅 get stranded on a shoal
【浅谈】qiǎntán〈名〉brief discussion [usu used in titles of books and articles]
【浅显】qiǎnxiǎn〈形〉simple: ～的科学读物 simple scientific literature ‖ 包含～的道理 embody a plain truth
【浅易】qiǎnyì〈形〉simple and easy: ～读物 easy readings
【浅斟低唱】qiǎnzhēn-dīchàng〈成〉enjoy oneself by drinking leisurely and singing softly
【浅种】qiǎnzhòng〈名〉shallow sowing
【浅子】qiǎnzi〈名〉shallow container

遣 qiǎn

〈动〉1（派遣）send: ～信使 send away a messenger ▸～送, 差～ 2（消除）expel: 无以自～ have no diversions ‖ 赋诗～怀 express oneself in verse ▸排～

【遣词】qiǎncí〈动〉 word: ～造句 wording and phrasing ‖ 他以～用字生动清新而见长。 His diction is noted for its vividness and freshness.
【遣返】qiǎnfǎn〈动〉 repatriate: ～难民 repatriate a refugee ‖ ～原籍 send sb. back to his native place
【遣怀】qiǎnhuái〈动〉〈书〉 give vent to one's feelings
【遣闷】qiǎnmèn〈动〉 divert oneself from boredom
【遣派】qiǎnpài = 派遣 pàiqiǎn
【遣散】qiǎnsàn〈动〉 1（旧）（解散） disband: ～军队 disband an army ‖ ～费 severance pay 2（指俘虏） send away: 全部敌军缴械～。 The enemy troops were disarmed and disbanded.
【遣送】qiǎnsòng〈动〉 send back: ～出境 deport ‖ ～回国 send sb. back to his country

谴（譴） qiǎn〈动〉 1（责备） reproach: 自～ blame oneself for one's error ▸～责 2〈书〉（获罪降职） be demoted and banished: ▸～谪
【谴责】qiǎnzé〈动〉 denounce: ～虐待妇女儿童的行径 condemn cruelty to women and children ‖ 他受到了良心的～。 His conscience plagued him.
【谴谪】qiǎnzhé〈动〉〈书〉 be demoted and banished

缱（繾） qiǎn
【缱绻】qiǎnquǎn〈形〉〈书〉 deeply attached to: ～柔情 deep attachment

qiàn

欠 qiàn〈动〉 1（打哈欠） yawn: ▸～伸 2（身体前倾） raise slightly: ～了～身子 bow slightly ▸～身 3（缺少） lack: ～考虑 without due consideration ‖ 文章～润色。 The article lacked final touches. ▸～佳, ～缺, ～妥 4（未还清） owe: ～人情 owe sb. a favour ‖ ～税 arrears of taxes ‖ 他所～的债永远也还不清。 The debt that he owed could never be paid. ▸～款, 亏～, 拖～
【欠安】qiàn'ān〈形〉〈旧〉 indisposed: 身体～ not feel well
【欠产】qiànchǎn〈动〉 have a shortfall in output: 今年严重～。 Crop shortfalls are severe this year.
【欠发达】qiànfādá〈形〉 less developed: ～国家 less developed country
【欠费】qiànfèi〈动〉 be in arrears
【欠火】qiànhuǒ〈动〉 be undercooked: 这馒头还欠点儿火。 The buns haven't been steamed long enough.
【欠佳】qiànjiā〈形〉 below par: 身体～ feel below par
【欠款】qiànkuǎn A〈动〉 owe money B〈名〉 balance due: 还清～ pay off one's debts ‖ 收回～ recover arrears
【欠情】qiànqíng〈动〉 be indebted to sb.: 咱俩谁也不欠谁的情。 Neither of us is indebted to the other.
【欠缺】qiànquē A〈动〉 lack: ～经验/资金 lack experience/funds B〈名〉 shortcoming: 事情办得很圆满，没有什么～。 It's perfect; I cannot find a thing wrong with it.
【欠伸】qiànshēn〈动〉 stretch oneself and yawn
【欠身】qiànshēn〈动〉 raise oneself slightly: ～表示敬意 lean forward to show respect
【欠条】qiàntiáo〈名〉 IOU (I owe you): 打～ give sb. an IOU
【欠妥】qiàntuǒ〈动〉 be not proper: 措词～ not properly worded ‖ 这事办得～。 The matter wasn't handled properly.
【欠项】qiànxiàng〈名〉 liabilities
【欠薪】qiànxīn A〈动〉 delay paying a salary B〈名〉 overdue salaries
【欠债】qiànzhài A〈动〉 be in debt: ～不还 not pay back the money one owes ‖ ～容易还债难。 It's easier to run into debt than to get out of it. B〈名〉 debt: 追讨～ demand payment of an old debt
【欠账】qiànzhàng = 欠债 qiànzhài
【欠资】qiànzī〈名〉 postage due: ～信 postage-due letter
【欠揍】qiànzòu〈动〉〈口〉 need a spanking: 他说这话真是～。 He deserves a good spanking for what he said.
【欠租】qiànzū〈动〉 be behind with one's rent: 欠一个月的租 owe sb. a month's rent

纤（縴） qiàn〈名〉 tow rope: ▸～绳
▸xiān
【纤夫】qiànfū〈名〉〈旧〉 boat tracker
【纤路】qiànlù〈名〉 towpath
【纤绳】qiànshéng〈名〉 tow rope
【纤手】qiànshǒu〈名〉 1〈旧〉（经纪人） estate agent 2 = 纤夫 qiànfū

芡 qiàn〈名〉 1［植物］ Euryale ferox 2（用于做菜） starch used in cooking
【芡粉】qiànfěn〈名〉 1（芡实粉） seed powder of Euryale ferox 2（淀粉） any starch used in cooking
【芡实】qiànshí〈名〉［植物］ Euryale ferox

茜 qiàn ▸p. 863〈名〉 1［植物］ madder 2（红色） rose madder: ～纱 red gauze
【茜草】qiàncǎo〈名〉［植物］ madder

倩¹ qiàn〈形〉〈书〉 beautiful: ▸～影

倩² qiàn〈动〉 ask sb. to do sth. on one's behalf: ～人执笔 ask sb. to write on one's behalf
【倩影】qiànyǐng〈名〉〈书〉 beautiful image (of a woman)
【倩装】qiànzhuāng〈名〉 beautiful dress

堑（塹） qiàn〈名〉 chasm: ▸吃一～，长一智，天～
【堑壕】qiànháo〈名〉［军事］ trench: ～工事 entrenchment works

绩（綪） qiàn〈名〉〈书〉 dark red silk

椠（槧） qiàn〈名〉〈书〉 1（指木板） board for taking notes in ancient China 2（指刻本） block-printed edition: 元～ Yuan Dynasty block-printed edition

嵌 qiàn〈动〉 inlay: ～宝石 set a jewel ‖ ～金/银 inlay sth. with gold/silver ‖ 戒指上～着一颗钻石。 The ring is set with a diamond. ▸镶～
【嵌板】qiànbǎn〈名〉 panel

慊 qiàn〈动〉〈书〉 regret
▸qiè

歉 qiàn〈动〉 1（指收成） have a poor harvest: 以丰补～ make up for a crop failure with a bumper harvest 2（指心情） be apologetic: 迟复为～ apologize for the late reply ▸抱～, 道～
【歉忱】qiànchén〈名〉〈书〉 apology
【歉疚】qiànjiù〈动〉 be sorry: 深感～ feel guilty
【歉年】qiànnián〈名〉 lean year
【歉然】qiànrán〈形〉〈书〉 apologetic: ～不语 apologetic and silent
【歉收】qiànshōu〈动〉 have a poor harvest: 因遭大旱而～ have a bad harvest due to a severe drought ‖ 今年庄稼～。 Crops are very scanty this year.
【歉岁】qiànsuì〈名〉 lean year
【歉意】qiànyì ▸p. 156〈名〉 apology: 深表～ apologize deeply to sb. ‖ 谨致～。 Please accept my apology.

q

qiāng

抢（搶） qiāng〈动〉〈书〉 knock: ▸呼天～地
▸qiǎng

呛（嗆） qiāng〈动〉 choke: 吃饭吃～了 choke on one's food ‖ 小孩喝水太猛，～着了。 The child took a big gulp and almost choked.
▸qiàng

羌 Qiāng〈名〉 1（指古代民族） Qiang 2（指民族） Qiang ethnic group: ▸～笛
【羌笛】qiāngdí ▸p. 929〈名〉 Qiang flute
【羌族】Qiāngzú〈名〉 Qiang ethnic group

玱（瑲） qiāng〈拟〉〈书〉 clink

枪（槍） qiāng
A〈名〉 1（指冷兵器） spear: ▸标～, 红缨～ 2（指火器） gun: 开～ fire a gun (at sb./sth.) ‖ 鸣～警告 fire a warning shot ‖ 自动步～ automatic rifle ▸手～, 冲锋～ 3（枪状物） gun-like thing: ▸喷～, 水～
B〈动〉 sit for an examination in place of sb. else: ▸～替
【枪靶】qiāngbǎ〈名〉 (shooting) target
【枪把】qiāngbà〈名〉 pistol grip
【枪毙】qiāngbì〈动〉 1〈本〉 execute by shooting: 他被当作叛徒～了。 He was shot as a traitor. 2〈喻〉（否定） turn down: 他的处女作被出版社～了。 His maiden work was rejected by the publisher.
【枪刺】qiāngcì〈名〉 bayonet
【枪打出头鸟】qiāng dǎ chūtóuniǎo〈俗〉〈喻〉 the person in the limelight bears the brunt of the attack
【枪弹】qiāngdàn〈名〉 1（弹药） cartridge 2（子弹） bullet: ～雨点般地落在我们周围。 Bullets rained about us.
【枪法】qiāngfǎ〈名〉 1（指射击） marksmanship: 他～高明，百发百中。 He is a crack shot and never misses the target. 2（指长枪） skills in using a spear: ～纯熟 be highly skilled in using a spear
【枪杆】qiānggǎn〈名〉 1（指杆子） barrel of a gun 2（指枪） rifle: 拿起～上前线 take up arms and go to the front ‖ ～子里面出政权。 Power comes from the barrel of a gun.
【枪杆子】qiānggǎnzi = 枪杆 qiānggǎn
【枪管】qiāngguǎn〈名〉 gun barrel

q

【枪击】qiāngjī〈动〉 shoot: 校园～事件 school shooting ‖ 遭～身亡 be shot dead
【枪机】qiāngjī〈名〉 rifle bolt
【枪架】qiāngjià〈名〉 rifle rack
【枪决】qiāngjué〈动〉 execute by shooting: 执行～ carry out a shooting
【枪口】qiāngkǒu〈名〉 muzzle: 把～对准敌人 point one's gun at the enemy
【枪林弹雨】qiānglín-dànyǔ〈成〉 heavy gunfire: 冒着敌人的～ under the enemy's heavy fire
【枪榴弹】qiāngliúdàn〈名〉 rifle grenade
【枪炮】qiāngpào〈名〉 guns
【枪杀】qiāngshā〈动〉 shoot dead: 遭到～ be shot dead
【枪伤】qiāngshāng ▸p. 50〈名〉 gunshot wound
【枪声】qiāngshēng〈名〉 shot
【枪手】qiāngshǒu〈名〉 1〈本〉 gunman: 神～ expert marksman 2〈喻〉 one who sits for an examination in place of sb. else
【枪栓】qiāngshuān〈名〉 rifle bolt
【枪膛】qiāngtáng〈名〉 gun bore
【枪替】qiāngtì〈动〉 sit for an examination in place of sb. else
【枪筒】qiāngtǒng〈名〉 gun barrel
【枪托】qiāngtuō〈名〉 rifle butt: 木～ wooden stock
【枪乌贼】qiāngwūzéi〈名〉［动物］ squid
【枪械】qiāngxiè〈名〉 firearms
【枪眼】qiāngyǎn〈名〉 1（射击孔） embrasure 2（子弹孔） bullet hole
【枪鱼】qiāngyú〈名〉［鱼类］ marlin
【枪战】qiāngzhàn〈名〉 gun battle: 激烈的～ fierce gunfight ‖ 在～中丧生 get killed in a gun battle
【枪支】qiāngzhī〈名〉 firearms: ～弹药 firearms and ammunition
【枪子儿】qiāngzǐr〈名〉〈口〉 bullet: 挨/吃～ get shot

戗（戧） qiāng
〈动〉 1（方向相对） go in an opposite direction: ▸～风 2（冲突） clash: 为小事说～了 clash over a trivial matter
▸qiàng
【戗风】qiāngfēng〈动〉 go against the wind: ～行船 sail against the wind

戕 qiāng
〈动〉〈书〉 kill: ▸自～
【戕害】qiānghài〈动〉 harm: ～身体 be harmful to sb.'s health ‖ ～无辜 harm the innocent
【戕贼】qiāngzéi〈动〉 harm: ～身体 harm sb.'s health

斨 qiāng
〈名〉〈古〉 a kind of axe

将（將） qiāng
〈动〉〈书〉 ask: ～进酒 please have a drink
▸jiāng, jiàng

跄（蹌） qiāng
▸qiàng
【跄跄】qiāngqiāng〈动〉 walk rhythmically in a prescribed manner

腔 qiāng
〈名〉 1（指动物体） cavity: ▸口～, 满～热忱, 胸～ 2（曲调） tune: 唱走了～儿 sing out of tune ▸花～ 3 ▸p. 918（语气） tone: 京～ Beijing accent ▸打官～, 油～滑调 4（话） speech: ▸答～, 开～
【腔肠动物】qiāngcháng dòngwù〈名〉 coelenterate
【腔调】qiāngdiào〈名〉 1（唱腔） tune: 豫剧～ Henan opera tunes 2〈贬〉（语调） tone of voice: 我不喜欢你说话的～。 I don't like the tone of your voice. 3 ▸p. 918（口音） accent: 他说英语带美国南部～。 He speaks English with a southern American accent. ‖ 听他说话的～是山东人。 Judging from his accent, he is from Shandong.
【腔骨】qiānggǔ〈名〉［食品］ spinal joints of pigs, sheep, etc.

蜣 qiāng
【蜣螂】qiāngláng〈名〉［昆虫］ dung beetle

锖（錆） qiāng
【锖色】qiāngsè〈名〉 tarnish

锵（鏘） qiāng
〈拟〉 clang: 锣声～～。 Gongs clanked.

蹡（蹌） qiāng
【蹡蹡】qiāngqiāng〈形〉〈书〉 trained performance moves

镪（鏹） qiāng
▸qiǎng
【镪水】qiāngshuǐ〈名〉〈口〉 strong acid

qiáng

强 qiáng
A〈形〉 1（健壮） strong: 身～体壮 healthy and strong ‖ 两～相遇，必有一场恶战。 There'll be a fierce battle between the two powers. ▸～大, ～国, 富～ 2（坚定） staunch: ▸～硬, 刚～, 坚～ 3（横暴） forceful: ～夺 wrench sth. out of sb.'s hand ‖ ～索钱财 take money by force ▸～渡, ～奸, ～占 4（好） high-standard: 能力～ be capable ‖ 责任心～ have a strong sense of responsibility ▸要～ 5（优越） superior: ～于对手 be better than one's opponent ‖ 他比我～得多。 He is way superior to me. 6（略多） slightly over: 四分之一～ slightly more than a quarter ‖ 实际产量超过原定计划10%～。 The actual output is a little more than 10 per cent beyond the original plan.
B〈动〉 strengthen: ▸～身, ～心剂, 富国～兵
▸jiàng, qiǎng
【强暴】qiángbào A〈形〉 brutal: ～的行为 act of violence B〈名〉 ferocious adversary: 不畏～ defy brute force C〈动〉 rape: 遭到～ be raped
【强大】qiángdà〈形〉 powerful: ～的攻势 powerful offensive ‖ 国力日益～。 The national power is increasing day by day. ‖ 这部影片演员阵容～。 The film has a strong cast.
【强档】qiángdàng〈名〉 high grade: ～财经类节目 effective financial programs
【强盗】qiángdào〈名〉 robber: 一伙～ a gang of robbers ‖ ～行径 act of robbery ‖ ～逻辑 gangster logic
【强敌】qiángdí〈名〉 formidable opponent
【强调】qiángdiào〈动〉 stress: 反复～ repeatedly emphasize ‖ 不要～客观原因。 Don't overemphasize the objective factors.
【强度】qiángdù〈名〉 1（指作用力） intensity: 辐射～ radiation intensity ‖ 劳动～ labour intensity ‖ 音响～ acoustic intensity 2（指抵抗力） strength: 抗压～ compressive strength ‖ 抗震～ shock strength
【强渡】qiángdù〈动〉［军事］ fight one's way across a river: ～大河 make a forced crossing of a big river
【强风】qiángfēng〈名〉［气象］ strong breeze
【强干】qiánggàn〈形〉 capable and experienced: 精明～ intelligent and capable
【强攻】qiánggōng〈动〉 take by storm: ～敌营 storm the enemy campsite ‖ ～篮下，投进一球。 He broke through the defence and made a shot.
【强固】qiánggù〈形〉 strong and solid: ～的工事 strong fortifications
【强国】qiángguó A〈名〉 powerful nation: 工业～ industrial power ‖ 体育～ sports power B〈动〉 build up national strength: ～之本在于发展经济。 Economic development is essential for building a powerful nation.
【强悍】qiánghàn〈形〉 fierce: ～好战 be fierce and warlike
【强横】qiánghèng〈形〉 rude and unreasonable: 态度～ rude and arrogant attitude ‖ ～无理 rude and unreasonable
【强化】qiánghuà〈动〉 strengthen: ～国家机器 strengthen the state apparatus ‖ ～税收管理 consolidate tax administration ‖ ～训练 intensify the training
【强化食品】qiánghuà shípǐn〈名〉 fortified food
【强击机】qiángjījī〈名〉 attack plane
【强加】qiángjiā〈动〉 force sth. on sb.: 把莫须有的罪名～在某人头上 bring a fabricated charge against sb. ‖ 将自己的意志～于人 impose one's will upon sb. else
【强奸】qiángjiān〈动〉 rape: ～未遂 be charged with attempted rape ‖ ～犯 rapist ‖ 熟人～ acquaintance rape
【强奸民意】qiángjiān-mínyì〈成〉〈喻〉 defile public opinion
【强碱】qiángjiǎn〈名〉［化学］ alkali
【强健】qiángjiàn〈形〉 sturdy: 身体～ be healthy and strong
【强将手下无弱兵】qiángjiàng shǒuxià wú ruòbīng〈俗〉 there are no poor soldiers under an able general
【强劲】qiángjìng〈形〉 forceful: ～的对手 formidable opponent ‖ 国家经济增长势头～。 The nation's economy is growing with increasing momentum.
【强劳动力】qiángláodònglì〈名〉 able-bodied labourer
【强力】qiánglì〈名〉 1（指能力） great force: ～夺取 seize with great force ‖ ～胶 super glue 2（指力量） strength
【强梁】qiángliáng〈形〉 brutal: 不畏～ defy brute force
【强烈】qiángliè〈形〉 1（激烈） strong: ～反对 strongly oppose ‖ ～要求 demand strongly ‖ ～的愿望 strong desire ‖ 发生了～地震。 A violent earthquake has erupted. 2（突出） sharp: 形成～的对比 pose a striking contrast
【强令】qiánglìng〈动〉 give a peremptory order: ～执行 deliver a peremptory order to carry out
【强龙难压地头蛇】qiánglóng nán yā dìtóushé〈俗〉〈喻〉 even a powerful outsider cannot crush a local bully
【强弩之末】qiángnǔzhīmò〈成〉 a spent force: 敌人已是～，不堪一击。 The enemy troops were exhausted and couldn't withstand a single blow.
【强强联合】qiángqiáng liánhé〈动〉 join

forces for strengthened collaboration: 兼并重组，～ merge and reorganize for added collaborative strength ‖ 两家大型国企实现了～。 The two large-scale state-owned enterprises have successfully merged into one powerful business.

【强取豪夺】 qiángqǔ-háoduó〈成〉exact by force

【强权】 qiángquán〈名〉 power: ～政治 power politics

【强人】 qiángrén〈名〉 **1**（能干的人）strong man: 我们经理是个女～。 Our manager is an iron lady. **2**（强盗） robber

【强如】 qiángrú = 强似 qiángsì

【强身】 qiángshēn〈动〉 improve one's physique: ～健体 build up a good physique and improve one's health ‖ 习武～ practise martial arts to improve one's health

【强盛】 qiángshèng〈形〉 powerful and prosperous: 国家～ powerful and prosperous country

【强势】 qiángshì〈名〉 **1**（指势头） strong rising tendency **2**（指势力） strength: ～地位 strong position

【强手】 qiángshǒu〈名〉master: 不畏～ not fear strong competition ‖ ～如林 plenty of master players

【强似】 qiángsì〈动〉〈书〉 be better than: 今年的收成又～去年。 This year's harvest is better than last year's.

【强酸】 qiángsuān〈名〉［化学］ strong acid

【强徒】 qiángtú〈名〉 bandit

【强袭】 qiángxí〈动〉 take by storm

【强项】 qiángxiàng **A**〈名〉 strength: 球类运动是他的～。 Ball games are his forte. **B**〈形〉〈书〉 upright and unyielding

【强心剂】 qiángxīnjì〈名〉 cardiotonic

【强行】 qiángxíng〈动〉 force: ～闯入 force an entrance ‖ ～登陆 force a landing

【强行军】 qiángxíngjūn〈动〉［军事］ force march

【强压】 qiángyā〈动〉 suppress: ～怒火 suppress one's anger

【强硬】 qiángyìng〈形〉 tough: 采取～措施 take tough measures ‖ 态度～ uncompromising stand ‖ ～派 hard-liner

【强有力】 qiángyǒulì〈形〉 strong

【强占】 qiángzhàn〈动〉 forcibly occupy: ～民宅 seize a private residence ‖ ～有利地形 seize a favourable position

【强震】 qiángzhèn〈名〉［地质］ strong shock

【强直】 qiángzhí **A** ▸**p. 50**〈名〉［医学］ rigidity **B**〈形〉〈书〉 firm and honest

【强制】 qiángzhì〈动〉 force: 采取～措施 resort to coercive measures ‖ ～执行 enforce

【强制性】 qiángzhìxìng〈名〉 compulsoriness: ～命令 mandatory order

【强中自有强中手】 qiángzhōng zìyǒu qiángzhōng shǒu〈俗〉 however strong you are, there is always someone stronger

【强壮】 qiángzhuàng **A**〈形〉 sturdy: 身体～ be physically strong ‖ ～的体魄 be of a strong physique **B**〈动〉 strengthen: 这药能～病人体质。 This drug can build up a patient's physique.

【强子】 qiángzǐ〈名〉［物理］ hadron

墙（牆） qiáng〈名〉 **1**（屏障）

wall: 挂在～上 hang (sth.) on the wall ‖ 隔音～ soundproof wall ‖ 土/砖～ earthen/brick wall ▸城～，防火～，围～ **2**（墙状物） anything shaped or functioning like a wall: ▸人～

【墙报】 qiángbào = 壁报 bìbào

【墙壁】 qiángbì〈名〉 wall: 粉刷～ whitewash a wall

【墙倒众人推】 qiáng dǎo zhòngrén tuī〈俗〉〈喻〉 everybody hits the man who is down

【墙根】 qiánggēn〈名〉 foot of a wall

【墙基】 qiángjī〈名〉 base of a wall

【墙角】 qiángjiǎo〈名〉 corner between walls: ～家具 corner furniture

【墙脚】 qiángjiǎo〈名〉 **1**（墙根） foot of a wall **2**〈喻〉（中坚力量） foundation: 挖～ pull the rug out from under sb.'s feet

【墙裙】 qiángqún〈名〉［建筑］ wainscot: 外～ outer wainscot

【墙头】 qiángtóu〈名〉 **1**（指顶部） top of a wall **2**（指墙围） short, low enclosing wall

【墙头草】 qiángtóucǎo〈名〉〈喻〉 fence-sitter

【墙垣】 qiángyuán〈名〉〈书〉 wall

【墙纸】 qiángzhǐ〈名〉 wallpaper: ～图案 patterns on wallpaper

蔷（薔） qiáng

【蔷薇】 qiángwēi〈名〉［植物］ rose

嫱（嬙） qiáng〈名〉〈古〉

woman court official

樯（檣） qiáng〈名〉〈书〉 mast:

帆～如林 forest of masts

qiǎng

抢¹（搶） qiǎng〈动〉 **1**（抢夺）

snatch: ～钱 rob sb. of his money ‖ ～座位 grab a seat ‖ 她的钱包被～了。 Her purse was snatched. ▸～劫 **2**（争先） compete for: ～生意 compete for business ‖ 大家都～着做志愿者。 All vie with each other to be volunteers. ▸～购，～先 **3**（抓紧） rush: ～时间 lose no time ▸～救，～修

抢²（搶） qiǎng〈动〉 scrape:

磨剪子～菜刀 sharpen scissors and kitchen knives ‖ 锅底～一～再洗。 Scrape the bottom of the pot before you wash it. ▸qiāng

【抢白】 qiǎngbái〈动〉 reprimand: 我被她～了。 I was told off by her.

【抢答】 qiǎngdá〈动〉 race to be the first to answer

【抢点】 qiǎngdiǎn〈动〉 **1**（指交通）make up time **2**（指球赛） race to a favourable position

【抢渡】 qiǎngdù〈动〉 speedily cross

【抢断】 qiǎngduàn〈动〉 intercept: ～球 intercept the ball

【抢夺】 qiǎngduó〈动〉 snatch: ～胜利果实 seize the fruits of victory

【抢购】 qiǎnggòu〈动〉 rush to purchase: ～短缺原材料 rush to buy scarce raw materials ‖ 音乐会的票被～一空。 The tickets for the concert have been sold out.

【抢婚】 qiǎnghūn = 抢亲 qiǎngqīn A

【抢劫】 qiǎngjié〈动〉 rob: ～银行 rob a bank ‖ 拦路～ mug ‖ ～案 robbery

【抢劫犯】 qiǎngjiéfàn〈名〉 robber

【抢截】 qiǎngjié〈动〉［体育］ intercept

【抢镜头】 qiǎng jìngtóu〈动〉 **1**〈本〉 fight for a vantage point from which to take a picture **2**〈喻〉（引人注意） steal the show: 她喜欢～，出风头。 She loves to steal the show and to be the centre of attention.

【抢救】 qiǎngjiù〈动〉 rescue: ～伤员 rescue the wounded ‖ ～措施 emergency measures ‖ ～无效。 All rescue efforts were in vain.

【抢掠】 qiǎnglüè〈动〉 plunder: 烧杀～ burn, kill and plunder

【抢跑】 qiǎngpǎo〈动〉［体育］ jump the gun

【抢七】 qiǎngqī〈动〉［体育］ tie-break: 通过～获胜 win on a tie-break

【抢亲】 qiǎngqīn **A**〈名〉 marriage ceremony in which the bridegroom pretends to kidnap his bride **B**〈动〉 grab a woman from her home to be one's wife with the help of others

【抢墒】 qiǎngshāng〈动〉 hurry to sow seeds while the soil is still moist

【抢时间】 qiǎng shíjiān〈动〉 lose no time

【抢收】 qiǎngshōu〈动〉 rush in the harvest

【抢手】 qiǎngshǒu〈形〉［of goods］ marketable in great demand: ～货 fast-selling goods ‖ 球赛门票十分～。 The tickets for the ball game are in great demand.

【抢滩】 qiǎngtān〈动〉 **1**［军事］ seize a beachhead **2**（抢占市场） race to capture a market: 世界各大银行～上海。 Major international banks are scrambling for the Shanghai market.

【抢先】 qiǎngxiān〈动〉 vie to be the first: ～发言 speak before everybody else ‖ 比对手～一步 forestall a competitor ‖ ～报道消息 vie to be the first to get the story

【抢险】 qiǎngxiǎn〈动〉 rush to deal with an emergency: 抗洪～ combat a flood and hurry to the rescue

【抢修】 qiǎngxiū〈动〉 do rush repairs: ～大坝 rush to repair the dam

【抢眼】 qiǎngyǎn〈形〉 conspicuous: 打扮得很～ be loudly dressed

【抢运】 qiǎngyùn〈动〉 rush transport

【抢占】 qiǎngzhàn〈动〉 **1**（抢先占领） race to seize: ～制高点 race to control a commanding point **2**（非法占有） unlawfully occupy: ～集体财产 unlawfully take possession of collective property

【抢种】 qiǎngzhòng〈动〉 plant in a hurry: ～冬小麦 lose no time in planting winter wheat

【抢注】 qiǎngzhù〈动〉 rush to register: 恶意～ have dubious motives for being the first to register ‖ ～域名 rush to register a domain name

【抢嘴】 qiǎngzuǐ〈动〉 **1**〈方〉（抢着说话） try to get the first word in: 别～。 Don't all try to speak at once. **2**（抢着吃） rush to eat up the food

羟（羥） qiǎng

【羟基】 qiǎngjī〈名〉［化学］ hydroxyl (group)

强 qiǎng〈动〉 **1**（迫使） force: ▸～迫

2（勉强） strive: ～忍眼泪 force back one's tears ‖ ～作笑颜 force a smile ▸jiàng, qiáng

【强逼】 qiǎngbī〈动〉 force: 自愿参加，不～。 Participation is voluntary, so nobody is to be forced.

【强辩】 qiǎngbiàn〈动〉 argue against all reason

【强不知以为知】 qiǎng bùzhī yǐwéi zhī〈成〉 pretend to know what one does not know

【强词夺理】 qiǎngcí-duólǐ〈成〉 resort to

sophistry: 明明是你错了，何必～。 You are evidently in the wrong, so what's the point in trying to defend yourself?

【强买强卖】qiǎngmǎi-qiǎngmài〈成〉force sb. to buy or sell

【强扭的瓜不甜】qiǎngniǔdeguā bù tián〈俗〉〈喻〉forcing one will not produce the desired results

【强迫】qiǎngpò〈动〉force: 个人意见不要～别人接受。 Don't force your opinions on others. ‖ 她在父母的～下嫁给了一个有钱人。 Coerced by her parents, she married a rich man.

【强迫症】qiǎngpòzhèng ▸**p. 50**〈名〉［医学］obsessive-compulsive disorder

【强求】qiǎngqiú〈动〉make peremptory demands: 写文章可以有各种风格，不必～一律。 No rigid format should be imposed on articles and the styles may vary.

【强人所难】qiǎngrénsuǒnán〈成〉force sb. to do what he is unwilling or unable to do: 他不会唱歌，不要～了。 He can't sing, so don't force him.

【强使】qiǎngshǐ〈动〉force: ～服从 force sb. to obey

【强颜欢笑】qiǎngyán-huānxiào〈成〉try to look happy

镪（鏹） qiǎng〈名〉〈书〉string of copper coins
▸qiāng

襁 qiǎng〈名〉straps for carrying a baby on the back

【襁褓】qiǎngbǎo〈名〉swaddling clothes: ～中的婴儿 baby in swaddling clothes ‖ 母亲千辛万苦地把他从～中抚育成人。 His mother went through all kinds of hardships in order to bring him up.

qiàng

呛（嗆） qiàng〈动〉irritate the respiratory organs: 辣椒味真～人。 The smell of chillies is very irritating. ‖ 烟～得他透不过气来。 The smoke almost choked him.
▸qiāng

戗（戧） qiàng
A〈动〉prop up: 用两根木头来～住这堵墙 brace the wall with two logs
B〈名〉［建筑］prop
▸qiāng

【戗面】qiàngmiàn **A**〈动〉knead flour into a dough **B**〈名〉leavened dough mixed with flour

炝（熗） qiàng〈动〉**1**（煮后拌）boil in water then dress with sauce: ～莲菜 quick-boiled lotus root dressed with soy and vinegar **2**（炒后煮）fry sth. quickly in hot oil, then cook it with sauce and water: ～锅肉丝面 noodles with quick-fried shredded pork ‖ 用葱花～～锅 fry chopped green onions in the pot

跄（蹌） qiàng
▸qiāng

【跄踉】qiàngliàng = 踉跄 liàngqiàng

qiāo

悄 qiāo
▸qiǎo

【悄悄】qiāoqiāo **A**〈形〉quiet: ▸静～ **B**〈副〉quietly: ～离开 slip away ‖ 他～地溜走了。 He crept off without being noticed.

【悄悄话】qiāoqiāohuà〈名〉private whisper: 说～ speak in whispers

硗（磽） qiāo〈形〉〈书〉[of land] hard and infertile

【硗薄】qiāobó〈形〉〈书〉barren: 土地～ infertile land

【硗瘠】qiāojí = 硗薄 qiāobó

雀 qiāo
▸qiǎo, què

【雀子】qiāozi〈名〉〈口〉freckles

跷（蹺） qiāo
A〈动〉**1**（抬）lift up: ～二郎腿 sit with one's legs crossed ‖ ～起大拇指 stick up one's thumb in approval **2**（踮）walk on tiptoe: ～起脚看墙上的布告 stand on tiptoe to look at the bulletin on the wall
B〈名〉stilts: 登在三尺多高的～上扭秧歌 do a *yangge* dance on three-*chi*-high stilts ▸高～

【跷跷板】qiāoqiāobǎn〈名〉seesaw: 玩～ play on a seesaw

锹（鍬） qiāo〈名〉shovel: 一～煤 a shovelful of coal ‖ 方头～ square spade ▸铁～

劁 qiāo〈动〉geld: ～猪 castrate a pig

敲 qiāo〈动〉**1**（击打）knock: ～锣打鼓 beat drums and gongs ‖ ～门 knock at the door ‖ 钟声～响了。 The clock struck. **2**（敲竹杠）overcharge: 他在馆子里狠狠～了我一顿。 He landed me in it when the bill came for the food.

【敲边鼓】qiāo biāngǔ〈惯〉back sb. up: 我给你～。 I'll back you up.

【敲打】qiāodǎ〈动〉**1**（击打）beat: 锣鼓～得很热闹。 Drums and gongs were beating loudly. ‖ 雨点～着窗子。 The rain lashed against the window. **2**（批评）say sth. to criticize or irritate sb.: 冷言冷语～人 irritate people with sarcasm **3**（提醒）pressurize and supervise sb.: 我这人缺点很多，往后还得请您常～着点儿。 I have many shortcomings and need your constant prodding.

【敲定】qiāodìng〈动〉〈口〉determine: ～人选 decide on the candidates ‖ 这事就这样～了。 That settles the matter.

【敲骨吸髓】qiāogǔ-xīsuǐ〈成〉〈喻〉suck the lifeblood

【敲击】qiāojī〈动〉strike

【敲警钟】qiāo jǐngzhōng〈动〉〈喻〉sound a warning

【敲门砖】qiāoménzhuān〈名〉〈喻〉stepping-stone to success: 旧文人把读书当成～。 Old men of letters saw reading as a means to promotion.

【敲诈】qiāozhà〈动〉blackmail: ～钱财 extort money (from sb.) ‖ ～勒索 extort

【敲竹杠】qiāo zhúgàng〈惯〉fleece: 这简直是～! This is sheer daylight robbery!

橇 qiāo〈名〉sledge: ▸雪～

缲（繰） qiāo〈动〉hem with invisible stitches: 给裤子～边儿 hem the trousers

qiáo

乔[1]（喬） qiáo〈形〉tall: ▸～木

乔[2]（喬） qiáo〈动〉disguise: ▸～装

【乔木】qiáomù〈名〉arbor: ～林 high forest

【乔其纱】qiáoqíshā〈名〉［纺织］georgette (crêpe)

【乔迁】qiáoqiān〈动〉move to a better place or get a promotion: ～新居 move to a new home

【乔迁之喜】qiáoqiānzhīxǐ〈成〉happy occasion of moving into a new home: 恭贺～ congratulations on your new home

【乔治敦】Qiáozhìdūn〈名〉Georgetown

【乔装】qiáozhuāng〈动〉disguise: 他用假胡须～起来。 He was disguised with a false beard.

【乔装打扮】qiáozhuāng-dǎbàn〈成〉disguise oneself: 他～混进了敌人中间。 He went among the enemy in disguise.

侨（僑） qiáo
A〈动〉reside abroad: ▸～民, ～胞
B〈名〉person residing abroad: ▸华～, 外～

【侨胞】qiáobāo〈名〉nationals residing abroad: 海外～ overseas nationals

【侨汇】qiáohuì〈名〉overseas remittance

【侨居】qiáojū〈动〉live abroad: ～海外 reside abroad

【侨眷】qiáojuàn〈名〉relatives of overseas Chinese: 华侨及～ overseas Chinese and their relatives

【侨民】qiáomín〈名〉national of a particular country residing abroad: 在华的外国～ foreign nationals in China

【侨商】qiáoshāng〈名〉overseas Chinese businessman

【侨属】qiáoshǔ = 侨眷 qiáojuàn

【侨务】qiáowù〈名〉overseas Chinese affairs: ～工作 overseas Chinese affairs ‖ ～政策 policy toward overseas Chinese affairs

【侨乡】qiáoxiāng〈名〉village or town inhabited by relatives of overseas Chinese and returned overseas Chinese

【侨资】qiáozī〈名〉investment by overseas Chinese: ～企业 overseas Chinese enterprise

荞（蕎） qiáo

【荞麦】qiáomài〈名〉buckwheat: ～面 buckwheat flour

峤（嶠） qiáo〈形〉〈书〉[of a mountain] high and pointed
▸jiào

桥（橋） qiáo〈名〉bridge: 架～ build a bridge ‖ 公路铁路两用～ rail and highway bridge ▸吊～, 独木～, 立交～

【桥洞】qiáodòng〈名〉bridge opening

【桥段】qiáoduàn〈名〉chapter of a film: 重点～ key chapter of a film ‖ 最精彩的～ the outstanding part of a film

【桥墩】qiáodūn〈名〉pier
【桥归桥，路归路】qiáoguīqiáo, lùguīlù〈惯〉〈喻〉you do your thing and I'll do mine
【桥拱】qiáogǒng〈名〉bridge arch
【桥涵】qiáohán〈名〉bridge and its culvert
【桥孔】qiáokǒng〈名〉bridge opening: 这桥有三个～。 The bridge rests on three arches.
【桥梁】qiáoliáng〈名〉bridge: 架设～ build a bridge ‖ ～建筑 bridge construction ‖〈喻〉连接政府与企业的～ bridge that links government and enterprises ‖〈喻〉友谊的～ bridge of friendship
【桥牌】qiáopái ▸p. 909〈名〉bridge: 打～ play bridge
【桥式起重机】qiáoshì qǐzhòngjī〈名〉bridge crane
【桥塔】qiáotǎ〈名〉［建筑］bridge tower
【桥头】qiáotóu〈名〉either end of a bridge
【桥头堡】qiáotóubǎo〈名〉1［军事］bridgehead: 攻占～ seize a bridgehead 2［建筑］bridge tower 3（指据点）stronghold for attack
【桥堍】qiáotù〈名〉either end of a bridge
【桥桩】qiáozhuāng〈名〉bridge pier

翘（翹）qiáo〈书〉

A〈动〉1（抬）raise: ▸～首，～望 2（不平）become twisted: 这块板～得厉害。 This board is badly warped.
B〈形〉outstanding: ▸～楚
▸qiào
【翘楚】qiáochǔ〈名〉〈书〉talented person: 医中～ eminent physician
【翘盼】qiáopàn〈动〉eagerly look forward to: ～春节到来 long for the Spring Festival
【翘企】qiáoqǐ〈动〉〈书〉eagerly look forward to: 不胜～ look forward to sth. with eager anticipation
【翘首】qiáoshǒu〈动〉〈书〉raise one's head and look: ～星空 look up at the starry sky ‖ ～瞻仰 look up at sth. with reverence ‖ ～以待 expect sth. to happen soon
【翘望】qiáowàng〈动〉1（抬头望）raise one's head and look 2（期盼）eagerly look forward to: ～亲人的到来 eagerly look forward to the arrival of one's family

谯（譙）qiáo

【谯楼】qiáolóu〈名〉〈古〉1（瞭望楼）watch tower 2（鼓楼）drum tower

鞒（鞽）qiáo〈名〉pommel and cantle of a saddle

憔 qiáo

【憔悴】qiáocuì〈形〉thin and pallid: 脸色～ haggard look ‖ 因过度劳累而形容～ look like a wreck from overwork

樵 qiáo

A〈名〉1〈书〉（木柴）firewood 2（打柴）woodcutter
B〈动〉〈书〉gather firewood: ▸～夫
【樵夫】qiáofū〈名〉woodcutter

瞧 qiáo〈动〉〈口〉look: ～一眼 have a look at ‖ ～，他来了！See, here he comes! ‖ 等着～吧。 Wait and see. ▸～见，～病

【瞧病】qiáobìng〈动〉〈口〉consult a doctor
【瞧不起】qiáobuqǐ〈动〉〈口〉look down on: ～别人 look down on other people ‖ 非常～ hold sb. in contempt ‖ 他～所有比他穷的人。 He treated everyone poorer than him with disdain.
【瞧不上眼】qiáobushàngyǎn〈动〉consider beneath one's notice
【瞧得起】qiáodeqǐ〈动〉〈口〉think highly of
【瞧见】qiáojiàn〈动〉〈口〉see: 我刚才～他出去了。 I saw him go out just now.
【瞧上】qiáoshang〈动〉〈口〉be to one's liking: 人家姑娘不一定瞧得上你。 The girl won't necessarily take a liking to you.

qiǎo

巧 qiǎo〈形〉1（有技术）clever: 这个机器人造得好～啊！What an ingenious robot this is! ▸～匠 2（灵巧）deft: 嘴～ be smooth-spoken ‖ 你的手很～。 You have deft hands. ▸心灵手～ 3（虚华）cunning: ▸～言令色，花言～语 4（正好）opportune: 来得真～ come just at the right time ‖ 在那儿遇到他真是～极了。 What a coincidence to meet him there! ▸～合

【巧辩】qiǎobiàn〈动〉argue skilfully or plausibly
【巧夺天工】qiǎoduó-tiāngōng〈成〉superb craftsmanship excelling nature: 这件象牙雕刻是～的珍品。 This ivory carving is an artistic treasure of supernatural workmanship.
【巧妇难为无米之炊】qiǎofù nán wéi wú mǐ zhī chuī〈俗〉〈喻〉one cannot make a silk purse out of a sow's ear
【巧干】qiǎogàn〈动〉work ingeniously
【巧合】qiǎohé〈动〉be coincidental: 如有雷同，纯属～。 Any similarity to real people is purely coincidental.
【巧计】qiǎojì〈名〉clever trick: 施～ use a clever trick
【巧匠】qiǎojiàng〈名〉master craftsman: ▸能工～
【巧劲儿】qiǎojìnr〈名〉〈方〉knack: 干这种活儿得使～。 There's a trick to the job.
【巧克力】qiǎokèlì〈名〉chocolate: ～蛋糕 chocolate cake ‖ 果仁～ nut chocolate
【巧立名目】qiǎolì-míngmù〈成〉concoct various excuses: ～乱收费 collect fees arbitrarily under all sorts of pretexts
【巧妙】qiǎomiào〈形〉clever: 构思～ be ingeniously conceived ‖ 对问题做出～的回答 give a neat reply to a question
【巧取豪夺】qiǎoqǔ-háoduó〈成〉take away by force or trickery
【巧舌如簧】qiǎoshé-rúhuáng〈成〉have a glib tongue: 这位政客～。 This politician is a smooth talker.
【巧手】qiǎoshǒu〈名〉1（指手）dexterous hands: 有一双～ be clever with one's hands 2（指人）dab hand: 绣花～ dab hand at embroidery
【巧言令色】qiǎoyán-lìngsè〈成〉flatter with artful speech and flashy manners: ～以惑众 mislead people with clever talk and an ingratiating manner
【巧遇】qiǎoyù〈动〉chance upon

悄 qiǎo〈形〉1（寂静）silent: ～无人迹 without a soul in sight ‖ 低声～语 speak in a low voice ▸～然 2〈书〉（担忧）sad

▸qiāo
【悄寂】qiǎojì〈形〉〈书〉quiet: 乡野一片～。 The countryside was completely still.
【悄然】qiǎorán〈形〉〈书〉1（忧愁）sad: ～落泪 shed tears of sorrow 2（寂静）quiet: ～离去 leave quietly
【悄声】qiǎoshēng〈名〉whisper: ～细语 talk in whispers ‖ 他蹑手蹑脚，～走进房间。 He tiptoed into the room.

雀 qiǎo〈名〉〈口〉sparrow: ▸家～儿

▸qiāo, què

愀 qiǎo

【愀然】qiǎorán〈形〉〈书〉1（严肃）stern: ～作色 become stern 2（不愉快）unhappy: ～不悦 look displeased

qiào

壳（殼）qiào〈名〉shell: ▸地～，金蝉脱～

▸ké
【壳菜】qiàocài〈名〉［动物］mussel

俏 qiào

A〈形〉1（好看）good-looking: 打扮得真～ be smartly dressed ‖ 她的发型做得很～。 Her hair is stylishly done. ▸～丽，俊～ 2（畅销）fast-selling: 行情看～。 A rising market is expected. ‖ 这种货卖得很～。 This product is in great demand. ▸～货，紧～，走～
B〈动〉〈方〉season: 给菜～点儿糖 season the dish with some sugar
【俏货】qiàohuò〈名〉fast-selling goods
【俏丽】qiàolì〈形〉good-looking: 容貌～ be good-looking
【俏皮】qiàopi〈形〉1（好看）good-looking: 这身装束使她看上去很～。 She looked smart in this dress. 2（机敏）witty: 他的话说得很～。 His remarks are full of wit and humour.
【俏皮话】qiàopihuà〈名〉1（指讽刺）sarcastic remarks 2（风趣）witty remarks: 他爱说～。 He loves to come out with wisecracks. 3 = 歇后语 xiēhòuyǔ
【俏头】qiàotou〈名〉1（指烹调）seasoning 2［戏曲］tricks to gain applause
【俏销】qiàoxiāo〈动〉sell well: ～全国 sell well all over the country ‖ ～商品 marketable commodity

诮（誚）qiào〈动〉〈书〉1（责备）blame: ～责 reproach 2（讥讽）ridicule: ▸讥～

帩 qiào

【帩头】qiàotóu〈名〉〈古〉scarf worn by men to tie up the hair

峭 qiào〈形〉1（陡峭）steep: ▸～壁，峻～ 2〈书〉（严厉）stern: ▸～直，冷～

【峭拔】qiàobá〈形〉1（指山）precipitous: 山峰～ towering peaks ‖ 山势～ high and precipitous mountains 2（指文笔）vigorous: 笔锋～ have a vigorous writing style
【峭壁】qiàobì〈名〉cliff: ▸悬崖～
【峭寒】qiàohán〈形〉chilly
【峭立】qiàolì〈动〉rise steeply: ～的山峰 steep mountain peak ‖ 岩石～ steep rock
【峭厉】qiàolì〈形〉〈书〉[of wind, cold air, etc.] bitter
【峭直】qiàozhí〈形〉〈书〉upright and stern: 秉性～ be upright and stern by nature

窍（竅） qiào〈名〉**1**（窟窿）aperture in the human body: 吓得灵魂出～ be scared out of one's wits ▸鬼迷心～, 七～ **2**〈喻〉（关键）knack: ▸～门, 诀～

【窍门】qiàomén〈名〉 knack: 找～ try to find the trick (to doing sth.) ‖ 做这事有个～。 There is a clever way to do this.

翘（翹） qiào〈动〉〈口〉stick up: 麻雀～起了尾巴。 The sparrow stuck its tail up. ‖ 她轻蔑地～起了嘴唇。 She curled up her lips in a sneer.
▸qiáo

【翘辫子】qiào biànzi ▸**p. 772**〈动〉〈诙〉 kick the bucket: 他说不定哪一天就会～。 He could kick the bucket any day now.

【翘尾巴】qiào wěiba〈动〉〈口〉〈喻〉become stuck-up: 不要取得一点成绩就～。 Don't let a little success go to your head.

撬 qiào〈动〉 prise: ～保险箱 crack a safe ‖ ～锁 pick a lock ‖ 用镐～起一块石头 prise up a stone with a pickaxe

【撬杠】qiàogàng〈名〉 crowbar

鞘 qiào〈名〉**1**（剑套）sheath: 把剑插入剑～ put a sword in its sheath ‖ 刀出～ take a knife out of a sheath **2**（鞘状物）sheath-shaped thing: ▸～翅, 腱～
▸shāo

【鞘翅】qiàochì〈名〉［昆虫］ elytron: ～甲虫 shard beetle

qiē

切 qiē〈动〉**1**（分割）cut: ～菜 cut up vegetables ‖ ～蛋糕 cut a cake ‖ 小心别～了手。 Be careful not to cut your hand. ▸～除, ～片, ～削 **2**（隔断）cut off: ～断电源 cut off the electricity ‖ ～断敌人的退路 cut short the enemy's retreat route **3**［数学］ be tangent: 两圆相～。 The two circles are tangent. ▸～点, ～线
▸qiè

【切变】qiēbiàn〈名〉［物理］ shear

【切菜板】qiēcàibǎn〈名〉 chopping board

【切草机】qiēcǎojī〈名〉 hay cutter

【切除】qiēchú〈动〉［医学］ excise: ～发炎的阑尾 remove an inflamed appendix ‖ ～手术 surgical resection ‖ 胃～ gastrectomy

【切磋】qiēcuō〈动〉 compare notes: 有空儿咱俩～～棋艺。 When you have time, let's play chess and see what we can learn from each other.

【切磋琢磨】qiēcuō-zhuómó〈成〉〈喻〉study and learn by mutual discussion

【切点】qiēdiǎn〈名〉［数学］ point of tangency

【切断】qiēduàn〈动〉 cut off: ～电力/食品/水的供应 cut off the electricity/food/water supply ‖ ～联系 cut off communication ‖ ～退路 cut off sb.'s retreat

【切分音】qiēfēnyīn〈名〉［音乐］ syncopation

【切腹自杀】qiēfù zìshā〈动〉 commit hara-kiri

【切糕】qiēgāo〈名〉 rice cake sold in sliced pieces

【切割】qiēgē〈动〉**1**（用刀具）cut: ～成片 cut into slices ‖ ～机 cutter **2**（用机床）cut metal: ～金属 cut through metal ‖ 电弧～ arc cutting

【切花】qiēhuā〈名〉cut flowers: 鲜～ freshly cut flowers

【切换】qiēhuàn〈动〉 cut: ～镜头 cut from one shot to another ‖ ～输入法 switch input modes

【切汇】qiēhuì〈动〉 deduct a sum by a black market money changer from a foreign exchange transaction

【切口】qiēkǒu〈名〉［印刷］ margin
▸qièkǒu

【切面】qiēmiàn〈名〉**1**（指面条）machine-made noodles **2** = 剖面 pōumiàn

【切片】qiēpiàn **A**〈动〉 cut into slices: 把羊肉～ slice mutton ‖ ～面包 sliced bread **B**〈名〉［医学］ section: 做～检查 cut sections of organic tissue for microscopic examination

【切片机】qiēpiànjī〈名〉slicer: 食品～ food slicer

【切入】qiērù〈动〉 penetrate: ～正题 come to the main theme ‖ ～点 point of penetration

【切线】qiēxiàn〈名〉［数学］tangent: ～坐标 tangential coordinates

【切削】qiēxiāo〈动〉［机械］ cut: ～工具 cutting tool ‖ 金属～ metal cutting

【切纸刀】qiēzhǐdāo〈名〉 paper cutter

qié

伽 qié
▸gā, jiā

【伽蓝】qiélán〈名〉 Buddhist temple

【伽南香】qiénánxiāng = 沉香 chénxiāng

茄 qié〈名〉 aubergine〈英〉; eggplant〈美〉: ～盒 stuffed aubergine slices ‖ ～泥 mashed aubergine
▸jiā

【茄子】qiézi〈名〉 aubergine〈英〉; eggplant〈美〉

qiě

且[1] qiě〈副〉**1**（暂且）for the time being: ～听下回分解 to be continued ‖ 价钱多少～不说，东西得好。 Let's not talk about the price for the time being, but the goods have got to be quality. ▸得过～过, 暂～ **2**〈口〉（长久）for a long time: 他～来不了呢。 It'll be a while before he comes.

且[2] qiě〈连〉**1**（表并列）both ... and ...: 她既漂亮～十分聪明。 She is both pretty and smart. ‖ 这本书既有趣～有教育意义。 The book is both interesting and instructive. ▸而～ **2**（表递进）moreover: 这衣服太贵，～尺寸也不合适。 This garment is too expensive and anyway it doesn't fit me. ▸况～ **3**（表同时）while: ～歌～舞 sing and dance at the same time ‖ ～战～退 keep fighting whilst beating a retreat **4**（表让步） even: 死～不怕，困难又算什么？ If even death holds no fear for us, how could mere difficulties? ▸尚～
▸jū

【且不说】qiěbùshuō〈惯〉 not to mention: ～你的本事有多大，就你这种态度人家也不会要你。 Even though you are so capable, they won't hire you because of your attitude.

【且慢】qiěmàn〈动〉 wait a moment: ～，请听我把话说完。 Wait a moment. Please hear me out.

【且说】qiěshuō〈动〉 let's begin with ... [a stock phrase used in old Chinese novels or stories to introduce a new episode]

qiè

切 qiè
A〈动〉**1**（靠近）be close to: ▸～肤之痛, ～身 **2**（符合）correspond to: 不～实际的要求 unrealistic request ▸～合, ～实, ～题 **3**（摸脉）feel the pulse: ▸～脉, 望闻问～
B〈形〉 eager: 回家心～ be anxious to get home ▸急～, 迫～
C〈副〉 must: ～不可粗心大意 be sure to be careful ‖ 对此～不可掉以轻心。 We must never treat this lightly. ▸～记, ～忌
D ▸反切 fǎnqiè

> 切
> ▸望、闻、问、切

▸qiē

【切齿】qièchǐ〈动〉 gnash one's teeth: ～痛恨 hate bitterly ‖ 令人～ make sb.'s blood boil ▸咬牙～

【切当】qièdàng〈形〉 appropriate: 措词～ be appropriately worded

【切肤之痛】qièfūzhītòng〈成〉 acute pain: 他对邪教的危害有～。 He has bitter memories of the harm caused by the evil cult.

【切骨】qiègǔ〈形〉 to the bone: ～之寒 piercing cold

【切骨之仇】 qiègǔzhīchóu 〈成〉 bitter hatred

【切合】qièhé〈动〉 fit in with: ～实际 be geared to actual circumstances ‖ ～消费者的需要 suit the needs of the consumers

【切记】qièjì〈动〉 be sure to bear in mind: ～不要骄傲。 Always guard against arrogance.

【切忌】qièjì〈动〉 be sure not to do sth.: ～盲目跟风 avoid blindly following the crowd ‖ ～饮酒过度。 Be sure to avoid excessive drinking.

【切近】qièjìn **A**〈形〉 close: 要实现远大的理想，必须从～处做起。 In order to realize long-term ambitions, it is necessary to start close to home first. **B**〈动〉 be close to: ～生活 be life-like ‖ 这样释义比较～原诗本意。 This paraphrasing seems closer to the original meaning of the poem.

【切口】qièkǒu〈名〉 jargon: 盗贼的～ thieves' slang
▸qiēkǒu

【切脉】qièmài〈动〉［中医］ feel the pulse: ～听诊 feel sb.'s pulse and listen to his breathing

【切莫】qièmò〈副〉〈书〉 sure not to do sth.

【切盼】qièpàn〈动〉 yearn for: ～回复。 I'm longing for your reply.

【切切】qièqiè **A**〈副〉 must: ～不可忘记。 Be sure not to forget. **B**〈形〉**1**（表再三告诫） serious: ～此令。 This order is to be strictly observed. **2**（诚恳） eager: ～请求 earnestly request **3** = 窃窃 qièqiè A

【切身】qièshēn〈形〉**1**（与己相关） personal: ～大事 matter of deep personal concern ‖ ～利益 immediate interests **2**（亲身） first-hand: ～体会 first-hand understanding ‖ ～体验 personal experience

【切实】qièshí〈形〉**1**（切合实际） practical: ～可行的解决办法 a down-to-earth, practical solution ‖ ～有效 be practical and effective **2**（实实在在） conscientious: ～做好工作 do one's job conscientiously ‖

～履行诺言 carry out one's promise in earnest

【切实可行】qièshí-kěxíng〈惯〉practicable: ～的解决办法 workable solution

【切题】qiètí〈动〉be relevant to the subject: 你的回答不～。 Your answer is beside the point. ‖ 这段文字不～。 This paragraph is off topic.

【切勿】qièwù〈副〉sure not to do sth.: ～酒后驾车 be sure not to drive after drinking

【切要】qièyào〈形〉〈书〉vital: ～之举 indispensable measure

【切音】qièyīn〈动〉［语言］use two Chinese characters to represent the pronunciation of a third character

【切诊】qièzhěn〈名〉［中医］pulse feeling and palpation

【切中】qièzhòng〈动〉hit the mark: ～要害 strike home ‖ 他的话～要害。 His remarks struck home.

【切中时弊】qièzhòng-shíbì〈成〉make a cutting analysis of current social evils: 这篇文章～。 The article made a cutting attack on present-day evils.

妾 qiè〈名〉1〈旧〉（小老婆）concubine: 纳～ take a concubine 2〈古〉〈谦〉（女子自称）（作主语）I;（作宾语）me

怯 qiè〈形〉1（胆小）timid: 她腼腆，～于开口。 Shyness inhibited her from speaking. ▸～场, ～懦, 胆～ 2〈口〉（俗气）vulgar: 这种颜色有点～。 This colour is a bit vulgar. 3〈方〉〈贬〉（指口音）rustic: 说话～ speak with a rustic accent 4〈方〉（外行）ignorant: ▸露～

【怯场】qièchǎng〈动〉suffer from stage fright: 她因为～而忘了台词。 She forgot her lines because of stage fright.

【怯懦】qiènuò〈形〉cowardly: 生性～ be timid by nature

【怯弱】qièruò〈形〉timid and weak-willed: 生性～ have a timid and weak-willed nature

【怯生】qièshēng〈形〉〈方〉shy with strangers: 孩子有点～。 Children are a bit shy of strangers.

【怯生生】qièshēngshēng〈形〉timid and shy: 一副～的样子 be timid-looking

【怯声怯气】qièshēng-qièqì〈成〉speak timidly and nervously: ～地说话 speak haltingly

【怯阵】qièzhèn〈动〉1〈本〉be battle-shy 2〈喻〉（怯场）have stage fright

窃（竊）qiè

A〈动〉1（偷）steal: ▸～案, 盗～, 行～ 2（非法占有）usurp: ▸～夺, ～取, 剽～
B〈名〉thief: ▸惯～
C〈副〉1〈书〉〈谦〉（表自己）personally: ～以为 in my humble opinion 2（暗中）secretly: ▸～听, ～喜, ～笑

【窃案】qiè'àn〈名〉burglary: ～发生后应尽快报警。 You should contact the police as soon as possible after a burglary.

【窃夺】qièduó〈动〉usurp: ～权力 usurp power

【窃国】qièguó〈动〉usurp state power: ～大盗 arch usurper of state power

【窃据】qièjù〈动〉usurp: ～要职 usurp a key post

【窃密】qièmì〈动〉steal secrets

【窃窃】qièqiè A〈形〉whispering: ～交谈 converse with sb. in whisper ▸～私语 B〈副〉secretly: ～自喜 feel secretly glad

【窃窃私语】qièqiè-sīyǔ〈成〉whisper: 对着某人的耳朵～ whisper into sb.'s ear

【窃取】qièqǔ〈动〉steal: ～国家机密 steal state secrets ‖ ～情报 steal secret information ‖ ～职位 usurp an official position

【窃听】qiètīng〈动〉eavesdrop: ～电话 bug a telephone ‖ ～器 tapping device

【窃喜】qièxǐ〈动〉be secretly delighted

【窃笑】qièxiào〈动〉chuckle to oneself

【窃贼】qièzéi〈名〉thief: 抓捕～ capture a thief

挈 qiè〈动〉〈书〉1（举）raise: ▸提纲～领 2（带领）take along: 他～眷返回故里。 He went back to his native place, taking his family along with him. ▸提～

【挈带】qièdài〈动〉take along: ～家眷 take one's family along

惬（愜）qiè〈形〉〈书〉1（满足）satisfied: ～如人意 be satisfactory ‖ 未～人意 be unsatisfactory ▸～意 2（恰当）appropriate: ▸～当

【惬当】qièdàng〈形〉〈书〉apt: 其言～ appropriate in language

【惬怀】qièhuái〈形〉〈书〉pleased: 甚为～ feel very satisfied

【惬意】qièyì〈形〉satisfied: ～的环境 agreeable environment ‖ 天气凉爽，让人感到～。 It was pleasantly cool.

趄 qiè

A〈动〉slant: ～着身子 lean sideways ‖ ～坡 slope
B ▸趔趄 lièqie

▸jū

慊 qiè〈动〉〈书〉be satisfied

▸qiàn

锲（鍥）qiè〈动〉〈书〉engrave

【锲而不舍】qiè'érbùshě〈成〉〈喻〉keep on chipping away: ～地致力于研究 keep plodding away at one's research

箧（篋）qiè〈名〉〈旧〉small suitcase: 藤～ wicker suitcase

qīn

钦（欽）qīn

A〈动〉respect: ▸～敬, ～佩, ～仰
B〈副〉by the emperor himself: ▸～差, ～定

【钦差】qīnchāi〈名〉imperial envoy

【钦差大臣】qīnchāi dàchén〈名〉1（钦差）imperial envoy 2（上级派来的人）nickname for a representative of the higher authorities with full powers

【钦定】qīndìng〈动〉be made by imperial order

【钦敬】qīnjìng〈动〉admire and respect: 令人～ command admiration and respect ‖ 向英雄们表示～之意 show respect and admiration to the heroes

【钦慕】qīnmù〈动〉respect and admire: 表达～之情 express admiration

【钦佩】qīnpèi〈动〉admire: 令人～ command respect ‖ 极为～ admire greatly

【钦羡】qīnxiàn〈动〉respect and admire: 对她的成就～不已 have enormous respect and admiration for her success ‖ 投以～的目光 cast sb. an admiring glance

【钦仰】qīnyǎng〈动〉〈书〉revere: 充满～之情 be filled with veneration

侵 qīn〈动〉1（侵入）invade: ▸～犯, ～蚀, 入～ 2〈书〉（接近）approach: ～晨 the approach of daybreak

【侵夺】qīnduó〈动〉seize by force: ～国有资产 encroach upon state assets

【侵犯】qīnfàn〈动〉1（损害他人权利）violate: ～人权 violate human rights ‖ ～新闻/出版自由 make inroads into the freedom of the press ‖ ～人身/财产罪 offences against the person/property 2（侵入）intrude into: ～别国领海/领空 encroach upon another nation's territorial waters/air space ‖ 我们的领土神圣不可～。 Our territory is sacred and safe from attack.

【侵害】qīnhài〈动〉encroach upon and damage: 防止棉铃虫～棉花 prevent ball worms from getting into and damaging the cotton ‖ 不得～公众利益。 Do not damage the interests of the populace.

【侵略】qīnlüè〈动〉invade: 保卫国家不受～ protect the country against invasion ‖ 经济/文化～ economic/cultural invasion ‖ 武装～ armed aggression ‖ ～者 invader

【侵权】qīnquán〈动〉［法律］infringe on sb.'s rights: ～行为 tort

【侵扰】qīnrǎo〈动〉invade and harass: ～边境 make border raids ‖ 受到蚊子～ be infested with mosquitoes

【侵人犯规】qīnrénfànguī〈名〉［体育］personal foul

【侵入】qīnrù〈动〉invade: ～别国领土 make incursions into another country's territory ‖ ～机体 invade an organism ‖ 外国资本的～ invasion of foreign capital

【侵蚀】qīnshí〈动〉1（腐蚀）corrode: 抵制腐朽思想的～ resist the corrosive influence of decadent ideology ‖ 遭到风雨～ suffer erosion from wind and rain ‖ 酸能～铁。 Acid corrodes iron. 2（一点点侵占）embezzle bit by bit, encroach upon/on: ～公款 embezzle public funds

【侵吞】qīntūn〈动〉1（指财产）embezzle: ～国家财产 embezzle state property 2（指国土）annex: ～别国领土 annex another country's territory

【侵袭】qīnxí〈动〉invade and attack: 遭受洪水/寒流/沙尘暴～ be hit by a flood/cold current/sandstorm ‖ 沿海地区常遭台风～。 The coastal areas are often hit by typhoons.

【侵越】qīnyuè〈动〉overstep one's authority

【侵占】qīnzhàn〈动〉1（占有）seize: ～他人财产 encroach on other people's property ‖ ～公有土地 seize public land ‖ ～他人权益 interlope 2（入侵）invade and occupy: ～别国领土 invade and occupy another country's territory

亲（親）qīn

A〈形〉1（亲密）close: 我和她很～。 She is very dear to me. ▸～爱, ～近 2（有血缘关系）related by blood: ～姐妹 blood sisters ‖ ～兄弟 blood brothers
B〈名〉1（父母）parent: ▸父～, 母～, 双～ 2（亲戚）relative: ▸～戚, 大义灭～ 3（婚姻）marriage: ▸～事, 定～ 4（新娘）bride: ▸娶～, 送～, 迎～
C〈动〉1〈书〉（亲近）fraternize with: ～华 pro-Chinese ‖ ～美 pro-American 2（亲吻）kiss: ～脸 kiss sb. on the cheek ▸～吻, ～嘴
D〈副〉personally: ～耳听见 hear with one's own ears ▸～口, ～手, ～自

▸qìng

q

q

【亲爱】qīn'ài〈形〉beloved: ～的祖国 one's beloved country/homeland ‖ ～的朋友 dear friend ‖ ～的 my dear

【亲本】qīnběn〈名〉［生物］ parent: ～鸟 parent bird

【亲笔】qīnbǐ **A**〈动〉write in one's own hand: ～签名 sign an autograph ‖ ～信 personally handwritten letter ‖ 这信是他～写的。He wrote the letter in/with his own hand. **B**〈名〉one's own handwriting: 这是他的～。This is his handwriting.

【亲传】qīnchuán〈动〉impart personally: ～弟子 one's own disciple

【亲代】qīndài〈名〉［生物］ parental generation

【亲睹】qīndǔ〈动〉witness personally

【亲骨肉】qīngǔròu〈名〉one's own flesh and blood: 他是我的～，我无法拒绝他。I couldn't reject him because he was my own flesh and blood.

【亲故】qīngù〈名〉relatives and old friends: 遍寻～ search everywhere for one's relatives and old friends

【亲和力】qīnhélì〈名〉affinity: 盐和水有～。Salt has an affinity for water. ‖ 她毫无～可言。Nobody is very drawn to her.

【亲近】qīnjìn **A**〈形〉intimate: ～的朋友 close friend ‖ 他跟爸爸最～。His closest relationship is with his father. **B**〈动〉try to be friends with sb.: 他设法～她，但屡遭拒绝。He tried to get friendly with her but was rejected every time.

【亲眷】qīnjuàn〈名〉**1**（亲戚）one's relatives **2**（眷属）one's family dependants

【亲口】qīnkǒu〈副〉personally: ～尝尝 taste with one's own mouth ‖ 这是她～告诉我的。She told this to me herself.

【亲历】qīnlì〈动〉〈书〉experience personally: 未曾～其境 have never had personal experience of the scene

【亲临】qīnlín〈动〉go to a place personally: ～现场 go personally to the scene ‖ ～指导 come personally to give guidance

【亲密】qīnmì〈形〉close: ～的战友 close comrade-in-arms ‖ 他俩关系越来越～。The two of them became more and more intimate.

【亲密无间】qīnmì-wújiàn〈成〉be on intimate terms with each other: ～的老朋友 old friends on very intimate terms

【亲昵】qīnnì〈形〉affectionate: ～的称呼 affectionate form of address

【亲朋】qīnpéng〈名〉relatives and friends: ～好友 one's relatives and close friends

【亲朋满座】qīnpéng-mǎnzuò〈成〉the place is thronged with relatives and friends

【亲戚】qīnqi〈名〉relative: 走～ go to see a relation ‖ 远房～ distant relative ‖ 我们两家是～。Our two families are related.

【亲启】qīnqǐ〈动〉[of letter] to be opened personally

【亲切】qīnqiè〈形〉**1**（亲密）dear: 他的话使我们感到很～。What he said touched our hearts. **2**（关切）kind: ～的关怀 loving care ‖ 会谈在～友好的气氛中进行。The talks were held in a cordial and friendly atmosphere.

【亲情】qīnqíng〈名〉affection: 骨肉～ affection between blood relations

【亲热】qīnrè **A**〈形〉warm-hearted: ～地问长问短 make affectionate inquiries about sb.'s health, etc. ‖ 我们都～地称她为大姐。We all affectionately refer to her as our elder sister. **B**〈动〉show affection through action: 每次回到家，他总要先和儿子～一会儿。Whenever he gets home, he likes first to give his son a little cuddle.

【亲人】qīnrén〈名〉**1**（有亲属关系）one's own flesh and blood: ～团聚 reunite with one's family and relatives ‖ 他除母亲外没有别的～。His only close relative is his mother. **2**〈喻〉（无亲属关系）beloved: 他一直像对待～一样待我。He's always treated me as if I were a member of his family.

【亲如手足】qīnrúshǒuzú〈成〉be as close as brothers

【亲如一家】qīnrúyījiā〈成〉be as dear to each other as members of one family

【亲善】qīnshàn〈形〉close and friendly: ～大使 goodwill ambassador ‖ 两邻国间的～睦邻关系 friendly relations between two neighbouring countries

【亲上加亲】qīnshàngjiāqīn〈名〉become more closely related through marriage

【亲身】qīnshēn〈形〉personal: ～经历 experience personally ‖ ～感受 first-hand experience

【亲生】qīnshēng〈形〉biological: ～父母 one's biological parents ‖ 他们把这个孩子当作自己的～子女来抚养。They have cherished the child as one of their own.

【亲事】qīnshi〈名〉marriage: 她妈同意了这门～。Her mother assented to the marriage.

【亲手】qīnshǒu〈副〉personally: ～处理此事 handle the work personally ‖ 我得～交给他。I have to hand it to him in person.

【亲疏】qīn-shū〈形〉[of relatives or social connections] close or distant: 不分～ make no distinction between close associates and mere acquaintances

【亲属】qīnshǔ〈名〉family: ～关系 family ties ‖ 她不是我的～。She isn't any relation to me. ▸旁系～, 直系～

【亲水】qīnshuǐ〈形〉**1**［化学］ hydrophilic **2**（指近水）by the water: ～住宅 waterfront housing

【亲水性】qīnshuǐxìng〈名〉［化学］ hydrophilicity

【亲痛仇快】qīntòng-chóukuài〈成〉grieve one's own people and gladden the enemy: 不做～之事 not to do anything that hurts your nearest and dearest and benefits the enemy only

【亲王】qīnwáng〈名〉prince: ～府 prince's residence ‖ 威尔士～ Prince of Wales

【亲吻】qīnwěn〈动〉kiss: ～脸颊 kiss sb. on the cheek ‖ 一次又一次的～ kiss again and again

【亲信】qīnxìn **A**〈动〉be close to and trust sb.: ～小人 be in cahoots with vile characters **B**〈名〉〈贬〉henchman: 培植～ cultivate one's favourite

亲属称谓

汉语和英语的亲属称谓有很大的不同。与汉语的称谓相比，英语的称谓要简单得多。这一方面反映了西方以小家庭为主的社会特征，另一方面也反映了西方的文化特点。英语亲属称谓只根据辈分、直系／旁系和男／女 3 个参数区分，对 cousin 这一组亲属的称谓，更连男／女都不再区分。汉语亲属称谓则有 5 个参数，包括辈分、直系／旁系、男／女、长／幼和父系／母系。下表给出了英汉亲属称谓的一些例子，以比较中西方文化中亲属称谓的不同：

汉语称谓	英语称谓
祖父／爷爷 外祖父／外公	grandfather
祖母／奶奶 外祖母／外婆	grandmother
孙子 外孙	grandson
孙女 外孙女	granddaughter
伯父 叔父 姑父 舅父 姨夫	uncle
伯母 叔母／婶 姑母／姑妈 舅母／舅妈 姨母／姨妈	aunt

汉语称谓	英语称谓
哥哥 弟弟	brother
姐姐 妹妹	sister
姐夫 妹夫	brother-in-law
嫂子 弟妹	sister-in-law

汉语称谓	英语称谓
堂哥 堂弟 堂姐 堂妹 姑表哥 姑表弟 姑表姐 姑表妹 舅表哥 舅表弟 舅表姐 舅表妹 姨表哥 姨表弟 姨表姐 姨表妹	cousin

【亲兄弟，明算账】qīnxiōngdì, míngsuànzhàng〈俗〉even among brothers, accounts should be settled without ambiguity
【亲眼】qīnyǎn〈副〉with one's own eyes: ～所见 see with one's own eyes
【亲眼目睹】qīnyǎn-mùdǔ〈成〉witness with one's own eyes: 要不是～，我还不信呢。If I had not seen it for myself, I wouldn't have believed it.
【亲友】qīnyǒu〈名〉friends and family: 已故～ relatives and friends who have passed away
【亲友团】qīnyǒutuán〈名〉group of friends and relatives: 到场助威的有粉丝团、～。Groups of fans, friends and relatives came to the scene to offer support.
【亲缘】qīnyuán〈名〉［生物］blood relation: ～关系 blood relationship
【亲者痛，仇者快】qīn zhě tòng, chóu zhě kuài = 亲痛仇快 qīntòng-chóukuài
【亲征】qīnzhēng〈动〉[of an emperor] personally lead a military expedition
【亲政】qīnzhèng〈动〉〈旧〉assume the reins of government upon coming of age
【亲子鉴定】qīnzǐ jiàndìng〈名〉paternity test
【亲自】qīnzì〈副〉personally: ～出马 attend to the matter personally ‖ ～动手 do the job oneself
【亲族】qīnzú〈名〉members of the same family: 柠檬和酸橙是～。There is a close affinity between lemons and limes.
【亲嘴】qīnzuǐ〈动〉kiss sb. on the lips

衾 qīn
〈名〉〈书〉**1**（被子）quilt **2**（裹尸布）cover for the dead

骎（駸）qīn
【骎骎】qīnqīn〈形〉〈书〉galloping:〈喻〉我国的现代化建设～日上。Our modernization drive is galloping ahead.

嵚 qīn
【嵚崟】qīnyín〈形〉〈书〉[of a mountain] high and steep

qín

芹 qín
〈名〉celery
【芹菜】qíncài〈名〉celery

芩 qín
▸黄芩 huángqín

矜 qín
〈名〉〈古〉handle of a spear ▸guān, jīn

秦 Qín
〈名〉**1**（指国名）Qin [state in the Zhou Dynasty] **2**（秦朝）Qin Dynasty: ～兵马俑 Terracotta Warriors and Horses of the Qin Dynasty **3** ▸**p. 661**（指地域）Qin [another name for Shaanxi (陕西) and Gansu (甘肃) provinces (esp Shaanxi)]: ～时明月汉时关。The age-old moon still shines over the ancient Great Wall. ▸～腔
【秦艽】qínjiāo〈名〉［植物］large-leaved gentian
【秦晋】Qín-Jìn〈名〉**1**（指国家）Qin and Jin [two states during the Eastern Zhou Dynasty] **2**〈喻〉（指婚姻）matrimonial alliance between two families
【秦晋之好】Qín-Jìn zhī hǎo〈成〉alliance formed between two families through marriage: 两家结了～。The two families formed a union through marriage.
【秦岭】Qínlǐng〈名〉Qinling Mountains
【秦楼楚馆】Qínlóu-Chǔguǎn〈成〉brothels
【秦腔】qínqiāng〈名〉Shaanxi opera

> **秦腔**
> *Qingqiang*, a traditional opera, popular in Shaanxi and Gansu as well as parts of neighbouring provinces. The opera features clappers called *bangzi* (梆子), which are used to beat time. The pitch of singing is high and intense, with a distinctive rhythm, and it displays a great range of emotions. The libretto consists of seven words to a line. Well-known traditional theatrical pieces include *Three Drops of Blood* (《三滴血》), and *The Orphan of Zhao Family* (《赵氏孤儿》), amongst others.

【秦始皇】Qín Shǐhuáng〈名〉［历史］Emperor Qin Shihuang [259-210 BC, the first emperor in Chinese history, who unified China in 221 BC]

> **秦始皇**
> The founding emperor of the Qin Dynasty who, between 230-221 BC, brought to an end the rivalries of the Warring States, establishing the first centrally-controlled kingdom in Chinese history. Qin Shihuang unified the legal system and standardized currency, weights and measures, as well as the written language. He also constructed the Great Wall (▸长城) that stretches from present-day Gansu Province to the area east of the Liao River. Qin Shihuang was notorious for burning many books, and for having more than 460 Confucian scholars and alchemists buried alive (known as 焚书坑儒).

【秦俑】Qínyǒng〈名〉Terracotta Warriors and Horses of the Qin Dynasty

琴 qín
〈名〉**1** = 古琴 gǔqín **2**（指乐器）certain musical instruments: ▸风～, 钢～, 提～
【琴拨】qínbō〈名〉plectrum
【琴凳】qíndèng〈名〉piano stool
【琴弓】qíngōng〈名〉bow
【琴拱】qíngǒng〈名〉arm of a stringed instrument
【琴键】qínjiàn〈名〉key: 钢琴～ piano keys
【琴马】qínmǎ〈名〉［音乐］bridge (of a stringed instrument)
【琴鸟】qínniǎo〈名〉［鸟类］lyrebird
【琴棋书画】qín-qí-shū-huà〈成〉music, chess, calligraphy, and painting [accomplishments of a scholar of the old school]
【琴瑟】qínsè〈名〉〈喻〉marital harmony: ～不调 discord between husband and wife ‖ ～和谐 live in wedded bliss
【琴师】qínshī ▸**p. 966**〈名〉fiddler
【琴书】qínshū〈名〉story-telling, mainly in songs, with musical accompaniment
【琴弦】qínxián〈名〉string of a musical instrument

禽 qín
〈名〉**1**〈书〉（鸟兽）birds and beasts: ▸五～戏 **2**（鸟类）fowl: ～蛋产品 poultry and egg products ▸家～, 珍～异兽
【禽流感】qínliúgǎn〈名〉bird flu: ～病毒 bird flu virus
【禽舍】qínshè〈名〉poultry housing
【禽兽】qínshòu〈名〉**1**〈本〉birds and beasts **2**〈喻〉beast: ～之行 beast conduct ▸衣冠～

勤 qín
A〈形〉**1**（辛劳）hard-working: ～于收集材料 be industrious in the collection of materials ▸～快, ～劳 **2**（频繁）frequent: ～查字典 constantly refer to the dictionary ‖ ～洗～换 change and wash regularly ‖ 来得～ come frequently
B〈名〉**1**（勤务）hard work: ▸～务, 后～ **2**（出席）attendance: ▸出～, 考～, 执～
【勤奋】qínfèn〈形〉hard-working: 工作～ work with diligence ‖ ～好学 be hard-working and eager to learn
【勤工俭学】qíngōng-jiǎnxué〈成〉**1**（工读）part-work and part-study: 靠～读完大学 work one's way through college **2**（指办学形式）work-study programme
【勤俭】qínjiǎn〈形〉hard-working and thrifty: ～过日子 lead an industrious and frugal life ‖ ～持家 manage one's household with industry and thrift
【勤俭节约】qínjiǎn-jiéyuē〈成〉be diligent and thrifty
【勤谨】qínjin〈形〉〈方〉hard-working: 他一向很～。He's always been a hard worker.
【勤恳】qínkěn〈形〉diligent and conscientious: 工作～ be painstaking with one's work ‖ 勤勤恳恳为人民服务 serve the people heart and soul
【勤苦】qínkǔ〈形〉diligent: ～练习 practise assiduously ‖ 他一天到晚在～工作。He plods away all day long.
【勤快】qínkuai〈形〉〈口〉hard-working: 他手脚～，一刻也不闲着。He is diligent and busy with work all the time.
【勤劳】qínláo〈形〉hard-working: ～勇敢的中国人民 hard-working and courageous Chinese people ‖ ～致富 become rich through hard work ‖ ～的双手 a pair of untiring hands
【勤勉】qínmiǎn〈形〉diligent: 工作～ be diligent about one's work ‖ ～好学 be hard-working and eager to learn
【勤能补拙】qínnéngbǔzhuō〈成〉hard work can make up for lack of talent
【勤朴】qínpǔ〈形〉industrious and simple
【勤王】qínwáng〈动〉〈古〉**1**（指援救）come to the rescue of the king: 发兵～ send troops to save the king **2**（指辅佐）do one's best to serve the king
【勤务】qínwù〈名〉**1**（指事务）public duties: 海上～ sea service ‖ ～兵 orderly **2**（指人）odd-job man in the army
【勤务员】qínwùyuán〈名〉**1** ▸**p. 966**〈本〉odd-job man **2**〈喻〉public servant: 人民的～ servant of the people
【勤学苦练】qínxué-kǔliàn〈成〉study diligently and train hard
【勤杂工】qínzágōng〈名〉odd-job man: 办公室的～ office boy
【勤杂人员】qínzá rényuán ▸**p. 966**〈名〉odd-job man
【勤政】qínzhèng〈动〉〈书〉practise diligent governance: ～为民 be diligent in government affairs and provide a good service for the people

嗪 qín
▸哌嗪 pàiqín

擒 qín
〈动〉capture: ▸～获, 生～, 束手就～
【擒获】qínhuò〈动〉capture: 当场～ catch sb. red-handed
【擒拿】qínná **A**〈名〉grip: ～技巧 wrestling hold **B**〈动〉capture: ～杀人犯 arrest the murderer

q

【擒贼擒王】qínzéi-qínwáng = 擒贼先擒王 qín zéi xiān qín wáng

【擒贼先擒王】qín zéi xiān qín wáng〈成〉if you want to round up the gang, you must get the chief first

【擒纵轮】qínzònglún〈名〉［机械］escape wheel

噙 qín〈动〉hold in the mouth/eyes: ～着烟袋 hold a pipe between one's lips ‖ 她眼里～着泪水。Her eyes were filled with tears.

檎 qín ▸ 林檎 línqín

qǐn

梫 qǐn〈名〉**1**〈古〉［植物］(Chinese) cinnamon tree **2** = 梫木 qǐnmù

【梫木】qǐnmù〈名〉Japanese andromeda

寝（寢） qǐn

A〈动〉**1**（睡）sleep: ▸～室，废～忘食 **2**〈书〉（停）end: 其事遂～。No more was heard of the matter thereafter.

B〈名〉**1**（卧室）bedroom: ▸就～, 寿终正～ **2**（坟墓）coffin chamber in an imperial mausoleum: ▸陵～

【寝车】qǐnchē〈名〉sleeper car

【寝宫】qǐngōng〈名〉**1**（指宫殿）sleeping quarters of the emperor and empress **2**（指坟墓）coffin chamber in an imperial mausoleum

【寝具】qǐnjù〈名〉〈书〉bedding

【寝食】qǐnshí〈名〉daily life: ～不安 have no peace of mind day or night

【寝室】qǐnshì〈名〉bedroom: 打扫～ clean one's room

qìn

吣 qìn〈动〉**1**（呕吐）vomit **2**〈方〉（谩骂）talk nonsense: 满嘴胡～ talk complete nonsense

沁 qìn〈动〉seep: 他的额上～出了汗珠。Beads of sweat oozed from his forehead. ▸～人心脾

【沁人肺腑】qìnrén-fèifǔ = 沁人心脾 qìnrén-xīnpí

【沁人心脾】qìnrén-xīnpí〈成〉be refreshing: 一大早空气清新，～。Fresh early morning air is so refreshing. ‖ 优美的乐曲～。The beautiful music puts everyone at ease.

【沁润】qìnrùn〈动〉permeate: 雨水～着大地。The rain soaked the earth.

揿（撳） qìn〈动〉〈方〉press: ～门铃 press a doorbell

qīng

青 qīng

A〈形〉**1** ▸**p. 863**（指颜色）**a**（蓝色）blue: 气得脸发～ be livid with rage ▸～出于蓝，～天，～苔 **b**（绿色）green **c**（黑色）black: ～布 black cloth ‖ 把某人打得～一块紫一块 beat sb. black and blue ▸～丝，～眼 **2**（年纪小）young: ▸～春，～年

B〈名〉**1**（指植物）sth. green: ▸返～，踏～ **2**（指年轻人）youth: ▸知～ **3** ▸**p. 661** Qīng（青海）Qing [another name for Qinghai Province]

【青帮】Qīngbāng〈名〉*Qingbang*, Green Gang [secret society in the Qing Dynasty]

【青碧】qīngbì ▸**p. 863**〈形〉**1**（深绿色）dark green: 峰峦～ dark green mountain peaks **2**（深蓝色）azure: 天空～ blue sky

【青菜】qīngcài〈名〉**1**（小白菜）a variety of Chinese cabbage **2**（蔬菜）greens

【青草】qīngcǎo〈名〉green grass

【青出于蓝】qīng chū yú lán〈成〉〈喻〉the pupil outdoes the teacher

【青出于蓝而胜于蓝】qīng chū yú lán ér shèng yú lán = 青出于蓝 qīng chū yú lán

【青春】qīngchūn〈名〉**1**（青年时期）youth: 把～献给祖国 dedicate one's youth to serving one's country ‖ 焕发～ regain one's youth ‖ ～常驻/永驻 permanent youthfulness ‖ ～依旧 keep one's youth **2**〈旧〉（指年龄）age of young people: 令爱～几何? How old is your daughter?

【青春痘】qīngchūndòu〈名〉acne

【青春饭】qīngchūnfàn〈名〉〈喻〉jobs appropriate for young people only

【青春偶像】qīngchūn ǒuxiàng〈名〉youth idol

【青春期】qīngchūnqī〈名〉puberty: 到～ reach puberty

【青瓷】qīngcí〈名〉celadon (ware)

【青葱】qīngcōng ▸**p. 863**〈形〉verdant: ～的草地 lush green meadows ‖ 山上草木～。The hills are covered with a lush green.

【青翠】qīngcuì ▸**p. 863**〈形〉verdant: 春天的山峦一片～。Spring green mantled the hills.

【青岛】Qīngdǎo〈名〉Qingdao

【青灯】qīngdēng〈名〉〈书〉oil lamp

【青豆】qīngdòu〈名〉green soya bean

【青蚨】qīngfú〈名〉〈书〉(copper) cash

【青光眼】qīngguāngyǎn ▸**p. 50**〈名〉［医学］glaucoma

【青果】qīngguǒ〈方〉= 橄榄 gǎnlǎn 1

【青海】Qīnghǎi ▸**p. 661**〈名〉Qinghai Province: ～湖 Qinghai Lake

【青红皂白】qīnghóng-zàobái〈成〉〈喻〉right and wrong: 警察不分～把他们统统抓走了。The police officers arrested all of them regardless of who was in the right or the wrong.

【青花瓷】qīnghuācí〈名〉blue-and-white porcelain

【青黄不接】qīnghuáng-bùjiē〈成〉〈喻〉temporary shortage of food, personnel, etc.: 现在科技人才～。There are not enough trained younger scientists ready to take over from the older experts.

【青灰】qīnghuī ▸**p. 863**〈名〉greenish lime

【青灰色】qīnghuīsè ▸**p. 863**〈名〉slate-grey

【青椒】qīngjiāo〈名〉green pepper: ～牛排 pepper steak

【青筋】qīngjīn〈名〉blue veins: ～暴突的双手 blue-veined hands

【青稞】qīngkē〈名〉**1**（指作物）highland barley **2**（指子实）seed of highland barley: ～酒 barley beer

【青睐】qīnglài〈动〉〈书〉show appreciation: 受到～ find favour with sb.

【青莲色】qīngliánsè ▸**p. 863**〈名〉pale purple

【青龙】qīnglóng〈名〉**1** = 苍龙 cānglóng 1 **2**（指神）Green Dragon [guardian spirit of the east in Taoism]

【青楼】qīnglóu〈名〉〈旧〉brothel: ～女子 prostitute

【青绿】qīnglǜ ▸**p. 863**〈形〉dark green: ～的松林 dark green pine forest

【青麻】qīngmá = 苘麻 qǐngmá

【青梅】qīngméi〈名〉green plum

【青梅竹马】qīngméi-zhúmǎ〈成〉childhood playmates: ～，两小无猜 be innocent playmates in childhood

【青霉素】qīngméisù〈名〉penicillin

【青面獠牙】qīngmiàn-liáoyá〈成〉hideous features: 露出～的凶相 reveal ferocious features

【青苗】qīngmiáo〈名〉unripe crops

【青年】qīngnián〈名〉**1** ▸**p. 526**（指年龄段）youth: ～时代 one's youth ‖ ～期 adolescence ‖ ～学生 young student **2**（指人）young people: 做～工作 do youth work ‖ ～志愿者 youth volunteers ‖ 好～ worthy young people ‖ 农村～ village youth

【青年节】Qīngniánjié〈简称〉= 五四青年节

【青年联合会】Qīngnián Liánhéhuì〈名〉Youth Federation

【青鸟】qīngniǎo〈名〉**1**〈本〉blue bird **2**〈喻〉messenger

【青色】qīngsè ▸**p. 863**〈名〉cyan

【青纱帐】qīngshāzhàng〈名〉green curtain of tall crops

【青山】qīngshān〈名〉green hills:〈喻〉～不老，绿水长存。Friendship lasts forever.

【青山绿水】qīngshān-lǜshuǐ〈成〉blue mountains and green waters

【青衫】qīngshān〈名〉**1**（指衣服）black gown **2**（指官职）lowly official position

【青少年】qīng-shàonián〈名〉teenagers: ～读物 teenage reading

【青少年犯罪】qīng-shàonián fànzuì〈名〉juvenile crime

【青少年时代】qīng-shàonián shídài〈名〉teenage

【青史】qīngshǐ〈名〉annals of history: 永垂～ go down in the annals of history

【青丝】qīngsī〈名〉**1**〈书〉（指头发）black hair (of a woman or girl): 一缕～ a wisp of black hair **2**（青梅丝）shredded green plums: 带～的点心 pastries with some shredded green plums

【青饲料】qīngsìliào〈名〉green fodder

【青松】qīngsōng〈名〉pine: ～翠柏 green pines and verdant cypresses

【青蒜】qīngsuàn〈名〉garlic shoots

【青苔】qīngtái〈名〉moss

【青檀】qīngtán〈名〉［植物］wingceltis

【青天】qīngtiān〈名〉**1**〈本〉blue sky **2**〈喻〉just and upright official: ～大老爷 my lord

【青天白日】qīngtiān-báirì〈成〉broad daylight: ～下，发生了劫案。The robbery took place in broad daylight.

【青田石】qīngtiánshí〈名〉Qingtian stone [from Qingtian County in Zhejiang Province, used to make seals]

【青铜】qīngtóng〈名〉bronze: ～像 bronze statue ‖ ～器 bronze ware

【青铜峡】Qīngtóngxiá〈名〉Qingtong Gorge: ～水利枢纽工程 Qingtongxia Key Water Control Project

【青蛙】qīngwā〈名〉frog: 蝌蚪长成～。Tadpoles grow into frogs.

【青虾】qīngxiā〈名〉freshwater shrimp

【青葙】qīngxiāng〈名〉［植物］feather cockscomb

【青眼】qīngyǎn〈名〉favour: 老板对他～相待。He was in his boss's good books.

> **青铜器**
>
> Bronze was widely used in the Shang and Zhou periods for farming implements, ritual vessels and ornaments. The most treasured ritual vessel was the *ding* (▸鼎). Many ancient bronze artefacts have cast or engraved inscriptions which provide valuable information about ancient politics, military events, economic affairs, and culture. During the Warring States period, the use of ritual bronze vessels declined, and iron replaced bronze in weapon-making.

【青衣】 qīngyī 〈名〉 **1**（指衣服） black clothing **2**〈古〉（指婢女） housemaid **3**（指旦角） *qingyi* [one of the main divisions of the *dan* (旦) or female roles in traditional Chinese opera, dressed in black]

【青鼬】 qīngyòu 〈名〉［动物］ yellow-throated marten

【青鱼】 qīngyú〈名〉 black carp

【青云】 qīngyún 〈名〉〈喻〉 high official position: ▸～直上, 平步～

【青云直上】 qīngyún-zhíshàng〈成〉 have a meteoric rise

【青藏高原】 Qīng-Zàng Gāoyuán 〈名〉 Qinghai-Tibet Plateau

【青贮】 qīngzhù〈动〉［农业］ ensile: ～饲料 ensilage

【青砖】 qīngzhuān〈名〉 grey brick

【青壮年】 qīng-zhuàngnián〈名〉 the young and the middle-aged

轻（輕） qīng

A〈形〉 **1**（重量小） light: 重量～ be light in weight ‖ 他比我～。 He weighs less than me. ▸～而易举, ～工业 **2**（灵巧） light: ▸～便, ～骑, ～盈, ～装 **3**（轻松） relaxed: ▸～闲, ～音乐, 无官一身～ **4**（不重要） unimportant: 礼物太～ very small gift ‖ 责任～ have minimal responsibilities ▸～贱, 掉以～心, 人微言～ **5**（不庄重） frivolous: ▸～薄, ～浮 **6**（轻率） rash: ～下结论 jump to a conclusion ▸～举妄动, ～率, ～信 **7**（程度浅） small in number, degree, etc.: 病得不～ be seriously ill ‖ 教学任务～ have a light teaching load ‖ 伤势较～ have a slight injury ▸～伤, ～微 **8**（用力小） gentle: ～拿～放 handle with care ‖ ～声说 speak in a soft voice ‖ ～～一推 give a gentle push ▸～柔

B〈动〉 think sth. unimportant: 把钱看得很～ care little for money ▸～敌, ～视, 重男～女

【轻便】 qīngbiàn〈形〉 **1**（分量轻） light;（便携） portable;（易于使用） convenient to use: ～灭火器 portable fire extinguisher ‖ ～自行车 lightweight bicycle **2**（轻松） easy: ～活儿 light work

【轻薄】 qīngbó〈形〉 frivolous: 态度～ frivolous attitude ‖ ～少年 flirtatious young man

【轻财重义】 qīngcái-zhòngyì〈成〉 value friendship more than money

【轻仓】 qīngcāng〈名〉［金融］ small holding (of shares or funds)

【轻车简从】 qīngchē-jiǎncóng〈成〉 [of officials] travel with little luggage and few attendants: 外出视察时, 他总是～。 During his inspection tour, he always travelled light.

【轻车熟路】 qīngchē-shúlù〈成〉〈喻〉 do sth. one knows well and can manage with ease

【轻淡】 qīngdàn〈形〉 **1**（不清晰） faint: ～的记忆 faint memory **2**（不重视） casual: 对名利看得很～ take a casual attitude towards fame and gain

【轻敌】 qīngdí〈动〉 underestimate the enemy: ～思想 tendency to take the enemy lightly

【轻度】 qīngdù〈形〉 minor: ～感染 mild infection ‖ ～烧伤 minor burn ‖ ～通货膨胀 moderate inflation

【轻而易举】 qīng'éryìjǔ〈成〉 be as easy as ABC: ～地击败对手 beat one's opponents hands down ‖ ～的事 a piece of cake

【轻纺】 qīngfǎng〈名〉 **1**（轻工业） textile and other light industries **2**（纺织业） textile industry: ～产品 textile products

【轻风】 qīngfēng〈名〉［气象］ light breeze: ～拂面。 A soft wind kisses the face.

【轻浮】 qīngfú〈形〉 frivolous: 举止～ behave frivolously ‖ ～的女人 flighty woman

【轻歌剧】 qīnggējù〈名〉 **1**［音乐］ operetta **2**［戏剧］ light opera

【轻歌曼舞】 qīnggē-mànwǔ〈成〉 soft music and graceful dance, sing merrily and dance gracefully

【轻工】 qīnggōng〈简称〉= 轻工业

【轻工业】 qīnggōngyè〈名〉 light industry

【轻骨头】 qīnggǔtou〈方〉 **A**〈形〉 smug and bloated **B**〈名〉 contemptible wretch

【轻轨】 qīngguǐ〈名〉 light rail: ～列车 light rail train ‖ ～铁路 light railway

【轻合金】 qīnghéjīn〈名〉 light alloy

【轻核】 qīnghé〈名〉［物理］ light nucleus

【轻忽】 qīnghū〈动〉 neglect: ～职守 neglect one's duty

【轻活】 qīnghuó〈名〉 light work

【轻机关枪】 qīngjīguānqiāng = 轻机枪 qīng-jīqiāng

【轻机枪】 qīngjīqiāng〈名〉 light machine gun

【轻贱】 qīngjiàn **A**〈形〉 mean and worthless: ～的行当 humble occupation **B**〈动〉 look down upon: 受人～ be looked down upon

【轻剑】 qīngjiàn〈名〉［体育］ sabre

【轻健】 qīngjiàn〈形〉 brisk: 步履～ walk with a spring in one's step

【轻捷】 qīngjié〈形〉 springy: 他～地跳上公共汽车。 He stepped lightly into a bus.

【轻金属】 qīngjīnshǔ〈名〉 light metal

【轻举妄动】 qīngjǔ-wàngdòng〈成〉 act rashly: 不要～。 Don't be reckless.

【轻看】 qīngkàn〈动〉 look down upon

【轻口薄舌】 qīngkǒu-bóshé = 轻嘴薄舌 qīngzuǐ-bóshé

【轻快】 qīngkuài〈形〉 **1**（敏捷） spry: ～的脚步 light footsteps ‖ 他步履～。 He is fleet of foot. **2**（轻松愉快） lively: ～的曲调 lively tune

【轻狂】 qīngkuáng〈形〉 extremely frivolous: 举止～ frivolous behaviour

【轻量级】 qīngliàngjí〈名〉［体育］ lightweight

【轻慢】 qīngmàn〈动〉 disrespect: 不许～无礼。 Don't be impertinent. ‖ 不可～客人。 Make sure to show the guests due respect.

【轻描淡写】 qīngmiáo-dànxiě〈成〉 play down: 把一个问题～地一带而过 play down a problem

【轻蔑】 qīngmiè〈动〉 disdain: ～地一笑 give a contemptuous smile ‖ 投以～的目光 give sb. a scornful look

【轻诺寡信】 qīngnuò-guǎxìn〈成〉 be quick to promise but slow to perform

【轻诺易忘】 qīngnuò-yìwàng〈成〉 a man apt to promise is apt to forget

【轻飘】 qīngpiāo〈形〉 **1**（轻） light: ～的雪花 snowflakes drifting slowly in the air **2**（轻浮） flighty: 作风～ frivolous style

【轻飘飘】 qīngpiāopiāo〈形〉 **1**（轻） light: 柳枝在微风中～地摆动。 Willow branches were swaying gently in the breeze. **2**（指动作） nimble;（指心情） relaxed: 脚底下～的 walk as if treading on air

【轻骑】 qīngqí〈名〉 **1**（指骑兵） light cavalry **2**（指摩托车） motorcycle

【轻巧】 qīngqiǎo〈形〉 **1**（灵便） light and handy: 身材～ be slim and light ‖ 这辆自行车真～。 This is a very nippy little bicycle. **2**（灵巧） agile: 动作～ be nimble in movement **3**（简单） simple: 说得～。 You talk as if it were just a walkover.

【轻轻】 qīngqīng〈形〉 gentle

【轻取】 qīngqǔ〈动〉 win an easy victory: 以3比0～对手 beat one's opponent easily by three to zero

【轻柔】 qīngróu〈形〉 gentle: ～地抚摸 caress gently ‖ 她说话～。 She is softly spoken.

【轻软】 qīngruǎn〈形〉 light and soft

【轻纱】 qīngshā〈名〉 fine gauze

【轻伤】 qīngshāng〈名〉 minor wound: ～不下火线 not leave the front line on account of minor wounds

【轻生】 qīngshēng ▸p. 772〈动〉〈婉〉 commit suicide

【轻声】 qīngshēng〈名〉 **1**（指声调） soft voice: ～细语 say under one's breath **2**［语言］ neutral tone

【轻世傲物】 qīngshì-àowù〈成〉 be full of conceit and defiant of convention

【轻视】 qīngshì〈动〉 look down upon: ～妇女 look down upon women ‖ 受到～ be held in contempt

【轻手轻脚】 qīngshǒu-qīngjiǎo〈成〉 move quietly: 母亲～地走来。 The mother crept over.

【轻率】 qīngshuài〈形〉 hasty: ～地下结论 jump to a conclusion ‖ 他一时～, 干了那事。 He did it in a rash moment.

【轻水】 qīngshuǐ〈名〉［化学］ light water

【轻水反应堆】 qīngshuǐ fǎnyìngduī〈名〉［物理］ light water reactor

【轻松】 qīngsōng **A**〈形〉 relaxed: 感到～ feel relaxed ‖ 心情～ have peace of mind ‖ ～的话题 light topic ‖ ～自如 free and relaxed ‖ 这工作决不～。 This work is not at all easy. **B**〈动〉 relax: 我们去看场电影～一下吧。 Let's go to the cinema to wind down.

【轻佻】 qīngtiāo〈形〉 frivolous: 举止～ skittish behaviour

【轻微】 qīngwēi〈形〉 light: 做些～的家务活儿 do some light housework ‖ ～污染 be slightly polluted ‖ 损失～。 The losses are slight.

【轻武器】 qīngwǔqì〈名〉［军事］ small arms

【轻侮】 qīngwǔ〈动〉 treat with disrespect: 国家的尊严岂容～。 The dignity of the state allows no slight and insult.

【轻雾】 qīngwù〈名〉 mist

【轻喜剧】 qīngxǐjù〈名〉 light comedy

【轻闲】 qīngxián〈形〉 **1**（不忙） leisurely: 过着～舒适的生活 lead a leisurely and comfortable life **2**（容易） easy: 编字典可不是什么～活儿。 Compiling a dictionary is no easy job at all.

【轻信】 qīngxìn〈动〉 be credulous: ～谣言 give ready credence to rumours ‖ 要重证据, 不要～口供。 Lay stress on evidence, and do not readily believe in confessions.

【轻型】 qīngxíng〈形〉 light-duty: ～机械 light-duty machinery ‖ ～武器 light weapon

【轻言】qīngyán〈动〉〈书〉speak without careful thought: ～细语 speak in a soft, gentle voice ‖ 他从不～失败。He is slow to admit defeat.

【轻扬】qīngyáng〈动〉 lightly drift: 旗帜在微风中～。The flag is floating in the breeze.

【轻易】qīngyì **A**〈形〉easy: 这些成绩不是～取得的。These achievements were not easily come by. **B**〈副〉rashly: ～下结论 jump to a conclusion ‖ 别～表示同意或反对。Do not express your approval or disapproval hastily.

【轻音乐】qīngyīnyuè〈名〉light music: 欣赏～ appreciate light music

【轻盈】qīngyíng〈形〉**1**（苗条）lithe: 体态～ of slender build ‖ 她步子～地走过来，向大家微笑致意。She breezed along, smiling at everyone. **2**（轻松）relaxed: 笑语～ talk and laugh merrily and lightheartedly

【轻悠悠】qīngyōuyōu〈形〉**1**（形容姿态）light: 蝴蝶在花丛中～地飞来飞去。Butterflies are fluttering lightly among the flowers. **2**（形容声音）gentle: 能够听到从远处传来的～的音乐。Soft music can be heard from the distance.

【轻于鸿毛】qīngyú-hóngmáo〈成〉〈喻〉be of no significance

【轻躁狂】qīngzàokuáng〈名〉hypomania

【轻重】qīngzhòng〈名〉**1**（指重量）weight: 用手掂掂～ weigh sth. in one's hand **2**（指程度）importance: ►～缓急, 举足～ **3**（指分寸）propriety: 说话不知～ not know the proper way to talk

【轻重倒置】qīngzhòng-dàozhì〈成〉lack a sense of priority

【轻重缓急】qīngzhòng-huǎnjí〈成〉relative importance: 解决问题应分～。Problems should be resolved in order of importance and urgency.

【轻重量级】qīngzhòngliàngjí〈名〉［体育］light heavyweight

【轻舟】qīngzhōu〈名〉〈书〉skiff

【轻装】qīngzhuāng〈名〉**1**（指行装）light pack(s): ～前进 march with light packs ‖ 放下包袱，～上阵 free oneself from worries and join the action without any sense of burden **2**（指装备）light equipment: ～部队 lightly-armed troops

【轻装简从】qīngzhuāng-jiǎncóng ＝ 轻车简从 qīngchē-jiǎncóng

【轻装上阵】qīngzhuāng-shàngzhèn〈成〉go into battle with a light pack

【轻嘴薄舌】qīngzuǐ-bóshé〈成〉make caustic remarks

【轻罪】qīngzuì〈名〉minor offence

氢（氫）qīng

〈名〉［化学］hydrogen (H): ～原子 hydrogen atom

【氢弹】qīngdàn〈名〉［军事］hydrogen bomb, H-bomb

【氢化钾】qīnghuàjiǎ〈名〉［化学］potassium hydride

【氢离子】qīnglízǐ〈名〉［化学］hydrogen ion

【氢气】qīngqì〈名〉hydrogen: ～球 hydrogen balloon

【氢燃料】qīngránliào〈名〉hydrogen fuel: ～电池 hydrogen fuel cell

【氢氧化钙】qīngyǎnghuàgài〈名〉calcium hydroxide

【氢氧化铝】qīngyǎnghuàlǚ〈名〉aluminium hydroxide

【氢氧化钠】qīngyǎnghuànà〈名〉sodium hydroxide

倾（傾）qīng

A〈动〉**1**（歪斜）lean: 身子向前～ bend forward ‖ ～斜 slant **2**（倒塌）collapse: ►～覆 **3**〈书〉（压倒）overwhelm **4**（倒出）empty out: ►～盆大雨 **5**（用尽）do all one can: ～全力 do all in one's power ‖ ～其所有 give away all one has ►～诉, ～吐, ～销
B〈名〉inclination: ►右～, 左～

【倾侧】qīngcè〈动〉tilt: 船向左/右舷～。The ship listed to port/starboard.

【倾巢】qīngcháo〈动〉〈贬〉turn out in full force

【倾巢出动】qīngcháo-chūdòng〈成〉turn out in full force

【倾城倾国】qīngchéng-qīngguó〈成〉devastatingly beautiful: 有～之貌 be of unmatched beauty

【倾倒】qīngdǎo〈动〉**1**（倒塌）overturn: 这座危房随时可能～。The house is in danger of collapsing at any moment. **2**（倾慕）greatly admire: 他们精彩的表演使观众为之～。Their brilliant performance took the audience by storm.

【倾倒】qīngdào〈动〉dump: 此处不准～垃圾。No dumping here.

【倾动】qīngdòng〈动〉move and win admiration: ～一时 cause a great sensation

【倾耳而听】qīng'ěr'értīng〈成〉prick up one's ears and listen attentively

【倾覆】qīngfù〈动〉**1**（倒塌）overturn: 船撞上冰山而～。The ship hit an iceberg and capsized. **2**（颠覆）overthrow: ～国家政权 overthrow a country's regime

【倾国倾城】qīngguó-qīngchéng ＝ 倾城倾国 qīngchéng-qīngguó

【倾家荡产】qīngjiā-dàngchǎn〈成〉bring a family to ruin: 赌得～ gamble away a family fortune

【倾角】qīngjiǎo〈名〉**1**［物理］dip **2**［数学］inclination

【倾力】qīnglì〈动〉do all one can: ～相助 try one's best to help

【倾慕】qīngmù〈动〉greatly admire: ～已久 have long admired sb. ‖ 相互～ have great admiration for each other

【倾囊相助】qīngnáng-xiāngzhù〈成〉empty one's purse to help

【倾盆大雨】qīngpén-dàyǔ〈成〉downpour: 遇上～ be caught in a downpour

【倾圮】qīngpǐ〈动〉〈书〉collapse: 古庙已经～。The ancient temple has fallen into ruin.

【倾情】qīngqíng〈动〉devote heart and soul to: ～之作 work that has been given heart and soul ‖ ～演唱 sing with all one's emotions

【倾洒】qīngsǎ〈动〉[of snow, tears, etc.] pour down

【倾诉】qīngsù〈动〉pour out: ～衷肠 pour out one's heart ‖ 我的哀怨和痛苦向谁～呢？To whom can I pour out my grievances and sufferings?

【倾塌】qīngtā〈动〉collapse

【倾谈】qīngtán〈动〉〈书〉have a good heart-to-heart talk

【倾听】qīngtīng〈动〉listen attentively to: ～群众的意见 listen attentively to the views of the masses

【倾吐】qīngtǔ〈动〉unload: ～苦水 pour out one's grievances ‖ 她向我～了她的伤心事。She unloaded all her grief on me.

【倾箱倒箧】qīngxiāng-dǎoqiè〈成〉〈喻〉give away all one has

【倾向】qīngxiàng **A**〈动〉incline towards: 他在政治上～于保守主义。Politically he leans towards conservatism. **B**〈名〉inclination: 纠正不良～ rectify unhealthy tendencies ‖ 思想～ ideological predisposition

【倾向性】qīngxiàngxìng〈名〉tendency: 表现出某种～ show a tendency ‖ 带有～的论文 tendentious thesis

【倾销】qīngxiāo〈动〉dump: 廉价～ dump sth. at a low price ‖ 反～ anti-dumping

【倾斜】qīngxié **A**〈形〉sloping: 古塔向西～。The old pagoda slants towards the west. **B**〈动〉give preferences to: 向教育～ favour education

【倾泻】qīngxiè〈动〉pour down: 山洪夹着泥沙～而下。Torrents of water and silt came rushing down the mountain.

【倾卸】qīngxiè〈动〉dump: 装载的东西被～在垃圾场上。The load is tipped out at the dumping site.

【倾心】qīngxīn〈动〉**1**（爱慕）adore: 一见～ fall in love at first sight **2**（诚心）pour out one's heart: ～交谈 have a heart-to-heart

【倾心吐胆】qīngxīn-tǔdǎn〈成〉pour out one's heart (to sb.)

【倾轧】qīngyà〈动〉jostle: 两派互相～。The two parties jostled with one another.

【倾注】qīngzhù〈动〉**1**（指流入）pour into: 一股泉水～入深潭。A gush of spring water streams into the deep pond. **2**（指集中）pour (one's feeling, energy, etc.) into: 把爱全部～在孩子身上 invest all one's love in one's child ‖ 为了事业而～全部精力 throw all one's energy into a career

卿 qīng

〈名〉〈古〉**1**（指官名）senior official: ～相 high court officials and chief ministers **2**（你）you [a form of address to friend] **3**（指夫妻间爱称）my dear: ►～～我我

【卿卿我我】qīngqīng-wǒwǒ〈成〉whisper sweet nothings to one another

清[1] qīng

A〈形〉**1**（无杂质）clear: 一池～水 a pool of clear water ►～澈, ～泉 **2**（纯洁）clean: ►～白, ～洁, 冰～玉洁 **3**（单纯）pure: ～咖啡 black coffee ►～唱, ～醇, ～一色 **4**（清楚）distinct: 解释不～ hard to explain ‖ 摸～情况 know a situation inside out ►～楚, 澄～ **5**（廉洁）fair and honest: ►～官, ～廉, ～正 **6**（清静）quiet: ►～静, 冷～
B〈动〉**1**（使洁净）clear: ～嗓子 clear one's throat ►～除, ～洗, 坚壁～野 **2**（结清）settle: 付～房租 square up one's rent ‖ 账已还～。All the accounts have been settled. ►～党, ～欠, 结～

清[2] Qīng

〈名〉Qing Dynasty

【清白】qīngbái〈形〉clean: 历史～ have a clean record ‖ 清清白白做人 live completely cleanly ‖ 事实证明他是～的。The facts prove that he is clean.

【清白无辜】qīngbái-wúgū〈成〉innocent

【清仓】qīngcāng〈动〉make an inventory of a warehouse: ～查库 make an inventory of a warehouse ‖ ～甩卖 clearance sale

【清册】qīngcè〈名〉detailed list: 财产～ inventory of one's possessions

【清茶】qīngchá〈名〉**1**（绿茶）green tea: 你喝～还是红茶？Which do you want, green tea or black tea? **2**（茶水）tea served without refreshments: 这里只有～一杯。There is nothing here but a cup of tea.

【清查】qīngchá〈动〉check: ～库存 make a stock check ‖ ～户口 check residency permits ‖ ～账目 audit the accounts
【清偿】qīngcháng〈动〉pay off: ～债务 clear a debt
【清场】qīngchǎng〈动〉clear a public place of people
【清唱】qīngchàng **A**〈动〉sing opera arias without make-up: ～剧 oratorio **B**〈名〉singing without musical accompaniment
【清澈】qīngchè〈形〉clear: 湖水～见底。The lake is so clear that you can see the bottom.
【清晨】qīngchén ▸**p. 669**〈名〉early morning: ～空气新鲜。The early morning air is very fresh.
【清除】qīngchú〈动〉get rid of: ～出党 expel sb. from a party ‖ ～垃圾 chuck away rubbish ‖ ～贪官 root out corrupt officials ‖ ～园子里的杂草 weed a garden
【清楚】qīngchu **A**〈形〉**1**（清晰、明白）clear: 把情况讲～ put the case clearly ‖ 字迹～ be written in a clear hand ‖ ～的电视图像 sharp TV picture **2**（理解透彻）clear-headed: 对投资风险很～ be very clear about the risks involved in investing ‖ 他头脑～。He is a clear thinker. **B**〈动〉be clear about: 你～事情的始末吗？ Do you know the whole story? ‖ 我不～你的想法。I can't see into your thoughts.
【清纯】qīngchún〈形〉**1**（指人）pretty and innocent **2**（指物）fresh and clear: 雨后空气～。The air is clear and fresh after the rain.
【清醇】qīngchún〈形〉pure and mellow: 这酒～可口。The wine is pure and mellow to the taste.
【清脆】qīngcuì〈形〉**1**（指声音）clear and melodious: 嗓音～ clear voice ‖ 黄莺～的鸣叫声 melodious notes of an oriole **2**（指食物）crisp: ～的黄瓜 crisp cucumber
【清单】qīngdān〈名〉detailed list: 材料～ inventory of materials ‖ 购物～ shopping list
【清淡】qīngdàn〈形〉**1**（指颜色、气味）delicate: ～的荷花香 delicate fragrance of lotus flowers ‖ ～的绿茶 weak green tea **2**（指食物）light: ～的食物 light food ‖ 味道～的菜 lightly seasoned dishes **3**（指风格）fresh and elegant: ～的艺术风格 fresh and elegant artistic style **4**（指生意）slack: 生意～ slack in business
【清党】qīngdǎng〈动〉purge a political party
【清道】qīngdào〈动〉**1**（指清扫）sweep the street **2**（指驱散行人）clear the way for the carriage of the emperor or high officials in ancient times
【清道夫】qīngdàofū〈名〉〈旧〉street sweeper:〈喻〉我愿意为这次谈判做～。I would like to clear the way for this negotiation.
【清点】qīngdiǎn〈动〉make an inventory of: ～存货 inventory a stock ‖ ～人数 count heads
【清炖】qīngdùn〈动〉boil in clear soup without soy sauce: ～鸡 stewed chicken without soy sauce
【清风】qīngfēng〈名〉cool breeze: ～徐来 fresh breeze blowing gently ‖ ～亮节 one's deportment being clear and bright
【清福】qīngfú〈名〉life of ease and leisure: 享～ enjoy the happiness of a leisurely life
【清辅音】qīngfǔyīn〈名〉[语言] unvoiced consonant
【清高】qīnggāo〈形〉**1**（纯洁高尚）virtuous: 他为人品德～，受人尊敬。He is respected for his lofty character. **2**〈贬〉（不合群）aloof: 自视～ think oneself morally superior to others
【清稿】qīnggǎo〈名〉clean copy: ～已交出版社。The clean copy has already been handed over to the publishing house.
【清官】qīngguān〈名〉honest and upright official
【清官难断家务事】qīngguān nán duàn jiāwùshì〈俗〉even a just official finds it hard to settle family disputes
【清规】qīngguī〈名〉Buddhist monastic rules
【清规戒律】qīngguī-jièlǜ〈成〉**1**（针对僧道）regulations, taboos and commandments for Buddhists/Taoists **2**（规章制度）restrictions and regulations: 打破一切～ break all taboos
【清锅冷灶】qīngguō-lěngzào〈成〉the pot is empty and the stove is cold:〈喻〉屋里一副～的样子，好像很久没人住了。The house looked completely disused and deserted, as if it had not been lived in for a long time.
【清寒】qīnghán〈形〉**1**（清贫）poor: 家境～ be born in a poor family **2**（清朗）cold and clear: 月色～ clear, cold moonlight
【清还】qīnghuán〈动〉pay off: ～欠款 pay off one's debts ‖ ～图书 return books to the library
【清火】qīnghuǒ〈动〉[中医] relieve inflammation
【清寂】qīngjì〈形〉〈书〉cold and silent: ～的秋夜 cold and quiet autumn night
【清剿】qīngjiǎo〈动〉clean up: ～土匪 clean out the bandits ‖ 下令～残敌 order a mop-up
【清教】Qīngjiào〈名〉Puritanism: ～徒 Puritan
【清洁】qīngjié〈形〉clean: 保持～ keep sth. clean ‖ 注意～卫生 pay attention to sanitation and hygiene ‖ ～能源 clean energy
【清洁袋】qīngjiédài〈名〉rubbish bag
【清洁队】qīngjiéduì〈名〉cleaning squad
【清洁工】qīngjiégōng〈名〉**1**（保洁员）cleaner **2**（清运垃圾者）dustman〈英〉; garbage collector〈美〉
【清洁剂】qīngjiéjì〈名〉detergent: 皮革～ leather cleaner
【清洁能源】qīngjié néngyuán〈名〉clean energy
【清净】qīngjìng〈形〉**1**（无人打扰）peaceful and quiet: 图～ seek a peaceful and quiet life ‖ 耳根～ peace of mind away from worldly discord **2**（清澈）clear: ～的泉水 clear spring water
【清净无为】qīngjìng-wúwéi〈成〉discard all desires and worries from one's mind
【清静】qīngjìng〈形〉tranquil: 环境～ peaceful surroundings ‖ 找个～的地方谈一谈 find a quiet place to talk
【清君侧】qīng jūncè〈成〉purge the emperor's court [often used as an excuse for staging a coup d'état or an armed rebellion]
【清客】qīngkè〈名〉〈旧〉hanger-on of rich and powerful families
【清口】qīngkǒu〈形〉tasty and refreshing: 这道凉拌菜吃着挺～的。The salad is tasty and refreshing.
【清苦】qīngkǔ〈形〉poor: 生活～ live in poverty
【清朗】qīnglǎng〈形〉**1**（凉爽晴朗）cool and bright: 天气～ cool and bright weather **2**（清净明亮）clear and bright: 眉目～ have clean-cut features **3**（清楚响亮）loud and clear: ～的笑声 resounding laughter **4**（清新明快）refreshing and lively: 笔调～ fresh and lucid writing style
【清冷】qīnglěng〈形〉**1**（清凉）chilly: ～的秋夜 chilly autumn night **2**（冷清）deserted: ～的街上 deserted street
【清理】qīnglǐ〈动〉put in order: ～档案 put the archives in order ‖ ～房间 tidy up one's room ‖ ～书桌 clear out a desk ‖ ～账目 straighten out one's accounts
【清丽】qīnglì〈形〉**1**（指景色）elegant and beautiful: 景色～ tranquil and beautiful scene **2**（指作品）lucid and graceful: ～的散文 chiselled essay
【清廉】qīnglián〈形〉honest and upright: 为官～ be fair and square in performing one's government functions
【清凉】qīngliáng〈形〉cool and refreshing: ～饮料 cold drink
【清凉油】qīngliángyóu〈名〉essential balm
【清亮】qīngliàng〈形〉clear and resounding: 嗓音～ clear voice
【清亮】qīngliang〈形〉clear: ～的溪水 clear stream ‖ 我心里一下子～了。Suddenly it all became clear to me.
【清冽】qīngliè〈形〉〈书〉chilly: ～的泉水 cool and fresh springs
【清零】qīnglíng〈动〉reset: ～不良记录 reset poor results to zero ‖ 选票～后进入新一轮投票 enter another round of voting after resetting the vote count
【清凌凌】qīnglínglíng〈形〉clear and rippling: 微风中，湖水～的。The lake is clear and rippling in the light breeze.
【清泠泠】qīnglínglíng = 清凌凌 qīnglínglíng
【清流】qīngliú〈名〉〈书〉clear stream
【清明】qīngmíng **A**〈形〉**1**（指政局）well regulated: 政治～ have a well-regulated political environment **2**（指思维）sober and calm: 神志～ be in one's right mind **3**（清澈明亮）clear and bright: ～的月光 bright moonlight **B** Qīngmíng〈名〉Pure Brightness [beginning of the 5th of the 24 solar terms]
【清明节】Qīngmíngjié〈名〉Tomb Sweeping Day

> **清明节**
>
> The 5th of the 24 solar terms, celebrated each year around the 4th or 5th of April. On this day people make offerings to their ancestors, sweep the family graves, and go on spring outings (▸踏青). *Qingming* is a statutory public holiday in China.

【清盘】qīngpán〈名〉[经济] liquidation: ～大拍卖 liquidation sale
【清贫】qīngpín〈形〉poor: 甘于～ be ready to lead a poor but honest life ‖ 家道～ come of an impoverished family
【清平】qīngpíng〈形〉peaceful: ～盛世 times of peace and prosperity ‖ ～世界 peaceful world
【清漆】qīngqī〈名〉varnish
【清讫】qīngqì〈动〉receive payment
【清欠】qīngqiàn〈动〉clear up one's debts
【清切】qīngqiè〈形〉**1**（清亮）clear: 他说话的声音太低，听不～。His voice is so low that I can't hear him clearly. **2**（凄切）mournful: 山谷中不时回响起孤雁～的哀鸣声。At times the valley resounded with the plaintive call of a lonely wild goose.
【清清白白】qīngqīng-báibái〈成〉lead a clean life
【清清楚楚】qīngqīng-chǔchǔ〈成〉be crystal clear
【清秋】qīngqiū〈名〉〈书〉clear autumn air

q

【清癯】qīngqú〈形〉〈书〉lean: 面容～ thin face
【清泉】qīngquán〈名〉fresh spring
【清热】qīngrè〈动〉［中医］relieve inflammation: ～解毒 clear heat and detoxicate
【清扫】qīngsǎo〈动〉thoroughly clean up: ～街道 sweep the street ‖ ～战场 clean up the battlefield
【清瘦】qīngshòu ▸p. 772〈形〉〈婉〉thin: 一场大病之后他～了许多。He was a lot thinner after a bout of serious illness.
【清爽】qīngshuǎng〈形〉1（清凉）fresh and cool: ～的空气 cool and refreshing air 2（轻松爽快）relieved: 作业做完了，真是～! I feel so relieved now that I have finished my homework! 3〈方〉（整洁）neat and tidy: 只要她在家，屋里总是清清爽爽的。The house is always tidy and clean as long as she is at home. 4〈方〉（清淡爽口）light and refreshing: 这菜吃起来很～。This dish is nice and light.
【清水衙门】qīngshuǐ-yámen〈成〉organization with limited funds and welfare facilities: 这里可是～。This is a place lacking in funds and benefits.
【清算】qīngsuàn〈动〉1（指财务）settle: ～账目 square accounts 2（指错误）settle the score: ～血债 straighten out blood debts ‖ 彻底～他的罪行 force him to make complete amendments for his crimes
【清算公司】qīngsuàn gōngsī〈名〉liquidation company
【清算银行】qīngsuàn yínháng〈名〉clearing bank
【清谈】qīngtán〈名〉1（指风气）discussions on impractical matters and pure philosophical theories among intellectuals 2（指议论）empty talk: 不尚～ have no respect for empty talk
【清汤】qīngtāng〈名〉light soup
【清汤寡水】qīngtāng-guǎshuǐ〈成〉watery
【清甜】qīngtián〈形〉refreshing and sweet: ～的山泉 cool and sweet mountain spring
【清通】qīngtōng〈形〉clear and coherent: 文章要写得～，必须下一番苦功。You must work hard to achieve unity and coherence in writing.
【清退】qīngtuì〈动〉check on and return: ～赃款赃物 check on and return stolen money and goods
【清玩】qīngwán A〈名〉elegant object for enjoyment B〈动〉delight in
【清婉】qīngwǎn〈形〉clear and sweet: 歌声～。The singing was clear and sweet.
【清晰】qīngxī〈形〉distinct: 口齿～ have clear articulation ‖ 思路～ lucidity of thought ‖ 图像～ sharp image
【清晰度】qīngxīdù〈名〉1（指图像）resolution 2（指声音）articulation: 高～电视 high-definition television
【清洗】qīngxǐ〈动〉1（洗涤）cleanse: ～伤口 cleanse a wound 2（清除）purge: ～党内腐败分子 purge corruption from within the party
【清闲】qīngxián〈形〉idle: 过着舒适～的生活 live a life of ease and idleness ‖ 我们难得～。We have very little leisure time.
【清香】qīngxiāng〈名〉delicate fragrance: ～扑鼻 be met with wafts of sweet scent
【清心】qīngxīn A〈形〉peaceful: 摆脱家务你就可以～了。You will feel at peace once you've dealt with all the household burdens. B〈动〉1（指心境）clear one's mind of worries: ～养性 clear one's head and cultivate one's moral character ▸～寡欲 2［中医］relieve internal heat
【清心寡欲】qīngxīn-guǎyù〈成〉have a pure heart and few worldly desires
【清新】qīngxīn〈形〉1（指空气）refreshing: 空气～ fresh air 2（指文笔）original: 文笔～ be written in a refreshingly lucid style ‖ ～雅致 have elegant and tasteful colour
【清新剂】qīngxīnjì〈名〉air freshener
【清馨】qīngxīn〈名〉〈书〉faint scent: 满园～。A delicate fragrance filled the garden.
【清醒】qīngxǐng A〈形〉clear-headed: 保持头脑～ keep a clear head ‖ 他对自己的错误有了～的认识。He was fully aware of his mistakes. B〈动〉regain consciousness: 病人～过来了。The patient has come to. ‖ 他的神志～了。He has regained consciousness.
【清秀】qīngxiù〈形〉pretty and refined: 眉目～ have fine, delicate features
【清雅】qīngyǎ〈形〉1（指风格）elegant and refined: 格调～ be elegant in style 2（指仪表）pretty and well-mannered: 仪容举止～大方 extremely handsome and well-mannered
【清样】qīngyàng〈名〉［印刷］final proof: 付印前的～ press proof
【清夜】qīngyè〈名〉quiet night: ～静思 be deep in thought in the still of night
【清一色】qīngyīsè A〈名〉（指麻将）all of one suit;（指扑克牌）flush B〈形〉identical: 穿着～的衣服 be all dressed alike ‖ 委员会～由女子组成。The committee consists of female members exclusively.
【清议】qīngyì〈名〉〈旧〉political criticism by scholars
【清逸】qīngyì〈形〉〈书〉fresh and refined: 文风～ fresh and elegant style of writing
【清音】qīngyīn〈名〉1［曲艺］a type of ballad-singing popular in Sichuan Province 2〈旧〉（指音乐）band music played at weddings or funerals 3［语言］voiceless sound
【清莹】qīngyíng〈形〉clear and glistening: ～的露珠 glistening dew
【清幽】qīngyōu〈形〉quiet and beautiful: ～的山谷 enchanting and secluded valley
【清油】qīngyóu = 素油 sùyóu
【清誉】qīngyù〈名〉〈旧〉untarnished reputation: 有损～ be damaging to one's spotless reputation
【清越】qīngyuè〈形〉clear and melodious: ～的歌声 clear and ringing singing
【清运】qīngyùn〈动〉clear away: ～垃圾 clear away the rubbish
【清早】qīngzǎo〈名〉early morning: 他一～就出去了。He went out very early in the morning.
【清湛】qīngzhàn〈形〉〈书〉crystal clear: 湖水～。The lake is crystal clear.
【清丈】qīngzhàng〈动〉measure a piece of land
【清账】qīngzhàng A〈动〉square an account: 与供应商～ settle accounts with a supplier B〈名〉detailed settled accounts
【清障】qīngzhàng〈动〉remove obstacles: 疏河～ remove obstacles from a river course
【清真】qīngzhēn〈形〉Muslim: ～食品 halal food ‖ ～食堂 Muslim canteen
【清真教】Qīngzhēnjiào = 伊斯兰教 Yīsīlánjiào
【清真寺】qīngzhēnsì〈名〉mosque
【清蒸】qīngzhēng〈动〉steam in clear soup without soy sauce: ～鱼 steamed fish
【清正】qīngzhèng〈形〉incorruptible and upright: 为官～ be upright and honest in performing one's official duties

蜻 qīng

【蜻蜓】qīngtíng〈名〉dragonfly
【蜻蜓点水】qīngtíng-diǎnshuǐ〈成〉〈喻〉scratch the surface

鲭（鯖）qīng〈名〉［鱼类］mackerel

▸zhēng

qíng

情 qíng〈名〉1（感情）feeling: 产生爱慕之～ form an attachment (to/for sb.) ‖ 以～动人 move people ▸～不自禁，～操 2（道理）reason: 合～合理 fair and reasonable ▸～理，常～ 3（情况）situation: ▸～况，～形 4（情欲）sexual desire: ▸～欲，春～，催～ 5（爱情）love: ▸～敌，～侣 6（情面）favour: ▸～面，讲～

【情爱】qíng'ài〈名〉1（爱情）love: ～甚笃 be deeply in love with each other 2（情谊）affection: 充满～的集体 a community filled with affection
【情报】qíngbào〈名〉information: 窃取秘密～ steal secret information ‖ 军事～ military intelligence ‖ ～员 intelligence agent ‖ 技术/商业～ technical/commercial information ‖ 美国中央～局 Central Intelligence Agency (CIA)
【情报检索】qíngbào jiǎnsuǒ〈名〉information retrieval (IR)
【情变】qíngbiàn〈名〉emotional break-up: 夫妻间的～ break-up between husband and wife
【情不自禁】qíngbùzìjīn〈成〉cannot help: ～哭了 cannot help crying
【情操】qíngcāo〈名〉sentiment: 陶冶～ nourish the human spirit ‖ 高尚的～ lofty sentiments
【情场】qíngchǎng〈名〉arena of love: ～得意 be lucky in love ‖ 赌场得意，～失意。Lucky in play, unlucky in love.
【情痴】qíngchī〈名〉love maniac
【情敌】qíngdí〈名〉rival in love
【情调】qíngdiào〈名〉sentiment: 具有异国～ be of exotic character ‖ 影片充满伤感～。This film is full of sentiment.
【情窦初开】qíngdòu-chūkāi〈成〉[esp of a young girl] be in one's first bloom of love
【情分】qíngfen〈名〉mutual affection: 夫妻～ marital affection ‖ 朋友～ friendship ‖ 兄弟～ fraternity
【情夫】qíngfū〈名〉lover of a married woman
【情妇】qíngfù〈名〉mistress
【情感】qínggǎn〈名〉1（情绪）emotion: 发泄～ let off steam 2（感情）affection: 加深相互间的～ deepen the mutual attachment
【情感剧】qínggǎnjù〈名〉romantic drama: 温情脉脉的～ sentimental romantic drama
【情歌】qínggē〈名〉love song: ～对唱 sing antiphonal love songs
【情话】qínghuà〈名〉sweet nothings: 在耳边轻声说～ whisper sweet nothings in sb.'s ear
【情怀】qínghuái〈名〉feelings: 抒发～ express one's thoughts and feelings ‖ 高尚的～ noble soul
【情急】qíngjí〈动〉feel anxious: ～之下 in one's eagerness
【情急智生】qíngjí-zhìshēng〈成〉hit on a good idea in a moment of desperation
【情节】qíngjié〈名〉1（指文学创作）plot: 构思小说的～ construct the plot of a novel ‖ ～曲折离奇 complicated and fantastic plot ‖ 故事～的发展 evolution of a story 2（情节）circumstances: 他的错误～严重。His error is serious.

【情节剧】qíngjiéjù〈名〉melodrama: ～片 action film
【情结】qíngjié〈名〉complex: 思乡～ homesickness ‖ 自卑～ inferiority complex
【情景】qíngjǐng〈名〉1▸（感情和景象）feelings and scenes: ▸～交融 2▸（景象）sight: 悲喜交集的～ half comic, half pathetic sight ‖ 分手时的～仍历历在目。The departure scene is still vivid in my memory.
【情景交融】qíngjǐng jiāoróng〈成〉successful blend of scenery and sentiment
【情景剧】qíngjǐngjù〈名〉sitcom:《我爱我家》是典型的国产～。'I Love My Home' is a typical Chinese sitcom.
【情景喜剧】qíngjǐng xǐjù〈名〉sitcom
【情境】qíngjìng〈名〉circumstances: 在那种～中我无话可说。I have nothing to say under these circumstances.
【情况】qíngkuàng〈名〉1▸（指状况）circumstances: 不了解～ be out of the picture ‖ 实际～ actual circumstances ‖ ～良好 be in a good condition ‖ ～急剧恶化。Things were deteriorating drastically. ‖ 她的～糟透了。Her affairs were in a terrible state. 2▸（指军事变化）military situation: 一有新～出现，就立即报告总部。Any change in the situation is to be reported immediately to headquarters.
【情郎】qíngláng〈名〉sweetheart
【情理】qínglǐ〈名〉reason: 不合～ be unreasonable ‖ 合乎～ stand to reason ‖ ～不通 beyond all reason ‖ ～难容 contrary to reason ‖ 这种要求也在～之中。This demand is within the bounds of reason.
【情侣】qínglǚ〈名〉sweethearts: 很般配的一对～ a well-matched couple
【情面】qíngmiàn〈名〉feelings: 碍于～ for fear of hurting sb.'s feelings ‖ ～难却 cannot cause sb. to lose face ‖ 不讲～。There is no place for sentiment.
【情趣】qíngqù〈名〉1▸（性情志趣）temperament and interest: ～相同 be in the same vein 2▸（情调趣味）taste: 高雅的艺术～ fine taste in art ‖ 他喜欢用有趣的例子给文章增添～。He likes to spice up his writing with amusing examples.
【情人】qíngrén〈名〉lover: 旧～ old flame ‖ 梦中～ dream lover
【情人节】Qíngrénjié〈名〉(Saint) Valentine's Day
【情人眼里出西施】qíngrén yǎnli chū Xīshī〈俗〉beauty is in the eye of the beholder: 老话说，～。The old dictum says that love is blind.
【情色】qíngsè〈名〉erotic: ～题材的影片 a film with an erotic theme
【情杀】qíngshā〈动〉murder for love: 遭～ be murdered for love
【情商】qíngshāng〈名〉［心理］emotional quotient (EQ)
【情深似海】qíngshēn-sìhǎi〈成〉one's love is as deep as the sea
【情深义重】qíngshēn-yìzhòng〈成〉deep affection and feelings
【情圣】qíngshèng〈名〉noble lover: 塑造一位～形象 create the image of a noble lover
【情诗】qíngshī〈名〉love poem
【情史】qíngshǐ〈名〉love affair: 她与黑道人物的～被曝光。The romantic attachment between her and an underground figure was revealed.
【情势】qíngshì〈名〉situation: 为～所迫 be under the force of circumstances ‖ 看来～不妙。Things don't look good.
【情书】qíngshū〈名〉love letter
【情丝】qíngsī〈名〉ties of love: 两人分手后～。The ties of love remained unbroken after they parted.
【情思】qíngsī〈名〉1▸（情感）affection: ～绵绵 everlasting affection 2▸（情绪）mood
【情愫】qíngsù〈名〉〈书〉1▸（感情）feelings: 合作共事增加了他们之间的～。Working together increased their good feeling for one other. 2▸（真情实意）innermost feelings: 披露～ reveal one's true feelings
【情随事迁】qíngsuíshìqiān〈成〉as times move on, people's affections change: 她一辞职则一切～。Her resignation puts everything in a different light.
【情态】qíngtài〈名〉spirit: 塑像～逼真。The statue is very life-like.
【情态动词】qíngtài dòngcí〈名〉［语法］modal verb
【情同骨肉】qíngtóng-gǔròu〈成〉as dear to sb. as one's own flesh and blood
【情同手足】qíngtóng-shǒuzú〈成〉feel a kinship with sb.: 他们～。They are like brothers.
【情投意合】qíngtóu-yìhé〈成〉find mutual affection and agreement: 两人～，一见如故。The two of them got on like a house on fire.
【情网】qíngwǎng〈名〉web of love: 堕入～ ensnarl oneself in a love affair
【情味】qíngwèi〈名〉flavour: 这篇散文富有中国乡村～。This essay gives a flavour of Chinese country life.
【情文并茂】qíng-wén bìngmào〈成〉be excellent in both content and language
【情形】qíngxing〈名〉circumstances: 在目前～下 under the present circumstances ‖ 看～要下雨。It looks like rain. ‖ 现在～完全不同了。Things now are completely different.
【情绪】qíngxù〈名〉1▸（指心理状态）mood: 发泄不满～ vent one's dissatisfaction ‖ 影响～ influence one's moods ‖ 滋长自满～ breed self-satisfaction ‖ ～高涨 morale is high ‖ ～消沉 get depressed ‖ 敌对～ feelings of hostility 2▸（不快的情感）moodiness: 有点儿～ be a bit moody ‖ 他今天闹～了。He's in a mood today.
【情义】qíngyì〈名〉ties of friendship: 重～ value friendship over sth. else ‖ 夫妻～ true feelings between husband and wife
【情谊】qíngyì〈名〉friendly feelings: 师生～ affection between teachers and students ‖ ～深厚 affection runs deep
【情意】qíngyì〈名〉affection: 表达友好～ express friendly sentiments ‖ ～绵绵 in everlasting love
【情由】qíngyóu〈名〉hows and whys: 不问～ without asking the ins and outs ‖ 解释～ explain the hows and whys of sth.
【情有独钟】qíngyǒudúzhōng〈成〉show special preference to: 她对绘画～。She has a particular love of painting.
【情有可原】qíngyǒukěyuán〈成〉excusable: 出点小差错，～。Small errors can be tolerated.
【情欲】qíngyù〈名〉sensual desire: 放纵～ indulge one's passion
【情缘】qíngyuán〈名〉predestined love: 他们～未了。Their love has not run its course.
【情愿】qíngyuàn A〈动〉be willing: 不～做 be unwilling to do sth. ▸两相～, 心甘～, 一相～ B〈副〉preferably: 他～出去吃，也不愿意自己做饭。He would rather eat out than cook for himself.
【情韵】qíngyùn〈名〉〈书〉charm: 这个舞蹈颇具东方～。This dance has Eastern charm.
【情真意切】qíngzhēn-yìqiè〈成〉genuine affection and sincere concern: 他的忠告～。His advice comes from a very genuine place.
【情知】qíngzhī〈动〉be fully aware of: ～有危险，他还是坚持要去。He insisted on going even though he was fully aware of the dangers involved.
【情致】qíngzhì〈名〉〈书〉interest: 别有～ have special appeal ‖ ～正高 be keenly interested
【情种】qíngzhǒng〈名〉sentimental type: 他是个～，极容易堕入爱河。He is the sentimental type; he falls in love easily.
【情状】qíngzhuàng〈名〉〈书〉situation: 见此～，他大为光火。He flared up at what he saw.

晴 qíng〈形〉clear: ～间多云 fine with occasional clouds ‖ ～转多云 [in weather forecast] fine to cloudy ‖ 雨过天～。The rain's stopped and the sky cleared up. ▸～空, ～朗, 放～
【晴好】qínghǎo〈形〉fine and clear: 天气～ beautiful day
【晴和】qínghé〈形〉sunny and bright: 天气～ bright sunny day
【晴空】qíngkōng〈名〉clear sky: ～万里 boundless stretch of blue sky
【晴朗】qínglǎng〈形〉fine: 天空～ sunny skies ‖ 天气～ fine sunny weather
【晴明】qíngmíng〈形〉〈书〉clear: 天气～。It's a sunny day.
【晴天】qíngtiān〈名〉sunny day: 今天是个大～。It's a glorious sunny day today.
【晴天霹雳】qíngtiān-pīlì〈成〉a bolt from the blue: 噩耗传来，真如～。The bad news hit us like a thunderbolt.
【晴雨表】qíngyǔbiǎo〈名〉barometer: 股市是商情的～。The stock market is a barometer of business conditions.

腈（腈） qíng〈动〉inherit: ▸～受
【腈受】qíngshòu〈动〉inherit: ～财产/遗产 inherit a property/legacy

氰 qíng〈名〉［化学］cyanogen
【氰化钾】qínghuàjiǎ〈名〉［化学］potassium cyanide

擎 qíng〈动〉support: ▸～天柱, 众～易举
【擎天柱】qíngtiānzhù〈名〉〈喻〉mainstay

黥 qíng〈动〉〈古〉1▸（指刑罚）brand the face (as a punishment) 2▸（刺青）tattoo

q

qǐng

苘 qǐng
【苘麻】qǐngmá〈名〉［植物］Indian mallow

顷[1]（頃） qǐng〈量〉*qing* [unit of area, equal to 6.6667 hectares]

顷[2]（頃） qǐng〈书〉
A〈名〉moment: ▸～刻, 少～
B〈副〉just: ～接来信 have just received a letter

【顷刻】qǐngkè〈名〉 instant: ～瓦解 collapse like a house of cards ‖ ～之间 in no time

请(請) qǐng〈动〉 1 (请求) ask: ～人帮助 ask sb. for help ‖ ～人指点 ask sb. for advice ▸～假, ～教, 申～ 2 (聘请、邀请) invite: ～不起家庭教师 cannot afford a private teacher ‖ ～人吃饭 invite sb. to dinner ‖ 不～自来 gatecrash ▸聘～, 邀～ 3 〈旧〉(买) buy holy sacrificial items: ～灶神 buy an image of the Kitchen God 4 〈敬〉(表示客气) please: ～稍候。Just a moment, please. ‖ ～坐。Please be seated. ‖ 敬～光临。Please oblige me with your presence.

【请安】qǐng'ān ▸**p. 780**〈动〉 pay respects to sb.: 给您～了。Wishing you good health.

【请便】qǐngbiàn〈动〉 do as you wish: 要去要留, ～。Stay or go as you choose.

【请调】qǐngdiào〈动〉 apply for a transfer: ～报告 application for a transfer

【请功】qǐnggōng〈动〉 ask the authorities to recognize sb.'s accomplishment

【请假】qǐngjià〈动〉 ask for leave (of absence): 请两天假 ask for two days off ‖ ～条 application for leave ‖ 向学校～ get leave from school ‖ 我请了一天病假。I've asked for a day's sick leave.

【请柬】qǐngjiǎn〈名〉 invitation: 发～ send out invitations

【请将不如激将】qǐngjiàng bùrú jījiàng〈俗〉 it's better to nudge sb. to do sth. than to beg them to do it

【请教】qǐngjiào〈动〉 ask for advice: 虚心向群众～ learn modestly from the masses ‖ 能向你～一个问题吗? May I have your advice on a problem?

【请君入瓮】qǐngjūnrùwèng〈成〉〈喻〉 give sb. a taste of his own medicine

【请客】qǐngkè〈动〉 invite sb. to dinner: ～送礼 give lavish dinner parties and gifts to sb. ‖ 这次我～。This is my treat.

【请命】qǐngmìng〈动〉 plead on sb.'s behalf: 为民～ plead on behalf of the people

【请求】qǐngqiú A〈动〉 request: ～援助 request sb.'s assistance ‖ 他～老板再给他一次机会。He asked his boss for another chance. B〈名〉 request: 批准～ approve sb.'s request ‖ 我有个小小的～。I have a small request.

【请赏】qǐngshǎng〈动〉 petition the authorities to grant a reward to sb. on account of their achievements: 为有功人员～ petition for a reward for those who have performed exploits/meritorious deeds

【请神容易送神难】qǐng shén róngyì sòng shén nán〈俗〉 it is easier to invite sb. in than to send them away

【请示】qǐngshì〈动〉 request instructions: 发急件～上级 write a dispatch to one's superiors asking for instructions ‖ 向上级～ ask those higher up for instructions

【请帖】qǐngtiě〈名〉 invitation: 婚礼～ wedding invitation

【请托】qǐngtuō〈动〉 ask sb. to do sth.: 这件事我只好～他人办理。I have to ask somebody else to handle this matter.

【请问】qǐngwèn〈动〉〈敬〉 excuse me: ～大名? Can you tell me your name, please? ‖ ～几点了? Excuse me, but could you tell me what time it is?

【请降】qǐngxiáng〈动〉 beg to surrender

【请缨】qǐngyīng〈动〉〈书〉 submit a request for a military assignment: ～杀敌 volunteer for battle

【请愿】qǐngyuàn〈动〉 petition: 向当局～ petition the authorities ‖ ～书 petition

【请战】qǐngzhàn〈动〉 ask for a battle assignment: ～书 written request for a battle assignment

【请罪】qǐngzuì〈动〉 apologize: ▸负荆～

庼(廎) qǐng〈名〉〈书〉 small hall

qìng

庆(慶) qìng

A〈动〉 celebrate: ～丰收 celebrate a bumper harvest ▸～典, ～功, 欢～

B〈名〉 celebration: ▸国～, 校～

【庆大霉素】qìngdàméisù〈名〉[药学] gentamicin

【庆典】qìngdiǎn〈名〉 celebration: 建校百年～ centennial celebration of the founding of a school ‖ 举行盛大～ hold a grand celebration

【庆父不死, 鲁难未已】Qìngfǔ bù sǐ, Lǔ nàn wèi yǐ〈成〉〈喻〉 there will always be trouble until its source is removed

【庆功】qìnggōng〈动〉 celebrate a victory: ～会 victory meeting

【庆贺】qìnghè〈动〉 congratulate: ～八十大寿 celebrate sb.'s 80th birthday ‖ 值得～的事 matter deserving of congratulation

【庆幸】qìngxìng〈动〉 thank one's lucky stars: ～自己脱险 consider oneself lucky to have escaped danger ‖ ～找到一份好工作 congratulate oneself on having found a good job ‖ ～的是, 我们身体还不错。Luckily, we enjoy good health.

【庆祝】qìngzhù〈动〉 celebrate: ～中华人民共和国成立60周年 celebrate the 60th anniversary of the founding of the People's Republic of China ‖ 举行盛大的～活动 throw a huge festival celebrating an event ‖ ～大会 celebration meeting

亲(親) qìng

▸qīn

【亲家】qìngjia〈名〉 1 (指关系) relatives by marriage 2 (指人) son's or daughter's parents-in-law

【亲家公】qìngjiagōng〈名〉 son's or daughter's father-in-law

【亲家母】qìngjiamǔ〈名〉 son's or daughter's mother-in-law

箐 qìng〈名〉〈方〉 bamboo groves in mountain valleys

磬 qìng〈名〉 1 (指曲尺形) chime stone 2 (指铜制钵形) inverted bell

罄 qìng〈动〉〈书〉 use up: 售～ be all sold out ‖ ～其所有 empty one's purse ▸～竹难书

【罄竹难书】qìngzhú-nánshū〈成〉[esp of crimes] be too many to mention

qióng

穷(窮) qióng

A〈动〉 1 (尽) having an end: ▸层出不～, 日暮途～ 2 (探究) thoroughly investigate: ▸～原竟委, 追本～源 3 (用尽) use up: ▸～兵黩武, 黔驴技～

B〈副〉 1 (极为) extremely: ▸～奢极欲, ～凶极恶 2 (彻底) thoroughly: ～究其因 probe deeply into sth. to find the cause ▸～追不舍 3 〈口〉(勉强) despite difficult conditions: ～讲究 be overly particular ‖ ～开心 be happy despite misery

C〈形〉 poor: ～国 poor country ‖ ～学生 poor student ▸～苦, ～困

【穷棒子】qióngbàngzi〈名〉 1 〈贬〉(穷人) poor peasant 2 (穷而有志气的人) poor person with high aspirations: ～精神 spirit of the hard-working poor peasants

【穷兵黩武】qióngbīng-dúwǔ〈成〉 be militaristic and aggressive

【穷愁】qióngchóu〈形〉 destitute and distressed: ～潦倒 be penniless and frustrated

【穷乏】qióngfá〈形〉 poor

【穷光蛋】qióngguāngdàn〈名〉〈口〉〈贬〉 pauper: 身无分文的～ poor devil without a penny in his pouch

【穷鬼】qióngguǐ〈名〉〈贬〉 poor wretch

【穷极无聊】qióngjí-wúliáo〈成〉 be bored out of one's mind: 她失业在家, 感到～。She lost her job and was hanging around at home, bored to death.

【穷尽】qióngjìn A〈动〉 use up: 群众的智慧是不会～的。The wisdom of the people is inexhaustible. B〈名〉 limit: 知识是没有～的。There is no limit to how much you can learn.

【穷举】qióngjǔ〈名〉[数学] exhaustion: ～法 method of exhaustion

【穷寇】qióngkòu〈名〉 hard-pressed enemy

【穷寇勿追】qióngkòu-wùzhuī〈成〉 do not pursue a hard-pressed enemy

【穷苦】qióngkǔ〈形〉 poor and miserable: 生活～ live in poverty and misery ‖ ～的人们 those who are poor and needy

【穷匮】qióngkuì〈动〉〈书〉 lack: 财用～ be short of money and goods

【穷困】qióngkùn〈形〉 poverty-stricken: 生活在～中 live in misery and want

【穷困潦倒】qióngkùn-liáodǎo〈成〉 be poor and wretched: 过着～的生活 lead a dog's life

【穷忙】qióngmáng〈动〉 1 〈旧〉(指为谋生) work hard to eke out a living 2 (因事务多) be awfully busy: 我一天到晚～。I'm rushed off my feet all the time.

【穷年累月】qióngnián-lěiyuè〈成〉 year in, year out

【穷人】qióngrén〈名〉 the poor: 帮助～ help the poor

【穷山恶水】qióngshān-èshuǐ〈成〉 barren hills and untamed rivers: 治理～ make barren hills fertile and check turbulent rivers

【穷奢极侈】qióngshē-jíchǐ = 穷奢极欲 qióngshē-jíyù

【穷奢极欲】qióngshē-jíyù〈成〉 live a life of wanton extravagance: 过着～的生活 wallow in luxury

【穷酸】qióngsuān〈形〉 poor and pedantic: 那时他只是个～的教书先生。At that time he was a mere impoverished pedant.

【穷途末路】qióngtú-mòlù〈成〉 have come to a dead end: 到了～ be driven into a tight corner

【穷乡僻壤】qióngxiāng-pìrǎng〈成〉 backwater: 昔日的～如今变成了繁华的城市。This once remote and backward place has now become a prosperous city.

【穷形尽相】qióngxíng-jìnxiàng〈成〉 1 (刻画生动) describe in minute, vivid detail 2 (丑态毕露) appear in all one's ugliness

【穷凶极恶】qióngxiōng-jí'è〈成〉 ferocious and wicked: ～的敌人 unscrupulous and

vicious enemy
【穷原竟委】qióngyuán-jìngwěi〈成〉get to the bottom of a matter
【穷源溯流】qióngyuán-sùliú = 穷原竟委 qióngyuán-jìngwěi
【穷则思变】qióngzésībiàn〈成〉poverty gives rise to a desire for change
【穷追不舍】qióngzhuībùshě〈成〉keep after: 警察～，终于抓到了他。The police kept after him until they finally captured him.
【穷追猛打】qióngzhuī-měngdǎ〈成〉hotly pursue and fiercely attack

茕（煢） qióng〈形〉〈书〉 1（孤单）solitary 2（忧愁）grieved
【茕茕】qióngqióng〈形〉〈书〉all alone
【茕茕孑立】qióngqióng jiélì〈成〉be solitary

穹 qióng〈书〉
A〈形〉domed: ～顶 dome
B〈名〉sky: ▸苍～
【穹苍】qióngcāng〈名〉〈书〉dome of the sky: 在茫茫～之下 under the canopy of heaven
【穹顶】qióngdǐng〈名〉［建筑］dome
【穹隆】qiónglóng〈形〉〈书〉domed
【穹庐】qiónglú〈名〉〈书〉yurt
【穹形】qióngxíng〈形〉vaulted

琼（瓊） qióng〈名〉 1〈书〉（美玉）fine jade: ～阁 jewelled palace ▸～浆 2 ▸**p. 661** Qióng（海南）Qiong [another name for Hainan Province]
【琼浆】qióngjiāng〈名〉〈书〉fine wine
【琼剧】qióngjù〈名〉Hainan opera
【琼楼玉宇】qiónglóu-yùyǔ〈成〉magnificent building
【琼脂】qióngzhī〈名〉agar
【琼州海峡】Qióngzhōu Hǎixiá〈名〉Qiongzhou Strait [separating Hainan Island from the mainland]

跫 qióng
【跫然】qióngrán〈拟〉〈书〉patter: 足音～ the footsteps pattered

銎 qióng〈名〉〈书〉hole in an axe for the handle

qiū

丘 qiū
A〈名〉 1（土堆）mound: 荒～ barren hillock ▸～陵，沙～，一～之貉 2（坟墓）grave: ▸～墓，坟～
B〈动〉place a coffin in a temporary shelter pending burial
C〈量〉〈方〉plot: 一～稻田 a paddy field
【丘八】qiūbā〈名〉〈旧〉〈贬〉soldier
【丘比特】Qiūbǐtè〈名〉Cupid: 被～之箭射中 be hit by Cupid's arrow
【丘陵】qiūlíng ▸**p. 164**〈名〉hills: ～起伏 rolling hills ‖ ～地带 hilly country
【丘墓】qiūmù〈名〉〈书〉grave
【丘疹】qiūzhěn ▸**p. 50**〈名〉［医学］pimple

邱 Qiū〈名〉Qiu [surname]

龟（龜） qiū
▸guī, jūn
【龟兹】Qiūcí〈名〉［历史］Qiuci [ancient state in present-day Xinjiang Uyghur Autonomous Region]

秋[1] qiū〈名〉 1（成熟的季节）harvest season: ▸大～，麦～ 2 ▸**p. 345**（秋天）autumn; fall〈美〉: ～雨 autumn rain ‖ ～去冬来。Winter follows autumn. ‖ ～冬之交 when autumn is changing to winter ▸～风，～高气爽，晚～ 3（年）year: ▸千～万代，一日三～ 4（时期）period of time: 危急存亡之～ most critical moment ▸多事之～ 5（收成）autumn crops: ▸护～，收～

秋[2]（鞦） qiū = 秋千 qiūqiān
【秋波】qiūbō〈名〉〈喻〉bright and clear eyes of a beautiful woman: 送～ cast amorous glances (at sb.) ‖（和某人）～传情 flash amorous glances (at sb.) ▸暗送～
【秋播】qiūbō〈动〉sow in autumn: ～作物 autumn-sown crops
【秋菜】qiūcài〈名〉autumn vegetables
【秋虫】qiūchóng〈名〉autumn insects
【秋分】Qiūfēn〈名〉Autumn Equinox [beginning of the 16th of the 24 solar terms]
【秋风】qiūfēng〈名〉autumn breeze: ～萧瑟。The autumn wind is whistling.
【秋风过耳】qiūfēng-guò'ěr〈成〉like an autumn breeze passing the ear
【秋风扫落叶】qiūfēng sǎo luòyè〈成〉〈喻〉sweep away all that is rotten
【秋高气爽】qiūgāo-qìshuǎng〈成〉invigorating autumn climate: 现在～，正是旅游的好时节。Clear and fresh, autumn is just the season for travelling.
【秋灌】qiūguàn〈动〉irrigate in autumn
【秋海棠】qiūhǎitáng〈名〉［植物］begonia
【秋毫】qiūháo〈名〉〈喻〉minute detail: ▸明察～
【秋毫无犯】qiūháo-wúfàn〈成〉not encroach on the interests of the people in the slightest degree
【秋后的蚂蚱】qiūhòude màzha〈歇后〉〈喻〉nearing one's end: 敌人像～，蹦跶不了几天了。The enemies are like grasshoppers in late autumn; their days are numbered.
【秋后算账】qiūhòu-suànzhàng〈成〉〈喻〉wait until sth. is over to settle accounts
【秋季】qiūjì ▸**p. 345**〈名〉autumn; fall〈美〉: ～商品交易会 autumn commodities fair
【秋景】qiūjǐng〈名〉 1（指景色）autumnal scenery: 春光～ spring scenes and autumnal scenery 2（指收成）autumn harvest: 今年～明显好于去年。This year's autumn harvest is better than last year's.
【秋老虎】qiūlǎohǔ〈名〉〈喻〉scorching heat in early autumn
【秋凉】qiūliáng〈名〉cool autumn days: 等～后再去南方吧。Don't go to the south until the end of autumn.
【秋粮】qiūliáng〈名〉autumn grain: 储存～ store up autumn grain
【秋令】qiūlìng〈名〉 1（指季节）autumn〈英〉; fall〈美〉: ～服装 autumn clothing 2（指气候）autumn weather: 冬行～。The winter weather is like that in autumn.
【秋千】qiūqiān〈名〉swing: 荡～ play on the swing
【秋色】qiūsè〈名〉autumn scenery: ～宜人 pleasant autumn scenery ‖ 满园～。The garden is filled with the beauty of autumn. ▸平分～
【秋试】qiūshì〈名〉〈旧〉Ming and Qing dynasties imperial examinations held in autumn
【秋收】qiūshōu A〈动〉gather in autumn crops: 农民们在忙着～。The farmers are all busy with the autumn harvest. B〈名〉autumn harvest: 今年～不错。This year's autumn crop is very good.
【秋霜】qiūshuāng〈名〉 1〈本〉autumn frost 2〈喻〉（白发）white hair: 染上～ get a touch of grey in one's hair 3〈喻〉（严厉）sternness
【秋水】qiūshuǐ〈名〉〈喻〉bright eyes: ▸望穿～
【秋水仙】qiūshuǐxiān〈名〉［植物］meadow saffron
【秋水仙碱】qiūshuǐxiānjiǎn〈名〉［药学］colchicine
【秋思】qiūsī〈名〉melancholy autumn thoughts
【秋天】qiūtiān ▸**p. 345**〈名〉autumn; fall〈美〉: ～即将来临。Autumn is on its way.
【秋汛】qiūxùn〈名〉autumn flood
【秋意】qiūyì〈名〉 1（指景色）autumn scene: ～萧瑟 bleak autumn scene 2（指气候）slight hint of autumn: 现在已有几分～。Autumn is in the air.
【秋游】qiūyóu〈动〉make an autumn excursion: 组织～ organize an autumn outing
【秋雨】qiūyǔ〈名〉autumn rain
【秋种】qiūzhòng〈动〉sow in autumn
【秋装】qiūzhuāng〈名〉autumn clothing

蚯 qiū
【蚯蚓】qiūyǐn〈名〉［动物］earthworm

湫 qiū〈名〉〈书〉pond: 山～ mountain pool

楸 qiū〈名〉［植物］Chinese catalpa

鳅（鰍） qiū ▸泥鳅 níqiū

鞧 qiū
A ▸后鞧 hòuqiū
B〈动〉〈方〉contract: ～眉头 contract the brows

qiú

仇 Qiú〈名〉Qiu [surname]
▸chóu

囚 qiú
A〈动〉imprison: 被～ be imprisoned ▸～禁
B〈名〉prisoner: ▸阶下～，死～
【囚车】qiúchē〈名〉prison van
【囚犯】qiúfàn〈名〉prisoner: 提审～ arraign a prisoner ‖ 被判长期徒刑的～ long-term convict
【囚房】qiúfáng〈名〉prison cell
【囚歌】qiúgē〈名〉prisoner's lament
【囚禁】qiújìn〈动〉imprison: 她被～三个月。She was held captive for three months.
【囚牢】qiúláo〈名〉〈旧〉prison: 被打入～ be thrown into prison
【囚笼】qiúlóng〈名〉〈古〉prisoner's cage: 关在～中的犯人 prisoner imprisoned in a cage
【囚室】qiúshì〈名〉prison cell

【囚首垢面】 qiúshǒu-gòumiàn 〈成〉 with unkempt hair and a dirty face
【囚徒】 qiútú 〈名〉 prisoner: 过～般的生活 live like a convict
【囚衣】 qiúyī 〈名〉 prison uniform

犰 qiú

【犰狳】 qiúyú 〈名〉 ［动物］ armadillo

求 qiú

〈动〉 **1**（追求） seek: ～进步 strive for further progress ‖ ～学问 seek knowledge ‖ 不～名，不～利。 Seek neither fame nor gain. ▸～同存异，～学，实事～是 **2**（请求） ask: ～您帮个忙，行吗？ May I ask you a favour? ‖ 我有事～你。 I have a request to make of you. ▸～情，～饶，央～ **3**（寻求） require: 所有动物都有～生存的本能。 All animals are endowed with an instinct for survival. ▸～全责备，精益～精，要～ **4**（需求） demand: ～大于供 demand exceeds supply ▸供不应～，供～
【求爱】 qiú'ài 〈动〉 court: 向某人～ make advances on sb.
【求大同，存小异】 qiú dàtóng, cún xiǎoyì 〈成〉 seek common ground on major issues while reserving differences on minor ones
【求告】 qiúgào 〈动〉 entreat: 苦苦～ entreat piteously ‖ ～无门 have nothing to turn to for help
【求购】 qiúgòu 〈动〉 seek to purchase: 高价～ offer high price to secure the purchase of sth. ‖ ～热线 buyer's hotline
【求和】 qiúhé 〈动〉 **1**（指作战） hold out an olive branch: 政府正在做出～的表示。 The government is making overtures for peace. **2**（指竞赛） try to equalize
【求欢】 qiúhuān 〈动〉 〈书〉 seek woman's consent for sexual intercourse
【求婚】 qiúhūn 〈动〉 make a proposal of marriage: 向一位姑娘～ propose to a girl ‖ 主动～ take the initiative in a proposal of marriage
【求婚者】 qiúhūnzhě 〈名〉 suitor
【求见】 qiújiàn 〈动〉 request an audience: 登门～ pay a personal call on sb. ‖ 他有急事～总统。 He requested an audience with the president on an urgent issue.
【求教】 qiújiào 〈动〉 ask for advice: 登门～ come to seek advice ‖ 虚心～ listen to advice with an open mind
【求解】 qiújiě 〈动〉 find the solution to a mathematical problem
【求借】 qiújiè 〈动〉 beg to borrow: ～无门 fail to find anyone that one can borrow something from
【求救】 qiújiù 〈动〉 ask for help: 发出～信号 signal an SOS
【求靠】 qiúkào 〈动〉 seek refuge with sb.: ～亲友 seek refuge with one's relatives and friends
【求偶】 qiú'ǒu 〈动〉 seek a mate: ～心切 be eager to find a husband or wife
【求乞】 qiúqǐ 〈动〉 beg: ～钱财 beg for money ‖ 沿街～ beg in the street
【求签】 qiúqiān 〈动〉 seek divine guidance by drawing lots
【求签问卜】 qiúqiān-wènbǔ 〈成〉 seek divine advice by drawing lot
【求亲】 qiúqīn 〈动〉 make an offer of marriage to another family on behalf of one's son or daughter
【求亲告友】 qiúqīn-gàoyǒu 〈成〉 ask favours from friends and relatives
【求情】 qiúqíng 〈动〉 plead: ～告饶 beg for leniency and mercy ‖ 替人～ plead on sb.'s behalf
【求全】 qiúquán 〈动〉 **1**（追求完美） demand perfection: ～之心 desire for perfection **2**（指成全某事） try to bring sth. to completion: ▸委曲～
【求全责备】 qiúquán-zébèi 〈成〉 demand perfection: 对别人不要～。 Don't nit-pick on others.
【求饶】 qiúráo 〈动〉 beg for mercy: 屈膝～ get on one's knees and beg for mercy
【求人】 qiúrén 〈动〉 ask for help: ～指教 go to sb. for advice
【求人不如求己】 qiú rén bùrú qiú jǐ 〈俗〉 God helps those who help themselves
【求荣】 qiúróng 〈动〉 seek personal glory: 卖国～ turn traitor for personal gain
【求神拜佛】 qiúshén-bàifó 〈成〉 ask for blessings from god and pray to Buddha for help
【求神问卜】 qiúshén-wènbǔ 〈成〉 seek divine advice
【求生】 qiúshēng 〈动〉 seek survival: ～的本能 survival instinct
【求胜心切】 qiúshèngxīnqiè 〈成〉 be eager to win
【求实】 qiúshí 〈动〉 be practical-minded: ～精神 realistic approach
【求是】 qiúshì 〈动〉 seek truth: ▸实事～
【求索】 qiúsuǒ 〈动〉 seek: ～新路子 seek new ways
【求同存异】 qiútóng-cúnyì 〈成〉 seek common ground leaving aside existing differences: 本着～的精神 in a spirit of seeking common ground whilst reserving differences
【求贤若渴】 qiúxián-ruòkě 〈成〉 hunger for talent
【求降】 qiúxiáng 〈动〉 beg to surrender
【求学】 qiúxué 〈动〉 **1**（上学） go to school: 到国外～ go abroad to study ‖ 在北大～之际 when studying at Peking University **2**（探索学问） seek knowledge: ～不辍 never stop seeking knowledge
【求爷爷告奶奶】 qiú yéye gào nǎinai 〈俗〉 go about begging for help
【求医】 qiúyī 〈动〉 seek medical advice: 到国外～ seek a cure in another country
【求雨】 qiúyǔ 〈动〉 〈旧〉 pray for rain
【求援】 qiúyuán 〈动〉 ask for help: 向友人～ turn to one's friend for help
【求战】 qiúzhàn 〈动〉 **1**（寻找战机） seek battle **2**（请求作战） ask to go into battle: ～心切 be itching for a fight
【求真务实】 qiúzhēn-wùshí 〈成〉 seeking truth and being pragmatic
【求证】 qiúzhèng 〈动〉 seek verification: 多方～ seek evidence from various sources
【求之不得】 qiúzhī-bùdé 〈成〉 more than one could wish for: 这真是～的好机会。 This is a most welcome opportunity.
【求知】 qiúzhī 〈动〉 seek knowledge: ～若渴 hunger for knowledge
【求知欲】 qiúzhīyù 〈名〉 desire to learn: 他的～很强。 He has a strong thirst for knowledge.
【求职】 qiúzhí 〈动〉 seek employment: 激烈的～竞争 intense competition for jobs ‖ ～面试 job interview
【求职信】 qiúzhíxìn 〈名〉 application for employment
【求职者】 qiúzhízhě 〈名〉 job applicant
【求治】 qiúzhì 〈动〉 seek a cure
【求助】 qiúzhù 〈动〉 seek help: ～于人 ask sb. for help ‖ ～热线 helpline

虬（虯） qiú

A = 虬龙 qiúlóng
B 〈形〉 〈书〉（拳曲） twisted: ▸～须
【虬龙】 qiúlóng 〈名〉 legendary small dragon with horns
【虬髯】 qiúrán 〈名〉 〈书〉 curly whiskers
【虬须】 qiúxū 〈名〉 〈书〉 curly beard

泅 qiú

〈动〉 swim: ～过河去 swim across the river
【泅渡】 qiúdù 〈动〉 swim across: 武装～ swim across fully armed
【泅水】 qiúshuǐ 〈动〉 swim
【泅泳】 qiúyǒng 〈动〉 swim

俅[1] Qiú

〈旧〉 = 独龙族 Dúlóngzú

俅[2] qiú

【俅俅】 qiúqiú 〈形〉 〈书〉 respectful and submissive

酋 qiú

〈名〉 chief: 匪～ bandit chief
【酋长】 qiúzhǎng 〈名〉 chief: 部落～ chief of a tribe
【酋长国】 qiúzhǎngguó 〈名〉 emirate: 阿拉伯联合～ United Arab Emirates

逑 qiú

〈名〉 〈书〉 spouse

尿 qiú

〈名〉 〈方〉 〈粗〉 cock 〈粗〉

球 qiú

〈名〉 **1**（球状物） ball: 火～ ball of fire ‖ 泥～ ball of clay ▸煤～，气～，雪～ **2**（地球） earth: ▸地～，寰～ **3**（体育用品） ball: 踢～ kick a ball ▸篮～，高尔夫～，传～，发～，弧圈～ **4**（球类运动） ball game: 上周末我们看了一场～。 We watched a ball game last weekend. ▸～迷，～赛 **5**（球体） sphere: ▸～面，～体，～心
【球棒】 qiúbàng 〈名〉 club: 板球～ cricket bat
【球操】 qiúcāo 〈名〉 ［体育］ ball exercises
【球场】 qiúchǎng 〈名〉（指足球、垒球） field; pitch 〈英〉;（指篮球、排球、网球等） court;（指高尔夫球） course: 棒球～ baseball field ‖ 高尔夫～ golf course
【球胆】 qiúdǎn 〈名〉 bladder of a ball
【球蛋白】 qiúdànbái 〈名〉 ［生化］ globulin
【球洞】 qiúdòng 〈名〉 golf hole
【球队】 qiúduì 〈名〉 team: 篮/足～ basketball/football team
【球阀】 qiúfá 〈名〉 ［机械］ ball valve
【球风】 qiúfēng 〈名〉 sportsmanship: ～不正 lack of sportsmanship
【球杆】 qiúgān 〈名〉 golf club
【球感】 qiúgǎn 〈名〉 feel for the ball
【球罐】 qiúguàn 〈名〉 ［石油］ sphere
【球果】 qiúguǒ 〈名〉 ［植物］ cone
【球技】 qiújì 〈名〉 ball skills: 展示高超的～ demonstrate superb ball skills
【球茎】 qiújīng 〈名〉 ［植物］ corm
【球茎甘蓝】 qiújīng gānlán 〈名〉 ［植物］ kohlrabi
【球菌】 qiújūn 〈名〉 ［医学］ coccus
【球类运动】 qiúlèi yùndòng 〈名〉 ball games
【球龄】 qiúlíng 〈名〉 number of years for which one has played a ball game
【球路】 qiúlù 〈名〉 tactics in ball games: 熟悉对方～ be familiar with one's opponent's tactics ‖ ～多变 use a variety of ball tricks
【球门】 qiúmén 〈名〉 goal: 把球踢进～ kick

a ball into the goal
【球门球】qiúménqiú〈名〉 goal kick
【球门区】qiúménqū〈名〉 goal area
【球门线】qiúménxiàn〈名〉 goal line
【球门柱】qiúménzhù〈名〉 goalpost
【球迷】qiúmí〈名〉 fan: 铁杆～ devoted fan ‖ ～协会 association of sports enthusiasts
【球面】qiúmiàn〈名〉［数学］ sphere
【球面度】qiúmiàndù〈名〉［数学］ steradian
【球面几何学】qiúmiàn jǐhéxué〈名〉［数学］ spherical geometry
【球面镜】qiúmiànjìng〈名〉［物理］ spherical mirror
【球墨铸铁】qiúmò zhùtiě〈名〉［冶金］ nodular cast iron
【球幕电影】qiúmù diànyǐng = 全景电影 quánjǐng diànyǐng
【球拍】qiúpāi〈名〉（指网球和羽毛球） racket;（指乒乓球） bat
【球票】qiúpiào〈名〉 ticket for a ball game: 倒卖～ tout tickets for a ball game
【球权】qiúquán〈名〉［体育］ right to the ball: 掌握～ get the ball
【球赛】qiúsài〈名〉 ball game: 看～ watch a ball game
【球市】qiúshì〈名〉 ball game market situation
【球手】qiúshǒu〈名〉 ballplayer
【球台】qiútái〈名〉 table
【球坛】qiútán〈名〉 ball-playing world: ～老将 veteran ballplayer ‖ ～新秀 new star player
【球探】qiútàn〈名〉 talent scout
【球体】qiútǐ〈名〉 sphere: 地球并不是一个很圆的～。 The earth is not a perfect sphere.
【球童】qiútóng〈名〉（指高尔夫球）caddie;（指网球）（指男性） ballboy;（指女性） ballgirl
【球王】qiúwáng〈名〉 ball king
【球网】qiúwǎng〈名〉 net (for a ball game)
【球鞋】qiúxié〈名〉 gym shoes
【球心】qiúxīn〈名〉 centre of a sphere
【球星】qiúxīng〈名〉 (ball-game) star, star player: 超级/职业～ super/professional star
【球形】qiúxíng〈名〉 sphericity
【球衣】qiúyī〈名〉 jersey
【球艺】qiúyì〈名〉 ball game skill: 切磋～ exchange ball-game techniques ‖ 高超的～ superb ball skills
【球员】qiúyuán ▸**p. 966**〈名〉 ballplayer: 最有价值～ most valuable player (MVP)
【球轴承】qiúzhóuchéng〈名〉［机械］ ball bearing
【球状】qiúzhuàng〈名〉 sphericity

遒 qiú〈形〉〈书〉 powerful
【遒劲】qiújìng〈形〉〈书〉 vigorous: 笔力～ write in a bold hand ‖ ～的苍松 sturdy green pine

巯（巰） qiú〈名〉［化学］ mercapto
【巯基】qiújī〈名〉［化学］ mercapto

裘 qiú〈名〉〈书〉 fur coat: ▸狐～, 集腋成～
【裘皮】qiúpí〈名〉 fur: ～大衣 fur coat

蝤 qiú
▸yóu
【蝤蛴】qiúqí〈名〉〈古〉 longicorn larva

qiǔ

糗 qiǔ
A〈名〉〈古〉 solid food prepared for a journey
B〈动〉〈方〉 [of noodles or porridge] become mushy: 面都煮～了，没法吃了。 The noodles had been boiled down into a mush, and were quite uneatable.

qū

区（區） qū
A〈名〉 **1**（区域） area: 产煤～ coal-producing region ‖ 工业～ industrial zone ‖ 金融～ financial district ‖ 危险～ danger zone ‖ 住宅～ residential area **2**（行政区划单位） district: ～政府 district government ▸军～, 特～, 行政～
B〈动〉 discriminate: ▸～别, ～分
▸Ōu
【区别】qūbié **A**〈动〉 differentiate: ～对待 deal with each case in its own way ‖ 把两者～开来 differentiate one from the other **B**〈名〉 difference: 两者没有～。 There is no difference between the two. ‖ 这两个词在意义上有很大～。 There is a big discrepancy in meaning between the two words.
【区段】qūduàn〈名〉 section
【区分】qūfēn〈动〉 differentiate: ～两类不同性质的矛盾 differentiate between the two different types of contradictions ‖ 你能～英国英语和美国英语吗? Can you tell the difference between British English and American English?
【区号】qūhào〈名〉 dialling code〈英〉; area code〈美〉
【区划】qūhuà〈名〉 division into districts: 行政～ administrative divisions
【区徽】qūhuī〈名〉 regional emblem: 澳门特别行政区的～ emblem of the Macao Special Administrative Region
【区间】qūjiān〈名〉 section of a normal route: ▸～车
【区间车】qūjiānchē〈名〉 bus or train travelling only part of a certain route
【区块】qūkuài〈名〉 block
【区片】qūpiàn〈名〉 block of land: 征地～综合地价 land expropriation parcel price
【区旗】qūqí〈名〉 regional flag: 香港特别行政区的～ the flag of the Hong Kong Special Administrative Region
【区区】qūqū〈形〉 trifling: ～薄礼，不成敬意。 Please accept this small gift as a token of my appreciation. ‖ ～小事，何足挂齿。 Such a trifling incident is hardly worth mentioning.
【区时】qūshí〈名〉［天文］ zone time
【区位】qūwèi〈名〉 area: ～优势 locational advantage
【区域】qūyù〈名〉 region: ～电网 regional power grid ‖ ～分工 regional division of work ‖ ～自治 regional autonomy
【区域合作】qūyù hézuò〈名〉 regional cooperation
【区域经济】qūyù jīngjì〈名〉 regional economy: ～一体化 integration of regional economies
【区长】qūzhǎng〈名〉 district head

曲[1] qū
A〈形〉 **1**（弯曲） bent: ～管 curved pipe ▸～径, ～折, 弯～ **2**（不公正） wrong: ▸～解, 歪～
B〈动〉 bend: ～肱而枕 bend one's arm to make a head rest
C〈名〉 **1**（弯曲处） bend: ▸河～ **2**（偏远之处） remote area

曲[2]**（麯）** qū〈名〉 yeast: ▸酒～
▸qǔ
【曲笔】qūbǐ〈名〉〈书〉 **1**（指歪曲事实） distortion of facts to hide the truth **2**（故意离题） deliberate digression in writing
【曲别针】qūbiézhēn〈名〉 paper clip
【曲柄】qūbǐng〈名〉［机械］ crank: ～钻 crank brace
【曲尺】qūchǐ〈名〉 carpenter's square
【曲拱】qūgǒng〈名〉 arch: ～桥 arched bridge
【曲棍球】qūgùnqiú〈名〉［体育］ **1** ▸**p. 909**（指运动） hockey〈英〉; field hockey〈美〉 **2**（指球） hockey ball
【曲解】qūjiě〈动〉 misinterpret: 你～了我的意思。 You have distorted my meaning. ‖ 她～了我的话。 She twisted what I said.
【曲尽其妙】qūjìn-qímiào〈成〉 demonstrate subtly and skilfully
【曲颈甑】qūjǐngzèng〈名〉［化学］ retort
【曲径】qūjìng〈名〉 winding path
【曲径通幽】qūjìng-tōngyōu〈成〉 winding path leading to seclusion
【曲里拐弯】qūliguǎiwān〈成〉〈口〉 zigzagging: ～的小路 zigzagging path ‖ 直说吧，别～地绕弯子。 Come straight to the point. Don't beat about the bush.
【曲率】qūlǜ〈名〉［数学］ curvature
【曲霉】qūméi〈名〉［医学］ aspergillus
【曲面】qūmiàn〈名〉 curved surface: 内/外～ negative/positive camber
【曲奇】qūqí〈名〉 biscuit〈英〉; cookie〈美〉
【曲曲弯弯】qūqū-wānwān〈成〉 winding: ～的海岸线 meandering coastline ‖ 公路～地穿过群山。 The road zigzags its way across the hills.
【曲蟮】qūshàn〈名〉〈方〉 earthworm
【曲射炮】qūshèpào〈名〉 curved-fire gun
【曲突徙薪】qūtū-xǐxīn〈成〉〈喻〉 take precautions against possible danger
【曲线】qūxiàn〈名〉 **1**（指轨迹） curve: 画一条～ draw a curve ‖ 标枪在空中呈～运动。 The javelin curved through the air. **2**（指人体线条） curves: 她很有～美。 She is curvaceous.
【曲线板】qūxiànbǎn〈名〉 curve ruler
【曲线救国】qūxiàn jiùguó〈动〉［历史］ save the nation in circuitous way
【曲线图】qūxiàntú〈名〉 curve chart
【曲线运动】qūxiàn yùndòng〈名〉［物理］ curvilinear motion
【曲意逢迎】qūyì-féngyíng〈成〉 go out of one's way to curry favour with sb.
【曲张】qūzhāng ▸**p. 50**〈形〉［医学］ cirsoid: ▸静脉～
【曲折】qūzhé〈形〉 **1**（弯曲） tortuous: 山路迂回～。 The mountain road is full of twists and turns. ‖ 前途是光明的，道路是～的。 The road is tortuous, but prospects are bright. **2**（复杂） complicated: 情节～的小说 novel with a complicated plot ‖ ～离奇 complicated and eccentric
【曲直】qūzhí〈名〉 right and wrong: 分清是非～ distinguish between right and wrong
【曲轴】qūzhóu〈名〉［机械］ crankshaft

岖（嶇） qū ▸崎岖 qíqū

q

诎（詘） qū〈动〉 1▸〈书〉（缩短） curtail 2▸〈书〉（言语迟钝） be slow of speech 3▸ = 屈 qū

驱（驅） qū〈动〉 1▸（驱赶）drive: 扬鞭～马 brandish a whip to urge on a horse ▸～策 2▸（驾驶） drive: ▸～车 3▸（快跑） run quickly: ▸并驾齐～，长～直入 4▸（赶走） expel: ～云防雹 disperse clouds to prevent a hailstorm ▸～寒，～散，～逐 5▸（迫使） compel: ▸～迫，～使

【驱策】 qūcè 〈动〉 1▸（驱赶） drive 2▸〈喻〉（使唤） compel: 任人～ allow oneself to be ordered about

【驱车】qūchē〈动〉 drive a vehicle: 她～前往机场迎接外宾。 She drove to the airport to meet the foreign guests.

【驱驰】qūchí〈动〉〈书〉1▸（驱马）gallop a horse 2▸（使唤） run about busily for others: 供～ be at sb.'s beck and call

【驱虫剂】qūchóngjì〈名〉 insect repellent: 喷洒～ spray insect repellent

【驱虫药】qūchóngyào〈名〉 vermifuge

【驱除】qūchú〈动〉 drive out: ～入侵者 drive out intruders ‖ ～害虫 get rid of annoying insects ‖ ～邪念 eliminate evil thoughts from one's mind

【驱动】qūdòng〈动〉 1▸（使运转） drive: 水力～ be driven by water power ‖ 磨是由电/水～的。 The mill is driven by electricity/water. 2▸（驱使） drive: 在暴利的～下 be driven by sudden excessive profits

【驱动程序】qūdòng chéngxù〈名〉［计算机］ driver

【驱动轮】qūdònglún〈名〉 driving wheel

【驱动器】qūdòngqì〈名〉［计算机］ drive: 软盘/硬盘～ soft/hard drive

【驱赶】qūgǎn〈动〉 1▸（使快走） drive: ～马车 drive a cart 2▸（使离开） drive away: ～苍蝇 shoo off flies

【驱寒】qūhán〈动〉 dispel cold

【驱迫】 qūpò 〈动〉 urge: 为良心～ be driven by one's conscience

【驱遣】qūqiǎn〈动〉 1▸（差遣） drive sb. to do sth. 2▸〈书〉（赶走） drive away: ～人群 disperse a crowd 3▸（消除） dispel: ～别情 dispel the sad feeling of parting ‖ ～烦闷 get rid of depression

【驱热解毒】qūrè-jiědú〈动〉［中医］ eliminate fever and detoxicate poison

【驱散】qūsàn〈动〉 1▸（赶走） disperse: ～围观人群 break up a crowd of onlookers 2▸（消除） dispel: 阳光～了薄雾。 The sun dispelled the mist. ‖ 她温柔的话语～了他的忧愁。 Her sweet words drove away his melancholy.

【驱使】 qūshǐ 〈动〉 1▸（指强迫） order about: 受人～ be ordered about 2▸（推动） drive: 为好奇心所～ be driven by curiosity ‖ 在贪婪的～下，人会做任何事情。 A man motivated by greed may do anything.

【驱蚊剂】qūwénjì〈名〉 mosquito repellent

【驱邪】qūxié〈动〉 banish evil spirits: ～降福 expel evil spirits and invoke blessings

【驱逐】qūzhú〈动〉 expel: ～外交官 expel a foreign diplomat ‖ ～出境 deport

【驱逐舰】 qūzhújiàn 〈名〉［海军］ destroyer

屈 qū〈动〉 1▸（弯曲） bend: ▸能～能伸 2▸（使弯曲） cause to bend: ▸～膝，～指可数 3▸（屈服） yield: 威武不能～ cannot be subdued by force ▸～从，～服 4▸（委屈） wrong: ▸～才，冤～ 5▸（理亏） be in the wrong: ▸～心，理～词穷

【屈才】qūcái〈动〉 not do justice to sb.'s talents: 让他当部门经理太～了。 It was a waste of his talent to appoint him as mere department manager.

【屈从】qūcóng〈动〉 yield to: ～他人意志 bend to sb.'s will ‖ ～于外来压力 bow to external pressure

【屈打成招】qūdǎ-chéngzhāo〈成〉confess to false charges under torture: 他是～的。 He made a spurious confession under coercion.

【屈服】qūfú〈动〉 yield to: 决不～ never yield (to sb./sth.) ‖ 困难并未使他～。 Hardships failed to make him submit.

【屈光度】 qūguāngdù 〈名〉 ［物理］ dioptre

【屈驾】qūjià〈动〉〈套〉 be kind enough to come: 敬请～光临指导。 Your presence and advice are cordially requested.

【屈节】qūjié〈动〉〈书〉 1▸（失去气节） humble oneself: ～事仇 forfeit one's honour by serving the enemy 2▸（降低身份） condescend: 卑躬～ act obsequiously/servilely

【屈就】 qūjiù 〈动〉〈套〉 condescend to take a post offered: 如蒙～，不胜荣幸。 We will be greatly honoured if you condescend to take this post.

【屈居】qūjū〈动〉 be reconciled to a lower position: ～亚军 have to settle for being the runner-up

【屈戌儿】qūqur〈名〉 metal fastening

【屈辱】qūrǔ 〈名〉 humiliation: 蒙受～ suffer humiliation

【屈死】qūsǐ〈动〉 be wronged and driven to death

【屈体】qūtǐ〈动〉［体育］ pike

【屈枉】qūwang〈动〉 treat unjustly: ～好人 wrong an innocent person

【屈膝】qūxī〈动〉1▸（下跪）kneel: ～求饶 go down on one's knees and beg for mercy 2▸〈喻〉（屈服）yield to: ～投降 go down on one's knees in surrender ▸卑躬～

【屈膝礼】qūxīlǐ〈名〉 curtsy: 向某人行～ curtsy to sb.

【屈心】qūxīn〈动〉〈口〉 have a guilty conscience: 这种～事我不干。 I wouldn't do a mean thing like that.

【屈戌】qūxū〈书〉= 屈戌儿 qūqur

【屈折】qūzhé〈动〉［语言］ inflect: 词形的～变化 the inflection of words

【屈折语】qūzhéyǔ〈名〉［语言］inflectional language

【屈指】qūzhǐ〈动〉 count on one's fingers: ～算来 count on one's fingers

【屈指可数】 qūzhǐ-kěshǔ 〈成〉 can be counted on one's fingers: 医生说她的日子～。 The doctor said that her days were numbered.

【屈尊】qūzūn〈动〉〈套〉condescend: ～求教 deign to ask for advice

胠 qū〈书〉
A〈名〉 sides
B〈动〉 open from the side: ～箧 steal

祛 qū〈动〉 dispel: ～病延年 eliminate disease and prolong life

【祛除】qūchú〈动〉 dispel: ～疾病 eradicate diseases ‖ ～疑虑 dispel sb.'s misgivings

【祛蠹除奸】qūdù-chújiān〈成〉 get rid of harmful elements and evil-doers

【祛风】 qūfēng 〈动〉［中医］ relieve rheumatic pains

【祛湿】qūshī〈动〉［中医］ clear dampness

【祛暑】qūshǔ〈动〉［中医］ drive away summer heat

【祛痰】qūtán〈动〉［中医］ clear phlegm

【祛邪】qūxié〈动〉 drive away evil

【祛疑】qūyí〈动〉〈书〉 dispel sb.'s doubts

【祛淤】qūyū〈动〉［中医］ remove blood stasis: ～活血 remove blood stasis and promote blood circulation

袪 qū〈书〉〈名〉 sleeve

蛆 qū〈名〉 maggot

【蛆虫】qūchóng〈名〉 1▸（指虫） maggot 2▸〈喻〉（指人） shameless person

躯（軀） qū 〈名〉 human body: ▸～体，身～，为国捐～

【躯干】qūgàn〈名〉 torso

【躯壳】qūqiào〈名〉 body [as opposed to soul]

【躯体】qūtǐ〈名〉 body: ～魁梧 be tall and sturdy

焌 qū〈动〉〈方〉 1▸（熄灭） extinguish a burning object: 把香烟在鞋底上～灭 put out a cigarette by stubbing it against the sole of one's shoe 2▸（烧） burn: 他的手让烟头～了一下。 A cigarette end burnt his hand. 3▸ a（炒） stir-fry after adding condiments to boiling oil: ～豆芽 stir-fried bean sprouts b（用热油浇） heat oil and then pour it on cooked food: 给凉拌莴笋～点香油 pour heated sesame oil on asparagus salad

趋（趨） qū 〈动〉 1▸（快走） hasten 2▸（追逐） pursue: ～名逐利 seek fame and fortune ▸～光性，～之若鹜 3▸（迎合） ingratiate oneself with: ▸～奉，～炎附势 4▸（趋向） tend towards: 局势～于明朗。 The situation is becoming clear. ‖ 双方意见～于一致。 The two look as if they are inclined to agree. ▸～势，～向，大势所～

【趋避】qūbì〈动〉 dodge: ～路旁 make a dodge to the side of the road

【趋奉】qūfèng〈动〉 fawn on: 阿谀～某人 curry favour with sb. ‖ 他是靠～领导获得提升的。 He got the promotion by toadying to the leaders.

【趋附】qūfù〈动〉 ingratiate oneself with: ～权贵 ingratiate oneself with dignitaries

【趋光性】 qūguāngxìng 〈名〉 ［生物］ phototaxis

【趋冷】qūlěng〈动〉 cool down gradually

【趋利避害】 qūlì-bìhài 〈成〉 seek advantages and avoid disadvantages

【趋时】qūshí〈动〉〈书〉 follow the fashion: 她衣着～。 She dresses trendily.

【趋势】qūshì〈名〉 trend: 当代教育发展～ contemporary trends in education ‖ 物价有上涨/下降～。 Prices tend to go up/down.

【趋水性】 qūshuǐxìng 〈名〉 ［生物］ hydrotaxis

【趋同】qūtóng〈动〉 tend to converge

【趋向】qūxiàng A〈动〉 tend towards: 国际形势～缓和。 The international situation is becoming more relaxed. ‖ 他的病情～好转。 His condition is taking a favourable turn. B〈名〉 tendency: 人过中年就有发胖的～。 People have a tendency to get fat when they pass middle age.

【趋炎附势】qūyán-fùshì〈成〉 fawn on the rich and powerful

【趋之若鹜】 qūzhī-ruòwù 〈成〉 〈贬〉

〈喻〉 scramble for sth.: 有些人对名利～，对工作则敷衍塞责。 Some people are grubbing for money and fame and can't even be bothered to do their jobs.

蛐 qū
【蛐蛐儿】qūqur〈名〉〈方〉 cricket: ～罐儿 cricket pot
【蛐蟮】qūshàn = 曲蟮 qūshàn

觑（覷） qū〈动〉 squint: 她～起眼睛看画。 She squinted at the pictures. ▸qù

黢 qū〈形〉 black: ▸黑～～
【黢黑】qūhēi〈形〉 pitch-black: ～一片，我们根本就看不见路。 We couldn't see our way at all in the pitch-dark.

曜 qū〈拟〉 whistle: 裁判～～地吹哨子。 The referee blew his whistle. ‖ 蟋蟀在草丛里～～地叫。 Crickets are chirping away in the grass.

qú

劬 qú〈形〉〈书〉 1（劳苦） fatigued 2（勤劳） industrious
【劬劳】qúláo〈形〉〈书〉 fatigued: 不辞～ spare no pains

鸲（鴝） qú
【鸲鹆】qúyù〈名〉［鸟类］ crested myna

渠[1] qú〈名〉 canal: 修水～ build a ditch ‖ 开～灌溉 open up a canal for irrigation ▸沟～，灌～，河～

渠[2] qú〈代〉〈方〉（用作主语） he;（用作宾语） him
【渠道】qúdào〈名〉 1（水道） canal: 灌溉～ irrigation channel ‖ 排水～ drainage ditch 2〈喻〉（途径） channel: 拓宽利用外资～ widen channels for using foreign capital ‖ 合法～ legal channel ‖ 外交/官方/私人～ diplomatic/official/private channel ‖ 信息～ conduit of information ‖ 书籍是获取知识的～。 Books are avenues to knowledge.

璩 Qú〈名〉 Qu [surname]

瞿 Qú〈名〉 Qu [surname]

鼩 qú
【鼩鼱】qújīng〈名〉［动物］ shrew

氍 qú
【氍毹】qúshū〈名〉 1〈本〉 wool carpet 2〈喻〉（舞台） stage: ～场中 on the stage ‖ 红～ stage

鸜（鸜） qú
【鸜鹆】qúyù = 鸲鹆 qúyù

癯（臞） qú〈形〉〈书〉 lean: ▸清～

衢 qú〈名〉〈书〉 thoroughfare: ▸通～

蠼（蠼） qú
【蠼螋】qúsōu〈名〉［昆虫］ earwig

qǔ

曲 qǔ〈名〉 1（指韵文） *qu* [type of verse for singing]: ▸～牌，散～，元～ 2（歌曲） tune: 高歌一～ belt out a song ‖ 名～ well-known tune ‖ ～不离口，拳不离手 song can't dispense with the mouth, nor boxing with the hand ‖ 主题～ theme song ▸～调，～子，插～ 3（歌谱） song music: ▸谱～，作～ ▸qū
【曲调】qǔdiào〈名〉 tune: ～优美 melodious tune
【曲高和寡】qǔgāo-hèguǎ〈成〉〈喻〉 be so highbrow that few people can enjoy or understand
【曲剧】qǔjù〈名〉 *quju* [opera derived from ballad singing]
【曲目】qǔmù〈名〉 repertoire: 他们有保留～二十多个。 They have a repertoire of over 20 songs. ‖ 他们能演奏很多～。 They have a wide repertoire.
【曲牌】qǔpái〈名〉 names of the tunes to which *qu* (曲) are composed
【曲谱】qǔpǔ〈名〉 1（辑录） collection of tunes of *qu* (曲) 2（乐谱） music score
【曲式】qǔshì〈名〉 musical form
【曲坛】qǔtán〈名〉 circles of *quyi* (曲艺) performers
【曲协】qǔxié〈简称〉= 曲艺家协会
【曲艺】qǔyì〈名〉 *quyi* [folk vocal art forms]
【曲艺家协会】qǔyìjiā xiéhuì〈名〉 Ballad Singers Association
【曲终人散】qǔzhōng-rénsàn〈成〉〈喻〉 sadness following a joyful reunion
【曲终奏雅】qǔzhōng-zòuyǎ〈成〉 brilliant conclusion of an essay or a performance
【曲子】qǔzi〈名〉 tune: 用口哨吹一首流行的～ whistle a popular tune

苣 qǔ ▸jù
【苣荬菜】qǔmǎicài〈名〉［植物］ endive

取 qǔ〈动〉 1（领取） take: ～汇款 draw one's remittance ‖ ～票 fetch a ticket ‖ ～行李 claim one's luggage ‖ ～邮件 collect the mail ‖ 从银行～钱 get money out from a bank 2（得到） obtain: ▸～暖，～信于民，咎由自～ 3（选择） choose: ～个吉利 for good luck ‖ ～平均数 take the mean ‖ 掐头去尾，只～中段 break off both ends and just keep the middle section ▸～道，～景，录～
【取保】qǔbǎo〈动〉［法律］ ask sb. to bail one out: ～就医 bail sb. out for medical treatment ‖ ～候审 be released upon bail
【取材】qǔcái〈动〉 select materials: 就地～ draw on local resources ‖ 小说～于一个山村的生活。 The novel draws on life in a mountain village.
【取长补短】qǔcháng-bǔduǎn〈成〉 make up for one's deficiencies by learning from others' strong points: ～，共同提高 learn from each other's good points to make common progress
【取代】qǔdài〈动〉 replace: 用天然气～烧煤 replace coal with natural gas ‖ 世界上有什么东西能～母亲的爱与关怀吗？ Can anything in the world take the place of a mother's love and care?
【取道】qǔdào〈动〉 pass through: 他们～伦敦去法国。 They went to France via London.
【取得】qǔdé〈动〉 gain: ～版权 secure a copyright ‖ ～长足的进步 make considerable progress ‖ ～成功 win success ‖ ～成就 make achievements ‖ ～信任 win sb.'s confidence ‖ ～学位 get a degree ‖ 通过实践～经验 gain experience through practice ‖ 他刚～律师资格。 He has just qualified as a lawyer.
【取灯儿】qǔdēngr〈名〉〈方〉 match
【取缔】qǔdì〈动〉 ban: ～非法组织 ban illegal organizations ‖ ～无证摊贩 ban unlicensed stalls
【取而代之】qǔ'érdàizhī〈成〉 take the place of: 他被他的助手～了。 He was replaced by his assistant.
【取法】qǔfǎ〈动〉 follow the example of
【取经】qǔjīng〈动〉 1［佛教］ go on a pilgrimage to India to acquire Buddhist scriptures: 去西天～ go West to acquire Buddhist scriptures 2〈喻〉（吸取他人经验） learn from sb. else's experience: 向先进企业～ follow the example of successful companies
【取精用宏】qǔjīng-yònghóng〈成〉 select the finest from a vast quantity
【取景】qǔjǐng〈动〉 find a view: 摄影～ find a view to photograph ‖ ～器 viewfinder
【取决】qǔjué〈动〉 depend (up)on: 成功与否～于你的努力和能力。 Success depends on your efforts and ability. ‖ 商品的价格主要～于供求关系。 The prices of commodities mainly hinge on the relation between demand and supply.
【取款】qǔkuǎn〈动〉 withdraw money
【取款机】qǔkuǎnjī〈名〉 automatic teller machine (ATM)
【取乐】qǔlè〈动〉 seek pleasure: 别拿我～。 Don't make fun of me.
【取名】qǔmíng〈动〉 give sb. a name: 给孩子～ name a child
【取闹】qǔnào〈动〉 1（吵闹） kick up a fuss: ▸无理～ 2（取乐） amuse oneself at sb. else's expense: 不应拿残疾人～。 You should not make fun of disabled people.
【取暖】qǔnuǎn〈动〉 warm oneself up: 烤火～ warm oneself by the fire ‖ ～器 heater
【取平】qǔpíng〈动〉 even up
【取齐】qǔqí〈动〉 1（与标准相同） even up: 把纸～后再裁。 Even up the edges of the sheets before cutting them. 2（聚齐） assemble: 上午九点～。 Let's get together at nine in the morning.
【取其精华】qǔqí-jīnghuá〈成〉 absorb what is best: ～，去其糟粕 absorb what is good and reject what is bad
【取巧】qǔqiǎo〈动〉 wangle: ～图便 choose the easy way for the sake of convenience ▸投机～
【取人之长，补己之短】qǔ rén zhī cháng, bǔ jǐ zhī duǎn = 取长补短 qǔcháng-bǔduǎn
【取舍】qǔshě〈动〉 make one's choice: 有批判地加以～ adopt and discard with a critical eye ‖ ～得当 make an appropriate choice
【取胜】qǔshèng〈动〉 score a success: 侥幸～ gain a victory by sheer luck ‖ 以智～ triumph through strategy
【取水口】qǔshuǐkǒu〈名〉［水利］ water intake
【取向】qǔxiàng〈名〉 tendency: 价值观～ orientation of one's values ‖ 审美～ aesthetic trend
【取消】qǔxiāo〈动〉 cancel: ～航班 cancel a flight ‖ ～合同/协议 cancel a contract/an

agreement ‖ ～会议 cancel a meeting ‖ ～资格 rescind sb.'s qualifications ‖ ～决定 revoke a decision ‖ 运动会因雨～。The sports meet was called off because of rain.

【取笑】qǔxiào〈动〉 laugh at: ～某人的口音 laugh at sb.'s accent ‖ 如今他已成为众人～的对象。Now he has become something of a laughing stock.

【取信】qǔxìn〈动〉 gain sb.'s confidence: ～于人 establish credibility among others

【取信于民】qǔxìnyúmín〈成〉 win the trust of the people

【取样】qǔyàng〈动〉 take a sample: ～检验 take a sample for examination and testing ‖ 随机～ random sampling

【取样器】qǔyàngqì〈名〉 sampler

【取悦】qǔyuè〈动〉 ingratiate oneself with: ～上司 play up to one's boss

【取证】qǔzhèng〈动〉 gather evidence: 调查～ conduct an investigation and obtain evidence ‖ 广泛～ gather evidence on an extensive basis

【取之不尽，用之不竭】qǔ zhī bù jìn, yòng zhī bù jié〈成〉 inexhaustible: ～的能源 inexhaustible energy

【取之于民，用之于民】qǔ zhī yú mín, yòng zhī yú mín〈成〉 what is taken from the people is to be used for the good of the people

娶 qǔ〈动〉 marry (a woman): ～媳妇 marry a woman ‖ 他～了个英国姑娘。He married an English girl.

【娶了媳妇忘了娘】qǔ le xífù wàng le niáng〈俗〉 once the son is married, the mother is forgotten

【娶妻】qǔqī〈动〉 take a wife: ～生子 get married and have children

【娶亲】qǔqīn〈动〉 **1**（娶妻） take a wife **2**（接新娘） go to pick up one's bride at her house

龋（齲） qǔ〈动〉 decay

【龋齿】qǔchǐ〈名〉 **1**（指病症） tooth decay: 预防～ prevention of tooth decay **2**（指牙齿） decayed tooth

qù

去[1] qù

A〈动〉 **1**（离开） leave: ▸～世，～职 **2**〈书〉（距离） be apart from in space or time: ～今六十余年 more than 60 years ago ‖ 两国相～万里。The two countries are ten thousand *li* apart. **3**（失掉） lose: 光阴一～不复返。Time once lost is never regained. ▸大势已～ **4**（除掉） get rid of: ～头屑 get rid of dandruff ‖ ～污渍 remove stains ▸～粗取精，～火，掐头～尾 **5** ▸**p. 772**〈婉〉（过世） die: 爷爷先奶奶～了。Granddad passed away before grandma. **6**（前往） go to: 从北京～上海 leave Beijing for Shanghai ‖ 她以前～过那里。She has been there before. ‖ 我给他～了一封信。I sent him a letter. ▸～处，～向 **7**（表目的） [used after a verbal phrase or prepositional phrase and before another verbal phrase or verb, indicating purpose] go in order to do sth.: 拿斧头～砍树 use an axe to cut a tree ‖ 上街～买菜 go to the market to buy some vegetables **8**（表去做某事） [used at the end of a sentence after a verb or verbal phrase, indicating purpose] go in order to do sth.: 他听讲座～了。He went to the lecture. ‖ 她上图书馆借书～了。She has gone to the library to borrow books. **9** **a**（表运动方向） [used after a verb, indicating motion away from the speaker]: 回家～ go home ‖ 朝大门外跑～ run towards the gate **b**（表动作结果） [used after a verb, indicating that sb./sth. is no longer in its original place]: 把这些话删～。Leave out these words. ‖ 她的父母相继死～。Her parents died one after the other. **c**（表动作持续） [used after a verb, indicating the continuation of an action, etc.]: 让他玩～。Let him go on playing. ‖ 随他说～。Let him say whatever he likes.

B〈形〉 previous: ～冬今春 last winter and this spring ▸～年

C〈副〉〈方〉 extremely: 操场上的人多了～了。There are quite a lot of people at the playground. ‖ 这几年变化可大了～了。There have been great changes these last few years.

D = 去声 qùshēng

去[2] qù〈动〉 play a part: 他在那出戏里～曹操。He played the part of Cao Cao in the play.

【去病】qùbìng〈动〉 prevent or cure a disease

【去臭】qùchòu〈动〉 deodorize

【去除】qùchú〈动〉 get rid of: ～衣服上的油渍 remove grease from one's clothes ‖ 彻底～恶习 do away with one's bad habits

【去处】qùchù〈名〉 **1**（去的地方） whereabouts: 她的～不明。Her whereabouts are unknown. **2**（场所） spot: 这是避暑的好～。This is a great summer spot.

【去磁】qùcí〈动〉［物理］ demagnetize: ～器 demagnetizer

【去粗取精】qùcū-qǔjīng〈成〉 separate the wheat from the chaff

【去钉器】qùdīngqì〈名〉 staple remover

【去恶从善】qù'è-cóngshàn〈成〉 exterminate the evil and follow the good

【去功能化】qù gōngnénghuà〈动〉 disable: 核设施～工作 the disabling of nuclear facilities

【去垢】qùgòu〈动〉 descale: 给水壶～ descale a kettle ‖ ～剂 detergent

【去骨】qùgǔ〈动〉 bone

【去火】qùhuǒ〈动〉［中医］ relieve inflammation or fever: 绿豆汤可帮助～。The mung bean soup helps to reduce internal heat.

【去就】qù-jiù〈动〉〈书〉 resign or remain in one's post: ～未定 not be certain whether to quit or stay

【去壳】qùké〈动〉 shell: 给鸡蛋～ peel boiled eggs ‖ ～的坚果 shelled nut

【去留】qù-liú〈动〉 go or stay: ～未决 hover between staying and going ‖ ～自便 be free to go or stay

【去路】qùlù〈名〉 way: 挡住～ block sb.'s way

【去你的】qùnǐde〈动〉〈粗〉 go to hell: ～! 我还不至于蠢到那个地步。Go on with you! I know better than that.

【去年】qùnián ▸**p. 618**〈名〉 last year: ～今日 a year ago today ‖ ～夏天 last summer

【去皮】qùpí〈动〉 remove the peel or skin: 把水果～ peel fruit ‖ ～猪肉 skinned pork ‖ 香蕉去了皮再吃。Peel the banana before you eat it.

【去皮器】qùpíqì〈名〉 peeler: 土豆～ potato peeler

【去任】qùrèn〈动〉 leave an official post

【去日】qùrì〈名〉〈书〉 the past: ～苦多 suffered a lot in the past

【去声】qùshēng〈名〉［语言］ **1**（指古汉语） falling tone [third of the four tones in classical Chinese pronunciation] **2**（指普通话） falling tone [fourth of the four tones in modern standard Chinese pronunciation]

【去世】qùshì ▸**p. 772**〈动〉 pass away: 因病～ die of an illness

【去势】qùshì〈动〉［畜牧］ geld

【去暑】qùshǔ〈动〉 dispel summer heat

【去岁】qùsuì〈名〉〈书〉 last year

【去痛】qùtòng〈动〉 kill a pain

【去痛片】qùtòngpiàn〈名〉 painkiller

【去伪存真】qùwěi-cúnzhēn〈成〉 discard what is false and keep what is genuine

【去污粉】qùwūfěn〈名〉 household cleaner

【去芜存精】qùwú-cúnjīng〈成〉 discard the dross and keep the essential

【去雾器】qùwùqì〈名〉 demister〈英〉; defogger〈美〉

【去向】qùxiàng〈名〉 whereabouts: 不知～ be nowhere to be found ‖ ～不明 sb.'s whereabouts are unknown

【去邪归正】qùxié-guīzhèng〈成〉 turn over a new leaf

【去雄】qùxióng〈动〉［植物］ emasculate

【去意】qùyì〈名〉 intention to leave: ～已决 be determined to leave

【去职】qùzhí〈动〉〈书〉 leave one's post: 因病～ resign on the grounds of ill health

【去中国化】qù zhōngguóhuà〈动〉 desinicize: ～的政策不得人心。The policy of desinicization is very unpopular.

阒（闃） qù〈形〉〈书〉 still: ～无一人。All was quiet and not a soul was to be seen.

【阒寂】qùjì〈形〉〈书〉 quiet

【阒然】qùrán〈形〉〈书〉 quiet: ～无声 absolutely still

趣 qù

A〈名〉 **1**（志向） inclination: ▸志～ **2**（趣味） interest: ▸风～，乐～，自讨没～

B〈形〉 interesting: ▸～闻

【趣话】qùhuà〈名〉 funny remark

【趣事】qùshì〈名〉 amusing incident: 童年～ amusing childhood incident

【趣谈】qùtán〈名〉 amusing remarks

【趣味】qùwèi〈名〉 **1**（乐趣） fun: ～无穷 be the best fun ‖ 增强～性 step up the fun value **2**（兴趣） taste: ～索然 dry as dust ‖ 低级～ poor tastes ‖ ～高雅 good taste

【趣味盎然】qùwèi-àngrán〈成〉 full of interest

【趣味相投】qùwèi-xiāngtóu〈成〉 be congenial to one's taste

【趣闻】qùwén〈名〉 interesting anecdote: 讲述旅途～ relate interesting travel tales

觑（覷） qù〈动〉〈书〉 steal a glance at: 冷眼相～ give sb. a cold look ▸面面相～，小～ ▸qū

【觑视】qùshì〈动〉〈书〉 look at

qu

戌 qu ▸屈戌儿 qūqur ▸xū

quān

卷 quān〈名〉〈书〉crossbow

悛 quān〈动〉〈书〉repent and mend one's ways: ▸怙恶不～

圈 quān

A〈名〉**1**（指环形）circle: 画个～儿 draw a circle ‖ 吐烟～ blow smoke rings ‖ 钥匙～ key ring ‖ 大家手拉着手，围成一个～儿。Everyone joined hands and formed a circle. ‖ 运动员已经跑了四～。The athletes have completed four circuits. ▸花～，救生～ **2**（指范围）circle: 生活～ circle of life ‖ 演艺～ theatrical circles ‖ 他不是～里人。He does not belong to the inner circle.

B〈动〉**1**（做标记）circle: 把你的选项～出来。Circle your choices. ‖ 老师用红笔把学生的错误～出来。The teacher circled the pupils' mistakes in red ink. ▸～点，～阅 **2**（加限制）encircle: 用绳子把事故现场～起来 rope off the scene of the accident ‖ 监狱被高墙～住了。The prison is enclosed by high walls. ▸～地

▸juān, juàn

【圈操】quāncāo〈名〉［体育］ ring exercise

【圈地】quāndì〈动〉 enclose land: 非法～ illegally enclose land

【圈点】quāndiǎn〈动〉**1**（表示句读） punctuate an ancient text with dots or small circles **2**（表示强调） mark words and phrases for special attention with dots and small circles

【圈定】quāndìng〈动〉 decide by marking a circle

【圈圈】quānquan〈名〉 circle

【圈套】quāntào〈名〉 trap: 设下～ set a trap

【圈外人】quānwàirén〈名〉 outsider

【圈椅】quānyǐ〈名〉round-backed armchair

【圈阅】quānyuè〈动〉 circle one's name on a document submitted for approval to show that one has read it

【圈占】quānzhàn〈动〉 enclose and occupy: ～农田 enclose farm land and claim ownership of it

【圈子】quānzi〈名〉 circle: 扩大生活～ widen one's circle ‖ 大家围成一个～。We formed a circle. ‖ 她的生活～很小。She moves in very small circles. ▸兜～，绕～

quán

权（權） quán

A〈名〉**1**〈书〉（秤锤） steelyard weight **2**（权变） adaptability: ▸～变，通～达变 **3**（权力） power: 决策～ decision-making power ‖ 掌握生杀大～ have the power over life and death ‖ ～钱交易 power-money deal ‖ 经理有～解雇职员。The manager has the power to fire an employee. ▸～限，当～，授～，政～ **4**（权利） right: 言论自由～ right of free speech ‖ 被告人有～保持沉默。The defendant has the right to remain silent. ‖ 她因出生在英国而有英国公民～。She is British by birthright. ▸版～，人～，特～ **5**（支配力量） advantageous position: 掌握主动～ have the initiative ▸霸～，制空～

B〈动〉 weigh: ▸～衡

C〈副〉 temporarily: ～充 act temporarily as ‖ ～作不知 pretend not to know for the moment ▸～且

【权变】quánbiàn〈动〉 act according to circumstances: 多智谋，善～ be resourceful and flexible

【权标】quánbiāo〈名〉 mace [symbol of authority]

【权柄】quánbǐng〈名〉 power: 掌握～ be in the saddle

【权臣】quánchén〈名〉 powerful and domineering minister: ～当道/用事 domineering ministers are in power

【权当】quándāng〈动〉 consider: 死马～活马医 not give it up for lost ‖ 你要是不听，就～我没说。If you won't listen, then forget it.

【权贵】quánguì〈名〉 powerful officials: 依附～ attach oneself to influential people

【权衡】quánhéng **A**〈名〉〈书〉 sliding weight and beam of a steelyard **B**〈动〉 weigh: ～得失 weigh up the costs and the benefits

【权衡利弊】quánhéng-lìbì〈成〉 weigh up the pros and cons

【权奸】quánjiān〈名〉 powerful and treacherous court official

【权力】quánlì〈名〉**1**（指强制力量） power: 国家～ state power ‖ ～机关 organ of power ‖ ～下放 transfer power to lower levels **2**（指支配权） authority: 滥用～ abuse one's power ‖ 行使～ exercise authority ‖ ～过分集中 excessive centralization of power ‖ 国会授予总统一切应变～。Congress delegated all the emergency powers to the president.

【权力斗争】quánlì dòuzhēng〈名〉 power struggle

【权利】quánlì〈名〉 right: 维护～ defend sb.'s right ‖ 享有～ enjoy a right ‖ 公民的基本～和义务 fundamental rights and duties of a citizen ‖ 受教育的～ right to education ‖ 人们享有生命、自由和人身安全的～。People have rights to life, liberty and security.

【权利能力】quánlì nénglì〈名〉［法律］ ability to exercise one's rights and honour one's obligations

【权门】quánmén〈名〉 families of influential officials: 依附～ attach oneself to the families of influential people

【权迷心窍】quánmíxīnqiào〈成〉 be obsessed with a lust for power

【权谋】quánmóu〈名〉 flexible tactics: ～多变 be resourceful

【权能】quánnéng〈名〉 powers and functions: 法院有这些～。The court has these powers and functions.

【权且】quánqiě〈副〉〈书〉 for the time being: ～如此吧。Let it be for the time being. ‖ ～吃几片饼干充饥。For now let's have a few biscuits to stave off our hunger.

【权时】quánshí **A**〈形〉 temporary **B**〈动〉〈书〉 size up the situation

【权势】quánshì〈名〉 power and influence: 倚仗～ rely on one's powerful connections ‖ 他利用自己的～为子女谋得好工作。He used his influence to get his children good jobs.

【权术】quánshù〈名〉 political machinations: 玩弄～ play politics

【权数】quánshù〈名〉〈书〉 resourcefulness

【权威】quánwēi〈名〉**1**（指力量、威望） authority: 维护政府机关的～ safeguard the authority of the government organs ‖ ～人士 authority ‖ ～著作 authoritative book **2**（指人、事物） authority: 学术～ academic authority ‖ 医学～ medical authority ‖ 公认的～ recognized authority

【权位】quánwèi〈名〉 power and position: 谋取～ seek power and position

【权限】quánxiàn〈名〉 jurisdiction: 超越～ overstep one's authority ‖ 此事不在我的～之内。This matter does not fall within my jurisdiction.

【权要】quányào〈名〉 influential people

【权宜】quányí〈形〉 expedient: 应急的～措施 expedient measure to meet an emergency

【权宜之计】quányízhījì〈成〉 expedient measure: 这是～。This is an expedient measure.

【权益】quányì〈名〉 rights: 维护妇女与儿童的合法～ defend the lawful rights and interests of women and children ‖ 消费者～保护 protect the rights of the consumers

【权欲】quányù〈名〉 hunger for power: ～膨胀使他走上了犯罪道路。His hunger for power led him down the criminal path.

【权欲熏心】quányù-xūnxīn〈成〉 be overcome by a lust for power

【权责】quánzé〈名〉 power and responsibility

【权诈】quánzhà〈形〉〈书〉 tricky

【权杖】quánzhàng〈名〉 staff: 国王的～ king's sceptre ‖ 主教的～ bishop's crosier

【权证】quánzhèng〈名〉［金融］ warrant

【权重】quánzhòng〈名〉 weight

全 quán

A〈形〉**1**（完备） complete: 店虽小，东西却很～。The store, though small, has a considerable variety of goods. ‖ 这本书不～。The book is incomplete. ▸残缺不～，健～ **2**（整个） whole: ～党 whole Party ‖ ～世界 the whole world ‖ ～中国 all of China ‖ ～书共十卷。The book comprises 10 volumes. ▸～部，～国

B〈动〉 make complete: ▸两～其美

C〈副〉**1**（所有） all: ～走了。All are gone. ‖ 他的孩子～是女孩。All his children are girls. **2**（完全） entirely: 他～是为了你好才做的。He did it entirely for your good. ▸～然，～新

【全般】quánbān〈形〉whole: ～工作 entire work

【全豹】quánbào〈名〉〈喻〉 full picture: 未窥～ fail to see the whole picture

【全本】quánběn **A**〈形〉 complete: 他们演出了～《哈姆雷特》。They performed the full version of *Hamlet*. **B** = 足本 zúběn

【全部】quánbù〈形〉 total: ～费用 total expenditure ‖ 承担～责任 shoulder the entire responsibility ‖ 贡献～力量 give one's all ‖ 设法了解～情况 try to find out about the whole situation

【全才】quáncái〈名〉 all-rounder: 文武～ be both a scholar and a warrior

【全长】quáncháng〈名〉 overall length: 新桥的～ whole length of the new bridge

【全场】quánchǎng〈名〉**1**（指人） whole audience;（指范围） the house: ～观众给演员们热烈鼓掌。The audience gave the actors a warm applause. **2**［体育］ all court: ～紧逼 full-court press

【全称】quánchēng〈名〉 full name: 美国的～是美利坚合众国。America's full name is the United States of America.

【全程】quánchéng〈名〉 whole journey: ～马拉松 full marathon ‖ ～陪同某人 be with sb. the whole time

【全等】quánděng〈形〉［数学］ congruent: ～三角形 congruent triangles

q

【全都】quándōu〈副〉 all: 一切～结束了。Everything is finished. ‖ 他把蛋糕～吃光了。He ate up every bit of the cake.

【全额】quán'é〈名〉 full amount

【全方位】quánfāngwèi〈名〉 all directions: ～出击 all-round attack ‖ ～开放格局 pattern of all-round opening-up

【全份】quánfèn〈名〉 complete set: ～表册 complete set of lists and forms

【全副】quánfù〈形〉 complete: ～武装 be armed to the teeth ‖ 他的～精力都放在工作上。He is completely taken up with his work.

【全国】quánguó〈名〉 whole country: 闻名～ be well-known throughout the country ‖ ～上下 all over the country ‖ ～一盘棋 coordinate all the activities of a nation like moves on a chessboard ‖ 居～之首 lead the nation

【全国人大】Quánguó Réndà〈简称〉= 全国人民代表大会

【全国人民代表大会】Quánguó Rénmín Dàibiǎo Dàhuì〈名〉 National People's Congress (NPC)

【全乎】quánhu〈形〉〈口〉 complete: 你收集的资料还挺～。The materials you collected are quite comprehensive.

【全会】quánhuì〈名〉 plenary session: 党的十一届三中～ Third Plenary Session of the Eleventh Central Committee of the Party

【全集】quánjí〈名〉 collected works: 《鲁迅～》 *The Complete Works of Lu Xun* ‖ 《莎士比亚戏剧～》 *A Complete Edition of Shakespeare's Plays*

【全家福】quánjiāfú〈名〉〈口〉 1〉(指照片) family photograph: 照张～ take a picture of the whole family 2〉(指菜肴) hodgepodge

【全价票】quánjiàpiào〈名〉 full fare ticket

【全歼】quánjiān〈动〉 wipe out: ～敌军 wipe out enemy forces down

【全景】quánjǐng〈名〉 panorama

【全景电影】quánjǐng diànyǐng〈名〉 Cinerama®

【全局】quánjú〈名〉 overall situation: 事关～ be of importance to the overall situation ‖ 总揽～ manage the overall situation ‖ 从～出发 in view of the overall situation

【全军覆没】quánjūn-fùmò〈成〉 the whole army is wiped out

【全开】quánkāi〈名〉［印刷］ standard-sized sheet: ～招贴画 full-size poster

【全科医生】quánkē yīshēng〈名〉 general practitioner

【全劳动力】quánláodònglì = 全劳力 quánláolì

【全劳力】quánláolì〈名〉 fully able-bodied farm worker

【全力】quánlì〈名〉 all one's strength: 竭尽～ spare no effort ‖ ～支持 support with all one's might

【全力以赴】quánlìyǐfù〈成〉 go all out: 这项任务需要我们～。The task demands all our power.

【全麻】quánmá〈名〉［医学］ general anaesthesia

【全麦】quánmài〈名〉 whole wheat: ～面包 wholemeal bread

【全貌】quánmào〈名〉 complete picture: 弄清问题的～ try to get a complete picture of the problem

【全面】quánmiàn A〈形〉 overall: 技术～ have all-round skills ‖ ～落实党的政策 implement the Party's policies in a comprehensive way ‖ 进行～检查 conduct an overall check-up ‖ 他叙述得很～。His account was most comprehensive. B〈名〉 comprehensiveness: ～情况还不清楚。The overall situation is still unclear.

【全面战争】quánmiàn zhànzhēng〈名〉 all-out war

【全面质量管理】quánmiàn zhìliàng guǎnlǐ〈名〉 total quality control

【全苗】quánmiáo〈名〉［农业］ full stand

【全民】quánmín〈名〉 entire nation: ～动员 mobilization of the entire nation ‖ ～健身运动 nationwide physical fitness campaign

【全民公决】quánmín gōngjué〈名〉 referendum: 进行～ hold a referendum

【全民皆兵】quánmín-jiēbīng〈成〉 an entire nation in arms

【全民所有制】quánmín suǒyǒuzhì〈名〉 ownership by all the people: ～企业 enterprise owned by the whole people

【全民投票】quánmín tóupiào〈名〉 referendum

【全名】quánmíng〈名〉 full name: 请写下～和详细地址。Please write down your full name and address.

【全能】quánnéng〈形〉［体育］ all-round: 男子个人～ men's individual all-round ‖ ～冠军 all-round champion

【全年】quánnián〈名〉 whole year

【全盘】quánpán〈形〉 overall: ～否定 complete negation ‖ 打乱～计划 disrupt an overall plan

【全陪】quánpéi A〈名〉 tour conductor B〈动〉 guide the whole tour

【全票】quánpiào〈名〉 1〉(指门票、车票等) full-fare ticket: 成人～，儿童半票。Adults are full price, children half price. 2〉(指选票) total votes: ～当选 be unanimously elected

【全勤】quánqín〈名〉 full attendance: 出～ have recorded full attendance ‖ 获～奖 win a prize for full attendance

【全球】quánqiú〈名〉 whole world: ～变暖 global warming ‖ ～财富论坛 Fortune Global Forum ‖ ～战略 global strategy

【全球定位系统】quánqiú dìngwèi xìtǒng〈名〉 Global Positioning System (GPS)

【全球化】quánqiúhuà〈名〉 globalization: 经济～ economic globalization

【全球通】quánqiútōng〈简称〉= 全球移动通信系统

【全球性】quánqiúxìng〈形〉 global: ～发展战略 global development strategy

【全球移动通信系统】quánqiú yídòng tōngxìn xìtǒng〈名〉 Global System for Mobile Communications (GSM)

【全权】quánquán〈名〉 full power: ～委托 entrust sb. with full responsibility ‖ 你～代表我们处理。We give you carte blanche to act for us.

【全权大使】quánquán dàshǐ〈名〉 ambassador plenipotentiary: 特命～ ambassador extraordinary and plenipotentiary

【全权代表】quánquán dàibiǎo〈名〉 plenipotentiary

【全然】quánrán〈副〉〈书〉 entirely: ～不顾个人安危 give no thought to one's own safety ‖ ～不知 have not the least idea of ‖ 我对此事～不知。I was totally ignorant of this matter.

【全日制】quánrìzhì〈形〉 full-time: ～学校 full-time school

【全乳】quánrǔ〈名〉［食品］ whole milk

【全色】quánsè〈名〉［摄影］ full colour

【全色胶片】quánsè jiāopiàn〈名〉 panchromatic film

【全色盲】quánsèmáng ▸p. 50〈名〉［医学］ total colour blindness: ～者 monochromat

【全身】quánshēn〈名〉 whole body: ～乏力 feel weak all over ‖ ～雕塑/照片 full-length statue/photo ‖ ～麻醉 general anaesthesia

【全身像】quánshēnxiàng〈名〉 full-length picture

【全神贯注】quánshén-guànzhù〈成〉 focus all one's attention on: ～地听讲 be all ears

【全胜】quánshèng A〈名〉 complete victory: 大获～ win a resounding victory B〈动〉 be all-victorious: 四战～ win all the four games

【全盛】quánshèng〈形〉 most flourishing: ～时期 zenith

【全食】quánshí〈名〉［天文］ total eclipse: 日/月～ total solar/lunar eclipse

【全始全终】quánshǐ-quánzhōng〈成〉 see sth. through

【全数】quánshù〈名〉 whole amount: 账已～付清。The bill has been paid in full.

【全速】quánsù〈名〉 full speed: 部队～前进。The troops were marching at top speed. ‖ 汽车以每小时120英里～行驶。The car was running at a top speed of 120 miles an hour.

【全损】quánsǔn〈名〉［经济］ total loss: ～险 total loss only

【全瘫】quántān ▸p. 50〈名〉［医学］ panplegia

【全套】quántào〈名〉 complete set: ～瓷器 whole set of china ‖ ～登山装备 mountain-climber's outfit ‖ ～家具 complete set of furniture

【全体】quántǐ〈名〉 whole: ～代表 all the representatives ‖ ～会议 plenary session ‖ ～教职员工 entire teaching, administrative and supporting staff ‖ ～起立默哀。Everyone rose to their feet in silent tribute.

【全天候】quántiānhòu〈形〉 all-weather: ～飞机 all-weather aircraft ‖ ～服务 24-hour service

【全托】quántuō〈名〉 full-time child-care: 你的孩子是～还是日托？ Is your child a boarder or a day pupil?

【全脱产】quántuōchǎn〈动〉 be fully released from one's regular work

【全维作战】quánwéi zuòzhàn〈名〉 integrated battle across varied terrain

【全文】quánwén〈名〉 full text: ～发表 be published in full ‖ 声明～如下。The following is the full text of the statement.

【全武行】quánwǔháng〈名〉 1〉(指武打表演) full-scale battle scene 2〉(指暴力行为) punch-up

【全息】quánxī〈形〉 holographic: ～电影 holographic film ‖ ～编码 hologram code

【全息照相】quánxī zhàoxiàng〈名〉 hologram: 激光～ laser hologram

【全线】quánxiàn〈名〉 1〉(指战线) all fronts: ～出击 launch an attack on all fronts ‖ 敌人已～崩溃。The enemy was routed on all fronts. 2〉(指路线) whole route: 这条高速公路已～通车。The whole highway has been opened to traffic.

【全向导航】quánxiàng dǎoháng〈名〉 omnirange

【全心全意】quánxīn-quányì〈成〉 heart and soul: ～为人民服务 serve the people with all one's heart

【全新】quánxīn〈形〉 brand-new

【全新世】Quánxīnshì〈名〉［地质］ Holocene

【全薪】quánxīn〈名〉 full pay

【全休】quánxiū〈动〉 take long-term sick leave: 医生建议～三个月。The doctor prescribed a complete rest of three months.

【全休止符】quánxiūzhǐfú〈名〉[音乐] whole rest
【全音】quányīn〈名〉[音乐] whole tone: ～符 semibreve〈英〉, whole note〈美〉
【全优】quányōu〈形〉all-round excellent: ～工程 all-excellent project meeting all quality standards ‖ 成绩～学生 straight-A student
【全员】quányuán〈名〉whole staff: ～培训 training programme for all staff members
【全运会】Quányùnhuì〈名〉National Games
【全知全能】quánzhī-quánnéng〈成〉be omniscient and omnipotent
【全脂奶粉】quánzhī nǎifěn〈名〉whole milk powder
【全职】quánzhí ▸**p. 966**〈形〉full-time: ～教师 full-time teacher
【全自动】quánzìdòng〈形〉fully automatic: ～洗衣机 fully automatic washing machine

诠（詮） quán〈书〉
A〈动〉explain: ▸～释, ～注
B〈名〉reason: 真～ truth
【诠释】quánshì〈动〉〈书〉elucidate: 详加～ explain in detail ‖ 文字艰深，颇费～。The writing is too difficult to interpret.
【诠注】quánzhù〈动〉〈书〉annotate

泉 quán〈名〉**1**（泉水）spring (water): 温～ hot spring ‖ 甘～ sweet spring water ▸矿～, 喷～ **2**（泉眼）mouth of a spring **3**〈古〉（钱币）coin: ～币 coin
【泉流】quánliú〈名〉spring-fed stream
【泉水】quánshuǐ〈名〉spring (water): ～潺潺。The spring is gurgling.
【泉眼】quányǎn〈名〉mouth of a spring
【泉涌】quányǒng〈动〉well up: 泪如～ tears gush like water from a spring
【泉源】quányuán〈名〉**1**（水源）wellhead: ～已经枯竭。The source has dried up. **2** = 源泉 yuánquán

辁（輇） quán〈古〉
A〈名〉wheel without spokes
B〈形〉shallow

拳 quán
A〈名〉**1**（拳头）fist: 挥～相向 come to blows ‖ 握～ clench one's fist ▸～击, 赤手空～, 摩～擦掌 **2**（拳术）Chinese boxing: 一套～ a shadow boxing set ‖ 练～ practise shadow boxing ▸～师, ～术
B〈动〉bend: ～着腿 with one's legs curled up ▸～曲
【拳棒】quánbàng〈名〉*wushu*, martial arts
【拳不离手，曲不离口】quán bù lí shǒu, qǔ bù lí kǒu〈俗〉practice makes perfect
【拳打脚踢】quándǎ-jiǎotī〈成〉punch and kick: 对人～ beat sb. up
【拳击】quánjī ▸**p. 909**〈名〉boxing: ～冠军 boxing champion ‖ ～手套 boxing glove ‖ ～手 boxer
【拳脚】quánjiǎo〈名〉**1**（拳头和脚）fists and feet: ～相加 cuff and kick **2**（拳术）Chinese boxing: 他学了几下～。He learned a few tricks in Chinese boxing.
【拳曲】quánqū〈动〉twist: 她的头发天生～。Her hair curls naturally.
【拳拳】quánquán〈形〉〈书〉sincere: ～之心 sincere heart ‖ ～服膺 have a sincere belief in
【拳师】quánshī ▸**p. 966**〈名〉boxing master
【拳手】quánshǒu〈名〉boxer: 职业～ prizefighter
【拳术】quánshù〈名〉Chinese boxing
【拳坛】quántán〈名〉boxing circles
【拳头】quántóu〈名〉fist: 挨一顿～ be beaten up ‖ 握紧～ clench one's fist
【拳头产品】quántóu chǎnpǐn〈名〉highly competitive product
【拳王】quánwáng〈名〉champion boxer: 赢得～称号 win a boxing title

铨（銓） quán〈动〉〈书〉
1（衡量轻重）weigh **2**（选拔）select: 考～ examine officials' work or knowledge ▸～叙
【铨度利弊】quánduó lìbì〈成〉weigh the pros and cons
【铨叙】quánxù〈动〉〈书〉examine the records and qualifications of officials in making appointments
【铨选】quánxuǎn〈动〉〈书〉select officials according to their qualifications

痊 quán〈动〉fully recover
【痊愈】quányù〈动〉be completely recovered: 妈妈做过手术后还没～。Mum is not yet fully recovered after the operation. ‖ 祝您早日～。I wish you a speedy recovery.

筌 quán〈名〉〈古〉bamboo fish trap: ▸得鱼忘～

蜷 quán〈动〉curl up: 孩子～在母亲身边。The child snuggled up to her mother. ‖ 他～身睡着。He curled up and slept.
【蜷伏】quánfú〈动〉curl up: 那只狗吓得～在桌子底下。The dog huddled under the table with fear.
【蜷曲】quánqū〈动〉curl up: 他～而卧。He was lying curled up.
【蜷缩】quánsuō〈动〉curl up: 刺猬受到攻击就～成一团。A hedgehog rolls itself into a ball when attacked. ‖ 小女孩把身体～起来。The little girl curled herself into a ball.

醛 quán〈名〉[化学] aldehyde: ▸甲～

鳈（鰁） quán〈名〉fat minnow [a kind of small edible freshwater fish, indigenous to eastern China]

鬈 quán〈形〉**1**〈书〉（美丽）[of hair] beautiful **2**（弯曲）[of hair] curly
【鬈发】quánfà〈名〉curly hair

颧（顴） quán
【颧骨】quángǔ ▸**p. 614**〈名〉[解剖] cheekbone: ～突起 have prominent cheekbones

quǎn

犬 quǎn〈名〉dog: 养～ have a dog ‖ 爱～ pet dog ‖ 狂～ rabid dog ▸警～, 猎～
【犬齿】quǎnchǐ〈名〉canine tooth
【犬马之劳】quǎnmǎzhīláo〈成〉be at sb.'s beck and call: 效～ be at sb.'s beck and call
【犬儒】quǎnrú〈名〉cynic: ～主义 cynicism
【犬牙】quǎnyá〈名〉**1** = 犬齿 quǎnchǐ **2**（尖牙）fang
【犬牙交错】quǎnyá-jiāocuò〈成〉interlocking: ～的战争态势 interlocking pattern of war
【犬子】quǎnzǐ〈名〉〈旧〉〈谦〉my son

绻（綣） quǎn ▸缱绻 qiǎnquǎn

quàn

劝（勸） quàn〈动〉**1**〈书〉（勉励）exhort: ～人为善 encourage people to do good ▸～善, ～学 **2**（劝说）urge: 好言相～ try to advise sb. with well-intentioned words ‖ 她～我别买那辆车。She advised me not to buy that car. ▸～告, ～说
【劝导】quàndǎo〈动〉advise: 经过妻子反复～，他终于戒了烟。He gave up smoking after repeated exhortations by his wife.
【劝服】quànfú〈动〉persuade
【劝告】quàngào **A**〈动〉advise: 再三～ advise repeatedly ‖ 医生～他不要吸烟。The doctor advised him not to smoke. **B**〈名〉advice: 不听～ reject sb.'s advice ‖ 他欣然接受了我的～。He took my advice cheerfully.
【劝和】quànhé〈动〉urge reconciliation
【劝化】quànhuà〈动〉**1**[佛教] exhort to do good: 不听～ repel exhortations to do good **2** = 募化 mùhuà
【劝驾】quànjià〈动〉urge sb. to accept a post or invitation
【劝架】quànjià〈动〉mediate between two quarrelling parties
【劝谏】quànjiàn〈动〉admonish
【劝解】quànjiě〈动〉**1**（劝导）mollify: 经我耐心～，她的情绪有所好转。After my patient talks with her, she cheered up a little bit. **2**（劝架）mediate: 我们～争吵双方重归于好。We reconciled the two quarrelling parties through mediation.
【劝诫】quànjiè〈动〉admonish: 她～丈夫改掉在床上吸烟的习惯。She argued with her husband about his habit of smoking in bed.
【劝酒】quànjiǔ〈动〉[at a banquet] urge sb. to drink more
【劝勉】quànmiǎn〈动〉advise and encourage: 相互～ help and encourage each other ‖ 他～我们要勤奋。He encouraged us to work hard.
【劝募】quànmù〈动〉solicit contributions by persuasion
【劝善】quànshàn〈动〉encourage people to do good
【劝说】quànshuō〈动〉persuade: 不听～ reject sb.'s advice ‖ 耐心～ patiently induce
【劝退】quàntuì〈动〉persuade sb. to withdraw from an organization or resign an official position: 公司给他～处分。As punishment, the company forced him to resign.
【劝慰】quànwèi〈动〉soothe
【劝降】quànxiáng〈动〉induce (the enemy) to surrender
【劝学】quànxué〈动〉encourage learning
【劝业场】quànyèchǎng〈名〉bazaar where general merchandise is sold
【劝诱】quànyòu〈动〉induce: ～某人信教 bring sb. round to religion
【劝止】quànzhǐ = 劝阻 quànzǔ
【劝阻】quànzǔ〈动〉dissuade sb. from doing sth.: 极力～ try very hard to dissuade sb. from doing sth. ‖ 尽管我再三～，他仍一意孤行。He went ahead in spite of my exhortations.

券 quàn〈名〉certificate: 百元～ hundred *yuan* note ‖ 就餐～ meal ticket ‖ 入

场～ entrance ticket ‖ 礼～ gift voucher ▸国库～, 奖～
▸xuàn
【券商】quànshāng〈名〉broker

quē

炔 quē〈名〉[化学] alkyne: ▸乙～

缺 quē
A〈形〉1（不完整）incomplete: 保存得完好无～ be kept intact ▸～口, 残～ 2（不完美）imperfect: ▸～点, ～憾
B〈动〉1（缺少）lack: ～人手 be short of manpower ‖ 他们什么都不～。They are lacking in nothing. ‖ 她～钙。She has a calcium deficiency. ‖ 我们～资金。We are short of funds. ▸～德, ～乏 2（缺席）be absent: 今天大家一个不～，都到齐了。Everyone is here today. Nobody is absent. ▸～课, ～勤, ～席
C〈名〉vacancy: ▸补～, 出～
【缺编】quēbiān〈动〉be short of staff: 目前我们严重～。We're dreadfully under-staffed at present.
【缺吃少穿】quēchī-shǎochuān〈成〉go short of food and clothes
【缺档】quēdàng〈动〉[of goods] be in short supply
【缺德】quēdé〈形〉wicked: 做～事 play a mean trick ‖ 这人多～! What a wicked man he is!
【缺点】quēdiǎn〈名〉shortcoming: 克服～ overcome a shortcoming ‖ 主要～ principal defect
【缺额】quē'é〈名〉vacancy: 该厂按编制还有二十名～。The factory is short of 20 workers.
【缺乏】quēfá〈动〉lack: ～诚意 lack sincerity ‖ ～蛋白质/维生素 be deficient in protein/vitamins ‖ ～教养 be ill-bred ‖ ～信心 lack confidence ‖ ～后劲 lack sustainable momentum ‖ 人才～ dearth of talent ‖ 师资～ teacher shortage
【缺憾】quēhàn〈名〉regret: 没赶上开幕式，实在是个～。I regret missing the opening ceremony.
【缺货】quēhuò〈动〉be out of stock
【缺斤短两】quējīn-duǎnliǎng = 缺斤少两 quējīn-shǎoliǎng
【缺斤少两】quējīn-shǎoliǎng〈成〉give short measure: 杜绝～现象 eliminate the problem of giving short weight
【缺考】quēkǎo〈动〉miss an exam
【缺课】quēkè〈动〉be absent from class: ～太多就跟不上了。If you miss class too much, it is hard to catch up.
【缺口】quēkǒu〈名〉1（指物体）gap: 堵住～ close up a gap ‖ 缸子上有一个～。The mug has a chip in it. 2（指经费、物资）shortfall: 资金～很大。There is a great deficiency of funds.
【缺漏】quēlòu〈名〉gaps and omissions: 弥缝～ fill in gaps and supply omissions
【缺略】quēlüè〈动〉be incomplete: 译文～ incomplete translation ‖ 文章的关键部分～了。The key part of the article was omitted.
【缺门】quēmén〈名〉gap: 这一学科在我们这里还是～。We have a gap in this branch of learning.
【缺欠】quēqiàn A〈名〉shortcoming: 这个计划有什么～，希望大家提出来。We hope that you will not hesitate to make us aware of any weaknesses in the plan. B〈动〉lack: ～科技人才 lack qualified scientists and technicians ‖ 因～资金，计划只得暂停。The plan has to be suspended because of a shortfall in funds.
【缺勤】quēqín〈动〉be absent from duty: 因病～ be off sick ‖ 降低～率 reduce the absentee rate
【缺少】quēshǎo〈动〉lack: ～训练 lack training ‖ ～证据 lack proof ‖ 不可～的条件 indispensable conditions
【缺省值】quēshěngzhí〈名〉[计算机] default value
【缺失】quēshī A〈名〉shortcoming: 弥补～ remedy a defect B〈动〉lack: 手稿～严重。There are a lot of pages missing in the manuscript.
【缺损】quēsǔn〈动〉1（破损）be damaged: 家具～严重。The damage to the furniture is severe. 2 ▸p. 50 [医学] be physiologically deficient: 后天～ acquired defect ‖ 先天～ congenital defect
【缺铁性贫血】quētiěxìng pínxuè ▸p. 50〈名〉iron-deficiency anaemia
【缺位】quēwèi A〈动〉1（职位空缺）fall vacant: 校长一职暂时～。The position of headmaster is still vacant. 2（达不到要求）fall short B〈名〉vacancy: 补～ fill a vacancy
【缺席】quēxí〈动〉be absent: 无故～ be absent without reason ‖ 因事～ be absent because of a separate engagement ‖ ～判决 judgement by default
【缺席者】quēxízhě〈名〉absentee
【缺陷】quēxiàn〈名〉defect: 弥补～ remedy a defect ‖ 生理～ physical defect ‖ 制度上的～ deficiencies in the system
【缺心眼儿】quēxīnyǎnr〈形〉〈口〉1（指头脑简单）simple-minded 2（指智力低下）dull-witted
【缺氧症】quēyǎngzhèng ▸p. 50〈名〉[医学] anoxia
【缺一不可】quēyī-bùkě〈成〉not a single one can be omitted
【缺衣少食】quēyī-shǎoshí〈成〉be short of food and clothing
【缺医少药】quēyī-shǎoyào〈成〉be short of medical services and supplies
【缺阵】quēzhèn〈动〉be absent: 主攻手～，导致球队失利。The absence of the ace striker led to the team's defeat.

阙（闕）quē〈书〉
A = 缺 quē
B〈名〉（过失）error
▸què
【阙如】quērú〈动〉〈书〉be deficient: 暂付～ be temporarily lacking
【阙失】quēshī〈名〉mistake
【阙疑】quēyí〈动〉leave a difficult question open

qué

瘸 qué〈动〉〈口〉be lame: 走路一～一拐 hobble along
【瘸腿】quétuǐ〈形〉〈口〉lame
【瘸子】quézi〈名〉〈口〉lame person: 变成～ go lame

què

却（卻）què
A〈动〉1（后退）withdraw: ▸退～, 望而～步 2〈书〉（使退却）drive back: ～敌 drive back an enemy 3（推辞）decline: ～而不受 refuse to accept ▸盛情难～, 推～ 4（去除）do away with: ▸冷～, 了～, 失～, 忘～
B〈副〉yet: 简单～有效的解决办法 simple but effective solution ‖ 她喜欢音乐，她丈夫～不喜欢。She likes music, but her husband doesn't.
【却病】quèbìng〈动〉〈书〉eliminate a disease: ～延年 prevent disease and prolong life
【却步】quèbù〈动〉〈书〉hang back: 因恐惧而～ shrink with fear ▸望而～
【却说】quèshuō〈动〉〈套〉we were at the point at which [used by story-tellers to resume narration where they had left off]
【却之不恭】quèzhī-bùgōng〈成〉it would be impolite to decline: ～，受之有愧。To decline would be disrespectful but to accept is embarrassing.

雀 què〈名〉[鸟类] sparrow
▸qiāo, qiǎo
【雀斑】quèbān〈名〉freckle: 长满～的脸 freckly face
【雀鹰】quèyīng〈名〉[鸟类] sparrow hawk
【雀跃】quèyuè〈动〉jump for joy: 欢呼～ shout and jump for joy
【雀噪】quèzào〈动〉〈喻〉enjoy loud fame

确（確）què
A〈形〉1（坚决）firm: ▸～保, ～认, ～守, ～信 2（真实）real: 其言甚～ what one says is quite true ‖ 消息不～。The news is not reliable. ▸～切, 明～, 千真万～, 准～
B〈副〉really: ～有其事。It's true.
【确保】quèbǎo〈动〉ensure: ～安全生产 ensure safety in production ‖ ～产品质量 guarantee product quality ‖ ～家庭与社会稳定 ensure family and social stability ‖ 只有一种办法可以～成功。There is only one sure way to succeed.
【确当】quèdàng〈形〉appropriate: 措词～ appropriate wording ‖ 结论～ fitting conclusion
【确定】quèdìng A〈形〉certain: ～的日期 fixed date ‖ 结果～无疑。The result is a foregone conclusion. B〈动〉determine: ～开会的时间和地点 fix the time and place for the meeting ‖ ～人选 decide on the candidates ‖ 警察尚不能～凶手的身份。The police are still uncertain of the murderer's identity.
【确乎】quèhū〈副〉〈书〉really: ～有效 really effective
【确乎不拔】quèhū-bùbá〈成〉firm and unshakeable
【确立】quèlì〈动〉establish: ～规章制度 set up rules and regulations ‖ 他们已经～了优势地位。They have already established their superiority.
【确切】quèqiè〈形〉1（准确）exact: ～的含义 precise meaning ‖ 告知～的日期 inform sb. of the exact date ‖ ～地说 to be precise 2（真实）real: 消息～ reliable information ‖ ～的保证 sure-fire guarantee
【确权】quèquán〈动〉affirm one's rights: 财产～案 property rights case ‖ 集体林地～到户。Collective forest property rights go to individual households.
【确认】quèrèn〈动〉confirm: ～预订 confirm a booking ‖ 得到～ be firmly established ‖ 警察～他是小偷。The police identified him as the thief.
【确实】quèshí A〈形〉real: ～的报道 reli-

q

able report ‖ 消息～无疑。 The news is unquestionably true. **B** 〈副〉 really: 你～爱他吗? Do you really love him? ‖ 我～去过，可他不在。 I really did go, but he wasn't in.

【确守】quèshǒu〈动〉 faithfully observe: ～和平共处五项原则 strictly abide by the five principles of peaceful coexistence ‖ ～诺言 be true to one's promise ‖ ～信义 act in good faith

【确信】quèxìn **A** 〈动〉 firmly believe: 我～你是无辜的。 I am convinced of your innocence. ‖ 我们～他有能力解决这个问题。 We are assured of his ability to solve the problem. **B** 〈名〉 reliable information: 何时来沪，请给我一个～。 Please let me know exactly when you are coming to Shanghai.

【确凿】quèzáo〈形〉 conclusive: 证据～ conclusive proof ‖ 目前尚未发现～证据。 No hard evidence has been found so far.

【确凿不移】quèzáo-bùyí〈成〉 absolutely true and irrefutable

【确诊】quèzhěn〈动〉 make a definite diagnosis: 他的病已～为癌症。 His illness has been diagnosed as cancer.

【确证】quèzhèng **A** 〈动〉 conclusively prove: 事实已经～了这个理论。 Facts have conclusively proved the theory. **B** 〈名〉 conclusive proof: 拿出～ provide conclusive proof

阕（闋） què

A 〈动〉〈书〉 end: 乐～。 The music ended. **B** 〈量〉 **1**（指歌或词） [for songs and *ci* poems]: 一～词 a *ci* poem ‖ 一～歌 a song **2**（指词的一段） [for divisions of a *ci* poem] stanza: 这首词分为两～。 This *ci* poem comprises two stanzas.

鹊（鵲） què

〈名〉［鸟类］ magpie: ▸喜～

【鹊巢鸠占】quècháo-jiūzhàn〈成〉〈喻〉 one person seizes another's territory

【鹊起】quèqǐ〈动〉 [of sb.'s fame] spread quickly: 他声誉～。 He quickly rose to fame. ‖ 这本书的出版使她文名～。 The publication of the book has greatly added to her literary fame.

【鹊桥】quèqiáo〈名〉 Magpie Bridge [bridge formed by magpies which the Weaving-Girl must cross in order to meet the Herdboy on the 7th evening of the 7th lunar month]:〈喻〉 ～相会 reunion of lovers after a long separation

阙（闕） què

〈名〉 **1**（指楼台） watchtowers on either side of a palace gate: ▸宫～ **2**（指石雕） stone carvings erected in front of a shrine or mausoleum ▸quē

榷¹ què

〈动〉〈书〉 monopolize: ～盐 monopoly on salt ‖ ～税 tax levied on monopolized trades

榷² què

〈动〉 discuss: ▸商～

qūn

囷 qūn

〈名〉〈古〉 round granary

逡 qūn

〈动〉〈书〉 draw back

【逡巡】qūnxún〈动〉〈书〉 hang back: ～不前 hesitate to move forward

qún

宭 qún

〈动〉〈书〉 live in groups

裙 qún

〈名〉 **1**（裙子） skirt: 长/短～ long/short skirt ‖ 超短～ miniskirt **2**（裙状物） skirt-shaped thing: ▸墙～, 围～

【裙钗】qúnchāi〈名〉 women

【裙撑】qúnchēng〈名〉 bustle

【裙带】qúndài〈形〉 related by marriage: 〈喻〉 ～关系 nepotism

【裙带风】qúndàifēng〈名〉 petticoat influence

【裙房】qúnfáng〈名〉 skirt building: ～内有餐厅。 There is a canteen in the skirt building.

【裙裤】qúnkù〈名〉 culottes

【裙子】qúnzi〈名〉 skirt

群（羣） qún

A 〈名〉 **1**（指聚在一起） crowd: 建筑～ groups of buildings ‖ 羊～ flocks of sheep ▸成～, 人～ **2**（指众多） multitude: ▸～众, 超～

B 〈形〉 numerous: ▸～岛, ～山

C 〈量〉 flock: 一～匪徒/强盗 a band of gangsters/robbers ‖ 一～鸽子 a flock of pigeons ‖ 一～孩子 a group of children ‖ 一～狼/猎狗 a pack of wolves/hounds ‖ 一～蜜蜂 a swarm of bees

【群策群力】qúncè-qúnlì〈成〉 work with collective wisdom and concerted efforts: 全厂工人～，大搞技术革新。 All the workers in the factory devoted their wisdom and energy to technological innovation.

【群唱】qúnchàng〈名〉 form of performance in which three or more people sing in turn

【群岛】qúndǎo ▸**p. 164**〈名〉 archipelago: 南沙～ Nansha Islands

【群雕】qúndiāo〈名〉 sculpture consisting of a number of statues: 一组～ a group of sculptures

【群而不党】qún'ér-bùdǎng〈成〉 keep company with all men, yet join no faction

【群芳】qúnfāng〈名〉〈喻〉 a multitude of pretty women: 技压～ have incomparable skills ‖ ～斗艳。 Flowers vie with each other for glamour.

【群婚】qúnhūn〈名〉 communal marriage

【群集】qúnjí〈动〉 assemble in large numbers: 抗议的人们～在大使馆前。 A multitude of protesters gathered in front of the embassy.

【群架】qúnjià〈名〉 gang fight: ▸打～

【群居】qúnjū〈动〉 **1**（指聚居） live in groups: ～穴处 be crude and ignorant **2**〈书〉（指聚集） assemble in large numbers: 爱～，不爱独处 prefer company to isolation

【群居动物】qúnjū dòngwù〈名〉 gregarious animal

【群口相声】qúnkǒu xiàngsheng〈名〉［曲艺］ group crosstalk

【群龙无首】qúnlóng-wúshǒu〈成〉〈喻〉 a group without a leader

【群论】qúnlùn〈名〉［数学］ group theory

【群落】qúnluò〈名〉 **1**［生物］ colony **2**（群体） group: 建筑～ groups of buildings

【群氓】qúnméng〈名〉〈书〉〈贬〉 common herd

【群魔乱舞】qúnmó-luànwǔ〈成〉〈喻〉 rogues of all kinds running wild

【群殴】qún'ōu〈名〉 gang fight: 一场～ a gang fight

【群起】qúnqǐ〈动〉 rally: ～响应 rally to respond

【群起而攻之】qúnqǐ ér gōng zhī〈成〉 all rise against sb./sth.

【群情】qúnqíng〈名〉 public sentiment: ～鼎沸 vast upsurge of public feeling ‖ ～振奋。 Everyone is exhilarated.

【群山】qúnshān〈名〉 chain of mountains: ～环绕 be surrounded by hills ‖ ～起伏 rolling mountains

【群生植物】qúnshēng zhíwù〈名〉 social plant

【群体】qúntǐ〈名〉 **1**［生物］ colony **2**（指整体） group: 低收入～ low-income group ‖ 古建筑～ collection of ancient buildings

【群体行为】qúntǐ xíngwéi〈名〉 group behaviour

【群威群胆】qúnwēi-qúndǎn〈成〉 mass heroism and daring spirit

【群舞】qúnwǔ〈名〉 collective dance

【群戏】qúnxì〈名〉［影视］ multi-character drama

【群星】qúnxīng〈名〉 **1**〈本〉 sea of stars: ～闪烁 a sea of stars twinkled **2**〈喻〉 heady array of stars: ～云集 a heady array of stars gathered together

【群星拱月】qúnxīng-gǒngyuè〈成〉 group of stars clustering around the moon

【群雄】qúnxióng〈名〉 warlord: ～割据 warlords carving up a country ‖ ～逐鹿 feudal lords vie for the throne

【群言堂】qúnyántáng〈名〉 rule by the voice of the majority: 要搞"～"，反对"一言堂" advocate 'letting everyone have their say' and oppose the practice of 'what I say goes'

【群英】qúnyīng〈名〉 galaxy of talents: ～欢聚 splendid gathering of talented people

【群英会】qúnyīnghuì〈名〉 gathering of heroes

【群众】qúnzhòng〈名〉 **1**（人民大众） the masses: 密切联系～ maintain close links with the masses ‖ 依靠～ rely on the masses ‖ 为～谋福利 work for the well-being of the people **2**（指非党员或团员） person without political affiliation: 他政治面貌是～。 He is non-partisan. **3**（指非领导） member of the rank and file

【群众关系】qúnzhòng guānxi〈名〉 relations with the masses: 搞好～ build good relations with the masses

【群众路线】qúnzhòng lùxiàn〈名〉 mass line: 走～ follow the mass line

【群众演员】qúnzhòng yǎnyuán〈名〉 extra

【群众运动】qúnzhòng yùndòng〈名〉 mass movement: 大搞～ unfold a mass movement on a large scale

【群众组织】qúnzhòng zǔzhī〈名〉 mass organization

【群租】qúnzū〈动〉 house-share in illegal numbers: 解决～顽症 stamp out the plague of house-sharing in illegal numbers

麇 qún

〈副〉〈书〉 in flocks

【麇集】qúnjí〈动〉〈书〉 flock together: ～周围 rally round sb./sth.

Rr

r

rán

蚺 rán

【蚺蛇】ránshé = 蟒蛇 mǎngshé

然 rán

A〈代〉so: 不尽～ not exactly the case ‖ 知其～，不知其所以～ have the knowledge but not know why it is so

B〈形〉correct: ►不以为～

C〈连〉〈书〉but: ►～而

D〈后缀〉[used to form an adjective or adverb]: ►安～，忽～，茫～，突～

【然而】rán'ér〈连〉but: 这件工作很辛苦，～很值得。It was hard work, but it was worthwhile. ‖ 她死了，～她的精神永存。She died, but her values endure.

【然后】ránhòu〈连〉then: 先朝前直走，～向左拐。Go straight forward and then turn left. ‖ 请听我把话说完，～再下结论。Please hear me out before you draw any conclusions.

【然诺】ránnuò〈动〉〈书〉make a promise: 重～ be serious about making and keeping one's promises

【然则】ránzé〈连〉〈书〉in that case: ～何时而乐耶？When, then, can they enjoy themselves in life?

髯 rán〈名〉〈书〉beard: 美～公 man with well-trimmed beard and moustache

【髯口】ránkou〈名〉［戏曲］false beard and whiskers: 挂～ wear a false beard and whiskers

燃 rán〈动〉1（燃烧）burn: 点～ set alight ‖ 严禁携带易～物品。Flammable items are forbidden. ►～烧 2（点燃）light: ～香 light incense ‖ ～起一堆篝火 light a bonfire ‖〈喻〉～起新的希望 rekindle a hope ►～放

【燃爆】ránbào〈动〉ignite and explode

【燃炽】ránchì〈动〉burn

【燃点】rándiǎn A〈动〉light: ～蜡烛 light a candle B〈名〉［化学］ignition point

【燃放】ránfàng〈动〉let off: ～烟火 set off fireworks

【燃耗】ránhào〈名〉fuel consumption

【燃具】ránjù〈名〉gas appliance

【燃料】ránliào〈名〉fuel: 节省～ save fuel ‖ ～短缺 fuel shortage ‖ ～附加费 bunker surcharge ‖ 矿物～ fossil fuel ►固体～，核～

【燃料库】ránliàokù〈名〉fuel depot

【燃料油】ránliàoyóu〈名〉fuel oil

【燃眉之急】ránméizhījí〈成〉be extremely urgent

【燃气】ránqì〈名〉fuel gas: ～热水器 gas heater

【燃气锅炉】ránqì guōlú〈名〉gas-fired burner

【燃气具】ránqìjù〈名〉1（指煤气灶）gas cooker 2（指燃气热水器）gas boiler

【燃气灶】ránqìzào〈名〉gas stove

【燃烧】ránshāo〈动〉burn: 烈火熊熊～。The raging fire burned vigorously. ‖ 那场森林大火～了好几天。The forest fire burned for days. ‖〈喻〉复仇的火焰在他胸中～。A desire for vengeance was burning within him.

【燃烧弹】ránshāodàn〈名〉fire bomb

【燃烧瓶】ránshāopíng〈名〉Molotov cocktail

【燃烧室】ránshāoshì〈名〉［机械］combustion chamber

【燃烧值】ránshāozhí〈名〉fuel value

【燃油】rányóu〈名〉fuel oil: ～锅炉 oil-burning boiler ‖ ～附加税 bunker surcharge

【燃油炉】rányóulú〈名〉oil burner

rǎn

冉 rǎn

【冉冉】rǎnrǎn〈书〉A〈副〉slowly: 国旗～升起。The national flag is rising slowly. ‖ 太阳从地平线上～升起。The sun gradually rose above the horizon. B〈形〉[of tree branches, etc.] hanging down loosely

苒 rǎn ►荏苒 rěnrǎn

染 rǎn〈动〉1（着色）dye: ～布 dye a piece of cloth ‖ ～成红色/绿色 dye sth. red/green ‖ 他把头发～得金黄。He dyed his hair blonde. ►蜡～，印～ 2（沾上）catch: ～上流感 catch the flu ‖ ～上坏习惯 fall into a bad habit ►～病，传～，沾～，污～

【染病】rǎnbìng〈动〉contract an illness: 身染重病 be seriously ill ‖ 他～在床。He's in bed with an illness.

【染厂】rǎnchǎng〈名〉dye-works

【染发】rǎnfà〈动〉dye one's hair: 去美发厅～ go to the hairdresser's to get one's hair coloured

【染发剂】rǎnfàjì〈名〉hair-dye

【染坊】rǎnfáng〈名〉dye-works

【染缸】rǎngāng〈名〉1〈本〉dye vat 2〈喻〉（指环境）corrupting environment

【染工】rǎngōng〈名〉dyer

【染疾】rǎnjí〈动〉contract a disease

【染剂】rǎnjì〈名〉［化工］dye: 酸性～ acid dye

【染料】rǎnliào〈名〉［化工］dye: 合成～ synthetic dye

【染色】rǎnsè〈动〉dye: ～剂 colouring agent

【染色法】rǎnsèfǎ〈名〉staining

【染色体】rǎnsètǐ〈名〉［生物］chromosome: ～基因 chromosome genetic ‖ ～疾病 chromosomal disorder ‖ ～减数 chromosome reduction ‖ ～突变 chromosomal mutation ‖ ～图谱 chromosome map

【染色质】rǎnsèzhì〈名〉chromatin

【染指】rǎnzhǐ〈动〉have a hand in: ～别国资源 encroach on another country's resources ‖ 绝无～之心 have no intention of profiting from sth.

【染指于鼎】rǎnzhǐyúdǐng〈成〉dip one's finger in

【染指择肥】rǎnzhǐ-zéféi〈成〉dip one's finger in the pie and claim the lion's share

rāng

嚷 rāng ►rǎng

【嚷嚷】rāngrang〈动〉〈口〉1（吵闹）yell: 请别大声～。Could you please speak quietly? 2（声张）shout about: 这件事你可别～出去。Don't let this out.

ráng

禳 ráng〈动〉〈书〉exorcize: ～灾 perform rituals or pray to gods to ward off calamities

【禳解】rángjiě〈动〉〈书〉ward off disaster or evil by praying to ghosts and gods

穰 ráng

A〈名〉1〈方〉（秸秆）grain stalks after thrashing: 豆～子 bean stalks after thrashing ►～草 2 = 瓤 ráng A

B〈形〉〈书〉bumper: ～岁 bumper harvest

【穰草】rángcǎo〈名〉rice or wheat straw

【穰穰】rángráng〈形〉〈书〉abundant: ～满家 with stores at home filled with a bumper grain harvest

瓤 ráng

A〈名〉1（瓜果肉）pulp: 红～ red flesh ‖ 柑橘～ pith of citrus fruit ‖ 西瓜～ watermelon pulp ►沙～ 2（瓤状物）interior: ►信～儿

B〈形〉1〈方〉（差）weak: 病后身体～ be weak after an illness ‖ 她开车的技术真不～。She is an excellent driver. 2〈口〉（松软）soft: 这块木头～了。This piece of wood has rotted.

【瓤子】rángzi〈名〉1（指瓜果肉）pulp 2 = 瓤 ráng A2

纕 ráng〈形〉〈旧〉dirty: 衣服～了。The clothes are dirty.

rǎng

壤 rǎng〈名〉① (土壤) soil: 沃～ rich soil ‖ 红～ red soil ▸～土, 土～ ② 〈书〉(大地) earth: 霄～ heaven and earth ▸天～之别 ③ (地区) land: ▸接～, 穷乡僻～

【壤土】 rǎngtǔ〈名〉① [地质] loam ② 〈书〉(土地) land

攘 rǎng

A 〈动〉〈书〉① (排斥) reject; (抵御) fend off: ～敌 resist the enemy ‖ ～外 resist external aggression ② (抢夺) seize: ▸～夺 ③ (捋起) roll up one's sleeves: ▸～臂

B 〈形〉 chaotic: ▸扰～

【攘臂】 rǎngbì〈动〉〈书〉 roll up one's sleeves in excitement: ～高呼 raise one's arms and shout

【攘除】 rǎngchú〈动〉〈书〉 cast out: ～奸邪 weed out crafty and evil people

【攘夺】 rǎngduó〈动〉〈书〉 seize: ～王位 usurp the throne

【攘攘】 rǎngrǎng〈形〉〈书〉 chaotic: 天下～ the hustle and bustle of the world

嚷 rǎng〈动〉① (叫喊) yell: 别～了, 影响他人睡觉。 Stop yelling. You'll disturb people sleeping. ② 〈口〉(吵闹) make a noise: 我气得跟他～了一顿。 I was so furious that I got into a row with him.
▸rāng

【嚷嘴】 rǎngzuǐ〈动〉〈口〉 bicker

ràng

让 (讓) ràng

A 〈动〉① (谦让) give way: 见困难就上, 见荣誉就～ step up to difficulties but be ever willing to let others take the glory ‖ 谁都～他三分。 Everybody yields to him somewhat. ▸～步, ～利, ～座, 退～ ② (给他人) offer: ～茶 offer tea ③ (出让) convey: ▸出～, 割～, 转～ ④ (使) let: ～窗子开着 leave the window open ‖ ～人失望 let people down ‖ ～一部分人先富起来。 Allow some people to prosper ahead of others. ‖ 谁～你来找我的? Who told you to come to me? ⑤ (让开) make way: 请～一～。 Excuse me. ▸～路

B 〈介〉〈口〉 [used as passive signifier]: 我的钱包～人偷了。 My wallet was stolen. ‖ 衣服～雨水打湿了。 The clothes were wet with rain.

【让步】 ràngbù〈动〉 give way: 不肯～ be unwilling to compromise ‖ 在原则问题上决不～ not compromise one's principles

【让车道】 ràngchēdào〈名〉[交通] passing lane

【让渡】 ràngdù〈动〉[法律] transfer

【让价】 ràngjià〈动〉 reduce the price

【让开】 ràngkāi〈动〉 step aside

【让利】 rànglì〈动〉 give a discount: 对企业～ allow enterprises to retain more profits ‖ ～销售 sell at reduced prices

【让路】 rànglù〈动〉 make way: 给救护车～ make way for an ambulance ‖ 〈喻〉其他工作都要为中心工作～。 The central task takes precedence over all other work.

【让位】 ràngwèi〈动〉① (指地位、职位) give up one's position: 军队控制了政权并迫使总统～。 The army took over and forced the president's abdication. ‖ 老干部应主动～, 退居二线。 Veteran cadres should retire voluntarily from their leading posts to assume advisory ones. ② (指座位) give up one's seat to sb.

【让贤】 ràngxián〈动〉 resign from one's post to make way for sb. better qualified: 主动～ step down in favour of a worthier candidate

【让座】 ràngzuò〈动〉 offer one's seat to sb.: 给孕妇～ offer one's seat to a pregnant woman

ráo

饶 (饒) ráo

A 〈形〉 plentiful: ～有情趣 be full of interest ▸丰～, 富～

B 〈动〉① (额外增添) give sth. extra: ▸～头 ② (饶恕) let sb. off: 这次～了你。 I'll let you off this time. ▸～恕, 求～

【饶命】 ráomìng〈动〉 spare sb.'s life: 乞求～ beg to be spared ‖ 请饶我一命。 Please spare me!

【饶人】 ráorén〈动〉 forgive sb.: 得理不～ not forgive when one is in the right ‖ 得～处且～ forgive when you can

【饶舌】 ráoshé〈动〉 be talkative: 请不要再～啦! Please stop gossiping.

【饶舌妇】 ráoshéfù〈名〉 gossipy woman

【饶恕】 ráoshù〈动〉 forgive: 不可～ unforgivable ‖ 请求～ ask for forgiveness

【饶头】 ráotou〈名〉〈口〉 freebie: 这是个～, 不要钱。 This one's a freebie. There is no charge.

【饶有风趣】 ráoyǒufēngqù〈成〉 full of wit and humour

娆 (嬈) ráo ▸娇娆 jiāoráo, 妖娆 yāoráo
▸rǎo

桡 (橈) ráo〈名〉〈书〉 oar

【桡动脉】 ráodòngmài〈名〉[生理] radial artery

【桡骨】 ráogǔ〈名〉[生理] radius

rǎo

扰 (擾) rǎo

A 〈动〉① (使混乱) disturb: ▸～乱, 打～, 干～, 庸人自～ ② 〈套〉(打搅) trespass on sb.'s hospitality: ▸叨～

B 〈形〉 confusing: ▸纷～

【扰动】 rǎodòng **A** 〈动〉 be in turmoil **B** 〈名〉① [物理] perturbation motion ② [地质] disturbance

【扰乱】 rǎoluàn〈动〉 upset: ～公共秩序 disturb public order ‖ ～民心 undermine the morale of the people ‖ ～视听 mislead public opinion ‖ ～思路 interrupt one's train of thought

【扰民】 rǎomín〈动〉 disturb the people: 在任何情况下都不可～。 Harassing people is never allowed under any circumstances. ‖ 噪声～。 The noise disturbed everyone.

【扰攘】 rǎorǎng〈名〉〈书〉 tumult: 十年～ ten years of turmoil

【扰扰】 rǎorǎo〈形〉〈书〉 confused: 纷纷～ chaotic

娆 (嬈) rǎo〈动〉〈书〉 harass
▸ráo

rào

绕¹ (繞) rào〈动〉① (缠) coil: ～线 wind wire ‖ 把绳子～在树上 coil a rope around a tree ▸盘～ ② (弄不清) confuse: 我让他给～住了。 I was baffled by him. ③ (使不顺畅) make difficult: ▸～口

绕² (遶) rào ① (围绕) move round: ～场三周 go around the track three times ‖ ～场一周向观众致意 run a lap of honour for the spectators ‖ 月亮～着地球转。 The moon revolves around the earth. ▸缭～ ② (迂回通过) go round: ～过暗礁 bypass a submerged reef ‖ 从后门～进去 make a detour through the back door ‖ 〈喻〉～过董事会, 擅自决定 get around the board of directors and make a decision for oneself ▸～道

【绕脖子】 rào bózi〈惯〉① (不直截了当) beat about the bush: 有话直说, 别～。 If you have something to say, then say it straight. Don't beat about the bush. ② (令人费解) tricky: ～的话 convoluted remarks ‖ 一道～的算术题 a tricky mathematical problem

【绕道】 ràodào〈动〉 make a detour: ～而行 make a detour

【绕过】 ràoguò〈动〉 bypass

【绕口】 ràokǒu〈形〉 tongue-twisting

【绕口令】 ràokǒulìng〈名〉 tongue twister

【绕梁三日】 ràoliáng-sānrì〈成〉 [of beautiful music, etc.] reverberate and linger in the air for a long time

【绕路】 ràolù = 绕道 ràodào

【绕圈子】 rào quānzi〈动〉① (指行程) make a detour: 绕了一千英里的大圈子 make a thousand-mile detour ② = 绕弯子 rào wānzi

【绕弯儿】 ràowānr〈动〉①〈口〉(散步) go for a stroll ② = 绕弯子 rào wānzi

【绕弯子】 rào wānzi〈动〉〈口〉 beat about the bush: 说话～ talk in a roundabout way ‖ 别～了。 Stop beating about the bush.

【绕行】 ràoxíng〈动〉 make a detour: 车辆～ traffic diversion〈英〉, traffic detour〈美〉

【绕远儿】 ràoyuǎnr **A** 〈动〉 go the long way round: 宁可～也不走小路 prefer to take the long way round and not the short cut **B** 〈形〉 circuitous: 走这条路太～了。 Taking this road is too tortuous.

【绕嘴】 ràozuǐ〈形〉 hard to pronounce: 这句话真～! What a mouthful!

rě

若 rě ▸般若 bōrě
▸ruò

喏 rě ▸唱喏 chàngrě
▸nuò

惹 rě〈动〉① (招引) invite: ～麻烦 invite trouble ▸～祸, ～事, 招～ ② (触犯) provoke: 此人可不好～。 This man is not easily offended. ‖ 此人可～不起。 Nobody dares to offend this man. ③ (使) cause: ～某人生气 ruffle sb. up the wrong way ‖ ～人讨厌 make a nuisance of oneself ‖ ～人注意 attract attention

【惹不起】 rěbùqǐ〈动〉 cannot afford to

offend: 我～他。 I can't afford to offend him.

【惹草拈花】 rěcǎo-niānhuā = 拈花惹草 niānhuā-rěcǎo

【惹火烧身】 rěhuǒshāoshēn〈成〉play with fire: 我才不会～。 I would never be so foolish as to invite trouble.

【惹祸】 rěhuò〈动〉court disaster: 这下你可～了。 You've really stirred things up now.

【惹乱子】 rě luànzi〈动〉 cause trouble

【惹恼】 rěnǎo〈动〉 irritate: 她的固执～了所有在场的人。 Her obstinacy irritated everybody present.

【惹气】 rěqì〈动〉 get angry: 不要为这种小事～。 Don't get yourself into a huff over such a trifle.

【惹事】 rěshì〈动〉 cause trouble: 别再给我～了。 Don't you go stirring up trouble for me any more.

【惹是非】 rě shìfēi〈动〉 stir up trouble: 他长大后成了个怕～的人。 He grew into a timid person who would avoid trouble at all costs.

【惹是生非】 rěshì-shēngfēi〈成〉 make mischief: 不要～。 Let sleeping dogs lie.

【惹眼】 rěyǎn〈形〉〈口〉 eye-catching

r

rè

热（熱） rè

A〈形〉 **1**（温度高） hot: 大～天 sizzling hot day ‖ 趁～吃。 Eat while it's hot. ‖ 我又～又渴。 I'm hot and thirsty. ▸～带, 滚～, 酷～ **2**（热情） warm-hearted: 他是个～心肠。 He has a warm heart. ▸～爱, ～烈, 亲～ **3**（羡慕） envious: ▸～衷, 眼～ **4**（时兴） popular: 爵士乐又～起来了。 Jazz is getting popular again. ▸～门, ～销 **5**（与热量相关） thermal: ～中子反应堆 thermal neutron reactor

B〈名〉 **1**（热量） heat: 生/传～ generate/conduct heat ‖ 太阳发出光和～。The sun gives off warmth and light. ▸地～ **2**（发烧） fever: 服药退～ take some medicine to bring down one's fever ‖ 清～解毒 relieve internal heat and expel poisons ▸发～ **3**（热潮） craze: 出国～正在降温。 The craze for going abroad is abating. ‖ 中国掀起了奥运～。 Olympic fever hit China in a big way.

C〈动〉 heat (up): 牛奶在炉子上～着呢。 The milk is warming on the stove. ‖ 水～得慢。 Water heats slowly.

【热爱】 rè'ài〈动〉 have a deep love for: ～本职工作 be devoted to one's work ‖ ～祖国 love one's country ardently

【热泵】 rèbèng〈名〉［机械］ heat pump

【热病】 rèbìng〈名〉［中医］ acute disease accompanied by fever

【热播】 rèbō〈动〉 broadcast a popular programme: ～剧 hit show

【热层】 rècéng〈名〉［气象］thermosphere

【热插拔】 rèchābá〈动〉［计算机］ hot-plug

【热潮】 rècháo〈名〉 craze: 掀起基本建设的新～ start a new upsurge in capital construction ‖ 生产～ upsurge in production

【热炒】 rèchǎo **A**〈名〉 quick stir-fry: 要了三个～ order three stir-fries **B**〈动〉〈喻〉 overexpose: 明星隐私被媒体～。 The media has infringed upon the star's privacy.

【热忱】 rèchén〈名〉 zeal: 爱国～ patriotic fervour ‖ 满腔～ full of eagerness and sincerity

【热诚】 rèchéng〈形〉 warm and sincere: 待人～ be cordial to others ‖ ～欢迎 cordially welcome

【热处理】 rèchǔlǐ〈动〉［机械］ treat with heat: ～金属 heat-treated metal

【热传导】 rèchuándǎo〈名〉［物理］ heat conduction

【热传递】 rèchuándì〈名〉［物理］ heat transmission

【热传感器】 rèchuángǎnqì〈名〉 thermal sensor

【热磁效应】 rècí xiàoyìng〈名〉 thermomagnetic effect

【热带】 rèdài〈名〉 tropical zone: ～风光 tropical scene

【热带风暴】 rèdài fēngbào〈名〉 tropical storm

【热带气旋】 rèdài qìxuán〈名〉tropical cyclone

【热带鱼】 rèdàiyú〈名〉 tropical fish

【热带雨林】 rèdài yǔlín〈名〉 tropical rain forest: 保护～ protect tropical rain forests

【热带植物】 rèdài zhíwù〈名〉 tropical plants

【热当量】 rèdāngliàng〈名〉［物理］ heat equivalent

【热导】 rèdǎo〈名〉［物理］ thermal conductance

【热导体】 rèdǎotǐ〈名〉［物理］ heat conductor

【热岛效应】 rèdǎo xiàoyìng〈名〉 tropical island effect

【热得快】 rèdekuài〈名〉〈口〉 immersion heater

【热点】 rèdiǎn〈名〉 hot spot: ～地区 flash point area ‖ 旅游～ tourist hot spot ‖ ～问题 central issue

【热电厂】 rèdiànchǎng〈名〉thermal power plant

【热电站】 rèdiànzhàn〈名〉 thermal power station

【热电阻】 rèdiànzǔ〈名〉 thermal resistance

【热动力】 rèdònglì〈名〉 thermal power

【热度】 rèdù〈名〉 **1**（指气温） degree of heat: ～降低了。 The heat has abated. **2**〈口〉（指体温） fever: ～退下来了。 The fever has abated. **3**（指热情） fad: 三分钟的～ passing fad

【热费】 rèfèi〈名〉 heating charges: ～补贴 heating subsidy ‖ ～定价 the fixing of heating charges

【热风】 rèfēng〈名〉 hot air

【热风炉】 rèfēnglú〈名〉 hot-blast furnace

【热封】 rèfēng〈名〉 heat seal

【热敷】 rèfū〈动〉［医学］ foment

【热辐射】 rèfúshè〈名〉 thermal radiation

【热功当量】 règōng dāngliàng〈名〉［物理］ Joule's equivalent

【热狗】 règǒu〈名〉［食品］ hot dog

【热管】 règuǎn〈名〉 heating pipe

【热锅上的蚂蚁】 règuōshangde mǎyǐ〈俗〉〈喻〉 like a cat on a hot tin roof: 考试前他急得像～。 He was extremely fidgety before the examination.

【热合金】 rèhéjīn〈名〉 thermalloy

【热核反应】 rèhé fǎnyìng〈名〉 thermonuclear reaction

【热核武器】 rèhé wǔqì〈名〉thermonuclear weapon

【热烘烘】 rèhōnghōng〈形〉 very warm: 暖气使房间里～的。 The room was quite warm because of the central heating.

【热红外】 rèhóngwài〈形〉［物理］thermal infra-red

【热乎乎】 rèhūhū〈形〉warm: ～的饭菜 hot meals ‖ 心里～的 feel warm at heart

【热乎】 rèhu〈形〉〈口〉 **1**（指温度） nice and warm: 屋里真～。 The room is so warm and cosy. **2**（指人际关系） chummy: 他们俩最近很～。 They have been quite chummy recently.

【热火朝天】 rèhuǒ-cháotiān〈成〉 be bustling with activity: 大家都在～地工作。 Everyone was working with great enthusiasm.

【热货】 rèhuò = 热门货 rèménhuò

【热火】 rèhuo〈形〉 **1**（热烈） exciting: ～的场面 scene of noisy hilarity **2** = 热和 rèhuo

【热和】 rèhuo〈形〉〈口〉 **1**（不凉） nice and warm: ～的饭菜 warm dishes **2**（亲热） warm and friendly: 谈得很～ have a very friendly chat

【热机】 rèjī〈名〉［机械］ heat engine

【热寂】 rèjì〈名〉［物理］ heat death

【热加工】 rèjiāgōng〈动〉［冶金］hot work

【热键】 rèjiàn〈名〉［计算机］ hotkey

【热交换】 rèjiāohuàn〈名〉［机械］ heat exchange: ～器 heat exchanger

【热解】 rèjiě〈名〉［化学］ thermolysis

【热裤】 rèkù〈名〉 hot pants

【热辣】 rèlà〈形〉 hot

【热辣辣】 rèlàlà〈形〉 burning hot: 觉得脸上～的 feel one's cheeks burning

【热浪】 rèlàng〈名〉 heat wave: 遭到～袭击 be hit by a heat wave ‖〈喻〉 一股抢购～ a wave of panic-buying

【热泪】 rèlèi〈名〉 hot tears: ～滚滚 hot tears rolling down one's cheeks

【热泪盈眶】 rèlèi-yíngkuàng〈成〉 dissolve into tears: 老兵的故事使孩子们～。 The old soldier's story brought tears to the eyes of the children.

【热离子】 rèlízǐ〈名〉［物理］ thermion

【热力】 rèlì〈名〉［机械］ heating power: ～学 thermodynamics

【热恋】 rèliàn〈动〉 be head over heels in love: 他们在～中。 They are very much in love.

【热量】 rèliàng〈名〉 quantity of heat: 释放～ give out heat

【热烈】 rèliè〈形〉 ardent: 气氛～ lively atmosphere ‖ ～的掌声 warm applause ‖ 表示～欢迎 give a warm welcome

【热流】 rèliú〈名〉 **1**（指感觉） warm current: 一股～涌上心头 a warm current of emotion rose in one's heart **2**［物理］ thermal current

【热卖】 rèmài〈动〉 sell like hot cakes: 汽车正在～。 Cars are selling briskly.

【热门】 rèmén〈名〉 trend: ～话题 hot topic ‖ 计算机现在是大学里的～专业。 Computer science is now a popular major at college.

【热门货】 rèménhuò〈名〉 hot commodity: 手机眼下在中国是～。 Mobile phones are now going like hot cakes in China.

【热敏电阻】 rèmǐn diànzǔ〈名〉［电气］ thermal resistor

【热敏纸】 rèmǐnzhǐ〈名〉 thermal paper

【热闹】 rènao **A**〈形〉 lively: ～的场面 noisy scene ‖ 早上八点，小镇开始～起来。 The town begins to bustle at eight o'clock. **B**〈动〉 liven up: 明天放假，咱们找个地方～～吧。 Tomorrow is a holiday. Let's go somewhere and have a good time. **C**〈名〉 lively scene: 看～ observe a lively scene

【热能】 rènéng〈名〉［物理］ thermal energy

【热盼】 rèpàn〈动〉 eagerly await: ～世博会的到来 eagerly await the World Expo ‖ ～已久 long-awaited

【热喷喷】 rèpēnpēn〈形〉 steaming hot

【热膨胀】rèpéngzhàng〈名〉［物理］thermal expansion: ～系数 thermal expansion coefficient
【热捧】rèpěng〈动〉have great admiration for: 受到～ be greatly admired
【热评】rèpíng〈名〉hot review
【热启动】rèqǐdòng〈名〉［计算机］warm start
【热气】rèqì〈名〉steam: 冒～ give off steam ‖〈喻〉～腾腾 overflowing with enthusiasm
【热气球】rèqìqiú〈名〉hot-air balloon
【热钱】rèqián〈名〉［金融］hot money: 加强对～的监管 step up the supervision of hot money
【热切】rèqiè〈形〉fervent: ～的希望 fervent hope ‖ 怀着～的心情 in an ardent mood
【热情】rèqíng **A**〈名〉enthusiasm: ～高涨 burning with ardour ‖ 爱国～ patriotic enthusiasm ‖ 工作～ enthusiasm for one's work ‖ 她的讲话缺乏～。 Her speech lacked passion. ‖ 工作～有余而计划不足 work with more enthusiasm than planning **B**〈形〉enthusiastic: ～款待 treat cordially ‖ 待人～ deal with people warmly
【热情洋溢】rèqíng-yángyì〈成〉overflow with enthusiasm
【热容量】rèróngliàng〈名〉calorific capacity
【热身】rèshēn〈动〉warm up: ～运动 warm-up exercise ‖ ～赛 warm-up match
【热水】rèshuǐ〈名〉hot water
【热水袋】rèshuǐdài〈名〉hot-water bottle
【热水瓶】rèshuǐpíng〈名〉〈口〉Thermos; (vacuum) flask〈英〉
【热水器】rèshuǐqì〈名〉water heater: 电～ electric heater ‖ 太阳能～ solar water heater
【热水浴】rèshuǐyù〈名〉hot bath
【热塑性】rèsùxìng〈名〉thermal plasticity
【热损耗】rèsǔnhào〈名〉［物理］deprivation of heat
【热汤面】rètāngmiàn〈名〉noodles in hot soup
【热腾腾】rèténgténg〈形〉steaming hot: 一盘～的饺子 a plate of steaming hot dumplings
【热天】rètiān〈名〉hot day: 大～ very hot day
【热土】rètǔ〈名〉**1**（故乡、祖国）native land **2**（热点地区）hot spot: 投资者的～ hot spot for investors
【热望】rèwàng〈书〉**A**〈动〉fervently hope: ～成为作家 aspire to become an author **B**〈名〉fervent hope
【热吻】rèwěn〈名〉passionate kiss
【热污染】rèwūrǎn〈名〉heat pollution
【热舞】rèwǔ〈名〉crazy dance: ～表演 a crazy dance performance ‖ 在台上高歌～。 There was loud singing and mad dancing on the stage.
【热线】rèxiàn〈名〉**1**（指电话）hotline: 服务～ service hotline ‖ 投诉～ hotline for complaints ‖ ～电话 hotline **2**（指交通）hot route: 旅游～ travelling hot route
【热线节目】rèxiàn jiémù〈名〉phone-in programme
【热销】rèxiāo〈动〉sell like hot cakes: ～商品 hot-selling goods
【热孝】rèxiào〈名〉〈旧〉mourning over the recent death of one's grandparents, parents or husband: ～在身 wear mourning
【热效率】rèxiàolǜ〈名〉thermal efficiency
【热效应】rèxiàoyìng〈名〉thermal effect
【热心】rèxīn〈形〉enthusiastic: ～公益 be public spirited ‖ ～助人 be forward in helping others ‖ 对她的建议不太～ show no enthusiasm for her suggestion
【热心肠】rèxīncháng〈名〉**1**（指心地）warm-heartedness **2**（指人）warm-hearted and helpful person
【热学】rèxué〈名〉thermology
【热血】rèxuè〈名〉**1**（指血）warm blood: ～动物 warm-blooded animal **2**〈喻〉（指热情）enthusiasm: ～青年 passionate youth ‖ 满腔～ full of enthusiasm
【热血沸腾】rèxuè-fèiténg〈成〉with one's blood boiling over: 每当唱起这首歌，他就觉得～。 Every time he sang the song, he felt as if his blood were boiling.
【热压】rèyā〈名〉hot pressing
【热议】rèyì〈动〉discuss in a lively fashion: 引起媒体～ give rise to a lively media debate
【热饮】rèyǐn〈名〉hot drinks
【热映】rèyìng〈动〉be frequently shown in cinemas: 这部动画片正在～。 This hit animated cartoon is being shown often across cinemas everywhere.
【热源】rèyuán〈名〉heat source
【热轧】rèzhá〈名〉［冶金］hot-rolling: ～钢 hot-rolled steel
【热战】rèzhàn〈名〉hot war
【热值】rèzhí〈名〉calorific value
【热衷】rèzhōng〈动〉**1**（指追求）crave: ～名利 hanker after fame and gain **2**（指喜好）be hot for sth.: ～足球 be crazy about football ‖ ～古典文学 be full of enthusiasm about classics ‖ ～流行音乐 be mad for pop music
【热作用】rèzuòyòng〈名〉heat utilization

rén

人 rén〈名〉**1**（人类）person: 五口～ five people in a family ‖ 有学问的～ learned people ‖ 普通～ ordinary people ‖ ～多好办事。 Many hands make light work. ▸成～ **2**（某种人）people of different kinds: ▸白～，军～，客～ **3**（每个人）everybody: ～手一册 one copy each ‖ ～各有所好。 There is no accounting for taste. ▸～所共知 **4**（成年人）adult: 长大成～ reach manhood **5**（所有人）someone: 待～诚恳 treat others with sincerity ▸助～为乐 **6**（为人）[referring to a person's character, reputation, etc.]: 她～好。 She is nice. ‖ 真丢～! It's really humiliating! **7**（身体）[referring to a person's physical or mental condition]: 他～已经不行了。 He is dying. ▸不省～事 **8**（人手）manpower: 缺～ be short of hands ▸～浮于事
【人本主义】rénběnzhǔyì〈名〉humanism
【人不犯我，我不犯人；人若犯我，我必犯人】rén bù fàn wǒ, wǒ bù fàn rén; rén ruò fàn wǒ, wǒ bì fàn rén〈成〉we will not attack unless we are attacked; if we are attacked, we will certainly counter-attack
【人不可貌相】rén bù kě mào xiàng〈俗〉don't judge by appearances: ～，海水不可斗量。 As the sea cannot be measured with a bushel, so people cannot be judged by their appearances.
【人不知，鬼不觉】rén bù zhī, guǐ bù jué〈俗〉done in complete secrecy
【人才】réncái〈名〉**1**（指人）talented person: 招募～ recruit people with talent ‖ ～难得 talent is hard to come by ‖ 引进～ introduce talent ‖ 高素质～ talents of high quality **2**（指容貌）distinguished appearance: ▸一表～
【人才辈出】réncái-bèichū〈成〉people of talent emerging in large numbers: 此地～。 There is no lack of talented people here.
【人才荟萃】réncái-huìcuì〈成〉galaxy of talented persons
【人才济济】réncái-jǐjǐ〈成〉wealth of talents
【人才交易会】réncái jiāoyìhuì〈名〉talent fair
【人才库】réncáikù〈名〉brain bank
【人才流入】réncái liúrù〈名〉brain gain
【人才流失】réncái liúshī〈名〉brain drain
【人才市场】réncái shìchǎng〈名〉employment market
【人财两空】rén-cái liǎngkōng〈成〉lose both the person and the money
【人财两旺】rén-cái liǎngwàng〈成〉be blessed with a large family and a large fortune
【人潮】rénchāo〈名〉flood of people: ～涌动。 Huge crowds of people surged forwards.
【人臣】rénchén〈名〉〈古〉minister
【人称】rénchēng〈名〉［语言］person: 第一/二/三～ the first/second/third person ‖ ～代词 personal pronoun
【人次】réncì〈量〉person-time: 五十～ 50 person-times
【人丛】réncóng〈名〉crowd
【人大】Réndà〈简称〉= 人民代表大会
【人大常委会】Réndà Chángwěihuì〈名〉Standing Committee of the People's Congress
【人大代表】Réndà dàibiǎo〈名〉deputy to the People's Congress
【人代会】réndàihuì〈简称〉= 人民代表大会
【人道】réndào **A**〈名〉humanity: 以～的名义 in the name of humanity **B**〈形〉humane: 不～ inhuman
【人道主义】réndào zhǔyì〈名〉humanitarianism: ～精神 spirit of humanism ‖ ～援助/救助 humanitarian aid/assistance
【人地生疏】rén-dì shēngshū〈成〉be unfamiliar with the people and the place
【人丁】réndīng〈名〉**1**〈旧〉（成年男子）adult males **2**（人口）population: ～兴旺 be growing in number
【人盯人防守】réndīngrén fángshǒu〈名〉［体育］man-to-man defence
【人定胜天】réndìngshèngtiān〈成〉humans will triumph over nature
【人堆儿】rénduīr〈名〉〈口〉crowd
【人盾】réndùn〈名〉human shield
【人多好办事】rénduō hǎo bànshì〈俗〉many hands make the job easy
【人多势众】rénduō-shìzhòng〈成〉dominate by sheer force of numbers
【人多智广】rénduō-zhìguǎng〈成〉more people, greater wisdom
【人多嘴杂】rénduō-zuǐzá **1**（指说法多）many voices **2**（指易泄密）it's difficult to keep a secret when lots of people already know it
【人犯】rénfàn〈名〉criminal
【人贩子】rénfànzi〈名〉human trafficker
【人防工程】rénfáng gōngchéng〈名〉air defence works
【人非草木】rén fēi cǎomù〈成〉human beings are not without feelings
【人非圣贤，孰能无过】rén fēi shèngxián, shú néng wú guò〈成〉to err is human
【人份】rénfèn〈量〉person-share: 十万～牛痘疫苗 doses of bovine vaccines for 100,000 people

r

【人粪尿】rénfènniào〈名〉［农业］ night soil

【人逢喜事精神爽】rén féng xǐshì jīngshén shuǎng〈俗〉 joyous occasions brace the spirit

【人浮于事】rénfúyúshì〈成〉be over-staffed: ～的行政机构 bloated and top-heavy administrative organ

【人高马大】réngāo-mǎdà〈成〉 be tall and strong

【人格】réngé〈名〉 1（指品格、个性等） personality: ～高尚 have a noble character ‖ 双重～ split personality ▸～分裂 2（指权利、资格） human dignity: 侮辱～ insult sb.'s dignity ‖ 尊重～ respect one's dignity ‖ 以～担保 on one's honour

【人格分裂】réngé fēnliè〈名〉［心理］personality split

【人格化】réngéhuà〈动〉 personify

【人格权】réngéquán〈名〉 right to human dignity

【人各有志】réngèyǒuzhì〈成〉 everyone has his own ambition

【人工】réngōng A〈形〉 man-made: ▸～湖 B〈名〉 1（指用人力） manual work: ～打包 hand press-packing ‖ ～电话交换机 manual switchboard 2（指工作量计算单位） person-day: 完成这项工程一定花了不少～。 It must have taken a lot of person-days to complete the project.

【人工操作】réngōng cāozuò〈名〉 manual operation

【人工岛】réngōngdǎo〈名〉 man-made island

【人工繁殖】réngōng fánzhí〈名〉 artificial propagation

【人工喉】réngōnghóu〈名〉artificial larynx

【人工呼吸】réngōng hūxī〈名〉 artificial respiration: 做～ give sb. artificial respiration ‖ ～器 artificial respirator

【人工湖】réngōnghú〈名〉 man-made lake

【人工降水】réngōng jiàngshuǐ〈名〉 artificial precipitation

【人工降雨】réngōng jiàngyǔ〈名〉 artificial rainfall

【人工流产】réngōng liúchǎn〈名〉 induced abortion

【人工受孕】réngōng shòuyùn〈名〉 artificial insemination

【人工授粉】réngōng shòufěn〈名〉 artificial pollination

【人工授精】réngōng shòujīng〈名〉 artificial insemination: 接受～ undergo artificial insemination

【人工引产】réngōng yǐnchǎn〈名〉induced labour

【人工影响天气】réngōngyǐngxiǎng tiānqì〈名〉 weather modification

【人工语言】réngōng yǔyán〈名〉 artificial language

【人工照明】réngōng zhàomíng〈名〉 artificial lighting

【人工智能】réngōng zhìnéng〈名〉［计算机］ artificial intelligence (AI): ～语言 artificial intelligence language

【人公里】réngōnglǐ〈量〉［交通］ passenger-kilometre

【人贵有自知之明】rén guì yǒu zìzhīzhīmíng〈惯〉 it is important to know one's own limitations

【人海】rénhǎi〈名〉 1（指人群） sea of people: 消失在～之中 disappear into the crowd ‖ 茫茫～ vast sea of people ▸人山～ 2〈书〉〈喻〉（指社会） human world: ～沧桑 vicissitudes of life

【人海战术】rénhǎi zhànshù〈名〉 huge-crowd strategy

r

【人和】rénhé〈名〉 harmony among people: 天时、地利、～ favourable climatic, geographical and human conditions ▸政通～

【人话】rénhuà〈名〉 sensible talk: 你这还算说了句～。 Now you are talking sense.

【人欢马叫】rénhuān-mǎjiào〈成〉〈喻〉 a busy, prosperous country scene

【人寰】rénhuán〈名〉〈书〉 human world: ▸惨绝～

【人祸】rénhuò〈名〉 man-made disaster: ▸天灾～

【人机对话】rén-jī duìhuà〈名〉 human-computer interaction

【人际】rénjì〈形〉 interpersonal: ～交往 interpersonal communication ‖ ～关系 interpersonal relationships

【人迹】rénjì〈名〉 human footprints

【人迹罕至】rénjì-hǎnzhì〈成〉 off the beaten track

【人家】rénjiā〈名〉 1（住户） household: 十户～ ten households 2（家庭） family: 富裕～ well-to-do family 3（婆家） family of a girl's betrothed: 她已经有～了。 She is engaged to be married.

【人家】rénjia〈代〉 1（别人） everybody else: ～都不怕，就你怕。 Nobody is afraid except you. ‖ 别让～笑话。 Don't let yourself be made a mockery of. 2（他） he;（她） she;（他们） they: 别等了，～不会来了。 Don't wait any more. They won't come. ‖ 瞧～新买的大奔! Look at the big Mercedes Benz he's just bought! 3（我）（用作主语） [often used playfully] I;（用作宾语） me: 等一会儿， 没看见～忙着呢。 Wait a minute. Can't you see I am busy? ‖ 别急，听～说嘛。 Be patient. Just listen to me.

【人尖子】rénjiānzi〈名〉〈口〉 pick of the crop

【人间】rénjiān〈名〉 the world: ～奇迹 the wonders of the world ‖ ～悲剧 human tragedy ‖ ～天堂 heaven on earth

【人间沧桑】rénjiān-cāngsāng〈成〉 vicissitudes of life

【人间地狱】rénjiān-dìyù〈名〉〈喻〉 living hell

【人见人爱】rénjiànrén'ài〈成〉 be loved by all

【人杰】rénjié〈名〉〈书〉 outstanding personality: 生为～，死为鬼雄 live and die like a hero

【人杰地灵】rénjié-dìlíng〈成〉the greatness of a person lends glory to a place

【人尽其才】rénjìnqícái〈成〉 bring out the best in people: 我们必须做到～，物尽其用。 We must tap manpower and material resources to the full.

【人精】rénjīng〈名〉〈口〉1（指成年人） bright spark 2（指孩子） child genius

【人居】rénjū〈形〉 people-inhabited: ～环境 human settlement

【人均】rénjūn〈形〉 per capita: ～产值 per capita output value ‖ ～消费 per capita consumption ‖ ～住房面积 per capita housing space

【人均国民生产总值】rénjūn guómín shēngchǎn zǒngzhí〈名〉 per capita GNP

【人均国内生产总值】rénjūn guónèi shēngchǎn zǒngzhí〈名〉 per capita GDP

【人均收入】rénjūn shōurù〈名〉 per capita income

【人靠衣裳马靠鞍】rén kào yīshang mǎ kào ān〈俗〉 clothes make the person

【人孔】rénkǒng〈名〉［建筑］ manhole

【人口】rénkǒu〈名〉 1（指宏观） human population: 控制～ control population growth ‖ 农业～ farming population ‖ ～稀少 be sparsely populated ▸城市～ 2（指家庭） family size: 我们家～多/少。 I have a big/small family. 3（人） person: 拐卖～ kidnap and sell people

【人口爆炸】rénkǒu bàozhà〈名〉 population explosion

【人口高峰】rénkǒu gāofēng〈名〉 population peak

【人口红利】rénkǒu hónglì〈名〉 demographic dividend

【人口结构】rénkǒu jiégòu〈名〉 demographic structure

【人口密度】rénkǒu mìdù〈名〉 population density

【人口普查】rénkǒu pǔchá〈名〉 census: 进行～ conduct a census

【人口统计】rénkǒu tǒngjì〈名〉demographic statistics: ～表 census report ‖ ～学 demography ‖ ～资料 demographic data

【人口学】rénkǒuxué〈名〉 demography: ～家 demographer

【人口意识】rénkǒu yìshi〈名〉 awareness of the population problem

【人口增长】rénkǒu zēngzhǎng〈名〉 population growth: 控制～ control the population growth ‖ ～率 rate of population growth ‖ 人口负增长 negative population growth

【人口组成】rénkǒu zǔchéng〈名〉 demographic composition

【人困马乏】rénkùn-mǎfá〈成〉 be completely worn out

【人来疯】rénláifēng〈形〉 [of children] showing off in the presence of visitors

【人来人往】rénlái-rénwǎng〈成〉 people are hurrying to and fro

【人浪】rénlàng〈名〉 Mexican wave

【人老心不老】rén lǎo xīn bù lǎo〈俗〉 be young in heart though old in age

【人老珠黄】rénlǎo-zhūhuáng〈成〉〈喻〉 lose one's looks in old age

【人类】rénlèi〈名〉 mankind: ～的进步 human progress ‖ ～的起源 origin of man ‖ ～灵魂的工程师 [architects of the human spirit] teachers ‖ 为了全～的利益 in the interest of all humanity

【人类工程学】rénlèi gōngchéngxué〈名〉 ergonomics

【人类基因组】rénlèi jīyīnzǔ〈名〉 human genome: ～工程 human genome project ‖ ～研究 human genome research

【人类起源】rénlèi qǐyuán〈名〉 anthropogeny

【人类迁徙】rénlèi qiānxǐ〈名〉 human migration

【人类社会】rénlèi shèhuì〈名〉human society

【人类学】rénlèixué〈名〉 anthropology: ～家 anthropologist

【人力】rénlì〈名〉 manpower: ～不足 shortage of manpower ‖ 给予财力和～上的支持 support with money and people

【人力车】rénlìchē〈名〉 1（指使用人力） man-powered cart 2〈旧〉（指人拉车） rickshaw: ～夫 rickshaw driver

【人力资本】rénlì zīběn〈名〉［经济］ human capital

【人力资源】rénlì zīyuán〈名〉 human resources: ～部 human resources department

【人流】rénliú A〈名〉（指人群） stream of people: 疏散～ evacuate a crowd B〈简称〉= 人工流产

【人流如潮】rénliúrúcháo〈成〉 sea of faces

【人伦】rénlún〈名〉 human relations [according to feudal ethics]

【人马】rénmǎ〈名〉 1（部队） forces: 全

部～ all the troops **2**（人员） staff: 全部～ all staff members ‖ 原班～ original team

【人马座】Rénmǎzuò〈名〉［天文］Sagittarius

【人脉】rénmài〈名〉connections: ～很广 have extensive connections

【人满为患】rénmǎnwéihuàn〈成〉be overcrowded: ～的地铁 overcrowded subway

【人们】rénmen〈名〉people: ～的品味各有不同。Everybody's tastes are different.

【人面兽心】rénmiàn-shòuxīn〈成〉the face of a human but the heart of a beast

【人民】rénmín〈名〉the people: 为～服务 serve the people ‖ 劳动～ working people

【人民币】rénmínbì ▸**p. 328**〈名〉*Renminbi* (RMB)

【人民大会堂】Rénmín Dàhuìtáng〈名〉the Great Hall of the People

【人民大众】rénmín dàzhòng〈名〉the general public

【人民代表大会】Rénmín Dàibiǎo Dàhuì〈名〉People's Congress: ～制度 the system of the People's Congress

【人民法院】rénmín fǎyuàn〈名〉people's court: ～院长 president of the people's court

【人民公敌】rénmín gōngdí〈名〉public enemy

【人民公社】rénmín gōngshè〈名〉people's commune

【人民检察院】rénmín jiǎncháyuàn〈名〉people's procuratorate: ～检察长 chief procurator of the people's procuratorate

【人民解放军】Rénmín Jiěfàngjūn〈名〉People's Liberation Army (PLA)

【人民警察】rénmín jǐngchá〈名〉people's police

【人民来信来访】rénmín láixìn láifǎng〈名〉letters and visits from the masses

【人民民主专政】rénmín mínzhǔ zhuānzhèng〈名〉people's democratic dictatorship

【人民内部矛盾】rénmín nèibù máodùn〈名〉contradictions among the people: 正确处理～ correctly handle the contradictions among the people

【人民陪审员】rénmín péishěnyuán〈名〉［法律］people's assessor

【人民群众】rénmín qúnzhòng〈名〉the masses

【人民日报】Rénmín Rìbào〈名〉*People's Daily*

> **《人民日报》**
>
> The official organ of the Central Committee of the Chinese Communist Party, and China's most authoritative and influential daily newspaper. Founded in 1948, its editorials and commentaries on theory and policy are regarded as the direct voice of the Party. Its masthead was inscribed by Mao Zedong (毛泽东). An international edition, launched in 1985, is distributed in over 80 countries and regions, with a worldwide circulation of three to four million.

【人民团体】rénmín tuántǐ〈名〉mass organization

【人民武装】rénmín wǔzhuāng〈名〉people's armed forces

【人民武装部】rénmín wǔzhuāngbù〈名〉people's armed forces department

【人民英雄纪念碑】Rénmín Yīngxióng Jìniànbēi〈名〉the Monument to the People's Heroes

【人民战争】rénmín zhànzhēng〈名〉people's war: 打一场～ wage a people's war

【人民政府】rénmín zhèngfǔ〈名〉people's government

【人名】rénmíng〈名〉person's name

【人命】rénmìng〈名〉human life: 夺去两条～ claim two lives

【人命关天】rénmìng-guāntiān〈成〉matter of life and death

【人模狗样】rénmó-gǒuyàng〈俗〉〈贬〉pretend to be a person of some worth

【人莫予毒】rénmòyúdú〈成〉be so confident of his power as to think no one can do harm to him

【人脑】rénnǎo〈名〉human brain

【人年】rénnián〈名〉person-year

【人偶】rénǒu〈名〉figure

【人怕出名猪怕壮】rén pà chūmíng zhū pà zhuàng〈俗〉fame can be a double-edged sword

【人品】rénpǐn〈名〉**1**（指品格）character: ～不佳 person of disreputable character ‖ ～好 person of fine character **2**〈口〉（指外表）looks: ～出众 be extraordinarily good-looking

【人气】rénqì〈名〉popularity: ～旺 be popular

【人强马壮】rénqiáng-mǎzhuàng〈成〉strong workforce

【人墙】rénqiáng〈名〉**1**（指在足球赛中）the wall: 球打在～上，飞出场外。The ball hit the wall and flew out of the field. **2**（用于阻拦）human shield: 搭起～ form a human barricade

【人勤地不懒】rén qín dì bù lǎn〈俗〉where the tiller is hard-working, the land is productive

【人禽流感】rénqínliúgǎn ▸**p. 50**〈名〉Avian influenza (Bird flu) in humans

【人情】rénqíng〈名〉**1**（指感情）human feelings: 不近～ be heartless ‖ 违背～ be unnatural and abnormal **2**（指情分）feelings: 讲/重～ set great store by friendship ‖ 欠～ owe sb. a debt of gratitude **3**（指恩惠）favour: 做个～ do sb. a favour ‖ 空头～ empty promise **4**（指习俗）courtesy: 迫于～ out of a sense of obligation ‖ 随～ follow the customary practice ‖ 行～ observe etiquette **5**（指礼物）gift: 送～ give sb. a gift

【人情冷暖】rénqíng-lěngnuǎn〈名〉social snobbery

【人情练达】rénqíng-liàndá〈成〉be worldly-wise

【人情世故】rénqíng-shìgù〈成〉ways of the world: 不懂～ be ignorant of the ways of the world

【人情味】rénqíngwèi〈名〉human feeling: 富于～ have a strong human touch ‖ 没有一点～ be devoid of human kindness

【人情债】rénqíngzhài〈名〉debt of gratitude

【人穷志短】rénqióng-zhìduǎn〈成〉poverty stifles ambition

【人去楼空】rénqù-lóukōng〈成〉old sights recall to mind loved ones who are gone

【人权】rénquán〈名〉human rights: 保障～ guarantee human rights ‖ 侵犯～ violate human rights

【人权记录】rénquán jìlù〈名〉human rights record

【人权宣言】Rénquán Xuānyán〈名〉Universal Declaration of Human Rights (of the United Nations, 1948)

【人权组织】rénquán zǔzhī〈名〉human rights group

【人群】rénqún〈名〉crowd: 驱散～ disperse a crowd ‖ 愤怒/欢呼的～ angry/cheering crowds

【人人】rénrén〈名〉everybody: ～有责 everyone is responsible ‖ 法律面前～平等。All people are equal in the eyes of the law.

【人人为我，我为人人】rénrén wèi wǒ, wǒ wèi rénrén〈惯〉all for one and one for all

【人人自危】rénrén-zìwēi〈成〉everyone feels insecure

【人日】rénrì〈名〉〈旧〉seventh of the first lunar month of the Chinese calendar

【人瑞】rénruì〈名〉〈书〉respected person of venerable age

【人山人海】rénshān-rénhǎi〈成〉huge crowds of people

【人蛇】rénshé〈名〉〈方〉illegal immigrant

【人身】rénshēn〈名〉person: ～不可侵犯 inviolability of the person ‖ ～安全 personal safety ‖ ～攻击 personal attack

【人身保险】rénshēn bǎoxiǎn〈名〉life insurance: ～合同 personal life insurance contract

【人身迫害】rénshēn pòhài〈名〉physical persecution

【人身侵犯】rénshēn qīnfàn〈名〉physical abuse

【人身权】rénshēnquán〈名〉personal right

【人身伤害】rénshēn shānghài〈名〉bodily harm

【人身事故】rénshēn shìgù〈名〉accident involving casualties

【人身意外伤害保险】rénshēn yìwài shānghài bǎoxiǎn〈名〉personal accident insurance

【人身自由】rénshēn zìyóu〈名〉personal freedom: ～不可侵犯权 inviolability of personal freedom ‖ ～权 right of personal freedom

【人参】rénshēn〈名〉ginseng

【人生】rénshēng〈名〉life: 享受～ enjoy one's life ‖ ～大事 the most important event in one's life

【人生地不熟】rén shēng dì bù shú〈惯〉be a stranger in a strange place

【人生观】rénshēngguān〈名〉life outlook: 树立正确的～ establish a positive outlook on life

【人生如梦】rénshēng-rúmèng〈成〉life is but a dream

【人生一世，草木一春】rénshēng-yīshì, cǎomù-yīchūn〈成〉〈喻〉life is but a short span

【人生朝露】rénshēng-zhāolù〈成〉a person's life is like the morning dew

【人声】rénshēng〈名〉human voice

【人声鼎沸】rénshēng-dǐngfèi〈成〉hubbub

【人时】rénshí〈名〉person-hour

【人士】rénshì〈名〉public figure: 党外～ non-Party personages ‖ 权威～ authoritative sources ‖ 知名～ well-known figures

【人氏】rénshì〈名〉〈旧〉people native to a place: 当地～ native-born ‖ 您贵姓？何方～？What's your surname? Where do you come from?

【人世】rénshì〈名〉the human world: 不久于～ be dying ‖ 他已不在～。He is no longer alive.

【人世沧桑】rénshì-cāngsāng〈成〉great changes in the world

【人世间】rénshìjiān = 人世 rénshì

【人事】rénshì〈名〉**1**（指事情）human affairs **2**（指人员变动事宜）personnel matters: ～变动 personnel changes ‖ ～任免 personnel appointment and removal ‖ 做～工作 manage people **3**（指事理）ways of the world: 不懂～ not know the ways of the world **4**（指知觉）consciousness of the outside world: ▸不省～ **5**（尽力）what is humanly possible: 尽～ do one's best

【人事部】rénshì bù〈名〉personnel department

【人事档案】rénshì dàng'àn〈名〉personal file
【人事关系】rénshì guānxì〈名〉organizational affiliation
【人事科】rénshìkē〈名〉personnel section
【人事制度】rénshì zhìdù〈名〉personnel system
【人手】rénshǒu〈名〉manpower: ～不足 be short of hands
【人寿保险】rénshòu bǎoxiǎn〈名〉life insurance: 参加～ take out a life insurance policy
【人寿年丰】rénshòu-niánfēng〈成〉good health amid bountiful harvests
【人数】rén shù〈名〉number of people
【人算不如天算】rén suàn bùrú tiān suàn〈俗〉man proposes, God disposes
【人所共知】rén suǒ gòng zhī〈成〉it is common knowledge
【人梯】réntī〈名〉**1**（人搭成的梯子）human ladder **2**〈喻〉（为他人成功而奉献的人）person who makes sacrifices for the success of others: 甘当～ be willing to act as a stepping stone for others
【人体】réntǐ〈名〉human body: ～解剖 human anatomy ‖ ～炸弹 human bomb
【人同此心，心同此理】rén tóng cǐ xīn, xīn tóng cǐ lǐ〈俗〉people feel the same way about this matter
【人头】réntóu〈名〉**1**（人的头）head of a person **2**（人数）number of people: 按～分配 distribute sth. equally per head ‖ ～税 poll tax **3**（人际关系）relations with people: ～儿熟 know a lot of people
【人头攒动】réntóu cuándòng〈成〉be thronging with people
【人往高处走，水往低处流】rén wǎng gāochù zǒu, shuǐ wǎng dīchù liú〈俗〉people want to move up as water has to flow down
【人望】rénwàng〈名〉〈书〉prestige
【人微言轻】rénwēi-yánqīng〈成〉the words of the lowly carry little weight
【人为】rénwéi **A**〈动〉do: ▸事在～ **B**〈形〉man-made: ～因素 human factor ‖ ～障碍 man-made barrier
【人为刀俎，我为鱼肉】rén wéi dāozǔ, wǒ wéi yúròu〈成〉〈喻〉be at sb.'s mercy
【人为财死，鸟为食亡】rén wèi cái sǐ, niǎo wèi shí wáng〈俗〉people will die for wealth, as birds for food
【人文】rénwén〈名〉humanities: ▸～科学
【人文奥运】rénwén Àoyùn〈名〉People's Olympics
【人文景观】rénwén jǐngguān〈名〉human landscape
【人文科学】rénwén kēxué〈名〉humanities
【人文学科】rénwén xuékē〈名〉humanities
【人文主义】rénwén zhǔyì〈名〉humanism
【人无远虑，必有近忧】rén wú yuǎnlǜ, bì yǒu jìnyōu〈俗〉unpreparedness spells trouble
【人五人六】rénwǔ-rénliù〈俗〉be conceited
【人武部】rénwǔbù〈简称〉= 人民武装部
【人物】rénwù〈名〉**1**（指人）figure: 传奇～ living legend ‖ 杰出～ remarkable personality ‖ 神秘～ mystic figure ‖ 重要～ VIP ▸风云～ **2**（指作品形象）character: 刻画～ depict a character ‖ ～塑造 characterization ‖ 典型～ typical character
【人物画】rénwùhuà〈名〉figure painting
【人像】rénxiàng〈名〉portrait
【人心】rénxīn〈名〉**1**（众人的愿望）public feeling: 收买～ try to buy people over ‖ 稳定～ reassure the public ▸大快～, 得～ **2**（人性）moral nature
【人心不古】rénxīn-bùgǔ〈成〉public morality is not what it used to be
【人心不足蛇吞象】rénxīn bù zú shé tūn xiàng〈俗〉a person in a permanent state of dissatisfaction is like a snake trying to swallow an elephant
【人心大快】rénxīn dàkuài = 大快人心 dàkuài-rénxīn
【人心隔肚皮】rénxīn gé dùpí〈俗〉you can never tell what's going on in other people's minds
【人心惶惶】rénxīn-huánghuáng〈成〉everyone is in a state of anxiety

ℹ 与人体有关的语句

■ 英语里，当主语本身是动词所述动作的施动者时，表示身体部位的名词前要用形容词性物主代词或名词所有格：

请举手
= Raise your hand, please
或 Put up your hand, please

请把嘴张大
= Open your month wide, please

她闭上了眼睛
= She closed her eyes

我弄断了左脚
= I broke my left foot

她用手托住脸颊
= She is holding her cheeks

她揉了揉眼
= She rubbed her eyes

父亲把我搂入怀中
= My father held me in his arms

他把手插进了口袋
= He put his hands in his pockets

■ 无论是动作的施动者还是动作的接受者，表示身体部位的名词前都要用所有格修饰语：

他把手放在我的额头上
= He put his hand on my forehead

她轻柔地用手指头抚摸猫的脸
= She tenderly stroked the cat's face with her fingertips

■ 在英语中，表示打、碰、抓、拉等动作的动词，一般以接受该动作的人作为其宾语，另用介词短语来说明是身体的哪一部位，而表示身体部位的名词前要用定冠词 the，不用所有格修饰语：

我打了他的脸
= I hit him in the face

石头打中了小王的头
= The stone hit Xiao Wang on the head

他碰了一下我的肩膀
= He touched me on the shoulder

姑娘拉着她奶奶的手
= The girl took her grandmother by the hand

警察抓住了他的衣领
= The policeman grabbed him by the collar

但

他握住了妻子的手
= He held his wife's hands

■ 注意下面例子的翻译：

她弄断了双腿
= She broke her legs

她双腿断了
= Her legs are broken

描述五官

■ 头发：

她留着短发
= She has short hair

她的头发很短
= Her hair is very short

一位短发女士
= a lady with short hair
或 a short-haired lady

■ 眼睛：

他有双蓝眼睛
= He has blue eyes

他的眼睛是蓝色的
= His eyes are blue

蓝眼睛的男人
= a blue-eyed man
或 a man with blue eyes

■ 其他部位：

他鼻子扁平
= His nose is flat
或 He has a flat nose

鼻子扁平的男人
= a man with a flat nose
或 a flat-nosed man

他有双大耳朵
= He has big ears

她颧骨高
= She has high cheek-bones

她的脸颊红扑扑的
= She has rosy cheeks
或 She is rosy-cheeked

她有一张漂亮的脸
或 她的脸很漂亮
= She has a pretty face

她有一张圆圆的脸
= She has a round face

她有张樱桃小口
= She has a small mouth

■ 汉语可以用"大"或"宽"形容某人的嘴，英语可用 big 或 wide。英语里 she is/has a big mouth 有两个意思：字面意思是她有张大嘴巴，比喻意思是她嘴不严，保不住秘密。汉语中说某人嘴不严时，一般说"她是个大嘴巴"：

她有张大嘴
= She has a wide mouth
或 She has a big mouth

但

她是个大嘴巴
= She is a big mouth
或 She has a big mouth

【人心叵测】rénxīn-pǒcè〈成〉one's heart is past finding out
【人心齐，泰山移】rénxīn qí, Tàishān yí〈俗〉when people act with one mind, they can work wonders
【人心如面】rénxīn-rúmiàn〈成〉so many faces, as many hearts
【人心所向】rénxīn-suǒxiàng〈成〉accord with public sentiment: 统一祖国是～。The unification of the country is in keeping with the will of the people.
【人心向背】rénxīn-xiàngbèi〈成〉will of the people: 战争的胜败取决于～。Victory or defeat in war depends on who has popular support.
【人心果】rénxīnguǒ〈名〉［植物］sapodilla
【人行道】rénxíngdào〈名〉pavement〈英〉; sidewalk〈美〉
【人行横道】rénxíng héngdào〈名〉pedestrian crossing〈英〉; crosswalk〈美〉
【人行天桥】rénxíng tiānqiáo〈名〉footbridge
【人性】rénxìng〈名〉**1**（人的特性）human nature: ～论 theory of human nature **2**（良知）reason: 不通～ be unfeeling and unreasonable ‖ 灭绝～ be utterly inhuman
【人选】rénxuǎn〈名〉candidate: 物色～ try to find a suitable candidate ‖ 最佳～ the best candidate
【人烟】rényān〈名〉sign of human habitation: ～稀少 be sparsely populated ‖ 有～的地方 populated area ‖ 荒无～ desolate and uninhabited
【人言可畏】rényán-kěwèi〈成〉gossip is a fearful thing
【人仰马翻】rényǎng-mǎfān〈成〉suffer a crushing defeat
【人样】rényàng〈名〉proper conduct required of a person: 穿得像个～ dress properly ‖ 活出个～来 make something of oneself
【人妖】rényāo〈名〉（变性人）transsexual
【人意】rényì〈名〉one's will: 不尽～ be not quite up to one's expectations ‖ 善解～ kind and considerate
【人影儿】rényǐngr〈名〉**1**（指影子）human shadow: 黑暗中看见一个模糊的～ make out a figure in the darkness **2**（指踪迹）trace of human presence: 不见～ not a soul to be seen ‖ 教室里连个～都没有。There's no one to be found in the classroom.
【人鱼】rényú〈名〉〈口〉［动物］manatee
【人欲】rényù〈名〉〈书〉human desires
【人欲横流】rényù-héngliú〈成〉be overflowing with human desires
【人员】rényuán〈名〉personnel: ～安排 personnel placement ‖ 机关工作～ office worker ‖ 教学～ teaching staff
【人员编制】rényuán biānzhì〈名〉staffing quota
【人员调动】rényuán diàodòng〈名〉transfer of personnel
【人员配备】rényuán pèibèi〈名〉staffing
【人缘儿】rényuánr〈名〉relations with people: 没～ be unpopular ‖ ～好 enjoy great popularity
【人猿】rényuán〈名〉anthropoid (ape)
【人云亦云】rényún-yìyún〈成〉parrot others' words: 他没有自己的主见，只会～。He had no opinions of his own but simply followed the herd.
【人赃俱获】rénzāng-jùhuò〈成〉catch sb. red-handed: 警察将他～。The police nailed him with the goods.
【人造】rénzào〈形〉artificial
【人造大理石】rénzào dàlǐshí〈名〉scagliola
【人造地球卫星】rénzào dìqiú wèixīng〈名〉artificial earth-orbiting satellite
【人造革】rénzàogé〈名〉imitation leather
【人造黄油】rénzào huángyóu〈名〉margarine
【人造棉】rénzàomián〈名〉［纺织］artificial cotton
【人造丝】rénzàosī〈名〉rayon
【人造卫星】rénzào wèixīng〈名〉artificial satellite
【人造纤维】rénzào xiānwéi〈名〉synthetic fibre
【人造橡胶】rénzào xiàngjiāo〈名〉artificial rubber
【人渣】rénzhā〈名〉dregs
【人证】rénzhèng〈名〉［法律］witness testimony: ～物证俱全 have both witness testimony and material evidence
【人之常情】rénzhīchángqíng〈成〉human nature: 同情弱者，这是～。It is human nature to sympathize with the weak.
【人质】rénzhì〈名〉hostage: 释放～ release hostages ‖ （把某人）扣为～ take (sb.) hostage
【人治】rénzhì〈名〉rule of man: 要搞法治，不搞～。We must observe the rule of law and get rid of the rule of man.
【人中】rénzhōng〈名〉［生理］philtrum
【人种】rénzhǒng〈名〉race: 黑色/黄色/白色～ black/Mongoloid/white people
【人种学】rénzhǒngxué〈名〉ethnology: ～家 ethnologist
【人字呢】rénzìní〈名〉herringbone (weave)
【人字式拖鞋】rénzìshì tuōxié〈名〉flip-flops
【人自为战】rénzìwéizhàn〈成〉everyone fighting by themselves
【人走茶凉】rénzǒu-cháliáng〈成〉out of sight, out of mind

壬 rén〈名〉ninth of the ten Heavenly Stems (天干)

仁 rén
A〈形〉compassionate: ▸～爱, 为富不～
B〈名〉**1**（指道德观念）benevolence: ▸～至义尽 **2**（用于尊称）kind [used in polite address for a male friend]: ▸～弟, ～兄 **3**（果核）stone: 核桃～ walnut kernel ▸杏～ **4**（仁儿状物）meat from a nut-like fruit: ▸虾～
【仁爱】rén'ài〈形〉kind-hearted: ～之心 kind heart
【仁慈】réncí〈形〉benevolent: ～的老人 benevolent old man
【仁德】réndé〈名〉magnanimity
【仁弟】réndì〈名〉〈书〉〈敬〉[address for a younger male friend or former male student] my dear friend
【仁厚】rénhòu〈形〉benevolent and generous: 待人～ treat people with kindness and generosity
【仁人君子】rénrén-jūnzǐ〈成〉benevolent gentlemen
【仁人志士】rénrén-zhìshì〈成〉kind and upright persons
【仁兄】rénxiōng〈名〉〈书〉〈敬〉[address for a male friend] my dear friend
【仁义】rényì **A**〈名〉justice and humanity: ～道德 humanity, justice and virtue **B**〈形〉amiable
【仁者见仁，智者见智】rénzhě jiàn rén, zhìzhě jiàn zhì〈成〉different people have different views on the same thing
【仁政】rénzhèng〈名〉policy of benevolence: 施行～ implement a policy of benevolence
【仁至义尽】rénzhì-yìjìn〈成〉do one's very best in helping others

任 Rén〈名〉Ren [surname]
▸rèn

rěn

忍 rěn〈动〉**1**（忍耐）bear: ～不住笑了起来 unable to suppress a smile ▸～辱负重, ～痛 **2**（忍心）have the heart (to do sth.): ▸于心不～
【忍冬】rěndōng〈名〉［植物］honeysuckle
【忍饥挨饿】rěnjī-ái'è〈成〉suffer starvation
【忍俊不禁】rěnjùn-bùjīn〈成〉cannot help laughing: 使观众～ evoke laughter from the audience
【忍耐】rěnnài〈动〉exercise restraint: 无法～ run out of patience ‖ ～是有限度的。There are limits to one's patience.
【忍气吞声】rěnqì-tūnshēng〈成〉swallow one's pride
【忍让】rěnràng〈动〉exercise self-control: 相互～ show mutual restraint
【忍辱负重】rěnrǔ-fùzhòng〈成〉endure humiliation for the sake of a higher objective
【忍辱含垢】rěnrǔ-hángòu〈成〉swallow insults and suffer indignity
【忍辱偷生】rěnrǔ-tōushēng〈成〉endure humiliation in order to survive
【忍受】rěnshòu〈动〉bear: ～艰难困苦 endure hardships ‖ 难以～ be unbearable
【忍痛】rěntòng〈动〉do sth. very reluctantly: ～割爱 part reluctantly with sth. one treasures
【忍无可忍】rěnwúkěrěn〈成〉reach the limit of one's patience: 到了～的地步 reach the limit of one's patience
【忍心】rěnxīn〈动〉be hard-hearted: 不～拒绝 not have the heart to refuse
【忍者】rěnzhě〈名〉ninja

荏[1] rěn = 白苏 báisū

荏[2] rěn
A〈形〉weak: ▸色厉内～
B = 荏苒 rěnrǎn
【荏苒】rěnrǎn〈动〉〈书〉pass quickly: 光阴～ time is slipping by

稔 rěn〈书〉
A〈动〉ripen: ～年 year of bumper harvest
B〈名〉year: 五～ five years
C〈形〉familiar: ▸～知
【稔知】rěnzhī〈动〉〈书〉know quite well

rèn

刃 rèn
A〈名〉**1**（刀口）blade: 双～剑 double-edged sword ▸刀～ **2**（剑）sword; （刀）knife: ▸白～, 利～
B〈动〉〈书〉kill with a sword or knife
【刃钢】rèngāng〈名〉shear steel
【刃具】rènjù〈名〉［机械］cutting tool: ～厂 cutting instrument factory
【刃口】rènkǒu〈名〉edge (of a knife, sword, etc.)

认（認） rèn〈动〉**1**（辨别）recognize: ～笔迹 identify handwriting ‖ 好/难～ be easy/hard to read ▸～领，辨～ **2**（承认）admit: ▸～错，默～ **3**（确立关系）adopt: ～敌为友 take a foe for a friend ‖ 他～了个干女儿。He took on a god daughter. **4**（承认价值）undertake to do sth.: ▸～购，～股，～捐 **5**（接受）[followed by 了] resign oneself to sth.: 该我倒霉，我～了。It's my bad luck and I have to resign myself to it.

【认不是】rèn bùshi〈动〉〈口〉admit one's fault

【认出】rènchū〈动〉recognize

【认错】rèncuò〈动〉own up to a mistake: 公开～ openly acknowledge a mistake

【认得】rènde〈动〉recognize: 你还～我吗？ Do you still recognize me? ‖ 你～回家的路吗？ Do you know your way home?

【认定】rèndìng〈动〉**1**（坚信）maintain: 我们～他是无辜的。We firmly believe him to be innocent. **2**（确立）establish: ～事实 establish a fact

【认罚】rènfá〈动〉be ready to accept a punishment

【认购】rèngòu〈动〉subscribe for: ～公债 subscribe for government bonds ‖ ～国库券 subscribe for state treasury bonds

【认沽】rèngū〈动〉［金融］sell shares at a fixed price

【认股】rèngǔ〈动〉subscribe for shares

【认股权】rèngǔquán〈名〉stock option: ～证 stock warrant

【认捐】rènjuān〈动〉offer to donate: ～一万元 pledge a donation of 10,000 *yuan*

【认可】rènkě〈动〉approve: 得到～ receive recognition ‖ 公众～ public approbation

【认可度】rènkědù〈名〉level of recognition: 裁决的～ the degree of recognition of the ruling ‖ 候选人的～ the candidate's level of recognition

【认领】rènlǐng〈动〉**1**（辨认领取）claim: ～失物 claim a lost article **2** = 认养 rènyǎng 1

【认命】rènmìng〈动〉be resigned to one's fate

【认生】rènshēng〈动〉[of a child] be shy with strangers: 这孩子不～。The child is not shy with strangers.

【认识】rènshi **A**〈动〉know: ～某人 become acquainted with sb. ‖ 他们从小就～。They've known each other since childhood. **B**〈名〉knowledge: ～来源于实践。Knowledge originates in practice. ▸感性～

【认识论】rènshilùn〈名〉theory of knowledge: 唯心主义～ idealistic cognition theory

【认输】rènshū〈动〉admit defeat: 我～。I give up.

【认死理】rèn sǐlǐ〈动〉〈口〉be stubborn: 他可是个～的人。He is a very stubborn person.

【认同】rèntóng〈动〉**1**（赞同）approve: 和谈的原则已得到双方政府的～。The principles for the peace talks have been approved by the two governments. **2**（认为有共同之处）identify

【认为】rènwéi〈动〉think: 我～该计划不可行。I think that the plan cannot work.

【认养】rènyǎng〈动〉**1**（针对人）adopt and support through a children's foundation: ～一个孤儿 promise to support an orphan **2**（针对花草、动物）assume the responsibility of raising flowers, trees or animals: ～几棵树 promise to take care of several trees

【认贼作父】rènzéizuòfù〈成〉regard the enemy as one's kith and kin

【认账】rènzhàng〈动〉**1**（指债务）acknowledge a debt: 他借了我的钱，还不～。He borrowed money from me but he no longer acknowledges it. **2**〈喻〉（指言行）admit what one has said or done: 说过的话就得～。You can't go back on your word.

【认真】rènzhēn **A**〈形〉serious: ～对待 take sth. seriously ‖ 做出～而非敷衍的检讨 make genuine, not superficial self-criticisms **B**〈动〉be serious: 对她的话不要太～。Don't take her remarks too much to heart.

【认证】rènzhèng〈动〉［法律］certify: ～签名 authenticate a signature ‖ ～遗嘱 attest a will ‖ ～机构 certification body

【认证书】rènzhèngshū〈名〉certification: 安全食品～ safe food certification

【认知】rènzhī〈动〉［心理］be cognitive: ～能力 cognitive ability

【认准】rènzhǔn〈动〉set one's mind on

【认字】rènzì〈动〉learn to read

【认罪】rènzuì〈动〉admit one's guilt: 低头～ hang one's head and plead guilty ‖ ～态度 attitude toward one's guilt

仞 rèn〈量〉〈古〉measure of length equal to seven or eight *chi* (尺)

任[1] rèn

A〈动〉**1**（任命）appoint: 被～为校长 be made principal of a school ▸～人唯贤 **2**（担任）assume: ～系主任 be the department chair ‖ 连～总统 assume a second presidency **3**（担负）bear: ▸～劳～怨

B〈名〉official post: ▸到～，就～

C〈量〉[the number of terms one served on a post]: 做过两～总统 served two terms as president ‖ 第二～妻子 second wife

任[2] rèn

A〈动〉allow: ～人宰割 (cannot but) allow oneself to be walked all over ▸～性，～意，放～自流

B〈连〉no matter (how, what, etc.): ～别人怎么说，他也不动摇。He won't budge no matter what others say.

▸Rén

【任便】rènbiàn〈动〉as you please: 我今天不想跟你一起去。——哦，那就～吧。I don't want to go with you today. — Well, do as you please.

【任从】rèncóng〈动〉let sb. do as they please

【任何】rènhé〈代〉any: 没有～理由 have absolutely no reason ‖ ～人不得凌驾于法律之上。No one should place themselves above the law.

【任教】rènjiào〈动〉take up teaching: 他在中学～。He is a high school teacher.

【任课】rènkè〈动〉teach a course: ～老师 teacher of the course

【任劳任怨】rènláo-rènyuàn〈成〉work hard and not be upset by criticism: 十年来，她一直在～地工作。She has been a willing and uncomplaining worker for ten years.

【任免】rènmiǎn〈动〉appoint and dismiss: ～领导干部 appoint and remove leading cadres ‖ ～名单 list of appointments and removals ‖ ～状 commission

【任命】rènmìng〈动〉appoint sb.: ～他为校长 appoint him to school principal ‖ 新～的总理 newly appointed premier

【任凭】rènpíng **A**〈动〉allow sb. do as they please: ～法院裁定 leave to the discretion of the court ‖ ～你挑选 choose whatever you like **B**〈连〉no matter what, how, etc.: ～他怎么劝说，她也不听。No matter how hard he tried, she wouldn't listen.

【任期】rènqī〈名〉term of office: ～届满 one's tenure of office has expired ‖ ～内 during one's term of office ‖ 校长的～为五年。The tenure of the presidency is five years.

【任其泛滥】rènqífànlàn〈成〉be left unchecked

【任其自流】rènqízìliú〈成〉let things run their natural course

【任其自然】rènqízìrán〈成〉let things run their natural course

【任情】rènqíng〈书〉**A**〈副〉to one's heart's content **B**〈形〉capricious

【任人唯亲】rènrén-wéiqīn〈成〉make appointments by favouritism

【任人唯贤】rènrén-wéixián〈成〉make appointments on merit

【任所】rènsuǒ〈名〉place of office

【任务】rènwu〈名〉task: 布置～ give sb. a task ‖ 完成～ complete an assignment ‖ 执行～ carry out one's mission ‖ 工作/学习～ work/study assignments

【任性】rènxìng〈形〉wilful: ～的孩子 headstrong child ‖ 做事不能太～。You shouldn't do things merely according to your own will.

【任选】rènxuǎn〈动〉pick freely: 两者～一个 take either of the two

【任意】rènyì **A**〈副〉wantonly: ～歪曲 wilfully distort ‖ ～涨价 raise prices arbitrarily **B**〈形〉unconditional: ～三角形 arbitrary triangle

【任意球】rènyìqiú〈名〉［体育］**1**（足球）free kick: 发～ take a free kick ‖ 获得～ win a free kick **2**（手球）free throw

【任用】rènyòng〈动〉employ sb. as: ～贤能 use the wise and employ the capable

【任职】rènzhí〈动〉hold a position: ～资格 qualifications for a job ‖ 在一家公司～ be employed in a firm

【任重道远】rènzhòng-dàoyuǎn〈成〉there is tough work ahead and a long way to go

纫（紉） rèn〈动〉**1**（穿针）thread a needle: ～针 thread a needle **2**（缝缀）sew: ▸缝～ **3**〈书〉（感激）feel grateful: ～佩 feel gratitude and admiration

韧（韌） rèn〈形〉tough: ▸坚～

【韧带】rèndài〈名〉ligament: ～撕裂 torn ligament

【韧度】rèndù〈名〉tenacity

【韧劲】rènjìn〈名〉tenacity: 他有股～。He has a tenacious streak.

【韧皮】rènpí〈名〉［植物］bast

【韧性】rènxìng〈名〉**1**（指物）toughness: 这块皮子～好。This piece of leather is very tough. **2**（指人）tenacity: 缺乏～ lack tenacity

轫（軔） rèn〈名〉〈书〉log used to stop wheels: ▸发～

饪（飪） rèn〈动〉cook: ▸烹～

妊 rèn〈动〉be pregnant: ▸～妇
【妊妇】rènfù〈名〉pregnant woman
【妊娠】rènshēn〈名〉pregnancy: ～反应 morning sickness ‖ 足月～ full-term pregnancy
【妊娠期】rènshēnqī〈名〉gestation period

纴（紝） rèn〈动〉〈书〉weave

衽 rèn〈名〉〈书〉**1**（衣襟）one or two pieces making up the front of a Chinese gown **2**（席子）sleeping mat

rēng

扔 rēng〈动〉**1**（用大力甩）hurl: ～手榴弹 throw a hand grenade ‖ 把毛巾～给我。Throw me the towel. **2**（丢弃）throw away: 不要乱～果皮纸屑。No littering. ‖ 她～下手里的活儿走了。She dropped what she was doing and left.
【扔弃】rēngqì〈动〉abandon

réng

仍 réng
A〈动〉〈书〉remain: ▸～旧
B〈形〉〈书〉frequent: ▸频～
C〈副〉still: ～有希望。There is still hope. ‖ 手术～在进行。The operation is still going ahead.
【仍旧】réngjiù **A**〈动〉remain the same: 规矩～。The regulations remain unchanged. **B** = 仍然 réngrán
【仍然】réngrán〈副〉still: 问题～没有解决。The issue is yet to be solved. ‖ 这些合同～有效。These contracts still stand.

rì

日 rì
A〈名〉**1**（太阳）sun: 看～出 see the sun rise ▸～光, 烈～ **2**（白天）daytime: 整～整夜 all day and all night ▸～场, ～托 **3**（日子）day: 接连数～ for days on end ‖ 去年的今～ this day last year **4**（每天）every day: ～产量 daily output ▸～报, 蒸蒸～上 **5**（时候）time: 夏～ summertime ‖ 昔～ the past ▸来～, 往～ **6**（某一天）particular day: 发薪～ pay day ‖ 纪念～ anniversary ▸节～, 生～ **7** Rì（日本）Japan: ▸～语, ～圆
B〈量〉day: 事隔多～, 想不起来了。That was many days ago and I don't remember it.
【日班】rìbān〈名〉day shift: 上～ be on the day shift
【日斑】rìbān = 太阳黑子 tàiyáng hēizǐ
【日报】rìbào **A**〈名〉daily: 《人民～》*Renmin Ribao (People's Daily)* ‖ 《中国～》*China Daily* **B**〈动〉report daily: 现金～ daily cash report ‖ 延迟工作～表 daily delay report
【日本】Rìběn〈名〉Japan: ～人 Japanese ‖ ～语 Japanese
【日本广播协会】Rìběn Guǎngbō Xiéhuì〈名〉Nippon Hoso Kyokai (NHK)
【日本料理】Rìběn liàolǐ〈名〉Japanese cuisine
【日薄西山】rìbóxīshān〈成〉〈喻〉be in the evening of one's life
【日不暇给】rìbùxiájǐ〈成〉be fully occupied from morning to night
【日常】rìcháng〈形〉day-to-day: ～维护 daily maintenance ‖ ～工作 routine work ‖ ～生活 everyday life
【日常开支】rìcháng kāizhī〈名〉daily expenditure
【日常事务】rìcháng shìwù〈名〉daily routine
【日常用品】rìcháng yòngpǐn〈名〉articles for daily use
【日常用语】rìcháng yòngyǔ〈名〉everyday words
【日场】rìchǎng〈名〉day show: ～电影 film matinée
【日程】rìchéng〈名〉schedule: 比赛～ match schedule ‖ 提到议事～上 put sth. on the agenda ‖ ～安排 scheduling arrangements
【日程表】rìchéngbiǎo〈名〉schedule
【日出】rìchū〈名〉sunrise
【日戳】rìchuō〈名〉date stamp: 盖上～ stamp with the date
【日耳曼人】Rì'ěrmànrén〈名〉Germanic people
【日耳曼语族】Rì'ěrmàn Yǔzú〈名〉Germanic languages
【日珥】rì'ěr〈名〉［天文］solar prominence
【日复一日】rìfùyīrì〈成〉day after day
【日工】rìgōng〈名〉**1**（指工作）day work **2**（指人）day labourer
【日光】rìguāng〈名〉sunlight
【日光灯】rìguāngdēng〈名〉day lamp
【日光浴】rìguāngyù〈名〉sunbath: 洗～ sunbathe
【日晷】rìguǐ〈名〉sundial
【日后】rìhòu〈名〉future: 我～再报答你的恩情。Some day I'll repay you for your kindness.
【日华】rìhuá〈名〉solar halo
【日环食】rìhuánshí〈名〉［天文］annular eclipse of the sun
【日积月累】rìjī-yuèlěi〈成〉by gradual accumulation: 学习是～的过程。Learning is a process of accumulation.
【日记】rìjì〈名〉diary: 记～ keep a diary ‖ 旅行～ travel diary
【日记本】rìjìběn〈名〉notebook
【日记账】rìjìzhàng〈名〉journal
【日间】rìjiān〈名〉daytime: ～航班 day flight
【日见】rìjiàn〈副〉day by day: ～好转 be getting better every day
【日渐】rìjiàn〈副〉day by day: ～消瘦 be getting thinner and thinner
【日界线】rìjièxiàn〈名〉International Date Line
【日经指数】Rìjīng Zhǐshù〈名〉［金融］Nikkei Index
【日久见人心】rìjiǔ jiàn rénxīn〈成〉time reveals a person's heart
【日久天长】rìjiǔ-tiāncháng〈成〉as time goes by
【日均】rìjūn〈名〉daily average: ～客流量 average daily passenger numbers
【日K线】rì K xiàn〈名〉［金融］daily K-line
【日来】rìlái〈名〉the past few days: ～生意冷清。Business has been down in the last few days.
【日理万机】rìlǐ-wànjī〈成〉be busy with a myriad of state affairs every day
【日历】rìlì〈名〉calendar
【日凌】rìlíng〈名〉sun outage: ～会造成卫星传输信号的短暂中断。Sun outage can cause brief interruptions in satellite signal transmission.
【日落】rìluò〈名〉sunset: ～西方, 红霞满天。The sunset glows to the west.
【日冕】rìmiǎn〈名〉［天文］solar corona
【日暮途穷】rìmù-túqióng〈成〉〈喻〉be nearing the end of one's days
【日内】rìnèi〈名〉a couple of days: 伤口～就会愈合。The wound will heal in a couple of days.
【日内瓦】Rìnèiwǎ〈名〉Geneva
【日偏食】rìpiānshí〈名〉［天文］partial solar eclipse
【日期】rìqī ▸**p. 618**〈名〉date: 电告～ telegraph a date ‖ 截止～ closing date
【日期变更线】rìqī biàngēngxiàn〈名〉Date Line: 国际～ International Date Line
【日前】rìqián〈名〉a few days ago
【日趋】rìqū〈副〉day by day: 国家～繁荣。The country is getting more prosperous with each passing day. ‖ 该地区局势～紧张。Tensions are mounting in the area.
【日全食】rìquánshí〈名〉［天文］total solar eclipse
【日日夜夜】rìrì-yèyè〈成〉day and night
【日上三竿】rìshàng-sāngān〈成〉it's quite late in the morning [usu referring to getting up late]
【日食】rìshí〈名〉［天文］solar eclipse
【日蚀】rìshí = 日食 rìshí
【日思夜想】rìsī-yèxiǎng〈成〉long for day and night
【日坛】Rìtán〈名〉Altar to the Sun [in Beijing]
【日头】rìtou〈名〉〈方〉sun: ～落山了。The sun has set.
【日托】rìtuō〈名〉day care
【日文】Rìwén ▸**p. 918**〈名〉Japanese
【日夕】rìxī〈名〉〈书〉day and night
【日息】rìxī〈名〉per diem interest
【日心说】rìxīnshuō〈名〉［天文］heliocentric theory
【日新月异】rìxīn-yuèyì〈成〉change rapidly: 世界形势～。The world changes every day.
【日薪】rìxīn〈名〉daily wage
【日行夜宿】rìxíng-yèsù〈成〉travel during the day and sleep at night
【日夜】rìyè〈名〉day and night: ～操劳 toil day in and day out ‖ ～兼程 travel day and night
【日夜商店】rìyè shāngdiàn〈名〉round-the-clock shop
【日以继夜】rìyǐjìyè = 夜以继日 yèyǐjìrì
【日益】rìyì〈副〉increasingly: ～繁荣 become more flourishing with each passing day ‖ 矛盾～尖锐。The contradictions are becoming increasingly intense.
【日用】rìyòng **A**〈名〉daily expenses: 这些钱给你做～吧。This money is for your daily expenses. **B**〈形〉of daily use: ～消费品 goods for everyday consumption ‖ ～小商品 small articles for everyday use
【日用品】rìyòngpǐn〈名〉daily necessities
【日用杂货】rìyòng záhuò〈名〉various household needs
【日语】Rìyǔ ▸**p. 918**〈名〉Japanese
【日元】rìyuán = 日圆 rìyuán
【日圆】rìyuán ▸**p. 328**〈名〉Japanese yen
【日月】rìyuè〈名〉**1**（太阳、月亮）the sun and the moon **2**（岁月）life: 艰苦的～ hard life **3**（时间）time: ～蹉跎 time slips by without anything being accomplished
【日月如梭】rìyuè-rúsuō〈成〉time flies
【日月潭】Rìyuètán ▸**p. 305**〈名〉Sun Moon Lake [the biggest lake in Taiwan]

【日晕】rìyùn〈名〉［气象］solar halo
【日杂】rìzá〈简称〉= 日用杂货
【日杂店】rìzádiàn〈名〉general store
【日照】rìzhào〈名〉sunshine: ～时间 sun time
【日臻】rìzhēn〈副〉day by day: ～完善 gradually approaching perfection
【日志】rìzhì〈名〉daily record: 工作～ work log ‖ 航海～ maritime log
【日中】rìzhōng〈名〉noon
【日子】rìzi〈名〉**1**（日期）day: 定～ set a date ‖ 大喜的～ wedding day **2**（时间）time: 过些～你再来。Come again in a few days' time. ‖ 我好些～没见他了。I haven't seen him for quite some time. **3**（生活）life: 过上好～ live a happy life ‖ 他们的～越来越不好过。They are finding it harder and harder to get by.

róng

戎[1] róng〈名〉〈书〉**1**（兵器）weaponry: ▸兵～相见 **2**（军队）army;（军事）military affairs: ▸～装, 投笔从～

戎[2] Róng〈名〉the Rongs [generic term for the tribes in the west of ancient China]
【戎行】rónghàng〈名〉〈书〉army: 久历～ have served in the army for a long time
【戎机】róngjī〈名〉〈书〉**1**（指军事）military affairs: 通晓～ be well-versed in the art of war **2**（指战机）good opportunity for winning a battle: 贻误～ forfeit a winning battle opportunity
【戎马】róngmǎ〈名〉〈书〉army horse: ～一生 serve in the army one's whole life
【戎马倥偬】róngmǎ-kǒngzǒng〈成〉hectic military career
【戎装】róngzhuāng〈名〉〈书〉battle attire

茸 róng
A〈形〉[of grass or hair] fine and soft: ▸绿～～, 毛～～
B〈名〉young pilose antler: ▸鹿～
【茸毛】róngmáo〈名〉（指植物）fuzz;（指人或动物）fine hair
【茸茸】róngróng〈形〉[of grass, hair, etc.] fine, soft and thick: 绿草～ carpet of green grass ‖ 一头～的头发 a head of soft, thick hair

荣（榮） róng〈形〉**1**（草木茂盛）thriving: 本固枝～ when the root is firm, the branches flourish **2**（兴盛）prosperous: ▸繁～昌盛 **3**（光荣）glorious: 不以为耻，反以为～ take it as an honour rather than as a disgrace ▸～誉, 光～

r

日期

■ 英语和汉语在表达日期中的年、月、日时有不同的顺序。汉语的顺序是：年、月、日；英语的顺序是：日、月、年（英式英语）或月、日、年（美式英语）。

■ 无论是读还是写，汉语的日期都用基数词。英语在书写日期时可用基数词也可用序数词，但在读日期时必须用序数词（first、second 等）。

■ 英语表达日期有几种不同的方式：
23 March 2007 或 23rd March 2007（英）
March 23 2007 或 March 23rd 2007（美）

也可将整个日期都用数字来表达。这常用于书信或表格中：
23.03.07 或 23/03/07（英）
03.23.07 或 03/23/07（美）

■ 如果包括星期几的话，英语把星期放在最前面：

2008 年 8 月 13 号星期三
= Wednesday 13 August 2008（英）
或 Wednesday August 13 2008（美）

7 月 4 日星期五
= Friday 4th July（英）
或 Friday July 4th（美）

9 月 9 日星期六
写：Saturday 9 September（英）
或 Saturday September 9（美）
读：Saturday, the ninth of September
或 Saturday, September the ninth

2008 年 8 月 8 号
写：8 August 2008（英）
或 August 8 2008（美）
读：August the eighth two thousand and eight
或 the eighth of August two thousand and eight

1997.07.31
写：31.07.1997（英）
或 07.31.1997（美）
读：July the thirty-first nineteen ninety-seven
或 the thirty-first of July nineteen ninety-seven

公元 500 年
写：AD 500
读：AD five hundred

公元前 2000 年
写：2000 BC
读：two thousand BC

公元前 5 世纪
写：the 5th/fifth century BC
读：the fifth century BC

读写日期

■ 问日期：

今天几号？—— 15 号
= What's the date today? — It's the fifteenth

上周三是几号？—— 8 月 20 号
= What was the date last Wednesday?
— It was August the twentieth
或 It was the twentieth of August

■ 读写日期：

10 月 2 号
写：2nd October（英）
或 October 2nd（美）
读：the second of October
或 October the second

日期前的介词

■ 英语在表示具体的某一天时用介词 on，在表示某一年或某一月时用介词 in：

我 2005 年 9 月 9 号来过这儿
= I came here on 9 September 2005

我 11 月 5 号拜访你
= I will visit you on 5th November

她 20 号到
= She will arrive on the twentieth

我每月 15 号付账单
= I pay the bill on the 15th of every month

我 1987 年 5 月去过北京
= I went to Beijing in May 1987

我生在 1966 年
= I was born in 1966

那件事发生在 6 月
= That happened in June

其他短语

■ 注意下面例句中英语介词的使用：

我 12 月初 / 底出国
= I am going abroad at the beginning/end of December

他 11 月中旬要度假
= He will be on holiday in the middle of November

她 10 月 11 日前后临产
= She will give birth around October 11th

我到 4 月 10 号才回来
= I won't come back until 10th April

我会待到月底
= I will stay till the end of this month

在 3 月上旬
= in early March

在 5 月中旬
= in the middle of May
或 in mid-May

在 4 月下旬
= in late April

在 30 年代
= in the 30s
或 in the thirties

在 20 世纪
= in the twentieth century
或 in the 20th century

在 19 世纪 40 年代
= in the 1840s
而不是
in the 1940s

在 18 世纪早期
= in the early 18th century

在 18 世纪晚期
= in the late 18th century

在 16 世纪中叶
= in the middle of the 16th century

在 16 世纪上半叶
= in the first half of the 16th century

在 16 世纪下半叶
= in the latter half of the 16th century
或 in the second half of the 16th century

【荣光】róngguāng〈形〉〈书〉glorious: 无上～ most glorious
【荣归】róngguī〈动〉return in glory: ～故里 return to one's hometown with honour
【荣华富贵】rónghuá-fùguì〈成〉high position and great wealth: 享不尽的～ enjoy no end of wealth and honour
【荣获】rónghuò〈动〉have the honour to win: ～冠军 win the honoured title of champion ‖ ～最佳女演员奖 win the best actress award
【荣立】rónglì〈动〉be honoured for: ～一等功 be cited for meritorious service, first class
【荣任】róngrèn〈动〉be honoured with an appointment to a post
【荣辱】róngrǔ〈名〉honour or disgrace: 不计～进退 be heedless of personal ups and downs
【荣辱观】róngrǔguān〈名〉concept of honour and shame
【荣辱与共】róngrǔ-yǔgòng〈成〉share honour or disgrace: 肝胆相照，～ be loyal and open-hearted to each other and share weal or woe
【荣升】róngshēng〈动〉be honoured with promotion
【荣幸】róngxìng〈形〉〈套〉honoured: 深感～ feel greatly honoured ‖ 承蒙光临，不胜～。We are greatly honoured by your presence.
【荣耀】róngyào〈形〉glorious: 他被评为劳动模范，深感～。It was the greatest honour for him to be named a model worker.
【荣膺】róngyīng〈动〉〈书〉be honoured with: ～战斗英雄称号 be honoured with the title of combat hero
【荣誉】róngyù〈名〉honour, credit, glory: ～称号 honorary title ‖ 最高～ highest honour ‖ 为祖国的～而战 fight for the honour of one's country
【荣誉感】róngyùgǎn〈名〉sense of honour: 有集体/民族～ have a sense of collective/national honour
【荣誉军人】róngyù jūnrén〈名〉disabled soldier honourably discharged from military service
【荣誉学位】róngyù xuéwèi〈名〉honorary degree
【荣誉证书】róngyù zhèngshū〈名〉certificate of honour

狨 róng〈名〉［动物］marmoset

绒（絨） róng〈名〉**1**（指体毛）fine hair: ▸鹅～，驼～，羽～ **2**（指纺织品）cloth with a nap surface on one or either side: ▸法兰～，丝～ **3**（指绒线）fine floss for embroidery
【绒布】róngbù〈名〉flannelette
【绒花】rónghuā〈名〉［美术］velvet flowers, birds, etc.
【绒裤】róngkù〈名〉sweat pants
【绒毛】róngmáo〈名〉**1**（指体毛）fine hair **2**［纺织］nap
【绒面革】róngmiàngé〈名〉suede (leather)
【绒球】róngqiú〈名〉pompom
【绒毯】róngtǎn〈名〉woollen blanket: 地上铺着～。The floor is covered with a woollen rug.
【绒线】róngxiàn〈名〉**1**（粗丝线）crewel **2**〈方〉（毛线）knitting wool: 用～织毛衣 knit a sweater with knitting wool
【绒线刺绣】róngxiàn cìxiù〈名〉crewelwork
【绒线帽】róngxiànmào〈名〉knitted woollen cap
【绒绣】róngxiù〈名〉［美术］woollen embroidery: ～地毯 finished needlepoint carpet
【绒衣】róngyī〈名〉sweatshirt

容[1] róng
A〈动〉**1**（盛）contain: 这个锅能～两加仑水。The pan can hold two gallons of water. ▸～量，～器 **2**（谅解）tolerate: 情理难～ be contrary to reason ‖ 她～不得别人比她好。She can't stand anybody being better than her. ▸～忍，宽～ **3**（允许）allow: 不～分说 not allow others to explain ‖ 事实不～歪曲。The facts brook no distortion. ▸～许
B〈副〉〈书〉perhaps: ▸～或

容[2] róng〈名〉**1**（神色）look: ▸病～，笑～ **2**（相貌）appearance: ▸～貌，遗～ **3**（状态）bearing: ▸军～，市～
【容差】róngchā〈名〉allowance
【容错】róngcuò〈名〉［计算机］fault-tolerance: ～软件 fault-tolerant software
【容光】róngguāng〈名〉radiant facial expression
【容光焕发】róngguāng-huànfā〈成〉glowing with health
【容或】rónghuò〈副〉〈书〉perhaps: ～有之 that might be the case
【容积】róngjī〈名〉volume: 这个储藏室的～为100立方米。The storeroom has a volume of 100 cubic metres.
【容积率】róngjīlǜ〈名〉Floor Area Ratio (FAR): 提高土地～ increase the Floor Area Ratio of the plot
【容量】róngliàng〈名〉capacity: 这个桶～为50升。This barrel holds 50 litres.
【容留】róngliú〈动〉take in: 我们绝对不能～一个犯罪分子。We could never take in a criminal.
【容貌】róngmào〈名〉facial features: ～端庄 have regular features ‖ ～娇美 look sweet and charming
【容纳】róngnà〈动〉**1**（盛下）hold: 鸟巢可～八万名观众。The Bird's Nest has a seating capacity of 80,000 spectators. **2**（接受）tolerate: 能～不同意见 can tolerate dissenting views
【容器】róngqì〈名〉container
【容情】róngqíng〈动〉[usu used in the negative] show forgiveness: 对坏人决不～ never show any mercy to evildoers
【容人】róngrén〈动〉be tolerant of others: 不～ be intolerant of others
【容忍】róngrěn〈动〉tolerate: 无法～这种态度 cannot put up with that kind of attitude ‖ 令人难以～ be beyond endurance
【容身】róngshēn〈动〉take shelter: 无处～ find no place to shelter ‖ 无～之地 have no place to stay
【容受】róngshòu〈动〉endure
【容恕】róngshù〈动〉tolerate and forgive
【容限】róngxiàn〈名〉［物理］tolerance
【容许】róngxǔ **A**〈动〉allow: 决不～外来干涉 forbid outside interference ‖ ～负荷 allowable load ‖ ～剂量 permissible dose ‖ 每位乘客只～带一件手提行李。The passengers are allowed only one item of hand luggage each. **B**〈副〉〈书〉perhaps: 此类事件十年前～有之。This kind of thing could perhaps have happened ten years ago.
【容许误差】róngxǔ wùchā〈名〉permissible error
【容颜】róngyán〈名〉appearance: ～憔悴 look haggard
【容易】róngyì〈形〉**1**（不难）easy: 非常～ as easy as pie ‖ 说起来～做起来难。It's easier said than done. **2**（易于）liable: ～混淆 be liable to get mixed up ‖ 冬天～感冒。It is easy to catch cold in winter.
【容止】róngzhǐ〈名〉〈书〉demeanour
【容装】róngzhuāng〈名〉appearance and dress
【容姿】róngzī〈名〉〈书〉features

嵘（嶸） róng ▸峥嵘 zhēngróng

蓉 róng〈名〉**1**（指粉状物）mashed fruit flesh, seeds, etc.: ▸豆～，椰～ **2** ▸芙蓉 fúróng **3** Róng（成都）Rong [another name for Chengdu]

溶 róng〈动〉dissolve: 盐可～于水。Salt dissolves in water.
【溶洞】róngdòng〈名〉limestone cave
【溶化】rónghuà〈动〉**1**（指在液体里）dissolve: 糖在水中～。Sugar dissolves in water. **2** = 融化 rónghuà
【溶剂】róngjì〈名〉［化学］solvent
【溶胶】róngjiāo〈名〉［化学］sol
【溶解】róngjiě〈动〉dissolve: ～度 solubility ‖ 水能～盐。Water dissolves salt.
【溶解热】róngjiěrè〈名〉heat of a solution
【溶媒】róngméi = 溶剂 róngjì
【溶溶】róngróng〈形〉〈书〉vast: ～月色 soothing flood of moonlight ‖ 江水～。The broad expanse of water in the river is flowing gently.
【溶蚀】róngshí〈动〉［地质］**1**（指金属）corrode **2**（指岩石等）erode
【溶体】róngtǐ〈名〉［化学］solution
【溶血】róngxuè ▸**p. 50**〈名〉［医学］haemolysis: ～病 haemolytic disease
【溶液】róngyè〈名〉solution: 稀释～ dilute a solution
【溶质】róngzhì〈名〉［化学］solute: 把食盐溶解于水中时，水是溶剂，食盐是～。When salt is dissolved in water, water is the solvent and salt is the solute.

榕 róng〈名〉**1**（指树）banyan tree **2** Róng（福州）Rong [another name for Fuzhou]

熔 róng〈动〉melt: ▸～点，～铸
【熔点】róngdiǎn〈名〉［物理］melting point
【熔断器】róngduànqì〈名〉fuse box
【熔锅】róngguō〈名〉melting pot
【熔合】rónghé〈动〉fuse: 将锌与铜～成黄铜 fuse zinc and copper to make brass
【熔化】rónghuà〈动〉fuse: ～金属 melt down metals
【熔剂】róngjì〈名〉［冶金］flux
【熔接】róngjiē〈动〉weld
【熔解】róngjiě〈动〉［物理］fuse
【熔炼】róngliàn〈动〉**1**（指冶炼）smelt **2**〈喻〉（指锻炼）temper: 在战斗中～自己 temper oneself in combat
【熔炉】rónglú〈名〉furnace: 在生活的～中得到锻炼 be tempered in the crucible of life
【熔融】róngróng〈动〉melt
【熔丝】róngsī〈名〉［电气］fuse
【熔岩】róngyán〈名〉［地质］lava
【熔冶】róngyě〈动〉［冶金］smelt
【熔铸】róngzhù〈动〉found

蝾（蠑）róng

【蝾螈】róngyuán〈名〉［动物］salamander

镕（鎔）róng = 熔 róng

融 róng

〈动〉 **1**（融化）melt: 积雪消～。The snow build-up melted away. ▸～化 **2**（混合）blend: 海天似乎～为一体了。Sea and sky seemed to blend. ‖ 油水不相～。Water does not mix with oil. ▸～合, 水乳交～ **3**（流通）circulate: ▸金～

【融合】rónghé〈动〉mix together: 种族～ racial integration ‖ 这种装饰完美地～了传统与现代的特色。The decor is a harmonious blend of traditional and modern features.

【融和】rónghé **A**〈形〉**1**（暖和）pleasantly warm: 天气～。The weather is pleasantly warm. **2**（和谐）harmonious: 气氛～。The atmosphere is harmonious. **B** = 融合 rónghé

【融化】rónghuà〈动〉melt: 积雪～了。The snow has thawed. ‖ 蜡开始～。The wax began to run.

【融会】rónghuì〈动〉mix together

【融会贯通】rónghuì-guàntōng〈成〉gain a thorough understanding of sth.

【融解】róngjiě〈动〉melt: 冰块在热水中～了。The ice cubes melted in the hot water.

【融洽】róngqià〈形〉harmonious: 感情～ harmonize in feeling ‖ 他们相处得很～。They are on good terms with each other.

【融券】róngquàn〈名〉［金融］securities loan

【融融】róngróng〈形〉**1**（和睦欢乐）happy and harmonious: 其乐～ be in a joyous atmosphere **2**（暖和）warm: 春光～。Spring fills the air with warmth. ‖ 屋子里暖～的。It was warm and cosy in the room.

【融通】róngtōng〈动〉**1**（融合流通）circulate: ～资金 circulate funds **2**（贯通）gain a thorough understanding: ～古今 gain a thorough understanding of the past and the present **3**（使融洽）harmonize

【融资】róngzī〈动〉raise funds: 扩大～规模 expand the scale of capital circulation ‖ 为一项工程～ raise funds for a project ‖ ～租赁 financial lease

【融资渠道】róngzī qúdào〈名〉financing channel

rǒng

冗 rǒng〈书〉

A〈形〉**1**（闲散）superfluous: ▸～长, ～员 **2**（繁琐）full of trivial details: ▸～务, ～杂
B〈名〉busy routine: ▸拨～

【冗笔】rǒngbǐ〈名〉superfluous words or strokes

【冗长】rǒngcháng〈形〉long-winded: ～的讲话 long and tedious speech

【冗词】rǒngcí〈名〉superfluous word

【冗词赘句】rǒngcí-zhuìjù〈成〉redundant words and repetitive expressions

【冗繁】rǒngfán〈形〉miscellaneous and tedious: ～的琐事 trivial and complicated matters

【冗务】rǒngwù〈名〉miscellaneous affairs: ～缠身 be tied up with small routine affairs

【冗余】rǒngyú〈名〉redundancy

【冗员】rǒngyuán〈名〉superfluous staff: 裁减～ reduce redundant personnel

【冗杂】rǒngzá〈形〉miscellaneous: ～的事务 miscellaneous affairs

【冗赘】rǒngzhuì〈形〉verbose: 行文～ verbose writing style

róu

柔 róu

A〈形〉**1**（软）soft, supple: ▸～嫩, ～软 **2**（温和）gentle: ▸～顺, 温～
B〈动〉soften: ～麻 soften hemp

【柔板】róubǎn〈名〉［音乐］adagio

【柔肠】róucháng〈名〉tender feelings

【柔肠寸断】róucháng-cùnduàn〈成〉be heart-broken

【柔道】róudào〈名〉［体育］judo: ～运动员 judoka

【柔和】róuhé〈形〉gentle: ～的光线 soft light ‖ 色调～ the colour is of subdued tone

【柔滑】róuhuá〈形〉soft and smooth: ～的肌肤 soft skin ‖ 手感～ be soft and smooth to the touch

【柔静】róujìng〈形〉gentle and peaceful

【柔美】róuměi〈形〉soft and graceful: 音色～ soft and exquisite timbre ‖ 舞姿～ graceful dance

【柔媚】róumèi〈形〉gentle and charming: 目光～ eyes sparkling with tenderness and charm ‖ ～的女子 lovely girl

【柔嫩】róunèn〈形〉tender: ～的皮肤 delicate skin ‖ ～的幼芽 tender shoots

【柔能克刚】róu néng kè gāng〈成〉the soft can overcome the hard

【柔情】róuqíng〈名〉tender feelings: ～似水 be deeply attached

【柔情蜜意】róuqíng-mìyì〈成〉tenderness and affection

【柔情侠骨】róuqíng-xiágǔ〈成〉a tender heart and a chivalrous spirit

【柔韧】róurèn〈形〉pliable: ～的皮革 supple leather ‖ ～性 pliability

【柔茹刚吐】róurú-gāngtǔ〈成〉bully the weak and dread the strong

【柔软】róuruǎn〈形〉soft: 质地～ soft to the touch ‖ ～的四肢 supple limbs ‖ ～剂 softening agent

【柔软体操】róuruǎn tǐcāo〈名〉callisthenics

【柔润】róurùn〈形〉tender and smooth: 皮肤～ delicate skin ‖ 嗓音～ soft and mellow voice

【柔弱】róuruò〈形〉weak: 身体～ be in frail health ‖ 生性～ have a weak character

【柔术】róushù〈名〉［体育］jujitsu

【柔顺】róushùn〈形〉meek: 性情～ be of a gentle disposition

【柔顺剂】róushùnjì〈名〉［化工］softener: 衣物～ fabric softener

【柔婉】róuwǎn〈形〉**1**（柔和婉转）soft and agreeable: ～的嗓音 soft and pleasing voice **2**（柔和温顺）gentle and yielding: 性情～ be of gentle disposition

【柔细】róuxì〈形〉soft and fine: ～的柳枝 delicate twigs of willow ‖ ～的嗓音 soft and thready voice

【柔性】róuxìng **A**〈名〉［物理］flexibility: ～路面 flexible pavement **B**〈形〉flexible: ～处理 handle flexibly

【柔中有刚】róuzhōng-yǒugāng〈成〉have a hard core in a mild exterior

揉 róu

〈动〉**1**（反复擦、搓）massage: ～眼睛 rub one's eyes **2**（团弄）knead: ～面 knead dough **3**〈书〉（使弯曲）bend

【揉搓】róucuo〈动〉**1**（反复摩擦）rub and knead with the hands **2**〈方〉（折磨）torture: ～人 torment sb.

糅 róu

〈动〉mix: ▸杂～

【糅合】róuhé〈动〉mix together: 两种观点不能～在一起。You can't combine the two points of view.

【糅杂】róuzá〈动〉mix

蹂 róu

〈动〉〈书〉trample

【蹂躏】róulìn〈动〉ravage: ～别国主权 ravish the sovereignty of another country ‖ 惨遭～ be ruthlessly trampled on

【蹂踏】róutà〈动〉trample

鞣 róu

〈动〉tan: ～皮子 tan a hide

【鞣料】róuliào〈名〉tanning material

【鞣酸】róusuān〈名〉［化学］tannic acid

【鞣制】róuzhì〈动〉tan hides

ròu

肉 ròu

A〈名〉**1**（指动物）meat;（指人）flesh: 生/熟～ raw/cooked meat ‖ 少吃～多吃蔬菜 eat less meat and more vegetables ▸烤～, 熏～, 腌～ **2**（指瓜果）pulp: 桂圆～ longan pulp ‖ 桃子的果～ flesh of a peach ‖ 椰～ coconut meat
B〈形〉〈方〉**1**（指瓜果）mushy: 这瓜太～。This melon is too spongy. **2**（指人）slow-moving: 他是个～脾气。He is phlegmatic.

【肉包子】ròubāozi〈名〉steamed bun with stuffing of minced meat

【肉饼】ròubǐng〈名〉meat pie

【肉搏】ròubó〈动〉fight hand-to-hand

【肉搏战】ròubózhàn〈名〉hand-to-hand combat: 展开～ engage in hand-to-hand combat

【肉菜】ròucài〈名〉meat dishes

【肉畜】ròuchù〈名〉livestock raised for meat

【肉垂】ròuchuí〈名〉［鸟类］wattle

【肉苁蓉】ròucōngróng〈名〉［中药］saline cistanche

【肉弹】ròudàn〈名〉**1**（人体炸弹）human bomb **2**（性感美女）sex-bomb

【肉丁】ròudīng〈名〉diced meat

【肉嘟嘟】ròudūdū〈形〉〈口〉plump: ～的脸 chubby face

【肉毒杆菌】ròudúgǎnjūn〈名〉［医学］botulinum toxin (Botox)

【肉墩墩】ròudūndūn〈形〉〈口〉pudgy: ～的手 pudgy hands

【肉墩子】ròudūnzi〈名〉chopping block

【肉感】ròugǎn〈形〉voluptuous and sexy

【肉冠】ròuguān〈名〉［鸟类］comb

【肉桂】ròuguì〈名〉［植物］cassia-bark tree

【肉红】ròuhóng〈形〉pinkish red

【肉乎乎】ròuhūhū〈形〉fleshy

【肉鸡】ròujī〈名〉roasting chicken

【肉夹馍】ròujiāmó〈名〉meat bun [consisting of hot chopped meat inside a baked bun]

【肉酱】ròujiàng〈名〉minced meat: 剁成～ chop into mince

【肉卷】ròujuǎn〈名〉mince roll

【肉类】ròulèi〈名〉meats: ～加工厂 meat-processing factory

【肉瘤】ròuliú〈名〉sarcoma

【肉麻】ròumá〈形〉sickening: ～的恭维 nauseating compliments
【肉糜】ròumí = 肉末儿 ròumòr
【肉末儿】ròumòr〈名〉minced meat〈英〉; ground meat〈美〉
【肉牛】ròuniú〈名〉beef cattle
【肉排】ròupái〈名〉steak
【肉泡眼】ròupāoyǎn〈名〉pouchy eyes
【肉皮】ròupí〈名〉pork skin
【肉皮冻】ròupídòng〈名〉pork skin jelly
【肉片】ròupiàn〈名〉sliced meat
【肉票】ròupiào〈名〉hostage: 撕～ kill a hostage
【肉禽】ròuqín〈名〉table poultry
【肉色】ròusè〈名〉flesh colour: ～长袜 flesh-coloured stockings
【肉身】ròushēn〈名〉［佛教］mortal body
【肉食】ròushí **A**〈形〉carnivorous: ～动物 carnivore **B**〈名〉edible meat
【肉丝】ròusī〈名〉shredded meat
【肉松】ròusōng〈名〉fry-dried meat floss
【肉汤】ròutāng〈名〉meat broth
【肉体】ròutǐ〈名〉human body: 出卖～ sell one's body
【肉头】ròutóu〈形〉〈方〉**1**（软弱无能）indecisive and incompetent **2**（傻）foolish **3**（迟缓）sluggish
【肉头】ròutou〈形〉〈方〉plump and soft: 这孩子的一双小手又白又～。The child's little hands are plump and white.
【肉丸子】ròuwánzi〈名〉meatball
【肉馅儿】ròuxiànr〈名〉minced meat stuffing: 香肠～ sausage meat
【肉刑】ròuxíng〈名〉corporal punishment
【肉性子】ròuxìngzi〈名〉〈口〉phlegmatic temperament
【肉芽】ròuyá〈名〉［医学］granulation
【肉眼】ròuyǎn〈名〉**1**（指眼睛）naked eye: 细菌用～看不见。Bacteria are invisible to the naked eye. **2**（指视力）vision of a mortal person: ～凡胎 ordinary mortal
【肉眼泡儿】ròuyǎnpāor〈名〉puffy eyelids
【肉用鸡】ròuyòngjī = 肉鸡 ròujī
【肉欲】ròuyù〈名〉sexual desire: 放纵～ indulge in carnal pleasures
【肉汁】ròuzhī〈名〉gravy
【肉制品】ròuzhìpǐn〈名〉meat products
【肉质植物】ròuzhì zhíwù〈名〉succulent
【肉中刺】ròuzhōngcì〈名〉〈喻〉thorn in one's side
【肉猪】ròuzhū〈名〉slaughter pig
【肉赘】ròuzhuì〈名〉wart

rú

如[1] rú

A〈动〉**1**（符合）comply with: ▸～期, ～愿 **2**（好像）be like: ～我所说 as I have said ‖ 数十年～一日地工作 work for decades as if it were only one day ▸～同, 胆小～鼠, 犹～ **3**（比得上）[used in the negative] be as good as: 天时不～地利，地利不～人和。The right time isn't as important as the right place, but the right place isn't as important as harmony among the people. ▸百闻不～一见 **4**（书）（往）go to: ～厕 go to the toilet
B〈介〉**1**（引进对象）[introducing the surpassed object]: 光景一年强～一年。Life is getting better year by year. **2**（例如）such as: 他去过许多国家，～日本、美国、加拿大等。He has been to many countries, such as Japan, the United States and Canada.
C ▸**p. 350**〈连〉if: ～不同意，请告诉我。If you disagree, please let me know.

如[2] rú

〈后缀〉[used after some adjectives to indicate the state of things or an action]: ▸空空～也, 突～其来
【如臂使指】rúbìshǐzhǐ〈成〉be in perfect command of sth.
【如厕】rúcè〈动〉go to the toilet
【如常】rúcháng〈动〉be as usual: 一切～ everything is normal ‖ 健康～ be in one's usual good health
【如出一辙】rúchūyīzhé〈成〉be identical: 两人的论调～。Their two views are identical.
【如初】rúchū〈动〉be as before: 他们又和好～。They are great friends once again.
【如此】rúcǐ〈代〉such: ～昂贵 so expensive ‖ ～等等 and so on and so forth ‖ 事已～ such being the case
【如此而已】rúcǐ'éryǐ〈成〉that is all there is to it
【如次】rúcì〈动〉〈书〉be as follows: 全文～。The full text is as follows.
【如堕五里雾中】rú duò wǔlǐwù zhōng〈成〉be utterly bewildered
【如法炮制】rúfǎ-páozhì〈成〉follow a set pattern
【如风过耳】rúfēngguò'ěr〈成〉turn a deaf ear to
【如鲠在喉】rúgěngzàihóu〈成〉〈喻〉having a criticism one must express
【如故】rúgù〈动〉**1**（像原先一样）be as before: 依然～ remain unchanged **2**（像老朋友一样）be like old friends: ▸一见～
【如果】rúguǒ ▸**p. 350**〈连〉if: ～一切顺利，我们将提前完工。If all goes well, we'll be able to complete the project ahead of schedule.
【如何】rúhé〈代〉how: 你近况～? How are things going with you? ‖ 这可～是好? What shall I do then?
【如虎添翼】rúhǔtiānyì〈成〉〈喻〉with redoubled efforts
【如花似锦】rúhuā-sìjǐn〈成〉**1**（指风景）beautiful **2**（指前途）bright: ～的前程 brilliant prospects **3**（指装饰）magnificent
【如花似玉】rúhuā-sìyù〈成〉be exquisitely beautiful
【如火如荼】rúhuǒ-rútú〈成〉grow vigorously: 改革正～地开展着。Reform is in full swing.
【如获至宝】rúhuòzhìbǎo〈成〉seize sth. as heaven-sent
【如饥似渴】rújī-sìkě〈成〉with great eagerness: ～地探求真理的人 voracious seeker of the truth
【如胶似漆】rújiāo-sìqī〈成〉be deeply attached to one another
【如今】rújīn ▸**p. 618**〈名〉nowadays: ～坐飞机是平常事。Air travel is a commonplace nowadays.
【如旧】rújiù〈动〉be as before
【如来】Rúlái ▸**p. 274**〈名〉［佛教］Buddha
【如狼似虎】rúláng-sìhǔ〈成〉as ferocious as wolves and tigers
【如雷贯耳】rúléiguàn'ěr〈成〉reverberate like thunder: 久闻大名，～。Your great name has long resounded in my ears.
【如临大敌】rúlíndàdí〈成〉take every precaution as if anticipating a fierce enemy attack
【如临深渊】rúlínshēnyuān〈成〉as though on the edge of an abyss
【如履薄冰】rúlǚbóbīng〈成〉〈喻〉act with utmost caution
【如芒在背】rúmángzàibèi〈成〉〈喻〉be on tenterhooks
【如梦初醒】rúmèngchūxǐng〈成〉〈喻〉begin to see the light
【如鸟兽散】rúniǎoshòusàn〈成〉〈贬〉run off in complete disorder
【如期】rúqī〈副〉on schedule: ～交货 deliver the goods on schedule ‖ 四方会谈将～举行。The four-party talks will go ahead as planned.
【如其】rúqí〈连〉if
【如泣如诉】rúqì-rúsù〈成〉be plaintive
【如日方升】rúrìfāngshēng〈成〉〈喻〉with boundless prospects
【如日中天】rúrìzhōngtiān〈成〉〈喻〉be at the height of one's power, career, etc.: 成就～ be in the full flush of success
【如入无人之境】rú rù wú rén zhī jìng〈成〉march through without encountering any significant resistance
【如若】rúruò〈书〉= 如果 rúguǒ
【如丧考妣】rúsàngkǎobǐ〈成〉〈贬〉be utterly wretched: 他的垮台使其追随者～。His downfall left his followers feeling as if they had been orphaned.
【如上】rúshàng〈动〉be as above: ～所述 as stated/mentioned above ‖ ～所说 as stated above
【如实】rúshí〈副〉truthfully: ～反映 report accurately ‖ ～交待 make a clean breast of things
【如释重负】rúshìzhòngfù〈成〉feel as if a weight has been lifted from one's shoulders: 我～，倍感轻松。That's a great weight off my mind.
【如数家珍】rúshǔjiāzhēn〈成〉be very familiar with and proud of what one is talking about
【如数】rúshù〈副〉in full: ～偿还 pay back the whole amount ‖ ～交纳 pay in full
【如汤沃雪】rútāngwòxuě〈成〉〈喻〉easily and speedily done
【如同】rútóng〈动〉be like: ～白昼 as bright as daylight ‖ ～亲人 like one's own kith and kin
【如下】rúxià〈动〉as follows: 声明～ issue the following statement ‖ 全文～。The full text follows.
【如心】rúxīn〈形〉gratified
【如许】rúxǔ〈代〉〈书〉**1**（这么多）so much: 枉费～工夫。So much time has been wasted. **2**（如此）so: 行路～难。The journey was so difficult.
【如一】rúyī〈动〉be consistent: 始终～ consistent ‖ 表里～ think and act as one
【如蚁附膻】rúyǐfùshān〈成〉〈贬〉**1**（追求恶劣的事物）running after unwholesome things **2**（指趋炎附势）attaching oneself to influential people for personal gain
【如意】rúyì **A**〈动〉be satisfactory: 顺心～ be happy and satisfied ‖ 祝万事～。May everything you want come your way. **B**〈名〉ornamental sceptre
【如意算盘】rúyì-suànpán〈成〉wishful thinking: 打～ indulge in wishful thinking
【如影随形】rúyǐngsuíxíng〈成〉be inseparable
【如鱼得水】rúyúdéshuǐ〈成〉take to sth. like a duck to water: 进入公司，他～，成绩显著。He took to the company like a duck to water and was highly successful there.
【如愿】rúyuàn〈动〉get what one wished for: 未能～ unable to obtain one's heart's desire

【如愿以偿】rúyuàn-yǐcháng〈成〉obtain one's heart's desire
【如醉如痴】rúzuì-rúchī〈成〉〈喻〉be enraptured
【如坐针毡】rúzuòzhēnzhān〈成〉like a cat on a hot tin roof: 接到恐吓电话后，他整日～。After receiving the threatening phone call, he was on edge all day.

茹 rú〈动〉〈书〉eat: ～素 be a vegetarian
【茹苦含辛】rúkǔ-hánxīn = 含辛茹苦 hánxīn-rúkǔ
【茹毛饮血】rúmáo-yǐnxuè〈成〉live a primitive life

铷（鉫） rú〈名〉［化学］rubidium (Rb)

儒 rú〈名〉**1**（指思想流派）Confucianism **2**〈旧〉（指人）scholar: 腐～ pedant
【儒艮】rúgèn〈名〉［动物］dugong
【儒家】Rújiā〈名〉Confucian school: ～思想 Confucianism

> **儒家**
>
> A school of thought founded by Confucius (▸孔子). Confucianism emphasizes character-building and an ethical education, with benevolence (仁) and righteousness (义) as criteria for behaviour. It upholds the relationship between sovereign and subject, father and son, husband and wife, brothers etc. Mencius (孟子) is another important figure in Confucianism, and the names of Confucius and Mencius are often combined as Kong Meng (孔孟). From the Han Dynasty, Confucianism became the dominant ideology in Chinese feudal society. This lasted for over 2,000 years.

【儒将】rújiàng〈名〉scholar-general
【儒教】Rújiào〈名〉Confucianism
【儒林】rúlín〈名〉**1**（儒家学者）Confucian scholars **2**（知识界）scholars: 《～外史》*Unofficial History of the Literati*
【儒商】rúshāng〈名〉scholarly businessman
【儒生】rúshēng〈名〉**1**（儒家学者）Confucian scholar **2**（读书人）scholar
【儒术】rúshù〈名〉Confucianism
【儒学】rúxué〈名〉**1**（指学说）Confucian teachings **2**（指学校）government-run Confucian schools at county, prefecture or province level during the Yuan, Ming and Qing dynasties
【儒雅】rúyǎ〈形〉〈书〉**1**（指学识）erudite **2**（指气度）scholarly and refined: ～风度 scholarly bearing
【儒医】rúyī〈名〉scholar-physician

薷 rú ▸香薷 xiāngrú

嚅 rú
【嚅动】rúdòng〈动〉move one's lips as if to say sth.
【嚅嗫】rúniè〈书〉= 嗫嚅 nièrú

濡 rú〈动〉〈书〉**1**（沾湿）immerse: ～笔 dip one's pen ▸耳～目染 **2**（迟滞）linger: 行动～滞 be slow in action
【濡染】rúrǎn〈动〉〈书〉immerse
【濡湿】rúshī〈动〉soak

孺 rú〈名〉child
【孺子】rúzǐ〈名〉〈书〉child: 黄口～ mere child
【孺子可教】rúzǐ-kějiào〈成〉the boy is worth teaching
【孺子牛】rúzǐniú〈名〉〈喻〉servant of the people

襦 rú〈名〉〈书〉short jacket: 绣～ short embroidered upper garment

颥（顬） rú ▸颞颥 nièrú

蠕 rú〈动〉wriggle
【蠕变】rúbiàn **A**〈动〉change slowly **B**〈名〉［冶金］creep (deformation)
【蠕虫】rúchóng〈名〉worm
【蠕动】rúdòng〈动〉**1**（扭动）wriggle: 蚯蚓～着钻出小洞。The earthworm wriggled out of a small hole. **2**（爬行）creep: 向前～ inch along
【蠕蠕】rúrú〈副〉in a wriggly manner: ～前行 wriggle along

rǔ

汝 rǔ〈代〉〈书〉you: ～辈 you people

乳 rǔ
A〈动〉**1**〈书〉（喂奶）feed with milk **2** give birth to
B〈名〉**1**（乳房）（指人）breast;（指牲口）udder: 双～ breasts ▸～罩 **2**（乳汁）milk: ▸母～ **3**（奶状物）milk-like liquid: ▸～胶
C〈形〉（初生）newborn: ▸～燕, ～牙
【乳癌】rǔ'ái ▸**p. 50**〈名〉breast cancer
【乳白】rǔbái〈形〉creamy: ～灯泡 opal bulb ‖ ～色的地毯 cream-coloured carpet
【乳钵】rǔbō〈名〉mortar
【乳齿】rǔchǐ = 乳牙 rǔyá
【乳畜】rǔchù〈名〉dairy animal
【乳儿】rǔ'ér〈名〉sucking baby
【乳房】rǔfáng〈名〉breast: 丰满的～ full breasts
【乳峰】rǔfēng〈名〉breasts
【乳鸽】rǔgē〈名〉squab
【乳沟】rǔgōu〈名〉cleavage
【乳化】rǔhuà〈动〉emulsify: ～液 emulsion
【乳黄】rǔhuáng〈形〉creamy
【乳剂】rǔjì〈名〉［化学］emulsion: 感光～ sensitive emulsion
【乳胶】rǔjiāo〈名〉［化学］emulsion: ～漆 emulsion paint
【乳酪】rǔlào〈名〉cheese
【乳糜】rǔmí〈名〉［生物］chyle
【乳名】rǔmíng〈名〉child's pet name
【乳母】rǔmǔ〈名〉wet nurse
【乳娘】rǔniáng〈名〉wet nurse
【乳牛】rǔniú〈名〉dairy cow
【乳品】rǔpǐn〈名〉dairy product: ～厂 creamery
【乳酸】rǔsuān〈名〉［生化］lactic acid
【乳酸钙】rǔsuāngài〈名〉calcium lactate
【乳糖】rǔtáng〈名〉［化学］lactose
【乳头】rǔtóu〈名〉**1**（奶头）nipple **2**［解剖］papilla: 视神经～ optic papilla
【乳突】rǔtū〈名〉mastoid process
【乳腺】rǔxiàn〈名〉mammary gland
【乳腺癌】rǔxiàn'ái ▸**p. 50**〈名〉breast cancer
【乳腺炎】rǔxiànyán ▸**p. 50**〈名〉［医学］mastitis
【乳臭未干】rǔxiù-wèigān〈成〉be wet behind the ears
【乳牙】rǔyá〈名〉baby tooth
【乳燕】rǔyàn〈名〉baby swallow
【乳液】rǔyè〈名〉emulsion
【乳晕】rǔyùn〈名〉areola
【乳罩】rǔzhào〈名〉bra
【乳汁】rǔzhī〈名〉milk: 甘甜的～ sweet milk
【乳脂】rǔzhī〈名〉butterfat
【乳制品】rǔzhìpǐn〈名〉dairy product
【乳猪】rǔzhū〈名〉suckling pig: 烤～ roasted suckling pig

辱 rǔ
A〈名〉disgrace: ▸奇耻大～, 屈～
B〈动〉**1**（使受辱）humiliate: ▸～骂, 凌～, 丧权～国 **2**（玷污）disgrace: 不～使命 not fail a mission ▸～没
C〈副〉〈书〉gratefully: ～承赐教。I am indebted to you for your instruction.
【辱骂】rǔmà〈动〉abuse
【辱命】rǔmìng〈动〉fail a mission: 幸不～。Luckily I accomplished the mission.
【辱没】rǔmò〈动〉bring disgrace on sb./sth.: ～集体荣誉 disgrace the good name of the collective

擩 rǔ〈动〉〈方〉put in: 把刀～进草垛里 thrust a sword in the haystack

rù

入 rù
A〈动〉**1**（进入）enter: 陷～ fall into ‖ ～春 enter into spring ‖ 外人莫～。No admittance to non-members. ▸～场, 病从口～, 祸从口出, 渐～佳境 **2**（使进入）put in: 放～ put into ▸～库, ～账, 纳～ **3**（加入）join: ～中国籍 be naturalized as a Chinese citizen ▸～伍, 加～ **4**（合乎）conform to: ▸～时, ～情～理
B〈名〉**1**（收入）income: ▸～不敷出, 收～, 岁～ **2** = 入声 rùshēng
【入不敷出】rùbùfūchū〈成〉live beyond one's means: 我经常～。I often spend more than I actually have.
【入仓】rùcāng〈动〉put in storage
【入常】rùcháng〈动〉become a permanent member of the UN Security Council: 日本的"～"愿望非常强烈。Japan is extremely keen to become a permanent member of the UN Security Council .
【入场】rùchǎng〈动〉enter an arena: 凭票～ admission by ticket only ‖ ～式 march-in ceremony ‖ 运动员～。The athletes are entering the arena.
【入场券】rùchǎngquàn〈名〉**1**〈本〉entrance ticket: 音乐会～ ticket for a concert **2**〈喻〉（指参与资格）qualification: 争取奥运会的～ strive to qualify for the Olympic Games
【入超】rùchāo〈名〉［经济］trade deficit
【入党】rùdǎng〈动〉become a member of a political party: ～申请书 application for Party membership
【入定】rùdìng〈动〉［佛教］sit in meditation
【入耳】rù'ěr〈形〉easy on the ear: 不堪～的话 offensive-sounding language
【入伏】rùfú〈动〉enter the hottest days of the year: 今天～。The hottest days begin today.
【入港】rùgǎng〈动〉**1**（指船舶）enter a port: 船～了。The ship sailed into the port. **2**〈旧〉（指交谈投机）be in perfect harmony: 二人谈得～。The two of them were in deep conversation and in full

agreement with each other.

【入彀】rùgòu〈动〉〈书〉1（受人掌握）play into sb.'s hands 2（入神）be concentrated 3〈喻〉（合乎标准）conform to a normal standard

【入股】rùgǔ〈动〉buy shares

【入骨】rùgǔ〈动〉reach the marrow: ▸恨之～

【入关】rùguān〈动〉1（指关口）enter one of the gates of the Great Wall from the outside 2（指关贸总协定）be admitted to the General Agreement on Tariffs and Trade (GATT): ～后，进口商品大幅降价。After the country was admitted to GATT, the price of imported goods was greatly reduced.

【入国问禁】rùguó-wènjìn〈成〉on entering a foreign country, enquire about its prohibitions

【入海口】rùhǎikǒu〈名〉［地理］estuary

【入画】rùhuà〈动〉be picturesque

【入会】rùhuì〈动〉become a member: ～费 admission fee

【入伙】rùhuǒ〈动〉1（指团伙）join a gang 2（指伙伴关系）join in partnership: 同意某人～ admit sb. into a partnership 3（指集体伙食）share a meal

【入籍】rùjí〈动〉acquire citizenship

【入寂】rùjì〈动〉［佛教］pass away

【入教】rùjiào〈动〉be converted to a religion

【入静】rùjìng〈动〉［宗教］sit in meditation and achieve absolute mental tranquillity

【入境】rùjìng〈动〉enter a country: ～签证 entry visa

【入境手续】rùjìng shǒuxù〈名〉entry formalities

【入境问俗】rùjìng-wènsú〈成〉when in Rome, do as the Romans

【入镜】rùjìng〈动〉record on camera

【入口】rùkǒu A〈动〉1（指嘴）enter the mouth: 不可～! Not to be taken orally! 2（指口岸）import: ～检查处 check-in counter B〈名〉entrance: 大厦～ entrance to a building ‖ 地铁～ subway entrance

【入寇】rùkòu〈动〉〈旧〉invade

【入库】rùkù〈动〉be put in storage: 粮食～ put the grain into storage

【入殓】rùliàn〈动〉put a corpse in a coffin

【入列】rùliè〈动〉［军事］take one's place in the ranks

【入流】rùliú〈动〉be qualified: 不～ not qualified

【入梅】rùméi〈动〉enter the rainy season

【入寐】rùmèi〈动〉〈书〉fall asleep: 不能～ cannot go to sleep

【入门】rùmén A〈动〉learn the fundamentals of sth.: 他们的学习才刚刚～。Their studies have only just begun. ‖ 计算机我还没～呢。I haven't even grasped the basics of how to use a computer. B〈名〉primer: 《汉语语法～》*The ABC of Chinese Grammar*

【入梦】rùmèng〈动〉1（睡着）fall asleep 2（进入某人梦境）appear in one's dream

【入迷】rùmí〈动〉be lost in sth.: 他们看电影入了迷。They were lost in the magic of the film.

【入眠】rùmián〈动〉1（指人）fall asleep 2（指蚕）neither move nor eat

【入魔】rùmó〈动〉be entranced: 他赌博入了魔。He is addicted to gambling.

【入木三分】rùmù-sānfēn〈成〉1（指书法）having forceful strokes 2（指见解、议论）penetrating: ～的分析 incisive analysis

【入侵】rùqīn〈动〉invade: 大举～ carry out a full-on invasion ‖ ～之敌 invaders ‖ 军事～ military incursion ‖ ～病毒 intrusive virus ‖ ～者 invader

【入情入理】rùqíng-rùlǐ〈成〉be fair and reasonable

【入神】rùshén A〈动〉be entranced: 我们听着她的故事入了神。We listened, enthralled by her story. B〈形〉exquisite: ～的画 exquisite picture

【入声】rùshēng〈名〉［语言］entering tone [fourth of the four tones in classical Chinese pronunciation]

【入时】rùshí〈形〉fashionable: 打扮～ be fashionably dressed

【入世】rùshì〈动〉1（指社会）enter society: ～不深 have little experience of the world 2（指世贸组织）enter the World Trade Organization (WTO)

【入室】rùshì〈动〉1（进入房内）enter sb.'s house: ～行窃 burgle ▸引狼～ 2（指成就）gain mastery of: ～弟子 well-accomplished student

【入室操戈】rùshì-cāogē〈成〉〈喻〉turn sb.'s argument against himself

【入手】rùshǒu〈动〉start with: 不知从何～ not know where to start

【入睡】rùshuì〈动〉fall asleep

【入土】rùtǔ〈动〉be buried: ～为安 burial brings peace to the deceased

【入团】rùtuán〈动〉join the Youth League

【入托】rùtuō〈动〉start going to a nursery: 把孩子～ place a child in day care

【入网】rùwǎng〈动〉（指通信设备）link up to a telecommunications network;（指电脑）connect to the Internet

【入微】rùwēi〈副〉in every possible detail: 体贴～ show sb. great consideration

【入围】rùwéi〈动〉qualify for: 本次锦标赛八强产生，中国有三名选手～。Three players from China were among the eight who qualified for the quarter-finals.

【入闱】rùwéi〈动〉1〈旧〉（进入殿试）enter the imperial examination hall 2（被选上）be selected

【入味儿】rùwèir〈形〉1（有滋味）tasty: 这菜挺～。The dish is quite tasty. 2（有趣味）be interested: 越看越～ get more and more absorbed the more one sees

【入伍】rùwǔ〈动〉enlist: 应征～ be called up

【入席】rùxí〈动〉take one's seat: 请各位～。Please be seated.

【入宪】rùxiàn〈动〉enter into the constitution: 人权和社会保障～。Human rights and social security are written into the constitution.

【入乡随俗】rùxiāng-suísú〈成〉conform to local practices

【入选】rùxuǎn〈动〉be selected

【入学】rùxué〈动〉1（指小学）start school: 我七岁时～。I started school at seven. 2（指大学）matriculate: ～考试 entrance examination ‖ ～通知书 notice of admission

【入眼】rùyǎn〈形〉easy on the eye: 看不～ not to one's liking

【入药】rùyào〈动〉be used as medicine: 这种草可～。This herb can be used as medicine.

【入夜】rùyè〈动〉fall (of night)

【入狱】rùyù〈动〉be sent to jail: 锒铛～ be put in chains and thrown into prison

【入院】rùyuàn〈动〉be admitted to hospital: ～治疗 be hospitalized for treatment

【入账】rùzhàng〈动〉enter an item in an account: 货款已经～。Payment for goods has already been entered into the accounts.

【入蛰】rùzhé〈动〉go into hibernation

【入主】rùzhǔ〈动〉become the master: ～白宫 take the helm at the White House

【入住】rùzhù〈动〉move into: 小区八月竣工，年底～。The residential quarter will be completed in August, and residents will be able to move in towards the end of the year.

【入住率】rùzhùlǜ〈名〉occupancy rate: "十一"黄金周期间，酒店～高达90%以上。During the National Day Golden Week, hotel occupancy rates were over 90%.

【入赘】rùzhuì〈动〉[of a man] marry into and live with the bride's family

【入座】rùzuò〈动〉take one's seat: 对号～ take the seat numbered on one's ticket

溽 rù〈形〉〈书〉humid

【溽热】rùrè〈形〉muggy

【溽暑】rùshǔ〈名〉sweltering summer weather

缛（縟）rù〈形〉〈书〉elaborate: ▸繁文～节

蓐 rù〈名〉〈书〉straw mat

褥 rù〈名〉cotton-padded mattress: ▸被～

【褥疮】rùchuāng ▸p. 50〈名〉［医学］bedsore

【褥单】rùdān〈名〉bed sheet

【褥套】rùtào〈名〉1（指棉絮）bedding sack 2（指布套）mattress cover

【褥子】rùzi〈名〉cotton-padded mattress

ruǎn

阮 ruǎn

【阮咸】ruǎnxián ▸p. 929〈名〉［音乐］four- or three-stringed plucked musical instrument

软（軟）ruǎn〈形〉1（不硬）soft: ～胶底 soft rubber soles ‖ ～木料 soft wood ▸～糖, ～席, 松～ 2（柔和）gentle: ▸～风, ～语 3（无力）weak: 两腿发～ one's legs feel weak ‖ 身子～得坐不起来 be too feeble to sit up ▸酥～ 4（不强硬）soft: 对某人太～ be too soft on sb. ‖ ～的不行来硬的 use hard tactics when soft ones do not effect ‖ 欺～怕硬 bully the weak and fear the strong ▸吃～不吃硬 5（不坚决）easily influenced: 心肠～ be soft-hearted ▸耳朵～, 心～ 6（差）inferior: 工夫～ incompetent skill ‖ 货色～ poor-quality goods

【软包装】ruǎnbāozhuāng〈名〉soft package: ～牛奶 soft-packaged milk ‖ ～饮料 drinks in soft packages

【软尺】ruǎnchǐ〈名〉tape measure

【软处理】ruǎnchǔlǐ〈动〉handle a matter in a calm atmosphere

【软磁盘】ruǎncípán = 软盘 ruǎnpán

【软蛋】ruǎndàn〈名〉〈口〉〈喻〉coward

【软刀子】ruǎndāozi〈名〉〈喻〉imperceptible harmful means: 用～杀人 murder with an invisible knife

【软底鞋】ruǎndǐxié〈名〉soft-soled shoe

【软钉子】ruǎndīngzi〈名〉polite snub: 碰～ be politely rejected

【软毒品】ruǎndúpǐn〈名〉soft drugs

r

【软缎】ruǎnduàn〈名〉silk fabric woven like satin but soft and supple
【软腭】ruǎn'è〈名〉［生理］soft palate
【软耳朵】ruǎn'ěrduo〈名〉credulous, indecisive person
【软风】ruǎnfēng〈名〉① (柔风) gentle breeze ②［气象］force 1 wind
【软钢】ruǎngāng〈名〉［冶金］mild steel
【软膏】ruǎngāo〈名〉cream
【软骨】ruǎngǔ〈名〉［生理］cartilage
【软骨病】ruǎngǔbìng〈名〉chondropathy
【软骨鱼】ruǎngǔyú〈名〉fish whose skeleton may be calcified but not ossified
【软骨头】ruǎngǔtou〈名〉〈喻〉coward
【软管】ruǎnguǎn〈名〉hose: ～接头 hose connection
【软罐头】ruǎnguàntou〈名〉food packed in cartons
【软广告】ruǎnguǎnggào〈名〉soft advertisement
【软化】ruǎnhuà〈动〉① (指水) soften: 使硬水～ soften hard water ② (指态度等) persuade by soft tactics: 态度开始～ one's attitude is beginning to soften ③ (指物体) bate
【软化剂】ruǎnhuàjì〈名〉softener
【软话】ruǎnhuà〈名〉conciliatory words
【软环境】ruǎnhuánjìng〈名〉soft environment: 大力改善外商投资的～ make great efforts to improve the soft environment for the convenience of foreign investors
【软和】ruǎnhuo〈形〉① (柔软) soft: ～的被子 soft quilt ② (温和) gentle: ～话 kind words
【软技术】ruǎnjìshù〈名〉soft technology
【软件】ruǎnjiàn〈名〉①［计算机］software: 开发～ develop software ‖ 防病毒/杀病毒～ anti-virus software ‖ 游戏～ games software ‖ 正版/盗版～ genuine/pirated software ② (非设备性因素) quality of personnel, management and service, etc.
【软件包】ruǎnjiànbāo〈名〉software package
【软禁】ruǎnjìn〈动〉put (sb.) under house arrest: 他被～了。He is under house arrest.
【软科学】ruǎnkēxué〈名〉soft science: 心理学被认为是一种～。Psychology is considered one of the soft sciences.
【软肋】ruǎnlèi〈名〉〈喻〉weak point: 数学是她的～。Maths is her weakness.
【软媚】ruǎn mèi〈形〉gentle and lovable
【软绵绵】ruǎnmiānmiān〈形〉① (柔软) soft: ～的手套 soft gloves ② (无力) weak: 她饿得浑身～的。She felt weak all over with hunger. ③ (情意绵绵) sentimental: ～的歌曲 sentimental song
【软磨硬泡】ruǎnmó-yìngpào〈成〉tiresomely pursue sth.
【软木】ruǎnmù〈名〉cork: ～塞 cork stopper
【软盘】ruǎnpán〈名〉floppy disk: 格式化～ format a disk
【软片】ruǎnpiàn〈名〉(roll of) film
【软钱】ruǎnqián〈名〉soft money [unrestricted donation in election]
【软驱】ruǎnqū〈名〉(floppy) disk drive
【软弱】ruǎnruò〈形〉weak: 她病后身体～无力。The illness had left her feeling tired and weak. ‖ 领导～无能。The leader is weak and incompetent. ‖ 别以为我们～可欺。Don't think of us as easy prey.
【软杀伤】ruǎnshāshāng〈名〉［军事］soft destruction
【软设备】ruǎnshèbèi〈名〉〈喻〉service, management and labour quality
【软实力】ruǎnshílì〈名〉soft power
【软食】ruǎnshí〈名〉soft diet
【软式】ruǎnshì〈形〉soft: ～排球/网球 soft volleyball/tennis
【软水】ruǎnshuǐ〈名〉soft water
【软酥酥】ruǎnsūsū〈形〉〈口〉limp
【软糖】ruǎntáng〈名〉soft sweets
【软梯】ruǎntī〈名〉rope ladder
【软体动物】ruǎntǐ dòngwù〈名〉mollusc〈英〉; mollusc〈美〉
【软通货】ruǎntōnghuò〈名〉soft currency
【软卧】ruǎnwò〈名〉soft sleeper [first-class sleeper on train]: ～车厢 soft sleeper carriage
【软武器】ruǎnwǔqì〈名〉［军事］soft weapon
【软席】ruǎnxí〈名〉cushioned seat: ～车厢 soft seat compartment
【软新闻】ruǎnxīnwén〈名〉soft news
【软性读物】ruǎnxìng dúwù〈名〉light reading
【软饮料】ruǎnyǐnliào〈名〉soft drinks
【软硬不吃】ruǎn-yìng bùchī〈成〉yield to neither persuasion nor coercion
【软硬兼施】ruǎn-yìng jiānshī〈成〉use both hard and soft tactics
【软语】ruǎnyǔ〈名〉gentle and sweet words: 吴侬～ dialects of southern Jiangsu/northern Zhejiang
【软玉】ruǎnyù〈名〉［矿业］nephrite
【软玉温香】ruǎnyù-wēnxiāng〈成〉〈喻〉feminine charm
【软指标】ruǎnzhǐbiāo〈名〉soft target
【软着陆】ruǎnzhuólù〈动〉①［航空］soft-land: 月球车在月球～。The moon rover made a soft landing on the moon. ②［经济］soft-land: 中国经济已经实现～。The Chinese economy has achieved a soft landing.
【软资源】ruǎnzīyuán〈名〉soft resources
【软组织】ruǎnzǔzhī〈名〉［生理］soft tissue: ～损伤 soft tissue injury
【软座】ruǎnzuò〈名〉soft seat [first-class seat on train]

ruí

蕤 ruí ▸葳蕤 wēiruí

ruǐ

蕊(蘂) ruǐ〈名〉stamen: 雌～ pistil ‖ 雄～ stamen

ruì

芮 Ruì〈名〉Rui [surname]

枘 ruì〈名〉〈书〉tenon: ▸方～圆凿

蚋 ruì〈名〉buffalo gnat

锐(鋭) ruì
A〈形〉sharp: ▸～利, 敏～
B〈名〉vitality: ▸养精蓄～
C〈副〉rapidly: ▸～减
【锐不可当】ruìbùkědāng〈成〉be irresistible: 以～之势 with irresistible force
【锐减】ruìjiǎn〈动〉drop sharply
【锐角】ruìjiǎo〈名〉［数学］acute angle: ～三角形 acute triangle
【锐利】ruìlì〈形〉① (尖而快) sharp: ～的猎刀 razor-sharp hunting knife ② (敏锐有力) penetrating: 目光～ have a sharp eye ‖ 文笔～ write in a pithy style
【锐敏】ruìmǐn = 敏锐 mǐnruì
【锐气】ruìqì〈名〉dash: 挫敌～ humble one's enemies ‖ ～正盛 one's drive has reached its height
【锐器】ruìqì〈名〉sharp tool
【锐舞】ruìwǔ〈名〉rave
【锐眼】ruìyǎn〈名〉sharp eyes
【锐意】ruìyì〈副〉firmly: ～改革 carry out reforms with keen determination ‖ ～进取 be determined to make progress
【锐增】ruìzēng〈动〉increase dramatically

瑞 ruì〈形〉auspicious: ▸～雪, 祥～
【瑞典】Ruìdiǎn〈名〉Sweden: ～人 the Swedish ‖ ～王国 Kingdom of Sweden ‖ ～语 Swedish
【瑞士】Ruìshì〈名〉Switzerland: ～联邦 Swiss Confederation ‖ ～人 Swiss
【瑞雪】ruìxuě〈名〉timely snow: 普降～ have an auspicious snowfall over a large area
【瑞雪兆丰年】ruìxuě zhào fēngnián〈俗〉timely snow augurs a good harvest

睿 ruì〈形〉〈书〉far-sighted
【睿智】ruìzhì〈形〉wise and prescient

rùn

闰(閏) rùn〈名〉［天文］intercalation
【闰年】rùnnián〈名〉leap year
【闰日】rùnrì〈名〉February 29 in a leap year
【闰月】rùnyuè〈名〉leap month

润(潤) rùn
A〈动〉① (滋润) moisten: ～～喉咙 moisten one's throat ‖ ～肠茶 tea for easing constipation ② (修饰) polish: ▸～色
B〈形〉smooth: 墨色很～ in dark full-bodied ink ▸～泽, 湿～, 珠圆玉～
C〈名〉profit: ▸利～
【润笔】rùnbǐ〈名〉payment for painting/writing
【润肠】rùncháng〈动〉［中医］ease constipation
【润肺】rùnfèi〈动〉［中医］facilitate expectoration (by moistening the lungs)
【润肤】rùnfū〈动〉moisturize the skin: ～露 skin lotion ‖ ～霜 moisturizing cream
【润格】rùngé〈名〉〈旧〉rate of pay of a writer, painter or calligrapher
【润喉片】rùnhóupiàn〈名〉［药学］throat tablet
【润滑】rùnhuá **A**〈动〉lubricate: ～剂 lubricant **B**〈形〉smooth and silky: ～的肌肤 silky-smooth skin
【润滑油】rùnhuáyóu〈名〉lubricating oil
【润色】rùnsè〈动〉polish: 文章还需～。The essay still needs some polishing.
【润湿】rùnshī **A**〈动〉moisten: 在动手塑造前得把泥～。Wet the clay before you start to mould it. **B** = 湿润 shīrùn A
【润饰】rùnshì = 润色 rùnsè
【润泽】rùnzé **A**〈形〉sleek: ～的肌肤 smooth skin **B**〈动〉moisten: ～轴承 lubricate the bearing
【润资】rùnzī = 润笔 rùnbǐ

ruó

挼 ruó〈动〉〈书〉knead

【挼搓】ruócuo〈动〉rub

ruò

若[1] ruò

A〈动〉be like: ▸大智～愚，寥～晨星，～无其事，旁～无人

B ▸**p. 350**〈连〉〈书〉if: ～有问题，请及时与我电话联系。If there are any questions, please don't hesitate to call me.

若[2] ruò〈代〉〈书〉you: ～辈 people like you
▸rě

【若不然】ruòbùrán〈连〉if not

【若虫】ruòchóng〈名〉［昆虫］nymph

【若非】ruòfēi ▸**p. 350**〈连〉〈书〉but for: ～亲眼所见，我是不会相信的。I wouldn't have believed it if I hadn't seen it with my own eyes.

【若干】ruògān **A** ▸**p. 927**〈数〉several: ～年后 a couple of years later **B**〈代〉how many/much: 关于市场管理的～问题 a few questions about market management ‖ 所剩还有～? How much is left?

【若何】ruòhé〈代〉〈书〉how: 近况～? 望告。How have you been recently? Please drop me a line.

【若即若离】ruòjí-ruòlí〈成〉keep sb. at arm's length

【若明若暗】ruòmíng-ruò'àn〈成〉**1**（不清晰）have a hazy notion about **2**（不明确）be ambiguous: 态度～ have an ambiguous attitude

【若是】ruòshì ▸**p. 350**〈连〉if: ～我，我就不去。If it were me, I wouldn't go.

【若无其事】ruòwúqíshì〈成〉as if nothing had happened: ～的样子 look as if nothing had happened

【若要人不知，除非己莫为】ruò yào rén bù zhī, chúfēi jǐ mò wéi〈俗〉what is done by night appears by day

【若隐若现】ruòyǐn-ruòxiàn〈成〉appear indistinctly

【若有所失】ruòyǒusuǒshī〈成〉feel distracted

【若有所思】ruòyǒusuǒsī〈成〉look pensive

偌 ruò〈代〉such

【偌大】ruòdà〈形〉so big: ～的宫殿 such a big palace ‖ ～年纪 so old

弱 ruò〈形〉**1**（不强）weak: 身体～ physically weak ‖ 光线～ weak light ‖ 电视信号很～。The television signal is quite weak. ▸～小 **2**（年幼）young: ▸老～ **3**（差）inferior: 我的能力比她～。I am not as capable as she is. ‖ 她的智力不比谁的～。She is intellectually inferior to no one. **4**（少于）a little less than: 五分之三～ a little less than three-fifths

【弱不禁风】ruòbùjīnfēng〈成〉be extremely frail

【弱点】ruòdiǎn〈名〉weakness: 利用对方的～ take advantage of the other side's weakness ‖ 致命～ Achilles' heel

【弱冠】ruòguàn〈名〉〈书〉the approach of adulthood [20 years of age]

【弱化】ruòhuà〈动〉weaken: ～乡土观念 weaken provincialism ‖ 强化宏观调控，～微观管理 strengthen macro-adjustment and control and weaken micro-management

【弱碱】ruòjiǎn〈名〉［化学］weak base

【弱柳扶风】ruòliǔfúfēng〈成〉like a willow branch trembling in the wind

【弱旅】ruòlǚ〈名〉〈书〉weak team

【弱能】ruònéng〈形〉mentally or physically handicapped

【弱肉强食】ruòròu-qiángshí〈成〉the law of the jungle

【弱势】ruòshì〈名〉**1**（指趋势）comparatively weak position: 改变～ turn around a losing streak **2**（指势力）the disadvantaged: 处于～ be disadvantaged ‖ ～群体 disadvantaged group

【弱视】ruòshì〈名〉lazy eye

【弱手】ruòshǒu〈名〉incompetent person

【弱酸】ruòsuān〈名〉［化学］weak acid

【弱听】ruòtīng〈形〉hard of hearing

【弱项】ruòxiàng〈名〉weak point

【弱小】ruòxiǎo〈形〉small and weak: ～民族 small and weak ethnic group

【弱音器】ruòyīnqì〈名〉［音乐］mute

【弱者】ruòzhě〈名〉the weak: 同情～ sympathize with the weak

【弱智】ruòzhì〈形〉have learning disabilities: ～儿童 child with learning disabilities

箬（篛） ruò

【箬帽】ruòmào〈名〉broad-rimmed bamboo hat with conical crown

【箬竹】ruòzhú〈名〉indocalamus [kind of bamboo with broad leaves]

Ss

sā

仨 sā ▸**p. 691**〈数〉〈方〉 three: ～馒头 three rolls of steamed bread ‖ 姐儿～ three sisters ‖ 他们～是一个单位的。 The three of them belong to the same work unit.

【仨瓜俩枣】 sāguā-liǎzǎo〈惯〉〈喻〉odds and ends

挲 sā ▸摩挲 māsā
▸suō

撒[1] sā 〈动〉 **1**（抛） cast;（松开） release: ～开绳子 let go of the rope ‖ ～(开)手 let go ▸～手, ～腿, ～网 **2**〈口〉（排泄）piss;（泄漏）leak: ▸～尿, ～气 **3**〈贬〉（放纵） let oneself go: ▸～娇, ～酒疯

撒[2] Sā = 撒拉族 Sālāzú
▸sǎ

【撒旦】 Sādàn〈名〉［基督教］ Satan [the Devil]

【撒刁】 sādiāo〈动〉 act in a slick and shameless way: 别～, 没人吃你那一套。 Don't be so underhand. No one's going to buy it.

【撒哈拉沙漠】 Sāhālā shāmò〈名〉 Sahara (Desert)

【撒哈拉以南地区】 Sāhālā yǐnándìqū〈名〉 Sub-Sahara

【撒欢儿】 sāhuānr〈动〉〈方〉 gambol: 小羊羔在草地上～。 The lambs are frisking about in the meadow. ‖ 一群孩子在海滩上～。 A group of children are frolicking around on the beach.

【撒谎】 sāhuǎng〈动〉〈口〉 lie: 存心/故意～ intentionally lie ‖ 当面～ lie through one's teeth ‖ 靠～骗得一份好工作 lie one's way into a good job

【撒娇】 sājiāo〈动〉 act in a spoilt way: 她经常在男朋友面前～。 She often acts spoilt in front of her boyfriend.

【撒娇卖俏】 sājiāo-màiqiào〈成〉 act spoilt and flirtatiously

【撒酒疯】 sā jiǔfēng〈动〉 be drunk and disorderly: 他一端起杯子就～。 He gets drunk and out of control as soon as his lips touch alcohol.

【撒拉族】 Sālāzú〈名〉 Salar ethnic group

【撒赖】 sālài〈动〉 kick up a fuss: 她又哭又闹, 躺在地上～。 She cried and swore. Then she lay on the ground and wouldn't get up.

【撒尿】 sāniào〈动〉〈口〉 pee

【撒泼】 sāpō〈动〉 throw a tantrum: 在公共场合这样～很丢脸。 It's disgraceful making such a scene in public.

【撒泼放刁】 sāpō-fàngdiāo〈成〉 act in an unreasonably perverse way: 她在～呢, 别理她。 She is making a scene. Just ignore her.

【撒气】 sāqì〈动〉 **1**（漏气） go flat: 车胎～了。 I've got a flat tyre. **2**（发泄怒气） vent one's anger: 你不高兴, 也别拿孩子～。 Don't take it out on the kid when you are unhappy.

【撒手】 sāshǒu〈动〉 **1**（放手） loosen one's hold (of/on): 你拿好, 我～了。 Hold it tight. I'm going to let go. ‖ 千万别～。 Whatever you do, don't let it go. **2** ▸**p. 772**〈婉〉（去世） die: ▸～人世

【撒手不干】 sāshǒu-bùgàn〈成〉 chuck in/up one's job

【撒手锏】 sāshǒujiǎn〈名〉 trump card: 使出～ play one's trump card

【撒手人世】 sāshǒu-rénshì ▸**p. 772**〈成〉 pass away

【撒腿】 sātuǐ〈动〉 take to one's heels: 歹徒看到警察, ～就跑。 The gangsters broke into a run at the sight of policemen.

【撒网】 sāwǎng〈动〉 cast a net: ～捕鱼 cast for fish ‖〈喻〉～捉犯人 trap a criminal

【撒丫子】 sā yāzi〈动〉〈方〉 make a dash (for): ～就跑 beat it double-quick

【撒鸭子】 sā yāzi = 撒丫子 sā yāzi

【撒野】 sāyě〈动〉 behave wildly: 对人～ be rude to sb. ‖ 当她听到要受惩处时便撒起野来。 She went crazy when she heard that she would be punished.

sǎ

洒[1] sǎ ▸洒家 sǎjiā

洒[2]（灑） sǎ〈动〉 **1**（喷洒） spray;（泼） sprinkle: ～农药 spray pesticide **2**（散落在地）（指固体） scatter;（指液体） spill;（指光线） spread: 为革命事业抛头颅、～热血 shed blood and sacrifice one's life for the revolutionary cause ‖ 别把汤～了。 Don't spill the soup. ‖ 阳光～满大地。 The land is bathed in sunshine. ‖〈喻〉 把欢乐～向人间 shed happiness on the human world ▸～泪, ～扫, ～水

【洒家】 sǎjiā〈名〉〈旧〉 [a term from a northern dialect used by a man to refer to himself]（主格） I;（宾格） me: 店小二, 给～拿酒来。 Waiter, bring me some wine.

【洒泪】 sǎlèi〈动〉 shed tears: 洒了几滴眼泪 shed a few tears ‖ 我们怀着沉重的心情和他～而别。 With heavy hearts, we took a tearful leave of him.

【洒落】 sǎluò〈动〉 **1**（指固体） trickle: 盐从盒子的小孔中～出来。 Salt trickled from a hole in the box. **2**（指液体） drip: 汗珠大滴大滴地从他的脸上～下来。 Sweat dripped in big drops from his face.

【洒扫】 sǎsǎo〈动〉 sweep

【洒水】 sǎshuǐ〈动〉 sprinkle water: 给花上洒些水 sprinkle some water on the flowers ‖ 自动～装置 automatic sprinkler

【洒水车】 sǎshuǐchē〈名〉 sprinkler

【洒水壶】 sǎshuǐhú〈名〉 sprinkling can

【洒脱】 sǎtuō〈形〉 natural: 举止～ have a natural manner ‖ 她很～。 She is a free spirit.

靸 sǎ〈动〉〈方〉 wear cloth shoes with the back part of the uppers trodden down: ～着拖鞋 be in one's slippers

撒 sǎ〈动〉 **1**（撒布）（指粉末、种子） scatter;（指沙、盐） sprinkle: ～种子 scatter seeds ‖ 把骨灰～入大海 scatter sb.'s ashes over the sea ‖ 往汤里～些胡椒粉 pepper the soup ‖ 飞机给庄稼～农药。 The plane dusted the crops with an insecticide. **2**（散落） spill: 盐～了一地。 Salt spilled all over the floor. ‖ 水～了出来。 The water has spilt out.
▸sā

【撒播】 sǎbō〈动〉 scatter: 在田里～种子 sow the field with seeds

【撒种】 sǎzhǒng〈动〉 spread seeds evenly in the field

sà

卅 sà ▸**p. 691**〈数〉〈书〉 thirty: ～载 thirty years ▸五～运动

飒（颯） sà

【飒然】 sàrán〈形〉〈书〉 whistling: 风～而至。 A whistling wind sprang up.

【飒飒】 sàsà〈拟〉 pitter-patter: ～雨声 the pitter-patter of rain ‖ 树叶在微风中～作声。 The leaves rustled in the breeze.

【飒爽】 sàshuǎng〈形〉〈书〉 valiant: ～英姿 take a courageous stance

脎 sà〈名〉［化学］ osazone

萨（薩） Sà

【萨尔瓦多】 Sà'ěrwǎduō〈名〉 El Salvador: ～人 Salvadorean

【萨福克郡】 Sàfúkèjùn〈名〉 Suffolk

【萨克拉门托】 Sàkèlāméntuō〈名〉 Sacramento

【萨克斯管】 sàkèsīguǎn ▸**p. 929**〈名〉［音乐］ saxophone: 吹～ play the saxophone ‖ ～吹奏者 saxophonist

【萨拉热窝】 Sàlārèwō〈名〉 Sarajevo

【萨里郡】 Sàlǐjùn〈名〉 Surrey

【萨满】 sàmǎn〈名〉 shaman: ～教 shamanism

【萨摩亚】 Sàmóyà〈名〉 Samoa: ～人 Samoan ‖ ～语 Samoan
【萨默塞特郡】Sàmòsàitèjùn〈名〉 Somerset
【萨那】Sànà〈名〉Sana'a
【萨其马】 sàqímǎ 〈名〉 *saqima* [a sweet pastry of Manchu origin]
【萨瑟兰郡】Sàsèlánjùn〈名〉 Sutherland

sāi

腮 sāi〈名〉 cheek: 两～红润 have rosy cheeks ▸～帮子, 尖嘴猴～
【腮帮子】sāibāngzi〈名〉〈口〉 cheek: 鼓起～ puff out one's cheeks
【腮红】sāihóng〈名〉 rouge, blush
【腮颊】sāijiá〈名〉 cheek
【腮托】sāituō〈名〉［音乐］ chin rest (of a violin or viola)
【腮腺】 sāixiàn 〈名〉［生理］ parotid (gland)
【腮腺炎】 sāixiànyán ▸p. 50 〈名〉 parotiditis: 流行型～ mumps

塞 sāi
A〈动〉 **1**（堵住） block: ～老鼠洞 stop up a mouse hole ‖ 管子～住了。The pipe is blocked. **2**（填入） cram: ～饱肚子 fill one's stomach ‖ 把衣服～进包里 stuff clothes into a bag ‖ 他嘴里～满了面包。His mouth was crammed full of bread.
B〈名〉 stopper: 暖瓶～ Thermos stopper ▸耳～, 活～
▸sài, sè
【塞车】sāichē〈动〉 be caught in a traffic jam: 塞了一个小时的车 be stuck in heavy traffic for an hour
【塞条】sāitiáo〈名〉［医学］ tent
【塞牙】sāiyá〈动〉 get stuck between the teeth
【塞子】sāizi〈名〉 cork: 拔掉～ uncork ‖ 给瓶子塞上～ cork a bottle

噻 sāi
【噻吩】sāifēn〈名〉［化学］ thiophene
【噻唑】sāizuò〈名〉［化学］ thiazole

鳃（鰓） sāi〈名〉 gill: 鱼～ fish gills

sài

塞 sài〈名〉 stronghold: ▸～翁失马，焉知非福, 边～, 要～
▸sāi, sè
【塞北】Sàiběi〈名〉 area north of the Great Wall: ～江南 lush southern-type fields north of the Great Wall
【塞尔扣克郡】Sài'ěrkòukèjùn〈名〉Selkirkshire
【塞尔维亚】Sài'ěrwéiyà〈名〉 Serbia: ～克罗地亚语 Serbo-Croatian ‖ ～人 Serb
【塞拉利昂】Sàilālì'áng〈名〉 Sierra Leone: ～人 Sierra Leonian
【塞纳河】Sàinàhé ▸p. 294〈名〉 Seine
【塞内加尔】Sàinèijiā'ěr〈名〉 Senegal: ～人 Senegalese
【塞内加尔共和国】Sàinèijiā'ěr Gònghéguó〈名〉 Republic of Senegal
【塞浦路斯】Sàipǔlùsī〈名〉 Cyprus: ～人 Cypriot
【塞舌尔】Sàishé'ěr〈名〉 Seychelles: ～人 Seychellois
【塞舌尔共和国】 Sàishé'ěr Gònghéguó〈名〉 Republic of Seychellois
【塞外】Sàiwài〈名〉 area beyond the Great Wall: ～风光 northern-frontier scenery
【塞翁失马，焉知非福】sàiwēng shī mǎ, yān zhī fēi fú〈成〉〈喻〉 a blessing in disguise

赛¹（賽） sài
A〈动〉 **1**（竞技） contest: ～篮球 have a basketball match ‖ ～出水平，～出风格 give of your best and do it in style ‖ 如果你愿意，我来和你～一～。 I will play with you, if you like. ▸～场, 比～, 竞～ **2**（比得上） be as good as: 这些小伙子干活一个～过一个。These young men are equally competent in their work.
B〈名〉 competition: 公开～ open competition ‖ 世界杯～ World Cup tournament ‖ 加时～ play-off match ‖ 足球～ football game ▸决～, 联～, 越野～

赛²（賽） sài〈动〉〈古〉 offer sacrifice to gods
【赛场】sàichǎng〈名〉 venue
【赛车】sàichē〈名〉［体育］ **1**（指比赛）（汽车） motor race;（自行车） cycle race: 以～为职业 race cars professionally **2**（指车）（汽车） racing car〈英〉; race car〈美〉;（自行车） racing bike
【赛程】sàichéng〈名〉［体育］ **1**（指距离） race distance **2**（指过程） order of play: ～过半。 The game is past the midway point.
【赛船】sàichuán〈名〉［体育］ **1**（指比赛） boat race **2**（指船） racing boat
【赛点】sàidiǎn〈名〉［体育］ match point
【赛风】sàifēng〈名〉 sportsmanship: 强调良好的～ underline the importance of good sportsmanship
【赛狗】sàigǒu〈名〉 dog race
【赛过】sàiguò〈动〉 surpass: 在技术/力量/速度上～对手 surpass one's rivals in skill/strength/speed ‖ 这姑娘干活～小伙子。This girl is more efficient at work than a young man.
【赛季】sàijì〈名〉［体育］ season: 新～下周开始。The new season begins next week.
【赛龙舟】sàilóngzhōu〈名〉 dragon boat race
【赛璐玢】sàilùfēn〈名〉［化学］cellophane
【赛璐珞】sàilùluò〈名〉［化学］ celluloid
【赛马】sàimǎ〈名〉 **1**（指比赛） horse race: 赌～ play the races ‖ 去看～ go to the races **2**（指马匹） racehorse
【赛马场】sàimǎchǎng〈名〉racetrack; racecourse〈英〉
【赛马大会】sàimǎ dàhuì〈名〉 race meeting (in Britain): ～的常客 racegoer ‖ 你打算参加下周的～吗? Are you going to race your horse next week?
【赛马总会】 sàimǎ zǒnghuì 〈名〉 jockey club
【赛跑】sàipǎo〈动〉 race: 参加～ run a race ‖ 马拉松～ Marathon ‖ 越野～ cross-country race ‖〈喻〉与时间～ race against time
【赛区】sàiqū〈名〉 zone: 上海～ Shanghai venue
【赛时】sàishí〈名〉 game time
【赛事】sàishì〈名〉 sporting event: 奥运会是世界上收视率最高的体育～。 The Olympic Games are the sports event with the highest audience rating in the world. ‖ 他们最近～繁忙。They've been very busy with competitions lately.
【赛艇】sàitǐng〈名〉［体育］ **1**（指比赛） rowing: 剑桥大学～队 Cambridge crew **2**（指艇） rowing boat〈英〉; racing shell〈美〉: 单人～ single ‖ 单人双桨～ scull
【赛艇俱乐部】sàitǐng jùlèbù〈名〉 yacht club
【赛制】sàizhì〈名〉 competition rules

sān

三 sān ▸p. 691〈数〉 **1**（表数目） three: ～把伞/头牛/匹马 three umbrellas/cattle/horses ‖ ～件套的衣服 three-piece suit ‖ ～室一厅 [of a flat] three bedrooms and one living room ‖ 增加到～倍 increase threefold ‖ ～～得九。 Three times three is nine. ‖ 将本表格填写一式～份。 Fill in the form in triplicate. ‖ 他敲了～次。 He knocked three times. ▸～角形, ～棱镜, 第～者 **2**（表示多数） several: ▸～令五申, ～心二意 **3**（表示少数） a few: ▸～～两两, ～言两语
【三八国际劳动妇女节】 Sān-Bā Guójì Láodòng Fùnǚjié〈名〉 International Working Women's Day [March 8]
【三八红旗手】sān-bā hóngqíshǒu〈名〉 'March 8th' red banner winner: 荣获～称号 be awarded the title of March 8th Red-Banner Pace-setter
【三八式】sānbāshì〈名〉 **1**（指枪） 38-rifle [a Japanese rifle made in the 38th year of Showa (昭和)]: 两支～ two 38-rifles **2**（指人） thirty-eighter [of a person who joined the revolution around 1938]
【三八线】sānbāxiàn〈名〉38th parallel [38° north latitude on the Korean Peninsula, which serves as the military demarcation line between north and south Korea]
【三百六十行】sānbǎi liùshí háng〈成〉 all trades and professions: ～，行行出状元 each and every profession produces its top experts
【三班倒】sānbāndǎo〈动〉 work in three shifts: 工人实行～。 Workers work in three shifts.
【三包】sānbāo〈名〉 **1**（指保修） triple guarantee service [ie guarantee for repair, refund and change of goods sold to customers]: 厂家应对自己售出的产品实行～。 Producers should provide purchasers with three levels of guarantee. **2**（指卫生） three-fold responsibility (for keeping the area in front of one's door/shop sanitary and green and free of lawlessness)
【三胞胎】sānbāotāi〈名〉 triplets
【三宝】 sānbǎo 〈名〉 **1**（指物产） The Three Treasures: 东北有～：人参、貂皮、乌拉草。 There are three treasures in north-east China: ginseng, marten and sedge. **2**（指宗教） Triratna [ie the Buddha, the dharma, and the sangha in Buddhism; the Tao, scriptures and masters in Taoism]
【三北地区】 Sānběi dìqū 〈名〉 northern China
【三边】sānbiān〈名〉 trilaterality: ～会谈 trilateral talks ‖ ～协定 trilateral agreement
【三不管】sānbùguǎn〈名〉（指地区） area without jurisdiction;（指事情） event without jurisdiction: 你这地方是个～地区。 Yours is an unsupervised area.
【三不知】 sānbùzhī 〈动〉 be completely ignorant: 一问～ unable to give any answer to the question

S

【三步并做两步】sān bù bìng zuò liǎng bù〈惯〉go in a hurry

【三步一岗，五步一哨】sān bù yī gǎng, wǔ bù yī shào〈成〉〈喻〉be heavily guarded

【三部曲】sānbùqǔ〈名〉trilogy: ～的第一/二/三部 first/second/third part of a trilogy ‖ 他以描写工人阶级生活的～而闻名。He is best known for his trilogy on working-class life.

【三彩】sāncǎi〈名〉three-colour glazed pottery [esp of the Tang Dynasty, 618-907]: ▶唐～

【三叉戟】sānchājǐ〈名〉trident: ～导弹核潜艇 Trident nuclear missile submarine ‖ ～飞机 Trident

【三叉神经】sānchā shénjīng〈名〉［解剖］trigeminal nerve: ～痛 trigeminal neuralgia

【三岔路口】sānchà lùkǒu〈名〉fork (in the road)

【三产】sānchǎn〈简称〉= 第三产业

【三长两短】sāncháng-liǎngduǎn〈成〉mishap: 万一他有个～ if anything untoward should happen to him

【三朝元老】sāncháoyuánlǎo〈成〉**1**〈本〉minister serving three successive emperors **2**〈喻〉the most senior employee

【三重】sānchóng〈形〉triple: ～压迫 threefold oppression ‖ 他以副校长、英语系系主任和捐赠人的～身份出席。He attended in his capacity as vice-president, dean of the English department and donor.

【三重唱】sānchóngchàng〈名〉trio: 这首歌排成～。This song is arranged for singing in three voices.

【三重奏】sānchóngzòu〈名〉trio

【三春】sānchūn〈名〉〈书〉the three months of spring

【三从四德】sāncóng-sìdé〈成〉three obediences and four virtues for a woman according to Confucian ethics [ie obedience to one's father before marriage, to one's husband after marriage, and to one's son after one's husband's death; morality, proper speech, modest manner, and diligent work]

【三寸不烂之舌】sāncùn bù làn zhī shé〈成〉〈喻〉glib tongue: 凭着～ with the help of some smooth talk

【三寸金莲】sāncùn jīnlián〈名〉〈旧〉three-*cun* lily feet [formerly laudatory term used by men to describe women's bound feet]

【三大差别】sān dà chābié〈名〉three major distinctions [between town and country, industry and agriculture, physical and mental labour]

【三大纪律，八项注意】sān dà jìlǜ, bā xiàng zhùyì〈名〉[of the Chinese People's Liberation Army] Three Main Rules of Discipline and Eight Points for Attention [The Three Main Rules of Discipline are: 1. Obey orders in all your actions. 2. Don't take a single needle or piece of thread from the masses. 3. Turn in everything captured. The Eight Points for Attention are: 1. Speak politely. 2. Pay fairly for what you buy. 3. Return everything you borrow. 4. Pay for anything you damage. 5. Don't hit or swear at people. 6. Don't damage crops. 7. Don't take liberties with women. 8. Don't ill-treat captives.]

【三大球】sāndàqiú〈名〉football, basketball and volleyball

【三大战役】sān dà zhànyì〈名〉three major campaigns [the three biggest campaigns launched in 1948 and 1949 by the People's Liberation Army against KMT troops]: 反映～的小说 novel on the three major campaigns

【三等兵】sānděngbīng〈名〉（美国陆军）basic private;（美国海军）apprentice seaman;（美国空军）airman third class

【三点式】sāndiǎnshì〈名〉bikini

【三叠纪】Sāndiéjì〈名〉［地质］Triassic Period

【三叠系】Sāndiéxì〈名〉［地质］Triassic System

【三冬】sāndōng〈名〉**1**（三年）three years **2**（泛指冬天）winter

【三段论】sānduànlùn〈名〉［逻辑］syllogism

【三番两次】sānfān-liǎngcì = 三番五次 sānfān-wǔcì

【三番五次】sānfān-wǔcì〈成〉over and over again: ～地强调 emphasize repeatedly ‖ 他～地看这部影片。He saw the film over and over again.

【三废】sānfèi〈名〉three wastes in industrial production [ie waste gas, water, and industrial residue]: 回收～ recycle the three wastes

【三分】sānfēn **A**〈副〉somewhat: 怕他～ be a little afraid of him ‖ 让他～ let him have his way ▶入木～ **B**〈名〉（指考试）a mark of C **C**〈动〉be divided into three parts: ～天下 split the country into three

【三分法】sānfēnfǎ〈名〉trichotomy

【三分球】sānfēnqiú〈名〉[of basketball] three pointer: 投中～ make a three pointer

【三分像人，七分像鬼】sānfēn xiàng rén, qīfēn xiàng guǐ〈俗〉look more like a ghost than a human being

【三伏】sānfú〈名〉**1**（初伏、中伏、末伏合称）three *fu* [three hottest ten-day periods of the hot season] **2**（末伏）third *fu* [third ten-day period of the hot season]

【三副】sānfù〈名〉［航海］third mate

【三纲五常】sāngāng-wǔcháng〈成〉three cardinal guides and five constant virtues as specified in the Confucian ethical code [ie ruler guides subject, father guides son, and husband guides wife; benevolence, righteousness, propriety, wisdom and fidelity]

【三个代表】sānge dàibiǎo〈名〉Three Represents [The guiding ideology of the Communist Party of China adopted in 2002 at the 16th Party Congress, upholding continued economic and cultural development and the fundamental interests of the Chinese people.]

【三个臭皮匠，顶个诸葛亮】sānge chòupíjiàng, dǐnggè Zhūgě Liàng〈俗〉〈喻〉the wisdom of the masses exceeds that of the wisest individual

【三个和尚没水吃】sānge héshang méi shuǐ chī〈俗〉〈喻〉two's company, three's a crowd

【三个世界理论】sāngè shìjiè lǐlùn〈名〉theory of the three worlds [a theory put forward by Mao Zedong which divides the world into three categories: the first world, the second world and the third world]

【三更】sāngēng〈名〉midnight: 正值～时刻。It was just midnight.

【三更半夜】sāngēng-bànyè = 半夜三更 bànyè-sāngēng

【三宫六院】sāngōng-liùyuàn〈成〉**1**〈本〉three palaces and six chambers **2**〈喻〉imperial harem

【三姑六婆】sāngū-liùpó〈成〉**1**〈本〉three kinds of nuns and six kinds of old women [ie nuns (尼姑), Taoist nuns (道姑), nun fortune-tellers (卦姑); women traffickers (牙婆), women matchmakers (媒婆), witches (师婆), procuresses (虔婆), women who are believed to have magic powers and the ability to cure people of diseases (药婆) and midwives (稳婆)] **2**〈喻〉women of dubious character making a living by dishonest means

【三股势力】sāngǔ shìlì〈名〉the 'Three Evil Forces' (of terrorism, separatism and extremism): 中俄共同打击～。China and Russia are mounting a joint attack on the 'Three Evil Forces'.

【三顾茅庐】sāngù-máolú〈成〉〈喻〉repeatedly request sb. to take up a post: ～，老先生才答应做我们的学术顾问。It was only after our repeated requests that the old scholar agreed to be our academic counsellor.

【三光】sānguāng〈名〉〈书〉[three luminaries] the sun, the moon, and the stars

【三光政策】sānguāng zhèngcè〈名〉policy of 'burn all, kill all, loot all' [pursued by the Japanese invaders in China]

【三跪九叩】sānguì-jiǔkòu〈成〉three times kneeling and nine times kowtowing [a sign of respect that was made to the emperor in old times]

【三国】Sānguó〈名〉Three Kingdoms [ie Wei (魏), Shu (蜀), and Wu (吴)]: 《～演义》*The Romance of the Three Kingdoms* ‖ 《～志》*History of the Three Kingdoms*

> 《三国演义》
>
> One of the four great classical works of Chinese literature that include *A Dream of the Red Mansions* (▶《红楼梦》), *Journey to the West* (▶《西游记》) and *The Water Margin* (▶《水浒传》). The author is generally believed to be Luo Guanzhong (罗贯中), who lived at the end of the Yuan Dynasty and the beginning of the Ming Dynasty. The novel describes the period from 169 to 280 AD and the turbulent political, foreign and military affairs of the Wei, Shu and Wu kingdoms.

【三过其门而不入】sān guò qí mén ér bù rù〈成〉be too busy to go home even when you are right on the doorsteps

【三好学生】sānhǎo xuéshēng〈名〉merit student [an honourable title for outstanding students who are good in study, morality, and health]: 被评为～ be selected as a merit student

【三合板】sānhébǎn〈名〉a three-ply board: 一张～ sheet of three-ply board

【三合土】sānhétǔ〈名〉［建筑］lime-sand-clay mixture

【三合一】sānhéyī〈形〉three-in-one: ～洗发精 three-in-one shampoo

【三花脸】sānhuāliǎn〈名〉clown [comic role in Chinese opera]

【三皇五帝】Sānhuáng-Wǔdì〈名〉**1**〈本〉Three Sovereigns and Five Emperors [Fuxi (伏羲/天皇), Suiren (燧人/地皇) and Shennong (神农/人皇); Huangdi (黄帝), Zhuanxu (颛顼), Di Ku (帝喾), Tang Yao (唐尧), and Yu Shun (虞舜)] **2**〈喻〉legendary rulers of China in ancient times

【三级片】sānjípiàn〈名〉X-rated film [HK film classification; for viewers 18 and above]

【三级跳远】sānjí tiàoyuǎn〈名〉triple jump

【三极管】sānjíguǎn〈名〉radio triode: 晶体～ transistor

【三家村】sānjiācūn〈名〉〈喻〉small remote hamlet

【三夹板】sānjiábǎn = 三合板 sānhébǎn

【三价】sānjià〈名〉［化学］trivalence: ～元素 triad

【三驾马车】sānjià mǎchē〈名〉**1**〈本〉carriage drawn by three horses **2**〈喻〉three main driving forces

S

【三尖瓣】sānjiānbàn〈名〉［生理］ tricuspid (valve)

【三缄其口】sānjiān-qíkǒu〈成〉 refuse to speak, keeping one's mouth shut more than once

【三件套】sānjiàntào〈名〉 three-piece suit

【三键】sānjiàn〈名〉［化学］ triple bond

【三焦】sānjiāo〈名〉［中医］ three visceral cavities housing the internal organs

【三角】sānjiǎo〈名〉 1［数学］ trigonometry: ～方程 trigonometric equation ‖ ～函数 trigonometric function 2（三角形物） triangle: ～插头 three-pin plug ‖ ～刀 V-shaped gouge ▸～洲

【三角板】sānjiǎobǎn〈名〉 set square

【三角测量】sānjiǎo cèliáng〈名〉 triangulation

【三角锉】sānjiǎocuò〈名〉 triangle file

【三角帆】sānjiǎofān〈名〉［航海］ lateen

【三角关系】sānjiǎo guānxi〈名〉 triangular relationship: 一个女孩与两名男子的～ triangular relationship between a girl and two men

【三角肌】 sānjiǎojī〈名〉［生理］ deltoid muscle

【三角架】sānjiǎojià〈名〉 triangular frame

【三角巾】sānjiǎojīn〈名〉 sling

【三角裤】sānjiǎokù〈名〉（女用） panties; knickers〈英〉;（通用） briefs

【三角恋爱】sānjiǎo liàn'ài〈名〉 love triangle

【三角旗】sānjiǎoqí〈名〉 pennant

【三角兽】sānjiǎoshòu〈名〉 tricorne

【三角铁】sānjiǎotiě〈名〉 1 ▸p. 929［音乐］ triangle: 演奏～ play the triangle 2［建筑］ angle iron

【三角形】sānjiǎoxíng〈名〉 triangle: 不等边/等边/等腰～ scalene/equilateral/isosceles triangle ‖ 直角～ right-angled triangle

【三角学】 sānjiǎoxué〈名〉［数学］ trigonometry

【三角债】sānjiǎozhài〈名〉 debt chain: 清理～ clear the debt chain

【三角洲】sānjiǎozhōu〈名〉 delta: ～地区 deltaic area ‖ 长江～ Yangtze River Delta

【三脚架】sānjiǎojià〈名〉 tripod: 照相机～ camera tripod

【三教九流】sānjiào-jiǔliú〈成〉 1〈本〉 three religions and nine schools of thought [ie Confucianism (儒教), Taoism (道教) and Buddhism (佛教); the Confucians (儒家), the Taoists (道家), the *Yin-Yang* (阴阳家), the Legalists (法家), the Logicians (名家), the Mohists (墨家), the Political Strategists (纵横家), the Eclectics (杂家) and the Agriculturists (农家)] 2〈贬〉（指流派） various religious sects and academic schools 3〈贬〉（指人） people of various trades: 他和～的人都有来往。 He has dealings with people of every sort.

【三街六巷】sānjiē-liùxiàng〈成〉〈喻〉 all over the city

【三节】sānjié〈名〉 three festivals [ie the Dragon Boat Festival, the Mid-Autumn Festival and the Spring Festival — three traditional festivals in China]

【三节棍】 sānjiégùn〈名〉［武术］ three-sectioned cudgel

【三结合】sānjiéhé〈名〉 three-in-one combination: 老中青～的领导班子 leading body composed of the old, the middle-aged and the young

【三进制】sānjìnzhì〈名〉［数学］ ternary: ～运算 ternary arithmetic

【三九】sānjiǔ〈名〉 mid-winter: ～天气 bitterly cold weather ‖ 夏练三伏，冬练～ practice in the hardest condition yields the best results

【三局两胜】sānjúliǎngshèng［体育］ best of three

【三句半】 sānjùbàn〈名〉［曲艺］ three-sentence-and-a-half ballad

【三句话不离本行】sān jù huà bù lí běnháng〈俗〉 hardly be able to open one's mouth without talking shop: 那位商人～，句句都是生意经。 That businessman never opens his mouth without talking shop.

【三聚氰胺】sānjùqíng'àn〈名〉［化学］ Melamine

【三军】sānjūn〈名〉 1（指军种） three services [ie ground force, air force and navy] 2〈旧〉（泛指军队） military forces: 犒赏～ reward the army

【三军仪仗队】sānjūn yízhàngduì〈名〉 tri-service guard of honour

【三K党】Sānkèidǎng〈名〉 Ku Klux Klan (KKK)

【三棱尺】sānléngchǐ〈名〉 triangular scale

【三棱镜】sānléngjìng〈名〉［物理］ triangular prism

【三棱锥】sānléngzhuī〈名〉 triangular pyramid

【三连音符】 sānlián yīnfú〈名〉［音乐］ triplet

【三联单】sānliándān〈名〉 triplicate form

【三令五申】sānlìng-wǔshēn〈成〉 warn and order repeatedly: 政府～，要杜绝党内一切腐败现象。 The government has repeatedly warned against all kinds of corruptions within the party.

【三流】 sānliú〈形〉 third-rate: ～演员 third-rate actor

【三六九等】 sān-liù-jiǔděng〈成〉 various grades and ranks: 人不能分为～，大家都是平等的。 Human beings cannot be divided into different categories. They are all equal.

【三轮车】sānlúnchē〈名〉 tricycle: 骑～的人 tricyclist ‖ 手摇～ hand tricycle [used by disabled people]

【三轮儿】sānlúnr〈口〉= 三轮车 sānlúnchē

【三昧】sānmèi〈名〉 1［佛教］ Samadhi 2（精髓） knack: 深得其中～ master the secrets of an art

【三门峡】Sānménxiá〈名〉 Sanmen Gorge [a gorge in the middle reaches of the Yellow River, located between Henan (河南) and Shanxi (山西) provinces]

【三秒区】sānmiǎoqū〈名〉 [of basketball] foul lane

【三秒违例】sānmiǎo wéilì〈名〉 [of basketball] 3-second-rule violation

【三民主义】sānmínzhǔyì〈名〉 Three Principles of the People

> **三民主义**
>
> Political philosophy developed by Sun Yat-sen (孙中山). The three principles are 'Nationalism' (民族主义), 'Democracy' (民权主义) and 'the People's Livelihood' (民生主义). 'Nationalism' involved freedom and independence for the Chinese people; 'Democracy' the replacing of the feudal political system with a constitutional government, and 'the People's Livelihood' the equal right to land and economic and social development.

【三明治】sānmíngzhì〈名〉 sandwich: 吃/做～ eat/make sandwiches ‖ 火腿/乳酪/果酱～ ham/cheese/jam sandwich

【三目显微镜】 sānmù xiǎnwēijìng〈名〉 trinocular microscope

【三年五载】sānnián-wǔzǎi〈成〉〈喻〉 in a few years

【三农】sānnóng〈名〉 agriculture, rural areas and farmers: ～问题 issues concerning agriculture and farmers

【三陪】sānpéi〈动〉 provide intimate escort services: ～女 call girl

【三七】sānqī〈名〉［中药］ pseudo-ginseng

【三七开】sān-qīkāi〈名〉 a ratio of seventy to thirty: 赢利～ divide the profits seventy-thirty

【三栖明星】sānqī míngxīng〈名〉 star of screen, video and music

【三亲六故】 sānqīn-liùgù〈成〉 relatives, friends and acquaintances

【三秋】 sānqiū〈名〉 1［农业］ three autumn jobs (of harvesting, ploughing and sowing): 日夜奋战抢～ work around the clock to harvest, plough and sow 2〈书〉（秋季第三个月） third month of autumn [ie the ninth month in the lunar calendar] 3（秋季三个月） three autumn months 4（三年） three years: ▸一日～

【三权分立】sānquán fēnlì〈名〉 division of legislative, executive and judicial powers

【三拳两脚】sānquán-liǎngjiǎo〈成〉 cuffs and kicks: 他～就把小偷打倒在地。 He knocked the thief to the ground with a few cuffs and kicks.

【三人成虎】sānrén-chénghǔ〈成〉〈喻〉 repeated false reports sound convincing

【三人行，必有我师】sān rén xíng, bì yǒu wǒ shī〈成〉 if there are three men walking together, one of them must be qualified to be my teacher

【三三两两】 sānsān-liǎngliǎng〈成〉 in twos and threes: 他们～地出去了。 They went out in twos and threes. ‖ ～的人在酒店外面争论着。 People are arguing outside the pub in little groups.

【三色版】sānsèbǎn〈名〉［印刷］ three-colour block: ～印刷 three-colour printing

【三色堇】sānsèjǐn〈名〉［植物］ pansy

【三生】sānshēng〈名〉［佛教］ the three stages of life [one's present, previous and future life]

【三生有幸】 sānshēng-yǒuxìng〈成〉 be lucky enough: 能与这些成功人士交往，他感到～。 He considered himself most fortunate to have been able to rub shoulders with such successful people.

【三牲】sānshēng〈名〉〈旧〉 three domestic animals [ie cattle, sheep and pigs, formerly used as sacrificial offerings]

【三十而立】sānshí-érlì〈成〉 a man should be independent at the age of thirty

【三十二开】sānshí'èrkāi〈名〉［印刷］ thirty-two mo: ～纸 32 mo paper

【三十六计，走为上计】sānshíliù jì, zǒu wéi shàngjì〈成〉〈喻〉 the best thing to do now is to quit

【三十年河东，三十年河西】sānshí nián hé dōng, sānshí nián hé xī〈俗〉〈喻〉 life is full of ups and downs

【三熟制】sānshúzhì〈名〉［农业］ triple-cropping system

【三思】sānsī〈动〉 think carefully: 这事很重要，你可得～啊! This is very important. You must think it over.

【三思而后行】sānsī'érhòuxíng = 三思而行 sānsī'érxíng

【三思而行】sānsī'érxíng〈成〉〈喻〉 look before you leap

【三天打鱼，两天晒网】sān tiān dǎ yú, liǎng tiān shài wǎng〈成〉〈喻〉 flit in and out: 她～，怎么能把学习搞好? She's always flitting in and out of things. How on earth is she supposed to succeed in her studies?

【三天两头】sāntiān-liǎngtóu〈成〉 almost every day: ～光顾酒吧 frequent bars

【三通】sāntōng〈名〉 1［机械］ three-way: ～阀门/管道/龙头 three-way valve/pipe/tap 2（特指大陆与台湾之间） the three direct

S

links of trade, travel and post across the Taiwan Straits

> 三通
>
> Postal, trade and transportation links between the Chinese mainland and Taiwan, proposed in 1979 following the 30-year military stand-off between the two sides. Limited postal and trade links (the 'three small links') were introduced in 2001 between Kinmen and Matsu islands and the Fujian coast. Limited cross-straits direct flights were introduced in 2006. In 2008 an agreement was signed between the mainland and Taiwan on daily direct flights and cargo routes.

【三头六臂】sāntóu-liùbì〈成〉〈喻〉superhuman powers: 这件事要不是集体的力量，纵有～，也难以办成。 If there hadn't been a collective effort, even superhuman powers wouldn't have seen us through this one.

【三推六问】sāntuī-liùwèn〈成〉criminal interrogations

【三围】sānwéi〈名〉vital statistics [ie chest, waist and seat/hip measurements of a woman]

【三维】sānwéi〈形〉three-dimensional (3-D): ～动画片 three-dimensional animation ‖ ～空间 three-dimensional space

【三位数】sānwèishù ▸**p. 691**〈名〉three digits

【三位一体】sānwèi-yītǐ〈名〉**1**［基督教］Trinity **2**〈喻〉（三合一） trinity: 旅游开发、生态建设、环境保护，这是～的方针。 The three ways forward are to open up tourism, improve the ecology, and environment protection.

【三无产品】sānwú chǎnpǐn〈名〉unmarked product

【三五成群】sānwǔ-chéngqún〈成〉in threes and fours: 人们～地聊天。 People stood around in small groups, chatting.

【三峡】Sānxiá〈名〉Three Gorges: ～大坝 Three Gorges Dam ‖ ～工程 Three Gorges Project

【三下五除二】sān xià wǔ chú èr〈惯〉deft: 警察～就制伏了劫匪。 The policeman subdued the robber with a few swift cuffs and kicks. ‖ 她～就把零乱的房子收拾得干净整齐。 She tidied and cleaned the messy room in no time at all.

【三下乡】sānxiàxiāng〈动〉bring culture, science and technology, and health care to the countryside

【三夏】sānxià〈名〉**1**［农业］three summer jobs (of harvesting, planting and field management): 支援～ help peasants to harvest, plant, and manage the fields **2**〈书〉（夏季三个月） three summer months [April, May and June in the lunar calendar] **3**（夏季第三个月） the last month of summer

【三鲜】sānxiān〈名〉three delicacies [a combination of delicacies such as sea slug, squid, shrimp, and chicken, used as ingredients of a dish]: 炒～ stir-fried three delicacies

【三弦】sānxián〈名〉［曲艺］*sanxian* [three-stringed plucked instrument]

【三项全能】sānxiàng quánnéng〈名〉［体育］triathlon

【三相】sānxiàng〈名〉［电气］three-phase: ～电炉 three-phase electric furnace

【三硝基甲苯】sānxiāojījiǎběn〈名〉［化学］trinitrotoluene (TNT)

【三心二意】sānxīn-èryì〈成〉flit from one thing to another: 别再～，就这样去办吧。 Stop dilly-dallying. Go ahead and do it. ‖ 他做事总是～。 He can never make up his mind what to do.

【三星】sānxīng〈名〉**1**（指猎户座）Orion's belt **2**（福、禄、寿） Gods of happiness, wealth and longevity in Chinese folklore

【三言两语】sānyán-liǎngyǔ〈成〉in one or two words: 他无法用～表达自己的感情。 He couldn't put his feelings into a few words.

【三叶草】sānyècǎo〈名〉clover

【三叶虫】sānyèchóng〈名〉［生物］trilobite

【三元】sānyuán〈名〉[under the former imperial examination system] academic titles conferred on the three candidates who came out first at examinations held at three levels [*Jieyuan* (解元) for the winner at the provincial level, *Huiyuan* (会元) for the winner at the national level, and *Zhuangyuan* (状元) for the winner at the Imperial Palace level]: ▸连中～

【三元及第】sānyuán-jídì〈成〉come out first at all the three levels of the imperial examinations held at the provincial capital, national capital and the palace

【三月】sānyuè ▸**p. 928**〈名〉**1**（阳历） March: ～五日举行 be held on March 5th **2**（阴历） third month of the lunar year

【三灾八难】sānzāi-bānàn〈成〉disaster upon disaster

【三藏】Sānzàng〈名〉［佛教］Tripitaka [the three categories of the Buddhist classics: doctrinal records, writings on discipline, and writings on metaphysics]

【三只手】sānzhīshǒu〈名〉〈方〉pickpocket

【三资企业】sānzī qǐyè〈名〉three kinds of foreign-invested enterprises [ie Sino-foreign joint ventures, Sino-foreign cooperative enterprises and exclusively foreign-funded enterprises]

【三字经】Sānzìjīng〈名〉*Three Characters Classic*

> 《三字经》
>
> Basic reader for children dating from the 13th century (Song Dynasty), with supplementary material added in the Ming and Qing dynasties. Written in triplets, and designed to be recited aloud, it taught children basic Confucian morality, history, geography, astronomy, and the value of study. It continues to circulate in various parts of the Chinese-speaking world.

【三足鼎立】sānzú-dǐnglì〈成〉〈喻〉triangular balance of power

【三座大山】sānzuòdàshān〈名〉three big mountains [said to have weighed down the Chinese people before 1949 — imperialism, feudalism and bureaucrat-capitalism]

叁 sān

▸**p. 691**〈名〉three [used for the numeral 三 on cheques, etc. to avoid alterations or mistakes]

sǎn

伞（傘） sǎn

〈名〉**1**（遮挡物） umbrella: 一把～ an umbrella ‖ 撑～ open an umbrella ‖ 带把～，以防下雨。 Take an umbrella with you in case it rains. ▸保护～，雨～，折叠～ **2**（伞状物） umbrella-shaped thing: ▸降落～，跳～

【伞包】sǎnbāo〈名〉［军事］pack

【伞兵】sǎnbīng〈名〉paratrooper

【伞兵部队】sǎnbīng bùduì〈名〉paratroops

【伞兵服】sǎnbīngfú〈名〉parasuit

【伞骨】sǎngǔ〈名〉rib

【伞架】sǎnjià〈名〉umbrella stand

【伞降】sǎnjiàng〈名〉parachuting: ～训练任务 training programme in parachuting

【伞面儿】sǎnmiànr〈名〉canopy

【伞投】sǎntóu〈动〉parachute: ～炸弹 parachute bomb ‖ 救援物资已～到震区。 Relief supplies have been parachuted into the earthquake zone.

【伞形花序】sǎnxíng huāxù〈名〉［植物］umbel

散 sǎn

A〈形〉**1**（不紧密） loose;（无拘束） free: ▸～漫，松～，一盘～沙 **2**（不集中） scattered: 住/坐得很～ live/sit far apart from one another ▸～居，～页，～装

B〈名〉［中药］medicinal powder: 中药有汤、～、丸等不同剂型。 Traditional Chinese medicine may be in liquid, powder or pill form. ▸～剂

C〈动〉（松开） become loose;（解体） fall apart: 背包～了。 The blanket roll has come loose. ‖ 那本旧书～了。 The old book fell apart.

▸sàn

【散板】sǎnbǎn〈名〉［戏曲］free measure

【散兵】sǎnbīng〈名〉［军事］skirmisher

【散兵游勇】sǎnbīng-yóuyǒng〈成〉**1**〈本〉stragglers and disbanded soldiers **2**〈喻〉people who belong to no organization and act on their own

【散打】sǎndǎ〈名〉［体育］*sanda* [free-style grappling or confrontational boxing]

【散工】sǎngōng = 零工 línggōng ▸sàngōng

【散光】sǎnguāng〈名〉astigmatism: ～远视 hypermetropic astigmatism

【散光灯】sǎnguāngdēng〈名〉floodlight

【散户】sǎnhù〈名〉［经济］private investor: 股市～ individual investor in the stock market

【散货】sǎnhuò〈名〉bulk cargo

【散记】sǎnjì〈名〉random notes: 旅行～ travel notes

【散剂】sǎnjì〈名〉［中医］powder medicine

【散架】sǎnjià〈动〉**1**（散开） fall apart: 马车被撞得散了架。 The carriage was smashed to pieces. ‖ 她浑身酸疼，骨头像散了架似的。 Aching all over, she felt as if all her limbs were out of joint. **2**（解体） disband: 这个小组要不是你们撑着，早就～了。 This group would have broken up long ago had it not been for your support.

【散件】sǎnjiàn〈名〉part

【散居】sǎnjū〈动〉live scattered: 一些学生～在附近的村子里。 Some students live here and there in the nearby villages.

【散客】sǎnkè〈名〉individual tourist

【散乱】sǎnluàn〈形〉straggly: ～的头发 straggly hair ‖ 有许多～的东西要清理。 There's a lot of mess to clear up.

【散漫】sǎnmàn〈形〉**1**（不守纪律） undisciplined **2**（随便） slack: ～的行为 lax behaviour ‖ 他越来越～，出了些荒谬的错误。 He's been getting slack and making silly mistakes. **3**（不集中） scattered: 这篇文章写得～芜杂。 This article is loosely organized and lacking in order.

【散曲】sǎnqǔ〈名〉*sanqu*, non-dramatic song [a type of song/tune popular in the Yuan, Ming and Qing dynasties]

【散射】sǎnshè〈动〉［物理］scatter

【散体】sǎntǐ〈名〉simple, direct prose style

【散文】sǎnwén〈名〉**1**（指传统文体） literary writings that do not observe the rules

S

of rhyming [common in ancient China] 2 (指现代文体) prose: 用～体写作 write in prose ‖ 她的～写得很优美。 She writes beautiful prose.
【散文诗】sǎnwénshī〈名〉 prose poem
【散养户】sǎnyǎnghù〈名〉backyard farmer: 从～手中收购牛奶/家禽 purchase milk/poultry from backyard producers
【散页】sǎnyè〈名〉 loose page
【散装】sǎnzhuāng〈形〉 in bulk: ～饼干/咖啡 loose biscuits/coffee ‖ ～水泥 loose cement
【散座】sǎnzuò〈名〉 1 〈旧〉(指在剧场) orchestra seat 2 (指在饭店) seats for individual customers

糁（糝）sǎn〈名〉〈方〉 grains of cooked rice
▸shēn

馓（饊）sǎn
【馓子】sǎnzi〈名〉〈方〉 deep-fried dough twist

sàn

散 sàn〈动〉 1 (分开) break up: ～会。 The meeting is over. ▸～伙, 解～ 2 (消散) disperse: 乌云已经～去。 The dark clouds have already scattered. ▸烟消云～ 3 (分发) disseminate: ～传单 give out leaflets ▸～布, ～发 4 (排遣) get rid of: ▸～闷, ～心
▸sǎn
【散播】sànbō〈动〉［农业］ sow: ～种子 sow seeds
【散布】sànbù〈动〉 spread: ～假消息 put out false information ‖ ～流言蜚语 spread gossip ‖ 羊群～在山坡上吃草。 A flock of sheep are grazing here and there on the hillside. ‖ 犹太人～在世界各地。 Jewish people can be found all over the world.
【散步】sànbù〈动〉 take a stroll: 去～ go for a walk ‖ 沿海岸有几处宜人的～场所。 There are several pleasant walks along the coast.
【散场】sànchǎng〈动〉 be over: 电影～了。 The film is over. ‖ 球赛要到九点才能～。 The match wouldn't be over until nine.
【散发】sànfā〈动〉(分发) distribute; (发出) give out: ～救济品/文件 distribute relief materials/papers ‖ 花儿～着阵阵清香。 The flowers have a beautiful, strong smell.
【散工】sàngōng = 放工 fànggōng
▸sǎngōng
【散会】sànhuì〈动〉 [of a meeting] be over: 快～了。 The meeting is ending. ‖ 现在～。 The meeting is over.
【散伙】sànhuǒ〈动〉 1 (解体) disband: 公司～了。 The company is dissolved. ‖ 他和他的代理人～了。 He has parted company with his agent. 2 (分裂) break up: 他们俩口子～已经好几年了。 They have been divorced for several years. ‖ 夫妻俩经常吵架，早晚要～。 The couple are always fighting. They will break up sooner or later.
【散开】sànkāi〈动〉 disperse: 向两边～给车队让路 disperse to make way for the motorcade ‖ 士兵迅速～，消失在树林中。 The soldiers rapidly dispersed and vanished into the wood.
【散落】sànluò〈动〉 1 (指落下) fall here and there: 捡起～在地上的东西 pick up the things scattering on the ground ‖ 把～在地上的叶子耙在一起 rake up the loose leaves 2 (指分散) be scattered 3 (失散) lose contact after being scattered
【散闷】sànmèn〈动〉 keep oneself occupied: 看电视～ watch TV as an escape from boredom
【散热】sànrè〈动〉 1 (指消除) dissipate heat 2 (指辐射) radiate heat
【散失】sànshī〈动〉 1 (丢失) be missing: 她和家人在战争中～了。 She lost her family in the war. ‖ 有些书稿在战乱中～了。 Some of the manuscripts of the book went missing during the war. 2 (消散) disappear: 防止热量的～ stop the heat from being lost ‖ 水分在夏天～得很快。 Moisture disappears quickly in summer.
【散摊儿】sàntānr = 散摊子 sàn tānzi
【散摊子】sàn tānzi〈动〉〈口〉(指人) break up; (指组织) disband; (指经济实体) bankrupt: 他俩过不到一块儿，最后只好～。 Unable to get along well with each other, they had to divorce in the end. ‖ 一场争吵之后，这个组织就～了。The organization was disbanded after the quarrel.
【散席】sànxí〈动〉 [of a dinner party or banquet] be over: ～了吗? Has the banquet ended? ‖ 席还没散。 The banquet is not over yet.
【散戏】sànxì〈动〉 [of a show, play, opera, etc.] be over: 他没等～就走了。 He left before the play ended.
【散心】sànxīn〈动〉 relieve oneself of worry: 听音乐～ relieve boredom by listening to music ‖ 她走了走亲戚，散了散心。 She went and visited some of her relatives to keep her mind off things.
【散学】sànxué〈动〉〈方〉 [of a school] be over: ～回家 go home after school
【散瘀消肿】sànyūxiāozhǒng〈动〉［中医］ dissipate blood stasis and promote the subsidence of swelling

sāng

丧（喪）sāng〈名〉(葬礼) funeral; (丧事) mourning: 国～ national mourning ‖ 服～一年 be in mourning for a year ▸～事, ～钟, 吊～
▸sàng
【丧服】sāngfú〈名〉 mourning clothes: 她身穿黑色～。 She was dressed in funeral black.
【丧假】sāngjià〈名〉 compassionate leave
【丧礼】sānglǐ〈名〉 funeral: 参加/举行/主持～ attend/hold/conduct a funeral
【丧乱】sāngluàn〈名〉〈书〉 calamity
【丧事】sāngshì〈名〉funeral affairs: 料理～ attend to/conduct/undertake funeral affairs
【丧葬】sāngzàng〈名〉 funeral affairs: ～仪式花了两天时间。 The funeral arrangements took two days.
【丧葬费】sāngzàngfèi〈名〉 funeral expenses: 减少/支付～ reduce/cover the funeral expenses
【丧钟】sāngzhōng〈名〉 death knell: 敲～ toll the death knell ‖ 敲响旧时代的～ ring the knell for the old era

桑 sāng〈名〉 mulberry tree
【桑巴】sāngbā〈名〉 samba: ～舞 samba
【桑蚕】sāngcán〈名〉 silkworm: ～丝 mulberry silk
【桑寄生】sāngjìshēng〈名〉［中药］ parasitic loranthus
【桑拿】sāngná〈名〉 sauna: 洗～ take a sauna ‖ ～浴 Turkish bath ‖ 我每周洗～并按摩一次。 I have a sauna and massage every week.
【桑拿天】sāngnátiān〈名〉［气象］ hot and humid weather
【桑葚】sāngshèn〈名〉mulberry: ～汁 mulberry juice
【桑树】sāngshù〈名〉 mulberry (tree)
【桑叶】sāngyè〈名〉 mulberry leaf
【桑榆】sāngyú〈名〉〈书〉 1 〈本〉 mulberry and elm tree 2 〈喻〉(日暮) sunset 3 〈喻〉(暮年) old age
【桑榆暮景】sāngyú-mùjǐng〈成〉 old age: 他父亲已到～之年。 Her father is in the final years of his life.
【桑梓】sāngzǐ〈名〉〈书〉 native land: 服务～ serve one's native land

sǎng

搡 sǎng〈动〉〈方〉 push violently: 把他～个跟头 give him a good push

嗓 sǎng〈名〉 1 (喉咙) throat: ▸～音, ～子 2 (声音) voice: 尖/小/哑～儿 shrill/low/hoarse voice
【嗓门儿】sǎngménr〈名〉 voice: 提高～ raise one's voice ‖ 扯起～喊 shout at the top of one's voice
【嗓音】sǎngyīn〈名〉 voice: ～圆润 have a mellow voice ‖ 动听/清脆/柔和的～ musical/clear/gentle voice ‖ 他～洪亮。His voice carries well.
【嗓子】sǎngzi〈名〉 1 (喉咙) throat: 清～ clear one's throat ‖ ～疼 have a sore throat 2 (声音) voice: 吊～ sing scales ‖ 放开～唱 sing powerfully ‖ 她～喊哑了。 She shouted herself hoarse.
【嗓子眼儿】sǎngziyǎnr〈名〉 throat: 饱到～ be full to bursting

颡（顙）sǎng〈名〉〈书〉 forehead

sàng

丧（喪）sàng〈动〉 1 (失去) lose: ▸～家之犬, ～尽天良, 玩物～志 2 (死) die: ～妻 to lose one's wife ‖ 孩子们因～父而成为孤儿。 The children were orphaned after the death of their father. ▸～命, ～亡 3 (情绪低落) be disappointed: ▸懊～, 沮～
▸sāng
【丧胆】sàngdǎn〈动〉 be terror-stricken: ▸闻风～
【丧魂落魄】sànghún-luòpò = 失魂落魄 shīhún-luòpò
【丧家之犬】sàngjiāzhīquǎn〈成〉stray dog: 惶惶如～ very frightened ‖ 被追捕的罪犯到处逃窜，成了～。 The hunted criminal fled in panic.
【丧尽天良】sàngjìn-tiānliáng〈成〉 be heartless: 这种人～，无恶不作。 This kind of person has no conscience and stops at no evil.
【丧门星】sàngménxīng〈名〉 one who brings bad luck
【丧命】sàngmìng〈动〉 lose one's life: 差点儿～ come within an inch of one's life ‖

S

三人在这起车祸中～。 Three people died in the car accident.

【丧偶】sàng'ǒu〈动〉〈书〉 lose one's spouse: 中年～ lose one's spouse in middle age

【丧气】sàngqì〈动〉 lose heart: 目前的结果令人～。 The current results are discouraging. ‖ 他的话使我们感到很～。 We were greatly discouraged by his words. ▸垂头～, 灰心～

【丧气】sàngqi〈形〉〈口〉 unlucky: ～话 discouraging remarks ‖ 不能走，真～! We're not allowed to leave. How unlucky!

【丧权辱国】sàngquán-rǔguó〈成〉 surrender a country's sovereign rights under humiliating terms: ～的条约 treaty of national betrayal and humiliation

【丧生】sàngshēng〈动〉 get killed: 寒流袭来，使许多人～。 The cold snap claimed many lives.

【丧失】sàngshī〈动〉 lose: ～机会/领土/信心 lose opportunity/territory/confidence ‖ ～理智 be bereft of reason ‖ 记忆力的～ memory loss

【丧亡】sàngwáng〈动〉〈书〉 meet one's end

【丧心病狂】sàngxīn-bìngkuáng〈成〉 frenzied: ～地进行破坏活动 engage in destructive activities in a frenzied manner

【丧志】sàngzhì〈动〉 lose one's ambition

S

sāo

搔 sāo〈动〉 scratch: ▸～首弄姿, ～痒

【搔到痒处】sāodào-yǎngchù〈成〉 hit the nail on the head: 他对我说的一番话，正好～。 What he said to me hit the nail right on the head.

【搔首弄姿】sāoshǒu-nòngzī〈成〉 be coquettish: 她在公众场合～，实在令人作呕。 She was nauseatingly flirtatious in public.

【搔头】sāotóu〈动〉 scratch one's head: 为难地～ scratch one's head as if in a dilemma

【搔痒】sāoyǎng〈动〉 scratch an itch: 猫在～。 The cat's having a scratch.

骚[1]（騷） sāo〈动〉 disturb: ▸～动, ～乱, ～扰

骚[2]（騷） sāo〈名〉（诗文） poetry: ▸～客, ～人墨客

骚[3]（騷） sāo〈形〉（放荡） coquettish: 那个～女人! What a tart she is! ▸～货, 风～

【骚动】sāodòng〈动〉 **1**（动荡） cause a commotion: 引起～ cause a commotion ‖ 大规模的～ large-scale chaos ‖ ～稍稍平静了一些。 The commotion subsided a bit. **2**（无秩序） become restless: ～的人群 riotous crowd ‖ 人群～起来。 The crowd was in tumult.

【骚货】sāohuò〈名〉〈贬〉 tart

【骚客】sāokè〈名〉〈书〉 poet: 文人～ men of letters

【骚乱】sāoluàn〈名〉 riot: 发动～ start a riot ‖ 平息～ calm a disturbance ‖ 政治/宗派～ political/factional turmoil ‖ 这个国家的～是由总统遇刺触发的。 The country's turmoil was caused by the assassination of the president.

【骚扰】sāorǎo〈动〉 harass: 不断受到恐怖分子的～ be constantly harassed by terrorists ‖ 他不停地～我。 He kept disturbing me. ▸性～

【骚扰电话】sāorǎo diànhuà〈名〉 nuisance call

【骚人墨客】sāorén-mòkè〈成〉 men of letters

缫（繅） sāo〈动〉 reel (silk)

【缫丝】sāosī〈动〉 reel silk: ～厂 reeling mill

臊 sāo〈形〉 [of smell] foul: 屋子里有股～味。 There is a smell of urine in the room. ▸～气, 狐～, 腥～

▸sào

【臊气】sāoqì〈名〉 foul smell: 尿～ foul smell of urine ‖ 一身～ stink from head to toe

▸sào

sǎo

扫（掃） sǎo

A〈动〉 **1**（打扫） sweep: ～地板/院子 sweep the floor/yard ‖ 地～过了吗? Have you swept the floor? ▸～地, 打～, 祭～ **2**（去除） clear away: 秋风～落叶 autumn wind sweeping away fallen leaves ▸～雷, ～盲, ～兴 **3**（快速掠过） dart: 向听众～了一眼 dart one's eyes over the audience ‖ 探照灯～过夜空。 The searchlights swept across the night sky.

B〈形〉 total: ▸～数

▸sào

【扫除】sǎochú〈动〉 **1**（打扫） clean up: ～垃圾 sweep away rubbish ‖ ～积雪 shift the snow that has accumulated ‖ 大～ a big clean-up **2**（清除） eradicate: ～前进路上的障碍 sweep obstacles from one's path ‖ ～文盲 wipe out illiteracy

【扫荡】sǎodàng〈动〉 **1**（用武力肃清） mop up: 粉碎敌人的～ smash the enemy's mopping-up operations **2**（彻底清除） eliminate: ～歪风邪气 wipe out evil trends and unhealthy practices

【扫地】sǎodì〈动〉 **1**〈本〉 sweep the floor: ～抹桌 sweep the floor and clean the tables **2**〈喻〉（尽失） reach rock bottom: 名誉～ be thoroughly discredited ‖ 威信～ lose all prestige ▸斯文～

【扫地出门】sǎodì-chūmén〈成〉 be driven out: 他被老板～。 He was kicked out by his boss.

【扫黑】sǎohēi〈动〉 combat crime: ～行动 anti-crime operations

【扫黄】sǎohuáng〈动〉 launch a crackdown on pornography: ～打非 crack down on pornography and illegal publications

【扫雷】sǎoléi〈动〉 clear mines: ～舰 minesweeper ‖ ～器 mine-sweeping apparatus

【扫路机】sǎolùjī〈名〉 street sweeper: 小型～ mini-roadsweeper

【扫盲】sǎománg〈动〉 eradicate illiteracy: ～计划 literacy programme ‖ ～运动 literacy campaign ‖ 国际～日 International Literacy Day

【扫描】sǎomiáo〈动〉 **1**［电子］ scan: ～检查脑瘤 scan the brain for tumours **2**［计算机］ scan **3**（扫视） glance around

【扫描器】sǎomiáoqì〈名〉［电子］scanner: 条形码～ bar code scanner

【扫描仪】sǎomiáoyí〈名〉 scanner: 彩色～ colour scanner

【扫墓】sǎomù〈动〉 pay tribute to a dead person at his tomb: ～活动 grave-sweeping activity ‖ 去烈士陵园～ go to the revolutionary martyrs' cemetery to pay one's respects

【扫平】sǎopíng〈动〉 crush: ～叛乱 put down a rebellion

【扫清】sǎoqīng〈动〉 clear away: ～港湾里的水雷 clear a harbour of mines ‖ ～前进道路上的一切绊脚石 clear all obstacles on the road to progress

【扫射】sǎoshè〈动〉 **1**（用武器） machine-gun from the air: 架起机枪～ set up the machine-guns and open fire ‖ 敌人疯狂地向房子里～。 The enemy strafed the house wildly. **2**（用灯光） scan: 探照灯在夜空～。 The spotlights flooded the night sky.

【扫视】sǎoshì〈动〉 sweep: ～一张名单 cast one's eyes over a list of names ‖ 他用尖锐的目光～着房间。 His keen eyes swept the room.

【扫数】sǎoshù〈副〉 totally: ～还清。 The debt was paid off in full. ‖ ～入库。 Everything was put into storage.

【扫榻以待】sǎotà-yǐdài〈成〉 look forward to sb.'s visit: 我们～，期望能早日见到你们。 We are looking forward to your visit and wish to see you as soon as possible.

【扫堂腿】sǎotángtuǐ〈名〉［武术］ way to topple an opponent by a vigorous sweeping movement of the leg

【扫尾】sǎowěi〈动〉 round off: ～工程 final phase of a project

【扫兴】sǎoxìng〈动〉 spoil the fun: 使人～ rain on sb.'s parade ‖ 公众的冷淡使他很～。 His enthusiasm was dampened by the apathy of the public.

【扫雪车】sǎoxuěchē〈名〉 snowplough〈英〉; snowplow〈美〉

嫂 sǎo〈名〉 **1**（哥哥的妻子） sister-in-law **2**（称呼年纪相仿的已婚妇女） Madame: 大～ elder sister ‖ 王～ Mrs Wang **3**（指称已婚的某种职业妇女） 军～ wife of an officer ‖ 空～ married air hostess

【嫂夫人】sǎofūren〈名〉〈尊〉 your wife: 请代问～好。 Please extend my regards to your wife.

【嫂嫂】sǎosao〈名〉〈方〉 **1**（哥哥的妻子） sister-in-law **2**（称呼年纪相仿的已婚妇女） sister

【嫂子】sǎozi〈名〉 **1** ▸**p. 588**〈口〉（哥哥的妻子） sister-in-law **2**（朋友的妻子） wife of one's friend

sào

扫（掃） sào = 扫 sǎo [only used in words like 扫帚 and 扫把]

▸sǎo

【扫把】sàobǎ〈方〉= 扫帚 sàozhou

【扫帚】sàozhou〈名〉 broom: 一把～ a broom ‖ 用～扫院子 sweep the yard with a broom

【扫帚星】sàozhouxīng〈名〉 **1**〈旧〉（彗星） comet **2**（指人） jinx

瘙 sào〈名〉 scabies: ▸～痒

【瘙痒】sàoyǎng〈动〉 itch: ～难熬 unbearable itch ‖ 老年（性）～ senile pruritus

臊 sào〈动〉 feel shy: ～得脸通红 go bright red ‖ 没羞没～ be shameless ▸害～

▸sāo

【臊子】sàozi〈名〉〈方〉 cooked minced

meat to be added to noodles or other food before serving: 羊肉~面 noodles with diced mutton

sè

色 sè〈名〉**1**（脸色）look: 喜怒不形于~ not show one's feelings ▸~厉内荏, 察言观~, 面不改~ **2**（景象）scene: ▸湖光山~, 景~, 暮~ **3**（种类）kind: ▸花~, 货~ **4** ▸p. 863（颜色）colour: 中国烹饪讲求~、香、味、形俱佳。Chinese cuisine demands that the colour, smell, taste and appearance of every dish be superb. ▸冷~, 上~, 退~ **5**（容貌）feminine charms: ▸国~, 姿~ **6**（质量）quality: ▸成~, 音~ **7**（性欲）sexual desire: ▸好~, 贪~, 桃~
▸shǎi

【色标】sèbiāo〈名〉colour code

【色不迷人人自迷】sè bù mí rén rén zì mí〈俗〉lust doesn't blind, one blinds oneself

【色彩】sècǎi〈名〉**1**（颜色）colour: 增添~ add colour (to) ‖ ~鲜艳 of bright colours **2**〈喻〉（指情调）tone: 具有神秘~ have an air of mystery ‖ 地方~ local flavour ‖ 这部电影带有极强的感情~。The film is very sentimental in tone.

【色彩层次】sècǎi céngcì〈名〉gradation

【色彩亮度】sècǎi liàngdù〈名〉chromaluminance

【色差】sèchā〈名〉**1**［物理］chromatic aberration **2**［纺织］off colour **3**［摄影］chromatic effect

【色带】sèdài〈名〉ribbon: 打印机~ printer ribbon

【色胆】sèdǎn〈名〉lust: ~包天 go to any lengths for sex

【色调】sèdiào〈名〉**1**（指颜色）tone: 冷/暖~ cool/warm tone ‖ 使画面~明亮/柔和 tone up/down a picture ‖ 主~ dominant hue **2**（指思想）sentiment: 这篇散文~明快。The prose is lively in tone.

【色度】sèdù〈名〉**1**［物理］chrominance **2**（色彩）shade of colour

【色度计】sèdùjì〈名〉［物理］colorimeter: 光电~ photoelectric colorimeter

【色光】sèguāng〈名〉coloured light

【色鬼】sèguǐ〈名〉lecher: 老~ dirty old man

【色觉】sèjué〈名〉sense of colour: ~测验 colour vision test

【色拉】sèlā〈名〉salad: 拌~ prepare a salad ‖ ~调味品 salad dressing ‖ 水果~ fruit salad ‖ ~酱 salad cream

【色拉油】sèlāyóu〈名〉**1**（拌色拉用）salad oil **2**（炒菜用）cooking oil

【色狼】sèláng〈名〉lecher

【色厉内荏】sèlì-nèirěn〈成〉fierce of mien but faint of heart: 他~。He looks like a force to be reckoned with but actually he's very weak.

【色盲】sèmáng ▸p. 50〈名〉colour blindness: 先天性~ congenital colour blindness

【色盲检查镜】sèmáng jiǎnchájìng〈名〉anomaloscope

【色盲检查图】sèmáng jiǎnchátú〈名〉colour test chart

【色眯眯】sèmīmī〈形〉lecherous: 那个色狼~地看着她。The lecher looked at her with lustful eyes.

【色谱】sèpǔ〈名〉［物理］colour spectrum: ~分析/功能 chromatographic analysis/function ‖ ~仪 chromatograph

【色情】sèqíng〈名〉pornography: ~电影 pornographic film ‖ ~小说 erotic novel ‖ 提供~服务 provide sex

【色情狂】sèqíngkuáng〈名〉**1** ▸p. 50［心理］erotomania **2**（指人）sex maniac

【色情文学】sèqíng wénxué〈名〉erotica

【色球】sèqiú〈名〉［天文］chromosphere

【色弱】sèruò ▸p. 50〈名〉colour weakness: ~患者 tritanope

【色散】sèsàn〈名〉［物理］chromatic dispersion

【色素】sèsù〈名〉pigment: 皮肤的~ skin pigment ‖ 人造~ artificial colouring

【色素沉着】sèsù chénzhuó〈名〉［医学］pigmentation

【色相】sèxiàng〈名〉**1**（指色彩）colour **2**［佛教］appearance **3**（指姿色）sexual appeal: 出卖~ sell one's charms

【色艺】sèyì〈名〉look and skill: ~绝伦 be unparalleled both in looks and skills

【色欲】sèyù〈名〉sexual desire

【色泽】sèzé〈名〉colour and lustre: ~鲜亮 bright and lustrous ‖ 金属的~ lustre of metals

【色织布】sèzhībù〈名〉yarn-dyed fabric

【色纸】sèzhǐ〈名〉coloured paper

【色痣】sèzhì〈名〉pigmented mole

涩（澀） sè〈形〉**1**（不光滑）rough: 摸着发~ not feel smooth ‖ 轮轴太~，该上油了。The wheel axle does not work smoothly. It needs oiling. ▸干~, 枯~ **2**（指味道）sharp: 这些柿子特别~。The persimmons are very tart. ▸苦~ **3**（难懂）obscure: ▸晦~, 艰~, 生~

【涩脉】sèmài〈名〉［中医］uneven pulse

【涩滞】sèzhì〈形〉rough going: 他文笔~。His writing reads very unevenly.

啬（嗇） sè〈形〉stingy: 他太~了，不愿捐钱行善。He is too stingy to give money to charity. ▸吝~

【啬刻】sèke〈形〉〈方〉stingy: ~鬼 miser ‖ 他花钱~。He is stingy with his money.

铯（銫） sè〈名〉［化学］cesium (Cs)

塞 sè〈动〉block up: ▸闭~, 茅~顿开, 堵~
▸sāi, sài

【塞责】sèzé〈动〉perform one's duties perfunctorily: 心不在焉地敷衍~ perform duties in a perfunctory and absent-minded way

瑟 sè ▸p. 929〈名〉［音乐］*se* [a twenty-five-stringed or sixteen-stringed plucked instrument, similar to the zither]: 鼓~ play the *se* ▸胶柱鼓~

【瑟瑟】sèsè **A**〈拟〉[of the wind] rustle: 微风~ rustle of the breeze **B**〈形〉[of a person] trembling: 一想起要见他的老板，他就~发抖。He trembled at the thought of seeing his boss.

【瑟缩】sèsuō〈动〉cower: 那个人~在墙角。That man cowered in a corner.

穑（穡） sè ▸稼穑 jiàsè

sēn

森 sēn〈形〉**1**（树木多）full of trees: 松柏~~ dense pine and cypress trees ▸~林 **2**〈书〉（众多）in profusion: ▸~罗万象 **3**（幽暗）dark: ▸~然, 阴~ **4**（严格）strict: ▸~严

【森林】sēnlín〈名〉forest: 一片~ an expanse of forest ‖ 保护~ preserve the forests ‖ 砍伐~ cut down a forest ‖ 原始~ primeval forests

【森林防火】sēnlín fánghuǒ〈名〉forest fire control

【森林覆盖率】sēnlín fùgàilǜ〈名〉forest coverage

【森林覆盖面积】sēnlín fùgài miànjī〈名〉forested area

【森林公园】sēnlín gōngyuán〈名〉forest park: 国家~ national forest park

【森林火灾】sēnlín huǒzāi〈名〉forest fire: 扑灭~ extinguish a forest fire

【森林看守员】sēnlín kānshǒuyuán〈名〉forest ranger

【森林学】sēnlínxué〈名〉forestry

【森罗殿】sēnluódiàn〈名〉palace of the King of Hell

【森罗万象】sēnluó-wànxiàng〈成〉all-inclusive: 这个博物馆里展出的东西~，令人目不暇接。The items exhibited in this museum are a feast for the eyes.

【森然】sēnrán〈形〉**1**（数木茂密）dense: 那个公园林木~。The park is thick with tall trees. **2**（阴森可怕）awesome: ~可怖 awesome and terrifying

【森森】sēnsēn〈形〉**1**（数木茂密）dense: 松柏~ dense pine and cypress trees **2**（阴森可怕）gloomy: ▸阴~

【森严】sēnyán〈形〉strict: 等级~ form a strict hierarchy ‖ 戒备~ be heavily guarded

【森严壁垒】sēnyán-bìlěi〈成〉**1**（戒备严密）be closely guarded **2**（界线分明）be sharply divided

S

sēng

僧 sēng〈名〉bonze: 大唐高~ eminent Tang monk ▸~人

【僧多粥少】sēngduō-zhōushǎo = 粥少僧多 zhōushǎo-sēngduō

【僧服】sēngfú = 僧衣 sēngyī

【僧侣】sēnglǚ〈名〉clergy: ~生活 monastic life ‖ ~政治 theocracy ‖ ~主义 fideism

【僧尼】sēng-ní〈名〉Buddhist monks and nuns

【僧伽】sēngqié〈名〉［佛教］sangha

【僧伽罗语】Sēngqiéluóyǔ ▸p. 918〈名〉Sinhalese

【僧人】sēngrén〈名〉Buddhist monk

【僧俗】sēng-sú〈名〉clergy and laity

【僧徒】sēngtú〈名〉Buddhist believers

【僧衣】sēngyī〈名〉monastic habit

【僧院】sēngyuàn〈名〉Buddhist monastery

【僧众】sēngzhòng〈名〉Buddhist monks

shā

杀（殺） shā〈动〉**1**（杀死）kill: ~光 kill off ▸他~, 误~, 自~ **2**（战斗）fight: ~出一条血路 carve out a route through the enemy ‖ 双方~得难分难解。The two sides are locked in fierce fighting. ▸冲~, 刺~ **3**（削减）abate: 你最好~~他的威风。You'd better try to kill his arrogance. ‖ 这场雨可以大~暑气。This rain can really reduce the summer heat greatly. ▸~价, ~气 **4**（破坏）spoil: ▸~风景 **5**（表示程度深）气~ hopping mad ‖ 这出有趣的戏笑~我了。The play was so funny it nearly killed me. **6** = 煞 shā 1

7〉〈方〉（疼痛） sting: 伤口用酒精消毒～得很。 Alcohol smarts when it is used to sterilize a cut.

【杀虫剂】shāchóngjì〈名〉 insecticide

【杀虫药】shāchóngyào〈名〉 pesticide: 杀蛔虫药 ascaricide ‖ 杀寄生虫药 parasiticide

【杀敌】shādí〈动〉 fight the enemy: ～本领 combat skills ‖ 他们在战场上英勇～。 They fought the enemy heroically on the battlefield.

【杀毒】shādú〈动〉［计算机］ destroy a computer virus: 计算机～工具 scan and kill virus tools ‖ ～软件 antivirus software ‖ 此病毒已经杀除。 The virus has been removed.

【杀风景】shā fēngjǐng〈惯〉 be a wet blanket: 大～ utterly spoil the fun ‖ 不要做～的人。 Don't be a wet blanket.

【杀富济贫】shāfù-jìpín〈成〉 kill the rich and help the poor

【杀害】shāhài〈动〉 kill: ～无辜平民 slaughter innocent civilians ‖ 惨遭～ be brutally killed

【杀回马枪】shā huímǎqiāng〈惯〉 wheel around and hit back

【杀机】shājī〈名〉 intent to kill: 他心怀～。 He harbours some murderous intentions.

【杀鸡给猴看】shā jī gěi hóu kàn = 杀鸡吓猴 shājī-xiàhóu

【杀鸡取卵】shājī-qǔluǎn〈成〉 kill the goose that lays the golden egg: 滥伐林木，无异于～。Deforestation is very short-sighted.

【杀鸡吓猴】shājī-xiàhóu〈成〉 punish one person as a warning to the masses

【杀鸡焉用牛刀】shājī yān yòng niúdāo〈成〉 no need to go to town over a small issue

【杀价】shājià〈动〉 slash the price: 他们很会～。 They are good at slashing prices. ‖ 这辆汽车他要价400英镑，但是我们～杀到350英镑。 He was asking 400 pounds for the car, but we cut/beat him down to 350 pounds.

【杀戒】shājiè〈名〉 prohibition against taking life [one of the ten Buddhist prohibitions]: 大开～ butcher in large numbers

【杀菌】shājūn〈动〉 sterilize: ～肥皂 germicidal soap ‖ ～剂 germicide ‖ ～作用 sterilization

【杀戮】shālù〈动〉 massacre: ～无辜 slaughter innocent people ‖ 惨遭～ be massacred in cold blood

【杀卵剂】shāluǎnjì〈名〉［农业］ ovicide

【杀螨剂】shāmǎnjì〈名〉［农业］ acaricide

【杀气】shāqì **A**〈名〉 murderous look: 满脸～ with a murderous look on one's face ‖ ～腾腾 murderous **B**〈动〉 vent one's anger: 不要拿别人～。 Don't vent your anger on others. ‖ 你不能老拿太太孩子～。 You can't always blow steam off at your wife and kids.

【杀亲】shāqīn **A**〈动〉 kill one's parent **B**〈名〉 parenticide: ～罪 parenticide

【杀青】shāqīng〈动〉 1〉（指竹简） heat bamboo strips for writing 2〉（指作品） finalize a piece of work: 她的处女作现已～。 She has already finished her maiden work. ‖ 这部影片将于明年～。 The film will be completed next year. 3〉（指茶叶） heating process

【杀人】shārén **A**〈动〉 kill a person: ～偿命 a life for a life **B**〈名〉［法律］ homicide: 故意～ intentional homicide, murder in the second degree ‖ 过失～ involuntary manslaughter, murder in the third degree

【杀人不见血】shārén bù jiàn xiě〈成〉 kill by subtle means

【杀人不眨眼】shārén bù zhǎyǎn〈成〉 kill a person without batting an eyelid: ～的杀人犯 ruthless murderer

【杀人偿命，欠债还钱】shārén chángmìng, qiànzhài huánqián〈俗〉 a debtor must pay with money, a murderer with life

【杀人犯】shārénfàn〈名〉 murderer: 处决～ a murderer ‖ 女～ murderess

【杀人放火】shārén-fànghuǒ〈成〉 slaughter people and set fire to houses: 他们～，无恶不作。 They committed murder, arson and every crime imaginable.

【杀人灭口】shārén-mièkǒu〈成〉 kill sb. to keep his mouth shut

【杀人如麻】shārén-rúmá〈成〉 kill people like flies

【杀人嫌疑犯】shārén xiányífàn〈名〉 murder suspect

【杀人越货】shārén-yuèhuò〈成〉 murder sb. for his property

【杀人罪】shārénzuì〈名〉 homicide: 被控犯有～ be accused of homicide

【杀伤】shāshāng〈动〉 kill and wound: ～大批敌军 inflict heavy casualties on enemy troops ‖ 对野生动物有～性的影响 have a damaging effect on wildlife

【杀伤力】shāshānglì〈名〉［军事］ power of destruction: ～大的步枪 high-powered rifle ‖ 大规模～武器 weapon of mass destruction

【杀伤性武器】shāshāngxìng wǔqì〈名〉［军事］ anti-personnel weapon

【杀身成仁】shāshēn-chéngrén〈成〉 die for a righteous cause

【杀身之祸】shāshēnzhīhuò〈名〉 fatal disaster: 遭～ meet with a fatal disaster ‖ 招来～ court one's own destruction

【杀生】shāshēng〈动〉［佛教］ take the life of an animal: 不～。 Do not kill living things.

【杀手】shāshǒu〈名〉 1〉（杀人者） killer: 职业～ professional killer ‖ ～已被抓住。 The murderer has been caught. 2〉［体育］ formidable player: 她是中国队最具威力的锋线～。 She is the most powerful forward in the Chinese team. 3〉〈喻〉（致死因素） things that kill: 心脏病是美国的头号～。 Heart disease is America's number one killer disease.

【杀手锏】shāshǒujiǎn = 撒手锏 sāshǒujiǎn

【杀头】shātóu〈动〉 decapitate: 他因叛国罪被～。 He was beheaded for high treason.

【杀一儆百】shāyī-jǐngbǎi〈成〉 punish one as a deterrent to others

杉 shā〈名〉 China fir
▸shān

【杉篙】shāgāo〈名〉 fir pole: 一根～ a fir pole

【杉木】shāmù〈名〉 fir wood

沙[1] shā〈名〉 1〉（沙子） sand: 粗/细～ coarse/fine sand ‖ 黄～ yellow sand ‖ 航道被～淤塞。 The channel sanded up. ▸流～, 泥～ 2〉（沙状物） sth. granular: ▸蚕～, 豆～ 3〉（指器皿） utensils made of sand or pottery clay: ▸～锅

沙[2] shā〈形〉 [of voice] husky: 把嗓子都喊～了 shout oneself hoarse ▸～哑

沙[3] shā = 沙皇 shāhuáng
▸shà

【沙包】shābāo〈名〉 1〉（沙丘） sand dune 2〉（沙袋） sandbag

【沙场】shāchǎng〈名〉 battleground: 久经～ be an experienced soldier ‖ 他战死～。 He was killed in battle.

【沙尘】shāchén〈名〉 dust and sand: ～飞扬。 A cloud of dust filled the air.

【沙尘暴】shāchénbào〈名〉 sandstorm: ～席卷华北。 The sandstorm has swept across North China.

【沙城堡】shāchéngbǎo〈名〉 sandcastle: 堆～ build a sandcastle

【沙袋】shādài〈名〉 1〉（用于防洪） sandbag: 在河堤上堆置～以防洪水泛滥 sandbag the riverbanks to prevent flooding 2〉（用于锻炼）（拳击） punchbag;（负重） sandbag: 击打～ hit a punchbag

【沙雕】shādiāo〈名〉 sand sculpture

【沙丁鱼】shādīngyú〈名〉 sardine

【沙俄】Shā-É〈名〉 tsarist Russia

【沙发】shāfā〈名〉 sofa: 一对～ a pair of armchairs ‖ 一套～ a three-piece suite ‖ 单人～ (upholstered) armchair

【沙发床】shāfāchuáng〈名〉 sofa bed

【沙锅】shāguō = 砂锅 shāguō

【沙果】shāguǒ〈名〉 Chinese pear-leaved crabapple

【沙害】shāhài〈名〉 disastrous sandstorm

【沙化】shāhuà〈动〉 desertify: ～土壤 desertified soil

【沙荒】shāhuāng〈名〉 sandy wasteland: 改造～ reclaim a sandy wasteland

【沙皇】shāhuáng〈名〉 tsar, czar: ～政权 tsarist regime

【沙棘】shājí〈名〉 sea buckthorn

【沙浆】shājiāng = 砂浆 shājiāng

【沙金】shājīn〈名〉 placer gold

【沙坑】shākēng〈名〉 1〉（供儿童游戏用） sandpit〈英〉; sandbox〈美〉 2〉［体育］ jumping pit 3〉（特指高尔夫） bunker〈英〉; sand trap〈美〉

【沙拉】shālā = 色拉 sèlā

【沙里淘金】shālǐ-táojīn〈成〉〈喻〉 1〉（精选） sift diamonds from the rough: 本次竞选是采用～的办法，从几千人中挑出人来。 The election was won by the one good candidate out of thousands of pretenders. 2〉（费力却收效甚微） expend great efforts to no avail

【沙丽】shālì = 莎丽 shālì

【沙砾】shālì〈名〉 gravel

【沙粒】shālì〈名〉 grains of sand: 潮湿的～会粘在一起。 Wet sand grains stick together.

【沙疗】shāliáo〈名〉 sand bath treatment

【沙龙】shālóng〈名〉 salon: 社交/文学～ social/literary salon

【沙漏】shālòu〈名〉 sandglass: ～计时 use an hourglass for marking the time

【沙门】shāmén〈名〉［佛教］ Buddhist monk

【沙门氏菌】shāménshìjūn〈名〉salmonella

【沙弥】shāmí〈名〉 Buddhist novice

【沙漠】shāmò ▸**p. 164**〈名〉 desert: 一大片～ a vast expanse of desert ‖ 改造～ reclaim a desert ‖ 变～为绿洲 turn a desert into green land ‖〈喻〉文化～ cultural desert

【沙漠化】shāmòhuà〈名〉 desertification

【沙漠学】shāmòxué〈名〉 eremology

【沙漠之舟】shāmòzhīzhōu〈名〉〈喻〉 camel

【沙鸥】shā'ōu〈名〉［鸟类］ shorebird

【沙盘】shāpán〈名〉［军事］ sand table: 制作～ make a sand table ‖ ～作业 sand table exercise
【沙丘】shāqiū〈名〉 dune: 流动～ moving dune
【沙瓤】shāráng〈名〉 mushy pulp: ～西瓜 mushy watermelon
【沙壤土】shārǎngtǔ〈名〉 sandy loam
【沙沙】shāshā〈拟〉 rustle: ～的雨声 the pitter patter of rain ‖ 树林中微风～作响。 A breeze murmured through the trees. ‖ 树叶在微风中发出～声。 Leaves rustled in the breeze.
【沙参】 shāshēn 〈名〉［中药］ straight ladybell root
【沙生植物】 shāshēng zhíwù 〈名〉 psammophyte
【沙滩】shātān〈名〉 beach: 金色的～ golden sands ‖ 我们躺在～上享受日光浴。 We lay on the sand and sunbathed.
【沙滩排球】shātān páiqiú ▸**p. 909**〈名〉 beach volleyball
【沙特阿拉伯】 Shātè Ālābó 〈名〉 Saudi Arabia: ～人 Saudi Arabian
【沙特阿拉伯王国】Shātè Ālābó Wángguó〈名〉 Kingdom of Saudi Arabia
【沙田】shātián〈名〉 sandy land
【沙土】shātǔ〈名〉 sandy soil: ～淤积于麦田上。 Sandy soil silted over the wheat fields.
【沙土植物】shātǔ zhíwù ＝ 沙生植物 shāshēng zhíwù
【沙文主义】Shāwénzhǔyì〈名〉chauvinism: 大国～ big-power chauvinism
【沙哑】shāyǎ〈形〉 hoarse: 声音～ have a husky voice ‖ 他唱了一小时后嗓子都～了。 He became hoarse after singing for an hour. ‖ 他最近得过感冒，声音还有些～。 He is still a bit husky after his recent cold.
【沙岩】shāyán ＝ 砂岩 shāyán
【沙眼】shāyǎn〈名〉 trachoma: 患～ be infected with trachoma ‖ ～性结膜炎 trachomatous conjunctivitis
【沙浴】shāyù〈名〉 sandbath: ～疗法 sand treatment
【沙灾】shāzāi〈名〉 sandstorm disaster: 植树造林可以预防～。 Afforestation can prevent sandstorm disasters.
【沙枣】shāzǎo〈名〉 narrow-leaved wild olive: ～树 desert date
【沙洲】shāzhōu〈名〉 sandbank
【沙子】shāzi〈名〉 sand: 一粒～ a grain of sand ‖ 给结冰的路面撒～ spread grit on an icy road ‖ 他眼里容不下一粒～。 He cannot tolerate anything tainted.

纱（紗）shā〈名〉

1（纱状物） gauze: ▸～窗, ～门 **2**（指纺织品） textile: ▸泡泡～, 乔其～, 羽～ **3**（纱线） yarn: 粗支/细支～ low/fine count yarn ‖ 他们把棉花纺成～。 They spin cotton into yarn. ▸～厂, 纺～, 棉～
【纱包线】shābāoxiàn〈名〉 cotton-covered wire: 纱包绝缘线 cotton insulated wire
【纱布】shābù〈名〉 gauze: 一卷～ a roll of gauze ‖ ～绷带 gauze bandage ‖ 消毒～ sterilized gauze
【纱厂】shāchǎng〈名〉 cotton mill
【纱橱】shāchú〈名〉 screen cupboard
【纱窗】shāchuāng〈名〉 screen: 安装～ screen a window
【纱灯】shādēng〈名〉 gauze lantern: 一盏～ a gauze lantern
【纱锭】shādìng〈名〉［纺织］ spindle
【纱巾】shājīn〈名〉 gauze scarf
【纱笼】shālóng〈名〉 sarong
【纱帽】shāmào〈名〉 **1**（官帽） gauze hat worn by officials in feudal society **2**（官职） public office: 丢了～ to lose office ▸乌～ **3**（凉帽） gauze hat worn in summer
【纱门】shāmén〈名〉 screen door: 安装～ have screen doors fitted ‖ 单扇/双扇～ single/double leaf screen door
【纱线】shāxiàn〈名〉 yarn: ～支数 count of yarn
【纱罩】shāzhào〈名〉 **1**（用于遮盖食物） gauze covering **2**（灯罩） mantle
【纱支数】shāzhīshù〈名〉［纺织］ count

刹 shā〈动〉

check: ～住车 brake a car ‖ ～歪风 check unhealthy tendencies ▸～车
▸chà
【刹把】shābà〈名〉 **1**［机械］brake crank **2**（刹车的把手） handbrake
【刹车】shāchē **A**〈名〉 brake: 使用紧急～ apply the emergency brake ‖ ～失灵了。 The brakes failed. ‖ 他猛踩～。 He stepped hard on the brake. **B**〈动〉 **1**（停止车辆） apply the brakes: 遇上红灯时～ apply the brakes at a red light ‖ 她紧急～，避免了一场交通事故。 She braked sharply and avoided a traffic accident. ‖ ～灯 brake light ‖ ～踏板 brake pedal **2**（停止某事） put the brakes on sth.

砂 shā〈名〉

1（石粒） sand: ～斗 sand hopper ▸～轮, 翻～ **2**（砂状物） grit: ▸～糖, 矿～
【砂布】shābù〈名〉 abrasive cloth: ～用于抛光金属。 Emery cloth is used to polish metal.
【砂带】shādài〈名〉 abrasive cloth: ～磨削 abrasive belt grinding
【砂锅】shāguō〈名〉 earthenware pot: ～豆腐 bean curd stewed in an earthenware pot ‖ ～鸡 chicken casserole
【砂浆】shājiāng〈名〉［建筑］ mortar: 石灰/水泥～ lime/cement mortar
【砂礓】shājiāng〈名〉［地质］ gravel
【砂礁】shājiāo〈名〉［地质］ cay
【砂金】shājīn〈名〉 gold dust: ～石 aventurine
【砂矿】 shākuàng 〈名〉 placer: ～开采 placer mining
【砂砾】shālì ＝ 沙砾 shālì
【砂轮】 shālún 〈名〉［机械］ grinding wheel: ～切割机 abrasive wheel cutting machine ‖ 电动～ sanding machine ‖ ～机 grinder
【砂囊】shānáng〈名〉［动物］ gizzard
【砂皮】shāpí〈名〉〈方〉 emery cloth
【砂壤土】shārǎngtǔ〈名〉 sandy loam
【砂仁】 shārén 〈名〉 ［中药］ villous amomum fruit
【砂糖】shātáng〈名〉 granulated sugar
【砂洗】shāxǐ〈动〉 stone wash: ～布 stone-washed cloth ‖ ～牛仔裤 stone-washed jeans
【砂箱】shāxiāng〈名〉［冶金］sandbox: ～铸造 flask casting
【砂屑岩】shāxièyán〈名〉［地质］ arenite
【砂型】shāxíng〈名〉［冶金］ sand mould: ～铸造 sand casting
【砂岩】shāyán〈名〉［地质］ sandstone
【砂眼】shāyǎn〈名〉［冶金］ blowhole
【砂样】shāyàng〈名〉［石油］ drilling
【砂纸】shāzhǐ〈名〉 sand paper: 一张～ a sheet of sand paper ‖ ～打磨 sand papering ‖ 先用～把门磨光再上漆。Sandpaper the door before you paint it.

莎 shā

▸suō
【莎鸡】shājī〈名〉［昆虫］ long-horned
【莎丽】shālì〈名〉 sari

铩（鎩）shā

A〈名〉〈古〉 spear
B〈动〉〈书〉 wound: ▸～羽
【铩羽】shāyǔ〈动〉〈书〉 be defeated: ～而归 come back crestfallen

痧 shā〈名〉

［中医］ acute diseases such as cholera and sunstroke: ▸刮～
【痧子】 shāzi 〈名〉〈方〉 measles: 出～ have measles

煞 shā〈动〉

1（结束） bring to a close: ▸～尾, ～账 **2**（勒紧） bind: ～一～腰带 tighten one's belt **3**（停止） halt: 他开始发言， 但又忽然～住了。 He began to speak, but suddenly stopped. **4** ＝ 杀 shā 3, 5
▸shà
【煞笔】shābǐ **A**〈动〉 write concluding words: 到此还不能～。 I can't very well end here. **B**〈名〉 the end of a piece of writing: 这篇散文的～很精彩。 The concluding remarks of this prose are wonderful.
【煞车】shāchē〈动〉 **1**（固定） fasten a load **2** ＝ 刹车 shāchē
【煞风景】shā fēngjǐng ＝ 杀风景 shā fēngjǐng
【煞尾】shāwěi **A**〈动〉 finish off: 事情不多了，马上就可以～了。There isn't much left. We'll soon be winding up. ‖ 这部电影以一首歌～。 The film was rounded off with a song. **B**〈名〉 ending: ～部分需要重写。 The ending needs rewriting. ‖ 这出戏的～不够有力。 The ending of this play is not forceful enough.
【煞账】shāzhàng〈动〉 close accounts

裟 shā ▸袈裟 jiāshā

鲨（鯊）shā〈名〉

shark: 食人～ man-eating shark
【鲨鱼】shāyú〈名〉 shark

shá

啥 shá〈代〉〈方〉

what: 到～地方去? Where are you going? ‖ 那有～关系? What does it matter? ‖ 你～时候回来? When will you come back? ‖ 你来有～事? Why are you here?
【啥子】sházi〈代〉〈方〉 what: 你说～? What did you say?

shǎ

傻（儍）shǎ〈形〉

1（愚笨） stupid: 干～事 act the fool ‖ ～小子/丫头 silly boy/girl ▸犯～, 装～ **2**（不灵活） inflexible: 别一个劲儿～干，讲究一点方法。 Don't get stuck in just one way. Make sure to seek out other options.
【傻不愣登】shǎbulèngdēng〈形〉 stupid: 这个孩子看起来～的。 The child looks dumb.

S

【傻瓜】shǎguā〈名〉 idiot: 大～ big fool ‖ 十足的～ complete idiot ‖ 天生的～ natural fool ‖ 把某人当～看 take sb. for a fool
【傻瓜相机】shǎguā xiàngjī〈名〉 automatic camera
【傻呵呵】shǎhēhē〈形〉 naive: 别看他～的，心里可有数。 Maybe he doesn't look very smart, but he knows what's what. ‖ 他～地笑了笑，一句话也没说。 He smiled naively without saying a word.
【傻乎乎】shǎhūhū〈形〉 silly: 不要这样～的。 Don't be so foolish. ‖ 那个～的男孩是班上的尖子。 That silly-looking boy is top of his class.
【傻话】shǎhuà〈名〉 nonsense: 别讲～。 Don't talk rubbish.
【傻劲儿】shǎjìnr〈名〉 1（笨） foolishness: 他有一股子～。 There was a kind of stupidity in him. 2（蛮劲） sheer enthusiasm: 光靠～蛮干是不行的，要学会巧干。 Enthusiasm alone won't do. You have to be savvy in your work.
【傻乐】shǎlè〈动〉〈方〉 giggle: 你们在～什么呢？ What are you smirking at?
【傻里呱唧】shǎliguājī〈形〉〈方〉 foolish: 在我听来那句话～的。 That remark sounds stupid to me.
【傻帽儿】shǎmàor〈口〉 A〈名〉（笨蛋） idiot: 他真是个～，什么也不懂。 What an idiot he is! He doesn't know anything. B〈形〉（心眼儿实） naive: 你真～，为什么不阻止他？ Why didn't you stop him, you fool?
【傻气】shǎqì〈形〉 silly: 你也太～了！ You are silly! ‖ 他有点～。 He looks a bit dumb.
【傻人有傻福】shǎ rén yǒu shǎ fú〈俗〉 fortune favours fools
【傻事】shǎshì〈名〉 silly thing: 我昨晚喝醉了，但愿没干什么～。 I was very drunk last night. I hope I didn't do anything stupid.
【傻头傻脑】shǎtóu-shǎnǎo〈形〉 foolish-looking: 他还～的。 He's a simpleton.
【傻小子】shǎxiǎozi〈名〉〈诙〉 silly boy: 你这个～！ You silly boy!
【傻笑】shǎxiào〈动〉 smirk: 一阵～ a giggling fit ‖ 孩子们，别～，这是件严肃的事。 Stop giggling, children. This is a serious matter.
【傻眼】shǎyǎn〈动〉〈口〉 be dumbfounded: 得知面试没通过，她～了。 She was dumfounded when she heard that she had failed the interview. ‖ 这下他可～了。 He got a really nasty shock this time.
【傻样】shǎyàng〈名〉〈口〉 foolish look
【傻子】shǎzi〈名〉 idiot: 一生下来就是个～ be born an idiot ‖ ～都能看出这副画是假的。 Even an fool can see that the painting is a fake.

shà

沙 shà〈动〉〈方〉 sieve: 把米里的沙子～一～ sift the grains from the rice
▸shā

厦（廈） shà〈名〉 1（大楼） mansion: 广～ tall buildings ▸大～ 2（屋后的廊子） porch: 前廊后～ front and back verandas
▸xià

嗄 shà〈形〉〈书〉 hoarse: 号而不～ yelled but did not get hoarse

歃 shà〈动〉〈书〉 suck
【歃血】shàxuè〈动〉 smear the blood of a sacrifice on one's mouth [an ancient form of swearing an oath]
【歃血为盟】shàxuè-wéiméng〈成〉 smear one's mouth with blood in an oath of alliance

煞 shà
A〈名〉 evil spirit: ▸凶神恶～
B〈副〉 extremely: ～是好看 very nice indeed ▸～费苦心
▸shā
【煞白】shàbái〈形〉 deathly pale: 脸色～ look deathly pale ‖ 她吓得脸色～。 He turned pale with fright.
【煞费苦心】shàfèi-kǔxīn〈成〉 make a painstaking effort: 他们～，讨好老板。 They were falling over backwards to please the boss.
【煞气】shàqì A〈名〉 1（凶相） fierce look 2（邪气） evil spirit B〈动〉 have a flat tyre: 车胎～了。 The tyre is leaking.
【煞有介事】shàyǒujièshì〈成〉 take sth. seriously

霎 shà〈名〉 instant: ▸～时，一～
【霎时】shàshí = 霎时间 shàshíjiān
【霎时间】shàshíjiān〈名〉 instant: ～，乌云密布，大雨倾盆。 All of a sudden black clouds filled the sky and it poured with rain.

shāi

筛[1]（篩） shāi
A〈名〉 sieve: 粗/细～ coarse/fine sieve ‖ 煤～ coal screen ‖ 面粉～ flour sifter
B〈动〉 1（过滤） sift: ～麦壳 sift the wheat from the chaff ‖ ～煤 screen coal ‖ ～米 sift rice 2（倒） pour (wine) into a glass: 小二，给洒家～一碗酒。 Waiter, pour a bowl of wine for me. 3（加热） warm up (wine) over a fire: 把酒～一～再喝。 Warm the wine before drinking.

筛[2]（篩） shāi〈动〉〈方〉 beat (a gong): 打鼓～锣 beating drums and striking gongs
【筛板】shāibǎn〈名〉［化学］ sieve plate
【筛布】shāibù〈名〉 bolting cloth
【筛查】shāichá〈名〉［医学］ screening
【筛管】shāiguǎn〈名〉［植物］ sieve tube
【筛糠】shāikāng〈动〉〈口〉〈喻〉 shudder: 冻得全身～ shiver all over with cold ‖ 吓得～ shiver with fright
【筛选】shāixuǎn〈动〉 sift: ～出几名候选人 sift out a few candidates ‖ 经过严格～ through strict screening
【筛子】shāizi〈名〉 sieve: 用～筛面粉 sieve flour

shǎi

色 shǎi〈名〉 1〈口〉= 色 sè 2（指赌具） dice: ▸～子
▸sè
【色酒】shǎijiǔ〈名〉〈方〉 wine
【色子】shǎizi〈名〉 dice: 一颗/枚～ dice ‖ 摇/掷～ shake/throw dice

shài

晒（曬） shài〈动〉 1（太阳照射） shine on: 这几天～得要命。 There is too much sun these days. ‖ 太阳把他的脸～成了古铜色。 The sun made his face go brown. ▸风吹日～ 2（使干燥） dry in the sun: ～粮食 dry grain in the sun 3（接受光照） sunbathe: ～被子 air a quilt ‖ ～太阳 sunbathe 4（公开） expose: ～工资 expose wages
【晒斑】shàibān ▸p. 50〈名〉［医学］ sunburn
【晒版】shàibǎn〈名〉［印刷］ printing down
【晒场】shàichǎng〈名〉 drying yard
【晒垡】shàifá〈动〉［农业］ air the upturned soil
【晒干】shàigān〈动〉 dry in the sun: 那些衣服已经～了。 The clothes have dried in the sun.
【晒台】shàitái〈名〉 terrace
【晒图】shàitú A〈动〉 make a blueprint B〈名〉 blueprint
【晒烟】shàiyān〈名〉 sun-cured tobacco
【晒盐】shàiyán〈动〉 dry brine in the sun to obtain salt: ～场 salt field ‖ ～池 salt pan

shān

山 shān〈名〉 1［地质］（小山） hill;（大山） mountain: 登～ climb a mountain ‖ 翻过一座～ cross a hill ‖ 大/高～ huge/tall mountain ‖ 群～之间 in the mountains ▸～城，～庄，火～ 2（山区） mountainous area: ▸～货，～珍海味 3（山状物） anything resembling a mountain: ▸冰～，文～会海 4（蚕蔟） bunch of straw in which silkworms spin cocoons: 蚕上～了。 The silkworms have gone into the straw bundles to spin their cocoons. 5（指山墙） gable: 房～ gable
【山隘】shān'ài〈名〉 mountain pass
【山坳】shān'ào〈名〉 col: 这座电厂建在一个～里。 The power plant was built in a pass.
【山包】shānbāo〈名〉〈方〉 hillock
【山崩】shānbēng〈名〉 landslide
【山崩地裂】shānbēng-dìliè〈成〉 earth-shattering noise
【山不在高，有仙则灵】shān bù zài gāo, yǒu xiān zé líng〈成〉 any mountain, high or low, can be given spirit by a god: ～；水不在深，有龙则灵。 Any mountain, high or low, can be given spirit by a god; any waters, deep or shallow, can be given spirit by a dragon.
【山不转水转】shān bù zhuàn shuǐ zhuàn〈俗〉 nothing ever stays the same
【山茶】shānchá〈名〉［植物］ camellia: ～花 camellia
【山城】shānchéng〈名〉 mountain city: 重庆是一座美丽的～。 Chongqing is a beautiful mountain city.
【山重水复】shānchóng-shuǐfù〈成〉 [of a place] surrounded by mountain ranges and girdled by winding rivers:〈喻〉 ～疑无路，柳暗花明又一村 an abrupt turn to a new hopeful prospect
【山川】shānchuān〈名〉 1（山和河流） mountains and rivers 2（景色） landscape: ～壮丽 beautiful landscape
【山村】shāncūn〈名〉 mountain village: 一个遥远的小～ a small remote mountain

S

village ‖ 他出生在一个偏僻的～里。He was born in a remote mountain village.

【山大王】shāndàiwang〈名〉bandit leader on a mountain

【山丹】shāndān〈名〉［植物］morningstar lily

【山地】shāndì〈名〉**1**（多山地带）hilly country: 光秃秃的～ bare hilly area ‖ 树木繁多的～ heavily timbered mountainous region **2**（指农用地）hillside field: ～草原 upland meadow

【山地车】shāndìchē〈名〉mountain bike

【山地气候】shāndì qìhòu〈名〉mountain climate

【山地战】shāndìzhàn〈名〉mountain warfare

【山巅】shāndiān〈名〉〈书〉peak: 雾深深地罩住～。The fog hung heavily on the mountains.

【山顶】shāndǐng〈名〉**1**（山巅）peak: 到达～ reach the summit ‖ 登上～ go to the top of a hill **2**［解剖］culmen

【山顶洞人】Shāndǐngdòngrén〈名〉［考古］Upper Cave Man [a type of primitive human who lived ten to twenty thousand years ago and whose fossil remains were found in 1933 at Zhoukoudian near Beijing]

【山东】Shāndōng ▸**p. 661**〈名〉Shandong Province: ～半岛 Shandong Peninsula ‖ ～快书 Shandong clapper ballad

【山洞】shāndòng〈名〉cave

【山峰】shānfēng〈名〉mountain peak: 攀登～ ascend a mountain peak ‖ 白雪皑皑的～ snowy peak

【山旮旯儿】shāngālár〈名〉〈方〉remote mountain area

【山冈】shāngāng〈名〉hillock: 一道～ a low hill ‖ 高高的～ tall hill

【山岗子】shāngǎngzi〈名〉〈口〉hillock

【山高皇帝远】shān gāo huángdì yuǎn〈俗〉〈喻〉beyond the reach of the government

【山高水长】shāngāo-shuǐcháng〈成〉[of sb.'s moral integrity or the friendship between people or nations etc.] big as mountains, long as rivers

【山高水低】shāngāo-shuǐdī〈成〉（意外）unexpected misfortune: 如果他有个～ if anything untoward happens to him

【山高水远】shāngāo-shuǐyuǎn〈成〉**1**（遥远）far away **2** = 山高水低 shāngāo-shuǐdī

【山歌】shāngē〈名〉folk song: 唱～ sing a folk song

【山根】shāngēn〈名〉〈口〉foot of a hill: 在～下 at the foot of a mountain

【山沟】shāngōu〈名〉**1**（水沟）gully: 汽车突然转向掉进～里,导致21人死亡。The bus swerved into a ravine, killing 21 people. **2**（山谷）valley **3**（偏远山区）remote mountain area: 我生长在一个穷～里。I was born and brought up in a poor and remote mountain area.

【山沟沟】shāngōugou = 山沟 shāngōu

【山谷】shāngǔ〈名〉mountain valley: 风景如画的～ picturesque valley ‖ 住在～里 live down the valley

【山国】shānguó〈名〉**1**（指国家）mountainous country: 尼泊尔是一个～。Nepal is a mountainous country. **2**（指地区）hilly region

【山海关】Shānhǎiguān〈名〉Shanhaiguan Pass [the strategic pass at the eastern end of the Great Wall]

【山海经】Shānhǎijīng〈名〉**1**〈本〉*Classic of Mountains and Seas* **2**〈喻〉idle chat: 大谈～ idly chat

【山河】shānhé〈名〉**1**（山川和河流）mountains and rivers **2**（国家）territory: 锦绣～ beautiful land

【山核桃】shānhétao〈名〉**1**［植物］hickory **2**（果实）hickory nut

【山洪】shānhóng〈名〉mountain torrents: ～暴发。Torrents of water rushed down the mountain.

【山花】shānhuā〈名〉mountain flower: ～烂漫 mountain flowers are in full blossom

【山环水抱】shānhuán-shuǐbào〈成〉[of a resort] surrounded by hills and water

【山回路转】shānhuí-lùzhuǎn〈成〉**1**〈本〉winding paths along mountain ridges **2**〈喻〉（转机）a turn for the better

【山火】shānhuǒ〈名〉bush fire

【山货】shānhuò〈名〉**1**（指土产）mountain produce **2**（指日用品）household utensils

【山鸡】shānjī〈名〉〈方〉pheasant

【山积】shānjī〈动〉〈书〉be piled mountain high

【山脊】shānjǐ〈名〉mountain ridge

【山涧】shānjiàn〈名〉mountain stream: 一条～ a mountain creek

【山脚】shānjiǎo〈名〉foot of a hill: ～的小溪 stream at the bottom of a mountain ‖ 在～下 at the foot of the mountain

【山景】shānjǐng〈名〉mountain scenery

【山径】shānjìng〈名〉mountain path

【山口】shānkǒu〈名〉mountain pass

【山岚】shānlán〈名〉〈书〉mountain mists

【山梨】shānlí〈名〉［植物］sorb

【山梨酸】shānlísuān〈名〉［食品］sorbic acid

【山里红】shānlihóng〈名〉［植物］large-fruited Chinese hawthorn

【山梁】shānliáng〈名〉mountain ridge

【山林】shānlín〈名〉**1**（树林）forest **2**（山区）wooded mountain: ～文学 reclusive literature

【山陵】shānlíng〈名〉**1**〈书〉（山岳）lofty mountain **2**〈旧〉（坟墓）imperial tomb

【山岭】shānlǐng〈名〉mountain range: ～起伏 rising and falling mountain ranges

【山路】shānlù〈名〉mountain path: 崎岖的～ rough mountain path

【山麓】shānlù〈名〉〈书〉foot of a mountain: ～冲积平原 compound alluvial fan ‖ ～丘陵 foothill

【山峦】shānluán〈名〉range of mountains: ～重叠 range upon range of mountains ‖ ～起伏 rolling hills

【山脉】shānmài ▸**p. 164**〈名〉mountain range: 落基～ Rocky Mountains ‖ 秦岭～ Qinling Mountains ‖ 喜马拉雅～ Himalayas

【山猫】shānmāo〈名〉［动物］lynx

【山毛榉】shānmáojǔ〈名〉［植物］beech

【山门】shānmén〈名〉**1**（寺门）gate of a Buddhist temple **2**（寺庙）Buddhist temple **3**（佛教）Buddhism

【山盟海誓】shānméng-hǎishì〈成〉solemn pledge of love: 立下～ swear eternal love

【山民】shānmín〈名〉mountain inhabitant

【山明水秀】shānmíng-shuǐxiù = 山清水秀 shānqīng-shuǐxiù

【山姆大叔】Shānmǔ Dàshū〈名〉Uncle Sam [popular name for US or its government]

【山南海北】shānnán-hǎiběi〈成〉**1**〈本〉remote places: 祖国的～，到处都有勘探人员的足迹。The explorers have left their footprints all over the country. **2**〈喻〉chat aimlessly: 他们～地聊了半天。They talked for ages about everything under the sun.

【山难】shānnàn〈名〉mountain tragedy: 几名队员在～中受伤。Several team members were injured in the mountain disaster.

【山炮】shānpào〈名〉mountain cannon

【山坡】shānpō〈名〉mountain slope: 崎岖的～ rugged hillside ‖ ～筑成了梯田。The hillside has been terraced.

【山葡萄】shānpútáo〈名〉［中药］Amur Ampelopsis stem

【山墙】shānqiáng〈名〉gable: 有～的房子 gabled house

【山清水秀】shānqīng-shuǐxiù〈成〉picturesque mountain scenery

【山穷水尽】shānqióng-shuǐjìn〈成〉reach the limit of one's resources

【山丘】shānqiū〈名〉hillock: 荒芜的～ barren hill

【山区】shānqū〈名〉mountainous region: 建设/开发/支援～ develop/explore/support mountainous areas ‖ ～风光 mountain scenery ‖ ～牧场 mountain farm

【山泉】shānquán〈名〉mountain spring: 一股清澈的～ a clear mountain spring

【山雀】shānquè〈名〉［鸟类］tit

【山人】shānrén〈名〉hermit

【山色】shānsè〈名〉mountain scene: ～秀丽 beautiful mountain scene ▸湖光～

【山神】shānshén〈名〉mountain deity: ～庙 mountain deity temple

【山势】shānshì〈名〉mountain features

【山水】shānshuǐ〈名〉**1**（指水）mountain water: 引～灌溉农田 channel mountain water to irrigate fields **2**（风景）scenery: 热爱家乡的～ love the mountains and rivers in one's hometown **3**（指画）Chinese landscape painting: 泼墨～ splashed-ink landscape

【山水画】shānshuǐhuà〈名〉Chinese landscape painting: 他擅长～。He is an expert in Chinese landscape painting.

【山桃】shāntáo〈名〉mountain peach

【山桐子】shāntóngzǐ〈名〉［植物］idesia

【山头】shāntóu〈名〉**1**（山顶）hilltop: 一座～ a mountain top ‖ 占领～ occupy a hill **2**（势力）faction: 拉～ form a faction ‖ ～主义 factionalism

【山洼】shānwā〈名〉mountain valley

【山外有山，天外有天】shān wài yǒu shān, tiān wài yǒu tiān〈俗〉〈喻〉there's always something better out there

【山窝】shānwō〈名〉remote mountainous area: 到一个穷～蹲点 go and work in a poor remote mountainous area

【山窝窝】shānwōwo = 山窝 shānwō

【山坞】shānwù〈名〉nook in the hills

【山西】Shānxī ▸**p. 661**〈名〉Shanxi Province: ～梆子 Shanxi clapper opera

【山溪】shānxī〈名〉mountain stream

【山系】shānxì〈名〉mountain system: 喜马拉雅～ Himalayan Range

【山峡】shānxiá〈名〉gorge

【山险】shānxiǎn〈名〉perilous mountain pass

【山乡】shānxiāng〈名〉mountain village

【山响】shānxiǎng〈形〉thunderous: 把鞭子甩得～ make a loud crack of the whip ‖ 把鼓敲得～ beat the drums noisily

【山魈】shānxiāo〈名〉**1**［动物］mandrill **2**（鬼怪）legendary mountain spirit

【山鸦】shānyā〈名〉［鸟类］chough

【山崖】shānyá〈名〉cliff

【山阳】shānyáng〈名〉〈书〉sunny side of a mountain

【山羊】shānyáng〈名〉 1［动物］ goat 2［体育］ buck
【山羊胡子】shānyáng húzi〈名〉 goatee
【山羊绒】shānyángróng〈名〉 cashmere
【山腰】shānyāo〈名〉 hillside: 半～ halfway up the mountain ‖ 士兵们在～上呈扇形散开。The soldiers fanned out on the hillside.
【山摇地动】shānyáo-dìdòng〈成〉 earth-shattering
【山药】shānyao〈名〉［植物］ 1（薯蓣）Chinese yam 2〈方〉（甘薯） sweet potato
【山药蛋】shānyaodàn〈名〉〈方〉 potato
【山野】shānyě〈名〉 1（山岭原野）mountains and fields 2（民间） countryside: ～之民 rustic countryman
【山阴】shānyīn〈名〉〈书〉 shady side of a mountain
【山友】shānyǒu〈名〉 fellow mountaineer
【山雨欲来风满楼】shānyǔ yù lái fēng mǎn lóu〈成〉〈喻〉 a big event is always preceded by some kind of omen: ～。该国目前正处在这样的局势。There is something in the air. That is the situation in which the country finds itself today.
【山芋】shānyù〈名〉〈方〉 sweet potato
【山岳】shānyuè〈名〉〈书〉 lofty mountain: ～冰川 alpine glacier
【山楂】shānzhā〈名〉 1（指植物） hawthorn 2（指果实） haw: ～糕/露/酒 haw jelly/syrup/wine
【山楂片儿】shānzhāpiànr〈名〉 haw flake
【山寨】shānzhài A〈名〉 1（指据点） mountain stronghold 2（指村庄） mountain village: 苗家～ a Miao mountain village B〈形〉knock-off: ～手机 knock-off phone
【山珍海味】shānzhēn-hǎiwèi〈成〉 delicacies of every kind
【山中无老虎，猴子称大王】shānzhōng wú lǎohǔ, hóuzi chēng dàiwang〈俗〉 when the cat's away, the mice will play
【山茱萸】shānzhūyú〈名〉 1［植物］ cornel 2［中药］ medicinal cornel fruit
【山庄】shānzhuāng〈名〉 1（指村庄） mountain village 2（指别墅） mountain villa: 避暑～ summer retreat in the mountains
【山嘴】shānzuǐ〈名〉 spur (of a hill)

芟 shān〈动〉〈书〉 1（除草） mow 2（消灭） exterminate: ▸～除
【芟除】shānchú〈动〉 1（除草） mow: ～杂草 weed 2（删除） eliminate: ～冗词赘句 delete reduntant words and sentences

杉 shān〈名〉 China fir: ▸红～，冷～，云～
▸shā
【杉科】shānkē〈名〉 Taxodiaceae

删 shān〈动〉 cut: ～去文章中的无关细节 cut out irrelevant details from an essay ‖ 他的名字被从名单上～掉了。His name was deleted from the list. ‖ 这一段可以～去。This paragraph can be crossed out. ▸～繁就简，～改
【删除】shānchú〈动〉 cut out: ～程序/文件 delete a program/file ‖ ～多余的内容 delete anything superfluous
【删除键】shānchújiàn〈名〉［计算机］ delete key
【删定】shāndìng〈动〉 revise and finalize: ～文稿 revise and finalize a manuscript
【删繁就简】shānfán-jiùjiǎn〈成〉 simplify sth. by cutting out the superfluous
【删改】shāngǎi〈动〉 revise: 大加～ make radical changes ‖ 稿子几经～才定下来。The draft was revised several times before it was finalized.
【删减】shānjiǎn〈动〉 cut: ～文章 shorten an essay ‖ ～预算 cut a budget
【删节】shānjié〈动〉 abridge: 做一些～ make some retrenchments ‖ ～本 abridged version ‖ 它由原著～而成。It was abridged from the original work.
【删节号】shānjiéhào〈名〉 ellipsis
【删略】shānlüè〈动〉 leave out
【删汰】shāntài〈动〉〈书〉 eliminate: ～冗词赘句 eliminate redundancies
【删削】shānxuē〈动〉 cut: ～不重要的细节 cut out unimportant details

苫 shān〈名〉 1（指遮盖物） straw cover: 草～子 straw cover 2（指垫子） straw mat
▸shàn

钐（釤） shān〈名〉［化学］ samarium (Sm)
▸shàn
【钐中毒】shānzhòngdú〈名〉 samarium poisoning

衫 shān〈名〉 1（上衣） top: ▸衬～ 2（衣服） clothes: ▸衣～

姗 shān
【姗姗】shānshān〈形〉 leisurely: ～而入 amble in
【姗姗来迟】shānshān-láichí〈成〉 be slow in coming: 今年春天～。Spring is late this year. ‖ 他不太守时，开会总是～。He is not a punctual person. He is always late for meetings.

珊 shān
【珊瑚】shānhú〈名〉 coral: ～项链 coral necklace
【珊瑚虫】shānhúchóng〈名〉 coral polyp
【珊瑚岛】shānhúdǎo〈名〉 coral island
【珊瑚礁】shānhújiāo〈名〉 coral reef

栅 shān
▸zhà
【栅极】shānjí〈名〉［电子］ grid (electrode)

舢 shān
【舢板】shānbǎn〈名〉 sampan

扇 shān〈动〉 1（鼓风） fan: ～火 fan a fire ‖ 把炭火～旺 fan coal into a blaze 2（鼓动） agitate 3（用手打） slap
▸shàn
【扇动】shāndòng〈动〉 1（摇动） fan: ～翅膀 flap the wings 2 = 煽动 shāndòng

跚 shān ▸蹒跚 pánshān

煽 shān〈动〉 1 = 扇 shān 1 2（鼓动） agitate: ▸～动，～惑
【煽动】shāndòng〈动〉 stir up: ～罢工 instigate a strike ‖ ～暴力 incite violence ‖ ～民族仇恨 stir up national hatred ‖ ～排外情绪 whip up anti-foreign sentiment ‖ 这场暴乱是在一些别有用心的人的～下发生的。The riot broke out at the instigation of a few people with ulterior motives.
【煽动性】shāndòngxìng〈名〉 inflammatory nature: ～的演说/言论 inflammatory remarks ‖ ～宣传 seditious propaganda
【煽风点火】shānfēng-diǎnhuǒ〈成〉 stir up trouble: 乘机～ seize the opportunity to stir up trouble ‖ ～，制造不和 foment discord
【煽惑】shānhuò〈动〉 incite: ～人心 agitate public will ‖ 不受～ reject an instigation ‖ 他的谎言～了我。His lies misled me.
【煽情】shānqíng〈动〉 arouse enthusiasm: ～电影 sensational film ‖ 他的讲座太～了，没有一人中途退场。His lecture so engaged the audience that no one left early. ‖ 这部电影很～，赢得了不少观众的眼泪。The film was so moving that a number of people shed tears.
【煽阴风，点鬼火】shān yīnfēng, diǎn guǐhuǒ〈俗〉 stir up trouble

潸 shān〈形〉〈书〉 tearful
【潸然】shānrán〈形〉〈书〉 tearful: ～泪下 with tears trickling down one's cheeks
【潸潸】shānshān〈形〉〈书〉 1（指流泪） full of tears: 不禁～ unable to control one's tears ‖ 热泪～ tears streaming down one's cheeks 2（指下雨） relentless: 大雨～。It was raining non-stop.

膻（羶） shān〈形〉 smelling of mutton: ～羊肉 strong-smelling mutton ‖ 这羊肉太～。The mutton has got a strong smell. ▸如蚁附～，腥～
【膻气】shānqì〈名〉 mutton smell
【膻味】shānwèi〈名〉 mutton smell

shǎn

闪（閃） shǎn
A〈动〉 1（闪避） dodge: ～到一边 move quickly to one side ▸～开，躲～ 2（突然出现） appear suddenly: 黑暗里突然～出一个人来。Someone suddenly darted out of the darkness. ‖ 他脑子里～过一个念头。An idea flashed into his mind. ‖ 她脸上～过一丝微笑。A faint smile flickered across her face. 3（晃动） sway: 汽车一个急刹车，～了我一个跟头。The bus stopped suddenly, throwing me to the floor. ‖ 他身子～了一下，像是要跌倒。He swayed a little, as if about to fall. 4（扭伤） sprain: ～了腰 sprain one's back 5（闪耀） flash: ～金光 flashing golden rays ‖ 灯一～就灭了。The light flickered and went out. ‖ 钻石在阳光下～～发光。The diamond sparkles in the sunshine.
B〈名〉（闪电） lightning: ▸～电，打～
【闪避】shǎnbì〈动〉 dodge: ～目光 avoid sb.'s eyes ‖ ～不及 be too late to dodge
【闪变】shǎnbiàn〈动〉 flicker
【闪存】shǎncún〈名〉［计算机］ flash memory
【闪存盘】shǎncúnpán〈名〉 flash memory disk
【闪电】shǎndiàn〈名〉 lightning: 被～击伤 be struck by lightning ‖ 以～般的速度 with lightning speed ‖ 一道～照亮了天空。A flash of lightning lit the sky.
【闪电式】shǎndiànshì〈形〉 lightning: ～罢工 lightning strike ‖ ～访问 flying visit ‖ ～恋爱 instant romance ‖ ～入侵 speedy attack
【闪电战】shǎndiànzhàn〈名〉 blitz: 发动一场～ carry out a blitz
【闪动】shǎndòng〈动〉 flash: 操场上有个人影在～。Someone's shadow flickered on

the playground. ‖ 灯光～。 Lights flashed. ‖ 群星～。 Stars twinkled.
【闪躲】shǎnduǒ〈动〉 dodge: ～某人的拳头 dodge sb.'s blows ‖ ～到一旁 dodge to one side
【闪光】shǎnguāng **A**〈名〉 flash of light: 流星像一道～，划过夜空。 The meteor shot across the night sky like a flash of lightning. **B**〈动〉 glisten:〈喻〉～的事迹/行为 exemplary deeds/behaviour ‖〈喻〉～的语言 illuminating remarks
【闪光灯】shǎnguāngdēng〈名〉 **1**［摄影］ flashlight: 给相机安上～ mount a flashgun on a camera ‖ 内置～ built-in flash **2**（交通灯） blinker
【闪光灯泡】shǎnguāng dēngpào〈名〉 flashbulb
【闪光点】shǎnguāngdiǎn〈名〉 highlight
【闪光交通灯】shǎnguāng jiāotōngdēng〈名〉 blinker
【闪光器】shǎnguāngqì〈名〉 flash
【闪光信号】shǎnguāng xìnhào〈名〉blinking signal: ～灯 blinker lamp
【闪婚】shǎnhūn〈动〉 have a shotgun wedding
【闪击】shǎnjī〈动〉 make a surprise attack: 进行～ launch a surprise attack ‖ 遭到～ come under a surprise attack
【闪击战】shǎnjīzhàn = 闪电战 shǎndiànzhàn
【闪开】shǎnkāi〈动〉 jump aside: ～一击 dodge a blow ‖ 人们纷纷向两边～。 People quickly stepped aside.
【闪亮】shǎnliàng〈形〉 sparkling: ～的灯光 flashing lights ‖ ～的露珠 glistening dewdrops ‖ ～登场 come on to the stage in grandeur
【闪米特人】shǎnmǐtèrén〈名〉 Semite
【闪念】shǎnniàn〈动〉 flash across one's mind: 脑子一～ an idea flashes across one's mind
【闪闪】shǎnshǎn〈形〉 glittering: ～的红星 sparkling red star ‖ 金子在阳光下～发亮。 Gold glitters in the sunshine. ‖ 钻石～发光。 Diamonds have a bright sparkle.
【闪射】shǎnshè〈动〉 shine: 他的眼睛～出智慧的光芒。 His eyes sparkled with wisdom.
【闪身】shǎnshēn〈动〉 **1**（躲避） dodge: ～躲进屋里 duck into a room **2**（侧身） walk sideways: 请～让她过去。 Please turn to let her pass.
【闪失】shǎnshī〈名〉 mishap: 万一有个～，后悔就晚了。 If anything goes wrong, it will be too late for regrets. ‖ 这事决不会有～的。 Nothing can go wrong with this.
【闪烁】shǎnshuò〈动〉 **1**（指光亮） twinkle: 眼睛里～着泪花 eyes glistening with tears ‖ 灯光～不定。 The light kept flickering. ‖ 星星在天空中～。 Stars twinkle in the sky. **2**（吞吞吐吐） be evasive: 他对问题闪闪烁烁，不做正面回答。 He hummed and hawed, giving no direct reply to the question. ▸～其词
【闪烁其词】shǎnshuò-qící〈成〉equivocate: ～的答复 evasive answer ‖ 别～，给我们一个明确的答复。 Don't skirt around the issue. Give us a clear answer.
【闪现】shǎnxiàn〈动〉 appear in a flash: 她的心中～出一线希望。 A flicker of hope flashed within her. ‖ 一个荒唐的念头在他脑海里～。 An absurd idea suddenly flashed in his mind.
【闪耀】shǎnyào〈动〉glitter: 繁星～。 The stars are twinkling.
【闪熠】shǎnyì〈动〉〈书〉 glitter: 远处灯火～。 The lights glittered in the distance.
【闪音】shǎnyīn〈名〉［语言］ flap

陕（陝） Shǎn ▸p. 661〈名〉

Shan [another name for Shaanxi Province (陕西)]: 川～公路 Sichuan-Shaanxi Highway ‖ ～北 Northern Shaanxi ▸～西
【陕西】Shǎnxī ▸p. 661〈名〉Shaanxi Province
【陕西梆子】Shǎnxī bāngzi = 秦腔 qínqiāng

掺（摻） shǎn〈动〉〈书〉 grasp:

～手 shake hands
▸càn, chān

睒（睒） shǎn〈动〉 blink:

一～眼就不见了 disappear in the blink of an eye ‖ 一～眼的功夫 in the blink of an eye

shàn

讪（訕） shàn

A〈动〉 mock: ▸～笑, 搭～
B〈形〉 embarrassed: 脸上发～ look embarrassed ‖ ～～地走开 walk away in embarrassment
【讪脸】shànliǎn〈动〉〈方〉 grin mischievously: 不准在大人面前～。 Don't act up in front of adults.
【讪讪】shànshàn〈形〉 embarrassed: 他～地走开了。 He walked away, looking embarrassed.
【讪笑】shànxiào〈动〉 mock: 继续努力，不要怕别人～。 Keep trying; don't let others put you off. ‖ 他的预言遭到大家的～。 His prophecy was greeted with a good deal of ridicule.

汕 Shàn

【汕头】Shàntóu〈名〉 Shantou

苫 shàn〈动〉 cover:

用席把麦子～上 cover the wheat with straw mats ‖ 房顶～了一块油布。 The roof was covered with a tarpaulin.
▸shān
【苫背】shànbèi〈动〉 cover straw or mat with plaster as the foundation of a roof
【苫布】shànbù〈名〉 tarpaulin
【苫席】shànxí〈名〉 mat cover

钐（釤） shàn

A〈名〉 scythe
B〈动〉 cut with a scythe: ～草 cut grass with a scythe ‖ ～麦子 cut wheat with a big sickle
▸shān
【钐刀】shàndāo = 钐镰 shànlián
【钐镰】shànlián〈名〉 scythe

疝 shàn〈名〉 hernia:

腹股沟～ inguinal hernia ▸～气
【疝气】shànqì ▸p. 50〈名〉［医学］ hernia

单（單） Shàn〈名〉Shan [surname]

▸chán, dān

扇 shàn

A〈名〉 **1**（扇子） fan: ～骨 fan ribs ‖ ～面儿 fan cover ‖ ～坠 fan pendant ‖ 排气～ ventilation fan ‖ 台～ table fan ▸芭蕉～, 电～, 吊～, 落地～, 折～ **2**（遮挡物） leaf: 四～屏风 four-leaf screen ▸隔～, 门～, 磨～
B〈量〉 leaf: 一～门 a door leaf ‖ 他打开了一～窗户。 He opened a window leaf.
▸shān
【扇贝】shànbèi〈名〉［动物］ scallop
【扇区】shànqū〈名〉［计算机］ sector: ～是磁盘上的最小物理存储单位。 A sector is the smallest physical storage unit on a disk.
【扇形】shànxíng〈名〉 **1**（指形状） fan: 孔雀把尾羽展成～。 The peacock fanned its tail. ‖ 士兵们在山腰上呈～散开。 The soldiers fanned out on the hillside. **2**［数学］ sector
【扇形图】shànxíngtú〈名〉［数学］fan diagram
【扇状】shànzhuàng〈名〉 fan shape: ～分布 fan-like distribution
【扇子】shànzi〈名〉 fan: 一把～ a fan ‖ 不停地扇～ keep fanning oneself

墠（壇） shàn〈名〉 sacrificial place

禅（撣） Shàn〈名〉

1［历史］（指傣族） Shan **2**（指掸人） Shan [ethnic group in Burma]
▸dǎn

善 shàn

A〈形〉 **1**（好） good: ～策 wise policy ▸改～, 完～ **2**（善良） kind: 相～ be kind to each other ▸慈～, 和～, 面～ **3**（友好） friendly: ▸亲～, 友～
B〈名〉 benevolence: ▸～举, 行～
C〈动〉 **1**（做好） do well: ▸～后, ～始～终 **2**（擅长） be good at: ～交际 be a good mixer ▸能歌～舞, 循循～诱 **3**（易于） be likely to: ▸～变, 多愁～感
D〈副〉 well: ▸～罢甘休
【善罢甘休】shànbà-gānxiū〈成〉 [usu used in the negative or interrogative] leave it at that: 我想他不会～。 I don't think he'll let it go that easily.
【善报】shànbào〈名〉 positive reward: ▸善有～，恶有恶报
【善本】shànběn〈名〉 [of ancient books] best edition: ～书 rare book
【善变】shànbiàn〈动〉 be changeable
【善处】shànchǔ〈动〉〈书〉 deal properly (with)
【善待】shàndài〈动〉 treat well: ～员工 be good to one's employees ‖ 全社会都应当～老人。 Society should take good care of its senior citizens.
【善恶】shàn'è〈名〉 good and evil: ～不分 unable to tell good from evil
【善感】shàngǎn〈形〉 sensitive: ▸多愁～
【善后】shànhòu〈动〉 deal effectively with the aftermath of a situation: ～物资 relief goods and materials
【善举】shànjǔ〈名〉〈书〉 charitable act: 希望工程是一大～。 The Hope Project is a charitable activity. ‖ 他的～使许多穷孩子能够上大学。 His benevolence made it possible for many poor children to attend college.
【善类】shànlèi〈名〉〈书〉 [usu used in the negative] good people: 此人面目凶恶，定非～。 He looks ferocious and cannot possibly be a good man.
【善良】shànliáng〈形〉 kind-hearted: 本性～ be kind by nature ‖ ～的人们 good and honest people ‖ 她心地～。 She is kind-hearted.

S

【善男信女】shànnán-xìnnǚ〈成〉 Buddhist believers: 这座佛寺每天都有许多～来上香。 Everyday many Buddhists make pilgrimages to this temple.
【善人】shànrén〈名〉 well-doer
【善始善终】shànshǐ-shànzhōng〈成〉 do a good job from beginning to end: 我们无论干什么事情都要～。 Whatever we do, we should do it well from start to finish.
【善事】shànshì〈名〉 good deed: 做一件～ do a good deed ‖ 建学校是件～。 Building a school is an act of charity.
【善忘】shànwàng〈动〉 be forgetful: 他很～。 He is very forgetful.
【善心】shànxīn〈名〉 benevolence: 发～ show mercy
【善行】shànxíng〈名〉 kind deed
【善意】shànyì〈名〉 good will: 出于～ out of good will ‖ ～的批评 constructive criticism ‖ ～的忠告 well-meaning advice
【善有善报，恶有恶报】shàn yǒu shànbào, è yǒu èbào〈成〉 good is rewarded with good, and evil with evil: ～；不是不报，时候未到。 Good will be rewarded with good sooner or later, and the same is true of evil.
【善于】shànyú〈动〉 be good at: ～辞令 be very articulate ‖ ～交际 be good at socializing ‖ ～用人 know how to choose the right person for the right job
【善战】shànzhàn〈动〉 be good in battle: 勇敢～ be brave and good in battle
【善者不来，来者不善】shànzhě bù lái, láizhě bù shàn〈成〉 if your enemy comes to your door, it is advisable to prepare for the worst
【善终】shànzhōng〈动〉 1（老死） die a natural death 2（圆满结束） end well: ▸善始～

禅（禪）

shàn〈动〉 abdicate: 受～ accept the abdicated throne ▸～让, ～位 ▸chán
【禅让】shànràng〈动〉 abdicate: ～制 system of abdication
【禅位】shànwèi〈动〉 abdicate the throne

骟（騸）

shàn〈动〉 castrate: ～马 castrate a horse

缮（繕）

shàn〈动〉 1（修补） mend: ～甲兵 repair armour and weapons ▸修～ 2（抄写） copy: ▸～发, ～写
【缮发】shànfā〈动〉〈书〉 copy and send out: ～文件 copy a document and send it out
【缮写】shànxiě〈动〉 copy: ～员 copyist

擅

shàn〈动〉 1（专有） appropriate: ▸～权 2（擅自） do sth. on one's own authority: ～作主张 make a decision without authorization ▸～离职守 3（善于） be good at: ～辞令 be refined in one's speech ▸～长
【擅长】shàncháng〈动〉 be good at: ～刺绣 be good at embroidery ‖ ～花样滑冰 be an expert figure skater ‖ ～书画 be good at painting and calligraphy
【擅离职守】shànlí-zhíshǒu〈成〉 be absent without leave: ～20分钟 go AWOL for 20 minutes
【擅权】shànquán〈动〉 have sole power
【擅自】shànzì〈动〉 act without authorization: ～决定 make arbitrary decisions ‖ ～挪用公款 misappropriate public funds without authorization ‖ ～行动 act presumptuously ‖ 不得～改变操作规程。 The operation rules mustn't be changed without permission.

膳

shàn〈名〉 meal: 进/用～ take/eat one's meal ‖ 晚～ supper ▸～食, 御～
【膳费】shànfèi〈名〉 board expenses: ～自理 handle one's own board expenses
【膳食】shànshí〈名〉 meals: 改善学校～ improve school meals ‖ 合理的～结构 proper diet ‖ ～津贴 food subsidy
【膳宿】shànsù〈名〉 board and lodging: 提供～ provide food and lodgings

嬗

shàn〈动〉〈书〉 transform: ▸～变
【嬗变】shànbiàn A〈动〉〈书〉 evolve: 研究中国书法的～ study the evolution of Chinese calligraphy B〈名〉［物理］ transmutation: 核～ nuclear transmutation

赡（贍）

shàn〈动〉 support: ▸～养
【赡养】shànyǎng〈动〉 support: ～父母 provide for one's parents ‖ ～义务 duty to support ‖ ～费 support payments (for one's parents)

蟮

shàn ▸曲蟮 qūshàn

鳝（鱔）

shàn
【鳝鱼】shànyú〈名〉 eel

shāng

伤（傷）

shāng
A〈名〉 wound: 治～ treat a wound ‖ 眼～ eye injury ‖ 她的头部受了轻～。 She received a minor injury to her head. ▸暗～, 工～, 养～
B〈动〉 1（伤害） injure: ～身体 injure one's health ‖ ～了和气 injure a friendship ‖ 他～了腿。 He hurt his leg. ‖ ～感情 hurt sb.'s feelings ‖ 你～了他的自尊心。 You've damaged his ego. 2（致病） develop an illness: ▸～风, ～寒 3（指过度） get sick of sth.: 喝酒喝～了 get sick of drinking 4（妨碍） harm: 无～大雅 not matter much
C〈形〉 distressed: ▸～怀, 悲～
【伤疤】shāngbā〈名〉 1（疤痕） scar: 留下～ leave a scar ‖ 旧～ old scar ‖ 好了～忘了疼 forget the pain when the wound has healed 2〈喻〉 past mistake: 揭他的～是不对的。 It's not right to expose the mistakes he made in the past.
【伤悲】shāngbēi〈形〉 sad: ▸少壮不努力，老大徒～
【伤兵】shāngbīng〈名〉 wounded soldier
【伤病】shāngbìng〈名〉 injury and sickness: ～员 the sick and wounded ‖ 由于～太多，我们输了这场比赛。 We lost the match because a number of players in our team were injured or sick.
【伤财】shāngcái〈动〉 waste money: ▸劳民～
【伤残】shāngcán A〈动〉 1（指人） be disabled: 终身～ be permanently disabled ‖ 他是在一次车祸中～的。 He was disabled in a traffic accident. 2（指物） be defective B〈名〉 1（指人） disability: 身体有～ be physically disabled 2（指物） defect: 这个陶罐有明显～。 This earthenware pot is clearly defective.
【伤残保险】shāngcán bǎoxiǎn〈名〉 disability insurance
【伤悼】shāngdào〈动〉〈书〉 mourn sorrowfully
【伤风】shāngfēng ▸p. 50 A〈名〉 cold: 患～ catch a cold ‖ 治愈～ shake off a cold B〈动〉 have a cold: 她～头痛。 She has a head cold. ‖ 我大概～了。 Maybe I've got a cold.
【伤风败俗】shāngfēng-bàisú〈成〉 offend public decency
【伤感】shānggǎn〈形〉 sentimental: ～的歌曲/音乐 sentimental song/music
【伤害】shānghài〈动〉 hurt: ～感情 hurt sb.'s feelings ‖ ～他人身体 do an injury to sb. ‖ ～自尊心 wound sb.'s pride ‖ 免受～ escape injury
【伤害保险】shānghài bǎoxiǎn〈名〉 injury insurance
【伤害罪】shānghàizuì〈名〉［法律］ crime of inflicting bodily harm
【伤寒】shānghán ▸p. 50〈名〉 1［医学］ typhoid: ～杆菌 typhoid bacillus ‖ 副～ paratyphoid 2［中医］ fevers
【伤耗】shānghao〈动〉 damage: 运输中的～ shipping damage
【伤痕】shānghén〈名〉 bruise: 满身～ be covered in cuts and bruises ‖ 心灵上的～很难愈合。 Psychological scars are difficult to heal.
【伤痕文学】shānghén wénxué〈名〉 trauma literature [literature represented by the short story *Scar*, depicting the tragic experiences and spiritual wounds suffered by people in the Cultural Revolution]
【伤怀】shānghuái〈形〉〈书〉 distressed
【伤筋动骨】shāngjīn-dònggǔ〈成〉 have a sprain or fracture: 他摔了一跤，但并未～。 He tripped and fell, but didn't break any bones. ‖ ～一百天。 It usually takes about 100 days to recover from a fracture.
【伤口】shāngkǒu〈名〉 wound: 包扎～ dress a wound ‖ 为～消毒 disinfect a cut
【伤脑筋】shāng nǎojīn〈动〉 cause trouble: 为某事～ trouble one's mind about sth. ‖ ～的问题 knotty problem
【伤情】shāngqíng A〈名〉 state of an injury: 查看～ check on sb.'s wound B〈动〉 be sad: 女儿死去已一年多了，但他们还很～。 Their daughter died over a year ago, but they are still grieving.
【伤人】shāngrén〈动〉 1（伤害精神） hurt sb.'s feelings: ～的话 injurious remarks 2（伤害身体） inflict injuries: 我们可以和他们论理，但绝对不许～。 We can reason with them, but can never injure anyone.
【伤神】shāngshén〈动〉 1（费心） be nerve-racking: 他的父母为他上学很～。 His parents worried a lot about his schooling. 2〈书〉（伤心） feel sad: 挚友去世，他倍感～。 He grieved over the death of his close friend.
【伤生】shāngshēng〈动〉 1（杀害） kill: ～害命 kill living things 2（伤害身体） sap one's vitality: 积劳成疾，久郁～。 Constant overwork can make you ill.
【伤势】shāngshì〈名〉 state of an injury: 他头部的～很重。 He has suffered a severe injury to the head.
【伤逝】shāngshì〈动〉 1（哀悼） mourn sb.'s death 2（伤感） grieve
【伤天害理】shāngtiān-hàilǐ〈成〉 be ruthless and devoid of human feelings: 他岂敢做出如此～的事来？ How could he have the nerve to do something so inhuman?
【伤停补时】shāngtíng bǔshí〈名〉［足球］ injury time

S

【伤痛】shāngtòng〈名〉**1** (指感情) grief: 中年丧妻，～万分。It can be devastating to lose one's wife in middle age. **2** (指身体) pain: 身体的～ bodily pain

【伤亡】shāngwáng **A**〈动〉be injured or killed: ～惨重 incur heavy casualties ‖ 火灾造成47人～。The fire claimed 47 lives. **B**〈名〉casualties: 使敌人遭到重大～ inflict great losses on the enemy ‖ 双方都有～。There were casualties on both sides.

【伤心】shāngxīn〈动〉grieve: ～而死 die of a broken heart ‖ ～落泪 cry with grief ‖ 触到～处 hit a nerve ‖ 不要太～。Don't take it too much to heart. ‖ 他那些无情的话伤透了她的心。His cruel remarks cut her deeply.

【伤员】shāngyuán〈名〉wounded personnel: 抢救～ rescue the wounded

汤（湯）shāng

▸tāng

【汤汤】shāngshāng〈形〉〈书〉torrential: 浩浩～，横无际涯 torrential and boundless

殇（殤）shāng

A〈动〉〈书〉die young
B〈名〉a person who dies in battle: ▸国～

商[1] shāng

〈名〉**1** Shāng (商朝) Shang Dynasty **2** (商人) businessman: 古董～ antiques dealer ‖ 杂货～ grocer ▸奸～, 客～, 外～ **3** (商业) business: 弃～ stop trading ‖ ～用电脑 commercial computer ▸～场, 经～, 通～ **4** (指星宿) fifth of the 28 constellations in ancient Chinese astronomy

商[2] shāng

〈动〉discuss: 有要事相～ have important matters to discuss ▸～谈, 磋～, 协～

商[3] shāng

〈名〉［音乐］note on the ancient Chinese pentatonic (五音) scale, corresponding to 2 in *jianpu* (简谱) numbered musical notation

商[4] shāng ［数学］

A〈名〉quotient: 10 除以 2 的～是 5。If ten is divided by two, the quotient is five. ▸情～, 智～
B〈动〉use a number as a quotient: 10 除以 2～5。Ten divided by two is five.

【商标】shāngbiāo〈名〉brand: 著名～ famous brand ‖ 注册～ register a trademark ‖ 名牌～ well-known brand

【商标法】shāngbiāofǎ〈名〉trademark law

【商标侵权】shāngbiāo qīnquán〈名〉trademark infringement

【商标权】shāngbiāoquán〈名〉trademark rights

【商标注册】shāngbiāo zhùcè〈名〉trademark registration: ～费 trademark registration fee ‖ ～申请书 application to register a trademark

【商标专用权】shāngbiāo zhuānyòngquán〈名〉sole rights to a trademark

【商标转让】shāngbiāo zhuǎnràng〈名〉assignment of trademark

【商埠】shāngbù〈名〉〈旧〉trading port

【商场】shāngchǎng〈名〉**1** (市场) market **2** (大商店) department store: 一家灯火辉煌的大～ a brightly-lit mega-mall **3** (商界) business world: ～如战场。Competition in the market place is as fierce as that in war.

【商城】shāngchéng〈名〉shopping centre

【商店】shāngdiàn〈名〉shop〈英〉; store〈美〉: 儿童用品～ children's shop ‖ 日夜～ 24-hour shop ‖ 自助～ self-service shop ‖ 在一家～工作 work in a shop

【商调】shāngdiào〈动〉negotiate a transfer: 从其他院校～两名教授参与此项科研 negotiate the transfer of two professors from other universities for the research project

【商调函】shāngdiàohán〈名〉letter requesting transfer of personnel

【商定】shāngdìng〈动〉agree: ～婚期 collectively decide upon a wedding date ‖ 经～ it has been decided through consultation ‖ 两国～建立大使级的外交关系。The two countries have agreed to establish diplomatic relations at the ambassadorial level.

【商队】shāngduì〈名〉group of travelling salesmen

【商法】shāngfǎ〈名〉［法律］commercial law

【商贩】shāngfàn〈名〉small retailer: 不法～ law-breaking pedlar ‖ 个体～ self-employed vendor ‖ 路边～ street trader ‖ 小～ petty dealer

【商港】shānggǎng〈名〉commercial port

【商贾】shānggǔ〈名〉〈书〉merchant

【商海】shānghǎi〈名〉commercial world

【商行】shāngháng〈名〉business establishment

【商号】shānghào〈名〉business establishment: 历史悠久的～ firm of long standing ‖ 他已把～交给儿子经营。He has handed over his business to his son.

【商会】shānghuì〈名〉chamber of commerce: ～会长 chairperson of the chamber of commerce

【商机】shāngjī〈名〉business opportunity: 提供巨大～ offer huge commercial opportunities

【商检】shāngjiǎn〈简称〉= 商品检验

【商检局】shāngjiǎnjú〈名〉commodity inspection bureau

【商界】shāngjiè〈名〉business circles: 步入～ enter the commercial world ‖ 立足～ establish oneself in business ‖ ～巨子 business tycoon

【商籁体】shānglàitǐ = 十四行诗 shísìhángshī

【商量】shāngliang〈动〉talk over: ～对策 talk through counter measures ‖ 共同～ discuss together ‖ 他被请来～此事。He was called in for consultation over the matter. ‖ 这事好～。This can be settled through discussion.

【商路】shānglù〈名〉trade route

【商旅】shānglǚ〈名〉travelling merchants

【商贸】shāngmào〈名〉business and trade: ～机构 commercial and trading establishments ‖ ～集团 commercial conglomerate

【商品】shāngpǐn〈名〉goods: 陈列/出售/生产～ display/sell/produce goods ‖ 抵制外国～ boycott foreign merchandise ‖ 购买廉价～ buy bargain goods ‖ 内销～ commodities for the home market ‖ 清仓处理～ clearance goods

【商品房】shāngpǐnfáng〈名〉commercial housing: 开发～ develop commercial buildings

【商品化】shāngpǐnhuà〈动〉commercialize: 加速科研成果～ accelerate the commercialization of scientific and technological achievements

【商品价格】shāngpǐn jiàgé〈名〉commodity price

【商品检验】shāngpǐn jiǎnyàn〈名〉goods inspection: ～法 Commodity Inspection Law ‖ ～局 goods inspection and testing bureau

【商品交易】shāngpǐn jiāoyì〈名〉commodity transaction: 举办～会 hold a trade fair

【商品经济】shāngpǐn jīngjì〈名〉cash economy: 发展～ develop a cash economy

【商品粮】shāngpǐnliáng〈名〉marketable grain

【商品流通】shāngpǐn liútōng〈名〉commodity circulation: ～渠道 commodity circulation channel

【商品期权】shāngpǐn qīquán〈名〉commodity option

【商品生产】shāngpǐn shēngchǎn〈名〉commodity production: ～基地 commodity production base ‖ ～者 commodity producer

【商品市场】shāngpǐn shìchǎng〈名〉commodity market

【商品条形码】shāngpǐn tiáoxíngmǎ〈名〉bar code

【商品销售市场】shāngpǐn xiāoshòu shìchǎng〈名〉goods market

【商品学】shāngpǐnxué〈名〉merchandising

【商品展销会】shāngpǐn zhǎnxiāohuì〈名〉trade show

【商洽】shāngqià〈动〉consult and discuss: 具体业务请与对口单位～。For any specific business, please discuss with your counterparts.

【商情】shāngqíng〈名〉market conditions: ～预测 business forecasting ‖ ～晴雨表 business barometer

【商榷】shāngquè〈动〉deliberate: 文中的有些论点值得～。Some of the points in this essay are open to question. ‖ 这个问题如何处理，有待～。This problem must be discussed before it can be solved.

【商人】shāngrén〈名〉business person: 零售～ retail trader

【商厦】shāngshà〈名〉business plaza

【商社】shāngshè〈名〉commercial company: 外国～ foreign company

【商数】shāngshù〈名〉［数学］quotient: 智力～ intelligence quotient (IQ)

【商谈】shāngtán〈动〉negotiate: ～国家大事 discuss state affairs ‖ ～交接事宜 talk through matters relating to the handover ‖ ～一笔生意 negotiate a business deal

【商讨】shāngtǎo〈动〉discuss: ～共同关心的问题 confer upon matters of mutual concern ‖ ～合同 discuss a contract ‖ 我们愿意～。We are ready for discussions.

【商亭】shāngtíng〈名〉vendor's kiosk

【商务】shāngwù〈名〉commercial affairs: 洽谈～ negotiate business ‖ ～报告 business report ‖ ～活动 commercial activity

【商务参赞】shāngwù cānzàn〈名〉commercial attaché

【商务舱】shāngwùcāng〈名〉business class: 他决定乘坐～。He decided to go business class.

【商务车】shāngwùchē〈名〉business car

【商务代办】shāngwù dàibàn〈名〉commercial agent

【商务会谈】shāngwù huìtán〈名〉business negotiations

【商务旅游】shāngwù lǚyóu〈名〉business trip

【商务秘书】shāngwù mìshū〈名〉commercial secretary

【商务中心】shāngwù zhōngxīn〈名〉business centre

【商学院】shāngxuéyuàn〈名〉business school

【商业】shāngyè〈名〉commerce: 发展～ develop trade ‖ ～不景气 commercial slump ‖ ～对手 business rival ‖ ～情报/信息 business intelligence ‖ ～繁荣。Business is booming.
【商业部】shāngyèbù〈名〉ministry of commerce: ～长 minister of commerce
【商业炒作】shāngyè chǎozuò〈名〉commercial speculation
【商业广告】shāngyè guǎnggào〈名〉commercial advertising: 电视～ TV commercials
【商业化】shāngyèhuà〈动〉commercialize: 现在圣诞节已经非常～了。Christmas has become very commercialized these days.
【商业间谍】shāngyè jiàndié〈名〉corporate spy: ～活动 corporate spying
【商业街】shāngyèjiē〈名〉shopping street
【商业经济】shāngyè jīngjì〈名〉business economy: ～学 business economics
【商业竞争】shāngyè jìngzhēng〈名〉commercial competition: 缓和/加剧～ ease/intensify competition in business ‖ 激烈的～ fierce commercial competition
【商业片】shāngyèpiàn〈名〉commercial film
【商业区】shāngyèqū〈名〉business quarter: 建立～ establish a commercial district ‖ 去～购物 go shopping downtown
【商业网】shāngyèwǎng〈名〉business network: 扩大～ broaden a business network ‖ ～点 network of trading establishments ‖ ～站 business website
【商业信贷】shāngyè xìndài〈名〉commercial credit: 提供～ grant commercial credit
【商业银行】shāngyè yínháng〈名〉commercial bank
【商业用语】shāngyè yòngyǔ〈名〉business jargon
【商业中心】shāngyè zhōngxīn〈名〉business centre
【商议】shāngyì〈动〉discuss: ～重大问题 confer (with sb.) on a weighty issue ‖ 我们下周再～此事。We will talk about this matter next week.
【商誉】shāngyù〈名〉business reputation
【商约】shāngyuē〈名〉commercial treaty
【商栈】shāngzhàn〈名〉inn for caravans
【商战】shāngzhàn〈名〉trade war
【商住楼】shāngzhùlóu〈名〉office building
【商酌】shāngzhuó〈动〉〈书〉deliberate over: 计划有待进一步～。The plan needs further discussion and consideration.

觞（觴） shāng〈名〉〈古〉drinking vessel: 举～称贺 raise one's glass in praise of sb.

墒 shāng〈名〉［农业］moisture in the soil: ▸～情, 保～
【墒情】shāngqíng〈名〉soil moisture content: 这场雨后，～很好。There is adequate moisture in the soil after this rainfall.

熵 shāng〈名〉［物理］entropy

shǎng

上 shǎng
▸shàng, shang
【上声】shǎngshēng〈名〉［语言］1 （指古汉语） rising tone [second of the four tones in classical Chinese pronunciation] 2 （指普通话） falling-rising tone [third of the four tones in modern standard Chinese pronunciation]

垧 shǎng〈量〉*shang* [an area of land equal to fifteen *mu* in most parts of north-east China and three or five *mu* in north-west China]

晌 shǎng〈名〉1 （指时间段） certain time of day: 后半～儿 afternoon ‖ 前半～儿 morning 2 〈方〉（中午） noon: 歇～ take a midday nap
【晌午】shǎngwu〈名〉〈口〉midday: 都～了，该吃饭了。It's already twelve. It's time for lunch.

赏（賞） shǎng
A 〈动〉1 （奖赏） award: ～一件礼物 reward sb. with a gift ‖ ～一千元 award sb. 1,000 *yuan* ▸～罚分明, 奖～, 论功行～ 2 （赏识） appreciate: ▸称～, 赞～ 3 （欣赏） enjoy: 尽～美景 feast one's eyes upon a beautiful scene ▸观～, 欣～, 雅俗共～ 4 （给予） honour sb. with one's presence: ▸～光, ～脸
B 〈名〉award: 领～ claim an award ‖ 提供银行抢劫案线索者有～。Rewards will be given to anyone who can offer information about the bank robbery. ▸悬～, 重～
【赏赐】shǎngcì A〈动〉award: ～一大笔钱 give sb. a large sum of money ‖ ～一匹马 reward sb. with a horse B〈名〉reward: 得到很多～ receive a handsome reward
【赏罚】shǎngfá〈动〉reward and punish: 得到应有的～ get what one deserves ‖ ～分明
【赏罚分明】shǎngfá-fēnmíng〈成〉be fair in meting out rewards and punishments
【赏封】shǎngfēng〈名〉〈旧〉gift money in a red envelope (given to children or servants on festive occasions): 准备～ prepare gift money in red envelopes ‖ 这是舅舅给我的～。This red envelope was given to me by my uncle.
【赏格】shǎnggé〈名〉size of a reward: 警方悬出10万元～捉拿罪犯。The police are offering a reward of 100,000 *yuan* for the capture of the criminal.
【赏功罚罪】shǎnggōng-fázuì〈成〉reward those who have rendered outstanding services and punish those who have committed crimes
【赏光】shǎngguāng〈动〉〈套〉honour sb. with one's presence: 承蒙诸位～，不胜荣幸。Your presence is our greatest honour. ‖ 敬请～。We request the honour of your company.
【赏鉴】shǎngjiàn〈动〉appreciate and evaluate: ～字画 appreciate works of calligraphy and painting
【赏金】shǎngjīn〈名〉financial reward: 领取～ claim a reward ‖ 丰厚的～ handsome reward
【赏赉】shǎnglài〈动〉〈书〉grant a reward
【赏脸】shǎngliǎn〈动〉〈套〉1 （指答应要求） honour sb. with one's presence: 可否～与我一起吃饭？Will you do me the honour of dining with me? 2 （指接受赠品） please accept my present: 小礼物一件，请～笑纳。Please accept this small gift.
【赏钱】shǎngqián〈名〉financial reward: 一笔丰厚的～ a handsome reward ‖ 给～ grant a reward
【赏识】shǎngshí〈动〉appreciate: ～某人的才能 appreciate sb.'s abilities ‖ 教授非常～这篇博士论文。The professor thinks highly of the doctoral dissertation.
【赏玩】shǎngwán〈动〉enjoy: ～古董 delight in appreciating antiques ‖ ～山景 enjoy mountain scenery
【赏析】shǎngxī〈动〉〈书〉analyse appreciatively: 名篇～ analyse appreciatively classical works
【赏心乐事】shǎngxīn-lèshì〈成〉happy event
【赏心悦目】shǎngxīn-yuèmù〈成〉pleasing both the eye and the mind: ～的比赛 entertaining match ‖ ～的景物 feast for the eyes ‖ 桂林山水令人～。The scenery of Guilin delights both the eye and the mind.
【赏月】shǎngyuè〈动〉enjoy the moon: 中秋～ enjoy a full bright moon at Mid-Autumn Festival
【赏阅】shǎngyuè〈动〉read for pleasure: ～一篇散文 read a piece of prose for pleasure

shàng

上[1] shàng
A 〈名〉1 （高处） high place: ～部 upper part ‖ 往～看 look up ▸～有老，下有小，高高在～ 2 （皇帝） emperor: ▸～谕, 皇～ 3 （指地位等级） superior: ▸～行下效, ～级, ～将, 犯～作乱 4 （指顺序） last time: ～次 last time ‖ ～周 last week ‖ 今年～半年 first half of this year ▸～集, ～届, ～联 5 （指质量） thing of higher rank: ▸～等
B 〈动〉1 （登乘） ascend: ～船/飞机/火车 board a ship/an aircraft/a train ‖ ～楼 go upstairs ▸～马, ～山 2 （进行） advance: ～项目 launch a project ‖ 见困难就～ face up to difficulties ▸～升, 扶摇直～ 3 （呈递） submit: ▸～供, ～书, ～交, ～缴 4 （前往） go to: ～厕所 go to the toilet ‖ ～火线 go to the battle front ‖ 你～哪儿（去）？Where are you going? ▸～街 5 （达到） be up to: 比赛吸引了～万观众。The match attracted over 10,000 spectators. ▸～年纪, 日～三竿 6 （登台） appear on the stage; （上场） enter the court/field: 换人! 10号下，8号～。Substitution: Player No 8 for No 10. ‖ 前半场你们五人～。The five of you will play in the first half. ▸～场, ～演, ～阵 7 （添加） add: ▸～货, ～水 8 （登载） be recorded: 他的名字～了光荣榜。His name featured in the roll of honour. ‖ 这个故事～了晚间新闻。The story made the evening news. ▸～报, ～账 9 （安装） fit: ～刺刀 fix a bayonet ‖ ～螺丝 fix a screw 10 （拧紧） tighten: ～发条 wind a spring ‖ 螺丝没有～紧。The screw hasn't been tightened. 11 （涂抹） apply: ～药 apply medicine ‖ 给机器～油 oil the machine 12 （开始） do sth. at a fixed time: ～晚班 work the night shift ‖ ～英语课 have an English class ▸～学 13 （遭遇） come across: ▸～当, ～圈套 14 （端送） serve: ～汤 serve soup ‖ 你们要的菜全～齐了。All the dishes you ordered have been served. 15 （表由低到高） move upward: 登～山顶 reach the peak ‖ 飞～蓝天 soar into the sky ‖ 跟～时代步伐 keep up with the times 16 （表结果） [used after a verb indicating the attainment of an objective]: 当～人大代表 be elected as a deputy to the National People's Congress ‖ 考～大学 be admitted to a university 17 （表开始并继续） [used after a verb indicating the beginning and continuation of an action]: 她爱～了一位足球

运动员。She has fallen in love with a football player. ‖ 院子里种~了树。Trees have been planted in the courtyard. **18**（表数量）[used after a verb indicating an amount, value or extent reached or to be reached]: 多呆~几天 stay a few more days ‖ 下~几盘象棋 have a few games of chess

C〈副〉upward: ▸~进, ~涨

上² shàng〈名〉[音乐] note on the *gongche* (工尺) scale, corresponding to 1 in *jianpu* (简谱) numbered musical notation ▸shǎng, shang

【上班】shàngbān〈动〉go to work: ~时间 office hours ‖ 下午不~。No work this afternoon. ‖ 他~去了。He has gone to work.

【上班族】shàngbānzú〈名〉wage earners

【上半场】shàngbànchǎng〈名〉first half: ~的最后一个节目 the last item on the first half of the programme ‖ ~该队以7分领先。The team led by seven points at the half-way point.

【上半年】shàngbànnián ▸**p. 618**〈名〉first half of a year: 去年~ first half of last year ‖ 他今年~赚了一大笔钱。He made a large sum of money in the first half of this year.

【上半身】shàngbànshēn〈名〉upper part of the body

【上半时】shàngbànshí = 上半场 shàngbànchǎng

【上半天】shàngbàntiān〈名〉morning: ~经理有时间。The manager will be free in the morning.

【上半夜】shàngbànyè〈名〉first half of the night: 外面很吵，~我没睡着。It was so noisy outside that I didn't sleep until after midnight.

【上报】shàngbào〈动〉**1**（呈报）report to: ~国务院 report to the State Council ‖ 将计划~审批 submit a plan for approval **2**（登报）appear in the newspapers: 他的事迹~了。His feat made the papers.

【上辈儿】shàngbèir〈名〉**1**（祖先）ancestors: 我们的~到这里定居，已经三百多年了。It is over three hundred years since our ancestors settled here. **2**（长辈）elders

【上辈子】shàngbèizi〈名〉**1**（祖先）ancestors: 我们家~在明末从山西迁到陕西。My ancestors moved from Shanxi to Shaanxi in the late Ming Dynasty. **2** ▸**p. 618**（前世）previous life: ~造孽，下辈子遭报应。If you do wrong in this life, you will pay for it in the next.

【上臂】shàngbì〈名〉upper arm

【上边】shàngbian〈名〉**1**（指方位）higher place: 洗脸池~有一面镜子。There is a mirror above the wash basin. **2**（指级别）higher authority: ~派人来调查事故。The authorities have sent someone to investigate the accident. ‖ 这是~的命令。This is an order from the authorities.

【上膘】shàngbiāo〈动〉[of animals] get fat: 精心饲养，牲畜就会~。Livestock will fatten up if they are carefully raised.

【上宾】shàngbīn〈名〉guest of honour: 待为~ treat sb. like a distinguished guest ‖ 敬为~ regard sb. as a distinguished guest

【上不封顶，下不保底】shàng bù fēngdǐng, xià bù bǎodǐ〈惯〉impose neither an upper nor a lower limit: 对员工的奖金~ have neither an upper nor a lower limit on employee bonuses

【上不着天，下不着地】shàng bù zháo tiān, xià bù zháo dì〈惯〉be suspended in mid-air

【上苍】shàngcāng〈名〉Heaven: 感谢~。Praise be to Heaven.

【上操】shàngcāo〈动〉do exercises: 上早操 do morning exercises

【上策】shàngcè〈名〉best policy: 这绝非~。This is definitely not the best policy.

【上层】shàngcéng〈名〉**1**（指等级）upper levels: ~管理人员 top manager ‖ ~领导 leadership at the upper levels **2**（指船）upper deck;（指公共汽车）top deck: 我们的船舱在~。Our cabin is on the upper deck. ‖ 孩子们在乘双层车时喜欢坐~。The kids love riding on the top deck. **3**（指建筑）higher floor

【上层建筑】shàngcéng jiànzhù〈名〉superstructure: 经济基础决定~。Economic basis determines superstructure.

【上层路线】shàngcéng lùxiàn〈名〉high-up paths: 走~ get things done through the influence of one's higher connections

【上层社会】shàngcéng shèhuì〈名〉upper society

【上场】shàngchǎng〈动〉**1**［戏剧］enter the stage: 演出结束后全体演员都~谢幕。The cast took to the stage for curtain calls after the performance. **2**［体育］enter the court/field: 今天轮到你~。Today it's your turn to take to the stage. ‖ 运动员都已~。All the players are already on the field.

【上场阵容】shàngchǎng zhènróng〈名〉first team

【上朝】shàngcháo〈动〉〈旧〉**1**（指臣子）go to court **2**（指君主）hold court

【上乘】shàngchéng〈名〉**1** = 大乘 dàchéng **2**（上等）first-class literary/artistic work: ~之作 first-class work ‖ 质量~ first-class quality

【上床】shàngchuáng〈动〉go to bed: 安顿孩子们~睡觉 put the children to bed ‖ 我要~睡觉了。I'm going to bed. ‖〈喻〉他绝对不会与妻子以外的女人~。He will never go to bed with women other than his wife.

【上窜下跳】shàngcuàn-xiàtiào〈成〉**1**（指动物）run and jump all over the place: 猴子在假山里~。Monkeys are jumping up and down in the rockery. **2**〈贬〉（指人）run around on dubious missions: 他~，到处煽风点火。He ran about and stirred up trouble all over the place.

【上达】shàngdá〈动〉〈书〉reach the higher authorities: 下情~ inform the higher authorities of the situation at lower levels

【上代】shàngdài〈名〉previous generation

【上当】shàngdàng〈动〉be taken in: 上坏人的当 be fooled by bad people ‖ 容易~ be taken in easily ‖ 我~受骗，以为他爱我。I was fooled into thinking that he loved me.

【上等】shàngděng〈形〉first-class: ~产品 choice product ‖ ~货 quality goods ‖ 质量~ of top quality

【上等兵】shàngděngbīng〈名〉**1**［陆军］first-class soldier **2**［海军］first-class seaman **3**［空军］first-class pilot

【上帝】Shàngdì〈名〉**1**［基督教］God **2**〈喻〉（主宰者）god: 顾客就是~。The customer is king.

【上吊】shàngdiào〈动〉hang oneself: 她一时悔恨竟~自杀了。She hanged herself in a fit of remorse.

【上调】shàngdiào〈动〉**1**（指人）transfer to a higher post: 从省里~到中央 be transferred from provincial government to central government **2**（指物）transfer to a unit at a higher level: 这些物资将被~。These materials will be transferred to superior units. ▸shàngtiáo

【上冻】shàngdòng〈动〉freeze: ~前完工 finish the work before the freeze sets in ‖ 河已经~了。The river has frozen over. ‖ 路~了。The roads are iced up.

【上颚】shàng'è〈名〉**1**（指节肢动物）mandible **2**（指脊椎动物）upper jaw

【上方宝剑】shàngfāng bǎojiàn〈名〉**1**〈本〉imperial sword **2**〈喻〉mandate from above: 领导给了他~，所以他在关键时刻处理问题能当机立断。With the leaders' mandate, he could act promptly and deal with problems at critical junctures.

【上房】shàngfáng = 正房 zhèngfáng

【上访】shàngfǎng〈动〉visit a higher authority to voice one's grievances and ask for help: 到省里~ visit the provincial authorities to voice one's grievances and ask for help

【上坟】shàngfén〈动〉pay homage at a grave

【上风】shàngfēng〈名〉**1**〈本〉the direction from which the wind is coming: 站在~头 stand on the side the wind is coming from **2**〈喻〉（优势）advantage: 上半时中国队占~。The Chinese team had the upper hand at half time.

【上峰】shàngfēng〈名〉〈旧〉superior: 接到~的命令 receive an order from one's superior

【上浮】shàngfú〈动〉increase: 工资~一级。Wages went up by one notch. ‖ 物价~。The price has risen.

【上纲】shànggāng〈动〉elevate an issue to the level of principle: ~上线 elevate matters to the level of principle and ideology ‖ 这个问题上不了纲。This is not a matter of principle.

【上岗】shànggǎng〈动〉**1**（执勤）go on duty: 交警~指挥交通。The policeman is at his duty, directing traffic. **2**（被聘用）take up a job: 择优~ select the best for the post ‖ 导游人员应当持证~。Tour guides should take their certificates when working.

【上岗证】shànggǎngzhèng〈名〉job qualification certificate: 会计~ accountant's certificate

【上告】shànggào〈动〉**1**（告状）appeal to higher authorities: ~到中央 appeal to the Central Government **2**（报告）report to a higher body: ~卫生部 report to the Ministry of Public Health

【上工】shànggōng〈动〉**1**（上班）go to work: 今天有两个人~迟到了。Two people were late for work today. ‖ 她患了重感冒，今天上不了工。She cannot go to work today because she has a bad cold. **2**（开始工作）start work: 新来的工人下周一~。The new worker will start work next Monday.

【上供】shànggòng〈动〉**1**（供奉）offer a sacrifice: 给祖先~ offer up a sacrifice to one's ancestors ‖ 烧香~ burn incense and lay offerings at the altar **2**（送礼）slip someone some cash: 不~是办不成事的。Without handing over cash, nothing gets done.

【上钩】shànggōu〈动〉**1**（指鱼）take the hook: 鱼~了。A fish has taken the bait. **2**（指人）rise to a bait: 他没有~。He wasn't drawn in.

【上钩拳】shànggōuquán〈名〉［体育］uppercut

【上古】shànggǔ ▸p. 618〈名〉ancient times: ～时代 ancient times

【上光】shàngguāng **A**〈动〉**1**［印刷］varnish **2**［摄影］ferrotype **B**〈名〉［纺织］lustring

【上光蜡】shàngguānglà〈名〉wax polish

【上轨道】shàng guǐdào〈动〉〈口〉proceed smoothly: 经济改革已～。Economic reform is right on track. ‖ 生产已～。Production is on track.

【上海】Shànghǎi ▸p. 661〈名〉Shanghai

【上海公报】Shànghǎi Gōngbào〈名〉Shanghai Communiqué [concluded in Shanghai on Feb 28, 1972]

【上海证券交易所】Shànghǎi Zhèngquàn Jiāoyìsuǒ〈名〉Shanghai Stock Exchange

【上好】shànghǎo〈形〉first-class: ～的茶叶 first-class tea ‖ ～的钢材 premium quality steel

【上颌】shànghé〈名〉［生理］upper jaw

【上呼吸道】shànghūxīdào〈名〉［生理］upper respiratory tract

【上呼吸道感染】shànghūxīdào gǎnrǎn〈名〉infection of the upper respiratory tract

【上回】shànghuí〈名〉〈口〉last time: ～我来的时候没见到你。I didn't see you last time I came here.

【上火】shànghuǒ〈动〉**1**［中医］suffer from excessive internal heat: 他鼻子流血，准是～了。His nose is bleeding. He must be suffering from excessive internal heat. **2**〈方〉（生气）get angry: 他又～了。He's got mad again.

【上货】shànghuò〈动〉**1**（进货）replenish stocks for sale **2**（摆上货物）display goods on shelves: ～要及时。Goods must be put on shelves in good time.

【上机】shàngjī〈动〉operate a computer: ～时间 computer operation time

【上级】shàngjí〈名〉**1**（指级别）higher level: ～组织 superior organization **2**（指人）superior: 报告～ report to a higher authority ‖ 讨好～ curry favour with one's superior

【上级机关】shàngjí jīguān〈名〉higher authority/body

【上级领导】shàngjí lǐngdǎo〈名〉leading body at a higher level

【上集】shàngjí〈名〉first part: 电视剧/电影的～ first part of a TV series/a film

【上家】shàngjiā〈名〉preceding player

【上浆】shàngjiāng〈动〉starch: ～布 starched cloth ‖ 这块布料要～。This cloth needs starching.

【上将】shàngjiàng〈名〉**1**［陆军］general **2**［海军］admiral **3**［空军］（美国）general;（英国）air chief marshal

【上交】shàngjiāo〈动〉hand in: ～报告 submit a report to a higher authority

【上缴】shàngjiǎo〈动〉turn over to a higher authority: ～战利品 hand over the spoils of war ‖ ～国库 hand in to the exchequer ‖ 向国家～利税 turn tax payments and profit turnovers to the state

【上街】shàngjiē〈动〉**1**（购物）go shopping: 他～去了。He went shopping. **2**（去街上）take to the streets: ～示威 demonstrate in the streets

【上届】shàngjiè〈名〉previous term: ～毕业生 last year's graduates ‖ ～乒乓球冠军 defending ping-pong champion ‖ ～总统 former president

【上界】shàngjiè〈名〉world above

【上进】shàngjìn〈动〉make progress: 不求～ have no desire to make progress ‖ ～心 desire to go forward

【上劲儿】shàngjìnr〈动〉〈口〉do sth. with great vigour: 越说越～ get more and more excited in talking ‖ 他工作比别人都～。He works more energetically than the others.

【上镜】shàngjìng〈动〉be photogenic: ～的女演员 photogenic actress ‖ 她很～。She photographs well.

【上客】shàngkè〈名〉distinguished guest

【上课】shàngkè〈动〉（指学生）attend a class;（指老师）teach a class: 上地理课 take a geography class ‖ ～时间 school hours ‖ 用英语～ conduct a lesson in English ‖ 正在～ be in class ‖ 学校八点开始～。Classes begin at eight.

【上空】shàngkōng〈名〉sky above: 飞过太平洋～ fly across the Pacific Ocean ‖ 五彩缤纷的气球漂浮在广场～。Multicoloured balloons are floating in the sky above the square.

【上口】shàngkǒu〈动〉**1**（流利）be able to read aloud fluently: 把一首唐诗念得琅琅～ recite a Tang poem very fluently **2**（易读）be easy to read: 这篇文章很～。This article makes very smooth reading.

【上款】shàngkuǎn〈名〉name of the recipient [inscribed on a painting or a calligraphic scroll presented as a gift]

【上蜡】shànglà〈动〉wax: 地板需要～。The floor needs waxing.

【上来】shànglái〈动〉**1**（开始）begin, start: 一～就有劲 be very energetic from the start **2**（到高处）come up: 这山太高了，我爬了两个多钟头才～。This mountain is too high. It took me more than two hours to get to the top. ‖ 这些干部刚从基层～。These cadres have just come from grass-roots units.

【上来】shànglai〈动〉**1**（表由远及近）[used after a verb, indicating a movement either upward or from afar]: 把饭端～ serve up a meal **2**（表成功）[used after a verb, indicating success in doing sth.]: 这个问题你一定答得～。I'm sure you can come up with an answer to this question. **3**〈方〉（表程度加深）[used after adjectives indicating intensification]: 秋天到了，天气慢慢凉～。Autumn is here and the cold is slowly setting in.

【上联】shànglián〈名〉first half of a couplet: 我出～，你对下联。I'll come up with the first line of the couplet and you give the second.

【上脸】shàngliǎn〈动〉turn red: 他酒量不大，喝几口就～。He can't take more than a few sips of alcohol without going red.

【上梁不正下梁歪】shàngliáng bù zhèng xiàliáng wāi〈俗〉when those above behave badly, those below will follow suit: ～，他的所作所为把孩子引上了邪路。It was his bad example that led his son astray.

【上列】shàngliè〈形〉the above-mentioned: 在～例句中 in the sample sentences listed above ‖ ～人员都要参加明天的会议。All the above are asked to attend tomorrow's meeting.

【上流】shàngliú **A**〈名〉upper reaches: 黄河～ upper reaches of the Yellow River **B**〈形〉upper-class: ～人物 people from high society

【上流社会】shàngliú shèhuì〈名〉upper classes: 与～交往 mix in good society

【上楼】shànglóu〈动〉go upstairs: 急忙～ rush upstairs

【上路】shànglù〈动〉**1**（出发）set out: 你几点～的？What time did you set out? ‖ 休息半小时后我们又～了。After half an hour's rest, we were on our way again. **2**（入门）get on the right track: 她英语学习还没有～。She still hasn't found her feet when it comes to learning English.

【上马】shàngmǎ〈动〉**1**（骑马）mount a horse **2**（开始）start: 这项工程即将～。The project will start soon. ‖ 三峡工程于1997年～。The Three Gorges Project was launched in 1997.

【上门】shàngmén〈动〉**1**（登门）visit: ～服务 provide home service ‖ 免费送货～ do free home delivery **2**（锁门）bolt a door: 睡觉前别忘了～。Don't forget to lock the door before you go to bed. **3**（停止营业）close up **4**（入赘）marry into the bride's family: ▸～女婿

【上门女婿】shàngmén nǚxu〈名〉live-in son-in-law

【上面】shàngmian〈名〉**1**（高处）higher place: 飞机在云层～飞行。The plane is flying above the clouds. ‖ 护城河～有一座吊桥。There is a drawbridge across the city moat. **2**（上述）the above-mentioned: ～列举的几个实例 above-mentioned examples ‖ 财产属于～所说的王先生。The property belongs to the aforementioned Mr Wang. **3**（指表面）surface of an object: 墙～贴着一些画。There are some pictures on the wall. **4**（方面）aspect: 在学习～他下了很多功夫。He has taken great pains with his studies. ‖ 在这～，他比我强。He is better than me in this respect. **5**（上级）higher authority: ～的指示 instructions from above ‖ ～要来人检查工作。Some people from above are coming to inspect our work. ‖ ～有人在帮他。Somebody high up is trying to help him. **6**（长辈）elders

【上年】shàngnián ▸p. 618〈名〉last year

【上年纪】shàng niánji〈动〉be advanced in years: 虽然上了年纪，他腿脚还相当灵便。Even though he's getting on a bit, he's pretty sure on his feet.

【上皮组织】shàngpí zǔzhī〈名〉epithelial tissue

【上品】shàngpǐn〈名〉top quality: ～名瓷 top-grade porcelain ‖ 龙井是茶中～。*Longjing* is a top-grade tea.

【上坡】shàngpō **A**〈名〉uphill **B**〈动〉go uphill

【上坡路】shàngpōlù〈名〉**1**〈本〉road uphill: 走～ walk uphill **2**〈喻〉（指趋势）upward trend: 生产走～。Production is on the up.

【上铺】shàngpù〈名〉upper berth: 她订了一张从西安到北京的～票。She has booked an upper berth on the train from Xi'an to Beijing. ‖ 我睡双层床的～。I'm sleeping on the top bunk of the bed.

【上气不接下气】shàngqì bù jiē xiàqì〈惯〉out of breath: 跑得～ out of breath from running

【上情】shàngqíng〈名〉wishes of higher authorities: ～下达 transmit the views of the high-ups to the lower levels

【上去】shàngqù〈动〉**1**（到高处）go up: 登着梯子～ go up a ladder ‖ 这楼太高了，没有电梯怎么～？This is a very tall building. How can we get to the top without a lift? **2**（到他处）[used with an object, indicating appearance]: ～两个人帮他提行李。Two of you go and help him with the luggage.

【上去】shàngqu〈动〉**1**（上前）[used after a verb, indicating outward or forward

direction]: 走～和客人一一握手 walk up and shake hands with each of the guests ‖ 大家连忙迎～。 Everyone rushed up to greet them. **2**（向上）[used after a verb, indicating a rise in level]: 把工人的意见反映～ make the views of the workers known to those above ‖ 把生产搞～ expand production **3**（表添加或合拢）[used after a verb, indicating addition or adhesion]: 请帮我把这颗螺丝拧～。 Please give me a hand getting this screw in.

【上圈套】 shàng quāntào〈惯〉 fall into a trap: 上了人家的圈套 fall into sb.'s trap ‖ 敌人终于上我们的圈套了。 The enemy finally fell into our trap.

【上任】 shàngrèn **A**〈动〉 take office: 新厂长～不久厂子便破产了。 The new director had not been in post long when the factory went bankrupt. ▸走马～ **B**〈名〉 predecessor: ～总统 former president

【上色】 shàngshǎi〈动〉 colour: 把门上成红色。 Paint this door red. ‖ 他先画了一头大象，然后给它上了色。 First he drew an elephant and then he coloured it in.

【上山】 shàngshān〈动〉 **1**（爬山） go to the mountains: ～植树 go to the mountains to plant trees **2**〈方〉（特指蚕） go up small straw bundles (to spin cocoons)

【上山下乡】 shàngshān-xiàxiāng [of educated urban youth] go and work in rural areas (during the Cultural Revolution): ～知识青年 educated urban youth working in rural areas

【上上】 shàngshàng〈形〉 **1**（最好） very best: ～策 best plan **2**（前一个时期之前） before last: ～星期 the week before last

【上上下下】 shàngshàng-xiàxià〈成〉 everybody: 她的举止使～都喜欢她。 Her manner recommend her to high and low alike.

【上身】 shàngshēn **A**〈名〉 **1**（上体） upper part of the body: 光着～ be stripped to the waist ‖ 他～穿着白衬衣。 He is wearing a white shirt. **2**（上衣） top: 她穿着白～，花裙子。 She is wearing a white blouse and a brightly-coloured skirt. **B**〈动〉 start wearing: 天气暖了， 裙子该～了。 It's getting warmer. Time to start wearing a skirt.

【上升】 shàngshēng〈动〉 **1**（指位置） move upward: 烟在空中袅袅～。 The smoke is rising slowly into the sky. **2**（指等级、程度、数量） be on the rise: ～0.18% be up 0.18% ‖ 把会谈～为部长级 take talks to the ministerial level ‖ 湖泊水位继续～。 The level of the lake continues to rise.

【上士】 shàngshì〈名〉 **1**［陆军］ staff sergeant **2**［海军］ chief petty officer **3**［空军］ flight sergeant

【上市】 shàngshì〈动〉 **1**（指农产品） go on the market: 西瓜～了。 Watermelons have appeared on the market. ‖ 下星期鲜黄瓜将～。 Fresh cucumbers will be available for purchase next week. **2**（去市场） go shopping: 他一大早就～买菜去了。 He went to the vegetable market early this morning. **3**［经济］ list: 允许～ allow a listing ‖ ～流通 be traded on the market ‖ 在纽约～ be listed on New York market

【上市公司】 shàngshì gōngsī〈名〉 listed company

【上世】 shàngshì〈名〉 last generation

【上手】 shàngshǒu **A**〈名〉 **1**（上首） seat of honour **2** = 上家 shàngjiā **B**〈动〉 **1**〈方〉（动手） get to work: 这事我一个人处理就行了，你们不用～了。 I can handle the matter by myself. You don't have to bother about it. **2**（开始） get started: 这场球一～就打得很顺利。 Everything went smoothly from the beginning of the match.

【上首】 shàngshǒu〈名〉 seat of honour: 我父亲坐在～。 My father took his place at the head of the table.

【上书】 shàngshū〈动〉〈书〉 submit a written statement to a higher authority: ～中央 submit a petition to the Central Government

【上述】 shàngshù〈形〉〈书〉 above-mentioned: ～规定 aforementioned regulations ‖ 严格遵守～原则 strictly abide by the above-mentioned principle ‖ ～情况属实。 The aforementioned situation proved to be true.

【上水】 shàngshuǐ **A**〈名〉 upper reaches **B**〈动〉 **1**（逆水） sail upstream: 这艘船在～而行。 This ship is sailing upstream. **2**（加水） top up with water: 给水箱～ fill the tank with water

【上司】 shàngsi〈名〉 superior: 巴结～ fawn on one's superior ‖ 顶头～ one's immediate boss ‖ 看～的眼色行事 take one's cue from the boss

【上诉】 shàngsù〈动〉［法律］ appeal: 驳回～ reject an appeal ‖ 提出～ lodge an appeal ‖ 向上一级法院～ appeal to a higher court

【上诉法院】 shàngsù fǎyuàn〈名〉 court of appeal

【上诉判决】 shàngsù pànjué〈名〉 decision on an appeal

【上诉人】 shàngsùrén〈名〉 appellant

【上溯】 shàngsù〈动〉 **1**（逆流而上） go upstream: 从宜昌乘船～到重庆 sail upstream from Yichang to Chongqing **2**（向上追溯） date back to: 有文字可考的中国历史可～到五千多年以前。 China's written history can be traced back over five thousand years.

【上算】 shàngsuàn〈形〉 worthwhile: 钱花得～ get one's money's worth ‖ 烧煤气比烧煤～。 It's more economical to use gas than coal.

【上岁数】 shàng suìshu〈动〉〈口〉 be advanced in years: 人上了岁数，身体一年不如一年。 When people start getting old, their health gradually deteriorates. ‖ 我们俩现在都～了。 We're both getting on now.

【上台】 shàngtái〈动〉 **1**（登台） take to the stage: ～表演 take to the stage and perform **2**（掌权） come to power: 重新～ return to power ‖ ～执政 assume office ‖ 谁将～领导国家? Who will take power and lead the nation?

【上台阶】 shàng táijiē〈动〉 reach new heights: 农业生产又上新台阶。 Agricultural production once again rose to new heights.

【上膛】 shàngtáng〈动〉［军事］ load a gun: 一支上了膛的枪 a loaded gun ‖ 子弹～了。 The gun is loaded.

【上套】 shàngtào〈动〉 **1**（上马具） harness **2**（进圈套） fall into a trap: 我相信他这次会～的。 I believed that he would fall into the trap this time.

【上体】 shàngtǐ〈名〉 upper part of the body

【上天】 shàngtiān **A**〈动〉 **1**（升入天空） go up into the sky: 气球～不久就破了。 The balloon burst soon after it rose into the sky. ‖ 无人宇宙飞船～了。 The unmanned spacecraft has been launched. **2** ▸**p. 772**〈婉〉（死亡） die: 一颗子弹送他上了天。 He was killed by a bullet. **B**〈名〉 Heaven: ～不容 Heaven forbid

【上天入地】 shàngtiān-rùdì〈成〉 be extremely capable: 就是有～的本领，这个任务你一个人也无法完成。 No matter how capable you are, you won't be able to accomplish this task on your own.

【上天无路，入地无门】 shàngtiān wú lù, rù dì wú mén〈俗〉 be in dire straits

【上调】 shàngtiáo〈动〉 raise: 原油价格已～了。 The price of crude oil has risen. ▸shàngdiào

【上头】 shàngtóu〈动〉 **1**〈旧〉（指女子） start wearing one's hair in a bun **2**（指喝酒） go to one's head: 这酒一喝就～。 The wine went straight to my head.

【上头】 shàngtou〈名〉 **1**（上级） higher authority: ～批准了这个计划。 The project has been approved by the authorities. **2**（上面） higher place: 我们的办公室就在餐馆～。 Our office is above the restaurant.

【上吐下泻】 shàngtù-xiàxiè〈动〉 suffer from both vomiting and diarrhoea

【上推下卸】 shàngtuī-xiàxiè〈成〉 shift blame to higher-ups or one's subordinates

【上网】 shàngwǎng〈动〉 go online: 免费～ have free access to the Internet ‖ 他正在～。 He's surfing the net.

【上尉】 shàngwèi〈名〉 **1**［陆军］ captain **2**［海军］ lieutenant **3**［空军］ flight lieutenant

【上文】 shàngwén〈名〉 preceding text: 见～ see above

【上无片瓦，下无立锥之地】 shàng wú piàn wǎ, xià wú lì zhuī zhī dì〈成〉 be completely destitute

【上午】 shàngwǔ ▸**p. 669**〈名〉 morning: ～六点 six o'clock in the morning ‖ 第二天～ next morning ‖ 今天/昨天～ this/yesterday morning

【上西天】 shàng xītiān ▸**p. 772**〈动〉〈婉〉 die: 他去年就～了。 He died last year.

【上下】 shàngxià **A**〈名〉 **1**（所有人） everybody: 举国～ whole nation **2**（从上到下） up and down: ～打量 look sb. up and down ‖ 他浑身～都是血。 He was covered in blood. **3**（高低） relative superiority/inferiority: 这两个球队难分～。 It is hard to tell which team is the stronger of the two. **4**（上层和下层） high and low: ～脱节 dislocation of higher and lower organizations ▸不相～ **5** ▸**p. 927**（左右）[used after a numeral or numeral-measure word to indicate a rough number]: 此人五十～。 This man is about fifty years old. ‖ 今天的气温有二十摄氏度～。 It's 20°C or so today. **B**〈动〉 go up and down: 楼梯太窄了，～很不方便。 It's not easy going up and down these narrow stairs.

【上下其手】 shàngxiàqíshǒu〈成〉 distort facts to suit one's own purpose

【上下文】 shàngxiàwén〈名〉 context: 根据～确定词义 determine the meaning of a word from its context ‖ 联系～看，他的话有一定的意思。 Taken in context, his remarks make some sense.

【上弦】 shàngxián **A**〈动〉 wind (up) a clock/watch: 钟该～了。 The clock needs winding. **B**〈名〉［天文］ first quarter (of the moon): ～月 new moon

【上限】 shàngxiàn〈名〉 upper limit: 奖金的～ bonus ceiling

【上线】 shàngxiàn〈动〉 meet the pass mark: 今年他们班的同学高考全都～了。 Everyone in his class made the grade in this year's national college entrance examination.

【上香】shàngxiāng〈动〉burn incense and worship: 每年春季来这儿～的人很多。In spring a lot of people come here to burn incense.
【上相】shàngxiàng〈动〉be photogenic: 不～ photograph badly
【上校】shàngxiào〈名〉1 ［陆军］colonel 2 ［海军］captain 3 ［空军］colonel
【上鞋】shàngxié = 绱鞋 shàngxié
【上心】shàngxīn〈动〉be diligent: 他无论干什么事都很～。He takes great care in whatever he does. ‖ 他学习很～。He works very hard at his studies.
【上星】shàngxīng〈动〉satellite-broadcast: ～频道 satellite TV channel ‖ 我国已有100多套电视节目～。China broadcasts over 100 TV programs via satellite.
【上刑】shàngxíng〈动〉torture
【上行】shàngxíng〈动〉1 (指火车) go up to the capital from other part of the country: ～列车 train going up-country 2 (指船) go upstream: ～船 boat going upstream 3 (指公文) submit to higher authorities: ～公文 documents to be submitted to the upper levels
【上行下效】shàngxíng-xiàxiào〈成〉follow bad examples of those above
【上旋】shàngxuán〈名〉［体育］topspin
【上旋球】shàngxuánqiú〈名〉topspin ball: 发～ serve a topspin ball
【上学】shàngxué〈动〉1 (去学校) go to school: 开车送孩子～ drive children to school ‖ 她今天没～。She's not at school today. 2 (开始小学教育) start school: 中国儿童通常七岁开始～。Chinese children usually start school at the age of seven.
【上旬】shàngxún ▸p. 618〈名〉first ten-day period of a month: 在五月～ in early May
【上演】shàngyǎn〈动〉stage: 本地戏院有新戏要～。A new play is coming to the local theatre. ‖ 今晚～什么节目? What's on tonight?
【上扬】shàngyáng〈动〉go up: 股票价格今日～。Share prices went up today. ‖ 上海股市在低迷了几周之后今天～了将近三个百分点。The Shanghai stock market surged by nearly three per cent today after being stagnant for several weeks.
【上夜】shàngyè〈动〉〈口〉be on night duty
【上衣】shàngyī〈名〉jacket: 花呢～ tweed jacket ‖ 做工极好的～ well-made coat
【上议院】shàngyìyuàn〈名〉upper house: ～议员 the Lords
【上瘾】shàngyǐn〈动〉be addicted (to sth.): 喝酒～ be addicted to drinking ‖ 玩电脑游戏～ be hooked on computer games ‖ 吸毒～ have a drug habit
【上映】shàngyìng〈动〉screen: 国庆节期间将～几部国产影片。Several Chinese films will be shown during the National Day holidays. ‖ 新影片将在全国～。The new film will be screened nationwide.
【上游】shàngyóu〈名〉1 (指河流) upper reaches: 黄河～ upper reaches of the Yellow River ‖ 船在向～行进。The ship is making its way upstream. 2〈喻〉(指顺序) advanced position: ▸力争～
【上有老，下有小】shàng yǒu lǎo, xià yǒu xiǎo〈俗〉have both parents and young children to take care of
【上有天堂，下有苏杭】shàng yǒu tiāntáng, xià yǒu Sū-Háng〈俗〉just as there is paradise in heaven, so on earth there are Suzhou and Hangzhou
【上有政策，下有对策】shàng yǒu zhèngcè, xià yǒu duìcè〈俗〉policies from on high will always be countered by strategies from down below
【上谕】shàngyù〈名〉〈书〉imperial edict
【上元节】Shàngyuánjié = 元宵节 Yuánxiāojié
【上载】shàngzài〈动〉［计算机］upload
【上涨】shàngzhǎng〈动〉rise: ～5% rise by 5% ‖ ～24点 gain 24 points ‖ ～到124点 be up to 124 points ‖ ～行情 bull market ‖ 地皮价格急剧～。The land appreciated rapidly. ‖ 股票价格不断～。Share prices are rising steadily. ‖ 河水正在～。The river is rising. ‖ 物价～太快。Prices have gone up very rapidly.
【上账】shàngzhàng〈动〉enter in an account
【上照】shàngzhào〈方〉= 上相 shàngxiàng
【上阵】shàngzhèn〈动〉1 (上战场) go into battle: ～杀敌 enter battle to fight the enemy 2 (参加) take part in: 他们一起～，工作很快就完成了。They all pitched in and soon finished the job. ‖ 下午的比赛你要～。You are going to play in this afternoon's match.
【上肢】shàngzhī〈名〉upper limbs: 我的～有点麻木。I felt a little numb in my upper limbs.
【上装】shàngzhuāng A〈动〉make oneself up: 演员们正在后台～。The actors and actresses are making themselves up backstage. B〈名〉jacket: 身穿白色～ wear a white jacket ‖ 她的～与裙子不配。Her top doesn't go with her skirt.
【上座】shàngzuò〈名〉seat of honour: 在～就坐 take one's seat at the head of the table ‖ 请坐～。Please take the seat of honour.
【上座率】shàngzuòlǜ〈名〉performance at the box-office: 提高～ increase attendance figures ‖ 这部电影～创了新高。This film has hit new box office highs.
【上座儿】shàngzuòr〈动〉1 (指餐馆) draw customers 2 (指剧场) draw an audience: 戏院里～不到五成。Less than fifty per cent of the theatre's seats have been booked. 3 (指电影等) be a box-office success: 那部电影不～。That film has done badly at the box office.

尚[1] shàng

A〈形〉noble: ▸高～
B〈动〉value: ～贤使能 value the virtuous and employ the able ▸～武, 崇～
C〈名〉prevailing custom: ▸风～, 时～

尚[2] shàng

〈副〉〈书〉1 (还) still: ～待解决的问题 problem yet to be solved ‖ 事实～待证明。The fact remains to be proved. ‖ 现在下结论为时～早。It's still too early to draw a conclusion at the moment. 2 (尚且) even: 庸人～且羞之，况于将相乎? Even a commoner would be ashamed of such a thing, let alone ministers and generals.
【尚方宝剑】shàngfāng bǎojiàn = 上方宝剑 shàngfāng bǎojiàn
【尚且】shàngqiě〈连〉even: 我们～不行，更何况他了。If we can't do it, then surely he can't either.
【尚书】shàngshū〈名〉〈古〉minister [in the Ming and Qing dynasties]: ～省 Department of State Affairs ‖ 吏部～ Minister of Personnel
【尚未】shàngwèi〈副〉〈书〉not yet: ～完成的任务 unfinished task ‖ ～获得正式批准。Official sanction has not yet been given. ‖ 问题～解决。The problem is still not resolved.
【尚武】shàngwǔ〈动〉encourage a martial spirit: 斯巴达是～的民族。Sparta was a warfaring nation.

绱（鞝） shàng

〈动〉sole a shoe: ▸～鞋
【绱鞋】shàngxié〈动〉sole a shoe: 她正忙着～。She is busy soling a pair of shoes.

shang

上 shang

〈名〉1 (表位置) [used after a noun, indicating position]: 脸～ on one's face ‖ 桌子～ on the table 2 (表范围) [used after a noun, indicating place]: 报～ in the newspaper ‖ 课堂～ in class ‖ 书～ in the book 3 (表方面) [used after a noun, indicating certain aspect]: 事实～ in fact ‖ 思想～ ideologically ‖ 在数量～占优势 excel at numbers 4 (表年龄) [used after words denoting age, indicating time]: 他十岁～死了父亲。He lost his father at the age of ten.
▸shǎng, shàng

裳 shang

▸衣裳 yīshang
▸cháng

shāo

烧（燒） shāo

A〈动〉1 (燃烧) burn: 把木头～成木炭 burn wood for charcoal ‖ 火～得正旺。The fire is ablaze. ‖ 木房子很快就～起来了。The wooden house caught fire quickly. ‖ 这只炉子是～油的。This stove is an oil-burner. ▸～荒 2 (加热) heat: ～砖 fire bricks ‖ 水～开了。The water is boiling. ‖ 陶器是用文火焙～的。Pottery is fired at a moderate heat. 3 (腐蚀) burn: 硫酸～坏了他的手。His hands were burnt by sulphuric acid. 4 (指肥料) damage by excessive use of fertilizer: 施肥过多会～坏庄稼。The crops will be damaged by excessive application of fertilizer. 5 (烹饪) a (烹煮) cook: 饭～好了没有? Is dinner ready? ‖ 他～一手地道的中国菜。He cooks Chinese food well. b (炖) stew after frying; (炸) fry after stewing: ～茄子 stewed eggplant c (烤) roast, braise: ～鹅 braised goose ‖ ～土豆 roast potato 6 (发烧) run a fever: ～到39℃ have a temperature of 39℃ ‖ 他现在～得很厉害。He is burning up. 7 (熔断) blow: 空调的保险丝～了。The fuse of the air conditioner blew.
B〈名〉fever: ～正在退。The fever is abating.
C〈形〉〈口〉big-headed: 钱使她～得慌。Money has given her a big head. ‖ 他买彩票中了头彩，～得不知怎么好了。He's become full of himself since hitting the jackpot.
【烧包】shāobāo〈动〉〈方〉get a big head: 发了一笔小财，他就～了。He made a bit of money and it went to his head.
【烧杯】shāobēi〈名〉beaker
【烧饼】shāobing〈名〉sesame seed bun
【烧高香】shāo gāoxiāng〈惯〉express thanks: 你只要不出去惹是生非，我就～了。I'd be very grateful if you could go out without making trouble.

【烧锅】shāoguō〈名〉enamel cooking pot
【烧锅】shāoguo〈名〉distillery
【烧化】shāohuà〈动〉 **1**（指尸体） cremate **2**（指祭品） burn as an offering
【烧荒】shāohuāng〈动〉 burn grass and bushes on wasteland (for reclamation): 山火是由～引起的。 The mountain fire was caused by the burning of grass and bushes.
【烧毁】shāohuǐ〈动〉 destroy by fire: ～秘密文件 burn secret documents ‖ 房子被大火～。 The house was destroyed by the fire.
【烧火】shāohuǒ〈动〉 light a fire: ～做饭 light a fire to cook food
【烧鸡】shāojī〈名〉 grilled chicken
【烧碱】shāojiǎn〈名〉［化学］ sodium hydroxide
【烧结】shāojié〈动〉 sinter: ～玻璃/磁铁/坩埚 sintered glass/magnet/crucible
【烧酒】shāojiǔ〈名〉spirits: 喝～取暖 drink spirits to keep warm
【烧烤】shāokǎo **A**〈动〉 barbecue: ～羊肉 barbecued lamb **B**〈名〉 barbecue: 取缔街头～ ban street barbecues ‖ 韩国～ Korean barbecue ‖ ～架 barbecue
【烧卖】shāomai〈名〉 *shaomai* [steamed dumpling with dough gathered at the top]
【烧瓶】shāopíng〈名〉 flask: ～不能直接接触火焰。 The flask shouldn't come into direct contact with the flame.
【烧钱】shāoqián〈动〉 burn money: ～买官 roll out the cash for an official post
【烧伤】shāoshāng **A**〈动〉 burn: 施肥过量会～植物。 Over-fertilization might scorch the plants. ‖ 他全身都被～了。 He received burns all over his body. **B** ▸**p. 50**〈名〉 burn: 包扎/治愈～ dress/heal a burn ‖ 轻度/中度～ minor/moderate burn ‖ 大面积～ extensive burns
【烧香】shāoxiāng〈动〉 **1**〈本〉 burn incense (before an idol): ～拜佛 burn incense and pray to Buddha ‖ 在庙里～ burn incense at a temple **2**〈喻〉（送礼） bribe: 给上司～ bribe one's superior
【烧心】shāoxīn〈动〉 **1**（指胃） cause a stomach upset: 柿饼吃多了～。 Excessive consumption of dried persimmons will cause a stomach upset. **2**〈方〉（指菜心） turn yellow at the core: 萝卜～了。 The radish has turned yellow in the middle.
【烧纸】shāozhǐ **A**〈动〉 burn paper money for the dead **B**〈名〉 paper money burnt as an offering to the dead
【烧灼】shāozhuó〈动〉 burn: 她的手上有～的疤痕。 Her hands are scarred with burns.

捎 shāo ▸**p. 145**〈动〉 take sth. to sb.: ～个口信 take sb. a message ‖ 请把这把伞～给我儿子。 Take this umbrella to my son, please. ‖ 这些苹果是我从老家～来的。 I've brought these apples from my hometown.
▸shào
【捎带】shāodài〈副〉 in passing: 你去文具店时请～给我买瓶墨水。 Please buy a bottle of ink for me when you go to the stationer's.
【捎话】shāohuà〈动〉〈口〉 deliver a message to sb.: 请给你父亲捎个话，说他要的票我买到了。 Please tell you father that I've bought the ticket he wants.
【捎脚】shāojiǎo〈动〉 give sb. a lift: 要求～ hitch a ride ‖ 你能捎个脚儿吗？ Could you give me a lift?

梢 shāo〈名〉 **1**（树梢） thin end of a twig: ▸树～ **2**（条状物） thin end of sth. long and narrow: 鞭～ whiplash ‖ 辫～ end of a plait ▸眉～
【梢公】shāogōng = 艄公 shāogōng
【梢头】shāotóu〈名〉 tip of a branch: 月到柳～。 The moon rose to the top of the willow tree.

稍 shāo〈副〉 a little: ～暗 a bit dark ‖ ～等片刻 wait a moment ‖ ～事休息 take a short rest
▸shào
【稍稍】shāoshāo〈副〉 a little: ～休息一下 take a little rest
【稍胜一筹】shāoshèng-yīchóu = 略胜一筹 lüèshèng-yīchóu
【稍微】shāowēi〈副〉 a little: ～不同 be slightly different ‖ 地板～有些倾斜。 The floor is on a slight slope. ‖ 他～有点头痛。 He had a slight headache.
【稍为】shāowéi = 稍微 shāowēi
【稍许】shāoxǔ = 稍微 shāowēi
【稍纵即逝】shāozòng-jíshì〈成〉 fleeting: 这种机会～，可不要错过了。These kinds of opportunities are fleeting. Don't let them pass.

蛸 shāo ▸蟏蛸 xiāoshāo
▸xiāo

筲 shāo
A〈名〉 bucket: 水～ pail
B〈量〉 bucketful: 两～水 two buckets of water
【筲箕】shāojī〈名〉 bamboo basin [kitchen utensil for washing rice or vegetables]

艄 shāo〈名〉 **1**（船尾） stern: ▸船～ **2**（舵） helm: 掌～ take the helm
【艄公】shāogōng〈名〉 helmsman: 一个/名/位～ a helmsman

鞘 shāo〈名〉 whiplash: 鞭～ tip of a whip
▸qiào

sháo

勺（杓） sháo〈名〉 **1**（指器具） spoon: 不锈钢～ stainless steel spoon ‖ 长柄～ ladle ‖ 水～ water ladle ‖ 小～儿 little spoon ▸漏～, 汤～, 掌～儿 **2**（勺状物） ladle-like object: ▸后脑～儿
【勺斗】sháodǒu〈名〉 scoop
【勺子】sháozi〈名〉spoon: 用～舀糖 spoon out some sugar

芍 sháo = 芍药 sháoyao
【芍药】sháoyao〈名〉 **1**（指植物） Chinese herbaceous peony **2**（指花） flower of the Chinese herbaceous peony

苕 sháo〈名〉〈方〉 sweet potato: ▸红～
▸tiáo

韶 sháo〈形〉〈书〉 splendid, beautiful: ▸～光
【韶光】sháoguāng〈名〉〈书〉 **1**（春光） beautiful springtime **2**（时间） time: ～荏苒，转瞬已是寒冬。Time flies and winter is coming on. **3**〈喻〉（青春） glorious youth: ～易逝。 Youth passes quickly.
【韶华】sháohuá〈名〉〈书〉 **1**（春光） springtime **2**（青春） youth: 虚度～ idle away one's youth
【韶山】Sháoshān〈名〉 Shaoshan [a county town in Hunan Province, noted as the birthplace of Mao Zedong]

shǎo

少 shǎo
A〈形〉 little: ～吃多餐 have many meals but little food at each ‖ ～花钱多办事 get more done on less money ‖ 我们得到的消息很～。 The information we have is very sketchy. ‖ 五月以来，雨愈来愈～了。 It's been raining less and less since May.
B〈动〉 **1**（缺乏） lack: 缺医～药 be short of doctors and medicine ‖ 这本字典～了五页。 This dictionary is missing five pages. **2**（亏欠） owe: 还～十元。 Ten dollars is still due. ‖ 我还～你三个月的房租。 I still owe you three months' rent. **3**（丢失） be missing: 我钱包里～了五十元。 Fifty *yuan* is missing from my wallet. ‖ 什么都在，就～了钥匙。 Everything is here except the keys. **4**（禁止） cease: ～跟我谈他! Stop talking about him to me! ‖ 课堂上～废话! Don't talk rubbish in class!
C〈副〉a moment: 请～候。Wait a moment, please. ▸～安毋躁
▸shào
【少安毋躁】shǎo'ān-wúzào〈成〉 be patient: 请诸位～，晚会很快就要开始了。 Please relax for a while. Tonight's party will start soon.
【少不得】shǎobudé〈动〉 can't do without: 生命～空气。 Air is indispensable to life. ‖ 日后～要向你讨教。 I may have to ask for your advice later on.
【少不了】shǎobuliǎo〈动〉〈口〉 **1**（不能缺） can't do without: 办这件事可～你。 We can't handle the matter without you. **2**（难免） be unavoidable: 初学者～犯错误。 Beginners are bound to make some mistakes. **3**（不会少） be bound to be a lot: 眼前的困难看来～。 It appears that there will be a lot of difficulties.
【少得了】shǎodeliǎo〈动〉〈口〉 [used in rhetorical questions] can do without: 我们做生意～电话吗? Can we do without a telephone in our business?
【少而精】shǎo'érjīng〈形〉 smaller in quantity but better in quality: 办事机构要～。 There should be fewer but more efficient management mechanisms.
【少汗症】shǎohànzhèng ▸**p. 50**〈名〉［医学］ hypohidrosis
【少见】shǎojiàn **A**〈动〉〈套〉 [a form of greeting] I haven't seen you for ages **B**〈形〉 rare: 当时，职业妇女很～。 At the time there were very few career women. ‖ 这种树种越来越～。This tree is becoming increasingly rare.
【少见多怪】shǎojiàn-duōguài〈成〉 be easily surprised because of ignorance
【少礼】shǎolǐ〈动〉〈套〉 **1**（别多礼） dispense with formalities **2**（失礼） excuse oneself for one's lack of manners: 恕我～。 Please excuse my poor manners.
【少量】shǎoliàng〈形〉 a little: ～现金 a small amount of cash ‖ ～杂质 minute traces of impurities ‖ 吃～食物 have a light meal

【少尿症】shǎoniàozhèng ▸p. 50 〈名〉［医学］oliguria
【少陪】shǎopéi〈动〉〈套〉[used to excuse oneself for parting company] I am afraid I must be going now: 对不起，～了。I'm sorry. I must be leaving now.
【少顷】shǎoqǐng = 少时 shǎoshí
【少生优生】shǎoshēng-yōushēng〈成〉[of family planning] have fewer but healthier babies
【少时】shǎoshí〈名〉〈书〉moment: ～雨过天晴。The rain soon cleared.
【少数】shǎoshù〈名〉few: ～派 minority group ‖ 占极～ be very much in the minority ‖ ～服从多数。The minority yields to the majority. ‖ 只有～人出席了会议。Attendance for the meeting is poor.
【少数民族】shǎoshù mínzú〈名〉ethnic minority: ～地区 minority nationality area ‖ ～干部 ethnic minority cadres ‖ ～语言 languages of ethnic minorities ‖ 要注意搞好汉族和～的关系。Attention must be paid to the fostering of good relations between Han Chinese and ethnic minorities.
【少说】shǎoshuō〈动〉say the least: 这块石头～也有两吨重。This stone weighs two tons at the very least. ‖ 他～也有四十岁了。He is forty years old at least.
【少许】shǎoxǔ〈形〉〈书〉a little: ～胡椒面 a dash of pepper ‖ 加入～调味品 add a little bit of seasoning
【少言寡语】shǎoyán-guǎyǔ〈成〉scarcely speak: 她天生～，即使跟好朋友在一起也是如此。She is naturally reticent, even with some of her closest friends.
【少有】shǎoyǒu〈形〉rare: ～的拜访 infrequent visits ‖ 就业机会现在真是～。Job opportunities are few and far between at the moment.
【少云】shǎoyún〈形〉［气象］partly cloudy

S

shào

少 shào

A〈形〉young: 他比我年～。He is younger than me. ▸～年, ～壮, 男女老～
B〈名〉son of a rich family: 恶～ young ruffian ‖ 阔～ son of a rich family
▸shǎo
【少白头】shàobáitóu **A**〈动〉be prematurely grey **B**〈名〉young person with greying hair
【少不更事】shàobùgēngshì〈成〉young and inexperienced: ～者 novice ‖ 年轻人～，要多向前辈学习。Young people are lacking in experience and have a lot to learn from the elders.
【少东家】shàodōngjia〈名〉〈旧〉young master
【少儿】shào'ér〈名〉children: ～读物 children's book ‖ ～不宜 not fit for children ▸少年儿童
【少妇】shàofù〈名〉young married woman
【少管所】shàoguǎnsuǒ〈名〉young offenders' institution
【少将】shàojiàng〈名〉**1**［陆军］major general **2**［海军］rear admiral **3**［空军］air vice-marshal〈英〉; major general〈美〉
【少教所】shàojiàosuǒ = 少管所 shàoguǎnsuǒ
【少林拳】shàolínquán〈名〉Shaolin boxing
【少林寺】Shàolínsì〈名〉Shaolin Monastery

> **少林**
>
> The birthplace of *Zen* (禅) Buddhism and the Shaolin style of martial arts. Shaolin Temple is situated in Henan Province, in the Song Mountain. It was founded in the Northern Wei Dynasty by the Emperor Xiaowen, after the arrival in China of the Indian dhyana master Fotuo (佛陀), who later became the temple's first abbot. The temple is notable for its large collection of Tang Dynasty stupas. The Shaolin form of boxing is the most influential school of Chinese boxing arts.

【少奶奶】shàonǎinai〈名〉〈旧〉**1**（少爷的妻子）young mistress **2**〈尊〉（别人的儿媳）daughter-in-law
【少男少女】shàonán-shàonǚ〈名〉teenagers
【少年】shàonián〈名〉**1** ▸p. 526（指年龄段）early youth: ～时代 childhood **2**（指人）teenager: ～男子/女子单打冠军 boy's/girl's singles champion **3**（青年男子）young man: 翩翩～ elegant young man
【少年儿童】shàonián értóng〈名〉children: ～出版社 children's publishing house
【少年法庭】shàonián fǎtíng〈名〉juvenile court
【少年犯】shàoniánfàn〈名〉juvenile offender: ～管教所 young offenders' institution
【少年夫妻老来伴】shàonián fūqī lǎo lái bàn〈俗〉a man and his wife are lovers when they are young, companions when they are old
【少年宫】shàoniángōng〈名〉children's palace

> **少年宫**
>
> Centres for extracurricular activities for children and young people, established by the China Youth League in many Chinese cities. The centres house science and technology activity areas, arts facilities, electronic games rooms, and indoor and outdoor sports facilities.

【少年老成】shàonián-lǎochéng〈成〉have an old head on young shoulders
【少年先锋队】Shàonián Xiānfēngduì〈名〉Young Pioneers
【少女】shàonǚ〈名〉young girl: ～时期 in one's maiden years ‖ 摩登～ modern young girl
【少帅】shàoshuài〈名〉young commander-in-chief
【少尉】shàowèi〈名〉second lieutenant
【少先队】shàoxiānduì〈简称〉= 少年先锋队

> **少先队**
>
> A patriotic children's organization led by the Chinese Communist Youth League. Young Pioneers wear a red scarf, and their pennant is a red flag with a torch and a five-pointed star. The emblem of the Young Pioneers is a red ribbon with a five-pointed star, a torch, and the words 'China Young Pioneers'. The team song is 'We are the heirs of Communism'. Young people between the ages of 6 and 14 may apply to become members, and once they are admitted they take part in a special ceremony.

【少校】shàoxiào〈名〉major
【少爷】shàoye〈名〉**1**（主人的儿子）young master [a form of address formerly used by servants to the master's son]: 活像个～ look very much like a spoiled young man **2**〈旧〉〈尊〉（指别人的儿子）son
【少壮】shàozhuàng〈形〉young and strong
【少壮不努力，老大徒伤悲】shàozhuàng bù nǔlì, lǎodà tú shāngbēi〈成〉a lazy youth makes for a regretful old age
【少壮派】shàozhuàngpài〈名〉rising stars

邵 Shào〈名〉Shao [surname]

劭 shào〈书〉

A〈动〉encourage: 先帝～农。The late emperor encouraged farming.
B〈形〉admirable: 年高德～ be of venerable age and eminent virtue

绍[1]（紹）shào〈动〉**1**〈书〉（继承）carry forward **2**（介绍）introduce: ▸介～

绍[2]（紹）Shào〈名〉Shaoxing: ▸～剧, ～酒

【绍介】shàojiè〈书〉= 介绍 jièshào
【绍酒】shàojiǔ = 绍兴酒 shàoxīngjiǔ
【绍剧】shàojù〈名〉Shaoxing opera
【绍兴酒】shàoxīngjiǔ〈名〉Shaoxing rice wine

捎 shào〈动〉**1**（倒退）move backwards **2**（退色）fade: ▸～色

▸shāo
【捎色】shàoshǎi〈动〉fade: ～的牛仔裤 faded jeans ‖ 衣服在强烈的阳光下会～。Clothes will fade when exposed to strong sunlight.

哨[1] shào

A〈动〉patrol: ▸巡～
B〈名〉post: 观察～ observation post ‖ 换～ relieve a sentry ▸～兵, 放～

哨[2] shào

A〈动〉chirp: 那鸟～得真好听。That bird has a lovely call.
B〈名〉whistle: 吹～儿 blow a whistle ‖ 裁判鸣～宣布比赛结束。The referee whistled the end of the match.
【哨兵】shàobīng〈名〉sentry: 入口处有～把守。The entrance was guarded by sentries.
【哨笛】shàodí ▸p. 929〈名〉［音乐］flageolet
【哨卡】shàoqiǎ〈名〉checkpoint: 边防～ border sentry post
【哨所】shàosuǒ〈名〉sentry post: 边防～ frontier guard post ‖ 前沿～ outpost
【哨位】shàowèi〈名〉sentry post
【哨子】shàozi〈名〉whistle: 吹～ blow a whistle ‖ 裁判吹响了～，比赛结束。The referee blew the whistle and the game was over.

稍 shào

▸shāo
【稍息】shàoxī〈动〉stand at ease: ～! At ease!

潲[1] shào〈动〉**1**（指雨水）fall at an angle: 快关窗户，别让雨水～进来。Close the windows quickly so that the rain doesn't get in. **2**〈口〉（洒水）sprinkle: 往花上～水 sprinkle water on flowers ‖ 扫地前先～点儿水。Please sprinkle some water on the ground before you sweep it.

潲[2] shào〈名〉〈方〉swill: 猪～ hogwash

【潲水】shàoshuǐ〈名〉〈方〉 swill: 收～养猪 collect pigswill to raise pigs ‖ 我们用～喂猪。 We feed slops to the pigs.

shē

畲（畬） Shē = 畲 Shē

奢 shē〈形〉**1**（奢侈） extravagant: 由～入俭难。It's difficult to adapt to a simple life after living a luxurious one. ▸～侈, ～华, 穷～极欲 **2**（过分） excessive: ▸～求, ～望, ～想

【奢侈】shēchǐ〈形〉 extravagant: 反对～和铺张 object to extravagance and ostentation ‖ 生活～ live in luxury ‖ 对我来说那是一种～。 As far as I'm concerned that's a luxury.

【奢侈品】shēchǐpǐn〈名〉 luxury goods: 很少有人买得起这种～。 Few people can afford this kind of luxury.

【奢华】shēhuá〈形〉 luxurious: 陈设～ be sumptuously furnished ‖ 我们一度过着极～的生活。 For a time we lived in great luxury.

【奢糜】shēmí = 奢靡 shēmí

【奢靡】shēmí〈形〉 extravagant

【奢念】shēniàn〈名〉 excessive expectations

【奢求】shēqiú〈动〉 make excessive demands: 无所～ have no unreasonable demands

【奢谈】shētán〈动〉 talk in an exaggerated and irresponsible way

【奢望】shēwàng〈名〉 extravagant hopes: 我对此不抱～。 I entertain no high hopes about this.

【奢想】shēxiǎng = 奢望 shēwàng

赊（賒） shē〈动〉（指买） buy on credit; （指卖） sell on credit: ～些必需品 buy some essentials on credit ▸～购, ～销

【赊购】shēgòu〈动〉 purchase on credit: 拒绝/允许～ refuse/grant sb. credit

【赊欠】shēqiàn〈动〉（指买） buy on credit; （指卖） sell on credit: 允许～ grant credit ‖ 本店概不～。 Credit is not given at this shop.

【赊售】shēshòu = 赊销 shēxiāo

【赊销】shēxiāo〈动〉 sell on credit: 我们不～。 We don't sell on credit.

【赊账】shēzhàng **A**〈动〉（指买） buy on credit; （指卖） sell on credit: 靠～度日 live on credit ‖ 恕不～。 No credit. **B**〈名〉 outstanding bills: 还有几笔～未清。 Some bills still haven't been paid.

猞 shē

【猞猁】shēlì〈名〉［动物］ lynx

畲 Shē

【畲族】Shēzú〈名〉 She ethnic group

畬 shē〈动〉［农业］ slash and burn
▸yú

shé

舌 shé〈名〉**1**（指人体器官） tongue: ▸～苔, ～头 **2**（舌状物） tongue-shaped object: 鞋～ tongue of a shoe ▸喉～, 火～ **3**（锤） clapper

【舌背】shébèi〈名〉 tongue dorsum

【舌敝唇焦】shébì-chúnjiāo〈成〉 talk oneself hoarse

【舌疮】shéchuāng〈名〉［中医］ tongue sore

【舌根】shégēn〈名〉 root of the tongue: ～音 velar [such as g, k, h in standard Chinese pronunciation]

【舌耕】shégēng〈动〉〈书〉 make a living by teaching

【舌簧】shéhuáng〈名〉 reed

【舌尖】shéjiān〈名〉 tip of the tongue

【舌剑唇枪】shéjiàn-chúnqiāng = 唇枪舌剑 chúnqiāng-shéjiàn

【舌面】shémiàn〈名〉 front of the tongue

【舌黏膜】shéniánmó〈名〉 periglottis

【舌巧如簧】shéqiǎo-rúhuáng = 巧舌如簧 qiǎoshé-rúhuáng

【舌苔】shétāi〈名〉 tongue coating: ～厚 furred tongue

【舌头】shétou〈名〉**1**（指器官） tongue: 伸～ stick out one's tongue ‖ 长～ be fond of gossip **2**（指人） enemy soldier captured to extract information: 抓～ capture an enemy soldier to solicit information

【舌位图】shéwèitú〈名〉 linguagram

【舌战】shézhàn〈动〉 have a heated argument: ～群儒 have a heated dispute with a group of scholars ‖ 展开～ engage in a battle of words

折 shé〈动〉**1**（断） snap: 树枝～了。 The branch snapped. **2**（亏损） lose one's capital: 他把老本都～光了。 He has lost all his capital. ▸～本, ～耗
▸zhē, zhé

【折本】shéběn〈动〉 lose money: 我们卖那些货折了本。 We made a loss on those goods.

【折本买卖】shéběn mǎimai〈名〉 loss-making business: 没有人愿意做这种～。 No one is willing to engage in such loss-making business. ‖ 这可真是一笔～。 This is really a bad deal.

【折秤】shéchèng〈动〉 lose weight in the course of reweighing: 水果一般都会～。 Fruits usually lose weight when they are weighed.

【折耗】shéhào〈名〉 damage and loss: 这批蔬菜在长途运输中～很大。 The vegetables were badly damaged during transit.

佘 Shé〈名〉 She [surname]

蛇 shé〈名〉 snake: 捕～ trap a snake ‖ 那条～游走了。 The snake slithered away. ▸打草惊～, 地头～, 眼镜～
▸yí

【蛇胆】shédǎn〈名〉 snake gall bladder

【蛇豆】shédòu = 蛇瓜 shéguā

【蛇毒】shédú〈名〉 snake venom

【蛇瓜】shéguā〈名〉［植物］ snake gourd

【蛇馆】shéguǎn〈名〉 serpentarium

【蛇管】shéguǎn〈名〉［机械］ hosepipe

【蛇麻】shémá〈名〉［植物］ golden hop

【蛇皮】shépí〈名〉 snakeskin: ～钱包 snakeskin purse

【蛇皮管】shépíguǎn〈名〉［电气］ flexible metal conduit

【蛇头】shétóu〈名〉 snakehead [ringleader of organized illegal immigration]: 警察逮捕了～，但释放了其他人。 Police arrested the ringleaders but let the others go free.

【蛇蜕】shétuì〈名〉 snake slough

【蛇纹石】shéwénshí〈名〉［矿业］ serpentine

【蛇无头不行】shé wú tóu bù xíng〈俗〉 nothing can be accomplished without a leader

【蛇蝎】shéxiē〈名〉〈喻〉 snakes and scorpions: 毒如～ as vicious as a viper

【蛇蝎心肠】shéxiē-xīncháng〈成〉 as venomous as snakes and scorpions: 这个人～，你最好离他远点。 This person is vicious. You'd better stay away from him.

【蛇行】shéxíng〈动〉**1**（指人） crawl: 他们匍匐～，迅速穿过封锁线。 They crawled across the blockade very quickly. **2**（指交通工具） snake: 火车在山间～前进。 The train snaked its way through the mountains.

【蛇形】shéxíng〈形〉 S-shaped: ～队形 S-shaped formation ‖ ～航线 zigzag course

【蛇形管】shéxíngguǎn〈名〉 coiled pipe

【蛇药】shéyào〈名〉 snakebite antidote

【蛇足】shézú〈名〉 superfluity

阇（闍） shé
▸dū

【阇梨】shélí〈名〉［佛教］ monk

shě

舍（捨） shě〈动〉**1**（放弃） give up: ▸～弃, 割～, 锲而不～ **2**（给予） give alms: ～药 come off medicine ▸施～
▸shè

【舍本逐末】shěběn-zhúmò〈成〉 dwell on side issues: 恐怕我们到目前为止一直在做一些～的事情。 I am afraid that so far we have been pursuing unimportant issues.

【舍不得】shěbude〈动〉**1**（不忍离开） loath to part with: ～离开父母 find it hard to part from one's parents **2**（吝惜） begrudge: ～花钱 be loath to spend one's money ‖ 她～穿那件新裙子。 She begrudged wearing her new skirt.

【舍得】shěde〈动〉 not begrudge: 练字必须～下功夫。 To acquire good handwriting one mustn't begrudge practice time. ‖ 你～把这本书送给别人吗? Are you willing to give the book to somebody else?

【舍得一身剐，敢把皇帝拉下马】shěde yīshēn guǎ, gǎn bǎ huángdì lāxià mǎ〈俗〉 be so fearless that one is willing to unhorse the emperor

【舍己救人】shějǐ-jiùrén〈成〉 save sb. else's life at the risk of one's own

【舍己为公】shějǐ-wèigōng〈成〉 sacrifice one's own interests for the sake of the public: 在抗洪中，他是～的英雄。 He proved a selfless hero who distinguished himself during the flood fighting.

【舍己为人】shějǐ-wèirén〈成〉 sacrifice one's own interests for the sake of others

【舍近求远】shějìn-qiúyuǎn〈成〉 ignore what is close at hand in favour of the far afield: 原料不必～进口，国产的就足够了。 We needn't take the trouble to import. We have enough domestically.

【舍车马保将帅】shějūmǎ-bǎojiàngshuài〈成〉 make minor sacrifices to safeguard major interests

【舍命】shěmìng〈动〉 risk one's life: ～救人 risk one's life to save another's

【舍命陪君子】shěmìng péi jūnzǐ〈俗〉〈诙〉 make sacrifices for the sake of keeping sb.'s company: 今天我～，陪你走一

趟。 Today I'll go with you even at the risk of my own life.

【舍弃】shěqì〈动〉 give up: ～财产 abandon one's estate

【舍入】shěrù〈动〉［数学］ round off

【舍身】shěshēn〈动〉 lay down one's life: ～救人 save sb. else's life at the risk of one's own ‖ ～为国 sacrifice oneself for one's country

【舍生取义】shěshēng-qǔyì〈成〉 lay down one's life for a noble cause: 为了中国革命的成功，无数革命党人～，英勇献身。 Countless revolutionaries laid down their lives in order for the Chinese revolution to succeed.

【舍生忘死】shěshēng-wàngsǐ〈成〉 risk one's life

【舍我其谁】shěwǒqíshuí〈成〉 if I cannot do it, who can?

shè

厍（厙） Shè〈名〉 She [surname]

设（設） shè

A〈动〉 **1**（安置） set: ～岗哨 station a sentinel ‖ ～圈套 lay a trap ‖ 总部～在莫斯科。 The headquarters is based in Moscow. ▸安～，陈～，架～ **2**（开办） establish: 新～机构 newly founded institution ‖ 本市下～六个区。 This city is divided into six districts. ▸～立，建～，开～ **3**（筹划） work out: ▸～法，～计 **4**（假想） presume: ～长方形的宽是 x 米。 Suppose the width of a rectangle is x metres. ▸～想，假～

B ▸**p. 350**〈连〉〈书〉 supposing: ～有困难，当尽力相助。 In case of difficulties you can count on me to help.

【设备】shèbèi〈名〉 equipment: 安装新～ install new equipment ‖ 办公/家用～ office/household equipment ‖ 供暖～ heating installation ‖ 生产～ production facilities ‖ 通讯～ communication equipment ‖ 消防～ fire-fighting equipment

【设得兰群岛郡】Shèdélánqúndǎojùn〈名〉 Shetland Islands

【设定】shèdìng〈动〉 set: 把闹钟～在六点 set the alarm for six

【设法】shèfǎ〈动〉 do what one can: ～克服困难 manage to overcome difficulties ‖ 我们正在～解决这一问题。 We are trying to find a solution to the problem. ▸想方～

【设防】shèfáng〈动〉 set up defences: 层层～ set up solid defences ‖ ～的城市 fortified city

【设伏】shèfú〈动〉〈书〉 lay an ambush: 在山口～ lay an ambush at a mountain pass

【设岗】shègǎng〈动〉 post a sentry: 在门口～ post a sentry at the gate

【设计】shèjì〈动〉 **1**（规划） design: ～版面 lay out a printed page ‖ 服装/建筑/课程～ dress/architectural/course design ‖ 最佳～ best design **2**（定下计谋） hatch a plot: ～陷害 frame a case

【设计师】shèjìshī ▸**p. 966**〈名〉 designer: 服装～ fashion designer ‖ 总～ chief architect

【设计院】shèjìyuàn〈名〉 design institute

【设计者】shèjìzhě〈名〉 designer: 博物馆的～ museum designer ‖ 自己命运的～ architect of one's own fortunes

【设立】shèlì〈动〉 establish: ～常委会 set up a standing committee ‖ ～基金 set up a fund ‖ 这是一个新～的研究机构。 This is a newly established research institute.

【设若】shèruò ▸**p. 350**〈连〉〈书〉 if

【设色】shèsè〈动〉 colour: ～柔和 be painted in quiet colours

【设身处地】shèshēn-chǔdì〈成〉 put oneself in sb. else's position: 请您～地为我想一想。 Please put yourself in my shoes.

【设施】shèshī〈名〉 facilities: 公共～ public facilities ‖ 防洪～ flood control facilities ‖ 这家旅馆具备各种现代化～。 This hotel is equipped with every modern amenity. ▸基础～

【设使】shèshǐ ▸**p. 350**〈连〉〈书〉 supposing: ～能解决这个问题，我们就成功了。 If we can solve this problem, we will surely succeed.

【设问】shèwèn〈名〉［语言］ rhetorical question

【设想】shèxiǎng〈动〉 **1**（假设） assume: 大胆地～ make a bold assumption ‖ 初步～ tentative plan ‖ 他们的工程耗资比原先～的要多。 Their project is more costly than they had envisaged. **2**（着想） have consideration for: 处处替国家～ have absolute consideration for the state ‖ 为学生～ take the interests of the students into consideration

【设宴】shèyàn〈动〉 hold a banquet: ～欢迎 give sb. a welcome banquet ‖ ～招待客人 host a dinner party in honour of one's guests ‖ 设寿宴/喜宴 give a birthday/wedding feast (to)

【设营】shèyíng〈动〉［军事］ encamp

【设置】shèzhì **A**〈动〉 **1**（建立） set up: ～警卫 mount sentries ‖ ～骗局 lay a trap ‖ ～专门机构 set up a special organization **2**（设立） put up: ～路障 set up road blocks ‖ ～障碍 erect barriers **B**〈名〉［计算机］ configuration

社 shè〈名〉 **1**（土神） god of land: 春～ spring sacrifice ▸～稷 **2**（集体组织） society: ▸～团，合作～，结～ **3**（用于机构名） agency, service: ▸报～，出版～，旅～

【社保费】shèbǎofèi〈名〉 social security fee: 企业不得拒缴、欠缴～。 Companies may not withhold social security fees.

【社保卡】shèbǎokǎ〈名〉 social security card

【社工】shègōng ▸**p. 966**〈名〉 social worker: 有知识有经验的～ a knowledgeable and experienced social worker

【社会】shèhuì〈名〉 society: ～动乱 social unrest ‖ 当今～ present-day society ‖ 国际～ international community

【社会办学】shèhuì bànxué〈名〉 schools run by non-governmental sectors: 鼓励～ encourage non-governmental sectors to run educational institutions

【社会保险】shèhuì bǎoxiǎn〈名〉 social insurance

【社会保障】shèhuì bǎozhàng〈名〉 social security: ～措施 social security measures

【社会变革】shèhuì biàngé〈名〉 social changes

【社会财富】shèhuì cáifù〈名〉 wealth of society

【社会地位】shèhuì dìwèi〈名〉 social status: ～高/低 have high/low social status ‖ ～不如/高于自己的人 one's social inferior/superior

【社会分工】shèhuì fēngōng〈名〉 social division of labour

【社会福利】shèhuì fúlì〈名〉 social welfare: ～彩票 social welfare lottery ticket ‖ ～机构 social welfare agency ‖ ～事业 social welfare services

【社会各界】shèhuì gèjiè〈名〉 all sectors of society: ～人士 people from all sectors of society

【社会公德】shèhuì gōngdé〈名〉 public morality

【社会购买力】shèhuì gòumǎilì〈名〉 society's purchasing power

【社会关系】shèhuì guānxi〈名〉 **1**（指生产关系） social ties **2**（指亲朋关系） one's friends and relatives

【社会化】shèhuìhuà〈动〉 socialize: ～大生产 large-scale socialized production ‖ 劳动～ socialization of labour

【社会活动】shèhuì huódòng〈名〉 public activities: 参加各种～ take part in all kinds of social activities

【社会集团购买力】shèhuì jítuán gòumǎilì〈名〉 institutional purchasing power

【社会科学】shèhuì kēxué〈名〉 the social sciences：～家 social scientist ‖ ～研究 social studies

【社会科学院】Shèhuì Kēxuéyuàn〈名〉 Academy of Social Sciences

【社会名流】shèhuì míngliú〈名〉 eminent person

【社会企业家】shèhuì qǐyèjiā〈名〉 social entrepreneur

【社会青年】shèhuì qīngnián〈名〉 unemployed youth: 给～提供更多的就业机会 provide more job opportunities for unemployed young people

【社会实践】shèhuì shíjiàn〈名〉 exposure to real life: 从事～ participate in real life activity

【社会效益】shèhuì xiàoyì〈名〉 social benefits: 正确处理经济效益和～的关系 handle correctly the relationship between economic returns and social benefits

【社会形态】shèhuì xíngtài〈名〉 social form

【社会学】shèhuìxué〈名〉 sociology: ～家 sociologist

【社会意识】shèhuì yìshi〈名〉 social awareness

【社会舆论】shèhuì yúlùn〈名〉 public opinion: 诉诸～ appeal to public opinion

【社会语言学】shèhuì yǔyánxué〈名〉 sociolinguistics

【社会渣滓】shèhuì zhāzi〈名〉 dregs of society

【社会治安】shèhuì zhì'ān〈名〉 public order: 扰乱/维持/维护～ disrupt/maintain/preserve public order ‖ ～管理条例 regulations on maintenance of public order ‖ ～情况 public security situation

【社会制度】shèhuì zhìdù〈名〉 social system: 建立/完善～ establish/improve a social system ‖ 消灭一切不合理的～ abolish all unreasonable social systems

【社会秩序】shèhuì zhìxù〈名〉 social order: 扰乱/维护/整顿～ disturb/preserve/improve social order

【社会资源】shèhuì zīyuán〈名〉 social resources

【社会总产值】shèhuì zǒngchǎnzhí〈名〉 aggregate social product

【社会主义】shèhuìzhǔyì〈名〉 socialism: 建设～ build socialism ‖ ～初级阶段 primary stage of socialism ‖ 科学/空想～ scientific/utopian socialism

【社会主义道路】shèhuìzhǔyì dàolù〈名〉 socialist road: 走～ follow the socialist road

【社会主义法制】shèhuìzhǔyì fǎzhì〈名〉 socialist legal system: 健全～ perfect the socialist legal system

【社会主义建设】shèhuìzhǔyì jiànshè〈名〉

socialist construction: ～总路线 general line for socialist construction

【社会主义精神文明】shèhuìzhǔyì jīngshén wénmíng〈名〉 socialist culture and ideology: 建设～ build a socialist society that is culturally and ideologically advanced

【社会主义市场经济】 shèhuìzhǔyì shìchǎng jīngjì〈名〉socialist market economy

【社会主义所有制】shèhuìzhǔyì suǒyǒuzhì〈名〉 socialist ownership

【社会主义物质文明】shèhuìzhǔyì wùzhì wénmíng〈名〉 socialist material civilization

【社会主义现代化】shèhuìzhǔyì xiàndàihuà〈名〉 socialist modernization

【社会主义制度】shèhuìzhǔyì zhìdù〈名〉 socialist system: 坚持～ adhere to the socialist system

【社火】shèhuǒ〈名〉〈旧〉 traditional festivities (such as lion dance, dragon lantern dance, 'land boat' dance, etc. in China): 玩～ hold traditional merry-making activities

【社稷】shèjì〈名〉 1（土神和谷神） gods of earth and grain 2（国家） country

【社交】shèjiāo〈名〉 social contact: ～活动 social activities ‖ ～礼节 social etiquette ‖ 她～活动频繁。 She lives a busy social life.

【社交界】shèjiāojiè〈名〉 society: 出入～ mix in society ‖ ～名人 socialite in society

【社科院】Shèkēyuàn〈简称〉= 社会科学院

【社论】shèlùn〈名〉 editorial; leading article〈英〉: 发表～ carry an editorial ‖ 措词强硬的～ strong editorial

【社评】shèpíng〈名〉 editorial

【社情】shèqíng〈名〉 social conditions: 了解～民意 get to know social conditions and public opinions

【社情民意】shèqíng mínyì〈名〉 social conditions and public opinion

【社区】 shèqū〈名〉 community: ～服务 community service ‖ ～活动中心 community centre ‖ 华人～ Chinese community

【社团】shètuán〈名〉 mass organization: 组织～ form a mass organization

【社戏】shèxì〈名〉〈旧〉 village theatrical performance (given on religious festivals)

【社员】 shèyuán〈名〉 1（指社团） member 2〈旧〉（指公社） commune member: 召开全体～大会 hold a general meeting of commune members

舍 shè

A〈名〉 1（房屋） house: ▸旅～, 宿～, 校～ 2〈谦〉（家） my place: 敝～ my place ▸～下, 寒～ 3（家畜的圈）（指鸡） fold;（指猪） sty;（指狗） house

B〈量〉 *she* [an ancient unit of distance, equal to 30 *li*]: ▸退避三～

C〈形〉 [used before relatives younger than or junior to oneself] my: ～弟/妹 my younger brother/sister ‖ ～侄 my nephew

▸shě

【舍间】 shèjiān〈名〉〈谦〉 my humble abode: 请到～一叙。 Please come to my place for a chat.

【舍利】shèlì〈名〉［佛教］ sarira [relics left after the cremation of the Buddha or a saintly monk deposited in a stupa for worship]: ～塔 stupa

【舍利子】shèlìzǐ = 舍利 shèlì

【舍亲】shèqīn〈名〉〈谦〉 my relative

【舍下】shèxià = 舍间 shèjiān

拾 shè〈动〉〈书〉 ascend in light steps

▸shí

【拾级而上】shèjí'érshàng〈动〉 ascend a flight of steps

射 shè〈动〉

1（指箭、子弹等） shoot: ～中靶心 hit the bull's eye ‖ 在距球门三十米外～进一球 score a goal from 30 metres away ‖ 箭～中了目标。 The arrow hit the target. ▸～箭, ～门, 扫～ 2（指液体） spout: ▸喷～, 注～ 3（指光、热等） emit: 太阳透过晨雾～出光芒。 The sun's rays shone through the morning mist. ▸～线, 辐～, 照～ 4（有所指） refer to: ▸暗～, 影～

【射程】shèchéng〈名〉 firing range: 进入～ come within range ‖ 有效～ effective range ‖ 在大炮～之内/外 within/beyond the range of the cannons

【射电】shèdiàn〈名〉 radio: ～望远镜 radio telescope

【射击】shèjī **A**〈动〉 shoot: 停止～ hold one's fire ‖ 实弹～ solid shot ‖ 用手枪～ fire one's pistol **B** ▸p. 909〈名〉［体育］ shooting: ～比赛 shooting match ‖ 飞碟～ clay-pigeon shooting

【射击场】shèjīchǎng〈名〉 shooting range

【射极】shèjí〈名〉［物理］ emitter: ～电流 emitter current ‖ ～电阻 emitter current ‖ ～脉冲/引线 emitter pulse/terminal

【射箭】shèjiàn **A**〈动〉 shoot an arrow **B** ▸p. 909〈名〉［体育］ archery: 室内/室外～ indoor/outdoor archery

【射箭场】shèjiànchǎng〈名〉archery range

【射界】shèjiè〈名〉 field of fire

【射精】shèjīng〈动〉［生理］ ejaculate

【射孔】shèkǒng〈动〉 perforate: ～器 perforator

【射猎】shèliè〈动〉 hunt: ～高手 excellent hunter

【射流】shèliú〈名〉［物理］ jet: ～电路 fluidic circuit ‖ ～装置 fluidic device

【射门】shèmén〈动〉 shoot: ～得分 score a goal ‖ 鱼跃～ dive shot ‖ 他的～偏右了。 His shot went to the right of the goal.

【射频】shèpín〈名〉［电子］ radio frequency (RF): ～放大器 radio frequency amplifier ‖ ～信号/装置 radio frequency signal/unit

【射人先射马，擒贼先擒王】shè rén xiān shè mǎ, qín zéi xiān qín wáng〈俗〉 when catching robbers, seize the leader first

【射手】shèshǒu〈名〉 1（指用枪炮或箭） marksman: 机枪～ machine gunner ‖ 神～ sharpshooter 2［体育］ striker: 本赛季最佳～ best striker of the season

【射手座】Shèshǒuzuò〈名〉［天文］ Sagittarius

【射线】shèxiàn〈名〉 ray: 伽马～ gamma ray ‖ X光～ X-ray

【射影】shèyǐng〈名〉［数学］ projecting: ～法 projective method ‖ ～函数 mapping function ‖ ～坐标 projective coordinates

涉 shè〈动〉

1（徒步过水） wade: ～过沼泽地 wade through marshland ▸跋山～水 2（经历） experience: ▸～世, ～险 3（牵涉） involve: ▸～及, 牵～, ～外

【涉案】shè'àn〈动〉 be involved in a case: ～人员 people involved in a case

【涉黑】shèhēi〈动〉 be Triad-related: 侦办～案件 investigate Triad-related cases ‖ ～犯罪集团 Triad-related criminal gang

【涉及】 shèjí〈动〉 involve: ～很多问题 cover a wide range of issues ‖ ～许多人的利益 affect the interests of many people ‖ 所～的问题 issues involved ‖ 他的研究～范围极广。 His research covers broad ground.

【涉猎】shèliè〈动〉 dabble in: ～文学 dabble in literature ‖ ～政治 dip into politics ‖ 他广泛～了文学作品。 He read literary works extensively.

【涉禽】shèqín〈名〉［鸟类］ wading bird

【涉世】shèshì〈动〉 gain life experience: ～不深 have little experience of life

【涉水】shèshuǐ〈动〉 wade through water: ～过河 wade a stream

【涉讼】shèsòng〈动〉〈书〉 be involved in a lawsuit

【涉外】shèwài〈形〉 concerning foreign affairs: ～活动 activities involving foreign countries/nationals ‖ ～婚姻 marriage between people of different nationalities

【涉外案件】shèwài ànjiàn〈名〉 foreign-related case

【涉外婚姻】 shèwài hūnyīn〈名〉 international marriage

【涉外经济纠纷】shèwài jīngjì jiūfēn〈名〉 economic dispute involving foreign entities

【涉外劳务合作】shèwài láowù hézuò〈名〉 foreign service cooperation

【涉外刑事案件】shèwài xíngshì ànjiàn〈名〉 criminal case involving foreign elements

【涉嫌】shèxián〈动〉 be a suspect: ～受贿 be suspected of taking bribes ‖ ～人犯 suspect ‖ 他～参与了那次抢劫。 He was suspected of having taken part in the robbery.

【涉险】shèxiǎn〈动〉 experience dangers: ～过关 have a brush with danger

【涉足】shèzú〈动〉〈书〉 set foot in : ～财经/政界 dip one's toe in finance/politics

S

赦 shè〈动〉 pardon: ▸～免, 大～, 十恶不～

【赦令】shèlìng〈名〉 amnesty: 他们是根据大～而获释的。 They were released under an amnesty.

【赦免】shèmiǎn〈动〉 pardon: ～罪犯 offer an amnesty to criminals ‖ 无条件～ unconditional pardon ‖ 他在服刑五年后被～。 He was pardoned after serving five years of his sentence.

【赦免令】shèmiǎnlìng〈名〉 pardon

【赦罪】shèzuì〈动〉 give/grant absolution

摄¹（攝） shè〈动〉 act for: ▸～政

摄²（攝） shè〈动〉

1（吸取） absorb: ▸～取, ～食 2（摄影） take a photograph of: ▸～制, 拍～

摄³（攝） shè〈动〉〈书〉 keep healthy: ▸～生, 珍～

【摄魂钩魄】shèhún-gōupò〈成〉 hold sb. spellbound

【摄录机】shèlùjī〈名〉 video camera recorder (VCR)

【摄谱仪】shèpǔyí〈名〉［物理］ spectrograph

【摄取】shèqǔ〈动〉 1（吸收） take in: ～营养 absorb nourishment 2（拍摄） take a photograph of: ～几个镜头 take several shots

【摄生】shèshēng〈动〉〈书〉 keep healthy: ～之道 way to keep fit

【摄食】shèshí〈动〉 feed: ～行为 feeding behaviour

【摄氏度】Shèshìdù ▸p. 776〈名〉 Celsius, centigrade (°C): 30～ 30 degrees Celcius/centigrade (30°C)

【摄氏温标】Shèshì wēnbiāo〈名〉 Celsius/centigrade temperature scale

【摄氏温度】Shèshì wēndù ▸p. 776〈名〉centigrade/Celsius degree (°C): ～计 centigrade/Celsius thermometer
【摄像】shèxiàng〈动〉make a video recording
【摄像机】shèxiàngjī〈名〉video camera: 电视～ television/TV camera ‖ 医用～ medical video camera
【摄影】shèyǐng〈动〉1 (照相) take a photograph (of): ～留念 take a picture as a souvenir ‖ ～比赛 photographic competition ‖ 新闻～ reportage photography 2 (拍电影) film: 内景/外景现场～ interior/exterior/location shooting
【摄影场】shèyǐngchǎng〈名〉studio
【摄影机】shèyǐngjī〈名〉1 (照相机) camera 2 (摄像机) video camera
【摄影记者】shèyǐng jìzhě ▸p. 966〈名〉press photographer, cameraman
【摄影棚】shèyǐngpéng〈名〉film studio
【摄影师】shèyǐngshī ▸p. 966〈名〉1 (指照相) photographer 2 (指拍摄影片) cameraman
【摄影室】shèyǐngshì〈名〉photo studio
【摄影展览】shèyǐng zhǎnlǎn〈名〉photo exhibition
【摄政】shèzhèng〈动〉act as regent
【摄政王】shèzhèngwáng〈名〉prince regent
【摄制】shèzhì〈动〉produce: ～电影 produce a film
【摄制组】shèzhìzǔ〈名〉production crew: 电影～ film production crew

慑（懾） shè〈动〉〈书〉awe: ～于某人的淫威 be cowed by someone's arbitrariness ‖ ～人魂魄 awe-inspiring ▸威～
【慑服】shèfú〈动〉〈书〉1 (顺服) submit in fear 2 (使屈服) cow sb. into submission

麝 shè〈名〉1 (动物) musk deer 2 = 麝香 shèxiāng
【麝牛】shèniú〈名〉musk ox: 雌/母～ musk cow
【麝鼠】shèshǔ〈名〉muskrat
【麝香】shèxiāng〈名〉musk

shéi

谁（誰） shéi〈代〉1 (用作疑问代词) (作主语) who; (作宾语) whom; (表所有格) whose: ～打破了杯子? Who broke the cup? ‖ 你找～? Who are you looking for? ‖ 这是～的书? Whose book is this? 2 (表虚指) somebody, someone: 是不是有～来过这儿? Has someone come here before? 3 (表泛指) anybody, anyone, everybody, everyone: ～来都欢迎。Anyone who comes is welcome. ‖ ～准备好～发言。Whoever's ready may take the floor. 4 (没有人) [used in rhetorical questions to indicate no one] nobody, no one: ～能比得上你呀! Nobody can compare with you! ‖ ～都不怀疑他的能力。No one will doubt his ability.
【谁个】shéigè〈代〉〈方〉who: 此事～不知, ～不晓。This matter is known to all.
【谁人】shéirén〈代〉who: ～不知, 她是这方面的专家。Everybody knows that she is an expert in this field.
【谁谁】shéishéi〈代〉[dual interrogative pronoun to indicate people whose names need not be mentioned]: 大家纷纷谈论着～已在本届奥运会上夺得了冠军。Everyone was talking about who had won gold medals in this Olympic Games.

shēn

申[1] shēn〈动〉1 (展开) extend: ▸引～ 2 (说明) explain: 重～我们的立场 reaffirm our stand ▸～辩, ～明, 三令五～

申[2] Shēn〈名〉Shen [another name for Shanghai (上海)]

申[3] shēn〈名〉ninth of the twelve Earthly Branches (地支)
【申奥】shēn'ào〈动〉bid to host the Olympics: 庆祝北京～成功 celebrate Beijing's successful bid for the Olympics
【申办】shēnbàn〈动〉bid: ～奥运会 bid to host the Olympic Games
【申报】shēnbào〈动〉1 (报告) report to a higher body: ～财产 submit a report on one's property 2 (申请) apply (for): ～户口 apply for residence registration 3 (指纳税) declare: ～关税 make a customs declaration 4 (指返税) file: ～收入 declare one's income
【申报表】shēnbàobiǎo〈名〉declaration form
【申辩】shēnbiàn〈动〉defend oneself: 允许～ allow sb. to argue their case ‖ 有～的权利 have the right to defend oneself ‖ 被告未作～。The accused made no defence.
【申斥】shēnchì〈动〉〈书〉rebuke: 予以～ deliver a rebuke ‖ 他因失职受到上司的严厉～。He was sternly reprimanded by his superiors for a breach of duty.
【申饬】shēnchì〈动〉〈旧〉1 (告诫) admonish: ～下级谨慎行事 warn one's subordinates to act with caution 2 = 申斥 shēnchì
【申敕】shēnchì = 申饬 shēnchì 1
【申购】shēngòu〈动〉apply to purchase: ～新股 apply for the purchase of new stocks
【申令】shēnlìng〈动〉〈书〉decree: ～全国 issue orders to all parts of the country
【申论】shēnlùn A〈动〉expound: ～自己的观点 defend one's point of view B〈名〉Shenlun [a written examination undertaken by candidates of the state civil service exams, in which examinees are required to read a passage of text and articulate their views]
【申明】shēnmíng〈动〉declare: ～观点 state one's opinion ‖ ～理由 give one's reasons ‖ 公开～ openly declare
【申请】shēnqǐng〈动〉apply for: ～护照/签证 apply for a passport/visa ‖ ～奖学金 apply for a scholarship ‖ ～破产 file for bankruptcy ‖ 撤回～ withdraw one's application ‖ 递交～ submit an application
【申请表】shēnqǐngbiǎo〈名〉application form: 填写～ fill in an application (form)
【申请人】shēnqǐngrén〈名〉applicant
【申请书】shēnqǐngshū〈名〉application: 递交～ submit an application ‖ 填写～ fill in an application (form)
【申曲】shēnqǔ = 沪剧 hùjù
【申时】shēnshí〈名〉〈旧〉period of the day from 3 p.m. to 5 p.m.
【申述】shēnshù〈动〉state: ～观点 expound one's views ‖ ～意见 express one's opinion
【申说】shēnshuō〈动〉state: ～迟到的原因 explain why one was late
【申诉】shēnsù〈动〉1 (向上级机关或处理机关) appeal for justice: ～冤屈 complain of an injustice against oneself ‖ 驳回～ ignore a complaint ‖ 向当局～ file a complaint with the authorities 2 (向法院或检察院) appeal: 向上级法庭提出～ appeal to a higher court ‖ 法院驳回其～。The court rejected his appeal. ‖ 他们不服判决, 决定～。Not satisfied with the verdict, they decided to make an appeal.
【申诉书】shēnsùshū〈名〉[法律] letter of appeal: 递交～ submit a letter of appeal
【申讨】shēntǎo〈动〉condemn: ～敌人的罪行 denounce the crimes of the enemy
【申谢】shēnxiè〈动〉〈书〉express one's gratitude
【申雪】shēnxuě = 申冤雪耻 shēnyuān-xuěchǐ
【申遗】shēnyí〈动〉compete for nomination for World Heritage Site status
【申冤】shēnyuān〈动〉1 (纠正) redress an injustice: 给某人～ redress a wrong done to sb. 2 (申诉) appeal to redress an injustice
【申冤雪耻】shēnyuān-xuěchǐ〈成〉redress a grievance and wipe out a disgrace: 为遭受迫害的人～ redress the grievance and wipe out the disgrace for those persecuted

伸 shēn〈动〉1 (展开) extend: ～长脖子 stretch one's neck out ‖ ～出援助的手 extend a helping hand ‖ 把头～出窗外 stick one's head out of the window ▸～手, 延～ 2 (申诉) report: ▸～冤
【伸懒腰】shēn lǎnyāo〈动〉stretch: 她下床痛痛快快地伸了个懒腰。She got out of bed and gave a long stretch.
【伸手】shēnshǒu〈动〉1 (伸出手) stretch out one's hand: 你～能够到那本书吗? Can you reach for the book? ▸～不见五指 2 (要求钱物等) ask for handouts: 不要一有困难就～向国家要钱。Don't be asking for assistance from the state as soon as you run into difficulties. 3 (干预) meddle in: 你的手伸得太长了吧。You're too greedy.
【伸手不见五指】shēnshǒu bùjiàn wǔzhǐ〈成〉pitch-black: 外面很黑, ～。It was so dark outside that you couldn't see your hand in front of your face.
【伸缩】shēnsuō〈动〉1 (伸和缩) expand and contract: 一些照相机的镜头可以～。Some cameras have collapsible lenses. 2 (变动) be flexible: 留有～的余地 leave some room for flexibility
【伸缩性】shēnsuōxìng〈名〉flexibility
【伸腿】shēntuǐ〈动〉1 (舒展腿) stretch one's legs 2 (插足) step in 3〈口〉〈诙〉(死亡) kick the bucket
【伸雪】shēnxuě = 申雪 shēnxuě
【伸延】shēnyán = 延伸 yánshēn
【伸腰】shēnyāo〈动〉straighten oneself up
【伸冤】shēnyuān = 申冤 shēnyuān 1
【伸展】shēnzhǎn〈动〉stretch: 向远方～ stretch into the distance ‖ 他～着身子躺在草地上睡着了。He stretched himself out on the lawn and fell asleep.
【伸张】shēnzhāng〈动〉promote: ～正义 uphold justice
【伸直】shēnzhí〈动〉stretch (out): 把腰～ straighten one's back

身 shēn
A〈名〉1 (身体) body: ～患重病 be seriously ill ‖ ～着便装 be dressed in civilian clothing ‖ 转过～去 turn around ‖ 他在岩洞里栖～。He lived in a cave. ▸～体, 强～, 挺～而出 2 (主体) body: ▸车～, 船～ 3 (自身) oneself: ～兼数职 wear

S

several different hats ‖ ～居高位 hold a high office ▸～临其境，以～作则 **4**（生命） life: ▸奋不顾～，舍～，献～ **5**（人生） one's entire life: ▸～后，终～ **6**（品格修养） one's moral character and conduct: ▸洁～自好，立～处世，修～ **7**（地位） social status: ▸～败名裂，～份，出～

B〈量〉 [of clothes] suit: 一～新衣裳 a new suit

【身败名裂】shēnbài-mínglìè〈成〉 be utterly discredited: 政治上～ be finished in politics

【身板】shēnbǎn〈名〉〈方〉 constitution: ～结实 be sturdily built ‖ ～硬朗 have a strong constitution

【身边】shēnbiān〈名〉 **1**（周围） one's side: 把所有的人都叫到～ summon everyone to one's side ‖ 你年纪大了，～没人可不行。 You are too old to live alone. ‖ 他对～的一切漠不关心。 He was totally indifferent to what was going on around him. **2**（随身） one's person: 我～没钱。 I have no money on me.

【身不由己】shēnbùyóujǐ〈成〉 in spite of oneself: 他太累了，～地倒在地上。 He was so tired that he just fell to the ground. ‖ 人在江湖，～。 Sometimes one has to do something despite oneself.

【身不由主】shēnbùyóuzhǔ ＝ 身不由己 shēnbùyóujǐ

【身材】shēncái〈名〉 figure: ～矮小 of small stature ‖ 中等～ of average stature ‖ 她～苗条。 She has a slender figure.

【身残志坚】shēncán-zhìjiān〈成〉 disabled in body but firm in spirit

【身长】shēncháng〈名〉 **1**（身高） height **2**（指衣服） length

【身段】shēnduàn〈名〉 figure: 那件裙子显出了她优美的～。 The skirt showed off her lovely figure.

【身分】shēnfèn ＝ 身份 shēnfèn

【身份】shēnfèn〈名〉 **1**（地位） status: 暴露～ reveal one's identity ‖ 符合～ be suitable to one's status ‖ 双重～ dual capacity **2**（特指地位高贵） honourable position: 显赫的～ distinguished position ‖ 有～的人 person of position ‖ 这样的行为有失你的～。 Such an act would be beneath your dignity.

【身份盗窃】shēnfèn dàoqiè〈名〉 identity theft

【身份证】shēnfènzhèng〈名〉identity card, ID (card): 随身携带～ take one's ID ‖ 请出示～! Please show your ID!

【身负重任】shēnfù-zhòngrèn〈成〉 be charged with important tasks/heavy responsibilities

【身高】shēngāo〈名〉 height: 他～两米。 He is two metres tall.

【身故】shēngù〈动〉〈书〉 die: 他祖父于去年～。 His grandfather died last year.

【身后】shēnhòu〈名〉**1**（身体后面）place behind one: 他在我～站着。 He is standing behind me. **2**（死后） time after death: ～事 posthumous affairs ‖ 他～留下两个孩子。 When he died, he left behind two children.

【身怀六甲】shēnhuái-liùjiǎ〈成〉 be pregnant: 她现在～，不能再干重活。 She is pregnant and can't do heavy work any more.

【身家性命】shēnjiā-xìngmìng〈成〉 one's personal safety and that of one's family

【身价】shēnjià〈名〉 **1**（价格） person's sale price: ～很高的选手 high-priced player **2**（地位） social status: 他的～正在提高。 His prestige is rising.

【身价百倍】shēnjià-bǎibèi〈成〉 have a meteoric rise in social status

【身教】shēnjiào〈动〉〈书〉teach others by one's own example: ～胜于言传 example is better than precept

【身经百战】shēnjīngbǎizhàn〈成〉 be a veteran of many battles: ～的老战士 seasoned veteran

【身历】shēnlì〈动〉〈书〉 have personal experience of sth.: ～第二次世界大战 have personal experience of World War II

【身临其境】shēnlínqíjìng〈成〉 be personally on the scene: 只有～，才能有深切的感受。 You can have the feel of something only when you have personally experienced it.

【身强力壮】shēnqiáng-lìzhuàng〈成〉 healthy and strong

【身躯】shēnqū〈名〉 stature: ～高大 be tall in stature ‖ 健壮的～ strong body

【身上】shēnshang〈名〉 **1**（身体） on one's body: 他～穿着一件白衬衣。 He is wearing a white shirt. ‖ 我～不舒服。 I'm not feeling well. **2**（随身） with one: 你～有钢笔吗? Do you have a pen with you? ‖ 我～没零钱。 I haven't got any change on me.

【身世】shēnshì〈名〉 one's lot: 滔滔不绝地诉说自己的～ reel off the story of one's life ‖ 这个人～很凄凉。 This person has had a miserable life.

【身手】shēnshǒu〈名〉 talent: 大显～ display one's ability to the full ‖ ～不凡 have extraordinary talent

【身首异处】shēn-shǒuyìchù〈成〉 be beheaded: 历史上许多犯人在这儿～。 In times gone by, many criminals were beheaded here.

【身受】shēnshòu〈动〉 have personal experience of sth.: ～其害 suffer a lot from sth. ‖ 感同～ be personally very grateful for something

【身体】shēntǐ〈名〉 **1**（躯体） body: 检查～ have a check-up ‖ 健康的～ healthy body **2**（健康） health: ～强壮 healthy and strong ‖ ～每况愈下 be in declining health

【身体素质】shēntǐ sùzhì〈名〉 constitution: ～很差 poor constitution

【身体力行】shēntǐ-lìxíng〈成〉 practise what one preaches: 领导干部必须～，才能赢得群众的支持。 Senior leaders will only win the support of the people if they practise what they preach.

【身外之物】shēnwàizhīwù〈成〉 material wealth: 富贵功名乃～。Fortune, rank, success and fame are merely material things.

【身亡】shēnwáng〈动〉〈书〉 die: 遇刺～ be assassinated ‖ 自杀～ commit suicide

【身无分文】shēnwúfēnwén〈成〉 penniless: 他一夜之间变得～。 He became destitute overnight.

【身先士卒】shēnxiānshìzú〈成〉 take the lead in doing sth.: 领导干部要～。 Leaders must take charge.

【身心】shēnxīn〈名〉 body and mind: ～健康 be sound in body and mind ‖ ～愉快 feel well both physically and mentally ‖ 全～投入 be completely devoted

【身心交瘁】shēnxīn-jiāocuì〈成〉 worn out both physically and mentally: 这次失败使他～。 This time the failure truly broke him.

【身影】shēnyǐng〈名〉 silhouette: 一个高大的～ a tall figure ‖ 她的～被黑暗吞没了。 Her silhouette vanished in the darkness.

【身孕】shēnyùn〈名〉 pregnancy: 她有五个月的～。 She is five months pregnant.

【身在曹营心在汉】 shēn zài Cáoyíng xīn zài Hàn〈成〉 **1**（不忠诚） appear to be dutiful but in fact remain loyal to someone else **2**（不专心） be half-hearted

【身在福中不知福】shēn zài fú zhōng bù zhī fú〈俗〉 not appreciate one's own luck

【身正不怕影子斜】 shēn zhèng bùpà yǐngzi xié〈俗〉 an honest person fears no gossip

【身姿】shēnzī〈名〉 carriage: ～绰约 graceful demeanour

【身子】shēnzi〈名〉 **1**（身体） body: 光着～ be naked ‖ ～不大舒服 not feel well **2**（怀孕） pregnancy: 有了三个月的～ be three months pregnant

【身子骨儿】shēnzigǔr〈名〉〈方〉 health: 爷爷的～还挺结实。 Grandpa is still enjoying good health.

呻 shēn

【呻吟】shēnyín〈动〉 moan: 发出绝望的～ give a groan of despair ‖ 痛苦地～ groan with pain ▸无病～

参[1]（參） shēn〈名〉 one of the 28 constellations in ancient Chinese astronomy

参[2]（參） shēn〈名〉 ginseng

▸cān, cēn

【参商】shēnshāng〈名〉〈书〉〈喻〉 **1**（指不能会面） friends who are permanently estranged **2**（指感情不和） people who are not able to get on

绅（紳） shēn〈名〉〈旧〉 gentleman: 富～ wealthy gentleman ‖ 劣～ evil gentry ▸豪～，乡～

【绅士】shēnshì〈名〉 gentleman: 当地～ local gentry ‖ ～风度 gentility

莘 shēn

【莘莘】shēnshēn〈形〉〈书〉 numerous: ～学子 students in large numbers

砷 shēn〈名〉［化学］ arsenic (As)

【砷化物】shēnhuàwù〈名〉 arsenide

娠 shēn〈动〉〈书〉 be pregnant: ▸妊～

深 shēn

A〈形〉 **1**（垂直间距大） deep: ～埋 bury sth. deep ‖ ～～地鞠了一躬 make a low bow ‖ ～呼吸 deep breathing ‖ 这湖～不见底。 The lake was so deep that we could not see the bottom. ▸～层，～海，水～火热 **2**（深奥） abstruse: 这本书对他来说太～了。 The book is too difficult for him. ▸～入浅出 **3**（透彻） thorough: ▸～刻，～思熟虑，发人～省 **4**（密切） intimate: 他俩的关系已经很～了。 The two of them are already very close. ▸一往情～ **5** ▸**p. 863**（颜色浓） deep: ～蓝/绿 dark blue/green **6**（时间久） late: 夜～了。 It was deep into the night. ▸～更半夜，～秋

B ▸**p. 82**〈名〉 depth: 测量水～ plumb the depth of the water ‖ 这口井有多～? How deep is the well? ▸进～，纵～

C〈副〉 very: ～表同情 show deep sympathy ‖ ～受感动 be deeply moved ‖ 他～陷爱河。 He is head over heels in love. ‖ 这部电影～受欢迎。 The film has been very well received. ▸～恶痛绝，～信

S

【深奥】shēn'ào〈形〉 profound: ～的道理 profound theory ‖ 他的著作太～，我看不懂。 His writings are too profound for me to understand.

【深不可测】shēnbùkěcè〈成〉 unfathomable: ～的海洋 fathomless ocean ‖ 此人～。 He is an enigma.

【深藏若虚】shēncáng-ruòxū〈成〉 be modest about one's talent

【深层】shēncéng A〈名〉 depth B〈形〉 thorough: ～分析 in-depth analysis ‖ ～含义 deeper implications ‖ ～结构 deep structure

【深长】shēncháng〈形〉 profound: 寓意～ with much meaning

【深沉】shēnchén〈形〉 1（指程度）deep: 暮色～。 The dusk is deepening. 2（指声音） deep: ～的声音 deep voice 3（含蓄） reserved: ～的微笑 meaningful smile ‖ 这人很～。 He is very deep.

【深仇大恨】shēnchóu-dàhèn〈成〉 intense hatred: 怀有～ harbour a deep-seated hatred (of/for)

【深处】shēnchù〈名〉depth: 大海～ depths of the ocean ‖〈喻〉 灵魂～ deep in one's psyche

【深度】shēndù ▸p. 82〈名〉 depth: ～报道 in-depth report ‖ 改革的广度和～ breadth and depth of the reform ‖ ～昏迷 deep coma ‖ ～近视 extremely near-sighted ‖ 她的论文很有～。 Her thesis has remarkable depth. ‖ 这条河的～为五十米。 The river is 50 metres deep.

【深幅】shēnfú〈副〉 drastically: 股指～下挫/波动。 The stock index fell/fluctuated drastically.

【深更半夜】shēngēng-bànyè〈成〉 deep into the night: 他们一直工作到～。 They worked deep into the night. ‖ ～的，你在干什么呀? What are you doing at such a late hour?

【深耕】shēngēng〈名〉［农业］ deep ploughing: ～细作 deep ploughing and intensive cultivation

【深沟高垒】shēngōu-gāolěi〈成〉 1〈本〉 deep trenches and high ramparts 2〈喻〉（防御坚固） strong defence

【深谷】shēngǔ〈名〉 deep and secluded valley

【深广】shēnguǎng〈形〉 deep and wide: 见识～ have wide experience and deep knowledge ‖ 影响～ be of wide and profound influence

【深闺】shēnguī〈名〉〈旧〉 boudoir: 独处～ live in the seclusion of one's boudoir

【深海】shēnhǎi〈名〉 deep sea: ～采矿/捕鱼/钻探 deep-sea mining/fishing/drilling ‖ ～动物 deep sea creatures

【深海测量】shēnhǎi cèliáng〈名〉 bathymetry

【深海潜水艇】shēnhǎi qiánshuǐtǐng〈名〉 bathyscaphe

【深海潜望镜】shēnhǎi qiánwàngjìng〈名〉 bathyscope

【深海区】shēnhǎiqū〈名〉 abyssal region

【深海生物】shēnhǎi shēngwù〈名〉 hyperbenthos

【深海探测仪】shēnhǎi tàncèyí〈名〉 bathometer

【深厚】shēnhòu〈形〉 1（浓厚） deep: ～的感情 profound feelings 2（坚实） deep-seated: 基础～ have a solid foundation

【深化】shēnhuà〈动〉 deepen: ～改革，扩大开放 further reforms and open up more widely to the outside world ‖ 认识～ deepen one's understanding (of sth.)

【深加工】shēnjiāgōng〈名〉 deep processing: ～产品 deep-processed products

【深涧】shēnjiàn〈名〉 ravine

【深交】shēnjiāo A〈名〉 intimate friendship: ～甚少 have few close friends B〈动〉 have close relations: 此人不可～。 This is not someone to trust.

【深井】shēnjǐng〈名〉 deep well: ～泵 deep-well pump

【深究】shēnjiū〈动〉 go deep into sth.: 不要在细枝末节上～。 Don't delve too deep into unimportant matters.

【深居简出】shēnjū-jiǎnchū〈成〉 lead a secluded life: 他现在过着～的生活。 He is now living the life of a retreat.

【深刻】shēnkè〈形〉 deep: ～的变化/教训 profound changes/lessons ‖ 对问题有～的理解 have a profound understanding of the problem

【深明大义】shēnmíng-dàyì〈成〉 know clearly what is right and proper

【深谋远虑】shēnmóu-yuǎnlǜ〈成〉 think deeply and plan carefully

【深浅】shēnqiǎn〈名〉 1（指水深）depth: 没人知道这湖的～。 Nobody knows how deep the lake is. 2 ▸p. 863（指颜色） shade: 颜色～不同 be of different shades 3〈喻〉（指分寸） sense of propriety: 说话没～ speak inappropriately

【深切】shēnqiè〈形〉 1（充分） thorough: ～地感受到事态的严重性 fully realize the seriousness of the situation ‖ ～体会 profound experience 2（深挚） deep: 表达～的谢意 extend one's profound thanks (to) ‖ 表示～的关怀 show one's deep concern (over)

【深情】shēnqíng A〈名〉 deep affection: 她非常珍惜丈夫的一片～。 She cherishes her husband's affection for her. B〈形〉 affectionate: ～地接吻 exchange affectionate kisses

【深情厚谊】shēnqíng-hòuyì〈成〉profound friendship

【深秋】shēnqiū〈名〉 late autumn

【深入】shēnrù A〈动〉 go deep into: ～国境线 be deep beyond the frontier ‖ ～基层 go down to the grass roots ‖ ～生活 plunge into life B〈形〉 in-depth: ～开展一项运动 launch an intensive campaign ‖ ～研究事物本质 probe into the essence of things ‖ 做～分析 make an in-depth analysis

【深入浅出】shēnrù-qiǎnchū〈成〉 explain the profound in simple terms

【深入人心】shēnrù-rénxīn〈成〉 strike a deep chord in the hearts of the people: 新思想逐渐～。 New ideas are slowly filtering into people's minds.

【深山】shēnshān〈名〉 remote mountains: 住在～里 live deep in the mountains ‖ ～老林 remote mountains and virgin forests

【深深】shēnshēn〈副〉 deeply: 她～地爱上了他。 She is head over heels in love with him.

【深水】shēnshuǐ〈名〉 deep water: ～池 swimmer's pool ‖ ～港 deep-water harbour

【深水码头】shēnshuǐ mǎtou〈名〉 deep-water wharf

【深水炸弹】shēnshuǐ zhàdàn〈名〉 depth bomb

【深思】shēnsī〈动〉 think deeply (about): 值得～ deserve careful thinking ‖ 做出决定前要～。 You must think the matter over before deciding.

【深思熟虑】shēnsī-shúlǜ〈成〉 deliberate carefully: ～的计划 mature scheme ‖ 做出～的决定 make a deliberate decision

【深邃】shēnsuì〈形〉 1（指空间） deep: ～的山谷 deep valley 2（深奥） profound: 寓意～ carry a profound message

【深谈】shēntán〈动〉 have an in-depth discussion: 这件事我已经和他～过一次。 I have already had an in-depth discussion with him over this matter.

【深通】shēntōng〈动〉 be thoroughly versed in: 他～三门外语。 He has a good command of three foreign languages.

【深透】shēntòu〈形〉 profound: 老师把课文分析得很～。 The teacher has made a deep and thorough analysis of the text.

【深望】shēnwàng〈动〉〈书〉 sincerely wish: ～诸位通力合作。 We sincerely hope for your cooperation.

【深文周纳】shēnwén-zhōunà〈成〉 convict someone unfairly by deliberately stretching the law

【深恶痛绝】shēnwù-tòngjué〈成〉 detest: 对腐败现象～ abhor corruption

【深信】shēnxìn〈动〉 firmly believe: ～不疑 believe beyond a shadow of doubt ‖ 她～自己将来能够成功。 She is convinced that she will be successful in the future.

【深夜】shēnyè ▸p. 669〈名〉 late night: 工作/谈话到～ work/talk deep into the night

【深意】shēnyì〈名〉 profound meaning

【深渊】shēnyuān〈名〉 abyss: 掉进～ fall into the abyss ‖ 陷入罪恶的～ sink into the depths of vice

【深源地震】shēnyuán dìzhèn〈名〉 earthquake occurring at great depth

【深远】shēnyuǎn〈形〉 far-reaching: 影响～ have far-reaching influence ‖ 具有～的历史意义 have profound historic significance

【深造】shēnzào〈动〉 pursue advanced studies: 继续～ continue one's study ‖ 去英国～ go to Britain for advanced study

【深宅大院】shēnzhái-dàyuàn〈成〉 mansion

【深湛】shēnzhàn〈形〉 profound and thorough: 功夫～ consummate skill

【深挚】shēnzhì〈形〉〈书〉 deep and sincere: ～的友情 close friendship

【深重】shēnzhòng〈形〉 extremely serious: 罪孽～ be guilty of heinous crimes ‖ 灾难～ long-suffering

糁（糝） shēn〈名〉 crushed grain: 玉米～儿 crushed corn
▸sǎn

鲹（鰺） shēn〈名〉［鱼类］ carangid

shén

什（甚） shén
▸shí

【什么】shénme〈代〉 1（表疑问） [used before a noun or by itself to indicate who or what]: 你找～? What are you looking for? ‖ ～人? Who is it? ‖ 我们～时候出发? When shall we set out? 2（虚指） [used to refer to things indefinite] something, anything: 我想吃点～。 I want to have something to eat. ‖ 你在北京有～亲戚吗? Do you have any relatives in Beijing? 3（任指） [used before 也 or 都 to indicate there is no exception within the limits mentioned] any, every: 他～也不怕。 He is not afraid of anything. ‖ 学

S

习比～都重要。 Nothing is more important than study. 4（表前者决定后者） [used correlatively with another 什么 to indicate that the first one determines the other] whatever: 我想～就说～。 I'll say whatever is in my mind. 5（表惊讶或不满） [used to express anger, surprise, censure or negation]: ～! 都九点了! What! It's already nine o'clock! ‖ 你装～哑巴! Stop playing dumb. ‖ 你知道～! What the hell do you know? 6（表责难） [used to express disapproval or disagreement]: 给你添麻烦了! ——麻烦～。 Sorry to trouble you so much! — My pleasure. 7（列举） [used to indicate an incomplete list] such as: ～送个信呀，跑个腿儿啦,他都干得了。 He can do things like delivering letters, running errands and so on.

【什么的】shénmede〈代〉 and so on: 修个机器，换个零件～，他都能对付。He can cope with things like repairing a machine or replacing a part.

神 shén

A〈名〉 1 ▸p. 274（神灵） god: 土地～ god of land ▸～灵, 财～ 2（精神） spirit: ▸～往, 愣～儿 3（神气） expression: ▸～采, 眼～

B〈形〉 supernatural: ▸～奇, ～医, 出～入化

【神兵天将】shénbīng-tiānjiàng〈成〉 army from heaven

【神不守舍】shénbùshǒushè〈成〉 be distracted

【神不知，鬼不觉】shén bù zhī, guǐ bù jué〈成〉 without anybody knowing: 他已～地来了她跟前。 Unknown to anybody, he had already come to her side.

【神采】shéncǎi〈名〉 expression: 这女人～动人。 The woman has an attractive countenance.

【神采飞扬】shéncǎi-fēiyáng〈成〉 in high spirits

【神采奕奕】shéncǎi-yìyì〈成〉 brim with energy and vitality: 他身着新装，显得～。 Dressed in a new suit, he looked smart and brimming with health.

【神差鬼使】shénchāi-guǐshǐ = 鬼使神差 guǐshǐ-shénchāi

【神驰】shénchí〈动〉 [of one's thoughts] skip around

【神出鬼没】shénchū-guǐmò〈成〉 come and go like a shadow

【神道】shéndào〈名〉 1 ▸p. 274（鬼神祸福） way of the gods [belief in ghosts and gods, fortune and misfortune] 2（墓道） tomb passage 3 Shéndào（指宗教） Shinto [native religion of Japan]: ～教 Shintoism ‖ ～碑 stone tablet at a tomb passage

【神道】shéndao〈形〉〈口〉 1（精神旺盛） vigorous 2（举止异常） weird

【神父】shénfu = 神甫 shénfu

【神甫】shénfu〈名〉 Father

【神怪】shénguài〈名〉 gods and spirits: ～故事 teratology

【神汉】shénhàn〈名〉〈旧〉 sorcerer

【神乎其神】shénhūqíshén〈成〉 fantastic: 吹得～ boast outrageously

【神户】Shénhù〈名〉 Kobe

【神化】shénhuà〈动〉 deify: ～国王 deify a king

【神话】shénhuà〈名〉 1（故事） mythology: 古代～ ancient mythology ‖ 希腊～ Greek mythology 2（奇迹） myth: 创造～ perform a miracle ‖ 戳穿～ explode a myth

【神魂】shénhún〈名〉 state of mind: ～不定 distraught

【神魂颠倒】shénhún-diāndǎo〈成〉 be infatuated: 爱得～ be completely infatuated

【神机妙算】shénjī-miàosuàn〈成〉 brilliant intelligence: 诸葛亮以其～而著称。Zhuge Liang is well-known for his brilliant foresight.

【神交】shénjiāo **A**〈名〉 friends who are on the same wavelength **B**〈动〉 admire (sb.) out of mutual understanding and trust without having met: 他们虽未谋面，但～已久。 Though they have never met, they have had a mutual understanding and trust for a long time.

【神经】shénjīng〈名〉 1（指身体组织） nerve: 感觉/视觉/听觉～ sensory/optical/auditory nerve ‖ ～处于紧张状态 in a state of nerves 2（精神失常） mental disorder: ～错乱 mental disorder ‖ 她有点～。 She is rather disturbed.

【神经病】shénjīngbìng ▸p. 50〈名〉 1（指神经系统） neuropathy 2（精神病） mental disorder: 他有～。 He is not quite right in the head.

【神经毒气】shénjīng dúqì〈名〉 nerve gas

【神经官能症】shénjīng guānnéngzhèng〈名〉 neurosis

【神经过敏】shénjīng guòmǐn **A**〈名〉 neuroticism **B**〈形〉 neurotic: 提起此事，他就～。 He gets oversensitive whenever anyone mentions it.

【神经末梢】shénjīng mòshāo〈名〉 nerve-end

【神经衰弱】shénjīng shuāiruò ▸p. 50〈名〉 neurosism

【神经痛】shénjīngtòng ▸p. 50〈名〉［生理］ neuralgia

【神经外科】shénjīng wàikē〈名〉 neurosurgery

【神经兮兮】shénjīng-xīxī〈形〉〈方〉 neurotic: 他～的，根本无法与人相处。 He's a real nerd and lacks any kind of social skills.

【神经细胞】shénjīng xìbāo〈名〉 nerve cell

【神经系统】shénjīng xìtǒng〈名〉 nervous system

【神经性皮炎】shénjīngxìng píyán ▸p. 50〈名〉 neurodermatitis

【神经性厌食症】shénjīngxìng yànshízhèng ▸p. 50〈名〉 anorexia nervosa

【神经语言学】shénjīng yǔyánxué〈名〉 neurolinguistics

【神经元】shénjīngyuán〈名〉 neuron: ～性关节病 neurogenic arthropathy

【神经质】shénjīngzhì〈名〉 nervousness: ～的老太太 nervous old lady ‖ 他有点～。 He has a nervous temperament.

【神经中枢】shénjīng zhōngshū〈名〉 nerve centre: 大脑是人体的～。 The brain is the human body's nerve centre. ‖〈喻〉华尔街是美国金融的～。 Wall Street is the financial nerve centre of America.

【神龛】shénkān〈名〉 shrine for ancestral tablets

【神来之笔】shénláizhībǐ〈成〉 inspired writing

【神聊】shénliáo〈动〉 engage in chit-chat: 他没事就找人～。 He likes to chat with people when he's got nothing else to do.

【神灵】shénlíng ▸p. 274〈名〉 gods: 祈求～的帮助 pray to the gods for help

【神秘】shénmì〈形〉 mysterious: ～的宇宙 mysterious universe ‖ ～电话 crank phone call ‖ 为晚会增添～色彩 give a little mystery to the party ‖ 他是个～人物。 He is a mystery.

【神秘化】shénmìhuà〈动〉 mystify: 把自然现象～ mystify natural phenomena

【神秘莫测】shénmì-mòcè〈成〉 be shrouded in mystery: ～的现象 inexplicable phenomenon ‖ 这一案件～。 The case is shrouded in mystery.

【神妙】shénmiào〈形〉 wonderful: ～的笔法 ingenious brushwork ‖ ～的技艺 marvellous skill

【神明】shénmíng ▸p. 274〈名〉 gods: 奉若～ worship sb. as a god

【神女】shénnǚ ▸p. 274〈名〉 goddess

【神炮手】shénpàoshǒu〈名〉 crack gunner

【神品】shénpǐn〈名〉 masterpiece

【神婆】shénpó〈名〉〈旧〉 sorceress

【神奇】shénqí〈形〉 magical: ～的效果 miraculous effect

【神祇】shénqí ▸p. 274〈名〉〈书〉 deities

【神气】shénqì **A**〈名〉 manner: 他说话的～很严肃。 He has a very serious expression when he talks. **B**〈形〉 1（精神） spirited: 看起来很～ look quite impressive ‖ 孩子们个个一身新衣服，可～了。The children were all in high spirits in their new clothes. 2（傲慢） cocky: 你有什么可～的呢? What makes you so pleased with yourself? ‖ 她获奖后就～起来了。 She became all high-and-mighty after she won the prize.

【神气活现】shénqì-huóxiàn〈成〉 high-and-mighty: 他～，似乎不屑和咱们一般人打交道。 He acts as if he's too good to associate with us ordinary folk.

【神气十足】shénqì-shízú〈成〉 looking very dignified

【神枪手】shénqiāngshǒu〈名〉 crack shot: 百发百中的～ spot-on shooter

【神情】shénqíng〈名〉 expression: ～不安 look worried ‖ ～忧郁 have a melancholy air ‖ 惊恐的～ startled expression ‖ ～恍惚 have a roving eye

【神权】shénquán〈名〉 1（指鬼神） religious authority 2（指统治权） divine right

【神人】shénrén〈名〉 1（指神） spiritual being 2（指人） exceptional person

【神色】shénsè〈名〉 expression: 面带鄙夷的～ wear a disdainful expression ‖ ～慌张 look flustered

【神伤】shénshāng〈形〉〈书〉 dejected: 黯然～ feel depressed

【神社】shénshè〈名〉 1（祭神场所） shrine 2（指日本神道教） Shinto shrine

【神神叨叨】shénshen-dāodāo = 神神道道 shénshen-dāodāo

【神神道道】shénshen-dāodāo〈形〉 bizarre: 他这个人有时候～的。 He is very odd sometimes.

【神圣】shénshèng〈形〉 holy: ～的领土 sacred territory ‖ ～的职责 sacred duty ‖ ～不可侵犯 be sacred and inviolable

【神思】shénsī〈名〉 mental state: ～不定 be distracted ‖ ～恍惚 be distracted

【神似】shénsì〈动〉 be an excellent likeness: 好的译文不仅要形似，而且要～。A good translation should be similar to the original text not only in form but also in spirit. ‖ 他画的鸟极其～。 The birds he paints are extremely lifelike.

【神速】shénsù〈形〉 marvellously quick: 进展～ make speedy progress

【神算】shénsuàn〈名〉 1（指推算） accurate prediction 2（指计谋） marvellous stratagem

【神态】shéntài〈名〉 manner: ～傲慢 have a proud air ‖ ～悠闲 look perfectly relaxed

【神通】shéntōng〈名〉 magic power: ▸大显～

【神通广大】shéntōng-guǎngdà〈成〉 possess unusual powers: 孙悟空～。 The

S

Monkey King had vast untold magical powers.
【神童】shéntóng〈名〉prodigy
【神往】shénwǎng〈动〉be carried away: 美丽壮观的景色令我～。I was blown away by the beauty and grandeur of the scenery.
【神威】shénwēi〈名〉invincible might: 子弟兵大显～。The people's army made a big show of its martial prowess.
【神位】shénwèi〈名〉spirit tablet
【神物】shénwù〈名〉〈书〉 1（神奇的事物）wonder 2（神灵）supernatural being: 非洲许多部落仍把蛇视为～。In Africa, the snake is still sacred to many peoples.
【神仙】shénxiān〈名〉 1 ▸p. 274（仙人）immortal: ～下凡 the immortals descended into the mortal world 2（料事如神的人）clairvoyant 3（超脱的人）person free from worldly cares: 真是～过的日子！What a comfortable life!
【神仙鱼】shénxiānyú〈名〉angelfish
【神像】shénxiàng〈名〉divine image
【神效】shénxiào〈名〉miraculous effect
【神学】shénxué〈名〉theology: ～院 college of theology
【神医】shényī〈名〉highly skilful doctor
【神异】shényì A〈名〉gods and spirits B〈形〉magical
【神勇】shényǒng〈形〉extraordinarily brave: 在战斗中表现～ be extraordinarily brave in battle
【神游】shényóu〈动〉〈书〉make a spiritual tour: ～故土 make a mental tour to one's homeland
【神韵】shényùn〈名〉[of literature and art] romantic charm: 保持原文的～ retain the romantic charm of the original text
【神职人员】shénzhí rényuán〈名〉clergy
【神志】shénzhì〈名〉consciousness: ～不清 be in a coma ‖ ～昏迷 lose consciousness ‖ 直到临终老人的～一直很清楚。The old man was completely conscious to the last.
【神智】shénzhì〈名〉intellect: ～十分清醒 be in full possession of one's senses
【神州】Shénzhōu〈名〉Divine Land [a poetic name for China]
【神主】shénzhǔ〈名〉ancestral tablet

shěn

沈（瀋） shěn
【沈阳】Shěnyáng ▸p. 661〈名〉Shenyang [capital of Liaoning Province (辽宁)]
▸chén

审¹（審） shěn
A〈动〉1（审查）examine: ～稿 go over a manuscript ▸～查, 政～ 2（审讯）try: ～案 try a case ‖ 他申请重～。He applied for a fresh trial. ▸～判, 提～
B〈形〉meticulous: ▸～慎, ～视

审²（審） shěn〈副〉〈书〉indeed: ～如其言。It is indeed as it is said.
【审办】shěnbàn〈动〉investigate and handle: 负责～大案 be responsible for the investigation and trial of major cases
【审查】shěnchá〈动〉examine: ～干部 look into leaders' pasts ‖ ～账目 audit accounts ‖ 接受～ undergo examination ‖ ～属实。The fact was established after investigation. ‖ 该案件正在～之中。The case is under investigation.
【审查制度】shěnchá zhìdù〈名〉censorship: 新闻～ press censorship
【审察】shěnchá〈动〉1（观察）observe closely: ～气候变化 observe climate change 2（审查）investigate: ～各种年度报表 scrutinize various annual reports
【审处】shěnchǔ〈动〉1（审判处理）try and punish: 交高级法院～ hand over to the supreme court for trial 2（审查处理）deliberate and decide: 这件事将由主管部门～。This matter will be dealt with by the authorities concerned.
【审订】shěndìng〈动〉revise: ～教材 revise teaching material
【审定】shěndìng〈动〉examine and approve: ～文件 finalize a document ‖ ～预算 finalize a budget ‖ 交上级～ submit to a higher body for examination and approval
【审读】shěndú = 审阅 shěnyuè
【审改】shěngǎi〈动〉revise: ～文稿 revise a manuscript
【审核】shěnhé〈动〉check: ～预算 check a budget ‖ ～账目 audit accounts
【审计】shěnjì〈动〉audit: ～监督 auditing supervision ‖ 财务～ financial audit ‖ ～报告 audit report
【审计处】shěnjìchù〈名〉auditing division
【审计机构】shěnjì jīgòu〈名〉auditing body
【审计机关】shěnjì jīguān〈名〉auditing organ
【审计局】shěnjìjú〈名〉auditing office
【审计师】shěnjìshī ▸p. 966〈名〉auditor
【审计员】shěnjìyuán ▸p. 966〈名〉auditor
【审计长】shěnjìzhǎng〈名〉chief auditor
【审计制度】shěnjì zhìdù〈名〉auditing system
【审校】shěnjiào〈动〉revise
【审结】shěnjié〈动〉try and close: ～刑事案件 try and close a criminal case
【审理】shěnlǐ〈动〉try: ～案件 hear a case ‖ 在～中 be under trial ‖ 该案即将～。The case will be brought to trial soon.
【审美】shěnměi〈动〉appreciate the beautiful: ～标准 aesthetic standards ‖ 他很有～眼光。He has an aesthetic eye.
【审美观】shěnměiguān〈名〉concept of the aesthetic
【审判】shěnpàn〈动〉try and sentence: ～经济案件 try an economic case ‖ 得到公正的～ get a fair trial ‖ 接受～ undergo a trial
【审判机关】shěnpàn jīguān〈名〉judicial organ
【审判厅】shěnpàntīng〈名〉court of law
【审判员】shěnpànyuán ▸p. 966〈名〉judge
【审判长】shěnpànzhǎng〈名〉chief judge
【审批】shěnpī〈动〉examine and approve: 报上级～ submit to a higher level for examination and approval
【审慎】shěnshèn〈形〉cautious: ～处理 handle with caution ‖ 处理这个问题必须～。The matter has to be handled carefully.
【审时度势】shěnshí-duóshì〈成〉make a correct assessment of the situation
【审视】shěnshì〈动〉〈书〉examine: ～一幅画 scrutinize a painting ‖ ～片刻 look at sth. carefully for a while
【审题】shěntí〈动〉carefully consider a topic: 作文～不准 inaccurate understanding of the subject of the piece
【审问】shěnwèn〈动〉question: ～犯人 interrogate a prisoner ‖ 受到警察的～ be questioned by the police
【审讯】shěnxùn〈动〉try: ～囚犯 interrogate a prisoner ‖ 公开的～ open trial ‖ 经过～，他被判有罪。He was tried and found guilty.
【审验】shěnyàn〈动〉inspect: ～驾驶证 check sb.'s driving licence
【审议】shěnyì〈动〉review: ～工作报告 review a work report ‖ 提交全国人民代表大会～ submit sth. to the National People's Congress for review ‖ 那些提议仍在～中。The proposals are still under consideration.
【审阅】shěnyuè〈动〉read over: ～稿件 go over a manuscript ‖ 未经作者～，不得再版。Not to be reprinted without the review of the author.

哂 shěn〈动〉〈书〉1（微笑）smile: ▸～纳 2（讥笑）ridicule: ▸～笑
【哂纳】shěnnà〈动〉〈套〉kindly accept
【哂笑】shěnxiào〈动〉〈书〉ridicule: 遭行家～ be ridiculed by experts
【哂正】shěnzhèng〈动〉〈谦〉comment and revise: 敬请～。You are kindly invited to make comments and revisions.

谂（諗） shěn〈动〉〈书〉1（知道）know: ▸～悉 2（劝告）advise
【谂熟】shěnshú〈动〉〈书〉be familiar with
【谂悉】shěnxī〈动〉〈书〉know

婶（嬸） shěn〈名〉1（有亲戚关系）aunt 2（无亲戚关系）auntie
【婶母】shěnmǔ〈名〉aunt
【婶娘】shěnniáng〈方〉= 婶母 shěnmǔ
【婶婶】shěnshen〈口〉= 婶母 shěnmǔ
【婶子】shěnzi〈口〉= 婶母 shěnmǔ

shèn

肾（腎） shèn〈名〉1 [生理] kidney: ～动脉 renal artery 2 [中医] testicle
【肾癌】shèn'ái ▸p. 50〈名〉renal carcinoma
【肾病】shènbìng ▸p. 50〈名〉nephrosis
【肾功能】shèngōngnéng〈名〉kidney function: ～衰竭 renal failure
【肾积水】shènjīshuǐ ▸p. 50〈名〉[医学] hydronephrosis
【肾结石】shènjiéshí ▸p. 50〈名〉[医学] renal calculus/stone
【肾亏】shènkuī ▸p. 50〈名〉[中医] renal weakness
【肾瘤】shènliú ▸p. 50〈名〉[医学] nephroma
【肾囊】shènnáng〈名〉[解剖] capsulae renis
【肾囊肿】shènnángzhǒng ▸p. 50〈名〉renal cyst
【肾切除术】shènqiēchúshù〈名〉[医学] nephrectomy
【肾上腺】shènshàngxiàn〈名〉[生理] adrenal (gland)
【肾上腺素】shèngshàngxiànsù〈名〉adrenalin
【肾衰竭】shènshuāijié ▸p. 50〈名〉[医学] renal failure
【肾透析】shèntòuxī〈名〉[医学] renal dialysis
【肾下垂】shènxiàchuí ▸p. 50〈名〉[医学] nephroptosis
【肾炎】shènyán ▸p. 50〈名〉nephritis
【肾移植】shènyízhí〈名〉kidney transplant
【肾硬化】shènyìnghuà ▸p. 50〈名〉[医学] nephrosclerosis

S

【肾盂】shènyú〈名〉［生理］ renal pelvis: ～肾炎 pyelonephritis
【肾脏】shènzàng〈名〉 kidney

甚[1] shèn〈书〉
A〈形〉serious: ▸欺人太～
B〈副〉 extremely: 来宾～多。 A lot of people came. ‖ 知者～少。 Very few people knew about it.
C〈动〉exceed: 旱情日～一日。The draught is getting worse with each passing day.

甚[2] shèn〈代〉〈口〉 what: 你想要～? What do you want? ‖ 他姓～名谁? What's his name?
【甚而】shèn'ér 〈连〉 so much so that: 有人说他是傻子，～说他是疯子。 Some people say he is a fool; some even say he is insane.
【甚而至于】shèn'érzhìyú = 甚至 shènzhì
【甚或】shènhuò〈书〉 = 甚至 shènzhì
【甚为】shènwéi〈副〉〈书〉 extremely: ～不安 be most concerned ‖ ～得意 be very pleased with oneself ‖ ～恼火 be extremely angry
【甚嚣尘上】shènxiāo-chénshàng〈成〉 be very much talked about
【甚至】shènzhì〈连〉 even to the extent that: 他～没说再见就走了。 He left without even saying goodbye.
【甚至于】shènzhìyú = 甚至 shènzhì

胂 shèn〈名〉［化学］ arsine

渗（滲） shèn〈动〉 ooze: 水从裂缝中～进来。 Water seeped in through a crack.
【渗出】shènchū〈动〉 seep: 泉水从岩石中～。 The spring seeps out of the rocks. ‖ 血不停地从伤口～。 Blood was oozing from the wound.
【渗出液】shènchūyè〈名〉［医学］exudate
【渗沟】shèngōu〈名〉 sewer
【渗井】shènjǐng = 渗坑 shènkēng
【渗坑】shènkēng〈名〉 seepage pit
【渗流】shènliú〈动〉 seep
【渗漏】shènlòu〈动〉 effuse
【渗滤】shènlǜ〈名〉［化学］percolation: ～器 percolator
【渗入】shènrù〈动〉 **1**（指液体） permeate: 雨水～地下。 The rain seeped into the ground. **2**〈贬〉（指势力） penetrate: 防止恐怖分子～我国 prevent the infiltration of terrorists into our country
【渗透】shèntòu **A**〈名〉［物理］ osmosis **B**〈动〉 **1**（指液体） permeate: ～到泥土中 seep through the soil **2**〈喻〉（指思想或力量） infiltrate: 思想/文化/政治～ ideological/cultural/political infiltration ‖ 恐怖分子已～进该国的警察队伍。 Terrorists have already penetrated the police force of that country.
【渗析】shènxī〈名〉［化学］ dialysis: ～器 dialyser
【渗血】shènxuè ▸**p. 50**〈名〉［医学］ staxis

葚 shèn ▸桑葚 sāngshèn

椹 shèn = 葚 shèn

蜃 shèn〈名〉［动物］ clam
【蜃景】shènjǐng〈名〉 mirage

瘆（瘮） shèn〈形〉 frightening: 夜里走山路真～得慌。 Travelling on mountain roads at night time is very frightening.

慎 shèn〈形〉 careful: ▸～重，谨～，审～
【慎独】shèndú〈动〉〈书〉 take care of oneself when alone: 君子必慎其独。 A gentleman must take care of his behaviour even when he is alone.
【慎密】shènmì 〈形〉〈书〉 cautious and meticulous
【慎言慎行】shènyán-shènxíng〈动〉 exercise caution in speech and conduct
【慎之又慎】shènzhīyòushèn〈成〉 exercise maximum caution: 在处理国际关系时，要～。 One cannot be too careful when dealing with international relations.
【慎重】shènzhòng 〈形〉 careful: ～处理 handle with care ‖ ～行事 act with discretion ‖ 态度～ a cautious attitude

shēng

升[1]（昇、陞） shēng〈动〉
1（指空间位置） ascend: ～旗 hoist a flag ‖ 气球缓缓～上天空。 The balloon rose up slowly into the air. ‖ 死亡人数～至900人。 The death toll has risen to 900. ▸上～
2（指等级） promote: 他已～为销售经理。 He has been promoted to sales manager. ▸～级，提～

升[2] shēng
A〈名〉 *sheng* [instrument for measuring grain]
B〈量〉 **1**（指市制） *sheng* [unit of capacity, equal to 1 litre]: 五～黄豆 five *sheng* of soya bean **2**（指公制） litre: 两～啤酒 two litres of beer
【升班】shēngbān〈动〉〈口〉go up a grade
【升班马】shēngbānmǎ〈名〉［体育］ promoted team
【升调】shēngdiào〈名〉［语言］rising tone
【升幅】shēngfú〈名〉 extent of increase: ～较大 rise by a big margin
【升高】shēnggāo〈动〉 rise: 血压～ rise in blood pressure ‖ 气温～到零度以上。 The temperature rose above freezing.
【升格】shēnggé〈动〉 promote: 该领事馆已经～为大使馆。 The consulate has been upgraded to embassy status.
【升官】shēngguān〈动〉 be promoted to a higher official post: ～发财 win promotion and get rich
【升号】shēnghào〈名〉［音乐］ sharp (#)
【升华】shēnghuá〈动〉 **1**［化学］ sublimate: 使硫～ sublimate sulphur **2**〈喻〉 raise to a higher level: 艺术是现实生活的～。 Art is the distillation of real life.
【升级】shēngjí〈动〉 **1**（指等级） go up a grade: 考试及格的学生将～。 Pupils who pass this test will be promoted to the next grade. ‖ 该软件需要不断～。 This software needs to be upgraded constantly. ‖ 他已经～为将军。 He has been promoted to general. **2**（指严重性） escalate: 不断～的紧张关系 mounting tension ‖ 阻止战争的～ prevent the escalation of war
【升级换代】shēngjí-huàndài〈动〉 update and upgrade: 产品的～ updating and upgrading of products
【升降】shēng-jiàng〈动〉 go up and down: ～摄影车 camera crane ‖ ～输送机 lift and conveyor
【升降机】shēngjiàngjī〈名〉 lift, elevator
【升降台】shēngjiàngtái〈名〉elevating platform
【升降梯】shēngjiàngtī〈名〉 elevator, lift
【升空】shēngkōng〈动〉 rise into the sky: ～入轨 lift off into orbit
【升力】shēnglì〈名〉［航空］ lift
【升幂】shēngmì〈名〉［数学］ ascending power
【升幂级数】shēngmì jíshù〈名〉 ascending power series
【升平】shēngpíng〈名〉〈书〉 peace: ～气象 peaceful times ▸歌舞～
【升旗】shēngqí〈动〉 raise a flag: ～仪式 flag-raising ceremony
【升起】shēngqǐ〈动〉 rise: 房顶上～一股黑烟。 A pillar of black smoke rose over the building.
【升迁】shēngqiān〈动〉 be transferred and promoted: 放弃～的机会 pass up the chance for promotion
【升任】shēngrèn〈动〉 be promoted to the post of: ～市长 be promoted to mayor
【升水】shēngshuǐ〈名〉［经济］ premium
【升堂】shēngtáng〈动〉〈旧〉 hold a court trial
【升堂入室】shēngtáng-rùshì〈成〉 become highly proficient (in)
【升腾】shēngténg〈动〉 rise: 火焰～。 Flames leapt up. ‖ 山谷里雾气～。 Fog rose in the valley.
【升天】shēngtiān〈动〉 **1**（升到天空）rise into the sky: 卫星～了。 The satellite has risen into the sky. **2**（死亡） die: 他昨晚～了。 He died last night.
【升位】shēngwèi〈动〉 add another digit to telephone numbers: 电话号码～ expand the telephone numbering system
【升温】shēngwēn〈动〉 heat up: 两国之间的舌战～。 The war of words between the two countries heated up.
【升息】shēngxī 〈动〉 raise interest rates: 投资者期待美元～。 Investors expect the US dollar to rise.
【升学】shēngxué〈动〉enter a higher grade school: ～考试 entrance examination ‖ ～率 rate of admission into higher grade schools
【升压】shēngyā〈动〉［电气］ boost: ～泵 booster pump
【升帐】shēngzhàng〈动〉〈旧〉 call officers together and give orders in a military tent
【升值】shēngzhí〈动〉［经济］ appreciate: 日元已～到历史最高水平。 The yen has hit a record high. ‖ 这幅画～了。 The painting gained in value.

生[1] shēng
A〈动〉 **1**（生长） grow: 这块地只～野草，不长庄稼。 Nothing can grow on this piece of land but grass. ▸～长，野～ **2**（生育） give birth to: ～孩子 have a baby ▸～儿育女，亲～ **3**（出生） be born: 他～在美国。 He was born in America. ▸～老病死，诞～，降～ **4**（产生） breed: 一闲～百邪。 An idle brain is the devil's workshop. ▸～效，急中～智 **5**（点燃） light: ～炉子 light a stove ▸～火 **6**（活着） exist: ▸～还，起死回～
B〈名〉 **1**（读书人） scholar: ▸儒～，书～ **2**（学生） student: ▸考～，招～ **3**［戏曲］ *sheng* [the male role, one of the four main roles in traditional Chinese opera]: ▸～旦净丑，武～，小～ **4**（指专业人员） people taking up certain jobs as their occupation: ▸学～，医～ **5**（生命） life: ▸轻～，丧～ **6**（一

S

辈子) one's life: ▸今～, 终～ 7 (生计) means to maintain life: 以打鱼为～ depend on fishery for one's livelihood ▸谋～, 营～ 8 (陌生人) stranger: ▸欺～, 认～

C 〈形〉 1 (活的) alive: ▸～龙活虎, ～物 2 (指食物) uncooked; (指果实) unripe: ～鸡蛋 raw egg ‖ ～苹果 unripe apple ‖ 黄瓜可以～吃。 Cucumbers can be eaten raw. ▸夹～饭 3 (未加工的) unrefined: ▸～漆, ～铁 4 (陌生) strange: 刚到这里, 工作很～。 I'm new here, so I'm not familiar with the work. ▸～僻, 陌～

D 〈副〉 1 (生硬) stiffly: ▸～搬硬套, ～硬 2 〈口〉 (硬是) just: 事情～让他们搅和坏了。 They had actually messed it up. 3 (非常) very: ～痛 ache terribly ▸～怕

生² shēng 〈后缀〉 ▸好生 hǎoshēng

【生搬硬套】 shēngbān-yìngtào 〈成〉 apply blindly: 学习国外经验时, 切忌～。 Whilst we must learn from foreign countries, we mustn't copy indiscriminately.

【生变】 shēngbiàn 〈动〉 bring trouble: 日久～。 Delay means trouble.

【生病】 shēngbìng 〈动〉 fall ill: 接二连三地～ have one illness after another ‖ 他生了一场重病。 He got sick with something serious.

【生不逢时】 shēngbùféngshí 〈成〉 be born at the wrong time

【生财】 shēngcái 〈动〉 make money: ▸和气～

【生财有道】 shēngcái-yǒudào 〈名〉 know how to make money: 他真是～, 不到两年家里的房子就盖起来了。 He knew how to make money and earned enough to build a house for his family within two years.

【生财之道】 shēngcáizhīdào 〈名〉 means of making money

【生菜】 shēngcài 〈名〉 1 [植物] (莴苣类) lettuce 2 (未煮熟) raw vegetable

【生产】 shēngchǎn 〈动〉 1 (产出) produce: 增加工业品～ boost the production of manufactured goods ‖ 粮食/棉花～ grain/cotton production ‖ 批量～ mass production 2 (分娩) give birth to a baby: 她快～了。 She's going to give birth very soon.

【生产成本】 shēngchǎn chéngběn 〈名〉 manufacturing cost: 降低～ lower the cost of production

【生产队】 shēngchǎnduì 〈名〉 〈旧〉 production team

【生产方式】 shēngchǎn fāngshì 〈名〉 mode of production

【生产工具】 shēngchǎn gōngjù 〈名〉 production tool

【生产关系】 shēngchǎn guānxì 〈名〉 production relations

【生产规模】 shēngchǎn guīmó 〈名〉 production scale

【生产过剩】 shēngchǎn guòshèng 〈名〉 overproduction

【生产建设兵团】 shēngchǎn jiànshè bīngtuán 〈名〉 production and construction corps

【生产力】 shēngchǎnlì 〈名〉 productive forces

【生产率】 shēngchǎnlǜ 〈名〉 productivity: 工业～的增长 increases in industrial productivity

【生产能力】 shēngchǎn nénglì 〈名〉 production capacity: ～过剩 overcapacity

【生产商】 shēngchǎnshāng 〈名〉 manufacturer

【生产手段】 shēngchǎn shǒuduàn 〈名〉 means of production

【生产线】 shēngchǎnxiàn 〈名〉 production line: 计算机～ computer production line

【生产销售一体化】 shēngchǎn xiāoshòu yītǐhuà 〈名〉 integration of production and marketing

【生产效率】 shēngchǎn xiàolǜ 〈名〉 production efficiency: 提高～ increase production efficiency

【生产要素】 shēngchǎn yàosù 〈名〉 essential factors in production: ～市场 market for production essentials

【生产指标】 shēngchǎn zhǐbiāo 〈名〉 production target

【生产资料】 shēngchǎn zīliào 〈名〉 means of production: 必要的～ necessary means of production

【生产自救】 shēngchǎn zìjiù 〈动〉 [usu used after a natural disaster] restore production and make a living with one's own hands

【生产总值】 shēngchǎn zǒngzhí 〈名〉 total output value: ～翻两番 double the total output value

【生辰】 shēngchén 〈名〉 〈书〉 birthday

【生辰八字】 shēngchén-bāzì 〈名〉 Eight Chinese Characters used to represent time, dates, and in fortune telling

【生成】 shēngchéng 〈动〉 1 (产生) bring into being: 雨的～需要一定的湿度。 A certain amount of moisture is essential to the formation of rain. 2 (具有) be born with: 他～一双巧手。 He is naturally good with his hands.

【生成程序】 shēngchéng chéngxù 〈名〉 [计算机] generating program

【生成语法】 shēngchéng yǔfǎ 〈名〉 [语言] generative grammar

【生词】 shēngcí 〈名〉 new word: 课文中～太多。 There are too many new words in the text.

【生词表】 shēngcíbiǎo 〈名〉 list of new words

【生存】 shēngcún 〈动〉 survive: 为～而斗争 fight for survival ‖ 没有空气我们不能～。 We cannot survive without air.

【生存环境】 shēngcún huánjìng 〈名〉 living environment

【生存竞争】 shēngcún jìngzhēng 〈名〉 struggle for survival

【生存空间】 shēngcún kōngjiān 〈名〉 living space

【生存能力】 shēngcún nénglì 〈名〉 viability

【生旦净丑】 shēng-dàn-jìng-chǒu 〈名〉 *sheng*, *dan*, *jing* and *chou* [the four main roles in Chinese traditional opera, ie the male role, the female role, the painted-face role, and the comic role]

【生地】 shēngdì 〈名〉 1 (不熟悉) alien land 2 (未开垦) virgin soil 3 [中药] dried rhizome of rehmannia

【生动】 shēngdòng 〈形〉 vivid: ～的描写 vivid description ‖ 文笔～ picturesque style ‖ 语言～ colourful language

【生动活泼】 shēngdòng-huópo 〈形〉 lively: 这场晚会开得～。 The party was very lively.

【生儿育女】 shēng'ér-yùnǚ 〈动〉 give birth to babies and bring them up

【生发剂】 shēngfàjì 〈名〉 hair regrowth liniment

【生分】 shēngfen 〈形〉 estranged: 我们之间有些～了。We are not as close as before.

【生俘】 shēngfú 〈动〉 capture alive: ～叛军头目 capture the rebel leader

【生父】 shēngfù 〈名〉 biological father

【生根】 shēnggēn 〈动〉 take root: 这种植物～很快。 This plant takes root very quickly.

【生花妙笔】 shēnghuā-miàobǐ 〈成〉 brilliant pen

【生化】 shēnghuà 〈简称〉 = 生物化学

【生化武器】 shēnghuà wǔqì 〈名〉 biochemical weapons

【生还】 shēnghuán 〈动〉 survive: 此次海难中无一～。 No one survived the shipwreck.

【生还者】 shēnghuánzhě 〈名〉 survivor: 他是事故中惟一的～。 He was the only survivor of the accident.

【生荒】 shēnghuāng = 生荒地 shēnghuāngdì

【生荒地】 shēnghuāngdì 〈名〉 [农业] uncultivated land: ～里的庄稼长不好。 Crops can't grow very well in virgin soil.

【生活】 shēnghuó A 〈名〉 1 (日常活动) life: 过单身～ live alone ‖ 热爱～ love life ‖ ～简朴 live a simple existence ‖ 靠工资～ live on one's wages 2 〈方〉 (工作) work: 做～ do one's work ‖ ～忙 be busy with one's work B 〈动〉 live: 他们～得很幸福。 They lived very happily.

【生活必需品】 shēnghuó bìxūpǐn 〈名〉 daily necessities

【生活补助】 shēnghuó bǔzhù 〈名〉 allowance for living expenses

【生活方式】 shēnghuó fāngshì 〈名〉 way of life: 改变～ change one's life style ‖ 坚持传统的～ cling to one's traditional way of life

【生活费】 shēnghuófèi 〈名〉 living expenses

【生活费用】 shēnghuó fèiyong 〈名〉 cost of living

【生活环境】 shēnghuó huánjìng 〈名〉 living environment

【生活垃圾】 shēnghuó lājī 〈名〉 consumer waste

【生活来源】 shēnghuó láiyuán 〈名〉 source of income

【生活能力】 shēnghuó nénglì 〈名〉 [生物] viability

【生活水平】 shēnghuó shuǐpíng 〈名〉 standard of living: 提高～ boost one's standard of living

【生活条件】 shēnghuó tiáojiàn 〈名〉 living conditions: 改善～ improve living conditions

【生活污水】 shēnghuó wūshuǐ 〈名〉 domestic sewage

【生活习惯】 shēnghuó xíguàn 〈名〉 habits and customs

【生活用品】 shēnghuó yòngpǐn 〈名〉 articles for daily use

【生活用水】 shēnghuó yòngshuǐ 〈名〉 domestic water

【生活质量】 shēnghuó zhìliàng 〈名〉 quality of life

【生活资料】 shēnghuó zīliào 〈名〉 means of subsistence

【生活作风】 shēnghuó zuòfēng 〈名〉 conduct: ～有问题 lead a dissipated life

【生火】 shēnghuǒ 〈动〉 light a fire: ～做饭 light a fire to cook

【生机】 shēngjī 〈名〉 1 (生存机会) life force: 一线～ a glimmer of hope 2 (活力) vigour: 恢复～ regain one's vitality ‖ ～盎然 full of life ‖ 自然界充满着～。 Nature is full of life.

【生计】 shēngjì 〈名〉 livelihood: 另谋～ try to find other means of living ‖ 维持～ make a living

【生姜】 shēngjiāng 〈名〉 〈口〉 ginger

【生胶】 shēngjiāo 〈名〉 raw rubber

【生津】 shēngjīn 〈动〉 [中药] promote the secretion of saliva or body fluid

【生境】 shēngjìng 〈名〉 [生物] habitat

【生就】shēngjiù〈动〉 be born with: 他～一张利嘴。 He has the gift of the gab.
【生角】shēngjué〈名〉［戏曲］role of *sheng* [usu refers to *laosheng* in traditional Chinese opera]
【生客】shēngkè〈名〉 new guest: 今晚我们有几位～来吃饭。 We are having some new people to dinner tonight.
【生恐】shēngkǒng〈动〉 be very afraid: ～再遭失败 fear further failure
【生拉硬扯】shēnglā-yìngchě〈成〉 1（用力拉扯） drag sb. against his will: 把他～向外拖 drag him outside by force 2（牵强附会） make a far-fetched comparison
【生拉硬拽】shēnglā-yìngzhuài = 生拉硬扯 shēnglā-yìngchě
【生来】shēnglái〈动〉 be born with: ～记性好 be gifted with a good memory ‖ 我～就不是那种人。 I'm just not that kind of person.
【生老病死】shēng-lǎo-bìng-sǐ〈成〉 birth, old age, sickness and death
【生冷】shēnglěng〈名〉 raw or cold food: 忌食～ avoid eating anything raw or cold
【生离死别】shēnglí-sǐbié〈成〉 be parted forever
【生理】shēnglǐ〈名〉 physiology: ～缺陷 physical defect ‖ ～现象 physiological phenomenon
【生理心理学】shēnglǐ xīnlǐxué〈名〉physiological psychology
【生理学】shēnglǐxué〈名〉 physiology
【生理盐水】shēnglǐ yánshuǐ〈名〉 physiological saline solution
【生力军】shēnglìjūn〈名〉 1（指部队） fresh troops 2（指主力） fresh force: 他们是电信领域的一支～。 They are a vital new force in the field of telecommunications.
【生料】shēngliào〈名〉 raw material
【生灵】shēnglíng〈名〉〈书〉 1（百姓） common people: ►～涂炭 2（生命） life: 可爱的小～ lovely little creature
【生灵涂炭】shēnglíng-tútàn〈成〉 the people are plunged into an abyss of misery
【生龙活虎】shēnglóng-huóhǔ〈成〉 full of energy: 这些年轻人干起活来真是～。 These young people have so much energy about their work.
【生路】shēnglù〈名〉 means of making a living: 自谋～ seek a living for oneself ‖ 你本该给他留条～。 You should have left him a way out.
【生猛】shēngměng〈形〉 1（指海鲜） live 2（威猛有力） full of life: ～的武打动作 action-packed fighting movements
【生猛海鲜】shēngměng hǎixiān〈名〉〈方〉 fresh seafood
【生米煮成熟饭】shēngmǐ zhǔchéng shúfàn〈俗〉 the die is cast
【生命】shēngmìng〈名〉 life: 献出～ lay down one's life ‖ ～垂危 be nearing one's end ‖ 冒～危险 risk one's life ‖ 政治～ political career
【生命科学】shēngmìng kēxué〈名〉 life science
【生命力】shēngmìnglì〈名〉 life force: 富有～ be full of life
【生命线】shēngmìngxiàn〈名〉 lifeline: 交通干线是经济繁荣的～。 Lines of communications are the lifeblood of a prosperous economy.
【生母】shēngmǔ〈名〉 birth mother
【生怕】shēngpà〈动〉 fear: ～伤害别人的感情 be afraid of hurting other people's feelings
【生皮】shēngpí〈名〉 rawhide
【生啤】shēngpí〈名〉 draught beer
【生僻】shēngpì〈形〉 rare: ～的典故 obscure allusion ‖ ～的字眼 rarely used word
【生平】shēngpíng〈名〉 all one's life: 作者～简介 brief account of the author's life ‖ ～第一次 first time in one's life
【生漆】shēngqī〈名〉 raw lacquer
【生气】shēngqì A〈动〉 get angry: 生自己的气 be angry with oneself ‖ 无缘无故地～ get angry about nothing ‖ 她动不动就～。 She is quick to take offence. B〈名〉 vitality: 毫无～ be lethargic ‖ 他充满～。 He is full of life.
【生气勃勃】shēngqì-bóbó〈成〉 full of vim and vigour: ～的城市/孩子 lively city/children
【生前】shēngqián〈名〉 time before one's death: ～愿望 unfulfilled wish
【生擒】shēngqín〈动〉 capture alive: ～活捉 capture alive
【生趣】shēngqù〈名〉 joy of life: 富有～ be full of the pleasures of life
【生人】shēngrén〈名〉 stranger: 别让～进来。 Don't let any strangers in.
【生日】shēngrì〈名〉 birthday: ～蛋糕 birthday cake ‖ ～卡片 birthday card ‖ ～晚会 birthday party ‖ 过～ celebrate one's birthday ‖ 祝你～快乐! Happy birthday to you! ‖ 七月一日是中国共产党的～。 July 1 is the birthday of the Communist Party of China.
【生色】shēngsè〈动〉 add colour to: 他的精彩表演使晚会～不少。 His excellent performance added a real something to the party.
【生涩】shēngsè〈形〉 jarring: 文字～ jerky style of writing
【生杀予夺】shēngshā-yǔduó〈成〉have sb. completely in one's power
【生身父母】shēngshēn fùmǔ〈名〉 birth parents
【生生不息】shēngshēng-bùxī〈成〉 multiply in an endless succession
【生生世世】shēngshēng-shìshì〈成〉 for generations: ～永不忘 remember for generations
【生石膏】shēngshígāo〈名〉 plaster stone
【生石灰】shēngshíhuī〈名〉 quicklime
【生事】shēngshì〈动〉 make trouble: 他脾气很坏, 容易～。 He has a bad temper and tends to create trouble.
【生手】shēngshǒu〈名〉 beginner: ～难免出错。 Novices are likely to make mistakes. ‖ 他在业务上还是个～。 He is still new to his job.
【生疏】shēngshū〈形〉 1（不熟）unfamiliar: 人地～ be a stranger to the surroundings ‖ 业务～ not know the ropes 2（荒废） out of practice: 他的棋艺有点～了。 He's a little rusty at chess. 3（疏远） not as close as before: 她与家人的关系～了。 She's grown distant from the family.
【生水】shēngshuǐ〈名〉 unboiled water: 别喝～。 Don't drink unboiled water.
【生丝】shēngsī〈名〉 raw silk
【生死】shēngsǐ A〈动〉 live and die: ～关头 critical juncture B〈形〉 life-and-death: ►～之交
【生死存亡】shēngsǐ-cúnwáng〈成〉 life and death: ～的关头 point where one's very existence is at stake
【生死未卜】shēngsǐ-wèibǔ〈成〉 hang between life and death
【生死攸关】shēngsǐ-yōuguān〈成〉 a matter of life and death
【生死与共】shēngsǐ-yǔgòng〈成〉 go through thick and thin together: ～的朋友 friends through thick and thin ‖ ～, 休戚相关 hold together in life and death, sharing good times and bad
【生死之交】shēngsǐzhījiāo〈成〉 friends that are ready to die for one another: 他俩是～。 They are sworn friends.
【生态】shēngtài〈名〉 ecology
【生态变异】shēngtài biànyì〈名〉 ecocline
【生态工程】shēngtài gōngchéng〈名〉eco-engineering
【生态环境】shēngtài huánjìng〈名〉 eco-environment
【生态建筑】shēngtài jiànzhù〈名〉 ecological architecture
【生态林】shēngtàilín〈名〉 ecological forest
【生态旅游】shēngtài lǚyóu〈名〉 ecotourism
【生态灭绝】shēngtài mièjué〈名〉 ecocide
【生态农业】shēngtài nóngyè〈名〉 ecoagriculture
【生态平衡】shēngtài pínghéng〈名〉 ecological balance: 保持～ maintain the ecological balance
【生态圈】shēngtàiquān〈名〉 ecosphere
【生态危机】shēngtài wēijī〈名〉 eco-crisis
【生态系统】shēngtài xìtǒng〈名〉 ecosystem
【生态学】shēngtàixué〈名〉 ecology: ～家 ecologist
【生态园】shēngtàiyuán〈名〉 ecological park
【生铁】shēngtiě = 铸铁 zhùtiě
【生铜】shēngtóng〈名〉 pig copper
【生土】shēngtǔ〈名〉［农业］ immature soil
【生吞活剥】shēngtūn-huóbō〈成〉 accept sth. uncritically: ～地照搬外国经验 accept uncritically the experience of foreign countries
【生物】shēngwù〈名〉 living thing: 海洋～ marine life ‖ 保护～的多样性 protect biological diversity ►浮游～, 微～
【生物安全】shēngwù ānquán〈名〉 biosafety
【生物催化剂】shēngwù cuīhuàjì〈名〉 biocatalyst
【生物带】shēngwùdài〈名〉 biozone
【生物地理学】shēngwù dìlǐxué〈名〉 biogeography
【生物电】shēngwùdiàn〈名〉 bioelectricity
【生物多元化】shēngwù duōyuánhuà〈名〉 biodiversity
【生物防治】shēngwù fángzhì〈名〉［农业］ biological control
【生物工程学】shēngwù gōngchéngxué〈名〉 biological engineering, bioengineering
【生物工艺学】shēngwù gōngyìxué〈名〉 biotechnology
【生物光】shēngwùguāng〈名〉 bioluminescence
【生物化学】shēngwù huàxué〈名〉 biochemistry
【生物环】shēngwùhuán〈名〉 biocycle
【生物技术】shēngwù jìshù〈名〉 biotechnology
【生物碱】shēngwùjiǎn〈名〉［化学］ alkaloid
【生物节律】shēngwù jiélǜ〈名〉 biorhythm
【生物进化】shēngwù jìnhuà〈名〉 organic evolution: ～史 biogenesis
【生物科学】shēngwù kēxué〈名〉 biologic science
【生物控制】shēngwù kòngzhì〈名〉 biocontrol

【生物起源】shēngwùqǐyúan〈名〉biogenesis
【生物区】shēngwùqū〈名〉bioregion
【生物圈】shēngwùquān〈名〉biosphere: 生物保护圈 biosphere reserve
【生物生态学】shēngwù shēngtàixué〈名〉bioecology
【生物体】shēngwùtǐ〈名〉organism
【生物武器】shēngwù wǔqì〈名〉biological weapons
【生物芯片】shēngwù xīnpiàn〈名〉biological chip
【生物学】shēngwùxué〈名〉biology: ～家 biologist
【生物制品】shēngwù zhìpǐn〈名〉biological products
【生物钟】shēngwùzhōng〈名〉biological clock: 打乱/调节～ upset/regulate one's biological clock
【生息】shēngxī〈动〉1（取得利息）bear interest: ～资本 interest-bearing capital 2（生存）live: 我们的祖先曾在这块土地上劳动～。Our ancestors have laboured and lived on this land.
【生相】shēngxiàng〈名〉appearance: 他～好。He is good-looking.
【生橡胶】shēngxiàngjiāo〈名〉raw rubber
【生肖】shēngxiào〈名〉any of the 12 symbolic animals associated with a 12-year cycle, often used to denote the year of a person's birth [the 12 animals are: rat, ox, tiger, rabbit, dragon, snake, horse, sheep, monkey, rooster, dog, and pig]
【生效】shēngxiào〈动〉take effect: 立即～ come into force immediately ‖ 自签字之日起～ go into effect as from the date of signing
【生性】shēngxìng〈名〉one's natural disposition: ～多疑 have a suspicious mind ‖ ～争强好胜 have a competitive personality ‖ 她～活泼。She is lively in disposition.
【生锈】shēngxiù〈动〉rust: 防止～ prevent rust ‖ 容易～ get rusty easily
【生涯】shēngyá〈名〉career: 政治～ political career ‖ 舞台～ stage career
【生养】shēngyǎng〈动〉〈口〉give birth to: 她难道不能～? Isn't she able to have children?
【生药】shēngyào〈名〉dried medicinal herbs
【生疑】shēngyí〈动〉become suspicious: 使人～ arouse suspicion
【生意】shēngyì〈名〉〈书〉life: 春回大地，～蓬勃。With the arrival of spring, the earth is filled with vitality.
【生意】shēngyi〈名〉business: 做～ be engaged in business ‖ ～清淡 business is slack ‖ ～兴隆 business is thriving ‖ 赚钱的～ good bargain ‖ ～不景气。Business is in a slump.
【生意经】shēngyijīng〈名〉〈方〉shrewd business sense
【生意人】shēngyirén〈名〉business person
【生硬】shēngyìng〈形〉1（不自然）awkward: 措词～ awkward wording 2（不柔和）stiff: 态度～ have a stiff manner
【生鱼片】shēngyúpiàn〈名〉sashimi
【生育】shēngyù〈动〉bear: ～第一胎 give birth to a child for the first time ‖ ～高峰 baby boom ▸计划～
【生育能力】shēngyùnénglì〈名〉fertility
【生育年龄】shēngyù niánlíng〈名〉child-bearing age
【生员】shēngyuán〈名〉〈古〉one who passed the imperial examination at the county level (in the Ming and Qing dynasties)
【生源】shēngyuán〈名〉supply of students: 扩大～ expand the source of students ‖ ～不足 short supply of students
【生造】shēngzào〈动〉coin (words and expressions)
【生造词】shēngzàocí〈名〉coinage
【生长】shēngzhǎng〈动〉1（成长）grow: ～在田地里 grow in the fields ‖ 花园里～着许多玫瑰花。In the garden roses grew in abundance. 2（出生长大）be born and brought up: 他～在这座城市。He was born and brought up in this city.
【生长点】shēngzhǎngdiǎn〈名〉［植物］growing point
【生长激素】shēngzhǎng jīsù〈名〉［生理］growth hormone
【生长期】shēngzhǎngqī〈名〉growing period
【生长素】shēngzhǎngsù〈名〉［农业］auxin
【生殖】shēngzhí〈动〉reproduce: 无性～ asexual reproduction
【生殖泌尿系统】shēngzhí mìniào xìtǒng〈名〉urogenital system
【生殖能力】shēngzhí nénglì〈名〉reproductive capacity
【生殖器】shēngzhíqì〈名〉reproductive organs: ～发育不全 agenosomia ‖ ～机能障碍 dysgonesis
【生殖腺】shēngzhíxiàn〈名〉genital gland
【生殖学】shēngzhíxué〈名〉study of reproduction
【生猪】shēngzhū〈名〉pig: 饲养～ raise pigs
【生字】shēngzì〈名〉new word/character: 记～ memorize new characters

声（聲）shēng

A〈名〉1（声音）sound: 呼救～ cry for help ‖ 脚步/雨～ sound of footsteps/rain ‖ 小～说话 speak in a low voice ▸歌～，异口同～ 2（消息）news: ▸无～无息，销～匿迹 3（名声）reputation: ▸～望，名～ 4（声母）initial of a Chinese syllable: ▸～母 5（音调）tone: 普通话有四～。Standard Chinese has four tones. ▸平～，上～
B〈动〉state: ▸～称，～讨
C〈量〉[used for sounds]: 大喝一～ shout loudly ‖ 听到一～枪响 hear a shot
【声辩】shēngbiàn〈动〉argue: 不容～ leave no room for argument ‖ 为被告～ plead for the accused
【声波】shēngbō〈名〉［物理］sound wave: ～探测器 acoustical detector
【声部】shēngbù〈名〉［音乐］part
【声称】shēngchēng〈动〉claim: ～对爆炸/谋杀负责 claim responsibility for the explosion/assassination ‖ ～自己无罪 profess one's innocence ‖ 两党都～取得了胜利。Both parties claimed victory.
【声带】shēngdài〈名〉1［生理］vocal cords: ～振动 vibration of vocal cords 2（指电影）soundtrack
【声道】shēngdào〈名〉sound track: 单/双～ single/double sound track
【声调】shēngdiào〈名〉1（声音）note: ～低沉 in a low, sad voice ‖ 模仿某人的～讲话 imitate the pitch of sb.'s voice 2（音调）tone: 这两个字的～不一样。These two characters have different tones.
【声东击西】shēngdōng-jīxī〈成〉cry in one direction but attack another
【声光】shēngguāng〈名〉1（名声）reputation 2（声和光）sound and light: ～表演 sound-and-light show
【声卡】shēngkǎ〈名〉［计算机］sound card
【声控】shēngkòng〈形〉sound-activated
【声控机器人】shēngkòng jīqìrén〈名〉televox
【声控装置】shēngkòng zhuāngzhì〈名〉sound-activated apparatus
【声浪】shēnglàng〈名〉uproar: 喝彩/抗议的～ the clamour of acclaim/protest
【声泪俱下】shēnglèi-jùxià〈成〉in a tearful voice: ～地诉说自己的不幸遭遇 tearfully relate one's misfortunes
【声门】shēngmén〈名〉［生理］glottis
【声名】shēngmíng〈名〉reputation: ～显赫 be of great renown ‖ ～远扬 win far-flung fame
【声名狼藉】shēngmíng-lángjí〈成〉fall into disrepute: 经理因受贿把自己弄得～。The manager got himself a bad reputation for taking bribes.
【声明】shēngmíng A〈动〉declare: ～自己与此事无关 state that one has nothing to do with the matter ‖ 公开/事先～ state openly/beforehand B〈名〉declaration: 发表～ issue a statement ‖ 联合～ joint statement ‖ 竞选～ election manifesto
【声母】shēngmǔ〈名〉［语言］initial of a Chinese syllable
【声呐】shēngnà〈名〉［物理］sonar
【声旁】shēngpáng〈名〉［语言］phonetic element of a Chinese pictophonetic character
【声频】shēngpín〈名〉［物理］audio frequency
【声谱】shēngpǔ〈名〉［物理］sound spectrum: ～仪 sound spectrograph
【声气】shēngqì〈名〉1〈书〉（消息）information: 互通～ exchange information 2〈口〉（声音）tone: 听他说话的～像是很不高兴。He sounded quite unhappy.
【声腔】shēngqiāng〈名〉［戏曲］operatic tune
【声强】shēngqiáng〈名〉［物理］sound intensity
【声情并茂】shēngqíng-bìngmào〈成〉be remarkable for both voice and expression
【声色】shēngsè〈名〉1（声音和表情）voice and countenance: ▸～俱厉，不动～ 2（特点）style: 他的演出别具～。He performed with a style of his own. 3（活力）vigour: 新领导给我们学院增添了不少～。The new leader brought great energy to our institute. 4〈书〉（歌舞和女色）sensual pleasures: 沉溺于～ abandon oneself to sensual pleasures
【声色俱厉】shēngsè-jùlì〈成〉stern in voice and countenance
【声色犬马】shēngsè-quǎnmǎ〈成〉sensual pleasures
【声势】shēngshì〈名〉influence: 扩大～ extend one's power ‖ ～浩大 powerful and dynamic ▸虚张～
【声嘶力竭】shēngsī-lìjié〈成〉shout oneself hoarse
【声速】shēngsù〈名〉［物理］speed of sound
【声讨】shēngtǎo〈动〉condemn
【声望】shēngwàng〈名〉fame: 提高～ enhance sb.'s reputation ‖ 国际～ international fame ‖ 学术～ academic prestige
【声威】shēngwēi〈名〉1（名声）prestige: ～大震 gain fame and prestige 2（权力）power
【声息】shēngxī〈名〉1（声音）sound: 没有一点儿～ not a squeak 2（消息）information: ～相通 keep in touch with one another
【声响】shēngxiǎng〈名〉sound: 发出～

S

make a noise
【声像】shēngxiàng〈名〉[物理] sound image
【声学】shēngxué〈名〉acoustics
【声讯】shēngxùn〈名〉telephone information service: ～台 telephone information station
【声音】shēngyīn〈名〉(指物) sound; (指人) voice: 发出～ make a sound ‖ 降低～ lower one's voice ‖ 刺耳的～ ear-splitting sound ‖ 洪亮的～ sonorous voice
【声域】shēngyù〈名〉vocal range
【声誉】shēngyù〈名〉reputation: 享有国际～ enjoy international fame ‖ 维护国家的～ defend the honour of one's country ‖ 严重损害学校的～ do incalculable harm to a school's reputation ‖ 他是个～极好的商人。He has a good reputation as a businessman.
【声誉鹊起】shēngyù-quèqǐ〈成〉rise to fame quickly
【声援】shēngyuán〈动〉support: ～正义战争 voice one's support for a just war ‖ 给予道义上的～ administer moral support
【声源】shēngyuán〈名〉sound source
【声乐】shēngyuè〈名〉[音乐] vocal music: ～家 vocalist
【声韵学】shēngyùnxué = 音韵学 yīnyùnxué
【声张】shēngzhāng〈动〉disclose: 这件事不要～出去。Don't breathe a word of this to anyone.

牲 shēng〈名〉**1** (指祭品) animal sacrifice: 献～ offer an animal sacrifice ▸三～ **2** (指家畜) domestic animal: ▸～畜, ～口
【牲畜】shēngchù〈名〉domestic animals: 饲养/繁殖～ raise/breed livestock ‖ 屠宰～ kill animals
【牲口】shēngkou〈名〉draught animal: 养～ keep draught animals
【牲口棚】shēngkoupéng〈名〉livestock shed

笙 shēng ▸p. 929〈名〉*sheng* [a reed pipe wind instrument]
【笙歌】shēnggē〈名〉〈书〉music and singing

甥 shēng〈名〉nephew [sister's son]: ▸外～
【甥女】shēngnǚ〈名〉niece [sister's daughter]

shéng

绳（繩） shéng
A〈名〉**1** (绳子) rope: 棉纱～ cotton rope ‖ 用～捆住 tie with a rope ▸缰～, 跳～ **2** (墨绳) carpenter's line marker: ▸～墨 **3** (标准) criterion: ▸准～
B〈动〉restrain: ▸～之以法
【绳操】shéngcāo〈名〉[体育] cord dance
【绳技】shéngjì〈名〉[杂技] tightrope walking
【绳锯木断】shéngjù-mùduàn〈成〉little strokes fell great oaks
【绳墨】shéngmò〈名〉〈书〉〈喻〉rules and regulations: 拘守～ stick to the rules
【绳索】shéngsuǒ〈名〉rope: 解开～ untie a rope knot
【绳套】shéngtào〈名〉**1** (指套) cord loop **2** (指绳具) lasso
【绳梯】shéngtī〈名〉rope ladder
【绳之以法】shéngzhīyǐfǎ〈成〉bring sb. to justice: 罪犯终于被～。The criminal was brought to justice at last.
【绳子】shéngzi〈名〉rope: 拉紧～ tighten a rope

shěng

省[1] shěng〈动〉**1** (省略) omit: ～去麻烦 save trouble ‖ 这些词不能～。These words cannot be left out. ▸～略 **2** (节省) save: ～时间 save time ‖ 既～工又～料 economize on labour as well as materials ▸～吃俭用, 节～

省[2] shěng〈名〉**1** (省份) province: 东北三～ three provinces in the northeastern part of China ‖ 河北～ Hebei Province ▸～会, ～长 **2** (省会) provincial capital: 去～里开会 go to the provincial capital for a meeting
▸xǐng
【省便】shěngbiàn〈形〉convenient: 怎么～就怎么做吧。Just do it in the easiest way.
【省城】shěngchéng〈名〉provincial capital: 这条公路直通～。This road leads straight to the provincial capital.
【省吃俭用】shěngchī-jiǎnyòng〈成〉live frugally: 为送孩子上学，他们不得不～。They had to live a frugal life in order to afford their child's tuition.
【省得】shěngde〈连〉lest: 我把它带过来，～邮寄了。I'll bring it round to save the trouble of putting it through the post.
【省份】shěngfèn〈名〉province: 受灾～ disaster-stricken province
【省会】shěnghuì〈名〉provincial capital: ～城市 provincial capital city
【省界】shěngjiè〈名〉provincial boundaries
【省劲】shěngjìn = 省力 shěnglì
【省力】shěnglì〈动〉save labour: 得想一个～的办法。We must find a way to save on labour.
【省略】shěnglüè〈动〉leave out: 第一段可以～。The first paragraph can be deleted.
【省略号】shěnglüèhào〈名〉ellipsis
【省钱】shěngqián〈动〉save money: 在这里生活很～。It's quite cheap to live here. ‖ 我设法～，但就是省不下。I tried to save money; but I just couldn't.
【省却】shěngquè〈动〉**1** (减少) save: ～时间 save time **2** (免除) rid sb. of sth.: ～繁文缛节 dispense with formalities
【省事】shěngshì〈动〉save trouble: 看起来～，其实很费事。It looks easy, but in fact it's quite troublesome. ‖ 在食堂吃饭～。It's more convenient to eat in the canteen.
【省委】shěngwěi〈名〉provincial Party committee: ～书记 secretary of a provincial Party committee ‖ ～委员 member of a provincial Party committee
【省心】shěngxīn〈动〉spare sb. worry: 孩子听话，家长～。Well-behaved children can save their parents a lot of worry.
【省油灯】shěngyóudēng〈名〉person who doesn't make trouble: 他可不是省油的灯。He is a typical trouble-maker.
【省长】shěngzhǎng〈名〉governor of a province

眚 shěng〈书〉
A〈动〉have a cataract
B〈名〉error: 不以一～掩大德。Don't let one mistake obscure great virtue.

ℹ 省份名称/地名

■ 翻译汉语的省名和地名时，可全用汉语拼音，也可将其中的“省”、“市”、“地区”等用英语来表达。“自治区”一词一般翻译成 autonomous region:

陕西省
= Shaanxi Sheng
或 Shaanxi Province

北京市
= Beijing Shi
或 the City of Beijing

景德镇
= Jingde Zhen
或 Jingde Town

广西壮族自治区
= Guangxi Zhuang Autonomous Region

■ 在不引起误解的情况下，地名中的省、市、地区、镇等可省略不译:

深圳
= Shenzhen

湖南
= Hunan

但

周口地区
= Zhoukou District

周口市
= the City of Zhoukou

■ 固定短语里的省、自治区及直辖市的简称一定用全名来翻译:

京广铁路
= Beijing-Guangzhou Railway

豫剧
= Henan opera

粤菜
= Guangdong cuisine

蜀绣
= Sichuan embroidery

■ 写地址时，英语的顺序和汉语完全相反：汉语是从大到小，英语是从小到大:

英国
爱丁堡
爱丁堡大学
文学、语言及文化学院
欧洲语言和文化系

= Department of European Languages and Cultures
School of Literatures, Languages and Cultures
The University of Edinburgh
Edinburgh
UK

shèng

圣（聖）shèng

A〈形〉**1**（超凡）noble: ▸～明，～人 **2**（神圣）sacred: ▸～地，神～
B〈名〉**1**（圣人）sage: ▸～贤，超凡入～ **2**（大师）master: 画/乐～ painting/music master ▸棋～ **3**（圣上）emperor: ▸～旨 **4**［宗教］[form of address for the respected]: 《～经》*Holy Bible* ‖ ～灵 Holy Spirit

【圣保罗】Shèngbǎoluó〈名〉São Paulo

【圣餐】shèngcān〈名〉［宗教］Holy Communion

【圣代】shèngdài〈名〉［食品］sundae: 草莓/巧克力～ strawberry/chocolate sundae

【圣诞】shèngdàn〈名〉Christmas: ～快乐 Merry Christmas

【圣诞节】Shèngdànjié〈名〉Christmas

【圣诞卡】shèngdànkǎ〈名〉Christmas/Xmas card

【圣诞老人】Shèngdàn Lǎorén〈名〉Santa Claus; Father Christmas〈英〉

【圣诞树】shèngdànshù〈名〉Christmas tree

【圣地】shèngdì〈名〉**1**［宗教］Holy Land **2**〈喻〉sacred place: 延安是中国革命的～。Yan'an is a sacred place of the Chinese revolution.

【圣地亚哥】Shèngdìyàgē〈名〉Santiago

【圣多美】Shèngduōměi〈名〉São Tomé

【圣多美和普林西比】Shèngduōměi Hé Pǔlínxībǐ〈名〉São Tomé and Príncipe

【圣多明各】Shèngduōmínggè〈名〉Santo Domingo

【圣何塞】Shènghésài〈名〉San José

【圣胡安】Shènghú'ān〈名〉San Juan

【圣火】shènghuǒ〈名〉holy fire: ▸奥运～

【圣基茨和尼维斯联邦】Shèngjīcí Hé Níwéisī Liánbāng〈名〉Federation of St Kitts and Nevis

【圣洁】shèngjié〈形〉holy and pure: ～的爱 pure love

【圣经】Shèngjīng〈名〉［基督教］the Bible

【圣灵】Shènglíng〈名〉［基督教］Holy Spirit

【圣灵节】Shènglíngjié〈名〉［基督教］Whit Sunday〈英〉, Whitsunday〈美〉*also called* Pentecost

【圣卢西亚】Shènglúxīyà〈名〉Saint Lucia

【圣马力诺】Shèngmǎlìnuò〈名〉San Marino: ～人 San Marinese

【圣庙】shèngmiào〈名〉Confucian temple

【圣明】shèngmíng〈形〉〈旧〉capable and virtuous

【圣母】shèngmǔ〈名〉**1**（女神）goddess **2** Shèngmǔ（耶稣之母）Blessed Mother, Madonna: 巴黎～院 Notre Dame de Paris

【圣女果】shèngnǚguǒ〈名〉cherry tomato

【圣乔治】Shèngqiáozhì〈名〉St George's

【圣人】shèngrén〈名〉**1**（品格才智极高）sage **2**〈旧〉（君主）[way to address a monarch by his officials in feudal China] Your Majesty

【圣萨尔瓦多】Shèngsà'ěrwǎduō〈名〉San Salvador

【圣上】shèngshàng〈名〉Your Majesty, His/Her Majesty

【圣诗班】shèngshībān〈名〉choir

【圣手】shèngshǒu〈名〉〈旧〉master

【圣水】shèngshuǐ〈名〉**1**（用于治病、驱魔）sacred water **2**（用于宗教仪式）holy water

【圣坛】shèngtán〈名〉chancel

【圣徒】shèngtú〈名〉［基督教］saint

【圣文森特和格林纳丁斯】Shèngwénsēntè Hé Gélínnàdīngsī〈名〉St Vincent and the Grenadines

【圣贤】shèngxián〈名〉saint: 人非～，孰能无过？Men are not saints, so how can they be free from faults?

【圣训】shèngxùn〈名〉〈旧〉**1**（指皇帝）imperial decree **2**（指圣贤）admonitions of a sage

【圣谕】shèngyù〈名〉imperial decree

【圣战】shèngzhàn〈名〉holy war

【圣旨】shèngzhǐ〈名〉imperial edict

> **圣旨**
>
> An imperial edict, signifying the emperor's wishes and commands. The term was already in use in the Han Dynasty, and came into formal use in the Song Dynasty. Edicts were written on a scroll, the type of handle and colour of which were strictly ordained according to the rank of the recipient. Three, five or seven colours were used: the more colours the higher the rank. Today, scrolls are produced as works of art, and usually display the phrase 奉天承运，皇帝诏曰 ('By virtue of the Mandate of Heaven, the Emperor decrees').

胜（勝）shèng

A〈动〉**1**（能承担）be equal to: ▸～任，不～枚举，数不～数 **2**（胜利）win: 三战三～ have three wins and no defeats ‖ 这场比赛他们～了。They won the match. ▸百战百～，决～，险～ **3**（击败）defeat: 以少～多 use a small force to defeat a large one ‖ 他在选举中～了对手。He defeated his opponent in the election. ▸战～，制～ **4**（超过）be superior to: 比先辈们更～一筹 surpass one's predecessors
B〈副〉completely: ▸美不～收
C〈形〉superb: ▸～地，～景
D〈名〉place of natural beauty: ▸名～

【胜败】shèng-bài〈名〉victory or defeat: ～未卜。The outcome is hanging in the balance.

【胜败乃兵家常事】shèng-bài nǎi bīngjiā chángshì〈成〉a temporary setback means nothing in war

【胜不骄，败不馁】shèng bù jiāo,bài bù něi〈成〉neither made dizzy with success, nor discouraged by failure

【胜场】shèngchǎng〈名〉winning match

【胜出】shèngchū〈动〉defeat one's rival: 在比赛中以2比0～ win a game 2 : 0

【胜地】shèngdì〈名〉place of natural beauty: 避暑～ summer resort ‖ 旅游～ tourist mecca

【胜负】shèng-fù〈名〉victory or defeat: 比赛～难分。The match is too close to call.

【胜负手】shèngfùshǒu〈名〉**1**（指围棋）deciding move **2**（指球员）key player

【胜过】shèngguò〈动〉prevail over: ～对手 be superior to one's opponent ‖ 盟军在数量上～敌军。The allies outnumbered their enemies.

【胜机】shèngjī〈名〉chance of winning: 把握～ seize the chance to win

【胜迹】shèngjì〈名〉famous historical site: 名山～ famous mountains and historical sites

【胜绩】shèngjì〈名〉win: 到目前为止，主队尚无～。The host team has had no wins so far.

【胜景】shèngjǐng〈名〉beautiful scenery: 浏览几处～ tour several resorts

【胜境】shèngjìng〈名〉**1**（指地方）scenic spot **2**（指境界）beautiful conception

【胜局】shèngjú〈名〉success, victory: ～已定 victory is a foregone conclusion

【胜利】shènglì〈动〉**1**（胜出）be victorious: 获得～ win a victory ‖ 庆祝～ celebrate a win ‖ ～在望。Victory is in sight. **2**（成功）attain a goal as planned: ～完成任务 successfully carry out a task ‖ 大会～闭幕。The conference has concluded successfully.

【胜利果实】shènglì guǒshí〈名〉fruits of victory: 保卫～ defend the fruits of victory

【胜利者】shènglìzhě〈名〉winner

【胜率】shènglǜ〈名〉**1**（指机会）winning chance **2**（指比例）winning rate

【胜券】shèngquàn〈名〉confidence in victory: ～在握 guaranteed victory ▸稳操～

【胜任】shèngrèn〈动〉be competent at sth.: ～工作 be up to a job ‖ 基本/完全～ basically/perfectly competent ‖ 他不能～这项工作。He is inadequate for the task.

【胜似】shèngsì〈动〉surpass: ～亲人 be dearer than one's own family members

【胜诉】shèngsù〈动〉win a case

【胜算】shèngsuàn〈名〉stratagem which ensures success: 稳操～ be sure of success ‖ 没有～ be out of the running

【胜选】shèngxuǎn〈动〉win an election: 没有～可能 have no chance of winning the election

【胜仗】shèngzhàng〈名〉victory: 打～ win a battle

乘 shèng〈古〉

A〈量〉兵车二百～ two hundred war chariots ‖ 千～之国 state of a thousand chariots
B〈名〉historical records: 史～ history
▸chéng

盛 shèng〈形〉

1（繁荣）flourishing: 由～转衰 go from prosperity to decline ‖ 樱花开得很～。The cherry trees are in full bloom. ▸～开，繁～，兴～ **2**（充足）plentiful: ▸～产，丰～ **3**（巨大）great: ▸～名，～大，～会，～况 **4**（普遍）popular: ▸～传，～行 **5**（极力）sparing no effort: ～夸 laud to the skies ▸～赞 **6**（深厚）deep: ▸～情，～意 **7**（强烈）vigorous: 年轻气～ young and aggressive ‖ 牢骚太～ too many complaints
▸chéng

【盛产】shèngchǎn〈动〉abound in: ～石油 be rich in oil ‖ ～水果 abound with fruit

【盛传】shèngchuán〈动〉spread far and wide: 当地～着他的英雄事迹。His heroic deeds are widely known in this area.

【盛大】shèngdà〈形〉magnificent: ～的节日 grand festival ‖ ～的庆祝活动 huge celebration

【盛典】shèngdiǎn〈名〉grand ceremony: 举行～ hold a grand ceremony

【盛服】shèngfú〈名〉〈书〉splendid attire

【盛会】shènghuì〈名〉magnificent gathering: 体育～ magnificent sports meet ‖ 团结的～ grand gathering of unity

【盛极一时】shèngjí-yīshí〈成〉be in fashion for a time: 这本书当年～。The book was all the rage then.

【盛举】shèngjǔ〈名〉worthy project: 共襄～ cooperate in a great project

【盛开】shèngkāi〈动〉be in full bloom: ～的玫瑰 roses in full bloom ‖ 玫瑰花已经～。The roses have come to bloom.

【盛况】shèngkuàng〈名〉spectacular event: 国庆节的～ spectacular National Day events ‖ ～空前 unprecedented grandeur

【盛名】shèngmíng〈名〉glorious name: 享有～ have an excellent reputation

【盛名之下，其实难副】shèngmíng zhī xià, qí shí nán fù〈成〉it is hard to live up to a great reputation

【盛年】shèngnián〈名〉prime of life: 正值～ in one's prime

【盛怒】shèngnù〈动〉〈书〉be furious: ～之下 in a fury

【盛气凌人】shèngqì-língrén〈成〉high and mighty

【盛情】shèngqíng〈名〉great kindness: ～款待 lavish hospitality

【盛情难却】shèngqíng-nánquè〈成〉not-to-be-refused hospitality

【盛世】shèngshì〈名〉period of prosperity: 太平～ times of peace and prosperity

【盛事】shèngshì〈名〉grand occasion: 皇室婚礼是喜庆的～。The royal wedding was an occasion of great festivity.

【盛暑】shèngshǔ〈名〉sweltering summer heat

【盛衰】shèng-shuāi〈名〉prosperity and decline

【盛衰荣辱】shèngshuāi-róngrǔ〈成〉vicissitudes of life

【盛夏】shèngxià ▸p. 345〈名〉high summer: ～时节 height of summer

【盛行】shèngxíng〈动〉be in fashion: ～起来 come into fashion ‖ ～一时 prevail for a time ‖ 这首歌～不衰。The song has remained popular.

【盛宴】shèngyàn〈名〉grand banquet: 设～招待客人 hold a grand banquet in honour of the guests

【盛意】shèngyì〈名〉great kindness

【盛誉】shèngyù〈名〉excellent reputation: 享有～的学校 prestige school

【盛赞】shèngzàn〈动〉extol: ～中国的经济发展 be full of praise for China's economic development

【盛装】shèngzhuāng〈名〉splendid attire: 穿上节日～ be dressed in one's festive best

剩（賸）

shèng〈动〉be left over: ～菜～饭 leftovers ‖ 屋里只～他们俩。Only two of them were left in the room. ▸～余, 过～

【剩女】shèngnǚ〈名〉old spinster

【剩下】shèngxia〈动〉be left (over): ～多少? How much is left? ‖ 大家都走了，只～他一个人。They have all gone. He is the only one left.

【剩余】shèngyú〈动〉be left (over): ～库存 residue stock ‖ ～粮食 food surplus

【剩余价值】shèngyú jiàzhí〈名〉［经济］surplus value: 创造～ produce surplus value

【剩余劳动】shèngyú láodòng〈名〉surplus labour

【剩余劳动力】shèngyú láodònglì〈名〉surplus work force

shī

尸[1]

shī〈名〉〈古〉person sitting behind the altar at a memorial ceremony, acting as the deceased during the performance of sacrificial rites

尸[2]（屍）

shī〈名〉corpse: 认～ identify a corpse ▸～首, 毁～灭迹, 僵～

【尸斑】shībān〈名〉［医学］post-mortem lividity

【尸骨】shīgǔ〈名〉1（骨头）skeleton: 挖出～ dig up a skeleton ‖ 掩埋～ bury bones 2（尸体）dead body: ～未寒 when sb. has just passed away

【尸骸】shīhái = 尸骨 shīgǔ

【尸横遍野】shīhéngbiànyě〈成〉be strewn with corpses

【尸检】shījiǎn〈名〉［医学］autopsy

【尸蜡】shīlà〈名〉1（指蜡状尸体）well-preserved corpse 2［医学］grave wax

【尸身】shīshēn = 尸体 shītǐ

【尸首】shīshou〈名〉corpse

【尸体】shītǐ〈名〉corpse: 辨认～ identify a corpse ‖ 掩埋/埋葬～ bury a dead body ‖ ～火化 cremation

【尸体解剖】shītǐ jiěpōu〈名〉autopsy

【尸位素餐】shīwèi-sùcān〈成〉hold office without doing a stroke of work

失

shī

A〈动〉1（丢失）lose: ～民心 lose the support of the people ‖ ～体面 lose face ▸～败, 损～ 2（找不到）cannot find: ▸～踪, 迷～ 3（失控）lose control of: ▸～手, ～足 4（失常）become abnormal: ▸～神, ～态 5（未达到）fail to achieve one's end: ▸～望, ～意 6（违背）violate: ▸～礼, ～约

B〈名〉error: ▸～误, 过～

【失败】shībài〈动〉1（被击败）be defeated: 屡遭～ suffer repeated defeats ‖ 外交上的～ diplomatic setback 2（未成功）fail: 导致～ lead to failure ‖ 部分～ partial failure ‖ 两国间的和谈～了。Peace talks between the two countries have failed.

【失败是成功之母】shībài shì chénggōng zhī mǔ〈俗〉failure is the mother of success

【失败者】shībàizhě〈名〉loser

【失败主义】shībàizhǔyì〈名〉defeatism

【失策】shīcè〈动〉be unwise: 计划/指挥～ be unwise in one's planning/command ‖ 这样做非常～。It was a very unwise move.

【失察】shīchá〈动〉neglect one's supervisory duties: 一时～ make a momentary oversight ‖ 对下属～ fail to supervise one's subordinates

【失常】shīcháng〈形〉abnormal: 精神～ not in one's right mind ‖ 举止～ act oddly

【失宠】shīchǒng〈动〉〈贬〉fall into disfavour: ～于领导 fall out of favour with the leadership

【失传】shīchuán〈动〉no longer exist: ～的药方 lost prescription ‖ 这种技艺已～了。The art was lost to the world.

【失磁】shīcí〈名〉［物理］loss of excitation: ～继电器 excitation-loss relay

【失聪】shīcōng〈动〉〈书〉lose one's hearing: 双耳～ become deaf in both ears

【失措】shīcuò〈动〉lose one's head: 茫然～ be at a total loss as to what to do ‖ 惊慌～ be scared out of one's wits

【失单】shīdān〈名〉list of lost/stolen property: 向警方提供～ provide the police with a lost property list

【失当】shīdàng〈形〉inappropriate: 处理～ be improperly handled ‖ 举止～ behave inappropriately ‖ 言语～ make inappropriate remarks

【失道寡助】shīdào-guǎzhù〈成〉an unjust cause finds scant support: ▸得道多助, ～

【失地】shīdì A〈动〉lose territory: ～千里 lose a vast expanse of land B〈名〉lost territory: 收复～ recover lost territory

【失掉】shīdiào〈动〉1（丢失）lose: ～磁性 lose magnetism ‖ ～联络 lose contact 2（错过）miss: ～机会 miss an opportunity ‖ ～战机 fail to grasp a battle-winning opportunity

【失读症】shīdúzhèng ▸p. 50〈名〉［医学］alexia: 患～ suffer from alexia

【失而复得】shī'érfùdé〈成〉regain what is lost

【失范】shīfàn〈动〉1（违背）go against the grain 2（丧失）forfeit: 严重的市场～ serious non-standard market operations

【失分】shīfēn〈名〉points lost: 我在翻译题上～最多。I lost most of my marks in the translation part.

【失和】shīhé〈动〉become estranged: 与父母～ become estranged from one's parents

【失衡】shīhéng〈动〉lose balance: 比例～ be disproportionate ‖ 供求～ imbalance between supply and demand

【失悔】shīhuǐ〈动〉〈书〉regret: 深感～ bitterly regret

【失婚】shīhūn〈动〉〈旧〉1（丧偶）lose one's spouse 2（离婚）divorce and remain unmarried

【失魂落魄】shīhún-luòpò〈成〉be panic-stricken: 吓得～ be scared/frightened out of one's wits/life

【失火】shīhuǒ〈动〉（指动态）catch fire;（指状态）be on fire: ～地点 fire scene/spot ‖ 仓库～了! The store house is on fire!

【失计】shījì = 失策 shīcè

【失检】shījiǎn〈动〉be indiscreet: 行为～ be indiscreet in one's actions

【失节】shījié〈动〉1（丧失节气）be disloyal 2（特指妇女）be unchaste: 宽恕妻子的～ condone the disloyalty of one's wife

【失禁】shījìn ▸p. 50〈动〉［医学］be incontinent: 大小便～ suffer from incontinence of faeces and urine

【失敬】shījìng〈动〉〈套〉excuse me for my lack of manners: 没能去机场接您，～，～。Sorry for being unable to meet you at the airport.

【失控】shīkòng〈动〉get out of control: 局势～。The situation got out of control. ‖ 汽车～了。The car went out of control.

【失礼】shīlǐ〈动〉1（粗鲁）commit a breach of etiquette: 对顾客～ be impolite to customers ‖ 他生气时有些～。He's rather curt when he is angry. 2 ▸p. 156〈套〉（失敬）excuse me for my lack of manners: 对不起，～了。Pardon me for my lack of manners.

【失利】shīlì〈动〉be defeated: 谈判～ suffer a setback in negotiation ‖ 在首场比赛中～ lose the first game ‖ 军事上的～ military setback

【失恋】shīliàn〈动〉be disappointed in love: ～的痛苦 bitter taste of disappointed love ‖ 他～了。He was jilted.

【失灵】shīlíng〈动〉be out of order: 开关～。The switch is not working. ‖ 刹车～了。The brakes failed.

【失落】shīluò〈动〉1〈书〉（丢失）lose: 不慎～ lose sth. through carelessness 2（迷茫）feel lost: ～的一代 lost generation

【失落感】shīluògǎn〈名〉sense of loss: 下岗后，她有一种强烈的～。She felt completely lost after she was laid off.

【失密】shīmì〈动〉leak a secret: 谨防～ guard against the leaking of secrets ‖ 怎么～的? How did the secret get out?

【失眠】shīmián〈动〉suffer from insomnia: 老是～ be plagued by insomnia ‖ ～患者 insomniac ‖ ～症 insomnia ‖ 昨晚他～了。He was unable to fall asleep last night.

【失明】shīmíng〈动〉lose one's eyesight: 双目～ be blind in both eyes

【失陪】shīpéi ▸p. 156〈动〉〈套〉please excuse me: 对不起，～了，我还要参加一个重要会议。Excuse me, I have to leave for an important meeting.

【失窃】shīqiè〈动〉be burgled: ～的珠宝 lost jewels ‖ 警察追回了～的手表。The police recovered the stolen watch. ‖ 家中～了。My house was burgled.

【失去】shīqù〈动〉lose: ～机会 miss an opportunity ‖ ～警觉 relax one's vigilance ‖ ～理智 lose one's senses ‖ ～时效 be no longer effective/valid ‖ ～信心 lose confidence ‖ ～知觉 lose consciousness

【失却】shīquè〈动〉〈书〉lose

【失群】shīqún〈动〉stray from one's flock: 一只～的大雁 a lost wild goose

【失认症】shīrènzhèng〈名〉agnosia

【失散】shīsàn〈动〉stray: ～多年 go years without any news

【失色】shīsè〈动〉1（指颜色） fade: 年久～ lose colour with the passage of time ‖ 丝绸容易～。Silk fades easily. 2（指脸色） turn pale: 惊慌～ turn pale with panic

【失闪】shīshan〈名〉mishap: 要是有个～，可不是闹着玩的。There would be serious consequences if anything went wrong.

【失墒】shīshāng〈动〉lose moisture

【失身】shīshēn〈动〉lose one's virginity

【失神】shīshén〈动〉1（走神）be absent-minded: 上课～ not pay attention in class 2（精神不振） be out of sorts: 她～地坐在那里，望着远方。She sat there in low spirits, staring into the distance.

【失慎】shīshèn〈动〉〈书〉be inattentive: 我一时～打翻了架上的花瓶。I inadvertently knocked a vase off the shelf.

【失声】shīshēng〈动〉〈书〉1（失控出声） burst out: ～大笑 burst out laughing, burst into laughter ‖ ～喊叫 exclaim ‖ ～痛哭 burst into tears 2（哭不出声） cry so much that one loses one's voice: 痛哭～ cry oneself hoarse 3（无法出声） be unable to speak

【失时】shīshí〈动〉miss an opportunity: 播种不能～。Don't miss the sowing season.

【失时效】shīshíxiào〈形〉［法律］stale: ～的债务 stale debt

【失实】shīshí〈动〉be inconsistent with the facts: 报道～。The report was inaccurate. ‖ 传闻～。The rumour was unfounded.

【失势】shīshì〈动〉lose power: ～隐退 lose power and retire ‖ 暂时～ temporary loss of power

【失事】shīshì〈动〉have an accident: 轮船在非洲海岸～了。The ship was wrecked off the coast of Africa. ‖ 一百多人在这次飞机～中丧生。More than 100 people were killed in the plane crash.

【失收】shīshōu〈动〉〈书〉1（无收成） fail: 今年夏季作物因干旱～。The summer crops failed this year because of the drought. 2（未收录） not be included: ～的文章 unanthologized article

【失手】shīshǒu〈动〉1（指不小心） do sth. accidentally: ～打碎了茶杯 accidentally drop a cup and break it 2（失利） be defeated unexpectedly

【失守】shīshǒu〈动〉fall: 该城在遭受猛烈炮击后～。The city fell after heavy bombardment.

【失水】shīshuǐ ▸p. 50〈名〉［医学］dehydration

【失速】shīsù〈动〉［航空］stall: 进入～下降状态 go into a stall

【失算】shīsuàn〈动〉miscalculate: 有点～ make a small miscalculation ‖ 这一次他可～了。He miscalculated this time.

【失态】shītài〈动〉lose control of oneself: 酒后～ lose control under the influence of alcohol

【失调】shītiáo〈动〉1（失去平衡） lose balance: 比例～ disproportion ‖ 雨水～ abnormal rainfall ‖ 供求严重～。There is a serious imbalance between supply and demand. 2（调养不当） be lacking in proper care: 产后～ lack proper care after childbirth ‖ 先天不足，后天～ be born weak and be ill cared for after birth

【失望】shīwàng A〈动〉lose heart: 从不～ never give up hope ‖ 别～! Don't lose heart! B〈形〉disappointed: 感到～ be disappointed ‖ 令人～ be disappointing

【失物】shīwù〈名〉lost property: 归还～ return lost property to its owner ‖ 认领～ claim one's lost property ‖ ～招领处 lost and found

【失误】shīwù〈动〉make a mistake: 发球～ serve a fault ‖ 判断～ error of judgement ‖ 重大～ serious mistake ‖ 工作中难免会有～。It is hard to avoid mistakes in one's work.

【失陷】shīxiàn〈动〉fall: 小镇最终～，落入敌人手中。The town finally fell into enemy hands.

【失效】shīxiào〈动〉lose effectiveness: 自动～ automatically lose effectiveness ‖ ～支票 stale cheque ‖ 这药已经～。The medicine no longer has any effect. ‖ 他的保险单已～。His insurance policy has become invalid.

【失写症】shīxiězhèng ▸p. 50〈名〉［医学］anorthography

【失信】shīxìn〈动〉go back on one's word: ～于民 lose the confidence of the people

【失修】shīxiū〈动〉fall into disrepair: 年久～ be neglected for years

【失序】shīxù〈动〉lose order: 管理～ lose administrative control

【失学】shīxué〈动〉be deprived of schooling: ～儿童 (school) dropout ‖ 她十岁就～了。She dropped out of school at the age of ten.

【失血】shīxuè〈动〉lose blood: ～过多 excessive loss of blood

【失血性休克】shīxuèxìng xīukè ▸p. 50〈名〉［医学］haemorrhagic shock

【失言】shīyán〈动〉make an indiscreet remark: 酒后～ make an indiscreet remark under the influence of alcohol ‖ 那不过是一时～。That's just a slip of the tongue.

【失业】shīyè ▸p. 966〈动〉be out of work: 面临～ face unemployment ‖ ～工人 unemployed/jobless worker ‖ 季节性/结构性/全国性～ seasonal/structural/nationwide unemployment ‖ 工厂的倒闭使许多人～。The bankruptcy of the factory put many people out of work.

【失业保险】shīyè bǎoxiǎn〈名〉unemployment insurance

【失业救济金】shīyè jiùjìjīn〈名〉unemployment benefit: 接受～ be on the dole

【失业率】shīyèlǜ〈名〉unemployment rate: 控制～ check unemployment ‖ 急剧上升的～ surging joblessness

【失业者】shīyèzhě〈名〉the unemployed: 帮助～再就业 help the unemployed find work again

【失宜】shīyí〈形〉〈书〉inappropriate: 处置～ handle improperly

【失意】shīyì〈动〉be frustrated: 克服～情绪 get over one's disappointment ‖ 情场～ be disappointed in love

【失迎】shīyíng〈动〉〈套〉please excuse me: ～! ～! So sorry! So sorry!

【失语症】shīyǔzhèng ▸p. 50〈名〉［医学］aphasia

【失约】shīyuē〈动〉fail to keep an appointment: 第一次和朋友约会你可不能～。You must not miss your first appointment with a friend.

【失责】shīzé〈动〉be derelict in one's duty

【失着】shīzhāo〈动〉make a careless move

【失真】shīzhēn〈动〉1（指声音、图像等） not be true to the original: 影片情节～。The plot of the film is not true to the original. 2［电子］distort: 图像～ image distortion

【失之东隅，收之桑榆】shī zhī dōngyú, shōu zhī sāngyú〈成〉make up on the roundabouts what one loses on the swings

【失之毫厘，谬以千里】shī zhī háolí, miù yǐ qiānlǐ〈成〉a small discrepancy leads to a great error

【失之交臂】shīzhī-jiāobì〈成〉just miss an opportunity

【失职】shīzhí〈动〉be derelict in one's duty: 严重～ seriously fail in one's duty

【失重】shīzhòng〈动〉［物理］be weightless: 宇宙飞船中的～状态 weightlessness in a spacecraft

【失主】shīzhǔ〈名〉owner of lost property: 将失物归还～ return lost property to its owner

【失踪】shīzōng〈动〉go missing: ～士兵 missing soldier ‖ 地震中有两百多人～。More than 200 people are missing in the earthquake.

【失足】shīzú〈动〉1（跌倒） miss one's step: ～落水 slip and fall into the water ‖ 她～滚下楼梯。She tripped and tumbled down the stairs. 2〈喻〉（堕落） take a false step: ～青年 juvenile delinquent

师（師）shī

A〈名〉1［军事］division: 步兵/骑兵～ infantry/cavalry division ‖ 装甲～ armoured division ‖ 一二五～ Division 125 ▸～部，～长 2（部队） troops: 雄～ mighty army ‖ 正义之～ army dedicated to a just cause ▸班～，出～不利，挥～ 3（老师） teacher: 尊～爱生 respect teachers and cherish students ‖ 严～出高徒。Strict teachers produce excellent students. ▸～长，教～，良～益友 4（榜样） model: ▸前事不忘，后事之～ 5（职业人员） person skilled in a certain profession: ▸厨～，工程～，律～ 6〈尊〉（大师） master: ▸禅～，法～ 7（同门） [a form of address derived from the relationship between teachers and students or between masters and apprentices]: ▸～母，～兄

B〈动〉〈书〉learn: ～从张大千 taught by Zhang Daqian ▸～承，～法

【师表】shībiǎo〈名〉〈书〉person of exemplary virtue: ▸为人～

【师部】shībù〈名〉［军事］division headquarters

【师承】shīchéng〈书〉A〈动〉study under B〈名〉transmission from master to disciple: 这些艺人各有自己的～。These artists have each inherited the traditions of their respective masters.

【师出无名】shīchū-wúmíng〈成〉do sth. without a proper reason

【师出有名】shīchū-yǒumíng〈成〉do sth. with good reason

【师道尊严】shīdào-zūnyán〈成〉dignity of the teaching profession

【师德】shīdé〈名〉teaching ethics: ～高尚 be an ethical teacher

【师弟】shīdì〈名〉**1**（指同一师门）junior male fellow apprentice/student **2**（指师傅的儿子） son of one's tutor (younger than oneself) **3**（指父亲的徒弟） father's (male) apprentice/student (younger than oneself) **4**（老师和弟子） teacher and student

【师法】shīfǎ〈书〉**A**〈动〉 model oneself after a great master: ～前辈 follow the example of the older generation **B**〈名〉 knowledge or skill passed down by one's master: 不失～ not forget the skill taught by one's master

【师范】shīfàn〈名〉**1**（指学校） teacher-training school: 幼儿～ school for teachers of preschool children ►～学校 **2**〈书〉（榜样） model

【师范大学】shīfàn dàxué〈名〉 teacher's university

【师范教育】shīfàn jiàoyù〈名〉 teacher-training

【师范学校】shīfàn xuéxiào〈名〉 teacher-training school

【师范学院】shīfàn xuéyuàn〈名〉 teacher's college

【师范专科学校】shīfàn zhuānkē xuéxiào〈名〉 teacher-training school

【师父】shīfu〈名〉**1** = 师傅 shīfu **2**〈尊〉（称呼出家人） master

【师傅】shīfu〈名〉**1**（老师） mentor: 他是我在厂里的～。 He was my mentor when I was a worker in the factory. **2**〈尊〉（工匠） master: 工人～ master workman ‖ 木匠～ carpenter

【师傅领进门，修行在个人】shīfu lǐngjìn mén, xiūxíng zài gèrén〈俗〉 the master teaches the trade, but the apprentice's skill is self-made

【师姐】shījiě〈名〉**1**（指同一师门）senior female fellow apprentice/student **2**（指师傅的女儿） daughter of one's tutor (older than oneself) **3**（指父亲的徒弟） father's female apprentice/student (older than oneself)

【师妹】shīmèi〈名〉**1**（指同一师门） junior female fellow apprentice/student **2**（指师傅的女儿） daughter of one's tutor (younger than oneself) **3**（指父亲的徒弟） father's female apprentice/student (younger than oneself)

【师母】shīmǔ〈名〉 wife of one's teacher

【师娘】shīniáng〈口〉= 师母 shīmǔ

【师生】shīshēng〈名〉 teachers and students: ～比例 ratio of teachers to students ‖ ～关系 relationship between teachers and students ‖ ～员工 teachers, students, administrative personnel and workers

【师事】shīshì〈动〉〈书〉 acknowledge sb. as one's teacher

【师徒】shītú〈名〉 master and apprentice: ～合同 indentures ‖ ～关系 master-apprentice relationship

【师心自用】shīxīn-zìyòng〈成〉 unwilling to listen to advice

【师兄】shīxiōng〈名〉**1**（指同一师门） senior male fellow apprentice/student **2**（指师傅的儿子） son of one's tutor (older than oneself) **3**（指父亲的徒弟） father's male apprentice/student (older than oneself)

【师兄弟】shīxiōngdì〈名〉**1**（指同一师傅） fellow (male) apprentices **2**（指同一老师） fellow (male) students

【师训】shīxùn〈名〉 teacher's instructions: 遵循～ follow the teacher's instructions

【师训班】shīxùnbān〈名〉 teacher-training class

【师爷】shīye〈名〉〈旧〉 private adviser: 钱粮～ private assistant attending to economic and financial affairs ‖ 刑名～ private adviser on legal matters

【师友】shīyǒu〈名〉 teachers and friends

【师院】shīyuàn〈简称〉= 师范学院

【师长】shīzhǎng〈名〉**1**〈尊〉（老师） teacher: 尊敬～ have respect for teachers **2**［军事］ division commander

【师专】shīzhuān〈简称〉= 师范专科学校

【师资】shīzī〈名〉 teaching staff: 培训～ train teachers ‖ ～力量不足 be short of teachers ‖ ～质量 professional competence of teaching staff

诗（詩） shī〈名〉 poetry: 朗诵～ recite a poem ‖ 抒情/叙事～ lyric/narrative poetry ‖ 古体～ classical poetry ►～人, 打油～, 古～

【诗风】shīfēng〈名〉 poetic style

【诗歌】shīgē〈名〉 poem: 朗诵～ recite poems ‖ ～集 anthology of poems ‖ ～语言 poetic diction

【诗歌朗诵】shīgē lǎngsòng〈名〉 poetry reading: ～比赛 poetry reading competition ‖ ～会 poetry recital

【诗行】shīháng〈名〉 verse

【诗话】shīhuà〈名〉**1**（指评论） poetry criticism **2**（指文学作品） vernacular stories interspersed with poems

【诗集】shījí〈名〉 anthology of poems: 出版～ publish an anthology of verse ‖ 《郭沫若～》 *Collected Poems of Guo Moruo*

【诗节】shījié〈名〉 verse: 第二～ second stanza

【诗经】shījīng〈名〉 *Book of Songs*

> **《诗经》**
>
> The earliest collection of poems and songs in China. 305 pieces were collected over 500 years, from the beginning of the Western Zhou to the middle of the Spring and Autumn period. The collection was called *Poems* (《诗》) or *Three Hundred Poems* (《诗三百》) in the pre-Qin period. In the Western Han they were acknowledged as Confucian classics, and acquired the title *Book of Songs* (《诗经》). Most of the poems have four lines, and are divided into three categories: *feng* (风), *ya* (雅) and *song* (颂) poems. *Feng* poems are mostly folk songs from 15 states. *Ya* poems are songs for royal banquets and gatherings. *Song* poems are sung to dance music while offerings are made at the royal ancestral shrines, and mostly praise the exploits of the ancestors.

【诗句】shījù〈名〉 verse: 引用～ quote verses ‖ 莎士比亚的～ lines of Shakespeare

【诗剧】shījù〈名〉 poetic drama: 现代～ modern verse drama

【诗律】shīlǜ〈名〉 prosody

【诗篇】shīpiān〈名〉**1**〈本〉 poetry: 爱情～ love poems **2**〈喻〉 inspirational piece of writing: 光辉/壮丽的～ glorious/magnificent epic ‖ 英雄的～ heroic epic

【诗情画意】shīqíng-huàyì〈成〉 poetic charm: 富有～的景色 idyllic scene

【诗人】shīrén〈名〉 poet: 当代～ poet of the age ‖ 浪漫主义/现实主义～ romantic/realistic poet ‖ 田园～ pastoral poet

【诗社】shīshè〈名〉 poetry club: 成立～ establish a poetry club ‖ 加入～ join a poetry club

【诗史】shīshǐ〈名〉**1**（指发展史） history of poetry: 中国～ history of Chinese poetry **2**（指诗歌） poems that mirror the times in which they were written

【诗书】shīshū〈名〉 Confucian classics: 出身～名门 come from a family of Confucian scholars

【诗坛】shītán〈名〉 poetic circles: ～领袖 dean of poetry ‖ ～新秀 new poetry star

【诗兴】shīxìng〈名〉 poetic inspiration: ～大发 be in a poetic mood

【诗选】shīxuǎn〈名〉 selected poems

【诗学】shīxué〈名〉 poetics

【诗意】shīyì〈名〉 poetic sentiment: 富有～ be rich in poetic flavour ‖ ～盎然 be brimming with poetic sentiment ‖ 过着充满～的生活 live a quite poetic life

【诗韵】shīyùn〈名〉**1**（韵律） rhyme **2**（韵书） rhyming dictionary

【诗章】shīzhāng〈名〉 canto

【诗作】shīzuò〈名〉 poetry

虱（蝨） shī〈名〉 louse

【虱多不痒，债多不愁】shī duō bù yǎng, zhài duō bù chóu〈俗〉 when one is up to one's ears in debt, one stops worrying

【虱子】shīzi〈名〉 louse: 头上有～ have lice in one's hair

狮（獅） shī〈名〉 lion: 驯～ tame a lion ‖ 母～ lioness ‖ 雄～ lion ‖ ～吼。 A lion roars.

【狮虎】shīhǔ〈名〉［动物］ liger

【狮身人面像】shīshēn-rénmiànxiàng〈名〉 sphinx

【狮子】shīzi〈名〉 lion: 把～关进笼子 cage a lion

【狮子搏兔】shīzi-bótù〈成〉 do one's best even when performing a minor task

【狮子大开口】 shīzi dà kāikǒu〈俗〉 demand an exorbitant price: 她可真是～。 She's demanding an excessive price.

【狮子狗】shīzigǒu〈名〉 pug-dog

【狮子头】shīzitóu〈名〉［食品］large meatballs [usu deep-fried before being braised with vegetables]: 红烧～ large meatballs braised in soy sauce

【狮子舞】shīziwǔ〈名〉 lion dance: 表演～ perform a lion dance

【狮子座】Shīzizuò〈名〉［天文］ Leo

施 shī〈动〉**1**（给予） bestow: ►～恩, ～加, ～礼 **2**（特指财物） give alms: ►～药, ～主, 乐善好～ **3**（加） use: ～底肥 apply fertilizer to the subsoil ‖ ～脂粉 apply cosmetics, wear make-up ►～肥 **4**（实行） carry out: 略～小计 play a little trick on sb. ►～行, 措～, 软硬兼～

【施暴】shībào〈动〉**1**（施加暴力） take violent action **2** ►p. 772〈婉〉（强奸） rape

【施恩】shī'ēn〈动〉 grant favours: ～于人 bestow favours on others

【施放】shīfàng〈动〉 discharge: ～催泪弹 fire shells of tear gas ‖ ～毒气 discharge poisonous gas ‖ ～烟幕 lay a smokescreen

【施肥】shīféi〈动〉 apply fertilizer: 给庄稼～ fertilize crops with manure ‖ 合理～ adequate fertilization

【施工】shīgōng〈动〉 carry out a construction project: 加紧～ speed up construction ‖ 道路～，车辆绕行。 Detour. Road under construction.

【施工单位】shīgōng dānwèi〈名〉 unit undertaking the construction (of)

【施工进度】shīgōng jìndù〈名〉 progress of construction

【施工图】shīgōngtú〈名〉 working drawing: 绘～ make a working drawing ‖ 看～ read project drawings

【施惠】shīhuì〈动〉grant favours
【施加】shījiā〈动〉impose: ～压力 put pressure ‖ ～影响 exercise one's influence
【施教】shījiào〈动〉〈书〉instruct: ▸因材～
【施救】shījiù〈动〉〈书〉rescue: 紧急～ carry out an emergency rescue
【施礼】shīlǐ〈动〉〈书〉salute: 弯腰～ bow to salute
【施虐狂】shīnüèkuáng〈名〉[心理] 1（指病）sadism 2（指人）sadist
【施舍】shīshě〈动〉give alms: ～食品 give food in charity ‖ 接受～ accept charity ‖ 没有人愿意靠别人～生活。No one really wants to live off charity.
【施事】shīshì〈名〉[语法] agent
【施威】shīwēi〈动〉throw one's weight about: 向百姓～ exercise one's power over the common people
【施洗】shīxǐ〈名〉[基督教] baptize: 给基督徒～ baptize a Christian
【施刑】shīxíng〈动〉1（指刑罚）impose a penalty 2（指体罚）torture: ～逼供 use torture to extract a confession ‖ 禁止对犯人～。Torturing prisoners is forbidden.
【施行】shīxíng〈动〉1（生效）put into force: 开始～ go into effect ‖ 本条例自公布之日起～。These regulations come into force upon proclamation. 2（进行）perform: ～急救 administer emergency treatment ‖ ～手术 perform a surgical operation
【施药】shīyào〈动〉give free medicine to the poor
【施医】shīyī〈动〉give free medical treatment to the poor
【施用】shīyòng〈动〉employ: ～化肥/农家肥 apply fertilizer/farmyard manure ‖ ～药物 administer a drug
【施与】shīyǔ〈动〉grant: ～钱财 grant sb. some money ‖ 慷慨～ grant liberally
【施斋】shīzhāi〈动〉provide monks with free food
【施展】shīzhǎn〈动〉display: ～本领/才能 demonstrate one's ability ‖ ～阴谋诡计 carry out plots and schemes ‖ 充分～ give full play to
【施诊】shīzhěn〈动〉provide free medical service for the poor
【施政】shīzhèng〈动〉manage government affairs: ～方针 principles for running an institution or government ‖ ～纲领 administrative programme
【施政演说】shīzhèng yǎnshuō〈名〉policy speech
【施主】shīzhǔ〈名〉[a form of address used by Buddhist monks and Taoist priests] patron: 女～ lady patron

湿（濕、溼）shī

A〈形〉wet: ～毛巾 damp towel ‖ ～衣服 wet clothes ▸～度, ～润, 加～器
B〈名〉[中医] humidity [one of the six external factors which cause diseases, namely, wind, cold, summer heat, humidity, dryness and fire]: ▸风～
【湿病】shībìng ▸p. 50〈名〉[中医] damp-induced disease
【湿材】shīcái〈名〉[林业] green lumber
【湿答答】shīdādā〈形〉〈方〉dripping wet: 衣服还～的。The clothes are still dripping wet.
【湿地】shīdì〈名〉wetland: 保护～ preserve wetland
【湿度】shīdù〈名〉moisture content: 减少/增加空气～ decrease/increase air humidity ‖ 绝对/相对～ absolute/relative humidity ‖ 土壤～ soil moisture ‖ 这儿～很大。There is a lot of moisture here.
【湿度表】shīdùbiǎo〈名〉moisture meter
【湿度记录器】shīdù jìlùqì〈名〉hygrograph
【湿度调节器】shīdù tiáojiéqì〈名〉humidity regulator
【湿度仪】shīdùyí〈名〉hygronom
【湿法】shīfǎ〈名〉wet method
【湿法抛光】shīfǎ pāoguāng〈名〉wet polishing
【湿法冶金】shīfǎ yějīn〈名〉hydrometallurgy: ～处理 wet metallurgical processing
【湿敷】shīfū〈名〉[医学] wet dressing
【湿乎乎】shīhūhū〈形〉damp
【湿呼呼】shīhūhū = 湿乎乎 shīhūhū
【湿货】shīhuò〈名〉wet goods
【湿季】shījì〈名〉wet season
【湿季风】shījìfēng〈名〉[气象] wet monsoon
【湿剂】shījì〈名〉[中医] moist formula
【湿津津】shījīnjīn〈形〉sweaty: ～的衬衣 sweaty shirt
【湿冷】shīlěng〈形〉damp and chilly: ～的天气 cold and damp weather
【湿淋淋】shīlínlín〈形〉dripping wet: 浑身～的 be drenched through ‖ ～的衣服 sopping wet clothes
【湿漉漉】shīlùlù〈形〉damp: ～的台阶 wet steps ‖ ～的衣服 damp clothes ‖ 床单摸上去还～的。The sheet still feels damp.
【湿气】shīqì〈名〉1 [中医] fungus infection 2（潮湿度）moisture: 空气中的～ moisture in the air
【湿热】shīrè〈形〉hot and humid: ～的天气 sticky weather
【湿润】shīrùn A〈形〉moist: ～的空气 humid air ‖ ～的土壤 moist soil ‖ 她的眼睛～了。Her eyes were moist with tears. B〈动〉wet: 他不停地用舌头～嘴唇。He kept moistening his lips with his tongue.
【湿透】shītòu〈形〉wet through: 浑身～ be wet through ‖ 汗水把他全身～了。Sweat drenched his body. ‖ 这孩子的衣服被雨水～了。The boy's clothing was wet through with rain.
【湿疣】shīyóu〈名〉moist wart: 尖锐～ pointed wart
【湿疹】shīzhěn〈名〉eczema
【湿重】shīzhòng〈名〉wet weight
【湿租】shīzū〈动〉wet-lease: ～飞机 wet-lease an aircraft

蓍 shī〈名〉[植物] common yarrow

酾[1]（釃）shī〈动〉〈书〉1（过滤）filtrate 2（斟）pour

酾[2]（釃）shī〈动〉〈书〉dredge

嘘（噓）shī〈叹〉[used to stop sb. from doing sth., or to drive sb. or sth. away] sh: ～，小点声! Sh! Keep quiet!
▸xū

鲺（鰤）shī〈名〉yellowtail

鳋（鯴）shī〈名〉fish louse

shí

十 shí

A ▸p. 691〈数〉ten: ～大新闻 top ten news stories ‖ ～点～分 ten past ten ‖ ～倍 tenfold ▸～进制
B〈形〉topmost: ▸～分, ～足
【十八般武艺】shíbā bān wǔyì〈名〉versatile: ～，样样精通 all-rounder
【十八层地狱】shíbā céng dìyù〈名〉the depths of hell
【十八罗汉】shíbā luóhàn〈名〉[佛教] eighteen arhats: ～的塑像 statues of the eighteen arhats
【十病九痛】shíbìng-jiǔtòng〈成〉get all kinds of aches and pains
【十冬腊月】shídōng-làyuè〈名〉coldest months of the year
【十恶不赦】shí'è-bùshè〈成〉guilty beyond forgiveness: ～的人 atrocious person ‖ ～的罪犯/罪行 heinous criminal/crime
【十二分】shí'èrfēn〈副〉exceedingly: ～满意 more than satisfied ‖ 我有～把握。I am more than 100 per cent sure.
【十二生肖】shí'èr shēngxiào〈名〉twelve symbolic animals associated with a 12-year cycle

> **十二生肖**
>
> The twelve animals of the Chinese zodiac, corresponding to the twelve Earthly Branches (▸天干地支). Each Earthly Branch represents an individual's year of birth, and has a corresponding animal. These are, in order, the rat (鼠), ox (牛), tiger (虎), rabbit (兔), dragon (龙), snake (蛇), horse (马), sheep (羊), monkey (猴), rooster (鸡), dog (狗) and pig (猪). Therefore, people born in the 子 year have the rat as their animal. The birth year, known as the '*benmingnian*' (本命年), returns in a twelve-year cycle. Each animal has a particular character, and it is believed that personality traits are determined by one's birth year.

【十二月】shí'èryuè ▸p. 928〈名〉1（阳历）December 2（阴历）twelfth month of the lunar year
【十二指肠】shí'èrzhǐcháng〈名〉[生理] duodenum: ～溃疡 duodenal ulcer
【十番】shífān = 十番乐 shífānyuè
【十番锣鼓】shífān luógǔ = 十番乐 shífānyuè
【十番乐】shífānyuè〈名〉music played by a band with the ten traditional percussion instruments
【十方】shífāng〈名〉[佛教] ten directions [north, south, east, west, north-east, north-west, south-east, south-west, above and below]
【十分】shífēn〈副〉very: ～宝贵 extremely valuable ‖ ～高兴 very pleased ‖ ～害怕 be mortally afraid ‖ ～肯定 be absolutely sure ‖ ～有害 extremely harmful ‖ ～重视 attach great importance (to)
【十个指头有长短】shígè zhǐtou yǒu chángduǎn〈俗〉you can't expect everybody to be all the same
【十环】shíhuán〈名〉bullseye: 击中～ hit the bullseye
【十佳】shíjiā〈名〉ten best: ～运动员 top ten athletes
【十戒】shíjiè〈名〉[佛教] Ten Prohibitions
【十诫】shíjiè〈名〉[宗教] Ten Commandments
【十锦】shíjǐn = 什锦 shíjǐn
【十进法】shíjìnfǎ〈名〉[数学] decimal numeration
【十进位】shíjìnwèi〈形〉[数学] decimal
【十进制】shíjìnzhì〈名〉[数学] decimal system
【十六分音符】shíliùfēn yīnfú〈名〉[音乐] semiquaver〈英〉; sixteenth note

S

〈美〉

【十六进制】shíliùjìnzhì〈名〉 sexadecimal number system

【十六开】shíliùkāi〈名〉［印刷］sixteenmo, 16mo

【十目所视，十手所指】shí mù suǒ shì, shí shǒu suǒ zhǐ〈成〉 wrong doings never go unnoticed

【十拿九稳】shíná-jiǔwěn〈成〉 practically certain: 这事～能成。A hundred to one, it will be a success.

【十年动乱】shínián dòngluàn〈名〉 decade of turmoil [referring to the 1966-1976 Cultural Revolution]

【十年寒窗】shínián hánchuāng〈成〉years of perseverance in one's studies despite great hardships

【十年浩劫】shínián hàojié〈名〉 ten-year catastrophe [referring to the 1966-1976 Cultural Revolution]

【十年九不遇】shí nián jiǔ bù yù〈成〉 be very rare

【十年树木，百年树人】shí nián shù mù, bǎi nián shù rén〈成〉 it takes a long time for people to come into their own

【十全十美】shíquán-shíměi〈成〉 perfect: ～的产品 perfect product ‖ 他绝非～。He is far from perfect.

【十三点】shísāndiǎn〈方〉**A**〈形〉 foolish **B**〈名〉 nitwit

【十三经】Shísānjīng〈名〉 Thirteen Classics of Confucianism

【十三辙】shísānzhé〈名〉 thirteen rhyme schemes

【十室九空】shíshì-jiǔkōng〈成〉 scene of desolation

【十四行诗】shísìhángshī〈名〉 sonnet: 莎士比亚的～ Shakespearean sonnet

【十万八千里】shíwàn bāqiān lǐ〈成〉 poles apart: 离题～ be completely off the point

【十万火急】shíwàn-huǒjí〈成〉 very urgent: ～的电报 urgent telegram

【十位】shíwèi〈名〉［数学］tens place

【十位数】shíwèishù ▸**p. 691**〈名〉［数学］tens digit

【十项全能运动】shíxiàng quánnéng yùndòng〈名〉 decathlon: ～员 decathlete

【十一】Shí-Yī〈名〉**1**（十月一日）October 1st **2**（国庆节）National Day [of the People's Republic of China]

【十一月】shíyīyuè ▸**p. 928**〈名〉**1**（阳历）November **2**（阴历）eleventh month of the lunar year

【十有八九】shíyǒubājiǔ = 十之八九 shízhībājiǔ

【十月】shíyuè ▸**p. 928**〈名〉**1**（阳历）October **2**（阴历） tenth month of the lunar year

【十月革命】Shíyuè Gémìng〈名〉 October Revolution [which occurred in Russia in 1917]

【十之八九】shízhībājiǔ〈成〉 in all likelihood: ～明天会下雪。Ten to one it will snow tomorrow. ‖ ～他会迟到。It's very likely that he'll be late.

【十指连心】shízhǐ-liánxīn〈成〉be intimately connected

【十字】shízì〈名〉 cross: ▸红～会

【十字架】shízìjià〈名〉 crucifix: 钉死在～上 die on the Cross

【十字街头】shízì-jiētóu〈名〉 busy city streets

【十字军】Shízìjūn〈名〉**1**（指11至13世纪）the Crusades [eight expeditions by European Christians to recover Jerusalem from Muslims, 1096-1270] **2**（指中世纪）crusade: ～战士 crusader

【十字路口】shízì lùkǒu〈名〉 intersection: 处于～ be at a crossroads ‖ 徘徊于～ hesitate at the crossroads ‖ 这是我人生的～。It was a crossroads in my life.

【十字星】shízìxīng〈名〉［金融］cross sign [in MACD indicating that opening and closing prices are at the same level]

【十足】shízú〈形〉**1**（成色纯） pure: ～的黄金 solid gold **2**（完全） sheer: 干劲/信心～ be full of energy/confidence ‖ ～的笨蛋 perfect fool

什 shí

A ▸**p. 691**〈数〉〈书〉 ten: ～一 one tenth ‖ ～百 tenfold

B〈形〉 assorted: ▸～锦

C〈名〉 sundries: ▸家～

▸shén

【什件儿】shíjiànr〈名〉**1**（鸡鸭内脏） giblets: 炒～ fried giblets **2**〈方〉（金属器物） metal accessories: 黄铜～ brass accessories

【什锦】shíjǐn **A**〈形〉 assorted: ～饼干 assorted biscuits ‖ ～糖 assorted sweets **B**〈名〉 mix: 素～ vegetable medley

【什罗普郡】shíluópǔjùn〈名〉 Shropshire

【什物】shíwù〈名〉 odds and ends: 家用～ household sundries

【什叶派】Shíyèpài〈名〉［伊斯兰教］Shia

石 shí

〈名〉**1**（石头） stone: 一～二鸟 kill two birds with one stone ▸～雕, 矿～, 水落～出 **2**（石刻） stone inscription: ▸金～ **3**（做药材） medicinal minerals: 药～ medical treatment **4**（石针） stone needles [for acupuncture]

▸dàn

【石斑鱼】shíbānyú〈名〉 grouper

【石板】shíbǎn〈名〉**1**（指建材）slabstone: 一块～ a slab of stone **2**（指文具） slate: 记事～ slate for memos

【石板路】shíbǎnlù〈名〉 flagging

【石板瓦】shíbǎnwǎ〈名〉 roofing slate: ～屋顶 slate roof

【石版】shíbǎn〈名〉［印刷］stone plate

【石版画】shíbǎnhuà〈名〉 lithograph

【石碑】shíbēi〈名〉 stone tablet, stele

【石壁】shíbì〈名〉**1**（岩石） cliff **2**（石墙） stone wall

【石材】shícái〈名〉 stone material: ～加工厂 stoneworks

【石沉大海】shíchéndàhǎi〈成〉never to be seen or heard of again

【石刁柏】shídiāobǎi〈名〉［植物］asparagus

【石雕】shídiāo〈名〉**1**（指雕刻） stone carving;（指塑像） stone sculpture **2**（指艺术品） carved stone

【石碓】shíduì〈名〉 pestle

【石墩】shídūn〈名〉 stone seat

【石方】shífāng〈名〉 cubic metre of stonework: 三千～ three thousand cubic metres of stonework

【石坊】shífāng〈名〉 stone memorial arch

【石舫】shífǎng〈名〉 marble boat

【石膏】shígāo〈名〉 gypsum: 腿上上了～ have a plaster cast on one's leg

【石膏雕刻】shígāo diāokè〈名〉 art or act of engraving on gypsum

【石膏粉】shígāofěn〈名〉 gesso

【石膏像】shígāoxiàng〈名〉 plaster statue

【石工】shígōng〈名〉**1**（指工作） masonry **2**（石匠） stonemason

【石拱桥】shígǒngqiáo〈名〉 stone arch bridge

【石鼓文】shígǔwén ▸**p. 918**〈名〉［考古］**1**（指铭文） inscriptions on drum-shaped stone blocks from the Warring States Period **2**（指字体） script used for such inscriptions

【石棺】shíguān〈名〉 sarcophagus

【石磙】shígǔn = 碌碡 liùzhou

【石斛】shíhú〈名〉**1**［植物］dendrobium **2**［中药］stem of dendrobium

【石花菜】shíhuācài〈名〉［植物］agar-agar

【石化产品】shíhuà chǎnpǐn〈名〉 petrochemicals

【石化厂】shíhuàchǎng〈简称〉= 石油化工厂

【石灰】shíhuī〈名〉 lime: ▸生～, 熟～

【石灰厂】shíhuīchǎng〈名〉 limeworks

【石灰池】shíhuīchí〈名〉 lime pit

【石灰石】shíhuīshí〈名〉 limestone

【石灰水】shíhuīshuǐ〈名〉 lime water

【石灰岩】shíhuīyán〈名〉 limestone

【石级】shíjí〈名〉 stone step

【石家庄】Shíjiāzhuāng ▸**p. 661**〈名〉 Shijiazhuang [capital of Hebei Province (河北)]

【石匠】shíjiang = 石工 shígōng 2

【石决明】shíjuémíng〈名〉［中药］shell of abalone or sea-ear

【石刻】shíkè〈名〉**1**（指石碑或石壁） carved stone **2**（指文字或图画） stone inscription

【石窟】shíkū〈名〉 grotto: 龙门～ Longmen Grottoes

【石块】shíkuài〈名〉 stone block: 一群示威者向派出所扔～。A crowd of demonstrators threw rocks at the police station.

【石蜡】shílà〈名〉［材料］paraffin

【石料】shíliào〈名〉 stone material: 加工～ work the stone

【石料加工厂】shíliào jiāgōngchǎng〈名〉 stoneworks

【石林】shílín〈名〉 stone forest

【石榴】shíliu〈名〉 pomegranate

【石榴裙】shíliuqún〈名〉**1**（指裙子） pomegranate-red skirt **2**〈喻〉（女子） woman: 拜倒在～下 be infatuated with a woman

【石榴石】shíliushí〈名〉［矿业］garnet

【石绿】shílǜ〈名〉 malachite green

【石煤】shíméi〈名〉 bone coal

【石棉】shímián〈名〉 asbestos: ～制品 asbestos product ‖ ～板 asbestos board

【石棉瓦】shímiánwǎ〈名〉［建筑］asbestos tile

【石墨】shímò〈名〉 graphite: ～块/片/球 graphite block/flake/pebble

【石墨粉】shímòfěn〈名〉 powdered graphite

【石墨坩埚】shímò gānguō〈名〉 graphite crucible

【石磨】shímò〈名〉 millstone

【石女】shínǚ〈名〉 woman with a non-perforated hymen

【石破天惊】shípò-tiānjīng〈成〉remarkably original and forceful

【石器】shíqì〈名〉 stone artefact

【石器时代】shíqì shídài〈名〉 Stone Age: 旧～ Palaeolithic Period ‖ 新～ Neolithic Period ‖ 中～ Mesolithic Period

【石蕊】shíruǐ〈名〉**1**［植物］reindeer lichen/moss **2**［化学］litmus

【石蕊试纸】shíruǐ shìzhǐ〈名〉［化学］litmus paper

【石首鱼】shíshǒuyú〈名〉［鱼类］sciaenoid

【石笋】shísǔn〈名〉［地质］stalagmite

【石锁】shísuǒ〈名〉［体育］stone dumbbell carved in the form of an old-fashioned padlock

【石炭】shítàn〈名〉〈旧〉 coal

S

【石炭纪】Shítànjì〈名〉［地质］Carboniferous Period
【石炭酸】shítànsuān〈名〉carbolic acid
【石炭系】Shítànxì〈名〉［地质］Carboniferous System
【石头】shítou〈名〉stone: 一块～ a piece of stone ‖ 凿～ cut stone ‖ 像～一样坚硬 be as hard as rock
【石头子儿】shítouzǐr〈名〉〈口〉pebble: ～铺的路 cobbled street
【石硪】shíwò〈名〉circular stone rammer with ropes attached at the sides
【石羊】shíyáng〈名〉［动物］bharal
【石印】shíyìn〈名〉lithography
【石英】shíyīng〈名〉quartz
【石英表】shíyīngbiǎo〈名〉quartz watch
【石英电子表】shíyīng diànzǐ biǎo = 石英表 shíyīngbiǎo
【石英电子钟】shíyīng diànzǐzhōng = 石英钟 shíyīngzhōng
【石英岩】shíyīngyán〈名〉quartzite
【石英钟】shíyīngzhōng〈名〉quartz clock
【石油】shíyóu〈名〉petroleum: 开采～ tap oil ‖ 提炼～ refine petroleum
【石油储量】shíyóu chǔliàng〈名〉oil reserves/deposits
【石油化工厂】shíyóu huàgōngchǎng〈名〉petrochemical works
【石油气】shíyóuqì〈名〉petroleum gas
【石油输出国组织】shíyóu shūchūguó zǔzhī〈名〉Organization of Petroleum Exporting Countries (OPEC)
【石油冶炼厂】shíyóu yěliànchǎng〈名〉oil refinery
【石钟乳】shízhōngrǔ = 钟乳石 zhōngrǔshí
【石竹】shízhú〈名〉［植物］China pink
【石柱】shízhù〈名〉**1**［地质］stone pillar **2**（柱子）stele
【石子儿】shízǐr = 石头子儿 shítouzǐr

S

时（時）shí

A〈名〉**1**（季节）season: ►～令，农～，应～ **2**（时间）time: 等候多～ have waited for a long time ►～不我待，～差，～过境迁 **3**（时段）a period of time: 在空闲～ at one's leisure ‖ ～近黄昏。The day is almost out. ►平～ **4**（时点）fixed time: 准～到达 arrive on time ►按～，及～，届～ **5**〈旧〉（时辰）[one of the twelve two-hour periods into which the day was divided in China before the introduction of western chronology, each being given the name of one of the 12 Earthly Branches (地支)]: ►丑～，寅～ **6**（点钟）hour: 上午九～ nine o'clock in the morning ‖ 下午六～十分 ten past six in the afternoon ►～速，～钟 **7**（时机）opportunity: ►～来运转，背～，失～ **8**［语法］tense: 过去/将来/现在～ past/future/present tense
B〈形〉**1**（当前）current, present: ►～事，～务，～下 **2**（一时）momentary: 他一～糊涂偷了钱。He stole the money in a moment of aberration. ►～机，～运，～装
C〈副〉**1**（时常）from time to time: 学而～习之。Review what you have learned from time to time. ►～～ **2**（时而）occasionally: ～醒～睡 sleep on and off ‖ ～隐～现 appear and disappear ‖ 他的身体～好～坏。He has been ill on and off.
【时弊】shíbì〈名〉social evils of the day: 抨击～ lash out at social evils
【时不可失】shíbùkěshī〈成〉seize the time
【时不时】shíbùshí〈副〉every now and then: 他～来看我。He comes to see me from time to time.
【时不我待】shíbùwǒdài〈成〉time waits for no man
【时不宜迟】shíbùyíchí〈成〉there is no time to lose
【时不再来】shíbùzàilái〈成〉the opportunity may never come again
【时差】shíchā〈名〉**1**（时间差）jet lag: 倒～ recover from jet lag **2**［天文］equation of time
【时差反应】shíchā fǎnyìng〈名〉jet lag
【时常】shícháng〈副〉often: ～发生 occur frequently ‖ 我～去那儿。I often go there.
【时辰】shíchen〈名〉**1**〈旧〉（计时单位）double-hour [one of the 12 two-hour periods into which the day was divided in the past before the introduction of western chronology, each being given the name of one of the 12 Earthly Branches (地支)]: 约莫半个～ about an hour **2**（时候）time for sth.: ～到了。The time has come. ‖ ～未到。It is not yet time.
【时代】shídài〈名〉**1**（指时期）times: 跟不上～ be out of step with the times ‖ 开创新～ usher in a new era ‖ 历史～ historical era ‖ 信息～ information age ‖ ～不同，风气不同。There are different ways of doing things for different times. **2**（人生阶段）period in one's life: 儿童～ childhood ‖ 青年～ youth hood ‖ 学生～ school days
【时代潮流】shídài cháoliú〈名〉trends of the times: 符合～ conform to the trends of the times ‖ 顺应～ adapt to the times
【时代精神】shídài jīngshén〈名〉spirit of the times: 体现～ embody the spirit of the times
【时代脉搏】shídài màibó〈名〉pulse of the times
【时代气息】shídài qìxī〈名〉spirit of the times: 富有～ be full of the spirit of the times
【时点】shídiǎn〈名〉point in time
【时调】shídiào〈名〉popular tunes of a particular locality: 天津～ Tianjin tunes
【时段】shíduàn〈名〉period of time: 黄金～ prime time
【时而】shí'ér〈副〉**1**（表重复发生）now and then: ～外出购物 go shopping from time to time ‖ 天空～飘过几朵薄薄的白云。Every now and then fleecy clouds floated across the sky. **2**（表交替发生）now ... now ...: ～好，～坏 be good one moment and bad the next ‖ ～晴天，～下雨 fine one moment, raining the next
【时分】shífēn〈名〉〈书〉time: 黄昏～ at dusk ‖ 三更～ at the third watch ‖ 深夜～ in the dead of night
【时乖命蹇】shíguāi-mìngjiǎn = 时乖运蹇 shíguāi-yùnjiǎn
【时乖运蹇】shíguāi-yùnjiǎn〈成〉have the hand of fate against one
【时光】shíguāng〈名〉**1**（时间）time: 浪费～ waste one's time ‖ 虚度～ idle away one's time ‖ ～流逝。Time is flying. **2** = 时期 shíqī **3**（时段）times: 度过一段欢乐～ have a nice time ‖ 一生中最美好的～ best years of one's life
【时过境迁】shíguò-jìngqiān〈成〉things have changed with the passing of time
【时候】shíhou〈名〉time: 农忙～ busy farming season ‖ 每天这个～ at this time every day ‖ 在任何～ at any moment ‖ 你来了多少～了? How long have you been here? ‖ ～不早了。It's getting late. ‖ 是采取行动的～了。Now is the time to act.
【时或】shíhuò〈副〉〈书〉at times
【时机】shíjī〈名〉opportunity: 错过～ miss an opportunity ‖ 等待～ bide one's time ‖ 抓住～ seize an opportunity ‖ 有利～ favourable opportunity ‖ ～不成熟。The time is not yet ripe.
【时价】shíjià〈名〉current price: 高于～ be higher than the market price
【时间】shíjiān〈名〉time: ～与空间 time and space ‖ 赶～ pushed for time ‖ 浪费～ waste one's time ‖ 延长～ extend the time ‖ 珍惜～ value time ‖ 办公～ office hours ‖ 交通高峰～ rush hour ‖ 业余～ spare time ‖ ～紧迫。Time is pushing on. ‖ ～就是生命，浪费时间就是浪费生命。One's time is one's life, wasting time means wasting one's life. ‖ 北京/格林尼治～ Beijing/Greenwich time ‖ 出发/到达～ departure/arrival time ‖ 截止～ deadline
【时间表】shíjiānbiǎo〈名〉schedule: 落后于～ lag behind schedule
【时间差】shíjiānchā〈名〉time difference
【时间词】shíjiāncí〈名〉［语言］temporal word
【时间性】shíjiānxìng〈名〉timeliness: 这项任务～很强。This task must be done on time.
【时节】shíjié〈名〉**1**（季节）season: 春耕～ season for spring ploughing ‖ 金秋～ golden autumn season **2**（时候）occasion: 那～他还是个孩子。He was still a child then.
【时局】shíjú〈名〉current political situation: ～动荡不安。The situation is volatile.
【时刻】shíkè **A**〈名〉moment: 处在重要的历史～ be at a critical historical juncture ‖ 非常幸福的～ moment of great happiness ‖ 在此关键～ at this crucial hour **B**〈副〉always: ～保持清醒的头脑 always keep a cool head ‖ ～准备保卫祖国 be ready to defend the country at any moment
【时刻表】shíkèbiǎo〈名〉schedule: 列车/火车～ train timetable ‖ 作息～ daily schedule
【时空】shíkōng〈名〉space and time
【时来运转】shílái-yùnzhuǎn〈成〉the luck has turned in one's favour: ～，我们赢了。Our fortune turned and we won.
【时令】shílìng〈名〉season: 苹果正当～。Apples are in season now. ‖ ～已是初春。It is already early spring.
【时髦】shímáo〈形〉fashionable: 追求～ seek out the fashionable ‖ 穿着～ be fashionably dressed ‖ 又～起来 be back in fashion again
【时髦词】shímáocí〈名〉buzzword
【时评】shípíng〈名〉editorial
【时期】shíqī〈名〉period: 关键～ crucial period ‖ 和平～ time of peace ‖ 历史～ period of history
【时区】shíqū〈名〉time zone: 标准～ standard time zone ‖ 地球被分为二十四个～。The earth is divided into 24 time zones.
【时人】shírén〈名〉〈书〉contemporaries: ～有诗为证。There is a poem by a contemporary poet which testifies to this.
【时日】shírì〈名〉**1**（时间和日期）time: 没有多少～ have little time ‖ 延误～ miss a deadline **2**（一段时间）relatively long period of time: 工程完工尚需～。The project will need a little longer before it's finished.
【时尚】shíshàng **A**〈名〉fashion: 合于～ be in fashion ‖ 流行音乐的新～ new fad in pop music **B**〈形〉fashionable: 这种款式很～。This style is very fashionable.

ℹ 时间

问时间

几点了？
= What time is it?
或 What's the time?

你能告诉我几点了吗？
= Could you tell me the time?

你知道几点了吗？
= Have you got the time on you?
或 Do you know what time it is?
或 Do you have the time?

你的表几点了？
= What time is it by your watch?

6 点了
= It is 6 o'clock

大约 4 点钟
= It is about 4

刚好 3 点 / 3 点整
= It is exactly 3 o'clock
或 It is 3 sharp

将近 8 点
= It is nearly 8 o'clock

就要到 8 点了
= It's just before 8

刚过 9 点
= It's just after 9

表示时间

■ 英语里，书写一个具体时间的时候可用小数点，也可用冒号。

■ 在书写时间的时候，a.m. 或 am 指午夜到中午之间的时间，p.m. 或 pm 指中午到午夜之间的时间。在读出时间的时候，午夜到中午之间的时间可说 in the morning，中午到午夜之间的时间根据不同的时间段可用 in the afternoon、in the evening 及 at night。

■ 3:40 可以说 twenty to four 或 three forty。英国英语用 to，美国英语用 of。

3:04 可以说 four minutes past three 或 four minutes after three。英国英语用 past，美国英语用 after。如果表示过了某个整点的几分钟，英语习惯加上 minutes。在有必要的情况下，也可用 minutes 来精确地表示时间，如 twenty minutes past three。

■ o'clock 只用于整点，但也可省去不用，如晚上 7 点可以说 seven o'clock in the evening 或 seven in the evening，但 7:10 不能说 ten past seven o'clock。

■ 下面以英国英语为例：

	写	读
早上 6 点	6 am 6 o'clock in the morning six in the morning	six (o'clock) in the morning
下午 3 点	3 pm 3 o'clock in the afternoon three in the afternoon	three (o'clock) in the afternoon
晚上 8 点	8 pm 8 o'clock in the evening eight in the evening	eight (o'clock) in the evening
晚上 11 点	11 pm 11 o'clock at night eleven at night	eleven (o'clock) at night
5 点零 3 分	three minutes past five 5.03	three minutes past five five oh three
6 点 10 分	ten past six six ten 6.10	ten past six six ten
7 点一刻	a quarter past 7 seven fifteen 7.15	a quarter past seven seven fifteen
5 点半	half past five five thirty 5.30	half past five five thirty
5:40	twenty to six five forty 5.40	twenty to six five forty
差一刻 6 点	a quarter to six five forty-five 5.45	a quarter to six five forty-five
6.48	twelve minutes to seven twelve to seven 6.48	twelve minutes to seven twelve to seven six forty-eight

午夜
= midnight

凌晨 12 点 / 零点
= 12 midnight

中午 12 点
= 12 noon
或 midday

介词的使用

■ 用 what time 提问的时候用不用 at 都可以：

火车什么时候到达？
= What time will the train arrive (at)?

他什么时候离开？
= What time will he leave?

■ 表示时间的时候，汉语有时用介词“在”、“于”，有时什么介词都不用，而英语中使用 at 或 in：

那件事大约发生在 9 点钟
= That happened at about 9

火车将在上午 10 点半到达
= The train will arrive at half past 10 in the morning
或 The train will arrive at 10.30 am

公交车在整点差五分到达，整点过一刻开走
= Buses arrive at five minutes to the hour and leave at a quarter past the hour

会议将于两个小时之后开始
= The meeting will start in two hours' time

我常在午饭时给朋友发短信
= I often send text messages to my friends in my lunch hour

■ 注意下面介词的使用：

护士每到整点来看他
= The nurse sees him every hour on the hour

午饭将在 12 点钟之前准备好
= The lunch will be ready by 12

老板上午 10 点才到
= The boss won't come until 10 am

我会待到半夜 12 点
= I will stay until 12 midnight

这家商店从早上 10 点开到晚上 8 点
= The shop is open from 10 am to 8 pm

【时尚界】shíshàngjiè〈名〉 fashion world: 从时装秀中可以看出，黑白两色依然是～的最爱。 Looking at fashion shows, you can see that black and white are still the favourites of the fashion world.

【时尚专家】shíshàng zhuānjiā ▸p. 966〈名〉 style guru

【时时】shíshí〈副〉 always: ～处处严格要求自己 be strict with oneself in all matters

【时时刻刻】shíshí-kèkè〈副〉 at every moment: ～为人民利益着想 always keep the people's interests in mind

【时世】shíshì〈名〉 1（时代） times: 艰难～ hard times 2（当今社会） present-day society

【时式】shíshì〈名〉 latest style: ～领带 a tie in the latest fashion

【时势】shíshì〈名〉 current situation: 认清～ see the way things are going

【时势造英雄】shíshì zào yīngxióng〈成〉 circumstances create heroes

【时事】shíshì〈名〉 current affairs: ～评论 news commentaries

【时蔬】shíshū〈名〉 seasonal vegetable

【时俗】shísú〈名〉 custom of the time

【时速】shísù〈名〉 speed per hour: ～80公里 80 kilometres per hour

【时态】shítài〈名〉［语言］ tense: 过去/将来/进行～ past/future/continuous tense

【时务】shíwù〈名〉 trend of the times: ▸不识～, 识～者为俊杰

S

【时下】shíxià ▸p. 618〈名〉 now: ～正是旅游旺季。 Now is the busiest tourist season.

【时鲜】shíxiān〈名〉 fresh food in season: ～果品 fresh fruits and nuts ‖ ～蔬菜 vegetables in season

【时限】shíxiàn〈名〉 time limit: 定出～ set a deadline ‖ 在规定～内 within the prescribed time

【时效】shíxiào〈名〉 1（指效用） effectiveness for a given period of time: 失去～ lose effectiveness ‖ 药品～ expiry dates of medicines 2［法律］ limitation: 诉讼～ limitation of actions

【时新】shíxīn〈形〉 trendy: ～货物 fashion goods ‖ ～式样 up-to-date style ‖ 他穿着最～的衣服。 He wears very trendy clothes.

【时兴】shíxīng A〈动〉 be in fashion: 现在不～留长发了。 Long hair is no longer in fashion. ‖ 这种式样已经不再～了。 This style is no longer in vogue. B〈形〉 popular: 滑板运动是～的玩意儿。 Skateboarding is the latest craze.

【时行】shíxíng = 时兴 shíxīng

【时序】shíxù〈名〉 sequential timing

【时宜】shíyí〈名〉 that which is appropriate to the occasion: 不合/切合～ be inappropriate/appropriate ‖ 不合～的话 mistimed remarks

【时疫】shíyì〈名〉 epidemic

【时运】shíyùn〈名〉 luck: ～不济 misfortune ‖ ～倒转 suffer a reversal of fortune

【时针】shízhēn〈名〉 1（钟表指针） hands of a clock/watch 2（钟表的短针） hour hand (of a clock/watch)

【时政】shízhèng〈名〉 political situation of the time: ～要闻 pressing political news

【时钟】shízhōng〈名〉 clock: ～收音机 clock radio

【时装】shízhuāng〈名〉 1（指式样新颖） latest fashion: 春季～ spring fashions ‖ 夏季流行～ hot fashions for summer 2（指当代通行） contemporary wear

【时装表演】shízhuāng biǎoyǎn〈名〉 fashion show: ～队 modelling team

【时装模特儿】shízhuāng mótèr〈名〉 fashion model

【时装设计师】shízhuāng shèjìshī〈名〉 fashion designer

【时装秀】shízhuāngxiù〈名〉 fashion show

识（識）shí

A〈动〉 1（知道） have a sense of: ▸～趣 2（认得） know: ～水性 be good at swimming ‖ 一字不～ be completely illiterate ▸～别, 素不相～

B〈名〉 knowledge: ▸才～, 胆～ ▸zhì

【识别】shíbié〈动〉 identify: ～骗子 spot a swindler ‖ ～善恶 discern good from evil ‖ ～颜色 judge colours ‖ 善于～真伪 know how to tell the real from the fake

【识别力】shíbiélì〈名〉 discernment: 培养～ cultivate one's power of discrimination

【识货】shíhuò〈动〉 know what's what

【识家】shíjiā〈名〉 discerning customer

【识见】shíjiàn〈名〉〈书〉 knowledge and experience

【识破】shípò〈动〉 see through: ～诡计 be wise to a trick ‖ ～骗局 spot a fraud

【识谱】shípǔ〈动〉 be able to read music

【识趣】shíqù〈动〉 know how to behave in a delicate situation

【识时务者为俊杰】shí shíwù zhě wéi jùnjié〈俗〉 he who understands the times is a wise man

【识文断字】shíwén-duànzì ▸p. 999〈成〉 be literate

【识相】shíxiàng〈形〉〈方〉 show good sense: 他这个人不～，自讨没趣。 He was tactless and got the snub that he deserved.

【识字】shízì ▸p. 999〈动〉 learn to read: 不～ be illiterate ‖ 读书～ read and write ‖ 他还识几个字。 He can read a little.

【识字班】shízìbān〈名〉 literacy class

【识字课本】shízì kèběn〈名〉 elementary textbook

实（實）shí

A〈形〉 1（不空） full: 把窟窿填～ fill up a hole ‖ 里面是～的。 It's solid inside. ▸充～, 厚～, 坚～ 2（富裕） wealthy: 丰～ be well-off ▸殷～ 3（具体） concrete: ▸～词, ～惠, ～力, ～效 4（实在） sincere: 寻找不～的借口 look for a phoney excuse ‖ ～利 tangible benefits ▸～事求是, 诚～

B〈名〉 1（实际） reality: ▸名副其～, 如～, 事～ 2（种子） seed: 开花结～ blossom and bear fruit ▸子～

C〈副〉 truly: ▸～不相瞒

D〈动〉 fill: ▸荷枪～弹

【实报实销】shíbào-shíxiāo〈动〉 be reimbursed for actual expenses: 出差费用～。 All the expenses incurred during the business trip can be reimbursed.

【实不相瞒】shíbùxiāngmán〈成〉 to be frank: ～，你这次考试又没及格。 To be honest with you, you have failed the exam again this time.

【实测】shícè〈动〉 measure with instruments

【实诚】shícheng〈形〉〈方〉 honest: ～话 frank words

【实处】shíchù〈名〉 where it really counts: 把措施落到～ put the measure into practice

【实词】shící〈名〉［语言］ notional word

【实打实】shídǎshí〈惯〉 genuine: ～的生意人 real business person ‖ 掌握～的本领 grasp real skills

【实弹】shídàn A〈名〉 live ammunition: ～射击 combat firing ‖ ～演习 exercises with live ammunition B〈动〉 be loaded: ▸荷枪～

【实得】shídé〈动〉 actually get: ～报酬 net earnings ‖ ～工资 take-home pay

【实地】shídì〈副〉 1（在现场） on the spot: ～了解施工情况 learn on site how construction is proceeding 2（实实在在） practically: ～去做 do sth. in a down-to-earth manner

【实地调查】shídì diàochá〈动〉 make a site inspection

【实地考察】shídì kǎochá〈动〉 make an on-the-spot investigation

【实感】shígǎn〈名〉 genuine feelings

【实干】shígàn〈动〉 do solid work

【实干家】shígànjiā〈名〉 man of action

【实话】shíhuà〈名〉 truth: 说～ tell the truth ‖ 他说的没有一句是～。 There is not a syllable of truth in what he said.

【实话实说】shíhuà-shíshuō〈成〉 talk straight

【实惠】shíhuì A〈名〉 material benefits: 得到～ get real benefit ‖ 没有一点～ receive no material benefits B〈形〉 substantial: 经济～ inexpensive but substantial

【实际】shíjì A〈名〉 reality: 符合～ correspond to reality ‖ 脱离～ be out of touch with reality ‖ 理论联系～ integrate theory with practice ‖ 从～出发 be realistic B〈形〉 1（具体） practical: ～工作 practical work ‖ ～经验 hands-on experience ‖ 不～的想法 impractical idea 2（真实） real: ～高度 true height ‖ ～年龄 physical age ‖ ～损失 actually caused loss ‖ ～成本 actual cost ‖ ～工资 actual wages

【实际控制线】shíjì kòngzhìxiàn〈名〉［军事］ line of actual control

【实际情况】shíjì qíngkuàng〈名〉 facts: 合乎～ accord with actual conditions

【实际伤害】shíjì shānghài〈名〉［法律］ actual harm

【实际上】shíjìshàng〈副〉actually: 这个问题～从来没有讨论过。 As a matter of fact the question was never discussed.

【实寄封】shíjìfēng〈名〉 cover [envelope with stamp affixed and franked]

【实绩】shíjì〈名〉 concrete results: 他为官多年，无～可言。 He had nothing tangible to show for his years of office.

【实价】shíjià〈名〉 actual price: ～五元 at five *yuan* net

【实践】shíjiàn A〈动〉 put into practice: ～诺言 keep one's word ‖ ～自己的主张 put one's ideas into practice B〈名〉 practice: 理论与～相结合 combine theory with practice ‖ 这在～中毫无用处。 It has no practical use.

【实践出真知】shíjiàn chū zhēnzhī〈俗〉 one learns by doing

【实践经验】shíjiàn jīngyàn〈名〉 practical experience: 缺乏～ lack practical experience

【实景】shíjǐng〈名〉 realistic view

【实据】shíjù〈名〉 substantial proof: 提供～ produce factual evidence ‖ 真凭～ ironclad evidence ▸查无～

【实况】shíkuàng〈名〉 what is actually happening: 转播开幕式～ broadcast the opening ceremony live ‖ 奥运会～报道 live coverage of the Olympic Games

【实况录像】shíkuàng lùxiàng〈名〉 live videotaping

【实况转播】shíkuàng zhuǎnbō〈名〉 live broadcast: ～车 outside broadcast (OB) van

‖ ～时间 live time

【实力】shílì〈名〉strength: 增强～ build up one's strength ‖ 经济～ economic power

【实例】shílì〈名〉living example

【实录】shílù **A**〈名〉**1**（记录） faithful record **2**（史书） veritable records [annalistic history narrating the events of an emperor's reign] **B**〈动〉record facts

【实脉】shímài〈名〉［中医］strong pulse

【实名】shímíng〈名〉real name: ►～制

【实名制】shímíngzhì〈名〉personal banking real name system

【实木】shímù〈名〉timber: ～地板/家具 wooden floor/furniture

【实盘】shípán〈名〉［金融］trading: ～交易 actual trading

【实情】shíqíng〈名〉actual situation: 道出～ tell the truth ‖ 了解～ know the true state of affairs ‖ 掩盖～ hide the facts

【实权】shíquán〈名〉real power: 他没有～。He has no real power.

【实生】shíshēng〈形〉raised directly from planted seeds: ～苗 seedling

【实施】shíshī〈动〉put into effect: ～改革 initiate a reform ‖ ～计划 carry out a plan ‖ 付诸～ put sth. into effect ‖ 检查政策的～情况 check up on the implementation of a policy ‖ 暂不～这项规定 suspend this regulation

【实施细则】shíshī xìzé〈名〉rules for implementation

【实时】shíshí〈副〉in real time: 进行～报道 give a report in real time

【实实在在】shíshí-zàizài〈形〉true: ～的好处 tangible benefits ‖ 给予～的评价 give an objective appraisal ‖ 有～的本事 have real ability

【实事】shíshì〈名〉**1**（真实的事） fact **2**（实在的事） practical things: 多做～ perform more actual deeds

【实事求是】shíshì-qiúshì〈成〉be true to facts: 采取～的态度 take a realistic approach ‖ ～的工作作风 practical and realistic style of work

【实数】shíshù〈名〉**1**（真实的数字） actual amount **2**［数学］real number

【实说】shíshuō〈动〉speak frankly: ～了吧，我根本不喜欢那份工作。To be frank, I don't like the job at all. ‖ 这件事你就给我们～吧。Just tell us the truth about it. ►实话～

【实体】shítǐ〈名〉**1**［哲学］substance: ～形式 substantial form **2**（机构或组织） entity: 经济/政治～ economic/political entity

【实物】shíwù〈名〉**1**（物体） material object: 展出～ display objects **2**（非货币） goods in place of money: ～津贴/捐献 allowance/contribution in kind **3**［物理］matter

【实物地租】shíwù dìzū〈名〉rent in kind

【实物工资】shíwù gōngzī〈名〉wages in kind: ～制 truck system

【实物交易】shíwù jiāoyì〈名〉barter (trade)

【实物资本】shíwù zīběn〈名〉material capital

【实物资产】shíwù zīchǎn〈名〉material assets

【实习】shíxí〈动〉practise: 毕业～ graduation fieldwork ‖ 临床～ do clinical practice

【实习法庭】shíxí fǎtíng〈名〉moot court

【实习护士】shíxí hùshi〈名〉trainee nurse

【实习记者】shíxí jìzhě〈名〉student journalist

【实习期】shíxíqī〈名〉internship

【实习生】shíxíshēng〈名〉trainee

【实习医生】shíxí yīshēng〈名〉intern; house officer〈英〉

【实习医院】shíxí yīyuàn〈名〉training hospital

【实现】shíxiàn〈动〉realize: ～抱负/愿望 realize one's ambitions/wishes ‖ ～和平统一 bring about peaceful reunification ‖ ～小康 attain a fairly comfortable level of life ‖ ～祖国统一 unify the motherland ‖ 他的期望未能～。His expectation has failed to materialize.

【实线】shíxiàn〈名〉real line

【实像】shíxiàng〈名〉［物理］real image

【实效】shíxiào〈名〉effect: 讲求～ strive for substantial results ‖ 确有～ prove to be effective ‖ 注重～ emphasize practical results

【实心】shíxīn〈形〉**1**（真诚） sincere: ～话 words spoken from the heart **2**（非空心） solid: ～轮胎 solid tyre

【实心球】shíxīnqiú〈名〉［体育］medicine ball

【实心实意】shíxīn-shíyì = 真心实意 zhēnxīn-shíyì

【实心眼儿】shíxīnyǎnr **A**〈形〉honest and serious-minded **B**〈名〉honest person

【实行】shíxíng〈动〉put into practice: ～按劳分配原则 apply the principle of distribution according to work ‖ ～封锁 enforce a blockade ‖ ～改革开放政策 implement the policies of reform and opening up ‖ ～集体领导 exercise collective leadership ‖ ～经济制裁 invoke economic sanctions

【实学】shíxué〈名〉real learning: 有虚名而无～ have a false reputation and no real learning ►真才～

【实验】shíyàn **A**〈动〉test: ～新配方 experiment with a new formula ‖ 用动物～ experiment on animals **B**〈名〉experiment: 做～ conduct an experiment ‖ 科学～ scientific experiment ‖ ～剧院 experimental theatre ‖ ～影院 cinematheque

【实验器材】shíyàn qìcái〈名〉experimental apparatus

【实验室】shíyànshì〈名〉laboratory (lab): 建造～ build a laboratory ‖ ～试验 laboratory test

【实验数据】shíyàn shùjù〈名〉experimental data

【实验学校】shíyàn xuéxiào〈名〉experimental school: 创办～ found an experimental school

【实验式】shíyànshì〈名〉chemical equation

【实业】shíyè〈名〉business: ～公司 industrial corporation ‖ ～家 businessman

【实意】shíyì〈名〉sincerity: 实心～为人民服务 serve the people with sincerity

【实义词】shíyìcí〈名〉［语言］content word

【实用】shíyòng **A**〈动〉apply (sth.) in practice **B**〈形〉practical: 既美观，又～ be both beautiful and practical

【实用标准】shíyòng biāozhǔn〈名〉practical standard

【实用程序】shíyòng chéngxù〈名〉utilities

【实用性】shíyòngxìng〈名〉practicability

【实用主义】shíyòng zhǔyì〈名〉pragmatism: ～者 pragmatist

【实在】shízài **A**〈形〉real: 说话～ talk straight ‖ 内容～。The content is substantial. **B**〈副〉**1**（的确） really: ～太好了 very good indeed ‖ ～为难 be in a genuine dilemma ‖ 我～不能干那件事。I can't bring myself to do it. **2**（其实） actually **C**〈名〉［哲学］reality: 客观/主观～ objective/subjective reality

【实在论】shízàilùn〈名〉［哲学］realism

【实在】shízai〈形〉〈方〉done carefully: 工作做得～。The work is well done.

【实则】shízé〈副〉actually

【实战】shízhàn〈名〉actual combat: ～训练 exercise under battle conditions

【实战演习】shízhàn yǎnxí〈名〉field combat exercise

【实证】shízhèng〈名〉［法律］concrete evidence: 缺乏～ lack concrete evidence

【实证论】shízhènglùn〈名〉positivism: ～者 positivist

【实证主义】shízhèng zhǔyì〈名〉［哲学］positivism: ～法学 positive jurisprudence ‖ ～者 positivist

【实症】shízhèng〈名〉［中医］excess syndrome: ～为主，兼有虚症 excess syndrome complicated with deficiency symptoms

【实职】shízhí〈名〉position with real power and responsibility

【实至名归】shízhì-míngguī〈成〉fame follows merit

【实质】shízhì〈名〉essence: 抓住问题的～ get to the heart of a problem ‖ ～部分 substantive part ‖ ～问题 issue of substance ‖ 问题的～ crux of a matter

【实质性】shízhìxìng〈名〉materiality: 取得～进展 make substantial progress ‖ ～问题 problem of substance ‖ 条约已做了～修改。The treaty underwent substantial modification.

【实字】shízì〈名〉［语言］notional word

【实足】shízú〈形〉full: ～两个小时 two solid hours ‖ 这袋麦子～100斤。This sack of wheat is a full 100 *jin*.

【实足年龄】shízú niánlíng〈名〉exact age

拾¹

shí〈动〉**1**（捡） pick up off the ground: ～麦穗 glean ‖ ～破烂儿 search a rubbish heap for odds and ends ‖ 在街上～到一个钱包 pick up a purse on the street ►～取，路不～遗 **2**（收拾） tidy: ►～掇，收～

拾²

shí ►**p. 691**〈数〉ten [used for the numeral 十 on cheques, etc. to avoid alterations or mistakes]

►shè

【拾波】shíbō〈名〉［物理］pick-up: ～器 adaptor

【拾掇】shíduo〈动〉**1**（收拾） put in order: ～屋子 tidy up a room **2**（修理） mend: ～洗衣机 fix a washing machine **3**〈口〉（教训） punish: 把流氓狠狠地～了一顿 give the rascals a good beating

【拾荒】shíhuāng〈动〉live off odds and ends

【拾金不昧】shíjīn-bùmèi〈成〉not pocket the money one picks up

【拾零】shílíng〈动〉put together bits and pieces about sth.: 赛场～ titbits from the competition

【拾取】shíqǔ〈动〉collect: 在麦田里～麦穗 collect wheat ears in the field

【拾趣】shíqù〈动〉〈书〉collect titbits

【拾人牙慧】shírényáhuì〈成〉appropriate other people's ideas and pass them off as one's own

【拾物】shíwù〈名〉found lost article: ～招领 lost and found ‖ ～招领处 lost property office

【拾遗】shíyí〈动〉**1**（拾取） appropriate lost property: ►路不～ **2**（补充） make up for omissions: ►～补阙

【拾遗补阙】shíyí-bǔquē〈成〉make up for omissions and deficiencies

【拾音】shíyīn〈名〉pick-up: ～话筒 pick-up transmitter ‖ ～器 pick-up

食[1] shí

A〈名〉(食物) food: 觅～ look for food ‖ 喂～ feed ‖ 狗/猫～ dog/cat food ▸～量, 丰衣足～, 面～
B〈动〉eat: ～素 have a vegetarian diet ‖ 多～蔬菜 eat lots of vegetables ‖ 少～多餐 have more meals but less food at each ▸～堂, 废寝忘～, 绝～
C〈形〉**1**(供食用) edible: ▸～物 **2**(供烹调用) cooking: ▸～盐

食[2] (蚀) shí〈动〉eclipse: ▸日～, 月～
▸sì

【食补】shíbǔ〈动〉eat nutritious food
【食不甘味】shíbùgānwèi〈成〉have no appetite
【食不果腹，衣不蔽体】shí bù guǒ fù, yī bù bì tǐ〈成〉have not enough to eat and wear
【食不厌精，脍不厌细】shí bù yàn jīng, kuài bù yàn xì〈成〉be particular about one's food
【食草动物】shícǎo dòngwù〈名〉herbivore
【食道】shídào = 食管 shíguǎn
【食而不化】shí'érbùhuà〈成〉**1**〈本〉eat without digesting **2**〈喻〉read without taking anything in
【食分】shífēn〈名〉[天文] degree of obscuration
【食古不化】shígǔ-bùhuà〈成〉pedantic
【食管】shíguǎn〈名〉[生理] oesophagus
【食积】shíjī〈名〉[中医] indigestion
【食既】shíjì〈名〉[天文] second contact of a total eclipse
【食具】shíjù = 餐具 cānjù
【食客】shíkè〈名〉**1**〈旧〉(门客) hanger-on of an aristocrat **2**(餐馆的顾客) restaurant customer
【食粮】shíliáng〈名〉food: ～供应 food supplies ‖ 精神～ spiritual food
【食量】shíliàng〈名〉appetite: ～大 have a big appetite
【食疗】shíliáo **A**〈动〉treat with food therapy **B**〈名〉food therapy
【食品】shípǐn〈名〉foodstuffs: ～卫生检查 food hygiene inspection ‖ ～质量管理 quality control of food ‖ 保健～ health food ‖ 罐头～ canned food ‖ 婴儿～ baby food
【食品厂】shípǐnchǎng〈名〉food factory
【食品防腐剂】shípǐn fángfǔjì〈名〉preservative
【食品柜】shípǐnguì〈名〉cupboard
【食品加工】shípǐn jiāgōng〈名〉food processing
【食品添加剂】shípǐn tiānjiājì〈名〉food additive
【食谱】shípǔ〈名〉**1**(菜谱) recipe: 大众/家常～ popular/everyday recipe **2**(菜单) menu: 一周～ menu of the week
【食人鲨】shírénshā〈名〉man-eating shark
【食肉动物】shíròu dòngwù〈名〉carnivorous animals
【食甚】shíshèn〈名〉[天文] middle phase of an eclipse
【食宿】shísù〈名〉board and lodging: ～自理 pay one's own board and lodging
【食堂】shítáng〈名〉dining hall: 员工～ staff canteen
【食糖】shítáng〈名〉sugar
【食物】shíwù〈名〉food: 储藏/供应～ preserve/supply food ‖ 冷冻～ frozen food
【食物链】shíwùliàn〈名〉food chain
【食物中毒】shíwù zhòngdú〈名〉food poisoning
【食相】shíxiàng〈名〉[天文] phases of an eclipse
【食性】shíxìng〈名〉**1**[动物] feeding habits **2**(指人) eating habits
【食言】shíyán〈动〉break one's promise: 绝不～ never go back on one's word
【食言而肥】shíyán'érféi〈成〉fail to keep one's word
【食盐】shíyán〈名〉salt
【食蚁兽】shíyǐshòu〈名〉anteater
【食用】shíyòng〈动〉**1**(吃) eat: 适合～ be fit for consumption **2**(用于吃) be edible: ～鱼 edible fish
【食用菌】shíyòngjūn〈名〉edible fungus
【食用油】shíyòngyóu〈名〉cooking oil
【食油】shíyóu = 食用油 shíyòngyóu
【食欲】shíyù〈名〉appetite: 刺激/满足～ whet/appease sb.'s appetite ‖ ～不振 have a poor appetite ‖ ～旺盛 have a good appetite ‖ ～缺乏症 anorexia
【食欲障碍】shíyù zhàng'ài ▸p. 50〈名〉[医学] dysorexia
【食之无味，弃之可惜】shí zhī wúwèi, qì zhī kěxī〈成〉it isn't great but it would be a shame to give it away
【食指】shízhǐ〈名〉index finger
【食茱萸】shízhūyú〈名〉[植物] ailanthus prickly ash

蚀 (蝕) shí〈动〉**1**(损失) lose: ▸～本, 亏～, 偷鸡不着～把米 **2**(蛀) eat into: ▸蛀～ **3**(腐蚀) corrode: ▸腐～, 侵～, 锈～ **4** = 食[2] shí
【蚀本】shíběn〈动〉lose one's capital: ～出售 sell at a loss ‖ ～生意 loss-making business
【蚀刻】shíkè〈动〉etch: ～玻璃 etched glass ‖ ～艺术 art of etching
【蚀刻法】shíkèfǎ〈名〉etching

炻 shí
【炻器】shíqì〈名〉stoneware

埘 (塒) shí〈名〉〈书〉chicken roost built into a wall

莳 (蒔) shí
▸shì
【莳萝】shíluó〈名〉[植物] dill

鲥 (鰣) shí
【鲥鱼】shíyú〈名〉hilsa herring

鼫 shí〈名〉〈古〉flying squirrel

shǐ

史 shǐ〈名〉**1**(历史) history: 医学～ medical annals ‖ 世界～ world history ▸～无前例, 病～, 家～ **2**〈古〉(史官) official historian: ▸～官
【史部】shǐbù〈名〉history as the second of the four divisions of the ancient Chinese library collection
【史册】shǐcè〈名〉historical records: 载入～ go down in history
【史官】shǐguān〈名〉〈古〉official historian
【史话】shǐhuà〈名〉historical account
【史籍】shǐjí〈名〉historical records
【史迹】shǐjì〈名〉historical relics
【史料】shǐliào〈名〉historical data: 收集～ collect historical data
【史略】shǐlüè〈名〉brief history: 《中国小说～》*A Brief History of Chinese Fiction*
【史论】shǐlùn〈名〉historical essays
【史评】shǐpíng〈名〉historical criticism
【史前】shǐqián〈名〉prehistory: ～动物 prehistoric animal
【史前时代】shǐqián shídài〈名〉prehistoric age
【史诗】shǐshī〈名〉epic: 荷马～《伊利亚特》Homer's epic *The Iliad*
【史实】shǐshí〈名〉historical facts: 该书内容与～不符。The book is historically inaccurate.
【史书】shǐshū〈名〉historical records: 博览～ read history extensively ‖ 据～记载 according to historical records
【史无前例】shǐwúqiánlì〈成〉unprecedented in history: ～的壮举 unprecedented feat
【史学】shǐxué〈名〉history: ～家 historian

矢[1] shǐ〈名〉〈书〉arrow: 飞～ flying arrow ▸流～, 无的放～

矢[2] shǐ〈动〉vow: ▸～口, ～志不移

矢[3] shǐ〈名〉faeces: 遗～ empty one's bowels
【矢车菊】shǐchējú〈名〉[植物] cornflower
【矢口】shǐkǒu〈动〉state categorically: ～抵赖 categorically deny ‖ ～否认 make a flat denial
【矢量】shǐliàng〈名〉[数学] [物理] vector: 风～ wind vector ‖ ～比 vector ratio ‖ ～分析 vector analysis
【矢志】shǐzhì〈动〉〈书〉pledge one's devotion: ～于医学 pledge to devote one's life to medicine
【矢志不移】shǐzhì-bùyí = 矢志不渝 shǐzhì-bùyú
【矢志不渝】shǐzhì-bùyú〈成〉be unswerving: ～的共产主义者 committed Communist

豕 shǐ〈名〉〈书〉swine
【豕突狼奔】shǐtū-lángbēn = 狼奔豕突 lángbēn-shǐtū

使 shǐ

A〈动〉**1**(派遣) send: ～人去打听消息 send sb. to make enquiries ▸～唤, 鬼～神差, 支～ **2**(让) cause: ～人落泪 make sb. cry ‖ 这只会～事情更糟。This will only make things worse. **3**(用) use: 这支笔很好～。This pen writes well. ▸～劲 **4**(出使) be sent abroad on official mission: ▸出～
B〈连〉〈书〉supposing: ▸假～
C〈名〉envoy: ▸～馆, 大～, 特～
【使绊儿】shǐbànr〈动〉**1**(使摔跤) trip sb. up in wrestling **2**〈喻〉(暗算) injure sb. by underhand means: 背后给人～ stab sb. in the back
【使绊子】shǐ bànzi = 使绊儿 shǐbànr
【使不得】shǐbude〈动〉**1**(不能使用) be unusable: 这只手表～了。The watch can't be used any more. **2**(不行) be unworkable: 明天要考试，今晚看电影可～。There's an exam tomorrow, so we really can't go to the film tonight.
【使臣】shǐchén〈名〉〈旧〉diplomatic

envoy

【使出】shǐchū〈动〉 exert: ～浑身解数 do all that one is capable of ‖ ～最后一点力气 exert one's last bit of strength

【使得】shǐde〈动〉 **1**（可以使用） be usable: 这台电脑～使不得? Does this computer work all right? **2**（可以） be feasible: 你不去如何～? How can it be feasible if you don't go? ‖ 我拟的计划～吗? Is my plan workable? **3**（让） render: ～家喻户晓 make known to everyone

【使馆】shǐguǎn〈名〉 diplomatic mission: ～工作人员 embassy personnel ►大～, 公～

【使馆区】shǐguǎnqū〈名〉 diplomatic quarters

【使坏】shǐhuài〈动〉〈口〉 play dirty: 这孩子又～了。 The child was up to mischief again.

【使唤】shǐhuan〈动〉 **1**（支使） order about: 听人～ be at sb.'s beck and call ‖ 爱～人 be bossy **2**〈口〉（使用） use: 新工具～起来方便吗? Are the new tools easy to handle?

【使假】shǐjiǎ〈动〉 practise fraudulence

【使节】shǐjié〈名〉 diplomatic envoy: 接待外国友好～ receive a goodwill envoy of a foreign country ‖ 各国驻华～ diplomatic envoys to China

【使劲】shǐjìn〈动〉 exert all one's strength: ～蹬车 pedal a bicycle furiously ‖ ～喊 shout at the top of one's voice ‖ ～跑 run as quickly as one can ‖ 再使把劲 put in more effort

【使君子】shǐjūnzǐ〈名〉［中药］ fruit of Rangoon creeper

【使领馆】shǐlǐngguǎn〈名〉 embassies and consulates

【使命】shǐmìng〈名〉 mission: 身负特别～ on a special mission ‖ 外交～ diplomatic mission

【使命感】shǐmìnggǎn〈名〉 calling

【使女】shǐnǚ〈名〉〈旧〉 housemaid

【使气】shǐqì〈动〉 lose one's temper: 别拿孩子～。 Don't vent your anger on the child.

【使然】shǐrán〈动〉 make it so

【使团】shǐtuán〈名〉 diplomatic corps: ～团长 dean of the diplomatic corps

【使性子】shǐ xìngzi〈动〉 get angry: 无缘无故～ lose one's temper for no reason

【使眼色】shǐ yǎnsè〈动〉 wink: 给同伴～ wink at one's companion

【使役】shǐyì〈动〉 work: ～牲口不能过度。 Don't overwork draught animals.

【使用】shǐyòng〈动〉 use: ～暴力 resort to violence ‖ ～假币 pass counterfeit money ‖ ～武力 use force ‖ 不再～ be no longer in use ‖ 广泛～ be in general use ‖ 这本字典～起来很方便。 This dictionary is very easy to use.

【使用价值】shǐyòng jiàzhí〈名〉［经济］ use value

【使用率】shǐyònglǜ〈名〉 rate of utilization

【使用年限】shǐyòng niánxiàn〈名〉 service life

【使用期】shǐyòngqī〈名〉 term of service

【使用权】shǐyòngquán〈名〉 right of use: 土地～ land use rights

【使用手册】shǐyòng shǒucè〈名〉 user's manual

【使用说明书】shǐyòng shuōmíngshū〈名〉 instructions for use

【使者】shǐzhě〈名〉 envoy: 派遣～ dispatch an envoy ‖ 友好～ messenger of friendship

始 shǐ

A〈名〉 beginning, start: 有～就该有终。 If you start something, you should finish it. ►～末, 自～至终 **B**〈动〉 begin, start: 不知～于何时 not know exactly when this came into being ►周而复～ **C**〈副〉 only then: 坚持学习，～能不断进步。 Steady progress can only be achieved through persistent study.

【始创】shǐchuàng〈动〉 initiate: ～阶段 initial stage

【始发港】shǐfāgǎng〈名〉 port of departure

【始发期】shǐfāqī〈名〉 initial phase: 疾病的～ initial phase of a disease

【始发站】shǐfāzhàn〈名〉 departure station

【始料不及】shǐliào-bùjí〈成〉 unforeseen: ～的结果 unexpected results

【始料所及】shǐliào-suǒjí〈成〉 as expected: 非～ beyond one's expectations

【始乱终弃】shǐluàn-zhōngqì〈成〉 seduce a woman and then abandon her

【始末】shǐmò〈名〉 beginning and end: 事情的～ whole story ‖ 请详述事故的～。 Please tell us in detail everything about the accident.

【始新世】Shǐxīnshì〈名〉［地质］ Eocene Epoch

【始业】shǐyè〈动〉 begin a school year

【始终】shǐzhōng **A**〈名〉 entire process: 政策必须得贯彻～。 The policy must be fully implemented from start to finish. **B**〈副〉 from beginning to end: 会谈～在友好的气氛中进行。 The talks were carried out in a friendly manner throughout. ‖ 我将～支持你。 I'll back you all the way.

【始终不渝】shǐzhōng-bùyú〈成〉 steadfast: 对共产主义～ be committed to communism ‖ 他们的友谊～。 Their friendship was consistent.

【始祖】shǐzǔ〈名〉 **1**（祖先） earliest ancestor: 人类的～ earliest ancestor of mankind **2**（创始人） founder

【始祖鸟】shǐzǔniǎo〈名〉 archaeopteryx

【始作俑者】shǐzuòyǒngzhě〈成〉 creator of a bad precedent

驶（駛） shǐ

〈动〉 **1**（快跑） go fast: 救护车飞速～往医院。 The ambulance sped to the hospital. ‖ 一辆火车呼啸～过。 An express train hurtled past. ►疾～ **2**（开动） move: 迎面～来的一辆汽车 an oncoming car ‖ 船～进了港口。 The ship sailed into the port. ‖ 列车～出车站。 The train pulled out of the station. ►驾～, 行～

屎 shǐ

〈名〉 **1**（排泄物） excrement: 拉～ empty one's bowels ‖ ～尿 stools and urine ‖ 鸡～ chicken droppings ‖ 牛～ cow dung **2**（分泌物） secretion: ►耳～, 眼～

【屎壳郎】shǐkelàng〈名〉〈方〉 dung beetle

【屎坑】shǐkēng〈名〉 dung pit

【屎盆子】shǐpénzi〈名〉〈方〉 evildoing: 别把～往我身上扣。 Don't try to shift the blame onto me.

shì

士 shì

〈名〉 **1**〈古〉（未婚男子） bachelor: ►～女 **2**〈古〉（指阶层） social stratum between senior officials (大夫) and the common people (庶民) **3**（书生） scholar: ～农工商 scholars, peasants, workers and business people ►寒～, 名～ **4**（表美称） person: ►烈～, 有识之～, 壮～ **5**（技术人员） skilled person: ►护～, 院～, 助产～ **6**（军人） soldier: ►～兵, ～气, 将～ **7**（指军衔） non-commissioned officer: ►上～, 下～, 中～ **8**（指象棋） guard

【士别三日，刮目相看】shì bié sān rì, guā mù xiāng kàn〈成〉 after three days of absence, the scholar has to be looked at with new eyes

【士兵】shìbīng〈名〉 soldier: 出口处均由～把守。 All the exits were guarded by soldiers.

【士大夫】shìdàfū〈名〉〈旧〉 scholar-officials

【士多店】shìduōdiàn〈名〉〈方〉 grocery store

【士官】shìguān〈名〉 warrant officer: ～的军衔分为三等六级。 Warrant officers are classified into three grades and six classes.

【士可杀，不可辱】shì kě shā, bù kě rǔ〈成〉 a scholar would rather die than be humiliated

【士女】shìnǚ〈名〉 **1**〈旧〉（男女） young men and women **2** = 仕女 shìnǚ 2

【士气】shìqì〈名〉 morale: 保持旺盛的～ maintain a high morale ‖ 鼓舞～ boost sb.'s morale ‖ ～低落 sagging morale

【士人】shìrén〈名〉〈旧〉 scholar

【士绅】shìshēn〈名〉〈旧〉 gentry

【士为知己者死】shì wèi zhījǐzhě sǐ〈成〉 a true gentleman dies for a bosom friend

【士卒】shìzú〈名〉〈旧〉 soldiers: ►身先～

【士族】shìzú〈名〉〈旧〉 influential and privileged family of scholar-officials

氏 shì

〈名〉 **1**（姓氏） surname: 王～兄弟 Wang brothers **2**（对妇女的称呼） née: 张王～ Mrs Zhang, née Wang **3**〈书〉（指亲属） one's kinsfolk: 舅～ maternal uncle ►zhī

【氏族】shìzú〈名〉 clan: 父系/母系～ patrilineal/matrilineal clan

【氏族公社】shìzú gōngshè〈名〉 clan community

示 shì

〈动〉 show: 如表1所～ as indicated in table 1 ‖ 盼速～知。 I hope you will notify me soon. ►～范, 启～, 请～, 展～

【示爱】shì'ài〈动〉 show one's love: 以山歌～ sing folk songs as an expression of love

【示波】shìbō〈名〉［电气］ oscillography

【示波器】shìbōqì〈名〉 oscilloscope

【示波仪】shìbōyí〈名〉 oscillograph

【示范】shìfàn〈动〉 demonstrate: ～计算机的操作 demonstrate how the computer works ‖ 做～ give a demonstration

【示范店】shìfàndiàn〈名〉 exemplary shop [one that does not sell counterfeit goods, and which is honest and reliable]

【示范田】shìfàntián〈名〉 model field

【示警】shìjǐng〈动〉 warn: 鸣锣～ give a warning by beating a gong ‖ 鸣枪～ fire a warning shot

【示例】shìlì〈动〉 give a demonstration

【示人】shìrén〈动〉 show sth. to others: 此物珍藏多年，从不轻易～。 I have kept this for many years but I rarely show it to others.

【示弱】shìruò〈动〉 display weakness: 不甘～ be unwilling to be outdone

【示威】shìwēi〈动〉**1**（显示力量） display one's prowess **2**（指集体行动） hold a demonstration: 举行～ stage a demonstration (against sth./sb.) ‖ ～群众 demonstrators ‖ 反战～ demonstrate against war

【示威游行】shìwēi yóuxíng〈动〉 demonstration: 举行～ stage a demonstration ‖ 反战～ anti-war rally

【示威者】shìwēizhě〈名〉demonstrator

【示意】shìyì〈动〉 signal: ～某人出去 motion to sb. to go out ‖ 以目～ wink at sb. ‖ 他招手～我坐在他旁边。 He beckoned to me to sit beside him.

【示意图】shìyìtú〈名〉sketch map

【示众】shìzhòng〈动〉exhibit to the public: 游街～ parade sb. through the streets

【示踪】shìzōng〈名〉［物理］ tracing: ～元素 tracer element

世 shì〈名〉**1**（代） generation: 第十～后裔 10th generation descendants ▸～代 **2**（一代又一代） from generation to generation: ～爵 hereditary rank of nobility ▸～仇, ～传, ～袭 **3**（表尊称） [a form of address used among old family friends]: ～伯 uncle **4**（一生） life: 一～ all one's life ‖ 在～期间 during one's life time ▸今～, 来～, 永～ **5**（时代） age: 当今之～ at present ‖ 盛～ flourishing era ▸近～ **6**（世界） world: 不久于人～ will die soon ‖ ～上没有十全十美的事。 There is no rose without a thorn. ▸～间, 举～闻名, 问～ **7**［地质］ epoch: ▸全新～

【世弊】shìbì〈名〉〈书〉 social evils

【世变】shìbiàn〈名〉〈书〉 vicissitudes: ～人亦变。 Society has changed and so have the people.

【世博会】Shìbóhuì〈简称〉= 世界博览会

【世仇】shìchóu〈名〉 **1**（冤仇） feud: 部落/家族～ tribal/family feud **2**（指人或家族） hereditary enemy

【世传】shìchuán〈动〉 hand down through generations: ～秘方 secret recipe handed down from generation to generation

【世代】shìdài〈名〉 **1**（指年代） long period of time **2**（好几辈） generations: ～相传 pass on from generation to generation ‖ ～书香门第 generations of scholar families

【世代交替】shìdài jiāotì〈名〉［生物］ alternation of generations

【世道】shìdào〈名〉ways of the world

【世风】shìfēng〈名〉〈书〉 public morals and mores

【世风日下】shìfēng-rìxià〈成〉 public morals are declining day by day

【世故】shìgù〈名〉ways of the world: 人情～ worldly wisdom

【世故】shìgu〈形〉 worldly-wise: 想不到他年纪轻轻的却这么～。 I never realized that a man so young could be so sophisticated.

【世纪】shìjì ▸**p. 618**〈名〉 century: 跨～ span centuries ‖ 迎接新～ usher in a new century ‖ ～之交 at the turn of the century ‖ 20～40年代 1940's ‖ 本～最杰出的艺术家 foremost artist of this century

【世纪末】shìjìmò〈名〉**1**〈本〉 end of a century **2**〈喻〉 declining stage of a society

【世家】shìjiā〈名〉**1**（旺族） family holding high office for generations: 名门～ highly respectable family **2**（指有某种专长） family in which a special skill has been handed down from generation to generation: 出身于演员～ come from a family with a long line of actors ‖ 中医～ family skilled in traditional Chinese medicine

【世间】shìjiān〈名〉 world: ～少有 rarely seen

【世交】shìjiāo〈名〉 **1**（指人或家族） old family friends: 两家是～。 The two families are old friends. **2**（指友谊） long-standing friendship between families

【世界】shìjiè〈名〉 **1**（一切事物） world: 创造新～ create a new world ‖ ～闻名 be world-famous ‖ ～头号强国 dominant world power **2**［佛教］ universe: ▸大千～ **3**（全球） all parts of the world: 他们的产品经销～各地。 Their products are sold worldwide. **4**（风气） mores of the world **5**（领域） realm: 儿童～ world of children ‖ 科学～ scientific realms

【世界版权公约】Shìjiè Bǎnquán Gōngyuē〈名〉 Universal Copyright Convention [1952]

【世界杯】Shìjièbēi〈名〉 World Cup: 国际足联～ FIFA World Cup

【世界波】shìjièbō〈名〉［足球］ world ball: 一脚势大力沉的～，攻破了对方的球门。 A spectacular shot went right into the opponent's goal.

【世界博览会】Shìjiè Bólǎnhuì〈名〉 World Expo

【世界产业工人联盟】Shìjiè Chǎnyègōngrén Liánméng〈名〉 Industrial Workers of the World (IWW)

【世界大学生运动会】Shìjiè Dàxuéshēng Yùndònghuì〈名〉Universiade

【世界大战】shìjiè dàzhàn〈名〉world war: 第一/二次～ First/Second World War, World War I/II

【世界工会联合会】Shìjiè Gōnghuì Liánhéhuì〈名〉World Federation of Trade Unions

【世界观】shìjièguān〈名〉world view: ～、人生观和价值观 outlooks on the world, life and values

【世界冠军】 shìjiè guànjūn〈名〉 world champion

【世界纪录】shìjiè jìlù〈名〉 world record: 打破～ break a world record ‖ ～保持者 world record holder

【世界锦标赛】shìjiè jǐnbiāosài〈名〉［体育］World Championships

【世界劳工联合会】Shìjiè Láogōng Liánhéhuì〈名〉World Confederation of Labour (WCL)

【世界粮食计划署】Shìjiè Liángshi Jìhuàshǔ〈名〉World Food Programme (WFP)

【世界贸易组织】Shìjiè Màoyì Zǔzhī〈名〉 World Trade Organization (WTO)

【世界气象组织】Shìjiè Qìxiàng Zǔzhī〈名〉World Meteorological Organization (WMO)

【世界人权宣言】Shìjiè Rénquán Xuānyán〈名〉 Universal Declaration of Human Rights [1948]

【世界时】shìjièshí〈名〉［天文］ universal time

【世界市场】shìjiè shìchǎng〈名〉 global market: 打入～ break into the world market

【世界水平】shìjiè shuǐpíng〈名〉 world standard

【世界卫生组织】Shìjiè Wèishēng Zǔzhī〈名〉World Health Organization (WHO)

【世界屋脊】shìjiè wūjǐ〈名〉 Qinghai-Tibet Plateau

【世界舞台】shìjiè wǔtái〈名〉world arena

【世界银行】Shìjiè Yínháng〈名〉 World Bank

【世界语】Shìjièyǔ ▸**p. 918**〈名〉 Esperanto

【世界知识产权组织】Shìjiè Zhīshi Chǎnquán Zǔzhī〈名〉 World Intellectual Property Organization (WIPO)

【世锦赛】shìjǐnsài〈简称〉= 世界锦标赛

【世局】shìjú〈名〉 international situation

【世贸组织】Shìmào Zǔzhī〈简称〉= 世界贸易组织

【世面】shìmiàn〈名〉 life: 见过～ have experienced life

【世情】shìqíng〈名〉 ways of the world: 不懂～ be unsophisticated

【世人】shìrén〈名〉 common people: 仍在～记忆中 still within living memory ‖ 为～所知 be in the public eye ‖ 在～眼中 in the eyes of the world

【世上】shìshàng〈名〉on earth

【世上没有不透风的墙】shìshàng méiyǒu bù tòufēng de qiáng〈俗〉 all walls have ears

【世上无难事，只怕有心人】shìshàng wú nánshì, zhǐ pà yǒuxīnrén〈俗〉 where there is a will, there is a way

【世事】shìshì〈名〉 worldly affairs: 饱经～ have experienced many vicissitudes of life ‖ ～沧桑 the world is changing all the time

【世世代代】shìshì-dàidài〈副〉 from generation to generation

【世俗】shìsú〈名〉 **1**（流俗） social conventions: ～之见 common views ‖ ～之人 man of the world **2**［宗教］ anything secular/worldly

【世态】shìtài〈名〉 ways of the world: ～人情 ways of the world

【世态炎凉】shìtài-yánliáng〈成〉fickleness of human relationships

【世外桃源】shìwài-táoyuán〈成〉 Land of Peach Blossom [a haven of peace]

【世袭】shìxí〈动〉 be hereditary: ～爵位 hereditary title ‖ ～领地 free hold estate ‖ ～权力 hereditary right

【世袭制】shìxízhì〈名〉 hereditary system

【世系】shìxì〈名〉 pedigree

【世兄】shìxiōng〈名〉〈旧〉 young sir

【世医】shìyī〈名〉〈书〉 doctor of traditional Chinese medicine whose family has practised the trade for generations

【世族】shìzú〈名〉〈书〉 influential family going back generations

仕 shì〈动〉fill official office: ▸～途, 出～

【仕宦】shìhuàn〈动〉〈书〉 be in government service: ～之家 official family ‖ ～子弟 sons of an official family

【仕进】shìjìn〈动〉〈书〉 pursue an official career: 不求～ give up the thought of pursuing an official career

【仕女】shìnǚ〈名〉 **1**（宫女） maid in an imperial palace **2**（指中国画） traditional Chinese painting of beautiful women

【仕女图】shìnǚtú〈名〉 painting of beautiful women

【仕途】shìtú〈名〉〈书〉 official career: ～沉浮 ups and downs of an official career ‖ ～捷径 short cut to officialdom

市 shì

A〈名〉 **1** （市场） market: 金～ gold market ▸～场, 门庭若～, 夜～ **2**（行情） market price: ▸行～ **3**（城市） city: ▸～民, ～容, 城～ **4**（行政区划单位） municipality: 北京～ Beijing Municipality ▸～长, ～政 **5**（市制） the traditional Chinese system of weights and measures: ▸～尺, ～斤, ～亩

B〈动〉〈书〉 trade: ～马 deal in horses ‖

S

～惠 curry favour with sb.

【市场】shìchǎng〈名〉marketplace: 国内外～ domestic and foreign markets ‖ 开辟～ open up a market ‖ 垄断～ corner the market ‖ 投放～ put on the market ‖ 占领～ capture a market ‖ 农贸～ market selling farm produce ‖ 人才～ talent market ‖ ～萧条/繁荣。The market is depressed/booming. ▸跳蚤～

【市场部】shìchǎngbù〈名〉marketing department

【市场调查】shìchǎng diàochá〈名〉market investigation

【市场动态】shìchǎng dòngtài〈名〉market trend

【市场份额】shìchǎng fèn'é〈名〉market share: 增加～ increase one's market share

【市场管理】shìchǎng guǎnlǐ〈名〉market control

【市场机制】shìchǎng jīzhì〈名〉market mechanism

【市场价格】shìchǎng jiàgé〈名〉market rate

【市场经济】shìchǎng jīngjì〈名〉market economy

【市场调节】shìchǎng tiáojié〈名〉market readjustment: ～价 market-regulated price

【市场销售】shìchǎng xiāoshòu〈名〉marketing: ～管理 marketing management

【市场学】shìchǎngxué〈名〉marketing

【市场占有率】shìchǎng zhànyǒulǜ〈名〉market share

【市场秩序】shìchǎng zhìxù〈名〉market order

【市场准入】shìchǎng zhǔnrù〈名〉market access

【市秤】shìchèng〈名〉traditional Chinese scale of weights

【市尺】shìchǐ〈量〉*chi* [a traditional unit of length, equivalent to 0.333 metre or 1.094 feet]

【市花】shìhuā〈名〉city flower: 西安市的～是石榴花。Xi'an's city flower is the pomegranate flower.

【市话】shìhuà〈简称〉= 市内电话

【市徽】shìhuī〈名〉city emblem

【市级】shìjí〈名〉municipal level: ～以上干部 officials above the municipal level

【市集】shìjí〈名〉1▸（集市）marketplace 2▸（小镇）small town

【市际】shìjì〈形〉intercity: ～交通 intercity traffic

【市价】shìjià〈名〉market price: 高于/低于～ above/below the market price ‖ 按～出售 sell at market price

【市郊】shìjiāo〈名〉suburb: 住在～ live on the outskirts of a town ‖ 在～ in the suburbs (of)

【市斤】shìjīn ▸**p. 978**〈量〉*jin* [a traditional unit of weight, equivalent to 0.5 kilogram or 1.102 pounds]

【市井】shìjǐng〈名〉〈旧〉marketplace: ～小人 philistine

【市净率】shìjìnglǜ〈名〉［金融］price-to-book ratio (P/B)

【市侩】shìkuài〈名〉sordid merchant: ～习气 philistinism ‖ ～哲学 philistinism

【市况】shìkuàng〈名〉〈书〉business situation: 水果～趋好。The fresh fruit trade is getting better.

【市里】shìlǐ〈量〉*li* [a traditional unit of length, equivalent to 0.5 kilometre or 0.311 mile]

【市立】shìlì〈形〉municipal: ～学校/医院 municipal school/hospital

【市面】shìmiàn〈名〉1▸（市场）market: 这种东西在～上买不到。We can't get this on the market. 2▸（经济）market conditions: ～繁荣。Trade is flourishing. ‖ ～萧条。Business is slack.

【市民】shìmín〈名〉city residents

【市亩】shìmǔ〈量〉*mu* [a traditional unit of area, equivalent to 6.667 ares or 0.165 acre]

【市内电话】shìnèi diànhuà〈名〉local phone call

【市内交通】shìnèi jiāotōng〈名〉urban transport

【市容】shìróng〈名〉appearance of a city: 保持～整洁 keep the city clean and tidy ‖ 浏览～ go on a sightseeing tour round the city

【市区】shìqū〈名〉city proper

【市委】shìwěi〈名〉municipal communist party committee: ～机关 municipal communist party organizations

【市盈率】shìyínglǜ〈名〉［金融］price-earning ratio

【市长】shìzhǎng〈名〉mayor: 竞选～ run for mayor ‖ 宣誓就任～ swear in as mayor

【市镇】shìzhèn〈名〉town

【市政】shìzhèng〈名〉municipal administration: ～当局 municipal authorities

【市政工程】shìzhèng gōngchéng〈名〉municipal engineering: ～局 bureau of public works

【市政建设】shìzhèng jiànshè〈名〉public works construction

【市政府】shìzhèngfǔ〈名〉municipal government

【市值】shìzhí〈名〉market value

【市制】shìzhì〈名〉traditional Chinese system of weights and measures [with *chi* (市尺) as its basic unit of length, *jin* (市斤) as its basic unit of weight, and *sheng* (市升) as its basic unit of capacity]

【市中心】shìzhōngxīn〈名〉city centre〈英〉; downtown〈美〉

式 shì

式 shì〈名〉1▸（标准）standards: ▸程～, 格～ 2▸（样式）type: ▸老～, 形～, 中～ 3▸（仪式）ceremony: ▸闭幕～, 仪～, 阅兵～ 4▸（符号组）formula: ▸方程～ 5▸［语言］mood: 命令～ imperative ‖ 虚拟～ subjunctive

【式微】shìwēi〈形〉〈书〉declining

【式样】shìyàng〈名〉model: 设计新～ design a new model ‖ 传统/流行～ prevailing fashion ‖ 最新～ latest style

【式子】shìzi〈名〉1▸（姿势）posture 2▸（符号组）formula

似 shì

▸sì

【似的】shìde〈助〉be like: 白得像雪～ as white as snow ‖ 看上去很伤心～ seem to be very sad ‖ 像个孩子～可爱 as lovable as a child

事 shì

A〈名〉1▸（事情）thing: 这～不容易办。This is no easy job. ‖ 大家～大家管。Public affairs are everybody's affairs. ‖ 跟你说件～。I have something to tell you. ‖ 今日～今日毕。Never put off till tomorrow what can be done today. ‖ 那是另一回～。That's another matter. ‖ 什么～? What's up? ▸公～, 国～, 好人好～ 2▸（工作）work: 谋个～儿 look for a job ‖ 做～ do work ▸差～ 3▸（事故）trouble: 惹～ make trouble ‖ 平安无～。All is well. ▸出～ 4▸（责任）responsibility: 靠交罚金了～ get off with a fine ‖ 不关我的～。It has nothing to do with me.

B〈动〉〈书〉1▸（侍奉）serve: ～父母 wait upon one's parents 2▸（从事）be engaged in: 不～生产 lead an idle life ‖ 大～宣传 launch a vigorous propaganda campaign ▸无所～～

【事半功倍】shìbàn-gōngbèi〈成〉get twice the result with half the effort

【事倍功半】shìbèi-gōngbàn〈成〉labour hard to little avail

【事必躬亲】shìbìgōngqīn〈成〉attend to everything oneself

【事变】shìbiàn〈名〉1▸（政治、军事事件）incident: 七七～ July 7th incident (of 1937) 2▸（政治、军事变化）emergency: 突发～ unexpected emergencies 3▸（事物变化）events

【事不关己，高高挂起】shì bù guān jǐ, gāogāo guàqǐ〈俗〉adopt a nonchalant attitude towards things of no personal interest

【事不过三】shìbùguòsān〈成〉one shouldn't make the same mistake more than three times

【事不宜迟】shìbùyíchí〈成〉there's no time to be lost

【事出有因】shìchū-yǒuyīn〈成〉everything has a wherefore

【事到临头】shìdàolíntóu〈成〉when things come to a head

【事典】shìdiǎn〈名〉1▸（书）（指类书）encyclopedia 2▸（指工具书）reference book

【事端】shìduān〈名〉incident: 挑起～ stir up troubles ‖ 制造～ create disturbances

【事非经过不知难】shì fēi jīngguò bù zhī nán〈俗〉you never know how hard a task is until you have done it yourself

【事故】shìgù〈名〉accident: 交通～ traffic accidents ‖ 遭遇意外～ meet with an accident

【事故多发区】shìgù duōfāqū〈名〉black spot

【事故责任】shìgù zérèn〈名〉liability for an accident

【事关重大】shìguānzhòngdà〈成〉it's most important

【事过境迁】shìguò-jìngqiān〈成〉events have passed and times have changed

【事后】shìhòu〈名〉afterwards: ～调查 subsequent investigation ‖ ～的想法 afterthought

【事后诸葛亮】shìhòu Zhūgě Liàng〈成〉second guesser

【事机】shìjī〈名〉1▸（秘密）secret 2▸（时机）opportunity

【事迹】shìjì〈名〉deed: 歌颂某人的～ praise sb.'s good deeds ‖ 英雄～ heroic deeds ‖ 先进～报告会 public lectures on exemplary deeds

【事假】shìjià〈名〉leave of absence: 请几天～ ask for a few days' leave

【事件】shìjiàn〈名〉incident: 遭遇突发～ be overtaken by unforeseen events ‖ 历史/政治～ historical/political event

【事理】shìlǐ〈名〉reason: 不合～ be unreasonable ‖ 不明～ lack common sense

【事例】shìlì〈名〉example: 列举～ give an example

【事略】shìlüè〈名〉〈书〉biographical sketch

【事前】shìqián〈名〉before the event: ～你应该向我说一声。You should have told me about it beforehand. ‖ ～我一无所知。Before it happened I knew nothing about it.

【事情】shìqing〈名〉1▸（事务）affair: 严肃的～ serious matter ‖ ～的经过是这样的。This is what happened. ‖ ～做了就做了。What's done is done. ‖ 她有许多～

S

要办。 She has many things to attend to. **2**（工作） job: 假期我想找个～做。 I want to find work for the vacation. **3**（差错） mistake: 他工作中从来没有出过什么～。 He has never made a mistake in his work.

【事实】shìshí〈名〉 fact: 讲出～ tell the truth ‖ ～婚姻 de facto union ‖ 歪曲～ distort the facts ‖ 没有～依据 have no factual basis ‖ ～恰恰相反。 The opposite is true. ‖ 这是～。 It's the truth.

【事实上】shìshíshàng〈副〉 actually: 名义上和～ both in name and in reality ‖ ～并非如此 In fact it's not like that at all.

【事实胜于雄辩】shìshí shèngyú xióngbiàn〈成〉 facts speak louder than words

【事事】shìshì **A**〈名〉 everything: ～顾全大局 take the public interests into account in whatever one does **B**〈动〉〈书〉 be engaged: ▸无所～

【事态】shìtài〈名〉 state of affairs: 控制～的发展 control the development of the situation ‖ ～在恶化。 The situation is deteriorating.

【事体】shìtǐ〈名〉〈方〉 **1**（差错） accident **2**（工作） work, job

【事无巨细】shìwú-jùxì〈成〉 all matters, big or small: ～, 他都很认真。 He sets his mind to everything he does. ‖ 我可不能～地都揽下来。 I can't take charge of everything.

【事务】shìwù〈名〉 **1**（事情） work: ～性工作 routine work ‖ 国际～ international affairs ‖ 日常～ day-to-day routine ‖ 行政～ administration **2**（总务） general affairs: ▸～员

【事务所】shìwùsuǒ〈名〉 office: 纽约～ New York office

【事务员】shìwùyuán ▸**p. 966**〈名〉 office clerk

【事务主义】shìwù zhǔyì〈名〉 pettiness: ～者 person bogged down in routine matters

【事物】shìwù〈名〉 thing: 客观～ objective reality

【事先】shìxiān〈名〉 beforehand: ～警告 forewarn ‖ ～通知 give advance notice ‖ 你本该～告诉我的。 You ought to have told me in advance.

【事项】shìxiàng〈名〉matter: 保密～ security regulations ‖ 有关～ relevant issues ‖ 注意～ points for attention

【事业】shìyè〈名〉 **1**（工作） undertaking: 开创一项～ launch a career ‖ 献身于～ dedicate oneself to a cause ‖ ～有成 get ahead in one's career ‖ 文化教育～ cultural and educational undertakings **2**（非企业） institution: 公用～ public utilities ‖ 集体福利～ collective welfare services

【事业单位】shìyè dānwèi〈名〉 independent non-profit institution

【事业费】shìyè fèi〈名〉 operating expense

【事业心】shìyèxīn〈名〉 dedication to one's work: ～强 devote oneself to one's work

【事宜】shìyí〈名〉〈书〉 relevant matters

【事由】shìyóu〈名〉 **1**（原委） particulars of a matter: 问清～ gain a clear idea of the whys and wherefores of a matter **2**（主要内容） main content **3**（理由） excuse: 找个～离开 find an excuse to leave

【事与愿违】shìyǔyuànwéi〈成〉 fail to obtain the desired result: 我们的生活中有不少～的情况。 Many events in our lives do not go according to plan.

【事在人为】shìzàirénwéi〈成〉 man is the determining factor

【事主】shìzhǔ〈名〉 victim of a crime: ～要求索赔损失。 The injured party asked for compensation for his loss.

势（勢） shì

〈名〉 **1**（势力） power: ▸权～, 失～, 仗～欺人 **2**（气势） momentum: 以排山倒海之～ with the momentum of an avalanche ▸～如破竹, 气～, 声～ **3**（形貌） outward appearance of an object: 山～ mountain range ▸地～ **4**（姿态） posture: ▸架～, 装腔作～, 姿～ **5**（情势） situation: ▸局～, 时～, 形～ **6**（雄性生殖器） male genitals: ▸去～

【势必】shìbì〈副〉 inevitably: 敌人～要失败。 The enemy is bound to fail. ‖ 他路过这里时～要来拜访你。 He will certainly come to visit you when he passes by.

【势不可当】shìbùkědāng〈成〉overwhelming

【势不可挡】shìbùkědǎng = 势不可当 shìbùkědāng

【势不两立】shìbùliǎnglì〈成〉 be irreconcilable

【势单力薄】shìdān-lìbó〈成〉 not have enough manpower or resources

【势均力敌】shìjūn-lìdí〈成〉 be equally matched: ～的比赛 tight match ‖ ～的对手 close rival

【势力】shìlì〈名〉 force: 很有～ have great influence

【势力范围】shìlì fànwéi〈名〉 sphere of influence: ～之内 within sb.'s sphere of influence

【势利】shìli〈形〉 snobbish: 头号～ prime snob

【势利眼】shìliyǎn **A**〈形〉 snobbish **B**〈名〉 snob

【势能】shìnéng〈名〉［物理］ potential energy

【势如累卵】shìrúlěiluǎn〈成〉 in a precarious position

【势如燎原】shìrúliáoyuán〈成〉 spreading like wildfire

【势如破竹】shìrúpòzhú〈成〉 with crushing force

【势态】shìtài〈名〉 situation

【势头】shìtóu〈名〉 **1**（形势） momentum: 保持强劲的～ maintain a strong momentum ‖ 物价上涨的～ upward tendency in prices **2**〈口〉（情势） look of things: 见～不对 find the situation unfavourable to oneself

【势焰】shìyàn〈名〉〈贬〉 influence and power: ～万丈 aggressively powerful ‖ ～熏天 earth-shattering power

【势在必行】shìzàibìxíng〈成〉 imperative under the circumstances: 改革～。 The reform must be enforced.

侍 shì

〈动〉 serve: ▸服～

【侍从】shìcóng〈名〉 attendant: ～副官 aide-de-camp

【侍奉】shìfèng〈动〉 tend to: ～父母 look after one's parents

【侍候】shìhòu〈动〉 serve: ～病人 look after a patient ‖ ～老人 look after one's aged parents ‖ 把他～得很周到 take good care of him

【侍郎】shìláng〈名〉［历史］ vice-president of one of the Six Boards (六部) [in Ming and Qing dynasties]

【侍立】shìlì〈动〉 stand in attendance: ～两旁 stand on both sides in attendance

【侍弄】shìnòng〈动〉 **1**（养） tend with care: ～一盆金鱼 take care of a bowl of gold fish ‖ ～庄稼 attend to one's crops **2**（修理） repair: ～收音机 fix a radio

【侍女】shìnǚ〈名〉 maid

【侍卫】shìwèi **A**〈动〉 guard **B**〈名〉 bodyguard

【侍养】shìyǎng〈动〉 attend to

【侍者】shìzhě〈名〉〈书〉 attendant

饰（飾） shì

A〈动〉 **1**（装饰） adorn: 油～门窗 paint doors and windows ▸修～, 装～ **2**（掩饰） cover up: ▸文过～非, 掩～ **3**（扮演） play the role of: 在剧中～主角 play the major role in the opera ▸～演 **4**（润饰） polish: ▸润～, 藻～
B〈名〉 decorations: 窗～ window decorations ▸服～, 首～

【饰板】shìbǎn〈名〉 plaque

【饰词】shìcí〈名〉〈书〉 pretext: ～诬告 invent a story and make a false accusation

【饰品】shìpǐn〈名〉 ornaments: 黄金/钻石～ gold/diamond jewels

【饰物】shìwù〈名〉 **1**（首饰） jewellery **2**（装饰品） decorations: 华丽的～ gay decorations ‖ 衣服上的～ adornments on clothes

【饰演】shìyǎn〈动〉 play: ～坏蛋 play a villain

【饰针】shìzhēn〈名〉 stickpin

试（試） shì

〈动〉 **1**（尝试） try: ～衣服 try on a dress ‖ ～一～ have a try ‖ 你要～一～吗? Do you want to give it a crack? ‖ 让我～一下。 Let me have a go. ▸～点, ～验, ～用 **2**（考查） test: ▸～题, 复～, 口～, 应～

【试办】shìbàn〈动〉 run on a trial basis: ～工厂 run a pilot plant

【试杯】shìbēi〈名〉 test glass

【试笔】shìbǐ〈动〉 try one's hand at writing or painting: ～之作 one's first attempt at writing/painting

【试表】shìbiǎo〈动〉 take sb.'s temperature: 给病人～ take the patient's temperature

【试播】shìbō〈动〉 pilot

【试产】shìchǎn〈动〉 trial-manufacture

【试场】shìchǎng〈名〉〈旧〉 examination hall

【试车】shìchē〈动〉 test-drive: 我去试一下新车。 I'm going to try out the new car.

【试穿】shìchuān〈动〉 try on: 这件外套你最好～一下再买。 You'd better try on the coat before you buy it.

【试点】shìdiǎn **A**〈动〉 launch a pilot project: 搞～ conduct experiments ‖ ～计划 pilot project ‖ ～项目 pilot programme **B**〈名〉 experimental unit: ～学校 experimental school

【试电笔】shìdiànbǐ〈名〉［电气］ test pencil

【试读】shìdú〈动〉 be admitted on a probational basis: 允许进入学校～ be admitted to school on a probational basis

【试读生】shìdúshēng〈名〉 student on probation

【试飞】shìfēi〈动〉test-fly: 进行～ carry out a trial flight

【试飞员】shìfēiyuán ▸**p. 966**〈名〉 test pilot

【试岗】shìgǎng〈动〉 work on probation

【试工】shìgōng〈动〉 be on probation: 通过～ pass one's probation ‖ ～半年 be on a six-month probation

【试工期】shìgōngqī〈名〉 probation period: ～三个月 be on a three-month probation

【试管】shìguǎn〈名〉 test tube

【试管受精】shìguǎn shòujīng〈名〉 in vitro fertilization (IVF)

S

【试管婴儿】shìguǎn yīng'ér〈名〉test-tube baby

【试航】shìháng〈动〉shake down a ship or plane: 船舶～ trial voyage

【试婚】shìhūn〈动〉marry on a trial basis

【试剂】shìjì〈名〉reagent: 化学～ reagent chemicals

【试讲】shìjiǎng〈动〉give a trial lecture

【试金石】shìjīnshí〈名〉touchstone: 友谊的～ the measure of friendship

【试镜】shìjìng〈动〉screen test: 让演员～ screen test an actor/actress

【试举】shìjǔ〈动〉［体育］make an attempt lift: 第一次～ first attempt

【试卷】shìjuàn〈名〉examination paper: 一份～ an examination paper ‖ 批改～ mark papers ‖ 地理/历史～ geography/history paper

【试刊】shìkān〈名〉pilot issue

【试看】shìkàn〈动〉① (指非正式) test out: ～电视 try out a TV set ② (请看) wait and see: ～哪个队能夺冠? Let's wait and see which team will win the championship.

【试鸣】shìmíng〈动〉test an alarm: ～防空警报 test out an air-raid siren

【试射】shìshè〈动〉［军事］test-fire

【试生产】shì shēngchǎn〈名〉trial production

【试手】shìshǒu〈动〉① (试工) be on probation ② (试做) have a try

【试探】shìtàn〈动〉probe: ～水的深浅 fathom the depth of the water

【试探法】shìtànfǎ〈名〉heuristics

【试探性】shìtànxìng〈形〉exploratory: ～攻击 feeler attacks ‖ ～谈判 exploratory talks

【试探】shìtan〈动〉sound sb. out (about sth.): ～反应 test out a reaction ‖ ～民意 sound out public opinion

【试题】shìtí〈名〉examination item: 答完所有～ answer all the test questions

【试跳】shìtiào〈动〉［体育］① (指田径) make a trial jump ② (指跳水) do a trial dive

【试图】shìtú〈动〉try: ～逃跑 make an attempt at escaping ‖ ～找到答案 try to find the answer

【试问】shìwèn〈动〉may we ask: ～谁为这件事负责? May we ask who is responsible for it?

【试想】shìxiǎng〈动〉try to imagine: ～, 还有谁能干这件事? Have a think about who else can do this?

【试销】shìxiāo〈动〉place goods on trial sale: ～产品 trial-sale product

【试行】shìxíng〈动〉try out: ～条例 proposed regulations

【试演】shìyǎn〈动〉audition: ～新角色 audition for a new part

【试验】shìyàn〈动〉test: 做皮肤～ do a skin test ‖ 科学～ scientific experiment

【试验报告】shìyàn bàogào〈名〉test report

【试验场】shìyànchǎng〈名〉testing ground: 导弹～ missile test site

【试验堆】shìyànduī〈名〉［物理］test reactor

【试验农场】shìyàn nóngchǎng〈名〉experimental farm

【试验品】shìyànpǐn〈名〉experimental article

【试验田】shìyàntián〈名〉① ［农业］experimental plot ② 〈喻〉(试点) experiment

【试验性】shìyànxìng〈形〉pilot: ～飞弹 experimental missile

【试样】shìyàng A〈名〉sample: ～材料 sample material ‖ ～检验 test check B〈动〉try on a partly finished garment

【试衣室】shìyīshì〈名〉fitting room

【试营业】shì yíngyè〈动〉be in trial operation: 本店～期间 during the trial operation of the shop

【试映】shìyìng〈动〉preview (a film, etc.)

【试用】shìyòng〈动〉be on probation: ～人员 person on probation ‖ 你～过那种牙膏吗? Have you tried that toothpaste? ‖ 我将～你的儿子。I'll give your boy a trial.

【试用本】shìyòngběn〈名〉trial edition

【试用品】shìyòngpǐn〈名〉trial product: 赠送～ give away sample products

【试用期】shìyòngqī〈名〉probation period: 通过～ pass one's probation period ‖ 在～内被解雇 be fired during probation

【试院】shìyuàn〈名〉〈旧〉imperial examination hall

【试运行】shìyùnxíng〈动〉operate on a trial basis

【试运转】shìyùnzhuǎn〈动〉［机械］test-run

【试纸】shìzhǐ〈名〉［化学］reagent paper

【试制】shìzhì〈动〉trial-manufacture: ～小组 trial-production group

【试种】shìzhòng〈动〉plant experimentally: ～水稻 grow rice on a trial basis

视（視）

shì〈动〉① (看) look at: ▸～力, 虎～眈眈, 注～ ② (考察) inspect: ▸～察, 审～, 巡～ ③ (看待) regard: 他～世间的功名成就如粪土。He considered worldly success as beneath contempt. ▸～死如归, 仇～, 重～

【视差】shìchā〈名〉① (误差) visual error ② ［天文］parallax: ～角 angle of parallax

【视察】shìchá〈动〉① (检查) inspect: 每周～两次 carry out two inspections a week ② (察看) examine: ～地形 survey the terrain ‖ ～现场 inspect the scene ‖ ～灾情 investigate the afflicted areas

【视察员】shìcháyuán〈名〉inspector

【视唱】shìchàng〈动〉sight-sing

【视唱练耳】shìchàng liàn'ěr〈动〉sing a solfeggio

【视程】shìchéng〈名〉［气象］visual range

【视窗操作系统】shìchuāng cāozuò xìtǒng〈名〉［计算机］Windows

【视点】shìdiǎn〈名〉perspective

【视地平】shìdìpíng〈名〉［天文］apparent horizon

【视而不见】shì'érbùjiàn〈成〉look without seeing: 对腐败～ turn a blind eye to corruption ‖ 她双眼盯着电话, 其他一律～。Her eyes were taking in nothing but the telephone.

【视而不见, 听而不闻】shì'érbùjiàn, tīng'érbùwén〈成〉turn a blind eye and a deaf ear to sth.

【视级】shìjí〈名〉scale of visibility

【视角】shìjiǎo〈名〉① ［物理］angle of view ② (指镜头) optic angle ③ (观察角度) perspective

【视界】shìjiè〈名〉event horizon

【视距】shìjù〈名〉range of visibility: ～测高 stadia levelling

【视距测量】shìjù cèliáng〈名〉tachymetering: ～法 tacheometry

【视觉】shìjué〈名〉vision: ～敏锐 have keen eyesight

【视觉传感器】shìjué chuángǎnqì〈名〉vision sensor

【视觉器官】shìjué qìguān〈名〉visual organ

【视觉缺失】shìjué quēshī〈名〉blindness

【视觉神经】shìjué shénjīng〈名〉optic nerve

【视觉误差】shìjué wùchā〈名〉collimation error

【视觉障碍】shìjué zhàng'ài〈名〉vision disorder

【视力】shìlì〈名〉eyesight: ～差/好 have poor/good eyesight ‖ ～检查 eye test ‖ 你的～已减退到0.7。Your vision has dropped to 0.7.

【视力表】shìlìbiǎo〈名〉eye-chart

【视亮度】shìliàngdù〈名〉［天文］apparent luminance

【视盘】shìpán〈名〉video compact disc (VCD)

【视盘机】shìpánjī〈名〉VCD player: 数字～ DVD player

【视频】shìpín〈名〉［物理］video frequency: 输入/输出～ video input/output

【视频博客】shìpín bókè〈名〉video blog

【视频放大器】shìpín fàngdàqì〈名〉video amplifier

【视频显示器】shìpín xiǎnshìqì〈名〉visual display unit

【视频信号】shìpín xìnhào〈名〉video signal: ～接收 video reception

【视如敝屣】shìrú-bìxǐ〈成〉regard as of no importance

【视如粪土】shìrú-fèntǔ〈成〉consider as beneath contempt

【视如己出】shìrú-jǐchū〈成〉regard sb. as one's own child

【视若无睹】shìruòwúdǔ〈成〉turn a blind eye

【视神经】shìshénjīng〈名〉［生理］optic nerve: ～萎缩 optic atrophy

【视事】shìshì〈动〉〈书〉attend to one's duties after assuming office

【视死如归】shìsǐrúguī〈成〉face death unflinchingly

【视听】shìtīng A〈名〉what is seen and heard: 混淆～ confuse the public ‖ 以正～ so as to clarify matters to the public B〈形〉audio-visual

【视听电话】shìtīng diànhuà〈名〉videophone

【视听教材】shìtīng jiàocái〈名〉audio-visual teaching materials

【视听器】shìtīngqì〈名〉audio-visual aids

【视同儿戏】shìtóng-érxì〈成〉not take sth. seriously

【视同路人】shìtóng-lùrén〈成〉regard as a stranger: 你不应该把他们～。You shouldn't have treated them like strangers.

【视图】shìtú〈名〉［机械］view: 侧/前～ side/front view

【视网膜】shìwǎngmó〈名〉［生理］retina

【视网膜脱离】shìwǎngmó tuōlí〈名〉［医学］detached retina

【视为】shìwéi〈动〉regard as: ～例外 treat as an exception ‖ ～莫大的荣誉 regard as a great honour ‖ ～知己 consider sb. to be a close friend

【视为畏途】shìwéi-wèitú〈成〉consider as dangerous

【视线】shìxiàn〈名〉① (指眼睛) line of vision: 挡住～ block sb.'s view ‖ 扰乱～ interfere with sb.'s view ‖ 在～内 within one's view ② 〈喻〉(注意力) attention: 转移人们的～ divert people's attention

【视野】shìyě〈名〉field of vision: 进入～ come into view ‖ 开阔～ broaden one's view ‖ ～宽广 have a wide field of vision

【视域】shìyù = 视阈 shìyù 2

【视阈】shìyù〈名〉 1 [生理] visual threshold: ～测量 measurement of visual area 2 (视野) field of vision: 挡住～ obstruct the view
【视障】shìzhàng〈名〉 visual impairment: ～歌手/运动员 a visually impaired singer/athlete

贳（貰） shì〈动〉〈书〉 1 (出借) hire out 2 (赊) buy on credit: ～酒 buy wine on credit 3 (赦免) pardon: 对犯法者不稍～ show no mercy to offenders

柿 shì〈名〉 persimmon
【柿饼】shìbǐng〈名〉 dried persimmon
【柿霜】shìshuāng〈名〉[中药] persimmon frost
【柿子】shìzi〈名〉 1 (指树) persimmon (tree) 2 (指果实) persimmon (fruit): 涩～ tart persimmon
【柿子椒】shìzijiāo〈名〉 bell pepper

拭 shì〈动〉 wipe (away): ～泪 wipe away tears ▸～目以待, 擦～, 揩～
【拭目以待】shìmùyǐdài〈成〉 wait and see

是 shì
A〈代〉 1〈书〉(这) this, that: ～日 that day ‖ 如～ like this ▸～可忍，孰不可忍 2 (复指宾语) [used to introduce the verb]: ▸唯利～图, 唯命～从
B〈动〉 1 (联系两种事物) a (表判断) be: 他～工人，我～学生。 He is a worker and I am a student. b (表分类) [used with 的 at the end of the sentence, to indicate category, characteristic, etc.]: 她～教师。 She is a teacher. ‖ 屋子里全～人。 The room is full of people. c (表明确) [used to indicate actuality]: 事实总～事实，谁也否认不了。 Facts are facts, and no one can deny them. d (表让步) [to indicate concession]: 东西好～好，就是太贵。 It is good, but it is too expensive. e (表适合) [to indicate suitability]: 你来得正～时候。 You came at just the right time. ‖ 这衣柜放得不～地方。 This is not the place for a clothes cabinet. 2 (凡是) [used before a noun to indicate each and every one of the kind]: ～学生就得好好学习。 To be a student is to study hard. 3 (的确) [used to indicate certainty, usu stressed]: 这屋子当教室～太小了。 This room is really too small for a classroom. ‖ 昨天我～病了。 I really was ill yesterday. 4 (表强调) [used at the beginning of a sentence to stress the word after it]: ～父母把我们养育大的。 It is our parents who brought us up. ‖ ～我。 It's me. 5 (表选择) [used in an alternative or a negative question]: 你～喝咖啡还～喝茶? What would you like to drink, coffee or tea? ‖ 他不～来了吗? Hasn't he come? 6〈书〉(肯定) be certain: ～古非今 praise the past and condemn the present 7 (表答应) [used to indicate promise]: ～，我马上就去。 OK, I'll go at once. ‖ ～，我明白了。 Yes, I've got it.
C〈形〉 correct: 你说得～。 You're right. ‖ 你应该来早一点才～。 You should have come a little bit earlier. ▸似～而非, 一无～处, 自以为～
D〈名〉 truth: ▸各行其～, 实事求～
【是的】shìde = 似的 shìde
【是非】shìfēi〈名〉 1 (对错) right and wrong: 不明～ be unable to tell right from wrong ‖ 混淆～ confuse right with wrong ‖ 明辨～ tell right from wrong 2 (纠纷) dispute: 搬弄～ tell tales
【是非题】shìfēití〈名〉 true or false question
【是非曲直】shìfēi-qūzhí〈成〉 merits and demerits: 每个事件将根据其～做出决定。 Each case will be decided on its merits.
【是非窝】shìfēiwō = 是非之地 shìfēizhīdì
【是非之地】shìfēizhīdì〈名〉 place where one is apt to get into trouble
【是非自有公论】shìfēi zìyǒu gōnglùn〈俗〉 the public are the best judge
【是否】shìfǒu〈副〉 whether (or not): ～属实 whether or not it is true ‖ 她～愿意，我还不清楚。 I am not yet clear whether she is willing or not. ‖ 我不知道～应该告诉你。 I wonder if I ought to tell you.
【是可忍，孰不可忍】shì kě rěn,shú bùkě rěn〈成〉 if this can be tolerated, what cannot
【是味儿】shìwèir〈动〉〈口〉 1 (地道) taste good: 这饭做的真～。 The dinner is delicious. 2 (舒服) feel good: 这场电影看得很～。 It was an experience to watch this film.
【是样儿】shìyàngr〈动〉〈口〉 look right/good

适¹（適） shì〈动〉〈书〉 1 (前往) go: 离京～沪 leave Beijing for Shanghai ▸～可而止 2 (出嫁) marry: ～人 [of a girl] marry

适²（適） shì
A〈动〉 suit: ▸～龄, ～用, 削足～履
B〈副〉 just: ～因此故 just for this reason ‖ ～逢"五一节"放假。 It happened to be the Labour Day holiday. ▸～得其反, ～逢其会
C〈形〉 comfortable: 感到不～ not feel well ▸舒～, 闲～
【适才】shìcái〈副〉 just now: ～还想去看你。 I thought of paying you a visit only a moment ago.
【适当】shìdàng〈形〉 appropriate: ～的安排 proper arrangements ‖ ～的人选 suitable candidate ‖ 采取～的措施 take adequate measures ‖ 以～形式 in appropriate form ‖ 在～的时候 at the right moment
【适得其反】shìdé-qífǎn〈成〉 have an opposite effect: 本想说服他，结果～。 The attempts to persuade him seem to have backfired. ‖ 他的威胁产生了～的结果。 His threat has worked against him.
【适度】shìdù〈形〉 appropriate: 长短～ be of the right length ‖ 批评～ be temperate in one's criticism ‖ ～的体育活动 moderate amount of physical exercise ‖ ～的营养 proper nutrition
【适逢其会】shìféng-qíhuì〈成〉 happen to be present at the right moment: ～，我参加了这次聚会。 I happened to be present at the gathering.
【适合】shìhé〈动〉 suit: ～做这项工作 be suitable for the job ‖ 他～当教师。 He was cut out to be a teacher. ‖ 这气候对我不～。 The climate doesn't agree with me.
【适婚】shìhūn〈形〉 of marriageable age: ～青年 young people of a marriageable age
【适可而止】shìkě'érzhǐ〈成〉 know how far to go
【适量】shìliàng〈形〉 of right amount: ～饮酒 drink in moderation
【适龄】shìlíng〈形〉 of the right age: ～青年 young people of the right age ‖ ～儿童 children of school age
【适时】shìshí〈形〉 timely: ～播种 sow in good time
【适销】shìxiāo〈形〉 marketable: ～商品 saleable/marketable goods ‖ ～对路 suitable for the market
【适宜】shìyí〈形〉 suitable: ～搞教学工作 be suited to teaching ‖ 气候～ favourable climate ‖ 寒冷的气候～于种小麦。 Wheat is suited to a cold climate. ‖ 那里的气候对他的健康更～。 The climate there is better for his health.
【适意】shìyì〈形〉 agreeable: ～的环境 congenial environment
【适应】shìyìng〈动〉 be suited to: ～当地条件 adapt to local conditions ‖ ～时代要求 keep abreast of the times ‖ ～新环境 adjust to the new environment ‖ ～市场需要 meet the needs of the market ‖ 对大城市的生活不～ not suited to city life ‖ 她是个能够～环境的人。 She is an adaptable person.
【适应性】shìyìngxìng〈名〉 adaptability
【适用】shìyòng〈动〉 suit: ～于每个人 can be applied to everyone ‖ 普遍～ be universally applicable ‖ 仍然～ still hold good
【适用范围】shìyòng fànwéi〈名〉 scope of application
【适用性】shìyòngxìng〈名〉 applicability
【适者生存】shìzhěshēngcún〈成〉 survival of the fittest
【适值】shìzhí〈副〉〈书〉 just when: ～收获季节 just during the harvest season
【适中】shìzhōng〈形〉 1 (指程度) moderate: 长短/大小～ be of appropriate length/size ‖ 价格/雨量～ moderate price/rainfall 2 (指位置) well situated: 地点～ be well located

恃 shì〈动〉 rely on: ▸～才傲物, 有～无恐
【恃才傲物】shìcái-àowù〈成〉 be inordinately proud of one's ability
【恃强凌弱】shìqiáng-língruò〈成〉 play the bully

室 shì〈名〉 1 (房间) room: 会客～ reception room ‖ 307 ～ Room 307 ▸～内, 教～, 卧～ 2 (指星宿) one of the 28 constellations in ancient Chinese astronomy 3 (家族) clan: ▸皇～, 王～, 宗～ 4 (家属) family member or wife: ▸继～, 家～, 妻～ 5 (室状器官) cavity: ▸脑～, 心～ 6 (工作单位) administrative unit: ▸办公～, 收发～, 资料～
【室内】shìnèi〈名〉 interior: ～温度 indoor temperature ‖ 他搞～布景极为出色。 He does the most divine interiors.
【室内赛】shìnèisài〈名〉[体育] indoor tournament
【室内天线】shìnèi tiānxiàn〈名〉 indoor antenna
【室内田径运动会】shìnèi tiánjìng yùndònghuì ▸**p. 909**〈名〉 indoor track meet
【室内网球】shìnèi wǎngqiú ▸**p. 909**〈名〉 indoor tennis: ～场 indoor tennis court
【室内乐】shìnèiyuè〈名〉 chamber music: ～队 chamber orchestra
【室女座】Shìnǚzuò〈名〉[天文] Virgo
【室外】shìwài〈名〉 exterior: ～活动 outdoor activities ‖ ～温度 outdoor temperature
【室温】shìwēn〈名〉 room temperature
【室友】shìyǒu〈名〉 room-mate

莳（蒔） shì〈动〉 1〈书〉(种植) cultivate: 播～五谷 grow food crops ‖ ～花 grow flowers 2〈方〉(移栽)

S

transplant: ～秧 transplant rice seedlings ▸shí

逝 shì〈动〉**1**（消失）pass: 时光易～。Time flies. ▸流～，消～ **2**（去世） pass away: ▸～世，病～，长～

【逝世】shìshì ▸**p. 772**〈动〉 pass away: 为某人的～而悲伤 lament the death of sb. ‖ 举世哀悼他的～。 The whole world mourned his death.

铈（鈰） shì〈名〉［化学］ cerium (Ce)

舐 shì〈动〉〈书〉 lick

【舐犊情深】shìdú-qíngshēn〈成〉 parental love

弑 shì〈动〉〈书〉 murder: ～母 matricide ‖ ～君 regicide

释[1]（釋） shì〈动〉**1**〈书〉（松开） be relieved of **2**（放走） release: 得到开～ win an acquittal **3**（解除） dispel: ▸～怀，～然 **4**（解说） explain: ▸～文，解～，注～ **5**（放开） lay down: ▸爱不～手

释[2]（釋） Shì〈名〉**1**（释迦牟尼） Sakyamuni Buddha **2**（佛教） Buddhism: ▸～典，～教

【释典】shìdiǎn〈名〉 Buddhist Scripture

【释读】shìdú〈动〉 conduct research on and explain the texts of ancient writings

【释法】shìfǎ〈动〉 interpret a law: 以案～宣传法律知识 use the interpretation of the case to disseminate legal knowledge

【释放】shìfàng〈动〉 release: ～人质 free hostages ‖ 刑满～ be released upon completion of a sentence ‖ ～气球中的空气 let the air out of a balloon

【释怀】shìhuái〈动〉〈书〉 dismiss from one's mind: 那件往事让我久久不能～。 For ages I couldn't stop thinking about what had happened.

【释迦牟尼】Shìjiāmóuní〈名〉 Sakyamuni Buddha [565-486BC]

【释教】Shìjiào〈名〉 Buddhism

【释老】Shì-Lǎo〈名〉 Buddhism and Taoism

【释然】shìrán〈形〉〈书〉 relieved

【释手】shìshǒu〈动〉 let go: ▸爱不～

【释文】shìwén **A**〈动〉 transcribe the text of ancient writings **B**〈名〉 annotations

【释疑】shìyí〈动〉 remove doubts: ～解难 explain difficult points

【释义】shìyì〈动〉 paraphrase

【释子】shìzǐ〈名〉〈书〉 Buddhist monk

谥（謚、諡） shì

A〈名〉 posthumous title

B〈动〉 name: ～之为保守主义 call it conservatism

嗜 shì〈动〉 be addicted to: ～烟 be addicted to smoking ‖ ～赌成性的人 compulsive gambler ▸～好，～酒，～杀成性

【嗜好】shìhào〈名〉 hobby: 唯一的～ only indulgence ‖ 我没有什么～。 I have no hobby.

【嗜痂成癖】shìjiā-chéngpǐ〈成〉 acquire a strange addiction (to)

【嗜酒】shìjiǔ〈动〉 be addicted to alcohol: ～狂 alcoholic

【嗜眠症】shìmiánzhèng ▸**p. 50**〈名〉［医学］ lethargy

【嗜杀成性】shìshā-chéngxìng〈成〉 bloodthirsty: ～的匪徒 bloodthirsty gangsters

【嗜血】shìxuè〈动〉 be bloodthirsty: ～成性 be bloodthirsty

【嗜欲】shìyù〈名〉 desire for the satisfaction of the senses: 满足～ satisfy one's sensual desires

筮 shì〈动〉〈书〉 practise divination by means of the milfoil: ▸卜～

誓 shì

A〈动〉 pledge: ～报此仇 swear vengeance ‖ ～守秘密 be sworn to secrecy ▸～不两立，～师，～言

B〈名〉 vow: 发过～ be under oath ▸立～，起～，信～旦旦，宣～

【誓不罢休】shìbùbàxiū〈成〉 swear not to give up: 不达目的，～。 We'll never stop until we reach our goal.

【誓不两立】shìbùliǎnglì〈成〉 resolve to destroy sb. or die in the attempt

【誓词】shìcí〈名〉 oath: 立下～ take a vow ‖ 宣读～ read out an oath

【誓师】shìshī〈动〉**1**（特指军队） rally to pledge a resolution **2**（指群众） take a mass pledge: ～大会 oath-taking rally

【誓死】shìsǐ〈动〉 pledge one's life: ～保卫祖国 be ready to die in defence of one's country

【誓死不二】shìsǐ-bù'èr〈成〉 swear to be loyal forever

【誓死不屈】shìsǐ-bùqū〈成〉 swear to die rather than to submit

【誓同生死】shìtóng-shēngsǐ〈成〉pledge to live and die together

【誓言】shìyán〈名〉 pledge: 立下～ swear an oath ‖ 违背～ go back on one's word ‖ 信守～ keep one's pledge

【誓愿】shìyuàn〈名〉 vow: 许下～ make a pledge

【誓约】shìyuē〈名〉 pledge: 履行～ fulfil a pledge

噬 shì〈动〉〈书〉 bite: ▸吞～

【噬菌体】shìjūntǐ〈名〉［生物］ bacteriophage: ～形态 morphology of phages

【噬细胞】shìxìbāo〈名〉［生物］phagocyte

【噬脂】shìzhī〈名〉 lipophagia: ～细胞 lipophage

螫 shì〈动〉〈书〉 sting

【螫针】shìzhēn〈名〉 sting (of a bee, etc.)

shi

匙 shi ▸钥匙 yàoshi ▸chí

殖 shi ▸骨殖 gǔshi ▸zhí

shōu

收 shōu〈动〉**1**（拘禁） detain: ▸～监，～审，～押 **2**（收拢） put sth. away: 把耳机～起来 put away the earphones ‖ 把玩具～起来 put the toys away ‖ 把晒洗的衣服～进来 get the washing in ▸～藏，～集，～拾 **3**（获得） gain: ▸～入，～益，坐～渔利 **4**（收获） gather in: ～麦子 harvest wheat ‖ ～庄稼 reap crops ▸～成，抢～，秋～ **5**（收取） collect: ～作业 collect homework ▸～费，～税 **6**（接受） accept: ～礼物 accept a gift ‖ ～信 receive a letter ▸～礼，～留，～养 **7**（约束） restrain: ～住脚步 stop walking ▸～敛，～心 **8**（结束） bring to an end: ▸～工，～兵，～盘，～尾

【收报】shōubào〈动〉 receive a telegram: ～机 telegraphic receiver ‖ ～员 telegrapher

【收编】shōubiān〈动〉 incorporate into one's own force: ～地方部队 incorporate local armed forces

【收兵】shōubīng〈动〉**1**（撤军） withdraw troops: 不获全胜，决不～。 We will not withdraw our forces until a complete victory is assured. ▸鸣金～ **2**〈喻〉（结束） finish up: 草率～ declare a matter closed before it is thoroughly settled

【收藏】shōucáng〈动〉 collect: ～古董/邮票 collect antiques/stamps ‖ 图书馆里～着大批书籍。 The library has a large collection of books.

【收藏家】shōucángjiā ▸**p. 966**〈名〉 collector: 艺术～ art collector

【收藏癖】shōucángpǐ〈名〉 collectomania

【收藏品】shōucángpǐn〈名〉 collection: 充实～ enrich one's collection

【收操】shōucāo〈动〉 end a drill: 吹～号 sound the recall

【收场】shōuchǎng **A**〈名〉 ending: 不会有好～ will come to no good end ‖ 出乎意料的～ unexpected denouement **B**〈动〉 end up: 草草～ wind sth. up hastily ‖ 比赛以平局～。 The game ended in a draw.

【收车】shōuchē〈动〉 return vehicle to terminal: 太晚了，公共汽车肯定～了。 There won't be any buses running at this time of day.

【收成】shōucheng〈名〉 yield: ～好 have a bumper harvest ‖ 今年小麦～将创新记录。 This year's wheat crop will set a new record.

【收存】shōucún〈动〉 receive and keep: 把谷物～起来留作种子 keep grain for seed ‖ 把那幅油画～在博物馆里 keep that oil painting in the museum

【收到】shōudào〈动〉 receive: ～请帖 receive an invitation ‖ ～预期效果 achieve the expected results

【收低】shōudī〈动〉［金融］ close low

【收发】shōufā **A**〈动〉receive and dispatch: ～文件 receive and dispatch documents ‖ ～开关 transmit-receive switch ‖ ～装置 transmitter-receiver set (T-R unit) **B**〈名〉 dispatcher

【收发报机】shōufābàojī〈名〉 transmitter-receiver

【收发室】shōufāshì〈名〉 mail room: ～工作人员 dispatcher

【收方】shōufāng〈名〉 debit side: 把钱记入～ put money on the debit side

【收费】shōufèi〈动〉 charge: ～道路/桥梁 toll road/bridge ‖ 额外～ additional charge

【收费厕所】shōufèi cèsuǒ〈名〉 pay toilet

【收费处】shōufèichù〈名〉 toll gate

【收费电视】shōufèi diànshì〈名〉 pay-TV

【收费区】shōufèiqū〈名〉 toll area

【收费亭】shōufèitíng〈名〉 tollbooth

【收费员】shōufèiyuán ▸**p. 966**〈名〉 toll collector

【收费站】shōufèizhàn〈名〉 toll station

【收蜂箱】shōufēngxiāng〈名〉 swarm box

【收伏】shōufú = 收服 shōufú

【收服】shōufú〈动〉 reduce to submission: ～叛乱分子 bring the rebels under control

【收抚】shōufǔ〈动〉**1**（安抚）take in and

S

comfort: ～难民 take in refugees and comfort them **2**（抚养） take in and bring up: ～孤儿 adopt an orphan ‖ ～烈士遗孤 foster the children of martyrs

【收复】 shōufù 〈动〉 recover: ～失地 recover lost territory ‖ 他们～了落入敌手的小镇。 They recapture the town lost to the enemy.

【收高】 shōugāo 〈动〉［金融］ close high: 道琼斯工业平均指数～3%。 The Dow Jones Industrial Average is up 3%.

【收割】 shōugē 〈动〉 reap: ～水稻 harvest rice ‖ ～期 harvest time ‖ 帮助～ help with the harvest ‖ 小麦已经～。 The wheat has been cut.

【收割机】 shōugējī 〈名〉 harvester: 联合～ combine harvester

【收割脱粒机】 shōugē tuōlìjī 〈名〉 harvester-thresher

【收工】 shōugōng 〈动〉 stop work for the day: 按时～ stop work on time ‖ 他们迟迟不能～。 They could not wrap up on time.

【收购】 shōugòu 〈动〉 purchase: ～二手设备 purchase second-hand equipment ‖ ～旧家具 buy used furniture ‖ 他们决定～这家公司。 They decided to buy out this company.

【收购站】 shōugòuzhàn 〈名〉 purchasing station

【收官】 shōuguān 〈动〉 **1**（指围棋） close a game: 棋局已到～阶段。 The 'go' game has already reached its final stages. **2**〈喻〉 finish up: 京沪铁路建设的～之战 the final stages of the construction of the Beijing-Shanghai railway

【收归】 shōuguī 〈动〉 reclaim: ～国有 be taken over by the government

【收回】 shōuhuí 〈动〉 **1**（取回） recover: ～贷款 recall a loan ‖ ～投资 recoup one's investment ‖ ～主权 regain sovereignty **2**（取消） withdraw: ～报价 withdraw an offer ‖ ～承诺 retract one's promise ‖ 说出口的话收不回。 You can't take back what you have said.

【收回成命】 shōuhuí-chéngmìng 〈成〉 revoke a command

【收活】 shōuhuó 〈动〉 **1**（接受活计） accept orders for repairs or processing: 我们已经不～了。 We have stopped accepting orders. **2**〈方〉（收工） knock off (work): 他们早早就～回家了。 They packed up early and went home.

【收货人】 shōuhuòrén 〈名〉 consignee

【收获】 shōuhuò **A**〈动〉 harvest: ～机具 harvesting machinery ‖ ～季节 harvest season ‖ 春天播种，秋天～ sow in spring and reap in autumn **B**〈名〉 results: 不下苦功，便无～。 No pain, no gain. ‖ 我们的访问很有～。 Our visit was duly rewarded.

【收集】 shōují 〈动〉 collect: ～钱币/邮票 collect coins/stamps ‖ ～情报/资料 gather information/material ‖ 多方面～信息 collect information from many sources

【收监】 shōujiān 〈动〉 imprison: ～候审 take into custody to await trial

【收件人】 shōujiànrén 〈名〉 addressee

【收缴】 shōujiǎo 〈动〉 **1**（缴获） confiscate **2**（征收） collect: ～税款 levy taxes

【收旧利废】 shōujiù-lìfèi 〈成〉 recycle

【收据】 shōujù 〈名〉 receipt: 开～ make out a receipt ‖ 正式～ formal receipt

【收看】 shōukàn 〈动〉 tune in to: ～电视 watch television ‖ 请继续～。 Please stay tuned.

【收口】 shōukǒu 〈动〉 **1**（指编织） cast off **2**（指伤口） close up: 他胳膊上的伤已～了。 The wound in his arm has begun to heal.

【收款】 shōukuǎn 〈动〉 collect money: ～处 cashier desk ‖ ～台 cashier desk

【收款方】 shōukuǎnfāng 〈名〉 payee

【收款机】 shōukuǎnjī 〈名〉 cash register

【收款人】 shōukuǎnrén 〈名〉 payee

【收款通知书】 shōukuǎn tōngzhīshū 〈名〉 advice of collection

【收款员】 shōukuǎnyuán ▸p. 966 〈名〉 receiving teller

【收揽】 shōulǎn 〈动〉 **1**〈贬〉（笼络） buy over: ～人心 buy people over **2**〈书〉（承揽） keep within one's grasp

【收礼】 shōulǐ 〈动〉 accept a gift: 拒绝～ refuse to accept gifts

【收镰】 shōulián 〈动〉 finish the harvest

【收敛】 shōuliǎn 〈动〉 **1**（消失） disappear: 他～了笑容。 His smile vanished. **2**（约束） pull back: ～行为 rein oneself in ‖ 有所～ pull back somewhat **3**［医学］ make astringent: ～膏 astringent cream ‖ ～药 astringent

【收殓】 shōuliàn 〈动〉 lay a body in a coffin: ～入葬 place a corpse in a coffin and bury it

【收留】 shōuliú 〈动〉 take in: ～孤儿 take in an orphan

【收拢】 shōulǒng 〈动〉 **1**（聚合） gather together: 把雨伞～ close an umbrella ‖ 把网～ draw in a net **2**〈贬〉（笼络） win over: ～人心 buy popular support

【收录】 shōulù 〈动〉 **1**（雇用） recruit: ～职员 recruit office workers ‖ 公司今年～了许多大学毕业生。 The company has employed many college graduates this year. **2**（采用） include: 这本书～了他的全部作品。 This book incorporates all of his works. **3**（录制） record: ～广播音乐会 make a recording of a radio concert ‖ ～英语节目 record an English-language programme

【收录机】 shōulùjī 〈名〉 radio-cassette recorder

【收罗】 shōuluó 〈动〉 gather: ～材料/资料 collect materials/data ‖ ～人才 recruit qualified personnel

【收买】 shōumǎi 〈动〉 **1**（购买） purchase: ～股票 buy stocks **2**（贿赂） bribe: ～证人 buy off a witness ‖ ～人心 buy sb. over

【收没】 shōumò = 没收 mòshōu

【收纳】 shōunà 〈动〉 take in: 如数～ receive in full

【收拍】 shōupāi 〈动〉［体育］ **1**（指球类运动） close: 今天世界羽毛球锦标赛在上海～。 The World Badminton Championships conclude today in Shanghai. **2**（指选手） retire: 奥运会后她将～。 She will retire after the Olympics.

【收盘】 shōupán 〈动〉［经济］ close: ～时增长了 6.2个点 close 6.2 points up

【收盘价】 shōupánjià 〈名〉 closing price

【收讫】 shōuqì 〈动〉 be duly received: 全部付款～ received in full ‖ ～章 receipt stamp ‖ 费用～。 Expenses paid.

【收清】 shōuqīng 〈动〉 receive in full

【收秋】 shōuqiū 〈动〉 gather in autumn crops: 是～的时间了。 It is time to gather in the autumn crops.

【收取】 shōuqǔ 〈动〉 charge: ～附加费 impose a surcharge ‖ ～手续费 charge commission

【收容】 shōuróng 〈动〉 take in: ～难民 house refugees

【收容所】 shōuróngsuǒ 〈名〉 temporary shelter: 难民～ refugee camp

【收入】 shōurù **A**〈动〉 take in **B**〈名〉 income: 增加～ increase one's income ‖ ～来源 source of income ‖ 票房～ box-office receipts ‖ 月/周/年～ monthly/weekly/yearly revenue

【收入调节税】 shōurù tiáojiéshuì 〈名〉 regulatory income tax

【收审】 shōushěn 〈动〉 detain for interrogation: 犯罪嫌疑人已被公安机关～。 The suspect has been detained by the public security agency.

【收生】 shōushēng 〈动〉〈旧〉 deliver a baby: ～婆 midwife

【收尸】 shōushī 〈动〉 identify and bury the dead

【收市】 shōushì 〈动〉 close for the day: ～后的交易 after hours trading ‖ 大部分股票～较低。 Most stocks closed lower.

【收市价】 shōushìjià 〈名〉 closing price

【收视】 shōushì 〈动〉 watch: ～效果 viewing effect

【收视率】 shōushìlǜ 〈名〉 audience rating: 这个节目的～相当高。 This programme has very high ratings.

【收拾】 shōushi 〈动〉 **1**（整理） put in order: ～床铺 make one's bed ‖ ～屋子 tidy up a room ‖ ～行李 pack one's luggage **2**（修理） repair: ～鞋子 mend shoes **3**〈口〉（教训） deal with: 明天我再～你。 I'll deal with you tomorrow. **4**〈口〉（消灭） wipe out

【收受】 shōushòu 〈动〉 accept: ～贿赂 take a bribe

【收税】 shōushuì 〈动〉 collect taxes

【收缩】 shōusuō 〈动〉 **1**（变小或短） contract: ～肌肉 contract a muscle ‖ 因冷而～ shrink in the cold **2**（缩减） tighten up: ～部队 concentrate the troops ‖ ～开支 cut expenditure

【收缩尺】 shōusuōchǐ 〈名〉 contraction gauge

【收缩肌】 shōusuōjī 〈名〉［解剖］ contractor

【收缩量】 shōusuōliàng 〈名〉 shrinkage

【收缩率】 shōusuōlǜ 〈名〉 shrinkage

【收缩性】 shōusuōxìng 〈名〉 contractability

【收缩压】 shōusuōyā 〈名〉［生理］ systolic pressure

【收缩应力】 shōusuō yìnglì 〈名〉［物理］ contraction stress

【收摊儿】 shōutānr 〈动〉〈口〉 wind up business for the day

【收条】 shōutiáo 〈名〉 receipt: 打个～ make out a receipt ‖ 在～上签名 sign a receipt

【收听】 shōutīng 〈动〉 listen in to: ～广播 listen to broadcasts ‖ 请继续～。 Please stay tuned.

【收听率】 shōutīnglǜ 〈名〉 ratings

【收尾】 shōuwěi **A**〈动〉 bring to a conclusion: 做～工作 wind up a job ‖ 工程接近～。 The project is approaching its completion. **B**〈名〉 ending

【收文】 shōuwén 〈名〉 incoming dispatch: ～簿 register of incoming dispatches ‖ ～篮 in-tray

【收悉】 shōuxī 〈动〉 be received and read

【收夏】 shōuxià 〈动〉 harvest summer crops

【收降】 shōuxiáng 〈动〉 accept surrender

【收效】 shōuxiào **A**〈动〉 get results: ～快 get quick returns ‖ ～甚微 bear little fruit **B**〈名〉 return: 投资少，～大 make small investments that return good profits ‖ 这项计划有～。 This plan is bearing fruit.

【收心】 shōuxīn 〈动〉 get into a serious frame of mind: 你得让孩子们收收心。 You've got to get the children into a more serious frame of mind.

【收信人】shōuxìnrén〈名〉 addressee: 寄信前请在信封上写上～的姓名和地址。 Please address your letters before you send them.
【收押】shōuyā〈动〉 detain: ～嫌疑犯 detain a suspect
【收押所】shōuyāsuǒ〈名〉 detention house
【收阳】shōuyáng〈动〉［金融］ close high
【收养】shōuyǎng〈动〉adopt: ～关系 adoptive relationship ‖ ～公证 notarization of adoption ‖ ～继承人 heir by adoption
【收养法】shōuyǎngfǎ〈名〉 adoption law
【收养人】shōuyǎngrén〈名〉 adopter
【收益】shōuyì〈名〉 profit: 增加～ increase one's income ‖ ～递增 increasing returns ‖ ～可观 handsome profit
【收益分配】shōuyì fēnpèi〈名〉 distribution of income
【收益股票】shōuyì gǔpiào〈名〉 income stock
【收益率】shōuyìlǜ〈名〉 rate of return
【收音】shōuyīn〈动〉 1（指声音） have good acoustics: 这座剧场不～。 This theatre has bad acoustics. 2（指广播） receive radio waves: ～接线 receiver connection ‖ 极佳的～效果 excellent reception
【收音机】shōuyīnjī〈名〉 radio; wireless〈英〉: 便携式～ portable radio ‖ 短波～ short-wave receiver ‖ 调频～ FM receiver
【收银】shōuyín〈动〉 collect money
【收银机】shōuyínjī〈名〉 cash register
【收银台】shōuyíntái〈名〉 cashier desk
【收银员】shōuyínyuán ▸p. 966〈名〉 cashier〈英〉; teller〈美〉
【收摘】shōuzhāi〈动〉 pick: ～棉花/苹果 pick cotton/apples
【收债】shōuzhài〈动〉 collect debts
【收账】shōuzhàng〈动〉 1（记入账簿） charge to accounts 2（讨回欠账） collect debts
【收针】shōuzhēn〈动〉 cast off
【收支】shōuzhī〈名〉 income and expenses: ～平衡 balance between income and expenditure ‖ 财政～ budgetary revenues and expenditures ‖ ～两抵。 The account balances out.
【收支逆差】shōuzhī nìchā〈名〉 balance of payments deficit: 国际～ unfavourable balance of international payments
【收支顺差】shōuzhī shùnchā〈名〉balance of payments surplus
【收支预算】shōuzhī yùsuàn〈名〉 budget for revenue and expenditure
【收执】shōuzhí A〈动〉 receive and keep: 交有关人员～ be given to the person concerned for safe-keeping B〈名〉 receipt issued by a government agency
【收治】shōuzhì〈动〉［of a hospital］ accept and treat (a patient)

shóu

熟 shóu〈形〉〈口〉 cooked: 饭～了。 The food is done.
▸shú

shǒu

手 shǒu
A〈名〉 1 ▸p. 614（指人的上肢末端） hand: 一双～ pair of hands ‖ ～捧鲜花 hold flowers ‖ 一～交钱，一～交货 cash on delivery ▸～拉～, ～忙脚乱, 赤～空拳, 招～ 2（技艺） skill: ▸妙～回春, 心灵～巧, 眼高～低 3（有特长的人） person good at sth.: ▸多面～, 歌～, 选～ 4（做某种事的人） person engaging in a certain activity: ▸帮～, 打～, 扒～
B〈动〉 hold in one's hand
C〈形〉 1（便携） handy: ～镜 hand-mirror ▸～册, ～炉, ～枪 2（亲手） handwritten: ▸～笔, ～稿, ～令
D〈副〉 personally: ▸～书, ～植
E〈量〉 1（指技艺）［for skill of proficiency］: 烧得一～好菜 be good at preparing dishes ‖ 写一～好字 write well ‖ 有两～ know one's stuff ▸留一～, 露一～ 2（指经手次数）［used in first-hand, second-hand, etc.］: 一～资料 first-hand data ‖ 二～货 second-hand goods ‖ 二～房 previously owned house
【手把手】shǒubǎshǒu〈副〉 in person: 他～地教我。 I was taught by him personally.
【手把】shǒubà = 手柄 shǒubǐng
【手包】shǒubāo〈名〉 handbag
【手背】shǒubèi〈名〉 back of a hand
【手笔】shǒubǐ〈名〉 1（手迹） hand: 鲁迅的～ the hand of Lu Xun 2（造诣） skill: 大～ be worthy of a well-known writer 3（排场） style: 阔～ be liberal with money
【手臂】shǒubì〈名〉 1（胳膊） arm: 折断～ break one's arm ‖ ～上挎着一个篮子 have a basket on one's arm ‖ 他～受了伤。He was wounded in the arm. 2〈喻〉（帮手） helper: 得力～ right-hand man
【手边】shǒubiān〈名〉 at hand: ～备些钱 keep some money in hand ‖ ～备有参考书 have reference books near at hand ‖ 把词典放在～ keep a dictionary to hand ‖ 使用～最容易得到的材料。 Use the material close at hand.
【手表】shǒubiǎo〈名〉 watch: 戴～ wear a watch ‖ ～指针 watch hand
【手柄】shǒubǐng〈名〉 hand lever: ～断了。 The handle has broken off.
【手播】shǒubō〈动〉 sow by hand
【手不释卷】shǒubùshìjuàn〈成〉diligent in one's studies
【手册】shǒucè〈名〉 1（说明书） handbook: 安装～ installation manual ‖ 旅游～ tourist guide ‖ 《英语语法～》 *A Handbook of English Grammar* 2（记事本） workbook: 工作～ workbook
【手抄】shǒuchāo〈动〉 copy by hand
【手抄本】shǒuchāoběn〈名〉 handwritten copy
【手创】shǒuchuàng〈动〉 create with one's own hands
【手锤】shǒuchuí〈名〉 light hammer
【手戳】shǒuchuō〈名〉〈口〉 private seal
【手锉】shǒucuò〈名〉［机械］ hand file
【手搭凉棚】shǒudā liángpéng〈成〉 shade one's eyes from the sun by placing one's hand horizontally against the forehead
【手大】shǒudà〈形〉 careless with money: 他这个人～。 He always spends more than is necessary.
【手袋】shǒudài〈名〉 handbag
【手到病除】shǒudào-bìngchú〈成〉 1（指医治） have exceptional medical skills 2（指解决问题） solve problems quickly
【手到擒来】shǒudào-qínlái〈成〉 snap one's fingers and get what one wants
【手倒立】shǒudàolì〈名〉［体育］ handstand: 做～ do a handstand
【手底下】shǒudǐxia = 手下 shǒuxià
【手电】shǒudiàn〈口〉= 手电筒 shǒudiàntǒng
【手电筒】shǒudiàntǒng〈名〉 torch〈英〉; flashlight〈美〉
【手动】shǒudòng〈形〉［机械］ manual
【手动挡】shǒudòngdǎng〈名〉 manual transmission: ～汽车 car with manual transmission
【手动阀】shǒudòngfá〈名〉 hand operated valve
【手动装置】shǒudòng zhuāngzhì〈名〉［机械］ hand-gear
【手段】shǒuduàn〈名〉 1（方法） means: ～高明 play one's cards well ‖ 必要～ necessary actions ‖ 法律～ legal measure ▸不择～ 2（本领） skill 3（贬）（特指不正当） trick: 要～ play tricks
【手法】shǒufǎ〈名〉 1（技巧） technique: ～独特 unique skill ‖ 写作～ writing method ‖ 艺术表现～ means of artistic expression 2（特指不正当） trick: 卑劣的～ dirty tricks ‖ ～高明 play a good game ‖ 巧妙的～ sleight of hand
【手风琴】shǒufēngqín ▸p. 929〈名〉 accordion
【手扶拖拉机】shǒufú tuōlājī〈名〉 walking tractor
【手感】shǒugǎn〈名〉 feel: ～平滑的布料 cloth that is smooth to the touch
【手稿】shǒugǎo〈名〉 manuscript: 查阅～ consult a manuscript
【手工】shǒugōng A〈名〉 1（指工艺） handwork 2〈口〉（指报酬） charge for a piece of handwork: 你这件外套～多少? How much did you pay for the tailoring of this overcoat? B〈形〉 manual: ～操作 do by hand ‖ ～制造 handmade ‖ ～编织的毛衣 hand-knitted sweater
【手工费】shǒugōngfèi〈名〉 payment for handwork
【手工活】shǒugōnghuó〈名〉 handwork
【手工课】shǒugōngkè〈名〉 manual training
【手工劳动】shǒugōng láodòng〈名〉 manual labour
【手工业】shǒugōngyè〈名〉 handicraft: ～者 craftsman
【手工艺】shǒugōngyì〈名〉 handicraft: ～工人 craftsman ‖ ～品 handicrafts
【手鼓】shǒugǔ ▸p. 929〈名〉 tabor
【手黑】shǒuhēi〈形〉〈口〉 wicked: 心狠～ be cruel and vicious
【手机】shǒujī〈名〉 mobile/cellular phone: ～入网费 mobile access fee
【手机卡】shǒujīkǎ〈名〉 SIM card
【手疾眼快】shǒují-yǎnkuài〈成〉 sharp of eye and deft of hand
【手记】shǒujì A〈动〉 take notes: 我自己～了一些会议要点。 I have taken notes on some of the important points of the meeting myself. B〈名〉 notes: 你可以看看我的～。 You can have a look at my notes.
【手技】shǒujì〈名〉 1（手艺） craftsmanship 2［杂技］ juggling
【手迹】shǒujì〈名〉 original hand
【手脚】shǒujiǎo〈名〉 1（手和脚） hands and feet 2（指动作） movements of hands or feet: ～利落 agile ‖ 放不开～ be restrained 3（贬）（不正当行为） trick: 肯定有人从中做了～。 Someone has messed around here.
【手脚不干净】shǒujiǎo bù gānjìng ▸p. 772〈惯〉 light-fingered
【手巾】shǒujīn〈名〉 towel: 一块/条～ a towel
【手紧】shǒujǐn〈形〉 1（控制严） tight-fisted: 我们的钱不多了，得～点。 As we're short of money, we need to tighten

S

our purse strings a little. 2 (缺钱) be hard up

【手劲儿】shǒujìnr〈名〉grip

【手锯】shǒujù〈名〉handsaw: ～条 hand-saw blade

【手卷】shǒujuàn〈名〉［美术］hand scroll

【手绢】shǒujuàn〈名〉handkerchief

【手铐】shǒukào〈名〉handcuffs

【手快】shǒukuài〈形〉deft of hand: 他手好快。He is quick with his hands. ▸眼疾～

【手拉手】shǒulāshǒu〈动〉hold hands: 她俩～走了进来。They came in hand in hand.

【手辣】shǒulà〈形〉vicious: ▸心狠～

【手雷】shǒuléi〈名〉［军事］anti-tank grenade

【手力千斤顶】shǒulì qiānjīndǐng〈名〉［机械］hand jack

【手链】shǒuliàn〈名〉bracelet

【手铃】shǒulíng〈名〉handbell

【手令】shǒulìng〈名〉handwritten order

【手榴弹】shǒuliúdàn〈名〉1［军事］grenade: 一颗/枚～ a grenade 2［体育］hand grenade

【手笼】shǒulóng〈名〉muff

【手炉】shǒulú〈名〉hand warmer

【手轮】shǒulún〈名〉［机械］hand wheel

【手锣】shǒuluó〈名〉small gong

【手慢】shǒumàn〈形〉slow

【手忙脚乱】shǒumáng-jiǎoluàn〈成〉be flustered

【手模】shǒumó〈名〉handprint

【手帕】shǒupà = 手绢 shǒujuàn

【手旗】shǒuqí〈名〉［军事］hand flag

【手气】shǒuqì〈名〉luck: ～正好 be on a winning streak ‖ 你昨天打牌的～如何? How was your luck at cards yesterday?

【手枪】shǒuqiāng〈名〉handgun: 拔出～ draw a pistol ‖ 自动～ automatic pistol ‖ 左轮～ revolver ‖ ～射程 pistol shot ‖ ～射击场 pistol range ‖ ～套 holster

【手巧】shǒuqiǎo〈形〉deft: ▸心灵～

【手勤】shǒuqín〈形〉diligent: ～手快 be keen and quick in one's work

【手轻】shǒuqīng〈形〉gentle: 这东西不结实，～点。This article breaks easily. Please handle with care.

【手球】shǒuqiú〈名〉［体育］1 (指球类运动) handball: 打～ play handball 2 (指犯规) handball

【手软】shǒuruǎn〈形〉soft-handed: ▸心慈～

【手勺】shǒusháo〈名〉ladle

【手勺取样】shǒusháo qǔyàng〈名〉［冶金］spoon test

【手生】shǒushēng〈形〉out of practice

【手势】shǒushì〈名〉gesture: 打/做～ make a gesture

【手势语】shǒushìyǔ〈名〉sign language: ～学 study of gestures

【手书】shǒushū A〈动〉write in one's own hand B〈名〉personal letter: 顷接～。I have just received your letter.

【手术】shǒushù〈名〉surgery: 给某人动/做～ operate on sb. ‖ 接受～ have an operation ‖ ～器械 surgical instrument ‖ 整形～ plastic/cosmetic surgery

【手术刀】shǒushùdāo〈名〉scalpel

【手术室】shǒushùshì〈名〉operating room

【手术台】shǒushùtái〈名〉operation table

【手松】shǒusōng〈形〉liberal: 他～。He is free with his money.

【手谈】shǒután〈动〉〈书〉play *weiqi*

【手套】shǒutào〈名〉glove: 一副/双～ a pair of gloves ‖ 无指～ mittens

【手提】shǒutí A〈动〉carry with one's hand B〈形〉portable: ～电脑 portable computer ‖ ～摄影机 hand-held camera ‖ ～式灭火机 portable extinguisher

【手提包】shǒutíbāo〈名〉handbag; purse〈美〉

【手提步话机】shǒutí bùhuàjī〈名〉walkie-talkie

【手提电话】shǒutí diànhuà〈名〉cellular/mobile phone

【手提箱】shǒutíxiāng〈名〉suitcase

【手头】shǒutóu〈名〉1 (手边) place within one's reach: ～的工作 work at hand ‖ ～的资料 available materials ‖ 他～有很多现金。He's got a lot of cash at hand. 2 (经济状况) financial situation: ～拮据 be hard up ‖ ～宽裕 be quite well off

【手推搬运车】shǒutuī bānyùnchē〈名〉hand truck

【手推车】shǒutuīchē〈名〉pushcart; barrow〈英〉

【手推磨】shǒutuīmò〈名〉quern

【手推婴儿车】shǒutuī yīng'érchē〈名〉pushchair〈英〉; stroller〈美〉

【手腕】shǒuwàn〈名〉1 (指人体部位) wrist: 掰～ do arm wrestling 2 (手段) stratagem: 耍～ play tricks ‖ 他很有外交～。He has excellent diplomatic skills.

【手腕子】shǒuwànzi〈名〉wrist

【手纹】shǒuwén〈名〉handprint: ～鉴定 verification of handprint

【手无寸铁】shǒuwúcùntiě〈成〉completely unarmed: ～之人 unarmed person

【手无缚鸡之力】shǒu wú fù jī zhī lì〈成〉be very weak

【手舞足蹈】shǒuwǔ-zúdǎo〈成〉leap for joy

【手下】shǒuxià A〈名〉1 (管辖下) under the direction of: 我们在他的～工作。We work under him. ▸强将～无弱兵 2 = 手头 shǒutóu 1 3 = 手头 shǒutóu 2 B〈动〉take action: ▸～留情

【手下败将】shǒuxià-bàijiàng〈成〉one's defeated opponent

【手下留情】shǒuxià-liúqíng〈成〉show mercy

【手下人】shǒuxiàrén〈名〉1 (部下) subordinates 2 (仆人) servants

【手相】shǒuxiàng〈名〉palmistry: 看～ read sb.'s palm

【手写】shǒuxiě〈动〉write by hand: ～输入 input by hand ‖ ～体 handwritten form

【手心】shǒuxīn〈名〉1 (掌心) palm 2 (掌控) control: 落入敌人的～ fall into the enemy's power

【手性】shǒuxìng〈名〉［化学］chirality: ～分子/药物 chiral molecule/drugs

【手续】shǒuxù〈名〉procedure: 办～ go through the formalities ‖ 履行～ follow procedures ‖ 法律～ legal formalities

【手续费】shǒuxùfèi〈名〉commission

【手癣】shǒuxuǎn ▸p. 50〈名〉［医学］tinea manuum

【手眼】shǒuyǎn = 手段 shǒuduàn 3

【手眼通天】shǒuyǎn-tōngtiān〈成〉be exceptionally sycophantic

【手痒】shǒuyǎng〈形〉itchy: 如果你～难耐，不妨试一试。If you're getting itchy to do it, have a go.

【手摇】shǒuyáo〈形〉hand-operated: ～风琴 hand organ ‖ ～喷雾器 hand-operated duster ‖ ～铡草机 hand-operated chopper ‖ ～钻 brace

【手艺】shǒuyì〈名〉craftsmanship: 学～ learn a trade ‖ 掌握一门～ master a craft

【手艺人】shǒuyìrén〈名〉craftsman

【手淫】shǒuyín〈动〉masturbate

【手印】shǒuyìn〈名〉1 (手掌印) handprint 2 (指纹) fingerprint: 按～ put one's thumbprint (on a document, etc.)

【手语】shǒuyǔ〈名〉sign language

【手谕】shǒuyù〈名〉〈旧〉handwritten directive

【手泽】shǒuzé〈名〉〈书〉handwriting or articles left by one's ancestors

【手札】shǒuzhá〈名〉〈旧〉personal letter

【手掌】shǒuzhǎng〈名〉palm

【手掌心】shǒuzhǎngxīn〈名〉〈口〉1 (手心) centre of the palm 2〈喻〉(控制) control: 他逃不出我的～。He couldn't free himself of my control.

【手杖】shǒuzhàng〈名〉walking stick

【手植】shǒuzhí〈动〉personally plant

【手纸】shǒuzhǐ〈名〉〈口〉toilet paper

【手指】shǒuzhǐ〈名〉finger

【手指甲】shǒuzhǐjia〈名〉fingernail

【手指头】shǒuzhǐtou〈名〉〈口〉finger

【手指字母】shǒuzhǐ zìmǔ〈名〉manual alphabet

【手重】shǒuzhòng〈形〉heavy-handed

【手镯】shǒuzhuó〈名〉bracelet

【手足】shǒuzú〈名〉1 (手和脚) hands and feet 2〈喻〉(兄弟) brothers: 亲如～ as close as brothers ▸情同～

【手足无措】shǒuzú-wúcuò〈成〉at a loss as to what to do

【手足之情】shǒuzúzhīqíng〈成〉brotherly affection: 请念及～，不要因我没有出息，就把我抛弃。Please remember our affection as siblings. Don't abandon me because I have no prospects.

【手钻】shǒuzuàn〈名〉hand drill

守

shǒu〈动〉1 (保持) maintain: ～秘密 keep a secret ▸～业, ～旧, 保～ 2 (遵守) observe: ～规矩 play by the rules ‖ ～纪律 abide by the discipline ‖ ～信用 keep one's promise ▸～法, ～信 3 (守卫) defend: ～边疆 guard the frontier ‖ ～球门 be in goal ▸～卫, 镇～ 4 (看护) keep watch: ～着病人 watch over a patient ‖ 两只虎形石兽为他～墓。His tomb is watched over by two tiger-like stone statues. ▸～护, ～株待兔, 看～ 5 (靠近) be close to: ～着炉子取暖 get warm by a stove ‖ ～着水的地方 a place near water

【守备】shǒubèi〈动〉perform garrison duty: 加强～ strengthen the garrison ‖ ～任务 garrison duty ‖ ～部队 garrison (force) ‖ ～区 garrison command

【守财奴】shǒucáinú〈名〉miser

【守常不变】shǒucháng-bùbiàn〈成〉be conservative and opposed to change

【守场员】shǒuchǎngyuán〈名〉［体育］fielder

【守车】shǒuchē〈名〉［铁路］guard's van〈英〉; caboose〈美〉: ～车长 vanguard

【守敌】shǒudí〈名〉enemy troops guarding a place

【守法】shǒufǎ〈动〉be law-abiding: 奉公～ carry out official duties and observe laws ‖ ～公民 law-abiding citizen

【守服】shǒufú〈动〉〈旧〉observe mourning for one's parent

【守宫】shǒugōng〈旧〉= 壁虎 bìhǔ

【守寡】shǒuguǎ〈动〉remain a widow

【守恒】shǒuhéng〈名〉［物理］conservation

【守恒定律】shǒuhéng dìnglǜ〈名〉conservation law

【守候】shǒuhòu〈动〉1 (等待) wait for 2 (看护) keep watch: ～病人 watch over

a patient
【守护】shǒuhù〈动〉guard
【守护神】shǒuhùshén〈名〉［宗教］patron saint
【守节】shǒujié〈动〉〈旧〉1（保持节操）remain loyal 2（指妇女）remain unmarried [after the death of her husband or her betrothed]
【守旧】shǒujiù〈形〉sticking to old ways: 在婚姻问题上思想～ conservative about marriage
【守旧派】shǒujiùpài〈名〉old fogey
【守军】shǒujūn〈名〉defence force
【守空房】shǒu kōngfáng〈动〉be left alone at home by one's husband
【守口如瓶】shǒukǒu-rúpíng〈成〉keep tight-lipped: 对自己的事～ keep one's cards close to one's chest ‖ 他要我们～。He asked us to keep our mouths shut.
【守垒员】shǒulěiyuán〈名〉［体育］baseman
【守林人】shǒulínrén〈名〉ranger
【守灵】shǒulíng〈动〉keep vigil beside a coffin
【守门】shǒumén〈动〉1［体育］keep goal 2（看门）guard a door: ～人 gate keeper
【守门员】shǒuményuán〈名〉［体育］goalkeeper
【守丧】shǒusāng = 守灵 shǒulíng
【守身如玉】shǒushēn-rúyù〈成〉preserve one's integrity
【守时】shǒushí〈动〉be on time: 这次你可得～。You must be punctual this time.
【守势】shǒushì〈名〉defensive: 采取～ be on the defensive
【守岁】shǒusuì〈动〉stay up to see in the new year: ～迎新 ring in the New Year
【守望】shǒuwàng〈动〉keep watch: ～台 watchtower
【守望相助】shǒuwàng-xiāngzhù〈成〉keep watch for and help defend one another
【守卫】shǒuwèi〈动〉guard: ～祖国边疆 defend the frontiers of one's country
【守孝】shǒuxiào〈动〉〈旧〉observe a period of mourning for one's deceased parent
【守信】shǒuxìn〈动〉keep one's word
【守业】shǒuyè〈动〉safeguard one's heritage: 创业难，～更难。It is difficult to set up a business and even harder to keep one going.
【守夜】shǒuyè〈动〉keep watch at night: 通宵～ keep vigil throughout the night ‖ ～人 night-watchman
【守约】shǒuyuē〈动〉1（指协议）abide by an agreement 2（指约定）keep an appointment
【守约方】shǒuyuēfāng〈名〉observant party
【守则】shǒuzé〈名〉regulations: 维修～ service manual
【守正不阿】shǒuzhèng-bù'ē〈成〉be just and impartial
【守职】shǒuzhí〈动〉take one's duties seriously
【守株待兔】shǒuzhū-dàitù〈成〉wait around aimlessly for a windfall that is unlikely to come

首 shǒu

A〈名〉1（头）head: ▸～饰，叩～，斩～ 2（首领）leader: 匪～ bandit chief ▸～长，群龙无～，罪魁祸～ 3（开头）beginning: ▸岁～
B〈副〉initially: ▸～创，～屈一指
C ▸**p. 691**〈数〉first: ▸～次，～届
D〈形〉supreme: ▸～都，～席
E〈动〉bring charges against sb.: ▸出～，自～
F〈量〉[for poems or songs]: 两～诗 two poems ‖ 五～歌 five songs ‖ 一～乐曲 a piece of music
【首班车】shǒubānchē〈名〉first bus (of a regular service)
【首播】shǒubō〈动〉broadcast for the first time
【首倡】shǒuchàng〈动〉initiate: ～者 initiator
【首创】shǒuchuàng〈动〉pioneer: 这个项目是全国～。The programme was the first of its kind in the country.
【首创精神】shǒuchuàng jīngshén〈名〉pioneering spirit
【首次】shǒucì〈名〉first time: ～亮相 make one's debut ‖ ～公演 premiere
【首当其冲】shǒudāng-qíchōng〈成〉bear the brunt: 在战斗中～ bear the brunt of a battle ‖ 他们村在那次水灾中～。Their village was the first to be hit by the flood waters.
【首都】shǒudū〈名〉capital
【首恶】shǒu'è〈名〉chief criminal: ～必办。The principal culprits must be punished.
【首发】shǒufā〈动〉1（指出版）publish for the first time: 百科全书的～仪式 ceremony marking the publication of the encyclopedia 2（指公共汽车）dispatch 3（指发行）issue for the first time 4［体育］start: ～阵容 starting line-up
【首发式】shǒufāshì〈名〉launch ceremony
【首发团】shǒufātuán〈名〉first tour group: 赴台旅游～ the first tour group to Taiwan
【首犯】shǒufàn〈名〉chief criminal
【首府】shǒufǔ〈名〉1〈旧〉（指省会）prefecture 2（指自治区或自治州）capital city
【首付款】shǒufùkuǎn〈名〉down payment: 购房～比例为20%。Down payment on a house is 20% of the purchase price.
【首富】shǒufù〈名〉richest person in the locality
【首功】shǒugōng〈名〉first-class merit
【首航】shǒuháng〈动〉make a maiden voyage
【首航式】shǒuhángshì〈名〉launching ceremony
【首户】shǒuhù〈名〉wealthiest family in the locality
【首级】shǒují〈名〉〈旧〉severed head
【首季】shǒujì〈名〉first quarter of the year
【首届】shǒujiè〈名〉first occasion: ～选举 first election
【首肯】shǒukěn〈动〉nod one's approval: 得到上级～ get approval of one's superiors
【首领】shǒulǐng〈名〉leader: 工会～ trade union chief ‖ 叛乱～ ringleader of a revolt
【首轮】shǒulún〈名〉first round: ～谈判 first round of talks
【首脑】shǒunǎo〈名〉head: 公司～ person at the helm of a company
【首批】shǒupī〈名〉first batch
【首屈一指】shǒuqū-yīzhǐ〈成〉be second to none: 他的古玩收藏堪称～。His collection of curios is unparalleled.
【首任】shǒurèn〈名〉first appointee to an office: ～大使 first ambassador
【首日封】shǒurìfēng〈名〉first-day cover
【首饰】shǒushi〈名〉1（头饰）head ornaments 2（珠宝）jewellery: 戴～ wear jewels
【首鼠两端】shǒushǔ-liǎngduān〈成〉be in two minds
【首尾】shǒuwěi〈名〉1（前后）front and back: ～夹攻 attack at the front and at the rear 2（从始到终）period from beginning to end: 装修～花了一个多月。The renovation lasted over a month.
【首尾相应】shǒuwěi-xiāngyìng〈成〉1（指文章）the beginning and the ending complement one another 2（指队伍）the vanguard and the rear are working together
【首位】shǒuwèi〈名〉first place: 放在～ give first priority ‖ 居～ rank first ‖ 我们应该把国家利益放在～。We should put national interests above everything else.
【首乌】shǒuwū = 何首乌 héshǒuwū
【首席】shǒuxí〈名〉1（指席位）head of the table: 坐～ take the seat of honour 2（指职位）chief: ～顾问 chief adviser
【首席大法官】shǒuxí dàfǎguān〈名〉chief justice
【首席检察官】shǒuxí jiǎncháguān〈名〉chief prosecutor
【首席小提琴手】shǒuxí xiǎotíqínshǒu〈名〉first violinist: 担任～ play first violin
【首席行政长官】shǒuxí xíngzhèng zhǎngguān〈名〉commissioner
【首席执行官】shǒuxí zhíxíngguān〈名〉chief executive officer (CEO)
【首先】shǒuxiān **A**〈副〉first: ～要讲质量 put quality above everything else **B**〈连〉first of all: ～，你必须坦诚。Above all else, you must be frank. ‖ ～，我们的路子对头。To start with, we are on the right track.
【首相】shǒuxiàng〈名〉prime minister: ～职位 premiership ‖ ～府 residence of the prime minister
【首项】shǒuxiàng〈名〉first item: 本月～足球赛事 the first football match of the month
【首选】shǒuxuǎn〈动〉be the first to be selected: ～职业 first choice of profession
【首演】shǒuyǎn〈动〉give the first performance
【首要】shǒuyào **A**〈形〉key: ～规则 cardinal rule ‖ ～任务 chief task ‖ ～条件 most important condition ‖ ～问题 number one problem ‖ ～职责 first duty **B** = 首脑 shǒunǎo
【首要分子】shǒuyàofènzǐ〈名〉ringleader
【首义】shǒuyì〈动〉〈书〉be the first to rise in revolt
【首映】shǒuyìng〈动〉premiere (of a film)
【首映式】shǒuyìngshì〈名〉premiere (of a film)
【首战】shǒuzhàn〈名〉first battle: ～告捷 win the very first battle
【首长】shǒuzhǎng〈名〉senior official: 老～ old chief ‖ 团～ commanders of a regiment
【首长席】shǒuzhǎngxí〈名〉VIP seats
【首字母】shǒuzìmǔ〈名〉initial
【首字母缩略词】shǒuzìmǔ suōlüècí〈名〉acronym
【首坐】shǒuzuò = 首座 shǒuzuò
【首座】shǒuzuò〈名〉1（指席位）seat of honour 2（指僧人）abbot

艏 shǒu〈名〉bow

shòu

寿（壽）shòu

A〈形〉1（长寿）long: ▸～星，人～年丰

2 ▸**p. 772**〈婉〉（指装殓用品） funerary: ▸～材，～衣
B〈名〉 **1**（生命） life: ▸～比南山，～命，长～ **2**（生日） birthday: ▸～礼，～面，祝～
【寿斑】shòubān〈名〉 age spot
【寿比南山】shòubǐ-nánshān〈成〉 many happy returns of the day
【寿材】shòucái ▸**p. 772**〈名〉〈旧〉coffin prepared before one's death
【寿辰】shòuchén〈名〉 [of elderly people] birthday
【寿诞】shòudàn = 寿辰 shòuchén
【寿酒】shòujiǔ〈名〉 birthday feast
【寿礼】shòulǐ〈名〉 birthday present [for an elderly person]
【寿联】shòulián〈名〉 birthday couplets
【寿面】shòumiàn〈名〉 longevity noodles [eaten on one's birthday]
【寿命】shòumìng〈名〉 **1**（生命）lifespan: 延长～ increase longevity ‖ 平均～ life expectancy **2**〈喻〉（使用年限） service life: 汽车～ life of a car
【寿木】shòumù = 寿材 shòucái
【寿山石】shòushānshí〈名〉 *Shoushan* stone [translucent stone found at Shoushan, Fujian Province, prized as a precious material for seals]
【寿数】shòushu〈名〉 allotted lifespan: ～已尽 one's days are drawing to a close
【寿司】shòusī〈名〉 [食品] sushi
【寿桃】shòutáo〈名〉 **1**（桃） peach [given as a birthday present] **2**（点心） peach-shaped birthday cake
【寿险】shòuxiǎn〈名〉 life insurance
【寿星】shòuxing〈名〉 **1**（指神） god of longevity **2**（指人） person whose birthday is being celebrated
【寿穴】shòuxué〈名〉〈旧〉grave prepared before one's death
【寿筵】shòuyán〈名〉 birthday feast
【寿衣】shòuyī ▸**p. 772**〈名〉 shroud
【寿终】shòuzhōng〈动〉 die of old age
【寿终正寝】shòuzhōng-zhèngqǐn〈成〉 die a natural death

受 shòu〈动〉 **1**（接受） receive: 我不愿～人指挥。 I will not be dictated to. **2**（遭受） suffer: ～处罚 receive a punishment ‖ ～打击 sustain a blow ‖ ～法律制裁 be punished by law ‖ ～损害 come to harm ‖ ～委屈 be wronged ‖ ～限制 be subject to restrictions ▸～苦，～罪，自作自～ **3**（忍受） bear: 我～够了。 I've had enough of it. ▸～不了，～苦～难 **4**〈口〉（适合） suit: ▸～用
【受保人】shòubǎorén〈名〉 the insured
【受不了】shòubuliǎo〈动〉〈口〉be unable to endure: 冷/热/疼得～ can't stand the cold/heat/pain
【受潮】shòucháo〈动〉 be affected with damp: 切勿～! Keep dry!
【受宠】shòuchǒng〈动〉 be in sb.'s favour
【受宠若惊】shòuchǒng-ruòjīng〈成〉 be overwhelmed by sb.'s flattery
【受挫】shòucuò〈动〉 suffer a setback: 在事业上～ have a setback in one's career ‖ 计划～。 The plan was foiled. ‖ 和平进程～。 The peace process has been thwarted.
【受到】shòudào〈动〉 receive: ～热烈欢迎 be warmly welcomed ‖ ～严厉批评 come in for severe criticism ‖ ～应有的赏罚 get one's just desserts ‖ ～直接攻击 come under direct attack
【受得了】shòudeliǎo〈动〉〈口〉can bear: 你怎能～这样的羞辱? How could you stand such humiliation?
【受敌】shòudí〈动〉 come under enemy attack: 四面～ be attacked by the enemy on all sides
【受冻挨饿】shòudòng-ái'è〈动〉 go cold and hungry
【受罚】shòufá〈动〉 be punished: 司机因违反交通规则而～。 The driver was fined for violation of traffic rules.
【受粉】shòufěn〈动〉 [植物] be pollinated
【受雇】shòugù〈动〉 be employed: ～于人 hire oneself out to sb. ‖ ～人 employee
【受过】shòuguò〈动〉 take the blame: 代人～ take responsibility for sb. else's wrong doing
【受害】shòuhài〈动〉 fall victim to: ～不浅 suffer a lot ‖ ～最大 be hardest hit ‖ 首先～的是欧洲。 Europe bore the brunt of it.
【受害人】shòuhàirén〈名〉 [法律] aggrieved party
【受害者】shòuhàizhě〈名〉 sufferer: 成为～ fall victim to ‖ ～家属 family of the victim
【受贿】shòuhuì〈动〉 take bribes: 坚拒～ fight against corruption
【受贿者】shòuhuìzhě〈名〉 bribe taker
【受惠】shòuhuì〈动〉 receive benefits
【受惠国】shòuhuìguó〈名〉 [外交] beneficiary country
【受夹板气】shòu jiābǎnqì〈惯〉 be caught in a cross fire
【受奖】shòujiǎng〈动〉be granted an award
【受戒】shòujiè〈动〉 [佛教] be initiated into monkhood/nunhood
【受尽】shòujìn〈动〉 have one's fill of: ～煎熬 suffer all kinds of torments
【受惊】shòujīng〈动〉 take fright: 孩子～了。 The child was frightened. ‖ 这匹马容易～。 The horse startles easily.
【受精】shòujīng〈动〉 be fertilized
【受精卵】shòujīngluǎn〈名〉 spermatovum
【受精体】shòujīngtǐ〈名〉 receptive body
【受窘】shòujiǒng〈动〉 feel embarrassed: 我的坦率使他～。 My frankness made him uneasy.
【受苦】shòukǔ〈动〉 suffer
【受苦受难】shòukǔ-shòunàn〈成〉 be downtrodden
【受累】shòulěi〈动〉〈书〉 get involved: 他也在该案中～。 He was also dragged into the case.
【受累】shòulèi〈动〉 be put to a lot of trouble: 叫您～了。 I'm sorry to have put you to so much trouble.
【受礼】shòulǐ〈动〉 accept a gift: 他一生从不～。 He never accepted a gift in his life.
【受理】shòulǐ〈动〉 **1**（办理） accept and attend to: ～托运业务 handle a consignments of goods **2**（审理） hear a case: ～申诉 hear a claim
【受凉】shòuliáng〈动〉 catch (a) cold
【受命】shòumìng〈动〉 be commissioned
【受难】shòunàn〈动〉 suffer calamities: ～者 disaster victim ‖ 战争～者 war victim
【受骗】shòupiàn〈动〉 be deceived: ～上当 be taken in
【受聘】shòupìn〈动〉 **1**（指聘礼） [of a woman] accept betrothal gifts **2**（指工作） accept a job offer
【受气】shòuqì〈动〉 be bullied
【受气包】shòuqìbāo〈名〉〈口〉 whipping boy
【受穷】shòuqióng〈动〉 live in poverty: 一辈子～ have been poor all one's life
【受屈】shòuqū〈动〉 suffer an injustice
【受权】shòuquán〈动〉 be authorized: ～使用武力 be authorized to use force
【受热】shòurè〈动〉 **1**（指高温） be exposed to heat: 切勿～! Keep cool! **2**（中暑） have heatstroke
【受人一饭，听人使唤】shòu rén yī fàn, tīng rén shǐhuan〈俗〉 There is no such thing as a free lunch
【受人之托】shòu rén zhī tuō〈成〉 receive a request
【受辱】shòurǔ〈动〉 be humiliated: 当众～ suffer public humiliation
【受伤】shòushāng〈动〉 be injured: 颈部/膝部/胸部～ have a neck/knee/chest injury ‖ ～致死 receive fatal wounds ‖ 在火灾中～ be injured in a fire
【受赏】shòushǎng〈动〉 be rewarded: 立功～ be cited for one's merits
【受审】shòushěn〈动〉 stand trial: 因谋杀罪～ be on trial for murder ‖ 在法庭～ be tried in court
【受事】shòushì〈名〉 [语法] object
【受试人】shòushìrén〈名〉 **1**（指考试） examinee **2**（指试验） testee
【受损】shòusǔn〈动〉 be damaged: ～程度 extent of damage
【受胎】shòutāi〈动〉 become pregnant
【受托】shòutuō〈动〉 be entrusted with: ～照顾孩子 be entrusted with the care of a child
【受托方】shòutuōfāng〈名〉 trustee: 担当慈善基金～ act as trustee of a charity
【受托国】shòutuōguó〈名〉 [外交] mandatory power
【受托人】shòutuōrén〈名〉 [法律] trustee
【受洗】shòuxǐ〈动〉 [基督教] be baptized
【受限】shòuxiàn〈动〉 be limited
【受降】shòuxiáng〈动〉 accept a surrender
【受刑】shòuxíng〈动〉 be tortured
【受训】shòuxùn〈动〉 receive training: 严格～ be strictly disciplined
【受业】shòuyè **A**〈动〉〈书〉 receive instruction **B**〈名〉〈尊〉（我） I [a form of self-address used by a student when speaking to the teacher]
【受益】shòuyì〈动〉 benefit from: ～于某人的忠告 profit from sb.'s advice
【受益方】shòuyìfāng〈名〉 benefiting party
【受益继承人】shòuyì jìchéngrén〈名〉 heir beneficiary
【受益人】shòuyìrén〈名〉 beneficiary: ～利益 beneficial interest
【受用】shòuyòng〈动〉 benefit from: ～不尽 benefit from sth. all one's life
【受用】shòuyong〈形〉 feeling good: 我今天身体不～。 I don't feel well today.
【受援】shòuyuán〈动〉 receive help: ～国 recipient country
【受灾】shòuzāi〈动〉 suffer a disaster: ～地区 disaster area ‖ ～群众 people affected by a natural disaster
【受之无愧】shòuzhī-wúkuì〈成〉 deserve: ～的诺贝尔奖获得者 worthy winner of the Nobel Prize ‖ 英雄称号他～。 He fully deserves the title of hero.
【受之有愧】shòuzhī-yǒukuì〈成〉 be unworthy of sth.: 我～。 I don't deserve it.
【受制】shòuzhì〈动〉 be controlled: ～于人 be under sb.'s control
【受众】shòuzhòng〈名〉 audience
【受阻】shòuzǔ〈动〉 be hindered: 救援物资进城～。 Relief supplies have been blocked from entering the city.
【受罪】shòuzuì〈动〉 **1**（受折磨） endure hardships **2**（令人烦恼） meet with sth. unpleasant: 和他在一起真～。 It's most unpleasant to be with him.

S

狩 shòu〈动〉hunt: ▸～猎

【狩猎】shòuliè〈动〉hunt: ～工具 hunting tool

授 shòu〈动〉**1**（给予）award: ～博士学位 confer doctor's degree on sb. ▸～奖, ～衔, ～意 **2**（教）teach: ▸～课, 函～, 讲～

【授粉】shòufěn〈动〉［植物］pollinate: 人工～ artificial pollination ‖ 异花～ cross-pollination

【授粉媒介】shòufěn méijiè〈名〉pollinator

【授奖】shòujiǎng〈动〉grant an award: 给某人授一等奖 award sb. with a top prize

【授奖仪式】shòujiǎng yíshì〈名〉award ceremony

【授精】shòujīng〈动〉inseminate: 人工～ artificial insemination

【授课】shòukè〈动〉deliver a lecture: ～计划 course plan ‖ 教授每周给学生～两次。 The professor gives two lectures a week to his students.

【授命】shòumìng〈动〉**1**（下令）authorize **2**〈书〉（献出生命）lay down one's life

【授权】shòuquán〈动〉authorize: 得到政府～ get a government endorsement

【授权书】shòuquánshū〈名〉letter of attorney

【授人以柄】shòurényǐbǐng〈成〉give sb. the upper hand

【授受】shòushòu〈动〉give and accept: 私相～ deal under the table

【授受不亲】shòushòu-bùqīn〈成〉not allow direct contact between men and women

【授衔】shòuxián〈动〉confer a title: 给某人授军衔 confer a military rank on sb.

【授信】shòuxìn〈动〉extend credit: 银行～数千万，解决中小企业资金不足问题。 The bank has extended credit by several million in order to resolve the financial deficit for small and medium-sized companies.

【授信额度】shòuxìn édù〈名〉credit line

【授勋】shòuxūn〈动〉confer a medal on sb.

【授意】shòuyì〈动〉inspire: 由某人～散布的谣言 a rumour instigated by sb. ‖ 那封信是在小王的～下写的。 That letter was written at Xiao Wang's suggestion.

【授予】shòuyǔ〈动〉award: ～某人奖学金 grant sb. a scholarship ‖ ～某人学位 confer a degree upon sb. ‖ 被～劳模称号 be given the title of model worker

售 shòu〈动〉**1**（卖）sell: ～完 be sold out ▸～货, 零～, 销～ **2**〈书〉（实现）make sth. work: 以～其奸 in order to achieve a treacherous purpose

【售后服务】shòuhòu fúwù〈名〉after-sales service

【售货】shòuhuò〈动〉sell goods: ～经理 sales manager

【售货机】shòuhuòjī〈名〉vending machine

【售货亭】shòuhuòtíng〈名〉kiosk

【售货员】shòuhuòyuán ▸**p. 966**〈名〉shop assistant〈英〉; sales clerk〈美〉

【售价】shòujià〈名〉price

【售卖】shòumài〈动〉sell

【售票】shòupiào〈动〉sell tickets: ～设备 ticket issuing equipment ‖ ～窗口 ticket window

【售票处】shòupiàochù〈名〉ticket office; booking office〈英〉: 代理～ ticket agency

【售票厅】shòupiàotīng〈名〉booking hall

【售票员】shòupiàoyuán ▸**p. 966**〈名〉[of a bus] conductor

【售罄】shòuqìng〈动〉sell out

兽（獸） shòu

A〈名〉animal: ▸～医, 野～

B〈形〉bestial: ▸～性

【兽环】shòuhuán〈名〉animal-shaped door knocker

【兽类】shòulèi〈名〉animals

【兽力车】shòulìchē〈名〉animal-drawn cart

【兽皮】shòupí〈名〉hide

【兽王】shòuwáng〈名〉king of animals [lion or tiger]

【兽行】shòuxíng〈名〉**1**（野蛮行为）savagery **2**（淫秽行为）act of lust

【兽性】shòuxìng〈名〉barbarity

【兽医】shòuyī〈名〉vet

【兽医学】shòuyīxué〈名〉veterinary medicine

【兽医站】shòuyīzhàn〈名〉veterinary station

【兽疫】shòuyì〈名〉epizootic disease

【兽欲】shòuyù〈名〉animal desire

绶（綬） shòu〈名〉silk ribbon attached to an official seal or a medal

【绶带】shòudài〈名〉ribbon attached to an official seal or a medal

瘦 shòu〈形〉**1**（指人）thin: 又高又～ tall and skinny ‖ 他～了。He has lost weight. ‖ 这匹马～得可怜。 The poor horse was all skin and bone(s). ▸骨～如柴, 面黄肌～ **2**（指书法）thin: 字体～硬 handwriting with thin but powerful strokes **3**（指肉）lean: ▸～肉, 挑肥拣～ **4**（指衣服）tight: 她的新裙子有点～。 Her new dress is a bit tight. **5**（指土地）infertile: ～田 barren land

【瘦瘪】shòubiě〈形〉thin and hollow

【瘦长】shòucháng〈形〉long and thin: 身材～ tall and slender figure

【瘦骨嶙峋】shòugǔ-línxún〈成〉all skin and bones: 那时他～。 He was like a walking skeleton then.

【瘦骨伶仃】shòugǔ-língdīng〈成〉thin and weak

【瘦果】shòuguǒ〈名〉［植物］achene

【瘦猴儿】shòuhóur〈名〉〈口〉waif

【瘦瘠】shòují〈形〉**1**（指人）thin and weak **2**（指土地）infertile: ～的土壤 sterile soil

【瘦肉】shòuròu〈名〉lean meat

【瘦肉精】shòuròujīng〈名〉clenbuterol [used in animal feed to promote lean meat]

【瘦肉型】shòuròuxíng〈名〉animals bred for their lean meat

【瘦弱】shòuruò〈形〉emaciated: 身体～ weak health

【瘦身】shòushēn = 减肥 jiǎnféi

【瘦死的骆驼比马大】shòusǐde luòtuo bǐ mǎ dà〈俗〉when the mighty fall, they still command more respect than the man in the street

【瘦小】shòuxiǎo〈形〉thin and small: 身材～ be slight of figure

【瘦削】shòuxuē〈形〉gaunt: 身体～ be skinny

【瘦子】shòuzi〈名〉skinny person

shū

殳 shū〈名〉〈古〉weapon made of bamboo

书（書） shū

A〈动〉write: ▸～写, 罄竹难～

B〈名〉**1**（字体）script: ▸草～, 隶～ **2**（著作）book **3**（文件）document: ▸申请～, 说明～, 证～ **4**（信件）letter: ▸～信, 家～

【书案】shū'àn〈名〉〈旧〉desk

【书包】shūbāo〈名〉school bag: 小学生～ schoolboy's satchel

【书报】shūbào〈名〉books, newspapers, and periodicals: ～费 allowance for buying books and periodicals

【书背】shūbèi〈名〉book spine

【书本】shūběn〈名〉books: 啃～ delve into books

【书不尽言】shūbùjìnyán〈成〉I could write more, but I must stop here

【书场】shūchǎng〈名〉hall for storytelling performers

【书痴】shūchī〈名〉bookworm

【书橱】shūchú〈名〉bookcase

【书呆子】shūdāizi〈名〉swot〈英〉; grind〈美〉

【书单】shūdān〈名〉book list

【书挡】shūdǎng〈名〉bookend

【书到用时方恨少】shū dào yòng shí fāng hèn shǎo〈俗〉you never realize the value of books until you need them

【书店】shūdiàn〈名〉bookshop〈英〉; bookstore〈美〉

【书法】shūfǎ〈名〉calligraphy: 学习～ practise calligraphy

> **书法**
>
> The art of writing Chinese characters. Calligraphy requires a brush, ink, paper and an inkstone. These are known collectively as the four treasures of the study (▸文房四宝). The main calligraphic styles are seal script (篆书), official script (隶书), cursive script (草书), regular or model script (楷书) and running script (行书).

【书法家】shūfǎjiā〈名〉calligrapher

【书坊】shūfāng〈名〉〈旧〉bookshop with a printing workshop

【书房】shūfáng〈名〉study

【书稿】shūgǎo〈名〉literary manuscript: 手写～ handwritten manuscript

【书柜】shūguì〈名〉bookcase

【书函】shūhán〈名〉**1** = 书套 shūtào **2**（书信）correspondence: 商业～ commercial letters

【书号】shūhào〈名〉book number: 国际标准～ International Standard Book Number (ISBN)

【书后】shūhòu〈名〉postscript (PS)

【书画】shūhuà〈名〉painting and calligraphy: ～大师 master of painting and calligraphy

【书画展】shūhuàzhǎn〈名〉exhibition of painting and calligraphy

【书籍】shūjí〈名〉books: 文学～ works of literature

【书脊】shūjǐ〈名〉spine

【书记】shūji〈名〉**1**（负责人）secretary: 总～ general secretary **2**〈旧〉（文书）clerk

【书记处】shūjichù〈名〉secretariat: 联合国～ United Nations Secretariat

【书记员】shūjiyuán ▸**p. 966**〈名〉clerk

【书架】shūjià〈名〉bookshelf: 固定式～ built-in bookcase

【书柬】shūjiǎn = 书简 shūjiǎn

【书简】shūjiǎn〈名〉〈书〉letters: 商务～ business correspondence

【书局】shūjú〈名〉publishing house

【书卷】shūjuàn〈名〉〈书〉books
【书卷气】shūjuànqì〈名〉bookishness
【书刊】shūkān〈名〉books and periodicals: 黄色～ pornographic material
【书刊审查制度】shūkān shěnchá zhìdù〈名〉print media censorship
【书库】shūkù〈名〉stack room
【书立】shūlì = 书挡 shūdǎng
【书眉】shūméi〈名〉top of a page
【书迷】shūmí〈名〉**1**（指看书）bookworm **2**（指听书）storytelling fan
【书面】shūmiàn〈形〉written: ～凭证 written confirmation
【书面保证】shūmiàn bǎozhèng〈名〉written guarantee
【书面声明】shūmiàn shēngmíng〈名〉written statement
【书面体】shūmiàntǐ〈名〉literary style
【书面形式】shūmiàn xíngshì〈名〉written form
【书面语】shūmiànyǔ〈名〉written language: 用～表达 express in literary language
【书名】shūmíng〈名〉book title
【书名号】shūmínghào〈名〉book title mark (《》)
【书目】shūmù〈名〉book list: 参考～ bibliography
【书目分类法】shūmù fēnlèifǎ〈名〉bibliographic classification
【书皮】shūpí〈名〉**1**（封面）book cover **2**（保护层）dust jacket: ～纸 paper book cover
【书评】shūpíng〈名〉book review
【书签】shūqiān〈名〉**1**（指夹在书中）bookmark **2**（指封面上）title label
【书商】shūshāng〈名〉bookseller
【书社】shūshè〈名〉**1**〈旧〉（指文人团体）literary club **2**（指出版机构）publishing house
【书生】shūshēng〈名〉scholar
【书生气】shūshēngqì〈名〉bookishness: ～十足 bookish and naive
【书生之见】shūshēngzhījiàn〈成〉pedantic view
【书市】shūshì〈名〉book fair
【书摊】shūtān〈名〉book stand
【书坛】shūtán〈名〉**1**（指书法）calligraphers' circles: ～新秀 promising calligrapher **2**（指说书）storytelling circles: ～奇才 storytelling talent
【书套】shūtào〈名〉cover: 装入～ mount in a slipcase
【书体】shūtǐ〈名〉script style: 斜～ italicized calligraphy
【书亭】shūtíng〈名〉bookstall
【书童】shūtóng〈名〉〈旧〉page boy
【书屋】shūwū〈名〉**1**〈旧〉（看书用）study **2**（书店）bookshop〈英〉; bookstore〈美〉
【书香】shūxiāng〈名〉literary family: ～世家 eminent family of intellectuals ‖ ～门第 scholar family ‖ 她家世代～。She comes from a long line of scholars.
【书写】shūxiě〈动〉write: 用铅笔～ write with a pencil ‖ ～错误 clerical error
【书写格式】shūxiě géshi〈名〉form of a certain type of writing
【书信】shūxìn〈名〉letter: 和某人保持～往来 keep up correspondence with sb. ‖ ～格式 form of a letter
【书信集】shūxìnjí〈名〉collected letters
【书信体】shūxìntǐ〈名〉epistolary style: ～诗歌 epistolary poem
【书页】shūyè〈名〉page: 散～ loose page
【书影】shūyǐng〈名〉sample pages
【书友会】shūyǒuhuì〈名〉book club
【书院】shūyuàn〈名〉〈旧〉academy of classical learning
【书札】shūzhá〈名〉〈书〉letters
【书斋】shūzhāi〈名〉〈书〉study
【书展】shūzhǎn〈名〉**1**（指图书）book fair **2**（指书法）calligraphy exhibition
【书证】shūzhèng〈名〉［法律］documentary evidence
【书桌】shūzhuō〈名〉desk

抒 shū〈动〉express: ▸～怀, ～情, 各～己见

【抒发】shūfā〈动〉express: ～感情 express one's feelings
【抒怀】shūhuái〈动〉〈书〉pour out one's heart
【抒情】shūqíng〈动〉express one's emotions: ～歌曲 lyric song ‖ ～散文 lyric prose
【抒情诗】shūqíngshī〈名〉lyric
【抒写】shūxiě〈动〉express in writing: 这本书～了他在中国的所见所闻。The book describes what he saw and heard in China.

纾（紓）shū

A〈形〉〈书〉comfortably off
B〈动〉**1**（使宽裕）improve sb.'s lot **2**〈书〉（解除）relieve: ▸～祸, ～难
【纾祸】shūhuò〈动〉〈书〉alleviate calamities
【纾难】shūnàn〈动〉〈书〉relieve sb.'s distress

枢（樞）shū〈名〉**1**（转轴）pivot: ▸流水不腐，户～不蠹 **2**（中心）centre: ▸～纽 **3**〈旧〉（要职）key government department: ▸～要

【枢机】shūjī〈名〉**1**〈旧〉（指政府部门）key government post **2**〈书〉（指问题）heart of the matter
【枢机主教】shūjī zhǔjiào〈名〉［宗教］cardinal
【枢密院】Shūmìyuàn〈名〉Privy Council: ～官员 privy councillor
【枢纽】shūniǔ〈名〉hub: ～工程 key project
【枢要】shūyào〈名〉〈书〉central administration: ～部门 department of the central administration

叔 shū〈名〉**1**〈书〉（排行老三）third among brothers: ▸伯仲～季 **2**（丈夫的弟弟）husband's younger brother: ～嫂 brother-in-law and sister-in-law ▸小～子 **3**（父亲的弟弟）father's younger brother: ～侄 uncle and nephew ‖ 小～ father's youngest brother ▸～父 **4**（父辈男性）uncle **5**（表尊称）uncle: 张～ Uncle Zhang

【叔伯】shūbai〈名〉cousins of the same grandfather or great-grandfather
【叔父】shūfù ▸**p. 588**〈名〉uncle [father's younger brother]
【叔公】shūgōng ▸**p. 588**〈名〉**1**（丈夫的叔叔）husband's uncle **2**〈方〉（父亲的叔叔）paternal great-uncle
【叔母】shūmǔ ▸**p. 588**〈名〉aunt [wife of father's brother]
【叔婆】shūpó ▸**p. 588**〈名〉**1**（丈夫的婶母）husband's uncle's wife **2**〈方〉（叔祖母）paternal great-aunt
【叔叔】shūshu〈名〉**1** ▸**p. 588**（指亲戚）uncle [father's younger brother] **2**（指父辈男性）uncle: 警察～ Mr Policeman ‖ 李～ Uncle Li
【叔祖】shūzǔ ▸**p. 588**〈名〉great-uncle
【叔祖母】shūzǔmǔ ▸**p. 588**〈名〉great-aunt (wife of paternal grandfather's younger brother)

姝 shū〈书〉

A〈形〉[of a lady] pretty
B〈名〉beauty: 绝代之～ lady of unparalleled beauty

殊 shū

A〈动〉die: ▸～死
B〈形〉**1**（不同）different: ▸～途同归, 悬～ **2**（特别）remarkable: ～誉 special honour ‖ ～勋 distinguished service
C〈副〉〈书〉extremely: ～难相信 very difficult to believe
【殊不知】shūbùzhī〈动〉〈书〉**1**（指知道）who knows that ... **2**（指想到）hardly imagine: 我以为她没考上大学，～她都要大学毕业了。I thought she had failed in the college entrance exam. I never dreamed that she was about to graduate from college.
【殊荣】shūróng〈名〉special honour
【殊死】shūsǐ〈形〉desperate: ～搏斗 life-and-death battle
【殊途同归】shūtú-tóngguī〈成〉all roads lead to Rome
【殊效】shūxiào〈名〉〈书〉remarkable efficacy

倏 shū〈副〉〈书〉quickly

【倏地】shūdì〈副〉suddenly
【倏尔】shū'ěr〈副〉〈书〉suddenly
【倏忽】shūhū〈副〉suddenly
【倏然】shūrán〈副〉〈书〉**1**（突然）suddenly: ～消失 disappear abruptly **2**（快）quickly

菽 shū〈名〉〈书〉beans: 不辨～麦 lack everyday knowledge

【菽粟】shūsù〈名〉beans and crops: 布帛～ cloth and grain

梳 shū

A〈名〉comb: ▸～篦, ～子
B〈动〉comb: 你的头发得～一～了。Your hair needs a bit of a comb. ‖ 小女孩把头发～成辫子。The little girl wears her hair in plaits. ▸～洗, ～妆
【梳篦】shūbì〈名〉thick and fine-toothed comb
【梳辫子】shū biànzi〈动〉**1**〈本〉braid one's hair **2**〈喻〉（分析归类）sort sth. out
【梳理】shūlǐ〈动〉**1**［纺织］card: 将羊毛～成毛线 card wool into thread **2**（整理）comb: ～思路 organize one's ideas
【梳毛机】shūmáojī〈名〉carding machine
【梳棉】shūmián〈动〉［纺织］card: ～机 carding machine
【梳头】shūtóu〈动〉comb one's hair
【梳洗】shūxǐ〈动〉wash and dress
【梳妆】shūzhuāng〈动〉get dressed and do one's make-up: ～打扮 get dressed up
【梳妆台】shūzhuāngtái〈名〉dressing table
【梳子】shūzi〈名〉comb

淑 shū〈形〉pretty: ▸～静, ～女, 贤～

【淑静】shūjìng〈形〉[of a woman] refined and gentle
【淑女】shūnǚ〈名〉fair maiden: ～装 young ladies' fashion

舒 shū

A〈动〉 stretch: ～了一口气 give a sigh of relief ▸～筋活络, ～眉展眼
B〈形〉 **1**〈书〉（慢） slow: ▸～缓 **2**（轻松） leisurely: ▸～服, ～适, ～坦
【舒畅】shūchàng〈形〉 at ease: 心情～ feel happy
【舒服】shūfu〈形〉 **1**（舒适） comfortable: 躺在被窝里～极了。 It was so nice and cosy tucked up in bed. **2**（健康） well: 感觉不～ feel very bad ‖ 今天我有点不～。 I don't feel too great today.
【舒缓】shūhuǎn〈形〉 **1**（缓慢） leisurely: 节奏～ slow pace **2**（缓和） mild: 语气～ relaxed tone **3**（坡度小） gentle
【舒筋活络】shūjīn-huóluò〈动〉［中医］ stimulate blood circulation and relax muscles and joints
【舒筋活血】shūjīn-huóxuè〈动〉［中医］ soothe the sinew and quicken the blood
【舒卷】shūjuǎn〈动〉〈书〉 [of clouds or smoke] roll and unroll
【舒眉展眼】shūméi-zhǎnyǎn〈成〉 beam with joy: 成功使她～。 Success brought a smile to her face.
【舒散】shūsàn〈动〉 **1**（指肢体） stretch: ～筋骨 relax one's muscles ‖ ～四肢 stretch one's limbs **2**（指心绪） shake off: ～心中的郁闷 express one's displeasure
【舒适】shūshì〈形〉 cosy: 感到很～ feel very snug ‖ ～的生活 comfortable life
【舒适度】shūshìdù〈名〉 comfort level: 提高硬座车厢的～ improve the level of comfort in hard-seat compartments
【舒松】shūsōng〈形〉 relieved and relaxed: 大脑～ relax one's mind
【舒坦】shūtan〈形〉 comfortable: 浑身～ feel at ease
【舒心】shūxīn〈形〉 contented: ～地一笑 smile cheerfully ‖ 工作～ work is going smoothly
【舒展】shūzhǎn〈动〉 **1**（展开） extend: ～眉头 unknit one's brows **2**（拉伸） limber up: ～筋骨 stretch one's muscles and joints ‖ 在沙发上～一下身子 stretch out on the sofa
【舒张】shūzhāng〈名〉［生理］ diastole: ～压 diastolic pressure

疏¹ shū〈名〉 **1**〈旧〉（条陈） memorial to the emperor **2**（注解） annotation: ▸注～

疏² shū

A〈动〉 **1**（疏通） dredge: ▸～导, ～浚, ～通 **2**（分散） scatter: ～财 disperse aid ▸～剪, ～散
B〈形〉 **1**（不密） sparse: ～星 scattered stars ▸～密 **2**（疏远） distant: 别久情～。 Out of sight, out of mind. ▸～远, 亲～ **3**（不熟练） unskilful: ▸荒～, 生～ **4**（空虚） hollow: ▸才～学浅, 空～, 志大才～ **5**（疏忽） negligent: ～于照顾 be ill cared for ‖ ～于职守 neglect one's duties ▸～忽, ～漏
【疏财仗义】shūcái-zhàngyì = 仗义疏财 zhàngyì-shūcái
【疏导】shūdǎo〈动〉 **1**（疏通水道） dredge **2**（引导） guide: ～交通 relieve traffic congestion
【疏放】shūfàng〈形〉 unconventional
【疏肝理气】shūgān-lǐqì〈动〉［中医］ soothe the liver and regulate the circulation of vital energy
【疏忽】shūhu〈动〉 overlook: 那一点我～了。 That point slipped my attention. ‖ 事故是由于～而造成的。 The accident was due to negligence. ‖ 我一时～用了这个词。 I used the word in carelessness.
【疏忽保险单】shūhu bǎoxiǎndān〈名〉 negligence policy
【疏忽大意】shūhu-dàyi〈成〉 be careless
【疏剪】shūjiǎn〈动〉 prune: ～树枝 prune off branches
【疏解】shūjiě〈动〉 **1**（解决） mediate **2**（开导） alleviate: ～忧虑 relieve anxiety
【疏浚】shūjùn〈动〉 dredge: ～工程 dredging work
【疏狂】shūkuáng〈形〉〈书〉 unrestrained: 举止～ wanton behaviour
【疏阔】shūkuò〈形〉〈书〉 **1**（不周密） rough: 立论～ loosely conceived argument **2**（迂阔） unrealistic **3**（分别） separated: ～数年 years of separation **4**（疏远） distant: 交往～ have a casual association with sb.
【疏懒】shūlǎn〈形〉〈书〉 indolent: 生性～ be inherently lazy
【疏朗】shūlǎng〈形〉〈书〉 **1**（稀疏而清晰） thin and clear **2**（开朗） cheerful
【疏离】shūlí〈动〉 maintain a separation
【疏漏】shūlòu **A**〈动〉 make an oversight: 书写～ slip of the pen **B**〈名〉 oversight: 明显的～ an obvious omission
【疏略】shūlüè〈书〉 **A**〈形〉 rough **B**〈动〉 be inaccurate: ～之处甚多 have quite a few inaccuracies
【疏落】shūluò〈形〉 scattered: 广场上到处坐着疏疏落落的人群。 There were people sitting dotted all around the square.
【疏密】shūmì〈名〉spacing: 行距的～ space between the lines
【疏散】shūsàn **A**〈形〉 scattered: ～的人群 dispersed crowds **B**〈动〉 evacuate: 被～人员 evacuee ‖ 警察要求人们～。 The police asked everyone to disperse.
【疏失】shūshī〈名〉 careless mistake
【疏松】shūsōng **A**〈形〉 loose **B**〈动〉 loosen
【疏通】shūtōng〈动〉**1**（疏浚）dredge: ～港口 dredge a harbour **2**（沟通） mediate
【疏远】shūyuǎn **A**〈形〉alienated **B**〈动〉 distance oneself from: 互相～ be estranged from one another

摅（攄） shū〈动〉〈书〉 express: ～怀 express one's feelings ‖ 略～已意 offer one's humble opinion

输（輸） shū〈动〉 **1**（运送） transport: ▸～出, ～送, 灌～ **2**〈书〉（捐献） donate **3**（失败） lose: ～了一个球 concede a goal ‖ A～给了B。 A lost to B. ▸～家, 认～

【输诚】shūchéng〈动〉〈书〉 **1**（表示诚心） express one's sincerity: ～结交 make friends in sincerity **2**（投降） surrender
【输出】shūchū〈动〉 **1**（外送） send out **2**（出口） export: 禁止高科技产品～ prohibit the export of high-tech products **3**［电气］［计算机］ output: ～电压 output voltage ‖ ～装置 output device
【输出端子】shūchūduānzǐ〈名〉 output
【输出港】shūchūgǎng〈名〉 port of export
【输出许可证】shūchū xǔkězhèng〈名〉 export permit
【输电】shūdiàn〈动〉 transmit electricity: ～线路 transmission line
【输电量】shūdiànliàng〈名〉 transmission capacity
【输电网】shūdiànwǎng〈名〉 grid system: 建造～ construct a power transmission network
【输电线路】shūdiàn xiànlù〈名〉 transmission line
【输家】shūjiā〈名〉 loser: 同情～ sympathize with a loser
【输精管】shūjīngguǎn〈名〉 seminal duct: ～结扎术 vasoligation ‖ ～切除术 vasectomy
【输理】shūlǐ〈动〉 be in the wrong
【输卵管】shūluǎnguǎn〈名〉Fallopian tube: ～结扎术 tubal ligation ‖ ～绝育 tubal sterilization
【输尿管】shūniàoguǎn〈名〉 ureter: ～囊肿 ureterocele
【输入】shūrù〈动〉 **1**（送入） bring in: 把血液～病人体内 give a patient a blood transfusion ‖ ～管道 inlet pipe **2**（进口） import: ～税 import duty **3**［电气］［计算机］ input: 用键盘～ key sth. in ‖ ～装置 input device
【输入端子】shūrùduānzǐ〈名〉 input
【输入港】shūrùgǎng〈名〉 port of entry
【输入许可证】shūrù xǔkězhèng〈名〉 import licence
【输送】shūsòng〈动〉 transport: ～技术工人 provide technical personnel ‖ ～新鲜血液 inject fresh blood
【输送带】shūsòngdài〈名〉 conveyor belt
【输送机】shūsòngjī〈名〉 conveyor
【输血】shūxuè〈动〉 transfuse blood: 给某人～ give sb. a blood transfusion
【输血者】shūxuèzhě〈名〉 blood donor
【输氧】shūyǎng〈动〉 treat with oxygen therapy
【输液】shūyè〈动〉 have an infusion: 静脉～ intravenous infusion
【输液管】shūyèguǎn〈名〉 infusion/drip tube
【输液架】shūyèjià〈名〉 infusion support
【输赢】shūyíng〈名〉 **1**（胜负） victory or defeat: 不计～ disregard winning or losing ‖ 我们有输有赢。 We have won some and lost some. **2**（指赌博） gains and losses
【输油】shūyóu〈动〉 transport oil: ～设备 oil transporting appliance
【输油管道】shūyóu guǎndào〈名〉oil pipeline

毹 shū ▸氍毹 qúshū

蔬 shū〈名〉 vegetables

【蔬菜】shūcài〈名〉 vegetables
【蔬果】shūguǒ〈名〉 fruit and vegetables: 多食～有益健康。 Plenty of fruit and vegetables are good for your health.

shú

秫 shú〈名〉 sorghum

【秫秸】shújiē〈名〉 sorghum stalk
【秫米】shúmǐ〈名〉 husked sorghum

孰 shú〈代〉〈书〉 **1**（谁） who: ▸人非圣贤, ～能无过 **2**（哪个） who, which: 吾与徐公～美? Who is more handsome, me or Master Xu?

赎（贖） shú〈动〉**1**（指抵押品） redeem: ～回典当品 redeem pawned items ▸～当, ～金, ～身 **2**（弥补） atone for: ▸～罪, 将功～罪

【赎当】shúdàng〈动〉 redeem sth. pawned
【赎回】shúhuí〈动〉 redeem: ～被绑架的

S

男孩 ransom the kidnapped boy ‖ 从当铺～戒指 redeem one's ring from the pawnshop
【赎回价】shúhuíjià〈名〉redemption price
【赎回票据】shúhuí piàojù〈名〉redeemed bill
【赎回证书】shúhuí zhèngshū〈名〉ransom
【赎金】shújīn〈名〉ransom: 绑匪索要两百万～。The kidnappers demanded a ransom of two million dollars.
【赎款】shúkuǎn = 赎金 shújīn
【赎买】shúmǎi〈动〉redeem: ～抵押财产 redeem a mortgage
【赎买政策】shúmǎi zhèngcè〈名〉buy-out policy
【赎身】shúshēn〈动〉buy back one's freedom
【赎刑】shúxíng〈动〉redeem sb. from punishment by paying a ransom
【赎罪】shúzuì〈动〉atone for one's crime
【赎罪金】shúzuìjīn〈名〉blood money
【赎罪券】shúzuìquàn〈名〉［宗教］ indulgence: 出售～ sell indulgences
【赎罪日】Shúzuìrì〈名〉［宗教］ Day of Atonement
【赎罪者】shúzuìzhě〈名〉expiator

塾 shú〈名〉〈旧〉private school: ▸私～
【塾师】shúshī〈名〉〈旧〉private tutor

S

熟 shú〈形〉1（指烹调）cooked: ～肉 cooked meat ▸～食，生米煮成～饭 2（指生长）ripe: 菜园子里的番茄～了。The tomatoes in the kitchen garden are ripe. ▸成～，瓜～蒂落，早～ 3（指加工）processed: ▸～料，～铁，～橡胶 4（熟悉）familiar: 我跟他不～。I'm not personally acquainted with him. ‖ 这地方我很～。I know this place very well. ▸～人，～视无睹，耳～ 5（熟练）practised: ▸～练，～能生巧 6（指程度）deep: 睡得～ sleep soundly ▸～睡，深思～虑
▸shóu
【熟谙】shú'ān〈动〉〈书〉be familiar with: ～民间小调 know folk tunes ‖ ～天象 be well acquainted with astronomical phenomena
【熟菜】shúcài〈名〉cooked food
【熟道】shúdào = 熟路 shúlù
【熟地】shúdì〈名〉1（指土地）cultivated land 2 = 熟地黄 shúdìhuáng
【熟地黄】shúdìhuáng〈名〉［中药］ prepared rhizome of rehmannia
【熟化】shúhuà〈动〉1［农业］ cultivate: ～过的地 cultivated land 2（指果蔬）ripen 3（指材料）cure
【熟荒】shúhuāng〈名〉［农业］abandoned cultivated land
【熟荒地】shúhuāngdì = 熟荒 shúhuāng
【熟记】shújì〈动〉learn by heart: ～台词 memorize one's lines
【熟客】shúkè〈名〉frequent visitor: 一家饭店的～ frequent customer of a restaurant
【熟练】shúliàn〈形〉skilled: ～工 skilled worker ‖ 技术～ skilled technician
【熟料】shúliào〈名〉fired refractory material
【熟路】shúlù〈名〉familiar road
【熟门熟路】shúmén-shúlù〈成〉things that one knows well
【熟能生巧】shúnéngshēngqiǎo〈成〉practice makes perfect
【熟年】shúnián〈名〉bumper year
【熟皮】shúpí A〈动〉tan hides B〈名〉tanned hide
【熟漆】shúqī〈名〉lacquer
【熟人】shúrén〈名〉acquaintance: 老～ old acquaintance ‖ 新闻界你有～吗? Do you know anybody in the news media?
【熟稔】shúrěn〈动〉〈书〉be familiar with
【熟石膏】shúshígāo〈名〉plaster of Paris
【熟石灰】shíshíhuī〈名〉slaked lime
【熟食】shúshí〈名〉cooked food: ～店 delicatessen
【熟视无睹】shúshì-wúdǔ〈成〉turn a blind eye to a familiar sight
【熟识】shúshi〈动〉know well: 彼此～ be well acquainted with one another
【熟手】shúshǒu〈名〉old hand: 木雕～ old hand at woodcarving
【熟睡】shúshuì〈动〉sleep soundly: 孩子们～了。The children fell fast asleep.
【熟丝】shúsī〈名〉［纺织］ boiled silk
【熟思】shúsī〈动〉deliberate: 未经～ without fully considering the question
【熟铁】shútiě〈名〉wrought iron
【熟铜】shútóng〈名〉wrought copper
【熟土】shútǔ〈名〉［农业］ mellow soil
【熟悉】shúxī〈动〉be familiar with: ～当地情况 familiarize oneself with the local conditions ‖ ～的面孔 familiar face ‖ 他们彼此很～。They know each other very well.
【熟习】shúxí〈动〉be practised in: ～业务 be practised in one's business
【熟橡胶】shúxiàngjiāo〈名〉vulcanized rubber
【熟油】shúyóu〈名〉boiled oil
【熟语】shúyǔ〈名〉idiom
【熟知】shúzhī〈动〉know very well
【熟字】shúzì〈名〉familiar word

shǔ

暑 shǔ
A〈形〉hot: ▸～气，～天
B〈名〉1（热）heat: ▸～假，寒来～往 2［中医］ summer heat [one of the six external factors which cause disease — wind, cold, summer heat, humidity, dryness and fire]
【暑假】shǔjià〈名〉summer holiday〈英〉; summer vacation〈美〉: 你打算在哪儿过～? Where are you going to spend your summer vacation?
【暑期】shǔqī〈名〉summer: ～学校 summer school
【暑气】shǔqì〈名〉summer heat
【暑热】shǔrè〈名〉summer heat: ～难耐 unbearably hot summer
【暑天】shǔtiān〈名〉hot summer: 炎热的～ sweltering summer days

黍 shǔ〈名〉broomcorn millet
【黍类】shǔlèi〈名〉millet
【黍子】shǔzi〈名〉broomcorn millet

属（屬）shǔ
A〈动〉1（隶属）be subordinate to: 我们学校～教育部直接领导。Our university is under the direct leadership of the Ministry of Education. ▸附～，直～ 2（归属）belong to: ～某一类 come under a category 3〈书〉（是）be: 此事纯～虚构。This is sheer fabrication. ▸～实 4（指属相）be born in the year of (one of the twelve symbolic animals associated with a 12-year cycle): ～马/虎 be born in the year of the horse/tiger
B〈名〉1（类别）category: ▸金～ 2（亲属）family members: ▸家～，烈～，亲～ 3［生物］ genus: 种～ species and genera
▸zhǔ
【属地】shǔdì〈名〉dependency: ～管辖权 territorial jurisdiction
【属地化】shǔdìhuà〈动〉localize: ～管理 localized management
【属国】shǔguó〈名〉dependent state
【属实】shǔshí〈动〉be true
【属下】shǔxià〈名〉subordinate
【属相】shǔxiang〈口〉= 生肖 shēngxiào
【属性】shǔxìng〈名〉attribute: 物理～ physical attribute ‖ 自然～ natural properties
【属于】shǔyú〈动〉belong to: ～个人财产 be part of one's individual wealth ‖ 我们～同一个世界。We belong to one world.
【属员】shǔyuán〈名〉〈旧〉staff: 全体～ all staff members

署¹ shǔ
A〈动〉1（安排）arrange: ▸部～ 2（代理）handle by proxy: ▸～理
B〈名〉office: ▸公～，官～，行～

署² shǔ〈动〉sign: 在稿件的末尾～上笔名 write one's pen name at the bottom of a manuscript ▸～名，签～
【署理】shǔlǐ〈动〉〈旧〉handle by proxy
【署名】shǔmíng〈动〉sign: 有本人～ bear one's own signature ‖ 在文件上～ put one's name to a document ‖ 亲笔～ genuine signature
【署名文章】shǔmíng wénzhāng〈名〉signed article

蜀 Shǔ〈名〉1（指国名）Shu [state in the Zhou Dynasty State] 2（指三国之一）Kingdom of Shu 3 ▸**p. 661**（四川）Shu [another name for Sichuan Province]: ▸～锦，～绣
【蜀汉】Shǔ Hàn〈名〉Kingdom of Shu Han
【蜀锦】shǔjǐn〈名〉Sichuan brocade
【蜀犬吠日】Shǔquǎn-fèirì〈成〉make fuss about small things
【蜀黍】shǔshǔ〈名〉sorghum
【蜀绣】shǔxiù〈名〉Sichuan embroidery

鼠 shǔ〈名〉rat
【鼠辈】shǔbèi〈名〉scoundrel
【鼠标】shǔbiāo〈名〉［计算机］ mouse
【鼠标手】shǔbiāoshǒu〈名〉carpal tunnel syndrome (CTS)
【鼠窜】shǔcuàn〈动〉scurry away like a frightened rat
【鼠窜狼奔】shǔcuàn-lángbēn〈成〉run in all directions
【鼠胆】shǔdǎn〈形〉cowardly
【鼠肚鸡肠】shǔdù-jīcháng = 小肚鸡肠 xiǎodù-jīcháng
【鼠害】shǔhài〈名〉plague of rats
【鼠夹】shǔjiā〈名〉mousetrap
【鼠科动物】shǔkē dòngwù〈名〉murid
【鼠目寸光】shǔmù-cùnguāng〈成〉see only what is under one's nose
【鼠窃狗盗】shǔqiè-gǒudào〈成〉petty theft
【鼠蹊】shǔxī〈名〉［生理］ groin
【鼠疫】shǔyì〈名〉plague

数（數）shǔ〈动〉1（查点）count: ～零钱 count the change 2（比较起来）be reckoned as: ～他年龄最小。He is the youngest. ▸～得着，～一～二 3（责备）scold: ▸～落，～说
▸shù, shuò

【数不胜数】 shǔbùshèngshǔ〈成〉 countless: 书中错误～。 There are countless mistakes in the book.
【数不上】 shǔbushàng〈动〉 not make the ranks: 要说足球明星，现在他还～。 He can't be counted as a football star yet.
【数得上】 shǔdeshàng〈动〉 make the ranks: 他可～是个有名的画家。 He's up there amongst famous painters.
【数得着】 shǔdezháo〈动〉 be reckoned among
【数典忘祖】 shǔdiǎn-wàngzǔ〈成〉 forget one's own origins
【数伏】 shǔfú〈动〉 come into the hottest days of the year
【数九】 shǔjiǔ〈动〉 come into the coldest days of the year
【数九寒天】 shǔjiǔ-hántiān〈成〉 coldest days of the year
【数来宝】 shǔláibǎo〈名〉［曲艺］ rhythmic storytelling to the accompaniment of clappers
【数落】 shǔluo〈动〉〈口〉 1（责备） rebuke: ～某人失职 reproach sb. for neglect of duty ‖ 她老是～自己的丈夫。 She goes on at her husband all the time. 2（列举） list
【数米而炊】 shǔmǐ'érchuī〈成〉 1（表不必要） fuss over small things 2（指生活困窘） be impoverished 3（吝啬） be extremely stingy
【数秒】 shǔmiǎo〈动〉 count down the seconds
【数说】 shǔshuō〈动〉 1（列举叙述） list 2（责备） rebuke
【数数儿】 shǔshùr〈动〉 count: 扳着手指～ count on one's fingers
【数往知来】 shǔwǎng-zhīlái〈成〉 draw inference about the future from the past
【数一数二】 shǔyī-shǔ'èr〈成〉 count among the best: 他是本世纪～的舞蹈家之一。 He is among the greatest dancers of the century.

薯 shǔ
〈名〉 general designation of crops such as potato and yam: ►白～, 甘～
【薯莨】 shǔliáng〈名〉［植物］ 1（指植物） dye yam 2（指块茎） tuber of this plant
【薯莨绸】 shǔliángchóu〈名〉［纺织］ gambiered Guangdong gauze
【薯片】 shǔpiàn〈名〉 potato crisps
【薯蓣】 shǔyù〈名〉［植物］ Chinese yam
【薯蓣豆】 shǔyùdòu〈名〉 yam bean

曙 shǔ
〈名〉〈书〉 dawn: ►～光, ～色
【曙光】 shǔguāng〈名〉 dawn sunshine: ～初照 at the crack of dawn ‖ 见到胜利的～ see the dawn of victory
【曙色】 shǔsè〈名〉 early dawn light

shù

术（術） shù
〈名〉 1（方法） method: ►权～, 战～ 2（技艺） art: ►不学无～, 剑～, 医～
►zhú
【术科】 shùkē〈名〉 technical courses offered in military or physical training
【术士】 shùshì〈名〉〈旧〉 1（指读书人） Confucian scholar 2（方士） alchemist
【术语】 shùyǔ〈名〉 term: 法律～ legal terminology ‖ 军事～ military term

戍 shù
〈动〉 defend: ►～守, 卫～
【戍边】 shùbiān〈动〉 defend the border
【戍守】 shùshǒu〈动〉〈书〉 defend: 加强～ strengthen the garrison
【戍卒】 shùzú〈名〉〈旧〉 garrison soldier

束 shù
A〈动〉 1（系） bind: ～发 tie up one's hair ‖ ～皮带 wear a belt ►～手待毙, ～之高阁 2（约束） control: ►管～, 拘～, 约～
B〈名〉 beam: ►电子～, 光～
C〈量〉 bundle: 一～花 a bunch of flowers ‖ 一～箭 a bundle of arrows
【束腹裤】 shùfùkù〈名〉 girdle
【束缚】 shùfù A〈动〉 1（捆绑） bind: ～手脚 tie sb.'s hands and feet 2（约束） restrain: 受家庭～ have ties to home B〈名〉 shackles
【束射】 shùshè〈名〉 beam: ～管 beam tube
【束身】 shùshēn〈动〉 1（约束） restrain oneself 2（捆绑） bind oneself
【束身自爱】 shùshēn-zì'ài〈成〉 maintain one's standards
【束手】 shùshǒu〈动〉 have one's hands tied
【束手待毙】 shùshǒu-dàibì〈成〉 resign oneself to defeat
【束手就擒】 shùshǒu-jiùqín〈成〉 offer no resistance
【束手束脚】 shùshǒu-shùjiǎo = 缩手缩脚 suōshǒu-suōjiǎo 2
【束手无策】 shùshǒu-wúcè〈成〉 be at a loss at what to do
【束胸】 shùxiōng〈名〉〈旧〉 breast girdle
【束脩】 shùxiū〈名〉〈书〉 a private tutor's remuneration
【束腰】 shùyāo A〈动〉 girdle the waist B〈名〉 girdle
【束之高阁】 shùzhīgāogé〈成〉 shelve and forget sth.
【束装】 shùzhuāng〈动〉〈书〉 pack up

述 shù
〈动〉 relate: 略～一二 give a brief account ►～说, 口～, 叙～
【述而不作】 shù'érbùzuò〈成〉 expound the works of one's predecessors without adding anything new to them
【述怀】 shùhuái〈动〉〈书〉 pour out one's feelings
【述评】 shùpíng A〈名〉 commentary: 时事～ news commentaries B〈动〉 review
【述说】 shùshuō〈动〉 give an account of: ～经历 recount one's experiences ‖ ～事实真相 state the true facts
【述位】 shùwèi〈名〉［语言］ rheme
【述职】 shùzhí〈动〉 report on one's work: 回国～ return to one's country for consultations ‖ ～报告 progress report

树（樹） shù
A〈动〉 1（种植） plant: ►十年～木，百年～人 2（建立） establish: ～雄心 have lofty ambitions ‖ ～正气 uphold healthy tendencies ►～碑立传, 独～一帜, 建～
B〈名〉 tree: 苹果～ apple tree ►～林, 松～, 植～
【树碑立传】 shùbēi-lìzhuàn〈成〉 glorify sb. (in a permanent way)
【树杈】 shùchà〈名〉 crotch, fork (of a tree)
【树丛】 shùcóng〈名〉 grove: 在～中 among the trees
【树大根深】 shùdà-gēnshēn〈成〉〈喻〉 very influential
【树大招风】 shùdà-zhāofēng〈成〉〈喻〉 those in high positions are liable to be attacked
【树袋熊】 shùdàixióng〈名〉［动物］ koala
【树倒猢狲散】 shù dǎo húsūn sàn〈成〉 when an influential person falls from power, those beneath him tend to flee
【树敌】 shùdí〈动〉 make an enemy: ～太多 make too many enemies
【树墩】 shùdūn〈名〉 tree stump
【树墩子】 shùdūnzi = 树墩 shùdūn
【树干】 shùgàn〈名〉 trunk
【树高千丈，叶落归根】 shù gāo qiānzhàng, yè luò guī gēn〈成〉 a person residing away from home eventually returns to his native soil
【树根】 shùgēn〈名〉 tree root
【树挂】 shùguà = 雾凇 wùsōng
【树冠】 shùguān〈名〉 crown
【树行子】 shùhàngzi〈名〉 woods
【树胶】 shùjiāo〈名〉 gum (of a tree)
【树懒】 shùlǎn〈名〉［动物］ sloth
【树篱】 shùlí〈名〉 hedge
【树立】 shùlì〈动〉 establish: ～榜样 set an example ‖ ～良好的企业形象 foster a good company image ‖ ～雄心壮志 aim high and have lofty ambitions
【树林】 shùlín〈名〉 wood [forest]
【树林子】 shùlínzi = 树林 shùlín
【树龄】 shùlíng〈名〉 age of a tree
【树苗】 shùmiáo〈名〉 sapling
【树木】 shùmù〈名〉 trees
【树皮】 shùpí〈名〉 bark
【树人】 shùrén〈动〉〈书〉 cultivate the young
【树梢】 shùshāo〈名〉 treetop
【树身】 shùshēn〈名〉 tree trunk
【树突】 shùtū〈名〉［解剖］ dendrite
【树形】 shùxíng〈名〉 tree shape: ～图 arborescence
【树丫】 shùyā〈名〉 crotch, fork (of a tree)
【树桠】 shùyā = 树丫 shùyā
【树叶】 shùyè〈名〉 tree leaf: 一片～ a leaf
【树荫】 shùyīn〈名〉 shade of a tree: 坐在～下 sit in the shade of a tree
【树欲静而风不止】 shù yù jìng ér fēng bù zhǐ〈成〉 things take their own course regardless of one's will
【树葬】 shùzàng〈名〉 tree burial
【树枝】 shùzhī〈名〉 branch
【树脂】 shùzhī〈名〉 resin: 天然～ natural resin
【树脂胶合板】 shùzhī jiāohébǎn〈名〉 compo board
【树脂漆】 shùzhīqī〈名〉 lacquer-type organic coating
【树脂涂料】 shùzhī túliào〈名〉 resinous varnish
【树脂粘合剂】 shùzhī zhānhéjì〈名〉 resin binder
【树种】 shùzhǒng〈名〉 1（种类） kind of tree: 针叶～ coniferous trees 2（种子） tree seeds
【树桩】 shùzhuāng〈名〉 tree stump

竖（竪、豎） shù
A〈动〉 erect: 把梯子靠墙～着 stand a ladder up against a wall ►～立
B〈形〉 vertical: ～线 vertical line
C〈名〉 [in Chinese characters] vertical stroke: 两横一～ two horizontal strokes and one vertical stroke
【竖笛】 shùdí ►p. 929〈名〉 clarinet
【竖脊肌】 shùjǐjī〈名〉［解剖］ erector spinae
【竖井】 shùjǐng〈名〉［矿业］ shaft: ～矿 shaft mine
【竖立】 shùlì〈动〉 erect: 人民英雄纪念碑

～在天安门广场上。The Monument to the People's Heroes stands on Tian'anmen Square.

【竖起】shùqǐ〈动〉stick up: ～大拇指 stick one's thumb up ‖ ～电视天线 erect a television antenna ‖ ～耳朵 prick up one's ears

【竖琴】shùqín ▸**p. 929**〈名〉harp: ～演奏者 harpist

【竖蜻蜓】shù qīngtíng〈方〉= 倒立 dàolì 2

【竖向】shùxiàng〈形〉vertical: ～百叶窗 vertical blind

【竖子】shùzǐ〈名〉〈书〉**1**（童仆）lad **2**〈贬〉（小子）mean fellow: ～不足与谋。That brute doesn't deserve our confidence.

恕 shù

〈动〉**1**（体贴）show consideration for others **2**（原谅）pardon: ▸～罪, 宽～, 饶～ **3**〈套〉（请原谅）excuse me: ～我直言。Excuse me for speaking bluntly. ▸～不奉陪

【恕不奉陪】shùbùfèngpéi〈成〉excuse me for not keeping you company

【恕难从命】shùnáncóngmìng〈成〉I regret that I cannot comply with your wishes

【恕罪】shùzuì〈动〉pardon an offence

庶 shù

A〈形〉numerous: ▸～务, 富～

B〈名〉**1**〈书〉（平民）common people: ▸～民, 黎～ **2**〈旧〉（妾生）children born to a concubine: ▸～子

C〈副〉〈书〉if only: ～免于难 if only one could avoid dangers

【庶出】shùchū〈动〉be born to a concubine

【庶乎】shùhū〈书〉= 庶几 shùjī

【庶几】shùjī〈连〉〈书〉thereby

【庶民】shùmín〈名〉〈书〉common people

【庶母】shùmǔ〈名〉madam [term of address for a concubine of one's father]

【庶人】shùrén〈名〉〈书〉common people

【庶务】shùwù〈名〉〈旧〉**1**（指事）general affairs **2**（指人）person in charge of business matters or general affairs

【庶子】shùzǐ〈名〉son of a concubine

腧（俞）shù

【腧穴】shùxué〈名〉［中医］acupuncture point

数（數）shù

A〈名〉**1**（数字）number: 两位～ double-digit figure ‖ 学生～ number of students ‖ 你要多少, 说个～? Tell us how many you want. ▸～目, ～字, 岁～ **2**（天命）fate: ▸定～, 气～, 天～ **3**［数学］number: ▸小～, 有理～, 整～ **4**［语法］number: ▸单～, 复～

B ▸**p. 927**〈数〉several: ～次 several times ‖ ～人 a few people

▸shǔ, shuò

【数表】shùbiǎo〈名〉mathematical table

【数词】shùcí〈名〉［语言］numeral

【数额】shù'é〈名〉number: ～不大 be small in number ‖ 规定～ required amount

【数积】shùjī〈名〉［数学］scalar product

【数据】shùjù〈名〉data: ～传输 data transmission ‖ 科学～ scientific data

【数据处理】shùjù chǔlǐ〈名〉data processing

【数据存储系统】shùjù cúnchǔ xìtǒng〈名〉data-storage system

【数据分析】shùjù fēnxī〈名〉data analysis

【数据管理】shùjù guǎnlǐ〈名〉data management

【数据加密】shùjù jiāmì〈名〉data encryption

【数据库】shùjùkù〈名〉database: ～处理机 database machine

【数据库存】shùjù kùcún〈名〉［计算机］data warehousing

【数控】shùkòng〈简称〉= 数字控制

【数理逻辑】shùlǐ luójí〈名〉mathematical logic

【数量】shùliàng〈名〉quantity: ～控制 quantity control

【数量词】shùliàngcí〈名〉［语言］numeral-classifier compound

【数量级】shùliàngjí〈名〉［物理］order of magnitude

【数列】shùliè〈名〉［数学］ordered series of numbers

【数论】shùlùn〈名〉［数学］number theory

【数码】shùmǎ **A**〈名〉**1**（数字）numeral **2**（数量）number: 今天销售的～比昨天多。We have sold more today than we did yesterday. **B**〈形〉digital

【数码激光视盘】shùmǎ jīguāng shìpán〈名〉digital video disc (DVD): ～机 DVD player

【数码相机】shùmǎ xiàngjī〈名〉digital camera

【数目】shùmù〈名〉number: ～不详。The amount is unknown.

【数目字】shùmùzì = 数字 shùzì

【数位】shùwèi〈名〉［数学］digit

【数学】shùxué〈名〉mathematics: 高等～ higher mathematics ‖ 应用～ applied mathematics ‖ 有～头脑 have a mathematical mind

【数学公式】shùxué gōngshì〈名〉mathematical formula

【数学家】shùxuéjiā ▸**p. 966**〈名〉mathematician

【数值】shùzhí〈名〉［数学］numerical value: ～天气预报 numerical weather forecast

【数制】shùzhì〈名〉number representation system

【数轴】shùzhóu〈名〉［数学］number axis

【数字】shùzì〈名〉**1**（指文字）characters that denote amounts **2**（数据）figure: 人口统计～ population figures ‖ 根据官方～ according to official figures **3**（数量）quantity

【数字编码】shùzì biānmǎ〈名〉digital coding

【数字电视】shùzì diànshì〈名〉digital TV

【数字鸿沟】shùzì hónggōu〈名〉digital divide

【数字化】shùzìhuà〈动〉digitize: ～战场 digital battlefield

【数字技术】shùzì jìshù〈名〉digital technology

【数字计算机】shùzì jìsuànjī〈名〉digital computer

【数字控制】shùzì kòngzhì〈名〉numeral control (NC): ～装置 numerical control device

【数字录音】shùzì lùyīn〈名〉digital sound recording

【数字签名】shùzì qiānmíng〈名〉digital signature

【数字通信】shùzì tōngxìn〈名〉digital communication

【数字相机】shùzì xiàngjī = 数码相机 shùmǎ xiàngjī

【数字移动电话】shùzì yídòng diànhuà〈名〉digital mobile telephone

【数罪并罚】shùzuì bìngfá〈成〉mete out sentence for more than one crime

墅 shù

〈名〉villa: ▸别～

漱 shù

〈动〉rinse: ▸～口

【漱口】shùkǒu〈动〉gargle: 用盐水～ gargle with salt water

【漱口杯】shùkǒubēi〈名〉mug

【漱口液】shùkǒuyè〈名〉gargle

澍 shù

〈名〉〈书〉timely rain: ▸～雨

【澍雨】shùyǔ〈名〉〈书〉timely rain

shuā

刷[1] shuā

A〈名〉brush: 鞋～ shoe brush ‖ 油漆～ paintbrush ▸牙～

B〈动〉**1**（涂抹）paint with a brush: ～墙 whitewash a wall ‖ ～油漆 apply paint to **2**（清理）scrub: ～地板 brush the floor ‖ ～锅 scour the pots ‖ ～鞋 brush one's shoes ▸～牙 **3**〈口〉（淘汰）eliminate: 他在第一轮比赛中就被～下来了。He was eliminated in the first round of the game.

刷[2] shuā

〈拟〉rustle: ～～的雨声 pitter-patter of rain ‖ 树叶在风中～～作响。The tree leaves were rustling in the wind.

▸shuà

【刷卡】shuākǎ〈动〉swipe a card: ～上班/下班 swipe one's card to clock in/out

【刷卡机】shuākǎjī〈名〉debit card reader

【刷卡族】shuākǎzú〈名〉cardholders

【刷拉】shuālā〈拟〉swish: 风吹杨柳刷拉拉。The willow twigs rustled in the wind.

【刷洗】shuāxǐ〈动〉scrub: ～地板 scrub the floor

【刷新】shuāxīn〈动〉**1**（使焕然一新）renovate: ～记忆 refresh one's memory ‖ ～家具 repaint the furniture **2**（突破）surpass: ～纪录 break a record **3**［计算机］refresh: ～页面 refresh a page

【刷牙】shuāyá〈动〉brush one's teeth

【刷子】shuāzi〈名〉brush: 一把～ a brush

shuǎ

耍 shuǎ

〈动〉**1**（玩）play: ▸玩～ **2**（戏弄）play tricks: 我被人～了。I've been fooled. ▸～弄, ～笑 **3**（表演）play with: ～剑 flourish a sword **4**〈贬〉（施展）display: ▸～笔杆子, ～滑, ～手段

【耍把戏】shuǎ bǎxì〈惯〉**1**（指杂技）give an acrobatics performance **2**〈方〉〈喻〉（指手段）play tricks

【耍笔杆子】shuǎ bǐgǎnzi〈惯〉〈贬〉be skilled in literary tricks

【耍横】shuǎhèng〈动〉〈方〉be rude and unreasonable

【耍猴儿】shuǎhóur〈动〉**1**（指杂技）put on a monkey show **2**〈喻〉（戏弄）tease: 别拿我～玩了。Don't mess with me.

【耍花腔】shuǎ huāqiāng〈惯〉sweet-talk: 别在我面前～。Don't try to sweet-talk me.

【耍花招】shuǎ huāzhāo〈惯〉play tricks

【耍滑】shuǎhuá〈动〉shirk responsibility

【耍滑头】shuǎ huátóu = 耍滑 shuǎhuá

【耍奸】shuǎjiān = 耍滑 shuǎhuá

【耍赖】shuǎlài〈动〉act without shame: ～

数字

英语基数词

■ 读或写一百、一千等时，有些情况下用 one 或 a 都可以。注意下面例子里它们的用法：

0	zero	16	sixteen
1	one	17	seventeen
2	two	18	eighteen
3	three	19	nineteen
4	four	20	twenty
5	five	21	twenty-one
6	six	29	twenty-nine
7	seven	30	thirty
8	eight	40	forty
9	nine	50	fifty
10	ten	60	sixty
11	eleven	70	seventy
12	twelve	80	eighty
13	thirteen	90	ninety
14	fourteen	99	ninety-nine
15	fifteen	100	one/a hundred

101	one/a hundred and one
109	one/a hundred and nine
110	one/a hundred (and) ten
119	one/a hundred (and) nineteen
120	one/a hundred (and) twenty
199	one/a hundred (and) ninety-nine
200	two hundred
300	three hundred
900	nine hundred
999	nine hundred and ninety-nine
1,000	one/a thousand
1,001	one/a thousand and one
1,090	one/a thousand and ninety
1,900	one/a thousand nine hundred
2,000	two thousand
9,000	nine thousand
10,000	ten thousand
10,001	ten thousand and one
10,010	ten thousand and ten
10,100	ten thousand and one hundred
11,000	eleven thousand
20,000	twenty thousand
100,000	one/a hundred thousand
200,000	two hundred thousand
1,000,000	one/a million
2,000,000	two million
10,000,000	ten million
20,000,000	twenty million
100,000,000	a hundred million
900,000,000	nine hundred million
1,000,000,000	one/a billion

英语序数词

■ 英语序数词有两种形式：缩略形式和全称。缩略形式多用于书写日期。读序数词时，所有的序数词都要读全称，包括缩略形式。

■ 20 以上而又不是 10 的倍数的序数词，是由基数词加 1 到 9 的序数词构成的。注意在这种情况下，英语要用连字号。

■ 在百位和十位之间，可以用 and 连接，也可以不用：

缩略形式	全称
1st	first
2nd	second
3rd	third
4th	fourth
5th	fifth
6th	sixth
7th	seventh
8th	eighth
9th	ninth
10th	tenth
11th	eleventh
12th	twelfth
19th	nineteenth
20th	twentieth
21st	twenty-first
25th	twenty-fifth
30th	thirtieth
90th	ninetieth
92nd	ninety-second
100th	hundredth
101st	hundred and first
110th	hundred and tenth
199th	hundred and ninety-ninth
999th	nine hundred and ninety-ninth
1000th	thousandth
1030th	thousand and thirtieth

他在这场赛跑中名列第四
= He came fourth in the race

剧院的第 5 排
= the fifth row in the theatre

千分之一秒
= a thousandth of a second

他是第 151 名参加这场考试的人
= He was the one hundred and fifty-first candidate to take the exam

英语的分数

■ 分数中的分子读基数词，分母读序数词。如果分母是 4，用 quarter。如果分子大于 1，用作分母的序数词要加 s。分子是 1 时，一般可用 a，但在书面语或强调时，要用 one：

	读
1/2	a/one half
2/3	two thirds
3/4	three quarters
1/8	a/one eighth
3/8	three eighths

英语的小数和百分比

■ 用英语读小数点之前和之后的数时，各个数位可看作一个个的整数单独读出：

	读
0.003	zero point zero zero three
0.34	zero point three four
3.58	three point five eight
88.66	eight eight point six six
266.99	two six six point nine nine

■ 在读百分比的时候，percent 要放在数的后面：

	读
19%	nineteen percent
99%	ninety-nine percent

电话号码

■ 读电话时，单独读出每个数字，0 可读作 zero 或 oh。如果某个数字连着重复，可用 double（重复两次）及 triple（重复三次）。像 800 和 3000 的数字，可分别读作 eight double oh 和 three triple zero，也可读作 eight hundred 和 three thousand：

	读
001 222 888	double zero one triple two triple eight
01224 711 552	oh one double two four seven double one double five two
0044 131 322 669	zero zero four four one three one three two two six six nine
0800 55 3000	oh eight hundred double five three thousand 或 zero eight double zero double five three triple zero

多少个？

屋子里有多少人？—— 有 130 人
= How many people are there in the room?
— There are a hundred and thirty people

你们中有多少人要来参加我的聚会？—— 我们有 20 人要来
= How many of you are coming to my party?
— Twenty of us are coming

定了多少张电影票？—— 10 张
= How many film tickets have been booked?
— Ten

■ 注意下面例子 and 的使用：

105 个学生
= 105 students（书写）
= a hundred and five students（写或读）

150 个参加者
= 150 participants（书写）
= one hundred and fifty participants（写或读）

1,007 张书桌
= 1,007 desks（书写）
= a thousand and seven desks（写或读）

1,030 张选票
= 1,030 votes（书写）
= a thousand and thirty votes（写或读）

1,400 个座位
= 1,400 seats（书写）
= one thousand four hundred seats（写或读）

■ 关于约数，参见语用信息框“约数”。

撒泼 act be unreasonable and make a scene
【耍赖皮】shuǎ làipí = 耍赖 shuǎlài
【耍流氓】shuǎ liúmáng〈惯〉act indecently
【耍闹】shuǎnào〈动〉lark about
【耍弄】shuǎnòng〈动〉1（施展）resort to: ～花招 play tricks 2（戏弄）make a fool of sb.: 你是不是在～我？Are you pulling my leg?
【耍盘子】shuǎ pánzi〈动〉［杂技］do plate-spinning
【耍脾气】shuǎ píqi〈惯〉put on a show of bad temper: 他爱～。He gets into a huff easily.
【耍贫嘴】shuǎ pínzuǐ〈惯〉prattle: 别再～了，咱们开始干活吧。Stop prattling and let's get on with it.
【耍钱】shuǎqián〈动〉〈方〉gamble: 他～把家产输光了。He gambled away all his family property.
【耍人】shuǎrén〈动〉make fun of sb.: 他经常～。He often plays tricks on others.
【耍手段】shuǎ shǒuduàn = 耍手腕 shuǎ shǒuwàn
【耍手腕】shuǎ shǒuwàn〈惯〉play tricks: 他为卖掉那批货耍了些手腕。He took a bit of license in order to make the sale.
【耍手艺】shuǎ shǒuyì〈惯〉make a living as a craftsman
【耍死狗】shuǎ sǐgǒu〈惯〉〈方〉act shamelessly
【耍态度】shuǎ tàidu〈惯〉lose one's temper
【耍坛子】shuǎ tánzi〈动〉［杂技］do a jar balancing act
【耍威风】shuǎ wēifēng〈惯〉throw one's weight about
【耍无赖】shuǎ wúlài = 耍赖 shuǎlài
【耍笑】shuǎxiào〈动〉1（说笑）laugh and joke 2（戏弄）play a joke on
【耍心眼儿】shuǎ xīnyǎnr〈惯〉resort to clever tricks
【耍嘴皮子】shuǎ zuǐpízi〈惯〉1〈贬〉（卖弄口才）be a smooth talker 2（只说不做）be all talk and no action

shuà

刷 shuà〈动〉〈方〉select
▸shuā
【刷白】shuàbái〈形〉pale: 他脸色吓得～。He was pale with fear.

shuāi

衰 shuāi〈动〉decline: 老人病体日～。The old man was fading fast. ▸～败，～弱，未老先～
▸cuī
【衰败】shuāibài〈动〉run to seed: 草木～the plants and trees have all withered and died ‖ 家业～ the family business is in decline
【衰变】shuāibiàn〈动〉［物理］decay
【衰变期】shuāibiànqī〈名〉decay period
【衰草】shuāicǎo〈名〉〈书〉withering grass: ～败叶 withered grass and wilted leaves
【衰减】shuāijiǎn〈动〉1（减弱）weaken: 我的体力日渐～。I'm getting gradually weaker. 2［物理］attenuate
【衰减量】shuāijiǎnliàng〈名〉decrement
【衰竭】shuāijié A〈动〉be prostrated: 心力～ have a heart failure B ▸p. 50〈名〉［医学］prostration
【衰竭综合征】shuāijié zōnghézhēng ▸p. 50〈名〉［医学］exhaustion syndrome
【衰老】shuāilǎo A〈形〉old and feeble: 几年不见，他显得～多了。In the years since I last saw him, he had clearly aged. B ▸p. 50〈名〉senility
【衰落】shuāiluò〈动〉decline: 罗马帝国的～ decline of the Roman Empire
【衰迈】shuāimài〈形〉〈书〉senile
【衰弱】shuāiruò A〈形〉weak: 久病后身体～ be emaciated after a long illness B〈动〉weaken: 敌军攻势已经～。The enemy offensive is petering out. C ▸p. 50〈名〉［医学］asthenia: ▸神经～
【衰颓】shuāituí〈形〉〈书〉[of body, spirit etc.] weak and degenerate
【衰退】shuāituì〈动〉decline: 记忆力～ be losing one's memory ‖ 经济～ economic recession ‖ 他的视力在～。His eyesight is failing.
【衰亡】shuāiwáng〈动〉become feeble and die: 罗马帝国的～ decline and fall of the Roman Empire
【衰微】shuāiwēi〈动〉〈书〉[of a country, a nation] decline
【衰萎】shuāiwěi〈动〉wither
【衰朽】shuāixiǔ〈形〉〈书〉feeble and decaying: ～残年 declining years

摔 shuāi〈动〉1（扔）fling: 把书～到桌上 throw a book on the table 2（跌落）fall down: 从梯子上～下来 fall off a ladder 3（使破损）break: 盘子掉在地上～碎了。The plate smashed on the floor. 4（下落）lose one's balance: ～一跤 have a fall ‖ ～倒在地 fall to the ground ‖ 他在冰上滑倒了，～断了腿。He slipped on the ice and broke his leg. 5 = 摔打 shuāida 1
【摔打】shuāida〈动〉1（拍打）beat: 把鞋底上的泥～掉。Beat the dirt off the sole of your shoes. 2（锻炼）toughen up: 青年人应该到艰苦的环境中去～。Young people should temper themselves in difficult circumstances.
【摔跟头】shuāi gēntou〈惯〉1（摔倒）trip and fall 2〈喻〉（受挫）trip up: 他没有经验，～不可避免。Inexperienced as he is, a few slip-ups are inevitable.
【摔跤】shuāijiāo A〈动〉1（摔倒）trip and fall: 重重地摔了一跤 have a nasty fall ‖ 来时路太滑，摔了我一跤。The road was so slippery that I took a tumble on my way here. 2〈喻〉（受挫）trip up B ▸p. 909〈名〉［体育］wrestling: 古典式～ classical wrestling ‖ 自由式～ free-style wrestling
【摔跤运动员】shuāijiāo yùndòngyuán〈名〉wrestler

shuǎi

甩 shuǎi〈动〉1（抡）swing: ～胳膊 swing one's arms ‖ 把鞭子一～ crack a whip ‖ 狮子的尾巴～来～去。The lion's tail lashed to and fro. 2（扔）toss: ～石子 throw stones 3（抛开）brush off: ～掉跟踪者 shake off a pursuer ‖ 她的男朋友把她～了。Her boyfriend dumped her.
【甩包袱】shuǎi bāofu〈惯〉〈喻〉cast off a burden
【甩车】shuǎichē〈动〉［铁路］uncouple
【甩掉】shuǎidiào〈动〉cast off: ～包袱 cast off a burden ‖ ～尾巴 throw off a tail
【甩开膀子】shuǎikāi bǎngzi〈惯〉go all out: ～大干 go full steam ahead with one's work
【甩卖】shuǎimài A〈动〉sell at reduced prices: 清仓大～ clearance sale B〈名〉markdown sale: 歇业～ closing sale
【甩手】shuǎishǒu〈动〉1（抡）swing one's arms 2〈喻〉（不管）wash one's hands of: 这事你可不能～不管! You can't wash your hands of this!
【甩手掌柜】shuǎishǒu zhǎngguì〈名〉1（指丈夫）husband who cares little about housework 2（指领导）hands-off leader: 戒除～的作风 eliminate the hands-off style of management

shuài

帅[1]（帥）shuài〈名〉［军事］commander-in-chief: ▸统～，元～

帅[2]（帥）shuài〈形〉〈口〉handsome: 字写得～ write beautifully ‖ 这小伙子真～。This guy is really good-looking. ▸～气
【帅才】shuàicái〈名〉born commander
【帅哥】shuàigē〈名〉〈口〉good-looking young man
【帅旗】shuàiqí〈名〉flag of a commander-in-chief
【帅气】shuàiqi〈形〉handsome
【帅印】shuàiyìn〈名〉seal of a commander-in-chief

率[1] shuài
A〈动〉1（带领）lead: ～部起义 lead one's troops in revolt ▸～领，统～ 2〈书〉（顺着）follow: ▸～由旧章
B〈名〉example: ▸表～

率[2] shuài
A〈形〉1（不慎重）rash: ▸草～，轻～ 2（直爽）frank: ▸坦～，直～
B〈副〉〈书〉generally: 大～如此。This is usually the case.
▸lǜ
【率尔】shuài'ěr〈形〉〈书〉rash
【率领】shuàilǐng〈动〉lead: ～代表团 head a delegation
【率然】shuàirán〈副〉〈书〉hastily
【率先】shuàixiān〈副〉taking the lead: ～行动 take the lead in an operation
【率由旧章】shuàiyóujiùzhāng〈成〉follow the established pattern
【率真】shuàizhēn〈形〉frank and sincere: 为人～ be straight with people
【率直】shuàizhí〈形〉straightforward: 说话～ speak frankly

蟀 shuài ▸蟋蟀 xīshuài

shuān

闩（閂）shuān
A〈名〉bolt: 上～ fasten with a bolt ▸门～
B〈动〉bolt: 把门～上 bolt the door

拴 shuān〈动〉tie: 把两条绳子～到一起 hitch two ropes together ‖ 用绳把船～在树上 fasten a boat to a tree with a rope ‖ 我们被一大堆工作给～住了。We were tied up with a large piece of work.

【拴马桩】shuānmǎzhuāng〈名〉 hitching post

栓 shuān〈名〉1▸（指机件） plug: ▸枪～, 消火～ 2▸（塞状物） stopper: ▸～剂, 血～

【栓剂】shuānjì〈名〉［药学］ suppository

【栓皮】shuānpí〈名〉［林业］ cork

【栓皮栎】shuānpílì〈名〉 oriental oak

【栓塞】shuānsè ▸**p. 50**〈名〉［医学］ embolism: 脑～ cerebral embolism

【栓子】shuānzǐ〈名〉［医学］ embolus

shuàn

涮 shuàn〈动〉1▸（清洗） rinse: 把瓶子～一下 rinse out a bottle ▸洗～ 2▸（指吃法） instant-boil: ▸～锅, ～羊肉 3▸〈口〉（耍弄） fool: 他叫人给～了。He has been made a fool of.

【涮锅】shuànguō〈动〉 have a hotpot

【涮羊肉】shuànyángròu A〈动〉 have mutton hotpot B〈名〉 mutton hotpot

shuāng

双（雙） shuāng

A〈形〉1▸（两） two: ～脚 both feet ‖ 闭紧～唇 compress one's lips ‖ 粮食、棉花～丰收 reap bumper harvests of both grain and cotton ▸～边, ～方, ～职工 2▸（偶数） even: ▸～号, ～日 3▸（加倍） double: 付～薪 pay double ▸～倍, ～层, ～重

B〈量〉 pair: 三～袜子 three pairs of socks ‖ 一～筷子 a pair of chopsticks

【双胞胎】shuāngbāotāi〈名〉 twins: ～姐妹/兄弟 twin sisters/brothers

【双倍】shuāngbèi ▸**p. 31**〈名〉 double: 付～的钱 pay double ‖ ～偿还 pay in twice the amount

【双臂】shuāngbì〈名〉 both arms

【双边】shuāngbiān〈形〉 bilateral: ～关系 bilateral relations ‖ ～贸易 bilateral trade ‖ ～协定 bilateral agreement

【双宾语】shuāngbīnyǔ〈名〉［语法］ double object

【双层】shuāngcéng〈形〉 double-layered: ～玻璃窗 double-glazed window ‖ ～床 double-bunk ‖ ～公共汽车 double-decker ‖ ～列车 double-decker train

【双铲犁】shuāngchǎnlí〈名〉［农业］ double-bladed plough

【双程票】shuāngchéngpiào〈名〉 return ticket

【双重】shuāngchóng〈形〉 double: ～打击 double blow

【双重标准】shuāngchóng biāozhǔn〈名〉 double standards

【双重否定】shuāngchóng fǒudìng〈名〉 double negative

【双重关税】shuāngchóng guānshuì〈名〉 dual tariff

【双重国籍】shuāngchóng guójí ▸**p. 279**〈名〉 dual nationality

【双重领导】shuāngchóng lǐngdǎo〈名〉 dual leadership

【双重人格】shuāngchóng réngé〈名〉〈贬〉 dual personality

【双唇音】shuāngchúnyīn〈名〉［语言］ bilabial

【双打】shuāngdǎ〈名〉［体育］ doubles: ～比赛 doubles match ‖ 男子/女子～ men's/women's doubles

【双底】shuāngdǐ〈名〉［金融］ double bottom

【双方】shuāngfāng〈名〉 both sides: ～当事人 both litigants ‖ ～利益 interests of both sides ‖ ～犯规 double foul ‖ 劳资～ both labour and capital ‖ 男女～ both the female and male sides ‖ ～互不相让。Neither side was willing to give in.

【双飞】shuāngfēi〈名〉 round trip flight

【双峰驼】shuāngfēngtuó〈名〉 Bactrian camel

【双幅】shuāngfú〈名〉 double width: ～布料 double-width cloth

【双缸发动机】shuānggāng fādòngjī〈名〉 twin-cylinder engine

【双缸洗衣机】shuānggāng xǐyījī〈名〉 twin-tub washing machine

【双杠】shuānggàng〈名〉［体育］ parallel bars

【双关】shuāngguān〈动〉 have a double meaning: ▸一语～

【双关语】shuāngguānyǔ〈名〉 pun

【双管】shuāngguǎn〈名〉 double barrels: ～猎枪 double-barrelled shotgun

【双管齐下】shuāngguǎn-qíxià〈成〉 work along two lines at the same time: 控制人口增长和提高人口素质要～。We should control population growth and at the same time promote population quality.

【双规】shuāngguī〈动〉 be subject to investigation at a designated time and place: 因涉嫌受贿被纪委～ be investigated by the Discipline Inspection Commission at a designated time and place on suspicion of taking bribes

【双轨】shuāngguǐ〈名〉 dual-track: ～铁路 double-track railway

【双轨制】shuāngguǐzhì〈名〉 dual-track system: 价格～ double-track pricing system

【双号】shuānghào〈名〉 even number

【双核】shuānghé〈名〉1▸［金融］ two core: ～平衡基金 two-core balanced fund 2▸［计算机］ core duo: ～笔记本电脑 core duo laptop computer

【双簧】shuānghuáng〈名〉 two-man comic show: ▸演～

【双簧管】shuānghuángguǎn ▸**p. 929**〈名〉［音乐］ oboe

【双极】shuāngjí〈形〉 bipolar

【双季稻】shuāngjìdào〈名〉 double-crop rice

【双肩挑】shuāngjiāntiāo〈惯〉 shoulder the responsibility for both professional and administrative work: ～干部 cadres assuming administrative as well as professional responsibilities

【双联单】shuāngliándān〈名〉 duplicate form: ～汇票 drafts in duplicate

【双料】shuāngliào〈形〉 of superior quality: ～脸盆 superior quality basin ‖〈喻〉～冠军 double champion

【双轮】shuānglún〈名〉1▸［体育］ double round 2▸（指轮子） two wheels: ～马车 two-wheeled cab

【双轮双铧犁】shuānglún shuānghuálí〈名〉 two-wheeled double-share plough

【双面】shuāngmiàn〈形〉 two-sided: ～唱片 double-sided record ‖ ～刀片 double-edged razor blade ‖ ～夹克 reversible jacket ‖ ～提花地毯 ingrain carpet

【双面绣】shuāngmiànxiù〈名〉 double-faced embroidery

【双面织物】shuāngmiàn zhīwù〈名〉 reversible cloth

【双模】shuāngmó〈名〉 dual mode: 混合动力和电动～新能源汽车 dual-mode hybrid and electric car ‖ ～手机 dual-mode mobile phone

【双目】shuāngmù A〈名〉 both eyes: ～失明 be blind in both eyes B〈形〉 binocular: ～显微镜 binocular microscope

【双年展】shuāngniánzhǎn〈名〉 biennial exhibition: 北京国际美术～ Beijing International Biennial Art Exhibition

【双抢】shuāngqiǎng〈动〉 rush through harvesting and planting: ～季节 rush-harvesting and rush-planting season

【双亲】shuāngqīn〈名〉 parents

【双球菌】shuāngqiújūn〈名〉［生物］ diplococcus: ～素 diplococcin

【双曲拱桥】shuāngqū gǒngqiáo〈名〉 double-vaulted arch bridge

【双曲线】shuāngqūxiàn〈名〉［数学］ hyperbola

【双全】shuāngquán〈动〉 have both: 父母～。Both parents are alive. ▸才貌～, 文武～, 智勇～

【双人床】shuāngrénchuáng〈名〉 double bed

【双人房】shuāngrénfáng〈名〉 double room

【双人滑】shuāngrénhuá〈名〉［体育］ pair skating

【双人舞】shuāngrénwǔ〈名〉 pas de deux

【双刃剑】shuāngrènjiàn〈名〉 double-edged sword

【双日】shuāngrì〈名〉 even-numbered day

【双身子】shuāngshēnzi〈名〉〈口〉 pregnant woman

【双生】shuāngshēng〈形〉 twins: ～姐妹 twin sisters ‖ ～子 twins

【双声】shuāngshēng〈名〉［语言］ alliterative compound

【双声道】shuāngshēngdào〈名〉 dual track

【双手】shuāngshǒu〈名〉 both hands: 反绑～ tie sb.'s hands behind their back ‖ ～抱头 bury one's head in one's hands ‖ ～合十 put one's palms together ‖ 举～赞成 support wholeheartedly

【双输】shuāngshū〈动〉 both sides concerned lose

【双数】shuāngshù ▸**p. 691**〈名〉 even number: ～日 even-numbered day

【双双】shuāngshuāng〈形〉 both: 兄弟俩～获奖。Both brothers won a prize.

【双双对对】shuāngshuāng-duìduì〈成〉 in pairs: ～的青年男女 young men and young women in pairs

【双糖】shuāngtáng〈名〉［化学］ disaccharide

【双体船】shuāngtǐchuán〈名〉 catamaran

【双筒望远镜】shuāngtǒng wàngyuǎnjìng〈名〉 binoculars: 一副～ a pair of binoculars

【双喜临门】shuāngxǐ-línmén〈成〉 two happy events come together

【双响】shuāngxiǎng〈名〉 double-bang firecracker

【双向】shuāngxiàng〈形〉 two-way: ～贸易与投资 bilateral trade and investment ‖ ～收费 dual-way charging

【双向飞碟射击】shuāngxiàng fēidié shèjī〈名〉［体育］ skeet shooting

【双向选择】shuāngxiàng xuǎnzé〈名〉 two-way selection

【双薪】shuāngxīn〈名〉 double pay: 发～ pay double time

【双星】shuāngxīng〈名〉1▸［天文］ binary star 2▸（牛郎星和织女星） Altair and Vega

【双休日】shuāngxiūrì〈名〉 two-day weekend

【双学位】shuāngxuéwèi〈名〉 dual degree

【双眼皮】shuāngyǎnpí〈名〉double-fold eyelid
【双氧水】shuāngyǎngshuǐ〈名〉［药学］hydrogen peroxide solution
【双翼机】shuāngyìjī〈名〉biplane
【双音节词】shuāngyīnjiécí〈名〉［语言］disyllabic word
【双引号】shuāngyǐnhào〈名〉double quotation mark (“”)
【双赢】shuāngyíng〈动〉have a victory for both sides: ～局面 win-win situation
【双拥】shuāngyōng〈动〉support the army and government and cherish the people
【双鱼座】Shuāngyúzuò〈名〉［天文］Pisces
【双语】shuāngyǔ〈形〉bilingual: ～词典 bilingual dictionary
【双语制】shuāngyǔzhì〈名〉bilingualism
【双元音】shuāngyuányīn〈名〉［语言］diphthong
【双月刊】shuāngyuèkān〈名〉bimonthly
【双职工】shuāngzhígōng〈名〉working couple: ～家庭 double-income family
【双周刊】shuāngzhōukān〈名〉biweekly
【双绉】shuāngzhòu〈名〉［纺织］crêpe de Chine
【双子叶植物】shuāngzǐyè zhíwù〈名〉dicotyledon
【双子座】Shuāngzǐzuò〈名〉［天文］Gemini

S

霜 shuāng

A〈名〉1（霜冻）frost: 严寒使窗子结了～。The cold has frosted the windows. ▸～冻，～降，冰～，除～ 2（霜状物）frost-like powder: ▸柿～，糖～，盐～
B〈形〉〈书〉hoary: 两鬓微～ with a touch of grey at the temples ▸～鬓
【霜鬓】shuāngbìn〈名〉〈书〉grey hair on the temples
【霜晨】shuāngchén〈名〉frosty morning
【霜冻】shuāngdòng〈名〉frost: 严重～ heavy frost
【霜害】shuānghài〈名〉［气象］frostbite: 遭受～的农作物 frost-bitten crops
【霜花】shuānghuā〈名〉rime: 结着～的窗户 windows covered with frost
【霜降】Shuāngjiàng〈名〉Frost's Descent [beginning of the 18th of the 24 solar terms]
【霜期】shuāngqī〈名〉［气象］season of frost
【霜天】shuāngtiān〈名〉frosty weather
【霜叶】shuāngyè〈名〉autumn leaves

孀 shuāng

A〈名〉widow: ▸～妇，遗～
B〈动〉live in widowhood: ▸～居
【孀妇】shuāngfù〈名〉〈书〉widow
【孀居】shuāngjū〈动〉〈书〉live as a widow: ～多年 be widowed for years

shuǎng

爽[1] shuǎng〈形〉1（明朗）bright: ▸清～，秋高气～ 2（爽快）frank: ▸～快，豪～，直～ 3（舒服）well: 身体不～ not feeling well ▸人逢喜事精神～

爽[2] shuǎng〈动〉deviate: ▸～约，屡试不～

【爽脆】shuǎngcuì〈形〉1（指声音）sharp and clear: 说话～ speak clearly 2（指个性、动作）straightforward: 他干活向来～。He always works with enthusiasm. 3（指食物）crisp: 新鲜的苹果吃起来很～。Fresh apples are crisp to the taste.
【爽健】shuǎngjiàn〈形〉〈书〉healthy and strong
【爽口】shuǎngkǒu〈形〉tasty and refreshing: 这种饮料喝着很～。This kind of drink is very refreshing.
【爽快】shuǎngkuai A〈形〉1（舒坦）refreshed: 心里～ be delighted 2（直爽）straightforward: 说话～ be outspoken B〈副〉readily: ～地接受了任务 readily accept the task
【爽朗】shuǎnglǎng〈形〉1（明朗）bright and clear 2（开朗）candid: 性格～ have a frank and open personality ‖ ～的笑声 hearty laughter
【爽利】shuǎnglì〈形〉efficient and able: 办事～ be efficient in one's work ‖ 动作～ be agile in one's movements
【爽目】shuǎngmù〈形〉easy on the eye
【爽气】shuǎngqì A〈名〉〈书〉cool and refreshing air B〈形〉〈方〉frank: 他为人～。He's a straightforward man.
【爽然】shuǎngrán〈形〉〈书〉perplexed
【爽然若失】shuǎngrán-ruòshī〈成〉be at a loss
【爽身粉】shuǎngshēnfěn〈名〉talcum powder
【爽心悦目】shuǎngxīn-yuèmù〈成〉refreshing for the mind and pleasing to the eye: 山中美景～。The beautiful mountain scenery is a refreshing and heartening sight.
【爽信】shuǎngxìn〈动〉〈书〉fail to keep one's promise
【爽性】shuǎngxìng〈副〉just as well: 太晚了，咱们～别去了。It's too late. We might just as well not go.
【爽约】shuǎngyuē〈动〉fail to keep an appointment: ～于人 fail to keep an appointment with sb.
【爽直】shuǎngzhí〈形〉straightforward: 生性～ candid by nature ‖ ～一点说 to put it bluntly

shuí

谁（誰）shuí = 谁 shéi

shuǐ

水[1] shuǐ

A〈名〉1（指物质）water: 一杯～ a cup of water ‖ 喝～ drink water ▸～质，淡～，海～ 2（河）river: 渭～ Weihe River 3（水域）waters: 三面环～ be surrounded by water on three sides ▸～域，跋山涉～ 4（洪水）flood: 这个地方去年发了～。A big flood struck this area last year. 5（液体）liquid: 墨～ ink ▸花露～，酒～，药～ 6（指钱）extra income: ▸升～，贴～，外～ 7（体液）body fluid: ▸口～，羊～
B〈动〉〈口〉swim: 你会～吗？Can you swim? ▸～性
C〈量〉washes: 洗过几～就会褪色。After several washes the colour will fade.

水[2] Shuǐ ▸水族 Shuǐzú

【水按摩】shuǐ'ànmó〈名〉［医学］hydromassage
【水吧】shuǐbā〈名〉water bar
【水坝】shuǐbà〈名〉dam: 在河上修筑～ build a dam across a river
【水斑】shuǐbān〈名〉［摄影］water spot
【水泵】shuǐbèng〈名〉water pump
【水笔】shuǐbǐ〈名〉1（写字用）stiff-haired writing brush 2（绘画用）water-colour paintbrush 3〈方〉（自来水笔）fountain pen: 一支～ a pen
【水标】shuǐbiāo〈名〉watermark: ～尺 river gauge
【水表】shuǐbiǎo〈名〉water meter
【水鳖】shuǐbiē〈名〉［植物］frogbit
【水鳖子】shuǐbiēzi〈名〉〈口〉［动物］tadpole shrimp
【水滨】shuǐbīn〈名〉water front: ～旅馆 waterside hotel
【水兵】shuǐbīng〈名〉bluejacket
【水波】shuǐbō〈名〉ripple
【水采】shuǐcǎi〈名〉［矿业］hydraulic mining
【水彩】shuǐcǎi〈名〉watercolour
【水彩画】shuǐcǎihuà〈名〉watercolour painting: 画～ paint in watercolour ‖ ～家 watercolourist
【水槽】shuǐcáo〈名〉water channel
【水草】shuǐcǎo〈名〉1（水和草）water and grass: ～丰茂 have plenty of water and lush grass 2（指水生植物）aquatic plants
【水层】shuǐcéng〈名〉aqueous layer: ～带 pelagic zone
【水产】shuǐchǎn〈名〉aquatic products: ～品 aquatic product
【水产养殖】shuǐchǎn yǎngzhí〈名〉aquatic farming: ～场 aquafarm ‖ ～业 aquaculture
【水产业】shuǐchǎnyè〈名〉aquatic industry
【水车】shuǐchē〈名〉1〈旧〉（指灌溉工具）waterwheel: 手摇～ manual waterwheel 2（运水车）water wagon 3〈方〉（消防车）fire engine
【水成岩】shuǐchéngyán〈名〉［地质］aqueous rock
【水城】shuǐchéng〈名〉city surrounded by water
【水程】shuǐchéng〈名〉voyage: 船行了六七里～就靠了岸。The ship reached the bank after a journey of six or seven miles.
【水池】shuǐchí〈名〉pond
【水池草】shuǐchícǎo〈名〉pondweed
【水池子】shuǐchízi = 水池 shuǐchí
【水尺】shuǐchǐ〈名〉［水利］water gauge
【水处理】shuǐchǔlǐ〈名〉water treatment: ～厂 water treatment plant
【水床】shuǐchuáng〈名〉waterbed
【水淬】shuǐcuì〈名〉quench hardening (by water)
【水到渠成】shuǐdào-qúchéng〈成〉success is assured when conditions are ripe
【水道】shuǐdào〈名〉1［水文］stream 2［航海］channel 3［建筑］waterway 4［地理］canal 5［体育］lane 6［航空］water lane
【水稻】shuǐdào〈名〉paddy: 种～ grow rice
【水滴石穿】shuǐdī-shíchuān〈成〉constant effort brings success
【水底】shuǐdǐ〈名〉bottom of water
【水底电缆】shuǐdǐ diànlǎn〈名〉underwater cable
【水底生物】shuǐdǐ shēngwù〈名〉benthos
【水底植物】shuǐdǐ zhíwù〈名〉phytobenthon
【水地】shuǐdì〈名〉1 = 水浇地 shuǐjiāodì 2（水田）paddy field
【水电】shuǐdiàn〈名〉1（水和电）water and electricity 2（用水发电）hydroelectricity: ～资源 hydroelectric resource
【水电费】shuǐdiànfèi〈名〉charges for water and electricity

【水电气】shuǐ diàn qì〈名〉 water, power and gas: ～基础设施齐全。 Utilities infrastructure is complete.
【水电站】shuǐdiànzhàn〈名〉 hydroelectric power station
【水貂】shuǐdiāo〈名〉 mink: ～皮 mink (fur)
【水动力学】shuǐdònglìxué〈名〉 hydrodynamics
【水痘】shuǐdòu ▸p. 50〈名〉［医学］chickenpox
【水碓】shuǐduì〈名〉 water-powered triphammer for husking rice
【水发】shuǐfā〈动〉 steep in water: ～海产 soaked sea cucumber ‖ ～香菇 shiitake mushrooms soaked in water
【水法】shuǐfǎ〈名〉 water law
【水肥】shuǐféi〈名〉 liquid manure
【水费】shuǐfèi〈名〉 water rate
【水粉】shuǐfěn〈名〉 1（指粉条） soaked bean noodle 2（化妆粉） liquid powder
【水粉画】shuǐfěnhuà〈名〉 gouache
【水分】shuǐfèn〈名〉 1（水） moisture content: 从土壤中吸收～ absorb moisture from the soil ‖ ～充足 abundant water 2〈喻〉（不真实的成分） exaggeration
【水浮莲】shuǐfúlián〈名〉［植物］ water lettuce
【水缸】shuǐgāng〈名〉 water vat
【水阁】shuǐgé〈名〉 waterside pavilion
【水耕法】shuǐgēngfǎ〈名〉［农业］ water culture
【水工】shuǐgōng〈名〉 1 = 水暖工 shuǐnuǎngōng 2 = 水利工程 shuǐlì gōngchéng
【水沟】shuǐgōu〈名〉 drain: 跳过一条小～ jump over a small ditch
【水垢】shuǐgòu = 水碱 shuǐjiǎn
【水垢净化器】shuǐgòu jìnghuàqì〈名〉 scaler
【水鸪鸪】shuǐgūgū〈口〉= 鹁鸪 bógū
【水管】shuǐguǎn〈名〉 water pipe
【水罐】shuǐguàn〈名〉 water jug
【水龟虫】shuǐguīchóng〈名〉［昆虫］ water scavenger beetle
【水柜】shuǐguì〈名〉 water tank
【水果】shuǐguǒ〈名〉 fruit
【水果冻】shuǐguǒdòng〈名〉 fruit jelly
【水果罐头】shuǐguǒ guàntou〈名〉 tin of fruit
【水果糖】shuǐguǒtáng〈名〉 fruit drops
【水害】shuǐhài〈名〉 flood
【水旱】shuǐ-hàn〈名〉 1（水涝和干旱） flood and drought 2（水陆） water and land
【水合】shuǐhé〈名〉［化学］ hydration
【水合物】shuǐhéwù〈名〉［化学］ hydrate
【水红】shuǐhóng〈形〉 bright pink
【水壶】shuǐhú〈名〉 1（烧水用） kettle 2（盛水用） water bottle 3（浇水用） watering can
【水葫芦】shuǐhúlu〈名〉［植物］water hyacinth
【水浒传】shuǐhǔzhuàn〈名〉 *The Water Margin*
【水花】shuǐhuā〈名〉 spray: 银色的～ silvery spray
【水华】shuǐhuá〈名〉 water bloom [algae]
【水环境】shuǐhuánjìng〈名〉 water environment: ～治理 management of the water environment
【水患】shuǐhuàn〈名〉 flood
【水荒】shuǐhuāng〈名〉 acute water shortage

《水浒传》

The Water Margin, also known as *Outlaws of the Marsh*, one of the four great works of Chinese classical literature. There is disagreement over the authorship of the book, although it is generally believed to have been written by Shi Nai'an (施耐庵), who lived at the end of the Yuan and beginning of the Ming Dynasty. The 'water margin' refers to the edge of the Liang Mountain lake (in Liang Mountain County, present-day Shandong Province). The story relates the exploits of 108 heroic characters, exposing the brutality and corruption of the ruling classes, and the vicissitudes and desires of ordinary people. The idiom '*bi shang Liangshan*' (逼上梁山, 'be driven to extremities') derives from the story of the hero Lin Chong and others who fled to the Liang Mountain to rebel against the local authorities.

【水火】shuǐhuǒ〈名〉 1（水和火）fire and water 2〈喻〉（对立） opposites: 势如～ be incompatible 3〈喻〉（灾难） extreme misery: 生活在～之中 live in misery
【水火不容】shuǐhuǒ-bùróng = 水火不相容 shuǐhuǒ bù xiāng róng
【水火不相容】shuǐhuǒ bù xiāng róng〈成〉 be utterly incompatible: 那两个人～。 Those two people are completely incompatible.
【水火无情】shuǐhuǒ-wúqíng〈成〉 flood and fire have no mercy for anybody
【水货】shuǐhuò〈名〉 contraband goods
【水迹】shuǐjì〈名〉 water stain
【水迹线】shuǐjìxiàn〈名〉 waterline
【水煎包】shuǐjiānbāo〈名〉 lightly fried stuffed bread
【水碱】shuǐjiǎn〈名〉 scale: 锅炉～ boiler scale
【水浇地】shuǐjiāodì〈名〉 irrigated land
【水饺】shuǐjiǎo〈名〉 boiled *jiaozi* /dumpling
【水窖】shuǐjiào〈名〉 water cellar
【水解】shuǐjiě〈动〉［化学］ hydrolyze
【水解蛋白】shuǐjiě dànbái〈名〉 protein hydrolysate
【水解酶】shuǐjiěméi〈名〉［生化］ hydrolase
【水介质】shuǐjièzhì〈名〉［化学］ aqueous medium
【水晶】shuǐjīng〈名〉 crystal
【水晶包】shuǐjīngbāo〈名〉 steamed dumpling containing pig fat and sugar
【水晶玻璃】shuǐjīng bōli〈名〉 crystal
【水晶宫】shuǐjīnggōng〈名〉 Crystal Palace (of the Dragon King in ancient Chinese mythology)
【水晶婚】shuǐjīnghūn〈名〉 crystal wedding anniversary
【水晶体】shuǐjīngtǐ〈名〉［解剖］ crystalline lens
【水井】shuǐjǐng〈名〉 well
【水景】shuǐjǐng〈名〉 waterscape
【水景房】shuǐjǐngfáng〈名〉 house with water features
【水警】shuǐjǐng〈名〉 coast guard
【水酒】shuǐjiǔ〈名〉〈谦〉 watery wine
【水军】shuǐjūn〈名〉〈旧〉 waterborne troops
【水坑】shuǐkēng〈名〉 puddle: 小～ little pools
【水库】shuǐkù〈名〉 reservoir
【水牢】shuǐláo〈名〉 water dungeon
【水涝】shuǐlào〈动〉 waterlog
【水雷】shuǐléi〈名〉［军事］ underwater mine: ～区 submarine mine zone ‖ 船触～沉没了。 The ship struck a mine and sank.
【水冷】shuǐlěng〈形〉 water-cooling
【水力】shuǐlì〈名〉 hydraulic power: ～采矿 hydraulic mining
【水力发电】shuǐlì fādiàn〈名〉 hydraulic power generation: ～厂 hydraulic power plant ‖ ～机 hydroelectric generator
【水力工程学】shuǐlì gōngchéngxué〈名〉 hydrotechnics
【水利】shuǐlì〈名〉 1（指自然能源）water conservancy 2（指设施） water conservancy project: 兴修～ build irrigation works
【水利工程】shuǐlì gōngchéng〈名〉 hydraulic works: ～学 hydraulic engineering
【水利灌溉网】shuǐlì guàngàiwǎng〈名〉 irrigation network
【水利枢纽】shuǐlì shūniǔ〈名〉 key water control project
【水量】shuǐliàng〈名〉 volume of water
【水疗】shuǐliáo〈名〉［医学］hydrotherapy: ～法 hydrotherapy
【水淋淋】shuǐlínlín〈形〉 dripping wet
【水灵】shuǐling〈形〉〈口〉 1（鲜美多汁） fresh and juicy: 这种桃儿很～。 This kind of peach is fresh and juicy. 2（有神采） radiant: 一双～的大眼睛 a pair of bright and beautiful eyes
【水流】shuǐliú〈名〉 1（江河） general term for rivers and streams 2（流动的水） current: ～湍急 have a rapid flow
【水龙】shuǐlóng〈名〉 hose: 消防～ fire hose
【水龙带】shuǐlóngdài〈名〉 hose: 卷～ reel a hose
【水龙卷】shuǐlóngjuǎn〈名〉［气象］ waterspout
【水龙头】shuǐlóngtóu〈名〉 tap〈英〉; faucet〈美〉: 打开/关上～ turn on/off the tap
【水漏】shuǐlòu〈名〉 clepsydra
【水陆】shuǐlù〈名〉 1（水上和陆地上） waterway and land: ～交通 land and water transportation 2〈书〉（山珍海味） delicacies from land and sea: ～俱陈 have all kinds of delicacies
【水陆联运】shuǐlù liányùn〈名〉 water-land transport: ～码头 dock for joint land and water transportation service
【水陆两用】shuǐlù liǎngyòng〈形〉 amphibious: ～船 alligator
【水陆坦克】shuǐlù tǎnkè〈名〉［军事］ amphibious tank
【水路】shuǐlù〈名〉 waterway: 走～ go by water ‖ ～运输 water transportation ‖ ～图 hydrographic chart
【水绿】shuǐlǜ〈名〉 aquamarine
【水轮】shuǐlún〈名〉 waterwheel
【水轮泵】shuǐlúnbèng〈名〉 water pump
【水轮发电机】shuǐlún fādiànjī〈名〉 hydrogenerator
【水轮机】shuǐlúnjī〈名〉 hydraulic turbine
【水落管】shuǐluòguǎn〈名〉［建筑］downpipe〈英〉; downspout〈美〉
【水落石出】shuǐluò-shíchū〈成〉everything will come to light
【水幔】shuǐmàn〈名〉 screen of water
【水煤气】shuǐméiqì〈名〉［化学］ water gas
【水门】shuǐmén〈名〉 1（阀） sluice 2〈方〉= 水闸 shuǐzhá
【水蜜桃】shuǐmìtáo〈名〉 honey peach
【水面】shuǐmiàn〈名〉 1（水的表面） water surface: 浮出～ surface ‖ 鲸鱼突然露出～。 The whale suddenly surfaced. 2（水域面积） area of a body of water
【水磨】shuǐmó〈动〉 polish with water stone: ～石 terrazzo
▸shuǐmò

S

【水磨功夫】shuǐmó gōngfu〈成〉painstaking work
【水墨画】shuǐmòhuà〈名〉wash painting
【水磨】shuǐmò〈名〉watermill ▸shuǐmó
【水母】shuǐmǔ〈名〉［动物］jellyfish
【水幕】shuǐmù〈名〉1 ［矿业］water curtain 2（指屏幕）water screen
【水难】shuǐnàn〈名〉shipwreck
【水囊肿】shuǐnángzhǒng ▸p. 50〈名〉［医学］hydrocele
【水能】shuǐnéng〈名〉hydroenergy
【水能动力学】shuǐnéng dònglìxué〈名〉hydrodynamics
【水能载舟，亦能覆舟】shuǐ néng zài zhōu, yì néng fù zhōu〈成〉popular support is of overriding importance to a government
【水泥】shuǐní〈名〉cement: 搅拌～ mix cement ‖ ～地面 cement flooring ‖ ～板 cement plate ‖ ～瓦 cement tile ‖ ～砖 cement brick
【水泥标号】shuǐní biāohào〈名〉cement grade
【水泥厂】shuǐníchǎng〈名〉cement plant
【水泥钉】shuǐnídīng〈名〉cement nail
【水泥灌浆】shuǐní guànjiāng〈名〉［建筑］grouting: ～泵 grout pump
【水泥浆】shuǐníjiāng〈名〉cement slurry
【水泥搅拌机】shuǐní jiǎobànjī〈名〉cement mixer
【水泥砂浆】shuǐní shājiāng〈名〉cement mortar
【水碾】shuǐniǎn〈名〉water-powered roller
【水鸟】shuǐniǎo〈名〉［鸟类］aquatic bird
【水牛】shuǐniú〈名〉buffalo
【水暖】shuǐnuǎn〈名〉1（指供暖系统）hot water central heating system: ～系统 water-heating system 2（自来水和暖气设备）water supply and heating
【水暖工】shuǐnuǎngōng〈名〉plumber
【水牌】shuǐpái〈名〉notice board
【水泡】shuǐpào〈名〉bubble: 池塘里冒出～。Water bubbled up through the pond.
【水疱】shuǐpào〈名〉blister: 手上出了～ get blisters on one's hands
【水漂】shuǐpiāo〈名〉ducks and drakes: ▸打～
【水平】shuǐpíng A〈名〉level: 提高生活～ improve a standard of living ‖ ～参差不齐 be varied in standard ‖ 文化～ level of education B〈形〉horizontal: ～方向 horizontal direction
【水平测试】shuǐpíng cèshì〈名〉proficiency test
【水平分布】shuǐpíng fēnbù〈名〉horizontal distribution
【水平面】shuǐpíngmiàn〈名〉1（指水形成的）water level 2（与水面相平的面）horizontal plane
【水平线】shuǐpíngxiàn〈名〉horizontal line
【水平仪】shuǐpíngyí〈名〉spirit level
【水瓶座】Shuǐpíngzuò〈名〉［天文］Aquarius
【水汽】shuǐqì〈名〉steam: 擦掉窗玻璃上的～ wipe off the moisture from the panes
【水枪】shuǐqiāng〈名〉1（指消防用具）water pistol 2 ［矿业］hydraulic monitor
【水橇】shuǐqiāo〈名〉water ski
【水芹】shuǐqín〈名〉［植物］water parsnip
【水禽】shuǐqín = 水鸟 shuǐniǎo
【水情】shuǐqíng〈名〉［水利］regimen
【水球】shuǐqiú ▸p. 909〈名〉［体育］water polo
【水曲柳】shuǐqūliǔ〈名〉［植物］Manchurian ash
【水渠】shuǐqú〈名〉canal
【水圈】shuǐquān〈名〉［水文］hydrosphere
【水权】shuǐquán〈名〉water rights
【水溶胶】shuǐróngjiāo〈名〉hydrosol
【水溶性】shuǐróngxìng〈名〉water-solubility
【水溶液】shuǐróngyè〈名〉［化学］aqueous solution
【水乳交融】shuǐrǔ-jiāoróng〈成〉get along swimmingly
【水杉】shuǐshān〈名〉［植物］dawn redwood
【水上芭蕾】shuǐshàng bālěi〈名〉［体育］synchronized swimming
【水上飞机】shuǐshàng fēijī〈名〉seaplane
【水上交通】shuǐshàng jiāotōng〈名〉waterborne traffic
【水上警察】shuǐshàng jǐngchá〈名〉water police
【水上运动】shuǐshàng yùndòng〈名〉aquatic sports: 游泳和划船都是～。Swimming and rowing are both aquatic sports.
【水蛇】shuǐshé〈名〉water snake
【水蛇腰】shuǐshéyāo〈名〉slim waist
【水深火热】shuǐshēn-huǒrè〈成〉〈喻〉extreme misery: 处在～之中 be plunged into an abyss of suffering
【水深图】shuǐshēntú〈名〉bathygram
【水神】shuǐshén〈名〉water deity
【水生】shuǐshēng〈形〉aquatic
【水生动物】shuǐshēng dòngwù〈名〉aquatic animal
【水生生物】shuǐshēng shēngwù〈名〉aquatic life: ～学 hydrobiology
【水生植物】shuǐshēng zhíwù〈名〉aquatic plant
【水师】shuǐshī〈名〉〈旧〉navy
【水虱】shuǐshī〈名〉［昆虫］beach louse
【水蚀】shuǐshí〈动〉water erosion
【水势】shuǐshì〈名〉1（水流）flow of water: ～湍急 rushing current 2（潜能）water potential
【水手】shuǐshǒu〈名〉seaman: ～长 boatswain
【水松】shuǐsōng〈名〉［植物］China cypress
【水塔】shuǐtǎ〈名〉water tower
【水獭】shuǐtǎ〈名〉［动物］otter
【水潭】shuǐtán〈名〉pool
【水塘】shuǐtáng〈名〉pond
【水体】shuǐtǐ〈名〉waters
【水田】shuǐtián〈名〉paddy field
【水桶】shuǐtǒng〈名〉pail
【水头】shuǐtóu〈名〉［水利］1（水源）head 2（指洪峰）flood peak 3（指来势）oncoming force of water
【水土】shuǐtǔ〈名〉1（自然环境）natural environment: ▸～不服 2（水和土）water and soil
【水土保持】shuǐtǔ bǎochí〈名〉［农业］water and soil conservancy
【水土不服】shuǐtǔ-bùfú〈成〉not be acclimatized
【水土流失】shuǐtǔ liúshī〈名〉soil erosion
【水豚】shuǐtún〈名〉［动物］water hog
【水汪汪】shuǐwāngwāng〈形〉1（形容土地）waterlogged: 下过雨后，地里～的。The fields were submerged after the rain. 2（形容眼睛）watery
【水网】shuǐwǎng〈名〉network of rivers: ～遍布 criss-crossed with rivers, rivulets, lakes and ponds
【水位】shuǐwèi〈名〉1（指水面）water level: 河水已经超出正常～。The river has risen above the normal level. 2（指地下水）water table
【水位差】shuǐwèichā〈名〉hydraulic gradient
【水温】shuǐwēn〈名〉water temperature: ～表 water temperature gauge
【水文】shuǐwén〈名〉hydrology: ～预报 hydrologic forecast ‖ ～资料 hydrological data
【水文地理学】shuǐwén dìlǐxué〈名〉hydrography
【水文地质】shuǐwén dìzhì〈名〉hydrographical geology: ～勘探 hydrogeologic prospecting ‖ ～学 hydrogeology
【水文工作者】shuǐwén gōngzuòzhě ▸p. 966〈名〉hydrologist
【水文气象学】shuǐwén qìxiàngxué〈名〉hydrometeorology
【水文气象站】shuǐwén qìxiàngzhàn〈名〉hydrometeorological station
【水文学】shuǐwénxué〈名〉hydrology: ～家 hydrographer
【水文站】shuǐwénzhàn〈名〉hydrologic station
【水纹】shuǐwén〈名〉［工程］water wave
【水污染】shuǐwūrǎn〈名〉water pollution: 防止～ prevent contamination of water
【水雾】shuǐwù〈名〉water fume
【水螅】shuǐxī〈名〉［动物］hydroid
【水洗】shuǐxǐ〈名〉1（用水洗）rinsing 2 ［摄影］wash
【水洗布】shuǐxǐbù〈名〉washed cloth
【水系】shuǐxì〈名〉water system: 长江～ Yangtze River System
【水下】shuǐxià〈形〉underwater: ～作业 works under water
【水仙】shuǐxiān〈名〉narcissus
【水线】shuǐxiàn〈名〉waterline
【水乡】shuǐxiāng〈名〉region of rivers and lakes
【水箱】shuǐxiāng〈名〉water tank
【水泻】shuǐxiè ▸p. 50〈名〉［医学］watery diarrhoea
【水泄不通】shuǐxiè-bùtōng〈成〉〈喻〉densely packed: 围得～ be hemmed in
【水榭】shuǐxiè〈名〉waterside pavilion
【水星】Shuǐxīng〈名〉［天文］Mercury
【水性】shuǐxìng〈名〉1（游水的技能）swimming ability: 识～ swim like a duck 2（特点）regimen: 熟悉长江～ know the characteristics of the Yangtze River
【水性涂料】shuǐxìng túliào〈名〉［材料］water-based paint
【水性杨花】shuǐxìng-yánghuā〈成〉[of a woman] of easy virtue: ～的女人 woman of loose morals
【水袖】shuǐxiù〈名〉long white silky sleeves worn in traditional Chinese performances
【水锈】shuǐxiù〈名〉1 = 水碱 shuǐjiǎn 2（痕迹）watermark
【水循环】shuǐxúnhuán〈名〉1（指大自然）hydrologic cycle 2（指系统）water circulation
【水压】shuǐyā〈名〉hydraulic pressure
【水压机】shuǐyājī〈名〉hydraulic press
【水鸭】shuǐyā〈名〉teal
【水烟】shuǐyān〈名〉shredded tobacco for water pipe: 抽～ smoke a water pipe
【水烟袋】shuǐyāndài〈名〉hookah
【水烟筒】shuǐyāntǒng = 水烟袋 shuǐyāndài
【水眼】shuǐyǎn〈名〉mouth of a spring
【水杨柳】shuǐyángliǔ〈名〉［植物］bigcatkin willow
【水杨酸】shuǐyángsuān〈名〉［化学］salicylic acid: ～钠 sodium salicylate
【水样】shuǐyàng〈名〉water sample
【水样便】shuǐyàngbiàn〈名〉［医学］watery stool
【水妖】shuǐyāo〈名〉water sprite
【水舀子】shuǐyǎozi〈名〉〈方〉ladle
【水翼】shuǐyì〈名〉hydrofoil

S

【水翼船】shuǐyìchuán = 水翼艇 shuǐyìtǐng
【水翼艇】shuǐyìtǐng〈名〉hydrofoil
【水银】shuǐyín〈名〉［化学］mercury
【水银灯】shuǐyíndēng〈名〉mercury lamp
【水银温度计】shuǐyín wēndùjì〈名〉mercury thermometer
【水银中毒】shuǐyín zhòngdú〈名〉mercurial poisoning
【水银柱】shuǐyínzhù〈名〉mercury column: ～血压计 mercurial sphygmomanometer
【水印】shuǐyìn〈名〉1（美术）watercolour block printing 2（指纹理）watermark 3（痕迹）water stain
【水有源，树有根】shuǐ yǒu yuán, shù yǒu gēn〈俗〉everything has its origin
【水域】shuǐyù〈名〉waters: 国际～ international waters
【水源】shuǐyuán〈名〉1（发源地）headspring 2（来源）source of water: 寻找新的～ seek new sources of water
【水运】shuǐyùn〈动〉transport by water: ～物资 transport supplies by water ‖ ～码头 dock
【水灾】shuǐzāi〈名〉flood disaster: 遭～ be hit by a flood
【水葬】shuǐzàng〈名〉water burial
【水蚤】shuǐzǎo〈名〉［动物］water flea
【水藻】shuǐzǎo〈名〉algae
【水泽】shuǐzé〈名〉〈书〉region of rivers, lakes and marshes
【水闸】shuǐzhá〈名〉sluice
【水战】shuǐzhàn〈名〉battle on the water
【水站】shuǐzhàn〈名〉water kiosk: 拿水桶到～灌装纯净水 take the jug to the water station and fill it with purified water
【水涨船高】shuǐzhǎng-chuángāo〈成〉particular things improve with the improvement of the general situation
【水蒸气】shuǐzhēngqì〈名〉steam: ～含量 water vapour content
【水至清则无鱼】shuǐ zhì qīng zé wú yú〈成〉it is best not to criticize other people too much, or you'll end up with no friends at all
【水质】shuǐzhì〈名〉water quality
【水蛭】shuǐzhì〈名〉［动物］leech
【水中捞月】shuǐzhōng-lāoyuè〈成〉make vain efforts
【水肿】shuǐzhǒng ►**p. 50**〈名〉［医学］oedema: 膝关节～ water on the knee
【水珠】shuǐzhū〈名〉drop of water
【水柱】shuǐzhù〈名〉column of water
【水准】shuǐzhǔn〈名〉1（水平面）water level 2（水平）level: 保持某一～ maintain a standard ‖ 提高生产～ increase the standard of production ‖ 按照国际～ on the international level
【水准点】shuǐzhǔndiǎn〈名〉bench mark
【水准面】shuǐzhǔnmiàn〈名〉level surface
【水准仪】shuǐzhǔnyí〈名〉［工程］level
【水资源】shuǐzīyuán〈名〉water resources: 征收～费 impose a water tax ‖ 许多城市～严重匮乏。Many cities face a serious water shortage.
【水渍】shuǐzì〈名〉water damage
【水族】Shuǐzú〈名〉Sui ethnic group
【水族】shuǐzú〈名〉aquatic animals: ～馆 aquarium
【水钻】shuǐzuàn〈名〉artificial diamond

shuì

说（説） shuì〈动〉persuade: ►游～
►shuō, yuè
【说客】shuìkè〈旧〉= 说客 shuōkè

帨 shuì〈名〉〈古〉scarf

税 shuì〈名〉tax: 缴所得～ pay tax on one's earnings ‖ 逃～/漏～ defraud the revenue ►关～, 纳～, 收～
【税单】shuìdān〈名〉tax receipt
【税额】shuì'é〈名〉amount of tax
【税法】shuìfǎ〈名〉tax law
【税负】shuìfù〈名〉tax burden
【税改】shuìgǎi〈名〉reform of tax systems
【税基】shuìjī〈名〉tax base
【税金】shuìjīn = 税款 shuìkuǎn
【税捐】shuìjuān〈名〉〈旧〉duty
【税款】shuìkuǎn〈名〉taxation: 交纳/免除～ render/remit a tax
【税利】shuìlì〈名〉taxes and profits
【税率】shuìlǜ〈名〉rate of taxation: 比例/累进～ proportional/progressive tax rate ‖ 双重～ dual tariff
【税目】shuìmù〈名〉taxable item
【税票】shuìpiào〈名〉tax receipt
【税卡】shuìqiǎ〈名〉〈旧〉checkpoint for tax collection
【税收】shuìshōu〈名〉revenue: 加强～ tighten tax collection ‖ 国内～ inland revenue
【税务】shuìwù〈名〉tax administration: 加强～管理 reinforce tax management ‖ ～支付 revenue payment
【税务机关】shuìwù jīguān〈名〉tax authorities
【税务局】shuìwùjú〈名〉tax bureau
【税务师】shuìwùshī ►**p. 966**〈名〉tax agent: 注册～ registered tax agent
【税务员】shuìwùyuán ►**p. 966**〈名〉tax collector
【税源】shuìyuán〈名〉source of tax: 开发新～ tap new sources of taxes
【税则】shuìzé〈名〉tax regulations
【税制】shuìzhì〈名〉tax system: ～改革 taxation reform
【税种】shuìzhǒng〈名〉categories of taxes

睡 shuì〈动〉1（睡觉）sleep: ～地板 sleep on the floor ‖ ～午觉 take an afternoon nap ‖ ～得很晚 stay up very late ‖ 早～早起 early to bed and early to rise ►～衣, ～意, 酣～ 2（容纳）sleep: 这个屋子～四个人没问题。The room can sleep four easily. ‖ 这张床～不下三个人。The bed is not big enough for three people.
【睡袋】shuìdài〈名〉sleeping bag
【睡觉】shuìjiào〈动〉sleep: ～晚 stay up late ‖ 上床～ go to bed ‖ 睡一个安稳觉 have a good sleep ‖ 该～了。It's time to go to bed.
【睡裤】shuìkù〈名〉pyjama bottoms
【睡懒觉】shuì lǎnjiào〈动〉get up late: 明天休假，你可以～了。It's a holiday tomorrow, so you can sleep in.
【睡莲】shuìlián〈名〉［植物］water lily
【睡帽】shuìmào〈名〉nightcap
【睡美人】shuìměirén〈名〉sleeping beauty
【睡梦】shuìmèng〈名〉sleep: 把某人从～中惊醒 startle sb. out of his sleep
【睡眠】shuìmián〈名〉sleep: ～失调 sleep disorder ‖ 你打搅了我的～。You disturbed my sleep. ‖ 他～不足。He did not get enough sleep.
【睡眠疗法】shuìmián liáofǎ〈名〉sleep therapy
【睡眠障碍】shuìmián zhàng'ài ►**p. 50**〈名〉［医学］dyssomnia
【睡魔】shuìmó〈名〉〈喻〉extreme sleepiness
【睡袍】shuìpáo〈名〉nightgown
【睡乡】shuìxiāng〈名〉dreamland: 进入～ fall into the land of Nod
【睡相】shuìxiàng〈名〉posture in sleep
【睡醒】shuìxǐng〈动〉wake up: 七点钟～ wake up at seven o'clock
【睡眼】shuìyǎn〈名〉sleepy eyes: ～惺忪 be sleepy-eyed
【睡衣】shuìyī〈名〉pyjamas〈英〉; pajamas〈美〉
【睡椅】shuìyǐ〈名〉deck chair: 躺在～上 lie back in a reclining chair
【睡意】shuìyì〈名〉sleepiness: 毫无～ not at all sleepy ‖ ～正浓 be dead to the world
【睡着】shuìzháo〈动〉fall asleep: 看书时～了 fall asleep whilst reading ‖ 我睡不着。I couldn't sleep.

shǔn

吮 shǔn〈动〉suck
【吮乳】shǔnrǔ〈动〉suckle (at) the breast
【吮吸】shǔnxī〈动〉suck: 用吸管～ suck with a straw ‖ 婴儿正在～母亲的乳汁。The baby was suckling at its mother's breast.
【吮痈舐痔】shǔnyōng-shìzhì〈成〉〈喻〉be sycophantic: 对老板～ suck up to one's boss

楯 shǔn〈名〉〈书〉banisters
►dùn

shùn

顺（順） shùn
A〈动〉1（顺从）yield to: 别什么事都～着孩子。Don't give your children everything they want. ►归～, 孝～ 2（朝同一方向）follow: ～风 go with the wind ►～流, ～时针 3（使有条理）put in order: 用手～一～头发 smooth down one's hair 4（使方向同）turn round: 把车～过来 turn a car around 5（符合）suit: 不～他的心 not to his liking
B〈形〉1（方向相同）along with: ～船 downstream boat 2（通顺）fluent: 文字通～ have a smooth writing style ‖ 她英语讲得很～。She speaks very fluent English. 3（顺利）smooth: 爱情上不～ be unlucky in love ‖ 一切都很～。Everything went off without a hitch. ►～当 4（适宜）harmonious: ►风调雨～
C ►**p. 781**〈介〉along: ～着河边走 walk along a river ‖ ～着走廊走过来 come along the corridor
【顺变】shùnbiàn〈动〉〈书〉be accommodating: ►节哀～
【顺便】shùnbiàn〈副〉in passing: ～去一趟商店 drop in at a shop ‖ ～说一下 by the way ‖ 我妈妈昨天～来看我。My mother dropped round yesterday.
【顺差】shùnchā〈名〉surplus: 贸易～ favourable balance of trade
【顺产】shùnchǎn〈名〉［医学］normal childbirth
【顺畅】shùnchàng〈形〉smooth: 文笔～ smooth style of writing ‖ 交通～。The traffic is moving steadily.
【顺磁】shùncí〈名〉［物理］paramagnetic: ～性 paramagnetism
【顺次】shùncì〈副〉in proper sequence: ～进入教室 go into the classroom in order
【顺从】shùncóng〈动〉submit to: ～父亲

的意见 comply with one's father's wishes ‖ 对某人表示～ render obedience to sb.

【顺带】shùndài = 顺便 shùnbiàn

【顺当】shùndang〈形〉smooth: 日子过得顺顺当当 lead a smooth existence ‖ 办事不～ have trouble in dealing with a matter

【顺道】shùndào〈副〉on the way: ～看望老朋友 visit an old friend on one's way

【顺耳】shùn'ěr〈形〉pleasing to the ear: 听起来不～ be harsh on the ear

【顺风】shùnfēng **A**〈名〉［气象］tailwind **B**〈动〉［航空］［航海］go with the wind: ～航行 sail with the wind ‖ 祝你一路～! Bon voyage!

【顺风吹火】shùnfēng-chuīhuǒ〈成〉〈喻〉achieve sth. easily by going with the flow

【顺风耳】shùnfēng'ěr〈名〉**1**（指听力好）person with good hearing **2**（指消息灵通）well-informed person

【顺风转舵】shùnfēng-zhuǎnduò〈成〉go with the flow

【顺服】shùnfú〈动〉submit to: ～的孩子 docile child

【顺竿儿爬】shùngānrpá〈惯〉follow sb.'s cue

【顺和】shùnhe〈形〉affable: 态度～的老人 genial old man ‖ 语气～ speak in gentle tones

【顺价】shùnjià〈名〉favourable price: 实行粮食～销售 sell grain at favourable prices

【顺脚】shùnjiǎo **A**〈副〉**1**（顺便）on the way: ～捎回来一些菜 get some vegetables on the way back **2** = 顺路 shùnlù A **B** = 顺路 shùnlù B

【顺境】shùnjìng〈名〉favourable circumstances: 他逐渐进入～。The circumstances began to favour him.

【顺口】shùnkǒu **A**〈形〉**1**（流畅）easy to read: 经他一改，读起来～多了。It is much easier to read since his revision. **2**〈口〉（指口味）agreeable to one's taste: 这道菜真～。The dish is really tasty. **B**〈副〉thoughtlessly: ～答应 say 'yes' without much thought

【顺口溜】shùnkǒuliū〈名〉doggerel

【顺理成章】shùnlǐ-chéngzhāng〈成〉**1**（顺着条理）follow a logical course **2**（合乎情理）follow as a matter of course

【顺利】shùnlì〈形〉smooth: ～进行 go well ‖ ～通过考试 sail through one's exams

【顺溜】shùnliu〈形〉〈方〉**1**（有条理）well ordered: 文章写得很～。This essay is well-organized. **2**（乖）well behaved: 孩子今天很～。The child has been very well behaved today. **3**（顺畅）smooth: 日子过得挺～ live a trouble-free existence

【顺流】shùnliú〈副〉downstream: ～而下 go downstream

【顺路】shùnlù **A** ▸**p. 781**〈副〉on the way: 回家时～给儿子买个玩具 buy a toy for one's son on the way home **B**〈形〉direct: 这么走太绕远儿，不～。This is a roundabout way, not the shortest.

【顺民】shùnmín〈名〉〈贬〉obedient person

【顺时针】shùnshízhēn〈形〉clockwise: ～旋转 clockwise rotation

【顺势】shùnshì〈副〉at an opportunity: ～离开办公室 take the opportunity to leave the office ‖ ～批评他几句 make incidental criticisms of him

【顺手】shùnshǒu **A**〈形〉without a hitch: 第一次试验不太～是很自然的。It is natural that the first experiment did not go altogether smoothly. **B**〈副〉**1**（顺便）without any extra effort: ～从树上摘下一个苹果 pick an apple off a branch with great ease **2**（附带）at one's own convenience: 请～关门。Please close the door after you.

【顺手牵羊】shùnshǒu-qiānyáng〈成〉walk off with: ～的小偷 sneak thief ‖ 那贼～拿走了桌上的一块金表。The thief made off with a gold watch on the table.

【顺水】shùnshuǐ〈动〉go downstream: ～而下的小船 boat drifting downstream

【顺水人情】shùnshuǐ-rénqíng〈成〉favour done at little cost

【顺水推舟】shùnshuǐ-tuīzhōu〈成〉seize an opportunity to attain one's goal

【顺遂】shùnsuì〈形〉smooth: 处境～ be in a good situation

【顺藤摸瓜】shùnténg-mōguā〈成〉follow a clue to get results: 他们～，终于找到了罪犯的下落。They tracked the criminal down by following the clues.

【顺位】shùnwèi〈名〉rank: 第二～继承人 person ranked second in succession

【顺心】shùnxīn〈形〉satisfactory

【顺序】shùnxù **A**〈名〉order: ～颠倒 in reverse order ‖ 按时间～ in chronological order ‖ 按字母～ in alphabetical order **B**〈副〉in proper sequence

【顺延】shùnyán〈动〉postpone: ～三天 be postponed for three days

【顺眼】shùnyǎn〈形〉easy on the eye: 看着不～ be an eyesore

【顺意】shùnyì〈形〉agreeable: 祝你万事～! Hope everything goes well for you! ‖ 我们做什么事都得顺他的意。Whatever we do must be agreeable to him.

【顺应】shùnyìng〈动〉comply with: ～历史潮流 conform to historical trends ‖ ～民意 comply with the will of the people

【顺之者昌，逆之者亡】shùn zhī zhě chāng, nì zhī zhě wáng〈成〉those who bow before it will prosper, those who resist shall perish

【顺嘴】shùnzuǐ = 顺口 shùnkǒu A1, B

瞬

瞬 shùn〈动〉blink: ▸～时, 转～

【瞬间】shùnjiān〈名〉instant: ～消失 vanish in an instant ‖ 转～ for one fleeting moment ‖ 一～ in the blink of an eye

【瞬刻】shùnkè = 瞬息 shùnxī

【瞬时】shùnshí〈名〉instant: ～即逝 vanish in the twinkling of an eye

【瞬时电压】shùnshí diànyā〈名〉［电气］instantaneous voltage

【瞬时功率】shùnshí gōnglǜ〈名〉［物理］instantaneous power

【瞬时强度】shùnshí qiángdù〈名〉instantaneous strength

【瞬时速度】shùnshí sùdù〈名〉instantaneous velocity

【瞬时值】shùnshízhí〈名〉［物理］instantaneous value

【瞬息】shùnxī〈名〉twinkle: ～之间 in the twinkling of an eye

【瞬息万变】shùnxī-wànbiàn〈成〉undergo rapid change

shuō

说（説）shuō

A〈动〉**1**（表达）speak: ～实话 tell the truth ‖ ～英语 speak English ‖ 开玩笑地～ speak in jest ‖ 总的～来 generally speaking ‖ ～得太多，做得不够。There's too much talk and not enough action. ‖ 我不知道该怎么～。I don't know how to put it. ▸～谎 **2**（解释）explain: 把话～清楚 make it clear **3**（批评）criticize: 挨～了 be scolded ‖ 他又迟到了，你得～～他。He was late again. It's time you had a word with him. **4**（劝说）persuade: ▸～媒, ～情 **5**（指）refer to: 你们在～谁? Who are you talking about? ‖ 你是在～我吗? Do you mean me? **6**（表演）perform: ～相声 perform a comic dialogue **B**〈名〉theory: ▸邪～, 学～

▸shuì, yuè

【说白】shuōbái〈名〉［戏曲］spoken part

【说白了】shuōbáile〈动〉〈口〉tell it straight

【说不定】shuōbudìng〈副〉〈口〉perhaps: ～还是你对呢。Maybe you were right after all.

【说不过去】shuōbuguòqù〈动〉be unable to explain away: 借钱不还，那也太～了。To borrow money and then not give it back, that's just too much.

【说不来】shuōbulái〈动〉**1**〈口〉（无法相处）not be able to get along with: 我和他一点也～。He and I just can't get along at all. **2**〈方〉（无法表达）be unable to express oneself

【说不上】shuōbushàng〈动〉**1**（因不知道）be unable to say: 她也～去书店的路怎么走。She doesn't know how to get to the bookshop either. **2**（不值一提）be not worth mentioning: 这些伪制品～有什么收藏价值。These fakes will not help to enrich your collection.

【说曹操，曹操就到】shuō Cáo Cāo, Cáo Cāo jiù dào〈成〉speak of the devil

【说长道短】shuōcháng-dàoduǎn〈成〉indulge in idle gossip: 她喜欢对邻居～。She loves to gossip about her neighbours.

【说唱】shuōchàng〈名〉**1**（指曲艺）talking and singing **2**（指唱歌）rap: ～歌手 rapper

【说唱文学】shuōchàng wénxué〈名〉prosimetric literature

【说穿】shuōchuān〈动〉reveal

【说辞】shuōcí〈名〉excuse

【说大话】shuō dàhuà〈动〉talk up: 一味～ indulge in big talk

【说到做到】shuōdào-zuòdào〈成〉live up to one's word

【说道】shuōdào〈动〉say: 技术员～: "只有那么办了。" 'That's the only way out,' said the technician.

【说道】shuōdao〈方〉**A**〈动〉**1**（说出来）say: 你把刚才讲的在会上～～。Tell us what was said at the meeting. **2**（讨论）discuss: 这件事我们得～～。We have to talk this matter over. **B**〈名〉reason: 她为什么突然改变主意，这里头肯定有～。There must be some reason why she changed her mind so suddenly.

【说得过去】shuōdeguòqù〈动〉be passable: 她的英语马马虎虎，还～。She speaks passable English.

【说得来】shuōdelái〈动〉**1**〈口〉（有共同话题）be able to get along: 他跟所有的邻居都～。He gets along well with all his neighbours. **2**〈方〉（会说）have the gift of the gab

【说定】shuōdìng〈动〉agree upon: 价钱你们～了吗? Have you agreed on the price yet?

【说东道西】shuōdōng-dàoxī〈成〉talk about everything under the sun

【说短论长】shuōduǎn-lùncháng = 说长道短 shuōcháng-dàoduǎn

【说法】shuōfǎ〈动〉expound Buddhist doctrine

【说法】shuōfa〈名〉 1 (措词) way of saying things: 换一个～ in other words ‖ 这个意思可以有两种～。 This meaning can be expressed in two ways. 2 (见解) story: 关于她的死有各种～。 There are different versions of her death. ‖ 这种～现在已经没人相信了。 This argument is no longer accepted now. 3 (理由) explanation: 讨个～ demand an explanation ‖ 我要讨个～。 I want justice.
【说服】shuōfú〈动〉 persuade: ～某人 talk sb. round ‖ ～丈夫不再抽烟 convince one's husband to give up smoking ‖ 她容易被～。 She is easily persuaded.
【说服教育】shuōfú jiàoyù〈动〉 persuade and educate
【说服力】shuōfúlì〈名〉 persuasiveness: 缺乏～ lack persuasion ‖ 有～ be convincing
【说古道今】shuōgǔ-dàojīn〈成〉 talk about the past and the present
【说好】shuōhǎo〈动〉 come to an agreement: 我们已经～了。 We have come to an agreement already.
【说合】shuōhe〈动〉 1 (撮合) bring parties together: ～亲事 act as a matchmaker ‖ ～人 go-between 2 (讨论) discuss: 这件事得～～。 We have to talk it over. 3 = 说和 shuōhe
【说和】shuōhe〈动〉 settle a quarrel: 在吵架的双方中间～ mediate in a quarrel
【说话】shuōhuà A〈动〉 1 (说) speak: 爱～ be talkative ‖ ～太随便 have a loose tongue 2 (闲聊) chat: 说了一晚上话儿 talk the night away 3 (责怪) scold: 要按时到，否则人家要～了。 You'd better come on time, or you will be told off. B〈名〉〈方〉 an instant: 你稍等一等，我～就来。 Wait a minute. I'll come right away.
【说谎】shuōhuǎng〈动〉 tell a lie: 他从不～。 He never lies.
【说教】shuōjiào〈动〉 1 [宗教] preach 2 (讲大道理) lecture: 别对我～了。Stop lecturing me.
【说开】shuōkāi〈动〉 1 (解释清楚) explain sth. clearly: 还是把话～了好。 It would be better to explain it clearly. 2 (流行) come into popular use: 这个词在年轻人中间已经～了。 This word has become popular among young people.
【说客】shuōkè〈名〉 1 (劝说者) good talker 2〈贬〉(游说者) lobbyist ▸shuìkè
【说来话长】shuōlái-huàcháng〈成〉 it's a long story
【说来说去】shuōlái-shuōqù〈惯〉 after so much talking: ～你是不想跟我去? You mean you won't go with me even after so much explanation?
【说理】shuōlǐ〈动〉 1 (评理) argue: 找他～去 go and reason things out with him ‖ 文章～透彻。 The essay has a very clear argument. 2 (讲道理) be reasonable
【说漏嘴】shuōlòuzuǐ〈动〉 let slip: 他只是～了。 He just made a slip of the tongue.
【说媒】shuōméi〈动〉 act as a matchmaker
【说梦话】shuō mènghuà〈动〉 1〈本〉 talk in one's sleep 2〈喻〉 propose absurd ideas
【说明】shuōmíng A〈动〉 1 (解释) explain: ～理由 give reasons ‖ 加以～ make an explanation ‖ 举例～ illustrate by example 2 (证明) show: 事实～我们是正确的。 The fact proves that we are right. B〈名〉 explanation: 保养～ maintenance instructions ‖ 用法～ directions for use
【说明书】shuōmíngshū〈名〉 instructions: 使用～ user's guide
【说明文】shuōmíngwén〈名〉 expository writing
【说破】shuōpò〈动〉 reveal
【说亲】shuōqīn = 说媒 shuōméi
【说情】shuōqíng〈动〉 speak for
【说三道四】shuōsān-dàosì〈成〉gossip: 这不关你的事，你无权在这儿～。 This has nothing to do with you. You've no right to gossip about it here.
【说时迟，那时快】shuō shí chí, nàshí kuài〈惯〉 before you can say 'knife'
【说书】shuōshū〈动〉 tell a story: ～的人 storyteller

> **说书**
> A popular vocal art form involving the recitation of long stories such as Suzhou *pinghua* (苏州评话, ▸评弹) and *pingshu* (评书, storytelling in north China). Broadly speaking, this may include singing as well as speaking, and sometimes the accompaniment of musical instruments.

【说头儿】shuōtour〈名〉 1 (值得讨论) something worth talking about: 关于谁错谁对的问题已经没什么～了。 There is no point in talking about who's right and who's wrong. 2 (理由) excuse: 他每次迟到总有～。 He's always got an excuse for being late.
【说妥】shuōtuǒ〈动〉 come to an agreement: 发货日期你们～了吗? Have you agreed on the delivery date?
【说戏】shuōxì〈动〉 explain a play to an actor/actress
【说闲话】shuō xiánhuà〈动〉 1 (闲聊) chat: 和某人～ have a chat with sb. 2 (抱怨) gossip: 我不愿别人说我的闲话。 I don't want to be talked about.
【说项】shuōxiàng〈动〉 speak for sb.
【说笑】shuōxiào〈动〉 talk and laugh: 又说又笑 chatting and laughing
【说笑话】shuō xiàohua〈动〉 joke: 我只是跟她～。 I was only pulling her leg.
【说一不二】shuōyī-bù'èr〈成〉 mean what one says: 在这件事上我是～的。 I stand by my word on this matter.
【说着玩儿】shuōzhewánr〈动〉〈口〉 say sth. for fun: 我这话是～的。 I am saying it just for fun.
【说嘴】shuōzuǐ〈动〉 brag: 那没什么可～的。 That's nothing to boast about.

shuò

妁 shuò ▸媒妁 méishuò

烁（爍） shuò〈形〉 bright: ▸闪～
【烁烁】shuòshuò〈形〉sparkling: 繁星～。 The stars are twinkling.

铄（鑠） shuò A〈动〉〈书〉 1 (熔化) melt: ▸～石流金，众口～金 2 (削弱) weaken B = 烁 shuò
【铄石流金】shuòshí-liújīn = 流金铄石 liújīn-shuòshí

朔 shuò〈名〉 1 (指月相) phase of the moon on the first day of each lunar month 2 ▸p. 618〈书〉(朔日) first day of each lunar month: ▸～望 3 (指方向) north: ▸～方, ～风
【朔方】shuòfāng〈名〉〈书〉 north
【朔风】shuòfēng〈名〉〈书〉 north wind
【朔日】shuòrì ▸p. 618〈名〉 first days of each lunar month
【朔望】shuòwàng〈名〉 1 ▸p. 618 (指农历) first and fifteenth days of each lunar month 2 [天文] new moon and full moon
【朔望月】shuòwàngyuè〈名〉[天文] lunar month
【朔月】shuòyuè〈名〉 new moon

硕（碩） shuò〈形〉 large: ▸丰～
【硕大】shuòdà〈形〉 huge
【硕大无比】shuòdà-wúbǐ = 硕大无朋 shuòdà-wúpéng
【硕大无朋】shuòdà-wúpéng〈成〉gigantic: 地球像一个～的磁铁。 The earth is like a gigantic magnet.
【硕导】shuòdǎo〈简称〉= 硕士研究生导师
【硕果】shuòguǒ〈名〉 great achievements: 结～ bear rich fruits
【硕果仅存】shuòguǒ-jǐncún〈成〉 one of the few still left
【硕果累累】shuòguǒ-léiléi〈成〉 1〈本〉 be heavy with fruit: ～，树枝都压弯了。 The fruit was so heavy that it weighed the branches down. 2〈喻〉 achieve great success: 科研上～ impressive accomplishments in academic research
【硕士】shuòshì〈名〉master: 理学～ Master of Science (MSc) ‖ 文学～ Master of Arts (MA) ‖ 医学～ Master of Medical Science (MSc Med) ‖ 工商管理～ Master of Business Administration (MBA)
【硕士学位】shuòshì xuéwèi〈名〉 master's degree
【硕士研究生】shuòshì yánjiūshēng〈名〉 postgraduate student
【硕士研究生导师】shuòshì yánjiūshēng dǎoshī〈名〉 academic adviser to master's degree candidate

搠 shuò〈动〉 thrust: 用剑～敌人胸膛 thrust one's sword through an enemy's chest

蒴 shuò
【蒴果】shuòguǒ〈名〉[植物] capsule

数（數） shuò〈副〉〈书〉 frequently: ▸频～
▸shǔ, shù
【数见不鲜】shuòjiàn-bùxiān〈成〉 very common

槊 shuò〈名〉 ancient spear

sī

司 sī
A〈动〉 manage: 各～其职 each attends to their own duties ▸～机, ～令
B〈名〉 department: 人事～ personnel department ▸～长
【司铎】sīduó = 神甫 shénfu
【司舵】sīduò A〈动〉 be at the helm B〈名〉 helmsman
【司法】sīfǎ〈名〉 judicatory: 妨碍～ obstruct justice ‖ ～人员 judicial member
【司法部】sīfǎbù〈名〉department of justice
【司法部门】sīfǎ bùmén〈名〉 judiciary
【司法程序】sīfǎ chéngxù〈名〉judicial process
【司法机关】sīfǎ jīguān〈名〉 judicial organ
【司法鉴定】sīfǎ jiàndìng〈名〉 appraisal of justice

S

【司法界】sīfǎjiè〈名〉judicial circles
【司法权】sīfǎquán〈名〉jurisdiction
【司法审查】sīfǎ shěnchá〈名〉judicial review
【司法系统】sīfǎ xìtǒng〈名〉judicatory
【司法援助】sīfǎ yuánzhù〈名〉judicial aid
【司法制度】sīfǎ zhìdù〈名〉judiciary
【司号】sīhào **A**〈动〉sound a bugle **B**〈名〉trumpeter
【司号员】sīhàoyuán〈名〉trumpeter
【司机】sījī〈名〉driver: 出租车～ taxi driver
【司空见惯】sīkōng-jiànguàn〈成〉be a common sight: ～的现象 common occurrence
【司库】sīkù〈名〉treasurer
【司令】sīlìng〈名〉commander
【司令部】sīlìngbù〈名〉headquarters
【司令员】sīlìngyuán〈名〉commander
【司炉】sīlú〈名〉fireman
【司马昭之心，路人皆知】Sīmǎ Zhāo zhī xīn, lùrén jiē zhī〈歇后〉the villain's ambition is obvious
【司南】sīnán〈名〉〈古〉compass
【司售人员】sī shòu rényuán ►**p. 966**〈名〉bus crew
【司务长】sīwùzhǎng〈名〉［军事］company quartermaster
【司线员】sīxiànyuán〈名〉［体育］linesman
【司药】sīyào〈名〉pharmacist
【司仪】sīyí〈名〉master of ceremonies (MC): 在婚礼上做～ officiate at a wedding
【司长】sīzhǎng〈名〉director general of a department
【司职】sīzhí〈动〉take up a position or responsibility: ～前锋 play up front

S

丝（絲）sī

A〈名〉**1**（蚕丝）silk: ►～线, ～织品, 蚕～ **2**（丝状物）anything thread-like: 土豆～ shredded potato ‖ 蜘蛛～ spider yarn ►钢～, 铁～, 钨～ **3**（弦乐器）stringed instrument
B〈量〉whisker: 一～光线 a thread of light ‖ 一～微笑 a trace of smile ‖ 他身上没有一～浪漫情调。There's not a whisker of romance in him.
【丝虫】sīchóng〈名〉［动物］filaria
【丝虫病】sīchóngbìng ►**p. 50**〈名〉filariasis
【丝绸】sīchóu〈名〉silk: ～厂 silk mill
【丝绸之路】sīchóu zhī lù〈名〉Silk Road

> **丝绸之路**
>
> The Silk Road, also known as 丝路 in Chinese. From the 2nd century BC to the 13th and 14th centuries, this was an overland trade route from China through to central Asia, south and west Asia, Europe, and north Africa. It was called the Silk Road because of the vast quantities of Chinese silk and silk products that were traded westward along this route. It is generally considered that the route started at Chang'an (present-day Xi'an). Many Chinese technological innovations were transmitted westward along the Silk Road, including paper-making, gunpowder, printing, compasses, and ceramics, while Buddhism and Islam were transmitted eastward to China. The 13th century Italian adventurer Marco Polo is said to have travelled to China along the Silk Road.

【丝带】sīdài〈名〉silk ribbon
【丝糕】sīgāo〈名〉steamed corn cake
【丝瓜】sīguā〈名〉towel gourd: ～络 loofah
【丝光】sīguāng〈名〉mercerization: ～棉/羊毛 mercerized cotton/wool
【丝毫】sīháo〈形〉tiny: 没有～证据 not have a shred of evidence ‖ ～不能放松警惕 must not relax one's vigilance in the slightest ‖ 没有～的兴趣 not the least bit interested
【丝绵】sīmián〈名〉silk floss: ～被 silk-floss wadded quilt
【丝绒】sīróng〈名〉velvet
【丝丝入扣】sīsī-rùkòu〈成〉with meticulous care and flawless artistry
【丝袜】sīwà〈名〉silk stockings
【丝弦】sīxián〈名〉**1**（琴弦）silk string **2**（指地方剧）*sixian* opera [popular in Shijiazhuang, Hebei Province]
【丝线】sīxiàn〈名〉silk thread
【丝织画】sīzhīhuà〈名〉Stevengraph
【丝织品】sīzhīpǐn〈名〉silk product
【丝竹】sīzhú〈名〉traditional Chinese stringed and woodwind instruments: 江南～ southern Yangtze musical instruments
【丝状】sīzhuàng〈形〉thread-like
【丝锥】sīzhuī〈名〉tap

私 sī

A〈形〉**1**（私人）private: ►～生活, ～事, ～交 **2**（自私）selfish: ►～心, 自～ **3**（不公开）secret: 公款～用 illegitimate use of public funds ►～货
B〈名〉**1**（个人）something personal: ►公而忘～ **2**（私利）personal interest: ►铁面无～, 假公济～ **3**（违法购运）contraband: ►走～, 贩～
C〈副〉secretly: ►～奔, ～了
【私奔】sībēn〈动〉elope: 她跟情人～了。She eloped with her lover.
【私弊】sībì〈名〉corrupt practice
【私藏】sīcáng〈动〉**1**（指收藏）privately possess **2**（指藏匿）illegally keep: ～枪支弹药 illegally store guns and ammunition
【私产】sīchǎn〈名〉personal property
【私车】sīchē〈名〉private car
【私仇】sīchóu〈名〉personal grudge: 报～ settle personal scores
【私处】sīchù ►**p. 772**〈名〉〈婉〉private parts
【私党】sīdǎng〈名〉**1**（指党派）clique **2**（指成员）member of a clique
【私德】sīdé〈名〉personal morality: ～失检 be loose
【私邸】sīdǐ〈名〉private abode
【私底下】sīdǐxia〈副〉privately: 在～说坏话 speak ill of sb. behind their back
【私第】sīdì〈名〉〈书〉private residence
【私法】sīfǎ〈名〉［法律］private law
【私方】sīfāng〈名〉private side of a joint public-private enterprise
【私房】sīfáng〈名〉private house
【私访】sīfǎng〈动〉〈旧〉make an anonymous tour of inspection
【私房】sīfang〈形〉**1**（私下积蓄）private: ～钱 private savings **2**（私人之间）secret: ～话 confidence
【私分】sīfēn〈动〉divide privately: ～公款 divide public funds in secret
【私愤】sīfèn〈名〉personal spite: 出于～ out of spite
【私话】sīhuà〈名〉confidence: 这是咱俩的～，你可别往外说。This is just between you and me. Don't tell anybody else about it.
【私活】sīhuó〈名〉personal business: 上班时间干～ do one's personal business during office hours
【私货】sīhuò〈名〉contraband: 偷运～ smuggle goods
【私家】sījiā〈名〉something private: ～车 private car
【私见】sījiàn〈名〉**1**（偏见）prejudice: 不存～ have no personal bias **2**（个人意见）personal opinion
【私交】sījiāo〈名〉personal friendship
【私立】sīlì〈形〉private: ～学校 private school
【私利】sīlì〈名〉personal gain: 为了一己～ in one's own (private) interest
【私了】sīliǎo〈动〉settle privately: ～还是公了？Would you prefer to settle the matter in court or out of court?
【私密】sīmì **A**〈形〉private and personal **B**〈名〉privacy: 窥探他人～ stick one's nose into sb. else's business
【私囊】sīnáng〈名〉private purse: 中饱～ fatten one's own pocket
【私念】sīniàn〈名〉selfish motive
【私企】sīqǐ〈名〉private enterprise
【私情】sīqíng〈名〉**1**（个人交情）personal relationship: 不徇～ not be swayed by personal considerations **2**（男女感情）love affairs
【私权】sīquán〈名〉private right: 个人身份信息属于～。An individual's personal information is his or her own private right.
【私人】sīrén〈形〉**1**（个人）private: ～财产 private property ‖ ～信件 personal correspondence **2**（个人之间）interpersonal: ～关系 interpersonal relationships
【私人代表】sīrén dàibiǎo〈名〉personal representative
【私人访问】sīrén fǎngwèn〈名〉private visit
【私人侦探】sīrén zhēntàn〈名〉private investigator: 雇用～ hire a private detective
【私人住宅】sīrén zhùzhái〈名〉private house
【私商】sīshāng〈名〉**1**（指企业）private shop **2**（指经营者）businessman
【私设公堂】sīshè gōngtáng〈成〉set up a kangaroo court
【私生活】sīshēnghuó〈名〉private life: 名人的～ private life of a famous person
【私生子】sīshēngzǐ〈名〉illegitimate child
【私事】sīshì〈名〉private concern: 这是我的～，与你无关。This is my private business. It has nothing to do with you.
【私淑】sīshū〈动〉〈书〉regard an academically accomplished person as one's teacher though one has never studied under him: ～弟子 self-styled disciple
【私塾】sīshú〈名〉〈旧〉private school: ～先生 private tutor
【私通】sītōng〈动〉**1**（私下勾结）engage to secret communication **2**（通奸）commit adultery: 与人～ commit adultery with sb.
【私吞】sītūn〈动〉embezzle: ～公司资金 misappropriate company funds
【私下】sīxià〈副〉**1**（背地里）in private: 那是别人～告诉我的。I was told about that matter in secret. ‖ 我想和他～谈谈。I wish to talk with him privately. **2**（自己进行）without appropriate procedure: ～调解 secretly mediate
【私相授受】sīxiāngshòushòu〈成〉engage in private dealing
【私心】sīxīn〈名〉**1**（内心）inner world **2**（利己心）selfish motive: ～太重 be too selfish
【私心杂念】sīxīn-zániàn〈成〉selfish ideas and personal considerations
【私刑】sīxíng〈名〉lynching
【私蓄】sīxù〈名〉personal savings
【私学】sīxué〈名〉private school
【私营】sīyíng〈动〉privately operate: ～商店 privately-owned shop

【私营经济】sīyíng jīngjì〈名〉private sector of the economy
【私营企业】sīyíng qǐyè〈名〉private enterprise
【私有】sīyǒu〈动〉privately own: ～观念 private ownership mentality
【私有财产】sīyǒu cáichǎn〈名〉private property
【私有化】sīyǒuhuà〈动〉privatize
【私有制】sīyǒuzhì〈名〉private ownership
【私语】sīyǔ **A**〈动〉whisper: ▸窃窃～ **B**〈名〉confidence
【私欲】sīyù〈名〉selfish desire
【私怨】sīyuàn〈名〉personal grudge: 了结～ settle a personal grudge
【私运】sīyùn〈动〉smuggle
【私章】sīzhāng〈名〉personal seal
【私衷】sīzhōng〈名〉〈书〉innermost thought
【私自】sīzì〈副〉secretly: ～过户 illegal transfer ‖ ～放走犯人 release a criminal without official permission ‖ ～挪用公款 illegitimately use public funds

咝(噝) sī〈拟〉hiss: 炉子上的水壶发出～～的声音。The kettle was whistling on the stove.

思 sī
A〈动〉**1**（考虑）think: ▸～考, 沉～, 构～ **2**（想念）miss: ▸～乡, ～念, 相～ **3**（希望）hope: ～归 wish to return ▸穷则～变
B〈名〉**1**（心绪）feeling: ▸愁～, 哀～ **2**（思路）thinking: ▸文～
【思辨】sībiàn **A**〈动〉speculate: ～能力 ability to analyse **B**〈名〉[哲学] reasoning
【思潮】sīcháo〈名〉**1**（思想潮流）ideological trend: 当代科学～ modern scientific thought **2**（思潮活动）thoughts: ～起伏 thoughts surging in one's mind
【思春】sīchūn〈动〉[of a young girl] have thoughts of love
【思忖】sīcǔn〈书〉= 思量 sīliang
【思过】sīguò〈动〉reflect on one's faults
【思旧】sījiù〈动〉**1**（指旧事）recall the past **2**（指旧友）think of an old friend
【思考】sīkǎo〈动〉consider: 不加～ without due consideration ‖ 长期反复～ ponder long and deeply ‖ 独立～ think one's own thoughts
【思恋】sīliàn〈动〉long for: ～故乡 yearn for one's home town
【思量】sīliang〈动〉reflect (upon/on)
【思路】sīlù〈名〉train of thought: ～清晰 think clearly
【思虑】sīlǜ〈动〉〈书〉consider
【思谋】sīmóu〈动〉〈书〉think about: 昨晚我将他的话反复～了好久。I turned his remarks over in my mind for a long time last night.
【思慕】sīmù〈动〉admire: ～之情 yearning
【思念】sīniàn〈动〉long for: ～故土 long for one's homeland ‖ ～亲人 miss one's nearest and dearest
【思前想后】sīqián-xiǎnghòu〈成〉turn sth. over in one's mind
【思如泉涌】sīrúquányǒng〈成〉be brimming with ideas
【思索】sīsuǒ〈动〉ponder: ～问题 reflect on a question ‖ 不假～ without much thinking
【思维】sīwéi〈名〉thinking: ～方式 way of thinking ‖ ～模式 thought pattern ‖ ～能力 faculty of thinking
【思乡】sīxiāng〈动〉be homesick
【思想】sīxiǎng **A**〈名〉**1**（指理性认识）thought: 有～准备 be mentally prepared ‖ ～跟不上 lag behind in one's understanding ‖ 共产主义～ communist ideology ‖ 儒家～ Confucian ideas **2**（念头）idea: 我根本没有出国的～。I have absolutely no intention of going abroad. **B** = 思量 sīliang
【思想包袱】sīxiǎng bāofu〈名〉mental burden
【思想斗争】sīxiǎng dòuzhēng〈名〉**1**（指思想意识）ideological struggle **2**（指个人内心）mental struggle: 经过一番～, 他做出了正确的选择。Having weighed up the alternatives in his mind, he made the right choice.
【思想方法】sīxiǎng fāngfǎ〈名〉method of thinking
【思想负担】sīxiǎng fùdān〈名〉mental burden
【思想改造】sīxiǎng gǎizào〈名〉ideological reform
【思想工作】sīxiǎng gōngzuò〈名〉ideological work
【思想家】sīxiǎngjiā ▸**p. 966**〈名〉thinker
【思想教育】sīxiǎng jiàoyù〈名〉ideological education
【思想觉悟】sīxiǎng juéwù〈名〉political awareness
【思想路线】sīxiǎng lùxiàn〈名〉ideological line
【思想认识】sīxiǎng rènshi〈名〉ideological understanding
【思想史】sīxiǎngshǐ〈名〉history of thought
【思想体系】sīxiǎng tǐxì〈名〉ideology: 马克思主义～ Marxist ideology
【思想性】sīxiǎngxìng〈名〉ideological level
【思想意识】sīxiǎng yìshi〈名〉ideology
【思想作风】sīxiǎng zuòfēng〈名〉ideological style
【思绪】sīxù〈名〉〈书〉**1**（思路）thinking: 整理～ marshal one's thoughts ‖ ～万千 be lost in a myriad of thoughts **2**（情绪）feelings: ～不宁 one's mind is in turmoil

鸶(鷥) sī ▸鹭鸶 lùsī

斯 sī〈代〉〈书〉this: ～人 this person ‖ ～时 at this moment ‖ 生于～, 长于～ be born and brought up here
【斯德哥尔摩】Sīdégē'ěrmó〈名〉Stockholm
【斯芬克斯】Sīfēnkèsī〈名〉Sphinx
【斯堪的纳维亚】Sīkāndínàwéiyà〈名〉Scandinavia
【斯拉夫】Sīlāfū〈名〉Slav: ～人 Slav ‖ ～语 Slavic ‖ ～字母 Cyrillic alphabet
【斯里兰卡】Sīlǐlánkǎ〈名〉Sri Lanka: ～民主社会主义共和国 Democratic Socialist Republic of Sri Lanka ‖ ～人 Sri Lankan
【斯洛伐克】Sīluòfákè〈名〉Slovakia: ～共和国 Republic of Slovakia ‖ ～人 Slovak ‖ ～语 Slovak
【斯洛文尼亚】Sīluòwénníyà〈名〉Slovenia: ～共和国 Republic of Slovenia ‖ ～人 Slovene
【斯塔福德郡】Sītǎfúdéjùn〈名〉Staffordshire
【斯特灵郡】Sītèlíngjùn〈名〉Stirlingshire
【斯瓦希里语】Sīwǎxīlǐyǔ ▸**p. 918**〈名〉Swahili
【斯威士兰】Sīwēishìlán〈名〉Swaziland: ～人 Swazi
【斯文】sīwén〈名〉〈书〉**1**（文化人）scholar: 敬重～ hold the literati in high regard **2**（文雅）learning: ▸～扫地
【斯文扫地】sīwén-sǎodì〈成〉**1**（指自甘堕落）disgrace one's scholarly dignity **2**（指蔑视学问）hold learning in contempt
【斯文】sīwen〈形〉refined: 假～ shabby gentility

蛳(螄) sī ▸螺蛳 luósī

厮[1](廝) sī〈名〉〈旧〉**1**（男仆）male servant: 小～ boy servant **2**〈贬〉（人）guy

厮[2](廝) sī〈副〉with each other: ▸～打, ～混
【厮打】sīdǎ〈动〉exchange blows: 相互～ tear into each other
【厮混】sīhùn〈动〉**1**〈贬〉（鬼混）associate with: 跟有夫之妇～ fool about with a married woman ‖ 这个姑娘和一帮坏人～。The girl was mixing with a bad set. **2**（混杂）mix
【厮杀】sīshā〈动〉fight at close quarters: ～声 sounds of battle

锶(鍶) sī〈名〉[化学] strontium (Sr)

撕 sī〈动〉tear: ～成碎片 rip sth. into shreds ‖ ～下副券 tear off a coupon ‖ 把一张纸～成两半 tear a sheet of paper in half ‖ ～下假面具 unmask sb.
【撕扯】sīchě〈动〉tear: 互相～头发 tear at each other's hair
【撕毁】sīhuǐ〈动〉rip into pieces: ～协议 tear up an agreement
【撕裂】sīliè〈动〉rip (up): ～肌肉 tear a muscle ‖ ～伤 lacerated wound
【撕票】sīpiào〈动〉kill a hostage
【撕破脸】sīpòliǎn〈惯〉not spare sb.'s feelings
【撕碎】sīsuì〈动〉tear into pieces: 把信～ tear up a letter

嘶 sī
A〈动〉〈书〉neigh: ▸～鸣
B〈形〉hoarse: ▸～哑, 声～力竭
C = 咝 sī
【嘶喊】sīhǎn〈动〉shout
【嘶叫】sījiào〈动〉**1**（尖叫）scream: 吓得～起来 scream with fright **2** = 嘶鸣 sīmíng
【嘶鸣】sīmíng〈动〉（指马）neigh;（指驴）bray
【嘶哑】sīyǎ〈形〉hoarse: 把嗓子喊～了 shout oneself hoarse

sǐ

死 sǐ
A〈动〉**1**（死亡）（指动作）die;（指状态）be dead: ～得很惨 die a cruel death ‖ ～于心脏病 die from a heart attack ‖ 被打～ be beaten to death ‖ 酗酒致～ drink oneself to death ▸～尸, ～讯, 找～ **2**（不顾性命）do sth. to the death: ～战 fight to the death ▸～守
B〈形〉**1**（坚决）unyielding: ～不放手 hold on to the death ▸～不改悔, ～心塌地 **2**（不改变）inflexible: 把日期定～ fix a precise date ‖ 我们很难说～。It is hard for us to say for sure. ▸～火山 **3**（不可调

和） irreconcilable: ▸～敌，～对头 4（不通） impassable: ▸～胡同，～水 5（死板） inflexible: ～规定 rigid rules ▸～脑筋，～心眼儿 6（极端） extreme: ～要面子 save face at all costs ‖ 高兴～了 be tickled to death ‖ 笑～我啦！ I'm dying of laughing! ‖ 我头痛～了。 I've got a terrible headache.

【死板】sǐbǎn〈形〉 rigid: ～的规定 rigid rules ‖ 他这个人太～。 He's too inflexible.

【死不改悔】sǐbùgǎihuǐ〈成〉 incorrigible

【死不瞑目】sǐbùmíngmù〈成〉 die discontent

【死不足惜】sǐbùzúxī〈成〉 sb.'s death is not to be regretted

【死产】sǐchǎn〈名〉［医学］ stillbirth

【死党】sǐdǎng〈名〉 1（指党羽） diehard follower 2（指集团） diehard reactionary clique

【死到临头】sǐdàolíntóu〈成〉 be on one's deathbed

【死得其所】sǐdéqísuǒ〈成〉 die a worthy death

【死敌】sǐdí〈名〉 sworn enemy

【死地】sǐdì〈名〉 fatal situation: 置之～而后快 be satisfied with nothing but sb.'s death

【死点】sǐdiǎn〈名〉 1［机械］ dead centre 2［生物］ dead point 3［电气］ dead spot

【死对头】sǐduìtou〈名〉 sworn enemy

【死而后已】sǐ'érhòuyǐ〈成〉 to the end of one's days

【死而无悔】sǐ'érwúhuǐ〈成〉 die without remorse

【死而无怨】sǐ'érwúyuàn〈成〉 die without a grudge

【死鬼】sǐguǐ〈名〉 1（家伙） devil 2〈旧〉（死人） dead person

【死海】Sǐhǎi〈名〉 Dead Sea

【死胡同】sǐhútòng〈名〉 1〈本〉 blind alley 2〈喻〉 dead end: 走进～ reach a dead end

【死缓】sǐhuǎn〈名〉［法律］ stay of execution [two-year probation under a suspended death sentence]

【死灰】sǐhuī〈名〉 cold ashes: 心如～ be completely disheartened

【死灰复燃】sǐhuī-fùrán〈成〉〈贬〉〈喻〉 rise again from the ashes: 防止纳粹主义～ prevent the resurgence of Nazism

【死活】sǐhuó A〈名〉 fate B〈副〉 in any case: 经理～不答应我们的要求。 At any rate the manager refused to agree to our request.

【死火山】sǐhuǒshān〈名〉 extinct volcano

【死机】sǐjī〈动〉［计算机］ crash: 他的计算机～了。 His computer crashed.

【死记】sǐjì〈动〉 learn by rote

【死记硬背】sǐjì-yìngbèi〈成〉 learn by rote

【死寂】sǐjì〈形〉 deathly still: 四下里一片～。 All around was deadly silent.

【死角】sǐjiǎo〈名〉 1［军事］ dead space 2〈喻〉 untouched area

【死结】sǐjié〈名〉 fast knot: 没有人能够打开她心里的那个～。 No one can untie the knot in her heart.

【死劲儿】sǐjìnr A〈名〉 all one's strength B〈副〉 with all one's strength: ～盯住某人 fix one's eyes on sb.

【死局】sǐjú〈名〉 no-win situation

【死扣儿】sǐkòur〈口〉= 死结 sǐjié

【死牢】sǐláo〈名〉 death house

【死老虎】sǐlǎohǔ〈名〉〈贬〉 person who has lost his power

【死里逃生】sǐlǐ-táoshēng〈成〉 escape by the skin of one's teeth

【死力】sǐlì A〈名〉 all one's strength: 出～ give it all one has B〈副〉 with all one's strength: ～战斗 fight to the death

【死路】sǐlù〈名〉 dead end: 这样做只有～一条。 This is sure to be nothing but a dead end.

【死马当做活马医】sǐmǎ dàngzuò huómǎ yī〈俗〉 make a last attempt to save a hopeless situation

【死面】sǐmiàn〈名〉 unleavened dough

【死命】sǐmìng A〈名〉 doom B〈副〉 desperately

【死难】sǐnàn〈动〉 die in an accident: ～烈士 martyr

【死脑筋】sǐnǎojīn A〈形〉 stereotyped B〈名〉 person with a one-track mind

【死皮赖脸】sǐpí-làiliǎn〈成〉 be utterly shameless

【死期】sǐqī〈名〉 doom

【死棋】sǐqí〈名〉 1〈本〉（指棋子） dead piece; （指棋局） hopeless game 2〈喻〉（指局面） hopeless case

【死气沉沉】sǐqì-chénchén〈成〉 lifeless: 这支足球队～的。 The football team lacks vigour.

【死乞白赖】sǐqibáilài〈成〉 continuously pester sb.

【死气白赖】sǐqibáilài = 死乞白赖 sǐqibáilài

【死契】sǐqì〈名〉 irrevocable contract

【死钱】sǐqián〈名〉 1（不生息的钱） money that does not yield interest 2（固定收入） regular income

【死囚】sǐqiú〈名〉 condemned prisoner

【死球】sǐqiú〈名〉［体育］ dead ball

【死去活来】sǐqù-huólái〈成〉 hover between life and death: 哭得～ cry one's eyes out ‖ 被打得～ be thrashed to within an inch of one's life

【死人】sǐrén〈名〉 1（死者） dead people 2（尸体） corpse 3〈诙〉 devil

【死伤】sǐshāng〈动〉 be hurt or killed: 那次事故中～五十人。 There were fifty casualties in the accident.

【死神】sǐshén ▸**p. 274**〈名〉 Death: ～夺去了他的爱妻。 Death robbed him of his wife.

【死尸】sǐshī〈名〉 corpse: 火化/掩埋～ cremate/bury a dead body

【死守】sǐshǒu〈动〉 1（拼死防守） defend to the last 2（固执地遵守） stick to: ～传统 cling to tradition

【死水】sǐshuǐ〈名〉 stagnant water: 一潭～ a stagnant pool of water

【死胎】sǐtāi〈名〉 stillbirth

【死亡】sǐwáng〈动〉 die: 勇敢地面对～ look death calmly in the face ‖ 走向～ march to one's doom ‖ 意外事故造成的～ death by misadventure ‖ 因病～ die from an illness

【死亡保险】sǐwáng bǎoxiǎn〈名〉 insurance against death

【死亡鉴定】sǐwáng jiàndìng〈名〉 verification of death

【死亡率】sǐwánglǜ〈名〉 mortality rate: 降低婴儿～ reduce infant mortality ‖ 高～ high mortality rate

【死亡线】sǐwángxiàn〈名〉 verge of death: 把病人从～上救了回来 save a patient from the jaws of death

【死亡证明】sǐwáng zhèngmíng〈名〉 evidence of death: ～书 death certificate

【死无对证】sǐwúduìzhèng〈成〉 the dead cannot bear witness

【死无葬身之地】sǐ wú zàngshēn zhī dì〈成〉 die a cruel death

【死心】sǐxīn〈动〉 give up hope

【死心塌地】sǐxīn-tādì〈成〉 hell-bent: ～地跟某人走 be dead set on following sb. ‖ ～的追随者 diehard follower

【死心眼儿】sǐxīnyǎnr A〈形〉 stubborn B〈名〉 stubborn person

【死信】sǐxìn〈名〉 1（指信件） dead letter 2（指消息） news of sb.'s death

【死刑】sǐxíng〈名〉 death penalty: 废除～ abolish capital punishment ‖ 执行～ carry out a death sentence

【死刑犯】sǐxíngfàn〈名〉 condemned criminal

【死讯】sǐxùn〈名〉 news of sb.'s death

【死因】sǐyīn〈名〉 cause of death

【死硬】sǐyìng〈形〉 1（生硬） stiff 2（顽固） stubborn: ～分子 diehard

【死有余辜】sǐyǒuyúgū〈成〉 even death would be too good for sb.

【死于非命】sǐyú-fēimìng〈成〉 die a violent death

【死战】sǐzhàn A〈名〉 life-and-death battle: ▸决一～ B〈动〉 fight to the death: ～到底 fight to the bitter end

【死账】sǐzhàng〈名〉 dead loan

【死者】sǐzhě〈名〉 the dead: ～家属 family members of the deceased

【死罪】sǐzuì〈名〉 1（死刑罪） capital offence 2〈套〉（指过失） extremely serious blunder

sì

巳 Sì〈名〉 sixth of the twelve Earthly Branches (地支)

【巳时】sìshí〈名〉〈旧〉 period of the day from 9 am to 11 am

四[1] sì ▸**p. 691**〈数〉 four: 第～次 fourth time ‖ 三加一等于～。 Three plus one is four.

四[2] sì ▸**p. 929**〈名〉［音乐］ note on the *gongche* (工尺) scale, corresponding to a low 6 in *jianpu* (简谱) numbered musical notation

【四胞胎】sìbāotāi〈名〉 quadruplet

【四倍体】sìbèitǐ〈名〉［生物］ tetraploid

【四边】sìbiān〈名〉 all sides: ～围着墙 be enclosed by walls

【四边形】sìbiānxíng〈名〉 quadrilateral

【四不像】sìbùxiàng〈名〉〈俗〉 1 = 麋鹿 mílù 2〈喻〉（不伦不类） nondescript

【四步舞】sìbùwǔ〈名〉 foxtrot

【四部】sìbù〈名〉 four bibliographic categories [the four traditional divisions of a Chinese library, including Confucian classics (经), history (史), philosophy and arts and sciences (子), and collected literary works (集)]

【四重唱】sìchóngchàng〈名〉 vocal quartet

【四重奏】sìchóngzòu〈名〉 instrumental quartet

【四出】sìchū〈动〉 go from place to place: ～乞讨 go around begging

【四处】sìchù〈名〉 all places: ～奔忙 be rushed on one's feet ‖ ～漂泊 drift about ‖ ～逃窜 flee in all directions

【四川】Sìchuān ▸**p. 661**〈名〉 Sichuan Province

【四大发明】sì dà fāmíng〈名〉 four great Chinese inventions

【四大皆空】sìdà-jiēkōng〈成〉［佛教］ the physical world is illusory

【四大金刚】Sì Dà Jīngāng = 四大天王 Sì Dà Tiānwáng
【四大天王】Sì Dà Tiānwáng〈名〉Devaraja [the four heavenly guardians]
【四方】sìfāng **A**〈名〉all sides: ～响应 response from every quarter ‖ 好男儿志在～。A good man should have lofty aspirations. **B**〈形〉square: ～木块 wooden cube ‖ 四四方方的大脸 big broad face
【四方步】sìfāngbù〈名〉leisurely and measured pace
【四方联】sìfānglián〈名〉[of stamp collecting] block of four
【四分五裂】sìfēn-wǔliè〈成〉fall apart: 那个党已经～了。The party split up into groups.
【四分音符】sìfēn yīnfú〈名〉[音乐] crotchet〈英〉; quarter note〈美〉
【四分之一决赛】sìfēnzhīyī juésài〈名〉quarter-finals: 进入～ advance to the quarter-finals
【四伏】sìfú〈动〉lurk everywhere
【四个现代化】sìgè xiàndàihuà〈名〉Four Modernizations [ie the modernization of industry, agriculture, defence, and science and technology]
【四顾】sìgù〈动〉look around
【四海】sìhǎi〈名〉〈书〉whole world: 畅游～ travel around the world
【四海升平】sìhǎi-shēngpíng〈成〉peace reigns in the world
【四海为家】sìhǎi-wéijiā〈成〉make one's home wherever one is
【四海之内皆兄弟】sìhǎi zhī nèi jiē xiōngdì〈成〉all people in the world are brothers
【四合院】sìhéyuàn〈名〉courtyard dwelling [traditional residential compound in north China]

> **四合院**
> Traditional Chinese courtyard residence, typically found in the *hutongs* of Beijing (▸胡同), and also in Hebei and Shandong provinces and north-east China. The characteristic arrangement is an open courtyard, flanked on all sides by rooms with windows opening in towards the courtyard, rather than outwards towards the street. The residences usually contain two courtyards separated by a festooned gate (垂花门). The inner courtyard is the heart of the living area. Larger residences typically contain a number of courtyards. Just inside the main entrance to the house is a carved wall (影壁), which screens the courtyard from outside view.

【四化】sìhuà〈简称〉= 四个现代化
【四环素】sìhuánsù〈名〉[药学] tetracycline
【四季】sìjì〈名〉four seasons: ～如春 be like spring all the year round ‖ ～宜人 be pleasant in all seasons ▸一年～
【四季豆】sìjìdòu〈名〉French bean〈英〉; string bean〈美〉
【四季青】sìjìqīng〈名〉[植物] Chinese holly leaf
【四郊】sìjiāo〈名〉suburbs
【四角号码】sìjiǎo hàomǎ〈名〉four-corner system [a system of coding Chinese characters in dictionaries]
【四脚八叉】sìjiǎo-bāchā〈俗〉lie on one's back with arms and legs stretched out
【四脚朝天】sìjiǎo-cháotiān〈成〉fall backwards with one's arms and legs in the air: 把某人摔了个～ send sb. sprawling
【四脚蛇】sìjiǎoshé〈名〉〈口〉lizard
【四近】sìjìn〈名〉surrounding area: ～里静悄悄的 All around was very quiet.
【四开本】sìkāiběn〈名〉[印刷] quarto
【四库全书】sìkùquánshū〈名〉Complete Library in Four Branches of Literature [imperial library of manuscripts in the Qing Dynasty]
【四联单】sìliándān〈名〉quadruplicate form
【四邻】sìlín〈名〉one's neighbours: ▸街坊～
【四轮驱动】sìlún qūdòng〈名〉four-wheel drive (4WD)
【四面】sìmiàn〈名〉all sides: ～环山 be hemmed in by mountains
【四面八方】sìmiàn-bāfāng〈成〉all sides: 从～奔赴现场 rush to the place from every direction
【四面楚歌】sìmiàn-Chǔgē〈成〉find oneself under attack from all quarters
【四面受敌】sìmiàn-shòudí〈成〉lay exposed to attacks on all sides
【四面体】sìmiàntǐ〈名〉tetrahedron
【四拍子】sìpāizi〈名〉[音乐] quadruple time
【四旁】sìpáng〈名〉all sides: ～一个人也没有。There is not a single person in sight.
【四平八稳】sìpíng-bāwěn〈成〉play safe: 这篇文章写得～。The essay is well organized.
【四起】sìqǐ〈动〉rise from all directions: 谣言～。Rumours circulated widely.
【四人帮】sìrénbāng〈名〉the Gang of Four
【四散】sìsàn〈动〉scatter in all directions
【四舍五入】sìshě-wǔrù〈名〉[数学] rounding off
【四声】sìshēng〈名〉[语言] four tones in Chinese pronunciation: 普通话有～。Standard Chinese has four phonetic tones.
【四时】sìshí = 四季 sìjì
【四时八节】sìshí-bājié〈成〉four seasons and eight solar terms
【四书】Sìshū〈名〉Four Books [ie *The Great Learning* (《大学》), *The Doctrine of the Mean* (《中庸》), *The Analects of Confucius* (《论语》) and *Mencius* (《孟子》)]
【四书五经】Sìshū Wǔjīng〈名〉Confucian classics
【四体】sìtǐ〈名〉**1**〈书〉(四肢) four limbs **2** = 四体书 sìtǐshū
【四体不勤，五谷不分】sìtǐ bù qín, wǔgǔ bù fēn〈成〉can neither do physical work nor distinguish rice from wheat
【四体书】sìtǐshū〈名〉four scripts [ie regular script (正书), cursive script (草书), official script (隶书), and seal script (篆书)]
【四通八达】sìtōng-bādá〈成〉extend in all directions: 公路～。The highways open out in all directions.
【四外】sìwài〈名〉all directions: ～无人 not a single soul in sight
【四围】sìwéi〈名〉all sides: 在花园～修围墙 build walls around a garden ‖ 这个池塘～都是树。The pond was surrounded by trees.
【四下】sìxià = 四下里 sìxiàli
【四下里】sìxiàli〈名〉surrounding area: ～看看 look around
【四仙桌】sìxiānzhuō〈名〉small square table
【四乡】sìxiāng〈名〉countryside around a town
【四项基本原则】sìxiàng jīběn yuánzé〈名〉Four Cardinal Principles [ie adherence to the socialist road, the people's democratic dictatorship, the leadership of the Communist Party, and Marxism-Leninism and Mao Zedong Thought]
【四言诗】sìyánshī〈名〉four-character verse
【四仰八叉】sìyǎng-bāchā = 四脚八叉 sìjiǎo-bāchā
【四野】sìyě〈名〉〈书〉vast expanse of open countryside
【四月】sìyuè ▸**p. 928**〈名〉**1**(阳历) April **2**(阴历) fourth month of the lunar year
【四则】sìzé〈名〉four fundamental arithmetic operations [ie addition, subtraction, multiplication and division]: ～运算 arithmetic calculation
【四诊】sìzhěn〈名〉[中医] four methods of diagnosis [ie observation (望), auscultation and olfaction (闻), interrogation (问), and pulse feeling and palpation (切)]
【四肢】sìzhī〈名〉four limbs: ～发达 have strong arms and legs
【四周】sìzhōu〈名〉all sides: ～都是树 be surrounded with trees
【四周围】sìzhōuwéi = 四周 sìzhōu
【四座】sìzuò〈名〉all the people present

寺 sì
〈名〉**1**[佛教] temple: ▸～庙, 少林～ **2**[伊斯兰教] mosque: ▸清真～ **3**〈旧〉(官署名) ministry: 大理～ Imperial Court of Justice
【寺观】sìguàn〈名〉**1**(佛寺和道观) Buddhist and Taoist temples **2**(庙宇) temples
【寺庙】sìmiào〈名〉temple
【寺院】sìyuàn〈名〉temple

S

似 sì
A〈动〉be like: 晚霞恰～一幅彩绸。The afterglow is just like a piece of coloured silk. ▸酷～, 如花～玉, 类～
B〈副〉seemingly: ～懂非懂 not fully/thoroughly understand ‖ ～笑非笑 wear a faint/slight smile ‖ 你的观点～欠妥当。I'm afraid your point of view is not right. ▸～曾相识
C〈介〉[used for comparison]: 我的身体一天胜～一天。I'm getting better every day. ▸shì
【似曾相识】sìcéngxiāngshí〈成〉seem to have met before
【似乎】sìhū〈副〉as if: ～要下雨了。It looks as if it might rain. ‖ 我～感冒了。I seem to have caught a cold.
【似是而非】sìshì'érfēi〈成〉specious
【似水流年】sìshuǐliúnián〈成〉time flies

兕 sì
〈名〉〈古〉female rhinoceros

伺 sì
〈动〉**1**(侦察) spy on/into: ▸窥～ **2**(守候) wait for: ▸～机 ▸cì
【伺服】sìfú〈名〉[电气] servo: ～定位 servo positioning ‖ ～电动机 servomotor
【伺机】sìjī〈动〉wait for an opportunity

祀 sì
〈动〉offer sacrifices: ～祖 offer sacrifices to one's ancestors ▸祭～

姒 sì
〈名〉〈古〉**1**(姐姐) elder sister **2**(兄妻) sister-in-law [wife of husband's elder brother]

饲（飼）sì
〈动〉rear: ▸～料, ～养
【饲草】sìcǎo〈名〉forage grass
【饲料】sìliào〈名〉fodder: 鸡/猪～ chicken/pig feed ‖ 精～ fodder concentrate
【饲养】sìyǎng〈动〉rear: ～家畜 raise livestock
【饲养场】sìyǎngchǎng〈名〉farm

【饲养员】 sìyǎngyuán ▸**p. 966** 〈名〉 breeder

泗[1] sì 〈名〉〈书〉（鼻涕） nasal mucus

泗[2] Sì

【泗河】 Sìhé ▸**p. 294** 〈名〉 Si River

驷（駟） sì 〈名〉 **1**〈古〉（驷马） team of four horses **2**〈书〉（马） horse

【驷马】 sìmǎ 〈名〉〈古〉 team of four horses: ▸君子一言，～难追

俟 sì 〈动〉〈书〉 wait: ▸～机

【俟机】 sìjī 〈动〉 wait for an opportunity

食 sì 〈动〉〈书〉 feed
▸shí

涘 sì 〈名〉〈书〉 water margin

耜 sì 〈名〉〈古〉 spade-shaped farm tool

笥 sì 〈名〉〈书〉 square bamboo-plaited utensil

肆[1] sì 〈动〉 be unrestrained: ▸～无忌惮，放～

肆[2] sì 〈名〉〈书〉 shop 〈英〉; store 〈美〉: ▸酒～

肆[3] sì ▸**p. 691** 〈数〉 four [used for the numeral 四 on cheques, etc. to avoid alterations or mistakes]

【肆虐】 sìnüè 〈动〉 wreak havoc: 洪水～ the flood wreaked havoc

【肆无忌惮】 sìwújìdàn 〈成〉 stop at nothing: ～的侵略行为 act of wanton aggression

【肆行】 sìxíng 〈动〉〈书〉 be wanton: ～无忌 act in a reckless way

【肆意】 sìyì 〈副〉 recklessly: ～攻击 make an unbridled attack ‖ ～挥霍公款 freely squander public funds ‖ ～歪曲事实 wilfully distort facts

嗣 sì

A 〈动〉〈书〉 inherit: ▸～位

B 〈名〉 heir: 无～ without issue

【嗣后】 sìhòu 〈副〉〈书〉 subsequently

【嗣位】 sìwèi 〈动〉 succeed to the throne

【嗣子】 sìzǐ 〈名〉 son of a wife [as compared with the son of a concubine]

sōng

忪 sōng ▸惺忪 xīngsōng
▸zhōng

松[1] sōng 〈名〉 pine tree

松[2]**（鬆）** sōng

A 〈形〉 **1**（宽松） slack: 对学生管得太～ be too lax with the students ‖ 鞋穿穿会～的。 Shoes loosen up with wear. ▸～～垮垮，～弛，～懈 **2**（酥） light: 这种饼子又～又脆。 This cake is light and fluffy. **3**（宽裕） not hard up: 手头～了一点 have a bit more cash in one's pockets

B 〈动〉 **1**（放松） relax: ～一口气 heave a sigh of relief ▸～劲 **2**（松开） loosen: ～一～螺丝 loosen the screw ▸～绑，～手

C 〈名〉 dried minced meat: ▸肉～，鱼肉～

【松绑】 sōngbǎng 〈动〉 **1**（指绳子） untie **2**〈喻〉（指约束） give sb. free rein: 给国有企业～ relax control of state-owned enterprises

【松弛】 sōngchí **A** 〈形〉 **1**（不结实） slack: 缺乏运动，肌肉变得～了。 The muscles have got soft through lack of exercise. **2**（放松） relaxed **3**（松懈） sluggish: ～的安全措施 lax security **B** 〈动〉 relax

【松动】 sōngdòng **A** 〈动〉 **1**（不牢固） come loose: 他有一颗牙齿～了。 He has got a wobbly tooth. **2**（不拥挤） become less crowded **3**〈喻〉（变得灵活） become flexible: 口气有所～ speak in a less resolute tone **B** 〈形〉 not strapped for cash: 这个月我们手头稍微有些～。 We are not so strapped for cash this month.

【松糕鞋】 sōnggāoxié 〈名〉 platform shoes

【松果】 sōngguǒ 〈名〉 pine cone

【松花蛋】 sōnghuādàn 〈名〉 preserved egg

【松花江】 Sōnghuājiāng ▸**p. 294** 〈名〉 Sungari River

【松缓】 sōnghuǎn **A** 〈形〉 relaxed **B** 〈动〉 relax

【松鸡】 sōngjī 〈名〉［鸟类］ grouse

【松节油】 sōngjiéyóu 〈名〉［化工］ turpentine

【松紧】 sōngjǐn 〈名〉 elasticity

【松紧带】 sōngjǐndài 〈名〉 elastic (cord)

【松劲】 sōngjìn 〈动〉 slack off: 尽管我们赢了也不能～。 Even though we're winning we mustn't ease off.

【松开】 sōngkāi 〈动〉 release hold of: ～车闸 release the brakes ‖ ～绳子 let go of the rope ‖ ～螺丝 loosen a screw

【松口】 sōngkǒu 〈动〉 **1**（张嘴放开） relax one's bite **2**（不再坚持） loosen up: 不管我说什么，他就是不～。 In spite of all that I said, he remained intransigent.

【松快】 sōngkuai 〈形〉 **1**（舒畅） relieved **2**（放松） relaxed **3**（不拥挤） less crowded

【松林】 sōnglín 〈名〉 pinewood [forest]

【松毛虫】 sōngmáochóng 〈名〉 pine caterpillar

【松明】 sōngmíng 〈名〉 pine torches

【松木】 sōngmù 〈名〉 pinewood [material]

【松墙】 sōngqiáng 〈名〉 wall of pine trees

【松球】 sōngqiú = 松果 sōngguǒ

【松仁】 sōngrén 〈名〉 pine nut

【松软】 sōngruǎn 〈形〉 **1**（蓬松柔软） spongy: ～的面包 fluffy bread ‖ ～的泥土 soft soil **2**（无力） weak

【松散】 sōngsǎn 〈形〉 **1**（指结构） loosely organized: ～的国际财团 loose international consortium ‖ 这篇文章结构～。 The essay is all over the place. **2**（指注意力） absent-minded

【松手】 sōngshǒu 〈动〉 **1**（放手） let go: 他抓住我的胳膊不肯～。 He caught my arm and would not let it go. **2**（松懈） relax in one's efforts

【松鼠】 sōngshǔ 〈名〉 squirrel

【松树】 sōngshù 〈名〉 pine tree: ～林 pinewood [forest]

【松松垮垮】 sōngsōng-kuǎkuǎ 〈形〉 **1**（松散） loose: 这辆自行车～的。 The bike hardly holds together. **2**（懈怠） slack

【松涛】 sōngtāo 〈名〉〈书〉 whistling of the wind in the pines

【松土】 sōngtǔ 〈动〉 loosen the soil: ～机 scarifier

【松香】 sōngxiāng 〈名〉 rosin

【松懈】 sōngxiè **A** 〈动〉 be slack: 他在思想上一刻也没有～过。 His mind never let up for an instant. **B** 〈形〉 **1**（懈怠） undisciplined **2**（不紧密） not well organized: ～的组织 loose organization

【松心】 sōngxīn 〈动〉 feel relaxed: 孩子们结婚后，父母～多了。 The parents were much relieved after their children got married.

【松烟】 sōngyān 〈名〉 pine soot: ～墨 pine-soot ink

【松针】 sōngzhēn 〈名〉 pine needle

【松脂】 sōngzhī 〈名〉 pine resin

【松子】 sōngzǐ 〈名〉 **1**（指种子） pine nut **2**〈方〉= 松仁 sōngrén

【松嘴】 sōngzuǐ = 松口 sōngkǒu

凇 sōng 〈名〉 rime: ▸雾～，雨～

菘 sōng 〈名〉〈古〉 Chinese cabbage

【菘菜】 sōngcài 〈名〉〈方〉 Chinese cabbage

嵩 sōng 〈形〉 **1**（指山岳） tall **2**〈书〉（高土） lofty

【嵩山】 Sōngshān 〈名〉 Mount Song

sóng

㞞（屣） sóng 〈口〉

A 〈名〉 semen

B 〈形〉〈贬〉 weak by nature: 那家伙真～。 He's a real coward.

【㞞包】 sóngbāo 〈名〉〈贬〉 coward

sǒng

怂（慫） sǒng

【怂恿】 sǒngyǒng 〈动〉 incite: 在某人的～下 at sb.'s instigation

耸[1]**（聳）** sǒng 〈动〉 terrify: ▸～人听闻，危言～听

耸[2]**（聳）** sǒng 〈动〉 **1**（矗立） soar high: ▸～立 **2**（向上动） shrug: ▸～肩

【耸动】 sǒngdòng 〈动〉 **1**（向上动） shrug **2**（捏造或夸大事实） create a sensation: ～视听 shock the public

【耸肩】 sǒngjiān 〈动〉 shrug one's shoulders: ～作答 answer a question with a shrug ‖ 他无奈地耸了耸肩。 He gave a shrug of helplessness.

【耸立】 sǒnglì 〈动〉 tower: 雕塑高高～在港口。 The statue towers above the harbour.

【耸人听闻】 sǒngréntīngwén 〈成〉 be sensational: ～的报道 sensational report

【耸入云霄】 sǒngrù-yúnxiāo 〈成〉 tower into the sky

【耸峙】 sǒngzhì 〈动〉〈书〉 tower aloft

悚 sǒng 〈形〉〈书〉 terrified: ▸～然

【悚然】 sǒngrán 〈形〉 terrified: ▸毛骨～

竦 sǒng 〈形〉〈书〉 respectful: ～然肃立 stand in respect

S

sòng

讼（訟） sòng〈动〉 1 〈书〉（争辩） contend 2 （打官司） bring to court: ▸～词，诉～

【讼词】sòngcí〈名〉 legal case

【讼棍】sònggùn〈名〉〈旧〉 shyster

【讼师】sòngshī〈名〉〈旧〉 legal counsel

宋[1] Sòng〈名〉 1 （指国名） Song [state in the Zhou Dynasty] 2 （南朝之一） Song Dynasty 3 （北宋和南宋） Song Dynasty

宋[2] sòng〈量〉 sone: 1～等于1,000毫～。 One sone is equal to 1,000 millisones.

【宋词】sòngcí〈名〉 poetry of the Song Dynasty

> 宋词
> ▸唐诗

【宋体字】sòngtǐzì〈名〉 Song typeface

送 sòng〈动〉 1 （陪同） see sb. off: 接～孩子上学 drop off children at school and pick them up ‖ ～朋友上火车 see sb. onto a train ‖ 把客人～到门口 see a guest to the door ‖ 让我～你一程。 Let me go a little way with you. ▸～别，护～，押～ 2 （赠予） give: ～某人生日礼物 give sb. a birthday present ▸～礼，陪～ 3 （拿给） deliver: ～报/奶/信 deliver newspaper/milk/letters ‖ 请把我的早餐～上来。 Send my breakfast up, please. ▸～货 4 （丧失） lose: ▸～命，～死，断～，葬～

【送变电】sòngbiàndiàn〈名〉 electricity supply and transformation

【送别】sòngbié〈动〉 1 （送行） see sb. off: ～晚会 farewell party 2 （送殡） pay one's last respects

【送殡】sòngbìn〈名〉 attend a funeral

【送风】sòngfēng〈名〉［冶金］ blowing-in: ～机 blower

【送佛送到西天】sòng fó sòng dào xītiān〈俗〉 not do a good deed by half measures

【送还】sònghuán〈动〉 return

【送货】sònghuò〈动〉 deliver goods: ～上门 provide home delivery service ‖ ～升降机 dumb waiter

【送交】sòngjiāo〈动〉 hand over: ～警方 hand over to the police

【送君千里，终有一别】sòng jūn qiānlǐ, zhōng yǒu yī bié〈成〉 no matter how far you escort a guest, at some point you have to part ways

【送客】sòngkè〈动〉 see off a visitor: ～到车站 see a guest off at the station

【送礼】sònglǐ〈动〉 give sb. a present

【送料】sòngliào〈动〉 feed

【送料槽】sòngliàocáo〈名〉 feed chute

【送料斗】sòngliàodǒu〈名〉 hopper

【送命】sòngmìng〈动〉 get killed

【送气】sòngqì〈动〉［语言］ aspirate: ～音 aspirated sound

【送亲】sòngqīn〈动〉 escort a bride to the home of the bridegroom

【送人】sòngrén〈动〉 give away: 他把自己的大部分钱财都～了。 He gave away most of his fortune.

【送人情】sòng rénqíng〈动〉 1 （讨好） ingratiate oneself with sb. by doing favours 2 〈方〉= 送礼 sònglǐ

【送丧】sòngsāng = 送殡 sòngbìn

【送上门】sòngshàngmén〈动〉 deliver to the door: 您的定货我们～! We deliver your order to your door. ‖ 没有～的好事。 You can't expect things to just land in your lap.

【送上西天】sòngshàng-xītiān〈成〉 send sb. to his death

【送审】sòngshěn〈动〉 submit to a superior for approval

【送死】sòngsǐ〈动〉〈口〉 court death

【送往迎来】sòngwǎng-yínglái〈成〉 see off those who depart and welcome those who arrive

【送温暖】sòng wēnnuǎn〈动〉 offer help to the needy

【送信儿】sòngxìnr〈动〉〈口〉 send word: 给经理送个信儿,说客人八点到。 Go and tell the manager that the guests will arrive at eight.

【送行】sòngxíng〈动〉 1 （告别） see sb. off 2 （饯别） give a send-off party

【送葬】sòngzàng〈动〉 attend a funeral

【送站】sòngzhàn〈动〉 see sb. off at a station

【送终】sòngzhōng〈动〉 1 （指照顾） look after a dying family member 2 （指办丧事） bury a senior family member

诵（誦） sòng〈动〉 1 （朗读） read aloud: ▸～读，朗～ 2 （述说） recount: ▸传～ 3 （背诵） recite: ▸背～，过目成～

【诵读】sòngdú〈动〉 read aloud

颂（頌） sòng

A 〈动〉 1 （赞扬） praise: ▸～词，～扬，传～，歌～ 2 （祝愿） wish: 敬～近安! All the best!

B 〈名〉 1 （赞歌） song of praise:《橘～》 *In praise of the Orange Tree* 2 （《诗经》的一部分） one of the three sections of *The Book of Songs*, consisting of sacrificial songs

【颂词】sòngcí〈名〉 1 （溢美之词） eulogy 2 ［外交］（大使讲话） speech delivered by an ambassador

【颂歌】sònggē〈名〉 song of praise

【颂扬】sòngyáng〈动〉 sing praises: ～某人的功绩 laud sb.'s merits

sōu

搜 sōu〈动〉 1 （盘查） search: 全身上下被～了个遍 be subjected to an all-over body search ‖ 警察将所有的屋子～了又～。 The police searched all the rooms again and again. ▸～身，～捕 2 （寻找） look for: ▸～集，～寻

【搜捕】sōubǔ〈动〉 seek and arrest: 警方开始～罪犯。 The police began a search for a criminal.

【搜查】sōuchá〈动〉 search: ～违禁品 rummage for contraband ‖ 挨家挨户～ house-to-house search

【搜查令】sōuchálìng〈名〉 search warrant

【搜查证】sōucházhèng〈名〉 search warrant

【搜肠刮肚】sōucháng-guādù〈成〉 rack one's brains

【搜刮】sōuguā〈动〉 expropriate: 向百姓～钱财 extort money from the common people

【搜集】sōují〈动〉 collect: ～情报 collect information ‖ ～大量第一手资料 gather a large amount of first-hand information

【搜剿】sōujiǎo〈动〉 seek out and exterminate

【搜缴】sōujiǎo〈动〉 seek out and confiscate

【搜罗】sōuluó〈动〉 scout out: ～人才 scout for talent ‖ ～史料 collect historical data

【搜拿】sōuná〈动〉 seek out and arrest: ～逃犯 seek out and arrest an escaped criminal

【搜求】sōuqiú〈动〉 seek

【搜身】sōushēn〈动〉 give sb. a body search: 被强行～ be subjected to an enforced body search

【搜索】sōusuǒ〈动〉 1 （寻找） seek: 四处～ have a scout about ‖ ～范围 hunting zone 2 ［计算机］ search: ～引擎 search engine

【搜索枯肠】sōusuǒ-kūcháng〈成〉 rack one's brains

【搜寻】sōuxún〈动〉 search for: ～幸存者 search for survivors

蒐 sōu = 搜 sōu 2

嗖 sōu〈拟〉 whizz: 公路上汽车从我们身边～～驶过。 Cars whizzed past us on the highway. ‖ 子弹从我们耳边～～飞过。 Bullets hissed past our ears.

馊（餿） sōu

A 〈动〉 turn sour: 牛奶不冷藏会～的。 If you don't keep milk in the fridge it will go off.

B 〈形〉〈口〉 lousy: ▸～主意

【馊点子】sōudiǎnzi = 馊主意 sōuzhǔyi

【馊主意】sōuzhǔyi〈名〉 lousy idea: 出个～ give sb. lousy advice

廋 sōu〈动〉〈书〉 hide

溲 sōu〈动〉〈书〉 urinate: ～便 excrete stools and urine

飕（颼） sōu〈拟〉〈书〉 whistle: 风在他们耳边～～地吹。 The wind whistled round them.

锼（鎪） sōu〈动〉〈方〉 engrave: 在钢笔上～上名字 carve one's name on a pen

螋 sōu ▸蠼螋 qúsōu

艘 sōu〈量〉 [used for a boat or ship]: 一～大船 a ship of great bulk ‖ 一～小船/油轮 a boat/tanker

sǒu

叟 sǒu〈名〉〈书〉 old man: ▸童～无欺

嗾 sǒu

A 〈拟〉 whistle

B 〈动〉 1 〈书〉（驱使狗） whistle to a dog 2 （教唆） instigate: ▸～使

【嗾使】sǒushǐ〈动〉 instigate

擞（擻） sǒu ▸抖擞 dǒusǒu ▸sòu

薮（藪） sǒu〈名〉〈书〉 1 （野草丛生的湖泽） marsh overgrown with wild plants 2 （指聚集地） haunt: ▸渊～

S

sòu

嗽 sòu〈动〉 cough: ～了～嗓子 clear one's throat

擞（擻） sòu〈动〉〈方〉 rake the ashes off a stove fire: ～火 stoke a fire ▸sǒu

sū

苏¹（蘇） sū〈名〉［植物］ perilla: ▸白～，紫～

苏²（蘇） sū〈名〉 tassel: ▸流～

苏³（蘇、甦） sū〈动〉 regain consciousness: ▸～醒，复～

苏⁴（蘇） Sū〈名〉 1 ▸p. 661 （江苏） Su [another name for Jiangsu Province (江苏)] 2（苏州） Su [another name for Suzhou (苏州)]: ▸～绣

苏⁵（蘇） Sū〈名〉 Soviet Union

苏⁶（蘇、囌） sū ▸噜苏 lūsū

【苏白】sūbái〈名〉 1 ▸p. 918 （苏州话） Suzhou dialect 2（指道白） spoken part in Suzhou dialect in Beijing opera or *kunqu*

【苏必利尔湖】Sūbìlì'ěrhú ▸p. 305 〈名〉 Lake Superior

【苏打】sūdá〈名〉 soda: 小～ baking soda

【苏打水】sūdáshuǐ〈名〉 soda (water)

【苏丹】sūdān〈名〉 1（指国君） sultan 2 Sūdān（指国家） the Sudan: ～共和国 Republic of the Sudan ‖ ～人 Sudanese ‖ ～语 Sudanic

【苏丹红】sūdānhóng〈名〉 Sudan red

【苏俄】Sū-É〈名〉 Soviet Russia

【苏格兰】Sūgélán〈名〉 Scotland: ～威士忌 Scotch whisky ‖ ～人 Scot

【苏黎世】Sūlíshì〈名〉 Zurich

【苏里南】Sūlǐnán〈名〉 Surinam: ～人 Surinamese

【苏联】Sūlián〈名〉 Soviet Union: ～人 Soviet

【苏门答腊】Sūméndálà〈名〉 Sumatra: ～人 Sumatran

【苏区】sūqū〈名〉〈旧〉 Chinese Soviet Area

【苏铁】sūtiě〈名〉［植物］ sago cycas

【苏瓦】Sūwǎ〈名〉 Suva

【苏维埃】sūwéi'āi〈名〉 Soviet: ～政府 Soviet government

【苏醒】sūxǐng〈动〉 regain consciousness: 突然～过来 come round suddenly

【苏绣】sūxiù〈名〉 Suzhou embroidery

【苏伊士运河】Sūyīshì Yùnhé ▸p. 294 〈名〉 Suez Canal

酥 sū

A〈名〉 1〈旧〉（酥油） butter 2（指点心） shortbread

B〈形〉 1（松软） flaky and crispy: 这饼子很～。 The cake is nice and spongy. 2（无力） weak: 累得浑身都～了 be tired out

【酥脆】sūcuì〈形〉 crunchy: ～的饼干 crispy crackers

【酥麻】sūmá〈形〉 numb

【酥软】sūruǎn〈形〉 sluggish: 两腿～ feel limp in one's legs

【酥松】sūsōng〈形〉 loose: ～的泥土 soft soil

【酥糖】sūtáng〈名〉 crunchy candy

【酥胸】sūxiōng〈名〉〈书〉 soft and fair-skinned breast

【酥油】sūyóu〈名〉 butter

【酥油茶】sūyóuchá〈名〉 buttered tea: ～壶 butter-tea pot

【酥油花】sūyóuhuā〈名〉 coloured butter sculpture [Tibetan work of art]

稣 sū

A = 苏³ sū

B ▸耶稣 Yēsū

窣 sū ▸窸窣 xīsū

sú

俗 sú

A〈名〉 1（风俗） custom: ▸民～，习～，移风易～ 2（未出家的人） layman: ▸还～

B〈形〉 1（俗气） vulgar: 房子布置得很～。 The house is furnished in poor taste. ‖ 她衣着不～。 She dresses well. ▸～气，庸～ 2（大众化） popular: ▸～语，通～

【俗不可耐】súbùkěnài〈成〉 be unbearably vulgar

【俗称】súchēng A〈动〉 be known colloquially as: "脚气"～"香港脚"。 'Beriberi' is commonly known as 'Hong Kong foot'. B = 俗名 súmíng 1

【俗话】súhuà〈名〉 proverb: ～说 as the saying goes

【俗家】sújiā〈名〉 1（僧尼等称其父母的家） my parents' home 2（未出家的人） layman: 佛教的～弟子 lay Buddhist follower

【俗名】súmíng〈名〉 1（通俗的名称） popular name: 氯化钠～食盐。 Sodium chloride is commonly known as salt. 2（出家前的名字） secular name

【俗气】súqi〈形〉 vulgar: 打扮～ dress in poor taste

【俗人】súrén〈名〉 1（庸俗的人） vulgar person 2（世俗之人） layman

【俗尚】súshàng〈名〉〈书〉 conventional practice: 拘于～ be constrained by convention

【俗套】sútào〈名〉 1（指礼节） boring convention 2（指格调） set practice: 过时的～ outdated convention ▸不落～

【俗体字】sútǐzì〈名〉 non-standard forms of Chinese characters

【俗文学】súwénxué〈名〉 popular literature

【俗务】súwù〈名〉 routine business

【俗物】súwù〈名〉 vulgar/uncouth person or thing

【俗语】súyǔ〈名〉 common saying: ～说 as the saying goes

【俗子】súzǐ〈名〉〈书〉 layman: ▸凡夫～

【俗字】súzì = 俗体字 sútǐzì

sù

夙 sù

A〈名〉〈书〉 morning

B〈形〉 old: ▸～敌，～愿

【夙仇】sùchóu = 宿仇 sùchóu

【夙敌】sùdí = 宿敌 sùdí

【夙世】sùshì〈名〉［佛教］ previous incarnation: ～冤家 predestined enemy

【夙嫌】sùxián = 夙怨 sùyuàn

【夙兴夜寐】sùxīng-yèmèi〈成〉 be hard-working

【夙夜】sùyè〈名〉〈书〉 day and night: ～忧国 be always concerned with one's country

【夙怨】sùyuàn〈名〉 old grudge: 了结～ settle old scores

【夙愿】sùyuàn〈名〉 long-cherished dream

诉（訴） sù〈动〉 1（告诉） tell: ▸告～ 2（倾诉） speak out one's mind: 互～衷情 open up to one another ▸～苦，倾～ 3（控告） accuse: ▸～讼，上～

【诉苦】sùkǔ〈动〉 vent one's grievances: ～叫冤 complain of injustice ‖ 无处～ have nowhere to air one's sufferings

【诉求】sùqiú A〈动〉 petition B〈名〉 demand

【诉权】sùquán〈名〉 right to sue

【诉述】sùshù = 诉说 sùshuō

【诉说】sùshuō〈动〉 recount: ～苦衷 pour out one's woes ‖ ～事情的经过 give an account of an event ‖ ～自己的不幸 relate one's misfortune

【诉讼】sùsòng〈动〉［法律］ bring a lawsuit (against sb.): 撤回～ drop a case ‖ 对某人提起～ take legal proceedings against sb. ‖ 民事～ civil suit

【诉讼程序】sùsòng chéngxù〈名〉 legal process

【诉讼当事人】sùsòng dāngshìrén〈名〉 litigant

【诉讼法】sùsòngfǎ〈名〉 procedural law

【诉讼费】sùsòngfèi〈名〉 cost of a lawsuit: 承担～ bear the litigation expenses

【诉讼权】sùsòngquán〈名〉 right of action

【诉讼时效】sùsòng shíxiào〈名〉 limitation of action

【诉冤】sùyuān〈动〉 air one's grievances

【诉愿】sùyuàn〈动〉 lodge a disciplinary complaint

【诉诸法律】sùzhū-fǎlǜ〈动〉 take to court

【诉诸武力】sùzhū-wǔlì〈动〉 resort to force

【诉状】sùzhuàng〈名〉 indictment: 向法院递交～ file a complaint at court

肃（肅） sù

A〈形〉 1（恭敬） respectful: ▸～立，～然起敬 2（庄严） solemn: ▸～穆，～静

B〈动〉 1（整饬） tighten: 整～军纪 tighten military discipline 2（清除） eliminate: ▸～清，～反

【肃反】sùfǎn〈动〉 purge counter-revolutionaries: ～运动 crackdown on counter-revolutionaries

【肃静】sùjìng〈形〉 solemnly still: 请保持～! Please keep quiet!

【肃立】sùlì〈动〉 stand in solemn silence: ～致敬 stand in salute

【肃穆】sùmù〈形〉 1（安静） solemnly silent: 神情～ look solemn 2（庄严） solemnly harmonious

【肃清】sùqīng〈动〉 eliminate: ～封建思想 eradicate feudal ideas

【肃然起敬】sùrán-qǐjìng〈成〉 feel deep reverence: 令人～ command respect ‖ 我对他～。 I felt deep reverence for him.

【肃杀】sùshā〈形〉〈书〉 cold and lifeless

素 sù

A〈名〉 1（指丝织品） natural-coloured silk 2（基本成分） basic constituent: ▸色～，要～，元～ 3（无荤腥） vegetarian

S

food: 吃～ be a vegetarian ‖ 每餐一荤两～ one meat dish and two vegetable dishes for each meal
B 〈形〉 **1** (本色) white: ▸～白, ～服 **2** (色彩单纯) plain: ▸～净, ～雅 **3** (未加修饰) unprocessed: ▸～材, ～质
C 〈副〉 usually: 昆明～称"春城"。 Kunming is often called 'Spring City'. ▸～不相识, ～常, ～来
【素白】sùbái〈形〉 plain and white: ～裙子 plain white skirt
【素不相识】sùbùxiāngshí 〈成〉 be strangers to one another: 我与他～。 He is a perfect stranger to me.
【素材】sùcái〈名〉 source material: 写作～ writing materials
【素菜】sùcài 〈名〉 vegetable dish: ～馆 vegetarian restaurant
【素餐】sùcān **A**〈名〉 vegetarian meal: ～餐馆 vegetarian restaurant **B**〈动〉 **1** (吃素) be a vegetarian **2**〈书〉(白吃不干) eat the bread of idleness: ▸尸位～
【素常】sùcháng〈名〉 normal situation: 比～更卖力 work harder than usual ‖ 和～一样 as usual
【素淡】sùdàn〈形〉 plain: 穿着～ be plainly dressed
【素服】sùfú〈名〉 white mourning clothes
【素洁】sùjié〈形〉 white and plain: ～的莲花 plain white lily
【素净】sùjing〈形〉 plain and neat: 花色～ be simple in colour
【素来】sùlái〈副〉 usually: 他～很严肃。 He is always serious.
【素昧平生】sùmèi-píngshēng 〈成〉 be strangers to one another
【素描】sùmiáo〈名〉 sketch: 黑白～ black and white sketch ‖ ～簿 sketchbook
【素朴】sùpǔ〈形〉 **1** (朴素) simple and unadorned: ～的风格 beautiful simplicity of style **2** (不成熟) undeveloped
【素日】sùrì〈名〉 most occasions: 他～不大爱讲话。 He is a man of few words.
【素什锦】sùshíjǐn〈名〉 assorted vegetarian delicacies
【素食】sùshí **A**〈名〉 vegetarian meal: 严格～者 vegan ‖ 他现在只吃～。 He is on a vegetarian diet. **B**〈动〉 be a vegetarian
【素食者】sùshízhě〈名〉 vegetarian
【素数】sùshù ▸**p. 691** 〈名〉 [数学] prime number
【素昔】sùxī〈副〉〈书〉 usually: ～无多往来 seldom see each other
【素席】sùxí〈名〉 vegetarian feast
【素馨】sùxīn〈名〉 [植物] jasmine
【素性】sùxìng〈名〉 nature: ～开朗 have a cheerful temperament ‖ ～善良 be kind by nature
【素雅】sùyǎ〈形〉 simple but elegant
【素养】sùyǎng〈名〉 accomplishment: 很有音乐～ be well versed in music ‖ 文学～ literary attainments ‖ 有～的人 cultured mind
【素油】sùyóu〈名〉 vegetable oil
【素愿】sùyuàn〈名〉 long-cherished wish
【素志】sùzhì〈名〉〈书〉 long-cherished ambition: ～不改 keep to one's life-long ambition
【素质】sùzhì 〈名〉 **1** (本来的性质) nature **2** (素养) disposition: 她具备当一位好律师的～。 She has the makings of a good lawyer. **3** [医学] diathesis
【素质教育】sùzhì jiàoyù〈名〉 education for all-round development: 由应试教育向～转变 shift from examination-oriented education to quality-oriented education
【素装】sùzhuāng〈名〉 **1** (白色服装) white dress **2** (淡雅的装束) plain dress

速[1] sù

A〈形〉 fast: ～去～回 go and return quickly ▸～效, 迅～
B〈名〉 speed: 因超～被罚款 be fined for speeding ▸风～

速[2] sù〈动〉〈书〉 invite: ▸不～之客

【速成】sùchéng〈动〉 accelerate (an educational programme): ～班 crash course
【速递】sùdì **A**〈动〉 deliver quickly **B**〈名〉 express mail service
【速冻】sùdòng〈动〉 freeze: ～食品 frozen food
【速度】sùdù〈名〉 **1** [物理] velocity: 恒定～ constant speed ▸加～ **2** (快慢程度) speed: 放慢～ slacken the pace ‖ 加快～ speed up ‖ 经济增长～ rate of economic growth ‖ 以每小时60英里的～ at a speed of 60 mph
【速度滑冰】sùdù huábīng〈名〉 [体育] speed skating
【速滑】sùhuá〈简称〉= 速度滑冰
【速记】sùjì〈动〉 write in shorthand: 会～ know shorthand ‖ ～电话 dictograph ‖ ～员 shorthand typist〈英〉, stenographer〈美〉
【速决】sùjué〈动〉 decide quickly: ～战 quick and decisive battle
【速率】sùlǜ〈名〉 speed
【速溶】sùróng〈形〉 instant: ～咖啡 instant coffee
【速射】sùshè〈名〉 [军事] [体育] rapid fire
【速食面】sùshímiàn〈方〉= 方便面 fāngbiànmiàn
【速算】sùsuàn〈动〉 calculate quickly
【速效】sùxiào **A**〈名〉 instantaneous effect **B**〈形〉 instant: ～肥 quick-acting fertilizer ‖ ～药 quick-acting medicine
【速写】sùxiě **A**〈动〉 sketch **B**〈名〉 literary sketch
【速战速决】sùzhàn-sùjué〈成〉 **1** (指打仗) fight a quick battle **2** (指做事) solve a problem quickly

宿 sù

A〈动〉 stay overnight: 借～一晚 ask for a night's lodging ▸～舍, 住～
B〈形〉 **1** (时间久) long-standing: ▸～疾, ～愿, ～志 **2**〈书〉(经验丰富) experienced: ▸～将, ～儒
C〈名〉〈书〉 eminent person: ▸名～
▸xiǔ, xiù
【宿弊】sùbì〈名〉〈书〉 chronic malady: 革除～ eradicate long-standing abuses
【宿娼】sùchāng〈动〉〈书〉 visit prostitutes
【宿仇】sùchóu〈名〉 **1** (指仇恨) enmity **2** (指仇人) long-time enemy
【宿敌】sùdí〈名〉 long-time enemy
【宿根】sùgēn〈名〉 [植物] perennial root: ～植物 perennial plant
【宿疾】sùjí〈名〉 chronic disease
【宿将】sùjiàng〈名〉 veteran general
【宿命论】sùmìnglùn〈名〉 fatalism: ～者 fatalist
【宿儒】sùrú〈名〉〈旧〉 experienced and learned scholar
【宿舍】sùshè〈名〉 hall of residence〈英〉; dormitory〈美〉: 学生～ students' dormitory ‖ 职工～ staff quarters
【宿世】sùshì = 夙世 sùshì
【宿土】sùtǔ〈名〉 earth on the root of a plant
【宿营】sùyíng〈动〉 camp out: 露天～ camp overnight in the open
【宿营地】sùyíngdì〈名〉 camp site
【宿缘】sùyuán〈名〉 [佛教] predestined cause: 前世～ cause going back to a previous incarnation
【宿怨】sùyuàn = 夙怨 sùyuàn
【宿愿】sùyuàn = 夙愿 sùyuàn
【宿债】sùzhài 〈名〉 **1** (旧债) long-standing debt: 偿还～ pay an old debt **2** [佛教] original sin
【宿志】sùzhì〈名〉〈书〉 long-cherished dream
【宿主】sùzhǔ〈名〉 [生物] host

粟 sù〈名〉 millet

【粟米】sùmǐ〈名〉〈方〉 maize
【粟子】sùzi〈名〉〈方〉 millet

谡(謖) sù〈动〉〈书〉 stand up

【谡谡】sùsù〈形〉〈书〉 tall and straight

嗉(膆) sù ▸嗉子 sùzi

【嗉囊】sùnáng = 嗉子 sùzi
【嗉子】sùzi〈名〉 crop (gullet): 鸡～ crop of a chicken

塑 sù

A〈动〉 mould: 用泥～人像 mould a figure out of clay ▸～像, ～造, 可～性
B〈名〉 plastic: ▸～胶, ～料
【塑封】sùfēng〈动〉 coat with plastic: ～卡片 plastic-coated card
【塑钢】sùgāng〈名〉 plastic and steel frame
【塑胶】sùjiāo〈名〉 plastic cement: ～跑道 plastic cement race track
【塑料】sùliào〈名〉 plastic: ～玩具 plastic toy
【塑料薄膜】sùliào bómó〈名〉 plastic film
【塑料袋】sùliàodài〈名〉 plastic bag
【塑像】sùxiàng **A**〈动〉 mould a statue **B**〈名〉 statue: 为～揭幕 unveil a statue
【塑性】sùxìng〈名〉 plasticity: ～黏土 plastic clay
【塑造】sùzào〈动〉 **1** (塑制) mould: ～孔子像 mould a statue of Confucius **2** (刻画) portray: ～英雄形象 portray the image of a hero

溯 sù

〈动〉 **1**〈书〉(逆流而上) go against the stream: ～江行舟 row against the stream **2** (回想) recall: ▸回～, 上～, 追～
【溯源】sùyuán〈动〉 trace to the source: 追根～ trace sth. to its source

愫 sù〈名〉〈书〉 true feelings: ▸情～

蔌 sù〈名〉〈书〉 vegetable: 野～ wild vegetables

傈 sù ▸傈僳族 Lìsùzú

缩 sù

▸suō
【缩砂蜜】sùshāmì〈名〉 [植物] cocklebur-like amomum fruit

簌 sù

【簌簌】sùsù **A**〈拟〉 rustle: 树叶在微风中～作响。 Leaves rustled in the breeze. **B**〈形〉 **1** (形容眼泪) streaming: 泪水

S

从她的脸上～淌下。Tears streamed down her face. 2 (形容肢体) trembling

suān

酸[1] suān
A〈形〉 1 (指味道或气味) sour: 天气太热，牛奶变～了。 The hot weather has turned the milk sour ▸～菜，～枣 2 (悲痛) sad: 心里发～ feel very distressed ▸～楚，悲～，辛～ 3 (迂腐) rigid: ～秀才 rigid pedant ▸寒～，穷～
B〈名〉 acid: ▸～性，～雨，硫～

酸[2] **(痠)** suān〈形〉aching: 两腿发～ have a tingle in one's legs ▸腰～背痛

【酸败】suānbài〈动〉turn sour

【酸不溜丢】suānbuliūdiū〈形〉〈方〉 1〈本〉 unpleasantly sour 2〈喻〉 jealous

【酸菜】suāncài〈名〉 pickled Chinese cabbage: 腌～ make pickles ‖ ～汤 Chinese pickled vegetable soup

【酸沉降】suānchénjiàng〈名〉 acid deposition

【酸楚】suānchǔ〈形〉 distressed: 没人能理解他的～。 No one can understand his misery.

【酸度】suāndù〈名〉 acidity

【酸腐】suānfǔ〈形〉 1 (指气味) rotten and sour: ～变质 go bad 2 (迂腐) pedantic

【酸腐蚀】suānfǔshí〈名〉acid corrosion

【酸酐】suāngān〈名〉［化学］ acid anhydride

【酸根】suāngēn〈名〉［化学］acid radical

【酸碱度】suānjiǎndù〈名〉pH value

【酸碱中和】suānjiǎn zhōnghé〈名〉 acid-base neutralization

【酸懒】suānlǎn〈形〉〈方〉 aching and limp: 浑身～ be aching all over and overcome with fatigue

【酸溜溜】suānliūliū〈形〉 1 (指味道) sour: 这菜吃起来～的，挺好吃。 The dish tastes pleasantly sour. 2 (酸痛) aching: 网球比赛后，我感觉两臂～的。 My arms ached after the tennis match. 3 (妒忌或难过) slightly sad: 看到别人成功心里～的 be a bit envious of sb.'s success 4 (迂腐) pedantic: 他作了一场～的讲演。 He made a bookish speech.

【酸梅】suānméi〈名〉 smoked plum: ～汤 sweet-sour plum juice

【酸奶】suānnǎi〈名〉 yogurt

【酸软】suānruǎn〈形〉 aching and limp: 四肢～ have aching limbs

【酸甜】suāntián〈形〉 sour-sweet: ～味 sour-sweet taste

【酸甜苦辣】suān-tián-kǔ-là〈成〉 the highs and lows of life: 饱尝人生的～ drink the cup of life to the bottom

【酸痛】suāntòng〈形〉 aching: 我累得浑身～。 My whole body aches with weariness.

【酸味】suānwèi〈名〉 sour odour

【酸心】suānxīn〈动〉 1 (胃发酸) sour the stomach, suffer from heartburn: 这种水果吃多了～。 Eating too much of this fruit sours the stomach. 2 (心酸) feel sad: 她生活放荡，让她的朋友们～。 Her wild living brought grief to her friends.

【酸性】suānxìng〈名〉 acidity

【酸性土】suānxìngtǔ〈名〉 acid soil

【酸血症】suānxuèzhèng ▸p. 50〈名〉［医学］ acidaemia

【酸雨】suānyǔ〈名〉 acid rain

【酸枣】suānzǎo〈名〉 wild jujube

suàn

蒜 suàn〈名〉 garlic: 一瓣～ a clove of garlic ▸大～，糖～

【蒜瓣儿】suànbànr〈名〉 garlic clove

【蒜毫】suànháo = 蒜薹 suàntái

【蒜黄】suànhuáng〈名〉 blanched garlic leaf

【蒜苗】suànmiáo〈名〉 garlic shoot

【蒜泥】suànní〈名〉 mashed garlic: 捣～ crush garlic

【蒜皮】suànpí〈名〉 garlic skin

【蒜薹】suàntái〈名〉 garlic shoot

【蒜头】suàntóu〈名〉 garlic bulb

【蒜头鼻子】suàntóu bízi〈名〉 pug nose

算 suàn
A〈动〉 1 (计算) calculate: 扳着指头～ count on one's fingers ‖ ～一～你一共有多少钱 figure out how much money you've got ▸～账，结～，预～ 2 (计划) project: ▸～计，打～，盘～ 3 (估计) guess: 我～准她今天会来。 I reckon she will come today. 4 (包括) factor in: ～在总数内 include in the total ‖ 你把邮费～在内了吗? Have you factored in the cost of postage? ‖ 我也～一个。 Count me in. 5 (认作) regard as: 从年龄看，我的身体还～好。 My health is good for my age. ‖ 他根本～不上一个诗人。 He really isn't a poet. ‖ 他～是个好人。 You could say he's a good man. 6 (表示不计较) let it pass: ～了，我们走吧。 That's enough! Let's go. ‖ 我们就这样～了吗? Shall we let it go at that? 7 (算数) count: 我的损失跟你的相比根本～不了什么。 My losses are nothing to yours. ‖ 这里我说了不～。 What I say doesn't count here.
B〈副〉 finally: 到月底才～有了结果。 There was no result until the end of the month. ‖ 我儿子总～回来啦! My son is home at last!

【算草】suàncǎo〈名〉 rough calculation formula

【算尺】suànchǐ = 计算尺 jìsuànchǐ

【算得】suàndé〈动〉 reckon as: 他们俩真～上是一对好夫妻。 They really are a very nice couple.

【算法】suànfǎ〈名〉 1［数学］ algorithm 2 (计算方法) way of solving a mathematical problem: 这道题有两种～。 There are two ways to solve this problem.

【算法语言】suànfǎ yǔyán〈名〉［计算机］ algorithmic language (ALGOL)

【算卦】suànguà〈动〉 read sb.'s fortune

【算计】suànji〈动〉 1 (计算) calculate: 我～了一下，一共二十个。 I totted them up and altogether there were 20 of them. 2 (计划) consider: 让我先～～，然后再给你答复。 Let me think it over before I give you an answer. ‖ 他～着买一辆新车。 He is planning to buy a new car. 3 (估计) reckon: 我～他不会来了。 I guess he won't come. 4 (暗中损害他人) plot: ～某人 scheme against sb.

【算旧账】suàn jiùzhàng〈动〉 settle an old score: 跟某人～ settle old scores with sb.

【算命】suànmìng〈动〉 read sb.'s fortune

【算命先生】suànmìng xiānsheng〈名〉 fortune-teller

【算盘】suànpán〈名〉 1 (指运算用具) abacus: 打～ calculate on an abacus 2 (打算) plan: 心里有自己的～ have an axe to grind ‖ 这次他打错了～。 This time he miscalculated. ▸如意～

【算式】suànshì〈名〉 equation

【算是】suànshì〈副〉 at last: 他在床上翻来覆去，后来～睡着了。 He tossed and turned and finally got to sleep.

【算术】suànshù〈名〉 arithmetic: 他～很好。 He is good at sums.

【算术题】suànshùtí〈名〉 arithmetic problem: 做～ do sums

【算数】suànshù〈动〉 1 (承认有效) count: 初试不～。 The first attempt won't count. ‖ 我们说话～。 We mean what we say. 2 (完结) be over: 光会说还不～，还得会做。 Talk is not the end of it. We need action.

【算学】suànxué〈名〉〈旧〉 1 (数学) mathematics 2 (算术) arithmetic

【算账】suànzhàng〈动〉 1 (计算账目) balance accounts: ～算得好 be good at accounts ‖ 服务员算错了账。 The waiter got his arithmetic wrong. 2 (追究责任) get even with sb.: 跟某人算总账 settle all accounts with sb. ‖ 你回来我再跟你～。 I'll deal with you when you get home.

【算子】suànzǐ〈名〉［数学］ operator

suī

尿 suī〈名〉〈口〉 wee-wee: 孩子又尿了一泡～。 The baby did a wee-wee again. ▸niào

【尿泡】suīpāo = 尿脬 suīpāo

【尿脬】suīpāo〈方〉= 膀胱 pángguāng

虽 (雖) suī〈连〉 1 (虽然) although: 他～穷，却活得很快活。 Though he is poor, he is quite happy. 2 (即使) even though: ～败犹荣 be a glorious defeat ▸～死犹生

【虽然】suīrán〈连〉 although: ～只有五岁，但他经常帮妈妈做家务。 Even though he is only five, he often helps his mother with housework.

【虽说】suīshuō〈连〉 though: 车～旧点，却很好开。 The car is old, but it runs well.

【虽死犹生】suīsǐ-yóushēng〈成〉 even if one dies, one's name will still live on in the hearts of the people

【虽则】suīzé = 虽然 suīrán

荽 suī ▸芫荽 yánsuī

睢 suī ▸恣睢 zìsuī

suí

绥 (綏) suí〈书〉
A〈动〉 placate: ▸～靖
B〈形〉 peaceful

【绥靖】suíjìng〈动〉 pacify: ～政策 policy of appeasement

隋 Suí〈名〉 Sui Dynasty

随 (隨) suí
A〈动〉 1 (跟着) follow: 紧～其后 follow on the heels of sb./sth. ▸～从，～后，尾～ 2 (依从) comply with: 不管你说什么，我都～你。 I'm happy with whatever you say. ▸～顺，客～主便，入乡～俗 3 (任凭) let sb. do as he likes: ～你说什

么，我都要去。 Whatever you say, I will go. ‖ 干不干～你。 It's up to you to decide whether to do it or not. ▸～便，～意 **4**〈口〉（像） look like: 她长得～她爸。 She takes after her father.

B〈介〉 **1**（依赖） with: ～风飘扬 fly with the wind ▸～机应变，～声附和 **2**（顺便） along with: ～手关门。 Close the door after you.

C〈副〉 雪～下～化。 The snow melts as it falls.

【随笔】 suíbǐ 〈名〉 **1**（散文） sketch **2**（笔记） jottings

【随便】 suíbiàn **A**〈动〉 do as one pleases: 随你的便。 Do as you like, please. ‖ 卖还是不卖，随你的便。 Sell or don't sell, whatever you think is best. **B**〈形〉 casual: ～说几句 make a random comment ‖ 不～发表意见 not offer opinions casually ‖ ～一些，这不是正式场合。 Relax a bit. This isn't a formal occasion. ‖ 说话不要随随便便。 Be careful what you say. ‖ 他穿得很～。 He was casually dressed. **C**〈连〉 no matter: ～别人在背后说什么，他都不在乎。 He doesn't care at all what others say behind his back. ‖ ～多远，我去定了。 I don't care how far it is. I'll have to go.

【随波逐流】 suíbō-zhúliú〈成〉 go with the tide: 在这件事上，你绝对不能～。 You really can't follow the crowd in this matter.

【随常】 suícháng〈形〉 everyday: ～的饭菜 ordinary meal

【随处】 suíchù〈副〉 anywhere: ～可见 be very common

【随从】 suícóng **A**〈动〉 accompany: ～部长访问日本 accompany the minister on a visit to Japan **B**〈名〉 entourage: 有大批～陪同 be accompanied by a large entourage

【随大流】 suí dàliú = 随大溜 suí dàliù

【随大溜】 suí dàliù〈惯〉 follow the crowd: 我爱干啥就干啥，从不～。 I do what I like and never follow the crowd.

【随带】 suídài〈动〉 **1**（附有） go along with: 信外～磁带一盒。 Along with the letter there is a tape. **2**（随身携带） take along: ～雨伞一把 take an umbrella along

【随地】 suídì 〈副〉 anywhere: ～核查 inspect anywhere one wishes ‖ 请勿～吐痰。 No spitting.

【随访】 suífǎng 〈动〉 **1**（随同访问） accompany: ～记者 accompanying journalist **2**（追踪访问） pay a follow-up visit: 对出院病人给予～治疗 provide follow-up care for a discharged hospital patient

【随风倒】 suífēngdǎo〈惯〉 be easily swayed

【随风转舵】 suífēng-zhuǎnduò = 顺风转舵 shùnfēng-zhuǎnduò

【随感】 suígǎn〈名〉 random thoughts

【随行就市】 suíháng-jiùshì〈成〉 sell at the market price

【随和】 suíhe〈形〉 easy-going

【随后】 suíhòu〈副〉 soon afterwards: 你先走，我们～就到。 You go ahead, and we'll be there shortly.

【随机】 suíjī **A**〈动〉 happen randomly: ～调整政策 revise policies in a random way **B**〈形〉 stochastic: ～采访过路行人 conduct random interviews with passers-by

【随机存取】 suíjī cúnqǔ〈名〉［计算机］ random access: ～存储器 random-access memory (RAM) ‖ ～文件 random access file

【随机应变】 suíjī-yìngbiàn 〈成〉 adjust according to changing circumstances: 你要～处理好这件事。 You should handle this matter as the circumstances require.

【随即】 suíjí〈副〉 immediately afterwards: 一阵大风过后，～就是一场大雨。 A gale was immediately followed by a heavy rain. ‖ 主席～又提出另外一个建议。 The president immediately followed up with yet another proposal.

【随记】 suíjì〈名〉 random notes: 参观～ random notes on the visit

【随叫随到】 suíjiào suídào〈惯〉 be at sb.'s beck and call

【随军】 suíjūn〈动〉 be with an army

【随军记者】 suíjūn jìzhě ▸**p. 966** 〈名〉 war correspondent

【随口】 suíkǒu〈副〉 casually: ～作答 make a casual reply

【随群儿】 suíqúnr〈动〉 go with the flow/stream, follow the herd/crowd: 他性格古怪，从不～。 He is eccentric and never follows the crowd.

【随身】 suíshēn〈动〉 have sth. with oneself: ～用品 personal necessities ‖ 他总是～带着身份证。 He carries his identification card with him all the time.

【随身听】 suíshēntīng〈名〉 Walkman: CD～ Discman ‖ MP3～ MP3 player

【随身行李】 suíshēn xíngli〈名〉 hand luggage

【随声附和】 suíshēng-fùhè〈成〉 echo what others say: 他在会上只是～。 During the meeting he just agreed with what everyone else said.

【随时】 suíshí〈副〉 **1**（任何时候） at any time: 你～都可以离开。 You are free to leave at any time. ‖ 汽车～都会来。 The bus may come at any moment. ‖ 死亡～都可能降临到她头上。 Death lay in wait for her at every turn. **2**（需要时） whenever necessary: 该表扬的就应～给予表扬。 Give credit where credit is due.

【随时随地】 suíshí-suídì〈成〉 at any time and in any place: 这种事～都可能发生。 This kind of thing can happen any time any place.

【随手】 suíshǒu〈副〉 without any extra effort: 请～关门。 Please close the door behind you.

【随顺】 suíshùn〈动〉 comply with: 她没多加思考就～朋友的建议。 She went along with her friend's suggestion without thinking about it much.

【随俗】 suísú〈动〉 follow the customs: ▸入乡～

【随同】 suítóng〈动〉 accompany: ～总统访问 accompany the president on a visit

【随喜】 suíxǐ〈动〉 **1**［佛教］ take part in charitable acts **2**（从众） be willing to join others in entertainment or in presenting a gift **3**〈旧〉（游览寺院） visit a temple

【随想】 suíxiǎng〈名〉 random thought: ～曲 caprice

【随心】 suíxīn〈动〉 **1**（听凭心意） follow one's own inclinations: ▸～所欲 **2**（满意） find sth. satisfactory: ～如意 be perfectly satisfied ‖ 这套房子不随他的心。 The house doesn't live up to his expectations.

【随心所欲】 suíxīnsuǒyù〈成〉 do as one pleases: 他们～，想来就来，想去就去。 They come and go as they wish.

【随行】 suíxíng〈动〉 accompany sb. on a trip: ～人员 entourage

【随意】 suíyì〈形〉 do as one pleases: ～停下来 stop at one's own convenience ‖ 让某人～使用某物 put sth. at sb.'s disposal

【随意肌】 suíyìjī 〈名〉［生理］ voluntary muscle

【随遇而安】 suíyù'ér'ān〈成〉 take things as they come

【随员】 suíyuán 〈名〉 **1**（随行人员） entourage: 由助手和翻译组成的大批～ large retinue of aides and interpreters **2**［外交］ attaché

【随葬】 suízàng〈动〉 be buried with the dead: ～品 funerary object

【随着】 suízhe〈介〉 along with: ～时间的推移 as time goes on ‖ 人的体力～年龄的增长而衰退。 Man's strength reduces with age.

遂 suí ▸半身不遂 bànshēn-bùsuí ▸suì

suǐ

髓 suǐ〈名〉 **1**（骨髓） marrow: ▸骨～ **2**［解剖］ marrow: ▸脑～ **3**［植物］ pith **4**〈喻〉（精华） pith: ▸精～

suì

岁（歲） suì

A〈名〉 **1**（年） year: 今～ this year ‖ ～末 end of a year ▸～月，守～ **2**〈书〉（年成） year: 丰～ bumper year ‖ 歉～ lean year **3**〈书〉（时间） time: ～不我与。 Time and tide wait for no man.

B ▸**p. 526**〈量〉 year: 超过/不到50～ over/under 50 ‖ 长某人一～ be one year older than sb. ‖ 他似乎年轻了10～。 He looked as if he had lost 10 years. ▸虚～，周～

【岁差】 suìchā〈名〉［天文］ precession of the equinoxes

【岁出】 suìchū〈名〉 annual expenditure

【岁初】 suìchū〈名〉 beginning of a year

【岁除】 suìchú〈名〉〈书〉 New Year's Eve

【岁寒三友】 suìhán-sānyǒu〈成〉 the three winter companions [ie pine, bamboo and plum]

【岁寒知松柏】 suìhán zhī sōngbǎi 〈成〉 adversity reveals virtue

【岁口】 suìkǒu〈名〉 age of draught animals

【岁暮】 suìmù〈名〉〈书〉 **1**（年末） close of the year **2**〈喻〉（年老） advanced age: ～之人 person of an advanced years

【岁入】 suìrù〈名〉 annual revenue: 增加～ increase revenues

【岁首】 suìshǒu〈名〉〈书〉 beginning of a year

【岁数】 suìshu ▸**p. 526**〈名〉〈口〉 age: 上了～ be getting on ‖ 您多大～？ How old are you?

【岁星】 suìxīng〈名〉〈旧〉 planet Jupiter

【岁序】 suìxù〈名〉〈书〉 sequence of years: ～更新 change of years

【岁月】 suìyuè〈名〉 years: 难忘的～ unforgettable years ‖ ～不我待 time and tide wait for no man ‖ ～流逝。 The years flew by.

谇（誶） suì 〈动〉〈书〉 **1**（责骂） scold **2**（劝告） counsel a sovereign against a royal decision

祟 suì〈名〉 **1**（灾害） disaster brought by spirits **2**（指行为） secretive behaviour: ▸鬼～，作～

遂 suì

A〈动〉 **1**（成功） succeed: 所谋不～ fail

S

in one's attempt ▸未～ 2（如愿） satisfy: ▸～心如意, ～愿, 顺～
B〈副〉〈书〉 thereupon
▸suí
【遂心】suìxīn〈形〉 have one's wish fulfilled: 他诸事～。 Everything goes his way.
【遂心如意】 suìxīn-rúyì 〈成〉 be perfectly satisfied
【遂心所欲】 suìxīn-suǒyù 〈成〉 do as one pleases
【遂意】suìyì = 遂心 suìxīn
【遂愿】 suìyuàn 〈动〉 have one's desire fulfilled: 她事事不～。 Everything goes against her will.

碎 suì

A〈动〉 smash into pieces: 打～ break into pieces ‖ 粉身～骨 be crushed to a pulp ‖ 杯子掉到地板上～了。 The cup dropped on the floor and smashed. ‖ 知道了事情真相后，她的心都～了。 Her heart broke when she learned the truth. ▸破～, ～纸机
B〈形〉 1（不完整） broken: ～玻璃 bits of broken glass ‖ ～纸片 shreds of paper 2（唠叨） long-winded: ▸闲言～语
【碎布】suìbù〈名〉 rag
【碎步儿】suìbùr〈名〉 quick short step
【碎花】suìhuā〈名〉 dense flower pattern
【碎矿机】suìkuàngjī〈名〉 ore crusher
【碎裂】suìliè〈动〉 break into pieces
【碎煤机】suìméijī〈名〉 coal breaker
【碎片】suìpiàn〈名〉 fragment: 砸/打成～ break/smash sth. into pieces
【碎尸】suìshī A〈动〉 dismember a body B〈名〉 dismembered body
【碎尸案】suìshī'àn〈名〉 case of a dismembered body
【碎尸万段】suìshī-wànduàn〈成〉 dismember sb.
【碎石】suìshí A〈名〉 1（石子） broken stone 2［地质］ spall B〈动〉 1［医学］ pulverize gallstones 2（指石子） crush stones
【碎石机】suìshíjī〈名〉 stone crusher
【碎屑】suìxiè〈名〉 piece: 面包～ scraps of bread
【碎纸机】suìzhǐjī〈名〉 shredder
【碎嘴子】suìzuǐzi〈名〉〈方〉 1（唠叨） chatter: 别犯～! Stop your prattle! 2（唠叨的人） chatterbox

隧 suì〈名〉 tunnel: ▸～道, ～洞

【隧道】suìdào〈名〉 tunnel: 英吉利海底～ Channel Tunnel
【隧道掘进机】suìdào juéjìnjī〈名〉 tunnel borer
【隧洞】suìdòng = 隧道 suìdào

燧 suì〈名〉 1（燧石） flint: ▸～石 2〈古〉（烽火） daytime beacon fire: 烽～ beacon

【燧石】suìshí〈名〉 flint

穗[1] suì〈名〉 1（指植物） ear of grain: 玉米正在抽～。 The corn is tasselling. ▸麦～ 2（指装饰品） tassel

穗[2] Suì〈名〉 Sui [another name for Guangzhou (广州)]

【穗选】suìxuǎn〈名〉［农业］ ear selection
【穗子】suìzi〈名〉 1（指植物） ear of grain 2（指装饰品） tassel

邃 suì〈形〉〈书〉 1（深远） remote: ▸深～ 2（精深） profound

【邃密】suìmì〈形〉〈书〉 1（深远） deep 2（精深周密） profound: ～的哲学理论 profound philosophical theory

sūn

孙（孫） sūn〈名〉 1（儿子的子女） grandchild: ▸～女, 子～ 2（孙子辈亲属） relative of one's grandchildren's generation: ▸外～, 侄～ 3（孙子辈以下各代） generations below that of one's grandchildren: ▸曾～, 重～ 4（指植物） second growth of plants: ▸～竹

【孙女】sūnnǚ ▸**p. 588**〈名〉 granddaughter
【孙女婿】sūnnǚxu ▸**p. 588**〈名〉 grandson-in-law
【孙媳妇】sūnxífu ▸**p. 588**〈名〉 granddaughter-in-law
【孙竹】sūnzhú〈名〉 new shoots of bamboo from an old stump
【孙子】sūnzi ▸**p. 588**〈名〉 grandson

荪（蓀） sūn〈名〉〈古〉 aromatic plant

狲（猻） sūn ▸猢狲 húsūn

飧（飱） sūn〈名〉〈书〉 supper

sǔn

损（損） sǔn

A〈动〉 1（减少） decrease: ▸～兵折将, ～失, 亏～ 2（使受损） harm: ▸～公肥私, ～人利己 3〈口〉（讥讽） mock: ～某人 make a mockery of sb. 4（破坏） damage: 有～于双方的相互信任 undermine the trust between two parties ▸～坏, 残～, 破～
B〈形〉 sarcastic: 说话太～ make caustic remarks
【损兵折将】sǔnbīng-zhéjiàng〈成〉 suffer heavy casualties
【损公肥私】 sǔngōng-féisī〈成〉 feather one's nest at public expense
【损害】sǔnhài〈动〉 harm: ～国家声誉 harm the national honour ‖ ～健康 be harmful to one's health ‖ ～人民的利益 jeopardize the interests of the people ‖ 造成～ cause damage ‖ 两国的关系会受到～。 The relationship between the two countries will suffer.
【损耗】sǔnhào〈动〉 cause wear and tear: 降低摩擦～ reduce friction loss
【损耗率】sǔnhàolǜ〈名〉［经济］ proportion of goods damaged
【损坏】sǔnhuài〈动〉 harm: ～形象 tarnish an image ‖ 船的龙骨严重～。 The steamer sustained serious damage to her keel.
【损毁】sǔnhuǐ〈动〉 destroy
【损人】sǔnrén〈动〉 1〈口〉（讥讽别人） ridicule: 他总爱～。 He is given to using sarcasm. 2（损害别人） cause damage to others
【损人利己】sǔnrén-lìjǐ〈成〉 profit at the expense of others
【损伤】sǔnshāng A〈动〉 damage: 衣服用热水洗会受到～。 The clothes will be damaged if they are washed in hot water. B〈名〉 1 ▸**p. 50**［医学］ trauma: 脑部～ brain damage ‖ 致命的～ lethal injury ‖ 心脏及神经～ heart and nerve tissue damage 2（伤亡） loss: 敌人兵力～很大。 The enemy forces suffered heavy losses.
【损失】sǔnshī A〈动〉 lose: ～大量外汇 suffer heavy losses in foreign exchange ‖ 这场火灾～惨重。 The fire has caused severe damage. B〈名〉 loss: 避免经济～ avert economic losses ‖ 赔偿～ recover a loss ‖ 遭受重大～ suffer heavy losses ‖ 他的逝世是我们事业的一个重大～。 His death is a great loss to our cause.
【损益】sǔnyì A〈动〉〈书〉 increase and decrease B〈名〉 profit and loss: ～相抵。 The gains are balanced by the losses.
【损益表】 sǔnyìbiǎo〈名〉［经济］ profit and loss statement

笋（筍） sǔn

A〈名〉 bamboo shoot: ▸春～, 竹～
B〈形〉 tender: ▸～鸡
【笋鞭】sǔnbiān〈名〉 subterranean stem of bamboo
【笋干儿】 sǔngānr〈名〉 dried bamboo shoots
【笋瓜】 sǔnguā〈名〉［植物］ winter squash
【笋鸡】sǔnjī〈名〉 young chicken
【笋尖】sǔnjiān〈名〉 tips of bamboo shoots

隼 sǔn〈名〉［鸟类］ falcon: 雌～ female falcon

榫 sǔn〈名〉 tenon

【榫眼】sǔnyǎn〈名〉 mortise
【榫子】sǔnzi〈名〉 tenon

suō

莎 suō

▸shā
【莎草】 suōcǎo〈名〉［植物］ nutgrass flatsedge

唆 suō〈动〉 instigate: ▸～使, 教～

【唆使】suōshǐ〈动〉 instigate: ～某人犯罪 abet sb. in crime ‖ ～谋杀 instigate a murder ‖ 受人～ at sb.'s instigation

娑 suō

【娑罗树】suōluóshù〈名〉［植物］ sal tree

桫 suō

【桫椤】suōluó〈名〉［植物］ spinulose tree fern

梭 suō〈名〉 shuttle: 无～织机 shuttleless loom ▸穿～, 日月如～

【梭镖】suōbiāo〈名〉 spear
【梭巡】suōxún〈动〉〈书〉 patrol to and fro
【梭鱼】suōyú〈名〉 red-eye mullet
【梭子】suōzi A〈名〉 1（指纺织工具） shuttle 2（弹匣） cartridge clip B〈量〉 [used for bullets]: 一～子弹 a clip of bullets
【梭子蟹】suōzixiè〈名〉 swimming crab
【梭子鱼】suōziyú〈名〉 barracuda

挲 suō ▸摩挲 mósuō

▸sā

睃 suō〈动〉〈方〉 look askance: ～了某人一眼 give sb. a sideways glance

蓑（簑）suō

【蓑笠】suōlì〈名〉large straw or palm-bark rain hat

【蓑衣】suōyī〈名〉straw or palm-bark raincoat

嗦 suō ▸哆嗦 duōsuo, 啰嗦 luōsuo

嗍 suō〈动〉〈口〉suck: ～奶头 suck (at) the breast

羧 suō

【羧基】suōjī〈名〉［化学］carboxyl

缩（縮）suō〈动〉1（收缩）contract: 裤子洗了以后～短了。The trousers shrank in the wash. ▸～小, 收～ 2（蜷缩）recoil: 吓得～作一团 shrink into oneself with fear ‖ 把手～了回去 pull back one's hand ▸龟～, 畏～ 3（减少）economize: ▸～编, 节衣～食, 紧～, 压～ ▸sù

【缩编】suōbiān〈动〉1（指编制）reduce the size of the staff: ～武装部队 streamline the armed forces ‖ 政府机构要～减员 government departments want to streamline 2（指篇幅）shorten

【缩尺】suōchǐ〈名〉shrinkage scale

【缩短】suōduǎn〈动〉cut down: ～工作时间 reduce the working hours ‖ ～假期 cut short a holiday ‖ 把发言～到二十分钟 curtail a speech to 20 minutes

【缩放仪】suōfàngyí〈名〉pantograph

【缩合】suōhé〈名〉［化学］condensation

【缩减】suōjiǎn〈动〉reduce: ～费用 keep costs down ‖ ～开支 cut expenses

【缩聚】suōjù〈名〉［化学］condensation polymerization

【缩量】suōliàng〈动〉［金融］reduce in quantity: 股市～下跌。The stock market took a tumble. ‖ 成交明显～。The deal that was clinched was clearly much lower.

【缩略语】suōlüèyǔ〈名〉abbreviation

【缩手】suōshǒu〈动〉1（收回手）draw back one's hand 2〈喻〉（不再参与）shrink from doing sth.

【缩手缩脚】suōshǒu-suōjiǎo〈成〉1（手脚蜷缩）shrink with cold: 冻得～ be huddled up with cold 2（顾虑多）be overcautious

【缩水】suōshuǐ〈动〉1〈本〉shrink: 这种布洗后会～。This cloth shrinks in the wash. 2〈喻〉fall: 股市市值大幅～ The stock market has fallen sharply in value

【缩头缩脑】suōtóu-suōnǎo〈成〉1（畏缩）recoil in fear: 在困难面前～ recoil from difficulties 2（怕担责任）shrink from responsibility

【缩微】suōwēi〈动〉miniaturize

【缩微复制品】suōwēi fùzhìpǐn〈名〉microform

【缩微胶卷】suōwēi jiāojuǎn〈名〉microfilm: ～阅读器 microfilm reader

【缩微照片】suōwēi zhàopiàn〈名〉microphotograph

【缩位拨号】suōwèi bōhào〈名〉speed dialling

【缩小】suōxiǎo〈动〉reduce: ～范围 reduce the scope ‖ ～贫富差距 narrow the gap between rich and poor

【缩小率】suōxiǎolǜ〈名〉minification

【缩写】suōxiě A〈动〉abbreviate: 由原著～而成 be abridged from the original work B〈名〉abbreviation: OPEC是石油输出国组织的～。OPEC is an abbreviation of Organization of Petroleum Exporting Countries.

【缩写本】suōxiěběn〈名〉abridged version

【缩写词】suōxiěcí〈名〉abbreviation

【缩衣节食】suōyī-jiéshí = 节衣缩食 jiéyī-suōshí

【缩印】suōyìn〈动〉reprint in reduced size: ～本 reduced size edition

【缩影】suōyǐng〈名〉miniature: 作品主人公的遭遇是当时农民生活的～。The experiences of the protagonist reflect the lives of farmers at that time.

【缩约词】suōyuēcí〈名〉［语言］contraction

suǒ

所 suǒ

A〈名〉1（地方）place: ▸处～, 哨～ 2（机构）institution: ▸派出～, 研究～

B〈助〉1（用于动词前构成名词性词组）[used before a verb to form a noun phrase]: 非人力～能及 beyond the sweep of human power ‖ 我们～面临的困难 difficulties we are facing ‖ 他～说的与事实不符。His story did not tie in with facts. 2（表示被动）[used in the construction 为…所… to indicate passive voice]: 不为困难～吓倒 not recoil from difficulties ‖ 为表面现象～迷惑 be misled by appearances

C〈量〉[used for building, school, hospital, etc.]: 一～楼房 a building ‖ 三～大学 three universities ‖ 一～医院 a hospital

【所部】suǒbù〈名〉troops under one's command

【所长】suǒcháng〈名〉forte: 各有～ each has their strong points ‖ 烹饪是她～。Cooking is her forte. ▸suǒzhǎng

【所得】suǒdé〈名〉income: 非法～ illicit gains ‖ 劳动～ earned income

【所得税】suǒdéshuì〈名〉income tax: 交纳/收取～ pay/collect income tax

【所见即所得】suǒjiàn jí suǒdé〈名〉［计算机］WYSIWYG (what you see is what you get)

【所见所闻】suǒjiàn-suǒwén〈名〉what one sees and hears

【所罗门群岛】Suǒluómén Qúndǎo〈名〉Solomon Islands

【所属】suǒshǔ〈形〉1（指机构）subordinate: 总公司～各连锁店 each chain store affiliated to the company headquarters ‖ 沈阳军区～某部 PLA unit under the command of the Shenyang Military Region 2（指人）personal: 在～医院登记 register at one's own hospital

【所谓】suǒwèi〈形〉1（表解释）what is known as: ～语言学是指对语言的科学研究。By linguistics we mean the scientific study of language. 2（表否定）so-called: ～的自由主义者 so-called liberal ‖ 被～的朋友所欺骗 be deceived by a so-called friend

【所向披靡】suǒxiàng-pīmǐ〈成〉be invincible: 在足球联赛中～ sweep a football league series

【所向无敌】suǒxiàng-wúdí〈成〉be invincible

【所以】suǒyǐ A〈连〉so: 因为找不到你，～我走了。I couldn't find you so I left. ‖ 我今天上班～迟到，是因为我的表今早停了。The reason why I was late for work today is that my watch stopped this morning. ‖ 他在美国呆了四年，这就是他～英语讲得如此流利的原因。He was in America for four years. That's why he speaks English so fluently. ‖ ～呀，要不我就不请你啦。That's just it, otherwise I wouldn't have invited you. B〈名〉real situation: ▸忘乎～

【所以然】suǒyǐrán〈名〉reason: 看不出个～ not be able to see the whys and wherefores (of) ‖ 知其然不知其～ know what it is but not know why it is so

【所有】suǒyǒu A〈动〉possess: 那所房子现归一位老太太～。That house is now in the possession of an old lady. ‖ 这块土地依法归国家～。The land belongs legally to the state. B〈名〉possessions: ▸一无～ C〈形〉all: ～的朋友/时间/精力 all one's friends/time/energy ‖ 回答～的问题 answer all the questions ‖ 他个子比其他～人都高。He is taller than everyone else.

【所有格】suǒyǒugé〈名〉［语法］possessive case: ～代词 possessive pronoun

【所有权】suǒyǒuquán〈名〉possession: 重新获得～ recover possession ‖ 土地～ land ownership

【所有人】suǒyǒurén〈名〉owner

【所有制】suǒyǒuzhì〈名〉ownership: 集体～ collective ownership

【所在】suǒzài〈名〉1（表处所）place: 寻找舒适的～居住 look for a comfortable place to live 2（表存在）the essence of sth.: 病因～ cause of the disease ‖ 这就是要害～。Here lies the point.

【所在地】suǒzàidì〈名〉site: 博物馆的～ location of a museum

【所长】suǒzhǎng〈名〉head: 研究所～ director of a research institute ‖ 派出所～ head of a police station ▸suǒcháng

【所致】suǒzhì〈动〉〈书〉be caused by: 由疏忽～ caused by negligence ‖ 企业的不景气是管理不善～。The business's slump was caused by poor management.

【所作所为】suǒzuò-suǒwéi〈成〉what one does and how one behaves: 他的～有损军人的形象。His conduct has injured the reputation of a soldier.

索¹ suǒ〈名〉rope: ▸绞～, 绳～, 铁～

索² suǒ〈动〉1（寻找）look for: ▸搜～ 2（探求）probe: ▸摸～, 思～ 3（讨取）ask for: ▸～赔, 勒～

索³ suǒ〈形〉〈书〉1（孤独）lonely: ▸离群～居 2（没兴趣）uninteresting: ▸～然寡味

【索偿】suǒcháng〈动〉demand compensation: 向保险公司～ claim damages from an insurance company

【索道】suǒdào〈名〉cableway: 在河上架～ build a cableway across a river

【索尔兹伯里】Suǒ'ěrzībólǐ〈名〉Salisbury

【索非亚】Suǒfēiyà〈名〉Sofia

【索贿】suǒhuì〈动〉solicit a bribe: ～受贿100万元 demand and accept one million *yuan* in bribes

【索价】suǒjià〈动〉ask a price: ～过高 demand an unreasonable price ‖ 每吨煤～80元 charge coal at 80 *yuan* a ton

【索马里】Suǒmǎlǐ〈名〉Somalia: ～共和国 Somali Republic ‖ ～人 Somali ‖ ～语 Somali

【索寞】suǒmò〈形〉〈书〉1（消沉）depressed 2（凄凉）desolate: 洪水过后，这个国家一片～的景象。After the flood the country was completely desolate.

【索赔】suǒpéi〈动〉make a claim: ～精神

S

损失费 demand compensation for emotional loss ‖ 提出巨额～ claim a huge indemnity ‖ 向保险公司～ claim on an insurance company

【索赔时限】suǒpéi shíxiàn〈名〉 time limit for filing claims

【索取】suǒqǔ〈动〉 demand: ～高额报酬 extort high payment ‖ ～1,000元赔偿费 claim 1,000 *yuan* compensation

【索然】suǒrán〈形〉〈书〉 dull: ～无味的谈话 insipid conversation

【索然寡味】suǒrán-guǎwèi〈成〉 insipid: ～的笑话 pointless joke

【索索】suǒsuǒ **A**〈拟〉 rustle: 把报纸弄得～响 make a rustling sound with the newspaper ‖ 微风中树枝发出的～声 the rustle of branches in the breeze **B**〈形〉 trembling: 孩子们看见警察吓得～发抖。 The children trembled with fear when they saw the policeman.

【索性】suǒxìng〈副〉既然你赢不了，～退出比赛算了。 Since you can't win the game, you might as well quit. ‖ 既然已经做了，～就把它做完。 Since we've already started it, we'd better finish it.

【索要】suǒyào〈动〉 demand: ～收据 ask for a receipt

【索引】suǒyǐn〈名〉 index: 编～ compile an index ‖ 所有的人名都将编入～。 All the personal names will be indexed.

唢（嗩）suǒ

【唢呐】suǒnà ▸**p. 929**〈名〉 *suona* horn [a Chinese brass trumpet-like wind instrument]

琐（瑣）suǒ

〈形〉 **1**（零碎） trivial: ▸～事，繁～ **2**（卑微） humble: ▸猥～

【琐事】suǒshì〈名〉 trifling matter: ～缠身 be taken up with small things

【琐碎】suǒsuì〈形〉trivial: ～的细节 inconsequential details

【琐闻】suǒwén〈名〉〈书〉 bits of news

【琐细】suǒxì = 琐碎 suǒsuì

【琐屑】suǒxiè〈形〉〈书〉 trifling: ～事务 trivialities

【琐议】suǒyì〈名〉〈书〉 trivial comments

锁（鎖）suǒ

A〈名〉 **1**（器具） lock: 弹簧～ Yale lock ‖ 制～厂/工人 lockmaker **2**（锁状物） lock-shaped thing: ▸长命～，石～ **3**（锁链） chain: ▸～链，拉～

B〈动〉 **1**（用锁关住） lock up: ～门 lock a door ‖ 这门～不上。 The door won't lock. **2**（缝纫方法） lock-stitch: ～扣眼 buttonhole ▸～边儿

【锁边儿】suǒbiānr〈动〉 lock-stitch: ～机 lock-stitching machine

【锁匙】suǒchí〈方〉= 钥匙 yàoshi

【锁定】suǒdìng **A**〈名〉［电子］ locking **B**〈动〉 **1**（确定不变） lock up: ～利率 have interest rates locked up **2**（保持在） keep to: ～体育频道 log on to the sports channel ‖ 只要有NBA比赛，他就会～电视体育频道。 Whenever there is an NBA match, he stays tuned to the sports channel. **3**（最终确定） finally decide: 终场前主队前锋打进一球，把比分～在1比0上。 A goal by a host team striker just before the whistle sealed the match at 1 : 0.

【锁骨】suǒgǔ〈名〉［解剖］ collarbone

【锁国】suǒguó〈动〉 close a country to the outside world: ～政策 closed-door policy ▸闭关～

【锁匠】suǒjiàng〈名〉 locksmith

【锁具】suǒjù〈名〉 set of locks

【锁孔】suǒkǒng〈名〉 keyhole: 从～偷看 spy through the keyhole

【锁链】suǒliàn〈名〉 shackles: 戴上～ be chained up ‖ 砸碎封建制度的～ break the chains of feudalism

【锁舌】suǒshé〈名〉 bolt

【锁眼】suǒyǎn = 锁孔 suǒkǒng

【锁钥】suǒyuè〈名〉 **1**（锁和钥匙） lock and key **2**〈喻〉（关键） key: 有规律的饮食和睡眠是身体健康的～。Regular diet and sleep are the keys to good health. **3**〈喻〉（军事要地） strategic place

S

Tt

tā

他 tā〈代〉**1**（人称代词）**a**（男性第三人称）（作主语） he;（作宾语） him;（所有格） his: ～父母 his parents ‖ ～是我兄弟。 He is my brother. ‖ 非～莫属。 No one else is fit for that but him. ‖ 给～一本书。 Give him a book. **b**（泛指） [used for sb. whose gender is either unknown or unimportant]: 每个人都有～的长处和短处。 Everyone has their merits and demerits. **c**（表强调） [used in apposition to the subject or a sentence for emphasis]: 小马～可是个实在人。 Xiao Ma is an honest and trustworthy man. **2**〈书〉（指示代词） **a**（另外的） other: 别无～求 have no other request ‖ 留作～用 reserve for other uses ▸～人, ～日, ～乡 **b**（其他） other things: ▸其～ **3**（任指） [used in the pattern 你也…, 他也… to express the idea of everybody]: 你也喊，～也叫，教室里一片混乱。 With everyone crying and yelling, the classroom was in a state of chaos. **4**（虚指） [used after a verb as a meaningless mock object]: 查～个一清二楚 make a thorough investigation ‖ 好好吃～一顿 have a good meal ‖ 再试～一次。 Let's have another go.

【他动】tādòng〈动〉 be propelled by an external force

【他方】 tāfāng 〈名〉 elsewhere: 远走～ leave for a faraway place

【他加禄人】Tājiālùrén〈名〉 Tagalog

【他加禄语】Tājiālùyǔ〈名〉 Tagalog

【他俩】tāliǎ〈代〉 they two: ～是双胞胎兄弟。 They are twin brothers.

【他律】tālǜ〈名〉 heteronomy

【他们】tāmen〈代〉（作主语） they;（作宾语） them: ～家离学校不远。 Their home is not far from the school. ‖ ～都说一种新电脑马上就要上市。 They all say that a new type of computer is coming on the market soon. ‖ ～英国人认为问人家年龄很不礼貌。 British people consider it impolite to ask people about their age. ‖ 老张、老李～都同意。 Both Lao Zhang and Lao Li agreed. ‖ 老王～不愿意去。 Lao Wang's lot don't want to go.

【他年】tānián〈名〉 some day in the future: ～我一定会回来的。 I'm sure to return some day.

【他人】tārén〈代〉 others: 关心～ be concerned about others ‖ 尊重～就等于尊重自己。 To respect others is to respect oneself.

【他日】tārì〈名〉〈书〉 some day: ～再议吧。 Let's discuss it some other time.

【他杀】tāshā〈名〉［法律］ homicide: 警方认定是～，不是自杀。 The law determined that it was homicide and not suicide.

【他山之石，可以攻玉】tā shān zhī shí, kěyǐ gōng yù〈成〉〈喻〉 advice from others may help one overcome his shortcomings

【他乡】tāxiāng〈名〉 alien land: 作客～ sojourn in a strange land ‖ 流落～ be stranded in a strange land

它[1] tā〈代〉 [referring to a thing] it: 这款手机～的功能不少。 This mobile phone has many different functions. ‖ 钥匙在包里，当心别把～丢了。 The key is in the bag. Be careful not to lose it.

它[2]（**牠**） tā〈代〉 [referring to an animal] it: 狗在找～的主人。 The dog is looking for its master.

【它们】tāmen〈代〉 [plural of 它]（作主语） they;（作宾语） them: 农场有五百多头猪，～都是同一品种。 There are over 500 pigs on the farm and they are all the same breed.

她 tā〈代〉（女性第三人称）（作主语） she;（作宾语或所有格） her: ～儿子/丈夫 her son/husband ‖ ～回娘家去了。 She returned to her parents' home. ‖ 我们热爱祖国，愿意为～贡献智慧和力量。 We love our motherland and we are willing to give her the benefit of all our wisdom and hard work.

【她们】tāmen〈代〉 [referring to female humans];（作主语） they;（作宾语） them: 他有两个姐姐，～都是医生。 He's got two sisters. They are both doctors.

趿 tā

【趿拉】tāla〈动〉 wear shoes with the backs trodden down: 他～着拖鞋走过来。 He came in in slippers.

【趿拉板儿】tālabǎnr〈名〉〈方〉 clogs

铊（**鉈**） tā〈名〉［化学］ thallium (Tl): ～中毒 thallium poisoning ▸tuó

塌 tā〈动〉**1**（塌陷） collapse: 地震把屋顶震～了。 The roof caved in because of the earthquake. ‖ 墙～了。 The wall collapsed. ‖ 天不会～下来。 The sky is not going to fall down. ▸～方，～陷，倒～ **2**（凹下） sink: ～鼻子 flat nose ‖ 她瘦得两腮都～下去了。 She is so thin that her cheeks have become sunken. **3**（安定） have peace of mind: ～下心来好好工作/学习 settle down to one's work/studies

【塌方】tāfāng〈动〉 collapse: 堤坝～。 The dam has caved in. ‖ 火车因～受阻。 The train was held up by a landslide.

【塌架】tājià〈动〉**1**〈本〉 collapse: 黄瓜架被风刮～了。 The cucumber trellis toppled in the wind. **2**〈喻〉（垮台） fall from power: 那个恶霸终于～了。 That local tyrant has fallen from power at last.

【塌棵菜】tākēcài〈名〉〈方〉［植物］ broadleaf mustard

【塌台】tātái〈动〉 fall from power: 他因性丑闻而～。 He was forced out of office because of a sex scandal.

【塌陷】tāxiàn〈动〉 cave in: 地基～。 The foundations have subsided. ‖ 墙壁上的裂缝是由地面～引起的。 The crack in the wall was caused by subsidence in the ground.

【塌心】tāxīn〈动〉〈方〉 have peace of mind: 任务不完成，我不～。 I cannot set my mind at ease until the task is accomplished. ‖ 问题一解决，就～了。 I was relieved as soon as the matter was settled.

【塌秧】tāyāng〈方〉**A**〈动〉 [of vegetables, plants, etc.] droop: 园子里的蔬菜在烈日下都～了。 The vegetables in our garden have drooped in the sweltering sun. **B**〈形〉 downcast: 想到考试不及格，他就～了。 He was crestfallen at failing the exam.

遢 tā ▸邋遢 lāta

溻 tā〈动〉〈方〉 become soaked with sweat: 运动员的汗衫全～了。 The players' sweaters were all drenched in sweat.

踏 tā

【踏实】tāshi〈形〉**1**（不浮躁） solid: 工作～ be a steady worker ‖ 他是个很～的人。 He is a very reliable person. **2**（安稳） relaxed: 睡得～ have a good, sound sleep ‖ 你回来了，我心里就～了。 I can put my mind at rest now that you are home. ▸tà

褟 tā

A〈名〉 undershirt

B〈动〉 hem (with lace or ribbons): 给衬衣领口～上花边 edge the collar of a shirt with lace

tǎ

塔[1] tǎ〈名〉**1**（指佛教建筑） pagoda: 佛～ Buddhist pagoda ‖ 舍利～ stupa ▸～林，宝～ **2**（指塔形建筑） tower: 伦敦～ Tower of London ▸灯～，电视～，水～ **3**［化学］ column: 蒸馏～ distillation tower

塔[2] Tǎ ▸塔吉克族 Tǎjíkèzú, 塔塔尔族 Tǎtǎ'ěrzú

【塔吊】tǎdiào〈名〉［机械］ tower crane

【塔夫绸】tǎfūchóu〈名〉［纺织］ taffeta

【塔吉克人】Tǎjíkèrén〈名〉 Tajik

【塔吉克斯坦】Tǎjíkèsītǎn〈名〉Tajikistan: ～人 Tajik ‖ ～语 Tajik
【塔吉克语】Tǎjíkèyǔ ▸p. 918〈名〉Tajik
【塔吉克族】Tǎjíkèzú〈名〉Tajik ethnic group
【塔克拉玛干沙漠】Tǎkèlāmǎgān Shāmò〈名〉Taklimakan Desert
【塔里木河】Tǎlǐmùhé ▸p. 294〈名〉Tarim River
【塔里木盆地】Tǎlǐmù Péndì〈名〉Tarim Basin
【塔林】tǎlín〈名〉forest of pagodas (under which Buddhist abbots were buried)
【塔楼】tǎlóu〈名〉1（指楼房）tower block 2（指顶部小楼）turret
【塔桥】Tǎqiáo〈名〉Tower Bridge (in London)
【塔什干】Tǎshígān〈名〉Tashkent
【塔斯社】Tǎsīshè〈名〉TASS [official news agency of the former Soviet Union]
【塔塔尔族】Tǎtǎ'ěrzú〈名〉Tatar ethnic group
【塔塔尔语】Tǎtǎ'ěryǔ ▸p. 918〈名〉Tatar
【塔台】tǎtái〈名〉［航空］control tower
【塔希提岛】Tǎxītídǎo〈名〉Tahiti
【塔钟】tǎzhōng〈名〉tower clock

獭（獺） tǎ 1 = 水獭 shuǐtǎ 2 = 旱獭 hàntǎ 3 = 海獭 hǎitǎ

鳎（鰨） tǎ〈名〉［鱼类］sole
【鳎目鱼】tǎmùyú〈名〉sole

tà

拓（搨） tà〈动〉make rubbings from inscriptions on stone tablets or bronze vessels: ～碑文 make rubbings from inscriptions on a stone tablet ▸～本, ～片
▸tuò
【拓本】tàběn〈名〉book of rubbings
【拓片】tàpiàn〈名〉rubbing from a stone tablet or bronze vessel

沓 tà〈形〉1〈书〉（繁多）numerous: ▸纷至～来, 杂～ 2（迟缓）sluggish: ▸拖～
▸dá

挞（撻） tà〈动〉〈书〉flog: ▸鞭～
【挞伐】tàfá〈动〉〈书〉1〈本〉send troops to suppress: 朝廷出兵～叛军。The imperial government sent troops to attack rebelling forces. 2〈喻〉（抨击）criticize

闼（闥） tà〈名〉〈书〉small door: 排～直入 push the door open and go straight in

嗒 tà
▸dā
【嗒然】tàrán〈形〉〈书〉dejected: ～而归 return dejected
【嗒丧】tàsàng〈形〉despondent: ～而返 come away disappointed

阘（闒） tà
【阘懦】tànuò〈形〉〈书〉mean and cowardly
【阘茸】tàróng〈形〉〈书〉mean and low: 为人～ be mean and low

榻 tà〈名〉couch: 藤～ rattan couch ‖ 竹～ bamboo couch ▸病～, 卧～, 下～
【榻榻米】tàtàmǐ〈名〉tatami

踏 tà〈动〉1（踩）tread: ～上故土 set foot on one's native land ‖ ～上新的工作岗位 take up a new job ‖ ～破门槛 visit sb. much too frequently ‖ 请勿践～草地。Please keep off the grass. ‖ 球场发生踩～事件。There was a stampede at the stadium. ▸～步, ～青 2（在现场）go to the scene: ▸～访, ～看
▸tā
【踏板】tàbǎn〈名〉1（用于船）gangplank;（用于车）ramp 2（指附属家具）footstool in front of a bed 3［体育］springboard: 跳远～ long jump take-off board 4（指操纵装置）pedal: 缝纫机～ treadle of a sewing machine ‖ 刹车～ brake pedal
【踏步】tàbù〈动〉mark time: ～不前 mark time and make no headway ‖ 原地～ march in place
【踏春】tàchūn〈动〉go hiking on a spring day
【踏访】tàfǎng〈动〉make an on-the-spot investigation: ～古迹 pay a visit to historic sites
【踏歌】tàgē〈名〉singing accompanied by stamping of feet or rhythmic dancing [peculiar to the Miao and Yao ethnic groups]
【踏脚石】tàjiǎoshí〈名〉stepping stone
【踏勘】tàkān〈动〉1（指勘察地形、地质）conduct a field survey: ～油田 survey an oilfield 2（查看）make an on-the-spot investigation: ～现场 make an investigation on the scene
【踏看】tàkàn〈动〉make an on-the-spot investigation: ～地形 survey the terrain
【踏空】tàkōng〈动〉1（失足）miss one's step: 他下地窖时一脚～跌了下去。When he went down into the cellar, he missed his step and fell. 2［金融］lose the chance to buy shares at a low price
【踏破铁鞋】tàpò-tiěxié〈成〉spare no efforts in searching for sth.
【踏青】tàqīng〈动〉go hiking on a spring day

> **踏青**
>
> Also known as *chunyou* (春游). The term generally refers to an outing to the countryside during spring. Traditionally, the outing takes place around the Qingming Festival（▸清明节）. '*Qing*' (青, green) refers to '*qingcao*' (青草, green grass).

【踏雪】tàxuě〈动〉walk in the snow
【踏月】tàyuè〈动〉take a walk in the moonlight
【踏足】tàzú〈动〉〈书〉set foot in/on: ～其间 step into the middle of sth. ‖ ～商界 gain a foothold in the world of business

蹋 tà〈动〉1（踩）tread: ▸糟～ 2〈书〉（踢）kick: ～鞠 kick a ball

tāi

苔 tāi ▸舌苔 shétāi
▸tái

胎¹ tāi
A〈名〉1（指幼体）fetus: 怀～ be pregnant ▸～儿, ～教, 堕～ 2（填充物）padding: ▸棉花～ 3（粗坯）roughcast: ▸～具, 泥～ 4〈喻〉（根源）source: ▸祸～
B〈量〉birth: 我家的猫一～生了五只小猫。Our cat gave birth to five kittens in one litter. ▸头～

胎² tāi〈名〉tyre: 备用～ spare tyre ‖ 爆～ burst a tyre ▸车～, 轮～
【胎动】tāidòng〈名〉［医学］fetal movement
【胎毒】tāidú〈名〉［中医］skin infections of newborn infants
【胎儿】tāi'ér〈名〉fetus: ～发育正常。The fetus is developing normally.
【胎发】tāifà〈名〉lanugo hair
【胎记】tāijì〈名〉birthmark: 他背上有块黑色～。He has a black birthmark on his back.
【胎教】tāijiào〈名〉antenatal training
【胎具】tāijù〈名〉mould
【胎里素】tāilǐsù〈名〉born vegetarian
【胎毛】tāimáo〈名〉lanugo hair
【胎膜】tāimó〈名〉［医学］fetal membrane
【胎盘】tāipán〈名〉［医学］placenta
【胎气】tāiqì〈名〉［中医］1（指征状）nausea, vomiting and oedema of legs during pregnancy 2（养胎之气）nourishing ether for the fetus: 动～ disturb the fetus
【胎生】tāishēng〈形〉［动物］viviparous: ～动物 viviparous animal
【胎死腹中】tāisǐfùzhōng〈成〉1〈本〉a fetus dies in the womb 2〈喻〉（指计划等）a plan is aborted
【胎位】tāiwèi〈名〉［医学］fetal position: 矫正～ correct the fetal position ‖ ～不正 abnormal fetal position
【胎衣】tāiyī = 胞衣 bāoyī
【胎痣】tāizhì = 胎记 tāijì

tái

台¹ tái〈名〉〈书〉〈敬〉you: ▸～驾, ～鉴

台²（臺） tái
A〈名〉1（用于远望）raised large building or structure: ▸近水楼～ 2（指基座）stand: 火箭发射～ missile launch pad ▸灯～, 蜡～, 炮～ 3（指设备）stage: 登～演讲 mount the platform and deliver a speech ‖ ～上只有一个演员。There was only one actor on the stage. ▸讲～, 舞～, 主席～ 4（台状物）platform-shaped thing: ▸窗～, 锅～ 5（指服务台）station: 国际～ international broadcasting service ▸查号～, 气象～ 6（指掌权）power: 在上次大选中，工党上了～，保守党下了～。In the last general election, Labour got in and the Conservatives went out. ▸倒～, 垮～ 7 Tái（指台湾）Taiwan: 港～地区 Hong Kong and Taiwan regions ▸～胞, ～盟, ～资
B〈量〉1（用于戏剧、歌舞）a whole set of items performed on a single occasion: 一～文艺晚会 a theatrical performance ‖ 一～戏 a performance 2（指机器、仪器）[used for certain machinery, apparatus, etc.]: 一～车床 a lathe ‖ 一～联合收割机 a combine harvester ‖ 两～发电机 two power generators

台³（檯、枱） tái〈名〉table: 乒乓球～ table-tennis table ▸柜～, 梳妆～

台[4]（颱）tái ▸台风 táifēng

【台胞】Táibāo〈名〉 Taiwanese compatriots

【台刨】táibào〈名〉［机械］ bench plane

【台北】Táiběi ▸**p. 661**〈名〉 Taipei

【台本】táiběn〈名〉 script of a play with stage directions

【台笔】táibǐ〈名〉 desk pen

【台标】táibiāo〈名〉 logo of a TV station

【台布】táibù〈名〉 tablecloth: 塑料～ plastic tablecloth

【台步】táibù〈名〉［戏曲］ theatrical stage walk: ～轻盈 graceful stage walk

【台秤】táichèng〈名〉 **1**（磅秤） platform scale **2**〈方〉（案秤） counter scale

【台词】táicí〈名〉 actor's lines: 背～ recite one's lines ‖ 她的～不多。 She had just a few lines. ▸潜～

【台灯】táidēng〈名〉 reading lamp

【台地】táidì〈名〉［地质］ platform

【台独】Táidú〈名〉 Taiwan independence movement: ～分子 advocates of Taiwanese independence ‖ ～势力 forces that advocate Taiwanese independence

【台风】táifēng〈名〉 **1**［气象］ typhoon: ～警报 typhoon warning ‖ 强～ violent typhoon **2**（指表演） stage demeanour: ～稳健 calm and steady stage demeanour

【台甫】 táifǔ〈名〉〈旧〉〈敬〉 [used in asking the name of the person spoken to] your name: 请教～? May I have your name?

【台海】Táihǎi〈简称〉= 台湾海峡

【台基】táijī〈名〉 base of a structure above ground

【台驾】táijià〈名〉〈旧〉〈敬〉you: 恭候～光临。 I will wait respectfully for your visit.

【台鉴】táijiàn〈动〉〈旧〉〈套〉 [used in an old-fashioned letter right after the name of the addressee in the salutation] please read my letter: 张先生～ For the attention of Mr Zhang

【台阶】táijiē〈名〉 **1**〈本〉 steps: 水泥～ concrete steps **2**〈喻〉（指阶段） step: 生产跃上新的～。 Output has climbed to new levels. **3**〈喻〉（指机会）opportunity to extricate oneself from an awkward position: 给他们一个～下。 Give them an out.

【台历】táilì〈名〉 desk calendar

【台盟】 Táiméng 〈简称〉= 台湾民主自治同盟

【台面】táimiàn〈名〉 **1**（桌儿面） tabletop: 我们把事情拿到～上来说。 Let's bring this issue to the table. **2**〈方〉（赌金总额） all the money on a gambling table

【台盘】 táipán 〈名〉〈方〉 **1**（席面） tabletop: 这是宴席，家常菜上不了～。 This is a banquet. Home-style cooking is inappropriate for the occasion. **2**〈喻〉（公开场合） public occasions: 此人上不了～。 This person is unable to rise to the occasion.

【台钳】táiqián〈名〉［机械］ bench vice

【台球】táiqiú〈名〉 **1** ▸**p. 909**（指运动） billiards: 打～ play billiards **2**（指球） billiard ball **3**〈方〉（乒乓球） table tennis

【台球杆】táiqiúgān〈名〉 cue

【台球台】táiqiútái〈名〉 billiards table

【台扇】táishàn〈名〉 table fan

【台商】táishāng〈名〉 Taiwanese businessman

【台式】táishì〈形〉 table-top

【台式计算机】táishì jìsuànjī〈名〉 desktop computer

【台式机】táishìjī〈简称〉= 台式计算机

【台属】Táishǔ〈名〉 relatives of Taiwanese compatriots

【台田】táitián〈名〉［农业］ raised fields

【台湾】Táiwān ▸**p. 661**〈名〉 Taiwan

【台湾海峡】Táiwān Hǎixiá〈名〉 Taiwan Straits

【台湾民主自治同盟】Táiwān Mínzhǔ Zìzhì Tóngméng〈名〉 Taiwan Democratic Self-Government League

【台砧】táizhēn〈名〉 bench anvil

【台钟】táizhōng〈名〉〈方〉 desk clock

【台柱子】táizhùzi〈名〉 **1**（指演员） star of a theatrical troupe **2**〈喻〉（骨干） backbone: 他是我们篮球队的～。 He is the backbone of our basketball team.

【台资】táizī〈名〉 investment from Taiwan: ～企业 Taiwanese-funded enterprise

【台子】táizi〈名〉 **1**（桌子） table **2**（平台）platform: 窗～ windowsill ‖ 戏～ stage

邰 Tái〈名〉 Tai [surname]

抬（擡）tái

A〈动〉 **1**（举起） lift: ～胳膊/腿 raise one's arm/leg ‖ 把头～起来 lift up one's head ‖〈喻〉 哄～物价 raise prices ‖〈喻〉 自～身价 put higher value on oneself ▸～价，高～贵手 **2**（共同搬） [of two or more persons] carry: ～担架 carry a stretcher ‖ 把钢琴～到楼上去 carry a piano upstairs ▸～轿子 **3**〈口〉（争辩） bicker: ▸～杠 1
B〈量〉 [used for things carried by two persons]: 八～妆奁 eight boxes of dowry

【抬爱】tái'ài〈动〉〈书〉 favour: 多蒙～ have enjoyed many favours from you

【抬秤】 táichèng 〈名〉 huge steelyard [usu worked by three people]

【抬杠】 táigàng 〈动〉 **1**〈口〉（争辩） bicker: 他是故意和你～。 He's just arguing with you for the sake of argument. ‖ 先别和我～，回去好好想想。 Think it over before you come and pick quarrels with me. **2**〈旧〉（抬灵柩） [of four or more persons] carry a coffin on stout poles

【抬高】táigāo〈动〉 raise: ～物价 raise prices ‖ 打击别人，～自己 attack others in order to elevate oneself

【抬价】táijià〈动〉 raise prices: ～出售 sell sth. at raised prices

【抬轿子】tái jiàozi〈惯〉〈喻〉〈贬〉 fawn on

【抬举】táiju〈动〉 praise or promote sb. to show favour: 多谢您的～。 Thank you very much for your kind words. ‖ 这是在～我。 You are flattering me. ▸不识～

【抬升】táishēng〈动〉 rise: 物价逐步～。 Prices are rising steadily.

【抬手】táishǒu〈动〉 **1**〈本〉 lift up one's hand: 她轻轻地一～，把他打发走了。 With a slight lift of her hand, she dismissed him. **2**〈喻〉 not be too hard on sb.: 你们这次就抬抬手，放过我吧。 Please stretch a point in my case this time.

【抬头】táitóu **A**〈动〉 **1**〈本〉 raise one's head: ～看 look up ‖ ～挺胸 with one's chin up and chest out **2**〈喻〉 gain ground: 受处分后，他在同事面前总是抬不起头来。 He couldn't look his colleagues in the eye after receiving the dressing down. ‖ 我们绝不能让奢靡之风重新～。 We will not allow overindulgence to take hold once again. **B**〈名〉 space on receipts, bills, etc. for names of the buyer or payee: 这张支票～写谁? To whom is this cheque payable?

【抬头不见低头见】táitóu bùjiàn dītóu jiàn〈俗〉 run into one another frequently

【抬头纹】táitóuwén〈名〉 wrinkles on one's forehead

苔 tái〈名〉［植物］ liverwort: 青～ moss ▸tāi

【苔藓植物】táixiǎnzhíwù〈名〉 bryophyte

【苔原】táiyuán〈名〉［地理］ tundra

炱 tái〈名〉 soot: 松～ pine soot

跆 tái〈动〉〈书〉 tread

【跆拳道】 táiquándào 〈名〉［体育］ tae kwon do

鲐（鮐）tái 〈名〉［鱼类］ chub mackerel

薹[1] tái〈名〉［植物］sedge: ～笠 rain hat made of sedge

薹[2] tái〈名〉 bolt of garlic, rape, etc.: 韭～ stalks of Chinese chives ▸蒜～

tài

太 tài

A〈形〉 **1**（高） greatest: ▸～空，～学 **2**（身份高） senior (in generational hierarchy): ～老伯 great-uncle ‖ ～奶奶 great-grandmother ▸～公，～上皇 **3**（久远） remotest: ▸～古
B〈副〉 **1**（表赞叹） so: 那场篮球赛～吸引人了。 That basketball match was spectacular. ‖ 他和他爸爸的性格～像了。His temperament is very like his father's. ‖ 这个小女婴～可爱了。 This baby girl is so adorable. **2**（表程度过分） too: 别～担心。 Don't be overanxious about it. ‖ 你～自信了。 You are too sure of yourself. **3**（用于缓和否定语气） too: 妈妈不～愿意。 Mum is not that keen. ‖ 他今天感觉不～好。 He is not feeling too well today.

【太白星】Tàibáixīng〈古〉= 金星 jīnxīng

【太仓一粟】 tàicāng-yīsù 〈成〉〈喻〉 a drop in the ocean

【太妃】tàifēi〈名〉 imperial concubine of the late emperor

【太妃糖】tàifēitáng〈名〉 toffee

【太公】 tàigōng 〈名〉〈方〉 great-grandfather

【太古】tàigǔ〈名〉 remote antiquity: ～代 Archaean (Era)

【太行山】 Tàihángshān 〈名〉 Taihang Mountains

【太和殿】Tàihédiàn〈名〉 Hall of Supreme Harmony [in the Palace Museum in Beijing]

【太后】tàihòu〈名〉 empress dowager

【太湖】Tàihú ▸**p. 305**〈名〉 Taihu Lake

【太湖石】tàihúshí〈名〉 Taihu rocks

【太极】tàijí〈名〉 Supreme Ultimate

> **太极**
>
> *Taiji* (also *t'ai chi*, 'Supreme Ultimate'), the ultimate origin of the cosmos in Chinese philosophy. According to the *Yijing* (▸《易经》), *Taiji* is the primordial source of activity and creativity from which *yin* and *yang* arise. Philosophers are divided over whether *Taiji* is material or immaterial. A martial arts master in the Qing Dynasty adopted the concepts of *yin* and *yang* to introduce a style of martial arts known as *taijiquan* (太极拳).

【太极拳】 tàijíquán 〈名〉［体育］ *t'ai chi*: 打～ do *t'ai chi*

【太极图】tàijítú〈名〉 yin-yang symbol

【太监】tàijiān〈名〉court eunuch
【太君】tàijūn〈名〉〈旧〉 1（指老夫人）title granted to the mother of a feudal official 2（指日本军人）term forced upon Chinese to address Japanese in occupied areas during Japanese aggression against China
【太空】tàikōng〈名〉(outer) space: ～行走 space walk ‖ ～实验室 spacelab ‖ 向～发射火箭 launch a rocket into outer space
【太空病】tàikōngbìng ▸p. 50〈名〉space sickness
【太空船】tàikōngchuán〈名〉spaceship
【太空服】tàikōngfú〈名〉spacesuit
【太空人】tàikōngrén〈名〉 1（宇航员）astronaut 2（外星人）extraterrestrial being (ET)
【太空时代】tàikōng shídài〈名〉space age
【太空站】tàikōngzhàn〈名〉space station
【太庙】tàimiào〈名〉Imperial Ancestral Temple
【太平】tàipíng〈形〉 1（安定）peaceful and tranquil: ～盛世 times of peace and prosperity ‖ 天下并不～。The world is far from tranquil. 2（平安）safe: ▸～门, ～梯
【太平斧】tàipíngfǔ〈名〉hydrant hatchet
【太平鼓】tàipínggǔ〈名〉 1 ▸p. 929（指乐器）drum with sheepskin membranes stretched over its ends and iron rings attached to its handle, beaten with a long thin drumstick 2（指舞蹈）folk dance in which women beat the drum while dancing
【太平间】tàipíngjiān〈名〉mortuary
【太平门】tàipíngmén〈名〉emergency exit
【太平梯】tàipíngtī〈名〉fire escape
【太平天国】Tàipíng Tiānguó〈名〉［历史］Heavenly Kingdom of Great Peace [1851-1864]
【太平花】tàipínghuā〈名〉［植物］Beijing mock orange
【太平洋】Tàipíngyáng〈名〉Pacific (Ocean): ～战争 War of the Pacific
【太婆】tàipó〈名〉〈方〉great-grandmother
【太上皇】tàishànghuáng〈名〉 1〈本〉title assumed by the reigning emperor's father who abdicated in favour of his son 2〈喻〉overlord
【太师椅】tàishīyǐ〈名〉old-fashioned wooden armchair
【太守】tàishǒu〈名〉〈旧〉prefect
【太岁】tàisuì〈名〉 1（指木星）Master of the Year [ancient name for Jupiter] 2 ▸p. 274（指凶神）God of the Year [legendary god supposed to change his dwelling on earth every year and to allow no construction work where he happens to dwell and presides]: ▸～头上动土 3〈贬〉（指人）local tyrant: 花花～ King of Lechers ‖ 镇山～ brigand chief
【太岁头上动土】tàisuì tóushang dòng tǔ〈俗〉〈喻〉beard the lion in his den
【太太】tàitai〈名〉 1〈旧〉（妻子）wife of an official or officer: 军官～ wife of an officer ‖ 市长～ wife of the mayor 2〈旧〉（女主人）mistress of a household: "是，～。"女佣答道。'Yes, madam,' said the maid. 3〈尊〉（指已婚女子）Mrs: 王/张～ Mrs Wang/Zhang 4（别人的妻子）wife: 你～我见过。I've met your wife. 5〈尊〉（指年长女子）lady: 老～ old lady
【太尉】tàiwèi〈名〉〈旧〉supreme government official in charge of military affairs
【太息】tàixī〈动〉〈书〉heave a deep sigh: 仰天～ look up to heaven and sigh deeply
【太学】tàixué〈名〉〈古〉Imperial College
【太阳】tàiyáng〈名〉 1（指恒星）sun: ～从东方升起。The sun rises in the east. 2（指阳光）sunshine: 晒～ sunbathe ‖ 今天～真好。It's a lovely sunny day.
【太阳风暴】tàiyáng fēngbào〈名〉solar storm
【太阳黑子】tàiyáng hēizǐ〈名〉［天文］sunspot: ～活动 sunspot activity
【太阳镜】tàiyángjìng〈名〉sunglasses
【太阳历】tàiyánglì = 阳历 yánglì
【太阳帽】tàiyángmào〈名〉sun hat
【太阳能】tàiyángnéng〈名〉solar power: ～电池 solar battery ‖ ～发电厂 solar power plant ‖ ～热水器 solar water heater
【太阳年】tàiyángnián = 回归年 huíguīnián
【太阳神】tàiyángshén ▸p. 274〈名〉sun god [used as Apollo, Sol, etc.]
【太阳系】tàiyángxì〈名〉［天文］solar system
【太阳穴】tàiyángxué〈名〉［解剖］temple: 他一拳打在对手的～上。He punched his opponent on the temple.
【太爷】tàiyé〈名〉 1〈方〉（曾祖父）great-grandfather 2〈旧〉（长官）county magistrate: 县～ county magistrate
【太医】tàiyī〈名〉 1（御医）imperial physician 2〈方〉（医生）doctor
【太阴】tàiyīn〈名〉〈方〉moon
【太阴历】tàiyīnlì = 阴历 yīnlì
【太原】Tàiyuán ▸p. 661〈名〉Taiyuan [capital of Shanxi Province (山西)]
【太子】tàizǐ〈名〉crown prince: 立/废～ designate/depose the crown prince
【太子港】Tàizǐgǎng〈名〉Port-au-Prince

汰 tài〈动〉discard: ▸淘～

态（態） tài〈名〉 1（形状）appearance: ▸～度, 固～ 2［语法］voice: 被动/主动～ passive/active voice ▸语～
【态度】tàidu〈名〉 1（举止神情）manner: ～和蔼可亲 have a kind manner ‖ ～温和 mild-mannered ‖ 耍～ get into a huff 2（看法、行为）attitude: 保持良好的工作～ maintain a good work attitude ‖ 持观望～ take a wait-and-see attitude ‖ 端正学习～ take a correct attitude towards one's studies ‖ ～暧昧 sit on the fence ‖ ～坚决 take a firm stance
【态势】tàishì〈名〉state: 分析～ size up a situation ‖ 扭转被动～ put an end to the passive state of affairs

肽 tài〈名〉［化学］peptide

钛（鈦） tài〈名〉［化学］titanium (Ti): ～箔 titanium foil ‖ ～合金 titanium alloy

泰 tài
A〈形〉 1（平安）safe: ▸～然自若, 国～民安 2〈书〉（最）extreme: ▸～西
B〈副〉〈书〉excessively: 简略～甚 overly concise
【泰斗】tàidǒu〈名〉〈喻〉leading authority: 京剧～ foremost actor of Beijing opera ‖ 文坛～ lord of the literary world
【泰恩－威尔郡】Tài'ēn-Wēi'ěrjùn〈名〉Tyne and Wear
【泰国】Tàiguó〈名〉Thailand: ～人 Thai
【泰姬陵】Tàijīlíng〈名〉Taj Mahal
【泰拳】tàiquán〈名〉Thai boxing
【泰然】tàirán〈形〉self-possessed: ～处之 take sth. calmly
【泰然自若】tàirán-zìruò〈成〉be composed and calm: 当时我表面上还～，心里却很焦急。Calm as I appeared, I was very anxious at the time.
【泰山】Tàishān〈名〉 1〈本〉Mount Tai; 〈喻〉symbol of great weight or importance: 死或重于～，或轻于鸿毛。Death could either be of great importance or completely insignificant. ▸有眼不识～ 2（岳父）father-in-law
【泰山北斗】Tàishān-Běidǒu〈成〉〈喻〉leading authority: 中国科学界之～ foremost scientist in China
【泰山压顶】Tàishān-yādǐng〈成〉〈喻〉create overwhelming pressure: ～不弯腰 not yield to any pressure
【泰晤士报】Tàiwùshìbào〈名〉*The Times* [UK newspaper]
【泰晤士河】Tàiwùshìhé ▸p. 294〈名〉The Thames (River)
【泰西】Tàixī〈名〉〈旧〉West: ～各国 Western countries
【泰语】Tàiyǔ ▸p. 918〈名〉Thai
【泰铢】tàizhū ▸p. 328〈量〉Baht [unit of currency in Thailand]

酞 tài〈名〉［化学］phthalein

tān

坍 tān〈动〉collapse: 地震将一些建筑物震～了。The earthquake toppled a number of buildings. ‖ 墙随时会～。The wall is likely to collapse at any time. ▸～塌, ～陷
【坍方】tānfāng = 塌方 tāfāng
【坍缩】tānsuō〈动〉[of a celestial body] shrink
【坍塌】tāntā〈动〉collapse: 大桥被山洪冲得～了。The bridge gave way under the mountain torrents. ‖ 窑顶～了。The kiln caved in.
【坍台】tāntái〈动〉〈方〉 1（垮台）fold: 没有名演员，剧团就要～。Without eminent actors the troupe is likely to fold. 2（丢脸）lose face: 当众～ make a spectacle of oneself in public
【坍陷】tānxiàn〈动〉sink: 地基～了。The foundations have subsided.

贪（貪） tān〈动〉 1（寻求）hanker after: ～安逸 seek ease and comfort ‖ ～小利 hanker after petty gains ▸～财, ～恋, ～生怕死 2（贪污）embezzle: 倡廉肃～ promote honest and clean government and eliminate corruption ▸～官污吏, ～污 3（贪图）have an insatiable desire: ～女色 be a womanizer ▸～得无厌, ～婪
【贪杯】tānbēi ▸p. 772〈动〉be excessively fond of drinking: 好酒～ take to drink
【贪财】tāncái〈动〉be greedy for money: ～丧生 lose one's life in the pursuit of wealth
【贪大求全】tāndà-qiúquán〈成〉go in for grandiose projects
【贪得无厌】tāndé-wúyàn〈成〉have an insatiable greed: 你越迁就他，他越～。The more you give in to him, the greedier he will get.
【贪多嚼不烂】tānduō jiáo bù làn〈俗〉bite off more than one can chew
【贪官】tānguān〈名〉corrupt official
【贪官污吏】tānguān-wūlì〈成〉corrupt officials: 严惩～ mete out severe punishment to corrupt officials
【贪贿】tānhuì〈动〉bribe greedily: ～数额巨大 demand an extortionate bribe
【贪婪】tānlán〈形〉 1〈贬〉（贪得无厌）

avaricious: ～的目光 voracious gaze ‖ ～成性 be greedy by nature **2**（渴求） greedy: ～地汲取知识 have an insatiable appetite for learning
【贪恋】tānliàn〈动〉 feel reluctant to part with: ～舒适的生活 be reluctant to give up a life of comfort
【贪墨】tānmò〈动〉〈书〉 embezzle
【贪念】tānniàn〈名〉 covetous thoughts: 不要对别人的钱财起～。 Never covet the wealth of others
【贪便宜】tān piányi〈动〉 be keen on gaining petty advantages: 贪小便宜吃大亏 gain petty advantages only to suffer heavy losses
【贪求】tānqiú〈动〉 seek: ～安逸 seek ease and comfort ‖ ～富贵 covet wealth and power
【贪权】tānquán〈动〉 covet power
【贪色】tānsè〈动〉 be a womanizer
【贪生怕死】tānshēng-pàsǐ〈成〉 cravenly cling to life instead of braving death
【贪天之功】tāntiānzhīgōng〈成〉 claim credit for other people's achievements
【贪图】tāntú〈动〉 covet: ～安逸 seek ease and comfort ‖ ～钱财 seek wealth ‖ ～享乐 seek a life of pleasure
【贪玩】tānwán〈动〉 be excessively fond of having a good time
【贪污】tānwū〈动〉 embezzle: ～公款 embezzle public funds ‖ ～受贿 embezzle money and take bribes ‖ ～分子 embezzler
【贪污犯】tānwūfàn〈名〉 embezzler
【贪污腐化】tānwū-fǔhuà〈成〉 corruption and degeneration
【贪小】tānxiǎo〈动〉 seek petty gains: ～失大 seek small gains but incur big losses
【贪心】tānxīn **A**〈名〉 greed: ～不足 be insatiably greedy **B**〈形〉 greedy
【贪欲】tānyù〈名〉 avarice
【贪赃】tānzāng〈动〉 take bribes
【贪赃枉法】tānzāng-wǎngfǎ〈成〉 take bribes and stretch the law
【贪占】tānzhàn〈动〉 embezzle: ～公款 embezzle public funds
【贪嘴】tānzuǐ〈动〉 have a voracious appetite

摊（攤）tān

A〈动〉 **1**（铺平） spread out: 禁止在公路上～晒麦子。 It is forbidden to spread wheat out to dry on highways. ‖ 他的工具～了一地。 His tools were strewn all over the floor. ▸～场, ～牌 **2**（分担） share: 领导分～了责任。 The leadership shared the responsibility. ‖ 每村需～十个工日。 Each village will have to contribute 10 workdays. ▸～派, 分～, 均～ **3**（碰到） befall: 这么倒霉的事怎么～到我们头上了! Why has such an unfortunate thing happened to us! **4**（指烹调方法） fry a thin layer of batter : ～煎饼 make pancakes ▸～鸡蛋 **B**〈名〉 stall: 水果～ fruit stand ‖ 书报～ news-stand ▸地～ **C**〈量〉 [for paste or thick liquid]: 一～水/血 a pool of water/blood ‖ 一～泥 a mud puddle
【摊薄】tānbáo〈动〉 spread thinly
【摊场】tāncháng〈动〉 spread grain that has just been gathered on a threshing ground
【摊点】tāndiǎn〈名〉 stall: 设～ set up a stand ‖ 流动～ mobile stall
【摊贩】tānfàn〈名〉 street vendor: 流动～ mobile street vendor ‖ 无证～ unlicensed street pedlar
【摊鸡蛋】tānjīdàn〈名〉 omelette
【摊开】tānkāi〈动〉 unfold: 他把书～放在书桌上。 He laid the book open on the desk.
【摊牌】tānpái〈动〉〈喻〉 lay one's cards on the table: 末了，他们只得～。 In the end, they had to lay their cards on the table.
【摊派】tānpài〈动〉 apportion: ～费用 apportion expenses ‖ ～任务 apportion tasks (to sb.)
【摊售】tānshòu〈动〉 sell goods
【摊位】tānwèi〈名〉 stall: 集市～ market stall ‖ 书展上有很多～。 There were many stands at the book fair.
【摊位费】tānwèifèi〈名〉 **1**（指市场） stall fee **2**（指会展） booth fee
【摊主】tānzhǔ〈名〉 stall owner
【摊子】tānzi〈名〉 **1**（铺子） stall: 旧书～ second-hand bookstall ‖ 他靠在集市上摆～过活。 He made a living by running a stand at the bazaar. **2**〈喻〉（局面） set-up: 他们错在把～铺得过大。 Their mistake was that they tried to go about it on too large a scale. ▸烂～

滩（灘）tān〈名〉

1（指水流急） shoal: 急流险～ rapids and shoals **2**（指水浅） beach: ▸～地, 海～, 沙～
【滩地】tāndì〈名〉 beach (by lake, along river)
【滩簧】tānhuáng〈名〉［曲艺］ *tanhuang* [a kind of storytelling in rhymes popular in southern Jiangsu and northern Zhejiang provinces]
【滩头】tāntóu〈名〉 beach: ～阵地 beachhead position
【滩涂】tāntú〈名〉 tidal land
【滩羊】tānyáng〈名〉 a kind of sheep known for its fine pelt

瘫（癱）tān〈动〉

1（瘫痪） be paralysed: 他完全～了。 He was completely paralysed. ▸截～, 偏～ **2**（瘫软） become weak: 吓～了 be paralysed with fright ‖ 他累得一回家就～在床上。 He was so tired that he threw himself in bed as soon as he returned home. ▸～软
【瘫痪】tānhuàn〈动〉 **1**（指身体） be paralysed: ～病人 paralytic ‖ 他下肢～。 He is paralysed from the waist down. **2**〈喻〉（指组织、系统等） break down: 工厂因罢工而陷入～。 The factory was paralysed by the strike. ‖ 交通陷于～。 Traffic had come to a standstill.
【瘫软】tānruǎn〈动〉 become weak and limp: 浑身～ feel weak all over ‖ 两腿～ feel weak in one's legs
【瘫子】tānzi〈名〉 paralytic

tán

坛[1]（壇）tán〈名〉

1（指高台） altar: ▸祭～, 天～ **2**（指平台） raised plot of land for planting flowers, etc.: ▸花～ **3**（指领域） circles: ▸棋～, 体～, 文～ **4**（指讲演台） forum: ▸讲～, 论～ **5**（指组织） organization set up by a secret society to worship gods in a rally

坛[2]（罎）tán〈名〉

earthenware jar: 酒～ wine jug ‖ 一～泡菜 a jar of pickles
【坛坛罐罐】tántán-guànguàn〈成〉 personal belongings: 橱柜里塞满了各式各样的～。 The cupboards are stacked with all sorts of things.
【坛子】tánzi〈名〉 earthenware jar: ▸醋～

昙[1]（曇）tán〈名〉〈书〉

thick clouds: ～～ overcast with clouds

昙[2]（曇）tán ▸昙花 tánhuā

【昙花】tánhuā〈名〉［植物］ broad-leaved epiphyllum
【昙花一现】tánhuā-yīxiàn〈成〉〈喻〉 be a flash in the pan: ～的人物 transient figure

谈（談）tán

A〈动〉 talk: ～正事 talk business ‖ 他跟我～过此事。 He spoke to me about this. ‖ 咱们边喝茶边～。 Let's talk over a cup of tea. ▸～话, ～判, 会～ **B**〈名〉 remark: ▸街～巷议, 奇～, 笑～
【谈柄】tánbǐng〈名〉 laughing stock: 传为～ become a standing joke
【谈不来】tánbulái〈动〉 not get along well (with sb.)
【谈不拢】tánbulǒng〈动〉 not agree with each other
【谈不上】tánbushàng〈动〉 be out of the question: 离开了稳定，就～改革开放。 Without stability, reform and opening up would be out of the question. ‖ 若果真如此，其他一切都～了。 If so, what's the point of talking about anything else?
【谈得来】tándelái〈动〉 get along well (with sb.)
【谈锋】tánfēng〈名〉 eloquence: ～甚健 be a good talker
【谈古论今】tángǔ-lùnjīn〈成〉 talk about the past and the present
【谈何容易】tánhé-róngyì〈成〉 it is easier said than done
【谈虎色变】tánhǔ-sèbiàn〈成〉〈喻〉 get anxious at the mere mention of sth. scary
【谈话】tánhuà **A**〈动〉 talk: 我无意中听到了他们的～。 I inadvertently overheard what they were saying. ‖ 老师要找你～。 The teacher wants to talk to you. **B**〈名〉 statement: 外交部发言人就中美关系发表～。 The spokesperson of the Foreign Ministry issued a statement on Sino-US relations.
【谈恋爱】tán liàn'ài〈动〉 court: 你们俩在～吗? Are you two going out? ‖ 他俩谈了四年恋爱才决定结婚。 They had been dating for four years before they decided to get married.
【谈论】tánlùn〈动〉 discuss: ～国家大事 discuss state affairs ‖ ～往事 talk about the old days
【谈判】tánpàn〈动〉 negotiate: 与某人～ negotiate with sb. ‖ 恢复～ resume talks ‖ 贸易～ trade talks ‖ 通过～达成协议 negotiate an agreement ‖ ～破裂/失败。 The negotiations broke down/failed.
【谈情说爱】tánqíng-shuō'ài〈成〉 be dating: 这是年轻人～的地方。 This is a place where young people come on dates.
【谈天】tántiān〈动〉 chat
【谈天说地】tántiān-shuōdì〈成〉 chat: 我们坐在茶馆里～。 We sat around in the teahouse, chatting about this and that.
【谈吐】tántǔ〈名〉 conversational style: ～不俗 have an elegant style of conversation ‖ ～优雅 have a refined way of talking
【谈笑风生】tánxiào-fēngshēng〈成〉 talk and laugh cheerfully
【谈笑自若】tánxiào-zìruò〈成〉 keep talking and laughing as if nothing had happened: 沉着镇静，～ go on talking and laughing without turning a hair ‖ 临危不惧，～ talk and laugh imperturbably in face of danger

t

【谈心】tánxīn〈动〉 have a *tête-à-tête*: 促膝～ have a heart-to-heart talk

【谈兴】tánxìng〈名〉 mood for conversation: ～正浓 talk in an animated way

【谈言微中】tányán-wēizhòng〈成〉 speak with tact but to the point

【谈资】tánzī〈名〉 topic of conversation

弹（彈） tán〈动〉 **1**（弹射） catapult: 用弹弓～石子 shoot pebbles with a catapult ‖ 盒子～开了。The box sprang open. ▸～射 **2**（弹掉） flick: ～烟灰 flick ash from a cigarette ‖ 他～掉袖子上的土。He flicked the dust off his sleeve. ▸～冠相庆 **3**（演奏） play: ～钢琴 play the piano ‖ ～琵琶 pluck the *pipa* ▸～奏，对牛～琴 **4**（抨击） accuse: ▸～劾 **5**（有弹性） be elastic: ▸～簧，～力，～性 **6**（使松软） tease: ～棉花 fluff cotton ▸dàn

【弹拨乐器】tánbō yuèqì〈名〉 stringed instrument

【弹唱】tánchàng〈动〉 sing while playing a stringed instrument

【弹词】táncí〈名〉［曲艺］ **1**（指曲艺形式） *tanci* [storytelling to the accompaniment of stringed instruments and drums] **2**（指底本） script for *tanci*

【弹冠相庆】tánguān-xiāngqìng〈成〉 congratulate each other on the prospect of getting good appointments

【弹劾】tánhé〈动〉 **1**（指君主时代） report on the crimes of officials **2**（指议会） impeach: 国会成功地～了总统。The Congress successfully impeached the President.

【弹花机】tánhuājī〈名〉 cotton fluffer

【弹簧】tánhuáng〈名〉 spring

【弹簧秤】tánhuángchèng〈名〉 spring balance

【弹簧床】tánhuángchuáng〈名〉 spring bed

【弹簧刀】tánhuángdāo〈名〉 flick knife〈英〉; switchblade〈美〉

【弹簧夹】tánhuángjiā〈名〉 spring clip

【弹簧门】tánhuángmén〈名〉 swing door

【弹簧锁】tánhuángsuǒ〈名〉 spring lock

【弹力】tánlì〈名〉elasticity: 这根橡皮筋已失去～。The stretch has gone out of the rubber band.

【弹力裤】tánlìkù〈名〉 stretch pants

【弹力袜】tánlìwà〈名〉 stretch sock

【弹琴】tánqín〈动〉 play stringed musical instruments

【弹射】tánshè〈动〉 **1**（射出） shoot out: ～器 ejector **2**〈书〉（指摘） find fault with: ～时弊 criticize present-day social evils and malpractices

【弹射座椅】tánshè zuòyǐ〈名〉［航空］ ejector seat

【弹跳】tántiào〈动〉 bounce: ～力 bounce capacity

【弹性】tánxìng〈名〉 **1**（指恢复原状） elasticity: ～绷带 stretchy bandage ‖ ～好的跳板 springboard with a lot of give ‖ 运动员的肌肉有～。The sportsman's muscles were very springy. **2**〈喻〉（灵活性） flexibility: ～工资 flexible pay ‖ ～外交 flexible/elastic diplomacy ‖ 这些标准～太大，操作有困难。These criteria are too broad to handle.

【弹性碰撞】tánxìng pèngzhuàng〈名〉［物理］ elastic collision

【弹压】tányā〈动〉 quell

【弹指】tánzhǐ〈动〉〈书〉〈喻〉 [of time] pass quickly: ～之间 in the twinkling of an eye

【弹奏】tánzòu〈动〉 **1**（演奏） play: ～钢琴 play the piano ‖ ～一支曲子 play a tune **2**〈书〉（指检举） impeach an official

覃 tán〈形〉〈书〉 profound: ～思 be deep in thought

痰 tán〈名〉 phlegm: 吐～ spit ‖ ～中带血 with blood in the sputum

【痰气】tánqì〈名〉〈方〉 **1**（精神病） mental disorder **2**（中风） apoplexy

【痰桶】tántǒng〈名〉〈口〉 spittoon

【痰盂】tányú〈名〉 spittoon

谭（譚） tán〈古〉= 谈 tán

潭 tán〈名〉 **1**（深水池） deep pool: 深～ deep pond ▸龙～虎穴 **2**〈方〉（坑） pit: ▸泥～

【潭府】tánfǔ〈名〉〈书〉 **1**（深水池） deep pool **2**〈尊〉（指住宅） your house

檀 tán〈名〉［植物］ sandalwood: ▸紫～

【檀板】tánbǎn〈名〉 hardwood clappers (used for keeping rhythm in Chinese operas)

【檀香】tánxiāng〈名〉［植物］ white sandalwood: ～扇 sandalwood fan

【檀香木】tánxiāngmù〈名〉 sandalwood

【檀香皂】tánxiāngzào〈名〉 sandalwood soap

【檀香山】Tánxiāngshān〈名〉 Honolulu

【檀越】tányuè〈名〉［佛教］ [used by a Buddhist monk or nun to address a lay person] benefactor

tǎn

忐 tǎn

【忐忑】tǎntè〈形〉 perturbed: ～不安 restless

坦 tǎn〈形〉 **1**（平而宽） broad and level: ▸～途，平～ **2**（安定） calm: ▸～然，舒～ **3**（坦白） straightforward: ▸～白，～率

【坦白】tǎnbái **A**〈形〉 straightforward: 胸怀～ open-hearted ‖ 让我～地告诉你 let me tell you frankly **B**〈动〉 confess: ～自首 give oneself up ‖ ～从宽，抗拒从严 leniency to those who confess their crimes and severity to those who refuse to

【坦陈】tǎnchén〈动〉 state frankly: ～自己的观点 state one's views frankly

【坦称】tǎnchēng〈动〉 state frankly

【坦承】tǎnchéng〈动〉 acknowledge frankly: 她～自己想结婚了。She was very straight about wanting to get married.

【坦诚】tǎnchéng〈形〉 open and sincere: ～相见 be open and sincere with sb. ‖ ～的话语 candid remarks ‖ 他为人～。He is frank with people.

【坦荡】tǎndàng〈形〉 **1**（平坦广阔） broad and level: ～的马路 wide and smooth road **2**（胸怀宽阔） magnanimous: 胸怀～ have largeness of mind ‖ 君子坦荡荡，小人长戚戚。The gentleman is easy of mind, while the petty man is always full of anxiety.

【坦缓】tǎnhuǎn〈形〉 [of land] level

【坦克】tǎnkè〈名〉 tank: 两栖～ amphibious tank ‖ 轻型/重型～ light/heavy tank

【坦克兵】tǎnkèbīng = 装甲兵 zhuāngjiǎbīng

【坦克车】tǎnkèchē = 坦克 tǎnkè

【坦克手】tǎnkèshǒu〈名〉 tank soldier

【坦露】tǎnlù〈动〉 express frankly: 真情～ express one's true feelings openly

【坦然】tǎnrán〈形〉 calm: 神色～ look unperturbed ‖ ～自若 completely at ease

【坦桑尼亚】Tǎnsāngníyà〈名〉 Tanzania: ～人 Tanzanian

【坦率】tǎnshuài〈形〉 candid: ～地说 to put it bluntly ‖ 他说话很～。He is rather blunt in speech. ‖ 她是个～的人。She is a frank person.

【坦途】tǎntú〈名〉 smooth road:〈喻〉人生无～。No one's life is without twists and turns.

【坦言】tǎnyán **A**〈动〉 speak candidly: 他～是他的错。He was candid enough to admit his mistake. **B**〈名〉 honest words: ～相告 to be honest with you

【坦直】tǎnzhí〈形〉 **1**（指人） candid: 为人～ be an outspoken person **2**（指道路） smooth and straight

【坦挚】tǎnzhì〈形〉 frank and open

钽（鉭） tǎn〈名〉［化学］ tantalum (Ta)

袒 tǎn〈动〉 **1**（露出） be stripped to the waist: ▸～露 **2**（袒护） shield: ▸～护，偏～

【袒护】tǎnhù〈动〉 shield: 家长～孩子是没有好处的。Parents who shield their children are not doing them any good. ‖ 他竟公开～违纪者。He openly shielded the offender.

【袒露】tǎnlù〈动〉 expose: 袒胸露背 be décolleté ‖〈喻〉 ～心声 reveal one's innermost thoughts

毯 tǎn〈名〉 blanket, rug, carpet: 飞～ flying carpet ‖ 魔～ magic carpet ‖ 军用～ army blanket ▸壁～，地～，毛～

【毯子】tǎnzi〈名〉 blanket, rug, carpet: 地板上铺着～。The floor is covered with a carpet.

tàn

叹（嘆、歎） tàn〈动〉 **1**（叹气） sigh in lament: 一声长～ heave a long sigh ▸～气，哀～ **2**（吟咏） chant: ▸咏～ **3**（赞美） exclaim in admiration: ～为奇观 acclaim sth. as a wonder ▸～服，赞～

【叹词】tàncí〈名〉［语法］ exclamation

【叹服】tànfú〈动〉 gasp in admiration: 令人～ command admiration

【叹号】tànhào〈名〉［语法］ exclamation mark

【叹绝】tànjué〈动〉〈书〉 acclaim sth. to be the best: 令人～ impress as the best

【叹气】tànqì〈动〉 heave a sigh: 他伤心地叹了一口气，转身走了。With a sigh of sadness, he turned and left. ▸唉声～

【叹赏】tànshǎng〈动〉 express admiration: ～不绝 praise profusely

【叹惋】tànwǎn〈动〉〈书〉 sigh with regret

【叹为观止】tànwéi-guānzhǐ〈成〉 acclaim sth. to be the best

【叹息】tànxī〈动〉 heave a sigh: 为自己的不幸/失败而～ sigh over one's misfortune/failure

【叹惜】tànxī〈动〉 sigh with regret: 为失

t

去大好机会而～。 sigh with regret over lost opportunities

炭 tàn

〈名〉 **1**（木炭） charcoal: ►木～ **2**〈方〉（煤） coal: ►焦～，煤～ **3**（炭状物） coal-like substance: 山楂～ hawthorn charcoal

【炭棒】 tànbàng〈名〉 carbon rod

【炭笔】 tànbǐ〈名〉 charcoal pencil: ～素描 charcoal sketch

【炭黑】 tànhēi〈名〉［化工］(carbon) black

【炭化】 tànhuà〈动〉 carbonize

【炭画】 tànhuà〈名〉［美术］ charcoal drawing

【炭火】 tànhuǒ〈名〉 charcoal fire

【炭精】 tànjīng〈名〉 **1**（炭制品） charcoal products **2**〈方〉（人造炭和石墨） artificial charcoal and graphite

【炭疽】 tànjū ►**p. 50**〈名〉［医学］anthrax: 牛～ anthrax of cattle ‖ 皮肤～ cutaneous anthrax ‖ ～病 anthracnose

【炭盆】 tànpén〈名〉 charcoal brazier

【炭窑】 tànyáo〈名〉 charcoal kiln

探 tàn

A〈动〉 **1**（用手摸取） dip one's hand into sth.: 他把手～进口袋，摸出一把糖来。 He dipped his hand into his pocket and fished out a handful of sweets. ►～囊取物 **2**（探寻） try to find out: ►～测，钻～ **3**（刺探） pry into: ～秘密 pry into sb.'s secrets ‖ ～情况 try to find out about the situation ►刺～，窥～ **4**（看望） visit: ►～病，～监，～亲 **5**（伸出） stretch forward: ►～身

B〈名〉 detective: ►暗～，敌～，密～

【探案】 tàn'àn〈动〉 investigate a case: ～小说 detective story

【探本穷源】 tànběn-qióngyuán〈成〉 get to the root of the matter

【探本溯源】 tànběn-sùyuán = 探本穷源 tànběn-qióngyuán

【探病】 tànbìng〈动〉 visit a sick person

【探测】 tàncè〈动〉 survey: ～地雷 detect a mine ‖ ～石油储量 survey for petroleum deposits ‖ 高空～ aerial survey ‖〈喻〉～某人的想法 probe sb.'s mind

【探测器】 tàncèqì〈名〉 detector: 月球～ lunar probe ‖ 电子～ electronic detector

【探查】 tànchá〈动〉 probe: ～敌情 gather intelligence about the enemy ‖ ～事故原因 look into an accident ‖ ～胃部肿瘤 examine a stomach tumour

【探察】 tànchá〈动〉 survey: ～地形 survey the terrain ‖ 实地～ make an on-the-spot investigation

【探访】 tànfǎng〈动〉 **1**（寻访） seek out: ～丢失孩子的下落 inquire into the whereabouts of the lost child **2**（拜访） visit: ～亲友 visit one's relatives and friends

【探风】 tànfēng〈动〉 fish for information

【探戈】 tàngē〈名〉 tango

【探花】 tànhuā〈名〉〈古〉 *tanhua* [title conferred on the third-place winner in the highest imperial examination in the Ming and Qing dynasties]

【探家】 tànjiā〈动〉 make a brief trip home

【探监】 tànjiān〈动〉 visit a prisoner

【探井】 tànjǐng〈名〉 **1**［矿业］ test pit **2**［石油］ exploratory well

【探究】 tànjiū〈动〉 probe into: ～原因 explore the causes ‖ ～战争根源 probe the roots of war

【探看】 tànkàn〈动〉 pay a visit to: ～病人 visit a patient

【探空】 tànkōng〈名〉［气象］ sounding: ～气球 sounding balloon

【探空仪】 tànkōngyí〈名〉［气象］ sonde: 雷达～ radar sonde

【探口风】 tàn kǒufēng = 探口气 tàn kǒuqi

【探口气】 tàn kǒuqi〈惯〉 sound sb. out: 让我们先探探他的口气。 Let's sound him out about it first.

【探矿】 tànkuàng〈动〉 prospect: 探金矿 prospect for gold

【探雷】 tànléi〈动〉 detect a mine: ～器 mine detector

【探骊得珠】 tànlí-dézhū〈成〉 [of writing] bring out the important points from amongst a mass of facts

【探路】 tànlù〈动〉 explore the way

【探马】 tànmǎ〈名〉〈旧〉 mounted scout

【探秘】 tànmì〈动〉 explore the mysteries: 太空～ exploration of space mysteries

【探明】 tànmíng〈动〉 **1**（指打听） find out: ～敌人的虚实 find out the true situation of the enemy **2**（指勘探） ascertain: ～煤储量 ascertain coal deposits

【探囊取物】 tànnáng-qǔwù〈成〉〈喻〉 as easy as falling off a log

【探亲】 tànqīn〈动〉 go home to see one's relatives: 回乡～ go home to see one's relatives ‖ ～假 home leave

【探亲流】 tànqīnliú〈名〉 flow of people travelling to visit their relatives: ～高峰期 peak season to visit relatives

【探求】 tànqiú〈动〉 pursue: ～人生真谛 search for the true meaning of life ‖ ～宇宙奥秘 explore the secrets of the universe

【探伤】 tànshāng〈动〉［冶金］ detect a flaw: ～仪 flaw detector

【探身】 tànshēn〈动〉 lean forward: ～窗外 lean out of the window

【探胜】 tànshèng〈动〉〈书〉 make an excursion to scenic spots

【探视】 tànshì〈动〉 **1**（看望） visit: ～病人 visit a patient **2**（察看） watch: 向窗外～ look out of the window

【探索】 tànsuǒ〈动〉 explore: ～大自然的奥秘 explore the secrets of nature ‖ 他们在～解决问题的新办法。 They are groping for a new solution to the problem.

【探讨】 tàntǎo〈动〉 inquire into: 我们～了几种解决问题的方法。 We explored several solutions to the problem. ‖ 这一领域中有许多问题还没有人～过。 Much of this field is still unexplored.

【探听】 tàntīng〈动〉 sound sb. out: ～消息 fish for information ‖ ～虚实 try to sound out the other party's position ‖ 我去～一下。 I'll go and make some investigations.

【探头】 tàntóu **A**〈动〉 crane one's neck: ～张望 crane one's neck and look around ‖ ～探脑 pop one's head in and look around **B**〈名〉［电子］ probe: 安装～ install a probe

【探望】 tànwàng〈动〉 **1**（张望） look in order to find out: 四处～ look around ‖ 他不时向窗外～。 He looked out of the window every now and then. **2**（看望） visit: ～住院病人 visit the sick in hospital ‖ 回乡～亲友 return home and visit one's relatives and friends

【探问】 tànwèn〈动〉 **1**（询问） sound sb. out: ～失踪儿童的下落 enquire about the whereabouts of missing children ‖ ～对方的意图 sound out the intentions of the other party **2**（看望问候） visit: ～病人 visit a sick person

【探析】 tànxī〈动〉 explore and analyse

【探悉】 tànxī〈动〉 ascertain: 从有关方面～ learn from those concerned

【探险】 tànxiǎn〈动〉 explore: 去北极～ explore the Arctic regions ‖ ～队 expedition ‖ ～家 explorer

【探寻】 tànxún〈动〉 search for: ～矿藏 prospect for mineral deposits ‖ ～人生真谛 search for the true meaning of life ‖ ～真理 seek truth

【探询】 tànxún = 探问 tànwèn

【探幽】 tànyōu〈动〉〈书〉 **1**（指道理） delve into the abstruse **2**（指地方） look for scenic spots

【探月】 tànyuè〈动〉 go on a lunar probe

【探赜索隐】 tànzé-suǒyǐn〈成〉 unravel mysteries

【探照灯】 tànzhàodēng〈名〉 searchlight: ～灯光 searchlight beam

【探针】 tànzhēn〈名〉 probing pin: 离子～ ion probe

【探知】 tànzhī〈动〉 learn

【探子】 tànzi〈名〉〈旧〉 **1**（指人） scout **2**（指用具） thin tube used to extract samples of food grains, etc.

碳 tàn

〈名〉［化学］ carbon (C): ～同位素 carbon isotope

【碳电极】 tàndiànjí〈名〉［电气］ carbon electrode

【碳关税】 tànguānshuì〈名〉 carbon tariff

【碳黑】 tànhēi〈名〉［化学］ carbon black

【碳弧】 tànhú〈名〉［电气］ carbon arc: ～切割 carbon arc cutting ‖ ～灯 carbon arc lamp

【碳化】 tànhuà〈动〉 carbonize: ～物 carbide

【碳截存】 tànjiécún〈名〉 carbon sequestration

【碳排放】 tànpáifàng〈名〉 carbon dioxide emissions

【碳氢化合物】 tànqīng huàhéwù〈名〉［化学］ hydrocarbon

【碳融资】 tànróngzī〈名〉 carbon financing: 世行～基金 World Bank Carbon Fund

【碳14断代法】 tàn-shísì duàndàifǎ〈名〉［考古］ carbon dating

【碳刷】 tànshuā〈名〉［电气］carbon brush

【碳水化合物】 tànshuǐ huàhéwù〈名〉［化学］ carbohydrate

【碳丝】 tànsī〈名〉［电气］ carbon filament: ～灯 carbon lamp

【碳素钢】 tànsùgāng〈名〉［冶金］ carbon steel

【碳素墨水】 tànsù mòshuǐ〈名〉 high carbonic ink

【碳酸】 tànsuān〈名〉［化学］carbonic acid

【碳酸钙】 tànsuāngài〈名〉 calcium carbonate

【碳酸镁】 tànsuānměi〈名〉magnesium carbonate

【碳酸钠】 tànsuānnà〈名〉 sodium carbonate, soda

【碳酸气】 tànsuānqì = 二氧化碳 èryǎnghuàtàn

【碳酸氢氨】 tànsuānqīng'ān〈名〉 ammonium hydrogen carbonate

【碳酸氢钠】 tànsuānqīngnà〈名〉 sodium bicarbonate

【碳酸盐】 tànsuānyán〈名〉 carbonate

【碳纤维】 tànxiānwéi〈名〉 carbon fibre

tāng

汤（湯） tāng

〈名〉 **1**（开水） boiling water: ►赴～蹈火 **2**（指药液） decoction of Chinese medicine: 当归补血～ Chinese angelica decoction for replenishing the blood ►～剂，换～不换药 **3**（菜汤）

t

soup: 牛肉～ beef broth ‖ 浓～ thick soup ‖ 酸辣～ sour and spicy soup ▸菜～, 高～ 4 (煮食物的水) water in which sth. has been boiled: 饺子～ *jiaozi* water ▸面～ ▸shāng

【汤包】tāngbāo〈名〉 steamed dumplings filled with juicy meat

【汤池】tāngchí〈名〉 1 (护城河) city moat: ▸金城～ 2 (浴池) hot water bathing pool (in a public bath-house) 3 (温泉) hot spring

【汤匙】tāngchí〈名〉 tablespoon

【汤锅】tāngguō〈名〉 1 (指大锅) butcher's cauldron in a slaughterhouse 2 (指屠宰场) slaughterhouse

【汤壶】tānghú〈名〉 metal, earthenware or plastic hot-water bottle for warming up a bed

【汤剂】tāngjì〈名〉[中医] decoction of herbal medicine

【汤加】Tāngjiā〈名〉 Tonga: ～人 Tongan ‖ ～语 Tongan

【汤料】tāngliào〈名〉 soup stock: 浓缩～ concentrated soup

【汤面】tāngmiàn〈名〉 noodles in soup

【汤婆子】tāngpózi〈方〉= 汤壶 tānghú

【汤泉】tāngquán〈名〉〈古〉 hot spring

【汤勺】tāngsháo〈名〉 soup ladle

【汤水】tāngshuǐ〈名〉 1 (指汤) soup 2〈方〉(指水) boiling water

【汤头】tāngtóu〈名〉[中药] prescription for a medical decoction: ～歌诀 prescriptions in rhyme

【汤团】tāngtuán = 汤圆 tāngyuán

【汤药】tāngyào〈名〉[中药] decoction of medicinal ingredients: 服～ take a decoction of Chinese medicinal herbs

【汤圆】tāngyuán〈名〉 sweet dumplings made of glutinous rice flour served in the water they are boiled in

> **汤圆**
>
> Round dumplings, traditionally eaten on the 15th day of the new lunar year, and known as *yuanxiao* (元宵) in north China (▸元宵节). They symbolize reunion and success. The dumplings are made of glutinous rice, and contain a sweet or savoury filling. They are usually boiled in water. Southern dumplings are made by adding a filling to a ball of dough. Northern dumplings are made by putting damp fillings into dry glutinous rice flour, and shaking the flour until the fillings are covered and a ball has formed. These kind of dumplings are known as '*shaken yuanxiao*' (摇元宵).

耥 tāng〈动〉 weed and loosen the soil (in a paddy field): 把地～平 rake the soil smooth

【耥耙】tāngbà〈名〉 paddy-field harrow

嘡（鏜） tāng〈拟〉 clang: ～～敲钟 clang a bell

趟（蹚） tāng〈动〉 1 (走过浅水) wade: ～水过河 wade across a river ‖ 在草地上～出一条路 tread a path across the grass 2 (翻地除草) turn the soil and dig up weeds: ～地 turn the soil and weed ▸tàng

【趟道】tāngdào〈动〉〈喻〉 try to find out about a situation

【趟浑水】tāng húnshuǐ〈惯〉〈喻〉 follow sb.'s example in doing evil

【趟路】tānglù = 趟道 tāngdào

羰 tāng〈名〉[化学] carbonyl

táng

饧（餳） táng〈书〉= 糖 táng ▸xíng

唐¹ táng〈形〉 boastful: ▸荒～

唐² Táng〈名〉 1 (指上古时期) dynasty established by Emperor Yao (尧): ～虞之世 time of Emperor Yao (唐帝尧) and Emperor Shun (虞帝舜) 2 (唐朝) Tang Dynasty: ▸～三彩 3 (后唐) Later Tang Dynasty

【唐古拉山】Tánggǔlāshān〈名〉 Tanggula Mountains

【唐花】tánghuā〈名〉 hothouse flowers

【唐郡】Tángjùn〈名〉 County Down

【唐宁街】Tángníngjiē〈名〉 Downing Street

【唐人街】Tángrénjiē〈名〉 Chinatown

【唐三彩】tángsāncǎi〈名〉[考古] Tang tricolour

> **唐三彩**
>
> Tricoloured glazed pottery from the Tang Dynasty. Found predominantly in Luoyang and Xi'an, it includes coloured and glazed ceramic figurines, animals and utensils, used as burial objects. The raw material used was a clay that turned white or reddish after firing. At this point it was painted in the three main colours of red, green and white. Blue, yellow, brown and purple were also used. It was then heated for a second time in the kiln. Tricoloured glazed pottery flourished in the Tang Dynasty and the beginning of the Yuan Dynasty. By the Ming and Qing dynasties, tricoloured glaze was used mainly for tiles and roof ridges.

【唐诗】tángshī〈名〉 Tang poetry: 《～三百首》 *Three Hundred Tang Poems*

> **唐诗**
>
> Poems (诗), lyric poems (词) and *qu* (曲) are representative literary forms of the Tang, Song and Yuan dynasties. Tang poetry is considered to be the Golden Age of Chinese poetry. *The Collected Tang Poems*, published in the Qing Dynasty, included over 48,000 poems, written by more than 2,200 poets. The two most influential Tang poets are Li Bai (李白) and Du Fu (杜甫). A famous collection of Tang poetry is the *Three Hundred Tang Poems* (《唐诗三百首》), compiled in the Qing Dynasty, and still widely read today. The Song period is known for its lyric poems, which were originally sung to a musical accompaniment. In style this form was either graceful and constrained, or bold and unconstrained. The representative literary form of the Yuan Dynasty is the *yuanqu*, drama consisting of song, operatic dialogue and movement. Guan Hanqing (关汉卿) is the most widely known of the *yuanqu* masters. His surviving plays include *The Injustice Suffered by Dou E* (《窦娥冤》).

【唐宋八大家】Táng-Sòng bādàjiā〈名〉 eight prose masters of the Tang-Song period [Han Yu (韩愈), Liu Zongyuan (柳宗元), Ouyang Xiu (欧阳修), Su Xun (苏洵), Su Shi (苏轼), Su Zhe (苏辙), Zeng Gong (曾巩), and Wang Anshi (王安石)]

【唐突】tángtū A〈动〉〈书〉 offend: ～圣人 disrespect a sage B〈形〉 offensive: 行为～ presumptuous act ‖ 恕我～。Excuse my bluntness.

【唐装】tángzhuāng〈名〉 traditional Chinese-style attire

堂 táng

A〈名〉 1 (厅堂) main room of a house: ▸～屋 2〈旧〉(指办案处) courtroom in a *yamen*: ▸公～, 过～ 3 (专用地) room for a specific purpose: ▸祠～, 教～, 食～ 4 (用于厅堂名称) hall: 三松～ Hall of Three Pines 5 = 堂房 tángfáng 6 (用于商店名称) hall: 同仁～ Tongrentang Pharmacy 7 (母亲) mother: ▸高～, 令～

B〈量〉 1 (用于家具) set: 一～家具 a set of furniture 2 (用于课时) period: 上两～课 have two classes 3〈旧〉(用于审案次数) [used for court sessions]: 过了两～ have been tried in court twice 4 (用于场景、壁画等) [used for scenes, murals, etc.]: 两～壁画 two murals ‖ 三～内景 three indoor scenes

C ▸堂堂 tángtáng

【堂奥】táng'ào〈名〉〈书〉 1 (房屋深处) innermost recess of a house 2 (内陆) hinterland 3〈喻〉(深奥的道理) depth of thought or knowledge

【堂弟】tángdì〈名〉 cousin on the paternalside

【堂而皇之】táng'érhuángzhī〈成〉 1 (满不在乎) openly 2 (有气派) in a grand style

【堂房】tángfáng〈形〉 [relationship between cousins etc.] of the same paternal grandfather or great-grandfather: ～弟兄/姐妹 cousins on the paternal side

【堂鼓】tánggǔ〈名〉 barrel-shaped drum used in traditional opera

【堂倌】tángguān〈名〉〈旧〉 waiter

【堂皇】tánghuáng〈形〉 1 (气势宏大) magnificent: ～的建筑 stately buildings ▸富丽～ 2 (冠冕堂皇) high-sounding: ～的理由 high-sounding reason ▸冠冕～

【堂会】tánghuì〈名〉〈旧〉 performance for home celebrations

【堂姐】tángjiě〈名〉 cousin on the paternal side

【堂客】tángkè〈名〉 1 (女客人) lady guest 2〈方〉(女人) woman 3〈方〉(妻子) wife

【堂妹】tángmèi〈名〉 cousin on the paternal side

【堂上】tángshàng〈名〉 1 (父母) parents 2〈旧〉(长官) Your Honour 3〈旧〉(正厅上) courtroom

【堂堂】tángtáng〈形〉 1 (形容仪表) impressive: 相貌～ be impressive-looking 2 (形容志气) ambitious and daring: ～男子汉 ambitious and daring man ‖ ～中华儿女 sons and daughters of the Chinese nation with high aspirations and boldness of vision 3 (形容阵势) formidable: ～大国 great power ‖ ～军威 formidable prestige of an army

【堂堂正正】tángtáng-zhèngzhèng〈成〉 1 (光明正大) open and above board: ～做人 be upright of character 2 (仪表出众) [of a man's appearance] impressive: 相貌～ be impressive-looking

【堂屋】tángwū〈名〉 1 (正房居中的一间屋) central room of a one-storey traditional Chinese house 2 (正房) principal rooms in a courtyard

【堂戏】tángxì〈名〉 1 (指堂会上演的戏) performance by hired actors and actresses at home celebrations 2 (指剧种) Tang opera [local opera in Hubei Province]

t

【堂兄】 tángxiōng〈名〉 cousin on the paternal side
【堂子】 tángzi〈名〉 1 (指祭神场所) [in Qing Dynasty] imperial sacrificial temple 2 (澡堂) public baths: 去~里洗个澡 go to the bathhouse 3 〈方〉〈旧〉(妓院) brothel

棠 táng〈名〉[植物] birchleaf pear
【棠棣】 tángdì〈名〉[植物] 1 〈古〉(指植物) a kind of white poplar 2 〈书〉〈喻〉(指兄弟) brother
【棠梨】 tánglí〈名〉[植物] birchleaf pear

塘 táng〈名〉 1 (水池) pond: ▸池~, 鱼~ 2 (堤岸) embankment: ▸~堰, 海~, 河~ 3 (坑状物) pit-shaped thing: 火~ fireplace ▸澡~
【塘坝】 tángbà = 塘堰 tángyàn
【塘泥】 tángní〈名〉 pond sludge
【塘堰】 tángyàn〈名〉 small reservoir in a hilly area

搪[1] táng〈动〉 1 (抵挡) keep out: ~风 keep the wind out ‖ ~寒 fend off the cold ‖ ~饥饿 allay one's hunger 2 (应付) do sth. perfunctorily: ~差事 perform one's duty perfunctorily ‖ ~账 stall payment of a debt ▸~塞

搪[2] táng〈动〉 daub: ~炉子 line a stove with clay ▸~瓷
【搪瓷】 tángcí〈名〉 enamel: ~缸子/脸盆 enamel mug/basin ‖ ~器皿 enamelware
【搪塞】 tángsè〈动〉 do sth. perfunctorily: ~差事 perform one's duty perfunctorily ‖ 她转换话题想把我的询问~过去。 She guided the conversation to another subject in order to distract from my enquiry.

溏 táng〈形〉 viscous
【溏便】 tángbiàn〈名〉[中医] semi-liquid stool
【溏心】 tángxīn〈形〉 soft-boiled: ~儿鸡蛋 soft-boiled egg

樘 táng
A〈名〉 frame: 窗/门~ window/door frame
B〈量〉 [used for a door or window and its frame]: 两~门 two doors ‖ 四~窗 four windows

膛 táng〈名〉 1 (指体腔) chest: ▸开~, 胸~ 2 (指器物) chamber: 子弹上了~。 The gun is loaded. ▸炉~, 枪~
【膛径】 tángjìng〈名〉 bore
【膛线】 tángxiàn〈名〉[军事] rifling

镗(鏜) táng〈动〉[机械] bore
【镗床】 tángchuáng〈名〉[机械] boring machine: 卧式~ horizontal boring machine

糖 táng〈名〉 1 (指甜味剂) sugar: 蔗~ cane sugar ‖ 无~食品 food with no added sugar ‖ 她喝咖啡喜欢放~。 She likes to add sugar to her coffee. ▸白~, 冰~ 2 (糖果) sweet: 什锦~ assorted sweets ‖ 水果~ fruit drops ‖ 椰子~ coconut candy ▸奶~ 3 [化学] carbohydrate: ▸单~, 多~, 双~
【糖炒栗子】 tángchǎolìzi〈名〉 chestnuts roasted in sand with sugar
【糖醋】 tángcù〈名〉 sweet-and-sour sauce: ~排骨 sweet-and-sour spare ribs ‖ ~鱼 fish in sweet-and-sour sauce
【糖甙】 tángdài〈名〉[生化] glycoside
【糖苷】 tánggān〈名〉[生化] glycoside
【糖果】 tángguǒ〈名〉 sweets〈英〉; candy〈美〉: 他的口袋里塞满了~。 His pocket was bulging with sweets.
【糖果店】 tángguǒdiàn〈名〉 sweet shop〈英〉; candy store〈美〉
【糖葫芦】 tánghúlu〈名〉 candied haws on a stick
【糖姜】 tángjiāng〈名〉 sugared ginger
【糖浆】 tángjiāng〈名〉 1 (用于冲淡苦味) medicinal syrup: 止咳~ cough syrup 2 (用于制糖果) syrup; treacle〈英〉
【糖精】 tángjīng〈名〉 saccharin
【糖精钠】 tángjīngnà〈名〉 sodium saccharin
【糖萝卜】 tángluóbo〈名〉 1 (甜菜) beet 2 〈方〉(指蜜饯) preserved carrot
【糖尿病】 tángniàobìng ▸p. 50〈名〉[医学] diabetes: ~患者 diabetic
【糖人】 tángrén〈名〉 sugar figurine
【糖色】 tángshǎi ▸p. 863〈名〉 half-burnt brown sugar used to colour meat: 给肉上~ colour meat with half-burnt brown sugar
【糖霜】 tángshuāng〈名〉 icing; frosting〈美〉
【糖水】 tángshuǐ〈名〉 syrup: ~梨/桃 pears/peaches in syrup
【糖蒜】 tángsuàn〈名〉 sweetened garlic
【糖稀】 tángxī〈名〉 malt sugar
【糖衣】 tángyī〈名〉 sugar coating
【糖衣炮弹】 tángyī pàodàn〈喻〉 sugar-coated bullet
【糖原】 tángyuán〈名〉[生化] glycogen
【糖纸】 tángzhǐ〈名〉 sweet wrapper

醣 táng〈形〉 [of sb.'s complexion] red: 紫~脸 purplish brown complexion

螳 táng〈名〉 mantis
【螳臂当车】 tángbì-dāngchē〈成〉〈喻〉 overestimate one's own strength
【螳臂挡车】 tángbì-dǎngchē = 螳臂当车 tángbì-dāngchē
【螳螂】 tángláng〈名〉[昆虫] mantis
【螳螂捕蝉，黄雀在后】 tángláng bǔ chán, huángquè zài hòu〈成〉〈喻〉 covet gains ahead, unaware of the danger behind

tǎng

帑 tǎng〈名〉〈书〉 state treasury funds: 公~ public funds ‖ 国~ funds in the state treasury

倘 tǎng ▸p. 350〈连〉〈书〉 if: ~能如此，就最好不过了。 It would be best if it could be done like this. ‖ ~有不测，要及时报警。 If anything untoward should happen, you should contact the police immediately.
▸cháng
【倘或】 tǎnghuò ▸p. 350〈连〉〈书〉 supposing: ~发生意外，要保持镇静。 Keep calm in the face of the unexpected.
【倘来之物】 tǎnglái-zhīwù〈成〉 windfall
【倘若】 tǎngruò ▸p. 350〈连〉〈书〉 if: ~嫌疑犯开枪，就当场击毙他。 Should the suspect open fire, shoot him dead right away. ‖ ~不信，你就亲自去看看。 Go and look if you don't believe me.
【倘使】 tǎngshǐ ▸p. 350〈连〉〈书〉 in case: ~失败，也不要灰心。 Don't get down if you fail.

淌 tǎng〈动〉 drip: ~口水 slaver ‖ ~眼泪 shed tears ‖ 工人们~着汗干活。 The workers worked up a sweat. ‖ 河水~得很慢。 The river is running very slowly. ▸流~

傥(儻) tǎng ▸倜傥 tìtǎng

锐(钂) tǎng〈名〉 fork-shaped weapon used in ancient times

躺 tǎng〈动〉 lie: ~在床上 lie in bed ‖ ~倒不干 shirk one's obligations ‖ ~在过去的功劳簿上 rest on one's laurels ‖ 不要~着看书。 Don't read while you're lying down.
【躺柜】 tǎngguì〈名〉 chest
【躺椅】 tǎngyǐ〈名〉 deck chair

tàng

烫(燙) tàng
A〈动〉 1 (灼痛) scald: 手上~了一个泡 get a blister on one's hand from a burn ‖ 当心，别让开水~着了! Be careful not to get scalded by the boiling water! ▸~伤 2 (使升温) warm: ~衣服 iron clothes ‖ 用热水~脚 warm one's feet up in hot water 3 (烫发) perm: ▸电~, 冷~
B〈形〉 boiling hot: 这汤太~，还不能喝。 This soup is too hot to drink. ▸滚~
【烫发】 tàngfà〈动〉 have one's hair permed
【烫花】 tànghuā〈名〉 pyrography
【烫金】 tàngjīn〈动〉[印刷] gild: ~封面 gilt cover ‖ ~字 gold-stamped characters
【烫酒】 tàngjiǔ〈动〉 heat wine (by putting the container in hot water)
【烫蜡】 tànglà〈动〉 wax
【烫面】 tàngmiàn〈名〉 dough kneaded with boiling water: ~卷儿 steamed rolls
【烫伤】 tàngshāng A〈动〉 scald: 被严重~ get severely scalded B ▸p. 50〈名〉 scald: 造成深度~ produce a deep scald
【烫手山芋】 tàngshǒu shānyù〈成〉〈喻〉 hot potato: 由抢手货变成了~ go from being an item in demand to being a hot potato
【烫头】 tàngtóu = 烫发 tàngfà
【烫衣板】 tàngyībǎn〈名〉 ironing board

趟 tàng
A〈名〉 sth. that is proceeding: 年轻人学得快，我老了，跟不上~。 Young people pick up things easily. At my age, I can't hope to keep up with them.
B〈量〉 1 (用于来往次数) [used for a round trip]: 他那里我去过一~。 I have been to his place once. ‖ 从这里到北京每天有两~火车。 There are two trains a day from here to Beijing. 2 〈方〉(用于成行的东西) [used for a street or things arranged in a row]: 半~街 half way up the street ‖ 两~椅子 two rows of chairs
▸tāng
【趟马】 tàngmǎ〈名〉[戏曲] set of stage motions symbolizing trotting or galloping

t

tāo

叨 tāo〈动〉get the benefit of: ►～光 ►dāo, dáo

【叨光】tāoguāng〈动〉〈套〉be much obliged to you: 我今晚～坐你的车回家。I am much obliged to you for the lift home tonight.

【叨教】tāojiào〈动〉〈套〉have the benefit of your instruction: ～了。Thank you very much for your advice.

【叨扰】tāorǎo ►p. 156〈动〉〈套〉thank you for your hospitality: ～了。Thank you ever so much.

涛（濤） tāo〈名〉**1**（大浪）billows: ►波～, 惊～骇浪 **2**（指声音）sound of the sea: ►林～, 松～

绦（縧） tāo〈名〉silk ribbon: 丝～ silk ribbon

【绦虫】tāochóng〈名〉tapeworm: 驱～药 medicine for expelling tapeworms

【绦子】tāozi〈名〉silk ribbon

掏 tāo〈动〉**1**（挖）dig: 在墙上～个洞。Make a hole in the wall. **2**（往外拿）fish out: ～鼻孔 pick one's nose ‖ ～鸟窝 fish young birds or eggs out of a bird's nest ‖ 在手提包里～钥匙 dig around in one's handbag for one's keys

【掏底】tāodǐ〈名〉try to find out the real situation

【掏心】tāoxīn〈动〉be from the bottom of one's heart: 说句～的话，你真不该告诉她。To be frank, you shouldn't have told her that.

【掏心窝子】tāo xīnwōzi〈惯〉confide in sb.

【掏腰包】tāo yāobāo〈惯〉**1**（付钱）pay out of one's own pocket: 今天这顿饭轮到谁～? Whose turn is it to foot the bill for today's meal? **2**（扒窃）pick sb.'s pocket: 有人掏了我的腰包! My wallet has been stolen!

滔 tāo〈形〉flooding

【滔滔】tāotāo〈形〉**1**（形容波浪）torrential: 白浪～ whitecaps surging **2**（形容说话）jabbering

【滔滔不绝】tāotāo-bùjué〈成〉talk nineteen to the dozen: ～地足足讲了一个小时 jabber on in unsparing detail for a whole hour

【滔天】tāotiān〈形〉**1**（形容水势）billowing: 小船被～巨浪卷走了。The small boat was washed away by huge waves. **2**（形容罪恶、灾祸）heinous: 罪恶～ be guilty of the most heinous crimes ‖ 闯下～大祸 stir up appalling trouble

韬（韜） tāo
A〈名〉**1**〈书〉（剑套）sheath;（弓套）bow case **2**（谋略）military strategy: ►～略
B〈动〉hide: ►～晦

【韬光养晦】tāoguāng-yǎnghuì〈成〉conceal one's strengths and bide one's time

【韬晦】tāohuì〈动〉〈书〉lie low: ～之计 trick of concealing one's true intentions

【韬略】tāolüè〈名〉〈旧〉military strategy: ～过人 excel in military strategy

饕 tāo〈动〉〈书〉be gluttonous: 老～ voracious eater

【饕餮】tāotiè〈名〉**1**（指兽）*taotie* [name of a ferocious legendary animal] **2**〈喻〉（凶恶贪婪的人）fierce and greedy person **3**〈喻〉（贪吃的人）voracious eater

táo

逃 táo〈动〉**1**（逃跑）run away: ～进丛林 take to the jungle ‖ ～到国外去了 flee abroad ►～犯, ～跑, ～亡 **2**（躲避）evade: 罪责难～ hard to get away with sth. ‖ 什么事都～不过他的眼睛。Nothing escaped his eyes. ►～避, ～税

【逃奔】táobèn〈动〉run away: ～他乡 run away to a place far from home ‖ 敌人四处～。The enemy fled in all directions.

【逃避】táobì〈动〉escape: ～法律制裁 evade the law ‖ ～现实 refuse to face reality ‖ ～责任 shirk one's responsibility

【逃兵】táobīng〈名〉**1**〈本〉deserter **2**〈喻〉one who flinches from their duty in face of difficulties: 登山队的向导头一夜就当了～。The local guides deserted the mountaineering team the very first night.

【逃窜】táocuàn〈动〉[of bandits, rebel forces, etc.] flee in disorder: 狼狈～ flee helter-skelter ‖ 叛匪仓皇～。The rebels fled in panic helter-skelter.

【逃遁】táodùn〈动〉flee: 罪犯无处～。The criminal could find no refuge.

【逃犯】táofàn〈名〉escaped criminal: 通缉～ order the arrest of a criminal at large

【逃荒】táohuāng〈动〉flee from famine

【逃汇】táohuì〈动〉evade foreign exchange

【逃婚】táohūn〈动〉escape from one's marriage

【逃课】táokè〈动〉cut class: 他经常～。He often plays truant.

【逃离】táolí〈动〉run away: ～危险 flee from danger

【逃命】táomìng〈动〉run for one's life: ～他乡 flee to an alien land

【逃难】táonàn〈动〉flee from a calamity: ～在外 flee to a distant place to escape calamity

【逃匿】táonì〈动〉go into hiding: ～山林 hide away in forests and mountains

【逃跑】táopǎo〈动〉make one's getaway: 越狱～ escape from prison ‖ 她一看有危险就～了。She fled away at the first sign of danger.

【逃票】táopiào〈动〉sneak through without a ticket: 抓住几个～的人 apprehend several people without tickets

【逃散】táosàn〈动〉become separated after an escape: 寻找～的亲人 search for loved ones who one lost during an escape

【逃生】táoshēng〈动〉run for one's life: ►死里～

【逃税】táoshuì〈动〉dodge a tax: ～伎俩 tax dodges

【逃脱】táotuō〈动〉**1**（跑掉）run away: ～虎口 flee from the jaws of death ‖ 囚犯从看守手中～了。The prisoner broke away from his guards. **2**（摆脱）evade: ～罪责 evade one's responsibility for an offence ‖ ～不了法律的制裁 unable to escape punishment by law

【逃亡】táowáng〈动〉go into exile: ～国外 flee to a foreign country ‖ 他过了十年～生活。He spent 10 years in exile.

【逃席】táoxí〈动〉leave a feast without saying goodbye: 借故～ excuse oneself from the table

【逃学】táoxué〈动〉play truant: 孩子们经常装病～。Children often avoid school by pretending to be ill.

【逃逸】táoyì〈动〉〈书〉abscond: 畏罪～ abscond to avoid punishment ‖ 肇事司机～了。The hit-and-runner fled.

【逃逸速度】táoyìsùdù〈名〉[航天] escape velocity

【逃债】táozhài〈动〉dodge a creditor

【逃之夭夭】táozhīyāoyāo〈成〉〈诙〉take to one's heels

【逃走】táozǒu〈动〉take to one's heels: 昨晚一个囚犯～了。A prisoner got out last night.

洮 Táo ►p. 294〈名〉Taohe River

桃 táo〈名〉**1**[植物] peach tree **2**（指果实）peach: 罐头～ tinned peaches ►蟠～, 水蜜～, 投～报李 **3**（核桃）walnut **4**（桃状物）peach-shaped thing: ►棉～

【桃符】táofú〈名〉〈旧〉**1**（桃木板）peach wood charms (hung on the door of a house) **2**（春联）Spring Festival couplets (posted on the door)

【桃脯】táofǔ〈名〉preserved peach

【桃红】táohóng ►p. 863〈名〉peach pink: ～衬衣 pink shirt

【桃红柳绿】táohóng-liǔlǜ〈成〉beautiful spring scene

【桃花】táohuā〈名〉peach blossom

【桃花雪】táohuāxuě〈名〉spring snow

【桃花汛】táohuāxùn〈名〉spring flood

【桃花源】táohuāyuán = 世外桃源 shìwàitáoyuán

【桃花运】táohuāyùn〈名〉[of a man] luck in love: 走～ be lucky in love

【桃花心木】táohuāxīnmù〈名〉mahogany

【桃李】táolǐ〈名〉〈喻〉one's pupils: ～盈门 have numerous disciples

【桃李不言，下自成蹊】táolǐ bù yán, xià zì chéng xī〈成〉〈喻〉men of true worth need not speak, yet they will win admiration

【桃李满天下】táolǐ mǎn tiānxià〈成〉have pupils everywhere

【桃仁】táorén〈名〉**1**[中药] peach kernel **2**（核桃仁）walnut kernel

【桃色】táosè **A** ►p. 863〈名〉peach-blossom pink **B**〈形〉illicit: ～事件 love affair ‖ ～新闻 sex scandal

【桃子】táozi〈名〉peach

陶[1] táo
A〈名〉earthenware: ～罐 earthen jug ‖ ～制器皿 earthenware vessel ►～瓷, ～器, 彩～, 黑～
B〈动〉**1**〈本〉make pottery **2**〈喻〉（培育）cultivate: ►～冶 2, 熏～

陶[2] táo〈形〉contented: ►～然, ～醉

【陶吧】táobā〈名〉pottery cafe

【陶瓷】táocí〈名〉ceramics: ～器皿 porcelain ware

【陶雕】táodiāo〈名〉pottery sculpture

【陶管】táoguǎn〈名〉[建筑] earthenware pipe

【陶器】táoqì〈名〉earthenware

【陶然】táorán〈形〉〈书〉happy and carefree: ～自得 be happy and content ‖ ～亭 Pavilion of Happiness and Ease

【陶塑】táosù〈名〉pottery figure

【陶陶】táotáo〈形〉cheerful

【陶土】táotǔ〈名〉potter's clay

【陶文】táowén ►p. 918〈名〉[考古]

inscription on pottery

【陶冶】táoyě〈动〉1〈本〉 make pottery and smelt metal 2〈喻〉（影响） mould: ～情操 shape one's values ‖ ～性情 cultivate the mind

【陶艺】táoyì〈名〉 ceramics

【陶俑】táoyǒng〈名〉［考古］ terracotta figure

【陶铸】táozhù〈动〉〈书〉 1（烧制） mould 2〈喻〉（造就） train: ～贤才 train talent

【陶醉】táozuì〈动〉 be carried away: 他的表演令人～。 Everyone was enchanted by his performance. ‖ 我们不能～于已有的成绩。 We must not get carried away by our success. ►自我～

萄 táo〈名〉 grape: ►葡～

梼（檮） táo

【梼昧】táomèi〈形〉〈书〉〈谦〉 ignorant: 自惭～ have a sense of inferiority

【梼杌】táowù〈名〉〈书〉 fierce person

啕 táo ►号啕 háotáo

淘¹ táo〈动〉 1（淘洗） rinse out gravel, sand, etc.: ～米 wash rice ►～金, ～汰 2（舀出） dredge: ～井 dredge a well ‖ ～下水道 clean out a sewer 3〈方〉（购买） search out and buy: ～旧书 seek out and purchase second-hand books ‖ ～便宜货 look out and purchase used goods

淘² táo

A〈动〉 be taxing: ►～神

B〈形〉 mischievous: 这孩子可真～。 This child is really naughty.

【淘河】táohé〈名〉［鸟类］ pelican

【淘金】táojīn〈动〉 1［矿业］ pan 2〈喻〉（设法赚钱） try to make high profits: 去大城市～ go to the big city to try to strike it rich ‖ ～梦 dream of hitting the big time

【淘金热】táojīnrè〈名〉 gold rush

【淘箩】táoluó〈名〉 basket for washing rice in

【淘气】táoqì〈形〉 naughty: ～的孩子 mischievous child

【淘气包】táoqìbāo = 淘气鬼 táoqìguǐ

【淘气鬼】táoqìguǐ〈名〉 rascal: 你这个～把我的眼镜藏哪儿去了？ Where have you hidden my glasses, you little rascal?

【淘神】táoshén〈动〉〈口〉 be trying: 再别为那孩子～了。 Don't let that child bother you any more.

【淘汰】táotài〈动〉 1［体育］ knock out: 该队已经被～出局。 This team was knocked out of the event. ‖ 三名种子选手在第一轮便遭～。 The three seeded players were eliminated in the first round of the competition. 2（废弃） fall into disuse: ～陈旧设备 eliminate obsolete equipment ‖ ～产品 disused products

【淘汰赛】táotàisài〈名〉［体育］ knockout tournament

tǎo

讨¹（討） tǎo〈动〉 1（攻打） send armed forces to suppress: ►～伐, 征～ 2（谴责） denounce: ►申～, 声～ 3（研究） discuss: ►～论, 研～

讨²（討） tǎo〈动〉 1（索要） beg for: ～些吃的 beg for some food ‖ ～回公道 request a return to justice ►～饭, ～债 2（娶） marry (a woman): ～老婆 get married 3（引起） invite: ～人喜欢的孩子 lovable child ►～厌, 自～苦吃 4（有成效） achieve: 吃力不～好 put in a lot of effort to no avail

【讨伐】tǎofá〈动〉 send troops to suppress: ～叛军 crush rebel forces

【讨饭】tǎofàn〈动〉 beg for food: ～为生 get by by begging

【讨好】tǎohǎo〈动〉 1（求取好感） ingratiate oneself with: ～上司 ingratiate oneself with one's superior ‖ 说些～的话 make flattering remarks 2（取得好效果） [used in the negative] have one's labour rewarded: 这种费力而不～的事我不干。 I don't want to engage in activities that take a lot out of me but fail to produce results.

【讨还】tǎohuán〈动〉 demand the return of sth.: ～血债 demand payment of a blood debt ‖ ～欠款 demand repayment of a debt

【讨价】tǎojià〈动〉 name a price: 店主～太高。 The shop owner's asking price was too high.

【讨价还价】tǎojià-huánjià〈成〉 bargain: 本店拒绝～。 The shop refuses to bargain over the price. ‖〈喻〉 经过长时间的～，他们终于达成了协议。 After a lot of haggling, they finally reached an agreement.

【讨教】tǎojiào〈动〉 seek advice: 当面～ ask sb. for advice face to face

【讨论】tǎolùn〈动〉 discuss: ～工作计划 discuss a work plan ‖ 课堂/学术～ class/academic discussion ‖ 小组～ panel discussion ‖ 他们就该问题进行热烈的～。 They had a lively discussion on the issue.

【讨论会】tǎolùnhuì〈名〉 discussion: 中外经济合作问题～ symposium on China's economic cooperation with foreign countries

【讨没趣】tǎo méiqù〈动〉 invite the cold shoulder: 自～ ask for a snub

【讨便宜】tǎo piányi〈动〉 try to gain sth. at the expense of others: 想从我这儿～，没门儿。 If you're trying to take advantage of me, you can get lost!

【讨平】tǎopíng〈动〉〈旧〉 send troops to suppress: ～叛乱 put down a rebellion

【讨乞】tǎoqǐ〈动〉 beg: 四处～ go around begging

【讨巧】tǎoqiǎo〈动〉 try to get sth. for nothing

【讨俏】tǎoqiào〈动〉 try to be witty

【讨情】tǎoqíng〈动〉〈方〉 plead for mercy: ～告饶 plead for leniency

【讨饶】tǎoráo〈动〉 beg for mercy: 下跪～ go down on one's knees and beg for mercy

【讨扰】tǎorǎo〈动〉〈套〉 thank you for your hospitality: ～了。 Thank you ever so much.

【讨生活】tǎo shēnghuó〈动〉 1（寻求生计） seek a living 2（闲逛） loaf around

【讨喜】tǎoxǐ〈形〉 pleasant

【讨嫌】tǎoxián〈形〉 disagreeable: 你再这样下去，就讨人嫌了。 If you go on like that, people are going to get very annoyed with you. ‖ 她真～，整天说东家道西家。 She is a sheer nuisance, gossiping all day long.

【讨厌】tǎoyàn A〈形〉 1（令人厌烦） nasty: ～的气味/味道 repulsive smell/taste ‖ 多～的家伙! What a nasty man! 2（让人心烦） troublesome: 这事有点～，恐怕不好办。 This is a bit of a tricky issue, and I'm afraid it might be difficult to resolve. ‖ 这种病比较～，很难根治。 This kind of illness is quite awkward and is very difficult to cure. B〈动〉 hate: 真～这种潮湿的天气。 I'm completely sick of this wet weather. ‖ 吸烟让我特别～。 Smoking is one of my pet hates. ‖ 我一见他就十分～。 The sight of him is completely repulsive to me.

【讨债】tǎozhài〈动〉 demand the payment of a debt

【讨债公司】tǎozhài gōngsī〈名〉 debt-recovery firm

【讨债鬼】tǎozhàiguǐ〈名〉 1（指小孩） child who dies young 2（讨债人） nuisance 3（浪子） spendthrift

【讨账】tǎozhàng〈动〉 1 = 讨债 tǎozhài 2〈方〉（讨还欠款） ask for payment for goods/services

tào

套 tào

A〈名〉 1（外罩） case: 沙发～ sofa cover ‖ 椅垫～ cushion cover ►笔～, 手～, 枕～ 2（棉絮） cotton padding: 袄～ padded lining of a traditional Chinese jacket ►被～ 3（成套） set: 两件～泳衣 two-piece bathing suit ‖ 整～家具 whole set of furniture ‖ 这上衣和裤子不配～。 The jacket and trousers do not match. ►～装, 成～, 全～ 4（固定的格式或办法） formula: ►～话, 客～, 俗～ 5（结） knot: 活～儿 slip knot ‖ 死～儿 fast knot ►绳～ 6（指绳具） harness: 牲口～ harness for a draught animal 7（圈套） trick: 落入～中 fall into a trap ‖ 下个～ set a trap ►圈～ 8（常用于地名） bend of a river or curve in a mountain range: ►河～

B〈动〉 1（罩外罩） cover with: ～枕套 put the pillow in the pillowcase ‖ 今天早上很冷，你最好～上一件毛衣。 It's cold this morning. You'd better put a sweater on. 2（相互衔接） overlap: 一环～一环 one ring linked with another ►～间, ～色, ～种 3（套用） model sth. on sth.: ～公式 apply a formula ►～用, 生搬硬～ 4（用绳拴系） harness: ～马 lasso a horse ‖ 把钥匙～在钥匙环上。 Put the keys on a ring. ‖〈喻〉 我的钱大部分都～在股票市场上了。 Most of my money is tied up in the stock market. ►～车 5（拉拢） try to win sb.'s friendship, favour, etc.: ►～交情, ～近乎 6（引出） coax sth. out of sb.: 别来～我的话。 Don't try to coax the secret out of me. ‖ 你得用好话～出他掌握的情况。 You have to coax the information out of him. 7（不正当购买） buy illegally: ►～购, ～汇

C〈形〉 covering: ►～裤, ～袖

D〈量〉 [used for books, furniture, rooms, methods, etc.] set: 两～衣服 two suits of clothes ‖ 一～瓷器 a set of china ‖ 一～课本 a set of textbooks ‖ 他做事自有一～办法。 He has his own special way of doing things.

【套版】tàobǎn［印刷］ A〈动〉 arrange process plates on a printing machine B〈名〉 process plate

【套包】tàobāo〈名〉 collar

【套包子】tàobāozi = 套包 tàobāo

【套播】tàobō〈动〉 1 = 套种 tàozhòng 2（重复播放） repeatedly broadcast: ～广告 repeatedly broadcast advertisements

【套裁】tàocái〈动〉 cut several pieces out

of one piece of cloth so as to make the best use of the material

【套餐】tàocān〈名〉1▸（指饮食） set meal 2▸〈喻〉（指产品） package product;（指服务） package service

【套车】tàochē 〈动〉 harness a draught animal to a cart

【套瓷】tàocí〈动〉〈口〉 cosy up (to): 公事公办，少来～。Business is business. Don't try to butter me up.

【套房】tàofáng 〈名〉 1▸（套间） inner room: 一个小～ a small inner room 2▸（成套住房） suite: 商务/总统～ business/presidential suite

【套服】tàofú = 套装 tàozhuāng

【套改】tàogǎi〈动〉 reform in accordance with corresponding regulations

【套购】tàogòu〈动〉 illegally buy up: ～外汇 buy foreign exchange by illegal means

【套管】tàoguǎn〈名〉 casing: 绝缘～ insulating bush

【套红】tàohóng〈动〉［印刷］ chromatograph part of a page red: ～标题 news headline in red

【套话】tàohuà〈名〉 1▸（客套话） conventionalism: 说几句～ make a few conventional remarks 2▸（空话） stereotyped expressions: 说话要开门见山，不要讲～、空话。Come straight to the point when you speak, avoiding clichés and empty words.

【套汇】tàohuì 〈动〉 1▸（非法购买外汇） buy foreign exchange by illegal means 2▸［经济］ arbitrage

【套间】tàojiān 〈名〉 1▸（配间） inner room: 一个小～ a small inner room 2▸（指一套房） apartment

【套交情】tào jiāoqing〈动〉 try to establish friendship with sb.

【套近乎】tào jìnhu〈动〉〈贬〉 try to be friendly with: 咱们按原则办事，别来～。We must act according to protocol, so don't come cosying up to me.

【套裤】tàokù〈名〉 leggings

【套牢】tàoláo〈动〉［经济］ hung up

【套利】tàolì〈名〉［经济］ arbitrage: ～公司 arbitrage house ‖ 股票～ arbitrage of stocks

【套路】tàolù〈名〉 1▸（指武术动作） established series of skills and tricks in *wushu* 2▸〈口〉（指思路） systemized methods: 医疗改革有什么新～吗？ Are there any new systematic methods in the medical reforms?

【套马索】tàomǎsuǒ〈名〉 lasso

【套牌车】tàopáichē 〈名〉 vehicle with fake license plates: 用～从事非法营运 use a car with fake license plates for illegal dealings

【套票】tàopiào〈名〉complete set of tickets

【套期保值】tàoqī bǎozhí 〈动〉［金融］ hedge: ～机制 hedging mechanism

【套曲】tàoqǔ〈名〉［音乐］ divertimento: ～形式 cyclical form

【套圈】tàoquān〈动〉 hoop

【套裙】tàoqún〈名〉 woman's suit

【套色】tàosè 〈名〉［印刷］ chromatography: ～版 process plate ‖ ～木刻 coloured woodcut

【套衫】tàoshān〈名〉 pullover: 女士紧身～ jersey

【套数】tàoshù〈名〉1▸［戏曲］ a sequence of songs with one rhyme and a common set of melodies 2▸〈喻〉（指技巧、方法） established series of skills and tricks in *wushu*, boxing, etc. 3▸ = 套子 tàozi 3

【套索】tàosuǒ〈名〉 lasso

【套套】tàotao〈名〉〈方〉 ways: 老～ same old ways

【套筒】tàotǒng〈名〉［机械］ sleeve

【套问】tàowèn〈动〉 find out by asking seemingly casual questions

【套鞋】tàoxié〈名〉 overshoes: 长筒～ long overshoes

【套袖】tàoxiù〈名〉 oversleeve

【套印】tàoyìn〈动〉［印刷］chromatograph: 彩色～ process printing

【套用】tàoyòng〈动〉 apply mechanically: 胡乱～公式 apply a formula indiscriminately ‖ 不加区别地～别人的经验 copy other people's experience indiscriminately

【套语】tàoyǔ〈名〉 1▸（客套话） conventionalism 2▸（空话） stereotyped expressions: ～滥调 platitudes

【套种】tàozhòng〈动〉［农业］ interplant: 实行间作～ adopt intercropping and interplanting ‖ 棉花地里～红薯 interplant sweet potatoes with cotton

【套住】tàozhù〈动〉 trap up

【套装】tàozhuāng〈名〉 suit: 两件/三件式～ two-piece/three-piece suit

【套子】tàozi〈名〉 1▸（外罩） case: 沙发～ sofa cover 2▸〈方〉（棉絮） cotton padding: 棉花～ cotton padding 3▸（定势） conventionality: 老～ same old story ‖ 俗～ social conventions 4▸（圈套） trap: 下～ set a trap ‖ 陷进～ fall into a trap

【套作】tàozuò = 套种 tàozhòng

tè

忑 tè ▸忐忑 tǎntè

忒 tè〈名〉〈书〉 error ▸tuī

特 tè

A〈形〉 special: ▸～别, ～权, 奇～

B〈副〉 1▸a（特地） specially: 她～为你而来。She's come specially for you. ‖ 这些房子是～为老年人设计的。These houses are specifically designed for old people. ▸～此, ～地, ～意 b〈口〉（非常） particularly: 今天～冷。It's particularly cold today. ‖ 她～能干。She is exceptionally capable. ‖ 这孩子的模仿能力～强。This child is an extremely good mimic. 2▸〈书〉（只） only: 此～匹夫之勇耳。This is nothing but sheer foolhardiness.

C〈名〉 secret agent, spy: ▸～工, ～务, 敌～

【特奥会】Tè'àohuì〈名〉 Special Olympics

【特别】tèbié A〈形〉 special: 受到～关怀 receive special care ‖ 他的脾气很～。He has a peculiar temperament. ‖ 有什么～之处吗？ Is there anything special about it? B〈副〉 1▸（异常） particularly: 去年夏天～热。It was particularly hot last summer. ‖ 她今天～激动。She is especially excited today. 2▸（专门） specially: 这是～为你准备的。This is especially for you. 3▸（尤其） especially: 他喜欢体育，～是足球。He likes sports, particularly football. ‖ 我喜爱乡村，～是春天的乡村。I love the country, especially in spring.

【特别监护病房】tèbié jiānhù bìngfáng〈名〉 intensive care unit (ICU)

【特别快车】tèbié kuàichē〈名〉 express train

【特别联大】tèbié liándà〈名〉 special session of the UN General Assembly

【特别提款权】tèbié tíkuǎnquán〈名〉［经济］ special drawing rights (SDR)

【特别行政区】tèbié xíngzhèngqū〈名〉 special administrative region (SAR): ～首席执行官 chief executive of Hong Kong or Macao Special Administrative Region ‖ 澳门～ Macao Special Administrative Region ‖ 香港～ Hong Kong Special Administrative Region

【特产】tèchǎn〈名〉 speciality: 地方～ local speciality ‖ 这种水果是热带地区的～。This fruit is particular to the tropics.

【特长】tècháng〈名〉 specialty: 充分发挥～ bring one's special skill into full play ‖ 你有什么～？ What are your special areas?

【特长生】tèchángshēng〈名〉 student exceptionally skilled in sth.: 他是作为体育～被录取的。He was admitted to the school because he was especially good at sports.

【特出】tèchū〈形〉 outstanding: 培养～的人才 train outstanding talents ‖ 做出～的成绩 make remarkable achievements

【特此】tècǐ〈副〉〈书〉 [in documents or formal letters] hereby: ～通告 notice is hereby given ‖ ～证明 hereby testify

【特大】tèdà〈形〉 extra large: ～号服装 extra large size (XL) ‖ ～洪水 catastrophic flood ‖ ～城市 megalopolis

【特等】tèděng〈形〉 top-grade: ～战斗英雄 first-class combat hero ‖ ～舱 de luxe cabin ‖ ～奖 special award

【特地】tèdì〈副〉 specially: 我～来向你请教。I came especially in order to seek your advice.

【特点】tèdiǎn〈名〉 distinguishing feature: 时代～ characteristic of the times ‖ 强节奏是爵士乐的～。Heavily accented rhythm is a characteristic of jazz music.

【特定】tèdìng〈形〉 1▸（特别指定） specially designated: 他是～的候选人。He was the specially appointed candidate. 2▸（某一具体的） specific: ～场合 specific occasion ‖ 在～的条件下 under specified conditions ‖ 这笔钱有～用途。The money is to be used for a specific purpose.

【特富龙】tèfúlóng〈名〉 Teflon: ～不粘锅 Teflon nonstick pan

【特工】tègōng〈名〉 1▸（指工作） secret service: ～人员 special agent 2▸（指人） secret agent: 受过特别训练的联邦调查局～ specially trained FBI agent

【特供】tègōng〈形〉 specially supply: ～商品 specially supplied goods

【特护】tèhù A〈动〉 give special nursing care: 医院给重危病人以～。Intensive care is given to the seriously ill. B〈名〉 special duty nurse

【特护病房】tèhù bìngfáng〈名〉 intensive care unit

【特惠】tèhuì〈形〉［经济］ specially preferential: ～价 specially preferential prices ‖ ～关税 preferential tariff

【特混舰队】tèhùn jiànduì〈名〉 naval task force

【特级】tèjí〈形〉special-grade: ～大师 grand master ‖ ～教师 teacher of a special classification ‖ ～绿茶 superfine green tea

【特急】tèjí〈形〉 extra urgent: ～电报 super urgent telegram

【特辑】tèjí〈名〉 1▸（指报刊） special issue 2▸（指电影） special collection of short films

【特技】tèjì〈名〉 1▸（指技巧） stunt: 飞行～表演 flying stunt ‖ ～跳伞 skydiving 2▸［影视］ special effects: ▸～镜头

【特技镜头】tèjì jìngtóu〈名〉 trick shot

【特技摄影】tèjì shèyǐng〈名〉 trick photography: ～师 trick photographer

【特技演员】tèjì yǎnyuán ▸p. 966〈名〉（指男性）stuntman; （指女性）stunt woman
【特价】tèjià〈名〉special offer: ～商品 goods on special offer ‖ ～书 discounted book
【特警】tèjǐng〈名〉special police: ～部队 special forces
【特刊】tèkān〈名〉special issue: 元旦～ New Year's Day special
【特快】tèkuài **A**〈形〉express: ～邮件 express post ‖ ～列车 express train **B** = 特别快车 tèbié kuàichē
【特快专递】tèkuài zhuāndì〈名〉special delivery: 邮政～ Express Mail Service (EMS)
【特困】tèkùn〈形〉poverty-stricken: ～户 poverty-stricken family ‖ ～生 destitute student
【特拉华州】Tèlāhuázhōu〈名〉Delaware
【特立独行】tèlì-dúxíng〈成〉be independent in mind and action
【特立尼达和多巴哥】Tèlìnídá Hé Duōbāgē〈名〉Trinidad and Tobago
【特例】tèlì〈名〉special case
【特洛伊】Tèluòyī〈名〉Troy: ～木马 Trojan horse ‖ ～战争 Trojan War
【特卖】tèmài〈名〉special sale: 空调～ a special sale for air conditioners ‖ ～会 special sale
【特命全权大使】tèmìng quánquán dàshǐ〈名〉ambassador extraordinary and plenipotentiary
【特命全权公使】tèmìng quánquán gōngshǐ〈名〉envoy extraordinary and minister plenipotentiary
【特派】tèpài〈动〉specially appoint: ～专人调查此案 specially appoint sb. to investigate the case ‖ ～记者 special correspondent
【特派员】tèpàiyuán〈名〉commissioner: ～公署 commissioner's office
【特批】tèpī〈动〉specially approve
【特聘】tèpìn〈动〉specially hire: ～教授 specially hired professor
【特遣部队】tèqiǎn bùduì〈名〉task force
【特区】tèqū〈名〉**1**（指地区）special zone: 贸易～ special trade zone ‖ 经济～ special economic zone **2** = 特别行政区 tèbié xíngzhèngqū
【特权】tèquán〈名〉privilege: 享有～ enjoy privileges ‖ 行使～ exercise one's prerogative ‖ 外交～ diplomatic privilege
【特色】tèsè〈名〉characteristic: 民族～ distinctive national characteristic ‖ 建设有中国～的社会主义 build socialism with Chinese characteristics ‖ 表演各有～。Each performance has its own distinguishing characteristic.
【特色菜】tèsècài〈名〉speciality: 我们餐馆的～是烤鸭。Roast duck is a speciality of our restaurant.
【特赦】tèshè〈动〉grant a special pardon: 获得～ be under an amnesty ‖ ～令 decree of special pardon
【特使】tèshǐ〈名〉special envoy: 联合国～ UN emissary ‖ 总统～ presidential envoy
【特首】tèshǒu〈名〉chief executive of Hong Kong or Macao Special Administrative Regions
【特殊】tèshū〈形〉special: 给于～照顾 give special treatment ‖ 享受～待遇 enjoy preferential treatment ‖ ～情况 special circumstances
【特殊化】tèshūhuà〈动〉〈贬〉[of those in positions of authority] start receiving privileges: 搞～ use one's power to seek privileges
【特殊教育】tèshū jiàoyù〈名〉special education
【特殊性】tèshūxìng〈名〉peculiarity: 这工作有它的～。The job has its peculiarities.
【特斯拉】tèsīlā〈量〉［物理］tesla
【特体】tètǐ〈形〉[of human body] unusual in size: 加工～服装 make garments of special sizes
【特为】tèwèi〈副〉specially: 我～感谢你而来。I've come specially to thank you.
【特务】tèwù〈名〉［军事］special duties: ～营 special task battalion
【特务】tèwu〈名〉special/secret agent, spy: 老牌～ experienced secret agent ‖ 潜伏～ mole
【特嫌】tèxián〈名〉**1**（指嫌疑）suspicion of being a spy: ～分子 person suspected of being a spy **2**（指嫌疑人）person suspected of being a spy
【特效】tèxiào〈名〉special efficacy: 有～ be especially effective ‖ ～药 effective cure
【特写】tèxiě〈名〉**1**（指新闻体裁）feature article: 人物～ feature article on a person ‖ 新闻～ news feature **2**［影视］close-up: 面部～ face close-up ‖ ～镜头 close-up
【特型】tèxíng〈名〉**1**（指材质）special type: ～钢材 special types of steel **2**（指人）special kind: ～演员 typecast actor
【特性】tèxìng〈名〉characteristic: 具有某种～ have a particular characteristic ‖ 民族～ national traits ‖ 对物质是根据其～进行描述的。Matter is described in terms of its properties.
【特需】tèxū〈形〉specially needed: ～供应 specially needed commodity supply ‖ ～商品 specially needed commodity
【特许】tèxǔ〈动〉specially permit: ～经销权 franchise ‖ ～通行证 franchising permit
【特许权】tèxǔquán〈名〉franchise
【特许状】tèxǔzhuàng〈名〉charter
【特邀】tèyāo〈动〉specially invite: ～代表 specially invited representative ‖ ～嘉宾 specially invited guest of honour
【特异】tèyì〈形〉**1**（特别优异）excellent: 成绩～ outstanding achievements **2**（特殊）distinctive: 风格～ distinctive style
【特异功能】tèyì gōngnéng〈名〉supernatural power
【特意】tèyì〈副〉specially: 我是～来看你的。I've come here specially to see you. ‖ 这蛋糕是她～为庆祝你的生日做的。She made this cake specially for your birthday.
【特有】tèyǒu〈形〉characteristic: 本地～的物种 species peculiar to this place ‖ 他说话带着南方～的口音。He speaks with an accent peculiar to the South.
【特约】tèyuē〈动〉engage by special arrangement: ～评论员 special commentator ‖ ～演员 guest actor
【特约记者】tèyuē jìzhě〈名〉special correspondent
【特招生】tèzhāoshēng〈名〉specially enrolled student
【特征】tèzhēng〈名〉characteristic: 地理/地质～ geographical/geological feature ‖ 面部～ facial characteristic ‖ 时代～ characteristics of the times ‖ 性格～ personality trait ‖ 艺术～ artistic feature
【特指】tèzhǐ〈动〉refer in particular to: 人们用"超级大国"～美国。By 'super power' people refer specifically to the United States of America.
【特制】tèzhì〈动〉be custom-made; be bespoke〈英〉: 他们穿～的潜水服潜水。They dive in custom-made suits.
【特质】tèzhì〈名〉distinguishing characteristic
【特种】tèzhǒng〈形〉special
【特种兵】tèzhǒngbīng〈名〉special technical troops
【特种部队】tèzhǒng bùduì〈名〉special forces: 美国陆军～ US Army Special Forces
【特种工艺品】tèzhǒng gōngyìpǐn〈名〉special handicraft products
【特种邮票】tèzhǒng yóupiào〈名〉special stamp

铽（鋱） tè〈名〉［化学］terbium (Tb)

tēng

熥 tēng〈动〉heat up by steaming: ～馒头 heat up steamed buns

鼟 tēng〈拟〉[sound of drumbeat] thump: 鼓声～～ thumping drumbeats

téng

疼 téng〈动〉**1**（感到疼痛）pain: 止～ kill the pain ‖ 胃～ have a stomach ache ‖ 牙～ have a toothache ‖ 发炎的伤口很～。The inflamed wound is giving me a lot of pain. ▸头～ **2**（喜爱）dote on: 妈妈最～小儿子。Mother dotes on her youngest son. ‖ 这孩子招人～。The child is very lovable. ▸～爱
【疼爱】téng'ài〈动〉love dearly: 爷爷最～小孙女。Grandpa really dotes on his granddaughter. ‖ 这个小女孩真惹人～。This little girl is really adorable.
【疼痛】téngtòng〈名〉pain: 减轻～ relieve pain ‖ 剧烈的～ intense pain
【疼惜】téngxī〈动〉love tenderly

腾（騰） téng〈动〉**1**（上升）soar: ▸～空, ～云驾雾, 升～ **2**（跳起）jump: ～身跃过 leap over sth. ▸～越, 奔～, 欢～ **3**（空出来）clear out: ～房子给客人住 vacate one's own room in order to put up a visitor ‖ 她每天～出时间给孩子辅导英语。She sets aside some time every day to coach her child in English. **4**（表反复、连续）[used after certain verbs to indicate repeated actions]: ▸倒～, 闹～, 折～
【腾达】téngdá〈动〉〈书〉**1**（上升）soar **2**（发迹）rise to power and position: ▸飞黄～
【腾飞】téngfēi〈动〉**1**（腾空飞起）soar: 壁画里有～的龙。There are flying dragons in the mural. **2**（快速发展）make rapid progress: 中国的经济在～。China's economy is really taking off.
【腾格里沙漠】Ténggélǐ Shāmò〈名〉Tengger Desert
【腾空】téngkōng〈动〉rise high into the air: 烈焰～。Raging flames soared into the air. ‖ 火箭～而起。The rocket soared into the sky.
【腾挪】téngnuó〈动〉**1**（挪用）reassign: 专款专用，不得任意～。Funds earmarked for specific purposes are not to be transferred to other use without due authorization. **2**（挪动）move sth. to make room for sth. else: 他为摆放新书，把架子上的东西～了一下。He moved the things on the shelf to make room for his new books.

【腾让】téngràng〈动〉make room (for sth.)

【腾闪】téngshǎn〈动〉dodge: ～不及 be too late to avoid dodge

【腾腾】téngténg〈形〉steaming: 烟雾～ smoke-laden ‖ 热气～ steaming hot

【腾涌】téngyǒng〈动〉[of water currents] surge

【腾跃】téngyuè〈动〉**1**（奔跑跳跃）gallop: 万马～ horses are galloping about **2**〈书〉（快速上升）soar: 近来油价～。The price of oil is skyrocketing.

【腾越】téngyuè〈动〉jump over: ～障碍物 jump over an obstacle

【腾云驾雾】téngyún-jiàwù〈成〉**1**〈本〉mount the clouds and ride the mist **2**〈喻〉feel giddy: 过山车让他们感到犹如～。The roller coaster made them feel giddy. ‖ 他喝了威士忌感到～一般。The whisky made him go dizzy.

誊（謄）

téng〈动〉write out: 照底稿～一遍 make a clean copy of the draft

【誊抄】téngchāo〈动〉copy out

【誊录】ténglù〈动〉copy out: ～文稿 copy out a manuscript

【誊清】téngqīng〈动〉make a clean copy: ～稿 clean copy ‖ 这是底稿，还没有～呢! This is the draft. It hasn't been transcribed yet.

【誊写】téngxiě〈动〉write out: ～讲课笔记 transcribe lecture notes ‖ ～员 copyist

【誊印社】téngyìnshè〈名〉mimeograph service

滕

téng〈名〉*teng* [name of a vassal state of the Zhou Dynasty]

藤（籐）

téng〈名〉**1**（指茎蔓）vine: 葡萄/西瓜～ grape/watermelon vine ▸顺～摸瓜 **2**（指植物）rattan: ～椅 rattan chair

【藤本植物】téngběn zhíwù〈名〉［植物］liana

【藤编】téngbiān〈名〉rattan work

【藤壶】ténghú〈名〉［动物］barnacle

【藤萝】téngluó〈名〉［植物］Chinese wisteria

【藤牌】téngpái〈名〉cane shield

【藤球】téngqiú ▸**p. 909**〈名〉［体育］kick volleyball

【藤圈】téngquān〈名〉rattan hoop: ～操 hoop exercises

【藤条】téngtiáo〈名〉cane

【藤蔓】téngwàn〈名〉vine: 黄瓜的～爬满了架。Cucumber vines are climbing all over the trellis.

【藤箱】téngxiāng〈名〉rattan suitcase

【藤子】téngzi〈名〉〈口〉**1**（指茎蔓）vine **2**（指植物）rattan

tī

体（體）

tī

▸tǐ

【体己】tīji **A**〈形〉intimate: ～话 words spoken in confidence ‖ ～人 bosom friend **B**〈名〉private savings: 攒～钱 scrape together one's private savings ‖ 这家每个成员都有自己的～。Each member of the family has his or her own private savings.

剔

tī **A**〈动〉**1**（刮下来）pick meat from bones: ～排骨上的肉 pick meat from the ribs ‖ 把骨头～净 pick a bone clean **2**（往外挑）clean with a pointed instrument: ～牙 pick one's teeth ‖ ～指甲 clean one's fingernails **3**（拣出去）weed out: 把残次品～出来 weed out inferior goods ‖ 把烂苹果～出去 pick out the rotten apples ▸～除, 挑～ **B**〈名〉rising stroke [in a Chinese character]

【剔除】tīchú〈动〉eliminate: 吸取精华，～糟粕 absorb the essence and reject the dross

【剔骨肉】tīgǔròu〈名〉meat with the bones removed

【剔红】tīhóng〈名〉carved lacquerware

【剔透】tītòu〈形〉transparent: ▸玲珑～

梯

tī〈名〉**1**（梯子）ladder: 伸缩～ extension ladder ▸电～, 阶～ **2**（梯状物）sth. shaped like a ladder: ▸～队, ～田

【梯次】tīcì〈名〉division: 教师年龄结构～合理。There is a good balance of ages amongst the teachers.

【梯度】tīdù〈名〉**1**［物理］gradient **2** = 梯次 tīcì

【梯队】tīduì〈名〉**1**［军事］echelon formation: 成～飞行 fly in echelon formation ‖ ～阵列 echelon **2**（指人员结构层次）group of persons of one level or grade in an organization, kept for use when needed: 形成人才～ form an echelon of qualified personnel

【梯恩梯】tī'ēntī〈名〉［化学］trinitrotoluene (TNT): ～当量 TNT equivalent

【梯级】tījí〈名〉**1**（指阶梯）step **2**（指水利工程）system of irrigation dams

【梯己】tīji = 体己 tīji

【梯田】tītián〈名〉［农业］terraced fields: 修～ terrace mountain slopes

【梯形】tīxíng〈名〉［数学］trapezium〈英〉; trapezoid〈美〉

【梯子】tīzi〈名〉ladder

锑（銻）

tī〈名〉［化学］antimony: ～中毒 antimony poisoning

踢

tī〈动〉kick: ～毽子 kick a shuttlecock ‖ ～足球 kick a football ‖ 把门～开 kick the door open ‖〈喻〉她被公司～出了门。She was kicked out of the company.

【踢跶】tīdā〈拟〉[sound of footsteps] patter: 她～～地在地板上走过。She tapped across the floor.

【踢蹬】tīdeng〈动〉**1**（又踢又蹬）kick at random: 孩子仰面躺在那里，双腿不停地向上～。The baby was lying on its back, kicking its legs in the air. **2**（挥霍）squander: 他已经把这个月的工资～完了。He has already squandered away his entire month's salary. **3**（处理）deal with: 我花了整整一星期才把搬家后那些家务～完。It took me a whole week to sort out all the stuff from the move.

【踢脚板】tījiǎobǎn〈名〉［建筑］skirting board〈英〉; baseboard〈美〉

【踢脚线】tījiǎoxiàn = 踢脚板 tījiǎobǎn

【踢皮球】tī píqiú〈惯〉〈喻〉pass the buck: 互相～ pass the buck to each other

【踢踏舞】tītàwǔ〈名〉tap dance: 表演～ perform a tap dance

【踢腾】tīteng = 踢蹬 tīdeng

【踢腿】tītuǐ〈动〉［体育］split kick

鹛（鷈）

tī ▸䴘鹛 pìtī

擿

tī〈动〉〈书〉expose: 发奸～伏 openly expose sb.'s evildoing

tí

荑

tí〈名〉〈书〉**1**（嫩叶）sprout: 新～ tender bud **2**（稗子）tare

▸yí

绨（綈）

tí〈名〉〈书〉thick silk: ～袍 silk gown

▸tì

提

tí

A〈动〉**1**（垂着手拿）carry in one's hand: ～行李 carry one's luggage in one's hand ‖ 我去～水。I'll go and fetch water. ▸～心吊胆 **2**（升高）lift: ～薪 raise sb.'s salary ‖ ～价 raise prices ‖ 将某人～到领导岗位上来 promote sb. to a position of leadership ▸～拔, ～高, ～升 **3**（提前）move forward: ▸～前, ～早 **4**（举出）put forward: ～意见 offer an opinion ‖ ～建议 make a suggestion ‖ ～条件 put forward conditions ‖ ～要求 present one's demands ‖ 把某事～上日程 put sth. on the agenda ▸～名, ～示, ～醒 **5**（取出）extract: 从银行～现金 withdraw cash from a bank ‖ 我要去邮局～包裹。I'm going to collect a parcel at the post office. ▸～成, ～货, ～炼 **6**（带出）summon for interrogation: ～犯人 fetch a prisoner for interrogation ▸～审, ～讯 **7**（提及）mention: 不值一～ not worth mentioning ‖ 旧事重～ bring up a matter of the past ▸只字不～ **B**〈名〉**1**（提勺）ladle: ▸酒～, 油～ **2**（指笔画）[in Chinese characters] rising stroke

▸dī

【提案】tí'àn〈名〉proposal: 撤回～ withdraw a proposal ‖ 反对～ oppose a motion ‖ 提交～ submit a proposal ‖ 赞成～ second a motion ‖ ～国 sponsor country (of a resolution) ‖ ～审查委员会 motions examination committee

【提拔】tíbá〈动〉promote: ～到领导岗位 promote sb. to a position of leadership

【提包】tíbāo〈名〉handbag

【提笔】tíbǐ〈动〉start writing

【提倡】tíchàng〈动〉advocate: ～勤俭节约 advocate thrift and frugality ‖ ～晚婚晚育 advocate late marriage and late birth

【提成】tíchéng **A**〈动〉draw a percentage **B**〈名〉commission: 拿到了百分之三的～ get a 30% commission

【提出】tíchū〈动〉put forward: ～抗议 lodge a protest ‖ ～一系列整顿措施 formulate a series of rectification measures ‖ ～意见 offer a suggestion

【提纯】tíchún〈动〉purify: ～金属 refine metals ‖ ～酒精 purify alcohol

【提词】tící〈动〉［戏剧］prompt: 给演员～ prompt an actor

【提存】tícún〈名〉deposit

【提单】tídān〈名〉bill of lading: 凭～提货 use a bill of landing to take delivery of goods

【提到】tídào〈动〉mention

【提调】tídiào **A**〈动〉supervise: 他的工作就是～这个车站所有的车辆。His job is to supervise all the vehicles in this depot. **B**〈名〉supervisor: 舞台～ stage manager ‖ 总～ supervisor general

【提兜】tídōu〈名〉handbag: 拎着～去购物

go shopping with a bag

【提督】tídū〈名〉〈旧〉provincial military commander in imperial China

【提法】tífǎ〈名〉wording: ～不妥 improper wording ‖ 我不能同意你的～。I can't agree with the way that you're putting it.

【提干】tígàn〈动〉**1**（提拔干部）promote a cadre to a higher position: 突击～ promote a cadre in a rush **2**（提为干部）promote sb. to the rank of cadre: 他参军不到两年就～了。Having served in the army for less than two years, he was promoted to cadre.

【提纲】tígāng〈名〉outline: 草拟/起草～ draw up/draft an outline ‖ 发言～ outline for a speech ‖ 写作文前先拟～。Before trying to write a composition, make an outline first.

【提纲挈领】tígāng-qièlǐng〈成〉〈喻〉bring out the essentials: 他在发言中只～地谈及自己的计划。He only touched upon the essentials of his plan in his speech.

【提高】tígāo〈动〉raise: ～产品和服务质量 improve the quality of products and services ‖ ～警惕 sharpen one's vigilance ‖ ～嗓门 raise one's voice ‖ ～业务水平 improve one's professional skill ‖ 你的英语有待进一步～。There is room for further improvement in your English.

【提供】tígōng〈动〉provide: ～贷款 provide sb. with a loan ‖ ～日常生活必需品 supply daily necessities ‖ ～食宿 provide board and lodging ‖ ～信息 furnish sb. with information ‖ ～援助 render assistance ‖ ～证据 produce evidence

【提灌】tíguàn〈动〉pump water for irrigation

【提行】tíháng〈动〉begin a new line

【提盒】tíhé〈名〉tiered lunch box with a handle

【提花】tíhuā〈名〉［纺织］jacquard weave: ～浴巾 jacquard bath towel

【提货】tíhuò〈动〉take delivery of goods: ～通知 cargo delivery notice

【提货单】tíhuòdān = 提单 tídān

【提及】tíjí〈动〉mention: 顺便～此事 mention this thing in passing

【提级】tíjí〈动〉promote: 又加薪又～ receive a rise not only in salary but also in position ‖ 本产品～不提价。This product has been upgraded but its price hasn't been put up.

【提价】tíjià〈动〉raise prices: 食用油已多次～。The price of cooking oil has gone up several times.

【提交】tíjiāo〈动〉submit: ～辞呈 hand in one's resignation ‖ ～仲裁 submit to arbitration ‖ 把决议草案～大会讨论 submit the draft resolution to the congress for discussion ‖ 他被～军事法庭审判。He was handed over to the military tribunal for trial.

【提款】tíkuǎn〈动〉withdraw money from a bank: 预约～ arrange a withdrawal

【提篮】tílán〈名〉hand-basket

【提炼】tíliàn〈动〉extract and purify: 从芬香植物中～香精 abstract flavouring essence from fragrant plants ‖ 将生活素材～加工 [of literary writing] refine raw material gathered from life

【提梁】tíliáng〈名〉handle

【提留】tíliú〈动〉retain part of a sum: ～部分款项作为奖励基金 keep back some of the money for a reward

【提名】tímíng〈动〉nominate: ～为候选人 put sb. in for nomination ‖ 获得百花奖～的有三部电影。Three films have been nominated for the Hundred Flowers Prize.

【提名奖】tímíngjiǎng〈名〉nomination: 奥斯卡～ nomination for an Oscar

【提起】tíqǐ〈动〉**1**（谈到）mention: ～诗人的早逝，没有一个人不感到惋惜。No one ever spoke of the untimely death of the poet without regret. **2**（奋起）exert oneself: ～精神 brace oneself ‖ ～注意力 attract sb.'s attention **3**（提出）put forward: ～诉讼 bring a case (against sb.)

【提前】tíqián〈动〉do sth. ahead of time: ～获释 be released ahead of time ‖ ～完成任务 complete the task ahead of schedule ‖ 他们的婚期～了。Their wedding date has been moved forward.

【提前量】tíqiánliàng〈名〉［军事］lead

【提挈】tíqiè〈动〉**1**（统帅）lead: ～全军 marshal all one's forces **2**（帮助）guide and support: ～后辈 guide and help younger people ‖ 承蒙～，我才有今日。I owe everything to your patronage.

【提亲】tíqīn〈动〉propose a marriage alliance

【提琴】tíqín ▸p. 929〈名〉［音乐］violin family: 小～ violin

【提请】tíqǐng〈动〉submit: ～大会讨论 submit sth. to the congress for discussion ‖ ～各位注意 call everyone's attention ‖ ～仲裁 submit to arbitration

【提取】tíqǔ〈动〉**1**（取回）draw: ～银行存款 withdraw bank deposits ‖ 从机场～行李 collect one's luggage at the airport **2**（提炼）extract: 从油页岩中～石油 extract oil from oil shale

【提取物】tíqǔwù〈名〉extract

【提神】tíshén〈动〉refresh: ～健脑 refresh oneself and invigorate the brain ‖ 喝杯咖啡来～ give oneself a lift with a cup of coffee

【提审】tíshěn〈动〉**1**（针对人）bring to trial: ～犯人 bring a prisoner to trial **2**（针对案件）review: ～悬案 review an unsettled law case

【提升】tíshēng〈动〉**1**（指职位级别）promote: 他做了十多年的助理经理应该～了。After being assistant manager for over ten years, it's time he was promoted. ‖ 他被～为这所大学的校长。He was promoted to the presidency of the university. **2**（指位置水平）elevate: ～生活水平 raise living standards

【提升机】tíshēngjī〈名〉hoist: 斗式～ bucket elevator

【提示】tíshì〈动〉prompt: 给学生～课文要点 give students the gist of the text ‖ 如果我忘记了台词，请你～我一下好吗？Will you prompt me if I forget my lines?

【提手】tíshǒu〈名〉handle

【提速】tísù〈动〉speed up: 火车～了。The train picked up speed.

【提桶】títǒng〈名〉pail

【提味】tíwèi〈动〉flavour: 往汤里放味精～ flavour the soup with MSG

【提问】tíwèn〈动〉ask a question: 老师就课文～，但全班没有一个人能够回答。The teacher put a number of questions about the text to the class, but no one knew the answers.

【提息】tíxī〈动〉raise interest rates: 近期不会～。Interest rates will not rise in the near future.

【提现】tíxiàn〈动〉withdraw cash

【提线木偶】tíxiàn mù'ǒu〈名〉stringed puppets

【提箱】tíxiāng〈名〉suitcase

【提携】tíxié〈动〉**1**（牵扶）lead by the hand **2**（提拔）guide and support: 多蒙～。I'm grateful to you for your guidance. **3**〈书〉（合作）cooperate: 他们在生意中互相～。They helped each other in business.

【提心吊胆】tíxīn-diàodǎn〈成〉have one's heart in one's mouth: 每次飞机着陆，她都～。She has her heart in her mouth every time the plane lands.

【提薪】tíxīn〈动〉raise the salary

【提醒】tíxǐng〈动〉remind: 请你～我饭前吃药。Please remind me to take the medicine before each meal. ‖ 我会～他注意此事。I'll call his attention to the matter.

【提讯】tíxùn〈动〉bring to trial: 犯人被～。The prisoner was brought to court for the trial.

【提要】tíyào **A**〈动〉summarize **B**〈名〉summary: 论文～ abstract of a thesis ‖ 新闻～ news headlines ‖ 《英语语法～》*The Essentials of English Grammar*

【提议】tíyì **A**〈动〉propose: 姐姐～我们乘火车去。My sister suggested that we go by train. ‖ 她～由张先生任主席。She proposed that Mr Zhang be chairman. **B**〈名〉proposal: 他的～以多数票通过。His proposal was adopted by a majority. ‖ 她公开反对我的～。She was openly opposed to my proposal.

【提早】tízǎo〈动〉do sth. in advance: ～出发 set out earlier than planned ‖ ～通知 notify in advance

【提制】tízhì〈动〉extract: 麻黄素是从麻黄中～的。Ephedrine is extracted from ephedra.

【提子】tízi〈名〉grape

猑 tí〈名〉hound ▸灵～

啼 tí〈动〉**1**（鸣叫）caw: 鸡～。Cocks crow. ‖ 月落乌～。The crows caw when the moon goes down. **2**（出声哭）cry: ▸～哭, ～笑皆非

【啼号】tíháo〈动〉wail

【啼饥号寒】tíjī-háohán〈成〉wail with hunger and cold

【啼哭】tíkū〈动〉cry: 大声～ weep aloud

【啼泣】tíqì〈动〉cry

【啼天哭地】títiān-kūdì〈成〉wail with great sorrow

【啼笑皆非】tíxiào-jiēfēi〈成〉not know whether to laugh or cry: 你这事办得让人～。About what you did, I really don't know whether to laugh or cry.

鹈（鵜）tí

【鹈鹕】tíhú〈名〉［鸟类］pelican

缇（緹）tí〈形〉〈书〉orange red

题（題）tí

A〈名〉**1**（题目）subject: 讨论～ topic for discussion ‖ 作文～ topic of a composition ▸～目, 标～, 文不对～ **2**（问题）question: 三道算术～ three mathematical problems ▸出～, 试～, 习～

B〈动〉inscribe: 在墓碑上～诗 inscribe verses on a tombstone ▸～名

【题跋】tíbá〈名〉preface and postscript

【题壁】tíbì **A**〈动〉write on the wall **B**〈名〉inscriptions on a wall: 文人墨客的～ inscriptions by literary men

【题材】tícái〈名〉subject matter: ～新颖 novel subject matter ‖ 历史～ historical theme

【题材股】tícáigǔ〈名〉［金融］theme stock: 高科技～ high-technology theme stocks

t

【题词】tící A〈动〉write words of commemoration, encouragement or appreciation: ～留作纪念 write an inscription for commemoration B〈名〉1（表示留念的话）dedication: 书前有～"献给亲爱的父亲"。The book's dedication reads 'To my dear father'. 2（序文）foreword

【题额】tí'é〈动〉write inscriptions on a horizontal board

【题海】tíhǎi〈名〉〈喻〉question bank: ～战术 the approach of using a question bank

【题花】tíhuā〈名〉title design

【题记】tíjì〈名〉notes preceding the text of a book or following the title of an article

【题解】tíjiě〈名〉1（指解释性文字）explanatory notes 2（指详细解题过程）key to exercises or problems:《平面几何～》*Key to Exercises in Plane Geometry*

【题库】tíkù〈名〉examination question bank: 建～ establish an examination question bank

【题名】tímíng A〈动〉autograph: 请～留念。Please leave your autograph as a memento. B〈名〉autograph

【题目】tímù〈名〉1（标题）subject: 作文～ composition subject ‖ 这篇文章～为《论教育》。The article is entitled '*On Education*.' 2（问题）examination question

【题签】tíqiān A〈动〉write a book title on a label to be stuck on the cover B〈名〉label with a book title on it

【题外话】tíwàihuà〈名〉digression

【题写】tíxiě〈动〉inscribe

【题型】tíxíng〈名〉type of items in an examination paper

【题字】tízì A〈动〉inscribe: 请来宾在纪念册上～。Visitors are invited to sign guest book. B〈名〉autograph: 书上有作者的亲笔～。The book is signed by the author.

t

醍 tí

【醍醐】tíhú〈名〉〈书〉1（指牛奶精华）finest cream 2［佛教］〈喻〉（指最高佛法）supreme truth: ～灌顶 be enlightened

蹄 tí〈名〉hoof: ▸马不停～, 猪～

【蹄筋】tíjīn〈名〉tendons: 红烧～ tendons stewed in soy sauce

【蹄髈】típǎng〈名〉〈方〉upper part of a leg of pork

【蹄铁】títiě〈名〉horseshoe

【蹄子】tízi〈名〉1（兽足）hoof 2〈方〉（肘子）upper part of a leg of pork 3〈旧〉〈粗〉（指女人）bitch〈粗〉: 小～ little bitch

鳀（鯷）tí〈名〉［鱼类］anchovy

tǐ

体（體）tǐ

A〈名〉1（身体）body: ～长 body height ‖ ～弱多病 have a weak constitution ▸～检, ～重, 身～ 2（身体的一部分）part of the body: ▸五～投地, 肢～ 3（整体）mass: ▸～积, 集～, 整～ 4（形态）shape or state of a substance: ▸固～, 气～, 液～ 5［语法］aspect of a verb: 进行～ progressive aspect ‖ 完成～ perfect aspect 6（系统）system: ▸～例, ～系, 政～ 7（风格）style: ▸～裁, 草～, 文～

B〈动〉1（体验）experience sth. personally: ▸～会, ～验 2（为他人着想）put oneself in sb. else's position: ▸～谅, ～贴, ～恤

▸tī

【体表】tǐbiǎo〈名〉body surface: ～面积 body surface area ‖ ～温度 body surface temperature

【体裁】tǐcái〈名〉literary form

【体彩】tǐcǎi〈名〉sports lottery

【体操】tǐcāo ▸**p. 909**〈名〉gymnastics: 竞技～ competitive gymnastics ‖ 器械～ apparatus gymnastics ▸艺术～, 自由～

【体操服】tǐcāofú〈名〉gym outfit

【体操馆】tǐcāoguǎn〈名〉gym

【体操器械】tǐcāo qìxiè〈名〉gymnastic apparatus

【体操鞋】tǐcāoxié〈名〉gym shoes

【体操运动员】tǐcāo yùndòngyuán ▸**p. 966**〈名〉gymnast

【体测】tǐcè〈名〉physical examination

【体察】tǐchá〈动〉experience and observe: ～民情 try to find out and understand how ordinary people feel

【体尝】tǐcháng〈动〉savour: ～到成功/失败的滋味 taste success/failure ‖ ～人生的辛酸 taste the bitterness of life

【体词】tǐcí〈名〉［语法］[in Chinese grammar] general term for nouns, pronouns, numerals and measure words

【体大思精】tǐdà-sījīng〈成〉[of a book] extensive in scope and brilliant in conception

【体罚】tǐfá〈动〉mete out physical punishment: 老师不该～学生。Teachers should not punish their students by beating them.

【体改】tǐgǎi〈简称〉= 体制改革

【体改委】tǐgǎiwěi〈简称〉= 体制改革委员会

【体格】tǐgé〈名〉1（指体质）physique: ～强健 have a strong physique ‖ 他生就一副强壮的～。Nature favoured him with a cast-iron constitution. 2（指体形）build: ～粗壮/瘦小/匀称 be of heavy/slight/proportional build

【体工队】tǐgōngduì〈名〉professional sports team

【体会】tǐhuì A〈动〉learn from experience: 参观了这个展览会，使我～到现代技术的威力。My visit to the exhibition enlightened me on the power of modern technology. ‖ 只有深入群众，才能～他们的真实思想感情。You won't be able to understand the true thoughts and feelings of the masses unless you go deep among them. B〈名〉understanding: 读了这本书你有什么～? What have you learned from the book? ‖ 让我谈谈个人的～。I'd like to say a few words about how I feel about it.

【体绘】tǐhuì〈名〉body painting

【体积】tǐjī〈名〉bulk: ～大 be bulky

【体积吨】tǐjīdūn〈量〉measurement ton

【体检】tǐjiǎn〈名〉physical examination: 定期～ have a regular health check-up ‖ 全面～ general physical examination

【体力】tǐlì〈名〉physical strength: 恢复～ recover one's strength ‖ ～不支 feel run down ‖ ～充沛 be full of physical strength

【体力劳动】tǐlì láodòng〈名〉manual labour: 参加～ take part in manual labour ‖ 从事～ do hard labour

【体例】tǐlì〈名〉style: 编写～ compile stylistic rules

【体谅】tǐliang〈动〉give sympathetic consideration to: 你应该充分～他人的难处。You should make full allowances for other people's difficulties. ‖ 她心肠好，能～人。She is kind-hearted and shows great empathy with others.

【体貌】tǐmào〈名〉general physical appearance: ～相似 resemble each other in bearing and looks ‖ ～特征 physical features

【体面】tǐmian A〈名〉dignity: 有失～ lose face B〈形〉1（光彩）honourable: 行为不～ disgraceful conduct ‖ 好吃懒做是不～的事。Being gluttonous and lazy is disgraceful. 2（好看）good-looking: 穿着～ be well-dressed ‖ 长得～ be good-looking

【体内】tǐnèi〈形〉internal

【体能】tǐnéng〈名〉physical strength: ～训练 strength training ‖ ～下降 one's physical strength is declining ‖ ～测试 test of stamina

【体念】tǐniàn〈动〉show understanding and sympathy for: ～他人难处 make allowances for others' difficulties

【体魄】tǐpò〈名〉physique: ～健壮 have a powerful physique ‖ 他有一副强健的～。He has a strong healthy body.

【体腔】tǐqiāng〈名〉［动物］coelom: ～造影术 endoradiography

【体热】tǐrè〈名〉body heat

【体认】tǐrèn〈动〉experience and understand: 亲身～ get to know personally

【体弱多病】tǐruò-duōbìng〈成〉weak and ill

【体式】tǐshì〈名〉1（字体式样）form of characters and letters: 拼音字母有印刷和手写两种～。Phonetic letters can be printed or handwritten. 2〈书〉（体裁格式）literary style

【体态】tǐtài〈名〉posture: ～轻盈 have a lithe and graceful carriage ‖ 她～优美。She carries herself well.

【体坛】tǐtán〈名〉sports world: ～盛会 grand sports meet ‖ ～新秀 new sports star

【体贴】tǐtiē〈动〉be considerate: 他很～他年迈的母亲。He's very considerate to his aged mother. ‖ 他对妻子～不够。He doesn't show enough consideration for his wife's needs.

【体贴入微】tǐtiē-rùwēi〈成〉be extremely considerate

【体统】tǐtǒng〈名〉propriety: 有失～ be scandalous ‖ 成何～! What a disgrace! ▸不成～

【体外】tǐwài〈形〉external

【体外受精】tǐwài shòujīng〈名〉external fertilization

【体外碎石术】tǐwài suìshíshù〈名〉extracorporeal shock-wave lithotripsy (ESWL)

【体外循环】tǐwài xúnhuán〈名〉extracorporeal circulation: ～心脏手术 open-heart surgery

【体委】tǐwěi〈简称〉= 体育运动委员会

【体位】tǐwèi〈名〉posture

【体味】tǐwèi A〈动〉savour: ～成功的快乐 taste the joy of success ‖ ～人生苦乐 savour the joys and sorrows of life B〈名〉body odour (BO): 除～剂 (body odour) deodorant

【体温】tǐwēn ▸**p. 776**〈名〉body temperature: 他的～在升高。His temperature is going up. ‖ 人的正常～为37摄氏度左右。The normal temperature of the human body is about 37℃.

【体温表】tǐwēnbiǎo = 体温计 tǐwēnjì

【体温计】tǐwēnjì〈名〉thermometer

【体无完肤】tǐwúwánfū〈成〉1〈本〉have cuts and bruises all over one's body: 被打得～ be beaten black and blue 2〈喻〉be torn to pieces: 他的学说被批驳得～。His doctrine was refuted down to the last point.

【体悟】tǐwù〈动〉have a thorough understanding of: ～其中道理 have a thorough

grasp of the reasoning

【体惜】tǐxī〈动〉 understand and sympathize with: ～下属 show sympathetic understanding towards one's subordinates

【体系】tǐxì〈名〉 system: 中国特色社会主义理论～ the system of socialism with Chinese characteristics ‖ 防御～ defence system ‖ 哲学～ philosophical system

【体细胞】tǐxìbāo〈名〉［生物］ somatic cell: ～基因治疗 somatic cell gene therapy ‖ ～染色体 somatic chromosome

【体现】tǐxiàn〈动〉 embody: 该项法律真正～"一国两制"的构想。 This law truly embodies the concept of 'one country, two systems.' ‖ 这本书～了作者的观点。 The book reflected the author's views.

【体校】tǐxiào〈简称〉= 体育运动学校

【体协】tǐxié〈名〉 sports association

【体形】tǐxíng〈名〉 1（指人或动物）figure: 我们俩～偏瘦。 Both of us are a little underweight. 2（指机器） shape: 机器～美观。 The machine has a nice shape.

【体型】tǐxíng〈名〉 body type: 成年人和儿童在～上有显著的区别。 Adults and children are quite different in build. ‖ 她的～适合跳芭蕾舞。 She has a good body for ballet.

【体恤】tǐxù〈动〉 understand and sympathize with: ～孤寡老人 show empathy for the orphaned and widowed, the lonely and aged

【体癣】tǐxuǎn ▸**p. 50**〈名〉［医学］ ringworm (of the body)

【体循环】tǐxúnhuán〈名〉［生理］systemic circulation

【体验】tǐyàn〈动〉 learn through personal experience: ～到死亡的恐惧 taste the fear of death ‖ 我～到了读书的乐趣。 I savoured the pleasures of reading. ‖ 作家应该到群众中去～生活。 Writers should go among the masses to observe and learn from real life.

【体液】tǐyè〈名〉 body fluid

【体育】tǐyù〈名〉 1（指教育） physical education (PE): ～锻炼 physical exercise ‖ 我们下午有两节～课。 We have two hours of PE this afternoon. 2（指运动） sports: ～新闻 sports news ‖ ～节目 sports programme ‖ ～专栏 sports section ‖ 群众性～活动 mass sporting activities

【体育彩票】tǐyù cǎipiào〈名〉 sports lottery

【体育场】tǐyùchǎng〈名〉 1（比赛场地） sports ground 2（体育馆） stadium: 奥林匹克～ Olympic Stadium ‖ 北京工人～ Beijing Workers' Stadium

【体育道德】tǐyù dàodé〈名〉 sportsmanship

【体育馆】tǐyùguǎn〈名〉 gymnasium

【体育界】tǐyùjiè〈名〉 sports world

【体育学院】tǐyù xuéyuàn〈名〉 sports institute/college

【体育用品】tǐyù yòngpǐn〈名〉 sporting goods: ～商店 sports shop

【体育运动】tǐyù yùndòng〈名〉 sports: 爱好～ enjoy sports

【体育运动委员会】tǐyù yùndòng wěiyuánhuì〈名〉 sports commission

【体育运动学校】tǐyù yùndòng xuéxiào〈名〉 sports school

【体院】tǐyuàn〈简称〉= 体育学院

【体征】tǐzhēng〈名〉［医学］ pathological sign: ～平稳 stable pathological signs

【体制】tǐzhì〈名〉 1（指组织制度）system: 管理～ managerial structure ‖ 经济～ economic system ‖ 政治～ political set-up 2（指体裁） style of literary writing: 五言诗的～在汉代就形成了。 The five characters to a line style of poetry appeared as early as the Han Dynasty.

【体制改革】tǐzhì gǎigé〈名〉 institutional reform

【体制改革委员会】tǐzhì gǎigé wěiyuánhuì〈名〉 commission for structural reforms

【体制性】tǐzhìxìng〈形〉 institutional: 提供～保障 provide institutional safeguards ‖ ～矛盾 institutional conflict

【体质】tǐzhì〈名〉constitution: 增强～ build up a strong constitution ‖ ～虚弱 have a weak constitution ‖ 增强人民～ build up people's health

【体重】tǐzhòng〈名〉 (body) weight: 一个星期～减轻五斤 sweat off five *jin* in a week

tì

屉（屜） tì〈名〉 1（抽屉）drawer: 三～桌 three-drawer desk 2（笼屉） steamer tray: 一～馒头 a trayful of steamed buns 3（可活动部分） removable part of a bed or chair usu made of rattan, wire, etc.

【屉子】tìzi〈名〉 1（笼屉） food steamer of several trays 2（可活动部分） removable part of a bed or chair usu made of rattan, wire, etc. 3〈方〉（抽屉） drawer

剃 tì〈动〉 shave: ～胡子 have a shave ‖ 他～了个平头。 His hair was shaved in a crew cut.

【剃刀】tìdāo〈名〉 razor: 锋利的～ sharp razor

【剃刀鲸】tìdāojīng = 蓝鲸 lánjīng

【剃度】tìdù〈动〉［佛教］ shave off hair: ～为尼/僧 take the tonsure and become a Buddhist nun/monk ‖ ～修行 have one's hair cut and become a Buddhist monk/nun

【剃光头】tì guāngtóu〈动〉 1〈本〉 have one's head shaved clean 2〈喻〉 score no points: 去年这个中学在全国高考中被剃了光头。 Not a single student from this middle school passed the national college entrance examination last year.

【剃头】tìtóu〈动〉 have one's hair cut: 他们的头都剃了。 Their heads were shaven.

【剃头挑子一头热】tìtóu tiāozi yī tóu rè〈歇后〉〈喻〉 be the only one to take the initiative

【剃头店】tìtóudiàn〈名〉 barber's

【剃头匠】tìtóujiàng〈名〉 barber

【剃须】tìxū〈动〉 have a shave

【剃须刀】tìxūdāo〈名〉 razor: 电动～ electric razor

【剃须膏】tìxūgāo〈名〉 shaving cream

倜 tì

【倜傥】tìtǎng〈形〉〈书〉unconstrained: 风流～ unconventional and romantic ‖ ～不羁 unconventional and unconstrained

涕 tì〈名〉 1〈书〉（泪） tear: ▸破～为笑，痛哭流～ 2（鼻涕） mucus of the nose: ▸鼻～

【涕泪】tìlèi〈名〉 1（泪） tears 2（泪和鼻涕） tears and snivel: ～俱下 stream with tears

【涕零】tìlíng〈动〉 weep: ▸感激～

【涕泣】tìqì〈动〉〈书〉 sob

【涕泗滂沱】tìsì-pāngtuó〈成〉 be drenched with tears and snivel

悌 tì〈动〉〈书〉 have love and respect for one's elder brother: ▸孝～

绨（綈） tì〈名〉〈书〉 silk and cotton fabric ▸tí

惕 tì〈形〉〈书〉 watchful: ▸警～

【惕厉】tìlì〈形〉〈书〉 watchful and frightened

替[1] tì〈形〉〈书〉 waning: 衰～ decline ▸兴～

替[2] tì

A〈动〉 take the place of: 今天我～你开车。 Today I'll drive the car for you. ‖ 他今天不来了，你～他吧。 He isn't coming today. Will you take his place? ▸～班，交～，接～

B〈介〉for: 别～我担心。 Don't worry about me. ‖ 我～她预订了旅馆房间。 I've reserved a room for her at the hotel.

【替班】tìbān〈动〉 take sb. else's place in a work shift: 他今天请病假，我们得找个人～。 He is on sick leave today. We have to find somebody to take his place.

【替补】tìbǔ〈动〉 substitute for: ～队员 substitute ‖ 每个队都有几名～队员。 There are several substitutes on each team.

【替补席】tìbǔxí〈名〉［体育］ bench: 因伤不能上场的主力中锋也坐在～上。 Due to injury, the lead centre is also sitting out on the bench.

【替代】tìdài〈动〉 substitute for: 用天然气～煤作燃料 substitute natural gas for coal ‖ 不可～的人 irreplaceable person ‖ 她外出时她的助手将～她处理事务。 Her assistant will stand in for her while she is away.

【替代燃料】tìdài ránliào〈名〉 alternative fuel

【替工】tìgōng A〈动〉 fill in for: 我明天有事，请你给我替一下工。 I have an appointment tomorrow. Would you please fill in for me? B〈名〉 temporary substitute worker: 找个～ get a replacement

【替换】tìhuàn〈动〉 replace: 多带一些～的衣服 take some more changes of clothes ‖ 主力中锋被～下场。 The top centre-forward was substituted.

【替考】tìkǎo〈动〉 take an examination for sb. else

【替身】tìshēn〈名〉 1（替罪羊） scapegoat 2（替代者） substitute: ～演员 stunt double ‖ 他拍电影从来不用～。 When he makes a film, he never uses stand-ins.

【替死鬼】tìsǐguǐ〈名〉〈口〉 scapegoat

【替罪羊】tìzuìyáng〈名〉 scapegoat

嚏 tì

【嚏喷】tìpen = 喷嚏 pēntì

tiān

天 tiān

A〈名〉 1（天空） sky: 蓝～白云 blue sky and white clouds ‖ 明朗的～ clear sky ‖ 太阳一出满～红。 The sky is aglow with the rising sun. ▸～昏地暗，苍～ 2（上帝） God: ～哪! My God! ▸～机，～意 3（天堂） heaven: ▸～国，～堂 4（自然界） nature: ▸～灾人祸，人定胜～ 5（天

t

气）weather: 雨～ rainy weather ‖ ～晴了。The sky has cleared. ‖ ～热起来了。It's become hot. ▸晴～, 阴～ **6**（季节）season: 冷～ cold season ‖ 三伏～ dog days ▸春～ **7**（日子）day: 第二～ second day ‖ 每～ every day ‖ 八月有三十一～。There are thirty-one days in August. ▸今～, 昨～ **8**（时辰）period of time in a day: 五更～ around four o'clock in the morning ‖ ～还早呢。It's still early.

B〈形〉**1**（天然）natural: ▸～赋, ～堑, ～性 **2**（架在空中）overhead: ▸～窗, ～桥, ～线

【天安门】Tiān'ānmén〈名〉Tian'anmen [Gate of Heavenly Peace]: ～城楼 Tian'anmen gate tower ‖ ～广场 Tian'anmen Square

【天半】tiānbàn〈名〉mid-air: 悬在～ be suspended in mid-air

【天崩地裂】tiānbēng-dìliè〈成〉earth-shattering event

【天边】tiānbiān〈名〉**1**（天涯）ends of the earth: ▸远在～, 近在眼前 **2**（天际）horizon

【天兵】tiānbīng〈名〉**1**（神兵）divine troops: ～天将 divine troops descending from Heaven **2**（指军队）imperial troops **3**（无敌的军队）invincible troops

【天禀】tiānbǐng〈名〉〈书〉natural endowments: ～聪颖 be naturally bright and talented

【天波】tiānbō〈名〉［通信］sky wave

【天不怕，地不怕】tiān bù pà, dì bù pà〈俗〉fear nothing on earth

【天不作美】tiānbùzuòměi〈惯〉the weather is not good

【天才】tiāncái〈名〉**1**（指才能）genius: ～的发明家/科学家/音乐家 inventive/scientific/musical genius ‖ 大家公认他有艺术～。Everyone recognizes his artistic talent. **2**（指人）genius: 军事/数学/艺术/音乐～ military/mathematical/artistic/musical genius ‖ 莎士比亚是伟大的文学～。Shakespeare was a great literary genius.

【天蚕】tiāncán〈名〉［昆虫］giant silkworm

【天差地远】tiānchā-dìyuǎn〈成〉be poles apart

【天长地久】tiāncháng-dìjiǔ〈成〉everlasting and unchanging: 愿我们的友谊～。May our friendship last forever.

【天长日久】tiāncháng-rìjiǔ〈成〉as time goes by: 起初，她不喜欢这里这么潮湿。～，也就习惯了。At the beginning, she didn't like the humidity here, but she got used to it as time went by.

【天车】tiānchē〈名〉［机械］overhead travelling crane: ～滑道 crane runway

【天成】tiānchéng〈动〉〈书〉be made by nature: 佳偶～ heaven-made couple ‖ 美丽～ endowed with natural beauty

【天秤座】Tiānchèngzuò〈名〉［天文］Libra

【天池】Tiānchí ▸**p. 305**〈名〉Tianchi Lake [any of the lakes on Tianshan (天山) in Xinjiang, Baitou Mountains (白头山) in Jilin, or Guancen Mountains (管涔山) in Shanxi]

【天窗】tiānchuāng〈名〉skylight

【天赐】tiāncì〈动〉be sent by heaven: ～良机 god-sent opportunity ‖ ～良缘 marriage sent from heaven

【天从人愿】tiāncóngrényuàn〈成〉by the grace of God

【天打雷轰】tiāndǎ-léihōng〈成〉[usu used in swearing] be punished by God

【天打雷劈】tiāndǎ-léipī = 天打雷轰 tiāndǎ-léihōng

【天打五雷轰】tiāndǎ wǔléihōng = 天打雷轰 tiāndǎ-léihōng

【天大】tiāndà〈形〉as big as the heavens: ～的笑话 outrageous joke ‖ 你就是有～的本事，也难把他教育过来。However clever you are, you can't make him mend his ways.

【天道】tiāndào〈名〉〈古〉［哲学］Way of Heaven

【天敌】tiāndí〈名〉natural enemy: 猫是老鼠的～。The cat is the natural enemy of the mouse.

【天底下】tiāndǐxia〈名〉〈口〉the world: ～哪有这种道理! How preposterous! ‖ 我是～最幸福的人。I am the happiest man on earth.

【天地】tiāndì〈名〉**1**（天和地）universe: ～万物 everything in the world ‖ ～之大，无奇不有。On this vast earth there is no shortage of miracles. **2**（范围）scope: 开辟合作的新～ open up a new field for collaboration ‖ 另有一番～ have a different field of activity **3**〈方〉（境地）plight: 他不料走错一步，竟落到这般～。He didn't expect that this one wrong move would land him in such a predicament.

【天地不容】tiāndì-bùróng〈成〉neither god nor man can forgive

【天地良心】tiāndì-liángxīn〈成〉in all honesty: ～，她和这事真的一点关系都没有。In all fairness, I have to make it clear that she has nothing to do with the matter.

【天地头】tiāndìtóu〈名〉［印刷］top and bottom margins of a page

【天帝】tiāndì〈名〉〈古〉Celestial Ruler

【天电】tiāndiàn〈名〉［电气］static: ～干扰 static interference

【天顶】tiāndǐng〈名〉［天文］zenith

【天鹅】tiān'é〈名〉swan: 小～ cygnet

【天鹅绒】tiān'éróng〈名〉［纺织］velvet: ～织物 velvet stuff

【天鹅座】Tiān'ézuò〈名〉［天文］Cygnus

【天蛾】tiān'é〈名〉hawkmoth

【天翻地覆】tiānfān-dìfù〈成〉**1**（形容变化大）earth-shaking changes: 这几年，村里起了～的变化。The village has witnessed tremendous changes over the years. **2**（形容混乱）total disorder: 他们闹得～，四邻不安。They almost turned the house upside down, creating great disturbance in the neighbourhood.

【天方】Tiānfāng〈名〉〈旧〉Arab countries in the Middle East: ～国 Arab countries

【天方夜谭】Tiānfāng-yètán〈名〉**1**（指故事集）*The Arabian Nights* **2**〈喻〉（指传闻）cock-and-bull story

【天分】tiānfèn〈名〉talent: ～高 be highly talented ‖ 他很有音乐～。He has a gift for music.

【天府之国】tiānfǔzhīguó〈成〉land of abundance [usu referring to Sichuan Province]

【天赋】tiānfù **A**〈动〉be endowed by nature **B**〈名〉natural gift: ～聪颖 be gifted with intelligence ‖ 那家人都有音乐～。A gift for music runs in that family.

【天干】tiāngān〈名〉Heavenly Stems

【天罡】Tiāngāng〈名〉［天文］**1**（北斗星）Big Dipper **2**（北斗星的柄）handle of the Big Dipper

【天罡星】Tiāngāngxīng〈名〉［天文］Big Dipper

【天高地厚】tiāngāo-dìhòu〈成〉**1**（指恩情）profound **2**（指复杂艰巨程度）immensity of the universe: ▸不知～

【天高皇帝远】tiān gāo huángdì yuǎn〈俗〉**1**（指不公正）justice is late in coming **2**（指无人管）when the cat's away, the mice will play

> **天干地支**
>
> Two cycles, known in shortened form as 干支, that form a system that was traditionally used to mark the passing of time. 干支 were already widely used as early as the Western Han period. The ten Heavenly Stems combine with the twelve Earthly Branches in a fixed order to form a 60-year cycle known as 六十甲子. The Heavenly Stems are, in order: 甲、乙、丙、丁、戊、己、庚、辛、壬、癸. The Earthly Branches are, in order: 子、丑、寅、卯、辰、巳、午、未、申、酉、戌、亥. The first year of the 60-year cycle is 甲子, the second 乙丑, and so on. Each Earthly Branch is associated with one of the twelve animals of the Chinese zodiac (▸十二生肖). The year 2009, for example, is the 己丑 Ox year, and so is 2069, 60 years later. The 干支 system was also used to denote months and times of the day.

【天高气爽】tiāngāo-qìshuǎng〈成〉fine autumn weather

【天鸽座】Tiāngēzuò〈名〉［天文］Columba

【天各一方】tiāngèyīfāng〈成〉live far apart from each other

【天公】tiāngōng〈名〉God

【天公地道】tiāngōng-dìdào〈成〉fair and reasonable: 多劳多得，是～的事儿。More pay for more work is absolutely fair.

【天宫】tiāngōng〈名〉heavenly palace: 孙悟空大闹～ the Monkey King wreaking havoc in the Heavenly Palace

【天沟】tiāngōu〈名〉［建筑］gutter

【天光】tiānguāng〈名〉**1**（天色）time of the day: ～不早了。It's getting late. ‖ ～还早。It's still early. **2**（日光）sunlight: ～渐渐隐去。The sunlight gradually faded away.

【天癸】tiānguǐ〈名〉［中医］menstruation

【天国】tiānguó〈名〉**1**［基督教］Heaven: 愿他的灵魂在～安息。May his soul rest in Heaven. **2**（天堂）paradise: 人间～ paradise on earth

【天寒地冻】tiānhán-dìdòng〈成〉it is so cold that the earth is frozen solid

【天河】Tiānhé〈名〉［天文］Milky Way

【天黑】tiānhēi〈名〉deepening dusk

【天候】tiānhòu〈名〉［气象］weather: ▸全～

【天花】tiānhuā ▸**p. 50**〈名〉［医学］smallpox: ～病毒 variola virus

【天花板】tiānhuābǎn〈名〉ceiling

【天花乱坠】tiānhuā-luànzhuì〈成〉wild boast about sth.: 吹得～ make a wild boast about sb./sth.

【天荒地老】tiānhuāng-dìlǎo〈成〉for all eternity

【天皇】tiānhuáng〈名〉**1**（皇帝）emperor **2**（日本天皇）emperor of Japan

【天昏地暗】tiānhūn-dì'àn〈成〉**1**（天气阴暗）dark all around: 一阵狂风刮得～。A gust of wind darkened the sky and obscured everything. **2**（社会黑暗）in a state of chaos and darkness: 军阀混战，闹得全国～。The fighting among the warlords plunged the country into complete chaos. **3**（程度剧烈）to an extreme degree: 母亲去世时，她哭了个～。She cried her heart out when her mother passed away.

【天昏地黑】tiānhūn-dìhēi = 天昏地暗 tiānhūn-dì'àn

【天火】tiānhuǒ〈名〉fire caused by lightning or other natural phenomena

【天机】tiānjī〈名〉**1**（天意）God's design **2**〈喻〉（机密）great secret: 一语道破

～ expose a secret with one remark ‖ ～不可泄漏。 Heaven's secrets must not be divulged.

【天极】tiānjí〈名〉1 ［天文］ celestial pole 2〈书〉（天边） horizon

【天际】tiānjì〈名〉 horizon: 在遥远的～ on the distant horizon

【天价】tiānjià〈名〉 exorbitant price: 这幅古画以～成交。 This ancient painting is being sold at an exorbitant price.

【天骄】tiānjiāo〈名〉 God's favoured son [first referring to *chanyu* (单于), monarch of the Xiongnu (匈奴) ethnic group in the Han Dynasty and later to rulers of minority peoples]: 一代～成吉思汗 Genghis Khan, proud son of Heaven of his time

【天津】Tiānjīn ▸**p. 661**〈名〉 Tianjin

【天经地义】tiānjīng-dìyì〈成〉 in line with the principles of heaven and earth: 杀人偿命，～。 It is only right and proper that murder should be punishable by death.

【天井】tiānjǐng〈名〉 1（院中露天空地） courtyard 2［矿业］ raise: 通风～ air raise 3［建筑］ sunk panel

【天九牌】tiānjiǔpái〈名〉Chinese dominoes

> **天九牌**
>
> *Tianjiu*, a game usually played by four players using 32 tiles divided into 2 suits, civilian and military, with 'Heaven' (天) and 'nine' (九) being the biggest piece in each suit, hence the name. There are 11 types of civilian tiles, with 2 of each kind, making 22 pieces altogether. There are 10 military tiles: 2 are completely different, while the other 8 fall into 4 pairs, each pair having the same number, but different images. The first player leads by playing a piece, or a combination of pieces, from either suit or both suits. In order to win the round, other players must put down the same type and number of pieces but with a higher value. The player who takes the last round wins the game.

【天空】tiānkōng〈名〉 sky: 仰望～ look up at the sky ‖ ～乌云密布。 The sky clouded over. ‖ 雄鹰在～翱翔。 An eagle is hovering in the sky.

【天籁】tiānlài〈名〉〈书〉 sounds of nature: ～之音 sounds of nature

【天蓝】tiānlán〈名〉 sky blue

【天狼星】Tiānlángxīng〈名〉［天文］Sirius

【天朗气清】tiānlǎng-qìqīng〈成〉the sky is clear and the air is crisp

【天老爷】tiānlǎoye〈名〉 God

【天理】tiānlǐ〈名〉 1（道德法则） heavenly principles [feudal ethics as propounded by the Confucianists in the Song Dynasty]: 存～，灭人欲 maintain the heavenly principles and eradicate human desires 2（正义） justice: ～难容 heaven forbids

【天理教】Tiānlǐjiào〈名〉 Heavenly Principles religious sect

【天理昭彰】tiānlǐ-zhāozhāng〈成〉 Heaven's laws are fully manifest

【天良】tiānliáng〈名〉 conscience: 丧尽～ have no conscience whatsoever

【天亮】tiānliàng〈动〉 dawn: ～以前 before dawn ‖ 我一觉睡到～。 I did not wake up until daybreak.

【天灵盖】tiānlínggài〈名〉 crown of the head

【天龙座】Tiānlóngzuò〈名〉［天文］ Draco

【天炉座】Tiānlúzuò〈名〉［天文］ Fornax

【天伦】tiānlún〈名〉 natural bonds and ethical relationships between family members

【天伦之乐】tiānlúnzhīlè〈成〉 family happiness: 共叙～ enjoy family happiness together

【天罗地网】tiānluó-dìwǎng〈成〉 tight encirclement: 布下～ spread a dragnet from which there is no escape

【天麻】tiānmá〈名〉［植物］ rhizoma gastrodiae

【天马行空】tiānmǎ-xíngkōng〈成〉〈喻〉 [of writing, calligraphy, etc.] powerful and unconstrained in style: ～，笔意纵横 write in a free and powerful style

【天门】tiānmén〈名〉 1〈旧〉（天宫的门） gate to the Heavenly Palace 2（宫门） gate to an imperial palace 3（前额中央） centre of the forehead

【天门冬】tiānméndōng〈名〉［中药］ lucid asparagus

【天明】tiānmíng〈名〉 daybreak

【天命】tiānmìng〈名〉 God's will: 这是～。 This is fate. ‖ ～难逃。 It's difficult to escape from one's fate.

【天幕】tiānmù〈名〉 1（天空）sky 2［戏剧］ backdrop

【天南地北】tiānnán-dìběi〈成〉 1（形容遥远） far apart: ～，各在一方 be far apart 2（指不同地方） all over the country: 来自～ come from all over the country 3（形容漫无边际） a wide range of things: 两个人～地说了半天。 The two of them talked about everything under the sun for a long time.

【天南海北】tiānnán-hǎiběi ＝ 天南地北 tiānnán-dìběi

【天年】tiānnián〈名〉 natural span of one's life: 颐养～ take good care of oneself so as to live out one's years to the fullest ‖ 我母亲享尽～而逝。 My mother died after a long and full life.

【天牛】tiānniú〈名〉［昆虫］ long-horned beetle

【天怒人怨】tiānnù-rényuàn〈成〉 widespread indignation and discontent

【天女】tiānnǚ〈名〉 heavenly maid: ～散花 heavenly maids strewing flowers

【天疱疮】tiānpàochuāng ▸**p. 50**〈名〉［医学］ pemphigus

【天棚】tiānpéng〈名〉 1［建筑］ ceiling: ～灯 ceiling lamp 2（凉棚） awning or canopy

【天平】tiānpíng〈名〉 balance

【天气】tiānqì〈名〉 1（气象变化） weather: ～预报 weather forecast ‖ ～恶劣 bad weather ‖ 好～ fine weather ‖ 坏～ bad weather ‖ 今天～很好。 It is a fine day today. 2（时间） time of the day: ～不早了，快回家吧! It's getting late and we'd better hurry home.

【天气预报】tiānqì yùbào〈名〉 weather forecast

【天堑】tiānqiàn〈名〉 chasm: ～变通途 turn a deep chasm into a thoroughfare ‖ 长江～ natural chasm in the Yangtze

【天桥】tiānqiáo〈名〉 1（人行桥） overpass 2［体育］ bridge

【天琴座】Tiānqínzuò〈名〉［天文］ Lyra

【天青】tiānqīng〈形〉 reddish black

【天青石】tiānqīngshí〈名〉 celestite

【天穹】tiānqióng〈名〉 firmament

【天球】tiānqiú〈名〉［天文］ heavenly sphere

【天球仪】tiānqiúyí〈名〉［天文］ celestial globe

【天趣】tiānqù〈名〉 natural charm: ～盎然 instinct with a natural charm

【天阙】tiānquè〈名〉 1（天上宫阙） heavenly palace 2（皇宫） imperial palace

【天然】tiānrán〈形〉 natural: ～牧场 natural pasture ‖ ～屏障 natural barrier ‖ ～港 natural harbour

【天然气】tiānránqì〈名〉 natural gas: 液化～ liquefied natural gas

【天然食品】tiānrán shípǐn〈名〉 natural food

【天然丝】tiānránsī〈名〉 natural silk

【天然橡胶】tiānrán xiàngjiāo〈名〉 natural rubber

【天壤之别】tiānrǎngzhībié〈成〉 poles apart: 兄弟二人一个勤奋，一个懒惰，真有～。 One of the brothers is diligent and the other is lazy. There is really a world of difference between them.

【天人合一】tiānrénhéyī〈名〉 Human beings are an integral part of nature

【天日】tiānrì〈名〉〈喻〉 light: ▸暗无～，重见～

【天色】tiānsè〈名〉 colour of the sky: ～阴沉 gloomy sky ‖ ～已晚。 It's getting late.

【天上】tiānshàng〈名〉 sky: 鸟在～飞。 Birds were flying in the sky. ‖〈喻〉～人间 a world of difference

【天神】tiānshén〈名〉 god

【天生】tiānshēng〈形〉 natural: ～的一对 match made in heaven ‖ ～丽质 be a natural beauty ‖ 他是～胖不起来的那种人。 He is the type who can't get fat.

【天时】tiānshí〈名〉 1（适时） timeliness: ～、地利、人和 favourable timing, geographical and human conditions 2（季节） season: 农耕必须趁～，早不得，晚不得。 Farming should be done in season, neither too early nor too late. 3（时间） time: ～已晚。 It's getting late.

【天使】tiānshǐ〈名〉 1［宗教］ angel: 复仇～ avenging angel ‖〈喻〉 白衣～ nurse ‖ 大家都叫她小～。 Everybody calls her a little angel. 2（指使者） imperial or heavenly envoy

【天授】tiānshòu〈动〉 be endowed by nature

【天书】tiānshū〈名〉 1（难懂的文章） abstruse or illegible writing 2（诏书） imperial edict

【天数】tiānshù〈名〉 fate: ～已尽 be nearing one's fated end

【天塌地陷】tiāntā-dìxiàn〈成〉〈喻〉 violent social upheavals

【天坛】Tiāntán〈名〉 Temple of Heaven

> **天坛**
>
> The largest extant altar and temple structure in China, located in south-eastern Beijing. Ming and Qing emperors came here to offer sacrifices to heaven and pray for a good harvest. Construction started in 1420 in the reign of the Emperor Yongle, with reconstruction in the Qing Dynasty. In 1998 it was designated a UNESCO World Heritage Site.

【天堂】tiāntáng〈名〉 1（极乐世界） heaven: ～地狱 heaven and hell 2（美好的地方） paradise: 人间～ paradise on earth ‖ 这里是购物者的～。 This place is a shopper's paradise.

【天梯】tiāntī〈名〉 tall ladder on high buildings or structures

【天体】tiāntǐ〈名〉［天文］ celestial body: ～动力学 astrodynamics

【天体力学】tiāntǐ lìxué〈名〉 celestial mechanics

【天天】tiāntiān〈名〉 every day: ～向上 make progress every day

【天条】tiāntiáo〈名〉 the will of Heaven: 触犯～ violate Heaven's will

【天庭】tiāntíng〈名〉 1（前额中央） middle of the forehead: ～饱满 full forehead 2（天帝的宫殿） court of the Lord of Heaven 3（皇宫） imperial court

【天头】tiāntóu〈名〉 top margin

【天外】tiānwài〈名〉 remotest place: ～来客 extraterrestrial being

【天外有天】tiānwài-yǒutiān〈成〉 there is

t

no limit to the universe: ～，学无止境 knowledge knows no bounds

【天王】tiānwáng〈名〉1▸（皇帝） emperor 2▸（洪秀全的称号） Heavenly King 3▸（天神） name for certain deities

【天王老子】tiānwáng lǎozi〈俗〉〈喻〉〈口〉 person of supreme power

【天王星】Tiānwángxīng〈名〉［天文］Uranus

【天网恢恢】tiānwǎng-huīhuī〈成〉 God's justice is inescapable: ～，疏而不漏 justice has a long arm

【天威】tiānwēi〈名〉〈书〉 heavenly might

【天文】tiānwén〈名〉 astronomy: ～观测 astronomical observation

【天文单位】tiānwén dānwèi〈名〉 astronomical unit

【天文馆】tiānwénguǎn〈名〉 planetarium

【天文年】tiānwénnián〈名〉［天文］natural year

【天文数字】tiānwén shùzì〈名〉 astronomical figure

【天文台】tiānwéntái〈名〉 observatory

【天文望远镜】tiānwén wàngyuǎnjìng〈名〉 space telescope

【天文学】tiānwénxué〈名〉 astronomy: ～家 astronomer

【天文仪】tiānwényí〈名〉 astroscope

【天文钟】tiānwénzhōng〈名〉 chronometer

【天无绝人之路】tiān wú jué rén zhī lù〈俗〉 there is always a way out

【天无宁日】tiānwúníngrì〈成〉 not have a day of peace

【天下】tiānxià〈名〉1▸（世界） the world; （全国） the whole country: ～太平 the world is at peace 2▸（国家政权） state power: 打～ seize state power ‖ 新中国是人民的～。 In new China the people are the masters.

【天下本无事，庸人自扰之】tiānxià běn wú shì, yōngrén zì rǎo zhī〈俗〉 there is nothing wrong with the world, and, if there is trouble, it is because foolish people look for it

【天下大乱】tiānxià-dàluàn〈成〉 the world is in chaos

【天下奇闻】tiānxià-qíwén〈名〉 most fantastic tale

【天下为公】tiānxià-wéigōng〈成〉 the whole world as one community

【天下乌鸦一般黑】tiānxià wūyā yībān hēi〈俗〉〈喻〉 evil people are the same the world over

【天下无不散的筵席】tiānxià wú bù sàn de yánxí〈俗〉 all good things must come to an end

【天下无敌】tiānxià-wúdí〈成〉 invincible

【天下无难事，只怕有心人】tiānxià wú nánshì, zhǐpà yǒuxīnrén〈俗〉 where there is a will, there is a way

【天下兴亡，匹夫有责】tiānxià xīngwáng, pǐfū yǒu zé〈成〉 everyone has a duty to their country

【天仙】tiānxiān〈名〉〈喻〉 goddess: 貌似～ be as beautiful as a goddess

【天险】tiānxiǎn〈名〉 natural barrier: 长江～ natural barrier of the Yangtze River

【天线】tiānxiàn〈名〉aerial; antenna〈美〉: 架设～ put up an aerial ‖ 拉杆～ telescopic aerial

【天象】tiānxiàng〈名〉1▸（天文现象） celestial phenomenon: 观测～ observe celestial bodies 2▸（天气征兆） meteorological phenomenon: 人们常根据～预测天气的变化。 People can often predict changes in the weather based on their observations of meteorological phenomena.

【天象馆】tiānxiàngguǎn〈名〉 planetarium

【天象仪】tiānxiàngyí〈名〉 planetarium

【天晓得】tiānxiǎode〈方〉= 天知道 tiānzhīdao

【天蝎座】Tiānxiēzuò〈名〉［天文］Scorpio

【天幸】tiānxìng〈名〉〈书〉 lucky escape

【天性】tiānxìng〈名〉 nature: ～善良 be kind-hearted ‖ 母亲的～ maternal instinct ‖ 他～不爱说话。 He is quiet by nature.

【天悬地隔】tiānxuán-dìgé = 天差地远 tiānchā-dìyuǎn

【天旋地转】tiānxuán-dìzhuǎn〈成〉1▸（重大变化） fundamental changes 2▸（眩晕） dizzy: 昏沉沉，只觉得～ feel faint and dizzy as if the sky and the earth were spinning round 3▸（闹得很凶） kick up a fierce row: 他们吵了个～。 They had a hell of a row.

【天涯】tiānyá〈名〉 end of the world: 浪迹～ rove all over the world ‖ 远在～，近在咫尺 seemingly as far away as the remotest corner on earth, but actually as close as just a few feet

【天涯海角】tiānyá-hǎijiǎo〈成〉 ends of the earth: 我要跟随你到～。 I shall follow you to the ends of the earth.

【天涯知己】tiānyá zhījǐ〈成〉 bosom friend

【天摇地动】tiānyáo-dìdòng〈成〉as though heaven and earth were shaken

【天衣无缝】tiānyī-wúfèng〈成〉〈喻〉flawless

【天意】tiānyì〈名〉 God's will: 这是～。 It is Heaven's will.

【天鹰座】Tiānyīngzuò〈名〉［天文］Aquila

【天有不测风云】tiān yǒu bùcè fēngyún〈俗〉 sth. unexpected may happen at any time: ～，人有旦夕祸福 in nature there are unexpected storms and in life unpredictable vicissitudes

【天宇】tiānyǔ〈名〉1▸（天空） sky: 歌声响彻～。 Singing fills the air. 2▸〈书〉（天下） world

【天渊之别】tiānyuānzhībié = 天壤之别 tiānrǎngzhībié

【天灾】tiānzāi〈名〉 natural disaster: 遭受～ suffer a natural calamity

【天灾人祸】tiānzāi-rénhuò〈成〉 natural and man-made calamities

【天葬】tiānzàng〈名〉 sky burial

【天造地设】tiānzào-dìshè〈成〉 heavenly: 这里物产丰富，山水秀丽，四季如春，真是～的好地方。 This is a really good place, with rich natural resources, beautiful scenery and a spring-like climate all the year round. ‖ 他们真是～的一对好夫妻。 They make a perfect match.

【天真】tiānzhēn〈形〉1▸（朴实） simple and unaffected: ～可爱的女孩子 sweet innocent girl 2▸〈贬〉（幼稚） naive: 这种想法过于～。 This is too naive an idea.

【天真烂漫】tiānzhēn-lànmàn〈成〉 [usu of children] simple and unaffected

【天真无邪】tiānzhēn-wúxié〈成〉 innocent

【天之骄子】tiānzhījiāozǐ〈成〉〈喻〉 God's favoured one

【天知道】tiānzhīdao〈惯〉 God knows: ～他要干什么! Heaven knows what he's trying to do!

【天职】tiānzhí〈名〉 vocation: 服从命令是军人的～。 It is a soldier's bounden duty to obey orders.

【天诛地灭】tiānzhū-dìmiè〈成〉 [usu used in cursing or taking vows] may God strike one dead

【天竺】Tiānzhú〈名〉〈古〉 India

【天竺葵】tiānzhúkuí〈名〉［植物］pelargonium

【天竺鼠】tiānzhúshǔ〈名〉［动物］guinea pig

【天主】Tiānzhǔ〈名〉［宗教］God

【天主教】Tiānzhǔjiào〈名〉 Catholicism

【天主堂】tiānzhǔtáng〈名〉Catholic church

【天姿国色】tiānzī-guósè〈成〉 exceptional beauty

【天资】tiānzī〈名〉 natural endowments: ～聪颖 be naturally bright and talented

【天子】tiānzǐ〈名〉 the emperor: 朝见～ have an audience with the emperor ▸一朝～一朝臣

【天字第一号】tiānzì-dì-yī hào〈惯〉 number one

【天足】tiānzú〈名〉〈旧〉 unbound feet

【天尊】tiānzūn〈名〉〈尊〉1▸［道教］deity 2▸［佛教］Buddha

【天作之合】tiānzuòzhīhé〈成〉match made in heaven [usu used in congratulations on marriage]: 他俩真可谓～。 The two of them are really a match made in heaven.

添 tiān〈动〉1▸（添加） add: ～几件家具 add a few pieces of furniture ‖ ～衣服 put on more clothes ‖ 对不起，给你～麻烦了。 Sorry to have troubled you. ▸～砖加瓦，锦上～花，如虎～翼 2▸〈口〉（生育） give birth to: 他盼着～个小孙子。 He is looking forward to having a grandson.

【添补】tiānbu〈动〉 add to one's possessions: ～夏装 add to one's summer wardrobe

【添彩】tiāncǎi〈动〉 add glory to: 中国奥运健儿为祖国增光～。 The Chinese Olympic athletes brought glory and honour to their motherland.

【添丁】tiāndīng〈动〉〈旧〉 have a baby born into the family

【添堵】tiāndǔ〈动〉〈口〉 be annoying

【添加】tiānjiā〈动〉 add: ～人手 increase manpower

【添加剂】tiānjiājì〈名〉［化学］additive: 食品～ food additive

【添乱】tiānluàn〈动〉 give sb. more trouble: 人家这是在谈正事，别在一旁～了。 We are talking business here, so don't you go making trouble!

【添油加醋】tiānyóu-jiācù = 添枝加叶 tiānzhī-jiāyè

【添枝加叶】tiānzhī-jiāyè〈成〉〈喻〉 add colour: 把发生的事情照实告诉她，可别～。 Tell her exactly what has happened and don't embellish your story.

【添置】tiānzhì〈动〉 add to one's possessions: ～家具 buy more furniture ‖ ～衣服 add to one's wardrobe

【添砖加瓦】tiānzhuān-jiāwǎ〈成〉〈喻〉 do one's bit: 我们要为国家的经济建设～。 We should do our bit to help develop our country's economy.

黇 tiān

【黇鹿】tiānlù〈名〉 fallow deer

tián

田 tián〈名〉1▸（庄稼地） field: 麦～ wheat fields ‖ 在～里劳动 do farm work ▸～野，种～ 2▸（矿区） field: ▸煤～，气～，油～

【田产】tiánchǎn〈名〉 estate: 变卖～ sell one's estate ‖ 购置～ buy an estate

【田塍】tiánchéng〈名〉〈方〉 ridge between fields

【田畴】tiánchóu〈名〉〈书〉 farmland

【田地】tiándì〈名〉1▸（庄稼地） farmland: 耕种～ till the fields 2▸（境地） wretched situation: 谁也没想到事情会弄到这步～。 Who could have guessed that things

could get as bad as this?

【田赋】tiánfù〈名〉〈旧〉land tax: 征收～ collect land tax

【田埂】tiángěng〈名〉ridge between fields

【田鸡】tiánjī〈名〉frog

【田家】tiánjiā〈名〉farming family: ～情趣 countryside charm

【田间】tiánjiān〈名〉❶（田地里）field: ～地头 everywhere on the farm ‖ ～管理 field management ❷（乡间）countryside: 来自～ come from the countryside

【田径】tiánjìng ▸**p. 909**〈名〉［体育］track and field; athletics〈英〉: 我喜欢看～比赛。I like watching field and track events.

【田径赛】tiánjìngsài〈名〉track and field meet

【田径运动】tiánjìng yùndòng〈名〉track and field; athletics〈英〉: ～会 track and field meet

【田坎】tiánkǎn〈名〉ridge between fields

【田垄】tiánlǒng〈名〉❶（田埂）ridge between fields ❷（垄）raised strip of land for planting crops

【田螺】tiánluó〈名〉［动物］river snail

【田亩】tiánmǔ〈名〉field

【田纳西州】Tiánnàxīzhōu〈名〉Tennessee

【田七】tiánqī = 三七 sānqī

【田契】tiánqì〈名〉land deed

【田赛】tiánsài〈名〉［体育］field event competition: ～项目 field event

【田舍】tiánshè〈名〉〈书〉❶（田地和房屋）farm ❷（农舍）farmhouse ❸（农家）farming family: ～郎 young farmer

【田鼠】tiánshǔ〈名〉field mouse

【田坛】tiántán〈名〉track and field circles

【田野】tiányě〈名〉open country: 广阔的～ vast expanse of farmland ‖ ～工作 fieldwork

【田园】tiányuán〈名〉countryside: ～风光 rural scenery ‖ ～生活 idyllic life

【田园诗】tiányuánshī〈名〉pastoral poetry: ～人 pastoral poet

【田庄】tiánzhuāng〈名〉❶（指田地）country estate ❷〈方〉（指农村）countryside

【田租】tiánzū〈名〉farm rent

佃 tián〈动〉〈书〉cultivate: ～作 cultivate
▸diàn

恬 tián〈形〉❶（安静）tranquil: ▸～静, ～适 ❷〈书〉（淡泊）indifferent to fame or wealth: ▸～淡 ❸（坦然）indifferent: ▸～不知耻

【恬不知耻】tiánbùzhīchǐ〈成〉be devoid of all sense of shame

【恬淡】tiándàn〈形〉❶（淡泊）indifferent to fame or gain: 心怀～ be quiet in mind with few desires ‖ ～寡欲 be contented and indifferent to worldly gain ❷（清静）tranquil: ～的生活 peaceful life

【恬静】tiánjìng〈形〉quiet: 环境幽雅～ quiet and peaceful environment ‖ ～的生活 peaceful life

【恬谧】tiánmì〈形〉〈书〉tranquil

【恬然】tiánrán〈形〉〈书〉unperturbed: 处之～ remain unruffled ‖ ～自若 calm and at ease

【恬适】tiánshì〈形〉〈书〉quiet and comfortable

钿（鈿） tián〈名〉〈方〉money: 几～? How much is it?
▸diàn

甜 tián〈形〉❶（指味道）sweet: 这西瓜真～。This watermelon is really sweet. ▸～食, ～滋滋, 甘～ ❷（指感受）pleasant: 日子过得～ lead a happy life ‖ 她笑得多～! What a sweet smile she has! ❸（指睡眠）sound: 他睡得真～。He was sound asleep.

【甜菜】tiáncài〈名〉❶（指植物）beet ❷（指块根）beetroot〈英〉; beet〈美〉

【甜橙】tiánchéng〈名〉sweet orange

【甜点】tiándiǎn〈名〉dessert; sweet〈英〉: 餐后～ dessert

【甜度】tiándù〈名〉sweetness

【甜瓜】tiánguā〈名〉sweet melon

【甜活儿】tiánhuór〈名〉〈口〉cushy job

【甜椒】tiánjiāo〈名〉sweet pepper

【甜津津】tiánjīnjīn〈形〉pleasantly sweet

【甜酒】tiánjiǔ〈名〉sweet wine

【甜美】tiánměi〈形〉❶（味道甜）sweet: 味道～ have a sweet taste ‖ 这种橙子多汁而～。These oranges are juicy and sweet. ❷（舒适美好）happy: 生活～ lead a happy life ‖ 音色～ have a sweet voice

【甜蜜】tiánmì〈形〉sweet: ～的生活 happy life ‖ 孩子们笑得那么～。How sweetly the children laughed!

【甜蜜素】tiánmìsù〈名〉［食品］（味道甜）cyclamate [artificial sweetener]: ～超标 exceed the permitted cyclamate level

【甜面酱】tiánmiànjiàng〈名〉sweet sauce made of fermented flour

【甜品】tiánpǐn〈名〉dessert

【甜情蜜意】tiánqíng-mìyì〈成〉deep affection

【甜润】tiánrùn〈形〉sweet and pleasant: 嗓音～ have a sweet voice ‖ 清凉～的空气 cool and refreshing air

【甜食】tiánshí〈名〉dessert; sweet〈英〉: 爱吃～ have a sweet tooth

【甜水】tiánshuǐ〈名〉fresh water: ～井 fresh water well

【甜丝丝】tiánsīsī〈形〉❶（味道甜）pleasantly sweet: 这种菜～的，很好吃。This kind of vegetable is sweet and tasty. ❷（幸福、愉快）happy: 心里感到～的 feel happy

【甜头】tiántou〈名〉❶（甜味）sweet taste ❷（好处、利益）good: 尝到了炒股的～ become aware of the benefits of speculating in stocks and shares

【甜言蜜语】tiányán-mìyǔ〈成〉sweet talk: 他被她的～给骗了。He was deceived by her honeyed words.

【甜滋滋】tiánzīzī = 甜丝丝 tiánsīsī

填 tián〈动〉❶（塞满）fill: ～饱肚子 fill the stomach ‖ ～坑 fill a pit ▸欲壑难～ ❷（补充）make up a deficiency: ▸～补, ～充 ❸（填写）fill out: ～表 fill out a form ▸～报, ～写

【填报】tiánbào〈动〉fill in a form and submit it: 每周～工程进度 complete a weekly progress report on the project

【填补】tiánbǔ〈动〉fill: ～空缺 fill a vacancy ‖ ～亏空 make up a deficit ‖ 他的发现～了科学技术领域的一项空白。His discovery filled in a gap in the fields of science and technology.

【填充】tiánchōng〈动〉❶（塞满）stuff: 用羽毛～被子/枕头 stuff a quilt/pillow with feathers ❷（填空）fill in the blanks: ～题 cloze test

【填词】tiáncí〈动〉fill in words to fit a given tune

【填房】tiánfáng〈动〉[of a woman] marry a widower

【填房】tiánfang〈名〉wife taken by a widower after the death of his first wife

【填海造地】tiánhǎi-zàodì〈惯〉reclaim land from the sea

【填空】tiánkòng〈动〉❶（指职位）fill a vacancy: ～补缺 fill in what is needed ❷ = 填充 tiánchōng 2

【填窟窿】tián kūlong〈惯〉〈喻〉make up a deficit

【填料】tiánliào〈名〉filling

【填权】tiánquán〈动〉［金融］have a higher trading price than the total price of a stock's ex-rights and ex-dividends

【填塞】tiánsè〈动〉stop up: ～洞隙 stop up holes

【填写】tiánxiě〈动〉fill out: ～汇款单 fill in a money order ‖ ～履历表 write out a curriculum vitae

【填鸭】tiányā **A**〈动〉force-feed a duck **B**〈名〉force-fed duck: ～式教学法 force-feeding teaching method

【填字游戏】tiánzì yóuxì〈名〉crossword puzzle

阗（闐） tián〈动〉〈书〉be filled with: 宾客～门。The house is full of guests.

tiǎn

忝 tiǎn〈副〉〈书〉〈谦〉unworthily: ～列其中 have the honour to be one of them

殄 tiǎn〈动〉exterminate: ～灭匪徒 wipe out the bandits ▸暴～天物

悿 tiǎn〈形〉〈书〉ashamed

觍（覥） tiǎn〈动〉❶〈书〉（面露愧色）be ashamed: ▸～颜 ❷〈口〉（厚着脸皮）brazen: ～着脸 brazen it out

【觍颜】tiǎnyán〈动〉〈书〉❶（面露愧色）be shamefaced ❷（厚着脸皮）be shameless: ～惜命 save one's life at the cost of one's honour

腆 tiǎn
A〈形〉〈书〉sumptuous
B〈动〉〈口〉bulge: ～着肚子 bulge one's belly ‖ ～着胸脯 stick out one's chest

靦（靦） tiǎn
A〈形〉〈书〉（形容人脸）facial
B = 觍 tiǎn

舔 tiǎn〈动〉lick: ～去伤口的血 lick blood from a cut ‖ ～嘴唇 lick one's lips ‖ 猫在～爪子。The cat is licking its paw.

【舔屁股】tiǎn pìgu〈俗〉〈粗〉lick sb.'s arse〈粗〉

【舔食】tiǎnshí〈动〉lap up

tiàn

掭 tiàn〈动〉❶（指用毛笔）dip a writing brush in ink and work it on an ink stone

t

2〈方〉(拨动) prop up: ～灯心 raise the wick of an oil lamp

tiāo

佻 tiāo〈形〉 frivolous: ▸～薄, 轻～

【佻薄】tiāobó〈形〉〈书〉 skittish: 举止～ behave in a frivolous manner

挑[1] tiāo

A〈动〉 shoulder: ～担 carry a load with a shoulder pole ‖ ～两桶水 shoulder two buckets ▸～担子

B〈名〉 shoulder pole with its load: 挑～儿 carry a load on a shoulder pole ▸～子

C〈量〉 load carried on a shoulder pole: 两～菜 two baskets of vegetables carried on a shoulder pole

挑[2] tiāo〈动〉 1 (选择) select: ～个好日子成亲 choose a propitious day for the wedding ‖ ～几个身强力壮的小伙子干这活。 Select a few strong young men for the job. ▸～肥拣瘦, ～选 2 (挑剔) nit-pick: ～毛病 pick holes ▸～刺儿, ～剔

▸tiǎo

【挑刺儿】tiāocìr〈动〉 pick holes: 故意～ find fault deliberately ‖ 他就爱挑别人的刺儿。 He is fond of finding fault with people.

【挑错】tiāocuò〈动〉 find fault (with)

【挑担子】tiāodànzi〈动〉〈喻〉 assume responsibility: 勇于～ be brave enough to take on the responsibility

【挑肥拣瘦】tiāoféi-jiǎnshòu〈成〉 choose whatever is to one's own advantage: 她对分派的工作总是～。 She is always very choosy about work assignments.

【挑夫】tiāofū〈名〉 porter

【挑拣】tiāojiǎn〈动〉 pick and choose: 多数女人买东西时总喜欢挑挑拣拣。 Most women are fastidious about their shopping.

【挑脚】tiāojiǎo〈动〉〈旧〉 carry loads on a shoulder pole

【挑礼】tiāolǐ〈动〉 be fastidious about etiquette

【挑三拣四】tiāosān-jiǎnsì〈成〉 be choosy: 他对工作从不～。 He is never particular when it comes to work.

【挑食】tiāoshí〈动〉 be particular about what one eats: 这孩子不～。 The child doesn't mind what he eats.

【挑剔】tiāoti〈动〉 nit-pick: 过分～ be overly particular ‖ 他吃东西很～。 He is fussy about his food. ‖ 她过于～，跟谁也合不来。 She is so hypercritical that she can hardly get on with anybody.

【挑选】tiāoxuǎn〈动〉 select: 精心～ select meticulously ‖ 国家队成员都是经过严格～的。 The national team has gone through a strict selection process.

【挑眼】tiāoyǎn〈动〉〈方〉 find fault

【挑字眼儿】tiāo zìyǎnr〈动〉 be fastidious about the choice of words

【挑子】tiāozi〈名〉 carrying pole with its load: ▸剃头～一头热

【挑嘴】tiāozuǐ = 挑食 tiāoshí

祧 tiāo〈书〉

A〈名〉 ancestral temple for remote ancestors

B〈动〉 1 (移祖先神位) move an ancestor's memorial tablet to the memorial temple for remote ancestors: 不～之祖 revered earliest ancestor 2 (继承上代) become heir to

tiáo

条（條） tiáo

A〈名〉 1 (枝条) twig: ▸柳～, 枝～ 2 (细长物) strip: 把布撕成～儿 tear a piece of cloth into strips ‖ 他不在家，我给他留了个～儿。 He wasn't in so I left him a note. ▸便～, 金～, 链～, 面～ 3 (长条形) stripe: 花～布 striped cloth ▸～案, ～幅, ～纹 4 (条理) order: ▸井井有～, 有～不紊 5 (分项) item: ▸～款, ～目

B〈量〉 1 (用于细长物) [for sth. long, narrow or thin]: 两～腿 two legs ‖ 一～裤子 a pair of trousers ‖ 一～毛巾 a towel 2 (用于条状物) [for bar-shaped objects]: 两～肥皂 two bars of soap ‖ 一～烟 a carton of cigarettes 3 (用于人) [for people]: 三～人命 three human lives ‖ 父子俩两～心。 The father and the son were not of one mind. 4 (用于逐条罗列) [for sth. that can be listed item by item]: 几～理由 several reasons ‖ 三～新闻 three pieces of news

【条案】tiáo'àn〈名〉 long, narrow table

【条播】tiáobō〈名〉［农业］ drilling: ～行距 drill spacing

【条畅】tiáochàng〈形〉〈书〉 [of writing] smooth and well-organized: 文笔～ write in a clear and smooth style

【条陈】tiáochén A〈动〉〈书〉 state point by point B〈名〉〈旧〉 itemized memorandum: 上～ submit an itemized memorandum

【条凳】tiáodèng〈名〉 bench

【条分缕析】tiáofēn-lǚxī〈成〉 make a clear and detailed analysis

【条幅】tiáofú〈名〉 wall scroll: 一轴绘画/书法～ a painting/calligraphy scroll

【条规】tiáoguī〈名〉 rules

【条几】tiáojī = 条案 tiáo'àn

【条件】tiáojiàn〈名〉 1 (因素) condition: 气候/自然～ weather/natural conditions ‖ 利用有利～ take advantage of the favourable conditions 2 (标准要求) requirement: 符合招工～ meet the requirements of the job ‖ 在同等～下外语流利者优先录用 those fluent in another language will receive preferential treatment under equal conditions ‖ 做这项工作需要具备什么～? What qualifications do you need for the job? 3 (情况) circumstances: 工作/生活～ working/living conditions ‖ 他的身体～很好。 He is in good physical condition. ‖ 这个工厂的～很好。 This factory has very good conditions.

【条件从句】tiáojiàn cóngjù ▸**p. 350**〈名〉［语法］ conditional clause

【条件反射】tiáojiàn fǎnshè〈名〉［生理］ conditioned response

【条件句】tiáojiànjù ▸**p. 350**〈名〉［语法］ conditional sentence

【条块】tiáokuài〈名〉 management of departments at different levels and of regions at the same level: ～结合 integration of departments and regions at different levels

【条款】tiáokuǎn〈名〉 provision: 违反协议～ violate an agreement ‖ 法律～ legal provision ‖ 附加～ additional clause

【条理】tiáolǐ〈名〉 orderliness: 你的生活安排得很有～。 You've organized your life very well. ‖ 这篇论文～清楚。 The dissertation is well organized.

【条例】tiáolì〈名〉 regulation: 奖惩～ regulations regarding rewards and penalties ‖ 现行～ existing regulations ‖ 治安管理～ public security codes

【条令】tiáolìng〈名〉［军事］ regulation: 纪律～ disciplinary regulations ‖ 内务～ routine service regulations (for barracks)

【条码】tiáomǎ = 条形码 tiáoxíngmǎ

【条目】tiáomù〈名〉 1 (条款) clauses and sub-clauses 2 (词条) entry

【条屏】tiáopíng = 屏条 píngtiáo

【条绒】tiáoróng = 灯芯绒 dēngxīnróng

【条条大路通罗马】tiáotiáo dàlù tōng Luómǎ〈俗〉 all roads lead to Rome

【条条框框】tiáotiao-kuàngkuang〈成〉〈贬〉 rules and regulations: 受～的束缚 be hedged in with rules and regulations

【条文】tiáowén〈名〉 clause: 法律～ legal clause

【条纹】tiáowén〈名〉 stripe: 一条有蓝白～的床单 a blue and white striped bed sheet ‖ 老虎身上有～。 Tigers have stripes.

【条形码】tiáoxíngmǎ〈名〉 bar code: ～标记 bar code label ‖ 印有～的商品 bar-coded commodity

【条约】tiáoyuē〈名〉 treaty: 缔结～ conclude a treaty ‖ 不平等～ unequal treaty ‖ 互不侵犯～ non-aggression pact

【条子】tiáozi〈名〉 1 (狭长物) strip: 布～ strip of cloth 2 (便条) note: 递～ pass sb. a note 3〈方〉(金条) gold bar

苕 tiáo = 凌霄花 língxiāohuā

▸sháo

迢 tiáo

【迢迢】tiáotiáo〈形〉 remote: ▸千里～

调[1]（調） tiáo

A〈形〉 harmonious: ▸风～雨顺, 失～, 协～

B〈动〉 1 (调整) mix: ～工资 adjust wages ‖ ～颜色 blend colours ‖ 把电视机的音量～低 turn down the volume on the TV ▸～节, ～味, 烹～, 众口难～ 2 (调解) mediate: ▸～处, ～解, ～停

调[2]（調） tiáo〈动〉 1 (嘲弄) tease: ▸～戏, ～笑 2 (挑拨) incite: ▸～唆

▸diào

【调处】tiáochǔ〈动〉 mediate: ～争端 mediate a dispute

【调幅】tiáofú〈名〉［通信］ amplitude modulation (AM)

【调羹】tiáogēng〈名〉 spoon

【调和】tiáohé A〈动〉 1 (掺和并搅拌) mix: ～油 ready-mixed oil ‖ 把两种颜料～在一起 mix two colours together 2 (使和解) mediate: 从中～ act as mediator 3 (妥协) [usu used in the negative] reconcile: 不可～的矛盾 irreconcilable conflicts ‖ 在原则问题上没有～的余地。 There is no room for compromise on a question of principle. B〈形〉 harmonious: 色彩～。 The colours go well.

【调和漆】tiáohéqī〈名〉 ready-mixed paint

【调护】tiáohù〈动〉 nurse: 精心～病人 nurse a patient with meticulous care

【调级】tiáojí〈动〉 adjust a wage scale [usu upwards]

【调剂】tiáojì〈动〉 1 (配制药剂) make up a prescription 2 (适当调整) adjust: ～劳动力 redistribute manpower ‖ ～余缺 regulate supply and demand ‖ 听听音乐，以～生活。 Listening to music will

help to break the monotony of life.

【调剂商店】tiáojì shāngdiàn〈名〉second-hand shop that buys and sells goods

【调价】tiáojià〈动〉adjust prices: 季节性～ seasonal price adjustment

【调教】tiáojiào〈动〉**1**（调理教养）discipline: 不服～ disregard discipline **2**（训练）feed and train: ～烈马 tame a fierce horse ‖ ～鹦鹉 train a parrot

【调节】tiáojié〈动〉regulate: ～室温 regulate the room temperature ‖ ～水流 regulate the flow of water ‖ 对货币流通进行～ adjust the amount of money in circulation

【调节器】tiáojiéqì〈名〉regulator

【调节税】tiáojiéshuì〈名〉regulatory tax

【调解】tiáojiě〈动〉mediate: ～争端 mediate a dispute ‖ 在劳资之间进行～ mediate between labour and management ‖ 原告主动提出进行～。The plaintiff offered mediation.

【调解员】tiáojiěyuán〈名〉mediator

【调经】tiáojīng〈动〉［中医］regulate the menstrual function

【调酒师】tiáojiǔshī ▸**p. 966**〈名〉cocktail waiter

【调侃】tiáokǎn〈动〉ridicule: 互相～ poke fun at one another

【调控】tiáokòng〈动〉regulate and control: ～地下水的水位 regulate and control the underground water level ‖ 加强经济的宏观～ increase macro control of the economy

【调理】tiáolǐ〈动〉**1**（调养护理）nurse one's impaired health: 病刚好，要注意～。You should take good care of yourself since you've only just got better. **2**（照料）take care of: ～伙食 take care over what one eats ‖ ～牲口 look after livestock **3**（教育训练）discipline: 这些男孩子真难～。These boys are impossible.

【调料】tiáoliào〈名〉seasoning: 这菜～放得太多。There is too much flavouring in this dish.

【调料瓶】tiáoliàopíng〈名〉cruet

【调弄】tiáonòng〈动〉**1**（戏弄）make fun of: ～妇女 flirt with a woman **2**（拨弄调整）arrange: ～琴弦 tune a stringed instrument **3**（调唆）stir up: ～是非 stir up trouble

【调配】tiáopèi〈动〉mix: ～颜色 mix colours ‖ 照药方～药剂 make up a prescription
▸ diàopèi

【调皮】tiáopí〈形〉**1**（淘气）naughty: ～的孩子 naughty child **2**（不驯服）unruly: ～的牲口 wilful draught animal **3**（做事不老实）tricky

【调皮捣蛋】tiáopí-dǎodàn〈成〉be mischievous: 孩子都～。Children are always getting into mischief.

【调皮鬼】tiáopíguǐ〈名〉mischief-maker: 你真是个～。What a mischief you are!

【调频】tiáopín［电气］**A**〈动〉adjust the frequency **B**〈名〉frequency modulation (FM): ～立体声 FM stereo

【调情】tiáoqíng〈动〉flirt: 他在和一个漂亮姑娘～。He was flirting with a pretty girl.

【调三窝四】tiáosān-wōsì〈成〉sow discord

【调三斡四】tiáosān-wòsì = 调三窝四 tiáosān-wōsì

【调色板】tiáosèbǎn〈名〉painter's palette

【调适】tiáoshì〈动〉fine-tune: 学会自我心理～ learn how to adjust one's own psychology

【调试】tiáoshì〈动〉have a trial run: ～新设备 test-run new equipment

【调速】tiáosù〈动〉regulate the speed: ～杆 speed control rod

【调唆】tiáosuō〈动〉incite: ～是非 stir up trouble

【调停】tiáotíng〈动〉mediate: 居中～ act as mediator ‖ 他们通过～解决了劳资纠纷。They mediated a settlement between labour and management.

【调味】tiáowèi〈动〉flavour: 花椒、八角都可以～。Both Chinese prickly ash and anise can add flavour to food.

【调味品】tiáowèipǐn〈名〉seasoning: 胡椒粉是一种～。Pepper is a kind of seasoning.

【调温】tiáowēn〈动〉regulate the temperature

【调戏】tiáoxì〈动〉take liberties with: ～妇女 flirt with a woman

【调笑】tiáoxiào〈动〉make fun of: ～为乐 mock for fun

【调协】tiáoxié〈动〉harmonize: 不相～ be not in harmony

【调谐】tiáoxié **A**〈形〉harmonious: 色彩～ be harmonious in colour **B**〈动〉［电气］resonate: ～旋钮 tuning knob

【调谑】tiáoxuè〈动〉make fun of

【调压】tiáoyā〈动〉regulate pressure: ～器 voltage regulator

【调养】tiáoyǎng〈动〉build up one's health by rest and through nourishing food: ～身体 build up one's health

【调音】tiáoyīn〈动〉［音乐］tune

【调音师】tiáoyīnshī ▸**p. 966**〈名〉sound mixer: 钢琴～ piano tuner

【调匀】tiáoyún **A**〈动〉mix well: 把颜料～ mix the colours well **B**〈形〉balanced: 雨水～ well-distributed rainfall

【调整】tiáozhěng〈动〉adjust: ～计划 revise a plan ‖ ～物价 regulate prices ‖ ～作息时间 adjust the work schedule

【调治】tiáozhì〈动〉recuperate under medical treatment

【调制】tiáozhì **A**〈名〉［电子］modulation: 音频～ audio modulation **B**〈动〉mix: ～鸡尾酒 mix cocktails

【调制解调器】tiáozhì jiětiáoqì〈名〉modem

【调资】tiáozī〈动〉adjust a wage: 评级～ make adjustments to rank and salary

【调嘴弄舌】tiáozuǐ-nòngshé = 调嘴学舌 tiáozuǐ-xuéshé

【调嘴学舌】tiáozuǐ-xuéshé〈成〉tittle-tattle

笤 tiáo

【笤帚】tiáozhou〈名〉small broom

龆（齠） tiáo

〈动〉〈书〉lose one's milk teeth: ～龀 childhood

蜩 tiáo

〈名〉〈书〉［昆虫］cicada

髫 tiáo

〈名〉〈书〉child's hanging hair: ～龄 childhood

鲦（鰷） tiáo

【鲦鱼】tiáoyú〈名〉sharpbelly

tiǎo

挑 tiǎo

A〈动〉**1**（拨）poke: ～刺 pick out a splinter ‖ ～水疱 prick a blister **2**（挑拨）provoke: ～是非 stir up trouble ‖ 我俩吵了一架，都是他～起的。He instigated a quarrel between us. ▸～逗，～衅，～战 **3**（支起）lift up with a pole: 把帘子～起来 raise the curtain ▸～灯 **4**（指刺绣）cross-stitch: ▸～花

B〈名〉rising stroke [in a Chinese character]
▸ tiāo

【挑拨】tiǎobō〈动〉instigate: ～民族关系 sow discord among minority groups ‖ ～是非 stir up trouble

【挑拨离间】tiǎobō-líjiàn〈成〉sow discord: 他老是在朋友中间～。He often sowed discord among his friends.

【挑大梁】tiǎo dàliáng〈惯〉play an important role: 小字辈～ the younger generation is shouldering heavy responsibilities

【挑灯】tiǎodēng〈动〉**1**（指油灯）raise the wick of an oil lamp **2**（指灯笼）hang up a lantern: ～夜战 burn the midnight oil

【挑动】tiǎodòng〈动〉**1**（引起）arouse: ～好奇心 arouse one's curiosity ‖ ～是非 lead to a dispute **2**（挑拨煽动）instigate: ～罢工 instigate a strike ‖ ～民众闹事 incite the populace to stir up trouble

【挑逗】tiǎodòu〈动〉tease: ～妇女 flirt with a woman ‖ 他这人～不得。You'd better not provoke him.

【挑花】tiǎohuā〈名〉cross-stitch work

【挑明】tiǎomíng〈动〉bring into the open: 把事情～ bring sth. into the open

【挑弄】tiǎonòng〈动〉**1**（挑唆）stir up: ～是非 stir up trouble **2**（戏弄）make fun of

【挑起】tiǎoqǐ〈动〉provoke: ～冲突 provoke a conflict ‖ ～是非 sow discord

【挑唆】tiǎosuō〈动〉incite: ～俩人不和 sow discord between the two people ‖ ～青少年犯罪 abet teenagers in a crime ‖ 暗中～ stir up trouble behind the scenes

【挑头】tiǎotóu〈动〉take the lead: 他～给领导提意见。He took the lead in criticizing the leadership. ‖ 这件事由你来～吧。It's over to you to take the lead on this one.

【挑衅】tiǎoxìn〈动〉provoke: 武装～ armed provocation ‖ 公然～ flagrant provocation ‖ 严重～ severe provocation

【挑战】tiǎozhàn〈动〉**1**（指作战）throw down the gauntlet: 接受～ take up the gauntlet ‖ ～书 challenge **2**（指竞赛）challenge: 迎接～ rise to a challenge

窕 tiǎo

▸ 窈窕 yǎotiǎo

tiào

眺 tiào

〈动〉look into the distance from a high place: 远～ overlook

【眺望】tiàowàng〈动〉look into the distance from a high place: 凭栏～ lean against the railings to take in the view ‖ 站在山顶～ gaze into the distance from a hilltop

粜（糶） tiào

〈动〉〈旧〉sell: ～米 sell rice

跳 tiào

〈动〉**1**（向上蹦）jump: ～过壕沟 hop over a ditch ‖ ～上车 jump into a car ‖ 高兴得～起来 jump for joy ‖ 妹妹连蹦带～地跑进来。My little sister came bouncing in. ‖ 小偷～窗逃走。The thief escaped through the window. ▸～高，～伞 **2**（弹起）bounce: 新皮球～得高。The new ball is very bouncy. **3**（振动）throb: 她心～加快。Her heart beat faster. ‖ 我眼皮直～。My eyes kept twitching.

4 (越过) skip: ～至第三章 skip to Chapter 3 ‖ 从一个话题～到另一个话题 jump from one subject to another ▸～级
【跳班】tiàobān = 跳级 tiàojí 1
【跳板】tiàobǎn 〈名〉 1 (用于上下船) gangplank 2 (用于跳水) springboard: 一米/三米～ one-metre/three-metre springboard 3 〈喻〉 (用于过渡) springboard: 把婚姻作为～ use one's marriage as a springboard
【跳布扎】tiào bùzhá 〈名〉 [宗教] dance performed by Tibetan monks at religious festivals to exorcize demons
【跳槽】tiàocáo 〈动〉 1 (指牲口) leave one trough to eat at another 2 〈喻〉 (指人) hop from job to job: 工作不到三个月就～去另一个单位了 do a job for barely three months before hopping into something else
【跳动】tiàodòng 〈动〉 pulsate: 他的心脏停止了～。 His heart stopped beating. ‖ 她的脉搏～正常。 Her pulse was of normal frequency.
【跳发球】tiàofāqiú 〈名〉 [排球] jump-service
【跳房子】tiào fángzi 〈名〉 hopscotch: 玩～的游戏 play hopscotch
【跳高】tiàogāo ▸p. 909 〈名〉 [体育] high jump: 背越式～ Fosbury flop ‖ ～运动员 high jumper
【跳行】tiàoháng 〈动〉 1 (漏行) skip a line: 她跳着行看完了这本书。 She skipped through the book. 2 (另起一行) start a new paragraph 3 (改行) jump from one profession to another
【跳级】tiàojí 〈动〉 1 (指学生) skip a year: ～生 accelerated student 2 (越级) jump a rank
【跳脚】tiàojiǎo 〈动〉 stamp one's feet: 气得～ stamp with rage
【跳进黄河洗不清】tiàojìn Huánghé xǐbuqīng 〈俗〉〈喻〉 find it hard to clear oneself of a charge
【跳梁小丑】tiàoliáng-xiǎochǒu 〈成〉 buffoon
【跳羚】tiàolíng 〈名〉 [动物] springbok
【跳楼】tiàolóu 〈动〉 commit suicide by jumping off a building
【跳楼价】tiàolóujià 〈名〉 distress price
【跳马】tiàomǎ 〈名〉 [体育] 1 (指器械) vaulting horse 2 (指运动) horse-vaulting
【跳皮筋儿】tiào píjīnr 〈名〉 rubber band skipping
【跳棋】tiàoqí 〈名〉 Chinese checkers: 西洋～ draughts 〈英〉, checkers 〈美〉
【跳伞】tiàosǎn 〈动〉 parachute: ～训练 parachute training
【跳伞塔】tiàosǎntǎ 〈名〉 parachute tower
【跳神】tiàoshén 〈名〉 1 (指迷信活动) sorcerer's dance in a trance 2 = 跳布扎 tiào bùzhá
【跳绳】tiàoshéng A 〈动〉 skip rope B 〈名〉 skipping rope 〈英〉; jump rope 〈美〉
【跳水】tiàoshuǐ 〈动〉 1 ▸p. 909 [体育] dive: ～表演 diving exhibition ‖ ～池 diving pool 2 〈喻〉 (急速下跌) dive: 开盘不久，一些蓝筹股便大幅～。 Not long after the market opened some blue chip stocks took a dive.
【跳台】tiàotái 〈名〉 [体育] diving platform: 十米～ ten-metre platform ‖ ～跳水 platform diving
【跳台滑雪】tiàotái huáxuě 〈名〉 ski jumping
【跳投】tiàotóu 〈动〉 [篮球] jump to shoot
【跳舞】tiàowǔ 〈动〉 dance: 她的舞跳得好极了。 Her dancing is superb. ‖ 能否赏光与我～? Can you honour me with a dance? ‖ 这个周末去～吗? Are you going to the dance this weekend?
【跳箱】tiàoxiāng 〈名〉 [体育] 1 (指器械) box horse 2 (指运动) box vaulting
【跳鞋】tiàoxié 〈名〉 spiked jumping shoes
【跳远】tiàoyuǎn ▸p. 909 〈名〉 [体育] long jump: 三级～ triple jump ‖ ～运动员 long jumper
【跳月】tiàoyuè 〈名〉 moon dance [folk dance popular among the Miao and Yi ethnic groups]
【跳跃】tiàoyuè 〈动〉 jump: ～前进 bound forward ‖ ～运动 leaping exercise
【跳跃器】tiàoyuèqì 〈名〉 [体育] buck
【跳蚤】tiàozao 〈名〉 flea
【跳蚤市场】tiàozao shìchǎng 〈名〉 flea market
【跳闸】tiàozhá 〈动〉 [电气] trip: 过载～ overload trip ‖ 自动～ automatic tripping

tiē

帖 tiē
A 〈形〉 well-placed: ▸妥～
B 〈动〉 be submissive: ▸服～, 俯首～耳
▸tiě, tiè

贴¹ (貼) tiē
A 〈动〉 1 (粘) paste: ～布告 put up a notice ‖ ～邮票 stick on a stamp ‖ 墙上～满了广告。 The wall was covered with advertisements. ▸剪～, 张～ 2 (紧挨) keep close to: ～着墙走 walk along the wall ‖ 孩子紧～在妈妈身边。 The child snuggled up against its mother. ▸～身, ～心 3 (补贴) give financial assistance: 哥哥每月～他零用钱。 His elder brother gives him a monthly allowance. ▸～补, 倒～
B 〈名〉 allowance: 房～ housing subsidies ‖ 米～ food allowance ▸补～, 津～
C 〈量〉 [for medicated plaster] piece: 一～膏药 a piece of medicated plaster

贴² (貼) tiē = 帖 tiē A
【贴吧】tiēbā 〈名〉 message forum: 在～上发布虚假信息 post false information on a message forum
【贴边】tiēbiān A 〈动〉〈口〉 be relevant: 尽说些不～的话 come up with nothing but irrelevancies ‖ 别问我，我可与这事不～。 Don't ask me. I have nothing to do with this. B 〈名〉 hem
【贴标签】tiē biāoqiān 〈动〉 label: 给行李贴上标签 put labels on one's luggage ‖ 〈喻〉 坏人脸上又没有～，谁能一眼认出来? Bad guys don't come with labels attached to their faces, so how is it possible to spot one at a glance?
【贴饼子】tiēbǐngzi A 〈动〉 bake corn cakes B 〈名〉 corn cakes cooked in a pan
【贴补】tiēbǔ 〈动〉 help to support financially: 他假期打零工～家用。 He helped support the family by doing odd jobs during his holidays. ‖ 他每月～弟弟一些钱。 He helps his younger brother out by giving him some money each month.
【贴花】tiēhuā 〈名〉 [纺织] appliqué
【贴画】tiēhuà 〈名〉 1 (年画) picture poster: 百寿图～ picture of longevity 2 (画片) pictorial label
【贴己】tiējǐ 〈形〉 intimate: 互相说～话 share confidences ‖ 有个可以说～话的人 have sb. one can confide in ‖ 当成～的人 take sb. into one's confidence
【贴金】tiējīn 〈动〉 touch up: 给佛像～ cover the statue of Buddha with gold foil ‖ 〈喻〉 别给自己脸上～。 Don't blow your own trumpet.
【贴近】tiējìn A 〈动〉 keep close to: ～生活 life-like B 〈形〉 close: 找～的人说说心里话 find sb. one is close to and get some things off one's chest
【贴面】tiēmiàn 〈名〉 face: 塑料～ Formica ‖ 大理石～圆柱 marble-faced column ‖ ～砖 face tile
【贴面舞】tiēmiànwǔ 〈名〉 cheek-to-cheek dancing: 跳～ dance cheek to cheek
【贴谱】tiēpǔ 〈形〉〈口〉 appropriate: 话说得不～ having made some irrelevant remarks ‖ 你的分析很～。 Your analysis is quite sound.
【贴切】tiēqiè 〈形〉 apt: 措词～ be aptly worded ‖ 比喻要用得～。 Metaphors should be apt.
【贴身】tiēshēn 〈形〉 1 (紧挨身体) body-hugging: ～衣服 underwear 2 (合身) nicely-fitting: 这件衣服穿着～。 The dress fits well. 3 (跟随身边) constantly accompanying: ～丫鬟 personal maid ‖ ～保镖 personal bodyguard
【贴水】tiēshuǐ [金融] A 〈动〉 pay agio B 〈名〉 agio
【贴题】tiētí 〈形〉 pertinent: 着墨不多，但是十分～ brief but very much to the point ‖ 他的发言不太～。 His speech had little relevance.
【贴息】tiēxī [金融] A 〈动〉 pay interest in the form of a deduction B 〈名〉 deducted interest
【贴现】tiēxiàn 〈动〉 [金融] discount: ～率 discount rate
【贴心】tiēxīn 〈形〉 close: ～的朋友 close friend ‖ ～话 words spoken in confidence ‖ ～人 confidant

萜 tiē 〈名〉 [化学] terpene

tiě

帖 tiě
A 〈名〉 1 (请柬) invitation: ▸请～, 喜～ 2 (指写有生辰八字) card containing details of a person's name, age, birthplace, etc.: ▸庚～
B 〈量〉 [for herbal medicine] dose: 一～药 a dose of herbal medicine
▸tiē, tiè
【帖子】tiězi = 帖 tiě A

铁 (鐵) tiě
A 〈名〉 1 [化学] iron: ～会生锈。 Iron rusts. ▸趁热打～, 废～ 2 (武器) arms: ▸手无寸～
B 〈形〉 1 (确定不移) ironclad: ～的纪律 iron discipline ‖ ～的事实 hard fact ▸～案如山, ～证 2 (坚硬) unyielding: 他有着～一般的意志。 He is a man of iron will. ▸～拳, ～人, ～腕 3 (无情) ruthless: ▸～面无私, ～石心肠, ～蹄
【铁案】tiě'àn 〈名〉 clear-cut case: 把案子办成～ make a case ironclad
【铁案如山】tiě'àn-rúshān 〈成〉 ironclad case
【铁板钉钉】tiěbǎn-dìngdīng 〈成〉〈喻〉 that clinches it: 主队的胜利已是～。 There's already no doubt about the home team's victory.
【铁板一块】tiěbǎn-yīkuài 〈成〉 monolithic bloc: 不要以为敌人是～，他们是可以分

音 节 表
Pinyin Index

（音节右边的数字指《汉英词典》正文部分的页码）
(The number to the right of the Pinyin indicates the page number in the Chinese-English Dictionary)

Measure words in Chinese 汉语量词

Hanyu Pinyin 汉语拼音	Chinese character 汉字	Description and example 说明和示例
mén	门	1. for academic courses, subjects or disciplines, crafts: 一门课程/科学/专业/手艺 2. for cannons, guns: 一门炮
miàn	面	for flat, smooth objects, such as mirrors, flags, etc.: 一面红旗/镜子/墙/锣
míng	名	for persons with professional or prominent social identities: 七名学生/医生/士兵/工人
pái	排	for things or people grouped or set in rows: 一排座位/树/房子/人
pán	盘	1. for flat things: 一盘录像带/菜 2. for board games: 一盘棋
pī	批	for people or goods: 一批人、两批货物
pǐ	匹	1. for horses, mules: 三匹马/骡子 2. for bolts of cloth: 一匹布
piān	篇	for papers, articles, written versions of a speech: 一篇课文/论文/日记/社论
piàn	片	1. for flat, thin things or things in slices: 三片肉/面包、两片药/饼干/叶子/瓦 2. for expanses or stretches of ocean, desert, mist, fog, etc.: 一片沙滩/树林/田野 3. for atmospheres, moods, etc.: 一片欢乐/心意
qī	期	for issues of periodicals, magazines, journals, etc.: 一期杂志/国债
qún	群	for a group, crowd, herd, or flock: 一群孩子/鸟/羊
shàn	扇	for doors, windows, etc.: 两扇门、一扇窗
shēng	声	for counting cries, shouts, or other utterances: 一声雷/炮响/她喊了我两声、你走以前喊我一声
shǒu	首	for songs, poems, music: 六首歌/诗/曲子
shù	束	= bunch: 一束花
shuāng	双	for things that come in twos, such as shoes, socks, chopsticks, etc., = pair: 一双鞋/袜子/眼睛
sōu	艘	for ships: 三艘船/油轮/军舰
suǒ	所	for buildings, houses, schools, etc.: 两所医院/学校/房子
tái	台	for stage performances, machines, equipment, etc.: 一台戏、九台电视机/洗衣机/计算机
táng	堂	for classes or periods at school or university: 四堂课
tàng	趟	1. for scheduled services of public transportation: 去北京的下一趟火车 2. for trips, journeys, visits, etc.: 上个月我去了三趟北京、昨天她到我房间来了两趟
tào	套	for sets of books, clothing, tools, furniture, etc.: 一套邮票/规则/课本/茶具
tiáo	条	1. for long, narrow things: 一条毛巾/船/裤子/裙子/河/路/街/蛇/虫/烟/肥皂 2. for items of news, laws, ideas, views: 三条消息/法律/意见/路线/理由 3. for limbs of the human body: 两条腿/胳膊 4. for human lives: 四条人命
tīng	听	= tin, can: 一听啤酒、罐头
tóu	头	1. for certain animals: 五头牛/猪/羊/象/狮子 2. for garlic bulbs: 一头蒜
tuán	团	for certain round things: 一团毛线/纸/火
wèi	位	a polite measure word for people: 一位先生/女士/老师/教授/师傅
xià	下	for brief actions, = time: 敲三下门、点几下头
xiàng	项	1. for work, projects, tasks, requirements, etc.: 一项工作/工程 2. for decisions or announcements: 一项决定/声明
yàng	样	for kinds of things in general: 三样工具/礼物
zé	则	for items of writing: 笑话五则、一则新闻
zhǎn	盏	for lamps: 一盏灯
zhāng	张	1. for flat things such as paper, paintings, tables, maps, etc.: 两张纸/报/桌子/床/画/票/邮票 2. for faces, mouths: 一张脸/嘴
zhèn	阵	for events or states of short duration: 一阵大雨/风/咳嗽
zhī	支	1. for stick-like things: 一支笔/筷子/蜡烛/笛子/枪 2. for music, songs, or teams: 一支曲子/歌/队伍 3. for army: 一支军队
zhī	只	1. for one of a pair: 一只鞋/眼睛/耳朵/手/脚 2. for some animals: 一只鸡/羊/猴子/鸟/猫/螃蟹 3. for boats: 一只小船
zhī	枝	for branches or branches with flowers: 一枝玫瑰花
zhǒng	种	= kind, type, sort: 两种人/植物/衣服/字典/主张/思想/意见
zuò	座	for mountains, buildings, structures, etc.: 一座山/桥/楼/宫殿/电影院

Measure words in Chinese

Hanyu Pinyin 汉语拼音	Chinese character 汉字	Description and example 说明和示例
fā	发	for bullets, artillery shells: 一发子弹/炮弹
fān	番	to indicate the number of times: 一番话/工夫/道理、研究了一番
fēn	分	1. = one-tenth: 七分成绩、三分错误 2. for units of currency: 一分钱
fèn	份	1. = portion, share: 一份饭/菜/礼物 2. for copies of newspapers, magazines, or manuscripts: 两份文件/报纸/计划/材料/试卷
fēng	封	for letters, telegrams: 八封信/电报
fú	幅	for paintings, works of calligraphy, fabrics, maps: 一幅山水画/花布/地图/照片
fù	副	1. for things that come in pairs or sets: 一副象棋/牌、一副手套/眼镜/筷子 2. for facial expressions: 一副笑脸/严肃的表情/面孔
gè	个	for various concrete and abstract nouns: 一个孩子/问题/月/杯子/鸡蛋/句子
gēn	根	for long, thin objects: 一根绳子/针/柱子/香肠/草/筷子/面条
háng	行	for things that form a line: 两行汉字/树/诗/泪
hù	户	for households: 五户人家
huí	回	for times, occurrences: 我要再试/去/来两回
huǒ	伙	for groups or bands of people: 一伙人/强盗/流氓
jiā	家	for families, enterprises, restaurants, hotels, etc.: 十二家住户/工厂/银行/商店/医院
jià	架	for aeroplanes, pianos, cameras, etc.: 六架飞机/钢琴/照相机
jiān	间	for rooms: 一间屋子/办公室/厨房
jiàn	件	for luggage, clothes, furniture, matters, etc.: 一件行李/衬衫/事/衣物/家具
jié	节	1. for sections of things, = section, length, segment: 一节竹子 2. for torch batteries, railway carriages, class periods at school: 四节车厢/电池/课
jié	截	= section, chunk: 一截木头/粉笔
jiè	届	1. for regular sessions, conferences, sports tournaments, terms of office, etc.: 第十届联合国大会/农业会议/总统 2. for students graduating in the same year, = year, class, grade: 第四届毕业班/毕业生
jù	句	for lines, sentences, units of speech, poetry, etc.: 一句话/诗
kē	棵	for trees, plants: 一棵树/草/水仙花/白菜
kē	颗	1. for small, round things such as pearls, teeth and hearts; also for things that appear small such as stars, satellites and planets: 一颗珠子/豆子/心/星/牙 2. for bullets, bombs, etc: 一颗子弹/炸弹
kǒu	口	1. for the number of people in a family or village: 八口人 2. for spoken languages, used with the verb 'speak' and with the number 'one' (一): 说一口北京话 3. for wells, pots: 一口井/锅 4. for things related to the mouth: 一口气
kuài	块	1. for things that come in chunks or solid pieces: 三块肥皂/糖/石头/手表 2. for things that are shaped like sheets: 五块桌布/木板/手绢 3. for slices, sections, divisions, etc.: 四块蛋糕/布/地
lèi	类	= kind of, sort of: 这类东西/问题
lì	粒	for very small, round things, such as peas, peanuts or grains: 一粒米/沙子、三粒药/种子
liàng	辆	for vehicles: 十辆汽车/自行车/卡车
liè	列	for trains: 一列火车
liǔ	绺	= tuft, lock, skein: 一绺头发/线
lún	轮	1. for round objects such as the sun, the moon: 一轮明月 2. = round: 第二轮会谈
luò	摞	= pile, stack: 一摞书/报/碗
méi	枚	for objects such as stamps, safety pins, bombs: 几枚邮票/回形针/炸弹

汉语量词

Hanyu Pinyin 汉语拼音	Chinese character 汉字	Description and example 说明和示例
bǎ	把	1. for objects with a handle or with something a person can hold: 三把刷子/刀/钥匙/雨伞/椅子/牙刷 2. for things that can be grouped in bunches or bundles: 一把筷子/草 3. = handful: 一把沙子/大米/豆子
bān	班	for scheduled services of public transportation: 下一班飞机/公交车
bāng	帮	for groups of people: 一帮人/孩子/学生
bāo	包	= package, packet, bundle: 一包香烟/糖果/药/衣服/点心
běn	本	for things that are bound, such as books, magazines, etc.: 五本书/杂志/画册
bǐ	笔	1. for sums of money: 那笔钱/账/债 2. for deals in business or trade: 这笔交易/生意
biàn	遍	to indicate the number of times an action or state occurs, = time: 看/写/说/唱/叫了两遍
bù	部	1. for novels, films, machines, vehicles, etc.: 三部小说/电影 2. for machines, vehicles, etc.: 两部电话、一部汽车
cè	册	1. for books or volumes of books: 这部小说有两册 2. for copies of books: 十万册书
céng	层	1. = storey, floor: 一座五层大楼/塔 2. for a layer, coat, sheet: 一层油漆/薄冰/雪/土/皮/灰尘
cháng	场	1. for the whole process of being ill: 一场病 2. for a natural disturbance, war, disaster, etc.: 一场雨/雪/战争/灾难
chǎng	场	for a show, performance, game, or debate: 一场电影/京剧/辩论、两场足球比赛/篮球比赛
chū	出	for plays: 一出戏
chuàn	串	= string, bunch, cluster: 一串钥匙/葡萄/珍珠
chuáng	床	for quilts, blankets, sheets: 三床被子/毯子/床单
cì	次	1. to indicate the number of times an action or state occurs, = time: 他来了三次、唱/说/写了两次 2. for events such as examinations, accidents, experiments, etc.: 两次考试/事故/实验/访问
cù	簇	= bunch, cluster: 一簇花
dá	打	= dozen: 一打鸡蛋/铅笔
dá	沓	= pad: 一沓报纸/钞票
dào	道	1. for orders issued by an authority, questions on an examination: 一道命令/算术题 2. for things in the shape of a line: 一道裂缝/光线/皱纹/门/沟 3. for courses in a meal: 有三道菜的午饭 4. for stages in a precedure: 一道工序
dī	滴	= drop: 一滴血/水/酒/泪
diǎn	点	for suggestions, requirements, ideas, opinions: 两点建议/要求/意见/变化
dǐng	顶	for hats, caps, or things with a top: 一顶帽子/帐篷
dòng	栋	for buildings: 十栋楼房
dǔ	堵	for walls: 一堵墙
duàn	段	1. for lengths of road, cable, etc., = section, segment: 一段公路 2. for periods of time, = period, length: 那一段历史/时间/婚姻 3. for units of writing, articles, speeches, etc., = piece, passage, paragraph: 一段音乐/发言/讲话/日记
duī	堆	= pile: 一堆书/衣服/雪/垃圾
duì	对	= pair, couple: 一对夫妻/花瓶/矛盾/眼珠
dùn	顿	1. for meals: 每天三顿饭 2. for actions that take place in single sessions: 他被批评了/骂了/说了/打了一顿
duǒ	朵	for flowers, clouds: 几朵花/云

Kinship terms

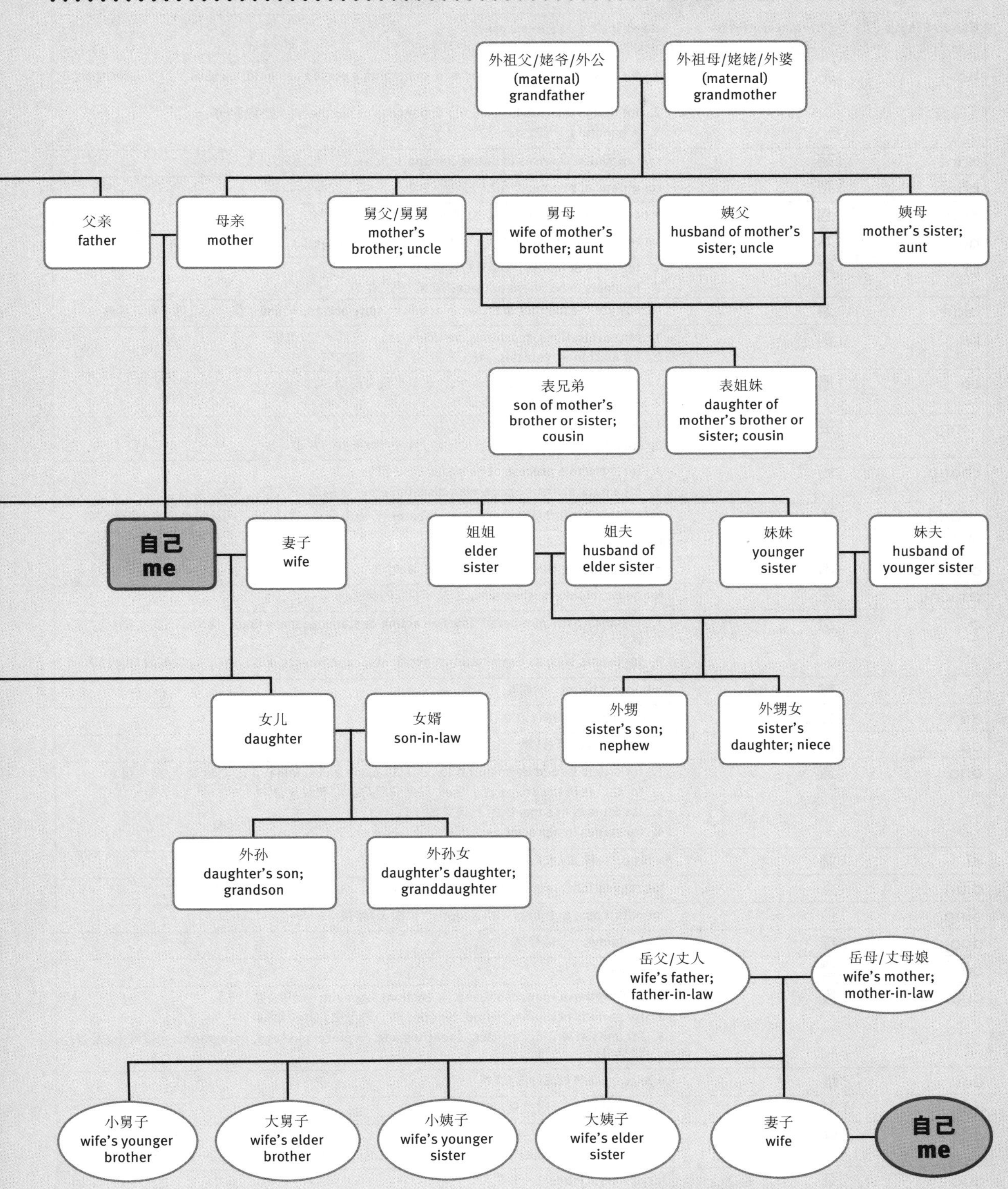

亲属称谓

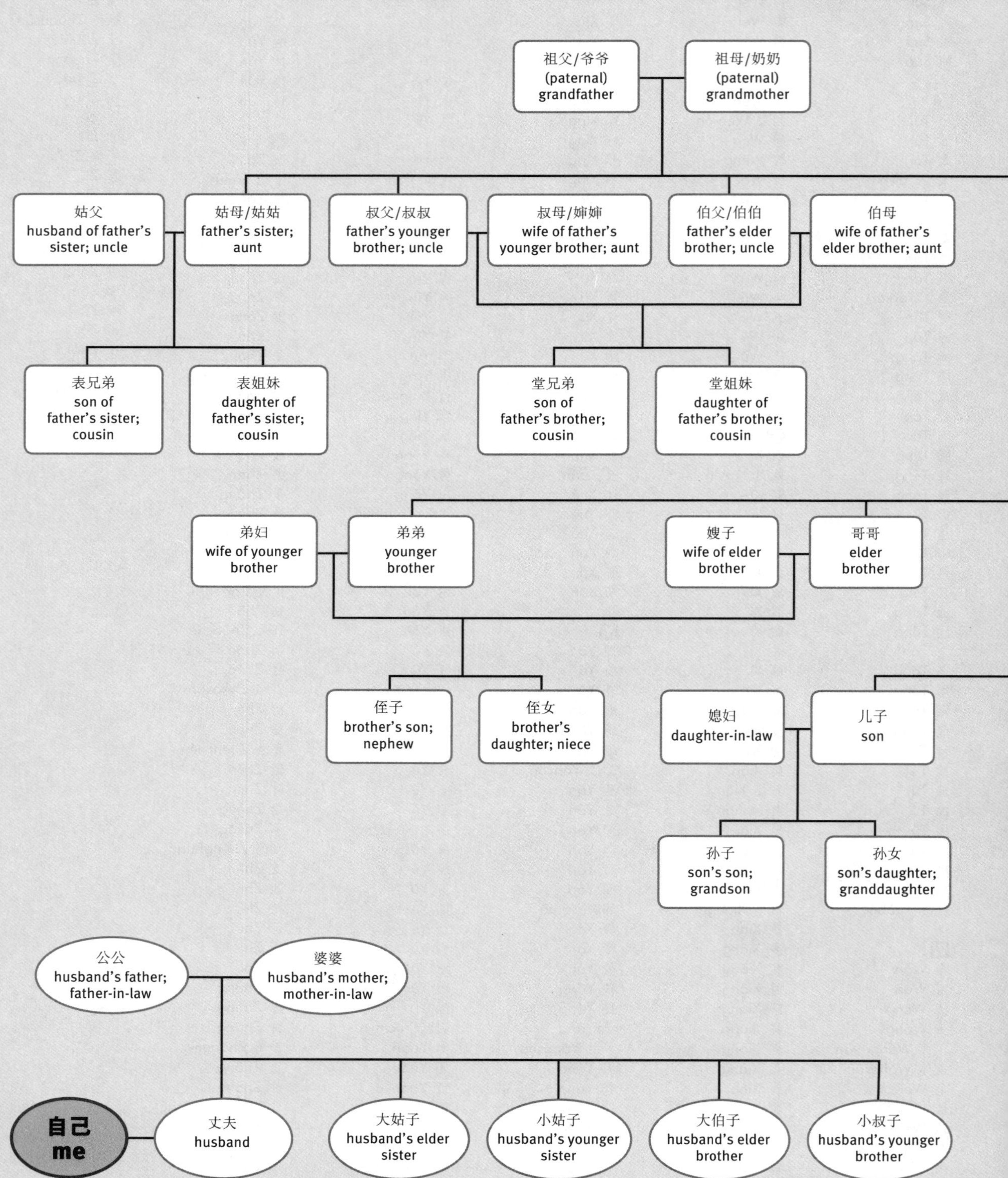

祖父/爷爷
(paternal)
grandfather
祖母/奶奶
(paternal)
grandmother
姑父
husband of father's sister; uncle
姑母/姑姑
father's sister; aunt
叔父/叔叔
father's younger brother; uncle
叔母/婶婶
wife of father's younger brother; aunt
伯父/伯伯
father's elder brother; uncle
伯母
wife of father's elder brother; aunt
表兄弟
son of father's sister; cousin
表姐妹
daughter of father's sister; cousin
堂兄弟
son of father's brother; cousin
堂姐妹
daughter of father's brother; cousin
弟妇
wife of younger brother
弟弟
younger brother
嫂子
wife of elder brother
哥哥
elder brother
侄子
brother's son; nephew
侄女
brother's daughter; niece
媳妇
daughter-in-law
儿子
son
孙子
son's son; grandson
孙女
son's daughter; granddaughter
公公
husband's father; father-in-law
婆婆
husband's mother; mother-in-law
自己
me
丈夫
husband
大姑子
husband's elder sister
小姑子
husband's younger sister
大伯子
husband's elder brother
小叔子
husband's younger brother

眭 Suī
睢 Suī
睢阳 Suīyáng
隋 Suí
随 Suí
孙 Sūn
所 Suǒ
索 Suǒ
锁 Suǒ

T

台 Tái
邰 Tái
太 Tài
太叔 Tàishū
泰 Tài
谈 Tán
覃 Tán
谭 Tán
潭 Tán
澹台 Tántái
檀 Tán
镡 Tán
汤 Tāng
唐 Táng
堂 Táng
桃 Táo
陶 Táo
腾 Téng
滕 Téng
藤 Téng
提 Tí
逓 Tí
田 Tián
铁 Tiě
邒 Tíng
通 Tōng
同 Tóng
仝 Tóng
佟 Tóng
彤 Tóng
童 Tóng
痛 Tòng
钭 Tǒu
凃 Tú
徒 Tú
涂 Tú
屠 Tú
土 Tǔ
庹 Tuǒ
拓 Tuò
拓拔 Tuòbá

W

宛 Wǎn
万 Wàn
汪 Wāng
王 Wáng
王官 Wángguān
王孙 Wángsūn
危 Wēi
威 Wēi
微 Wēi
微生 Wēishēng
韦 Wéi
维 Wéi
伟 Wěi
隗 Wěi
卫 Wèi
未 Wèi
位 Wèi
畏 Wèi
尉 Wèi
魏 Wèi
温 Wēn
文 Wén
闻 Wén
闻人 Wénrén
问 Wèn
翁 Wēng
沃 Wò
乌 Wū
邬 Wū
巫 Wū
巫马 Wūmǎ
毋 Wú
吴 Wú
五 Wǔ
午 Wǔ
伍 Wǔ
仵 Wǔ
武 Wǔ

X

西 Xī
西门 Xīmén
郗 Xī
息 Xī
奚 Xī
奚容 Xīróng
溪 Xī
巂 Xī
习 Xí
席 Xí
袭 Xí
郤 Xì
下 Xià
夏 Xià
夏侯 Xiàhóu
先 Xiān
鲜 Xiān
鲜仪 Xiānyí
鲜于 Xiānyú
贤 Xián
咸 Xián
冼 Xiǎn
洗 Xiǎn
洗辜 Xiǎngū
羡 Xiàn
乡 Xiāng
相 Xiāng
香 Xiāng
降 Xiáng
祥 Xiáng
向 Xiàng
项 Xiàng
肖 Xiāo
萧 Xiāo
小 Xiǎo
晓 Xiǎo
孝 Xiào
校 Xiào
效 Xiào
颉 Xié
谢 Xiè
解 Xiè
燮檀 Xiètán
忻 Xīn
辛 Xīn
忻 Xīn
新 Xīn
信 Xìn
刑 Xíng
邢 Xíng
行 Xíng
形 Xíng
幸 Xìng
熊 Xióng
修 Xiū
修敬 Xiūjìng
吁 Xū
须 Xū
胥 Xū
徐 Xú
许 Xǔ
绪 Xù
续 Xù
轩 Xuān
轩辕 Xuānyuán
宣 Xuān
禤 Xuān
玄 Xuán
还 Xuán
薛 Xuē
雪 Xuě
寻 Xún
郇 Xún
荀 Xún

Y

押 Yā
衙 Yá
轧 Yà
烟 Yān
焉 Yān
鄢 Yān
鄢楚 Yānchǔ
燕 Yān
延 Yán
闫 Yán
严 Yán
言 Yán
阎 Yán
阎法 Yánfǎ
颜 Yán
彦 Yàn
晏 Yàn
秧 Yāng
扬 Yáng
羊 Yáng
羊舌 Yángshé
阳 Yáng
杨 Yáng
仰 Yǎng
养 Yǎng
幺 Yāo
要 Yāo
尧 Yáo
姚 Yáo
药 Yào
野 Yě
业 Yè
叶 Yè
夜忽 Yèhū
伊 Yī
衣 Yī
依 Yī
仪 Yí
夷 Yí
宜 Yí
扆 Yǐ
弋 Yì
弋郅 Yìzhì
易 Yì
奕 Yì
羿 Yì
益 Yì
阴 Yīn
殷 Yīn
银 Yín
尹 Yǐn
印 Yìn
应 Yīng
英 Yīng
营 Yíng
嬴 Yíng
雍 Yōng
勇 Yǒng
用 Yòng
用火 Yònghuǒ
尤 Yóu
由 Yóu
油 Yóu
游 Yóu
有 Yǒu
酉 Yǒu
於 Yū
纡 Yū
纡涂 Yūtú
于 Yú
余 Yú
鱼 Yú
俞 Yú
虞 Yú
宇 Yǔ
宇文 Yǔwén
禹 Yǔ
瘐 Yǔ
玉 Yù
郁 Yù
预 Yù
喻 Yù
愈 Yù
蔚 Yù
豫 Yù
尉迟 Yùchí
渊 Yuān
元 Yuán
袁 Yuán
原 Yuán
源 Yuán
远 Yuǎn
苑 Yuàn
院 Yuàn
乐 Yuè
乐正 Yuèzhèng
岳 Yuè
越 Yuè
云 Yún
芸 Yún
负 Yùn
运 Yùn
员 Yùn
恽 Yùn
郓 Yùn

Z

宰 Zǎi
宰父 Zǎifǔ
载 Zài
昝 Zǎn
臧 Zāng
造 Zào
迮 Zé
笮 Zé
曾 Zēng
查 Zhā
翟 Zhái
祭展 Zhàizhǎn
占 Zhān
詹 Zhān
展 Zhǎn
战 Zhàn
湛 Zhàn
张 Zhāng
章 Zhāng
彰 Zhāng
长孙 Zhǎngsūn
仉 Zhǎng
仉督 Zhǎngdū
钊 Zhāo
钊佘 Zhāoshé
招 Zhāo
赵 Zhào
召郇 Zhàoxún
折 Zhé
真 Zhēn
真谌 Zhēnchén
甄 Zhēn
阵 Zhèn
正 Zhèng
郑 Zhèng
郑宦 Zhènghuàn
支 Zhī
职 Zhí
植 Zhí
芷 Zhǐ
郅 Zhì
智 Zhì
中 Zhōng
忠 Zhōng
钟 Zhōng
钟离 Zhōnglí
衷 Zhōng
仲 Zhòng
仲长 Zhòngcháng
仲孙 Zhòngsūn
周 Zhōu
朱 Zhū
邾 Zhū
诸 Zhū
诸葛 Zhūgě
竹 Zhú
竺 Zhú
住 Zhù
祝 Zhù
颛孙 Zhuānsūn
壮 Zhuàng
庄 Zhuāng
卓 Zhuó
禚 Zhuó
资 Zī
訾 Zī
子车 Zǐchē
紫 Zǐ
自 Zì
字 Zì
宗 Zōng
宗政 Zōngzhèng
纵 Zòng
邹 Zōu
俎 Zǔ
祖 Zǔ
左 Zuǒ
左丘 Zuǒqiū
左人 Zuǒrén
佐 Zuǒ
座 Zuò

翦 Jiǎn
蹇 Jiǎn
见 Jiàn
建 Jiàn
江 Jiāng
将 Jiāng
姜 Jiāng
蒋 Jiǎng
焦 Jiāo
矫 Jiǎo
敫 Jiǎo
缴 Jiǎo
佼隽 Jiǎojuàn
徼 Jiào
接 Jiē
揭 Jiē
节 Jié
介 Jiè
戒 Jiè
金 Jīn
晋 Jìn
晋楚 Jìnchǔ
晋伯 Jìnbó
靳 Jìn
经 Jīng
荆 Jīng
京臬 Jīngniè
井 Jǐng
景 Jǐng
敬 Jìng
靖 Jìng
酒 Jiǔ
居 Jū
琚 Jū
鞠 Jū
菊 Jú
巨 Jù
具 Jù
剧 Jù
隽 Juàn
君 Jūn

K

开 Kāi
勘 Kān
阚 Kàn
康 Kāng
亢 Kàng
抗 Kàng
抗铁 Kàngtiě
柯 Kē
科 Kē
可 Kě
克 Kè
客 Kè
空 Kōng
孔 Kǒng
寇 Kòu
库 Kù
蒯 Kuǎi
刽 Kuài
匡 Kuāng
邝 Kuàng
旷 Kuàng
况 Kuàng
况阎 Kuàngyán
隗 Kuí
葵 Kuí
夔 Kuí

L

来 Lái
赖 Lài
兰 Lán
蓝 Lán
郎 Láng
劳 Láo
老 Lǎo
乐 Lè
泐 Lè
勒 Lè
雷 Léi
冷 Lěng
梨 Lí
黎 Lí
李 Lǐ
力 Lì
历 Lì
厉 Lì
励 Lì
利 Lì
荔 Lì
郦 Lì
栗 Lì
连 Lián
莲 Lián
廉 Lián
练 Liàn
练达 Liàndá
炼 Liàn
梁 Liáng
梁丘 Liángqiū
粱 Liáng
廖 Liào
列 Liè
林 Lín
吝 Lìn
赁 Lìn
蔺 Lìn
令狐 Línghú
伶 Líng
灵 Líng
凌 Líng
泠 Líng
苓舜 Língshùn
令 Lìng
刘 Liú
留 Liú
柳 Liǔ
龙 Lóng
隆 Lóng
娄 Lóu
楼 Lóu
卢 Lú
芦 Lú
鲁 Lǔ
陆 Lù
录 Lù
鹿 Lù
逯 Lù
禄 Lù
路 Lù
闾 Lǘ
闾丘 Lǘ qiū
吕 Lǚ
侣 Lǚ
律 Lǜ
栾 Luán
滦 Luán
伦 Lún
罗 Luó
洛 Luò
骆 Luò
雒 Luò

M

麻 Má
马 Mǎ
祃 Mà
麦 Mài
满 Mǎn
忙 Máng
毛 Máo
茆 Máo
茅 Máo
卯 Mǎo
冒 Mào
枚 Méi
梅 Méi
美 Měi
门 Mén
蒙 Méng
孟 Mèng
祢 Mí
糜 Mí
米 Mǐ
芈 Mǐ
弭 Mǐ
宓 Mì
密 Mì
密商 Mìshāng
秘衷 Mìzhōng
苗 Miáo
妙 Miào
庙 Miào
缪 Miào
闵 Mǐn
明 Míng
谬 Miù
万俟 Mòqí
莫 Mò
墨 Mò
默 Mò
牟 Móu
母 Mǔ
木 Mù
沐 Mù
沐赏 Mùshǎng
牧 Mù
墓 Mù
睦 Mù
慕 Mù
慕容 Mùróng
穆 Mù

N

那 Nā
纳 Nà
佴 Nài
南 Nán
南宫 Nángōng
南门 Nánmén
南岳 Nányuè
能 Néng
尼 Ní
兒 Ní
倪 Ní
年 Nián
念 Niàn
乜 Niè
聂 Niè
宁 Níng
牛 Niú
钮 Niǔ
农 Nóng
那 Nuó

O

区 Ōu
欧 Ōu
欧阳 Ōuyáng

P

潘 Pān
盘 Pán
泮 Pàn
庞 Páng
逄 Páng
逢 Páng
裴 Péi
彭 Péng
皮 Pí
便 Pián
片 Piàn
朴 Piáo
朴谕 Piáoyù
票 Piào
平 Píng
繁 Pó
莆 Pú
蒲 Pú
濮 Pú
濮阳 Púyáng
浦 Pǔ
普 Pǔ

Q

戚 Qī
漆 Qī
漆雕 Qīdiāo
漆胶 Qījiāo
亓 Qí
亓官 Qíguān
亓壹 Qíyī
齐 Qí
祁 Qí
耆 Qí
綦 Qí
綦蹇 Qíjiǎn
蕲 Qí
圻木 Qímù
岂 Qǐ
杞 Qǐ
卡 Qiǎ
千 Qiān
谦 Qiān
骞 Qiān
钱 Qián
潜 Qián
羌 Qiāng
强 Qiáng
墙 Qiáng
乔 Qiáo
桥 Qiáo
谯 Qiáo
谯洛 Qiáoluò
郄 Qiè
钦 Qīn
钦萨 Qīnsà
秦 Qín
琴 Qín
覃 Qín
禽潜 Qínqián
青 Qīng
卿 Qīng
庆 Qìng
丘 Qiū
邱 Qiū
秋 Qiū
仇 Qiú
酋 Qiú
裘 Qiú
曲 Qū
麴 Qū
屈 Qū
屈突 Qūtū
渠 Qú
璩 Qú
瞿 Qú
权 Quán
全 Quán
泉 Quán
阕 Què
阙 Què

R

冉 Rǎn
壤驷 Rǎngsì
荛 Ráo
饶 Ráo
绕 Rào
壬 Rén
仁 Rén
任 Rén
戎 Róng
荣 Róng
容 Róng
融 Róng
茹 Rú
汝 Rǔ
阮 Ruǎn
芮 Ruì
瑞 Ruì
闰 Rùn

S

洒 Sǎ
萨 Sà
赛 Sài
伞 Sǎn
桑 Sāng
僧 Sēng
沙 Shā
山 Shān
钐 Shān
闪 Shǎn
陕 Shǎn
单 Shàn
善 Shàn
商 Shāng
赏 Shǎng
上官 Shàngguān
尚 Shàng
韶 Shào
邵 Shào
绍 Shào
折 Shé
佘 Shé
厍 Shè
申 Shēn
申屠 Shēntú
莘 Shēn
神 Shén
沈 Shěn
慎 Shèn
生 Shēng
绳 Shéng
圣 Shèng
胜 Shèng
盛 Shèng
师 Shī
施 Shī
石 Shí
时 Shí
史 Shǐ
侍 Shì
守 Shǒu
寿 Shòu
殳 Shū
舒 Shū
叔孙 Shūsūn
疏邝 Shūkuàng
束 Shù
树 Shù
庶 Shù
帅 Shuài
帅揭 Shuàijiē
率 Shuài
双 Shuāng
水 Shuǐ
税 Shuì
硕 Shuò
司 Sī
司空 Sīkōng
司寇 Sīkòu
司马 Sīmǎ
司士 Sīshì
司徒 Sītú
思 Sī
斯 Sī
松 Sōng
宋 Sòng
苏 Sū
素 Sù
宿 Sù
粟 Sù

中国百家姓
Chinese surnames

按汉语拼音排序 *Arranged in Pinyin order*

A

艾 Ài
爱 Ài
安 Ān
昂 Áng
敖 Áo
傲 Ào
奥 Ào

B

巴 Bā
芭 Bā
白 Bái
百里 Bǎilǐ
柏 Bǎi
拜 Bài
班 Bān
邦 Bāng
包 Bāo
宝 Bǎo
保 Bǎo
鲍 Bào
暴 Bào
北宫 Běigōng
北郭 Běiguō
贝 Bèi
贲 Bēn
毕 Bì
秘 Bì
边 Biān
卞 Biàn
别 Bié
宾 Bīn
滨 Bīn
邴 Bǐng
秉 Bǐng
伯 Bó
柏 Bó
博 Bó
薄 Bó
卜 Bǔ
补 Bǔ
布 Bù
步 Bù
步叔 Bùshū

C

才 Cái
材 Cái
采 Cǎi
菜 Cài
蔡 Cài
仓 Cāng
苍 Cāng
藏 Cáng
操 Cāo
曹 Cáo
岑 Cén
茶 Chá
柴 Chái
缠 Chán
单于 Chányú
产 Chǎn
昌 Chāng
苌 Cháng
常 Cháng
畅 Chàng
钞 Chāo
晁 Cháo
巢 Cháo
朝 Cháo
车 Chē
陈 Chén
谌 Chén
成 Chéng
呈 Chéng
承 Chéng
程 Chéng
池 Chí
迟 Chí
迟介 Chíjiè
充 Chōng
种 Chóng
种繁 Chóngfán
崇 Chóng
丑 Chǒu
初 Chū
储 Chǔ
楚 Chǔ
褚 Chǔ
揣 Chuǎi
啜 Chuài
传 Chuán
春 Chūn
椿 Chūn
淳 Chún
淳于 Chúnyú
辞 Cí
慈 Cí
次 Cì
从 Cóng
丛 Cóng
爨 Cuàn
崔 Cuī
催 Cuī

D

达 Dá
达忽 Dáhū
笪 Dá
笪一 Dáyī
代 Dài
岱 Dài
戴 Dài
单 Dān
儋傜 Dānyáo
旦 Dàn
但 Dàn
淡 Dàn
党 Dǎng
刀 Dāo
邓 Dèng
狄 Dí
邸 Dǐ
底 Dǐ
第五 Dìwǔ
典 Diǎn
佃 Diàn
殿 Diàn
刁 Diāo
丁 Dīng
东 Dōng
东方 Dōngfāng
东宫 Dōnggōng
东郭 Dōngguō
东门 Dōngmén
冬 Dōng
董 Dǒng
懂 Dǒng
斗 Dòu
豆 Dòu
窦 Dòu
都 Dū
独孤 Dúgū
堵 Dǔ
杜 Dù
端 Duān
端木 Duānmù
段 Duàn
段干 Duàngān
顿 Dùn
多 Duō
朵 Duǒ

E

阿 Ē
鄂 È
恩 Ēn
恩随 Ēnsuí

F

法 Fǎ
法来 Fǎlái
藩 Fān
凡 Fán
樊 Fán
范 Fàn
方 Fāng
邡 Fāng
芳 Fāng
房 Fáng
斐 Fěi
翡 Fěi
费 Fèi
丰 Fēng
风 Fēng
风虎 Fēnghǔ
封 Fēng
酆 Fēng
冯 Féng
逢 Féng
凤 Fèng
奉 Fèng
鄜 Fū
弗 Fú
伏 Fú
扶 Fú
苻 Fú
服 Fú
洑 Fú
符 Fú
浮邱 Fúqiū
甫 Fǔ
辅 Fǔ
付 Fù
赴 Fù
副 Fù
傅 Fù
富 Fù

G

改 Gǎi
盖 Gài
干 Gān
甘 Gān
刚 Gāng
罡 Gāng
高 Gāo
高堂 Gāotáng
郜 Gào
戈 Gē
盖 Gě
葛 Gě
庚 Gēng
庚癸 Gēngguǐ
耿 Gěng
弓 Gōng
公 Gōng
公良 Gōngliáng
公明 Gōngmíng
公沙 Gōngshā
公孙 Gōngsūn
公西 Gōngxī
公晰 Gōngxī
公羊 Gōngyáng
公冶 Gōngyě
公仪 Gōngyí
供 Gōng
宫 Gōng
龚 Gōng
巩 Gǒng
贡 Gòng
勾 Gōu
句 Gōu
沟 Gōu
缑 Gōu
苟 Gǒu
苟恽 Gǒuyùn
辜 Gū
古 Gǔ
谷 Gǔ
谷梁 Gǔliáng
顾 Gù
雇 Gù
关 Guān
官 Guān
官覃 Guāntán
管 Guǎn
贯 Guàn
冠 Guàn
毌邱 Guànqiū
光 Guāng
广 Guǎng
归 Guī
归海 Guīhǎi
归牟 Guīmóu
规 Guī
邽 Guī
炅 Guì
炅过 Guìguò
贵 Guì
桂 Guì
过 Guō
呙 Guō
郭 Guō
国 Guó
果 Guǒ

H

哈 Hǎ
哈涂 Hǎtú
海 Hǎi
海门 Hǎimén
亥彘 Hàizhì
韩 Hán
闬 Hàn
杭 Háng
蒿 Hāo
郝 Hǎo
何 Hé
和 Hé
郃 Hé
贺 Hè
贺若 Hèruò
赫 Hè
赫连 Hèlián
黑 Hēi
衡 Héng
弘 Hóng
红 Hóng
宏 Hóng
洪 Hóng
鸿 Hóng
侯 Hóu
后 Hòu
郈 Hòu
厚 Hòu
候 Hòu
呼 Hū
呼延 Hūyán
轷 Hū
胡 Hú
胡母 Húmǔ
虎 Hǔ
户 Hù
扈 Hù
鄠 Hù
花 Huā
滑 Huá
化 Huà
华 Huà
怀 Huái
淮 Huái
环 Huán
环阿 Huán'ē
郇 Huán
桓 Huán
宦 Huàn
皇 Huáng
皇甫 Huángfǔ
黄 Huáng
辉 Huī
回 Huí
惠 Huì
魂 Hún
浑言 Húnyán
火 Huǒ
霍 Huò

J

姬 Jī
基 Jī
嵇 Jī
稽 Jī
吉 Jí
汲 Jí
姞 Jí
戢 Jí
藉 Jí
纪 Jǐ
计 Jì
记 Jì
季 Jì
冀 Jì
夹谷 Jiāgǔ
家 Jiā
葭 Jiā
郏 Jiá
荚 Jiá
甲 Jiǎ
甲锁 Jiǎsuǒ
贾 Jiǎ
菅 Jiān
简 Jiǎn

中国节日及假期
Chinese festivals and holidays

阴历 Lunar calendar

正月初一——春节 (1st of the first lunar month—Spring Festival)
Spring Festival, or Chinese New Year, occurs on the first day of the traditional Chinese lunar year (falling between the end of January and the end of February in the Gregorian calendar). People return home to be with their families. Traditions include cleaning the home; wearing new clothes; presenting gifts; pasting up auspicious couplets (对联) on either side of the front door; giving children small amounts of money in red envelopes (红包); in the North, making and eating boiled dumplings (饺子); and letting off firecrackers and fireworks. In business, all debts should be cleared at New Year. Celebrations can start late in the preceding month, and go on till the following Lantern Festival. The official holiday, however, is just three days.

正月十五——元宵节 (15th of the first lunar month—Lantern Festival)
The Lantern Festival falls on the first full moon of the lunar year. The main activity is watching lanterns and solving 'lantern riddles' (灯谜) written on them. The traditional food is round glutinous rice dumplings (元宵). The Lantern Festival marks the end of the New Year period.

四月初八——佛诞节 (8th of the fourth lunar month—Buddha's Birthday)
Buddha's Birthday is more popular in Hong Kong, and is especially celebrated in Buddhist temples.

五月初五——端午节 (5th of the fifth lunar month—Dragon Boat Festival)
A traditional festival, ostensibly commemorating the poet Qu Yuan (340-278 BC) of the state of Chu. Qu Yuan wrote what is regarded as some of the greatest poetry in Chinese history. On hearing the news of the defeat of Chu by Qin, he is said to have committed suicide by jumping into the Miluo River. The traditions of dragon-boat racing and eating glutinous rice pyramids (粽子) are meant to mark Qu Yuan's death—since supposedly at the time local people threw rice into the river to divert the fish from eating his body.

七月初七——七夕节 (7th of the seventh lunar month—Double Seventh Festival)
This festival is associated with the traditional love story of the mortal Cowherd and the celestial Weaving Girl. According to the story, the couple fell in love and she came down to earth to marry him. However, they were discovered by the Queen of Heaven, who separated them by creating the Milky Way and took the Weaving Girl back to heaven. Subsequently, magpies took pity on the pair and once a year form themselves into a bridge over the Milky Way so that the Cowherd and the Weaving Girl can be reunited. In contemporary China the festival is a day for lovers.

七月十五——中元节 (15th of the seventh lunar month—Hungry Ghost Festival)
Traditionally, the whole of the seventh month is Ghost Month, when spirits wander the earth. At the Hungry Ghost Festival, ritual food offerings are made and paper money burnt to appease these spirits. This festival is more popular in Hong Kong.

八月十五——中秋节 (15th of the eighth lunar month—Mid-Autumn Festival)
Another traditional festival when the moon is full. On this day people enjoy the moon, set out food, and in particular eat moon cakes (月饼). It is timed to celebrate the harvest.

九月初九——重阳节 (9th of the ninth lunar month—Double Ninth Festival)
The number nine symbolizes Yang (阳), the positive principle in nature. So, on the 9th day of the 9th month, this principle is at its strongest. Traditionally, people climb mountains on this day. The chrysanthemum is also symbolic of the festival.

阳历 Solar calendar

1 月 1 日——元旦 (1 January—New Year's Day)
Though it does not have traditional significance, this day is an official holiday in China.

3 月 8 日——国际劳动妇女节 (8 March—International Working Women's Day)
Women have a half or whole day's holiday.

3 月 12 日——植树节 (12 March—Tree-planting Day)
Begun in 1979, this is a day for planting trees and addressing ecological problems.

4 月初（4 至 6 日之间）——清明节 (early April, between 4th and 6th—Qingming Festival)
Linked to the early Chinese solar calendar, the traditional Qingming Festival marked an important transition to warmer weather in the agricultural year. It is now an official one-day holiday. The main activity is 'sweeping the tombs' of the ancestors. At gravesides people conduct a symbolic sweeping with new willow fronds; offer food, gifts and flowers; and burn incense and paper money. It is also a festival for spring outings and kite flying.

5 月 1 日——国际劳动节 (1 May—International Labour Day, (US) Labor Day)
As in other parts of the world, May Day has been denoted a day for workers. There is an official one-day holiday.

5 月 4 日——中国青年节 (4 May—Chinese Youth Day)
This day commemorates the May 4th Movement of 1919, when students in Beijing and across China demonstrated for nationalism and modernization. Today, young people under 28 have half a day's holiday.

6 月 1 日——国际儿童节 (1 June—International Children's Day)
On this day children are presented with gifts, and get free entrance to various kinds of entertainment.

7 月 1 日——七一建党节 (1 July—Founding of the Chinese Communist Party)
The CCP was founded in Shanghai in 1921.

8 月 1 日——中国人民解放军建军节 (1 August—Army Day)
A ceremonial day, it commemorates the founding of the People's Liberation Army and also emphasizes collaboration between the People's Liberation Army and the people.

9 月 10 日——教师节 (10 September—Teacher's Day)
The new official day for honouring teachers.

10 月 1 日——国庆节 (1 October—National Day)
This was the day that Chairman Mao proclaimed the founding of the People's Republic of China in 1949. Today, it is sometimes celebrated with grand processions of school children, workers, minority representatives and troops, and displays of military hardware. There are three days' official holiday.

12 月 22 日或 23 日——冬至 (mid-Winter, 22nd or 23rd December—Winter Solstice)
Another festival determined by the Chinese solar calendar. As the turning point away from winter, it marks the time in the year when the Yang (阳) principle is at its lowest. Various kinds of dumplings are eaten to build up strength.

Ethnic groups in China

中文 **Chinese**	汉语拼音 **Pinyin**	英文 **English**	人口(万人) **Population** **(x 10 000)**	主要分布地区 **Main distribution areas**
门巴族	Ménbāzú	Monba	0.9	西藏 Tibet
蒙古族	Měnggǔzú	Mongol	582.8	内蒙古、辽宁、吉林、河北、黑龙江、新疆 Inner Mongolia, Liaoning, Jilin, Hebei, Heilongjiang, Xinjiang
苗族	Miáozú	Miao	894.6	贵州、湖南、云南、广西、重庆、湖北、四川 Guizhou, Hunan, Yunnan, Guangxi, Chongqing, Hubei, Sichuan
仫佬族	Mùlǎozú	Mulam	20.7	广西 Guangxi
纳西族	Nàxīzú	Naxi	30.9	云南 Yunnan
怒族	Nùzú	Nu	2.9	云南 Yunnan
普米族	Pǔmǐzú	Primi, *also* Pumi	3.4	云南 Yunnan
羌族	Qiāngzú	Qiang	30.6	四川 Sichuan
撒拉族	Sālāzú	Salar	10.5	青海 Qinghai
畲族	Shēzú	She	71.0	福建、 浙江、 江西、 广东 Fujian, Zhejiang, Jiangxi, Guangdong
水族	Shuǐzú	Shui	40.7	贵州、广西 Guizhou, Guangxi
塔吉克族	Tǎjíkèzú	Tajik	4.1	新疆 Xinjiang
塔塔尔族	Tǎtǎ'ěrzú	Tatar	0.5	新疆 Xinjiang
土家族	Tǔjiāzú	Tujia	803.7	湖南、湖北、重庆、贵州 Hunan, Hubei, Chongqing, Guizhou
土族	Tǔzú	Tu	24.2	青海、甘肃 Qinghai, Gansu
佤族	Wǎzú	Va	39.7	云南 Yunnan
维吾尔族	Wéiwú'ěrzú	Uighur, *also* Uigur *or* Uygur	840.5	新疆 Xinjiang
乌孜别克族	Wūzībiékèzú	Uzbek	1.2	新疆 Xinjiang
锡伯族	Xībózú	Xibe	18.9	辽宁、新疆 Liaoning, Xinjiang
瑶族	Yáozú	Yao	263.9	广西、湖南、云南、广东 Guangxi, Hunan, Yunnan, Guangdong
彝族	Yízú	Yi	776.6	四川、云南、贵州、广西 Sichuan, Yunnan, Guizhou, Guangxi
裕固族	Yùgùzú	Yugur	1.4	甘肃 Gansu
藏族	Zàngzú	Tibetan	542.3	西藏、四川、青海、甘肃、云南 Tibet, Sichuan, Qinghai, Gansu, Yunnan
壮族	Zhuàngzú	Zhuang	1,618.7	广西、云南、广东 Guangxi, Yunnan, Guangdong

说明：本表中人口据《中国民族统计年鉴 2000》（民族出版社，2000 年）资料整理。

Note: The population figures shown in this table are based on *The Yearbook of Chinese Ethnic Groups Statistics 2000* (Ethnic Groups Publishing House, 2000).

中国各民族

按汉语拼音排序
Arranged in Pinyin order

中文 **Chinese**	汉语拼音 **Pinyin**	英文 **English**	人口(万人) **Population** (x 10 000)	主要分布地区 **Main distribution areas**
阿昌族	Āchāngzú	Achang	3.4	云南 Yunnan
白族	Báizú	Bai	186.2	云南、贵州、湖南 Yunnan, Guizhou, Hunan
保安族	Bǎo'ānzú	Bonan	1.7	甘肃 Gansu
布朗族	Bùlǎngzú	Blang, *also* Bulong	9.2	云南 Yunnan
布依族	Bùyīzú	Bouyei	297.3	贵州 Guizhou
朝鲜族	Cháoxiǎnzú	Korean	193.0	辽宁、吉林、黑龙江 Liaoning, Jilin, Heilongjiang
达斡尔族	Dáwò'ěrzú	Daur	13.3	内蒙古、黑龙江 Inner Mongolia, Heilongjiang
傣族	Dǎizú	Dai	115.9	云南 Yunnan
德昂族	Dé'ángzú	De'ang, *also* Deang	1.8	云南 Yunnan
东乡族	Dōngxiāngzú	Dongxiang	51.4	甘肃、新疆 Gansu, Xinjiang
侗族	Dòngzú	Dong	296.3	贵州、湖南、广西 Guizhou, Hunan, Guangxi
独龙族	Dúlóngzú	Derung, *also* Drung	0.7	云南 Yunnan
鄂伦春族	Èlúnchūnzú	Oroqen	0.8	黑龙江、内蒙古 Heilongjiang, Inner Mongolia
俄罗斯族	Èluósīzú	Russian	1.6	新疆、黑龙江 Xinjiang, Heilongjiang
鄂温克族	Èwēnkèzú	Ewenki, *also* Evenk	3.1	内蒙古 Inner Mongolia
高山族	Gāoshānzú	Gaoshan	0.4	台湾、福建 Taiwan, Fujian
仡佬族	Gēlǎozú	Gelao	58.0	贵州 Guizhou
哈尼族	Hānízú	Hani	144.0	云南 Yunnan
哈萨克族	Hāsàkèzú	Kazakh, *also* Kazak	125.1	新疆 Xinjiang
汉族	Hànzú	Han	115,940	遍布全国 throughout China
赫哲族	Hèzhézú	Hezhen	0.5	黑龙江 Heilongjiang
回族	Huízú	Hui	982.8	宁夏、甘肃、河南、新疆、青海、云南、河北、山东、安徽、辽宁、北京、内蒙古、天津、黑龙江、陕西、贵州、吉林、江苏、四川 Ningxia, Gansu, Henan, Xinjiang, Qinghai, Yunnan, Hebei, Shandong, Anhui, Liaoning, Beijing, Inner Mongolia, Tianjin, Heilongjiang, Shaanxi, Guizhou, Jilin, Jiangsu, Sichuan
基诺族	Jīnuòzú	Jino, *also* Jinuo	2.1	云南 Yunnan
京族	Jīngzú	Kinh, *also* Gin	2.3	广西 Guangxi
景颇族	Jǐngpōzú	Jingpo	13.2	云南 Yunnan
柯尔克孜族	Kē'ěrkèzīzú	Kirgiz	16.1	新疆 Xinjiang
拉祜族	Lāhùzú	Lahu	45.4	云南 Yunnan
黎族	Lízú	Li	124.8	海南 Hainan
傈僳族	Lìsùzú	Lisu	63.5	云南、四川 Yunnan, Sichuan
珞巴族	Luòbāzú	Lhoba	0.3	西藏 Tibet
满族	Mǎnzú	Manchu	1,070.8	辽宁、河北、黑龙江、吉林、内蒙古、北京 Liaoning, Hebei, Heilongjiang, Jilin, Inner Mongolia, Beijing
毛南族	Máonánzú	Maonan	10.7	广西 Guangxi

A chronology of historical and cultural events in China

公元 105 年 蔡伦改进造纸术，采用树皮、麻头、破布、旧鱼网为原料造出质地优良的植物纤维纸。造纸术和其后出现的印刷术、指南针和火药并称为中国古代四大发明。

AD 105. Cai Lun improved paper-making technology, using bark, hemp, rags and old fishing nets as materials to make fine-quality paper. Paper-making, printing, the compass and gunpowder were the four great discoveries of ancient China.

公元 132 年 张衡创制地动仪、浑天仪和指南车。

AD 132. Zhang Heng created the seismograph, the armillary sphere, and the south-pointing chariot (compass).

公元 219 年 医圣张仲景去世。曾穷毕生之力著《伤寒杂病论》。

AD 219. Death of the medical sage Zhang Zhongjing, author of *Treatise on Cold Pathogenic and Miscellaneous Diseases*.

公元 427 年 陶渊明去世。生前因厌倦仕宦生活而辞官归隐，成为田园诗人。

AD 427. Death of Tao Yuanming. Weary of the life of an official, he resigned from his official position to live in seclusion, becoming a pastoral poet.

公元 462 年 数学家祖冲之创"大明历"。他计算出的 π 值精确到小数点后第七位。

AD 462. The mathematician Zu Chongzhi created the Daming calendar. He accurately calculated π to seven decimal points.

公元约 533-554 年间 贾思勰撰写《齐民要术》，总结农作物、蔬果、竹木等的栽培技术，及家禽饲养、食品加工技术。

AD 533-554 (approx.). Jia Sixie wrote the *Main Techniques for the Welfare of the People*, summarizing information about the cultivation of crops, fruit, vegetables, trees and bamboo, the rearing of poultry, and food-processing.

公元 605 年 隋文帝分科取士，科举制度诞生。

AD 605. Emperor Suiwendi introduced the imperial civil service examination system for selecting the best scholars in different fields.

公元 629 年 玄奘赴天竺取经。著《大唐西域记》，将大量佛教经书译成中文。

AD 629. Xuan Zang went on a pilgrimage to India. He wrote the *Great Tang Records on the Western Regions* and translated many Buddhist scriptures into Chinese.

公元 725 年 僧一行卒。曾发起在多地点天文观测并测算出地球子午线长度，编制"大衍历"。

AD 725. Death of Seng Yixing. He conducted astronomical surveys in many different places to calculate the lengths of the earth's meridians and compiled the Dayan Calendar.

公元 762 年 诗人李白卒。其诗歌富有个性特色和浪漫精神，达到唐诗艺术高峰。唐朝还涌现出杜甫和白居易等著名诗人。

AD 762. Death of the poet Li Bai. His characterful and romantic poems marked the height of Tang dynasty poetry. Other important poets of the Tang dynasty were Du Fu and Bai Juyi.

公元 824 年 文学家韩愈卒。与柳宗元合倡古文运动，力反骈偶文风，提倡散体。韩愈、柳宗元和宋代的苏轼、苏洵、苏辙、欧阳修、王安石、曾巩并称为唐宋八大家。

AD 824. Death of the literary scholar, Han Yu. Together with Liu Zongyuan, he launched the classical Chinese movement, which opposed the parallel-prose writing style and advocated a direct prose style. Han Yu, Liu Zongyuan and (of the Song dynasty) Su Dongpo, Su Xun, Su Zhe, Ouyang Xiu, Wang Anshi and Zeng Gong were the Eight Great Men of Letters of the Tang and Song dynasties.

公元 1031 年 沈括出生。汇集前人科学成果，著《梦溪笔谈》。

AD 1031. Birth of Shen Kuo, who collected past scientific achievements in *The Dream Pool Essays*.

公元 1041 年 毕昇发明活字印刷术取代刻版印刷。

AD 1041. Bi Sheng invented the art of letter-press printing.

公元 1231 年 郭守敬出生。与他人共同编制"授时历"，创制多种天文仪器。

AD 1231. Birth of Guo Shoujing. Together with others he compiled the 'official calendar' and created many kinds of astronomical instruments.

公元 1405-1433 年 郑和七次下西洋，促进了中外文化交流。

AD 1405-1433. Zheng He sailed to the West seven times, promoting cultural links between China and the outside world.

公元 1593 年 李时珍去世。参考历代医书并结合自身实践经验，编成《本草纲目》。

AD 1593. Death of Li Shizhen, who compiled the *Compendium of Materia Medica* based on his own experience and the works of previous generations.

公元 1764 年 曹雪芹去世。所著长篇小说《红楼梦》规模宏大，结构严谨，语言生动优美，塑造了多个个性鲜明的人物形象，达到中国古代现实主义小说的巅峰。《红楼梦》和《三国演义》、《水浒传》、《西游记》并称为中国古典四大名著。

AD 1764. Death of Cao Xueqin, author of *Dream of the Red Mansions*. With its broad scope, compact structure, vivid and graceful language, and many strongly delineated characters, it represents the peak of classical realism in the Chinese novel. *Dream of the Red Mansions, Romance of the Three Kingdoms, The Water Margin,* and *Journey to the West* are the four great works of Chinese classical literature.

公元 1782 年《四库全书》修成，收录中国历代古籍，保存了大量文献。

AD 1782. The encyclopedic *Complete Library in Four Branches of Literature* was compiled. It included ancient works of past generations and preserved a great number of archived documents.

公元 1862 年 京师同文馆创办。为清末第一所外语专门学校，以培养外语翻译和洋务人才为目的，后并入京师大学堂（北京大学前身）。

AD 1862. Jingshi Tongwen Guan founded. It was the first foreign language college with the aim of training foreign language interpreters and experts in foreign affairs. It subsequently became part of Jingshi Daxuetang (later Peking University).

公元 1905 年 在中国延续 1,300 多年的科举制度被废除。

AD 1905. The imperial civil service examination was abolished after over 1,300 years.

公元 1911 年 辛亥革命爆发，次年中华民国成立，中国封建制度结束。

AD 1911. The 1911 Xinhai Revolution. The following year the Republic of China was established, bringing China's feudal system to an end.

公元 1915 年 新文化运动开始，陈独秀创办《新青年》，举起民主和科学的旗帜，倡导文学革命，提倡白话文。

AD 1915. New Culture Movement began. Chen Duxiu founded the *New Youth* magazine, raising the flag of democracy and science. The start of a literary revolution, advocating vernacular prose.

公元 1918 年 鲁迅发表了第一部白话小说《狂人日记》。

AD 1918. Lu Xun published the first novel written in the vernacular, *Diary of a Madman*.

公元 1919 年 "五四"运动爆发。

AD 1919. May 4th Movement.

中国历史文化事件年表

约 170 万年前 元谋人生活在云南元谋一带，开始直立行走，捕猎为生，能打造石器，可能已会使用火。

1.7 million years ago (approx.). Yuanmou Man (*Homo erectus yuanmouensis*) lived in the Yuanmou region of Yunnan. Began to walk upright, hunted for a living, could make stone implements and possibly make use of fire.

约 70-20 万年前 北京人生活在北京周口店一带，群居于洞穴中，以采集和狩猎为生，会使用石器和骨器。

700,000-200,000 years ago (approx.). Peking Man (*Homo erectus pekinensis*) lived in the Zhoukoudian area of Beijing. Lived in groups in caves as hunter-gatherers, could make stone and bone implements.

约 1.8 万年前 山顶洞人开始氏族公社的生活，按母系血统确立亲属关系，共同劳动，共同分配食物，以采集狩猎为生，会捕鱼，能人工取火。

18,000 years ago (approx.). Upper Cave Man began to live in communal, matriarchal kinship groups. Worked together, hunted and gathered for a living, and shared food. Could catch fish and make fire.

约 5,000-7,000 年前 河姆渡、半坡母系氏族公社时期，以种植水稻为主，兼营畜牧、采集、渔猎，会制陶和建筑房屋、酿酒等。

5,000-7,000 years ago (approx.). Hemudu and Banpo matriarchal communities. Planted rice and raised livestock, gathered plants, fished and hunted. Could make pottery, build houses and brew beer.

约 4,000-5,000 年前 大汶口文化中晚期，父系氏族公社时期，能制造精美工具及陶器，以农业生产为主，兼营畜牧、狩猎和捕鱼业。原始文字符号开始出现。

4,000-5,000 years ago (approx.). The middle and later period of the Dawenkou culture. A patriarchal community, with the ability to create fine tools and pottery. Mainly agricultural, they also raised livestock and hunted and fished. Appearance of the first written symbols.

约 4,000 多年前 传说中的炎帝、黄帝、尧、舜、禹时期，推广耕作农业，出现了国家职能的社会管理机构。

Over 4,000 years ago (approx.). The period of the five legendary emperors Yandi, Huangdi, Yao, Shun, and Yu. The emergence of farming techniques and a national social management structure.

约公元前 21 世纪 夏朝建立。中国进入奴隶社会时期。夏朝时创立了历法。

21st century BC (approx.). The founding of the Xia Dynasty. The beginning of the slave system in China. The calendar system was created.

约公元前 17 世纪 商朝建立。发明了文字，出现了甲骨文、瓷器，也是青铜文化的灿烂时期。

17th century BC (approx.). The founding of the Shang Dynasty. The invention of writing, the appearance of oracle bone inscriptions, porcelain and magnificent bronzeware.

公元前 1046 年 周朝建立。实行井田制，农业发达，发明冶铁技术。

1046 BC. The founding of the Zhou Dynasty. The beginning of the well-field system, the development of agriculture, and the invention of iron-smelting.

公元前 841 年 发生国人暴动，共和行政。中国历史开始有确切纪年。

841 BC. Insurrections and Gonghe administration. Chinese history began to be accurately recorded.

公元前 722 年 编年体史书《春秋》采用干支记日。这是世界上使用时间最长的记日法。

722 BC. The *Spring and Autumn Annals* used the Heavenly Stems and Earthly Branches to record days. This is the oldest method in the world used to record time.

公元前约 571 年 老子出生。他的《道德经》阐述了朴素的辩证法思想，成为道家主要经典。

571 BC (approx.). Birth of Laozi. His *Tao Te Ching* expounded simple dialectical thought, becoming the principal Taoist text.

公元前 551 年 孔子出生。他主张仁政、德治、忠孝的思想，一生仕途坎坷，后致力于著述和教育，开创私学，收弟子达三千人。据传《春秋》经其修订过。由其弟子编成的《论语》为儒家经典著作。

551 BC. Birth of Confucius. Advocated benevolent government, rule of virtue, loyalty and filial duty. Devoted himself to writing and teaching after a difficult official career. Set up a private school and had 3,000 disciples. Is said to have revised the *Spring and Autumn Annals*. The *Confucian Analects* collected by his disciples is a classical Confucian text.

公元前约 535 年 军事家孙武出生，所著《孙子兵法》对后世军事理论产生深远影响。

535 BC (approx.). Birth of the military strategist Sun Wu, whose work *The Art of War* had a profound influence on later generations of military theory.

公元前 475 年 战国时期开始，中国进入封建社会。

475 BC. The beginning of the Warring States period. China entered the age of feudalism.

公元前 356 年 商鞅变法。实行土地私有制，允许开荒，土地自由买卖，重农抑商，统一秦国度量衡。

356 BC. Shang Yang's political and agricultural reform. Introduced private ownership of land, permitted cultivation of virgin land, freedom to buy and sell land. Agriculture was encouraged and commerce frowned upon. Unified weights and measures within the Qin kingdom.

公元前 278 年 浪漫主义诗人屈原投江自尽。其主要作品有《离骚》、《九章》、《九歌》、《天问》。

278 BC. The romantic poet Qu Yuan committed suicide by drowning. His main works were *Encountering Sorrow, Nine Elegies, Nine Songs,* and *Inquiring Heaven*.

公元前 221 年 秦统一中国。秦王改称始皇帝，强化中央集权，统一文字、货币和度量衡，建立郡县制，修建长城。

221 BC. The Qin state unified China. The Qin king changed his name to 'the First Emperor', centralized power, unified the writing system, currency and weights and measures, established the system of prefectures and counties, and started the construction of the Great Wall.

公元前 213、前 212 年 秦始皇下令焚毁《秦记》以外的史书及诸子百家的著作，坑杀方士、儒生四百六十余人。

213, 212 BC. With the exception of the *Qin Records*, the First Emperor ordered the burning of historical books and the works of various schools of thought, and buried alive over 460 Confucian scholars and alchemists.

公元前 138、前 119 年 张骞两次出使西域，促进汉夷文化交往，中原文明通过"丝绸之路"传入中亚。

138, 119 BC. Zhang Qian was sent twice to western regions on diplomatic missions to promote contact between Han and western cultures. Chinese civilization spread into central Asia via the Silk Road.

公元前 99 年 司马迁下狱，后受宫刑，忍辱写成中国第一部纪传体通史《史记》。

99 BC. Sima Qian was imprisoned and castrated. He wrote China's first biographical general history *Historical Records*.

中国历史朝代表
A chronology of Chinese dynasties

五帝时代 Period of the Five Legendary Rulers (unverified) c.3000 BC – 2100 BC		黄帝 Huangdi (Yellow Emperor)	
		颛顼 Zhuanxu	
		帝喾 Diku (Emperor Ku)	
		唐尧 Yao of Tang	
		虞舜 Shun of Yu	
夏 Xia Dynasty (unverified)		c.2100 BC – 1600 BC	
商 Shang Dynasty		1600 BC – 1046 BC	
西周 Western Zhou Dynasty		1046 BC – 771 BC	
东周 Eastern Zhou Dynasty 770 BC – 256 BC	春秋 Spring and Autumn Period	770 BC – 476 BC	
	战国 Warring States Period	475 BC – 221 BC	
秦 Qin Dynasty		221 BC – 206 BC	
汉 Han Dynasty 206 BC – 220 AD	西汉 Western Han	206 BC – AD 25	
	东汉 Eastern Han	25 – 220	
三国 Three Kingdoms 220 – 280	魏 Wei	220 – 265	
	蜀汉 Shu Han	221 – 263	
	吴 Wu	222 – 280	
晋 Jin Dynasty 265 – 420	西晋 Western Jin	265 – 317	
	东晋 Eastern Jin	317 – 420	
南北朝 Northern and Southern Dynasties 420 – 589	南朝 Southern Dynasties	宋 Song	420 – 479
		齐 Qi	479 – 502
		梁 Liang	502 – 557
		陈 Chen	557 – 589
	北朝 Northern Dynasties	北魏 Northern Wei	386 – 534
		东魏 Eastern Wei	534 – 550
		北齐 Northern Qi	550 – 577
		西魏 Western Wei	535 – 556
		北周 Northern Zhou	557 – 581
隋 Sui Dynasty		581 – 618	
唐 Tang Dynasty		618 – 907	
五代十国 Five Dynasties and Ten Kingdoms	五代 Five Dynasties 907 – 960	后梁 Later Liang	907 – 923
		后唐 Later Tang	923 – 936
		后晋 Later Jin	936 – 947
		后汉 Later Han	947 – 950
		后周 Later Zhou	951 – 960
	十国 Ten Kingdoms 902 – 979	北汉 Northern Han	951 – 979
		吴 Wu	902 – 937
		吴越 Wuyue	907 – 978
		闽 Min	909 – 945
		南汉 Southern Han	917 – 971
		荆南（又称“南平”）Jingnan (also Nanping)	924 – 963
		楚 Chu	927 – 951
		南唐 Southern Tang	937 – 975
		前蜀 Former Shu	907 – 925
		后蜀 Later Shu	934 – 965
宋 Song Dynasty 960 – 1279	北宋 Northern Song	960 – 1127	
	南宋 Southern Song	1127 – 1279	
辽 Liao（契丹 Qidan, or Khitan）		907 – 1125	
金 Jin（女真 Nüzhen, or Jurchen）		1115 – 1234	
西夏 Xixia（党项 Dangxiang, or Tangut）		1038 – 1227	
元 Yuan Dynasty（蒙古 Menggu, or Mongol）		1206 – 1368	
明 Ming Dynasty		1368 – 1644	
清 Qing Dynasty（满洲 Manzhou, or Manchu）		1616 – 1911	
中华民国 Republic of China		1912 – 1949	
中华人民共和国 People's Republic of China		1949 –	

British and US festivals and holidays
英美节日及假期

1 January—New Year's Day (1月1日——元旦)
每年的第1天，为英美的公共假日。

The third Monday in January—Martin Luther King Jr. Day (US)
(1月第3个星期一——马丁·路德·金纪念日(美))
非暴力民权运动领袖马丁·路德·金的生日纪念日。马丁·路德·金公开反对联邦与州法律中的种族歧视，于1968年被暗杀。

2 February—Groundhog Day (US) (2月2日——土拨鼠日(美))
传说土拨鼠(一种体粗腿短的松鼠科动物)于当日结束冬眠，爬出洞穴。据说，如果当天天气晴朗，土拨鼠能看到自己的影子，就意味着冬季还将持续6个多星期。

The third Monday in February—President's Day (US)
(2月第3个星期一——总统日(美))
乔治·华盛顿(2月22日)与亚伯拉罕·林肯(2月12日)的生日纪念日。

14 February—St Valentine's Day (2月14日——情人节)
通常于当日向自己心仪的人赠送情人卡，情侣通常互赠贺卡或礼物。

1 March—St David's Day (3月1日——圣大卫节)
纪念威尔士的主保圣人圣大卫的基督教节日。当日许多威尔士人在衣领上佩戴黄水仙。

17 March—St Patrick's Day (3月17日——圣帕特里克节)
纪念爱尔兰的主保圣人圣帕特里克的基督教节日。

The Sunday before Easter—Palm Sunday
(复活节前的星期日——棕枝主日)
耶稣进入耶路撒冷城的纪念日。许多基督教教堂举行手持棕榈树枝的游行。

The Friday before Easter—Good Friday
(复活节前的星期五——耶稣受难日)
耶稣被钉死在十字架上的基督教纪念日，通常举行斋戒和忏悔，为英国的公共假日。

Easter Sunday (春分月满之后的第1个星期日——复活节)
耶稣复活纪念日。

Easter Monday (复活节星期一)
英国的公共假日。

The fourth Sunday in Lent—Mother's Day, Mothering Sunday (UK)
(大斋节的第4个星期日——母亲节，省亲星期日(英))
孩子们通常在当日向母亲赠送贺卡和礼物。

1 April—April Fool's Day (4月1日——愚人节)
通常人们会制造恶作剧骗人开玩笑。当受骗者发现上当时，骗人者会大叫"呆瓜!"

23 April—St George's Day (4月23日——圣乔治节)
纪念英格兰的主保圣人圣乔治的基督教节日。

1 May—May Day (5月1日——五朔节)
传统春季节日，也是向劳动人民表达敬意的国际节日。在英国，距5月1日最近的星期一是公共假日。

The second Sunday in May—Mother's Day (US)
(5月第2个星期日——母亲节(美))
孩子们通常在当日向母亲赠送礼物，并举家去餐馆就餐。

The last Monday in May—Memorial Day (US)
(5月最后1个星期一——阵亡将士纪念日(美))
战争死难者纪念日。

The last Monday in May—Late Spring Bank Holiday (UK)
(5月最后1个星期一——春末银行假日(英))
英国的公共假日。

14 June—Flag Day (US) (6月14日——国旗纪念日(美))
美国人于当日悬挂国旗，以纪念1777年6月14日采用星条旗为国旗。

The third Sunday in June—Father's Day
(6月第3个星期日——父亲节)
孩子们通常在当日向父亲赠送贺卡或礼物以表敬意。

4 July—Fourth of July, Independence Day (US)
(7月4日——独立纪念日(美))
纪念1776年7月4日大陆会议通过《独立宣言》的法定假日。

The Monday nearest to 31 August—August Bank Holiday (UK)
(距8月31日最近的星期一——8月银行假日(英))
英格兰、威尔士及北爱尔兰的8月最后1个星期日为公共假日。

The first Monday in September—Labor Day (US)
(9月第1个星期一——劳动节(美))
向劳动人民表达敬意的法定假日。

12 October—Columbus Day (US) (10月12日——哥伦布纪念日(美))
克里斯托弗·哥伦布发现美洲的纪念日。

31 October—Halloween (10月31日——万圣节前夕)
过去人们相信可以在万圣节前夜看见鬼魂。如今人们在当夜举行聚会，化装成幽灵或女巫，并用掏空的南瓜做成人脸灯笼。孩子们则玩"不请吃就捣蛋"游戏，挨家挨户去敲门，如果不给糖果吃就搞恶作剧。

5 November—Bonfire Night, Guy Fawkes' Night (UK)
(11月5日——篝火之夜，盖伊·福克斯之夜(英))
当夜燃放烟花，点燃篝火，焚烧盖伊·福克斯人像，以纪念于1605年11月5日国会开幕典礼时企图炸毁议会大楼的阴谋失败。

11 November—Veterans' Day (US) (11月11日——退伍军人节(美))
一战结束纪念日，纪念美国退伍老兵及战争死难者。

The Sunday nearest to 11 November—Remembrance Sunday, Remembrance Day (UK)
(距11月11日最近的星期日——阵亡将士纪念日(英))
以纪念仪式及宗教仪式纪念两次世界大战及其后的战争死难者，纪念者佩戴(人造)红罂粟。

The fourth Thursday in November—Thanksgiving (US)
(11月第4个星期四——感恩节(美))
一年一度的法定假日，纪念1621年清教徒移民欢庆丰收。当日会举行宗教仪式并食用传统食物。对于很多美国人来说，这是除圣诞节外最重要的节日。

30 November—St Andrew's Day (11月30日——圣安德烈日)
纪念苏格兰的主保圣人圣安德烈的基督教节日。

24 December—Christmas Eve (12月24日——圣诞节前夜)
儿童相信圣诞老人会在圣诞前夜将礼物放在他们悬挂在床边的袜子中。通常礼物用彩纸包装，放在圣诞树下。有些人会去教堂做子夜弥撒。

25 December—Christmas Day (12月25日——圣诞节)
庆祝耶稣诞生的纪念日。当日早晨，多数家庭聚在一起开拆礼物，晚上共进特别的圣诞晚餐，在英国通常包括烤火鸡或鹅，另配蔬菜。

26 December—Boxing Day (UK) (12月26日——节礼日(英))
英国的法定假日。许多体育赛事在当日举行，英美许多商店于当日开门营业。

31 December—New Year's Eve (12月31日——除夕，元旦前夜)
许多人当日举行聚会，按照习俗要唱《友谊地久天长》并互相祝福"新年快乐"。大城市里许多人会在伦敦特拉法加广场等公共场所聚集。苏格兰的除夕称为Hogmanay。

US states
美国各州名称

50 states and 1 district* 50州及1特区

State 州	Abbreviation (postal/traditional) 缩写（邮政缩写/传统缩写）	State capital 州首府
Alabama 亚拉巴马	*AL/Ala.*	Montgomery 蒙哥马利
Alaska 阿拉斯加	*AK/Alaska or Alas.*	Juneau 朱诺
Arizona 亚利桑那	*AZ/Ariz.*	Phoenix 菲尼克斯
Arkansas 阿肯色	*AR/Ark.*	Little Rock 小石城
California 加利福尼亚	*CA/Calif. or Cal.*	Sacramento 萨克拉门托
Colorado 科罗拉多	*CO/Colo. or Col.*	Denver 丹佛
Connecticut 康涅狄格	*CT/Conn.*	Hartford 哈特福德
Delaware 特拉华	*DE/Del.*	Dover 多佛
District of Columbia* 哥伦比亚特区	*DC/D.C.*	Washington, D.C. 华盛顿
Florida 佛罗里达	*FL/Fla. or Flor.*	Tallahassee 塔拉哈西
Georgia 佐治亚	*GA/Ga.*	Atlanta 亚特兰大
Hawaii 夏威夷	*HI/Hawaii or Hi.*	Honolulu 火奴鲁鲁
Idaho 爱达荷	*ID/Idaho or Id. or Ida.*	Boise 博伊西
Illinois 伊利诺伊	*IL/Ill.*	Springfield 斯普林菲尔德
Indiana 印第安纳	*IN/Ind.*	Indianapolis 印第安纳波利斯
Iowa 艾奥瓦	*IA/Iowa or Ia.*	Des Moines 得梅因
Kansas 堪萨斯	*KS/Kans. or Kan.*	Topeka 托皮卡
Kentucky 肯塔基	*KY/Ky. or Kent.*	Frankfort 法兰克福
Louisiana 路易斯安那	*LA/La.*	Baton Rouge 巴吞鲁日
Maine 缅因	*ME/Maine or Me.*	Augusta 奥古斯塔
Maryland 马里兰	*MD/Md.*	Annapolis 安纳波利斯
Massachusetts 马萨诸塞	*MA/Mass.*	Boston 波士顿
Michigan 密歇根	*MI/Mich.*	Lansing 兰辛
Minnesota 明尼苏达	*MN/Minn.*	St. Paul 圣保罗
Mississippi 密西西比	*MS/Miss.*	Jackson 杰克逊
Missouri 密苏里	*MO/Mo.*	Jefferson City 杰斐逊城
Montana 蒙大拿	*MT/Mont.*	Helena 海伦娜
Nebraska 内布拉斯加	*NE/Nebr. or Neb.*	Lincoln 林肯
Nevada 内华达	*NV/Nev.*	Carson City 卡森城
New Hampshire 新罕布什尔	*NH/N.H.*	Concord 康科德
New Jersey 新泽西	*NJ/N.J.*	Trenton 特伦顿
New Mexico 新墨西哥	*NM/N. Mex. or N.M.*	Santa Fe 圣菲
New York 纽约	*NY/N.Y.*	Albany 奥尔巴尼
North Carolina 北卡罗来纳	*NC/N.C.*	Raleigh 罗利
North Dakota 北达科他	*ND/N. Dak. or N.D.*	Bismarck 俾斯麦
Ohio 俄亥俄	*OH/Ohio or O.*	Columbus 哥伦布
Oklahoma 俄克拉何马	*OK/Okla.*	Oklahoma City 俄克拉何马城
Oregon 俄勒冈	*OR/Oreg. or Ore.*	Salem 塞勒姆
Pennsylvania 宾夕法尼亚	*PA/Pa. or Penna.*	Harrisburg 哈里斯堡
Rhode Island 罗得岛	*RI/R.I.*	Providence 普罗维登斯
South Carolina 南卡罗来纳	*SC/S.C.*	Columbia 哥伦比亚
South Dakota 南达科他	*SD/S. Dak. or S.D.*	Pierre 皮尔
Tennessee 田纳西	*TN/Tenn.*	Nashville 纳什维尔
Texas 得克萨斯	*TX/Tex. or Texas*	Austin 奥斯汀
Utah 犹他	*UT/Utah*	Salt Lake City 盐湖城
Vermont 佛蒙特	*VT/Vt.*	Montpelier 蒙彼利埃
Virginia 弗吉尼亚	*VA/Va.*	Richmond 里士满
Washington 华盛顿	*WA/Wash.*	Olympia 奥林匹亚
West Virginia 西弗吉尼亚	*WV/W. Va. or W.V.*	Charleston 查尔斯顿
Wisconsin 威斯康星	*WI/Wis. or Wisc.*	Madison 麦迪逊
Wyoming 怀俄明	*WY/Wyo.*	Cheyenne 夏延

UK counties
英国各郡名称

ENGLAND 英格兰

County 郡	Abbreviation 缩写	County town 郡首府
Bedfordshire 贝德福德郡	*Beds*	Bedford 贝德福德
Berkshire 伯克郡	*Berks*	Reading 雷丁
Buckinghamshire 白金汉郡	*Bucks*	Aylesbury 艾尔斯伯里
Cambridgeshire 剑桥郡	*Cambs*	Cambridge 剑桥
Cheshire 柴郡	*Ches*	Chester 切斯特
Cornwall 康沃尔郡	–	Truro 特鲁罗
Cumbria 坎布里亚郡	*Cumb*	Carlisle 卡莱尔
Derbyshire 德比郡	*Derbys*	Matlock 马特洛克
Devon 德文郡	–	Exeter 埃克塞特
Dorset 多塞特郡	–	Dorchester 多切斯特
Durham 达勒姆郡	–	Durham 达勒姆
East Sussex 东萨塞克斯郡	*E Sussex*	Lewes 刘易斯
Essex 埃塞克斯	–	Chelmsford 切姆斯福德
Gloucestershire 格洛斯特郡	*Gloucs, Glos*	Gloucester 格洛斯特
Hampshire 汉普郡	*Hants*	Winchester 温切斯特
Herefordshire 赫里福德郡	*Heref, Herefs*	Hereford 赫里福德
Hertfordshire 赫特福德郡	*Herts*	Hertford 赫特福德
Kent 肯特郡	–	Maidstone 梅德斯通
Lancashire 兰开夏郡	*Lancs*	Lancaster 兰开斯特
Leicestershire 莱斯特郡	*Leics*	Leicester 莱斯特
Lincolnshire 林肯郡	*Lincs*	Lincoln 林肯
Norfolk 诺福克郡	*Norf*	Norwich 诺里奇
Northamptonshire 北安普敦郡	*Northants*	Northampton 北安普敦
Northumberland 诺森伯兰郡	*Northd*	Morpeth 莫珀斯
North Yorkshire 北约克郡	*N Yorks*	Northallerton 诺萨勒顿
Nottinghamshire 诺丁汉郡	*Notts*	Nottingham 诺丁汉
Oxfordshire 牛津郡	*Oxon*	Oxford 牛津
Rutland 拉特兰郡	–	Oakham 奥克姆
Shropshire 什罗普郡	*Shrops*	Shrewsbury 什鲁斯伯里
Somerset 萨默塞特郡	*Som*	Taunton 汤顿
Staffordshire 斯塔福德郡	*Staffs*	Stafford 斯塔福德
Suffolk 萨福克郡	*Suff*	Ipswich 伊普斯威奇
Surrey 萨里郡	*Surr, Su*	Kingston-upon-Thames 泰晤士河畔金斯顿
Warwickshire 沃里克郡	*Warks*	Warwick 沃里克
West Sussex 西萨塞克斯郡	*W Sussex*	Chichester 奇切斯特
Wiltshire 威尔特郡	*Wilts*	Trowbridge 特罗布里奇
Worcestershire 伍斯特郡	*Worcs*	Worcester 伍斯特

Metropolitan counties 都市郡

Greater London 大伦敦郡
Greater Manchester 大曼彻斯特郡
Merseyside 默西塞德郡
South Yorkshire 南约克郡
Tyne and Wear 泰恩-威尔郡
West Midlands 西米德兰兹郡
West Yorkshire 西约克郡

Traditional counties 传统郡

Cumberland 坎伯兰郡
Ely, Isle of 伊利岛郡
Huntingdonshire 亨廷登郡
Middlesex 米德尔塞克斯郡
Westmorland 威斯特摩兰郡
Yorkshire 约克郡

WALES 威尔士

County 郡	County town 郡首府
Anglesey 安格尔西郡	Llangefni 兰盖夫尼
Carmarthenshire 卡马森郡	Carmarthen 卡马森
Ceredigion 锡尔迪吉恩郡	Aberaeron 阿伯赖伦
Denbighshire 登比郡	Ruthin 里辛
Flintshire 弗林特郡	Mold 莫尔德
Gwynedd 圭内斯郡	Caernarfon 卡那封
Monmouthshire 蒙茅斯郡	Monmouth 蒙茅斯
Pembrokeshire 彭布罗克郡	Haverfordwest 哈弗福韦斯特
Powys 波伊斯郡	Llandrindod Wells 兰德林多德韦尔斯

Former/Historical counties 旧郡

Breconshire, Brecknockshire 布雷肯郡
Caernarvonshire 卡那封郡
Cardiganshire 卡迪根郡
Clwyd 克卢伊德郡
Dyfed 达费德郡
East Glamorgan 东格拉摩根郡
Gwent 格温特郡
Merionethshire 梅里奥尼斯郡
Mid Glamorgan 中格拉摩根郡
Montgomeryshire 蒙哥马利郡
Radnorshire 拉德诺郡
South Glamorgan 南格拉摩根郡
West Glamorgan 西格拉摩根郡

SCOTLAND 苏格兰

Historical counties 旧郡

Aberdeenshire 阿伯丁郡
Angus 安格斯郡
Argyllshire 阿盖尔郡
Ayrshire 艾尔郡
Banffshire 班夫郡
Berwickshire 贝里克郡
Bute 比特郡
Caithness 凯斯内斯郡
Clackmannanshire 克拉克曼南郡
Cromartyshire 克罗默蒂郡
Dumfriesshire 邓弗里斯郡
Dunbartonshire 邓巴顿郡
East Lothian 东洛锡安郡
Fife 法夫郡
Hebrides 赫布里底郡
Inverness-shire 因弗内斯郡
Kincardineshire 金卡丁郡
Kinross-shire 金罗斯郡
Kirkcudbrightshire 柯库布里郡
Lanarkshire 拉纳克郡
Midlothian 中洛锡安郡
Moray 马里郡
Nairnshire 奈恩郡
Orkney Islands 奥克尼群岛郡
Peebleshire 皮布尔斯郡
Perthshire 珀斯郡
Renfrewshire 伦弗鲁希尔郡
Ross-shire 罗斯郡
Roxburgh 罗克斯堡郡
Selkirkshire 塞尔扣克郡
Shetland Islands 设得兰群岛郡
Stirlingshire 斯特灵郡
Sutherland 萨瑟兰郡
West Lothian 西洛锡安郡
Wigtownshire 威格敦郡

NORTHERN IRELAND 北爱尔兰

County 郡	County town 郡首府
Antrim 安特里姆郡	**Antrim** 安特里姆
Armagh 阿马郡	**Armagh** 阿马
Down 唐郡	**Downpatrick** 唐帕特里克
Fermanagh 弗马纳郡	**Enniskillen** 恩尼斯基林
Londonderry 伦敦德里郡	**Londonderry, Derry** 伦敦德里，德里
Tyrone 蒂龙郡	**Omagh** 奥马

美国历史年代简表

1898 ► The Spanish-American War, arising from the destruction of the US warship *Maine*, for which the US blamed Spain. The US won easily, and after this victory came to be recognized by other countries as a world power.
西班牙—美国战争。“缅因号”战舰被炸沉，美国认为是西班牙所为，美西战争爆发。美国轻松取得胜利，此后美国被列国视为世界强国。

1917 ► The US entered World War I.
美国参加第一次世界大战。

1919 ► Prohibition became law, so that it became illegal to produce or sell alcohol in the US until the repeal of the law in 1933.
禁酒令生效，在美国制造和销售酒类成为非法，直到 1933 年该法律才被废止。

1929 ► Women gained the right to vote.
妇女获得选举权。

1929–1939 ► The Great Depression, the financial and industrial slump that lasted from1929 until World War II.
大萧条。金融和工业衰退从 1929 年一直延续到二战时期。

1941–1945 ► The US joined World War II after the Japanese attack on Pearl Harbor. Americans fought in both Europe and the Pacific. The war ended after the US dropped atomic bombs on the Japanese cities of Hiroshima and Nagasaki.
日本袭击珍珠港后美国参加第二次世界大战。美国在欧洲和太平洋两线作战。美国在日本广岛和长崎投下原子弹后战争结束。

1950–1953 ► The Korean War, fought between North and South Korea. The US persuaded the UN to act on behalf of South Korea, while China intervened on the side of the North. The war ended with the restoration of previous boundaries.
朝鲜南北方之间发生朝鲜战争。美国说服联合国出兵加入韩国一方作战，中国加入朝鲜一方作战。战争结束后恢复到战前边界。

1954 ► The Supreme Court ruled in *Brown v Board of Education* that racial segregation in public schools was illegal.
最高法院在“布朗诉教育局”一案中判决在公立学校中实行种族隔离违宪。

1959 ► Alaska and Hawaii became the two last states to join the US.
阿拉斯加和夏威夷成为最后两个加入美国的州。

1961 ► President John F. Kennedy sent advisers to South Vietnam, beginning US military involvement in the Vietnam War.
总统约翰·F·肯尼迪向南越派遣顾问，美国军事介入越南战争。

1962 ► The Cuban Missile Crisis. When the US discovered Soviet nuclear missiles on Cuba, President John F. Kennedy demanded their removal. A nuclear war between the two countries seemed possible, however the Soviet leader, Nikita Khrushchev, acceded to US demands.
古巴导弹危机。美国发现苏联在古巴部署核导弹，总统约翰·F·肯尼迪要求其撤出。美苏核战一触即发之时，苏联领导人赫鲁晓夫接受了美国的要求。

1963 ► President Kennedy was assassinated. This event, along with the controversy within the US over its involvement in the Vietnam War and the assassination of Martin Luther King (1968) and Robert F. Kennedy (1968), had a profound effect on American society and optimism.
肯尼迪总统遇刺身亡。这一事件，加上美国介入越战的社会争议、马丁·路德·金和罗伯特·F·肯尼迪于 1968 年相继遇刺身亡，都对美国社会和其乐观态度产生了深远的影响。

1964–1965 ► The civil rights movement of the 1950s and 1960s led to the Civil Rights Act of 1964 and the Voting Rights Act of 1965, guaranteeing basic rights for African Americans and people of all races.
20 世纪 50 至 60 年代的民权运动促成了 1964 年《民权法案》和 1965 年《选举权法案》的诞生，保障了非洲裔美国人和各种族人的基本权利。

1969 ► Neil Armstrong became the first person to walk on the moon.
尼尔·阿姆斯特朗成为踏上月球的第一人。

1973 ► The US military involvement in Vietnam ended.
美国结束在越南的军事介入。

1973 ► The Supreme Court decision in *Roe v Wade* made abortion legal, a decision that continues to provoke great controversy in US politics.
最高法院对“罗伊诉韦德案”的判决导致堕胎合法化。这一判决至今仍在美国政界广受争议。

1974 ► The Watergate scandal forced President Richard Nixon to resign, making him the first president ever to do so.
水门丑闻迫使理查德·尼克松总统辞职，使他成为美国历史上第一位辞职的总统。

1979 ► Diplomatic relations between China and the US were formally established.
中国和美国正式建立外交关系。

2001 ► Terrorists flew planes into the World Trade Center and the Pentagon on September 11.
9 月 11 日，恐怖分子驾机撞击世界贸易中心和五角大楼。

2009 ► Barack Obama became the first African American president.
巴拉克·奥巴马成为第一位非洲裔美国总统。

A brief chronology of US history

Before 4000 BC ► Ancestors of modern Native Americans arrived in North America, probably by crossing the Bering Strait from Siberia.
公元前 4000 年之前 现代美洲原住民的祖先到达北美洲，很可能是从西伯利亚穿越白令海峡而来。

1492 AD ► Christopher Columbus reached the Bahamas. This led to European exploration and colonization of North and South America.
公元 1492 年 克里斯托弗・哥伦布到达巴哈马群岛，开启了欧洲对南北美洲的探险和殖民进程。

1607 ► The first permanent English colony in North America was established at Jamestown, Virginia.
英国在弗吉尼亚的詹姆斯敦建立了在北美的第一个永久殖民地。

1619 ► The first African slaves brought to North America landed at Jamestown.
第一批运往北美洲的非洲奴隶抵达詹姆斯敦。

1620 ► The Pilgrims arrived from England on the *Mayflower* at Massachusetts.
来自英国的朝圣者搭乘"五月花"号抵达马萨诸塞。

1664 ► The Dutch colony of New Amsterdam was taken by the British and renamed New York.
英国夺取荷兰殖民地新阿姆斯特丹，更名为纽约。

1754–1763 ► The French and Indian War gained new land for the American colonists.
法国—印第安人战争使美洲殖民者取得更多土地。

1773 ► The Boston Tea Party took place in Boston harbour. American colonists boarded ships and threw boxes of tea into the sea as a protest against the imposition of a tax on tea by the British parliament.
波士顿港发生波士顿倾茶事件。美洲殖民者登船将茶箱推入大海，抗议英国议会强征茶叶税。

1774 ► The first Continental Congress took place, making demands for more rights from Britain. The Continental Congress was the first governing body of the thirteen colonies which later became the United States.
第一次大陆会议召开，向英国要求更多权利。大陆会议是 13 个殖民地的第一个执政机构。这 13 个殖民地后来组成了美利坚合众国。

1775–1783 ► The American Revolution led to independence from Britain. The Declaration of Independence was signed in 1776.
独立战争使美国脱离英国获得独立。1776 年签署《独立宣言》。

1787–1791 ► The US Constitution and Bill of Rights were written and approved. The Constitution, which was signed in 1789, established the legislative, judicial, and executive branches of government and detailed the responsibilities of each. The Bill of Rights, consisting of the first ten amendments to the Constitution, was ratified two years later. George Washington became the first President of the United States in 1789.
《美国宪法》和《人权法案》起草并通过。宪法于 1789 年签署通过，建立了政府立法、司法和行政三大机构，并确定了各自的详细职责。由最初十条宪法修正案构成的《人权法案》，两年后获得通过。1789 年，乔治・华盛顿出任美国第一任总统。

1800 ► The seat of Government moved from Philadelphia to Washington D.C.
联邦政府所在地从费城迁往华盛顿哥伦比亚特区。

1803 ► The Louisiana purchase, whereby the US acquired from France over two million sq km (828,000 sq miles) of territory stretching north from the mouth of the Mississippi to its source and west to the Rockies.
路易斯安那购地案。美国从法国获得超过 200 万平方公里（828,000 平方英里）土地，从密西西比河河口向北延伸到其发源地，西至落基山脉。

1808 ► Importing slaves was banned but the trade in slaves in the country continued.
往美国贩运奴隶被禁止，但国内奴隶贸易依然存在。

1812–1815 ► The US fought Britain in the War of 1812. The British captured Washington, D.C. in 1814. American successes, however, led to the Treaty of Ghent (1814) which ended the war.
1812 年英美发生战争。英国于 1814 年占领华盛顿哥伦比亚特区，但美国随后取得一系列胜利，双方签署《根特条约》(1814)，战争结束。

1819 ► The Adams-Onís Treaty, an agreement made between the United States and Spain in which Spain ceded Florida to the United States and relinquished its claims to Oregon. Also known as the Transcontinental Treaty.
美国和西班牙签订《亚当斯—奥尼斯条约》，西班牙把佛罗里达割让给美国，并放弃对俄勒冈的主权要求。又称《贯洲条约》。

1848–1849 ► The California Gold Rush, during which some 40,000 people moved to the US state of California after gold was discovered there.
加利福尼亚淘金热。美国加州发现黄金，先后有约 4 万人前去淘金。

1861–1865 ► The Civil War was fought between the Union (= northern states) and the Confederate States (= southern states). The Union won. In 1863 President Abraham Lincoln signed the Emancipation Proclamation, abolishing slavery in the US.
美国联邦政府（北方各州）和邦联政府（南方各州）之间发生内战。联邦政府取得胜利。1863 年，林肯总统签署《解放宣言》，在美国废除了奴隶制。

1865 ► President Lincoln was assassinated.
林肯总统遇刺身亡。

1865–1867 ► Reconstruction in the South. Confederate states were brought back into the US. Laws were passed making slavery illegal and giving new rights to black people. The Ku Klux Klan was founded in opposition to these social changes.
南方重建。南方各州重返美国。立法规定奴隶制违宪，给予黑人多种权利。反对这些社会变革的三 K 党成立。

英国历史年代简表

1721 ► Sir Robert Walpole became the first Prime Minister in the modern sense.
罗伯特·沃波尔爵士成为英国历史上第一位首相。

1771 ► The 'factory age' began with the opening of Britain's first cotton mill.
英国第一家棉纱厂开工，开启了“工厂时代”。

1783 ► With the end of the American War of Independence Britain lost her American colonies.
美国独立战争结束，英国失去北美殖民地。

1800 ► The second Act of Union added Ireland to Great Britain to form the United Kingdom of Great Britain and Ireland.
第二部《合并法案》将爱尔兰纳入大不列颠，成立大不列颠及爱尔兰联合王国。

1805 ► The Royal Navy led by Admiral Lord Nelson commanded the British fleet that defeated a French and Spanish fleet at the Battle of Trafalgar.
皇家海军统帅纳尔逊率英国皇家舰队在特拉法尔加战役中打败法国和西班牙联合舰队。

1815 ► The Duke of Wellington defeated Napoleon at the Battle of Waterloo.
威灵顿公爵在滑铁卢战役中打败拿破仑。

1824 ► The first railway was built, part of the technological development that changed the face of Britain.
第一条铁路建成。这是改变英国面貌的技术进步之一。

1832 ► The first Reform Act created more seats in Parliament and gave more men the vote.
第一部《改革法案》新增部分议席，给更多男性以选举权。

1838 ► Slavery was abolished in the British Empire.
英帝国全面废除奴隶制。

1851 ► The Great Exhibition. The first international exhibition of the products of industry, promoted by Prince Albert and held in the Crystal Palace in London.
艾伯特亲王在伦敦水晶宫举办万国博览会。这是历史上第一次国际工业商品展览会。

1853–1856 ► The Crimean War, fought by Britain, France, and Turkey against Russia, which had ambitions to expand westward and southward. Florence Nightingale's work in the military hospitals was an important influence on the development of professional nursing.
为遏制俄国向西、南方扩张的野心，英、法和土耳其联合对俄发动克里米亚战争。弗洛伦丝·南丁格尔在军队医院的工作对后来职业护理的发展产生重大影响。

1880 ► It became compulsory for children between the ages of five and thirteen to go to school.
5 至 13 岁儿童强制接受义务教育。

1911 ► The National Insurance Act introduced sickness and unemployment insurance for workers.
《国民保险法案》颁布，为劳动者提供疾病和失业保险。

1914–1918 ► World War I, in which the Central Powers (Germany and Austria-Hungary, joined later by Turkey and Bulgaria) were defeated by the Allies (Britain, France, and Russia, joined later by Italy and the US).
第一次世界大战。同盟国（德国、奥匈帝国以及后来加入的土耳其和保加利亚）被协约国（英、法、俄和后来加入的意、美）打败。

1918 ► Women gained the right to vote from the age of 30.
年满 30 岁的妇女获得选举权。

1921 ► Ireland was divided into the Irish Free State and the Protestant counties in the north.
爱尔兰分裂为爱尔兰自由邦和北爱新教各郡。

1926 ► The General Strike, a strike by workers in all of Britain's important industries in support of the mineworkers, who were being asked to work for less money.
英国所有重要行业的工人举行大罢工，声援被降低工资的矿工。

1928 ► Women were allowed to vote from the age of 21, the same age as for men.
年满 21 岁妇女获得投票权，这一年龄与男性相同。

1939–1945 ► World War II, in which the Axis Powers (Germany, Italy, and Japan) were defeated by an alliance eventually including the United Kingdom and its dominions, the Soviet Union, and the US.
第二次世界大战。轴心国（德、意、日）被最终由英国及其属国、苏联和美国组成的同盟国打败。

1948 ► The National Health Service was set up by the Labour government, providing medical care that is paid for mainly by taxation.
工党政府建立国民保健体系，主要靠税收提供医疗服务。

1952 ► Elizabeth II succeeds her father, George VI, as British monarch.
伊丽莎白二世继承其父乔治六世的王位。

1973 ► Britain became a member of the European Economic Community.
英国成为欧洲经济共同体成员国。

1998 ► The first attempt to set up a Northern Ireland Assembly, as part of the Good Friday Agreement.
第一次尝试根据《受难日协议》建立北爱尔兰议会。

1999 ► The Welsh Assembly and the Scottish Parliament were set up.
威尔士议会和苏格兰议会成立。

A brief chronology of British history

Before 6500 BC ► 公元前 6500 年之前
Until the English Channel was formed, Britain was linked by land to Europe. Many different peoples lived in Britain as hunter-gatherers.
英吉利海峡形成之前，不列颠与欧洲大陆曾连为一体。这里生活着多个民族，靠采集和狩猎为生。

4000–1500 BC ► 公元前 4000 至 1500 年
By 4000 BC, the land was being farmed and we have evidence of settlements.
From about 2500 BC onwards, the Ancient Britons began constructing huge stone monuments.
到了公元前 4000 年，土地已有耕种，且有人类定居的遗迹。公元前 2500 年起，古布立吞人开始建造巨石阵。

500 BC ► 公元前 500 年
The Celts arrived in Britain. Celtic culture became established in Britain and continued during the Roman occupation.
凯尔特人到达不列颠。凯尔特文化在不列颠得以确立并一直延续到古罗马人统治时期。

55 BC–410 AD ► 公元前 55 年至公元 410 年
Julius Caesar invaded Britain in expeditions in 55 and 54 BC. Britain was now a recognized part of the Roman world.
尤利乌斯·恺撒于公元前 55 年和 54 年两次征伐不列颠。不列颠在此时期被纳入古罗马版图。

From 400 AD ► 公元 400 年起
Anglo-Saxon invaders settled in Britain and ruled over much of England.
盎格鲁—萨克逊入侵者在不列颠定居并统治英格兰大部分地区。

From 800 AD ► 公元 800 年起
Raids by Vikings from Denmark and Norway were followed in 865 by an invasion of Danes who by 877 controlled the eastern half of England.
英格兰受到来自丹麦和挪威的维京人掳掠。865 年丹麦人侵入，并于 877 年占领英格兰东半部。

1066 ►
The Norman duke who came to be known as William the Conqueror invaded England and defeated the English king, Harold. For the next few centuries England was ruled by Normans, and French became the language of the court.
以“征服者威廉”闻名后世的诺曼公爵入侵英格兰，打败英格兰国王哈罗德。在此后的几个世纪中，英格兰一直由诺曼人统治，法语成为宫廷语言。

1088 ►
The Domesday Book was completed, giving a comprehensive record of the ownership and value of land in England in 1086.
《最终税册》（又称《土地调查清册》）编成，全面记录了英格兰 1086 年土地权属及价值情况。

1215 ►
King John is forced to sign the Magna Carta, restricting his power and giving new rights to the barons and the people.
英王约翰被迫签署《大宪章》，限制国王自身的权力，给予贵族和人民以更多权利。

1283 ►
Wales was conquered by Edward I of England.
英王爱德华一世征服威尔士。

1314 ►
The Scots defeated an invading English army at the Battle of Bannockburn, allowing Scotland to remain an independent country.
苏格兰人在班诺克本战役中击败入侵的英军，使苏格兰得以继续保持独立。

1346 ►
The English defeated the French at the Battle of Crécy. It was the first major English victory of the Hundred Years War.
英军在克雷西战役中击败法军。这是百年战争时期英格兰首次重大胜利。

1455–1485 ►
The Wars of the Roses. Intermittent civil wars fought between members of the House of Lancaster and the House of York.
玫瑰战争。兰开斯特家族和约克家族之间断续发生多次内战。

1534 ►
King Henry VIII became the Head of the Church in England.
英王亨利八世成为英格兰教会最高领袖。

1564 ►
The birth of Shakespeare, English poet and playwright, the foremost figure in English literature and a primary influence on the development of especially the literary language.
诗人和剧作家莎士比亚诞生。他是英国最杰出的文学家，对文学语言的发展影响尤深。

1588 ►
The Spanish Armada, a fleet of ships sent to invade England, was defeated.
西班牙无敌舰队入侵英格兰，被击败。

1603 ►
King James VI of Scotland became King James I of England, Scotland, and Wales. His mother was Mary, Queen of Scots. Inheriting the throne after the death of Elizabeth I, he united Scotland and England under one government.
苏格兰国王詹姆士六世成为英格兰、苏格兰和威尔士的国王詹姆士一世。他的母亲是苏格兰女王玛丽。他在伊丽莎白一世去世后继位，统辖苏格兰和英格兰。

1605 ►
James I was hated by many Catholics and a group of them attempted to kill him when he was in Parliament.
许多天主教徒痛恨詹姆士一世，一伙人曾趁他出席议会会议时图谋刺杀他。

1642–1651 ►
The English Civil War. King Charles I's forces (the Royalists or Cavaliers) were decisively defeated by the parliamentary forces (or Roundheads) in 1645. Charles I was executed in 1649.
英格兰内战。1645 年，英王查理一世的军队（保王党人或骑士党人）被议会军（圆颅党人）彻底打败。查理一世于 1649 年被处决。

1653–1658 ►
Cromwell dismissed Parliament and ruled as Lord Protector of England, Scotland, and Ireland.
克伦威尔解散议会，以“护国公”的身份主政英格兰、苏格兰和爱尔兰。

1660 ►
The Restoration of the monarchy took place with the return of Charles II.
查理二世回朝执政，恢复君主制。

1689 ►
The Catholic James II was removed from the throne and the Protestant William of Orange and his wife Mary, James's daughter, were crowned instead.
信奉天主教的詹姆士二世被废黜，信奉新教的奥伦治亲王威廉及其妻詹姆士的女儿玛丽共同加冕。

1707 ►
The Act of Union joined England, Wales and Scotland as one kingdom called Great Britain.
根据《合并法案》，英格兰、威尔士和苏格兰统一为一个王国，称作大不列颠。

icon	图标
scrollbar	滚动条
to scroll up/down	向上/向下滚动屏幕
menu	菜单
pull-down menu	下拉式菜单
drop-down menu	下拉式菜单
to pop up	弹出
pop-up menu	弹出式菜单
server	服务器
network	网络
to network	连接成网络
to download	下载
downloadable	可下载的
to upload	上传
uploadable	可上传的
font	字体
software	软件
freeware	免费软件
shareware	共享软件
tutorial	教程
multi-user licence	多用户许可证
spell checker	拼写检查程序
anti-virus (software)	防病毒软件
plug-in (application)	插件式应用程序
(hypertext) link	（超文本）链接
hot link	热链接；友情链接
secured page	受保护网页
index	网站主页
help page	帮助页
help menu	帮助菜单

How to say a website address:
如何报出网址：

www.elviragraphics.co.uk/design_history is spoken as follows:
'w-w-w **dot** elviragraphics **dot** co **dot** u-k **forward slash** design **underscore** history'

www.elviragraphics.co.uk/design_history 应如下报出：
"w-w-w **点** elviragraphics **点** co **点** u-k **（正）斜杠** design **下画线** history"

http:// (for example, as in http://www.elviragraphics.co.uk) is spoken as follows:
'h-t-t-p **colon forward slash forward slash**'

http://（例如在 http://www.elviragraphics.co.uk 中）应如下报出：
"h-t-t-p **冒号（正）斜杠（正）斜杠**"

DOWNLOADING A PROGRAM
下载程序

Useful words and phrases 常用的单词和词组

software	软件
hard drive	硬盘（驱动器）
anti-virus software	防病毒软件
to download (a program)	下载（程序）
to upload (a file)	上传（文件）
to install a program	安装程序
to run a program	运行程序
to open a file	打开文件
user-friendly	用户友好的；操作简便的
USB (Universal Serial Bus)	USB（通用串行总线）端口

Using email and the Internet 电子邮件和互联网

Useful words and phrases 常用的单词和词组

to be on email	能收发电子邮件
email address	电子邮件地址
at sign (@)	"at"符号（@）
to compose/write an email	写电子邮件
to send/receive/forward an email	发送/接收/转发电子邮件
c.c. (carbon copy)	抄送
to copy sb. in/ to cc sb.	把某人加入抄送/ 把邮件抄送给某人
b.c.c (blind carbon copy)	密件抄送
emoticon	表情符号
smiley (☺)	笑脸符（☺）
to attach a file	添加附件
to receive an attachment	接收附件
to open/run an attachment	打开/运行附件
to delete/zap a message	删除一条信息
inbox	收件箱
outbox	发件箱
to send spam/junk mail	发送垃圾邮件
to get spam/junk mail	收到垃圾邮件
to block a sender	屏蔽一个发件人
address book	地址簿；通讯录
mailing list	发送名单
file	文件
signature file	签名文件
to save a message on the desktop/ hard disk	在桌面上/ 硬盘上保存一条信息
freemail	免费邮件
snail mail	平信（蜗牛邮件）
spamming	垃圾邮件发送
mail bomb	邮件炸弹
modem	调制解调器

How to say an email address:
如何报出电子邮件地址：

andrew.martin@sch.co.uk is spoken as follows:
'andrew **dot** martin **at** s-c-h **dot** co **dot** u-k'

andrew.martin@sch.co.uk 应如下报出：
"andrew **点** martin **at** s-c-h **点** co **点** u-k"

USING THE INTERNET
使用互联网

Useful words and phrases 常用的单词和词组

the (World Wide) Web	（万维）网
the Internet, the Net	互联网
to surf the Net	浏览互联网
online/offline	在线的/离线的
Internet café	网吧
Internet Service Provider, ISP	互联网服务提供商；ISP
Online Service Provider, OSP	在线服务提供商；OSP
access provider	网络接入服务提供商
FTP (File Transfer Protocol)	文件传输协议；FTP
intranet	内部网
extranet	外部网
website	网站
web(site) address	网址
web page	网页
URL (Uniform Resource Locator)	URL 地址（统一资源定位地址）
webmaster	（万维网）站点管理员；版主
home page	主页；首页
home	主页
favourite	收藏页
bookmark	网络书签
to bookmark a site	把一个网站加入网络书签
hit	一次点击
to browse	浏览
a browser	浏览器
portal	门户网站
search engine	搜索引擎
web crawler	网络搜索器
quicksearch	快速搜索
advanced search	高级搜索
exact match	精确匹配
to match case	区分大小写
to google (sb./sth.)	用谷歌搜索（某人/某物）
dot-com	网络公司
newsgroup	（网络）新闻组
chatgroup, chatroom	（网络）聊天群，聊天室
chat	（网络）聊天
cookie	网上信息块
netiquette	网络礼仪
dialogue box	对话框
to highlight	加亮标注
to be highlighted	被加亮标注
to click (on sth.)	点击（某物）
to double-click	双击
to drag and drop	拖放
to copy and paste	复制并粘贴

Using email and the Internet
电子邮件和互联网

SENDING AN EMAIL
发送电子邮件

To : Andrew.martin@sch.co.uk
c.c. :
Subject : cool website!
Attach : annajoke.doc

Hi, Andy!

I've just bought a wireless router so now I can go on line in any room in the flat. I'm writing this in the kitchen! It's great – much better than sitting at my desk all the time!

Anyway, I wanted to tell you about a good website I found: http://www.what's-up.com. You should bookmark it. You remember we were wondering where to eat when we go to Manchester? Well, on the home page you can enter any name of a road in Manchester and it gives all the bars/restaurants/concert venues etc. on the road you choose. When you click on the name of a bar, a map automatically pops up and the place you've selected is highlighted. Mail me when you've had a chance to browse. I'm sure we'll be able to find somewhere for the coming holiday.

I also attach a joke that Anna sent me this morning. It really made me laugh. Don't worry about opening the file. I ran my anti-virus over it and it got the all-clear!

Speak to you soon!

Sallie ☺

PS: Could you forward this to Mark? I'm sure he'll love the joke! I wanted to copy him in but can't find his email address as I zapped his email from my inbox by mistake.

收件人: Andrew.martin@sch.co.uk
抄送:
主题: 很酷的网站!
附件: annajoke.doc

安迪，你好!

我刚刚买了个无线路由器，现在可以在家里的任何一个房间上网了。我正在厨房里写这封邮件!这实在是太棒了——比总是坐在书桌前好多了!

反正，我是想告诉你我发现了一个很好的网站：http://www.what's-up.com。你应该把它加入网络书签。还记得我们去曼彻斯特的时候不知道去哪里吃饭吗？好了，在这个主页上，你可以输入曼彻斯特任何一条街道的名字，它就会给你列出所有在你选的这条街道上的酒吧、饭店、音乐厅等等。点击一个酒吧的名字，一张地图便会自动弹出来，然后选择的地方会被加亮标注出来。等你有机会浏览了这个网页，就发封邮件给我。我敢肯定我们能为下个假日找到些可以去的地方。

我还把一个笑话放在了附件里，是安娜今天早上发给我的，真让我好好笑了一回。打开文件时不必顾虑，我用防病毒软件扫描过了，完全无毒!

再聊!

萨莉 ☺

又及：你能把这个转发给马克吗？我肯定他会喜欢这个笑话！我原本想把邮件抄送给他，但是因为我不小心从收件箱里删除了他的邮件，我找不到他的电子邮件地址了。

SMS (text message) abbreviations 短信息中的缩略语

汉语短信息中的缩略语 Chinese SMS abbreviations

缩略语 Abbreviation	全称 Full form	英文 English
BB	宝贝	baby
	情人	darling
	孩子	kid
	再见	bye bye
bf	男友	boyfriend
BS	鄙视	despise
BT	变态	warped
DD	弟弟	brother (younger)
dd	东东	thing
FB	腐败	corrupt
gf	女友	girlfriend
GG	哥哥	brother (elder)
gx	恭喜	congratulations
haha	哈哈	haha
hehe	呵呵	hehe
high	兴奋	excited
in	时尚	in (fashionable)
JJ	姐姐	sister (older)
JS	奸商	profiteer
MF	麻烦	nuisance
MM	妹妹	sister (younger)
	美眉	pretty girl
PLMM	漂亮美眉	beautiful girl
PF	佩服	admire
PP	漂漂	pretty
	片片	picture
	屁屁	bum
Q	求人	beg
	可爱	cute
	用 ICQ message 聊天工具呼叫	message sb. on ICQ
RPWT	人品问题	personality problem
sg, ssgg	帅哥	cute guy; seriously hot guy
3x, 3Q	谢谢	thank you
4242	是啊是啊	totally!
555	呜呜呜（哭）	sob sob
84	不是	no
848	不是吧	no
886, 88	拜拜喽！	bye bye
8 错	不错	pretty good
9494	就是就是	exactly!
+U	加油	go for it

短信息中的缩略语

Abbreviation 缩略语	Full form 全称	Chinese 中文
MYOB	mind your own business	管好你自己的事
NE	any	任何
NE1	anyone	任何人
NHOH	never heard of him/her	从来没听说过这个人
NOYB	none of your business	你别管
NO1	no one	没有人
OIC	oh, I see	哦，明白了
OTOH	on the other hand	从另一方面来说
PCM	please call me	请打电话给我
PLS	please	请
PPL	people	人
R	are	是
ROFL	rolling on the floor, laughing	地上打滚，大笑中
RU	are you	你是不是…；你是不是在…
RUOK	are you ok?	你还好吗？
SIT	stay in touch	保持联系
SOM1	someone	某人；有人
SOW	speaking of which	谈到这儿
SPK	speak	说
THKQ	thank you	谢谢
TTYL	talk to you later	待会儿跟你聊
TX	thanks	谢谢
U	you	你
UR	you are	你是
W/	with	和
WAN2	want to	想要
WAN2TLK	want to talk?	想聊聊吗？
WERV U BIN	where have you been?	你去哪儿了？
WKND	weekend	周末
WOT	what	什么
WU	what's up?	怎么了？
X	kiss	吻
XLNT	excellent	棒极了
XOXOX	hugs and kisses	抱抱亲亲
YR	your	你的
1	one	一
2	to, too	去，也
2DAY	today	今天
2MORO	tomorrow	明天
2NITE	tonight	今晚
3SUM	threesome	三个
4	for	为了

SMS (text message) abbreviations

English SMS abbreviations 英语短信息中的缩略语

Abbreviation 缩略语	Full form 全称	Chinese 中文
@	at	在；@符号
AAMOF	as a matter of fact	事实上
ADN	any day now	没几天；很快
AFAIK	as far as I know	据我所知
ATB	all the best	祝一切顺利
B	be	是；在
B4	before	之前
B4n	bye for now	再见啦
BBL	be back late(r)	待会儿回来；晚（些）回来
BCNU	be seeing you	再会
BFN	bye for now	再见啦
BRB	be right back	马上回来
BTW	by the way	顺便说一声
BWD	backward	向后
C	see	看见
CU	see you	回见
CUL8R	see you later	待会儿见
F2F	face-to-face	面对面
FWD	forward	转发；向前
FWIW	for what it's worth	不论好坏
FYI	for your information	仅供参考
GAL	get a life	做些有意义的事
GR8	great	太棒了
H8	hate	讨厌
HAND	have a nice day	祝你有美好的一天
HSIK	how should I know	我怎么会知道
HTH	hope this helps	希望这能有所帮助
IC	I see	明白了
ILUVU	I love you	我爱你
IMHO	in my humble opinion	依鄙人拙见
IMO	in my opinion	依我之见
IOW	in other words	换句话说
JIC	just in case	以防万一
JK	just kidding	开玩笑而已
KIT	keep in touch	保持联系
KWIM	know what I mean	知道我什么意思吗
L8	late	晚
L8R	later	稍后
LOL	lots of love/laughing out loud	非常爱你/大笑中
MOB	mobile	手机
MSG	message	信息；短信

打电话

Calling a company 给公司打电话

A. Good afternoon, Modern Living Magazine, Joanna speaking. How may I help you? B. Could you put me through to the sales department, please. A. Please hold on a moment while I transfer your call.	甲：下午好。这里是《现代生活》杂志社，我是乔安娜。有什么能帮您的吗？ 乙：请帮我接销售部，谢谢。 甲：我会帮您转接，请稍等。
A. Good morning, Oxford Office Suppliers. B. May I speak to the manager, please. A. Certainly. I'll put you through to her office now.	甲：早上好，这里是牛津办公用品公司。 乙：请帮我接通经理的电话，谢谢。 甲：好的。我现在就帮您接到她的办公室。
A. Good afternoon, this is Frank Phillips. Can you put me through to James Miller, please. B. Mr Miller is not in the office today. Would you like to leave a message for him? A. Yes, please. Next Friday's meeting has been postponed. Could you ask him to call me to arrange a new time? A. No, thank you. Can you tell me when he'll be back in the office? A. No, thank you. I'll call back later.	甲：下午好，我是弗兰克·菲利普斯。请帮我接詹姆斯·米勒，谢谢。 乙：米勒先生今天不在办公室。您想给他留个言吗？ 甲：好的。下周五的会议推迟了。您能让他给我打电话安排个新时间吗？ 甲：不用了，谢谢。您能告诉我他什么时候回办公室吗？ 甲：不用了，谢谢。我以后再打。

Using the answer(ing) machine (voice mail) 使用答录机（语音邮件）

Leaving a message for a friend: Hi Julie, it's Elisabeth here. Just phoning to say that I'll see you tomorrow morning at 8.30. Call me back if that doesn't suit you. Bye!	*给朋友留言：* 嗨，朱莉。我是伊丽莎白。我打电话来就是想告诉你我明天早上8:30和你见面。如果不行的话，请给我回个电话。再见！
Leaving a message for a colleague: Hello, this is a message for James Miller. It's 10 am Friday, this is Frank Phillips. I need to speak to you urgently about the deal with Simcom, as there have been some new developments. Could you please call me on my mobile. The number is …	*给同事留言：* 您好，这是给詹姆斯·米勒的一条留言。弗兰克·菲利普斯于周五上午10点留言：由于有了一些新进展，我急需和你商量一下和Simcom公司的生意。你能打我的手机吗？我的号码是…

Calling an extension number 拨打分机

A. Could you put me through to extension 510, please. Could I have extension 510, please. B. Connecting you. B. I'm sorry. All the lines are engaged.	甲：请帮我接510分机，谢谢。 乙：正在帮您转接。 乙：很抱歉，所有电话都占线了。

Calling a call centre 拨打声讯电话服务中心

A. Good afternoon. I have a query about my bill. B. Could I have your account number and full name, please. B. Could I have your postcode (*Brit*)/zip code (*Amer*), please. B. I'm sorry to keep you waiting. B. I'm trying to connect you. B. I'm sorry, there's no answer.	甲：下午好。我想查询一下我的账单。 乙：请告诉我您的账户号和全名。 乙：请告诉我您的邮政编码。 乙：很抱歉让您久等。 乙：正在帮您转接。 乙：很抱歉，电话无人接听。

Using a mobile phone 使用移动电话

A. Hello, it's Anna. I just phoned for a chat and to give you the telephone number you asked for. B. I'm sorry, this isn't a good time to talk. Can I call you back in an hour or so? A. Don't worry. I'll text you the number now.	甲：喂，我是安娜。我打电话来就是想和你聊聊天，并把你要的那个电话号码给你。 乙：不好意思。我现在不方便讲话。我大约一个小时以后再打给你好吗？ 甲：不要紧。我现在把号码用短信发给你。
When the signal is failing: We're losing the signal. I'm going into a tunnel. I'm about to lose the signal. You're breaking up.	*信号变弱的时候：* 快没信号了。 我要进隧道了，快没信号了。 你要没信号了。

Using a computer as a phone 使用电脑打电话

A. What's the best way of getting in touch with you this evening? B. I'll be at my computer till late, so the best thing would be to call me on line.	甲：今天晚上怎么跟你联系最好？ 乙：我会用电脑到很晚，所以你最好在网上打电话给我。

Using the telephone

Useful words and phrases 常用的单词和词组

land line (telephone) fixed line (telephone)	固定电话
mobile phone (*Brit*) mobile (*Brit*) cell phone (*Amer*)	移动电话；手机
local call	本地通话
long-distance call	长途电话
conference call	电话会议
to make a telephone call to sb. to make a phone call to sb. to call *or* telephone *or* phone sb.	打电话给某人
to answer the phone to pick up the phone	接电话
to hang up	挂断
to send sb. a text message to text sb.	给某人发短信
extension (phone)	分机
telephone number	电话号码
extension (number)	分机号码
business number	公司电话
residential number	住宅电话
to be ex-directory	未列入电话簿；加入黑名单
Freephone® number (*Brit*) toll-free number (*Amer*)	免费电话号码
hot line	热线电话
area/country code	区号/国家号
dialling tone	拨号音
to dial a number	拨号
the number is engaged (*Brit*) the number is busy (*Amer*)	该号码正在通话中
operator	电话接线员
switchboard	总机
fax machine	传真机
answer(ing) machine	答录机
voice mail	语音邮件
to make a reverse-charge call (*Brit*) to make a collect call (*Amer*)	打对方付费电话
to make an online call to sb. to call sb. on line	给某人打网络电话
phone card	电话卡
phone book	电话簿
telephone directory	通讯录
the Yellow Pages®	黄页

Common phrases used on the phone 电话交际常用表达

Hello!	喂?
Hold the line, please.	请别挂。
I'll put you on to him/her.	我把电话给他/她。
Who's calling, please?	请问是哪位?
May I take a message?	您要留言吗?
One moment, please.	请稍等。
May I speak to ..., please?	请问我能和…讲话吗?
I'll call back later.	我待会儿打过来。
It's a personal call.	这是个私人电话。
Mr. Williams is on the phone.	威廉斯先生正在打电话。
It's Jane (speaking).	我是简。
Speaking!	我就是!

Phoning a friend 给朋友打电话

A. Hello. B. Hi, Nick. It's Julie. A. Hello.	甲：喂? 乙：喂，尼克，我是朱莉。 甲：你好。
A. Hello, is that Emma? B. Speaking! A. Oh, hello. This is James.	甲：喂，是埃玛吗? 乙：我就是! 甲：哦，你好，我是詹姆斯。
A. Hello, this is Amy. Can I speak to Susan, please? B. Susan's not in at the moment. Can I take a message? A. No, thank you. I'll call again later.	甲：喂，我是埃米。请问我能和苏珊通话吗? 乙：苏珊这会儿不在。需要我留个言吗? 甲：不用了，谢谢。我待会儿再打过来。

D. Personal business correspondence

Complaint about negligence

漕泾家具店
吕总经理:

2月22日晚上贵店的一场大火，造成一死三伤的惨剧，经济损失达数千万。身为顾客，我们认为这次重大事故的发生，与主管安全生产的人员失职渎职有关，必须严肃处理。

漕泾家具店早就存在安全隐患。上月下旬，我们到贵家具店采购时，已发现贵店多处已老化的电线外露，走火通道也没有放置灭火器材，对店内工作人员及顾客造成危险。我们已向店员反映有关问题，但相信有关人员接获有关投诉后，没有作出适当处理，其后电线短路，火灾由此发生。

我们希望贵公司追究有关人员的责任，严肃处理这种失职渎职行为。此致
敬礼

顾客 杨秉义 杜宣 舒同和等
2010年2月25日

Responding to a complaint

施晓东先生:

来信收悉。由于我公司职工在邮件递送途中不慎把您的包裹丢失，多方寻找无着，给您造成经济损失和不快，对此我们表示深深的歉意！根据公司规定，我们将按保价金额全额赔偿，不知这样处理您是否满意。

特此致歉。

腾飞快递公司
2010年5月5日

Warning letter

宏达计算机公司执行总裁:

两个月前，我购买了贵公司生产的迅捷530型计算机一台，使用中不断出现故障，不仅启动速度太慢，有时还突然死机或出现黑屏；光驱的刻录功能也有问题。为此，我已先后两次去指定维修部维修，都没能修好。不得已我携机到销售商店要求退货，但销售员只答应可以送修，不同意退货。

我认为这台计算机存在严重的质量问题，我坚决要求退货。请总裁先生在一周内给我一个明确答复(电话：535246XX)，否则，我将通过法律途径解决此事。

消费者 梅伯乐
2010年10月8日

Letter of commendation

南海炼油厂:

2010年8月5日，你厂一个油罐突然爆炸起火，当时我和一班同学及老师，一行二十人正好在厂内参观。现场值班工人林永被爆炸气浪击倒，头部、臂部、腿部多处受伤，鲜血直流。在这危急关头，林永为了在场工人及我们的安全，强忍剧痛，奋不顾身，冲入烈火之中，迅速关闭油罐阀门，并先后用了五个干粉灭火器灭火。在随后赶来的消防员的共同努力下，经过一个多小时的奋战，终于将大火扑灭，避免了大火的蔓延。为此，我代表全班同学及老师特致函贵公司，感谢林永的英勇行为，并希望贵公司能对他的表现作出嘉许。

永庆中学初三甲班
陈勇
2010年9月1日

D. 私人事务

投诉工程质量

112 Victoria Road
Chiswick
London W4 9PP

14/6/2010

Allan Deal Builders
35 Green St
Acton
London W3 4RT

ref. WL/45/LPO

Dear Sirs,

I confirm my phone call,[1] complaining that the work carried out by your firm on our patio last week is not up to standard. Large cracks have already appeared in the concrete area, and several of the slabs in the paved part are unstable. Apart from anything else, the area is now dangerous to walk on.

Please send someone round this week to re-do the work. In the meantime, I am of course withholding payment.

Yours faithfully,

W. Nicholas Cotton

W. Nicholas Cotton

[1] 投诉时应采用书信形式，日后若事件有所争议，信件可以作为该事件的记录。

对投诉的回复

Allan Deal | BUILDERS *35 Green St, Acton, London W3 4RT*

15 June 2010

Mr W. N. Cotton
112 Victoria Road
Chiswick
London W4 9PP

ref. WL/45/LPO

Dear Mr Cotton

Thank you for your phone call and letter of Monday informing us of your dissatisfaction as regards work undertaken by Allan Deal in laying a patio.

In the first instance, we suggest that our surveyor, Roger True, visits you to investigate the nature of the issues you describe, in order to make a recommendation as to whether remedial work may be required.[1] Mr True will telephone you this week to make an appointment at a time convenient to you.

We are sorry to learn you are unhappy with the patio work. Our aim is always to provide a good service to our clients, and we trust that we will be able to resolve this matter in an appropriate way.

Yours sincerely

Beatrice Small

Beatrice Small
Contracts Manager

[1] 机构以书面回应投诉时，一般不会直接承认责任，因为可能会引致法律后果。

投诉工作人员失职

76b Wellington Road
London E9 7AA

1 April 2010

Corporate Complaints Unit
Hackham Council
5 Beech Crescent
London E14 2VB

Complaint about flooding at 76b Wellington Road

Dear Sir or Madam,

I am writing to make a formal complaint about flooding at 76b Wellington Road, owing to Council negligence.

As outlined on the enclosed complaints form,[1] the flooding took place on 30 March. The Council's contractors, Johnsons, who were working in the flat upstairs, left a tap on overnight, and the resulting flood has caused considerable damage to our flooring and internal decoration.

We look forward to hearing from you as to the outcome of this complaint. As council tenants, we are particularly keen to learn when the damage will be made good.

Yours faithfully,

Mira Collins

Mira Collins

[1] 大型机构，如市政部门，通常有整套投诉流程。熟悉这些程序并填写必要的表格是很有用的。

表扬信

12 Upward Street
Archway
London, N19 2PK

7 February 2010

Dr M. Khan
Department of Paediatrics
The Samuel Johnson Hospital NHS Trust
Coleridge Way
London, N19 6ZP

Dear Dr Khan

This letter is to thank you and staff in the paediatrics department at the Samuel Johnson Hospital for your professionalism and care in looking after our little boy, James.

James was first admitted to your department suffering from meningitis in mid-December last year. As you know, the following six weeks were a worrying time for my husband and me. But throughout this period of James' treatment and operation, we were continually reassured by the medical expertise and fine bedside manner[1] of staff in the paediatrics department.

We are particularly grateful to you for your professional care, and your patience in explaining the medical options. We also extend our thanks to the nurses, Mary and Letitia, for their kindness and good humour throughout.

I am pleased to report that James now seems to be fully recovered. We feel very fortunate to have been looked after by such a wonderful team.

Yours sincerely

Meredith Eliot

Meredith Eliot

[1] bedside manner 是套语，指医护人员对待病人的态度。

D. Personal business correspondence

Bank balance enquiry

中国银行上海分行杨桥支行
庄经理:

你好！今有一事有劳大驾，请予协助为盼。

我在ATM机上查询我的银行卡结存款时发现，我于3月20日存入美金三万元，可今日显示的存款结余为两万一千元。在此期间，我并未动用该款项，不知为何少了九千美元。请你帮我查一下这九千美元的去向，并尽快告知查询结果。谢谢！

我的卡号：3030302-005600-6000452XX

我的电话：633025XX

谷世达 谨启
2010年4月21日

Lost pet notice

启事

我家宠物猫已丢失5天，至今不知去向。该猫是波斯猫，身长约30厘米，体重约2.5公斤，纯白色，蓝眼睛。有知情者请来电告知，必有重谢。电话：641055XX 刘女士。

2010年6月5日

Piano wanted[1]

本人欲购国产钢琴一架，八成新的即可，有意转让者请跟我联系（电话：583425XX 马先生）。价格面议。

Ordering a book

大家出版社发行部:

近从《读书》杂志新书预告栏中看到，贵社将于11月出版发行新编《汉英大辞典》，因工作关系，我非常想购买此书，今特函预订。书款及邮寄费近日将按"预告"中要求邮寄到贵部，请予查收。谢谢！此致
敬礼

孔仁德
2010年10月19日

邮寄地址：上海市黄浦区江西中路58号
邮编：200026

[1] This type of notice is often published in newspapers or on the internet.

D. 私人事务

银行转账

23 St John's Road
London, NW12 4AA
Mobile[1]: 07813 8557XX
30 November 2010

The Manager
Royal National Bank
75 Bow Place
London, WC2 5TG

Current account: 004987XX
Deposit account: 556767XX[2]

Dear Sir/Madam

Please find enclosed a cheque[3] for £550.00, which is to be paid into my current account, number 004987XX, at your branch.

I should also be grateful if you would transfer the sum of £1500 (one thousand five hundred pounds) from my current account to my deposit account, number 556767XX, on receipt of this letter. While writing, could I also ask you to send me a new cheque book at the above address?

Please confirm in due course that these instructions have been carried out.

Yours faithfully

R. Chatterjee

R. Chatterjee (Dr)

[1] 美式英语为 cell (phone)。
[2] 给银行、企业或其他大型机构的正式信件中，通常在信首列出参考信息，可能是相关银行账号或是一系列书信往来的字母数字编号。这将方便收信机构搜寻信中讨论事宜的相关信息。
[3] 美式英语为 check 。

个人养老金变更指示

14 Orchard Close
Uxbridge
Middlesex UB8 1UY
15 November 2010

The Manager
Prudent Life
44 Queen's Street
Edinburgh EH1 1AB

Policy number: PPP897840XX

Dear Sir/Madam

I am writing to you in respect of my contributions to my personal pension[1] with Prudent Life, policy number PPP897840XX.

Currently, I am paying £350 net[2] per month by direct debit into the Cautious Managed Fund. I would like to request that as from next month my contributions are paid instead into the Ethical Fund. I believe the next payment is due on 6 December 2010.

Thank you for your attention. I look forward to receiving confirmation from you that these instructions have been carried out.

Yours faithfully

Jonah Smith

Jonah Smith

[1] 个人养老金指的是个人申领的养老金，通常养老金申领人可选择资金的投向。其他种类的养老金还包括公司养老金和国家养老金。
[2] net 表示“（所得）税后”。gross 表示“税前”。

致函订酒

27 Midnight Terrace
Oxford
OX4 4DP

11 March 2010

Regular Wine Merchants
High Street
Oxford OX1 4NN

Dear Sir/Madam

I wish to take advantage of your promotional offer on Spanish wine.

Please could you send me a case of Campo Grande 2006 Rioja Tempranillo (12 bottles) to the above address. I understand you are offering a 15 % discount on Rioja this month, so enclose a cheque for £ 46.75 (£ 55.00 less 15%).

Yours faithfully

Stephen Ball

Stephen Ball

致函订书

14 The Slope
Cardiff, CF1 7DF

10 March 2010

Snail's Bookshop
12 Church Street
Hay-on-Wye
HR3 5DN

Dear Mr Grey

Further to our telephone conversation this morning, I wish to order the 1950 edition (Allen and Unwin) of Arthur Waley's *The Poetry and Career of Li Po, 701-762 A.D.*

I enclose a cheque for £60, and would be grateful if you could send the book to me at the above address. In addition, I would be glad to receive a copy of your latest catalogue.

Many thanks for your assistance in finding this book.[1]

Yours sincerely

Rhian Lloyd

Rhian Lloyd

[1] 专门的二手书店能帮助顾客找到书籍的早期版本。

D. Personal business correspondence

Apartment wanted

本人因工作需要，急需在本小区征租住房一套，一室或两室均可，有独用卫生间和厨房，家具、家电全配。租金面议。有意者请电告本人：136254848XX史先生。

Writing to an estate agent about a house purchase

上海绿地集团售楼部：

近从《房地产报》上看到，贵集团新开发的“海上明珠”楼盘即将公开出售，我有购买意向。但对该楼盘的具体情况不甚了解，请函复我以下问题：

1、该楼盘是毛坯房[1]还是全装修房？

2、该楼盘有哪几种房型？

3、该楼盘的销售均价是多少？

4、若是一次性付款，有无折扣优惠？

盼复。此致

敬礼

王亦兵

2010年2月6日

联系地址：杭州市山林路379号。邮编：300093

电话：541832XX

[1] This term means 'roughcast house'.

Ending a tenancy agreement

董建国先生：

今年三月，我与您签署了丹桂花园25号301室的租赁合同，租赁期为一年。近日，公司决定调我到广州分公司工作，不日即将南下[1]。事出突然，不得已只能与董先生提前终止租约，望能谅解。临行前，我会付清五个月的房租及水、煤、电等一应费用，并按合同规定再给两千元作为提前终止租约的补偿[2]。不知您意下如何，请回复。专此

奉达

承租人 陈晓东启

2010年7月20日

[1] Good reasons must be given to terminate the tenancy.

[2] If wishing to terminate the tenancy prior to the expiry of the term, you should expect to pay a certain amount in compensation. This amount will depend on the terms of the contract.

Schools enquiry

上海市教委：

我是浦东西门子公司的德国专家。我和我的太太及两个孩子都生活在上海。我的大儿子格拉斯今年已满 6 周岁，到了入学年龄。我想让他就读上海某所小学，但不知教委在接纳外国孩子入学方面有哪些政策规定，需要办理哪些手续。请你们拨冗给予答复为盼。此致

敬礼！

鲁道夫

2010年5月20日

D. 私人事务

致函律师有关购买房屋事宜

63 Bramley Road
Wandsworth
London SW6 5UN

4.5.2010

Ms Roberta Ellison
Smithers & Pair, Solicitors[1]
16 Vanley Road
London SW3 9LX

Dear Ms Ellison,

You have been recommended to me by Mr Francis Jackson of Alfriston, and I am writing to ask if you would be willing to act for me in my purchase of a house in Battersea. I enclose the estate agent[2]'s details of the property, for which I have offered £565,000. The offer is under consideration.

Please would you let me have an estimate of the total cost involved, including all fees.

I should be grateful to learn that you are willing to represent me in this matter.

Yours sincerely,

Li Encheng

Li Encheng

[1] 美式英语中，这类律师称为 attorney。
[2] 美式英语中称为 Realtor。

房子粉饰费用估价

JIM BRISTOL
PAINTER AND DECORATOR

26 Fitzgerald Street
Tottenham
London, N17 9NG

14 July 2010

Anna Gibson
44 Prestwick Gardens
Stoke Newington
London, N16 4EQ

Dear Ms Gibson

Further to my visit on 10 July, my estimate (inclusive of work and materials[1]) is as follows:

1. To paint living room, matt and eggshell, colour(s) of choice £ 300
2. To paint two bedrooms, matt and eggshell, colour(s) of choice £ 500
3. To make good water damage in the kitchen, white £ 125
4. To paint front door, gloss, colour of choice, and sand/varnish step £ 160

As we discussed, my earliest availability is likely to be the first half of September.

Yours sincerely

Jim Bristol

[1] 估价应指明是否已经包括材料费用。

终止租约

2 Grampian Close
HELENSBURGH
G84 7PP

30th June 2010

Caledonian Property Services Ltd
3 Union Terrace
GLASGOW
G12 9PQ

Dear Sirs,

2 Grampian Close, Helensburgh

I wish to inform you of my intention to terminate the tenancy agreement for the above property signed on 1st April 2008. In accordance with the terms of the agreement, I am giving three months' notice[1] of my proposed date of departure, 1st October 2010.

Please could you let me know the arrangements for checking the inventory[2], returning the keys and reclaiming my deposit[3].

Yours faithfully,

V.F. Cassels

V. F. Cassels

[1] 租赁合约通常规定一个通知期限，即房客必须在搬离前通知房主的时限。
[2] 清单是指由房主提供给房客使用的家具及其他家居用品的列表。
[3] 签署房屋租赁合约时，通常要向房主付押金，作为房屋损毁的保证金。押金在租赁期满时退还。

邮寄支票缴付房子粉饰工程费用

44 Prestwick Gardens
Stoke Newington
London, N16 4EQ

2 October 2010

Dear Jim

Enclosed please find my cheque for £ 925 for painting and decorating work undertaken at 44 Prestwick Gardens in September.

As per your estimate, this amount represents the work done on the living room, the main bedroom, the second bedroom and the kitchen. Owing to poor weather, in the event you were unable to paint the front door, and we agreed that you would fit this in before the end of the year and bill separately for it.

Thank you for doing an excellent job.

Regards and best wishes

Anna

C. The world of work

Accepting a job offer

赵春熙先生:

来函敬悉。十分荣幸。承蒙厚爱，聘用我为贵设计院桥梁设计所高级设计师。我定会努力工作，尽职尽力，决不辜负您对我的信任[1]。贵设计院人才济济，我会与各位专家和谐相处，合作共事，为贵院增光添彩。敬祈

万事顺遂

蒋永和 谨启

2010年6月25日

[1] The organization employing you will expect to know your attitude towards the job once you have accepted it.

Declining a job offer

圣明兄:

来信收悉。承蒙关照，向贵校举荐我任英文教师，我深以为谢。你我同窗挚友，倘能在一校任教，合作共事，乃求之不得。无奈我已接受本校为期一年的续聘，因而难以如愿。事已至此，身不由己，还望你多多原谅。特此敬复。并祝

教安[1]

弟 海英 上

2010年7月5日

[1] 即颂　教安/文安/撰安 etc. may be used as closing words, according to the occupation of the addressee.

Resigning from a job[1]

深津贸易有限公司

人事部[2]:

我在本公司会计部担任会计工作已二十余年。二十多年来，我在工作上一向任劳任怨，公司对我也关怀备至。日前经医院检查，我患有严重高血压、心脏病，医生嘱咐不能再继续工作，要好好休息，接受治疗。考虑到我已年过五十，身体确实大不如前，加上家中尚有八旬老母需有人照料，因此决定辞去公司会计一职，请予允准。体恤之情，铭记在心。此请

台祉

公司会计

高 明

2010年2月20日

[1] The reasons for wishing to resign should be given. Expressions of gratitude and good wishes should be included at the end of the letter.

[2] A letter of resignation is handed to the human resources department or to your supervisor.

Letter requesting leave of absence

王奎主任[1]:

昨晚我突发高烧，立即去医院挂了急诊，经医生诊断为急性病毒性感冒，今明两天无法前来上班，特请假两天，请予批准。此致

敬礼

附医院证明一张[2]

司徒汉

2010年3月11日

[1] The name of the addressee is usually written in full to show formality.

[2] A sick note (from the doctor) should be attached when asking for a sick leave.

II 检字表

Characters Organized by Radicals

（字右边的数字指《汉英词典》正文部分的页码，带圆括号的字是繁体字或异体字）
(The number to the right of each character indicates the page number in the Chinese-English Dictionary. Characters in parentheses are the complex forms or variant forms)

I 部首目录

List of Radicals

(部首右边的数字指检字表的页码)
(The number to the right of each radical indicates the page number in the Characters Organized by Radicals)

部首检字表
Radical Index

检字方法说明:

1. 先在“部首目录”，按待检索字的部首笔画找出所属部首页码。画数相同的部首按起笔“—”(横)、“丨”(直)、“丿”(撇)、“丶”(点)、“乛”(折，包括 亅𠃌乚𡿨等笔形)的顺序排列。

2. 然后根据页码到“检字表”中，按待检索字其余笔画找出该字。画数相同的字也是按起笔“—”(横)、“丨”(直)、“丿”(撇)、“丶”(点)、“乛”(折，包括 亅𠃌乚𡿨等笔形)的顺序排列。

3. 对于未能确定部首的字，可到“难检字笔画索引”，按笔画检索。

How to use this index:

1. When you are looking up an unknown character, first refer to the ‘List of Radicals’ to find the radical of the character you are looking up. You do this by counting the number of strokes in the radical. The radicals in the ‘List of Radicals’ are organized by the number of strokes they contain. Once you have found the radical you are looking for, you will be sent to a page number in the second part of this index (the ‘Characters Organized by Radicals’ section). For each radical there is a long list of all the characters that contain it, organized by the number of strokes in the character. To search for a character, count up the number of strokes that it contains in addition to its radical. Radicals with the same number of strokes are listed according to the sequence of ‘—’ (horizontal line), ‘丨’ (vertical line), ‘丿’ (left slash), ‘丶’ (dot), ‘乛’ (straight stroke with a bendin g tip, or with an extended bending stroke such as 亅𠃌乚𡿨).

2. In the ‘Characters Organized by Radicals’ section, all the characters in the dictionary are listed under their radicals, according to the number of strokes they contain, not counting the strokes in their radicals. There are headings, in Chinese, that group the characters by this number. For example, characters with an additional one to three strokes are listed under the heading ‘一至三画’; characters with an additional four strokes are listed under the heading ‘四画’, and so on. Note that characters with the same number of strokes are listed according to the sequence of strokes as mentioned above.

3. For those characters with radicals that are difficult to classify, search for them in the ‘Index of Characters with Radicals Difficult to Classify’ by counting the total number of strokes in the character.

化的。 Don't think the enemy is monolithic. They can be split up.
【铁笔】tiěbǐ〈名〉 1 (用于刻图章) cutting tool 2 (用于刻蜡纸) stencil pen
【铁箅子】tiěbìzi〈名〉 1 (炉架等) grate (of a stove, etc.) 2 (烤架) grill
【铁壁铜墙】tiěbì-tóngqiáng = 铜墙铁壁 tóngqiáng-tiěbì
【铁饼】tiěbǐng〈名〉［体育］ 1 (指运动) discus throw 2 (指器械) discus: 扔～ throw a discus
【铁杵磨成针】tiěchǔ móchéng zhēn〈成〉〈喻〉 steady efforts can work miracles: 只要功夫深，～。 So long as you work hard enough, victory will be yours.
【铁窗】tiěchuāng〈名〉 prison: 五年的～生活使他改变了很多。 Five years behind bars changed him dramatically.
【铁搭】tiědā〈名〉〈方〉 iron rake with three to six teeth
【铁打】tiědǎ〈形〉〈喻〉unshakeable: ～的汉子 man of iron ‖ ～的江山 unshakeable state power
【铁道】tiědào〈名〉 railway: ～部 ministry of railways
【铁道兵】tiědàobīng〈名〉 railway engineering corps: 中国人民解放军～ the PLA railway engineering corps
【铁定】tiědìng〈形〉 ironclad: ～的事实 irrefutable evidence
【铁饭碗】tiěfànwǎn〈名〉〈喻〉 secure job: 打破～ abolish the system of lifetime employment
【铁杆】tiěgǎn〈形〉 1 (极忠诚) loyal and reliable: ～球迷 diehard football fans 2 (顽固不化) diehard: ～汉奸 out-and-out traitor
【铁哥们儿】tiěgēmenr〈名〉〈口〉 faithful friend
【铁公鸡】tiěgōngjī〈名〉〈喻〉 miser
【铁公鸡，一毛不拔】tiěgōngjī, yī máo bùbá〈歇后〉〈喻〉 miser
【铁骨铮铮】tiěgǔ-zhēngzhēng〈成〉 firm and unyielding
【铁观音】tiěguānyīn〈名〉 *Tieguanyin* [a variety of oolong tea]
【铁轨】tiěguǐ = 钢轨 gāngguǐ
【铁柜】tiěguì〈名〉 strongbox
【铁汉】tiěhàn〈名〉 man of steel: 他是条～。 He is a man of steel.
【铁汉子】tiěhànzi = 铁汉 tiěhàn
【铁画】tiěhuà〈名〉 1 (指笔画) forceful strokes 2［美术］ iron openwork
【铁环】tiěhuán〈名〉 iron hoop: 滚～ play with a hoop
【铁灰】tiěhuī〈名〉 iron-grey
【铁蒺藜】tiějíli〈名〉［军事］ caltrop
【铁甲】tiějiǎ〈名〉 1 (指战衣) armour: ～骑兵 armoured cavalry 2 (指外壳) outer shell: ～车 armoured car
【铁将军】tiějiāngjūn〈名〉〈诙〉 door lock: ～把门 the door is padlocked
【铁匠】tiějiang〈名〉 blacksmith
【铁脚板】tiějiǎobǎn〈名〉〈喻〉 person with toughened feet
【铁军】tiějūn〈名〉〈喻〉 invincible army
【铁矿】tiěkuàng〈名〉 1 (指矿石) iron ore: ～石 iron ore 2 (指矿藏) iron mine: 开采～ work an iron mine
【铁力木】tiělìmù〈名〉［植物］ ferreous mesua
【铁路】tiělù〈名〉 railway〈英〉; railroad〈美〉: ～运输 railway transportation ‖ 电气化～ electric railway
【铁律】tiělǜ〈名〉 unchanging law: 不忘科学发展的～ not to forget the iron law of scientific development
【铁马】tiěmǎ〈名〉 1 (铁骑) strong mounted forces: ▸金戈～ 2 (金属片) tinkling pieces of metal hanging from the eaves of pagodas, temples, etc.
【铁面无私】tiěmiàn-wúsī〈成〉 strictly impartial
【铁木】tiěmù〈名〉［植物］ ironwood
【铁幕】tiěmù〈名〉 Iron Curtain
【铁娘子】tiěniángzi〈名〉 iron lady
【铁牛】tiěniú〈名〉〈喻〉 tractor
【铁皮】tiěpí〈名〉 iron sheet: 白～ tin plate ‖ 黑～ black sheet iron
【铁骑】tiěqí〈名〉〈书〉 strong cavalry
【铁器】tiěqì〈名〉 ironware
【铁器时代】tiěqì shídài〈名〉［考古］ Iron Age
【铁锹】tiěqiāo〈名〉 spade
【铁青】tiěqīng〈形〉 ashen: 气得脸色～ turn pale with rage
【铁拳】tiěquán〈名〉〈喻〉 iron fist
【铁人】tiěrén〈名〉〈喻〉 iron man
【铁人三项】tiěrén sānxiàng〈名〉［体育］ iron man triathlon
【铁三角】tiěsānjiǎo〈名〉 powerful trio: 女篮的"～" the unbeatable women's basketball trio
【铁纱】tiěshā〈名〉 wire gauze: ～网 wire gauze screen
【铁砂】tiěshā〈名〉 1［矿业］ iron sand 2 (作为子弹) pellet
【铁杉】tiěshān〈名〉［植物］Chinese hemlock
【铁石心肠】tiěshí-xīncháng〈成〉 be hard-hearted
【铁树】tiěshù〈名〉［植物］ sago cycas
【铁树开花】tiěshù-kāihuā〈成〉〈喻〉 something barely possible
【铁水】tiěshuǐ〈名〉［冶金］ molten iron
【铁丝】tiěsī〈名〉 iron wire
【铁丝网】tiěsīwǎng〈名〉 1 (指网子) wire netting 2 (指障碍物) wire entanglement: 有刺～ barbed wire entanglement
【铁算盘】tiěsuànpán〈名〉〈喻〉 1 (指计算) careful calculation and strict budgeting 2 (指人) financial wizard
【铁索】tiěsuǒ〈名〉 iron chain: ～吊车 cable car
【铁索桥】tiěsuǒqiáo〈名〉 chain bridge
【铁塔】tiětǎ〈名〉 1 (指塔) iron tower: 埃菲尔～ Eiffel Tower 2［电气］ pylon
【铁蹄】tiětí〈名〉〈喻〉 tyrannical rule
【铁腕】tiěwàn〈名〉 1 (指人) iron hand: ～人物 tyrannical person 2 (指统治) strong rule: ～统治 rule with an iron fist
【铁锨】tiěxiān〈名〉 shovel
【铁心】tiěxīn〈动〉 be unshakeable in one's determination: ～经商 be determined to enter into business ‖ 这回他可是铁了心啦。 He is unshakeable in his determination this time.
【铁锈】tiěxiù〈名〉 rust
【铁血】tiěxuè〈形〉 having strong will and readiness to sacrifice: ～男儿 strong-willed and valiant man ‖ ～青年 courageous and upright youth
【铁则】tiězé〈名〉〈书〉 iron rule
【铁砧】tiězhēn〈名〉 anvil
【铁铮铮】tiězhēngzhēng〈形〉 staunch: ～的汉子 man of iron will
【铁证】tiězhèng〈名〉 ironclad evidence: ～如山 conclusive evidence
【铁中铮铮】tiězhōng-zhēngzhēng〈成〉〈喻〉 outstanding person
【铁嘴】tiězuǐ〈名〉〈喻〉 eloquent tongue: ～钢牙 having a ready and eloquent tongue

tiè

帖 tiè〈名〉 book containing models of calligraphy or painting for learners to copy: 临～ practise calligraphy/painting after a model ▸碑～, 画～, 字～
▸tiē, tiě

餮 tiè〈形〉〈书〉 gluttonous: ▸饕～

tīng

厅（廳） tīng〈名〉 1 (指部门) government department: 民政～ department of civil administration ‖ 省教育～ provincial department of education ▸办公～, 财政～ 2 (指大厅) hall: 会议～ conference hall ‖ 歌舞～ singing and dancing hall ‖ 展览～ exhibition hall ‖ 三室一～ three bedrooms and a sitting room ▸餐～, 客～
【厅堂】tīngtáng〈名〉 hall

汀 tīng〈名〉〈书〉 low, level land along a river
【汀线】tīngxiàn〈名〉 line track
【汀洲】tīngzhōu〈名〉 sand bar

听[1]（聽） tīng〈动〉 1 (用耳朵接受声音) listen to: ～广播 listen to the radio ‖ ～音乐 listen to music ‖ 我没～懂。 I didn't understand. ‖ 这名字～起来耳熟。 The name rings a bell. ‖ 这主意～起来不错。 The idea sounds good. 2 (听从) heed: 一切行动～指挥 act on every order ‖ 我劝他，但他不～。 I tried to persuade him, but he wouldn't listen. ▸言～计从 3 (任凭) allow: ▸～其自然, ～任, 悉～尊便 4 (治理) administer: ▸～讼, ～证, ～政

听[2] tīng〈名〉 tin: 两～啤酒 two tins of beer ‖ 三～咖啡 three tins of coffee ▸～装
【听壁脚】tīng bìjiǎo〈动〉〈方〉 eavesdrop
【听便】tīngbiàn〈动〉 do as one pleases: 去留～。 You may go or stay as you please.
【听差】tīngchāi〈旧〉 A〈动〉 run errands: 他曾在衙门～。 He used to run errands in the *yamen*. B〈名〉 man servant
【听从】tīngcóng〈动〉 obey: ～劝告 take sb.'s advice ‖ ～指挥 obey sb.'s order
【听到风就是雨】tīng dào fēng jiùshì yǔ = 听风是雨 tīngfēng-shìyǔ
【听而不闻】tīng'érbùwén〈成〉 take no notice of: 对别人的批评，她总是～。 She always turns a deaf ear to other people's criticism.
【听风是雨】tīngfēng-shìyǔ〈俗〉〈喻〉 speak or act on hearsay
【听骨】tīnggǔ〈名〉［生理］ ear bones
【听候】tīnghòu〈动〉 await: ～处理 await punishment ‖ ～分配/派遣 wait for orders of dispatch/assignment ‖ ～上级指示 pending further instructions from higher authorities ‖ ～通知 wait for sb.'s notification
【听话】tīnghuà〈动〉 1 (听声音) hear: 他耳朵有点聋，～有困难。 He is a bit deaf and doesn't hear very well. 2 (顺从) be obedient: ～的学生 obedient pupil ‖ ～，快去睡觉。 Be good and go to bed now. ‖ 他把手下不～的人都辞退了。 He fired all those who did not obey his orders.

t

【听话儿】tīnghuàr〈动〉 wait for a reply: 过两天～吧。 You'll be informed of our reply in a couple of days.
【听话听音儿】tīnghuà-tīngyīnr〈俗〉 listen for the meaning behind sb.'s words
【听会】tīnghuì〈动〉 be a visitor at a meeting: 今天来～的人很多。 There was a large audience at the meeting today.
【听见】tīngjiàn〈动〉 hear: 观众静得连根针落地的声音都能～。 The audience was so quiet you could have heard a pin drop. ‖ 她说话声音小得几乎听不见。 Her voice was scarcely audible. ‖ 我～有人在隔壁房间说话。 I heard someone talking in the next room. ‖ 我什么也没有～。 I heard nothing.
【听见风就是雨】tīng jiàn fēng jiùshì yǔ = 听风是雨 tīngfēng-shìyǔ
【听讲】tīngjiǎng〈动〉 listen to a talk: 专心～ listen attentively to a lecture
【听觉】tīngjué〈名〉 sense of hearing: ～灵敏 have sharp ears ‖ ～有问题 have a hearing problem ‖ ～器官 auditory organ
【听课】tīngkè〈动〉 attend a class: 专心～ listen intently in class
【听力】tīnglì〈名〉 hearing: 恢复/丧失～ regain/lose one's hearing ‖ 我的一只耳朵～很差。 My hearing is bad in one ear.
【听命】tīngmìng〈动〉 obey orders: ～于人 be at sb.'s beck and call ‖ 俯首～ bow and scrape ‖ 你不应该要别人～于你。 You shouldn't expect others to dance to your tune.
【听凭】tīngpíng〈动〉allow: ～他人摆布 be at the mercy of others ‖ 去留～她决定。 It's up to her whether to stay or leave.
【听其言而观其行】tīng qí yán ér guān qí xíng〈成〉 listen to what someone says and watch what they do
【听其自然】tīngqízìrán〈成〉let nature take its course: 一切都～吧。 Let everything take its own course.
【听取】tīngqǔ〈动〉 listen to: ～汇报 debrief ‖ 虚心～群众的意见 listen to the opinions of the masses with an open mind
【听任】tīngrèn = 听凭 tīngpíng
【听审】tīngshěn〈动〉［法律］ wait for a trial
【听说】tīngshuō〈动〉 1（听和说） listen and speak: 提高～能力 improve one's listening and speaking skills 2（听人说） hear of: ～那是部好电影。 I've heard that it's a good film. ‖ ～她已经结婚了。 It is said that she is married.
【听讼】tīngsòng〈动〉〈书〉［法律］ hear a case
【听天由命】tīngtiān-yóumìng〈成〉 be reconciled to one's lot: 到了这一步，你只好～。 At this stage there's nothing you can do but resign yourself to your fate.
【听筒】tīngtǒng〈名〉 1（电话机受话器） telephone receiver: 拿起～ pick up the receiver 2 = 听诊器 tīngzhěnqì
【听闻】tīngwén〈名〉〈书〉 what one hears: 以广～ in order to widen one's knowledge ▸骇人～
【听写】tīngxiě〈动〉 dictate: ～单词 dictate words ‖ ～练习 dictation exercise
【听信】tīngxìn〈动〉 1（等候消息） wait for news: 录取与否，回去～儿吧。 Go home and wait for our notification as to whether you are admitted or not. 2（相信） believe what one hears: ～谣言 believe rumours ‖ ～一面之词 believe the one-sided story
【听者】tīngzhě〈名〉〈书〉 listener: ～甚众。 There was a large audience.
【听诊】tīngzhěn〈动〉［医学］ auscultate
【听诊器】tīngzhěnqì〈名〉 stethoscope
【听证】tīngzhèng〈动〉 hear the evidence: ～会 hearing
【听政】tīngzhèng〈动〉hold court: ▸垂帘～
【听之任之】tīngzhī-rènzhī〈成〉 let things pass: 对违法行为不能～。 We cannot shut our eyes to illegal acts.
【听众】tīngzhòng〈名〉 audience: 广播～ radio listener ‖ ～热线 audience hotline ‖ 演讲深深地打动了～。 The speaker moved the audience deeply.
【听装】tīngzhuāng〈形〉 tinned: ～饼干 tinned biscuits ‖ ～奶粉 tinned milk powder

烃（烴） tīng〈名〉［化学］ hydrocarbon: ～基 hydrocarbon radical

桯 tīng〈名〉 shaft of an awl
【桯子】tīngzi〈名〉 1（指锥子） shaft of an awl: 锥～ shaft of an awl 2（指花轴） floral axis of a plant

tíng

廷 tíng〈名〉 government: 清～ Qing government ▸朝～, 宫～

莛 tíng〈名〉 stem: 麦～ wheat stem

亭[1] tíng〈名〉 1（亭子） pavilion: 八角～ octagonal pavilion 2（小房子） kiosk: 书报～ news-stand ‖ 售票～ ticket booth ▸电话～, 岗～

亭[2] tíng〈形〉〈书〉 well-balanced: ▸～午
【亭台楼阁】tíngtái-lóugé〈名〉 pavilions, terraces and towers
【亭亭】tíngtíng〈形〉〈书〉 1（高耸） towering 2 = 婷婷 tíngtíng
【亭亭玉立】tíngtíng-yùlì〈成〉 1（形容女子） [of a woman] tall, slim and graceful: ～的身段 slender figure 2（形容树） [of a tree, etc.] tall and straight
【亭午】tíngwǔ〈名〉〈书〉 noon
【亭子】tíngzi〈名〉 pavilion
【亭子间】tíngzijiān〈名〉〈方〉 small back room

庭 tíng〈名〉 1（厅堂） hall: ▸大～广众 2（院子） front yard: 前～后院 front yard and back garden ▸～院, 门～若市 3（法庭） law court: ▸出～, 开～ 4［中医］ middle of the forehead: ▸天～
【庭除】tíngchú〈名〉〈书〉 courtyard: 黎明即起，洒扫～ rise at dawn and sweep the courtyard
【庭审】tíngshěn〈动〉 hear a case: ～日 court day
【庭外和解】tíngwài héjiě〈名〉［法律］ out-of-court settlement
【庭讯】tíngxùn〈动〉 summon for investigation: 进行～ issue a court summons
【庭园】tíngyuán〈名〉 garden
【庭院】tíngyuàn〈名〉 front courtyard: ～绿化 planting of trees, flowers etc. in a front courtyard

停[1] tíng
A〈动〉 1（停止） stop: ～下脚步 stop walking ‖ ～发工资 stop paying wages ‖ 雨～了。 The rain has stopped. ▸～顿, ～火, ～止 2（逗留） stop over: 列车在小站只～了两分钟。 The train stopped at the station for only two minutes. ‖ 我在杭州～了三天，才去上海。 I stopped over at Hangzhou for three days before I went on to Shanghai. 3（停泊） park: 车～在大门前。 The car is parked in front of the gate. ‖ 这条船在港口～了好几天。 The ship has been lying at anchor in the harbour for quite a few days. ▸～泊, ～放, ～灵
B〈形〉 settled: ▸～当, ～妥

停[2] tíng〈量〉 portion: 三～儿去了两～儿，还剩一～儿。 When two thirds are taken away, there is only one third left. ‖ 五～儿苹果有三～儿是坏的。 Three out of five apples are rotten.
【停摆】tíngbǎi〈动〉 1（指钟摆） stop: 钟～了。 The clock has stopped. 2〈喻〉（指事情） come to a standstill: 因原料跟不上，生产已～了两天。 Production has been held up for two days because of lack of a raw materials.
【停板】tíngbǎn〈动〉［金融］ stop trading: 涨～ limit up ‖ 跌～ limit down
【停办】tíngbàn〈动〉 close down: 一些企业已经～。 Some firms have been closed down.
【停泊】tíngbó〈动〉 anchor: 那里～着很多渔船。 Many fishing boats were moored over there. ‖ 这座码头可以～远洋轮。 Ocean-going ships can lie at anchor in this harbour.
【停产】tíngchǎn〈动〉 halt production: ～整顿 suspend operations pending consolidation ‖ 勒令～ issue a compulsory order to stop production
【停车】tíngchē〈动〉 1（逗留） stop a car: 我们在下一站～十分钟。 We'll stop for 10 minutes at the next station. ‖ 列车临时～。 The train made an incidental stop. 2（泊车） park: 违章～罚款单 parking ticket ‖ 此处禁止～! No parking! 3（停止转动） stop working: ～保养 shutdown maintenance ‖ 我们车间～维修。 Our workshop has ceased operations in order to undergo repairs.
【停车场】tíngchēchǎng〈名〉 car park〈英〉; parking lot〈美〉: 多层～ multi-storey car park
【停当】tíngdang〈形〉ready: 行李收拾～。 The luggage is packed and ready.
【停顿】tíngdùn〈动〉 1（暂停） halt: 罢工使生产陷于～状态。 Production came to a standstill because of the strike. 2（语音上有间歇） pause: 稍作～之后说道 say after a moment's pause ‖ 她～了好长时间才接着把信读下去。 She paused for a long while before going on to read the rest of the letter.
【停放】tíngfàng〈动〉 place: 棺材～在大厅中央。 The coffin was placed in the middle of the hall. ‖ 此处不许～车辆。 Parking is forbidden here.
【停工】tínggōng〈动〉 stop work: 经济萧条期间，许多工厂～了。 Many factories were shut down during the recession. ‖ ～待料 close down for lack of materials
【停航】tíngháng〈动〉 suspend service: 班机因气候恶劣～。 The scheduled flight was suspended due to bad weather.
【停火】tínghuǒ〈动〉 cease fire: 签订～协定 sign a truce ‖ 单方面宣布～ declare a unilateral ceasefire
【停机】tíngjī〈动〉 1（拍摄结束） finish shooting 2（停放飞机） park: ▸～坪

3 (停止运作) stop a machine: 该机器可自动～。The machine shuts off automatically. ‖ 他的手机已经～。His mobile phone service has been suspended.
【停机坪】tíngjīpíng〈名〉parking apron
【停建】tíngjiàn〈动〉stop construction: 这个项目已经～。The project has been suspended.
【停经】tíngjīng〈名〉[医学] menolipsis
【停刊】tíngkān〈动〉stop publication: 杂志～了。Publication of the magazine has been suspended.
【停靠】tíngkào〈动〉(指火车) stop; (指船) berth; (指飞机) pull in: 北京方向来的快车～二号站台。The express train from Beijing will stop at Platform 2. ‖ 一艘货轮～在码头。A freighter berthed at the dock.
【停课】tíngkè〈动〉suspend classes: 学校明天～开运动会。Classes will be suspended tomorrow for the school sports meet.
【停灵】tínglíng〈动〉rest a coffin temporarily in a place before burial or cremation
【停留】tíngliú〈动〉1 (逗留) stop over: 作短暂～ make a brief stop ‖ 代表团在北京～了一周。The delegation stopped over in Beijing for a week. ‖ 去纽约的途中，他们在东京～了一下。They stopped over in Tokyo on their way to New York. ‖ 她的目光～在婴儿身上。Her eyes settled on the baby. ‖ 我们径直去了那里，途中未作～。We went straight there without making any stops along the way. 2 (不发展) stagnate: 我们不能～在目前的水平上。We cannot call a stop at the present level.
【停牌】tíngpái〈动〉[金融] suspend trading
【停赛】tíngsài〈动〉suspend an athlete: ～两场 two-match suspension ‖ 她因药检呈阳性而被～两年。She was suspended for two years for testing positive.
【停尸房】tíngshīfáng〈名〉mortuary
【停食】tíngshí〈动〉[中医] have indigestion
【停手】tíngshǒu〈动〉stop what one is doing
【停水】tíngshuǐ〈动〉cut off the water (supply)
【停妥】tíngtuǒ〈形〉〈书〉in (good) order: 收拾～。Everything is in order. ‖ 一切准备～。All set.
【停息】tíngxī〈动〉stop: 暴风雨～了。The storm has subsided. ‖ 江水奔流，永无～。The river flows continuously.
【停歇】tíngxiē〈动〉1 (歇业) close down: 小店因亏本而～。The small store lost money and went out of business. 2 (停止) stop: 大风直到天亮才～。The wind did not let up until dawn. 3 (休息) stop for a rest: 队伍～在小树林里。The troops stopped in a wood for a rest.
【停薪】tíngxīn〈动〉suspend payment to an employee: ～留职 be on leave with pay suspension
【停学】tíngxué〈动〉drop out of school: 因病～一年 give up school for a year on account of illness
【停业】tíngyè〈动〉1 (指暂时不营业) stop doing business temporarily: ～整顿 suspend business in order to consolidate ‖ 超市晚上十点钟～。The supermarket closes at 10 o'clock. 2 (指歇业) close business: ～甩卖 closing down sale
【停战】tíngzhàn〈动〉suspend hostilities: ～协定 armistice
【停诊】tíngzhěn〈动〉stop receiving outpatients: 节日～，急诊例外。Emergency cases only during holidays.
【停职】tíngzhí〈动〉suspend sb. from office: ～停薪 suspend sb. from his duties and stop his pay
【停止】tíngzhǐ〈动〉1 (不再进行) stop: ～敌对行动 cease hostilities ‖ ～工作 stop working ‖ ～广播 go off the air ‖ 将军命令～进攻。The general called a halt to attacks. ‖ 他的心脏已～跳动。His heart stopped beating. 2 (停留) stagnate: 我们的认识不能总～在目前的水平上。Our knowledge should not stagnate at the present level.
【停滞】tíngzhì〈动〉be at a standstill: 生产处于～状态。Production is in a state of stagnation.
【停滞不前】tíngzhì-bùqián〈成〉remain stagnant: 经济发展～。The economy has stagnated.

蜓 tíng ▸ 蜻蜓 qīngtíng

婷 tíng
【婷婷】tíngtíng〈形〉〈书〉graceful and erect: ～玉立 delicate and graceful

霆 tíng〈名〉thunderbolt: ▸ 雷～

tǐng

町 tǐng〈名〉〈书〉1 (田界) raised path between farm fields 2 (旧地) farmland

挺 tǐng
A〈形〉1 (硬而直) upright: ▸～立，笔～ 2 (特出) outstanding: ▸～拔，～秀
B〈动〉1 (突出) stick out: ～起腰板来 straighten up ‖ 抬头～胸 with one's chin up and chest out 2 (勉强支撑) endure: 他发着烧还～着上课。He has come to class in spite of his fever. ‖ 我困得～不住了。I was too sleepy to hold out any longer. ▸ 硬～ 3 (支持) support: 力～张总连任总经理 enthusiastically support the re-election of Chief Zhang as general manager
C〈量〉[for machine guns]: 二十～机关枪 20 machine guns
D〈副〉〈口〉very: ～好 pretty good ‖ 他学习～努力。He studies very hard. ‖ 这花～香。This flower has quite a sweet smell.
【挺拔】tǐngbá〈形〉1 (直立高耸) tall and straight: 峰峦～ towering mountain ridges and peaks ‖ 青松～ tall and straight pine trees 2 (强劲) vigorous: 笔力～ vigorous strokes
【挺括】tǐngguā〈形〉[of cloth, paper, etc.] stiff and smooth
【挺进】tǐngjìn〈动〉press onward: 部队马不停蹄地向前～。The troops pressed onward without a rest.
【挺举】tǐngjǔ〈动〉[体育] clean and jerk [in weightlifting]
【挺立】tǐnglì〈动〉stand straight: 昂首～ stand erect with one's chin up ‖ 两棵松树～在山坡上。Two pine trees stand firm on the hillside.
【挺身】tǐngshēn〈动〉straighten one's back: ～反抗 rise in resistance
【挺身而出】tǐngshēn'érchū〈成〉step forward bravely: 在危急时刻，他～。At the critical moment he stepped forward bravely.
【挺尸】tǐngshī〈动〉〈粗〉lie sleeping like a corpse
【挺秀】tǐngxiù〈形〉〈书〉tall and graceful: 字体～ write an elegant hand
【挺直】tǐngzhí A〈形〉erect: ～的鼻梁 straight nose B〈动〉straighten up (physically): 把身子～ hold one's body erect

珽 tǐng〈名〉〈书〉jade tablet [held by an emperor on ceremonial occasions as a sign of power]

梃 tǐng〈名〉1〈方〉(花梗) stem: 独～儿 single stem ‖ 花～ stalk of a flower 2〈书〉(木棍) club: ～击 beat with a club 3 (边框) frame: 窗/门～ window/door frame
▸ tìng
【梃子】tǐngzi〈名〉frame

铤（鋌） tǐng〈形〉〈书〉fast-paced
▸ dìng
【铤而走险】tǐng'érzǒuxiǎn〈成〉make a reckless move: 被迫～ be forced into taking a risk

颋（頲） tǐng〈形〉〈书〉upright

艇 tǐng〈名〉1 (指民用) light boat: ▸ 救生～，汽～，游～ 2 (指军用) naval vessel: ▸ 炮～，潜水～

tìng

梃 tìng
A〈动〉poke an iron rod into a slaughtered pig in order to pump up the skin to clean it
B〈名〉iron rod
▸ tǐng

tōng

恫 tōng〈名〉〈书〉sickness
▸ dòng

通 tōng
A〈动〉1 (达到) lead to: 直～北京 lead directly to Beijing ‖ 条条大路～罗马。All roads lead to Rome. ▸ 四～八达 2 (可通行) be open: 此路不～! No through road! ‖ 电话～了。The line has gone through. ‖ 山洞快要打～了。The tunnel is about to be bored through. ▸～行，畅～ 3 (了解) know: ～多种外语 know several foreign languages ‖ 不～人情 be unreasonable ▸～情达理，精～，无师自～ 4 (使不堵塞) open up or clear out by poking or jabbing: ～炉子 poke a fire ‖ ～下水道 unblock a sewer ▸ 疏～ 5 (连接) connect: 互～信息 exchange information ‖ 这两间房是～着的。The two rooms open into each other. ▸～商，串～，沟～ 6 (传达) tell: ～个电话 phone sb. ▸～报，～知
B〈名〉authority: 美国～ expert on the US ‖ 中国～ old China hand ▸ 万事～
C〈形〉1 (通顺) coherent: 这个句子不～。The sentence is ungrammatical and incoherent. ▸～顺 2 (普通) general: ▸～病，～常，～则 3 (整个) whole: ▸～盘，～宵
D〈量〉〈书〉[for letters, telegrams, etc.]: 两

t

～电报 two telegrams ‖ 一～电话 a phone call ‖ 一～文书 one document
▸tòng

【通报】tōngbào **A**〈动〉①（书面通知）circulate a notice: ～表扬/批评 circulate a notice of commendation/criticism ‖ ～各军兵种 circulate a dispatch to all military divisions ②（告知）notify: 随时～ keep sb. closely informed ‖ 请～总经理一声，门外有人求见。 Please tell the general manager that someone here requests to see him. ③（说出）give one's name: 请～各自的姓名。 Everyone, please tell us your names. **B**〈名〉①（指通知文件）circular: 关于台湾问题的～ circular on the Taiwan issue ②（指刊物）bulletin: 《经济～》 *Economic Journal* ‖ 《物理～》 *Physics Bulletin*

【通便】tōngbiàn〈动〉［医学］ relax the bowels: 润肠～ ease constipation

【通病】tōngbìng〈名〉 common fault: 语言学习的～ common errors in language learning ‖ 固执是他们家人的～。 Stubbornness is one of his family's traits.

【通才】tōngcái〈名〉 all-rounder

【通常】tōngcháng〈形〉 usual: ～的方法 usual way ‖ 在～情况下 under normal circumstances ‖ 他～六点起床。 He usually gets up at six.

【通畅】tōngchàng〈形〉①（运行无阻）clear: 保持交通～ keep traffic going ‖ 血液循环～ free blood circulation ‖ 道路～。 The road is clear. ‖ 水流～。 The water is flowing smoothly. ②（顺畅）easy and smooth: 文笔～。 He writes with ease and grace.

【通车】tōngchē〈动〉①（开始行车）be open to traffic: ～典礼 unveiling ceremony ‖ 我们期望这条铁路早日建成～。 We hope that the railway will be built and put into operation as early as possible. ‖ 这条公路将在国庆前～。 This highway will be open to traffic by the National Day. ②（有车往来）have a transport service: 我的老家在山区，现在也通了车。 Transportation services are now available even in my home town, a small mountain village.

【通彻】tōngchè〈动〉 understand thoroughly

【通称】tōngchēng **A**〈动〉 be generally known as: 汞～水银。 Mercury is generally known as quicksilver. **B**〈名〉 common term: 水银是汞的～。 Quicksilver is the popular name for mercury.

【通存通兑】tōngcún-tōngduì〈名〉［金融］ nationwide deposit and cash withdrawal: 办理～业务 manage a nationwide deposit and cash withdrawal service

【通达】tōngdá〈动〉 understand: ～人情 be understanding and considerate ‖ ～事理 understand the ways of the world

【通道】tōngdào〈名〉 passageway: 地下～ underground passage ‖ 绿色～ green channel ‖ 贸易～ trade channel

【通敌】tōngdí〈动〉 collude with the enemy

【通电】tōngdiàn **A**〈动〉①（输送电）set up an electric circuit: 村村～。 Electricity has reached every village. ②（公开用电报告知）publish an open telegram: ～全国 publish an open telegram to the whole nation **B**〈名〉 circular: 发出～ issue an open telegram ‖ 大会～ conference circular

【通牒】tōngdié〈名〉 diplomatic note: ▸最后～

【通读】tōngdú〈动〉①（阅读全文）read through: ～课文 read the text through ②（读懂）understand what one reads

【通分】tōngfēn〈名〉［数学］ reduction of fractions to a common denominator

【通风】tōngfēng〈动〉①（使空气流通）ventilate: ～设备 ventilating equipment ‖ 把窗子打开，通通风。 Open the windows to let in some fresh air. ②（透气儿）be well ventilated: 火炉～不好。 The stove does not draw well. ‖ 这屋子不～。 This room is poorly ventilated. ③（透露消息）disclose information: ▸～报信

【通风报信】tōngfēng-bàoxìn〈成〉 divulge secret information: 要不是他～，我们还蒙在鼓里呢。 Had he not furnished us with the information, we would have still been in the dark.

【通稿】tōnggǎo〈名〉 wire copy: 新闻～ news wire copy

【通告】tōnggào **A**〈动〉 announce: 谨此～ it is hereby announced that **B**〈名〉 announcement: 发布防火～ issue a circular on fire prevention ‖ 布告栏里贴着一张～。 There is a notice on the bulletin board.

【通共】tōnggòng〈副〉 altogether: ～有八个队参加比赛。 There are altogether eight teams participating in the tournament.

【通古斯人】Tōnggǔsīrén〈名〉 Tungus

【通古斯语】Tōnggǔsīyǔ ▸**p. 918**〈名〉 Tungus

【通关】tōngguān〈动〉 clear sth. through customs: 办理～手续 clear customs procedures ‖ 提高～速度 speed up the customs process

【通关节】tōng guānjié〈惯〉 offer bribes to facilitate one's operations: 靠～进了公司 bribe one's way into the company

【通观】tōngguān〈动〉 take an overall view: ～全局 take a comprehensive view of the situation

【通过】tōngguò **A**〈动〉①（经过）pass (through): ～敌人的封锁线 get through the enemy blockage ‖ 队伍～了沙漠。 The troops crossed the desert. ‖ 路太窄，汽车不能～。 The road is too narrow for motor vehicles to pass along. ②（成立生效）pass: ～决议 pass a resolution ‖ 举手～提案 pass a motion by a show of hands ‖ 他的发明～了专家/技术鉴定。 His invention has passed the experts' appraisal /technical tests. ③（经由）request approval: ～领导 be approved by the authorities ‖ 这个问题要～群众，不能作出决定。 The decision should not be made until the masses have been consulted. **B**〈介〉 through: ～对话解决争端 settle a dispute through dialogue ‖ ～外交途径协商解决 make a compromise settlement through diplomatic channels

【通航】tōngháng〈动〉 be open to navigation or air traffic: 直接～ direct air/sea service ‖ 枯水期间船只不能～。 During dry spells ships are not able to pass through.

【通好】tōnghǎo〈动〉〈书〉［of nations］ have friendly relations

【通红】tōnghóng〈形〉 very red: 脸颊～ burning cheeks ‖ 夕阳把天空映得～。 The sky glowed red in the setting sun.

【通话】tōnghuà〈动〉①（指打电话）communicate by telephone: 她正在跟妈妈～。 She is on the phone with her mother. ②（指对话）converse: 他和那个法国人用英语～。 He conversed with the French person in English.

【通婚】tōnghūn〈动〉 be related by marriage: 异族～ transracial marriage

【通货】tōnghuò〈名〉［经济］ currency: ～贬值/升值 depreciation/appreciation of currency ‖ 硬～ hard currency

【通货紧缩】tōnghuò jǐnsuō〈名〉 deflation: ～政策 policy of deflation

【通货膨胀】tōnghuò péngzhàng〈名〉 inflation: 遏制～ check inflation

【通货膨胀率】tōnghuò péngzhànglǜ〈名〉 rate of inflation

【通缉】tōngjī〈动〉 put sb. on the wanted list: ～犯 criminal wanted by the police ‖ ～令 order for the arrest of a criminal at large

【通家】tōngjiā〈名〉①〈书〉（指家庭）families: ～之谊 long established friendship between two families ②（指姻亲）relation by marriage ③（指专家）expert

【通假】tōngjiǎ〈名〉 interchangeability of Chinese characters

【通奸】tōngjiān〈动〉 commit adultery: ～行为 adultery

【通解】tōngjiě〈动〉〈书〉understand thoroughly

【通经】tōngjīng〈动〉①（指儒家经典）be well versed in the Confucian classics ②［中医］ stimulate the menstrual flow: ～止痛 induce menstruation to relieve menalgia

【通栏】tōnglán〈名〉 layout of a page without columns: ～标题 banner

【通览】tōnglǎn〈动〉take an overall view of

【通力】tōnglì〈动〉 make a concerted effort: ～合作 make a concerted effort

【通例】tōnglì〈名〉①（常规）common practice: 周末休息是机关的～。 It is a general rule that offices are closed at weekends. ②〈书〉（普遍规律）universal law

【通连】tōnglián〈动〉 lead to: 跟接待室～的还有一间小屋子。 There is a small room leading to the reception room.

【通亮】tōngliàng〈形〉 well-lit: 灯火把广场照得～。 The square was ablaze with lights.

【通令】tōnglìng **A**〈动〉 issue a general order: ～嘉奖 issue an order of commendation ‖ ～全国 issue a general order to the whole nation **B**〈名〉 general order: 发布～ issue a general order

【通路】tōnglù〈名〉①（指道路）thoroughfare: 在人群中挤出一条～ force one's way through the crowd ②（指途径）channel: 电流的～ electricity circuit

【通路子】tōng lùzi〈惯〉 find means to meet one's goal

【通论】tōnglùn〈名〉①〈书〉（指议论）well-rounded argument ②（指论述）general introduction: 《化学～》 *General Chemistry*

【通名】tōngmíng **A**〈动〉 introduce oneself: ～报姓 give one's name **B**〈名〉 common term

【通明】tōngmíng〈形〉 brightly-lit: 灯火～ be ablaze with lights

【通盘】tōngpán〈形〉 overall: ～安排 make a comprehensive arrangement ‖ ～考虑 take the overall situation into account

【通票】tōngpiào〈名〉 through ticket

【通铺】tōngpù〈名〉 wide bed for several people (in hostels and barracks)

【通气】tōngqì〈动〉①（通风）ventilate: 使房间～ ventilate a room ②（互通声气）be in touch with each other: 上下不～。 There is a lack of communication between the leaders and those below. ‖ 这件事你得跟他通个气。 You should let him know about it.

【通窍】tōngqiào〈动〉 be sensible: 他是个榆木脑袋，不～。 He is a blockhead and doesn't understand a thing.

【通勤】tōngqín〈名〉 commuter service: ～车 commuter train

【通情达理】tōngqíng-dálǐ〈成〉 have good sense: 他是个～的人。 He is a very reasonable person.

t

【通衢】tōngqú〈名〉〈书〉thoroughfare: 南北～ highway running from north to south

【通权达变】tōngquán-dábiàn〈成〉be adaptable to changing circumstances

【通人】tōngrén〈名〉〈书〉erudite person

【通融】tōngróng〈动〉1（变通办法）bend the rules: 这事我们可以～。We can make an exception in this case. 2（短期借钱）accommodate sb. with a short-term loan: 我想跟你～三百块钱。I wonder if you could lend me 300 *yuan*.

【通商】tōngshāng〈动〉have trade relations: ～协定 trade agreement ‖ ～口岸 trading port

【通身】tōngshēn〈名〉entire body: ～乏力 feel weak all over ‖ ～湿透 be soaked to the skin

【通史】tōngshǐ〈名〉general history:《中国～》*General History of China*

【通式】tōngshi〈名〉［化学］general formula

【通顺】tōngshùn〈形〉clear and coherent: 这篇短文写得很～。This essay reads smoothly.

【通俗】tōngsú〈形〉common: ～读物 popular literature ‖ 用～的语言来说明深刻的道理 expound a profound truth in simple language

【通俗歌曲】tōngsú gēqǔ〈名〉pop song: 原创～ original pop song

【通俗易懂】tōngsú-yìdǒng〈成〉easy to understand

【通缩】tōngsuō〈简称〉= 通货紧缩

【通泰】tōngtài〈形〉refreshed

【通体】tōngtǐ〈名〉1（整个）whole thing: 这块钻石～透明。The diamond is entirely transparent. 2（全身）entire body: ～湿透 get soaked through

【通天】tōngtiān〈动〉1（极大）be exceedingly great: 罪恶～ monstrous crime ‖ ～的本领 superhuman skill 2（指人际关系）have direct access to the highest authorities: ～人物 person who has friends in high places

【通条】tōngtiáo〈名〉1（用于炉子）poker 2（用于枪）cleaning rod

【通通】tōngtōng〈副〉all: 这些书你～拿去吧! Take all these books away!

【通同】tōngtóng〈动〉collude: 分明是你和他～作弊。I'm certain that you must have been in collusion with him.

【通统】tōngtǒng = 通通 tōngtōng

【通透】tōngtòu A〈动〉penetrate: 南北～的房间 a room with light flooding through from south to north B〈形〉thorough: 道理讲得很～。The argument was explained thoroughly.

【通途】tōngtú〈名〉〈书〉thoroughfare

【通脱】tōngtuō〈形〉〈书〉unconventional: ～不拘 be flexible and unrestrained

【通宵】tōngxiāo〈名〉whole night: ～未眠 lie awake all night ‖ 工作了一个～ work all night

【通宵达旦】tōngxiāo-dádàn〈成〉all night (long): ～工作/学习 work/study all night

【通晓】tōngxiǎo〈动〉have a good command of: ～多种语言 have a good command of several languages ‖ ～英国文学 be well versed in British literature

【通心粉】tōngxīnfěn〈名〉macaroni

【通信】tōngxìn〈动〉1（指用书信）correspond: （与某人）保持～联系 keep up correspondence (with sb.) ‖ ～地址 postal address 2（指用电波、光波）communicate: 海底～电缆 undersea communication cable ‖ ～设备 communication apparatus ‖ 数字～ digital communication

【通信兵】tōngxìnbīng〈名〉1（指兵种）signal corps 2（指人）signalman

【通信费】tōngxìnfèi〈名〉call charge: 每月的～支出 monthly call expenses

【通信卫星】tōngxìn wèixīng〈名〉telecommunication satellite

【通信员】tōngxìnyuán〈名〉messenger

【通行】tōngxíng〈动〉1（通过）pass through: 自由～ pass freely ‖ 禁止机动车辆～。No vehicles. ‖ 前方施工，停止～。Road works ahead. Closed to traffic. 2（通用）be in common use: 这是全国各处～的办法。This is the current practice throughout the country.

【通行费】tōngxíngfèi〈名〉toll

【通行证】tōngxíngzhèng〈名〉pass: 出示～ show one's pass ‖ 边境～ border pass ‖ 临时～ provisional pass

【通宿】tōngxiǔ〈名〉whole night

【通讯】tōngxùn A = 通信 tōngxìn 2 B〈名〉news dispatch: ～报道 news report ‖ 新华社～ Xinhua dispatch

【通讯录】tōngxùnlù〈名〉address book

【通讯社】tōngxùnshè〈名〉news agency: 外国～ foreign news agency ‖ 新华～ Xinhua News Agency

【通讯网】tōngxùnwǎng〈名〉communication network

【通讯员】tōngxùnyuán ▸p. 966〈名〉reporter: 特约～ special correspondent ‖ 战地～ war correspondent

【通夜】tōngyè〈名〉whole night: 母亲～守在女儿床边。The mother sat by her daughter's bed all night long.

【通用】tōngyòng〈动〉1（普遍使用）be commonly used: 全国～教材 national textbook ‖ 公制世界～。The metric system is commonly used all over the world. 2（可替换）be interchangeable: 这两个词可以～。These two words are interchangeable.

【通用货币】tōngyòng huòbì〈名〉current money

【通用语言】tōngyòng yǔyán〈名〉language in common use

【通邮】tōngyóu〈动〉be accessible by postal communication

【通则】tōngzé〈名〉general rule: 民法～ general rules of civil law

【通胀】tōngzhàng〈简称〉= 通货膨胀

【通胀率】tōngzhànglǜ〈简称〉= 通货膨胀率

【通知】tōngzhī A〈动〉notify: ～某人来开会 notify sb. about coming to the meeting ‖ 等候～ wait for sb.'s notification ‖ 预先～某人 give sb. advance notice ‖ 若地址有变，请～我。Please let me know if there is any change of address. B〈名〉notification: 口头～ verbal notice ‖ 医生一接到～马上就赶来了。The doctor came as soon as he received the news.

【通知单】tōngzhīdān〈名〉letter of advice: 取货～ delivery notice

【通知书】tōngzhīshū〈名〉notice: 录取～ enrolment notification

嗵 tōng

〈拟〉thud: 我的心～～直跳。My heart was thumping. ‖ 他～的一声跪在地上。He flopped down on his knees.

tóng

仝 tóng = 同 tóng

同 tóng

A〈动〉1（相似）be similar: 条件不～ under different conditions ‖ 我们就读于～一所学校。We studied at the same school. ▸～类, ～样, 大～小异 2（相同）be the same as: "贰"～"二"。贰 is the same as 二. ▸～上

B〈副〉together: ～乘一架飞机 be on the same flight ‖ ～吃～住 live under the same roof and eat at the same table ▸～甘共苦, ～学, 会～, 陪～

C〈介〉a（表示一起）with: ～父母住在一起 live with one's parents ‖ 她～他一起去看电影了。She went to the cinema with him. ‖ 这事～我没有任何关系。This has nothing to do with me. b（表示比较）[used to show comparison, etc.] like: ～去年相比，我国国民生产总值增长了百分之八。Our country's GNP has increased by 8% over the last year. ‖ 今年的气候～往年差不多。The weather this year is more or less the same as it used to be.

D ▸p. 448〈连〉and: 当时屋里只有他～我两个人。Only he and I were in the room at that time. ‖ 你～他都答对了。Both you and he gave the correct answer. ▸tòng

【同案犯】tóng'ànfàn〈名〉accomplice

【同班】tóngbān A〈动〉be in the same class: ～同学 classmate ‖ ～战友 comrade-in-arms from the same squad B〈名〉classmate: 他是我～同学。He is my classmate.

【同伴】tóngbàn〈名〉companion: 志趣相投的～ congenial companion

【同胞】tóngbāo〈名〉1（有血缘关系）sibling: ～兄弟/姐妹 full brothers/sisters 2（无血缘关系）compatriot: 港澳～ compatriots in Hong Kong and Macao

【同胞手足】tóngbāo-shǒuzú〈名〉siblings

【同辈】tóngbèi A〈动〉be of the same generation: 他俩同岁但不～。The two of them are the same age but of different generations. B〈名〉peer: ～人 contemporary ‖ 我们是～。We are of the same generation.

【同比】tóngbǐ〈副〉compared to the same period of the previous year: ～销售额/增长 like-for-like sales/growth ‖ 第四季度食品价格～增长了8%。The price of food products rose 8% on the fourth quarter of last year.

【同病相怜】tóngbìng-xiānglián〈成〉〈喻〉fellow sufferers have mutual sympathy

【同步】tóngbù〈动〉1［物理］synchronize: ～传输 synchronous transmission ‖ ～加速器 synchronous accelerator ‖ 进入地球～轨道 enter the earth's synchronous orbit 2（步调一致）keep pace with: 使产值、利润和财政收入～增长 maintain a synchronized increase in output value, profit and revenue

【同步轨道】tóngbù guǐdào〈名〉synchronous orbit

【同步回旋加速器】tóngbù huíxuán jiāsùqì〈名〉［物理］synchrocyclotron

【同步技术】tóngbù jìshù〈名〉synchronization

【同步通信卫星】tóngbù tōngxìn wèixīng〈名〉synchronous communications satellite

【同步卫星】tóngbù wèixīng〈名〉geosynchronous satellite

【同侪】tóngchái = 同辈 tóngbèi B

【同仇敌忾】tóngchóu-díkài〈成〉be united as one against the common enemy: ～，共

t

御外侮 share a bitter hatred and rise in a united resistance against foreign aggressors

【同出一辙】tóngchū-yīzhé〈成〉be of an identical nature

【同窗】tóngchuāng **A**〈动〉study in the same class or school: ～三载 study in the same school for three years ‖ ～好友 good friend from the same school **B**〈名〉classmate: 他是我旧日的～。He is an old schoolmate of mine.

【同床异梦】tóngchuáng-yìmèng〈成〉〈喻〉hide different purposes behind the semblance of accord: ～，各怀鬼胎 strange bedfellows, each harbouring their own sinister design

【同党】tóngdǎng〈名〉confederate

【同道】tóngdào **A**〈名〉**1**（志同道合者）people engaged in the same pursuit **2**（同行业者）people of the same trade: 新闻界的～ fellow journalist **B**〈动〉take the same path: ～南下 go down south together

【同等】tóngděng〈形〉equal: ～重要 be of equal importance ‖ 享受～待遇 enjoy equal treatment

【同等学历】tóngděng xuélì〈名〉same educational level: 具有～ have the same educational level ‖ 具有～者 holder of general equivalency diploma

【同调】tóngdiào〈名〉〈喻〉people with the same interests: 引为～ regard sb. as sharing one's ideas

【同恶相济】tóng'è-xiāngjì〈成〉the wicked help the wicked

【同犯】tóngfàn〈名〉accomplice

【同房】tóngfáng〈动〉**1**（同住一屋）share a room **2** ▸**p. 772**〈婉〉（过性生活）sleep together **3**（同一家族分支）be of the same branch of an extended family: ～兄弟 brothers of the same extended family

【同父异母】tóngfù-yìmǔ〈动〉be born of the same father but a different mother

【同甘共苦】tónggān-gòngkǔ〈成〉share joys and sorrows: ～的战友 comrades-in-arms sharing weal and woe

【同甘苦，共患难】tóng gānkǔ, gòng huànnàn = 同甘共苦 tónggān-gòngkǔ

【同感】tónggǎn〈动〉have the same feeling: 他认为玛丽很刻苦，我也有～。He thinks Mary is very hard-working, and so do I.

【同庚】tónggēng〈动〉be the same age: 咱俩～。We are the same age.

【同工同酬】tónggōng-tóngchóu〈成〉equal pay for equal work: 法律规定男女必须～。The law stipulates that men and women must be paid equally for performing the same job.

【同工异曲】tónggōng-yìqǔ = 异曲同工 yìqǔ-tónggōng

【同归】tóngguī〈动〉reach the same goal: ▸殊途～

【同归于尽】tóngguīyújìn〈成〉meet one's death together

【同行】tóngháng **A**〈动〉engage in the same trade: 他俩～，都是学医的。Both of them are in the same profession — medicine. **B**〈名〉people of the same trade: ～是冤家。People of the same trade can never agree. ‖ 他们是～。They are in the same profession.
▸tóngxíng

【同好】tónghào〈名〉people with similar interests

【同呼吸，共命运】tóng hūxī, gòng mìngyùn〈成〉share a common fate

【同化】tónghuà〈动〉assimilate: 民族～ assimilation of ethnic groups ‖ 长期接触才会发生～。Assimilation occurs only after long contact.

【同化政策】tónghuà zhèngcè〈名〉policy of national assimilation

【同化作用】tónghuà zuòyòng〈名〉［生物］assimilation

【同伙】tónghuǒ **A**〈动〉collude: ～作案 collude in a case **B**〈名〉accomplice: 供出～ name one's accomplice

【同居】tóngjū〈动〉**1**（同住）live together: 父母死后，他和奶奶～。He lived with his grandma after his parents died. **2**（指男女）cohabit: 他们～一年之后才结婚。They were cohabiting for one year before they got married.

【同类】tónglèi **A**〈形〉similar: ～案件 cases of a similar nature ‖ ～产品 like product **B**〈名〉people/things of the same kind: ～相残 kill one's own kind ‖ 他们是～。They are of the same type.

【同类项】tónglèixiàng〈名〉［数学］similar terms

【同僚】tóngliáo〈名〉〈旧〉colleague

【同龄】tónglíng ▸**p. 526**〈动〉be the same age: ～人 contemporary ‖ 我和新中国～。I was born in the same year that new China was founded. ‖ 他们几个是～人。They are all the same age.

【同流合污】tóngliú-héwū〈成〉join sb. in their evildoing: 别跟他们～。Don't get dragged into their evil deeds.

【同路】tónglù〈动〉go the same way: 你俩和他～，跟他走吧。You two go with him.

【同路人】tónglùrén〈名〉fellow traveller:〈喻〉革命的～ revolutionary companion

【同门】tóngmén〈书〉**A**〈动〉study under the same teacher: ～弟子 disciples of the same master **B**〈名〉fellow disciple

【同盟】tóngméng **A**〈动〉form an alliance: ～罢工 joint strike ▸～国 **B**〈名〉alliance:（与某人）结成～ form an alliance (with sb.) ‖ 军事～ military alliance ▸攻守～

【同盟国】tóngméngguó〈名〉**1**（缔约国）ally **2**（特指一战）the Central Powers **3**（特指二战）the Allies

【同盟会】Tóngménghuì〈名〉United League of China [the predecessor of the Kuomintang]

【同盟军】tóngméngjūn〈名〉allied forces

【同名】tóngmíng〈动〉have the same name: ～异姓 have the same given name but a different family name ‖ 这部电影是根据～小说改编的。This film is based on a novel of the same title.

【同谋】tóngmóu **A**〈动〉conspire: ～作案 conspire to commit a crime ‖ ～犯 accessory **B**〈名〉accomplice: 供出～ confess one's accomplice

【同母异父】tóngmǔ-yìfù〈动〉be born of the same mother but a different father

【同年】tóngnián **A**〈名〉**1**（指年份）same year: 新火车站～十月建成。The new railway station was completed in October of that same year. **2**〈旧〉（指人）candidates who passed the imperial examination in the same year **B** ▸**p. 526**〈动〉be the same age: 我俩～。We are the same age.

【同期】tóngqī〈名〉**1**（同一时期）same period: 与去年～相比 compared with the corresponding period last year ‖ 产量超过历史～最高水平。The output reached a new high for the same period. **2**（同一届）same school year: ～毕业 graduate in the same year

【同衾共枕】tóngqīn-gòngzhěn〈成〉sleep together

【同情】tóngqíng〈动〉**1**（指怜悯）sympathize with: ～受害者及其家属 feel for the victims and their families ‖ 深表～ show deep sympathy for ‖ 他出于～给了那乞丐一些钱。He gave the beggar some money out of pity. **2**（指赞成）sympathize with: 我们～你们的正义事业。We offer our sympathy to your just cause.

【同情心】tóngqíngxīn〈名〉sympathy: 缺乏～ lack sympathy

【同人】tóngrén〈名〉〈书〉colleague

【同仁】tóngrén = 同人 tóngrén

【同日而语】tóngrì'éryǔ〈成〉[usu used in the negative] be mentioned in the same breath: 这座城市的今昔不可～。The city's past and present cannot be mentioned in the same breath.

【同上】tóngshàng〈动〉be the same as the above: 出处～ ibid.

【同生共死】tóngshēng-gòngsǐ〈成〉live and die together

【同声】tóngshēng〈动〉say in unison: ～呼喊 shout in unison

【同声传译】tóngshēng chuányì〈名〉simultaneous interpretation

【同声相应，同气相求】tóngshēng xiāngyìng, tóngqì xiāngqiú〈成〉like attracts like

【同时】tóngshí **A**〈名〉same time: ～发生 happen at the same time ‖ 他们是～复员的。They were demobilized at the same time. **B**〈连〉furthermore: 这任务非常重要，～也非常艰巨。It is a task of great importance and, moreover, it is an arduous one.

【同事】tóngshì **A**〈动〉work together: 我们～已经多年。We have been working together for many years. **B**〈名〉colleague: 老～ former colleague ‖ 与～关系融洽 get on well with one's workmates

【同室操戈】tóngshì-cāogē〈成〉〈喻〉internal strife

【同岁】tóngsuì ▸**p. 526**〈动〉be the same age: 他俩～。They are the same age.

【同位角】tóngwèijiǎo〈名〉［数学］corresponding angle

【同位素】tóngwèisù〈名〉［化学］isotope: 放射性～治疗 radioisotope treatment

【同位语】tóngwèiyǔ〈名〉［语言］appositive: ～从句 appositive clause

【同温层】tóngwēncéng〈旧〉= 平流层 píngliúcéng

【同喜】tóngxǐ〈动〉〈套〉thank you for your congratulations

【同乡】tóngxiāng〈名〉person from the same village/town/province: ～会 association of people from the same province town

【同心】tóngxīn〈动〉be of one mind: ～协力 work together with one heart

【同心结】tóngxīnjié〈名〉lovers' knot

【同心锁】tóngxīnsuǒ〈名〉lovers' lock

【同心同德】tóngxīn-tóngdé〈成〉be of one heart and one mind

【同心圆】tóngxīnyuán〈名〉［数学］concentric circles

【同行】tóngxíng〈动〉travel together: ～伙伴 travel companion ‖ 与他～的还有两位同学。Two of his classmates travelled with him.
▸tóngháng

【同性】tóngxìng **A**〈形〉same-sex: ▸～恋 **B**〈名〉things of the same nature: 异性电荷互相吸引，～电荷互相排斥。Unlike electric charges attract but two like electric charges repel.

【同性恋】tóngxìngliàn〈名〉homosexuality: ～男子 gay ‖ ～女子 lesbian ‖ ～者 homosexual

【同姓】tóngxìng〈动〉have the same surname: 同名～的人很多。Lots of people have the same names.

【同学】tóngxué **A**〈动〉study in the same school: 他和她～五年。He and she studied in the same school for five years. ‖ 我们自幼～。We studied in the same school when we were young. **B**〈名〉**1**（指同校或同班）classmate: 老/新～ former/new schoolmate ‖ 她和我在大学里是同班～。She and I were classmates at college. **2**（用于称呼）[form of address when speaking to a student]: ～, 请问去博物馆怎么走？Excuse me, could you tell me the way to the museum?

【同学会】tóngxuéhuì〈名〉alumni association: 欧美～ European/American alumni association

【同样】tóngyàng〈形〉same: ～大小 be of the same size ‖ 作～处理 treat in the same way ‖ 他们做～的工作。They do similar work. ‖ 她的英语说得和汉语～流利。She speaks English as fluently as she does Chinese.

【同业】tóngyè〈名〉**1**（指行业）same business **2**（指人）person of the same profession

【同业公会】tóngyè gōnghuì〈名〉〈旧〉guild

【同一】tóngyī〈形〉same: ～目标 same goal ‖ 持～观点 share the same point of view ‖ 他们都朝～方向奔去。They all ran in one direction.

【同一律】tóngyīlǜ〈名〉［逻辑］law of identity

【同义词】tóngyìcí〈名〉synonym: 这两个词是～。These two words are synonyms.

【同意】tóngyì〈动〉agree: 他～我的观点。He agreed with me. ‖ 他们～了我们的建议。They agreed to our suggestion. ‖ 您的意见我不能～。I don't share your opinion. ‖ 上级已经～我们的计划。The higher authorities have approved our plan. ‖ 点头表示～, 摇头表示不～。Nod to show you agree, shake your head to show you disagree.

【同音词】tóngyīncí〈名〉homonym

【同源词】tóngyuáncí〈名〉cognate words

【同志】tóngzhì〈名〉**1**（用作称呼）comrade: ～关系 comradeship ‖ 老～ old comrade ‖ 女～ female comrade **2**〈口〉（同性恋者）homosexual

【同质化】tóngzhìhuà〈动〉homogenize: 超市～现象严重。The homogenization of supermarkets is widespread.

【同舟共济】tóngzhōu-gòngjì〈成〉pull together in times of trouble: 在困难面前, 我们要～。We must join hands in face of difficulty.

【同轴电缆】tóngzhóu diànlǎn〈名〉coaxial cable

【同桌】tóngzhuō **A**〈动〉share a desk: ～吃饭 eat at the same table ‖ 我们曾～三年。We shared the same desk for three years. **B**〈名〉person sharing the same desk

【同宗】tóngzōng〈动〉be of the same clan: 他们俩同姓不～。The two of them have the same surname but are of different clans.

【同族】tóngzú〈动〉be of the same clan: 两家是同宗～。The two families share a common ancestry.

彤 tóng〈形〉〈书〉red

【彤云】tóngyún〈名〉**1**（红霞）red clouds **2**（阴云）dark clouds: ～密布。The sky is overcast.

侗 tóng〈形〉〈书〉ignorant ▸Dòng

茼 tóng

【茼蒿】tónghāo〈名〉［植物］crown daisy

桐 tóng〈名〉［植物］**1**（泡桐）paulownia **2**（梧桐）phoenix tree **3**（油桐）tung oil tree

【桐油】tóngyóu〈名〉tung oil

砼 tóng〈名〉concrete

铜（銅）tóng〈名〉copper: ～具有良好的导电性。Copper is a good conductor. ▸黄～, 青～

【铜板】tóngbǎn〈名〉**1**（铜钱）copper coin **2**（铜制快板）copper clappers **3**（铜制板材）copper sheet

【铜版】tóngbǎn〈名〉［印刷］copperplate: ～印刷 copperplate printing

【铜版画】tóngbǎnhuà〈名〉copperplate

【铜版纸】tóngbǎnzhǐ〈名〉art paper

【铜币】tóngbì〈名〉copper (coin)

【铜鼓】tónggǔ ▸**p. 929**〈名〉bronze drum

【铜管乐】tóngguǎnyuè〈名〉music produced by brass instruments: ～器 brass instrument

【铜壶滴漏】tónghú dīlòu〈名〉［考古］copper clepsydra

【铜婚】tónghūn〈名〉copper wedding

【铜匠】tóngjiang〈名〉coppersmith

【铜筋铁骨】tóngjīn-tiěgǔ〈成〉〈喻〉strong and solid body

【铜镜】tóngjìng〈名〉［考古］bronze mirror

【铜矿】tóngkuàng〈名〉**1**（指矿藏）copper mine **2**（指矿石）copper ore

【铜绿】tónglǜ〈名〉［化学］verdigris

【铜锣】tóngluó〈名〉bronze gong

【铜模】tóngmú = 字模 zìmú

【铜牌】tóngpái〈名〉bronze (medal): ～得主 bronze medallist

【铜器】tóngqì〈名〉bronze ware

【铜器时代】tóngqì shídài〈名〉［考古］Bronze Age

【铜钱】tóngqián〈名〉copper coin

> **铜钱**
>
> Copper coins were already being produced at the end of the Spring and Autumn period. From the Qin to the Qing dynasties, most of the coins were round with a square hole in the middle. This is why money in China is sometimes humorously referred to as *kongfangxiong* (孔方兄, literally 'a brother with a square hole'). Being of low value, coins were usually strung together to create higher denominations. Because of the inscriptions on the reverse side, each coin was known as a 'wen' (文, meaning 'word'), and this gave rise to expressions such as '*bu ming yi wen*' (不名一文, 'penniless'). Coins without holes were introduced at the end of the Qing Dynasty and were known as *tongyuan* (铜元) or *tongban* (铜板).

【铜墙铁壁】tóngqiáng-tiěbì〈成〉〈喻〉bastion of iron: 我们的政权是牢不可破的～。Our political power is truly an impregnable bastion of iron.

【铜丝】tóngsī〈名〉copper wire

【铜钿】tóngtián〈名〉〈方〉money

【铜像】tóngxiàng〈名〉bronze statue

【铜臭】tóngxiù〈名〉stench of money: 满身～ be filthily rich

【铜锈】tóngxiù = 铜绿 tónglǜ

【铜元】tóngyuán = 铜圆 tóngyuán

【铜圆】tóngyuán〈名〉copper (coin)

【铜子儿】tóngzǐr〈口〉= 铜圆 tóngyuán

童 tóng

A〈名〉**1**（小孩儿）child: ～裤/帽/鞋 children's trousers/cap/shoes ▸～年, 儿～, 牧～, 神～ **2**（未成年男仆）boy servant: ▸书～

B〈形〉**1**（处子）virgin: ▸～男, ～女, ～贞 **2**（秃）bare: ▸～山

【童车】tóngchē〈名〉**1**（坐式婴儿车）buggy〈英〉; stroller〈美〉**2**（儿童脚踏车）child's bicycle

【童工】tónggōng〈名〉child labour

【童话】tónghuà〈名〉children's fairy tale: 女儿总是让我给她讲～故事。My daughter always asks me to tell her fairy tales.

【童蒙】tóngméng〈名〉〈书〉innocent and ignorant child

【童男】tóngnán〈名〉**1**（指无性经历）virgin boy **2**（指未成年）boy

【童年】tóngnián ▸**p. 526**〈名〉childhood: ～时代 childhood days

【童女】tóngnǚ〈名〉**1**（指无性经历）virgin girl **2**（指未成年）girl

【童趣】tóngqù〈名〉childish delight

【童山】tóngshān〈名〉bare hill: ～秃岭 barren hills and mountains

【童身】tóngshēn〈名〉maidenhood

【童声】tóngshēng〈名〉child's voice: ～合唱 children's chorus

【童叟无欺】tóngsǒu-wúqī〈成〉[often in shop advertisements] cheat neither the old nor the young

【童心】tóngxīn〈名〉childlike innocence: ～未泯 still retain one's childlike innocence

【童星】tóngxīng〈名〉child star

【童言无忌】tóngyán-wújì〈成〉a child says what it thinks

【童颜鹤发】tóngyán-hèfà = 鹤发童颜 hèfà-tóngyán

【童养媳】tóngyǎngxí〈名〉〈旧〉child bride

【童谣】tóngyáo〈名〉nursery rhyme

【童贞】tóngzhēn〈名〉virginity

【童真】tóngzhēn〈名〉naivety: 歌中充满了～的感情。The song is full of childlike simplicity.

【童装】tóngzhuāng〈名〉children's wear

【童子】tóngzǐ〈名〉boy: ～军 boy scout

【童子鸡】tóngzǐjī〈名〉〈方〉young chicken

酮 tóng〈名〉［化学］ketone

橦 tóng〈名〉〈古〉kapok tree

曈 tóng

【曈昽】tónglóng〈形〉〈书〉[of the rising sun] turning bright: 旭日～ twilight of daybreak

【曈曈】tóngtóng〈形〉〈书〉**1**（指日出）bright **2**（指眼睛）shining

朣 tóng

【朣朦】tóngméng〈形〉〈书〉dim

t

瞳 tóng〈名〉pupil
【瞳孔】tóngkǒng〈名〉pupil: ～放大 have dilated pupils
【瞳人】tóngrén〈名〉pupil
【瞳仁】tóngrén = 瞳人 tóngrén

tǒng

统[1]（統） tǒng
A〈名〉interconnected system: ▸传～, 系～
B〈副〉in unity: ▸～筹, ～购
C〈动〉control: ～兵 command troops ‖ 上级主管部门不要对企业～得过死。 Higher authorities should not exercise rigid and excessive control over enterprises. ▸～辖, ～治

统[2]（統） tǒng = 筒 tǒng 3
【统编】tǒngbiān〈动〉compile consistently: ～教材 consolidated teaching materials
【统舱】tǒngcāng〈名〉steerage: 坐～ travel steerage
【统称】tǒngchēng **A**〈动〉be collectively named: 绘画、雕塑、建筑等～为造型艺术。 Painting, sculpture and architecture are collectively called the plastic arts. **B**〈名〉general term: 陶瓷是陶器和瓷器的～。 Ceramics is a general term for pottery and porcelain.
【统筹】tǒngchóu〈动〉make overall plans: ～全局 take the whole situation into account and plan accordingly ‖ ～安排 make an overall arrangement
【统筹兼顾】tǒngchóu-jiāngù〈成〉unified planning with due consideration for all concerned
【统分结合】tǒngfēn jiéhé〈名〉[in farming] individual household contract responsibility system integrated with a collective management system
【统共】tǒnggòng〈副〉altogether: 这所大学～有八个学院。 There are eight schools in the university in all.
【统购】tǒnggòu〈动〉monopolize purchasing: ～统销 monopolize purchasing and marketing
【统观】tǒngguān〈动〉make an overview: ～全局 take an overview of a situation
【统管】tǒngguǎn〈动〉administer in an overall manner: 学校的行政和教学工作都由校长～。Both the administrative work and teaching affairs are in the charge of the principal.
【统货】tǒnghuò〈名〉ungraded and uniformly-priced goods
【统计】tǒngjì〈动〉**1**（计算）count: ～人数 count heads ‖ ～选票 count votes **2**（做统计工作）do statistics: ～结果 statistical result ‖ 人口～ census ‖ ～资料 statistics
【统计局】tǒngjìjú〈名〉statistics bureau
【统计数字】tǒngjì shùzì〈名〉statistics
【统计学】tǒngjìxué〈名〉statistics
【统计员】tǒngjìyuán ▸p. 966〈名〉statistician
【统建】tǒngjiàn〈动〉construct in a systematic way
【统考】tǒngkǎo〈名〉standardized examination: 全国～ nationwide uniform examination
【统揽】tǒnglǎn〈动〉assume overall responsibility: ～全厂工作 take full charge of factory work
【统领】tǒnglǐng **A**〈动〉command: ～全军 command the whole army **B**〈名〉commander
【统配】tǒngpèi〈动〉monopolize distribution: ～物资 materials earmarked for unified distribution
【统摄】tǒngshè〈动〉〈书〉exercise control over: ～三军 command the armed services
【统收统支】tǒngshōu-tǒngzhī〈名〉unified collection and allocation of funds (of the state)
【统属】tǒngshǔ〈动〉be subordinate: ～关系 subordinate relations ‖ 彼此不相～。 Neither is subordinate to the other.
【统帅】tǒngshuài **A**〈名〉commander-in-chief: 三军～ commander of the armed forces ‖ 最高～ supreme commander ‖ ～部 supreme command **B** = 统率 tǒngshuài
【统率】tǒngshuài〈动〉command: ～全军 command the armed forces
【统体】tǒngtǐ〈名〉whole body
【统统】tǒngtǒng = 通通 tōngtōng
【统辖】tǒngxiá〈动〉exercise control over: 这个团归司令部直接～。 This regiment is under the direct command of the headquarters.
【统销】tǒngxiāo〈动〉monopolize marketing
【统一】tǒngyī **A**〈动〉unify: ～行动 act in unison ‖ 促进祖国和平～ promote the peaceful reunification of the motherland ‖ 意见不～ differ in opinion ‖ 纸张大小必须～。 The papers must be of uniform size. **B**〈形〉unified: ～标准 uniform standard ‖ ～指挥 central command ‖ 在～领导下 under the unified leadership
【统一发票】tǒngyī fāpiào〈名〉uniform invoice
【统一体】tǒngyītǐ〈名〉［哲学］entity
【统一战线】tǒngyī zhànxiàn〈名〉united front: 爱国～ patriotic united front
【统战】tǒngzhàn〈简称〉= 统一战线
【统战部】tǒngzhànbù〈名〉Department of United Front Work
【统制】tǒngzhì〈动〉control: ～军用物资 exercise control over military supplies ‖ 经济～ economic control
【统治】tǒngzhì〈动〉**1**（掌控管理）rule: 独裁～ dictatorial rule ‖ 封建～ feudal rule ‖ 殖民～ colonial rule ‖ 国家是阶级～的机器。 The state is an organ of class domination. **2**（控制）dominate: 在外语教学中，英语占～地位。 In foreign language teaching, English is the dominant language.
【统治阶级】tǒngzhì jiējí〈名〉ruling class
【统治者】tǒngzhìzhě〈名〉ruler: 暴虐的～ despotic ruler

捅 tǒng〈动〉**1**（戳）poke;（刺）stab: 用匕首～人 stab sb. with a dagger ‖ 他把纸～了一个大洞。 He poked a big hole in the paper. **2**（碰）nudge: 别用胳膊肘～我。 Stop jabbing me with your elbow. ‖ 他睡着了，～他一下。 He's falling asleep. Give him a nudge. **3**（揭露）give away: 你不该把这个秘密～出去。 You shouldn't have let the secret out.
【捅娄子】tǒng lóuzi〈惯〉〈喻〉make a mess of sth.: 看，这回～了吧。 Look, you've really done it this time!
【捅漏子】tǒng lòuzi = 捅娄子 tǒng lóuzi
【捅马蜂窝】tǒng mǎfēngwō〈惯〉stir up a hornet's nest

桶 tǒng〈名〉bucket: 汽油～ petrol tank ▸饭～, 垃圾～, 马～
【桶装】tǒngzhuāng〈形〉packed in barrels: ～啤酒 draught beer

筒 tǒng〈名〉**1**（粗竹管）section of thick bamboo: ▸竹～ **2**（筒状物）thick tube-shaped object: 茶叶～ tea caddy ▸笔～, 手电～, 烟～, 邮～ **3**（筒状部分）tube-shaped part of an article or clothing, etc.: 高～靴 high-leg boots ▸袖～
【筒管】tǒngguǎn〈名〉［纺织］bobbin
【筒裤】tǒngkù〈名〉straight-legged trousers
【筒裙】tǒngqún〈名〉straight skirt
【筒瓦】tǒngwǎ〈名〉semicircular tile
【筒状花】tǒngzhuànghuā〈名〉［植物］tubular flower
【筒子】tǒngzi〈名〉tube: 枪～ barrel of a gun ‖ 靴～ boot leg
【筒子楼】tǒngzilóu〈名〉block of flats with rooms on either side of the hallway, and without private kitchens or toilets

tòng

同（衕） tòng ▸胡同 hútòng ▸tóng

恸（慟） tòng〈动〉〈书〉feel deep sorrow: ▸悲～

通 tòng〈量〉[for a complete course of activity]: 挨一～骂 get a dressing-down ‖ 发一～牢骚 utter a torrent of complaints ▸tōng

痛 tòng
A〈动〉**1**（感到疼）pain: 止～ relieve a pain ‖ 肚子～ have a stomach ache ‖ 关节～ have joint pains ‖ 伤口～不～? Does the wound hurt? ▸酸～, 头～, 胃～ **2**（悲伤）be sad: ▸哀～, 悲～
B〈副〉deeply: ▸～打, ～哭, ～饮
【痛不欲生】tòngbùyùshēng〈成〉be so overwhelmed with grief as to wish one were dead
【痛斥】tòngchì〈动〉bitterly attack: ～卖国贼 bitterly denounce the traitor ‖ ～歪理邪说 lash out at fallacies and false reasoning
【痛楚】tòngchǔ〈形〉〈书〉painful
【痛处】tòngchù〈名〉sore spot: 这话触到他的～。 The remarks touched his sore spot.
【痛打】tòngdǎ〈动〉give sb. a good beating: ～落水狗 be merciless with bad people even if they are down ‖ ～一顿 give sb. a sound thrashing
【痛悼】tòngdào〈动〉express profound condolences: ～烈士 mourn the martyrs deeply
【痛定思痛】tòngdìng-sītòng〈成〉draw a lesson from a bitter experience
【痛风】tòngfēng ▸p. 50〈名〉［医学］gout: ～性关节炎 gouty arthritis
【痛改前非】tònggǎi-qiánfēi〈成〉make a clean break with one's past errors: ～，重新做人 sincerely mend one's ways and turn over a new leaf
【痛感】tònggǎn **A**〈动〉feel strongly: 他～自己知识贫乏。 He feels his lack of knowledge keenly. **B**〈名〉sense of pain: 针灸时有轻微的～。 Acupuncture causes slight

discomfort.

【痛恨】tònghèn〈动〉 hate bitterly: ～吸烟 detest smoking

【痛悔】tònghuǐ〈动〉 deeply regret: 为自己的劣迹感到～ feel remorse for one's bad deeds

【痛击】tòngjī〈动〉 deliver a heavy blow: 迎头～ strike at sb. head-on

【痛经】tòngjīng ▸**p. 50**〈名〉［医学］ dysmenorrhoea

【痛觉】tòngjué〈名〉［生理］ algesthesia: ～神经 pain nerve

【痛哭】tòngkū〈动〉 sob one's heart out: ～一场 have a good cry ‖ 放声～ wail with grief

【痛哭流涕】tòngkū-liútì〈成〉 cry one's heart out: 他悔恨地～，表示愿意改邪归正。 He wept bitter tears of remorse, saying he would mend his ways.

【痛苦】tòngkǔ〈形〉 painful: ～的表情 pained expression ‖ 精神上/肉体上的～ mental/ physical suffering ‖ 给某人带来～ inflict pain on sb.

【痛快】tòngkuài〈形〉 **1**（高兴） happy: 人家没邀请他，他很不～。 He was upset at not being invited. ‖ 一切都按时完成了，我感到很～。 Having everything done on time, I feel delighted. **2**（尽兴） sated: 玩个～ have a heavenly time ‖ 我们在游乐场玩得很～。 We had a whale of a time at the pleasure ground. **3**（爽快） candid: 说话～ not mince one's words ‖ 这人很～，心里有什么就说什么。 This person is very direct and says whatever comes to mind.

【痛快淋漓】tòngkuài-línlí〈成〉impassioned and forceful

【痛骂】tòngmà〈动〉 scold severely

【痛切】tòngqiè〈形〉 most sorrowful: ～地认识自己的错误 come to recognize one's own mistake with feelings of deep remorse

【痛入骨髓】tòngrùgǔsuǐ〈成〉 hurt sb. to the very marrow of their bones

【痛失】tòngshī〈动〉 lose regretfully: ～良机 be so sorry to have missed a golden opportunity

【痛恶】tòngwù〈动〉 bitterly detest: 人民～官僚主义。 Bureaucracy is detested by the people. ‖ 腐败之风令人～。 The tendency towards corruption is bitterly detested.

【痛惜】tòngxī〈动〉 deeply regret: 诗人英年早逝，令人～。 It is deeply regrettable that the talented poet died in the flower of youth.

【痛心】tòngxīn〈动〉 be distressed: 失去夺金牌的机会真叫人～。 It was terrible to have missed the chance to win the gold medal. ‖ 做出这种事，真令人～。 What a shame to have done something like this.

【痛心疾首】tòngxīn-jíshǒu〈成〉with bitter resentment

【痛痒】tòngyǎng〈名〉〈喻〉 **1**（疾苦） hardships: 关心群众的～ be concerned about the well-being of the masses **2**（紧要的事） importance: 无关～ be of little account

【痛饮】tòngyǐn〈动〉 drink one's fill: 开怀～ drink to one's heart's content

【痛责】tòngzé〈动〉 severely rebuke

tōu

偷 tōu

A〈动〉 **1**（窃取） steal: ～东西是违法的。 Stealing is illegal. ‖ 我的钱包被～走了。 My purse was stolen. **2**（挤出） find (time): ▸～空，忙里～闲 **3**（只顾眼前） loaf around: ▸～安

B〈名〉 thief: ▸惯～，小～

C〈副〉 stealthily: ～吃 take food on the sly

【偷安】tōu'ān〈动〉 seek temporary ease: ▸苟且～

【偷盗】tōudào〈动〉steal: ～财物 steal sb.'s property ‖ 他因～而坐牢。 He is in prison for theft.

【偷渡】tōudù〈动〉 slip out of a blockade in an area with water: ～出境 steal out of a country

【偷工减料】tōugōng-jiǎnliào〈成〉 do shoddy work and use inferior materials

【偷换】tōuhuàn〈动〉 surreptitiously substitute one thing for another: ～概念 sneakily replace a concept

【偷鸡不着蚀把米】tōu jī bùzháo shí bǎ mǐ〈俗〉〈喻〉 seek to better oneself but end up losing what one already had

【偷鸡摸狗】tōujī-mōgǒu〈成〉〈喻〉 **1**（小偷小摸） go pilfering **2**（偷情） have illicit relations with women

【偷看】tōukàn〈动〉 steal a glance (at)

【偷空】tōukòng〈动〉 grab a moment: ～打个盹儿 grab a little sleep ‖ 我前两天曾～去看过他一次。 I took time off work to visit him just the other day.

【偷懒】tōulǎn〈动〉 be lazy: 她做事从不～。 She always goes all out, whatever she is doing.

【偷垒】tōulěi〈动〉［体育］ steal a base

【偷梁换柱】tōuliáng-huànzhù〈成〉〈喻〉 perpetrate a fraud

【偷猎】tōuliè〈动〉 poach

【偷拍】tōupāi〈动〉 take a photo without permission

【偷跑】tōupǎo〈动〉［体育］ jump the gun

【偷巧】tōuqiǎo〈动〉 resort to trickery to serve oneself or avoid a difficulty

【偷窃】tōuqiè〈动〉 steal: ～情报 steal information ‖ ～行为 theft

【偷情】tōuqíng〈动〉 carry on an illicit love affair

【偷人】tōurén〈动〉 [of a married woman] commit adultery

【偷生】tōushēng〈动〉 drag out an ignoble existence: ～苟安 be content with temporary ease and comfort ‖ 忍辱～ live in humiliation ▸苟且～

【偷税】tōushuì〈动〉 evade taxes: ～漏税 defraud the revenue

【偷天换日】tōutiān-huànrì〈成〉〈喻〉 perpetrate a gigantic fraud

【偷听】tōutīng〈动〉 eavesdrop

【偷偷】tōutōu〈副〉 secretly: 趁人没注意，他～地溜走了。 He sneaked away while nobody was watching. ‖ 我～塞给他一张纸条。 I slipped him a note.

【偷偷摸摸】tōutōu-mōmō〈成〉 surreptitious

【偷袭】tōuxí〈动〉 make a surprise attack: ～敌营 make a surprise attack on an enemy camp

【偷闲】tōuxián〈动〉 **1**（抽空） snatch some time off: 忙里～ steal a moment of leisure **2**〈方〉（偷懒） be lazy

【偷香窃玉】tōuxiāng-qièyù〈成〉indulge in secret relations with women

【偷眼】tōuyǎn〈副〉 stealthily: 她～看了一下母亲的神色。 She stole a glance at her mother's face.

【偷营】tōuyíng〈动〉 make a surprise attack on an enemy camp

【偷越】tōuyuè〈动〉 slip through: ～国境 sneak across the border

【偷运】tōuyùn〈动〉 transport by stealth

【偷嘴】tōuzuǐ〈动〉 take food on the sly

tóu

头（頭）tóu

A〈名〉 **1** ▸**p. 614**（头部） head: 点～ nod one's head ‖ 摇～ shake one's head ‖ 一～浓发 a thick head of hair ‖ 小心碰～。 Mind your head. ▸～痛，～重脚轻，光～，抬～ **2**（头发） hair: 把～剃光 shave one's head ‖ 学生～ student's haircut ▸寸～，梳～，洗～ **3**（首领） head: ▸～领，～目，～羊，工～ **4**（顶端或末梢） end: 火柴～ match head ‖ 一根绳子有两个～儿。 A rope has two ends. ▸案～，地～，桥～，山～，源～ **5**（起点或终点） beginning or end: 一年到～ all the year round ‖ 妈妈一旦起个～儿，小姑娘就能把故事讲下来。 If her mother can start things off for her, the little girl is able to tell the whole story. ▸从～ **6**（残余部分） end: 蜡烛～ candle stump ‖ 铅笔～ pencil stub ▸布～，烟～ **7**（方面） side: 分～寻找 search in different directions ‖ 两～讨好 try to please both sides ‖ 只顾一～ pay attention to only one aspect of the matter ▸两～

B ▸**p. 691**〈数〉 first: ～班车 first bus ‖ 在进攻中打～阵 spearhead the offensive ▸～版，～等，～号，～胎

C〈形〉 **1**（最初） [used before a numeral] first: ～半个月 first half of the month ‖ ～十名 top ten ‖ ～一次 first time **2**〈方〉（之前） [used before 年 or 天] last: ～两天 last two days ‖ ～几年 last few years ▸～年，～天

D〈介〉〈方〉 before: ～进考场，他把书又看了一遍。 He leafed through the book once again before entering the examination hall. ‖ 他每天～七点就到。 He comes before seven o'clock every day.

E〈量〉 **1**（用于牲口） [for certain domestic animals]: 二十～牛 twenty head of cattle ‖ 三～驴 three donkeys ‖ 五～猪 five pigs **2**（用于蒜、洋葱等） [for garlic, etc.]: 两～蒜 two bulbs of garlic

▸tou

【头版】tóubǎn〈名〉 front page: ～新闻 front-page news ‖ ～头条 front-page headline

【头半天】tóubàntiān〈名〉 forenoon

【头部】tóubù〈名〉 head: ～中弹 be shot in the head

【头彩】tóucǎi〈名〉 first prize in a lottery: 中～ win first prize in a lottery

【头筹】tóuchóu〈名〉 first place: 在百米赛中拔取～ take first place in the 100m

【头寸】tóucùn〈名〉［金融］ **1**（指银根） money supply: ～紧/松。 Money is tight/easy. **2**〈旧〉（指款项） cash: ～缺 be out of cash

【头等】tóuděng〈形〉first-class: ～舱 first-class cabin ‖ ～大事 matter of prime importance ‖ ～重要任务 task of prime importance

【头发】tóufa ▸**p. 614**〈名〉 hair: 把～染黑 dye one's hair black

【头伏】tóufú = 初伏 chūfú

【头盖骨】tóugàigǔ〈名〉［生理］ skull

【头功】tóugōng〈名〉 highest merit: 立～ render the greatest service

【头骨】tóugǔ〈名〉［生理］ skull

【头号】tóuhào〈形〉 **1**（第一号） number one: ～政敌 top political rival ‖ ～字 size one type **2**（最好的） first-class: ～棉花 top-quality cotton

t

【头回生，二回熟】tóu huí shēng, èr huí shóu〈俗〉strangers the first time, friends the second

【头昏】tóuhūn〈形〉dizzy: 我～。I feel giddy.

【头昏脑涨】tóuhūn-nǎozhàng〈成〉feel dizzy: 事情太多，搞得我～的。There's too much going on. It's making my head spin.

【头昏眼花】tóuhūn-yǎnhuā〈成〉feel one's head swimming and one's vision blurred: 饿得～ be faint with hunger

【头婚】tóuhūn〈口〉= 初婚 chūhūn 1

【头家】tóujiā〈名〉**1**（聚赌抽头的人）organizer of a gambling party who takes a percentage of the winnings **2**（庄家）banker in a gambling party **3**（上家）player whose turn comes just before

【头角】tóujiǎo〈名〉talent: ▸崭露～

【头角峥嵘】tóujiǎo-zhēngróng〈成〉[of a young person] prominent

【头巾】tóujīn〈名〉headdress

【头颈】tóujǐng〈名〉〈方〉neck

【头盔】tóukuī〈名〉helmet: 防撞～ crash helmet

【头里】tóuli〈名〉〈口〉**1**（前面）place in front: 您～走。Please go ahead. ‖ 她在学习和工作中都走在～。She takes the lead in work as well as in study. **2**（事前）advance position: 让我们把话说在～，可别事后反悔。Let's make it clear in advance so that neither of us can regret afterwards.

【头脸】tóuliǎn〈名〉**1**（面貌）face: 走到跟前，我才看清他的～。I didn't see him clearly until I came up close. **2**（面子）prestige: 他在地方上是个有～的人物。He is quite a prominent figure in his community.

【头领】tóulǐng〈名〉leader

【头颅】tóulú〈名〉head: ▸抛～，洒热血

【头马】tóumǎ〈名〉lead horse

【头面人物】tóumiàn rénwù〈成〉prominent figure

【头目】tóumù〈名〉〈贬〉ringleader: 土匪～ bandit chief

【头脑】tóunǎo〈名〉**1**（脑筋）head: 有商业/政治～ be commercially/politically minded ‖ 有数学～ have a head for mathematics ‖ ～灵活 be quick-witted ‖ ～清醒 keep a clear head ‖ 被胜利冲昏～ be dizzy with success ‖ 头头脑脑 bigwig **2**（头绪）main gist: 他的话让人摸不着～。No one could understand a word of what he said. **3**〈口〉（首领）head

【头年】tóunián〈名〉**1**（第一年）first year: 三年看～。The first year is the most important out of the three years. **2**（上一年）previous/last year: ～春节 last Spring Festival ‖ ～他曾回过家。He had been home the previous year.

【头牌】tóupái〈名〉［戏曲］plate with the name of a star actor on it

【头皮】tóupí〈名〉**1**（头顶及周围皮肤）scalp: 搔～ scratch one's head ‖ 他挠着～想主意。He is scratching his head for ideas. **2** = 头屑 tóuxiè

【头皮屑】tóupíxiè = 头屑 tóuxiè

【头破血流】tóupò-xuèliú〈成〉be beaten to a pulp

【头前】tóuqián〈名〉〈方〉**1**（前头）place in front: 他在～引路。He walked in front to show us the way. **2**（从前）previous time: ～，这里是一片稻田。Previously this was a rice paddy.

【头钱】tóuqián〈名〉commission taken from the winnings of a gambling party

【头球】tóuqiú〈名〉［足球］header: ～破门 head the ball into the goal

【头儿】tóur〈名〉〈口〉chief: 谁是你们的～? Who is your boss?

【头人】tóurén〈名〉chieftain

【头生】tóushēng **A**〈形〉firstborn: ～的孩子 firstborn child **B**〈名〉firstborn child

【头绳】tóushéng〈名〉string for binding one's hair: 在辫子上扎一根红～ tie one's plait with a piece of red yarn

【头虱】tóushī〈名〉head louse

【头式】tóushì〈名〉hairstyle

【头饰】tóushì〈名〉headdress

【头胎】tóutāi〈名〉firstborn child: 她～生了双胞胎。Her first born were twins.

【头套】tóutào〈名〉［戏曲］wig

【头疼】tóuténg〈口〉= 头痛 tóutòng

【头疼脑热】tóuténg-nǎorè〈成〉ailment

【头天】tóutiān〈名〉〈方〉**1**（昨天）previous day **2**（第一天）first day

【头童齿豁】tóutóng-chǐhuō〈成〉**1**〈本〉hair gone and teeth falling out **2**〈喻〉（衰老）senile

【头痛】tóutòng **A** ▸p. 50〈动〉have a headache: ～得厉害 have a terrible headache ‖ 这种药治疗～很有效。The medicine is an effective cure for a headache. **B**〈形〉troublesome: 这孩子真让他父亲～。The child is a real headache for his father.

【头痛医头，脚痛医脚】tóutòng yī tóu, jiǎotòng yī jiǎo〈成〉〈喻〉apply palliative remedies

【头头是道】tóutóu-shìdào〈成〉clear and logical: 他说得倒是～，可做起来根本不是那么回事。What he said was clear and logical, but what he did turned out completely differently.

【头头儿】tóutour〈名〉〈口〉boss: 他是这家企业的～。He is the boss of this enterprise.

【头陀】tóutuó〈名〉［佛教］mendicant Buddhist monk

【头衔】tóuxián〈名〉title: 学术～ academic title ‖ 少将～ the title of major general

【头像】tóuxiàng〈名〉sculpture of a head: 铜制～ bronze head

【头屑】tóuxiè〈名〉dandruff: 去～ get rid of dandruff

【头绪】tóuxù〈名〉main threads: 理不出个～来 be unable to get things into shape ‖ ～纷繁 have too many irons in the fire

【头雁】tóuyàn〈名〉lead wild goose

【头羊】tóuyáng〈名〉lead sheep

【头油】tóuyóu〈名〉hair oil

【头晕】tóuyūn〈形〉dizzy

【头晕目眩】tóuyūn-mùxuàn〈成〉feel dizzy

【头重脚轻】tóuzhòng-jiǎoqīng〈成〉be top-heavy

【头子】tóuzi〈名〉〈贬〉ringleader: 黑社会～ gang leader ‖ 土匪～ bandit chief

投[1] tóu〈动〉**1**（扔）hurl: ～标枪 throw the javelin ‖ 把球～进篮筐 toss the ball into the basket ‖ 他被～进监狱。He was thrown into prison. ▸～笔从戎，～掷 **2**（跳入）throw oneself into: ▸～河，自～罗网 **3**（放进去）drop: ▸～放，～票，～资 **4**（相合）fit in with: ▸～缘，情～意合 **5**（寄送）send: ▸～递，～稿 **6**（投射）cast: ～下影子 cast a shadow ‖ ～以爱慕的眼光 give sb. an adoring look ‖ 把目光～向远方 cast one's eyes into the distance ▸～影 **7**（投靠）go to: ▸～奔，～宿，弃暗～明

投[2] tóu〈动〉〈口〉rinse: 把衣服～干净。Rinse the washing out. ‖ 先用清水～一～，再打肥皂。Dip it into water before applying soap.

【投案】tóu'àn〈动〉turn oneself in to the police: ～自首 turn oneself in to the police

【投保】tóubǎo〈动〉insure: ～人寿 take out life insurance ‖ ～金额 insured amount ‖ ～人 policy-holder

【投奔】tóubèn〈动〉seek refuge: ～亲戚 go to one's relatives for help ‖ ～革命 join in the revolution

【投笔从戎】tóubǐ-cóngróng〈成〉forsake the pen for the sword

【投币式】tóubìshì〈形〉coin-operated: ～公用电话 pay phone

【投畀豺虎】tóubì-cháihǔ〈成〉feel strong indignation against evildoers

【投鞭断流】tóubiān-duànliú〈成〉〈喻〉[of an army] mighty and strong

【投标】tóubiāo〈动〉make a bid: 参加～ put in a tender ‖ ～建造公路 submit a tender for road construction ‖ 竞价～ competitive tender

【投产】tóuchǎn〈动〉go into operation: 化肥厂去年建成～。The chemical fertilizer plant went into production last year.

【投诚】tóuchéng〈动〉switch allegiances: 敌军纷纷起义～。Many enemy soldiers revolted and came over to our side.

【投弹】tóudàn〈动〉**1**（指炸弹）bomb **2**（指手榴弹）throw a hand grenade: ～训练 train in grenade-throwing

【投档】tóudàng〈动〉submit students' files

【投档线】tóudàngxiàn〈名〉admissions cut-off mark: 已达重点大学～ meet the admissions cut-off mark for a key university

【投敌】tóudí〈动〉defect to the enemy: 叛国～ commit treason and defect to the enemy

【投递】tóudì〈动〉deliver: ～报纸 deliver newspapers ‖ 无法～的信件 dead letter

【投递员】tóudìyuán ▸p. 966〈名〉postman

【投毒】tóudú〈动〉poison: 往井里～ poison a well

【投放】tóufàng〈动〉**1**（放进）throw in: ～鱼饵 throw in the bait **2**（用于）put into circulation: ～资金 invest ‖ 为兴修水利，～了大量劳力。A lot of labour has been put into water conservancy projects. **3**（供应）launch: 将新产品～市场 launch a new product

【投稿】tóugǎo〈动〉submit a piece of writing for publication: 向杂志～ submit a contribution to a magazine

【投稿人】tóugǎorén〈名〉contributor

【投工】tónggōng〈动〉contribute labour: 修这个水库需要投多少工? How many workdays are needed to build the reservoir?

【投合】tóuhé〈动〉**1**（合得来）agree: 他俩性情很～。The two of them are very similar. **2**（迎合）cater to: ～顾客的口味 cater to the tastes of customers

【投河】tóuhé〈动〉jump into a river to drown oneself

【投机】tóujī **A**〈形〉agreeable: 话不～ disagreeable conversation ‖ 他俩越谈越～。The more they talked, the more they felt attracted towards each other. **B**〈动〉speculate: ～钻营 speculate and secure personal gains ‖ 在股票交易市场上～ play the stock market

【投机炒作】tóujī chǎozuò〈动〉speculate: 房地产市场中的～行为 real estate speculation

【投机倒把】tóujī-dǎobǎ〈成〉play the market: 取缔～ ban speculation and profiteering
【投机取巧】tóujī-qǔqiǎo〈成〉be opportunistic
【投机商】tóujīshāng〈名〉speculator
【投寄】tóujì〈动〉post: ～包裹 send a parcel by post ‖ ～信件 send a letter
【投井下石】tóujǐng-xiàshí = 落井下石 luòjǐng-xiàshí
【投军】tóujūn〈动〉〈旧〉join the army
【投考】tóukǎo〈动〉sign up for an examination: ～大学 sign up for a college entrance examination
【投靠】tóukào〈动〉go and seek refuge: ～亲友 go and seek refuge with one's relatives and friends ‖ ～有权势的人 seek the patronage of those in power ▸卖身～
【投篮】tóulán〈动〉sink a shot: ～不准 inaccurate shooting ‖ ～命中 make a basket
【投料】tóuliào〈名〉feeding
【投拍】tóupāi〈动〉start shooting (a film, etc.)
【投票】tóupiào〈动〉cast a vote: ～表决 decide by ballot ‖ 无记名～ vote by secret ballot ‖ ～站 polling station ‖ ～权 right to vote
【投其所好】tóuqísuǒhào〈成〉cater to sb.'s tastes
【投契】tóuqì〈形〉〈书〉congenial
【投枪】tóuqiāng〈名〉javelin
【投亲】tóuqīn〈动〉go and live with one's relatives: ～靠友 seek refuge with one's relatives and friends
【投球】tóuqiú〈动〉［体育］pitch (a ball)
【投入】tóurù **A**〈动〉**1**（参加）put into: ～生产 go into operation ‖ ～使用 be put into use ‖ ～战斗 go into battle **2**（全神贯注）be absorbed in: 她干什么事都很～。She concentrates on whatever she does. **3**（投放资金）invest: 各级政府应增加农业～。Governments at different levels should increase their investment in agriculture. **B**〈名〉investment: 教育～逐年增加。The input in education is increasing year on year.
【投射】tóushè〈动〉**1**（投掷）throw: 紧握标枪用力～ hold the javelin tight and throw it with all one's might **2**（射向）cast: 太阳从云海中升起，金色的光芒～在平静的海面上。The sun rises from a mass of clouds, casting its golden rays on the calm waters.
【投身】tóushēn〈动〉throw oneself into: ～革命 join in the revolution ‖ ～国防事业 dedicate oneself to national defence
【投生】tóushēng = 投胎 tóutāi
【投师】tóushī〈动〉seek instruction from a master: ～学艺 learn a trade from a master
【投石问路】tóushí-wènlù〈成〉sound out
【投手】tóushǒu〈名〉［体育］pitcher: ～犯规 baulk
【投书】tóushū〈动〉write a letter: ～报社 write to a newspaper
【投鼠忌器】tóushǔ-jìqì〈成〉〈喻〉hold back from taking action against an evildoer for fear of involving good people
【投诉】tóusù〈动〉complain: ～法院 appeal to a court ‖ 向消保委～产品质量问题 appeal to the consumer rights board about product quality ‖ ～电话 telephone complaint ‖ ～热线 complaint hotline
【投宿】tóusù〈动〉put up for the night: 到朋友处～数日 put up at a friend's place for a few nights
【投胎】tóutāi〈动〉be reincarnated
【投桃报李】tóutáo-bàolǐ〈成〉exchange gifts
【投降】tóuxiáng〈动〉surrender: 缴械～ lay down one's arms and surrender ‖ 无条件～ unconditional surrender
【投降派】tóuxiángpài〈名〉capitulator
【投向】tóuxiàng〈名〉orientation for: 优化贷款～ optimize the loan orientation
【投效】tóuxiào〈动〉〈书〉go and offer one's services: ～祖国 serve one's motherland
【投药】tóuyào〈动〉apply poison
【投医】tóuyī〈动〉see a doctor: ～求药 seek medical treatment ‖ 病急乱～。When a man is mortally ill, he will try any remedy.
【投影】tóuyǐng **A**〈动〉project: ～电视 projection television ‖ ～仪 projector **B**〈名〉shadow
【投影机】tóuyǐngjī〈名〉projector
【投映】tóuyìng〈动〉reflect: 月亮～在平静的湖面上。The moon was reflected in the calm surface of the lake.
【投缘】tóuyuán〈形〉agreeable: 他们俩一见面就很～。The two of them hit it off as soon as they met. ‖ 他们越谈越～。As they talked, they found that they got along better and better.
【投掷】tóuzhì〈动〉throw: ～标枪/手榴弹/铁饼 throw a javelin/hand grenade/discus ‖ ～硬币 toss a coin
【投注】tóuzhù **A**〈动〉**1**（倾注）throw oneself into: 把全副精力～到工作里 throw all one's energies into one's work **2**（投进去财物）lay down a stake **B**〈名〉lottery money: 本期体彩～总额为九千余万元。The total amount in the sports lottery is over 90 million *yuan*.
【投注站】tóuzhùzhàn〈名〉lottery booth: 福利彩票～ welfare lottery ticket booth
【投资】tóuzī **A**〈动〉invest: ～一百万元 invest a million *yuan* ‖ ～意向 investment intention ‖ 招商～ invite outside investment **B**〈名〉investment: 撤回～ withdraw an investment ‖ ～总额 gross investment ‖ 智力～ intellectual investment
【投资公司】tóuzī gōngsī〈名〉investment company
【投资环境】tóuzī huánjìng〈名〉investment climate
【投资基金】tóuzī jījīn〈名〉investment fund
【投资品】tóuzīpǐn〈名〉investments: 黄金～正在受到热捧。Gold investments are pretty hot right now.
【投资信托公司】tóuzī xìntuō gōngsī〈名〉investment trust company
【投资银行】tóuzī yínháng〈名〉investment bank; merchant bank〈英〉

骰 tóu

【骰子】tóuzi〈方〉= 色子 shǎizi

tǒu

钭（鈄） Tǒu〈名〉Tou [surname]

tòu

透 tòu

A〈动〉**1**（通过）penetrate: ～过现象看本质 see through appearances to get to the essence ‖ 玻璃能～光。Glass is pervious to light. **2**（泄露）reveal: ～个信儿 disclose a piece of information ‖ 有关会谈情况能～点消息吗? Can you let us know if there was anything that came out of the meeting? **3**（露出）show: 脸色白里～红 rosy-white complexion ‖ 他身上～着一股英雄气概。He looks like he has a heroic spirit.
B〈形〉**1**（透彻）clear: 把道理讲～ explain one's reasons clearly ‖ 谁也猜不～她的心事。Nobody is able to work out what's on her mind. ‖ 我把他的脾气摸～了。I know his moods inside out. **2**（极度）complete: 糟～了 be extremely bad ‖ 他浑身湿～了。He was wet through. ‖ 庄稼熟～了。The crops are quite ripe.
【透彻】tòuchè〈形〉thorough: 她对形势有～的了解。She has a thorough understanding of the situation. ‖ 演讲者把观点讲得很～。The speaker drove his point home.
【透底】tòudǐ〈动〉reveal the ins and outs of a matter: 这件事不能向任何人～。Do not reveal the ins and outs of this matter to just anyone.
【透雕】tòudiāo〈名〉［美术］fretwork
【透顶】tòudǐng〈副〉〈贬〉thoroughly: 腐败～ be rotten to the core ‖ 我竟然做出这等事情，真是糊涂～! How stupid of me to have done such a thing.
【透风】tòufēng〈动〉**1**（漏风）air: 门缝～儿。The cracks in the door let the air in. **2**（让风吹）dry in the air: 把箱子打开，让衣服透透风。Open the trunk and air the clothes. **3**（透露消息）leak: 关于这件事，他给我透了一点儿风。He gave me a tip off about it.
【透汗】tòuhàn〈名〉good sweat: 出一身～ sweat all over
【透镜】tòujìng〈名〉［物理］lens: 凹～ concave lens ‖ 凸～ convex lens
【透亮】tòuliang〈形〉**1**（明亮）bright: 新建的办公楼既～又宽敞。The newly-built office buildings are bright and spacious. **2**（清楚明白）perfectly clear: 经你这么一解释，我心里就～了。Thanks to your explanation, it's perfectly clear to me now.
【透漏】tòulòu〈动〉reveal: ～消息 leak information
【透露】tòulù〈动〉reveal: ～风声 disclose information ‖ ～真相 reveal the truth ‖ 我向他～过这一打算。I let him in on my plan.
【透明】tòumíng〈形〉**1**（可透过光线）transparent: 半～ translucent ‖ 玻璃是一种～材料。Glass is a transparent material. **2**〈喻〉（公开）open: 评选活动公正、～。The election was fair and transparent.
【透明度】tòumíngdù〈名〉**1**（可透过光线）transparency: 增加～ increase transparency **2**（公开）openness: 政策的～ openness of policies
【透辟】tòupì〈形〉sharp: ～的分析 incisive analysis ‖ 道理讲得很～。The logic was explained very thoroughly.
【透气】tòuqì〈动〉**1**（通气）air: 我有点头晕，开窗透点气好吗? I'm a bit dizzy. Shall we open the windows and let in some fresh air? **2**（自由呼吸）breathe freely: 他被卡住脖子，透不过气来。He was strangled and couldn't breathe. **3**（通声气）disclose information: 公司里上下不～，工作很难开展。There is a lack of communication between senior and lower levels of the company.
【透气性】tòuqìxìng〈名〉［纺织］(air) permeability
【透视】tòushì **A**〈名〉**1**（指表现立体空间）perspective: ～图 scenograph **2**［医

t

学] fluoroscopy: X光～ X-ray examination **B**〈动〉〈喻〉 see clearly

【透视镜】tòushìjìng〈名〉 perspective glass

【透熟】tòushú〈动〉 know thoroughly: 对数据～ have the data at one's fingertips ‖ 这本书的内容他～。 He is very familiar with the contents of this book.

【透水层】tòushuǐcéng〈名〉［地质］ permeable stratum

【透析】tòuxī **A**〈名〉［医学］ dialysis: 肾～ renal dialysis **B**〈动〉 make a thorough analysis: 本月国际形势～ penetrating analysis of the international affairs in this month

【透心儿凉】tòuxīnrliáng〈形〉〈口〉 be cold to the marrow

【透信儿】tòuxìnr〈动〉 leak information

【透雨】tòuyǔ〈名〉 soaking rain: 下了一场～。 It was a real downpour.

【透支】tòuzhī〈动〉 **1**［金融］ get an overdraft: 你的账户～了。 Your account is overdrawn. **2**（入不敷出） overspend: 他月月～。 Every month his expenditure exceeds his income. **3**（预支工资） draw one's salary in advance **4**〈喻〉（超出极限） surpass: 身心严重～ to burn the candle at both ends

tou

头（頭） tou〈后缀〉 **1**（用于名词后） [added to a noun]: ▸锄～, 骨～, 木～, 石～ **2**（用于方位名词后） [added to a word of location]: ▸后～, 里～, 上～, 下～ **3**（用于动词后） [added to a verb to form a noun]: ▸看～, 盼～, 想～ **4**（用于形容词后） [added to an adjective to form a noun]: ▸苦～, 甜～, 准～
▸tóu

tū

凸 tū〈形〉 protruding: 地面凹～不平。 The surface is bumpy.

【凸版】tūbǎn〈名〉［印刷］ relief printing plate: ～胶印 letterset

【凸轮】tūlún〈名〉［机械］ cam: ～传动 cam drive

【凸面镜】tūmiànjìng〈名〉［物理］ convex mirror

【凸透镜】tūtòujìng〈名〉［物理］ convex lens

【凸显】tūxiǎn〈动〉 show clearly: 矛盾已～出来。 The contradictions have already become apparent.

【凸现】tūxiàn〈动〉 appear distinctly

秃 tū〈形〉 **1**（没头发） bald: 他的头有点～了。 He's going bald. ▸～鹫, ～头 **2**（没枝叶） bare: ～树 leafless tree ‖ 荒山～岭 barren, untouched hill **3**（钝） blunt: 手钻磨～了。 This hand drill has become blunt. ‖ 这支铅笔～了。 This pencil is not sharp any more. **4**（不完整） unsatisfactory: 这剧本结尾有点～。 The play ends rather abruptly.

【秃笔】tūbǐ〈名〉〈喻〉 poor writing ability: 我这支～不行。 I'm no good at writing.

【秃疮】tūchuāng = 黄癣 huángxuǎn

【秃顶】tūdǐng **A**〈动〉 go bald: 他四十刚出头就开始～了。 He started to go bald in his early forties. **B**〈名〉 bald head

【秃鹫】tūjiù〈名〉 (cinereous) vulture

【秃瓢儿】tūpiáor〈名〉〈口〉 shaven head: 那男孩剃了个～。 The boy has a clean-shaven head.

【秃头】tūtóu **A**〈动〉 not have a hat on: 他在冬天也秃着头。 He doesn't wear a hat in winter. **B**〈名〉 **1**（指头） bald head: ～的老人 bald old man **2**（指人） bald-headed person: 你见过那个～吗? Have you seen that bald-headed man?

【秃子】tūzi〈名〉 baldy

【秃子头上的虱子——明摆着】 tūzi tóu-shàngde shīzi—míngbǎizhe〈歇后〉 it goes without saying

突¹ tū
A〈副〉 suddenly: ▸～变, ～然, 唐～, 异军～起
B〈动〉 **1**（猛冲） dash forward: ▸～击, ～破, 狼奔豕～ **2**（高于周围） stick out: 礁石～出水面。 The reef protrudes from the water.
C〈名〉〈书〉 chimney: ▸曲～徙薪

突² tū〈拟〉 **1**（指机器声响） chug: 我听见拖拉机爬坡时～～的响声。 I heard the chug-chug of the tractor as it struggled up the hill. **2**（指心脏跳动） pit-a-pat: 他的心脏～～直跳。 His heart went pit-a-pat.

【突变】tūbiàn〈动〉 **1**（突然改变） change suddenly: 神色/天气～ sudden change of look/weather ‖ 形势～ unexpected turn of events **2**［哲学］ leap **3**［生物］ mutate: 基因～ gene mutation

【突出】tūchū **A**〈动〉 **1**（冲出） break through: ～重围 break through a tight encirclement **2**（鼓出来） stick out: 颧骨～ prominent cheekbones ‖ 太阳穴处的青筋～。 The veins stood out at the temples. **3**（强调） stress: ～重点 lay emphasis on the key points ‖ 他从不～自己。 He never places himself in the spotlight. **B**〈形〉 outstanding: 成绩～ outstanding achievements ‖ 作出～的贡献 make remarkable contributions ‖ 他的作品比别人～。 His work stands out from those of others.

【突发】tūfā〈动〉 erupt: ～事件 unexpected event ‖ ～奇想 hit upon a strange idea ‖ 心脏病～ have a heart attack

【突飞猛进】tūfēi-měngjìn〈成〉 advance by leaps and bounds: 该国经济发展～。 The nation's economy has developed by leaps and bounds. ‖ 来这儿以后, 她的英语～。 Her English has improved enormously since she came.

【突击】tūjī〈动〉 **1**（指作战） make a raid: 我们向敌人左翼发起～。 We made a sudden charge on the enemy's left wing. ▸～队 **2**（指做事） do a rush job: ～检查 make a surprise inspection ‖ ～上项目 rush into a project ‖ ～花钱 rush to spend surplus funds ‖ 他为考试在～英语。 He's doing some cramming for his English exam.

【突击部队】tūjī bùduì〈名〉 shock troops

【突击队】tūjīduì〈名〉 commando

【突厥】Tūjué〈名〉 Tujue [ethnic group in ancient China]

【突尼斯】Tūnísī〈名〉 **1**（指国家） Tunisia: ～人 Tunisian **2**（指城市） Tunis

【突破】tūpò〈动〉 **1**（攻破） break through: ～防线 break through a line of defence **2**（打破） surmount: ～难关 overcome a tough job ‖ ～记录 break a record ‖ 在动物克隆方面取得重大～ make a big breakthrough in animal cloning **3**［体育］ break through the opponent's defence

【突破口】tūpòkǒu〈名〉［军事］ breach: 〈喻〉 找到解决污染问题的～ crack the pollution problem

【突起】tūqǐ〈动〉 break out: 狂风～。 A fierce gale sprang up. ‖ 异军～ a new force suddenly coming to the fore

【突然】tūrán〈形〉 sudden: ～死亡 sudden death ‖ 她听到这消息感到很～。 The news took her by surprise.

【突然死亡法】tūránsǐwáng fǎ〈名〉［体育］ sudden death

【突然袭击】tūrán-xíjī〈成〉 surprise attack

【突如其来】tūrúqílái〈成〉 appear out of nowhere: ～的变化 sudden change

【突审】tūshěn〈动〉 subject a suspect to a surprise interrogation: ～犯罪嫌疑人 bring a suspect to a sudden trial

【突突】tūtū〈拟〉 [sound of a running engine] chug: 发动机～地发动起来了。 The engine started chugging.

【突围】tūwéi〈动〉 make a sortie: ～成功 make a successful sortie

【突兀】tūwù〈形〉 **1**（高耸） towering: 山石～ lofty crags **2**（出乎意外） sudden: 事情来得如此～, 他简直不知所措了。 It all happened so suddenly that he had no idea what to do.

【突袭】tūxí = 突然袭击 tūrán-xíjī

【突显】tūxiǎn〈动〉 protrude conspicuously

【突现】tūxiàn〈动〉 **1**（突然显现） appear suddenly **2**（突出显现） show distinctly

葖 tū ▸蓇葖 gūtū

tú

图（圖） tú
A〈名〉 **1**（图画） picture: 绘～ draw a picture ‖ 看～识字 learn characters with the aid of pictures ▸～画, 插～ **2**（计划） plan: 别无他～ have no other intention ▸宏～, 意～
B〈动〉 **1**（谋划） plan: ▸～谋, 企～, 妄～ **2**（贪图） seek: ～安逸 seek ease and comfort ‖ 不～名, 不～利。 Seek neither fame nor wealth. ▸贪～, 惟利是～

【图案】tú'àn〈名〉 pattern: ～设计 pattern design ‖ 花卉～ floral design

【图版】túbǎn〈名〉［印刷］ plate

【图表】túbiǎo〈名〉 chart: 统计～ statistical chart

【图财害命】 túcái-hàimìng = 谋财害命 móucái-hàimìng

【图钉】túdīng〈名〉 drawing pin〈英〉; thumbtack〈美〉

【图画】túhuà〈名〉 drawing: 画～ draw a picture ‖ ～课 drawing class

【图画文字】túhuà wénzì〈名〉［语言］ pictography

【图画纸】túhuàzhǐ〈名〉 drawing paper

【图籍】tújí〈名〉〈书〉 maps of territory and census registers

【图记】tújì〈名〉 **1**（图章） seal **2**（标志） sign

【图鉴】tújiàn〈名〉 [usu used in book titles] illustrated handbook: 《鸟类动物～》 *Illustrated Handbook of Birds*

【图解】tújiě〈名〉 diagram: 用～说明 explain through a diagram

【图景】tújǐng〈名〉 **1**（指景物） scene in a picture **2**（指景象） prospect: 新的工作为他展现出光明的～。 The new job gives him bright prospects.

【图卷】tújuàn〈名〉 picture scroll

【图例】túlì〈名〉 legend

【图谋】túmóu **A**〈动〉 plot: ～夺权 contrive a plot to seize power ‖ ～私利 seek personal gains **B**〈名〉 plot: 粉碎敌对势力的～ smash the conspiracy of hostile forces ‖ 另有～ have other plans

【图谋不轨】túmóu-bùguǐ〈成〉hatch a plot: 一个～的危险人物 a dangerous figure given to hatching unlawful plots

【图片】túpiàn〈名〉 picture: ～展 photo exhibition ‖ ～社 picture service

【图谱】túpǔ〈名〉 collection of illustrative plates: 中草药～ an atlas of Chinese medicines

【图穷匕首见】tú qióng bǐshǒu xiàn〈成〉〈喻〉hidden intentions are always exposed in the end

【图穷匕见】túqióngbǐxiàn = 图穷匕首见 tú qióng bǐshǒu xiàn

【图书】túshū〈名〉 books: ～交易会 book fair ‖ ～目录 library catalogue ‖ 科技～ science books ‖ 外文～ foreign language books ‖ ～管理员 librarian

【图书馆】túshūguǎn〈名〉 library: 国家/公共～ national/public library

【图说】túshuō〈名〉 illustrated handbook

【图腾】túténg〈名〉 totem: ～崇拜 totem worship

【图瓦卢】Túwǎlú〈名〉 Tuvalu

【图文并茂】túwén-bìngmào〈成〉 be excellent in both illustrations and text

【图文电视】túwén diànshì〈名〉 teletext

【图像】túxiàng〈名〉 image: ～清晰 the image is clear

【图形】túxíng〈名〉 graph: 绘制～ draw a graph

【图样】túyàng〈名〉 design: 车床～ design for a lathe

【图章】túzhāng〈名〉 stamp: 加盖～ affix a seal ‖ 橡皮～ rubber stamp

【图纸】túzhǐ〈名〉 blueprint: 工程～ project blueprint ‖ 施工～ blueprint

荼 tú

〈名〉〈古〉 **1**（指苦菜） bitter edible plant **2**（指白花） white flowers of reeds, etc.: ▸如火如～

【荼毒】túdú〈动〉〈书〉 torment: ～生灵 plunge the people into the depths of suffering

【荼蘼】túmí〈名〉［植物］ roseleaf raspberry

徒 tú

A〈动〉 be on foot: ▸～步

B〈名〉 **1**（徒弟） disciple: 尊师爱～ respect teachers and love students ▸～弟, ～工, 门～, 学～ **2**〈贬〉（指某种人） character: ▸赌～, 匪～, 叛～ **3**（指宗教信徒） religious follower: ▸教～, 信～ **4**〈书〉（指刑罚） prison sentence: ▸～刑

C〈形〉 bare: ▸～手

D〈副〉 **1**（仅仅） merely: ▸～有虚名, 家～四壁 **2**（枉然） in vain: ～费心机 rack one's brains in vain ‖ ～费唇舌 waste one's breath ▸～劳

【徒步】túbù〈动〉 be on foot: ～旅行 travel on foot ‖ ～探险 walking expedition

【徒弟】túdì〈名〉 disciple: 收～ take an apprentice

【徒费唇舌】túfèi-chúnshé〈成〉waste one's breath

【徒工】túgōng = 学徒工 xuétúgōng

【徒唤奈何】túhuàn-nàihé〈成〉 cry in vain

【徒劳】túláo〈动〉 work to no avail: ～之举 futile effort ‖ ～往返 make a trip in vain

【徒劳无功】túláo-wúgōng〈成〉 work to no avail

【徒然】túrán〈副〉 **1**（枉然） in vain: ～耗费精力 waste one's energy **2**（仅仅） merely

【徒手】túshǒu〈形〉 unarmed: ～格斗 fight with bare fists

【徒手操】túshǒucāo〈名〉 free-standing exercises

【徒托空言】tútuō-kōngyán〈成〉 make empty promises: 相信我，我绝不是～。 Trust me. I'm not making empty promises.

【徒刑】túxíng〈名〉［法律］ prison sentence: 判两年～，缓期两年执行 sentence sb. to two years' imprisonment suspended for two years ▸有期～, 无期～

【徒有其表】túyǒu-qíbiǎo〈成〉 be good in appearance only

【徒有其名】túyǒu-qímíng = 徒有虚名 túyǒu-xūmíng

【徒有虚名】túyǒu-xūmíng〈成〉 not live up to one's name: 民主变得～。 Democracy has become just a name.

【徒子徒孙】túzǐ-túsūn〈成〉 **1**（徒弟和徒孙） disciples and followers **2**〈贬〉（党羽） hangers-on and their spawn

途 tú

〈名〉 road: 长～汽车 coach ‖ 路～遥远 far away ▸前～

【途程】túchéng〈名〉 way: 革命～ course of a revolution ‖ 人类进化的～ the evolution of the human species

【途次】túcì〈名〉〈书〉 travellers' lodging

【途经】tújīng〈动〉 pass by: ～香港到达广州 pass through Hong Kong on the way to Guangzhou

【途径】tújìng〈名〉 way: 寻求解决问题的～ find a solution to the problem ‖ 外交～ diplomatic channel

涂（塗） tú

A〈名〉 **1**〈书〉（泥） mud: ▸～炭 **2**（海涂） shoal: ▸滩～

B〈动〉 **1**（涂抹） apply: ～药膏 apply some ointment ‖ 在表面～上胶水 apply some glue to the surface ▸～饰, ～脂抹粉 **2**（抹去） cross out: 把写错的字～掉 cross out wrong characters ▸～改 **3**（乱涂乱画） scribble: 不要在文物上乱～。 Don't scribble on the artefacts. ‖ 这书～得乱七八糟。 The book was scrawled all over. ▸～鸦

【涂层】túcéng〈名〉 coating: 特氟隆～ Teflon coating

【涂改】túgǎi〈动〉 alter: ～账目 tamper with the accounts ‖ ～无效 invalid if altered

【涂改液】túgǎiyè〈名〉 correction fluid

【涂料】túliào〈名〉 coating: 防腐～ anticorrosive paint

【涂抹】túmǒ〈动〉 **1**（抹） apply: ～药膏 apply some ointment **2**（乱涂乱画） scribble: 信笔～ doodle

【涂片】túpiàn〈名〉［医学］ smear: 血样～ blood smear

【涂饰】túshì〈动〉 **1**（涂上） paint: ～家具 paint furniture **2**（粉刷） whitewash: ～墙壁 whitewash a wall

【涂炭】tútàn **A**〈名〉〈书〉 utter misery: ▸生灵～ **B**〈动〉 tyrannize: ～百姓 wreak havoc among the people

【涂写】túxiě〈动〉 scribble: 禁止～! No scribbling! ‖ 他们把标语～在墙上。 They scrawled their slogans on the walls.

【涂鸦】túyā〈名〉〈谦〉 scrawl: 信笔～ write at random

【涂乙】túyǐ〈动〉〈书〉 prune

【涂泽】túzé〈动〉〈书〉 whitewash

【涂脂抹粉】túzhī-mǒfěn〈成〉〈喻〉 prettify: 别为自己～。 Don't be glossing over your faults.

菟 tú

▸於菟 wūtú ▸tù

屠 tú

〈动〉 **1**（宰杀） slaughter: ～狗 butcher a dog ▸～夫, ～宰 **2**（残杀） massacre: ▸～城, ～戮, ～杀

【屠场】túchǎng〈名〉 slaughterhouse

【屠城】túchéng〈动〉 massacre the inhabitants of a conquered city

【屠刀】túdāo〈名〉 butcher's knife

【屠夫】túfū〈名〉 **1**〈旧〉（宰杀牲畜者） butcher **2**〈喻〉（残杀人民者） ruthless ruler

【屠户】túhù〈名〉〈旧〉 butcher

【屠戮】túlù〈动〉〈书〉 massacre

【屠杀】túshā〈动〉 massacre: 叛军～了该城无数无辜居民。 The rebel troops massacred numerous innocent residents of the city.

【屠苏】túsū〈名〉〈古〉 *tusu* [ancient wine, usu drunk on lunar New Year's Day]

【屠宰】túzǎi〈动〉 butcher: ～牲畜 slaughter animals

【屠宰场】túzǎichǎng〈名〉 slaughterhouse

酴 tú

〈名〉〈书〉 distiller's yeast

【酴醾】túmí〈名〉 **1**〈古〉（指酒） double-fermented wine **2** = 荼蘼 túmí

tǔ

土[1] tǔ

A〈名〉 **1**（土壤） earth: 红～地 red earth ‖ ～墙 earthen wall ‖ 瘠～ poor soil ▸～坯, 黏～, 沃～ **2**（土地） land: ▸～地, 国～ **3**（故土） hometown: 热～难离 it's hard to depart from one's hometown ▸本～, 故～ **4**（指鸦片） crude opium: ▸烟～

B〈形〉 **1**（本地） native: ▸～产, ～著 **2**（不合潮流） unrefined: ▸～包子 **3**（自制） home-made: ～设备 home-made equipment ▸～布

土[2] Tǔ

▸土家族 Tǔjiāzú, 土族 Tǔzú

【土邦】tǔbāng〈名〉 native state

【土包子】tǔbāozi〈名〉〈贬〉 (country) bumpkin

【土崩瓦解】tǔbēng-wǎjiě〈成〉disintegrate: 一个泱泱大国一夜之间～。 A once great power collapsed overnight.

【土鳖】tǔbiē〈名〉［昆虫］ ground beetle

【土拨鼠】tǔbōshǔ〈名〉 marmot

【土布】tǔbù〈名〉 handwoven cloth

【土产】tǔchǎn **A**〈形〉 local: ～品 local produce **B**〈名〉 local produce: 经销～ sell local products

【土地】tǔdì〈名〉 **1**（土壤） land: ～肥沃 fertile soil ‖ ～开发 land development ‖ ～资源 land resources **2**（领土） territory: ～广阔，物产丰富 vast territory with abundant resources

【土地承包制】tǔdì chéngbāozhì〈名〉land contract system

【土地改革】tǔdì gǎigé〈名〉 land reform

【土地】tǔdi ▸**p. 274**〈名〉 village god

【土地庙】tǔdìmiào〈名〉 temple housing the village god

【土豆】tǔdòu〈名〉 potato

【土耳其】Tǔ'ěrqí〈名〉 Turkey: ～人 Turk ‖ ～语 Turkish
【土法】tǔfǎ〈名〉 indigenous method: ～打井 dig a well using indigenous methods ‖ ～上马 start by using indigenous methods
【土方】tǔfāng〈名〉1（指计量单位）cubic metre of earth 2（指土方工程） earthwork
【土肥】tǔféi〈名〉 farmyard manure
【土匪】tǔfěi〈名〉 bandit
【土改】tǔgǎi〈简称〉= 土地改革
【土岗】tǔgǎng〈名〉 mound
【土埂】tǔgěng〈名〉 bank of earth between fields
【土棍】tǔgùn〈名〉 local bully
【土豪】tǔháo〈名〉 local tyrant
【土豪劣绅】tǔháo-lièshēn〈成〉 local tyrants and evil gentry
【土话】tǔhuà〈名〉 local dialect
【土皇帝】tǔhuángdì〈名〉 local tyrant
【土黄】tǔhuáng〈形〉 yellowish brown
【土货】tǔhuò〈名〉 local produce
【土籍】tǔjí〈名〉 native place of one's ancestors
【土家族】Tǔjiāzú〈名〉 Tujia ethnic group
【土建】tǔjiàn〈名〉 civil engineering: ～工程 civil engineering project
【土库曼斯坦】Tǔkùmànsītǎn〈名〉 Turkmenistan: ～人 Turkmen ‖ ～语 Turkmen
【土牢】tǔláo〈名〉 dungeon
【土老帽儿】tǔlǎomàor〈名〉〈口〉(country) bumpkin
【土老儿】tǔlǎor〈名〉〈旧〉 clodhopper
【土礼】tǔlǐ〈名〉 gift of local produce
【土里土气】tǔli-tǔqì〈形〉 uncouth: 打扮得～ be unrefined in one's dress
【土楼】tǔlóu〈名〉 tamped earth circular building
【土霉素】tǔméisù〈名〉［药学］ oxytetracycline
【土木】tǔmù〈名〉 building: 大兴～ go in for large-scale construction
【土木工程】tǔmù gōngchéng〈名〉 civil engineering: ～师 civil engineer
【土牛木马】tǔniú-mùmǎ〈成〉〈喻〉 thing/person of no value
【土偶】tǔ'ǒu〈名〉 clay idol
【土坯】tǔpī〈名〉 adobe
【土气】tǔqì A〈名〉 rustic style B〈形〉 rustic
【土丘】tǔqiū〈名〉 mound
【土壤】tǔrǎng〈名〉 soil: ～肥沃 fertile soil ‖ ～改良 soil improvement
【土壤污染】tǔrǎng wūrǎn〈名〉 soil contamination
【土壤学】tǔrǎngxué〈名〉 soil science: ～家 pedologist
【土人】tǔrén〈名〉 native: 澳大利亚～ Australian aborigine
【土色】tǔsè ►p. 863〈形〉 ashen: 面如～ turn deadly pale
【土生土长】tǔshēng-tǔzhǎng〈成〉 be locally born and bred: 他是～的福建人。He is a Fujian man born and bred.
【土石方】tǔshífāng〈名〉 cubic metre of earth and stone
【土司】tǔsī〈名〉1（指体系） system of appointing hereditary chieftains from minority ethnic groups in the Yuan, Ming and Qing dynasties 2（指人） national minority hereditary chieftain
【土俗】tǔsú A〈名〉 native custom: ～淳朴 simple native custom B〈形〉 vulgar: ～的语言 vulgar language
【土特产】tǔtèchǎn〈名〉 local speciality

【土头土脑】tǔtóu-tǔnǎo〈成〉 rustic
【土戏】tǔxì〈名〉1（土家族戏曲） Tujia opera 2（壮族戏曲） Zhuang opera
【土星】Tǔxīng〈名〉［天文］ Saturn: ～光环 Saturn's rings
【土腥气】tǔxīngqì〈名〉 smell of the soil
【土腥味儿】tǔxīngwèir = 土腥气 tǔxīngqì
【土洋结合】tǔ-yáng jiéhé〈成〉 combine traditional and modern methods
【土仪】tǔyí〈名〉〈书〉gift of local produce
【土语】tǔyǔ = 土话 tǔhuà
【土葬】tǔzàng〈动〉 bury in the ground
【土政策】tǔzhèngcè〈名〉 local policy
【土质】tǔzhì〈名〉 quality and composition of the soil: ～肥沃 fertile soil
【土著】tǔzhù〈名〉 aborigine: 澳大利亚～ Australian aborigines ‖ 印第安～部落 native Indian tribe
【土专家】tǔzhuānjiā〈名〉 self-taught expert
【土族】Tǔzú〈名〉 Tu ethnic group

吐 tǔ〈动〉1（从口中出来） spit: ～舌头 stick out one's tongue ‖ ～唾沫 spit out saliva ‖ 不准随地～! No spitting! 2（说） tell: ～出一肚子苦水 pour out all one's grievances ‖ ～怨气 vent one's grievances ►～露，谈～ 3（长出来） put forth: 蚕～丝。Silkworms spin out silk. ►～穗，～絮
►tù
【吐蕃】Tǔbō〈名〉 Tubo [ethnic group once inhabiting the Qinghai-Tibetan plateau]
【吐翠】tǔcuì〈动〉〈书〉 look fresh and green
【吐故纳新】tǔgù-nàxīn〈成〉 get rid of the old and take in the new
【吐口】tǔkǒu〈动〉 tell: 问了半天，他就是不～。He refused to utter a word even after repeated questioning.
【吐露】tǔlù〈动〉 reveal: ～内心深处的想法 reveal one's innermost thoughts ‖ ～心声 disclose one's heartfelt wishes ‖ ～真情 unbosom oneself
【吐气】tǔqì〈动〉 feel elated: ►扬眉～
【吐绶鸡】tǔshòujī = 火鸡 huǒjī
【吐司】tǔsī〈名〉 toast
【吐穗】tǔsuì〈动〉［农业］ put forth ears: 玉米和小米正在～。The maize and millet are forming ears.
【吐絮】tǔxù〈动〉［农业］ [of bolls] open
【吐谷浑】Tǔyùhún〈名〉 Kokonor [ethnic group of ancient times living in present-day Gansu and Qinghai provinces]
【吐字】tǔzì〈动〉 enunciate: ～清楚 pronounce clearly

钍（釷） tǔ〈名〉［化学］ thorium (Th)

tù

吐 tù〈动〉1（指从口中） throw up: 恶心得想～ feel sick ►～血，呕～ 2〈喻〉（指被迫退还） give up unwillingly: ～出全部赃款 hand over all the dirty money
►tǔ
【吐沫】tùmo〈名〉 saliva
【吐血】tùxiě〈动〉 spit blood

兔 tù〈名〉 rabbit: ►家～，野～
【兔唇】tùchún = 唇裂 chúnliè
【兔毫】tùháo〈名〉 writing brush made of rabbit's hair
【兔儿爷】tùryé〈名〉 clay figurine with the head of a rabbit [a toy for the Mid-Autumn Festival]
【兔死狗烹】tùsǐ-gǒupēng〈成〉〈喻〉 trusted aids are eliminated when they have outlived their usefulness
【兔死狐悲】tùsǐ-húbēi〈成〉〈喻〉 like feels for like
【兔脱】tùtuō〈动〉〈书〉 flee
【兔崽子】tùzǎizi〈名〉〈粗〉bastard〈粗〉
【兔子】tùzi〈名〉 rabbit
【兔子不吃窝边草】tùzi bùchī wōbiāncǎo〈俗〉 even a villain doesn't harm the next door neighbours
【兔子尾巴长不了】tùzi wěiba chángbuliǎo〈歇后〉〈贬〉 won't last long

堍 tù〈名〉 ramp of a bridge

菟 tù
►tú
【菟丝子】tùsīzǐ〈名〉［中药］ seed of Chinese dodder

tuān

湍 tuān
A〈名〉〈书〉 rapids: ►急～
B〈形〉 torrential: ►～急
【湍急】tuānjí〈形〉 rapid: 水流～。The current is rapid.
【湍流】tuānliú〈名〉〈书〉 rapids
【湍流层】tuānliúcéng〈名〉［气象］ turbosphere

tuán

团[1]（團） tuán
A〈形〉（圆形） round;（环形） circular: ～城 round city ‖ ～脸 round face ►～扇
B〈动〉1（使成球状） roll sth. into a ball: ～饭团 make rice balls ‖ ～煤球儿 make egg-shaped briquettes 2（会聚） assemble: ►～结，～聚，～圆
C〈名〉1［军事］ regiment 2（团队） group: 考察～ observation group ‖ 旅游～ tour group ►财～，剧～ 3（共青团） Communist Youth League of China: ～中央 Central Committee of the Communist Youth League of China ►～员，入～ 4（球状物） ball-shaped thing: 缩成一～ curl up into a ball ‖ 线～ ball of thread ►蒲～
D〈量〉 [for sth. in the shape of a ball]: 一～废纸 a ball of waste paper ‖ 一～乱麻 a knot of entangled hemp ‖ 一～毛线 a ball of knitting wool

团[2]（糰） tuán〈名〉stuffed dumpling made of glutinous rice flour: ►汤～
【团拜】tuánbài〈动〉 gather together to exchange greetings
【团部】tuánbù〈名〉［军事］ regiment headquarters
【团队】tuánduì〈名〉 team: 体育～ sports team ‖ ～精神 team spirit
【团费】tuánfèi〈名〉 League membership fees
【团粉】tuánfěn〈名〉 cooking starch
【团购】tuángòu〈动〉 group-purchase: 建材～ group purchase of building materials
【团徽】tuánhuī〈名〉 Youth League badge
【团伙】tuánhuǒ〈名〉〈贬〉 gang: 犯罪～ criminal gang ‖ 贩毒～ drug ring ‖ 流氓

～ gang of hoodlums

【团结】tuánjié A〈动〉 unite: ～一切爱国人士 unite all patriots ‖ ～一致 unite as one ‖ ～就是力量。 Unity is strength. B〈形〉 harmonious: 大家很～。 Everybody is very friendly.

【团聚】tuánjù〈动〉 1（相聚） have a reunion: 家庭～ family reunion ‖ 与亲人～ be reunited with one's family and relatives 2（团结） assemble: ～千千万万的民众 gather thousands upon thousands of people

【团粒】tuánlì〈名〉［农业］ granule: ～结构 granular structure

【团练】tuánliàn〈名〉〈旧〉 local militia organized by the landlords to suppress peasant rebellions

【团圞】tuánluán A〈形〉 [of the moon] round: ～明月 bright full moon B〈动〉 have a reunion: 合家～ family reunion

【团脐】tuánqí〈名〉 1（圆形蟹甲） round abdomen of a female crab 2（雌蟹） female crab: 人们喜欢～胜过尖脐。People prefer female crabs to male ones.

【团扇】tuánshàn〈名〉 round fan

【团体】tuántǐ〈名〉 organization: 民间～ non-governmental organization ‖ 学术～ academic association ‖ 宗教～ religious organization

【团体操】tuántǐcāo〈名〉 group callisthenics: ～表演 group callisthenics performance

【团体冠军】tuántǐ guànjūn〈名〉 team title

【团体旅游】tuántǐ lǚyóu〈名〉 group tour

【团体票】tuántǐpiào〈名〉 group ticket

【团体赛】tuántǐsài〈名〉 team competition

【团体项目】tuántǐ xiàngmù〈名〉 team event

【团团】tuántuán〈形〉 1（圆形） round: ～的小脸 round little face 2（环绕的样子） all-round: 被～围住 be completely surrounded

【团团转】tuántuánzhuàn〈动〉 go round and round: 急得～ pace up and down in agitation ‖ 忙得～ be up to one's ears with things

【团鱼】tuányú = 鳖 biē

【团员】tuányuán〈名〉 1（团体成员） member of a group: 代表团～ member of a delegation ‖ 文工团～ member of an art troupe 2（共青团员） member of the Communist Youth League of China: 共青～ Communist Youth League member

【团圆】tuányuán A〈动〉 have a reunion: ～饭 family reunion dinner ‖ 夫妻～ reunion of husband and wife ‖ 骨肉～ family reunion ‖ 作者设计了一个大～的结局。 The writer contrived a happy ending. B〈形〉 round: 这个人～脸，大眼睛。 This person has a round face and large eyes.

【团圆节】Tuányuánjié〈名〉 Mid-Autumn Festival

【团章】tuánzhāng〈名〉 constitution of the Communist Youth League

【团长】tuánzhǎng〈名〉 1［军事］ regimental commander 2（指代表团） head of a delegation: 代表团～ chief of the delegation

【团支部】tuánzhībù〈名〉 Communist Youth League branch

【团中央】tuánzhōngyāng〈名〉 Communist Youth League Central Committee

【团子】tuánzi〈名〉 dumpling: 菜～ cornmeal dumpling with vegetable stuffing ‖ 糯米～ dumpling made of glutinous rice

【团总支】tuánzǒngzhī〈名〉general branch of the Communist Youth League

【团组织】tuánzǔzhī〈名〉 organization of the Communist Youth League

【团坐】tuánzuò〈动〉 sit in a circle

抟（摶） tuán = 团¹ tuán B1

tuǎn

曈 tuǎn〈名〉 village: 走村串～ wander from village to village ‖ 贾～ Jia Village

tuī

忒 tuī〈副〉〈方〉 too: 那件裙子～贵。 That dress is too expensive. ‖ 你骑车骑得～慢。 You are riding the bicycle so slowly. ▸tè

推 tuī〈动〉 1（往外用力） push: ～车 push a cart ‖ ～铅球 throw the shot put ‖ 他从后面～了我一把。 He gave me a push from behind. ‖ 他用力一～，门就开了。 He gave the door a mighty push and it opened. ▸～倒，顺水～舟 2（削剪） pare: ～草坪 mow the lawn ‖ 用刨子把桌面～平 smooth out a table top with a plane ▸～头 3（碾磨） grind: ～点儿白面 grind some wheat into flour 4（使事情开展） push forward: ～向极端 push to the extreme ‖ 把反贪污运动～向高潮 propel the anti-corruption drive to a climax ▸～动，～广，～销 5（推迟） postpone: ～后几天 postpone for a few days ‖ 今天能做的事绝不要～到明天。 Never put off till tomorrow what can be done today. ▸～迟，～延 6（推举） elect: ～为首领 elect sb. as leader ▸～荐，～举 7（推崇） praise highly: ▸～崇，～许，～重 8（推断） infer: ▸～测，～论，类～ 9（辞让） decline: ▸～辞，～让 10（推诿） refuse on a certain pretext: ～病不去 refuse to go on the pretext of illness ‖ ～来～去 make all sorts of excuses

【推本溯源】tuīběn-sùyuán〈成〉 ascertain the cause

【推波助澜】tuībō-zhùlán〈成〉 add fuel to the fire

【推测】tuīcè〈动〉 infer: 根据案发现场～ make speculations based on the scene of the crime

【推陈出新】tuīchén-chūxīn〈成〉 weed through the old to bring forth the new

【推诚相见】tuīchéng-xiāngjiàn〈成〉 deal with sb. in good faith

【推迟】tuīchí〈动〉 delay: ～行期 postpone one's departure until a later date ‖ ～选举 put off an election

【推崇】tuīchóng〈动〉 praise highly: ～备至 praise sb. to the skies ‖ 大家都十分～他的教学方法。 Everybody has a lot of respect for his teaching method.

【推出】tuīchū〈动〉 release: ～新产品 launch a new product ‖ 隆重～ promote in a grand way ‖ 新近～的电影 recently released film

【推辞】tuīcí〈动〉 decline: 我们诚心邀请你当顾问，你就别～了。 We cordially invite you to consult for us, please do not turn us down.

【推戴】tuīdài〈动〉〈书〉 support sb. in assuming leadership: 竭诚～ support sb. wholeheartedly

【推挡】tuīdǎng〈名〉［体育］ half volley

【推宕】tuīdàng〈动〉〈书〉 put off

【推导】tuīdǎo〈动〉 derive: 你的方程式～有毛病。 There are flaws in your derivation of the equations.

【推倒】tuīdǎo〈动〉 1（使倒） push over: ～土墙 push down an earthen wall ‖ 把某人/某物～在地 push sb./sth. to the ground 2（使不成立） reverse: ～前人的学说 reverse the previous theory ‖ 这个方案要～重来。 The proposal has to be reworked.

【推倒重来】tuīdǎo-chónglái〈成〉 make a new start

【推定】tuīdìng〈动〉 1（推举） elect: 大家～他为下次会议主席。 He was elected chairman of the next meeting. 2（推测断定） infer: 无罪/有罪～ presumption of innocence/guilt ‖ 我们还难以～他变卦的原因。 It's hard for us to tell why he's changed his mind.

【推动】tuīdòng〈动〉 drive: ～经济增长和社会的全面进步 promote economic growth and all-round social progress ‖ 科学技术～生产力的发展。 Science and technology propel productivity.

【推断】tuīduàn〈动〉 infer: 从前因～后果 deduce effect from cause ‖ 只有经过周密的调查和分析才能作出正确的～。 Correct inferences can be drawn only from careful investigation and analysis.

【推度】tuīduó〈动〉 infer

【推而广之】tuī'érguǎngzhī〈成〉 likewise

【推翻】tuīfān〈动〉 1（使垮台） overturn: ～反动政府 overthrow the reactionary government 2（使不成立） reverse: ～法院判决 overturn the court verdict ‖ ～原计划 cancel the original plan

【推高】tuīgāo〈动〉 push up: ～油价/房价 push up oil/housing prices

【推故】tuīgù〈动〉 give a pretext

【推广】tuīguǎng〈动〉 popularize: ～应用 popularize and apply ‖ ～普通话 popularize standard Chinese ‖ ～先进的工作方法 spread progressive working methods ‖ 大力～节能减排技术 vigorously promote techniques to conserve energy and reduce emissions

【推及】tuījí〈动〉 reach by analogy

【推己及人】tuījǐ-jírén〈成〉 put oneself in somebody else's shoes

【推见】tuījiàn〈动〉 imagine: 看书名和封面，就不难～这本书的类型。 By looking at its title and cover, it is not hard for you to tell what kind of book it is.

【推荐】tuījiàn〈动〉 recommend: 他经常向学生～优秀的科普作品。 He often recommends outstanding popular scientific works to his students. ‖ 我～她来当秘书。 I put her forward for secretary.

【推荐生】tuījiànshēng〈名〉 recommended student [not required to take an entrance exam]: ～名额 the quota of recommended students

【推荐信】tuījiànxìn〈名〉 letter of recommendation

【推介】tuījiè〈动〉 recommend and introduce: ～新书 recommend and introduce a new book ‖ ～会 promotion meeting

【推襟送抱】tuījīn-sòngbào〈成〉〈喻〉 treat sb. with sincerity

【推进】tuījìn〈动〉 1（使有进展） give impetus to: ～和平进程 advance the peace process ‖ ～政治体制改革 further the reform of the political system 2［军事］ advance: 部队正在向前～。 The troops are advancing.

【推究】tuījiū〈动〉 examine: ～缘由 study the whys and wherefores of things

【推举】tuījǔ〈动〉 elect: 大家～他为小组长。 They elected him group leader.

【推理】tuīlǐ〈动〉reason: 间接/直接～ indirect/direct inference ‖ 类比～ reasoning by analogy ‖ 演绎～ deductive reasoning
【推理小说】tuīlǐ xiǎoshuō〈名〉inference novel
【推力】tuīlì〈名〉1（指力量）driving force 2（指物理力）propulsion: 喷气发动机～ jet thrust
【推论】tuīlùn A〈动〉deduce B〈名〉deduction: 你的～缺乏说服力。Your deduction is not convincing enough.
【推磨】tuīmò〈动〉turn a millstone
【推拿】tuīná = 按摩 ànmó
【推铅球】tuīqiānqiú〈名〉［体育］shot put
【推敲】tuīqiāo〈动〉deliberate: ～词句 measure one's words ‖ 你的论点经不起～。Your argument doesn't stand up. ‖ 这一结论是经过仔细～的。The conclusion was reached with great deliberation.
【推情度理】tuīqíng-duólǐ〈成〉consider the circumstances and infer the reasons
【推求】tuīqiú〈动〉ascertain: ～对方的动机 try to find out what the other is after
【推却】tuīquè〈动〉decline: 借故～ decline with an excuse
【推让】tuīràng〈动〉decline out of modesty
【推人犯规】tuīrén fànguī〈名〉［体育］pushing [in basketball, etc.]
【推三阻四】tuīsān-zǔsì〈成〉decline with all sorts of excuses
【推射】tuīshè〈动〉［体育］push shoot: 一脚～，球应声入门。One push-shot, and the ball went in.
【推算】tuīsuàn〈动〉reckon: 我～他应该六十岁刚出头。I reckon he should be in his early sixties. ‖ 气象学家可以～日食发生的时间。Meteorologists can calculate when a solar eclipse will occur.
【推涛作浪】tuītāo-zuòlàng〈成〉stir up trouble
【推头】tuītóu〈动〉〈口〉1（给人理发）cut sb.'s hair 2（理发）have a haircut
【推土机】tuītǔjī〈名〉bulldozer
【推托】tuītuō〈动〉plead: 他～有事，没有参加会议。He made an excuse and did not attend the meeting.
【推脱】tuītuō〈动〉evade: ～责任 shirk a responsibility
【推诿】tuīwěi〈动〉pass the buck: 互相～ shift the blame onto one another
【推问】tuīwèn〈动〉interrogate
【推贤让能】tuīxián-ràngnéng〈成〉recommend the worthy and give way to the able
【推想】tuīxiǎng〈动〉imagine
【推销】tuīxiāo〈动〉promote sales: ～产品 push products ‖ ～员 salesperson
【推卸】tuīxiè〈动〉shirk: ～责任，委过于人 shirk responsibilities and shift the blame onto others
【推谢】tuīxiè〈动〉find an excuse to decline
【推心置腹】tuīxīn-zhìfù〈成〉bare one's soul: ～地谈话 have a heart-to-heart talk
【推行】tuīxíng〈动〉push: ～新的招生制度 push for a new enrolment system
【推许】tuīxǔ〈动〉commend: 他得到众人交口～。Everybody holds him in high regard.
【推选】tuīxuǎn〈动〉elect: ～某人为工会主席 elect sb. chairman of the union
【推延】tuīyán〈动〉postpone: 会议因故～五天。For some reason, the meeting has been postponed for five days.
【推演】tuīyǎn〈动〉deduce
【推移】tuīyí〈动〉1（指时间）elapse: 随着时间的～，情况会改善的。Things will get better with time. 2（指情形）develop
【推展】tuīzhǎn〈动〉1（推进）promote: 双边关系持续～。Relations between the two sides have continued to develop. 2（推介展销）recommend and exhibit for sale: ～一款新车 hold a promotional exhibition of a new car
【推知】tuīzhī〈动〉deduce: 由此可～其余。The rest may be deduced by analogy.
【推重】tuīzhòng〈动〉have a high regard for: 人们不仅～他的作品，更～他的人品。He is respected not just for his work but also his character.
【推子】tuīzi〈名〉clippers

tuí

颓（頹）tuí

A〈动〉1〈书〉（坍塌）collapse: ▸～垣断壁 2（衰败）decline: ▸～败
B〈形〉dejected: ▸～废, ～丧
【颓败】tuíbài〈形〉〈书〉decayed
【颓废】tuífèi〈形〉decadent: ～情绪 dispirited state of mind ‖ ～派 the decadents school
【颓风】tuífēng〈名〉〈书〉depraved customs: ～败俗 degenerate practice and depraved customs
【颓靡】tuímǐ〈形〉〈书〉downcast: 有些青年因未能考上大学而～。Some young people were devastated at not being admitted to college.
【颓然】tuírán〈形〉〈书〉dejected
【颓丧】tuísàng〈形〉despondent: 失败使他～。Defeat filled him with gloom. ‖ 他下岗后精神～。After he was laid off, he was really down in the dumps.
【颓势】tuíshì〈名〉declining tendency: 扭转～ retrieve a hopeless situation
【颓唐】tuítáng〈形〉dejected: 神情～ look depressed
【颓萎】tuíwěi〈形〉dejected
【颓垣断壁】tuíyuán-duànbì = 残垣断壁 cányuán-duànbì

tuǐ

腿 tuǐ

〈名〉1 ▸p. 614（指肢体）leg: 两～交叉 cross one's legs ‖ 鸡～ chicken leg ▸大～, 飞毛～, 小～ 2（指支撑部分）leg-shaped support: 桌子/椅子～ table/chair leg 3（指火腿）ham: 云～ Yunnan ham
【腿肚子】tuǐdùzi〈名〉〈口〉calf (of leg)
【腿脚】tuǐjiǎo〈名〉ability to walk: ～不便 have difficulty walking ‖ 老人～还很利落。The old man can walk briskly.
【腿勤手快】tuǐqín-shǒukuài〈成〉deft of hand and tireless in running around
【腿腕子】tuǐwànzi〈名〉ankle
【腿子】tuǐzi〈名〉〈口〉henchman: ▸狗～

tuì

退 tuì

〈动〉1（向后移动）move backwards: 只能前进，不能后～ must go forwards, not backwards ‖ ～一步说 even so ▸～缩, 撤～, 进～两难 2（使向后移）cause to move back: 把子弹～出来 unload a gun 3（退出）withdraw from: ▸～场, ～位, ～伍, ～休, 隐～ 4（减退）recede: 潮水～了。The tide is out. ‖ 洪水～了。The floods have subsided. ▸～潮, ～色, 衰～ 5（退还）return: ～礼 return a gift ‖ 三日内商品包～包换。The goods can be returned or exchanged within three days. ▸～还, ～票 6（取消）cancel: ～掉订货 cancel a goods order ▸～婚
【退保】tuìbǎo〈动〉surrender one's insurance policy: ～金额 surrender value
【退避】tuìbì〈动〉keep away: ～不及 be unable to get out of the way in time ‖ 他～一旁，静观动静。He stepped aside and watched which way the wind was blowing.
【退避三舍】tuìbì-sānshè〈成〉give way to avoid a conflict
【退兵】tuìbīng〈动〉1（撤退军队）withdraw: 下令～ order a retreat ‖ 全线～ be in full retreat 2（使敌军撤退）force the enemy to retreat: ～之计 stratagem for repelling the enemy
【退步】tuìbù A〈动〉1（落后）fall behind: 学习～了 fall down in one's studies ‖ 这位舞蹈演员疏于练习，技艺～了。With insufficient practice the dancer is not up to speed. 2（退让）yield B〈名〉leeway: 留个～ leave some leeway
【退场】tuìchǎng〈动〉make one's exit: 运动员～式 players' exit ceremony ‖ 电影结束后，观众纷纷～。When the film was over, the audience made their exit.
【退朝】tuìcháo〈动〉〈书〉adjourn an imperial court session
【退潮】tuìcháo〈动〉ebb: ～后，海滩上留下许多贝壳。As the tide went out, many shells were left behind.
【退出】tuìchū〈动〉1（离开）leave: ～会场 walk out of a meeting 2（脱离）withdraw from: ～比赛 withdraw from a competition ‖ ～交易 back out of a deal ‖ 他宣布～篮坛。He announced his retirement from basketball.
【退磁】tuìcí〈动〉［物理］demagnetize
【退党】tuìdǎng〈动〉withdraw from a political party
【退敌】tuìdí〈动〉drive the enemy back
【退而求其次】tuì ér qiú qícì〈成〉have to put up with the second best
【退岗】tuìgǎng〈动〉retire from a post: 单位的一些元老已陆续～。Some of the company's old timers have already retired one after another.
【退稿】tuìgǎo〈动〉reject sb.'s article contribution to a newspaper/magazine
【退格键】tuìgéjiàn〈名〉backspace (key)
【退耕】tuìgēng〈动〉convert farmland to other purposes: ～还林 allow cultivated land to return to woodland
【退股】tuìgǔ〈动〉withdraw shares
【退化】tuìhuà〈动〉1［生物］degenerate: 机能～ functional retrogradation 2（由好变坏）deteriorate: 社会风气～ deteriorating social morals
【退还】tuìhuán〈动〉return: ～公物 return public property ‖ ～押金 return a deposit
【退换】tuìhuàn〈动〉exchange a purchase: 货物售出，恕不～。Goods sold are not returnable.
【退回】tuìhuí〈动〉1（退还）return: ～押金 return a deposit ‖ 无法投递，～原处。Undeliverable, returned to sender. 2（返回）go back: 队伍从原路～。The troops went back by the same route.
【退婚】tuìhūn〈动〉break off an engagement
【退火】tuìhuǒ〈动〉［冶金］anneal: 材料应～以消除应力。Material should be annealed to relieve stress.
【退伙】tuìhuǒ〈动〉withdraw from a secret society or an underworld gang
【退货】tuìhuò〈动〉return goods

【退居】tuìjū〈动〉step down: ～二线 retire from active life and take up a nominal post ‖ ～幕后 withdraw behind the scenes
【退款】tuìkuǎn **A**〈动〉refund **B**〈名〉returned money
【退路】tuìlù〈名〉**1**（指道路）route of retreat: 切断敌人的～ cut off the enemy's retreat **2**（指余地）leeway: 留个～ leave some leeway
【退赔】tuìpéi〈动〉return what has been misappropriated: 如数～ compensate in full
【退票】tuìpiào **A**〈动〉get a refund for a ticket: 去～窗口办理～手续 go to the ticket returns window for a refund **B**〈名〉returned/unused ticket: 等～ look for a returned ticket ‖ 买了两张～ bought two returned tickets
【退坡】tuìpō〈动〉〈喻〉fall off: 思想～ easing off of revolutionary will
【退亲】tuìqīn = 退婚 tuìhūn
【退却】tuìquè〈动〉**1**（指军队）retreat: 全线～ be in full retreat ‖ 战略～ strategic retreat **2**（畏缩）hang back: 临危～ flinch from danger ‖ 困难再大，也不该～。No matter how difficult things get there can be no shying away.
【退让】tuìràng〈动〉**1**（向后退）step aside: 他来不及～，结果被车撞倒。Before he had time to make way for the car, it knocked him down. **2**（让步）concede: 在原则问题上决不～ never make concessions on issues of principle
【退热】tuìrè = 退烧 tuìshāo
【退色】tuìshǎi = 褪色 tuìshǎi
【退烧】tuìshāo〈动〉allay a fever: ～药 antifebrile ‖ 他～了。His temperature has come down.
【退市】tuìshì〈动〉withdraw from the market
【退守】tuìshǒu〈动〉retreat and stand on the defensive: ～待命 retreat and wait for further orders
【退税】tuìshuì〈动〉［经济］refund a tax: 出口～ export tax rebate
【退缩】tuìsuō〈动〉flinch: 不在困难面前～ never flinch from difficulty
【退堂】tuìtáng〈动〉〈旧〉dismiss a court: 打～鼓 beat a retreat
【退庭】tuìtíng〈动〉dismiss a court
【退团】tuìtuán〈动〉withdraw from the League
【退位】tuìwèi〈动〉abdicate
【退伍】tuìwǔ〈动〉be discharged from active military service: ～军人 ex-serviceman
【退席】tuìxí〈动〉**1**（指宴席）leave a banquet **2**（指会场）walk out: ～以示抗议 walk out in protest
【退行】tuìxíng〈动〉retrograde: ～性变态 change for the worse
【退休】tuìxiū〈动〉retire: ～职工/人员 retired worker/people ‖ 60岁快～了。60 is close to retirement age.
【退休金】tuìxiūjīn〈名〉pension: 领取～ draw one's pension
【退学】tuìxué〈动〉drop out of school: 勒令～ expel a student from school ‖ 因病～ discontinue one's schooling for reasons of bad health
【退押】tuìyā〈动〉return a deposit
【退养】tuìyǎng〈动〉take early retirement
【退役】tuìyì〈动〉**1**（指军人）be discharged from active military service: ～军人 ex-serviceman **2**（指武器）be out of service: 这种老式战机早该～了。These old-fashioned fighter planes should be withdrawn as soon as possible. **3**（指运动员）retire from sport: 老运动员纷纷～。The old athletes have been retiring one by one.
【退隐】tuìyǐn〈动〉[of an official] go into retirement: ～山林 retire deep into the mountains from public life
【退赃】tuìzāng〈动〉surrender one's booty
【退职】tuìzhí〈动〉leave office: 申请～ request to resign ‖ 因病～ resign on the grounds of ill health
【退走】tuìzǒu〈动〉retreat

蜕 tuì
A〈名〉exuviation: ▸蝉～, 蛇～
B〈动〉**1**（脱皮）exuviate: ▸～皮 **2**（变化）degenerate: ▸～变, ～化 **3**（换毛）moult
【蜕变】tuìbiàn **A**〈动〉transform: 由公务员～为罪犯 go from civil servant to criminal **B**〈名〉［物理］decay
【蜕化】tuìhuà〈动〉**1**（脱皮）exuviate **2**〈喻〉（堕落）degenerate: 思想～ become corrupt ideologically ‖ ～变质分子 degenerate element
【蜕皮】tuìpí〈动〉［动物］shed a skin: 蛇定期～。Snakes regularly shed their skin.

煺 tuì〈动〉remove the hairs/feathers of a slaughtered animal/bird by scalding: ～毛 remove the hairs/feathers of an animal/bird

褪 tuì〈动〉**1**〈书〉（指衣服）take off: 今日暖和，不妨～去毛衣。It's warm today, so you can take your sweater off. **2**（指颜色）fade, discolour: ▸～色 **3**（指羽毛）shed hairs/feathers: 母鸡～毛了。The hen has shed her feathers.
▸tùn
【褪色】tuìshǎi〈动〉fade

tūn

吞 tūn〈动〉**1**（整个地咽）swallow: ～药丸 swallow pills ▸～食, 狼～虎咽, 囫囵～枣 **2**（并吞）seize: ▸～并, 独～, 侵～
【吞并】tūnbìng〈动〉seize: ～别国领土 seize another country's territory ‖ 个体小商业常遭大公司～。Small private businesses are often gobbled up by larger firms.
【吞吃】tūnchī〈动〉swallow up
【吞金】tūnjīn〈动〉swallow gold: ～自杀 commit suicide by swallowing gold
【吞灭】tūnmiè〈动〉conquer and annex
【吞没】tūnmò〈动〉**1**（据为己有）embezzle: ～公款 embezzle public funds **2**（淹没）engulf: 洪水～了村庄。The flood engulfed the town.
【吞声】tūnshēng〈动〉〈书〉swallow one's tears: ▸忍气～
【吞食】tūnshí〈动〉devour: 大鱼～小鱼。Big fish eat small fish. ‖ 蛇把鸡蛋～到肚子里。The snake devoured an egg.
【吞噬】tūnshì〈动〉swallow: 洪水～了成千上万人的生命。Thousands of people lost their lives in the flood.
【吞吐】tūntǔ〈动〉**1**（大量进出）take in and send out in large quantities: 港口的年～量 annual amount of goods going in and out of the harbour **2**（含混不清）mumble: ～其词 mumble one's words
【吞吐量】tūntǔliàng〈名〉handling capacity (of a harbour)
【吞吞吐吐】tūntūn-tǔtǔ〈成〉humming and hawing: 有话就说，别～。Speak up! No humming and hawing, please.
【吞咽】tūnyàn〈动〉swallow: 他咽喉疼，～困难。He is suffering from a sore throat and has difficulty swallowing. ‖ 她还想说点什么，却又把话～了回去。She wanted to say something else, but she bit her tongue.
【吞云吐雾】tūnyún-tǔwù〈成〉smoke
【吞占】tūnzhàn〈动〉**1**（据为己有）embezzle: ～公款 embezzle public funds **2**（侵占）seize: ～别国领土 seize another country's territory

暾 tūn〈名〉〈书〉newly-risen sun: 朝～ early morning sun

tún

屯 tún
A〈动〉**1**（储存）store up: ～货 store up goods ‖ ～粮 store up grain **2**（驻扎）station troops: ▸～兵, ～田, ～扎
B〈名〉[usu used in a village name] village: ▸～子
▸zhūn
【屯兵】túnbīng〈动〉station (troops): ～戍边 station troops to guard the frontier
【屯集】túnjí〈动〉gather: ～粮草 collect together grain and fodder for an army
【屯聚】túnjù〈动〉assemble: ～兵马 assemble military troops
【屯垦】túnkěn〈动〉station troops to open up wasteland: ～戍边 station troops at the frontier to open up wasteland
【屯落】túnluò〈名〉〈方〉village
【屯守】túnshǒu〈动〉garrison: ～边陲 defend the frontier
【屯田】túntián〈动〉have garrison troops or peasants open up wasteland and grow food grain
【屯扎】túnzhā〈动〉station troops
【屯子】túnzi〈名〉〈方〉village

囤 tún〈动〉store up: ～货 store up goods ‖ ～粮 store up grain
▸dùn
【囤积】túnjī〈动〉hoard for speculation: ～垄断小麦市场 corner the wheat market
【囤积居奇】túnjī-jūqí〈成〉hoarding and profiteering
【囤聚】túnjù〈动〉store up: ～木材 store up timber

饨（飩） tún ▸馄饨 húntun

豚 tún〈名〉suckling pig: ▸海～
【豚鼠】túnshǔ〈名〉［动物］guinea pig

鲀（魨） tún〈名〉globefish

臀 tún〈名〉［生理］buttocks
【臀部】túnbù〈名〉buttocks
【臀尖】túnjiān〈名〉rump
【臀鳍】túnqí〈名〉［鱼类］anal fin
【臀围】túnwéi〈名〉hip measurement

tǔn

汆 tǔn〈动〉〈方〉**1**（漂浮）float: 稻草在水上～。The straw drifted on the water. **2**（用油炸）deep-fry: 油～肉丸 deep-fried meat balls

t

tùn

褪 tùn〈动〉 slip out of sth.: 护士让他～下一只袖子给他打针。 The nurse asked him to slip one arm out of his sleeve for the injection.
▸tuì

tuō

托[1] tuō
A〈动〉 **1**（向上支撑） hold in the palm: ～着下巴 cup one's chin in one's hands ‖ 用盘子～着几杯酒 hold a tray with several glasses of wine on it ▸～盘 **2**（陪衬） set off: ▸衬～, 烘～
B〈名〉 **1**（支撑物） something serving as a support: ▸～子, 茶～ **2**（衬托者） foil: 医～ medical profiteer

托[2]（託） tuō〈动〉 **1**（依赖） rely on: ▸～庇, ～福 **2**（推托） give as a pretext: ▸～病, ～词, 假～ **3**（委托） entrust: ～人办事 ask sb. to do sth. ‖ 她～我照看一天孩子。 She's entrusted her child to me for the day. ▸～儿所, ～付, ～运, 拜～, 嘱～

托[3] tuō〈名〉［物理］ torr [unit of pressure]

【托庇】tuōbì〈动〉〈书〉 rely on sb. for protection: ～平安。 All is well, thanks to your protection.
【托病】tuōbìng〈动〉 plead illness: 他想～辞职。 He wanted to resign on the pretext of illness.
【托钵僧】tuōbōsēng〈名〉 mendicant monk
【托词】tuōcí **A**〈动〉 make an excuse: ～不见 refuse to see sb. on some pretext ‖ ～婉拒 graciously decline with an excuse **B**〈名〉 excuse: 寻找～ look for an excuse ‖ 他说对此事闻所未闻，那不过是～而已。 His claim that he had heard nothing about it was nothing but an excuse.
【托辞】tuōcí = 托词 tuōcí
【托儿所】tuō'érsuǒ〈名〉 nursery
【托福】tuōfú **A**〈动〉〈套〉 be owing to: 托您的福，一切顺利。 Things are fine, thank you. **B**〈名〉 TOEFL [Test of English as a Foreign Language]: ～考试 TOEFL
【托付】tuōfù〈动〉 entrust: 把孩子～给某人照料 entrust one's child to sb.'s care
【托孤】tuōgū〈动〉 [usu of a dying emperor] entrust one's young son to the care of (usu a minister)
【托故】tuōgù〈动〉 find an excuse: ～谢绝 decline on some pretext ‖ ～早退 take an early leave under some pretext
【托管】tuōguǎn〈动〉 **1**（委托管理） entrust: 这笔遗产暂由银行～。 This heirloom is in the care of the bank. **2**（在联合国监管下管理） trust: ～地 mandated/trust territory
【托管人】tuōguǎnrén〈名〉 custodian: 基金～ fund custodian
【托拉斯】tuōlāsī〈名〉［经济］ trust
【托老所】tuōlǎosuǒ〈名〉 retirement home
【托门子】tuō ménzi〈惯〉〈口〉 solicit help from potential backers
【托梦】tuōmèng〈动〉 [of the spirit of one's deceased] appear in one's dream to deliver a message or make a request
【托名】tuōmíng〈动〉 do sth. in somebody else's name
【托派】Tuōpài〈名〉 Trotskyist
【托盘】tuōpán〈名〉 serving tray
【托腔】tuōqiāng〈名〉 musical accompaniment suitable as complement to the singing of an actor or actress
【托情】tuōqíng = 托人情 tuō rénqíng
【托儿】tuōr〈名〉〈方〉 bait: 那家私人诊所雇了个～从大医院招揽病人。 The private clinic hired someone as bait to lure patients from large hospitals.
【托人情】tuō rénqíng〈动〉 seek the good offices of sb.: ～，找工作 look for a job with the help of sb.'s connections
【托身】tuōshēn〈动〉 find a place to live in: 无处～ unable to find a lodgings
【托收】tuōshōu〈名〉［经济］ collection: ～银行 remitting bank
【托运】tuōyùn〈动〉 consign for shipment: ～行李 check in one's luggage
【托运单】tuōyùndān〈名〉consignment bill
【托运人】tuōyùnrén〈名〉 consignor
【托子】tuōzi〈名〉 base: 花瓶～ vase support

拖 tuō〈动〉 **1**（拉） drag: ～地板 mop the floor ‖ ～网捕鱼 haul in a fishing net ‖ 撞坏了的车被～到附近一家修理厂。 The damaged car was towed to a nearby repair shop. ▸～车, ～船 **2**（耷拉着） hang down: 衣裙～在地上 dress trailing on the floor ‖ 小松鼠～着个大尾巴。 The little squirrel has a bushy tail. **3**（拖延） delay: ～时间 play for time ‖ 这工程～了一年才完成。 This project was completed one year behind schedule. ‖ 这件事不能再～了。 This matter cannot be put off any longer. ▸～拉, ～欠, ～延 **4**（牵制） encumber: 把大家～垮 wear everyone down ‖ 把敌人死死～住 pin down the enemy
【拖把】tuōbǎ〈名〉 mop
【拖驳】tuōbó〈名〉 barge towed by a tugboat or motor boat
【拖布】tuōbù = 拖把 tuōbǎ
【拖车】tuōchē〈名〉 trailer
【拖船】tuōchuán〈名〉 **1**（拖轮）tow boat **2**〈方〉（木船）small wooden boat towed by a tugboat
【拖宕】tuōdàng〈动〉〈书〉 postpone
【拖儿带女】tuō'ér-dàinǚ〈成〉be tied down by small children
【拖后腿】tuō hòutuǐ〈惯〉 hold sb. back: 你放心去吧，我决不会拖你的后腿。 You go on ahead, I don't want to hold you back. ‖ 我这是为大家办事，你可不能～。 I've done this for everyone, so don't you go getting in the way.
【拖家带口】tuōjiā-dàikǒu = 拉家带口 lājiā-dàikǒu
【拖拉】tuōlā〈形〉 sluggish: 作风～ sluggish working style ‖ 做事～ let grass grow under one's feet
【拖拉机】tuōlājī〈名〉 tractor: 履带式～ caterpillar tractor ‖ 手扶～ walking tractor
【拖累】tuōlěi〈动〉 **1**（牵累） be a burden to: 受家务～ be tied down by household chores ‖ 无儿女～ without encumbrance ‖ 孩子多了是个～。 Too many children are a burden. **2**（影响） involve: ～家人 implicate one's family ‖ 他的供状～了不少官员。 His confession implicated numerous other officials.
【拖轮】tuōlún〈名〉 tow boat
【拖泥带水】tuōní-dàishuǐ〈成〉 sloppy: 他办事～。 He does things very sloppily. ‖ 这篇文章写得～。 This article is verbose and carelessly written.
【拖欠】tuōqiàn〈动〉 be in arrears: ～房租 be behind with one's rent ‖ ～税款 be in arrears with a tax payment ‖ ～的工资 overdue wages
【拖腔】tuōqiāng〈动〉［戏曲］ draw out a word in singing
【拖人下水】tuōrén-xiàshuǐ〈成〉 drag sb. into the fray
【拖三拉四】tuōsān-lāsì〈成〉 put off one's work with all sorts of excuses
【拖沓】tuōtà〈形〉 sluggish: 作风～ sluggish working style ‖ 办事～ dilly-dally about things ‖ 行文～ write in a long-winded way
【拖堂】tuōtáng〈动〉not dismiss class when time is already up: 我们那位老师几乎每次都～。 That teacher of ours ran over time almost every class.
【拖网】tuōwǎng〈名〉 dragnet: ～鱼船 trawler
【拖尾巴】tuō wěiba〈惯〉〈喻〉 leave sth. unfinished
【拖鞋】tuōxié〈名〉 slippers: 夹趾/人字～ flip-flops ‖ 塑料～ plastic thongs
【拖延】tuōyán〈动〉 put off: ～时间 play for time ‖ 期限快到，不能再～了! The deadline is drawing near; it can't be delayed any more.
【拖曳】tuōyè〈动〉 tow
【拖油瓶】tuōyóupíng〈名〉〈贬〉 child of a preceding marriage living with its mother in her second marriage

脱 tuō〈动〉 **1**（脱落） come off: ～发 lose one's hair ▸～落, ～皮 **2**（除去） take off: ～衣/鞋 take off one's clothes/shoes ‖ 他～光了衣服。 He took all his clothes off. ▸～帽 **3**（掉） remove: ▸～色, ～水, ～脂 **4**（脱离） get out of: ～出樊笼 shake off the shackles ▸～产, ～节, ～贫 **5**（漏掉） leave out: 这个句子肯定有～字。 There must be some words missing in this sentence. ▸～漏, ～误
【脱靶】tuōbǎ〈动〉 miss the target
【脱班】tuōbān〈动〉 be late
【脱产】tuōchǎn〈动〉be released from one's regular work to take on other duties: ～进修 go on block release ‖ ～学习 be given study leave
【脱党】tuōdǎng〈动〉 leave a political party
【脱档】tuōdàng〈动〉 be out of stock: 紧俏商品有时出现～是正常的。 It's normal for goods that are in great demand to be out of stock from time to time.
【脱发】tuōfà〈动〉 lose one's hair
【脱肛】tuōgāng ▸**p. 50**〈名〉［医学］ prolapse of the anus
【脱岗】tuōgǎng〈动〉 **1**（指擅自离岗） leave one's post without permission **2**（指暂时离岗） leave one's post temporarily: ～培训 off-the-job training
【脱稿】tuōgǎo〈动〉 [of a manuscript] be completed: 已～付印。 The manuscript has been completed and sent to press.
【脱钩】tuōgōu〈动〉 cut ties: 政企要～。 Politics must be kept separate from business.
【脱谷机】tuōgǔjī〈名〉 threshing machine
【脱轨】tuōguǐ = 出轨 chūguǐ
【脱货】tuōhuò〈动〉 be out of stock
【脱机】tuōjī〈动〉［计算机］ be off-line: ～处理 off-line process
【脱缰之马】tuōjiāngzhīmǎ〈成〉〈喻〉 uncontrollable: 物价飞涨，有如～。 Prices were running wild.
【脱胶】tuōjiāo〈动〉 **1**（开胶） come

unstuck: 这双胶鞋的底子~了。The soles of these rubber boots have come unstuck. 2 〔化学〕 degum: ~丝 degummed silk
【脱节】tuōjié〈动〉 come apart: 理论不能与实践~。Theory must not be divorced from practice. ‖ 产销~ stalling between production and marketing
【脱臼】tuōjiù = 脱位 tuōwèi
【脱壳机】tuōkéjī〈名〉 huller
【脱口】tuōkǒu〈动〉 blurt out: 在气头上，他~说出了个脏字。In his rage he unwittingly let out an obscenity.
【脱口而出】tuōkǒu'érchū〈成〉 blurt sth. out
【脱口秀】tuōkǒuxiù〈名〉 talk show: ~主持人 chat show host
【脱困】tuōkùn〈动〉 get out of a difficult situation
【脱蜡】tuōlà〈动〉〔石油〕 dewax
【脱离】tuōlí〈动〉 break away from: ~群众 cut oneself off from the masses ‖ 理论~实际 theory divorced from practice ‖ 病人尚未~危险。The patient is not yet out of danger.
【脱离速度】tuōlí sùdù〈名〉〔航天〕 second cosmic velocity
【脱粒】tuōlì〈动〉〔农业〕 thresh: ~机 threshing machine
【脱磷】tuōlín〈动〉〔化学〕 dephosphorize
【脱硫】tuōliú〈动〉〔化学〕 desulphurize
【脱漏】tuōlòu〈动〉 be left out: 她打毛衣时~了一针。She dropped a stitch in her knitting. ‖ 这里可能~了几个字。A few words have probably been left out here.
【脱落】tuōluò〈动〉 1 （掉下） shed: 毛发~ lose hair ‖ 桌面上的油漆~了。The paint on the tabletop has come off. 2 （漏掉） be omitted
【脱盲】tuōmáng〈动〉 eliminate illiteracy: 他到二十好几才~。He didn't learn to read and write until he was in his late twenties.
【脱毛】tuōmáo〈动〉 moult: 这件毛皮大衣~。The fur coat moults. ‖ 这只猫~脱得厉害。The cat is shedding badly.
【脱帽】tuōmào〈动〉 doff one's hat: ~致敬 raise one's hat in salute
【脱敏】tuōmǐn〈动〉〔医学〕 desensitize: ~牙膏 desensitizing toothpaste
【脱坯】tuōpī〈动〉 mould adobe blocks
【脱皮】tuōpí〈动〉 shed skin: 他的脸~了。His face is peeling.
【脱贫】tuōpín〈动〉 lift oneself out of poverty: ~致富 shake off poverty and build up a fortune ‖ 许多农民已经~。Many farmers have lifted themselves out of poverty.
【脱期】tuōqī〈动〉 miss a deadline: ~交货 delay delivery ‖ 工程~。The project is running behind schedule.
【脱色】tuōsè〈动〉 1 （使无颜色） decolour 2 （掉色） fade: 若在冷水里洗这衣服，就不~。If you wash the dress in cold water, the colour won't run.
【脱涩】tuōsè〈动〉 remove the tart taste from persimmons
【脱身】tuōshēn〈动〉 extricate oneself: ~之计 plan of escape ‖ 工作忙得脱不开身 be tied down to one's job
【脱手】tuōshǒu〈动〉 1 （脱开手） slip out of the hand: 我的杯子~打碎了。The cup slipped out of my hand and broke. 2 （处理完） dispose of: 稿子已~，我马上寄出。I have finished the manuscript and will post it out right away. ‖ 这些股票得立即~，不然要亏。To cut our losses, we must get these stocks off our hands immediately.
【脱水】tuōshuǐ〈动〉 1 ▸p. 50 〔医学〕 lose body fluids: 严重~ serious dehydration 2 〔化学〕 dehydrate
【脱水机】tuōshuǐjī〈名〉 hydroextractor
【脱水蔬菜】tuōshuǐ shūcài〈名〉 dehydrated vegetable
【脱水桶】tuōshuǐtǒng〈名〉 spin-dryer (of a washing machine)
【脱俗】tuōsú〈形〉 refined: 这女孩清新~。The girl is pure and free of all vulgarity.
【脱酸】tuōsuān〈动〉〔化学〕 deacidify
【脱榫】tuōsǔn〈动〉 [of furniture] be out of joint
【脱胎】tuōtāi〈动〉 1 〔美术〕 make bodiless lacquerware: ~漆器 bodiless lacquerware 2 （衍变） be born out of: 封建社会是从奴隶社会~而来的。Feudal society was born out of the slave society.
【脱胎换骨】tuōtāi-huàngǔ〈成〉 1 〈本〉 be reborn 2 〈喻〉 undergo a complete transformation: ~，重新做人 turn over a new leaf
【脱逃】tuōtáo〈动〉run away: 临阵~ sneak away at a critical juncture
【脱位】tuōwèi ▸p. 50 〈动〉〔医学〕 dislocate: 他的右肘~了。He dislocated his right elbow.
【脱误】tuōwù〈名〉 omissions and errors
【脱险】tuōxiǎn〈动〉 escape danger: 安然~ come through without so much as a scratch ‖ 经急诊抢救，孩子~了。The emergency treatment has brought the child out of danger.
【脱销】tuōxiāo〈动〉 be sold out: 这本书已~。This book is out of stock.
【脱卸】tuōxiè〈动〉 evade
【脱氧】tuōyǎng〈动〉〔化学〕deoxidize: ~剂 deoxidant
【脱氧核糖核酸】tuōyǎng hétáng hésuān〈名〉〔生化〕deoxyribonucleic acid (DNA)
【脱衣舞】tuōyīwǔ〈名〉 striptease: 表演~ do a striptease ‖ ~女 striptease artist
【脱颖而出】tuōyǐng'érchū〈成〉〈喻〉 talent reveals itself: 一些年轻科学家~。A few young scientists are coming through.
【脱羽】tuōyǔ〈动〉 shed feathers
【脱脂】tuōzhī〈动〉 degrease: ~棉/纱布 absorbent cotton/gauze ‖ ~奶粉 non-fat milk powder

tuó

驮（馱） tuó〈动〉 carry on the back: 老师~着学生过河。The teacher helped his pupil cross the river by carrying him piggyback.
▸duò
【驮鞍】tuó'ān〈名〉 pack saddle
【驮畜】tuóchù〈名〉 pack animal
【驮轿】tuójiào〈名〉 sedan chair carried by a mule
【驮马】tuómǎ〈名〉 packhorse
【驮运】tuóyùn〈动〉 transport on the back of a pack animal: 粮食主要靠毛驴~。Grain was mainly transported on the back of a donkey.

陀 tuó
【陀螺】tuóluó〈名〉 1 （指玩具） top: 抽~ whip a top 2 = 陀螺仪 tuóluóyí
【陀螺仪】tuóluóyí〈名〉〔航空〕 gyroscope

坨 tuó
A 〈名〉 lump: 泥~ lump of mud
B 〈动〉 [of cooked food] stick together: 面条~了。These noodles are sticking together.
【坨子】tuózi〈名〉 lump: 泥~ lump of mud

沱 tuó〈名〉〈方〉 [often used in place names] small bay in a river
【沱茶】tuóchá〈名〉 bowl-shaped compressed mass of tea leaves

驼（駝） tuó
A 〈名〉 camel: ▸~峰, 骆~
B 〈动〉 be hunchbacked: 爷爷的背~了。My grandpa's back has become bent.
【驼背】tuóbèi A 〈动〉 be hunchbacked: ~由脊椎畸形所致。Hunchbacks are caused by a deformity of the spine. B 〈名〉 hunchback, humpback: 他是个~。He has a hunchback/humpback.
【驼峰】tuófēng〈名〉 1 （指骆驼） camel hump 2 〔铁路〕 hump: ~调车场 hump yard
【驼铃】tuólíng〈名〉 camel bell
【驼鹿】tuólù〈名〉 elk
【驼绒】tuóróng〈名〉 1 （骆驼的绒毛） camel's hair 2 = 骆驼绒 luòtuoróng
【驼色】tuósè ▸p. 863 〈名〉 camel colour
【驼子】tuózi〈名〉〈口〉〈粗〉 hunchback

柁 tuó〈名〉〔建筑〕 girder
▸duò

砣¹ tuó
A 〈名〉 stone roller
B 〈动〉 cut jade with an emery wheel

砣² tuó〈名〉 sliding weight of a steelyard
【砣子】tuózi〈名〉 emery wheel for cutting jade

铊（鉈） tuó = 砣² tuó
▸tā

鸵（鴕） tuó〈名〉 ostrich
【鸵鸟】tuóniǎo〈名〉 ostrich
【鸵鸟政策】tuóniǎo zhèngcè〈名〉 ostrich policy

酡 tuó〈形〉〈书〉 flushed with drink: ~颜 face flushed from drinking

跎 tuó ▸蹉跎 cuōtuó

橐¹ tuó〈名〉〈古〉 bag

橐² tuó〈拟〉 sound of footsteps
【橐驼】tuótuó〈名〉〈书〉 camel

鼍（鼉） tuó〈名〉〔动物〕Chinese alligator
【鼍龙】tuólóng = 扬子鳄 yángzǐè

tuǒ

妥 tuǒ〈形〉 1 （妥当） appropriate: ~为保存 take good care of ‖ 报告~否，请指示。Please indicate whether the reports are sound. ▸~当, ~善, 欠~, 稳~ 2 （齐备） ready: 事已办~。The matter has

t

been settled. ‖ 条件已谈～。 These terms have been agreed upon.
【妥当】tuǒdang〈形〉 appropriate: 这事你办得很～。 You've handled it well.
【妥善】tuǒshàn〈形〉 appropriate: ～保管 take good care of ‖ 这件事需要～处理。 This issue calls for careful and skilful handling.
【妥实】tuǒshí〈形〉 proper
【妥帖】tuǒtiē〈形〉 fitting: 安排得妥妥帖帖 be well arranged ‖ 你用词似乎不大～。 Your wording doesn't seem to be very appropriate.
【妥协】tuǒxié〈动〉 meet sb. halfway: 老板同意向罢工者～。 The boss agreed to meet the strikers halfway. ‖ 原则问题不能～。 On questions of principle there are no compromises.

椭（橢） tuǒ〈形〉 oval-shaped

【椭圆】tuǒyuán〈名〉［数学］ 1►（指椭圆形） oval 2►（指椭圆体） ellipsoid

tuò

拓 tuò〈动〉 open up: ►开～

►tà
【拓荒】tuòhuāng〈动〉 reclaim wasteland: ～者 trailblazer
【拓宽】tuòkuān〈动〉 widen: ～道路 widen a road ‖ ～思路 broaden one's thinking ‖ ～研究领域 broaden the scope of research
【拓扑学】tuòpūxué〈名〉［数学］ topology
【拓销】tuòxiāo〈动〉 expand the market
【拓展】tuòzhǎn〈动〉 expand: ～市场 expand the market ‖ ～业务 develop a business

柝 tuò〈名〉〈书〉 watchman's clapper

唾 tuò

A〈名〉 saliva: ►～沫, ～液
B〈动〉 1►（吐唾沫） spit: ►～手可得 2►（鄙视） spit with contempt: ►～骂, ～弃
【唾骂】tuòmà〈动〉 revile: 为世人所～ be spurned by society
【唾面自干】tuòmiàn-zìgān〈成〉 swallow humiliation
【唾沫】tuòmo〈名〉 saliva: 吐～ spit out saliva ‖ ～星子 spray of saliva
【唾弃】tuòqì〈动〉 spurn
【唾手可得】tuòshǒu-kědé〈成〉〈喻〉 get sth. with extreme ease
【唾腺】tuòxiàn = 唾液腺 tuòyèxiàn
【唾液】tuòyè〈名〉 saliva: 分泌～ secrete saliva
【唾液腺】tuòyèxiàn〈名〉 salivary gland
【唾余】tuòyú〈名〉〈书〉 trivial remarks: 拾人～ repeat other people's trivial remarks

魄 tuò variant for pò as in 落魄 luòpò

►bó, pò

wā

凹 wā〈方〉= 洼 wā
▸āo

挖 wā〈动〉**1**（用手或工具掘）dig: ～耳朵 pick one's ears ‖ ～洞 dig a hole ‖ ～防空洞/战壕 dig an air-raid shelter/a trench ‖ ～塘泥 dredge up sludge from a pond **2**（发现）discover: ～出隐藏的敌人 ferret out the hidden enemy ‖ ～潜力 tap the potential (of sb./sth.) ‖ ～人才 steal sb.'s best people **3**〈方〉（用指甲抠）scratch with fingernails

【挖补】wābǔ〈动〉mend by replacing a damaged part: ～衣服 patch up worn-out clothes

【挖东墙，补西墙】wā dōngqiáng, bǔ xīqiáng = 拆东墙，补西墙 chāi dōngqiáng, bǔ xīqiáng

【挖耳勺】wā'ěrsháo〈名〉〈方〉ear pick

【挖改】wāgǎi〈动〉out and correct: 本次重印对错字进行了～。The misspelt words were corrected before this reprint.

【挖掘】wājué〈动〉**1**（指具体物品）excavate: ～地下宝藏 unearth buried treasures ‖ ～古物 excavate ancient relics **2**（指抽象事物）probe: ～潜力 tap all potentialities ‖ ～人才 exploit talents ‖ ～机 excavator

【挖空心思】wākōng-xīnsī〈成〉〈贬〉rack one's brains: ～替自己辩解 rack one's brains trying to find a way to justify oneself

【挖苦】wāku〈动〉make a dig: ～别人 dig at sb. ‖ ～话 ironical remark ‖ ～嘲笑朋友 mock and make jibes at one's friends ‖ 他惯于～人。He was given to sarcasm.

【挖泥船】wāníchuán〈名〉dredger

【挖潜】wāqián〈动〉tap latent potential

【挖墙脚】wā qiángjiǎo〈惯〉pull the rug from under: 你抽走了所有的资金，这是在挖我们公司的墙脚。By withdrawing funding from our company, you are pulling the rug out from under our feet.

【挖人】wārén〈动〉poach

【挖肉补疮】wāròu-bǔchuāng = 剜肉补疮 wānròu-bǔchuāng

【挖土机】wātǔjī〈名〉excavator

哇 wā〈拟〉sound of crying or vomiting
▸wa

【哇啦】wālā〈拟〉hullabaloo

【哇喇】wālā = 哇啦 wālā

【哇赛】wāsài〈叹〉〈口〉wow [an exclamation of admiration, amazement, etc.]

【哇哇】wāwā〈拟〉wailing of a child: ～大哭 sob one's heart out ‖ ～叫 shriek for sb.

洼（窪） wā

A〈名〉depression: 水～ water-logged depression

B〈形〉hollow: 这一带地势太～。This plot of land is too hollow. ▸坑坑～～

【洼地】wādì〈名〉lowland: 填平～ fill up a depression ‖ ～改造 improvement of low-lying land ‖ 大雨过后，几处～都积了水。After the heavy rain, water collected in several depressions.

【洼陷】wāxiàn〈动〉sink: 路面～了。The road surface has caved in.

娲（媧） wā ▸女娲 Nǚwā

蛙 wā〈名〉frog

【蛙人】wārén〈名〉frogman

【蛙泳】wāyǒng〈名〉［体育］breaststroke

wá

娃 wá〈名〉〈方〉**1**（小孩）baby: 把～搂在怀里 hold a baby in one's arms ‖ 生～ give birth to a child **2**（小动物）newborn: 一窝狗/猫/猪～ a litter of puppies/kittens/piglets

【娃娃】wáwa〈名〉baby: 泥～ clay doll ‖ 洋～ doll ‖ 芭比～ Barbie doll ‖ 足球应该从～抓起。Footballers have to start young.

【娃娃兵】wáwabīng〈名〉**1**（指战士）child soldier: 禁止招募年龄不到18岁的～参战。Enlistment of child soldiers under 18 years of age is prohibited. **2**（指球员）junior player: 在少年足球训练基地上，可以看到～刻苦训练的身影。At youth football training camps you can see junior players training hard.

【娃娃脸】wáwaliǎn〈名〉baby face: 长了张～ be baby-faced

【娃娃亲】wáwaqīn〈名〉〈旧〉betrothal of a boy and a girl arranged by the parents of both sides: 定～ be betrothed in childhood

【娃娃生】wáwashēng〈名〉baby *sheng* [subdivision of the *xiaosheng* (小生) role in traditional Chinese opera, representing loud-voiced boys]

【娃娃鱼】wáwayú〈名〉［动物］giant salamander

【娃子】wázi〈名〉〈方〉**1**（小孩）child **2**（小动物）newborn animal cub: 猪～ piglet

wǎ

瓦 wǎ〈名〉**1**（指瓦片）tile: ～房 tile-roofed house ‖ 水泥～ cement tile ▸琉璃～ **2**（指器具）earthenware: ～器 earthenware **3** = 瓦特 wǎtè
▸wà

【瓦当】wǎdāng〈名〉［考古］eaves tile

【瓦釜雷鸣】wǎfǔ-léimíng〈成〉〈喻〉unworthy man in a high position

【瓦工】wǎgōng〈名〉**1**（指工作）bricklaying **2**（指人）bricklayer

【瓦罐】wǎguàn〈名〉earthenware jar

【瓦灰】wǎhuī〈形〉dark grey

【瓦匠】wǎjiang〈名〉bricklayer

【瓦解】wǎjiě〈动〉disintegrate: ～敌军 disintegrate the enemy forces ‖ 敌人的战线全面～了。The enemy front has completely crumbled. ▸土崩～

【瓦块】wǎkuài = 瓦片 wǎpiàn

【瓦蓝】wǎlán〈形〉sky-blue: 天空～～的，不见一丝云彩。The sky is a cloudless blue.

【瓦楞】wǎléng〈名〉rows of tiles on a roof

【瓦楞纸】wǎléngzhǐ〈名〉corrugated paper: ～盒 corrugated paper box

【瓦砾】wǎlì〈名〉debris: 大楼被炸成了一堆～。The building was reduced to rubble by bombing.

【瓦亮】wǎliàng〈形〉shiny: 枪擦得锃光～。The gun was polished to a shine.

【瓦垄】wǎlǒng = 瓦楞 wǎléng

【瓦努阿图】Wǎnǔ'ātú〈名〉Vanuatu

【瓦盆】wǎpén〈名〉earthen basin

【瓦片】wǎpiàn〈名〉broken tile pieces

【瓦圈】wǎquān〈名〉wheel rim

【瓦全】wǎquán〈动〉〈喻〉live in dishonour: ▸宁为玉碎，不为～

【瓦斯】wǎsī〈名〉gas: ～爆炸 gas explosion ‖ 催泪～ tear gas

【瓦特】wǎtè〈量〉［电气］watt

【瓦特计】wǎtèjì〈名〉wattmeter

【瓦窑】wǎyáo〈名〉tile kiln

佤 Wǎ

【佤族】Wǎzú〈名〉Va ethnic group

wà

瓦 wà〈动〉tile: 屋顶可以～了。The roof is ready to be tiled.
▸wǎ

【瓦刀】wàdāo〈名〉bricklayer's cleaver

袜（襪） wà〈名〉socks: 尼龙/丝/毛～ nylon/silk/woollen socks ‖ 网眼长～ mesh stockings ‖ ～厂 hosiery

【袜裤】wàkù〈名〉pantyhose

【袜套】wàtào〈名〉ankle socks

【袜筒】wàtǒng〈名〉stocking leg

【袜子】wàzi〈名〉socks: 穿上/脱下～ put on/take off one's socks ‖ 她的～抽丝了。She got a ladder in her stockings.

腽 wà

【腽肭】wànà〈形〉〈书〉obese
【腽肭兽】wànàshòu〈名〉［动物］fur seal

wa

哇 wa〈助〉[used in place of 啊 after a word ending in u or ao]: 你怎么还不走～? Why haven't you left yet, eh? ‖ 你好～? Well, how are you?
▸wā

wāi

歪 wāi

A〈形〉**1**（不正）askew: 把画挂～了 hang a picture askew ‖ 这堵墙有点～。This wall is at a slight slant. **2**（不正确）improper: ～点子 evil ideas ‖ 不要把我的话想～了。Don't take my words the wrong way.
B〈动〉〈方〉recline: 她把头～在我肩上。She leant her head on my shoulder.
【歪脖】wāibó〈名〉wryneck: 他是个～儿。He has a wryneck.
【歪才】wāicái〈名〉**1**（指才能）unique talent in a certain field **2**（指人）freak
【歪缠】wāichán〈动〉nag
【歪打正着】wāidǎ-zhèngzháo〈成〉〈喻〉score a lucky hit: 他～，投篮命中了。His shot was a sheer fluke.
【歪道】wāidào〈名〉**1**（邪路）evil ways: 她不在的那三年，儿子走上了～。It was during her three-year absence that her son went astray. ▸邪门～ **2**（坏主意）wicked idea: 满脑子的～ be full of wicked ideas
【歪风】wāifēng〈名〉unhealthy trend: 打击～，发扬正气 combat evil trends and foster a spirit of uprightness
【歪风邪气】wāifēng-xiéqì〈成〉unhealthy trends and evil practices: 有力地打击～ lash out against evil trends
【歪话】wāihuà〈名〉untruth: 别教小孩说～。Don't lead the child to tell lies.
【歪理】wāilǐ〈名〉false reasoning: ～邪说 heresies and sophistries
【歪门邪道】wāimén-xiédào ＝ 邪门歪道 xiémén-wāidào
【歪七扭八】wāiqī-niǔbā〈成〉crooked: ～地写几个字 scrawl a few words
【歪曲】wāiqū〈动〉distort: ～历史 distort history ‖ ～某人的观点/原话 twist sb.'s views/words ‖ ～事实 bend the truth
【歪歪扭扭】wāiwāi-niǔniǔ〈形〉shapeless and twisted: 字写得～ scrawl
【歪斜】wāixié〈形〉crooked: 口眼～ have a slanting mouth and eyes
【歪嘴和尚】wāizuǐ héshang〈成〉person who unscrupulously distorts principles for their own benefits

㖞（喎）wāi〈形〉wry-mouthed

喎 wāi〈叹〉hey: ～，你能听到我的声音吗? Hey, can you hear me?

wǎi

搋 wǎi〈动〉〈方〉scoop out: 从缸里～了一勺水 scoop up a ladle of water

崴 wǎi ＝ 踒 wǎi
▸wēi
【崴泥】wǎiní〈动〉fall through: 因款项不足，计划～了。Owing to lack of funds, the plan fell through.
【崴子】wǎizi〈名〉〈方〉[usu used in place names] bend

踒 wǎi〈动〉sprain: 我从台阶上下来，不小心～了脚。I sprained my ankle coming downstairs without looking.

wài

外 wài

A〈名〉**1**（外边）exterior: ～包装 outer packaging ‖ 内～有别 distinguish between one's own people and outsiders ‖ 意料之～ contrary to one's expectations ▸～伤，～貌 **2**（外国）foreign country: 促进对～贸易 promote foreign trade ‖ 利用～资 make use of foreign investment ▸～币，～宾
B〈形〉**1**（其他）other: ～单位/省 other units/provinces ‖ ～系 other departments **2**（额外）additional: ▸～带，～加 **3**（非正式）unofficial: ▸～史，～号 **4**（关系远）distantly related: ▸～人，见～ **5**（女方家）of one's mother, sisters or daughters: ▸～公，～甥，～孙
【外办】wàibàn〈名〉foreign affairs office
【外包】wàibāo〈动〉outsource: ～服务 outsourcing service ‖ 人事～ personnel outsourcing ‖ 法务～ legal outsourcing
【外包装】wàibāozhuāng〈名〉packaging: 食品～ food packaging
【外币】wàibì〈名〉foreign currency: 持有～ possess foreign currency ‖ 兑换～ exchange foreign currency
【外边】wàibian〈名〉**1**（某一范围之外）outside: 在～等 wait outside ‖ ～很冷。It's cold outdoors. **2**（外地）place other than where one lives or works: 暑假去～走走 travel somewhere during the summer vacation **3**（表面）exterior: 粉刷房子～ whitewash the exterior of a house
【外表】wàibiǎo〈名〉outward appearance: ～老实 look honest ‖ ～美观 look nice ‖ 建筑物的～是玻璃幕墙。The exterior of the building is all glass.
【外宾】wàibīn〈名〉foreign visitor: 陪同～游览西安 escort foreign guests around Xi'an ‖ 设宴招待～ treat foreign guests to dinner
【外部】wàibù〈名〉**1**（某一范围之外）outside: ～环境 external environment ‖ ～条件 external conditions **2**（外表）exterior: ～装修 exterior decoration ‖ 事物的～特征 the external characteristics of things
【外埠】wàibù〈名〉〈旧〉towns or cities other than one's home: ～新闻 news from other cities ‖ ～邮件 out-of-town mail
【外财】wàicái〈名〉extra income
【外侧】wàicè〈名〉outer flank: ～行车道 outside lane
【外层】wàicéng〈名〉outer layer
【外层空间】wàicéng kōngjiān〈名〉outer space
【外场】wàichǎng〈名〉**1**（指行事）sociability: 她是个～人，人头儿挺广。She is sociable and has a large circle of acquaintances. **2**［体育］outfield: ～防守员 the covers
【外钞】wàichāo〈名〉foreign banknote
【外车道】wàichēdào〈名〉outside lane
【外城】wàichéng〈名〉outer city
【外弛内张】wàichí-nèizhāng〈成〉controlled tension
【外出】wàichū〈动〉go out: ～度假 be away on vacation ‖ ～访问 go out for a visit ‖ ～游玩 go on an outing ‖ ～几天 be away for a few days ‖ 禁止～ no exit
【外出血】wàichūxuè ▸**p. 50**〈名〉［医学］external haemorrhage
【外传】wàichuán〈动〉**1**（向外散布）leak: 绝密文件，不得～。Highly confidential document. Not for dissemination. ‖ 此事不宜～。This is not to be leaked out. **2**（外界传言）be said: ～他有可能成为下一届总理。It is rumoured that he will be the next Prime Minister.
▸wàizhuàn
【外存储器】wàicúnchǔqì〈名〉［计算机］external storage
【外带】wàidài **A**〈名〉tyre: ～和里带都扎穿了。The tyre and the inner tube are both punctured. ‖ ～爆了。The tyre burst. **B**〈动〉do as well: 她要做饭、洗衣，～照顾老人，忙得不可开交。What with cooking, washing as well as taking care of the old people, she was very busy.
【外道】wàidào〈名〉**1**［佛教］unorthodox sect **2**［体育］outside lane
【外道】wàidao〈形〉〈口〉over-polite: 你再客气，就显得～了。If you are any more polite, it would be over the top.
【外敌】wàidí〈名〉foreign enemy: 抵御～ resist foreign enemies ‖ ～入侵 foreign invasion
【外地】wàidì〈名〉other places: 去～打工 go to work in other places ‖ 这位小说家将去～体验生活。The novelist will leave for other parts of the country in order to experience life there.
【外电】wàidiàn〈名〉dispatch from a foreign news agency: 据～报道 according to a foreign news agency
【外调】wàidiào〈动〉**1**（指调用）transfer to other localities or institutions: ～物资 materials to be transferred to other places ‖ 他已～北京。He has been transferred to Beijing. **2**（指调查）go out to another unit on an investigative mission: 内查～ make both internal and external investigations
【外耳】wài'ěr〈名〉outer ear: ～道 external auditory meatus
【外藩】wàifān〈名〉〈旧〉**1**（指人）vassal **2**（指领土）vassal state: 削减～的权利 reduce the power of the vassal states
【外访】wàifǎng〈动〉visit a foreign country
【外分泌】wàifēnmì〈名〉［生理］exocrine: ～腺 exocrine gland ‖ ～学 exocrinology
【外敷】wàifū〈动〉apply externally: 用于～ for external application ‖ ～药 medicine for external application
【外感】wàigǎn **A**〈动〉be affected by: ～风寒 be affected by the cold **B**〈名〉［中医］disease caused by external factors
【外港】wàigǎng〈名〉outport: ～区 outer harbour area
【外公】wàigōng ▸**p. 588**〈名〉maternal grandfather
【外功】wàigōng〈名〉external exercises [*wushu* exercises]
【外挂】wàiguà〈动〉**1**（指空调）hang outside: 空调～机 external air-conditioner unit **2**（指软件）extension: ～软件程序 secretly install one's own plug-in software programs ‖ "～"网站 website add-on
【外观】wàiguān〈名〉outward appearance:

W

房子的～ exterior of a house ‖ 从～看，它就像一只普通的箱子。 From the outside, it looks like an ordinary box.

【外国】wàiguó〈名〉 foreign country: ～军事基地 foreign military base ‖ ～留学生/友人 foreign student/friend ‖ ～人 foreigner

【外国腔】wàiguóqiāng〈名〉 outlandish way of talking

【外国文学】wàiguó wénxué〈名〉 foreign literature

【外国语】wàiguóyǔ ▸p. 918〈名〉 foreign language: ～学院 foreign language institute

【外国租界】wàiguó zūjiè〈名〉 foreign concession

【外海】wàihǎi〈名〉 open sea

【外行】wàiháng **A**〈名〉 layman: 谈到法律，我是个～。 Where the law is concerned, I am only a layman. **B**〈形〉 lay: ～话 lay language ‖ 搞工程他可不～。 He's no amateur when it comes to engineering.

【外行看热闹，内行看门道】wàiháng kàn rènao, nèiháng kàn méndao〈俗〉 connoisseurs appraise and appreciate whereas laymen merely watch the fun with the crowd

【外号】wàihào〈名〉 nickname: 给某人起～ give sb. a nickname

【外话】wàihuà〈名〉〈方〉 unduly polite words (that a friend is not expected to say): 谢谢你! ——别说～了! Thank you! — Don't mention it.

【外患】wàihuàn〈名〉〈旧〉 foreign aggression: ～频仍 be subjected to repeated foreign invasion ‖ 内忧～ anxiety arising from within and trouble coming from without

【外汇】wàihuì〈名〉 foreign currency: ～储备 foreign currency reserve ‖ 倒卖～ speculate in foreign currency

【外汇兑换率】wàihuì duìhuànlǜ〈名〉 foreign exchange rate

【外汇管理局】Wàihuì Guǎnlǐjú〈名〉 Administration of Foreign Exchange

【外汇行情】wàihuì hángqíng〈名〉 exchange quotations

【外汇汇率】wàihuì huìlǜ〈名〉 exchange rate

【外汇牌价】wàihuì páijià〈名〉 foreign exchange quotation

【外汇清算】wàihuì qīngsuàn〈名〉 foreign exchange clearing

【外汇业务】wàihuì yèwù〈名〉 foreign exchange business

【外货】wàihuò〈名〉 imported goods: ～进口报单 declaration for importation of foreign goods

【外祸】wàihuò〈名〉 external aggression

【外籍】wàijí ▸p. 279〈名〉 foreign nationality: ～华人 foreign national of Chinese descent ‖ ～教练 foreign coach ‖ ～教师 foreign teacher ‖ ～劳工 foreign labour ‖ ～专家 foreign expert

【外加】wàijiā〈动〉 plus: 这是～的东西。 This is an additional thing. ‖ 给你们两台电脑，～一台录音机。 Here you are. Two computers, plus a tape-recorder.

【外家】wàijiā〈名〉 **1**（外祖父母家） maternal grandparents' home **2**〈方〉（娘家） family of a married woman's parents **3**〈书〉（岳父母家） home of one's husband's parents-in-law **4**〈旧〉（情妇） mistress **5**〈旧〉（外室） outside family (with a mistress or concubine)

【外间】wàijiān〈名〉 **1**（指房间） outer room **2**〈书〉（指世界） outside world: ～传闻，别往心里去。 Don't take the rumours to heart.

【外交】wàijiāo〈名〉 diplomacy: 通过～途径解决纷争 settle disputes through diplomatic channels ‖ ～谈判 diplomatic negotiation ‖ 穿梭～ shuttle diplomacy

【外交庇护】wàijiāo bìhù〈名〉 diplomatic asylum: ～权 right of diplomatic sanctuary

【外交部】wàijiāobù〈名〉 ministry of foreign affairs: ～发言人 foreign ministry spokesperson

【外交部长】wàijiāo bùzhǎng〈名〉 foreign minister

【外交程序】wàijiāo chéngxù〈名〉 diplomatic procedure

【外交辞令】wàijiāo cílìng〈名〉 diplomatic language: 这位官员善用～。 The official is very diplomatic in public discourse.

【外交大臣】Wàijiāo Dàchén〈名〉 Foreign Secretary [UK]

【外交关系】wàijiāo guānxì〈名〉 diplomatic relations: 断绝～ sever diplomatic relations ‖ 建立大使级～ establish diplomatic relations at the ambassadorial rank

【外交官】wàijiāoguān〈名〉 diplomat: 职业～ career diplomat

【外交惯例】wàijiāo guànlì〈名〉 diplomatic practice

【外交豁免权】wàijiāo huòmiǎnquán〈名〉 diplomatic immunity

【外交家】wàijiāojiā ▸p. 966〈名〉 diplomat

【外交礼节】wàijiāo lǐjié〈名〉 diplomatic protocol

【外交使节】wàijiāo shǐjié〈名〉 diplomatic envoy: 派遣～ dispatch a diplomatic envoy

【外交事务】wàijiāo shìwù〈名〉 foreign affairs

【外交特权】wàijiāo tèquán〈名〉 diplomatic privilege: 行使～ exercise diplomatic prerogatives

【外交团】wàijiāotuán〈名〉 diplomatic corps

【外交学院】wàijiāo xuéyuàn〈名〉 foreign affairs college

【外交照会】wàijiāo zhàohuì〈名〉 diplomatic note

【外交政策】wàijiāo zhèngcè〈名〉 foreign policy: 调整～ adjust the foreign policy

【外教】wàijiào〈名〉 **1**（指教师） foreign teacher **2**（指教练） foreign coach

【外界】wàijiè〈名〉 outside world: ～干扰 external interference ‖ 与～隔绝 be hedged off from the outside world

【外借】wàijiè〈动〉 **1**（借出） lend: 工具书恕不～。 Reference books are not for lending. **2**（借入） borrow: 这些桌椅是～的。 These desks and chairs are borrowed.

【外景】wàijǐng〈名〉 exterior: 选～ look for exteriors ‖ ～拍摄 location shooting

【外景地】wàijǐngdì〈名〉 location: 在～拍摄 shoot on location

【外径】wàijìng〈名〉 outside diameter: 齿轮～ outside diameter of gear ‖ ～千分尺 outside micrometer

【外舅】wàijiù〈名〉〈书〉 father-in-law

【外卡】wàikǎ〈名〉［体育］ wild card

【外科】wàikē〈名〉［医学］surgical department: ～手术 surgical operation ‖ 整形～ plastic surgery ‖ ～病房 surgical ward ‖ ～手术式打击 surgical strike

【外科学】wàikēxué〈名〉 surgery [branch of medicine]

【外科医生】wàikē yīshēng〈名〉 surgeon

【外壳】wàiké〈名〉 outer casing: 电视机/手表～ case of a TV set/wrist watch ‖ 这种甲虫有坚硬的～。 This kind of beetle has a hard shell.

【外客】wàikè〈名〉 distantly-related guest

【外寇】wàikòu〈名〉〈旧〉 invading army

【外快】wàikuài〈名〉〈口〉 extra income: 挣～ make some extra cash

【外来】wàilái〈形〉 external: ～务工人员 external labour force ‖ 他的早期绘画受到不少～影响。 His early paintings show much external influence.

【外来词】wàiláicí〈名〉 loan word: 源于拉丁语的～ words of Latin origin

【外来户】wàiláihù〈名〉 sb. from out of town

【外来妹】wàiláimèi〈名〉 female migrant worker

【外来移民】wàilái yímín〈名〉 immigrant

【外来语】wàiláiyǔ = 外来词 wàiláicí

【外力】wàilì〈名〉 **1**（外部力量） outside force **2**［物理］ external force: 在～的作用下，一个运动物体可能会改变其运动方向。 When acted upon by an external force, a moving object may change its path.

【外联网】wàiliánwǎng〈名〉 extranet

【外流】wàiliú〈动〉 outflow: 资金～ capital outflow ‖ 人才～ brain drain

【外路】wàilù〈形〉 outside: ～货 non-local goods ‖ ～人 non-local person

【外露】wàilù〈动〉 reveal: 他感情从不～。 He never reveals his true feelings.

【外轮】wàilún〈名〉 foreign vessel

【外卖】wàimài **A**〈动〉 provide a takeout service: 提供～服务的餐馆 takeaway restaurant ‖ 本店～烤鸭。 This restaurant offers takeaway roast duck. **B**〈名〉 takeaway〈英〉; carryout〈美〉: 吃～ have a takeaway ‖ 送～ deliver takeaways

【外贸】wàimào〈名〉 foreign trade

【外貌】wàimào〈名〉 appearance: ～特征 external feature

【外面】wàimiàn〈名〉 **1**（外部） exterior: 这件大衣里面是毛，～是布。 This coat has fur on the inside and cloth on the outside. **2**（室外） outside: ～很冷。 It's cold outside. ‖ 不接触社会怎么会了解～的事儿? Without contact with society, how can you hope to understand the outside world?

【外面儿光】wàimiànrguāng〈惯〉〈方〉 outward appearance: 做事要考虑实际效果，不能追求～。 In handling such matters, we must pay attention to actual results and not try to show off.

【外聘】wàipìn〈动〉 employ from a unit other than one's own: 该校老师70%都是从周围院校～的。 Seventy per cent of the teachers at this school are employed from colleges or universities nearby.

【外婆】wàipó ▸p. 588〈名〉 maternal grandmother

【外戚】wàiqī〈名〉 relative of a king or emperor on the side of his mother or wife

【外企】wàiqǐ〈名〉 foreign enterprise

【外墙】wàiqiáng〈名〉 outer wall

【外强中干】wàiqiáng-zhōnggān〈成〉 outwardly strong but inwardly weak: 一切反动派都是～的纸老虎。 All reactionaries are paper tigers. They look strong, but are actually weak.

【外侨】wàiqiáo〈名〉 foreign national

【外切】wàiqiē〈形〉［数学］ circumscribed: ～圆 excircle

【外勤】wàiqín〈名〉 **1**（指工作） fieldwork: 跑～ do fieldwork **2**（指人） fieldworker

【外人】wàirén〈名〉 **1**（不相干的人） stranger: 别客气，我又不是～。 No need for formalities. I'm no stranger. ‖ 在婆婆家她总感觉自己像是～。 She always feels like an outsider at her mother-in-law's. **2**（外国人） foreigner

【外柔内刚】wàiróu-nèigāng〈成〉 soft on the outside but firm on the inside
【外伤】wàishāng〈名〉 external injury: 医生认为她的伤都是～。 The doctor thinks her injuries are all external.
【外商】wàishāng〈名〉 foreign businessman: ～来料加工 process materials for foreign businessmen
【外商独资企业】wàishāng dúzī qǐyè〈名〉 exclusively foreign-owned enterprise
【外生殖器】wàishēngzhíqì〈名〉［生理］ external genital organs
【外甥】wàisheng〈名〉 nephew [sister's son]
【外甥打灯笼——照舅(旧)】wàisheng dǎ dēnglong—zhàojiù〈歇后〉 the same as before
【外甥女】wàishengnǚ〈名〉 niece [sister's daughter]
【外史】wàishǐ〈名〉 unofficial history:《儒林～》*Unofficial History of the Scholars*
【外事】wàishì〈名〉 **1**（外交事务） foreign affairs: 他今晚有～活动。 He has an appointment with some foreign visitors this evening. **2**（外边的事） outside affairs: 妻子一心操持家务，不问～。 The wife concentrates on household affairs and doesn't enquire about what goes on outside.
【外事办公室】wàishì bàngōngshì〈名〉 foreign affairs office
【外事部门】wàishì bùmén〈名〉 foreign affairs department
【外室】wàishì〈名〉〈旧〉 mistress
【外水】wàishuǐ〈名〉 extra income
【外孙】wàisūn ▸**p. 588**〈名〉 grandson [daughter's son]
【外孙女】wàisūnnǚ ▸**p. 588**〈名〉 granddaughter [daughter's daughter]
【外孙子】wàisūnzi〈名〉〈口〉 grandson [daughter's son]
【外胎】wàitāi = 外带 wàidài A
【外逃】wàitáo〈动〉 **1**（逃往外地） flee to another place **2**（逃往国外） flee the country: 携款～ abscond with the cash
【外套】wàitào〈名〉 **1**（大衣） overcoat **2**（外衣） outer garment
【外听道】wàitīngdào〈名〉［生理］ external auditory meatus
【外头】wàitou〈名〉〈口〉 outside: ～很黑。 It's dark outside.
【外围】wàiwéi〈名〉 periphery: 建于城市～的工厂 factory built on the periphery of the town ‖ ～人员 subsidiary staff ‖ ～组织 peripheral organization
【外文】wàiwén ▸**p. 918**〈名〉 foreign language: 学习～ learn a foreign language ‖ ～报纸 foreign language newspaper
【外屋】wàiwū〈名〉 outer room
【外侮】wàiwǔ〈名〉〈书〉 foreign aggression: 抵御～ resist foreign aggression
【外务】wàiwù〈名〉 **1**（本职以外的事） matters external to one's job **2**〈旧〉（外交事务） foreign affairs
【外务大臣】wàiwù dàchén〈名〉 minister of foreign affairs
【外务省】Wàiwùshěng〈名〉 Ministry of Foreign Affairs [in Japan]
【外骛】wàiwù〈动〉〈书〉 get involved in things that are not one's business: 他心无～。 His heart is in his work.
【外线】wàixiàn〈名〉 **1**［军事］ exterior lines: ～作战 fight on exterior lines **2**（指电话线） outside line: 让接线生接～ ask the switchboard operator for an outside line
【外乡】wàixiāng〈名〉 another part of the country: ～口音 non-local accent ‖ ～人 non-native
【外向】wàixiàng〈形〉 **1**［心理］ extroverted: 性格～ have an outgoing personality **2**（面向国外市场） export-oriented: ～型经济 export-oriented economy
【外相】wàixiàng〈名〉 foreign minister: 日本～ Japanese Foreign Minister
【外销】wàixiāo〈动〉 sell abroad or in another part of the country: ～物资 materials for export ‖ 产品全部～。 All the products are for export.
【外心】wàixīn〈名〉 **1**（不忠之心） unfaithful intentions: 自从见了这位迷人的姑娘，他便有了～。 The sight of the charming girl seduced him into unfaithful thoughts. **2**［数学］ circumcentre
【外星人】wàixīngrén〈名〉 extraterrestrial being
【外形】wàixíng〈名〉 appearance: ～美观大方 elegant and graceful in appearance ‖ ～设计 contour design
【外姓】wàixìng〈名〉 **1**（指姓氏） surname other than one's own **2**（指人） people of a clan other than one's own
【外需】wàixū〈名〉 international market demand
【外延】wàiyán〈名〉［逻辑］ denotation: Plant 这个词～很大。 'Plant' is a word with wide extension.
【外扬】wàiyáng〈动〉 spread: ▸家丑不可～
【外衣】wàiyī〈名〉 **1**〈本〉 coat: 穿上/脱掉～ put on/take off one's jacket **2**〈喻〉（伪装） appearance: 他披着天使的～，却心如魔鬼。 He looks like an angel but has the heart of a devil.
【外溢】wàiyì〈动〉 **1**（指液体） spill over: 杯中啤酒～。 The beer in the cup spilled over. **2**（指财富） outflow: 资金～ funding drain ‖ ～效应 spillover effect
【外因】wàiyīn〈名〉［哲学］ external cause: 把自己的失败归咎于～ blame external factors for one's inability to succeed
【外阴】wàiyīn〈名〉［生理］ vulva: ～搔痒 itchy vulva
【外引】wàiyǐn〈动〉 introduce (foreign funds, technology, talent, etc.) from abroad or other parts of the country: ～内联 absorb investment from abroad and establish cooperative relations at home
【外用】wàiyòng〈名〉［医学］ external use: ～药 medicine for external use ‖ ～药水 lotion
【外语】wàiyǔ ▸**p. 918**〈名〉 foreign language: 精通一门～ be good at a foreign language ‖ 学习～ learn a foreign language
【外域】wàiyù〈名〉〈书〉 foreign land
【外遇】wàiyù〈名〉 extramarital relations: 她怀疑丈夫有～。 She suspected her husband of having an affair.
【外圆内方】wàiyuán-nèifāng〈成〉〈喻〉 outwardly flexible but inwardly strict
【外援】wàiyuán〈名〉 **1**（国外援助） external assistance: 需要～ need outside help **2**（外籍运动员） international player: 每支足球队最多只能有三名～。 Each soccer team is allowed to have a maximum of three foreign players.
【外在】wàizài〈形〉 external: ～因素/原因 external factor/cause
【外在世界】wàizài shìjiè〈名〉［哲学］ external world
【外债】wàizhài〈名〉 foreign debt: 偿还～ repay external debts ‖ ～累累 be immobilized by foreign debt
【外长】wàizhǎng〈简称〉= 外交部长
【外罩】wàizhào〈名〉 **1**（指衣服） overall **2**（指套子） cover
【外痔】wàizhì ▸**p. 50**〈名〉［医学］ external haemorrhoid
【外置式】wàizhìshì〈形〉 outboard
【外传】wàizhuàn〈名〉 unauthorized biography
▸wàichuán
【外资】wàizī〈名〉 foreign investment: 吸引～ attract foreign capital
【外资企业】wàizī qǐyè〈名〉 foreign-owned enterprise
【外子】wàizǐ〈名〉〈书〉 my husband
【外族】wàizú〈名〉 **1**（本家族以外的人） people not of the same clan **2**（外国人） foreigner **3**（其他民族） other peoples
【外祖父】wàizǔfù ▸**p. 588**〈名〉 maternal grandfather
【外祖母】wàizǔmǔ ▸**p. 588**〈名〉 maternal grandmother

wān

弯（彎） wān

A〈形〉 curved: ～～的月亮 crescent moon ‖ 厚厚的积雪把树枝都压～了。 The branches are weighed down by a heavy layer of snow. ▸～路，～曲
B〈动〉 bend: 把金属线～成环状 bend a wire into a loop
C〈名〉 turn: 拐～儿 turn a corner ‖ 跑道转～处 bend of a race course
【弯道】wāndào〈名〉 bend
【弯度】wāndù〈名〉 curvature
【弯路】wānlù〈名〉 **1**〈本〉 winding road: 汽车在～处放慢了速度。 The car slowed down at the bends in the road. **2**〈喻〉（冤枉路） roundabout way: 我们工作走了～。 We were sidetracked in our work.
【弯曲】wānqū〈形〉 zigzagging: ～的小道 winding path
【弯头】wāntóu〈名〉［机械］ elbow joint: 水管～ bend in a water pipe
【弯腰】wānyāo〈动〉 bend down
【弯子】wānzi〈名〉〈口〉 bend: 绕～ go a roundabout way ‖〈喻〉 脑子一时转不过～来 not be able to get one's head around something

剜 wān

〈动〉 gouge out: ～眼睛 gouge out sb.'s eyes ‖ 把苹果烂的地方～掉。 Scoop out the rotten part of the apple.
【剜肉补疮】wānròu-bǔchuāng〈成〉〈喻〉 resort to a stopgap measure detrimental to long-term interests

塆 wān

〈名〉 small piece of flat land in a mountain gully

湾（灣） wān

A〈名〉 **1**（水流弯曲处） bend in a stream: 河～ river bend **2** ▸**p. 164**（海湾） gulf: 波斯～ Persian Gulf ‖ 渤海～ Bohai Bay ‖ 墨西哥～ Gulf of Mexico ▸港～，海～
B〈动〉 moor: 把小船～在大树下。 Moor the boat under the tree.
【湾泊】wānbó〈动〉 anchor

蜿 wān

【蜿蜒】wānyán〈形〉〈书〉 **1**（指爬行） wriggling: 一条蛇～爬过道路。 A snake wriggled across the road. **2**（指延伸） zigzagging: ～曲折的道路 winding road ‖ 一条小溪从草地～流过。 A brook winds its way through the meadow.

W

豌 wān

【豌豆】wāndòu〈名〉pea

wán

丸 wán

A〈名〉**1**（球状物）ball: 泥～ mud ball ‖ 肉～ meatball ▸弹～, 睾～, 药～ **2**（丸药）pill

B〈量〉[used for pills of Chinese medicine]: 每次服两～ take two pills each time ‖ 一盒十～ ten pills in each box

【丸剂】wánjì〈名〉pill

【丸药】wányào〈名〉Chinese medicine pill

【丸子】wánzi〈名〉**1**（指食物）ball: 鱼～ fish ball **2**（指药丸）Chinese medicine pill

刓 wán

〈动〉〈书〉**1**（削去棱角）whittle edges and corners **2**（挖）carve

纨（紈） wán

〈名〉〈书〉fine white silk fabrics: ～扇 round silk fan

【纨绔】wánkù〈名〉〈书〉sons of rich families: ～子弟 dandy

完 wán

A〈形〉whole: ▸～好

B〈动〉**1**（完成）finish: 等一等，我还没～呢! Wait. I haven't finished yet. ▸～成, ～稿, ～婚 **2**（完结）end: 修～大学课程 complete college courses ‖ 她话未说～，他就把她打断了。 He interrupted her before she had finished what she was saying. ‖ 这事还没～。 This is not the end of the matter. **3**（用尽）use up: 牙膏用～了。 We are out of toothpaste. ‖ 米吃～了。 We have run out of rice. **4**（交纳）pay: ～粮 pay the grain tax

【完败】wánbài〈动〉be thrashed: 客队以零比五～。 The visiting team were thrashed 0 : 5.

【完备】wánbèi〈形〉complete: 设施～ be well-equipped ‖ ～的检测手段 perfect inspection facilities ‖ 这部宪法还有不够～的地方。 This constitution still requires some fine-tuning.

【完毕】wánbì〈动〉complete: 实弹演习～。 The live ammunition manoeuvre is completed. ‖ 一切准备～。 Everything is ready.

【完璧归赵】wánbì-guīzhào〈成〉〈喻〉return sth. to its owner in perfect condition

【完成】wánchéng〈动〉accomplish: ～计划 carry out a plan ‖ ～任务 accomplish a task ‖ ～学业 finish with school ‖ ～作业/工作 finish one's homework/work ‖ 尚未～ be not yet complete ‖ 提前～ finish ahead of time

【完成时态】wánchéngshítài〈名〉[语法] perfect tense

【完蛋】wándàn〈动〉〈口〉be done for: 这计划注定要～。 The plan is a lost cause.

【完稿】wángǎo〈动〉finish a piece of writing: 该书已经～，即可付印。 The book has been completed and is ready to go to print.

【完工】wángōng〈动〉complete a project: 按期～ complete on schedule ‖ 这座过街天桥将于下月底～。 This overpass is to be completed by the end of next month.

【完好】wánhǎo〈形〉intact: 保存～ be kept in good condition ‖ 瓷器～无损。 The porcelain remained intact.

【完婚】wánhūn〈动〉〈书〉[of a man] get married: 择日～ fix a date for the wedding

【完结】wánjié〈动〉finish: 此事还没有～。 This is not the end of the matter.

【完聚】wánjù〈动〉〈书〉reunite: 春节期间，合家～。 The entire family reunited for Spring Festival.

【完竣】wánjùn〈动〉〈书〉be completed: 古城墙修复工作业已～。 Renovation of the old city walls is now complete.

【完了】wánliǎo〈动〉end: 比赛～后，出现了戏剧性的变化。 Dramatic changes took place after the end of the game.

【完满】wánmǎn〈形〉satisfactory: ～的结局 satisfactory end ‖ 问题终于～解决了。 The problem has been solved satisfactorily at last.

【完美】wánměi〈形〉perfect: 不够～ be imperfect ‖ 达到～ achieve/attain perfection ‖ 接近～ be almost perfect ‖ 力求～ strive for perfection ‖ ～的婚姻/人生/演出 perfect marriage/life/performance ‖ ～无缺 perfect

【完美主义】wánměizhǔyì〈名〉perfectionism: ～者 perfectionist

【完全】wánquán **A**〈形〉complete: 设施～。 The facilities are complete. ‖ 他话没说～。 He didn't give a full picture. **B**〈副〉completely: ～不同 be totally different ‖ ～没必要 be entirely unnecessary ‖ 与事实～相反 be in complete opposition to the facts ‖ ～正确 be absolutely correct

【完全小学】wánquán xiǎoxué〈名〉primary school with the full six grades

【完全中学】wánquán zhōngxué〈名〉combined middle and high school

【完人】wánrén〈名〉perfect man: 人无～。 No one is perfect.

【完赛】wánsài〈动〉finish a competition: F1上海站顺利～。 The Shanghai F1 event came to a smooth completion.

【完善】wánshàn **A**〈形〉perfect: 设备～ be very well-equipped ‖ 新制度难免有不够～的地方。 Imperfections are almost unavoidable. **B**〈动〉perfect: ～工业体系 perfect the industrial system ‖ ～法制 improve the legal system

【完胜】wánshèng〈动〉win a clear victory: 主队昨天～客队。 The home team thrashed the guest team yesterday.

【完事】wánshì〈动〉finish: 你以为道过歉就～了吗? Do you think your apology can bring the matter to an end?

【完税】wánshuì〈动〉pay tax: ～凭证 tax payment receipt

【完小】wánxiǎo〈简称〉= 完全小学

【完整】wánzhěng〈形〉complete: 结构～ be complete in structure ‖ 领土～ territorial integrity

【完中】wánzhōng〈简称〉= 完全中学

玩[1] wán

A〈动〉**1**（玩耍）hold and fondle: ▸～物丧志, 把～ **2**（观赏）enjoy: ▸游～ **3**（深究）probe: 细～文义 probe (into) a piece of writing for its message ▸～味 **4**（轻慢）play around with: ▸～弄, ～世不恭

B〈名〉object for appreciation: ▸古～

玩[2] wán

〈动〉**1**（使用）employ: ～花招 play tricks ‖ ～手腕 play tricks **2**（从事）have fun: ～牌 play cards ‖ ～游戏 play a game ‖ ～杂耍 practise juggling ‖ ～得很痛快 enjoy oneself to the full ‖ 孩子们都喜欢～儿。 All children love to play. ‖ 她只是说着～儿的。 She only said it as a joke. ▸贪～

【玩忽职守】wánhū-zhíshǒu〈成〉neglect one's duty

【玩火】wánhuǒ〈动〉play with fire: 这场森林大火是由孩子～引起的。 This devastating forest fire was caused by children messing around with fire. ‖ 你可千万不能再～了。 Don't go playing with fire again.

【玩火自焚】wánhuǒ-zìfén〈成〉he who plays with fire will get burnt

【玩家】wánjiā〈名〉gamer: 游戏～ computer gamer

【玩具】wánjù〈名〉toy: ～枪/汽车 toy gun/car ‖ 电动～ electric toy

【玩乐】wánlè〈动〉have fun

【玩弄】wánnòng〈动〉**1**（摆弄）play with: ～手枪 mess about with a pistol ‖ ～钢笔 play with a pen **2**（戏弄）dally with: ～感情 play around with sb.'s affections ‖ ～女性 womanize **3**（搬弄）play with: ～词藻 play with words **4**（施展）employ: ～两面派手法 engage in double-dealing ‖ ～权术 play politics ‖ ～阴谋诡计 resort to schemes and intrigues

【玩偶】wán'ǒu〈名〉doll

【玩儿不转】wánr bu zhuàn〈惯〉cannot manage: 你这点小事都～? You can't handle a small thing like this?

【玩儿得转】wánr de zhuàn〈惯〉can manage: 你一个人能～吗? Can you handle this by yourself?

【玩儿命】wánrmìng〈动〉〈口〉〈诙〉gamble with one's life: ～地干 work like hell ‖ 把车开到每小时170公里简直是在～。 Driving at 170 kilometres an hour is playing with one's life.

【玩儿票】wánrpiào〈动〉〈口〉do a job as a sideline: 这位画家教书纯粹是～。 This painter is taking teaching merely as a sideline.

【玩儿完】wánrwán〈动〉〈口〉〈诙〉be done for

【玩赏】wánshǎng〈动〉enjoy: ～风景 admire the scenery ‖ ～邮票 enjoy collecting stamps

【玩世不恭】wánshì-bùgōng〈成〉be cynical: ～的行为 cynical behaviour

【玩耍】wánshuǎ〈动〉have fun: 在户外～ play outdoors

【玩味】wánwèi〈动〉ponder: 值得～ be worth pondering

【玩物】wánwù〈名〉plaything: 她似乎满足于做大款的～。 She seemed content with her life as a rich man's plaything.

【玩物丧志】wánwù-sàngzhì〈成〉pursuit of petty pleasures thwarts high aims

【玩笑】wánxiào **A**〈动〉joke with: 我很清楚他说娶我只是～而已。 I'm sure he was joking when he asked me to marry him. **B**〈名〉joke: 爱开～ enjoy cracking jokes ‖ 拿生命开～ trifle with sb.'s life

【玩艺儿】wányìr = 玩意儿 wányìr

【玩意儿】wányìr〈名〉〈口〉**1**（玩具）toy **2**（曲艺、杂技等）performance **3**（事物）thing: 收集各种各样的小～ collect all sorts of little gadgets ‖ 新鲜～ something new ‖ 他是什么～? What a louse he is!

顽（頑） wán

〈形〉**1**（顽固）obstinate: ～匪 stubborn ruffian ▸～敌, ～固 **2**（傻）stupid: ▸冥～不灵, 愚～ **3**（淘气）naughty: ▸～劣, ～皮, ～童

【顽敌】wándí〈名〉stubborn enemy: 歼灭～ destroy the stubborn enemy

【顽钝】wándùn〈形〉〈书〉**1**（愚笨）stupid: 资质～ be obtuse by nature **2**（无

节气）lacking moral courage 3（不锋利）blunt
【顽梗】wángěng〈形〉〈书〉obstinate
【顽固】wángù〈形〉1（指思想）stubborn: ～地坚持错误立场 stubbornly cling to the wrong position ‖ 思想～ stubborn thinking 2（指立场）diehard: ～分子 diehard element 3（指疾病、行为等）chronic: 这种病很～。This type of illness can be very persistent.
【顽固不化】wángù-bùhuà〈成〉incorrigibly obstinate
【顽固派】wángùpài〈名〉diehard
【顽疾】wánjí〈名〉persistent ailment
【顽抗】wánkàng〈动〉stubbornly resist: 对改革采取～态度 show stubborn resistance to reform ‖ 敌人负隅～。The enemy tried to put up a stubborn resistance.
【顽劣】wánliè〈形〉〈书〉mischievous and wilful: 秉性～ be stubborn and mischievous by nature
【顽皮】wánpí〈形〉naughty: ～的孩子 naughty child
【顽强】wánqiáng〈形〉indomitable: ～拼搏 keep pressing on with one's work no matter how hard things get ‖ 同自然灾害进行～的斗争 carry on a tenacious struggle against natural calamity
【顽石点头】wánshí-diǎntóu〈成〉very persuasive
【顽童】wántóng〈名〉naughty boy
【顽症】wánzhèng = 顽疾 wánjí
【顽主】wánzhǔ〈名〉cynical and disaffected person

烷 wán〈名〉［化学］alkane: ▸甲～, 乙～

wǎn

宛 wǎn
A〈形〉winding: ▸～转
B〈副〉〈书〉seemingly: 音容～在 as if the deceased were still alive
【宛然】wǎnrán〈副〉〈书〉as if: ～在目 as if before one's very eyes
【宛如】wǎnrú〈副〉〈书〉just like: 起伏的麦田～大海的波涛。The flowing wheat in the field is like the waves in the sea.
【宛若】wǎnruò = 宛如 wǎnrú
【宛若天仙】wǎnruòtiānxiān〈成〉look like a heavenly goddess
【宛似】wǎnsì = 宛如 wǎnrú
【宛转】wǎnzhuǎn A = 辗转 zhǎnzhuǎn B = 婉转 wǎnzhuǎn

挽[1] wǎn〈动〉1（拉）pull: ～弓搭箭 fit an arrow and draw one's bow ‖ 手～手 hand in hand 2（往上卷）roll up: ～起袖子 roll up one's sleeves 3（扭转）retrieve: ～狂澜于既倒 do one's utmost to save the desperate situation ▸～救, 力～狂澜

挽[2]（輓）wǎn〈动〉1（牵引）draw: ～车 draw a carriage 2（哀悼）lament: ▸～歌, 敬～

挽[3] wǎn = 绾 wǎn
【挽词】wǎncí〈名〉memorial speech
【挽歌】wǎngē〈名〉elegy: 唱～ chant a dirge ‖ 旧制度的～ elegies on the old system
【挽回】wǎnhuí〈动〉1（扭转）retrieve: ～败局 retrieve a defeat ‖ ～面子 save one's face ‖ 形势已无法～。The situation is now beyond redemption. 2（收回）take back: ～经济损失 recover financial losses ‖ 已说的话无法～。It is not possible to take back what has already been said.
【挽救】wǎnjiù〈动〉rescue: ～病人的生命 save the life of a patient ‖ ～失足青少年 rescue juvenile delinquents
【挽具】wǎnjù〈名〉harness: 给马套上～ harness a horse
【挽联】wǎnlián〈名〉elegiac couplet
【挽留】wǎnliú〈动〉persuade sb. to stay: 苦苦/执意～ repeatedly/insistently urge sb. to stay ‖ ～某人吃饭 ask sb. to stay for dinner
【挽幛】wǎnzhàng〈名〉large, oblong sheet of silk, usually blue, with inscriptions, presented at a funeral

莞 wǎn
▸guān
【莞尔】wǎn'ěr〈形〉〈书〉with a smiling air: ～一笑 give a soft smile

菀 wǎn ▸紫菀 zǐwǎn
▸yù

晚 wǎn
A〈名〉1（晚上）evening: ～风 evening breeze ‖ 今～ this evening ‖ 从早到～ from morning till night ▸傍～ 2（晚年）old age: ▸～节, ～境
B〈形〉1（迟）late: ～十五分钟/一个小时/一天 be fifteen minutes/an hour/a day late ‖ 饭吃～了 be late with a meal 2（后期）late: ～草莓/番茄 late strawberries/tomatoes ‖ ～唐 the late Tang Dynasty 3（后来）succeeding: ▸～辈
【晚安】wǎn'ān ▸p. 780〈形〉〈套〉good night
【晚班】wǎnbān〈名〉night shift: 上～ work the night shift
【晚报】wǎnbào〈名〉evening paper
【晚辈】wǎnbèi〈名〉younger generation
【晚餐】wǎncān〈名〉〈书〉dinner: 与某人共进～ share a dinner with sb.
【晚场】wǎnchǎng〈名〉evening show: ～演出 evening performance
【晚车】wǎnchē〈名〉night train
【晚春】wǎnchūn ▸p. 345〈名〉late spring: 时值～。It was late spring.
【晚祷】wǎndǎo〈名〉vespers: 参加～ attend vespers
【晚稻】wǎndào〈名〉late rice
【晚点】wǎndiǎn〈动〉be behind schedule: 飞机～两个小时才起飞。There was a two-hour delay before the plane took off. ‖ 火车～了。The train is late.
【晚饭】wǎnfàn〈名〉dinner: ～吃什么? What's for supper?
【晚会】wǎnhuì〈名〉evening party: 春节联欢～ Spring Festival get-together ‖ 篝火～ campfire party ‖ 生日～ birthday party
【晚婚】wǎnhūn〈动〉marry late: 提倡～ advocate late marriage ‖ ～晚育 late marriage and late childbirth
【晚间】wǎnjiān〈名〉evening: ～新闻 Evening News
【晚节】wǎnjié〈名〉integrity in one's later years: ～不保 lose one's virtue in old age
【晚景】wǎnjǐng〈名〉1（指景色）evening scene: 田园～ evening pastoral scene 2（指景况）one's circumstances in old age: ～凄凉 lead a miserable and dreary life in old age
【晚境】wǎnjìng〈名〉conditions in old age
【晚礼服】wǎnlǐfú〈名〉evening dress
【晚年】wǎnnián〈名〉old age: 安度～ live out one's remaining years in peace and quiet ‖ 过着幸福的～ enjoy a happy old age
【晚娘】wǎnniáng〈名〉〈方〉stepmother
【晚期】wǎnqī ▸p. 618〈名〉later period: ～作品 later works ‖ 十九世纪～ late 19th century ‖ 他的肝癌已到～。His liver cancer has reached an advanced stage.
【晚秋】wǎnqiū ▸p. 345〈名〉late autumn: ～作物 late-autumn crop ‖ 时值～。It was late autumn.
【晚上】wǎnshang ▸p. 669 ▸p. 780〈名〉evening: 乘～的列车 travel on the night train ‖ ～好。Good evening. ‖ 她白天做文秘，～到酒吧唱歌。She's a secretary by day and a singer in a bar by night.
【晚生】wǎnshēng〈名〉〈旧〉〈谦〉I
【晚世】wǎnshì〈名〉〈旧〉modern times
【晚熟】wǎnshú〈动〉［农业］mature late: ～品种 late variety ‖ ～作物 late-maturing crop
【晚霜】wǎnshuāng〈名〉1（指霜）late frost 2（指护肤品）night cream
【晚霞】wǎnxiá〈名〉sunset glow: ～满天。The setting sun kindled the sky. ‖ ～红似火。The evening sky is as red as fire.
【晚香玉】wǎnxiāngyù〈名〉［植物］tuberose
【晚宴】wǎnyàn〈名〉dinner: 参加～ participate in a banquet
【晚育】wǎnyù〈动〉have a child late in life
【晚造】wǎnzào〈名〉late crop

脘 wǎn〈名〉gastric cavity: 胃～不适 have a queasy stomach

惋 wǎn〈动〉〈书〉sigh: 叹～ sigh in lament
【惋惜】wǎnxī〈动〉regret: 这小伙子没考上大学，真让人～。It's a great pity that this young man failed to get into college.

婉 wǎn〈形〉1（柔顺）mild: ▸～和, ～顺 2（婉转）tactful: ▸～辞, ～拒 3〈书〉（美好）elegant: ▸～丽
【婉词】wǎncí = 婉辞 wǎncí A
【婉辞】wǎncí A〈名〉gentle words B〈动〉refuse politely: 他～了对方的邀请。He declined the invitation.
【婉和】wǎnhé〈形〉tactful: ～的语气 mild tone
【婉拒】wǎnjù〈动〉decline politely: ～邀请 decline an invitation
【婉丽】wǎnlì〈形〉〈书〉1（指容貌）beautiful 2（指诗文）graceful
【婉顺】wǎnshùn〈形〉〈书〉[of a woman] meek: 性情～ be meek by nature
【婉谢】wǎnxiè〈动〉politely refuse: ～邀请 decline sb.'s invitation
【婉言】wǎnyán〈名〉gentle words: ～拒绝 politely refuse ‖ ～相劝 gently persuade
【婉约】wǎnyuē〈形〉〈书〉graceful and restrained
【婉转】wǎnzhuǎn〈形〉1（指说话）tactful: 尽量～地解释 explain as tactfully as possible ‖ 说得～些 put it mildly 2（指歌声、鸟叫等）sweet and agreeable: ～的歌喉 sweet voice

绾（綰）wǎn〈动〉coil up: ～个扣儿 tie a knot ‖ ～头发 coil one's hair

W

琬 wǎn〈名〉〈书〉fine jade

皖 Wǎn ▸**p. 661**〈名〉Wan [another name for Anhui Province (安徽)]: ～南 Southern Anhui

碗 wǎn〈名〉**1**（指器皿）bowl: 洗～ wash up ▸饭～ **2**（碗状物）bowl-like object: 轴～儿 axle bowl

【碗橱】wǎnchú = 碗柜 wǎnguì

【碗柜】wǎnguì〈名〉kitchen cupboard

【碗碗腔】wǎnwǎnqiāng〈名〉*wanwanqiang* [local opera in Shaanxi Province]

wàn

万（萬） wàn

A〈数〉**1** ▸**p. 691**（一万）ten thousand: ～米跑 ten-thousand-metre race ‖ 百～ million **2**（大量）myriad: ～里长空 vast clear skies ‖ ～事～物 myriads of things ▸～众一心, ～紫千红

B〈副〉absolutely: 此事～不可泄漏出去。Be sure not to let it out. ▸～恶, ～幸

【万般】wànbān **A**〈形〉multifarious: ～无奈 have no alternative whatsoever **B**〈副〉extremely: ～惆怅 be completely disconsolate

【万宝全书】wànbǎoquánshū〈名〉walking encyclopedia

【万变不离其宗】wàn biàn bù lí qí zōng〈成〉remain essentially the same despite all apparent changes

【万不得已】wànbùdéyǐ〈成〉out of absolute necessity: 不是～，我们不会出此下策。If we'd had any other choice, we would not have taken such an unwise decision.

【万代】wàndài = 万世 wànshì

【万端】wànduān〈形〉〈书〉multifarious: 变化～ kaleidoscopic changes ‖ 感慨～ all sorts of feelings welling up in one's mind

【万恶】wàn'è **A**〈形〉extremely evil: ～不赦 be unpardonably vicious **B**〈名〉all evils: ～之源 root of all evils

【万恶淫为首】wàn'è yín wéi shǒu〈俗〉lewdness is the worst of all vices

【万方】wànfāng **A**〈名〉〈旧〉all places: ～同贺。Congratulations flooded in from all directions. **B**〈形〉〈书〉of various different postures: 仪态～的女士 lady of graceful carriage

【万分】wànfēn〈副〉very much, extremely: 悲痛～ be overwhelmed by grief ‖ ～感激 extremely grateful

【万夫莫当】wànfū-mòdāng〈成〉[of a brave warrior] any number of men cannot withstand him

【万夫莫当之勇】wànfū-mòdāng zhī yǒng〈成〉strength and bravery which ten thousand men cannot resist

【万福】wànfú ▸**p. 780**〈名〉〈旧〉wishing you all happiness [form of greeting by women with traditional Chinese curtsy]: 道～ curtsy

【万古】wàngǔ〈名〉aeons: ～不变 forever immutable ‖ ～长存 be everlasting

【万古长青】wàngǔ-chángqīng〈成〉be everlasting: 祝两国人民的友谊～! May the friendship between our two peoples last forever.

【万古流芳】wàngǔ-liúfāng〈成〉achieve immortal fame

【万贯】wànguàn〈名〉〈旧〉great wealth: 他有～家财。He is extremely wealthy.

【万国】wànguó〈名〉〈旧〉all nations: ～博览会 international exhibition

【万国邮政联盟】Wànguó Yóuzhèng Liánméng〈名〉Universal Postal Union (UPU)

【万户侯】wànhùhóu〈名〉〈旧〉high official

【万花筒】wànhuātǒng〈名〉kaleidoscope

【万机】wànjī〈名〉〈书〉numerous state affairs: 日理～ be taken up with important matters

【万家灯火】wànjiā-dēnghuǒ〈成〉dazzling city lights: 漫步街头，但见～，一片灿烂。Walking down the street, we were greeted with a sea of lights.

【万箭穿心】wànjiàn-chuānxīn〈成〉〈喻〉grief-stricken

【万劫不复】wànjié-bùfù〈成〉lost forever: 陷于～之地 be doomed forever

【万金油】wànjīnyóu〈名〉**1**（指药油）Tiger Balm **2**〈喻〉（指人）Jack of all trades and master of none

【万籁俱寂】wànlài-jùjì〈成〉silence reigns supreme

【万里长城】Wànlǐ Chángchéng〈名〉Great Wall of China: ～今犹在，不见当年秦始皇。The Great Wall is still in existence, but its builder Qin Shihuang is no more.

【万里长空】wànlǐchángkōng〈名〉boundless sky

【万里长征】Wànlǐ Chángzhēng〈名〉Long March [1934-1935]

【万里无云】wànlǐ-wúyún〈成〉cloudless sky

【万灵药】wànlíngyào〈名〉panacea

【万隆】Wànlóng〈名〉Bandung: ～会议 Bandung Conference

【万马奔腾】wànmǎ-bēnténg〈成〉all going full steam ahead: 长江以～之势滚滚向前。The Yangtze River surges onward like ten thousand horses galloping.

【万马齐喑】wànmǎ-qíyīn〈成〉〈喻〉lifeless atmosphere

【万民】wànmín〈名〉broad mass of the populace: ～拥戴 broad support

【万难】wànnán〈书〉**A**〈副〉impossibly: ～从命 impossible to comply with sb.'s request ‖ ～推辞 be extremely difficult to say 'No' **B**〈名〉all sorts of difficulties: 排除～ surmount all difficulties

【万能】wànnéng〈形〉**1**（无所不能）omnipotent: ～的主 Almighty God ‖ 金钱不是～的。Money is not all-powerful. **2**（多功能）universal: ～胶 all-purpose glue ‖ ～钥匙 master key

【万年】wànnián〈名〉eternity: 遗臭～ leave a bad name for all eternity

【万年历】wànniánlì〈名〉perpetual calendar

【万年青】wànniánqīng〈名〉[植物] **1**（指木本植物）evergreen **2**（指草本植物）rohdea japonica

【万念俱灰】wànniàn-jùhuī〈成〉be reduced to despair: 极度贫困使他～。Extreme poverty had reduced him to a state of apathy.

【万千】wànqiān〈形〉multifarious: 变化～ change all the time ‖ 思绪～ myriads of thoughts welling up in one's mind ‖ 气象～ be spectacular

【万顷】wànqǐng〈名〉〈书〉vast expanse: ～碧波 vast expanse of water

【万全】wànquán〈形〉sure-fire: ～之策 sure-fire plan

【万儿八千】wànrbāqiān〈惯〉〈口〉about ten thousand

【万人坑】wànrénkēng〈名〉mass grave

【万人空巷】wànrén-kōngxiàng〈成〉a full turnout

【万圣节】Wànshèngjié〈名〉[基督教] All Saints' Day: ～前夕 Halloween

【万世】wànshì〈名〉generation after generation: ～不衰 last forever ‖ ～师表 Model Teacher of all eternity [honorific title for Confucius]

【万世流芳】wànshì-liúfāng〈成〉be remembered forever

【万事】wànshì〈名〉all things: ～万物 myriads of things ‖ ～顺利 everything fares well

【万事大吉】wànshì-dàjí〈成〉everything is just fine: 他一完婚，他妈就～了。As soon as her son gets married, she will feel that all is well with the world.

【万事亨通】wànshì-hēngtōng〈成〉everything goes smoothly

【万事俱备，只欠东风】wànshì jù bèi, zhǐ qiàn dōngfēng〈成〉〈喻〉all is ready except what is crucial

【万事开头难】wànshì kāitóu nán〈俗〉everything's hard in the beginning

【万事如意】wànshì-rúyì〈套〉have all that one desires: 祝你～! May you have all that you desire!

【万事通】wànshìtōng〈名〉know-all

【万寿菊】wànshòujú〈名〉marigold

【万寿无疆】wànshòu-wújiāng〈套〉〈旧〉(may you enjoy) boundless longevity

【万水千山】wànshuǐ-qiānshān〈成〉the trials of a long and arduous journey: 踏遍～ travel widely

【万死】wànsǐ〈动〉die ten thousand deaths: 罪该～ deserve to die ten thousand deaths

【万死不辞】wànsǐ bùcí〈成〉willing to risk any danger

【万岁】wànsuì **A**〈动〉long live: 祖国～! Long live my fatherland! **B**〈名〉Your Majesty

【万万】wànwàn **A**〈副〉[used in negative sense] absolutely: ～不可掉以轻心 must never be negligent ‖ 这一点我～没有想到。This idea never occurred to me. **B** ▸**p. 691**〈数〉hundred million

【万维网】Wànwéiwǎng〈名〉World Wide Web (WWW)

【万位】wànwèi〈名〉[计算器] myriabit

【万无一失】wànwúyīshī〈成〉perfectly safe: 确保火箭发射～ ensure the successful launch of a rocket

【万物】wànwù〈名〉everything on earth: ～丛生 grow in great variety and profusion ‖ ～生长靠太阳。All things on earth depend on the sun for their growth.

【万向】wànxiàng〈形〉[机械] universal: ～轮 universal wheel

【万象】wànxiàng〈名〉**1**〈书〉（一切事物或景象）all manifestations of nature: 包罗～ be all-inclusive **2** Wànxiàng（老挝首都）Vientiane

【万象更新】wànxiàng-gēngxīn〈成〉everything looks new and fresh: 春回大地，～。With the coming of spring, everything looks fresh and new again.

【万幸】wànxìng〈形〉very fortunate: 不幸中的～ great fortune in the midst of bad ‖ 他能从地震中逃生，真是～。He is so lucky to have survived the earthquake!

【万一】wànyī **A**〈连〉just in case: ～有紧急情况，请按红色按钮以切断电源。Should there be an emergency, please press the red button to cut off the electricity. **B**〈名〉**1**（意外）eventuality: 防备～ be prepared for all eventualities **2**〈书〉

（极小部分） tiny percentage: 笔墨不能形容其～。 It's simply beyond description.
【万应灵丹】wànyìng-língdān〈名〉cure-all
【万用表】wànyòngbiǎo〈名〉［电气］multimeter
【万有引力】wànyǒu yǐnlì〈名〉［物理］gravitational force
【万丈】wànzhàng〈数量〉〈喻〉towering: ～高楼 skyscraper ‖ ～深渊 bottomless chasm ‖ 光芒～ shine with boundless radiance
【万众】wànzhòng〈名〉the multitude: 喜讯传来，～欢腾。 Millions of people rejoiced at the happy news.
【万众一心】wànzhòng-yīxīn〈成〉all people of one heart and one mind: 中国人民～为实现四化而奋斗。 All Chinese people are united in the modernization drive.
【万状】wànzhuàng〈形〉〈书〉extreme: 惊恐～ be frightened out of one's wits
【万紫千红】wànzǐ-qiānhóng〈成〉blaze of colour: 百花盛开，～。 Flowers of all sorts are blooming in a riot of colour.

忨 wàn〈动〉〈书〉covet

腕 wàn〈名〉wrist: 将某人的双～反拷在背后 handcuff sb.'s wrists behind them ▸护～, 脚～, 手～
【腕表】wànbiǎo〈名〉〈口〉wristwatch
【腕骨】wàngǔ〈名〉carpal bone: ～骨折 fracture of carpal bone
【腕关节】wànguānjié〈名〉wrist joint
【腕力】wànlì〈名〉**1**〈本〉wrist strength **2**〈喻〉（能力） ability: 佩服他的胆识和～ admire his courage, insight and competence
【腕儿】wànr〈名〉big shot: 大～明星 megastar
【腕饰】wànshì〈名〉wristlet
【腕子】wànzi〈名〉wrist: 用绷带包住～ wrap a bandage around the wrist
【腕足】wànzú〈名〉peduncle: ～动物 brachiopod

蔓 wàn〈名〉tendrilled vine: 南瓜爬～了。 The pumpkin plant is climbing. ▸mán, màn

wāng

汪¹ wāng
A〈形〉〈书〉deep and vast: ～洋 vast ocean **B**〈名〉〈方〉pond: 村边有个小水～。 There was a small pool near the village. **C**〈动〉accumulate: 眼里～着泪水 have tears in one's eyes **D**〈量〉pool: 一～血水 a pool of blood ‖ 一～雨水 a puddle of rainwater

汪² wāng〈拟〉bark
【汪汪】wāngwāng **A**〈形〉**1**（充满水或泪的样子） tearful: 泪～ with tears pouring down ‖ 水～的眼睛 bright and intelligent eyes **2**〈书〉（水面宽广） vast **B**〈拟〉bark: 狗～地叫。 A dog is barking.
【汪洋】wāngyáng〈形〉**1**（水势浩大） vast: 一片～ a vast expanse of water **2**〈书〉（气度宏大）magnanimous: 大度～ with immense generosity
【汪洋大海】wāngyángdàhǎi〈成〉boundless ocean

wáng

亡 wáng
A〈动〉**1**（逃跑） flee: ▸流～, 逃～ **2**〈书〉（丢失） lose: ～失 disappear ▸唇～齿寒, 歧路～羊 **3**（灭亡） perish: ～我之心不死 not give up on the desire to subjugate our country ‖ 国破家～。 The nation and the family perished. ▸存～, 衰～, 兴～ **4**（死亡） die: 夭～ die young ‖ 遇刺身～ be assassinated **B**〈形〉deceased: 悼～ mourn for the dead ‖ ～妻 late wife ▸伤～
【亡故】wánggù〈动〉〈书〉die: 他的双亲～多年了。 His parents have been dead for many years.
【亡国】wángguó **A**〈动〉cause a nation to perish: 亡了国，哪里还有家？ How can a family survive if the nation perishes? **B**〈名〉〈书〉fallen nation
【亡国奴】wángguónú〈名〉conquered people: 誓死不做～ would rather die than be conquered
【亡国之君】wángguózhījūn〈名〉**1**（指使国家灭亡） king who causes the collapse of a nation **2**（指国家被征服） king of a conquered nation
【亡魂】wánghún〈名〉soul of a deceased person
【亡魂丧胆】wánghún-sàngdǎn〈成〉be scared out of one's wits
【亡灵】wánglíng〈名〉soul of a deceased person: 超度～ release the soul of a deceased person from suffering
【亡命】wángmìng〈动〉**1**（逃亡） flee: ～天涯 seek refuge in remote areas **2**（绝望） be desperate: ～之徒 desperado
【亡失】wángshī〈动〉〈书〉be lost: ～多年 have been lost for ages
【亡羊补牢】wángyáng-bǔláo〈成〉〈喻〉lock the stable door after the horse has bolted: ～，犹未为晚。 Better late than never.

王 wáng
A〈名〉**1**（君王） king: ▸～朝, ～位, 国～ **2**（最高爵位） duke: ▸亲～ **3**（首领） chief: 占山为～ lead a gang of outlaws in the mountains **4**（同类之首） largest, best or strongest of its kind: 百兽～ king of the beasts ‖ 拳～ boxing champion **B**〈形〉〈书〉great: ～父 grandfather ▸wàng
【王八】wángba〈名〉**1**（乌龟） tortoise **2**（妻子有外遇的人） cuckold **3**（开妓院的男子） male brothel-owner
【王八蛋】wángbadàn〈名〉〈粗〉son of a bitch〈粗〉
【王不留行】wángbùliúxíng〈名〉［中药］seed of cowherb
【王朝】wángcháo〈名〉**1**（指朝廷） imperial court **2**（指朝代） dynasty: ～更迭 dynastic succession ‖ 封建～ feudal dynasty ‖ 清～ Qing Dynasty
【王储】wángchǔ〈名〉crown prince
【王道】wángdào〈名〉benevolent government: 行～ rule the country benevolently
【王法】wángfǎ〈名〉**1**（国家法律）law of the land **2**（政策法规） state law and policy: 目无～ have no respect for laws and policies
【王妃】wángfēi〈名〉**1**（太子之妻） princess **2**（帝王之妾） concubine of a king
【王府】wángfǔ〈名〉prince's residence
【王公】wánggōng〈名〉nobility: ～大臣 princes, dukes and ministers ‖ ～贵族 princes, dukes and aristocrats
【王宫】wánggōng〈名〉imperial palace
【王冠】wángguān〈名〉crown: 戴着一顶镶有钻石的～ wear a crown encrusted with diamonds
【王国】wángguó〈名〉**1**（指国家） kingdom: 丹麦～ Kingdom of Denmark ‖ 摩洛哥～ Kingdom of Morocco ‖〈喻〉动物～ animal kingdom ‖ 这个国家被称为足球～。 This country is known as the kingdom of football. **2**（指领域） realm: 从必然～到自由～ from the realm of necessity to the realm of freedom
【王侯】wánghóu〈名〉princes and marquises
【王后】wánghòu〈名〉queen consort
【王浆】wángjiāng〈名〉royal jelly
【王莲】wánglián〈名〉［植物］Amazon royal water lily
【王母娘娘】Wángmǔ Niángniang〈名〉Queen Mother of the Western Heavens
【王牌】wángpái〈名〉**1**〈本〉trump card **2**〈喻〉most powerful figure or means: 握有克敌制胜的～ hold a trump card that will defeat one's opponent and win the game ‖ ～军 crack troops
【王婆卖瓜，自卖自夸】Wángpó mài guā, zì mài zì kuā〈歇后〉blow one's own trumpet
【王权】wángquán〈名〉monarchical power: 维护～ defend the monarchy ‖ ～至上论 regalism
【王师】wángshī〈名〉〈旧〉royal troops
【王室】wángshì〈名〉**1**（王族） royal family: ～成员 member of the royal family ‖ ～继承人 heir to the throne **2**（朝廷） imperial court
【王水】wángshuǐ〈名〉［化学］aqua regia
【王孙】wángsūn〈名〉prince's offspring
【王太后】wángtàihòu〈名〉queen mother
【王位】wángwèi〈名〉throne: 登上～ take the throne ‖ 争夺～ contend for the throne ‖ ～继承人 heir to the throne
【王爷】wángye〈名〉His/Your Highness
【王子】wángzǐ〈名〉prince: ▸白马～
【王子犯法与庶民同罪】wángzǐ fànfǎ yǔ shùmín tóng zuì〈俗〉all persons are equal in the eyes of law
【王族】wángzú〈名〉royal clan

wǎng

网（網） wǎng
A〈名〉**1**（指器具） net: 撒～ cast a net ‖ 织～ knit/weave a net ‖ 渔～ fishing net **2**（网状物） net-like object: 头球入～ head the ball into the net ‖ 铁丝～ wire mesh ‖ 蜘蛛～ a spider's web ▸发～ **3**（指系统、体系） network: 落入法～ be caught in the net of justice ‖ 高速公路～ highway network ‖ 通信～ communications network ‖ 有线电视～ cable TV network **4**（因特网） Internet: 上～ get online ‖ ～上购物 shop online ‖ 从～上下载 download from the Internet ▸互联～, 因特～ **B**〈动〉**1**（笼罩） cover or enclose: 眼里～着红丝 have bloodshot eyes **2**（用网捕捉） catch with a net: ～了满满一网鱼 net a good haul of fish
【网吧】wǎngbā〈名〉Internet cafe
【网虫】wǎngchóng〈名〉Internet buff
【网点】wǎngdiǎn〈名〉network of commercial establishments: 增设服务～ establish a network of service centres ‖ 商业～

W

commercial network
【网店】wǎngdiàn〈名〉online shop: ～经营缺乏政策监管。Online shopping is lacking in policy control.
【网兜】wǎngdōu〈名〉string bag
【网格】wǎnggé〈名〉1（格子）grid 2［计算机］great global grid (GGG)
【网格化】wǎnggéhuà〈动〉divide into grids: 对社区服务工作进行～管理 apply a gridded management structure to community service work
【网购】wǎnggòu〈动〉shop online: ～已成为颇受欢迎的消费新模式。Online shopping has become the new model of consumption.
【网管】wǎngguǎn〈名〉1（指工作）network management 2（指人）network administrator
【网警】wǎngjǐng〈简称〉= 网络警察
【网具】wǎngjù〈名〉fishing gear
【网卡】wǎngkǎ〈名〉network (interface) card
【网开一面】wǎngkāiyīmiàn〈成〉be lenient
【网篮】wǎnglán〈名〉basket with netting on top
【网恋】wǎngliàn〈名〉cyber romance
【网龄】wǎnglíng〈名〉number of weeks, months or years since first starting to surf the Internet
【网罗】wǎngluó A〈名〉〈喻〉（针对人）trap B〈动〉gather: ～人才 enlist people of ability
【网络】wǎngluò〈名〉1（因特网）network: ～地址 network address ‖ ～系统 network system ‖ ～新闻 cyber news ‖ ～中心 network hub 2（系统）network: 有源～电学 active network ‖ 计算机～ computer network ‖ 销售～ marketing network
【网络版】wǎngluòbǎn〈名〉publishing version for the Internet
【网络大学】wǎngluò dàxué〈名〉e-college
【网络电话】wǎngluò diànhuà〈名〉Internet phone
【网络犯罪】wǎngluò fànzuì〈名〉cybercrime
【网络服务器】wǎngluò fúwùqì〈名〉network server
【网络化】wǎngluòhuà〈动〉cyberize
【网络教育】wǎngluò jiàoyù〈名〉e-schooling
【网络经济】wǎngluò jīngjì〈名〉cybereconomy
【网络警察】wǎngluò jǐngchá〈名〉net police
【网络空间】wǎngluò kōngjiān〈名〉cyberspace
【网络日志】wǎngluò rìzhì〈名〉［计算机］blog
【网络世界】wǎngluò shìjiè〈名〉cyberworld
【网络讨论区】wǎngluò tǎolùnqū〈名〉talkboard
【网络文化】wǎngluò wénhuà〈名〉cyberculture
【网络营销】wǎngluò yíngxiāo〈名〉online marketing
【网络杂志】wǎngluò zázhì〈名〉webzine
【网迷】wǎngmí〈名〉Internet addict
【网民】wǎngmín〈名〉netizen
【网名】wǎngmíng〈名〉username: 她以"秋水"的～与丈夫在网上"相遇"。She met her husband online under the username "Autumn Water".
【网膜】wǎngmó〈名〉［生理］1（指大肠表面）omentum: ～切除术 omentectomy 2 = 视网膜 shìwǎngmó
【网球】wǎngqiú〈名〉1 ▸p. 909（指运动）tennis: 打～ play tennis ‖ ～公开赛 open tennis championship ‖ ～场 tennis court 2（指球）tennis ball
【网球拍】wǎngqiúpāi〈名〉tennis racket
【网球选手】wǎngqiú xuǎnshǒu〈名〉tennis player
【网上购物】wǎngshàng gòuwù〈名〉Internet shopping
【网上录取】wǎngshàng lùqǔ〈名〉Internet enrolment
【网上银行】wǎngshàng yínháng〈名〉online bank: 通过～转账方便又实惠。Online banking makes transfers convenient and affordable.
【网式足球】wǎngshì zúqiú〈名〉soccer tennis
【网速】wǎngsù〈名〉network speed: ～快/慢 fast/slow network speed
【网坛】wǎngtán〈名〉tennis circles
【网线】wǎngxiàn〈名〉internet cable
【网箱】wǎngxiāng〈名〉net cage: ～养殖 net-cage culture
【网眼】wǎngyǎn〈名〉mesh: 细～长丝袜 stockings made of fine silk mesh
【网页】wǎngyè〈名〉web page: 设计～ design a web page ‖ 个人～ personal home page
【网银】wǎngyín〈简称〉= 网上银行
【网瘾】wǎngyǐn〈名〉Internet addiction: ～和毒瘾一样积习难改。Internet addiction, like drug addiction, is hard to kick.
【网游】wǎngyóu〈名〉online games: ～产业方兴未艾。The online games industry is in the ascendant.
【网友】wǎngyǒu〈名〉web friend
【网站】wǎngzhàn〈名〉website: 登陆～ log into a website ‖ 建立免费～ build a free website
【网址】wǎngzhǐ〈名〉website: 搜索～ search for a website
【网状】wǎngzhuàng〈名〉reticulation: ～细胞 reticulocyte ‖ ～组织 reticular tissue
【网子】wǎngzi〈名〉〈口〉1（网状物）net 2（发网）hairnet

枉 wǎng

A〈形〉1（错误）crooked: ▸矫～过正 2（冤屈）unjust: ▸冤～
B〈动〉twist: ▸贪赃～法
C〈副〉in vain: ～担虚名 the name falls short of the reality ‖ ～活一世 have wasted one's life ▸～费心机，～然
【枉法】wǎngfǎ〈动〉stretch the law: 贪赃～ take bribes and take the law into one's own hands
【枉费】wǎngfèi〈动〉waste: ～唇舌 waste one's breath
【枉费心机】wǎngfèi-xīnjī〈成〉rack one's brains to no avail
【枉然】wǎngrán〈形〉futile: 跟他讲理纯属～。It is no use reasoning with him.
【枉死】wǎngsǐ〈动〉die without being cleared of a false charge: ～于一场无谓的争斗 die in vain in an unnecessary combat
【枉自】wǎngzì〈副〉in vain: ～开了多次会，还是毫无结果。We have had quite a few meetings, but to no avail.

罔[1] wǎng

〈动〉〈书〉deceive: 欺～ cheat

罔[2] wǎng

〈动〉〈书〉no, not: ▸置若～闻

往 wǎng

A〈动〉go: 寒来暑～ as winter comes and summer goes ▸～返，来～，勇～直前
B ▸p. 781〈介〉in the direction of: ～东走 head east ‖ 劲～一处使 all directing their efforts towards the same goal ‖ ～前看 look forward ‖ 从北京飞～西安 fly from Beijing to Xi'an
C〈形〉past: ▸～年，～事
【往常】wǎngcháng〈名〉former times: 比～忙 be busier than usual ‖ 她又恢复了～的样子。She's back to her former self again.
【往返】wǎngfǎn〈动〉travel to and fro: ～要两个小时 take two hours to get there and back ‖ 乘公共汽车～于办公室与住所之间 commute by bus between one's office and one's home ‖ ～票 return ticket〈英〉, round-trip ticket〈美〉
【往复】wǎngfù〈动〉1（来回）move back and forth: 循环～，以至无穷 repeat itself in endless cycles 2（联系）contact: 书信～ exchange letters
【往后】wǎnghòu〈名〉the future: ～的日子会越来越好。The future will be better and better.
【往还】wǎnghuán〈动〉contact: 经常有书信～ write to each other regularly
【往届】wǎngjiè〈形〉previous: ～毕业生 previous graduates
【往来】wǎnglái〈动〉1（去和来）come and go: 大街上～车辆很多。There is a lot of traffic in the streets. 2（交际）communicate: 友好～ friendly exchange ‖ 礼尚～。Courtesy demands reciprocity. ‖ 这俩姐妹～密切。The two sisters see a lot of each other.
【往来账目】wǎnglái zhàngmù〈名〉current account
【往年】wǎngnián〈名〉previous years: ～这时候西瓜已经上市了。In previous years watermelons were already on the market by this time. ‖ 今年不同于～。This year is different from previous years.
【往日】wǎngrì〈名〉former times: ～的情谊，记忆犹新。Our friendship from all those years ago is still fresh in the mind.
【往时】wǎngshí〈名〉former times: 他和～大不一样了。He is very different from the way he used to be.
【往事】wǎngshì〈名〉the past: 回忆～ recall the past ‖ ～不堪回首。It's sad to reflect on the past.
【往往】wǎngwǎng〈副〉often: ～如此 this happens often ‖ 事情～不像人们想象的那么简单。Things are often not as simple as people expect.
【往昔】wǎngxī〈名〉the past: 一如～ be as usual
【往者不可谏，来者犹可追】wǎngzhě bùkě jiàn, láizhě yóu kě zhuī〈成〉that which has passed cannot be mended, but that which is in the future can be prepared for

惘 wǎng

〈形〉frustrated: ▸怅～，迷～
【惘然】wǎngrán〈形〉〈书〉frustrated: ～若失 feel lost and puzzled

辋（輞）wǎng

〈名〉wheel rim

蝄 wǎng

【蝄蜽】wǎngliǎng = 魍魉 wǎngliǎng

W

魍 wǎng

【魍魉】wǎngliǎng〈名〉 demons and monsters

wàng

王 wàng

〈动〉〈旧〉 govern: ～天下 govern all under heaven ▸wáng

妄 wàng

〈形〉 **1**（荒谬）absurd: ▸～自尊大 **2**（胡乱） reckless: ～加猜测 make wild guesses ‖ ～加评论 make improper comments ‖ ～作主张 make a rash decision

【妄称】wàngchēng〈动〉 claim to be: 他只不过粗通文墨，竟也～作家。He barely knows the rudiments of writing, yet passes himself off as a professional writer.

【妄动】wàngdòng〈动〉 act impulsively: ▸轻举～

【妄断】wàngduàn〈动〉 jump to a conclusion: 真相大白之前你不能～。 You can't jump to conclusions before the case becomes entirely clear.

【妄念】wàngniàn〈名〉 wild idea: 消除～ give up an unpractical idea

【妄求】wàngqiú〈动〉 make an improper request: ～物质享受 seek unreasonable material comforts

【妄取】wàngqǔ〈动〉 take the liberty of using: 任何人不能～当地群众的财物。 No one is allowed to take away anything belonging to the local people.

【妄人】wàngrén〈名〉〈书〉 arrogant and presumptuous person

【妄说】wàngshuō〈动〉 talk irresponsibly: 情况不明，我不敢～。 As I'm not clear about it, I don't dare comment.

【妄图】wàngtú〈动〉 make a futile attempt: ～颠覆现政权 attempt in vain to subvert government power ‖ 罪犯～畏罪潜逃。 The criminal foolishly attempted to escape unpunished.

【妄为】wàngwéi〈动〉 act recklessly: ▸胆大～

【妄下雌黄】wàngxià-cíhuáng〈成〉 **1**（乱发议论） make irresponsible comments **2**（乱改文字） make wrong corrections in others' writing

【妄想】wàngxiǎng **A**〈动〉 vainly hope to do sth.: ～挽回败局 make a vain attempt to turn the tables ‖ ～一步登天 vainly hope for a meteoric rise **B**〈名〉 **1**（无法实现的想法） vain hope: 痴心～ wishful thinking **2** ▸**p. 50** ［医学］ delusion: ～狂 paranoid delusion

【妄言】wàngyán = 妄语 wàngyǔ

【妄语】wàngyǔ **A**〈动〉 talk nonsense **B**〈名〉 wild talk

【妄自菲薄】wàngzì-fěibó〈成〉 humble oneself unduly: 不要自高自大，也不要～。 One must be neither conceited nor overly modest.

【妄自尊大】wàngzì-zūndà〈成〉 be self-important: 跟人交往切勿～。 Never act with self-importance in one's interactions with others.

忘 wàng

〈动〉 forget: ～得一干二净 clean forget ‖ 好了伤疤～了疼 forget the pain when the wound has healed ‖ 喝水不～挖井人。 When you drink the water, think of those who sank the well. ‖ 前事不～后事之师。 The past not forgotten is a guide for the future. ‖ 我～带钥匙了。 I forgot my key. ‖ 我的包～在公共汽车上了。 I left my bag on the bus. ▸淡～, 废寝～食, 健～

【忘本】wàngběn〈动〉 forget one's past suffering: 我们不能因为过上了好日子就忘了本。 We must not forget where we have come from simply because our lives are happy now.

【忘掉】wàngdiào〈动〉 forget: ～烦恼 put one's worries out of one's mind ‖ 我把学过的英语单词几乎都～了。 I have forgotten almost all the English words I learned.

【忘恩负义】wàng'ēn-fùyì〈成〉 forget sb.'s kindness and turn one's back on him in return: 不要～。 Don't bite the hand that feeds you.

【忘乎所以】wànghū-suǒyǐ〈成〉 forget oneself: 在成功面前不要～。 Don't be carried away by success.

【忘怀】wànghuái〈动〉 forget: 难以～ be difficult to forget ‖ 那种感人的场面令我久久不能～。 For a long time afterwards I could not get the moving scene out of my mind.

【忘记】wàngjì〈动〉 forget: ～以前发生的事 forget all about the past ‖ ～关灯了 forget to turn the light off ‖ 你对我的帮助，我永远不会～。 I shall never forget the help you have given me.

【忘年交】wàngniánjiāo〈名〉 **1**（指交情） friendship between generations **2**（指人） good friends despite great difference in age

【忘其所以】wàngqí-suǒyǐ = 忘乎所以 wànghū-suǒyǐ

【忘情】wàngqíng〈动〉 **1**（不留恋） be indifferent: 不能～ remain emotionally attached **2**（不控制） let oneself go: ～地歌唱 abandon oneself in song

【忘却】wàngquè〈动〉 forget: 初恋是永远无法～的。 One never forgets one's first love.

【忘我】wàngwǒ〈动〉 be selfless: ～地工作 work selflessly ‖ ～的精神 spirit of selflessness

【忘形】wàngxíng〈动〉 be beside oneself: ▸得意～

【忘性】wàngxing〈名〉 forgetfulness: 人老了～大。 One tends to get forgetful in one's old age.

旺 wàng

〈形〉 flourishing: 人气很～ enjoy great popularity ‖ 火烧得很～。 The fire is raging. ‖ 购销两～。 Buying and selling are both brisk. ‖ 人畜两～。 Both men and livestock are flourishing. ▸～盛, 兴～

【旺季】wàngjì〈名〉 peak period: 草莓～ strawberry season ‖ 五月份是旅游～。 May is the peak tourist month.

【旺健】wàngjiàn〈形〉 vigorous

【旺盛】wàngshèng〈形〉 vigorous: 精力～ be full of vigour ‖ 在创作能力最～的时期 be at one's creative best ‖ 秧苗长势～。 The rice seedlings are growing luxuriantly.

【旺市】wàngshì〈名〉 **1**（指市场） brisk market **2**（指行市） brisk market business

【旺势】wàngshì〈名〉 upward trend

【旺销】wàngxiāo〈动〉 sell well: ～季节 peak sales period ‖ 夏季空调～。 Air-conditioners sell well in summer.

【旺月】wàngyuè〈名〉 busy month

望 wàng

A〈动〉 **1**（远眺） gaze into the distance: 登山远～ climb a mountain and gaze far afield ‖ 放眼～去 look ahead as far as the eye can see ▸凝～, 守～ **2**（观察） observe: ▸～风, ～闻问切, 观～ **3**（希望） expect: ～回信。 Awaiting your reply. ‖ ～速归。 Hoping you'll return as soon as possible. ▸～子成龙, 渴～, 期～ **4**（探视） pay a visit: ▸拜～, 看～, 探～ **5**〈书〉（怨恨） hate: 怨～ nurse a grudge

B〈名〉 **1**（月圆的一天） full moon **2** ▸**p. 618**（农历每月15日） 15th (sometimes the 16th or the 17th) day of a lunar month: ▸～日, 朔～ **3**（声望） reputation: ▸德高～重, 名～ **4**（店铺标志） shop sign in the form of a streamer: ▸酒～ **5**（盼头） range of vision, imagination, hope or expectation: 丰收在～。 A bumper harvest is in sight. ‖ 胜利在～。 Victory is in sight. ▸厚～, 失～

C〈形〉 reputable: ▸～族

D〈介〉 towards: ～窗外看 look out of the window ‖ ～前看 look ahead ‖ 拖着疲惫的身子～家里走 drag oneself home

【望尘莫及】wàngchén-mòjí〈成〉〈喻〉 too far behind to catch up: 她网球打得很棒，我～。 She can beat me hands down at tennis.

【望穿秋水】wàngchuān-qiūshuǐ〈成〉 await with baited breath

【望穿双眼】wàngchuān-shuāngyǎn〈成〉 be on the edge of one's seat

【望断】wàngduàn〈动〉〈书〉 watch sth. in the distance until it vanishes: ～南飞雁 watch the wild geese vanish southward

【望而却步】wàng'érquèbù〈成〉 stand in awe: 这房子摇摇欲坠，我们大家都～。 The house looked as if it would collapse, and we all hung back in fear.

【望而生畏】wàng'ér-shēngwèi〈成〉 be overawed by the sight of sb. or sth.: 那只老虎样子凶恶，令人～。 The tiger looked fierce and awesome.

【望风】wàngfēng〈动〉 keep watch: 派人～ post a lookout

【望风捕影】wàngfēng-bǔyǐng = 捕风捉影 bǔfēng-zhuōyǐng

【望风而逃】wàngfēng'értáo〈成〉 flee at the mere sight of an oncoming force: 敌军～。 The enemy fled pell-mell at the sight of our advancing force.

【望风披靡】wàngfēng-pīmǐ〈成〉 flee helter-skelter at the mere sight of sb.

【望楼】wànglóu〈名〉 watchtower

【望梅止渴】wàngméi-zhǐkě〈成〉〈喻〉 console oneself with false hopes

【望门】wàngmén〈名〉 prominent family

【望门寡】wàngménguǎ〈名〉 unmarried woman widowed by her betrothed

【望其项背】wàngqíxiàngbèi〈成〉 [usu used in the negative] be a match for sb.: 无人可以～。 No one can compare with him.

【望日】wàngrì ▸**p. 618**〈名〉 (usu) 15th day of a lunar month

【望文生义】wàngwén-shēngyì〈成〉 take words too literally: 翻译时切勿～。 When translating a text, do not make overly literal interpretations.

【望闻问切】wàng-wén-wèn-qiè〈成〉［中医］ observation, auscultation and smelling, interrogation, and palpitation

【望眼欲穿】wàngyǎn-yùchuān〈成〉 keep gazing anxiously till one's eyes are strained: 妻子盼望丈夫归来，真是～。 The wife was anxiously awaiting the return of her husband.

【望洋兴叹】wàngyáng-xīngtàn〈成〉〈喻〉 bemoan one's insignificance in the face of sth. great

望、闻、问、切

Four basic methods of diagnosis used in traditional Chinese medicine (▸中医), known collectively as the '*si zhen*' (四诊, four methods of diagnosis). '*Wang*' (望, observation) refers to observation of the patient's mental state, skin, complexion, etc. Looking at the patient's tongue is an important part of this. '*Wen*' (闻, auscultation and olfaction) involves listening to any sounds and smells produced by the patient. '*Wen*' (问, interrogation) means asking patients questions about their condition. '*Qie*' (切, palpitation) mainly involves taking the patient's pulse.

【望远镜】wàngyuǎnjìng〈名〉telescope: 射电～ radio telescope ‖ 天文～ astronomical telescope

【望月】wàngyuè〈名〉full moon

【望诊】wàngzhěn〈名〉［中医］observation (of the patient's complexion, tongue, expression, behaviour, etc.) as one of the four basic methods of diagnosis in traditional Chinese medicine

【望子成龙】wàngzǐ-chénglóng〈成〉have high expectations of one's children

【望子】wàngzi〈名〉shop sign in the form of a streamer

【望族】wàngzú〈名〉〈书〉prominent family: 名门～ notable family and great clan

wēi

危 wēi

A〈形〉**1**〈书〉（高耸）precipitous: ～峰 towering peak ‖ ～崖 precipitous cliff **2**〈书〉（端正）proper: ▸正襟～坐 **3**（危险）dangerous: ▸～房，～在旦夕 **4**（垂死）dying: ▸病～，垂～ **5**（恐惧）frightening: 人人自～。Everyone had a sense of insecurity. ▸～言耸听 **B**〈动〉endanger: ▸～害 **C**〈名〉one of the 28 constellations in ancient Chinese astronomy

【危城】wēichéng〈名〉**1**（指城墙高）city with high walls **2**（指被围困）besieged city

【危殆】wēidài〈形〉〈书〉perilous: 病势～ be critically ill ‖ 情势～ be in great peril

【危地马拉】Wēidìmǎlā〈名〉Guatemala: ～共和国 Republic of Guatemala ‖ ～人 Guatemalan

【危笃】wēidǔ〈形〉〈书〉critically ill

【危房】wēifáng〈名〉dilapidated building: 改造～ renovate a run-down building

【危害】wēihài〈动〉endanger: ～国家安全 endanger national security ‖ ～社会治安 jeopardize public security ‖ ～健康 be detrimental to health ‖ ～农作物 harm the crops ‖ ～青少年的身心健康 damage the physical and mental health of youngsters ‖ 吸烟～健康。Smoking is harmful to health.

【危害性】wēihàixìng〈名〉harmfulness

【危机】wēijī〈名〉crisis: 政治～ political crisis ‖ 经济～ economic crisis ‖ 能源/石油～ energy/oil crisis

【危机感】wēijīgǎn〈名〉sense of crisis

【危机四伏】wēijī-sìfú〈成〉be crisis-ridden

【危及】wēijí〈动〉endanger: ～国家安全 endanger national security ‖ ～生命 place sb.'s life in danger

【危急】wēijí〈形〉critical: ～关头 critical juncture ‖ 病人情况～。The patient's condition is critical.

【危局】wēijú〈名〉desperate situation: 力挽～ do one's utmost to save a critical situation ‖ 应付～ meet the crisis

【危惧】wēijù〈动〉be apprehensive: 心存～ be filled with apprehension

【危楼】wēilóu〈名〉〈书〉**1**（高楼）tall building **2**（有倒塌危险的楼）dilapidated building: 拆除～ demolish a dilapidated building

【危难】wēinàn〈名〉jeopardy: 处于～之中 be in dire peril

【危浅】wēiqiǎn〈形〉〈书〉critically ill: 人命～ be critically ill

【危如累卵】wēirúlěiluǎn〈成〉be in an extremely precarious situation: 局势～，令人堪忧。The situation is very precarious and worrying.

【危亡】wēiwáng〈动〉be critical: 民族～的时刻 when the fate of the nation hangs in the balance

【危险】wēixiǎn〈形〉dangerous: ～地带 danger zone ‖ ～人物 dangerous person ‖ ～因素 hazards ‖ 她的处境非常～。She is in great peril. ‖ 他有生命～。His life is in danger.

【危险品】wēixiǎnpǐn〈名〉dangerous articles: 严禁携带～上车。It is strictly forbidden to take dangerous articles aboard.

【危险期】wēixiǎnqī〈名〉critical period: 已经渡过了～。The critical period has already passed.

【危险性】wēixiǎnxìng〈名〉danger

【危言耸听】wēiyán-sǒngtīng〈成〉say frightening things just to cause alarm: 你不要～吓唬人。You shouldn't go around talking wildly just to frighten people.

【危在旦夕】wēizàidànxī〈成〉be in imminent danger: 他的生命～。His life is in imminent peril.

【危重】wēizhòng〈形〉critically ill: ～病人 critically ill person

【危坐】wēizuò〈动〉〈书〉sit in state: 正襟～ straighten out one's dress and sit in state

委 wēi

▸wěi

【委蛇】wēiyí〈书〉**A** = 逶迤 wēiyí **B**〈动〉accede to: ▸虚与～

威 wēi

A〈名〉awesome might: ～震四方 known far and wide for one's military prowess ▸～力，～信，权～ **B**〈动〉threaten by force: 声～天下。One's might is felt across the country. ▸～逼，～迫，～胁

【威逼】wēibī〈动〉intimidate: ～手段 means of intimidation

【威逼利诱】wēibī-lìyòu〈成〉use both coercion and bribery

【威尔士】Wēi'ěrshì〈名〉Wales: ～人 Welsh ‖ ～语 Welsh ‖ ～亲王 Prince of Wales

【威尔特郡】Wēi'ěrtèjùn〈名〉Wiltshire

【威风】wēifēng **A**〈名〉power and prestige: 大显～ make an impressive show of one's courage and power ‖ 长自己的～ boost one's own morale **B**〈形〉awe-inspiring: 她穿上军装很是～。She looks impressive in military uniform.

【威风八面】wēifēng-bāmiàn = 八面威风 bāmiàn-wēifēng

【威风凛凛】wēifēng-lǐnlǐn〈成〉awe-inspiring

【威格敦郡】Wēigédūnjùn〈名〉Wigtownshire

【威吓】wēihè〈动〉intimidate: ～目击证人 intimidate the witness ‖ 用枪～ threaten with a gun

【威赫】wēihè〈形〉powerful and influential: ～一时 be powerful and influential for a time

【威力】wēilì〈名〉might: 巨大的～ powerful drive ‖ 舆论的～ force of public opinion

【威力无比】wēilì-wúbǐ〈成〉be extremely powerful

【威猛】wēiměng〈形〉brave and fierce

【威名】wēimíng〈名〉fame: ～传天下。One's fame has spread far and wide. ‖ ～远扬。One's reputation spreads extensively.

【威尼斯】Wēinísī〈名〉Venice: ～人 Venetian ‖ ～方言 Venetian

【威迫】wēipò〈动〉intimidate: ～利诱 practise intimidation and bribery

【威权】wēiquán〈名〉authority

【威慑】wēishè〈动〉terrorize with military force: ～力量 deterrent ‖ 核～ nuclear deterrence

【威士忌】wēishìjì〈名〉whisky

【威势】wēishì〈名〉power and influence: 倚仗～ rely on others' power and influence

【威斯康星州】Wēisīkāngxīngzhōu〈名〉Wisconsin

【威斯特摩兰郡】Wēisītèmólánjùn〈名〉Westmorland

【威望】wēiwàng〈名〉prestige: 享有很高的国际～ enjoy high international prestige

【威武】wēiwǔ **A**〈名〉might **B**〈形〉mighty: ～之师 mighty army ‖ ～雄壮 be full of power and grandeur

【威武不屈】wēiwǔ-bùqū〈成〉unyielding in the face of force

【威胁】wēixié〈动〉threaten: ～某人做某事 intimidate sb. into doing sth. ‖ 构成～ pose a threat ‖ 以武力相～ resort to threats of force

【威信】wēixìn〈名〉prestige: 树立～ build up one's prestige ‖ 他在群众中享有很高的～。He enjoys high prestige among the masses.

【威信扫地】wēixìn-sǎodì〈成〉be completely discredited: 丧失人心，～ forfeit popular support and prestige

【威严】wēiyán **A**〈形〉dignified: ～的神态 commanding look ‖ 他的举止毫无～。His appearance was anything but dignified. **B**〈名〉dignity: 摆出审判长的～ assume the dignity of the chief justice ‖ 维护法律的～ defend the dignity of the law

【威仪】wēiyí〈名〉impressive and dignified manner: ～凛然 awe-inspiring manner ‖ 帝王的～ awesome regal bearing

逶 wēi

【逶迤】wēiyí〈形〉winding: ～的山路 winding mountain path ‖ 群山～。The mountain range is winding.

偎 wēi

〈动〉snuggle up to: ～着母亲 snuggle up to one's mother ‖ ～着取暖 cuddle up to sb. to get warm ▸依～

【偎傍】wēibàng〈动〉lean on: 她～在情人的手臂上。She leaned on her lover's arm.

【偎抱】wēibào〈动〉hug: 把孩子～在怀中 cuddle the baby in one's arms

【偎依】wēiyī〈动〉snuggle up to: ～在母亲的怀里 snuggle up in one's mother's arms ‖ 她的脸～在他的肩上。She snuggled her cheek against his shoulder.

W

隈 wēi 〈名〉〈书〉 1 (水流弯曲处) river bend 2 (山边弯曲处) mountain recess

搣 wēi 〈动〉〈口〉 bend: 把树枝～成个圆圈 bend the twig into a circle

葳 wēi

【葳蕤】wēiruí 〈形〉〈书〉 exuberant

崴 wēi

▸wǎi

【崴嵬】wēiwéi 〈形〉〈书〉 [of mountains] towering

微 wēi

A 〈形〉 1 (细小) tiny: 相差甚～。The difference is negligible. ▸～风，略～ 2 (地位低) humble: ▸～贱，卑～ 3 (深奥) profound: ▸～妙，～言大义

B 〈量〉 micro: ▸～安，～米

C 〈动〉 decline: ▸式～，衰～

D 〈副〉 slightly: ～热 rather hot ‖ ～感不适 feel a bit off colour ▸～笑

【微安】wēi'ān 〈量〉［电气］ microampere

【微波】wēibō 〈名〉［电子］ microwave: ～遥感器 microwave remote sensor ‖ ～通信 microwave communication

【微波接收机】wēibō jiēshōujī 〈名〉 microwave receiver

【微波炉】wēibōlú 〈名〉 microwave oven

【微薄】wēibó 〈形〉 meagre: 尽～的力量 exert what little strength one has ‖ 靠～收入为生 live on a meagre income

【微不足道】wēibùzúdào 〈成〉 insignificant: ～的差别 inappreciable difference ‖ ～的人物 person of no consequence

【微车】wēichē 〈名〉 minicar

【微处理机】wēichǔlǐjī 〈名〉［计算机］ microprocessor: ～开发系统 microprocessor development system

【微创手术】wēichuāng shǒushù 〈名〉 minimally invasive surgery

【微词】wēicí 〈名〉〈书〉 veiled criticism: 人们对他的表现颇有～。People muttered their disapproval of his behaviour.

【微辞】wēicí = 微词 wēicí

【微电机】wēidiànjī 〈名〉 micromotor

【微电子】wēidiànzǐ 〈名〉 microelectronics: ～技术 microelectronic technology

【微雕】wēidiāo 〈名〉 carving in miniature

> **微雕**
>
> A traditional Chinese craft, also known as rice-carving (米刻) or detailed carving (细刻). The craft involves carving words or images on materials such as a grain of rice, strand of hair, or sliver of ivory. Carving in miniature combines the skills of traditional Chinese calligraphy, painting and carving. There are three kinds of carving: on a surface, in three dimensions, and in relief. Miniature carvings are often enjoyed with the use of a magnifying glass or a microscope.

【微法拉】wēifǎlā 〈量〉［电气］ microfarad

【微分】wēifēn 〈名〉［数学］ differential: ～方程 differential equation

【微风】wēifēng 〈名〉 1 ［气象］ gentle breeze 2 (轻风) breeze: ～掠过树梢。A soft wind brushes the treetops.

【微伏】wēifú 〈量〉［电气］ microvolt

【微服】wēifú 〈动〉 [of officials] be in disguise: ～私访 travel incognito

【微幅】wēifú 〈副〉 small extent: 股指～上扬。The share index was slightly higher.

【微观】wēiguān 〈形〉 microscopic: ～世界 microcosm ‖ ～经济 micro economy ‖ ～搞活，宏观控制 micro-flexibility with macro-control

【微观结构】wēiguān jiégòu 〈名〉 microstructure

【微观经济学】wēiguān jīngjìxué 〈名〉 microeconomics

【微亨】wēihēng 〈量〉［电气］ microhenry

【微乎其微】wēihūqíwēi 〈成〉 next to nothing: ～的进步 minute improvement ‖ 双方达成协议的可能性～。There is hardly any possibility of the two parties reaching an agreement.

【微火】wēihuǒ 〈名〉 gentle heat

【微机】wēijī 〈名〉 1 (微型计算机) microcomputer 2 (计算机) computer: ～操作 computer operation

【微积分】wēijīfēn 〈名〉［数学］ calculus

【微贱】wēijiàn 〈形〉 humble: 出身～ be of humble origin

【微晶片】wēijīngpiàn 〈名〉 microchip

【微克】wēikè 〈量〉 microgram

【微刻】wēikè 〈名〉 miniature carving

【微利】wēilì 〈名〉 small profit

【微粒】wēilì 〈名〉 1 (微小颗粒) microscopic particle 2 ［物理］ corpuscle

【微量】wēiliàng 〈名〉 trace: ～元素 trace element

【微茫】wēimáng 〈形〉〈书〉 hazy

【微米】wēimǐ 〈量〉 micrometre: ～汞柱 micrometre of mercury

【微秒】wēimiǎo 〈量〉 microsecond

【微妙】wēimiào 〈形〉 delicate: ～的暗示 subtle hint ‖ ～的关系 delicate relations ‖ 目前的政治形势极其～。The current political situation is very delicate.

【微末】wēimò 〈形〉 insignificant: ～的成就 insignificant achievement

【微软】Wēiruǎn 〈名〉 Microsoft: ～磁盘操作系统 Microsoft Disk Operating System (MS-DOS) ‖ ～公司 Microsoft Corporation

【微弱】wēiruò 〈形〉 faint: 以～多数当选 be elected by a narrow majority ‖ 光线～ dim light ‖ 呼吸～ faint breathing

【微生物】wēishēngwù 〈名〉 microorganism: ～农药 microbial pesticide

【微缩】wēisuō 〈名〉 microform: ～胶卷 microfilm ‖ ～景观 miniature landscape

【微调】wēitiáo A 〈名〉［电子］ trimming: ～装置 vernier arrangement B 〈动〉 adjust slightly: 工资～ slight adjustment of salary

【微微】wēiwēi A 〈副〉 slightly: ～泛起红晕 develop a slight flush ‖ ～一笑 smile faintly B 〈形〉 tiny: ～细雨 fine rain

【微细】wēixì 〈形〉 tiny: ～的区别 fine distinction ‖ ～的血管 very small blood vessel

【微系统】wēixìtǒng 〈名〉 microsystem: ～技术 microsystems technology

【微小】wēixiǎo 〈形〉 small: 抱有～的希望 cherish slim hopes ‖ 极其～的变化 slightest nuance of change

【微笑】wēixiào A 〈名〉 smile: 面带～ wear a smile ‖ 她脸上露出一丝～。A faint smile crept across her face. B 〈动〉 smile: 幸福地～ smile happily ‖ 〈喻〉 幸运之神向我们～了。Fortune smiled upon us.

【微笑服务】wēixiào fúwù 〈名〉 service with a smile

【微笑圈】wēixiàoquān 〈名〉 smiley

【微行】wēixíng 〈动〉 travel incognito

【微型】wēixíng 〈形〉 miniature: ～汽车 compact car ‖ ～小说 mini-story

【微型计算机】wēixíng jìsuànjī 〈名〉 microcomputer

【微血管】wēixuèguǎn 〈名〉 capillary

【微循环】wēixúnhuán 〈名〉［生理］ microcirculation

【微言大义】wēiyán-dàyì 〈成〉 subtle words with profound meaning

煨 wēi 〈动〉 1 (小火炖) cook over a slow fire: ～牛肉 stewed beef 2 (烤) roast in cinders: ～白薯/板栗 roast sweet potatoes/chestnuts in cinders

薇 wēi ▸蔷薇 qiángwēi

鳂（鰃） wēi 〈名〉［鱼类］ holocentridae

巍 wēi 〈形〉 lofty

【巍峨】wēi'é 〈形〉 lofty: ～的群山 lofty mountains ‖ ～壮丽 solemn and magnificent

【巍然】wēirán 〈形〉 towering: ～屹立 stand lofty and firm ‖ 大桥～横跨在江上。The bridge spans the river majestically.

【巍巍】wēiwēi 〈形〉 towering: ～昆仑山 towering Kunlun Mountains

wéi

为¹（為、爲） wéi 〈动〉 1 (做) do: 敢作敢～ act with daring ‖ 尽力而～ try one's best ‖ 何乐而不～。Why not go ahead with it? ▸见义勇～ 2 (作为) act as: 推举某人～代表 delegate sb. ‖ 以某人～首的代表团 delegation led by sb. ‖ 有诗～证。A poem testifies to that. ▸不足～凭 3 (成为) become: 变沙漠～良田 turn the desert into arable land ‖ 化～乌有 vanish into nothing ‖ 化悲痛～力量 turn grief into strength ‖ 化整～零 break up the whole into parts ‖ 沦～乞丐 be reduced to begging ‖ 一分～二 divide into two ▸先入～主 4 〈书〉 (是) be: 试用期～三个月。The probation period lasts three months. ‖ 一公里～二华里。One kilometre is equivalent to two *li*.

为²（為、爲） wéi 〈介〉〈书〉 [often used with 所 in a passive sentence]: ～好奇心所驱使 be prompted by curiosity ‖ ～人民所爱戴 be loved and respected by the people ‖ 不～所动 be unmoved ‖ 不～表面现象所迷惑 not be seduced by superficial phenomena

为³（為、爲） wéi 〈助〉〈书〉 [used in a rhetorical question with 何]: 何以家～? What need have I of a home? [usu said during a national crisis]

为⁴（為、爲） wéi 〈后缀〉 1 (表副词化) [used after a single-character adjective to form an adverb]: 大～不满 be most displeased ‖ 广～流传 be widely spread 2 (表强调) [used after a single-character adverb for emphasis]: 极～重视这次比赛 attach great importance to this competition ‖ 颇～得意 be extremely conceited ‖ 尤～出色 be particularly outstanding

▸wèi

【为非作歹】wéifēi-zuòdǎi 〈成〉 commit crimes

【为富不仁】wéifù-bùrén 〈成〉 be rich and cruel

【为害】wéihài 〈动〉 harm: ～不浅 be very

detrimental ‖ ～一方 cause damage in the neighbourhood

【为荷】wéihè〈动〉〈书〉thank [usu used at the end of a letter]: 现将校样奉上，希认真审读～。The proofs are submitted for your kind revision.

【为患】wéihuàn〈动〉bring trouble: 洪水～ be scourged by floods ‖ 人满～ overcrowded with people

【为难】wéinán〈动〉**1**（感到难办）feel embarrassed: 使人～ embarrass sb. ‖ 左右～ be in a dilemma ‖ 你不知道这让我有多～。You can't understand how awkward this is for me. **2**（刁难）make things difficult for: 故意～我 deliberately make things difficult for me ‖ 她的前夫处处～她。Her ex-husband made things as awkward for her as he could.

【为期】wéiqī〈动〉last for a certain period of time: 举行～一周的罢工 stage a one-week strike ‖ 会议～三天。The meeting is scheduled to last three days. ‖ 圣诞节已～不远。Christmas is just around the corner.

【为人】wéirén **A**〈动〉conduct: ～之道 rules of conduct ‖ ～处世 the way one conducts oneself in society **B**〈名〉conduct: ～厚道 behave with great kindness ‖ 他～正派。He is a man of integrity. ‖ 我不了解她的～。I know nothing of her character.

【为人不齿】wéirén-bùchǐ〈成〉be spoken of only to one's shame

【为人师表】wéirén-shībiǎo〈成〉be a paragon of virtue and learning

【为生】wéishēng〈动〉earn a living: 无以～ live off nothing ‖ 以捕鱼～ make one's living as a fisherman

【为时】wéishí〈动〉last: ～三天 last three days ‖ ～过早 premature ‖ ～已晚 too late

【为首】wéishǒu〈动〉serve as the head: 以总统～的代表团 delegation led by the president

【为数】wéishù〈动〉amount to: ～不多 have only a small number ‖ 他给基金会捐了一笔～可观的钱。He contributed quite a lot of money to the foundation.

【为所欲为】wéisuǒyùwéi〈成〉do whatever one likes: 侵略者～的日子已经一去不复返。The days when the invaders could do precisely what they pleased are gone forever.

【为伍】wéiwǔ〈动〉associate with: 耻与某人～ feel ashamed to associate with sb. ‖ 与坏人～ associate with bad elements

【为限】wéixiàn〈动〉be within the limit of: 有效期以一年～ be valid for one year ‖ 载重以五吨～。The load is limited to five tons.

【为政】wéizhèng〈动〉**1**（处理政事）manage state affairs: ～清廉 manage state affairs honestly and incorruptibly **2**（做事）do things in a certain way: ▸各自～

【为之动容】wéizhī-dòngróng〈成〉cannot help but be moved

【为之神往】wéizhī-shénwǎng〈成〉be fascinated

【为止】wéizhǐ〈动〉be up to: 到发稿时～ up to the stage of going to press ‖ 迄今～ up to now ‖ 我们的关系到此～。Our relationship is over.

【为重】wéizhòng〈动〉attach greatest importance to: 以大局～ put the general interest first ‖ 以人民的利益～ value the interests of the people above everything else ‖ 以友谊～ value friendship highly

【为主】wéizhǔ〈动〉give priority to: 以自力更生～ rely mainly on one's own efforts ‖ 疾病应该以预防～。Emphasis should be put on the prevention of disease.

韦（韋）wéi〈名〉〈古〉leather

【韦编三绝】wéibiān-sānjué〈成〉be diligent in one's studies

圩 wéi〈名〉dyke: 筑～ build dykes ‖ ～堤 dyke combatting low-land flooding ▸xū

【圩岸】wéi'àn〈名〉dyke

【圩田】wéitián〈名〉polder

【圩垸】wéiyuàn〈名〉protective embankments in lakeside areas

【圩子】wéizi〈名〉**1**（防水堤岸）protective embankments surrounding low-lying fields **2** = 围子 wéizi 1

违（違）wéi〈动〉**1**（不依从）violate: ～者罚款。Any violator will be fined. ‖ ～者必究。Violations will not be tolerated. ▸～背，～法 **2**（离别）part: ▸久～

【违碍】wéi'ài〈动〉〈旧〉violate a taboo: ～字句 taboo words and expressions

【违拗】wéi'ào〈动〉defy: ～父亲的心愿 defy one's father's wishes

【违背】wéibèi〈动〉breach: ～规章制度 violate the rules and regulations ‖ ～良心 act against one's conscience ‖ ～人民的意志 go against the will of the people ‖ ～誓言 breach an oath

【违法】wéifǎ〈动〉break the law: 干～的事 do sth. illegal ‖ ～犯罪分子 offenders and criminals ‖ ～活动 illegal activity

【违法乱纪】wéifǎ-luànjì〈成〉commit malfeasance: 对于～者定要严惩。Those who break the law and violate discipline should be severely punished.

【违反】wéifǎn〈动〉violate: ～国际法 contravene international law ‖ ～国际惯例 commit a breach of international practice ‖ ～规定 contravene a regulation

【违犯】wéifàn〈动〉violate: ～交通规则 violate traffic regulations ‖ ～宪法 act contrary to the constitution ‖ ～校纪 violate school discipline

【违规】wéiguī〈动〉break the rules: ～操作 go against the rules ‖ ～停车 parking violation ‖ ～现象 violations of the regulations and rules

【违和】wéihé〈形〉〈旧〉〈婉〉indisposed: 近闻贵体～，深为不安。I've been very worried to hear that you've not been feeling well recently.

【违纪】wéijì〈动〉violate a discipline: ～人员 breakers of discipline ‖ ～行为 breach of discipline

【违禁】wéijìn〈动〉violate a ban: ～品 contraband

【违抗】wéikàng〈动〉disobey: ～命令 disobey an order ‖ 他们～父母的意愿结婚了。They got married against the wishes of their parents.

【违例】wéilì〈动〉**1**（违反常例）be contrary to the usual practice: 不得～ should not deviate from the usual practice **2**［体育］break the rules: 构成～ constitute a breach of the rules

【违逆】wéinì〈动〉〈书〉violate

【违忤】wéiwǔ〈动〉〈书〉violate

【违误】wéiwù〈动〉〈书〉[used in official documents] disobey orders and cause delay: 迅速办理，不得～。This is to be acted upon without delay.

【违宪】wéixiàn〈动〉be unconstitutional: ～行为 unconstitutional act

【违心】wéixīn〈动〉be contrary to one's convictions: 说几句～的话 say a few words against one's conscience ‖ 做～事 act against one's conscience

【违约】wéiyuē〈动〉**1**（指合约）break a contract: ～当事人 delinquent party **2**（指许诺）break one's promise

【违章】wéizhāng〈动〉break rules and regulations: ～操作 operate a machine contrary to its instructions ‖ ～行驶 drive against traffic regulations ‖ ～建筑 illegally built constructions

围（圍）wéi

A〈动〉enclose: ～海造田 reclaim land from the sea ‖ 他被来访者团团～住。He was besieged by visitors. ‖ 一家人都～着宝宝转。The whole family gathered around the baby. ▸包～，解～，突～

B〈名〉**1**（四周）all sides: ▸外～，周～ **2**（周长）girth: ▸胸～，腰～

C〈量〉**1**（指臂长）arm span: 树大十～ tree trunk with a circumference of ten arm spans **2**（指手长）hand span: 腰细两～ have a slender waist of only two hand spans

【围抱】wéibào〈动〉surround: 树木～的房子 house surrounded with trees

【围脖儿】wéibór〈名〉〈方〉muffler: 系着～ wear a scarf around one's neck

【围捕】wéibǔ〈动〉round up: ～逃犯 close in on an escaped prisoner

【围场】wéichǎng〈名〉hunting ground

【围城】wéichéng **A**〈动〉besiege a city: ～打援 besiege the enemy in order to strike at its reinforcements **B**〈名〉besieged city: 困守～ be entrenched in a besieged city

【围堵】wéidǔ〈动〉besiege and intercept

【围攻】wéigōng〈动〉**1**〈本〉besiege: ～要塞 lay siege to a fortress ‖ 发动～ launch a siege **2**〈喻〉（泛指攻击）jointly attack sb.: 多次遭到媒体的～ face repeated media attacks

【围观】wéiguān〈动〉surround and watch: ～的人群 crowd of onlookers

【围击】wéijī〈动〉besiege and attack

【围歼】wéijiān〈动〉surround and annihilate: ～敌军 destroy the enemy by encircling them

【围剿】wéijiǎo〈动〉encircle and suppress: ～残敌 encircle and annihilate the remaining enemy

【围巾】wéijīn〈名〉scarf: 系着～ have a scarf around one's neck

【围聚】wéijù〈动〉crowd around: ～在老师身旁 gather around a teacher

【围垦】wéikěn〈动〉build dykes to reclaim land from marshes: ～地 innings

【围困】wéikùn〈动〉hem in: 抢救被洪水～的村民 rescue villagers stranded by the floodwater

【围栏】wéilán〈名〉fence: 设置～ put a railing around

【围猎】wéiliè〈动〉round up and hunt

【围拢】wéilǒng〈动〉crowd around: 街上一发生意外，人们很快就～过来。People quickly crowd around when there is an incident in the street.

【围屏】wéipíng〈名〉folding screen

【围棋】wéiqí ▸**p. 909**〈名〉go [game]: 九段～大师 level 9 go master

【围墙】wéiqiáng〈名〉enclosure

【围裙】wéiqún〈名〉apron: 系着～ wear an apron

【围绕】wéirào〈动〉**1**（围在四周）encircle: 月亮～着地球旋转。The moon revolves around the earth. **2**（以某事为中

心) centre on: ～中心任务安排其他工作 arrange other work around the central task ‖ 故事的情节～着两个家庭之间的矛盾展开。 The plot of the story centres on the conflict between the two families.

> **围棋**
> A traditional Chinese board game for two players with a history, it is believed, of more than 2,000 years. The board is crossed with 19 lines, forming 361 intersections. Pieces are placed in turn on the intersections, one at a time. The aim is to encircle and wipe out one's opponent's pieces. The winner is the player who finally occupies the greatest number of positions.

【围网】wéiwǎng〈名〉 purse seine: ～渔船 purse boat

【围魏救赵】wéiWèi-jiùZhào〈成〉 relieve the besieged by besieging the base of the besiegers

【围堰】wéiyàn〈名〉 coffer

【围追堵截】wéizhuīdǔjié〈成〉 encirclement, pursuit, obstruction, and interception

【围子】wéizi〈名〉 1（防护墙） defensive wall surrounding a village: 土～ fortified village 2（帷子） curtain: 床～ bed curtain 3（圩子） protective embankments surrounding low-lying fields

【围嘴儿】wéizuǐr〈名〉 bib [for baby]

【围坐】wéizuò〈动〉 sit around: 客人们～在餐桌旁。 The guests sat around the dining table.

帏（幃） wéi〈名〉〈古〉 1（香袋） perfume bag 2 = 帷 wéi

闱（闈） wéi〈名〉 1（宫门） side gate of an imperial palace: ▸宫～ 2（科举考场） imperial examination hall: ▸入～

【闱墨】wéimò〈名〉〈旧〉 selections from the papers of successful candidates at the imperial palace

桅 wéi〈名〉 mast: ～顶 masthead

【桅灯】wéidēng〈名〉 1（航行信号灯） masthead light 2（马灯） barn lantern

【桅杆】wéigān〈名〉 mast: 爬上～ climb up a mast ‖ 把旗子升上～ run a flag up a mast

【桅樯】wéiqiáng〈名〉 mast

唯[1] wéi〈叹〉〈书〉 [used to answer in the affirmative] yea

唯[2] wéi

A〈副〉 only: ～愿 only wish ‖ ～你是问。 You alone will be held responsible.

B〈连〉〈书〉 but: 他学识渊博，～不善言谈。 He is learned, but taciturn.

▸wěi

【唯独】wéidú〈副〉 only: 大家都回家了，～他还在工作。 He kept on working when all the others had gone home.

【唯恐】wéikǒng〈动〉 fear that ...: 他们低声耳语，～别人听到。 They spoke in whispers lest they should be heard.

【唯利是图】wéilì-shìtú〈成〉 be intent on nothing but profit: ～的思想 profit-first mentality

【唯美主义】wéiměizhǔyì〈名〉aestheticism: ～者 aesthete

【唯命是从】wéimìng-shìcóng = 唯命是听 wéimìng-shìtīng

【唯命是听】wéimìng-shìtīng〈成〉 comply with the exact order

【唯我独尊】wéiwǒ-dúzūn〈成〉be extremely conceited: ～的架势 behave in an overbearing manner

【唯物辩证法】wéiwù biànzhèngfǎ〈名〉［哲学］ materialist dialectics

【唯物论】wéiwùlùn〈名〉［哲学］ materialism: ～的反映论 materialist theory of reflection ‖ 机械～ mechanical materialism

【唯物史观】wéiwù shǐguān〈名〉［哲学］ historical materialism

【唯物主义】wéiwù zhǔyì〈名〉［哲学］ materialism: ～者 materialist ‖ 机械～ mechanical materialism ▸辩证～, 历史～

【唯心论】wéixīnlùn〈名〉［哲学］ idealism

【唯心史观】wéixīn shǐguān〈名〉［哲学］ historical idealism

【唯心主义】wéixīn zhǔyì〈名〉［哲学］ idealism: ～者 idealist ▸历史～, 主观～

【唯一】wéiyī〈形〉 only: ～的办法 only way ‖ ～的继承人 sole heir ‖ ～合法的政府 sole legitimate government ‖ 实践是检验真理的～标准。 Practice is the sole criterion of truth.

【唯有】wéiyǒu A〈副〉 only: ～他留了下来。 Only he remained. B〈连〉 only: ～努力学习，才会取得进步。 You can only make progress by studying hard.

惟[1] wéi = 唯[2] wéi

惟[2] wéi〈助〉〈书〉 [used before a year, month or day]: ～二月既望 on the 16th of the second lunar month

惟[3] wéi〈名〉 thinking

【惟独】wéidú = 唯独 wéidú

【惟恐】wéikǒng = 唯恐 wéikǒng

【惟恐天下不乱】wéikǒng tiānxià bù luàn〈成〉 be anxious to see the world in disorder

【惟利是图】wéilì-shìtú = 唯利是图 wéilì-shìtú

【惟妙惟肖】wéimiào-wéixiào〈成〉 remarkably lifelike: 模仿得～ mimic perfectly ‖ 这部小说中的人物形象描绘得～。 The characters in the novel were very vividly depicted.

【惟命是从】wéimìng-shìcóng = 唯命是听 wéimìng-shìtīng

【惟命是听】wéimìng-shìtīng = 唯命是听 wéimìng-shìtīng

【惟其】wéiqí〈连〉〈书〉 precisely because: ～不懂，我们才要研究它。 It is precisely because we don't understand it that we must work on it.

【惟我独尊】wéiwǒ-dúzūn = 唯我独尊 wéiwǒ-dúzūn

【惟一】wéiyī = 唯一 wéiyī

【惟有】wéiyǒu = 唯有 wéiyǒu

维[1]**（維）** wéi〈动〉 1（连接） tie up: ▸～系 2（保持） maintain: ▸～持, ～护

维[2] wéi〈名〉［数学］ dimension: 三～空间 three-dimensional space

维[3] wéi〈名〉 thinking: ▸思～

【维持】wéichí〈动〉 1（保持） maintain: ～和平 keep the peace ‖ ～生活 support oneself or one's family ‖ ～生计 maintain one's livelihood ‖ 靠水～生命 subsist on water ‖ ～现状 maintain the status quo ‖ ～秩序 keep order ‖ 勉强～生活 scrape a living 2（保护） protect and support: 由于该官员的～，那个罪犯得以逍遥法外。 Due to the official's cover-up, the criminal went unpunished.

【维和】wéihé〈动〉 keep the peace: ～部队 peace-keeping force ‖ ～行动 peace-keeping operation

【维护】wéihù〈动〉 safeguard: ～国家主权 defend national sovereignty ‖ ～消费者权益 safeguard the rights and interests of consumers ‖ ～祖国统一 safeguard the unity of the motherland

【维纶】wéilún〈名〉［纺织］ polyvinyl alcohol fibre

【维纳斯】Wéinàsī〈名〉 Venus

【维尼龙】wéinílóng〈名〉 vinylon

【维尼纶】wéinílún = 维尼龙 wéinílóng

【维权】wéiquán〈动〉 safeguard legal rights and interests: ～意识 the concept of defending legal rights and interests ‖ ～行动 action to safeguard legal rights and interests

【维生素】wéishēngsù〈名〉 vitamin: 富含～ be rich in vitamins ‖ ～E/D vitamin E/D ‖ 孕妇通常需要补充～。Pregnant women often take vitamin supplements.

【维他命】wéitāmìng〈旧〉= 维生素 wéishēngsù

【维吾尔语】Wéiwú'ěryǔ ▸p. 918〈名〉 Uygur

【维吾尔族】Wéiwú'ěrzú〈名〉 Uygur ethnic group

【维系】wéixì〈动〉 maintain: ～人心 maintain popular morale ‖ 靠血缘来～ be tied by blood

【维新】wéixīn〈动〉 reform: 日本明治～ Meiji Reform of Japan

【维修】wéixiū〈动〉 maintain: ～房屋 maintain houses and buildings ‖ 进行～ conduct repairs ‖ 设备的～ upkeep of equipment

【维修费】wéixiūfèi〈名〉 maintenance cost

【维修工】wéixiūgōng〈名〉 maintenance worker

【维也纳】Wéiyěnà〈名〉 Vienna: ～人 Viennese

【维族】Wéizú〈简称〉= 维吾尔族

帷 wéi〈名〉 curtain

【帷幔】wéimàn = 帷幕 wéimù

【帷幕】wéimù〈名〉 heavy curtain: 冬奥会落下～。 The curtain descends on the Olympic Winter Games.

【帷幄】wéiwò〈名〉〈书〉 army tent: 运筹～ devise strategies within the command tent

【帷子】wéizi〈名〉curtain: 床～ bed curtain

嵬 wéi〈形〉〈书〉 lofty

【嵬嵬】wéiwéi〈形〉 towering

鮠（鮠） wéi〈名〉［鱼类］ leiocassis

wěi

伪（偽、僞） wěi〈形〉 1（虚假） fake: 去～存真 eliminate the false and retain the true ▸～钞, ～造, 虚～ 2（非法） illegal: ～宗教机构 pseudo-religious organizations ▸～政权

【伪币】wěibì = 伪钞 wěichāo

【伪钞】wěichāo〈名〉 counterfeit banknote

【伪称】wěichēng〈动〉 claim falsely

【伪军】wěijūn〈名〉 puppet army

W

【伪君子】wěijūnzǐ〈名〉 hypocrite: 圆滑的～ oily hypocrite
【伪科学】wěikēxué〈名〉 pseudoscience
【伪劣】wěiliè〈形〉 shoddy: ～产品/商品 shoddy products/goods
【伪善】wěishàn〈形〉 hypocritical: ～的人/行为/言辞 hypocritical person/behaviour/words
【伪书】wěishū〈名〉 ancient books of dubious authenticity
【伪托】wěituō〈动〉 forge ancient works
【伪造】wěizào〈动〉 falsify: ～历史 falsify history ‖ ～签名/证件 forge a signature/certificate
【伪造品】wěizàopǐn〈名〉 counterfeit
【伪造者】wěizàozhě〈名〉 counterfeiter
【伪造罪】wěizàozuì〈名〉 forgery: 犯～ perpetrate forgery
【伪证】wěizhèng〈名〉 perjury: 做～ commit perjury
【伪政权】wěizhèngquán〈名〉 puppet regime
【伪装】wěizhuāng **A**〈动〉 **1**（假装） pretend: ～进步/虔诚 pretend to be progressive/pious ‖ 他～成妇女，企图逃跑。He disguised himself as a woman and attempted to escape. **2**［军事］ camouflage: 用树枝～ use branches as camouflage **B**〈名〉 **1**（假的装扮） disguise: 剥去～ strip away sb.'s disguise ‖ 许多动物有天然的～使它们躲过敌人。 Many animals have a natural camouflage which conceals them from their enemies. **2**［军事］ camouflage: ～篷布 camouflage canopy ‖ ～网 camouflage net
【伪足】wěizú〈名〉［动物］ pseudopodium
【伪作】wěizuò **A**〈名〉 counterfeit: 那幅画被证明纯系～。 The painting proved to be pure counterfeit. **B**〈动〉 counterfeit

伟（偉） wěi〈形〉 **1**（高大） tall and big: ▸～岸, 宏～, 雄～ **2**（壮美） great: ▸～人, ～业, 丰功～绩

【伟岸】wěi'àn〈形〉〈书〉 tall and sturdy: 身材～ be of great height and powerful build ‖ ～的身材 towering figure
【伟大】wěidà〈形〉 great: ～的成就/胜利 great achievement/victory ‖ ～的国家/领袖/人民 great country/leader/people
【伟哥】wěigē〈名〉 Viagra
【伟绩】wěijì〈名〉〈书〉 brilliant achievement: ▸丰功～
【伟举】wěijǔ〈名〉 great undertaking
【伟力】wěilì〈名〉〈书〉 mighty force
【伟人】wěirén〈名〉 great man/woman: 当代～ great man/woman of our time ‖ 世纪～ man/woman of the century
【伟业】wěiyè〈名〉〈书〉 **1**（指事业） great undertaking: 千秋～ the greatest undertaking in centuries **2**（指业绩） great achievement: 丰功～ great achievements and heroic exploits

苇（葦） wěi〈名〉 reed: ▸芦～

【苇箔】wěibó〈名〉 reed curtain
【苇荡】wěidàng〈名〉 reed marsh
【苇塘】wěitáng〈名〉 reed pond
【苇席】wěixí〈名〉 reed mat
【苇子】wěizi〈名〉 reed: 用～编席 weave reeds into a mat

纬（緯） wěi

A〈名〉 **1**［纺织］ weft: ▸～纱, 经～ **2**［地理］ latitude: ▸～度, 北～, 南～
B〈简称〉= 纬书

【纬度】wěidù〈名〉［地理］ latitude: ～越高，天气越冷。 The higher the latitude, the colder it is.
【纬纱】wěishā〈名〉［纺织］ weft
【纬书】wěishū〈名〉〈古〉 augury book of the Han Dynasty
【纬线】wěixiàn〈名〉 **1**［纺织］ weft **2**［地理］ latitude line

尾 wěi

A〈名〉 **1**（尾巴） tail: 马～ horsetail ▸摇～乞怜 **2**（指星宿） sixth of the 28 constellations in ancient Chinese astronomy **3**（尾部） tail: ～螺旋 tailspin ‖ （减速）～伞 tail parachute ▸机～, 首～ **4**（末尾阶段） end: 年～ year end ‖ 信～ end of a letter ▸有头有～ **5**（未了结部分） remaining part: 烂～楼 unfinished building ▸扫～, 收～
B〈量〉 [used for fish]: 两～鱼 two fish
▸yǐ

【尾巴】wěiba〈名〉 **1**（指动物体） tail: 牛～ ox tail ‖ 狗摇～。 The dog is wagging its tail. ▸翘～ **2**（指物体） tail: 飞机～ tail of a plane ‖ 彗星～ tail of a comet ‖ 汽车～ rear bumper of a car **3**（无主见的人） servile adherent: 你怎么老做别人的～? Why are you always acting as other people's appendage? **4**（残留部分） remaining part: 他干活从不留～。 He never leaves jobs unfinished. **5**（盯梢的人） shadow: 甩掉～ throw off one's tail
【尾巴工程】wěiba gōngchéng〈名〉 project with a small part remaining unfinished for a long time
【尾大不掉】wěidà-bùdiào〈成〉〈喻〉 [of an organization] too cumbersome to be effective
【尾灯】wěidēng〈名〉 rear light: 打～ turn on the tail lights
【尾骨】wěigǔ〈名〉［生理］ coccyx
【尾号】wěihào〈名〉 tail number: 车牌～ tail number of the number plate ‖ 她手机～是2531。 The last few digits of her mobile number are 2531.
【尾花】wěihuā〈名〉 tailpiece [decorative pattern at the end of a piece of writing]
【尾迹】wěijì〈名〉 **1**（指飞机） vapour trail **2**（指舰船） wake
【尾款】wěikuǎn〈名〉 remaining balance: ～尚未结清。 The remaining balance still hasn't been settled.
【尾矿】wěikuàng〈名〉［矿业］ tailings
【尾流】wěiliú〈名〉［物理］ wake flow
【尾轮】wěilún〈名〉 tailwheel (of an aircraft)
【尾盘】wěipán〈名〉 late trading: ～略有上扬。Late trading has seen some small gains.
【尾鳍】wěiqí〈名〉 tail fin, caudal fin
【尾气】wěiqì〈名〉 tail gas: ～排放标准 exhaust emissions standards
【尾欠】wěiqiàn **A**〈动〉 owe a small balance **B**〈名〉 balance due
【尾声】wěishēng〈名〉 **1**（指乐曲、乐章） epilogue: 序幕和～ prologue and epilogue **2**（指活动） end: 晚会已接近～。 The party is drawing to an end.
【尾市】wěishì〈名〉 end of the market
【尾数】wěishù ▸p. 691〈名〉 **1**（指小数点后） number after the decimal point **2**（指结算账目） odd amount in addition to the round number **3**（指多位数中） last number of a multidigital figure
【尾随】wěisuí〈动〉 tail: 派人～ send sb. to tail sb./sth. ‖ 有些孩子～在游行队伍后面。 Some children followed the parade.
【尾翼】wěiyì〈名〉 tail surface of an aircraft
【尾音】wěiyīn〈名〉［语言］ last or end syllable
【尾蚴】wěiyòu〈名〉［动物］ cercaria
【尾羽】wěiyǔ〈名〉 tail feather: 孔雀展开艳丽的～。 The peacock spreads its splendid tail.
【尾注】wěizhù〈名〉 end note
【尾追】wěizhuī〈动〉 pursue: ～敌人 be in hot pursuit of the enemy
【尾椎】wěizhuī〈名〉［解剖］ caudal vertebra

玮（瑋） wěi〈书〉

A〈名〉 kind of jade
B〈形〉 valuable: ～宝 rare treasure

炜（煒） wěi〈形〉〈书〉 bright

委[1] wěi

A〈动〉 **1**（任命） entrust: ～以重任 entrust with an important task ▸～派, ～任, ～托 **2**〈书〉（丢弃） cast aside: ～之于地 cast to the ground ▸～弃 **3** = 诿 wěi
B〈名〉 **1**（委员） committee member: ▸常～, 政～ **2**（委员会） committee: 党～ Party committee ‖ 军～ military commission ‖ 省～ provincial committee

委[2] wěi〈形〉 indirect: ▸～曲, ～婉

委[3] wěi〈书〉

A〈动〉 gather: ～积 pile up
B〈名〉 lower reaches of a river: ▸穷原竟～, 原～

委[4] wěi〈形〉 dejected: ▸～顿, ～靡

委[5] wěi〈副〉〈书〉 indeed: ～系实情。 This is the true story. ▸～实
▸wēi

【委顿】wěidùn〈形〉〈书〉 weary: 精神～ be listless
【委过】wěiguò = 诿过 wěiguò
【委积】wěijī〈动〉〈书〉 accumulate: ～如山 pile up like a mountain
【委决不下】wěijué-bùxià〈成〉 be hesitant in making a decision
【委靡】wěimǐ = 萎靡 wěimǐ
【委内瑞拉】Wěinèiruìlā〈名〉 Venezuela: ～共和国 Republic of Venezuela ‖ ～人 Venezuelan
【委派】wěipài〈动〉 appoint: ～某人做某事 designate sb. to do sth. ‖ 他们～他为代表。 They appointed him as their representative.
【委培】wěipéi〈动〉 consign the training of personnel to a certain institution: ～生 student trainees entrusted to an institution other than their own
【委弃】wěiqì〈动〉〈书〉 abandon
【委曲】wěiqū〈书〉 **A**〈形〉 winding: ～的溪流 winding stream **B**〈名〉 all the details: 详述～ get to the details
【委曲求全】wěiqū-qiúquán〈成〉 make concessions for the sake of overall interests
【委屈】wěiqu **A**〈形〉 wronged: 感到很～ feel very aggrieved ‖ 满腹～ be full of grievances **B**〈动〉 put sb. to great inconvenience: 对不起，～你了。 Sorry to have put you to such inconvenience.
【委任】wěirèn〈动〉 appoint: ～某人为首席顾问/驻联合国大使 appoint sb. as chief adviser/ambassador to the United Nations
【委任书】wěirènshū〈名〉 certificate of appointment
【委任状】wěirènzhuàng〈名〉 certificate of appointment

W

【委身】wěishēn〈动〉 submit to: ～事人 submit oneself to the service of sb.
【委实】wěishí〈副〉〈书〉 indeed: ～不易 by no means easy ‖ ～可怜 be pitiful indeed ‖ 我～不知道。 I really don't know.
【委琐】wěisuǒ〈形〉 1〈书〉(琐碎) trifling: ～之事 trivial matters 2 = 猥琐 wěisuǒ
【委托】wěituō〈动〉 entrust: ～朋友照看孩子 entrust one's child to a friend's care ‖ 有关法律事务，～法律顾问办理。 All legal matters will be entrusted to our legal adviser.
【委托人】wěituōrén〈名〉 consignor
【委托书】wěituōshū〈名〉 power of attorney
【委婉】wěiwǎn〈形〉tactful: ～的语气 mild tone ‖ 他话说得很～。 He made his remarks very tactfully.
【委婉语】wěiwǎnyǔ〈名〉 euphemism
【委员】wěiyuán〈名〉 committee member: 中央～ member of the central committee
【委员会】wěiyuánhuì〈名〉 committee: 中央～ central committee ‖ 常务～ standing committee ‖ 顾问～ advisory committee ‖ 纪律检查～ commission for inspecting discipline ‖ 校务～ school board ‖ 仲裁～ arbitration board
【委员长】wěiyuánzhǎng〈名〉 chairman of the committee
【委罪】wěizuì = 诿罪 wěizuì

韡（韡） wěi〈形〉〈书〉 [of light] bright and rich

诿（諉） wěi〈动〉 shift
【诿过】wěiguò〈动〉 shift the blame onto others: ～于人 shift the blame onto sb. else
【诿卸】wěixiè〈动〉〈书〉 shirk
【诿罪】wěizuì〈动〉shift blame onto sb. else

娓 wěi
【娓娓】wěiwěi〈形〉 tireless in talking: ～而谈 talk in a kindly and informal fashion
【娓娓动听】wěiwěi-dòngtīng〈成〉pleasant to the ear

萎 wěi〈动〉 wither: ▸枯～
【萎顿】wěidùn = 委顿 wěidùn
【萎落】wěiluò〈动〉 1（枯萎败落） wither and fall 2（衰落） decline
【萎靡】wěimǐ〈形〉 dispirited: 精神～ be in listless spirits
【萎靡不振】wěimǐ-bùzhèn〈成〉 be in low spirits: 一次挫折使他～。 One setback put him in really low spirits.
【萎蔫】wěiniān〈动〉［植物］ wilt
【萎缩】wěisuō A〈动〉 1（枯萎） wither: 叶子因霜打而～了。 The leaves shrivelled up with the frost. 2（衰退） shrink: 出口贸易出现～。 There has been some shrinkage in export trade. ‖ 市场～。 The market is sagging. B ▸p. 50〈名〉［医学］ atrophy: 肌肉～ muscular atrophy

委婉语

■ 英语和汉语都有极为丰富的委婉语，都会采用委婉、含蓄的说法来表达敏感、令人难堪或不愉快的话题。两种语言的委婉语一方面反映各自的民族文化特征，另一方面又有许多相似之处。

■ 注意下面有些例子的英文翻译只是大致对应，有些表达法在两种语言里没有对应语。

死亡

■ 在英语里，表达"死"的委婉语很多，最常用的有：

他突然去世
= He passed away suddenly

他咽气了
= He breathed his last

老人已归天
= The old man is in heaven
或 The old man is with God

老太太早上 8 点闭了眼
= The old lady closed her eyes at 8 am

他母亲已不在了
= His mother is no more
或 His mother is gone

战士英勇牺牲了
= The soldier laid down his life
或 The solider made the ultimate sacrifice

■ 其他表示"死亡"的委婉语还有：

to have found rest
to have had the final sleep
to kick the bucket (俚语)
to turn up one's toes (俚语)

疾病

她有智力障碍
= She is mentally handicapped

我奶奶手脚不便
= My granny is physically handicapped

他视觉不好
= He is visually impaired

她耳朵背
= She is hard of hearing

■ 英语用 the Big C 指癌症：

他得了癌症
= He's got the Big C（口语）

贫穷

我手头紧
= I am badly-off
或 I am hard up

她生活不宽裕
= She is down on her luck
或 She is financially embarrassed（正式）

■"穷人"的委婉说法有：

a person of modest means
the disadvantaged

老人

■ 年龄在英语里是个敏感的话题，指老人时，通常说：

senior citizens
people of advanced years
elderly people

■ 如果你感觉你已老了，可委婉地说：

I feel my age

■ 养老院的委婉说法有：

rest home
nursing home

生理现象

■ 上厕所：

我可以用你的卫生间吗？
= Can I use your bathroom?

洗手间在哪儿？
= Where can I wash my hands?

■ 其他指"厕所"的委婉语还有：

the ladies' room
the gentlemen's room
the little girls' room
the little boys' room

■ 解大便：

解大手／去大号
= to do a number 2

■ 解小便：

解小手／去小号
= to relieve oneself
或 to pass water
或 to do a number 1

■ 月经：

我倒霉了／来例假了
= It's my time of the month
或 It's my period

其他话题

■ 失业：

他下岗了
= He is between jobs
或 He's resting

■ 垃圾清运工：

环卫工人
= sanitation workers
或 waste disposal workers

■ 色情：

黄色杂志／电影
= adult magazines/movies

■ 肥胖：

她很丰满
= She is full-figured
或 She is chubby
或 She is plump

他块儿头大
= He's big

她骨架大
= She is a big woman
或 She is big-boned
或 She is large-boned

■ 怀孕：

她有喜了／她有了
She is in the family way
或 She is expecting

W

【萎谢】wěixiè〈动〉 wither: ～的花 withered flowers

唯 wěi〈叹〉〈旧〉 yea ▸wéi

【唯唯诺诺】wěiwěi-nuònuò〈成〉 be a yes-man: ～的人 yes-man

隗 Wěi〈名〉 Wei [surname] ▸Kuí

猥 wěi〈形〉 1（多而杂） multifarious 2（鄙贱） obscene: ▸～琐, ～亵

【猥词】wěicí = 猥辞 wěicí

【猥辞】wěicí〈名〉 obscene language

【猥贱】wěijiàn〈形〉 lowly

【猥劣】wěiliè〈形〉〈书〉 abject: 行为～ behave in a base manner

【猥琐】wěisuǒ〈形〉 boorish: 举止～ conduct oneself very boorishly

【猥亵】wěixiè A〈形〉 lewd: 心怀～的念头 harbour indecent ideas ‖ ～的表情/目光/动作 lewd expression/glance/gesture ‖ ～的语言 filthy language B〈动〉 molest: ～妇女 harass a woman

韪（韙） wěi ▸不韪 bùwěi

艉 wěi〈名〉 stern: ～锚 stern anchor

痿 wěi〈动〉 be paralysed: ～痹 suffer paralysis ‖ 下～ be paralysed in the legs ▸阳～

鲔（鮪） wěi〈名〉［鱼类］ 1〈古〉（鲟鱼） sturgeon 2（指热带鱼） yaito tuna

wèi

卫[1]（衛、衞） wèi

A〈动〉 defend: 保家～国 protect our homes and defend our country ▸～戍, 防～, 自～

B〈名〉 1（指人） security guard: ▸后～, 警～, 门～ 2（指地方） place for stationing troops

卫[2]（衛、衞） Wèi〈名〉 Wei [state in the Zhou Dynasty]

【卫兵】wèibīng〈名〉 guard: 在大门周围布置～ place guards around the gate ‖ 总统的～ presidential bodyguard

【卫道】wèidào〈动〉 defend traditional moral principles

【卫道士】wèidàoshì〈名〉〈贬〉 apologist: 封建主义的～ apologist of feudalism

【卫队】wèiduì〈名〉 squad of bodyguards: 在～的护送下 be escorted by a group of guards

【卫护】wèihù〈动〉 protect: ～祖国的尊严 protect the dignity of the motherland

【卫冕】wèimiǎn〈动〉 defend one's title: ～成功 successfully defend one's title ‖ ～冠军 defending champion

【卫生】wèishēng A〈形〉 hygienic: ～知识 knowledge of hygiene ‖ ～检查 sanitary inspection ‖ ～洁具 toilet utensils ‖ ～陶瓷 sanitary porcelain ‖ ～裤 sweatpants ‖ ～筷子 disposable chopsticks ‖ 不良的～习惯 unclean sanitary practices ‖ 厨房环境不太～。 Conditions in the kitchen were not very sanitary. B〈名〉 hygiene: 讲～ pay attention to hygiene ‖ 公共～ public health ‖ 环境～ environmental hygiene

【卫生带】wèishēngdài〈名〉 sanitary towel

【卫生防疫站】wèishēng fángyìzhàn〈名〉 sanitation and anti-epidemic station

【卫生间】wèishēngjiān〈名〉 bathroom: 上～ go to the bathroom ‖ 公共～ public toilet

【卫生巾】wèishēngjīn〈名〉 sanitary towel〈英〉; sanitary napkin〈美〉

【卫生棉】wèishēngmián〈名〉 cotton wool〈英〉; absorbent cotton〈美〉

【卫生棉球】wèishēng miánqiú〈名〉 cotton wool ball

【卫生棉条】wèishēng miántiáo〈名〉 tampon

【卫生球】wèishēngqiú〈名〉 mothball

【卫生设备】wèishēng shèbèi〈名〉 sanitary facilities

【卫生室】wèishēngshì〈名〉 clinic (of an organization)

【卫生所】wèishēngsuǒ〈名〉 clinic

【卫生学校】wèishēng xuéxiào〈名〉 medical school

【卫生员】wèishēngyuán ▸p. 966〈名〉 health worker

【卫生院】wèishēngyuàn〈名〉 health centre

【卫生纸】wèishēngzhǐ〈名〉 toilet paper

【卫士】wèishì〈名〉 guard

【卫视】wèishì〈简称〉= 卫星电视

【卫戍】wèishù〈动〉 garrison: ～部队 garrison force ‖ 北京～区 Beijing Garrison Command

【卫校】wèixiào〈简称〉= 卫生学校

【卫星】wèixīng A〈名〉 1（指天体） satellite 2（人造卫星） man-made satellite: 发射～ launch an artificial satellite ‖ 环球～定位系统 Global Positioning System (GPS) ‖ 间谍/军用/气象/通信～ spy/military/weather/communications satellite ‖ 人造（地球）～ man-made (earth) satellite ‖ ～导航 satellite navigation B〈形〉 satellite: ～城市 satellite town

【卫星测控中心】wèixīng cèkòng zhōngxīn〈名〉 satellite monitoring and control centre

【卫星城】wèixīngchéng〈名〉 satellite town

【卫星导航】wèixīng dǎoháng〈名〉 satnav

【卫星地面站】wèixīng dìmiànzhàn〈名〉 ground satellite station

【卫星电视】wèixīng diànshì〈名〉 satellite television

【卫星发射中心】wèixīng fāshè zhōngxīn〈名〉 satellite launch centre

【卫星通信】wèixīng tōngxìn〈名〉 satellite communication: ～地面站 satellite ground station

【卫星云图】wèixīng yúntú〈名〉［气象］ satellite cloud picture

【卫浴】wèiyù〈名〉 sanitation: ～设备 sanitation equipment

为（為、爲） wèi

A〈动〉〈书〉 help

B〈介〉 1（替） for: ～国争光 struggle for the glory of the motherland ‖ ～后代着想 for the sake of future generations ‖ ～人民服务 serve the people ‖ ～运动员加油 cheer the players on 2（为了） for the purpose of: ～方便顾客 for the convenience of the customers ‖ ～生存而斗争 struggle to survive ‖ ～祖国的繁荣而努力工作 work hard for the prosperity of the country 3（因为） because: ～胜利而欢呼 hail a victory 4（对） to: 不足～外人道 not worth saying to outsiders ▸wéi

【为此】wèicǐ〈连〉 for this end

【为公】wèigōng〈副〉 for public good

【为国捐躯】wèiguó-juānqū〈成〉 lay down one's life for one's country

【为何】wèihé〈副〉〈书〉 why: ～冒险犯法? Why risk breaking the law? ‖ 你～如此高兴? Why do you look so happy?

【为虎傅翼】wèihǔ-fùyì = 为虎添翼 wèihǔ-tiānyì

【为虎添翼】wèihǔ-tiānyì〈成〉〈喻〉 aid an already powerful evil-doer

【为虎作伥】wèihǔ-zuòchāng〈成〉〈喻〉 help a villain to do evil

【为了】wèile〈介〉 for the sake of: ～和平做出让步 make concessions for the sake of peace ‖ ～求知而学习 study in order to acquire knowledge ‖ ～准确起见，我再次核查了所有数据。 To make sure, I checked all the figures over again.

【为民除害】wèimín-chúhài〈成〉 rid the people of a scourge: 他杀死了那个恶棍，其实是～。 He actually rid the people of an evil by doing away with that thug.

【为民请命】wèimín-qǐngmìng〈成〉 plead in the name of the people: 打着～的幌子 pose as a spokesperson of the people

【为民造福】wèimín-zàofú〈成〉 work for the well-being of the people

【为人作嫁】wèirén-zuòjià〈成〉〈喻〉 doing work for others with no benefit to oneself

【为什么】wèishénme〈副〉 why: ～不试一试? Why not have a try? ‖ ～犹豫不决呢? Why hesitate?

【为渊驱鱼，为丛驱雀】wèi yuān qū yú, wèi cóng qū què〈成〉〈喻〉 drive friends over to the side of the enemy

【为着】wèizhe = 为了 wèile

未[1] wèi ▸p. 221〈副〉 1（没） not yet: ～被采纳 unauthorized ‖ ～成年 not yet adult ‖ 价格～定。 The price is not yet set. ▸防患～然 2（不） not: ～知可否 not know whether sth. can be done ‖ 地址～详。 The address is unknown to me. ▸～必

未[2] wèi〈名〉 eighth of the twelve Earthly Branches (地支)

【未必】wèibì〈副〉 not necessarily: ～都对。 Everything is not necessarily correct. ‖ 他～知道。 He doesn't necessarily know.

【未便】wèibiàn〈副〉〈书〉 finding it hard (to do sth.): ～立即答复 find it difficult to give an immediate reply ‖ ～擅自处理 cannot do sth. without authorization

【未卜】wèibǔ〈动〉 be uncertain: 前途～ have a precarious future ‖ 胜负～ cannot predict who will be the winner ▸生死～

【未卜先知】wèibǔ-xiānzhī〈成〉 have foresight: 可惜我们不能～。 It's a shame we are not prophets.

【未曾】wèicéng ▸p. 221〈副〉〈书〉 not: ～谋面 have never seen each other before ‖ 暑假期间，我～休息过一天。 I have not had even one day off in the whole summer holiday.

【未尝】wèicháng ▸p. 221〈副〉 1（未曾） not: 走前人～走过的路 walk a path no one has ever walked before ‖ 她一夜～合眼。 She didn't get a wink of sleep the whole night. 2（未必） [used before a negative word, denoting a mild affirmative]: ～不可 have no reason not to ‖ 这～不是好主意。 That might not be a bad idea.

【未偿】wèicháng〈动〉 be outstanding

【未偿贷款】wèicháng dàikuǎn〈名〉 outstanding loan

【未偿债务】wèicháng zhàiwù〈名〉 outstanding debt
【未成年人】wèichéngniánrén〈名〉 minor: ～不得入内。No admission to minors.
【未定】wèidìng〈动〉 be undecided: 行期～。The departure date is yet to be decided. ‖ 比赛胜负～，我们不能贸然下结论。The game is not over yet, so who knows who will emerge the winner.
【未定稿】wèidìnggǎo〈名〉 draft
【未果】wèiguǒ〈动〉〈书〉 fail to realize
【未婚】wèihūn〈动〉 be unmarried: ～先孕 premarital pregnancy ‖ ～男子 bachelor
【未婚夫】wèihūnfū〈名〉 fiancé
【未婚妻】wèihūnqī〈名〉 fiancée
【未及】wèijí〈动〉 have no time (to do sth.)
【未几】wèijǐ〈副〉〈书〉 ❶（不久） before long ❷（不多） not many
【未竟】wèijìng〈动〉〈书〉 be unfinished: 继承～之业 take on unfinished work ‖ ～之志 unfulfilled ambition
【未决】wèijué〈动〉 ❶（未决定） be outstanding: 胜负～ be still difficult to tell who will win ‖ 议而～ be still under discussion ▸悬而～ ❷（未判决） have not yet faced trial: ～案件 pending case
【未决犯】wèijuéfàn〈名〉 prisoner awaiting trial
【未可】wèikě〈动〉〈书〉 not be able to: ～乐观 give no cause for optimism ‖ ～逆料 cannot foretell
【未可厚非】wèikě-hòufēi = 无可厚非 wúkě-hòufēi
【未窥全豹】wèikuī-quánbào〈成〉 fail to have the full picture
【未来】wèilái **A**〈形〉 coming: ～的事情 future events ‖ ～二十四小时内将有暴雨。There will be a rainstorm within the next 24 hours. **B**〈名〉 the future: 面向～ face the future ‖ 展望～ look into the future ‖ ～是属于年轻人的。Tomorrow belongs to the youth.
【未老先衰】wèilǎo-xiānshuāi〈成〉 be prematurely senile
【未了】wèiliǎo〈动〉 be unfinished: ～事宜 unfinished business ‖ ～的心愿 unfulfilled wish
【未免】wèimiǎn〈副〉 ❶（实在是） rather too: 这～太过份了。This is really going too far. ‖ 他～太多心了。He's a bit oversensitive. ‖ 你这样做～操之过急了。You were a bit hasty in doing that. ❷（不免） unavoidably: 这样说话～要得罪人。Such remarks are bound to offend others.
【未能】wèinéng〈动〉 fail to: ～达到目的 fail to achieve one's goal ‖ ～进入半决赛 unable to reach the semi-final ‖ 阴谋～得逞 be frustrated in one's plot
【未能免俗】wèinéng-miǎnsú〈成〉 be unable to rise above convention
【未然】wèirán〈动〉〈书〉 be as yet unfulfilled: ▸防患～
【未时】wèishí〈名〉〈旧〉 period of the day from 1 p.m. to 3 p.m.
【未始】wèishǐ = 未尝 wèicháng 2
【未遂】wèisuì〈动〉 fail to accomplish: 心愿～ fail to fulfil one's wishes ‖ 自杀/强奸/抢劫～ attempted suicide/rape/robbery
【未遂罪】wèisuìzuì〈名〉 attempted crime
【未亡人】wèiwángrén〈名〉 ❶〈旧〉（寡妇自称） I [said by a widow suggesting she is due to die but hasn't yet] ❷（寡妇） widow
【未详】wèixiáng〈动〉〈书〉 be unknown: 作者生卒～。The dates of the author's birth and death are unknown. ‖ 死因～。The cause of death is not clear.
【未央】wèiyāng〈动〉〈书〉 have not ended yet: 夜～。The night is not yet over.
【未雨绸缪】wèiyǔ-chóumóu〈成〉〈喻〉 take preventive measures
【未知数】wèizhīshù〈名〉 ❶［数学］ unknown number: X 和 Y代表两个～。X and Y are unknowns. ❷（还不知道的事情） unknown: 计划能否成功还是个～。Nobody is sure if the plan can be a success.
【未知项】wèizhīxiàng〈名〉 unknown term
【未置一词】wèizhì-yīcí〈成〉 make no comment

位 wèi

A〈名〉 ❶（地方） place: 把这些东西都各归其～ put all these things back in their place ‖ 椎骨错～ spinal displacement ▸方～，席～ ❷（地位） position: 在世界上排第三～ rank third in the world ‖ 不在其～，不谋其政。He who does not hold official position is not qualified to discuss policy. ▸岗～，学～，职～ ❸（王位） throne: ▸篡～，即～，退～ ❹［数学］ place: 计算到小数点后三～ calculate to three decimal places ‖ 两/三/四～数 double/three/four figures ▸个～，十～
B〈量〉〈套〉 [used to refer to people]: 一～代表 a representative ‖ 四～客人 four guests ‖ 各～来宾，晚上好！Good evening to all guests!
【位次】wèicì〈名〉 ❶（座次） rank: 按～排座 arrange the seats in order of rank ❷（等次） place: 该国贸易额在世界的～是11。The country's trade volume ranks 11th in the world.
【位及人臣】wèijírénchén〈成〉 rise to be an official of the highest rank
【位居】wèijū〈动〉 rank: ～前列 rank up top
【位居要津】wèijūyàojīn〈成〉 occupy a key position
【位数】wèishù ▸**p. 691**〈名〉 number of digits
【位移】wèiyí〈名〉［物理］ displacement: ～共振 displacement resonance
【位于】wèiyú〈动〉 be situated: ～车站附近 be situated near a station ‖ ～太平洋沿岸 be located on the Pacific coast
【位置】wèizhi〈名〉 ❶（地方） place: 按指定～就座 take one's designated seat ‖ 放回原来的～ put sth. back in its place ‖ 地理～ geographical position ‖ 你来晚了，没有你的～了。You are late and there's no room for you. ❷（地位） place: 把环保放在首要～ prioritize environmental protection ‖ 在当代文学史上占有重要～ hold an important place in the records of contemporary literature ❸（职位） position: 申请销售经理的～ apply for the position of marketing manager ‖ 替代某人的～ take sb.'s place
【位子】wèizi〈名〉 ❶（座位） place: 换～ change places ‖ 让～ make room ‖ 回到你的～上去。Go back to your seat. ❷（职位） position: 院长的～迄今还空着。The position of president remains vacant. ‖ 好些人在竞争这个～。Quite a few people are vying for the post.

味 wèi

A〈名〉 ❶（味道） taste: 淡而无～ lack flavour ‖ 有很浓的蒜～ have a strong taste of garlic ‖ 无～的液体 tasteless liquid ▸～觉，滋～ ❷（气味） smell: 香水～ perfume odour ‖ 他从宴会上回来身上全是酒～儿。He smelled of alcohol when he returned from the banquet. ‖ 屋子里有油漆～。The house smells of paint. ▸气～，香～ ❸〈口〉（意味） interest: 他的英语说得不是～儿。He speaks odd English. ‖ 这部电影真够～儿。This film is really interesting. ▸人情～，趣～ ❹（食物） food: ▸美～，野～
B〈动〉〈书〉 reflect on: 细～其言 chew over sb.'s words ▸耐人寻～，品～
C〈量〉 [for ingredients of a Chinese medicine prescription]: 这个方子共有七～药。The prescription specifies seven medicinal herbs.
【味道】wèidao〈名〉 ❶（口味） taste: 尝～ taste the flavour ‖ ～不正 be off in flavour ‖ 我不喜欢洋葱的～。I don't like the taste of onions. ❷（意味） particular sense or feeling: 有点装模做样的～ smack of affectation ‖ 他的话有点讽刺的～。There's a touch of sarcasm in his remarks. ❸（兴趣） interest: 这本书我越看越有～。This book gets more and more interesting the further I get into it. ❹〈方〉（气味） smell
【味精】wèijīng〈名〉 monosodium glutamate (MSG)
【味觉】wèijué〈名〉 sense of taste: 失去～ lose one's sense of taste
【味蕾】wèilěi〈名〉［生理］ taste bud
【味美思】wèiměisī〈名〉〈口〉 vermouth
【味素】wèisù = 味精 wèijīng
【味同嚼蜡】wèitóngjiáolà〈成〉 be as insipid as chewing wax: 这首诗读来～。This poem is totally insipid.

畏 wèi

〈动〉 ❶（害怕） fear: 不～强敌 not be fearful of a formidable enemy ▸望而生～ ❷（佩服） admire: ▸后生可～，敬～
【畏避】wèibì〈动〉 avoid out of fear: 孩子们不再～我了。The children don't flinch from me any more.
【畏光】wèiguāng〈名〉［医学］ photophobia
【畏忌】wèijì〈动〉 harbour suspicions: 相互～ be suspicious of each other
【畏惧】wèijù〈动〉 fear: 使某人～ inspire sb. with fear ‖ 毫无～ show no signs of fear
【畏难】wèinán〈动〉 fear difficulties: 克服～情绪 overcome the fear of difficulty
【畏怯】wèiqiè〈动〉 be timid: 毫无～之心 have no fear at all ‖ 令人～ frightening
【畏首畏尾】wèishǒu-wèiwěi〈成〉 be full of misgivings: ～的人最终将一事无成。Success does not favour a coward.
【畏缩】wèisuō〈动〉 recoil: ～不前 recoil in fear ‖ 在困难面前从不～ never shrink from difficulty
【畏途】wèitú〈名〉〈书〉 dangerous undertaking: 视为～ regard as dangerous
【畏葸】wèixǐ〈动〉〈书〉 be timid/afraid/frightened
【畏友】wèiyǒu〈名〉 revered friend: 严师～ strict teacher and esteemed friend
【畏罪】wèizuì〈动〉 dread punishment for one's crime: ～潜逃 flee to escape punishment ‖ ～自杀 commit suicide to escape punishment

胃 wèi

〈名〉 ❶（指器官） stomach: ～寒 stomach cold ▸～出血 ❷（指星宿） one of the 28 constellations in ancient Chinese astronomy
【胃癌】wèi'ái ▸**p. 50**〈名〉 stomach cancer: 死于～ die of cancer of the stomach
【胃病】wèibìng ▸**p. 50**〈名〉 gastrosis
【胃肠】wèicháng〈名〉［生理］ stomach and intestines
【胃出血】wèichūxiě ▸**p. 50**〈名〉［医学］ gastrorrhagia

W

【胃穿孔】wèichuānkǒng ▸p. 50〈名〉［医学］gastric perforation
【胃窦】wèidòu〈名〉gastric antrum: ～炎 antral gastritis
【胃分泌】wèifēnmì〈名〉［生理］stomachic secretion
【胃镜】wèijìng〈名〉gastroscope: ～检查 gastroscopy
【胃口】wèikǒu〈名〉appetite: 没有～ have no appetite ‖ ～不好/很好 have a poor/good appetite ‖ 对海鲜没～ have no stomach for sea food ‖ 炒股的～越来越大 have an insatiable appetite for speculation in stocks and shares ▸倒～
【胃窥镜】wèikuījìng = 胃镜 wèijìng
【胃溃疡】wèikuìyáng ▸p. 50〈名〉［医学］gastric ulcer
【胃扩张】wèikuòzhāng ▸p. 50〈名〉［医学］gastric dilatation
【胃切除术】wèiqiēchúshù〈名〉［医学］gastrectomy
【胃舒平】wèishūpíng〈名〉［药学］gastropine
【胃酸】wèisuān〈名〉［生理］gastric acid: ～过多 gastric hyperacidity
【胃痛】wèitòng ▸p. 50〈名〉［医学］stomach ache
【胃脘】wèiwǎn〈名〉［中医］gastric cavity
【胃下垂】wèixiàchuí ▸p. 50〈名〉［医学］ptosis of the stomach
【胃腺】wèixiàn〈名〉［生理］gastric gland
【胃炎】wèiyán ▸p. 50〈名〉［医学］gastritis: 萎缩性～ atrophic gastritis
【胃液】wèiyè〈名〉［生理］gastric juice

谓（謂） wèi〈动〉〈书〉**1**（说）say: 勿～言之不预。Don't say that I didn't warn you. ▸可～ **2**（称呼）call: ～之爱情 call it love ▸称～, 何～, 所～
【谓词】wèicí〈名〉**1**［逻辑］predicate: ～演算 predicate calculus **2** = 谓语 wèiyǔ
【谓语】wèiyǔ〈名〉［语言］predicate: ～性名词/形容词 predicate noun/adjective ‖ 复合～ compound predicate

尉 wèi〈名〉**1**（军衔名）junior officer: ▸上～, 少～, 中～ **2**（古）（古官名）official title in ancient China: ▸太～
【尉官】wèiguān〈名〉junior officer

遗（遺） wèi〈动〉〈书〉bestow: ～之豪宅 bestow a luxury abode on sb. ▸yí

喂[1]（餵） wèi〈动〉**1**（指对动物）feed: ～猪 feed pigs ‖ 用肉～狗 feed meat to a dog **2**（饲养）raise: ～七只母鸡 raise seven hens **3**（指对人）feed: 给病人/小孩～饭 feed a patient/baby ‖ 给婴儿～奶 give milk to a baby

喂[2] wèi〈叹〉hello: ～, 能找一下王先生吗? Hello, may I speak to Mr Wang? ‖ ～, 你的轮胎没气啦! Hey, you've got a flat tyre!
【喂奶】wèinǎi〈动〉feed (a baby)
【喂食】wèishí〈动〉feed: 定时～ feed regularly ‖ 给鸟～ put out food for the birds
【喂养】wèiyǎng〈动〉**1**（指对动物）raise: ～牲口 keep domestic animals **2**（指对人）feed: 母乳～ breast-feed

猬（蝟） wèi〈名〉［动物］hedgehog: ▸刺～
【猬集】wèijí〈形〉〈书〉〈喻〉numerous as the spines of a hedgehog: 诸事～ have too many irons in the fire

蔚 wèi〈形〉〈书〉**1**（茂盛）exuberant: 茂树荫～。A flourishing tree has luxuriant foliage. **2**（弥漫）magnificent: 云蒸霞～。Colourful clouds are slowly rising. ▸～为大观 ▸Yù
【蔚蓝】wèilán〈形〉deep blue: ～的天空 bright blue sky ‖ ～的大海 blue sea
【蔚然】wèirán〈形〉〈书〉luxuriantly: ～成林 grow into an exuberant forest
【蔚然成风】wèirán-chéngfēng〈成〉become common practice: 保护环境～。Protecting the environment is the order of the day.
【蔚为大观】wèiwéi-dàguān〈成〉make a magnificent sight: 陈列的艺术品～。The artwork in the exhibition made for a splendid sight.

慰 wèi〈动〉**1**（使人安适）comfort: ▸～问, 安～, 自～ **2**（心安）be relieved: 来函敬悉, 甚～。I'm glad to get your letter. ▸快～, 欣～
【慰安妇】wèi'ānfù〈名〉comfort woman [in Second World War]
【慰抚】wèifǔ〈动〉comfort: 用～的口吻说 speak in a soothing tone
【慰藉】wèijiè〈动〉〈书〉console: 给以精神上的～ give spiritual comfort
【慰劳】wèiláo〈动〉bring gifts or entertainment in recognition of services rendered: ～解放军战士 bring gifts, entertainment and greetings to the PLA soldiers ‖ ～品 gifts expressing one's appreciation for services rendered
【慰勉】wèimiǎn〈动〉〈书〉comfort and encourage
【慰问】wèiwèn〈动〉extend one's regards to: ～灾区人民 express sympathy with the people of disaster-stricken areas ‖ 对遇难者家属表示～ express one's condolences to the victims' family on their misfortune
【慰问团】wèiwèntuán〈名〉group sent to convey greetings and appreciation
【慰问信】wèiwènxìn〈名〉letter of sympathy
【慰唁】wèiyàn〈动〉〈书〉express one's condolences: ～死者家属 express one's condolences to the bereaved family

罻 wèi〈名〉〈书〉small net for catching birds

魏 Wèi〈名〉**1**（指国名）Wei [state in the Zhou Dynasty] **2**（指三国之一）Kingdom of Wei **3**（北魏）Northern Wei Dynasty
【魏碑】wèibēi〈名〉**1**（指碑刻）tablet inscriptions of the Northern Dynasties **2**（指书法字体）model calligraphy represented by Northern Dynasties inscriptions
【魏阙】wèiquè〈名〉〈古〉**1**（指建筑）gate of the imperial palace where imperial edicts were issued **2**（指朝廷）imperial court

鳚（鰄） wèi〈名〉［鱼类］blenny

wēn

温 wēn
A〈形〉**1**（暖）tepid: 粥还～着呢。The porridge is still warm. ▸～带, ～水 **2**（和顺）gentle: ▸～情, ～顺, ～驯 **3** = 瘟 wēn B
B〈名〉**1**（温度）temperature: ▸～度, 气～, 体～ **2** = 瘟 wēn A
C〈动〉**1**（适当加热）warm up: 把奶～热 warm up the milk **2**（温习）review: ～功课 go over one's lessons ‖ 重～旧交 brush up one's acquaintance with sb. ▸～故知新, 重～旧梦
【温饱】wēnbǎo〈名〉state of having enough to eat and wear: ～工程 programme for adequate food and clothing ‖ 终年劳累, 不得～ toil all year round without enough to eat and wear ‖ 提高人民生活水平, 从～达到小康 raise living standards from a basic state of having enough to eat and wear to leading a relatively comfortable life
【温标】wēnbiāo〈名〉［物理］thermometric scale: 华氏～ Fahrenheit thermometric scale ‖ 摄氏～ Celsius thermometric scale
【温差】wēnchā〈名〉difference in temperature: 昼夜～不大。The temperature changes little from day to night.
【温床】wēnchuáng〈名〉hotbed: ～栽培 hotbed culture ‖ 官僚主义是贿赂和腐败的～。Bureaucracy is a hotbed of bribery and corruption. ‖ 这地方是产生疟疾的～。The place is a hotbed of malaria.
【温存】wēncún **A**〈动〉be attentive: 百般～ shower attentions on sb. **B**〈形〉kind: 性格～ be tender in nature ‖ 她～和蔼。She is all tenderness and kindness.
【温带】wēndài〈名〉temperate zone: ～气候 temperate climate ‖ ～雨林 temperate rainforest ▸北～, 南～
【温度】wēndù ▸p. 776〈名〉temperature: 室内/室外～ indoor/outdoor temperature ‖ 最低/最高～ lowest/highest temperature ‖ ～降至零下20摄氏度。The temperature dropped to -20℃.
【温度表】wēndùbiǎo = 温度计 wēndùjì
【温度计】wēndùjì〈名〉thermograph: 水银～ mercury thermometer
【温哥华】Wēngēhuá〈名〉Vancouver
【温故知新】wēngù-zhīxīn〈成〉review the past helps one to understand the present
【温和】wēnhé〈形〉**1**（指气候）temperate: 气候～ temperate climate **2**（指态度、力量等）gentle: 措词～ be temperate in one's language ‖ 态度～ be mild in manner ‖ 性情～ have a gentle disposition ▸wēnhuo
【温和派】wēnhépài〈名〉moderate
【温厚】wēnhòu〈形〉gentle and kind: 为人～ be kind and sincere
【温乎】wēnhu = 温和 wēnhuo
【温和】wēnhuo〈形〉warm: 趁汤还～着, 快喝吧! Please help yourself to the soup while it is still warm. ▸wēnhé
【温居】wēnjū〈动〉have a house-warming (party): 你去参加他的～宴吗? Are you going to his house-warming party?
【温控】wēnkòng〈形〉temperature-controlled: ～装置 temperature-controlled equipment
【温良】wēnliáng〈形〉gentle and kind-hearted: 性情～ be gentle in disposition
【温良恭俭让】wēn-liáng-gōng-jiǎn-ràng

〈成〉 be kind and gentle in disposition and refined in manner

【温暖】wēnnuǎn **A**〈形〉 warm: 感到家庭的～ feel the warmth of one's family ‖ ～如春 be as mild as spring ‖ ～的阳光 warm sunshine **B**〈动〉 warm: ～人心 warm the cockles of the heart

【温情】wēnqíng〈名〉 tender loving care: ～满怀 be extremely affectionate ‖ 你对他太～了。 You're too lenient with him.

【温情脉脉】wēnqíng-mòmò〈成〉 be full of tenderness

【温情主义】 wēnqíng zhǔyì 〈名〉 undue leniency

【温泉】wēnquán〈名〉 hot spring: ～浴场 spa

【温柔】wēnróu〈形〉[usu of a woman] gentle and soft: 性情～ be of mild disposition ‖ 对某人～体贴 be tender and considerate towards sb.

【温柔敦厚】 wēnróu-dūnhòu 〈成〉 gentle and kindly

【温柔乡】wēnróuxiāng〈名〉〈喻〉 a place where a man can find solace in feminine charms

【温润】wēnrùn〈形〉 **1**（温和） gentle: ～的面容 kindly features **2**（温暖湿润） mild and moist: ～的气候 temperate and humid climate **3**（细润） fine and smooth: 玉质～ fine jade

【温湿】 wēnshī 〈形〉 temperate: ～计 hygrothermograph

【温室】wēnshì〈名〉 greenhouse: ～栽培 glasshouse culture ‖ 在～种植西红柿 grow tomatoes in a greenhouse

【温室气体】wēnshì qìtǐ〈名〉 greenhouse gases: ～排放 greenhouse gas emissions

【温室效应】wēnshì xiàoyìng〈名〉 **1**［农业］ greenhouse effect **2**（大气保温效应） global warming

【温水】wēnshuǐ〈名〉 warm water: ～游泳池 heated swimming pool

【温顺】wēnshùn〈形〉 docile: ～的妻子 submissive wife ‖ 像他这样～的男人不多。 Not many men are as meek as he is.

【温汤】wēntāng〈名〉 **1**（温水） warm water: ～浸种 hot water seed treatment **2**〈书〉（温泉） hot spring

【温吞水】wēntūnshuǐ〈名〉〈方〉 **1**（指水）lukewarm water **2**〈喻〉（指人） wet fish

【温文尔雅】wēnwén-ěryǎ〈成〉 refined: 言谈举止～ be gentle and refined in both speech and deportment

【温习】wēnxí〈动〉 review: ～功课 review one's lessons

【温馨】wēnxīn〈形〉 pleasant and sweet: ～的家 happy family ‖ ～的夜晚 pleasant evening ‖ 卧室布置得很～。 The bedroom was cosily furnished.

【温煦】 wēnxù 〈形〉〈书〉 **1**（暖和） pleasantly warm: ～的阳光 warm sunlight ‖ ～的气候 warm weather **2**（温和亲切） gentle and kind: ～的目光 gentle and kind look

【温血动物】wēnxuè dòngwù〈名〉 warm-blooded animal

【温驯】 wēnxùn 〈形〉 docile: ～的羔羊 meek lamb

榅 wēn

【榅桲】 wēnpo 〈名〉 **1**［植物］ quince **2**（指果实） quince

辒（轀） wēn

【辒辌】wēnliáng〈名〉〈古〉 sleeping carriage [also used as a hearse]

瘟 wēn

A〈名〉［中医］ acute epidemic: 春～ spring epidemic ▸～疫, 鸡～, 牛～

B〈形〉 [of the performance of traditional Chinese operas] dull and insipid: 跟以前的戏相比，这出戏有些～。 The opera was tame in comparison to previous ones.

【瘟病】 wēnbìng 〈名〉［中医］ seasonal febrile disease

【瘟神】wēnshén〈名〉 god of plague: 人们像躲～似的躲着他。 People shunned him like the plague.

【瘟疫】wēnyì〈名〉 pestilence: 防止～蔓延 avert the spread of the pestilence ‖ ～流行的地区 plague-ridden area

蕰 wēn

【蕰草】wēncǎo〈名〉〈方〉［植物］ water weed

鳁（鰛） wēn

【鳁鲸】wēnjīng〈名〉［动物］ sea whale

wén

文 wén

A〈名〉 **1**（字） character: ▸梵～, 甲骨～, 钟鼎～ **2**（书面语言） written language: ▸外～, 语～ **3**（文章） literary composition: 著～ write an article ▸～不对题, 散

ℹ 温度及天气

■ 常用的温度单位:

摄氏度	degrees Celsius/centigrade	(°C)
华氏度	degrees Fahrenheit	(°F)

■ 用英语表达温度（关于如何用英语表达数字，参见语用信息框“数字”）:

	读	写
100 摄氏度	a hundred degrees Celsius	100°C
0 摄氏度	zero degree centigrade	0°C
零下 100 摄氏度	minus a hundred degrees Celsius	–100°C
212 华氏度	two hundred and twelve degrees Fahrenheit	212°F
零下 200 华氏度	minus two hundred degrees Fahrenheit	–200 °F

超过 37 摄氏度
= above 37°C

在 40 华氏度以上
= over 40°F

在 100 度以下
= below 100°

摄氏温度计
= Celsius thermometer

华氏温度计
= Fahrenheit thermometer

温度计显示 55 摄氏度
= The thermometer says/shows 55°C

体温

人的正常体温接近 37 摄氏度或 98 华氏度
= The normal human body temperature is close to 37°C or 98°F

她的体温是多少? —— 是 38.5 摄氏度
= What is her temperature?
— Her temperature is 38.5°C

医生给我量了体温
= The doctor took my temperature

物体的温度

粥有多热? —— 大约 90 摄氏度
= How hot is the porridge?
或 What temperature is the porridge?
— It's about 90°C

水在什么温度下沸腾?
—— 水在 100 摄氏度或 212 华氏度下沸腾
= What temperature does water boil at?
— It boils at 100°C or 212°F

水在 0 摄氏度或在 32 华氏度结冰
= Water freezes at a temperature of 0°C or 32°F

炒锅被加热到了 120 摄氏度
= The wok was heated to a temperature of 120°C

A 比 B 热
= A is hotter than B

B 比 A 凉
= B is colder/cooler than A

A 和 B 温度相同
= A is the same temperature as B
或 A and B are the same temperature

天气

今天的气温是多少?
= What's the temperature today?

今天是 15 摄氏度
= It is 15 degrees centigrade

最高温度是 35 摄氏度，最低温度是零下 12 摄氏度
= The maximum temperature is 35°C and the lowest is –12°C

从上周起，气温逐渐下降
= There has been a gradual decrease in temperature since last week

今天非常热，气温是 45 摄氏度
= It's roasting/boiling today. It's 45°C

今天非常冷，气温是零下 25 华氏度
= It's freezing today. The temperature is –25°F

青岛比大连暖和
= Qingdao is warmer than Dalian

黑龙江冬天比北京冷
= Heilongjiang is colder in winter than Beijing

海口和广州的气温相同
= It's the same temperature in Haikou as in Guangzhou

～, 韵～ **4**（文言） literary language: 半～半白 half literary and half vernacular ‖ 别看他没读过多少书，说起话来还挺～的。 Despite his limited education, he sounds very cultured when he talks. ►～绉绉 **5**（文明） culture: ►～化, ～明, ～物 **6**（文科） humanities: 你是学～的，还是学理的？ Do you major in arts or science? **7**（礼节） etiquette: ►繁～缛节, 虚～ **8**（自然界现象） certain natural phenomena: ►水～, 天～

B〈形〉 **1**（非军事） civil: ►～官, ～职, ～武 **2**（柔和） gentle: ►～火, ～弱, ～雅

C〈动〉 **1**（掩盖） gloss over: ►～过饰非 **2**（指刺花纹或字） tattoo: ～了双颊 get one's cheeks tattooed ‖ 在背上～了一条龙 have a dragon tattooed on one's back ►～身

D〈量〉 [used for copper cash in old times]: 一～钱 one cent ►一～不名

【文案】wén'àn〈名〉 copy: 广告～ ad copy

【文本】wénběn〈名〉 text: 协议的正式～ official text of an agreement ‖ 本合同中英两种～具有同等效力。The Chinese and English texts of the contract are equally valid.

【文本输入】wénběn shūrù〈名〉 text input

【文本文件】wénběn wénjiàn〈名〉 text file

【文笔】wénbǐ〈名〉 style of writing: ～简洁 write in a concise style ‖ ～犀利 wield a trenchant pen ‖ 她以～细腻见长。 She has an exquisite style of writing.

【文不对题】wénbùduìtí〈成〉 be beside the point: 你的回答～。 Your answer is beside the point.

【文不加点】wénbùjiādiǎn〈成〉 never make the slightest change or revision in one's writing: ～，一挥而就 quickly compose an article that is free of mistakes

【文才】wéncái〈名〉 literary talent: ～出众 be of eminent literary talent

【文采】wéncǎi〈名〉 **1**（指色彩） rich and bright colours **2**（指才华） literary grace: 颇具～ be a literary talent **3**（指艺术魅力） ornate wording: 讲究～ have a preference for ornate wording ‖ 缺少～的文章 dull and prosaic article

【文昌鱼】wénchāngyú〈名〉［动物］ lancelet

【文场】wénchǎng〈名〉 **1**（指管弦乐器） civil division [referring to stringed and wind instruments as opposed to percussion instruments (武场)] **2**［曲艺］ *wenchang* [folk art popular in Guilin (桂林) and Liuzhou (柳州) of Guangxi Zhuang Autonomous Region]

【文抄公】wénchāogōng〈名〉〈贬〉 plagiarist

【文丑】wénchǒu〈名〉［戏曲］ clown skilled in dialogue and acting

【文词】wéncí = 文辞 wéncí

【文辞】wéncí〈名〉 **1**（指遣词造句） diction: ～华丽/优美 flowery language **2**（指文章） essay: 以善～出名 be famous for writing essays

【文从字顺】wéncóng-zìshùn〈成〉 coherent and smooth: 要做到～，必须千锤百炼。 Practise a lot in order for one's language to become idiomatic and one's wording apposite.

【文代会】wéndàihuì〈名〉 congress of writers and artists

【文旦】wéndàn〈名〉〈方〉［植物］ shaddock

【文档】wéndàng〈名〉 **1**（文字档案） document **2**［计算机］ document: 保存～ save a document ‖ 打开～ open a document ‖ 复制/拷贝～ copy a file

【文斗】wéndòu〈名〉 verbal arguing

【文牍】wéndú〈名〉 **1**（指公文、书信） official documents and correspondence: ～主义 red tape **2**〈旧〉（指人） scribe

【文法】wénfǎ〈名〉〈旧〉 grammar: ～错误 grammatical mistake

【文房四宝】wénfáng sìbǎo〈名〉 four treasures of the study

> **文房四宝**
>
> The tools and materials used in traditional Chinese painting and calligraphy. The four treasures are the writing brush (笔), ink (墨), paper (纸) and inkstone (砚). The brush is made up of a shaft and a head made of weasel hair, etc. The ink is made from a black lump of coal or pine soot. The most famous paper is *xuan* paper (宣纸), produced in Xuancheng in Anhui Province. The inkstone is made of stone and is used as a surface for grinding the soot with water to make ink.

【文风】wénfēng〈名〉 style of writing: 整顿～ rectify a style of writing ‖ ～朴实 have a simple writing style

【文稿】wéngǎo〈名〉 manuscript: 誊写～ copy a manuscript

【文告】wéngào〈名〉 proclamation: 发布～ issue a proclamation

【文革】Wéngé〈简称〉= 文化大革命

> **文化大革命**
>
> A political movement launched by Mao Zedong from 1966-76 in order to 'purify' Chinese Communism, and to strengthen his own political and ideological position. The full name is the Great Proletarian Cultural Revolution（"无产阶级文化大革命"）, often shortened to "文革". The period, sometimes referred to today as the 'ten years of chaos' (十年动乱), was characterized by the violent activities of the Red Guards (红卫兵), the enforced displacement of educated people to rural areas, and social and economic turmoil. The Gang of Four（"四人帮"）, a radical faction led by Mao's wife, Jiang Qing, played a key role in directing the excesses of the Cultural Revolution. Its members were arrested and sentenced in 1976.

【文蛤】wéngé〈名〉［动物］ clam

【文工团】wéngōngtuán〈名〉 cultural troupe

【文官】wénguān〈名〉 civil servant: ～政府 civil government

【文过饰非】wénguò-shìfēi〈成〉 cover up one's mistakes: 不要～ do not try to cover up your mistakes

【文翰】wénhàn〈名〉 **1**〈书〉（文章） essay **2**〈旧〉（公文信札） official documents and correspondence

【文豪】wénháo〈名〉 literary giant: 他被公认为20世纪30年代的大～。 He was generally regarded as one of the great writers of the 1930's.

【文化】wénhuà〈名〉 **1**（指物质与精神） civilization: 促进～交流 promote cultural exchanges ‖ 整理～遗产 sort out cultural heritages ‖ 传统～ traditional culture ‖ 民族～ national culture ‖ 物质～ material culture **2**（知识、文字能力） education: 学～ acquire an elementary education ‖ 有～ be educated ‖ ～修养很高的人 man of considerable education and upbringing ‖ ～程度 educational level **3**（特指精神） culture: 丰富～生活 enrich cultural life ‖ 提供～娱乐设施 provide cultural and recreational facilities **4**［考古］ ancient culture or civilization: 玛雅～ Mayan civilization ‖ 龙山～ Longshan Culture ‖ 仰韶～ Yangshao Culture

【文化部】wénhuàbù〈名〉 ministry of culture

【文化参赞】wénhuà cānzàn〈名〉 cultural attaché

【文化层】wénhuàcéng〈名〉［考古］ cultural stratum

【文化产业】wénhuà chǎnyè〈名〉 culture industry

【文化大革命】Wénhuà Dàgémìng〈名〉 'Great Cultural Revolution' [1966-1976]

【文化宫】wénhuàgōng〈名〉 cultural palace

【文化馆】wénhuàguǎn〈名〉 cultural centre

【文化教育】wénhuà jiàoyù〈名〉 culture and education: ～事业 cultural and educational undertakings

【文化界】wénhuàjiè〈名〉 cultural circles: ～名流 cultural figures

【文化课】wénhuàkè〈名〉 literacy class

【文化年】wénhuànián〈名〉 culture year: 中国将举办法国～。 China is going to hold a French Culture Year.

【文化品位】wénhuà pǐnwèi〈名〉 standing of culture

【文化侵略】wénhuà qīnlüè〈名〉 cultural aggression

【文化人】wénhuàrén〈名〉 **1**（专门从事文化工作的人） cultural worker **2**（知识分子） intellectual

【文化人类学】wénhuà rénlèixué〈名〉 cultural anthropology

【文化沙漠】wénhuà shāmò〈名〉 cultural desert: 这个镇子有点像～。 This town is a bit of a cultural desert.

【文化衫】wénhuàshān〈名〉 T-shirt printed with writing or pictures

【文化渗透】wénhuà shèntòu〈名〉 cultural infiltration

【文化史】wénhuàshǐ〈名〉 cultural history

【文化水平】wénhuà shuǐpíng〈名〉 schooling

【文化素养】wénhuà sùyǎng〈名〉 artistic appreciation

【文化遗产】wénhuà yíchǎn〈名〉 cultural heritage

【文化用品】wénhuà yòngpǐn〈名〉 stationery

【文化娱乐】wénhuà yúlè〈名〉 enjoyment of culture

【文化站】wénhuàzhàn〈名〉 cultural centre

【文化周】wénhuàzhōu〈名〉 culture week: 在德国举办中国西藏～。 A Tibetan Culture Week is being held in Germany.

【文火】wénhuǒ〈名〉 low heat: ～焖牛肉 simmer beef over a gentle heat

【文集】wénjí〈名〉 collected works: 《鲁迅～》 *Collected Works of Lu Xun*

【文件】wénjiàn〈名〉 **1**（公文、信件） document: 官方/正式～ official document ‖ 机密～ confidential document **2**［计算机］ file: 打开～ open a document ‖ 复制/拷贝～ copy a file ‖ ～备份 file backup ‖ ～管理器 file manager

【文件格式】wénjiàn géshi〈名〉［计算机］ file format

【文件共享】wénjiàn gòngxiǎng〈名〉［计算机］ file sharing

【文件夹】wénjiànjiā〈名〉 file folder

【文件名】wénjiànmíng〈名〉［计算机］ file name

【文教】wénjiào〈名〉 culture and education: ～界 cultural and educational circles

【文静】wénjìng〈形〉 quiet and refined: ～的女孩 quiet girl

【文句】wénjù〈名〉 diction: ～通顺 the language is coherent

【文具】wénjù〈名〉 stationery: ～店 stationer's ‖ ～盒 pencil case

W

【文据】wénjù〈名〉written pledge
【文科】wénkē〈名〉liberal arts: ～大学 liberal arts university ‖ 他是学～的。 He majors in liberal arts.
【文科博士】wénkē bóshì〈名〉doctor of arts
【文科硕士】wénkē shuòshì〈名〉master of arts (MA)
【文科学士】wénkē xuéshì〈名〉bachelor of arts (BA)
【文库】wénkù〈名〉library:《万有～》*Everyman's Library*
【文侩】wénkuài〈名〉literary scavenger
【文莱】Wénlái〈名〉Brunei
【文理】wénlǐ〈名〉**1**（指条理）unity and coherence in writing: ～不通 be incoherent ‖ ～通顺 make for smooth reading **2**（文科和理科）liberal arts and science: ～兼修 study both liberal arts and science
【文联】wénlián〈名〉literary federation: 中国～ China Federation of Literature and Art
【文盲】wénmáng〈名〉illiterate: 扫除～ wipe out illiteracy ‖ 半～ semi-literate
【文眉】wénméi〈动〉tattoo the eyebrows
【文秘】wénmì〈名〉scribe and secretary: ～工作 secretarial work
【文庙】wénmiào〈名〉Confucian temple
【文明】wénmíng **A**〈名〉civilization: 物质/精神～ material/spiritual civilization ‖ 印加～ Inca civilization ‖ 中原地区是中华～的摇篮。 The central plains are the cradle of Chinese civilization. **B**〈形〉**1**（指发展程度）civilized: ～国家/社会 civilized country/society ‖ ～村 model village **2**（指言行举止）civilized: ～经商 do business with civility ‖ 说话～点! Watch your language! **3**（有现代色彩）modern: ～婚礼 modern wedding
【文明棍】wénmínggùn〈名〉〈旧〉walking stick
【文明史】wénmíngshǐ〈名〉history of civilization: 人类～ history of human civilization
【文明戏】wénmíngxì〈名〉〈旧〉early form of modern drama
【文墨】wénmò〈名〉**1**（写作）writing: 粗通～ barely know the rudiments of writing **2**（文化知识）writing activities
【文痞】wénpǐ〈名〉literary scoundrel
【文凭】wénpíng〈名〉diploma: 颁发～ issue a diploma ‖ 大学～ college diploma
【文气】wénqì〈名〉vigour of a piece of writing: 该书～劲健。 The book was written with great vigour.
【文契】wénqì〈名〉contract: 在～上签字 sign a contract
【文气】wénqi〈形〉gentle and reserved: 她看上去挺～。 She looks very gentle.
【文情并茂】wénqíng-bìngmào〈成〉[of writing] elegant in style and rich in sentiment
【文曲星】wénqǔxīng〈名〉**1**（指神）legendary god in charge of imperial examinations and literary affairs **2**〈喻〉〈旧〉（指人）renowned man of letters
【文人】wénrén〈名〉man of letters: ～墨客 literati
【文人相轻】wénrén-xiāngqīng〈成〉writers often disparage one another: 摈弃～的陋习。 Scholars should get rid of the bad habit of belittling each other.
【文人雅士】wénrén yǎshì〈成〉refined scholars
【文如其人】wénrúqírén〈成〉the writing mirrors the writer
【文弱】wénruò〈形〉gentle and frail: ～书生 frail-looking scholar
【文山会海】wénshān-huìhǎi〈成〉mountains of papers and numerous meetings: 从～中摆脱出来 free oneself from office work and meetings
【文身】wénshēn〈动〉tattoo
【文史】wénshǐ〈名〉culture and history: ～资料 historical accounts of past events ‖ ～馆 research institute of culture and history
【文饰】wénshì〈动〉**1**（用文辞修饰）polish: 不加～的叙述 narration with no polish **2**（掩饰）gloss over: ～自己的错误 gloss over one's own faults
【文书】wénshū〈名〉**1**（指公文、函件等）documents: ～工作 clerical work ‖ 司法～ judicial documents **2**（指人）secretary
【文殊】Wénshū〈名〉[佛教] Manjusri [Bodhisattva, personifying supreme wisdom and depicted as seated on a lion or on a lotus]
【文思】wénsī〈名〉thread of ideas in writing: ～枯竭 run out of ideas to write about ‖ ～敏捷 have a ready pen
【文坛】wéntán〈名〉literary world: 震惊～ shock literary circles ‖ ～巨擘 literary mogul
【文韬武略】wéntāo-wǔlüè〈成〉military strategy: 谙熟～ be well-versed in military strategy
【文体】wéntǐ〈名〉**1**（文章体裁）literary form: 用正式的～写作 write in a formal style **2**（文娱和体育）recreation and sports: ～活动 recreational and sporting activities
【文体学】wéntǐxué〈名〉stylistics: ～家 stylist
【文恬武嬉】wéntián-wǔxī〈成〉the entire officialdom, both civil and military, wallows in luxury and dissipation
【文武】wénwǔ〈名〉**1**（文才和武艺）intellectual pursuits and martial arts **2**〈书〉（文治和武功）civil and military rule: ～并用 combine force with non-violence **3**〈书〉（文官和武将）ministers and generals: ～百官 civil officials and military officers
【文武双全】wénwǔ shuāngquán〈成〉be well-versed in both polite letters and martial arts
【文物】wénwù〈名〉cultural artefact: 出土～ protect unearthed cultural artefacts ‖ 走私～ smuggle cultural artefacts ‖ 国家重点～保护单位 major historic and cultural sites under state protection
【文戏】wénxì〈名〉gentle show [Chinese traditional opera focusing on singing and acting rather than martial arts]
【文献】wénxiàn〈名〉literature: 科技～ scientific and technological data ‖ 历史～ historical documents ‖ 医学～ medical literature
【文献记录片】wénxiàn jìlùpiàn〈名〉documentary film
【文献检索】wénxiàn jiǎnsuǒ〈名〉documentation retrieval
【文献搜集】wénxiàn sōují〈名〉literature search
【文献资料】wénxiàn zīliào〈名〉documentation
【文胸】wénxiōng〈名〉bra
【文选】wénxuǎn〈名〉selected works: 活页～ loose-leaf literary selections ‖《邓小平～》*Selected Works of Deng Xiaoping*
【文学】wénxué〈名〉literature: ～名著 literary classic ‖ 比较～ comparative literature ‖ 民间～ folk literature ‖ 古代/现代/当代～ ancient/modern/contemporary literature
【文学家】wénxuéjiā〈名〉man/woman of letters
【文学界】wénxuéjiè〈名〉literary world
【文学流派】wénxué liúpài〈名〉schools of literature
【文学批评】wénxué pīpíng〈名〉literary criticism
【文学史】wénxuéshǐ〈名〉history of literature
【文学艺术】wénxué yìshù〈名〉literature and art
【文学语言】wénxué yǔyán〈名〉**1**（标准语）standard speech **2**（文学作品使用的语言）literary language
【文雅】wényǎ〈形〉elegant: 举止～ have refined manners ‖ 谈吐～ be elegant in speech
【文言】wényán〈名〉classical Chinese: 这本小说用～写成。 This novel was written in classical Chinese.
【文言文】wényánwén〈名〉classical Chinese

> **文言文**
>
> Classical Chinese refers to the language used by past generations of scholars who modelled their language on the vernacular used by pre-Qin Dynasty writers. Early classical Chinese and the pre-Qin vernacular are basically the same. For example, the dialogues recorded in *The Analects of Confucius* (《论语》) are written mostly in the vernacular. Over time, the vernacular changed but the written form remained the same. After the Vernacular Movement of the early 20th century, modern vernacular Chinese (▶白话文) gradually replaced classical Chinese in writing.

【文以载道】wényǐzàidào〈成〉the function of literature is to convey the truth or moral values
【文艺】wényì〈名〉literature and art: ～创作 literary and artistic creation ‖ ～工作者 writers and artists ‖ ～团体 theatre company ‖ ～会演 theatre festival
【文艺复兴】Wényì Fùxīng〈名〉Renaissance: ～时期的艺术/音乐/绘画 Renaissance art/music/painting
【文艺界】wényìjiè〈名〉world of literature and art
【文艺批评】wényì pīpíng〈名〉literary and art criticism: ～家 literary/art critic
【文艺学】wényìxué〈名〉study of art and literature
【文友】wényǒu〈名〉literary associate
【文娱】wényú〈名〉cultural recreation: ～活动 recreational activities ‖ ～节目 entertainment programme
【文员】wényuán ▶**p. 966**〈名〉clerical worker: 他当了十年～。 He worked as a clerk for ten years.
【文苑】wényuàn〈名〉〈书〉**1**（文学界）literary circles **2**（文艺界）literary and art world
【文约】wényuē〈名〉contract
【文责】wénzé〈名〉author's responsibility for his or her writings: ～自负 the author takes sole responsibility for his views
【文摘】wénzhāi〈名〉**1**（指扼要摘录）abstract: 报刊～ newspaper and magazine digest ‖《读者～》*Reader's Digest* **2**（指文章片段）extract
【文章】wénzhāng〈名〉**1**（单篇作品）article: 写～ write an article ‖ 评论～ critical essay **2**（著述）literary works: ～写得好 have a deft pen **3**（暗含的意思）hidden meaning: 他的话里有～。 There is an insinuation in his remarks. ‖ 她说话躲躲闪闪，其中一定有～。 Her evasive remarks indicated there must be something going on. **4**（关于事情的做法）way: 做表面～ do sth. for the sake of appearances ‖ 在枝节问题上大做～ kick up a rumpus over some side issues
【文职】wénzhí〈名〉civilian post: ～人员

W

civil servant
【文治】wénzhì〈名〉〈书〉civil administration: ～武功 political and military achievements
【文质彬彬】wénzhì-bīnbīn〈成〉quiet and scholarly: 一个～的小伙子 a bookish young man
【文绉绉】wénzhōuzhōu〈形〉bookish: 说话～的 speak in a genteel manner
【文竹】wénzhú〈名〉［植物］asparagus fern
【文字】wénzì ▸p. 999〈名〉1▸（指语言符号）script: 表形～ hieroglyph ‖ 表意～ ideography ‖ 拼音～ alphabetic system of writing 2▸（书面语言）written language: 玩～游戏 play on words ‖ 有～可考的历史 recorded history 3▸（文章）writing: ～简练 be succinct in wording ‖ ～通畅 easy and smooth writing style
【文字材料】wénzì cáiliào〈名〉written material
【文字处理】wénzì chǔlǐ〈名〉［计算机］word processing: ～系统 word-processing system
【文字学】wénzìxué〈名〉philology
【文字狱】wénzìyù〈名〉［历史］literary punishment [of an author for writing something deemed to be offensive to the rulers]
【文宗】wénzōng〈名〉〈书〉acclaimed literary figure: 一代～ most outstanding literary figure of the time

纹（紋）wén

〈名〉1▸（纹路）vein: 细～木 fine-grained wood ▸皱～, 裂～, 螺～ 2▸（花纹）pattern: ▸花～
【纹风不动】wénfēng-bùdòng = 纹丝不动 wénsī-bùdòng
【纹理】wénlǐ〈名〉grain: 逆着木材的～刨木头 plane wood against the grain ‖ 有粉红色～的大理石 pink-veined marble
【纹路】wénlu〈名〉lines: 条形～ stripy lines
【纹饰】wénshì〈名〉engraved pattern
【纹丝】wénsī〈形〉[usu used in the negative] slightest: 使不受～干扰 not disturb sb. in the slightest
【纹丝不动】wénsī-bùdòng〈成〉completely motionless: 没有一点风，柳条儿～。There wasn't a breath of wind and the willow branches were perfectly still.
【纹银】wényín〈名〉〈旧〉fine silver
【纹玉】wényù〈名〉veined jade

炆 wén

〈动〉〈方〉simmer

闻（聞）wén

A〈动〉1▸（听到）hear: 听而不～ turn a deaf ear ‖ 早有所～ have heard a long time ago ▸～所未～, 充耳不～ 2▸（用鼻子嗅）smell: ～～这种香水 smell the perfume ‖ 我～到腥臭味儿了。I smelled something bad.
B〈名〉1▸（消息）news: ▸奇～, 新～, 逸～ 2▸（名声）reputation: 秽～ ill repute ‖ 令～ good reputation
C〈形〉〈书〉celebrated: ▸～人, 默默无～

> 闻
> ▸望、闻、问、切

【闻达】wéndá〈名〉〈书〉eminence: 不求～ seek for neither fame nor position
【闻风而动】wénfēng'érdòng〈成〉act without delay upon receiving a call
【闻风而逃】wénfēng'értáo〈成〉flee upon learning the news
【闻风丧胆】wénfēng-sàngdǎn〈成〉be alarmed at a mere rumour: 大军所到之处，土匪～。The bandits trembled with fear wherever they got wind of the army's advance.
【闻过则喜】wénguò-zéxǐ〈成〉be glad to have one's errors pointed out
【闻鸡起舞】wénjī-qǐwǔ〈成〉〈喻〉be diligent and self-disciplined
【闻见】wénjiàn〈名〉〈旧〉knowledge: ～广博 be knowledgeable ‖ 鄙人～有限。My knowledge is limited.
【闻名】wénmíng〈动〉1▸（有名）be well-known: ～全国 be well-known throughout the country ‖ ～的风景区 famous scenic spot ‖ 西安以兵马俑而～世界。Xi'an is world-famous for its terracotta warriors and horses. 2▸（听到名声）know sb. by repute: ～已久 have heard of sb. a long time ago ‖ ～不如见面。It is better to see a person in the flesh than to know him by repute.
【闻名遐尔】wénmíng-xiá'ěr〈成〉be well-known far and near: 这位医生35岁就开始～了。The doctor became famous far and near at the age of 35.
【闻人】wénrén〈名〉〈书〉celebrity: 最受爱戴的～之一 one of the best-loved personalities
【闻所未闻】wénsuǒwèiwén〈成〉unheard of: 这件事我～。I have never heard of it.
【闻讯】wénxùn〈动〉hear the news: ～赶来看演出 come to see the performance as soon as one hears the news
【闻一知十】wényī-zhīshí〈成〉be good at drawing analogies
【闻诊】wénzhěn〈名〉［中医］auscultation and olfaction [one of the four methods of diagnosis]

蚊 wén

〈名〉mosquito: 灭～ kill mosquitoes ▸疟～
【蚊虫】wénchóng〈名〉mosquito: ～叮咬 mosquito bite
【蚊香】wénxiāng〈名〉mosquito coil
【蚊帐】wénzhàng〈名〉mosquito net
【蚊子】wénzi〈名〉mosquito

雯 wén

〈名〉〈书〉patterned cloud

wěn

刎 wěn

〈动〉cut one's throat: ▸自～
【刎颈之交】wěnjǐng-zhījiāo〈成〉friends who are ready to die for one another

抆 wěn

〈动〉〈书〉wipe: ～泪 wipe one's tears

吻 wěn

A〈名〉1▸（唇）lip: ▸接～ 2▸［动物］animal's mouth
B〈动〉kiss: ～面颊/手/嘴唇 kiss sb. on the cheek/hand/lips ▸飞～, 亲～
【吻别】wěnbié〈动〉kiss sb. good-bye
【吻合】wěnhé〈动〉1▸（完全符合）tally: 意见～ have identical views ‖ 他对事件的描述与证人的陈述不～。His version of the event doesn't tally with the witnesses' statements. 2▸［医学］join by anastomosis: 进行血管～ join two parts of a vessel by anastomosis

紊 wěn

〈形〉disorderly: ▸有条不～
【紊流】wěnliú〈名〉［物理］turbulence
【紊乱】wěnluàn〈形〉chaotic: 秩序～ in chaos ‖ 肠胃功能～ gastrointestinal functional disorder

稳（穩）wěn

A〈形〉1▸（稳固）steady: 立场很～ have a firm stand ‖ 坐～ sit tight ‖ 这孩子走不～。The baby is not very steady on its feet yet. 2▸（稳重）reliable: ▸～重, 沉～, 四平八～ 3▸（稳妥）sure: ～拿金牌 be certain to win the gold medal ▸十拿九～
B〈动〉stabilize: ～～神儿! Steady your nerves! ‖ 先～住他，别让他跑了。In the first place, keep him where he is. Don't let him run off.
【稳便】wěnbiàn〈形〉convenient and reliable: ～的办法 safe and convenient method
【稳步】wěnbù〈名〉steady steps: ～发展 develop steadily ‖ ～增长 experience a steady growth
【稳操胜券】wěncāo-shèngquàn〈成〉be sure of success: 上半场射进三球后，我们已～。The three goals we scored in the first half gave us a useful cushion against defeat.
【稳产】wěnchǎn〈名〉stable output: ～高产田 field with high and stable yields
【稳当】wěndang〈形〉1▸（稳重妥当）reliable: 他办事～。He is a trustworthy man. ‖ 这个办法～不～? Is this a reliable method? 2▸（稳固牢靠）stable: 把桌子放～。Make the table steady.
【稳定】wěndìng A〈形〉stable: 情绪/政局/社会～ enjoy emotional/political/social stability ‖ ～的工作/收入 stable job/income ‖ 物价～。The price remains stable. B〈动〉stabilize: ～局势 stabilize the situation ‖ ～情绪 set sb.'s mind at rest ‖ ～物价 stabilize prices ‖ 病情～了下来。The patient's condition has stabilized.
【稳定剂】wěndìngjì〈名〉［化学］stabilizer
【稳定性】wěndìngxìng〈名〉［物理］stability: 三角形的～ stability of a triangle
【稳固】wěngù A〈形〉stable: 地位～ stable position ‖ 建立～的政权 establish a stable government B〈动〉stabilize: ～政权 stabilize a government
【稳获】wěnhuò〈动〉be sure to get: ～冠军 be sure to win the championship
【稳健】wěnjiàn〈形〉1▸（稳重）steady: 办事～ go about things steadily 2▸（稳而有力）firm: 迈着～的步子 walk with steady steps
【稳居】wěnjū〈动〉hold steady: ～前十名 hold a steady position among the top ten
【稳流】wěnliú〈名〉［物理］steady flow
【稳如泰山】wěnrú-Tàishān〈成〉firm as a rock
【稳妥】wěntuǒ〈形〉reliable: 制定～的计划 formulate a safe plan ‖ 这件事交给他办，就再～不过了。The matter will be in safe hands if we entrust it to him. ‖ 这样做更～。It is even safer to do it this way.
【稳压】wěnyā〈名〉［电气］voltage regulation: ～电源 regulated power supply ‖ ～变压器 voltage stabilizing transformer
【稳压器】wěnyāqì〈名〉1▸［电气］voltage regulator 2▸［物理］manostat
【稳扎稳打】wěnzhā-wěndǎ〈成〉1▸（指打仗）stand firmly and fight steadily 2▸〈喻〉（指做事）go about things steadily and surely: 干任何事情都要～。Whatever we do, we should take it step by step.
【稳中求进】wěnzhōng qiújìn〈成〉seek further progress on the basis of stability
【稳重】wěnzhòng〈形〉steady: 她儿子现在～多了。Her son is a lot steadier now. ‖ 新来的秘书既～又热情。The new secretary is both steady and warm-hearted.

【稳住阵脚】wěnzhù-zhènjiǎo〈惯〉 secure one's position

【稳准狠】wěn-zhǔn-hěn〈形〉 sure, accurate and relentless: ～地打击犯罪分子 strike at criminals in a sure, precise and unremitting fashion

【稳坐钓鱼船】wěn zuò diàoyúchuán〈俗〉〈喻〉 remain steady in the midst of a storm

wèn

问（問）wèn

A〈动〉**1**（提问） ask: ～老师问题 ask the teacher a question ‖ ～他明天有没有空。 Ask if he is free tomorrow. ‖ 有问题随时～。 Feel free to ask if you have any questions. ▸答非所～, 询～ **2**（问候） enquire after: 他信里～起你。 He asked after you in his letter. **3**（审讯） interrogate: ～明底细 get to the bottom of a matter ▸盘～, 审～, 质～ **4**（追究） hold responsible: 出了事惟你是～。 You'll be held responsible if anything goes wrong. ▸～罪 **5**（管） care: 亲自过～ take up a matter personally ‖ 这件事你不必过～了。 You needn't bother about this. ▸不闻不～

B〈介〉（引导动作对象）[indicating the object of an action] to;（引出间接宾语） [usu followed by an indirect object] from: ～老师要答案 ask the teacher for the answer ‖ ～她借点钱 go and borrow some money from her

> 问
>
> ▸望、闻、问、切

【问安】wèn'ān〈动〉 wish sb. good health

【问案】wèn'àn〈动〉 hear a case

【问卜】wènbǔ〈动〉 consult a fortune-teller: 求神～ beseech a deity and seek advice from divination

【问长问短】wèncháng-wènduǎn〈成〉 ask about this and that: 一见面总是～的 ask various questions immediately upon meeting

【问答】wèndá〈动〉 question and answer: ～奥运知识 questions and answers on Olympic topics ‖ ～题 essay question

【问道于盲】wèndàoyúmáng〈成〉〈喻〉 seek advice from one who can offer none

【问鼎】wèndǐng〈动〉**1**（谋取政权） aspire to the throne **2**（夺冠） compete for first prize: 仍有～的机会 there is still a chance to take the championship

【问寒问暖】wènhán-wènnuǎn〈成〉 enquire after sb.'s well-being

【问好】wènhǎo〈动〉 give one's regards to: 他向你～。 He sends you his regards.

❶ 问候

见面时问候

■ 遇到某人:

你好！/您好！
= Hello!

你好，见到你真高兴
= Hello! It's nice to see you
或 Hello! I'm pleased to meet you
或 Hi! Nice to see you（非正式）
或 Hi! Pleased to meet you（非正式）

嗨！
= Hi!

你好，李丽！真没想到会遇见你！
= Hi, Li Li! What a pleasant surprise!

嗨！今天是什么风把你吹来的？
= Hi! What brings you here today?

你好吗？
= How are you?

你过得怎么样？
= How are you doing?

好久不见了！你最近怎么样？
= Long time no see. How have you been?（非正式）

早上好！/早！
= Good morning!
或 Morning!（非正式）

下午好！
= Good afternoon!
或 Afternoon!（非正式）

晚上好！
= Good evening!

■ 对问候的应答:

我很好，谢谢。你/您怎么样？
= I'm fine, thanks. How are you?

我好极了，谢谢
= I'm just great, thanks
或 I'm good, thanks（俚语）

我确实很好，谢谢你/您
= I'm very well indeed, thank you

还不算太坏，谢谢
= Not too bad, thanks

马马虎虎，你呢？
= So-so. And you?

还可以，谢谢
= I'm OK, thanks

还凑合，谢谢
= Surviving, thanks

和以前一样，谢谢
= Same as ever, thanks

很好，从来都没这么好过！
= Very well. I've never been better!

■ 节日里或特殊场合碰到某人:

生日快乐！
= Happy Birthday!

新年快乐！
或 **新年好！**
= Happy New Year!

复活节快乐！
= Happy Easter!

恭喜恭喜！（婚礼、毕业典礼等）
= Congratulations!

写问候卡

■ 生日:

生日快乐！
= Happy Birthday!
或 Wishing you a happy birthday!

愿你的生日充满无穷的快乐！愿你美梦成真！
= I wish you a very happy birthday! May all your wishes come true!

■ 婚礼:

在你俩大喜之日，谨致最诚挚的祝贺
= My heartfelt congratulations on your wedding day

祝愿你们生活美满幸福
= I wish you both all the luck and happiness life can offer

■ 圣诞节/新年:

圣诞快乐！
= Merry Christmas!
或 Happy Christmas!

在圣诞节送上最美好的祝愿！
= With best wishes at Christmas!

圣诞快乐，新年愉快！
= A Merry Christmas and a Happy New Year!

■ 祝愿康复:

祝你早日康复！
= Hope you will get well soon!
或 Hope you will get better soon!
或 Wishing you a quick return to good health!
或 Best wishes for a speedy recovery!

衷心祝愿你早日康复！
= (My) heartfelt wishes that you will recover soon!

■ 父亲节:

父亲节快乐！
= Happy Father's Day!
或 Have a very happy Father's Day!

在父亲节献上最美好的祝愿！
= Best wishes on Father's Day!

有你这样的父亲，我是如此幸运！
= I'm so lucky to have a father like you!

■ 母亲节:

母亲节快乐！
= Happy Mother's Day!
或 Best wishes for a happy Mother's Day!

你是女儿心中最好的妈妈！
= You are the best mother a daughter can ever have

把我所有的爱献给您——世上最好的母亲！
= All my love to the best mother in the world!

■ 情人节:

情人节快乐，我的爱！
= Best wishes for a very happy Valentine's Day, my darling

你永远是我最亲爱的，我爱你到永远！
= You'll always be the most important person in my life. I love you forever and ever

你是我的一切，我爱你胜过所有！
= You mean the world to me. I love you more than anything!

■ 感谢卡:

你给我的礼物很美，非常感谢！
= It was a terrific gift. A big thank you!

谢谢你的支持。没有你，我不会成功！
= Thank you for your support. I couldn't have done it without you

【问号】 wènhào〈名〉 1▸(指标点符号) question mark 2▸(指不确定的事) unknown factor: 他到底能不能康复还是个～。 There is still some doubt as to whether or not he will recover.
【问候】 wènhòu〈动〉 send one's regards: 互致～ exchange greetings ‖ (向某人)致以诚挚的～ extend one's regards (to sb.)
【问话】 wènhuà〈动〉 ask about
【问津】 wènjīn〈动〉〈书〉 [usu used in the negative] make enquiries: 不敢～ not dare to make enquiries ‖ 乏人～。 Few people make enquiries about it.
【问卷】 wènjuàn〈名〉 questionnaire: ～调查 questionnaire survey
【问路】 wènlù〈动〉 ask for directions
【问难】 wènnàn〈动〉 raise difficult questions for discussion: ▸质疑～
【问世】 wènshì〈动〉 1▸(出版) be published: 这本书终于～了。 This book is finally out. 2▸(进入市场) be on the market: 又有一种新型电脑～。 Another new type of computer is now available on the market.
【问事】 wènshì〈动〉 1▸(询问) ask: 找他问个事 ask him about sth. ‖ ～到问讯处。 Enquiries should be directed to the information desk. 2▸〈书〉(过问事务) concern oneself with sth.: 市长一上任, 就开始～了。 The mayor began attending to his duties as soon as he took office.
【问题】 wèntí〈名〉 1▸(指题目) question: 回答～ answer a question ‖ 提～ raise a question ‖ 经常问到的～ frequently asked question (FAQ) 2▸(指待解决的矛盾、疑难) problem: 解决～ solve a problem ‖ 能源～ energy question ‖ 体制、机制方面的～ systemic and mechanical problems 3▸(麻烦) trouble: 她的汽车出了～。 She's got a problem with her car. ‖ 扬声器有～。 There is something wrong with the loudspeaker. 4▸(关键) crucial point: ～在于你是否重视这次会议。 The question is whether you've attached enough importance to the meeting. ‖ 这种牌子的车的确好, ～是大多数人买不起。 This make of car is really good. The problem is that it's beyond the reach of most people. 5▸(重要之点) point: 我今天谈四个～。 I'd like to make four points today.
【问题儿童】 wèntí értóng〈名〉 problem child
【问心无愧】 wènxīn-wúkuì〈成〉 have a clear conscience: 在这件事上我自觉～。 I don't think I've done anything to be ashamed of over this matter.
【问心有愧】 wènxīn-yǒukuì〈成〉 be guilt-ridden
【问询】 wènxún〈动〉 enquire about
【问讯】 wènxùn〈动〉 1▸(询问) enquire: ～处 information desk 2▸(问候) extend one's regards 3▸(指僧尼) greet by putting

ℹ 问路

如何问路

请问到火车站怎么走?
= Excuse me. Could you tell me the way to the railway station?
或 Excuse me. How can I get to the railway station?

劳驾, 你能否告诉我到爱丁堡大学怎么走?
= Excuse me. Can you direct me to the University of Edinburgh?

劳驾了, 你能告诉我天安门广场在哪儿吗?
= Excuse me. Can you tell me where Tian'anmen Square is?

我在找公证处。是不是快到了?
= I'm looking for the notary office. Am I anywhere near?

请问书店是一直往前吗?
= Excuse me. Is the bookshop straight ahead?

从这儿去友谊宾馆该是哪个方向?
= Which way is the Friendship Hotel from here?

到汽车站走这条路对吗?
= Is this the right way to the bus station?
或 Am I going the right way to the bus station?

你能告诉我往植物园是这个方向吗?
= Can you please tell me if I'm in the right direction for the botanical gardens?

附近有家饭店吗?
= Is there a restaurant near here?

请问最近的公园在哪?
= Excuse me, please. Where is the nearest park?

对不起, 打扰了。到游乐场怎么去最好?
= Sorry to trouble you, but which is the best way to the fun fair?

从这到体育场有多远?
= How far is it from here to the stadium?
或 How far is the stadium from here?

走着去银行需要多长时间?
= How long will it take to get to the bank on foot?
或 How long will it take to walk to the bank?

到警察局要坐哪路车?
= Which bus should I take to get to the police station?

如何指路

乘 3 或 47 路公共汽车, 从这里要坐 5 站
= Take bus No. 3 or 47. It is five stops from here

天河广场? 就在这儿不远。穿过马路, 马上往右拐, 左手边便是正门
= Tianhe Plaza? It's right near here. Just cross the street, and immediately take a right. The main entrance is just on the left

离这儿挺远的。你可以乘公共汽车到那儿, 但打的要容易得多
= It's quite far from here. You could get there by bus, but taking a taxi will be a lot easier

离这儿不远。沿这条街走大约 10 分钟, 然后往右拐
= It's not far from here. Continue on this street for about ten minutes, and then turn right

穿过购物中心, 走出去就是火车站
= Cut through the shopping mall, and then you exit into the train station

对不起, 我对这里不熟
= I'm sorry. I am new to this place myself
或 Sorry. I'm a stranger here myself

我住那儿。如果跟着我, 我指给你植物园在哪儿
= I live there. If you follow me, I will show you where the botanical gardens are

继续走 1 英里, 博物馆在你左手边
= Keep going straight for one mile. The museum is on your left

从这穿过马路, 然后在右手的第 3 个拐弯处转弯
= Cross here, and then take the third turning on the right

是的, 一直往前走。书店在街左边
= Yes, go straight ahead. The bookshop is on the left-hand side of the street

恐怕你走错方向了
= I'm afraid you are going in the wrong direction

是另外一条路。往回走, 在十字路口往右拐
= It's the other way. Turn round and then at the crossroads turn right

离这 200 米有家饭店。我陪你走到那儿吧, 我顺路
= There is a restaurant two hundred metres away. I'll walk you there. It's on my way

最近的公园就在拐角处
= The nearest park is just round the corner

最好是乘地铁。最近的地铁站是西站。从这儿左转, 然后在交通灯处再左转
= The best way is to take the underground. The nearest underground station is West Station. Turn left here. Take a left again at the traffic lights

很近, 走着去就行
= It's within walking distance

大约 1 英里
= It's about one mile away

一点都不远
= It's no distance at all

太远了, 不能走。你最好叫出租车或乘公共汽车
= It's too far to walk. You'd better take a taxi or bus

大约走 30 分钟
= It's about 30 minutes' walk

30 分钟内你可以走到
= You can walk it in 30 minutes
或 It'll take you no more than 30 minutes to walk there

你可以乘坐 29、37、或 42 路车。这些车次都是直达的
= You can take buses No. 29, 37, or 42. They are all direct buses

你需要先乘地铁, 然后换乘公交车。穿过马路就有一个地铁站。先乘坐地铁二号线, 在复兴门下车, 然后换乘地铁一号线, 坐到公主坟下车。从那儿走出地铁站, 换乘 363 路公交车。那趟车会把你直接送到目的地
= You need to take the underground and then transfer to a local bus. There is a underground station just across the road. First of all, take Line 2 to Fuxingmen, then change to Line 1 and get off at Gongzhufen. From there, take the exit for the bus station and get on the No. 363 bus. The bus will take you directly to your destination

one's palms together in front of oneself: 打个～ greet with one's palms together
【问斩】wènzhǎn〈动〉〈古〉 sentence to death by beheading
【问责】wènzé〈动〉 call to account
【问责制】wènzézhì 〈名〉 accountability system: 实行～ implement the accountability system
【问诊】wènzhěn 〈名〉［中医］ interrogation [one of the four methods of diagnosis]
【问罪】wènzuì〈动〉 denounce: ▸兴师～

揾 wèn〈动〉〈书〉 1（用手指按） press with the fingers 2（擦） wipe: ～泪 wipe away tears

wēng

翁 wēng〈名〉 1（老头儿） old man: ▸塞～失马，焉知非福，渔～ 2（旧）（父亲） father: 尊～ your father 3（岳父） father-in-law: ▸～姑，～婿
【翁姑】 wēnggū 〈名〉〈书〉 woman's father-in-law and mother-in-law
【翁婿】 wēngxù 〈名〉〈书〉 father-in-law and son-in-law
【翁仲】 wēngzhòng 〈名〉 stone statue placed in front of a tomb

嗡 wēng 〈拟〉 buzz: ～～响 buzzing ‖ 蜜蜂～～地飞。 Bees are buzzing all around.

wěng

蓊 wěng〈形〉〈书〉 lush
【蓊郁】wěngyù〈形〉〈书〉 lush: 山上满布～的森林。 Luxuriant forests cover the hills.

wèng

瓮（甕、罋） wèng 〈名〉 earthen jar: 腌菜～ jar for pickling vegetables ‖ 水～ water jar ▸请君入～
【瓮城】wèngchéng〈名〉 enclosure outside a city gate
【瓮棺】wèngguān〈名〉 funeral urn
【瓮声瓮气】wèngshēng-wèngqì〈形〉 in a low muffled voice
【瓮中之鳖】wèngzhōngzhībiē〈成〉〈喻〉 be trapped
【瓮中捉鳖】 wèngzhōng-zhuōbiē 〈成〉〈喻〉 be sure of success

蕹 wèng
【蕹菜】wèngcài〈名〉 water spinach

齆 wèng
【齆鼻儿】wèngbír A〈动〉 speak with a twang due to a stuffy nose B〈名〉 person who speaks with a twang

wō

挝（撾） wō ▸老挝 Lǎowō ▸zhuā

莴（萵） wō
【莴苣】wōjù〈名〉［植物］ lettuce
【莴笋】wōsǔn〈名〉 asparagus lettuce

倭 wō
A〈形〉 1（矮小） dwarf 2（短小） short: ～刀 short sword
B Wō〈名〉〈古〉 Japan
【倭瓜】wōguā〈名〉〈方〉 pumpkin
【倭寇】Wōkòu〈名〉［历史］ Japanese pirates [in Chinese coastal waters from the 14th century to the 16th century]

涡（渦） wō 〈名〉 whirlpool: 水～ whirls of water ▸旋～
【涡虫】wōchóng〈名〉［动物］turbellarian worm
【涡流】 wōliú 〈名〉 1（指流动） eddy 2（涡旋） vortex: 翼梢～ wing tip vortex 3［物理］ vortex: ～损耗 eddy-current loss 4［电气］ eddy current: ～加热 eddy-current heating
【涡轮机】wōlúnjī〈名〉 turbine: 燃气～ gas turbine
【涡旋】 wōxuán 〈名〉［物理］［气象］ vortex: 大气～ atmospheric vortex

喔[1] wō〈拟〉 [of a cock] crow: 公鸡在～～地叫。 The cock is crowing.

喔[2] wō〈叹〉 [used as an interjection to indicate understanding]: ～，我明白了。 Oh, I see.

窝（窩） wō
A〈名〉 1（动物的巢穴） nest: 黄蜂/蚂蚁～ wasps'/ants' nest ‖ 燕子～ swallow's nest ▸鸡～，鸟～ 2〈喻〉（坏人聚居处） den: 匪～ gangsters' hideout ‖ 强盗～ den of robbers 3〈喻〉（安身之处） place: 把小茅舍变成一个温暖的～ turn a cottage into a cosy nest ‖ 你该有自己的～了。 You should have a home of your own. 4（像窝的地方） thing or place resembling a nest: ▸～棚，被～儿 5（凹陷处） pit: 夹肢～ armpit ▸酒～，山～，眼～
B〈动〉 1（使弯曲） bend: 用铁丝～个钩子 bend the wire into a hook 2（藏匿） harbour: ▸～藏，～赃 3〈口〉（呆） stay: ～在家里不出门 shut oneself away ‖ ～在角落里 huddle in a corner 4（情绪郁积） check: ▸～火，～气，～心 5（闲置） lay idle: 我们库里～的货物太多，卖不出去。 We have too large a stock to dispose of. ▸～工
C〈量〉 litter: 一～小狗/小猫 a litter of puppies/kittens ‖ 一～小鸡/小鸭 a brood of chickens/ducklings
【窝藏】wōcáng〈动〉 harbour: ～罪犯 harbour a criminal ‖ ～赃物 conceal a booty
【窝点】wōdiǎn〈名〉 den: 捣毁走私～ destroy a smugglers hideout ‖ 制假～ counterfeiting den
【窝工】wōgōng〈动〉 lie idle: 原料供应不足，我们又～了。 We were held up again because of a lack of supplies of raw materials.
【窝火】wōhuǒ = 窝气 wōqì
【窝里斗】 wōlidòu 〈名〉〈惯〉 infighting: 挑起～ stir up an internal strife
【窝里横】wōlihèng〈动〉 be a lord at home (but a coward outside of it)
【窝囊】 wōnang 〈形〉 1（指因受委屈） frustrated: 受～气 be subjected to petty annoyances ‖ 这事实在叫人觉得～。 It's really annoying. 2（指胆小怕事） good-for-nothing: 他太～了。 He's really useless.
【窝囊废】wōnangfèi〈名〉〈口〉 good-for-nothing
【窝棚】wōpeng〈名〉 shack: 搭建～ make a shack ‖ 临时～ makeshift shed
【窝铺】wōpù〈名〉 shack for sleeping in
【窝气】wōqì〈动〉 be choked with resentment: 窝了一肚子气 have pent-up grievances ‖ 没来由地挨了骂，他心里～。 Blamed for no reason, he felt vexed and resentful.
【窝头】wōtóu〈名〉 steamed cone-shaped bun of corn, sorghum, etc.: 啃～ eat a corn bun
【窝窝头】wōwotóu = 窝头 wōtóu
【窝心】wōxīn〈形〉〈方〉 pent up: 她对他的无理指责感到～。 She was depressed over his groundless censure.
【窝赃】wōzāng〈动〉 harbour stolen goods
【窝主】wōzhǔ〈名〉 harbourer of criminals

蜗（蝸） wō〈名〉 snail
【蜗居】wōjū〈书〉 A〈名〉 humble abode: 栖身～ live in a humble abode B〈动〉 live in a small place: ～斗室 live in a small room
【蜗轮】wōlún〈名〉［机械］ worm gear
【蜗牛】wōniú〈名〉 snail
【蜗行牛步】 wōxíng-niúbù 〈成〉〈喻〉 move very slowly
【蜗旋】wōxuán〈动〉 spiral: 楼梯～而上。 The stairs spiral up.

踒 wō〈名〉 sprain: ～了脚脖子 sprain one's ankle

wǒ

我 wǒ〈代〉 1（指一人）（用作主语） I;（用作宾语） me;（表所属关系） my: 告诉～ tell me ‖ ～为人人，人人为～ one for all and all for one ‖ ～爸/妈 my father/mother ‖ ～的祖国 my homeland ‖ ～现在没空。 I am busy at the moment. ‖ 我认为～行! I think I can manage it. 2（指两人或以上）（用作主语） we;（用作宾语） us;（表所属关系） our: ～厂/国/校/军 our factory/country/school/army ‖ 敌军被～全歼。 The enemy was annihilated by us. ▸～方， 敌～矛盾 3（表泛指） [used together with 你 in parallel structures] anyone: 大家你一言，～一语，献计献策。 They had a brainstorming session with anyone and everyone joining in. ‖ 市场里你来～往非常热闹。 The market is bustling with people coming and going. ▸尔虞～诈，你死～活 4（指自我） self: ▸忘～，自～
【我辈】wǒbèi〈代〉〈书〉 we
【我方】wǒfāng〈名〉 we: ～认为 we think ‖ 在这一点上，～持不同意见。 We disagree with you on this point.
【我见】wǒjiàn〈名〉 my opinion: 依我之见 in my opinion
【我们】wǒmen〈代〉 1（"我"的复数形式）（用作主语） we;（用作宾语） us;（表所属关系） our: ～村里 our village ‖ ～的父母/祖国 our parents/homeland ‖ ～自己去。 We'll go by ourselves. ‖ 胜利属于～。 The victory is ours. 2〈口〉（指"我"）（用作主语） I;（用作宾语） me: ～那口子 my hubby/wife 3（用于报告、文章中，表委婉） we: 本文将列举～不同意其观点的几点理由。 The article lists the reasons for our disagreement with him.

W

【我行我素】wǒxíng-wǒsù〈成〉 stick to one's old way of doing things: 尽管老师一再警告，可他还是～。 In spite of the teacher's repeated warnings, he went and did things in his own way anyway.

wò

沃 wò

A〈动〉 irrigate: ～田 irrigate a field ▸如汤～雪

B〈形〉 fertile: 肥田～地 fertile fields and rich soil ▸～土, 肥～

【沃里克郡】Wòlǐkèjùn〈名〉 Warwickshire

【沃土】wòtǔ〈名〉 fertile soil: 良田～ fecund soil and rich farmland

【沃野】wòyě〈名〉 fertile land: ～千里 vast expanse of fertile land

卧 wò

A〈动〉 **1**（指人） lie down: 老人在炕上～着。 The old man is lying on the *kang*. ▸～病, 仰～, 坐～不安 **2**（指动物） crouch: ～虎 crouching tiger ‖ 母鸡～在窝里。 The hen sat in the coop. ‖ 小猫～在火炉旁。 A kitten is crouching at the side of a stove. **3**〈方〉（煮） poach: ～个蛋 poach an egg

B〈形〉 sleeping: ▸～房, ～铺

C〈名〉 sleeper: ▸软～, 硬～

【卧病】wòbìng〈动〉 be laid up: ～在床 be ill in bed ‖ 他因癌症～不起。 He is bed-ridden with cancer.

【卧车】wòchē〈名〉 **1**（指火车车厢） sleeper: 他通常乘～去北京。 He usually goes to Beijing on the sleeper. **2**（指小型汽车） car

【卧床】wòchuáng〈动〉 be confined to bed: ～不起 be bedridden ‖ 医生嘱他～休息。 The doctor told him to stay in bed.

【卧倒】wòdǎo〈动〉 lie prone: ～射击 lie prone ready to fire ‖ ～! Lie down!

【卧底】wòdǐ **A**〈动〉 work as a secret agent: 派人～ plant an undercover agent **B**〈名〉 mole

【卧房】wòfáng = 卧室 wòshì

【卧佛】wòfó〈名〉 recumbent Buddha: ～寺 Temple of the Recumbent Buddha

【卧轨】wòguǐ〈动〉 lie on railway tracks: ～自杀 commit suicide by lying on the railway line

【卧虎藏龙】wòhǔ-cánglóng = 藏龙卧虎 cánglóng-wòhǔ

【卧具】wòjù〈名〉 bedding

【卧铺】wòpù〈名〉 berth: 软席～ soft-class sleeper ‖ ～票 sleeper ticket

【卧铺车】wòpùchē〈名〉 sleeper car

【卧射】wòshè〈名〉［军事］ horizontal fire

【卧式】wòshì〈形〉［机械］ horizontal: ～车床 horizontal lathe

【卧室】wòshì〈名〉 bedroom: 有三个～的公寓 three-bedroom(ed) flat

【卧榻】wòtà〈名〉〈书〉 bed: ～之侧，岂容他人鼾睡 how can one tolerate others encroaching on one's space

【卧薪尝胆】wòxīn-chángdǎn〈成〉 endure hardships and temper oneself in order to accomplish one's goal: 他～，以期在下届奥运会上夺回冠军。 He endured great hardship in his quest to regain the title at the upcoming Olympic Games.

涴 wò

〈动〉〈方〉 stain: 衬衣～上了血迹。 The shirt was stained with blood.

握 wò

〈动〉 **1**（用手抓） hold: ～笔 hold a pen ‖ 紧～手中枪 grip the gun in one's hands ‖ 她～着他的手说… She grabbed his hand and said ... ▸～手, ～拳 **2**（掌握） possess: ～有生杀大权 have the power of life and death ‖ 大权在～ wield great power

【握别】wòbié〈动〉〈书〉 shake sb.'s hand in farewell: 他挥泪与我～。 Wiping away tears, he shook my hand in farewell.

【握力】wòlì〈名〉 grip: ～器 spring-grip dumb-bells

【握拳】wòquán〈动〉 clench one's fist: 他～而立，咄咄逼人。 With his fists clenched, he appeared aggressive and threatening.

【握手】wòshǒu〈动〉 shake hands: ～道贺 shake hands with sb. in congratulation ‖ 热情～表示欢迎 welcome with a warm handshake ‖ 一一～ shake hands with everyone

【握手言和】wòshǒu-yánhé〈成〉 shake hands and make up: 他俩拌过嘴，但已经～了。 They quarrelled, but they shook hands and made it up.

硪 wò

〈名〉 flat stone or iron rammer with ropes attached to the sides: 打～ operate a rammer

幄 wò

〈名〉〈书〉 tent: ▸运筹帷～

渥 wò

〈书〉

A〈动〉 moisten

B〈形〉 strong: 优～ liberal

【渥太华】Wòtàihuá〈名〉 Ottawa

斡 wò

〈动〉〈书〉 revolve

【斡旋】wòxuán〈动〉 mediate: 在两国之间～ mediate between two nations ‖ 他们的～无果而终。 Their mediation came to no avail.

龌（齷） wò

【龌龊】wòchuò〈形〉 **1**（脏） dirty: 房间～不堪 the room is disgustingly dirty ‖ 语言～ be foul-mouthed **2**〈喻〉（卑劣） despicable: 卑鄙～ foul

wū

兀 wū

▸wù

【兀秃】wūtu = 乌涂 wūtu

乌[1]（烏） wū

A〈名〉 crow: ▸爱屋及～

B〈形〉 black: ～眉大眼 dark eyebrows and big eyes ▸～黑, ～梅, ～云

乌[2]（烏） wū

〈代〉〈书〉 [used in rhetorical questions] what: ～足道哉? What's there worth mentioning about it?

乌[3]（烏） Wū

▸乌孜别克族 Wūzībiékèzú

▸wù

【乌尔都语】Wū'ěrdūyǔ ▸**p. 918**〈名〉 Urdu

【乌飞兔走】wūfēi-tùzǒu〈成〉 time flies: ～，你我一别已有两年。 How time flies. It's two years since I last saw you.

【乌干达】Wūgāndá〈名〉 Uganda: ～共和国 Republic of Uganda ‖ ～人 Ugandan

【乌骨鸡】wūgǔjī〈名〉 black-boned chicken

【乌龟】wūguī〈名〉 **1**（指动物） tortoise: ～壳 tortoise shell **2**（指人） cuckold

【乌合之众】wūhézhīzhòng〈成〉 rabble: 这些匪徒是一群～。 These bandits are just a disorderly mob.

【乌黑】wūhēi〈形〉 jet-black: ～的头发 jet-black hair

【乌鸡】wūjī = 乌骨鸡 wūgǔjī

【乌金】wūjīn〈名〉 **1**（煤） coal **2**［中药］ ink

【乌桕】wūjiù〈名〉［植物］ Chinese tallow tree

【乌克兰】Wūkèlán〈名〉 Ukraine: ～人 Ukrainian ‖ ～语 Ukrainian

【乌拉】wūlā〈名〉 **1**（指劳役） *wula* [corvée labour formerly imposed on Tibetan serfs] **2**（指人） *wula* labourer

▸wùla

【乌喇】wūlā = 乌拉 wūlā

【乌拉圭】Wūlāguī〈名〉 Uruguay: ～东岸共和国 Oriental Republic of Uruguay ‖ ～人 Uruguayan

【乌兰巴托】Wūlánbātuō〈名〉 Ulan Bator

【乌兰牧骑】wūlánmùqí〈名〉 Ulan Muqir [mounted artistic troupe in Inner Mongolia]

【乌鳢】wūlǐ〈名〉［鱼类］ snakehead

【乌亮】wūliàng〈形〉 lustrous black: ～的头发 glossy black hair

【乌溜溜】wūliūliū〈形〉 [of eyes] dark and sparkling: 一双～的大眼睛 big sparkling black eyes

【乌龙茶】wūlóngchá〈名〉 *oolong* (tea)

【乌龙球】wūlóngqiú〈名〉 own goal

【乌鲁木齐】Wūlǔmùqí ▸**p. 661**〈名〉 Urumqi [capital of Xinjiang (新疆)]

【乌梅】wūméi〈名〉 dark plum

【乌木】wūmù〈名〉［植物］ ebony

【乌篷船】wūpéngchuán〈名〉 boat with a black awning

【乌七八糟】wūqībāzāo〈成〉 **1**（杂乱） awfully messy: 把浴室搞得～ make a dreadful mess of the bathroom ‖ 案头～的。 The desk is horribly untidy. **2**（下流） filthy: 电视上怎么会播放这些～的东西。 I don't know how such filth can be shown on TV. ‖ 这部剧里全是些～的东西。 The play is filled with filth.

【乌漆墨黑】wūqī-mòhēi〈成〉 pitch-black: 晚上～的，什么也看不见。 We couldn't see anything in the pitch-darkness of the night.

【乌青】wūqīng〈形〉 dark blue: 他气得脸色～。 His face was black with rage.

【乌纱帽】wūshāmào〈名〉 **1**〈本〉 black gauze cap [worn by feudal officials] **2**〈喻〉 official post: 保住～ try to retain one's official position ‖ 丢了～ be removed from office

【乌苏里江】Wūsūlǐjiāng ▸**p. 294**〈名〉 Ussuri River

【乌涂】wūtu〈形〉 **1**（不热也不凉） tepid: ～水 lukewarm water **2**（不利索） sluggish: 他办事太～，当不了好领导。 He's too indecisive to make a good leader.

【乌托邦】wūtuōbāng〈名〉 Utopia: ～思想 Utopianism ‖ ～式社会 Utopian society

【乌鸦】wūyā〈名〉 crow: ～的翅膀遮不住太阳的光芒。 The wings of a crow cannot block out the radiance of the sun. ▸天下～一般黑

【乌鸦嘴】wūyāzuǐ〈名〉 mouth from which inauspicious remarks are uttered: 闭上你的～! Don't say such unlucky things!

【乌烟瘴气】wūyān-zhàngqì〈成〉 **1**（指

空气污浊） foul atmosphere: 他们不停地抽烟，弄得屋子里～的。 They puffed away at their pipes, filling the room with a foul stench. **2**（形容秩序混乱） foul atmosphere of ignorance and confusion: 搞得～ create a foul atmosphere

【乌药】wūyào〈名〉［中药］ root of three-nerved spicebush

【乌油油】wūyóuyóu〈形〉 glossy black: ～的头发 black and glossy hair ‖ ～的泥土 black and fertile soil

【乌有】wūyǒu〈名〉〈书〉 naught: ▸化为～, 子虚～

【乌鱼】wūyú = 乌鳢 wūlǐ

【乌鱼蛋】wūyúdàn〈名〉 egg gland of the cuttlefish [as food]

【乌云】wūyún〈名〉 **1**（指云） dark cloud: ～蔽日 murky clouds obscure the sun ‖ ～笼罩 be covered with dark clouds **2**〈喻〉（指形势） dark cloud: 战争的～ dark clouds of war **3**〈喻〉（指头发） women's dark hair

【乌枣】wūzǎo〈名〉 black jujube

【乌贼】wūzéi〈名〉［动物］ cuttlefish

【乌鲗】wūzéi = 乌贼 wūzéi

【乌兹别克斯坦】Wūzībiékèsītǎn〈名〉 Uzbekistan: ～共和国 Republic of Uzbekistan

【乌孜别克族】Wūzībiékèzú〈名〉 Uzbek ethnic group

圬（杇） wū〈书〉

A〈名〉 plastering trowel
B〈动〉 plaster

邬（鄔） Wū〈名〉 Wu [surname]

污 wū

A〈名〉 dirt: 排～ discharge waste ‖ 去～ remove dirt ▸藏～纳垢, 血～, 油～
B〈形〉 **1**（脏） dirty: 咖啡弄～了我的新地毯。 The coffee stained my new carpet. ▸～秽, ～泥, ～水 **2**（腐败） corrupt: ▸贪官～吏
C〈动〉 **1**（弄脏） make dirty: ▸～染, ～损, 玷～ **2**（侮辱） insult: ▸～蔑, 奸～

【污点】wūdiǎn〈名〉 stain: 洗刷～ wash out a stain ‖〈喻〉 历史上的～ blot on sb.'s past

【污垢】wūgòu〈名〉 dirt: 擦掉/洗掉～ wash off the dirt ‖ 浴盆上积了厚厚的一层～。 The bathtub is covered with a thick layer of dirt.

【污痕】wūhén = 污迹 wūjì

【污秽】wūhuì〈书〉 **A**〈形〉 dirty: 语言～ filthy language ‖ 化工厂排放的～废物会污染河流。 The filthy waste from chemical factories will pollute rivers. **B**〈名〉 dirt: 洗刷掉～ wash away the filth

【污迹】wūjì〈名〉 stain: 洗掉～ wash off a stain ‖ 墙纸上～斑斑。 The wallpaper had smudges all over it.

【污吏】wūlì〈名〉 corrupt official: ▸贪官～

【污蔑】wūmiè〈动〉 vilify: ～人格 slander sb.'s character ‖ ～名声 tarnish sb.'s reputation

【污泥】wūní〈名〉 mire: 出～而不染 unstained from the filth

【污泥浊水】wūní-zhuóshuǐ〈成〉〈喻〉 filth and mire: 荡涤旧社会遗留下来的～ clean up the filth left by the old society

【污七八糟】wūqībāzāo = 乌七八糟 wūqībāzāo

【污染】wūrǎn〈动〉 pollute: ～环境 pollute the environment ‖ ～水源 contaminate water sources ‖ 大气～ atmospheric pollution ‖ 环境～ environmental pollution ‖ 噪声～ noise pollution ‖ 水井被附近工厂排出的废物～了。 The well was contaminated by the waste discharge of the factories nearby. ‖〈喻〉 ～社会风气 debase social morals ‖〈喻〉 精神/文化～ spiritual/cultural pollution

【污染标准指数】wūrǎn biāozhǔn zhǐshù〈名〉 pollution standard index

【污染物】wūrǎnwù〈名〉 pollutant: ～排放标准 pollutant discharge standard ‖ 化学～ chemical contaminant

【污染源】wūrǎnyuán〈名〉 source of pollution

【污辱】wūrǔ〈动〉 **1**（侮辱） insult: ～妇女 insult women ‖ 遭受～ suffer a humiliation **2**（玷污） sully: 丑闻～了他的好名声。 The scandal tarnished his good reputation.

【污水】wūshuǐ〈名〉 waste water: 生活～ domestic sewage ‖ ～处理 sewage disposal ‖ ～排放标准 sewage discharge standard

【污水管】wūshuǐguǎn〈名〉 sewer pipe: ～道 sewage channel ‖ ～干管 trunk sewer

【污水净化】wūshuǐ jìnghuà〈名〉 sewage purification: ～池 sewage purifier

【污损】wūsǔn〈动〉 deface: ～书籍 deface books

【污物】wūwù〈名〉 dirt: 地板上净是～。 The floor is covered with filth.

【污言秽语】wūyán-huìyǔ〈成〉 filthy language: 讲了一连串的～ come out with a stream of abuse

【污浊】wūzhuó〈形〉 dirty: ～的空气 foul air

【污渍】wūzì〈名〉 stain: 洗掉～ wash off a stain ‖ 难以去除的～ stubborn stain

巫 wū〈名〉 witch: ▸女～, 小～见大～

【巫婆】wūpó〈名〉 witch

【巫神】wūshén = 巫师 wūshī

【巫师】wūshī〈名〉 wizard

【巫术】wūshù〈名〉 witchcraft

呜（嗚） wū〈拟〉 toot: ～～地哭个没完 sob uncontrollably ‖ 火车～的一声飞驰而过。 The train zoomed past.

【呜呼】wūhū **A**〈叹〉 alas: ▸～哀哉 **B**〈动〉 die: ▸一命～

【呜呼哀哉】wūhū-āizāi **A**〈叹〉〈旧〉 [used in funeral orations] alas, it is sad indeed **B**〈动〉〈诙〉 kick the bucket: 那老家伙～了。 The old wretch has kicked the bucket.

【呜咽】wūyè〈动〉 sob: 呜呜咽咽地哭个没完 sob uncontrollably ‖ 远处箫声～。 The mournful music of a bamboo flute whimpered from afar.

於 wū〈叹〉〈书〉 alas

▸Yū

【於菟】wūtú〈名〉〈古〉 tiger

钨（鎢） wū〈名〉［化学］ tungsten (W)

【钨灯】wūdēng〈名〉 tungsten lamp: ～丝 tungsten filament

【钨钢】wūgāng〈名〉［冶金］ tungsten steel

【钨丝】wūsī〈名〉［电气］ tungsten filament

【钨铁】wūtiě〈名〉［冶金］ ferrotungsten

【钨铁矿】wūtiěkuàng〈名〉［矿业］ ferberite

诬（誣） wū〈动〉 falsely accuse: ～良为盗 accuse an innocent person of theft ▸～告, ～蔑

【诬告】wūgào〈动〉 make a false accusation: ～好人 falsely accuse an innocent person ‖ ～罪 crime of false charge ‖ 我相信她是被人～的。 I am convinced she has been falsely charged.

【诬害】wūhài〈动〉 malign: ～忠良 frame loyal and upright people

【诬赖】wūlài〈动〉 falsely incriminate: ～好人 frame innocent people

【诬蔑】wūmiè〈动〉 slander: ～人格 smear sb.'s character ‖ 大肆造谣～ heap calumnies upon ‖ 这纯属～。 This is pure slander.

【诬陷】wūxiàn〈动〉 bring a false charge against sb.: ～好人 frame an innocent person ‖ 遭人～ be set up

【诬栽】wūzāi〈动〉 fabricate a charge: 把毒品～到她身上 plant drugs on her

屋 wū〈名〉 **1**（房子） house: 一座小～ a small house ‖ 出租～ put a house up for rent ‖ 草/木～ thatched/wooden house ‖ 邻～ neighbouring house ▸～顶, ～脊 **2**（房间） room: 一间小～ a small room ‖ 一～的客人 a roomful of guests ‖ 在隔壁～里 in the next room ▸～子, 里～, 外～

【屋顶】wūdǐng〈名〉 roof: ～漏雨 rain is coming through the roof ‖ ～花园 roof garden ‖ 狂风掀掉了～。 The roof was brought down in a gale.

【屋脊】wūjǐ〈名〉 roof: 青藏高原有世界～之称。 The Qinghai-Tibet Plateau is known as the roof of the world.

【屋架】wūjià〈名〉［建筑］ roof truss

【屋里的】wūlide = 屋里人 wūlirén

【屋里人】wūlirén〈名〉〈方〉 wife

【屋漏偏遭连夜雨】wū lòu piān zāo liányèyǔ〈俗〉〈喻〉 it never rains but it pours

【屋面】wūmiàn〈名〉［建筑］ roofing: 瓦～ tile roofing

【屋上架屋】wūshàng-jiàwū〈成〉〈喻〉 needless duplication

【屋檐】wūyán〈名〉 eaves: 生活在同一个～下 live under the same roof

【屋宇】wūyǔ〈名〉〈书〉 house: 声震～ the sound shook the house

【屋子】wūzi〈名〉 room: 打扫～ clean up a room ‖ 整理～ tidy a room ‖ 满～的人都回头看她。 The whole room turned and looked at her.

恶（噁） wū〈书〉

A〈代〉 what: 路～在? Which way shall I go?
B〈叹〉 [used to express surprise] oh: ～, 是何言也! Oh! What a thing to say!
▸ě, è, wù

wú

无（無） wú ▸p. 221

A〈动〉 not have: ～副作用 have no side effect ‖ 从～到有 grow out of nothing ▸～能, ～限
B〈副〉 not: ～碍大局 not affect the situation as a whole ▸～妨, ～须
C〈连〉 no matter: 事～大小，他都关心。 Everything, big and small, is of concern to him.
▸mó

【无碍】wú'ài〈动〉 not harm: ～大局 exert

W

no negative effect on the entire matter

【无伴奏】wúbànzòu〈形〉［音乐］ unaccompanied: ～合唱 a cappella chorus

【无比】wúbǐ〈动〉be incomparable: 英勇～ be unsurpassed in valour ‖ ～幸福 be incomparably happy ‖ ～自豪 be infinitely proud ‖ 他力大～。He is unparalleled in physical strength.

【无边】wúbiān〈形〉boundless: ～的沙漠 vast expanse of desert ‖ 一望～ stretch as far as the eye can see

【无边无际】wúbiān-wújì〈成〉boundless: ～的大海 boundless ocean ‖ ～的沙漠 vast expanse of desert

【无标题音乐】wúbiāotí yīnyuè〈名〉absolute music

【无病呻吟】wúbìng-shēnyín〈成〉**1**（指人）moan and groan with an imaginary illness **2**（指文艺作品）adopt a sentimental style

【无补】wúbǔ〈动〉be of no avail: 于事～ be of no use

【无不】wúbù〈副〉〈书〉without exception: ～称快。All without exception, were happy. ‖ 大家～为之感动。No one could not be moved.

【无产阶级】wúchǎn jiējí〈名〉proletariat

【无产者】wúchǎnzhě〈名〉proletarian: 全世界～，联合起来! Workers of the world, unite!

【无常】wúcháng **A**〈形〉changeable: 天气变化～。The weather is unpredictable. ▸反复～ **B** ▸**p. 274**〈名〉demon regarded as the messenger of death **C** ▸**p. 772**〈动〉〈婉〉pass away: 一旦～万事休。When death comes, everything is over.

【无偿】wúcháng〈形〉free: ～服务 provide service without pay ‖ ～献血 donate blood ‖ 提供～经济援助 give free financial assistance

【无偿劳动】wúcháng láodòng〈名〉unpaid labour

【无成】wúchéng〈动〉achieve nothing: 一世/终生～ accomplish nothing in one's entire life ▸一事～

【无耻】wúchǐ〈形〉shameless: ～透顶 be completely brazen ‖ ～之徒 shameless person ‖ 你这～小人! You rat! ▸厚颜～, 荒淫～

【无耻之尤】wúchǐzhīyóu〈成〉height of shamelessness: 这些家伙可以算是～了。These guys appear to be completely devoid of shame.

【无出其右】wúchūqíyòu〈成〉second to none

【无从】wúcóng〈副〉no way: ～说起 not know where to begin ‖ ～下手 not know where to start

【无担保贷款】wúdānbǎo dàikuǎn〈名〉［经济］ unsecured loan

【无党派】wúdǎngpài〈形〉non-party: ～民主人士 democrat without party affiliation

【无敌】wúdí〈形〉unrivalled: ～于天下 unmatched anywhere in the world ▸所向～

【无底洞】wúdǐdòng〈名〉bottomless pit:〈喻〉他简直是个～，不管你给他多少钱，他都不满足。He was like a bottomless pit: no matter how much money you gave him, it was never enough.

【无地自容】wúdì-zìróng〈成〉feel too ashamed to show one's face

【无的放矢】wúdì-fàngshǐ〈成〉〈喻〉shoot at random: 批评要有针对性，不要～。Criticisms must be aimed at a definite target; shooting at random should be avoided.

【无调性】wúdiàoxìng〈名〉［音乐］ atonality

【无动于衷】wúdòngyúzhōng〈成〉unmoved: 对某人的痛苦～ show no concern for sb.'s suffering ‖ 我劝了他半天，他却～。I tried for a long time to make him listen to reason, but he remained aloof and indifferent.

【无毒不丈夫】wúdú bù zhàngfū〈俗〉all great men are ruthless

【无独有偶】wúdú-yǒu'ǒu〈成〉it is not unique, but has its counterpart

【无度】wúdù〈动〉be excessive: 荒淫～ be excessively depleted ‖ 挥霍～ wantonly squander

【无端】wúduān〈副〉unwarrantedly: ～解雇 dismiss sb. without grounds ‖ ～生事 make trouble out of nothing ‖ ～受责 be falsely accused and condemned

【无恶不作】wú'è-bùzuò〈成〉one's evil doings know no bounds: 杀人放火，～ commit murder, arson and every crime imaginable

【无法】wúfǎ〈动〉have no way: ～辨认 undecipherable ‖ ～忍受 unable to stand ‖ ～想象 beyond the imagination ‖ 该问题～解决。The problem is unsolvable.

【无法无天】wúfǎ-wútiān〈成〉be completely lawless: ～的恶棍 lawless ruffian

【无方】wúfāng〈动〉be not in the proper way: 教子～ be unable to educate one's child in a proper way ‖ 经营～ mismanage

【无房户】wúfánghù〈名〉(urban) residents who do not have their own living quarters

【无妨】wúfáng **A**〈动〉would do no harm: 问他一下倒也～。There's no harm in asking him. **B**〈副〉no harm in: ～再试一次。There's no harm in having another go.

【无纺织布】wúfǎngzhībù〈名〉［纺织］ non-woven fabric

【无非】wúfēi〈副〉nothing but: 他想做的～就是这件事。This is all that he wants to do. ‖ 我来找你，～是想请你帮个忙。I have come to you with nothing other than a request for help.

【无风不起浪】wúfēng bù qǐ làng〈俗〉〈喻〉there's no smoke without fire

【无峰骆驼】wúfēng luòtuo〈名〉llama

【无缝钢管】wúfèng gāngguǎn〈名〉［冶金］ seamless steel tube

【无福消受】wúfú-xiāoshòu〈成〉not have the luck to enjoy

【无干】wúgān〈动〉have nothing to do with: 是我的错，与他人～。I am to blame; nobody else is involved. ‖ 这事与你～。It has nothing to do with you.

【无告】wúgào〈形〉〈书〉completely helpless: 孤苦～ forlorn and helpless

【无公害】wúgōnghài〈形〉pollution-free: ～蔬菜 pollution-free vegetables

【无功而返】wúgōng-érfǎn〈成〉return without accomplishing anything

【无功受禄】wúgōng-shòulù〈成〉get an unmerited reward: ～，于心有愧 feel ashamed to receive undeserved reward

【无辜】wúgū **A**〈动〉be innocent: ～受害者 innocent victim ‖ 我是～的。I'm innocent. **B**〈名〉innocent person: 陷害～ frame an innocent person ‖ 株连～ implicate an innocent person

【无故】wúgù〈副〉for no reason: ～迟到/缺席 be late/absent without good reason ‖ 任何一方均不得～解除合同。Neither party shall cancel the contract without sufficient cause or reason. ▸平白～, 无缘～

【无怪】wúguài〈副〉no wonder: 路上堵车，～你来晚了。Given the traffic, it's no wonder that you were late.

【无怪乎】wúguàihū = 无怪 wúguài

【无关】wúguān〈动〉have nothing to do with: ～大局 of little account ‖ 这事跟我～。It has nothing to do with me.

【无关宏旨】wúguān-hóngzhǐ〈成〉not matter much

【无关紧要】wúguān-jǐnyào〈成〉insignificant: 别人说什么～。What others say makes no difference. ‖ 这些事情其实～。Such things are actually of little importance.

【无关痛痒】wúguān-tòngyǎng〈成〉〈喻〉of no consequence: ～的自我批评 pointless self-criticism ‖ 说些～的话 make irrelevant remarks

【无官一身轻】wú guān yīshēn qīng〈俗〉happy is the man who is relieved of his office: ～，乐得自在 delighted is the man who has cast aside official duty

【无轨电车】wúguǐ diànchē〈名〉trolleybus

【无国籍】wúguójí〈动〉be stateless

【无过错责任】wúguòcuò zérèn〈名〉［法律］ liability without fault

【无害】wúhài〈动〉be harmless

【无核】wúhé〈动〉**1**（指核武器）be nuclear-free: 朝鲜半岛～化 denuclearization of the Korean Peninsula **2**（指果核）be seedless: ～水果 stoneless fruit

【无核区】wúhéqū〈名〉nuclear-free zone

【无后】wúhòu〈动〉〈旧〉have no male offspring: 不孝有三，～为大。Having no male heir is the gravest of the three cardinal offences against filial piety.

【无花果】wúhuāguǒ〈名〉［植物］ fig

【无华】wúhuá〈形〉simple and unadorned: 他的文章朴实～。He writes with a simplicity of style.

【无话不谈】wúhuà-bùtán〈成〉keep no secrets from each other

【无话可说】wúhuà-kěshuō〈成〉have nothing to say

【无悔】wúhuǐ〈动〉feel no regret: 青春～ have no regrets about one's youth

【无机】wújī〈形〉［化学］ inorganic: ～肥料 mineral fertilizer ‖ ～盐 inorganic salt

【无机化合物】wújī huàhéwù〈名〉mineral compound

【无机化学】wújī huàxué〈名〉inorganic chemistry

【无机物】wújīwù〈名〉inorganic substance

【无稽】wújī〈动〉be groundless: 荒诞～ absurd and unfounded

【无稽之谈】wújīzhītán〈成〉unfounded rumour: 这完全是～! This is sheer nonsense!

【无及】wújí〈动〉〈书〉be too late: 后悔～ too late to repent

【无级】wújí〈形〉［机械］ stepless: ～变速 stepless speed change

【无疾而终】wújí'érzhōng〈成〉[of an old person] pass away without illness

【无几】wújǐ〈动〉have very few: 两人的年岁相差～。The two are almost the same age. ▸寥寥～

【无脊椎动物】wújǐzhuī dòngwù〈名〉invertebrate

【无计可施】wújì-kěshī〈成〉at a loss as to what to do: 对此我已～。There is nothing I can do about it.

【无记名投票】wújìmíng tóupiào〈名〉secret ballot: 通过～选举 elect by ballot

【无际】wújì〈动〉be boundless: 无边～ boundless ‖ 一望～ stretch as far as the eye can see

【无济于事】wújì-yúshì〈成〉in vain: 我们试了又试，可全都～。We tried and tried, but it was all to no avail.

【无家可归】wújiā-kěguī〈成〉be homeless: ～的孩子 waif

【无价】wújià〈动〉be priceless: 情义～ priceless affection

【无价之宝】wújiàzhībǎo〈成〉invaluable asset: 这古董可是～。This antique is priceless.

【无坚不摧】wújiān-bùcuī〈成〉be all-conquering: 我们的军队显示了～的战斗力。Our army displayed invincible military strength.

【无间】wújiàn〈动〉〈书〉**1**（没有间隙）be very close to each other: ～可乘 there is no loophole to take advantage of ‖ 亲密～ be on intimate terms **2**（不间断）be continuous: 坚持晨练，风雨～。Keep on doing morning exercises in spite of bad weather. **3**（不区分）make no distinction: ～是非 make no distinction between right and wrong

【无疆】wújiāng〈动〉〈书〉be limitless: ▸万寿～

【无尽】wújìn〈动〉be endless: ～的宝藏 inexhaustible treasures ‖ 无穷～ endless

【无精打采】wújīng-dǎcǎi〈成〉in low spirits: 他整个上午都～的。He was out of sorts all morning.

【无拘无束】wújū-wúshù〈成〉unrestrained: ～的生活 free and easy life

【无菌包装】wújūn bāozhuāng〈名〉aseptic package

【无可比拟】wúkě-bǐnǐ〈成〉incomparable: 这是有史以来～的大变化。This is an unprecedented change.

【无可辩驳】wúkě-biànbó〈成〉irrefutable: ～的事实 indisputable fact ‖ ～的证据 incontestable evidence

【无可非议】wúkě-fēiyì〈成〉irreproachable: 他这样做，我觉得～。I don't think his conduct reproachable.

【无可奉告】wúkě-fènggào〈成〉no comment: 对于这一点，我～。As far as this is concerned, I have no comment.

【无可估量】wúkě-gūliáng〈成〉immeasurable

【无可厚非】wúkě-hòufēi〈成〉give no cause for criticism: 她的品行～。Her morals are above reproach.

【无可讳言】wúkě-huìyán〈成〉there is no denying the fact that ...: 事实俱在，～。None of the facts have been left out, and nothing can be covered up.

【无可救药】wúkě-jiùyào = 不可救药 bùkě-jiùyào

【无可奈何】wúkě-nàihé〈成〉there is nothing to be done: 他～，只好让步。He had no alternative but to make some concessions. ‖ 他整天游手好闲，母亲对他～。He just fools around all day long, and his mother can do nothing about it.

【无可匹敌】wúkě-pǐdí〈成〉incomparable

【无可挽回】wúkě-wǎnhuí〈成〉irretrievable: ～的损失 irremediable loss ‖ 过去的事情～。The past is not recoverable.

【无可无不可】wúkě wú bùkě〈成〉make little difference: 采取～的态度 take an indifferent attitude

【无可限量】wúkě-xiànliàng〈成〉immeasurable: 前途～的年轻人 promising young person

【无可争辩】wúkě-zhēngbiàn〈成〉indisputable: ～的事实 incontestable fact

【无可置疑】wúkě-zhìyí〈成〉unquestionable: ～，他是英格兰最优秀的板球选手。He is unquestionably the best cricketer in England.

【无孔不入】wúkǒng-bùrù〈成〉seize every opportunity: 小偷～，让人防不胜防。The thief took every opportunity that came his way, and there was no stopping him.

【无愧】wúkuì〈动〉have a clear conscience: 她～于先进工作者的称号。She was worthy of the title of model worker. ▸当之～, 问心～

【无赖】wúlài **A**〈形〉rascally: 耍～ act shamelessly **B**〈名〉rascal: 十足的～ veritable scoundrel ‖ 他是个～。He is a real rascal.

【无礼】wúlǐ〈动〉be discourteous: 不得～! None of your impudence!

【无理】wúlǐ〈动〉be unreasonable: 提出～要求 make an unreasonable demand ‖ 遭到～指责 be unjustly accused

【无理搅三分】wúlǐ jiǎo sānfēn〈俗〉unreasonable: 这个人～，很难对付。He is unreasonable and difficult to deal with.

【无理取闹】wúlǐ-qǔnào〈成〉be deliberately provocative: 她简直是～。She's being difficult on purpose.

【无理数】wúlǐshù〈名〉［数学］irrational number

【无力】wúlì〈动〉**1**（指能力）be powerless: ～养活全家 be unable to support the family ‖ 领导软弱～ have weak leadership **2**（指力气）be lacking in strength: 浑身～ feel weak all over ‖ 他因久病而虚弱～。He was feeble from a long illness. ▸有气～

【无立锥之地】wú lìzhuīzhīdì〈成〉have not even enough land to stick an awl into: 天下之大，而我却～。There is no place for me in the whole wide world.

【无利可图】wúlì-kětú〈成〉unprofitable

【无量】wúliàng〈动〉be immeasurable: 前途～ have boundless prospects

【无聊】wúliáo〈形〉**1**（空虚烦闷）dull: 闲得～，咱们去看电影吧。I'm tired of doing nothing. Let's go to the cinema. **2**（令人厌烦）tiresome: 说些～的话 make silly remarks ‖ 内容太～了。The content is too idiotic.

【无路可走】wúlù-kězǒu〈成〉have no alternative: 他被逼得～。He was driven to despair.

【无论】wúlùn〈连〉whatever: ～你到哪里，我都跟你在一起。No matter where you go, I will be with you.

【无论如何】wúlùnrúhé〈副〉in any event: ～，他不会放弃他的计划。He wouldn't give up his plan for love or money. ‖ ～，我都要把钱付给你。Whatever happens, I'll see that you get paid.

【无米之炊】wúmǐzhīchuī〈成〉〈喻〉lack the basic essentials: ▸巧妇难为～

【无冕之王】wúmiǎnzhīwáng〈成〉king without a crown

【无名】wúmíng〈形〉**1**（无姓名）nameless: 阵亡的～战士 unknown soldiers who laid down their lives in the war ▸～氏 **2**（不出名）unknown: ～作家 unknown writer ‖ 他们都是～之辈。They are all unknown people. ▸～小卒, ～英雄 **3**（没有来由）indescribable: 产生一种～的恐惧 generate an indescribable terror

【无名火】wúmínghuǒ = 无明火 wúmínghuǒ

【无名氏】wúmíngshì〈名〉anonymous person: 这本小说系～所作。This novel was written by an anonymous author.

【无名小卒】wúmíngxiǎozú〈成〉nobody: 他竟然两次败在～的手下。He was defeated twice by a complete nobody.

【无名英雄】wúmíngyīngxióng〈惯〉**1**（指英雄）unknown hero: 甘当～ be ready to be an unknown hero **2**（指战士）unknown soldier: ～纪念碑 monument to the unknown fallen soldiers

【无名指】wúmíngzhǐ〈名〉ring finger

【无明火】wúmínghuǒ〈名〉flames of anger: ～起 fly into a rage

【无奈】wúnài **A**〈动〉have no alternative: ～只得去做不想做的工作 have no alternative but to do the work one doesn't want to do ‖ 他出于～，只得让步。He had no choice but to give in. **B**〈连〉but: 我本应帮你，～当时手头很紧。I would have helped you, but I was short of money at the time.

【无奈何】wúnàihé **A**〈动〉have no choice but to: 敌人～，只得悄悄撤走。The enemy had no choice but to withdraw. **B** = 无可奈何 wúkě-nàihé

【无能】wúnéng〈形〉incapable: ～之辈 incompetent people ‖ 那个经理因～而被解雇。The manager was discharged for incompetence.

【无能为力】wúnéngwéilì〈成〉be in no position to do sth.: 这事我～。I'm not in a position to deal with this.

【无偏无党】wúpiān-wúdǎng〈成〉unbiased

【无期徒刑】wúqī-túxíng〈名〉life imprisonment: 被判处～ be sentenced to life imprisonment ‖ ～犯人 lifer

【无奇不有】wúqí-bùyǒu〈成〉strange things of every description: 大千世界，～ in this boundless universe there is no lack of strange things

【无牵无挂】wúqiān-wúguà〈成〉have no cares

【无铅汽油】wúqiān qìyóu〈名〉unleaded petrol

【无巧不成书】wú qiǎo bù chéng shū〈俗〉as luck would have it: ～，我又在宴会上碰见他。As luck would have it, I met him again at a dinner party.

【无亲无故】wúqīn-wúgù〈成〉with neither family nor friends

【无情】wúqíng **A**〈动〉be ruthless: 冷酷～ merciless ▸～无义 **B**〈形〉rigid: 法律是～的。The law is inexorable. ▸翻脸～, 水火～

【无情无义】wúqíng-wúyì〈成〉heartless: 想不到他对我如此～。I could never have expected that he could be so heartless towards me.

【无穷】wúqióng〈形〉be infinite: ～的烦恼 endless worries ‖ 言有尽而意～。There is an end to the words, but not to their message.

【无穷大】wúqióngdà〈名〉［数学］infinite greatness

【无穷无尽】wúqióng-wújìn〈成〉inexhaustible: ～的智慧和力量 inexhaustible wisdom and power

【无穷小】wúqióngxiǎo〈名〉［数学］infinitesimal

【无缺】wúquē〈形〉remain intact: 完好～ be completely intact

【无人机】wúrénjī〈名〉unmanned aerial vehicle (UAV)

【无人驾驶】wúrén jiàshǐ〈动〉be pilotless: ～飞机 pilotless plane

【无人区】wúrénqū〈名〉depopulated zone

【无人问津】wúrén-wènjīn〈成〉nobody is interested in: 这种蹩脚货现在～。Nobody is interested in this kind of shoddy commodity now.

【无任】wúrèn〈副〉〈书〉immensely: ～感激 be deeply grateful

【无任所大使】wúrènsuǒ dàshǐ〈名〉［外交］ambassador-at-large

【无日】wúrì〈副〉all the time: 我～不忙。There is not a single day when I am not busy.

【无如】wúrú = 无奈 wúnài B

【无伤大雅】wúshāng-dàyǎ 〈成〉 not matter much: 孩子们的话～。 What the children said matters little.

【无上】wúshàng 〈形〉 supreme: ～光荣 glorious ▸至高～

【无神论】wúshénlùn 〈名〉 atheism: ～者 atheist

【无生物】wúshēngwù 〈名〉 inanimate object

【无声】wúshēng〈动〉 be silent: ～的反抗 silent protest ‖ 悄然～ be quiet and silent ‖ ～手枪 pistol with a silencer

【无声电影】wúshēng diànyǐng〈名〉 silent movie

【无声片儿】wúshēngpiānr = 无声片 wúshēngpiàn

【无声片】wúshēngpiàn〈名〉 silent film

【无声无息】wúshēng-wúxī〈成〉 1（很寂静）silent 2〈喻〉（默默无闻）unknown: ～地生活一辈子 remain in obscurity all one's life

【无绳电话】wúshéng diànhuà〈名〉 cordless phone

【无师自通】 wúshī-zìtōng 〈成〉 be self-taught: ～的作家 self-taught writer

【无时无刻】wúshí-wúkè〈成〉 all the time: 他～不在想着她。 He thinks of her every minute of the day.

【无事不登三宝殿】wú shì bù dēng sānbǎodiàn〈俗〉〈喻〉 one only goes to sb.'s place when one is in need of help

【无事生非】 wúshì-shēngfēi 〈成〉 create trouble out of nothing: 这场争论完全是～。 The whole controversy is a huge fuss about nothing.

【无视】wúshì〈动〉 disregard: ～别国主权 disregard the sovereignty of other countries ‖ ～法律 defy laws ‖ ～某人的权利 ignore sb.'s rights

【无数】wúshù A〈形〉 innumerable: 死伤～ countless casualties ‖ 我告诉过你～次了，你就是不听。 I've told you countless times, but you just wouldn't listen. B〈动〉 not know for certain: 这场比赛结果如何，我心中～。 I can't be sure of the result of this game.

【无双】wúshuāng〈动〉 be unparalleled: 神勇～ be unsurpassed in valour ▸盖世～, 举世～

【无霜期】 wúshuāngqī 〈名〉 frost-free period

【无私】wúsī〈形〉 selfless: ～奉献 selfless devotion ‖ 给予～的援助 provide assistance out of the goodness of one's heart ‖ ～才能无畏。 Only the selfless can be fearless. ▸大公～, 铁面～

【无损】wúsǔn〈动〉 1（不造成损害） do no harm: ～政府形象 do no harm to the government's image ‖ 毫发～ have not hurt in the least 2（未损坏） remain intact: 一箱瓷器完好～。 The case of crockery was completely intact.

【无所不能】wúsuǒbùnéng〈成〉 completely versatile: 他琴棋书画，～。 He was thoroughly accomplished in music, chess, calligraphy and painting.

【无所不为】wúsuǒbùwéi〈成〉 commit all manner of crimes: 为达到目的，他～。 He went to great lengths to accomplish his purpose.

【无所不用其极】wú suǒ bù yòng qí jí〈成〉 go to great lengths: 贪婪的老板为了攫取利润而～。The greedy boss stopped at nothing in his pursuit of profit. ‖ 为了博取上级的欢心，他～。 He used every trick in the book in order to win the favour of his superiors.

【无所不有】 wúsuǒbùyǒu 〈成〉 want for nothing

【无所不在】wúsuǒbùzài〈成〉omnipresent: ～的上帝 omnipresent God ‖ 商业欺诈～。 Commercial fraud is a common phenomenon.

【无所不知】 wúsuǒbùzhī 〈成〉 know all there is to know: 他～。 There is nothing he does not know.

【无所不至】wúsuǒbùzhì〈成〉 1（没有达不到的地方） be all-pervasive: 毒气扩散范围很广，几乎～。 Poisonous gas is spreading practically everywhere. 2（能做的都做了） stop at nothing: 吃喝嫖赌，～ commit all evils under the sun

【无所措手足】wú suǒ cuò shǒu zú〈成〉 be at a loss as to what to do: 问题问得突然，我一时～。 The question was so unexpected that, for a moment, I didn't know what to do.

【无所顾忌】wúsuǒgùjì〈成〉 stop at nothing: 为了多捞点钱，他～。 He would stop at nothing to get more money for himself.

【无所事事】wúsuǒshìshì〈成〉 idle away one's time: 他看不得别人～地打发时间。 He cannot bear to see others messing about.

【无所适从】wúsuǒshìcóng〈成〉 be at a loss as to what to do: 政策多变，下面～。 The policies have changed so much that the people don't know what to do.

【无所畏惧】wúsuǒwèijù〈成〉 be fearless: 面对死亡,他～。 He was undaunted in the face of death.

【无所谓】 wúsuǒwèi 〈动〉 1（说不上） cannot be called: 这是随便说的，～什么建议。 It was a passing remark; I didn't mean it as a suggestion. 2（不在乎） not mind one way or the other: 金钱对他来说～。 Money means nothing to him. ‖ 他们赞成不赞成，我都～。 I really don't care if they agree or not.

【无所用心】wúsuǒyòngxīn〈成〉 not exert one's mind: 他在家闲住多日，～。 He stayed at home for several days without stretching his mind on any particular subject.

【无所作为】 wúsuǒzuòwéi 〈成〉 attempt nothing and accomplish nothing: 他一辈子～。 He accomplished nothing in his whole life.

【无题】wútí〈形〉 untitled: ～诗 untitled poem

【无条件】wútiáojiàn〈动〉be unconditional: ～的爱/接受 unconditional love/acceptance ‖ ～服从命令 obey orders to the letter ‖ ～投降 unconditional surrender

【无条件撤军】 wútiáojiàn chèjūn 〈名〉 unconditional withdrawal

【无痛拔牙】 wútòng báyá 〈名〉 painless extraction

【无痛手术】wútòng shǒushù〈名〉 painless surgery

【无头案】wútóu'àn〈名〉 unsolved mystery: 那件凶杀案仍是一桩～。 The murder remains an unsolved mystery.

【无头苍蝇】wútóu cāngying〈惯〉〈喻〉 a headless chicken

【无头公案】wútóu gōng'àn = 无头案 wútóu'àn

【无土栽培】wútǔ zāipéi〈名〉 soilless cultivation

【无往不利】wúwǎng-bùlì〈成〉 succeed at whatever one does: 才艺出众，工作～ have unparalleled talent and succeed at whatever one turn one's hand to

【无往不胜】 wúwǎng-bùshèng 〈成〉 be all-conquering: ～的神话被打破了。 The myth of its invincibility was shattered.

【无妄之灾】wúwàngzhīzāi〈成〉 unexpected turn for the worse: 遭遇～ suffer from an unexpected misfortune

【无望】wúwàng〈动〉〈书〉 be hopeless: 成功～。 There is no chance of success. ‖ 这种病治愈～。 This disease is beyond cure.

【无微不至】wúwēi-bùzhì〈成〉 meticulously: ～地照料 look after sb. meticulously ‖ 她对孩子们的关怀～。 She takes the greatest possible care of the children.

【无为】wúwéi〈动〉 1［道教］ take no action: ～而治 govern by non-interference ‖ ～而无不为。 A wise inaction smooths the way for efficient actions. 2（无所作为） accomplish nothing

【无味】wúwèi A〈动〉 be tasteless: 食物～ tasteless food ‖ 嘴里～，一点东西也不想吃。 I have no appetite, and I don't want to eat anything. ▸淡而～ B〈形〉〈喻〉 dull: 语言平淡～ flat, colourless language ‖ 读来索然～ read flatly and insipidly

【无畏】wúwèi〈动〉 be fearless: ～的英雄 intrepid hero

【无谓】wúwèi〈形〉 senseless: ～的牺牲 senseless sacrifice ‖ ～的争吵 pointless quarrel

【无物】wúwù〈形〉 empty: 言之～ empty talk

【无误】wúwù〈动〉 be faultless: 数据要确保准确～。 The data must be correct.

【无息】wúxī〈动〉［经济］ be interest-free

【无息贷款】wúxī dàikuǎn〈名〉 free loan

【无隙可乘】wúxì-kěchéng〈成〉 no loophole to exploit

【无瑕】wúxiá〈形〉〈书〉 flawless: 白璧～ flawless integrity ‖ 完美～ perfect

【无暇】wúxiá〈动〉〈书〉 have no time: ～过问 have no time to attend to ‖ ～照料年迈的双亲 be too busy to look after one's elderly parents

【无限】wúxiàn〈形〉 unlimited: ～热爱某人/某事物 have boundless love for sb./sth. ‖ ～的创造力 inexhaustible creative power ‖ ～光明的前途 future of incomparable brightness ‖ ～上纲 exaggerate sb.'s mistakes to the maximum

【无限大】wúxiàndà = 无穷大 wúqióngdà

【无限小】wúxiànxiǎo = 无穷小 wúqióngxiǎo

【无限责任公司】wúxiàn zérèn gōngsī〈名〉 unlimited liability company

【无限期】wúxiànqī〈动〉 be of indefinite duration: ～休会 adjourn indefinitely ‖ 举行～罢工 go on a strike of indefinite duration

【无线】wúxiàn〈形〉 wireless

【无线电】wúxiàndiàn〈名〉 radio: 听～播送新闻 listen to the news on the radio

【无线电报】wúxiàn diànbào〈名〉 wireless telegraph: 发～ send a message by wireless

【无线电导航】wúxiàndiàn dǎoháng〈名〉［航空］ radio navigation

【无线电广播】wúxiàndiàn guǎngbō〈名〉 radio broadcast: ～发射台/中心 radio broadcast transmitting station/centre

【无线电话】 wúxiàn diànhuà 〈名〉 radiotelephone

【无线电收发两用机】wúxiàndiàn shōufā liǎngyòngjī〈名〉 transceiver

【无线电收音机】 wúxiàndiàn shōuyīnjī〈名〉 radio receiver

【无线电通信】 wúxiàndiàn tōngxìn〈名〉 radio communication

【无线电通信卫星】 wúxiàndiàn tōngxìn

W

wèixīng〈名〉radio communication satellite

【无线电转播】wúxiàndiàn zhuǎnbō〈名〉wireless relay broadcasting: ～卫星 radio relay satellite

【无线话筒】wúxiàn huàtǒng〈名〉wireless microphone

【无线通信】wúxiàn tōngxìn〈名〉wireless communication

【无线网卡】wúxiàn wǎngkǎ〈名〉wireless LAN card

【无线寻呼】wúxiàn xúnhū〈名〉radio paging: 自动～ automatic radio paging

【无效】wúxiào〈动〉be invalid: 宣布选举～ nullify an election ‖ 医治～ fail to respond to medical treatment ‖ 逾期～ be invalid after the specified date

【无效婚姻】wúxiào hūnyīn〈名〉invalid marriage

【无效劳动】wúxiào láodòng〈名〉fruitless labour

【无效票】wúxiàopiào〈名〉**1**（指投票）invalid ballot **2**（指票据）invalid ticket

【无邪】wúxié〈形〉innocent: 天真～ innocent and naive

【无懈可击】wúxiè-kějī〈成〉unassailable: 他的推理～。His reasoning can't be flawed.

【无心】wúxīn〈动〉**1**（没有心思）not be in the mood for: ～恋战 have no desire to continue fighting ‖ 根本～干任何事情 have no inclination to do any work ‖ 她作业还没做完，～去听音乐会。She was in no mood to go to the concert, as she hadn't finished her homework. **2**（无意）be inadvertent: 他是出于好意，根本～伤害谁。He was well-intentioned and he didn't mean any harm. ▶言者～，听者有意

【无行】wúxíng〈动〉〈书〉be a man of loose virtue: 文人～ men of letters are lacking in moral character

【无形】wúxíng **A**〈形〉intangible: 摆脱～的枷锁 throw off invisible shackles ‖ 施加～的压力 impose an indefinable pressure (on sb.) **B**〈副〉unconsciously: 人总会有形～地受到环境的影响。Man is always consciously or unconsciously influenced by his surroundings.

【无形财产】wúxíng cáichǎn〈名〉intangible property

【无形损耗】wúxíng sǔnhào〈名〉non-physical wear

【无形投资】wúxíng tóuzī〈名〉intangible investment

【无形之中】wúxíngzhīzhōng = 无形中 wúxíngzhōng

【无形中】wúxíngzhōng〈副〉imperceptibly: 国王处处受到王后的支配，～她成了国家的统治者。The king was heavily influenced by his wife, which made her the virtual ruler. ‖ 这～成了风气。This has imperceptibly become common practice.

【无形资产】wúxíng zīchǎn〈名〉invisible assets: 公司的～ intangible assets of a company

【无性】wúxìng〈形〉［生物］asexual

【无性繁殖】wúxìng fánzhí〈名〉［植物］cloning

【无性生殖】wúxìng shēngzhí〈名〉［生物］asexual reproduction

【无性系】wúxìngxì〈名〉［生物］clone

【无性杂交】wúxìng zájiāo〈名〉［生物］asexual hybridization

【无休止】wúxiūzhǐ〈动〉never end: 受到～的指责 be the subject of perpetual criticism ‖ ～的争吵/争论 endless quarrelling/arguing

【无须】wúxū〈动〉have no need to: ～大惊小怪 need not make a fuss ‖ ～考虑 need not take into consideration

【无须乎】wúxūhū = 无须 wúxū

【无需】wúxū〈动〉not need: 一切靠自力更生，～外援 totally self-sufficient and do not need any outside help

【无涯】wúyá〈动〉be boundless

【无烟】wúyān〈形〉smoke-free: ～家庭 non-smoking family

【无烟车厢】wúyān chēxiāng〈名〉non-smoking (railway) carriage

【无烟煤】wúyānméi〈名〉anthracite

【无烟区】wúyānqū〈名〉no smoking area

【无言】wúyán〈动〉have nothing to say: 羞愧～ be abashed into silence ▶哑口～

【无言以对】wúyányǐduì〈成〉words fail one

【无颜见人】wúyánjiànrén〈成〉not have the face to appear in public

【无氧运动】wúyǎng yùndòng〈名〉anaerobic exercise

【无恙】wúyàng ▶**p. 780**〈动〉〈书〉be in good health: 安然～ safe and sound ‖ 别来～ trust that all has been well since our last meeting

【无业】wúyè〈动〉**1**（指工作）be out of work: ～人员 unemployed people ‖ ～游民 vagrant **2**（指产业）have no property: 无家～ have neither family nor property

【无依无靠】wúyī-wúkào〈成〉have no one to turn to: ～的孤儿 helpless orphan

【无遗】wúyí〈动〉have nothing left: 暴露～ be completely exposed ‖ 一览～ take in everything at a glance

【无疑】wúyí〈形〉undoubted: 确凿～ be well established and irrefutable ‖ 深信～ firmly believe

【无已】wúyǐ〈动〉〈书〉be endless: 苛责～ criticize incessantly

【无以复加】wúyǐfùjiā〈成〉in the extreme: 荒谬到了～的地步 be absurd in the extreme

【无以为报】wúyǐwéibào〈成〉be unable to repay a kindness

【无以为继】wúyǐwéijì〈成〉unable to continue

【无以为生】wúyǐwéishēng〈成〉have no livelihood

【无以自容】wúyǐzìróng〈成〉be ashamed of oneself

【无异】wúyì〈动〉be no different from: ～于破产 be tantamount to bankruptcy ‖ 大小/形状/颜色～ be identical in size/shape/colour

【无益】wúyì〈动〉have no beneficial effect: ～于和平解决 not be favourable to a peaceful settlement ‖ 对身体～ have no health benefits ‖ 非但～反而有害 do harm instead of good

【无意】wúyì **A**〈动〉have no intention: ～参加 have no intention of taking part ‖ ～介入 have no intention of intervening **B**〈副〉inadvertently: ～中得罪了人 offend sb. unintentionally ‖ 我～中发现了他们的秘密。I discovered their secret by chance.

【无意识】wúyìshí **A**〈形〉unconscious: ～的动作 unconscious act ‖ 她的错误是～的，但给她带来了麻烦。Her blunder, though unwitting, landed her in trouble. **B**〈名〉［心理］unconsciousness

【无意之中】wúyìzhīzhōng〈副〉unintentionally

【无翼鸟】wúyìniǎo〈名〉kiwi

【无垠】wúyín〈动〉〈书〉be boundless: 一望～的草原 vast prairie

【无影灯】wúyǐngdēng〈名〉［医学］shadowless lamp

【无影无踪】wúyǐng-wúzōng〈成〉disappear without a trace: 消失得～ vanish into thin air ‖ 事故发生后，肇事司机逃得～。After the accident the hit-and-run driver disappeared without a trace.

【无庸讳言】wúyōng-huìyán = 毋庸讳言 wúyōng-huìyán

【无庸赘述】wúyōng-zhuìshù = 毋庸赘述 wúyōng-zhuìshù

【无用】wúyòng〈形〉useless

【无忧无虑】wúyōu-wúlǜ〈成〉not have a care in the world: 过着～的生活 live a care-free life

【无由】wúyóu〈副〉〈书〉no way: 问题～解决 find no way of solving a problem

【无余】wúyú〈动〉〈书〉have nothing left: 揭露～ completely expose ‖ 一览～ take in everything at a glance

【无与伦比】wúyǔlúnbǐ〈成〉unparalleled: ～的贡献 unparalleled contribution ‖ 莎士比亚的戏剧天才迄今～。Shakespeare's genius as a dramatist is still unsurpassed.

【无欲则刚】wúyùzégāng〈成〉one can be austere if he has no selfish desires

【无冤无仇】wúyuān-wúchóu〈成〉bear each other no grudges

【无援】wúyuán〈动〉have no support: 孤立～ be isolated and cut off from help

【无缘】wúyuán〈动〉be predestined not to: 我和烟酒～。Smoking and drinking don't appeal to me. ‖ 我俩～相见。We were not meant to meet.

【无缘无故】wúyuán-wúgù〈成〉for no reason at all: ～被开除 be dismissed without good reason ‖ ～地发脾气 fly into a rage over nothing

【无源之水，无本之木】wú yuán zhī shuǐ, wú běn zhī mù〈成〉things without a solid foundation

【无怨无悔】wúyuàn-wúhuǐ〈成〉have neither complaints nor regrets

【无韵诗】wúyùnshī〈名〉blank verse

【无章可循】wúzhāng-kěxún〈成〉have no rules and regulations to abide by

【无障碍设施】wúzhàng'ài shèshī〈名〉barrier-free facilities

【无照】wúzhào〈动〉not have a licence: ～营业 do business without a licence

【无政府主义】wúzhèngfǔzhǔyì〈名〉anarchism

【无政府状态】wúzhèngfǔ zhuàngtài〈名〉anarchy

【无知】wúzhī〈形〉ignorant: 年幼～ young and ignorant ‖ 请原谅我的～，我不知道那是什么。Forgive my ignorance. I have no idea what that is.

【无止境】wúzhǐjìng〈动〉have no limits: ～的欲望 endless desire

【无纸贸易】wúzhǐ màoyì〈名〉electronic data interchange (EDI)

【无中生有】wúzhōng-shēngyǒu〈成〉fabricate out of thin air: 他的话全是～。What he said was sheer fabrication.

【无主语句】wúzhǔyǔjù〈名〉［语法］sentence with no subject

【无着】wúzhuó〈动〉be uncertain: 经费～ no funds available ‖ 生活～ not assured of an adequate livelihood

【无籽西瓜】wúzǐ xīguā〈名〉seedless watermelon

【无足挂齿】wúzúguàchǐ = 不足挂齿 bùzúguàchǐ

【无足轻重】wúzúqīngzhòng〈成〉be of little significance: ～的问题 petty problem ‖ ～的小人物 person of no consequence

W

【无阻】wúzǔ〈动〉 be clear of obstructions: 风雨～ regardless of the weather ‖ 畅通～ proceed without hindrance

【无罪】wúzuì〈动〉 be innocent: 宣告～ acquit sb. of a crime ‖ ～释放 release without charge

毋 wú〈书〉〈副〉 not: ～自欺 do not deceive yourself ▸宁缺～滥, 少安～躁

【毋宁】wúnìng〈副〉〈书〉 rather ... (than): 不自由，～死。 Give me liberty, or give me death. ‖ 这与其说是奇迹，～说是历史的必然产物。 This is not so much a miracle as the inevitable outcome of historical development.

【毋庸】wúyōng〈动〉〈书〉 need not: ～置疑 without doubt

【毋庸讳言】wúyōng-huìyán〈成〉 there is no need for reticence

【毋庸赘述】wúyōng-zhuìshù〈成〉need not elaborate: 这一点～。 It is not necessary to elaborate on this point.

吾 wú〈代〉〈书〉 I: ～国 my country ‖ ～辈 we

【吾人】wúrén〈代〉〈书〉 we: ～当自强。 We should strive to improve ourselves constantly.

芜（蕪）wú〈书〉

A〈形〉 **1**（指草） overgrown with weeds: ▸荒～ **2**（指文辞） mixed and disorderly: ～词 superfluous words

B〈名〉 land overgrown with weeds: 平～ open grassland

【芜鄙】wúbǐ〈形〉〈书〉[of writing] confused and disorderly

【芜秽】wúhuì〈形〉 overgrown

【芜菁】wújīng〈名〉［植物］ turnip

【芜杂】wúzá〈形〉 [of writing] jumbled

吴（吳）Wú〈名〉 **1**（指国名） Wu [state in the Zhou Dynasty] **2**（指三国之一） Kingdom of Wu **3**（指江苏南部和浙江北部） a name for the area comprising southern Jiangsu and northern Zhejiang provinces and Shanghai

【吴哥窟】Wúgēkū〈名〉 Angkor Wat

【吴牛喘月】Wúniú-chuǎnyuè〈成〉（指人） fear of sth. born out of a misunderstanding;（指天气） scorching hot

【吴语】Wúyǔ **▸p. 918**〈名〉 *Wu* dialect [dialect of Chinese spoken in Jiangsu and Zhejiang provinces and in Shanghai]

梧 wú〈名〉 Chinese parasol: ▸魁～

【梧桐】wútóng〈名〉［植物］ Chinese parasol (tree)

鹀（鵐）wú〈名〉［鸟类］ bunting

蜈（蜈）wú

【蜈蚣】wúgōng〈名〉［昆虫］ centipede

鼯 wú

【鼯鼠】wúshǔ〈名〉［动物］ flying squirrel

wǔ

五[1] wǔ **▸p. 691**〈数〉 five: ～分之一 one fifth ‖ 一周工作～天 work five days a week ▸～颜六色, 三令～申

五[2] wǔ〈名〉［音乐］ note on the *gongche* (工尺) scale, corresponding to 6 in *jianpu* (简谱) numbered musical notation

【五爱】wǔ'ài〈名〉 Five Loves [programme for social morality issued by the Chinese government in 1949 which referred to love for the motherland, the people, physical labour, science and public property (the last changed to 'socialism' in 1982]: ～教育 education concerning the Five Loves

【五百年前是一家】wǔbǎi nián qián shì yījiā〈惯〉 we share the same surname and so may be descendants of the same ancestors: 我们都姓赵，你我～。 Since we share the same surname Zhao, we must have belonged to the same family five hundred years ago.

【五保户】wǔbǎohù〈名〉 five-guarantee household [those living in rural areas with old, weak, orphaned, widowed, ill relatives or relatives with disabilities who are beneficiaries of the five guarantees of food, clothing, housing, medical care and burial expenses]

【五倍子】wǔbèizǐ〈名〉［中药］ Chinese gall

【五棓子】= 五倍子 wǔbèizǐ

【五笔字型】wǔbǐzìxíng〈名〉［计算机］ Five-Stroke Structure [for entering Chinese characters by numbered strokes]

【五边形】wǔbiānxíng〈名〉 pentagon

【五步蛇】wǔbùshé〈名〉 long-nosed pit viper

【五彩】wǔcǎi〈名〉 [five colours blue, yellow, red, white and black] multicoloured: ～的旗帜 colourful banners

【五彩缤纷】wǔcǎi-bīnfēn〈形〉 full of bright colours

【五彩斑斓】wǔcǎi-bānlán〈成〉 riot of colour

【五常】wǔcháng〈名〉 five constant virtues in traditional Chinese ethics [benevolence (仁), righteousness (义), propriety (礼), wisdom (智) and fidelity (信)]: ▸三纲～

【五重唱】wǔchóngchàng〈名〉［音乐］ (vocal) quintet

【五重奏】wǔchóngzòu〈名〉［音乐］ (instrumental) quintet

【五大三粗】wǔdà-sāncū〈成〉 big and tall: ～的汉子 tall and sturdy fellow

【五帝】Wǔdì〈名〉 Five Lords [the five legendary rulers in prehistoric China: Huangdi (黄帝), Zhuanxu (颛顼), Di Ku (帝喾), Tang Yao (唐尧) and Yu Shun (虞舜)]: ▸三皇～

【五斗橱】wǔdǒuchú = 五斗柜 wǔdǒuguì

【五斗柜】wǔdǒuguì〈名〉 chest of drawers; dresser〈美〉

【五毒】wǔdú〈名〉 five poisonous creatures [scorpion, viper, centipede, house lizard and toad]:〈喻〉 ～俱全 engaged in all kinds of unlawful acts

【五短身材】wǔduǎn-shēncái〈成〉 [of a man] short in stature: 他是个～的中年人。 He is a short middle-aged man.

【五方杂处】wǔfāng-záchǔ〈成〉be inhabited by people from all parts: 上海是一个～、万商云集的大都市。 Shanghai is a big cosmopolitan city with businesses from all over the world.

【五分制】wǔfēnzhì〈名〉 five-grade marking system [5, 4, 3, 2 and 1 are used to represent respectively 'excellent', 'good', 'fair', 'poor' and 'very poor']

【五分钟热度】wǔfēnzhōng rèdù〈惯〉 short-lived enthusiasm: 他又喜欢打乒乓球了，不过也就是～。 His current thing is table tennis, but his enthusiasm will soon wear off.

【五更】wǔgēng〈名〉〈旧〉 **1**（指五个时间段） five periods of the night **2**（指第五更） just before dawn: ～天 just before dawn ‖ 起～，睡半夜 go to bed at midnight and rise before dawn

【五古】wǔgǔ〈简称〉= 五言诗

【五谷】wǔgǔ〈名〉 **1**（指五种谷类） five cereals [rice, millet, broomcorn millet, wheat and beans]: 四体不勤，～不分 lazy and ignorant **2**（泛指粮食作物） food crops: ▸～丰登

【五谷丰登】wǔgǔ-fēngdēng〈成〉 bumper grain harvest: ～，天下太平。 The crops were abundant, and peace reigned.

【五官】wǔguān〈名〉 **1**（五种器官） five sense organs [usu referring to ears, eyes, mouth, nose and tongue in traditional Chinese medicine or eyes, ears, nose, throat and mouth in western medicine]: ～科 ear, nose and throat department **2**（面部器官） facial features: ～端正 have regular features

【五光十色】wǔguāng-shísè〈成〉 **1**（形容色彩） multicoloured: ～的宝石 multicoloured gem stones **2**（形容式样） varied: ～的工艺品 a great variety of handicrafts

【五行八作】wǔháng-bāzuò〈成〉 all trades and professions: 这条街上汇聚着～的人们。 People of all trades and professions gathered in the street.

【五好家庭】wǔhǎo jiātíng〈名〉 five virtues family [outstanding in being law-abiding and hard-studying, and in family planning, harmony and thrift]

【五湖四海】wǔhú-sìhǎi〈成〉 all corners of the land: 来自～ come from all corners of the country

【五花八门】wǔhuā-bāmén〈成〉 of a wide variety: 他们的爱好～。 Their hobbies are many and various.

【五花大绑】wǔhuā dàbǎng〈成〉 tie sb.'s hands and arms tightly behind with a rope looped round his neck

【五花肉】wǔhuāròu〈名〉 streaky pork

【五环旗】Wǔhuánqí〈名〉 Olympic Flag

【五加皮】wǔjiāpí〈名〉 **1**［中药］ bark of the slender acanthopanax **2**（指药酒） medicinal wine made by soaking the bark of the slender acanthopanax in liquor

【五讲四美】wǔjiǎng-sìměi〈成〉 five stresses and four beauties [norms advocated in the movement to build socialist ethics in China in the 1980's]

【五角大楼】Wǔjiǎo Dàlóu〈名〉 Pentagon [building in Washington DC that houses the headquarters of the US Department of Defence]

【五角星】wǔjiǎoxīng〈名〉 five-pointed star

【五角形】wǔjiǎoxíng〈名〉 pentagon

【五金】wǔjīn〈名〉 **1**（五种金属） five metals [gold, silver, copper, iron and tin] **2**（泛指金属制品） hardware; ironmongery〈英〉: ～厂 hardware factory ‖ ～店 hardware store

【五经】Wǔjīng〈名〉 Five Classics [*The Book of Songs* (诗经), *The Book of History* (书经), *The Book of Changes* (易经), *The Book of Rites* (礼记), and *The Spring and Autumn Annals* (春秋)]

【五局三胜制】wǔ jú sān shèng zhì〈名〉 best of five games, three out of five sets

【五绝】wǔjué〈简称〉= 五言绝句

【五劳七伤】wǔláo-qīshāng **A**〈名〉［中医］ 'five lesions' and 'seven injuries' [as caused to the spleen by overeating, to the liver by rage, to the kidneys by lifting heavy weights and sitting too long on wet ground, to the lungs by wearing too little and taking cold food and drinks, to the heart by sorrow and anxiety, to the body by abrupt weather changes, and to the consciousness by immoderate fear] **B**〈成〉〈喻〉prone to various diseases

【五雷轰顶】wǔléi-hōngdǐng〈成〉be thunderstruck: 他儿子在车祸中罹难的消息对他犹如～。The news that his son had been killed in a traffic accident came to him like a bolt from the blue.

【五里雾】wǔlǐwù〈成〉〈喻〉utter bewilderment: 我觉得如同在～中，不知所措。I felt as if I had been caught in a heavy fog and had no idea what to do next.

【五敛子】wǔliǎnzǐ〈名〉［植物］**1**（阳桃树）carambola **2**（阳桃）star fruit

【五粮液】Wǔliángyè〈名〉Five-Grain Liquor [brand of liquor distilled from five kinds of grain]

【五岭】Wǔ Lǐng〈名〉Five Ridges [across the borders between Hunan and Jiangxi, and between Guangdong and Guangxi provinces]

【五律】wǔlǜ〈简称〉= 五言律诗

【五伦】wǔlún〈名〉〈古〉five human relationships in ethics [between ruler and subject (君臣), father and son (父子), husband and wife (夫妻), brothers (兄弟), and friends (朋友)]

【五内】wǔnèi〈名〉〈书〉**1**（五脏）viscera **2**（内心）heart: 铭感～ feel grateful from the bottom of one's heart

【五内俱裂】wǔnèi-jùliè〈成〉feel a sharp, stabbing pain: 听到孩子受虐，真让人～。It was heart-breaking to hear how the child had been abused.

【五内如焚】wǔnèi-rúfén〈成〉be torn apart with anxiety: 听说母亲垂危，她～。Hearing that her mother was on her deathbed, she was torn apart with anxiety.

【五年计划】wǔnián jìhuà〈名〉five-year plan: 第十个～ the Tenth Five-Year Plan

【五七干校】Wǔ-Qī gànxiào〈名〉［历史］May Seventh Cadre School [farm-school for government officials, college teachers and students, etc., named after Mao Zedong's May 7 Directive of 1966]

【五禽戏】wǔqínxì〈名〉Five-Animal Exercise [modelled upon the movements of the tiger, deer, bear, ape and bird]

【五人制足球】wǔrénzhì zúqiú〈名〉［体育］five-a-side

【五日京兆】wǔrì-jīngzhào〈成〉lame-duck official

【五卅运动】Wǔ-Sà Yùndòng〈名〉May 30th Movement [1925]

【五色】wǔsè = 五彩 wǔcǎi

【五十步笑百步】wǔshí bù xiào bǎi bù〈成〉the pot calling the kettle black

【五四青年节】Wǔ-Sì Qīngniánjié〈名〉Youth Day [May 4]

【五四运动】Wǔ-Sì Yùndòng〈名〉［历史］May 4th Movement (of 1919) [anti-imperialist, anti-feudal, political and cultural movement]

【五台山】Wǔtáishān〈名〉Mount Wutai [a mountain in Shanxi Province, noted for Buddhist shrines]

【五体投地】wǔtǐ-tóudì〈成〉be awestruck with admiration: 佩服得～ be blown away with admiration and respect

【五味】wǔwèi〈名〉**1**（五种味道）five flavours [sweet, sour, bitter, pungent and salty] **2**（各种味道）all sorts of flavours: ～俱全 all kinds of flavours

【五味子】wǔwèizǐ〈名〉［中药］fruit of Chinese magnolia vine

【五线谱】wǔxiànpǔ〈名〉［音乐］staff

【五香】wǔxiāng〈名〉five spices [fennel, cinnamon, clove, star aniseed and prickly ash]: ～豆 spiced beans ‖ ～粉 spice powder

【五项全能运动】wǔxiàng quánnéng yùndòng〈名〉［体育］pentathlon: 现代～ modern pentathlon

【五星红旗】Wǔxīng Hóngqí〈名〉Five-Star Red Flag [national flag of the People's Republic of China]: ～徐徐升起。The Five-Star Red Flag is steadily rising up the pole.

【五星级】wǔxīngjí〈形〉five-star: ～宾馆 five-star hotel

【五星上将】wǔxīng shàngjiàng〈名〉five-star general [US General of the Army, Fleet Admiral, General of the Air Force]

【五刑】wǔxíng〈名〉〈古〉five chief forms of punishment [tattooing the face (墨), cutting off the nose (劓), cutting of the feet (剕), castration (宫) and decapitation (大辟)]

【五行】wǔxíng〈名〉［哲学］five elements [metal, wood, water, fire and earth, held by the ancients to make up the physical universe and later used in traditional Chinese medicine to explain various physiological and pathological phenomena]: ～学说 theory of the five elements

【五言绝句】wǔyán juéjù〈名〉classical poem with four five-character lines

【五言律诗】wǔyán lǜshī〈名〉classical poem with eight five-character lines

【五言诗】wǔyánshī〈名〉ancient poem with five characters to each line

【五颜六色】wǔyán-liùsè〈成〉multicoloured: ～的花 colourful flowers ‖ ～旗帜 multicoloured flags

【五羊城】Wǔyángchéng〈名〉City of Five Rams [another name for Guangzhou (广州)]

【五一】Wǔ-Yī〈简称〉= 五一国际劳动节

【五一国际劳动节】Wǔ-Yī Guójì Láodòngjié〈名〉May Day: 过～ celebrate May Day

【五一劳动奖章】Wǔ-Yī Láodòng Jiǎngzhāng〈名〉'May 1' Labour Award

【五音】wǔyīn〈名〉**1**〈古〉［音乐］five notes of the pentatonic scale: ～不全 sing out of tune **2**〈旧〉［语言］five points of consonant articulation

【五月】wǔyuè ▸**p. 928**〈名〉**1**（阳历）May: 去年～ last May **2**（阴历）fifth month of the lunar year

【五月节】Wǔyuèjié = 端午节 Duānwǔjié

【五岳】Wǔyuè〈名〉Five Sacred Mountains [Taishan Mountain (in Shandong Province, 东岳泰山); Hengshan Mountain (in Hunan Province, 南岳衡山); Huashan Mountain (in Shaanxi Province, 西岳华山); Hengshan Mountain (in Shanxi Province, 北岳恒山); and Songshan Mountain (in Henan Province, 中岳嵩山)]

【五脏】wǔzàng〈名〉［中医］five internal organs [heart, liver, spleen, lungs and kidneys]

【五脏六腑】wǔzàng-liùfǔ〈成〉internal organs of the body: 他咳得快把～都咳出来了。He was coughing his insides up.

【五指】wǔzhǐ〈名〉five fingers: 伸手不见～ so dark that one cannot see one's hand in front of one's face

【五中】wǔzhōng〈名〉〈书〉five internal organs [heart, liver, spleen, lungs and kidneys]: 铭感～ feel grateful from the bottom of one's heart

【五洲】wǔzhōu〈名〉[five continents] the whole world: ～四海 the whole world

【五子棋】wǔzǐqí〈名〉gobang: 一盘～ a game of gobang ‖ 下～ play gobang

午 wǔ

〈名〉**1**（指地支）seventh of the twelve Earthly Branches **2**（中午）midday: ▸晌～, 正～

【午餐】wǔcān〈名〉lunch: （与某人）共进～ have lunch (with sb.) ‖ 工作～ working/business lunch, staff meal

【午餐肉】wǔcānròu〈名〉luncheon meat: 火腿～ ham luncheon meat

【午饭】wǔfàn〈名〉lunch: 吃～ have lunch

【午后】wǔhòu〈名〉afternoon

【午间】wǔjiān〈名〉midday: ～新闻 midday news

【午觉】wǔjiào〈名〉afternoon siesta: 睡～ take a siesta

【午盘】wǔpán〈名〉［金融］noon market: ～点评 noon market commentary

【午前】wǔqián〈名〉late morning: 务必在～赶回来。Do come back before noon.

【午时】wǔshí〈名〉period of the day from 11 a.m. to 1 p.m.

【午市】wǔshì〈名〉**1**（指集市）midday business: 餐饮一条街的～与晚市一样热闹。Food Street is as busy at lunchtime as it is at dinner. **2**（指股市）midday (stock) market: ～后股指一路震荡上扬。Stocks shot up after the noon break.

【午睡】wǔshuì **A**〈动〉take a nap after lunch: 他有～的习惯。He is in the habit of napping after lunch. **B**〈名〉afternoon siesta

【午休】wǔxiū〈动〉take a nap after lunch

【午宴】wǔyàn〈名〉luncheon: 设～ hold a luncheon

【午夜】wǔyè ▸**p. 669**〈名〉midnight: ～电影 midnight film

伍 wǔ

A〈名〉**1**（指古代军队单位）basic five-man unit of the army in ancient China [used today as a term of general reference]: 入～ join the army ‖ 退～ retire from active military service ▸队～, 行～, 落～ **2**（同伴）company: 与某人为～ keep company with sb. ‖ 羞与某人为～ be ashamed of sb.'s company ‖ 不与犯罪分子为～ not associate with criminals
B ▸**p. 691**〈数〉five [used for the numeral 五 on cheques, etc. to avoid alterations or mistakes]

【伍斯特郡】Wǔsītèjùn〈名〉Worcestershire

仵 wǔ

〈名〉〈旧〉coroner

【仵作】wǔzuò〈名〉〈旧〉coroner

庑（廡）wǔ

〈名〉〈书〉side room or building in a traditional compound house: 西～ west wing

怃（憮）wǔ

〈书〉
A〈动〉caress
B〈形〉disappointed

【怃然】wǔrán〈形〉〈书〉disappointed: 情极～ look very disappointed

忤 wǔ

〈动〉**1**（不顺从）violate: ▸～逆 **2**（不和睦）be on bad terms: 与人无～ bear no ill will against anybody

【忤逆】wǔnì〈形〉unfilial: ～不孝 filial impiety

迕 wǔ

〈动〉〈书〉**1**（遇见）meet: 相～ meet with **2**（违背）go against: 违～ disobey

妩（嫵）wǔ

【妩媚】wǔmèi〈形〉attractive: ～动人 be charming and enchanting

武 wǔ

A〈名〉**1**（武力）(military) force: 动～ use force ‖ 尚～ emphasize military affairs ‖ 任命文～官员 appoint civil officials and

W

military officers ▸～力, 穷兵黩～ **2**（武术） *wushu*, martial arts: 比～ engage in a kung fu fight ‖ 习～ practise *wushu* ▸～打, ～功 **3**〈书〉（半步） half a step;（脚步） footstep: 继～ follow close on sb.'s heels

B〈形〉（勇猛） valiant;（猛烈） fierce: ▸～夫, ～火, 威～

【武昌鱼】wǔchāngyú〈名〉 blunt-snout bream

【武场】wǔchǎng〈名〉［戏曲］ percussion instrument accompaniment in traditional Chinese opera

【武丑】wǔchǒu〈名〉 acrobatic-fighting clown in traditional Chinese opera

【武打】wǔdǎ〈动〉 do kung fu: ～片 kung fu film

【武旦】wǔdàn〈名〉（指角色）female martial role [in traditional Chinese opera];（指演员） martial *dan* [one of the main divisions of the *dan* in traditional Chinese opera]

【武当拳】Wǔdāngquán〈名〉 *Wudang* boxing

【武德】wǔdé〈名〉 martial ethics

【武斗】wǔdòu **A**〈动〉 resort to violence (in a debate, dispute, etc.) **B**〈名〉 violent clash

【武断】wǔduàn **A**〈动〉 make an arbitrary decision: 做决定时要防止～。 We should avoid making arbitrary decisions. **B**〈形〉 arbitrary, subjective: 行事～ act arbitrarily ‖ 主观～的决定 subjective and arbitrary decision

【武夫】wǔfū〈名〉 **1**（有勇力的人） man of great physical prowess **2**〈旧〉（军人） soldier: 一介～ a military man

【武工】wǔgōng〈名〉 [in traditional opera] acrobatic skill: ～很好 be well-trained in acrobatic skills

【武工队】wǔgōngduì〈名〉 armed working team [operating under the leadership of the Chinese Communist Party in enemy-occupied areas during the War of Resistance Against Japan, 1937-1945]

【武功】wǔgōng〈名〉 **1**〈书〉（指功绩） military exploits: ～显赫 outstanding military exploits ‖ 文治～ political and military achievements **2**（指功夫） *wushu*, martial arts: ～高强 be good at martial arts **3** = 武工 wǔgōng

【武官】wǔguān〈名〉 **1**（军官） military officer **2**［外交］ military attaché

【武官处】wǔguānchù〈名〉［外交］ military attaché's office

【武馆】wǔguǎn〈名〉 *wushu* centre: 开设～ start a *wushu* centre

【武汉】Wǔhàn ▸**p. 661**〈名〉 Wuhan [capital of Hubei Province (湖北)]

【武行】wǔháng〈名〉 [in traditional Chinese opera] acrobatic actor playing a supporting role

【武火】wǔhuǒ〈名〉 high heat: ～用于烹炸。 A high heat is used for stir-frying and deep-frying.

【武将】wǔjiàng〈名〉 general

【武警】wǔjǐng〈简称〉= 武装警察

【武库】wǔkù〈名〉 armoury: 核～ nuclear arsenal

【武力】wǔlì〈名〉 **1**（暴力） force: 教师不得使用～来控制学生。 Teachers are not allowed to use force to control their students. **2**（军事力量） military force: 动用/诉诸～ resort to military force ‖ ～征服 conquer by force ‖ 以～进行威胁 resort to the threat of force

【武林】wǔlín〈名〉 kung fu world: ～高手 kung fu master

【武庙】Wǔmiào〈名〉 temple to the God of War

【武器】wǔqì〈名〉 weapon: 放下～ lay down one's arms ‖ 常规～ conventional weapon ‖ 大规模杀伤性～ weapon of mass destruction ‖ 化学/核/生物～ chemical/nuclear/biological weapon ‖ 思想～ ideological weapon

【武器核查】wǔqì héchá〈名〉 weapons inspection

【武器禁运】wǔqì jìnyùn〈名〉 arms embargo

【武器装备】wǔqì zhuāngbèi〈名〉 weaponry

【武生】wǔshēng〈名〉 male martial role in traditional Chinese opera

【武师】wǔshī〈名〉 kung fu master

【武士】wǔshì〈名〉 **1**（指古代宫廷卫兵） palace guard **2**（有勇力的人） warrior **3**（指在日本） samurai

【武士道】wǔshìdào〈名〉bushido [in ancient and medieval Japan]

【武术】wǔshù〈名〉 *wushu*: ～表演 martial arts performance ‖ ～大师 kung fu master

【武戏】wǔxì〈名〉 [in traditional Chinese opera] military acrobatic play: 今晚的压轴戏是～。 The grand finale tonight is a piece full of acrobatic fighting.

【武侠小说】wǔxiá xiǎoshuō〈名〉 martial arts novel

> **武侠小说**
>
> The martial arts novel, a major genre in Chinese fiction. It has its origins in the knight-errant stories found in Sima Qian's *Records of the Grand Historian* (《史记》). The genre developed in maturity from the supernatural stories of the Wei-Jin and Six dynasties periods to the short stories of the Tang Dynasty. After the Song Dynasty, vernacular forms began to emerge, and by the end of the Yuan Dynasty and the beginning of the Ming, longer stories in the vernacular were beginning to appear. These included *The Water Margin* (▸《水浒传》). The genre reached its height in the Qing Dynasty. Today, knight-errant fiction is found mostly in the works of Hong Kong and Taiwanese writers. Stories typically feature martial arts, military prowess, weaponry, and a spirit of chivalry that embodies a strong sense of social justice.

【武艺】wǔyì〈名〉 martial arts skill: ～高强 be highly skilled in martial arts

【武职】wǔzhí〈名〉 military post

【武装】wǔzhuāng **A**〈名〉 **1**（指装备） armed forces: ～部队 armed forces ‖ 人民～ people's armed forces ‖ 反政府～ anti-government forces **2**（指队伍） military equipment: 解除～ disarm ‖ 全副～ fully armed **B**〈动〉 arm: ～到牙齿 be armed to the teeth ‖ 用科学的理论～人的头脑 arm people's minds with scientific theories

【武装冲突】wǔzhuāng chōngtū〈名〉 military clash

【武装犯罪】wǔzhuāng fànzuì〈名〉 armed crime

【武装干涉】wǔzhuāng gānshè〈名〉armed intervention

【武装警察】wǔzhuāng jǐngchá〈名〉armed police: ～部队 armed forces

【武装力量】wǔzhuāng lìliàng〈名〉 armed forces

【武装起义】wǔzhuāng qǐyì〈名〉 armed uprising

【武装人员】wǔzhuāng rényuán〈名〉 military personnel

侮

侮 wǔ〈动〉 insult: 不可～ not to be bullied or insulted ▸～辱, 欺～

【侮骂】wǔmà〈动〉 speak insultingly or cruelly: 劈头盖脸地～ shower sb. with abuse

【侮慢】wǔmàn〈动〉 humiliate: 不得～使者。 Envoys should not be treated disrespectfully.

【侮蔑】wǔmiè〈动〉 treat with contempt: ～的眼光 scornful look ‖ 不得～长者。 Do not look down on the elderly.

【侮辱】wǔrǔ〈动〉 insult: ～妇女 insult a woman ‖ ～人格 commit an affront to sb.'s dignity ‖ 遭到～ suffer an affront ‖ 他一辈子都没受过这样的～。 He's never been so insulted in his whole life.

捂

捂 wǔ〈动〉 cover: ～着耳朵 block one's ears ‖ 双手～着脸哭 cry in one's hands ‖ 用手帕～住嘴 put a handkerchief over one's mouth ‖〈喻〉 丑闻是～不住的。 The scandal cannot be hushed up.

【捂盖子】wǔ gàizi〈惯〉 try to keep the lid on sth.: ～只能蒙蔽一时。 By covering up the truth, you can only fool people for so long.

牾

牾 wǔ〈动〉〈书〉 contradict: ～意 contravene sb.'s wishes ▸抵～

鹉（鵡）

鹉（鵡） wǔ ▸鹦鹉 yīngwǔ

舞

舞 wǔ

A〈名〉 dance: 跳一个～ have a dance ‖ 独～ solo dance ‖ 民间～ folk dance ‖ 双人～ pas de deux ▸芭蕾～, 交谊～

B〈动〉 **1**（跳舞） dance: ▸手～足蹈, 载歌载～ **2**（拿着东西跳舞）dance with sth. in one's hands: ～剑 perform a swordplay ‖ ～龙/狮 perform a dragon/lion dance **3**（挥舞） wield: ～枪弄棒 brandish spears and sticks ‖ 挥～帽子 wave one's cap **4**（玩弄） play with: ▸～文弄墨

【舞伴】wǔbàn〈名〉 dancing partner

【舞弊】wǔbì〈动〉 engage in fraudulent practices: ～行为 fraudulent behaviour ‖ 严禁考试～。 No cheating in the examination will be tolerated. ▸营私～

【舞步】wǔbù〈名〉 dance step: ～轻盈 dance gracefully ‖ 华尔兹～ steps of the waltz

【舞场】wǔchǎng〈名〉 dance hall: 开～ run a commercial dance hall

【舞池】wǔchí〈名〉 dance floor

【舞蹈】wǔdǎo〈名〉 dance: 设计～动作 choreograph ‖ 学习～ learn a dance ‖ 民间～ folk dance ‖ ～家 dancer

【舞动】wǔdòng〈动〉 **1**（挥舞） wave **2**（摇摆） sway: 柳枝随风～。 The willows swayed in the breeze.

【舞会】wǔhuì〈名〉 dance: 参加～ go to a dance ‖ 化装～ costume ball

【舞技】wǔjì〈名〉 dancing skill

【舞剧】wǔjù〈名〉 dance drama: 芭蕾～ ballet ‖ 民间～ folk dance drama

【舞美】wǔměi〈简称〉= 舞台美术

【舞男】wǔnán〈名〉 gigolo

【舞弄】wǔnòng〈动〉 wield: ～刀枪 brandish swords and spears

【舞女】wǔnǚ〈名〉 dancing girl

【舞曲】wǔqǔ〈名〉 dance music: 快三步/慢四步～ Viennese waltz/blues music

【舞台】wǔtái〈名〉 stage: 搬上～ stage ‖ 告别～（生涯） retire from the stage ‖ 旋转～ revolving stage ‖ 退出历史～

retire from the stage of history ‖ 走上政治～ enter the arena of politics
【舞台布景】wǔtái bùjǐng〈名〉 stage scenery
【舞台灯光】wǔtái dēngguāng〈名〉 stage lighting
【舞台剧】wǔtáijù〈名〉 stage production
【舞台美术】wǔtái měishù〈名〉 stage art, stagecraft
【舞坛】wǔtán〈名〉 dance circles: ～新星 rising star in the dance circles
【舞厅】wǔtīng〈名〉 **1**（指大厅） ballroom: 旋转～ revolving ballroom **2**（指舞场） dance hall: 迪斯科～ disco hall
【舞文弄法】wǔwén-nòngfǎ〈成〉 pervert the law by playing with legal phraseology
【舞文弄墨】wǔwén-nòngmò〈成〉 **1**（歪曲法律条文作弊） pervert the law by lexical chicanery **2**（玩弄文字技巧） play with words
【舞鞋】wǔxié〈名〉 dancing shoes
【舞榭歌台】wǔxiè-gētái〈成〉 entertainment set-up
【舞星】wǔxīng〈名〉 dance star
【舞艺】wǔyì〈名〉 dancing skill
【舞姿】wǔzī〈名〉 dancer's posture and movement: ～轻盈 dance gracefully

wù

兀 wù〈形〉〈书〉 **1**（高耸） lofty: ▸～立, 突～ **2**（秃） bald: ▸～鹫
▸wū
【兀傲】wù'ào〈形〉〈书〉 haughty: 性情～ be arrogant by nature
【兀鹫】wùjiù〈名〉［鸟类］ griffon vulture
【兀立】wùlì〈动〉〈书〉 stand erect: ～于上海的摩天大楼 skyscrapers that tower over Shanghai
【兀臬】wùniè = 杌陧 wùniè
【兀鹰】wùyīng〈名〉［鸟类］ buzzard
【兀自】wùzì〈副〉〈方〉 still: ～呆想 mooch about on one's own ‖ ～一人 all alone by oneself

乌（烏） wù
▸wū
【乌拉】wùla〈名〉 leather boots lined with *wula* sedge
▸wūlā
【乌拉草】wùlacǎo〈名〉［植物］ *wula* sedge

勿 wù ▸**p. 221**〈副〉 [used in prohibitions, admonitions, etc.] not: 请～践踏! Keep off! ‖ 请～触摸! Please do not touch! ‖ 请～入内! No entry!
【勿忘我】wùwàngwǒ〈名〉［植物］ forget-me-not
【勿谓言之不预】wù wèi yán zhī bù yù〈成〉 do not say that you have not been forewarned

戊 wù〈名〉 **1**（指天干） fifth of the ten Heavenly Stems (天干) **2**（第五） fifth
【戊肝】wùgān ▸**p. 50**〈名〉［医学］ viral hepatitis type E
【戊戌变法】Wùxū Biànfǎ〈名〉 Reform Movement of 1898 [also known as the Hundred Days Reform]

务（務） wù
A〈名〉 task: 俗～缠身 be confined to worldly affairs ▸公～, 内～, 总～
B〈动〉 be engaged in: ▸～农, ～虚, 不～正业
C〈副〉〈书〉 must: 除恶～尽 must thoroughly exterminate an evil ‖ ～请光临。 You are cordially invited. ‖ ～须周知。 Be sure to make it known to everyone. ▸陈言～去
【务必】wùbì〈副〉〈书〉 must: 此事你～帮忙。 You must help us with it. ‖ ～准时到场。 Be sure to arrive on time.
【务工】wùgōng ▸**p. 966**〈动〉 **1**（从事工业或工程工作） be engaged in industrial or engineering work **2**（打工） put in labour and effort: 外出～ go elsewhere for work
【务农】wùnóng ▸**p. 966**〈动〉 be a farmer: 回乡～ return to the countryside and do farm work
【务期】wùqī〈动〉〈书〉 be sure to: ～按时返校。 Be sure to come back to school on time.
【务求】wùqiú〈动〉〈书〉 ensure: 此问题～妥善解决。 We must find a satisfactory solution to the problem.
【务实】wùshí **A**〈动〉 deal with concrete matters **B**〈形〉 pragmatic: 采取～的态度 adopt a down-to-earth attitude ‖ ～的作风 practical style of work
【务使】wùshǐ〈动〉〈书〉 make sure
【务须】wùxū = 务必 wùbì
【务虚】wùxū〈动〉 discuss principles or ideological guidelines: ～会 meeting to discuss principles ‖ ～是为了统一认识。 We discuss principles in order to reach a consensus.
【务正】wùzhèng〈动〉〈书〉 [usu used in the negative] take up a proper job: 回心～ switch to a proper job

坞（塢） wù〈名〉 **1**（中间凹陷的地方） hollow: 村～ hamlet ▸山～ **2**〈书〉（防御性建筑物） fortified building: 筑～ build a castle **3**（挡风的建筑物） structure with high sides to keep the wind out: ▸船～, 花～

芴 wù〈名〉［化学］ fluorene

杌 wù〈名〉 square stool: ▸～凳, ～子
【杌凳】wùdèng = 杌子 wùzi
【杌陧】wùniè〈形〉〈书〉 **1**（指形势） unstable **2**（指心情） disturbed
【杌子】wùzi〈名〉 square stool

物 wù〈名〉 **1**（东西） thing: ▸～尽其用, ～品 **2**（外界） the outside world: ▸超然～外, 待人接～ **3**（内容） content: ▸言之无～
【物产】wùchǎn〈名〉 product: ～丰富 have a variety of products
【物阜民丰】wùfù-mínfēng〈成〉〈书〉 goods are abundant and the people live in plenty
【物故】wùgù〈动〉〈书〉 pass away
【物归原主】wùguī yuánzhǔ〈成〉 return sth. to its rightful owner
【物候】wùhòu〈名〉 phenology: 观察～ observe various phenomena
【物华天宝】wùhuá-tiānbǎo〈成〉 good products from the earth are nature's treasures
【物化】wùhuà **A**〈动〉〈书〉 pass away **B**〈形〉 physico-chemical: ～分析 physico-chemical analysis
【物化劳动】wùhuà láodòng〈名〉 materialized labour
【物换星移】wùhuàn-xīngyí〈成〉 **1**（时间推移） things change with the passing of the years **2**（节令变化） change of the seasons
【物极必反】wùjí-bìfǎn〈成〉 no extreme will hold strong for long
【物价】wùjià〈名〉 price: 哄抬/压低～ whoop up/force down prices ‖ 调整/稳定～ regulate/stabilize prices
【物价指数】wùjià zhǐshù〈名〉 price index: 物价上涨指数 rising price index
【物件】wùjiàn〈名〉 thing: 零碎～ odds and ends ‖ 小～ small objects
【物尽其用】wùjìnqíyòng〈成〉 let all things serve their proper purpose
【物镜】wùjìng〈名〉［物理］ object lens
【物理】wùlǐ〈名〉 **1**（指物理学） physics **2**（指内在规律） innate laws of things
【物理疗法】wùlǐ liáofǎ〈名〉 physiotherapy
【物理性质】wùlǐ xìngzhì〈名〉 physical property
【物理学】wùlǐxué〈名〉 physics: 高能～ high energy physics ‖ 地球～ geophysics ‖ 理论/应用～ theoretical/applied physics ‖ 原子/核～ atomic/nuclear physics
【物力】wùlì〈名〉 material resource: 爱惜/浪费人力～ treasure/waste manpower and material resources
【物流】wùliú〈名〉 logistics: ～中心 logistics centre
【物美价廉】wùměi-jiàlián = 价廉物美 jiàlián-wùměi
【物品】wùpǐn〈名〉 article: 贵重～ valuables ‖ 易损～ flimsy article ‖ 缴获违禁～ seize contraband
【物权】wùquán〈名〉 rights to things: ～法 property law
【物色】wùsè〈动〉 seek out: ～人才 look for qualified personnel ‖ ～演员 scout out actors
【物伤其类】wùshāngqílèi〈成〉〈喻〉 like feels for like
【物事】wùshì〈名〉 **1**〈书〉（事情） matter **2**〈方〉（物品） tangible thing
【物是人非】wùshì-rénfēi〈成〉 things are still there, but the people have changed
【物态】wùtài〈名〉 state of matter: ～变化 change of state
【物探】wùtàn〈名〉 physical exploration
【物体】wùtǐ〈名〉 substance: 放射性/有毒～ radioactive/toxic substance ‖ 透明～ transparent substance
【物外】wùwài〈名〉〈书〉 something beyond worldly affairs: 超然～ transcend worldly considerations
【物象】wùxiàng〈名〉 **1**（指现象） visible phenomena: 根据～预测天气 predict weather according to visible phenomena **2**（指形象） image: 摹写～ depict an image
【物像】wùxiàng〈名〉 image: 湖/镜中的～ reflection in the lake/mirror
【物业】wùyè〈名〉 property: ～管理 property management
【物业税】wùyèshuì〈名〉 property tax
【物以类聚，人以群分】wù yǐ lèi jù, rén yǐ qún fēn〈成〉 like attracts like
【物以稀为贵】wù yǐ xī wéi guì〈俗〉 the rarer a thing is, the more it is worth
【物议】wùyì〈名〉〈书〉 public criticism: 免遭～ avoid public censure
【物语】wùyǔ〈名〉 story: 爱的～ love story ‖ 校园～ campus story
【物欲】wùyù〈名〉 material or human desire: ～横流 overflow of material or human desires

【物证】wùzhèng〈名〉material evidence: 搜集/提供～ collect/provide material evidence
【物质】wùzhì〈名〉1（指客观实在）substance: 精神与～的关系 relation between matter and spirit ‖ 有毒～ toxic substance 2（指金钱、生活资料等）material: 给予～刺激 offer material incentive
【物质财富】wùzhì cáifù〈名〉material wealth: 拥有～ possess material wealth
【物质基础】wùzhì jīchǔ〈名〉material base: 打下～ lay the material base
【物质奖励】wùzhì jiǎnglì〈名〉material reward: 给予～ provide a material reward
【物质利益】wùzhì lìyì〈名〉material benefits
【物质名词】wùzhì míngcí ▸p. 411〈名〉［语法］material noun
【物质生活】wùzhì shēnghuó〈名〉material life: 提高人民的～水平 raise the people's material living standards
【物质条件】wùzhì tiáojiàn〈名〉material conditions: 改善～ better material conditions
【物质文明】wùzhì wénmíng〈名〉material civilization: ～和精神文明一起抓 attend to both spiritual and material civilization
【物种】wùzhǒng〈名〉［生物］species: 濒危～ endangered species ‖ 灭绝/稀有的～ extinct/rare species ‖《～起源》*The Origin of Species*
【物主】wùzhǔ〈名〉owner
【物主代词】wùzhǔ dàicí〈名〉［语法］possessive pronoun
【物资】wùzī〈名〉goods and materials: 出口/进口～ exported/imported goods ‖ 救灾～ disaster relief supplies ‖ 军用～ goods or materials for military purpose ‖ ～交流 interflow of commodities
【物资调拨】wùzī diàobō〈名〉delivery of goods and materials
【物资消耗】wùzī xiāohào〈名〉consumption of materials: ～增大 increase the consumption of materials

误（誤）wù

A〈形〉incorrect: 人们～以为… People are under the mistaken impression that... ▸～差, ～导, ～会, ～解
B〈动〉1（错过）miss: ～了火车 miss a train ‖ ～了农时 miss the farming season ▸～点, ～事, 耽～, 延～ 2（使受损害）hinder: ▸～人子弟
C〈副〉mistakenly: ～伤 accidentally injure ‖ ～报会议日期 misinform sb. over the date of a meeting ▸～判, ～入歧途
【误差】wùchā〈名〉error: 减少～ decrease errors ‖ ～不超过一毫米 with an error margin of less than one millimetre
【误场】wùchǎng〈动〉[of an actor] miss a performance
【误导】wùdǎo〈动〉mislead: ～消费者 mislead consumers
【误点】wùdiǎn〈动〉be behind schedule: ～二十分钟 be 20 minutes late ‖ 火车～了。The train is overdue.
【误工】wùgōng〈动〉be absent from work: 无故～ be absent from work without good reason ‖ 记好上班时间，注意别～! Remember the time for work. Don't be late.
【误国】wùguó〈动〉be detrimental to the nation: 空谈～。Empty talk will endanger the country.
【误会】wùhuì A〈动〉misunderstand: 他完全～了我的意思。He mistook my meaning entirely. B〈名〉misunderstanding: 消除～ clear up a misunderstanding ‖ 引起～ cause misunderstanding
【误解】wùjiě A〈动〉misunderstand: 容易引起～ be easily misconstrued ‖ 你一定～了我的意思。You must have misunderstood my meaning B〈名〉misunderstanding: 消除～ clear up a misunderstanding ‖ 这是一种～。This is just a kind of misunderstanding.
【误判】wùpàn〈动〉make an erroneous judgement: 由于裁判～，他们输了这场比赛。They only lost the game because of the erroneous judgement of the referee.
【误期】wùqī〈动〉exceed the time limit: 这项工程不能～。The project must not run behind schedule.
【误区】wùqū〈名〉myth: 走出～ get rid of long-standing myths
【误人子弟】wùrénzǐdì〈成〉lead young people astray: 不合格的老师只能～。Unqualified teachers can do nothing but damage to their students.
【误入歧途】wùrù-qítú〈成〉slip off the right track: 小心不要～。Be careful not to lose the way.
【误杀】wùshā〈动〉［法律］manslaughter
【误伤】wùshāng〈动〉accidentally injure: ～无辜 harm the innocent by mistake
【误事】wùshì〈动〉hold things up: 瞧我这记性，差点误了你的事。What a bad memory I have! I almost messed things up for you! ‖ 酗酒会～。Drunks can cause disturbances.
【误算】wùsuàn〈动〉miscalculate
【误译】wùyì〈动〉mistranslate
【误用】wùyòng〈动〉misuse
【误诊】wùzhěn〈动〉1（错误地诊断）misdiagnose: 由于～，他差点丢了性命。Due to the doctor's incorrect diagnosis, he almost lost his life. 2（延误诊治）miss the chance for a timely diagnosis or treatment

悟 wù

〈动〉realize: ～出其中的道理 awaken to reason ‖ 若有所～ seem to have understood ▸顿～, 领～, 醒～
【悟道】wùdào〈动〉awake to truth: ～之言 enlightened views
【悟性】wùxìng〈名〉comprehension: ～好/差的人 person of quick/slow comprehension

恶（惡）wù

〈动〉hate: ▸好～, 好逸～劳, 可～ ▸ě, è, wū

晤 wù

〈动〉〈书〉meet: 匆匆一～ have a brief meeting ‖ 来访未～ come to visit but fail to see sb. ▸～面, ～谈
【晤面】wùmiàn〈动〉〈书〉meet: 初次～ meet for the first time ‖ 久未～，近来可好？ I haven't seen you for a long time. How have you been?
【晤谈】wùtán〈动〉〈书〉have a talk: ～良久 have a long talk

焐 wù

〈动〉warm up: 把被褥～热 warm up the bedding ‖ 用热水袋～手 warm one's hands with a hot-water bottle

靰 wù

【靰鞡】wùla = 乌拉 wùla

痦 wù

【痦子】wùzi〈名〉［医学］mole

婺 Wù

〈名〉1 ▸p. 294（婺江）Wujiang River [in Jiangxi Province] 2〈旧〉（婺州）Wuzhou [old prefecture in and around present-day Jinhua in Zhejiang Province]
【婺剧】wùjù〈名〉*Wuju opera* [local opera popular in Jinhua Prefecture, Zhejiang Province]

骛（騖）wù

〈动〉〈书〉1（奔驰）move about freely and quickly 2（追求）go after: ▸好高～远

雾（霧）wù

〈名〉1（雾气）fog: 一场大～ a heavy fog ‖ 浓～ thick fog ‖ 机场因～关闭。Flights have been grounded due to fog. ▸～气, 腾云驾～, 云～ 2（雾状水滴）fine spray: ▸喷～器
【雾霭】wù'ǎi〈名〉fog: 江面上～蒙蒙。The river is covered in mist.
【雾沉沉】wùchénchén〈形〉foggy: 这儿冬天经常～的。It's often foggy here in winter.
【雾灯】wùdēng〈名〉fog lamp
【雾都】wùdū〈名〉foggy city
【雾化】wùhuà〈动〉atomize
【雾里看花】wùlǐ-kànhuā〈成〉〈喻〉blurred vision
【雾茫茫】wùmángmáng〈形〉foggy: ～的大海/山谷 foggy sea/valley
【雾气】wùqì〈名〉fog: 山谷里～腾腾。Mists arose from the valley. ‖ 她的眼镜上蒙了一层～。Her glasses fogged up.
【雾凇】wùsōng〈名〉［气象］rime
【雾锁迷障】wùsuǒmízhàng〈成〉be shrouded in a milky-white mist
【雾消云散】wùxiāo-yúnsàn〈成〉the fog lifted and the clouds dispersed

寤 wù

〈形〉〈书〉awake
【寤寐不忘】wùmèi bùwàng〈成〉not to forget sth., asleep or awake

鹜（鶩）wù

〈名〉〈书〉wild duck: ▸趋之若～

鋈 wù

〈名〉〈书〉1（白铜）white copper 2（镀）plating

W

xī

夕 xī〈名〉1 (傍晚) sunset: ▸~阳, ~照 2 (晚上) evening: 风雨之~ stormy night ▸朝不保~, 朝发~至

【夕烟】xīyān〈名〉evening smoke and haze: ~袅袅。Evening smoke curled upward.

【夕阳】xīyáng A〈名〉1〈本〉setting sun: 看~西下 watch the sunset ‖ ~无限好，只是近黄昏。The sunset is so beautiful but it will soon be dusk. 2〈喻〉(指晚年) final stage of a person's life: 老人很清楚自己已~无多。The old man knows that he is in the twilight of his life. B〈形〉〈喻〉fading, declining: ~产业 sunset industry

【夕照】xīzhào〈名〉〈书〉evening glow: ~中，田园更富有诗情画意。In the evening glow, the pastoral scene is just like a painting or a poem.

兮 xī〈助〉〈书〉[an exclamatory or emotive word, used in the middle of or at the end of a line of poetry in a way similar to the modern 啊, to mark a pause or some emotion]: 风萧萧~易水寒，壮士一去~不复还。The wind is wailing and the River Yi is cold; a hero sets forth, never to return.

【兮兮】xīxī〈后缀〉〈方〉very: 一副可怜~的样子 have a wretched look

西 xī〈名〉1 ▸**p. 205** (指方向) west: ~海岸 west coast ‖ ~偏北/南 west by north/south ‖ ~去的列车 westbound train ‖ 面朝~的阳台 west-facing balcony ‖ 淮河以~ to the west of the Huaihe River ‖ 由~向东流 flow from west to east ▸~半球, 声东击~ 2 (极乐世界) Western Paradise [in Buddhism]: 撒手~去 pass away ‖ 一命归~ go west 3 Xī (欧美各国) Western world: 中~文化交流 cultural exchange between China and the West ▸~化, ~医, 学贯中~

【西安】Xī'ān ▸**p. 661**〈名〉Xi'an [capital of Shaanxi Province (陕西)]

【西安事变】Xī'ān Shìbiàn〈名〉Xi'an Incident [1936, when Generals Zhang Xueliang (张学良) and Yang Hucheng (杨虎城) took Chiang Kai-shek (蒋介石) hostage and forced him to unite with the Communist Party in a national war against the Japanese invaders]

【西澳大利亚州】Xī'àodàlìyàzhōu〈名〉Western Australia

【西班牙】Xībānyá〈名〉Spain: ~人 Spaniard ‖ ~王国 Kingdom of Spain ‖ ~语 Spanish ‖ ~斗牛士 Spanish matador

【西半球】xībànqiú〈名〉western hemisphere

【西北】xīběi〈名〉1 ▸**p. 205** (指方向) north-west: 面朝/向~ face north-west ‖ ~角 north-western corner 2 Xīběi (特指中国西北地区) North-west China: 开发大~ develop North-west China

【西北风】xīběifēng〈名〉north-westerly wind: 一阵阵~ blasts of north-westerly winds ‖〈喻〉喝~ go hungry

【西边】xībian ▸**p. 205**〈名〉west: 甘肃在陕西的~。Gansu is west of Shaanxi.

【西伯利亚】Xībólìyà〈名〉Siberia: ~人 Siberian ‖ ~寒流 Siberian cold current

【西部】xībù ▸**p. 205**〈名〉western part: ~大开发 large-scale development of China's western region ‖ 青海位于中国的~。Qinghai is in the west of China.

【西部边陲】xībù biānchuí〈名〉western frontier

【西部片】xībùpiàn〈名〉western (film)

【西餐】xīcān〈名〉Western food: 吃~ eat Western food ‖ ~馆 Western food restaurant

【西德】Xīdé〈名〉West Germany

【西点】xīdiǎn〈名〉Western-style pastry

【西点军校】Xīdiǎn Jūnxiào〈名〉West Point Military Academy

【西电东送】xī diàn dōng sòng〈名〉West-to-East Power Transfer

【西番莲】xīfānlián〈名〉[植物] 1 (指草本植物) passion flower 2 (指果实) passion fruit 3 (大丽花) dahlia

【西方】xīfāng〈名〉1 ▸**p. 205** (指方向) west: 正~ due west 2 (指资本主义发达国家) the West: ~国家 Western countries ‖ ~文化/价值观念/文明/哲学 Western culture/values/civilization/philosophy ‖ ~人 Westerner 3 [佛教] Western Paradise: ~极乐世界 Western Paradise

【西非】Xī Fēi〈名〉West Africa: ~国家 West African countries

【西风】xīfēng〈名〉1 (指风) westerly wind: 寒冷的~ chilly west wind 2 (指文化、风俗) Western social mores and culture: ~东渐。Western culture is gradually spreading East. 3〈喻〉(指势力) decaying influences

【西弗吉尼亚州】Xīfújíníyàzhōu〈名〉West Virginia

【西服】xīfú〈名〉suit: 三件套~ three-piece suit

【西格拉摩根郡】Xīgélāmógēnjùn〈名〉West Glamorgan

【西宫】xīgōng〈名〉〈旧〉1 (指宫殿) residence of imperial concubine or concubines 2 (指妃子) imperial concubine: ~娘娘 Lady of the Western Palace [complimentary term for the emperor's secondary wife, next in importance to the first wife living in the Eastern Palace]

【西瓜】xīguā〈名〉watermelon: 无籽~ seedless watermelon ‖ ~子 watermelon seed

【西汉】Xī Hàn〈名〉Western Han Dynasty

【西河大鼓】xīhé dàgǔ〈名〉[曲艺] *xihe dagu* [a kind of *dagu* (大鼓) drum popular in Hebei and Henan provinces]

【西红柿】xīhóngshì〈名〉tomato: ~炒鸡蛋 scrambled eggs with tomatoes

【西葫芦】xīhúlu〈名〉[植物] courgette〈英〉; zucchini〈美〉

【西湖】Xīhú ▸**p. 305**〈名〉West Lake: ~美景 enchanting scenery of the West Lake

【西化】xīhuà〈动〉westernize: 全盘~ wholesale westernization

【西画】xīhuà〈简称〉= 西洋画

【西晋】Xī Jìn〈名〉Western Jin Dynasty

【西经】xījīng〈名〉[地理] west longitude: 我们目前位于~20°，北纬30°。Our current position is longitude 20° W, latitude 30° N.

【西口】xīkǒu〈名〉passes in the western sections of the Great Wall: 走~ go to make a living in the west beyond the Great wall

【西裤】xīkù〈名〉suit trousers

【西兰花】xīlánhuā〈名〉[植物] broccoli

【西历】xīlì ▸**p. 618**〈名〉〈旧〉Gregorian calendar

【西洛锡安郡】Xīluòxī'ānjùn〈名〉West Lothian

【西米】xīmǐ〈名〉sago: ~淀粉 sago starch ‖ ~粉 sago flour

【西米德兰兹郡】Xīmǐdélánzījùn〈名〉West Midlands

【西面】xīmiàn ▸**p. 205**〈名〉west: ~临海 border on the sea in the west

【西南】xīnán〈名〉1 ▸**p. 205** (指方向) southwest: ~方向 in a south-westerly direction ‖ ~角 south-west corner 2 Xīnán (特指中国西南地区) South-west China

【西宁】Xīníng ▸**p. 661**〈名〉Xining [capital of Qinghai Province (青海)]

【西欧】Xī Ōu〈名〉1 (指地区) Western Europe: ~国家 Western European countries 2 (指国家) Western European countries

【西皮】xīpí〈名〉[戏曲] *xipi* [basic group of operatic tunes usu accompanied by *huqin* (胡琴)]

【西气东输】xī qì dōng shū〈名〉West-to-East Gas Transfer

【西撒哈拉】Xīsāhālā〈名〉Western Sahara

【西萨摩亚】Xīsàmóyà〈名〉Western Samoa

【西萨塞克斯郡】Xīsàsàikèsījùn〈名〉West Sussex

【西沙群岛】Xīshā Qúndǎo〈名〉Paracel Islands [called 'Xisha Islands' in China]

【西晒】xīshài〈动〉have a western exposure to the sun: 那是间~的房子。That room faces west with exposure to the sun.

【西山】xīshān〈名〉1 (西边的山) western mountains 2 Xīshān (指景点) Western Hills [famous scenic spot to the west of Beijing]

【西施】Xīshī〈名〉1 (春秋越国一美女) Xishi [name of a beauty in the State of Yue during the late Spring and Autumn Period]

2▶（泛指美女） beautiful woman: ▸情人眼里出～

【西式】 xīshì 〈形〉 Western-style: ～家具 Western-style furniture ‖ ～甜点 Western-style dessert

【西天】 xītiān 〈名〉［佛教］ 1▶（极乐世界） Buddhist Paradise: ▸上～ 2▶（印度） India: ～取经 journey westwards to India in order to obtain Buddhist's scriptures

【西王母】 Xīwángmǔ 〈名〉 Queen Mother of the West [mythological figure, usu described as a beautiful immortal]

【西魏】 Xī Wèi 〈名〉 Western Wei Dynasty

【西文】 xīwén ▸p. 918 〈名〉 western languages: ～图书 western language books

【西席】 xīxí 〈名〉〈旧〉 1▶（宾客） guest 2▶（家庭教师） private tutor

【西夏】 Xī Xià 〈名〉 Western Xia regime

【西学】 xīxué 〈名〉 Western learning [late Qing Dynasty term for Western natural and social sciences]: 崇尚～ advocate Western learning ‖ ～东渐。 Western learning was progressively spreading East.

【西亚】 Xī Yà 〈名〉 South-west Asia

【西洋】 Xīyáng 〈名〉〈旧〉 1▶（指国家） Western world: ～文学/艺术 Western literature/art ‖ ～音乐 Western music 2▶（指海洋） Western Seas [referring to the region west of the South China Sea]: 郑和七下～ Zheng He's seven voyages to the Western Seas

【西洋红】 xīyánghóng 〈名〉 carmine

【西洋画】 xīyánghuà 〈名〉 Western painting

【西洋景】 xīyángjǐng 〈名〉 1▶（指文娱器具） peep show 2▶（指外来新奇事物） trickery: 戳穿～ expose sb.'s tricks

【西洋镜】 xīyángjìng = 西洋景 xīyángjǐng

【西洋参】 xīyángshēn 〈名〉 American ginseng

【西药】 xīyào 〈名〉 Western medicine

【西医】 xīyī 〈名〉 1▶（指医学） Western medicine: 中～结合 combine traditional Chinese medicine and Western medicine 2▶（指人） doctor trained in Western medicine: 看～ see a doctor trained in Western medicine

【西印度群岛】 Xīyìndù Qúndǎo 〈名〉 West Indies

【西游记】 Xīyóujì 〈名〉 *Journey to the West*

> **《西游记》**
>
> *Journey to the West*, a mythical story from the Ming Dynasty, and one of the four famous Chinese classical works. Authorship is ascribed to Wu Cheng'en (吴承恩). The story, told in 100 chapters, is based on folk legends about the monk Tang Seng's journey to the west to bring back Buddhist scriptures. The story of Tang Seng is based on real events. In 603 AD the Tang Dynasty monk, Xuan Zang, travelled from Chang'an (present-day Xi'an) to India, in order to obtain a fuller understanding of Buddhist doctrine. After an arduous journey, he returned with over 600 volumes of Buddhist texts. The four characters in the story are Tang Seng, Sun Wukong (Monkey), Zhu Bajie (Pigsy) and Sha Seng (Friar Sand). On the way to the west these characters vanquish numerous demons and monsters, encounter 81 trials and difficulties, before finally returning with the scriptures.

【西语】 xīyǔ ▸p. 918 〈名〉 1▶（欧美语言） Western language: ～系 department of Western languages 2▶（西班牙语） Spanish

【西域】 Xīyù 〈名〉 Western Regions [Han Dynasty term for the area, including present-day Xinjiang, parts of Central Asia and beyond]: 张骞通～ Zhang Qian's missions to the Western Regions

【西元】 xīyuán ▸p. 618 〈名〉〈旧〉 Gregorian calendar

【西约克郡】 Xīyuēkèjùn 〈名〉 West Yorkshire

【西乐】 xīyuè 〈名〉 Western music: 通晓～ be well-versed in Western music

【西岳】 Xīyuè 〈名〉 Western Sacred Mountain [Huashan Mountain (华山) in Shaanxi Province]

【西藏】 Xīzàng ▸p. 661 〈名〉 Tibet: ～自治区 Tibet Autonomous Region ‖ ～高原 Tibet plateau

【西周】 Xī Zhōu 〈名〉 Western Zhou Dynasty

【西装】 xīzhuāng = 西服 xīfú

【西子】 Xīzǐ = 西施 Xīshī

【西子湖】 Xīzǐhú = 西湖 Xīhú

吸

xī 〈动〉 1▶（引入体内） breathe in: ～气 take in some air ‖ ～一口新鲜空气 get a breath of fresh air ‖ 深～一口烟 suck/pull deeply on a cigarette ▸呼～, 吮～ 2▶（吸收） absorb: 海绵～水。 A sponge absorbs water. ‖ 软纸容易～墨水。 Soft paper tends to blot. 3▶（吸引） attract: 异性相～。 Opposite sexes are attracted to one another. ▸～力, ～铁石, ～引

【吸潮】 xīcháo 〈动〉 absorb moisture

【吸尘器】 xīchénqì 〈名〉 vacuum cleaner; Hoover 〈英〉

【吸虫】 xīchóng 〈名〉［动物］ fleece worm: 肝～ liver fluke ‖ ～病 fluke disease

【吸筹】 xīchóu 〈动〉［金融］ accumulate: 在股指处于低位时～，期待反弹时获利。 Buy low and reap profits on the rebound.

【吸储】 xīchǔ 〈动〉 [of banks, credit unions, etc.] attract deposits: 扩大～渠道 expand channels of attracting deposits

【吸顶灯】 xīdǐngdēng 〈名〉 ceiling lamp

【吸毒】 xīdú 〈动〉 take drugs: ～成瘾 be addicted to drugs ‖ ～者 drug user

【吸附】 xīfù 〈动〉［化学］ adsorb: ～毒气和杂质 adsorb poisonous gases and foreign matter ‖ ～剂 adsorbent

【吸管】 xīguǎn 〈名〉 1▶（指细管） straw: 弯曲～ curly straw 2▶［化学］ pipette

【吸汗】 xīhàn 〈动〉 absorb sweat: ～袜 sweat socks

【吸力】 xīlì 〈名〉 attraction: 磁性～ magnetic attraction

【吸墨纸】 xīmòzhǐ 〈名〉 blotting paper

【吸纳】 xīnà 〈动〉 1▶（吸入） inhale: ～新鲜空气 take in fresh air 2▶（接纳） absorb: ～别人的长处 absorb others' good qualities ‖ ～存款 accept savings deposits ‖ ～劳动力 absorb a labour force 3▶（采纳） accept: ～合理化建议 accept rationalization proposals ‖ ～先进技术 adopt advanced technology

【吸奶器】 xīnǎiqì 〈名〉 breast pump

【吸泥泵】 xīníbèng 〈名〉 dredge pump

【吸泥船】 xīníchuán 〈名〉 hydraulic suction dredge

【吸盘】 xīpán 〈名〉［机械］［动物］ sucker: 用橡皮～把衣钩吸在墙上 fix a hook to the wall with a sucker ‖ 章鱼的腕足有～。 An octopus has suckers on its tentacles.

【吸气】 xīqì 〈动〉 inhale: 用嘴～ breathe through one's mouth ‖ 深～ inhale deeply

【吸取】 xīqǔ 〈动〉 draw: ～教训 learn a lesson ‖ ～精华 absorb the quintessence ‖ ～水分 draw water ‖ ～养料 draw nourishment

【吸入】 xīrù 〈动〉 inhale: ～新鲜空气 breathe in the fresh air

【吸声】 xīshēng 〈名〉［建筑］ sound absorption: ～器 sound absorber

【吸食】 xīshí 〈动〉 suck: ～毒品 take drugs ‖ 用吸管～果汁 suck fruit juice through a straw

【吸收】 xīshōu 〈动〉 1▶（指机体） take in: ～养分 absorb nutrients ‖ 有些食物很容易被～。 Some food is easy to ingest. ‖ 树从土壤中～大量水分和营养。 Trees absorb large amounts of water and nutrients from the soil. 2▶（泛指吸入） absorb: ～光线/声音/热量 absorb light rays/sound/heat ‖ ～外资 absorb foreign capital ‖ ～新思想/知识 assimilate new ideas/knowledge 3▶（接纳） admit: ～新成员 admit new members ‖ ～入党 admit into the Party ‖ ～下岗工人 provide employment to laid-off workers ‖ ～中国加入世贸组织 admit China to the WTO

【吸收塔】 xīshōutǎ 〈名〉［化工］ absorption tower

【吸水】 xīshuǐ 〈动〉 absorb water: ～纸 absorbent paper

【吸吮】 xīshǔn 〈动〉 suck: ～母乳 nurse at the mother's breast ‖ ～拇指 suck one's thumb

【吸铁石】 xītiěshí 〈名〉 magnet: 用～吸出 extract with a magnet

【吸血鬼】 xīxuèguǐ ▸p. 274 〈名〉 1▶〈本〉 vampire 2▶〈喻〉 parasite

【吸烟】 xīyān 〈动〉 smoke: 禁止～ ban smoking ‖ 请勿～。 No smoking. ‖ ～有害健康。 Smoking is harmful to one's health.

【吸烟室】 xīyānshì 〈名〉 smoking room

【吸氧】 xīyǎng 〈动〉 take in oxygen

【吸音板】 xīyīnbǎn 〈名〉［建筑］ acoustic board

【吸引】 xīyǐn 〈动〉 attract: ～外资 attract foreign capital ‖ ～注意力 attract sb.'s attention ‖ 这部电影很～人。 This film is really drawing the crowds.

【吸引力】 xīyǐnlì 〈名〉 appeal: 侦探小说对我很有～。 I am especially fond of detective novels. ‖ 这部电影对年轻人有极大的～。 The film has a great attraction for young people.

【吸脂】 xīzhī 〈动〉 perform liposuction: ～减肥 liposuction weight loss

【吸脂术】 xīzhīshù 〈名〉［医学］ liposuction

【吸嘴】 xīzuǐ 〈名〉 suction nozzle

汐

xī 〈名〉 evening tide: ▸潮～

希[1]

xī = 稀 xī A2

希[2]

xī 〈动〉 hope: ～准时与会。 Please attend the meeting on time. ‖ 微薄之礼，敬～笑纳。 I hope you will accept this small gift from me. ▸～冀, ～图, ～望

【希伯来语】 Xībóláiyǔ ▸p. 918 〈名〉 Hebrew

【希罕】 xīhan = 稀罕 xīhan

【希冀】 xījì 〈书〉 = 希望 xīwàng

【希腊】 Xīlà 〈名〉 Greece: ～悲剧/喜剧 Greek tragedy/comedy ‖ ～共和国 Hellenic Republic ‖ ～人 Greek ‖ ～语 Greek

【希腊字母】 Xīlà zìmǔ 〈名〉 Greek alphabet

【希奇】 xīqí = 稀奇 xīqí

【希求】 xīqiú A 〈动〉 hope for: ～得到经济援助 hope to get financial support B 〈名〉 hope: 他们对谈判成功不抱任何～。 They

X

didn't hold out any hope for the success of the negotiation.

【希少】xīshǎo = 稀少 xīshǎo

【希世】xīshì = 稀世 xīshì

【希图】xītú〈动〉 have wild hopes for: ～蒙混过关 try to wangle one's way out of a bad situation ‖ ～逃跑 attempt to escape

【希望】xīwàng **A**〈动〉 hope: ～奇迹出现 hope for a miracle ‖ ～你常来做客。Please drop in whenever you have time. ‖ 他非常～能上大学。He has fervent hopes of going to university. **B**〈名〉 **1**（愿望） hope: 一线～ a glimmer of hope ‖ 把～变成现实 turn hopes into reality ‖ 一切～都破灭了。All hopes were dashed. **2**（寄托的对象） hope: 他是我们队获胜的唯一～。He is our team's only hope for victory.

【希望工程】Xīwàng Gōngchéng〈名〉 Project Hope [project helping children from poor families to receive education]

【希望小学】Xīwàng Xiǎoxué〈名〉 Hope Primary School [primary school funded by Project Hope]

【希有】xīyǒu = 稀有 xīyǒu

昔

xī〈名〉 former times: 抚今追～ reflect on the past in the light of the present ‖ 今胜于～。The present is superior to the past. ►今非～比, 往～

【昔年】xīnián〈名〉〈书〉 former years: ～同窗 former classmates

【昔日】xīrì〈名〉 former times: ～的风俗 former customs ‖ ～的荒山如今变成了果园。The barren hills of former times have become the orchards of today.

【昔时】xīshí〈名〉〈书〉 former times: 他们～是朋友。They were formerly friends.

析

xī〈动〉 **1**（分开） divide: ►分崩离～, 条分缕～ **2**（辨别） dissect: ►辨～, 分～

【析产】xīchǎn〈动〉 [of family members] divide up family property

【析出】xīchū〈动〉 **1**（分析出来） abstract **2**［化学］ separate out: 海水可以～盐。Salt may be separated from seawater.

【析居】xījū〈动〉〈书〉 [of family members] live separately: 兄弟～。The brothers lead separate lives in their own houses.

【析疑】xīyí〈动〉〈书〉 clear up a doubt

矽

xī〈名〉〈旧〉［化学］ silicon (Si)

【矽肺】xīfèi ►**p. 50**〈名〉［医学］ silicosis

【矽钢】xīgāng〈名〉［冶金］ silicon steel: ～片 silicon steel sheet

郗

Xī〈名〉 Xi [surname]
►Chī

恓

xī

【恓惶】xīhuáng〈形〉〈书〉 alarmed and vexed

栖

xī
►qī

【栖栖】xīxī〈形〉〈书〉 restless

唏

xī〈叹〉 humph: 那你就别来! ～, 谁稀罕似的! Don't come, then! Humph, see if I care!

【唏嘘】xīxū = 欷歔 xīxū

牺（犧）

xī〈名〉〈书〉 sacrifice: ～牛/羊 sacrificial ox/goat

【牺牲】xīshēng **A**〈名〉 sacrificial beast **B**〈动〉 **1** ►**p. 772**（指舍弃生命） make the supreme sacrifice: ～生命 sacrifice one's life ‖ 光荣～ die a glorious death ‖ 为国～ make the supreme sacrifice for one's country **2**（指放弃） sacrifice: ～个人利益 sacrifice one's personal interest ‖ ～休息时间 give up one's leisure time ‖ ～原则 sacrifice one's principles

【牺牲品】xīshēngpǐn〈名〉 prey: 成了包办婚姻的～ fall prey to the arranged marriage system

息

xī

A〈名〉 **1**（呼吸） breath: 战斗到最后一～ fight to one's last breath ‖ 一～尚存 there is still a breath left in sb. ►鼻～, 喘～, 叹～ **2**〈书〉（子女） children: 弱～ little sons or daughters ►子～ **3**（利息） interest: 还本付～ return the capital and pay the interest ‖ 低/高～贷款 loan at low/high interest ‖ 年/月～ annual/monthly interest ►股～, 利～ **4**（消息） news: 互通声～ keep each other informed ►消～, 信～

B〈动〉 **1**（休息） have a rest: ►安～, 稍～, 歇～, 休～ **2**（停止） cease: 生命不～, 战斗不止 go on fighting until one's last breath ‖ 掌声经久不～。The applause was prolonged. ►～怒 **3**（滋生） multiply: ►～肉, 蕃～, 生～

【息兵】xībīng〈动〉 stop fighting

【息肩】xījiān〈动〉〈书〉 have a rest: 他年事已高, 该～了。As he is advanced in age, he should be allowed to take breaks.

【息怒】xīnù〈动〉 cease to be angry: 请～, 这事可以商量着办。Calm down, please. The matter can be settled through discussion.

【息肉】xīròu ►**p. 50**〈名〉［医学］ polyp: 直肠～ rectal polyp

【息事宁人】xīshì-níngrén〈成〉 **1**（指从中调解） reconcile a dispute: 他左劝右说, 才得以～。It took him a lot of talking to bring about a reconciliation. **2**（指自行让步） make concessions to avoid further trouble: 为了～, 这事就别再提了。To avoid further dispute, let's let the matter drop.

【息讼】xīsòng〈动〉〈旧〉 drop a lawsuit: 只要他能答应我提出的条件, 我可以～。So long as he accepts my condition, I can drop the lawsuit.

【息息相关】xīxī-xiāngguān〈成〉 be closely linked: 祖国的命运与个人的命运～。The fate of the country is bound up with the fate of the individual.

【息息相通】xīxī-xiāngtōng = 息息相关 xīxī-xiāngguān

【息心】xīxīn〈动〉 **1**〈方〉（心情放松） feel relieved: 听说他伤势很轻, 全家人都～。The family were relieved to learn that his injury was only minor. **2**〈书〉（除去杂念） set one's mind at rest

【息影】xīyǐng〈动〉 **1**〈书〉（退隐闲居） retire from public life: ～乡间 go into seclusion in the countryside ‖ 杜门～ shut oneself away and live a private life **2**（不再拍戏） stop acting: 她已～三年。She stopped doing films three years ago.

【息止】xīzhǐ〈动〉 cease: 永不～地工作 work tirelessly

奚

xī〈代〉〈书〉（为何） why;（如何） how;（哪个） which;（什么） what;（哪里） where: 此～疾哉? What's the disease?

【奚落】xīluò〈动〉 sneer at: 别再～他了。Stop ridiculing him.

菥

xī

【菥蓂】xīmì〈名〉［植物］ penny cress

硒

xī〈名〉［化学］ selenium (Se)

晞

xī〈书〉

A〈形〉 dry: 晨露未～。The dew is still damp.

B〈动〉 dawn: 东方渐～。The day was dawning.

欷

xī

【欷歔】xīxū〈动〉〈书〉 sob: 掩面～ hide one's face in one's hands and weep

悉

xī

A〈动〉 specify: 来函敬～。I've read your letter. ►获～, 惊～, 熟～

B〈副〉 completely: ～已渡河 everyone has made it across the river ►～力, ～数, ～心

【悉力】xīlì〈动〉〈书〉 go all out: ～以赴, 追求卓越 not spare oneself in the pursuit of excellence

【悉尼】Xīní〈名〉 Sydney: ～歌剧院 Sydney Opera House

【悉数】xīshǔ〈动〉〈书〉 enumerate in full: 种类繁多, 不可～。There are too many varieties to list.

【悉数】xīshù〈名〉 full amount: ～奉还 gratefully return all that has been borrowed ‖ ～上缴 turn over every single one

【悉听尊便】xītīng-zūnbiàn〈成〉 you are at liberty to do whatever you please

【悉心】xīxīn〈动〉 devote all one's attention: ～研究 devote oneself to the study of sth. ‖ 他～照料病榻上的妻子。He is taking the utmost care of his wife who is confined to a sickbed.

烯

xī〈名〉［化工］ alkene: ►乙～

淅

xī〈动〉〈书〉 wash rice in a pan or basket

【淅沥】xīlì〈拟〉 [referring to the sound of a drizzle, a breeze, or falling leaves] patter: 秋风～。The autumn wind is rustling. ‖ 小雨淅淅沥沥地下了一整天。The rain has been pattering down all day.

【淅飒】xīsà〈拟〉 [referring to the sound of a breeze, a drizzle, etc.] rustle

【淅淅】xīxī〈拟〉 [referring to the quiet irregular sound of a drizzle, a breeze, etc.] rustle: 微风～。The breeze is rustling.

惜

xī〈动〉 **1**（珍惜） cherish: ～寸阴 treasure every moment ►爱～, 怜～, 珍～ **2**（吝惜） grudge: 不～工本 spare no expense ►吝～, 在所不～ **3**（可惜） pity: ►可～, 叹～, 痛～

【惜败】xībài〈动〉［体育］ be unfortunate to lose by just a small margin

【惜别】xībié〈动〉 be reluctant to part: 依依～ be reluctant to part ‖ ～之情 reluctance to part

【惜贷】xīdài〈动〉 be reluctant to lend: 国有商业银行的～是民营企业发展的瓶颈。The state-owned commercial banks' reluctance to lend is a bottleneck in the development of private enterprises.

【惜福】xīfú〈动〉 cherish one's blessings and use them sparingly: 老人生平省俭～。The old man refrains from leading an excessively comfortable life.

【惜老怜贫】xīlǎo-liánpín〈成〉 have compassion for the old and the poor
【惜力】xīlì〈动〉 not slack: 干活不~ spare no effort in one's work
【惜墨如金】xīmò-rújīn〈成〉 be scrupulous and succinct in writing or painting
【惜时】xīshí〈动〉 cherish one's time: ~如金 treasure one's time more than anything else
【惜售】xīshòu〈动〉 be unwilling to sell: 由于~造成积压。 The stocks have been piling up owing to the reluctance to sell.
【惜阴】xīyīn〈动〉〈书〉 make good use of every moment: 他是个~之士。 He is a person who makes the most of every single minute.
【惜玉怜香】xīyù-liánxiāng = 怜香惜玉 liánxiāng-xīyù

晰 xī〈形〉 clear: ►明~, 清~

晞 xī〈动〉〈书〉 ①(瞭望) look into the distance ②(仰慕) look up to

稀 xī
A〈形〉 ①(疏松) sparse: 头发~ be thin on top ‖ 月明星~。 The moon is bright and the stars are few. ►地广人~ ②(罕见) rare: 人生七十古来~。 Since ancient times, men have rarely lived to the age of seventy. ►~客, ~少, 物以~为贵 ③(含水多) thin: ~硫酸 dilute sulphuric acid ‖ ~泥/粥 thin mud/gruel ‖ 面和得太~。 The dough is too watery. ►~饭
B〈名〉 thin thing: ►拉~, 糖~
C〈副〉 very: ►~烂
【稀巴烂】xībalàn = 稀烂 xīlàn 2
【稀薄】xībó〈形〉 thin: ~气体 rarefied gas ‖ 高海拔地区空气~。 The air is thin at high altitudes.
【稀饭】xīfàn〈名〉 rice or millet gruel: 熬~ make gruel
【稀罕】xīhan A〈形〉 rare: 这里下雪是~事。 Snow is rare in this region. B〈动〉 value highly: 我才不~你的臭钱! I couldn't care less about your lousy money! C〈名〉 rarity: 看~ enjoy a rare sight
【稀客】xīkè〈名〉 rare visitor: 你是~。 Your visits are infrequent.
【稀拉】xīla〈形〉 ①(稀疏) sparse: ~的枯草 sparse withered grass ‖ ~的白发 thin white hair ②〈方〉(散漫) sloppy: 作风~ sloppy way of doing things
【稀烂】xīlàn〈形〉 ①(极烂) pulpy: 鸡炖得~。 The chicken was stewed to a pulp. ②(极碎) smashed to smithereens: 他把店窗砸了个~。 He shattered the shop window to smithereens. ‖ 一篮子鸡蛋摔了个~。 The basket of eggs was completely smashed.
【稀朗】xīlǎng〈形〉 [of lights or stars] sparse or scattered but bright: 星光~之夜 a night with a few stars shining brightly in the sky
【稀里糊涂】xīlihútú〈形〉 ①(迷糊) muddle-headed: 这道算术题他讲了两遍, 我还是~的。 He explained the maths problem twice, but I was none the wiser. ②(马虎) careless: ~地答应 make a casual promise ‖ 想都没想, 我就~地接受了这份工作。 Without a second thought I agreed to take the job.
【稀里哗啦】xīlihuālā A〈拟〉 crash: 那座楼~地坍塌了。 The building collapsed like a house of cards. ‖ 雨~地下了起来。 The rain came down in buckets. B〈形〉 ①(粉碎) shattered: 餐馆里的家具被砸了个~。 All the furniture in the restaurant was smashed. ②(七零八落) scattered in disorder: 旧书旧报~堆了一地。 Old books and newspapers were scattered about on the floor.
【稀里马虎】xīli-mǎhu〈形〉 careless: 他的工作有些~。 His work is somewhat slipshod.
【稀料】xīliào〈名〉 solvent: 汽油是一种能去除油污的~。 Petrol is a solvent that removes grease spots.
【稀溜溜】xīliūliū〈形〉 watery: 喝碗~的粥 have a bowl of watery porridge
【稀泥】xīní〈名〉 watery mud: 抹~ plaster watery mud
【稀奇】xīqí〈形〉 strange: 这东西并不~。 There's nothing strange about this at all.
【稀奇古怪】xīqí-gǔguài〈成〉 peculiar: ~的旧风俗 quaint old custom ‖ ~的念头 odd idea
【稀缺】xīquē〈形〉 scarce: ~商品 commodity in short supply ‖ ~资源 resources in short supply
【稀少】xīshǎo〈形〉 sparse: 人口/人烟~ be sparsely populated ‖ 街上车辆/行人~。 There was little traffic/there were few people in the street.
【稀世】xīshì〈形〉 rare: ~之才 rare genius ‖ ~珍宝 rare treasure
【稀释】xīshì〈动〉 dilute: ~剂 thinning agent
【稀释液】xīshìyè〈名〉［化学］ dilution
【稀疏】xīshū〈形〉 few and far between: ~的枪声 sporadic gunfire ‖ 树木~。 The trees are becoming sparse. ‖ 他的头发变~了。 His hair is thinning.
【稀松】xīsōng〈形〉 ①(懒散) lax: 作风~ sloppy style of work ②(差劲) bad: 服务~。 The service was not up to much. ‖ 由于管理~, 公司陷入了财政困境。 Bad management has put the company in a difficult financial position. ③(无关紧要) trivial: 那些~小事不值一提。 Such trivial matters are not worth talking about.
【稀土金属】xītǔ jīnshǔ〈名〉［冶金］ rare-earth metal
【稀土元素】xītǔ yuánsù〈名〉［化学］ rare-earth element
【稀稀拉拉】xīxilālā〈形〉 sparse: 他头顶上长了~的几根头发。 He's thin on top. ‖ 与会者~。 The meeting was poorly attended.
【稀稀落落】xīxīluòluò = 稀稀拉拉 xīxilālā
【稀有】xīyǒu〈形〉 rare: ~的珍品 rare treasure ‖ ~物种/资源 rare species/resource
【稀有金属】xīyǒu jīnshǔ〈名〉［化学］ scarce metal
【稀有气体】xīyǒu qìtǐ〈名〉 noble gas
【稀有元素】xīyǒu yuánsù〈名〉［化学］ rare element
【稀粥】xīzhōu〈名〉 thin gruel

傒 xī
【傒倖】xīxìng〈形〉 [often seen in early vernacular] vexed

翕 xī〈书〉
A〈形〉 amiable and compliant
B〈动〉 furl: ►~动, ~张
【翕动】xīdòng〈动〉〈书〉 [of lips, nostrils, etc.] open and close: ~翅膀 flap the wings ‖ 她嘴唇~了几下, 却没有说什么。 She moved her lips but did not say anything.
【翕然】xīrán〈形〉〈书〉 ①(言行一致) unanimous: ~反对 be unanimously opposed ‖ ~从之 follow in unison ②(安定) stable: 境内~ stable domestic situation
【翕张】xīzhāng〈动〉〈书〉 furl and unfurl: 双目~ with one's eyes opening and closing alternately

腊 xī〈名〉〈书〉 dry meat
►là

粞 xī〈名〉 ①〈书〉(碎米) crushed rice: 糠~ bran ②〈方〉(米糠) chaff

犀 xī〈名〉［动物］ rhinoceros
【犀角】xījiǎo〈名〉 rhinoceros horn
【犀利】xīlì〈形〉 sharp: 文笔~ wield a caustic pen ‖ ~的目光 sharp eyes
【犀牛】xīniú〈名〉［动物］ rhinoceros

皙 xī〈形〉〈书〉 [of skin] fair: ►白皙

锡（錫） xī〈名〉［化学］ stannum (Sn)
【锡伯族】Xībózú〈名〉 Xibe ethnic group
【锡箔】xībó〈名〉 tinfoil paper [formerly used as a funeral offering]
【锡尔迪吉恩郡】Xī'ěrdíjí'ēnjùn〈名〉 Ceredigion
【锡匠】xījiang〈名〉 tinsmith
【锡金】Xījīn〈名〉 Sikkim: ~人 Sikkimese
【锡剧】xījù〈名〉 Wuxi opera
【锡矿】xīkuàng〈名〉 tin ore
【锡器】xīqì〈名〉 tinware
【锡杖】xīzhàng〈名〉［宗教］ monk's staff
【锡纸】xīzhǐ〈名〉 tinfoil

溪 xī〈名〉 brook: 清~ clear stream ‖ ~声潺潺。 The brook warbled. ►~流, 小~
【溪谷】xīgǔ〈名〉 gully
【溪涧】xījiàn〈名〉 mountain stream
【溪流】xīliú〈名〉 brook: 波光粼粼/潺潺/弯弯曲曲的~ sparkling/babbling/meandering stream ‖ 山间~ mountain stream

裼 xī〈动〉〈书〉 unbutton or divest one's upper garment: 袒~裸裎 stark naked

熙 xī〈形〉〈书〉 bright and sunny
【熙和】xīhé〈形〉〈书〉 ①(和乐) congenial and happy ②(温暖) pleasantly warm: ~的风/空气 genial wind/air
【熙来攘往】xīlái-rǎngwǎng = 熙熙攘攘 xīxī-rǎngrǎng
【熙攘】xīrǎng = 熙熙攘攘 xīxī-rǎngrǎng
【熙熙攘攘】xīxī-rǎngrǎng〈成〉 bustling with activity: ~的闹市区 bustling downtown area ‖ ~的行人 hustling and bustling pedestrians

豨 xī〈名〉〈古〉 swine
【豨莶】xīxiān〈名〉［植物］ common St. Paul's wort

蜥 xī〈名〉 lizard
【蜥蜴】xīyì〈名〉 lizard

僖 xī〈形〉〈书〉 joyful

熄 xī〈动〉 extinguish
【熄灯】xīdēng〈动〉 turn off a light: 宿舍晚上十一点~。 Dormitory lights are switched off at 11 p.m.
【熄灯号】xīdēnghào〈名〉 lights-out

【熄火】xīhuǒ〈动〉1（停止燃烧）go out: ～后，炉温逐渐下降。The furnace cooled down slowly after the fire was put out. 2（停止运转）go dead: 不要让引擎～。Keep the engine running.

【熄灭】xīmiè〈动〉1（使停止燃烧）extinguish: ～蜡烛 blow out a candle 2（停止发光、发热）go out: 火炬渐渐～。The torch gradually died out. ‖ 山火已～。The mountain fire has gone out.

嘻 xī

A〈叹〉〈书〉[used when exclaiming in admiration, wonder, etc.]: 他惊羡地"～"了一声。He gave a gasp of admiration.
B〈拟〉giggle: 她～～地笑了。She burst into giggles.

【嘻哈】xīhā〈名〉hip-hop: ～文化/歌手 hip-hop culture/singer

【嘻皮笑脸】xīpí-xiàoliǎn = 嬉皮笑脸 xīpí-xiàoliǎn

【嘻嘻哈哈】xīxī-hāhā〈形〉1（形容欢笑快乐）laughing and joking: 我们办公室的人成天都～的。There is always a lot of joking and laughter in our office. 2（形容不认真）facetious: 探穴运动可不是～闹着玩的。It is no joke to go potholing.

噏 xī〈动〉1〈旧〉= 吸 xī 2〈书〉（收敛）contract

【噏动】xīdòng = 翕动 xīdòng

膝 xī〈名〉knee: 双～跪下 kneel down on both knees ‖ 水深过～。The water came above the knees. ►卑躬屈～

【膝盖】xīgài〈名〉knee: ～受伤 hurt one's knee

【膝关节】xīguānjié〈名〉knee joint: ～脱臼了。The knees were dislocated.

【膝下】xīxià〈名〉〈书〉1（子女）at one's knees [used in saying whether one has children or not] 2（用于称呼）[used in the salutations of letters to one's parents or grandparents as a sign of respect]: 父母亲大人～ Dear Father and Mother

瘜 xī

【瘜肉】xīròu = 息肉 xīròu

嬉 xī〈动〉〈书〉play: ►～闹，～皮笑脸，～戏

【嬉闹】xīnào〈动〉laugh and frolic: 在草地/海滩上～ frolic in the meadow

【嬉皮士】xīpíshì〈名〉hippy: ～用语 hippy saying

【嬉皮笑脸】xīpí-xiàoliǎn〈成〉grin mischievously

【嬉耍】xīshuǎ〈动〉play: 孩子们在草坪上～。The children were playing on the grass.

【嬉戏】xīxì〈动〉〈书〉frolic: 在草地上/水中～ frolic in the meadow/water

【嬉笑】xīxiào〈动〉laugh and play: 快乐的～声 happy laughter

【嬉笑怒骂】xīxiào-nùmà〈成〉laugh merrily or curse angrily: ～，皆成文章。Any emotion, from a merry laugh to an angry curse can make good reading.

【嬉笑颜开】xīxiào-yánkāi〈成〉be wild with joy

熹 xī〈形〉〈书〉bright: 星～。Stars are bright. ►～微

【熹微】xīwēi〈形〉〈书〉[of sunlight at dawn] faint: ►晨光～

樨 xī ►木樨 mùxi

螅 xī ►水螅 shuǐxī

歙 xī〈动〉〈书〉breathe in: ～风吐雾 breathe in air and puff out fog

窸 xī

【窸窣】xīsū〈拟〉swish: 听到一阵～声 hear a rustle ‖ 树叶在微风中～作响。The leaves rustled gently in the breeze.

【窸窸窣窣】xīxī-sūsū〈形〉rustle: 她走路时，裙子～的。Her skirt swished as she walked.

蹊 xī〈名〉〈书〉footpath: ►～径，桃李不言，下自成～
►qī

【蹊径】xījìng〈名〉〈书〉path: 另辟～ adopt a new approach ►独辟～

蟋 xī

【蟋蟀】xīshuài〈名〉cricket

【蟋蟀草】xīshuàicǎo〈名〉［植物］yard grass

豀 xī = 溪 xī

【豀壑】xīhè〈名〉〈书〉ravine

【豀卡】xīkǎ〈名〉manor [in Tibet formerly]

曦 xī〈名〉〈书〉sunlight of the early morning: 春～ spring sunlight ►晨～

巇 xī〈形〉〈书〉precipitous: ►险～

鼷 xī

【鼷鼠】xīshǔ〈名〉［动物］the smallest species of rat

xí

习（習）xí

A〈动〉1（学习）study: ～文 study literature ‖ ～武 practise martial arts ‖ 跟宫廷画师～画 study painting under court painters ‖ 学而时～之 study and make regular reviews ►～字，实～，学～ 2（习惯）get used to: 不～水性 have no training in swimming ►～非成是，～以为常
B〈名〉custom: ►～俗，恶～，陋～

【习得】xídé〈动〉acquire: 语言～ language acquisition

【习非成是】xífēi-chéngshì〈成〉get accustomed to what is wrong and accept it as right: 谬种流传，～。The diffusion of errors has the effect of making people accustomed to things that are wrong.

【习惯】xíguàn A〈动〉be accustomed to: ～早起 be used to getting up early ‖ 我～于开夜车。It is a habit with me to work late into the night. B〈名〉custom: 纠正不良～ correct a bad habit ‖ 养成良好的～ develop a good habit ‖ 生活～ way of life ‖ 他有午休的～。He is in the habit of taking a nap after lunch.

【习惯成自然】xíguàn chéng zìrán〈俗〉habit is second nature

【习惯法】xíguànfǎ〈名〉common law, customary law: ～要求人们先结婚后生子。Custom demands that people get married before having children.

【习惯性】xíguànxìng〈形〉habitual: ～动作 habitual movement

【习惯性流产】xíguànxìng liúchǎn ►**p. 50** 〈名〉［医学］habitual abortion

【习好】xíhào〈名〉〈书〉inveterate habit: ～饮酒 be addicted to drinking

【习见】xíjiàn〈动〉be commonly seen: ～不鲜 frequently seen ‖ 这种情况在当地已为人们所～。This is no uncommon occurrence to the local people.

【习气】xíqì〈名〉bad habit: 沾染坏～ be tainted by a bad habit ‖ 流氓～ hooliganism

【习染】xírǎn〈书〉A〈动〉fall into a bad habit: ～毒瘾 fall into the habit of taking drugs ‖ ～市侩作风 fall into bad ways B〈名〉bad habit: 革除～ get rid of a bad habit

【习尚】xíshàng〈名〉common practice: 传统/当地的～ traditional/native custom

【习俗】xísú〈名〉custom: 民间～ folk customs ‖ 本地的～ indigenous custom ‖ 春节互相拜年是中国的传统～。It is a traditional Chinese custom to exchange visits at Spring Festival time.

【习题】xítí〈名〉exercise: 布置～ assign exercises ‖ 做～ do exercises ‖ ～答案 key to the exercises ‖ 算术/物理～ arithmetic/physics exercises

【习习】xíxí〈形〉〈书〉breezy: 微风～。A gentle breeze is blowing.

【习性】xíxìng〈名〉trick: 动物的～ habits and characteristics of an animal

【习焉不察】xíyān-bùchá〈成〉be too accustomed to sth. to call it into question: 人们对于常见的事物往往～。People usually do not question what they are accustomed to.

【习以为常】xíyǐwéicháng〈成〉be used to sth.: 受冷遇对他来说已经～了。He has become used to receiving a cold welcome.

【习艺】xíyì〈动〉learn a trade, skill, or handicraft: 拜师～ learn a skill as an apprentice to a master

【习用】xíyòng〈动〉〈书〉frequently use: 这种词语搭配习见～。This word collocation is frequently found in everyday life.

【习用语】xíyòngyǔ〈名〉idiom: 用英语～表达 express in English idiom

【习与性成】xíyǔxìngchéng〈成〉grow into the habit of doing sth.

【习字】xízì〈动〉do exercises in calligraphy

【习字帖】xízìtiè〈名〉calligraphy model

【习作】xízuò A〈动〉do exercises in composition: 刻苦～ work hard to improve through practice B〈名〉exercise in composition, drawing, etc.: 这些是画家早年的～。They are the painter's early exercises.

席[1]（蓆）xí〈名〉mat: 一领/张/卷～ a mat ►草～，凉～，苇～

席[2] xí

A〈名〉1（座位）seat: 被告～ defendant's seat ‖ 来宾～ seats for guests ‖ 大厅里座无虚～。There are no empty seats in the hall. ►出～，入～，退～ 2（议会席位）seat: 在议会中占有42～ have 42 seats in Parliament 3（酒筵）feast: 摆一桌～ set out a great spread ‖ 吃～ attend a banquet ‖ ～间谈笑风生。It was a merry and cheerful feast. ►酒～，宴～
B〈量〉[used for banquets, talks, etc.]: 一～菜 a dinner ‖ 一～话 a conversation

【席箔】xíbó〈名〉matting

【席不暇暖】xíbùxiánuǎn〈成〉be rushed off one's feet: 她终日奔忙，～。She was rushed off her feet all day long and could

X

hardly snatch any rest.
【席次】xícì〈名〉 seating arrangement: 安排～ organize seating arrangements ‖ 请各位按指定～入座。 Please take your designated seats.
【席地】xídì〈动〉 sit or lie on the ground: ～而坐 sit on the floor
【席间】xíjiān〈介〉 during a feast: ～觥筹交错。 Glasses kept clinking at the feast.
【席卷】xíjuǎn〈动〉 1（卷走）carry everything with one: ～而逃 make off with everything 2（横扫） sweep across: 金融危机～全球。 The financial crisis has swept the globe. ‖ 暴风雨～滨海城市。 The storm ravaged the coastal cities.
【席梦思】xímèngsī〈名〉 inner-spring mattress
【席面】xímiàn〈名〉 1（筵席） feast: 婚宴的～非常丰盛。 The wedding banquet is a feast for the gods. 2（酒菜） food presented at dinner: ～精美无比，宾客赞不绝口。 Guests praised the superb food served at dinner.
【席篾】xímiè〈名〉 thin bamboo strip
【席棚】xípéng〈名〉 mat shed
【席位】xíwèi〈名〉 seat: 拥有议会中的多数～ hold a majority in Parliament ‖ 合法～ lawful seat
【席子】xízi〈名〉〈口〉 mat: 编织～ weave a mat

觋（覡） xí〈名〉〈书〉 wizard

袭[1]（襲） xí

A〈动〉 1（仿照） pattern after: ▸～用, 抄～, 沿～ 2（继承） inherit: ～位 succeed to the throne ▸世～

B〈量〉〈旧〉 suit or set of clothes: 一～薄纱 a piece of light veil ‖ 一～棉衣 a suit of cotton-padded clothes

袭[2] xí

〈动〉 make a surprise attack: 途中遭～ be ambushed midway ‖ 寒气～人。 There is a nip in the air. ▸～击, 空～
【袭故蹈常】xígù-dǎocháng〈成〉 follow the old rules and conventions
【袭击】xíjī〈动〉 make a surprise attack: ～敌军 conduct a raid on the enemy ‖ 遭受对方的突然～ be subjected to a surprise enemy raid ‖〈喻〉 受强台风的～ be hit by a violent typhoon
【袭取】xíqǔ〈动〉 1（指夺取） capture by a surprise attack: ～敌人的要塞 take the enemy's fort by a surprise attack 2（沿用） continue to use or employ: 他～小说内容，将其改编成电影。 He adapted the novel for the screen.
【袭扰】xírǎo〈动〉 harass: 遭蚊虫～ be pestered by mosquitoes ‖ 恐怖分子四处～。 The terrorists made repeated attacks all over the place.
【袭用】xíyòng〈动〉 follow: ～成说 follow an accepted theory or formulation ‖ ～宫廷食谱 follow imperial recipes
【袭占】xízhàn〈动〉 seize by surprise attack: ～机场 seize the airport in a surprise raid ‖ ～前沿基地 capture an outpost in an onslaught

媳 xí

〈名〉 1（媳妇） daughter-in-law: ▸儿～, 婆～, 童养～ 2（晚辈亲属的妻子） wife of a relative of the younger generation: ▸弟～, 孙～妇, 侄～妇
【媳妇】xífù〈名〉 1（儿子的妻子） daughter-in-law 2（晚辈亲属的妻子） wife of a relative of the younger generation: 孙～ grand-son's wife ‖ 侄～ nephew's wife
【媳妇儿】xífur〈名〉〈方〉 1（妻子） wife: 娶～ take a wife ‖ 她是我～。 She is my wife. ▸小～ 2（年轻已婚女子） young married woman

隰 xí

〈名〉〈书〉 1（低湿处） low-lying and damp place 2（新垦的田） newly reclaimed land

檄 xí

A〈名〉 war proclamation

B〈动〉〈书〉 make a proclamation of war: 严～诸将 strictly enlist and instruct generals
【檄文】xíwén〈名〉 war proclamation

xǐ

洗 xǐ

A〈动〉 1（去除污垢） wash: ～脸/手/头发 wash one's face/hands/hair ‖ ～掉衣服上的污垢 wash the dirt out of one's clothes ‖ 以泪～面 be bathed in tears ‖ 用肥皂/洗发液～ wash with soap/shampoo ▸冲～, 干～, 梳～ 2（除掉） clear: ～去被告的罪名 vindicate the defendant from a charge ‖ ～去罪孽 cleanse sb. from sin ▸～雪, ～冤 3（杀光或抢光） sack, devastate: ～城 massacre the inhabitants of a captured city ‖ 匪徒血～了整个村庄。 The bandits plunged the village into a bloodbath. ▸～劫 4（冲洗） develop: ～胶卷 have a film developed ‖ 所有照片都～得很清楚。 All the photographs came out clearly. 5（洗牌） shuffle: ～骨牌 shuffle the dominoes ‖ 把牌好好～一～ give the cards a good shuffle ▸～牌 6（清除） clean up: 清～ purge 7（抹去） erase: ～掉那段录音 erase a recording

B〈名〉 1 〈古〉（盥洗器皿） washing utensil: 笔～ basin for washing writing brushes 2（洗礼） baptism: 施～ baptize ‖ 受～为基督教徒 be baptized a Christian ▸领～
【洗车】xǐchē〈动〉 wash a car: ～场 car wash
【洗尘】xǐchén〈动〉 give a welcome dinner to a visitor from afar: 设便宴为某人～ give an informal dinner to welcome sb.
【洗涤】xǐdí〈动〉 wash: 彻底～ cleanse thoroughly ▸～剂
【洗涤剂】xǐdíjì〈名〉 cleanser: 合成～ synthetic detergents
【洗耳恭听】xǐ'ěr-gōngtīng〈成〉 listen carefully: 你有什么高见？我愿～。 Have you any opinion? I am all ears.
【洗发膏】xǐfàgāo〈名〉 cream shampoo
【洗发水】xǐfàshuǐ〈名〉 liquid shampoo
【洗劫】xǐjié〈动〉 loot: ～被占城市 sack a captured city ‖ ～美术馆 loot an art gallery ‖ 佛寺被～一空。 The temple was pillaged of all its Buddhist statuary.
【洗洁精】xǐjiéjīng〈名〉 dishwashing liquid; washing-up liquid〈英〉
【洗礼】xǐlǐ〈名〉 1［宗教］ baptism: 临终的～ clinical baptism 2〈喻〉（锻炼和考验） severe test: 接受战斗的～ go through the ordeal of battle
【洗脸盆】xǐliǎnpén〈名〉 washbasin〈英〉; sink〈美〉
【洗练】xǐliàn〈形〉 succinct: ～的风格/文笔 terse style/writing
【洗煤】xǐméi〈名〉 coal washing: ～厂 coal-cleaning plant
【洗面奶】xǐmiànnǎi〈名〉 facial cleanser
【洗脑】xǐnǎo〈动〉 brainwash
【洗牌】xǐpái〈动〉 1〈本〉 shuffle cards: 记住要先～，再发牌。 Remember to shuffle the cards before you deal. 2〈喻〉（格局变化）reshuffle: 房产开发商面临重新～的可能。 Real estate developers are facing a possible major reshuffle.
【洗盘】xǐpán〈动〉 [of stock market manipulating] wash sale
【洗钱】xǐqián〈动〉 launder money: 洗黑钱 launder illegal funds ‖ 反～法 anti-money laundering law
【洗染店】xǐrǎndiàn〈名〉 laundering and dyeing shop
【洗手】xǐshǒu〈动〉 1（清洗手） wash one's hands: 吃饭前先～ wash one's hands before eating 2 ▸p. 772〈婉〉（上厕所） go to the toilet 3（改邪归正） stop engaging in a criminal activity: 彻底～不干坏事 wash one's hands of the whole sordid business 4（彻底不干） wash one's hands of sth.: 这个工作她早就想～不干了。 She can't wait to wash her hands of this work.
【洗手间】xǐshǒujiān〈名〉 washroom; restroom〈美〉: 上～ go to the toilet
【洗手液】xǐshǒuyè〈名〉 liquid soap
【洗漱】xǐshù〈动〉 wash one's face and rinse one's mouth
【洗刷】xǐshuā〈动〉 1〈本〉 scrub: ～污垢 scrub off dirt ‖ 用刷子～卫生间 scrub the toilet with a brush 2〈喻〉（辩白） clear: ～耻辱/冤枉 clear oneself of opprobrium/a false accusation ‖ ～罪名 exculpate sb. from a charge
【洗涮】xǐshuàn〈动〉 rinse: 污迹～不掉。 The stain won't rinse out.
【洗头】xǐtóu〈动〉 wash one's hair
【洗碗机】xǐwǎnjī〈名〉 dishwasher
【洗胃】xǐwèi〈动〉［医学］have one's stomach pumped
【洗心革面】xǐxīn-gémiàn〈成〉〈喻〉 turn over a new leaf: 他将～，努力工作。 He is going to turn over a new leaf and work hard.
【洗雪】xǐxuě〈动〉 wipe out: ～沉冤 redress a deep grievance ‖ ～国耻 resolve a national disgrace
【洗眼剂】xǐyǎnjì〈名〉 eye wash
【洗液】xǐyè〈名〉 lotion
【洗衣店】xǐyīdiàn〈名〉 laundry
【洗衣粉】xǐyīfěn〈名〉 washing powder〈英〉; laundry detergent〈美〉
【洗衣机】xǐyījī〈名〉 washing machine
【洗印】xǐyìn〈动〉 process: ～胶卷 process a photographic film
【洗浴】xǐyù〈动〉 take a bath
【洗冤】xǐyuān〈动〉 right a wrong
【洗澡】xǐzǎo〈动〉 have a bath
【洗澡间】xǐzǎojiān〈名〉 bathroom
【洗澡盆】xǐzǎopén〈名〉 bath〈英〉; bathtub〈美〉
【洗濯】xǐzhuó〈动〉〈书〉 cleanse: ～污垢 wash the filth away

枲 xǐ

【枲麻】xǐmá〈名〉 male hemp plant

玺（璽） xǐ〈名〉 royal seal: ▸玉～

铣（銑） xǐ〈动〉［机械］ mill: 在工件上～个凹槽 mill a trough on the workpiece ▸～床, ～刀
▸xiǎn
【铣床】xǐchuáng〈名〉 milling machine

X

【铣刀】xǐdāo〈名〉［机械］ milling cutter: ～盘 facing cutter
【铣工】xǐgōng〈名〉 1（指工种） milling work: ～车间 milling shop 2（指工人） miller
【铣削】xǐxiāo〈动〉［机械］cut metals with miller

徙 xǐ

〈动〉 1（迁移） move: 流～ drift about ▸迁～ 2〈书〉（调动官职） transfer: ～任 be transferred to another post
【徙居】xǐjū〈动〉 move house: 举家～沿海城市。 The whole family moved to a coastal city.

喜 xǐ

A〈形〉 1（快乐） happy: ～获丰收 reap a bumper harvest ‖ ～迁新居 happily move into a new house ‖ 心中暗～ secretly feel pleased ▸～不自胜，欣～ 2（值得庆贺） joyful: ▸～事，～讯
B〈名〉 1（好事） happy event: ▸报～，贺～ 2（怀孕） pregnancy: 害～ show symptoms of pregnancy ‖ 她有～了。 She is pregnant.
C〈动〉 1（喜欢） like: ～读书 enjoy reading ▸～闻乐见，～好 2（适宜于） have an inclination for: ～光植物 sun plant ‖ 熊猫性～食竹。 Pandas are naturally inclined to eat bamboo. ‖ 兰花～温暖。 Orchids like warmth.
【喜爱】xǐ'ài〈动〉 like: ～打网球/篮球 enjoy playing tennis/basketball ‖ 惹人～ be adorable ‖ 他非常～小儿子。 He is very fond of his youngest son.
【喜报】xǐbào〈名〉 happy tidings: 贴～ post up some good news ‖ 立功～ citation of meritorious service ‖ ～频传。 Good news poured in.
【喜病】xǐbìng〈名〉 morning sickness due to pregnancy: 害～ show symptoms of early pregnancy
【喜不自胜】xǐbùzìshèng〈成〉be overjoyed: 听到喜讯～ be overjoyed at the good news
【喜车】xǐchē〈名〉 wedding car
【喜冲冲】xǐchōngchōng〈形〉 blissfully happy: ～地走来 walk over beaming with joy ‖ 他整天～的。 He has a sunny disposition.
【喜出望外】xǐchūwàngwài〈成〉 be pleasantly surprised: 这次成功让他～。 He felt elated by the unexpected success.
【喜果】xǐguǒ〈名〉assorted nuts and sweets [served to guests on the occasion of an engagement ceremony or a wedding]
【喜好】xǐhào〈动〉 like: ～钓鱼/游泳 like fishing/swimming ‖ ～音乐 be keen on music
【喜欢】xǐhuan A〈动〉 like: ～古典音乐 like classic music ‖ 你～她什么呢? What do you like about her? ‖ 我立刻就～上了她。 I warmed to her at once. ‖ 这个小女孩真讨人～。 The little girl is a real delight. B〈形〉 happy: 快去把这消息告诉你爷爷，叫他老人家也～～。 Go and give your grandpa the good news quickly, so that he can share in our joy. ‖ 看到孩子们学习有进步，他心里很～。 He was very pleased to see that the children had made progress at school.
【喜极而泣】xǐjí'érqì〈成〉 burst into tears of joy
【喜结良缘】xǐjiéliángyuán〈成〉 be happily married: 几年之后，他们终于～。 Several years later, they were happily married.
【喜酒】xǐjiǔ〈名〉 wedding feast: 喝～ attend a wedding feast
【喜剧】xǐjù〈名〉 comedy: 喜欢～而不喜欢悲剧 prefer comedy to tragedy ‖ ～演员 comedian
【喜剧片】xǐjùpiān〈名〉 comedy
【喜乐】xǐlè〈形〉 cheerful: 晚会充满了～气氛。 There was a really cheerful atmosphere at the party.
【喜联】xǐlián〈名〉 wedding scrolls
【喜马拉雅山】Xǐmǎlāyǎshān〈名〉 Himalayas
【喜眉笑眼】xǐméi-xiàoyǎn〈成〉 be all smiles
【喜娘】xǐniáng〈名〉 bridesmaid
【喜怒哀乐】xǐ-nù-āi-lè〈成〉 all human emotions: 她是个把～都挂在脸上的人。 She is a woman who shows her feelings openly.
【喜怒不形于色】xǐnù bù xíngyúsè〈成〉 show no anger or pleasure on one's face
【喜怒无常】xǐnù-wúcháng〈成〉be moody: 她是个～的女人。 She is a woman of incalculable moods.
【喜气】xǐqì〈名〉 cheerful atmosphere or expression: 她满脸～。 Her face is beaming with joy.
【喜气洋洋】xǐqì-yángyáng〈成〉be radiant with joy: 该队获胜后，球迷们～。 The fans were jubilant at the team's victory.
【喜钱】xǐqian〈名〉〈口〉 money given on a happy occasion
【喜庆】xǐqìng A〈形〉 joyous: ～的日子 happy occasion ‖ 红色显得～。 Red indicates joy. ‖ 晚会洋溢着～的气氛。 The mood of the party is joyful. B〈名〉 festive occasion: 结婚～ wedding festivities
【喜鹊】xǐquè〈名〉 magpie
【喜人】xǐrén〈形〉 pleasing: 一派～的丰收景象 the pleasant sight of a bumper harvest ‖ 麦苗长势～。 The wheat is coming on beautifully.
【喜丧】xǐsāng〈名〉 funeral for sb. who lived to a venerable age
【喜色】xǐsè〈名〉 cheerful look: 面带～ wear a cheerful smile
【喜上眉梢】xǐshàngméishāo〈成〉 be radiant with joy
【喜事】xǐshì〈名〉 1（令人开心的事） happy event: 有什么～? 看把你乐的。 What makes you so jubilant? ‖ 人逢～精神爽。 Happy occasions raise the spirits. 2（婚事） wedding: 你儿子什么时候办～? When will your son's wedding take place?
【喜糖】xǐtáng〈名〉 wedding sweets: 发～ hand out wedding sweets ‖〈喻〉 吃～ attend a wedding celebration
【喜帖】xǐtiě〈名〉 wedding invitation
【喜闻乐见】xǐwén-lèjiàn〈成〉 be delighted to see and hear: ～的艺术形式 popular art form
【喜相】xǐxiang〈名〉〈方〉 sunny disposition
【喜笑颜开】xǐxiào-yánkāi〈成〉be beaming with joy: 得知选举结果，他们～。 They were all smiles as they heard the results of the election.
【喜新厌旧】xǐxīn-yànjiù〈成〉 abandon the old for the new: 他是个～的花花公子。 He is a pleasure-seeker who is very fickle with his affections.
【喜形于色】xǐxíngyúsè〈成〉 be visibly pleased: 儿子考上了大学，父亲不禁～。 The father's face shone with joy when his son was admitted to university.
【喜讯】xǐxùn〈名〉 happy news: 接到～ get the good news ‖ ～频传。 Happy news keeps pouring in.
【喜宴】xǐyàn〈名〉 wedding feast: 办～ hold a wedding feast ‖ 赴～ attend a wedding banquet
【喜阳植物】xǐyáng zhíwù〈名〉 sun-loving plant
【喜洋洋】xǐyángyáng〈形〉 radiant: 孩子有出息了，父母心里～的。 The parents beamed with joy at their child's prospects.
【喜阴植物】xǐyīn zhíwù〈名〉 shade-loving plant
【喜盈盈】xǐyíngyíng〈形〉 beaming with joy: 她～地与我们打招呼。 She greeted us with a radiant smile.
【喜忧参半】xǐyōu-cānbàn〈成〉 have a mixed feeling of pleasure and foreboding
【喜雨】xǐyǔ〈名〉 welcome rain: 全省各地普降～。 There is widespread seasonable rain across the province.
【喜悦】xǐyuè〈形〉 delighted: 怀着～的心情 have a joyous feeling ‖ 无比～ be blissfully happy ‖ 他一脸～的神色。 His face radiated joy.
【喜滋滋】xǐzīzī〈形〉 blissfully happy: 她考试通过了，心里～的。 She was immensely pleased when she passed the exam.

葸 xǐ

〈动〉〈书〉 fear: 畏～不前 be too frightened to advance

屣 xǐ

〈名〉〈书〉 footwear: ▸敝～

禧 xǐ

〈名〉 happiness: 恭贺新～ Happy New Year!

镥（鑥） xǐ

〈名〉［化学］ seaborgium (Sg)

蟢 xǐ

【蟢子】xǐzi〈名〉 spider supposed to indicate the coming of some happy event

囍 xǐ

〈名〉 happiness

xì

卌 xì

▸p. 691〈数〉〈旧〉 forty: ～年婚庆 40th wedding anniversary

戏（戲） xì

A〈动〉 1（玩耍） play: 二龙～珠 two dragons playing with a huge pearl ▸～耍，儿～，游～ 2（嘲弄） make fun of: ▸～弄，～言，调～
B〈名〉 play: 看～ see a play ‖ 传统～ traditional play ‖ 古装～ costume drama ‖〈喻〉 好～还在后头。 The best part is yet to come. ‖〈喻〉 他有/没～。 He will/won't make it. ▸唱～，演～，京～
【戏班】xìbān〈名〉〈旧〉 theatrical troupe: 进～ join a theatrical troupe
【戏班子】xìbānzi = 戏班 xìbān
【戏本】xìběn〈名〉〈旧〉 opera script: 我国有些古代～已经失传。 Some of our most ancient librettos have been lost.
【戏称】xìchēng A〈动〉 nickname: 他很胖，大家～他为"肥肥"。 He is very fat, so he is nicknamed 'Fatty'. B〈名〉 nickname: "老夫子"是我们对他的～。 'Pedant' is our nickname for him.
【戏词】xìcí = 戏文 xìwén 1
【戏单】xìdān〈名〉 theatrical programme: 散发～ distribute programmes

X

【戏法】xìfǎ〈名〉 magic: 变～ perform a trick ‖ ～人人会变，各有巧妙不同。Magicians are many, but each has their own tricks.
【戏份儿】xìfènr〈名〉 1（指报酬） actor's remuneration 2（指表演工作量） workload: ～很重 huge workload
【戏服】xìfú〈名〉 stage costume: 穿上～ put on one's costume
【戏歌】xìgē〈名〉 artistic form combining opera singing with pop song
【戏馆】xìguǎn〈名〉 theatre
【戏剧】xìjù〈名〉 1（指艺术形式） drama: 把小说改编成～ dramatize a novel ‖ ～爱好者 drama lover ‖ ～晚会 theatre evening ‖ 古典/人间～ classical/human drama ‖ 莎士比亚～ Shakespeare drama 2（指剧本） script of a play
【戏剧化】xìjùhuà〈动〉 dramatize
【戏剧家】xìjùjiā ▸**p. 966**〈名〉 playwright
【戏剧效果】xìjù xiàoguǒ〈名〉 dramatic effect
【戏剧性】xìjùxìng〈名〉 dramatic nature: ～变化 dramatic change ‖ 这次事件极富～。The affair was most dramatic.
【戏路】xìlù〈名〉 range of roles: ～宽/窄 a big variety of/a limited number of roles
【戏码】xìmǎ〈名〉〈旧〉 repertoire
【戏迷】xìmí〈名〉 theatre fan: 吸引了众多～ attract a lot of theatre-goers
【戏目】xìmù〈名〉 theatrical programme
【戏弄】xìnòng〈动〉 tease: 爱～人 enjoy teasing people ‖ ～人的话 teasing remarks
【戏票】xìpiào〈名〉 theatre ticket
【戏曲】xìqǔ〈名〉 1（指戏剧形式） traditional opera [including *Kunqu*, Beijing opera and other local operas]: ～作品 works in traditional opera ‖ 传统/地方～ traditional/local opera 2（指文学形式） singing parts in a story
【戏曲片】xìqǔpiàn〈名〉 screen adaptation of a traditional or local opera
【戏耍】xìshuǎ〈动〉 1（戏弄） tease: 不要～别人。Don't tease others. 2（玩耍） enjoy oneself: 户外～ play outdoors
【戏水】xìshuǐ〈动〉 play in water: 鸳鸯～。Mandarin ducks are paddling in the water.
【戏说】xìshuō〈动〉 adapt a historical story by adding fabricated, comical plots: ～乾隆 relate playful stories about the Emperor Qian Long
【戏台】xìtái〈名〉 stage
【戏文】xìwén〈名〉 1（戏词） lines: 你的～记住了吗？ Have you learnt your lines yet? 2（戏曲） traditional opera 3（南戏） southern drama
【戏侮】xìwǔ〈动〉 mock: ～他口吃 tease him about his stutter
【戏谑】xìxuè〈动〉 banter: ～的口气 bantering voice
【戏言】xìyán A〈动〉 say in a joking way: 从不～ never joke B〈名〉 joke: 军中无～。There is no jesting in war.
【戏衣】xìyī = 戏服 xìfú
【戏园子】xìyuánzi〈名〉〈旧〉 theatre
【戏院】xìyuàn〈名〉 theatre: ～售票处 theatre box office
【戏照】xìzhào〈名〉 stage photo
【戏装】xìzhuāng〈名〉 theatrical costume: 穿～照相 have a photo taken in a stage costume
【戏子】xìzi〈名〉〈旧〉〈贬〉 actor

饩（餼） xì〈书〉

A〈名〉 grains and forage: ～食 cereals and food ‖ 马～ forage for horses B〈动〉 present (esp grains or forage) as a gift

系[1] xì〈名〉

1（系统） system: ▸派～, 水～ 2（指教学行政单位） department: 物理/哲学～ physics/philosophy department ‖ ～主任 head of a department 3［地质］ system: 奥陶～ Ordovician System

系[2]（繫） xì〈动〉

1（绑） tie: ～好安全带 have one's seat-belt fastened ‖ ～马 tether a horse ▸～缚 2〈书〉（扣押） incarcerate: ～囚 put in prison 3（挂念） miss: 他情～祖国。 His patriotism binds him to his motherland. ▸～恋, ～念 4（捆好后上提或下送） lower down or hoist up: 把桶～上井来 hoist a bucket up from a well

系[3]（係） xì〈动〉〈书〉

1（联结） relate to: 成败～于此举 stand or fall by this ‖ 名誉所～ have a direct bearing on one's reputation ▸维～ 2（是） be: 确～实情 be nothing but the truth ‖ 李白～唐代诗人。 Li Bai was a poet in the Tang Dynasty.
▸jì

【系词】xìcí〈名〉 1［逻辑］ copula 2［语言］ linking verb
【系缚】xìfù〈动〉〈书〉 fetter
【系恋】xìliàn〈动〉〈书〉 be reluctant to leave: ～故乡 can hardly tear oneself away from one's home place
【系列】xìliè〈名〉 series: ～报道 serial reports ‖ ～产品 series production ‖ ～讲座 series of lectures ‖ 一～问题 a series of problems
【系列化】xìlièhuà〈动〉 serialize: 产品～ serialization of products
【系列片】xìlièpiàn〈名〉 serial: 电视～ television series
【系念】xìniàn〈动〉〈书〉 concern oneself (with/about): ～父母的身体 feel concerned about one's parents' health
【系谱】xìpǔ〈名〉［生物］ pedigree
【系数】xìshù〈名〉［数学］ coefficient: 摩擦/膨胀～ coefficient of friction/expansion ‖ 安全～ safety factor
【系统】xìtǒng A〈名〉 system: 操作～ operating system ‖ 道路/灌溉/运输～ road/irrigation/transport system ‖ 消化～ digestive system ▸呼吸～, 神经～ B〈形〉 systematic: 进行～的规划/研究 make a systematic plan/study ‖ ～的训练 systematic training ‖ 内容很～。 The contents are arranged in a systematic way.
【系统工程】xìtǒng gōngchéng〈名〉［工程］ systems engineering
【系统化】xìtǒnghuà〈动〉 systematize
【系统论】xìtǒnglùn〈名〉 systems theory
【系统性】xìtǒngxìng〈名〉 systematic nature: 这套书编得很有～。 The layout in this set of books is systematic.

细（細） xì〈形〉

1（横截面小） fine: ～铁丝 fine wire ‖ 又长又～的棍子 long thin stick ▸～纱 2（微小） minute: 分工～ have an elaborate division of labour ▸～节, 事无巨～ 3（两边距离近） [of small distance between two sides] narrow: 她长得～眉～眼。 She has thin eyebrows and narrow eyes. 4（微弱） weak 5（声音小） soft: ～嗓子 have a soft voice ‖ ～声～气 be soft-spoken 6（颗粒小） fine: ～沙 fine sand 7（精致） exquisite: ～瓷器 fine porcelain ‖ 精米～面 refined rice and finely ground flour 8（详细周到） thorough: ～谈 talk in detail ‖ 工作做得很～ be meticulous in one's work ‖ 他心很～。 He is a very careful man.

【细胞】xìbāo〈名〉 cell: 癌～ cancer cells ‖ ～分裂 cell division ‖〈喻〉 有音乐～ have music in one's genes ▸白～
【细胞壁】xìbāobì〈名〉 cell wall
【细胞核】xìbāohé〈名〉 cell nucleus
【细胞膜】xìbāomó〈名〉［生化］ cell membrane
【细胞质】xìbāozhì〈名〉［生物］ cytoplasm: ～基因 cytogene
【细布】xìbù〈名〉 fine cloth
【细部】xìbù〈名〉 detail: ～图 detail drawing
【细菜】xìcài〈名〉 fine vegetable
【细察】xìchá〈动〉 scrutinize: ～究竟 probe for the real reasons ‖ 她的工作经不起～。Her work will not stand up to close scrutiny.
【细长】xìcháng〈形〉 tall and slender: 身材～ have a tall and slender figure ‖ ～的腿 long slender legs ‖ ～体 slender body
【细瓷】xìcí〈名〉 fine porcelain: 江西～ fine porcelain made in Jiangxi
【细大不捐】xìdà-bùjuān〈成〉 reject nothing, big or small
【细点】xìdiǎn〈名〉 delicacies
【细读】xìdú〈动〉 peruse
【细纺】xìfǎng〈动〉［纺织］ spin to a fine thread: ～亚麻 fine-spun linen
【细高挑儿】xìgāotiǎor〈名〉〈方〉 1（指形体） tall and slender figure 2（指人） tall and slender person
【细工】xìgōng〈名〉 fine workmanship
【细故】xìgù〈名〉 trivial matter: 我不因～与他争吵。 I don't quarrel with him over trivial matters. ▸毛举～
【细化】xìhuà〈动〉 go into full detail and further specification: 法规要进一步～，以便于操作。 The regulations must be further clarified in order for them to be operational.
【细活】xìhuó〈名〉 fine and delicate work: 慢工出～。Slow work yields fine products. ‖ 木工活是个～。Cabinet-making requires fine workmanship and meticulous care.
【细嚼慢咽】xìjiáo-mànyàn〈成〉 chew carefully and swallow slowly
【细节】xìjié〈名〉 detail: 补充～ furnish the details ‖ 略去～ omit the details ‖ ～描写 description of details
【细菌】xìjūn〈名〉 bacterium: 培养～ cultivate bacteria ‖ ～感染 bacterial contamination ‖ ～引起的疾病 microbial disease
【细菌肥料】xìjūn féiliào〈名〉 bacterial fertilizer
【细菌武器】xìjūn wǔqì〈名〉 germ weapon
【细菌性】xìjūnxìng〈形〉 bacterial: ～痢疾 bacillary dysentery ‖ ～胃肠炎 bacterial gastroenteritis
【细菌战】xìjūnzhàn〈名〉 germ warfare
【细粮】xìliáng〈名〉 fine food grains [wheat flour and rice]
【细流】xìliú〈名〉 trickle: 涓涓～ trickling stream
【细毛】xìmáo〈名〉 fine, soft and usu valuable fur
【细密】xìmì〈形〉 1（精细紧密） fine and close: 针脚～ with fine close stitches ‖ 质地～ be of close texture ‖ 布织得～。 The cloth was woven with a fine texture. 2（具体细致） detailed: 分工～ have a fine division of labour ‖ ～的分析 detailed analysis
【细目】xìmù〈名〉 detail: ～计划 detailed scheme ‖ ～卡片 detail card ‖ ～文件 detail file

【细嫩】xìnèn〈形〉 delicate: 肉质～ tender meat ‖ ～的皮肤 delicate skin
【细腻】xìnì〈形〉 1（细润光滑） fine and delicate: 瓷质～。 The porcelain is fine and glossy. 2（细致入微） exquisite: 感情～ be acutely sensitive ‖ 描写～而生动。 The description is minute and vivid.
【细皮嫩肉】xìpí-nènròu〈成〉 delicate skin and fair complexion
【细巧】xìqiǎo〈形〉 exquisite: ～的工艺 exquisite workmanship ‖ ～的图案 exquisite design
【细情】xìqíng〈名〉 details: 我不知～。 I know nothing of the details.
【细软】xìruǎn A〈名〉 valuables: 收拾～ collect up one's valuables B〈形〉 slender and soft: ～的手指 soft, slender fingers
【细润】xìrùn = 细腻 xìnì 1
【细弱】xìruò〈形〉 slender and weak: ～的声音 feeble voice
【细纱】xìshā〈名〉［纺织］ spun yarn
【细声细气】xìshēng-xìqì〈成〉softly-spoken: 他说话～。 He is softly-spoken.
【细水长流】xìshuǐ-chángliú〈成〉〈喻〉 1（节约使用） economize in order to avoid running short: 用钱要～。 Be economical with money, or it may run short. 2（坚持不懈） do sth. gradually and with perseverance: 学习不能突击，应该～，日积月累才行。 You can't expect to master everything quickly and in a rush. Instead, you've got to persist in your efforts.
【细说】xìshuō〈动〉 recount in detail: ～详情 relate in elaborate detail ‖ 没有时间～了。 There's no time for a lengthy account.
【细丝】xìsī〈名〉 filament: 蜘蛛网的～ delicate threads of a spider's web
【细碎】xìsuì〈形〉 small and irregular: ～的脚步声 sound of light and hurried footsteps
【细挑】xìtiao〈形〉 tall and slender
【细微】xìwēi〈形〉 slight: ～变化 slight change ‖ ～的区别 subtle distinction
【细小】xìxiǎo〈形〉 tiny: ～的事情 trivial matter ‖ 玻璃表面的～裂纹 tiny crack in the surface of the glass
【细心】xìxīn〈形〉careful: ～的管家 meticulous house-keeper ‖ ～照料 take meticulous care ‖ 做作业要～! Take care over your homework!
【细伢子】xìyázi〈名〉〈方〉 child
【细雨】xìyǔ〈名〉 drizzle: 下着蒙蒙～。 It was drizzling.
【细语】xìyǔ〈动〉 whisper: 低声～ speak in a soft voice
【细则】xìzé〈名〉 detailed rules and regulations: 合同～ detailed rules of the contract ‖ 管理～ detailed administration regulations
【细账】xìzhàng〈名〉 itemized account
【细针密缕】xìzhēn-mìlǚ〈成〉 1〈本〉 delicate and fine needlework 2〈喻〉（工作细致） meticulous in one's work: ～的校对 meticulous proof-reading 3〈喻〉（无懈可击） closely reasoned
【细枝末节】xìzhī-mòjié〈成〉 minor details: 略去～ omit details ‖ 他们尽扯些～的事。 Their talks were all about things of no consequence.
【细致】xìzhì〈形〉 1（精细周密） meticulous: 工作～ be careful with one's work ‖ ～周到 be meticulous in every minute detail 2（细腻精致） fine and delicate: ～的雕刻 exquisite sculpture ‖ ～的花纹 delicate decorative patterns
【细作】xìzuò〈名〉〈旧〉 secret agent

盻 xì〈动〉〈书〉 glare: 瞋目～之 glare at sb.

阋（鬩） xì〈动〉〈书〉 quarrel: ▸兄弟～墙

舄 xì〈名〉〈书〉 1（鞋） shoe 2 = 潟 xì

隙 xì〈名〉 1（缝隙） crack: 门/墙～ crack in the door/wall ‖ 蜥蜴跑进了石～。 A lizard darted into a crevice between two stones. ▸缝～，裂～ 2（间隙） gap: 空～ gap ‖ 农～ interval between busy seasons in farming ▸间～ 3（漏洞） loophole: ▸乘～ 4〈书〉（裂痕） rift: 与某人有～ bear ill will against sb. ‖ 这场婚姻导致他们兄弟生～。 The marriage caused a rift between the brothers. ▸嫌～
【隙地】xìdì〈名〉 unoccupied place: 林间～ clearing in the woods ‖ 在路旁的～种树 plant trees in the open space on the sides of the road
【隙缝】xìfèng〈名〉 crack: 悬崖峭壁的一道～ a rift in the cliff ‖ 有～的瓷花瓶 cracked china vase

潟 xì〈名〉〈书〉 saline land
【潟湖】xìhú〈名〉 lagoon
【潟卤】xìlǔ〈名〉〈书〉 saline-alkaline soil

xiā

呷 xiā〈动〉〈方〉 sip: ～茶聊天 chat over tea ‖ ～一口酒 take a sip of wine ▸gā

虾（蝦） xiā〈名〉 shrimp: 捕～ go shrimping ▸对～，龙～ ▸há
【虾兵蟹将】xiābīng-xièjiàng〈成〉〈喻〉 ineffective troops
【虾酱】xiājiàng〈名〉 salted shrimp paste
【虾米】xiāmi〈名〉 1（干虾） dried small shrimp 2〈方〉（小虾） small shrimp
【虾皮】xiāpí〈名〉 dried small shrimp
【虾片】xiāpiàn〈名〉 prawn-flavoured fried flour crisps
【虾仁】xiārén〈名〉 shelled fresh shrimp: 清炒～ sauté shrimps
【虾油】xiāyóu〈名〉 shrimp sauce
【虾子】xiāzǐ〈名〉 shrimp roe: ～酱 shrimp-roe paste ‖ ～酱油 shrimp roe soy sauce

瞎 xiā
A〈动〉 1（失明） be blind: ～了一只眼 be blind in one eye ‖ 又聋又～ be deaf and blind ‖ 我真～了眼，把她当好人。 I was blind to have taken her for a good person. 2〈方〉（损失） waste: 白～了一个名额 waste a candidature ‖ 一场暴风雨～了很多庄稼。 The storm destroyed a lot of crops. 3〈方〉（乱） become tangled: 毛线～成一团。 The wool is all in a tangle.
B〈副〉 vainly: ～操心 worry for nothing ‖ ～花钱 spend money foolishly ‖ 我自己的事不喜欢别人～掺和。 I don't like people meddling in my affairs.
C〈形〉 blind: ～弹 dud (bullet) ‖ 炮炮不～。 Not one of the shells failed to go off.
【瞎掰】xiābāi〈动〉〈口〉 1（白搭）make a futile effort: 所有这些努力似乎只是～而已。 All our efforts seem to be leading us down a blind alley. 2（胡说） talk nonsense: 别～了。 Stop talking nonsense. ‖ 我们不想听你～。 We want no more of your nonsense.
【瞎编】xiābiān〈动〉 fabricate: ～了一大堆理由 cook up a lot of excuses
【瞎猜】xiācāi〈动〉 make a wild guess
【瞎扯】xiāchě〈动〉 1（胡说） talk groundlessly or irresponsibly: 你对这事不清楚就不要～。 You know little about the matter, so don't talk groundlessly about it. 2（闲聊） natter: ～一晚上/一下午 natter away all evening/afternoon ‖ 别～了，快说正事吧。 Stop nattering. Let's get down to business.
【瞎吹】xiāchuī〈动〉 brag: 亩产一万斤，那是在～。 It is just a boast that the per *mu* yield reached 10,000 *jin*.
【瞎搞】xiāgǎo〈动〉 mess around with: ～一通 make a mess of
【瞎话】xiāhuà〈名〉 lie: 睁着眼睛说～ lie through one's teeth
【瞎混】xiāhùn〈动〉 mess about: 整天～ fool about all day
【瞎火】xiāhuǒ A〈名〉 dud (bullet): 打了五发炮弹，其中一发是～。 Five shells were fired and one of them was a dud. B〈动〉 fail to go off: 炮弹～了。 The shell failed to explode.
【瞎讲】xiājiǎng〈动〉 speak without any basis of fact
【瞎聊】xiāliáo〈动〉 make small talk: 围坐在一起～ sit around chatting idly
【瞎忙】xiāmáng〈动〉 potter about: 他整日～。 He just potters about all day.
【瞎猫逮死耗子】xiāmāo dǎi sǐhàozi〈俗〉〈喻〉 fluke: 你只不过是～而已。 It was a complete fluke.
【瞎蒙】xiāmēng〈动〉〈方〉 make a wild guess: 你不知道就是不知道，可别～。 If you don't know, say it. Don't just guess.
【瞎闹】xiānào〈动〉 1（胡闹） fool about: ～是闹不出个名堂来的。 Your rashness will get you nowhere. 2（无成效地乱做） act unreasonably: 不按章程办事，这是～! It's sheer madness to do things in disregard of the rules.
【瞎炮】xiāpào〈名〉 1（施工爆破中哑炮） dud 2（发射出去的哑弹） misfire
【瞎说】xiāshuō〈动〉 talk drivel: 别～了，快干正事。 Stop talking drivel and get down to business.
【瞎信】xiāxìn〈名〉 dead letter
【瞎眼】xiāyǎn〈形〉〈喻〉 blind: 我当初怎么就瞎了眼，竟然没看出他是个骗子。 I wonder why I was so blind as not to realize that he was a swindler.
【瞎折腾】xiāzhēteng〈动〉 act foolishly
【瞎指挥】xiāzhǐhuī〈惯〉 give arbitrary and impracticable instructions
【瞎抓】xiāzhuā〈动〉 work without any clear plan or system: 他复习时不得要领，～一气。 Without a methodical approach, he went about the revision in a haphazard manner.
【瞎子】xiāzi〈名〉〈贬〉 blind person: 生下来就是～ be blind from birth ‖ 他不戴眼镜就跟～一样。 He is as blind as a bat without glasses.
【瞎子点灯白费蜡】xiāzi diǎndēng báifèi là〈歇后〉 a sheer waste

xiá

匣 xiá〈名〉 casket: 首饰～ jewellery casket

X

【匣枪】xiáqiāng = 匣子枪 xiáziqiāng
【匣子】xiázi〈名〉small case: 正方形～ square casket
【匣子枪】xiáziqiāng〈名〉〈方〉Mauser pistol

侠（俠） xiá
A〈名〉chivalrous man: ▸游～
B〈形〉chivalrous: ～女 chivalrous lady ▸～肝义胆，～义
【侠盗】xiádào〈名〉chivalrous bandit [who robs the rich only to help the poor]
【侠肝义胆】xiágān-yìdǎn〈成〉chivalry and loyalty: 此人～，疾恶如仇。This man has a a strong sense of justice and a hatred of all forms of evil.
【侠骨】xiágǔ〈名〉chivalry: ～心肠 chivalrous frame of mind ‖ ～义胆 chivalry and loyalty
【侠客】xiákè〈名〉〈旧〉knight-errant
【侠气】xiáqì〈名〉chivalry
【侠士】xiáshì〈名〉chivalrous man
【侠义】xiáyì〈形〉chivalrous: ～行为 chivalrous act ‖ ～之士 chivalrous man

狎 xiá〈动〉〈书〉be inappropriately familiar with: ▸～妓，～昵
【狎妓】xiájì〈动〉visit prostitutes
【狎昵】xiánì〈形〉inappropriately familiar

柙 xiá〈名〉〈书〉wooden cage
【柙车】xiáchē〈名〉〈旧〉prison van

峡（峽） xiá〈名〉**1** ▸p. 164〔地理〕gorge: 长江三～ the Three Gorges on the Yangtze River ▸山～ **2**（海峡）strait: ▸海～
【峡沟】xiágōu〈名〉〔地理〕flume
【峡谷】xiágǔ ▸p. 164〈名〉gorge: 大～ the Grand Canyon
【峡湾】xiáwān〈名〉〔地理〕fjord

狭（狹） xiá〈形〉narrow: ～路 narrow path ‖ 坡陡路～。The slope is steep and the path narrow. ▸～隘，～长，～义
【狭隘】xiá'ài〈形〉**1**（窄）narrow: ～的山道 narrow mountain trail **2**（不宽广）parochial: 心胸～ be narrow-minded ‖ 走出～的家族小圈子 step out of the narrow confines of the family clan ‖ 此人眼界太～。The man is too parochial in his outlook.
【狭长】xiácháng〈形〉long and narrow: ～的山谷 long and narrow valley
【狭路相逢】xiálù-xiāngféng〈成〉come into unavoidable confrontation
【狭小】xiáxiǎo〈形〉narrow and small: 气量～ be closed-minded ‖ ～的空间 confined space
【狭义】xiáyì〈名〉narrow sense: ～的解释 narrow interpretation ‖ ～的文学 literature in the narrow sense of the word
【狭窄】xiázhǎi **A**〈形〉narrow: ～的小巷/人行道/走廊 narrow lane/pavement/corridor ‖ 心地/心胸～ be narrow-minded ‖ 知识面～ be limited in knowledge ‖ 此处河面～。The river narrows at this point. **B** ▸p. 50〈名〉〔医学〕stenosis, stricture: 骨盆/尿道～ stricture of pelvis/urethra

遐 xiá〈形〉〈书〉**1**（遥远）distant: ～布 spread far and wide ▸～想 **2**（长久）lasting: ～祚 enduring blessing or happiness
【遐迩】xiá'ěr〈形〉〈书〉far and wide: 闻名～ be known far and wide
【遐龄】xiálíng〈名〉〈书〉advanced age
【遐思】xiásī = 遐想 xiáxiǎng
【遐想】xiáxiǎng〈动〉daydream: 闭目～ be lost in thought with one's eyes closed ‖ 沉浸在～中 indulge in reveries

瑕 xiá〈名〉flaw in a piece of jade: 白玉微～ minute flaw in white jade
【瑕不掩瑜】xiábùyǎnyú〈成〉small defects cannot obscure great virtues
【瑕疵】xiácī〈名〉flaw: 留下～ leave a blemish ‖ 这颗祖母绿有一点～。This emerald jade has a flaw in it.
【瑕玷】xiádiàn〈名〉〈书〉blemish
【瑕瑜互见】xiáyú-hùjiàn〈成〉have both strong and weak points

暇 xiá〈名〉free time: 得～ have free time ‖ ～日 day of leisure ▸闲～，应接不～

辖（轄） xiá
A〈名〉linchpin
B〈动〉have jurisdiction over: 省～市 municipality or city directly under the jurisdiction of the provincial government ‖ 下～两个装甲师 have two armoured divisions under its command ▸管～，统～，直～
【辖区】xiáqū〈名〉area of jurisdiction: 那个市场不在该派出所的～之内。That market does not fall within the police station's jurisdiction.
【辖制】xiázhì〈动〉control: 香港的廉正公署不受任何个人的～。The Independent Committee of Anti-corruption in Hong Kong is not under the control of any individual.

霞 xiá〈名〉morning or evening glow of the sun: ▸彩～，晚～，朝～
【霞光】xiáguāng〈名〉rays of morning or evening sunlight: ～四射 magnificent beams of radiating sunshine ‖ ～万道 gorgeous rays of light
【霞帔】xiápèi〈名〉〈古〉embroidered ceremonial shawl of a noble woman

黠 xiá〈形〉〈书〉**1**（聪慧）clever: ▸～慧 **2**（狡诈）crafty: ▸狡～
【黠慧】xiáhuì〈形〉〈书〉shrewd

xià

下[1] xià
A〈名〉**1**（低处）low position or rank: 零～10度 ten degrees below zero ‖ 从桥～通过 pass beneath a bridge ‖ 上有老，～有小 have both parents and children to support ‖ 在山脚～ at the foot of a mountain ‖ 结果/摘要如～。The result/excerpt is as follows. ▸上有天堂，～有苏杭，自～而上 **2**（表属于一定范围、条件等）[used to indicate circumstance, extent, situation, etc.]: 在非常困难的情况～ under very difficult conditions ‖ 在交警的帮助～ with the help of the traffic policemen ‖ 在专家组的领导～ under the leadership of the expert group **3**（表方向或方位）[used after numerals, indicating position or direction]: 他把头伸出去，四～里看了看。He poked his head out and took a look around. ‖ 他俩～里都反对。Both of them opposed it. ▸普天之～ **4**（表当某个时间或时节）[used to indicate a certain time or season]: ▸节～，时～，眼～
B〈形〉**1**（处于低处）lower: ～嘴唇 lower lip ▸～层，～游，～肢 **2**（时间、顺序在后）next: 看～一场比赛 watch the next match ‖ ～个星期/世纪 next week/century ‖ ～一章/一站 next chapter/stop ‖ ～一步需要做的是找所房子。The next step is to find a house. **3**（等级低）lower: 分为上、中、～三等 be divided into three grades: the upper, the middle and the lower ▸～属

下[2] xià〈动〉**1**（低于）[usu used in the negative] be less than: 受伤者不～五十人。There were no less than fifty wounded. **2**（从高到低）go down: ～车 get out of a car ‖ ～床 get out of bed ‖ ～楼 go downstairs ‖ ～山 come down a mountain **3**（去）go down to: ～车间 go down to a workshop ‖ ～厨房 go into the kitchen to cook ‖ ～基层 go down to the grass roots ‖ 南～广州 go down to Guangzhou **4**（发布）issue: ～命令 issue orders ‖ ～通知 send out notices ‖ ～逐客令 show sb. the door **5**（离开）leave: ～火线 retreat from the front line ‖ 客队要求换人：3号上，7号～。The visiting team is requesting to substitute No 3 for No 7. ‖ 演出结束后从后门～。After the performance, please exit from the back door. ▸～岗 **6**（结束）stop: ～夜班 come off the night shift ▸～班，～课 **7**（降水）fall: ～霜。There is frost. ‖ 毛毛雨～个不停。A fine drizzle keeps falling. ‖ 雨～了一夜。Rain came down all night. ▸～雨 **8**（使用）begin to use: ～刀 stick a knife into sth. ‖ ～力气 exert oneself ▸～笔，～毒手 **9**（放入）put into: ～面条 put noodles into boiling water ‖ ～网 cast a net ‖ ～种 sow a field with seeds ‖ ～佐料 put in condiments **10**（进行）play: ～盘棋 have a game of chess **11**（取下）take down: 把门～下来 take down a door ‖ ～俘虏的枪 disarm a captive ‖ ～货 unload the cargo **12**（生产）give birth to: 刚～的蛋 newly laid egg ‖ 母猪要～崽了。The sow is about to give birth. ▸～蛋 **13**（做出）give: ～定义 give a definition ‖ ～结论 draw a conclusion ‖ ～判断 form an opinion **14**（攻陷）capture: 连～数城 capture several cities in succession **15**（退让）give in: 双方相持不～。Neither side would give in.

下[3] xià〈量〉**1**〈方〉（表容量）[used to indicate the amount of something in a container]: 瓶子里只有半～油。The bottle is half full of oil. **2**（表本领、技能）[used after 两 or 几, indicating one's ability or skill]: 真有两～子 have a special skill ‖ 他就这么几～子。That's all he can do. **3**（表动作次数）[used to indicate the repetition of an action]: 摆了～手 wave one's hand ‖ 看了一～ have a look ‖ 拍了一～肩膀 give sb. a pat on the shoulder ‖ 打扫一～房间 give the room a clean ‖ 钟敲了三～。The clock struck three times.
▸xia
【下奥陶纪】Xià Àotáojì〈名〉〔地质〕Lower Ordovician
【下巴】xiàba〈名〉**1**（下颌）chin: 翘起～ lift the chin ‖ 手托着～ cup one's chin in one's hand **2**（颏）lower jaw: 双～ double chin
【下巴颏儿】xiàbakēr〈名〉〈口〉chin
【下白垩纪】Xià Bái'èjì〈名〉〔地质〕Lower Cretaceous
【下摆】xiàbǎi〈名〉lower hem: ～开衩 side slit ‖ 长大衣的～ skirt of a long coat

【下拜】xiàbài〈动〉 kneel down to pay respect

【下班】xiàbān〈动〉 get off work: 已经～ be off duty ‖ 你什么时候～? What time do you finish work?

【下半辈子】xiàbànbèizi〈名〉 the rest of one's life: 他是我～的惟一依托。 He will be my sole support for the rest of my life.

【下半场】xiàbànchǎng〈名〉［体育］ second half of a game: 客队～又进一球。 The visiting team scored another goal in the second half.

【下半年】xiàbànnián ▸p. 618〈名〉 second half of a year: 为～做预算 budget for the second half of a year

【下半旗】xià bànqí〈动〉 fly a flag at half-mast: ～致哀 hang a flag at half mast to mourn the dead

【下半晌】xiàbànshǎng〈名〉〈口〉 afternoon: ～，天下起了大雪。 Snow began to fall heavily in the afternoon.

【下半身】xiàbànshēn〈名〉 lower part of the body: 她～瘫痪。 She is paralyzed in the lower part of her body.

【下半时】xiàbànshí = 下半场 xiàbànchǎng

【下半天】xiàbàntiān〈名〉 afternoon

【下半叶】xiàbànyè〈名〉 second half: 18世纪～ during the latter half of the 18th century

【下半夜】xiàbànyè〈名〉 latter half of the night: 他经常工作到～。 He often stayed up until the small hours.

【下半月】xiàbànyuè〈名〉 second half of a month: 呈交～的财务报表 submit the financial statements of the second half of the month

【下辈】xiàbèi〈名〉 1（子孙） future generations 2（下一代） younger generation of a family: ～尊敬长辈。 The younger generation should respect the elder generation.

【下辈子】xiàbèizi ▸p. 618〈名〉 next life: 我～一定报答你。 I will repay your kindness in the next life.

【下本钱】xià běnqian〈动〉 make an investment: 他急于赚钱，但不愿～。 He is eager to make a fortune, but is unwilling to invest anything. ‖ 要舍得～培养人才。 Don't begrudge the investment in training qualified personnel.

【下笔】xiàbǐ〈动〉 put pen to paper: 不知如何～。 I don't know how to start my piece. ‖ 你想好了再～。Think it out before you put pen to paper.

【下笔成章】xiàbǐ-chéngzhāng〈成〉 have literary ability

【下笔千言】xiàbǐ qiānyán〈成〉 write with amazing speed: ～，离题万里。 Write quickly but stray far off the point.

【下臂】xiàbì〈名〉 lower arm

【下边】xiàbian〈名〉 1（指方位） lower place: 大桥～ under the bridge ‖ 最～一个抽屉 bottom drawer 2（指顺序） next: ～轮到你了。 It's your turn next. ‖ ～请魏先生讲话。 May I now ask Mr Wei to speak? 3（指等级） subordinate: 倾听～的意见 listen attentively to the views of one's subordinates

【下拨】xiàbō〈动〉 allocate: ～旅行费用 disburse funds for travelling expenses

【下不为例】xiàbùwéilì〈成〉 not to be taken as a precedent: 我保证～。 I promise not to do it again.

【下不来】xiàbulái〈动〉 1（下降） be unable to come down: 孩子的体温～。 The child's temperature won't come down. 2（办不成） will not do: 这件衣服没有300美元～。 The dress isn't to be had for less than $300. 3（难堪） be embarrassed: 她的话让丈夫脸上～。 Her husband was visibly embarrassed at her remarks.

【下不来台】xiàbuláitái〈惯〉 be unable to dig oneself out of a hole: 让朋友～ be an embarrassment to a friend

【下不了台】xiàbuliǎotái = 下不来台 xiàbuláitái

【下操】xiàcāo〈动〉 1（出操） take exercises: 我们上午～，下午上课。 We have drills in the morning, and lectures in the afternoon. 2（收操） finish drilling: 他刚～回来。 He is just back from his workout.

【下策】xiàcè〈名〉 unwise decision: 不得已才出此～ have no alternative but to resort to this

【下层】xiàcéng〈名〉 1（指位置） lower levels: 公共汽车的～ lower deck of a double-decker bus ‖ 书架的～ lower levels of a bookshelf 2（指阶层） grass roots: 处于社会最～ be at the lowest stratum of society ‖ ～军官 junior officer

【下层社会】xiàcéng shèhuì〈名〉 lower stratum of society

【下场】xiàchǎng A〈动〉 1（离开舞台） exit from the stage: 谢完幕就～ go offstage after the curtain call 2（离开赛场） exit the playground, court, etc.: 客队5号被罚～之后，主队连入两球。 As soon as the visiting team's No. 5 was sent off, the home team scored two successive goals. B〈名〉 end: 为非作歹没好～。 Those who do evil will definitely come to a bad end.

【下场门】xiàchǎngmén〈名〉exit of a stage

【下车伊始】xiàchē-yīshǐ〈成〉 as soon as one takes office

【下沉】xiàchén〈动〉sink: 地基～了。 The foundations have subsided. ‖ 轮船慢慢～了。 The ship sank gradually.

【下沉气流】xiàchén qìliú〈名〉［气象］ downdraught

【下乘】xiàchéng A〈名〉［佛教］ Hinayana B〈形〉 shoddy: ～之作 artistic work of inferior quality

【下厨】xiàchú〈动〉 prepare food

【下处】xiàchu〈名〉 temporary lodging: 找个～ find a lodging

【下船】xiàchuán〈动〉 1（上岸） disembark: ～时，请带好自己的随身物品。 When you disembark, please make sure that you have all your belongings with you. 2（登船） get aboard: 旅客们剪票～。 All the passengers had their tickets punched and boarded the boat.

【下床】xiàchuáng〈动〉 get out of bed

【下垂】xiàchuí〈动〉 1（向下垂） hang down: 沉甸甸的稻穗～着。 The ears of rice drooped heavily. ‖ 她的头发～到肩头。 Her hair hung down on her shoulders. 2 ▸p. 50［医学］ prolapse: 子宫～ prolapse of the uterus ‖ 胃～ ptosis of the stomach

【下唇】xiàchún〈名〉 lower lip: 咬着～ bite one's lower lip ‖ 厚厚的～ full lower lip

【下次】xiàcì〈名〉 next time

【下存】xiàcún〈动〉 deposit a remaining sum: 取200元，～800元。 I'll withdraw 200 *yuan* and keep the remaining 800 *yuan* in my account.

【下挫】xiàcuò〈动〉 plummet: 股价大幅～。 Share prices plummeted.

【下达】xiàdá〈动〉 transmit: ～命令 issue orders ‖ ～任务 assign a task ‖ 直接～到基层 transmit directly to the basic level

【下蛋】xiàdàn〈动〉 lay eggs: 这些鸡冬天不～。 These hens don't lay eggs in winter.

【下等】xiàděng〈形〉 inferior: 质量～ be inferior in quality ‖ ～客房 cheap hotel room ‖ 开～酒吧 run a cheap bar ‖ ～人 person of the lower classes

【下地】xiàdì〈动〉 1（在田间） go to the fields: ～干活 go to work in the fields 2（下床活动） be up: 她能～走动了。 She is up and about. 3〈方〉（婴儿出生） be newborn

【下跌】xiàdiē〈动〉 drop: 股票价格骤然～。 Share prices plunged. ‖ 美元可能继续～。 The dollar may slump further.

【下定义】xiàdìngyì〈动〉 define

【下碇】xiàdìng〈动〉 cast anchor: 停船～ cast anchor

【下毒】xiàdú〈动〉 poison

【下毒手】xià dúshǒu〈动〉 deal (sb.) a deadly blow

【下蹲】xiàdūn〈动〉 squat down: ～姿势 squatting position

【下蹲式发球】xiàdūnshì fāqiú〈名〉［体育］ squatting service

【下颚】xià'è〈名〉 lower jaw

【下凡】xiàfán〈动〉 descend to earth: 天仙～。 A fairy descends to the mortal world.

【下饭】xiàfàn A〈动〉 have savoury dishes with one's staple food: 你拿什么～? What are you going to have with your rice? B〈形〉 good with staple food: 这个菜很～。 This dish goes very well with rice.

【下方】xiàfāng〈名〉 lower position: 左眼～有块伤疤 have a scar below one's left eye ‖ 在窗户～ beneath the window

【下房】xiàfáng〈名〉〈旧〉 servants' quarters: 几间～ several rooms for the servants

【下访】xiàfǎng〈动〉 consult with the masses: 开展多种形式的～活动 carry out a range of different activities in consultation with the masses

【下放】xiàfàng〈动〉 1（指权力） transfer to a lower level: 权力～ transfer authority to a lower level ‖ ～审批权限 delegate the power of examination and approval to the lower levels 2（指人） send officials to work in grass roots units or to do manual labour in the countryside or in a factory: ～劳动 transfer a cadre to do manual labour ‖ ～到农村 transfer sb. to work in the countryside

【下风】xiàfēng〈名〉 1（风吹去的方向） leeward: 他们住在一家养猪场的～处，有时味道很难闻。 They live downwind of a pig-farm and sometimes the smell is awful. 2〈喻〉（不利地位）disadvantageous position: 处于～ be at a disadvantage ▸甘拜～

【下浮】xiàfú〈动〉 drop: 利率～一个百分点。 The interest rate dropped by one per cent.

【下腹部】xiàfùbù〈名〉 underbelly

【下疳】xiàgān ▸p. 50〈名〉［医学］ chancre: 软性/硬性～ soft/hard chancre

【下岗】xiàgǎng〈动〉 1（换岗） go off sentry duty: 夜深了，交警仍未～。 It was late at night, but the traffic policemen were still on duty. 2 ▸p. 772 ▸p. 966（失业） be laid off: 安置～人员再就业 find jobs for laid-off workers ‖ ～分流 redistribute laid-off workers

【下工】xiàgōng〈动〉 knock off work: ～回家 get off work and go home ‖ 他们几点～? When will they knock off?

【下工夫】xià gōngfu〈动〉 put in time and energy: 想学好技术，就得～。 It takes time and effort to learn any skill.

【下馆子】xià guǎnzi〈动〉 dine out: 今晚我们～。 We're dining out tonight.

【下跪】xiàguì〈动〉kneel down: 双膝～ go down on one's knees ‖ 他向我～求饶。He begged me on his knees for forgiveness.

【下锅】xiàguō〈动〉put into the pot and start cooking: 豆角已经～了。The beans have already been put into the pan. ‖ 他家穷得没米～。His family is going hungry.

【下海】xiàhǎi〈动〉**1**（到海里去）go to sea: ～游泳 swim in the sea **2**（出海捕鱼）go fishing out at sea: 初次～，头晕呕吐是常事。You may very probably get sick and dizzy the first time you go out to sea. **3**（转为职业演员）turn professional **4**（离职经商）leave one's original profession and go into business: 他辞职～了。He resigned and went into commerce.

【下颌】xiàhé〈名〉［解剖］lower jaw

【下滑】xiàhuá〈动〉slide down: 防止山体～ prevent the mountain slope from sliding ‖ 她学习成绩～了。Her school marks have slipped.

【下怀】xiàhuái〈名〉〈谦〉one's heart's desire: ▸正中～

【下回】xiàhuí〈名〉next time

【下级】xiàjí〈名〉**1**（指级别）lower level: ～单位 subordinate unit ‖ ～服从上级。The lower level is subordinate to the higher level. **2**（指人）subordinate: 对～很粗暴 be rude to one's subordinates

【下集】xiàjí〈名〉**1**（指最后一部分）second part of a two-part programme or third part of a three-part programme **2**（指下一部分）next part (in a series)

【下家】xiàjiā〈名〉**1**（指打牌、行酒令等）next player: 该～出牌了。It is the next player's turn to play his card. **2**（指商业活动）next persons to whom goods are sold in a pyramid selling structure: 他的～催货很急。His client is very anxious to receive his goods.

【下嫁】xiàjià〈动〉〈旧〉marry beneath oneself: 宰相的女儿～给了一位农家子弟。The prime minister's daughter is married to a farmer's son.

【下贱】xiàjiàn〈形〉**1**〈旧〉（低贱）humble: 出身～ be of humble birth ‖ ～之人 person of humble origin **2**（卑劣）degrading: ～货 base person ‖ 我从未想到你会～到偷人家东西（的地步）。I never thought you would stoop to stealing.

【下江】xiàjiāng〈名〉lower reaches of the Yangtze River

【下降】xiàjiàng〈动〉fall: 质量～ fall in quality ‖ 成本～了4%。The cost was reduced by four per cent. ‖ 我的听力在～。My hearing is getting worse. ‖ 气温～了10度。The temperature fell by 10°C.

【下脚】xiàjiǎo〈动〉get a foothold: 没有地方～ be unable to gain a foothold ‖ 难以～ be difficult to get a footing

【下脚料】xiàjiǎoliào〈名〉scraps

【下届】xiàjiè〈名〉**1**（指会期）next session: ～联合国大会 next session of the UN General Assembly **2**（指任期）next term: 竞选～总统 run for the next presidency **3**（指学生）next year: ～毕业生 next year's graduate

【下界】xiàjiè **A**〈名〉human world **B** = 下凡 xiàfán

【下劲】xiàjìn〈动〉exert oneself: 他工作起来很～。He works like a demon.

【下九流】xiàjiǔliú〈名〉〈旧〉people from the lower walks of life: 这家小酒馆曾是各路～出没的地方。This small inn used to be frequented by people from the lower walks of life.

【下酒】xiàjiǔ **A**〈动〉go with wine: 用花生米～ serve the wine with peanuts **B**〈形〉going well with wine: 来点儿～的菜。Get some dishes that go well with wine.

【下酒菜】xiàjiǔcài〈名〉dish to go with wine

【下卷】xiàjuàn〈名〉the second volume of a two-volume book or the third of a three-volume book

【下课】xiàkè〈动〉**1**（上课结束）dismiss a class: ～铃响了。There goes the recess bell. ‖ 老师因为要开会，提前下了课。The teacher dismissed the class early because she had a meeting. **2**〈喻〉（被撤换）be fired: 球迷一再要求该队的主教练～。The football fans insistently demanded the dismissal of the team's head coach.

【下款】xiàkuǎn〈名〉signature

【下来】xiàlái〈动〉**1**（指从高处）come down: 从楼上～ come downstairs ‖ 他不好好学习，最近成绩～了。He hasn't been studying hard recently and his marks have dropped. **2**（指从上级部门）come down to a lower-level government office: 中央～了一个检查组。An inspection group came down from the central government. **3**（收获）be in season: 再有半个月桃就～了。Peaches will be in season in another half a month. **4**（时间结束）come to an end: 一年～，她学完了八门功课。After a year's study she completed eight courses. **5**（指动作趋向）[used after a verb to indicate a movement from a higher position to a lower position or from far to near]: 掉～ fall down ‖ 记～ take down ‖ 跳～ jump down ‖ 把李子从树上摘～。Pick the plums off the tree. **6**（指动作延续）[used after a verb to indicate a continuation from the past to the present or from the beginning to the end]: 坚持～ stick things out ‖ 一代一代传～ hand down from generation to generation **7**（指动作完成）[used after a verb to indicate the completion or result of an action]: 把车停～ bring a car to a stop ‖ 风停了～。The wind dropped. ‖ 我们的计划批～了。Our plan has been approved. **8**（指状态持续）[used after an adjective to indicate decrease of intensity]: 安静～ quiet down ‖ 灯光在渐渐暗～。The lights are dimming. ‖ 我对他的热情淡～了。My enthusiasm for him cooled off.

【下里巴人】xiàlǐ-bārén〈名〉**1**（指民间歌曲）Songs of the Rustic Poor [rustic folk songs popular among farmers in the State of Chu during the Warring States Period] **2**〈喻〉（通俗的文艺作品）popular literature or art: 这出戏虽然被称作～，但却很受欢迎。Though labelled as rustic, the play was very popular.

【下力】xiàlì〈动〉make efforts

【下联】xiàlián〈名〉the second line of a couplet: 你出上联，我对～。You offer the first line of the couplet, and I'll match it with a second.

【下列】xiàliè〈形〉following: 邀请～人员 invite those listed below ‖ 注意～几点。Pay attention to the following points.

【下令】xiàlìng〈动〉order: ～撤退/紧急着陆 order a retreat/an emergency landing

【下流】xiàliú **A**〈名〉**1**（下游）lower reaches of a river: 长江/黄河～ lower reaches of the Yangtze/Yellow River **2**〈旧〉（指地位）inferior rank: 位居～ be at the bottom of the hierarchy **B**〈形〉lewd: ～勾当 lewd act ‖ ～图片/网站 obscene picture/website ‖ 他讲的笑话很～。His jokes were really dirty.

【下楼】xiàlóu〈动〉go downstairs

【下落】xiàluò **A**〈名〉whereabouts: 丢失的货物有了～。The lost articles have been located. ‖ 她至今～不明。Her whereabouts are still unknown. **B**〈动〉drop: 热气球突然开始快速～。All of a sudden the hot-air balloon started to plummet.

【下马】xiàmǎ〈动〉**1**〈本〉dismount from a horse **2**〈喻〉call off: 工程～ discontinue a project

【下马看花】xiàmǎkànhuā〈成〉〈喻〉stay close to the action and investigate

【下马威】xiàmǎwēi〈名〉severity of a newly-appointed official: 给对手一个～ prevail over one's opponent from the very first encounter

【下毛毛雨】xià máomaoyǔ〈惯〉〈喻〉**1**（透露消息）impart: 先给她下点毛毛雨，让她思想有所准备。Break this to her gradually so that she can be mentally prepared. **2**（温和地批评）make a slight criticism: ～对他根本就没有用。Mild criticisms mean nothing to him.

【下面】xiàmian = 下边 xiàbian

【下品】xiàpǐn〈名〉thing of poor quality: 画中～ inferior painting

【下聘】xiàpìn〈动〉〈旧〉present betrothal gifts: ～娶亲 deliver betrothal gifts and marry

【下坡路】xiàpōlù〈名〉**1**（指坡路）downhill path: 这是一条～。The path slopes down. **2**〈喻〉（指趋势）downward slope: 他的身体一直在走～。His health has been on the decline. ‖ 学习上稍有放松，成绩就走～。If you slack off in your studies, your grades are going to suffer.

【下铺】xiàpù〈名〉**1**（指铺位）bottom berth **2**（指床）lower bunk

【下棋】xiàqí〈动〉play chess

【下欠】xiàqiàn **A**〈动〉still owe: 这辆车15万元，我们首付了5万，～10万。The price of the car is 150,000 *yuan*. We paid a 50,000 *yuan* down payment and still have 100,000 *yuan* owing. **B**〈名〉sum still owing: 你们全部还清了，并无～。The debt has been fully paid up. You don't owe anything.

【下情】xiàqíng〈名〉**1**（下级情况）grass roots conditions: ～上达 make the situation at the lower levels known to the higher levels ‖ 体察～ observe and understand the life and thoughts of ordinary people **2**（下级意见）grass roots opinion: ～上达 report grass roots opinions to the authority ‖ 了解～ find out what the masses are thinking **3**〈谦〉〈旧〉（自己的意思或心情）my situation

【下去】xiàqù〈动〉**1**（去低处）go down: 从山上～ go down the mountain ‖ 水很深，你敢～吗？Dare you go into such deep water? **2**（去基层）[of officials of higher ranks or positions] go down: 省长每年都要～搞调查。The governor goes down to the grass roots to make investigations every year. **3**（离职）step down: 乐意～，把位子让给年轻人 be willing to step aside in favour of a younger person **4**（离场）make an exit: 从舞台上～ go offstage ‖ 这位篮球运动员受伤～了。The basketball player got injured and went off the court. **5**（消退）return to a normal state: 他的气～了吗？Has he calmed down yet? ‖ 病人的烧～了。The patient's fever is down. **6**（消化）digest **7**（表动作趋向）[used after a verb, indicating a motion away from a higher place to a lower one or from the near to the far]: 把犯人押～ take the convict away ‖ 把药咽～ get the medicine down ‖ 洪水退～了。The flood has receded. **8**（表动作延续） [used after a verb, indicating the continuation of an action]: 继续干～ keep on working ‖ 请讲～。 Please carry on what you were saying. ‖ 再争吵～，对谁都没有好处。 It is in nobody's interests to continue arguing. ‖ 仗会一直打～。 The fighting will continue. **9**（表状态延续发展） [used after an adjective, indicating an increasing degree]: 瘦～ get thinner and thinner ‖ 选举失败后，她就消沉～了。 She got increasingly despondent after her defeat in the election.

【下人】xiàrén〈名〉〈旧〉 servant: 吩咐～去做 tell a servant to do it

【下三烂】xiàsānlàn **A**〈形〉 lacking in morals and honour: ～的动机 base motive ‖ ～的工作 degrading job **B**〈名〉 contemptible person: 村里的～ village riff-raff

【下山】xiàshān〈动〉 **1**（指人） go down a mountain **2**（指太阳） set

【下身】xiàshēn〈名〉 **1**（下半身） lower part of the body: 他～瘫痪。 The lower part of his body is paralysed. **2** ►**p. 772**〈婉〉（阴部） private parts **3**（指裙子） lower hem;（指裤子） trousers: 这套衣服～有些长。 The suit trousers are a bit long in the leg.

【下剩】xiàshèng〈动〉〈口〉 be left over: ～的粮食不多了。 There isn't much grain left. ‖ 我留下20块钱，～的给你。 I'll keep 20 *yuan* and the rest is for you.

【下士】xiàshì〈名〉 **1**［陆军］ corporal **2**［海军］ petty officer;（美国和中国） petty officer third class;（英国） petty officer second class **3**［空军］（美国和中国） sergeant;（英国） corporal

【下世】xiàshì **A**〈动〉 pass away: 他的父亲去年～了。 His father passed away last year. **B**〈名〉 next life: 真希望能有～，好重新做人。 How I wish I could have a next life so that I could begin again.

【下市】xiàshì〈动〉 **1**（已过产销旺季） come off the shelves: 立秋后西瓜～。 After the Beginning of Autumn, watermelons disappear from the market. **2**（结束一天的营业） be finished: 那些商店老早就～了。 The shops closed very early.

【下手】xiàshǒu **A**〈动〉 start doing sth.: 等到时机成熟再～ wait until the time is ripe to strike ‖ 无从～ not know where to start ‖ 他心太软，不敢～。 He is too soft-hearted to get it done. **B**〈名〉 **1**（指位置） seat of lower priority: 坐在老板～ sit to the right of the boss **2**〈口〉（助手） helper: 打～ act as an assistant ‖ 我们三人给你当～。 The three of us will act as your assistants. ‖ 她是那位厨师的得力～。 She is quite a help to the chef. **3** = 下家 xiàjiā

【下首】xiàshǒu = 下手 xiàshǒu B1

【下属】xiàshǔ〈名〉 subordinate: 把～当朋友一样 treat one's subordinates like friends ‖ 这个公司是我们的～单位。 This firm is our subsidiary.

【下水】xiàshuǐ〈动〉 **1**（指新船） be launched: 一艘新船～了。 A new ship was launched. **2**（指人、动物等） enter the water: ～游泳 go down to the water for a swim **3**（指纺织品等） shrink cloth or fabrics in water before use: 布料一经～，做成的衣服就不会缩水了。 The dress won't shrink in the wash because the fabric has been pre-shrunk. **4**〈喻〉（做坏事） fall into evil ways: 拉/拖～ lead sb. astray **5**（顺流而下） go downstream: ～船 downriver boat

【下水道】xiàshuǐdào〈名〉 sewer: 厨房～堵了。 The kitchen drain is blocked.

【下水管】xiàshuǐguǎn〈名〉 drainpipe

【下水】xiàshui〈名〉 offal: 猪～ pig's offal

【下榻】xiàtà〈动〉〈书〉 stay at: ～于钟楼饭店 stay at the Bell Tower Hotel

【下台】xiàtái〈动〉 **1**（离开舞台） go offstage: 把演员轰～ boo an actor off the stage **2**（交出权力） step down: 被迫～ be forced to step down ‖ 总统快～了。 The President will soon leave office. **3**〈喻〉（摆脱窘境） [usu used in the negative] get out of a predicament or an embarrassing situation: 使某人下不了台 put sb. on the spot ‖ 市长当时真有些没法～。 The mayor was really unable to deal with the embarrassing situation.

【下台阶】xiàtáijiē〈动〉〈喻〉 get out of a predicament or an embarrassing situation

【下体】xiàtǐ〈书〉= 下身 xiàshēn 1

【下田】xiàtián〈动〉 go to work in the (paddy) fields: ～插秧 go to the fields to transplant rice seedlings

【下调】xiàtiáo〈动〉 lower: ～价格 lower the price ‖ ～利率 lower the interest rate

【下同】xiàtóng〈名〉 [used in annotations] the same below

【下头】xiàtou = 下边 xiàbian 1, 3

【下网】xiàwǎng〈动〉 **1**（撒网） cast a net **2**［计算机］ go off line

【下文】xiàwén〈名〉 **1**（下面的文字） next part: 详见～ see below for details ‖ 听听～怎么说。 Let's stay and hear what's coming next. **2**〈喻〉（后续发展） outcome: 这件事后来就没有了～。 Nothing more has been heard about it since.

【下问】xiàwèn〈动〉 consult one's subordinate or a less learned person

【下午】xiàwǔ ►**p. 669**〈名〉 afternoon: ～三点 3 p.m. ‖ 今天/明天/昨天～ this/tomorrow/yesterday afternoon

【下下】xiàxià〈形〉 **1**（最差） worst: ～策 worst policy ‖ 抽了个～签 draw the worst of lots **2**（比后一个时期更往后） after next: ～个月 the month after next ‖ ～星期 the week after next

【下弦】xiàxián〈名〉［天文］ last or third quarter of the moon: ～月 waning moon

【下限】xiàxiàn〈名〉 floor: 工资/年龄～ minimum wage/age

【下线】xiàxiàn **A**〈动〉 come off the production line: 这车明年一月可以～。 The car will come off the line next January. **B**〈名〉 **1**（指贩卖） receiver of trafficked goods: 追查毒贩的～。 Track down the receivers of trafficked drugs. **2**（指传销） recruit into a pyramid scheme

【下陷】xiàxiàn〈动〉 sink, subside: 眼窝～ have sunken eyes ‖ 地基～了。 The foundations have subsided.

【下乡】xiàxiāng〈动〉 go down to the countryside: ～劳动 go to work in the country ‖ 文化、科技、卫生三～活动 activities to bring culture, science and technology, and medical and health care to the rural areas

【下泄】xiàxiè〈动〉 flow downstream: 洪峰正沿江～。 The flood peak is surging down the river.

【下泻】xiàxiè〈动〉 **1**（指水） flow downstream: ～不畅 be impeded in its downflow **2**（指价格） plummet: 汇率一路～。 The exchange rate dropped sharply. **3**（指腹泻） have loose bowels: ►上吐～

【下行】xiàxíng〈动〉 **1**（指火车） go down line: ～列车 down train ‖ ～线 down line **2**（指船） go downstream: ～船 downriver boat **3**（指文件） be sent to subordinate units: ～公文 documents to be delivered to the lower levels

【下旋球】xiàxuánqiú〈名〉［体育］ backspin

【下学】xiàxué〈动〉 finish school for the day: ～后步行回家 walk home after school

【下雪】xiàxuě〈动〉 snow: ～了! It's snowing!

【下旬】xiàxún ►**p. 618**〈名〉 last ten days of a month: 本月～ late this month

【下咽】xiàyàn〈动〉 swallow: 难以～的饭菜 unpalatable food

【下药】xiàyào〈动〉 **1**（开药方） prescribe medicines: 对症～ prescribe the right remedy for an illness **2**（下毒） put poison in, poison: 在咖啡里～ poison sb.'s coffee

【下野】xiàyě〈动〉 be forced to step down: 被迫～ be forced to relinquish power

【下一个】xiàyīgè〈代〉 next one

【下义词】xiàyìcí〈名〉［语言］ hyponym

【下议院】xiàyìyuàn〈名〉 lower house (of a parliament);（英国） House of Commons

【下意识】xiàyìshí **A**〈名〉 subconscious: 我的回答似乎是出自～。 My answer seemed to come from the subconscious. **B**〈副〉 subconsciously: 见到生人，她总是～低下头。 She'll always look down subconsciously when she sees a stranger.

【下影线】xiàyǐngxiàn〈名〉［金融］ lower shadow

【下游】xiàyóu〈名〉 **1**（指河流） lower reaches: 长江～（地区） lower reaches of the Yangtze **2**〈喻〉（指地位） backward position: 不可甘居～ must not resign oneself to lagging behind

【下游行业】xiàyóu hángyè〈名〉 downstream industry

【下雨】xiàyǔ〈动〉 rain: 下大雨。 It is raining hard.

【下狱】xiàyù〈动〉 imprison: ～六个月 be sent to prison for six months

【下院】xiàyuàn = 下议院 xiàyìyuàn

【下载】xiàzài〈动〉［计算机］ download: 从网上～到个人电脑 download sth. from the Internet onto one's personal computer ‖ 免费～ free download

【下葬】xiàzàng〈动〉 be buried: 择日～ choose a date for sb.'s interment

【下账】xiàzhàng〈动〉 enter into the account book: 这笔开销没有发票无法～。 The expenditure cannot be entered into the accounts without a formal invoice.

【下肢】xiàzhī〈名〉 legs: ～麻痹 paraplegia

【下种】xiàzhǒng〈动〉 sow: 什么时候～最好? When is the best time to sow?

【下注】xiàzhù〈动〉 make a bet: 拿手中一半钱～ stake half of one's money

【下箸】xiàzhù〈动〉〈书〉 start eating

【下装】xiàzhuāng〈动〉 remove theatrical make-up and costume

【下坠】xiàzhuì **A**〈动〉 fall: 跳伞人员向地面缓缓～。 The parachutists gradually dropped earthward. **B** ►**p. 50**〈名〉［医学］ strain tenesmus: 排尿～ vesical tenesmus

【下子】xiàzǐ〈动〉 **1**（播种） sow seeds **2**（下蛋） lay eggs

【下子】xiàzi = 下³ xià

【下作】xiàzuo〈形〉 mean: 无耻～的手段 mean trick

吓（嚇）

xià〈动〉 frighten: ～得脸色苍白 go white with fright ‖ 别～着孩子。 Don't scare the children. ‖ 你～了我一跳! You startled me!
►hè

【吓唬】xiàhu〈动〉 scare: 别担心，我只不过～～他。 Don't worry. I was only putting the wind up him.

【吓人】xiàrén〈形〉 scary: ～一跳 give sb. a fright ‖ 这片小树林天黑以后很～。 The wood is really spooky after it gets dark.

夏¹ xià ▸**p. 345**〈名〉 summer: 初～ early summer ‖ 盛～ high summer ▸～天，～至，立～，消～

夏² Xià〈名〉 1 (夏朝) Xia Dynasty 2 (中国) China: ▸华～

【夏布】xiàbù〈名〉 ramie cloth: ～衣服需要熨烫。 Garments made from ramie cloth need pressing.

【夏朝】Xiàcháo〈名〉 Xia Dynasty

【夏季】xiàjì ▸**p. 345**〈名〉 summer: 酷热/炎热的～ blazing hot summer

【夏季奥运会】 Xiàjì Àoyùnhuì〈名〉 Summer Olympic Games: 2008年～ 2008 Olympic Games

【夏历】xiàlì〈名〉 lunar calendar

【夏粮】xiàliáng〈名〉 summer grain crops: ～收购 summer grain purchases

【夏令】xiàlìng〈名〉 1 (夏季) summer: ～时装/衣服 summer fashions/clothes ‖ ～水果 summer fruit 2 (夏季的气候) summer weather: 春行～。 The spring weather feels like that of summer.

【夏令时】 xiàlìngshí〈名〉 summertime〈英〉; daylight-saving time〈美〉

【夏令营】xiàlìngyíng〈名〉 summer camp: 参加～ join a summer camp

【夏日】xiàrì〈名〉 summer

【夏收】xiàshōu **A**〈动〉 have the summer harvest **B**〈名〉 summer harvest

【夏天】xiàtiān ▸**p. 345**〈名〉 summer: 炎热的～ torrid summer

【夏娃】Xiàwá〈名〉 Eve [the first woman]

【夏威夷】 Xiàwēiyí〈名〉 Hawaii: ～人 Hawaiian

【夏威夷群岛】 Xiàwēiyí Qúndǎo〈名〉 Hawaiian Islands

【夏夜】xiàyè〈名〉 summer night

【夏衣】xiàyī〈名〉 summer clothes

【夏至】Xiàzhì〈名〉 Summer Solstice [beginning of the 10th of the 24 solar terms]

【夏种】xiàzhòng〈名〉 summer sowing: ～时节 summer sowing season

【夏装】xiàzhuāng〈名〉 summer clothing

唬 xià = 吓 xià
▸hǔ

厦（廈）xià
▸shà

【厦门】Xiàmén〈名〉 Xiamen

罅 xià〈名〉〈书〉 crack: 石～ crack in a rock ‖ 云～ break in the clouds

【罅漏】xiàlòu〈名〉〈书〉 loophole: 找出～ find loopholes ‖〈喻〉 这部法律还有很多～。 This law still has a number of loopholes.

【罅隙】xiàxì〈名〉〈书〉 rift:〈喻〉 两位好友之间出现了～。 Rifts began to form between the two friends.

xia

下 xia〈动〉 [used after a verb] 1 (指动作从高到低) [indicating a movement from the higher place to the lower]: 低～头 hang one's head ‖ 放～ put sth. down 2 (指动作完成) [indicating completion or result of an action]: 打～基础 lay a foundation ‖ 记～电话号码 note down a telephone number ‖ 留～姓名 write down sb.'s name 3 (指空间或容量) [indicating space or capacity]: 这屋子能坐～10人。 The room can seat ten people. ‖ 口袋太小，装不～这么多米。 The sack is too small to hold so much rice.
▸xià

xiān

仙 xiān〈名〉 1 (仙人) celestial being: 狐～ fox-fairy ▸～女，神～ 2 (出众的人) master: 酒～ great drinker ‖ 诗～ immortal poet

【仙丹】xiāndān〈名〉 elixir of life: ～妙药 elixir

【仙风道骨】 xiānfēng-dàogǔ〈成〉 divine demeanour

【仙姑】xiāngū〈名〉 1 (女仙人) goddess 2 (女巫师) sorceress

【仙鹤】xiānhè〈名〉［鸟类］Siberian white crane

【仙后座】Xiānhòuzuò〈名〉［天文］Cassiopeia

【仙界】xiānjiè〈名〉 fairyland: 身居～ live in fairyland

【仙境】xiānjìng〈名〉 wonderland

【仙客来】xiānkèlái〈名〉［植物］cyclamen

【仙女】xiānnǚ〈名〉 female divinity

【仙女座】 Xiānnǚzuò〈名〉［天文］Andromeda

【仙人】xiānrén〈名〉 immortal

【仙人球】xiānrénqiú〈名〉［植物］bulbous cactus

【仙人掌】 xiānrénzhǎng〈名〉［植物］cactus

【仙山琼阁】xiānshān-qiónggé〈名〉 fairyland

【仙逝】xiānshì ▸**p. 772**〈动〉〈婉〉 pass away

【仙子】xiānzǐ〈名〉 1 (仙女) fairy 2 (仙人) immortal

先 xiān

A〈名〉 1 (在前) first: ▸争～恐后，有言在～，～锋，～例 2〈书〉(先人) forefather: 不辱其～ not bring disgrace to one's ancestor ▸祖～ 3〈口〉(先前) beginning: 我～还以为她在开玩笑。 At first I thought she was joking.

B〈形〉〈敬〉 late: ～师 my late teacher ▸～烈

C〈副〉 1 (首先) first: ～拟个提纲 work out an outline first ‖ 他比我～到。 He arrived earlier than I did. ‖ 主队～入一球。 The home team scored a goal first. 2 (暂时) temporarily: 你～凑合着用吧! Just make do with it for the time being. ‖ 你～请坐，她马上就会回来。 Take a seat please! She will be back in a minute. ‖ 你散会后～别走。 Please don't go after the meeting is over.

【先辈】 xiānbèi〈名〉 1 (行辈在前的人) member of an older generation: ～的创业精神 pioneering spirit of the elder generation 2 (让人崇敬的前辈) forefather: 继承～遗志 carry on the unfinished task of one's forefathers ‖ 革命～ elder generation of revolutionaries

【先妣】xiānbǐ〈名〉〈旧〉〈书〉 my late mother

【先导】xiāndǎo **A**〈动〉 lead the way: 车队由摩托车～。 The motorcade was preceded by motorcycles. **B**〈名〉 guide: 做民众的～ be a guide for the masses ‖ 科研是实际应用的～。 Research precedes application.

【先睹为快】 xiāndǔ-wéikuài〈成〉 take delight in being the first to read or see sth.

【先发制人】 xiānfā-zhìrén〈成〉 gain the initiative by striking the first blow: 采取～的手段 take pre-emptive measures

【先锋】 xiānfēng〈名〉 pioneer: 起～作用 play a vanguard role ‖ 开路～ trail-blazing pioneer

【先锋队】xiānfēngduì〈名〉 vanguard: 共产党是工人阶级的～。 The Communist Party is the vanguard of the working class. ▸少年～

【先锋霉素】xiānfēngméisù〈名〉［药学］cephalosporin

【先锋派】xiānfēngpài〈名〉 avant-garde: ～艺术/文学/作家 avant-garde art/literature/writer

【先公后私】 xiāngōng-hòusī〈成〉 give public interests precedence over personal interests

【先河】xiānhé〈名〉〈喻〉precursor: 开妇女运动之～ be forerunners of the women's movement

【先后】xiānhòu **A**〈名〉 order of priority: 按～次序 according to the order of precedence ‖ 这些事办起来得有个～。All these matters should be taken up in order of priority. **B**〈副〉successively: 她～去过英国、德国和法国。 She went to Britain and afterwards to Germany and France.

【先见之明】xiānjiànzhīmíng〈成〉foresight: 佩服某人的～ admire sb.'s foresightedness ‖ 缺乏～ lack foresight

【先进】xiānjìn **A**〈形〉 advanced: 引进～设备 import sophisticated equipment ‖ 宣传～事迹 publicize sb.'s meritorious deeds ▸～工作者 **B**〈名〉 progressive individual or group: 表彰～ cite the progressive ‖ 学～ learn from the progressive

【先进工作者】 xiānjìn gōngzuòzhě〈名〉 advanced worker

【先决】 xiānjué〈形〉 prerequisite: ～条件 prerequisite

【先觉】xiānjué〈名〉 person of foresight

【先君子后小人】xiān jūnzǐ hòu xiǎorén〈俗〉 reason things out first and resort to force only when it is impossible to bring sb. to reason

【先考】xiānkǎo〈名〉〈书〉 my late father

【先来后到】 xiānlái-hòudào〈成〉 first come, first served: 买票应该有个～。 The tickets should be bought on a first come, first served basis.

【先礼后兵】xiānlǐ-hòubīng〈成〉 try peaceful means before resorting to force: 我们要～，如果劝降失败，就发动进攻。 Let us be gentlemen first and warriors second. We will launch the offensive only if we fail to persuade them to surrender.

【先例】 xiānlì〈名〉 precedent: 无～可循 have no precedent to go by ‖ 这件事没有～。 This matter is unprecedented.

【先烈】xiānliè〈名〉 martyr: 缅怀～ cherish the memory of our martyrs

【先令】xiānlìng ▸**p. 328**〈名〉 1 (英国) shilling [monetary unit of Britain until 1971] 2 (东非) shilling 3 (奥地利) schilling [former monetary unit of Austria, now replaced by the Euro]

【先民】xiānmín〈名〉〈书〉 1 (古人) the ancients: ～时代 ancient times 2 (古代贤人) ancient sages

【先破后立】xiānpò-hòulì〈成〉 destruction comes before construction
【先期】xiānqī〈名〉 1（某一日期前） earlier date: ～到达 arrive at an earlier time 2（前期） earlier stage: ～目标已经达到。 The targets set earlier on have already been reached.
【先前】xiānqián〈名〉 earlier times: ～的首席执行官 former chief executive officer ‖ 那首歌我～听过。 I've heard that song before. ‖ ～我和他同过学。 I used to study in the same school with him.
【先遣】xiānqiǎn〈形〉 sent in advance: ～部队 advance troops
【先秦】Xiān Qín〈名〉 the pre-Qin days [usually referring to the Spring and Autumn Period and the Warring States Period]
【先驱】xiānqū A〈动〉 lead: ▸～者 B〈名〉 forerunner: 做流行音乐的～ be the vanguard of popular music ‖ 现代文学的～ vanguard of modern literature
【先驱者】xiānqūzhě〈名〉 forefather
【先人】xiānrén〈名〉 1（祖先） ancestor: 不辱～ not bring shame on one's ancestors 2〈书〉（过世的父亲） sb.'s late father: 她的～也曾在这里工作。 Her late father also worked here.
【先人后己】xiānrén-hòujǐ〈成〉 put the interest of others above one's own
【先入为主】xiānrù-wéizhǔ〈成〉 be prejudiced by a first impression: 有了～的看法 harbour a preconceived idea
【先入之见】xiānrùzhījiàn〈成〉 preconception
【先声】xiānshēng〈名〉 first sign: 杜鹃鸟是春天的～。 The cuckoo is the harbinger of spring.
【先声夺人】xiānshēng-duórén〈成〉 forestall one's opponent by a show of strength: 她～，抢在各报之前报道了这一消息。 She acted swiftly and scooped all the other newspapers with the story.
【先生】xiānsheng〈名〉 1（老师） teacher: 要做好～，首先要做好学生。 To be a good teacher, one must first be a good pupil. 2（指成年男子） mister (Mr): 女士们，～们! Ladies and gentlemen! ‖ ～，你要点什么? Are you ready to order, sir? 3（指知识分子）（男） Mister;（女） Madame: 鲁迅～ Mr Lu Xun 4（丈夫） husband: 我/你（家）～ my/your husband ‖ 她～出差了。 Her husband is away on business. 5〈方〉（医生） doctor: 要不要请个～看看? Shall we send for a doctor? 6〈旧〉（管账的人） bookkeeper: 当账房～ work as a bookkeeper 7〈旧〉（说书人） storyteller;（算命者） fortune-teller: 说书～ storyteller ▸算命～
【先世】xiānshì〈名〉〈书〉 1（祖先） ancestors 2（前代） previous generation: ～名医 famed doctor of an elder generation
【先是】xiānshi〈连〉 before: 他～同意，后又反对。 Originally, he agreed but later he disagreed.
【先手】xiānshǒu〈名〉 offensive position: 占有～ have the initiative ‖ ～棋 offensive move
【先天】xiāntiān〈形〉 1（胚胎时期） congenital: ～缺陷 congenital defect 2［哲学］ innate: 知识是～固有的还是后天习得的? Is knowledge innate or acquired?
【先天不足】xiāntiān-bùzú〈成〉 have a congenital defect: ～，后天失调 be born weak and ill-cared for after birth ‖〈喻〉～的项目 project with some innate defects
【先天性】xiāntiānxìng〈名〉 innateness: ～失明 congenital blindness ‖ ～心脏病 congenital heart disease
【先头】xiāntóu A〈名〉 1（前部） front: 走在游行队伍的～ head a parade 2（早先） earlier time: 这件事他～讲过了。 He mentioned it before. ‖ ～，这个镇是个小村庄。 This town used to be a small village. B〈形〉 advance: ～部队 advance troops
【先下手为强】xiān xiàshǒu wéi qiáng〈俗〉 gain the upper hand by acting first: ～，后下手遭殃。 He who strikes first prevails, he who strikes late fails.
【先贤】xiānxián〈名〉〈书〉 ancient sage: ～遗训 teachings of an ancient sage ‖ 历代～ wise men of generations gone by
【先小人后君子】xiān xiǎorén hòu jūnzǐ〈俗〉 precede courtesy with impolite words
【先行】xiānxíng A〈动〉 1（走在前面） go in front: ▸兵马未动，粮草～ 2（预先进行） go beforehand: ～安排 make prior arrangements ‖ ～通知 notify in advance ‖ ～准备 make preparations beforehand B〈简称〉= 先行官
【先行官】xiānxíngguān〈名〉 commander of an advance unit
【先行先试】xiānxíng xiānshì〈动〉 pilot
【先行者】xiānxíngzhě〈名〉 forerunner: 革命～ revolutionary forerunner
【先验论】xiānyànlùn〈名〉［哲学］ transcendentalism: ～者 transcendentalist
【先意承志】xiānyì-chéngzhì〈成〉 anticipate and attend to the wishes of another person: 她极善～。 She is good at reading another's mind and then acting accordingly.
【先斩后奏】xiānzhǎn-hòuzòu〈成〉〈喻〉 act first and report afterwards
【先兆】xiānzhào〈名〉 1（征兆） omen: 暴风雨的～ signs of a storm ‖ 地震的～ indications of an impending earthquake 2［医学］ aura: ～症状 precursory symptoms ‖ 癫痫的～ epileptic aura
【先哲】xiānzhé〈名〉 ancient sage: 历代～ sages through the ages
【先知】xiānzhī〈名〉 1（指人） person of foresight: 人类的～ those with foresight 2［宗教］ prophet
【先祖】xiānzǔ〈名〉〈书〉 1（指祖父） my deceased grandfather 2（祖先） ancestry

纤（纖） xiān

A〈形〉 fine: ▸～尘, ～弱, ～细
B〈名〉 fibre: ▸化～
▸qiàn
【纤长】xiāncháng〈形〉〈书〉 slender and long: ～的手指 slender finger
【纤尘】xiānchén〈名〉〈书〉 fine dust: 室无～。 The room is spotlessly clean.
【纤尘不染】xiānchén-bùrǎn〈成〉 1〈本〉 not marred by a speck of dust: 件件家具～。 Every piece of furniture is spotlessly clean. 2〈喻〉（指品格） maintain one's original pure character: 洁身自爱，～ maintain one's moral integrity and pure character
【纤度】xiāndù〈名〉［纺织］ fibre number
【纤毫】xiānháo〈名〉 minutest detail: 人物形象在这些牙雕艺术品中刻绘得～毕现。 These ivory figures are so exquisitely carved that the finest details can be distinguished.
【纤毛】xiānmáo〈名〉［生物］ cilium
【纤毛虫】xiānmáochóng〈名〉 ciliophoran
【纤巧】xiānqiǎo〈形〉 fine and delicate: ～精致 dainty and delicate
【纤柔】xiānróu〈形〉 delicate and soft: ～的头发 fine soft hair
【纤弱】xiānruò〈形〉 delicate, slim and fragile: ～的身影 slim and fragile figure ‖ ～的体质 delicate constitution
【纤丝】xiānsī〈名〉 fibril
【纤维】xiānwéi〈名〉 fibre: 合成/人造/天然～ synthetic/man-made/natural fibre ‖ 植物～ plant fibre
【纤维板】xiānwéibǎn〈名〉［材料］ fibreboard
【纤维玻璃】xiānwéi bōli〈名〉 fibreglass
【纤维瘤】xiānwéiliú ▸p. 50〈名〉［医学］ fibroid (tumour)
【纤维素】xiānwéisù〈名〉［生物］ cellulose
【纤悉】xiānxī〈形〉〈书〉 extremely detailed, meticulous: ～无遗 no detail escapes notice
【纤细】xiānxì〈形〉 fine: 笔画～ written in a fine hand ‖ 身材～的少女 young girl of slight build
【纤纤】xiānxiān〈形〉〈书〉 long and slender: 十指～ have slim fingers
【纤小】xiānxiǎo〈形〉 fine: 身材～ be of slim physique

氙 xiān〈名〉［化学］ xenon (Xe)

【氙灯】xiāndēng〈名〉 xenon arc lamp

祆 xiān

【祆教】Xiānjiào〈名〉［宗教］ Zoroastrianism

籼（秈） xiān

【籼稻】xiāndào〈名〉 indica (rice cultivar)
【籼米】xiānmǐ〈名〉 polished indica rice

莶（薟） xiān ▸豨莶 xīxiān

掀 xiān〈动〉 1（揭开） raise: ～锅盖 take the lid off the pot ‖ ～门帘 lift the door curtain ‖〈喻〉～开历史新的一页 open a new leaf in history 2（翻腾） surge: 大海～起波涛。 Big waves surged on the sea. 3（使翻倒） topple: ～翻在地 push sb. over ‖ 他～倒了桌子。 He overturned the table. 4（吹掉） blow off: 台风把屋顶～了。 The typhoon blew the roof off the house.

【掀动】xiāndòng〈动〉 set in motion: 消息一传开，整个小城都～了。 The whole town stirred when the news spread.
【掀翻】xiānfān〈动〉 overturn: 一阵狂风把小船～了。 A gust of wind overturned the boat.
【掀风鼓浪】xiānfēng-gǔlàng〈成〉 stir up trouble
【掀盖式手机】xiāngàishì shǒujī〈名〉 clamshell phone
【掀开】xiānkāi〈动〉 open: ～盖子 take off the lid ‖ ～新娘的盖头 unveil a bride ‖ 在两国外交史上～新的一页 open a new chapter in the annals of diplomacy between the two countries
【掀起】xiānqǐ〈动〉 1（揭开） lift: ～面罩 raise a veil 2（翻腾） surge: 狂风～巨浪。 Wild winds raised up huge waves. 3（使兴起） set off: ～浪潮 start an onslaught

酰 xiān

【酰基】xiānjī〈名〉［化学］ acyl

跹（躚） xiān ▸蹁跹 piānxiān

锨（鍁） xiān〈名〉 shovel: 用～把雪铲走 clear the snow with a shovel ▸铁～

X

鲜（鮮）xiān

A〈形〉❶（新出产）fresh: ～肉/奶/鱼 fresh meat/milk/fish ❷（未枯萎） fresh: ～花/果 fresh flower/fruit ❸ ▸**p. 863**（鲜明） bright: 穿一件～红的外衣 wear a bright red coat ‖ 这条领带太～艳。This necktie is too loud. ▸～红, ～明, ～艳 ❹（鲜美） tasty: 味道～ delicious ‖ 这汤真～。The soup is really delicious. ▸～美
B〈名〉 ❶（鲜美的食物） delicious food, fruit etc.: 时～ seasonal vegetables or fruit ‖ 刚摘下来的葡萄，尝尝～吧。Have a taste of these freshly picked grapes. ❷（水产） seafood: ▸海～, 鱼～
▸xiǎn

【鲜卑】Xiānbēi〈名〉 Xianbei [ancient ethnic group in China]

【鲜贝】xiānbèi〈名〉 sea scallop

【鲜果】xiānguǒ〈名〉 fresh fruit

【鲜红】xiānhóng ▸**p. 863**〈形〉 bright red: ～的旗帜 bright red flag

【鲜花】xiānhuā〈名〉 fresh flower: 一束～ a bunch of flowers ‖ ～盛开。The flowers are in full bloom.

【鲜花插在牛粪上】xiānhuā chāzài niúfènshàng〈俗〉〈喻〉 an attractive woman married to a vulgar and usu ugly husband

【鲜活】xiānhuó〈形〉 ❶（新鲜） fresh: ～产品 fresh products ❷（鲜明生动） vivid: ～的人物形象 vividly-portrayed character

【鲜货】xiānhuò〈名〉 ❶（指果蔬） fresh fruit/vegetables ❷（指水产） fresh aquatic foods: 供应～ serve fresh aquatic foods ❸（指草药） fresh medicinal herbs

【鲜橘水】xiānjúshuǐ〈名〉 orange squash

【鲜丽】xiānlì〈形〉 dazzlingly beautiful: 衣着～ be beautifully dressed in bright colours ‖ ～的壁画 brightly-coloured mural

【鲜亮】xiānliang〈形〉❶（指色彩） bright: 色彩～ be in bright colours ‖ ～的粉红衬衣 bright pink shirt ❷〈方〉（指人） beautiful: 长得～ look very beautiful

【鲜灵】 xiānling〈形〉〈方〉 fresh and bright

【鲜美】xiānměi〈形〉 ❶（味道好） tasty: ～可口 fresh and tasty ❷〈书〉（新鲜美丽） fresh and beautiful: 芳草～。The grass is fresh and beautiful.

【鲜明】xiānmíng〈形〉❶（明艳）vivid: 色调～ be brightly coloured ❷（不含糊） distinct: 观点～ have a clear-cut viewpoint ‖ 富有～的地方特色 be characterized by a distinctive local style or flavour ‖ 形成～对照 pose a sharp contrast

【鲜奶】xiānnǎi〈名〉 fresh milk

【鲜嫩】xiānnèn〈形〉 fresh and tender: ～的竹笋 fresh and tender bamboo shoots

【鲜啤酒】xiānpíjiǔ〈名〉 draft beer

【鲜肉】xiānròu〈名〉 fresh meat

【鲜味】xiānwèi〈名〉 ❶（指味道） fresh flavour ❷（指蔬果） vegetables and fruit in season

【鲜血】xiānxuè〈名〉blood: ～淋漓 be dripping with blood

【鲜妍】xiānyán = 鲜艳 xiānyàn

【鲜艳】xiānyàn〈形〉 brightly-coloured: 身着～的节日盛装 wear brightly-coloured holiday clothes ‖ ～的五星红旗冉冉升起。The bright Five-Star Red Flag is rising slowly.

【鲜艳夺目】 xiānyàn duómù〈成〉 be attractively bright in colour

暹 xiān

【暹罗】Xiānluó〈名〉Siam [old name for Thailand]

xián

闲[1]（閑）xián

A〈名〉 fence
B〈动〉 defend: 防～ guard and hinder

闲[2]（閒）xián

A〈形〉 ❶（空闲） idle: ～着没事干 have nothing to do ‖ 这两天我都～着。I'm free for the next couple of days. ▸～居, 清～, 游手好～ ❷（闲置不用） vacant: 长年～着的房子 house left unoccupied for years ‖ 别让电脑～着。Don't let the computer stand idle. ▸～置 ❸（与正事无关） unimportant: 生～气 be annoyed over trivial things ▸～事, ～谈
B〈名〉free time: 他总是不得～。He never has any spare time. ▸忙里偷～

【闲步】xiánbù〈动〉〈书〉 take a stroll: ～林间 take a stroll through a forest

【闲不住】xiánbuzhù〈动〉〈口〉 be unable to remain idle

【闲扯】xiánchě〈动〉 chat: 你们在～些什么？What are you chatting about?

【闲荡】xiándàng〈动〉 saunter: 整天四处～ saunter about all day ‖ 在街上～ stroll through the streets

【闲工夫】xiángōngfu〈名〉 spare time: 我没～跟你争论。I have no time to argue with you.

【闲逛】xiánguàng〈动〉hang around: 我很忙，没时间陪你～。I'm too busy to hang out with you.

【闲花野草】 xiánhuā-yěcǎo〈名〉〈喻〉 women of easy virtue

【闲话】xiánhuà **A**〈名〉 ❶（指与正事无关） digression: ～少说，讨论具体问题吧！Enough of this digression; let's come to the point. ❷（指议论是非） gossip: 爱讲～ be fond of gossip ‖ 在背后说～ gossip about sb. behind their back **B**〈动〉〈书〉 chat: ～家常 small talk

【闲居】xiánjū〈动〉 stay at home with nothing to do

【闲空】xiánkòng〈名〉 free time: 没有一点～ not have a moment's leisure

【闲聊】xiánliáo〈动〉chat: 边喝茶边～ chat over tea ‖ 工作时不得～。No chatting during work hours.

【闲磨牙】 xiánmóyá〈动〉〈方〉 have an idle chat: 我这会儿烦着呢，没工夫跟你～。I'm not in the mood to indulge in idle argument with you right now.

【闲气】xiánqì〈名〉 annoyance over small things: 生～ lose one's temper over a trivial matter

【闲弃】xiánqì〈形〉 disused: ～的码头/铁路 disused dock/railway line ‖ 那一家搬走后，这座房子就～不用了。When the family moved away, the house fell into disuse.

【闲钱】xiánqián〈名〉〈口〉 spare cash: 他有了几个～就神气起来了。Having a bit of spare cash has made him cocky.

【闲情逸致】 xiánqíng-yìzhì〈成〉 leisurely and carefree mood: 没有那种～ be in no kind of leisurely mood

【闲人】 xiánrén〈名〉 ❶（指无事可做） idler: 他可是个大～。He never has anything to do. ❷（指不相干） person without concerns: ～免进 off limits to all unauthorized personnel

【闲散】xiánsǎn〈形〉 ❶（悠闲自在） free and leisurely: 过～日子 live a life of leisure ‖ 他～惯了。He is used to a free and easy life. ❷（闲置不用） idle: ～劳力 idle labour force ‖ ～人员 idle people ‖ ～资金 idle capital

【闲时】xiánshí〈名〉 free time: ～来玩。Please drop in when you're free.

【闲事】 xiánshì〈名〉 ❶（指与己无关） other people's business: 爱管～ like to poke one's nose into other people's business ❷（指无关紧要） unimportant matter

【闲是闲非】xiánshì-xiánfēi〈成〉idle gossip

【闲适】 xiánshì〈形〉〈书〉 leisurely and comfortable: 过～的生活 have an easy and carefree life

【闲书】xiánshū〈名〉 light reading: 看～ do some light reading

【闲谈】xiántán〈动〉 have a chat: 不拘礼节地～ have a casual conversation

【闲田】xiántián〈名〉 vacant field

【闲暇】xiánxiá〈名〉 leisure: ～无事 be free and at leisure

【闲心】xiánxīn〈名〉 ❶（指心情） leisurely mood: 我没有～开玩笑。I am in no mood for joking. ❷（指操心） unwarranted concern: 操不完的～ endless worries

【闲雅】xiányǎ〈形〉 refined, elegant

【闲言碎语】xiányán-suìyǔ〈成〉 idle tittle-tattle: 听到一些～ hear some rumours and gossip ‖ 不要听了几句～，就打退堂鼓。Don't give up just because of a few groundless rumours.

【闲员】 xiányuán〈名〉 surplus personnel: 裁汰～ reduce redundant personnel

【闲云野鹤】xiányún-yěhè〈成〉〈喻〉 carefree and unrestrained people: 退休后，他如～，自由自在。After he retired, he led a leisurely life, free from all worldly concerns.

【闲杂】xiánzá〈形〉 redundant: 裁减～人员 cut redundant staff

【闲章】xiánzhāng〈名〉 unofficial personal seal

【闲职】xiánzhí〈名〉 sinecure: 挂个～ have a nominal post

【闲置】 xiánzhì〈动〉 stand idle: ～不用 allow sth. to lie idle ‖ ～人员 idle hand ‖ 这条生产线～了三年。This production line has lain idle for three years.

贤（賢）xián

A〈形〉 ❶（德才兼备） worthy: ▸～良, ～明, ～士 ❷〈旧〉（用于称呼平辈或晚辈） [term of respectful address for a younger person]: ～弟 my worthy brother ‖ ～侄 my worthy nephew
B〈名〉 worthy person: 选～举能 recommend a virtuous and talented person for an office ▸见～思齐, 让～, 圣～

【贤达】xiándá〈名〉〈书〉 prominent and worthy person: 重用社会～ put prominent and worthy people in important positions

【贤德】xiándé **A**〈名〉 virtue **B**〈形〉 [of a woman] virtuous

【贤惠】xiánhuì〈形〉 [of a woman] virtuous: 他娶了位～的妻子。He married a virtuous wife.

【贤良】xiánliáng〈书〉 **A**〈形〉 able and virtuous: ～之士 person of integrity and ability **B**〈名〉 brilliant and virtuous person: 任用～ appoint people of virtue and talent

【贤路】xiánlù〈名〉〈书〉 opportunity for a worthy person to advance: 广开～ provide able people with wide access to leading positions

【贤明】xiánmíng **A**〈形〉 wise and able: ～的法官 sage judge ‖ ～的领袖 talented leader **B**〈名〉〈书〉 sage: 另聘～ employ another capable and wise [said when asking

X

to be allowed to refuse an appointment or to leave a post]
【贤内助】xiánnèizhù〈名〉good wife: 他有个～。He has a good wife.
【贤能】xiánnéng〈书〉**A**〈形〉able and virtuous: ～之士 virtuous and talented person **B**〈名〉able and virtuous person: 任用～ employ people of virtue and talent
【贤妻良母】xiánqī-liángmǔ〈成〉dutiful wife and loving mother: 她将来会是位～。She will make a good wife and mother.
【贤契】xiánqì〈名〉〈旧〉respectful address for a disciple or a son of a friend
【贤人】xiánrén〈名〉person of intelligence and integrity: 举用～ recruit persons of intelligence and integrity
【贤士】xiánshì = 贤人 xiánrén
【贤淑】xiánshū〈形〉[of a woman] virtuous and kind-hearted
【贤哲】xiánzhé〈书〉**A**〈形〉intelligent and virtuous: ～之士 intelligent and virtuous scholar **B**〈名〉person of outstanding intelligence and integrity

弦[1]（絃）
xián〈名〉**1**（指弓弦）string: 箭在～上。The arrow is on the string. ▸弓～ **2**（指乐器部件）string or cord of a musical instrument: 单～ a plucked instrument with one single string ▸～乐器, 琴～

弦[2]
xián **1**［数学］**a**（指三角形斜边）chord **b**（连接圆上任意两点的线段）hypotenuse **2**（指月相）crescent: 上～ the first quarter of the moon ‖ 下～ the last quarter of the moon **3**（发条）spring of a clock: 给闹钟上～ give the alarm clock a couple of winds ‖ 手表的～断了。The watch spring is broken.
【弦歌】xiángē〈动〉［音乐］sing to stringed accompaniment
【弦外之音】xiánwàizhīyīn〈成〉overtone: 难道他就听不出这话的～吗? Can't he comprehend the implication of the remarks?
【弦乐】xiányuè〈名〉［音乐］stringed instrument music: ～队 string orchestra
【弦乐器】xiányuèqì〈名〉stringed instrument: 她教小学生弹奏～。She teaches strings to schoolchildren.
【弦乐四重奏】xiányuè sìchóngzòu〈名〉string quartet
【弦子】xiánzi〈名〉three-stringed plucked musical instrument

挦（撏）
xián〈动〉pluck: ～鸡毛 pluck a chicken

X

咸[1]
xián〈副〉〈书〉all: 老少～宜 suit young and old alike ‖ ～受其益。All benefited from it.

咸[2]（鹹）
xián〈形〉salty: ～饼干 saltine ‖ 菜太～了。The dish is too salty.
【咸菜】xiáncài〈名〉salted vegetables: 腌～ pickle vegetables
【咸潮】xiáncháo〈名〉salt water intrusion: 上海再受～侵袭。Salt water intrusion hits Shanghai again.
【咸淡】xiándàn〈名〉degree of saltiness: ～正合适。The saltiness is just right.
【咸蛋】xiándàn〈名〉salted egg
【咸津津】xiánjīnjīn〈形〉having a nice salty taste
【咸肉】xiánròu〈名〉salted meat
【咸水湖】xiánshuǐhú〈名〉salt-water lake
【咸鸭蛋】xiányādàn〈名〉salted duck egg
【咸盐】xiányán〈名〉〈方〉salt
【咸鱼】xiányú〈名〉salted fish

涎
xián〈名〉saliva: 流～ salivate ▸馋～欲滴, 垂～三尺
【涎皮赖脸】xiánpí-làiliǎn〈成〉brazen-faced: 我们讨厌他那～的行为。We detested his shameless and loathsome behaviour.
【涎水】xiánshuǐ〈名〉〈口〉saliva: 流～ drool
【涎腺】xiánxiàn〈名〉［解剖］salivary gland
【涎着脸】xiánzheliǎn〈动〉〈方〉behave in a cheeky way

娴（嫺、嫻）
xián〈形〉**1**（文静）refined: ▸～静, ～雅 **2**（熟练）adept: ▸～熟
【娴静】xiánjìng〈形〉〈书〉gentle and refined: 举止～ be elegant in manner ‖ ～的微笑 demure smile
【娴淑】xiánshū〈形〉graceful and kind-hearted: ～端庄 be graceful and dignified in manner
【娴熟】xiánshú〈形〉skilled: 技术～ be skilled ‖ ～的技巧 consummate skill
【娴雅】xiányǎ〈形〉〈书〉refined and elegant: ～斯文 be quiet and gentle ‖ 举止～ behave gracefully

衔[1]（銜、啣）
xián〈动〉**1**（含）hold in the mouth: ～着烟斗 have a pipe between one's teeth ‖ 燕子～泥筑巢。The swallows are carrying bits of earth in their bills to build a nest. **2**（怀着）harbour: ～悲/恨 harbour sorrow/hatred ▸～冤 **3**〈书〉（接受）accept: ▸～命 **4**（相连）connect: 首尾相～。The head and the tail are connected. ▸～接

衔[2]（銜）
xián〈名〉rank: 公使～参赞 counsellor with the rank of minister ▸官～, 军～, 头～
【衔恨】xiánhèn〈动〉〈书〉harbour resentment: ～以终 nurse a deep resentment until the end
【衔级】xiánjí〈名〉title and rank
【衔接】xiánjiē〈动〉join: 与煤气管道～ connect with the gas-pipe ‖ 把两部分～起来 join the two sections together
【衔枚】xiánméi〈动〉〈古〉[of soldiers on the march] hold a wooden gag in the mouth (in order to maintain silence): ～疾走 march swiftly and silently
【衔命】xiánmìng〈动〉〈旧〉carry out an order: ～出使 go on a foreign mission according to the order
【衔铁】xiántiě〈名〉［电子］armature: ～簧/轴 armature spring/shaft
【衔头】xiántóu〈名〉title: 你现在什么～? What's your title now?
【衔冤】xiányuān〈动〉〈书〉nurse a bitter sense of wrong: ～负屈 be unjustly accused

舷
xián〈名〉side of a ship or aircraft: 右～ starboard ‖ 左～ port ▸船～
【舷窗】xiánchuāng〈名〉porthole
【舷墙板】xiánqiángbǎn〈名〉bulwark plating
【舷梯】xiántī〈名〉**1**（指船）gangplank: 登上～ mount the gangway ‖ 收起～ draw the gangplank in **2**（指飞机）ramp: 登上～ mount the ramp

痫（癇）
xián ▸癫痫 diānxián

鹇（鷴）
xián ▸白鹇 báixián

嫌
xián
A〈名〉**1**（嫌怨）resentment: 挟～报复 act in retaliation ▸～隙, ～怨, 前～ **2**（嫌疑）suspicion: 有杀人之～ be under suspicion of murder ‖ 有贪赃之～ be suspected of corruption ▸～疑, 避～, 涉～
B〈动〉**1**（厌恶）bear a grudge: ～麻烦 consider it troublesome ‖ 他～我话多。He doesn't like my talking so much. ‖ 她一直～我曾经反对过她。She always bore a grudge against me for having opposed her. ‖ 文字略～啰嗦。It is a bit wordy. **2**（怀疑）suspect: 猜～ be suspicious
【嫌犯】xiánfàn = 嫌疑犯 xiányífàn
【嫌贫爱富】xiánpín-àifù〈成〉despise the poor and curry favour with the rich
【嫌弃】xiánqì〈动〉cold-shoulder: 他虽有前科，但也不能～他。We mustn't forsake him even though he has a criminal record.
【嫌恶】xiánwù〈动〉loathe: 遭人～ be loathed by all ‖ 人人～的无耻之徒 shameless person universally detested
【嫌隙】xiánxì〈名〉animosity: 素有～ bear a grudge ‖ 与某人有～ feel animosity towards sb. ‖ ～冰消 the ill-feeling melted away like ice
【嫌疑】xiányí〈名〉suspicion: 排除～ remove suspicion ‖ 有犯罪～ be under suspicion of guilt ‖ 这篇论文有抄袭～。The essay is suspected to be a plagiarism.
【嫌疑犯】xiányífàn〈名〉suspect
【嫌疑人】xiányírén〈名〉suspect: 犯罪～ suspect in a crime ‖ 主要～ prime suspect
【嫌怨】xiányuàn〈名〉〈书〉grudge: 两国之间素有～。There is a long-standing animosity between the two countries. ‖ ～未消。The grudge has not gone away.
【嫌憎】xiánzēng〈动〉detest: 遭人～ be regarded with loathing ‖ 这使她更加～丈夫。This made her detest her husband all the more.

xiǎn

狝（獮）
xiǎn〈动〉〈古〉hunt in autumn: 秋～ autumn hunting

显（顯）
xiǎn
A〈形〉**1**（外露）obvious: 成效不～。The result is not so marked. ‖ 药效不～。The effect of the medicine is not noticeable. ▸～而易见, 明～, 浅～ **2**（盛大）great: ～宦 prominent official ▸～达, ～贵, ～赫
B〈动〉show: ～本领 go through one's paces ‖ 尽～英雄本色 fully display the true qualities of a hero ‖ 你穿这件衣服～得很年轻。This dress makes you look very young. ▸～露, ～示, ～现
【显摆】xiǎnbai〈动〉〈口〉show off: 别臭～，你以为你是谁? ! Stop showing off! Who do you think you are? ‖ 她送我回家只不过是要～她的新车。She only gave me a lift home in order to show off her new car.
【显鼻子显眼儿】xiǎnbízi-xiǎnyǎnr〈俗〉be very conspicuous: 他的婚事办得～。His wedding was completely ostentatious.
【显出】xiǎnchū〈动〉show, appear: ～诚意 show one's sincerity ‖ ～很高兴的样子

appear to be happy ‖ ～兴趣 manifest an interest (in) ‖ ～原形 show one's true colours ‖ 只有几处残垣断壁尚能～这座古城昔日的辉煌。 Only a few crumbling walls bear witness to the past greatness of the ancient city.

【显达】xiǎndá〈形〉〈书〉 eminent: 此人必有～之日。 This person will surely achieve power and fame some day.

【显得】xiǎnde〈动〉 appear: ～有点紧张 exhibit a slight nervousness ‖ 刮了胡子理了发，他～精神矍铄。 He looked hale and hearty after the haircut and shave.

【显而易见】xiǎn'éryìjiàn〈成〉 obviously: 战争造成的后果是～的。 The effects of the war were very much in evidence.

【显贵】xiǎnguì **A**〈形〉 noble and eminent **B**〈名〉 eminent personage: 傲视～ look down upon high officials ‖ 他祖上曾是朝中～。 His ancestors used to be high officials in the imperial court.

【显赫】xiǎnhè〈形〉 distinguished: 地位～ eminent position ‖ 声誉～ distinguished reputation ‖ ～一时 be glorious for a time

【显花植物】xiǎnhuā zhíwù〈名〉［植物］ phanerogam

【显豁】xiǎnhuò〈形〉〈书〉 bright and clear: 内容～，文笔生动 lucid in content and vivid in style

【显见】xiǎnjiàn〈动〉 be obvious: ～的理由/问题 obvious reason/problem ‖ ～她不愿帮忙。 It's evident that she is unwilling to help.

【显卡】xiǎnkǎ = 显示卡 xiǎnshìkǎ

【显灵】xiǎnlíng〈动〉 [of a ghost or spirit] reveal itself: 她不信神明真会～赐福。 She did not believe that deities can manifest their power and bestow blessings.

【显露】xiǎnlù〈动〉 appear: ～才华 reveal one's talent ‖ ～身份 reveal one's identity ‖ 他脸上～出慈祥的笑容。 A kind smile appeared on his face.

【显明】xiǎnmíng〈形〉 obvious: ～的道理 obvious truth ‖ ～的对比 sharp contrast

【显目】xiǎnmù〈形〉 conspicuous: 站在～的地方 stand in a conspicuous place

【显能】xiǎnnéng〈动〉 parade one's prowess: 在他面前，你就别～了。 Don't show off in front of him.

【显然】xiǎnrán〈副〉 obviously: 很～ it is clear that ... ‖ 他～醉了。 He was obviously drunk.

【显山露水】xiǎnshān-lùshuǐ〈成〉〈喻〉 [usu used in the negative] parade one's talent: 她武功高强，但从不～。 Although she excels in Chinese kung fu, she never shows off.

【显身手】xiǎn shēnshǒu〈动〉 display one's talent: 大～ cut a brilliant figure by a display of one's skill

【显圣】xiǎnshèng〈动〉 make one's presence felt

【显示】xiǎnshì〈动〉 show: ～才能 reveal one's talent ‖ ～威力 display one's tremendous strength ‖ ～自信 exhibit confidence

【显示卡】xiǎnshìkǎ〈名〉［计算机］ display card

【显示屏】xiǎnshìpíng〈名〉 display screen

【显示器】xiǎnshìqì〈名〉［计算机］display: 液晶～ LCD (liquid crystal display)

【显微镜】xiǎnwēijìng〈名〉 microscope: 高倍～ high power microscope

【显现】xiǎnxiàn〈动〉 appear: 她的形象总在我眼前～。 Her image often appears before me.

【显像管】xiǎnxiàngguǎn〈名〉［电子］picture tube: 彩色～ colour picture tube

【显效】xiǎnxiào **A**〈动〉 show an effect: ～快 produce a quick effect **B**〈名〉 tangible result: 未见～。 There has been no conspicuous effect.

【显形】xiǎnxíng〈动〉 reveal one's true colours: 他的丑恶嘴脸终于～了。 His hideous features were finally revealed. ‖ 鬼魂～。 The ghost revealed itself.

【显性】xiǎnxìng〈形〉 dominant: ～遗传 dominant inheritance

【显性基因】xiǎnxìng jīyīn〈名〉 dominant gene

【显学】xiǎnxué〈名〉〈书〉 **1**（著名学说、学派） famous theory or school of thought **2**（热门学科） popular subject of study

【显眼】xiǎnyǎn〈形〉 conspicuous: 陈列在～的位置 be displayed in a prominent position ‖ 她的红衣服在人群中很～。 Her red coat is very conspicuous in the crowd.

【显扬】xiǎnyáng〈动〉〈书〉 **1**（表彰） commend: ～美德 commend sb.'s virtues **2**（声誉著称） be celebrated: ～于天下 be well-known far and wide

【显要】xiǎnyào **A**〈形〉powerful and influential: ～人物 influential person **B**〈名〉 powerful and influential person: 政府～ eminent figure in the government

【显耀】xiǎnyào **A**〈形〉 celebrated: ～一时 enjoy popularity for a time **B**〈动〉 show off: ～财富 parade one's wealth ‖ ～身份 flaunt one's status

【显影】xiǎnyǐng〈动〉［摄影］ develop: ～不足 be underdeveloped ‖ ～液 developing solution

【显著】xiǎnzhù〈形〉 notable: 取得～成果 make remarkable achievements ‖ ～变化 marked change ‖ 该药疗效～。 The medicine produces notable results.

险（險）xiǎn

A〈形〉 **1**（地势险恶） perilous: ～道/坡 treacherous path/slope ▸～峰，～峻，～阻 **2**（狠毒） treacherous: ▸奸～，阴～ **3**（危险） dangerous: 这一手太～了! It is a very dangerous trick. ▸～情，艰～，惊～
B〈名〉 **1**（险要之地） treacherous place: 无～可守 have no tenable defence position ▸履～如夷，天～ **2**（危险） danger: 避～ avert danger ▸保～，冒～，脱～
C〈副〉 almost: ～遭杀害 be nearly killed ▸～胜

【险隘】xiǎn'ài〈名〉〈书〉strategic pass: 把守～ hold a strategic pass

【险地】xiǎndì〈名〉 **1**（指地势） strategic position **2**（指处境） perilous situation: 身处～ be in grave danger

【险恶】xiǎn'è〈形〉**1**（情况恶劣）dangerous: 病情～ be dangerously ill ‖ 环境～ be in a perilous situation **2**（阴险恶毒） malicious: 用心～ have sinister motives

【险峰】xiǎnfēng〈名〉 perilous peak: 攀登～ scale a perilous peak

【险固】xiǎngù〈形〉〈书〉 strategic and impregnable: 地势～ the terrain is unassailable

【险关】xiǎnguān〈名〉 perilous strategic pass: 一道～ a perilous pass ‖ 闯过～ pass a dangerous strategic pass

【险境】xiǎnjìng〈名〉 dangerous situation: 身处～ be in grave danger ‖ 脱离～ be out of danger

【险峻】xiǎnjùn〈形〉 **1**（指地势） precipitous: ～的悬崖 precipitous cliff **2**（指状况） dangerous: 形势～。 The situation is critical.

【险情】xiǎnqíng〈名〉 danger: 排除～ obviate a danger ‖ 不时出现～。 The situation turned dangerous at times.

【险胜】xiǎnshèng〈动〉［体育］ win by a narrow margin: 以微弱优势～ win by a nose ‖ 客队以95比94～。 The visiting team scraped a win 95-94.

【险滩】xiǎntān〈名〉 dangerous waters: 闯过急流～ shoot over rapids and shoals

【险巇】xiǎnxī〈形〉〈书〉 **1**（山路危险） perilous **2**（道路艰难） dangerous

【险象】xiǎnxiàng〈名〉 danger

【险象环生】xiǎnxiàng-huánshēng〈成〉 be fraught with dangers

【险些】xiǎnxiē〈副〉 narrowly: ～掉到河里 nearly fall into the river ‖ ～在空难中遇难 have a narrow escape in an air crash

【险要】xiǎnyào〈形〉strategic and inaccessible: 地势～ be in a strategically inaccessible place

【险遭】xiǎnzāo〈动〉 have a close call: ～不测 come within an inch of death ‖ ～毒手 have a narrow escape from attack

【险诈】xiǎnzhà〈形〉〈书〉 sinister and crafty: 行事～ be sinister and crafty

【险兆】xiǎnzhào〈名〉 evil omen

【险症】xiǎnzhèng〈名〉 dangerous illness: 身患～ be stricken with a dangerous disease

【险种】xiǎnzhǒng〈名〉 insurance type

【险阻】xiǎnzǔ〈形〉 dangerous and difficult: 崎岖～的山路 dangerous and difficult mountain path

蚬（蜆）xiǎn〈名〉［动物］ freshwater clam

铣（銑）xiǎn
▸xǐ

【铣铁】xiǎntiě〈名〉 cast iron

筅 xiǎn

【筅帚】xiǎnzhǒu〈名〉〈方〉 pot-scourer

跣 xiǎn〈动〉〈书〉 be barefoot: ～行 walk barefoot ‖ ～足 be barefooted

鲜（鮮）xiǎn〈形〉 rare: ～见 be rarely seen, be seldom met with ‖ ～有 few and far between ‖ ～为人知 little-known ▸寡廉～耻
▸xiān

藓（蘚）xiǎn〈名〉［植物］ class of bryophyte

燹 xiǎn〈名〉〈书〉 wild fire: 兵～ disaster of war

幰 xiǎn〈名〉〈书〉 curtain of a carriage

xiàn

见（見）xiàn〈动〉〈书〉 appear:
▸图穷匕首～
▸jiàn

苋（莧）xiàn〈名〉［植物］ amaranth

【苋菜】xiàncài〈名〉 three-coloured amaranth

县（縣） xiàn

〈名〉 county: ～人民代表大会 county people's congress ‖ ～政府 county government

【县城】xiànchéng〈名〉county town〈英〉; county seat〈美〉

【县官】xiànguān〈名〉〈旧〉county magistrate

【县级市】xiànjíshì〈名〉county-level city

【县令】xiànlìng〈名〉〈古〉county magistrate

【县委】xiànwěi〈名〉county Party committee

【县长】xiànzhǎng〈名〉county magistrate

【县志】xiànzhì〈名〉county annals: 据～记载 according to the county annals

【县治】xiànzhì〈名〉〈旧〉county seat

现（現） xiàn

A〈动〉appear: ～本性 reveal one's true colours ‖ ～原形 reveal one's true nature ▸表～, 出～, 昙花一～

B〈形〉**1**（现在）present: ～阶段 the present stage ‖ ～政府 the ruling government ‖ ～住所 current residence ▸～存, ～代, ～任 **2**（现成）ready: ▸～货, ～金, ～钱

C〈副〉impromptu: ～编一首诗 improvise a poem ‖ ～烤的蛋糕 newly baked cakes ‖ ～吃～做 cook for immediate consumption

D〈名〉cash: ▸兑～, 贴～

【现场】xiànchǎng〈名〉**1**（事件发生地）scene: 奔赴～ rush to the scene ‖ 事发～ scene of the event ‖ 作案～ scene of a crime ‖ 证明不在～的证据 evidence in support of alibi **2**（活动场所）site: 开～会 hold an on-the-spot meeting ‖ ～报道 live report ‖ ～直播 live coverage

【现场办公】xiànchǎng bàngōng〈动〉[of government officials] handle affairs on site

【现场保护】xiànchǎng bǎohù〈名〉［法律］crime scene protection

【现场调查】xiànchǎng diàochá〈名〉field survey

【现钞】xiànchāo ▸**p. 328**〈名〉cash

【现炒现卖】xiànchǎo-xiànmài〈惯〉〈喻〉apply a newly acquired skill: 我被迫当物理教师，只好～。 I have to teach physics and so will have to learn it as I go along.

【现成】xiànchéng〈形〉ready-made: 吃～的 eat a ready-made meal ‖ ～答案 ready answer ‖ 没有～经验可学。 There is no recorded experience to learn from.

【现成饭】xiànchéngfàn〈名〉**1**〈本〉ready meal **2**〈喻〉（指成果）unearned gain

【现存】xiàncún〈动〉be on hand: ～货物/商品 goods in stock

【现大洋】xiàndàyáng = 现洋 xiànyáng

【现代】xiàndài ▸**p. 618**〈名〉modern times: ～史 modern history ‖ ～作家 contemporary writer ‖ ～农业 modern agriculture

【现代化】xiàndàihuà〈动〉modernize: 使工业～ modernize an industry ‖ ～办公用品 modern office equipment ‖ ～管理 modernized management

【现代派】xiàndàipài〈名〉modernist school: ～艺术 modernist art ‖ ～作家 modernist writer

【现代五项】xiàndài wǔxiàng〈名〉［体育］modern pentathlon

【现代舞】xiàndàiwǔ〈名〉modern dance

【现代戏】xiàndàixì〈名〉modern drama

【现代主义】xiàndàizhǔyì〈名〉modernism: ～作家 modernist writer ‖ ～作品 modernist work

【现而今】xiàn'érjīn〈副〉〈方〉nowadays

【现房】xiànfáng〈名〉ready apartment

【现付】xiànfù〈动〉pay on ready cash

【现汇】xiànhuì〈名〉spot exchange: ～汇率 spot-exchange rate ‖ ～结算 cash settlement ‖ ～买入价 price of purchasing spot-exchange

【现货】xiànhuò〈名〉goods in stock: ～交易 spot trading ‖ 可供～。 Deliveries can be made off-the-shelf.

【现货市场】xiànhuò shìchǎng〈名〉cash market

【现浇混凝土】xiànjiāo hùnníngtǔ〈名〉cast-in-place concrete

【现今】xiànjīn ▸**p. 618**〈名〉nowadays: ～世界 present-day world

【现金】xiànjīn ▸**p. 328**〈名〉cash: 从取款机上取～ withdraw money from a cash dispenser ‖ 用～支付 pay by cash ‖ 我没带～。 I have no cash on me.

【现金流】xiànjīnliú〈名〉cash flow: ～充足 cash flow is sufficient ‖ ～急剧减少。 The cash flow is decreasing drastically.

【现款】xiànkuǎn〈名〉cash: 挪用～ embezzle cash ‖ ～短缺 run out of cash ‖ ～交易 cash transaction

【现年】xiànnián〈名〉present age: 他～18岁。 He is 18 years old this year.

【现钱】xiànqián〈口〉= 现款 xiànkuǎn

【现任】xiànrèn **A**〈形〉incumbent: ～领导 current leadership ‖ ～市长 incumbent mayor **B**〈动〉currently hold the office of: ～公司经理 currently hold the position of company manager ‖ 他～教育部长。 He is now Minister of Education.

【现如今】xiànrújīn〈副〉nowadays

【现身说法】xiànshēn-shuōfǎ〈成〉advise people by taking oneself as an example

【现时】xiànshí〈名〉the present time: ～售价 current selling price ‖ ～正是农忙时节。 It's the busy farming season now.

【现实】xiànshí **A**〈名〉reality: 成为～ become a reality ‖ 脱离～ be out of touch with reality ‖ 使某人面对～ bring sb. back to reality **B**〈形〉**1**（实际存在）real: 解决～问题 solve actual problems ‖ 源于～生活 originate in real life ‖ ～世界 the real world **2**（符合实际）realistic: 采取～的措施/态度 adopt a realistic measure/attitude ‖ 她做出这一决定显得很～。 In her decision she showed a down-to-earth realism. ‖ 这是个比较～的办法。 This is the more practical way.

【现实主义】xiànshízhǔyì〈名〉realism: ～小说/作家 realist novel/writer ‖ ～者 realist

【现世】xiànshì **A** ▸**p. 618**〈名〉this world **B**〈动〉bring shame on oneself

【现世报】xiànshìbào〈动〉receive immediate retribution

【现势】xiànshì〈名〉〈书〉present situation: ～不容乐观。 We are not optimistic about the present situation.

【现下】xiànxià〈副〉〈口〉nowadays

【现象】xiànxiàng〈名〉phenomenon: 被～所迷惑 be confused by the appearance of things ‖ 透过～看本质 see through appearances to grasp the essence ‖ 社会/天文/自然～ social/astronomical/natural phenomenon

【现行】xiànxíng〈形〉**1**（现时有效）current: ～法律 current law ‖ ～政策 current policy ‖ ～利率 prevailing rate of interest ‖ ～标准 currently effective standards ‖ ～制度 present system **2**（正在进行）active: 进行～破坏活动 engage in active sabotage

【现行法】xiànxíngfǎ〈名〉effective law: 违背～ violate effective laws

【现行犯】xiànxíngfàn〈名〉［法律］active criminal: 严惩～ mercilessly punish a criminal caught in the act

【现形】xiànxíng〈动〉reveal one's true colours

【现眼】xiànyǎn〈动〉make a spectacle of oneself: ▸丢人～

【现洋】xiànyáng〈名〉〈旧〉silver dollar

【现役】xiànyì **A**〈名〉active military service: 服～ be on active service **B**〈形〉active: ～军人 military personnel on active service

【现有】xiànyǒu〈形〉existing: ～技术 current technology ‖ ～资源 available resources

【现在】xiànzài ▸**p. 618**〈名〉present time: ～的男朋友 current boyfriend ‖ ～不谈此事。 Don't talk about it just now. ‖ ～是行动的时候了。 Now is the time for action. ‖ 她～在北京。 At present she is in Beijing.

【现在分词】xiànzài fēncí〈名〉［语法］present participle

【现在进行时】xiànzài jìnxíngshí〈名〉［语法］present progressive tense

【现在时】xiànzàishí〈名〉［语法］present tense

【现在式】xiànzàishì〈名〉［语法］present tense form

【现在完成时】xiànzài wánchéngshí〈名〉［语法］present perfect tense

【现职】xiànzhí〈名〉current position: ～官员 incumbent

【现状】xiànzhuàng〈名〉present situation: 安于～ be contented with the status quo ‖ 维持/改变～ maintain the status quo

限 xiàn

A〈名〉**1**（界限）limit: 以年底为～ set the end of the year as the deadline ▸界～, 期～, 权～ **2**〈书〉（门槛）threshold: 门～ threshold

B〈动〉limit: ～期完工。 This project must be completed within the specified time. ‖ 年龄不～。 There is no age limit. ‖ 本广告～印1,000份。 The advertisement is limited to 1,000 copies. ▸～定, ～量, ～制

【限产】xiànchǎn〈动〉limit output

【限定】xiàndìng〈动〉limit: ～时间 prescribe a time limit ‖ 由法律加以～ be circumscribed by laws ‖ 报名人数没有～。 There is no restriction on the number of applicants.

【限定词】xiàndìngcí〈名〉［语法］determiner

【限定动词】xiàndìng dòngcí〈名〉［语法］finite verb

【限定语】xiàndìngyǔ〈名〉［语法］qualifier

【限度】xiàndù〈名〉limit: 最低/高～ upper/lower limit ‖ 我的忍耐是有～的。 My patience has limits.

【限额】xiàn'é〈名〉limit: 超过～ exceed the quota ‖ 完成～ fulfil a quota ‖ 最低～ zero norm ‖ 最高～ ceiling ‖ 行李的重量～是多少? What's the luggage weight allowance?

【限高】xiàngāo〈名〉height limit

【限购】xiàngòu〈动〉limit a purchase: 开幕式门票每人～两张。 Tickets for the opening ceremony are limited to two per person.

【限价】xiànjià **A**〈动〉fix price: ～出售 sell at a prescribed price ‖ ～商品 commodities at set prices **B**〈名〉price limit: 最高/最底～ ceiling/floor price

X

【限价房】 xiànjiàfáng〈名〉 limited-price residential building: 增加～供应，解决低收入家庭的住房问题。 The provision of fixed-price commercial residential buildings should be stepped up as a means of solving the housing problem of low-income families.

【限界】 xiànjiè〈名〉 limit: ～利润 marginal profit ‖ ～信贷 marginal credit

【限量】 xiànliàng **A**〈动〉 limit the amount: ～发行 set limits to the issuance ‖ ～供应 limit the quantity of supply ‖ 前途不可～ have boundless prospects **B** = 限度 xiàndù

【限量版】 xiànliàngbǎn〈形〉 limited-edition: ～香水 limited-edition perfume ‖ ～新专辑 limited-edition new album

【限令】 xiànlìng **A**〈动〉 order sb. to do sth. within a certain time: ～三天之内拆除违章建筑 order sb. to tear down the unauthorized construction within three days ‖ ～该武官四十八小时内离境 give the military attaché 48 hours' notice to leave the country **B**〈名〉 orders to be carried out within a prescribed time limit: 放宽～ extend the deadline/time limit of orders to be carried out

【限期】 xiànqī **A**〈动〉 prescribe a time limit: ～偿还贷款 pay back loans within a set time ‖ ～整改 set a time limit for reform and consolidation **B**〈名〉 time limit: 给三天～ set a three-day time limit ‖ 在～内完成 finish within the specified time

【限时】 xiànshí〈动〉 set a time limit: ～完成 set a time limit for completion

【限售股】 xiànshòugǔ〈名〉［金融］ banned stocks: ～的解冻给市场带来压力。 Unfreezing banned shares puts pressure on the market.

【限速】 xiànsù〈名〉 speed limit: 超过～ exceed the speed limit

【限塑令】 xiànsùlìng〈名〉 plastic bag ban

【限薪】 xiànxīn〈动〉 limit excessive pay: ～规定/政策 pay limit stipulation/policy

【限行】 xiànxíng〈动〉 restrict access: 实施～措施，控制机动车流量 impose car restriction measures to control vehicle flow

【限养】 xiànyǎng〈动〉 restrict the rearing of certain animals: 制定～犬只的规定 make restrictions on keeping dogs

【限于】 xiànyú〈动〉 be limited to: ～思想水平 owing to one's limited ideological level ‖ ～篇幅，这些文章不能一一发表。 As space is limited, it is impossible to publish all the articles.

【限制】 xiànzhì **A**〈动〉 impose restrictions on: ～出口/进口 place restrictions on export/import ‖ ～开支/生产 place a restriction on spending/production ‖ ～时间 set a time limit (for) ‖ ～物价 put a ceiling on prices ‖ ～销售 restrict the sale ‖ 行动受到严格～ one's action is severely restricted ‖ ～自由 place restrictions on freedom ‖ 严格～数量 set a strict limit on the amount **B**〈名〉 restriction: 车速/年龄/时间～ speed/age/time limit ‖ 参赛人数有～。 There is a limit to the number of people who can compete.

线（綫、線） xiàn

A〈名〉 **1**（细长条状物）thread: 把珠子用～穿起来 thread the beads onto a length of string ‖ 棉/尼龙～ cotton/nylon thread ▸毛～, 丝～ **2**（线状物） wire: 电话～ telephone wire ‖ 漆包～ enamelled wire ▸电～ **3**（交通路线） traffic route: 供应～ supply route ‖ 京广～ Beijing-Guangzhou railway line ‖ 生产～ production line ‖ 运输～ transmission line ▸干～ **4**（线索） clue: ～索 **5**（内线） secret agent: ▸内～, 眼～ **6**［数学］ line: 画条～ draw a line ‖ 扫描～ scanning line ▸实～, 水平～, 直～ **7**（交界线） demarcation line: 罚球～ foul line ‖ 分界～ dividing line ▸海岸～, 前～ **8**（边际） brink: 录取分数～ pass mark ‖ 在死亡～上 on the verge of death ▸贫困～ **9**（思想、政治路线） ideological or political line

B〈量〉 [used to modify abstract nouns or numerals indicating few or little]: 一～生机 a chance of survival ‖ 一～希望 a ray of hope

【线报】 xiànbào〈名〉 inside information

【线材】 xiàncái〈名〉［冶金］ wire rod

【线虫】 xiànchóng〈名〉［昆虫］ roundworm

【线段】 xiànduàn〈名〉［数学］ line segment

【线缝】 xiànfèng〈名〉 seam

【线脚】 xiànjiǎo〈名〉 **1**〈方〉（针脚） stitch **2**［建筑］ skintled brickwork

【线粒体】 xiànlìtǐ〈名〉［生物］ chondriosome

【线路】 xiànlù〈名〉 **1**［电气］ circuit: 电话～ telephone line ‖ ～故障已有一周了。 The line has been out of order for a week. **2**（交通路线） route: 航空～ air route ‖ 公共汽车～ bus route

【线路故障】 xiànlù gùzhàng〈名〉 line fault

【线路图】 xiànlùtú〈名〉 circuit diagram

【线密度】 xiànmìdù〈名〉［纺织］ linear density

【线呢】 xiànní〈名〉 cotton suiting

【线圈】 xiànquān〈名〉［电气］ coil: 叠层～ band wound coil

【线人】 xiànrén〈名〉 spy, informant

【线绳】 xiànshéng〈名〉 cotton rope

【线速度】 xiànsùdù〈名〉［物理］ linear velocity

【线索】 xiànsuǒ〈名〉 clue: 发现～ unearth a clue ‖ 故事的～ thread of a story ‖ 破案～ clues for solving a case

【线毯】 xiàntǎn〈名〉 cotton blanket

【线膛】 xiàntáng〈名〉 rifled bore

【线条】 xiàntiáo〈名〉 **1**（指绘画） line: 用～勾画 line sth. **2**（指轮廓） figure: ～优美 have a good figure ‖ 流畅的～ sleek lines

【线条图】 xiàntiáotú〈名〉 line drawing

【线头】 xiàntóu〈名〉 **1**（线的一端） the end of a thread **2**（短线段） piece of short thread

【线团】 xiàntuán〈名〉 ball of string

【线下】 xiànxià〈名〉 offline: ～商贸运作 offline business operation

【线香】 xiànxiāng〈名〉 slender stick of incense

【线形虫】 xiànxíngchóng〈名〉 wireworm

【线形图】 xiànxíngtú〈名〉 string diagram

【线型】 xiànxíng〈名〉［物理］［电气］ type of line: ～分子链 linear chain

【线性】 xiànxìng〈形〉 linear: ～代数 linear algebra

【线性函数】 xiànxìng hánshù〈名〉［数学］ linear function

【线性扫描】 xiànxìng sǎomiáo〈名〉［电子］ linear scan

【线性思维】 xiànxìng sīwéi〈名〉 linear thinking

【线衣】 xiànyī〈名〉〈方〉 cotton knitwear

【线轴】 xiànzhóu〈名〉 spool of thread: 把线绕在～上 wind thread on the reel

【线装】 xiànzhuāng〈形〉 thread-bound: ～书 thread-bound Chinese book

> **线装书**
>
> *Xianzhuang* (线装) is a traditional method of bookbinding in which the pages are folded with the printed side outwards and the blank side inwards, the margins are aligned, covers added, the raw edges trimmed, and holes are made for the thread to pass through. Most thread-bound books have soft covers, and are often produced in a number of volumes, with a hard case added for protection. Thread-bound books flourished in the Ming and Qing dynasties. They are easy to browse through, do not come apart, and are still used today.

宪（憲） xiàn

〈名〉 **1**〈书〉（法令） decree: 布～ issue a decree **2**（宪法） constitution: ▸立～, 制～

【宪兵】 xiànbīng〈名〉 military policeman (MP): ～队 military police

【宪法】 xiànfǎ〈名〉 constitution: 违反～ violate the constitution ‖ 修订～ revise the constitution ‖ 遵守～ observe the constitution ‖ ～赋予的权利 constitutional right ‖ 中华人民共和国～ the Constitution of the People's Republic of China

【宪警】 xiànjǐng〈名〉 police

【宪章】 xiànzhāng〈名〉 **1**〈书〉（典章制度） decrees and regulations **2**（指文件） charter: 联合国～ the United Nations Charter

【宪政】 xiànzhèng〈名〉 constitutional government: 实行～ operate a constitutional government

陷 xiàn

A〈动〉 **1**（掉进） get stuck: ～在日常事务堆里 get bogged down in daily routine ‖ 公共汽车～在雪里动弹不得。 The bus got stuck in the snow. ▸沉～, 塌～, 下～ **2**（失守） be captured: ▸沦～, 失～ **3**（攻破） make a breakthrough: ▸冲锋～阵 **4**（陷害） frame: ～人于罪 frame sb. ▸诬～ **5**（凹进） sink: 深～的眼睛 deep-set eyes ‖ 他脚下的土地突然～了下去。 The ground suddenly sank under his feet. ▸凹～, 洼～

B〈名〉 **1**（陷阱） trap: ▸～阱, ～坑 **2**（缺点） defect: ▸缺～

【陷害】 xiànhài〈动〉 fabricate a charge: ～好人 frame an innocent person ‖ 政治～ political frame-up ‖ 谁都知道他是被～的。 Everybody knows he was wrongly accused.

【陷阱】 xiànjǐng〈名〉 trap: 落入～ be caught in a trap ‖ 设下～ set a trap

【陷坑】 xiànkēng = 陷阱 xiànjǐng

【陷落】 xiànluò〈动〉 **1**（下沉） subside: 地壳的～ subsidence of the earth's crust **2**（落入） sink into: ～重围 find oneself tightly encircled ‖ ～困境 land oneself in a predicament **3**（被攻占） fall into enemy hands: 许多城池～。 Many cities fell into enemy hands.

【陷入】 xiànrù〈动〉 **1**（落入） fall into: ～包围 be besieged ‖ ～困境 get into hot water ‖ ～僵局 come to a deadlock **2**〈喻〉（沉浸） be lost in: ～沉思 be lost in thought ‖ ～遐想 be deep in reverie

【陷身】 xiànshēn〈动〉〈书〉 fall into: ～囹圄 be thrown into prison

【陷于】 xiànyú〈动〉 fall into an unfavourable position: ～被动 lose the initiative ‖ 大雾使交通～混乱。 Fog disrupted the traffic.

【陷阵】xiànzhèn〈动〉 break into enemy ranks: ▸冲锋～

馅（餡） xiàn〈名〉 filling: 饺子～ stuffing for dumplings ‖ 枣泥～月饼 moon-cake with mashed date filling

【馅儿饼】xiànrbǐng〈名〉 pastry with filling

羡（羨） xiàn

A〈动〉 admire: ▸欣～, 艳～

B〈形〉〈书〉 superfluous: ▸～余

【羡慕】xiànmù〈动〉 envy: 受到很多人的～ get a lot of admiring glances ‖ 怀有～之情 possess feelings of admiration ‖ 令人～ enviable

【羡余】xiànyú〈形〉 surplus

献（獻） xiàn〈动〉 **1**（呈上） present: ～花圈 lay a wreath ‖ 把一生～给科研 dedicate one's life to scientific research ‖ 谨以此书～给先师。This book is hereby dedicated to my late teacher. ▸～血 **2**（展示） show: ～艺 give a performance ‖ ～一首歌 sing a song ▸～殷勤

【献宝】xiànbǎo〈动〉 **1**〈本〉 present a treasure **2**〈喻〉（指经验意见） offer one's valuable experience **3**〈喻〉（指新奇的东西） parade what one thinks valuable or novel

【献策】xiàncè〈动〉 offer advice: 问题如何解决得靠大家～。 To solve the problem, we need everyone to put forward their ideas.

【献丑】xiànchǒu〈动〉〈谦〉 show oneself up: 那我只好～，唱上一曲。 Well, here's my fumbling attempt to sing a song!

【献词】xiàncí〈名〉 congratulatory message: 新年～ New Year address

【献花】xiànhuā〈动〉 present a bouquet: 向老师～ present the teacher with flowers

【献计】xiànjì〈动〉 offer advice: ～献策 offer ideas

【献技】xiànjì〈动〉 show one's skill: 登台～ take to the stage to display one's skill

【献祭】xiànjì〈动〉 offer up as a sacrifice

【献礼】xiànlǐ〈动〉 present a gift: 国庆～片 film marking the anniversary of National Day

【献媚】xiànmèi〈动〉 curry favour: ～求宠 worm oneself into sb.'s favour

【献旗】xiànqí〈动〉 present a banner to express one's respect or appreciation

【献芹】xiànqín〈动〉〈书〉〈谦〉 offer my humble present/suggestion

【献身】xiànshēn〈动〉 devote oneself to: ～教育事业 devote oneself to the cause of education ‖ 为国～ give up one's life for one's country

【献血】xiànxiě〈动〉 donate blood: 义务～ give blood

【献血者】xiànxiězhě〈名〉 blood donor

【献言】xiànyán〈动〉〈书〉 offer advice

【献疑】xiànyí〈动〉〈书〉 put forward a question

【献艺】xiànyì〈动〉 show one's skill

【献殷勤】xiàn yīnqín〈动〉 ingratiate oneself: 向当权者大～ ingratiate oneself with people in authority

【献映】xiànyìng〈动〉 project for an audience

腺 xiàn〈名〉 gland: 蛇的毒～ viper's poison glands ▸汗～, 甲状～, 乳～

镍（鎳） xiàn〈名〉 metal wire

霰 xiàn〈名〉 graupel

xiāng

乡（鄉） xiāng〈名〉 **1**（指行政区划单位） township: ～政府 township government **2**（乡村） countryside: ▸～村 **3**（家乡） native place: 回～ come back to one's native place ▸背井离～, 故～, 同～

【乡巴佬】xiāngbalǎo〈名〉〈贬〉 country bumpkin

【乡愁】xiāngchóu〈名〉 homesickness: 她侨居国外，～与日俱增。 She has been homesick every day since she's been away.

【乡村】xiāngcūn〈名〉 village: ～风格 rustic style ‖ ～风光 rural scene ‖ ～学校 village school

【乡村音乐】xiāngcūn yīnyuè〈名〉 country music

【乡规民约】xiāngguī-mínyuē〈成〉 village rules and conventions

【乡间】xiāngjiān〈名〉 countryside: ～别墅/道路 country villa/road

【乡井】xiāngjǐng〈名〉〈书〉 native place: 远离～ be far away from home

【乡里】xiānglǐ〈名〉 **1**（指地方） hometown: 荣归～ return to one's native place with great honour **2**（指人） fellow villager: 看望～ visit a fellow villager

【乡里乡气】xiānglǐ-xiāngqì〈形〉 uncouth

【乡邻】xiānglín〈名〉 fellow villager

【乡亲】xiāngqīn〈名〉 **1**（同乡人） fellow villager **2**（当地乡民） local people: ～们都过上了好日子。 All the country folk are living a happy life.

【乡情】xiāngqíng〈名〉 affection for one's native place

【乡绅】xiāngshēn〈名〉 country gentleman

【乡试】xiāngshì〈名〉 triennial provincial civil service examination for the degree of *juren* (held in the provincial capital during the Ming and Qing dynasties)

【乡思】xiāngsī〈名〉 homesickness

【乡俗】xiāngsú〈名〉 rural custom

【乡谈】xiāngtán〈名〉 local dialect

【乡土】xiāngtǔ〈名〉 native soil: 摈弃～观念 cast away provincialism ‖ 具有～特色 possess local features

【乡土文学】xiāngtǔ wénxué〈名〉 native literature

【乡下】xiāngxia〈名〉 countryside: 住在～ live in the country ‖ ～佬 country bumpkin ‖ ～人 country folk

【乡谊】xiāngyì〈名〉〈书〉 close feelings of fellowship among people from the same locality

【乡音】xiāngyīn ▸**p. 918**〈名〉 local accent: 说话带着浓重的～ speak with a strong local accent

【乡邮】xiāngyóu〈名〉 rural postal service: ～员 rural postman

【乡长】xiāngzhǎng〈名〉 township head

【乡镇】xiāngzhèn〈名〉 **1**（乡和镇） villages and towns: ～公路 township road **2**（小市镇） small town

【乡镇企业】xiāngzhèn qǐyè〈名〉township enterprise: ～异军突起。 Township enterprises emerged as a new force.

【乡政府】xiāngzhèngfǔ〈名〉township government

【乡梓】xiāngzǐ〈名〉〈书〉 hometown

芗（薌） xiāng

A〈形〉〈书〉 fragrant: 芬～ aromatic scent

B〈名〉 fragrant herb in ancient Chinese books

【芗剧】xiāngjù〈名〉 Xiang opera [kind of local opera popular in the Xiangjiang area of Taiwan and Southern Fujian]

相[1] xiāng〈副〉 **1**（互相） mutually: ～视而笑 look and smile at each other ‖ 这两件事不～关联。 The two matters have nothing to do with each other. ▸～爱, ～距, ～像 **2**（表一方对另一方） toward: 实不～瞒 to tell you the truth ▸～劝

相[2] xiāng〈动〉 evaluate by seeing for oneself: ～女婿 assess the suitability of a prospective son-in-law or husband ‖ 这种款式我根本～不中。 This style is not at all to my liking. ▸～亲

▸xiàng

【相爱】xiāng'ài〈动〉 be in love with each other: 他俩～了。 They are in love.

【相安】xiāng'ān〈动〉 live together peacefully: 邻里～ get on well with one's neighbours ‖ ～无事 live in peace with each other

【相伴】xiāngbàn〈动〉 keep each other company: 在家呆一周与母亲～ stay home for a week to accompany one's mother

【相帮】xiāngbāng〈动〉 help: 这事得有朋友～。 This can only be done with the help of friends.

【相悖】xiāngbèi〈动〉 run counter to: 跟法律～ contradict the law

【相比】xiāngbǐ〈动〉 compare with each other: 二者不能～。 There is no comparison between the two. ‖ ～之下，我们的生活比他们富裕。 By contrast, we are better off than they are.

【相差】xiāngchà〈动〉 differ: ～无几 be almost the same ‖ 他俩～五岁。 They are five years apart.

【相称】xiāngchèn〈动〉 be suitable: 这件衣服与她年龄不～。 The dress is not appropriate for her age.

【相称】xiāngchēng〈动〉address each other as: 以兄妹～ address each other as brother and sister

【相成】xiāngchéng〈动〉 complement each other: ▸相辅～

【相承】xiāngchéng〈动〉 pass on from one to another: 世代～ pass on from generation to generation ‖ 一脉～ come down in one continuous line

【相乘】xiāngchéng〈动〉［数学］ multiply: 将7和8～ multiply 7 by 8

【相持】xiāngchí〈动〉 maintain a stand-off: 处于～阶段 be locked in a stalemate ‖ 双方在重要问题上仍然～不下。 The two parties have come to a deadlock on crucial issues.

【相持不下】xiāngchí-bùxià〈成〉 be locked in a stalemate

【相斥】xiāngchì〈动〉 repel each other: 同性～，异性相吸。 Like electric charges repel each other, while unlike ones attract each other.

【相处】xiāngchǔ〈动〉 get along: 和睦～ get along well with each other ‖ 难以～ be hard to get along with

【相传】xiāngchuán〈动〉 **1**（相互传说） according to legend: ～这件事发生在几百年前。 Tradition has it that the event took place hundreds of years ago. **2**（递相传授） pass on from one to another: 世代～ pass on from generation to generation

【相待】xiāngdài〈动〉 treat: 以礼～ treat sb. with courtesy

X

【相当】xiāngdāng **A**〈动〉 match: 收入与支出～。 Income is equal to expenditure. ‖ 两个队实力～。 The two teams are evenly matched. **B**〈形〉 appropriate: ～的人选 suitable person ‖ ～的字眼 appropriate word **C**〈副〉 considerably: ～成功 quite successful ‖ ～漂亮 very beautiful ‖ 一笔～可观的钱 a considerable sum of money ‖ 他考得～不错。 He did rather well in his exams.

【相当于】xiāngdāngyú〈动〉 correspond to: 你的工资～我的两倍。 Your salary is twice that of mine.

【相得益彰】xiāngdé-yìzhāng〈成〉 bring out the best in each other

【相等】xiāngděng〈动〉 be equal: 价值/重量～ be of equal value/weight

【相抵】xiāngdǐ〈动〉 **1**（指抵消） offset: 收支～，所剩无几。 When you offset income against expenditure, there is not much left over. **2**〈书〉（指抵触） be at variance with: 与法律～ contradict the law

【相对】xiāngduì **A**〈动〉 face each other: ～而坐 sit opposite each other ‖ 两塔遥遥～。 The two towers face one another over a distance. **B**〈形〉 relative: 保持～平衡 maintain a relative balance ‖ ～而言 relatively speaking ‖ 测出～高度 measure the relative altitude ‖ ～便宜些 be relatively cheap ‖ 高与低是～的。 'Being high' or 'being low' is relative. ▸～论

【相对多数】xiāngduì duōshù〈名〉 relative majority

【相对论】xiāngduìlùn〈名〉 theory of relativity: 广义/狭义～ general/special theory of relativity

【相对密度】xiāngduì mìdù〈名〉［物理］ relative density

【相对速度】xiāngduì sùdù〈名〉［物理］ relative velocity

【相对运动】xiāngduì yùndòng〈名〉［物理］ relative motion

【相对真理】xiāngduì zhēnlǐ〈名〉［哲学］ relative truth

【相烦】xiāngfán〈动〉〈书〉 trouble (you): 有事～ may I trouble you for sth.

【相反】xiāngfǎn **A**〈形〉 opposite: ～方向 opposite direction ‖ 事实恰恰～。 The opposite is the case. **B**〈连〉 instead: 他并没反对，～，他坚决支持。 He was not against it. On the contrary, he was strongly for it.

【相反相成】xiāngfǎn-xiāngchéng〈成〉 oppose and yet complement each other: 失败是成功之母，说明二者是～的。 It is a paradox that failure is the mother of success.

【相仿】xiāngfǎng〈形〉 similar: 年龄～ be almost of the same age ‖ 颜色～ be similar in colour

【相逢】xiāngféng〈动〉 chance upon: 异地～ meet in a strange land ‖ ～何必曾相识 now that destiny has brought us together, it matters little that we have never met before

【相符】xiāngfú〈动〉 tally with: 与事实/政策～ tally with the facts/policy ‖ 检查一下，看两组结果是否～。 Check the two sets of results to see if they tally.

【相辅而行】xiāngfǔ'érxíng〈成〉 complement each other: 国有企业和私有企业可以～。 State-owned enterprises and privately owned companies complement each other.

【相辅相成】xiāngfǔ-xiāngchéng〈成〉 complement each other: 民办学校可以与公办学校～。 Private and public schools complement one another.

【相干】xiānggān〈动〉 [usu used in the negative or interrogative sentence] be concerned with: 不～的事件 unrelated incidents ‖ ～性 coherence ‖ 这事与你不～。 This has nothing to do with you.

【相告】xiānggào〈动〉 tell: 我有要事～。 I have something important to tell you.

【相隔】xiānggé〈动〉 be apart: ～千山万水 be separated by numerous rivers and mountains ‖ ～一百年 be at an interval of 100 years

【相顾】xiānggù〈动〉〈书〉 look at each other: ～无言 look at each other in silence

【相关】xiāngguān〈动〉 be related: 密切～ be closely related ‖ 他们的命运休戚～。 Their fortunes were interlinked.

【相好】xiānghǎo **A**〈形〉 on intimate terms: 他们从小就～。 They have been bosom friends since their childhood. **B**〈动〉 have an affair with: 他们暗中～了三年。 Their secret love affair lasted three years. **C**〈名〉 **1**（情人） lover: 老～ old flame **2**（好友） good friend

【相互】xiānghù **A**〈副〉 each other: ～猜疑 be suspicious of each other ‖ ～依赖 depend on each other **B**〈形〉 mutual: 改善～间的关系 improve mutual relations

【相互代词】xiānghù dàicí〈名〉［语法］ reciprocal pronoun

【相互依存】xiānghù yīcún〈名〉 interdependence

【相互作用】xiānghù zuòyòng〈名〉 mutual effect

【相会】xiānghuì〈动〉 meet: 初次～ meet for the first time ‖ 二十年后再～ meet again after twenty years

【相继】xiāngjì〈副〉 in succession: ～发生 occur one after another ‖ ～离开 leave one after another

【相加】xiāngjiā〈动〉 add together: 5和4～等于9。 5 plus 4 is 9.

【相煎何急】xiāngjiān-héjí〈成〉 why such relentless infighting among brothers: 同室操戈，～! Why should brothers take up arms and fight each other with such hatred?

【相见】xiāngjiàn〈动〉 see each other: ▸仇人～，分外眼红

【相见恨晚】xiāngjiàn-hènwǎn〈成〉 regret not having met sooner

【相间】xiāngjiàn〈动〉 alternate with: 黑白～ black alternating with white

【相交】xiāngjiāo〈动〉 **1**（交叉） intersect: 该店位于两条街～的地方。 The shop is situated at the intersection of two streets. ‖ 这两条线～成角。 The two lines meet to form an angle. **2**（做朋友） be friends: ～多年 have been friends for many years

【相较见长】xiāngjiào jiànzhǎng〈成〉 gain by contrast or comparison

【相接】xiāngjiē〈动〉 join: 这座桥将那个岛屿与大陆～。 The bridge connects the island with the mainland.

【相近】xiāngjìn〈形〉 **1**（距离近） close: 比分～。 The score was very close. **2**（近似） similar: 年龄～ be almost the same age ‖ 这些词意义～。 These words are close in meaning.

【相敬如宾】xiāngjìng-rúbīn〈成〉 treat each other with the respect due to a guest: 夫妻二人～。 The couple treat each other with sincere respect.

【相救】xiāngjiù〈动〉 come to the rescue: 出手～ lend a hand in sb.'s rescue

【相距】xiāngjù〈动〉 be apart: ～不远 not far from one another ‖ ～甚远 be poles apart

【相聚】xiāngjù〈动〉 meet: ～一堂，共商国事 come together to discuss state affairs

【相看】xiāngkàn〈动〉 **1**（相对而视） look at each other: 含情脉脉～良久 look affectionately at each other for a long time **2**（对待） treat: 用老眼光～ be influenced by old views in one's treatment of sth. ▸另眼～

【相克】xiāngkè〈动〉 **1**［中医］ be mutually destructive **2**〈口〉（指运程） be ill-matched according to the horoscope

【相连】xiānglián〈动〉 be joined: 山水～ be joined by common mountains and rivers ‖ 心心～ hearts beating in harmony

【相联】xiānglián〈形〉［计算机］ associative: ～存储器 associative storage

【相邻】xiānglín〈动〉 neighbour: ～的两户人家 two adjoining families ‖ ～国家/地区 neighbouring country/area

【相骂】xiāngmà〈动〉 exchange insults

【相瞒】xiāngmán〈动〉 hold back: 实不～ to tell you the truth

【相陪】xiāngpéi〈动〉 accompany

【相配】xiāngpèi〈动〉 go well with: 他们是很～的一对。 They are a perfect match. ‖ 我要一条与这套衣服～的领带。 I want a tie that will go with this suit.

【相碰】xiāngpèng〈动〉 collide: 两辆车在十字路口～。 The two cars collided with each other at the crossroads.

【相扑】xiāngpū〈名〉［体育］ sumo wrestling: ～运动员 sumo wrestler

【相切】xiāngqiē〈动〉［数学］ be tangential to: 画一条与圆～的直线 draw a line tangential to the circle

【相亲】xiāngqīn〈动〉 see and assess the suitability of a prospective mate or son/daughter-in-law: 择日～ set a date for meeting a prospective mate

【相亲相爱】xiāngqīn-xiāng'ài〈成〉 love each other deeply

【相求】xiāngqiú〈动〉 entreat: 他有事～于我。 He asked a favour of me.

【相去】xiāngqù〈动〉 be separated: ～数千里 be thousands of kilometres apart ‖ ～甚远 be poles apart

【相去无几】xiāngqù-wújǐ〈成〉 there is hardly any difference (between)

【相劝】xiāngquàn〈动〉 persuade: 好言～ sweet-talk sb. into doing sth. ‖ 竭力～ do everything in one's power to persuade

【相让】xiāngràng〈动〉 **1**（忍让） make concessions: 各不～。 Neither will exercise forbearance. **2**（谦让） modestly decline: 礼貌～ defer to each other politely

【相扰】xiāngrǎo〈动〉〈书〉 **1**（干涉） interfere: 各不～ neither side interferes with the other **2**〈套〉（打扰） trouble: 有一事～。 Excuse me for bothering you with something.

【相忍为国】xiāngrěn-wèiguó〈成〉 exercise forbearance for the sake of the nation

【相认】xiāngrèn〈动〉 recognize: 离散多年以后，父子俩得以重新～。 The father and son resumed their relationship after a long separation.

【相容】xiāngróng **A**〈动〉 be compatible with one another **B**〈形〉［数学］ consistent

【相濡以沫】xiāngrúyǐmò〈成〉 help each other to pull through a crisis

【相若】xiāngruò〈形〉〈书〉 similar: 年龄～ be similar in age

【相商】xiāngshāng〈动〉 consult: 有要事～ have something important to discuss with you

【相生相克】xiāngshēng-xiāngkè〈成〉 mutual promotion and restraint

X

【相识】xiāngshí A〈动〉 get to know each other: 似曾～ seem familiar ‖ 早已～ have known each other a long time ▸素不～ B〈名〉 acquaintance: 老～ old friend
【相视】xiāngshì〈动〉 look at each other: ～而笑 look at each other and smile
【相率】xiāngshuài〈副〉〈书〉 in succession
【相思】xiāngsī〈动〉 1〈彼此思念〉 miss each other: 两地～ miss each other when far apart 2〈特指男女间〉 pine for a loved one: ～病 lovesickness ▸单～
【相思豆】xiāngsīdòu〈名〉 1〈指植物〉 Indian liquorice 2〈指种子〉 love pea
【相思子】xiāngsīzǐ〈名〉 1〈指植物〉 jequirity bean 2〈指种子〉 rosary pea
【相似】xiāngsì〈形〉 similar: 面貌～ look alike ‖ 颜色～ be similar in colour ‖ ～的观点/经历/情况 similar view/experience/case ‖ 他们的性格很～。They are quite alike in character.
【相似性】xiāngsìxìng〈名〉［物理］ similitude
【相送】xiāngsòng〈动〉 see sb. out/off: 到机场/车站～ see sb. off at the airport/station
【相随】xiāngsuí〈动〉 go with: 有警卫～ be escorted by a guard ‖ 他与父母～进了超市。He went to the supermarket with his parents.
【相谈】xiāngtán〈动〉 converse: ～甚欢 be in animated conversation
【相提并论】xiāngtí-bìnglùn〈成〉 [usu used in the negative] mention in the same breath: 两者不能～。The two of them cannot be mentioned in the same breath.
【相通】xiāngtōng〈动〉 be interlinked: 客厅与卧室～。The living room is connected to the bedroom. ‖ 虽然远隔重洋，但我们的心是～的。Though we are separated by seas and oceans, our hearts are linked.
【相同】xiāngtóng〈形〉 same: 大小/颜色～ be of the same size/colour ‖ 大不～ be completely different ‖ 有～的看法 see eye to eye with sb.
【相同点】xiāngtóngdiǎn〈名〉 similarity
【相投】xiāngtóu〈动〉 agree with each other: 趣味～ have similar tastes ▸臭味～
【相托】xiāngtuō〈动〉 entrust: 她将孩子～给妈妈照料。She has entrusted her child to her mother.
【相向】xiāngxiàng〈动〉 1〈面对面〉 face each other: ～而行 walk towards each other 2〈向着对方〉 target ...: 武力～ ready to use force against one's opponents
【相像】xiāngxiàng〈动〉 be similar: 面貌～ be alike in appearance ‖ 有～之处 bear a resemblance ‖ 他和妹妹十分～。He closely resembles his sister.
【相信】xiāngxìn〈动〉 believe: 没有理由不～某人/某事 have no reason not to believe sb./sth. ‖ 我说什么她都不～。She did not believe a word I said. ‖ 我～你是清白的。I believe in your innocence.
【相形见绌】xiāngxíng-jiànchù〈成〉 pale in comparison: 新电视机使原来那台～。The new TV set puts the old one in the shade. ‖ 我的画与他的相比～。My painting pales in comparison with his.
【相沿】xiāngyán〈动〉 pass down through long usage: ～成习 become common practice through long usage
【相依】xiāngyī〈动〉 depend on each other: 俩人～，共渡难关。They had only each other for company and shared the hardships together. ▸唇齿～
【相依为命】xiāngyī-wéimìng〈成〉 depend upon each other for survival: 父母去世后，姐弟俩～。After they were orphaned the sister and brother depended on each other for survival.
【相宜】xiāngyí〈形〉 appropriate: 采取～的行动 take appropriate action ‖ 她做这项工作很～。She is qualified to do the work.
【相异】xiāngyì〈形〉 different
【相迎】xiāngyíng〈动〉 welcome: 笑脸～ give sb. a smiling welcome
【相应】xiāngyìng〈动〉 be appropriate: 采取～的措施 take appropriate measures ‖ 做～改变/调整 make corresponding changes/adjustments
【相映】xiāngyìng〈动〉 provide a contrast: ～生辉 set each other off wonderfully
【相映成趣】xiāngyìng-chéngqù〈成〉 set each other off: 两位演员一俊一丑，～。Of the two actors, one is handsome and the other ugly, forming an amusing contrast.
【相与】xiāngyǔ A〈动〉 get on with: 他这个人极难～。He is extremely difficult to get along with. B〈副〉〈书〉 together: ～谈笑 talk and laugh together
【相遇】xiāngyù〈动〉 meet each other: 在机场～ meet at the airport
【相约】xiāngyuē〈动〉 reach an agreement: 他们～在门口见面。They made an appointment to meet at the gate.
【相悦】xiāngyuè〈动〉 love each other: 两心～。The two of them love each other very much.
【相赠】xiāngzèng〈动〉 present a gift
【相知】xiāngzhī A〈动〉 know each other well: ～多年 have known each other long B〈名〉 close friend
【相知恨晚】xiāngzhī-hènwǎn〈成〉 it is such a pity that we never met earlier: 他俩彻夜畅谈，～。The two of them talked from dusk to dawn, regretting that they had not known each other earlier.
【相中】xiāngzhòng〈动〉 take a fancy to: 这个女孩子是他一眼～的。This girl caught his fancy at first glance.
【相助】xiāngzhù〈动〉 help: 彼此～ help each other ‖ 鼎力～ go to great efforts to help
【相撞】xiāngzhuàng〈动〉 collide: 两列火车～。The two trains collided with one another.
【相左】xiāngzuǒ〈动〉〈书〉 1〈不相遇〉 fail to meet each other: 道中～，失之交臂。We failed to meet on the road and just missed each other. 2〈相反〉 disagree: 意见～ cannot see eye to eye

香 xiāng

A〈形〉 1〈气味好闻〉 fragrant: 稻～千里。The pleasant smell of ripening rice spread a thousand *lì*. ▸～瓜，～水 2〈味道好〉 delicious: 菜真～啊! What a delicious dish! 3〈胃口好〉 enjoyable: 吃得～ enjoy the food ‖ 吃饭不～ have no appetite 4〈受欢迎〉 popular: 这种货在农村很吃～。The merchandise is very popular in the countryside.
B〈副〉 soundly: 睡得～ sleep soundly
C〈名〉 1〈香料〉 perfume: ▸麝～，檀～ 2〈指掺香料的细条〉 incense: 一炷～ a stick of incense ‖ 烧～ burn incense ▸～灰，盘～，蚊～ 3〈女子〉 woman: ▸怜～惜玉
D〈动〉〈方〉 kiss: ～面孔 kiss sb.'s face
【香案】xiāng'àn〈名〉 incense table: ～上供着一尊佛像。A Buddha is enshrined on the table.
【香包】xiāngbāo〈名〉 scent bag
【香槟酒】xiāngbīnjiǔ〈名〉 champagne
【香波】xiāngbō〈名〉 shampoo
【香饽饽】xiāngbōbo〈名〉〈口〉〈喻〉 favourite thing: 高级管理人才成了企业的～。The senior administrators have become the darlings of the corporation.
【香菜】xiāngcài〈名〉 coriander〈英〉; cilantro〈美〉: ～叶 coriander leaves
【香草】xiāngcǎo〈名〉 1〈泛指草〉 sweetgrass 2〈特指香子兰〉 vanilla: ～冰激凌 vanilla ice-cream
【香肠】xiāngcháng〈名〉 sausage
【香臭不分】xiāng-chòu bùfēn〈成〉 be unable to tell good from bad
【香椿】xiāngchūn〈名〉 1［植物］ Chinese toon 2〈指嫩叶〉 tender leaves of Chinese toon [used as a vegetable]
【香醇】xiāngchún〈形〉 fragrant and pure: ～的酒 mellow wine
【香袋】xiāngdài〈名〉 perfume pouch
【香肚】xiāngdǔ〈名〉 cured pig bladder skin stuffed with spiced pork
【香榧】xiāngfěi〈名〉［植物］ Chinese torreya
【香粉】xiāngfěn〈名〉 cosmetic powder
【香干】xiānggān〈名〉 smoked and dried bean curd
【香港】Xiānggǎng ▸**p. 661**〈名〉 Hong Kong: ～特别行政区 Hong Kong Special Administrative Region (HKSAR)
【香港脚】xiānggǎngjiǎo ▸**p. 50**〈名〉 Hong Kong foot
【香格里拉】Xiānggélǐlā〈名〉 Shangri-La
【香菇】xiānggū〈名〉 wood mushroom
【香菰】xiānggū = 香菇 xiānggū
【香瓜】xiāngguā〈名〉 musk-melon
【香花】xiānghuā〈名〉 1〈本〉 fragrant flower: ～异草 fragrant flowers and exotic plants 2〈喻〉 writings or artistic works beneficial to the people: 这部小说是～而非毒草。This novel contributes to social good rather than to social harm.
【香灰】xiānghuī〈名〉 incense ash
【香会】xiānghuì〈名〉〈旧〉 group of pilgrims
【香火】xiānghuǒ〈名〉 1〈指香和灯烛〉 joss sticks and candles burning at a temple: ～甚盛 attract a large number of pilgrims 2〈庙祝〉 incense attendant in a temple 3〈子孙〉 continuance of a family line: 断了～ have no male heir 4〈指火〉 burning incense: 用～点燃爆竹 light a firecracker with a burning joss stick
【香火钱】xiānghuǒqián〈名〉 donations to a temple
【香蕉】xiāngjiāo〈名〉 1〈指植物〉 banana tree 2〈指果实〉 banana
【香蕉苹果】xiāngjiāo píngguǒ〈名〉 a species of apple with odour of banana
【香蕉球】xiāngjiāoqiú〈名〉［足球］ banana ball: 踢出一记～ kick a curve ball
【香蕉水】xiāngjiāoshuǐ〈名〉［化学］ banana oil
【香精】xiāngjīng〈名〉 flavouring essence: 食用～ flavouring essence
【香客】xiāngkè〈名〉［宗教］ pilgrim: 全国各地～络绎不绝。Pilgrims from all parts of the country came in endless streams.
【香料】xiāngliào〈名〉 perfume: 人造～ synthetic perfume
【香炉】xiānglú〈名〉 incense burner
【香茅】xiāngmáo〈名〉［植物］ lemon grass
【香米】xiāngmǐ〈名〉 fragrant rice
【香囊】xiāngnáng〈名〉 perfume pouch

X

【香喷喷】xiāngpēnpēn〈形〉1▸(指气味) fragrant: 一束~的花儿 a bundle of fragrant flowers 2▸(指味道) appetizing: ~的蛋糕/鸡汤 savoury cake/chicken soup
【香片】xiāngpiàn = 花茶 huāchá
【香蒲】xiāngpú〈名〉[植物] cat's tail grass
【香气】xiāngqì〈名〉aroma: ~扑鼻 a sweet smell assails one's nostrils ‖ ~四溢 an exquisite fragrance wafts all around
【香钱】xiāngqián〈名〉incense money [as a donation to a temple]
【香薷】xiāngrú〈名〉[植物] Elsholtzia cilita
【香山】Xiāngshān〈名〉Fragrant Hills [in west Beijing]
【香水】xiāngshuǐ〈名〉perfume: 法国~ French perfume
【香酥鸡】xiāngsūjī〈名〉crispy fried chicken
【香甜】xiāngtián〈形〉1▸(又香又甜) fragrant and sweet: ~的瓜果 sweet melons and fruits 2▸(踏实) sound: 睡得~ sleep soundly
【香味】xiāngwèi〈名〉fragrance: 闻到饭菜~ smell the delicious aroma of a meal ‖ 房间弥漫着玫瑰~。The room radiates the perfume of roses.
【香消玉殒】xiāngxiāo-yùyǔn〈成〉〈喻〉a beauty passes away
【香烟】xiāngyān〈名〉1▸(指烟) incense smoke: ~缭绕。Curls of smoke were rising from the joss sticks. 2▸〈旧〉= 香火 xiānghuǒ 3 3▸(纸烟) cigarette: 过滤嘴~ filter-tip cigarette ‖ 焦油含量低的~ low-tar cigarette
【香艳】xiāngyàn〈形〉〈旧〉1▸(指人) seductive: ~女子 girl of sensual charm 2▸(指作品) flowery: ~小说 amorous novel
【香油】xiāngyóu〈名〉sesame oil
【香橼】xiāngyuán〈名〉[植物] citron
【香云纱】xiāngyúnshā〈名〉[纺织] gambiered Guangdong gauze [silk fabric with a thin film of lacquer on the surface, used as summer dress material]
【香皂】xiāngzào〈名〉scented soap: 药用~ medicated toilet soap
【香脂】xiāngzhī〈名〉1▸(指护肤品) face cream: 搽~ put on face cream 2▸(指膏脂) balsam: ~树 balsam tree
【香烛】xiāngzhú〈名〉incense and candles

厢(廂) xiāng〈名〉1▸(厢房) wing: 东/西~ east/west wing 2▸(旁边) [usu used in traditional opera or fiction] side: 两~ both sides ‖ 这~ this side ▸一~情愿 3▸(整节火车车厢) railway carriage; (火车包间) train compartment; (剧院包间) box: ▸包~, 车~ 4▸(靠近城的地区) vicinity of a city: 城~ vicinity of a city
【厢房】xiāngfáng〈名〉wing: 东/西~ east/west wing (of a house)

葙 xiāng ▸青葙 qīngxiāng

湘 Xiāng〈名〉1▸ ▸p. 294 (指河流) Xiangjiang River 2▸ ▸p. 661 (湖南) Xiang [another name for Hunan Province (湖南)]: ▸~剧, ~绣
【湘菜】xiāngcài〈名〉Hunan cuisine
【湘妃竹】xiāngfēizhú〈名〉speckled bamboo
【湘剧】xiāngjù〈名〉Hunan opera
【湘莲】xiānglián〈名〉lotus seeds produced in Hunan
【湘绣】xiāngxiù〈名〉Hunan embroidery
【湘竹】xiāngzhú = 湘妃竹 xiāngfēizhú

缃(緗) xiāng〈形〉〈书〉light yellow: ~黄 pale yellow

箱 xiāng〈名〉1▸(箱子) chest: 弹药/工具~ ammunition/tool chest ‖ 木/柳条~ wooden/wicker case ‖ 樟木~ camphor wood box 2▸(箱状物) box-shaped thing: ▸风~, 信~
【箱底】xiāngdǐ〈名〉1▸(箱子底层) bottom of a chest 2▸(指财物) store of valuables: 他~厚。He is a man of considerable means.
【箱笼】xiānglóng〈名〉luggage
【箱式】xiāngshì〈形〉box-type: ~货车 box van
【箱子】xiāngzi〈名〉chest: 打开~ open a trunk ‖ 这~怕压。The chest won't stand much weight.

襄 xiāng〈动〉〈书〉assist: ~办 assist
【襄礼】xiānglǐ A〈动〉assist in a ceremony B〈名〉assistant master of ceremonies
【襄理】xiānglǐ〈书〉A〈动〉assist B〈名〉assistant manager
【襄助】xiāngzhù〈动〉〈书〉assist indirectly

骧(驤) xiāng〈动〉〈书〉1▸(奔跑) [of a horse] gallop with head held high 2▸(高举) raise: 高~ raise high

镶(鑲) xiāng〈动〉1▸(嵌入) inlay: ~假牙 have a false tooth put in one's mouth ‖ 给戒指~钻石 mount a diamond in a ring 2▸(外围加边) rim: 给裙子~花边 edge a skirt with lace
【镶边】xiāngbiān〈动〉border: 用缎子给旗袍~ edge a cheongsam with satin
【镶嵌】xiāngqiàn〈动〉inlay: ~银丝漆器 silver-inlaid lacquerware ‖ ~钻石的王冠 crown mounted with diamond
【镶牙】xiāngyá〈动〉put in a false tooth: 镶金牙 insert a gold tooth

xiáng

详(詳) xiáng
A〈形〉1▸(详细) detailed: ~禀 report in detail ‖ 不厌其~ go into minute detail ▸~尽, ~情, ~谈 2▸(清楚) clear: 他生卒年份不~。His date of birth and date of death are unknown.
B〈动〉〈书〉elaborate: 另~ will be explained elsewhere ‖ 内~ with the sender's name and address enclosed
【详备】xiángbèi〈形〉detailed and complete: 注释~ with extensive annotations
【详查】xiángchá〈动〉1▸(调查) investigate fully 2▸(检查) scrutinize: ~账目 check the accounts carefully
【详察】xiángchá〈动〉scrutinize
【详尽】xiángjìn〈形〉exhaustive: ~的记录/资料 exhaustive records/information
【详略】xiáng-lüè〈名〉treatment of or attention to detail: 注释正确, ~得当。The annotations are correct and sufficiently detailed.
【详密】xiángmì〈形〉meticulous: ~的分析 elaborate analysis ‖ ~的计划 meticulous plan
【详明】xiángmíng〈形〉detailed and lucid: 记述~ write down fully and clearly
【详情】xiángqíng〈名〉details: 告知~ tell sb. in detail ‖ ~面谈。I will give you the details when we meet in person.
【详实】xiángshí = 翔实 xiángshí
【详述】xiángshù〈动〉give an elaborate account
【详谈】xiángtán〈动〉expand on: 她希望与丈夫~。She wished she could talk things out with her husband.
【详图】xiángtú〈名〉detailed drawing: 发动机~ engine detail
【详悉】xiángxī〈书〉A〈动〉know the details: 信已收到, 内容~。I've got your letter and am aware of the details. B〈形〉detailed and exhaustive: 内容~, 笔调生动。It is detailed and thorough in content and vivid in style.
【详细】xiángxì〈形〉detailed: 打听~情况 request detailed information ‖ ~的描述/研究 detailed description/research

降 xiáng〈动〉1▸(投降) surrender: 宁死不~ would rather die than surrender ▸受~, 投~, 诈~, 招~ 2▸(使投降) subdue: 你这样的人~不住他。He shouldn't be suppressed by someone like you. ‖ 一物~一物。One thing always conquers the other. ▸~伏, ~龙伏虎 ▸jiàng
【降表】xiángbiǎo〈名〉〈旧〉letter of surrender
【降伏】xiángfú〈动〉tame: ~烈马 break in a wild horse
【降服】xiángfú〈动〉surrender: 率部~ surrender with one's army
【降龙伏虎】xiánglóng-fúhǔ〈成〉〈喻〉overcome formidable enemies
【降妖伏魔】xiángyāo-fúmó〈成〉vanquish demons and monsters

庠 xiáng〈名〉〈古〉country school
【庠生】xiángshēng〈名〉〈古〉student
【庠序】xiángxù〈名〉〈古〉school

祥 xiáng〈形〉auspicious: ▸吉~
【祥和】xiánghé〈形〉1▸(吉祥平和) peaceful and auspicious: 欢乐~的节日 blissful and auspicious festival 2▸(慈祥) amiable: 神情~ wear a kindly expression
【祥瑞】xiángruì〈名〉auspicious sign: ~之兆 good omen
【祥云】xiángyún〈名〉auspicious cloud
【祥兆】xiángzhào〈名〉auspicious omen: 丰收的~ omens for a good harvest

翔 xiáng
A〈动〉1▸(飞) fly: ▸翱~, 飞~, 滑~ 2▸〈书〉(游) swim: 鱼~浅底。The fish are swimming in shallow water.
B〈形〉detailed: ▸~实
【翔实】xiángshí〈形〉full and accurate: ~可信的叙述 elaborate and reliable account ‖ 材料~ full and accurate data

xiǎng

享 xiǎng〈动〉1▸〈书〉= 飨 xiǎng 2▸(享受) enjoy: ~清福 enjoy happy leisure time ‖ 共~胜利喜悦 share the joy of victory ▸坐~其成
【享福】xiǎngfú〈动〉enjoy a happy life: 老人现在可~了。These days the old one lives in ease and comfort.

X

【享乐】xiǎnglè〈动〉 lead a life of pleasure: 贪图～ seek a life of pleasure ‖ ～思想 preoccupation with pleasure-seeking
【享年】xiǎngnián〈动〉〈敬〉 live to the age of: ～八十 pass away at the age of eighty
【享受】xiǎngshòu〈动〉 enjoy: ～局级待遇 enjoy the rights and privileges of a bureau head ‖ ～权利 enjoy one's rights ‖ 贪图～ covet pleasure
【享用】xiǎngyòng〈动〉 enjoy the benefit of: ～自己的劳动果实 enjoy the fruits of one's own labour
【享有】xiǎngyǒu〈动〉 enjoy: ～国际声望 enjoy an international reputation ‖ ～平等权利/外交豁免权 enjoy equal rights/diplomatic immunity
【享誉】xiǎngyù〈动〉 enjoy fame: ～海内外 enjoy great prestige both at home and abroad

响（響）xiǎng

A〈名〉 **1**（回声） echo: ▸反～，回～，影～ **2**（声响） sound: 随着一声巨～ with a tremendous noise ‖ 一声炮～ the report of a cannon ▸声～，音～
B〈动〉 **1**（使发声） sound: ～锣 beat drums ‖ ～枪 sound a shot **2**（发声） make a sound: 全场～起了暴风雨般的掌声。 A storm of applause broke out in the hall. ‖ 他一声不～地离开了。 He left without saying a word. ‖ 门铃～了。 The door-bell rang.
C〈形〉 noisy: 电视太～。 The TV is too loud. ‖ 收音机放～点。 Turn the radio up loud.
【响板】xiǎngbǎn ▸p. 929〈名〉［音乐］ castanets
【响鼻】xiǎngbí〈动〉 [of a horse, etc.] snort
【响彻云霄】xiǎngchè-yúnxiāo〈成〉 resound across the heavens
【响当当】xiǎngdāngdāng〈形〉 **1**（声音响亮） loud **2**〈喻〉（出色有名） excellent: ～的律师 honest attorney ‖ ～的人物 outstanding personage
【响动】xiǎngdong〈名〉 noise: 屋里没有一点～。 There was no sound at all in the room.
【响度】xiǎngdù〈名〉［物理］ volume
【响遏行云】xiǎng'è xíngyún〈成〉 echo to the skies
【响箭】xiǎngjiàn〈名〉 whistling arrow
【响雷】xiǎngléi〈名〉 thunderclap: 震耳欲聋的～ deafening thunderclap
【响亮】xiǎngliàng〈形〉 loud and clear: ～的欢呼声/笑声 resounding cheers/laughs ‖ ～的回答 loud and clear reply ‖ 一记～的耳光 a thunderous slap in the face
【响铃】xiǎnglíng〈名〉 jingle bell
【响马】xiǎngmǎ〈名〉〈旧〉 mounted highwayman
【响器】xiǎngqì ▸p. 929〈名〉［音乐］ Chinese percussion instruments
【响晴】xiǎngqíng〈名〉〈方〉 clear and bright: ～的天空 cloudless sky
【响声】xiǎngshēng〈名〉 noise: 弄出～ make a sound ‖ 沙沙的～ rustle ‖ 震耳欲聋的～ deafening noise
【响头】xiǎngtóu〈名〉 kowtow with one's forehead knocking against the ground
【响尾蛇】xiǎngwěishé〈名〉 rattlesnake
【响吻】xiǎngwěn〈名〉 smack
【响应】xiǎngyìng〈动〉 answer: ～号召 respond to a call ‖ 她的提议得到积极～。 Her proposal was met with enthusiasm.
【响指】xiǎngzhǐ〈名〉 snapping of one's fingers: 打～ snap one's fingers

饷（餉）xiǎng

A〈名〉〈旧〉 pay: 发～ distribute pay ‖ 领～ receive pay ‖ 月～ monthly pay
B〈动〉〈书〉 entertain with food and drink: ～客 give dinner to guests
【饷银】xiǎngyín〈名〉〈旧〉 soldier's pay

飨（饗）xiǎng〈动〉〈书〉

1（宴请） treat to dinner: ～客 treat a guest to dinner **2**（请人享受） entertain: 以～读者 provide enjoyment for the reader

想 xiǎng〈动〉

1（思索） think: ～办法 think of a way ‖ ～问题 think over a problem ‖ ～主意 work out a solution ‖ ～来～去 turn sth. over in one's mind ‖ 仔细～～ think hard/carefully (about sth.) ‖ 你～得真周到。 You really think of everything. ‖ 让我～～。 Let me have a think about it. ▸冥思苦～ **2**（推测） suppose: 我～她只能当配角。 I reckon she will only have a supporting role. ‖ 没～到会在这里见到你。 I didn't expect to see you here. ▸～当然，猜～ **3**（希望） want: ～结婚 would like to get married ‖ ～试试 want to have a try ‖ 我很～去。 I have a good mind to go. **4**（想念） miss: ～父母 miss one's parents ‖ 我非常～家。 I am pining for home. ▸～念，朝思暮～ **5**（回想） remember: ～～看，是不是真的～不起当时的情况? Cast your mind back. Are you sure you can't recall what happened? ‖ 我～不起她的名字。 I can't remember what her name is.
【想必】xiǎngbì〈副〉 presumably: ～如此。 I presume so. ‖ ～你已听到这个消息了吧? Presumably you've heard the news?
【想不到】xiǎngbudào〈动〉 never expect: ～在这儿碰到你! Fancy meeting you here! ‖ ～你变化这么大! It's hard to believe that you have changed so much.
【想不开】xiǎngbukāi〈动〉 take things too hard: 别为小事～。 Don't take such trivial things to heart. ‖ 他遇事～，爱走极端。 He is unable to be philosophical and tends to take things to extremes.
【想不通】xiǎngbutōng〈动〉 can't get one's mind around: 我～她为什么不干了。 I never really worked out why she left her job.
【想当然】xiǎngdāngrán〈动〉 take sth. for granted: 每个细节都要认真检查核对，不要～。 Every detail should be carefully checked and verified; nothing should be taken for granted.
【想得到】xiǎngdedào〈动〉 [often used in rhetorical questions] imagine: 你怎能～他竟然是个骗子? Would you have imagined him to be a swindler?
【想得开】xiǎngdekāi〈动〉 be philosophical about sth.: 凡事还是～的好。 It's better not to take misfortunes to heart. ‖ 她似乎对这场灾难很～。 she seemed fairly philosophical about the calamity.
【想法】xiǎngfǎ **A**〈动〉 think of a way: ～弄点吃的 try to get something to eat ‖ ～取得联系 think of a way to establish contact **B**〈名〉 idea: 说出自己的～ air one's views ‖ 你有什么～? What do you think? ‖ 我的～和你一样。 I share your point of view.
【想方设法】xiǎngfāng-shèfǎ〈成〉 try every means: ～按时完成任务 do everything possible to fulfil a task as scheduled ‖ 我要～找到她的下落。 I'll do whatever I can to find out her exact whereabouts.
【想家】xiǎngjiā〈动〉 be homesick
【想见】xiǎngjiàn〈动〉 infer: 从她的表情，可以～她生我气了。 From the look on her face, I gathered that she was annoyed with me.
【想开】xiǎngkāi〈动〉 be philosophical about: 这事要～点。 Don't take it to heart.
【想来】xiǎnglái〈动〉 suppose: ～她不会来了。 I guess she is not coming. ‖ ～他会同意的。 Presumably he will agree.
【想来想去】xiǎngláixiǎngqù〈动〉 think it over and over again
【想念】xiǎngniàn〈动〉 miss: ～故乡/祖国/亲人 miss one's hometown/motherland/family ‖ ～去世的父亲 cherish the memory of one's late father
【想起】xiǎngqǐ〈动〉 remember: 这张照片使我～了老朋友。 This picture reminds me of my old friends. ‖ 我想不起收到过这封电子邮件。 I have no recollection of ever having received the e-mail.
【想入非非】xiǎngrù fēifēi〈成〉 indulge in wild daydreaming: 她爱～，希望能一举成名。 She lets her fancies run away with her a little, imagining that she can make it big just like that.
【想通】xiǎngtōng〈动〉 straighten out one's thinking: ～一个问题 think a problem through ‖ 你～了吗? ——我～了。 Are you convinced? — Yes, I've come around to the idea now.
【想头】xiǎngtou〈名〉〈口〉 **1**（想法） notion: 我有这样一个～。 This is the idea that I have. **2**（期望） hope: 想赢这场球根本就没～ not have a hope in hell of winning the game
【想望】xiǎngwàng〈动〉 long for: ～当一名宇航员 long to be an astronaut
【想象】xiǎngxiàng **A**〈名〉 imagination: 没留下任何～空间 leave no room for the imagination ‖ 丰富/奇妙的～ fertile/wonderful imagination **B**〈动〉 imagine: ～一个场景 picture a scene ‖ ～不到的困难 unimaginable difficulties ‖ 事情并不像我原先～的那样。 Things didn't turn out as I had expected them to.
【想象力】xiǎngxiànglì〈名〉 imagination: 发挥～ give free rein to one's imagination ‖ 富有～ be full of imagination ‖ ～丰富的设计家 imaginative designer
【想像】xiǎngxiàng = 想象 xiǎngxiàng
【想心事】xiǎngxīnshì〈动〉 ponder over sth.

鲞（鯗）xiǎng〈名〉

dried salted fish: 鳗～ dried eel

xiàng

向[1] xiàng

A〈动〉 **1**（面对） face: ～东 face east ▸～上，～阳 **2**（偏袒） side with: 我～理不～人。 I err on the side of reason, not letting personalities get in the way. ‖ 妈妈～着妹妹。 My mother favours my sister.
B〈名〉 **1**（方向） direction: ▸风～，去～ **2**（指趋向） inclination: ▸意～，志～
C〈介〉 [indicating direction or object of action] towards: ～东流 flow eastwards ‖ ～警方自首 surrender oneself to the police ‖ ～空中鸣枪 fire into the air ‖ ～上级汇报 report to one's superior

向[2]（嚮）xiàng〈书〉

A〈名〉 past: ～日 in the past

X

B〈动〉 approach: ▸～晚
C〈副〉 all along: ～无此例。 There is no precedent for this. ‖ 他对哲学～有研究。 He has always been devoted to the study of philosophy. ▸～来

【向背】xiàngbèi〈名〉 support and opposition: 人心～ support or disapproval of the people

【向壁虚构】xiàngbì-xūgòu〈成〉 fabricate out of thin air: ～故事 make up a story

【向壁虚造】xiàngbì-xūzào = 向壁虚构 xiàngbì-xūgòu

【向导】xiàngdǎo **A**〈动〉 guide **B**〈名〉 guide: 当～ act as a guide

【向光性】xiàngguāngxìng〈名〉［生物］ phototropism

【向后】xiànghòu〈副〉 backwards: ～撤 withdraw ‖ ～看 look back ‖ ～转! About turn!

【向来】xiànglái〈副〉 all along: ～不过问 never concern oneself with it ‖ 他做事～认真。 He is always conscientious about things.

【向例】xiànglì〈名〉〈书〉 convention: 打破～ break with usual practice

【向量】xiàngliàng〈名〉［数学］ vector: ～分析 vector analysis

【向慕】xiàngmù〈动〉 admire: 一片～之情 be full of admiration

【向内】xiàngnèi〈副〉 inward: ～跑 run inward

【向前】xiàngqián ▸**p. 781**〈副〉 forward: ～冲 rush ahead ‖ ～跑 run forward ‖ ～推 push forward ‖ ～推进 propel forward ‖ ～看的态度 forward-looking attitude ‖ ～看! Eyes front!

【向日】xiàngrì〈名〉〈书〉 former times: ～荣耀 former glory

【向日葵】xiàngrìkuí〈名〉 sunflower

【向善】xiàngshàn〈动〉 be charitable

【向上】xiàngshàng〈动〉 make one's way up: 努力～的热情 zeal for improvement

【向上爬】xiàngshàngpá〈惯〉 seek personal advancement: 挖空心思～ try whatever means possible to get ahead

【向晚】xiàngwǎn〈名〉 early evening: ～时分 at dusk

【向往】xiàngwǎng〈动〉 yearn for: ～幸福生活 look forward to a happy life ‖ ～自由 yearn for freedom ‖ 令人～ take sb.'s fancy

【向下】xiàngxià〈副〉 downwards: ～滑/看 slide/look downwards ‖ ～的压力 downward pressure

【向心力】xiàngxīnlì〈名〉 centripetal force: 〈喻〉 激发员工的～ enhance team feeling among employees

【向学】xiàngxué〈动〉〈书〉 pursue one's studies: 无心～ have no inclination to study ‖ 一心～ devote oneself to learning

【向阳】xiàngyáng〈动〉 face the sun: ～的房间 sunny room ‖ 葵花～。 Sunflowers always face the sun.

【向阳花】xiàngyánghuā〈名〉 sunflower

【向右】xiàngyòu ▸**p. 781**〈副〉 towards the right: ～转! Right turn!

【向隅】xiàngyú〈动〉〈书〉 feel left out: ～而泣 weep all alone in a corner

【向着】xiàngzhe〈动〉 **1**（朝着） face: 部队～南方急速挺进。 The troops pushed ahead towards the south. **2**〈口〉（偏袒） side with: 这个裁判～主队。 The referee was biased towards the home team.

【向左】xiàngzuǒ ▸**p. 781**〈副〉 towards the left: ～转! Left turn!

项[1]（項） xiàng

〈名〉 nape of the neck: ▸～背, ～链

项[2]（項） xiàng

A〈量〉 item: 两～开支 two expenses ‖ 四～原则 four principles ‖ 第八条第三款第二～ article eight, clause three, item two ‖ 一～工作/任务 a job/task ▸～目, 事～
B〈名〉 **1**（款项） sum of money: 用～ expenditures ▸进～, 欠～ **2**［数学］ term: 合并同类～ combine similar terms

【项背】xiàngbèi〈名〉〈书〉 back: 难以望其～ cannot compare with sb. in scholarly achievement

【项背相望】xiàngbèi-xiāngwàng〈成〉 walk one after another in close succession: 前来参观者～，络绎不绝。 There came an endless stream of visitors.

【项链】xiàngliàn〈名〉 necklace: 珍珠/钻石～ pearl/diamond necklace

【项目】xiàngmù〈名〉 **1**（指特定工作） project: ～经理 project manager ‖ ～管理 project management ‖ ～小组 project group ‖ 基建～ capital construction project ‖ 支出～ item of expenditure **2**［体育］ event: 男子～ men's event

【项圈】xiàngquān〈名〉 necklet

【项庄舞剑，意在沛公】Xiàng Zhuāng wǔ jiàn, yì zài Pèigōng〈成〉〈喻〉 act with a covert wicked motive

巷 xiàng

〈名〉 lane: 一条小～ a narrow alley ‖ ～尾 end of a lane
▸hàng

【巷陌】xiàngmò〈名〉〈书〉 streets and lanes

【巷战】xiàngzhàn〈名〉 street fighting: 激烈的～ fierce street fighting

【巷子】xiàngzi〈名〉〈方〉 lane: 住在一个～里 live in an alley

相 xiàng

A〈动〉 **1**（察看） appraise by scrutinizing closely: ～马 look a horse over to judge its worth ‖ 人不可貌～。 Never judge a person by his appearance. ▸～面 **2**〈书〉（辅助） assist: ～夫教子 help one's husband and bring up one's children ▸吉人天～
B〈名〉 **1**（容貌） looks: 一副狼狈～ a sorry figure ‖ 长得老～ look old for one's age ▸扮～, 福～, 长～ **2**（外观） exterior: ▸星～, 月～ **3**（姿态） carriage: 睡～不好 sleep sprawled all over the bed ‖ 站有站～，坐有坐～ have a graceful carriage **4**［物理］ phase: 三～电动机 three-phase motor **5**［地理］ facies: 海～ marine facies ‖ 煤～ coal facies **6**（宰相） prime minister: ▸丞～, 宰～ **7**（中央级官员） minister: ▸首～, 外～ **8**〈旧〉（帮助主人接待宾客的人） attendant: ▸傧～ **9**（指棋子） minister **10**（图像） image: 照～ take a picture
▸xiāng

【相册】xiàngcè〈名〉 photograph album: 把照片插进～ put a photo into an album

【相公】xiànggong〈名〉〈旧〉 **1**〈敬〉（丈夫） [form of address] husband **2**（年轻的读书人） [term common in traditional operas and old novels] young gentleman

【相国】xiàngguó〈名〉〈古〉 prime minister

【相机】xiàngjī **A**〈名〉 camera: 傻瓜～ point-and-shoot camera **B**〈动〉 bide one's time: ～而动 wait for an opportunity to act

【相机行事】xiàngjī-xíngshì〈成〉 act as one sees fit

【相貌】xiàngmào〈名〉 appearance: ～端正 have regular features ‖ ～堂堂 be noble in appearance

【相面】xiàngmiàn〈动〉 practise physiognomy

【相片儿】xiàngpiānr〈名〉〈口〉 photo

【相片】xiàngpiàn〈名〉 photograph: 洗～ have a film developed ‖ 彩色～ colour photograph

【相声】xiàngsheng〈名〉 crosstalk: 说～ perform a comic dialogue ‖ 单口～ comic monologue

> **相声**
>
> A traditional comic performance involving one, two or more performers who engage in rapid, bantering talk, imitation, song and satire. Usually there are two performers, one who makes the jokes, and the other who acts as a foil in order to heighten the comic effect. Xiangsheng originated in the Qing Dynasty, and is mainly performed in the Beijing dialect. It continues to enjoy great popularity today because of its entertainment value and its ability to reflect popular concerns.

【相时而动】xiàngshí'érdòng〈成〉 wait for the right time to take action

【相手术】xiàngshǒushù〈名〉 palmistry

【相术】xiàngshù〈名〉 physiognomy: ～精湛 be well versed in physiognomy

【相态】xiàngtài〈名〉［物理］ phase: 水蒸汽、水和冰是同一物质的三种～。 Steam, water and ice constitute the three phases of one and the same matter.

【相位】xiàngwèi〈名〉［物理］ phase: ～测量 phase difference measurement ‖ ～差 phase difference

【相纸】xiàngzhǐ〈名〉 photographic paper: 彩色/黑白～ colour/black-and-white printing paper

象 xiàng

A〈名〉 **1**（大象） elephant: 公～ bull ‖ 母～ cow ‖ 幼～ calf **2**（形态） appearance: ▸景～, 万～更新, 现～ **3**（指棋子） premier
B〈动〉 imitate: ▸～形

【象鼻】xiàngbí〈名〉 trunk

【象鼻虫】xiàngbíchóng〈名〉 snout beetle

【象海豹】xiànghǎibào〈名〉 sea elephant

【象棋】xiàngqí ▸**p. 909**〈名〉 Chinese chess: 下～ play chess ‖ 国际～ chess

> **象棋**
>
> A form of chess for two players, originating in China. The chess board has 9 vertical lines intersecting with 10 horizontal lines. The middle of the board, where there are no lines, is called the 'border river'. The squares where there are diagonally crossed lines are known as *jiugong* (九宫). There are 16 red and 16 black pieces. These pieces include the general (将 or 帅), two advisors (士 or 仕), two elephants (象 or 相), two chariots (车), two horses (马), two cannons (炮) and five soldiers (卒 or 兵). Red makes the first move, after which the players take turns to move their pieces. If one player attacks the other player's general, then in the next move the player can wipe the opponent off the board. This is known as 将军 or 将 ('check'). If the other player cannot defend the general, the game is over. If neither side can annihilate each other's generals, then the game results in a draw.

【象声词】xiàngshēngcí〈名〉 onomatopoetic word

【象限】xiàngxiàn〈名〉［数学］quadrant

【象形】xiàngxíng〈名〉［语言］pictograph [one of the six categories of Chinese characters]: ～字 pictographic character

【象形文字】xiàngxíng wénzì〈名〉pictograph

【象牙】xiàngyá〈名〉ivory: ～雕刻 ivory carving

> **象牙雕刻**
>
> The art of ivory-carving dates back 7,000 thousand years. The main areas of production are Beijing, Guangzhou and Suzhou. Carvings include figures, animals, flowers and plants, landscapes, seals, and brooches. The ivory used comes mainly from the tusks of African elephants. Today, ivory stocks are disappearing fast because of the international ban on ivory trading, and the craft of ivory-carving is facing extinction.

【象牙塔】xiàngyátǎ〈名〉ivory tower: 生活在～中 live in an ivory tower

【象牙之塔】xiàngyázhītǎ = 象牙塔 xiàngyátǎ

【象征】xiàngzhēng **A**〈动〉symbolize: 白色～纯洁。White stands for purity. **B**〈名〉symbol: 和平～ emblem of peace ‖ 剑是强权的～。A sword is the symbol of power gained by violence.

【象征性】xiàngzhēngxìng〈形〉symbolic: ～的收费 nominal fee

【象征主义】xiàngzhēngzhǔyì〈名〉symbolism

像 xiàng

A〈动〉**1**（类似）be like: ～落汤鸡 like a drowned rat ‖ 她长得～她母亲。She looks like her mother. **2**（比如）be like: ～大熊猫这样的珍稀动物要加以保护。Rare animals such as the giant panda should be given special protection. ‖ ～这种情况很少见。Such cases are rare.
B〈名〉**1**（指人物形象）picture: 父亲的一张～ a portrait of one's father ▸佛～, 画～, 铜～ **2**（指图景）image: ▸实～, 虚～
C〈副〉seemingly: ～是要下雨。It looks like rain. ‖ 她～是没明白。It seems that she could make no sense of it.

【像话】xiànghuà〈动〉[often used in the negative or interrogative sentences] be reasonable: 这么正式的场合，穿短裤去不～。It is improper to wear shorts to such a formal occasion. ‖ 你天天迟到，～吗? Aren't you ashamed to come late everyday?

【像回事儿】xiànghuíshìr〈惯〉just like the real thing: 她演得还真像（那么）回事儿。She performed like a professional actress.

【像模像样】xiàngmó-xiàngyàng〈成〉presentable: 收入虽不高，但俩人的日子还过得～。Although they don't earn much, they live quite well.

【像煞有介事】xiàng shà yǒu jiè shì〈成〉make a great show of being earnest

【像生】xiàngshēng〈名〉**1**（指物）lifelike imitation **2**（指人）female ballad singer [in the Song and Yuan dynasties]

【像素】xiàngsù〈名〉pixel

【像样】xiàngyàng〈形〉presentable: ～的饭菜/家具 decent meal/furniture ‖ ～的理由 sound reason

【像章】xiàngzhāng〈名〉badge with sb.'s likeness on it

橡 xiàng

〈名〉**1**（橡树）oak **2**（橡胶树）rubber tree

【橡胶】xiàngjiāo〈名〉rubber: 割～ tap rubber ‖ ～轮胎/制品 rubber tyre/goods ‖ 合成～ synthetic rubber

【橡胶垫】xiàngjiāodiàn〈名〉rubber cushion

【橡胶树】xiàngjiāoshù〈名〉rubber tree

【橡木】xiàngmù〈名〉oak: ～地板 oak floor

【橡皮】xiàngpí〈名〉**1**（指材质）vulcanized rubber: ～手套 rubber gloves **2**（指文具）eraser; rubber〈英〉

【橡皮膏】xiàngpígāo〈名〉adhesive plaster

【橡皮筋】xiàngpíjīn〈名〉elastic band〈英〉; rubber band〈美〉

【橡皮泥】xiàngpíní〈名〉plasticine

【橡皮圈】xiàngpíquān〈名〉**1**（救生圈）rubber ring **2**（橡皮筋）rubber band

【橡皮艇】xiàngpítǐng〈名〉rubber dinghy

【橡皮图章】xiàngpí túzhāng〈名〉rubber stamp: 一枚～ a rubber stamp ‖ 总裁拿主意，董事会只是盖个～而已。The chairman makes the decisions and the board just rubber-stamps them.

【橡实】xiàngshí = 橡子 xiàngzǐ

【橡子】xiàngzǐ〈名〉acorn

xiāo

枭（梟）xiāo

A〈动〉〈书〉hang up a decapitated head as a deterrent
B〈形〉〈书〉intrepid: ▸～将, ～雄
C〈名〉**1** = 鸺鹠 xiūliú **2**（首领）gang runner: 毒～ drug baron **3**〈书〉〈旧〉（指私贩食盐）smuggler: 盐～ salt smuggler

【枭将】xiāojiàng〈名〉〈书〉valiant general

【枭首】xiāoshǒu〈动〉〈旧〉display the head of a decapitated person: ～示众 expose a decapitated head to public view as a deterrent

【枭雄】xiāoxióng〈名〉intrepid and ambitious person

枵 xiāo〈形〉〈书〉hollow

【枵肠辘辘】xiāocháng-lùlù〈成〉have an empty rumbling stomach

【枵腹从公】xiāofù-cónggōng〈成〉attend to one's official duties on an empty stomach

削 xiāo

〈动〉**1**（指用刀）peel with a knife: ～苹果 peel an apple ‖ ～铅笔 sharpen a pencil **2**［体育］chop: ▸～球
▸xuē

【削笔刀】xiāobǐdāo〈名〉penknife

【削尖脑袋往里钻】xiāojiān nǎodai wǎnglǐ-zuān〈俗〉〈贬〉worm one's way in

【削皮】xiāopí〈动〉peel

【削皮器】xiāopíqì〈名〉peeler: 苹果/土豆～ apple/potato peeler

【削片】xiāopiàn〈动〉chip

【削球】xiāoqiú〈动〉［体育］chop: 擅长～ be good at cutting

哓（嘵）xiāo

【哓哓】xiāoxiāo〈形〉〈书〉**1**（指吵闹）noisy: ～不休 argue repeatedly and annoyingly **2**（指鸟鸣）frightened

骁（驍）xiāo〈形〉〈书〉valiant: ▸～将, ～勇

【骁悍】xiāohàn〈形〉valiant and strong

【骁将】xiāojiàng〈名〉〈书〉valiant general: 一员～ a valiant general

【骁骑】xiāoqí〈名〉〈书〉valiant cavalry

【骁勇】xiāoyǒng〈形〉intrepid: ～善战 be brave and experienced in battle

逍 xiāo

【逍遥】xiāoyáo〈形〉carefree

【逍遥法外】xiāoyáo-fǎwài〈成〉remain at liberty: 绝对不能让犯罪分子～。We must never allow a criminal to go unpunished.

【逍遥自在】xiāoyáo-zìzài〈成〉take life easy

鸮（鴞）xiāo ▸鸱鸮 chīxiāo

消 xiāo

〈动〉**1**（消失）disappear: 肿已～了。The swelling has gone down. ‖ 听了这席话，她的气～了。Her anger died down at these words. ▸～失, 烟～云散 **2**（消除）eliminate: 借酒～愁 drink away one's sorrows ▸～毒, 打～ **3**（度过）while away time: ▸～遣, ～闲 **4**（花费）spend money: ▸～费 **5**（需要）need: 不～说 needless to say ‖ 来回只～三天。It takes only three days to get there and back.

【消沉】xiāochén〈形〉downhearted: 意志～ be despondent

【消愁】xiāochóu〈动〉dispel worries: 借酒～愁更愁 try to drown one's sorrow in alcohol only to sink into greater sorrow

【消除】xiāochú〈动〉eliminate: ～腐败 stamp out corruption ‖ ～隔阂 clear away a misunderstanding ‖ ～疑虑 remove sb.'s doubts ‖ ～贫困 eliminate poverty ‖ ～歧视 eradicate discrimination ‖ ～隐患 remove a hidden danger ‖ 我们的分歧～了。Our differences melted away.

【消磁】xiāocí〈动〉demagnetize

【消毒】xiāodú〈动〉**1**（针对病原体）disinfect: 高温～ sterilize sth. at high temperature ‖ 给伤口～ disinfect a wound **2**（针对坏影响）decontaminate

【消毒剂】xiāodújì〈名〉disinfectant

【消毒棉】xiāodúmián〈名〉sterilized cotton

【消毒药】xiāodúyào〈名〉disinfectant

【消防】xiāofáng〈名〉fire fighting: ～设备 fire-fighting equipment ‖ ～队员 fire-fighter

【消防车】xiāofángchē〈名〉fire engine

【消防队】xiāofángduì〈名〉fire brigade〈英〉; fire department〈美〉

【消防龙头】xiāofáng lóngtóu〈名〉fire hydrant

【消防栓】xiāofángshuān〈名〉fire hydrant

【消防员】xiāofángyuán ▸**p. 966**〈名〉fire fighter

【消费】xiāofèi〈动〉consume: ～总量 total consumption ‖ 过度～ excessive consumption ‖ 人均食品～ per capita food consumption

【消费贷款】xiāofèi dàikuǎn〈名〉consumer loan

【消费合作社】xiāofèi hézuòshè〈名〉〈旧〉consumers' cooperative

【消费基金】xiāofèi jījīn〈名〉consumption fund

【消费开支】xiāofèi kāizhī〈名〉consumer spending

【消费品】xiāofèipǐn〈名〉consumer goods: 耐用～ consumer durables ‖ 日常～ daily commodities

【消费券】xiāofèiquàn〈名〉voucher: 发放旅游～以拉动内需 issue travel vouchers to boost domestic demand

【消费社会】xiāofèi shèhuì〈名〉consumer society
【消费水平】xiāofèi shuǐpíng〈名〉level of consumption
【消费税】xiāofèishuì〈名〉consumption tax
【消费物价指数】xiāofèi wùjià zhǐshù〈名〉consumer price index (CPI)
【消费信贷】xiāofèi xìndài〈名〉consumer credit
【消费者】xiāofèizhě〈名〉consumer: ～权益 rights and interests of consumers
【消费者协会】xiāofèizhě xiéhuì〈名〉consumers' association
【消费支出】xiāofèi zhīchū〈名〉consumer spending
【消费资料】xiāofèi zīliào〈名〉consumer goods
【消耗】xiāohào〈动〉1（减少）consume: ～弹药 expend ammunition ‖ ～精力 consume energy 2（使减少）drain: ～敌人的有生力量 drain the enemy troops of their strength ‖ 使能源～保持在最低水平 keep the expenditure of energy as low as possible
【消化】xiāohuà〈动〉1（针对食物）digest: 易～食品 digestible food ‖ ～不良 indigestion 2〈喻〉（针对知识内容）digest: ～学过的内容 digest the lessons of the past ‖ 这篇课文很难～。This text is difficult to digest. 3〈喻〉（针对成本费用）cope with: 商品运输增加的费用由企业～。Any increase in the cost of transporting goods shall be covered by the enterprise.
【消化道】xiāohuàdào〈名〉digestive tract
【消化器官】xiāohuà qìguān〈名〉digestive organ
【消化系统】xiāohuà xìtǒng〈名〉digestive system
【消魂】xiāohún = 销魂 xiāohún
【消火栓】xiāohuǒshuān〈名〉(fire) hydrant
【消极】xiāojí〈形〉1（反面）negative: 抱～态度 have a negative attitude ‖ ～因素 negative factor ‖ ～影响 negative influence 2（消沉）passive: 情绪～ be dispirited ‖ 态度～ take a passive attitude ‖ ～等待结果 wait passively
【消减】xiāojiǎn〈动〉diminish: ～10%的劳动力 trim the workforce by 10% ‖ 食欲～ diminished appetite ‖ 她的热情～了。Her enthusiasm waned.
【消解】xiāojiě〈动〉clear up: ～怒气 mollify sb.'s anger ‖ ～误会 clear up misunderstandings
【消渴】xiāokě〈名〉［中医］disease with the symptoms of frequent drinking and urination
【消弭】xiāomǐ〈动〉〈书〉put an end to: ～水患 prevent floods ‖ ～战患 prevent a war
【消灭】xiāomiè〈动〉1（绝迹）perish: 自行～ die out of itself ‖ 麻风病以及小儿麻痹症等病症几乎全部～了。Diseases such as leprosy and polio have almost completely died out. 2（铲除）eliminate: ～病虫害/侵略者 wipe out pests/invaders ‖ ～种族歧视 put an end to racial discrimination
【消磨】xiāomó〈动〉1（使逐渐消失）wear down: ～精力 fritter away sb.'s energy ‖ ～志气 sap sb.'s will 2（打发时间）kill time: 用打牌～时间 pass the time playing cards
【消纳】xiāonà〈动〉store for disposal: 垃圾～场 refuse disposal plant
【消气】xiāoqì〈动〉calm down: 他给她送了些花，想让她消消气。He tried to mollify her a little by sending her some flowers. ‖ 她不～就没法讨论。Discussion is impossible before she can calm down.
【消遣】xiāoqiǎn〈动〉kill time: 玩纸牌～ kill time by playing cards ‖ 下棋是我惟一的～。Playing chess is my only distraction.
【消溶】xiāoróng = 消融 xiāoróng
【消融】xiāoróng〈动〉melt: 春光明媚，冰雪～。The spring sun melted the ice and snow.
【消散】xiāosàn〈动〉dissipate: 晨雾～了。The morning mist lifted.
【消声器】xiāoshēngqì〈名〉muffler
【消失】xiāoshī〈动〉disappear: ～得无影无踪 vanish without trace ‖ 在视线中～ disappear from view ‖ 她脸上的笑容～了。The smile vanished from her face.
【消食】xiāoshí〈动〉help digestion: 开胃～ whet one's appetite and help digestion
【消逝】xiāoshì〈动〉die away: 随着时间的～ with the passing of time ‖ 最后一抹晚霞逐渐～在暮色之中。The last red streak of sunset faded away into the darkening sky.
【消释】xiāoshì〈动〉1〈书〉（溶化）melt 2（消除）remove: ～前嫌 dispel past grudges ‖ ～误会 iron out misunderstandings ‖ ～疑虑 dispel misgivings
【消受】xiāoshòu〈动〉1（享受）[often used in the negative] enjoy: 无福～ unable to enjoy 2（承受）bear: 我无法～他。I can't stand him.
【消瘦】xiāoshòu〈动〉lose weight: 她因久病而～了。Her long illness emaciated her.
【消暑】xiāoshǔ〈动〉1（解暑）alleviate the summer heat: ～止渴 relieve the summer heat and quench the thirst 2（消夏）take a summer vacation: 你准备去哪里～? Where are you going to spend the summer holiday?
【消损】xiāosǔn〈动〉1（逐渐减少）dwindle: 她的热情～了。Her enthusiasm has dwindled. 2（损耗）wear out: ～岁月 fritter away time ‖ 检查轮胎～情况 examine a tyre for wear and tear
【消停】xiāoting〈方〉A〈形〉peaceful: 过～日子 live a peaceful life ‖ 期待一个～的暑假 look forward to a quiet summer vacation B〈动〉take a rest: 周末我们也不得～。We don't get any leisure even at weekends. ‖ 他老惹事，让父母～不下来。He was a trouble-maker and never brought his parents a moment's peace.
【消退】xiāotuì〈动〉fade away: 潮水～了。The tide receded. ‖ 暑热～。The summer heat is fading.
【消亡】xiāowáng〈动〉die out: 国家的～ dying out of the state ‖ 恐龙数百万年前就～了。Dinosaurs became extinct millions of years ago.
【消息】xiāoxi〈名〉1（报道）news: 得到/等待～ receive/await news ‖ 小道～ news through the grapevine ‖ 最新～ latest news ‖ ～传出，无不惊讶。Everyone was surprised when the news broke. 2（音信）news: 杳无～ there has been no news ‖ 她几时来还没有～。There has been no news on when she will come.
【消息灵通人士】xiāoxi língtōng rénshì〈名〉well-informed source
【消夏】xiāoxià〈动〉take a summer holiday: 在海滨～ spend the summer at the seaside ‖ ～胜地 summer resort
【消闲】xiāoxián A〈动〉while away one's leisure time: ～解闷 relieve boredom B〈形〉carefree: 去年夏天他很～，度了一个月假。He went away for a month on holiday last summer in carefree comfort.
【消歇】xiāoxiē〈动〉〈书〉subside: 风雨～。The storm subsided.
【消协】xiāoxié〈简称〉= 消费者协会
【消炎】xiāoyán〈动〉alleviate inflammation: ～止痛 diminish inflammation and kill pain ‖ ～片 anti-inflammatory pill
【消炎药】xiāoyányào〈名〉anti-inflammatory drug
【消夜】xiāoyè A〈名〉midnight snack: 每次工作到深夜，他都要吃点～。Every time he worked into the night, he would have a little snack. B〈动〉have a midnight snack
【消音器】xiāoyīnqì〈名〉silencer〈英〉; muffler〈美〉
【消灾】xiāozāi〈动〉prevent calamities: ～免祸 avert calamities ‖ 破财～ pay one's way out of trouble
【消长】xiāozhǎng〈名〉rise and fall: 力量的～ growth and decline of relative strength
【消肿】xiāozhǒng〈动〉1〈本〉alleviate a swelling 2〈喻〉（精减）streamline: 给政府机构～ streamline government organizations
【消字灵】xiāozìlíng〈名〉ink eradicator

宵 xiāo〈名〉night: ▸春～, 良～, 通～

【宵禁】xiāojìn〈名〉curfew: 实行～ impose a curfew
【宵小】xiāoxiǎo〈名〉〈书〉villain: ～行径 criminal act
【宵夜】xiāoyè = 消夜 xiāoyè
【宵衣旰食】xiāoyī-gànshí〈成〉be diligent in discharging one's official duties: ～，日理万机 work conscientiously on a myriad of state affairs

绡（綃）xiāo〈名〉〈书〉1（生丝）raw silk 2（丝织品）raw silk fabric: ～帕 raw silk handkerchief

萧（蕭）xiāo〈形〉desolate: ▸～然, ～条

【萧规曹随】Xiāoguī-Cáosuí〈成〉follow the established rules
【萧墙】xiāoqiáng〈名〉〈书〉screen wall [usu facing the gate of a house]: 祸起～。Trouble arose at home.
【萧然】xiāorán〈形〉〈书〉1（寂寞冷清）desolate: 满目～ be a desolate sight 2（空虚）empty: 四壁～ have nothing but four bare walls
【萧飒】xiāosà〈书〉= 萧索 xiāosuǒ
【萧瑟】xiāosè A〈拟〉rustle: 秋风～。The autumn wind is soughing. B〈形〉desolate: ～景象 bleak scene
【萧森】xiāosēn〈形〉〈书〉1（草木衰败）bleak: 秋树～ desolate autumn trees 2（凄凉阴森）gloomy and desolate: 气象～ gloomy scene
【萧疏】xiāoshū〈形〉〈书〉1（萧条荒凉）desolate 2（稀疏）sparse: 白发～ with scant grey hair
【萧索】xiāosuǒ〈形〉bleak: ～的寒冬景色/景象 bleak cold winter scene
【萧条】xiāotiáo A〈形〉bleak: ～的码头/原野 desolate port/open country B〈名〉［经济］depression: 经济～ economic depression ‖ 市场～ slack market
【萧萧】xiāoxiāo A〈拟〉1〈书〉（指风声）whistle: 风～。The wind is rustling. 2（指马鸣声）whinny: 马～。The horse is neighing. B〈形〉sparse: 白发～ sparse grey hair

硝 xiāo

A〈名〉saltpetre: 墙～ wall saltpetre

B〈动〉 tan: ～革 tanned hide

【硝胺】xiāo'àn〈名〉～炸药 nitramine compound explosive

【硝化】xiāohuà〈动〉［化工］ nitrify

【硝化甘油】xiāohuà gānyóu〈名〉 nitroglycerine

【硝石】xiāoshí〈名〉［矿业］ nitre

【硝酸】xiāosuān〈名〉［化工］ nitric acid

【硝酸铵】xiāosuān'ān〈名〉 ammonium nitrate

【硝酸甘油】xiāosuān gānyóu〈名〉 nitroglycerine

【硝酸钾】xiāosuānjiǎ〈名〉 potassium nitrate

【硝酸钠】xiāosuānnà〈名〉 sodium nitrate

【硝酸盐】xiāosuānyán〈名〉 nitrate

【硝烟】xiāoyān〈名〉 gunpowder smoke: ～滚滚 billows of gunpowder smoke ‖ ～弥漫 be thick with gunpowder fumes

销（銷）xiāo

A〈动〉 **1**（熔化） melt: ～熔 melt **2**（解除） cancel: ～户口 cancel one's residence registration ‖ 把债务～掉 write off a debt ▸～账, 报～, 注～ **3**（消费） expend: ▸开～ **4**（销售） sell: ～完了 sell out of sth. ‖ 容易～ sell easily ▸～路, ～售, 畅～ **5**（插上销子） bolt: 把门～上 bolt the door

B〈名〉 bolt: 铁～ iron bolt ▸～钉, 插～

【销案】xiāo'àn〈动〉 close a case: 这个案子还没销。 The case has not yet come to a close.

【销钉】xiāodīng = 销子 xiāozi

【销户】xiāohù〈动〉 **1**（指账户） cancel one's account **2**（指户口） cancel one's household registration

【销毁】xiāohuǐ〈动〉 destroy: ～核武器 have the nuclear weapons destroyed ‖ ～罪证 destroy incriminating evidence

【销魂】xiāohún〈动〉 be overwhelmed with sorrow or joy: 让人～ give sb. a thrill ‖ 为离别而黯然～ feel great sorrow over a parting

【销魂夺魄】xiāohún-duópò〈成〉 bewitch the mind and intoxicate the sense

【销货】xiāohuò〈动〉 sell goods: ～合同 sales contract

【销假】xiāojià〈动〉 report one's return from leave

【销量】xiāoliàng〈名〉 sales volume: 煤炭/汽车～ coal/car sales ‖ 今年的～超过前两年之和。 Sales this year exceeded the total for the two previous years.

【销路】xiāolù〈名〉 sale: 打开～ secure a sale ‖ 没有～ find no market

【销纳】xiāonà = 消纳 xiāonà

【销声匿迹】xiāoshēng-nìjì〈成〉keep silent and lie low

【销蚀】xiāoshí〈动〉 corrode: ～剂 corrodant ‖ ～作用 corrosion

【销势】xiāoshì〈名〉 sales trend: ～很旺 sales are flourishing

【销售】xiāoshòu〈动〉 sell, market: ～淡季 slack sales season ‖ ～人员 sales staff ‖ ～渠道 distribution channel ‖ ～情况很好。 Sales held up well.

【销售部】xiāoshòubù〈名〉 marketing department

【销售代表】xiāoshòu dàibiǎo〈名〉 sales representative

【销售代理】xiāoshòu dàilǐ〈名〉 sales agency

【销售额】xiāoshòu'é〈名〉 sales

【销售价格】xiāoshòu jiàgé〈名〉 selling price

【销售目标】xiāoshòu mùbiāo〈名〉 sales target

【销售网点】xiāoshòu wǎngdiǎn〈名〉 commercial network

【销售网络】xiāoshòu wǎngluò〈名〉 sales network

【销售业绩】xiāoshòu yèjì〈名〉 sell-through

【销售总值】xiāoshòu zǒngzhí〈名〉 total sales value

【销行】xiāoxíng〈动〉 be on sale: ～全国 be on sale across the country

【销赃】xiāozāng〈动〉 **1**（指出售） deal in stolen goods **2**（指销毁） destroy stolen goods: ～灭迹 destroy incriminating evidence

【销账】xiāozhàng〈动〉 write off an account

【销子】xiāozi〈名〉 peg: 插上～ draw the bolt

蛸 xiāo ▸螵蛸 piāoxiāo ▸shāo

箫（簫）xiāo ▸p. 929〈名〉 *xiao* [vertical bamboo flute]

潇（瀟）xiāo〈形〉〈书〉deep and clear

【潇洒】xiāosǎ〈形〉 elegant and unconventional: 举止～ carry oneself with ease and natural poise ‖ 行文～自如 write with a pretty turn of phrase

【潇潇】xiāoxiāo〈形〉 **1**（形容刮风下雨） whistling and pattering: 风雨～。 The rain is pattering down and the wind is whistling. **2**（形容小雨） drizzly: 细雨～。 It's drizzling.

霄 xiāo〈名〉 **1**（云） clouds: ▸～汉, 云～ **2**（天空） sky: ▸～壤之别, 重～, 九～

【霄汉】xiāohàn〈名〉〈书〉 heavens: ▸气冲～

【霄壤之别】xiāorǎngzhībié〈成〉 as far apart as heaven and earth: 有～ be poles apart

魈 xiāo ▸山魈 shānxiāo

蟏（蠨）xiāo

【蟏蛸】xiāoshāo〈名〉［昆虫］ long-jawed orb weaver [a kind of spider]

嚣（囂）xiāo〈动〉 clamour: ▸叫～, 喧～

【嚣杂】xiāozá〈形〉〈书〉 clamorous: 从闹市传来的～声 clamour of voices from the noisy market

【嚣张】xiāozhāng〈形〉 aggressive: 气焰～ be puffed up with pride and arrogance

xiáo

淆 xiáo〈形〉 confused: ▸～杂, 混～

【淆惑】xiáohuò〈动〉〈书〉 bewilder: ～视听 mislead the public

【淆乱】xiáoluàn **A**〈形〉confused **B**〈动〉 confuse: ～社会秩序 disturb the social order

【淆杂】xiáozá〈形〉 mixed

xiǎo

小 xiǎo

A〈形〉 **1**（不大） small: ～房间 small room ‖ ～男孩 little boy ‖ ～问题 minor problem ‖ 她比我～两岁。 She is two years younger than I am. **2**（排行最末） youngest: ～妹 youngest sister ‖ ～女儿 youngest daughter **3**〈谦〉（我的） my, our: ～女 my daughter ‖ ～婿 my son-in-law ▸～弟 **4**（称呼年幼者） [used before the family name of a younger person as a form of familiar address]: ～王 Xiao Wang

B〈副〉 **1**（时间短） briefly: ～坐片刻 sit for a while ‖ ～住几天 stay for a few days ▸～睡 **2**（稍微） slightly: ～有名气 be somewhat popular ▸牛刀～试 **3**（将近） [used before a numeral] nearly: 结婚～50年了 have been married for nearly 50 years

C〈名〉 **1**（子女） children: 上有老, 下有～ have both parents and children to care for **2**（妾） concubine: 做～ be a concubine

【小巴】xiǎobā〈名〉〈口〉 minibus

【小白菜】xiǎobáicài〈名〉 variety of Chinese cabbage

【小白脸儿】xiǎobáiliǎnr〈名〉〈贬〉 pretty-faced young man: 他只不过是个小～。 He is just a pretty face.

【小百货】xiǎobǎihuò〈名〉 small daily necessities

【小摆设】xiǎobǎishe〈名〉 little curios

【小班】xiǎobān〈名〉 **1**（指孩子年岁小） bottom class in a kindergarten **2**（指人数少） small class

【小半】xiǎobàn ▸p. 927〈数〉 less than half: ～苹果 smaller half of an apple

【小包装】xiǎobāozhuāng〈名〉 package: ～食品 package food

【小保姆】xiǎobǎomǔ〈名〉 young housemaid

【小报】xiǎobào〈名〉 tabloid

【小报告】xiǎobàogào〈名〉 backbiting report: 向老师打同学的～ tell on one's classmate to the teacher

【小辈】xiǎobèi〈名〉 junior

【小本经营】xiǎoběn jīngyíng〈名〉 do business on a shoestring: 靠～为生 live on a shoestring

【小臂】xiǎobì〈名〉 forearm

【小便】xiǎobiàn **A**〈动〉 urinate: ～失禁 urinary incontinence **B**〈名〉 **1**（尿） urine: ～赤黄 dark urine **2**（男性生殖器） penis **3**（女性生殖器） vaginal orifice

【小便池】xiǎobiànchí〈名〉 urinal

【小辫儿】xiǎobiànr〈名〉 pigtail: 梳着～ wear one's hair in plaits

【小辫子】xiǎobiànzi〈名〉 **1** = 小辫儿 xiǎobiànr **2**〈喻〉（把柄） vulnerable point: 小心别让他抓住你什么～! Be careful not to let him get any evidence against you.

【小标题】xiǎobiāotí〈名〉 subheading

【小别重逢】xiǎobié chóngféng〈成〉 meet again after a short interval

【小别胜新婚】xiǎobié shèng xīnhūn〈俗〉 a brief separation makes the couple feel like honeymooners

【小病】xiǎobìng〈名〉 minor illness

【小不点儿】xiǎobudiǎnr **A**〈形〉 tiny **B**〈名〉 toddler

【小不忍则乱大谋】xiǎo bù rěn zé luàn dàmóu〈成〉 lack of forbearance in a trivial matter will spoil the whole

【小菜】xiǎocài〈名〉 **1**（凉菜） side dish

X

2〈口〉〈喻〉(小事) easy task: 这对他来说是～一碟。 That's a piece of cake for him.

【小册子】xiǎocèzi〈名〉 booklet

【小产】xiǎochǎn〈动〉 have a miscarriage: 引起～ cause a miscarriage

【小肠】xiǎocháng〈名〉[生理] small intestine

【小抄儿】xiǎochāor〈名〉〈口〉 small note secretly brought into an exam: 打～ pass a note

【小潮】xiǎocháo〈名〉 neap tide

【小炒】xiǎochǎo〈名〉 individually-cooked dish: 吃～ eat individually-cooked dishes

【小车】xiǎochē〈名〉 **1**(手推车) wheelbarrow **2**(小轿车) car; sedan〈美〉

【小乘】Xiǎochéng〈名〉[佛教] Hinayana: ～佛教 Hinayana Buddhism

【小吃】xiǎochī〈名〉 **1**(点心) snack: 风味～ local delicacy ‖ ～店 snack bar **2**(简单菜肴) small and cheap dishes: 经济～ economic food **3**(冷盘) [of Western food] cold dish

【小丑】xiǎochǒu〈名〉 **1**(滑稽演员) clown: 演～ play the clown ‖ 马戏团～ circus clown **2**(小人) vile character: ▸跳梁～

【小春】xiǎochūn〈名〉〈方〉 the 10th lunar month

【小词】xiǎocí〈名〉 **1**[语法] particle **2**[逻辑] minor term

【小葱】xiǎocōng〈名〉 **1**(指葱的一种) shallot **2**(幼嫩的葱) young onion

【小葱拌豆腐——一清二白】xiǎocōng bàn dòufu—yīqīng'èrbái〈歇后〉 be as clear as daylight

【小聪明】xiǎocōngming〈名〉〈贬〉 petty trick: 耍～ play petty tricks

【小打小闹】xiǎodǎ-xiǎonào〈惯〉 do sth. in dribs and drabs: 修个自行车,～挣几个钱 make a few bob out of a small business of fixing bicycles

【小大人儿】xiǎodàrénr〈名〉 precocious child

【小刀会】Xiǎodāohuì〈名〉 *Xiaodaohui*, Small-Sword Society [rebellious organization in late Qing Dynasty]

【小岛】xiǎodǎo〈名〉 islet

【小道】xiǎodào〈名〉 path: 羊肠～ winding path

【小道儿消息】xiǎodàor xiāoxi〈名〉 hearsay: 传播～ pass on news heard on the grapevine

【小的】xiǎode〈名〉 **1**(孩子) little one: 家里老的～都靠他。 All the family members, old or young, depend on him. **2**〈旧〉〈谦〉(我) I: ～不敢。 I don't dare.

【小弟】xiǎodì〈名〉 **1**(弟弟) little brother **2**〈书〉〈谦〉(我) I

【小调】xiǎodiào〈名〉 **1**(俚俗曲调) popular tune **2**[音乐] minor: C～交响曲 symphony in C minor

【小动作】xiǎodòngzuò〈名〉 petty trick/manoeuvre: 搞～ get up to mean, petty tricks

【小豆】xiǎodòu = 赤小豆 chìxiǎodòu

【小洞不补，大洞吃苦】xiǎodòng bù bǔ, dàdòng chīkǔ〈俗〉〈喻〉 a small leak will sink a great ship

【小肚鸡肠】xiǎodù-jīcháng〈成〉 narrow-minded

【小肚子】xiǎodùzi〈口〉= 小腹 xiǎofù

【小队】xiǎoduì〈名〉 team: 少先队～长 Young Pioneers team leader

【小额】xiǎo'é〈形〉 small amount: ～储蓄 small savings deposit ‖ ～贷款 petty loan

【小恩小惠】xiǎo'ēn-xiǎohuì〈成〉 petty favours: 以～拉拢某人 rope sb. in by giving petty favours

【小儿】xiǎo'ér〈名〉 **1**(孩子) children: ～疾病 paediatric disease **2**〈谦〉(我的儿子) my son

【小儿科】xiǎo'érkē **A**〈名〉 **1**(儿科) paediatrics: ～医生 paediatrician **2**〈喻〉(易办成的事) child's play: 这件事对他来说不过是～。 That's just child's play to him. **3**(不值得重视的事) insignificant thing **B**〈形〉〈方〉 stingy

【小儿麻痹症】xiǎo'ér mábìzhèng ▸**p. 50**〈名〉[医学] polio

【小而全】xiǎo ér quán〈形〉 small and all-inclusive

【小二】xiǎo'èr〈名〉〈旧〉 young waiter

【小贩】xiǎofàn〈名〉 pedlar〈英〉; pedlar〈美〉: 街头～ street vendor

【小费】xiǎofèi〈名〉 tip: 付/给5元～ tip sb. 5 *yuan* ‖ 收～ accept tips

【小分队】xiǎofēnduì〈名〉 detachment: 军事～ military detachment ‖ 医疗～ medical team

【小腹】xiǎofù〈名〉 lower abdomen: 感到～痛 feel pain in the lower abdomen

【小钢炮】xiǎogāngpào〈名〉 **1**[军事] small cannon **2**〈喻〉(指人) outspoken person

【小个子】xiǎogèzi〈名〉 small fellow

【小工】xiǎogōng〈名〉 unskilled labourer: 打/做～ work as an unskilled labourer

【小公共汽车】xiǎogōnggòngqìchē〈名〉 minibus

【小狗】xiǎogǒu〈名〉 puppy

【小姑子】xiǎogūzi〈名〉 husband's younger sister

【小广播】xiǎoguǎngbō〈名〉 **1**(指消息) gossip **2**(指人) sb. who gossips: 当～ tell tales

【小广告】xiǎoguǎnggào〈名〉 small ad: 清除街头～ remove the illegal ads in the street ‖ 乱贴～者 bill sticker

【小鬼】xiǎoguǐ〈名〉 **1**(指鬼) little devil **2**(指小孩) kiddie: 过来,～! Come here, you little imp!

【小孩儿】xiǎoháir〈名〉 **1**〈口〉(孩子) kid: 一群～ a group of children **2**(子女) child: 她结婚了,有三个～。 She is married with three young children.

【小寒】Xiǎohán〈名〉 Slight Cold [beginning of the 23rd of the 24 solar terms]

【小号】xiǎohào **A**〈形〉 small: ～字体 lower case letter ‖ 一件～的外衣 a small coat **B**〈名〉 **1**〈谦〉(我的铺子) my shop **2** ▸**p. 929** [音乐] trumpet: 吹～ play the trumpet

【小河】xiǎohé〈名〉 creek

【小胡桃】xiǎohútáo〈名〉〈方〉 hickory (nut)

【小户】xiǎohù〈名〉 **1**〈旧〉(指贫寒) family of humble means **2**(指人口少) small family

【小户型】xiǎohùxíng〈名〉 small-scale housing: ～商品房 small-scale commercial residential buildings

【小花脸】xiǎohuāliǎn〈名〉[戏曲] clown

【小环境】xiǎohuánjìng〈名〉 microenvironment

【小皇帝】xiǎohuángdì〈名〉 **1**(指皇帝) child emperor **2**〈喻〉(指孩子) spoiled child

【小黄鱼】xiǎohuángyú〈名〉[鱼类] little yellow croaker

【小惠】xiǎohuì〈名〉 petty favour

【小火】xiǎohuǒ〈名〉 slow fire

【小伙子】xiǎohuǒzi〈名〉〈口〉 lad

【小鸡】xiǎojī〈名〉 chick

【小集团】xiǎojítuán〈名〉 clique

【小家碧玉】xiǎojiā-bìyù〈成〉 pretty girl of humble birth

【小家电】xiǎojiādiàn〈名〉 small electrical appliance

【小家伙】xiǎojiāhuo〈名〉 kid

【小家庭】xiǎojiātíng〈名〉 small family

【小家子气】xiǎojiāziqì〈形〉 small-minded: 他那样做真～。 It was petty of him to do it that way.

【小建】xiǎojiàn〈名〉 lesser month of 29 days in the Chinese lunar calendar

【小将】xiǎojiàng〈名〉 **1**〈旧〉(年轻将领) young general **2**〈喻〉(能干的年轻人) outstanding young person: 乒坛～ top young player in the table tennis circles

【小脚】xiǎojiǎo〈名〉〈旧〉 bound feet: 〈喻〉～女人 narrow-minded person

【小节】xiǎojié〈名〉 **1**(琐碎小事) small matter: 拘泥于～ be a stickler for petty issues ‖ 生活～ matters concerning one's personal life ▸不拘～ **2**[音乐] bar: ～线 bar

【小结】xiǎojié **A**〈名〉 **1**(总结) brief summary: 年终～ year-end summary **2**[医学] nodule **B**〈动〉 summarize: ～上星期的工作 briefly summarize the work done last week

【小姐】xiǎojiě〈名〉 **1**〈旧〉(称主人的女儿) young lady **2**(未婚女子) miss **3**(用于称呼) Miss: 陈～ Miss Chen **4**(用于头衔) Miss: 世界/环球～ Miss World/Universe

【小姐妹】xiǎojiěmèi〈名〉 [of girls] buddy

【小解】xiǎojiě〈动〉 urinate

【小金库】xiǎojīnkù〈名〉 small exchequer: 私设～ set up one's own exchequer

【小尽】xiǎojìn = 小建 xiǎojiàn

【小径】xiǎojìng〈名〉〈书〉 path

【小九九】xiǎojiǔjiǔ〈名〉 **1**[数学] multiplication table **2**〈喻〉(算计) clear idea

【小舅子】xiǎojiùzi〈名〉 wife's younger brother

【小开】xiǎokāi〈名〉〈方〉 young master

【小楷】xiǎokǎi〈名〉 **1**[书法] small regular script **2**[印刷] lower-case letter

【小看】xiǎokàn〈动〉 look down upon: 可千万不能～这件事。 Don't underestimate the importance of this matter. ‖ 他这人可～不得。 He's not a man to be trifled with.

【小康】xiǎokāng〈形〉 comfortable: 过上～生活 be comfortably off ‖ ～之家 well-to-do family

【小康社会】xiǎokāng shèhuì〈名〉 well-off society: 全面建设～ build a well-off society in an all-round way

【小考】xiǎokǎo〈名〉 quiz: 我们每学五单元就有一个～。 We have a quiz on every five units.

【小可】xiǎokě **A**〈名〉〈谦〉 [often used in early vernacular] I **B**〈形〉 unimportant: ▸非同～

【小口径】xiǎokǒujìng〈形〉 small-calibre

【小口径步枪】xiǎokǒujìng bùqiāng〈名〉 small-calibre rifle

【小括号】xiǎokuòhào〈名〉 parentheses

【小老婆】xiǎolǎopo〈名〉 concubine

【小两口】xiǎoliǎngkǒu〈名〉〈口〉 young married couple: 那～又言归于好了。 The young couple have made it up after their quarrel.

【小量】xiǎoliàng = 少量 shǎoliàng

【小灵通】xiǎolíngtōng〈名〉 personal access system (PAS)

【小令】xiǎolìng〈名〉 **1**(指词调) short

tonal poem 2 (指散曲) shorter form of *sanqu* (散曲) poetry
【小流域】xiǎoliúyù〈名〉micro-watersheds
【小龙】xiǎolóng〈名〉snake [one of the 12 symbolic animals representing the Earthly Branches (地支) and used as birth signs]
【小笼包子】xiǎolóngbāozi〈名〉small steamed stuffed bun
【小炉匠】xiǎolújiàng〈名〉tinker
【小鹿】xiǎolù〈名〉fawn
【小萝卜】xiǎoluóbo〈名〉radish
【小萝卜头儿】xiǎoluóbotóur〈名〉1 (儿童) [endearing address] child 2 (小人物) small potato
【小锣】xiǎoluó ▸p. 929〈名〉[音乐] small gong
【小马】xiǎomǎ〈名〉pony
【小买卖】xiǎomǎimai〈名〉small business
【小麦】xiǎomài〈名〉wheat: ▸春～, 冬～
【小麦粉】xiǎomàifěn〈名〉wheat flour
【小卖】xiǎomài A〈名〉snack: 应时～ seasonal food B〈动〉do small business
【小卖部】xiǎomàibù〈名〉1 (小店) small shop 2 (小餐厅) canteen
【小满】Xiǎomǎn〈名〉Grain Full [beginning of the 8th of the 24 solar terms]
【小猫】xiǎomāo〈名〉kitten
【小猫熊】xiǎomāoxióng〈名〉lesser panda
【小毛头】xiǎomáotóu〈名〉〈方〉baby
【小门小户】xiǎomén-xiǎohù〈成〉poor and humble family
【小米】xiǎomǐ〈名〉millet: ～面 millet flour ‖ ～粥 millet gruel
【小蜜】xiǎomì〈名〉〈俗〉mistress
【小名】xiǎomíng〈名〉pet name
【小命儿】xiǎomìngr〈名〉〈口〉life: 差点儿丢了～ come within an inch of death
【小拇指】xiǎomuzhǐ〈名〉little finger
【小脑】xiǎonǎo〈名〉[生理] cerebellum
【小妮子】xiǎonīzi〈名〉〈口〉girlie
【小年】xiǎonián〈名〉1 (指年份) minor year 2 (指节日) Small Year [festival that falls on 23rd or 24th in the 12th lunar month] 3 [农业] off year
【小年轻】xiǎoniánqīng〈名〉〈口〉youngster
【小年夜】xiǎoniányè〈名〉1 (除夕前夜) night before the Eve of the Lunar New Year 2 (农历12月23日或24日) 23rd or 24th of the 12th month of the lunar year
【小鸟依人】xiǎoniǎo-yīrén〈成〉〈喻〉timid and lovable young woman
【小妞儿】xiǎoniūr〈名〉〈口〉girlie
【小牛】xiǎoniú〈名〉calf
【小农】xiǎonóng〈名〉individual farmer
【小农经济】xiǎonóng jīngjì〈名〉small-scale peasant economy
【小女】xiǎonǚ〈名〉〈谦〉my daughter
【小牌】xiǎopái〈名〉low card: 打出～ play low
【小盘股】xiǎopángǔ〈名〉[金融] small-cap stocks
【小跑】xiǎopǎo〈动〉〈口〉trot: 一路～ jog all the way
【小朋友】xiǎopéngyǒu〈名〉1 (儿童) kid 2 (用于称呼) little boy/girl/friend
【小便宜】xiǎopiányi〈名〉petty advantage: 爱占～ be keen on getting petty advantages ‖ 贪～ go after small gains
【小票】xiǎopiào〈名〉1 (指凭证) small note: 购物～ note of purchase 2 (指纸钞) banknote of small denomination
【小品】xiǎopǐn〈名〉short work: 演～ put on a short play ‖ ～演员 short play performer ‖ 讽刺～ satirical sketch
【小品文】xiǎopǐnwén〈名〉short essay
【小品词】xiǎopǐncí〈名〉[语言] particle
【小气候】xiǎoqìhòu〈名〉1 (指自然气候) microclimate 2〈喻〉(指政治、经济环境) particular environment or condition
【小汽车】xiǎoqìchē〈名〉car
【小憩】xiǎoqì〈动〉take a short rest: 躺下～ lie down and rest for a while
【小气】xiǎoqi〈形〉1 (吝啬) stingy; mean〈英〉: 花钱很～ be very tight with one's money ‖ ～鬼 penny-pincher 2〈方〉(气量小) petty: 他说这话未免太～了。It's so petty of him to have said that.
【小前提】xiǎoqiántí〈名〉[逻辑] minor premise
【小钱】xiǎoqián〈名〉small amount of money: 别在～上计较了。Stop niggling about every penny we spend.
【小瞧】xiǎoqiáo〈方〉= 小看 xiǎokàn
【小巧】xiǎoqiǎo〈形〉small and delicate: ～可爱的戒指 exquisite little ring
【小巧玲珑】xiǎoqiǎo línglóng〈成〉1 (形容女性) petite: ～的女孩 petite girl 2 (形容器物) small and exquisite: ～的饰物 small and exquisite ornament
【小青年】xiǎoqīngnián〈名〉youngster
【小秋收】xiǎoqiūshōu〈名〉small autumn harvest [harvest of wild plants, etc. that takes place after the main harvest]
【小球】xiǎoqiú〈名〉[体育] small ball sports
【小球藻】xiǎoqiúzǎo〈名〉[生物] chlorella
【小区】xiǎoqū〈名〉housing development: ～建设 housing estate construction ‖ 住宅～ housing estate
【小曲儿】xiǎoqǔr〈名〉ditty: 哼～ hum a tune
【小觑】xiǎoqù〈动〉belittle: 后生可畏，～不得。The young person shows great promise and should not be belittled.
【小圈子】xiǎoquānzi〈名〉1 (指社交圈) small social circle: 走出家庭的～ get out of the narrow family circle 2 (指小集团) clique: 搞～ form a small clique
【小人】xiǎorén〈名〉1〈旧〉(指地位低下) person of low position 2〈谦〉(称呼自己) I: ～不敢。I dare not. 3 (指人格卑鄙) vile character: 势利～ snob
【小人得志】xiǎorén-dézhì〈成〉a small person is intoxicated by success
【小人儿】xiǎorénr〈名〉〈口〉baby
【小人儿书】xiǎorénrshū〈名〉picture book
【小人物】xiǎorénwù〈名〉nonentity: 政坛～ political nonentity
【小日子】xiǎorìzi〈名〉easy life of a small family: 过着舒心的～ live a cosy and happy life
【小三】xiǎosān〈名〉〈口〉mistress (of a married man)
【小三通】xiǎosāntōng〈名〉Mini Three Links
【小嗓儿】xiǎosǎngr〈名〉[戏曲] falsetto
【小商贩】xiǎoshāngfàn〈名〉small tradespeople and pedlars
【小商品】xiǎoshāngpǐn〈名〉petty goods: ～市场 small commodity market
【小舌】xiǎoshé〈名〉[生理] uvula
【小生】xiǎoshēng〈名〉1 [戏曲] *xiaosheng* [young male character in traditional Chinese opera] 2〈旧〉〈谦〉(指称自己) [often used in early vernacular, self-address of a young scholar] I
【小生产】xiǎoshēngchǎn〈名〉small-scale production: ～观念 small producer's mentality ‖ ～者 small producer
【小声】xiǎoshēng〈名〉low voice
【小胜】xiǎoshèng〈动〉win by a narrow margin
【小时】xiǎoshí〈名〉hour: 按～付酬 pay by the hour ‖ 这家商店24～营业。The shop is open 24 hours.
【小时工】xiǎoshígōng〈名〉worker paid by the hour
【小时候】xiǎoshíhou〈名〉childhood: ～的梦想/相片 childhood dream/photo ‖ 他～身体很弱。He was very weak when he was a child.
【小食】xiǎoshí〈名〉〈方〉snack: ～铺 snack bar
【小市】xiǎoshì〈名〉marketplace for second-hand or small articles
【小市民】xiǎoshìmín〈名〉1 (指居民) urban petty bourgeois 2 (指好计较的人) plebeian: ～习气 plebeian habits
【小事】xiǎoshì〈名〉minor matter: 为～争吵 quarrel over petty things ‖ ～一桩 minor incident
【小试锋芒】xiǎoshì-fēngmáng〈成〉display only a small part of one's talent
【小视】xiǎoshì〈动〉look down upon: 不可～ cannot be taken lightly
【小手工业者】xiǎoshǒugōngyèzhě〈名〉small craftsman
【小手小脚】xiǎoshǒu-xiǎojiǎo〈形〉1 (指不大方) stingy 2 (指没魄力) timid: 别这么～的。Don't be so cautious.
【小叔子】xiǎoshūzi〈名〉brother-in-law
【小暑】Xiǎoshǔ〈名〉Slight Heat [beginning of the 11th of the 24 solar terms]
【小数】xiǎoshù ▸p. 691〈名〉1 [数学] decimal: ～表示法 fractional representation ‖ ～部分 fractional part ‖ 五分之三用～表示就是0.6。Three fifths expressed as decimal is 0.6. 2 (小的数目) small sum: 上万元的钱可不是个～。More than ten thousand yuan is no small sum.
【小数点】xiǎoshùdiǎn〈名〉decimal point: 计算到～后两位 calculate the result to two decimal places
【小睡】xiǎoshuì〈动〉have a nap: ～片刻 take a nap ‖ ～了一会儿，他的精神好多了。He felt refreshed after that little nap.
【小说】xiǎoshuō〈名〉novel: 长篇～ novel ‖ 短篇～ short story ‖ 获奖～ prize novel ‖ 科幻～ science fiction ‖ ～家 novelist
【小厮】xiǎosī〈名〉〈旧〉boy
【小苏打】xiǎosūdá〈名〉baking soda; bicarbonate of soda〈英〉
【小算盘】xiǎosuànpan〈名〉〈喻〉selfish calculation: 他很会打自己的～。He is very shrewd in looking after his own interests.
【小摊儿】xiǎotānr〈名〉stall: 摆～ set up a small stall ‖ 在～上出售 sell sth. at a stall
【小提琴】xiǎotíqín ▸p. 929〈名〉violin: 拉～ play the violin ‖ ～手 violinist
【小题大做】xiǎotí-dàzuò〈成〉make a mountain out of a molehill: 她就迟到了3分钟嘛，没必要～。She was only three minutes late! There is no need to make a mountain out of a molehill.
【小天地】xiǎotiāndì〈名〉small world: 生活在自己的～里 live in one's own little world
【小贴士】xiǎotiēshì〈名〉tip: 向乘客发放文明礼仪～ provide civility and etiquette tips to passengers
【小同乡】xiǎotóngxiāng〈名〉fellow villager
【小偷】xiǎotōu〈名〉petty thief: 抓～ catch a thief ‖ 当心～! Beware of pickpockets!
【小偷小摸】xiǎotōu-xiǎomō〈成〉petty theft

X

【小头】xiǎotóu〈名〉small part
【小腿】xiǎotuǐ〈名〉lower leg: ～抽筋 calf spasm
【小玩意儿】xiǎowányìr〈名〉1（指零散的东西）oddment 2（指小饰品）trinket
【小我】xiǎowǒ〈名〉self: 不要只考虑～。Don't just consider your own interests.
【小巫见大巫】xiǎowū jiàn dàwū〈成〉〈喻〉pale in comparison with: 我所做的，比起他来，只是～。What I have done is simply nothing compared with what he has done.
【小屋】xiǎowū〈名〉cabin
【小五金】xiǎowǔjīn〈名〉metal fittings
【小溪】xiǎoxī〈名〉brook: 趟过～ ford a stream ‖ 潺潺的～ babbling brook
【小媳妇儿】xiǎoxífur〈名〉1（新媳妇）young married woman 2〈喻〉（受气、受支使的人）person at others' beck and call
【小戏】xiǎoxì〈名〉playlet
【小先生】xiǎoxiānsheng〈名〉student teacher
【小巷】xiǎoxiàng〈名〉alley: 偏僻的～ back alley
【小小不言】xiǎoxiǎo-bùyán〈成〉〈口〉too petty to mention: ～的事，不要计较。There's no use niggling over such a trifling matter.
【小小说】xiǎoxiǎoshuō〈名〉flash fiction
【小小子】xiǎoxiǎozi〈名〉〈口〉young lad
【小鞋】xiǎoxié〈名〉1（指鞋）tight shoes 2〈喻〉（指刁难）difficulties deliberately created: ▸穿～
【小写】xiǎoxiě〈名〉1（指汉字）ordinary form of Chinese numerals: ～金额 amount in ordinary figures 2（指拼音字母）lower-case letter: ～字母 small letter
【小心】xiǎoxīn A〈动〉take care: ～说错话 be careful what one says ‖ ～碰头 mind your head ‖ 特别～ be extremely careful B〈形〉careful: ～轻放! Handle with care! ‖ 她开车很～。She is a careful driver.
【小心谨慎】xiǎoxīn-jǐnshèn〈成〉be cautious: 极为～地处理某事 handle sth. with the utmost discretion ‖ 强调～的必要性 stress the need for caution
【小心翼翼】xiǎoxīn-yìyì〈成〉with the utmost care: ～地开车 drive very carefully ‖ ～地做手术 carry out the operation with the utmost care
【小心眼儿】xiǎoxīnyǎnr A〈形〉petty: ～的人 narrow-minded person B〈名〉selfish scheming: 要～ pull a trick
【小行星】xiǎoxíngxīng〈名〉asteroid
【小型】xiǎoxíng〈形〉small-scale: ～电动机 miniature motor ‖ ～汽车 compact car ‖ ～运动会 small-scale sports meet
【小型化】xiǎoxínghuà〈动〉miniaturize
【小型张】xiǎoxíngzhāng〈名〉stamp sheetlet
【小性儿】xiǎoxìngr〈名〉〈方〉peevishness: 使～ be peevish
【小熊猫】xiǎoxióngmāo〈名〉lesser panda
【小熊座】Xiǎoxióngzuò〈名〉［天文］Little Bear
【小修】xiǎoxiū〈名〉minor repair: ～小补 make small repairs
【小学】xiǎoxué〈名〉1（指学校）primary school; grade school〈美〉: ～教师 primary-school teacher 2〈旧〉（指学问）philological studies
【小学生】xiǎoxuéshēng〈名〉1（指学生）pupil: 二年级的～ second-year pupil 2〈喻〉（指初学者）beginner: 翻译方面，我还是个～。I'm still a pupil when it comes to translation.
【小雪】xiǎoxuě〈名〉1 Xiǎoxuě（指节气）Slight Snow [beginning of the 20th of the 24 solar terms] 2（指降雪）light snow
【小循环】xiǎoxúnhuán〈名〉［生理］pulmonary circulation
【小鸭】xiǎoyā〈名〉duckling
【小羊】xiǎoyáng〈名〉lamb
【小阳春】xiǎoyángchūn〈名〉10th lunar month
【小样】xiǎoyàng A〈名〉1［印刷］galley proof 2〈方〉（样品）sample: 实物～ model of sth. B〈形〉〈方〉petty: 瞧他那～儿! What a petty person he is!
【小业主】xiǎoyèzhǔ〈名〉〈旧〉small proprietor
【小叶】xiǎoyè〈名〉［植物］small leaf
【小叶杨】xiǎoyèyáng〈名〉［植物］poplar
【小夜曲】xiǎoyèqǔ〈名〉serenade: 月光～ moonlight serenade
【小姨子】xiǎoyízi〈名〉〈口〉sister-in-law
【小意思】xiǎoyìsi〈名〉1（指心意）small gift: 你帮了我那么大的忙，这点～，还请笑纳。Please accept this small gift as a token of my gratitude for all the help that you have given me. 2（指微不足道的事）nothing important: 二百块钱，～，我掏了。Two hundred *yuan*, that's nothing. I will pay it. ‖ 这点活儿，～，一会儿就能干完。There isn't much to this job. I can finish it within minutes.
【小引】xiǎoyǐn〈名〉brief introductory note
【小影】xiǎoyǐng = 小照 xiǎozhào
【小语种】xiǎoyǔzhǒng〈名〉less commonly used language
【小雨】xiǎoyǔ〈名〉drizzle: 下～。It's drizzling.
【小月】xiǎoyuè A〈名〉lesser month [solar month of 30 days; lunar month of 29 days] B〈动〉have a miscarriage: 她第一个孩子～了。She suffered a miscarriage with her first child.
【小灶】xiǎozào〈名〉1（指伙食标准）small mess: 吃～ have special mess 2〈喻〉（指特殊对待）special treatment: 老师经常给他开～。The teacher often gives him extra help.
【小账】xiǎozhàng〈名〉tip
【小照】xiǎozhào〈名〉〈谦〉snapshot of oneself: 送一张～做纪念 give sb. one's picture as a keepsake
【小指】xiǎozhǐ〈名〉little finger
【小趾】xiǎozhǐ〈名〉little toe
【小众】xiǎozhòng〈名〉small group of people: 马术是"～"运动项目。Equestrianism is a select sporting event. ‖ 京剧观众有从大众变为～的趋势。Beijing Opera audiences are sliding in number from great packs to small groups.
【小猪】xiǎozhū〈名〉piglet
【小住】xiǎozhù〈动〉stay for a short time
【小注】xiǎozhù〈名〉〈旧〉note
【小传】xiǎozhuàn〈名〉profile: 作者～ short biographical sketch of the author
【小篆】xiǎozhuàn〈名〉［书法］lesser seal character
【小酌】xiǎozhuó〈名〉〈书〉drinks with snacks: ～两盏 drink a few glasses of wine
【小资】xiǎozī〈名〉1（小资产阶级）petit bourgeoisie 2（宽裕的人）fairly well-off people
【小资产阶级】xiǎozīchǎnjiējí〈名〉the petit bourgeoisie
【小子】xiǎozǐ〈名〉〈书〉young man: 后生～ young lad
【小字辈】xiǎozìbèi〈名〉youngster
【小子】xiǎozi〈名〉〈口〉1（儿子）boy: 他有两个～，一个丫头。He has two boys and one girl. 2〈贬〉（人）fellow: 这～一点也不讲理。This guy is totally unreasonable.
【小宗】xiǎozōng〈形〉small-scale: ～商品 small quantities of goods ‖ ～买卖 small deal
【小卒】xiǎozú〈名〉1〈旧〉（指士兵）private 2〈喻〉（无名小辈）nobody: 无名～ a mere nobody 3（指棋子）pawn
【小组】xiǎozǔ〈名〉small group: ～讨论 group discussion ‖ 领导～ leading group ‖ 专家～ panel of experts ‖ ～循环赛 group round robin
【小坐】xiǎozuò〈动〉sit for a short while: ～片刻 sit for a little while

晓（曉）xiǎo

A〈名〉dawn: ▸～行夜宿，报～，拂～
B〈动〉1（知道）know: 上通天文，下～地理 be a mine of information about all kinds of things ▸～得，家喻户～，知～ 2（告诉）inform: ～之以理 use reason to make sb. understand ‖ ～以大义 wake sb. up to the righteousness of sth. ▸揭～
【晓畅】xiǎochàng A〈动〉be knowledgeable about: ～英国文学 be well-versed in English literature B〈形〉clear and fluent: 文笔～ write in a smooth and clear style
【晓得】xiǎode〈动〉〈口〉know: 不～。I don't know. ‖ 天～。God knows.
【晓示】xiǎoshì〈动〉notify: ～民众 notify the public
【晓市】xiǎoshì〈名〉morning market
【晓行夜宿】xiǎoxíng-yèsù〈成〉travel by day and rest by night
【晓谕】xiǎoyù〈动〉〈书〉explicitly notify: ～百姓 inform the general public

筱 xiǎo

A〈名〉〈书〉bamboo twig
B〈形〉little [usu used in a person's name]

xiào

孝 xiào

A〈动〉do one's filial duty: ▸～顺，～子
B〈名〉1（指居丧礼俗）mourning: 守～ observe a period of mourning ‖ 有～在身 be in mourning ‖ ～满 go out of mourning 2（指服饰）mourning dress: ▸披麻戴～
【孝道】xiàodào〈名〉filial piety: 尽～ fulfil one's filial duty
【孝服】xiàofú〈名〉1（指衣服）mourning: 为逝去的父亲穿～ wear mourning for one's deceased father 2〈旧〉（指日子）mourning period: ～已满。The mourning is over.
【孝敬】xiàojìng〈动〉1（孝顺尊敬）perform one's filial duty: ～双亲 treat one's parents with filial respect 2（给尊长献礼）give a present: 她给母亲买了一件生日礼物以示～。She bought her mother a birthday present.
【孝女】xiàonǚ〈名〉filial daughter
【孝顺】xiàoshùn〈动〉show filial piety: ～父母 be filial to one's parents ‖ 她是个～女儿。She is a dutiful daughter.
【孝悌】xiàotì〈动〉pay both filial and fraternal duties
【孝心】xiàoxīn〈名〉filial piety: 一片～ one's single filial devotion ‖ 有～ have a filial heart
【孝养】xiàoyǎng〈动〉respect and support one's parents
【孝子】xiàozǐ〈名〉1（指孝顺）filial son/daughter 2（指居丧）son in mourning

X

【孝子贤孙】xiàozǐ-xiánsūn〈成〉filial children and virtuous grandchildren:〈喻〉反动阶级的～ worthy progeny of the reactionary class

肖 xiào〈动〉be like: ▸～像, 惟妙惟～

【肖像】xiàoxiàng〈名〉portrait: 伟人～ portrait of a great personage ‖ ～画家 portrait painter ‖ 奖章上有女王的～。The medal bears an effigy of the Queen.

【肖像画】xiàoxiànghuà〈名〉portrait-painting

【肖像权】xiàoxiàngquán〈名〉portraiture rights: 侵犯～ infringe sb.'s portraiture rights

校 xiào〈名〉1▸（学校）school: 按时到～ get to school on time ‖ 全～师生 the whole school ▸～庆, 母～ 2▸（校官）field officer: ▸～官, 上～
▸jiào

【校办】xiàobàn〈动〉run by a school: ～工厂 school-run factory

【校车】xiàochē〈名〉school bus

【校董】xiàodǒng〈名〉school trustee

【校方】xiàofāng〈名〉school authority

【校风】xiàofēng〈名〉school spirit: 整顿～ reform school spirit

【校服】xiàofú〈名〉school uniform

【校歌】xiàogē〈名〉school anthem

【校工】xiàogōng〈名〉school worker

【校官】xiàoguān〈名〉［军事］field officer

【校规】xiàoguī〈名〉school regulations: 遵守/违反～ observe/violate school regulations

【校花】xiàohuā〈名〉campus queen

【校徽】xiàohuī〈名〉school emblem: 佩戴～ wear a school badge

【校纪】xiàojì〈名〉school discipline: 破坏/违反～ undermine/violate school discipline

【校际】xiàojì〈形〉intercollegiate: ～比赛 intercollegiate match

【校刊】xiàokān〈名〉school magazine

【校历】xiàolì〈名〉academic calendar

【校旗】xiàoqí〈名〉school flag

【校庆】xiàoqìng〈名〉anniversary of the founding of a school: 百年～ school centenary

【校舍】xiàoshè〈名〉school building: ～建设 construction of a schoolhouse

【校外】xiàowài〈形〉off-campus: ～活动 extracurricular activity ‖ ～教育 after-school education

【校务】xiàowù〈名〉administrative affairs of a school: ～委员会 school council

【校训】xiàoxùn〈名〉school motto

【校友】xiàoyǒu〈名〉schoolmate: ～会 alumni association ‖ ～通讯录 alumni directory

【校园】xiàoyuán〈名〉school grounds: 美化～ beautify the campus ‖ ～歌曲 campus song

【校园网】xiàoyuánwǎng〈名〉campus network

【校园文化】xiàoyuán wénhuà〈名〉campus culture

【校长】xiàozhǎng〈名〉（指小学和中学）headmaster;（指大学）vice chancellor〈英〉; president〈美〉

【校址】xiàozhǐ〈名〉location of a school/college

哮 xiào
A〈动〉roar: ▸咆～
B〈名〉wheeze: ▸～喘

【哮喘】xiàochuǎn A〈动〉wheeze B ▸p. 50〈名〉asthma: 他患有～病。He suffers from asthma.

笑 xiào〈动〉1▸（露出笑容）laugh: ～得合不拢嘴 grin from ear to ear ‖ ～个不停 can't stop laughing ‖ 哈哈大～ roar with laughter ▸苦～, 微～ 2▸（讥笑）laugh at: 别～我，我英语不行。Don't laugh at me. My English is very poor. ▸～柄, 嘲～

【笑傲】xiào'ào〈动〉laugh proudly: ～人生 live a proud, successful life

【笑柄】xiàobǐng〈名〉laughing stock: 她的错误使她成为大家的～。Her mistakes have made her a laughing stock.

【笑场】xiàochǎng〈动〉corpse

【笑掉大牙】xiàodiào-dàyá〈惯〉laugh one's head off: 让人～的建议 laughable suggestion ‖ 这事要是传出去，肯定会让人～。If the story breaks, people will laugh their heads off.

【笑哈哈】xiàohāhā〈形〉laughing: 办公室里老是～的。There is always a lot of joking and laughter in the office.

【笑呵呵】xiàohēhē〈形〉happy and cheerful: 成天～的 be all smiles the whole time

【笑话】xiàohua A〈名〉joke: 闹～ make an exhibition of oneself ‖ 说～ crack a joke ‖ 天大的～ massive joke B〈动〉laugh at: 他因口吃而遭人～。He was laughed at because of his stammer.

【笑剧】xiàojù〈名〉farce: 一场～ a mere farce

【笑口常开】xiàokǒu chángkāi〈成〉always wear a smile

【笑里藏刀】xiàolǐ-cángdāo〈成〉have murderous intent behind one's smile: 他～。Malice lay behind his smile.

【笑脸】xiàoliǎn〈名〉smiling face: 陪～ put on a smile ‖ ～相迎 greet sb. with a smile

【笑料】xiàoliào〈名〉laughing stock: 爸爸的健忘成了全家人的～。My father's forgetfulness has become a standing joke in my family.

【笑骂】xiàomà〈动〉1▸（讥笑辱骂）taunt: 任人～ allow oneself to be taunted 2▸（开玩笑地骂）scold in jest: ～某人 blame sb. in a joking manner

【笑貌】xiàomào〈名〉〈书〉smiling face: 老人的音容～宛在眼前。The old man's voice and smiles are still fresh in my mind.

【笑眯眯】xiàomīmī〈形〉smiling: 她～地望着他。She looked at him with a bright smile.

【笑面虎】xiàomiànhǔ〈名〉〈喻〉person who is outwardly kind but inwardly cruel

【笑纳】xiàonà〈动〉〈套〉kindly accept: 这是我的一点小意思，请～。This small gift is just a token of my gratitude. Please do me the kindness of accepting it.

【笑破肚皮】xiàopò-dùpí〈惯〉burst one's sides with laughter

【笑气】xiàoqì〈名〉laughing gas

【笑容】xiàoróng〈名〉smile: 面带～ have a smile on one's face ‖ ～满面 be beaming with delight

【笑容可掬】xiàoróng-kějū〈成〉be all smiles: 装得～ put on one's best smile

【笑声】xiàoshēng〈名〉laughter

【笑谈】xiàotán A 1▸ = 笑柄 xiàobǐng 2▸ = 笑话 xiàohua A B〈动〉talk with a smile: ～人生 talk about life in a jocular fashion

【笑纹】xiàowén〈名〉laughter line: 眼角布满～ have lots of laughter lines around one's eyes

【笑窝】xiàowō〈名〉dimple

【笑嘻嘻】xiàoxīxī〈形〉grinning: 整天～的 be grinning all day

【笑星】xiàoxīng〈名〉comedian

【笑颜】xiàoyán〈名〉〈书〉smiling face: ～常开 be always smiling

【笑靥】xiàoyè〈名〉〈书〉1▸（酒窝）dimple 2▸（笑脸）smiling face

【笑一笑，十年少】xiào yī xiào, shínián shào〈俗〉smiles can take years off a person

【笑吟吟】xiàoyínyín〈形〉smiling: ～地说 say with a smile

【笑盈盈】xiàoyíngyíng〈形〉smiling: 他总是～的。He always wears a smile on his face.

【笑语】xiàoyǔ〈名〉〈书〉cheerful talk: ～满堂。There is a lot of joking and laughter in the room.

【笑逐颜开】xiàozhú-yánkāi〈成〉beam with joy: 不由得～ can't hold back a smile of joy

效[1]（傚） xiào〈动〉imitate: ▸～法, 仿～

效[2] xiào〈动〉devote: ▸～劳, ～命, ～忠

效[3] xiào〈名〉result: ▸～果, 成～, 无～

【效度】xiàodù〈名〉validity

【效法】xiàofǎ〈动〉follow the example of: 值得～ be worth following

【效仿】xiàofǎng〈动〉follow the example of

【效果】xiàoguǒ〈名〉1▸（结果）result: 取得～ achieve some results ‖ 治疗～ curative effect 2▸［戏剧］lighting or sound effect: 音响～ sound effect

【效绩】xiàojì = 绩效 jìxiào

【效劳】xiàoláo〈动〉serve: 甘愿～ be willing to offer one's service ‖ 随时为您～。I'm at your service all the time.

【效力】xiàolì A = 效劳 xiàoláo B〈名〉effect: 法律～ force of law ‖ 两种文本具有同等～。Both texts are equally authentic. ‖ 这种药～更好。This kind of medicine is even more effectivel.

【效率】xiàolǜ〈名〉efficiency: 提高工作～ improve one's efficiency in work ‖ 办事～高 be very efficient in business

【效命】xiàomìng〈动〉〈书〉go all out to serve: ～疆场 be ready to lay down one's life in battle

【效能】xiàonéng〈名〉efficiency: 充分发挥计算机的～ use the computer to its full capabilities ‖ 高～的设备 efficient equipment

【效颦】xiàopín〈动〉〈书〉imitate only to produce a ludicrous effect: ▸东施～

【效死】xiàosǐ〈动〉〈书〉go all out to serve: ～沙场 be willing to give one's life on the battlefield

【效验】xiàoyàn〈名〉desired result: 没有～ fail to produce the desired result

【效益】xiàoyì〈名〉benefit: 经济～ economic benefits ‖ 社会～ social benefits ‖ 以最小的代价取得最大的～ get the greatest return at the smallest cost

【效益分析】xiàoyì fēnxī〈名〉performance analysis

【效益工资】xiàoyì gōngzī〈名〉efficiency-related wage

【效益农业】xiàoyì nóngyè〈名〉profitable agriculture

【效应】xiàoyìng〈名〉1▸［物理］［化学］effect: 光电～ photoelectric effect ‖ 热对

金属产生的～ effects of heat on metal ▸温室～ ②〈喻〉（效果和反应） effect: 多米诺～ domino effect ‖ 明星～ celebrity pulling power

【效用】xiàoyòng〈名〉 effectiveness: 毫无～ to no avail ‖ 新药的～ effectiveness of a new drug

【效尤】xiàoyóu〈动〉〈书〉 knowingly follow a bad example: ▸以儆～

【效忠】xiàozhōng〈动〉 devote oneself heart and soul to: 发誓～祖国 pledge allegiance to the country

啸（嘯） xiào〈动〉 ①（指人） scream ②（指鸟兽） roar: 虎～ tigers roaring ③（指风、海） howl: 风～ howling wind ▸海～，呼～ ④（指子弹、飞机） whizz

【啸傲】xiào'ào〈动〉〈书〉 be unfettered by social conventions: ～林泉 live a hermit's life in the woods and by the brooks

【啸聚】xiàojù〈动〉〈书〉 band together: ～山林 band together and take to the woods

【啸鸣】xiàomíng **A**〈动〉 whistle: 汽笛～。 The siren is whistling. **B**〈名〉 whistling: 远处传来警笛的～ police sirens wailing in the distance

xiē

些 xiē〈量〉 ①（表数量） [used before nouns to indicate an indefinite amount] a few: 买～东西 do some shopping ‖ 好～人 quite a lot of people ‖ 前～日子 a few days ago ‖ 再给我～。 Give me some more. ②（表程度） [used after adjectives or verbs to indicate a very small amount, to a small degree, etc.] a little: 好～ be a little better ‖ 跑快～ run a little bit faster ‖ 有～冷 be a bit cold ‖ 早～来 come a little earlier

【些个】xiēge〈量〉〈口〉 some: 这～人 these people ‖ 他比你小，让他～。 He is younger than you, so humour him a little.

【些微】xiēwēi **A**〈形〉 slight: 秋风吹来，感到～凉意。 With the autumn wind coming I feel rather cold. **B**〈副〉 a little: 气温～下降。 There has been an appreciable drop in temperature. ‖ 伤口～有点儿疼。 The wound hurt a bit.

【些小】xiēxiǎo〈形〉 ①（一点儿） slight: 有了～进步 have made a little progress ②（细微） tiny: ～之事 trifling matter

【些许】xiēxǔ〈量〉 few: 加～盐 add a little salt ‖ ～小利 some small profits

揳 xiē〈动〉 drive: 把钉子～入木板 drive a nail into the plank ‖ 这扇窗户关不住，得用楔子～上。 The window doesn't stay closed unless you wedge it.

楔 xiē

A〈名〉（指木片） wedge: 木～ wedge ▸～子

B = 揳 xiē

【楔形文字】xiēxíng wénzì〈名〉 cuneiform

【楔子】xiēzi〈名〉 ①（指木片） wedge: 打进～ drive a wedge ‖ 用～固定某物 fasten sth. with a wedge ②（指钉子） peg: 把外衣挂在～上 hang one's coat on the peg ③（指文字片段） prologue

歇 xiē〈动〉 ①（休息） have a rest: ～口气 catch one's breath ‖ 躺下来～会儿 lie down and rest ‖ 坐下～～腿吧。 Sit down and rest your legs. ▸～伏，～脚 ②（停止） knock off: ▸～工，～业 ③〈方〉（睡） go to bed: 没～好 not sleep well ‖ 午饭后～一会儿 take a nap after lunch ‖ 在朋友家～一晚 sleep overnight at a friend's place

【歇班】xiēbān〈动〉 be off duty: 轮流～ have time off in turns ‖ ～的服务员 off-duty waiter ‖ 我今天～。 I am off duty today.

【歇顶】xiēdǐng〈动〉 go bald: 才20岁，他就～了。 At twenty he was already going bald. ‖ 他～了。 He is thin on top.

【歇乏】xiēfá〈动〉 rest after an exertion: 躺在草地上～ lie on the grass to rest

【歇伏】xiēfú〈动〉 suspend work during the hottest days of the year: 暑假给了我们愉快的～时间。 The summer holidays gave us a welcome break.

【歇工】xiēgōng〈动〉 ①（停工休息） finish work: ～吃午饭 knock off for lunch ②（停业）（指机构） close down;（指项目） be suspended

【歇后语】xiēhòuyǔ〈名〉 two-part allegorical saying [of which the first part, always stated, is descriptive, while the second part, sometimes unstated, clinches the point]

【歇肩】xiējiān〈动〉 rest one's shoulders

【歇脚】xiējiǎo〈动〉 rest one's feet: 咱们坐下来歇歇脚吧。 Let's sit down and rest our tired feet.

【歇凉】xiēliáng〈动〉 relax in a cool place: 在湖边～ enjoy the cool by the lake

【歇气】xiēqì〈动〉 have a rest: 她连续干了24个小时没～。 She's worked for 24 hours without a break.

【歇晌】xiēshǎng〈动〉〈方〉 have a siesta

【歇手】xiēshǒu〈动〉 stop doing: 先～吃点东西，然后再接着干。 Let's stop for a snack and then continue our work.

【歇斯底里】xiēsīdǐlǐ **A**〈名〉 hysterics: 患有～ have hysterics **B**〈形〉 hysterical: 近乎～的狂笑 hysterical laughter

【歇宿】xiēsù〈动〉 put up for the night: 在一家小客栈～ stop at an inn for the night

【歇腿】xiētuǐ = 歇脚 xiējiǎo

【歇息】xiēxi〈动〉 ①（休息） have a rest ②（住宿） put up for the night: 我能在你这儿～吗？ Could you put me up for the night?

【歇夏】xiēxià = 歇伏 xiēfú

【歇业】xiēyè〈动〉 go out of business: 这家超市明天～。 The supermarket will cease trading tomorrow.

【歇夜】xiēyè〈动〉〈口〉 put up for the night

蝎（蠍） xiē〈名〉 scorpion

【蝎虎】xiēhǔ〈名〉 gecko

【蝎虎座】Xiēhǔzuò〈名〉［天文］ Lizard

【蝎子】xiēzi〈名〉 scorpion

xié

叶 xié〈动〉 be in harmony: ▸～韵 ▸yè

【叶韵】xiéyùn〈动〉 rhyme

协（協） xié

A〈动〉 ①（共同） cooperate: ▸～定，～商，～力 ②（协助） assist: ▸～办，～助

B〈形〉 harmonious: ▸～和，～调

【协办】xiébàn〈动〉 assist: 本次研讨会由社科院主办，几家出版社～。 The symposium was sponsored by the Social Science Academy with the assistance of a few publishing houses.

【协查】xiéchá〈动〉 assist in an investigation

【协定】xiédìng **A**〈名〉 agreement: 缔结～ conclude a pact ‖ 贸易～ trade agreement ‖ 停战～ armistice agreement ▸君子～ **B**〈动〉 negotiate an agreement: ～一个项目 reach an agreement on a project

【协管】xiéguǎn〈动〉 help manage: 交通～员 traffic warden〈英〉, traffic cop〈美〉

【协和】xiéhé〈动〉 coordinate: ～劳资关系 harmonize the relationship between labour and capital

【协警】xiéjǐng〈名〉 police assistant: 交通～ traffic police assistant

【协会】xiéhuì〈名〉 association: 消费者/作家～ consumers'/writers' association

【协理】xiélǐ **A**〈动〉 assist in management: ～员 political assistant **B**〈名〉 assistant manager

【协力】xiélì〈动〉 join forces: 同心～ make concerted efforts towards a common purpose

【协拍】xiépāi〈动〉 assist in filming: 电视台～此片。 This film was made in association with the TV station.

【协商】xiéshāng〈动〉 consult: ～解决争端 settle a dispute through negotiation ‖ 同有关部门～ consult with the departments concerned ‖ 中国人民政治～会议 Chinese People's Political Consultative Conference (CPPCC)

【协调】xiétiáo **A**〈形〉 harmonious: ～的建筑群 harmonious group of buildings ‖ 色彩很～。 The colours are very harmonious. **B**〈动〉 coordinate: ～医患关系 harmonize patient-doctor relations ‖ ～国民经济各部门的发展 coordinate the development of different branches of the national economy

【协同】xiétóng〈动〉 cooperate with: ～作战 combine strengths to fight

【协议】xiéyì **A**〈动〉 negotiate: ～解除婚约 terminate a betrothal through discussion **B**〈名〉 agreement: 达成～ come to an agreement ‖ 撕毁～ tear up an agreement ‖ 口头/书面～ verbal/written agreement ‖ ～书 written statement of agreement

【协约】xiéyuē **A**〈动〉 negotiate **B**〈名〉 agreement

【协约国】Xiéyuēguó〈名〉 the Entente countries [in the First World War]

【协助】xiézhù〈动〉 assist: ～办理出国手续 help sb. deal with the paperwork for going abroad ‖ ～培养地方技术人员 assist in training local technical personnel

【协奏曲】xiézòuqǔ〈名〉 concerto: 钢琴～ piano concerto ‖ 小提琴～ violin concerto

【协作】xiézuò〈动〉 cooperate: 发扬～精神 bring into play the spirit of cooperation ‖ 经济技术～ economic and technical cooperation

邪 xié

A〈形〉 ①（不正当） evil: ▸～恶，～念，改～归正 ②（不正常） strange: 她的火发得可真～。 Her rages were really hard to understand. ‖ 这事真～了。 This is really strange. ▸～门儿

B〈名〉 ①（灾祸） disaster: ▸避～，驱～，中～ ②［中医］ unwholesome environmental factor: 风～ wind pathogen ‖ 寒～ cold pathogen ▸yé

【邪不压正】xiébùyāzhèng〈成〉 evil can never prevail over good

【邪财】xiécái〈名〉ill-gotten gains: 拒受～ refuse to accept any ill-gotten gains
【邪道】xiédào〈名〉evil ways: 走～ fall into evil ways
【邪恶】xié'è〈形〉evil: 善良与～的较量 battle between good and evil ‖ ～势力 evil forces
【邪乎】xiéhu〈形〉〈口〉**1**（超乎一般）extraordinary: 病得～ be seriously ill ‖ 天热得～。It is terribly hot. **2**（离奇）incredible: 她的故事～得可笑。Her story was so incredible that it was actually laughable.
【邪教】xiéjiào〈名〉cult: ～徒 heretic
【邪路】xiélù = 邪道 xiédào
【邪门儿】xiéménr〈形〉〈口〉odd: ～了，她刚才还好好的。It's strange. She was quite well a moment ago.
【邪门歪道】xiémén-wāidào〈成〉crooked ways: 靠～弄到一笔钱 get the money by dishonest means
【邪魔】xiémó〈名〉evil spirit
【邪魔外道】xiémó-wàidào〈成〉**1**［佛教］evil demons and heretics **2**（不正当途径）crooked means
【邪念】xiéniàn〈名〉wicked idea: 萌生～ conceive a wicked idea
【邪气】xiéqì〈名〉**1**（指风气）evil influence: 制止～上升 check unhealthy trends ▸歪风～ **2**［中医］pathogenic factor
【邪术】xiéshù〈名〉black magic
【邪说】xiéshuō〈名〉heresy: 受～的误导 be misled by some heresy ▸异端～
【邪祟】xiésuì〈名〉evil and mischievous being
【邪心】xiéxīn〈名〉wicked idea
【邪行】xiéxíng〈名〉wicked act

胁（脅）xié

A〈名〉flank: 两～疼痛 have a pain in both sides of the body
B〈动〉coerce: ▸～迫，威～
【胁持】xiéchí = 挟持 xiéchí
【胁从】xiécóng〈动〉be forced into evildoing: ～犯 person forced into criminal activity
【胁肩谄笑】xiéjiān-chǎnxiào〈成〉act obsequiously
【胁迫】xiépò〈动〉coerce: ～某人做某事 intimidate sb. into doing sth. ‖ ～妇女卖淫 force a woman into selling her body

挟（挾）xié

〈动〉**1**〈书〉（夹在腋下）hold under the arm: ～山超海 perform the impossible **2**（心怀）cherish: ～恨/怨 harbour hatred/a grudge ▸～嫌 **3**（挟持）coerce: ～天子以令诸侯 control the emperor and command the nobles in his name ▸～制，要～
【挟持】xiéchí〈动〉**1**（捉住）seize sb. on both sides by the arms **2**（迫使服从）take sb. by force: ～人质 take sb. hostage ‖ ～者 abductor
【挟带】xiédài〈动〉**1**（夹在腋下）carry under the arms **2**（随身带着）carry along
【挟权倚势】xiéquán-yǐshì〈成〉take advantage of one's power and position
【挟嫌】xiéxián〈动〉〈书〉bear a grudge: ～报复 bear resentment against sb. and retaliate
【挟制】xiézhì〈动〉force sb. to do one's bidding: 受人～ be forced into submission

偕 xié

〈副〉together with: ～夫人抵京 arrive in Beijing with one's wife ‖ ～游全国 travel across the country together
【偕老】xiélǎo〈动〉live together to a ripe old age: ▸白头～
【偕同】xiétóng〈动〉go together with: ～夫人前往伦敦 accompany one's wife to London
【偕行】xiéxíng〈动〉go together with

斜 xié

A〈形〉inclined: ～穿公路 angle across the road ‖ 这条线画～了。The line has been drawn askew. ▸～视，～线，倾～
B〈动〉slant: 把头～向一边 tip one's head to one side ‖ 太阳西～。The sun is setting in the west.
【斜边】xiébiān〈名〉［数学］hypotenuse
【斜度】xiédù〈名〉degree of inclination: ～为30度 slope of 30 degrees
【斜对面】xiéduìmiàn〈名〉diagonally opposite position: 她家就住在～。She lives diagonally across the street.
【斜晖】xiéhuī〈名〉〈书〉slanted rays of evening sunshine: ～从窗户洒了进来。The last few rays of evening sunshine slanted in through the window.
【斜井】xiéjǐng〈名〉［矿业］inclined shaft
【斜靠】xiékào〈动〉lean against: ～在沙发上 recline on the sofa
【斜拉桥】xiélāqiáo〈名〉cable-stayed bridge
【斜路】xiélù〈名〉**1**（指道路）ramp **2**〈喻〉（邪路）wrong track: 正路不走走～ veer from the straight and narrow
【斜面】xiémiàn〈名〉**1**［机械］oblique plane **2**（坡面）slope: 陡峭的～ steep slant
【斜坡】xiépō〈名〉slope: 爬～ climb up a slope
【斜射】xiéshè〈动〉shine at a slant: 阳光～树林。The sunlight slanted through the trees.
【斜视】xiéshì **A** ▸p. 50〈名〉［医学］squint: 矫正～ correct a squint **B**〈动〉cast a sidelong glance at: 目不～ not look sideways
【斜塔】xiétǎ〈名〉leaning tower
【斜体字】xiétǐzì〈名〉italic
【斜纹】xiéwén〈名〉［纺织］twill: ～布 twill
【斜线】xiéxiàn〈名〉diagonal
【斜眼】xiéyǎn〈名〉**1** = 斜视 xiéshì A **2**（指眼睛）cross-eye **3**（指人）cross-eyed person
【斜阳】xiéyáng〈名〉〈书〉setting sun
【斜照】xiézhào **A**〈动〉shine sideways **B**〈名〉〈书〉setting sun

谐（諧）xié

〈形〉**1**（协调）harmonious: ▸和～，～音 **2**〈书〉（办妥）settled: 事～。The matter has been settled. **3**（诙谐）humorous: ▸～谑，诙～
【谐波】xiébō〈名〉［物理］harmonic wave
【谐和】xiéhé **A**〈形〉harmonious: ～的气氛 harmonious atmosphere ‖ 合奏～。The instrumental ensemble is harmonious. **B**〈名〉［物理］consonance
【谐剧】xiéjù〈名〉comic opera [popular in Sichuan]
【谐美】xiéměi〈形〉concordant and euphonious
【谐趣】xiéqù〈名〉humour: ～横生 full of wit and humour
【谐声】xiéshēng = 形声 xíngshēng
【谐调】xiétiáo〈形〉harmonious: 这幅画色彩～。The painting has a nice balance of colours.
【谐谑】xiéxuè〈动〉banter
【谐谑曲】xiéxuèqǔ〈名〉［音乐］scherzo
【谐音】xiéyīn〈名〉**1**［语言］homophony **2**（指复合振动产生）euphony
【谐振】xiézhèn〈名〉［物理］resonance: ～频率 resonant frequency

絜 xié

〈动〉〈书〉**1**（指长度）measure the circumference **2**（指衡量）measure

颉（頡）xié

〈动〉〈书〉fly upwards
【颉颃】xiéháng〈动〉〈书〉**1**（鸟上下飞）fly up and down **2**（不相上下）rival: 二人学识相～。The two of them rival each other in knowledge.

携（攜）xié

〈动〉**1**（带）take along: ～款而逃 run off with the money ‖ 严禁～带易燃物品上车。It is strictly forbidden to take combustible goods on board. ▸扶老～幼 **2**（牵）take sb. by the hand: ▸～手
【携带】xiédài〈动〉**1**（带着）take along: ～家眷 take one's family along ‖ ～违禁品 carry contraband ‖ 随身～ carry sth. around ‖ 艾滋病病毒～者 HIV carrier **2**（提携）guide and support: 多承～。Many thanks for your support.
【携手】xiéshǒu〈动〉**1**（牵手）be hand in hand: ～并进/同行 go forward hand in hand **2**（合作）cooperate

鲑（鮭）xié

〈名〉〈旧〉fish dish ▸guī

鞋 xié

〈名〉shoe: 一双～ a pair of shoes ‖ 我穿9号的～。I take size nine shoes. ▸便～，凉～
【鞋拔子】xiébázi〈名〉shoehorn
【鞋帮】xiébāng〈名〉shoe upper
【鞋带】xiédài〈名〉shoelace; shoestring〈美〉: 系～ do up one's shoelaces
【鞋底】xiédǐ〈名〉sole: ～磨薄了。The soles are wearing thin.
【鞋店】xiédiàn〈名〉shoe shop
【鞋垫】xiédiàn〈名〉insole
【鞋跟】xiégēn〈名〉heel
【鞋匠】xiéjiang〈名〉cobbler
【鞋面】xiémiàn〈名〉instep
【鞋刷】xiéshuā〈名〉shoe brush
【鞋楦】xiéxuàn〈名〉shoe tree
【鞋样】xiéyàng〈名〉shoe pattern
【鞋印】xiéyìn〈名〉footprint
【鞋油】xiéyóu〈名〉shoe polish: 上～ apply shoe polish ‖ 黑色～ black polish
【鞋子】xiézi〈名〉shoe

撷（擷）xié

〈动〉〈书〉pick: ▸～取，采～
【撷长补短】xiécháng-bǔduǎn〈成〉learn from others' strong points to offset one's weaknesses
【撷取】xiéqǔ〈动〉pick: ～精华 select the best
【撷英】xiéyīng〈动〉〈书〉select the best

勰 xié

〈形〉〈书〉harmonious

xiě

写（寫）xiě

〈动〉**1**（画）draw: ▸～生，～真 **2**（书写）write: ～得一手好字 write a good hand ‖ 用钢笔/铅笔～

write with a pen/pencil ‖ 牌子上～着"请勿入内。" The sign says, 'No entry.' ▸默～, 书～, 听～ 3 (创作) compose: ～诗/文章 write a poem/an article ‖ ～作文 write a composition 4 (描写) describe: ～得很生动 give a vivid description ▸～景, ～实
▸xiè

【写本】xiěběn〈名〉handwritten copy

【写法】xiěfǎ〈名〉1 (写作方法) writing method: 文章的～很多。There are various approaches to writing articles. 2 (书写方法) way of writing characters: 这个字的～不对。This character has been written wrongly.

【写稿】xiěgǎo〈动〉1 (打草稿) draw up: 写个初稿 draw up a draft ‖ 写个演说稿 draft a speech 2 (写文章) write: 她经常给科普刊物～。She is a regular contributor to popular science magazines.

【写景】xiějǐng〈动〉describe the scenery

【写生】xiěshēng〈动〉sketch from life: 去户外～ go outdoors to draw from nature ‖ 静物～ still life drawing ‖ 人物～ still life portrait

【写生画】xiěshēnghuà〈名〉life drawing

【写实】xiěshí〈动〉write/paint realistically: ～手法 skill of writing realistically ‖ ～主义 realism

【写手】xiěshǒu ▸p. 966〈名〉writer: 网络～ writer for the Internet ‖ 青春小说～中的领军人物 a leading figure amongst writers of youth fiction

【写意】xiěyì〈名〉freehand brushwork: ～画 painting of freehand brushwork
▸xièyì

【写照】xiězhào A〈动〉portray: 传神～ give a vivid and lifelike portrayal B〈名〉portrayal: 真实的～ realistic portrayal

【写真】xiězhēn A〈动〉draw a portrait B〈名〉1 (指人像) portrait 2 (指描绘) faithful representation: ～之言 accurately descriptive words

【写真集】xiězhēnjí〈名〉photo album

【写字】xiězì〈动〉write: 学习～ learn to write

【写字间】xiězìjiān〈名〉〈方〉office

【写字楼】xiězìlóu〈名〉office building

【写字台】xiězìtái〈名〉writing desk

【写作】xiězuò〈动〉write: 从事～ take up writing as one's career ‖ ～技巧 writing techniques ‖ ～能力 writing ability ‖ ～班子 writing group

血 xiě〈名〉〈口〉blood: 流了好多～ bleed profusely ‖ ～的教训 lesson paid for in blood
▸xuè

【血糊糊】xiěhūhū〈形〉bloody: ～的伤口 bloody wound

【血淋淋】xiělínlín〈形〉1 (形容血流不断) bleeding: ～的尸体 bleeding body 2 (严酷) bloody: ～的教训 bitter lesson ‖ ～的事实 harsh fact

【血丝】xiěsī〈名〉trace of blood: 她的双眼布满了～。Her eyes were netted with little veins.

【血晕】xiěyùn〈名〉bruise
▸xuèyùn

xiè

写(寫) xiè
▸xiě

【写意】xièyì〈形〉〈方〉comfortable
▸xiěyì

灺(炧) xiè〈名〉〈书〉remaining ash or end of a candle or incense

泄(洩) xiè〈动〉1 (排出) let out: ▸～洪, 排～, 水～不通 2 (发泄) vent: ～私愤 give vent to one's personal spite ▸～恨, 发～ 3 (泄露) leak: ▸～露, ～密 4 (失去) lose: ▸～劲, ～气

【泄底】xièdǐ〈动〉reveal the inside story: 此事万万不可～。None of this must ever come out.

【泄愤】xièfèn〈动〉give vent to one's resentment: 你没必要拿我～。There's no need to vent your anger on me.

【泄恨】xièhèn = 泄愤 xièfèn

【泄洪】xièhóng〈动〉discharge a flood: 开闸～ open a sluice to release a flood

【泄洪闸门】xièhóng zhámén〈名〉floodgate

【泄劲】xièjìn〈动〉lose heart: 继续干, 别～。Keep going, don't lose heart.

【泄漏】xièlòu〈动〉1 (漏出) leak: 煤气～ gas leak 2 = 泄露 xièlòu

【泄露】xièlòu〈动〉disclose: ～国家机密 disclose a state secret ‖ ～消息 leak information ‖ 秘密已～出去了。The secret has slipped out.

【泄密】xièmì〈动〉divulge a secret: ～事件 leakage of a secret

【泄怒】xiènù〈动〉vent one's anger/rage (on sb.)

【泄气】xièqì A〈动〉lose heart: 不要～。Don't lose heart. ‖ 他虽然不断失败, 但并未～。After repeated failures, he was not in the least discouraged. B〈形〉pathetic: 这点小事你都干不了, 你也太～了。It's rather pathetic that you haven't managed to do even this small thing.

【泄水】xièshuǐ〈动〉sluice: ～工程 outlet works

【泄水阀】xièshuǐfá〈名〉sluice valve

【泄水闸】xièshuǐzhá〈名〉sluice gate

【泄欲】xièyù〈动〉gratify one's sexual desire

【泄殖腔】xièzhíqiāng〈名〉[动物] cloaca

泻(瀉) xiè〈动〉1 (快速地流) pour out: ▸流～, 倾～, 一～千里 2 (腹泻) have loose bowels: ▸～药, 上吐下～

【泻肚】xièdù〈动〉〈口〉have diarrhoea

【泻火】xièhuǒ〈动〉purge excessive internal heat

【泻药】xièyào〈名〉laxative

绁(紲) xiè〈书〉
A〈名〉rope: ▸缧～
B〈动〉tie

卸 xiè〈动〉1 (除下) unhitch: ～鞍 unsaddle ‖ ～牲口 untie a draught animal ▸～磨杀驴 2 (搬下来) unload: ～担子 lay down a burden ‖ 把这车砖～下来 unload the bricks from the truck ‖ ～船 unload a ship 3 (拆下来) disassemble: ～零件 disassemble the parts ‖ ～螺丝 remove a screw ▸拆～ 4 (解除) get rid of: ▸～任, ～责, 推～ 5 (取下来) remove: 把门从铰链上～下来 take the door off its hinges ▸～肩, ～妆

【卸包袱】xiè bāofu〈惯〉relieve oneself of a burden

【卸车】xièchē〈动〉unload a vehicle

【卸货】xièhuò〈动〉unload: 这条船正在～。The ship is being discharged of its cargo.

【卸肩】xièjiān〈动〉1 (放下肩头的东西) put down one's load 2〈喻〉(推卸责任) shirk one's responsibilities 3〈喻〉(辞职) resign

【卸磨杀驴】xièmò-shālǘ〈成〉〈喻〉get rid of sb. as soon as he outlives his usefulness

【卸任】xièrèn〈动〉leave office

【卸载】xièzài〈动〉1 (卸货) unload cargo 2 [计算机] uninstall: ～软件 uninstall a software

【卸责】xièzé〈动〉〈书〉shirk a responsibility: 推诿～ shirk the responsibility and shift it onto others

【卸职】xièzhí〈动〉leave office

【卸妆】xièzhuāng〈动〉[of a woman] remove one's make-up and dress

【卸装】xièzhuāng〈动〉remove one's stage make-up and costume

屑 xiè
A〈名〉scraps: 金属～ metal filings ‖ 面包～ breadcrumbs ‖ 木～ wood shavings ‖ 纸～ scraps of paper
B〈形〉trivial: ～～小事 trifling matter ▸琐～
C〈动〉consider worthwhile: ▸不～一顾

械 xiè〈名〉1〈书〉(刑具) shackles 2 (工具) tool: ▸机～, 器～ 3 (武器) weapon: ▸～斗, 缴～, 枪～

【械斗】xièdòu〈动〉fight with improvised weapons

亵(褻) xiè
A〈动〉〈书〉treat with irreverence: ～宠 favour sb. irreverently ▸～渎, ～慢
B〈形〉obscene: ～语 obscene language ▸猥～

【亵渎】xièdú〈动〉blaspheme: ～纪念碑 desecrate a monument ‖ ～神明 blaspheme the gods

【亵慢】xièmàn〈动〉〈书〉slight

渫 xiè〈动〉〈书〉1 (除去) get rid of 2 (疏通) dredge

谢(謝) xiè〈动〉1 (拒绝) decline: ▸～绝, 辞～, ～客 2 (辞别) depart: ▸～世 3 (凋落) wither: 花～了。The flowers have withered away. ▸凋～, 萎～ 4 (认错) excuse oneself: ▸～罪 5 (感谢) thank: 别～我, ～那些帮过忙的人。Don't thank me. Thank everyone who helped. ‖ 代我～～他。Thank him for me, please. ‖ 这件事你得～他才是。You have him to thank for it. ▸～幕, ～意

【谢忱】xièchén〈名〉〈书〉gratitude: 聊表～ express one's gratitude

【谢词】xiècí〈名〉thank-you speech

【谢辞】xiècí = 谢词 xiècí

【谢顶】xièdǐng〈动〉go bald: 他～了。He is getting thin on top.

【谢恩】xiè'ēn〈动〉reciprocate sb.'s kindness: 你救了这个孩子的命, 他今天特地赶来～。The boy has come specially to thank you for saving his life.

【谢过】xièguò〈动〉〈书〉apologize for a wrongdoing

【谢绝】xièjué〈动〉decline: ～帮助 decline sb.'s help ‖ 婉言～ decline with thanks

【谢客】xièkè〈动〉refuse to meet visitors: ▸闭门～

【谢礼】xièlǐ〈名〉1（指礼物） gift presented in gratitude 2（酬劳） honorarium
【谢幕】xièmù〈动〉 take a curtain call: 全体演员列队～。 The whole cast took a curtain call.
【谢却】xièquè〈动〉decline: ～邀请 decline an invitation
【谢世】xièshì ▸p. 772〈动〉〈书〉〈婉〉 pass away: 他于去年～。 He passed away last year.
【谢天谢地】xiètiān-xièdì〈成〉 thank heaven(s), praise the Lord: ～，你找到了我丢失的钥匙。 Thank goodness you found the key I lost.
【谢谢】xièxie ▸p. 236〈动〉 thank you: ～您的礼物 thank you for the present ‖ （向某人）道声～ say thank you (to sb.)
【谢意】xièyì〈名〉gratitude: 表示～ express one's gratitude ‖ 转达～ convey thanks
【谢罪】xièzuì〈动〉 apologize for an offence: 登门～ call on sb. to make an apology

塮 xiè〈名〉〈方〉 barnyard manure

解[1] xiè〈动〉〈口〉 get the point: 我就是～不开这个理。 I just couldn't see the point.

解[2] xiè〈名〉〈旧〉 acrobatic skills [esp those on horseback]
▸jiě, jiè
【解数】xièshù〈名〉1（武术招数） *wushu* movement 2（手段） skill: 使出浑身～ use all one's skills

榭 xiè〈名〉 pavilion built on a terrace: ▸舞～歌台

榍 xiè
【榍石】xièshí〈名〉［矿业］ titanite

薤 xiè〈名〉［植物］ Chinese onion

嶰 xiè〈名〉〈书〉 mountain brook: ～壑 deep ravine

獬 xiè
【獬豸】xièzhì〈名〉〈古〉 legendary one-horned beast

邂 xiè
【邂逅】xièhòu〈动〉〈书〉 encounter: ～一位著名学者 encounter a famous scholar ‖ 一次～ a chance meeting

廨 xiè〈动〉〈古〉 government office

澥 xiè〈动〉1（由稠变稀） thin down: 粥～了。 The porridge has lost its glueyness. 2〈方〉（使由稠变稀） cause to thin down: 把糨糊～一～再用。 Add water to the paste before using it.

懈 xiè〈形〉 slack: ▸松～, 无～可击
【懈怠】xièdài〈形〉 slack: 对工作从不～ never be slack about one's work
【懈气】xièqì〈动〉 slack off

燮 xiè〈动〉〈书〉 harmonize: ～理阴阳 harmonize *yin* and *yang*

蟹 xiè〈名〉 crab: ▸虾兵～将
【蟹粉】xièfěn〈名〉〈方〉 minced crab meat
【蟹黄】xièhuáng〈名〉 golden crab-spawn
【蟹獴】xièměng〈名〉［动物］ crab-eating mongoose
【蟹青】xièqīng〈名〉 greenish-grey
【蟹状星云】Xièzhuàng Xīngyún〈名〉［天文］ Crab Nebula

瀣 xiè ▸沆瀣 hàngxiè

躞 xiè
【躞蹀】xièdié = 蹀躞 diéxiè

xīn

心 xīn〈名〉1（心脏） heart: 他的～跳得很快。 His heart was beating fast. 2（大脑） mind: 眼不见，～不烦。 Out of sight, out of mind. 3（思想） thought: 定下～来 compose one's thoughts ‖ 赢得某人的～ win sb.'s heart ‖ 爱国之～ patriotic feelings ▸～烦意乱, ～情, 谈～ 4（图谋） intention: 出于好～ be well-meant ‖ 一～想留下 have every intention to stay 5（心地） heart: 好～人 kind-hearted person ‖ 人老～不老 be young at heart 6（中央） centre: 莴苣～ heart of a lettuce ▸重～, 核～, 圆～ 7（指星宿） one of the 28 constellations in ancient Chinese astronomy
【心爱】xīn'ài〈动〉 be beloved: ～的礼物 treasured gift ‖ ～的妻子 beloved wife
【心安理得】xīn'ān-lǐdé〈成〉 have an easy conscience: 如果你没做错什么，就应该～。 You should have a clear conscience if you didn't do anything wrong.
【心包】xīnbāo〈名〉［生理］ pericardium
【心包炎】xīnbāoyán ▸p. 50〈名〉［医学］ pericarditis
【心病】xīnbìng〈名〉1（指心情） anxiety: ～还需心药治。 Worry is only cured by heartening news. 2（指隐情） sore point: 不幸的婚姻成了她的～。 Her unhappy marriage is rather a sore point with her.
【心不在焉】xīnbùzàiyān〈成〉 absent-minded: 上课时～ be absent-minded in class
【心材】xīncái〈名〉［林业］ heartwood
【心裁】xīncái〈名〉 idea: ▸别出～
【心长力短】xīncháng-lìduǎn〈成〉 the heart holds the desire but the body is unable to fulfil it
【心肠】xīncháng〈名〉1（心地） heart: ～好 have a kind heart ‖ ～坏 have evil intentions 2（感情状态） state of mind, heart: ～软 be soft-hearted ‖ 妇人～ womanly heart ▸铁石～ 3（兴致） state of mind: 没有～去跳舞 be not in the mood to go dancing
【心潮】xīncháo〈名〉〈喻〉 surging thoughts and emotions: ～起伏 one's heart seems to rise and fall like waves
【心潮澎湃】xīncháo-péngpài〈成〉 be full of all kinds of thoughts and emotions
【心诚则灵】xīnchéngzélíng〈俗〉 sincerity works miracles
【心驰神往】xīnchí-shénwǎng〈成〉 have a deep longing for: 这就是我～的地方。 This is the place I've long hoped to visit.
【心传】xīnchuán A〈动〉［佛教］ pass from mind to mind B〈名〉 theory passed on from generation to generation
【心慈手软】xīncí-shǒuruǎn〈成〉 merciful: 对犯罪分子不能～。 We should not be soft on criminals.
【心粗气浮】xīncū-qìfú〈成〉 be hot-headed
【心存芥蒂】xīncúnjièdì〈成〉 bear a grudge
【心胆】xīndǎn〈名〉1（心和胆） heart and gall 2（意志和胆量） will and courage: 吓得～俱裂 frighten the life out of sb.
【心荡神摇】xīndàng-shényáo〈成〉 be in a confused mind
【心得】xīndé〈名〉 perception: 交换～ exchange perceptions ‖ 学习～ knowledge gained by study
【心底】xīndǐ〈名〉 bottom of one's heart: 她们的感激是发自～的。 Their gratitude came from the heart.
【心地】xīndì〈名〉1（内心） heart: ～纯洁 be pure at heart ‖ ～善良 be kind-hearted 2（心情） state of mind: ～轻松 be in light-hearted spirits
【心电图】xīndiàntú〈名〉electrocardiogram (ECG)
【心动】xīndòng A〈名〉 heartbeat: ～过缓 bradycardia ‖ ～过速 tachycardia B = 动心 dòngxīn
【心动图】xīndòngtú〈名〉［医学］ cardiogram
【心烦】xīnfán〈动〉 feel troubled: 这事真让人～。 This is really annoying. ‖ 你扰得我～。 You're getting on my nerves.
【心烦意乱】xīnfán-yìluàn〈成〉 be terribly upset: 他这阵子～。 He's got a lot on his mind at the moment.
【心房】xīnfáng〈名〉1［生理］ atrium: 右/左～ right/left atrium 2（内心） heart: 暖人～的话语 heart-warming remarks
【心扉】xīnfēi〈名〉〈书〉 heart of hearts: 敞开～ open one's heart ‖ 叩人～ tug at sb.'s heartstrings
【心服】xīnfú〈动〉 be genuinely convinced
【心服口服】xīnfú-kǒufú〈成〉 be utterly convinced: 他输得～。 He conceded defeat from the bottom of his heart.
【心浮气躁】xīnfú-qìzào〈成〉 flighty and impetuous: ～终将一事无成。 If you're impulsive, you'll accomplish nothing.
【心腹】xīnfù〈名〉1（心里头） confidence: ～朋友 confidant ‖ 说～话 confide in sb. 2（亲信的人） trustworthy person: 他是我的～之一。 He is one of my most trusted men.
【心腹之患】xīnfùzhīhuàn〈成〉 serious hidden danger: 除掉～ get rid of the thorn in one's side
【心腹之交】xīnfùzhījiāo〈成〉 bosom friend
【心甘】xīngān〈动〉 be willing: 死了也～ be prepared to die
【心甘情愿】xīngān-qíngyuàn〈成〉 be only too glad: 母亲为孩子做什么都～。 The mother is only too glad to do anything for her child.
【心肝】xīngān〈名〉1（良心） conscience: 没～ have no conscience 2（亲爱的人） darling: ～宝贝 one's sweetheart
【心高气傲】xīngāo-qì'ào〈成〉 ambitious and arrogant: ～的年轻人 young person with all sorts of airs and graces
【心梗】xīngěng〈简称〉= 心肌梗死
【心广体胖】xīnguǎng-tǐpán〈成〉 be carefree and contented: 他～。 He is fit and happy.
【心寒】xīnhán〈形〉1（失望） bitterly disappointed: 令人～ strike a chill into sb.'s heart 2（害怕） frightened: 胆战～ be scared out of one's wits
【心黑】xīnhēi〈形〉1（歹毒） vicious: 他的心可真黑呀。 He is really cruel. 2（贪心） greedy: 别那么～。 Don't be so greedy.
【心狠手辣】xīnhěn-shǒulà〈成〉 wicked

X

and merciless

【心花怒放】xīnhuā-nùfàng〈成〉 be beside oneself with joy: 听到这个消息，她～。She was overjoyed at the news.

【心怀】xīnhuái **A**〈动〉 harbour: ～不轨 harbour evil intentions ‖ 对老板～不满 harbour a grievance against the boss **B**〈名〉 **1**（心意） feeling: 抒发～ express one's feelings **2**（胸怀） nature: ～广阔 be broad-minded ‖ ～坦荡 be open-hearted

【心怀二意】xīnhuái'èryì〈成〉 harbour disloyal sentiments

【心怀鬼胎】xīnhuáiguǐtāi〈成〉 have sinister motives

【心怀叵测】xīnhuáipǒcè〈成〉 harbour sinister designs

【心慌】xīnhuāng **A**〈形〉（心里慌乱） flustered: 面试时我很～。 I was very nervous during the interview. **B**〈方〉= 心悸 xīnjì 1

【心慌意乱】xīnhuāng-yìluàn〈成〉 be confused and agitated

【心灰意懒】xīnhuī-yìlǎn〈成〉 be disheartened: 因～而放弃 feel disheartened and give up

【心灰意冷】xīnhuī-yìlěng = 心灰意懒 xīnhuī-yìlǎn

【心回意转】xīnhuí-yìzhuǎn = 回心转意 huíxīn-zhuǎnyì

【心火】xīnhuǒ〈名〉 **1**［中医］ internal heat: ～亢盛 excessive heart fire **2**（指怒气） hidden anger: 强按～ suppress one's anger

【心机】xīnjī〈名〉 thinking, scheming: 费尽～ rack one's brains ‖ 枉费～ rack one's brains in vain

【心肌】xīnjī〈名〉［生理］ myocardium: ～炎 myocarditis

【心肌梗死】xīnjī gěngsǐ〈名〉 myocardial infarction

【心急】xīnjí〈形〉 impatient: 这事不能～。You can't be impatient about it.

【心急火燎】xīnjí-huǒliǎo = 心急如焚 xīnjí-rúfén

【心急如焚】xīnjí-rúfén〈成〉 burn with impatience

【心计】xīnjì〈名〉 calculation: 很有～ be very calculating ▸工于～

【心迹】xīnjì〈名〉 true state of mind: 表明～ reveal one's true feelings

【心悸】xīnjì〈动〉 **1**（心跳加速） palpitate: 我跑得太快时就～。 I get palpitations if I run too fast. **2**〈书〉（害怕） be scared: 一想到要见上司我就～。 The prospect of meeting the boss is quite daunting.

【心尖】xīnjiān〈名〉 **1**［生理］ apex of the heart **2**（内心深处） bottom of one's heart **3**〈方〉（指人） sweetheart

【心间】xīnjiān〈名〉 mind: 记在～ bear in mind

【心骄气傲】xīnjiāo-qì'ào〈成〉arrogant and haughty

【心焦】xīnjiāo〈形〉 anxious: 为儿子的病～ worry about one's son's illness

【心绞痛】xīnjiǎotòng ▸p. 50〈名〉［医学］ angina pectoris

【心结】xīnjié〈名〉 complex

【心劲】xīnjìn〈名〉 **1**（想法） idea: 一个～搞研发 be of one mind in doing research and development ‖ 我妻子很对我的～。 My wife is a woman after my own heart. **2**（分析思考的能力） brains: 有～ to be analytical **3**（心气儿） spirit: ～儿十足 be enthusiastic ‖ 我对这个工作没～儿。 My heart is not in this job.

【心惊胆战】xīnjīng-dǎnzhàn〈成〉 tremble with fear: 令人～的噩梦 heart-stopping nightmare

【心惊肉跳】xīnjīng-ròutiào〈成〉 quake with terror

【心静】xīnjìng〈形〉 calm: ～神凝 keep calm with rapt attention ‖ ～的人 calm person ‖ ～自然凉。 A tranquil mind helps one to remain cool in the heat.

【心境】xīnjìng〈名〉 mood: ～极佳 in high spirits

【心坎】xīnkǎn〈名〉 **1** = 心口 xīnkǒu **2**（心灵深处） bottom of one's heart: 从～里佩服 stand in deep admiration ‖ 这话说到我～上了。 These words express perfectly what is in my heart.

【心口】xīnkǒu〈名〉 pit of the stomach: ～痛 have a pain in one's chest ‖ 把手放在～上 put one's hand on one's heart

【心口不一】xīnkǒu-bùyī〈成〉 say sth. different from what one thinks

【心口如一】xīnkǒu-rúyī〈成〉 speak one's mind: 他～。 His words are in complete accord with his thoughts.

【心宽】xīnkuān〈形〉 **1**（思想开放） open-minded **2**（心胸开阔） carefree

【心宽体胖】xīnkuān-tǐpán = 心广体胖 xīnguǎng-tǐpán

【心旷神怡】xīnkuàng-shényí〈成〉 carefree and happy: 一幅令人～的景象 a sight to gladden the heart

【心劳日拙】xīnláo-rìzhuō〈成〉 rack one's brains only to worsen the situation

【心理】xīnlǐ〈名〉 psychology: 理解学生的～ understand the students' psychology ‖ ～不平衡 mental instability ‖ ～健康 mental health ‖ ～压力 psychological pressure ‖ 逆反～ antagonistic psychology

【心理变态】xīnlǐ biàntài〈名〉 psychopathy

【心理分析】xīnlǐ fēnxī〈名〉 psychoanalysis: ～家 psychoanalyst

【心理活动】xīnlǐ huódòng〈名〉 mental activity

【心理矫正】xīnlǐ jiǎozhèng〈名〉 psychiatric correction

【心理年龄】xīnlǐ niánlíng〈名〉 mental age

【心理缺陷】xīnlǐ quēxiàn〈名〉 mental deficiency

【心理素质】xīnlǐ sùzhì〈名〉 psychological quality

【心理卫生】xīnlǐ wèishēng〈名〉 orthopsychiatry

【心理学】xīnlǐxué〈名〉 psychology: ～家 psychologist ‖ 普通～ general psychology

【心理医生】xīnlǐ yīshēng〈名〉 psychotherapist

【心理语言学】xīnlǐ yǔyánxué〈名〉 psycholinguistics

【心理战】xīnlǐzhàn〈名〉 psychological warfare

【心理障碍】xīnlǐ zhàng'ài〈名〉 psychological disorder

【心理咨询】xīnlǐ zīxún〈名〉 psychiatric consulting

【心里】xīnli〈名〉 **1**（胸口内部） chest: ～堵得慌 feel a tightness in the chest **2**（思想里） heart: ～明白 be clear in one's mind ‖ ～有数 know in one's heart ‖ 记在～ bear sth. in mind ‖ 你～有我吗? Is there a place for me in your heart?

【心里话】xīnlihuà〈名〉innermost thoughts and feelings: 说～ open one's heart ‖ 说～，我不喜欢他。 To be honest, I don't like him.

【心力】xīnlì〈名〉mental and physical effort: 费尽～ make strenuous efforts

【心力交瘁】xīnlì-jiāocuì〈成〉 be mentally and physically exhausted: 使人～ sap sb.'s energy and spirit

【心连心】xīnliánxīn〈惯〉 heart linked to heart: 全国人民～。 The hearts of the people across the country are all connected.

【心灵】xīnlíng〈名〉 heart: ～纯洁 have a pure heart ‖ ～高尚 have a noble mind ‖ ～创伤 psychological wound ‖ 眼睛是～的窗户。 The eyes are the window of the soul.

【心灵感应】xīnlíng gǎnyìng〈名〉 telepathy

【心灵美】xīnlíngměi〈动〉 have a noble heart

【心灵手巧】xīnlíng-shǒuqiǎo〈成〉 be clever and deft: 她真是～。 She is clever with her hands.

【心领】xīnlǐng〈动〉 **1**（理解） understand: ▸～神会 **2**〈套〉（用于谢绝馈赠） [used to appreciate sb.'s kind offer but have to decline]: 你的好意我～了。 I appreciate your kindness but must decline the offer.

【心领神会】xīnlǐng-shénhuì〈成〉 understand tacitly: 他对我们的暗示已～。 Our hints were not lost on him.

【心路】xīnlù〈名〉 **1**（心机） intelligence: 有～ have brains ‖ 斗～ fight a battle of wits **2**（气量） tolerance: ～窄 be narrow-minded **3**（居心） intention: ～不正 have bad intentions **4**（心思） thought: 这话说到我～上了。 The words touched the very core of my heart. **5**（心理变化过程） mental process: 她经历了一段从失落到重新找回自我价值的～历程。 She has been on a journey that has seen her come from feeling abandoned to regaining her self-esteem.

【心律】xīnlǜ〈名〉 heart rate: ～不齐 irregular heartbeat ‖ ～失常 arrhythmia

【心率】xīnlǜ〈名〉 heart rate: ～快 tachycardia

【心乱如麻】xīnluàn-rúmá〈成〉 be completely confused and disconcerted: 此时我～。 Disturbing thoughts are crowding my mind at the moment.

【心满意足】xīnmǎn-yìzú〈成〉 be perfectly content: 有了这份工作她就觉得～了。 Being offered the job gave her a tremendous sense of fulfilment.

【心明如镜】xīnmíng-rújìng〈成〉〈喻〉 be clear-headed

【心明眼亮】xīnmíng-yǎnliàng〈成〉see and think clearly: ～的读者肯定注意到了这幅照片名称搞错了。 Discerning readers would have noticed that the photograph was wrongly captioned.

【心目】xīnmù〈名〉 **1**（指感受） mood: 以娱～ amuse oneself **2**（思想） mind: 她在你～中如何? What is she to you?

【心平气和】xīnpíng-qìhé〈成〉 be even-tempered and good-humoured: ～地交换意见 exchange views calmly

【心魄】xīnpò〈名〉〈书〉 soul: 动人～ soul-stirring

【心气】xīnqì〈名〉 **1**（想法） intention: ～相通 be of the same mind **2**（志气） ambition: ～高 have lofty aspirations **3**（心情） mood: ～不顺 be in a bad mood **4**（气量） breadth of mind: ～窄 be narrow-minded

【心窍】xīnqiào〈名〉 capacity for clear thinking: 财迷～ be obsessed by a lust for money ‖ 他的一番话让我开了～。 His words cleared up my thinking.

【心切】xīnqiè〈形〉 eager: 回国～ can't wait to return to one's country ‖ 求胜～ be anxious to succeed

【心情】xīnqíng〈名〉 frame of mind: ～不

X

佳 be in a bad mood ‖ ～沉重 have a heavy heart ‖ ～复杂 have mixed feelings ‖ ～舒畅 enjoy ease of mind

【心曲】xīnqū〈名〉〈书〉1（内心）innermost being: 乱我～ disturb my peace of mind 2（心事）something weighing on one's mind: 畅叙～ pour out one's secret concern

【心如刀割】xīnrúdāogē〈成〉 feel as if a knife were piercing one's heart: 她悲痛得～。 Her heart is broken with grief. ‖ 儿子得了绝症，母亲～。 Her son's incurable disease was a dagger to the mother's heart.

【心如刀绞】xīnrúdāojiǎo = 心如刀割 xīnrúdāogē

【心如死灰】xīnrúsǐhuī〈成〉〈喻〉 lose heart completely

【心如铁石】xīnrútiěshí〈成〉 be hard-hearted

【心如止水】xīnrúzhǐshuǐ〈成〉 remain unmoved by the circumstances and stick to one's conviction

【心软】xīnruǎn〈形〉 soft-hearted: 对犯罪分子不能～。 We should not be soft on criminals. ‖ 他再三恳求，于是她～了。 She was moved to pity by his repeated imploring.

【心上人】xīnshàngrén〈名〉 beloved: 有了～ have a beloved one

【心上】xīnshang〈名〉 heart: 别把这事放在～。 Don't take it to heart.

【心神】xīnshén〈名〉1（心思精力）effort: 极耗～ be very taxing on sb.'s mind 2（精神状态） frame of mind: ～烦乱 be irritable

【心神不定】xīnshén-bùdìng〈成〉 feel unsettled: 显得～的样子 look restless

【心神不宁】xīnshén-bùníng = 心神不定 xīnshén-bùdìng

【心生一计】xīnshēngyījì〈成〉 hit upon an idea

【心声】xīnshēng〈名〉 innermost feelings: 表达～ speak out one's mind ‖ 反映人民的～ represent the true voice of the people

【心盛】xīnshèng〈动〉 be enthusiastic and energetic: 年轻～ be young and ambitious

【心事】xīnshì〈名〉 weight on one's mind: 了却一桩～ take a load off one's mind ‖ ～重重 be laden with anxiety

【心室】xīnshì〈名〉［生理］ ventricle: ～肥大 ventricular hypertrophy ‖ 左/右～ left/right ventricle

【心术】xīnshù〈名〉1（心思） design: ～不正 harbour evil intentions 2 = 心数 xīnshù

【心数】xīnshù〈名〉 scheming: 有～的人 calculating person

【心思】xīnsi〈名〉1（念头） thought: 猜不透他的～ cannot figure out what he is thinking about ‖ 她的～在别的事情上。 Her mind is elsewhere. 2（脑筋） thinking: 白费～ rack one's brains in vain ‖ 挖空～ rack one's brains ‖ 用～ think hard 3（心情） mood: 没有～读书 be in no mood to study ‖ 我现在没有～跟你开玩笑。 I am in no mood to joke with you right now.

【心酸】xīnsuān〈形〉 sad: 令人～的故事 heart-rending story

【心算】xīnsuàn〈名〉 mental arithmetic: 进行快速～ do a rapid mental calculation

【心碎】xīnsuì〈动〉 be heartbroken: 令人～的信 heart-rending letter

【心态】xīntài〈名〉 psychology: 理解国民的～ understand the mentality of the nation ‖ ～不平衡 feel hard done by

【心疼】xīnténg〈动〉1（疼爱）love dearly: ～孩子 show loving care for a child 2（怜惜） feel sorry: 她伤得很厉害，我们很～。 We felt sorry about her terrible injury. 3（舍不得） grudge: 我并不是～钱，只是觉得买这东西没多大用。 I'm not unwilling to spend money on it but I don't think it useful.

【心田】xīntián〈名〉〈书〉 heart: 暖人～的话语 heart-warming words

【心跳】xīntiào〈动〉 palpitate: ～停了一下 one's heart skipped a beat ‖ 病人的～很快。 The patient's heart is beating fast.

【心痛】xīntòng A〈动〉 feel sad: 令人～的消息 heart-rending news B ▸p. 50〈名〉 cardiac pain

【心头】xīntóu〈名〉 mind: 记在～ keep sth. in mind ‖ 往事涌上～ past memories flood back ‖ ～之恨 rankling hatred

【心头肉】xīntóuròu〈名〉〈喻〉 favourite: 她是妈妈的～。 She is her mother's pet.

【心窝儿】xīnwōr〈名〉1（心脏部位） precordium 2（内心） heart of hearts: 他的话句句说到了我的～里。 All his words were after my own heart.

【心无二用】xīnwú'èryòng〈成〉 one should concentrate on one thing at a time

【心细】xīnxì〈形〉 careful: 胆大～ bold but cautious ‖ 做任何事都极为～ do everything with the utmost care

【心弦】xīnxián〈名〉 heartstrings: 动人～ pull at sb.'s heartstrings ▸扣人～

【心想】xīnxiǎng〈动〉 think: 祝你～事成! May all your wishes come true!

【心心念念】xīnxīn-niànniàn〈成〉 set one's heart on: ～想当影星 dream of becoming a film star

【心心相印】xīnxīn-xiāngyìn〈成〉 be of the same mind: 小两口～，情投意合。 The young couple are of the same mind and disposition.

【心性】xīnxìng〈名〉 disposition: 陶冶～ cultivate the mind ‖ ～开朗 be of a cheerful disposition

【心胸】xīnxiōng〈名〉1（内心深处）heart of hearts: ～无忧 be free of worries 2（胸怀） breadth of mind: ～豁达/开阔 be broad-minded ‖ ～狭窄 be narrow-minded 3（抱负） aspiration: 有～ be very ambitious

【心秀】xīnxiù〈形〉 intelligent in unspoken ways

【心虚】xīnxū〈形〉1（指怕人知道） uneasy: 没做错什么，你～什么? Why are you feeling guilty if you have done nothing wrong? ▸做贼～ 2（缺少自信） diffident: 第一次求职面试时，我多多少少有些～。 I felt somewhat diffident when I had the first interview.

【心绪】xīnxù〈名〉〈书〉 state of mind: ～烦乱 be in an emotional turmoil ‖ ～不宁 feel unsettled

【心血】xīnxuè〈名〉 painstaking care: 花费很多～ take great pains ‖ ～的结晶 the fruit of one's painstaking work

【心血管】xīnxuèguǎn〈名〉heart and blood vessels: ～病 cardiovascular disease

【心血来潮】xīnxuè-láicháo〈成〉 be seized by a whim: ～想做某事 feel a sudden urge to do sth.

【心眼儿】xīnyǎnr〈名〉1（内心） heart: 一个～为国家 devote oneself heart and soul to one's country ‖ 他打～里喜欢这个孩子。 His heart was with this child. 2（心地） intention: 没安好～ be up to no good ‖ ～好 be kind-hearted 3（思维能力） intelligence: 缺～ be slow-witted ‖ 有～ have brains ▸要～ 4（不必要的疑虑） unfounded doubts: ～太多 have too many unnecessary misgivings 5（气量） tolerance: ～小 be petty-minded ‖ ～窄 be narrow-minded

【心痒】xīnyǎng〈动〉 itch to do sth.

【心仪】xīnyí〈动〉〈书〉 admire: （对某人）～已久 have long had a high regard (for sb.)

【心疑】xīnyí〈动〉1（猜测） suspect: 我～是他泄了密。 I suspected him of leaking the secret. 2（不相信） doubt: 她～他的能力。 She doubted his ability.

【心意】xīnyì〈名〉1（情意） regard: 一番/点/片～ a token of one's regard ‖ 表示～ express one's good will 2（意思） intention: 合大众的～ strike the popular fancy ‖ 他这人正合我的～。 He is a man after my own heart.

【心音】xīnyīn〈名〉1［生理］ cardiac sound: ～减弱 weakening of a heart beat ‖ ～亢进 accentuation of a heart beat 2 = 心声 xīnshēng

【心硬】xīnyìng〈形〉 hard-hearted

【心有灵犀一点通】xīn yǒu língxī yī diǎn tōng〈成〉 no hint will be lost on a kindred spirit

【心有余而力不足】xīn yǒuyú ér lì bùzú〈成〉 one's ability falls short of one's ambition

【心有余悸】xīnyǒuyújì〈成〉 have a lingering fear

【心语】xīnyǔ〈名〉 words from the heart: 倾听一个少女的～ listen attentively to the words from a girl's heart

【心猿意马】xīnyuán-yìmǎ〈成〉 restless of heart: 学习时要聚精会神，不要～。 You should be focused when you study and not allow yourself to be distracted.

【心愿】xīnyuàn〈名〉 dream: 符合人民的～ accord with the will of the people ‖ 共同～ common aspiration

【心悦诚服】xīnyuè-chéngfú〈成〉 lend heartfelt support: 我们对他的观点～。 We're completely convinced of his view.

【心杂音】xīnzáyīn ▸p. 50〈名〉［医学］ heart murmur

【心脏】xīnzàng〈名〉1（指器官） heart: ～病 heart disease ‖ ～移植 heart transplant 2〈喻〉（中心） centre: ～地带 heartland ‖ 北京是祖国的～。 Beijing is the heart of the motherland.

【心脏起搏器】xīnzàng qǐbóqì〈名〉［医学］ cardiac pacemaker

【心脏衰竭】xīnzàng shuāijié ▸p. 50〈名〉 cardiac failure

【心窄】xīnzhǎi〈形〉 narrow-minded

【心照不宣】xīnzhào-bùxuān〈成〉 have a tacit understanding: 彼此～ have a tacit understanding with each other

【心直口快】xīnzhí-kǒukuài〈成〉 be frank and outspoken: ～的人 forthright and outspoken person

【心志】xīnzhì〈名〉 will: ～坚强/薄弱之人 man of strong/weak will

【心智】xīnzhì〈名〉1（智慧） intellect: 启迪～ sharpen sb.'s intellect 2（心理） mind: 陶冶～ cultivate sb.'s intelligence ‖ ～健康 be mentally healthy

【心中无数】xīnzhōng-wúshù〈俗〉 not be clear in one's mind: 能否实现，～ be unsure about whether or not it can be realized

【心中有数】xīnzhōng-yǒushù〈俗〉be clear in one's mind: 对自己的所作所为～ be clear in one's mind about what one is doing

【心重】xīnzhòng〈动〉 be oversensitive

【心子】xīnzi〈名〉 heart: 白菜～ heart of a

X

Chinese cabbage
【心醉】xīnzuì〈动〉 be enchanted: 令人～的歌声 enchanting song
【心醉神迷】xīnzuì-shénmí〈成〉be in ecstasies over sth.

芯 xīn
〈名〉 1（草木的中心） rush pith 2（某些物体的中心部分） wick: ▸灯～，笔～
▸xìn
【芯片】xīnpiàn〈名〉［电子］chip

辛 xīn
A〈形〉 1（辣） pungent: ▸～辣，含～茹苦 2（辛苦） hard: ▸～苦，艰～ 3（痛苦） sad: ▸～酸
B〈名〉 eighth of the ten Heavenly Stems (天干)
【辛迪加】xīndíjiā〈名〉［经济］syndicate
【辛亥革命】Xīnhài Gémìng〈名〉 the 1911 Revolution
【辛苦】xīnkǔ A〈形〉 laborious: ～的工作 hard work ‖ 别太～了。Don't overwork yourself. B〈动〉〈套〉 go to great trouble: 你～了，非常感谢。Thank you for all the trouble you've taken. ‖ 能不能～你跑一趟? May I trouble you to go and see about it?
【辛苦费】xīnkǔfèi〈名〉 service charge
【辛辣】xīnlà〈形〉 bitter: ～的食品 spicy food ‖〈喻〉～的讽刺 biting sarcasm
【辛劳】xīnláo〈形〉 painstaking: 不辞～ spare no pains ‖ 日夜～ toil day and night
【辛勤】xīnqín〈形〉 hardworking: ～劳动 work hard
【辛酸】xīnsuān〈形〉bitter: ～的往事 bitter past ‖ ～泪 hot and bitter tears

忻 xīn = 欣 xīn

昕 xīn
〈名〉〈书〉 dawn: 自～至夕 from dawn till dusk

欣 xīn
〈形〉 glad: ▸～慰，～喜
【欣然】xīnrán〈副〉〈书〉 gladly: ～接受 readily accept ‖ ～同意 willingly agree
【欣赏】xīnshǎng〈动〉 1（享受） appreciate: ～风景 enjoy the scenery ‖ ～音乐 enjoy music ‖ 有高度～水平的观众 highly appreciative audience 2（喜欢） like: 自我～ self-appreciation ‖ 他很～这里宁静的环境。The peaceful surroundings are very much to his liking.
【欣慰】xīnwèi〈形〉 gratified: 感到～ feel gratified ‖ 令人～的消息 gratifying news
【欣闻】xīnwén〈动〉〈书〉 be delighted to hear
【欣悉】xīnxī〈动〉〈书〉 be happy to learn
【欣喜】xīnxǐ〈形〉 delighted: 因成功而～激动 be overjoyed at the success ‖ ～若狂 be beside oneself with joy
【欣羡】xīnxiàn〈动〉〈书〉 appreciate and admire: ～某人的人格魅力 admire sb.'s personal charm
【欣欣】xīnxīn〈形〉 1（形容高兴） happy 2（形容茂盛） thriving: ▸～向荣
【欣欣向荣】xīnxīn-xiàngróng〈成〉flourishing: 一派～的景象 a picture of prosperity

锌（鋅） xīn
〈名〉［化学］zinc (Zn)
【锌版】xīnbǎn〈名〉［印刷］ zinc plate

新 xīn
A〈形〉 1（刚出现） new: ～茶 newly picked tea leaves ‖ ～产品 new product ‖ ～世纪 new century ‖ 最～消息 latest news 2（未用过） new: ～车 new car ‖ ～鞋 new shoes 3（新婚） recently or just married: 一对～人 newly-weds ▸～郎，～娘
B〈动〉 make new: ▸耳目一～，改过自～
C〈名〉 the new: ▸推陈出～，尝～，迎～
D〈副〉 recently: ～当选的领导人 newly elected leadership ‖ ～粉刷的墙壁 recently painted wall
【新岸】xīn'àn〈名〉 road to a new life
【新版】xīnbǎn〈名〉 new edition
【新材料】xīncáiliào〈名〉 new material
【新潮】xīncháo A〈名〉 new trend: 赶～ follow the fashion B〈形〉 fashionable: ～服装 new fashions ‖ ～人物 swinger ‖ ～家具 stylish furniture
【新陈代谢】xīnchén-dàixiè〈成〉 1（指生物的基本特征） metabolism: ～过程 metabolic process 2〈喻〉（新旧替换） the new superseding the old
【新宠】xīnchǒng〈名〉new favourite: 这种品牌的葡萄酒已成为餐桌上的～。This brand of wine is a new favourite for the table.
【新仇旧恨】xīnchóu-jiùhèn〈成〉 new hatred piled on the old
【新春】xīnchūn〈名〉 new spring [10 or 20 days following the Spring Festival]: ～佳节 Spring Festival ‖ ～快乐! Happy New Year!
【新词】xīncí〈名〉 new word: ～新义 new words or new meanings ‖ 造～ coin a word
【新村】xīncūn〈名〉 new residential quarters
【新大陆】Xīndàlù〈名〉 New World [the Americas]: 发现～ discover the New World
【新低】xīndī〈名〉 new low: 创历史～ hit a new all-time low ‖ 跌至～ fall to a new low
【新房】xīnfáng〈名〉 1（指刚建成） new house: 搬进～ move into a new house 2（婚房） bridal chamber: 布置～ decorate the bridal chamber
【新风】xīnfēng〈名〉 new trend: 树～ set a new trend ‖ 校园～ new trend on campus
【新风尚】xīnfēngshàng〈名〉 new custom
【新妇】xīnfù〈名〉 bride
【新高】xīngāo〈名〉 new high: 创～ hit a new high ‖ 达到～ reach a new high
【新官上任三把火】xīnguān shàngrèn sān bǎ huǒ〈俗〉 new officials enforce strict measures
【新贵】xīnguì〈名〉 1（指显贵） parvenu 2（指官员） newly appointed high official
【新罕布什尔州】Xīnhǎnbùshí'ěrzhōu〈名〉 New Hampshire
【新华社】Xīnhuáshè〈名〉 Xinhua News Agency
【新欢】xīnhuān〈名〉〈贬〉 new lover: 另有～ be taken up with another woman
【新婚】xīnhūn〈动〉 be newly married: ～夫妇 newly-weds ‖ ～之夜 wedding night
【新婚燕尔】xīnhūn-yàn'ěr〈成〉 be newly married
【新几内亚】Xīn-Jǐnèiyà〈名〉 New Guinea: ～人 New Guinean
【新纪元】xīnjìyuán〈名〉 new era: 开创～ usher in a new epoch
【新加坡】Xīnjiāpō〈名〉 Singapore: ～人 Singaporean
【新疆】Xīnjiāng ▸**p. 661**〈名〉 Xinjiang: ～维吾尔自治区 Xinjiang Uygur Autonomous Region
【新交】xīnjiāo A〈动〉 become acquainted recently: ～的朋友 new friend B〈名〉 new acquaintance: 旧友～ old and new friends
【新教】Xīnjiào〈名〉 Protestantism: ～徒 Protestant
【新界】Xīnjiè〈名〉New Territories (of Hong Kong SAR)
【新近】xīnjìn〈副〉 recently
【新旧交替】xīnjiù-jiāotì〈成〉 transition from the old to the new
【新居】xīnjū〈名〉 new home: 迁入～ move into a new house
【新局面】xīnjúmiàn〈名〉 new situation: 打开～ open up new dimensions
【新来乍到】xīnlái-zhàdào〈成〉 new arrival: 她～，请多关照。She is a newcomer, so please help her.
【新郎】xīnláng〈名〉 bridegroom
【新郎官】xīnlángguān = 新郎 xīnláng
【新老交替】xīnlǎo-jiāotì〈成〉 replacement of the old by the new
【新绿】xīnlǜ〈名〉 light green
【新貌】xīnmào〈名〉 new look
【新民主主义】xīnmínzhǔzhǔyì〈名〉 new democracy: ～革命 new democratic revolution
【新墨西哥州】Xīn-Mòxīgēzhōu〈名〉 New Mexico
【新年】xīnnián〈名〉New Year: ～献词 New Year message ‖ ～快乐! Happy New Year!
【新娘】xīnniáng〈名〉 bride
【新娘子】xīnniángzi = 新娘 xīnniáng
【新派】xīnpài〈形〉 fashionable
【新篇章】xīnpiānzhāng〈名〉 new chapter
【新奇】xīnqí〈形〉 new: ～感 novel sensation ‖ ～的想法 novel idea ‖ ～的小玩意儿 newfangled gadget
【新气象】xīnqìxiàng〈名〉 new atmosphere
【新巧】xīnqiǎo〈形〉 novel and exquisite: 设计～ be novel and exquisite in design
【新秋】xīnqiū〈名〉〈书〉 early autumn
【新区】xīnqū〈名〉 newly developed area: 浦东～ Pudong Development Zone
【新人】xīnrén〈名〉 1（具有时代风貌的人） people of a new type: 一代～ a new generation ‖ 培养社会主义～ bring on fresh talents in the building of socialism 2（新出现的人才） new talent: 歌坛～ new singer ‖ 学术界涌现出大批～。A large number of new talents have emerged in the academic world. 3（新来的人） newcomer: 我们办公室来了几位～。There are a few newcomers in our office. 4（悔过自新的人） new person: 把失足青年改造成为～ make a new person out of a delinquent 5（新婚夫妇） newly married couple
【新人新事】xīnrén-xīnshì〈成〉 new people and new things
【新任】xīnrèn A〈形〉 newly appointed: ～校长 newly appointed president B〈名〉 new appointment: 赶赴～ go to take up a new post
【新锐】xīnruì A〈形〉 1（新奇锐利） new and sharp: ～武器 new and sharp weapon ‖ ～言论 incisive remarks 2（有锐气） spirited: ～作家 vivacious writer ‖ ～导演 spirited director B〈名〉 new talent: 棋坛～ new talent in chess circles
【新生】xīnshēng A〈形〉 newborn: ～事物 new things ‖ ～力量 new force ▸～儿 B〈名〉 1（指生命） rebirth: 获得～ be reborn 2（指学生） new student
【新生代】xīnshēngdài〈名〉 1［地质］ Cenozoic Era 2（新一代） new generation: ～导演 new generation director
【新生儿】xīnshēng'ér〈名〉 newborn: ～死亡率 infant mortality
【新生界】Xīnshēngjiè〈名〉［地质］ Cenozoic era

X

【新诗】xīnshī〈名〉 new verse [free verse written in the vernacular since the May 4th Movement]
【新石器时代】Xīnshíqì Shídài〈名〉 Neolithic Age
【新式】xīnshì〈形〉 latest: ～家具 modern furniture ‖ ～武器 modern weapon
【新手】xīnshǒu〈名〉 green hand: 雇用～ hire a new hand
【新书】xīnshū〈名〉 **1**（指崭新）new book **2**（指将出版） book to be published
【新四军】Xīnsìjūn〈名〉 New Fourth Army [led by the Chinese Communist Party during the War of Resistance Against Japan]
【新文化运动】Xīnwénhuà Yùndòng〈名〉 New Culture Movement [around the time of the May 4th Movement in 1919]
【新文学】xīnwénxué〈名〉 vernacular literature
【新闻】xīnwén〈名〉 **1**（报道的消息） news: 独家～ exclusive news report ‖ 国际/国内～ world/domestic news ‖ 现在报告～。 Here is the news. **2**（新近发生的事） news: 有什么～给我们说说? Do you have any news to share with us?
【新闻报道】xīnwén bàodào〈名〉 news report
【新闻采访】xīnwén cǎifǎng〈名〉 news-gathering
【新闻出版署】xīnwén chūbǎnshǔ〈名〉 press and publication administration
【新闻发布会】xīnwén fābùhuì〈名〉 press conference: 举行～ give a press briefing
【新闻发言人】xīnwén fāyánrén〈名〉 news spokesperson
【新闻稿】xīnwéngǎo〈名〉 press release
【新闻公报】xīnwén gōngbào〈名〉 press communiqué
【新闻记者】xīnwén jìzhě ▸**p. 966**〈名〉 journalist
【新闻简报】xīnwén jiǎnbào〈名〉 news bulletin
【新闻界】xīnwénjiè〈名〉 press circles
【新闻联播】xīnwén liánbō〈名〉 news hook-up
【新闻评论】xīnwén pínglùn〈名〉 news commentary: ～员 news analyst
【新闻人物】xīnwén rénwù〈名〉 person who makes the news
【新闻特写】xīnwén tèxiě〈名〉 news feature
【新闻线索】xīnwén xiànsuǒ〈名〉 news clue
【新闻纸】xīnwénzhǐ〈名〉 **1**〈旧〉（指报纸） newspaper **2**（指纸） newsprint
【新闻自由】xīnwén zìyóu〈名〉 freedom of the press: 遏制～ muzzle the press
【新闻周刊】Xīnwén Zhōukān〈名〉 *Newsweek*
【新西兰】Xīnxīlán〈名〉 New Zealand: ～人 New Zealander
【新媳妇儿】xīnxífur〈名〉〈口〉 bride
【新禧】xīnxǐ〈形〉 New Year greeting: 恭贺～! Happy New Year!
【新鲜】xīnxiān〈形〉 **1**（未变质、无杂质） fresh: ～面包 fresh bread ‖ ～蔬菜 fresh vegetable ‖ ～空气 fresh air **2**（出现不久） new: ～经验 new experience ‖ ～事 strange thing ‖ ～感很快消失。 The novelty soon wore off.
【新鲜出炉】xīnxiān chūlú〈动〉〈喻〉 be hot off the press: 产品国家标准～。 The national standard for products is just out.
【新鲜血液】xīnxiān xuèyè〈名〉 new blood:〈喻〉 吸收～ absorb some new blood ‖ 注入～ infuse new blood
【新新人类】xīnxīnrénlèi〈名〉 X Generation
【新兴】xīnxīng〈形〉 burgeoning: ～产业/工业 new industry ‖ ～城市 boom town ‖ ～力量 newly emerging force ‖ ～学科 new branch of science
【新星】xīnxīng〈名〉 **1**［天文］ nova **2**（指人） up-and-coming star: 体坛～ rising star in the world of sport ‖ 影坛～ up-and-coming film star
【新型】xīnxíng〈形〉 new-type: ～建筑材料 new building material ‖ ～劳动者 new type of worker
【新秀】xīnxiù〈名〉 up-and-coming star: 歌坛～ up-and-coming singer ‖ 体坛～ budding sportsperson ‖ 文坛～ rising star in the world of letters
【新学】xīnxué〈名〉 new learning [Western learning in late Qing Dynasty]
【新雅】xīnyǎ〈形〉 fresh and elegant
【新药】xīnyào〈名〉 **1**（刚研发的药） newly-developed medicine **2** = 西药 xīyào
【新义】xīnyì〈名〉 new meaning: 词的～ new sense of a word
【新异】xīnyì〈形〉 novel: 立意～ take a novel approach
【新意】xīnyì〈名〉 new idea: 他的论文没有什么～。 His thesis breaks no new ground.
【新颖】xīnyǐng〈形〉 novel: 款式～ have a novel style ‖ 构思～的作品 work original in its design ‖ ～的见解 original idea
【新约】Xīnyuē〈简称〉= 新约全书
【新约全书】Xīnyuē Quánshū〈名〉 *New Testament*
【新月】xīnyuè〈名〉 **1**（农历月初的弯月） crescent moon: 一弯～ a new moon **2**［天文］ new moon
【新泽西州】Xīnzéxīzhōu〈名〉 New Jersey
【新张】xīnzhāng〈形〉 [of a new shop] newly open: ～志喜 extend one's congratulations on the opening of a shop
【新正】xīnzhēng〈名〉 first month of the lunar year
【新知】xīnzhī〈名〉 **1**（指朋友） new friend: 旧友～ old and new friends **2**（指知识） new knowledge
【新殖民主义】xīnzhímínzhǔyì〈名〉 neocolonialism
【新址】xīnzhǐ〈名〉 new address
【新作】xīnzuò〈名〉 new artistic or literary work

歆 xīn〈动〉〈书〉 admire
【歆慕】xīnmù〈动〉〈书〉 admire: ～地看着某人 look at sb. with admiration
【歆羡】xīnxiàn〈动〉〈书〉 adore

薪 xīn〈名〉 **1**（柴火） firewood: ▸釜底抽～, 卧～尝胆 **2**（薪水） salary: 发～ pay out wages ‖ 调～ adjust a salary ‖ 高～工作 high-paying job ‖ 年/月～ annual/monthly salary
【薪酬】xīnchóu〈名〉 emolument
【薪俸】xīnfèng〈旧〉= 薪水 xīnshui
【薪金】xīnjīn = 薪水 xīnshui
【薪尽火传】xīnjìn-huǒchuán〈成〉〈喻〉 knowledge is passed on from one generation to another
【薪水】xīnshui〈名〉 salary: 要求增加～ demand a pay rise ‖ 相当可观的～ handsome salary
【薪饷】xīnxiǎng〈名〉〈旧〉 soldier's pay and rations
【薪资】xīnzī〈名〉 salary

馨 xīn〈名〉〈书〉 pervasive fragrance: ▸～香, 清～
【馨香】xīnxiāng〈名〉〈书〉 fragrance

鑫 xīn〈形〉〈书〉 prosperous

xìn

囟 xìn〈名〉［生理］ fontanelle
【囟门】xìnmén〈名〉［生理］ fontanelle

芯 xìn
▸xīn
【芯子】xìnzi〈名〉 **1**（捻子） fuse: 爆竹～ firecracker fuse ‖ 蜡烛～ candle wick **2**（蛇的舌头） forked tongue of a snake: 蛇嗖地吐出～。 The snake darted its tongue.

信 xìn
A〈形〉 **1**（确实） true: ～史 true history ▸～而有征 **2**（有信用） trustworthy: ▸～守, ～用
B〈名〉 **1**（凭据） sign: ▸～物, 印～ **2**（信息） information: 等着听～儿吧 just wait for the news ‖ 捎～ send word ▸～息, 口～ **3**（书信） letter: 回～ write back ‖ 寄～ post a letter ‖ （给某人）写～ write a letter to sb. ▸介绍～, 挂号～ **4**（信用） confidence: ▸失～, 守～ **5**（信石） arsenic: 白～ white arsenic ▸～石 **6**（引信） fuse: ▸～管
C〈动〉 **1**（相信） believe: ～不～由你 believe it or not ‖ 谁～你那一套! Tell that to the marines! ▸～赖, ～任 **2**（信奉） believe in: ～佛 have Buddhist beliefs ▸～奉, ～徒
D〈副〉 at random: ▸～笔, ～步, ～口开河
【信笔】xìnbǐ〈动〉 write at random: ～写来 write freely
【信笔涂鸦】xìnbǐ-túyā〈成〉 [used as self-effacing remark] write a poor hand
【信标】xìnbiāo〈名〉 beacon: ～跟踪 beacon tracking ‖ ～雷达显示 beacon radar presentation
【信步】xìnbù〈动〉 take a stroll
【信不过】xìnbuguò〈动〉 distrust: ～某人的话 cannot depend (up)on sb.'s word
【信差】xìnchāi〈名〉〈旧〉 **1**（送公文信件的人） messenger **2**（邮差） postman
【信从】xìncóng〈动〉 follow: 盲目～ follow advice blindly
【信贷】xìndài〈名〉 credit: 提供～ give credit ‖ 出口～ export credit ‖ ～员 credit person
【信贷公司】xìndài gōngsī〈名〉 finance company
【信贷业务】xìndài yèwù〈名〉 credit transaction/operation
【信得过】xìndeguò **A**〈动〉 trust: 我～你。 I have faith in you. **B**〈形〉 trustworthy: ～产品 trustworthy product
【信而有征】xìn'éryǒuzhēng〈成〉 be true and supported by evidence
【信访】xìnfǎng〈动〉 complain by letter or visits: 接待～群众 handle complaints lodged via letters or visits ‖ ～工作 correspondence and visitation work
【信访人】xìnfǎngrén〈名〉 petitioner: 不得打击迫害～。 Petitioners may not be attacked or persecuted.
【信风】xìnfēng〈名〉 trade wind
【信封】xìnfēng〈名〉 envelope: 在～上写姓名地址 address an envelope

【信奉】 xìnfèng〈动〉 **1**（信仰崇奉） believe in: ～佛教 believe in Buddhism ‖ ～上帝 believe in God **2**（奉行） pursue: ～社会主义 believe in socialism

【信服】 xìnfú〈动〉 be convinced: 令人～的理由 compelling reason

【信鸽】 xìngē〈名〉 homing pigeon

【信管】 xìnguǎn〈名〉 fuse: 炸药～ fuse in a blasting charge

【信函】 xìnhán〈名〉 letter: ～往来 exchange of letters ‖ 私人～ personal correspondence

【信号】 xìnhào〈名〉 signal: 发出求救～ signal for help ‖ 收到卫星～ receive a signal from a satellite ‖ 交通～ traffic signal

【信号弹】 xìnhàodàn〈名〉 signal flare

【信号灯】 xìnhàodēng〈名〉 signal lamp

【信号旗】 xìnhàoqí〈名〉 signal flag

【信号枪】 xìnhàoqiāng〈名〉 signal pistol

【信汇】 xìnhuì **A**〈动〉 send by money order **B**〈名〉 money order

【信笺】 xìnjiān〈名〉 writing paper

【信件】 xìnjiàn〈名〉 letter: 分拣～ sort letters ‖ 公务～ office mail ‖ 机密～ confidential letter ‖ 私人～ private letter

【信教】 xìnjiào〈动〉 profess a religion

【信口】 xìnkǒu〈动〉 speak casually: ～回答 answer casually ‖ ～说出 blurt out one's thoughts

【信口雌黄】 xìnkǒu-cíhuáng〈成〉 make irresponsible remarks

【信口开合】 xìnkǒu-kāihé = 信口开河 xìnkǒu-kāihé

【信口开河】 xìnkǒu-kāihé〈成〉 have a loose tongue: 不是～ not be just idle talk

【信赖】 xìnlài〈动〉 trust: 可～的同事 trustworthy colleague

【信马由缰】 xìnmǎ-yóujiāng〈成〉 **1**〈本〉 ride a horse without holding the reins **2**〈喻〉 do as one pleases

【信男】 xìnnán〈名〉 male devotee

【信念】 xìnniàn〈名〉 faith: 保持～ retain one's faith ‖ 坚定～ strengthen a conviction ‖ 坚持～ cling to one's belief ‖ 不可动摇的～ unshakeable faith ‖ 坚定的～ steadfast faith ‖ 政治～ political conviction

【信女】 xìnnǚ〈名〉 female devotee

【信皮儿】 xìnpír〈名〉〈口〉 envelope

【信瓤儿】 xìnrángr〈名〉〈方〉 letter enclosed in an envelope

【信任】 xìnrèn〈动〉 trust: 得到某人的～ gain sb.'s confidence ‖ 辜负某人的～ betray sb.'s trust ‖ 恢复～ restore confidence ‖ 缺乏～ lack confidence ‖ 对他失去～ lose faith in him ‖ 我完全～这位医生。 The doctor has my complete confidence.

【信任投票】 xìnrèn tóupiào〈名〉 vote of confidence: 赢得～ win a confidence vote

【信赏必罚】 xìnshǎng-bìfá〈成〉 due rewards and punishments will be meted out without fail

【信石】 xìnshí = 砒霜 pīshuāng

【信实】 xìnshí〈形〉〈书〉 **1**（诚实） trustworthy: 为人～ be trustworthy **2**（真实可靠） reliable: 资料～ reliable material

【信使】 xìnshǐ〈名〉 courier: 外交～ diplomatic messenger

【信士】 xìnshì〈名〉 **1**（信佛但未出家的男人） male Buddhist devotee **2**〈书〉（诚实的人） honest person

【信誓旦旦】 xìnshì-dàndàn〈成〉 make a solemn vow: ～地许诺 make a serious promise

【信手】 xìnshǒu〈副〉 conveniently: ～挥霍 squander money freely

【信手拈来】 xìnshǒu-niānlái〈成〉 wield a deft pen

【信守】 xìnshǒu〈动〉 abide by: ～合同 adhere to a contract ‖ ～诺言 keep one's word

【信天翁】 xìntiānwēng〈名〉［鸟类］ albatross

【信天游】 xìntiānyóu〈名〉 *xintianyou* [resonant folk songs of northern Shaanxi]

【信条】 xìntiáo〈名〉 tenet: 把医生的话当成～ take the doctor's words as gospel ‖ 经商～ business creed

【信筒】 xìntǒng〈名〉 letterbox

【信徒】 xìntú〈名〉 believer: 基督教～ Christian ‖ 狂热的～ fanatic believer

【信托】 xìntuō **A**〈动〉 entrust: 我们完全可以把这件事～给他。 We can entrust him with it. **B**〈形〉 trusted: ～业务 trust business ‖ ～投资公司 trust and investment company

【信托公司】 xìntuō gōngsī〈名〉 trust company

【信托基金】 xìntuō jījīn〈名〉 trust fund

【信望】 xìnwàng〈名〉〈书〉 prestige: ～卓著 enjoy high prestige

【信物】 xìnwù〈名〉 token: 交换～ exchange tokens ‖ 定情～ token of love

【信息】 xìnxī〈名〉 information: 得到～ acquire information ‖ 交换～ exchange information ‖ 科技～ technological information

【信息产业】 xìnxī chǎnyè〈名〉 IT industry

【信息处理】 xìnxī chǔlǐ〈名〉 information processing

【信息服务】 xìnxī fúwù〈名〉 information service: ～部 information services (IS) ‖ ～业 information service industry

【信息港】 xìnxīgǎng〈名〉 cyber port

【信息高速公路】 xìnxī gāosù gōnglù〈名〉 information superhighway: 建立～ build an information superhighway

【信息工程】 xìnxī gōngchéng〈名〉 information engineering

【信息化】 xìnxīhuà〈动〉 informationize: ～社会 information society

【信息技术】 xìnxī jìshù〈名〉 information technology (IT): ～产业 IT industry

【信息科学】 xìnxī kēxué〈名〉 information science

【信息库】 xìnxīkù〈名〉 information bank

【信息来源】 xìnxī láiyuán〈名〉 information source

【信息量】 xìnxīliàng〈名〉 amount of information

【信息流】 xìnxīliú〈名〉 information flow

【信息论】 xìnxīlùn〈名〉 information theory

【信息时代】 xìnxī shídài〈名〉 information age

【信息学】 xìnxīxué〈名〉 information science

【信息中心】 xìnxī zhōngxīn〈名〉 information centre: 国家～ State Information Centre

【信箱】 xìnxiāng〈名〉 **1**（用于投寄信件） postbox〈英〉; mailbox〈美〉 **2**（邮政专用信箱） post office box, PO box **3**（用于收信） letter box〈英〉; mailbox〈美〉

【信心】 xìnxīn〈名〉 confidence: 对未来充满～ be confident about the future ‖ 缺乏～ lack confidence ‖ ～很足 be brimming with confidence

【信心百倍】 xìnxīn-bǎibèi〈成〉 be full of confidence

【信仰】 xìnyǎng **A**〈名〉 faith: 坚持～ adhere to a belief ‖ 失去～ lose one's faith ‖ ～自由 freedom of belief ‖ 政治～ political conviction ‖ 宗教～ religious belief **B**〈动〉 believe in: ～危机 belief crisis ‖ ～上帝 believe in God ‖ 他～佛教。 He professed a belief in Buddhism.

【信以为真】 xìnyǐwéizhēn〈成〉 take what one hears at face value: 别人说什么他都～。 He believes whatever people say.

【信义】 xìnyì〈名〉 good faith: 不守～ break faith ‖ 讲～ act in good faith ‖ 重～ stand upon one's honour

【信用】 xìnyòng **A**〈名〉 trustworthiness: 讲～ keep one's word ‖ 没有～ have no credit ‖ 守～ keep a promise ‖ 守～的人 man of honour **B**〈形〉 creditable: ～贷款 unsecured loan ‖ ～状况 credit standing ‖ ～政策 credit policy ‖ 商业～ commercial credit **C**〈动〉〈书〉 trust and appoint: ～贤能 appoint people of virtue and talent

【信用等级】 xìnyòng děngjí〈名〉 credit rating

【信用额度】 xìnyòng édù〈名〉 credit limit

【信用风险】 xìnyòng fēngxiǎn〈名〉 credit risk

【信用合作社】 xìnyòng hézuòshè〈名〉 credit cooperative

【信用卡】 xìnyòngkǎ〈名〉 credit card: 用～付账 pay a bill with credit card

【信用评估】 xìnyòng pínggū〈名〉 credit rating

【信用社】 xìnyòngshè〈简称〉= 信用合作社

【信用危机】 xìnyòng wēijī〈名〉 credit crisis

【信用证】 xìnyòngzhèng〈名〉 letter of credit

【信誉】 xìnyù〈名〉 prestige: 建立良好～ establish credibility ‖ 享有很高的国际～ enjoy high international prestige ‖ ～好的公司 company with a sound credit record

【信札】 xìnzhá〈名〉 letters

【信纸】 xìnzhǐ〈名〉 writing paper

【信众】 xìnzhòng〈名〉 believers

衅（釁） xìn〈名〉 quarrel: ▸挑～, 寻～

xīng

兴（興） xīng

A〈动〉 **1**〈书〉（起来） get up: ▸夙～夜寐 **2**（发动） mobilize: ▸～师动众, ～妖作怪 **3**（开始出现） start: ▸～办, ～建, 大～土木 **4**（兴盛） prevail: 现在又～短发了。 Short hair is back in fashion again. ‖ 今年不～这种款式。 This style is no longer fashionable this year. ▸时～ **5**〈口〉（准许）[often used in the negative] allow: 不～大声嚷嚷。 Shouting is forbidden. ‖ 不～瞎说！ None of your nonsense!
B〈形〉 thriving: ▸～隆, ～盛
C〈副〉〈方〉 maybe: 明天旅游，他也～去，也～不去。 He may or may not come on the trip tomorrow. ▸～许
▸xìng

【兴办】 xīngbàn〈动〉 set up: ～合资企业 set up a joint venture ‖ ～学校 found a school

【兴兵】 xīngbīng〈动〉 send an army: ～讨伐 send out a punitive expedition

【兴废存亡】 xīngfèi-cúnwáng〈成〉 rise and fall

【兴奋】 xīngfèn〈形〉 excited: 感到～ feel excited ‖ 极度～ bubble over with excitement ‖ 酒后～ alcohol-induced frenzy ▸～剂

【兴奋剂】xīngfènjì〈名〉 stimulant: 服用～ use stimulants ‖ ～检测呈阳性 test positive for doping ‖ ～检测 doping test ‖ 反～机构/委员会 anti-doping agency/committee

【兴风作浪】xīngfēng-zuòlàng〈成〉〈喻〉 stir up trouble

【兴革】xīnggé〈动〉〈书〉 reform

【兴工】xīnggōng〈动〉 start construction: 破土～ break ground and start construction

【兴国】xīngguó〈动〉 rejuvenate a nation: ～安邦 make the country prosperous and stable ‖ 科教～ invigorate the country through science and education

【兴家立业】xīngjiā-lìyè〈成〉 make one's family prosper and establish a competency

【兴建】xīngjiàn〈动〉 build: ～发电厂 build a power plant

【兴利除弊】xīnglì-chúbì〈成〉 promote the beneficial and abolish the harmful

【兴隆】xīnglóng〈形〉 thriving: 买卖～。 The business is doing very well. ‖ 生意～。 Business is thriving.

【兴起】 xīngqǐ 〈动〉 1（出现并兴盛） spring up: 一场社会变革正在～。 A social transformation is in the making. 2〈书〉（奋起） rise in excitement: 闻风～ rise excitedly at the news

【兴盛】xīngshèng〈形〉 thriving: 国家～。 The country is prosperous.

【兴师】xīngshī〈动〉〈书〉 dispatch troops

【兴师动众】 xīngshī-dòngzhòng 〈成〉 mobilize a huge number of people: 这件事容易，没必要～。 It is just an easy job, so there is no need to drag in a lot of people.

【兴师问罪】xīngshī-wènzuì〈成〉 ask sb. to answer for a wrongdoing

【兴衰】xīngshuāi〈名〉 rise and fall: 大英帝国的～ rise and fall of the British Empire

【兴叹】xīngtàn〈动〉〈书〉 heave a sigh: ▸望洋～

【兴替】xīngtì〈动〉〈书〉 rise and fall

【兴亡】xīngwáng〈名〉 rise and fall: 国家～ rise and fall of a country

【兴旺】xīngwàng〈形〉 flourishing: 市场～ prosperous market ‖ 我们的事业～发达。 Our business is thriving.

【兴修】xīngxiū〈动〉 start construction: ～水利 build irrigation projects ‖ ～铁路 begin a railroad construction

【兴许】xīngxǔ〈副〉perhaps: ～你是对的。 Perhaps you are right.

【兴学】xīngxué〈动〉 establish schools to promote learning: 捐资～ donate money to set up a school

【兴妖作怪】 xīngyāo-zuòguài 〈成〉〈喻〉 stir up trouble

星 xīng〈名〉 1（星星） star: ～月交辉。 The stars and moon vied with each other in brightness. ▸～空, 流～, 披～戴月 2（星状物） star-shaped thing: 肩章上有两颗～。 There are two stars on the shoulder strap. ▸～号, 五角～ 3（小零碎） bit: 一～半点 a tiny bit ▸油～ 4（标记） weight marks on a steelyard: ▸秤～, 定盘～ 5（名人） celebrity: ▸歌～, 救～, 灾～ 6（指星宿） one of the 28 constellations in ancient Chinese astronomy

【星辰】xīngchén〈名〉 stars: 日月～ the sun, the moon and the stars

【星斗】xīngdǒu〈名〉 stars: 满天～ star-studded sky

【星冠】xīngguān〈名〉 astral crown

【星光】xīngguāng〈名〉 starlight: ～闪烁 glimmering starlight ‖ 今夜～灿烂。 The stars are shining brightly tonight.

【星汉】xīnghàn〈名〉〈旧〉 Galaxy

【星号】xīnghào〈名〉 asterisk (*): 加上～ add an asterisk

【星河】xīnghé〈名〉［天文］ Milky Way

【星火】xīnghuǒ〈名〉 1（微小的火）spark: ▸～燎原 2（流星） shooting star: ▸急如～

【星火计划】Xīnghuǒ Jìhuà〈名〉 Spark Programme [popular name for the Programme for the Promotion of Technological Development in Local Economies, initiated in China in 1985]

【星火燎原】 xīnghuǒ-liáoyuán ＝ 星星之火，可以燎原 xīngxīng zhī huǒ, kěyǐ liáoyuán

【星级】xīngjí A〈名〉 star: 四～酒店 4-star hotel B〈形〉 leading: ～服务 first-class service ‖ ～人物 prominent figure

【星际】xīngjì〈形〉 interplanetary: ～空间

ℹ 星期中的每天

■ 英语里只有全称和缩写两种形式表达一星期中的各天。缩写一般用于日历、日记、时间表或告示中，通常不用于正式文件或交流：

	全称	缩写
星期一	Monday	Mon
星期二	Tuesday	Tue
星期三	Wednesday	Wed
星期四	Thursday	Thu
星期五	Friday	Fri
星期六	Saturday	Sat
星期天	Sunday	Sun
星期	week	
工作日	weekday	
周末	weekend	

今天星期几？

今天星期几？—— 星期二
= What day is it? — It's Tuesday
或 What day is it today? — It is Tuesday
或 What's today? — Today is Tuesday

昨天礼拜几？—— 礼拜一
= What day was it yesterday?
— It was Monday

介词 on

■ 表示一周里特定的某一天、某一天的上、下午或晚上时，英语必须用介词 on:

她星期天到
= She will be arriving on Sunday

他星期六到这儿的
= He arrived here on Saturday

我周五下午去拜访
= I'll come round on Friday afternoon

我每个礼拜一的晚上看我母亲
= I visit my mother on Monday evenings
或 I visit my mother on a Monday evening
或 I visit my mother every Monday evening

我的英语课是在星期二
= My English class is on a Tuesday
或 My English class is on Tuesdays

我每月的第二个星期一付账单
= I pay the bills on the second Monday in the month

我在工作日跑步
= I go for a run on weekdays

礼拜天一大早
= early on Sunday

礼拜天晚点儿
= late on Sunday

其他介词

■ 在英语里根据语境所需，也可用其他介词:

从星期天起
= from Sunday onwards

在工作日期间
= during weekdays

在周末
= at the weekend（英）
或 on the weekend（美）

不用介词

■ 英语里，当 one、this/that、last/next、every/each、most、some 等与表示星期几的词连用时，则不使用任何介词:

一个星期五的下午
= one Friday afternoon
而不是
on one Friday afternoon

那个星期五晚上
= that Friday evening

这个星期五晚上
= this Friday evening

上个星期五
= last Friday

这个星期五
= this Friday

下个星期五
= next Friday

每星期五
= every/each Friday

隔周星期五
= every other Friday
而不是
on every other Friday

大部分星期五
= most Fridays

某些星期五
= some Fridays

每周
= every week

每隔一周 / 每两周
= every other week

每隔两周 / 每三周
= every third week

interstellar space ‖ ～旅行 space travel
【星空】xīngkōng〈名〉starry sky: 辽阔的～ vast starry sky
【星罗棋布】xīngluó-qíbù〈成〉be dotted with: 海岸上渔村～。Countless fishing villages dot the coast.
【星期】xīngqī〈名〉1（指一周）week: 上/下～ last/next week ‖ 一～之内 within a week 2（指一日）day of the week: 今天～几? Which day of the week is today? 3（星期日）Sunday
【星期二】xīngqī'èr〈名〉Tuesday
【星期六】xīngqīliù〈名〉Saturday
【星期日】xīngqīrì〈名〉Sunday
【星期三】xīngqīsān〈名〉Wednesday
【星期四】xīngqīsì〈名〉Thursday
【星期天】xīngqītiān = 星期日 xīngqīrì
【星期五】xīngqīwǔ〈名〉Friday
【星期一】xīngqīyī〈名〉Monday
【星球】xīngqiú〈名〉heavenly body
【星球大战】Xīngqiú Dàzhàn〈名〉[军事] Star Wars: ～计划 Star Wars
【星散】xīngsàn〈动〉〈书〉be scattered far and wide
【星术】xīngshù〈名〉astrology
【星探】xīngtàn〈名〉talent spotter
【星体】xīngtǐ〈名〉heavenly body
【星条旗】xīngtiáoqí〈名〉1（指国旗）Stars and Stripes [national flag of the United States] 2（指象征）Star-spangled Banner [national anthem of the United States]
【星图】xīngtú〈名〉star chart
【星团】xīngtuán〈名〉star cluster: 一个～ a cluster of stars
【星系】xīngxì〈名〉galaxy: 银河～ Galaxy
【星相】xīngxiàng〈名〉horoscope
【星象】xīngxiàng〈名〉astrology: ～占卜术 astromancy
【星星】xīngxīng〈名〉speck: 天空晴朗，一～云彩也没有。It is a fine day, and there is not a single cloud in the sky.
【星星点点】xīngxīng-diǎndiǎn〈形〉scrappy: 关于某事～知道一些 have only a sketchy knowledge of sth.
【星星之火，可以燎原】xīngxīng zhī huǒ, kěyǐ liáoyuán〈成〉a single spark can start a prairie fire
【星星】xīngxing〈名〉〈口〉star: 看～ watch stars ‖ ～闪烁 stars twinkle
【星宿】xīngxiù〈名〉constellation: 十二～ twelve constellations
【星夜】xīngyè〈名〉starry night: ～出发 set out by starlight ‖ ～行军 march on a starry night
【星移斗转】xīngyí-dǒuzhuǎn〈成〉passage of time
【星云】xīngyún〈名〉nebula: 环状～ ring nebula ‖ 网状～ network nebula ‖ 银河～ galactic nebula
【星子】xīngzi〈名〉speck: 唾沫～ spray of saliva
【星座】xīngzuò〈名〉[天文] constellation

猩 xīng〈名〉orang-utan
【猩红】xīnghóng〈形〉scarlet: ～的花朵 fiery red flowers
【猩红热】xīnghóngrè〈名〉scarlet fever
【猩猩】xīngxing〈名〉orang-utan

惺 xīng〈形〉〈书〉1（聪明）clever: ～悟 realize 2（清醒）drowsy-eyed
【惺忪】xīngsōng〈形〉drowsy-eyed: 睡眼～ eyes still heavy with sleep
【惺惺惜惺惺】xīngxīng xī xīngxīng〈成〉intelligent people like intelligence in others
【惺惺作态】xīngxīng-zuòtài〈成〉put on airs

腥 xīng
A〈名〉1（指食物）raw meat/fish: ▸荤～ 2（指气味）fishy smell: 做鱼放料酒可以去～。When cooking fish, add some cooking wine to get rid of the fishy smell. ▸～气
B〈形〉fishy: ▸～臭, ～臊
【腥臭】xīngchòu〈形〉smelly: 奶酪～了。The butter became rancid.
【腥风血雨】xīngfēng-xuèyǔ〈成〉carnage of war
【腥气】xīngqi A〈名〉fishy smell B〈形〉stinky: 这鱼多～! The fish really smells!
【腥臊】xīngsāo〈形〉smelly
【腥膻】xīngshān〈形〉fishy
【腥味儿】xīngwèir〈名〉fishy smell: 她手上有鱼～。Her hands smelt of fish.

xíng

刑 xíng〈名〉1（刑罚）punishment: 量～ determine a penalty ‖ 判～三年 be sentenced to three years' imprisonment ‖ ～满释放 be released after serving one's sentence ▸～罚, 服～, 死～ 2（体罚）torture: ▸动～, 酷～
【刑部】Xíngbù〈名〉[历史] Ministry of Punishments
【刑场】xíngchǎng〈名〉execution ground
【刑罚】xíngfá〈名〉punishment: 减轻～ mitigate punishment
【刑法】xíngfǎ〈名〉penal code: 触犯～ violate the criminal law
【刑法】xíngfa〈名〉〈旧〉corporal punishment: 动～ administer torture
【刑房】xíngfáng〈名〉torture room: 私设～ set up an illegal torture chamber
【刑警】xíngjǐng〈名〉criminal police: ～队 criminal police
【刑拘】xíngjū A〈名〉criminal detention B〈动〉detain on criminal charges
【刑具】xíngjù〈名〉instrument of torture
【刑律】xínglǜ〈名〉criminal law: 触犯～ violate the criminal law
【刑名】xíngmíng〈名〉1〈旧〉（法律）law 2（指名称）name of a punishment 3（指事务）official in charge of criminal prosecution [in the Qing Dynasty]
【刑期】xíngqī〈名〉prison term: ～已满 have served one's sentence
【刑事】xíngshì〈形〉[法律] criminal: ～案件 criminal case ‖ ～拘留 criminal custody ‖ ～犯罪 criminal offence
【刑事处罚】xíngshì chǔfá〈名〉criminal sanction
【刑事法规】xíngshì fǎguī〈名〉penal statute
【刑事法庭】xíngshì fǎtíng〈名〉criminal court
【刑事犯】xíngshìfàn〈名〉criminal
【刑事判决】xíngshì pànjué〈名〉penal sentence
【刑事审判】xíngshì shěnpàn〈名〉criminal trial: ～庭 tribunal
【刑事诉讼】xíngshì sùsòng〈名〉criminal prosecution: 提起～ bring criminal action
【刑事责任】xíngshì zérèn〈名〉criminal responsibility: 负有～ be criminally liable
【刑事侦查】xíngshì zhēnchá〈名〉criminal investigation
【刑讯】xíngxùn〈动〉exact a confession through torture: 禁止～逼供 extorting a confession through torture is forbidden
【刑侦】xíngzhēn = 刑事侦查

邢 Xíng〈名〉Xing [surname]

行 xíng
A〈动〉1（走）go: 缓步而～ walk at a leisurely pace ‖ 日～百里 travel a hundred *li* a day ▸～走, 寸步难～, 游～ 2（旅行）travel: 西安之～ trip to Xi'an ▸不虚此～, 旅～ 3（流通）be current: ～销全国 be on sale all over the country ▸～时, 流～ 4（做）do: ▸～礼, ～医 5（可以）be all right: 你今天晚上来，～吗? Is it all right for you to come tonight? ‖ 签上你的名字就～了。All you have to do is to sign your name. 6（进行）[used before a disyllabic verb, indicating the performance of certain action]: 另～通知 issue a separate notice
B〈形〉1（与旅行相关）travelling: ▸～程, ～装 2（临时性）temporary: ▸～宫, ～营 3（能干）competent: 我的口语不～。My oral English is poor. ‖ 小王，你真～! Xiao Wang, you are really terrific!
C〈名〉behaviour: ▸暴～, 品～, 言～
D〈副〉〈书〉soon: ▸～将就木
▸háng, hàng, héng
【行百里者半九十】xíngbǎilǐzhě bàn jiǔshí〈成〉〈喻〉the last bit of a task is the hardest to complete
【行板】xíngbǎn〈名〉[音乐] andante
【行不更名，坐不改姓】xíng bù gēngmíng, zuò bù gǎixìng〈成〉I will always be up front about my identity
【行不通】xíngbutōng〈动〉won't do: 你那一套～。Your method will get you nowhere.
【行藏】xíngcáng〈名〉〈书〉1（处世态度）conduct 2（底细）ins and outs: 查明～ ascertain sb.'s background ‖ 看破～ find out the ins and outs
【行草】xíngcǎo〈名〉[书法] running-cursive script [script between running and cursive scripts]
【行车】xíngchē〈动〉drive: 安全～十万公里 drive safely for 100,000 kilometres ‖ ～速度 driving speed ‖ ～执照 driving licence
▸hángchē
【行车道】xíngchēdào〈名〉1（指在马路上）traffic lane 2（指在公园中）drive
【行成于思】xíngchéngyúsī〈成〉success results from careful forethought
【行程】xíngchéng〈名〉1（路程）itinerary: 安排～ arrange a journey ‖ ～万里 travel 10,000 *li* ‖ 两天的～ two days' journey 2（进程）course: 历史～ course of history 3 = 冲程 chōngchéng
【行船】xíngchuán〈动〉navigate: 逆风～ sail against the wind ‖ 可～的河流 navigable river
【行刺】xíngcì〈动〉assassinate: ～总统 assassinate the President ‖ 图谋～ plot to assassinate
【行道树】xíngdàoshù〈名〉roadside tree
【行得通】xíngdetōng〈动〉will do: ～的计划 workable plan
【行动】xíngdòng A〈动〉1（走动）move about: ～不便 have difficulty moving about ‖ ～迟缓 move slowly 2（进行活动）take action: 付诸～ put into action ‖ 开始～ make a move ‖ ～起来 go into action
B〈名〉move: 有～自由 have freedom of movement ‖ ～诡秘 be furtive in one's movements
【行动计划】xíngdòng jìhuà〈名〉action plan

X

【行动准则】xíngdòng zhǔnzé〈名〉 operative norm
【行都】xíngdū〈名〉〈旧〉 provisional capital
【行方便】xíng fāngbian〈动〉 be accommodating: 请您行个方便! Please do me a favour.
【行房】xíngfáng ▸**p. 772**〈动〉〈婉〉have sex with one's spouse
【行宫】xínggōng〈名〉 temporary imperial abode
【行好】xínghǎo〈动〉 be charitable: 请行行好。 Please show your mercy.
【行贿】xínghuì〈动〉 bribe: 被指控～ be charged with bribery ‖ 向官员～ bribe an official
【行迹】xíngjì〈名〉 movements: ～不定 have no fixed whereabouts ‖ ～可疑 suspicious movements
【行将】xíngjiāng〈副〉〈书〉 soon: ～破产 be on the verge of bankruptcy ‖ ～消失的传统/习俗 dying tradition/custom
【行将就木】xíngjiāng-jiùmù〈成〉 have one foot in the grave
【行脚】xíngjiǎo〈动〉 [of a monk] travel far and wide on foot
【行脚僧】xíngjiǎosēng〈名〉 itinerant monk
【行劫】xíngjié〈动〉〈书〉 rob: 持械～ commit an armed robbery
【行进】xíngjìn〈动〉advance: 列队～ march in procession ‖ 全速～ travel at full speed
【行经】xíngjīng〈动〉 **1**（来月经） menstruate: ～规律 menstruate regularly **2**（途经） go by: ～西安去兰州 go to Lanzhou through Xi'an
【行径】xíngjìng〈名〉〈贬〉 act: 流氓～ rascality ‖ 侵略～ act of aggression ‖ 野蛮～ barbarous act
【行军】xíngjūn〈动〉 march: ～路线 route of a march ‖ ～途中 during the march ‖ 夜～ march by night ▸急～
【行军床】xíngjūnchuáng〈名〉 camp bed〈英〉; cot〈美〉
【行军壶】xíngjūnhú〈名〉 canteen
【行楷】xíngkǎi〈名〉［书法］ running-standard script [script between running and regular scripts]
【行乐】xínglè〈动〉〈书〉 seek amusement: 恣意～ indulge oneself in pleasure ▸及时～
【行礼】xínglǐ〈动〉 salute: 行注目礼 salute with one's eyes ‖ 向国旗～ salute the national flag
【行李】xíngli ▸**p. 411**〈名〉 luggage; baggage〈美〉: 领取～ claim one's luggage ‖ 收拾～ pack one's bags ‖ 托运～ check in one's luggage
【行李安全检查】xíngli ānquán jiǎnchá〈名〉 luggage check
【行李包】xínglibāo〈名〉 travelling bag
【行李车】xínglichē〈名〉 luggage van〈英〉; baggage car〈美〉
【行李房】xínglifáng〈名〉 luggage room
【行李寄存处】xíngli jìcúnchù〈名〉 left-luggage office〈英〉; baggage room〈美〉
【行李寄存柜】xíngli jìcúnguì〈名〉 luggage locker
【行李架】xínglijià〈名〉 luggage rack
【行李间】xínglijiān〈名〉 luggage compartment
【行李卷儿】xínglijuǎnr〈名〉 bedroll
【行李推车】xíngli tuīchē〈名〉 trolley
【行李托运】xíngli tuōyùn〈名〉luggage consignment
【行李箱】xínglixiāng〈名〉 boot (of car)〈英〉; trunk〈美〉
【行猎】xíngliè〈动〉〈书〉 go hunting
【行令】xínglìng〈动〉 play a drinking game: 猜拳～ be engaged in a finger-guessing game
【行旅】xínglǚ **A**〈名〉 traveller **B**〈动〉 travel: 记录下～途中的所见所闻 keep a record of what one has seen and heard on the road
【行囊】xíngnáng〈名〉〈书〉 travelling bag: 背着～ carry a travelling bag on one's back
【行骗】xíngpiàn〈动〉 cheat: 扮做记者～ deceive people by posing as a reporter
【行期】xíngqī〈名〉 departure date: 推迟～ postpone one's trip ‖ ～未定。 The departure date is yet to be decided.
【行乞】xíngqǐ〈动〉〈书〉 go begging: 靠～为生 live by begging ‖ 沿街～ beg in the street
【行腔】xíngqiāng〈动〉 [of traditional opera actors/actresses] handle tunes according to one's own understanding
【行窃】xíngqiè〈动〉 steal: ～时被抓获 be caught red-handed
【行箧】xíngqiè〈名〉〈旧〉 travelling suitcase
【行人】xíngrén〈名〉 pedestrian: 过往～ passers-by ‖ ～天桥 overpass
【行人情】xíng rénqíng〈动〉 give gifts to one's relatives and friends
【行若无事】xíngruòwúshì〈成〉 go about calmly as if nothing was the matter
【行色】xíngsè〈名〉〈书〉 scene at a departure: 以壮～ have sb. to leave in style ‖ ～匆匆 be in a hurry to set out
【行善】xíngshàn〈动〉 perform charitable deeds: 一生～ spend one's life doing good deeds
【行商】xíngshāng **A**〈动〉 do business: 下海～ go into business **B**〈名〉 travelling trader
【行赏】xíngshǎng〈动〉 dispense rewards: 论功～ mete out awards according to merit
【行尸走肉】xíngshī-zǒuròu〈成〉 **1**〈本〉 walking corpse **2**〈喻〉 layabout
【行时】xíngshí〈动〉 **1**（流行） be popular: ～一阵 be popular for a time ‖ 不再～ be no longer in fashion/vogue **2**（得势） be in the ascendant
【行使】xíngshǐ〈动〉 exercise: ～宪法赋予的权利 exercise one's constitutional rights ‖ ～职权 exercise one's functions and powers
【行驶】xíngshǐ〈动〉 [of vehicles or boats] go: 超速～ drive above the speed limit ‖ 这条船沿长江向上游～。 The ship sailed up the Yangtze River.
【行事】xíngshì **A**〈动〉 act: 谨慎～ play (it) safe ‖ 看人眼色～ take one's cue from others ▸见机～ **B**〈名〉 behaviour: 言谈～ speech and conduct
【行书】xíngshū〈名〉［书法］ running script
【行署】xíngshǔ〈简称〉= 行政公署
【行头】xíngtou〈名〉 **1**（戏服） costume and paraphernalia **2**〈诙〉（服装） outfit: ～多 have a large wardrobe
【行为】xíngwéi〈名〉 behaviour: ～不检 be indiscreet in one's conduct ‖ 不道德的～ unethical conduct ‖ 欺骗～ fraud ‖ ～规范 code of conduct
【行为能力】xíngwéi nénglì〈名〉 capacity
【行为人】xíngwéirén〈名〉 actor
【行为异常】xíngwéi yìcháng〈名〉 behaviour disorder
【行为主义】xíngwéizhǔyì〈名〉 behaviourism
【行为准则】xíngwéi zhǔnzé〈名〉 code of conduct
【行文】xíngwén〈动〉 **1**（写作） write: ～流畅 read smoothly **2**（发公文给） distribute an official document: ～各部委 send a document to all the ministries and commissions
【行侠仗义】xíngxiá-zhàngyì〈成〉 take action to uphold justice
【行销】xíngxiāo〈动〉 sell: ～全国 be on sale throughout the country
【行星】xíngxīng〈名〉 planet: 大/小～ major/minor planet
【行刑】xíngxíng〈动〉 execute: 因杀人而被～ be executed for murder ‖ ～队 executioners
【行凶】xíngxiōng〈动〉 assault: ～杀人 commit murder ‖ ～作恶 break the law and commit evils
【行医】xíngyī〈动〉 practise medicine: 世代～ practise medicine for generations
【行营】xíngyíng〈名〉〈旧〉 field headquarters
【行辕】xíngyuán = 行营 xíngyíng
【行云流水】xíngyún-liúshuǐ〈成〉 [of a writing style] natural and smooth: 他的文章如～，畅达自然。 He writes with natural grace.
【行者】xíngzhě〈名〉 **1**〈书〉（行人） pedestrian **2**［佛教］ untonsured monk
【行政】xíngzhèng **A**〈动〉 do administrative work: 依法～ administer according to law ‖ ～当局 executive authority ‖ ～机关 administrative organ **B**〈名〉 administration: ～费用 administrative expenses ‖ ～事务 administrative affairs ‖ ～主管 executive officer
【行政部门】xíngzhèng bùmén〈名〉administrative department
【行政处罚】xíngzhèng chǔfá〈名〉 administrative punishment
【行政处分】xíngzhèng chǔfèn〈名〉administrative sanction
【行政法规】xíngzhèng fǎguī〈名〉 administrative regulations
【行政复议】xíngzhèng fùyì〈名〉 administrative reconsideration
【行政公署】xíngzhèng gōngshǔ〈名〉 administrative office
【行政官员】xíngzhèng guānyuán〈名〉 administrator
【行政管理】xíngzhèng guǎnlǐ〈名〉 administration: ～费用 administration costs ‖ ～权 administrative power ‖ ～人员 administrative staff ‖ ～体制 system of administration
【行政拘留】xíngzhèng jūliú〈名〉 administrative attachment
【行政立法】xíngzhèng lìfǎ〈名〉 administrative legislation
【行政命令】xíngzhèng mìnglìng〈名〉 ministerial decree
【行政区】xíngzhèngqū〈名〉 administrative region: 香港特别～ Hong Kong Special Administrative Region (HKSAR)
【行政区划】xíngzhèng qūhuà〈名〉 administrative division
【行政事业单位】xíngzhèng shìyè dānwèi〈名〉 government departments and state institutions
【行政诉讼】xíngzhèng sùsòng〈名〉 administrative lawsuit: ～法 laws governing administrative procedure
【行政长官】xíngzhèng zhǎngguān〈名〉 chief executive
【行之有效】xíngzhī-yǒuxiào〈成〉 effective: ～的措施 effective measure
【行止】xíngzhǐ〈名〉〈书〉 **1**（行踪）

whereabouts: ～不明 sb.'s whereabouts are unknown **2**（行为）conduct: ～不端 be indiscreet in conduct
【行装】xíngzhuāng〈名〉baggage: 整理～ pack one's things
【行状】xíngzhuàng〈名〉〈书〉brief obituary
【行踪】xíngzōng〈名〉whereabouts: 隐匿～ cover one's tracks ‖ ～不定 be of no fixed whereabouts
【行走】xíngzǒu〈动〉walk: ～不便 walk with difficulty

饧（餳）xíng

A〈名〉〈书〉molasses: ～渣 molasses sediment
B〈动〉go soft: 糖～了。The sweets have gone soft and sticky. ‖ 这块面得～一～。The dough needs softening a bit.
C〈形〉drowsy-eyed: 两眼发～ be sleepy-eyed
▸táng

形 xíng

A〈名〉**1**（形体）body: ▸～影不离，无～ **2**（形状）shape: 不成～ be shapeless ▸长方～，菱～，奇～怪状
B〈动〉**1**（显露）appear: 他很难过，但毫不～之于色。He gave no outward sign of the sadness he felt. ▸喜～于色 **2**（比较）compare: ▸相～见绌
【形变】xíngbiàn〈名〉**1**［物理］deformation: ～张量 deformation tensor **2**［语言］declension
【形成】xíngchéng〈动〉take shape: ～独特风格 take on one's own unique style ‖ ～僵局 come to a deadlock ‖ ～鲜明对比 form a sharp contrast ‖ 这项计划已经～。The plan has already begun to take shape.
【形单影只】xíngdān-yǐngzhī〈成〉be all alone
【形而上学】xíng'érshàngxué〈名〉**1**（指哲学）metaphysics **2**（指世界观或方法论）world outlook or methodology that is opposed to dialectic materialism
【形符】xíngfú〈名〉pictogram
【形格势禁】xínggé-shìjìn〈成〉be hampered by circumstances
【形骸】xínghái〈名〉〈书〉human skeleton: 放浪～ refuse to be bound by convention
【形秽】xínghuì〈名〉vulgar appearance: ▸自惭～
【形迹】xíngjì〈名〉**1**（举动和神色）movements and expressions: 不露～ betray nothing in one's expressions and movements ‖ ～可疑 furtive behaviour **2**（痕迹）trace: 不留～ leave no trace **3**（礼貌）formality: 不拘～ without formality
【形旁】xíngpáng〈名〉［语言］pictographic element of a pictophonetic character
【形容】xíngróng **A**〈名〉〈书〉countenance: ～消瘦 look thin **B**〈动〉describe: 难以～ be beyond description ‖ 那情景无法用笔墨～。The scene defied all description.
【形容词】xíngróngcí〈名〉adjective
【形声】xíngshēng〈名〉pictophonetic character [usu made up of two elements, one of which indicates the meaning and the other the pronunciation]
【形式】xíngshì〈名〉form: 拘泥于～ observe the form ‖ 艺术～ art form ‖ ～和内容的统一 unity of form and content
【形式化】xíngshìhuà **A**〈动〉formalize **B**〈名〉formalization
【形式逻辑】xíngshì luójí〈名〉formal logic
【形式主义】xíngshìzhǔyì〈名〉formalism
【形势】xíngshì〈名〉**1**（外形结构）terrain: ～险要 be in a strategic inaccessible position ‖ 地理～ topographical features **2**（状态）situation: 国内/国际～ domestic/international situation ‖ 经济/政治～ economic/political situation ‖ ～逼人 the situation demands immediate action ‖ ～对你不利。The odds are against you.
【形似】xíngsì〈形〉similar in form: ～实非 be similar in form but different in kind ‖ 追求神似而非～ seek likeness in spirit rather than in appearance
【形态】xíngtài〈名〉**1**（外表体现）form: ～奇异 be strange in shape ‖ ～优美 have a beautiful shape ‖ 物质～ forms of matter ‖ 地球上的生命有很多～。Life on earth takes many shapes. ▸意识～ **2**［生物］［语言］morphology
【形态学】xíngtàixué〈名〉［生物］［语言］morphology
【形体】xíngtǐ〈名〉**1**（身体）figure: 保持～ keep one's figure ‖ ～苗条 have a slender physique **2**（形态结构）form and structure: 汉字的～ form of Chinese characters
【形体语言】xíngtǐ yǔyán〈名〉body language
【形同虚设】xíngtóngxūshè〈成〉exist in name only
【形象】xíngxiàng **A**〈名〉**1**（总体印象）image: 改善～ improve one's image ‖ ～良好 have a good image **2**（具体形状）imagery: 塑造人物～ create a character **B**〈形〉vivid: ～地描述 vividly describe ‖ 语言精练而～。The language is concise and vivid.
【形象大使】xíngxiàng dàshǐ〈名〉image representative
【形象代言人】xíngxiàng dàiyánrén〈名〉image spokesman
【形象工程】xíngxiàng gōngchéng〈名〉image project
【形象化】xíngxiànghuà〈动〉symbolize: ～的语言 symbolic language
【形象设计】xíngxiàng shèjì〈名〉image design
【形象思维】xíngxiàng sīwéi〈名〉thinking in images or symbols
【形销骨立】xíngxiāo-gǔlì〈成〉be nothing but skin and bones
【形形色色】xíngxíng-sèsè〈成〉assorted and varied: ～的货物 all kinds of goods ‖ ～的政客 politicians of various hues
【形影不离】xíngyǐng-bùlí〈成〉be inseparable: ～的朋友 inseparable friends
【形影相吊】xíngyǐng-xiāngdiào〈成〉be extremely lonely
【形影相随】xíngyǐng-xiāngsuí〈成〉be inseparable
【形制】xíngzhì〈名〉structure: ～优美 beautiful design
【形状】xíngzhuàng〈名〉shape: 保持原有的～ keep the original shape ‖ 改变～ change the shape ‖ ～不一 be differently shaped

陉（陘）xíng

〈名〉〈书〉mountain pass

型 xíng

〈名〉**1**（模具）mould: ▸模～ **2**（类型）model: 赛车～汽车 sports model ‖ 她不属于传统～妇女。She doesn't fit into the traditional mould of a woman. ▸～号，类～，血～ **3**（样式）form: 题～ question type ▸成～，定～，体～，造～ **4**（例子）example: ▸典～
【型材】xíngcái〈名〉［冶金］section bar
【型钢】xínggāng〈名〉shaped steel
【型号】xínghào〈名〉model: ～齐全 have a complete range of models ‖ 各种～的玩具汽车 toy cars of all shapes and sizes
【型男】xíngnán〈名〉stylish young man

xǐng

省 xǐng

〈动〉**1**（反思）examine oneself: ▸反～，内～ **2**〈书〉（探望）visit one's parents/elders: 归～ return home to visit one's parents ▸～亲 **3**（醒悟）become aware: 猛～ suddenly wake up to the truth ▸～悟，发人深～
▸shěng
【省察】xǐngchá〈动〉examine one's thoughts and conduct
【省亲】xǐngqīn〈动〉visit one's parents/elders
【省视】xǐngshì〈动〉call on: ～双亲 pay a visit to one's parents
【省悟】xǐngwù = 醒悟 xǐngwù

醒 xǐng

A〈动〉**1**（神志恢复正常）come round: 昏迷不～ remain unconscious ‖ 病人终于～过来了。The patient finally regained consciousness. ▸～酒，苏～ **2**（不在睡眠状态）wake up: 从睡梦中～来 awake from a dream ‖ 孩子～了。The children are awake. **3**（觉悟）become aware: ▸～悟，觉～，猛～
B〈形〉eye-catching: ▸～目
【醒豁】xǐnghuò〈形〉clear: 道理说得～ present one's argument clearly
【醒酒】xǐngjiǔ〈动〉sober up: 浓茶能帮他～。A cup of strong tea will sober him up.
【醒木】xǐngmù〈名〉story-teller's gavel
【醒目】xǐngmù〈形〉eye-catching: ～的标题 bold headline ‖ 红梅在白雪的衬托下显得格外～。Red plums stand out against the background of white snow.
【醒世】xǐngshì〈动〉〈书〉awaken the world: ～之言 words to arouse the public
【醒悟】xǐngwù〈动〉come to realize: 从错误中～过来 realize one's mistake

擤 xǐng

〈动〉blow one's nose: ～鼻涕 blow one's nose

xìng

兴（興）xìng

〈名〉interest: ～之所致 when one is in high spirits ‖ 乘～而去，败～而归。Leave in high spirits and come back disappointed. ▸～高采烈，～致，雅～
▸xīng
【兴冲冲】xìngchōngchōng〈形〉excited: ～地跑回家 run home in high spirits
【兴高采烈】xìnggāo-cǎiliè〈成〉jubilant: 听到我成功的消息他们～。They were immensely excited to learn of my success.
【兴会】xìnghuì〈名〉sudden flash of inspiration: 乘一时的～ on the spur of the moment
【兴趣】xìngqù〈名〉interest: 产生极大～ become very interested in (sb./sth.) ‖ 毫无～ be completely uninterested ‖ ～广泛 have broad interests

【兴头】xìngtóu〈名〉 enthusiasm: 看足球赛的～很大 be very keen on watching football games
【兴头儿上】 xìngtóurshang〈副〉 at the height of one's enthusiasm: 他正在～，别打扰他。 He is really enjoying himself. Leave him alone.
【兴味】xìngwèi〈名〉 interest: 饶有～ with great interest ‖ ～索然 be uninterested
【兴致】xìngzhì〈名〉 interest: ～不高 be not in the right mood
【兴致勃勃】xìngzhì-bóbó〈成〉 be in high spirits

杏 xìng〈名〉 apricot

【杏脯】xìngfǔ〈名〉 preserved apricot
【杏红】xìnghóng〈名〉 apricot pink
【杏核儿】xìnghúr〈名〉 apricot stone
【杏花】xìnghuā〈名〉 apricot blossom
【杏黄】xìnghuáng〈名〉 apricot yellow
【杏仁】xìngrén〈名〉 almond
【杏仁茶】xìngrénchá〈名〉 almond tea
【杏仁露】xìngrénlù〈名〉 almond milk
【杏树】xìngshù〈名〉 apricot tree
【杏眼】xìngyǎn〈名〉 almond-shaped eye: ～桃腮 large eyes and rosy cheeks
【杏子】xìngzi〈名〉 apricot: ～酱 apricot jam

幸[1] xìng

A〈形〉 fortunate: 有～见到你，我很高兴。 Pleased to meet you.
B〈副〉 **1**（侥幸） fortunately: ▸～亏，侥～ **2**〈书〉（希望） hopefully: ～勿推辞。 I hope that you will not refuse. ‖ ～勿见怪。 I hope that you will not be offended.
C〈动〉 rejoice: 欣～ be glad and thankful ▸～灾乐祸，庆～

幸[2]（倖） xìng〈动〉〈书〉

1（宠幸） favour: 得～ win favour ▸～臣，宠～ **2**〈旧〉（亲临某地） [of an emperor] grace with one's presence: ▸巡～
【幸臣】xìngchén〈名〉〈贬〉 court favourite
【幸存】xìngcún〈动〉 survive: 历经万险而～ survive all perils ‖ ～者 survivor
【幸而】xìng'ér〈副〉 luckily: ～你及时赶到帮我解了围。 Fortunately, you came in time to rescue me.
【幸福】xìngfú **A**〈名〉 happiness: 为人民谋～ work for the well-being of the people ‖ 追求～ seek happiness ‖ 婚姻～ have a happy marriage **B**〈形〉 happy: ～的回忆 happy memory ‖ ～的童年 happy childhood
【幸好】xìnghǎo = 幸亏 xìngkuī
【幸会】xìnghuì〈动〉〈套〉 be honoured to meet: ～，～。 It's a great honour to have met you.
【幸亏】xìngkuī〈副〉 luckily: ～抢救及时，他才保住了性命。 It was only thanks to the timely emergency treatment that his life was saved.
【幸免】 xìngmiǎn〈动〉 have a narrow escape: ～于难 escape death by a hair's breadth
【幸甚】xìngshèn〈动〉〈书〉 **1**（值得庆幸） be blessed: 如是则国家～，民族～。 If so, blessed indeed are both the country and the people. **2**〈套〉（非常荣幸） be honoured: 承不吝赐教，～，～。 We feel greatly honoured to be enlightened by your generous instructions.
【幸事】xìngshì〈名〉 good fortune: 意想不到的～ unexpected blessing
【幸运】xìngyùn **A**〈名〉 good fortune: ～之神 Lady Luck **B**〈形〉 lucky: 你大难不死可真～。 You're very lucky to have survived that tragic accident.
【幸运儿】xìngyùn'ér〈名〉 fortune's favourite: 你这～! You lucky dog!
【幸灾乐祸】xìngzāi-lèhuò〈成〉 be gratified by others' misfortunes: 对别人的失败～ smile smugly at the failures of others

性 xìng

A〈名〉 **1**（性格） nature: ～善 be good-natured ▸人～，兽～，野～ **2**（特性） character: ▸～格，秉～，耐～ **3**（性质） nature: ▸～能，词～，惯～ **4**（性别） sex: ▸男～，女～，雄～ **5**（与性相关） sexual intercourse: ～侵犯 sexual assault ‖ ～变态 sexual perversion ▸～病，～感 **6**［语法］ gender: ▸阳～，阴～，中～
B〈后缀〉 [used to form nouns and adjectives]: 独创～ originality ‖ 纪律～ discipline ‖ 科学～ scientific nature ▸可能～，弹～，特殊～
【性爱】xìng'ài〈名〉 sexual love
【性别】 xìngbié〈名〉 sex: 不分年龄和～ regardless of age or gender
【性别比】xìngbiébǐ〈名〉 sex ratio: 出生人口～ birth sex ratio ‖ 城市与农村人口～有差异。 The sex ratios of urban and rural populations vary.
【性别歧视】xìngbié qíshì〈名〉 sexism
【性病】xìngbing ▸**p. 50**〈名〉 venereal disease (VD)
【性传播】xìngchuánbō〈动〉 be sexually transmitted: ～疾病 sexually transmitted disease ‖ ～成为艾滋病的主要传播途径。 AIDS is spread primarily through sexual transmission.
【性犯罪】xìngfànzuì〈名〉 sex crime: ～分子 sex offender
【性感】xìnggǎn〈形〉sexy: ～明星 sexy star
【性高潮】xìnggāocháo〈名〉 orgasm: 达到～ reach orgasm
【性格】xìnggé〈名〉 nature: ～迥异 have very different characters ‖ ～开朗 be of a bright and cheerful disposition ‖ ～内向/外向 be introverted/extroverted
【性格演员】xìnggé yǎnyuán〈名〉 character actor/actress
【性功能障碍】 xìnggōngnéng zhàng'ài〈名〉 sexual dysfunction
【性关系】xìngguānxi〈名〉 sexual relations: 发生～ have sex
【性贿赂】xìnghuìlù〈名〉 sexual bribery
【性激素】xìngjīsù〈名〉 sex hormone
【性急】xìngjí〈形〉 short-tempered
【性价比】xìngjiàbǐ〈名〉 performance-price ratio
【性交】xìngjiāo〈动〉 have sex: 艾滋病病毒会通过～传染。 HIV can be transmitted through sexual intercourse.
【性教育】xìngjiàoyù〈名〉sex education: 接受～ receive sex education
【性解放】xìngjiěfàng〈名〉sexual liberation
【性冷淡】xìnglěngdàn〈名〉 frigidity
【性灵】xìnglíng〈名〉〈书〉 natural disposition: 陶冶～ mould one's temperament
【性命】 xìngmìng〈名〉 life: 险些丢了～ come to within an inch of one's life
【性命交关】 xìngmìng-jiāoguān〈成〉 of critical importance: 这是～的事情。 This is a matter of life and death.
【性命攸关】xìngmìng-yōuguān = 性命交关 xìngmìng-jiāoguān
【性能】xìngnéng〈名〉 natural capacity: ～不好/良好 perform poorly/well ‖ ～稳定 stable performance
【性虐待】xìngnüèdài〈名〉 sexual abuse, sadism
【性气】 xìngqì〈名〉 temperament: ～坏 have a bad disposition ‖ ～平和 be even-tempered
【性器官】xìngqìguān〈名〉 sex organ
【性侵犯】xìngqīnfàn〈动〉 sexually harass
【性情】xìngqíng〈名〉 disposition: ～柔顺 be of a yielding disposition ‖ ～随和 have an easy-going nature
【性取向】xìngqǔxiàng〈名〉 sexual orientation
【性染色体】xìngrǎnsètǐ〈名〉［生物］ sex chromosome
【性骚扰】xìngsāorǎo〈动〉 sexually harass: 起诉～ prosecute sb. for sexual harassment ‖ 遭受～ suffer sexual harassment
【性生活】xìngshēnghuó〈名〉 sex life
【性行为】xìngxíngwéi〈名〉 sexual behaviour: 非法～ illicit sexual act ‖ 婚前～ premarital sex ‖ 婚外～ extramarital sex
【性欲】xìngyù〈名〉 sex drive: 满足～ satisfy one's sexual desires ‖ ～冷淡/强烈 be under-sexed/over-sexed
【性质】xìngzhì〈名〉 nature: ～不同 be different in nature ‖ 化学～ chemical property ‖ 问题的～ nature of a problem
【性状】xìngzhuàng〈名〉 shape and properties: 土壤的理化～ physicochemical properties of the soil
【性子】xìngzi〈名〉 **1**（脾气） temper: 使～ get into a temper ‖ 由着～ give free rein to one's temper ‖ 急～ be short-tempered ‖ 慢～ have a sluggish disposition **2**（刺激性） strength: 这药～平和。 The drug is mild.

姓 xìng

A〈名〉 surname: 贵～? May I know your surname? ‖ 尊～大名。Your name, please. ▸～名，～氏，百家～
B〈动〉 be surnamed: 你～什么？——我～李。 What's your surname? — My surname is Li.
【姓名】xìngmíng〈名〉full name: ～权 right to one's name

> **姓名**
>
> In ancient times, a person was given a *ming* (名) at birth and was bestowed a *zi* (字) only at the age of 20, when he reached his maturity. He referred to himself by his *ming*, while addressing others by their *zi*. There was usually a connection in meaning between the *ming* and the *zi*. For instance, the *ming* of Zhuge Liang (诸葛亮), a politician who has become synonymous with resourcefulness in China, is *liang* (亮), which means 'bright'. His *zi* is Kongming (孔明), in which *ming* (明) also means 'bright'. Traditionally, one's *ming* or *zi* often reflected one's position in the family hierarchy. *Hao* (号) was originally an epithet one chose to describe oneself. Later on, it was also used at times to refer to *ming* or *zi*. Today, the word *mingzi* (名字) can mean either a person's full name (including surname), or just the given name. The surname (姓) designates the family clan, and comes before the given name.

【姓氏】xìngshì〈名〉 surname: 按～笔画排列 arranged according to the strokes in surnames

荇 xìng

【荇菜】xìngcài〈古〉= 莕菜 xìngcài

荇 xìng

【荇菜】xìngcài〈名〉［植物］floating heart

悻 xìng〈形〉〈书〉angry: ▸～然

【悻然】xìngrán〈形〉angry

【悻悻】xìngxìng〈形〉angry: ～而去 go off in a huff

婞 xìng〈形〉〈书〉obstinate

xiōng

凶[1] xiōng〈形〉1（不幸）inauspicious: ～事 inauspicious event ‖ ～讯 ominous news ▸～宅, ～兆 2〈书〉（年成很坏）detrimental to crops: ▸～年

凶[2]（兇）xiōng

A〈形〉1（凶恶）fierce: 样子很～ be fierce-looking ▸～恶, ～猛, 穷～极恶 2（厉害）terrible: 病势很～ be critically ill ‖ 抽烟很～ smoke a lot

B〈名〉1〈书〉（指人）ruffian: 四～ four ruffians ▸帮～, 元～ 2（指行为）act of violence: ▸～犯, ～器, 行～

【凶案】xiōng'àn〈名〉murder case

【凶暴】xiōngbào〈形〉fierce and brutal: 脾气～ be of fiendish temper

【凶残】xiōngcán〈形〉savage: ～成性 be cruel by nature ‖ ～的阴谋 fiendish plot

【凶多吉少】xiōngduō-jíshǎo〈成〉bode ill rather than well

【凶恶】xiōng'è〈形〉ferocious: ～的歹徒 vicious ruffians ‖ ～的样子 baleful look

【凶犯】xiōngfàn〈名〉criminal: 缉拿～ track down a murderer

【凶悍】xiōnghàn〈形〉ferocious

【凶耗】xiōnghào〈名〉news of sb.'s death

【凶狠】xiōnghěn〈形〉1（凶恶狠毒）ferocious: ～的表情 fierce look ‖ ～的歹徒 fiendish gangster 2（猛烈）powerful: 扣球/射门～ make powerful smashes/shots at the goal

【凶横】xiōnghèng〈形〉brutal and ferocious: 说话～ speak in a rude way

【凶狂】xiōngkuáng〈形〉fierce and ruthless

【凶戾】xiōnglì〈形〉〈书〉ruthless and tyrannical

【凶猛】xiōngměng〈形〉ferocious: 洪水来势～。The flood rushed down with a devastating force. ‖ 狮子～地扑向猎物。The lion attacked its victim ferociously.

【凶年】xiōngnián〈名〉famine year

【凶虐】xiōngnüè〈形〉tyrannical

【凶气】xiōngqì〈名〉ferocious expression: 一脸～ wear a murderous expression

【凶器】xiōngqì〈名〉lethal weapon: 杀人～ murder weapon

【凶杀】xiōngshā〈动〉murder: 描写～和暴力 describe killing and violence

【凶煞】xiōngshà = 凶神 xiōngshén

【凶神】xiōngshén〈名〉demon

【凶神恶煞】xiōngshén-èshà〈成〉evil spirits

【凶手】xiōngshǒu〈名〉killer

【凶死】xiōngsǐ〈动〉die a violent death

【凶嫌】xiōngxián〈名〉murder suspect

【凶险】xiōngxiǎn〈形〉1（危险）critical: 病情～ be critically ill 2（凶恶阴险）ruthless and treacherous: 用心～ be treacherous

【凶相】xiōngxiàng〈名〉ferocious look: 一脸～ with a fiendish look ‖ ～毕露 unleash all one's ferocity

【凶信】xiōngxìn〈名〉news of sb.'s death: 报～ give the news of sb.'s death

【凶焰】xiōngyàn〈名〉ferocity: ～万丈 be extremely ferocious

【凶宅】xiōngzhái〈名〉haunted house

【凶兆】xiōngzhào〈名〉evil omen

兄 xiōng〈名〉1（哥哥）elder brother: ～妹 brother and sister ‖ 长～ elder brother ▸父～ 2（同辈年长男子）elder male cousin: ▸表～, 内～ 3〈尊〉（男性朋友）[used between men]: ▸老～, 仁～

【兄弟】xiōngdì A〈名〉brothers: 孪生～ twin brothers ‖ 亲～ brothers born of the same parents ‖ 异父/异母～ half brothers B〈形〉fraternal

【兄弟单位】xiōngdì dānwèi〈名〉other units

【兄弟民族】xiōngdì mínzú〈名〉other ethnic groups

【兄弟阋墙】xiōngdì-xìqiáng〈成〉internal dispute: ～，外御其侮。Internal disunity dissolves at the threat of external invasion.

【兄弟】xiōngdi〈名〉1（弟弟）younger brother 2（称比自己年幼的男子）[familiar address for a man younger than oneself] 3〈谦〉（用于自称）I: ～不敢。I dare not.

【兄长】xiōngzhǎng〈名〉1 = 兄 xiōng 1 2（尊称男性朋友）respectful form of address for a male friend

芎 xiōng ▸川芎 chuānxiōng

匈 xiōng

【匈奴】Xiōngnú〈名〉Xiongnu [ancient nomadic peoples of Central Asia]

【匈牙利】Xiōngyálì〈名〉Hungary: ～人 Hungarian ‖ ～语 Hungarian

讻（訩）xiōng〈书〉

A〈动〉debate

B〈形〉tumultuous

【讻讻】xiōngxiōng〈形〉〈书〉tumultuous: 议论～ a flurry of discussion

汹（洶）xiōng〈形〉turbulent: ▸～涌澎湃

【汹汹】xiōngxiōng A〈拟〉〈书〉[sound of roaring waves]: 波浪～ surging waves B〈形〉〈贬〉truculent: ▸气势～

【汹涌】xiōngyǒng〈形〉tempestuous: 波涛～ turbulent waves ‖ ～而来的潮水 oncoming tide

【汹涌澎湃】xiōngyǒng-péngpài〈成〉sweeping and surging

胸 xiōng〈名〉1（胸部）chest: 挺～抬头 hold one's chest out and one's head high ‖ 突然感到一阵～痛 have a stabbing pain in one's chest ‖ 墙有齐～高。The wall is chest-high. ▸～腔, ～膛, 鸡～ 2（心里）heart: ▸～怀, ～襟, 心～

【胸部】xiōngbù〈名〉1（指躯干）chest: ～中弹 get a bullet in the breast ‖ 匕首刺入了他的～。The dagger pierced his breast. 2（指乳房）breasts: ～扁平 be flat-chested ‖ ～丰满 have a full bosom

【胸次】xiōngcì〈名〉〈书〉1（心情）mind: ～舒畅 have ease of mind 2（胸怀）breadth of mind: ～宽广 be broad-minded

【胸骨】xiōnggǔ〈名〉breast bone

【胸花】xiōnghuā〈名〉corsage

【胸怀】xiōnghuái A〈动〉cherish: ～大志 cherish high ideals ‖ ～全局 keep the overall situation in mind ‖ ～壮志 cherish high aspirations ‖ ～祖国 cherish one's motherland B〈名〉mind: ～磊落 be frank and honest ‖ ～坦白 be frank and open ‖ ～狭窄 be narrow-minded

【胸肌】xiōngjī〈名〉pectoral muscle

【胸襟】xiōngjīn〈名〉1（抱负）mind: ～开阔 be broad-minded ‖ ～狭窄 be narrow-minded 2（胸前）front: ～上戴着一朵大红花 wear a big red flower on one's front

【胸卡】xiōngkǎ〈名〉chest placard

【胸口】xiōngkǒu〈名〉chest: 感到～疼痛 feel unsettled in the pit of one's stomach ‖ ～堵得慌 feel a tightness in the chest

【胸毛】xiōngmáo〈名〉chest hair

【胸膜】xiōngmó〈名〉pleura: ～炎 pleurisy

【胸牌】xiōngpái〈名〉name badge: 挂着公司～的年轻白领 young professionals with company name badges

【胸脯】xiōngpú〈名〉breast: 拍～ beat one's chest ‖ 挺起～ puff out one's chest

【胸鳍】xiōngqí〈名〉pectoral fin

【胸腔】xiōngqiāng〈名〉chest cavity: ～外科 thoracic surgery

【胸墙】xiōngqiáng〈名〉1（矮墙）low wall up to the chest 2［军事］breastwork

【胸饰】xiōngshì〈名〉brooch

【胸膛】xiōngtáng〈名〉chest: 挺起～ throw out one's chest

【胸围】xiōngwéi〈名〉（指男性或女性）chest;（指女性）bust

【胸无城府】xiōngwúchéngfǔ〈成〉be simple and candid

【胸无大志】xiōngwúdàzhì〈成〉have no ambition at all

【胸无点墨】xiōngwúdiǎnmò〈成〉be unlearned: ～的商人 illiterate business person

【胸无芥蒂】xiōngwújièdì〈成〉bear no grudge

【胸像】xiōngxiàng〈名〉bust: 鲁迅/莎士比亚的～ bust of Lu Xun/Shakespeare

【胸臆】xiōngyì〈名〉〈书〉feelings: 直抒～ pour out one's heart

【胸有成竹】xiōngyǒuchéngzhú〈成〉〈喻〉have a well-thought-out plan

【胸章】xiōngzhāng〈名〉1（指标志）badge 2（指奖章）medal

【胸罩】xiōngzhào〈名〉bra

【胸针】xiōngzhēn〈名〉brooch

【胸中无数】xiōngzhōng-wúshù = 心中无数 xīnzhōng-wúshù

【胸中有数】xiōngzhōng-yǒushù = 心中有数 xīnzhōng-yǒushù

【胸椎】xiōngzhuī〈名〉sternal vertebra

xióng

雄 xióng

A〈形〉1（雄性）male: ▸～蜂, ～蕊, ～性 2（强有力）powerful: ▸～兵, ～才大略, ～劲 3（有气魄）grand: ▸～伟, ～壮

B〈名〉powerful and influential person/state: 战国七～ seven powerful states of the Warring States Period ▸奸～, 英～

【雄辩】xióngbiàn A〈名〉eloquence: 以～著称 have a reputation for powerful oratory ‖ ～是银，沉默是金。Speech is silver; silence is gold. ▸事实胜于～ B〈形〉eloquent: ～地证明 prove incontrovertibly

【雄兵】xióngbīng〈名〉crack troops: ～百万 hundreds of thousands of troops
【雄才大略】xióngcái-dàlüè〈成〉great talent and bold vision: 有～的人 person of rare and outstanding calibre
【雄风】xióngfēng〈名〉**1**〈书〉（强劲的风）strong wind **2**（威风）imposing manner: 重振～ restore power and prestige
【雄蜂】xióngfēng〈名〉drone
【雄关】xióngguān〈名〉〈书〉impregnable pass: 镇守～ garrison an impregnable pass
【雄厚】xiónghòu〈形〉abundant: 实力～ have enormous potential ‖ 资金～ abundant funds
【雄花】xiónghuā〈名〉staminate flower
【雄黄】xiónghuáng〈名〉realgar: ～酒 realgar liquor
【雄浑】xiónghún〈形〉forceful: ～的嗓音 strong voice ‖ ～的诗篇 powerful poem
【雄鸡】xióngjī〈名〉cock: ～报晓。The cock heralds the dawn.
【雄激素】xióngjīsù〈名〉androgen
【雄健】xióngjiàn〈形〉robust: ～的步伐 vigorous strides
【雄杰】xióngjié〈书〉**A**〈形〉exceptionally able: ～之士 man of great talent **B**〈名〉outstanding talent: 一代～ outstanding figure of the time
【雄劲】xióngjìn〈形〉majestic and powerful: 落笔～ write with great vigour
【雄赳赳】xióngjiūjiū〈形〉valiant: ～的列队士兵 soldiers in proud array ‖ ～，气昂昂 valiant and spirited
【雄踞】xióngjù〈动〉〈书〉be magnificently situated
【雄蕊】xióngruǐ〈名〉［植物］stamen
【雄师】xióngshī〈名〉powerful army: 百万～ a million bold troops
【雄图】xióngtú〈名〉grand plan: ～大略 great plan ‖ ～大业 great cause
【雄威】xióngwēi **A**〈名〉awesome bearing **B**〈形〉majestic
【雄伟】xióngwěi〈形〉**1**（雄壮）magnificent: ～壮丽 grand ‖ 气魄～ with great boldness and vision **2**（魁梧）tall and sturdy
【雄文】xióngwén〈名〉〈书〉profound and powerful literary work
【雄心】xióngxīn〈名〉great ambition: 缺乏～ lack ambition ‖ 他～依旧。His ambitions are still very much alive.
【雄心勃勃】xióngxīn-bóbó〈成〉cherish high aspirations: ～的计划 ambitious plan ‖ ～的年轻人 young man with grandiose ambitions
【雄心壮志】xióngxīn-zhuàngzhì〈成〉cherish lofty aspirations: 有～ have high aspirations
【雄性】xióngxìng〈名〉male: ～器官 male organ
【雄鹰】xióngyīng〈名〉strong and brave eagle
【雄壮】xióngzhuàng〈形〉**1**（强大）majestic: ～的军乐 majestic military music ‖ 威武～ mighty and powerful **2**（魁梧）tall and strong
【雄姿】xióngzī〈名〉majestic appearance: ～依旧 as heroic-looking as ever

熊 xióng

A〈名〉bear: ▸白～, 棕～
B〈形〉〈口〉useless: 你真～。You're pathetic. ▸～包
C〈动〉〈方〉scold: 挨～ get a scolding
【熊包】xióngbāo〈名〉〈口〉good-for-nothing
【熊胆】xióngdǎn〈名〉［中药］bear's gall
【熊猫】xióngmāo = 猫熊 māoxióng
【熊市】xióngshì〈名〉［金融］bear market
【熊瞎子】xióngxiāzi〈名〉〈方〉bear
【熊熊】xióngxióng〈形〉flaming: ～烈火 raging flames
【熊样儿】xióngyàngr〈名〉〈口〉pitiful/sheepish look
【熊掌】xióngzhǎng〈名〉bear's paw

xiū

休 xiū

A〈动〉**1**（休息）rest: ▸～假, ～息, 退～ **2**（停止）stop: ▸～会, 罢～, 喋喋不～ **3**〈旧〉（断绝夫妻关系）cast off one's wife and send her home: ～妻 divorce one's wife ▸～书
B〈副〉don't: ～怕。Don't be afraid. ▸～想
C〈形〉joyous: ～咎 good and bad fortune ▸～戚与共
【休兵】xiūbīng〈动〉stop fighting
【休耕】xiūgēng〈动〉［农业］rest: 这块地该～了。The field should be rested.
【休耕地】xiūgēngdì〈名〉fallow land
【休怪】xiūguài〈动〉don't blame (sb. for sth.): 他病了，～他旷课。Don't criticize him for skipping class. He was ill.
【休会】xiūhuì〈动〉adjourn a meeting: 宣布～ announce a recess ‖ ～一周 adjourn for a week ‖ ～期间 between sessions
【休会辩论】xiūhuì biànlùn〈名〉adjournment debate: 提议进行～ move an adjournment debate
【休假】xiūjià〈动〉go on holiday: 放弃～ give up one's holiday ‖ 休病假 be on sick leave ‖ 休产假 be on maternity leave ‖ 他可以带薪休假两周。He is entitled to two weeks' paid holiday.
【休克】xiūkè **A**〈名〉shock: 过敏性～ allergic shock **B**〈动〉go into shock: 他～了。He is suffering from shock.
【休克疗法】xiūkè liáofǎ〈名〉shock therapy: 实施～ apply shock therapy
【休眠】xiūmián〈动〉lie dormant: 冬天种子在土壤中～。Seeds remain dormant in the earth during winter. ‖ 冬季，蛇进入～状态。In winter, snakes go into a state of hibernation.
【休眠火山】xiūmián huǒshān〈名〉dormant volcano
【休眠期】xiūmiánqī〈名〉dormancy period
【休牧】xiūmù〈动〉suspend grazing
【休戚相关】xiūqī-xiāngguān〈成〉share joys and sorrows: ～，患难与共 be bound by a common cause and go through thick and thin together
【休戚与共】xiūqī-yùgòng〈成〉share weal and woe: ～，生死相依 share weal and woe, and stick together in life and death
【休憩】xiūqì〈动〉〈书〉take a rest
【休市】xiūshì〈动〉shut up shop
【休书】xiūshū〈名〉〈旧〉letter declaring one's decision to divorce one's wife
【休庭】xiūtíng〈动〉adjourn: 法官宣布～。The judge called a recess.
【休息】xiūxi〈动〉have a rest: 需要好好～ need a good rest ‖ ～片刻 take a breather ‖ 课间～ have a break between classes ‖ ～室 lounge
【休闲】xiūxián〈动〉**1**（休息）be at leisure: ～设施 leisure facilities ‖ ～装 casual wear **2**［农业］lie fallow: ～地 fallow land
【休闲装】xiūxiánzhuāng〈名〉casual wear: "80后"爱穿～。The 80s generation like wearing casual clothes.
【休想】xiūxiǎng〈动〉don't think about: 你～赖账。Don't think you can repudiate the debt. ‖ ～逃跑。Don't you dare think about trying to escape.
【休学】xiūxué〈动〉suspend schooling
【休养】xiūyǎng〈动〉**1**（指个人）recuperate: 去乡下～ go to the countryside to recuperate ‖ 长期～ long convalescence **2**（指国家）revitalize: ～国力 restore the national strength
【休养生息】xiūyǎng-shēngxī〈成〉recuperate and rebuild
【休业】xiūyè〈动〉**1**（指营业）close down: ～整顿 be closed for a shake-up ‖ 今天～。Closed today. **2**（指学习）complete one's studies
【休渔】xiūyú〈动〉suspend fishing
【休战】xiūzhàn〈动〉call a truce: 同意～ agree to a truce ‖ 宣布～ declare a ceasefire
【休整】xiūzhěng〈动〉rest and reorganize: 军队需要～。The troops need some time to rest and recuperate.
【休止】xiūzhǐ〈动〉stop: 无～地争论 argue endlessly
【休止符】xiūzhǐfú〈名〉［音乐］rest

咻 xiū

A〈动〉〈书〉make a din
B ▸咻咻 xiūxiū
【咻咻】xiūxiū〈拟〉**1**（形容喘气声）[sound of breathing]: ～地喘气 pant noisily ‖ ～的鼻息 noisy breathing through the nostrils **2**（形容叫声）cry of certain birds and animals: 小鸭～地叫着。The duckling is cheeping.

修 xiū

A〈动〉**1**（修饰）decorate: ▸～辞, ～饰, 不～边幅 **2**（修理）repair: ～表 repair a watch ‖ ～自行车 mend a bicycle ▸～复, ～缮, 维～ **3**（修建）build: ～路 build a road ‖ ～水库 construct a reservoir ‖ ～铁路 build a railway ▸～建, 兴～ **4**〈书〉（修编）write: ～史 write history ‖ ～志 compile local chronicles **5**（学习）study: ～完中学课程 complete high school courses ▸～身, ～养, 进～ **6**（修行）practise a religious doctrine: ▸～道, ～士 **7**（修剪）trim: ～草坪 mow a lawn ‖ ～树枝 prune off branches ‖ ～指甲 cut one's fingernails ▸～剪
B〈形〉long: ～竹 thin and long bamboo ▸～长
【修补】xiūbǔ〈动〉mend: ～旧鞋 mend old shoes ‖ ～篱笆 mend the fence ‖ ～破洞 fix a puncture ‖ ～屋顶 patch up a roof ‖ ～衣服 patch clothes
【修长】xiūcháng〈形〉slender: 身材～ slim build
【修船】xiūchuán〈动〉refit a ship
【修船厂】xiūchuánchǎng〈名〉shipyard
【修船坞】xiūchuánwù〈名〉repair dock
【修辞】xiūcí **A**〈动〉polish the language **B**〈名〉rhetoric: ～手法 rhetorical device
【修辞格】xiūcígé〈名〉［语言］figure of speech
【修辞学】xiūcíxué〈名〉［语言］rhetoric
【修道】xiūdào〈动〉［宗教］cultivate oneself according to a religious doctrine
【修道士】xiūdàoshì = 修士 xiūshì
【修道院】xiūdàoyuàn〈名〉（男修道院）monastery;（女修道院）convent
【修订】xiūdìng〈动〉revise: ～教学计划

X

revise a teaching plan ‖ ～本 revised edition

【修复】xiūfù〈动〉**1**（修理使复原）repair: ～关系 mend relations ‖ ～铁路 repair a railway ‖ ～一幅画 restore a painting **2**［计算机］fix: ～错误 fix a bug

【修改】xiūgǎi〈动〉alter: ～计划 revise a plan ‖ ～宪法 amend the constitution ‖ 提出～意见 propose an amendment ‖［计算机］～代码 modify the code

【修盖】xiūgài〈动〉build: ～教学楼 build a classroom building

【修函】xiūhán〈动〉〈书〉write a letter

【修好】xiūhǎo〈动〉**1**〈书〉（亲善友好）cultivate a friendship **2**〈方〉（行善）do good deeds

【修剪】xiūjiǎn〈动〉**1**（用剪刀修整）trim: ～果树 prune a fruit tree ‖ ～指甲 cut one's fingernails **2**（修改剪接）edit: ～影片 edit a film

【修建】xiūjiàn〈动〉build: ～机场 construct an airport ‖ ～桥梁 build a bridge

【修脚】xiūjiǎo〈动〉pedicure

【修旧利废】xiūjiù-lìfèi〈成〉repair and recycle

【修浚】xiūjùn〈动〉dredge: ～河道 dredge a river

【修理】xiūlǐ〈动〉**1**（使复原）repair: ～摩托车 fix a motorbike ‖ 汽车～厂 auto repair workshop **2** = 修剪 xiūjiǎn 1 **3**〈方〉（惩罚）punish: 把某人～一顿 mete out a punishment for sb.

【修理费】xiūlǐfèi〈名〉repair charge

【修理工】xiūlǐgōng〈名〉repairman

【修理行业】xiūlǐ hángyè〈名〉repairing trade

【修炼】xiūliàn〈动〉[of Taoists] practise asceticism

【修面】xiūmiàn〈动〉〈方〉shave

【修明】xiūmíng〈形〉〈书〉[of a government] honest and enlightened: 政治～ honest and enlightened politics

【修女】xiūnǚ〈名〉[of Roman Catholic and Greek Orthodox churches] nun

【修配】xiūpèi〈动〉make repairs and supply replacements: 汽车～厂 auto repair and assembly plant

【修葺】xiūqì〈动〉renovate: 房屋～一新。The house looks new after the renovation.

【修润】xiūrùn〈动〉revise and polish (a piece of writing)

【修缮】xiūshàn〈动〉renovate: ～房屋 do up a house

【修身】xiūshēn〈动〉cultivate one's moral character

【修身养性】xiūshēn-yǎngxìng〈成〉behave properly to cultivate oneself

【修史】xiūshǐ〈动〉〈书〉compile a history

【修士】xiūshì〈名〉monk

【修饰】xiūshì〈动〉**1**（修整装饰）decorate: ～一新 be fully decorated **2**（打扮）make oneself up and get dressed up: 出门前先～一番 make oneself up and get dressed up before going out **3**（润饰）polish: 对这份报告加以～ polish the report **4**［语言］modify: ～语 modifier

【修书】xiūshū〈动〉〈书〉**1**（编书）compile a book **2**（写信）write a letter: ～一封 write a letter

【修行】xiūxíng〈动〉practise Buddhism or Taoism: 出家～ become a monk/nun/Taoist

【修养】xiūyǎng〈名〉**1**（指水平）mastery: 有艺术～ be artistically accomplished ‖ 有文化～的人 person of culture **2**（指态度）self-cultivation: 没有～ be ill cultivated ‖ 四年的大学学习使他变得很有～。Four years of college study gave him considerable polish.

【修业】xiūyè〈动〉pursue one's studies: ～期满 finish school ‖ ～年限 length of schooling

【修造】xiūzào〈动〉**1**（修理制造）build and repair: ～船只 repair a ship ‖ ～农具 build and repair farm tools **2**（建造）build: ～花园 build a garden

【修整】xiūzhěng〈动〉**1**（修补整理）repair and maintain: ～农具 repair and maintain farm tools **2**（修饰打理）prune: ～耕地 level arable land ‖ ～树篱 trim a hedge

【修正】xiūzhèng〈动〉revise: ～错误 correct a mistake

【修正案】xiūzhèng'àn〈名〉amendment: 否决/提出～ veto/propose an amendment ‖ 宪法～ constitutional amendment

【修正主义】xiūzhèng zhǔyì〈名〉revisionism: ～思潮 revisionist trend

【修枝】xiūzhī〈动〉prune

【修治】xiūzhì〈动〉**1**（疏浚）dredge **2**（修理）repair and adjust

【修筑】xiūzhù〈动〉build: ～道路 build a road ‖ ～堤坝 erect a dam ‖ ～工事 put up fortifications

脩 xiū〈名〉〈旧〉dried meat, etc. presented in ancient China by pupils to their teachers at their first meeting: ▸束～

羞 xiū

A〈形〉shameful: ▸～耻, 遮～

B〈动〉**1**（感到羞耻）feel ashamed: ～于承认 be too ashamed to admit ▸～愧, ～与为伍 **2**（难为情）be shy: ～红脸 blush with embarrassment ‖ 她～得恨不得有个

修饰结构

■ 汉语中的结构助词“的”用在起修饰作用的词或短语后面，这些修饰语可以是名词或名词短语、代词、形容词、动词或动词短语及句子等。因此，在把“的”翻译成英语时，不可能总是翻译成英语的 of。下面的例子说明了“的”字修饰结构翻译成英语的多样性。

■ 当表示领属关系的名词或代词做定语时，汉语中用“的”字结构，而英语里可用前置修饰语（名词所有格及形容词性物主代词），或者后置修饰语（of + 名词 / 名词性物主代词）：

吉米的画
= Jimmy's painting

小王的车
= Xiao Wang's car

中国的文化生活
= China's cultural life

老师的女儿
= the daughter of the teacher

这所大学的雇员
= the employees of the university

我的那三个朋友
= those three friends of mine

他的那个聪明的儿子
= that clever son of his

■ 当汉语中表示领属关系的名词或代词后面不带“的”时，翻译成英语时仍照上面的方法：

我岳父的饭店
= my father-in-law's restaurant

她皮肤的颜色
= the colour of her skin

男士服装
= men's clothes

女子学校
= a girls' school

中华人民共和国主席
= the Chairman of the People's Republic of China

我儿子
= my son

我学校
= my school

我们国家
= our country

■ 英语的介词很丰富。下面用“的”字结构的汉语例子，在英语里使用了不同的介词：

电影院的入口
= the entrance to the cinema

我们去法国的旅行
= our trip to France

我办公室的钥匙
= the key to my office

绘画的才能
= a talent for drawing

穿白衣服的那位绅士
= the gentleman in white

戴眼镜的学生
= a student with glasses

桌子上的面包
= the bread on the table

关于汉语成语的文章
= a paper on Chinese idioms

关于幼儿教育的书
= a book about nursery education

关于现代中国生活的纪录片
= a documentary on Chinese modern life

飞机票的信息
= information on/about flight tickets

玩耍中的孩子
= children at play

你的电话
= a phone call for you

买书的钱
= money for books

上个月的账单
= bills for last month

待售的画
= a painting for sale

河边的树
= trees beside the river

地缝钻进去。She was so ashamed that she wished that the earth would open and swallow her up. ▸～涩, 害～, 怕～ 3 (使人难为情) embarrass: 伸手去～他的脸 stretch out a hand to shame him

C 〈书〉= 馐 xiū

【羞惭】xiūcán〈形〉 ashamed: ～满面 be overcome with shame ‖ 因～而脸红 flush with shame

【羞耻】xiūchǐ〈形〉 shameful: 不知～ be completely shameless

【羞答答】xiūdādā〈形〉 coy: 在生人面前～的 be bashful in the presence of strangers ‖ 别～的! Don't be shy!

【羞愤】xiūfèn〈形〉〈书〉 ashamed and resentful: ～不已 feel extremely ashamed and resentful

【羞口】xiūkǒu〈动〉 feel too shy to say sth.: ～难开 too shy to speak (out)

【羞愧】xiūkuì〈形〉 ashamed: 感到～ feel ashamed ‖ ～得低下头 hang one's head in shame ‖ ～难言 be ashamed beyond words

【羞赧】xiūnǎn〈形〉〈书〉 bashful: ～的新娘 blushing bride

【羞怯】xiūqiè〈形〉 timid: ～得说不出话来 too shy and nervous to utter a word

【羞人】xiūrén〈动〉 feel embarrassed: 别提了, 羞死人了。Don't mention it any more. It's so embarrassing.

【羞人答答】xiūrén-dādā〈形〉 bashful

【羞辱】xiūrǔ A〈名〉 humiliation: 屡遭～ suffer repeated humiliations ‖ 莫大的～ abominable humiliation B〈动〉 humiliate: ～对手 humiliate one's opponent

【羞臊】xiūsào〈动〉 1 (感到害臊) feel ashamed: ～得满脸通红 be puce with embarrassment 2 (使人害臊) shame: 别再～我了! Stop embarrassing me!

【羞涩】xiūsè〈形〉 bashful: ～的微笑 shy smile

【羞恶】xiūwù〈动〉〈书〉 be ashamed of one's misdemeanours: ～之心 sense of shame

【羞羞答答】xiūxiū-dādā = 羞答答 xiūdādā

【羞与为伍】xiūyǔ-wéiwǔ〈成〉 feel ashamed to associate with sb.

鸺 xiū

【鸺鹠】xiūliú〈名〉[鸟类] owl

貅 xiū ▸貔貅 píxiū

馐（饈） xiū〈名〉〈书〉 delicacy: ▸珍～

xiǔ

朽 xiǔ

A〈动〉 1 (腐烂) decay: 木头已完全～了。The wood has completely decayed. ▸腐～ 2 (磨灭) wear away: ▸不～

B〈形〉 decrepit: ▸～迈, 老～

【朽败】xiǔbài〈形〉 rotten

【朽腐】xiǔfǔ = 腐朽 fǔxiǔ

【朽坏】xiǔhuài〈动〉 decay

【朽烂】xiǔlàn〈动〉 rot: 木头～了。The wood is rotten.

【朽迈】xiǔmài〈形〉〈书〉 decrepit

【朽木】xiǔmù〈名〉 1 (指木头) rotten tree: ～枯株 rotten trees and withered stumps 2〈喻〉(指人) good-for-nothing: ～粪土之人 worthless person

【朽木不可雕也】xiǔmù bùkě diāo yě〈成〉 a congenital defeatist cannot be taught to succeed

宿 xiǔ〈量〉〈口〉 night: 聊了半～ chat till midnight ‖ 住一～ stay the night ▸sù, xiù

xiù

秀¹ xiù〈动〉 put forth: ～穗 put forth ears

秀² xiù

A〈形〉 1 (优异) outstanding: ▸优～ 2 (清秀) elegant: ▸～丽, ～气, 眉清目～ 3 (聪明) intelligent: ▸内～

B〈名〉 1 (指人) outstanding person: ▸后起之～, 新～ 2 (指表演) show: ▸脱口～, 作～

秀³ xiù〈名〉 show: ▸脱口～, 作～

【秀才】xiùcai〈名〉 1 (指明清生员) *xiucai* [scholar in the Ming and Qing dynasties who passed the imperial examination at county level] 2 (泛指读书人) scholar: 他是我们公司里的～。He is the scholar of our company.

【秀才人情纸半张】xiùcai rénqíng zhǐ bàn zhāng〈俗〉 a scholar's friendship finds expression in humble gifts such as a piece of paper

【秀场】xiùchǎng〈名〉 performance venue: 出现在～内 appear at a performance venue

【秀而不实】xiù'érbùshí〈成〉 1〈本〉 put forth flowers but bear no fruits 2〈喻〉 be fine in appearance but empty in substance

【秀发】xiùfà〈名〉 beautiful hair: 一头～ have a beautiful head of hair

【秀丽】xiùlì〈形〉 beautiful: ～的风景 beautiful landscape ‖ ～的姑娘 pretty girl

【秀美】xiùměi〈形〉 elegant: 山川～ the mountains and rivers are beautiful

【秀媚】xiùmèi〈形〉〈书〉 beautiful and charming: 容貌姣好～ lovely looks

【秀气】xiùqi〈形〉 1 (清秀) delicate: 长得～ have fine features ‖ 字迹～ write an elegant hand 2 (文雅) refined: 言谈～ speak in a refined manner 3 (小巧灵便) exquisite: ～的花瓶 delicate vase

【秀色】xiùsè〈名〉 1 (指景色) beautiful scenery 2 (指容貌) beauty

【秀色可餐】xiùsè-kěcān〈成〉 be ravishingly beautiful

【秀外慧中】xiùwài-huìzhōng〈成〉 elegant and intelligent

【秀雅】xiùyǎ〈形〉〈书〉 beautiful and refined: ～的装饰 elegant furnishings

【秀逸】xiùyì〈形〉〈书〉 elegant and graceful: 书法～ beautiful and free-flowing handwriting

岫 xiù〈名〉〈书〉 1 (山洞) cave, cavern 2 (山) mountain

臭 xiù

A〈名〉 odour: 空气无色无～。Air is colourless and odourless. ▸乳～未干

B〈动〉〈书〉 smell: ～出香水味 smell the fragrance of perfume

▸chòu

袖 xiù

A〈名〉 sleeve: 短～衬衣 short-sleeved shirt ▸～筒, 套～

B〈动〉 tuck inside the sleeve: ▸～手旁观

【袖标】xiùbiāo〈名〉 armband: 戴～ wear an armband

【袖管】xiùguǎn〈名〉 1 (袖子) sleeve 2〈方〉(袖口) cuff

【袖箭】xiùjiàn〈名〉 arrow hidden in the sleeve

【袖口】xiùkǒu〈名〉 cuff: ～钮 sleeve button

【袖手旁观】xiùshǒu-pángguān〈成〉 look on with folded arms: 他有困难, 我不能～。When he is in trouble, I can't just turn a blind eye.

【袖套】xiùtào〈名〉 oversleeve

【袖筒】xiùtǒng〈名〉 sleeve

【袖章】xiùzhāng〈名〉 armband: 戴～ wear an armband

【袖珍】xiùzhēn〈形〉 pocket: ～本 pocket edition ‖ ～收音机 pocket radio

【袖珍字典】xiùzhēn zìdiǎn〈名〉 pocket dictionary

【袖子】xiùzi〈名〉 sleeve: 卷起～ roll up one's sleeve

绣（綉、繡） xiù

A〈动〉 embroider: 在床单上～一朵花 embroider a flower on a bed sheet ‖ ～枕头 embroider a pillow

B〈名〉 embroidery: 苏～ Suzhou embroidery ‖ 湘～ Hunan embroidery

【绣房】xiùfáng〈名〉〈旧〉 young lady's chamber

【绣花】xiùhuā〈动〉 embroider: 在手绢上～ embroider a handkerchief ‖ ～被面 embroidered quilt cover ‖ ～箍 embroidery hoop ‖ ～架 embroidery frame

【绣花鞋】xiùhuāxié = 绣鞋 xiùxié

【绣花枕头】xiùhuā zhěntou〈成〉〈喻〉 outwardly attractive but inwardly empty person: 他不过是个～。He is just a pretty face.

【绣框】xiùkuàng〈名〉 embroidery frame

【绣球】xiùqiú〈名〉 ball of coloured silk strips

【绣球花】xiùqiúhuā〈名〉[植物] hydrangea

【绣像】xiùxiàng〈名〉 1 (绣成的人像) embroidered portrait 2 (指画像) exquisitely drawn portrait

【绣鞋】xiùxié〈名〉 embroidered shoes

宿 xiù〈名〉〈古〉 constellation: ▸星～ ▸sù, xiǔ

锈（銹、鏽） xiù

A〈名〉 1 (指氧化物质) rust: 生～ go rusty ‖ 铁～ iron rust ‖ 铜～ verdigris 2 (指附着物) encrustation: ▸茶～, 水～ 3 [农业] rust: 除～剂 rust remover ▸～病

B〈动〉 rust: ～得很厉害 be badly rusted ‖ 管子已经～坏了。The pipe has rusted away. ▸不～钢, 防～

【锈斑】xiùbān〈名〉 rust patch: 苹果上有～。The apples have rusty spots.

【锈病】xiùbìng〈名〉[农业] rust: 小麦～ wheat rust

【锈蚀】xiùshí〈动〉 corrode: 工具被雨水～了。The rain has rusted the tools.

嗅 xiù〈动〉 smell: ～到油漆味 smell fresh paint ‖ 东闻闻西～～ have a good sniff

【嗅觉】xiùjué〈名〉 sense of smell: ～灵敏 have a keen sense of smell ‖〈喻〉 他的政治～很灵敏。He is politically sharp.

【嗅觉器官】xiùjué qìguān〈名〉 olfactory organ

【嗅神经】xiùshénjīng〈名〉 olfactory nerve

溴 xiù〈名〉［化学］bromine (Br)
【溴化汞】xiùhuàgǒng〈名〉mercury bromide
【溴化钾】xiùhuàjiǎ〈名〉potassium bromide
【溴化钠】xiùhuànà〈名〉sodium bromide
【溴化氢】xiùhuàqīng〈名〉hydrogen bromide
【溴化物】xiùhuàwù〈名〉bromide
【溴化银】xiùhuàyín〈名〉silver bromide

xū

圩 xū〈名〉〈方〉country fair: 赶～ go to a fair ‖ ～场 country market
▸wéi

戌 xū〈名〉eleventh of the twelve Earthly Branches (地支)
▸qu
【戌时】xūshí〈名〉〈旧〉period of the day from 7 p.m. to 9 p.m.

吁 xū
A〈叹〉〈书〉why: ～，何其怪哉！ My! How strange it is!
B〈动〉sigh: ▸长～短叹
▸yū, yù
【吁吁】xūxū〈拟〉puff: 气喘～ puff and pant

盱 xū〈动〉〈书〉look up

须¹（須）xū〈动〉**1**〈书〉（等候）await **2**（必须）must: ～经预先批准 be subject to prior approval ▸～知，必～，务～

须²（鬚）xū〈名〉**1**（胡子）beard: ▸～发，～眉，胡～ **2**（胡须状物）feeler: ▸～根，～子，触～
【须发】xūfà〈名〉beard and hair: ～皆白 white hair and beard
【须根】xūgēn〈名〉［植物］fibrous root
【须鲸】xūjīng〈名〉［动物］baleen whale
【须眉】xūméi〈名〉**1**（胡须和眉毛）beard and eyebrows: ～皆白的老人 old man with a white beard and white eyebrows **2**（男子）man: 巾帼不让～。 Women refuse to be outdone by men.
【须弥座】xūmízuò〈名〉**1**（佛像底座）base of a Buddha's statue **2**（建筑物底座）base of a Buddhist pagoda
【须生】xūshēng＝老生 lǎoshēng
【须要】xūyào〈动〉must: 教育儿童～耐心。 It takes patience to educate children.
【须臾】xūyú〈名〉〈书〉instant: ～之间，雨过天晴。 In a flash the rain stopped and the sky cleared up.
【须知】xūzhī **A**〈名〉points for attention: 考试～ rules for the examination ‖ 旅客～ notice to travellers **B**〈动〉one should know that: ～"不劳则无获"。 The proverb 'no pain, no gain' must be borne in mind.
【须子】xūzi〈名〉**1**［动物］feelers: 虾～ feelers of a shrimp **2**［植物］tassel: 玉米～ tassels of maize

胥 xū〈书〉
A〈名〉petty official: ～吏 petty official
B〈副〉all: 万事～备。 Everything is ready.

虚（虛）xū
A〈形〉**1**（空）empty: ▸～无缥缈，空～，座无～席 **2**（虚心）humble: ▸～心，谦～ **3**（弱）weak: ▸～汗，～弱，～症 **4**（虚假）false: ▸～名，～情假意，～伪 **5**（胆怯）timid: ▸胆～
B〈名〉**1**（弱点）void: ▸避实击～，乘～而入 **2**（指导思想）guiding principle: 以～带实 let correct ideology guide practical work ▸务～ **3**（指星宿）one of the 28 constellations in ancient Chinese astronomy
C〈动〉〈书〉empty: ▸～位以待
D〈副〉vainly: 弹无～发。 Not a single bullet missed its target. ▸～度年华，不～此行
【虚报】xūbào〈动〉make a false report: ～年龄 lie about one's age ‖ ～收入 fail to disclose one's full income ‖ ～冒领 make a fraudulent application and claim
【虚词】xūcí〈名〉**1**［语言］function word **2**＝虚辞 xūcí
【虚辞】xūcí〈名〉〈书〉empty words
【虚度】xūdù〈动〉waste time: ～光阴 idle away one's time
【虚度年华】xūdù niánhuá〈成〉fritter away one's time
【虚浮】xūfú〈形〉superficial: 作风～ have a superficial style of work
【虚高】xūgāo〈形〉unreasonably high: 房价～ house prices are unreasonably high
【虚功】xūgōng〈名〉［物理］virtual work
【虚构】xūgòu〈动〉make up: 纯属～ sheer fabrication ‖ ～的故事 made-up story
【虚汗】xūhàn〈名〉abnormal sweating due to general debility: 冒～ perspire abnormal amounts of sweat
【虚怀若谷】xūhuái-ruògǔ〈成〉be extremely open-minded
【虚幻】xūhuàn〈形〉imaginary: ～感 imagination ‖ ～的景象/人物 illusory vision/figure
【虚晃一枪】xūhuǎng-yīqiāng〈惯〉feign an attack
【虚火】xūhuǒ〈名〉［中医］deficiency of fire: ～上升 escalation in fire deficiency
【虚假】xūjiǎ〈形〉false: ～广告/证明 misleading advertisement/testimony
【虚惊】xūjīng〈名〉false alarm: ～一场 merely a false alarm
【虚空】xūkōng〈形〉empty
【虚夸】xūkuā〈形〉exaggerated: ～的语言 exaggerated language
【虚礼】xūlǐ〈名〉insincere courtesy: 不拘～ not stand on ceremony
【虚名】xūmíng〈名〉false reputation: 徒有～ have an undeserved reputation
【虚拟】xūnǐ **A**〈形〉hypothetical: ～世界 virtual world ▸～语气 **B**〈动〉fabricate: ～的故事 fictitious story
【虚拟经济】xūnǐ jīngjì〈名〉virtual economy
【虚拟空间】xūnǐ kōngjiān〈名〉［计算机］cyberspace
【虚拟内存】xūnǐ nèicún〈名〉［计算机］virtual memory
【虚拟人】xūnǐrén〈名〉avatar: ～选美大赛 avatar beauty contest
【虚拟网】xūnǐwǎng〈名〉［计算机］virtual net
【虚拟现实】xūnǐ xiànshí〈名〉［计算机］virtual reality (VR)
【虚拟语气】xūnǐ yǔqì ▸**p. 350**〈名〉［语言］subjunctive mood
【虚胖】xūpàng〈形〉puffy: ～的人 bloated person
【虚飘飘】xūpiāopiāo〈形〉wobbly: 他喝了几杯酒，腿就～的了。 His legs began to feel wobbly after a few glasses of alcohol.
【虚情假意】xūqíng-jiǎyì〈成〉false display of affection: 看穿～ see through sb.'s false display of affection
【虚热】xūrè〈名〉asthenic fever
【虚荣】xūróng〈名〉vanity: 不慕～ not be vain
【虚荣心】xūróngxīn〈名〉vanity: 强烈的～ extreme vanity ‖ 出于～ out of vanity
【虚弱】xūruò〈形〉weak: 身体～ be in frail health ‖ 兵力～ be weak in military strength ‖ 国力～ have weak national strength
【虚设】xūshè〈动〉be nominal: ▸形同～
【虚实】xūshí〈名〉actual situation: 探听～ try to ascertain the strength of one's opponent
【虚数】xūshù〈名〉**1**［数学］imaginary number **2**（虚假数字）unreliable figure
【虚岁】xūsuì ▸**p. 526**〈名〉nominal age [according to Chinese tradition, a person is considered one year old at birth]: ～五岁 be at the nominal age of five
【虚套】xūtào＝虚套子 xūtàozi
【虚套子】xūtàozi〈名〉mere formalities: 不必来～。 There is no need to stand on ceremony.
【虚脱】xūtuō **A**〈名〉collapse **B**〈动〉collapse
【虚妄】xūwàng〈形〉unfounded: ～的计划 chimerical plan
【虚伪】xūwěi〈形〉sham: 他很～。 He is very hypocritical.
【虚位以待】xūwèiyǐdài〈成〉reserve a seat for sb.
【虚文】xūwén〈名〉**1**（具文）dead letter: 一纸～ a dead letter **2**（无意义的礼节）mere formalities: ～浮礼 mere formalities
【虚无】xūwú〈名〉nothingness: 梦想化为～。 Dreams melted into nothingness.
【虚无缥缈】xūwú-piāomiǎo〈成〉purely imaginary
【虚无主义】xūwú zhǔyì〈名〉nihilism: 采取～态度 adopt an attitude of nihilism
【虚席以待】xūxí yǐdài＝虚位以待 xūwèiyǐdài
【虚线】xūxiàn〈名〉dotted line
【虚像】xūxiàng〈名〉［物理］virtual image
【虚心】xūxīn〈形〉open-minded: ～好学 be modest and eager to learn ‖ ～接受批评 accept criticisms with an open mind
【虚虚实实】xūxū-shíshí〈成〉[of military tactics, etc.] combination of truth and falsehood
【虚悬】xūxuán〈形〉**1**（空缺）unsettled: 经理一职仍然～。 The post of manager is still vacant. **2**（凭空设想）imagined: ～的计划 fanciful plan
【虚掩】xūyǎn〈动〉**1**（指门窗）[of a closed door or window] be left unlocked: 房门～。 The door is on the latch. **2**（指衣襟）be unbuttoned
【虚应故事】xūyìng-gùshì〈成〉do sth. for the sake of form only: 我觉得他只是～。 I feel he is just going through the motions.
【虚有其表】xūyǒuqíbiǎo〈成〉look impressive but lack real worth: 他们的富有是～。 Their affluence is more apparent than real.
【虚与委蛇】xūyǔwēiyí〈成〉feign politeness and compliance: 对客人～ greet a guest with false civility
【虚造】xūzào〈动〉fabricate
【虚增】xūzēng〈动〉make false increases: ～指数 increase the index falsely ‖ ～银行

贷款规模 make insubstantial increases to the scale of bank loans
【虚张声势】xūzhāng-shēngshì〈成〉 make a false show of strength: ～的谈话 empty talk ‖ ～的威胁 empty threat ‖ ～的样子 swashbuckling posture ‖ 那不过是～而已。 It's merely a bluff.
【虚症】xūzhèng〈名〉［中医］asthenia syndrome
【虚职】xūzhí〈名〉 nominal position
【虚字】xūzì〈名〉［语言］ function word

谞（諝）xū 〈名〉〈书〉 1（才智） ability and wisdom 2（计谋） stratagem

欻 xū〈副〉〈书〉 suddenly
▸chuā

墟（墟）xū 〈名〉 1（荒废的地方） ruins: ▸废～, 殷～ 2〈书〉（村庄） village: ～里/落 hamlet 3 = 圩 xū

需 xū
A〈动〉 need: 各取所～。 Each receives according to his need. ‖ 尚～改进。 There is still room for improvement. ▸～求, 必～品, 急～
B〈名〉 needs: ▸军～
【需求】xūqiú〈名〉 need: 满足消费者的～ meet consumer demand ‖ 人才～ need for professional personnel
【需求量】xūqiúliàng〈名〉 demand: ～很大 be in great demand
【需要】xūyào A〈动〉 need: ～帮忙 need help ‖ ～大量时间和精力 require considerable time and energy ‖ 走到车站～十分钟。 It takes me ten minutes to walk to the bus stop. B〈名〉 need: 讲出～ voice one's needs ‖ 满足～ meet the demand ‖ 事业发展的～ career progression requirements

嘘（嘘）xū
A〈动〉 1（吐气） exhale slowly: ～了一口气 breathe out a slow breath 2〈书〉（叹气） sigh: 失望而～ sigh with disappointment 3（发出嘘声） hiss: ～下场 boo sb. off the stage ▸～声 4（用火或蒸气的热力加热） heat: 把饼放在炉子上～一～。 Put the pancake on the stove for a while.
B〈叹〉 shh: ～! 别把孩子吵醒了! Hush! You'll wake the baby!
▸shī
【嘘寒问暖】xūhán-wènnuǎn〈成〉 inquire after sb.'s well-being
【嘘声】xūshēng〈名〉 hiss: 发出～ utter a hiss ‖ 用～把某人轰下台 boo sb. off the stage
【嘘唏】xūxī = 歔欷 xūxī

魆 xū ▸黑魆魆 hēixūxū

歔（歔）xū
【歔欷】xūxī〈动〉〈书〉 sob

xú

徐 xú〈副〉 slowly: 春风～来。 The spring breeze is blowing gently. ▸～缓, ～图
【徐步】xúbù〈动〉〈书〉 saunter: 沿着小路～而行 walk slowly along a path
【徐缓】xúhuǎn〈形〉 unhurried
【徐娘半老】Xúniáng-bànlǎo〈成〉 attractive middle-aged woman
【徐图】xútú〈动〉〈书〉 adopt a gradual approach
【徐徐】xúxú〈副〉〈书〉 gently: 幕～落下。 The screen was gradually lowered. ‖ 飞机～降落在机场。 The plane landed slowly at the airport.

xǔ

许（許）xǔ
A〈动〉 1（允许） allow: 不～抽烟。 Smoking is not allowed. ‖ 展品只～看, 不～摸。 You are only permitted to look at the exhibits, not to touch them. ▸～可, 默～, 准～ 2（许诺） promise: ～下诺言 make a promise ‖ 以身～国 pledge one's life to one's country ▸～愿 3（许配） [of a girl] be betrothed: 姑娘已经～了人家。 The girl is already engaged to somebody. ▸～婚, ～配 4（称赞） praise: ～为佳作 be praised as a fine piece of writing ▸称～, 赞～
B〈副〉 1（可能） maybe: 他今天没来, ～是病了。 He is absent today; perhaps he's ill. ▸也～ 2（非常） so: ▸～多, ～久
C ▸p. 927 〈数〉〈书〉 approximately: 上午十时～ at about 10 am ▸几～, 少～, 些～
D〈名〉〈书〉 place: 她何～人? Where does she come from?
【许多】xǔduō〈数〉 many: ～变化/朋友 a lot of changes/friends ‖ ～麻烦 a good deal of trouble ‖ ～年前 many years ago
【许婚】xǔhūn〈动〉 [of a girl's parents or the girl herself] accept a proposal of marriage
【许久】xǔjiǔ〈形〉 long: 他～没来了。 It's been ages since he came last time.
【许可】xǔkě〈动〉 permit: 得到～ get permission ‖ 在条件～的情况下 when conditions allow ‖ 未经～不得入内。 No admittance without permission.
【许可证】xǔkězhèng〈名〉 permit: 出境/入境～ exit/entry permit ‖ 进口/出口～ import/export licence
【许诺】xǔnuò〈动〉 promise: ～多, 兑现少 all talk and no action ‖ 她父亲～给她买台电脑。 Her father promised to buy her a computer.
【许配】xǔpèi〈动〉 betroth a girl: 把女儿～给某人 betroth one's daughter to sb.
【许亲】xǔqīn〈动〉 accept a marriage proposal
【许愿】xǔyuàn〈动〉 1（指对神佛） make a vow: 烧香～ burn incense to make vows 2（指对人） promise sb. a reward: ～给儿子买辆自行车 promise one's son a bike

诩（詡）xǔ 〈动〉〈书〉 boast: ▸自～

栩 xǔ
【栩栩】xǔxǔ〈形〉 vivid: ▸～如生
【栩栩如生】xǔxǔ-rúshēng〈成〉 true to life: 把塑像做得～ breathe life into the statue ‖ ～的描写 vivid description

湑 xǔ〈书〉
A〈动〉 filter out wine sediment
B〈形〉 limpid

稰 xǔ〈名〉〈古〉 1（精米） fine rice used in worship 2（粮食） rations

醑 xǔ〈名〉 1〈书〉（美酒） fine wine 2［药学］ spirit: 樟脑～ camphor spirit
【醑剂】xǔjì〈名〉［药学］ spirit

xù

旭 xù〈名〉 brilliance of the rising sun: ▸～日
【旭日】xùrì〈名〉 rising sun: ～东升 the sun rising in the east

序 xù
A〈名〉 1（顺序） order: 以时间为～ in chronological order ‖ 以字母为～ in alphabetical order ▸程～, 秩～, 井然有～ 2（序文） preface: 写～ write a preface to a book ▸～言 3〈旧〉（指厢房） western and eastern wings of a house 4〈旧〉（指学校） school
B〈动〉〈书〉 arrange in order: ▸～齿, ～次
C〈形〉 introductory: 这几行诗是他那长篇叙事诗的～诗。 These lines form a prelude to his long narrative poem. ▸～幕, ～曲
【序跋】xùbá〈名〉 preface and postscript
【序齿】xùchǐ〈动〉〈旧〉 arrange in order of age
【序次】xùcì〈名〉 order
【序号】xùhào〈名〉 serial number
【序列】xùliè〈名〉 alignment: 不成～ out of alignment ‖ 战斗～ battle formation
【序论】xùlùn〈名〉 introduction
【序目】xùmù〈名〉 preface and table of contents
【序幕】xùmù〈名〉 1〈本〉 prologue 2〈喻〉 prelude: 抗日战争的～ prelude to the War of Resistance Against Japan
【序盘】xùpán〈名〉［体育］ opening [in chess or go]: 在～中优势明显。 The advantage was obvious at the opening.
【序曲】xùqǔ〈名〉 1［音乐］ overture 2〈喻〉 prelude
【序数】xùshù ▸p. 691 〈名〉 ordinal number
【序文】xùwén〈名〉 preface: ～作者 sb. who writes a preface
【序言】xùyán〈名〉 foreword: 为书写～ write a preface to a book

叙（敘、敍）xù
A〈名〉〈书〉 sequence
B〈动〉 1〈书〉（评定） assess: ▸～功 2（交谈） talk: ▸～旧 3（叙述） recount: ▸～事, ～述
【叙别】xùbié〈动〉〈书〉 have a farewell talk: ～以来, 倏忽三月。 Suddenly it's been three months since we said good-bye to each other.
【叙功】xùgōng〈动〉〈书〉 assess services: ～议赏 assess sb.'s achievements and decide on the awards
【叙旧】xùjiù〈动〉 reminisce about the past
【叙利亚】Xùlìyà〈名〉 Syria: ～人 Syrian ‖ ～语 Syrian
【叙事】xùshì〈动〉 narrate: 擅长～的作家 writer of great narrative power
【叙事曲】xùshìqǔ〈名〉［音乐］ ballade
【叙事诗】xùshìshī〈名〉 narrative poem
【叙事体】xùshìtǐ〈名〉 descriptive style
【叙述】xùshù〈动〉 recount: ～一段轶事 relate an anecdote ‖ 详细～ give a full account
【叙说】xùshuō〈动〉 narrate: ～冒险故事 narrate one's adventures

【叙谈】xùtán〈动〉 chat: 与朋友～ have a chat with one's friend
【叙文】xùwén = 序文 xùwén
【叙言】xùyán = 序言 xùyán
【叙用】xùyòng〈动〉〈书〉 appoint: 复职～ be reinstated in a post

洫 xù〈名〉〈书〉 field ditch

恤（卹）xù〈动〉 1（怜恤） sympathize: ▸怜～, 体～ 2（救济） compensate: ▸～金, 抚～
【恤金】xùjīn〈名〉 relief payment
【恤衫】xùshān〈名〉〈方〉 shirt

畜 xù〈动〉 raise
▸chù
【畜产品】xùchǎnpǐn〈名〉 animal product
【畜牧】xùmù〈动〉 raise livestock: ～业 animal husbandry
【畜养】xùyǎng〈动〉 raise: ～家畜 raise domestic animals

酗 xù
【酗酒】xùjiǔ〈动〉 drink excessively: ～滋事 get drunk and create a disturbance ‖ ～伤身。 Too much drink is not good for the health.

勖（勗）xù〈动〉〈书〉 encourage: ▸～勉
【勖勉】xùmiǎn〈动〉〈书〉 encourage: ～后生 give encouragement to a young man

绪（緒）xù〈名〉 1（开始） beginning: ▸～论, 千头万～, 头～ 2（心情） mental state: ▸情～, 思～, 心～ 3〈书〉（残余） remnants: ～年 remaining years ‖ ～余 surplus 4〈书〉（功业） undertaking: 缵～ carry on the cause of one's forefathers
【绪论】xùlùn〈名〉 introduction
【绪言】xùyán〈名〉 introduction

续（續）xù〈动〉 1（连接不断） be continuous: ▸持～, 连～ 2（接上） continue: 在杆子上～上一截绳子 join another piece of rope onto a pole ▸～编, ～集, 狗尾～貂 3〈口〉（添加） add: ～水 add some water
【续编】xùbiān〈名〉 sequel
【续貂】xùdiāo〈动〉〈谦〉 make a poor sequel to a fine work: ▸狗尾～
【续订】xùdìng〈动〉 renew a subscription: ～《读者文摘》 renew one's subscription to *Reader's Digest*
【续航】xùháng〈动〉 continue a journey without refuelling
【续集】xùjí〈名〉 sequel: 故事～ continuation of a story
【续假】xùjià〈动〉 extend one's leave of absence: ～一星期 have one's leave extended for another week
【续借】xùjiè〈动〉 renew a book: ～一个月 renew a book for another month
【续篇】xùpiān〈名〉 sequel: 小说的～ sequel to a novel
【续聘】xùpìn〈动〉 renew sb.'s employment contract: 他被公司～五年。 His employment contract was renewed by the company for another five years.
【续弦】xùxián〈动〉〈书〉 remarry after the death of one's wife
【续约】xùyuē A〈动〉 renew a contract B〈名〉 renewed contract

絮 xù
A〈名〉 1〈古〉（粗丝棉） coarse floss silk 2（絮状物） cotton-like thing: 芦～ reed catkin ▸柳～ 3（棉花胎） cotton wadding: ▸棉～
B〈动〉 pad with cotton: ～棉被 wad a quilt with cotton
C〈形〉 long-winded: ▸～叨, ～烦
【絮叨】xùdao A〈动〉 be long-winded: ～得烦死人了 nag sb. to death B〈形〉 long-winded: 说话太～ talk in an overly long-winded way
【絮烦】xùfan〈形〉 1（厌烦） fed up: 他没完没了的故事我都听得～了。 I was fed up with his endless stories. 2（啰嗦） wordy: 说话太～ be too long-winded
【絮聒】xùguō〈动〉 1（絮叨） be long-winded 2（添麻烦） bother
【絮棉】xùmián〈名〉 cotton for wadding
【絮窝】xùwō〈动〉 make a nest
【絮絮不休】xùxù-bùxiū〈成〉 talk ceaselessly
【絮絮叨叨】xùxù-dāodao〈形〉 jabbering
【絮语】xùyǔ〈书〉 A〈动〉 prattle on B〈名〉 prattle

婿 xù〈名〉 1（丈夫） husband: 夫～ husband ▸女～ 2（女婿） son-in-law: ▸乘龙快～, 翁～

蓄 xù〈动〉 1（储藏） store up: 水库～满了水。 The reservoir is fully stocked up with water. ▸～电池, 积～ 2（存有） harbour: ▸～念, ～意 3（留着） grow: ～发 wear one's hair long
【蓄电池】xùdiànchí〈名〉 storage battery: 给～充电 charge a battery
【蓄洪】xùhóng〈动〉 store flood water: ～区 flood storage area ‖ ～量 water storage capacity
【蓄积】xùjī〈动〉 store up: ～雨水 store up rainwater
【蓄谋】xùmóu〈动〉 premeditate: ～推翻政府 plot to overthrow the government ‖ ～已久 be long premeditated
【蓄念】xùniàn〈动〉 entertain an idea
【蓄水】xùshuǐ〈动〉 store water: 这个水库～多少? How much water can this reservoir hold?
【蓄水池】xùshuǐchí〈名〉 reservoir
【蓄养】xùyǎng〈动〉 store up: ～力量 build up strength
【蓄意】xùyì〈动〉 premeditate: ～谋杀/破坏 deliberately murder/sabotage ‖ ～挑衅 intentionally provoke
【蓄志】xùzhì〈动〉 have long cherished an ambition

煦 xù〈形〉〈书〉 warm: ～风 warm breeze ▸和～

xu

蓿 xu ▸苜蓿 mùxu

xuān

轩（軒）xuān
A〈名〉 1〈车〉 high-fronted, curtained carriage used in ancient times 2（小屋） small room or veranda with windows [used in names of studies, restaurants or teahouses in ancient times]
B〈形〉 lofty: ▸～昂, ～然大波
【轩昂】xuān'áng〈形〉 1（气度不凡） dignified: ▸气宇～ 2（高大） tall and big
【轩敞】xuānchǎng〈形〉〈书〉 spacious and bright
【轩然大波】xuānrán-dàbō〈成〉 mighty uproar: 引起一场～ cause a great stir
【轩轾】xuānzhì〈名〉〈书〉〈喻〉 superior or inferior: 不分～ be equal

宣 xuān
A〈动〉 1（传播） declare: ▸～布, ～誓, 心照不～ 2（疏通） drain off: ▸～泄
B = 宣纸 xuānzhǐ
【宣笔】xuānbǐ〈名〉 writing brush of high quality from Xuancheng (宣城), Anhui Province
【宣布】xuānbù〈动〉 announce: ～独立 declare independence ‖ ～进入紧急状态 declare a state of emergency ‖ ～开会 call a meeting to order
【宣称】xuānchēng〈动〉 declare: 法院～这项新法律违反宪法。 The court declared the new law to be unconstitutional.
【宣传】xuānchuán〈动〉 publicize: ～交通法规 publicize traffic regulations ‖ ～鼓动工作 propaganda and agitation
【宣传部】xuānchuánbù〈名〉 publicity department
【宣传画】xuānchuánhuà〈名〉 poster
【宣传教育】xuānchuán jiàoyù〈名〉 publicity and education
【宣传品】xuānchuánpǐn〈名〉 publicity material: 散发～ distribute promotional materials
【宣读】xuāndú〈动〉 read out: ～论文 present one's thesis ‖ 全文～ read out in full
【宣告】xuāngào〈动〉 declare: 公司～成立 announce the founding of a company ‖ ～破产 declare bankruptcy
【宣讲】xuānjiǎng〈动〉 preach: ～政策 publicize a policy ‖ ～团 publicity team
【宣教】xuānjiào〈动〉 publicize and educate
【宣礼】xuānlǐ〈名〉［伊斯兰教］ adhan [Islamic call to prayer]
【宣明】xuānmíng〈动〉 declare: ～立场 make one's position clear
【宣判】xuānpàn〈动〉 pronounce a judgement: ～无罪 declare sb. innocent ‖ 择日～ defer judgement to another day ‖ ～有罪 pronounce sb. guilty
【宣示】xuānshì〈动〉 announce
【宣誓】xuānshì〈动〉 make a vow: ～就职 take an oath of office ‖ ～入党 take the oath on being admitted to the Party ‖ 庄严～ make a solemn vow
【宣泄】xuānxiè〈动〉 1（排出） drain off: ～雨水 drain off rainwater 2（发泄） get sth. off one's chest: ～心中的愤懑 give vent to one's resentment 3〈书〉（泄露） disclose
【宣叙调】xuānxùdiào〈名〉［戏剧］ recitative
【宣言】xuānyán A〈名〉 declaration: 发表～ issue a manifesto ‖ 人权～ declaration of human rights B〈动〉 declare
【宣言书】xuānyánshū〈名〉 manifesto
【宣扬】xuānyáng〈动〉 publicize: ～好人好事 publicize good people and their good deeds ‖ 大肆～ publicize widely
【宣战】xuānzhàn〈动〉 1（指开战） declare war: 向侵略者～ declare war against the invaders 2（指开展大规模斗争） battle: 向癌症/贫困～ battle against cancer/poverty

【宣纸】xuānzhǐ〈名〉*Xuan* paper [high quality paper from Xuancheng (宣城), Anhui Province]

揎 xuān〈动〉〈书〉roll up one's sleeves: ～拳捋袖 stretch out one's hand and roll up one's sleeves

萱 xuān〈名〉**1**（萱草）tawny day lily **2**〈书〉（母亲）mother: ▸～堂

【萱草】xuāncǎo〈名〉［植物］day lily

【萱堂】xuāntáng〈名〉〈书〉mother

喧（諠） xuān〈形〉noisy: ▸～嚷，～嚣

【喧宾夺主】xuānbīn-duózhǔ〈成〉a minor issue takes precedence over a major one

【喧哗】xuānhuá **A**〈形〉uproarious: 住在～的大都市 live amid the hustle and bustle of a big city **B**〈动〉make an uproar: 请勿～。Please do not talk loudly.

【喧闹】xuānnào **A**〈形〉noisy: ～的商业中心 bustling business hub **B**〈动〉make a noise: 大声～ make a loud noise

【喧嚷】xuānrǎng〈动〉clamour: 人声～ a hubbub of voices ‖ ～的人群 clamorous crowd

【喧扰】xuānrǎo〈动〉make a commotion

【喧腾】xuānténg〈动〉be excited and noisy: 工地一片～。A hubbub filled the construction site.

【喧嚣】xuānxiāo **A**〈形〉uproarious: 车来人往的～声 roar of the traffic ‖ 会议在一片～声中结束。The meeting ended in an uproar. **B**〈动〉raise a racket: ～鼓噪 stir up a commotion ‖ ～一时 kick up a terrific racket for a while

【喧笑】xuānxiào〈动〉talk and laugh loudly

瑄 xuān〈名〉〈古〉round flat piece of jade with a hole in the centre

暄 xuān〈形〉**1**（温暖）warm: ▸寒～ **2**〈口〉（轻软）fluffy: 馒头特别～。The steamed bread is soft and light.

煊 xuān〈形〉eminent

【煊赫】xuānhè〈形〉eminent: ～一时 enjoy renown and influence for a time

儇 xuān〈形〉〈书〉**1**（轻浮）frivolous **2**（慧黠）cunning

【儇薄】xuānbó〈形〉〈书〉frivolous

【儇佻】xuāntiāo〈形〉〈书〉frivolous

xuán

玄 xuán〈形〉**1**（黑）black: ～玉 black jade ▸～狐，～青 **2**（远）distant: ▸～孙 **3**（深奥）profound: ▸～机，～妙 **4**〈口〉（不可靠）incredible: 这话真～。It's a pretty tall story. ▸～乎，故弄～虚

【玄奥】xuán'ào〈形〉abstruse

【玄关】xuánguān〈名〉**1**（门厅）hall **2**〈旧〉（大门）front door **3**［佛教］entry to Buddhism

【玄狐】xuánhú〈名〉black fox

【玄乎】xuánhu〈形〉〈口〉incredible: 他说得可真～。What he said sounds unbelievable.

【玄机】xuánjī〈名〉**1**［道教］mysteries of the universe **2**（深奥的道理）profound theory

【玄妙】xuánmiào〈形〉abstruse: ～莫测 difficult to guess

【玄青】xuánqīng〈形〉deep black

【玄参】xuánshēn〈名〉［中药］figwort

【玄孙】xuánsūn〈名〉great-great-grandson

【玄武】xuánwǔ〈名〉**1**（龟）tortoise **2**（指星宿）seven constellations of the northern sky **3**［道教］god of the northern sky

【玄武岩】xuánwǔyán〈名〉［地质］basalt

【玄想】xuánxiǎng〈名〉illusion

【玄虚】xuánxū **A**〈名〉ruse: 故弄～ play a trick **B**〈形〉incredible: 他话说得太～了。What he says is quite unbelievable.

【玄学】xuánxué〈名〉**1**（老庄哲学）*Xuanxue*, Dark Learning [3rd-4th century neo-Taoism] **2** = 形而上学 xíng'érshàngxué

【玄之又玄】xuánzhīyòuxuán〈成〉mystery of mysteries

悬（懸） xuán

A〈动〉**1**（吊挂）hang: ～在半空 be suspended in mid-air ‖ ～吊在天花板上的灯 lamp hung from the ceiling ▸～灯结彩，～梁刺股 **2**（公布）announce: ▸～赏 **3**（挂念）feel anxious: ▸～念，～望 **4**（假想）imagine: ▸～想 **5**（不着地）raise: ▸～浮，～空，～腕

B〈形〉**1**（远）far apart: ▸～隔，～殊，天～地隔 **2**（无结果）unsettled: 一直～着 remain unsettled ‖ 问题至今～而未决。The problem has not been resolved thus far. ▸～案 **3**〈口〉（危险）dangerous: 山路又陡又窄，走起来够～的。The mountain path is steep and narrow and very difficult to negotiate.

【悬案】xuán'àn〈名〉**1**（指案件）pending case: ～未结。The case is being suspended. **2**（指问题）outstanding issue

【悬臂】xuánbì〈名〉cantilever: ～起重机 cantilever crane

【悬揣】xuánchuǎi〈动〉speculate: ～来访的目的 speculate about the reasons for sb.'s visit

【悬垂】xuánchuí〈动〉hang down: 一串串～的葡萄 dangling clusters of grapes

【悬灯结彩】xuándēng-jiécǎi = 张灯结彩 zhāngdēng-jiécǎi

【悬而未决】xuán'érwèijué〈成〉be unsettled

【悬浮】xuánfú〈动〉suspend: ～在空中/水中 suspend in mid-air/water ‖ ～颗粒物 suspended particle matter ▸磁～

【悬浮液】xuánfúyè = 悬浊液 xuánzhuóyè

【悬隔】xuángé〈动〉be far apart: 两地～。The two places are far apart.

【悬挂】xuánguà〈动〉hang: ～国旗 fly the national flag ‖ 街上～着横幅。The banners stretch across the street.

【悬棺】xuánguān〈名〉hanging coffin [coffin placed in a cliff cave]: ～葬 hanging-coffin burial

【悬河】xuánhé〈名〉**1**（指河段）hanging river [with the riverbed higher than the surrounding countryside] **2**〈书〉（指瀑布）waterfall **3**（指言辞）torrent of words: ▸口若～

【悬壶】xuánhú〈动〉〈书〉practise medicine: ～济世 practise medicine to help the people

【悬乎】xuánhu〈形〉〈方〉dangerous: 叫他办事可有点～。It's a little risky to leave matters in his hands.

【悬空】xuánkōng〈动〉**1**（悬在空中）suspend in mid-air **2**〈喻〉（没着落）hang in the balance: 她工作还～着，所以生计得靠父母。Now that her job is hanging in the balance, she has to depend on her parents for a living.

【悬梁】xuánliáng〈动〉〈书〉hang from a beam: ～自尽 hang oneself from a beam

【悬梁刺股】xuánliáng-cìgǔ〈成〉〈喻〉grind away at one's studies

【悬铃木】xuánlíngmù〈名〉［植物］plane tree

【悬念】xuánniàn **A**〈动〉keep thinking about **B**〈名〉suspense: ～迭起的小说 suspense novel

【悬赏】xuánshǎng〈动〉offer a reward: ～缉拿逃犯 offer a reward for the capture of an escaped criminal

【悬殊】xuánshū〈形〉greatly disparate: 力量～ great disparity in strength ‖ 贫富～ wide gap between the rich and the poor

【悬索桥】xuánsuǒqiáo = 吊桥 diàoqiáo 1

【悬梯】xuántī〈名〉hanging ladder

【悬腕】xuánwàn〈动〉keep one's wrist raised when writing with a brush

【悬望】xuánwàng〈动〉look forward eagerly: 早去早回，免得让我～。You'd better come back early to save me from anxiety.

【悬想】xuánxiǎng〈动〉imagine: ～未来的幸福 dream of a happy future

【悬心】xuánxīn〈动〉worry: 父亲的病让他们很～。Their father's illness kept them in a state of suspense.

【悬心吊胆】xuánxīn-diàodǎn = 提心吊胆 tíxīn-diàodǎn

【悬崖】xuányá〈名〉precipice: 攀登～ scale a cliff

【悬崖勒马】xuányá-lèmǎ〈成〉〈喻〉ward off disaster at the critical moment

【悬崖峭壁】xuányá-qiàobì〈成〉steep cliff

【悬疑剧】xuányíjù〈名〉suspense drama

【悬肘】xuánzhǒu = 悬腕 xuánwàn

【悬浊液】xuánzhuóyè〈名〉turbid liquid

旋 xuán

A〈动〉**1**（旋转）revolve: ▸～转，盘～，天～地转 **2**（回来）return: ▸凯～

B〈副〉〈书〉immediately: ▸～即

C〈名〉**1**（圈儿）circle: ▸～涡，打～ **2**（指头发）whorled part of the scalp: 头顶上有两个～儿 have a double crown

▸xuàn

【旋即】xuánjí〈副〉promptly: 票～售罄。The tickets were soon sold out.

【旋律】xuánlǜ〈名〉melody: ～哀怨 doleful melody

【旋钮】xuánniǔ〈名〉knob: 调谐～ tuning knob ‖ 音量控制～ volume control knob

【旋绕】xuánrào〈动〉wind around: 把一串彩灯～在小树上 wind a string of coloured lights around a little tree ‖ 音乐在大厅里～。The music reverberated throughout the hall.

【旋塞】xuánsāi〈名〉turncock: 三通～ three-way cock

【旋梯】xuántī〈名〉spiral staircase

【旋涡】xuánwō〈名〉**1**〈本〉whirlpool: 被卷入～ be caught in a whirlpool **2**〈喻〉difficult situation: 战争～ maelstrom of war

【旋涡星云】xuánwō xīngyún〈名〉spiral nebula

【旋翼】xuányì〈名〉rotor

【旋踵】xuánzhǒng〈动〉〈书〉be quick: ～而至 arrive immediately ‖ ～即逝 vanish in a flash

【旋转】xuánzhuǎn〈动〉revolve: ～一周 make a complete rotation ‖ 逆时针/顺时针方向～ counterclockwise/clockwise rotation

【旋转餐厅】 xuánzhuǎn cāntīng〈名〉 revolving restaurant
【旋转门】 xuánzhuǎnmén〈名〉 revolving door
【旋转木马】 xuánzhuǎn mùmǎ〈名〉 merry-go-round; carousel〈美〉
【旋转乾坤】 xuánzhuǎn-qiánkūn〈成〉 turn the tide of world events
【旋转球】 xuánzhuǎnqiú〈名〉［体育］ spinning ball
【旋转舞台】 xuánzhuǎn wǔtái〈名〉 revolving stage
【旋子】 xuánzi〈名〉 circle: 打～ whirl around in a circle
▸xuànzi

漩 xuán〈名〉 whirlpool: ▸～涡
【漩涡】 xuánwō = 旋涡 xuánwō

璇 xuán〈名〉〈书〉 fine jade
【璇玑】 xuánjī〈名〉〈古〉 1 （指仪器） astronomical instrument [disc with serrated edge and central orifice] 2 （指星星） the first four stars of the Big Dipper

xuǎn

选（選） xuǎn
A〈动〉 1 （挑选） select: ～生日礼品 select a birthday present ‖ ～专业 choose a major ▸～修，～择，挑～ 2 （选举） elect: ～班长 elect a class monitor ‖ ～她担任主席 elect her president ‖ 被～入人大常委会 be elected into the Standing Committee of the National People's Congress ▸～举，～票
B〈名〉 1 （被挑中的） select: ▸人～，入～ 2 （选集） selection: 名家诗～ selections from great poets ‖ 小说～ anthology of novels ▸文～
【选拔】 xuǎnbá〈动〉 select: ～人才 select talented people ‖ ～运动员 select sportsmen
【选拔赛】 xuǎnbásài〈名〉 trials
【选本】 xuǎnběn〈名〉 selected works
【选编】 xuǎnbiān A〈动〉 select and compile: ～一本诗集 compile a selection of poems ‖ ～著名的演说 edit famous speeches B〈名〉 anthology: 散文～ collection of selected essays
【选材】 xuǎncái〈动〉 1 （指人） select a qualified person 2 （指物） select material: 这套家具～讲究。 This set of furniture is chosen for its top-quality material. 3 （指题材） select a topic: 这个故事～于传奇。 The story is culled from legend.
【选调】 xuǎndiào〈动〉 select and transfer: ～得力干部到基层工作 select competent cadres and have them transferred to grass-roots work
【选读】 xuǎndú A〈动〉 select and read: ～自己喜爱的作家作品 read selected works of one's favourite author B〈名〉 selected readings: 《英国文学～》 *Selected Readings in English Literature*
【选段】 xuǎnduàn〈名〉 selections: 京剧～ selections from Beijing opera
【选购】 xuǎngòu〈动〉 choose and buy: 有各种护肤品可供～ have a wide selection of skincare products
【选集】 xuǎnjí〈名〉 selected works: 鲁迅作品～ selected works of Lu Xun
【选辑】 xuǎnjí A〈动〉 select and compile B〈名〉 anthology
【选举】 xuǎnjǔ〈动〉 elect: ～学生会主席 elect sb. chair of the students' union ‖ 投票～ vote by ballot
【选举权】 xuǎnjǔquán〈名〉 right to vote: ～和被～ the right to vote and to stand for election
【选举人】 xuǎnjǔrén〈名〉 voter
【选举团】 xuǎnjǔtuán〈名〉 electoral college
【选举制度】 xuǎnjǔ zhìdù〈名〉 electoral system
【选刊】 xuǎnkān A〈动〉 select and publish B〈名〉 selected writings
【选矿】 xuǎnkuàng〈名〉 mineral separation: ～厂 separating plant
【选录】 xuǎnlù〈动〉 select and include: 名著～ extracts culled from the best authors
【选煤】 xuǎnméi〈名〉［矿业］ coal washing
【选美】 xuǎnměi〈名〉 beauty contest: 参加～活动 attend a beauty contest
【选民】 xuǎnmín〈名〉 voter: ～登记 voter registration ‖ ～证 voter registration card
【选派】 xuǎnpài〈动〉 select and send: ～留学生 select students for studying abroad ‖ ～代表参加会议 select representatives for a conference
【选票】 xuǎnpiào〈名〉 vote: 获得93%的～ capture 93% of the votes ‖ 拉～ canvass for votes
【选聘】 xuǎnpìn〈动〉 select for employment: ～教师 recruit teachers
【选区】 xuǎnqū〈名〉 electoral district
【选曲】 xuǎnqǔ〈名〉 selected tunes
【选取】 xuǎnqǔ〈动〉 select: 将从申请人中～五名。 Five of the applicants will be selected.
【选任】 xuǎnrèn〈动〉 select and appoint: ～管理人员 employ managerial personnel
【选手】 xuǎnshǒu〈名〉 contestant: 篮球/网球～ basketball/tennis player ‖ 优秀～ top-ranking athlete
【选送】 xuǎnsòng〈动〉 select and recommend sb.: ～优秀学生参加比赛 put the best students up for participation in the competition
【选题】 xuǎntí A〈动〉 select a topic B〈名〉 selected subject: 报～ submit one's topic
【选贤任能】 xuǎnxián-rènnéng〈成〉 select the worthy and promote the capable
【选项】 xuǎnxiàng A〈动〉 be an option B〈名〉 alternative
【选修】 xuǎnxiū〈动〉 take as an optional course of study: ～法语 take up French as an elective
【选修课】 xuǎnxiūkè〈名〉 optional course of study〈英〉; elective (course)〈美〉
【选秀】 xuǎnxiù〈动〉 draft
【选样】 xuǎnyàng〈名〉 sample
【选用】 xuǎnyòng〈动〉 select for employment: ～人才 recruit talents through a selection process
【选育】 xuǎnyù〈动〉［农业］ select and breed: ～良种小麦 develop improved varieties of wheat through selection
【选择】 xuǎnzé〈动〉 choose: ～学校 select a school ‖ 做出～ make a choice ‖ 别无～ have no alternative
【选择题】 xuǎnzétí〈名〉 multiple-choice question
【选择问句】 xuǎnzé wènjù〈名〉［语法］ alternative question
【选战】 xuǎnzhàn〈名〉 election war: 三大政党展开激烈的～。 The three parties set in motion a fierce election contest.
【选址】 xuǎnzhǐ A〈动〉 choose a site: ～建医院 choose a site for a hospital B〈名〉 selected address: 最合适的～ the best possible location
【选种】 xuǎnzhǒng〈动〉 select seeds: 选玉米种 select maize seeds

烜 xuǎn〈形〉〈书〉 magnificent: ▸～赫
【烜赫】 xuǎnhè〈形〉〈书〉 eminent: ～一时 be eminent for a time

癣（癬） xuǎn〈名〉 ringworm: 牛皮～ psoriasis

xuàn

券 xuàn〈名〉 arch
▸quàn

泫 xuàn〈动〉〈书〉 trickle
【泫然】 xuànrán〈形〉〈书〉 [of tears] trickling: ～泪下 tears trickling down one's cheeks

炫 xuàn〈动〉 1 （照射） dazzle: ▸～目 2 （夸耀） display: 自～其能 show off one's ability
【炫目】 xuànmù〈形〉 dazzling: 光彩～ blindingly bright
【炫弄】 xuànnòng〈动〉 show off: ～新车 show off one's new car
【炫示】 xuànshì〈动〉 show off: ～知识 parade one's knowledge
【炫耀】 xuànyào〈动〉 1 （照耀） dazzle 2 （夸耀） flaunt: ～财富 flaunt one's wealth ‖ ～武力 make a show of force ‖ ～学问 parade one's learning

绚（絢） xuàn〈形〉 gorgeous: ▸～烂，～丽
【绚烂】 xuànlàn〈形〉 splendid: ～的朝霞 gorgeous dawn clouds
【绚丽】 xuànlì〈形〉 gorgeous: ～的色彩 glorious colours ‖ ～多彩 bright and colourful

眩 xuàn
A〈形〉 dizzy: 头晕目～ feel dizzy ▸～晕
B〈动〉〈书〉 be dazzled: ～于名利 be dazzled by fame and wealth
【眩光】 xuànguāng〈名〉 dazzling light
【眩目】 xuànmù〈形〉 dazzling
【眩晕】 xuànyùn A〈动〉 feel dizzy: 一阵～ a fit of dizziness B ▸**p. 50**〈名〉［医学］ vertigo: 感到～ suffer from vertigo

铉（鉉） xuàn〈名〉 hooks used in ancient times for carrying tripod cooking vessels

旋[1] xuàn
A〈形〉 turning: ▸～风
B〈副〉〈口〉 at the time: ～用～学 learn for immediate use

旋[2] **（鏇）** xuàn
A〈动〉 pare: 把苹果皮～掉 peel an apple ▸～床
B = 旋子 xuànzi
▸xuán
【旋床】 xuànchuáng〈名〉［机械］ lathe
【旋风】 xuànfēng〈名〉 whirlwind: ～式访问 whirlwind visit ‖ ～式恋爱 whirlwind romance ‖ 奇异的～ freak whirlwind
【旋工】 xuàngōng〈名〉［机械］ turner

【旋子】xuànzi〈名〉hot water container for warming wine
▸xuánzi

渲 xuàn
【渲染】xuànrǎn〈动〉1（指国画技法）colour in 2〈喻〉（夸张地描述）play up: ～战争的恐怖 play up the horrors of war ‖ 大肆～ give a highly exaggerated account

楦 xuàn
A〈名〉（用于鞋）shoe last;（用于帽）hat block: ▸～头, 鞋～
B〈动〉shape with a last or block: ～一～新鞋 make new shoes on a last
【楦头】xuàntou = 楦子 xuànzi
【楦子】xuànzi〈名〉（鞋楦）shoe tree;（帽楦）hat block

碹 xuàn
A〈名〉arch
B〈动〉build an arch by laying stones

xuē

削 xuē〈动〉1（指用刀）[used in a compound word or phrase] pare: ▸～足适履 2（减少）reduce: ▸～价, ～减, ～弱 3（除去）remove: ▸～平, ～职 4（搜刮）plunder: ▸剥～
▸xiāo
【削壁】xuēbì〈名〉cliff
【削发】xuēfà〈动〉shave one's head: ～为尼/僧 take the tonsure and become a nun/monk
【削价】xuējià〈动〉cut the price: ～出售 sell at a reduced price ‖ ～处理 dispose of goods at a reduced price
【削减】xuējiǎn〈动〉cut down on: ～开支 cut down on expenditure ‖ ～预算 cut back a budget
【削平】xuēpíng〈动〉〈旧〉quell: ～叛乱 quell a rebellion
【削弱】xuēruò〈动〉weaken: ～当局的势力 weaken the might of the authorities ‖ ～敌人的有生力量 whittle down the enemy effectives ‖ 沉重的债务大大～了他们的经济。Huge debts are debilitating their economy.
【削铁如泥】xuētiě-rúní〈成〉be very sharp
【削职】xuēzhí〈动〉be dismissed from office: ～为民 demote an official to the rank of commoner
【削足适履】xuēzú-shìlǚ〈成〉〈喻〉do sth. in a perfunctory manner, regardless of specific conditions

靴 xuē〈名〉boots: 登山～ climbing boots ‖ 军～ army boots
【靴靿】xuēyào〈名〉boot leg
【靴子】xuēzi〈名〉boots: 穿上～ put on one's boots ‖ 脱掉～ take off one's boots

薛 Xuē〈名〉Xue [surname]

xué

穴 xué〈名〉1（洞）cave: ▸～居, 洞～, 孔～ 2（墓穴）grave: ▸墓～ 3（动物的窝）den: 蚁～ ant nest ▸龙潭虎～ 4（坏人盘踞地）lair: ▸匪～ 5（穴位）acupuncture point: ▸点～, 太阳～
【穴播】xuébō A〈动〉dibble B〈名〉dibbled planting
【穴道】xuédào = 穴位 xuéwèi 1
【穴居】xuéjū〈动〉live in caves
【穴居野处】xuéjū-yěchǔ〈成〉dwell in caves in the wilds
【穴头】xuétóu〈名〉organizer of informal theatrical or musical itinerant performances
【穴位】xuéwèi〈名〉1［中医］acupuncture point: ～按压疗法 acupressure therapy 2（墓穴的位置）location of a grave

茓 xué
A〈名〉coarse mat
B〈动〉store grain in a matting silo
【茓子】xuézi〈名〉coarse mat

学（學）xué
A〈动〉1（学习）study: ～本领 try and master skills ‖ ～文化 learn to read and write ‖ ～然后知不足 the more you learn, the less you feel you know ▸～校, 勤～苦练 2（仿照）imitate: ～鸡叫 copy the crowing of a cock ‖ 孩子～着大人的样子说话。The boy mimicked the adults' way of speaking. ▸鹦鹉～舌
B〈名〉1（学校）school: ▸大～, 入～, 上～ 2（学问）learning: ▸博～, 品～兼优, 治～ 3（学术）science: ▸汉～, 西～ 4（学科）subject of study: ▸经济～, 数～, 哲～
【学报】xuébào〈名〉academic journal
【学步】xuébù〈动〉learn to walk: ～的孩子 toddler ‖ ～车 baby walker
【学部】xuébù〈名〉departments of the Chinese Academy of Sciences: ～委员 academic committee member
【学潮】xuécháo〈名〉student unrest: 闹～ stir up student unrest
【学而不厌】xué'érbùyàn〈成〉have an insatiable desire to learn
【学而时习之】xué ér shí xí zhī〈成〉learn and review from time to time
【学而优则仕】xué ér yōu zé shì〈成〉a good scholar will make an official
【学阀】xuéfá〈名〉scholar-tyrant
【学非所用】xuéfēisuǒyòng〈成〉what one does has nothing to do with what one has learned
【学费】xuéfèi〈名〉1（指向学校缴纳）tuition fee: 交～ pay tuition fees ‖ ～全免 free tuition 2（指求学费用）education expenses
【学分】xuéfēn〈名〉credit: 三个～的课程 three-credit course ‖ ～制 credit system
【学风】xuéfēng〈名〉academic atmosphere: 整顿～ reorganize the study environment
【学府】xuéfǔ〈名〉institution of higher learning: 最高～ highest institution of learning
【学富五车】xuéfù-wǔchē〈成〉be well read
【学贯中西】xuéguàn-zhōngxī〈成〉well versed in the learning of both Chinese and western cultures
【学海】xuéhǎi〈名〉sea of learning: ～无涯 learning is an endless process
【学好】xuéhǎo〈动〉learn from good examples
【学坏】xuéhuài〈动〉follow bad examples: 我怕孩子会跟他～。I'm afraid the children will follow his bad example.
【学会】xuéhuì A〈动〉learn: ～弹钢琴 have learned to play the piano B〈名〉society: 申请加入～ apply for membership of an association ‖ 美国语言学～ Linguistic Society of America
【学籍】xuéjí〈名〉student status: ～管理 management of the student roll ‖ 保留～ retain one's student status ‖ 开除～ be expelled from school
【学监】xuéjiān〈名〉〈旧〉proctor
【学界】xuéjiè〈名〉academic circles
【学究】xuéjiū〈名〉pedant: ～气 pedantry
【学军】xuéjūn〈动〉learn military affairs
【学科】xuékē〈名〉1（指门类）branch of learning: ～带头人 leader of a field of learning ‖ ～评估 curriculum assessment 2（指科目）subject: 语文～ language course 3（指在军事或体育训练中）theoretical course in military/physical training
【学理】xuélǐ〈名〉scientific principle
【学力】xuélì〈名〉educational level: 具有同等～ have the same educational level
【学历】xuélì〈名〉academic background: 大学本科～ bachelor's diploma ‖ ～证书 academic certificate
【学历教育】xuélì jiàoyù〈名〉formal schooling
【学联】xuélián〈简称〉= 学生联合会
【学龄】xuélíng〈名〉school age: ～儿童 school-age child ‖ ～前儿童 preschool child
【学名】xuémíng〈名〉1（指人）formal name used at school 2（指物）scientific name
【学年】xuénián〈名〉academic year
【学农】xuénóng〈动〉learn farming
【学派】xuépài〈名〉school of thought: 创立～ found a school ‖ 弗洛伊德～ Freudian school
【学期】xuéqī〈名〉school term
【学前班】xuéqiánbān〈名〉preschool class: ～教师 preschool teacher
【学前教育】xuéqián jiàoyù〈名〉preschool education
【学前期】xuéqiánqī〈名〉preschool age
【学区】xuéqū〈名〉school district
【学人】xuérén〈名〉scholar
【学舌】xuéshé〈动〉parrot: ▸鹦鹉～
【学社】xuéshè〈名〉academic society
【学生处】xuéshēngchù〈名〉students' affairs division
【学生会】xuéshēnghuì〈名〉student union
【学生联合会】xuéshēng liánhéhuì〈名〉students' federation
【学生票】xuéshēngpiào〈名〉student ticket
【学生运动】xuéshēng yùndòng〈名〉student movement
【学生证】xuéshēngzhèng〈名〉student ID
【学生】xuésheng〈名〉1（在校读书的人）student: ～食堂 student cafeteria ‖ ～守则 rules and regulations for students ‖ 理科～ science student ‖ 文科～ arts and humanities student 2（向老师或前辈学习的人）follower: 他是梅兰芳先生的～。He is a disciple of Mei Lanfang.
【学识】xuéshí〈名〉learning: ～浅薄 have little learning ‖ ～渊博 be extremely learned
【学时】xuéshí〈名〉period
【学士】xuéshì〈名〉1（读书人）scholar: 文人～ scholar 2（指学位）bachelor: ～学位 bachelor's degree ‖ 法～ Bachelor of Law (LLB) ‖ 文～ Bachelor of Arts (BA)
【学术】xuéshù〈名〉learning: ～机构 academic institution ‖ ～会议 academic conference ‖ ～价值/交流 academic worth/exchange ‖ ～论文 thesis ‖ ～思想 academic ideas ‖ 这部著作～水平很高。This work is extremely scholarly.
【学术界】xuéshùjiè〈名〉academic circles: ～接受的观点 view accepted by academia
【学术性】xuéshùxìng〈名〉academic

X

nature: 这篇文章～很强。This article is of academic value.
【学说】xuéshuō〈名〉 theory: 向某一～挑战 challenge a doctrine ‖ 马克思主义～ Marxist theory
【学堂】xuétáng〈名〉〈方〉school
【学童】xuétóng〈名〉schoolchild
【学徒】xuétú A〈动〉serve an apprenticeship: ～两年 serve a two-year apprenticeship B〈名〉apprentice: 招～ take on an apprentice ‖ 在理发店当～ serve one's apprenticeship at a barber's
【学徒工】xuétúgōng〈名〉apprentice
【学徒期】xuétúqī〈名〉apprenticeship: ～满 have completed one's apprenticeship
【学位】xuéwèi〈名〉degree: 攻读～ study for a degree ‖ 博士/硕士～ doctoral/master's degree
【学位服】xuéwèifú〈名〉academic regalia
【学位论文】xuéwèi lùnwén〈名〉dissertation
【学位证书】xuéwèi zhèngshū〈名〉diploma
【学问】xuéwen〈名〉1（指系统知识）systematic learning: 新兴～ emergent branch of learning 2（学识）learning: ～渊博 profound learning ‖ 这里面大有～。There is much to learn from it.
【学无坦途】xuéwútǎntú〈成〉there is no royal road to learning
【学无止境】xuéwúzhǐjìng〈成〉knowledge is infinite
【学习】xuéxí〈动〉1（获取知识技能）study: ～文化 learn to read and write ‖ 在实践中～ learn through practice ‖ ～成绩 academic record ‖ ～方法 study method 2（吸取他人优点）follow the example of: ～别人的长处 emulate others' strong points ‖ ～他的为人 follow the way he conducts himself in society
【学习班】xuéxíbān〈名〉study class
【学习者】xuéxízhě〈名〉learner
【学衔】xuéxián〈名〉academic title: 她有副教授的～。She has the rank of associate professor.
【学校】xuéxiào〈名〉school: 开办～ set up a school ‖ 汽车驾驶～ driving school ‖ 中等专科～ technical secondary school
【学行】xuéxíng〈名〉scholarship and moral conduct
【学养】xuéyǎng〈名〉〈书〉scholarship and cultivation
【学业】xuéyè〈名〉studies: 完成～ finish one's studies ‖ ～成绩 academic achievements
【学以致用】xuéyǐzhìyòng〈成〉put into practice what one has learned
【学艺】xuéyì〈动〉learn a skill
【学用结合】xuéyòng jiéhé〈动〉integrate study with application
【学友】xuéyǒu〈名〉schoolmate: 同窗～ classmate
【学有专长】xuéyǒu zhuānchánɡ〈成〉have specialized knowledge of a subject
【学员】xuéyuán〈名〉student
【学院】xuéyuàn〈名〉college: 管理～ run a college ‖ 美术～ academy of fine arts ‖ 商～ business college ‖ 外语～ foreign language institute
【学院派】xuéyuànpài〈名〉academic group
【学杂费】xuézáfèi〈名〉tuition and miscellaneous fees
【学长】xuézhǎng〈名〉〈尊〉fellow student
【学者】xuézhě ▸p. 966〈名〉scholar: 访问～ visiting scholar ‖ 具有～风度的人 scholarly person
【学制】xuézhì〈名〉1（指制度）educational system: ～改革 reform in the educational system 2（指年限）length of schooling: 缩短～ shorten the period of schooling

> **中国学制**
>
> China's education system includes pre-school, primary, secondary, and higher education. Vocational, adult, and special education are also provided. Children usually go to kindergarten at about the age of three. Compulsory education starts at six or seven, and lasts nine years. This includes six years at primary school, and three years at junior high school, the first stage of secondary education. When compulsory education is completed, school leavers may go to vocational and technical schools. However, most will continue to senior high school, where they will study for a further three years. At the end of this time they will take the highly competitive college entrance examination (▸高考). Higher education institutions consist mainly of colleges and universities. Typically, it takes four years to get a Bachelor's degree, three years to get a Master's and another three years to get a PhD.

【学子】xuézǐ〈名〉〈书〉student: 海外～ overseas student

踅 xué〈动〉1（来回走）walk to and fro: ～来～去 wander hither and thither 2（盘旋）whirl: 树叶在风中～转。The leaves are whirling in the wind. 3（折回）turn back: ～回来看看 turn back and have a look

噱 xué〈动〉〈方〉laugh: 发～ make one laugh ▸～头
▸jué
【噱头】xuétóu〈方〉A〈名〉1（令人发笑的话或动作）wisecrack: 卖弄～ play to the gallery ‖ ～真多 be full of wisecracks 2（花招）tricks: 别摆～! Don't try any tricks! B〈形〉funny: ～极了。It is really funny.

xuě

雪 xuě
A〈名〉snow: 扫～ clear away the snow ▸～花, 暴风～, 瑞～
B〈动〉（指耻辱）wipe out;（指冤枉）avenge: ▸～耻, ～恨, ～冤
【雪白】xuěbái〈形〉snow-white: ～的衬衫 snow-white shirt
【雪豹】xuěbào〈名〉snow leopard
【雪暴】xuěbào〈名〉snowstorm
【雪崩】xuěbēng〈名〉avalanche
【雪冰】xuěbīng〈名〉snow and ice
【雪藏】xuěcáng〈动〉1〈方〉（冷藏）refrigerate: ～汽水 cold fizzy water 2〈喻〉（有意掩藏）intentionally withhold
【雪耻】xuěchǐ〈动〉avenge an insult: 报仇～ take revenge
【雪貂】xuědiāo〈名〉［动物］ferret
【雪雕】xuědiāo〈名〉snow sculpture
【雪糕】xuěgāo〈名〉1（冰棍）ice lolly 2〈方〉（冰激凌）ice cream
【雪恨】xuěhèn〈动〉avenge: 申冤～ revenge a wrong
【雪花】xuěhuā〈名〉snowflake: ～在空中飞舞。Snowflakes are dancing in the air.
【雪花膏】xuěhuāgāo〈名〉cream: 在脸上涂～ rub some cream on one's face
【雪茄】xuějiā〈名〉cigar: 哈瓦那～ Havana cigar
【雪晶】xuějīng〈名〉［气象］snow crystal
【雪景】xuějǐng〈名〉snowscape
【雪犁】xuělí〈名〉1（指工具）snowplough 2［体育］ski-bob: ～运动 ski-bobbing
【雪里红】xuělǐhóng〈名〉［植物］potherb mustard
【雪里蕻】xuělǐhóng = 雪里红 xuělǐhóng
【雪利酒】xuělìjiǔ〈名〉sherry
【雪莲】xuělián〈名〉snow lotus
【雪亮】xuěliàng〈形〉shiny: 把玻璃擦得～ polish the glass till it has a good shine ‖〈喻〉公众的眼睛是～的。The people have sharp eyes.
【雪柳】xuěliǔ〈名〉［植物］fontanesia
【雪盲】xuěmáng ▸p. 50〈名〉［医学］snow blindness
【雪泥鸿爪】xuění-hóngzhǎo〈成〉〈喻〉traces of the past
【雪片】xuěpiàn〈名〉snowflake: 鹅毛～ feathery snowflake ‖〈喻〉圣诞贺卡如～飞来。Christmas cards came snowing in.
【雪橇】xuěqiāo〈名〉sledge〈英〉; sled〈美〉: 狗拉～ dog-drawn sledge
【雪青】xuěqīng〈形〉lilac
【雪球】xuěqiú〈名〉snowball: ～越滚越大。A snowball gathers as it goes.
【雪人】xuěrén〈名〉1（用雪堆的人形）snowman: 堆～ build a snowman 2（指传说中的生物）Abominable Snowman [legendary man-like creature in the snows of the Himalayas]
【雪山】xuěshān〈名〉snow-capped mountain: ～草地 snow-capped mountains and marshlands
【雪上加霜】xuěshàng-jiāshuāng〈成〉〈喻〉rub salt into the wound: 她母亲的干预使他们的婚姻～。Her mother's interference exacerbated the difficulties in their marriage.
【雪松】xuěsōng〈名〉cedar
【雪兔】xuětù〈名〉［动物］snowshoe hare
【雪线】xuěxiàn〈名〉［地理］snow line
【雪野】xuěyě = 雪原 xuěyuán
【雪冤】xuěyuān〈动〉clear sb. of a false charge
【雪原】xuěyuán〈名〉snowfield: 茫茫～ a vast wilderness of snow
【雪灾】xuězāi〈名〉snow disaster
【雪仗】xuězhàng〈名〉snowball fight: 打～ have a snowball fight
【雪中送炭】xuězhōng-sòngtàn〈成〉〈喻〉render timely help

鳕（鱈） xuě〈名〉［鱼类］cod
【鳕鱼】xuěyú〈名〉cod

xuè

血 xuè
A〈名〉1（指液体组织）blood: 输～ transfuse blood ‖ 献～ donate blood ‖ ～常规检查 blood routine examination ▸～管, ～液, 呕心沥～ 2［中医］menstruation
B〈形〉1（有血缘关系）related by blood: ▸～亲, ～统 2〈喻〉（刚强热烈）energetic and high-spirited: ▸～气方刚, ～性
▸xiě
【血癌】xuè'ái ▸p. 50〈名〉〈俗〉leukaemia

X

【血案】xuè'àn〈名〉 murder case: ～在身 have committed a murder
【血本】xuèběn〈名〉 original capital: ～无归 fail to recover one's capital
【血崩】xuèbēng ▸p. 50〈名〉［中医］ metrorrhagia
【血沉】xuèchén〈名〉［医学］ erythrocyte sedimentation
【血仇】xuèchóu〈名〉 blood feud: 报～ square a blood debt
【血防】xuèfáng〈名〉［医学］ prevention and cure of schistosomiasis
【血管】xuèguǎn〈名〉 blood vessel: 使～扩张 distend a blood vessel ‖ ～硬化 vascular sclerosis
【血管扩张】xuèguǎn kuòzhāng〈名〉 vasodilatation
【血光之灾】xuèguāngzhīzāi〈成〉 disaster of being murdered
【血海深仇】xuèhǎi-shēnchóu〈成〉 profound hatred: 誓死要报～ swear to collect a blood debt
【血汗】xuèhàn〈名〉 sweat and toil: 榨取人民的～ get the people to sweat blood ‖ ～钱 hard-earned cash
【血红】xuèhóng〈形〉 blood-red: ～的夕阳 blood-red sunset
【血红蛋白】xuèhóng dànbái〈名〉［生化］ haemoglobin
【血红素】xuèhóngsù = 血红蛋白 xuèhóng dànbái
【血迹】xuèjì〈名〉 bloodstain: 沾有～的衬衣 bloodstained shirt ‖ ～斑斑 bloodstained
【血检】xuèjiǎn〈名〉 blood test
【血浆】xuèjiāng〈名〉 plasma
【血口喷人】xuèkǒu-pēnrén〈成〉 make an unfounded attack on sb.
【血库】xuèkù〈名〉 blood bank
【血块】xiěkuài〈名〉 blood clot
【血亏】xuèkuī ▸p. 50〈名〉［中医］ anaemia
【血泪】xuèlèi〈名〉 blood and tears: ～仇 deep-seated hatred ‖ ～史 history of blood and tears
【血流成河】xuèliú-chénghé〈成〉 bloodbath: 战场上～。 The battlefield was a bloodbath.
【血流漂杵】xuèliú-piāochǔ〈成〉 bloody massacre
【血流如注】xuèliú-rúzhù〈成〉 blood cascades down without stop
【血路】xuèlù〈名〉 bloody path: 杀出一条～ carve out a way through
【血脉】xuèmài〈名〉 1 (血管) blood vessels 2 (血统) blood relationship: ～相通 be of the same blood
【血尿】xuèniào ▸p. 50〈名〉 haematuria
【血浓于水】xuènóngyúshuǐ〈成〉 blood is thicker than water
【血盆大口】xuèpén-dàkǒu〈成〉 large fierce-looking mouth
【血拼】xuèpīn〈动〉 go on a spending spree
【血泊】xuèpō〈名〉 pool of blood: 倒在～中 lie in a pool of blood
【血气】xuèqì〈名〉 1 (精力) vigour: ▸～方刚 2 (血性) courage and uprightness: 有～的青年 courageous and upright youth
【血气方刚】xuèqì-fānggāng〈成〉 be full of vigour: ～的青年 hot-blooded youth
【血亲】xuèqīn〈名〉 blood relation: ～关系 blood relations ‖ 他们不是～。 They are not blood relatives.
【血清】xuèqīng〈名〉 serum: ～白蛋白 serum albumin ‖ ～蛋白 serum protein
【血球】xuèqiú = 血细胞 xuèxìbāo
【血肉】xuèròu〈名〉 1 (血和肉) flesh and blood: ～之躯 human body ‖ ～横飞 blood and flesh flying in all directions 2〈喻〉(密切的关系) close relationship: ～相连 be inseparably linked
【血肉模糊】xuèròu-móhu〈成〉 badly mangled: ～的尸体 mangled body
【血色】xuèsè〈名〉 complexion: ～很好 have a sanguine complexion ‖ 面无～ have no colour in one's cheeks
【血色素】xuèsèsù = 血红蛋白 xuèhóng dànbái
【血书】xuèshū〈名〉 letter written in one's own blood
【血栓】xuèshuān ▸p. 50〈名〉 thrombus: 脑～形成 cerebral thrombosis
【血水】xuèshuǐ〈名〉 thin blood
【血丝】xuèsī〈名〉 blood streak: 眼里充满～ one's eyes are bloodshot
【血糖】xuètáng〈名〉 blood sugar: 降低～ reduce the blood sugar ‖ ～浓度 sugar level in blood
【血统】xuètǒng ▸p. 279〈名〉 blood line: 有英国～ have British ancestry ‖ 贵族～ noble blood ‖ 有中国～的美国人 American of Chinese descent ‖ 她有法国～。 She is French by birth.
【血统论】xuètǒnglùn〈名〉 theory of the bloodline
【血污】xuèwū〈名〉 bloodstain: 擦去～ remove bloodstains
【血吸虫】xuèxīchóng〈名〉 schistosome
【血吸虫病】xuèxīchóngbìng〈名〉 schistosomiasis
【血洗】xuèxǐ〈动〉 kill all the inhabitants of a place in a bloody manner: 1937年12月日寇～南京城。 In December, 1937, the Japanese invaders drenched Nanjing in a bloodbath.
【血细胞】xuèxìbāo〈名〉 blood cell/corpuscle
【血象】xuèxiàng〈名〉 haemogram
【血小板】xuèxiǎobǎn〈名〉 platelet
【血腥】xuèxīng〈形〉 bloody: 遭到～镇压 be bloodily suppressed ‖ ～屠杀 bloody massacre ‖ ～统治 bloodthirsty rule
【血型】xuèxíng〈名〉 blood type: 你是什么～? What blood group are you?
【血性】xuèxìng〈形〉 courageous and upright: ～男儿 courageous and upright man
【血虚】xuèxū ▸p. 50〈名〉［中医］ deficiency of blood
【血循环】xuèxúnhuán〈名〉 blood circulation
【血压】xuèyā〈名〉 blood pressure: 量～ take sb.'s blood pressure ‖ 低～ low blood pressure ‖ 高～ high blood pressure
【血压计】xuèyājì〈名〉 sphygmomanometer
【血样】xuèyàng〈名〉 blood sample: 采集～ collect blood specimen
【血液】xuèyè〈名〉 1 (指血) blood: ～黏度 blood viscosity 2〈喻〉(指成分或力量) lifeblood: 输入/注入新鲜～ infuse with new blood ‖ 吸收新鲜～ absorb some fresh blood
【血液透析】xuèyè tòuxī〈名〉 haemodialysis
【血液循环】xuèyè xúnhuán〈名〉 blood circulation
【血衣】xuèyī〈名〉 bloodstained garment
【血印】xuèyìn〈名〉 bloodstain: 擦掉～ remove bloodstains
【血友病】xuèyǒubìng ▸p. 50〈名〉 haemophilia: ～患者 haemophiliac
【血雨腥风】xuèyǔ-xīngfēng = 腥风血雨 xīngfēng-xuèyǔ
【血缘】xuèyuán〈名〉 blood ties: ～关系 blood relationship
【血晕】xuèyùn〈名〉［中医］ coma induced by excessive loss of blood during the delivery of a child
▸xiěyùn
【血债】xuèzhài〈名〉 blood debt: 有～ have blood on one's hands ‖ ～累累 have heavy blood debts ‖ ～要用血来还 blood for blood
【血战】xuèzhàn A〈名〉 bloody battle B〈动〉 fight a fierce battle: ～到底 fight to the last drop of one's blood
【血证】xuèzhèng〈名〉 bloodstained evidence
【血脂】xuèzhī〈名〉 blood fat: 高～ hyperlipaemia
【血肿】xuèzhǒng ▸p. 50〈名〉 haematoma
【血渍】xuèzì = 血迹 xuèjì

谑（謔） xuè〈动〉〈书〉 banter: ～而不虐 tease without embarrassing ▸调～, 谐～

xūn

勋（勛、勳） xūn〈名〉 1 (功勋) meritorious service: ▸～劳, ～章, 功～ 2 (功劳大的人) person of great merit: ▸元～
【勋绩】xūnjì〈名〉 meritorious service: 光辉的～ glorious achievements
【勋爵】xūnjué〈名〉 1 (指爵位) feudal rank based on meritorious service 2 (指头衔) Lord
【勋劳】xūnláo〈名〉 meritorious service: ～卓著 be noted for meritorious service
【勋章】xūnzhāng〈名〉 medal: 授予～ award an order of merit

埙（塤） xūn〈名〉〈古〉 oval earthenware wind instrument with six holes

熏[1] **（燻）** xūn〈动〉 1 (指食品加工方法) smoke: ～肠/鸡/鱼 smoked sausage/chicken/fish ▸～肉, ～制 2 (用烟、气使变色或沾上气味) fumigate: ～房子 fumigate a room ‖ ～蚊子 smoke out mosquitoes ‖ 浓烟把墙都～黑了。 The wall is blackened by smoke. ‖ 他酒气～天。 He stank of alcohol.

熏[2] xūn
A〈动〉 influence: ▸～染, ～陶, 利欲～心
B〈形〉 warm: ▸～风
▸xùn
【熏风】xūnfēng〈名〉〈书〉 warm southerly breeze
【熏干儿】xūngānr〈名〉［食品］ smoke-dried bean curd
【熏染】xūnrǎn〈动〉 negatively influence
【熏肉】xūnròu〈名〉 smoked meat: 精致的～ well-cured meat
【熏陶】xūntáo〈动〉 nurture: 在父母的～下，他从小就喜爱音乐。 Nurtured by his parents, he has been interested in music since childhood.
【熏蒸】xūnzhēng〈动〉 be stifling: 暑气～ stifling summer heat
【熏制】xūnzhì〈动〉 fumigate

X

窨 xūn〈动〉 scent tea with jasmine ▸yìn

薰 xūn〈名〉 a kind of fragrant herb

【薰衣草】xūnyīcǎo〈名〉［植物］ lavender: ～油 lavender oil

【薰莸不同器】xūn-yóu bù tóng qì〈成〉〈喻〉 the good don't mix with the bad

曛 xūn〈书〉

A〈名〉 **1**（昏黑） dusk: ～晓 dawn and dusk **2**（日落余光） dim glow of the setting sun

B〈形〉 dim

醺 xūn〈形〉 drunk: 微～ tipsy ‖ 醉～～ inebriated

xún

旬 xún〈名〉 **1**（十日） ten-day period: ▸～刊，上～ **2**（十岁） ten-year period: 年满七～ have completed one's 70th year ‖ 九～老人 90-year-old man

【旬刊】xúnkān〈名〉publication that comes out every ten days

【旬日】xúnrì〈名〉 ten days

寻（尋） xún

A〈名〉〈古〉 *xun* [measure of length equal to about eight *chi* (尺)]

B〈动〉 look for: ▸～觅，搜～，自～烦恼

【寻查】xúnchá〈动〉 look for

【寻常】xúncháng〈形〉 ordinary: 不～ be unusual ‖ ～人家 ordinary family ‖ 今年春天异乎～的干燥。 It's unusually dry this spring.

【寻的】xúndì〈形〉［军事］ homing: ～导弹 homing missile ‖ ～鱼雷 target-seeking torpedo

【寻短见】xún duǎnjiàn〈动〉 commit suicide

【寻访】xúnfǎng〈动〉inquire about: ～故友 look for an old friend

【寻根】xúngēn〈动〉 **1**（指根源） probe to the bottom: ～溯源 make a thorough investigation into **2**（指祖籍） search out one's roots: ～文学 roots literature

【寻根究底】xúngēn-jiūdǐ〈成〉 investigate thoroughly

【寻根问底】 xúngēn-wèndǐ = 寻根究底 xúngēn-jiūdǐ

【寻呼】 xúnhū〈动〉 page: ～台 paging centre

【寻呼机】xúnhūjī〈名〉 pager

【寻花问柳】xúnhuā-wènliǔ〈成〉 frequent brothels

【寻欢作乐】xúnhuān-zuòlè〈成〉indulge in sensual pleasures

【寻机】xúnjī〈动〉 seek an opportunity: ～报复 seek one's revenge (on sb.)

【寻开心】xún kāixīn〈动〉〈方〉 joke: 为了～ for a laugh

【寻觅】xúnmì〈动〉 look for: ～知音 seek one's bosom friend ‖ 四处～ look everywhere

【寻求】xúnqiú〈动〉 seek: ～解决问题的办法 look for a solution to a problem ‖ ～真理/知识 seek truth/knowledge ‖ ～避难者 asylum seeker

【寻事】xúnshì〈动〉 stir up trouble: ～生非 make trouble

【寻死】xúnsǐ〈动〉 attempt suicide

【寻死觅活】 xúnsǐ-mìhuó〈成〉 make repeated suicide attempts

【寻思】xúnsi〈动〉 mull over: 我在～这件事该这么办。 I'm thinking about how we should handle this.

【寻索】xúnsuǒ〈动〉 **1**（寻找） look for **2**（探索）explore: ～答案 seek an answer

【寻味】xúnwèi〈动〉 think over: 他这番话耐人～。 What he has said gives much food for thought.

【寻问】xúnwèn〈动〉enquire about: ～消息 ask for news about

【寻隙】xúnxì〈动〉 **1**（故意挑剌） pick a quarrel: ～闹事 stir up trouble **2**（钻空子） seek an opportunity

【寻衅】xúnxìn〈动〉 pick a quarrel: ～闹事 pick a fight ‖ 蓄意～ pick a fight

【寻幽访胜】 xúnyōu-fǎngshèng〈成〉 visit scenic spots

【寻章摘句】xúnzhāng-zhāijù〈成〉 write in clichés and without originality

【寻找】xúnzhǎo〈动〉 look for: ～借口 look for an excuse ‖ ～线索 chase down clues ‖ 四处～ look about (for)

【寻踪觅迹】 xúnzōng-mìjì〈成〉 track sb. down

巡 xún

A〈动〉 patrol: 南～ go on an inspection tour to the south ▸～回，～行，～夜

B〈量〉 round of drinks: 酒过三～ the wine has gone round three times

【巡边员】xúnbiānyuán〈名〉［体育］ linesman

【巡捕】xúnbǔ〈名〉〈旧〉 police in former foreign concessions

【巡捕房】xúnbǔfáng〈名〉〈旧〉police station in former foreign concessions

【巡查】xúnchá〈动〉 make a tour of inspection: 边防战士日夜～。The frontier guards make their rounds day and night.

【巡察】xúnchá〈动〉 undertake an inspection tour: 去特区～ go to a special zone to conduct an inspection

【巡道】xúndào〈动〉 make one's rounds of the track: ～工 track walker

【巡风】xúnfēng〈动〉 keep watch

【巡抚】xúnfǔ〈名〉〈旧〉（在明朝） circuit inspector [in the Ming Dynasty];（在清朝） provincial governor [in the Qing Dynasty]

【巡航】xúnháng〈动〉 cruise: 在太平洋上～ take a cruise on the Pacific

【巡航导弹】xúnháng dǎodàn〈名〉 cruise missile: ～运载工具 cruise missile carrier

【巡回】xúnhuí〈动〉 make a circuit of: ～视察 make a tour of inspection

【巡回赛】xúnhuí sài〈名〉 tour match

【巡回大使】 xúnhuí dàshǐ〈名〉 roving ambassador

【巡回法庭】 xúnhuí fǎtíng〈名〉 circuit court

【巡回演出】xúnhuí yǎnchū〈名〉 performing tour: 做为期两天的～ play a two-day stand

【巡回演讲】xúnhuí yǎnjiǎng〈名〉speaking tour: 做～ be on the lecture circuit

【巡讲】xúnjiǎng〈动〉 conduct a speaking tour: 院士专家～活动 lecture tours by academy experts

【巡警】 xúnjǐng〈名〉 policeman〈英〉; patrolman〈美〉: 公路～ highway patrolman

【巡礼】xúnlǐ〈动〉 **1**（朝拜圣地） make a pilgrimage **2**（观光游览） tour

【巡逻】xúnluó〈动〉 patrol: 加强～ step up patrols ‖ 执行～任务 be on one's beat

【巡逻兵】xúnluóbīng〈名〉 patrol

【巡逻队】 xúnluóduì〈名〉 patrol: 海岸～ shore patrol

【巡逻哨】xúnluóshào〈名〉 patrol

【巡逻艇】xúnluótǐng〈名〉 patrol boat/craft

【巡哨】xúnshào〈动〉 go on patrol

【巡视】 xúnshì〈动〉 **1**（到各处视察） make an inspection tour: ～营地 make a circuit of the camp **2**（往四下看） cast one's eyes around

【巡天】xúntiān〈动〉 make an aerial tour

【巡行】xúnxíng〈动〉 tour: ～各地 make a tour of various places

【巡幸】xúnxìng〈动〉〈书〉go on an imperial inspection tour: ～江南 make an imperial inspection tour of the South

【巡演】xúnyǎn〈动〉 make a performing tour

【巡洋舰】xúnyángjiàn〈名〉cruiser: 导弹～ missile-carrying cruiser

【巡夜】 xúnyè〈动〉〈书〉 go on night patrol

【巡弋】xúnyì〈动〉〈书〉 cruise

【巡游】xúnyóu〈动〉 **1**（游逛） stroll: 环球～ world cruise **2**（巡行察看） make an inspection circuit: 在村外～ do the rounds outside the village

【巡展】xúnzhǎn〈动〉 hold an itinerant exhibition

【巡诊】 xúnzhěn〈动〉 [of a doctor] make one's rounds

询（詢） xún〈动〉 ask: ▸～问，查～

【询查】xúnchá = 查询 cháxún

【询问】xúnwèn〈动〉 ask about: ～年龄 ask sb.'s age ‖ ～姓名 ask sb.'s name ‖ ～学习情况 ask sb. about their studies

荀 Xún〈名〉 Xun [surname]

荨（蕁） xún ▸qián

【荨麻疹】xúnmázhěn〈名〉 nettle rash

峋 xún ▸嶙峋 línxún

洵 xún〈副〉〈书〉 truly: ～可宝贵 truly valuable

恂 xún

【恂恂】 xúnxún〈形〉〈书〉 **1**（恭顺） modest and prudent **2**（恐惧） fearful

珣 xún〈名〉〈书〉 jade

栒 xún〈名〉［植物］ cotoneaster

循 xún〈动〉 follow: ▸～例，～序渐进，遵～

【循规蹈矩】 xúnguī-dǎojǔ〈成〉 stick to convention: 他事事～。 He does everything by the book.

【循环】xúnhuán〈动〉 circulate: 促进血液～ stimulate blood circulation ‖ 恶性～ vicious circle ‖ ～往复 move in cycles

【循环经济】 xúnhuán jīngjì〈名〉 circular economy

【循环论证】 xúnhuán lùnzhèng〈名〉［逻辑］ circular argument

【循环赛】xúnhuánsài〈名〉［体育］ round-robin

【循环系统】xúnhuán xìtǒng〈名〉［生理］ circulatory system

【循环小数】xúnhuán xiǎoshù ▸p. 691〈名〉repeating decimal
【循例】xúnlì〈动〉follow convention
【循名责实】xúnmíng-zéshí〈成〉live up to one's name
【循序渐进】xúnxù-jiànjìn〈成〉make steady progress: ～地学习外语 learn a foreign language step by step
【循循善诱】xúnxún-shànyòu〈成〉give guidance in a skilful and systematic fashion

鲟（鱘） xún〈名〉［鱼类］sturgeon

xùn

训（訓） xùn
A〈动〉**1**（教导）lecture: 挨一顿～ get a talking to ▸～导, ～话, 教～ **2**（解释）explain: ▸～诂 **3**（训练）train: ▸～练, 集～, 军～
B〈名〉**1**（训诫的话）teachings: ▸家～, 遗～ **2**（准则）model: ▸不足为～
【训斥】xùnchì〈动〉scold: 受到～ get told off ‖ 严厉～ sternly reprimand
【训词】xùncí〈名〉admonition
【训导】xùndǎo〈动〉teach and guide: 宗教～ religious doctrines
【训诂】xùngǔ〈名〉commentary on ancient texts
【训诂学】xùngǔxué〈名〉critical interpretation of ancient texts
【训话】xùnhuà〈动〉admonish
【训诲】xùnhuì〈动〉〈书〉instruct
【训诫】xùnjiè **A**〈动〉admonish **B**〈名〉［法律］admonishing
【训练】xùnliàn〈动〉train: ～新兵 drill new recruits ‖ ～有素 well-trained ‖ 接受～ receive a training ‖ 进行～ undergo training ‖ 强化～ intensive training ‖ ～基地 training base ‖ 野外～ field training
【训令】xùnlìng〈名〉instruction
【训示】xùnshì〈名〉instruction
【训育】xùnyù〈名〉〈旧〉moral teachings
【训谕】xùnyù = 训喻 xùnyù
【训喻】xùnyù〈动〉〈书〉instruct

讯（訊） xùn
A〈动〉**1**（讯问）ask after: ▸问～ **2**（审问）question: ▸传～, 审～
B〈名〉information: 警察闻～立即赶到现场。On hearing the news, the police rushed to the scene. ▸电～, 通～
【讯号】xùnhào〈名〉signal
【讯问】xùnwèn〈动〉**1**（问）ask about: ～病情 ask about sb.'s illness ‖ ～事情的原委 enquire into the details **2**（审问）interrogate: ～案件 hear a case ‖ ～证人 examine a witness

汛 xùn〈名〉seasonal flood: ▸～期, 春～, 防～
【汛期】xùnqī〈名〉flood season
【汛情】xùnqíng〈名〉flood situation: ～严重。The flood is serious.

迅 xùn〈形〉fast: ▸～雷不及掩耳, ～速
【迅即】xùnjí〈副〉immediately: ～出发 set out at once ‖ 此事希～处理。It is hoped that immediate action will be taken on this matter.
【迅疾】xùnjí〈形〉swift: 动作～ be swift in motion
【迅捷】xùnjié〈形〉quick: 行动～ be quick in action
【迅雷不及掩耳】xùnléi bùjí yǎn ěr〈成〉〈喻〉with lightning speed: 以～之势 with the suddenness of a thunderbolt
【迅猛】xùnměng〈形〉swift and violent: ～发展 develop by leaps and bounds ‖ 水势～异常。The flood roared on swift and violent.
【迅速】xùnsù〈形〉swift: 动作～ be quick in action ‖ ～采取行动 swing into action ‖ ～做出反应 be prompt in one's response

驯（馴） xùn
A〈形〉tame: ▸～服, ～顺, 温～
B〈动〉tame: ～马 break in a horse ‖ ～兽师 animal trainer ▸～养
【驯服】xùnfú **A**〈形〉docile: 猫是很～的。Cats are very tame. **B**〈动〉tame: ～洪水 bring the flood under control ‖ ～烈马 break in a difficult horse
【驯化】xùnhuà〈动〉domesticate: 有些动物容易～。Some animals are easily domesticated.
【驯良】xùnliáng〈形〉tractable
【驯鹿】xùnlù〈名〉reindeer
【驯熟】xùnshú〈形〉**1**（驯顺）obedient **2**（熟练）skilled
【驯顺】xùnshùn〈形〉tame
【驯养】xùnyǎng〈动〉domesticate: ～动物 domesticate animals

徇 xùn〈动〉submit to: ▸～情, ～私舞弊
【徇情】xùnqíng〈动〉〈书〉practise favouritism
【徇情枉法】xùnqíng-wǎngfǎ〈成〉bend the law for the benefit of one's relatives or friends
【徇私舞弊】xùnsī-wǔbì〈成〉practise favouritism and engage in malpractices

逊（遜） xùn
A〈动〉**1**〈书〉（让出）abdicate: ▸～位 **2**（比不上）be inferior: 稍～一筹 be slightly inferior ▸～色
B〈形〉modest: ▸出言不～, 谦～
【逊尼派】Xùnnípài〈名〉［伊斯兰教］Sunni
【逊色】xùnsè〈形〉inferior: 毫不～ be by no means inferior
【逊位】xùnwèi〈动〉abdicate

殉 xùn〈动〉**1**（殉葬）be buried alive with the dead: ▸～葬 **2**（牺牲）sacrifice one's life for: ▸～国, ～职
【殉道】xùndào〈动〉die for a cause: ～者 martyr
【殉国】xùnguó〈动〉lay down one's life for one's country: 以身～ give oneself over to the service of one's country
【殉教】xùnjiào〈动〉die for a religious cause
【殉节】xùnjié〈动〉**1**（为国捐躯）die loyal to one's country **2**〈旧〉（因抗拒凌辱而死）die to preserve one's chastity **3**〈旧〉（因丈夫死而自杀）commit suicide after one's husband's death
【殉难】xùnnàn〈动〉die for a just cause: 不幸～ to die tragically for a just cause
【殉难者】xùnnànzhě〈名〉martyr
【殉情】xùnqíng〈动〉die for love
【殉葬】xùnzàng〈动〉be buried alive with the dead: ～的奴隶 slaves buried alive with their deceased master ‖ ～品 sacrificial object
【殉职】xùnzhí〈动〉die in the line of duty: 以身～ die a martyr at one's post

巽 xùn〈名〉one of the Eight Trigrams, symbolizing 'wind'

熏 xùn〈动〉〈口〉gas: 让煤气～死 be gassed
▸xūn

蕈 xùn〈名〉［植物］gill fungus

噀 xùn〈动〉〈书〉spurt liquid from the mouth: ～酒 spurt liquor from the mouth ‖ ～水 spout water from the mouth

Yy

yā

丫 yā〈名〉1（树杈） fork: ▸～杈，树～ 2（分支） fork: 五个指头四个～。Five fingers form four forks. ▸脚～子 3〈方〉（女孩） girl: 小～ little girl ‖ 潘家那～，长得和仙女一样。 The Pan family daughter is as beautiful as a fairy. ▸～环，～头

【丫杈】yāchà = 桠杈 yāchà

【丫环】yāhuan = 丫鬟 yāhuan

【丫鬟】yāhuan〈名〉〈旧〉 maidservant: 贴身～ personal maid

【丫髻】yājì〈名〉 girl's double-looped coiffure

【丫头】yātou〈名〉1（女孩） girl: 小～已长大成人。 The little girl has blossomed into a woman. ▸黄毛～ 2 = 丫鬟 yāhuan 3（女儿） daughter: 她的～ her daughter

压（壓）yā

A〈动〉1（施压力） press: 把子弹～进弹匣 press the cartridges into the magazine ‖ 累累的果实～弯了树枝。 The branches were weighed down by clusters of fruit. ‖〈喻〉 工作～得我们透不过气来。 We are swamped with work. ‖〈喻〉 这任务是从上面～下来的。 The task has come from above. 2（压制） suppress: 树正气，～邪气 encourage healthy trends and check unhealthy ones ‖ 以势～人 overwhelm people with one's power ‖ 别拿大帽子～我。 Don't intimidate me with unwarranted charges. ‖ 困难～不倒我们。 No difficulty can defeat us. ‖ 他又用顶头上司来～我了。 Once again he is trying to use our immediate superior to coerce me into submission. ▸～制，欺～，镇～ 3（使稳定） control: ～着怒火 control one's anger ‖ 把嗓门～得很低 lower one's voice to a hiss ‖ ～住阵脚 keep things under control ‖ 吃点药～～咳嗽。 Take some medicine to ease the cough. ▸～台，～阵 4（超越） prevail over: 在上半场比赛中，我们在比分上一直～着对方。 Throughout the first half of the game, our team was ahead of our opponents. 5（逼近） close in on: 敌军向我们的阵地～过来了。 The enemy troops were gaining on our position. ‖ 太阳～树梢了。 The setting sun is hovering over the treetops. ▸～境 6（积压） lay aside: 货～在仓库里。 The goods have piled up in the warehouse. ‖ 这份报告被～了半年。 This report was shelved for six months. ‖〈喻〉 这事一直～在我心上。 This has weighed heavily on my mind. ▸～库，积～ 7（赌） risk: 他把自己的前途～到这次考试上。 His future hinges on the result of this exam. ▸～宝，～题

B〈名〉 pressure: ▸加～，减～，变～器，低～，高～
▸yà

【压宝】yābǎo〈动〉 stake

【压编】yābiān〈动〉 cut staff

【压不住】yābuzhù〈动〉cannot keep under control: ～怒火 cannot control one's anger

【压仓】yācāng〈动〉 overstock

【压舱物】yācāngwù〈名〉［航海］ ballast

【压产】yāchǎn〈动〉 cut production: 限期～，减少库存 cut production to reduce stock over a limited period

【压场】yāchǎng〈动〉1（控制场面）keep a crowd under control: 他会讲话，能压住场。 He is a good speaker and will certainly be able to hold the attention of the audience. 2（节目排在最后） serve as the grand finale

【压场戏】yāchǎngxì = 压轴戏 yāzhòuxì

【压车】yāchē〈动〉1 = 押车 yāchē 2（指车辆） be jammed

【压秤】yāchèng〈动〉1（称起来分量大） be relatively heavy per unit volume: 干蘑菇不～，一斤就是一大堆。 Dried mushrooms don't weigh much. One *jin* of them is a lot. 2（故意压低分量） underweigh (in order to underpay)

【压船】yāchuán〈动〉［of cargo ships］ be held up in the harbour

【压担子】yā dànzi〈惯〉 charge sb. with heavy tasks: 给年轻人～，使他们得到锻炼。 Young people should be charged with heavy tasks in order to temper their characters.

【压倒】yādǎo〈动〉 overpower: ～性优势 overwhelming superiority ‖ 在人数上～对方 overwhelm one's opponent in numbers ‖ 以～多数击败对手 beat one's opponent by an overwhelming majority ‖ 以～性优势取胜 win a landslide victory ‖ 稳定是当前～一切的任务。 Stability is of overriding importance at present.

【压得住】yādezhù〈动〉 be able to keep under control

【压低】yādī〈动〉 reduce: ～价格 bring down prices ‖ ～声音 lower one's voice

【压顶】yādǐng〈动〉 bear down on one: 乌云～。Dark clouds hang overhead. ▸泰山～

【压锭】yādìng〈动〉［纺织］ reduce spindleage (to curtail production in a cotton mill)

【压队】yāduì = 押队 yāduì

【压发帽】yāfàmào〈名〉 slumber cap

【压风机】yāfēngjī〈名〉［矿业］ pressure fan

【压服】yāfú〈动〉 force into submission: 群众是压不服的。 The public cannot be forced to submit.

【压盖】yāgài〈名〉［机械］ gland

【压杆】yāgǎn〈名〉［机械］ pressure bar

【压港】yāgǎng〈动〉［of cargo on the wharf］ be held up

【压痕】yāhén〈名〉 impression

【压货】yāhuò〈名〉 cargo held up at loading point

【压价】yājià〈动〉 drive down a price: ～百分之五 force the price down by 5% ‖ ～销售 sell at a reduced price

【压肩迭背】yājiān-diébèi〈成〉very crowded

【压惊】yājīng〈动〉 help sb. get over a shock: 安排筵席，为友人～。 They held a banquet to help their friends get over the shock.

【压境】yājìng〈动〉［of enemy troops］ press on to the border: 大军～。 A large enemy force is bearing down upon the border.

【压酒】yājiǔ〈动〉 press fermented rice to make wine

【压卷】yājuàn〈名〉［used as a commendatory term for a poem, a book or a painting］ the best of all one's works: ～之作 the best work that has ever been written

【压库】yākù〈动〉1（积压） overstock: 店里自行车～严重。 The store is overstocked with bicycles. 2（减少库存） reduce the stocks: ～以增加效益 reduce an inventory to boost returns

【压垮】yākuǎ〈动〉 collapse under pressure: 被工作～ collapse under the pressure of work

【压力】yālì〈名〉1［物理］ pressure: 大气～ atmospheric pressure ‖ 深水处水的～ the pressure of water at great depths ‖ 每平方英寸的～为4千克。 It was a pressure of four kilos to the square inch. 2（负担） pressure: 顶住～ withstand pressure ‖ 施加～ exert pressure ‖ 人口～ population pressure ‖ 舆论～ pressure of public opinion

【压力表】yālìbiǎo = 压力计 yālìjì

【压力锅】yālìguō〈名〉 pressure cooker

【压力计】yālìjì〈名〉 pressure gauge

【压路机】yālùjī〈名〉 roller

【压面机】yāmiànjī〈名〉 noodle press

【压模】yāmó〈名〉 press mould: ～机 moulding press

【压平】yāpíng〈动〉 flatten out

【压迫】yāpò〈动〉1（强制别人服从） oppress: ～穷人 oppress the poor ‖ 反抗～ resist oppression ‖ 哪里有～哪里就有反抗。 Where there is oppression, there is resistance to oppression. 2［医学］ constrict: ～动脉 compress an artery ‖ ～止血 haemostasis by compression ‖ 肿瘤～神经。 The tumour is pressing on the nerves.

【压气】yāqì〈动〉1（指怒气） calm sb.'s anger: 说几句好话给他压压气儿。 Say a few agreeable words to calm him down. 2（指空气） compress air

【压强】yāqiáng〈名〉［物理］ pressure: ～计 pressure gauge

【压青】yāqīng〈名〉［农业］ green manuring

【压哨】yāshào〈动〉［体育］ come at the last second: 投入一个～球 score a last-second goal
【压舌板】yāshébǎn〈名〉［医学］ tongue depressor
【压岁钱】yāsuìqián〈名〉 money given to children as a lunar New Year gift: 给小孩发～ give lunar New Year money gifts to children

> **压岁钱**
>
> Money given at Chinese New Year by the older generation to the younger generation, usually after the New Year's Eve dinner or when paying visits during the Spring Festival period. 岁 (*sui*, 'year') has the same sound as 祟 (ghost), so in the past, copper coins were strung on a red string and hung on a child's chest as a way of driving out evil spirits. Today money is put into red paper envelopes for luck.

【压缩】yāsuō〈动〉**1**（使体积缩小）compress: 把气体～成液体 condense gas into liquid ‖ ～气体 compressed gas **2**（减少） cut down: ～办公费用 reduce office expenses ‖ ～开支 curb expenditure ‖ ～篇幅 cut short the text **3**［计算机］ compress: ▸～文件
【压缩饼干】yāsuō bǐnggān〈名〉 ship biscuit
【压缩格式】yāsuō géshi〈名〉［计算机］ packed format
【压缩机】yāsuōjī〈名〉 compressor: 空气～ air compressor
【压缩空气】yāsuō kōngqì〈名〉［物理］ compressed air: ～瓶 compressed air bottle
【压缩文件】yāsuō wénjiàn〈名〉［计算机］ zipped file
【压台】yātái〈动〉**1** = 压场 yāchǎng 2 **2**（稳住局面） stabilize a situation
【压题】yātí〈动〉**1** = 押题 yātí **2**（指排列） [of photographs or pictures] mix with headlines
【压条】yātiáo〈动〉［农业］ layer: ～法 layerage
【压痛】yātòng〈名〉［医学］ tender spot: ～点 pressure pain point ‖ 他的手腕肿了，而且还有～。 His wrist was swollen and tender.
【压腿】yātuǐ〈动〉［体育］ flex one's leg muscles
【压下】yāxià〈动〉**1**〈本〉 press down **2**〈喻〉 hold back
【压线球】yāxiànqiú〈名〉［体育］ line ball
【压抑】yāyì〈动〉 hold back: 精神～ feel oppressed ‖ ～不住内心的激动 be unable to restrain one's excitement
【压抑感】yāyìgǎn〈名〉 feeling of oppression: 减轻心中的～ unburden oneself of pent-up emotion ‖ 胸口有一种～ feel tight in the chest
【压榨】yāzhà〈动〉**1**（榨汁） press: ～橘子汁 squeeze the juice from oranges ‖ ～葡萄酿酒 press grapes to make wine **2**〈喻〉（剥削） exploit: ～穷人 fleece the poor ‖ 忍受残酷～ put up with ruthless exploitation
【压阵】yāzhèn〈动〉**1**（压队） bring up the rear: 骑兵在队伍后面～。 The mounted soldiers brought up the rear in the procession. **2**（稳住阵脚） keep a situation under one's control: 开会时老主任坐在新主任旁边～。 The former director sat beside the new chief to help keep order at the meeting.
【压枝】yāzhī〈动〉= 压条 yātiáo
【压制】yāzhì〈动〉**1**（抑制） suppress: ～民主 suppress democracy ‖ ～批评 suppress criticism ‖ 他的观点从一开始就受到～。 His ideas were stifled from the very beginning. **2**［军事］ neutralize: ～敌军炮火 neutralize enemy artillery fire **3**［机械］ press: ～成形 press sth. into shape ‖ ～唱片 press a phonograph record
【压轴】yāzhòu〈动〉 present the last but one item on a theatrical performance
【压轴戏】yāzhòuxì〈名〉 grand finale: 〈喻〉竞选刚刚开始，～还在后面呢。 The campaign has only just begun. Things haven't even begun to hot up yet.

呀 yā

A〈叹〉 oh: ～，孩子不见了！ Oh, the children have disappeared!
B〈拟〉 creak: 大门～的一声打开了。 The door creaked open.
▸ya

押¹ yā

A〈动〉**1**〈书〉（签字画符） sign: ～尾 mark in place of a signature **2**（抵押） pledge: 把房子～了出去 mortgage one's house ‖ 她把手表～在出租车司机那儿了。 She left her watch as a pledge with the taxi driver. ▸～金，抵～ **3**（拘禁） detain: 被～作人质 be detained as hostage ‖ 在～犯 criminal in custody ‖ 警方把他～起来了。 The police detained him. ▸关～，拘～，扣～ **4**（跟随看管） escort: 把罪犯～到监狱 escort the criminals to prison ‖ 他们把犯人～走了。 They marched the prisoner away. ▸～车，～解，～送
B〈名〉 signature: ▸画～

押² yā

〈动〉**1**（押韵） rhyme: ▸～韵 **2**（赌） stake: 你怎能把自己的前途～到这种冒险上面？ How can you risk your future on such an adventure? ▸～宝，～题
【押宝】yābǎo = 压宝 yābǎo
【押钞车】yāchāochē〈名〉 armoured car
【押车】yāchē〈动〉 escort a vehicle
【押当】yādàng **A**〈动〉 pledge: ～首饰 pawn jewellery ‖ 赎回～的物品 redeem a pledge ‖ 我把项链～了。 I have pawned my necklace. **B**〈名〉 small pawnshop
【押队】yāduì〈动〉 bring up the rear
【押解】yājiè〈动〉**1**（指人） take away under escort: ～出境 deport **2**（指物） escort sth. in transit: ～货物 escort goods in transit
【押金】yājīn〈名〉**1**（用于抵押） deposit: 交了10元钱～ leave 10 *yuan* as deposit ‖ 取回～ get back a deposit ‖ 收取/索要～ collect/demand a deposit **2**（用于预付） advance payment: 住院要先付～。 Hospitalization requires an advance payment.
【押禁】yājìn〈动〉 take into custody
【押款】yākuǎn **A**〈动〉 borrow money on security: 他用房产～创业。 He mortgaged his house in order to start a business. **B**〈名〉**1**（指贷款） secured loan **2** = 押金 yājīn 2
【押送】yāsòng〈动〉**1**（指人） escort: ～犯人 take a criminal away under escort ‖ 他被～到法庭受审。 He was escorted to the law court for trial. **2**（指物） convoy: 由士兵～军粮 transport army provisions under the convoy of troops
【押题】yātí〈动〉 study according to what one thinks or hopes will be in an exam: 考试靠猜题、～是没用的。 Preparing for what you guess is going to be in an exam is useless.
【押运】yāyùn〈动〉 convoy: ～军火 transport munitions under armed escort ‖ ～员 transport guard
【押韵】yāyùn〈动〉 rhyme: 这首诗不～。 This poem doesn't rhyme.
【押账】yāzhàng〈动〉 give (sth.) as security for a loan
【押租】yāzū〈名〉〈旧〉 rent deposit: 付～ pay a rent deposit

垭（埡） yā

〈名〉〈方〉 [used mainly in place names] mountain pass

鸦（鴉） yā

〈名〉 crow: ▸寒～，乌～
【鸦片】yāpiàn〈名〉 opium: 贩卖～ traffic in opium
【鸦片战争】Yāpiàn Zhànzhēng〈名〉 Opium War
【鸦雀无声】yāquè-wúshēng〈成〉 so silent as to be able to hear a pin drop

哑（啞） yā

= 呀 yā
▸yǎ
【哑哑】yāyā〈拟〉**1**（小儿学语声） babble **2**（乌鸦叫） caw

桠（椏） yā

〈名〉 fork of a tree
【桠杈】yāchà〈名〉 fork of a tree: 修剪～ prune a tree
【桠枝】yāzhī〈名〉 branch

鸭（鴨） yā

〈名〉 duck: 公～ drake ‖ 母～ duck ‖ 盐水～ salted duck ▸板～，烤～，填～
【鸭场】yāchǎng〈名〉 duck farm
【鸭蛋】yādàn〈名〉**1**（指蛋） duck's egg: 咸～ salted duck's egg **2**〈诙〉（指分数） goose egg
【鸭蛋脸】yādànliǎn〈名〉 oval face
【鸭蛋青】yādànqīng〈名〉 pale blue
【鸭梨】yālí〈名〉 *yali* [variety of Chinese pear from Hebei Province]
【鸭绿江】Yālùjiāng ▸**p. 294**〈名〉 Yalu River
【鸭棚】yāpéng〈名〉 duck coop
【鸭绒】yāróng〈名〉 duck down: ～被 eiderdown
【鸭舌帽】yāshémào〈名〉 duckbill cap
【鸭行鹅步】yāxíng-ébù〈成〉 waddle
【鸭掌】yāzhǎng〈名〉 duck's foot
【鸭胗】yāzhēn〈名〉 duck's gizzard
【鸭子】yāzi〈名〉〈口〉 duck
【鸭嘴笔】yāzuǐbǐ〈名〉 drawing pen
【鸭嘴兽】yāzuǐshòu〈名〉 duck-billed platypus

雅 yā

= 鸦 yā
▸yǎ
【雅片】yāpiàn = 鸦片 yāpiàn

yá

牙¹ yá

〈名〉**1**（牙齿） tooth: 拔～ extract a tooth ‖ 刷～ brush the teeth ‖ 蛀～ decayed tooth ▸补～，乳～ **2**（象牙） ivory: ～筷 ivory chopsticks ‖ ～章 ivory seal **3**（齿状物） tooth-like thing: ▸～轮

牙² yá

〈名〉〈旧〉 broker: ▸～行
【牙斑】yábān〈名〉［医学］ dental plaque
【牙病】yábìng ▸**p. 50**〈名〉 tooth disease
【牙槽】yácáo〈名〉［解剖］ tooth socket
【牙碜】yáchen〈形〉**1**（指食物） gritty: 菜没洗干净，有些～。 The vegetables

y

have not been washed properly. They seem gritty. 2〈喻〉（指语言） vulgar: 她说话真～。 She is coarse in speech.
【牙齿】yáchǐ〈名〉 tooth: 保护～ protect the health of one's teeth
【牙床】yáchuáng〈名〉 gum
【牙雕】yádiāo〈名〉 ivory carving
【牙缝】yáfèng〈名〉 gap between the teeth: 剔～ pick one's teeth ‖〈喻〉 父母用他们从～里挤出来的钱资助我读完大学。 My parents financed me through college with the money squeezed out of their tight food budget.
【牙缸】yágāng〈名〉 tooth mug
【牙膏】yágāo〈名〉 toothpaste: 药物～ medicinal toothpaste ▸挤～
【牙根】yágēn = 牙床 yáchuáng
【牙垢】yágòu〈名〉［医学］ tartar
【牙关】yáguān〈名〉 mandibular joint: 咬紧～ clench one's teeth
【牙行】yáháng〈名〉〈旧〉 1（指个人） broker 2（指商号） broker house
【牙慧】yáhuì〈名〉〈书〉 remarks made by others: ▸拾人～
【牙具】yájù〈名〉 tooth cleaning tools
【牙科】yákē〈名〉 dentistry department: ～医生 dentist ‖ ～诊所 dental clinic
【牙口】yákou〈名〉 1（指年龄） age of a draft animal as shown by the number of its teeth 2（指咀嚼能力） condition of one's teeth: 您这么大年纪，～可不错。 You certainly have good teeth for your age.
【牙轮】yálún〈名〉［机械］ cog
【牙买加】Yámǎijiā〈名〉 Jamaica: ～人 Jamaican
【牙牌】yápái = 骨牌 gǔpái
【牙婆】yápó〈名〉〈旧〉 middle-woman in human trafficking
【牙签】yáqiān〈名〉 toothpick
【牙石】yáshí〈名〉［医学］ tartar
【牙刷】yáshuā〈名〉 toothbrush
【牙髓】yásuǐ〈名〉［解剖］ dental pulp: ～炎 pulpitis
【牙线】yáxiàn〈名〉 dental floss
【牙牙】yáyá〈拟〉 [of baby] babble
【牙牙学语】yáyáxuéyǔ〈成〉 [of baby] babble out one's first words
【牙医】yáyī〈名〉 dentist
【牙龈】yáyín〈名〉 gum: ～出血 have bleeding gums
【牙龈萎缩】yáyín wěisuō〈名〉 gingival atrophy
【牙龈炎】yáyínyán ▸**p. 50**〈名〉 gingivitis
【牙釉质】yáyòuzhì〈名〉 dental enamel
【牙质】yázhì〈形〉 ivory: ～的刀把 ivory knife handle
【牙周炎】yázhōuyán ▸**p. 50**〈名〉 periodontitis

伢 yá〈名〉〈方〉 kid

【伢子】yázi〈名〉〈方〉 kid

芽 yá〈名〉

1（植物幼体） bud: 老树上长出了新～。 New buds sprouted from the old tree. ▸发～, 豆～儿 2（芽状物） bud-shaped thing: ▸肉～
【芽孢】yábāo〈名〉［生物］ spore
【芽茶】yáchá〈名〉 young tea leaves
【芽豆】yádòu〈名〉 sprouted broad bean
【芽眼】yáyǎn〈名〉［植物］ eye: 土豆的～ eye of a potato

蚜 yá〈名〉 aphid: 棉～ cotton aphid ‖ 烟～ tobacco aphid

【蚜虫】yáchóng〈名〉 aphid: 苹果～ apple aphid

崖 yá〈名〉

1（指陡立的侧面） edge of a cliff: ▸山～, 悬～, 云～ 2〈书〉（边际） boundary: ▸～略
【崖壁】yábì〈名〉 precipice
【崖画】yáhuà = 岩画 yánhuà
【崖刻】yákè〈名〉 cliff carving
【崖略】yálüè〈名〉〈书〉 outline
【崖葬】yázàng〈名〉 burial by placing coffins in niches dug in cliffs

涯 yá〈名〉

1〈书〉（水边） bank: 水～ river bank ▸～岸 2（边际） boundary: 一望无～ be boundless ▸天～海角, 生～
【涯岸】yá'àn〈名〉 embankment
【涯际】yájì〈名〉〈书〉 boundary: 漫无～的海洋 boundless sea

睚 yá〈名〉〈书〉 corner of the eye

【睚眦】yázì〈书〉 **A**〈动〉 stare angrily **B**〈名〉〈喻〉 small grievance
【睚眦必报】yázì-bìbào〈成〉 seek revenge for petty grievance
【睚眦之怨】yázìzhīyuàn〈成〉 petty grievance

衙 yá〈名〉 *yamen* [government office in feudal China]: ▸～门

【衙门】yámen〈名〉 *yamen* [government office in feudal China]
【衙内】yánèi〈名〉〈旧〉 1（官僚子弟） sons of high-ranking feudal officials 2（禁卫官） imperial bodyguard
【衙役】yáyi〈名〉 *yamen* runner

yǎ

哑（啞） yǎ〈形〉

1（不能说话） mute: 又聋又～ both deaf and dumb ‖ 喂，你～啦? Well? Have you lost your tongue? ‖ 两挺机关枪被打～了。 Two machine guns were put out of action. ▸～巴, 装聋作～ 2（无声） speechless: ▸～剧, ～口无言, ～谜 3（打不响） unexploded: ～弹 unexploded bomb ▸～火 4（沙哑） hoarse: 嗓子～了 lose one's voice ‖ 今天你声音有些～。 You sound a bit husky today. ‖ 她喊得嗓子～了。 She shouted herself hoarse. ▸沙～
▸yā
【哑巴】yǎba〈名〉 mute: 天生是～ be mute from birth
【哑巴吃黄连，有苦说不出】yǎba chī huánglián, yǒu kǔ shuōbuchū〈歇后〉 swallow one's bitterness
【哑巴亏】yǎbakuī〈惯〉 grievance that one has to keep to oneself: 吃～ have to grin and bear it
【哑场】yǎchǎng = 冷场 lěngchǎng
【哑火】yǎhuǒ〈形〉 1（打不响） unexploded 2（不说话） quiet
【哑剧】yǎjù〈名〉 mime: ～演员 mime artist
【哑口无言】yǎkǒu-wúyán〈成〉 be left speechless: 把对方驳得～ silence an opponent
【哑铃】yǎlíng〈名〉［体育］ dumb-bell: 举～ lift dumb-bells
【哑谜】yǎmí〈名〉 puzzling remark: 打～ keep sb. guessing
【哑炮】yǎpào〈名〉 dud [artillery shell]
【哑然】yǎrán〈形〉〈书〉 1（寂静） silent 2（形容惊异） dumbfounded
【哑然失笑】yǎrán-shīxiào〈成〉 cannot help laughing: 过了一会儿他又～了。 After a moment, he burst out laughing again.
【哑语】yǎyǔ〈名〉 sign language: 打～ use sign language

雅[1] yǎ

A〈形〉 1〈书〉（合乎规范） standard: ▸～言, ～正 2（高雅） elegant: 房间布置得很～。 The room is tastefully furnished. ▸～观, ～致, ～俗共赏, 文～ 3〈书〉〈套〉（用于称对方的情意、举动） your: ▸～教
B〈名〉 one of the three sections of *The Book of Songs*（《诗经》）, consisting of court hymns
C〈副〉〈书〉 unusually: ～以为善 truly consider sb. to be kind-hearted

雅[2] yǎ〈书〉

A〈名〉 acquaintance: 无一日之～ not have the pleasure of knowing sb. ‖ 一面之～ nodding acquaintance
B〈副〉 1（平素） usually: ～不相知 not be acquainted with each other 2（很） very: 情怀～合 very close feelings
▸yā
【雅典】Yǎdiǎn〈名〉 Athens
【雅典娜】Yǎdiǎnnà ▸**p. 274**〈名〉 Athena [goddess in Greek mythology]
【雅飞士】yǎfēishì〈名〉 useless Western youth
【雅观】yǎguān〈形〉 [usu used in the negative] tasteful: 姿势不～ carry oneself in an ungainly manner
【雅号】yǎhào〈名〉 1〈尊〉（名号） your name 2〈诙〉（绰号） nickname: 他有一个～叫"胖子"。 He is nicknamed 'Fatty'.
【雅加达】Yǎjiādá〈名〉 Jakarta
【雅教】yǎjiào〈名〉〈敬〉 your esteemed opinion
【雅静】yǎjìng〈形〉 1（幽雅宁静） refined and quiet: ～的房间 tasteful, quiet rooms 2（文静） gentle and quiet: 温文～的姑娘 gentle and quiet girl
【雅量】yǎliàng〈名〉 1（指气度） magnanimity: 王某向以～见称。 Wang has long been known for his generosity. 2（指酒量） high alcohol tolerance
【雅鲁藏布江】Yǎlǔzàngbùjiāng ▸**p. 294**〈名〉 Yarlung Zangbo River
【雅皮士】yǎpíshì〈名〉 yuppie
【雅气】yǎqì〈名〉 1（高雅不俗）（指环境） refined atmosphere;（指人） refined bearing 2〈书〉（正气） healthy trend
【雅趣】yǎqù〈名〉 refined taste: ～盎然 be in delightful taste
【雅人】yǎrén〈名〉 person of refined taste
【雅士】yǎshì〈名〉 person of refined taste: 文人～ men of letters and refined scholars
【雅思】Yǎsī〈名〉 IELTS (International English Language Testing System): 参加～考试 take part in the IELTS examination
【雅俗共赏】yǎsú-gòngshǎng〈成〉 appeal to both refined and popular tastes: 这出戏～，很受欢迎。 The play is very popular with both intellectuals and the general public.
【雅玩】yǎwán〈名〉 refined object for amusement
【雅温得】Yǎwēndé〈名〉 Yaoundé
【雅兴】yǎxìng〈名〉 aesthetic mood: 难得大家今天都有这～。 It's rare that everyone is in such a bright mood as today.

【雅言】yǎyán〈名〉〈书〉**1**〈旧〉（标准语） standard language **2**（正确的话） worthy opinion: 察纳～ seek good advice
【雅乐】yǎyuè〈名〉〈旧〉court music
【雅正】yǎzhèng **A**〈形〉〈书〉correct **B**〈动〉〈套〉[polite expression usu used in the inscription on sth. presented to sb. as a gift] please point out any inadequacy that you may find in my work
【雅致】yǎzhi〈形〉tasteful: 装饰～ be decorated in good taste
【雅座】yǎzuò〈名〉private room: 包～ hire a private room

yà

轧[1]（軋）
yà〈动〉**1**（碾）crush: ～棉花 gin cotton ‖ ～碎 crush to pieces ‖ 把路面～平 roll a road surface flat **2**（排挤） squeeze out: ▸倾～, 挤～

轧[2]（軋）
yà ▸轧轧 yàyà
▸gá, zhá
【轧板机】yàbǎnjī〈名〉［冶金］mangle
【轧场】yàcháng〈动〉**1**（指压平打谷场） level a threshing ground with a stone roller **2**（指辗压谷物） thresh grain on a threshing ground with a stone roller
【轧道车】yàdàochē〈名〉［铁路］track-testing trolley
【轧道机】yàdàojī = 压路机 yālùjī
【轧光机】yàguāngjī〈名〉calender
【轧花】yàhuā〈动〉［纺织］gin cotton
【轧花机】yàhuājī〈名〉cotton gin
【轧马路】yàmǎlù〈惯〉[of lovers] take a stroll
【轧轧】yàyà〈拟〉click: 缝纫机～地响着。 The sewing machine was clicking away. ‖ 铰链～作响。The hinges squeaked.

亚[1]（亞）
yà〈形〉inferior: 他的学问不～于任何人。 His knowledge is second to none. ▸～军, ～热带

亚[2]（亞）
Yà〈名〉Asia: ▸～太, ～洲
【亚当】Yàdāng〈名〉Adam
【亚得里亚海】Yàdélǐyàhǎi〈名〉Adriatic Sea
【亚的斯亚贝巴】Yàdìsī Yàbèibā〈名〉Addis Ababa
【亚非拉】Yà-Fēi-Lā〈名〉Asia, Africa and Latin America
【亚非会议】Yà-Fēi Huìyì〈名〉Asian-African Conference (1955)
【亚光速】yàguāngsù〈名〉［物理］subvelocity of light
【亚健康】yàjiànkāng ▸**p. 50**〈名〉［医学］poor health: 处于～状态 be in a state of poor health
【亚军】yàjūn〈名〉second place: 获得～ come (in) second
【亚拉巴马州】Yàlābāmǎzhōu〈名〉Alabama
【亚利桑那州】Yàlìsāngnàzhōu〈名〉Arizona
【亚硫酸】yàliúsuān〈名〉［化学］sulphurous acid
【亚麻】yàmá〈名〉**1**［植物］flax: ～纤维 flax ‖ ～籽 linseed **2**（指纤维） linen: ～布 linen
【亚马逊河】Yàmǎxùnhé ▸**p. 294**〈名〉Amazon River
【亚美尼亚】Yàměiníyà〈名〉Armenia: ～共和国 Republic of Armenia ‖ ～人 Armenian ‖ ～语 Armenian
【亚热带】yàrèdài〈名〉subtropical zone: ～气候 subtropical climate
【亚太】Yà-Tài〈形〉Asia-Pacific: ～地区 Asia-Pacific region
【亚太经合组织】Yà-Tài Jīnghé Zǔzhī〈简称〉= 亚洲太平洋经济合作组织
【亚特兰大】Yàtèlándà〈名〉Atlanta
【亚细亚】Yàxìyà〈名〉Asia
【亚硝酸】yàxiāosuān〈名〉［化学］nitrous acid
【亚型】yàxíng〈名〉subtype
【亚音速】yàyīnsù〈名〉subsonic speed: ～飞机 subsonic aircraft
【亚油酸】yàyóusuān〈名〉［化学］linoleic acid
【亚运村】Yàyùncūn〈名〉Asian Games Village
【亚运会】Yàyùnhuì〈名〉Asian Games
【亚种】yàzhǒng〈名〉［生物］subspecies
【亚洲】Yàzhōu〈名〉Asia: ～国家 Asian countries ‖ ～金融危机 financial crisis in Asia
【亚洲开发银行】Yàzhōu Kāifā Yínháng〈名〉Asian Development Bank (ADB)
【亚洲人】Yàzhōurén〈名〉Asian person
【亚洲四小龙】Yàzhōu sìxiǎolóng〈名〉the four little dragons of Asia [Taiwan, Hong Kong, the Republic of Korea and Singapore]
【亚洲太平洋经济合作组织】Yàzhōu Tàipíngyáng Jīngjì Hézuò Zǔzhī〈名〉Asia Pacific Economic Cooperation (APEC)
【亚洲小姐】Yàzhōu Xiǎojiě〈名〉Miss Asia

压（壓）
yà
▸yā
【压板】yàbǎn〈名〉〈方〉see-saw
【压根儿】yàgēnr〈副〉〈口〉[usu used in the negative] in the first place: 你持什么意见我～不在乎。 I do not care a damn about what you think. ‖ 我～不会唱歌。 I simply cannot sing.

讶（訝）
yà〈动〉〈书〉be surprised: ～然失色 turn pale with fright ▸惊～

迓
yà〈动〉〈书〉welcome: ▸迎～

砑
yà〈动〉press and smooth: 把皮子～光 press and smooth leather until it shines

娅（婭）
yà ▸姻娅 yīnyà

氩（氬）
yà〈名〉［化学］argon (Ar): ～气灯 argon lamp

揠
yà〈动〉〈书〉pull up
【揠苗助长】yàmiáo-zhùzhǎng〈成〉〈喻〉spoil things with excessive enthusiasm

ya

呀
ya〈助〉[used instead of 啊 after a syllable ending in a, e, i, o, or ü]: 快来～! Come quick.
▸yā

yān

咽
yān〈名〉［解剖］pharynx
▸yàn, yè
【咽喉】yānhóu〈名〉**1**［解剖］throat: ～痛 have a sore throat **2**〈喻〉（交通要道） key link: ～要地 strategic point
【咽喉炎】yānhóuyán ▸**p. 50**〈名〉［医学］pharyngolaryngitis
【咽痛】yāntòng ▸**p. 50**〈名〉sore throat
【咽头】yāntóu〈名〉［解剖］pharynx
【咽炎】yānyán ▸**p. 50**〈名〉［医学］pharyngitis

恹（懨）
yān
【恹恹】yānyān〈形〉run-down: 病～的 run-down with illness ‖ ～欲睡 feel weak and sleepy

殷
yān〈形〉dark red
▸yīn, yǐn
【殷红】yānhóng〈形〉dark red: ～的血迹 blackish red bloodstains

胭
yān〈名〉rouge: ▸～红
【胭红】yānhóng〈形〉cochineal
【胭脂】yānzhi〈名〉rouge: ～虫 cochineal ‖ 在脸上搽～ pat some rouge onto one's face
【胭脂鱼】yānzhiyú〈名〉［鱼类］mullet

烟（煙）
yān
A〈名〉**1**（气状物） smoke: 浓～缭绕上升。 Thick smoke spirals upward. ▸～筒, 炊～, 冒～ **2**（烟状物） smoke-like substance [mist, vapour, etc.]: ▸～霭, ～波, ～雾 **3**（烟子） soot: ▸松～ **4**（烟草） tobacco: ▸～农, ～叶, 烤～ **5**（香烟） tobacco product [cigarette or cigar]: 一条～ a carton of cigarettes ‖ 禁止吸～ No smoking ▸鼻～, 香～ **6**（鸦片） opium: ▸～枪, ～土
B〈动〉be irritated by smoke: ～得睁不开眼睛 can't open one's eyes for the smoke
【烟霭】yān'ǎi〈名〉〈书〉mist and cloud: ～朦胧 be misty
【烟波】yānbō〈名〉mist-covered waters
【烟波浩渺】yānbō-hàomiǎo〈成〉a vast expanse of misty, rolling waters: 远望大江东流，～。 Looking into the distance, we can see the great river flowing east, a vast expanse of mists and ripples.
【烟草】yāncǎo〈名〉tobacco: ～制品 tobacco product
【烟尘】yānchén〈名〉**1**（烟雾和尘埃） smoke and dust: ～弥漫 be enveloped in smoke and dust **2**〈旧〉（战火） flames of war: 无～之祸 be free from war
【烟囱】yāncōng〈名〉chimney: ～里冒出滚滚浓烟。 The chimney is spouting volumes of black smoke.
【烟袋】yāndài〈名〉Chinese tobacco pipe [small-bowled, long-stemmed tobacco pipe]: ▸水～
【烟袋锅儿】yāndàiguōr〈名〉pipe bowl
【烟道】yāndào〈名〉flue
【烟蒂】yāndì〈名〉cigarette butt: 不要乱扔～ No littering of cigarette butts
【烟斗】yāndǒu〈名〉pipe: 叼着～ have a pipe in one's mouth ‖ ～丝 pipe tobacco
【烟缸】yāngāng〈名〉ashtray
【烟垢】yāngòu〈名〉soot
【烟馆】yānguǎn〈名〉〈旧〉opium den
【烟鬼】yānguǐ〈名〉**1**（指吸鸦片） opium

addict 2（指抽烟） chain smoker: 老～ habitual smoker
【烟海】yānhǎi〈名〉 a sea of heavy fog: 如堕～ be utterly mystified as if lost in a fog ▸浩如～
【烟盒】yānhé〈名〉 cigarette case
【烟黑】yānhēi〈名〉 soot
【烟花】yānhuā〈名〉 1（书）（指春景） lovely spring scene 2（旧）（妓女） prostitute 3（焰火） fireworks: 禁止燃放～爆竹 No fireworks

> 烟花
> ▸鞭炮

【烟花女】yānhuānǚ〈名〉〈旧〉 prostitute
【烟花巷】yānhuāxiàng〈名〉〈旧〉 red-light district
【烟灰】yānhuī〈名〉 cigarette ash
【烟灰缸】yānhuīgāng〈名〉 ashtray
【烟火】yānhuǒ〈名〉 1（烟和火） smoke and fire: 严禁～! Smoking and fires are strictly forbidden. 2（指饮食） cooked food: 不食人间～ live the life of an immortal 3（书）（战火） flames of war 4（旧）（后嗣） descendants: 绝了～ have no male offspring
【烟火食】yānhuǒshí〈名〉 cooked food
【烟火】yānhuo〈名〉 fireworks: 燃放～ let off fireworks ‖ 盛大的～表演 magnificent fireworks display
【烟碱】yānjiǎn〈名〉［化学］ nicotine
【烟酒不沾】yānjiǔ bùzhān〈成〉 keep away from alcohol and tobacco
【烟具】yānjù〈名〉 smoking paraphernalia
【烟卷儿】yānjuǎnr〈名〉 cigarette: 嘴里叼着～ hold a cigarette between one's lips
【烟煤】yānméi〈名〉 bituminous coal
【烟民】yānmín〈名〉〈诙〉 smoker
【烟幕】yānmù〈名〉 smoke screen: 厚厚的一层～ a thick pall of smoke ‖〈喻〉为一项政策制造～ provide a smoke screen for a policy
【烟幕弹】yānmùdàn〈名〉 1［军事］ smoke bomb 2〈喻〉 smoke screen: 放～ put up a smoke screen
【烟农】yānnóng〈名〉 tobacco grower
【烟屁股】yānpìgu〈口〉= 烟头 yāntóu
【烟气】yānqì〈名〉［工程］ flue gas
【烟枪】yānqiāng〈名〉 opium pipe
【烟圈】yānquān〈名〉 smoke ring: 吐～ blow (smoke) rings
【烟色】yānsè ▸**p. 863**〈名〉 dark brown
【烟丝】yānsī〈名〉 pipe tobacco
【烟筒】yāntong〈名〉 chimney
【烟头】yāntóu〈名〉 cigarette end
【烟土】yāntǔ〈名〉 crude opium
【烟味】yānwèi〈名〉 cigarette breath: 他嘴里有～。 His breath stinks of cigarettes.
【烟雾】yānwù〈名〉 smoke: ～笼罩 be enveloped in a veil of mist ‖ ～弥漫 be enveloped in smoke
【烟雾报警器】yānwù bàojǐngqì〈名〉 smoke alarm
【烟雾腾腾】yānwù-téngténg〈成〉 be filled with smoke
【烟消云散】yānxiāo-yúnsàn〈成〉〈喻〉 vanish into thin air: 一切疑虑现在都～了。 All doubts have disappeared.
【烟熏火燎】yānxūn-huǒliǎo〈成〉〈喻〉 be restless: 急得～ be restless with worries
【烟叶】yānyè〈名〉 leaf tobacco: 烤～ cure tobacco leaves
【烟瘾】yānyǐn〈名〉 1（指香烟） cigarette habit: 过～ enjoy a cigarette ‖ ～大 be a heavy smoker 2（指鸦片烟） opium habit
【烟油】yānyóu〈名〉 tobacco tar
【烟雨】yānyǔ〈名〉 misty rain: ～蒙蒙。 Fine rain drizzles in the mist.
【烟云】yānyún〈名〉 smoke and clouds: ～缭绕。 Smoke and clouds are whirling around.
【烟柱】yānzhù〈名〉 column of smoke: 喷出一道～ emit a column of smoke
【烟子】yānzi〈名〉〈口〉 soot
【烟嘴儿】yānzuǐr〈名〉 cigarette holder

焉 yān〈书〉

A〈代〉 1（于此） [used to refer to the person, the thing, the place] here, this: 三人行，必有我师～。 Where there are three men walking together, one of them is bound to be able to teach me something. ‖ 罪莫大～。 There is no greater crime than this. ▸心不在～ 2（表反问） how, why: 不入虎穴，～得虎子? Nothing ventured, nothing gained.
B〈助〉〈书〉 [used at the end of a sentence for emphasis]: 幸勿哂～。 Please don't laugh at me.

崦 yān

【崦嵫】yānzī〈名〉〈古〉 place where the sun sets

阉（閹） yān

A〈动〉 castrate: ～猫 neuter a cat
B〈名〉〈书〉 eunuch: ～党 eunuch faction
【阉割】yāngē〈动〉 1〈本〉 castrate 2〈喻〉 emasculate: 由于删掉了实施条款，那项法案实际上被～了。 The bill was weakened by the removal of the enforcement clause.
【阉鸡】yānjī〈名〉 capon
【阉牛】yānniú〈名〉 bullock
【阉人】yānrén〈名〉 1（被阉割的人） castrated person 2（宦官） eunuch: 政治～ political eunuch
【阉羊】yānyáng〈名〉 wether
【阉猪】yānzhū〈名〉 barrow [castrated pig]

阏（閼） yān

▸è
【阏氏】yānzhī〈名〉 main wife of a Xiongnu chief

淹 yān

A〈动〉 1（淹没） flood: ～得半死 be half drowned ‖ 河水决堤，～了整个村子。 The river burst its banks, drowning the entire village. ‖ 许多房屋被～。 Many houses are under water. 2（刺激皮肤） irritate the skin: 被汗～得难受 be tingling from sweat
B〈形〉 1〈书〉（时间久） prolonged: ▸～留 2（深广） wide: ▸～博
【淹博】yānbó〈形〉〈书〉 wide: 学识～ have a broad knowledge
【淹灌】yānguàn〈名〉［农业］ basin irrigation
【淹留】yānliú〈动〉〈书〉 stay for a long period: ～他国 stay in a foreign country for years
【淹埋】yānmái〈动〉 submerge: 铁路线被流沙～了。 The railway line was buried in the drifting sands.
【淹没】yānmò〈动〉 drown: 洪水～了农田。 The flood submerged the fields. ‖〈喻〉 他的话被掌声～了。 His words were lost in the applause.

腌（醃） yān

〈动〉 pickle: ～菜 pickle vegetables ‖ ～黄瓜 pickled cucumber
▸ā
【腌菜】yāncài〈名〉 pickles
【腌肉】yānròu〈名〉 preserved meat
【腌鱼】yānyú〈名〉 preserved fish
【腌制】yānzhì〈动〉 pickle: ～酱菜 make pickles ‖ 用盐水～黄瓜 steep cucumbers in brine to pickle them
【腌渍】yānzì〈动〉 cure

湮 yān

〈动〉 1〈书〉（埋没） fall into oblivion: ▸～灭，～没 2（淤塞） clog up: 河道久～。 The river was clogged up for a long time.
【湮灭】yānmiè〈动〉 bury in oblivion
【湮没】yānmò〈动〉 fall into oblivion: ～无闻 disappear into oblivion ‖ 巴比伦的文明早已～。 The Babylonian civilization has long fallen into oblivion.

嫣 yān

〈形〉〈书〉 beautiful: ▸～然
【嫣红】yānhóng〈形〉 bright red: ▸姹紫～
【嫣然】yānrán〈形〉〈书〉 beautiful: ～一笑 give a sweet smile

燕 Yān

〈名〉 1（指国名） Yan [state in the Zhou Dynasty] 2〈旧〉（指地名） Hebei Province
▸yàn
【燕京】Yānjīng〈名〉〈旧〉 Beijing

yán

延 yán

〈动〉 1（延长） prolong: ▸～长，蔓～，绵～ 2〈书〉（聘请） engage: ～师 engage a teacher ‖ ～医 send for a doctor ▸～聘 3（推迟） postpone: ▸～期，顺～，拖～
【延挨】yán'ái〈动〉 stall: ～度日 endure hard times
【延安】Yán'ān〈名〉 Yan'an
【延边朝鲜族自治州】Yánbiān Cháoxiǎnzú Zìzhìzhōu〈名〉 Korean Autonomous Prefecture of Yanbian
【延长】yáncháng〈动〉 prolong: ～寿命 prolong life ‖ 会议～了两天。 The conference was extended for another two days.
【延长线】yánchángxiàn〈名〉 extension line
【延迟】yánchí〈动〉 delay: 会议～了。 The meeting has been postponed. ‖ 天气不好，预先安排好的活动～了。 Bad weather caused a delay in the scheduled activities.
【延宕】yándàng〈动〉〈书〉 procrastinate: ～时日 be delayed for days on end
【延搁】yángē〈动〉 postpone
【延缓】yánhuǎn〈动〉 delay: ～工作进度 delay the progress of work ‖ ～衰老 prevent premature senility
【延颈企踵】yánjǐng-qǐzhǒng〈成〉〈喻〉 be on tenterhooks
【延揽】yánlǎn〈动〉〈书〉 enlist the services of: ～人才 recruit talent
【延绵】yánmián〈动〉 stretch long and unbroken: ～不绝 stretch endlessly
【延纳】yánnà〈动〉〈书〉 receive: ～英才 receive talented people
【延年益寿】yánnián-yìshòu〈成〉 prolong life: 经常锻炼可以～。 Regular exercise can help you to live longer.
【延聘】yánpìn〈动〉 1〈书〉（聘用）

engage: ～法律顾问 engage sb. as one's legal adviser 2（续聘） prolong an employment period: 他被～两年。 He was employed for another two years after his retirement.

【延期】yánqī〈动〉 postpone: ～审理 postpone a trial ‖ 申请～ apply for a postponement ‖ ～数日 be postponed for a few days ‖ 运动会因雨～。 The sports meet was postponed on account of rain.

【延期交货】yánqī jiāohuò〈名〉 late delivery

【延期判决】yánqī pànjué〈名〉 deferred sentence

【延请】yánqǐng〈动〉 employ: ～法律顾问 engage sb. as one's legal adviser

【延烧】yánshāo〈动〉 [of fire] spread: 大火～了十几间房屋。 The fire destroyed more than a dozen houses.

【延伸】yánshēn〈动〉 extend: 厂区向东一直～到铁路边。 The factory compound extends eastward as far as the railway.

【延伸火力】yánshēn huǒlì〈名〉［军事］ creeping fire

【延时】yánshí〈动〉 delay

【延首远望】yánshǒu-yuǎnwàng〈成〉 stretch one's neck and look far ahead

【延髓】yánsuǐ〈名〉［生理］ medulla oblongata

【延误】yánwù〈动〉 incur loss through delay: ～工期 cause a delay in the time limit of a project ‖ ～时机 miss an opportunity because of a delay ‖ ～时日 lose time ‖ 不得～ no-delay basis

【延性】yánxìng〈名〉［物理］ ductility: ～铸铁 ductalloy

【延续】yánxù〈动〉 continue: 展览会将～两周。 The exhibition will last for a fortnight. ‖ 这种习俗在中国～了几千年。 The custom went on for thousands of years in China.

【延续性】yánxùxìng〈名〉 continuity

【延展】yánzhǎn〈动〉 stretch: 公路向山区～。 The motorway stretches all the way to the mountains.

【延展性】yánzhǎnxìng〈名〉［物理］ ductility

闫（閆） Yán〈名〉 Yan [surname]

芫 yán

►yuán

【芫荽】yánsui〈名〉［植物］ coriander〈英〉; cilantro〈美〉

严（嚴） yán

A〈形〉 1（严厉） solemn: ►～肃, 威～, 庄～ 2（严格） strict: 高标准, ～要求 high standards and strict demands ‖ 执法不～ be lax in enforcing the law ►～词, ～禁, ～峻 3（程度深） intense: ►～冬, ～刑峻法, ～重 4（紧密） tight: 门关得～～的。 The door was shut tight. ‖ 他的嘴不～。 He has got a big mouth. ►～紧, ～密

y

B〈名〉 father: 家～ my father

【严办】yánbàn〈动〉 punish with severity: ～肇事者 punish the troublemaker severely ‖ 依法～ punish severely according to the law

【严惩】yánchéng〈动〉 punish severely: ～干部违法乱纪行为 crack down on official malpractice ‖ ～罪犯 impose heavy penalties on criminals

【严惩不贷】yánchéngbùdài〈成〉 punish with severity: 违者～。 Those who disobey will be severely punished.

【严词】yáncí〈名〉 strong words: ～拒绝 give a stern rebuff ‖ ～谴责 denounce in strong terms

【严打】yándǎ A〈动〉 punish severely: ～经济犯罪行为 mete out severe punishment in economic criminal cases ‖ ～走私活动 crack down on smuggling B〈名〉 campaign to crack down on criminal activities

【严冬】yándōng〈名〉 severe winter: 熬过～ survive the harsh winter

【严防】yánfáng〈动〉 take strict precautions against: ～破坏 take strict precautions against sabotage ‖ 我们要～死守, 誓死保住大坝。 We'll fight to the death to ensure the safety of the embankments.

【严父慈母】yánfù-címǔ〈成〉 stern father and loving mother

【严格】yángé A〈形〉 strict: ～的纪律 firm discipline ‖ ～的训练 rigorous training ‖ ～要求自己 be strict with oneself ‖ ～执行规章制度 rigorously enforce rules and regulations ‖ 对质量～把关 make strict checks to guarantee quality ‖ 受到～训练 receive strict training ‖ 这是法律所～禁止的。 The law strictly forbids it. B〈动〉 rigorously enforce: ～组织纪律 rigidly enforce organizational discipline

【严固】yángù〈形〉 solid: 防守～ have a solid and impregnable defence

【严寒】yánhán〈形〉 bitterly cold: 冒着～ brave freezing temperatures ‖ ～的气候/天气 bitterly cold climate/weather

【严紧】yánjǐn〈形〉 1（严格） strict: 企业管理要～。 Management of the enterprise must be rigorous. 2（严密） tight: 窗户糊得挺～。 The windows are tightly sealed.

【严谨】yánjǐn〈形〉 1（指态度） rigorous: 办事～ be meticulous and precise in one's work ‖ 态度～ assume a rigorous attitude ‖ ～的治学态度 rigorous approach to scholarly research 2（指结构） compact: 这篇散文结构～。 The essay is tightly structured.

【严禁】yánjìn〈动〉 strictly prohibit: ～体罚学生 strictly forbid corporal punishment of pupils ‖ ～吸烟! No Smoking! ‖ ～携带易燃易爆物品上车! Taking combustible and explosive goods aboard are strictly prohibited!

【严峻】yánjùn〈形〉 severe: ～的考验 rigorous test ‖ ～的现实 hard rock of reality ‖ 他面色～。 There was a stern expression on his face. ‖ 国际形势已发展到极其～的程度。 The international situation has reached a point of extreme gravity.

【严控】yánkòng〈动〉 bring under strict control: ～物价 bring prices under strict control

【严酷】yánkù〈形〉 1（严厉） harsh: ～的教训 bitter lesson ‖ ～的现实 harsh reality 2（残酷） cruel: ～的剥削 cruel exploitation

【严厉】yánlì〈形〉 severe: 采取～措施 take drastic measures ‖ 态度～ be stern in manner ‖ ～惩罚 sternly punish ‖ ～斥责 scold sharply ‖ ～的批评 severe criticism ‖ ～谴责 denounce sb. bitterly ‖ ～制裁 impose stern sanctions

【严令】yánlìng〈动〉 give strict orders: ～禁止 be strictly forbidden according to orders

【严密】yánmì A〈形〉 1（无空隙） tight: ～防守 tight defence ‖ 封口～。 The seal is tight. 2（周密） strict: ～防范 take strict precautions ‖ ～封锁 impose a tight embargo ‖ ～监视 put under close surveillance ‖ 消息封锁得很～。 A strict blockade on the passage of information has been imposed. B〈动〉 tighten up: ～规章制度 tighten up rules and regulations

【严明】yánmíng A〈形〉 strict and impartial: 纪律～ observe strict discipline ‖ 执法～ be strict and impartial in law enforcement B〈动〉 strictly enforce: ～纪律 maintain strict discipline

【严命】yánmìng〈名〉〈书〉 strict order: ～缉拿凶手 give strict orders to apprehend the murderer

【严声厉色】yánshēng-lìsè〈成〉 be stern in voice and countenance

【严师】yánshī〈名〉 strict teacher

【严师出高徒】yánshī chū gāotú〈俗〉 a strict teacher produces brilliant disciples

【严师诤友】yánshī-zhèngyǒu〈成〉 strict teacher and outspoken friend

【严实】yánshi〈形〉〈方〉 1（无空隙） tight: 把自己裹得严严实实以抵御寒风 muffle oneself up against the freezing wind ‖ 把门关～点。 Shut the door tight. 2（不易找到） safe: 藏得很～ be well-hidden

【严守】yánshǒu〈动〉 1（指遵守） strictly observe: ～规章制度 be rigorous in one's observance of rules and regulations ‖ ～中立 strictly observe neutrality 2（指保守） guard closely: ～国家机密 strictly guard state secrets

【严霜】yánshuāng〈名〉 severe frost

【严丝合缝】yánsī-héfèng〈成〉〈喻〉 be watertight

【严肃】yánsù A〈形〉 1（使人敬畏） serious: 表情～ have a serious look on one's face ‖ ～的气氛 solemn atmosphere 2（严格认真） earnest: 态度～ be serious in attitude ‖ 此事要～处理。 This matter must be handled seriously. ‖ 领导～地指出了我们的问题。 The chief made an earnest attempt to point out our problems. B〈动〉 strictly enforce: ～党纪 enforce Party discipline ‖ ～法制 maintain the legal system

【严肃性】yánsùxìng〈名〉 austerity

【严刑】yánxíng〈名〉 torture: ～逼供 extort a confession by torture ‖ ～拷打 viciously attack

【严刑峻法】yánxíng-jùnfǎ〈成〉 draconian laws

【严以律己, 宽以待人】yányǐ-lǜjǐ, kuānyǐ-dàirén〈成〉 forgive others but be unsparing of oneself

【严阵以待】yánzhènyǐdài〈成〉 be at action stations: 我军在该地区～。 Our forces stand ready in the region.

【严整】yánzhěng〈形〉 1（严肃整齐） lined-up neatly 2（严谨） scrupulous

【严正】yánzhèng〈形〉 solemn and just: 发表～声明 solemnly declare ‖ 提出～交涉 lodge serious representations

【严重】yánzhòng〈形〉 serious: 病情～ be seriously ill ‖ ～失职 gross neglect of duty ‖ 造成～后果 produce grave consequences ‖ 问题越来越～。 The problems have worsened.

【严重性】yánzhòngxìng〈名〉 seriousness

言 yán

A〈动〉 say: 知而不～ be reticent to voice what one knows ‖ 一切尽在不～中。 Everything lies in what is left unsaid. ►不苟～笑, 不～而喻, 简而～之

B〈名〉 1（话语） speech: 常～道 as the saying goes ‖ 那是酒后之～。 It was the drink in him talking. ►留～, 序～, 名～ 2（字） word: 全书近十万～。 It is a book of nearly 10,000 words. ►千～万语

【言必信，行必果】yán bì xìn, xíng bì guǒ〈成〉one should always be true in word and resolute in action

【言必有中】yánbìyǒuzhòng〈成〉what one says is always to the point: 夫人不言，～。That man is no talker; but when he does say anything, he invariably hits the mark.

【言不及义】yánbùjíyì〈成〉talk only of trivialities

【言不尽意】yánbùjìnyì〈成〉**1**（所说未能表达全部意思）words cannot express what is on one's mind **2**（意犹未尽）[used to end a letter] I would like to say more, but I have to bring my letter to a close now

【言不由衷】yánbùyóuzhōng〈成〉not say what one thinks

【言差语错】yánchā-yǔcuò〈成〉mistakes or slips in speaking

【言出必行】yánchūbìxíng〈成〉be as good as one's word

【言出法随】yánchū-fǎsuí〈成〉once delivered, the orders shall be strictly enforced

【言传】yánchuán〈动〉express in words: ～不如身教。In teaching words are no substitute for example.

【言传身教】yánchuán-shēnjiào〈成〉teach by personal example as well as verbal instruction

【言词】yáncí = 言辞 yáncí

【言辞】yáncí〈名〉one's words: ～激烈 speak with indignation ‖ ～恳切 be sincere in what one says

【言多必失】yánduō-bìshī〈成〉one who talks too much is prone to error: 我害怕～，招来麻烦。I am afraid if I talk too much, I may make mistakes and bring trouble on myself.

【言而无信】yán'érwúxìn〈成〉go back on one's word: 他这个人总是～，出尔反尔。He never keeps his promises and is always going back on his word.

【言而有信】yán'éryǒuxìn〈成〉be true to one's word

【言归于好】yánguīyúhǎo〈成〉make up: 你同妻子～了吗？Have you made up with your wife?

【言归正传】yánguīzhèngzhuàn〈成〉get back to the point

【言过其实】yánguòqíshí〈成〉exaggerate: 这家报纸对事故的报道有点～。The newspaper's description of the accident was a bit over the top.

【言和】yánhé〈动〉make up: 握手～ shake hands and make it up

【言欢】yánhuān〈动〉talk cheerfully: 杯酒～ chat cheerfully over a glass of wine

【言简意赅】yánjiǎn-yìgāi〈成〉brief and to the point: 他的讲话～。His speech was short but to the point.

【言教】yánjiào〈动〉teach verbally: 父母应该既有～也有身教。Parents should teach by example as well as talk.

【言近旨远】yánjìn-zhǐyuǎn〈成〉simple in language but profound in meaning

【言路】yánlù〈名〉channels for communication with leadership: 广开～ encourage the airing of views

【言论】yánlùn〈名〉opinion on public affairs: 发表～ air one's views ‖ 散布错误～ spread wrong opinions ‖ ～自由 freedom of speech

【言情】yánqíng〈形〉romantic: ～小说 romantic fiction

【言情剧】yánqíngjù〈名〉romance: 日、韩的～颇受中国观众青睐。Japanese and Korean romances are popular with Chinese audiences.

【言情片】yánqíngpiān〈名〉romantic film

【言人人殊】yánrénrénshū〈成〉different people give different views

【言三语四】yánsānyǔsì〈成〉make irresponsible remarks

【言声儿】yánshēngr〈动〉〈口〉say: 需要什么，只管～。Just tell me if you need anything.

【言说】yánshuō〈动〉put to words: 不可～ be hard to put into words ‖ 难以～的痛苦 indescribable pain

【言谈】yántán **A**〈动〉have a way of talking: 不善～ be slow of speech **B**〈名〉speech: ～举止 speech and deportment ‖ ～得体 appropriate way of talking

【言听计从】yántīng-jìcóng〈成〉accept sb.'s advice without questioning: 对父亲，我一向～。When it comes to my father, I will do whatever it is he says.

【言外之意】yánwàizhīyì〈成〉hidden meaning

【言为心声】yánwéixīnshēng〈成〉what the heart thinks the tongue speaks

【言下之意】yánxiàzhīyì〈成〉undermeaning

【言笑】yánxiào〈动〉talk and laugh: ▶不苟～

【言行】yánxíng〈名〉words and actions: ～一致 be as good as one's word

【言犹在耳】yányóuzài'ěr〈成〉sb.'s words are still fresh in one's mind

【言语】yányǔ〈名〉**1**（说的话）speech: ～粗俗 be coarse and vulgar in speech ‖ ～能力 faculty of speech ‖ 我无法以～来表达我的感激之情。My gratitude is beyond words. **2**［语言］parole: 语言和～ language and speech

【言语机制】yányǔ jīzhì〈名〉［语言］speech mechanism

【言语器官】yányǔ qìguān〈名〉speech organ

【言语缺陷】yányǔ quēxiàn〈名〉speech defect

【言语障碍】yányǔ zhàng'ài ▶**p. 50**〈名〉［医学］speech disorder: ～矫正 speech therapy

【言喻】yányù〈动〉〈书〉[usu used in the negative] express: 不可～ cannot be explained in words ‖ 难以～ be difficult to describe

【言语】yányu〈动〉〈方〉speak: 他这个人不爱～。He is a man of few words. ‖ 你走的时候～一声。Let me know when you leave.

【言者无心，听者有意】yánzhě wúxīn, tīngzhě yǒuyì〈成〉a careless word may reveal much to an attentive listener

【言者无罪，闻者足戒】yánzhě wú zuì, wénzhě zú jiè〈成〉blame not the critics, but heed what they say

【言者谆谆，听者藐藐】yánzhě zhūnzhūn, tīngzhě miǎomiǎo〈成〉earnest words fall on deaf ears

【言之成理】yánzhī-chénglǐ〈成〉speak in a rational and convincing way

【言之过早】yánzhī-guòzǎo〈成〉make a premature statement

【言之无物】yánzhī-wúwù〈成〉be just empty talk: 他们话讲得很多，但～。They talked a great deal, but didn't really say much.

【言之有据】yánzhī-yǒujù〈成〉speak on sound authority

【言之有理】yánzhī-yǒulǐ = 言之成理 yánzhī-chénglǐ

【言之凿凿】yánzhī-záozáo〈成〉say sth. with certainty

【言中】yánzhòng〈动〉〈口〉[of one's word] be proved true: 不幸被～ one's prediction unfortunately proved true

【言重】yánzhòng〈动〉overstate: 如果我～了，请多担待。I hope you won't mind if I have overstated the case.

【言状】yánzhuàng〈动〉[usu used in the negative] describe: 难以～ be indescribable

妍 yán

〈形〉〈书〉beautiful: 百花争～。A hundred flowers contend in beauty. ▶～媸

【妍媸】yánchī〈形〉〈书〉beautiful and ugly: 不辨～ be unable to distinguish the beautiful from the ugly

【妍丽】yánlì〈形〉beautiful: 容貌～ beautiful looks

岩（巖）yán

〈名〉**1**（山峰）cliff: 七星～ Seven-Star Cliff [in Guangdong Province] **2**（岩石）rock: ▶～石, 沉积～, 花岗～

【岩层】yáncéng〈名〉［地质］rock layer

【岩洞】yándòng〈名〉grotto

【岩画】yánhuà〈名〉rock painting

【岩浆】yánjiāng〈名〉［地质］magma

【岩溶】yánróng〈名〉［地质］karst: ～地貌 karst topography

【岩石】yánshí〈名〉rock: 海浪冲蚀着～。Waves wear away rocks. ‖ 这儿的～风化了。The rock here is weathered.

【岩石圈】yánshíquān〈名〉lithosphere

【岩心】yánxīn〈名〉［地质］core: ～样品 core sample

【岩盐】yányán〈名〉rock salt

【岩羊】yányáng〈名〉［动物］blue sheep

炎 yán

A〈形〉scorching: ▶～热, ～夏

B〈名〉**1**〈喻〉（权势）power and influence: ▶趋～附势 **2** Yán（炎帝）*Yan Di* [legendary ruler of remote antiquity in Chinese history]: ▶～帝, ～黄子孙 **3**（炎症）inflammation: 嗓子发～ suffer from an inflammation of the throat ▶肺～, 消～

【炎帝】Yándì = 炎 yán B2

【炎黄】Yán-Huáng〈名〉*Yan Di* (炎帝) and *Huang Di* (黄帝) [two legendary rulers of remote antiquity, usu referred to as ancestors of the Chinese nation]

【炎黄子孙】Yán-Huáng zǐsūn〈名〉the Chinese people

【炎凉】yánliáng〈形〉snobbish: ▶世态～

【炎热】yánrè〈形〉scorching: ～的夏天 sweltering summer days

【炎日】yánrì〈名〉burning sun

【炎暑】yánshǔ〈名〉**1**（酷暑）hot summer: ～已至。Blazing hot summer has arrived. **2**（暑气）summer heat: ～逼人。The summer heat is stifling.

【炎夏】yánxià〈名〉boiling hot summer

【炎炎】yányán〈形〉**1**（形容阳光）sweltering: 烈日～。The sun is scorching. **2**（形容火势）raging: ～烈火 raging fire

【炎症】yánzhèng ▶**p. 50**〈名〉inflammation: 消除～ diminish an inflammation

沿 yán

A〈动〉**1**（遵循）follow: 世代相～ be handed down from generation to generation ▶～革, ～袭 **2**（镶边）border: ～鞋口 trim the top of a shoe ‖ ～有一道蓝边儿 be hemmed with a blue fringe

B ▶**p. 781**〈介〉along: ～门乞讨 go begging from door to door ‖ 泪水～着她的面

y

颊流下来。 Tears streamed down her cheeks.
C〈名〉 edge: 锅～ edge of a pan ‖ 缸/碗～儿 rim of a jar/bowl ▸床～
【沿岸】 yán'àn 〈名〉 coastland: 黄河～ Yellow River coastlands
【沿边儿】 yánbiānr〈动〉 hem: 用花边给衣服～ trim a dress with lace
【沿革】 yángé 〈名〉 evolution: 历史～ development of history ‖ 社会风俗的～ evolution of social customs
【沿海】 yánhǎi〈名〉 coastal areas: ～城市 coastal city ‖ ～水域 coastal waters ‖ ～地区 coastal area ‖ ～港口 coastal port
【沿海经济开发区】 yánhǎi jīngjì kāifāqū〈名〉 coastal economic development area
【沿河】 yánhé〈副〉 along the river: ～而上/而下 go upstream/downstream
【沿江】 yánjiāng〈名〉 areas along the Yangtze River: ～经济发展状况 economic development along the Yangtze River
【沿街】 yánjiē **A**〈副〉 along the street: ～叫卖 peddle along the street **B**〈名〉 the two sides of a street: ～有不少小吃店。 There are plenty of small eateries on both sides of the street.
【沿例】 yánlì〈动〉 follow common practice: ～办理 act according to established precedent
【沿路】 yánlù **A**〈副〉 on the way: ～寻找 look for sth. down the road **B**〈名〉 area beside a street: ～种了不少树。 Many trees have been planted along the road.
【沿途】 yántú **A** = 沿路 yánlù A **B**〈名〉 the course of a journey: ～风景优美。 The scenery along the road is very beautiful.
【沿袭】 yánxí〈动〉 continue: ～成说 follow an accepted theory ‖ 长期～的传统 long-standing tradition
【沿线】 yánxiàn〈副〉 along the line: 铁路～的村镇 villages and towns along the railway line
【沿用】 yányòng〈动〉 continue to use: ～原来的名称 continue to use the old name ‖ 这种做法就这样～了下来。 This old practice is still in use.

研 yán〈动〉

1（碾） grind: ～药 grind medicine ‖ ～成细末 grind into fine powder **2**（探究） research: ▸～讨, 钻～
【研读】 yándú〈动〉 study and read intensively: ～这篇著名文章的原文 make an intensive study of this well-known essay in its original form
【研发】 yánfā〈动〉 research and develop: ～新药 develop new drugs
【研究】 yánjiū〈动〉 **1**（探究） research: ～物种起源 research into the origin of species ‖ 从事～工作 engage in research ‖ ～报告 research report ‖ ～成果 research result ‖ ～对象 object of study ‖ ～机构 research institute ‖ ～计划 research proposal ‖ ～经费 research fund ‖ 申请～经费 apply for research funds ‖ 做基础～ pursue fundamental studies ‖ 潜心～ bury oneself in one's study **2**（商讨） discuss: 现场～ study on site ‖ 领导们～了该怎么解决这事。 The directors discussed what should be done to settle the matter. ‖ 这事正在～。 The matter is under discussion.
【研究课题】 yánjiū kètí〈名〉 research topic/project
【研究生】 yánjiūshēng〈名〉 postgraduate: 考～ take a postgraduate admission examination ‖ ～班 postgraduate class ‖ ～院 postgraduate department (of university research institute) ‖ 博士～ doctoral candidate ‖ 硕士～ MA candidate
【研究室】 yánjiūshì〈名〉 laboratory
【研究所】 yánjiūsuǒ〈名〉 research institute
【研究员】 yánjiūyuán〈名〉 research fellow
【研究院】 yánjiūyuàn〈名〉 research institute
【研磨】 yánmó〈动〉 **1**（使成细粉） grind: ～草药/咖啡 grind herbs/coffee **2**（使光滑） polish: 用沙子和水～玻璃 polish down glass with sand and water
【研判】 yánpàn〈动〉 study and judge: ～案情 study the details of a case
【研讨】 yántǎo〈动〉 deliberate: ～宇宙的奥秘 explore the secrets of the universe ‖ ～会 seminar
【研习】 yánxí〈动〉 research and study: ～法律 study law
【研修】 yánxiū〈动〉 research: 在大学～生物学 read biology at university
【研制】 yánzhì〈动〉 develop: ～新产品 research and develop new products ‖ ～新式武器 develop new weapons

盐（鹽） yán〈名〉

salt: 加点～ add a little salt ‖ 碱式～ basic salt ‖ 酸式～ acid salt ▸～场, 精～, 食～
【盐巴】 yánbā〈名〉〈方〉 table salt
【盐场】 yánchǎng〈名〉 saltworks
【盐池】 yánchí〈名〉 salt lake
【盐分】 yánfèn〈名〉 salt content
【盐湖】 yánhú〈名〉［地质］ salt lake
【盐湖城】 Yánhúchéng〈名〉 Salt Lake City
【盐花】 yánhuā〈名〉 pinch of salt: 汤里得加点～。 The soup should be lightly salted.
【盐碱地】 yánjiǎndì〈名〉 salt lick
【盐井】 yánjǐng〈名〉 salt well
【盐卤】 yánlǔ〈名〉［化学］ bittern
【盐瓶】 yánpíng〈名〉 salt cellar〈英〉; salt shaker〈美〉
【盐汽水】 yánqìshuǐ〈名〉 salt soda water
【盐霜】 yánshuāng〈名〉 salt frost
【盐水】 yánshuǐ〈名〉 salt solution: 输～ have an intravenous drip of saline solution ‖ 泡在～里 preserve in brine
【盐酸】 yánsuān〈名〉［化学］ hydrochloric acid
【盐滩】 yántān〈名〉 beach for making sea salt
【盐田】 yántián〈名〉 salt flat
【盐土】 yántǔ〈名〉 saline soil
【盐业】 yányè〈名〉 salt industry

阎（閻） yán〈名〉〈书〉

gate of a lane
【阎罗】 Yánluó ▸p. 274〈名〉［佛教］ Yama
【阎王】 Yánwang〈名〉 **1** ▸p. 274（阎罗） King of Hell (Yama): 见～ die ‖ ～殿 Yama's Palace **2**（凶残的人） tyrant: 活～ living King of Hell
【阎王好见，小鬼难缠】 Yánwang hǎo jiàn, xiǎoguǐ nán chán〈俗〉 the lackeys are even more difficult to deal with than their masters
【阎王爷】 Yánwangyé ▸p. 274〈名〉 King of Hell
【阎王债】 Yánwangzhài = 阎王账 Yánwangzhàng
【阎王账】 Yánwangzhàng〈名〉〈口〉 shark's loan

蜒 yán

▸海蜒 hǎiyán, 蜒蚰 yányóu, 蚰蜒 yóuyán
【蜒蚰】 yányóu〈名〉〈方〉［昆虫］ slug

筵 yán〈名〉

banquet: ▸婚～, 寿～
【筵席】 yánxí〈名〉 banquet: 大摆～ hold a feast ‖〈喻〉 天下没有不散的～。 Even the best of friends must part from time to time.

颜（顏） yán〈名〉

1（脸） face: ▸鹤发童～, 容～ **2**（表情） facial expression: ▸和～悦色, 喜笑～开 **3**（颜色） colour: ▸～料, 五～六色 **4**（面子） face: 无～见人 be too ashamed to face anyone ▸厚～无耻
【颜料】 yánliào〈名〉 paint: 调～ mix paints ‖ 人造/天然～ artificial/natural pigments ‖ 水彩～ water colour
【颜面】 yánmiàn〈名〉 **1** face: ～神经 facial nerve **2**（面子） face: 不顾～ have no concern for face ‖ ～扫地 be thoroughly discredited
【颜容】 yánróng〈名〉 countenance: ～枯槁 look haggard
【颜色】 yánsè〈名〉 **1**（色彩） colour: ～浅 be light in colour ‖ ～鲜艳 be bright in colour ‖ ～不协调。 The colours don't go together. **2**〈书〉（脸色） countenance: 这姑娘～憔悴。 The girl looks wan and sallow. **3**（表情） facial expression **4**（厉害的脸色或行动） intimidating appearance: 给他一点～看看。 Teach him a lesson.
【颜体】 Yántǐ〈名〉［书法］ Yan style [calligraphy of Yan Zhenqing (颜真卿) of the Tang Dynasty]

檐（簷） yán〈名〉

1（屋檐） eaves: 在～下筑巢 build a nest under the eaves ▸廊～, 屋～, 飞～走壁 **2**（边缘） edge: 宽～帽子 hat with a wide brim ▸帽～
【檐沟】 yángōu〈名〉 eaves gutter
【檐口】 yánkǒu〈名〉［建筑］ cornice
【檐子】 yánzi〈名〉 eaves

yǎn

奄 yǎn〈书〉

A〈动〉 cover: ～有四方 conquer the whole world
B〈副〉 all of a sudden: ▸～忽, ～然
【奄忽】 yǎnhū〈副〉〈书〉 suddenly
【奄然】 yǎnrán = 奄忽 yǎnhū
【奄然而逝】 yǎnrán'érshì〈成〉 die suddenly
【奄奄】 yǎnyǎn〈形〉 breathing feebly: 气息～ be fading away
【奄奄一息】 yǎnyǎn-yīxī〈成〉 be on the verge of death: 饿得～ be half dead from hunger ‖ 她被抬回家时，已经～。 She was brought back home more dead than alive.

俨（儼） yǎn

A〈形〉〈书〉 solemn
B〈副〉 just like: ～如白昼 be as bright as day
【俨然】 yǎnrán〈书〉 **A**〈形〉 **1**（庄重） solemn: 望之～。 He looks dignified from a distance. **2**（整齐） neatly arranged: 屋舍～ houses set out in neat order **B**〈副〉 just like: 说起话来～是个大人 speak just like a grown-up

衍 yǎn

A〈动〉〈书〉 **1**（繁衍） multiply: ▸繁～ **2**（多出来） be superfluous: ▸～文 **3**（开展） develop: ▸敷～

y

B〈名〉〈书〉 low-lying flatland
【衍变】yǎnbiàn = 演变 yǎnbiàn
【衍化】yǎnhuà〈动〉 develop and evolve
【衍射】yǎnshè〈动〉［物理］ diffract
【衍生】yǎnshēng〈动〉 **1**［化学］ derive **2**（演变发生） produce
【衍生品】yǎnshēngpǐn〈名〉derivatives: 金融～ financial derivatives
【衍生物】yǎnshēngwù〈名〉 derivative
【衍文】yǎnwén〈名〉 tautology due to misprinting or miscopying

弇 yǎn〈动〉〈书〉 cover: ～目 cover the eye ‖ ～日 blot out the sun
【弇陋】yǎnlòu〈形〉〈书〉 [of knowledge] superficial

剡 yǎn〈书〉
A〈动〉 chop: ～木为矢 slice wood into arrows
B〈形〉 sharp

扊（扊） yǎn〈名〉［动物］operculum

掩 yǎn〈动〉 **1**（遮蔽） cover: 用手～着脸 hide one's face in one's hands ▸～耳盗铃，～盖，遮～ **2**（关闭） close: ～门 shut the door ▸虚～ **3**〈口〉（夹住） get pinched: 小心门～了手。 Don't get your fingers caught in the door. **4**〈书〉（乘人不备） ambush and attack: ～捕 catch sb. off guard ▸～杀
【掩鼻】yǎnbí〈动〉 hold one's breath: ～而过 go past holding one's breath
【掩蔽】yǎnbì **A**〈动〉 cover: 分散～ scatter for cover ‖ ～目标 cover over the object **B**〈名〉 **1**（遮蔽处） screen: 堤埂很高，正好做我们的～。 The embankment was high enough to provide us with cover. **2**［物理］ audio masking
【掩蔽部】yǎnbìbù〈名〉［军事］shelter: 防空～ air-raid shelter
【掩藏】yǎncáng〈动〉 conceal: ～内心的忧虑 keep one's worries to oneself ‖ 把粮食～起来 conceal one's grain stores
【掩耳盗铃】yǎn'ěr-dàolíng〈成〉〈喻〉 bury one's head in the sand
【掩盖】yǎngài〈动〉 **1**（盖住） cover: 大雪～了田野。 The fields were covered in snow. **2**（隐藏） cover up: ～错误 gloss over one's mistakes ‖ ～事实 cover up the facts ‖ ～罪行 conceal a crime ‖ 他们之间的分歧太大，无法～。Their differences were too huge to paper over.
【掩护】yǎnhù **A**〈动〉 **1**［军事］ give cover: ～主力部队撤退 cover the retreat of the main forces ‖ 炮火～着我们。 The artillery gave us covering fire. **2**（暗中保护） shield: 用身体～孩子 shield the child with one's body ‖ 这家商店为非法活动打～。 This shop is a cover for unlawful activities. **B**〈名〉［军事］ blindage

颜色

■ 由于文化、语言习惯和社会背景的不同，英汉语里颜色词的用法也存在着差异。汉语的基本色是赤、橙、黄、绿、青、蓝、紫，英语的是 red、blue、green、yellow、purple、grey、brown、black 及 white。

颜色词

■ 注意英语里如何问颜色：

什么颜色？—— 白色
= What colour is it? — It's white

哪种绿？—— 墨绿
= What shade of green is it?
— It's dark green

■ 英语里表示颜色的词做形容词时，colour（色）一词不能加在颜色词后面：

我把椅子漆成了黑色
= I painted the chair black

她把头发染成了棕色
= She dyed her hair brown
或 She dyed her hair a shade of brown
而不是
She dyed her hair the colour of brown

一件白衬衣
= a white shirt

蓝天
= blue sky

■ 汉语里的颜色词是形容词， 而英语里的颜色词也可做名词：

我喜欢红色
= I like red

海军蓝很适合她
= Navy blue suits her

这是个很漂亮的黄色
= It is a pretty yellow
或 It is a pretty shade of yellow

他穿一身黑衣服
= He is dressed in black
或 He wears black

穿白衣服的女孩是我朋友
= The girl in white is my friend

■ 英语里，一些颜色词本身可做动词，如 yellow 和 grey。有些颜色词通过加上词尾 -en 变成动词，如 blacken 和 redden。当然，所有颜色词做形容词时，都可用在动词 become 或 turn 后面，构成系表结构：

这本书因年久已发黄
= The book has yellowed with age
或 The book has turned yellow with age
或 The book has become yellow with age

小丑涂黑了脸
= The clown blacked his face

窗帘布满了灰尘，成了黑色
= The curtain was blackened with dust

我刷白了我的运动鞋
= I whitened my trainers

■ 英汉语里，有些颜色词有时可以完全对应，有时却大相径庭：

灰色西装
= grey suits

他的头发已花白
= His hair has greyed
或 His hair has gone grey

白色衬衫
= a white shirt

他的脸变白了（害怕的样子）
His face turned white

她脸色发白（生病的样子）
= She is looking pale

白开水
= plain boiled water
而不是
white boiled water

棕色头发
= brown hair

红糖
= brown sugar

黑发
= black hair

红茶
= black tea

蓝色旗子
= blue flags

黄色电影
= blue movies
而不是
yellow movies

■ 注意英语里"颜色词 + 名词 + ed"（如 green-eyed）的用法：

棕色头发的女子
= a brown-haired girl

蓝眼睛的男孩
= a blue-eyed boy

色度

■ 汉语里表示色度的词如浅、淡、嫩等可以用英语的 pale 或 light 来表达；表示深、暗时可以用 dark 来表达；表示亮、明、鲜时可用 bright 来表达：

浅绿 / 嫩绿 / 淡绿
= pale green
或 light green

深绿 / 暗绿 / 墨绿
= dark green

亮黄 / 明黄 / 鲜黄
= bright yellow

■ 汉语里，表示一种颜色跟某种事物的颜色相似，该事物可直接加在颜色词之前，如"苹果绿"。在英语里，该事物既可加在 coloured 的前面（如 orange-coloured），也可加在颜色词前面（如 apple-green）。注意一般会用连字号：

橘黄色裙子
= orange-coloured skirts

苹果绿衬衫
= an apple-green shirt

巧克力色沙发
= chocolate-brown-coloured sofas

杏黄色外罩
= apricot-coloured coats

■ 英语后缀 -ish 可加在颜色词后面，相当于汉语里表示"接近"、"略带"或"发"某种颜色的意思：

这件衬衣发蓝
= The shirt is a bluish colour
或 The shirt is bluish in colour
或 The shirt is bluish

【掩埋】yǎnmái〈动〉 bury: ～尸体 bury a corpse ‖ ～在地下的城市 buried city

【掩面】yǎnmiàn〈动〉〈书〉 cover one's face: ～而泣 cover one's face with one's hands and start weeping

【掩人耳目】yǎnrén'ěrmù〈成〉 pull the wool over people's eyes: 那是～的幌子，人人都能识破。 That's a blind. Everyone can see through it.

【掩杀】yǎnshā〈动〉〈书〉make a surprise attack

【掩饰】yǎnshì〈动〉 cover up: ～过失 gloss over mistakes ‖ ～缺点 paint one's defects ‖ 他们一点也不～自己的喜悦。 They did nothing to conceal their joy.

【掩体】yǎntǐ〈名〉 1〔工程〕 blockhouse 2〔军事〕 bunker: 机枪～ machine-gun pit

【掩眼法】yǎnyǎnfǎ〈名〉 camouflage

【掩映】yǎnyìng〈动〉〈书〉set off: 竹木扶疏，交相～。 Bamboos and shady trees set each other off to advantage.

眼 yǎn

A〈名〉 1 ▸p. 614 （眼睛） eye: 闭～ close one's eyes ‖ 眯着～ narrow one's eyes ‖ 让我再看上一～。 Let me have another look. ▸～皮，眨～ 2（小孔） small hole: 打～ bore a hole ‖ 钻/扎一个～ drill/punch a hole ▸泉～，枪～，针～ 3（指围棋） trap: 做～ set a trap 4（见识） insight: ▸～浅，独具慧～ 5（关键） salient point: ▸节骨～ 6（节拍） unaccented beat: 一板三～ one accented and three unaccented beats in a bar ▸有板有～

B〈量〉 [used for wells, springs or cave-dwellings]: 一～井/泉 a well/spring

【眼巴巴】yǎnbābā〈形〉 1（形容急切盼望） anxious: 她～地期待着有关他的消息。 She is eager for news of him. 2（形容无奈） helpless: 他～地望着老鹰把小鸡抓走了。 He looked on helplessly as the hawk flew off with a chick clutched in its claws.

【眼白】yǎnbái〈名〉〈方〉 white of the eye

【眼保健操】yǎnbǎojiàncāo〈名〉 eye exercises

【眼病】yǎnbìng ▸p. 50〈名〉 eye disease

【眼波】yǎnbō〈名〉 [of young lady] glance: 迷人的～ bewitching glance

【眼不见为净】yǎn bù jiàn wéi jìng〈俗〉 what the eye doesn't see doesn't hurt

【眼不见，心不烦】yǎn bù jiàn, xīn bù fán〈俗〉 what the eye doesn't see, the heart doesn't grieve over

【眼馋】yǎnchán〈动〉〈方〉covet: 他那件明朝瓷瓶叫很多收藏家～。 His Ming vase is eagerly coveted by many collectors.

【眼眵】yǎnchī〈名〉 gum (in the eyes)

【眼袋】yǎndài〈名〉 bags under the eyes

【眼底】yǎndǐ〈名〉 1〔解剖〕 fundus of eye: 他～出血。 His eyes are bleeding. 2（眼中） view: 登楼一望，全城景色尽收～。 The top of the building gives us a panoramic view of the city.

【眼底下】yǎndixia〈名〉 1（跟前） right before one's eyes: 那事就发生在我的～。 It happened before my eyes. 2（眼前） the moment: 先处理～的事。 Let's settle the business at hand first.

【眼福】yǎnfú〈名〉 feast for the eyes: 这次画展让大家一饱～。 This painting exhibition is a real feast for the eyes.

【眼高手低】yǎngāo-shǒudī〈成〉have high standards but little ability: 他这个人～。 His ability doesn't match his aspirations.

【眼高心傲】yǎngāo-xīnào〈成〉 have a haughty look and a proud heart

【眼膏】yǎngāo〈名〉［药学］eye ointment

【眼格】yǎngé〈名〉〈方〉 field of vision

【眼骨】yǎngǔ〈名〉［动物］ ocular skeleton

【眼观六路，耳听八方】yǎn guān liùlù, ěr tīng bāfāng〈成〉 have sharp eyes and keen ears

【眼光】yǎnguāng〈名〉 1（目光） eye: 大家的～都集中到他身上。 All eyes were on him. 2（见识） sight: ～短浅 be short-sighted ‖ 他很有～。 He is a man of vision. 3（观点） view: 历史～ historical perspective ‖ 艺术家的～ artist's eye ‖ 把～放远一点 see things with a broader perspective ‖ 用老～看问题 judge things by old standards

【眼红】yǎnhóng〈形〉 1（羡慕） envious: 看他买辆新车，大家都很～。 His new car was an object of envy for everyone. 2（激怒） furious: ▸仇人相见，分外～

【眼花】yǎnhuā〈动〉 have blurred vision: 头晕～ be muddle-headed and bleary-eyed

【眼花缭乱】yǎnhuā-liáoluàn〈成〉 be dazed: 使人～的灯光 dazzling lights

【眼疾手快】yǎnjí-shǒukuài〈成〉 have sharp eyes and nimble fingers

【眼尖】yǎnjiān〈形〉 sharp-eyed: 这孩子～，一眼就认出了他。The sharp-eyed boy recognized him at once.

【眼睑】yǎnjiǎn〈名〉［解剖］ eyelid: ～浮肿 puffiness of the eyes

【眼见】yǎnjiàn〈副〉soon: ～就要过年了。 Spring Festival is just around the corner.

【眼见得】yǎnjiànde〈副〉〈方〉 evidently

【眼见为实】yǎnjiàn-wéishí〈成〉 seeing is believing

【眼角】yǎnjiǎo〈名〉［解剖］ canthus: 大/小～ inner/outer canthus

【眼睫毛】yǎnjiémáo〈名〉〈口〉 eyelash

【眼界】yǎnjiè〈名〉 field of vision: 开扩～ broaden one's outlook ‖ 这次访问真是大开～。 This visit was a real eye-opener.

【眼镜】yǎnjìng〈名〉 glasses: 戴～ wear glasses ‖ 老花～ presbyopic glasses ‖ 隐形～ contact lenses ‖ ～店 optician's ‖ ～盒 glasses case ‖ ～架 spectacle frame ‖ 弄断～架 break the frames of one's glasses ‖ ～框 spectacles frame ‖ ～链 spectacle string ‖ ～片 lens ‖ ～腿 earpiece ‖ 〈喻〉 戴着有色～看人 look at sb. through rose-tinted spectacles

【眼镜蛇】yǎnjìngshé〈名〉［动物］ cobra: ～毒 cobra venom

【眼睛】yǎnjing〈名〉 eye: 揉～ rub one's eyes

【眼睛里揉不进沙子】yǎnjing lǐ róu bù jìn shāzi〈俗〉 not tolerate blemishes or deceptions

【眼开眼闭】yǎnkāi-yǎnbì〈成〉turn a blind eye to: 对某人的错误～ turn a blind eye to sb.'s mistake

【眼看】yǎnkàn A〈副〉 in a moment: ～天就要下雨了。 It'll rain at any moment. B〈动〉 look on passively: 我们不能～着国家财产遭受损失。 We cannot look on passively while state property is damaged.

【眼科】yǎnkē〈名〉 department of ophthalmology: ～医生 ophthalmologist

【眼眶】yǎnkuàng〈名〉 1（眼球四周）eye socket: ～里含着泪水 with tears in one's eyes 2（眼睑周围） rim of the eye: ～发黑 have black rings round one's eyes

【眼泪】yǎnlèi〈名〉 tears: 擦干～ wipe the tears away ‖ 忍住～ choke back one's tears ‖ ～汪汪 tears well up in sb.'s eyes ‖ ～夺眶而出 tears stream down ‖ 流鳄鱼～ shed crocodile tears

【眼力】yǎnlì〈名〉 1（视力） eyesight: ～好/差 have good/poor eyesight 2（判断力） judgement: 他看人很有～。 He is good at sizing people up.

【眼帘】yǎnlián〈名〉 1（眼皮） eyelid: 垂下～ drop one's eyes 2（眼睛） eyes: 映入～ come into view

【眼面前】yǎnmiànqián〈名〉〈方〉1（跟前） before one's eyes: ～的问题 immediate problems ‖ 汽车就在我们～爆炸了。The car blew up before our very eyes. 2（常见） common: 虽然他没文化，～的几个字他还认识。 He hasn't had much schooling but recognizes quite a number of common everyday words.

【眼明手快】yǎnmíng-shǒukuài〈成〉 be sharp-eyed and agile

【眼目】yǎnmù〈名〉 1（眼睛） eyes: 耀人～ blind one's eyes 2（探子） spy: 敌人的～ enemy spy

【眼泡】yǎnpāo〈名〉 upper eyelid: 她～儿哭肿了。 Her eyes were swollen from crying.

【眼皮】yǎnpí〈名〉 eyelid: 单/双～ single-edged/double-edged eyelid

【眼皮底下】yǎnpí dǐxia = 眼底下 yǎndixia

【眼皮子】yǎnpízi〈名〉〈口〉 1（眼皮） eyelid: 我困得～都睁不开。 I was so sleepy I couldn't keep my eyes open. 2（见识） field of vision: 姑娘～高，看不上对方。 The girl has lofty ideals and doesn't think he is good enough for her. ‖ ～浅的人总是只顾眼前利益。 Short-sighted people think only of their immediate interests.

【眼前】yǎnqián〈名〉 1（近处） before one's eyes: ～是一片金黄的菜花。 Before our eyes was a vast stretch of golden rape flowers. 2（当下） the present: ～的问题 immediate problems ‖ ～利益 immediate interests

【眼前亏】yǎnqiánkuī〈名〉 immediate losses: ▸好汉不吃～

【眼浅】yǎnqiǎn〈形〉 short-sighted

【眼球】yǎnqiú〈名〉［生理］ eyeball

【眼圈】yǎnquān〈名〉 eye socket: 他累得～发黑。 His eyes were ringed with fatigue.

【眼热】yǎnrè〈形〉 envious: 见了某物～ eye sth. covetously

【眼色】yǎnsè〈名〉 meaningful glance: 使～ tip sb. the wink ‖ 看上司的～行事 take one's cue from one's superiors

【眼神】yǎnshén〈名〉 1（眼睛的神态） expression in one's eyes: 茫然若失的～ vacant-looking eyes 2〈口〉（视力） eyesight: ～儿不好 have poor eyesight

【眼生】yǎnshēng〈形〉 look unfamiliar: 这位客人很～。 The visitor is not remotely familiar to me.

【眼屎】yǎnshǐ〈名〉〈口〉 sand (in one's eyes)

【眼熟】yǎnshú〈形〉 familiar: 这人看着好～。 That person looks very familiar.

【眼霜】yǎnshuāng〈名〉 eye cream

【眼跳】yǎntiào〈动〉 [of one's eyes] twitch

【眼窝】yǎnwō〈名〉［解剖］ eye socket

【眼下】yǎnxià〈名〉 the moment: ～最畅销的书 book of the moment ‖ ～正是秋收大忙季节。 It's right in the autumn harvest rush.

【眼线】yǎnxiàn〈名〉 1（指线条） eyeline: 描～ apply eyeliner 2（指人） snitch: 安插～ plant an informer

【眼压】yǎnyā〈名〉 intraocular tension

【眼炎】yǎnyán ▸p. 50〈名〉［医学］ ophthalmia

【眼药】yǎnyào〈名〉medication for the eye: ～水 eye drops
【眼药膏】yǎnyàogāo〈名〉eye ointment
【眼影】yǎnyǐng〈名〉eyeshadow: ～粉 eyeshadow ‖ ～膏 eyeshadow
【眼晕】yǎnyùn〈动〉feel dizzy
【眼罩儿】yǎnzhàor〈名〉**1**（指物）blinkers〈英〉; blinders〈美〉**2**（指姿势）eyeshade: 打～ shade one's eyes with one's hands
【眼睁睁】yǎnzhēngzhēng〈形〉helpless: 他～地看着自己的房子被洪水卷走了。He watched his house being swept away in the flood, but there was nothing he could do.
【眼中钉】yǎnzhōngdīng〈名〉〈喻〉thorn in one's side
【眼中钉，肉中刺】yǎnzhōngdīng, ròuzhōngcì〈惯〉〈喻〉thorn in one's side: 除去～ rid oneself of a pest
【眼珠】yǎnzhū = 眼珠子 yǎnzhūzi 1
【眼珠子】yǎnzhūzi〈名〉**1**〈口〉（眼球）eyeball **2**〈喻〉（珍爱的人或物）apple of one's eye: 这孩子是他爷爷的～。The child has become the apple of his grandfather's eye.
【眼拙】yǎnzhuō〈形〉〈套〉forgetful: 恕我～，咱们在哪儿见过面？Please excuse my poor memory, but have we met before?

偃 yǎn〈书〉〈动〉**1**（仰面倒下）fall on one's back: ～卧 lie on one's back **2**（放倒）lay down: ▸～旗息鼓 **3**（停止）cease: ▸～武修文
【偃旗息鼓】yǎnqí-xīgǔ〈成〉cease hostilities: 慑于我军的强大攻势，敌人～，仓皇逃窜。Intimidated by our army's fierce attack, the enemy troops stopped fighting and beat a retreat.
【偃武修文】yǎnwǔ-xiūwén〈成〉stop war preparations and promote culture and education

琰 yǎn〈名〉〈书〉beautiful jade

晻 yǎn〈形〉〈书〉dim

罨 yǎn
A〈名〉〈书〉net for catching birds/fish
B〈动〉cover: 用纱布～伤口 cover a wound with gauze

演 yǎn〈动〉**1**（演变）develop: ▸～变, ～化 **2**（推演）deduce: ▸～绎, 推～ **3**（表演）perform: ～电影 show a film ‖ ～配角 play a supporting role ‖ 这出戏～了一个月。The play ran for a month. **4**（练习）practise: ▸～练, ～算
【演变】yǎnbiàn〈动〉evolve: 冲突～为内战。The conflict developed into civil war. ‖ 类人猿逐渐～成人。Humans gradually descended from apes.
【演播】yǎnbō〈动〉televise a performance: 联合～ joint broadcast ‖ ～室 studio
【演唱】yǎnchàng〈动〉perform a song: ～歌曲 sing a song ‖ ～京剧 act a part in a Beijing opera performance ‖ ～会 vocal concert
【演出】yǎnchū〈动〉perform: 参加～ take part in a performance ‖ 观看～ attend a performance ‖ 首场～ first show ‖ 巡回～ travelling show
【演出票】yǎnchūpiào〈名〉ticket (for a show)
【演化】yǎnhuà〈动〉evolve: ～过程 evolutionary process ‖ 生物的～ evolution of living things
【演技】yǎnjì〈名〉acting: 高超的～ high-quality acting
【演讲】yǎnjiǎng〈动〉give a lecture: 发表～ deliver a speech ‖ 巡回～ make a speaking tour ‖ ～比赛 speech contest ‖ ～稿 text of a speech ‖ ～技巧 speaking technique
【演进】yǎnjìn〈动〉evolve: 人类社会由低级向高级～。Human society evolves from a low to a high rank.
【演练】yǎnliàn〈动〉drill: ～战场救护 practise battlefield rescue work
【演示】yǎnshì〈动〉demonstrate: 用实物～ demonstrate using real objects
【演双簧】yǎn shuānghuáng〈动〉〈喻〉work on sth. in tandem
【演说】yǎnshuō **A**〈动〉make a speech: 即兴～ give an impromptu speech **B**〈名〉speech: 就职～ inaugural address ‖ 施政～ administrative policy speech
【演说词】yǎnshuōcí〈名〉text of a speech
【演说家】yǎnshuōjiā ▸**p. 966**〈名〉elocutionist
【演算】yǎnsuàn〈动〉make mathematical calculations: ～习题 do sums ‖ 概率～ calculus of probabilities
【演武】yǎnwǔ〈动〉practise *wushu* or traditional martial arts: ～场 martial arts arena
【演习】yǎnxí〈动〉exercise: 军事～ military manoeuvres ‖ 实弹～ live ammunition manoeuvres ‖ 消防～ fire drill
【演戏】yǎnxì〈动〉**1**（指表演）act in a play: 登台～ stage a play **2**〈喻〉（指骗人）play-act: 别～了，你这一套骗不了人。Stop that play-acting. You can't fool anyone.
【演义】yǎnyì **A**〈动〉extend the meaning on the basis of the text **B**〈名〉historical novel: 《三国～》*The Romance of the Three Kingdoms*
【演艺】yǎnyì〈名〉**1**（表演艺术）performing arts: ～界 performing art circles **2**（表演技巧）performing skill: ～精湛 accomplished performance
【演绎】yǎnyì **A**〈名〉［逻辑］deduction **B**〈动〉**1**（铺陈）narrate in detail: ～出感人的故事 relate a stirring story **2**（展现）elaborate: ～时尚潮流 expound on the fashion trend ‖ ～不同的风格 develop different styles
【演绎推理】yǎnyì tuīlǐ〈名〉deductive reasoning
【演员】yǎnyuán ▸**p. 966**〈名〉performer: 芭蕾舞～ ballet dancer ‖ 电影～ film actor ‖ 特技替身～ stuntman ‖ 相声～ cross-talk performer ‖ 性格～ character actor/actress ‖ 杂技～ acrobat
【演员表】yǎnyuánbiǎo〈名〉cast
【演奏】yǎnzòu〈动〉play a musical instrument: ～交响乐 perform a symphony ‖ ～钢琴 play the piano ‖ ～家 accomplished musician ‖ 乐队～得很出色。The band gave a magnificent performance.

魇（魘） yǎn〈动〉have a nightmare

蝘 yǎn
【蝘蜓】yǎntíng〈名〉［动物］gecko

黡（黶） yǎn〈名〉〈书〉black mole

甗 yǎn〈名〉〈古〉cooking utensil with a grid

鼹（鼴） yǎn〈名〉mole
【鼹鼠】yǎnshǔ〈名〉〈口〉mole

yàn

厌（厭） yàn〈动〉**1**（满足）be satisfied: ▸贪得无～, 学而不～ **2**（厌烦）be fed up with: 那本书让人生～。That book is a bore. ‖ 这首歌我都听～了。I am tired of listening to this song. ▸～烦, ～倦 **3**（嫌弃）detest: ▸～世, ～恶, 讨～
【厌烦】yànfán〈动〉be fed up with: 我对这些麻烦事～透了。I'm bored to death with all these troubles.
【厌恨】yànhèn〈动〉loathe: ～贪官污吏 loathe corrupt officials
【厌倦】yànjuàn〈动〉be tired of: 对单调的生活感到～ be tired of the dull life
【厌腻】yànnì〈动〉be fed up with
【厌弃】yànqì〈动〉cold-shoulder: 遭人～ be cold-shouldered
【厌食】yànshí〈动〉have a poor appetite: ～症 anorexia
【厌世】yànshì〈动〉be world-weary: 因～而轻生 despair of life and commit suicide
【厌恶】yànwù〈动〉detest: ～城市生活 hate town life ‖ 感到～ feel disgusted ‖ 令人～的陋习 disgusting bad habit ‖ 我一想起他就感到～。It makes me sick to think of him.
【厌学】yànxué〈动〉be tired of one's studies
【厌氧菌】yànyǎngjūn〈名〉anaerobe
【厌战】yànzhàn〈动〉be war-weary: ～情绪 war-weariness ‖ 官兵都～了。Both officers and soldiers have become weary of the war.

砚（硯） yàn〈名〉inkstone: 笔～ writing brush and inkslab
【砚池】yànchí〈名〉inkstone
【砚石】yànshí〈名〉stone suitable for making an ink slab
【砚台】yàntai〈名〉inkstone

咽（嚥） yàn〈动〉swallow: 这药难吃得很，我实在～不下去。I can't get this horrible medicine down. ‖〈喻〉～不下这口气 unable to take an insult ▸细嚼慢～
▸yān, yè
【咽气】yànqì ▸**p. 772**〈动〉breathe one's last breath

彦（彥） yàn〈名〉〈书〉man of virtue and ability

艳（艷、豔） yàn
A〈形〉**1** ▸**p. 863**（色彩明艳）gaudy: 这件衣服太～了。This dress is too gaudy. ▸～丽, 鲜～, 争奇斗～ **2**（香艳）romantic: ▸～福, ～情
B〈动〉〈书〉envy: ▸～羡
【艳福】yànfú〈名〉[of a man] luck in love: ～不浅 be lucky to be in love with a beautiful woman
【艳丽】yànlì ▸**p. 863**〈形〉gorgeous: 色彩～ be brightly-coloured ‖ 身穿～服装 be gorgeously dressed
【艳情】yànqíng〈形〉amorous: ～小说 erotic fiction
【艳如桃李，冷若冰霜】yànrútáolǐ, lěngruòbīngshuāng〈成〉[of a woman] be overwhelmingly beautiful but ice-cold

【艳诗】yànshī〈名〉love poem
【艳史】yànshǐ〈名〉love story
【艳羡】yànxiàn〈动〉〈书〉envy: 不胜～ admire immensely
【艳阳】yànyáng〈名〉bright sun: ～高照。The spring sun is shining high in the sky.
【艳阳天】yànyángtiān〈名〉bright sunny sky
【艳冶】yànyě〈形〉〈书〉pretty and coquettish
【艳照】yànzhào〈名〉romantic photo

晏 yàn
〈形〉〈书〉1▸（晚）late: ～起 get up late ▸～驾 2▸（平静）tranquil: ▸河清海～
【晏驾】yànjià〈动〉〈旧〉[of an emperor] pass away

唁 yàn
〈动〉extend one's condolences: ▸～电, 吊～
【唁电】yàndiàn〈名〉telegram of condolence: 发～ send a telegram of condolence
【唁函】yànhán〈名〉condolence letter

宴 yàn
A〈动〉entertain with wine and food: 大～宾客 entertain guests handsomely at a banquet ▸～请
B〈名〉feast: ▸国～, 赴～, 设～
C〈形〉〈书〉of ease and comfort
【宴安鸩毒】yàn'ān-zhèndú〈成〉seeking a life of pleasure is like drinking poisoned wine
【宴会】yànhuì〈名〉banquet: 设～ hold a banquet ‖ 告别/欢迎～ farewell/welcome banquet ‖ 盛大的～ sumptuous feast
【宴会厅】yànhuìtīng〈名〉banqueting hall
【宴请】yànqǐng〈动〉wine and dine: ～宾客 fête a guest
【宴席】yànxí〈名〉banquet: 大摆～ entertain guests at a sumptuous banquet ‖ 结婚～ wedding feast

验（驗）yàn
A〈动〉1▸（证实）prove effective through practice: ▸～方, ～证 2▸（检查）examine: ～血 take a blood test ‖ ～票 check tickets ▸～收, 检～, 试～ 3▸（产生预期效果）produce the desired effect: 屡试屡～ prove successful in every test ▸灵～, 应～
B〈名〉intended result: ▸效～
【验钞机】yànchāojī〈名〉banknote tester
【验方】yànfāng〈名〉［中医］proven recipe
【验关】yànguān〈动〉clear customs
【验光】yànguāng〈动〉have one's eyesight tested: ～配镜 have one's eyesight tested for glasses ‖ ～师 optometrist
【验核】yànhé〈动〉examine: ～驾驶执照 examine a driver's licence
【验货】yànhuò〈动〉inspect goods
【验看】yànkàn〈动〉examine: ～护照 examine a passport ‖ ～指纹 check sb.'s fingerprints
【验明正身】yànmíng-zhèngshēn〈成〉make a positive identification of a criminal before execution
【验枪】yànqiāng〈动〉［军事］inspect arms
【验伤】yànshāng〈动〉examine an injury
【验尸】yànshī〈动〉carry out/conduct a post-mortem examination, perform an autopsy on the remains (of): ～结果表明，那人死于中毒。The autopsy revealed that the dead man had been poisoned.
【验收】yànshōu〈动〉check upon delivery, inspect and approve, check and accept: ～工作 acceptance appraisal work ‖ 新楼已通过～。The new building has passed the acceptance test.
【验收单】yànshōudān〈名〉certification of inspection
【验收检查】yànshōu jiǎnchá〈名〉acceptance check
【验算】yànsuàn〈动〉check computations: 做～ make a checking calculation
【验血】yànxiě〈名〉blood test
【验资】yànzī〈动〉check and verify capital funds or assets
【验证】yànzhèng〈动〉test and verify: 有待～ remain to be tested

谚（諺）yàn
〈名〉saying: ▸古～, 民～
【谚语】yànyǔ〈名〉saying

堰 yàn
〈名〉dam
【堰塞湖】yànsèhú〈名〉［地理］barrier lake

雁 yàn
〈名〉wild goose
【雁过拔毛】yànguò-bámáo〈成〉〈喻〉snatch every opportunity possible
【雁行】yànháng〈名〉1▸（指鸿雁）line of wild geese flying 2▸〈喻〉（指弟兄）brothers: ～折翅 death of one's brother
【雁翎】yànlíng〈名〉wild goose down
【雁阵】yànzhèn〈名〉'V' formation [flying formation of wild geese]

焰 yàn
〈名〉1▸（火苗）blaze: ▸火～ 2▸〈喻〉（气势）arrogance: ▸气～, 凶～
【焰火】yànhuǒ〈名〉fireworks: 放～ let off fireworks
【焰口】yànkou〈名〉［佛教］ulka-mukha [flaming-mouth hungry ghost]: 放～ [of Buddhist monks] feed hungry ghosts

焱 yàn
〈名〉〈书〉flame

滟（灧、灩）yàn
▸潋滟 liànyàn

酽（釅）yàn
〈形〉strong: ～茶 strong tea

餍（饜）yàn
〈动〉1▸（吃饱）eat one's fill 2▸（满足）satisfy: 其求无～。His greed is never satisfied. ▸～足
【餍足】yànzú〈名〉〈书〉satisfy

谳（讞）yàn
〈动〉〈书〉sentence: 定～ pronounce a sentence

燕 yàn
A〈名〉［鸟类］swallow
B = 宴 yàn
▸Yān
【燕尔】yàn'ěr〈形〉1▸〈书〉（和乐）peaceful and happy 2▸（新婚）newly-married: ～之乐 happiness of newly-weds
【燕麦】yànmài〈名〉oats: ～片 oatmeal
【燕雀】yànquè〈名〉［鸟类］brambling
【燕雀安知鸿鹄之志】yànquè ān zhī hónghú zhī zhì〈成〉〈喻〉the lofty aims of a great man are beyond the understanding of a commoner
【燕尾服】yànwěifú〈名〉tailcoat
【燕窝】yànwō〈名〉esculent swift's nest: ～粥 bird's nest soup
【燕语莺声】yànyǔ-yīngshēng = 莺声燕语 yīngshēng-yànyǔ
【燕子】yànzi〈名〉swallow: ～呢喃。The swallow twitters.

赝（贋）yàn
〈形〉fake: ～钞 counterfeit bill
【赝本】yànběn〈名〉spurious edition: ～书籍 spurious copy of a book
【赝币】yànbì〈名〉〈书〉counterfeit coin
【赝品】yànpǐn〈名〉counterfeit: 那件古董是～。That antique is a fake.

yāng

央[1] yāng
〈名〉centre: ▸中～

央[2] yāng
〈动〉〈书〉end: 乐无～ enjoy infinite happiness ‖ 夜未～。The night is not yet spent.

央[3] yāng
〈动〉entreat: ▸～告, ～求
【央告】yānggao〈动〉beg: 苦苦～ beg piteously
【央行】yāngháng〈简称〉= 中央银行
【央亲告友】yāngqīn-gàoyǒu〈成〉turn to relatives and friends for help
【央求】yāngqiú〈动〉beg: ～某人 plead with sb. ‖ 苦苦～ implore persistently
【央视】Yāngshì〈简称〉= 中央电视台
【央托】yāngtuō〈动〉entreat sb. to do sth.
【央企】yāngqǐ〈名〉state-owned enterprise: ～高管 senior executive of a state-owned enterprise

泱 yāng
【泱泱】yāngyāng〈形〉1▸〈书〉（水面宽阔）vast: 江水～ mighty river 2▸（气势宏大）great: ～大国 great and impressive country

殃 yāng
A〈名〉disaster: ▸祸～, 灾～, 遭～
B〈动〉bring disaster to: ▸～及池鱼, 祸国～民
【殃及池鱼】yāngjí-chíyú〈成〉〈喻〉embroil innocent bystanders in a disturbance
【殃及无辜】yāngjí-wúgū〈成〉bring disaster upon innocent people

鸯（鴦）yāng
▸鸳鸯 yuānyāng

秧 yāng
A〈名〉1▸（幼苗）seedling: 萝卜～儿 radish seedling ‖ 树～ sapling ▸插～, 育～ 2▸（茎）vine: 瓜～ melon vine 3▸（幼仔）young: 鱼～ young fish ‖ 猪～ piglet
B〈动〉〈方〉breed: ～了一池鱼 have raised a pond of fish
【秧歌】yāngge〈名〉*yangge* [popular folk dance]: 扭～ do/perform *yangge*
【秧歌剧】yānggejù〈名〉Yangge opera
【秧苗】yāngmiáo〈名〉rice seedling
【秧田】yāngtián〈名〉rice seedling bed
【秧子】yāngzi〈名〉1▸（幼苗）seedling: 树～ sapling 2▸（茎）vine: 豆～ bean seedling ‖ 花生～ peanut seedling 3▸（幼仔）young: 猪～ piglet 4▸〈方〉〈喻〉〈贬〉（指人）sickly person: ▸病～

y

鞅 yāng〈名〉 1〈古〉（皮带） halter strap 2［统计］ martingale ▸yàng

yáng

扬¹（揚）yáng
A〈动〉 1（举起） raise: ～鞭 raise the whip ‖ ～起一片尘土 kick up a cloud of dust ▸～帆 2（向上撒） throw up and scatter: 晒干～净 dry and winnow thoroughly 3（传播） spread: ▸～名, ～言, 宣～ 4（称赞） praise: ▸表～, 赞～
B〈形〉 good-looking: 其貌不～ be of unfortunate appearance

扬²（揚）Yáng〈名〉Yang [another name for Yangzhou (扬州)]: ▸～剧

【扬长】yángcháng〈副〉 ostentatiously: ▸～而去

【扬长避短】yángcháng-bìduǎn〈成〉foster strengths and circumvent weaknesses

【扬长而去】yángcháng'érqù〈成〉 go off with a swagger: 话一说完，他便～。 He said what he had to say and strode off.

【扬场】yángcháng〈动〉［农业］winnow

【扬尘】yángchén A〈动〉 kick up dust B〈名〉 flying dust: 控制～污染 control flying dust pollution

【扬程】yángchéng〈名〉 pump lift: 高～水泵 high-lift pump

【扬帆】yángfān〈动〉 set sail: ～起航 set sail

【扬幡招魂】yángfān-zhāohún〈成〉〈喻〉 try to revive what is already dead

【扬花】yánghuā〈动〉 flower: 小麦正在～。 The wheat is in flower.

【扬剧】yángjù〈名〉 Yangzhou opera

【扬眉吐气】yángméi-tǔqì〈成〉 stand with one's head held high: 现在我们可以～地说，我们成功了。 Today we can hold our heads up and say that we have succeeded.

【扬名】yángmíng〈动〉 make a name for oneself: ～天下 make oneself known to the world

【扬旗】yángqí〈名〉［铁路］semaphore

【扬弃】yángqì〈动〉 1［哲学］ sublate 2（抛弃） discard: ～陋习 discard bad habits

【扬琴】yángqín ▸p. 929〈名〉［音乐］ dulcimer

【扬清激浊】yángqīng-jīzhuó = 激浊扬清 jīzhuó-yángqīng

【扬榷】yángquè〈动〉〈书〉expound briefly: ～古今 make a cursory review of the past and the present

【扬升】yángshēng〈动〉 increase

【扬声器】yángshēngqì〈名〉 loudspeaker: 低频～ woofer ‖ 高频～ tweeter

【扬水】yángshuǐ〈动〉 pump up water: ～灌溉 pump up water for irrigation ‖ ～泵 lift pump ‖ ～站 pumping station

【扬汤止沸】yángtāng-zhǐfèi〈成〉〈喻〉 adopt half-measures

【扬威】yángwēi〈动〉 flaunt one's strength: ～四海 flaunt one's might over the whole country ▸耀武～

【扬言】yángyán〈动〉〈贬〉 threaten: ～要进行报复 threaten to retaliate

【扬扬】yángyáng〈形〉 triumphant: ～自得 be very pleased with oneself

【扬扬得意】yángyáng-déyì〈成〉be puffed up with pride: 她找到工作后便～起来。 She was walking on air after she got the job.

【扬子鳄】yángzǐ'è〈名〉［动物］ Yangtze alligator

【扬子江】yángzǐjiāng ▸p. 294〈名〉 Yangtze River

羊 yáng〈名〉 sheep: 牧～ herd sheep ‖ ～群 a flock of sheep ▸羚～, 山～

【羊肠线】yángchángxiàn〈名〉［医学］ catgut suture

【羊肠小道】yángcháng-xiǎodào〈成〉 narrow winding path: 一条弯弯曲曲的～通向山顶。 A narrow meandering path winds its way to the mountain top.

【羊齿】yángchǐ〈名〉［植物］ fern

【羊癫风】yángdiānfēng ▸p. 50〈名〉［医学］ epilepsy: 突发～ have an epileptic fit

【羊羔】yánggāo〈名〉lamb: 产～ give birth to a lamb

【羊羹】yánggēng〈名〉 red-bean cake

【羊倌】yángguān〈名〉 shepherd

【羊毫】yángháo〈名〉 writing-brush made of goat's hair

【羊胡子草】yánghúzicǎo〈名〉［植物］ cotton grass

【羊角锤】yángjiǎochuí〈名〉 claw hammer

【羊角风】yángjiǎofēng ▸p. 50〈名〉［医学］ epilepsy

【羊圈】yángjuàn〈名〉 sheep pen

【羊落虎口】yángluòhǔkǒu〈成〉〈喻〉 be in a perilous position

【羊毛】yángmáo〈名〉 sheep's wool: 剪～ shear a sheep ‖ 纯～ pure wool ‖ ～衫 woollen sweater ‖ ～毯 woollen blanket

【羊毛出在羊身上】yángmáo chū zài yáng shēnshang〈俗〉〈喻〉 there is no such thing as a free lunch

【羊膜】yángmó〈名〉［解剖］ amnion

【羊奶】yángnǎi〈名〉 goat's milk

【羊排】yángpái〈名〉 lamb chop

【羊皮】yángpí〈名〉 sheepskin: ～袄 sheepskin coat ‖ ～手套 kid gloves

【羊皮筏子】yángpí fázi〈名〉 sheepskin raft

【羊皮纸】yángpízhǐ〈名〉 parchment

【羊绒】yángróng〈名〉 cashmere: ～衫 cashmere sweater

【羊肉】yángròu〈名〉 mutton: ～火腿 mutton ham

【羊肉没吃上，空惹一身膻】 yángròu méichīshàng, kōng rě yīshēn shān〈俗〉 bring trouble upon oneself without reaping any benefit

【羊肉串】yángròuchuàn〈名〉 roast skewered mutton: 烤～ roast lamb kebabs

【羊入虎口】yángrùhǔkǒu = 羊落虎口 yángluòhǔkǒu

【羊水】yángshuǐ〈名〉［生理］ amniotic fluid

【羊胎素】yángtāisù〈名〉 sheep placenta: ～胶囊 sheep placenta capsule

【羊桃】yángtáo〈名〉［植物］ starfruit

【羊驼】yángtuó〈名〉［动物］ alpaca

【羊痫风】yángxiánfēng = 羊癫风 yángdiānfēng

【羊脂玉】yángzhīyù〈名〉 white jade

阳（陽）yáng
A〈名〉 1（太阳） sun: ▸～光, 夕～, 向～ 2（山南水北） south of a hill or north of a river: 衡～ Hengyang [city situated on the south side of Mount Heng] ‖ 洛～ Luoyang [city north of the Luohe River in Henan Province] 3［哲学］ *yang* [the masculine or positive principle in nature in traditional Chinese philosophy]: ▸阴～ 4（人世） this world: ▸～间, ～世 5（正电） positive: ▸～极, ～离子, ～性 6（男性生殖器） male genitals: ▸壮～, ～痿
B〈形〉 1（公开） open: 阴一套，～一套 act one way in public and another in private ▸～奉阴违, ～沟 2（凸出） convex: ▸～文

【阳春】yángchūn〈名〉spring: ～三月 third lunar month in spring ‖ 十月小～ warm spell in the tenth lunar month

【阳春白雪】yángchūn-báixuě〈成〉 highbrow art and literature: 这位作家的许多作品被认为是～，读者甚少。 Many of this author's works are considered highbrow and are not widely read.

【阳春面】yángchūnmiàn〈名〉 noodles in plain sauce

【阳地植物】yángdì zhíwù〈名〉 sun plant

【阳电】yángdiàn〈名〉 positive electricity

【阳奉阴违】yángfèng-yīnwéi〈成〉 comply in public but oppose in private: ～，口是心非 feign compliance whilst opposing behind the scenes

【阳刚】yánggāng〈形〉 manly: ～之美 masculine beauty ‖ 有～之气的男人 manly man

【阳沟】yánggōu〈名〉 open drain

【阳关大道】yángguāndàdào = 阳关道 yángguāndào

【阳关道】yángguāndào〈名〉 broad road: 你走你的～，我过我的独木桥。 You go your way and I'll go mine.

【阳光】yángguāng A〈名〉 sunshine: ～充足 be full of sunlight ‖ ～明媚/灿烂 sunny/gloriously bright ‖ ～普照大地。 The sun illuminates every corner of the land. B〈形〉 1（公开） open: ～操作 transparent operation 2（开朗） cheery: ～少年 upbeat youth

【阳极】yángjí〈名〉［电子］［电气］anode

【阳间】yángjiān〈名〉 this world

【阳离子】yánglízǐ〈名〉［化学］ positive ion

【阳历】yánglì ▸p. 618〈名〉 solar calendar

【阳面】yángmiàn〈名〉 sunny side: 我的屋子在～。 My room is on the sunny side.

【阳平】yángpíng〈名〉［语言］ rising tone [second of the four tones in modern standard Chinese pronunciation]

【阳坡】yángpō〈名〉 hillside facing the sun

【阳畦】yángqí〈名〉［农业］ cold bed

【阳伞】yángsǎn〈名〉 parasol

【阳世】yángshì〈名〉 human world

【阳寿】yángshòu〈名〉〈旧〉 life span

【阳燧】yángsuì〈名〉〈古〉brass speculum [placed in the sun to generate heat high enough to ignite dry grass]

【阳台】yángtái〈名〉 balcony

【阳痿】yángwěi ▸p. 50〈名〉［医学］ impotence

【阳文】yángwén〈名〉 characters cut in relief: ～印章 seal in relief

【阳物】yángwù ▸p. 772〈名〉〈婉〉 penis

【阳线】yángxiàn〈名〉［金融］ positive line

【阳性】yángxìng A ▸p. 50〈形〉［医学］ positive: 艾滋病病毒检查呈～ be HIV-positive B〈名〉［语言］masculine gender

【阳虚】yángxū〈名〉［中医］ *yang* deficiency

【阳宅】yángzhái〈名〉 residence

玚（瑒）yáng〈名〉〈古〉 kind of jade

杨（楊）yáng〈名〉poplar: ▸白～

【杨辉三角】Yáng Huī sānjiǎo〈名〉 Yang

Hui's triangle [binomial array, known as Pascal's triangle in the West]
【杨柳】yángliǔ〈名〉1（杨树和柳树）poplar and willow 2（柳树）willow
【杨梅】yángméi〈名〉red bayberry
【杨梅疮】yángméichuāng〈名〉〈方〉syphilis
【杨树】yángshù〈名〉poplar
【杨桃】yángtáo〈名〉［植物］starfruit
【杨枝鱼】yángzhīyú〈名〉［鱼类］pipefish

旸（暘）yáng
A〈动〉〈书〉[of the sun] rise
B〈形〉clear
【旸谷】yánggǔ〈名〉〈古〉place where the sun rises

炀（煬）yáng〈书〉
A〈动〉smelt
B〈形〉roaring

佯 yáng〈动〉〈书〉feign: ～死 feign death ‖ ～为不见 shut one's eyes to sth. ▸～攻, ～狂
【佯称】yángchēng〈动〉tell lies: ～头疼 pretend to have a headache
【佯攻】yánggōng〈动〉［军事］feign an attack: 向敌人两侧发动～ feint at enemy flanks
【佯狂】yángkuáng〈动〉〈书〉feign madness
【佯言】yángyán〈动〉〈书〉tell a lie
【佯装】yángzhuāng〈动〉pretend: ～不知 feign ignorance ‖ ～有病 feign illness

疡（瘍）yáng
A〈名〉〈书〉sore
B〈动〉ulcerate: ▸溃～

垟 yáng〈名〉〈方〉field

徉 yáng ▸徜徉 chángyáng

洋 yáng
A〈形〉vast: ▸～～大观, ～溢
B〈名〉1 ▸p. 164（海洋）ocean: 四大～ four oceans ▸海～, 太平～ 2（外国）foreign country: 留～ study abroad ‖ ～办法 foreign method ▸～服, ～鬼子, 西～ 3〈旧〉（银币）silver dollar: 两块大～ two silver dollars
【洋八股】yángbāgǔ〈名〉foreign stereotyped writing
【洋白菜】yángbáicài〈名〉〈口〉cabbage
【洋布】yángbù〈名〉〈旧〉machine-woven cloth
【洋财】yángcái〈名〉1〈本〉profit gained in business with foreign companies 2〈喻〉（意外之财）windfall gain: 发～ have a windfall
【洋插队】yángchāduì〈动〉go abroad in droves to study or work
【洋场】yángchǎng〈名〉〈旧〉〈贬〉city overrun by foreign adventurers [usu referring to pre-liberation Shanghai]
【洋车】yángchē〈名〉〈口〉rickshaw: 拉～ pull a rickshaw
【洋瓷】yángcí〈名〉〈口〉enamel: ～缸/盆/碗 enamel mug/washbasin/bowl ‖ ～器皿 enamelware
【洋葱】yángcōng〈名〉onion: ～头 onion bulb
【洋地黄】yángdìhuáng〈名〉［植物］digitalis
【洋房】yángfáng〈名〉Western-style building
【洋服】yángfú〈名〉Western-style clothes
【洋镐】yánggǎo〈名〉pickaxe
【洋鬼子】yángguǐzi〈名〉〈贬〉foreign devil [term used in the past in China for foreign invaders]: 假～ imitation foreign devil
【洋行】yángháng〈名〉〈旧〉1（指由外商设立）foreign firm: 充当～买办 serve as compradors 2（指与外商做生意）firm doing business with foreigners

> **洋行**
>
> Foreign trading companies based in China from the late 18th century, some of which engaged in the opium trade. Their influence and size grew steadily in the 19th and early part of the 20th century, and they held a monopoly on Chinese foreign trade. Foreign managers were commonly known as *taipans* (▸大班), and the Chinese managers they hired were known as compradors (▸买办). After 1949, the activities of these companies on the Chinese mainland came to an end, although they continued to exist in Hong Kong and Taiwan.

【洋红】yánghóng ▸p. 863〈名〉1（指颜料）pink pigment 2（指颜色）carmine, deep pink
【洋槐】yánghuái〈名〉［植物］locust tree
【洋灰】yánghuī〈名〉〈旧〉cement
【洋火】yánghuǒ〈名〉〈旧〉matches
【洋货】yánghuò〈名〉imported goods: 抵制～ boycott foreign goods
【洋蓟】yángjì〈名〉［植物］artichoke
【洋泾浜】yángjīngbāng〈名〉pidgin: ～英语 pidgin English
【洋酒】yángjiǔ〈名〉foreign alcohol
【洋蜡】yánglà〈名〉〈旧〉candle
【洋里洋气】yánglǐyángqì〈形〉exotic: 打扮得～ be exotically dressed
【洋流】yángliú〈名〉［地理］ocean current
【洋楼】yánglóu〈名〉Western-style building of two storeys or more
【洋奴】yángnú〈名〉〈贬〉worshipper of everything foreign
【洋奴哲学】yángnú zhéxué〈名〉slavish comprador philosophy
【洋气】yángqì A〈名〉Western style: ～十足 completely Western in style B〈形〉stylish: 穿着不要太～，还是朴素一点好。Don't be too fashionable. It would be better to dress simply.
【洋钱】yángqián〈名〉silver dollar
【洋人】yángrén〈名〉foreigner [usu a Westerner]
【洋嗓子】yángsǎngzi〈名〉voice trained in the Western style of singing
【洋参】yángshēn〈名〉American ginseng: ～片 slices of ginseng
【洋铁】yángtiě〈名〉〈旧〉galvanized iron
【洋娃娃】yángwáwa〈名〉doll
【洋为中用】yángwéi-zhōngyòng〈成〉adapt foreign things to Chinese use
【洋文】yángwén〈名〉〈旧〉foreign language
【洋务】yángwù〈名〉1（指事务）foreign affairs [in late Qing Dynasty] 2（指行业）service trades intended for foreigners
【洋务运动】Yángwù Yùndòng〈名〉Westernization Movement [initiated by comprador bureaucrats in the latter half of the 19th century in order to preserve the rule of the Qing government]
【洋相】yángxiàng〈名〉funny manner: ▸出～
【洋烟】yángyān〈名〉imported cigarettes
【洋洋】yángyáng〈形〉1（众多）vast: ▸～大观 2 = 扬扬 yángyáng
【洋洋大观】yángyáng-dàguān〈成〉spectacular
【洋洋洒洒】yángyáng-sǎsǎ〈形〉write copiously and fluently: 这份报告～近900页。This lengthy report runs to nearly 900 pages.
【洋溢】yángyì〈动〉brim with: 热情～ glowing with enthusiasm ‖ 全国上下～着一片热烈的节日气氛。The whole country was brimming with the holiday spirit.
【洋油】yángyóu〈名〉〈方〉1（煤油）kerosene 2（进口油）imported oil
【洋芋】yángyù〈名〉〈方〉potato
【洋装】yángzhuāng A〈名〉Western-style clothes B〈形〉bound Western-style: ～书 books with Western-style binding

烊 yáng〈动〉〈方〉dissolve: 糖～了。The sweets have gone soft. ▸yàng

yǎng

仰 yǎng〈动〉1（脸向上）face upward: ～起头 raise one's head ‖ ～着睡 sleep on one's back ▸～望, ～卧, ～泳 2（敬慕）admire: ▸～慕, 信～, 瞻～ 3〈旧〉（表尊敬）[usu used in official letters from a government office at a higher level to an office at a lower level] be sure to: ～即遵照。We hope that you will act accordingly at once. 4（依靠）rely on: ▸～给, ～赖, ～仗
【仰承】yǎngchéng〈动〉1〈书〉（依靠）depend on 2〈敬〉（遵从）comply with: ～意旨 comply with your wishes
【仰光】Yǎngguāng〈名〉Yangon
【仰给】yǎngjǐ〈动〉rely on sb. for support: ～于人 rely on others for support
【仰角】yǎngjiǎo〈名〉［数学］angle of elevation
【仰赖】yǎnglài〈动〉rely on: 不能～他们。We can't rely on them.
【仰面】yǎngmiàn〈动〉face upward: 摔了个～朝天 fall flat on one's back
【仰慕】yǎngmù〈动〉admire: ～已久 have long been admiring
【仰人鼻息】yǎngrénbíxī〈成〉be at sb.'s beck and call: 我绝不～。I will never live at the mercy of others.
【仰韶文化】Yǎngsháo wénhuà〈名〉［考古］Yangshao Culture [Neolithic culture, named after Yangshao village, in Mianchi County, Henan Province]
【仰视】yǎngshì〈动〉look up at: ～天空 look up at the sky
【仰视图】yǎngshìtú〈名〉upward view
【仰首】yǎngshǒu〈动〉raise one's head
【仰天】yǎngtiān〈动〉look up at the sky: ～长叹 look up to heaven and sigh heavily ‖ ～大笑 look up at the sky and laugh loudly
【仰望】yǎngwàng〈动〉1（向上看）look up at: ～蓝天 look up at the blue sky 2〈书〉（期望）look to sb. for guidance or support: ～前辈指点 look to one's elders for guidance
【仰卧】yǎngwò〈动〉lie on one's back
【仰卧起坐】yǎngwò qǐzuò〈名〉［体育］sit-ups: 做～ do sit-ups
【仰泳】yǎngyǒng〈名〉［体育］backstroke
【仰仗】yǎngzhàng〈动〉depend on: 此事还得～诸位大力支持。I'll rely heavily on all of you for support in this matter.

养（養）yǎng

A〈动〉**1**（喂养）raise: ～蚕 breed silkworms ‖ ～花 grow flowers ‖ ～鸟 keep pet birds **2**（抚养）support: ～不起家 cannot afford to feed one's family ‖ 乡亲们把他～大成人。 He was raised by folks in the village. ▸抱～, 抚～ **3**（生育）give birth to: ～了个女孩 give birth to a daughter **4**（休养）convalesce: ～身体 recuperate one's health ▸～病, 疗～, 休～ **5**（养护）maintain: ▸～路 **6**（修养）cultivate: ▸涵～, 教～ **7**（培养）train: ▸～成, 培～ **8**（扶助）give aid to: 以进～出 use imports to serve the expansion of exports **9**（留长）let one's hair grow: 把头发～长了好梳辫子。 Let your hair grow long so that you can plait it.
B〈形〉adoptive: ▸～父, ～女

【养兵千日，用兵一时】yǎngbīng qiānrì, yòngbīng yīshí〈成〉soldiers are trained for use in time of crisis
【养病】yǎngbìng〈动〉convalesce: 在家～ convalesce at home
【养成】yǎngchéng〈动〉develop: ～习惯 form a habit ‖ ～优良的工作作风 cultivate a good style of work
【养地】yǎngdì〈动〉［农业］increase soil fertility
【养儿方知父母恩】yǎng ér fāng zhī fùmǔ ēn〈俗〉we can't really appreciate the great pains our parents have taken over us until we ourselves become parents
【养儿防老】yǎng ér fáng lǎo〈俗〉one brings up children in order to ease one's old age
【养分】yǎngfèn〈名〉nutrient: 吸收～ take in nutrients
【养蜂】yǎngfēng〈动〉keep bees: ～酿蜜 keep honey bees ‖ ～场 apiary ‖ ～人 bee-keeper
【养父】yǎngfù〈名〉foster/adoptive father
【养汉】yǎnghàn〈动〉[of a woman] commit adultery
【养虎贻患】yǎnghǔ-yíhuàn〈成〉〈喻〉appeasement brings disaster
【养护】yǎnghù〈动〉look after: ～公路 maintain public highways ‖ ～树苗 nurse young trees ‖ 铁路线必须经常～。 The railway lines have to be constantly maintained.
【养活】yǎnghuo〈动〉**1**（提供生活必需品）support: ～家室 feed one's family ‖ 要靠别人～ need other's support for a livelihood **2**（饲养）rear: 这家农场～了上万只鸡。 This farm raises over ten thousand chickens.
【养鸡场】yǎngjīchǎng〈名〉chicken farm
【养家】yǎngjiā〈动〉keep a family: 他连自己都养不活，更不用说～了。 He is not able to support himself, let alone a family.
【养家糊口】yǎngjiā-húkǒu〈成〉support one's family: 靠打工～ make a living by working as a hired labourer
【养精蓄锐】yǎngjīng-xùruì〈成〉conserve strength and build up one's energy: ～，以利再战 save one's strength for the next battle
【养老】yǎnglǎo〈动〉**1**（侍奉老人）provide for the aged: 给某人～ support sb. in his old age ‖ ～送终 look after one's parents in their old age and give them a proper burial after their death **2**（闲居休养）live out one's life in retirement: 攒钱～ save money for one's old age
【养老保险】yǎnglǎo bǎoxiǎn〈名〉endowment insurance
【养老金】yǎnglǎojīn〈名〉pension: 领取～ collect one's pension
【养老院】yǎnglǎoyuàn〈名〉nursing home
【养廉】yǎnglián〈动〉〈书〉restrain from graft and corruption: 俭以～ nourish honesty by living a frugal life
【养料】yǎngliào〈名〉nutrient: 从土壤中吸取～ draw nourishment from the soil
【养路】yǎnglù〈动〉maintain a road or railway: ～工 section hand
【养路费】yǎnglùfèi〈名〉road toll
【养母】yǎngmǔ〈名〉foster mother
【养女】yǎngnǚ〈名〉foster daughter
【养人】yǎngrén〈动〉be nutritious: 这东西很～。 This is very nutritious.
【养伤】yǎngshāng〈动〉nurse one's wound: 在家～ nurse an injury at home
【养神】yǎngshén〈动〉repose: 闭目～ sit and relax with one's eyes closed
【养生】yǎngshēng〈动〉keep in good health: ～之道 way to maintain good health
【养性】yǎngxìng〈动〉discipline one's temperament: ▸修身～
【养颜】yǎngyán〈动〉take care of one's complexion: 护肤～ look after one's skin
【养痈成患】yǎngyōng-chénghuàn〈成〉〈喻〉leaving evil unchecked spells ruin: 我们不应包庇坏人坏事，因为那样会～。 We should not harbour evil-doers and cover up their evil deeds, because leaving evil unchecked spells ruin.
【养痈遗患】yǎngyōng-yíhuàn = 养痈成患 yǎngyōng-chénghuàn
【养育】yǎngyù〈动〉bring up: ～子女 bring up children ‖ ～之恩 love and care received in one's upbringing as a child
【养殖】yǎngzhí〈动〉cultivate: ～海带/珍珠 cultivate kelp/pearl ‖ 淡水～ freshwater aquaculture ‖ 水产～场 aquatic farm
【养猪场】yǎngzhūchǎng〈名〉pig farm
【养子】yǎngzǐ〈名〉adopted son
【养尊处优】yǎngzūn-chǔyōu〈成〉enjoy a rich and comfortable lifestyle: ～的娇小姐 a little princess living the life of luxury

氧 yǎng

〈名〉［化学］oxygen (O): 缺～ lack oxygen ‖ 吸～ inhale oxygen ‖ 有～运动 aerobic exercise

【氧吧】yǎngbā〈名〉oxygen bar
【氧化】yǎnghuà〈动〉［化学］oxidize: ～作用 oxidation
【氧化剂】yǎnghuàjì〈名〉［化学］oxidant
【氧化铁】yǎnghuàtiě〈名〉［化学］ferric oxide
【氧化铜】yǎnghuàtóng〈名〉［化学］copper oxide
【氧化物】yǎnghuàwù〈名〉oxide
【氧气】yǎngqì〈名〉oxygen: ～袋 oxygen bag ‖ ～瓶 oxygen cylinder
【氧炔】yǎngquē〈名〉oxyacetylene: ～焊接/切割 oxyacetylene welding

痒（癢）yǎng

〈动〉**1**（指皮肤感觉）itch: 背上～得难受 have an unbearably itchy back ▸搔～ **2**（指愿望）itch for a try: 他看见别人踢球，心里就～了。 He can't resist the itch to play when he sees others playing football.

【痒痒】yǎngyang〈动〉〈口〉itch: 我感到喉咙～的。 I've got a tickle in my throat. ‖ 这羊毛衫扎得我脖子～的。 This woollen sweater is itching my neck. ‖ 他挠我～。 He tickled me.
【痒痒挠儿】yǎngyangnáor〈名〉itch scratcher

yàng

怏 yàng

【怏然】yàngrán〈形〉unhappy: ～不悦 be unhappy about sth.
【怏怏】yàngyàng〈形〉disgruntled: ～而归 go home in a sullen mood ‖ ～不乐 be in low spirits

样（樣）yàng

〈名〉**1**（形状）appearance: 装修后房间变～儿了。 The room looked different after it had been done up. ▸～子, 模～ **2**（外表）look: 几年没见，你还是老～儿。 It's several years since we last met, but you still look the same. **3**（样品）sample: 看～订货 place a sample order ▸～本, ～品, 榜～, 校～ **4**（趋势）tendency: 看～儿天要下雨了。 It looks as if it's going to rain. **5**（种类）kind: 三～菜 three different dishes ‖ 他～～都行。 He is an all-rounder.

【样板】yàngbǎn〈名〉**1**（样品）sample plate **2**［工程］template: ～刀 forming cutter **3**（榜样）model: ～房 show house ‖ ～工程 prototype project ‖ 树立～ set an example ▸～戏
【样板戏】yàngbǎnxì〈名〉model Beijing opera [term used during the Cultural Revolution]
【样本】yàngběn〈名〉**1**（指本子）sample book **2**［印刷］sample: 新书～ advance copy of a book
【样带】yàngdài〈名〉**1**［植物］belt transect **2**（指样品）sample tape
【样稿】yànggǎo〈名〉［印刷］sample manuscript
【样机】yàngjī〈名〉**1**（指机器）prototype of a machine **2**（指飞机）prototype aeroplane
【样片】yàngpiàn〈名〉sample copy of a film: 审看～ censor a sample film ‖ ～试映 preview a sample film
【样品】yàngpǐn〈名〉sample product: 检查～质量 test samples for quality
【样式】yàngshì〈名〉pattern: ～陈旧 be old-fashioned ‖ 各种～的打印机 printers in all styles
【样书】yàngshū〈名〉sample book
【样样】yàngyàng〈名〉every kind: 他～功课都好。 He is doing well in every course he takes.
【样张】yàngzhāng〈名〉**1**［印刷］specimen page: 打出一份～ pull a proof **2**（指纸样）pattern sheet: 衣服～ dress pattern sheet
【样子】yàngzi〈名〉**1**（模样）appearance: 你不像有病的～。 You don't look ill. ‖ 这件组合家具～很漂亮。 This set of furniture is beautifully styled. **2**（神情）air: 看他的～像是不久人世了。 By the looks of him, he won't live much longer. ‖ 他显出急于讨好的～。 He radiated anxiety to please. **3**（形状）model: 衣服～ clothes pattern ‖ 鞋～ shoe sample ‖ 你不要学他的～。 Don't take him as your example. **4**（形势）tendency: 看～天要下雨。 It looks like rain.

恙 yàng

〈名〉〈书〉ailment: 微～ indisposition ▸安然无～, 别来无～

烊 yàng

▸打烊 dǎyàng ▸yáng

鞅 yàng

▸牛鞅 niúyàng ▸yāng

漾 yàng〈动〉 **1**（水面微动） ripple: 湖面上～起层层波纹。 Ripples raced each other on the water's surface. ▸荡～ **2**（外溢） brim over: 脸上～出笑容 a smile comes over one's face ‖ 澡盆里的水～出来了。 The bathtub is overflowing.

【漾奶】yàngnǎi〈动〉 [of babies] throw up milk

yāo

幺（么） yāo

A〈形〉〈方〉youngest: ～妹 youngest sister ‖ ～叔 youngest uncle

B ▸**p. 691**〈数〉 one [used for the numeral '1' when speaking of figures]: 打～～零报警 dial 110 to call the police ‖ 报火警请拨～～九。 To report a fire, please dial 119.

【幺蛾子】yāo'ézi〈名〉〈方〉 wicked idea: 出～ make wicked suggestions

【幺麽】yāomó〈书〉 **A**〈形〉 petty: ～小丑 despicable wretch **B**〈名〉 vile person

夭[1] yāo〈动〉 die young: ▸～亡, ～折

夭[2] yāo〈形〉〈书〉 luxuriant

【夭亡】yāowáng〈动〉 die young

【夭折】yāozhé〈动〉 **1**〈本〉 die young: 七岁那年不幸～ die prematurely at the age of seven **2**〈喻〉（中途失败） meet an untimely end: 他的计划中途～。 His plan aborted midway.

吆 yāo〈动〉 bawl: 我们对被～来喝去有一肚子怨气。 We felt resentful at being shoved around. ▸～喝, ～五喝六

【吆喝】yāohe〈动〉 **1**（大喊） cry out: 到时候你在楼下～一声。 Give me a shout from downstairs when it is time. **2**（叫卖） cry one's wares: 卖什么，～什么。 Whatever you are selling, cry it out. ‖ 农贸市场上到处是～声。 The market was filled with farmers crying out their wares. **3**（赶牲口） urge a draft animal on with shouts: 就别～了，让牲口换口气吧。 Stop shouting at the animal and give it a break.

【吆五喝六】yāowǔ-hèliù〈成〉 **1**（赌博时的喧闹声） call out numbers, making a lot of noise **2**（盛气凌人的样子） shout overbearingly: 我不喜欢他对人～的。 I don't like the way he keeps snapping at people.

约（約） yāo〈动〉〈口〉 weigh: ～～这有多重。 See how much it weighs. ‖ 给我～三斤西红柿。 Weigh out three *jin* of tomatoes for me.
▸yuē

妖[1] yāo

A〈名〉 demon: ▸～精, ～魔鬼怪

B〈形〉 evil and fraudulent: ▸～术, ～言

妖[2] yāo〈形〉 gorgeous: ▸～娆, ～冶

【妖风】yāofēng〈名〉〈喻〉 evil trend: 刹住赌博的～。 Put an end to the evil trend of gambling.

【妖怪】yāoguài ▸**p. 274**〈名〉 demon

【妖精】yāojing ▸**p. 274**〈名〉 **1**（妖怪） demon **2**〈喻〉（指妖冶女子） seductress

【妖里妖气】yāoliyāoqì〈形〉〈贬〉 seductive and bewitching: 她把自己打扮得～。 She dressed like a whore.

【妖媚】yāomèi〈形〉 seductively charming

【妖魔】yāomó ▸**p. 274**〈名〉 evil spirit: ～乱舞。 Evil spirits of all kinds dance in joyous revelry.

【妖魔鬼怪】yāomó-guǐguài〈成〉〈喻〉 all forces of evil: 消灭一切～ wipe out all demons and ghosts

【妖魔化】yāomóhuà〈动〉 demonize: 被～了的山寨货 demonized knock-off goods

【妖孽】yāoniè〈名〉〈书〉 **1**（指事物） ill omens **2** ▸**p. 274**（指鬼怪） demons and ghosts **3**〈喻〉（指人） evil-doer

【妖娆】yāoráo〈形〉〈书〉 bewitching: 体态～ have an enchanting carriage

【妖人】yāorén〈名〉 sorcerer

【妖术】yāoshù〈名〉 witchcraft

【妖物】yāowù〈名〉 monster

【妖言】yāoyán〈名〉 heresy

【妖言惑众】yāoyán-huòzhòng〈成〉 deceive people with fallacies

【妖艳】yāoyàn〈形〉 gorgeous and flirtatious: 她穿得总是很～。 She always dresses in a gorgeous and flirtatious way.

【妖冶】yāoyě〈形〉 gorgeous and indecent

要 yāo〈动〉 **1**（要求） ask: ▸～求 **2**（强迫） force: ▸～挟
▸yào

【要求】yāoqiú **A**〈动〉 demand: ～赔偿 demand compensation ‖ 对他不要～过高。 Don't ask too much of him. ‖ 经理～大家都到会。 The manager requests everybody to attend the meeting. **B**〈名〉 requirement: 达到～ meet requirements ‖ 答应～ grant sb.'s demands ‖ 降低～ moderate one's demands ‖ 满足他的～ meet his requirements ‖ 应广大观众的～ at the request of the audience ‖ 所有产品都符合质量～。 All products meet quality requirements.

【要挟】yāoxié〈动〉 coerce: 以离婚相～ threaten with divorce

腰 yāo〈名〉 **1**（指身体部分） waist: 搂住～ put one's arms round sb.'s waist ‖ 弯～ bend down ‖ 笑得直不起～来 double up with laughter ▸～包, ～带 **2**〈口〉（肾脏） kidney: ▸～子 **3**（裤腰） waist: 把裙子的～放大/收小一点 let out/take in the waist of the skirt ▸裤～ **4**（腰包） purse: 她～里还有些钱。 She's got some money in her pockets. **5**（指地势） middle: 半山～ halfway up a mountain

【腰板儿】yāobǎnr〈名〉 **1**（腰和背）waist and back: 挺起～ straighten up **2**（体格） build: 老人八十多了～还挺硬朗。 The old man is well over eighty but still has a strong physique.

【腰包】yāobāo〈名〉 **1**（钱包） purse: 掏～ dip one's hand into one's purse ‖ 把钱装进自己的～ pocket the money **2**（系在腰间的钱包） bumbag

【腰部】yāobù〈名〉 waist: ～以下瘫痪 be paralysed from the waist down

【腰缠万贯】yāochán-wànguàn〈成〉 be very rich: 你以为我～吗? Do you think I'm made of money? ‖ 他～。 He is swimming in money.

【腰带】yāodài〈名〉 belt: 系紧～ tighten one's belt

【腰刀】yāodāo〈名〉 side-sword

【腰杆子】yāogǎnzi〈名〉 **1**（腰部） back: 挺起～ hold oneself tall and confident **2**〈喻〉（后台） support: ～不硬 have no strong backing ‖ ～硬 have strong backing

【腰鼓】yāogǔ〈名〉 **1** ▸**p. 929**（指鼓） waist drum **2**（指舞蹈） waist-drum dance

【腰锅】yāoguō〈名〉 waist cauldron [gourd-shaped cauldron used by some ethnic groups in Yunnan Province]

【腰果】yāoguǒ〈名〉［植物］ cashew nut

【腰花】yāohuā〈名〉 scallop-shaped kidney: 炒～ stir-fried kidney

【腰肌】yāojī〈名〉［解剖］ loin muscle: ～劳损 psoatic strain

【腰牌】yāopái〈名〉〈旧〉 pass worn at the waist

【腰身】yāoshēn〈名〉 waist: 她～纤细。 She has a slender waist. ‖ 这件衣服～太肥。 This dress is too loose in the waist.

【腰酸背痛】yāosuān-bèitòng〈成〉 have an aching back

【腰围】yāowéi〈名〉 **1**（指长度） waistline: 量～ take sb.'s waist measurement ‖ 你的～是多少? What size waist do you have? **2**（指带子） waistband

【腰眼】yāoyǎn〈名〉 **1**（指身体部位） either side of the small of the back **2**〈喻〉（要害） heart of a matter: 你的话点到～上了。 What you said hit the nail on the head.

【腰斩】yāozhǎn〈动〉 **1**（指酷刑） execute sb. by cutting him in two at the waist [capital punishment in ancient China] **2**〈喻〉（从中切断） cut sth. in half

【腰椎】yāozhuī〈名〉［生理］ lumbar vertebra

【腰子】yāozi〈名〉〈口〉 kidney: ～病 nephropathy

邀 yāo〈动〉 **1**〈书〉（求得） seek: ～准 seek approval ▸～功, ～赏 **2**（邀请） invite: 应～出席 be invited to attend ‖ 特～代表 specially invited representative **3**（拦住） intercept: ▸～击

【邀宠】yāochǒng〈动〉 curry favour with sb.

【邀功】yāogōng〈动〉〈书〉 take credit for someone else's achievements: ～请赏 take credit and seek rewards for someone else's achievements

【邀击】yāojī〈动〉〈书〉 ambush

【邀集】yāojí〈动〉 get together: ～各界民主人士共商国事 invite democratic personages from all walks of life to a meeting for consultation on state affairs

【邀买】yāomǎi〈动〉 buy over: ～人心 buy popular support

【邀请】yāoqǐng〈动〉 invite: ～朋友参加婚礼/聚会 invite friends to one's wedding/a party ‖ 发出～ issue an invitation ‖ ～书 invitation ‖ ～信 letter of invitation ‖ 接受～ accept an invitation ‖ 收到～ receive an invitation ‖ 谢绝～ decline an invitation

【邀请赛】yāoqǐngsài〈名〉 invitational tournament: 网球～ invitational tennis match

【邀赏】yāoshǎng〈动〉 seek rewards for one's achievements

【邀约】yāoyuē〈动〉〈书〉 invite: 盛情～ warmly invite

yáo

爻 yáo〈名〉 whole and broken linear symbols making up the Eight Trigrams in *I Ching*《易经》: 阳～ whole line ('—') ‖ 阴～ broken line ('--')

尧（堯） Yáo〈名〉 Yao [legendary sage king in ancient China, a model of wisdom and virtue]

【尧舜】Yáo-Shùn〈名〉 1〈本〉 Yao and Shun [legendary sage kings in ancient China] 2〈喻〉 ancient sages

【尧天舜日】 Yáotiān-Shùnrì 〈成〉〈喻〉 times of peace and prosperity

肴（餚） yáo〈名〉 meat and fish dishes: 佳～ delicious dishes ‖ 酒～ wine and meat dishes ▸菜～

【肴馔】 yáozhuàn〈名〉〈书〉 sumptuous courses

垚 yáo〈形〉〈书〉 high and steep [usu used in personal names]

姚 Yáo〈名〉 Yao [surname]

窑（窰、窯） yáo 〈名〉 1（指建筑物） kiln: 烧～ bake in a kiln ‖ 砖～ kiln-burnt brick ‖ 石灰～ limekiln 2（指煤矿） coal pit: 小煤～ small coal pit 3（窑洞） (dwelling) cave: ▸～洞 4〈口〉（妓院） brothel: ▸～子

【窑变】yáobiàn〈名〉［美术］ kiln transmutation: ～花瓶 flamed vase

【窑洞】yáodòng〈名〉 cave dwelling: 住～ live in a cave dwelling

> **窑洞**
>
> A type of housing found in the countryside on the loess plateau of north and north-west China. Cave dwellings are either dug out of a natural cliff face (靠崖窑) or out of the wall of a deep pit (地坑窑). They usually have an arched entrance, and extend back about three metres. Cave dwellings are simple and cheap to build. They are fire-proof and sound-proof, cool in summer and warm in winter.

【窑姐儿】yáojiěr〈名〉〈口〉 hooker

【窑子】yáozi〈名〉〈口〉whorehouse: 逛～ visit a brothel

谣（謠） yáo 〈名〉 1（歌谣） ballad: ▸歌～, 民～ 2（谣传） rumour: ▸～言, 辟～, 造～

【谣传】yáochuán A〈动〉 be rumoured: 外面～粮食又要涨价。 Rumour has it that there will be another rise in grain prices. B〈名〉 rumour: 毫无根据的～ wild rumour

【谣言】 yáoyán 〈名〉 rumour: 散布～ spread rumours ‖ 制造～ start a rumour ‖ ～传开了。 The rumour passed around.

【谣言惑众】yáoyán-huòzhòng〈成〉spread rumours and mislead the people

徭（傜） yáo〈名〉 corvée

【徭役】yáoyì〈名〉〈旧〉 corvée: 沉重的～ heavy corvée

摇（搖） yáo〈动〉 rock: ～船 row a boat ‖ ～橹 scull a boat ‖ ～扇子 wave a fan ‖ ～手柄 wind a handle ‖ ～镜头 pan the camera ‖ ～摇篮 rock a cradle ‖ 把车窗～下 roll down the car window ▸～摆, ～晃

【摇摆】yáobǎi〈动〉 sway: 荷叶迎风～。 The lotus leaves waved in the wind. ‖〈喻〉 政策～不定 policy vacillates

【摇摆舞】 yáobǎiwǔ 〈名〉 rock and roll (dance)

【摇臂】yáobì〈名〉［机械］ valve rocker

【摇唇鼓舌】 yáochún-gǔshé 〈成〉 engage in loose talk

【摇荡】yáodàng〈动〉 sway: 小船随波～。 The boat rolled over the waves.

【摇动】yáodòng〈动〉 1（使晃动） shake: ～旗帜 wave the banners 2（摇摆） rock: 他坐在椅子上前后轻轻地～。 He sat in the chair, gently rocking back and forth. 3（动摇） waver: 我的信念从未～过。 I've never wavered in my faith.

【摇鹅毛扇】 yáo émáoshàn 〈惯〉〈喻〉 mastermind a complicated operation: 他在公司里是～的人。 He is the brains of the company.

【摇滚】yáogǔn〈名〉 rock and roll

【摇撼】yáohàn〈动〉 1（晃动） shake violently: 地震时我感觉到整个房子在～。 I felt the whole house shake during the earthquake. 2〈喻〉（动摇） waver

【摇晃】yáohuàng〈动〉 shake: 船～得很厉害。 The ship rolled badly. ‖ 幼儿学步时总是摇摇晃晃的。 When a baby learns to walk it totters.

【摇惑】yáohuò〈动〉 1（动摇迷惑）waver: 人心～。 Popular feeling is wavering. 2（使动摇迷惑） cause to waver: ～军心 shake the army's morale

【摇奖】yáojiǎng〈动〉 shake out the winning number

【摇篮】yáolán〈名〉 1〈本〉 cradle: 摇～ rock a cradle 2〈喻〉 source: 中国革命的～ cradle of the Chinese revolution ‖ 黄河流域是中华文明的～。 The Yellow River region is the cradle of Chinese civilization.

【摇篮曲】yáolánqǔ〈名〉 lullaby: 唱～ sing a lullaby

【摇旗呐喊】yáoqí-nàhǎn〈成〉〈喻〉 beat the drum for sb.

【摇钱树】 yáoqiánshù 〈名〉〈喻〉 money tree

【摇身一变】 yáoshēn-yībiàn 〈成〉〈贬〉 suddenly change one's identity

【摇手】yáoshǒu A〈名〉 handle B〈动〉 wave one's hand to show disapproval

【摇头】yáotóu〈动〉 shake one's head: 他～一笑拒绝了。 He refused with a smile and a shake of the head.

【摇头摆尾】yáotóu-bǎiwěi〈成〉assume an air of complacency

【摇头晃脑】 yáotóu-huàngnǎo〈成〉 look pleased with oneself: ～地朗读诗文 read out poetry with an air of self-satisfaction

【摇头丸】yáotóuwán〈名〉 Ecstasy [a drug]

【摇尾乞怜】yáowěi-qǐlián〈成〉 fawn obsequiously

【摇摇欲坠】 yáoyáo-yùzhuì〈成〉 tremble in the balance: 大风中，广告牌～。 The advertising billboard teetered in the strong wind.

【摇曳】yáoyè〈动〉 flicker: ～的烛光 flickering light of a candle ‖ 树在风中轻轻～。 The trees are swaying gently in the wind.

【摇椅】yáoyǐ〈名〉 rocking chair

遥（遙） yáo 〈形〉 remote: 炸弹离我就三步之～。 The bomb lay just three paces away from me. ▸～控, ～望, ～相呼应

【遥测】yáocè〈名〉 telemetering: 卫星～获得的数据 data telemetered from a satellite

【遥感】yáogǎn〈名〉 remote sensing: ～仪 remote sensing instrument ‖ ～技术 remote sensing technique

【遥控】yáokòng〈动〉 1（远程指挥）keep remote control: ～指挥 pull the strings from behind the scenes 2（远程操作） control remotely: 电视～器 TV remote ‖ ～汽车 remote-controlled car ‖ ～器 remote control

【遥望】yáowàng〈动〉 look into the distance: ～星空 look up into the star-studded sky

【遥相呼应】 yáoxiāng-hūyìng 〈成〉 echo each other at a distance

【遥想】yáoxiǎng〈动〉 1（想象）imagine: ～未来 imagine the distant future 2（回想） recall: ～当年 reminisce about the past

【遥遥】yáoyáo〈形〉 1（指距离）far away: ～领先 hold a safe lead 2（指时间） distant: ～无期 in the distant future

【遥远】yáoyuǎn〈形〉 remote: 路途～ have a long journey ‖ ～的地方 faraway place ‖ ～的将来 remote future

瑶¹（瑤） yáo〈书〉

A〈名〉 beautiful jade: ～琴 fiddle inlaid with jade

B〈形〉 precious: ～浆 good wine

瑶²（瑤） Yáo ▸瑶族 Yáozú

【瑶池】Yáochí〈名〉 Jasper Lake [the place where the Queen Mother of the West (西王母) resided]

> **瑶池**
>
> In ancient Chinese mythology, the name of a lake in the Kunlun Mountain, the home of the Queen Mother of the West (西王母, also known as 王母娘娘). Legend has it that the Queen Mother often held banquets at the lake, treating her guests to immortalizing flat peaches, which ripen every 3,000 years.

【瑶族】Yáozú〈名〉 Yao ethnic group

鳐（鰩） yáo〈名〉［鱼类］ skate

yǎo

杳 yǎo〈形〉〈书〉 distant, profound and dim: ▸～无音信

【杳渺】 yǎomiǎo 〈形〉〈书〉 deep and remote

【杳然】yǎorán〈形〉〈书〉 quiet and still: 音信～ not be heard of again

【杳如黄鹤】yǎorúhuánghè〈成〉 be gone forever: 她已经一个月没露面了，～。She has not shown up for a month and is nowhere to be found.

【杳无人烟】yǎowúrényān〈成〉 there is no sign of human habitation

【杳无音信】 yǎowúyīnxìn 〈成〉 have not heard from sb.: 他去了那儿后，便～。 We have had no word from him since he went there.

咬 yǎo〈动〉 1（指用牙） bite: 被狗/蛇～了一口 get bitten by a dog/snake ‖ ～紧牙关 grit one's teeth 2（指用工具） grip: 一定要使锚～紧扎稳。 Be sure the anchor bites well. ‖〈喻〉 双方比分一直～得很紧。 The scores have been very close all through the match. 3（牵扯他人） implicate: 乱～好人 implicate innocent people indiscriminately ‖ 反～一口 make a false countercharge 4（发音） pronounce: ▸～字 5（过分计较） nit-pick over words: ▸～文嚼字 6（狗叫） bark: 鸡叫狗～。 Cocks crow and dogs bark. ‖ 狗对着陌生

Y

人～了几声。 The dog barked at the stranger several times.
【咬定】yǎodìng〈动〉 assert emphatically: 他一口～我没有付这本书的款。He insisted that I had not paid for the book.
【咬耳朵】yǎo ěrduo〈惯〉 whisper in sb.'s ear: 上课了，坐在窗口的那两个学生还在～。 When the class began, two students near the window were still whispering.
【咬合】yǎohé〈动〉 1（卡住） engage: 这两个齿轮相～。 These two gear wheels mesh. 2［医学］ articulate: 上下齿～情况良好 have a good bite
【咬紧牙关】 yǎojǐn yáguān 〈成〉 clench one's teeth
【咬群】 yǎoqún 〈动〉 1 （指家畜） be prone to fight within the group 2（指人） be apt to pick a quarrel within a group
【咬人狗儿不露齿】yǎo rén gǒur bù lù chǐ〈俗〉 a barking dog does not bite
【咬舌儿】yǎoshér A〈动〉 lisp: 她说话有点～。 She speaks with a slight lisp. B〈名〉 lisp
【咬文嚼字】yǎowén-jiáozì ▸p. 999〈成〉 be fastidious about wording: 说起话来～ speak with carefully-chosen words
【咬牙】yǎoyá〈动〉 1（咬紧牙齿） clench one's teeth: 恨得直～ gnash one's teeth in hatred ‖ 他咬着牙忍着痛苦。 He clenched his teeth, enduring the intense pain. ‖ 她咬咬牙一头扎进冰冷的水里。 She gritted her teeth and plunged into the cold water. 2（磨牙） grind one's teeth in one's sleep
【咬牙切齿】 yǎoyá-qièchǐ 〈成〉 clench one's teeth: ～地说 speak between clenched teeth ‖ 气得～ gnash one's teeth in anger
【咬字】yǎozì〈动〉 articulate: ～清晰 pronounce clearly
【咬字眼儿】yǎo zìyǎnr〈动〉 be fastidious about wording

舀 yǎo

〈动〉 ladle out: ～水 scoop out water ‖ 用匙～汤喝 spoon soup into one's mouth
【舀子】yǎozi〈名〉 ladle

窅 yǎo

〈形〉〈书〉 1（深陷） [of eyes] sunken: 他双目微～。 His eyes are rather sunken. 2（深远） deep and remote: ～不可测 too deep to be fathomed

窈 yǎo

〈形〉〈书〉 1（深远） profound 2（昏暗） dim
【窈窕】 yǎotiǎo 〈形〉〈书〉 1（美好） gentle and graceful: ～淑女 graceful maiden 2（幽深） secluded

yào

疟（瘧） yào

▸nüè
【疟子】yàozi ▸p. 50〈名〉〈口〉 malaria: 发～ get malaria

药（藥） yào

A〈名〉 1（药物） medicine: 吃/服～ take/have medication ‖ 补～ tonic ‖ 开～ prescribe medicine ‖ 外用～ external remedy ▸～材, 中～ 2（化学物质） certain chemicals: ▸焊～, 火～
B〈动〉 1〈书〉（治疗） cure: ▸不可救～ 2（毒死） kill with poison: ～老鼠 kill rats with rat poison ‖ ～死某人 kill sb. with poison
【药补】yàobǔ〈动〉 build up one's health by taking tonics: ～不如食补。 Diet helps more than medicine.
【药材】yàocái〈名〉 medicinal material: 名贵～ rare medicinal material
【药草】yàocǎo〈名〉 medicinal herb
【药单】yàodān〈名〉 medical prescription
【药典】yàodiǎn〈名〉 pharmacopoeia
【药店】yàodiàn〈名〉 1（指出售药品） chemist's〈英〉; drugstore〈美〉 2（指出售药材） herbal medicine shop
【药方】yàofāng〈名〉 1（指医生开的方子） prescription: 开～ write out a prescription ‖ 按～配药 fill out a prescription 2（指纸片） prescription paper
【药房】 yàofáng 〈名〉 1 （指商店） chemist's〈英〉; drugstore〈美〉 2（指医院部门） dispensary
【药费】yàofèi〈名〉 expenses for medicine: 报销～ reimbursement of medical expenses ‖ 负担不起～ cannot afford the cost of a medicine
【药膏】 yàogāo 〈名〉 ointment: 配制～ make up an ointment ‖ 上～ apply an ointment ‖ 把～敷在伤口上 apply ointment to a wound
【药罐子】 yàoguànzi 〈名〉 1（指罐子） pot for decocting herbal medicine 2〈喻〉（指人） chronic invalid
【药柜】yàoguì〈名〉 medicine cabinet
【药害】yàohài〈名〉 damage to crops caused by farm chemicals
【药衡】 yàohéng 〈名〉 apothecaries' measure
【药剂】yàojì〈名〉 medicament
【药剂师】yàojìshī ▸p. 966〈名〉 pharmacist; chemist〈英〉
【药检】yàojiǎn A〈动〉［药学］ test medicinal products for quality B〈名〉［体育］ drug testing: ～呈阳性 test positive for drugs
【药劲儿】yàojìnr〈口〉= 药力 yàolì
【药酒】yàojiǔ〈名〉 poisonous wine
【药理】yàolǐ〈名〉 pharmacodynamics
【药力】yàolì〈名〉 efficacy of a drug: ～发作。 The drug is taking effect.
【药棉】yàomián〈名〉 absorbent cotton
【药捻儿】yàoniǎnr = 药捻子 yàoniǎnzi
【药捻子】 yàoniǎnzi 〈名〉 slender roll of medicated gauze
【药片】yàopiàn〈名〉 medicinal tablet: 口服～ oral tablet
【药品】yàopǐn〈名〉 pharmaceutical products: ～管理 drug control ‖ 家庭备用～ family pharmacy
【药品检验】 yàopǐn jiǎnyàn 〈名〉 drug screening
【药铺】yàopù〈名〉〈旧〉 herbal medicine shop
【药企】yàoqǐ〈名〉 pharmaceutical business
【药膳】yàoshàn〈名〉 medicinal cuisine
【药石】yàoshí〈名〉［中医］ medicines and stone needles for acupuncture
【药石之言】yàoshízhīyán〈成〉 unpleasant but sincere advice: ～，不可不听。 Sincere advice, though seemingly unpalatable, must be followed.
【药水】yàoshuǐ〈名〉 liquid medicine: 眼～ eye drops
【药丸】yàowán〈名〉 pill
【药味】 yàowèi 〈名〉 1（指药） herbal medicines in a prescription 2（指气味） flavour of a drug: 医院的房间里有股～。 The hospital room smells of medicines.
【药物】 yàowù 〈名〉 medicines: 滥用～ abuse drugs ‖ ～过敏 drug allergy ‖ ～治疗 be on medication
【药物检查】yàowù jiǎnchá〈名〉 drug testing
【药物麻醉】yàowù mázuì〈名〉 drug anaesthesia
【药物学】yàowùxué〈名〉 pharmacology: ～家 pharmacologist
【药物牙膏】yàowù yágāo〈名〉 medicated toothpaste
【药箱】yàoxiāng〈名〉 medical kit: 急救～ first-aid kit
【药效】yàoxiào〈名〉 potency of a drug: ～很好。 The medicine is very effective.
【药械】yàoxiè〈名〉insecticide-spreading equipment
【药性】yàoxìng〈名〉 property of a medicine: ～平和/猛的药物 mild/strong medicine
【药学】yàoxué〈名〉 pharmacy: ～博士/硕士 Doctor/Master of Pharmacy
【药引子】 yàoyǐnzi 〈名〉［中医］ efficacy-enhancer added to medicine
【药用】yàoyòng〈形〉 medicinal: ～纱布 medicated gauze ‖ ～植物 medicinal plant
【药浴】yàoyù〈名〉 medicinal bath
【药皂】yàozào〈名〉 medicated soap
【药枕】yàozhěn〈名〉 medicinal pillow

要[1] yào

A〈名〉 main points: ▸扼～, 纪～, 摘～
B〈形〉 essential: ▸～紧, ～人, 次～

要[2] yào

〈动〉 1（想） want: 他～同律师谈一谈。 He would like to talk to the lawyer. ‖ 他～来就来，～去就去。 He comes and goes as he wishes. 2（希求） desire: 你～多少就拿多少。 Take as many as you want. ‖ 我们～和平，不～战争。 We desire peace, not war. 3（索求） ask for: 我只～了一瓶可乐。 I only asked for a bottle of cola. ▸～账 4（请求） request: 他再三～我帮忙。 He made repeated requests for my help. ‖ 我～他们在一小时内准备就绪。 I want them ready in one hour. 5（需要） need: 到那里～两个小时。 It takes two hours to get there. ‖ 一斤西红柿～多少钱? How much does a *jin* of tomatoes cost? 6（必须） must: 人～吃饭才能活。 Man has to eat to live. ‖ 一切行动～符合人民的利益。 Do everything in the interests of the people. 7（将要） be about to: 冬天～来了。 Winter is coming. ‖ 天～下雨了。 It is going to rain. 8（表估计） [used in comparisons to indicate an estimate] must: 我看你的工作～比我的轻松得多。 I believe you have got a much cushier job than me. 9（表决心） be determined: 我一定～在今晚完成此事。 I must finish this tonight. ‖ 如果你坚持～走，我也就不挽留了。 If you must go, I won't press you to stay.

要[3] yào

▸p. 350〈连〉 1（如果） if: 明天～下雨，我们就待在家里。 We'll stay at home tomorrow if it rains. ‖ 我～赶不来，请替我跟头儿打个招呼。 In case I can't come in time, please let the boss know. 2（要么） either ... or ...: ～就进来，～就出去。 Either come in or go out.
▸yāo
【要隘】yào'ài〈名〉 strategic pass: 扼守～ hold a strategic pass
【要案】yào'àn〈名〉 key criminal case: 查处大案～ investigate and deal with big and important cases
【要不】 yàobù 〈连〉〈口〉 1（否则） otherwise: 回家去吧，～你妈妈会担心

y

的。 Go home or your mother will be worried. **2**（要么） either ... or ...: 咱们～去跳舞，～去听音乐。 Let's either go dancing or to the concert.

【要不得】yàobude〈动〉 be inadvisable: 这样做～。 Such an act is inadvisable.

【要不是】yàobushì〈连〉 but for: ～你帮倒忙，我早就完成了。 If it had not been for your interference, I would have finished it.

【要冲】yàochōng〈名〉〈书〉 communications centre: 交通～ communications centre ‖ 军事～ strategic point

【要道】yàodào〈名〉 **1**（指道路） thoroughfare: 交通～ important line of communications **2**（指道理、方法） cardinal principle

【要得】yàodé〈形〉〈方〉fine: 这办法～。 This is a good idea.

【要地】yàodì〈名〉 strategic point: 战略～ strategic point

【要点】yàodiǎn〈名〉**1**（主要内容） main points: 领会/没有领会～ grasp/miss the main points ‖ 抓住～ get the gist ‖ 计划的～ essentials of a plan **2**（重要据点） key stronghold: 战略～ strategic point

【要端】yàoduān = 要点 yàodiǎn 1

【要犯】yàofàn〈名〉 most wanted criminal: 通缉～ order the arrest of the principal criminal at large

【要饭】yàofàn〈动〉 beg: ～的 beggar

【要害】yàohài〈名〉 **1**（致命部位） vital organ: 子弹未击中他的～部位。The bullet didn't hit his vital organs. **2**〈喻〉（关键）strategic point: ～部门 key department ‖ 回避～问题 evade the crucial question

【要好】yàohǎo〈形〉 **1**（关系好） close: ～的朋友 close friend **2**（力求上进） conscientious: 这孩子很～，从不耽误功课。 The child is eager to do well at school. He never misses his classes.

【要价】yàojià〈动〉**1**（指售价）charge: ～过高 demand an exorbitant price ‖ 她～九块钱一公斤，少了就不卖。 She wouldn't take less than 9 *yuan* for a kilo. **2**（指谈判条件） demand terms

【要件】yàojiàn〈名〉 **1**（指文件） important document **2**（指条件） essential condition

【要津】yàojīn〈名〉〈书〉**1**（指交通要道） vital water and land communications line **2**〈喻〉（指职位） key position: 身居～ hold a key post

【要紧】yàojǐn〈形〉 **1**（重要） important: 有～事商量 have an urgent matter to discuss with sb. **2**（严重） serious: 不过是轻伤，没什么～。 It's only a slight wound, nothing serious.

【要诀】yàojué〈名〉 tricks of a trade: 拍摄夜景的～ the secret of filming night scenes

【要脸】yàoliǎn〈动〉 care about one's reputation: 你不～别人可～。 You may have no sense of shame but that's not to say that others don't.

【要领】yàolǐng〈名〉 **1**（主要内容） main points: 不得～ miss the point ‖ 掌握～ get the drift **2**（基本要求） knack: 掌握动作～ grasp the essentials of a movement

【要略】yàolüè〈名〉 [usu used in the title of a book] summary

【要么】yàome〈连〉 either ... or ...: ～道歉，～滚出去。 Either say you are sorry or get out!

【要面子】yào miànzi〈动〉 be concerned about one's reputation: 他很～，害怕失败。 He was afraid of failure because he didn't want to lose face.

【要命】yàomìng〈动〉 **1**（致命） drive sb. to death: 一场重病，差点儿要了我的命。 A severe illness almost took my life. **2**（达到极点） be in the extreme: 吓得～ be frightened out of one's wits ‖ 天热得～。 It's incredibly hot. **3**（造成麻烦） be annoying: 真～，雨像是不会停了。 It seems the rain will never stop. What a nuisance!

【要目】yàomù〈名〉 principal items: 本报今日～ headlines in today's newspaper

【要强】yàoqiáng〈形〉 eager to excel: 他这个人太～了。 He is too eager to outdo others.

【要人】yàorén〈名〉 very important person (VIP): 政界～ eminent politician

【要塞】yàosài〈名〉 fortress: 攻占～ take a fortress

【要事】yàoshì〈名〉 important matter: 我来找你有～相商。 I have come to discuss an important matter with you.

【要是】yàoshi ▸**p. 350**〈连〉 if: ～发生火灾，就赶快按铃。 In case of fire, press the bell. ‖ 谁～考试作弊，都要受到警告处分。 Anyone caught cheating in the exam will be given a disciplinary warning.

【要死】yàosǐ〈动〉〈口〉be in the extreme: 疼得～ be unbearably painful ‖ 累得～ be dead tired

【要死要活】yàosǐ-yàohuó〈成〉 repeatedly threaten suicide

【要素】yàosù〈名〉 key element: 语言是一切文学作品的基本～。 Language is an essential factor of all literary works.

【要闻】yàowén〈名〉 important news: 国际～ major world news

【要务】yàowù〈名〉 important business: 处理～ attend to urgent business ‖ 发展是第一～。 Development is the most important thing.

【要想人不知，除非己莫为】 yào xiǎng rén bù zhī, chúfēi jǐ mò wéi〈俗〉 what is done by night appears by day

【要言不烦】 yàoyán-bùfán〈成〉 be succinct: 那本书真是～。 That book is very clear and to the point.

【要义】yàoyì〈名〉 essentials: 人生～ essentials of life

【要员】yàoyuán〈名〉 important official: 政界～ important political figure

【要账】yàozhàng〈动〉 demand payment of a debt

【要职】yàozhí〈名〉 important post: 担任～ hold a key position

【要旨】yàozhǐ〈名〉 main idea: 讲话～ gist of a speech

【要子】yàozi〈名〉 **1**（用于捆麦子等） straw rope for binding rice or wheat stalks **2**（用于打包） baling strap for binding packages

钥（鑰） yào〈名〉 key
▸yuè

【钥匙】yàoshi〈名〉 key: 配～ cut a key ‖ ～卡 key card ‖ 万能～ master key

靿 yào〈名〉 leg of a boot: 高～靴子 boots

鹞（鷂） yào〈名〉**1**（鹞鹰） sparrow hawk **2**（雀鹰） harrier

【鹞子】yàozi〈名〉 **1**（鹞鹰） sparrow hawk **2**〈方〉（风筝） kite: 放～ fly a kite

曜 yào〈书〉
A〈名〉**1**（日光） sunlight **2**（日、月、星辰） luminary [a collective term for the sun, the moon and five major stars in traditional Chinese astronomy, used in the past to form names of the days of the week]
B〈动〉 shine

耀 yào
A〈动〉 **1**（照射） shine: ▸～眼，闪～，照～ **2**（炫耀） laud: ▸～武扬威，炫～
B〈形〉 honourable: ▸荣～
C〈名〉 radiance: ▸光～

【耀斑】yàobān〈名〉［天文］ solar flare

【耀武扬威】 yàowǔ-yángwēi〈成〉 throw one's weight around: 别那么～，到时候你们会后悔的。 Don't swagger around like that. In time you will regret it.

【耀眼】yàoyǎn〈动〉 dazzle: ～的光 blinding light

yē

耶 yē
▸yé

【耶和华】Yēhéhuá〈名〉 Jehovah

【耶路撒冷】Yēlùsālěng〈名〉 Jerusalem

【耶稣】Yēsū〈名〉 Jesus

【耶稣教】Yēsūjiào〈名〉 Protestantism

掖 yē〈动〉 tuck in: 把餐巾～在下巴下 tuck a napkin under one's chin ‖ 母亲给他把被子～好。 Mother tucked him up in his quilt.
▸yè

椰 yē〈名〉［植物］ coconut tree

【椰雕】yēdiāo〈名〉 coconut shell carving

【椰壳】yēké〈名〉 coconut shell

【椰蓉】yēróng〈名〉 fine coconut mash [used as a filling for pies, mooncakes, etc.]

【椰汁】yēzhī〈名〉 coconut milk

【椰子】yēzi〈名〉 **1**（指植物） coconut tree **2**（指果实） coconut

噎 yē〈动〉 **1**（食物堵住食管） choke: 被食物～住了 choke on one's food ▸因～废食 **2**（呼吸困难） choke: 他哭得直～气。 He was choked up with tears. **3**（说话顶撞） render sb. speechless by saying sth. blunt: 我的一句话～得他满脸通红。 He blushed to the roots of his hair at my remark.

yé

邪 yé = 耶 yé
▸xié

爷（爺） yé〈名〉 **1**〈书〉（父亲） father: ▸～儿 **2**（祖父） grandfather: ～～奶奶 grandfather and grandmother ▸姥～，太～ **3**（尊称年长男子） grandpa: ▸大～ **4**〈旧〉（尊称官僚财主等） sir: ▸少～ **5**（尊称神佛） god: 财神～ God of Wealth

【爷们儿】yémenr〈名〉〈方〉 **1**（男人）(collective term for) men of two or more generations **2**（男人间互称） brother

【爷儿】yér〈名〉（父子辈） father and son;（叔侄辈） uncle and nephew;（祖孙辈） grandfather and grandson: ～俩在下棋。 Father and son are playing chess.

【爷儿们】yérmen〈名〉 (collective term for) men of two or more generations

Y

【爷爷】yéye〈名〉1 ▸p. 588 （祖父） paternal grandfather 2（尊称老年男子） grandpa

耶 yé〈助〉〈书〉[used at the end of a question]: 是～非～? Yes or no? ▸yē

揶 yé
【揶揄】yéyú〈动〉〈书〉 ridicule: 受人～ be in derision ‖ 屡遭～ be repeatedly ridiculed

yě

也[1] yě〈助〉1〈书〉（用于强调）[used at the end of a sentence indicating affirmation or used at the end of a question or an exclamatory sentence for emphasis]: 夫子曰: "小子识之，苛政猛于虎～!" Confucius said, 'You young people should know that tyranny is fiercer than a tiger!' ‖ 见义不为，无勇～。 To see what is right and not to do it is to lack courage. ‖ 后生可畏，焉知来者之不如今～? Respect the young. How do you know that they will not one day be all that you are now? 2（表停顿）[used in the middle of a sentence, marking off a sentence element about which there is to be a statement]: 民之于仁～，甚于水火。Goodness is more to the people than water and fire.

也[2] yě〈副〉1（表并列） also: 地～扫了，玻璃～擦了。 The ground has been swept, the windows have also been cleaned. ‖ 你不去，我～不去。 If you don't go, neither shall I. 2（表同样） too: 你可以坐在这儿，～可以坐在那儿。 You can sit here or you can sit there too. ‖ 她不聪明，～不漂亮。 She is neither smart nor pretty. ‖ 我～知道答案。 I know the answer, too. 3（表转折） even if: 即使失败十次，我～不灰心。 I'll never lose heart even if I should fail ten times. 4（表强调）[used for emphasis, often in a negative sentence]: 他连姓名～都不告诉我。 He won't even tell me who he is. ‖ 我一点～不累。 I am not tired at all. 5（表委婉） [used to soften up the tone]: 他来打了个照面，～算是给脸了。 He showed up briefly as a favour to us. ‖ 一个人拉扯大五六个孩子，～够难为她的。 It was quite a job for her bringing up half a dozen children all by herself.

【也罢】yěbà〈助〉1（表容忍） all right: ～，既然他不愿做，就不要勉强他。 All right, since he doesn't want to do it don't force him. 2（表同样） [used for reduplication] no matter whether: 他来～，不来～，对我无所谓。 It makes no difference to me whether he comes or not. ‖ 老师～，同学～，谁也说服不了他。 Neither his teachers nor his classmates could talk him round.

【也好】yěhǎo = 也罢 yěbà 2

【也门】Yěmén〈名〉 Yemen: ～共和国 Republic of Yemen ‖ ～人 Yemeni

【也许】yěxǔ〈副〉 perhaps: 那信今天～能到。 Perhaps the letter will come today. ‖ ～我能做这件事。 Maybe I can do it.

冶[1] yě〈动〉 smelt: ▸～金，～炼，陶～

冶[2] yě〈形〉〈书〉 seductively dressed or made up: ▸～容，妖～

【冶金】yějīn〈动〉 smelt: ～工业 metallurgical industry

【冶炼】yěliàn〈动〉 smelt: ～厂 smeltery

【冶容】yěróng〈书〉A〈形〉 seductively made up B〈名〉 seductive appearance

【冶铸】yězhù〈动〉 smelt and found

野 yě
A〈名〉1（野外） open country: ▸～外，旷～，原～ 2（不当政） state of being out of office: ▸朝～，下～ 3（界限） limit: ▸分～，视～
B〈形〉1（粗鲁）rough: 说话～ use coarse language ‖ 性子～ have a wild temper ▸粗～，撒～ 2（不受约束） unruly: 这些孩子～得很。 Those boys are completely wild. ▸～性 3（非人工饲养或培植） undomesticated: ～草 weeds ‖ ～果 wild fruit ▸～猪 4（不合法） illegal: ▸～合 5（无主人） stray: ～狗 stray dog

【野菜】yěcài〈名〉 edible wild herbs: 挖～ dig up edible wild herbs

【野餐】yěcān A〈动〉 go for a picnic: 他们正在草坪上～。 They are picnicking on the lawn. ‖ 我们常去海滨～。 We often have picnics at the beach. B〈名〉 picnic: 我们去时带上～。 We'll take a picnic with us.

【野炊】yěchuī〈动〉 cook in the open air

【野地】yědì〈名〉 wilderness

【野鸽】yěgē〈名〉 wild pigeon

【野汉子】yěhànzi〈名〉 lover (of a married woman)

【野合】yěhé〈动〉 commit adultery

【野花】yěhuā〈名〉1（指花）wild flower: 采～ pick wild flowers 2（指女人） woman of easy virtue

【野火】yěhuǒ〈名〉 bush fire: ～烧不尽，春风吹又生 the grass cannot be burned out even by a prairie fire but grows again with the spring breeze

【野鸡】yějī A〈名〉1（雉） pheasant 2〈旧〉（私娼） streetwalker B〈形〉 unauthorized: ～公司 unlicensed company ‖ ～大学 unlicensed university

【野驴】yělǘ〈名〉 kiang

【野马】yěmǎ〈名〉 wild horse

【野蛮】yěmán〈形〉1（不文明） uncivilized: 这些居民仍处于～状态。 The inhabitants were still uncivilized. 2（残暴） brutal: 犯下～暴行 commit barbarous acts ‖ ～屠杀 brutal massacre

【野猫】yěmāo〈名〉1（指猫） stray cat: 收养～ take in a wild cat 2〈方〉（指兔） hare

【野牛】yěniú〈名〉 wild ox

【野炮】yěpào〈名〉 field gun

【野禽】yěqín〈名〉 wild fowl

【野趣】yěqù〈名〉 rustic charm: 富有～ be full of rustic appeal

【野人】yěrén〈名〉1〈旧〉（平民） commoner 2（未开化的人） country bumpkin 3（粗野的人） savage

【野生】yěshēng〈形〉 wild: ～动物 wildlife ‖ ～植物 wild plant

【野食儿】yěshír〈名〉1〈本〉 food picked in the wild 2〈喻〉（外财） ill-gotten gains

【野史】yěshǐ〈名〉 unofficial history

【野兽】yěshòu〈名〉 wild beast: 捕猎～ hunt wild animals

【野兔】yětù〈名〉 hare

【野外】yěwài〈名〉 open country: ～工作 fieldwork ‖ 荒郊～ the wilderness

【野外作业】yěwài zuòyè〈名〉 fieldwork

【野味】yěwèi〈名〉 game: ～海鲜 game and seafood

【野心】yěxīn〈名〉 wild ambition: 否认自己有政治～ disavow one's own political ambitions ‖ 侵略～ ambition for aggression

【野心勃勃】yěxīn-bóbó〈成〉 be burning with ambition: 他～，想独揽大权。 He was burning with the ambition to arrogate all powers to himself.

【野心家】yěxīnjiā〈名〉 careerist

【野性】yěxìng〈名〉 wild nature: ～十足 be very wild

【野鸭】yěyā〈名〉 wild duck

【野营】yěyíng〈动〉 camp: 去～ go camping ‖ 他们在树林中～。 They camped out in the woods.

【野战】yězhàn〈动〉 engage in field operations: ～部队 field forces

【野战军】yězhànjūn〈名〉 field army

【野猪】yězhū〈名〉 wild boar

yè

业[1]（業）yè
A〈名〉1（学业） course of study: ▸毕～ 2（职业） occupation: 以教书为～ make teaching one's career ▸敬～，就～，失～ 3（行业） line of business: ▸行～，农～ 4（事业） cause: ▸～绩，创～，守～ 5（产业） estate: ▸家～，～主
B〈动〉〈书〉 engage in: ～农 be engaged in farming ‖ ～医 practise medicine

业[2]（業）yè〈副〉〈书〉 already: ～已核实 have already been verified

业[3]（業）yè〈名〉［佛教］ karma: ▸～障

【业大】yèdà〈简称〉= 业余大学

【业绩】yèjì〈名〉 outstanding achievement: 不朽的～ monumental achievement ‖ 光辉～ glorious achievement

【业界】yèjiè〈名〉 business circles: ～人士 industry insiders

【业经】yèjīng〈副〉〈书〉 already: ～呈报上级机关备案 have already reported the matter to higher-level authorities for the record

【业精于勤】yèjīngyúqín〈成〉 mastery of work comes from diligence

【业内】yènèi〈名〉 inside of the business: ～人士 industry insider

【业师】yèshī〈名〉〈书〉 my teacher

【业态】yètài〈名〉 form or state of business operation

【业外】yèwài〈名〉 beyond the scope a certain trade, business or profession: ～人士 outsider

【业委会】yèwěihuì〈简称〉= 业主委员会

【业务】yèwù〈名〉 business: ～水平 professional skill ‖ 发展～ expand one's business ‖ 钻研～ diligently study one's profession ‖ ～学习 vocational study ‖ 零售/批发～ retail/wholesale business ‖ 我们公司和贵公司有密切的～往来。 Our firm has close business ties with yours.

【业务班子】yèwù bānzi〈名〉 professional team

【业务范围】yèwù fànwéi〈名〉 scope of business: 扩大～ expand the scope of one's operation

【业务能力】yèwù nénglì〈名〉 professional

competence

【业务素质】yèwù sùzhì〈名〉 professional qualification

【业务知识】yèwù zhīshi〈名〉 professional knowledge

【业已】yèyǐ〈副〉〈书〉 already: ～完成 have already been completed ‖ ～准备就绪 ready-made

【业余】yèyú〈形〉 1（工作之余） after-hours: ～爱好 hobby ‖ ～时间 spare time 2（非专业） amateur: ～摄影师/演员/作家 amateur photographer/actor/writer

【业余大学】yèyú dàxué〈名〉 after-hours university

【业余教育】yèyú jiàoyù〈名〉 after-hours education

【业障】yèzhàng〈名〉 1［佛教］ sin that detracts from one's good works 2〈旧〉〈贬〉（指人）［said of one's inferiors］ vile spawn

【业者】yèzhě〈名〉 practitioner of a certain business

【业主】yèzhǔ〈名〉 proprietor: 企业～ business proprietor

【业主委员会】yèzhǔ wěiyuánhuì〈名〉 Property Owners' Committee: 成立～ set up a Proprietors' Committee ‖ ～和物业管理者常发生矛盾。 The Property Owners' Committee often has run-ins with property managers.

叶（葉） yè

〈名〉 1（叶子） leaf: 长出嫩～ put forth new leaves ‖ 落～ fallen leaves ‖ 残枝败～ dead twigs and withered leaves ▸～落归根，根深～茂 2（叶状物） leaf-like thing: 一～扁舟 a small boat ▸百～窗，合～ 3［生物］ lobe: ▸肺～ 4（时期） part of a historical period: 明朝末～ closing period of the Ming Dynasty ‖ 20世纪上/下半～ in the former/latter half of the 20th century ▸初～，末～，中～

▸xié

【叶柄】yèbǐng〈名〉 stalk of a leaf

【叶公好龙】Yègōng-hàolóng〈成〉〈喻〉 professed love of what one really fears

【叶猴】yèhóu〈名〉 langur

【叶绿素】yèlǜsù〈名〉 chlorophyll

【叶绿体】yèlǜtǐ〈名〉 chloroplast

【叶轮】yèlún〈名〉［机械］ impeller: 水泵～ water pump impeller

【叶落归根】yèluò-guīgēn〈成〉〈喻〉 a person residing elsewhere will eventually return to his ancestral home: 老华侨终于～，回到了阔别数十年的故乡。 Like fallen leaves returning to their roots, the old man finally returned to his hometown after several decades overseas.

【叶脉】yèmài〈名〉 leaf vein

【叶片】yèpiàn〈名〉 1［植物］ blade 2［机械］ blade: 涡轮～ turbine blade ‖ 螺旋桨～ propeller blade

【叶鞘】yèqiào〈名〉 leaf sheath

【叶酸】yèsuān〈名〉［生化］ folic acid

【叶序】yèxù〈名〉 arrangement of leaves on a stem

【叶芽】yèyá〈名〉 leaf bud

【叶腋】yèyè〈名〉 auxiliary bud

【叶枝】yèzhī〈名〉 leaf branch

【叶子】yèzi〈名〉 leaf: 长出～ come into leaf ‖ 树上的～全掉了。 The trees have lost all their leaves.

【叶子烟】yèziyān〈名〉 sun-cured tobacco leaves

页（頁） yè

A〈名〉 1（纸张） sheet: 散～ loose leaf ‖ 增～ supplementary sheet ▸插～，画～ 2［计算机］ page: 网～ web page **B**〈量〉 page: 二十～的小册子 twenty-page pamphlet ‖ 翻到第六～ turn to page 6 ‖〈喻〉 中国历史上光辉的一～ a glorious page in Chinese history

【页码】yèmǎ〈名〉 page number: ～错乱 the page numbers are all over the place

【页面】yèmiàn〈名〉［计算机］ page: ～显示 page display

【页心】yèxīn〈名〉 type page

【页岩】yèyán〈名〉［地质］ shale

曳 yè

〈动〉 drag: ▸弃甲～兵，摇～

【曳光弹】yèguāngdàn〈名〉［军事］ tracer bullet

夜 yè

A〈名〉 night: 昼短～长 short days and long nights ‖ 黑～ dark night ▸～宵，熬～，守～ **B**〈量〉 night: 他在旅馆住了三～。 He stayed three nights at the hotel.

【夜班】yèbān〈名〉 night shift: 上/值～ work the night shift ‖ ～费 night shift allowance

【夜班车】yèbānchē〈名〉 night bus

【夜半】yèbàn〈名〉 midnight: ～更深 late at night

【夜不闭户】yèbùbìhù〈成〉 law and order prevail

【夜不能寐】yèbùnéngmèi〈成〉 be unable to fall asleep all night

【夜餐】yècān〈名〉 night snack

【夜叉】yèchā〈名〉 1［佛教］ yaksha ［an evil spirit］ 2〈喻〉（指人） hideous monster: ▸母～

【夜长梦多】yècháng-mèngduō〈成〉〈喻〉 a long delay may mean trouble: 我们必须马上行动，否则～。 We must take action at once, otherwise something untoward may happen.

【夜场】yèchǎng〈名〉 evening performance: ～电影 late film

【夜车】yèchē〈名〉 night train

【夜大学】yèdàxué〈名〉 evening university

【夜店】yèdiàn〈名〉 late night entertainment venue: 逛～ go clubbing ‖ ～生意红火。 Business is booming in the late night entertainment venue.

【夜饭】yèfàn〈名〉 dinner: ▸年～

【夜工】yègōng〈名〉 evening job: 打～ do an evening job

【夜光杯】yèguāngbēi〈名〉 luminous wine glass

【夜光表】yèguāngbiǎo〈名〉 fluorescent watch

【夜航】yèháng〈动〉（指飞机） go on a night flight;（指船） take a night voyage

【夜壶】yèhú〈名〉〈旧〉 chamber pot

【夜话】yèhuà〈名〉〈书〉 evening talk

【夜间】yèjiān〈名〉 night time: ～施工 carry on construction work at night ‖ ～航班 night flight

【夜景】yèjǐng〈名〉 night scene: 拍摄～ film night scenes

【夜空】yèkōng〈名〉 night sky: 闪电划破乌云密布的～。 Lightning ripped the cloudy night sky. ‖ 一声爆炸响彻～。 An explosion ripped through the night sky.

【夜来】yèlái〈名〉〈书〉 1（昨天） yesterday 2（晚上） night: ～风雨声，花落知多少？ How much blossom was shed during the course of this turbulent night?

【夜来香】yèláixiāng〈名〉［植物］ tuberose

【夜阑人静】yèlán-rénjìng〈成〉 the dead of night

【夜郎自大】Yèláng-zìdà〈成〉〈喻〉 be blinded by presumptuous self-conceit

【夜里】yèli〈名〉 night: 昨天～下了一场雨。 It rained last night.

【夜盲症】yèmángzhèng ▸p. 50〈名〉［医学］ night blindness

【夜猫子】yèmāozi〈名〉〈方〉 1（猫头鹰） owl 2〈喻〉 night owl

【夜明珠】yèmíngzhū〈名〉 luminous pearl

【夜幕】yèmù〈名〉 gathering darkness: ～降临。 Night drew in. ‖ ～笼罩着大地。 The land is enveloped in a curtain of darkness.

【夜尿症】yèniàozhèng ▸p. 50〈名〉［医学］ nycturia

【夜色】yèsè〈名〉 night scene: 在茫茫～中 in the darkness of night ‖ ～降临了。 Darkness settled in.

【夜色阑珊】yèsè-lánshān〈成〉 the evening wears on

【夜深】yèshēn〈形〉 late at night: ～人静 in the quiet of the night

【夜生活】yèshēnghuó〈名〉 night life: 丰富多彩的～ rich and colourful night life

【夜市】yèshì〈名〉 night market: 逛～ shop at a night market

【夜视仪】yèshìyí〈名〉［军事］ night vision device

【夜晚】yèwǎn〈名〉 night: 满天星斗的～ starry night ‖ 漆黑的～ pitch-black night

【夜望镜】yèwàngjìng〈名〉［军事］ snooper-scope

【夜袭】yèxí〈动〉 carry out a night raid

【夜宵】yèxiāo〈名〉 midnight snack

【夜校】yèxiào〈名〉 night school: 上～ go to night school

【夜行】yèxíng〈动〉 travel by night

【夜行军】yèxíngjūn〈名〉 night march

【夜以继日】yèyǐjìrì〈成〉 round the clock: 大家都在～地苦干。 Everybody was working round the clock.

【夜莺】yèyīng〈名〉 nightingale

【夜鹰】yèyīng〈名〉 nightjar

【夜游症】yèyóuzhèng〈名〉 sleep-walking: ～患者 sleepwalker

【夜战】yèzhàn〈动〉 1［军事］ engage in night combat 2（夜间加班） work at night: 挑灯～ continue working by lamplight

【夜总会】yèzǒnghuì〈名〉 nightclub

咽 yè

〈动〉 choke with sobs: ▸悲～，哽～，呜～

▸yān, yàn

晔（曄） yè

〈形〉〈书〉 flourishing

烨（燁） yè

A〈名〉（日光） sunlight;（火光） firelight **B**〈形〉 bright

掖 yè

〈动〉〈书〉 prop up: ▸扶～，奖～

▸yē

液 yè

〈名〉 liquid: ▸～化，～态，血～

【液氮】yèdàn〈名〉［化学］ liquid nitrogen

【液化】yèhuà〈动〉 1（指气体） liquefy: 气体必须冷却到一定温度以下才能～。 Gas must be cooled before it can be liquefied below a certain temperature. 2（指机体） liquefy

Y

【液化气】yèhuàqì〈名〉 liquid gas: ～罐 gas bottle ‖ ～石油气 liquefied petroleum gas

【液晶】yèjīng〈名〉［物理］ liquid crystal: ～电视 liquid crystal TV ‖ ～显示屏 liquid crystal display (LCD)

【液态】yètài〈名〉 liquid state

【液态奶】yètàinǎi〈名〉 liquid milk

【液体】yètǐ〈名〉 liquid: 压缩成～ condense into liquid form ‖ ～燃料 liquid fuel

【液压】yèyā〈名〉［机械］ hydraulic pressure: ～锻造 hydrostatic forging ‖ ～机 hydraulic press

【液压泵】yèyābèng〈名〉 hydraulic pump

谒（謁） yè〈动〉〈书〉 call on: ～陵 pay homage at a mausoleum ▸拜～, 参～

【谒见】yèjiàn〈动〉 have an audience with

腋 yè〈名〉 **1**（腋窝） armpit: ▸～毛 **2**（狐狸腋下毛皮） finest fragments of fox fur: ▸集～成裘 **3**［植物］ axil: ▸～芽

【腋臭】yèchòu〈名〉 armpit odour

【腋毛】yèmáo〈名〉 armpit hair

【腋窝】yèwō〈名〉 armpit

【腋芽】yèyá〈名〉［植物］ axillary bud

靥（靨） yè〈名〉〈书〉 dimple: ▸酒～, 笑～

yī

一[1] yī

A ▸**p. 691** ▸**p. 882**〈数〉 **1**（表数目） one: ～百公斤 one hundred kilograms ‖ ～本书 a book ‖ 两万～ twenty-one thousand ‖ 五分之～ one-fifth **2**（同一） same: 我们坐～趟火车。 We rode on the same train. ‖ 咱们是～家人。 We are of the same family. **3**（整个） all: 他～身油泥。 He was covered in grime. ‖ 她～路哭到了家。 She cried the whole way home. **4**（每） each: ～人一只苹果 one apple each ‖ ～日三餐 three meals a day **5**（另一） another: 乌贼～名墨斗鱼。 The cuttlefish is also known as the inkfish. **6**（表动作短暂） [used in the middle of a reduplicated verb meaning a little, slightly]: 看～看 have a look ‖ 笑～笑 give a smile ‖ 坐下来想～想 sit down and have a think

B〈副〉 **1**（表猛然） [used before a verb or adjective, indicating the suddenness or thoroughness of an action or a change in the situation]: 大吃～惊 be startled ‖ 眼前～黑 be suddenly unable to see anything **2**（表前后动作间隔短） as soon as: 他～合眼就睡着了。 No sooner had he closed his eyes than he fell asleep. ‖ 这你～学就会。 You can learn it in no time at all. **3**（一旦） now that: ▸～失足成千古恨 **4**（专一） wholeheartedly: ▸～心～意

一[2] yī〈名〉［音乐］ note on the *gongche* (工尺) scale, corresponding to a low 7 in *jianpu* (简谱) numbered musical notation

【一把鼻涕一把眼泪】yī bǎ bítì yī bǎ yǎnlèi〈惯〉 sniffles and sobs: ～地诉说自己的不幸 pour out one's grief in sniffles and sobs

【一把屎一把尿】yī bǎ shǐ yī bǎ niào〈惯〉 burden (of bringing up one's children)

【一把手】yībǎshǒu〈名〉 **1**（一个成员） partner: 我们一起干，你也算～吧? We will pool our efforts. Can we count you in? **2**（能干的人） capable hand: 他里里外外都是～。 He is good at everything he puts his hand to. ‖ 要说刺绣，她可真是～。 She is excellent at embroidery. **3**（第一负责人） first in command: 她曾是我们厂的～。 She used to be the head of our factory.

【一把钥匙开一把锁】yī bǎ yàoshi kāi yī bǎ suǒ〈俗〉 use different methods to solve different problems

【一把抓】yībǎzhuā〈动〉 **1**（事事亲自管） take everything into one's own hands **2**（不分轻重缓急） tackle problems without prioritizing them

【一百八十度大转弯】yībǎi bāshí dù dà zhuǎnwān〈惯〉 U-turn: 在态度上突然来了个～ make a sudden U-turn in one's approach

【一败如水】yībài-rúshuǐ〈成〉 suffer a crushing defeat

【一败涂地】yībài-túdì〈成〉 suffer a crushing defeat: 敌军被打得～。 The enemy was completely routed.

【一班人】yībānrén〈名〉 a small body of people working together: 党委～ members of the Party committee

【一般】yībān **A**〈形〉 **1**（一样） same: 钢铁～的意志 iron will ‖ 哥俩～高。 The two brothers are the same height. **2**（普通） ordinary: ～情况 normal circumstances ‖ 收成～ average harvest ‖ ～来说 generally speaking ‖ 他的工作很～，谈不上出色。 His work is merely mediocre, certainly not distinguished. **B**〈数量〉 one kind: 别有～滋味 have the same taste

【一般规律】yībān guīlǜ〈名〉 general rule

【一般过去时】yībān guòqùshí〈名〉［语法］ simple past tense

【一般化】yībānhuà〈形〉 ordinary

【一般见识】yībān jiànshi〈成〉 let oneself sink to sb.'s level: 他是个有修养的人，不会和你～。 He is a man of honour and won't let himself sink to the likes of you.

【一般现在时】yībān xiànzàishí〈名〉［语法］ simple present tense

【一板一眼】yībǎn-yīyǎn〈成〉 be scrupulous and methodical: 她办事总是～的。 She is always very scrupulous and methodical in her work.

【一半】yībàn〈名〉 one half: 不到～ less than half ‖ 把费用削减～ cut the costs by half ‖ 现在付～，剩下的以后再付。 Pay half now and the rest later.

【一半天】yībàntiān〈名〉〈口〉 a day or two: 我出去～。 I'll be away for a couple of days.

【一报还一报】yī bào huán yī bào〈惯〉 return like for like

【一饱眼福】yībǎoyǎnfú〈成〉 feast one's eyes: 游行的盛况使我们～。 The grandeur of the parade was a feast on our eyes.

【一辈子】yībèizi〈名〉 lifetime: 婚姻是～的事。 Marriage is for life. ‖ 他干了～消防工作。 He has spent a lifetime fighting fires.

【一本万利】yīběn-wànlì〈成〉 make big profits with a small investment: 这是～的事情。 This is a highly profitable undertaking.

【一本正经】yīběn-zhèngjīng〈成〉 be dead serious: 装得～的样子 preserve a mask of solemnity

【一鼻孔出气】yī bíkǒng chūqì〈惯〉〈贬〉〈喻〉 be hand in glove with

【一笔带过】yībǐ-dàiguò〈成〉 mention in passing: 这一点可以～。 You can just touch upon this point.

【一笔勾销】yībǐ-gōuxiāo〈成〉 write off at one stroke: 所有欠账～。 All debts have been written off.

【一笔抹杀】yībǐ-mǒshā〈成〉 condemn out of hand: 你不能～他的优点。 You can't just dismiss his strong points out of hand.

【一笔抹煞】yībǐ-mǒshā = 一笔抹杀 yībǐ-mǒshā

【一臂之力】yībìzhīlì〈成〉 offer sb. a helping hand: 你有困难，我会助你～。 If you get into trouble, I'll do all I can to help.

【一边】yībiān **A**〈名〉 **1**（一面） one side: 这块木板～光滑，～毛糙。 The piece of wood is smooth on one side and rough on the other. ‖ 在这个问题上我站在你的～。 I am on your side in this issue. **2**（一侧） either side: 他～坐着一个小孩儿。 There is a child sitting on either side of him. **B**〈副〉 as: ～跑～喊 shout as one runs ‖ 他们～学习～工作。 They learn while they work. **C**〈形〉〈口〉 same: 他俩～高。 They are the same height.

【一边倒】yībiāndǎo〈动〉 **1**（倾向一方） lean to one side: 在是非问题上要～，不能骑墙。 One must take sides in issues concerning right and wrong and not sit on the fence. **2**（一方占绝对优势） be far superior: 比赛一开始就～。 The match was dominated by one side from the outset.

【一表非凡】yībiǎo-fēifán〈成〉 have very unusual looks

【一表人才】yībiǎo-réncái〈成〉 be of very striking appearance: 新来的人长得～。 The newcomer was a man of striking appearance.

【一并】yībìng〈副〉 along with everyone else: 书和有关资料～寄上。 Enclosed are the book and the relevant materials.

【一病不起】yībìng-bùqǐ〈成〉 fall ill and die: 他怎么忽然～? How was it that he died so suddenly after such a brief illness?

【一波三折】yībō-sānzhé〈成〉 be full of ups and downs: 谈判～。 There were all kinds of ups and downs in the negotiations.

【一波未平，一波又起】yī bō wèi píng, yī bō yòu qǐ〈成〉〈喻〉 hardly has one trouble passed than another rises

【一不做，二不休】yī bù zuò, èr bù xiū〈成〉 see sth. through to the finish: 到这地步，我们只好～。 Now that we've gone as far as this, we must either go the whole hog or drop it altogether.

【一步到位】yībù-dàowèi〈成〉 settle a matter at one go: 所需资金已～。 All the money needed has been put in place.

【一步登天】yībù-dēngtiān〈成〉 have a meteoric rise: 他是靠裙带关系～的。 He rose to the top through nepotism.

【一步裙】yībùqún〈名〉 pencil skirt

【一步一个脚印】yī bù yīge jiǎoyìn〈惯〉〈喻〉 make progress one step at a time: ～地获得成功 adopt a down-to-earth approach to success

【一草一木】yīcǎo-yīmù〈成〉〈喻〉 every little thing: 爱护自然保护区的～ treasure every tree and every blade of grass in the nature preserve

【一差二错】yīchā-èrcuò〈成〉 mishap: 他要是有个～，谁负责? Who will take responsibility if anything happens to him?

【一刹那】yīchànà〈名〉 instant: 就在她快要倒下的～，有人伸手扶住了她。 The moment she was about to fall, somebody came and caught her in their arms.

【一刬】yīchàn〈副〉 **1**〈方〉（一概） without exception: ～新式家具 completely new styles of furniture **2**（总是） always: 他开会～不说话。 He always keeps silent at meetings.

【一场空】yīchángkōng〈动〉 come to nothing: 辛苦一年结果还是～。 After a really difficult year, all efforts came to nothing. ▸竹篮打水～

【一倡百和】 yīchàng-bǎihè = 一唱百和 yīchàng-bǎihè

【一唱百和】yīchàng-bǎihè〈成〉meet with general approval: 他一提议，大家果然～。 As expected, his proposal met with widespread approval.

【一唱一和】yīchàng-yīhè〈成〉 sing the same tune: 那两个国家在中东问题上总是～。 Those two countries have always sung the same tune on the Middle East issue.

【一朝天子一朝臣】yī cháo tiānzǐ yī cháo chén〈俗〉〈喻〉 a new chief brings in new aides: 总统一就职，政府也跟着换人，可谓～。 As has always been the case with a new administration, the government was filled with new faces as soon as the new president was sworn in.

【一尘不染】 yīchén-bùrǎn〈成〉 **1**［佛教］ be unstained by an evil environment **2**（指人品） be incorruptible: 身居闹市，～ remain uncontaminated amidst the temptations of a big city **3**（指环境） be spotless: 深秋时节，蔚蓝色的天空～，晶莹透明。 In mid-autumn, the spotless blue sky is glittering and translucent.

【一成不变】 yīchéng-bùbiàn〈成〉 unchangeable: 世界上没有～的东西。 Nothing in the world is immutable.

【一程子】yīchéngzi〈数量〉〈方〉 period of time: 老太太的病这～大好了。 The old lady's condition has been improving over the past few days.

【一筹】yīchóu〈名〉 brilliant move: 略胜～ a notch above

【一筹莫展】yīchóu-mòzhǎn〈成〉 be at the end of one's tether: 警方因缺乏证据而～。 The police were completely baffled by the lack of evidence.

【一触即发】yīchù-jífā〈成〉 be on the verge of breaking out: 形势～。 It is an explosive situation.

【一触即溃】yīchù-jíkuì〈成〉 collapse at the first encounter: 纪律涣散的军队很可能会～。 An army that lacks discipline would most probably be routed at the first encounter with the enemy.

【一传】yīchuán〈名〉［排球］ first pass

【一传十，十传百】yī chuán shí, shí chuán bǎi〈成〉 spread far and wide

【一串红】yīchuànhóng〈名〉［植物］ scarlet sage

【一锤定音】 yīchuí-dìngyīn〈成〉 give the final word: 这事只能由你～。 It's up to you to make the final decision.

【一锤子买卖】yī chuízi mǎimai〈惯〉 one-off deal: 做生意决不能搞～。 A businessman should never fleece customers so much that they will never come again.

【一词多义】yīcí-duōyì〈名〉［语言］ polysemy

【一次方程】yīcì fāngchéng〈名〉［数学］ linear equation

【一次性】yīcìxìng〈形〉 one-time: ～补助 give sb. a lump-sum grant ‖ ～筷子 disposable chopsticks

【一蹴而就】yīcù'érjiù〈成〉 succeed at the first attempt: 这些问题的解决不可能～。 These problems can't be solved overnight.

【一寸光阴一寸金】yī cùn guāngyīn yī cùn jīn〈俗〉 time is money

【一大早】yīdàzǎo〈名〉〈口〉 early morning

【一代】 yīdài〈名〉 **1**（朝代） dynasty **2**（时代） era: ～名儒 celebrated scholar of his time **3**（一生） lifetime: 老～ older generation ‖ 下～ subsequent generation ‖ 青年～ young generation

【一带】 yīdài〈名〉 district: 这～人口稠密。 This is a densely populated region. ‖ 江南～雨量充沛。 The area south of the Yangtze River enjoys plentiful rainfall.

【一旦】yīdàn **A**〈名〉 very short time: 毁于～ be destroyed in one day ‖ 溃于～ collapse overnight **B**〈副〉 once: ～时机成熟 once the time is ripe ‖ 机会～错过，永远不会再来。 Once an opportunity slips away, it is gone for good.

【一刀两断】yīdāo-liǎngduàn〈成〉〈喻〉 make a clean break: 她和他已～了。 She is already completely finished with him.

【一刀切】yīdāoqiē〈惯〉〈喻〉 make hard-and-fast rules: 我们不能在这个问题上搞～。 We should allow some flexibility on this issue.

【一道】yīdào〈副〉 together: ～干活 work side by side ‖ 咱俩～走吧。 Let's go together.

【一得之功】yīdézhīgōng〈成〉just an occasional, minor success: 不要满足于～。 We mustn't be content with just a minor success.

【一得之愚】 yīdézhīyú〈成〉〈谦〉 my humble opinion: 我所谈的只不过是我个人的～。 What I said just now was only my humble opinion.

【一等】yīděng〈形〉 first-class: ～奖 first prize ‖ ～品 first-rate product

【一等兵】yīděngbīng〈名〉**1**［陆军］（英国） lance corporal;（美国）private, first class **2**［海军］（英国） able seaman;（美国） seaman, first class **3**［空军］（英国） senior craftsman;（美国）airman, first class

【一等一】yīděngyī〈形〉 foremost: 他不仅精通业务，玩网络游戏也是～的高手。 He's not only good at business, he's also the foremost expert at online games.

【一点儿】 yīdiǎnr〈数量〉 **1**（表很少量） some: 多带～钱 take some more money ‖ 给我～水喝。 Give me some water to drink. **2**（表程度轻） a bit: ～不错 be perfectly correct ‖ ～不知道 not have the faintest idea ‖ ～活都不干 not do a stitch of work ‖ ～用处也没有 be utterly useless

【一点一滴】yīdiǎn-yīdī〈成〉 every little bit

【一丁点儿】 yīdīngdiǎnr〈数量〉〈口〉 a tiny bit: ～小事 a trifle

【一定】yīdìng **A**〈形〉 **1**（确定） definite: ～的规章制度 specified rules and regulations ‖ 他上班时间不～。 He doesn't keep regular office hours. **2**（适当） certain: 保持～距离 maintain a certain distance ‖ 我对这个课题曾有～的了解。 I had some previous acquaintance with the subject. **3**（相当） fair: 达到～水平 reach a fairly high level ‖ 在市场上占有～的份额 occupy a fairly big share in the market **4**（特定） specific: ～的文化是～的社会现实的反映。 A particular culture is a reflection of particular social realities. **B**〈副〉certainly: 我猜想他～是迷了路。 I figured that he must have got lost. ‖ 下次我～把那本书给你带来。 I'll definitely bring that book for you next time.

【一定之规】yīdìngzhīguī〈名〉**1**（指规则） fixed pattern: 事物的发展有～。 Everything follows a fixed pattern in its development. **2**（指主意） fixed idea: 你有锦囊妙计，我有～。 You have your brilliant idea and I have my own way.

【一动】 yīdòng〈副〉 easily: ～就发脾气 lose one's temper easily

【一动不如一静】yī dòng bùrú yī jìng〈俗〉 it is better to stay put than to move

【一度】yīdù **A**〈副〉 once: 这部小说～很受欢迎。 The novel was once very popular. **B**〈数量〉 one occasion: 四年～的奥运会 the once in every four years occasion of the Olympics ‖ 一年～的春节快到了。 The once-a-year occasion of Spring Festival is soon upon us.

【一端】yīduān〈名〉 **1**（一头儿） one end (of an object): ～朝上 be up on end **2**（一方面） one aspect/side of the matter: 各执～ each sticking to his own argument

【一多半】yīduōbàn ▸**p. 927**〈数〉〈口〉 part, most: 小组成员～是年轻人。 Most of the group's members are young people.

【一而再，再而三】yī ér zài, zài ér sān〈成〉 again and again: 我～地警告过你不要那样做。 I've warned you over and over not to do that.

【一二】yī'èr ▸**p. 691**〈数〉 one or two: 略知～ have some idea about ‖ 邀请～知己小聚 invite one or two close friends for a get-together

【一二·九运动】Yī'èr-Jiǔ Yùndòng〈名〉the December 9th Movement [demonstration staged on December 9, 1935 by Beijing students under the leadership of the Chinese Communist Party calling for resistance to Japanese aggression and national salvation]

【一发】yīfā〈副〉 **1**（越发） all the more: 如果处理不当，就～不可收拾了。 If not handled properly, the situation could become even more hopeless. **2**（一起） together: 书和有关资料～寄上。 I am sending you the book along with the material concerned.

【一发千钧】 yīfà-qiānjūn = 千钧一发 qiānjūn-yīfà

【一帆风顺】yīfān-fēngshùn〈成〉〈喻〉 plain sailing: 他的生意做得～。 His business is doing very well.

【一反常态】yīfǎn-chángtài〈成〉 act out of character: 对方～，突然同意了我方的建议。 The other side acted out of character and suddenly agreed to our proposal.

【一方有难，八方支援】yīfāng yǒu nàn, bāfāng zhīyuán〈成〉 when disaster strikes, help comes from all sides

【一飞冲天】yīfēi-chōngtiān〈成〉 amaze the world with the first achievements: 立下～志 have lofty aspirations

【一分耕耘，一分收获】yī fēn gēngyún, yī fēn shōuhuò〈俗〉 no pain, no gain

【一分钱掰成两半花】yī fēn qián bāi chéng liǎngbàn huā〈俗〉 make a little money go a long way

【一分钱一分货】yī fēn qián yī fēn huò〈俗〉 you get what you pay for

【一分为二】yīfēnwéi'èr〈成〉 there are two sides to everything

【一风吹】yīfēngchuī〈惯〉〈喻〉 write off at one stroke: 旧账新账统统～ write off all the debts, old and new ‖ 过去的事情～。 Let bygones be bygones.

【一佛出世，二佛涅槃】yī fó chūshì, èr fó nièpán〈成〉 half dead

【一夫当关，万夫莫开】yī fū dāng guān, wàn fū mò kāi〈成〉 [of a pass] strategically located and difficult of access

【一夫多妻制】yīfū-duōqīzhì〈名〉polygamy

【一夫一妻制】yīfū-yīqīzhì〈名〉 monogamy

【一概】yīgài〈副〉 without exception: ～否

y

定 categorically deny ‖ ～拒绝 reject without exception ‖ 这事我～不知。 I know nothing whatsoever about this matter.

【一概而论】yīgài'érlùn〈成〉 treat indiscriminately: 不可～ not to be treated alike

【一干】yīgān〈形〉 related: ～人犯 a bunch of criminals

【一干二净】yīgān-èrjìng〈成〉 thoroughly: 把地面打扫得～ sweep the floor spotlessly clean ‖ 把责任推脱得～ clear oneself of all blame

【一竿子插到底】yī gānzi chā dào dǐ〈惯〉〈喻〉 carry sth. through to its roots: 传达文件要～。 The document should be relayed right down to the grass-roots level.

【一哥】yīgē〈名〉 **1**（指运动员） top-ranked male: 中国乒乓球队的"～"马琳 China's number one table tennis player Ma Lin **2**（指演员） male lead

【一个巴掌拍不响】yīge bāzhang pāibùxiǎng〈俗〉〈喻〉 it takes two to tango: ～，发生冲突双方都有责任。 It takes two to make a quarrel. Both sides are responsible for the conflict.

【一个鼻孔出气】yīge bíkǒng chūqì = 一鼻孔出气 yī bíkǒng chūqì

【一个唱红脸，一个唱白脸】yīge chàng hóngliǎn, yīge chàng báiliǎn〈俗〉 one coaxes and the other coerces

【一个劲儿】yīgejìnr〈副〉〈口〉 continuously: 他～地催我走。 He urged me over and over to leave. ‖ 他总是～地称赞你。 He is forever singing your praises.

【一个篱笆三个桩，一个好汉三个帮】yīge líba sān gè zhuāng, yīge hǎohàn sān gè bāng〈俗〉 as a fence needs the support of three stakes, so an able fellow needs the help of three other people

【一个萝卜一个坑】yīge luóbo yīge kēng〈俗〉〈喻〉 everybody has their own task and no one is idle

【一个心眼儿】yīge xīnyǎnr〈惯〉 **1**（一心一意） wholeheartedly: ～为集体 work wholeheartedly for the collective **2**（固执） be of one mind: 他就是～，不会随机应变。 He is of one mind that does not bend with the times.

【一根筋】yīgēnjīn〈形〉〈喻〉 inflexible: 像他这样～的人不多。 There aren't many people as stubborn as him.

【一根藤上的瓜】yī gēn téngshangde guā〈惯〉〈喻〉 people who share weal and woe: 我们是～，不要分什么你我。 We are part of each other, so what's the difference between yours and mine?

【一共】yīgòng〈副〉 altogether: 我～要付多少钱？ How much shall I pay in all? ‖ 我们班～三十人。 There are thirty people in our class altogether.

【一股脑儿】yīgǔnǎor〈副〉〈口〉 completely: 她终于开口说话了，把自己的烦恼～倒了出来。 Eventually she began to talk, and she poured out all her troubles.

【一鼓作气】yīgǔ-zuòqì〈成〉 press on to the finish without let-up: 他～完成了工作。 He has done all his work in one go.

【一官半职】yīguān-bànzhí〈成〉 some official post or other: 捞个～ get an official post of some kind

【一贯】yīguàn〈形〉 consistent: ～的思想/政策 consistent idea/policy ‖ ～的行为 consistent behaviour

【一棍子打死】yī gùnzi dǎsǐ〈惯〉 knock sb. down in one blow: 不能因为他有错误就将他～。 We can't write him off as worthless just because he has made some mistakes.

【一锅端】yīguōduān〈惯〉〈喻〉 **1**（全部消灭） wipe out: 把贩毒分子～ get rid of drug traffickers once and for all **2**（尽其所能） give one's all: 我把对事情的看法～地倒了出来。 I've said all I have to say about this.

【一锅粥】yīguōzhōu〈名〉〈喻〉 a complete mess: 离婚和破产后，他的个人生活乱成了～。 With divorce and bankruptcy, his personal life was in a complete mess.

【一锅煮】yīguōzhǔ〈惯〉 handle different problems in the same way: 这两个问题不能～。 These two problems mustn't be treated in the same way.

【一国两制】yīguó-liǎngzhì〈名〉 one country, two systems

> **一国两制**
>
> A policy developed in 1979 by the Chinese Communist Party under Deng Xiaoping. Its aim was to re-establish sovereignty over Taiwan, Hong Kong and Macao, and to enable a capitalist system to exist within the socialist system of the People's Republic of China. The policy was given constitutional status in 1982.

【一哄而起】yīhōng'érqǐ〈成〉 jump on the bandwagon

【一哄而散】yīhòng'érsàn〈成〉 disperse in a hubbub

【一呼百应】yīhū-bǎiyìng〈成〉 be able to rally multitudes at a single call

【一晃】yīhuǎng〈动〉 pass in a flash: 窗外有个人影，～就不见了。 A figure flashed past the window.

【一晃】yīhuàng〈副〉 [of time] passing in a flash: ～几年过去了。 Several years have passed by in a flash.

【一挥而就】yīhuī'érjiù〈成〉 [in writing or painting] finish at one go

【一回生，二回熟】yī huí shēng, èr huí shú〈俗〉 first time strangers, and second time friends: 咱们～。 Now that we have met for a second time, we have become friends.

【一会儿】yīhuìr **A**〈数量〉 **1**（很短时间） a little while: 过了～ after a while ‖ 歇～ rest for a while ‖ 请等～。 One moment, please. **2**（短时间内） soon: 他们～就把机器修理好了。 They repaired the machine in no time. ‖ 坐吧，我～就完。 Please be seated. I won't be a minute. **B**〈副〉 now ... then ...: ～这么说，～那么说 say one thing at one time and another thing at another ‖ 天气～晴～阴。 The weather is clear one moment, cloudy the next.

【一级】yījí〈形〉 **1**（指级别） first class: ～运动员 first grade sportsman **2**（指级数） one-level: ～火箭 one-stage rocket

【一级方程式赛车】yījí fāngchéngshì sàichē〈名〉 Formula One car racing

【一级市场】yījí shìchǎng〈名〉 primary market

【一级演员】yījí yǎnyuán〈名〉 A-list actor

【一级战备】yījí zhànbèi〈名〉 first-degree combat readiness

【一己】yījǐ〈形〉 private: ～之私 one's own selfish interest

【一计不成，又生一计】yī jì bùchéng, yòu shēng yī jì〈成〉 when one plot fails, one tries another

【一技之长】yījìzhīcháng〈成〉 proficiency in a particular field: 有～的人谋生就容易多了。 Those with professional skills find it much easier to make a living.

【一家之言】yījiāzhīyán〈成〉 one doctrine or school of thought: ～，仅供参考。 As one theory/view, this is only for reference.

【一见倾心】yījiàn-qīngxīn〈成〉 fall in love at first sight

【一见如故】yījiàn-rúgù〈成〉 become instant friends: 两人～，成了好朋友。 As soon as the two of them met, they became firm friends.

【一见钟情】yījiàn-zhōngqíng〈成〉 fall in love at first sight: 她对他～。 She fell in love with him at first sight.

【一箭双雕】yījiàn-shuāngdiāo〈成〉〈喻〉 kill two birds with one stone

【一箭之仇】yījiànzhīchóu〈成〉 loss or defeat to be retrieved

【一箭之遥】yījiànzhīyáo〈成〉 a stone's throw

【一姐】yījiě〈名〉 **1**（指运动员） top-ranked female: "～"张怡宁夺得单打冠军。 Number one player Zhang Yining took the singles title. **2**（指演员） female lead: 电影界的～ best female film star

【一经】yījīng〈副〉 as soon as: ～指点，我恍然大悟。 As soon as I was pointed in the right direction, I understood what was going on.

【一举】yījǔ **A**〈名〉 one action: 成败在此～。 Success or failure hinges on this one action. **B**〈副〉 at one swoop: ～歼灭来犯之敌 wipe out the enemy at one fell swoop ‖ 她的书使她～成名。 Her book skyrocketed her to fame.

【一举两得】yījǔ-liǎngdé〈成〉 kill two birds with one stone: ～的好机会 good chance to kill two birds with one stone

【一决雌雄】yījué-cíxióng = 决一雌雄 jué-yīcíxióng

【一蹶不振】yījué-bùzhèn〈成〉〈口〉 never be able to recover after a setback: 受了处分后，他便～。 He never recovered after receiving the punishment.

【一卡通】yīkǎtōng〈名〉 e-card: 交通～ public transport e-card

【一刻】yīkè〈数量〉 a short time: 他的双手～也不停。 His hands were never still.

【一刻千金】yīkè-qiānjīn〈成〉 time is precious

【一客不烦二主】yī kè bù fán èr zhǔ〈俗〉 a guest should not have to trouble two hosts

【一空】yīkōng〈形〉 empty: 将财物洗劫～ loot all the belongings

【一孔之见】yīkǒngzhījiàn〈成〉〈谦〉 limited view: 这是我的～，请你指教。 This is nothing but my humble opinion. I look forward to your instruction.

【一口】yīkǒu **A**〈名〉 real thing: 讲～纯正的英语 speak pure English **B**〈副〉 readily: ～答应 readily agree ‖ ～否认/回绝 flatly deny/refuse **C**〈数量〉 **1**（一嘴） a mouthful: 抽～烟 take a puff at a cigarette ‖ 今天我们～饭都没吃。 We have not had a bite to eat today. **2**（指刀、井） [used for knives, wells, etc.]: ～井 a well

【一口气】yīkǒuqì〈副〉 without a break: ～看完了这本书 finish the book in one go ‖ ～跑到家 rush home without stopping

【一口咬定】yīkǒu-yǎodìng〈俗〉 assert positively

【一块儿】yīkuàir **A**〈名〉 the same place: 他们在～上学。 They study at the same school. **B**〈副〉 together: 咱们～走吧。 Let's go together.

【一块石头落地】yī kuài shítou luò dì〈俗〉 feel at ease: 很高兴你告诉我这一切，我现在的心情好比是～了。 I'm glad you've told me everything. That sets my mind at ease.

【一窥全豹】yīkuīquánbào〈成〉 see the whole picture

【一来二去】yīlái-èrqù〈成〉 over the course of several encounters: 他们～成了要好的朋友。 They became close friends over the course of several encounters.

【一览】yīlǎn〈动〉have an overview

【一览表】yīlǎnbiǎo〈名〉schedule: 火车行车时间～ train timetable

【一览无遗】yīlǎn-wúyí〈成〉have an uninterrupted view: 对海上景色～ have an uninterrupted view of the sea ‖ 在塔上可将四周群山～。The tower provides an unobstructed view of the neighbouring hills.

【一揽子】yīlǎnzi〈形〉comprehensive: ～计划 package plan

【一劳永逸】yīláo-yǒngyì〈成〉get sth. done once and for all: ～的解决办法 solution that holds good for all time

【一力】yīlì〈副〉〈书〉to the best of one's ability: ～成全 do one's best to help

【一例】yīlì〈副〉alike: ～看待 treat all in the same way

【一连】yīlián〈副〉in succession: ～下了几天雨。It rained for several days running. ‖ 他～三次夺魁。He has won the championship three times in a row.

【一连串】yīliánchuàn〈形〉successive: ～的爆炸事件 a series of explosions ‖ ～的想法 a train of thoughts

【一了百了】yīliǎo-bǎiliǎo〈成〉all troubles end when the main trouble ends: 死了就～了。Death relieves one of all his troubles.

【一鳞半爪】yīlín-bànzhǎo〈成〉〈喻〉odd bits: ～的信息 fragments of information

【一流】yīliú A〈名〉the same kind: 他属于印象派～人物。He is an impressionist. B〈形〉first-class: ～作家 first-class writer ‖ 世界～水平的运动员 world-class athlete

【一溜风】yīliùfēng〈副〉in a flash: 他～地跑了。He ran off like the wind.

【一溜儿】yīliùr A〈数量〉row: ～房屋 a row of houses B〈名〉neighbourhood: 他家就在这～。He lives nearby.

【一溜烟】yīliùyān〈副〉in a flash: 她～跑去买了些面包。She nipped out and bought some bread. ‖ 小男孩～跑了。The boy ran away swiftly.

【一路】yīlù A〈名〉1（全程）the whole journey: ～平安 bon voyage ‖ 他们～上饱览了沿途的秀丽景色。They have greatly enjoyed the beautiful scenery along the way. 2（同一类）the same kind: 别把我看作他们～人。Don't count me as one of them. B〈副〉1（一起）together: 我也去公园，咱俩～走。I am also going to the park. Let's go together. 2（一直）always: ～领先 be in the lead all the way

【一路货色】yīlù-huòsè〈成〉be cut from the same cloth

【一律】yīlǜ A〈形〉same: 强求～ impose uniformity ▸千篇～ B〈副〉all: 除研究人员外，其他人～不得入内。No admittance except to research staff. ‖ 男女～平等。All men and women are equal.

【一落千丈】yīluò-qiānzhàng〈成〉suffer a drastic decline: 父亲去世之后他的家境～。His family financial situation has rapidly worsened since the death of his father. ‖ 由于丑闻，他的声望～。His prestige suffered a disastrous decline because of the scandal.

【一麻黑】yīmáhēi〈形〉〈口〉pitch-dark

【一马当先】yīmǎ-dāngxiān〈成〉take the lead: 不管任务多么艰巨，他总是～，抢挑重担。However difficult the task, he is always the first to assume the heavy responsibilities.

【一马平川】yīmǎ-píngchuān〈成〉a wide expanse of flat land: 眼前是～。Before our eyes is a wide stretch of flat country.

【一码事】yīmǎshì〈名〉one and the same thing

【一脉相承】yīmài-xiāngchéng〈成〉come down in one continuous line: 这两种说法其实是～的。In fact, these two views can be traced to the same origin.

【一脉相传】yīmài-xiāngchuán = 一脉相承 yīmài-xiāngchéng

【一毛不拔】yīmáo-bùbá〈成〉〈喻〉very stingy

【一门心思】yīmén-xīnsi〈成〉heart and soul: ～搞研究 devote oneself heart and soul to research

【一米线】yīmǐxiàn〈名〉one-metre mark

【一面】yīmiàn A〈名〉1（几个面之一）one side: 向阳的～ the side that is exposed to the sun ‖ 这块木板～光滑，～粗糙。The wooden board is smooth on one side and rough on the other. 2（一个方面）one section: 独当～ take charge of a department ‖ 这既有有利的～，也有不利的～。This has both advantages and disadvantages. B〈副〉simultaneously: ～教，～学 learn while teaching ‖ 她～工作，～照管生病的孩子。She kept an eye on the sick child as she worked. C〈动〉〈书〉meet once: 未尝～ have never met before ▸～之交

【一面倒】yīmiàndǎo〈动〉be overwhelmingly superior to the other side

【一面之词】yīmiànzhīcí〈成〉one-sided statement: 不可轻信～ do not believe one-sided accounts

【一面之交】yīmiànzhījiāo〈成〉nodding acquaintance: 我与他有～。He and I are passing acquaintances.

【一鸣惊人】yīmíng-jīngrén〈成〉take the world by storm with a single brilliant feat

【一命呜呼】yīmìng-wūhū〈成〉die: 没想到三天后他就～了。Who could have known that he would drop dead three days later?

【一模一样】yīmú-yīyàng〈成〉as like as two peas in a pod: 她和她母亲长得～。She is the spitting image of her mother.

【一木难支】yīmù-nánzhī = 独木难支 dúmù-nánzhī

【一目了然】yīmù-liǎorán〈成〉be clear at a glance: 此事～。This matter is clear at a glance.

【一目十行】yīmù-shíháng〈成〉read fast

【一男半女】yīnán-bànnǚ〈成〉a son or a daughter: 生个～ give birth to a child or two

【一年半载】yīnián-bànzǎi〈成〉in a year or so: 这项工程～不可能竣工。There is no way that this project can be completed in the space of a year.

【一年到头】yīnián-dàotóu〈成〉all the year round: ～总是忙 be busy all year round

【一年生】yīniánshēng〈形〉[of plants] annual: ～作物 annual crop

【一年四季】yīnián-sìjì〈成〉all year round

【一年一度】yīnián-yīdù〈成〉once a year

【一念之差】yīniànzhīchā〈成〉a wrong decision made on the spur of the moment: ～使他走上了犯罪的道路。A momentary slip led him down the path of crime.

【一诺千金】yīnuò-qiānjīn〈成〉be true to one's word: 他是个～的人。He is a man of his word.

【一拍即合】yīpāi-jíhé〈成〉make an easy fit: 两人～，决定合作办公司。The two of them hit it off immediately and decided to set up a company together.

【一派胡言】yīpài-húyán〈成〉sheer nonsense

【一盘棋】yīpánqí〈名〉〈喻〉overall situation: 树立～思想 establish the mentality of approaching every situation holistically

【一盘散沙】yīpán-sǎnshā〈成〉〈喻〉be in a state of disunity

【一旁】yīpáng〈名〉one side: 站在～观看 stand and watch from the sidelines

【一炮打响】yīpào-dǎxiǎng〈成〉〈喻〉get off to a good start

【一片冰心】yīpiàn-bīngxīn〈成〉be morally pure

【一票通】yīpiàotōng〈名〉thorough ticket

【一票制】yīpiàozhì〈名〉one-ticket system: 实行～，旅客凭船票乘坐转运车辆，无需另外买票。Under the one-ticket system a passenger with a ferry ticket can use other transport without having to buy another ticket.

【一瞥】yīpiē A〈动〉take a glance: 温柔的～ a tender glance B〈名〉a brief survey: 家电市场～ a brief glimpse at the household appliance market

【一贫如洗】yīpín-rúxǐ〈成〉as poor as a church mouse: 我～。I don't have a penny to my name.

【一品】yīpǐn〈名〉〈旧〉highest official rank in imperial China

【一品红】yīpǐnhóng〈名〉［植物］poinsettia

【一曝十寒】yīpù-shíhán〈成〉〈喻〉work in fits and starts: 学习要持之以恒，不能～。You must persevere with your studies rather than approach them in fits and starts.

【一妻多夫制】yīqī-duōfūzhì〈名〉polyandry

【一齐】yīqí〈副〉simultaneously: ～鼓掌 clap in unison ‖ ～努力 make a concerted effort

【一起】yīqǐ A〈名〉the same place: 住在～ live in the same place ‖ 把东西放在～ put things together B〈副〉together: 大家～唱。Everyone sang together. ‖ 你跟我～去。You go with me.

【一气】yīqì A〈副〉at one go: ～跑到路尽头 run to the end of the road without stopping ▸～呵成 B〈动〉be of the same gang: 串通～ work hand in glove C〈数量〉a spell: 胡吹～ tell tall stories ‖ 瞎闹～ kick up a row

【一气呵成】yīqì-hēchéng〈成〉〈喻〉1（指文章）flow smoothly 2（指工作）do sth. without interruption: 这项工作是～的。The work was done in one sitting.

【一钱不值】yīqián-bùzhí〈成〉not worth a penny

【一抢而空】yīqiǎng'érkōng〈成〉take everything away

【一窍不通】yīqiào-bùtōng〈成〉be completely ignorant: 他对语言学～。Linguistics is a closed book to him.

【一切】yīqiè〈代〉1（各种）all: 调动～积极因素 bring all positive factors into play ‖ 想尽～办法 do everything one can 2（全部事物）everything: ～从人民利益出发 proceed in all cases from the interests of the people ‖ ～缴获要归公 turn in everything captured ‖ 他已失去了～。He has already lost everything.

【一清二白】yīqīng-èrbái〈成〉perfectly clean: 我～，不怕别人说什么。I have a clear conscience and therefore do not care what others say about me.

【一清二楚】yīqīng-èrchǔ〈成〉as clear as daylight: 我对此事～，知道该怎么办。The whole thing was crystal clear to me: I had no doubts as to what to do.

【一清早】yīqīngzǎo〈名〉early morning: ～去上班 go to work early in the morning

【一穷二白】yīqióng-èrbái〈成〉[of a place] be both poor and backward: 毕业后他回到家乡，决心改变那里～的面貌。After graduation, he returned to his hometown, determined to help lift it from poverty and ignorance.

【一丘之貉】yīqiūzhīhé〈成〉〈贬〉rogues cut from the same cloth: 他们都是～。They are all tarred with the same brush.

【一去不复返】yī qù bù fù fǎn〈成〉gone for ever
【一瘸一拐】yīquéyīguǎi〈动〉hobble alone
【一人传虚，万人传实】yī rén chuán xū, wàn rén chuán shí〈俗〉one person circulates a false story and ten thousand tell it as a fact
【一人得道，鸡犬升天】yī rén dédào, jīquǎn shēngtiān〈俗〉〈喻〉when a man gets to the top, all his relatives also rise to power
【一人做事一人当】yī rén zuòshì yī rén dāng〈俗〉a man must bear the consequences of his own acts
【一任】yīrèn〈动〉〈书〉allow: ～胡为 let sb. run amok
【一仍旧贯】yīréng-jiùguàn〈成〉follow the old routine: 时代变了，我们就不能～。Times have changed, so we cannot stick to old practices.
【一日夫妻百日恩】yī rì fūqī bǎi rì ēn〈俗〉one day of married life fosters enduring affection
【一日千里】yīrì-qiānlǐ〈成〉by leaps and bounds: 科学技术的发展～。Science and technology is developing at a tremendous pace.
【一日三秋】yīrì-sānqiū〈成〉absence makes the heart grow fonder
【一日游】yīrìyóu〈名〉day trip
【一日之雅】yīrìzhīyǎ〈成〉casual acquaintance: 我与所有客人并无～。All the guests were perfect strangers to me.
【一如】yīrú〈动〉〈书〉be just like: ～所见 be just like what we have seen ‖ ～所述 be just as was stated
【一如既往】yīrú-jìwǎng〈成〉just as before: 我们将～坚持改革开放。We will continue to pursue the policy of reform and opening up.
【一扫而光】yīsǎo'érguāng = 一扫而空 yīsǎo'érkōng
【一扫而空】yīsǎo'érkōng〈成〉be swept clean away: 他积压在胸中的愁苦已经～。The grief and sorrow that had been weighing on his mind has already been completely lifted.
【一色】yīsè〈形〉**1**（颜色一样）of the same colour: 水天～。The water and the sky are of one hue. **2**（全部一样）uniform: ～的六层楼房 six-storeyed buildings of a uniform style
【一霎】yīshà〈名〉instant: ～工夫就不见他的影子了。He vanished in a flash.
【一身】yīshēn〈名〉**1**（全身）whole body: ～泥巴 be covered all over in mud ‖ ～是病 be afflicted by several ailments **2**（一个人）a single person: ～二任 hold two posts at the same time
【一身是胆】yīshēn-shìdǎn〈成〉know no fear
【一身正气】yīshēn-zhèngqì〈成〉be of absolute integrity
【一神教】yīshénjiào〈名〉［宗教］monotheism
【一审】yīshěn〈名〉**1**［法律］first trial **2**（指审读）preliminary appraisal (of a manuscript, thesis, etc.)
【一审法院】yīshěn fǎyuàn〈名〉court of first instance
【一审判决】yīshěn pànjué〈名〉judgement of first instance
【一生】yīshēng〈名〉all one's life: 虚度～ pass one's life in idleness ‖ ～坎坷 have a rough time in life ‖ ～受用 enjoy the benefit for one's whole life ‖ 平淡的～ uneventful life ‖ 他～从事医学研究。He devoted all his life to medical research.
【一声不吭】yīshēng-bùkēng〈成〉not say a word
【一失足成千古恨】yī shīzú chéng qiāngǔ hèn〈成〉one false move may cause lasting sorrow
【一时】yīshí **A**〈名〉**1**（一个时期）a period of time: 此～，彼～。Times have changed. **2**（短时间）a short while: 看一个人不要看他的～一事。Don't judge a person by a single factor in their life. ▸～半会儿，～半刻 **B**〈副〉**1**（偶尔）temporarily: ～冲动 act on a spur-of-the-moment impulse ‖ ～糊涂 get temporarily confused ‖ ～想不起来 can't recall it offhand **2**（时而）one moment ..., the next ...: 天气～冷，～热。The weather is cold one moment, hot the next. ‖ 他的病～好，～坏。His condition is sometimes good, sometimes bad.
【一时半会儿】yīshí-bànhuìr〈名〉〈口〉brief period of time: 恐怕他～回不来。I'm afraid he won't be back any time soon.
【一时半刻】yīshí-bànkè〈成〉a short time: 这事儿～办不成。This can't be done in a short time.
【一世】yīshì〈名〉**1**（一生）all one's life: ▸聪明～，糊涂一时 **2**（一个时代）one generation: ～之雄 hero of the times
【一事无成】yīshì-wúchéng〈成〉achieve nothing: 虽已两鬓斑白，却仍～。Though he is already getting old, he has accomplished nothing.
【一试身手】yīshì-shēnshǒu〈动〉try one's hand
【一视同仁】yīshì-tóngrén〈成〉treat all alike: 对学生们～ treat all students equally
【一是一，二是二】yī shì yī, èr shì èr〈成〉call a spade a spade: 男子汉大丈夫，～。A true man never equivocates.
【一手】yīshǒu **A**〈名〉**1**（本领）skill: 露～ show off one's skill ‖ 业务上有～ know one's stuff **2**（手段）trick: 他这～真毒辣! What a vicious trick he played! **B**〈副〉single-handed: ～策划 engineer single-handedly ‖ 把孩子～拉扯大 bring a child up all by oneself ‖ 他的婚事是父母～包办的。His marriage was stage-managed by his parents.
【一手遮天】yīshǒu-zhētiān〈成〉pull the wool over people's eyes: 岂能容忍他～? How can we put up with his hoodwinking?
【一瞬】yīshùn〈名〉the twinkling of an eye: ～即逝 vanish in a flash ‖ ～间 a fleeting moment
【一顺儿】yīshùnr〈形〉corresponding
【一丝】yīsī〈数量〉a tiny bit: 孩子脸上露出了～笑容。A trace of a smile appeared on the child's face.
【一丝不苟】yīsī-bùgǒu〈成〉be not in the least bit negligent: ～的工作作风 scrupulous working style
【一丝不挂】yīsī-bùguà〈成〉bestark-naked: 她全身赤条条的，～。She is stark naked.
【一丝一毫】yīsī-yīháo〈成〉a tiny bit
【一塌糊涂】yītāhútú〈成〉chaotic: 她在学校的成绩～。She got terrible results in school. ‖ 屋子乱得～。The room was in a complete mess.
【一胎率】yītāilǜ〈名〉one-child family ratio
【一潭死水】yītán-sǐshuǐ〈成〉〈喻〉lifeless condition
【一体】yītǐ〈名〉**1**（一个整体）an integral whole: 融为～ merge into an organic whole **2**（所有人）everyone: 望～遵照执行。It is hoped that everyone will abide by this.
【一体化】yītǐhuà〈名〉integration: 经济～ economic integration ‖ 城乡～ integration of urban and rural areas
【一体机】yītǐjī〈名〉multifunction (office) machine: 电话、打印、复印、传真～ all-in-one copier/printer/fax/phone
【一天到晚】yītiān-dàowǎn〈成〉from morning till night
【一条道走到黑】yī tiáo dào zǒu dào hēi〈俗〉stick obstinately to one course
【一条龙】yītiáolóng〈惯〉〈喻〉**1**（指队列）one continuous line: 十几辆车排成～，向前开动。A dozen trucks moved ahead one after another in a long line. **2**（指工作环节、程序）coordinated process: 实行产、运、销～ make production, transportation and marketing a coordinated process
【一条心】yītiáoxīn〈惯〉be of one mind: 军民～。Our army and the people are of one mind. ‖ 只要我们～，就没有克服不了的困难。So long as we are united as one, there will be no insurmountable difficulties for us.
【一通百通】yītōng-bǎitōng〈成〉grasp this one thing and you'll grasp everything
【一同】yītóng〈副〉together: ～工作 work together
【一统】yītǒng〈动〉unify: ～天下 unify the whole country
【一头】yītóu **A**〈副〉**1**（一面）[of several things happening at the same time]: 他～说，～朝门口走。As he talked, he headed for the door. **2**（径直）straight away: 门一开，他就～钻了进去。As soon as the door opened, he went in straight away. **3**（突然）unexpectedly: 我刚进门就～撞上了老板。I bumped into the boss the moment I came in. **4**（头部突然往下）headlong: ～扎进水里 plunge headlong into the water **B**〈名〉**1**（一端）one end: 我们从街道的～走到另～。We walked the street from end to end. **2**（一个头的高度）a head: 高出～ be taller by a head
【一头雾水】yītóu-wùshuǐ〈成〉be com pletely muddle-headed: 他讲了半天，我还是～。He talked and talked but I still couldn't figure out what he was driving at.
【一吐为快】yītǔ-wéikuài〈成〉feel relief after getting it all out
【一团和气】yītuán-héqì〈成〉keep on the right side of everyone
【一团麻】yītuánmá〈惯〉a complete mess: 心里乱成～ be in a completely confused state of mind
【一团漆黑】yītuán-qīhēi = 漆黑一团 qīhēi-yītuán
【一团糟】yītuánzāo〈形〉completely chaotic: 把事情弄得～ make a mess of sth. ‖ 瞧你把我的东西搞得～。Just look at what a mess you are making of my things.
【一退六二五】yī tuì liù èr wǔ〈惯〉evade all responsibility: 你是主管，出了问题哪能～? You are in charge, so how can you shirk responsibility when things go wrong?
【一拖再拖】yītuōzàituō〈动〉postpone again and again
【一碗水端平】yī wǎn shuǐ duānpíng〈惯〉be fair and impartial: 当领导的要～，不能搞亲亲疏疏。A leader must treat everyone equally and guard against favouritism.
【一网打尽】yīwǎng-dǎjìn〈成〉〈喻〉capture all in one haul: 警察一举将这个走私团伙～。The police captured all the members of the smuggling ring in one fell swoop.
【一往情深】yīwǎng-qíngshēn〈成〉be deeply attached: 他在国外居住了半个世纪，但对自己的祖国仍～。Although he has lived abroad for half a century, his love for his motherland has not diminished at all.
【一往无前】yīwǎng-wúqián〈成〉advance indomitably: ～的精神 indomitable spirit

【一望无际】yīwàng-wújì〈成〉stretch as far as the eye can see: 远处是~的麦田。Beyond there is a vast expanse of wheat fields.

【一望无垠】yīwàng-wúyín = 一望无际 yīwàng-wújì

【一维】yīwéi〈形〉one-dimensional

【一味】yīwèi〈副〉merely: ~迁就 make one concession after another ‖ ~追求数量 concentrate on quantity alone

【一文不名】yīwén-bùmíng〈成〉not have a penny to one's name

【一文不值】yīwén-bùzhí〈成〉completely worthless

【一问三不知】yī wèn sān bù zhī〈成〉be completely ignorant: 别问他了，他总是~。Don't ask him any questions. He never knows anything.

【一窝蜂】yīwōfēng〈副〉in a swarm: ~地去炒股 scramble to profiteer with stocks ‖ 学生们~似地奔向操场。The students swarmed towards the playground.

【一无是处】yīwú-shìchù〈成〉be devoid of any merit: 他总是把我说得~。He never has a good word to say about me.

【一无所长】yīwú-suǒcháng〈成〉have no special skill

【一无所成】yīwú-suǒchéng〈成〉have accomplished nothing

【一无所获】yīwú-suǒhuò〈成〉end up with nothing: 部队在森林里搜了15天，结果~。The troops searched the forest for fifteen days without result.

【一无所有】yīwú-suǒyǒu〈成〉not have a thing to one's name

【一无所知】yīwú-suǒzhī〈成〉know nothing about: 我对此~。I'm completely in the dark about this.

【一五一十】yīwǔ-yīshí〈成〉〈喻〉give a detailed account: 她把这事~地告诉了我。She told me everything that had happened.

【一物降一物】yī wù xiáng yī wù〈俗〉everything has its nemesis

【一息尚存】yīxī-shàngcún〈成〉till one's last gasp: ~，奋斗不止 keep on working till one's last gasp

【一席话】yīxíhuà〈名〉what one says in one conversation: 他的~使我茅塞顿开。His remarks made me see the light all of a sudden.

【一席之地】yīxízhīdì〈成〉niche: 在文坛上有~ have a proper place in the literary world

【一系列】yīxìliè〈形〉a series of: ~措施/讲座 a series of measures/lectures ‖ ~问题 a whole series of questions/problems

【一下】yīxià **A**〈数量〉[used after a verb as its complement, indicating an act or an attempt] once: 看~ have a look ‖ 试~ have a try ‖ 睡~ have a little sleep **B**〈副〉all at once: 他被~解除了所有职务。He was summarily stripped of all his official titles. ‖ 天~阴了下来。All of a sudden it became overcast.

【一下子】yīxiàzi = 一下 yīxià

【一线】yīxiàn **A**〈名〉front line: 抗击非典~医护人员 doctors and nurses in the front line of the fight against SARS ‖ 生产~工人 workers in the forefront of production **B**〈数量〉a ray of: ~生机 a slim chance of survival ‖ ~希望 a ray of hope

【一相情愿】yīxiāng-qíngyuàn〈成〉one's own wishful thinking: 这只是你的~。This is just your own wishful thinking.

【一厢情愿】yīxiāng-qíngyuàn = 一相情愿 yīxiāng-qíngyuàn

【一向】yīxiàng **A**〈名〉period of time in the past: 这~你到哪里去了? Where have you been lately? ‖ 前~雨水较多。There was quite a lot of rain earlier on. **B**〈副〉**1**（总是）always: 经理~善于用人。Our manager always gets the best out of people. ‖ 他~老实。He is always honest. **2**（最近）recently: 你~可好? How have you been lately?

【一小撮】yīxiǎocuō〈形〉a handful of: ~敌人 a handful of enemies

【一笑置之】yīxiào-zhìzhī〈成〉dismiss with a laugh: 大家对他们的那些议论~。We shrugged off their argument with a laugh.

【一些】yīxiē〈数量〉**1**（表不定数量）a few: ~国家 some countries ‖ 每个盘子里都盛~。Just put a little on each plate. **2**（不止一种）certain: 他担任过~重要职务。He has had a number of important positions. ‖ 有~问题还没搞清楚。Some problems have still not been resolved. **3**（略微）[placed after an adjective, indicating a slight change in degree]: 请走慢~。Please walk more slowly.

【一泻千里】yīxiè-qiānlǐ〈成〉**1**（指江河）flow with force: 长江水~，注入东海。The Yangtze River rushes down for ten thousand *li* and empties into the East China Sea. **2**（指写作风格）be bold and flowing: 他文笔流畅，~。He writes with great ease and his style is bold and flowing.

【一蟹不如一蟹】yī xiè bùrú yī xiè〈成〉〈喻〉each one is worse than the last

【一心】yīxīn **A**〈副〉heart and soul: ~为人民谋福利 work heart and soul in the interests of the people ‖ ~想出国留学 be intent on going abroad to study **B**〈形〉united as one: 万众~。Millions of people are all of one mind.

【一心不能二用】yī xīn bùnéng èr yòng〈俗〉you can't do two things at the same time

【一心一德】yīxīn-yīdé〈成〉be of one heart and one mind

【一心一意】yīxīn-yīyì〈成〉wholeheartedly: ~扑在工作上 devote oneself heart and soul to one's work

【一新】yīxīn〈形〉brand new: 房屋修缮~。The house has been completely renovated. ▸焕然~, 面目~

【一星半点儿】yīxīng-bàndiǎnr〈成〉a tiny bit: ~诚意也没有 lack an ounce of sincerity

【一行】yīxíng〈名〉a group travelling together: ~五十人的代表团 fifty-person delegation ‖ 他们~五人昨天到达北京。The five of them arrived in Beijing yesterday.

【一宿】yīxiǔ〈名〉〈口〉one night: ~没合眼 not sleep a wink the whole night

【一言半语】yīyán-bànyǔ〈成〉just a word or two

【一言不发】yīyán-bùfā〈成〉not utter a word

【一言既出，驷马难追】yī yán jì chū, sìmǎ nán zhuī〈成〉what is said cannot be unsaid

【一言九鼎】yīyán-jiǔdǐng〈成〉one's words carry great weight

【一言难尽】yīyán-nánjìn〈成〉it's a long story: 这几年你过得怎么样啊? ——~。How have you been doing all these years? — It's a long story.

【一言堂】yīyántáng〈名〉one person lays down the law: 要搞"群言堂"，不搞"~"。Let everyone have his say, not just one.

【一言为定】yīyán-wéidìng〈成〉it's a deal: ~，成本我们分摊。That's settled then. We'll divide the cost. ‖ ~，就这样办。It's a deal. We'll do it like this.

【一言一行】yīyán-yīxíng〈成〉what one says and does: 父母的~都会对孩子有影响。Everything parents say and do has an influence on their children.

【一言以蔽之】yī yán yǐ bì zhī〈成〉in a nutshell

【一氧化碳】yīyǎnghuàtàn〈名〉[化学] carbon monoxide

【一样】yīyàng〈形〉same: 你和我~，都与此事有关。You and I have equal stakes in this matter. ‖ 这么一来，问题的性质就不~了。This makes things look a little different. ▸一模~

【一叶蔽目，不见泰山】yī yè bì mù, bù jiàn Tàishān = 一叶障目，不见泰山 yī yè zhàng mù, bù jiàn Tàishān

【一叶障目，不见泰山】yī yè zhàng mù, bù jiàn Tàishān〈成〉〈喻〉cannot see the wood for the trees

【一叶知秋】yīyè-zhīqiū〈成〉**1**〈本〉the falling of one leaf is enough to tell of autumn's arrival **2**〈喻〉a small sign can indicate a great trend

【一夜情】yīyèqíng〈名〉one-night stand

【一一】yīyī〈副〉one by one: ~告别 say goodbye to everyone one by one ‖ 把你想到的~写下来。Write down everything that comes into your mind.

【一衣带水】yīyīdàishuǐ〈成〉separated only by a narrow strip of water: 日本同中国是~的邻邦。Japan is separated from China by a mere strip of water.

【一意孤行】yīyì-gūxíng〈成〉insist on doing things in one's own way: 我警告过他有危险，但他还是~。I had warned him of the danger, but he was determined to do things his own way.

【一饮而尽】yīyǐn'érjìn〈成〉finish off the drink with one gulp

【一应】yīyīng〈代〉all: ~花销我全包了。I will pay all the expenses.

【一应俱全】yīyīng-jùquán〈成〉well-stocked with everything one might need: 这家小商店各种电器~俱全。This small shop supplies all kinds of electrical appliances.

【一拥而上】yīyōng'érshàng〈成〉rush up in a crowd

【一隅】yīyú〈书〉**A**〈名〉corner: ~之地 very small area **B**〈形〉one-sided: ~之见 very limited view

【一隅三反】yīyú-sānfǎn = 举一反三 jǔyī-fǎnsān

【一语道破】yīyǔ-dàopò〈成〉hit the nail on the head

【一语破的】yīyǔ-pòdì〈成〉hit the nail on the head

【一语双关】yīyǔ-shuāngguān〈成〉pun

【一元方程】yīyuán fāngchéng〈名〉[数学] equation with one unknown quantity

【一元化】yīyuánhuà **A**〈动〉centralize **B**〈形〉unified: ~管理 unified management ‖ ~领导 unified leadership

【一元论】yīyuánlùn〈名〉[哲学] monism

【一月】yīyuè ▸**p. 928**〈名〉**1**（阳历）January **2**（阴历）first month of the lunar year **3**（一个月）a month

【一再】yīzài〈副〉again and again: ~警告某人 caution sb. repeatedly ‖ ~宣称 declare time and again ‖ 她~道歉。She was profuse in her apologies.

【一早儿】yīzǎor〈名〉〈口〉early morning: 他今天~就出去了。He went out early this morning.

【一站式】yīzhànshì〈形〉one-stop: ~服务 one-stop service

【一张一弛】yīzhāng-yīchí〈成〉tense up and relax alternately:〈喻〉~，劳逸结合 strike a balance between tension and relaxation, work and play

【一长制】yīzhǎngzhì〈名〉system of one-man leadership

【一招一式】yīzhāo-yīshì〈成〉[in martial arts or traditional opera] every posture and movement

【一着不慎，满盘皆输】yī zhāo bù shèn, mǎn pán jiē shū〈成〉〈喻〉one careless move and the whole game is lost

【一朝】yīzhāo〈副〉once: ～覆亡 collapse in one short day

【一朝被蛇咬，十年怕井绳】yīzhāo bèi shé yǎo, shí nián pà jǐngshéng〈俗〉once bitten, twice shy

【一朝一夕】yīzhāo-yīxī〈成〉one day: 非～之功 not the work of a single day

【一针见血】yīzhēn-jiànxiě〈成〉〈喻〉hit the nail on the head: 她的话～。What she said hit home.

【一针一线】yīzhēn-yīxiàn〈成〉a little property: 不拿群众～ never take the least items of property from the masses

【一枕黄粱】yīzhěn-huángliáng〈成〉pipe dream: 他的计划不现实，后来成了～。His plan was impractical and turned out to be nothing but a pipe dream.

【一阵】yīzhèn〈数量〉[used to indicate the duration of an action]: ～恶心 a rush of nausea ‖ ～狂风 a violent gust of wind ‖ ～掌声 a burst of applause

【一阵风】yīzhènfēng **A**〈副〉like a whirlwind: 她～似地跑来了。She came running over like a whirlwind. **B**〈动〉be transient: 反腐败不能～，要一抓到底。The anti-corruption campaign is a long-term undertaking and must be carried out to the end.

【一枝独秀】yīzhī-dúxiù〈成〉outshine others

【一知半解】yīzhī-bànjiě〈成〉have scanty knowledge: 满足于～ rest content with a smattering of knowledge

【一直】yīzhí〈副〉**1**（顺着一个方向）straight: ～往东 go straight eastward ‖ ～走 keep going straight **2**（持续不断）all along: 雨～下个不停。It kept on raining. ‖ 这个案子～无人过问。The case continues to go uninvestigated. **3**（强调所指范围）all the way: 他的一席话使我从心窝～热到全身。What he said made me feel warm all over.

【一纸空文】yīzhǐ-kōngwén〈成〉a mere scrap of paper: 该合同已成～。The contract has become nothing but scrap paper.

【一致】yīzhì **A**〈形〉identical: 步调～ act in unison ‖ 意见不～ do not share the same views ‖ 双方根本利益是～的。Both sides share the same fundamental interests. **B**〈副〉together: ～同意 agree unanimously ‖ ～反对 be unanimously opposed

【一掷千金】yīzhì-qiānjīn〈成〉spend money like water

【一柱擎天】yīzhù-qíngtiān〈成〉〈喻〉be capable of taking on important responsibilities

【一转眼】yīzhuǎnyǎn〈副〉in the turn of a hand

【一准】yīzhǔn〈副〉〈口〉certainly: 她～能来。She is definitely going to come.

【一字长蛇阵】yīzì chángshézhèn〈名〉single-line battle array: 摆开～ string out in a long line

【一字千金】yīzì-qiānjīn〈成〉highly finished artistic work

【一总】yīzǒng〈副〉**1**（总共）altogether: 她～儿花了五十元。She spent 50 *yuan* in all. **2**（全部）all: 这些任务～交给你干。We'll leave all the tasks to you.

【一醉方休】yīzuìfāngxiū〈成〉drink oneself into oblivion

伊[1] yī〈助〉〈书〉[used before a word or an expression for emphasis]: ～谁之力？To whom should the credit go?

伊[2] yī〈代〉**1**〈书〉（这）this;（那）that: ▶～人 **2**（她）she;（他）he

【伊甸园】Yīdiànyuán〈名〉［基督教］Garden of Eden

【伊拉克】Yīlākè〈名〉Iraq: ～共和国 Republic of Iraq ‖ ～人 Iraqi

【伊朗】Yīlǎng〈名〉Iran: ～人 Iranian ‖ ～伊斯兰共和国 Islamic Republic of Iran

【伊利岛郡】Yīlìdǎojùn〈名〉Isle of Ely

【伊利诺伊州】Yīlìnuòyīzhōu〈名〉Illinois

【伊妹儿】yīmèir〈名〉e-mail

【伊人】yīrén〈代〉〈书〉that person [esp a woman]

【伊始】yīshǐ〈名〉〈书〉beginning: 新年～ beginning of a new year ‖ 下车～ the moment one takes up a new post

【伊斯兰堡】Yīsīlánbǎo〈名〉Islamabad

【伊斯兰教】Yīsīlánjiào〈名〉Islam

【伊斯兰教教徒】Yīsīlánjiào jiàotú〈名〉Muslim

【伊斯兰教历】Yīsīlánjiàolì〈名〉Muslim calendar

【伊斯坦布尔】Yīsītǎnbù'ěr〈名〉Istanbul

【伊战】Yīzhàn〈名〉Iraq War

衣 yī〈名〉**1**（衣服）clothes: 更～ change one's clothes ‖ 有饭吃，有～穿，

---

i 一

a/an/one 等于汉语的"一"

■ 谈及整数、分数、金钱、度量衡时，a/an/one 相当于汉语的"一"，而且它们可互相代替：

一百
= a/one hundred

五分之一
= a/one fifth

一元
= a/one yuan

一便士
= a/one penny

一米
= a/one metre

一公斤
= a/one kilo

一升
= a/one litre

■ 算数或表达数量的概念时，one 相当于"一"，但这时不能用 a/an 代替：

我要了两个汉堡包，不是一个
= I asked for two burgers, not one

请给我一根香蕉
= Give me one banana, please

一加二等于三
= One plus two is three

他整整花了一百天游遍了整个欧洲
= He spent exactly one hundred days travelling all over Europe

我女儿刚满一岁
= My daughter is just one year old

桌子上有两个苹果和一个橘子
= There are two apples and one orange on the table

a/an/one 不等于汉语的"一"

■ 表示"…之一"或"其中一个…"时，英语要用 one，而不能用 a/an：

我其中一个儿子在读大学
= One of my sons is studying at university

李鸿是我们学校最帅的男孩之一
= Li Hong is one of the coolest boys in our school

■ 第一次提到某人或某物，或者不指定某个特定的人或物时，汉语用"(一) 个/位/件…"等（"一"可省去不用），而英语要用 a/an，不能用 one：

她买了条裤子，穿上很合身
= She bought a pair of trousers. They suit her well

我母亲给我买了（一）本书，这本书很有趣
= My mother bought me a book. The book is very interesting

他有个妻子
= He's got a wife

我有（一）只宠物猫
= I have a pet cat

■ 汉语用"每"的时候，英语可用 a/an，一般不用 one：

我每周看一次电影
= I see a film once a week

她每年挣一百万美元
= She earns a million dollars a year

她每天洗两次淋浴
= She has a shower twice a day

钢琴课一般是每小时 100 元
= The piano lesson is usually 100 yuan an hour

自助餐每位 6 镑
= The buffet is £6 a/per person

■ 谈及某类事物中的任何一个时，汉语不用任何冠词，而英语用 a/an，不能用 one：

她会骑马
= She can ride a horse

我很想喝啤酒
= I'd love a beer

■ 谈及职业时，英语要在表示职业的名词前用 a/an：

她是工程师
= She is an engineer

他是电脑专家
= He is a computer specialist

■ 汉语指某个"张先生"等时（说话者不认识），英语用 a/an：

有个杨小姐打过电话
= There was a call from a Miss Yang

一位姓张的先生想见你
= A Mr. Zhang wants to see you

有房子住 have food to eat, clothes to wear and a roof over one's head ▸～冠楚楚，丰～足食，棉～ 2（包在外面的一层东西）coating: 花生～ peanut skin ▸炮～，糖～ 3（胞衣）placenta: ▸～胞，胎～ ▸yì
【衣阿华州】Yī'āhuázhōu〈名〉Iowa
【衣摆】yībǎi〈名〉lower hem: 把～放长 let the hem down ‖ 把～改短 take the hem up
【衣胞】yībao〈名〉afterbirth
【衣钵】yībō〈名〉〈喻〉legacy: 继承～ inherit sb.'s mantle
【衣不蔽体】yībùbìtǐ〈成〉wear rags
【衣橱】yīchú〈名〉wardrobe
【衣兜】yīdōu〈名〉pocket
【衣服】yīfu〈名〉clothes: 叠～ fold up one's clothes ‖ 定做～ have clothes made to one's order ‖ 缝制～ sew clothes ‖ 晒～ hang out clothes ‖ 洗～ wash one's clothes ‖ 熨～ iron clothes ‖ 带上两件换洗的～。Take two changes of clothing with you.
【衣钩】yīgōu〈名〉clothes peg〈英〉; clothespin〈美〉
【衣冠楚楚】yīguān-chǔchǔ〈成〉be well dressed: 两人～。Both were well turned out.
【衣冠禽兽】yīguān-qínshòu〈成〉beast in human clothing
【衣冠冢】yīguānzhǒng〈名〉cenotaph
【衣柜】yīguì〈名〉wardrobe: 三门大～ three-door cabinet
【衣架】yījià〈名〉clothes rack
【衣架子】yījiàzi〈名〉1 = 衣架 yījià 2〈喻〉（好身材）good figure: 她是个天生的～。She's a born model (of clothes).
【衣襟】yījīn〈名〉front of a garment
【衣锦还乡】yījǐn-huánxiāng〈成〉return home after achieving wealth and power
【衣来伸手，饭来张口】yī lái shēnshǒu, fàn lái zhāngkǒu〈俗〉live off others' labour
【衣料】yīliào〈名〉dress material: ～考究 choice materials
【衣领】yīlǐng〈名〉collar: 翻上/下～ turn up/down a collar ‖ 竖/高/软～ stand-up/high/soft collar ‖ ～净 collar cleaner
【衣帽钩】yīmàogōu〈名〉hat-and-coat hook
【衣帽架】yīmàojià〈名〉clothes stand
【衣帽间】yīmàojiān〈名〉cloakroom; checkroom〈美〉
【衣衫】yīshān〈名〉clothing: ～褴褛 be shabbily dressed
【衣裳】yīshang〈名〉〈口〉clothes
【衣食】yīshí〈名〉clothes and food: ～丰足 ample clothing and food
【衣食父母】yīshí-fùmǔ〈成〉those on whom one's livelihood depends
【衣食住行】yī-shí-zhù-xíng〈成〉basic necessities of life
【衣饰】yīshì〈名〉clothes and jewellery
【衣物】yīwù〈名〉clothing and other articles of daily use: 收拾～ pack up one's bits and pieces
【衣箱】yīxiāng〈名〉suitcase
【衣袖】yīxiù〈名〉sleeve
【衣鱼】yīyú〈名〉silverfish
【衣原体】yīyuántǐ〈名〉［医学］chlamydia
【衣着】yīzhuó〈名〉clothing, headgear and footwear: ～寒酸/华丽 be shabbily/loudly dressed ‖ ～讲究 be particular about one's clothes ‖ ～整洁 be neatly dressed

医（醫）yī

A〈名〉1（医生）doctor: 四处求～ go all over looking for a cure ▸～生，军～ 2（医学）medical science, medicine: 学～ study medicine ▸中～，～学院
B〈动〉cure: 送～上门 treat patients in their homes ‖ 病还未～好。The illness still hasn't quite gone. ▸就～，行～
【医案】yī'àn〈名〉〈旧〉［中医］medical record
【医保】yībǎo〈名〉medical insurance: ～卡 Medicare card ‖ ～定点医院/药店 designated hospital/pharmacy for the medically insured
【医道】yīdào〈名〉［中医］medical expertise: ～高明 be a highly skilled doctor
【医德】yīdé〈名〉medical ethics: ～高尚 be an ethical doctor
【医改】yīgǎi〈简称〉= 医疗制度改革
【医护】yīhù〈动〉treat and nurse: ～人员 medical professionals
【医科】yīkē〈名〉medicine: ～大学 medical university
【医理】yīlǐ〈名〉medical knowledge: 精通～ have a good command of medicine
【医疗】yīliáo〈动〉give medical treatment: 享受公费～ enjoy a secure public health service ‖ ～器械 medical instruments, medical apparatus and instruments ‖ ～事故 medical malpractice
【医疗保险】yīliáo bǎoxiǎn〈名〉medical insurance: ～制度 medical insurance system
【医疗保障】yīliáo bǎozhàng〈名〉medical security
【医疗队】yīliáoduì〈名〉medical team
【医疗费用】yīliáo fèiyong〈名〉health expenses
【医疗服务】yīliáo fúwù〈名〉medical care
【医疗机构】yīliáo jīgòu〈名〉medical establishment
【医疗设施】yīliáo shèshī〈名〉medical facilities
【医疗制度改革】yīliáo zhìdù gǎigé〈名〉reform of medical system
【医生】yīshēng ▸**p. 966**〈名〉doctor: 临床～ clinician ‖ 内科～ physician ‖ 实习～ intern ‖ 外科～ surgeon ‖ 主治～ doctor in attendance
【医师】yīshī〈名〉certified doctor: 主任～ chief physician
【医士】yīshì〈名〉medical assistant
【医书】yīshū〈名〉medical book
【医术】yīshù〈名〉medical skill: 精通～ have excellent medical skills ‖ ～高明 have superb medical skills
【医托】yītuō〈名〉person acting as decoy for a doctor
【医务】yīwù〈名〉medical matters: ～工作 medical work ‖ ～人员 medical personnel
【医务室】yīwùshì〈名〉infirmary
【医学】yīxué〈名〉medical science: 传授～知识 impart medical knowledge ‖ 传统～ traditional medicine
【医学院】yīxuéyuàn〈名〉medical school
【医药】yīyào〈名〉medicine: ～常识 general medical knowledge ‖ ～用品商店 medical products store ‖ ～费 medical expenses
【医用】yīyòng〈形〉medical
【医院】yīyuàn〈名〉hospital: 到～看病 go to hospital ‖ 送往～ send sb. to the hospital ‖ 住进～ enter a hospital ‖ 附属～ affiliated hospital ‖ 专科～ specialized hospital
【医治】yīzhì〈动〉cure: ～疾病 treat a disease ‖ ～烧伤 heal burns ‖ ～无效 fail to respond to any medical treatment ‖ ～战争创伤 heal war wounds
【医嘱】yīzhǔ〈名〉doctor's instructions: 遵照～服药 take medicine as directed by the doctor
【医助自杀】yīzhù zìshā〈名〉doctor-assisted suicide

依 yī

A〈动〉1（紧挨着）lean on: ～山傍水 be near mountains and rivers 2（依赖）depend on: ▸～赖，相～为命 3（同意）comply with: 她要什么，她母亲都～她。Her mother complies with all her wishes. ▸～从，～顺
B〈介〉according to: ～法定程序处理 handle according to the law ‖ ～我看 as I see it
【依傍】yībàng〈动〉1（依靠）depend on: 互相～ depend on each other ‖ 无可～ without anyone to rely on 2（模仿）copy: ～前人 model oneself on one's predecessors
【依此类推】yīcǐ-lèituī〈成〉and so on and so forth
【依次】yīcì〈副〉successively: ～递补 fill vacancies in order of precedence ‖ ～入座 take one's seat in proper order ‖ ～上下车 get on and off one by one
【依从】yīcóng〈动〉comply with: ～父母 yield to one's parents ‖ 他们提出的某些条件难以～。Certain conditions of theirs are not easily met.
【依存】yīcún〈动〉depend on sb./sth. for existence: 相互～ be interdependent
【依存度】yīcúndù〈名〉interdependency: 中美经济发展的～日益加深。The interdependency of the China-U.S. economies is becoming increasingly acute.
【依法】yīfǎ〈动〉1（指成法）follow fixed rules: ～炮制 follow a prescribed method 2（指法律）abide by the law: ～办案 handle cases in conformity with legal provisions ‖ ～逮捕 arrest according to the law ‖ ～治国 manage state affairs under the rule of law
【依附】yīfù〈动〉1（附着）adhere to: 鲍鱼～在岩石上。The abalone is sticking to the rock. 2（依赖）depend on: ～权贵 attach oneself to bigwigs ‖ 决不～于大国 never become an appendage to big powers
【依归】yīguī A〈名〉starting point and destination: 以人民的利益为～ take the interests of the people as the starting and the end point for one's work B〈动〉depend on: 无所～ have nothing to rely on
【依葫芦画瓢】yī húlu huà piáo〈俗〉copy mechanically
【依旧】yījiù A〈动〉remain the same: 风景～。The scenery remained unchanged. B〈副〉still: 他～是老样子。He still looks like his old self.
【依据】yījù A〈介〉on the basis of: ～事实来判断 make judgement according to facts ‖ 你～什么得出这种结论？What's the basis for your conclusion? B〈名〉basis: 提供～ provide a basis for sth. ‖ 以事实为～ be based on fact
【依靠】yīkào A〈动〉rely on: ～父母 depend on one's parents for support ‖ ～自己的努力 rely on one's own effort B〈名〉backing: 生活有～ have one's livelihood assured
【依赖】yīlài〈动〉1（依靠）be dependent on: ～别人 be dependent on others ‖ ～进口 be reliant on imports ‖ ～性 dependence 2（不可分离）be dependent on each other: 相互～ be mutually dependent
【依赖思想】yīlài sīxiǎng〈名〉dependent mentality: 改变～ change dependent mentality
【依恋】yīliàn〈动〉be reluctant to leave: ～故乡 find it hard to leave one's hometown

【依凭】yīpíng〈书〉**A**〈动〉rely on: 无所～ have nothing to depend on **B**〈名〉proof

【依然】yīrán **A**〈动〉be the same as before: 风景～。The scenery remains unchanged. **B**〈副〉still: 和平和发展～是时代的主题。Peace and development are still the main themes of the day. ‖ 问题～没有解决。The question remains unsolved. ▸～如故

【依然故我】yīrán-gùwǒ〈成〉one's circumstances remain unchanged: 二十年过去了，我却～。Though twenty years have passed, I am still the same as I always was.

【依然如故】yīrán-rúgù〈成〉remain unchanged: 他总是起得很早，退休后也～。He has always been an early riser and still is in his retirement.

【依顺】yīshùn〈动〉submit to: 在家中他事事都～妻子。At home he defers to his wife in every matter.

【依随】yīsuí〈动〉comply with: 丈夫说什么她都～。She yields to her husband's every whim.

【依托】yītuō〈动〉**1**（依靠）rely on: ～权门 depend on powerful and influential families ‖ 无所～ have nothing to rely on **2**（假借名义）keep up a pretence: 他～鬼神，骗人钱财。He defrauded people of their money and belongings by claiming to understand the gods and spirits.

【依偎】yīwēi〈动〉nestle up against: 小女孩～在母亲身边。The little girl snuggled up to her mother. ‖ 他们～在一起取暖。They huddled together for warmth.

【依稀】yīxī〈形〉vague: 他～记得那个名字。He vaguely remembers the name. ‖ 在暮霭中，那座山峰～可见。The mountain peak was faintly discernible in the evening mist.

【依循】yīxún〈动〉follow: 有所～ have something to abide by

【依样画葫芦】yīyàng huà húlu〈成〉〈喻〉copy mechanically

【依依】yīyī〈形〉**1**〈书〉（形容树枝）swaying in the wind: 杨柳～。The willows are swaying in the breeze. **2**（不忍分离）reluctant to part: ▸～不舍

【依依不舍】yīyī-bùshě〈成〉cannot bear to part: 他们把他一直送到山口的大道上，这才～地告别。They escorted him all the way to the mountain pass for a reluctant farewell.

【依依惜别】yīyī-xībié〈成〉say goodbye reluctantly

【依允】yīyǔn〈动〉assent: 点头～ nod one's consent

【依仗】yīzhàng〈动〉count on: ～权势，欺压百姓 bully people on the back of one's powerful connections or position

【依照】yīzhào **A**〈动〉follow: 提拔干部要严格～有关规定。The promotion of cadres must be strictly in accordance with the relevant regulations. **B**〈介〉according to: ～情况而定 decide in accordance with circumstances

y

祎（禕）yī〈形〉〈书〉fine

咿 yī

【咿呀】yīyā〈拟〉**1**（指物体摩擦声）squeak: ～的桨声 the squeak of oars **2**（指小孩学语声）babble: ～学语 make babbling sounds like a small child

铱（銥）yī〈名〉［化学］iridium (Ir): ～金笔 iridium-point pen

猗 yī〈书〉

A〈助〉[used at the end of a sentence to express exclamatory feelings]: 河水清且涟～。The clear river ripples on. **B**〈叹〉[expressing praise]: ～欤盛哉! Magnificent!

壹 yī ▸**p. 691**〈数〉one [used for the numeral — on cheques, etc. to avoid alterations or mistakes]

揖 yī〈动〉bow: ～别 make a bow and say goodbye ▸打躬作～

漪 yī〈名〉〈书〉ripples: 清～ clear ripples

【漪澜】yīlán〈名〉〈书〉ripples and billows

噫 yī〈叹〉〈书〉alas

【噫嘻】yīxī〈叹〉〈书〉alas

繄 yī〈助〉〈书〉[used at the beginning of a sentence] only

yí

匜 yí〈名〉〈古〉gourd-shaped ladle

仪（儀）yí

A〈名〉**1**（礼节）ceremony: ▸礼～，司～ **2**（礼物）present: ▸贺～ **3**（外表）appearance: ▸～表堂堂，～容，威～ **4**（仪器）apparatus: ▸～表，～器，地球～ **B**〈动〉〈书〉admire: 心～已久 have long admired sb.

【仪表】yíbiǎo〈名〉**1**（外表）appearance: 讲究～ keep up appearances ‖ ～大方 be poised and graceful **2**（器具）instrument: 察看～ read an instrument ‖ 检查～ check a meter ‖ ～厂 instrument and meter plant

【仪表板】yíbiǎobǎn〈名〉**1**（指汽车）fascia〈英〉; dashboard〈美〉**2**（指飞机）instrument panel

【仪表盘】yíbiǎopán〈名〉instrument board

【仪表堂堂】yíbiǎo-tángtáng〈成〉be impressive-looking

【仪器】yíqì〈名〉instrument: 调试～ adjust an apparatus ‖ 光学～ optical apparatus ‖ 教学～ educational instrument ‖ 精密～ precision instrument

【仪容】yíróng〈名〉appearance: ～俊秀 be possessed of delicate beauty ‖ 端庄的～ dignified appearance

【仪式】yíshì〈名〉ceremony: 主持～ conduct a ceremony ‖ 签字～ ceremony for signing an agreement ‖ 升旗～ flag-raising ceremony ‖ 宗教～ religious ritual

【仪态】yítài〈名〉〈书〉bearing: ～优雅 have a graceful deportment

【仪态万方】yítài-wànfāng〈成〉be distinguished and elegant: 她身材非常优美，走起路来～。She has an excellent figure and walks with a distinguished and elegant air.

【仪态万千】yítài-wànqiān = 仪态万方 yítài-wànfāng

【仪仗】yízhàng〈名〉**1**（指古代帝王、官员出行用具）flags, weapons, etc. carried by guards before an emperor **2**（指国家大典、迎宾时用具）flags, weapons, etc. carried by guards of honour: 陆海空三军～队 guard of honour of the three armed forces

圯 yí〈名〉〈古〉bridge

夷[1] yí〈名〉**1**〈古〉（指民族）*yi* [tribes in east China] **2**〈旧〉（外国）foreign countries;（外国人）foreigners

夷[2] yí

A〈形〉safe: ▸化险为～ **B**〈动〉**1**（推倒）raze: ～为平地 raze to the ground **2**〈古〉（灭绝）exterminate: ～灭九族 exterminate the entire family of a criminal

诒（詒）yí〈动〉〈书〉present a gift

迤 yí ▸逶迤 wēiyí ▸yǐ

饴（飴）yí〈名〉maltose: ▸甘之如～

【饴糖】yítáng〈名〉maltose

怡 yí〈形〉〈书〉joyful: ▸～然自得，心旷神～

【怡和】yíhé〈形〉〈书〉affable

【怡情悦性】yíqíng-yuèxìng〈成〉cheer the heart and compose the mind

【怡然自得】yírán-zìdé〈成〉be happy and pleased with oneself: 安闲舒适，～ feel happy and contented with a leisurely and comfortable life ‖ 他听着风动树梢，小鸟欢唱，真是～。Listening to the breeze in the branches and the merry chirping of birds, he was filled with contentment.

【怡悦】yíyuè〈形〉happy: ～的心情 cheerful mood

宜 yí

A〈形〉suitable: 儿童不～ be unsuitable for children ‖ 这种食物～少吃。There is no benefit in eating too much of this food. ‖ 这种土壤～种花生。This kind of soil is good for planting peanuts. ▸得～，合～，适～，相～，因地制～ **B**〈动〉[often used in the negative] should: ～早不～晚。The sooner, the better. ‖ 不～操之过急。This should not be done in haste. ▸事不～迟 **C**〈副〉〈书〉certainly: ～其不从也。He will certainly not obey.

【宜人】yírén〈形〉pleasant: 景物～。The scenery is charming. ‖ 气候～。The weather is agreeable.

荑 yí〈动〉〈书〉weed ▸tí

咦 yí〈叹〉[expressing surprise or disapproval] why: ～，怎么孩子一转眼就不见了! What? How could the child have vanished so quickly? ‖ ～，这是怎么回事? Hey, what's all this about?

贻（貽）yí〈动〉〈书〉**1**（赠送）present sb. with a gift: ～赠 present **2**（遗留）bequeath: ▸～患，～人口实，～笑大方

【贻贝】yíbèi〈名〉［动物］mussel

【贻害】yíhài〈动〉 leave a legacy of trouble: ～无穷 lead to untold trouble
【贻患】yíhuàn〈动〉 sow the seeds of disaster: ▸养虎～
【贻人口实】yírén-kǒushí〈成〉 give occasion to gossip
【贻误】yíwù〈动〉 affect adversely: ～工作 affect the work adversely ‖ ～后人 mislead later generations ‖ ～战机 bungle the opportunity for combat
【贻笑大方】yíxiào-dàfāng〈成〉 make a laughing stock of oneself before experts: 我对此知之甚少，乱发议论，岂不～。I know very little about this and don't want to make a fool of myself by making random comments.

姨 yí〈名〉 1（妻子的姐妹） sister-in-law: ▸大～子，小～子 2（母亲的姐妹） one's mother's sister: ▸～妈 3（称母亲辈的妇女） aunt: 李～ Aunt Li
【姨表】yíbiǎo〈名〉 maternal cousin: ～姐妹 female maternal cousins ‖ ～兄弟 male maternal cousins
【姨夫】yífu ▸**p. 588**〈名〉 uncle [husband of one's maternal aunt]
【姨父】yífu = 姨夫 yífu
【姨姥姥】yílǎolao ▸**p. 588**〈名〉 great-aunt [sister of one's maternal grandmother]
【姨妈】yímā ▸**p. 588**〈名〉 aunt
【姨母】yímǔ ▸**p. 588**〈名〉 aunt
【姨奶奶】yínǎinai ▸**p. 588**〈名〉 1（祖母的姐妹） great-aunt [sister of one's paternal grandmother] 2（姨太太） concubine
【姨娘】yíniáng〈名〉〈旧〉 term of address for father's concubine
【姨太太】yítàitai〈名〉 concubine
【姨丈】yízhàng = 姨夫 yífu

胰 yí〈名〉［解剖］ pancreas
【胰岛素】yídǎosù〈名〉［医学］ insulin
【胰腺】yíxiàn〈名〉［解剖］ pancreas: ～癌 pancreatic cancer ‖ ～炎 pancreatitis
【胰脏】yízàng〈名〉［解剖］pancreas: ～切除术 pancreatectomy
【胰子】yízi〈名〉 1（猪羊的胰脏） pancreas 2〈方〉（肥皂） soap

宧 yí〈名〉〈古〉 north-east corner of a room

蛇 yí ▸委蛇 wēiyí
▸shé

移 yí〈动〉 1（移动）move: 把桌子往后～ move the table back ‖ 车站向南～了。The railway station moved south. ▸～动，迁～，转～ 2（改变） change: 我们立场坚定不～。Our standpoint is firm. ▸～风易俗，本性难～ 3（移栽） transplant: ～苗 transplant seedlings
【移东补西】yídōng-bǔxī〈成〉 rob Peter to pay Paul
【移动】yídòng〈动〉move: 向后/前～ move backwards/forwards ‖ ～PC mobile PC ‖ ～靶 moving target ‖ 一股冷气流正由西伯利亚向内蒙古～。A cold air mass is moving from Siberia to Inner Mongolia.
【移动电话】yídòng diànhuà〈名〉 mobile phone
【移动通信】yídòng tōngxìn〈名〉 mobile communication: 移动卫星通信 mobile satellite communication
【移防】yífáng〈动〉 be shifted elsewhere for garrison duty
【移风易俗】yífēng-yìsú〈成〉 change prevailing habits and customs
【移花接木】yíhuā-jiēmù〈成〉〈喻〉 stealthily substitute one thing for another: 这份报告～，歪曲事实。The report deliberately passes off falsehood as fact.
【移交】yíjiāo〈动〉 1（转交） transfer: 将小偷～警方 turn over a thief to the police ‖ 他被～军事法庭审判。He was handed over to a military tribunal for trial. 2（交接） devolve: ～工作 delegate work
【移解】yíjiè〈动〉 transfer a prisoner from one place to another under escort
【移居】yíjū〈动〉 migrate: ～海外 migrate overseas
【移民】yímín **A**〈动〉 migrate: 向海外/西部地区～ emigrate to a foreign country/western regions ‖ ～倾向 intention of immigrating **B**〈名〉 migrant: 安置～ resettle immigrants ‖ 非法～ illegal immigrants
【移民点】yímíndiǎn〈名〉 settlement
【移民法】yímínfǎ〈名〉 immigration law
【移民局】yímínjú〈名〉 immigration office
【移民政策】yímín zhèngcè〈名〉 immigration policy: 放宽～ liberalize an immigration policy
【移情】yíqíng **A**〈动〉 change one's affections: ～别恋 transfer one's affections to another person **B**〈名〉［心理］ transference: ～作用 empathy
【移山倒海】yíshān-dǎohǎi〈成〉 transform nature: ～之势 the power to transform nature
【移师】yíshī〈动〉 move forces elsewhere: 比赛结束后，篮球队将～上海。After the match, the basketball team will be transferred to Shanghai.
【移送】yísòng〈动〉 turn over: ～司法机关审理 turn over to the judicial system for trial
【移位】yíwèi〈名〉 1［计算机］ shift: ～功能 shifting function 2 ▸**p. 50**［医学］ translocation
【移徙】yíxǐ〈动〉〈书〉 migrate: 燕子于初秋开始向南～。Swallows begin their migration south in early autumn.
【移译】yíyì〈动〉〈书〉 translate
【移易】yíyì〈动〉〈书〉 change: 一字不可～。Not a word is to be altered.
【移用】yíyòng〈动〉 use elsewhere: ～公款 appropriate public funds
【移栽】yízāi〈动〉 transplant: ～树苗 transplant saplings
【移植】yízhí〈动〉 1（指植物） transplant: ～秧苗 transplant seedlings ‖〈喻〉 这个剧目是从京剧～过来的。This opera has been adapted from a Peking opera. 2 ▸**p. 50**［医学］ transplant: ～角膜/肾脏/心脏 transplant a cornea/kidney/heart ‖ 骨髓～ bone marrow transplant
【移植手术】yízhí shǒushù〈名〉 transplant operation: 做器官～ perform organ transplants ‖ 心脏～ heart transplant operation
【移樽就教】yízūn-jiùjiào〈成〉 go to sb. for advice

痍 yí〈名〉〈书〉 trauma: ▸满目疮～

遗（遺） yí
A〈动〉 1（丢失） lose: ▸～失 2（遗漏） leave out: 一览无～ in plain view ▸～漏，～忘 3（留下） leave behind: ▸～迹，～留，不～余力 4（死后留下）bequeath: ▸～容，～愿，～嘱 5（排泄） emit: ▸～精，梦～ **B**〈名〉 something lost: ▸路不拾～
▸wèi
【遗案】yí'àn〈名〉 unsolved case
【遗笔】yíbǐ〈名〉 writings of a deceased person
【遗产】yíchǎn〈名〉 legacy: 继承～ inherit a legacy ‖ 接受～ receive an inheritance ‖ 历史～ legacy of history ‖ 文化～ cultural legacy
【遗产继承权】yíchǎn jìchéngquán〈名〉 right to a legacy
【遗产继承人】yíchǎn jìchéngrén〈名〉heir to a property
【遗产税】yíchǎnshuì〈名〉 inheritance tax: 征收～ levy inheritance tax
【遗臭万年】yíchòu-wànnián〈成〉 go down in history as a byword for infamy: 大丈夫须求流芳后世，万不可～。A great man should hand down a good name to future generations, not a foul reputation.
【遗传】yíchuán〈动〉 pass on to the next generation: 隔代～ atavistic ‖ 她的蓝眼睛是母亲～给她的。She gets her blue eyes from her mother. ‖ 糖尿病有～性。Diabetes is hereditary.
【遗传病】yíchuánbìng ▸**p. 50**〈名〉 hereditary disease
【遗传工程】yíchuán gōngchéng〈名〉 genetic engineering
【遗传密码】yíchuán mìmǎ〈名〉 genetic code
【遗传物质】yíchuán wùzhì〈名〉 genetic material
【遗传性】yíchuánxìng〈名〉 heredity
【遗传学】yíchuánxué〈名〉 genetics: ～家 geneticist
【遗存】yícún **A**〈动〉 continue to exist: 这是～至今最早的希伯来文手稿。This is the oldest Hebrew manuscript in existence. **B**〈名〉 historical remains: 史前动物的化石～ fossil remains of a prehistoric animal
【遗毒】yídú〈名〉 evil legacy: 肃清～ wipe out all harmful traditions
【遗风】yífēng〈名〉 customs handed down from the past: 古代～ remnants of an ancient custom
【遗腹子】yífùzǐ〈名〉 child born after the death of its father: 领养～ adopt a child born after the death of its father
【遗稿】yígǎo〈名〉 posthumous manuscript
【遗孤】yígū〈名〉 orphan: 抚养～ foster an orphan ‖ 烈士～ orphan of a martyr
【遗骨】yígǔ〈名〉 remains of the dead: 动物～ animal remains ‖ 烈士～ remains of martyrs
【遗骸】yíhái〈名〉 remains: 烈士～ remains of martyrs ‖ 骆驼的化石～ fossilized remains of a camel
【遗憾】yíhàn **A**〈名〉 eternal regret: 终身～ lifelong regret **B** ▸**p. 156**〈动〉 regret: 很～，我不能和你同行了。I very much regret not being able to travel with you. ‖ 这是一件令人～的事情。It is a regrettable matter.
【遗恨】yíhèn〈名〉 eternal regret: 死无～ die without regrets ‖ ～终生 feel remorseful to the end of one's days
【遗迹】yíjì〈名〉 historical remains: 参观古罗马～ look around the remains of ancient Rome ‖ 古城～ remains of an ancient city
【遗精】yíjīng ▸**p. 50**〈名〉［生理］ nocturnal emission
【遗老】yílǎo〈名〉 1（指效忠前朝） adherent of a former dynasty: 前朝～ old adherent of an overthrown dynasty 2〈书〉

y

〈旧〉（指经历世变） old people who have witnessed big social changes
【遗留】yíliú〈动〉 leave behind: 解决历史～问题 resolve questions handed down in history ‖ 收拾前政府～下来的烂摊子 clear up the mess left by the previous government
【遗漏】yílòu〈动〉omit: 抄写时他～了整整一行。 He missed a line out when he was copying. ‖ 你在名单上～了我的名字。You have omitted my name from your list.
【遗民】yímín〈名〉 1（指效忠前朝的人） adherent of a former dynasty 2（指幸存者） survivor of a great upheaval
【遗墨】yímò〈名〉 posthumous papers, scrolls etc.: 收集～ collect sb.'s posthumous papers and scrolls
【遗尿】yíniào ▸p. 50〈名〉［医学］ bed-wetting
【遗篇】yípiān〈名〉 posthumous writings
【遗弃】yíqì〈动〉 1（指物） cast away: 敌军～的武器 weapons abandoned by the enemy troops 2（指人） abandon: ～妻子儿女 abandon one's wife and children ‖ 被社会～的人 social outcast
【遗弃罪】yíqìzuì〈名〉 crime of abandonment
【遗缺】yíquē〈名〉 vacancy: 他调走后办公室有个～。 His transfer causes a vacancy in the office.
【遗容】yíróng〈名〉 1（指容貌） remains: 瞻仰～ pay one's respects at sb.'s remains 2（指遗像） portrait of the deceased
【遗撒】yísǎ〈动〉 litter and leak
【遗少】yíshào〈名〉 young adherent of an overthrown dynasty
【遗失】yíshī〈动〉 lose: ～身份证 lose one's identity card ‖ ～不补 no reissue if lost
【遗失启事】yíshī qǐshì〈名〉 lost property notice
【遗事】yíshì〈名〉 1（前代的事迹） incidents of previous ages: 前朝～ incidents occurring in the previous dynasty 2（前人的事迹） deeds of those now dead
【遗书】yíshū〈名〉 1（指书信） note left by sb. immediately before death: 写～ write a letter before one's death 2（指遗作） [usu used in book titles] posthumous writings
【遗属】yíshǔ〈名〉 relatives and dependants of the deceased: 烈士～ dependants of a martyr
【遗孀】yíshuāng〈名〉 widow
【遗体】yítǐ〈名〉 mortal remains: 向～告别 pay one's last respects at sb.'s remains ‖ 他的～已被火化。 His remains were cremated.
【遗忘】yíwàng〈动〉 forget: 行李被～在车站月台上。 The luggage was left behind on the platform. ‖ 他的名字已经被人～了。His name has fallen into oblivion.
【遗闻】yíwén〈名〉 old-time tales: ～轶事 old-time tales and anecdotes
【遗物】yíwù〈名〉 things left behind by the deceased: 保留历史～ maintain historical relics ‖ 清理死者的～ go through the belongings of a deceased person
【遗像】yíxiàng〈名〉picture of the deceased
【遗训】yíxùn〈名〉 teachings of the deceased: 遵守～ follow teachings of the deceased
【遗言】yíyán〈名〉 one's last words: 留下～ leave words before one's death
【遗业】yíyè〈名〉 1（指事业） ancestral career: 继承先人～ carry on where one's ancestors left off 2 = 遗产 yíchǎn
【遗愿】yíyuàn〈名〉 deathbed behest: 实现先烈的～ carry out the behest of the martyrs ‖ 尊重死者～ respect the last wishes of the deceased
【遗赠】yízèng〈动〉 bequeath: ～尸体供科学研究 bequeath one's body to science
【遗诏】yízhào〈名〉 testamentary edict
【遗照】yízhào〈名〉 photograph of the deceased before death
【遗址】yízhǐ〈名〉 relics: 保护古城～ preserve the ruins of an ancient city ‖ 圆明园～ the remains of the old Summer Palace
【遗志】yízhì〈名〉 deathbed behest: 继承先烈～ carry out the behest of the martyrs
【遗嘱】yízhǔ〈名〉 will: 立～ make a will ‖ 写～ write a will
【遗著】yízhù〈名〉 posthumous works: 出版～ publish sb.'s posthumous works
【遗族】yízú〈名〉 family of the deceased
【遗作】yízuò〈名〉 posthumous work

颐（頤） yí〈书〉

A〈动〉 keep fit
B〈名〉 cheek: 支～ put one's cheek in one's palm ‖ 方额广～ square forehead and broad cheeks
【颐和园】Yíhéyuán〈名〉 Summer Palace
【颐养】yíyǎng〈动〉〈书〉 keep fit: ～天年 take good care of oneself so as to live out one's allotted life span
【颐指气使】yízhǐ-qìshǐ〈成〉 assume an air of command: 他～，盛气凌人。 He is arrogant and bossy.

疑 yí

A〈动〉 doubt: ～有埋伏/圈套 suspect an ambush/a trap ▸～惑, 无可置～, 怀～
B〈形〉 doubtful: ▸～点, ～问, ～云
C〈名〉 question: 存～ leave the question open ▸答～, 释～, 质～
【疑案】yí'àn〈名〉 1（指案件） disputed case: 解不开的历史～ unbreakable historical case 2（指秘密） mystery: ～终于告破。 The unsettled case was finally resolved.
【疑兵】yíbīng〈名〉 troops deployed to deceive the enemy
【疑点】yídiǎn〈名〉 questionable point: 这个案件还有几个～。 There are still a few questionable points in the case.
【疑窦】yídòu〈名〉〈书〉 cause for suspicion: 顿生～ suddenly feel suspicious
【疑犯】yífàn〈名〉 criminal suspect
【疑惑】yíhuò〈动〉 feel perplexed: ～不解 have doubts
【疑忌】yíjì〈名〉 suspicion: 无所～ have no suspicion ‖ 心怀～ harbour a suspicion
【疑惧】yíjù〈动〉 be apprehensive: 无端～ feel apprehensive without reason
【疑虑】yílǜ〈动〉 have misgivings: 消除～ clear up suspicions ‖ ～重重 be beset with doubts and worries
【疑难】yínán〈形〉 difficult: ～问题 knotty problem ‖ ～杂症 difficult and complicated cases
【疑人不用，用人不疑】yí rén bù yòng, yòngrén bù yí〈俗〉 never suspect the man you use and never use the man you suspect
【疑神疑鬼】yíshén-yíguǐ〈成〉 be extremely suspicious: 根本没那回事儿，别～的。 That's absolutely untrue. Don't be so suspicious.
【疑似】yísì〈形〉 doubtful: ～病例 suspected cases ‖ ～之词 ambiguous words
【疑团】yítuán〈名〉 doubts and suspicions: 解开～ clear up doubts and suspicions ‖ 满腹～ be full of doubts and suspicions
【疑问】yíwèn〈名〉 question: 提出～ raise a question ‖ 毫无～，他是全校最聪明的学生。 He is without question the brightest student in the school.
【疑问代词】yíwèn dàicí〈名〉［语法］ interrogative pronoun
【疑问副词】yíwèn fùcí〈名〉［语法］ interrogative adverb
【疑问句】yíwènjù〈名〉［语法］ interrogative sentence
【疑心】yíxīn A〈名〉 doubt: ～重 be too ready to suspect ‖ 他突然起了～。 A sudden doubt came to his mind. B〈动〉 suspect: 我早就～他可能吸毒。 I suspected from very early on that he was using drugs.
【疑心病】yíxīnbìng〈名〉 suspicious frame of mind: 犯～ be over-suspicious
【疑心生暗鬼】yíxīn shēng ànguǐ〈俗〉 suspicions create imaginary fears
【疑信参半】yíxìn-cānbàn〈成〉 half in belief and half in doubt
【疑凶】yíxiōng〈名〉 suspected murderer
【疑义】yíyì〈名〉 doubt: 毫无～ have no doubt
【疑云】yíyún〈名〉suspicions clouding one's mind: ～消散。 The misgivings have been dispelled.
【疑阵】yízhèn〈名〉［军事］ battle array to deceive and confuse enemies

彝[1] yí〈名〉〈古〉

1（祭器） bronze sacrificial utensils: ▸～器 2（法律） law

彝[2] Yí〈名〉 Yi ethnic group

【彝剧】yíjù〈名〉 Yi opera
【彝器】yíqì〈名〉 bronze sacrificial utensils
【彝族】Yízú〈名〉 Yi ethnic group

yǐ

乙[1] yǐ〈名〉

1（指天干） second of the ten Heavenly Stems（天干） 2（第二） second: ▸～等 3（指代另一） [used for an unspecified person or thing]: 甲队和～队 team A and team B

乙[2] yǐ〈名〉［音乐］

note on the *gongche*（工尺）scale, corresponding to a low 7 in *jianpu*（简谱）numbered musical notation

乙[3] yǐ〈名〉〈旧〉

[mark used to show where sth. is to be added in writing or to indicate where one stops in reading unpunctuated classical Chinese]
【乙部】yǐbù = 史部 shǐbù
【乙醇】yǐchún〈名〉［化学］ ethanol
【乙等】yǐděng〈名〉 second grade
【乙肝】yǐgān〈简称〉= 乙型肝炎
【乙肝病毒】yǐgān bìngdú〈名〉 hepatitis B virus
【乙醚】yǐmí〈名〉［化学］ ether
【乙脑】yǐnǎo〈简称〉= 乙型脑炎
【乙炔】yǐquē〈名〉［化学］ acetylene
【乙酸】yǐsuān〈名〉［化学］ acetic acid
【乙烷】yǐwán〈名〉［化学］ ethane
【乙烯】yǐxī〈名〉［化学］ ethylene: 聚～ polyethylene
【乙型肝炎】yǐxíng gānyán ▸p. 50〈名〉 hepatitis B
【乙型脑炎】yǐxíng nǎoyán ▸p. 50〈名〉 encephalitis B

已 yǐ

A〈动〉 stop: 感叹不～ keep sighing ▸死而后～

B〈副〉 already: ～成定局 be a foregone conclusion ‖ 名额～满。 The quota has been filled. ▸木～成舟

【已故】yǐgù〈动〉 be deceased: ～主席 late chairman

【已婚】yǐhūn〈动〉 be married: ～妇女/男子 married woman/man

【已经】yǐjing〈副〉 already: ～到夏天了。 It's summer already. ‖ 他～来了。 He has already come.

【已决犯】yǐjuéfàn〈名〉 convict

【已然】yǐrán〈书〉 **A**〈副〉 already so: 事情～如此，还是想开些吧。 Such being the case, don't take it to heart. **B**〈动〉 have already become a fact: 与其补救于～，不如防患于未然。Prevention is better than cure.

【已往】yǐwǎng〈名〉 the past: 今天的农村跟～大不一样。 Today's countryside is totally different from the countryside of the past. ‖ 她总是照～的方式办事。 She always does things according to how she did them before.

【已知】yǐzhī〈形〉 known: ～数 known number

以[1] yǐ

A〈介〉 **1**（用、拿） by means of: ～大局为重 put the general interest first ‖ ～教书为生 make a living by teaching ‖ ～事实为根据，～法律为准绳 take facts as the basis and the law as the criterion ‖ ～质量求生存、求发展 strive for survival and development on the basis of quality ▸～德报怨, ～毒攻毒, ～理服人 **2**（给予） to: 给敌人～沉重打击 deal a heavy blow to the enemy **3**（依照） according to: ～进价销售 sell goods at warehouse prices ‖ ～姓氏笔画为序 be listed according to the order of the number of strokes in surnames ▸～貌取人, 物～类聚，人～群分 **4**（因为） because of: 不～失败自馁，不～成功自满 not lose heart because of failure nor feel conceited because of success ‖ 古城西安～历史悠久闻名于世。 The ancient city of Xi'an is world-famous for its time-honoured history. **5**〈书〉（指具体时间） at;（指具体日期） on: 余～公元一九二五年八月六日生于广州。 I was born in Guangzhou on August 6,1925.

B〈连〉 so that: ～示区别 so as to show the difference ‖ ～正视听 in order to ensure correct understanding of the facts ▸～防万一

以[2] yǐ

〈连〉 from: ～下 below ‖ 二十年～前 20 years ago ‖ 十五岁～上 15 years and above

【以暴易暴】yǐbào-yìbào〈成〉 replace one tyranny with another

【以便】yǐbiàn〈连〉 so that: 写上邮编，～投递。 Write the postcode so as to ensure timely delivery.

【以不变应万变】yǐ bùbiàn yìng wànbiàn〈惯〉 meet all changes by remaining unchanged

【以诚相待】yǐchéng-xiāngdài〈成〉 be honest with

【以此类推】yǐcǐ-lèituī〈成〉 and so on and so forth

【以次】yǐcì **A**〈副〉 in proper order: ～入座 take one's seat in proper order **B**〈名〉 the following: ～各章 following chapters

【以次充好】yǐcì-chōnghǎo〈成〉 palm off shoddy goods as quality goods

【以德报怨】yǐdé-bàoyuàn〈成〉 recompense evil with good

【以德治国】yǐdé-zhìguó〈动〉 rule by virtue: 既要以法治国，也要～。 A country must be ruled according to law, but also with virtue.

【以点带面】yǐdiǎn-dàimiàn〈成〉 promote work in all areas by drawing upon experience gained at key points

【以毒攻毒】yǐdú-gōngdú〈成〉 **1**〈本〉 counteract one toxin with another **2**〈喻〉 repay evil with evil

【以讹传讹】yǐ'é-chuán'é〈成〉 disseminate falsehoods

【以防万一】yǐfáng-wànyī〈成〉be ready for anything

【以古讽今】yǐgǔ-fěngjīn〈成〉 use the past to mock the present

【以寡敌众】yǐguǎ-dízhòng〈成〉 pit few against many

【以观后效】yǐguān-hòuxiào〈成〉 lighten a punishment and see how the offender behaves: 给予警告处分，～ give sb. a disciplinary warning and see how they will behave

【以后】yǐhòu〈名〉 afterwards: 从今～ from now on ‖ 几天～ a few days later

【以货易货】yǐhuò-yìhuò〈动〉exchange one commodity for another

【以及】yǐjí ▸**p. 448**〈连〉 as well as: 评论家、艺术家～新闻工作者 critics, artists and journalists

【以己度人】yǐjǐ-duórén〈成〉 measure others according to one's own values

【以假乱真】yǐjiǎ-luànzhēn〈成〉 mix the false with the genuine: ～的仿制品 perfect copy

【以近】yǐjìn〈名〉 up to: 不售西安～的火车票。 Train tickets for stations before Xi'an are not available.

【以儆效尤】yǐjǐng-xiàoyóu〈成〉 punish sb. as a warning to others: 老师当着全班学生的面惩罚了那个学生，～。 The boy was made an example of in front of all the other pupils.

【以旧换新】yǐjiù-huànxīn〈成〉 trade in the old for the new

【以来】yǐlái〈名〉 period of ensuing time: 长期～ for a long time past ‖ 自古～ since ancient times ‖ 改革开放～中国的面貌发生了巨大变化。 Great changes have taken place in China since reform and opening up was initiated.

【以泪洗面】yǐlèi-xǐmiàn〈成〉 have a tearful face

【以礼相待】yǐlǐ-xiāngdài〈成〉 treat sb. with due respect

【以理服人】yǐlǐ-fúrén〈成〉 persuade through reasoning: 解决思想问题只能～。 We can only change people's thinking by reasoning.

【以粮为纲】yǐliáng-wéigāng〈成〉 take grain as the key link (to the national agriculture)

【以邻为伴】yǐlín-wéibàn〈动〉 enter into cooperative partnership with a neighbouring country: ～的外交政策 foreign policies of neighbouring partner countries

【以邻为壑】yǐlín-wéihè〈成〉〈喻〉 shift one's troubles onto others

【以卵击石】yǐluǎn-jīshí〈成〉 fight a hopeless battle

【以貌取人】yǐmào-qǔrén〈成〉 judge people by their appearance

【以免】yǐmiǎn〈连〉 lest: 仔细检查～出错 double check so as to avoid mistakes ‖ 他们三三两两地离开大厅，～引起注意。 They left the hall in twos and threes so as not to attract attention.

【以内】yǐnèi〈名〉 within a space or time: 长城～ inside the Great Wall ‖ 三年～ within three years ‖ 人员限制在500名～。 Personnel is limited to 500.

【以偏概全】yǐpiān-gàiquán〈成〉 generalize from isolated incidents: 不能抓住一个人的缺点，～，全盘否定。 We should not judge a person as completely worthless on the basis of his shortcomings alone.

【以期】yǐqī〈动〉〈书〉 be in the hope for: 再接再厉，～全胜 go all out for complete victory

【以其人之道，还治其人之身】yǐ qírén zhī dào, huán zhì qírén zhī shēn〈成〉 give sb. a taste of their own medicine

【以前】yǐqián〈名〉 earlier times: 很久～ a long time ago ‖ 她变了，不再是～的她了。 She has changed from the way she used to be.

【以强凌弱】yǐqiáng-língruò〈成〉 oppress the weak by sheer strength

【以勤补拙】yǐqín-bǔzhuō〈成〉 make up through hard work what one lacks in natural gifts

【以权谋私】yǐquán-móusī〈成〉 abuse power for personal gain

【以人废言】yǐrén-fèiyán〈成〉 reject an opinion because of the speaker: 君子不以言举人，不～。 The superior man does not promote a man simply on account of his words, nor does he reject good words because of the man.

【以人为本】yǐrén-wéiběn〈成〉 people-oriented

【以色列】Yǐsèliè〈名〉 Israel: ～国 State of Israel ‖ ～人 Israeli

【以上】yǐshàng〈名〉 **1** ▸**p. 927**（在某点之上） above: 价钱十元～ cost over 10 *yuan* ‖ 召集处级～干部开会 call a meeting of department chiefs and above **2**（前述内容） the above: ～所有的人都得参加明天的会议。 All the above are asked to attend tomorrow's meeting.

【以身试法】yǐshēn-shìfǎ〈成〉 challenge the law personally

【以身相许】yǐshēn-xiāngxǔ〈成〉 [of a girl] pledge to marry sb.

【以身殉职】yǐshēn-xùnzhí〈成〉die at one's post

【以身作则】yǐshēn-zuòzé〈成〉 lead by example: ～，身体力行 practise what one preaches

【以史为镜】yǐshǐ-wéijìng〈成〉 take history as a mirror

【以税代利】yǐshuì-dàilì〈动〉 substitute tax for profit

【以太网】yǐtàiwǎng〈名〉 Ethernet

【以退为进】yǐtuì-wéijìn〈成〉 make concessions in order to gain advantages

【以外】yǐwài〈名〉 beyond: 长城～ beyond the Great Wall

【以往】yǐwǎng〈名〉 the past: ～的经历 previous/past experiences

【以为】yǐwéi〈动〉 think: ～自己了不起 think oneself amazing ‖ 我～这不可能。 I don't think it's possible.

【以文会友】yǐwén-huìyǒu〈成〉 make friends through literary activities

【以下】yǐxià〈名〉 **1** ▸**p. 927**（在某点之下） below: 零度～ sub-zero temperatures ‖ 19岁～ 19 years or under ‖ 七岁～的儿童 children under seven **2**（下述内容）

the following: ～是我的观点。 My arguments are as follows.
【以小人之心，度君子之腹】yǐ xiǎorén zhī xīn, duó jūnzǐ zhī fù〈俗〉 measure the heart of a gentleman by the yardstick of a commoner
【以血还血】yǐxiě-huánxiě〈成〉 blood must be paid for with blood
【以眼还眼，以牙还牙】yǐ yǎn huán yǎn, yǐ yá huán yá〈成〉 an eye for an eye and a tooth for a tooth: 我将～向他报复。 I'll get him back for what he did to me.
【以一当十】yǐyī-dāngshí〈成〉fight bravely
【以逸待劳】yǐyì-dàiláo〈成〉 wait for one's opponent to tire themselves out
【以远】yǐyuǎn〈名〉 place beyond: 只售兰州～的车票。 Only tickets for Lanzhou and beyond are available.
【以怨报德】 yǐyuàn-bàodé 〈成〉 requite kindness with ingratitude: 我一向对他很好，他却～。 I have always been very good to him, but he repays my kindness with ingratitude.
【以正视听】yǐzhèng-shìtīng〈成〉 ensure a correct understanding of the facts
【以至】yǐzhì〈连〉 **1**（表延伸） up to: 循环往复，～无穷 repeat itself in endless cycles into infinity **2**（表结果） to such an extent that ...: 他们太虚弱了，～需要特殊治疗。 They were emaciated to such an extent that they needed special treatment.
【以致】 yǐzhì 〈连〉 with the result that: 大雨倾盆，～大坝倒塌，土地被淹。 The rain fell in torrents and as a result the dam broke and the land was flooded.
【以资】yǐzī〈动〉〈书〉 serve as a means of: ～比较 for the sake of comparison
【以子之矛，攻子之盾】 yǐ zǐ zhī máo, gōng zǐ zhī dùn〈成〉〈喻〉 refute sb. with their own argument

钇（釔） yǐ 〈名〉［化学］ yttrium (Y)

苡 yǐ〈名〉［植物］ Job's tears
【苡米】yǐmǐ = 薏米 yìmǐ
【苡仁】yǐrén = 薏米 yìmǐ

尾 yǐ〈名〉 **1**（马尾上的毛） hairs on a horse's tail **2**（蟋蟀等尾部的针状物） spikelets on a cricket's tail
▸wěi

矣 yǐ〈助〉〈书〉 **1**（了） [used at the end of a sentence like 了 to indicate completion of an action]: 悔之晚～。 It's too late to regret. **2**（表感叹） [used in exclamation]: 甚～，汝之不惠! How stupid you are!

迤 yǐ〈介〉 towards: 村庄～北是条小河。 To the north of the village is a small river.
▸yí
【迤逦】yǐlǐ〈形〉〈书〉 meandering

蚁（蟻） yǐ〈名〉 ant: 白～ termite ‖ 兵～ soldier ant ‖ 雌～ female ant ‖ 雄～ male ant ▸工～
【蚁蚕】yǐcán〈名〉newly-hatched silkworm
【蚁巢】yǐcháo〈名〉 ant nest
【蚁后】yǐhòu〈名〉 ant queen
【蚁丘】yǐqiū〈名〉 anthill
【蚁醛】yǐquán = 甲醛 jiǎquán
【蚁酸】yǐsuān〈名〉 formic acid

酏 yǐ
【酏剂】yǐjì〈名〉［药学］ elixir

倚 yǐ
A〈动〉 **1**（靠着） lean on: ～门而立 stand leaning against the door ‖ ～在栏杆上 lean against the railings ‖ 孩子把头～在妈妈的肩上。 The baby rested its head on its mother's shoulder. **2**（依仗） rely on: ▸～老卖老
B〈形〉〈书〉 partial: ▸不偏不～
【倚靠】 yǐkào 〈动〉 **1** = 依靠 yīkào A **2**（靠在） lean on: 她将头～在他的肩上。 She nestled her head against his shoulder.
【倚赖】yǐlài = 依赖 yīlài
【倚老卖老】yǐlǎo-màilǎo〈成〉exploit one's seniority: 他在对我～。 He is trying to beat me down with his seniority.
【倚马可待】 yǐmǎ-kědài 〈成〉 dash off a piece of writing
【倚势凌人】yǐshì-língrén〈成〉rely on one's position to bully others
【倚仗】yǐzhàng〈动〉 rely on: ～权势 rely on one's power and position
【倚重】yǐzhòng〈动〉 rely heavily on sb.'s service: 他德高望重，领导对他倍加～。 He has integrity and a good reputation and the leadership has the utmost confidence in him.

扆 yǐ〈名〉〈旧〉 screen between the window and the door of an old-style Chinese residence

椅 yǐ〈名〉 chair: 藤～ rattan chair ‖ 折～ folding chair ▸安乐～, 轮～, 转～
【椅垫】yǐdiàn〈名〉 chair cushion
【椅子】yǐzi〈名〉 chair: 一把～ a chair

蛾 yǐ〈书〉= 蚁 yǐ
▸é

旖 yǐ
【旖旎】 yǐnǐ 〈形〉〈书〉 charming and gentle: 风光～。 The scene is enchanting.

yì

乂 yì〈书〉
A〈动〉 administer
B〈形〉 stable

弋 yì〈古〉
A〈名〉 retrievable arrow with a string attached to it
B〈动〉 shoot a retrievable arrow
【弋获】yìhuò〈动〉〈书〉**1**（射中） shoot **2**（捕获） catch
【弋取】yìqǔ〈动〉〈书〉 seize

亿（億） yì ▸p. 691〈数〉 a hundred million: 中国有13～多人口。 China has a population of more than 1.3 billion.
【亿万】yìwàn ▸p. 691〈量〉 hundreds of millions: ～人民 hundreds of millions of people ‖ ～富翁 multimillionaire
【亿万斯年】yìwàn-sīnián〈成〉 aeons

义[1]（義） yì
A〈名〉 **1**（正义） justice: 见～不为，无勇也。 To see what is right and not to do it is cowardice. ▸～不容辞, 大～灭亲, 见～勇为 **2**（情谊） chivalry: ▸～气, 信～
B〈形〉 **1**（符合正义） righteous: ▸～举, ～卖, ～演 **2**（拜认） adopted: ▸～父, ～子 **3**（人造） artificial: ▸～齿, ～肢

义[2]（義） yì〈名〉 meaning: ▸词～, 定～, 歧～
【义薄云天】 yìbó-yúntiān 〈成〉 sky-high morality
【义不容辞】 yìbùróngcí 〈成〉 be duty-bound: ～的责任 obligation one can't shirk
【义齿】yìchǐ〈名〉 false tooth
【义地】yìdì〈名〉〈旧〉 free graveyard for the poor
【义断恩绝】yìduàn-ēnjué〈成〉 break off friendly ties (with sb.)
【义愤】 yìfèn 〈名〉 righteous indignation: 满腔～ be swollen with indignation ‖ 公众/强烈的～ public/strong indignation
【义愤填膺】yìfèn-tiányīng〈成〉 be filled with righteous indignation: 听到这一消息后，人人～。 After hearing the news everyone was burning with indignation.
【义父】yìfù〈名〉 adoptive father
【义工】 yìgōng 〈名〉 **1**（指工作） voluntary work without pay: 从事～ do voluntary work **2**（指人） volunteer: 当～ do volunteer work
【义和团】 Yìhétuán 〈名〉 Boxers: ～运动 Boxer Uprising

> **义和团运动**
>
> Chinese grass-roots movement at the end of the 19th and beginning of the 20th century. Originally known as 义和拳, the Boxers were a secret organization based in Shandong, Zhili (roughly present-day Hebei), and other places. They were later enlisted by the Qing government, and their name changed to 义和团. Their slogan was '*fu Qing mie yang*' (扶清灭洋, 'support the Qing and annihilate the Westerners'). Most of the Boxers were peasants and craftsmen. They were highly superstitious, believing that they were immune to swords and bullets. In 1900, the Eight-Power Allied Forces invaded China, and were resisted by the Boxers and Qing troops. The Boxer movement failed because of their inadequate strength, and because they were outlawed by the Qing government.

【义结金兰】yìjié-jīnlán〈成〉〈旧〉 vow to be sworn brothers or sisters
【义举】yìjǔ〈名〉 virtuous act: 扶弱济贫的～ the virtuous act of helping the weak and poor
【义捐】yìjuān〈动〉 make donations for a just cause: ～助学 donate money to poor students
【义军】yìjūn〈名〉 **1**（正义的军队） righteous army: 兴～，讨逆贼 raise a righteous army to suppress rebels **2**（起义军） uprising army
【义理】yìlǐ〈名〉 argumentation
【义卖】yìmài〈动〉 sell goods for worthy causes: ～活动 benefit sale activity ‖ 赈灾～ charity sales for disaster relief
【义母】yìmǔ〈名〉 adoptive mother
【义女】yìnǚ〈名〉 adopted daughter
【义拍】yìpāi〈动〉 hold a fund-raising auction
【义旗】yìqí〈名〉 banner of righteousness: 举～ rise against injustice
【义气】yìqi **A**〈名〉 code of brotherhood: 讲～ be loyal to one's friends ‖ 江湖～ code of brotherhood **B**〈形〉 loyal
【义赛】yìsài〈名〉 benefit match: 篮球～

basketball benefit
【义师】yìshī〈名〉army fighting a just war: 兴～ raise an army to fight for a just cause
【义士】yìshì〈名〉〈旧〉righteous man
【义无反顾】yìwúfǎngù〈成〉be duty-bound not to turn back
【义务】yìwù **A**〈名〉duty: 履行～ fulfil one's duty ‖ 道义/法律上的～ moral/legal obligation ‖ 纳税～ duty bound to pay taxes ‖ 公民都有服兵役的～。Serving in the army is obligatory for all citizens. **B**〈形〉voluntary: 参加～劳动 take part in voluntary labour ‖ 做～家教 volunteer as a tutor
【义务兵】yìwùbīng〈名〉compulsory serviceman
【义务兵役制】yìwù bīngyìzhì〈名〉compulsory military service: 你们国家实行～吗? Is military service compulsory in your country?
【义务教育】yìwù jiàoyù〈名〉compulsory education: 九年～ nine-year compulsory education
【义项】yìxiàng〈名〉item in a dictionary entry
【义形于色】yìxíngyúsè〈成〉be visibly indignant
【义学】yìxué〈名〉〈旧〉community school charging no tuition
【义演】yìyǎn〈动〉give a charity performance: 举行/组织～ give/organize a benefit performance
【义勇】yìyǒng〈形〉righteous and courageous
【义勇军】yìyǒngjūn〈名〉army of volunteers: 东北抗日～ anti-Japanese army of volunteers in North-east China
【义勇军进行曲】Yìyǒngjūn Jìnxíngqǔ〈名〉*March of the Volunteers* [national anthem of the People's Republic of China]
【义展】yìzhǎn〈动〉hold a benefit exhibition
【义诊】yìzhěn〈动〉**1**（指将诊疗所得捐出）set up a clinic to provide medical consultation to raise funds for justice and public welfare **2**（义务诊治）give free medical treatment: 几位著名专家将在诊所～。Several well-known specialists will see patients on a voluntary basis at the clinic.
【义正词严】yìzhèng-cíyán〈成〉speak sternly out of a sense of justice
【义肢】yìzhī〈名〉［医学］artificial limb
【义冢】yìzhǒng〈名〉〈旧〉burial place for paupers and strangers
【义子】yìzǐ〈名〉adopted child

艺（藝） yì〈名〉**1**（技能）skill: ▸多才多～, 工～, 手～ **2**（艺术）art: ▸～人, 曲～, 文～
【艺不压身】yìbùyāshēn〈成〉it will not burden you if you are proficient in many skills
【艺高人胆大】yì gāo rén dǎn dà〈俗〉boldness of execution stems from great skill
【艺伎】yìjì〈名〉geisha
【艺林】yìlín〈名〉**1**（图书荟萃的地方）place with great collections of classic books **2**（艺术界）art circles
【艺名】yìmíng〈名〉stage name
【艺人】yìrén〈名〉**1**（表演者）actor: 街头～ street entertainer ‖ 杂耍～ variety show artist **2**（手艺人）artisan
【艺术】yìshù **A**〈名〉**1**（指社会意识形态）art: 精湛的～ exquisite art ‖ 印象派～ impressionist art ‖ 戏剧/表演～ dramatic/performing arts ‖ 造型～ formative art **2**（技能）skill: 学会领导～ acquire the art of leadership ‖ 教学～ teaching skills **B**〈形〉tasteful: 这座建筑装饰得很～。The building is tastefully adorned.
【艺术家】yìshùjiā ▸**p. 966**〈名〉artist: 电影/摄影～ motion picture/photographic artist ‖ 表演～ performance artist
【艺术节】yìshùjié〈名〉art festival
【艺术界】yìshùjiè〈名〉art world
【艺术品】yìshùpǐn〈名〉work of art: ～收藏 art collection
【艺术体操】yìshù tǐcāo〈名〉［体育］artistic gymnastics
【艺术性】yìshùxìng〈名〉artistry
【艺术修养】yìshù xiūyǎng〈名〉artistic culture
【艺术院校】yìshù yuànxiào〈名〉art school
【艺术照】yìshùzhào〈名〉arty photo
【艺术指导】yìshù zhǐdǎo〈名〉art director
【艺术字】yìshùzì〈名〉character in a fancy style
【艺坛】yìtán〈名〉art world: 蜚声～ be famous in the art world ‖ ～新秀 new talent in the world of art
【艺校】yìxiào〈名〉art school
【艺员】yìyuán ▸**p. 966**〈名〉actor
【艺苑】yìyuàn〈名〉art and literary circles: ～奇葩 exquisite works of art

刈 yì〈动〉〈书〉mow: ～草/麦 mow grass/wheat ‖ ～草机 mower

忆（憶） yì〈动〉**1**（回想）recall: ▸回～, 追～ **2**（记起）remember: ▸记～
【忆旧】yìjiù〈动〉recall bygone days with nostalgia
【忆苦思甜】yìkǔ-sītián〈成〉recall the sorrows of the past and savour the joys of the present
【忆昔抚今】yìxī-fǔjīn〈成〉recall the past and compare it with the present

艾 yì〈动〉〈书〉repent: ▸自怨自～ ▸ài

仡 yì ▸gē
【仡仡】yìyì〈形〉〈书〉**1**（强壮勇敢）strong and brave: ～勇夫 strong and brave man **2**（高大）high

议（議） yì
A〈动〉**1**（商议）discuss: 我们把这个问题～一～。Let's exchange views on this problem. ▸计～, 商～, 审～ **2**（评论）comment: ▸非～, 公～, 评～
B〈名〉opinion: ▸倡～, 建～, 提～
【议案】yì'àn〈名〉bill: 撤销～ quash a bill ‖ 提交～ submit a proposal
【议程】yìchéng〈名〉agenda: 会议～ conference agenda
【议定】yìdìng〈动〉agree on
【议定书】yìdìngshū〈名〉protocol: 贸易～ trade protocol
【议而不决】yì'érbùjué〈成〉discuss without reaching a decision: ～, 决而不行 discussion leads to no decision and decision, if any, results in no action
【议购】yìgòu〈动〉buy at a negotiated price: ～议销 buy or sell at a negotiated price
【议和】yìhé〈动〉hold peace talks
【议会】yìhuì〈名〉parliament: 解散～ dissolve a parliament
【议会制】yìhuìzhì〈名〉parliamentary system
【议价】yìjià **A**〈动〉negotiate a price **B**〈名〉negotiated price: ～收购/销售 buy/sell at a negotiated price ‖ ～粮/油 grain/oil at a negotiated price
【议决】yìjué〈动〉pass a resolution
【议论】yìlùn **A**〈动〉discuss: 背后～ talk behind sb.'s back ‖ 我记得有人～过这件事。I remember people talking about the event. **B**〈名〉comment: 大发～ speak about sth. at great length
【议论纷纷】yìlùn-fēnfēn〈成〉be widely discussed
【议论文】yìlùnwén〈名〉argumentative writing
【议事】yìshì〈动〉discuss official business: ～规则 rules of procedure or debate ‖ 列入～日程 be put on the daily agenda
【议题】yìtí〈名〉topic for discussion: 中心～ central topic for discussion
【议席】yìxí〈名〉seat in a legislative assembly: 获得多数～ win the majority in the legislative assembly
【议员】yìyuán ▸**p. 966**〈名〉Member of Parliament (MP) [UK]: 当选～ win a seat in Parliament
【议院】yìyuàn〈名〉legislative assembly: 参～ senate
【议长】yìzhǎng〈名〉speaker: 美国众议院～ Speaker of the House of Representatives of the United States
【议政】yìzhèng〈动〉deliberate on state affairs

屹 yì〈形〉〈书〉towering like a mountain peak
【屹立】yìlì〈动〉stand erect
【屹然】yìrán〈形〉〈书〉towering: ～不动 stand firm and erect

亦 yì〈副〉〈书〉also: 反之～然 and vice versa ▸人云～云
【亦步亦趋】yìbù-yìqū〈成〉follow slavishly: 不要老跟着别人～。Don't always be copying other people.
【亦复如此】yìfùrúcǐ〈成〉in the same way
【亦即】yìjí〈动〉〈书〉be also known as: 鲁迅, ～周树人, 是中国现代文学的巨匠。Lu Xun, also known as Zhou Shuren, is a literary giant of modern China.
【亦庄亦谐】yìzhuāng-yìxié〈成〉be serious and comical at the same time

衣 yì〈动〉〈书〉be dressed in: ～布衣 wear cotton clothes ▸yī

异（異） yì
A〈动〉separate: ▸离～
B〈形〉**1**（不同）different: 口味因人而～。Everybody has different tastes. ▸～口同声, 求同存～ **2**（另外）other: ▸～地, ～国 **3**（特别）strange: ▸～味, ～香 **4**（惊奇）surprised: ▸诧～, 怪～, 惊～
【异邦】yìbāng〈名〉foreign land: 漂泊～ lead a wandering life in a foreign country
【异彩】yìcǎi〈名〉〈喻〉outstanding performance: ～纷呈 in varied colourful splendour ‖ 大放～ blossom in radiant splendour
【异常】yìcháng **A**〈形〉unusual: 表现～ show abnormality ‖ 神色～ not look one's usual self ‖ 没有～情况。There's nothing abnormal. ‖ 心肺未见～。There is no discernible abnormality of the heart or the lungs. **B**〈副〉extremely: 情绪～激动 be incredibly excited ‖ 她反应～机敏。She responded very wittily.

【异词】yìcí〈名〉words of dissent: 并无～。There is no disagreement.

【异地】yìdì〈名〉**1**（他乡） foreign land: 流落～ wander homeless in a strange land **2**（外地） place far away: ～取款 non-local withdrawal (of money)

【异读】yìdú〈名〉 variant pronunciation of a Chinese character

【异端】yìduān〈名〉 heresy: 视为～ regard as heresy

【异端邪说】yìduān-xiéshuō〈成〉 heretical beliefs: 鼓吹～ preach heresy

【异国】yìguó〈名〉 foreign country: ～情调 exotic atmosphere ‖ ～他乡 alien land

【异乎】yìhū〈形〉 different: ～寻常 out of the ordinary

【异花传粉】yìhuā chuánfěn〈名〉［植物］ cross-pollination

【异化】yìhuà〈动〉**1**（逐渐变得不同） alienate **2**［哲学］ alienate **3**［语言］ dissimilate

【异己】yìjǐ〈名〉 dissident: 排除～ exclude those who hold different views ‖ ～分子 dissident

【异教】yìjiào〈名〉 paganism: ～徒 pagan

【异军突起】yìjūn-tūqǐ〈成〉 a new force suddenly comes to the fore: 乡镇企业～。Township enterprises have emerged as a new force.

【异口同声】yìkǒu-tóngshēng〈成〉 in unison: ～地回答 answer in chorus ‖ 他们～地拒绝了。They refused with one voice.

【异类】yìlèi〈名〉 alien

【异曲同工】yìqǔ-tónggōng〈成〉〈喻〉 different in approach but equally satisfactory in result

【异趣】yìqù〈名〉**1**（指不同） different interests **2**（指特殊） special tastes

【异日】yìrì〈名〉〈书〉**1**（日后） some other day: 此事留待～再议。This will be discussed some other day. **2**（从前） former days: ～情谊，记忆犹新。Bygone friendships remain fresh in my mind.

【异体】yìtǐ **A**〈名〉［语言］ variant form of a Chinese character **B**〈形〉［生物］ of a different body: ～组织移植 alien tissue transplant

【异体字】yìtǐzì〈名〉［语言］ variant form of a Chinese character

【异同】yìtóng〈名〉 similarities and differences: 比较大麦和小麦的～ compare the similarities and differences between wheat and barley ‖ 分析两种社会制度的～ make an analysis of the similarities and differences between the two social systems

【异味】yìwèi〈名〉**1**（指美味） rare delicacy **2**（指气味） strange smell: 发出～ give off a peculiar smell ‖ 闻到～ smell a strange smell

【异物】yìwù〈名〉**1**（指物体） foreign matter: 胃中有～ have foreign matter in one's stomach **2**〈书〉（指人） ghost: 化为～ give up the ghost

【异乡】yìxiāng〈名〉 foreign land: 客居～ live in a foreign land ‖ ～人 stranger ‖ 独在～为异客，每逢佳节倍思亲。Alone in a strange land far away, one pines twice as much for one's kinsfolk during festival time.

【异香】yìxiāng〈名〉 rare fragrance: ～扑鼻。Strong whiffs of rare perfume assailed the nostrils.

【异想天开】yìxiǎng-tiānkāi〈成〉 indulge in wild fantasy: 别再～了，那是不可能的事。Stop letting your imagination run riot. That is never going to happen.

【异心】yìxīn〈名〉 disloyalty: 怀有～ harbour disloyalty

【异型】yìxíng〈形〉 special-shaped: ～钢材 special-shaped steel

【异性】yìxìng〈形〉**1**（指性别） opposite-sex: 交～朋友 make a friend of the opposite sex **2**（指性质） different in nature: 同性电荷相斥，～电荷相吸。Like electric charges repel each other and unlike ones attract each other.

【异姓】yìxìng〈名〉 different surname: 同名～ have the same first name but different surnames

【异言】yìyán〈名〉〈书〉 dissenting words: 并无～ raise no objection

【异样】yìyàng〈形〉**1**（不一样） different: 多年没见了，看不出他有什么～。We haven't seen each other for years, but I can't see any difference in him. **2**（奇怪） peculiar: 人们都用～的眼光打量他。Everybody sized him up curiously.

【异议】yìyì〈名〉 dissent: 提出～ raise an objection ‖ 对此我们没有～。We have no objection to this.

【异域】yìyù〈名〉**1**（外国） foreign country: ～文化 foreign culture **2**（外乡） alien land: ～孤魂 lonely soul far away from home

【异族】yìzú〈名〉 different race: ～通婚 mixed-race marriage

抑[1] yì〈动〉 curb: ～价 keep down prices ‖ ～恶扬善 condemn wickedness and commend morality ▸～制，压～

抑[2] yì〈连〉〈书〉**1**（或） or **2**（但是） but **3**（而且） moreover

【抑或】yìhuò〈连〉〈书〉 or: 他们是来，～不来，尚未可知。It's not clear yet whether they will come or not.

【抑强扶弱】yìqiáng-fúruò〈成〉 curb the strong and help the weak

【抑扬】yìyáng〈动〉 rise and fall

【抑扬顿挫】yìyáng-dùncuò〈成〉 in rhythmic tones: 他摇头晃脑～地背唐诗。He wagged his head as he recited a Tang poem, his voice rising, falling and pausing.

【抑郁】yìyù〈形〉 depressed: 精神～ feel low ‖ 心中～不平 feel disgruntled

【抑郁症】yìyùzhèng ▸**p. 50**〈名〉［医学］ depression

【抑止】yìzhǐ〈动〉 restrain: ～冲动 resist an impulse

【抑制】yìzhì〈动〉**1**［生理］ inhibit: ～正常的身体活动 inhibit normal bodily activity **2**（压下去） restrain: ～怒火 check one's anger ‖ ～通货膨胀 check inflation ‖ 我无法～自己的好奇心。I couldn't restrain my curiosity.

呓（囈） yì〈动〉 talk in one's sleep

【呓语】yìyǔ〈名〉 crazy talk: 狂人～ ravings of a madman

邑 yì〈名〉〈书〉**1**（城市） city: 通都大～ big city **2**〈古〉（县） county: ～令 county magistrate

佚 yì〈动〉 be lost: ～名 anonymous

【佚闻】yìwén〈名〉〈书〉 anecdote

役 yì

A〈动〉 use as a servant: ▸～畜，～使，奴～

B〈名〉**1**（兵役） military service: ▸兵～，服～，退～ **2**（苦力） forced labour: ▸劳～，徭～ **3**〈旧〉（仆人） servant: ▸仆～，衙～，杂～ **4**（战争） battle: ▸战～

【役畜】yìchù〈名〉 draught animal

【役龄】yìlíng〈名〉**1**（指年龄） enlistment age **2**（指年数） years of active service

【役使】yìshǐ〈动〉 work: ～家畜 work livestock

译（譯） yì〈动〉**1**（翻译） translate: 把英文～成中文 translate from English into Chinese ▸笔～，口～，意～ **2**（破译） decode: ～电码 decipher a code ▸破～

【译本】yìběn〈名〉translation:《红楼梦》英～ English translation of the *Dream of Red Mansions*

【译笔】yìbǐ〈名〉 quality or style of a translation: ～流畅。The translation reads smoothly.

【译稿】yìgǎo〈名〉 translated manuscript

【译介】yìjiè〈动〉 translate and introduce

【译名】yìmíng〈名〉 translated name

【译文】yìwén〈名〉 translated text: 对照原文核对～ check the translation against the original

【译意风】yìyìfēng〈名〉 simultaneous interpretation installation

【译音】yìyīn **A**〈动〉 transliterate: 这些外国人名和地名都译了音。These foreign names of people and places have all been transliterated. **B**〈名〉 transliteration: 这个词的～不够准确。The transliteration of this word is not accurate.

【译员】yìyuán〈名〉 interpreter: 当～ act as interpreter

【译者】yìzhě ▸**p. 966**〈名〉 translator

【译制】yìzhì〈动〉 dub: ～电影 dub a film ‖ 电影～厂 film dubbing studio

【译注】yìzhù〈动〉 translate and annotate: ～古籍 translate and annotate ancient books

【译著】yìzhù〈名〉 translation

【译作】yìzuò〈名〉 translation

易[1] yì〈动〉**1**（改变） change: 那所房子已几～其主。That house has already changed hands several times. ‖ ～地交货 deliver goods to a different place ▸～手，移风～俗 **2**（交换） exchange: 以货～货 exchange one thing for another ▸交～，贸～

易[2] yì〈形〉**1**（容易） easy: 严禁携带～燃～爆物品上车！Taking combustible and explosive goods aboard is strictly prohibited! ‖ 钱来之不～。Money doesn't grow on trees. ▸～如反掌，简～，轻而～举 **2**（平和） amiable: ▸平～近人

【易爆】yìbào〈形〉explosive: ～材料 explosive material ‖ ～气体 explosion hazard gases

【易北河】Yìběihé ▸**p. 294**〈名〉Elbe River

【易腐】yìfǔ〈形〉 perishable

【易攻难守】yìgōng-nánshǒu〈成〉 be easy to attack but hard to defend

【易货贸易】yìhuò màoyì〈名〉barter (trade)

【易拉罐】yìlāguàn〈名〉 ring-pull can

【易经】Yìjīng〈名〉 *I Ching*

【易燃】yìrán〈形〉 combustible: ～材料 flammable material

【易熔】yìróng〈形〉 fusible

【易如反掌】yìrúfǎnzhǎng〈成〉 be as easy as falling off a log: 对于你这样的聪明人来说，解决那个问题应该～。Solving that problem should be a piece of cake for a clever fellow like you.

【易手】yìshǒu〈动〉 change hands: 这幅画几经～。This painting has changed hands several times.

> **《易经》**
>
> *I Ching*, literally 'Classic of Changes' or 'Book of Changes', is China's first philosophical work, and one of the most important canons of Confucianism. It was originally entitled 《易》 or 《周易》. '*Yi*' can mean change, simplicity or invariability. '*Zhou*' can mean the Zhou Dynasty, referring to the period when the book was used as a text of divination. It can also mean 'all-inclusive'. Using *bagua* (▸八卦), *I Ching* describes the world as originating in the ceaseless dialectical interaction of two opposite forces, *yin* and *yang*.

【易碎】yìsuì〈形〉 breakable: ～品 breakable substance
【易性癖】yìxìngpǐ〈名〉 transsexualism
【易于】yìyú〈动〉 be easy to: ～接受 be easy to accept ‖ ～理解 be easy to understand
【易帜】yìzhì〈动〉〈书〉 change one's principles or allegiance

佾 yì〈名〉〈旧〉 ancient dance squad of eight people

怿（懌） yì〈形〉〈书〉 pleased

诣（詣） yì
A〈动〉 call on
B〈名〉 attainments: ▸苦心孤～, 造～

驿（驛） yì〈名〉〈旧〉 post station
【驿道】yìdào〈名〉 post road
【驿站】yìzhàn〈名〉 posthouse

绎（繹） yì〈动〉 unravel: ▸演～

轶（軼） yì〈动〉 **1**〈书〉（超过一般） excel: ～材 outstanding talent **2**（失传） be lost: ▸～事
【轶群超伦】yìqún-chāolún〈成〉 be head and shoulders above all others
【轶事】yìshì〈名〉 anecdote

昳 yì
▸dié
【昳丽】yìlì〈形〉〈书〉 beautiful

疫 yì〈名〉 epidemic disease: 防～ epidemic prevention ▸～情, 免～, 鼠～
【疫病】yìbìng〈名〉 epidemic disease: 控制～传播 control the spread of an epidemic
【疫点】yìdiǎn〈名〉 epidemic site
【疫苗】yìmiáo〈名〉 vaccine: 接种～ vaccinate sb. against a disease ‖ 流感～ influenza vaccine
【疫情】yìqíng〈名〉 epidemic situation: ～严重。 The epidemic situation was severe.
【疫区】yìqū〈名〉 epidemic-stricken area

弈 yì〈书〉
A〈名〉 *weiqi* ['go': game played with black and white pieces on a board of 361 crosses]: ▸博～
B〈动〉 play chess: 对～ play chess with sb.
【弈林】yìlín〈名〉 chess circles: ～高手 master chess player

奕 yì〈形〉〈书〉 grand
【奕奕】yìyì〈形〉 radiating power and vitality: ▸神采～

羿 Yì〈名〉 Yi [surname]

挹 yì〈动〉〈书〉 ladle out: ～取 ladle out
【挹彼注兹】yìbǐ-zhùzī〈成〉 draw from one to make good the deficit of another

益[1] yì
A〈动〉 increase: ▸延年～寿, 增～
B〈副〉 even more: ▸多多～善, 相得～彰

益[2] yì
A〈名〉 benefit: 得～于经验 profit by experience ▸开卷有～, 权～, 效～
B〈形〉 beneficial: ▸～鸟, 良师～友
【益虫】yìchóng〈名〉 beneficial insect
【益处】yìchu〈名〉 benefit: 带来～ bring benefits ‖ 得到～ gain profit
【益发】yìfā〈副〉 increasingly: ～困难 increasingly difficult ‖ ～漂亮 even more beautiful
【益母草】yìmǔcǎo〈名〉［中药］ motherwort
【益鸟】yìniǎo〈名〉 beneficial bird
【益生菌】yìshēngjūn〈名〉 probiotic: ～酸奶 probiotic yoghurt
【益友】yìyǒu〈名〉 friend and mentor: 良师～ good teacher and helpful friend
【益智】yìzhì〈动〉 be good for the brain: ～玩具 toys that are good for the brain

悒 yì〈形〉〈书〉 sad: ～郁 depressed ‖ ～～不乐 be depressed and unhappy

谊（誼） yì〈名〉 friendship: 尽地主之～ play the host ▸情～, 友～

埸 yì〈名〉〈书〉 **1**（田界） field boundary **2**（边界） border area

勚（勩） yì
A〈形〉〈书〉 toilsome: 劳～ toil
B〈动〉 be blunt: 螺丝扣～了。 The thread of the screw was worn out.

逸 yì
A〈动〉 **1**（逃跑） escape: ▸逃～ **2**〈书〉（隐居） be reclusive: ▸～民, 隐～ **3**（散失） be lost: ▸～闻 **4**（超过） surpass: ～群 be head and shoulders above all others
B〈形〉 leisurely: ▸安～, 好～恶劳, 一劳永～
【逸乐】yìlè〈形〉 comfortable and happy
【逸民】yìmín〈名〉〈旧〉 recluse
【逸趣】yìqù〈名〉 refined interest/taste
【逸史】yìshǐ〈名〉 unofficial history
【逸事】yìshì = 轶事 yìshì
【逸闻】yìwén〈名〉 anecdote: ～趣事 anecdotes and interesting episodes

翊 yì〈动〉〈书〉 assist: ～戴 assist and support (a ruler)

翌 yì〈形〉〈书〉 next: ～年 next year ‖ ～日 next day

嗌 yì〈名〉〈书〉 throat

肄 yì〈动〉 study
【肄业】yìyè〈动〉 **1**（修业） study at college **2**（中途离校） leave school before graduation

裔 yì〈名〉〈书〉 **1** ▸p. 279（后代） descendant: 华～美国人 American of Chinese descent **2**（边远的地方） borderland

意 yì
A〈名〉 **1**（心愿） desire: 合某人的～ find favour with sb. ‖ 这次最高级会议～在加强地区合作和团结。 The summit is designed to strengthen regional cooperation and unity. ▸恶～, 任～, 中～ **2**（意思） meaning: 段落大～ general idea of a paragraph ▸～义, 词不达～, 言外之～
B〈动〉 expect: ▸～料, ～外, 出其不～
【意表】yìbiǎo〈名〉〈书〉 what one does not expect: ▸出人～
【意大利】Yìdàlì〈名〉 Italy: ～共和国 Italian Republic ‖ ～人 Italian ‖ ～语 Italian
【意会】yìhuì〈动〉 sense: 只可～, 不可言传 can be grasped but not explained in words
【意见】yìjiàn〈名〉 **1**（看法） idea: 采纳～ adopt a view ‖ 持相同/相反～ take a similar/different view ‖ 发表～ say one's piece ‖ 交换～ exchange ideas ‖ 征求～ ask sb.'s opinion ‖ ～有分歧 opinions differ ‖ 反对～ objections ‖ 正反两方面的～都要听。 We must listen to both the pros and the cons. **2**（不满） differing opinion: 和人闹～ quarrel with sb. ‖ 提～ file a complaint ‖ 征求～ solicit criticisms ‖ 不少人对他的作风有～。 Lots of people object to his style. ‖ 有～拿到桌面上来。 If you have any objections, please bring them to the table for discussion.
【意见簿】yìjiànbù〈名〉 visitors' book
【意见箱】yìjiànxiāng〈名〉 suggestions box
【意境】yìjìng〈名〉 mood of a literary work
【意料】yìliào〈动〉 anticipate: 完全出乎～ beyond all expectations ‖ 这是～之中的事。 That's to be expected.
【意念】yìniàn〈名〉 idea: 他当时只有一个～。 At the time he had only one thought in his mind.
【意气】yìqì〈名〉 **1**（意志和气概） will and spirit: 失败使他～消沉。 Failure crushed his spirit. **2**（志趣和性格） disposition: ▸～相投 **3**（不良情绪） impulse: ▸～用事, 闹～
【意气风发】yìqì-fēngfā〈成〉 be daring and energetic
【意气相投】yìqì-xiāngtóu〈成〉 be alike in temperament: 他和我～。 He sees the world in the same way as I do.
【意气用事】yìqì-yòngshì〈成〉 act on impulse: 处理问题不要～。 Don't be impulsive when handling problems.
【意趣】yìqù〈名〉 interest and charm: ～盎然 be full of interest and charm
【意识】yìshí **A**〈名〉 consciousness: 增强法律～ increase the awareness of the law ‖ 存在决定～。 Existence determines consciousness. **B**〈动〉 be conscious of: 充分～到问题的严重性 be fully aware of the seriousness of the problem ‖ 他～到了其他许多人没有～到的问题。 He perceived what was not seen by many others.
【意识流】yìshíliú〈名〉［语言］ stream of consciousness: ～小说 stream-of-consciousness novel
【意识形态】yìshí xíngtài〈名〉［哲学］ ideology: ～领域 ideological field
【意思】yìsi **A**〈名〉 **1**（思想内容） meaning: 掌握文章的中心～ grasp the meaning of the article ‖ 你明白我的～吗? Do you understand what I mean? ‖ 这个单词有几个～。 This word has several meanings.

2（想法） view: 他一点也没有表示出要度假的～。 He showed not the slightest desire to go on holiday. ‖ 我的～还是不去为好。 In my opinion, it's better not to go. **3**（心意） token of appreciation: 一点儿小～，请收下吧。 Please accept this small gift as a token of our gratitude to you. **4**（迹象） hint: 天有点要下雨的～。 It looks like rain. **5**（趣味） fun: 电影的结尾很有～。 The film has a really great ending. ‖ 那事没多大～。 That is rather boring. **B**〈动〉 express one's gratitude, friendship, congratulations, etc.: 他们要结婚了，我们应该买件礼物～～。 They are going to get married. We should buy them a wedding present as a token of our congratulations.

【意图】yìtú〈名〉 intention: 表明～ make one's intention known ‖ 领会上级～ understand the intention of one's superior ‖ 透露～ reveal one's intention ‖ 他来的～是什么？ What is his purpose in coming?

【意外】yìwài **A**〈形〉 unexpected: 感到～ be taken by surprise ‖ 枪～走火。 The gun went off by accident. ‖ 这消息来的非常～。 The news came as a bolt from the blue. **B**〈名〉 accident: 避免～ avoid accidents ‖ 发生～ an accident happens

【意外事故】yìwài shìgù〈名〉［法律］accident

【意外收获】yìwài shōuhuò〈名〉 windfall

【意外死亡】yìwài sǐwáng〈名〉［法律］death by misadventure

【意味】yìwèi〈名〉 **1**（内涵） implication: 他的话～深长。 The implications of what he says are profound. **2**（情趣） interest: 富于文学～ be full of literary flavour

【意味着】yìwèizhe〈动〉 signify: 点头就～赞成 nod one's head to signify one's consent

【意下】yìxià〈名〉 opinion: 老兄～如何？ What's your opinion?

【意想】yìxiǎng〈动〉 imagine: ～不到的结局 unexpected result

【意向】yìxiàng〈名〉 intention: 双方都有扩大经济技术合作的～。 Both sides intend to extend economic and technological cooperation.

【意向金】yìxiàngjīn〈名〉 down payment: 购房～ down payment on a property

【意向书】yìxiàngshū〈名〉 letter of intent: 签订～ sign a statement of intent

【意象】yìxiàng〈名〉 image

【意兴】yìxìng〈名〉〈书〉 interest: ～勃勃 be highly enthusiastic ‖ ～索然 have not the least interest

【意义】yìyì〈名〉 **1**（包含的内容） meaning: 比喻～ figurative meaning ‖ 词汇/语法～ lexical/grammatical meaning **2**（价值） significance: 富有教育～ be very educational ‖ 中国入世具有重大的现实～和深远的历史～。 China's entry into WTO has great immediate and far-reaching significance.

【意译】yìyì〈动〉 **1**（相对"直译"） translate freely: 将诗～成散文 paraphrase poetry into prose **2**（相对"音译"） translate words of one language into another by similar meanings

【意欲】yìyù〈动〉 intend

【意愿】yìyuàn〈名〉 wish: 尊重他本人的～ respect his wishes ‖ 反映民众的～ reflect the wishes of the public

【意蕴】yìyùn〈名〉 implication: 反复琢磨，才能领会这首诗的～。The poem can be understood through deep investigation of its inner meaning.

【意在笔先】yìzàibǐxiān〈成〉 have an idea in mind before starting to write/paint

【意在言外】yìzàiyánwài〈成〉 meaning is implied: 古人为诗，贵于～。 Poets of ancient times made a point of implying their meaning rather than making it explicit.

【意旨】yìzhǐ〈名〉 intention: 秉承～ comply with sb.'s wishes

【意志】yìzhì〈名〉 will: ～薄弱 be weak-willed ‖ ～坚强 be strong-willed ‖ 钢铁般的～ iron will ‖ 不以人的～为转移 be independent of man's will

【意中人】yìzhōngrén〈名〉 one's beloved

溢 yì

A〈动〉 **1**（满出） overflow: 锅里的牛奶～出来了。 The milk spilled over out of the pot. ‖ 河水～过堤岸。 The river overflowed its banks. **2**（流露） reveal: ▸～于言表

B〈形〉〈书〉 excessive: ▸～美

【溢洪道】yìhóngdào〈名〉［水利］spillway

【溢价】yìjià〈名〉 [of stocks] excessive price

【溢价率】yìjiàlǜ〈名〉［金融］premium rate

【溢流】yìliú **A**〈动〉 overflow **B**〈名〉［水文］overflow stream

【溢美】yìměi〈动〉〈书〉 praise excessively: ～之词 fulsome compliments

【溢于言表】yìyú-yánbiǎo〈成〉 show clearly in one's words and manner: 愤激/感激之情～ indignation/gratitude is clearly revealed in one's words and manner

缢（縊） yì〈动〉〈书〉 hang: ▸自～

蓺 yì〈动〉〈书〉 grow

蜴 yì ▸蜥蜴 xīyì

毅 yì〈形〉 firm: ▸～力, ～然, 刚～

【毅力】yìlì〈名〉 willpower: 坚强的～ great willpower ‖ 惊人的～ amazing willpower

【毅然】yìrán〈形〉 firm: ～离家出走 leave home resolutely ‖ ～做出决定 be decisive in making a decision

【毅然决然】yìrán-juérán〈成〉 resolutely and determinedly: ～投身革命 resolutely plunge oneself into the revolutionary cause

鹝（鷊） yì〈名〉〈古〉 a kind of aquatic bird

熠 yì〈形〉〈书〉 brilliant

【熠熠】yìyì〈形〉〈书〉 glittering: ～生辉 sparkling and shining

薏 yì

【薏米】yìmǐ〈名〉 seed of Job's tears

【薏仁】yìrén = 薏米 yìmǐ

【薏苡】yìyǐ〈名〉［植物］Job's tears

殪 yì〈动〉〈书〉 **1**（死亡） die **2**（使死亡） kill

螠 yì〈名〉［动物］echiuroid

劓 yì〈动〉 cut off the nose as a punishment

翳 yì

A〈动〉〈书〉 conceal

B ▸**p. 50**〈名〉［医学］nebula

臆 yì

A〈名〉 chest: ▸胸～

B〈形〉 subjective: ▸～断, ～造

【臆测】yìcè〈动〉 guess: 不要武断～。 Please don't make wild guesses.

【臆断】yìduàn〈动〉 assume: 主观～ subjective assumptions

【臆度】yìduó〈动〉〈书〉 conjecture

【臆见】yìjiàn〈名〉 subjective view

【臆说】yìshuō〈名〉 assumption: 证实～ verify a hypothesis

【臆造】yìzào〈动〉 fabricate: 凭空～ fabricate without any basis

翼 yì

A〈名〉 **1**（翅膀） wing: 鼓～ flap the wings ▸蝉～, 如虎添～ **2**（阵地两侧） flank;（政治派别） wing: 部队的左右两～ both flanks of an army **3**（机翼） wing of an aeroplane: ▸机～ **4**（指星宿） one of the 28 constellations in ancient Chinese astronomy

B〈动〉〈书〉 assist

【翼侧】yìcè〈名〉［军事］flank: 从～迂回包抄敌人 go round the enemy's flank

【翼翅】yìchì〈名〉 wing

【翼轮】yìlún〈名〉［航空］wing wheel: ～推进器 vane propeller

【翼手动物】yìshǒu dòngwù〈名〉 chiropter

【翼翼】yìyì〈形〉 cautious: ▸小心～

镱（鐿） yì〈名〉［化学］ytterbium (Yb)

癔 yì

【癔病】yìbìng ▸**p. 50**〈名〉［医学］hysteria: ～患者 hysteric

【癔症】yìzhèng ▸**p. 50**〈名〉［医学］hysteria

懿 yì〈形〉〈书〉 exemplary: 嘉言～行 be careful in words and noble in conduct

【懿德】yìdé〈名〉〈书〉 moral excellence

【懿旨】yìzhǐ〈名〉 decree of an empress or empress dowager

yīn

因 yīn

A〈动〉 follow: ▸～袭, ～循守旧

B〈介〉 **1**（根据） on the basis of: ▸～材施教, ～地制宜, ～势利导 **2**（因为） because of: ～公外出 be away on business ‖ ～伤致残 become disabled through injury ‖ ～殉职 die in line of duty ‖ 比赛～雨而延期。 The match was postponed on account of rain. ▸～噎废食

C〈名〉 cause: 事出有～。 There is good reason for it. ▸内～, 外～

D〈连〉 because: 他～身体欠佳，不得不退休。 He had to retire because of ill health. ‖ ～天气恶劣，所有的飞机都停飞了。 All aircraft are grounded due to the bad weather.

【因材施教】yīncái-shījiào〈成〉 teach students according to their aptitude

【因此】yīncǐ〈连〉 therefore: 大坝倒塌了，土地～被淹。 The dam broke and the land was flooded. ‖ 工作太忙，～没来看

您。I was too busy to come to see you.

【因地制宜】yīndì-zhìyí〈成〉 suit measures to local conditions: 各地要～地发展经济。Local authorities should develop their economy in line with local conditions.

【因而】yīn'ér〈连〉 with the result that: 我因公出差，～未能出席那次重要会议。I was away on business, as a result of which I missed the important meeting.

【因弗内斯郡】Yīnfúnèisījùn〈名〉 Inverness-shire

【因故】yīngù〈副〉 for some reason

【因果】yīnguǒ〈名〉 1（原因和结果）cause and effect: ～关系 causality ‖ 颠倒～ invert cause and effect 2［佛教］karma: 受到～报应 suffer retribution for one's sins

【因果律】yīnguǒlǜ〈名〉 law of causation

【因祸得福】yīnhuò-défú〈成〉 benefit from a misfortune

【因利乘便】yīnlì chéngbiàn〈成〉 exploit the opportunity

【因陋就简】yīnlòu-jiùjiǎn〈成〉 make do with whatever is available

【因人成事】yīnrén-chéngshì〈成〉 rely on others for success

【因人而异】yīnrén'éryì〈成〉 differ from individual to individual: 疗效～。The curative effect varies from person to person.

【因人废言】yīnrén fèiyán〈成〉 deny what one says because of their unfavourable background

【因式】yīnshì〈名〉［数学］ factor: ～分解 factoring

【因势利导】yīnshì-lìdǎo〈成〉 guide action according to circumstances: 不管发生什么事，他总能～。Whatever happened to him, he always allows things to take their course a positive way.

【因素】yīnsù〈名〉 1（构成要素）element 2（原因或条件） factor: 调动一切积极～ bring every positive factor into play ‖ 决定性～ decisiveness factor ‖ 心理～ psychological factor

【因特网】Yīntèwǎng〈名〉 Internet: ～用户 Internaut ‖ 这些文章在～上可以查到。These articles can be found on the Internet.

【因为】yīnwèi A〈介〉 because of: 他～玩忽职守而被开除。He was sacked because of negligence of duty. B〈连〉 because: ～飞机晚点，我在机场多等了半个小时。I waited an extra half an hour at the airport because the flight was delayed.

【因袭】yīnxí〈动〉 follow: ～陈规 follow outmoded rules ‖ ～前人 follow in the footsteps of one's predecessors

【因小失大】yīnxiǎo-shīdà〈成〉 try to save a little only to lose a lot

【因循】yīnxún〈动〉 1（沿袭） follow the old routine: ～旧俗 follow old customs 2（迟延拖拉） procrastinate: ～坐误 fail to grasp an opportunity and let it pass by

【因循守旧】yīnxún-shǒujiù〈成〉 stay in the same old rut: 决不能～，固步自封。We mustn't get stuck, resting content with old practices.

【因噎废食】yīnyē-fèishí〈成〉〈喻〉 throw out the baby with the bathwater

【因应】yīnyìng〈动〉 1（应付） cope with: ～对手的挑战 respond to the challenges of one's opponent 2（适应） adapt oneself to: ～形势 act according to circumstances ‖ ～市场的需求 act according to the needs of the market

【因由】yīnyóu〈名〉 reason: 内中必有～。There must be some cause at heart.

【因缘】yīnyuán〈名〉 1［佛教］ principal and secondary causes 2（缘分） predestined relationship: 他俩好像～注定要成夫妻。They seemed to be destined to become husband and wife.

【因子】yīnzǐ = 因式 yīnshì

阴（陰）yīn

A〈形〉 1（云层密布） cloudy: ～转晴。The weather changed from cloudy to fine. ‖ 天气预报说～有小雨。The forecast is for overcast skies and a little rain. ►～雨 2（隐藏） concealed: ►阳奉～违 3（阴险） treacherous: 他这个人很～。He is a treacherous person. ►～谋，～险 4（凹下） in intaglio: ►～文
B〈名〉 1（日光照不到的地方） shade 2（山北水南） north of a hill or south of a river: 华～ Huayin [north of Huashan Mountain] ‖ 江～ Jiangyin [south of the Yangtze River] 3（生殖器） private parts 4［哲学］ *yin* [female/passive/negative principle in nature, as opposed to *yang* (阳)]: ►～阳 5（月亮） moon: ►～历 6（阴间） nether world: ►～间 7（带负电） negative: ►～离子

【阴暗】yīn'àn〈形〉 gloomy: ～的角落 dark corner ‖ 天色～。The weather is gloomy.

【阴暗面】yīn'ànmiàn〈名〉〈喻〉 dark side of things: 揭露～ reveal the dark side of things

【阴部】yīnbù〈名〉［生理］ genitals: ～瘙痒症 pruritus genitalium

【阴曹】yīncáo〈名〉 nether world

【阴曹地府】yīncáo-dìfǔ = 阴曹 yīncáo

【阴差阳错】yīnchā-yángcuò = 阴错阳差 yīncuò-yángchā

【阴沉】yīnchén〈形〉 gloomy: 脸色～ look glum ‖ 天色～。The sky is overcast.

【阴沉沉】yīnchénchén〈形〉 cloudy: 他脸色总是～的，从来不露出一丝笑容。He always looks glum and never cracks a smile. ‖ 天色～的，像要下雨。The sky is overcast as if it's going to rain.

【阴唇】yīnchún〈名〉［解剖］ labia

【阴错阳差】yīncuò-yángchā〈成〉 accidental error: 想不到会～，失去了与她见面的机会。I didn't expect that things would get messed up and so I would miss the opportunity of meeting up with her.

【阴丹士林】yīndānshìlín〈名〉 1［化学］ indanthrene 2（指布） cotton fabric dyed with indanthrene

【阴道】yīndào〈名〉［解剖］ vagina

【阴德】yīndé〈名〉 good deed done in secret: 积～ accumulate hidden merit

【阴蒂】yīndì〈名〉［解剖］ clitoris

【阴电】yīndiàn〈名〉［电子］ negative charge

【阴毒】yīndú〈形〉 sinister and ruthless: 生性～ be insidious in nature

【阴风】yīnfēng〈名〉 1（寒风） cold wind 2〈喻〉（邪恶的风潮） sinister trend: 煽～ secretly stir up trouble

【阴干】yīngān〈动〉 dry in the shade

【阴功】yīngōng = 阴德 yīndé

【阴沟】yīngōu〈名〉 sewer: 通～ unblock a drain

【阴沟里翻船】yīngōu lǐ fānchuán〈俗〉 suffer an unexpected setback: 他本想借这笔生意发财，不料～，反倒赔了一大笔钱。Instead of making money as he had expected, he failed miserably in the deal and lost a large amount of cash.

【阴河】yīnhé〈名〉 underground river

【阴户】yīnhù = 阴门 yīnmén

【阴晦】yīnhuì〈形〉 shady: 天色～ sombre sky

【阴魂】yīnhún〈名〉 soul:〈喻〉～不散 the ghosts remain

【阴极】yīnjí〈名〉 1［电气］ negative electrode 2［电子］ cathode

【阴极管】yīnjíguǎn〈名〉［电子］ cathode-ray tube

【阴极射线】yīnjí shèxiàn〈名〉［电子］ cathode ray

【阴间】yīnjiān〈名〉 nether world

【阴茎】yīnjīng〈名〉［解剖］ penis: ～勃起 get an erection

【阴茎包皮】yīnjīng bāopí〈名〉［解剖］ prepuce

【阴冷】yīnlěng〈形〉 1（指天气） gloomy and cold: ～的早晨 cold and gloomy morning ‖ 这几天～～的。It's been gloomy and cold these past few days. 2（指脸色） glum: 脸色～ be grim-faced

【阴离子】yīnlízǐ = 负离子 fùlízǐ

【阴历】yīnlì ►p. 618〈名〉 lunar calendar

【阴凉】yīnliáng A〈形〉 shady and cool: 到～处躲避烈日 step out of the sun into the cool B〈名〉 shady spot: 找一个～儿坐下来休息 seek out a shady spot where one can sit down and rest

【阴霾】yīnmái〈名〉〈书〉 haze

【阴毛】yīnmáo〈名〉 pubic hair

【阴门】yīnmén〈名〉［解剖］ vulva

【阴面】yīnmiàn〈名〉 shady side

【阴谋】yīnmóu A〈动〉 conspire: ～篡权 scheme to usurp power ‖ ～破坏 plot sabotage ‖ ～推翻政府 conspire to overthrow the government ‖ ～发动政变 scheme to stage a coup d'état B〈名〉 plot: 搞～ intrigue ‖ 识破了对方的～ see through one's opponent's plot ‖ 敌人的～破产了。The enemy's scheme fell apart.

【阴谋诡计】yīnmóu-guǐjì〈成〉 schemes and intrigues: 搞～ carry on an intrigue

【阴谋家】yīnmóujiā〈名〉 conspirator

【阴囊】yīnnáng〈名〉［解剖］ scrotum

【阴平】yīnpíng〈名〉［语言］ high and level tone [first of the four tones in modern standard Chinese pronunciation]

【阴柔】yīnróu〈形〉 graceful and restrained

【阴森】yīnsēn〈形〉 gloomy: ～可怖 ghastly and blood-curdling

【阴森森】yīnsēnsēn〈形〉 spooky

【阴盛阳衰】yīnshèng-yángshuāi〈成〉 1［中医］ *Yin* predominates over *Yang* 2（女的强过男的） women outdo men: 国家排球队一直是～。The national women's volleyball team has always been better than the men's.

【阴寿】yīnshòu〈名〉 1〈旧〉（纪念死者的诞辰） 10th posthumous birthday anniversary 2（人死后在阴间的年龄） age after death

【阴司】yīnsī = 阴间 yīnjiān

【阴私】yīnsī〈名〉 skeleton in the cupboard

【阴损】yīnsǔn A〈形〉 insidious and caustic B〈动〉 covertly harm

【阴天】yīntiān〈名〉 cloudy day

【阴文】yīnwén〈名〉 characters or designs cut in intaglio

【阴险】yīnxiǎn〈形〉 treacherous: 为人～ be treacherous ‖ ～狡猾 be evil and cunning

【阴线】yīnxiàn〈名〉 downward slope curve

【阴性】yīnxìng〈名〉 1 ►p. 50［医学］ negative: 药检呈～。The drug test was negative. 2［语言］ feminine gender

【阴虚】yīnxū〈名〉［中医］ deficiency of *Yin*

【阴阳】yīnyáng〈名〉 1［哲学］ *Yin* and *Yang* [the two opposing principles in nature, the former feminine and negative while the latter masculine and positive] 2（中国古代天文

学) ancient Chinese astronomy [esp the study of the movements of celestial bodies] 3 〈旧〉(星相、占卜等方术) occult arts such as astrology, divination, geomancy, etc. 4 = 阴阳生 yīnyángshēng

【阴阳怪气】yīnyáng-guàiqì〈成〉eccentric: 他这几天~的。He has been behaving rather peculiarly the last few days.

【阴阳历】yīnyánglì〈名〉lunisolar calendar: 农历是一种~。The traditional Chinese calendar is a kind of lunisolar calendar.

【阴阳人】yīnyángrén〈名〉(两性人) bisexual; (无两性特征) hermaphrodite

【阴阳生】yīnyángshēng〈名〉〈旧〉yin-yang geomancer

【阴阳先生】yīnyáng xiānsheng = 阴阳生 yīnyángshēng

【阴一套，阳一套】yīn yī tào, yáng yī tào〈俗〉act one way in public and another in private: 我就不信任那个~的家伙。I wouldn't trust that double-dealing fellow.

【阴翳】yīnyì = 荫翳 yīnyì

【阴影】yīnyǐng〈名〉shadow: 发现肺部有~ discover a shadow on one's lungs ‖〈喻〉死亡的~ shadow of death ‖〈喻〉不幸的消息给聚会蒙上了一层~。The sad news cast a shadow over the party.

【阴雨】yīnyǔ〈动〉be overcast and rainy: ~天 rainy day ‖ ~连绵 cloudy and drizzly for days on end

【阴郁】yīnyù〈形〉1 (阴暗沉闷) gloomy: 天色~。The weather is dismal. 2 (不开朗) depressed: 心情~ feel depressed ‖ ~的气氛 air of gloom

【阴云】yīnyún〈名〉dark clouds: 天空~密布。The sky was enveloped in dark clouds. ‖〈喻〉战争的~ war clouds

【阴宅】yīnzhái〈名〉grave

【阴招】yīnzhāo〈名〉treacherous act

茵

茵 yīn〈名〉mattress: 绿~场上 on the pitch ‖ 绿草如~。The green grass looks like a velvet carpet.

荫（蔭）

荫（蔭）yīn〈名〉shade: 林~道 boulevard ▸yìn

【荫蔽】yīnbì〈动〉1 (遮蔽) be shaded or hidden by foliage: ~在树丛中 lie hidden among the trees 2 (隐藏) conceal

【荫翳】yīnyì A = 荫蔽 yīnbì 1 B〈形〉with luxuriant foliage

音

音 yīn〈名〉1 (声音) note: 噪~ noise ‖ 超~速 supersonic speed ▸~响, ~乐 2 (音节) syllable: 读~不准 inaccurate pronunciation ‖ 一字一~。Each Chinese character has one syllable. ▸~标, ~译, 辅~ 3 (消息) news, tidings: ▸~信, 福~

【音爆】yīnbào〈名〉[航空] sonic boom

【音变】yīnbiàn〈名〉[语言] sound change

【音标】yīnbiāo〈名〉phonetic symbol: ▸国际~

【音波】yīnbō〈名〉[物理] sound wave

【音叉】yīnchā〈名〉[物理] tuning fork

【音长】yīncháng〈名〉duration of a sound

【音程】yīnchéng〈名〉[音乐] interval: 一个八度的~ an interval of one octave

【音带】yīndài〈名〉cassette tape

【音调】yīndiào〈名〉pitch: 降低/提高~ lower/raise the tone ‖ 他说话时~忽高忽低。When he speaks, his voice goes up and down.

【音碟】yīndié〈名〉audio CD

【音符】yīnfú〈名〉[音乐] musical note: 八分~ quaver〈英〉, eighth note〈美〉‖ 二分~ minim〈英〉, half note〈美〉‖ 三连~ triplet

【音高】yīngāo〈名〉[音乐] pitch

【音耗】yīnhào〈名〉〈书〉news: 久无~ have not heard from sb. for a long time

【音阶】yīnjiē〈名〉[音乐] (musical) scale

【音节】yīnjié〈名〉syllable: 重读~ stress a syllable

【音节文字】yīnjié wénzì〈名〉[语言] syllabic language

【音控开关】yīnkòng kāiguān〈名〉voice-operated switch

【音量】yīnliàng〈名〉volume: 调高/调低~ turn the sound up/down ‖ ~控制 volume control ‖ 电视机~已开到最大。The TV is at full volume.

【音律】yīnlǜ〈名〉[音乐] temperament

【音名】yīnmíng〈名〉1 = 律吕 lǜlǚ 2 [音乐] musical alphabet

【音频】yīnpín〈名〉[物理] audio frequency: ~信号 sound signal ‖ ~输出/输入 audio output/input

【音强】yīnqiáng〈名〉[音乐] intensity of a sound

【音区】yīnqū〈名〉[音乐] register: 低/中/高~ lower/medium/upper register

【音容】yīnróng〈名〉〈书〉voice and appearance: ~笑貌 voice and smiling face of the deceased

【音色】yīnsè〈名〉timbre: 这位歌唱家~悦耳。The singer's voice had a pleasant timbre.

【音素】yīnsù〈名〉[语言] phoneme

【音素文字】yīnsù wénzì〈名〉[语言] phonemic writing

【音速】yīnsù〈名〉speed of sound: ▸超~

【音位】yīnwèi〈名〉[语言] phoneme

【音问】yīnwèn = 音耗 yīnhào

【音箱】yīnxiāng〈名〉sound box

【音响】yīnxiǎng〈名〉1 (指声音效果) sound: ~效果 sound effects 2 (指设备) hi-fi: ~设备 stereo set

【音像】yīnxiàng〈名〉audio and video: ~制品 audio-video products

【音效】yīnxiào〈名〉[影视] sound effect

【音信】yīnxìn〈名〉news: ~全无 have not heard from sb. ‖ 她走后毫无~。There hasn't been any news of her since she went.

【音序】yīnxù〈名〉alphabetical order

【音讯】yīnxùn = 音信 yīnxìn

【音译】yīnyì〈动〉transliterate: Sofa 被~成"沙发"。'Sofa' is transliterated as 沙发.

【音域】yīnyù〈名〉[音乐] range: 那位歌手的~很宽。The singer's voice had a wide register.

【音乐】yīnyuè〈名〉music: ~伴奏 musical accompaniment ‖ ~晚会 musical evening ‖ 古典/流行/现代~ classical/pop/modern music ‖ ~家 musician

【音乐创作】yīnyuè chuàngzuò〈名〉musical composition

【音乐电视】yīnyuè diànshì〈名〉music television (MTV)

【音乐合成器】yīnyuè héchéngqì〈名〉music synthesizer

【音乐会】yīnyuèhuì〈名〉concert: 独唱~ vocal recital

【音乐记谱法】yīnyuè jìpǔfǎ〈名〉musical notation

【音乐剧】yīnyuèjù〈名〉musical

【音乐门铃】yīnyuè ménlíng〈名〉music bell

【音乐喷泉】yīnyuè pēnquán〈名〉dancing fountain

【音乐厅】yīnyuètīng〈名〉concert/philharmonic/music hall

【音乐学院】yīnyuè xuéyuàn〈名〉conservatoire

【音韵】yīnyùn〈名〉1 (声音的节奏旋律) rhyme and rhythm 2 (汉语字音的音、韵、调) sound, rhyme and tone of Chinese characters

【音韵学】yīnyùnxué〈名〉phonology

【音值】yīnzhí〈名〉[语言] phonetic value

【音质】yīnzhì〈名〉1 = 音色 yīnsè 2 (声音效果) acoustic fidelity

【音准】yīnzhǔn〈名〉[音乐] accuracy in pitch

洇

洇 yīn〈动〉[of ink] run and sink in: 这种纸~得很厉害。This kind of paper is very ink-absorbent.

姻

姻 yīn〈名〉1 (指婚姻) marriage: ▸~缘, 婚~, 联~ 2 (指亲戚) relation by marriage: ~兄弟 brothers-in-law

【姻亲】yīnqīn〈名〉relation by marriage: ~故旧 marriage connections and old friends

【姻娅】yīnyà〈名〉〈书〉relatives by marriage

【姻缘】yīnyuán〈名〉happy fate which brings lovers together: 缔结~ tie the marital knot ‖ 美满~ happy marriage ▸千里~一线牵

氤

氤 yīn

【氤氲】yīnyūn〈形〉〈书〉[of smoke, mist etc.] enshrouding

殷[1]

殷[1] yīn〈形〉1 (丰裕) abundant: ▸~富, ~实 2 (深厚) eager: ▸~切 3 (殷勤) hospitable: ▸~勤

殷[2]

殷[2] Yīn〈名〉Yin Dynasty [later period of the Shang Dynasty] ▸yān, yǐn

【殷富】yīnfù〈形〉wealthy: ~人家 wealthy family

【殷鉴】yīnjiàn〈名〉〈书〉negative example: 可资~ may serve as a negative example

【殷切】yīnqiè〈形〉eager: ~期望 ardent expectations

【殷勤】yīnqín〈形〉eagerly attentive: ~待客 attend to the visitors' every need ‖ 他向她献~。He was very attentive with her.

【殷实】yīnshí〈形〉well-off: ~人家 well-to-do family ‖ 家道~。The family is well-off.

【殷墟】Yīnxū〈名〉[考古] Yin ruins [in Henan Province]

【殷殷】yīnyīn〈形〉1 (殷切) ardent: ~期望 entertain an ardent expectation ‖ ~嘱咐 sincerely urge 2〈书〉(深重) worried and grieved: 忧心~ be heavy-hearted

【殷忧】yīnyōu〈动〉〈书〉be riddled with anxiety: 内怀~ be weighed down with worry

铟（銦）

铟（銦）yīn〈名〉[化学] indium (In)

堙

堙 yīn〈书〉

A〈动〉block up: 以石头~洪水 check a flood with stones

B〈名〉mound (of earth)

y

喑 yīn
A〈动〉 keep silent: ▸万马齐～
B〈形〉 mute: ▸～哑
【喑哑】yīnyǎ〈形〉 1（发不出声） mute and dumb 2（沙哑） hoarse

愔 yīn
【愔愔】yīnyīn〈形〉〈书〉 quiet

禋 yīn
A〈名〉〈古〉 sacrificial rites
B〈动〉 offer sacrifices

慇 yīn = 殷¹ yīn 3

yín

吟 yín
A〈动〉 1（吟咏） chant: ～诗作画 recite poetry and paint pictures ▸～诵, ～咏 2〈书〉（呻吟） groan: ▸呻～
B〈名〉 song [a type of classical poetry]
【吟唱】yínchàng〈动〉 chant: 小鸟儿在矮树丛中～。 The birds are singing on every bush.
【吟哦】yín'é〈动〉 recite poetry
【吟风弄月】yínfēng-nòngyuè〈成〉 write sentimental verse: 他的诗大多是～之作。 Most of his poems are sentimental pieces praising the wind and the moon.
【吟诵】yínsòng〈动〉 chant: ～诗词 recite poems
【吟味】yínwèi〈动〉〈书〉 recite with relish: 反复～ recite appreciatively over and over again
【吟咏】yínyǒng〈动〉 chant: 他的诗歌易上口～。 His poetry rolls off the tongue.

垠 yín〈名〉〈书〉 boundary: 无边无～的大草原 boundless stretch of prairie

狺 yín
【狺狺】yínyín〈拟〉〈书〉 yap: ～狂吠 bark frenziedly

崟 yín ▸嵚崟 qīnyín

银（銀） yín
A〈名〉 1［化学］ silver: ～手镯/项链 silver bracelet/necklace ‖ 纯～ pure silver 2（钱） money: ▸～根, ～行
B〈形〉 silver-coloured: 雪后树木披上了～装。 Snow tinselled the trees. ▸～发
【银白】yínbái〈形〉 silvery-white
【银杯】yínbēi〈名〉 silver cup
【银本位】yínběnwèi〈名〉［经济］ silver standard
【银币】yínbì〈名〉 silver coin
【银箔】yínbó〈名〉［冶金］ silver foil
【银川】Yínchuān ▸**p. 661**〈名〉 Yinchuan [capital of Ningxia (宁夏)]
【银弹】yíndàn〈名〉 silver bullet: ～外交 dollar diplomacy
【银锭】yíndìng〈名〉 1（银元宝） silver ingot 2（祭祀用假元宝） ingot made of silver paper used as offerings to ghosts and spirits
【银耳】yín'ěr〈名〉 tremella fungus: ～汤 tremella soup
【银发】yínfà〈名〉 white hair: ～老人 silver-haired old person
【银粉】yínfěn〈名〉 aluminium powder
【银根】yíngēn〈名〉［经济］ money supply: ～紧缩政策 tight money policy ‖ ～紧/松。 Money is tight/plentiful.
【银汉】yínhàn〈名〉〈书〉 Milky Way
【银行】yínháng〈名〉 bank: 把钱存入～ deposit money in a bank ‖ 世界～ World Bank ‖ 中国人民～ People's Bank of China
【银行存款】yínháng cúnkuǎn〈名〉 bank deposit: 冻结～ impound sb.'s bank account ‖ ～单 deposit receipt
【银行存折】yínháng cúnzhé〈名〉 passbook
【银行电汇】yínháng diànhuì〈名〉 bank cable transfer
【银行汇款】yínháng huìkuǎn〈名〉 bank remittance
【银行汇票】yínháng huìpiào〈名〉 bank draft
【银行家】yínhángjiā ▸**p. 966**〈名〉 banker
【银行卡】yínhángkǎ〈名〉 bank card
【银行票据】yínháng piàojù〈名〉 bank bill
【银行网点】yínháng wǎngdiǎn〈名〉 banking outlet
【银行业务】yínháng yèwù〈名〉 banking
【银行账户】yínháng zhànghù〈名〉 bank account: 开立/取消～ open/close a bank account
【银行支票】yínháng zhīpiào〈名〉 banker's cheque
【银行转账】yínháng zhuǎnzhàng〈名〉 bank transfer
【银毫】yínháo〈名〉 1（指毛发） fine long hair 2（小面值钱币） silver coin (of small denominations)
【银号】yínhào〈名〉〈旧〉 private banking house
【银河】Yínhé〈名〉［天文］ Milky Way
【银河系】Yínhéxì〈名〉［天文］ Galactic System
【银合欢】yínhéhuān〈名〉［植物］ silver wattle
【银红】yínhóng〈名〉 silver pink
【银狐】yínhú〈名〉 silver fox
【银环蛇】yínhuánshé〈名〉 silver-ringed snake
【银灰】yínhuī〈名〉 silvery grey
【银婚】yínhūn〈名〉 silver wedding anniversary [25th wedding anniversary]: ～纪念 silver wedding anniversary
【银监会】yínjiānhuì〈名〉 Banking Regulatory Commission
【银奖】yínjiǎng〈名〉 silver award
【银匠】yínjiàng〈名〉 silversmith
【银卡】yínkǎ〈名〉 silver card
【银矿】yínkuàng〈名〉 silver mine
【银联卡】yínliánkǎ〈名〉 UnionPay bank card
【银两】yínliǎng〈名〉〈旧〉 silver (as currency)
【银龄】yínlíng〈名〉 senior citizen: ～志愿者 elderly volunteer
【银楼】yínlóu〈名〉 jeweller's shop
【银幕】yínmù〈名〉 silver screen: 将小说搬上～ adapt a novel for the screen ‖ 宽～ wide screen
【银牌】yínpái〈名〉 silver medal: ～得主 silver medallist
【银屏】yínpíng〈名〉 TV screen
【银器】yínqì〈名〉 silverware
【银钱】yínqián〈名〉〈旧〉 money: ～交易 deal in cash
【银色】yínsè〈名〉 silver
【银团】yíntuán〈名〉 bank consortium
【银屑病】yínxièbìng ▸**p. 50**〈名〉［医学］ psoriasis
【银杏】yínxìng〈名〉［植物］ ginkgo: ～果/叶 ginkgo nut/leaf
【银洋】yínyáng〈名〉 silver dollar
【银样镴枪头】yínyàng làqiāngtóu〈成〉〈喻〉 good-looking but good-for-nothing person
【银鹰】yínyīng〈名〉〈喻〉 [Silver Eagle] fighter plane
【银鱼】yínyú〈名〉 whitebait
【银元】yínyuán = 银圆 yínyuán
【银圆】yínyuán〈名〉 silver dollar: ～外交 dollar diplomacy
【银针】yínzhēn〈名〉［中医］ silver acupuncture needle
【银证】yínzhèng〈名〉 bank securities
【银证通】yínzhèngtōng〈名〉 bank securities link
【银质奖章】yínzhì jiǎngzhāng〈名〉 silver medal
【银制品】yínzhìpǐn〈名〉 silverware
【银朱】yínzhū〈名〉［化学］ vermilion: ～涂料 vermilion paint
【银子】yínzi〈名〉 1（银） silver 2（钱） money

淫 yín〈形〉 1（过度） excessive: ▸～威, ～雨 2（放纵） unrestrained: ▸骄奢～逸 3（男女关系不正当） lascivious: 万恶～为首。 Lewdness is the worst of all vices. ▸～荡, ～秽, ～乱
【淫辞秽语】yíncí-huìyǔ〈成〉〈书〉 obscene language
【淫荡】yíndàng〈形〉 loose in morals: ～无耻 licentious and shameless
【淫妇】yínfù〈名〉 adulteress
【淫棍】yíngùn〈名〉 womanizer
【淫秽】yínhuì〈形〉 obscene: 查禁～录像 ban pornographic videotapes ‖ ～书刊 obscene publications
【淫乐】yínlè〈名〉 sexual indulgence
【淫乱】yínluàn〈形〉 sexually promiscuous
【淫书】yínshū〈名〉 erotica
【淫威】yínwēi〈名〉 despotic power: 横施～ abuse power
【淫猥】yínwěi〈形〉 obscene: ～下流的勾当 obscene and base acts
【淫雨】yínyǔ〈名〉 excessive rain: ～成灾。 The excessive rains became a calamity.
【淫欲】yínyù〈名〉 lust

寅 yín〈名〉 third of the twelve Earthly Branches (地支)
【寅吃卯粮】yínchī-mǎoliáng〈成〉 draw one's pay in advance: 工资微薄，常常是～。 With such a low salary we often end up using tomorrow's wages to feed today's needs.
【寅时】yínshí〈名〉 period of the day from 3 am to 5 am

龈（齦） yín〈名〉［解剖］ gum: ▸牙～

夤 yín〈书〉
A〈形〉 deep: ▸～夜
B〈动〉 seek connections in high places
【夤夜】yínyè〈名〉〈书〉 the dead of night
【夤缘】yínyuán〈动〉〈书〉〈喻〉 attach oneself to sb. powerful: ～得官 get an official post by courting powerful connections

yǐn

尹 yǐn〈名〉〈古〉 official title: 府～ prefectural magistrate

引 yǐn

A〈动〉 **1**〈书〉（拉弓） draw a bow: ▸～而不发 **2**（拉长） stretch out: ▸～吭高歌, ～桥, ～申 **3**（拉） pull: ▸～力, 穿针～线, 牵～ **4**（引导） lead: ～水灌田 draw water to irrigate the farmland ‖ 他把我～上了成功之路。 He set me on the road to success. ▸～导, ～狼入室, ～诱, 索～ **5**（招来） induce: 他的话～得大家哈哈大笑。 His words had everybody roaring with laughter. ▸抛砖～玉 **6**（推荐） recommend: ▸～荐 **7**（引用） quote: ▸～经据典, ～用, ～证 **8**（离开） leave: ▸～退
B〈量〉 *yin* [unit of length, equal to 33.3333 metres]

【引爆】yǐnbào〈动〉 **1**（使爆炸） ignite: ～炸弹 detonate a bomb ‖ ～装置 igniter **2**（使发生） trigger: ～价格大战 trigger off a price war
【引产】yǐnchǎn〈动〉［医学］ induce labour
【引导】yǐndǎo〈动〉 **1**（带领） lead: ～游客参观市容 take visitors round a city ‖ 老师要～学生独立思考。 Teachers should guide pupils to think for themselves. **2**［计算机］ boot: ～程序 boot loader
【引得】yǐndé〈名〉〈旧〉 index
【引动】yǐndòng〈动〉 cause: 一席话～我思乡的情怀。 A snatch of conversation filled me with longing for my hometown.
【引逗】yǐndòu〈动〉 **1**（逗弄） tease: 别～孩子，他该睡觉了。 Don't tease the child; it's time he went to bed. **2**（引诱） entice: 她在～他。 She was luring him.
【引渡】yǐndù〈动〉 **1**（引导渡水） lead across;（指引） guide: ～迷津 guide through a labyrinth **2**［法律］ extradite: ～程序 extradition proceedings ‖ ～条约 extradition treaty ‖ 他因谋杀罪而被从法国～到英国受审。 He was extradited from France to Britain to stand trial for murder.
【引而不发】yǐn'érbùfā〈成〉〈喻〉 **1**（善于引导） show people what to do instead of doing it on their behalf **2**（做好准备） be prepared to wait for an opportunity
【引发】yǐnfā〈动〉 trigger: ～暴乱 spark off a riot ‖ ～兴趣 arouse interest ‖ ～一场抛售风 trigger a selling spree
【引港】yǐngǎng = 领港 lǐnggǎng
【引吭高歌】yǐnháng-gāogē〈成〉 belt out a song
【引航】yǐnháng〈动〉 pilot a ship into/out of a harbour: ～员 pilot
【引号】yǐnhào〈名〉 quotation marks; inverted commas〈英〉: 单/双～ single /double quotation marks
【引河】yǐnhé〈名〉［水利］ irrigation channel
【引火】yǐnhuǒ〈动〉 ignite: 用木柴～ light a fire with firewood
【引火烧身】yǐnhuǒshāoshēn〈成〉 **1** = 惹火烧身 rěhuǒshāoshēn **2**〈喻〉（自己招惹批评） make a self-criticism to encourage criticism from others
【引火物】yǐnhuǒwù〈名〉 kindling
【引见】yǐnjiàn〈动〉 introduce: 他们把他～给来宾。 They introduced him to their visiting guests.
【引荐】yǐnjiàn〈动〉 recommend: 请某人出面～ ask sb. for a recommendation
【引介】yǐnjiè〈动〉 import and introduce: ～外国作品 import and introduce foreign works
【引进】yǐnjìn〈动〉 **1** = 引荐 yǐnjiàn **2**（引入） introduce: ～良种 introduce better strains of seeds ‖ ～人才 recruit talents ‖ ～外资 bring in foreign capital
【引经据典】yǐnjīng-jùdiǎn〈成〉 quote the classics: 不要～地为自己辩护。 Don't try to justify yourself by quoting from the classics.
【引颈】yǐnjǐng〈动〉〈书〉 crane one's neck: ～四望 crane one's neck to look around
【引咎】yǐnjiù〈动〉〈书〉 acknowledge one's mistake: ～辞职 acknowledge one's mistake and resign
【引狼入室】yǐnlángrùshì〈成〉〈喻〉 open the door to a dangerous enemy
【引力】yǐnlì〈名〉［物理］ gravitation: 地球～ terrestrial gravitation
【引力场】yǐnlìchǎng〈名〉［物理］ gravitational field
【引例】yǐnlì **A**〈动〉 cite **B**〈名〉 quotation: 通过～阐明词义 use citations to illustrate the meaning of words
【引领】yǐnlǐng〈动〉 **1**（带领） guide: ～来客就座 marshal the guests at a feast ‖ 由当地人～，我们穿过了树林。 Local people led us through the woods. **2**〈书〉（盼望殷切） eagerly look forward to sth.: ～而望 crane one's neck in anticipation
【引流】yǐnliú〈名〉［医学］ drainage: ～管 drain
【引路】yǐnlù〈动〉 guide: 盲人有时靠狗来～。 Blind people are sometimes guided by dogs.
【引路人】yǐnlùrén〈名〉 guide
【引起】yǐnqǐ〈动〉 give rise to: ～不满 stoke up resentment ‖ ～冲突 give rise to conflict ‖ ～大火 spark a fire ‖ ～反感 arouse antipathy ‖ ～反响 awaken a response ‖ ～关注 stir up concern ‖ ～好奇心 arouse curiosity ‖ ～轰动 cause a sensation ‖ ～怀疑 give rise to suspicion ‖ ～连锁反应 have ripple effect ‖ ～麻烦 stir up trouble ‖ ～同情 rouse pity ‖ ～误解 lead to misunderstanding ‖ ～轩然大波 set the fur flying ‖ ～争议 spark controversy ‖ ～注意 attract attention ‖ 这场争论是由他～的。 This debate was started by him.
【引桥】yǐnqiáo〈名〉［交通］ bridge approach: ～跨度 approach span
【引擎】yǐnqíng〈名〉 engine
【引擎罩】yǐnqíngzhào〈名〉 bonnet (of car)〈英〉; hood〈美〉
【引人入胜】yǐnrénrùshèng〈成〉 bewitching: 森林的景色～。 The forest has an enchanting air.
【引人深思】yǐnrénshēnsī〈成〉 be thought-provoking
【引人瞩目】yǐnrénzhǔmù〈成〉conspicuous
【引人注目】yǐnrénzhùmù〈成〉 be eye-catching: 她脸上最～的还是她那双动人的眼睛。 Her most striking feature was her eyes.
【引入】yǐnrù〈动〉 **1**（指引领） lead into: ～歧途 lead sb. astray **2**（指采用） introduce from elsewhere: ～竞争机制 introduce a competitive mechanism
【引蛇出洞】yǐnshé chūdòng〈成〉〈喻〉 lure evildoers into revealing their true colours
【引申】yǐnshēn〈动〉 extend the meaning of: ～义 extended meaning
【引述】yǐnshù〈动〉 quote: ～名家论点 quote an expert as saying
【引水槽】yǐnshuǐcáo〈名〉［矿业］ gutter
【引水工程】yǐnshuǐ gōngchéng〈名〉［水利］ water diversion project
【引水渠】yǐnshuǐqú〈名〉［水利］ feed canal
【引体向上】yǐntǐxiàngshàng〈名〉［体育］ pull-up
【引退】yǐntuì〈动〉 resign: 告老～ retire on account of old age
【引文】yǐnwén〈名〉 quotation: 查出～的出处 trace quotations to their original sources ‖ 核实～ verify a quotation
【引线】yǐnxiàn〈名〉 **1**［工程］ lead wire **2**（媒介） go-between **3**（引火线） fuse
【引信】yǐnxìn〈名〉 detonator: 拆除炸弹的～ defuse a bomb
【引言】yǐnyán〈名〉 forward
【引以为耻】yǐnyǐwéichǐ〈成〉 regard it as a disgrace
【引以为戒】yǐnyǐwéijiè〈成〉 learn lessons
【引以为荣】yǐnyǐwéiróng〈成〉 regard as a great honour
【引用】yǐnyòng〈动〉 **1**（用他人的话或事例做依据） quote: ～例子 quote examples ‖ ～数字来说明 explain by quoting figures ‖ 你错误地～了我的原话。 You misquoted me. **2**（任用） appoint
【引诱】yǐnyòu〈动〉 **1**（诱导） entice: ～未成年人犯罪 lure minors into committing crimes ‖ ～人上当受骗 lure sb. into a trap **2**（诱惑） tempt: 经不住金钱的～ yield to the temptations of money
【引语】yǐnyǔ = 引文 yǐnwén
【引玉之砖】yǐnyùzhīzhuān〈成〉〈谦〉〈喻〉 humble remarks offered to spark valuable opinions by others
【引证】yǐnzhèng〈动〉 cite as evidence: ～自己的看法 quote facts to support one's view
【引致】yǐnzhì〈动〉〈书〉 lead to: 过度砍伐～山洪暴发。 Excessive logging resulted in mountain torrents.
【引种】yǐnzhǒng〈动〉 introduce a new breed from elsewhere
【引种】yǐnzhòng〈动〉［农业］ plant an introduced variety
【引资】yǐnzī〈动〉 bring in capital from elsewhere: 招商～ invite outside investments
【引子】yǐnzi〈名〉 **1**［戏曲］（第一支曲子） first song in *Southern Song* (南曲) and *Northern Song* (北曲) **2**［戏曲］（开场白） actor's opening lines **3**［音乐］ prelude **4**（引出正文或用于启发的话） introductory remarks: 故事用一段～开头。 The story starts off with an introduction. **5**［中医］ added ingredient enhancing efficiency
【引座员】yǐnzuòyuán ▸p. 966〈名〉 usher

吲 yǐn

【吲哚】yǐnduǒ〈名〉［化学］ indole

饮（飲）yǐn

A〈动〉 **1**（喝） drink: ～茶/水 drink tea/water ‖ ～酒 drink alcohol ▸～料, ～水思源 **2**（心中怀有） nurse: ▸～恨
B〈名〉 **1**（饮料） drink: ▸冷～, 热～ **2**［中医］（饮子） decoction of Chinese medicine to be taken cold **3**［中医］（稀痰） watery sputum
▸yìn

【饮弹】yǐndàn〈动〉〈书〉 be hit by a bullet: ～身亡 be killed by a bullet
【饮恨】yǐnhèn〈动〉〈书〉 nurse a grievance: ～而终 die with bottled-up grievances
【饮恨吞声】yǐnhèn-tūnshēng〈成〉 endure insults and humiliations
【饮剂】yǐnjì〈名〉 potion
【饮料】yǐnliào〈名〉 drink
【饮片】yǐnpiàn〈名〉［中药］ shredded herbs ready for decoction

y

【饮品】yǐnpǐn〈名〉 beverage
【饮泣】yǐnqì〈动〉〈书〉 swallow one's tears: ～吞声 choke back one's sobs
【饮食】yǐnshí **A**〈名〉 food and drink: 保持均衡～ maintain a balanced diet ‖ 注意～卫生 be careful with food and drink hygiene ‖ ～文化 cooking culture ‖ ～习惯 dietary habit **B**〈动〉 eat and drink: ～起居 eating, drinking and living ‖ 不思～ forget to eat or drink
【饮食店】yǐnshídiàn〈名〉 snack bar
【饮食男女】yǐnshí-nánnǚ〈成〉 humanity's prime needs [food, drink and sex]
【饮食业】yǐnshíyè〈名〉 catering industry
【饮水不忘挖井人】yǐn shuǐ bù wàng wājǐngrén〈俗〉〈喻〉 do not forget the source of one's happiness
【饮水机】yǐnshuǐjī〈名〉 water dispenser
【饮水思源】yǐnshuǐ-sīyuán〈成〉 do not forget the source of one's happiness
【饮用水】yǐnyòngshuǐ〈名〉 drinking water: ～水质标准 drinking water standard
【饮誉】yǐnyù〈动〉〈书〉 be well-known: ～天下 enjoy a worldwide reputation ‖ ～文坛 be highly acclaimed in literary circles
【饮鸩止渴】yǐnzhèn-zhǐkě〈成〉〈喻〉 seek temporary relief regardless of the disastrous consequences
【饮子】yǐnzi〈名〉［中药］ decoction of Chinese medicine to be taken cold

蚓 yǐn〈名〉 earthworm: ▸蚯～

殷 yǐn〈拟〉〈书〉 rumble: 雷声～～。 The thunder rumbled.
▸yān, yīn

隐（隱）yǐn
A〈动〉 **1**（隐藏不露） hide from view: ▸～避，～藏，～匿 **2**（掩盖真相） cover up: ▸～瞒，～姓埋名
B〈形〉 **1**（不外露） latent: ▸～患，～情 **2**（不明显） indistinct
C〈名〉 secret: ▸～私，难言之～
【隐蔽】yǐnbì **A**〈动〉 take cover: 他们～在岩石下。 They sheltered themselves under a rock. **B**〈形〉 concealed: 十分～的位置 well-concealed position
【隐避】yǐnbì〈动〉 go into hiding: ～在山里 hide away in the mountains
【隐藏】yǐncáng〈动〉 hide: ～在树丛里 hide in the trees ‖ ～在心里的想法 idea lurking in one's mind
【隐恶扬善】yǐn'è-yángshàn〈成〉 cover up sb.'s faults and praise his merits
【隐伏】yǐnfú〈动〉 lie hidden: 蛇～在草丛中。 A snake is lurking in the grass. ‖ 该国经济～着危机。 Crisis lurks in this nation's economy.
【隐格纸】yǐngézhǐ〈名〉 feint-ruled paper
【隐含】yǐnhán〈动〉 imply: 他的缄默中～着怨恨。 His silence implied resentment.
【隐花植物】yǐnhuā zhíwù〈名〉 cryptogam
【隐患】yǐnhuàn〈名〉 hidden danger: 火灾～ hidden danger of fire ‖ 消除～ nip any trouble in the bud
【隐讳】yǐnhuì〈动〉 cover up: 对朋友毫无～ be completely frank with one's friends
【隐晦】yǐnhuì〈形〉 obscure: 这首诗有多处～难懂。 This poem is full of ambiguities.
【隐疾】yǐnjí〈名〉 unmentionable disease
【隐居】yǐnjū〈动〉 cut oneself off from the world: ～多年 spend many years in seclusion
【隐君子】yǐnjūnzǐ = 瘾君子 yǐnjūnzǐ
【隐括】yǐnkuò = 檃栝 yǐnkuò
【隐瞒】yǐnmán〈动〉 hold back: ～实情 conceal the truth ‖ ～罪行 hide one's guilt ‖ 毫不～ make no secret of sth.
【隐秘】yǐnmì **A**〈动〉 hide: ～真实身份 conceal one's true identity **B**〈形〉 hidden: ～的地方 hidden place **C**〈名〉 secret: 刺探～ pry into sb.'s secret
【隐没】yǐnmò〈动〉 hide: 轮船逐渐～在黑暗中。 The ship vanished into the darkness.
【隐匿】yǐnnì〈动〉 conceal: ～行踪 cover up one's tracks ‖ ～罪证 conceal criminal facts
【隐情】yǐnqíng〈名〉 unmentionable secret: 说出～ reveal a secret ‖ 其中必有～。 There must be some other reason behind it.
【隐忍】yǐnrěn〈动〉〈书〉 bear patiently: ～悲痛 bear sorrow with forbearance
【隐射】yǐnshè = 影射 yǐngshè
【隐身】yǐnshēn〈动〉 make oneself invisible: ～术 art of making oneself invisible
【隐士】yǐnshì〈名〉 recluse
【隐私】yǐnsī〈名〉 privacy: 侵犯～ invade sb.'s privacy ‖ 个人～ individual privacy ‖ ～权 right to privacy
【隐痛】yǐntòng〈名〉 **1**（指痛苦） secret anguish **2**（指疼痛） dull pain: 他感到胸部～。 He felt a dull ache in his bosom.
【隐退】yǐntuì〈动〉 **1**（逐渐消失） disappear: 往事渐渐从他的记忆中～。 Past events have gradually faded from his mind. **2**（退职隐居） withdraw from public life: 称病～ withdraw from public life on the pretext of illness
【隐现】yǐnxiàn〈动〉 be visible now and then: 对战争的恐惧～在他们心头。 The horrors of war hovered in their thoughts.
【隐形飞机】yǐnxíng fēijī〈名〉 stealth plane
【隐形轰炸机】yǐnxíng hōngzhàjī〈名〉 stealth bomber
【隐形技术】yǐnxíng jìshù〈名〉 stealth technology
【隐形眼镜】yǐnxíng yǎnjìng〈名〉 contact lens
【隐性】yǐnxìng〈形〉 recessive: ～基因 recessive gene ‖ ～亏损 invisible deficit ‖ ～杀手 hidden killer ‖ ～遗传 recessive inheritance
【隐性失业】yǐnxìng shīyè〈名〉 recessive unemployment
【隐性收入】yǐnxìng shōurù〈名〉 invisible income
【隐姓埋名】yǐnxìng-máimíng〈成〉 conceal one's identity: 罪犯～，藏匿国外。 The criminal lived in hiding overseas under an assumed name.
【隐血】yǐnxuè〈名〉［医学］ occult blood
【隐逸】yǐnyì〈书〉 **A**〈动〉 live in seclusion **B**〈名〉 recluse
【隐隐】yǐnyǐn〈形〉 faint: ～作痛 feel a dull ache ‖ 大雾弥漫，群山～。 Mist blurred the mountains.
【隐忧】yǐnyōu〈名〉 secret anxiety: 心怀～ have secret worries
【隐语】yǐnyǔ〈名〉 **1**（谜语） enigmatic language **2**（黑话） argot;（行话） jargon
【隐喻】yǐnyù〈名〉［语言］ metaphor
【隐约】yǐnyuē〈形〉 indistinct: 咚咚鼓声～可闻。 The faint roll of the drums could be heard. ‖ 树木在薄雾中～可见。 The trees could be seen faintly through the mist.
【隐约其辞】yǐnyuē-qící〈成〉 speak in ambiguities: 这篇文章对关键的问题～，叫人看了不痛快。 The article was evasive on key issues and left much to be desired.
【隐衷】yǐnzhōng〈名〉 feelings one wishes to keep to oneself

檃（檼）yǐn
【檃栝】yǐnkuò **A**〈名〉〈古〉 tool for straightening bent bamboo or wood **B**〈动〉〈书〉 prune or rewrite a piece of writing

瘾（癮）yǐn〈名〉 **1**（兴趣） strong interest: 棋～ passion for chess **2**（依赖性） addiction: 毒～ drug addiction ‖ 他酒～很大。 He is very fond of the bottle.
【瘾君子】yǐnjūnzǐ〈名〉 drug addict: 美沙酮用于帮助～戒毒。 Methadone is used to help addicts detoxify.
【瘾头】yǐntóu〈名〉 addiction: 他游泳的～儿不小。 He is completely obsessed with swimming.

yìn

印 yìn
A〈名〉 **1**（图章） seal: 盖～ affix a seal ▸～章，钢～ **2**（痕迹） trace: ▸～痕，脚～，手～
B〈动〉 **1**（符合） tally: ▸～证，心心相～ **2**（留下痕迹） engrave: 一个男人的鞋印清楚地～在湿泥上。 The mark of a man's shoe was printed clearly in the mud. ‖〈喻〉 往事深深地～在她的脑海里。 Memories of the past were stamped in her mind. **3**（印刷） print: 该书加～一千册。 Print off another thousand copies of this book. ▸～刷，排～，～染
【印把子】yìnbàzi〈名〉 seal of authority: ～掌握在人民手里。 Power is in the hands of the people.
【印本】yìnběn〈名〉 printed copy: 第一版～ first edition copy
【印鼻】yìnbí = 印纽 yìnniǔ
【印次】yìncì〈名〉［印刷］ impression: 这本词典已有二十个～。 This dictionary has had 20 impressions so far.
【印地语】Yìndìyǔ ▸**p. 918**〈名〉 Hindi
【印第安纳州】Yìndì'ānnàzhōu〈名〉 Indiana
【印第安人】Yìndì'ānrén〈名〉 American Indian〈英〉; Native American〈美〉
【印度】Yìndù〈名〉 India: ～共和国 Republic of India ‖ ～人 Indian
【印度教】Yìndùjiào〈名〉 Hinduism
【印度尼西亚】Yìndùníxīyà〈名〉 Indonesia: ～共和国 Republic of Indonesia ‖ ～人 Indonesian ‖ ～语 Indonesian
【印度洋】Yìndùyáng〈名〉 Indian Ocean
【印度支那】Yìndù-Zhīnà〈名〉 Indo-China
【印发】yìnfā〈动〉 print and distribute: ～传单 print and distribute leaflets
【印盒】yìnhé〈名〉 seal box
【印痕】yìnhén〈名〉 impression: 在橡皮泥上压出一个钥匙的～ imprint the shape of a key in Plasticine
【印花】yìnhuā **A**〈动〉［纺织］ print: ～布 cotton print **B**〈名〉 fiscal stamp
【印花税】yìnhuāshuì〈名〉 stamp duty: 征收～ levy a stamp tax
【印记】yìnjì **A**〈名〉 **1**〈旧〉（官印） stamp of a government organization **2**（痕迹） trace: 打有～ be marked with brands ‖〈喻〉 带有鲜明的时代～ with a marked imprint of the times **B**〈动〉 make a deep impression on one's mind: 这一场面深深地～在我的脑海里。 This scene left a very deep impression on my mind.

y

【印迹】yìnjì〈名〉 trace: 在泥地上留下～ leave impressions in the mud ‖ 苦难的经历在他的脸上留下了～。Suffering left its marks on his face.
【印加】Yìnjiā〈名〉 Inca: ～帝国 Inca Empire ‖ ～人 Inca
【印鉴】yìnjiàn〈名〉 specimen seal impression filed for checking: 在银行留有私人～ leave one's personal seal at the bank
【印模】yìnmó〈名〉 1（指模子） impression: 钥匙～ impression of a key 2［医学］impression: ～石膏 impression plaster
【印泥】yìnní〈名〉 Chinese vermilion seal paste
【印纽】yìnniǔ〈名〉knob of a seal (in animal shape)
【印钮】yìnniǔ = 印纽 yìnniǔ
【印欧语系】Yìn-Ōu Yǔxì〈名〉 Indo-European language family
【印谱】yìnpǔ〈名〉 album of seal impressions
【印染】yìnrǎn〈动〉［纺织］print and dye: ～厂 printing and dyeing mill
【印色】yìnsè = 印泥 yìnní
【印数】yìnshù〈名〉［印刷］impression
【印刷】yìnshuā〈动〉 print: ～错误 printing error ‖ 彩色～ colour printing ‖ ～厂 press
【印刷电路】yìnshuā diànlù〈名〉［电子］printed circuit
【印刷工】yìnshuāgōng〈名〉 printer
【印刷机】yìnshuājī〈名〉［印刷］printing press
【印刷品】yìnshuāpǐn〈名〉 printed matter
【印刷体】yìnshuātǐ〈名〉［印刷］block letter
【印台】yìntái〈名〉 ink pad
【印堂】yìntáng〈名〉 glabella
【印玺】yìnxǐ〈名〉 imperial seal
【印象】yìnxiàng〈名〉 impression: ～模糊 vague impression ‖ ～深刻 be deeply impressed with ‖ 第一～ first impression ‖ 你对这座城市的～如何? What's your impression of the city?
【印象派】yìnxiàngpài〈名〉 impressionist: ～画家 impressionist painter
【印信】yìnxìn〈名〉 official seal
【印行】yìnxíng〈动〉 publish: ～单行本 publish separate editions ‖ 此书限于国内～。The book is to be printed and distributed domestically only.
【印油】yìnyóu〈名〉 stamp-pad ink
【印张】yìnzhāng〈名〉［印刷］printed sheet
【印章】yìnzhāng〈名〉 seal: 盖～ affix a seal
【印证】yìnzhèng A〈动〉 confirm: 事实～了这一切。Facts have corroborated all of these. ‖ 这封信～了我的怀疑。This letter confirmed my doubt. B〈名〉 corroborating evidence: 这本圈点得密密麻麻的参考书是他刻苦学习的最好～。This densely marked reference book is the best testimony to his hard study.
【印制】yìnzhì〈动〉 print
【印子】yìnzi〈名〉 1（痕迹） mark: 脚～ footprint ‖ 手～ finger print 2 = 印子钱 yìnziqián
【印子钱】yìnziqián〈名〉〈旧〉 usury

饮（飲） yìn〈动〉 water: ～马 water a horse ‖ 牲口～过了吗? Have the cattle been watered?
▸yǐn

茚 yìn〈名〉［化学］indene: ～树脂 indene resin

荫¹（蔭） yìn〈形〉〈口〉 sunless: ▸～凉

荫²（廕） yìn〈动〉 1〈书〉（遮盖）shade: ▸～庇 2〈古〉（封赏） confer honours on one's descendants because of meritorious service: ▸封妻～子
▸yīn
【荫庇】yìnbì〈动〉〈书〉 1（遮蔽） cover with foliage 2（保佑庇护） protect
【荫凉】yìnliáng〈形〉 shady and cool: 小溪附近怡人的～处 pleasant shade near a brook

胤 yìn〈名〉〈书〉 offspring

鲫（鮣） yìn〈名〉［鱼类］remora

窨 yìn〈名〉 basement
▸xūn
【窨井】yìnjǐng〈名〉［建筑］inspection well

yīng

应¹（應） yīng〈动〉 should do: 决定～由他做出。The decision lies with him. ‖ 他积极努力，～得到奖赏。He deserves a reward for his efforts. ▸～有尽有, 理～, 罪有～得

应²（應） yīng〈动〉 promise: ▸～许
▸yìng
【应当】yīngdāng〈动〉 should: 这是我～做的。This is what I should do.
【应分】yīngfèn〈动〉 be part of one's job: 热情待客是我们～的事。It's our duty to receive guests warmly. ‖ 这是我～的事。This is my job.
【应付账款】yīngfù zhàngkuǎn〈名〉 accounts payable
【应该】yīnggāi〈动〉 should: 帮点忙是～的。We ought to help you. ‖ 我们不～做这种事情。We should not do such a thing.
【应计】yīngjì〈形〉［经济］accrued: ～成本 accrued cost ‖ ～利润/资产/债务 accrued profits/assets/liabilities ‖ ～收益 imputed income
【应届】yīngjiè〈形〉 of this year: ～毕业生 this year's graduating students
【应名儿】yīngmíngr A〈动〉 hold nominal power: 他当主席只是应了个名儿。He was chairperson only in name. B〈副〉 nominally: 他～是足球队员，实际上从来没上过场。He is a football player in name only. He has never played in a match.
【应声】yīngshēng〈动〉 answer: 我敲门敲了很长时间，但没人～儿。I've been knocking away for ages, but nobody has answered the door.
▸yìngshēng
【应收账款】yīngshōu zhàngkuǎn〈名〉 accounts receivable
【应税】yīngshuì〈形〉 taxable: ～商品 taxable goods
【应许】yīngxǔ〈动〉 1（答应） agree: 他～明天下午来。He promised to come tomorrow afternoon. 2（应允） allow: 这里不～抽烟。No smoking here.
【应有】yīngyǒu〈动〉 due: 做出～的贡献 make due contributions ‖ 你会得到～的惩罚。Justice will come your way.
【应有尽有】yīngyǒu-jìnyǒu〈成〉 have all that is necessary: 他的药店里各种各样贵重补药～。His shop had an abundant supply of rare and valuable medicines and tonics.
【应允】yīngyǔn〈动〉 agree: 欣然～ willingly consent

英¹ yīng
A〈名〉 1〈书〉（指花） flower: ▸落～ 2（指人） hero: ▸～豪, 精～, 群～会
B〈形〉 outstanding: ▸～才, ～俊, ～明

英² Yīng〈名〉 Britain: ▸～国, ～语
【英镑】yīngbàng ▸**p. 328**〈名〉 pound sterling: 可用～支付 be payable in sterling
【英才】yīngcái〈名〉 1（指人） person of outstanding ability: ～教育 elite education ‖ 社会～ greatest talents of society 2（指才能） talent
【英尺】yīngchǐ ▸**p. 82**〈量〉 foot
【英寸】yīngcùn ▸**p. 82**〈量〉 inch: 17～显示器 17-inch monitor
【英吨】yīngdūn〈量〉 gross ton
【英格兰】Yīnggélán〈名〉 England: ～人 English person
【英国】Yīngguó〈名〉 United Kingdom (UK): ～人 British person ‖ ～文学 English literature ‖ 她是～人。She is British.
【英国广播公司】Yīngguó Guǎngbō Gōngsī〈名〉 British Broadcasting Corporation (BBC)
【英汉词典】Yīng-Hàn cídiǎn〈名〉 English-Chinese dictionary
【英汉双解词典】Yīng-Hàn shuāngjiě cídiǎn〈名〉 dictionary of English with Chinese translation
【英豪】yīngháo〈名〉 heroes: 逞～ act heroically ‖ ～辈出 heroes come forth in large numbers
【英华】yīnghuá〈名〉 quintessence
【英魂】yīnghún = 英灵 yīnglíng 1
【英吉利海峡】Yīngjílì Hǎixiá〈名〉 English Channel
【英杰】yīngjié = 英豪 yīngháo
【英俊】yīngjùn〈形〉 1（才能出众） outstanding: ～有为 brilliant and promising 2（容貌俊秀） handsome: ～少年 handsome youth
【英里】yīnglǐ ▸**p. 82**〈量〉 mile: ～里程 mileage ‖ ～数 mileage ‖ 平方～ square mile
【英联邦】Yīngliánbāng〈名〉 British Commonwealth
【英烈】yīngliè A〈形〉 brave: ～女子 heroic woman B〈名〉 heroic martyr: 祭奠～ hold a memorial ceremony for the heroic martyrs ‖ 中华～ heroes of the Chinese nation
【英灵】yīnglíng〈名〉 1（指灵魂） spirit of a martyr: 告慰～ console the spirits of the martyrs ‖ ～永存。The martyrs are immortal. 2〈书〉（指人） person of outstanding talent
【英伦三岛】Yīnglún Sāndǎo〈名〉 British Isles [England, Scotland, Wales]
【英名】yīngmíng〈名〉 illustrious name: 使～永存 immortalize a heroic name ‖ ～远扬 establish one's illustrious name
【英明】yīngmíng〈形〉 wise: 决策～ make wise decisions ‖ ～的领导 brilliant leadership
【英模】yīngmó〈名〉 heroes and model

workers: ～报告会 public lecture of heroes and model workers ‖ ～事迹 exemplary deeds of heroes and model workers
【英亩】yīngmǔ〈量〉acre: ～数 acreage
【英年】yīngnián〈名〉youth: ～早逝 die in one's prime
【英气】yīngqì〈名〉heroic spirit: ～勃勃 be full of heroic spirit
【英石】yīngshí〈名〉limestone from Yingde (英德) County in Guangdong Province
【英式足球】yīngshì zúqiú〈名〉association football
【英特耐雄纳尔】Yīngtènàixióngnà'ěr〈名〉Internationale
【英文】Yīngwén ►p. 918〈名〉English: 讲～ speak English ‖ ～期刊 English periodicals
【英武】yīngwǔ〈形〉〈书〉soldierly
【英雄】yīngxióng A〈名〉hero: 巾帼～ heroine ‖ 民族～ national hero ‖ 战斗～ war hero B〈形〉heroic: ～事迹 heroic deeds ‖ ～行为 heroic act
【英雄所见略同】yīngxióng suǒjiàn lüè tóng〈俗〉great minds think alike
【英雄无用武之地】yīngxióng wú yòngwǔ zhī dì〈惯〉have no chance to exercise one's abilities
【英勇】yīngyǒng〈形〉heroic: ～牺牲 die heroically ‖ ～善战 be brave and skilful in battle
【英语】Yīngyǔ ►p. 918〈名〉English: ～国家 English-speaking country ‖ ～角 English corner ‖ 标准～ Queen's English
【英语水平考试】Yīngyǔ Shuǐpíng Kǎoshì〈名〉English Proficiency Test
【英制】yīngzhì〈名〉Imperial system (of weights and measures)
【英姿】yīngzī〈名〉heroic bearing: ～焕发 be dashing and spirited ‖ ～飒爽 be bold and brave

莺（鶯）

yīng〈名〉oriole
【莺歌燕舞】yīnggē-yànwǔ〈成〉joys of spring: 一片～的升平景象 a scene of peace and prosperity
【莺声燕语】yīngshēng-yànyǔ〈成〉[women's voices] as sweet asbirds twittering

婴[1]（嬰）

yīng〈名〉baby: 弃～ abandon a baby ‖ 母～平安。Both mother and baby are safe. ►～儿

婴[2]（嬰）

yīng〈动〉〈书〉harass
【婴儿】yīng'ér〈名〉baby: 新生～ new-born baby
【婴儿车】yīng'érchē〈名〉1（躺式）pram〈英〉; baby carriage〈美〉2（坐式）pushchair〈英〉; stroller〈美〉
【婴儿床】yīng'érchuáng〈名〉cot〈英〉; crib〈美〉
【婴孩】yīnghái〈名〉infant
【婴幼儿】yīng-yòu'ér〈名〉infants and preschool children: 重视～教育/营养 pay attention to the education/nutrition of infants and preschool children

瑛

yīng〈名〉〈书〉1（美玉）fine jade 2（玉的光彩）lustre of jade

锳（鍈）

yīng〈拟〉〈书〉tinkle

撄（攖）

yīng〈动〉〈书〉1（触犯）ruffle 2（扰乱）disturb

嘤（嚶）

yīng ►嘤嘤 yīngyīng
【嘤嘤】yīngyīng〈拟〉1〈书〉（鸟叫声）chirp: 鸟鸣～。Birds chirp. 2（哭泣声）sob: 她说着说着，～地哭了起来。As she spoke, she began to sob.

罂（罌）

yīng
A〈名〉〈古〉（指瓶子）small-mouthed jar
B ►罂粟 yīngsù
【罂粟】yīngsù〈名〉［植物］poppy: ～花 poppy flower

缨（纓）

yīng〈名〉1〈古〉（帽带）ribbon used to fasten the hat 2（带子）tassel: 帽～ hat tassel ►红～枪 3（穗状物）tassel-shaped thing: 玉米吐～了。The maize is putting forth tassels.
【缨子】yīngzi〈名〉1（帽带）hat tassels 2（穗状物）tassel-shaped vegetable leaves: 萝卜～ radish leaves

璎（瓔）

yīng〈名〉〈古〉jade-like stone
【璎珞】yīngluò〈名〉necklace of jade and pearls

樱（櫻）

yīng〈名〉1 = 樱花 yīnghuā 2 = 樱桃 yīngtáo
【樱花】yīnghuā〈名〉cherry blossom
【樱花树】yīnghuāshù〈名〉flowering cherry
【樱桃】yīngtáo〈名〉cherry
【樱桃树】yīngtáoshù〈名〉cherry tree

鹦（鸚）

yīng ►鹦鹉 yīngwǔ
【鹦哥】yīnggē = 鹦鹉 yīngwǔ
【鹦鹉】yīngwǔ〈名〉parrot: 长尾～ parakeet ‖ 虎皮～ budgerigar
【鹦鹉螺】yīngwǔluó〈名〉［动物］nautilus
【鹦鹉学舌】yīngwǔ-xuéshé〈成〉parrot talk: 他的这番话毫无新意，只是～而已。There is nothing new in what he said. It's mere parroting.

膺

yīng〈书〉
A〈名〉breast: ►义愤填～
B〈动〉1（承受）bear: 荣～英雄勋章 receive a hero's decoration ‖ 身～重任 hold a post of great responsibility 2（打击）strike: ►～惩
【膺惩】yīngchéng〈动〉〈书〉send a punitive expedition against
【膺选】yīngxuǎn〈动〉〈书〉be elected

鹰（鷹）

yīng〈名〉hawk
【鹰钩鼻子】yīnggōubízi〈名〉hooked nose
【鹰派】yīngpài〈名〉hawks: 一位～人物 a hawk
【鹰犬】yīngquǎn〈名〉1（指鹰和狗）hawks and hounds 2〈喻〉（指人）hired thug: 充当～ serve as sb.'s lackey
【鹰隼】yīngsǔn〈名〉〈书〉1（指鹰和隼）hawks and falcons 2〈喻〉（指人）fierce people
【鹰洋】yīngyáng〈名〉〈旧〉Mexican silver dollar
【鹰嘴豆】yīngzuǐdòu〈名〉［植物］chickpea

yíng

迎

yíng〈动〉1（迎接）welcome: ～来送往 welcome visitors and see them off ‖ ～新年 welcome in the New Year ►～接, 欢～, 辞旧～新 2（对着）meet face to face: ～着风浪前进 advance against the winds and waves ‖ ～着困难上 press forward in face of difficulties ►～风, ～击, ～面, ～头赶上
【迎宾】yíngbīn〈动〉greet guests: ～馆 guest house ‖ ～曲 welcome music
【迎春花】yíngchūnhuā〈名〉［植物］winter jasmine
【迎风】yíngfēng A〈动〉face the wind: ～挥舞旗帜 fling the banner to the wind ‖ ～使舵 luff the helm B〈副〉leeward: 红旗～招展 The red flag is fluttering in the wind ‖ 歌声～飘荡。The singing wafts on the breeze.
【迎合】yínghé〈动〉cater to: ～观众/上司 cater to the audience/one's superior ‖ ～时尚 cater to the current trend
【迎候】yínghòu〈动〉go and await the arrival of: 在门口～客人 await the arrival of a guest at the gate
【迎击】yíngjī〈动〉launch a head-on attack: ～来犯之敌 meet the invaders head-on
【迎接】yíngjiē〈动〉welcome: ～国庆节 welcome in National Day ‖ ～挑战 meet a challenge ‖ ～新生入学 greet the new students ‖ ～客人进来 usher guests inside
【迎面】yíngmiàn〈副〉head-on: 两辆卡车～相撞。Two trucks collided head-on. ‖ ～吹来刺骨的寒风。A cutting wind ripped into my face.
【迎亲】yíngqīn〈动〉go to meet the bride
【迎娶】yíngqǔ〈动〉go to fetch the bride
【迎刃而解】yíngrèn'érjiě〈成〉〈喻〉be easily solved: 思想问题解决了，矛盾也就～。Once the ideological problem is resolved, then the contradiction is solved.
【迎头】yíngtóu〈副〉head-on: 给某人～一棒 give sb. a blow to the head with a stick ‖ 两辆汽车～相撞。The two cars met each other head-on.
【迎头赶上】yíngtóu-gǎnshàng〈成〉try hard to catch up: 中国决心在信息高速公路方面～并与世界强国相抗衡。China is determined to catch up with its strong global competitors on the information highway.
【迎头痛击】yíngtóu-tòngjī〈成〉deal a severe blow: 我们要对各种流言飞语予以～。We must sternly repudiate all the rumours and slanders.
【迎新】yíngxīn〈动〉1（指新年）welcome in the new year: ►辞旧～ 2（指新人）welcome new arrivals: ～送旧 welcome in the new and send off the old
【迎迓】yíngyà〈动〉〈书〉welcome
【迎战】yíngzhàn〈动〉meet head-on: 他将～波兰选手。He will take on a Polish player.

茔（塋）

yíng〈名〉〈书〉grave: ～地 graveyard ‖ 祖～ ancestral grave

荧（熒）

yíng〈形〉〈书〉1（光亮微弱）glimmering: ～烛 glimmering candle light 2（眼光迷乱）dazzled: ►～惑
【荧光】yíngguāng〈名〉fluorescence: ～粉 fluorescent powder ‖ ～棒 light stick ‖ ～涂料 fluorescent coating

【荧光笔】 yíngguāngbǐ 〈名〉 highlighter (pen)
【荧光灯】 yíngguāngdēng 〈名〉 [电子] fluorescent lamp
【荧光屏】 yíngguāngpíng 〈名〉 [电子] viewing screen
【荧惑】 yínghuò 〈动〉 〈书〉 bewilder: ～人心 bewilder the people
【荧屏】 yíngpíng 〈名〉 **1** = 荧光屏 yíngguāngpíng **2** (电视) television: 这部电视连续剧下周将在～上再次和大家见面。 This TV series will be back on your screens next week.
【荧荧】 yíngyíng 〈形〉 twinkling

盈 yíng 〈动〉 **1** (充满) be full of: 她眼泪～眶。 Her eyes filled with tears. ▶恶贯满～ **2** (多余) have a surplus of: ▶～利, ～余
【盈亏】 yíngkuī 〈动〉 **1** (月圆和月缺) wax and wane **2** (赚钱和赔本) lose and gain: 自负～ be autonomous and responsible for one's own profit and losses ‖ ～平衡点 break-even point
【盈利】 yínglì = 赢利 yínglì
【盈盈】 yíngyíng 〈形〉 **1** (清澈) clear: 荷叶上露珠～。 The lotus leaves glittered with pearls of dew. ‖ 溪水～。 The stream is crystal clear. **2** (仪态美好) dainty: ～顾盼 look about gracefully **3** (到处洋溢) brimming over: 喜气～ brimming over with happiness **4** (动作轻盈) graceful: ～起舞 dancing gracefully
【盈余】 yíngyú **A** 〈动〉 have a surplus: ～两千元 have a surplus of 2,000 *yuan* **B** 〈名〉 surplus: 略有～ have a small surplus

莹 (瑩) yíng
A 〈形〉 〈书〉 lustrous and transparent
B 〈名〉 〈古〉 jade-like stone
【莹莹】 yíngyíng 〈形〉 sparkling and glistening: 泪水～ eyes glistening with tears

萤 (螢) yíng 〈名〉 firefly
【萤火虫】 yínghuǒchóng 〈名〉 firefly

营 (營) yíng
A 〈名〉 **1** (指驻扎地) barracks: ▶安～, 拔～, 露～ **2** (指军队编制单位) battalion: ～部 battalion headquarters
B 〈动〉 **1** (建造) construct: ▶～建, ～造 **2** (经营) manage: ▶～销, 经～ **3** (谋求) seek: ▶～救, ～生
【营办】 yíngbàn 〈动〉 manage
【营地】 yíngdì 〈名〉 campsite
【营房】 yíngfáng 〈名〉 barracks: 回～ return to barracks
【营火】 yínghuǒ 〈名〉 campfire
【营火会】 yínghuǒhuì 〈名〉 campfire party
【营建】 yíngjiàn 〈动〉 construct: ～校舍 construct school buildings
【营救】 yíngjiù 〈动〉 rescue: ～人质 rescue a hostage
【营垒】 yínglěi 〈名〉 **1** (军营) barracks and the enclosing walls: 设立～ set up camp **2** (阵营) camp: 极端右翼分子～ extreme right-wing camp
【营利】 yínglì 〈动〉 seek profits: ～性活动 profit-making activities
【营盘】 yíngpán 〈名〉 〈旧〉 military camp
【营生】 yíngshēng 〈动〉 earn a living: 靠稿费～ earn a living as a writer
【营生】 yíngsheng 〈名〉 〈旧〉 job: 没有一个正经的～ to have no serious job
【营私】 yíngsī 〈动〉 seek private gain: 结党～ form factions and seek private gain
【营私舞弊】 yíngsī-wǔbì 〈成〉 practise graft: 对那些～的人应该依法查处。 Those who engage in embezzlement and malpractice should be dealt with according to the law.
【营销】 yíngxiāo 〈名〉 marketing: ～观念 marketing concept ‖ ～策略 marketing strategy
【营销管理】 yíngxiāo guǎnlǐ 〈名〉 marketing management
【营销学】 yíngxiāoxué 〈名〉 marketing
【营销员】 yíngxiāoyuán ▶**p. 966** 〈名〉 salesperson
【营养】 yíngyǎng 〈名〉 nutrition: 富有～ be nutritious ‖ ～不良 dystrophy ‖ 严重缺乏～ be severely undernourished ‖ 增加～ have additional nutrients ‖ ～丰富 be highly nutritious
【营养钵】 yíngyǎngbō 〈名〉 [农业] nutritive bowl
【营养过剩】 yíngyǎng guòshèng 〈名〉 excessive nutrition
【营养价值】 yíngyǎng jiàzhí 〈名〉 nutritional value: ～高 be high in nutritional value
【营养品】 yíngyǎngpǐn 〈名〉 nutrient: 服用～ take nourishment
【营养师】 yíngyǎngshī ▶**p. 966** 〈名〉 dietitian
【营养失调】 yíngyǎng shītiáo 〈名〉 nutritional imbalance
【营养食品】 yíngyǎng shípǐn 〈名〉 health food
【营养素】 yíngyǎngsù 〈名〉 nutrient
【营养学】 yíngyǎngxué 〈名〉 nutriology: ～专家 nutritionist
【营养液】 yíngyǎngyè 〈名〉 [植物] nutrient solution
【营业】 yíngyè 〈动〉 do business: 开始～ start business ‖ 恢复正常～ reopen for business as usual ‖ 暂停～ suspend business ‖ ～利润 trading profit ‖ 我们今天照常～。 We are open for business as usual today.
【营业额】 yíngyè'é 〈名〉 turnover
【营业范围】 yíngyè fànwéi 〈名〉 business scope: 扩大～ expand the scope of business
【营业时间】 yíngyè shíjiān 〈名〉 business hours
【营业收入】 yíngyè shōurù 〈名〉 turnover
【营业税】 yíngyèshuì 〈名〉 sales tax: 交纳～ pay one's sales taxes
【营业许可证】 yíngyè xǔkězhèng 〈名〉 business permit
【营业员】 yíngyèyuán ▶**p. 966** 〈名〉 shop assistant
【营业执照】 yíngyè zhízhào 〈名〉 business licence: 办理～ take out a business permit
【营业总额】 yíngyè zǒng'é 〈名〉 business sales
【营运】 yíngyùn 〈动〉 **1** (运营) operate: 这条新船即将投入～。 This new ship will soon go into operation. **2** (经营) manage a business: 减少商业～成本 reduce the operational costs of a business
【营运车】 yíngyùnchē 〈名〉 vehicles in operation: 出租车行业的～数量大增。 The taxicab industry has seen a large increase in the number of vehicles in operation.
【营造】 yíngzào 〈动〉 construct: ～防风林 plant a windbreak forest ‖ ～节日气氛 create a holiday atmosphere
【营寨】 yíngzhài 〈名〉 〈旧〉 military camp: 偷袭～ launch a surprise attack on a military camp
【营长】 yíngzhǎng 〈名〉 battalion commander
【营帐】 yíngzhàng 〈名〉 tent: 搭～ pitch a tent

萦 (縈) yíng 〈动〉 〈书〉 entangle: 琐事～身 get bogged down with trivial matters
【萦怀】 yínghuái 〈动〉 〈书〉 occupy one's mind: 此事使人梦寐～。 This is the kind of thing that cannot be forgotten even in one's sleep.
【萦回】 yínghuí 〈动〉 〈书〉 hover: ～脑际 linger in one's mind
【萦绕】 yíngrào 〈动〉 linger: 那支新曲子一直～在我的脑海。 I've got that new tune in my head.
【萦系】 yíngxì 〈动〉 〈书〉 be preoccupied with: 思乡之念～他的心头。 He couldn't get thoughts of home out of his mind.

楹 yíng
A 〈名〉 principal columns of a hall
B 〈量〉 〈书〉 room
【楹联】 yínglián 〈名〉 antithetical couplet [written on scrolls, etc. and hung on the columns of a hall]

滢 (瀅) yíng 〈形〉 〈书〉 limpid

蝇 (蠅) yíng 〈名〉 fly: 灭～ kill a fly
【蝇拍】 yíngpāi 〈名〉 fly swatter
【蝇头】 yíngtóu 〈形〉 minuscule: 为～琐事争吵 quarrel over trivial matters hardly worth mentioning ‖ ～小楷 minuscule handwritten characters ‖ 追逐～小利 seek petty profits
【蝇营狗苟】 yíngyíng-gǒugǒu 〈成〉 〈喻〉 seek personal gain without shame
【蝇子】 yíngzi 〈名〉 〈口〉 fly

潆 (瀠) yíng 〈形〉 〈书〉 [of moving water] circuitous
【潆洄】 yínghuí 〈动〉 swirl
【潆绕】 yíngrào 〈动〉 wind: 小溪～ winding stream

嬴 Yíng 〈名〉 Ying [surname]

赢 (贏) yíng 〈动〉 **1** (获利) make a profit: ▶～利, ～余 **2** (获胜) win: ～了一场球 win a ball game ‖ 她十有八九要～。 The odds are ten to one that she will win.
【赢得】 yíngdé 〈动〉 win: ～观众的喝彩 win audience applause ‖ ～胜利 win a victory ‖ ～时间 gain time
【赢家】 yíngjiā 〈名〉 winner
【赢利】 yínglì **A** 〈动〉 profit: ～型企业 profit-making enterprise **B** 〈名〉 profit: 去年的～比前年翻了一番。 Last year's profit was double that of the year before.
【赢面】 yíngmiàn 〈名〉 chance to win: ～大 have a good chance of winning ‖ ～小 have a slim chance of winning
【赢余】 yíngyú = 盈余 yíngyú

瀛 yíng 〈名〉 〈旧〉 ocean: ▶东～
【瀛海】 yínghǎi 〈名〉 〈书〉 sea
【瀛寰】 yínghuán 〈名〉 〈书〉 whole world

yǐng

颖（穎） yǐng〈书〉

A〈名〉**1**（外壳） grain husk: ▸～果 **2**（尖端） tip

B〈形〉**1**（聪明） clever: ▸～悟，聪～ **2**（出色） extraordinary: ▸～异，新～

【颖果】yǐngguǒ〈名〉［植物］ caryopsis

【颖慧】yǐnghuì〈形〉〈书〉 [of a teenager] intelligent: 天资～ born with exceptional intelligence

【颖悟】yǐngwù〈形〉〈书〉 [of a teenager] clever

【颖异】yǐngyì〈形〉〈书〉 **1**（聪明过人） brilliant **2**（新颖奇特） new and unique: 设计～ original and unique in design

影 yǐng

A〈名〉**1**（阴影） shadow: ▸～子，剪～，皮～戏，投～ **2**（影像） reflection: ▸～像，倒～ **3**（迹象、印象） sign: 忘得连～儿都没了 clean forget sth. **4**（照片） photograph: ▸合～，留～，摄～ **5**（皮影戏） shadow play **6**（电影） film: ▸电～，息～

B〈动〉**1**（描摹） photoprint **2**〈方〉（隐藏） hide

【影壁】yǐngbì〈名〉**1**（用于屏蔽的墙壁） screen wall (facing the gate inside a traditional Chinese courtyard) **2** = 照壁 zhàobì **3**（塑有形象的墙壁） wall with carved murals

【影帝】yǐngdì〈名〉 king of the silver screen

【影碟】yǐngdié〈名〉〈方〉 VCD (visual compact disc): 激光～ compact video disc

【影碟机】yǐngdiéjī〈名〉〈方〉 VCD player: 数字式～ DVD player

【影后】yǐnghòu〈名〉 movie queen

【影集】yǐngjí〈名〉 photo album

【影剧院】yǐngjùyuàn〈名〉 theatre

【影楼】yǐnglóu〈名〉 photo studio: 在～拍艺术照 take some artistic pictures at a photo studio

【影迷】yǐngmí〈名〉 film fan

【影片儿】yǐngpiānr〈名〉〈口〉 film

【影片】yǐngpiàn〈名〉**1**（指胶片） film: 倒回～ rewind the film ‖ ～剪辑 film clips **2**（指电影） movie: 发行～ release a film ‖ 拍摄～ shoot a film ‖ 评论～ review a film ‖ 摄制～ produce a film ‖ 译制～ dub a film ‖ 获奖～ prize-winning film ‖ 这部～在北京举行首映。 The film had its premiere in Beijing.

【影评】yǐngpíng〈名〉 film review

【影射】yǐngshè〈动〉 insinuate: 他的话是在～上司。 His words implicate the boss.

【影视】yǐngshì〈名〉 film and television: ～作品 film and television product ‖ ～歌三栖明星 star of film, television and song ‖ ～新秀 new film and TV star

【影视剧】yǐngshìjù〈名〉 film for the big screen and television: 农村题材～ a film about the countryside for the big screen and television

【影坛】yǐngtán〈名〉 film world: ～新秀 new star in the world of film

【影厅】yǐngtīng〈名〉 cinema auditorium: 好的影片能吸引更多观众走进～。 A good film can get more bums on seats.

【影戏】yǐngxì〈名〉 shadow play

【影响】yǐngxiǎng **A**〈动〉 affect: ～工作 interfere with sb.'s work ‖ ～健康 affect health ‖ ～经济发展 hold up the growth of the economy ‖ ～情绪 influence one's moods ‖ ～群众积极性 dampen the enthusiasm of the masses ‖ ～士气 affect morale ‖ ～思想/行为 shape thoughts/actions ‖ ～威信 undermine one's prestige ‖ ～一代人 influence a generation **B**〈名〉 influence: 对…有～ have an influence on... ‖ ～深远 have a far-reaching influence ‖ 他对孩子造成了不良～。 He was a bad influence on children.

【影像】yǐngxiàng〈名〉**1**（肖像） portrait **2**（形象） image **3**（透过装置呈现的形象） silhouette: 高清电视机～清晰。 High resolution televisions have very clear images.

【影星】yǐngxīng〈名〉 film star〈英〉; movie star〈美〉: 超级～ great film star

【影印】yǐngyìn〈动〉［印刷］ photolithograph: ～本 facsimile ‖ ～件 photographic reproduction

【影影绰绰】yǐngyǐng-chuòchuò〈成〉 vague: 雾中～可以看到摩天大楼的轮廓。 We could just make out the shape of the skyscraper in the fog.

【影院】yǐngyuàn〈名〉 cinema; movie theater〈美〉: 家庭～ home cinema

【影展】yǐngzhǎn〈名〉**1**（照片展） photo exhibition **2**（电影展） film festival

【影子】yǐngzi〈名〉**1**（阴影） shadow: 投下～ cast a shadow **2**（映像） reflection: 倒映在湖中的～ reflections in the lake **3**（模糊的印象） vague impression: 那件事我连点儿～也记不得了。 I do not have the faintest recollection of it. **4**（人影） vestige: 整天不见某人的～ not catch a glimpse of a person for the whole day

【影子内阁】yǐngzi nèigé〈名〉 shadow cabinet

瘿（癭） yǐng〈名〉**1** ▸p. 50［医学］ goitre **2**［植物］ gall

yìng

应（應） yìng〈动〉

1（作出反应） answer: 我们回来时敲门没人～。 When we came back and knocked on the door, no one answered. ▸答～，响～，一呼百～ **2**（接受） grant, echo: 歌唱家～听众要求又唱了三首歌。 The singer gave three encores. ▸～聘，～邀，有求必～ **3**（适应、顺应） suit: ▸得心～手，～时 **4**（应付） deal with: ▸～变，～接不暇 **5**（验证） be confirmed: 今天的事可真～了他的话。 What happened today really confirmed what he had said. ▸～验

▸yīng

【应变】yìngbiàn〈动〉 handle an emergency: ～措施 emergency measure ▸随机～

【应承】yìngchéng〈动〉 promise: 满口～ make profuse promises ‖ 做不了的事就不要～。 Don't make promises you can't keep.

【应酬】yìngchou **A**〈动〉 be social: 忙于～ be busy with social activities ‖ ～几句 exchange a few polite words **B**〈名〉 social engagement: 今天晚上我有个～。 I have a dinner party to attend tonight.

【应从】yìngcóng〈动〉 agree: 父亲点点头，～了我的要求。Father quietly nodded his consent to my requests.

【应答】yìngdá〈动〉 reply: ～敏捷 be quick at repartee

【应答如流】yìngdá-rúliú〈成〉 reply readily and fluently

【应敌】yìngdí〈动〉 deal with the enemy: ～计划 battle plan

【应对】yìngduì〈动〉**1**（答对） reply: ～如流 reply readily and fluently **2**（采取对策） respond: 从容～突发事件 respond calmly in an emergency

【应付】yìngfù〈动〉**1**（应对） deal with: ～考试 cram for an examination ‖ ～困难 handle difficulties ‖ 难～的顾客 difficult customer ‖ 工作多得我～不过来。 There was more work than I could cope with. **2**（敷衍了事） go through the motions: 把客人～过去 handle a visitor in a routine manner ‖ ～的态度 perfunctory attitude **3**（将就） make do: 我们没有椅子坐，只能用旧箱子～一下。 We had no chairs, so we had to make do with old boxes. ‖ 我这件T恤衫今年还能～过去。 I'll make do with this T-shirt for this year.

【应付自如】yìngfù-zìrú〈成〉 handle with ease: 对复杂的局面能～ handle complicated situations with ease

【应和】yìnghè〈动〉〈书〉 echo: 同声～ respond with one voice

【应急】yìngjí〈动〉 deal with an emergency: 满足～需要 meet sb.'s pressing need ‖ 做好～准备 prepare for an emergency ‖ 采取～措施 adopt an emergency measure

【应急贷款】yìngjí dàikuǎn〈名〉 emergency loan

【应急灯】yìngjídēng〈名〉 emergency lamp

【应急计划】yìngjí jìhuà〈名〉 contingency plan

【应接不暇】yìngjiē-bùxiá〈成〉**1**（指景色） be more than one's eyes can take in: 一路上枝繁叶茂的春色使人～。The leafy beauty of spring along the road was more than the eye could take in. **2**（指人或事情） have more on than one can attend to: 他电话多得～。 He was swamped with telephone calls.

【应景】yìngjǐng〈动〉**1**（指勉强做） act out of formality: ～之作 do the necessary work **2**（适合节令） be in season: ～果品 seasonal fruits

【应举】yìngjǔ〈动〉〈古〉 take the imperial examination

【应考】yìngkǎo〈动〉 take an examination: ～人数大增 the number of entrants for the examination rose sharply

【应力】yìnglì〈名〉［物理］ strain

【应卯】yìngmǎo〈动〉〈旧〉 answer a roll call: 去应个卯就回来 go and sign in before coming back

【应门】yìngmén〈动〉〈书〉 answer the door: 无人～。 No one answered the door.

【应募】yìngmù〈动〉 enlist: ～从军 enlist in the army

【应诺】yìngnuò〈动〉〈书〉agree to do sth.: 连声～ make profuse promises

【应拍】yìngpāi〈动〉 answer a bid

【应聘】yìngpìn〈动〉 apply for an advertised post: 他～在我校执教一年。 He accepted a contract to teach at our university for one year.

【应声】yìngshēng〈副〉 at the sound of: ～开门 answer the door ‖ 一枪打去， 猛兽～而倒。 The wild beast fell at the sound of the gun going off.

▸yīngshēng

【应声虫】yìngshēngchóng〈名〉〈喻〉 yes-man

【应时】yìngshí **A**〈形〉 seasonable: ～水果 fruits in season ‖ ～蔬菜 vegetables in season **B**〈副〉 at once: 我脚底一滑，～就摔了个仰面朝天。 My foot slipped and I fell flat on my back.

【应市】yìngshì〈动〉 come onto the market to meet demand: 大批水产品节前～。 Large quantities of aquatic products will hit the market before the festival in order to meet demand.

【应试】yìngshì〈动〉 enter for an exam: 到场～ present oneself for an examination ‖ ～教育 examination-oriented education

【应税】yìngshuì〈动〉 be subject to tax: ～商品 taxable goods

【应诉】yìngsù〈动〉 respond to a charge

【应验】yìngyàn〈动〉 be confirmed: 药方～了。 The prescription is effective. ‖ 他的预言后来果然～了。 His prophecy was later fulfilled.

【应邀】yìngyāo〈动〉 accept an invitation: ～参加婚礼 be invited to a wedding party ‖ ～访问 pay a visit upon invitation

【应用】yìngyòng **A**〈动〉 apply: 推广～新技术 popularize the use of new technologies ‖ ～范围很广 be of very wide application **B**〈形〉 applied: ～化学 applied chemistry ‖ ～软件 application software

【应用科学】yìngyòng kēxué〈名〉 applied science

【应用文】yìngyòngwén〈名〉 practical writing

【应援】yìngyuán〈动〉 respond to a call for help

【应运】yìngyùn〈动〉 conform with the times

【应运而生】yìngyùn'érshēng〈成〉 emerge as the times demand

【应战】yìngzhàn〈动〉 **1**（指战争） meet an enemy attack: 沉着～ meet an attack calmly **2**（指挑战） rise to a challenge: 拒绝～ ignore a challenge

【应招】yìngzhāo〈动〉 respond to a call for recruits/candidates

【应召女郎】yìngzhào nǚláng〈名〉 call girl

【应诊】yìngzhěn〈动〉 see a patient: 外出～ be out seeing a patient ‖ ～时间 appointment hours

【应征】yìngzhēng〈动〉 **1**（响应征兵号召） be recruited: ～入伍 be conscripted **2**（响应征求或征集） respond to a call for contributions to a publication: ～投稿 submit a contribution at the editor's solicitation

映 yìng〈动〉

1（照） shine: 夕阳～红了天空。 The setting sun illuminated the skies. ▸～照 **2**（反射） reflect: ～出倒影 mirror a reflection ‖ 朝霞～在湖面上。 The glory of the morning is mirrored in the lake. ▸反～, 倒～ **3**（放映影片） project a film: 电影开～了。 The film has begun. ▸首～式

【映衬】yìngchèn **A**〈动〉 set off: 红梅在白雪的～下分外醒目。 Red plums stood out against a background of white snow. ‖ 在蓝天的～下，山峰的轮廓极为明显。 The peaks stood out in sharp relief against the azure sky. **B**〈名〉［语言］ antithesis

【映带】yìngdài〈书〉= 映衬 yìngchèn A

【映山红】yìngshānhóng〈名〉［植物］ azalea

【映射】yìngshè〈动〉 shine upon: 阳光～在水面上。 The sun is shining on the water.

【映现】yìngxiàn〈动〉 be present: 一幅生动的画面～在他眼前。 A vivid picture stands before his eyes.

【映像】yìngxiàng〈名〉 image

【映照】yìngzhào〈动〉 shine upon: 夕阳～，满天通红。 The sky was all aglow with the setting sun.

硬 yìng

A〈形〉 **1**（质地坚固） hard: ～领/纸板 stiff collar/cardboard ‖ ～塑料 inflexible plastic ▸僵～, 坚～, ～币 **2**（坚定） tough: 心肠～ be hard-hearted ‖ 既然软办法不行，那就来～的。 The kid-glove approach didn't work. It's time to get tough. **3**（好） good: 货色～ quality products ‖ 牌子～。 The trademark is prestigious. ▸～功夫

B〈副〉 forcibly: 他～缠着要和我们一块去。 He forced his company on us. ▸生搬～套

【硬邦邦】yìngbāngbāng〈形〉 **1**（坚硬结实） very hard: 冻得～的 be frozen stiff ‖ 那块面包摸起来～的。 The slice of bread was hard to the touch. **2**（话语生硬） unnatural

【硬包装】yìngbāozhuāng〈名〉 hard packaging

【硬笔】yìngbǐ〈名〉 hard-tipped writing instrument: ～书法 'hardpen' calligraphy

【硬币】yìngbì ▸**p. 328**〈名〉 coin: 一大把～ a fistful of coins ‖ 掷～ toss a coin

【硬撑】yìngchēng〈动〉 endure: ～着工作 force oneself to work

【硬充】yìngchōng〈动〉 pass oneself off as: ～好汉 act the hero

【硬磁盘】yìngcípán = 硬盘 yìngpán

【硬道理】yìngdàolǐ〈名〉 established truth: 发展是～。 Development is of paramount importance.

【硬地】yìngdì〈名〉 hard ground: ～网球场 hard court

【硬顶】yìngdǐng〈动〉 **1**（指做事） tough sth. out: ～着干 brace oneself to do **2**（指说话） talk back

【硬度】yìngdù〈名〉［物理］［化学］ hardness: 耐磨～ abrasive hardness

【硬腭】yìng'è〈名〉［解剖］ hard palate

【硬干】yìnggàn〈动〉 act recklessly

【硬功夫】yìnggōngfu〈名〉 mastery: 练就一身～ acquire a masterly skill through intensive training

【硬骨头】yìnggǔtou〈惯〉〈喻〉 **1**（指人） person of unyielding integrity **2**（指任务） hard nut

【硬汉】yìnghàn〈名〉 man of iron

【硬汉子】yìnghànzi = 硬汉 yìnghàn

【硬化】yìnghuà〈动〉 **1**（由软变硬） harden: 冷却～ be hardened by cooling ‖ 动脉～ hardening of the arteries ‖ 肝～ cirrhosis of the liver **2**〈喻〉（僵化） become rigid: 思想～ rigid thinking

【硬话】yìnghuà〈名〉 strong terms

【硬环境】yìnghuánjìng〈名〉 hard environment: 改善～ improve material working and living conditions

【硬件】yìngjiàn〈名〉 **1**［计算机］ computer hardware: 外围～ peripheral hardware **2**（有形条件） material conditions

【硬结】yìngjié **A**〈动〉 harden: 高温使陶土～。 High temperatures will harden clay. **B** ▸**p. 50**〈名〉［医学］ scleroma

【硬撅撅】yìngjuējuē〈形〉〈方〉 **1**（指物品） very tough: 那肉～的很难嚼。 The meat was very tough and hard to chew. **2**（指态度） stiff: 他答复的语气～的。 He replied in a stiff voice.

【硬科学】yìngkēxué〈名〉 hard science

【硬朗】yìnglang〈形〉 **1**（身体健壮） hale and hearty: 我父亲80岁了，身子还很～。 My father is 80 years old and still going strong. **2**（坚决有力） firm and powerful

【硬面】yìngmiàn〈名〉 stiff dough

【硬木】yìngmù〈名〉 hardwood: ～地板/家具 hardwood flooring/furniture

【硬目标】yìngmùbiāo〈名〉［军事］ hard target

【硬盘】yìngpán〈名〉［计算机］ hard disk: 把～格式化 format a hard disk ‖ ～空间 hard disk space

【硬碰硬】yìngpèngyìng〈惯〉 meet the tough with toughness

【硬气功】yìngqìgōng〈名〉 hard *qigong*

【硬气】yìngqi〈形〉〈方〉 **1**（刚强） be strong-willed **2**（理直气壮） self-possessed

【硬钱】yìngqián〈名〉 hard money [restricted donation in election]

【硬驱】yìngqū〈名〉［计算机］ hard disk drive

【硬任务】yìngrènwù〈名〉 hard task

【硬伤】yìngshāng〈名〉 **1**（指损伤） wound: 马腿有～。 The horse's leg is injured. **2**（指错误） obvious mistake: 这本小册子中有多处～。 There are a lot of glaring errors in this pamphlet.

【硬实力】yìngshílì〈名〉 hard power [obtained by military or economic coercion]: 在发展～的同时，也要发展软实力。 At the same time as developing hard power, it is also necessary to develop soft power.

【硬是】yìngshì〈副〉〈口〉 **1**（实在是） really: 我～拿他没办法。 I can really do nothing about him. **2**（就是） simply: 他～要钻牛角尖，气死我了。 His just wanting to split hairs is driving me mad.

【硬实】yìngshi〈形〉〈口〉 sturdy

【硬手】yìngshǒu〈名〉 skilled hand: 要说木雕，她算是～儿。 When it comes to wood carving, she is a dab hand.

【硬说】yìngshuō〈动〉 insist stubbornly: 他～自己是无辜的。 He insisted that he was innocent.

【硬水】yìngshuǐ〈名〉 hard water

【硬挺】yìngtǐng〈动〉 hold out with all one's might: 他虽然头疼得厉害，但还是～着做完了讲座。 In spite of his bad headache, he held on until he had finished his lecture.

【硬通货】yìngtōnghuò〈名〉 hard currency

【硬卧】yìngwò〈名〉 hard berth: ～车厢 hard sleeper

【硬席】yìngxí〈名〉 hard seat (on a train)

【硬性】yìngxìng〈形〉 rigid: ～规定 lay down hard and fast rules

【硬玉】yìngyù〈名〉［矿业］ jadeite

【硬仗】yìngzhàng〈名〉 tough battle: 打～ fight a hard battle ‖ 明天的比赛可是一场～。 Tomorrow's match is going to be a hard-fought battle.

【硬着头皮】yìngzhe tóupí〈惯〉 summon up courage: 他～又喝了一杯酒。 He braced himself to have another glass of wine.

【硬指标】yìngzhǐbiāo〈名〉 firm objective

【硬质合金】yìngzhì héjīn〈名〉［冶金］ hard alloys

【硬着陆】yìngzhuólù〈动〉 **1**［航空］ have a hard landing **2**［经济］ hard landing

【硬座】yìngzuò〈名〉 hard seat (on train): 预订～车票 reserve a hard-seat ticket

媵 yìng〈书〉

A〈动〉 escort a bride to her new home

B〈名〉 **1**（陪嫁的人） maid accompanying a bride to her new home **2**（妾） concubine

yō

哟（唷） yō〈叹〉

[used to express slight surprise]: ～，这几天你又胖了。 Oh! Looks like you've put on weight again lately. ▸yo

唷 yō ▸哼唷 hēngyō

yo

哟（喲） yo〈助〉 1（表祈使的语气）[used at the end of a sentence to urge sb. on]: 用力拉～! Heave ho! 2（用于歌中做衬字）[used as a syllable filler in a song]: 呼儿嗨～! Hu-er-hei-yo!
▸yō

yōng

佣（傭） yōng
A〈动〉 employ: ▸～工, 雇～
B〈名〉 servant: 女～ servant woman
▸yòng

【佣工】yōnggōng〈名〉 hired labour

拥（擁） yōng〈动〉 1（搂抱）embrace: ▸～抱 2（聚集）gather round: ～在入口处 gather around the entrance ‖ 人都～在门口。People crowded the gateway. ▸簇～, 前呼后～ 3（挤着走）crowd: ～成一团 squash together like sardines ‖ ～向大厅 swarm towards the lobby 4（拥护）support: ▸～戴, ～军优属, ～政爱民 5〈书〉（拥有）possess: ～军百万 have an army of one million strong

【拥抱】yōngbào〈动〉 hug: 紧紧～在一起 be locked in an embrace ‖ 热烈～ embrace warmly

【拥戴】yōngdài〈动〉 support: 深受～ enjoy support ‖ 大家～他担任领导职务。Everybody supported him in his bid for the leadership.

【拥堵】yōngdǔ〈名〉 traffic jam: 必须采取措施缓解市区交通～状况。Measures must be taken to relieve traffic jams in urban areas.

【拥护】yōnghù〈动〉 support: ～宪法 uphold the constitution ‖ ～真理 stand up for the truth ‖ ～政府的决策 support a government policy

【拥挤】yōngjǐ A〈动〉 push and squeeze: 请不要～。No pushing, please. B〈形〉 congested: 整顿～的交通状况 sort out badly congested traffic conditions ‖ ～不堪 be packed in like sardines

【拥军优属】yōngjūn-yōushǔ〈成〉 [of civilians] support the army and give preferential treatment to the families of soldiers and martyrs

【拥塞】yōngsè〈动〉 congest: 道路严重～。The road was heavily congested.

【拥有】yōngyǒu〈动〉 possess: ～版权 hold the copyright ‖ ～大量读者 enjoy a large readership ‖ ～丰富的矿藏资源 possess rich mineral deposits ‖ ～领土主权 have sovereignty over the land

【拥政爱民】yōngzhèng-àimín〈成〉 [of the army] support the government and cherish the people

痈（癰） yōng ▸p. 50〈名〉［医学］ carbuncle: ▸养～遗患

【痈疽】yōngjū ▸p. 50〈名〉 ulcer

邕 Yōng〈名〉 1 ▸p. 294（邕江）Yongjiang River [in Guangxi Zhuang Autonomous Region] 2（南宁）Yong [another name for Nanning]

【邕剧】yōngjù〈名〉 Yong opera [popular in the Cantonese-speaking areas of Guangxi Zhuang Autonomous Region]

庸[1] yōng〈书〉
A〈动〉 [usu used in negative expressions] need: ▸毋～讳言, 毋～赘述
B〈副〉 [used in rhetorical questions] how: ～可废乎? How could this possibly be relinquished?

庸[2] yōng〈形〉 commonplace: 平～ mediocre ▸～医

【庸才】yōngcái〈名〉 mediocre person: ～岂能成大事。How could someone so mediocre make big achievements?

【庸夫】yōngfū〈名〉 mediocre person

【庸碌】yōnglù〈形〉 mediocre and unambitious: ～无能 mediocre and incompetent ‖ ～之辈 second-raters

【庸人】yōngrén〈名〉 mediocre person

【庸人自扰】yōngrén-zìrǎo〈成〉 much ado about nothing: 事情已经解决，你就别～了。Everything is already sorted out, so there's no need for you to worry.

【庸俗】yōngsú〈形〉 vulgar: 趣味～ have vulgar tastes ‖ ～作风 vulgar style

【庸俗化】yōngsúhuà〈动〉 vulgarize: 把马克思主义～ popularize Marxism

【庸医】yōngyī〈名〉 quack: ～的疗法 quack treatment

【庸庸碌碌】yōngyōng-lùlù〈成〉 common and unremarkable: ～度过一生 have messed about to no end for one's whole life

【庸中佼佼】yōngzhōng-jiǎojiǎo〈成〉 be a giant amongst men

雍 yōng〈形〉〈书〉 harmonious: ▸～容

【雍和宫】Yōnghégōng〈名〉 Lamasery of Harmony and Peace (in Beijing)

【雍容】yōngróng〈形〉 elegant and poised: 风度～ be dignified in bearing ‖ ～不迫 poised and unhurried ‖ ～华贵 be poised and stately

墉 yōng〈名〉〈书〉 city wall

慵 yōng〈形〉〈书〉 weary: ～倦 tired and sleepy ‖ ～懒 lethargic

镛（鏞） yōng〈名〉〈古〉 large bell

壅 yōng〈动〉 1（堵塞）block: ▸～塞 2（堆积）heap fertilizer over and around the roots: ～肥 heap fertilizer around the roots ‖ ～土 earth up

【壅塞】yōngsè〈动〉 be clogged up: 水道被泥沙～。The waterway is clogged with silt.

臃 yōng〈形〉〈书〉 swelling

【臃肿】yōngzhǒng〈形〉 1（肥大）cumbersome: 穿着～ be encumbered by too much clothing ‖ ～的身子 obese body 2〈喻〉（庞大）overstaffed: 机构～。Departments are overstaffed.

鳙（鱅） yōng〈名〉［鱼类］ variegated carp

饔 yōng〈名〉〈书〉 1（熟食）cooked food 2（早餐）breakfast

【饔飧不继】yōngsūn-bùjì〈成〉〈书〉 not know where the next meal is coming from: 家道贫寒，～。The family was poor and lived from hand to mouth.

yóng

喁 yóng〈形〉〈书〉 respectful
▸yú

【喁喁】yóngyóng〈形〉〈书〉 respectful
▸yúyú

颙（顒） yóng〈动〉〈书〉 admire: ～望 look up to

yǒng

永 yǒng〈形〉 eternal: ～不称霸 never seek hegemony ‖ 学习～无止境。We are never too old to learn. ▸～久, ～恒

【永别】yǒngbié〈动〉 1（指分别）part forever 2 ▸p. 772（指人死）be parted by death

【永垂不朽】yǒngchuí-bùxiǔ〈成〉 be immortal: 人民英雄～。Eternal glory to the people's heroes!

【永垂青史】yǒngchuí-qīngshǐ〈成〉 go down in history: 他的名字将～。His name will go down in history.

【永磁】yǒngcí〈名〉［物理］ permanent magnetism

【永存】yǒngcún〈动〉 be eternal: 浩气～。Noble spirit is imperishable. ‖ 革命烈士的英名和业绩～。The memory of heroic names and the glorious achievements of our revolutionary martyrs will live forever in our hearts.

【永冻土】yǒngdòngtǔ〈名〉［地质］ permafrost

【永恒】yǒnghéng〈形〉 eternal: ～的爱 eternal love ‖ ～的信念 enduring faith ‖ ～的友谊 unfailing friendship ‖ 爱情是文学～的主题。Love is an eternal literary subject.

【永久】yǒngjiǔ〈形〉 everlasting: ～保存 preserve for all eternity ‖ ～居住权 permanent residency

【永久居留权】yǒngjiǔ jūliúquán〈名〉 permanent residency

【永久居留证】yǒngjiǔ jūliúzhèng〈名〉 permanent residence card

【永久居民】yǒngjiǔ jūmín〈名〉 permanent resident

【永居】yǒngjū A〈动〉 live permanently B〈名〉 permanent residency: 获得～ obtain permanent residency

【永诀】yǒngjué〈动〉〈书〉 part forever: 竟成～ never to meet again

【永乐大典】Yǒnglè Dàdiǎn〈名〉 Great Canon of the Yongle Era [encyclopedia of the Ming Dynasty, completed in 1408]

【永眠】yǒngmián ▸p. 772〈动〉〈书〉〈婉〉 pass away

【永生】yǒngshēng A〈名〉 1［基督教］ eternal life: 求得～ achieve immortality ‖ ～的灵魂 immortal soul 2（终生）lifetime: ～难忘的教训 lesson for life B〈动〉 [used in mourning for the dead] live forever: 为争取民族解放而牺牲的烈士们～! The memory of those who died for national liberation shall live forever in our hearts!

【永生永世】yǒngshēng-yǒngshì〈成〉 forever and ever: 英雄们将～为人们所怀念。People will cherish the memory of those heroes forever and ever.

Y

【永世】yǒngshì〈副〉 forever: ～不得翻身 be forever subjugated ‖ ～不忘 will never forget for the rest of one's life
【永逝】yǒngshì〈动〉 1 (指消失) be gone forever 2 (指逝世) pass away
【永无宁日】yǒngwúníngrì〈成〉 never will there be days of peace
【永远】yǒngyuǎn〈副〉 forever: ～相爱 have everlasting love for each other ‖ 他将～留在这里。 He will stay here for good.
【永驻】yǒngzhù〈动〉 stay forever: 青春～ stay young forever

甬[1] Yǒng〈名〉 1 ▸p. 294 (甬江) Yongjiang River [in Zhejiang Province] 2 (宁波) Yong [another name for Ningbo]

甬[2] yǒng ▸甬道 yǒngdào
【甬道】yǒngdào〈名〉 1 (指砖石路) paved path leading to a main hall or a tomb 2 (走廊) corridor
【甬剧】yǒngjù〈名〉 Yong opera [popular in Zhejiang Province]
【甬路】yǒnglù = 甬道 yǒngdào 1

咏（詠） yǒng〈动〉 1 (诵读) chant: ～诗 read poetry ▸～叹, 歌～, 吟～ 2 (用诗词叙述) express in poetic form: ～梅 ode to the plum blossom ▸～怀, ～史
【咏唱】yǒngchàng〈动〉 chant
【咏怀】yǒnghuái〈动〉 express one's feelings in poetic form: 借物～ use sth. to express one's sentiments and aspirations in poetic form ‖ ～诗 poems of the heart
【咏史】yǒngshǐ〈动〉 compose poems on history: ～诗 poems on history
【咏叹】yǒngtàn〈动〉 chant
【咏叹调】yǒngtàndiào〈名〉［音乐］ aria: 歌剧～ operatic aria
【咏赞】yǒngzàn〈动〉 sing the praise of

泳 yǒng〈动〉 swim: 侧～ sidestroke ‖ 冬～ winter swimming ▸游～, 蝶～, 仰～
【泳程】yǒngchéng〈名〉 swimming distance
【泳池】yǒngchí〈名〉 swimming pool
【泳道】yǒngdào〈名〉 swimming lane: 卫冕冠军在第五～。 The defending champion is swimming in lane five.
【泳裤】yǒngkù〈名〉 swimming trunks
【泳帽】yǒngmào〈名〉 swimming cap
【泳坛】yǒngtán〈名〉 swimming world: ～名将 star swimmer ‖ ～新秀 new star in the swimming world
【泳衣】yǒngyī〈名〉 swimsuit
【泳装】yǒngzhuāng〈名〉 bathing suit: 比基尼～ bikini

俑 yǒng〈名〉 tomb figure: 武士～ warrior figure ▸兵马～, 秦～, 陶～

勇 yǒng
A〈形〉 brave: 越战越～ mount in courage as the battle progresses ‖ 两军交战，～者胜。 In a set battle, the courageous side will win. ▸～往直前, 英～
B〈名〉 soldier: ▸散兵游～
【勇夫】yǒngfū〈名〉 brave man: 重赏之下，必有～。 When a reward is offered, brave men will be attracted to the prize.
【勇敢】yǒnggǎn〈形〉 brave: 机智～ be brave and resourceful ‖ ～善战 be courageous and skilful in battle
【勇冠三军】yǒngguàn-sānjūn〈成〉 distinguish oneself by peerless valour in battle
【勇悍】yǒnghàn〈形〉 bold and intrepid
【勇健】yǒngjiàn〈形〉 brave and strong
【勇猛】yǒngměng〈形〉 brave and fierce: ～果断 be brave and resolute in action ‖ ～前进 advance bravely
【勇气】yǒngqì〈名〉 courage: 鼓起～ pluck up courage ‖ 缺乏～ be spineless ‖ 丧失～ lose one's nerve/courage ‖ 非凡的～ strong nerves
【勇士】yǒngshì〈名〉 warrior
【勇挑重担】yǒngtiāo-zhòngdàn〈成〉 shoulder the heavy tasks with determination
【勇往直前】yǒngwǎng-zhíqián〈成〉 march forward without hesitation
【勇武】yǒngwǔ〈形〉 valiant: ～过人 surpass others in valour
【勇于】yǒngyú〈动〉 have the courage to do: ～承认错误 have the courage to admit one's mistakes ‖ ～创新 dare to be innovative ‖ ～负责 be brave in shouldering responsibilities ‖ ～克服困难 brave difficulties and hardships ‖ ～探索真理 be courageous enough to seek the truth ‖ ～自我批评 have the courage to criticize oneself

涌（湧） yǒng〈动〉 1 (水向上冒) gush: 水管破裂后，水～过街道。 When the pipes burst, water gushed across the street. ‖ 鲜血开始向外～。 The blood began to gush out. ▸风起云～ 2 (冒出) surge: 大批难民～入该国。 Refugees are now pouring into this country. ‖ 一连串的想法～上他的心头。 A whole host of thoughts besieged him.
▸chōng
【涌潮】yǒngcháo〈名〉 tidal wave
【涌浪】yǒnglàng〈名〉 turbulent waves
【涌动】yǒngdòng〈动〉 surge: 春潮～。 Spring tides came billowing. ‖ 激情～。 Passions ran high.
【涌流】yǒngliú〈动〉 gush: 泉水～。 The fountain gushed forth.
【涌泉】yǒngquán〈名〉 fountain
【涌现】yǒngxiàn〈动〉 emerge in large numbers: 群众中～了一大批先进人物。 A large number of advanced individuals have emerged from among the masses. ‖ 新生事物大量～。 New things sprang up in large numbers.

恿（慂） yǒng ▸怂恿 sǒngyǒng

蛹 yǒng〈名〉 pupa: 蝶～ chrysalis

踊（踴） yǒng〈动〉 leap up: ▸～跃
【踊跃】yǒngyuè A〈动〉 jump: ～欢呼 leap and cheer B〈形〉 eager: ～参军 vie with one another to join the army ‖ 会上人们～发言。 Everybody was eager to take the floor at the meeting.

鲬（鯒） yǒng〈名〉［鱼类］ flathead

yòng

用 yòng
A〈动〉 1 (使用) use: ～毛笔写字 write with a brush ‖ 节约～电 save electricity ‖ ～各种手段 use every trick in the book ‖ 可以～一下你的电话吗？ May I use your telephone? ▸学非所～ 2 (需要) [usu used in the negative] need: 花园不～浇水。 The garden doesn't need watering. ‖ 这事不～你帮忙。 There's no need for you to help out with this. 3 (敬) (吃) eat; (喝) drink: 请～茶。 Please help yourself to tea.
B〈名〉 1 (用处) use: 老而无～ outlive one's usefulness ‖ 与你争论没什么～。 It's no use arguing with you. ▸效～, 物尽其～ 2 (开支) expenses: 贴补家～ help out with the family expenses ▸费～
C〈连〉〈书〉 [used in letter writing] hence: ～特函答。 Hence this letter.
【用兵】yòngbīng〈动〉 use military force: 善于～ be well versed in the art of war ▸养兵千日，～一时
【用不了】yòngbuliǎo〈动〉 1 (指足够) have more than is needed 2 (指不超过) be less than: ～三天 in less than three days
【用不着】yòngbuzháo〈动〉 there is no need
【用材林】yòngcáilín〈名〉 timber forest
【用餐】yòngcān〈动〉 dine
【用场】yòngchǎng〈名〉〈口〉 use: 说不定哪天会派上～。 It may come in handy one day. ‖ 我拿它派不上～。 It was of no use to me.
【用处】yòngchu〈名〉 use: ～大 be of great use ‖ 目前没有～ be of little use at present
【用词】yòngcí〈名〉 wording: ～不当 use inappropriate wording
【用得着】yòngdezháo〈动〉 1 (有用) find sth. useful 2 (需要) there is need to
【用地】yòngdì〈名〉［建筑］ right of way: 建筑～ land used for construction
【用度】yòngdù〈名〉 expense: 他家人口多，～大。 He has a large family, so his outlays are huge.
【用法】yòngfǎ〈名〉 use: 说明～ illustrate uses ‖ 习惯～ usage
【用法说明】yòngfǎ shuōmíng〈名〉 directions for use
【用饭】yòngfàn〈动〉 eat a meal
【用非所长】yòngfēisuǒcháng〈成〉 unable to do what one is best at
【用费】yòngfèi〈名〉 expense: 负担一切会议～ take care of all the meeting expenses ‖ 日常～ everyday expenses
【用工】yònggōng〈动〉 recruit and use workers: ～制度 system of recruitment
【用功】yònggōng A〈动〉 work hard: 学习不～ be lazy with one's studies B〈形〉 hard-working: ～的学生 diligent student ‖ 极其～ be exceedingly hard-working
【用户】yònghù〈名〉 consumer: 竭诚为～服务 provide a loyal service for consumers ‖ 为～着想 be user-oriented ‖ 全球通～ GSM user
【用户界面】yònghù jièmiàn〈名〉［计算机］ user interface
【用户名】yònghùmíng〈名〉［计算机］ user name: 保存～ store user name ‖ 输入～ enter a user name
【用户群】yònghùqún〈名〉 user group
【用户识别卡】yònghù shíbiékǎ〈名〉［通信］ SIM card
【用户手册】yònghù shǒucè〈名〉 user guide
【用户账号】yònghù zhànghào〈名〉［计算机］ user account
【用尽】yòngjìn〈动〉 exhaust
【用劲】yòngjìn〈动〉 exert oneself: ～抓住 go all out to catch
【用具】yòngjù〈名〉 utensil: 厨房～ kitchen utensils
【用力】yònglì〈动〉 exert oneself: ～过猛

overexert oneself ‖ ～推 push with all one's might ‖ 全身～ use every ounce of one's strength
【用命】yòngmìng〈动〉〈书〉obey orders
【用能】yòngnéng〈动〉use energy: 节约～、用水 conserve energy and water
【用品】yòngpǐn〈名〉articles for use: 办公～ articles for office use ‖ 妇女～商店 boutique ‖ 生活～ articles for daily use
【用人】yòngrén〈动〉1（任用人员）make use of personnel: ～不当 not use the right person ‖ ～单位 employer 2（需要人手）need hands: 眼下正是～之际。Now is the time that we need qualified personnel.
【用人】yòngren〈名〉〈旧〉servant: 女～ woman servant, maid
【用事】yòngshì〈动〉1〈书〉（当权）be in power: 奸臣～。Treacherous court officials were in power. 2（办事）act: ▸感情～, 意气～
【用途】yòngtú〈名〉use: ～广泛 be widely used ‖ 有几种～的工具 tool with several uses
【用武】yòngwǔ〈动〉1（动用武力）use armed forces 2（施展才能）display one's abilities: 大有～之地 have ample scope to display one's abilities ‖ 没有～之地 unable to apply one's talents anywhere
【用项】yòngxiàng〈名〉expenditures: ～大 have many expenses
【用心】yòngxīn A〈动〉take care and thought over: ～听讲 listen attentively to a lecture ‖ ～学习 concentrate on one's studies B〈名〉motive, intention: ～险恶 have malicious intentions ▸别有～
【用心良苦】yòngxīn-liángkǔ〈成〉rack one's brains
【用刑】yòngxíng〈动〉torture
【用药】yòngyào〈动〉administer a medicine
【用药量】yòngyàoliàng〈名〉dosage
【用意】yòngyì〈名〉intention: 你这样做～何在? What's your purpose in doing this?
【用印】yòngyìn〈动〉affix an official seal
【用语】yòngyǔ〈名〉1（词语运用）wording: ～简洁 be neatly phrased ‖ 贴切的～ relevant wording 2（专用词语）term: 法律～ legal terms ‖ 外交～ diplomatic parlance ‖ 医学～ medical language
【用之不竭】yòngzhībùjié〈成〉be inexhaustible: 太阳能是一种～的能源。Solar energy is an inexhaustible energy source.

佣 yòng〈名〉commission
▸yōng
【佣金】yòngjīn〈名〉commission: 付～ pay commission ‖ 经纪人～ brokerage commission
【佣钱】yòngqian〈口〉= 佣金 yòngjīn

yōu

优[1]（優）yōu
A〈形〉1（丰厚）ample: ▸～厚, ～裕 2（非常好）excellent: ～缺点 merits and demerits ‖ 在考试成绩单上，A表示～，C表示及格。On the report card, A means excellent and C means pass. ▸～美, ～秀, 品学兼～
B〈动〉give preferential treatment: ▸～抚, ～遇, 拥军～属

优[2]（優）yōu〈名〉〈旧〉actor: ▸～伶, 名～
【优待】yōudài A〈动〉give preferential treatment: ～军属 give preferential treatment to the families of servicemen B〈名〉preferential treatment: 给予～ give sb. preferential treatment ‖ 受到～ receive preferential treatment ‖ 特殊～ special preference
【优待券】yōudàiquàn〈名〉complimentary ticket
【优等】yōuděng〈形〉first-rate: ～品 first-rate product ‖ ～生 first-class student
【优点】yōudiǎn〈名〉advantage: ～多于缺点。The merits outweigh the defects. ‖ 天然温泉水具有很多～。Natural thermal springs possesses many positive features.
【优抚】yōufǔ〈动〉give special care to: ～军烈属 give special care to family members of revolutionary martyrs and servicemen
【优厚】yōuhòu〈形〉munificent: 报酬～ be handsomely paid ‖ ～的待遇 favourable treatment ‖ ～的薪金 high salary
【优化】yōuhuà〈动〉optimize: ～产业结构 optimize industrial structures ‖ ～资源配置 optimize the allocation of resources
【优惠】yōuhuì〈形〉preferential: ～政策 preferential policy ‖ 给学生半价～ charge half-price for students ‖ 九折～ 10% discount
【优惠待遇】yōuhuì dàiyù〈名〉preferential treatment: 享受～ get preferential treatment
【优惠价格】yōuhuì jiàgé〈名〉preferential price
【优惠券】yōuhuìquàn〈名〉discount coupon
【优惠商品】yōuhuì shāngpǐn〈名〉bargain offer
【优惠条件】yōuhuì tiáojiàn〈名〉preferential terms
【优价】yōujià〈名〉1（高价）high price: 优质～ good quality products fetch high prices 2（廉价）favourable rates: ～处理库存商品 sell off goods in stock at clearance prices
【优良】yōuliáng〈形〉fine: 学习成绩～ good grades ‖ 发扬～传统 carry forward the fine tradition
【优良作风】yōuliáng zuòfēng〈名〉fine working style: 保持艰苦奋斗的～ maintain a good working style during difficulties
【优劣】yōuliè〈名〉good and bad: 难分～ be hard to distinguish good from bad ‖ 评判～ judge which is superior
【优伶】yōulíng〈名〉〈旧〉actor
【优美】yōuměi〈形〉exquisite: 舞姿～ dance with grace ‖ 浑厚而～的音色 rich melodic timbre ‖ 景色～。The scenery is beautiful.
【优盘】yōupán〈名〉USB stick: 存入～ save to a memory stick
【优缺点】yōuquēdiǎn〈名〉pluses and minuses
【优容】yōuróng〈动〉〈书〉treat with leniency
【优柔】yōuróu〈形〉1〈书〉（从容）leisurely: ～不迫 in a leisurely and unhurried manner 2〈书〉（平和）gentle 3（不果断）hesitant: ▸～寡断
【优柔寡断】yōuróu-guǎduàn〈成〉irresolute and hesitant: ～的人 timorous person
【优生】yōushēng〈动〉give birth to healthy babies: 提倡～、优育 promote healthy birthing and child rearing
【优胜】yōushèng〈形〉winning, superior: ～奖 winning prize
【优胜劣汰】yōushèng-liètài〈成〉survival of the fittest
【优势】yōushì〈名〉advantage: 竞争～ competitive edge ‖ 发挥～ make the most of oneself ‖ 失去～ lose the upper hand ‖ 占～ have the upper hand ‖ 以微弱的～险胜 win by a nose ‖ 微弱的～ narrow lead ‖ ～互补 have complementary strengths
【优渥】yōuwò〈形〉〈书〉munificent
【优先】yōuxiān〈动〉have priority: ～发展农业/教育 give priority to the development of agriculture/education ‖ ～录用 employ preferentially ‖ 女士～。Ladies first.
【优先股】yōuxiāngǔ〈名〉［金融］preference shares〈英〉; preferred stock〈美〉
【优先权】yōuxiānquán〈名〉right of priority: 获得～ receive priority ‖ 享有～ enjoy priority ‖ 掌握～ hold priority
【优秀】yōuxiù〈形〉outstanding: 成绩～ get excellent results ‖ 选拔～人才 select outstanding talents ‖ ～作品 works of high quality
【优选】yōuxuǎn〈动〉optimize
【优选法】yōuxuǎnfǎ〈名〉optimization
【优雅】yōuyǎ〈形〉1（雅致）elegant: 陈设～ be furnished with elegance and taste ‖ 穿着/服装～ be elegant in dress 2（高雅）tasteful: 举止～ be graceful and tasteful in manner ‖ ～的风度 elegant manners
【优异】yōuyì〈形〉outstanding: 考试成绩～ attain outstanding examination results ‖ ～的性能 excellent performance
【优游】yōuyóu〈书〉A〈形〉leisurely and carefree: ～岁月 pass one's days in carefree leisure ‖ ～自在 be leisurely and carefree B〈动〉leave one's life to fate
【优育】yōuyù〈动〉provide children with superior health care and education
【优裕】yōuyù〈形〉affluent: 享受～的生活 enjoy affluence ‖ 生活～ live in affluence
【优遇】yōuyù〈动〉give special treatment
【优越】yōuyuè〈形〉superior: 创造～条件 create favourable conditions ‖ ～的地理位置 advantageous geographical position ‖ ～感 sense of superiority ‖ ～性 superiority
【优哉游哉】yōuzāi-yóuzāi〈成〉leisurely and carefree: 过着～的日子 live a life of ease and leisure
【优质】yōuzhì〈形〉top-quality: ～产品 superior products ‖ ～服务 first-rate service

攸 yōu〈助〉〈书〉[used like the particle 所 in certain phrases]: 性命～关 be a matter of life and death

忧（憂）yōu
A〈形〉worried: ▸～愁, ～伤
B〈动〉be worried: ▸～国～民
C〈名〉1（忧愁）sorrow: ～乐与共 share joy and sorrow with each other ▸内～外患, 无～无虑 2〈书〉（丧事）funeral arrangements for one's parents: ▸丁～
【忧愁】yōuchóu〈形〉worried: 满腹～ be extremely worried
【忧烦】yōufán〈形〉worried: ～的神色 haunted look ‖ 你看上去愁眉苦脸，有什么事使你～? You look troubled. What's worrying you?
【忧愤】yōufèn〈形〉worried and indignant
【忧国忧民】yōuguó-yōumín〈成〉worry for the fate of one's country
【忧患】yōuhuàn〈名〉suffering: 饱经～ have experienced all sorts of untold hardships ‖ ～意识 sense of anxiety
【忧惧】yōujù〈动〉〈书〉be apprehensive: ～不安 worried and ill-at-ease
【忧虑】yōulǜ〈动〉be worried: 感到～ feel anxious ‖ 满怀～ be full of anxiety ‖ 深感～ be deeply anxious ‖ 消除～ quell sb.'s

y

anxieties ‖ 为某事/某人而～ be worried about sth./sb.
【忧闷】yōumèn〈形〉 depressed
【忧戚】yōuqī〈形〉〈书〉 distressed
【忧伤】yōushāng〈形〉 weighed down with grief: 减轻～ assuage one's grief ‖ 无比～ be incomparably grief-stricken ‖ 他面露～的神色。 He appeared to be consumed with grief.
【忧思】yōusī **A**〈动〉 be worried **B**〈名〉 troubled thoughts
【忧喜参半】yōuxǐ-cānbàn〈成〉be half sad, half pleased
【忧心】yōuxīn **A**〈动〉 be worried: 大家都替他的身体～。 Everybody was worrying about his fragile health. **B**〈名〉〈书〉 troubled heart: ▸～忡忡
【忧心忡忡】yōuxīn-chōngchōng〈成〉 be anxiety-ridden: 犯罪率太高,令人～。 The crime rate is depressingly high.
【忧心如焚】yōuxīn-rúfén〈成〉 be burning with anxiety: 他在屋里踱来踱去，～。 He paced up and down in the room eaten up with anxiety.
【忧悒】yōuyì〈形〉〈书〉 anxious and restless
【忧郁】yōuyù〈形〉 heavy-hearted: ～成疾 fall ill with sorrow ‖ ～的表情 sombre expression
【忧郁症】yōuyùzhèng ▸**p. 50**〈名〉［医学］ melancholia: ～患者 melancholic

呦

呦 yōu〈叹〉 **1**（表惊讶） [used to express surprise]: ～，饭糊了! Oh no, the rice is burnt. **2**（表突然发现） [used to express sudden awareness of sth.]: ～，忘带钥匙了。 Oh, dear! I forgot my key!
【呦呦】yōuyōu〈拟〉〈书〉 [used to refer to the cry of a deer] bleat

幽

幽 yōu
A〈形〉 **1**（昏暗） dim: ▸～暗 **2**（深远） deep and remote: ▸～谷，～邃 **3**（隐密） hidden: ▸～会 **4**（藏在心里） bottled-up: ▸～思，～怨 **5**（僻静） quiet: ▸～静，～雅
B〈动〉〈书〉 imprison: ▸～禁，～囚
C〈名〉 nether world: ▸～魂，～灵
【幽暗】yōu'àn〈形〉 gloomy: ～的房间 gloomy room ‖ ～的光线 poor light
【幽闭】yōubì〈动〉 **1**（软禁） be under house arrest **2**（在家不出） be housebound
【幽愤】yōufèn〈名〉 hidden resentment
【幽谷】yōugǔ〈名〉 deep and secluded valley
【幽会】yōuhuì〈动〉 rendezvous: 与情人～ have a rendezvous with one's lover
【幽魂】yōuhún〈名〉 spirit
【幽寂】yōujì〈形〉 secluded and lonely: ～的山谷 secluded valley
【幽禁】yōujìn〈动〉 imprison: ～终身 be imprisoned for life
【幽静】yōujìng〈形〉 quiet and secluded: ～的地方 peaceful and secluded place
【幽兰】yōulán〈名〉〈书〉 orchid
【幽灵】yōulíng〈名〉 spirit: ～般地出现在她的身边 appear like a ghost at her side
【幽美】yōuměi〈形〉 serene and beautiful: 景色～。 The scenery is secluded and beautiful.
【幽门】yōumén〈名〉［解剖］ pylorus: ～梗阻 pyloric stenosis
【幽明】yōumíng〈名〉〈书〉 the nether world and the earthly world: ～永隔。 The dead and the living will always be separated.
【幽冥】yōumíng〈书〉 **A**〈形〉 dim **B**〈名〉 nether world
【幽默】yōumò〈形〉 humorous: ～风趣 have a fine sense of humour ‖ ～的故事/话/趣闻 humorous story/remark/anecdote ‖ 他很～。 He has a great sense of humour.
【幽默感】yōumògǎn〈名〉sense of humour: 缺乏～ lack a sense of humour
【幽情】yōuqíng〈名〉 deep feelings: 发思古之～ ponder over the past
【幽囚】yōuqiú〈动〉〈书〉 imprison
【幽趣】yōuqù〈名〉 delightful serenity of seclusion
【幽深】yōushēn〈形〉 deep and serene
【幽思】yōusī **A**〈动〉 ponder **B**〈名〉 deep contemplation: 沉浸在对往事的～之中 be lost in quiet recollection of the past
【幽邃】yōusuì〈形〉〈书〉deep and unfathomable
【幽婉】yōuwǎn〈形〉〈书〉 subtle and delicate: ～的歌声 exquisite singing
【幽微】yōuwēi〈形〉〈书〉 **1**（不浓重） faint: ～的花香 delicate fragrance of flowers **2**（深奥） profound
【幽闲】yōuxián **1** = 幽娴 yōuxián **2** = 悠闲 yōuxián
【幽娴】yōuxián〈形〉 [of a woman] gentle and serene
【幽香】yōuxiāng〈名〉 delicate fragrance: ～四溢。 A delicate aroma fills the air.
【幽雅】yōuyǎ〈形〉 [of a place] quiet and tastefully put together: ～的环境 elegant and quiet surroundings
【幽咽】yōuyè〈形〉〈书〉 **1**（形容哭声） whimpering: ～的哭泣 whimpers **2**（形容流水声） murmuring
【幽忧】yōuyōu〈形〉〈书〉 distressed
【幽幽】yōuyōu〈形〉 **1**（轻微细弱） faint: ～啜泣 sob quietly ‖ ～的街灯 dim street lamps **2**〈书〉（深远） looming in the distance
【幽远】yōuyuǎn〈形〉 remote: ～的夜空 remote and tranquil night sky
【幽怨】yōuyuàn〈名〉 [of a young woman thwarted in love] hidden bitterness

悠¹

悠¹ yōu〈形〉 **1**（遥远、长久） remote: ▸～长，～久 **2**（闲适） leisurely: ▸～闲，～游

悠²

悠² yōu〈动〉 swing: 他抓住绳子～了过去。 He held on to the rope and swung across. ‖ 猴子在树枝上～来～去。 The monkey swung from branch to branch in the tree. ▸～荡，晃～
【悠长】yōucháng〈形〉 long-drawn-out: ～的汽笛声 long-drawn-out steam whistle ‖ ～的岁月 long-drawn-out years
【悠荡】yōudàng〈动〉 swing: 孩子们在秋千上来回～。 The children swung back and forth on the swings.
【悠久】yōujiǔ〈形〉 long-standing: 历史～ have a long history ‖ ～的传统 long-standing tradition ‖ 历史～的城市 city with an age-old history
【悠谬】yōumiù〈形〉〈书〉 absurd
【悠然】yōurán〈形〉 carefree and leisurely: ～自得 be carefree and content
【悠闲】yōuxián〈形〉 leisurely and carefree: ～的生活 life of leisure ‖ ～自在 leisurely and carefree
【悠扬】yōuyáng〈形〉 melodious: 笛声～ the flute is melodious ‖ ～的歌声 melodious singing
【悠悠】yōuyōu〈形〉 **1**（长久） long-drawn-out;（遥远） remote: ～长夜 night that seems to drag on ‖ ～山川 mountains and rivers far, far away ‖ 岁月～。 Years were dragging. **2**〈书〉（众多） numerous: ～万事 numerous events **3**（闲适） leisurely: ～自得 carefree and content ‖ 在街上慢～地逛来逛去 pace leisurely up and down the street
【悠游】yōuyóu **A**〈动〉 move about unhurriedly: 小船在荡漾的湖面上～。 The small boat was moving slowly over the rippling surface of the lake. **B**〈形〉 leisurely and carefree: ～自在 leisurely and carefree
【悠远】yōuyuǎn〈形〉 **1**（指时间） long-ago: ～的过去 remote past **2**（指距离） distant: 山川～。 Mountains and rivers are far away.
【悠着】yōuzhe〈动〉〈方〉 take things easy: ～劲儿，别太猛了。 Take things easy! Don't go at it so hard. ‖ 干活～点儿，别太累了。 Relax more when you work. Don't tire yourself out.

yóu

尤

尤 yóu〈书〉
A〈形〉 exceptional: ▸～物，无耻之～
B〈副〉 particularly: 对计算机～感兴趣 be particularly interested in computers ▸～其
C〈名〉 fault: ▸效～
D〈动〉 blame: ▸怨天～人
【尤伯杯】Yóubóbēi〈名〉［体育］ Uber Cup: 争夺～ compete for the Uber Cup
【尤里卡】Yóulǐkǎ〈名〉 EUREKA (European Research Coordination Agency)
【尤其】yóuqí〈副〉 especially: ～重要 be even more important ‖ 我喜欢喝茶，～是绿茶。 I like drinking tea, green tea in particular.
【尤甚】yóushèn〈形〉〈书〉 worst of all: 办公室里的人都很粗心，小李～。All the people in the office are careless, and no one is more so than Xiao Li.
【尤为】yóuwéi〈副〉〈书〉especially: 这一点～重要。 This point is especially important. ‖ 这使他～恼火。 This vexed him all the more.
【尤物】yóuwù〈名〉〈书〉 **1**（强调优异） distinguished person or thing **2**（强调貌美） [of a woman] rare beauty

由

由 yóu
A〈动〉 **1**（经过） pass through: ▸必～之路，言不～衷 **2**〈书〉（遵循） adhere to: ▸率～旧章 **3**（任由） follow: ～着性子 do as one pleases ‖ 信不信～你。 Believe it or not. ▸不～自主，听天～命
B〈介〉 **1**（经由） by: ～边门出/进 exit/enter by the side door ‖ ～此入内。 This way in. **2**（从） from: ～南往北 from south to north ‖ ～弱变强 go from weak to strong **3**（归） by: ～我请客。 This is my treat. ‖ 所有的维修费用～我公司承担。 All the costs of the repairs will be borne by our company. **4**（通过） by means of: ～前提推导出结论 draw conclusions from prerequisites ‖ ～此可见 thus it can be seen ‖ 代表～民主协商选举产生。 The representatives were elected after democratic consultation. **5**（因为） due to: 他的肺炎是～感冒引起的。 His pneumonia was caused by a common cold. ▸咎～自取
C〈名〉 cause: ▸理～，事～，缘～
【由表及里】yóubiǎo-jílǐ〈成〉 from the outside to the inside: 分析问题要～。 In analysing problems you should proceed from

the surface to what lies behind.

【由不得】yóubude **A**〈动〉 not be in one's power to decide **B**〈副〉 cannot help: 一句话叫人～笑了起来。 Just one sentence and no one could help laughing.

【由此】yóucǐ〈副〉 from this: ～看来 in view of this ‖ 你必须承担～产生的一切后果。 You must take all the consequences arising therefrom.

【由此及彼】yóucǐ-jíbǐ〈成〉 proceed from this to that

【由此可见】yóucǐ-kějiàn〈成〉 thus it can be seen

【由得】yóude〈动〉 allow: 国家的财物～你糟蹋吗? How can you be allowed to abuse the country's property?

【由俭入奢易，由奢入俭难】yóu jiǎn rù shē yì, yóu shē rù jiǎn nán〈俗〉 it is easy to go from thrift to luxury, but difficult to do vice versa

【由来】yóulái〈名〉 **1**（指时间） so far: ～已久 long-standing **2**（指原因） origin: 了解分歧的～ enquire into the source of the differences

【由浅入深】yóuqiǎn-rùshēn〈成〉 proceed from the elementary to the profound

【由头】yóutou〈名〉〈口〉 cause: 找个～ find a pretext

【由于】yóuyú **A**〈介〉 because of: ～健康原因，他提前退休了。 He retired early on the grounds of ill health. **B**〈连〉 since: ～时间晚了，我现在要回家了。 It's late, so I shall go home now.

【由衷】yóuzhōng〈形〉 heartfelt: 表示～的感谢 extend heartfelt thanks ‖ ～之言 sincere words

邮（郵）yóu

A〈动〉 post: 把信～走了 put the letter in the post ‖ 每月给家里～钱 send money to one's family every month

B〈名〉 **1**（邮政） post: ▸～费, ～局 **2**（邮票） postage stamp: ▸～市, 集～

【邮包】yóubāo〈名〉 package

【邮币卡】yóubìkǎ〈名〉 stamps, coins and telephone cards: ～市场 stamp, coin and telephone card market

【邮编】yóubiān〈简称〉= 邮政编码

【邮差】yóuchāi〈名〉〈旧〉 postman

【邮车】yóuchē〈名〉 post office van

【邮储】yóuchǔ〈简称〉= 邮政储蓄

【邮船】yóuchuán〈名〉 packet boat

【邮戳】yóuchuō〈名〉 postmark: 在信封上盖～ postmark an envelope ‖ 以～日期为准 verify by the date on the postmark

【邮袋】yóudài〈名〉 postbag

【邮递】yóudì〈动〉 mail; post〈英〉: 及时～信件/包裹 deliver a letter/package on schedule ‖ 他家住在山区，～不便。 Since he lives in the mountains, getting post to him is not easy.

【邮递员】yóudìyuán ▸**p. 966**〈名〉 postman〈英〉; mailman〈美〉

【邮电】yóudiàn〈名〉 post and telecommunications: ～部门 department of post and telecommunications ‖ ～业务 postal and telecommunication service

【邮电局】yóudiànjú〈名〉 post and telecommunication office

【邮费】yóufèi〈名〉 postal rates: ～付讫 postage paid

【邮购】yóugòu〈动〉 purchase by mail order: 提供～服务 mail-order service

【邮汇】yóuhuì〈动〉 send money by post: ～100元人民币 send a postal order for 100 *yuan*

【邮集】yóují〈名〉 stamp album

【邮寄】yóujì〈动〉 mail; post〈英〉: ～包裹/信件 mail a parcel/letter ‖ 挂号～ send by registered post

【邮件】yóujiàn〈名〉 **1**（信件、包裹） post〈英〉; mail〈美〉: 分拣～ sort out the post ‖ 投递～ deliver the mail ‖ 平寄/挂号/航空～ surface/registered/air mail **2**［计算机］ mail: 发～ send an e-mail ‖ 垃圾～ junk mail ▸电子～

【邮件炸弹】yóujiàn zhàdàn〈名〉［计算机］ letter bomb

【邮局】yóujú〈名〉 post office

【邮路】yóulù〈名〉 postal route

【邮轮】yóulún〈名〉 mail boat

【邮票】yóupiào〈名〉 postage stamp: 收集～ collect stamps ‖ 纪念～ memorial stamps

【邮品】yóupǐn〈名〉 postal items

【邮识】yóushí〈名〉 expertise in philately

【邮市】yóushì〈名〉 philatelic market

【邮亭】yóutíng〈名〉 postal kiosk

【邮筒】yóutǒng〈名〉 pillar box〈英〉; mailbox〈美〉

【邮箱】yóuxiāng〈名〉 **1**（信箱） letter box〈英〉; mailbox〈美〉 **2**［计算机］ mailbox

【邮展】yóuzhǎn〈名〉 philatelic exhibition

【邮政】yóuzhèng〈名〉 postal service: ～部门 postal department

【邮政包裹】yóuzhèng bāoguǒ〈名〉 postal parcel

【邮政编码】yóuzhèng biānmǎ〈名〉 postcode〈英〉; zip code〈美〉

【邮政储蓄】yóuzhèng chǔxù〈名〉 postal savings: 办理～业务 run a postal savings service

【邮政汇款】yóuzhèng huìkuǎn〈名〉 postal remittance

【邮政局】yóuzhèngjú〈名〉 post office: ～局长 postmaster

【邮政特快专递】yóuzhèng tèkuài zhuāndì〈名〉 express mail service (EMS)

【邮政信箱】yóuzhèng xìnxiāng〈名〉 postbox〈英〉; mailbox〈美〉

【邮资】yóuzī〈名〉 postage: ～已付 postage paid

犹（猶）yóu〈书〉

A〈动〉 be like: ▸～如, 过～不及, 虽死～生

B〈副〉 still: ～可挽回 be retrievable ‖ 春色～浓。 It is still the height of spring.

【犹大】Yóudà〈名〉［基督教］ Judas: ～之吻 Judas kiss

【犹如】yóurú〈动〉〈书〉 be like: 大厅里亮得～白昼。 It is as bright as daylight in the lobby. ‖ 他去世的消息～晴天霹雳。 The news of his death came as a bolt from the blue.

【犹他州】Yóutāzhōu〈名〉 Utah

【犹太复国主义】Yóutài fùguózhǔyì〈名〉 Zionism

【犹太教】Yóutàijiào〈名〉 Judaism: ～教士 rabbi ‖ ～教堂 synagogue

【犹太民族】Yóutàimínzú〈名〉 Jewish people

【犹太人】Yóutàirén〈名〉 Jew

【犹疑】yóuyí = 犹豫 yóuyù

【犹疑不决】yóuyi-bùjué〈成〉 not know one's own mind

【犹有余悸】yóuyǒu-yújì〈成〉 be still scared even now

【犹豫】yóuyù〈动〉 vacillate: 别再～了，打定主意吧。 Do stop dithering and make up your mind. ‖ 他～了一会儿才选了一本书。 He hesitated before choosing a book.

【犹豫不决】yóuyù-bùjué〈成〉 be in two minds: 她～，不知下一步该怎么办。 She was in two minds as to what to do next.

【犹豫期】yóuyùqī〈名〉 cooling-off period: 保险公司应在～内对投保人进行回访。 Insurance companies should pay return visits to policy holders during cooling-off periods.

【犹自】yóuzì〈副〉〈书〉 still: 现在提起那件事，～叫他心惊肉跳。 Even to this day, he can still feel a twinge of fear at the very mention of it.

油 yóu

A〈名〉 oil: 烹饪用～ cooking oil ‖ 汽～ petrol ‖ 柴～ diesel ‖ 加～站 petrol station ▸菜子～, 豆～, 橄榄～

B〈动〉 **1**（油漆） paint: ～家具 paint the furniture ‖ 地板刚～过。 The floor is freshly painted. **2**（被油弄脏） be grease-stained: 小心点，别弄～了我的衬衫。 Careful! You'll get grease on my shirt.

C〈形〉 glib: 他的嘴可～了。 He is very obsequious in speech. ‖ 这人太～了。 This person is too slippery. ▸～腔滑调

【油泵】yóubèng〈名〉［机械］ oil pump

【油饼】yóubǐng〈名〉 **1**［农业］ [used as animal feed/fertilizer] oil cake: ～类饲料 oil cake fodder **2**［食品］ deep-fried dough cake

【油布】yóubù〈名〉 oilskin: ～伞 oilskin umbrella

【油彩】yóucǎi〈名〉 greasepaint: 她的脸上涂了很重的～。 She has thick make up on her face.

【油菜】yóucài〈名〉 **1**（指油料作物） rape: ～籽 rapeseed **2**（指蔬菜） Chinese cabbage

【油层】yóucéng〈名〉［石油］ oil reservoir

【油茶】yóuchá〈名〉［植物］ **1** tea-oil tree **2**（指小吃） *youcha* [gruel of sweetened, fried flour]

【油船】yóuchuán〈名〉 oil tanker

【油灯】yóudēng〈名〉 oil lamp

【油底子】yóudǐzi〈名〉〈口〉 oil dregs

【油豆腐】yóudòufu〈名〉 fried tofu cube

【油坊】yóufáng〈名〉 oil mill

【油封】yóufēng〈名〉［机械］ grease seal

【油橄榄】yóugǎnlǎn〈名〉 olive

【油垢】yóugòu〈名〉 greasy dirt

【油管】yóuguǎn〈名〉 oil pipe

【油罐】yóuguàn〈名〉 oil tank: ～车 fuel tanker

【油光】yóuguāng〈形〉 shiny: 把皮鞋擦得～锃亮 polish leather shoes so they become really shiny

【油耗】yóuhào〈名〉 oil consumption: 降低机动车～ reduce vehicle oil consumption

【油乎乎】yóuhūhū〈形〉 oily: ～的抹布 oily rags

【油壶】yóuhú〈名〉 oilcan

【油葫芦】yóuhulǔ〈名〉［昆虫］ field cricket

【油花】yóuhuā〈名〉 blobs of fat

【油滑】yóuhuá〈形〉 slippery: 他这个人很～。 He is a very slippery character.

【油画】yóuhuà〈名〉 oil painting

【油画家】yóuhuàjiā ▸**p. 966**〈名〉 oil painter

【油灰】yóuhuī〈名〉［建筑］ putty

【油迹】yóujì〈名〉 oil stain

【油煎火燎】yóujiān-huǒliǎo〈成〉 be in a state of great agitation

【油井】yóujǐng〈名〉 oil well

【油库】yóukù〈名〉 oil depot

【油矿】yóukuàng〈名〉 **1**（指矿床） oil

deposit: 发现～ strike oil ‖ 开发～ open up oil deposits 2 (指场地) oilfield
【油老虎】 yóulǎohǔ 〈名〉 1 (指耗油量大) gas guzzler 2 〈喻〉 (指投机者) oil profiteer
【油亮】 yóuliàng 〈形〉 glossy: ～的叶子 shimmering leaves ‖ ～的皮鞋 shiny shoes
【油料作物】 yóuliào zuòwù 〈名〉 oil-plant
【油绿】 yóulǜ 〈形〉 glossy dark green
【油轮】 yóulún 〈名〉 oil tanker: 远洋～ ocean-going tanker
【油麻】 yóumá 〈名〉 batched jute
【油麦】 yóumài = 莜麦 yóumài
【油毛毡】 yóumáozhān 〈名〉 [建筑] asphalt felt
【油门】 yóumén 〈名〉 accelerator: 踩～ step on the accelerator ‖ 加大～ accelerate fast
【油焖】 yóumèn 〈动〉 braise in oil: ～茄子 braised aubergine slices
【油苗】 yóumiáo 〈名〉 [石油] oil seepage
【油墨】 yóumò 〈名〉 printing ink: 快干～ fast drying ink
【油泥】 yóuní 〈名〉 grease: 满是～的工作服 work clothes covered with grease dirt
【油腻】 yóunì A 〈形〉 oily: 这道菜太～了。 This dish is too oily. B 〈名〉 oily food: 忌食～ avoid oily food
【油品】 yóupǐn 〈名〉 petroleum products
【油漆】 yóuqī A 〈名〉 paint: ～未干 wet paint ‖ ～味 paint odour ‖ ～开始剥落。 The paint is beginning to flake away. B 〈动〉 paint: ～大门/房间 paint the gate/room ‖ ～家具 varnish furniture ‖ ～工/匠 painter
【油气】 yóuqì 〈名〉 oil and associated gas: ～资源 hydrocarbon resources
【油气田】 yóuqìtián 〈名〉 oil and gas field
【油腔滑调】 yóuqiāng-huádiào 〈成〉 frivolous and insincere in speech: 说起话来～ speak glibly
【油然】 yóurán 〈形〉 〈书〉 1 (自然而然) welling up spontaneously: 敬慕之心，～而生。 Admiration wells up in one's heart. 2 (云气上升) rising densely: 水汽～而升。 Vapours rose densely.
【油石】 yóushí 〈名〉 [机械] oilstone
【油饰】 yóushì 〈动〉 paint: ～一新 be freshly painted
【油水】 yóushui 〈名〉 1 (所含脂肪质) grease: 这道菜～很大。 This dish is very greasy. 2 〈喻〉 (好处) profit: 这工作没什么～可捞。 Nothing can be creamed off in this work.
【油松】 yóusōng 〈名〉 Chinese pine
【油酥】 yóusū 〈形〉 crispy: ～甜饼 shortcake
【油酸】 yóusuān 〈名〉 [化学] oleic acid: 亚～ linoleic acid
【油桃】 yóutáo 〈名〉 [植物] nectarine
【油提】 yóutí 〈名〉 oil dipper
【油田】 yóutián 〈名〉 [石油] oilfield: 开发新～ open (up) a new oilfield ‖ 海底～ undersea oil deposit
【油田伴生气】 yóutián bànshēngqì 〈名〉 [石油] associated gas
【油田气】 yóutiánqì 〈名〉 oil field gas
【油条】 yóutiáo 〈名〉 1 (指食品) deep-fried dough sticks 2 〈喻〉 (指人) sly person: 老～ sly old hand
【油桐】 yóutóng 〈名〉 [植物] tung tree
【油头粉面】 yóutóu-fěnmiàn 〈成〉 [usu of a man] hair slicked back and dressed like a dandy
【油头滑脑】 yóutóu-huánǎo 〈成〉 slippery: ～的家伙 shifty-looking fellow

> **油条**
>
> *Youtiao*, a traditional deep-fried breakfast food, usually made of two long strips of flour dough pressed together. They are believed to have originated in Hangzhou, Zhejiang Province. The story goes that in the Southern Song Dynasty, the famous General Yue Fei (岳飞) was falsely accused by the treacherous and universally hated Qin Hui (秦桧), and sentenced to death. One small restaurant made long strips of dough to represent Qin Hui and his wife. These were then fried and eaten. To this day, an untrustworthy person is colloquially known as a *youtiao*.

【油汪汪】 yóuwāngwāng 〈形〉 1 (油多) oily 2 (油光) shiny
【油污】 yóuwū 〈名〉 grease stain: 除去衣服上的～ remove grease from one's coat ‖ 分解～ dissolve grease stains
【油箱】 yóuxiāng 〈名〉 fuel tank: 给～加满汽油 fill up a tank with petrol ‖ 副～ auxiliary fuel tank
【油香】 yóuxiang 〈名〉 Muslim flour-and-salt cake fried in sesame oil
【油星】 yóuxīng = 油花 yóuhuā
【油性】 yóuxìng 〈名〉 oiliness: ～涂料 oil paint ‖ ～皮肤 oily skin ‖ 这种果仁～大。 This type of kernel is very oily.
【油烟】 yóuyān 〈名〉 soot: ～回收 oil fume recovery
【油盐酱醋】 yóu-yán-jiàng-cù 〈俗〉 basic necessities in cooking
【油页岩】 yóuyèyán 〈名〉 [地质] oil shale
【油印】 yóuyìn 〈动〉 mimeograph: ～讲义 mimeographed sheets ‖ ～机 mimeograph
【油渣】 yóuzhā 〈名〉 dregs of fat
【油炸】 yóuzhá 〈动〉 deep-fry: ～土豆片 potato crisp
【油毡】 yóuzhān = 油毛毡 yóumáozhān
【油脂】 yóuzhī 〈名〉 oil: 动物～ animal fat ‖ 植物～ vegetable fat
【油纸】 yóuzhǐ 〈名〉 oil paper: ～伞 oil-paper umbrella
【油渍】 yóuzì 〈名〉 grease stain: ～斑斑 be covered with grease spots
【油子】 yóuzi 〈名〉 1 (指物) black sticky substance: 烟袋～ tar inside a tobacco pipe 2 (指人) sly person: 老～ sly old hand
【油嘴】 yóuzuǐ A 〈形〉 glib: ▸～滑舌 B 〈名〉 1 (指人) glib talker 2 (指喷嘴) spray nozzle
【油嘴滑舌】 yóuzuǐ-huáshé 〈成〉 be glib-tongued: 老师见他～，非常气愤。 The teacher was angry at his smooth talking.

柚 yóu
▸yòu
【柚木】 yóumù 〈名〉 teak: ～地板 teak flooring

疣 yóu ▸p. 50 〈名〉 [医学] wart
【疣猪】 yóuzhū 〈名〉 [动物] warthog
【疣赘】 yóuzhuì ▸p. 50 〈名〉 wart

莜 yóu
【莜麦】 yóumài 〈名〉 [植物] naked oat

莸 (蕕) yóu 〈名〉 1 (有臭味的草) [in ancient books] stinking grass; (恶人) evil person: 薰～不同器 good people cannot get along with bad 2 [植物] common bluebeard

铀 (鈾) yóu 〈名〉 [化学] uranium (U): 浓缩～ enriched uranium
【铀浓缩】 yóunóngsuō 〈动〉 uranium enrichment

蚰 yóu
【蚰蜒】 yóuyán 〈名〉 [昆虫] common house centipede

鱿 (魷) yóu
【鱿鱼】 yóuyú 〈名〉 squid: ▸炒～

游[1] (遊) yóu 〈动〉 1 (流动) move about: ▸～动, ～击, ～移 2 (从容行走) travel: 一日～ go on a day excursion ‖ 那地方很值得一～。 The place is really worth a visit. ▸～览, ～山玩水, 旅～ 3 (玩) play: ▸～乐, ～戏, ～艺 4 〈书〉 (交往) associate with: ▸交～

游[2] yóu
A 〈动〉 swim: ～回岸边 swim back to the shore ‖ 金鱼在鱼缸里～来～去。 The goldfish swam up and down in the tank. ▸～泳, 畅～
B 〈名〉 part of a river: ▸上～, 下～
【游伴】 yóubàn 〈名〉 travel companion
【游标】 yóubiāo 〈名〉 [机械] vernier: ～尺 vernier scale
【游标卡尺】 yóubiāo kǎchǐ 〈名〉 vernier caliper
【游程】 yóuchéng 〈名〉 1 (游泳的距离) swimming distance: 她游完了一千米比赛的～。 She swam the 1,000 metres race. 2 (游玩的路程) route: 一日的～ a day's journey 3 (旅游日程) itinerary: 安排～ arrange one's itinerary
【游船】 yóuchuán 〈名〉 pleasure boat
【游荡】 yóudàng 〈动〉 1 (不务正业) loaf about: 四处～，无所事事 loiter around doing nothing 2 (游逛) wander: 孩子们放学后在街上～。 The children wandered the streets after school. 3 (漂浮晃荡) drift about: 船在湖心随波～。 The boat rolled with the waves in the middle of the lake.
【游动】 yóudòng 〈动〉 move about: ～目标 moving target ‖ 白云在空中徐徐～。 White clouds floated slowly across the sky.
【游动哨】 yóudòngshào 〈名〉 roving sentry
【游方】 yóufāng A 〈动〉 wander for religious purposes: ～僧 itinerant monk B 〈名〉 social gathering for boys and girls of the Miao ethnic group (苗族) during festivals or slack season
【游舫】 yóufǎng 〈名〉 pleasure boat
【游逛】 yóuguàng 〈动〉 go sightseeing: 出外～ go out sightseeing
【游击】 yóujī 〈动〉 engage in guerrilla warfare: ～战术 guerrilla tactics ▸打～
【游击队】 yóujīduì 〈名〉 guerrilla forces: ～员 guerrilla
【游击战】 yóujīzhàn 〈名〉 guerrilla warfare: 进行～ have a guerrilla war
【游记】 yóujì 〈名〉 travel notes: 写～ write an account of one's travels ‖ 《马可波罗～》 *The Travels of Marco Polo*
【游街】 yóujiē 〈动〉 1 (指押着犯人) parade an offender through the streets in order to subject him to public ridicule: 被抓获的罪犯带着镣铐列队～示众。 The captured criminals were paraded in chains through the streets. 2 (指簇拥着英雄) escort a hero through the streets so as to glorify him: 英雄们披红～。 Each draped with a band of red silk, the heroes were paraded through the streets.
【游客】 yóukè 〈名〉 tourist: 接待～ receive

y

tourists ‖ 招徕～ lure travellers ‖ ～止步! No Visitors.

【游览】yóulǎn〈动〉go sightseeing: ～名胜古迹 see the historical sights ‖ 观光～ take a sightseeing tour

【游览车】yóulǎnchē〈名〉tourist coach

【游览胜地】yóulǎn shèngdì〈名〉tourist attraction

【游览图】yóulǎntú〈名〉tourist map

【游廊】yóuláng〈名〉covered corridor linking two or more buildings

【游乐】yóulè〈动〉amuse oneself: 尽情～ enjoy oneself to one's heart's content

【游乐场】yóulèchǎng〈名〉playground; recreation ground〈英〉: 儿童～ children's playground

【游乐园】yóulèyuán〈名〉fun fair〈英〉; amusement park〈美〉

【游离】yóulí **A**〈形〉［化学］free: ～胆固醇/酸 free cholesterol/acid **B**〈动〉drift away: ～在集体之外 dissociate from the collective

【游历】yóulì〈动〉go travelling: ～名山大川 see the famous mountains and great rivers

【游轮】yóulún〈名〉tourist boat: 豪华～ luxury pleasure boat

【游民】yóumín〈名〉vagrant: 无业～ vagrant

【游民无产者】yóumín wúchǎnzhě〈名〉lumpen proletariat

【游牧】yóumù〈动〉live a nomadic life: ～民族 nomadic people ‖ ～生活 nomadic life

【游憩】yóuqì〈动〉〈书〉play and relax: 游客们～的好地方 a great place for tourists to enjoy themselves

【游禽】yóuqín〈名〉［鸟类］swimming bird

【游人】yóurén〈名〉tourist: 春暖花开，西子湖畔～如织。The warmth of spring and the blossoming flowers brought throngs of visitors to the shores of the West Lake.

【游刃有余】yóurèn-yǒuyú〈成〉〈喻〉be more than equal to a task: 他干厨师已经十年了，准备一顿午饭～。He has been a cook for ten years and he is more than equal to the task of preparing lunch.

【游山玩水】yóushān-wánshuǐ〈成〉make a sightseeing tour

【游手好闲】yóushǒu-hàoxián〈成〉eat the bread of idleness: ～之徒 people fooling around

【游水】yóushuǐ〈动〉swim

【游说】yóushuì〈动〉lobby: 他有几个朋友为他～宣传。He got a couple of friends to lobby for him.

【游丝】yóusī〈名〉**1**（蜘蛛丝）gossamer **2**［机械］hairspring

【游隼】yóusǔn〈名〉［鸟类］falcon

【游艇】yóutǐng〈名〉pleasure boat

【游玩】yóuwán〈动〉**1**（玩耍）play: 孩子们整个下午都在外边～。The children spent the whole afternoon playing outdoors. **2**（游览）go on an excursion: 去海边～ go on a visit to the seaside

【游戏】yóuxì **A**〈名〉game: 玩捉迷藏～ play hide-and-seek ‖ ～规则 rules of a game ‖ 文字～ play on words **B**〈动〉play: 孩子们在树下～。The children are playing under the tree.

【游戏机】yóuxìjī〈名〉video game machine

【游戏人生】yóuxì-rénshēng〈成〉treat life as a mere game

【游戏厅】yóuxìtīng〈名〉games hall

游戏及运动

踢足球、打篮球等

■ 汉语说踢足球、打篮球等，英语的 play 一词则几乎可以和所有表示游戏及运动的词搭配：

打网球
= to play tennis

踢足球
= to play football

打桥牌
= to play bridge

下象棋
= to play chess

玩捉迷藏
= to play hide-and-seek

■ 英语里表示游戏项目的词，有些以大写字母开头，有些用单数，又有些要用复数：

玩拼字游戏
= to play Scrabble

下双陆棋
= to play backgammon

下跳棋
= to play Chinese chequers

打弹子
= to play marbles

投飞镖
= to play darts

游戏者、运动员及赛事

■ 英语里 players 一词可表示汉语里的选手、运动员、参加者或游戏者等多个概念：

乒乓球选手
= a table tennis player

拼字游戏参加者
= a Scrabble player

棋手
= a chess player

网球运动员
= a tennis player

■ 有些表示运动项目的词后面还可跟后缀 -er 来表示 players：

足球运动员
= a footballer
或 a football player

高尔夫球运动员
= a golfer
或 a golf player

■ 注意下面例子的翻译：

4 到 6 人玩的游戏
= a game for four to six players

棋盘游戏
= board games

西洋跳棋
= a game of draughts

足球比赛
= a game of football

乒乓球世界冠军
= the table tennis champion of the world

奥运会冠军
= an Olympic champion

全国沙滩排球锦标赛
= the National Beach Volleyball Championship

奥林匹克运动会
= the Olympic Games
或 the Olympics

篮球比赛
= a basketball match

象棋联赛
= a chess tournament

世界拉力锦标赛
= the World Rally Championship

国际乒联职业巡回赛
= the International Table Tennis Federation Pro-Tour

美国高尔夫球公开赛
= the U.S. Open Golf Championship

世界排球大奖赛
= Volleyball World Grand Prix

其他短语

参加网球联赛
= to play a tennis tournament

参加足球赛
= to play in the football match

他代表哪个队参赛?
或 他为哪个队打比赛?
= Which team does he play for?

李维下周与刘立比赛
= Li Wei plays Liu Li next week

我与她赛过象棋
= I have played her at chess

广州队将与上海队比赛
= Guangzhou is going to play against Shanghai

广州队获胜
= Guangzhou won

我要和朋友下盘跳棋
= I'll play a game of Chinese chequers with my friends

黄阳获得了金牌
= Huang Yang won the gold medal

他赢了棋
= He won at chess

她输了棋
= She lost at chess

我下棋赢了他
= I beat him at chess

英格兰 1 比 1 战平意大利
= England drew 1–1 with Italy

曼联以 1 比 0 险胜利物浦
= Manchester United narrowly beat Liverpool one-nil

在与阿根廷的决赛中，法国遭遇惨败
= France suffered a bitter defeat in the final against Argentina

【游戏玩家】yóuxì wánjiā〈名〉 gamer: 网络～ online gamer
【游侠】yóuxiá〈名〉〈旧〉 knight-errant
【游行】yóuxíng〈动〉 demonstrate: ～示威 hold a demonstration ‖ ～队伍 parade procession ‖ 学生们上街～反对战争。 The students took to the streets to demonstrate against the war.
【游兴】yóuxìng〈名〉 itch to travel: ～大发 feel an itch to travel
【游学】yóuxué〈动〉〈旧〉study away from home
【游医】yóuyī〈名〉〈旧〉 travelling doctor
【游移】yóuyí〈动〉 1 (移动不定) move about: 浮云在空中～。 The clouds are drifting across the sky. 2 (迟疑) waver: ～观望 sit on the fence ‖ ～不定 dither
【游弋】yóuyì〈动〉 1 (巡逻) cruise: 航空母舰在地中海上～。 The aircraft carrier cruised in the Mediterranean. 2 (游动) swim: 几只野鸭在湖心～。 Several wild ducks were swimming around in the middle of the lake.
【游艺】yóuyì〈名〉 recreation: ～场 amusement park ‖ ～会 entertainment gathering
【游艺宫】yóuyìgōng〈名〉recreation centre
【游艺室】yóuyìshì〈名〉 recreation room
【游泳】yóuyǒng ▸**p. 909**〈动〉 swim: 去～ go for a swim ‖ ～裤 swimming trunks ‖ ～帽 bathing cap ‖ ～圈 water rings ‖ ～衣 swimwear ‖ ～健将 first-class swimmer ‖ ～比赛 swimming contest
【游泳池】yóuyǒngchí〈名〉swimming pool: 室内～ indoor swimming pool
【游泳馆】yóuyǒngguǎn〈名〉 natatorium
【游园】yóuyuán〈动〉 visit a park: 举行～庆祝活动 hold mass celebrations in parks
【游园会】yóuyuánhuì〈名〉 garden party
【游资】yóuzī〈名〉 floating capital: 利用～ make use of idle funds
【游子】yóuzǐ〈名〉〈书〉 traveller: 海外～ countrymen residing abroad ‖ 慈母手中线，～身上衣。 Mother's loving fingers sewed the coat worn by the wanderer.
【游走】yóuzǒu〈名〉［医学］ migration: ～性疼痛 wandering pain

鲉（鮋） yóu〈名〉［鱼类］ scorpionfish

猷 yóu〈名〉〈书〉 plan: 鸿～ great plan

蝣 yóu ▸蜉蝣 fúyóu

蝤 yóu ▸qiú

【蝤蛑】yóumóu〈名〉［动物］ swimming crab

yǒu

友 yǒu

A〈名〉 friend: 探亲访～ call on relatives and friends ‖ 交～ make friends ‖ 择～ choose one's friends ‖ 不分敌～ not distinguish friend from foe ▸良师益～
B〈形〉 1 (亲近) intimate: ▸～爱, ～善 2 (有友好关系) friendly: ▸～邦, ～军, ～人
【友爱】yǒu'ài〈形〉 affectionate: 互助～ help each other out of friendship ‖ 团结～ be united in brotherhood
【友邦】yǒubāng〈名〉 friendly nation
【友好】yǒuhǎo A〈名〉 close friend: 生前～ friends of the deceased B〈形〉 friendly: ～相处 be on friendly terms ‖ ～邻邦 friendly neighbouring country ‖ ～关系 friendly relations ‖ 热情～的讲话 warm and friendly speech
【友好城市】yǒuhǎo chéngshì〈名〉 twin cities: 北京与柏林结成了～。 Beijing was twinned with Berlin.
【友好条约】yǒuhǎo tiáoyuē〈名〉 friendship treaty
【友好往来】yǒuhǎo wǎnglái〈名〉 friendly exchanges
【友军】yǒujūn〈名〉 friendly troops
【友邻】yǒulín〈名〉 friendly neighbour
【友情】yǒuqíng〈名〉 friendship: 珍惜～ cherish a friendship ‖ 30年的～ 30 years of friendship
【友情客串】yǒuqíng kèchuàn〈动〉 be a guest performer for the sake of friendship
【友人】yǒurén〈名〉 friend: 国际～ international friends
【友善】yǒushàn〈形〉 amicable: ～相处 be on friendly terms
【友谊】yǒuyì〈名〉friendship: 保持～ maintain a friendship ‖ 增进～ promote friendship ‖ 诚挚/深厚的～ sincere/profound friendship ‖ 持久的～ enduring friendship
【友谊赛】yǒuyìsài〈名〉［体育］ friendly game: 足球～ friendly football match
【友谊商店】yǒuyì shāngdiàn〈名〉 friendship store [large retail store established in major cities in China to cater to foreign visitors]

有[1] yǒu

A〈动〉 1 (存在) exist: 车厢里只～我们两个人。 There were just two of us in the compartment. ‖ 这附近～商店吗? Are there any shops in the vicinity? 2 (拥有) have: ～本事 be capable ‖ ～独立工作能力 have the ability to work independently ‖ ～一分热，发一分光 do one's best, however little it may be ‖ ～中国特色的社会主义道路 road of socialism with Chinese characteristics ‖ 人贵～自知之明。 Self-knowledge is wisdom. ▸～罪 3 (表程度或数量) [used to indicate an estimate or a comparison]: 她身高～1.75米。 She is 1.75 metres in height. ‖ 问题～那么严重吗? Is the problem that serious? 4 (表时间长) [used to indicate having plenty of things or lasting a long period]: ～些日子了 for quite a few days ‖ 她干这一行可～年头了。 She has been doing this sort of work for years. 5 (出现) [used to indicate sth. that appears or occurs]: ～病 be sick ‖ 这孩子最近～点儿低烧。 Recently the child has had a mild fever. 6 (表应答) [used as a response]: "赵明!" "～!" 'Zhao Ming!' 'Yes!' 7 (表不定指) [used to express sth. indefinite] certain: 你不喜欢热闹，～人喜欢。 You don't like company, but others do. ‖ ～人打电话找你。 You are wanted on the phone. 8 (表一部分) [used before person, time or place indicating part of sth.]: ～人聪明，～人糊涂。 Some people are clever, others are confused. ‖ ～时候他也会大发脾气。 Sometimes he can also lose his temper.
B〈助〉〈套〉 [used before certain verbs in polite formulas]: ▸～劳, ～请

有[2] yǒu〈前缀〉〈书〉 [used before names of certain dynasties or certain nationalities]: ～苗 the Miao ethnic group ‖ 诗至～唐为极盛。 Poetry reached its acme during the Tang period.

【有碍】yǒu'ài〈动〉 get in the way: ～健康 affect health ‖ ～交通 hinder traffic ‖ ～观瞻 be an eyesore
【有案可查】yǒu'ànkěchá〈成〉 be on record
【有案可稽】yǒu'ànkějī = 有案可查 yǒu'ànkěchá
【有把握】yǒu bǎwò〈动〉 have the cards in one's hands: 绝对～成功 be absolutely certain ‖ 他接这活儿是～的。 He was confident of fulfilling the order.
【有百害而无一利】yǒu bǎi hài ér wú yī lì〈成〉 bring nothing but harm
【有百利而无一害】yǒu bǎi lì ér wú yī hài〈成〉 have everything to gain and nothing to lose
【有板有眼】yǒubǎn-yǒuyǎn〈成〉 methodical: 他说得～，我看可以相信。His words are very measured. I think we can believe him.
【有备无患】yǒubèi-wúhuàn〈成〉preparedness averts peril: 提前启动应急预案，做到～。 Having an emergency plan in advance will help if things do not go according to plan.
【有鼻子有眼儿】 yǒubízi-yǒuyǎnr〈惯〉 describe fictitious things in vivid and lifelike detail: 那个骗子说得～，蒙蔽了不少人。 The swindler described the whole thing in such vivid detail that many people were hoodwinked.
【有病乱投医】yǒubìng luàn tóuyī〈俗〉 in times of illness, people turn to any physician
【有产阶级】yǒuchǎnjiējí〈名〉 propertied class
【有产者】yǒuchǎnzhě〈名〉 man of property
【有偿】yǒucháng〈形〉 paid: ～服务 paid service ‖ ～使用 paid use
【有车族】yǒuchēzú〈名〉 car owner: 小区居民大多数是～。 Most people in this small residential community are car owners.
【有成】yǒuchéng〈动〉〈书〉 achieve success: 事业～ be successful in one's career
【有吃有穿】 yǒuchī-yǒuchuān〈动〉 have ample food and clothing
【有错必纠】yǒucuò-bìjiū〈成〉 right every wrong
【有待】yǒudài〈动〉 await: 工作方法～改进 the working style has yet to be improved ‖ 这件案子～进一步调查。 The case is awaiting further investigation.
【有袋动物】yǒudàidòngwù〈名〉marsupial
【有道理】yǒu dàolǐ〈动〉 be well founded: 你这么说～。 You are right in saying this.
【有得】yǒudé〈动〉 gain knowledge from learning: 学习～ have profited from one's studies
【有得必有失】yǒudé bì yǒushī〈成〉 you can't make an omelette without breaking eggs
【有的】yǒude〈代〉 some: ～人特别爱看电视。 Some people are crazy about watching TV.
【有的是】yǒudeshì〈动〉〈口〉have plenty of: 机会～。 There are ample opportunities available. ‖ 他～钱。 He has plenty of money.
【有底】yǒudǐ〈动〉 know one's own mind: 心中～ know what is what
【有的放矢】yǒudì-fàngshǐ〈成〉〈喻〉have a definite goal
【有点】yǒudiǎn A〈动〉 have a little: ～名气 enjoy some fame ‖ 锅里还～剩饭。 There is some leftover food in the pot. B〈副〉 somewhat: ～不好意思 be rather embarrassed ‖ ～过分 be a bit too much ‖

这老人耳朵～背。The old man is a little hard of hearing.

【有毒】yǒudú〈形〉poisonous: ～气体/物质 toxic gas/substance

【有法必依】yǒufǎ-bìyī〈惯〉ensure that laws are observed: ～，执法必严，违法必究。Laws must be observed and strictly enforced and violators must be brought to justice.

【有方】yǒufāng〈形〉appropriate: 教子～ have a fine way of educating one's children ‖ 领导～ exercise able leadership

【有夫之妇】yǒufūzhīfù〈名〉married woman

【有福同享，有难同当】yǒu fú tóng xiǎng, yǒu nàn tóng dāng〈俗〉share weal and woe

【有妇之夫】yǒufùzhīfū〈名〉married man

【有负众望】yǒufù-zhòngwàng〈成〉fall short of the expectations of the people

【有功】yǒugōng〈动〉have rendered great service: ～之臣 person who has rendered outstanding service

【有关】yǒuguān〈动〉**1**（有关系）have something to do with: 病因可能与吸烟～。The disease might have something to do with smoking. ‖ 这些问题与我们所有的人都～。These problems concern all of us. **2**（涉及到）be relevant: 研究物理及～学科 study physics and related subjects ‖ 邀请～方面前来参加会议 invite the relevant parties to the meeting

【有光纸】yǒuguāngzhǐ〈名〉cap paper

【有轨电车】yǒuguǐ diànchē〈名〉tram〈英〉; streetcar〈美〉

【有鬼】yǒuguǐ〈动〉smell fishy: 心中～ have dubious motives ‖ 这里面肯定～。There is something fishy about this.

【有过之无不及】yǒu guò zhī wú bù jí〈成〉surpass: 这次损失跟上次比是～。This loss is even greater than the last one.

【有害】yǒuhài〈动〉harm: ～健康 be detrimental to one's health

【有害气体】yǒuhài qìtǐ〈名〉poisonous gas

【有恒】yǒuhéng〈动〉〈书〉persevere: ～为成功之本。Perseverance is the mother of success.

【有机】yǒujī〈形〉**1**［化学］organic: ～肥料 organic fertilizer **2**（协调）organic: ～结合 be organically combined ‖ ～整体 organic whole

【有机玻璃】yǒujī bōli〈名〉［材料］perspex〈英〉; plexiglas〈美〉

【有机化学】yǒujī huàxué〈名〉organic chemistry

【有机农业】yǒujī nóngyè〈名〉organic farming

【有机食品】yǒujī shípǐn〈名〉organic food

【有机体】yǒujītǐ〈名〉organism

【有机物】yǒujīwù〈名〉organic compound

【有机质】yǒujīzhì〈名〉organic substance

【有机可乘】yǒujī-kěchéng〈成〉there is a loophole that can be taken advantage of

【有加无已】yǒujiā-wúyǐ〈成〉be on the increase

【有价无市】yǒujià-wúshì〈成〉[of a market] have only quotations but no actual trading

【有价证券】yǒujià zhèngquàn〈名〉securities

【有奖销售】yǒujiǎng xiāoshòu〈名〉prize-giving sales

【有教无类】yǒujiào-wúlèi〈成〉in education there should be no class distinction

【有劲】yǒujìn **A**〈动〉have great strength: 这人真～，能举起这块石头。This man is so strong that he can lift this stone. **B**〈形〉energetic: 大家谈得非常～。Everyone talked with great enthusiasm. ‖ 球赛非常精彩，他越看越～。The game was really exciting. The more he watched, the more enthusiastic he became.

【有旧】yǒujiù〈动〉〈书〉to have been friends in the past

【有救】yǒujiù〈动〉can be remedied: 有了这药，你的病就～了。With this medicine, your illness can be cured.

【有口皆碑】yǒukǒu-jiēbēi〈成〉be universally acclaimed: 她的敬业精神是～的。Her professionalism won universal acclaim.

【有口难辩】yǒukǒu-nánbiàn〈成〉find it hard to defend oneself

【有口难言】yǒukǒu-nányán〈成〉find it embarrassing to bring up a matter

【有口无心】yǒukǒu-wúxīn〈成〉not mean what one says: 他这个人～，你是了解的。You know what he is like. He says whatever enters his mind.

【有来有往】yǒulái-yǒuwǎng〈成〉have a reciprocal relation

【有赖】yǒulài〈动〉depend on: 这项任务的完成～于大家的努力。The completion of the task is dependent upon the efforts of everyone involved.

【有劳】yǒuláo〈动〉〈套〉please do me the favour of: ～你把这本书给他送去。Please do me the favour of delivering this book to him. ‖ 这事～您了。I'm sorry for giving you so much trouble.

【有了】yǒule〈动〉〈口〉**1**（有主意）[said when hitting upon a good idea] I've got it. **2** ▸**p. 772**〈婉〉（怀孕）be pregnant

【有了人家】yǒule rénjiā〈动〉[of a girl] be engaged

【有棱有角】yǒuléng-yǒujiǎo〈成〉〈喻〉have a forceful personality

【有理】yǒulǐ **A**〈动〉be reasonable: ～，有利，有节 on just grounds, to one's advantage and with restraint ‖ 她说得很～。She spoke a lot of sense. **B**〈名〉［数学］rational

【有理数】yǒulǐshù ▸**p. 691**〈名〉［数学］rational number

【有理走遍天下，无理寸步难行】yǒulǐ zǒubiàn tiānxià, wúlǐ cùn bù nán xíng〈俗〉with justice on your side, you can go anywhere; without it, you cannot take a step

【有力】yǒulì〈形〉powerful: 采取～措施 take strong measures ‖ 提供～的证据 provide compelling evidence

【有利】yǒulì〈形〉advantageous: ～于健康 be beneficial to one's health ‖ 抓住～时机 seize a favourable opportunity ‖ 对有关各方都～ benefit every side concerned

【有利可图】yǒulì-kětú〈成〉have good prospects of gain: 看到股市～，炒股的人越来越多。With the stock market looking promising, there are more and more investors.

【有利条件】yǒulì tiáojiàn〈名〉advantageous conditions

【有利有弊】yǒulì-yǒubì〈成〉have both pros and cons

【有脸】yǒuliǎn〈动〉have the face

【有两下子】yǒu liǎngxiàzi〈动〉〈口〉know one's stuff: 他在这方面～。When it comes to this point, he really knows his stuff.

【有零】yǒulíng〈名〉[used after round numbers] odd: 三十～ thirty-odd

【有令不行，有禁不止】yǒu lìng bù xíng, yǒu jìn bù zhǐ〈成〉orders are not carried out and prohibitions are not heeded

【有门儿】yǒuménr〈动〉〈口〉be hopeful: 这事看来～。This matter looks hopeful.

【有面子】yǒu miànzi〈动〉enjoy due respect

【有名】yǒumíng〈形〉famous: ～的外科医生 eminent surgeon ‖ ～的作家 well-known writer

【有名无实】yǒumíng-wúshí〈成〉in name but not in fact: 他这个主任～。He is a director in name only.

【有目共睹】yǒumù-gòngdǔ〈成〉be obvious to all: ～的事实 a fact that is obvious to all

【有目共赏】yǒumù-gòngshǎng〈成〉have universal appeal

【有奶便是娘】yǒu nǎi biànshì niáng〈俗〉〈喻〉lick the hand of anyone who throws a few crumbs

【有你的】yǒunǐde〈惯〉〈口〉[used to praise sb.] good for you: 真～！Great, good for you!

【有年】yǒunián〈副〉〈书〉for years: 习艺～ having practised the art for years

【有凭有据】yǒupíng-yǒujù〈成〉be furnished with proof and evidence

【有谱儿】yǒupǔr〈动〉〈口〉have confidence: 这事我心里早～了。I have felt confident about this for a long time.

【有期徒刑】yǒuqī-túxíng〈名〉［法律］fixed-term imprisonment: 被判处5年～ be sentenced to five years' imprisonment

【有其父，必有其子】yǒu qí fù, bì yǒu qí zǐ〈俗〉like father, like son

【有起色】yǒu qǐsè〈动〉pick up: 生意似乎～。Business appears to be picking up.

【有气无力】yǒuqì-wúlì〈成〉weak: 他讲起话来～。His voice is feeble when he speaks.

【有钱买马，没钱置鞍】yǒuqián mǎi mǎ, méiqián zhì ān〈俗〉spend extravagantly but grudge trifling expenses

【有钱难买老来瘦】yǒuqián nán mǎi lǎo lái shòu〈俗〉to be lean in old age is beyond all monetary value

【有钱能使鬼推磨】yǒuqián néng shǐ guǐ tuīmò〈俗〉〈喻〉money talks

【有钱人】yǒuqiánrén〈名〉the wealthy

【有钱有势】yǒuqián-yǒushì〈成〉be rich and powerful

【有情】yǒuqíng〈动〉be in love

【有情有义】yǒuqíng-yǒuyì〈成〉there are ties of friendship

【有顷】yǒuqǐng〈名〉〈书〉a short time afterwards

【有请】yǒuqǐng〈动〉〈套〉invite a guest in

【有求必应】yǒuqiú-bìyìng〈成〉grant whatever is requested: 她对孩子～。She doesn't deny her children anything.

【有求于人】yǒuqiúyúrén〈成〉have to look to sb. for help

【有去无还】yǒuqù-wúhuán〈成〉gone never to return again

【有趣】yǒuqù〈形〉interesting: ～的故事 interesting story ‖ 这笑话非常～。This joke is highly amusing.

【有染】yǒurǎn〈动〉have an affair: 他与老板的妻子～。He is having an affair with the boss's wife.

【有日子】yǒu rìzi〈动〉**1**（有好些天）for quite a while: 咱们～没见了。It's been a long time since we met last time. **2**（有确定的日子）have fixed a date: 公司开张～了吗？Has the company's opening date been decided yet?

【有如】yǒurú〈动〉be just like: 他待我们～贵宾。He treated us as honoured guests.

【有辱】yǒurǔ〈动〉 bring dishonour: ～家门 bring disgrace to one's family
【有色金属】yǒusè jīnshǔ〈名〉 non-ferrous metal
【有色人种】yǒusè rénzhǒng〈名〉 people of colour: 不要歧视～。Don't discriminate against people of colour.
【有色眼镜】yǒusè yǎnjìng〈名〉〈喻〉 rose-tinted spectacles: 戴着～看问题 look at things through rose-tinted spectacles
【有伤风化】yǒushāng-fēnghuà〈成〉 indecent: 你的行为～。Your behaviour is an offence against decency.
【有身孕】yǒu shēnyùn〈动〉 be pregnant
【有身子】yǒu shēnzi ▸**p. 772**〈动〉〈口〉 have a bun in the oven
【有神】yǒushén〈形〉 **1**（极佳） charmingly wonderful **2**（有神采） bright and piercing: 双目～ have sparkling eyes
【有神论】yǒushénlùn〈名〉 theism: ～者 theist
【有生力量】yǒushēng lìliàng〈名〉 **1**（指兵员和马匹） effective soldiers and horses **2**（指军队） effective troops: 集中～ concentrate one's effective strength ‖ 消灭敌人的～ enemy's effective forces
【有生以来】yǒushēng-yǐlái〈成〉 ever since one was born: 他～没有出过国。He's never been abroad in his life.
【有生之年】yǒushēngzhīnián〈成〉 one's remaining years: 在～为国多做贡献 contribute to one's country with the time one has left
【有声有色】yǒushēng-yǒusè〈成〉 full of sound and colour: 小说中的人物描绘得～。The characters in the novel are evoked with great vividness.
【有失】yǒushī〈动〉 lose: ～身份/尊严 be beneath one's rank/dignity
【有失体统】yǒushī tǐtǒng〈成〉be bad form: 你这种行为～。It's bad form for you to behave like this.
【有时】yǒushí〈副〉 sometimes: 天～热～冷。It is sometimes hot and sometimes cold.
【有识之士】yǒushízhīshì〈成〉 man of insight
【有史以来】yǒushǐyǐlái〈副〉 since the beginning of history: 获得～第一块金牌 win one's first ever gold medal ‖ ～最冷的冬天 coldest winter on record
【有始无终】yǒushǐ-wúzhōng〈成〉start sth. but fail to carry it through: 这项计划～。The programme began well but ended badly.
【有始有终】yǒushǐ-yǒuzhōng〈成〉 carry sth. through to the end: 我们无论做什么都要～，不要半途而废。Whatever we do, we must see it through to completion and not give up half way.
【有恃无恐】yǒushì-wúkǒng〈成〉〈贬〉 be emboldened by sb.'s support: 他们仗着人多势众，就～。They felt reassured and emboldened at the thought that they were stronger in number.
【有数】yǒushù **A**〈动〉 know exactly how things stand: 这事他心里～。He is quite sure about that. **B**〈形〉 limited in number: 没走的只剩下～的几个人了。Few people remained.
【有说有笑】yǒushuō-yǒuxiào〈成〉talk and laugh
【有损】yǒusǔn〈动〉 be harmful to: 吸烟～健康。Smoking is harmful to one's health.
【有所】yǒusuǒ〈动〉 have to some extent: ～顾忌 have certain misgivings ‖ ～作为 do sth. to one's credit ‖ 对他的评价我～保留。I have my reservations about him.
【有条不紊】yǒutiáo-bùwěn〈成〉 in perfect order: 做事～ do things systematically
【有头无尾】yǒutóu-wúwěi〈成〉 leave sth. unfinished
【有头有脸】yǒutóu-yǒuliǎn〈成〉 be prestigious: ～的人 prestigious figure
【有头有尾】yǒutóu-yǒuwěi〈成〉 see sth. through from beginning to end
【有望】yǒuwàng〈动〉 be promising: 成功～ show promise of success ‖ 价格～在第三季度降低10%。Prices were expected to be cut by as much as 10% in the third quarter.
【有为】yǒuwéi〈动〉 be promising: 奋发～ be industrious and promising ‖ 年轻～ be young and full of promise
【有闻必录】yǒuwén-bìlù〈成〉 record all that has been heard
【有喜】yǒuxǐ ▸**p. 772**〈动〉 be pregnant: 她～了。She is expecting.
【有戏】yǒuxì〈动〉〈口〉 **1**（有希望） be promising: 你的新房子～了。You are very likely to get the new house. **2**（富有戏剧性） become more complicated
【有隙可乘】yǒuxì-kěchéng〈成〉 there is a loophole to exploit: 精心安排，不让对方～。Arrange everything meticulously so as not to allow the other side to exploit any loophole.
【有限】yǒuxiàn〈形〉 limited: 能力～ limited in one's ability ‖ 一个人的知识是～的。There is a limit to a person's knowledge. ‖ 数量～，欲购从速。Quantities are limited, so order early.
【有限公司】yǒuxiàn gōngsī〈名〉 limited liability company (Ltd)
【有限责任】yǒuxiàn zérèn〈名〉 limited liability: ～股份公司 share-holding limited liability company
【有线电视】yǒuxiàn diànshì〈名〉 cable television
【有线广播】yǒuxiàn guǎngbō〈名〉wired broadcasting: ～网 wire broadcasting network
【有线通信】yǒuxiàn tōngxìn〈名〉 wire communication
【有效】yǒuxiào〈形〉 effective: ～措施 effective measure ‖ ～护照/证件 valid passport/documents ‖ 该协议仍然～。The contract still holds. ‖ 新药片非常～。The new tablets are extremely effective.
【有效期】yǒuxiàoqī〈名〉 **1**（指条约、合同等） validity period: ～为三个月 be valid for three months ‖ 延长护照的～ renew a passport **2**（指药品等） time of efficacy: 药的～已过。This medicine has passed its expiry date.
【有些】yǒuxiē **A**〈代〉 some: ～地方 some places ‖ ～人 some people ‖ ～鸟不会飞。Some birds cannot fly. **B**〈动〉 have some: 你说的～道理。There was an element of truth in what you said. ‖ 他思想～负担。He has something on his mind. **C**〈副〉 somewhat: ～口渴 feel rather thirsty ‖ 病人的情况～好转了。The patient's condition has improved somewhat.
【有心】yǒuxīn **A**〈动〉 have a mind to: 我～帮他一把。I've decided to give him a hand. **B**〈副〉 intentionally: ～捣乱 stir up trouble on purpose
【有心人】yǒuxīnrén〈名〉 person who sets their mind on doing something: 世上无难事，只怕～。Nothing in the world is difficult for one who sets their mind on it.
【有形】yǒuxíng〈形〉 tangible
【有形损耗】yǒuxíng sǔnhào〈名〉 material loss
【有形资产】yǒuxíng zīchǎn〈名〉 material assets
【有幸】yǒuxìng〈形〉〈谦〉 fortunate: ～参加代表大会 have the honour of attending the congress ‖ ～认识她 be lucky to know her
【有性】yǒuxìng〈形〉［生物］ sexual
【有性杂交】yǒuxìng zájiāo〈名〉［生物］ sexual hybridization
【有血有肉】yǒuxuè-yǒuròu〈成〉 lifelike: 小说中的主人公被描写得～。The portrayal of the hero in the novel is very lifelike.
【有言在先】yǒuyán-zàixiān〈成〉forewarn: 我们～，谁输了谁请客。We made it clear beforehand that the loser is to foot the bill.
【有眼不识泰山】yǒu yǎn bù shí Tàishān〈成〉〈喻〉 fail to recognize a person of eminence: 恕我～，冒犯了你。I hope you will forgive me for failing to recognize that you are a person of stature.
【有眼无珠】yǒuyǎn-wúzhū〈成〉〈喻〉 have eyes but no clarity
【有氧运动】yǒuyǎng yùndòng〈名〉 aerobic exercise
【有一搭没一搭】yǒu yīdā méi yīdā〈惯〉 **1**（没话找话） conversing for the sake of conversing: ～地说个不停 go on and on about nothing **2**（可有可无） dispensable
【有益】yǒuyì〈形〉 beneficial: ～健康 good for one's health ‖ 做出～的贡献 make valuable contributions
【有意】yǒuyì **A**〈动〉 **1**（有愿望） have a mind to: 双方～跟我们合作。Both sides are disposed towards cooperating with us. **2**（有爱慕之心） be attached to: 他对她～，可一直没有勇气表白。He is interested in her, but he is not brave enough to say it. **B**〈副〉 deliberately: ～刁难某人 deliberately make things difficult for sb. ‖ ～找茬 find mistakes by intent
【有意识】yǒu yìshí〈副〉 consciously: 他这样做完全是～的。He did it on purpose.
【有意思】yǒu yìsi〈动〉 **1**（耐人寻味） be meaningful: 他的演讲简短而～。Short as it is, his speech is significant. **2**（有趣） be interesting: 她这个人很～。She is great fun. **3**（有爱慕之心） be attached to: 你没看出他对你～？ Haven't you noticed that he likes you?
【有勇无谋】yǒuyǒng-wúmóu〈成〉be more brave than wise
【有余】yǒuyú **A**〈动〉 have a surplus: ▸绰绰～ **B**〈形〉 more than: 那人三十～。That man is thirty-odd.
【有缘】yǒuyuán〈动〉 be predestined: 他们结为夫妻算是前世～。Their getting married is the work of fate. ‖ 我们又见面了，真是～。It's our fate to meet each other again.
【有则改之，无则加勉】yǒu zé gǎi zhī, wú zé jiā miǎn〈成〉 correct mistakes if you have made any and guard against them if you have not
【有章可循】yǒuzhāng-kěxún〈成〉 there are rules and regulations to be followed
【有朝一日】yǒuzhāo-yīrì〈成〉 some day: ～我要跟你算账! One day I'll get even with you!
【有职无权】yǒuzhí-wúquán〈成〉 have a position without power
【有职有权】yǒuzhí-yǒuquán〈成〉 have both the post and the power
【有志不在年高】yǒu zhì bù zài nián gāo〈俗〉 those with determination will succeed regardless of their age
【有志者事竟成】yǒu zhì zhě shì jìng chéng

〈俗〉 where there is a will there is a way
【有致】yǒuzhì〈动〉 be interesting: 错落～ in picturesque disorder
【有种】yǒuzhǒng〈动〉〈口〉 be plucky
【有助于】yǒuzhùyú〈动〉 contribute to: ～消化 subserve digestion ‖ ～增进了解 contribute to better understanding ‖ ～增强体质 be conducive to good health
【有罪】yǒuzuì〈动〉［法律］ be guilty: 裁决～ find sb. guilty

酉 yǒu〈名〉 tenth of the twelve Earthly Branches (地支)
【酉时】yǒushí〈名〉〈旧〉 period of the day from 5 p.m. to 7 p.m.

卣 yǒu〈名〉〈古〉 small-mouthed wine vessel

莠 yǒu
A〈名〉 foxtail grass: ▸良～不齐
B〈形〉〈书〉（品质低下） mean

铕（銪） yǒu〈名〉［化学］ europium (Eu)

牖 yǒu〈名〉〈书〉 window

黝 yǒu〈形〉 dark
【黝黯】yǒu'àn〈形〉 dark: ～的角落里 in a dark corner
【黝黑】yǒuhēi〈形〉 dark: 皮肤～ dark-skinned

yòu

又 yòu〈副〉 1（表重复） [used for the repetition and continuation of an actual action happening again]: 他把机器装了～拆，拆了～装。 He repeatedly took the machine apart and then reassembled it. ‖ 他的哮喘病～犯了。 He has had another attack of asthma. ‖ 我们取得了一个～一个的胜利。 We have won one victory after another. 2（表同时存在） [expressing the coexistence of several conditions or qualities] both...: ～便宜～好 be cheap but good ‖ 母亲生病后，父亲既当爹～当妈。 When Mother was sick in bed, Father acted as both father and mother to us. ‖ 她有一头～长～密的黑发。 She has very long, thick black hair. 3（表更进一层） moreover: 那～是另一回事。 That is something else again. ‖ 她人漂亮，而且～聪明。 She is beautiful and furthermore she is intelligent. 4（表补充） in addition to: 工资之外，他～挣了不少版税。 In addition to his salary, he earns a lot from royalties. 5 ▸p. 448（表零数） [used between a whole number and a fraction] and: 十小时～五分钟 ten hours and five minutes ‖ 一～二分之一 one and a half 6（表转折） but: 我想去，～怕没时间. I'd like to go, but I'm not sure if I can find the time. ‖ 我想把实情告诉他，～怕他听了后难过。 I want to tell him the situation but am afraid that once he hears about it he'll be upset. 7（表强调） [used in a negative statement or a rhetorical question for emphasis]: 如果这是真的～怎样呢？ What if it's true? ‖ 再说，他那些话～有什么价值呢？ Then again, what do his fine words amount to?
【又当别论】yòudāngbiélùn〈成〉 be an exception to the rule
【又红又专】yòuhóng-yòuzhuān〈成〉 be both politically conscious and professionally competent
【又及】yòují〈动〉 postscript (PS)
【又惊又喜】yòujīng-yòuxǐ〈成〉 be pleasantly surprised: 给某人来个～ give sb. a pleasant surprise
【又要马儿好，又要马儿不吃草】yòu yào mǎr hǎo, yòu yào mǎr bù chī cǎo〈俗〉〈喻〉 have one's cake and eat it

右 yòu
A〈名〉 1 ▸p. 781（右边） right: ～臂 right arm ‖ 靠～走 keep to the right ‖ 在中国大陆，车辆一律靠～行驶。 On the Chinese mainland cars drive on the right. ▸～首，向～ 2〈旧〉（西） west: 山～ areas west of the Taihang Mountains 3〈古〉（较高位置） right side as the side of precedence: ▸无出其～
B〈形〉 right: 在政治上，她比她的前任更～。 Politically, she's further to the right than her predecessor. ▸～派，～倾，～翼
【右边】yòubian〈名〉 right-hand side: 请坐在我的～。 Please sit to my right.
【右侧】yòucè = 右边 yòubian
【右面】yòumiàn = 右边 yòubian
【右派】yòupài〈名〉 the Right: ～分子 rightist
【右前锋】yòuqiánfēng〈名〉［体育］ right forward
【右前卫】yòuqiánwèi〈名〉［体育］ right half-back
【右倾】yòuqīng〈名〉 Right deviation: 思想～的小说家 novelist with Right-deviationist thinking
【右倾机会主义】yòuqīng jīhuìzhǔyì〈名〉 Right opportunism
【右手】yòushǒu〈名〉 1（右边的手） right hand: 惯用～ be right-handed 2 = 右首 yòushǒu
【右首】yòushǒu〈名〉 right-hand side: 她坐在我～。 She is sitting on my right.
【右舷】yòuxián〈名〉 starboard
【右翼】yòuyì〈名〉 1［军事］ right flank: 攻击敌人的～ attack the enemy's right 2（指政党、阶级等） right wing: ～分子 right-winger
【右转弯】yòuzhuǎnwān〈名〉 right turn

幼 yòu
A〈形〉 young: ～鹿 fawn ‖ ～苗 sapling ‖ ～畜 young animal ▸～虫，～芽，年～无知
B〈名〉 the young: ▸扶老携～
【幼虫】yòuchóng〈名〉 larva
【幼雏】yòuchú〈名〉 young bird
【幼儿】yòu'ér〈名〉 infant: ～心理学 child psychology
【幼儿教育】yòu'ér jiàoyù〈名〉 preschool education: 从事～ be in preschool education
【幼儿师范】yòu'ér shīfàn〈名〉 kindergarten teacher-training college
【幼儿园】yòu'éryuán〈名〉 kindergarten: ～教师 kindergarten teacher
【幼发拉底河】Yòufālādǐhé ▸p. 294〈名〉 Euphrates
【幼教】yòujiào〈简称〉= 幼儿教育
【幼林】yòulín〈名〉［林业］ young growth
【幼苗】yòumiáo〈名〉 seedling: 培养～ grow seedlings
【幼年】yòunián〈名〉 childhood: ～丧母 lose one's mother in early childhood
【幼师】yòushī〈简称〉= 幼儿师范
【幼体】yòutǐ〈名〉［生物］ the young: 毛虫是蝴蝶的～。 Caterpillars are the larvae of butterflies.
【幼童】yòutóng〈名〉 young child
【幼小】yòuxiǎo〈形〉 young and small: ～的婴儿 small baby ‖ ～的植物 immature plants
【幼学壮行】yòuxué-zhuàngxíng〈成〉 learn while young and practise when strong
【幼芽】yòuyá〈名〉 young shoot: 掐掉～ nip the shoots off a plant ‖ 长出～ put out new shoots
【幼崽】yòuzǎi〈名〉 the young: 产下～ [of an animal species] produce young
【幼稚】yòuzhì〈形〉 1（幼小稚嫩） young 2（经验不足） childish: ～可笑 childish and ridiculous ‖ ～的想法 naive idea ‖ 政治上的～ political naivety
【幼稚园】yòuzhìyuán = 幼儿园 yòu'éryuán
【幼株】yòuzhū〈名〉 young plant
【幼子】yòuzǐ〈名〉 youngest son

佑[1] yòu〈动〉 assist: ～助 assist ▸庇～

佑[2]（祐） yòu〈动〉 bless: 菩萨保～ god bless

柚 yòu〈名〉［植物］ pomelo
▸yóu
【柚子】yòuzi〈名〉 pomelo

囿 yòu〈书〉
A〈名〉 enclosure: 鹿～ deer park ▸园～
B〈动〉 be fenced in: ～于成见 be blinded by prejudice

宥 yòu〈动〉〈书〉 pardon: 宽～ forgive

诱（誘） yòu〈动〉 1（引导） guide: ▸～导 2（引诱） lure: ～敌深入 entice the enemy in deep ‖ ～使某人上当受骗 lure sb. into a trap 3（引发） lead to: ▸～发，～因，～致
【诱逼】yòubī〈动〉 cajole and coerce
【诱变】yòubiàn〈名〉［生物］ mutagenesis
【诱捕】yòubǔ〈动〉 trap: ～老鼠 trap a mouse
【诱导】yòudǎo A〈动〉 induce: ～他改过自新 persuade him to mend his ways ‖ 细心～某人 guide sb. cautiously B〈名〉［物理］ induction
【诱饵】yòu'ěr〈名〉 bait: 在鱼钩上/兽夹里放～ put bait on a hook/in a trap ‖〈喻〉以金钱为～ use money as bait
【诱发】yòufā〈动〉 1（引导启发） bring out: ～联想 stir up associations 2（导致发生） induce: 有些癌症可在短时期内～显现。 Some cancers can manifest themselves very quickly.
【诱供】yògòng〈动〉 trap sb. into a confession
【诱拐】yòuguǎi〈动〉 abduct: ～儿童 abduct a child
【诱惑】yòuhuò〈动〉 1（使人迷惑上当） lure: 经不住～ surrender to temptation ‖ 金钱的～ lure of money ‖ 无法抗拒的～ irresistible temptation 2（吸引） attract: 窗外是一片～人的景色。 The window commands a charming view.
【诱奸】yòujiān〈动〉 seduce
【诱骗】yòupiàn〈动〉 trick: 他们把他～到一个死胡同。 They tricked him into a dead-end street.
【诱人】yòurén〈形〉 captivating: ～的美餐 inviting meal ‖ 一片～的景色 enchanting scenery

【诱杀】yòushā〈动〉 trap and kill: ～棉铃虫 lure boll-worms to their death
【诱使】yòushǐ〈动〉 trick into: ～某人干某事 entice sb. into doing sth.
【诱降】yòuxiáng〈动〉 lure into surrender
【诱因】yòuyīn〈名〉 predisposing cause
【诱致】yòuzhì〈动〉〈书〉 lead to: ～堕落 cause degeneration

蚴 yòu〈名〉 larva of a tapeworm or cercaria of a schistosome

釉 yòu〈名〉 glaze: 给瓷上～ glaze china
【釉面砖】yòumiànzhuān〈名〉 glazed tile
【釉陶】yòutáo〈名〉 glazed pottery
【釉质】yòuzhì〈名〉［生理］ enamel
【釉子】yòuzi〈名〉 glaze

鼬 yòu〈名〉［动物］ weasel: 白～ stoat
【鼬獾】 yòuhuān〈名〉［动物］ ferret-badger

yū

迂 yū〈形〉 **1**（曲折） circuitous: ▸～回, ～曲 **2**（迂腐） impractical: 这人～得很。 He is very impractical. ▸～腐, ～阔
【迂夫子】yūfūzǐ〈名〉 pedant
【迂腐】 yūfǔ〈形〉 pedantic: 脑筋～ be pedantically minded ‖ ～之谈/之论 pedantic remarks/views
【迂缓】yūhuǎn〈形〉 sluggish: 行动～ be slow to act
【迂回】yūhuí〈动〉 **1**（回旋） circle: 在人群中～穿行 twist one's way through a crowd ‖ ～的山道 circuitous mountain path **2**（绕到侧面或后面） circumvent: ～包抄 outflank and envelop ‖ ～战术 outflanking tactics ‖ 向敌人左侧～ outflank the enemy on the left
【迂阔】yūkuò〈形〉 high-sounding and impractical: ～之论 impractical view
【迂曲】yūqū〈形〉 winding: ～难行的山路 tortuous path over the mountain
【迂儒】 yūrú〈名〉 pedantic Confucian scholar
【迂执】yūzhí〈形〉〈书〉 impractical and stubborn
【迂拙】yūzhuō〈形〉〈书〉 impractical and foolish

吁 yū〈拟〉 [used as a command to animals to stop or slow down] whoa
▸xū, yù

纡（紆） yū〈书〉
A〈形〉 circuitous
B〈动〉 bind
【纡回】yūhuí〈书〉= 迂回 yūhuí
【纡徐】 yūxú〈形〉〈书〉 unhurried, leisurely

於 Yū〈名〉 Yu [surname]
▸wū

淤 yū
A〈名〉 silt: 引～肥田 fertilize the soil with silt ‖ 河～ sludge from a riverbed
B〈动〉 **1**（淤积） be choked with silt: 河里～了很多泥沙。 The river has become full of silt. **2**（血液不流通） stagnate: ▸～血
C〈形〉 silted (up): ▸～地, ～泥

【淤地】yūdì〈名〉 silt land
【淤灌】yūguàn〈名〉［农业］ warping
【淤积】yūjī〈动〉 silt up: ～平原 alluvial plain
【淤泥】yūní〈名〉 silt: 清除～ clean up muddy deposits
【淤塞】yūsè〈动〉 silt up: 航道被泥沙～。 The channel became choked with silt.
【淤沙】yūshā〈名〉 silt
【淤血】yūxuè〈名〉 extravasated blood
【淤滞】yūzhì〈动〉 flow slowly because of a silt build-up: 疏通～的河道 dredge a slow-flowing river

瘀 yū〈动〉 extravasate, stagnate: ▸～血
【瘀斑】yūbān ▸**p. 50**〈名〉［医学］ bruise
【瘀血】yūxuè ▸**p. 50**〈名〉［中医］ blood stasis

yú

于（於） yú
A〈介〉 **1**（在） [indicating time or place] at: 大会～昨天开幕。 The conference started yesterday. ‖ 他生～乌鲁木齐。 He was born in Urumqi. **2**（引进对象） [indicating the object of an action]: 满足～现状 be content with the status quo ‖ 求救～人 ask for help ‖ 热中～集邮 be keen on stamp collecting ▸嫁祸～人 **3**（从） [indicating beginning or source] from: 毕业～名牌大学 graduate from a prestigious university ‖ 死～矿井事故 die in a mine accident **4**（被） [indicating the performer of an action] by: 见笑～人 be laughed at by others ‖ 限～经济条件 be circumscribed by economical conditions **5**（表比较） [indicating comparison] than: 按低～成本价出售 sell below cost ‖ 上尉的军衔低～少校。 Captain is lower in rank than major.
B〈后缀〉 [used after a verb or adjective] with regard to: 忙～工作 be busy with one's work ‖ 股市趋～稳定。 The stock market is stabilizing.
【于今】yújīn **A**〈副〉 up to now: 我们相识～好几年了。 We have known each other for several years now. **B**〈名〉 now: ～, 他把对手已远远抛在后面。 These days he is way ahead of his rivals.
【于是】yúshì〈连〉 so: 大家一鼓励, 我～恢复了信心。 Everybody encouraged me, and so my confidence was restored.
【于是乎】yúshìhū = 于是 yúshì
【于事无补】yúshì-wúbǔ〈成〉 be of no use in terms of making things better
【于心不安】yúxīn-bù'ān〈成〉 feel uneasy about sth.
【于心不忍】yúxīn-bùrěn〈成〉 not have the heart to
【于心无愧】yúxīn-wúkuì〈成〉 not have a guilty conscience
【于心有愧】yúxīn-yǒukuì〈成〉have a guilty conscience

予 yú〈代〉〈书〉 I: ▸～取～求
▸yǔ
【予取予求】yúqǔ-yúqiú〈成〉 make unlimited demands: 我们要保护地球的资源, 不能总是对它～。 We should conserve the earth's resources, and not take from it at will.

余[1] yú〈代〉〈书〉 I: ～幼年丧母。 I lost my mother when I was a child.

余[2]（餘） yú
A〈动〉 remain: 身上已无～钱 have no more money on one ‖ 除去营业税, 还～5万元。 After business tax, there is 50 thousand *yuan* left. ▸～党, ～粮, 不遗～力
B〈名〉 time after an event: 工作之～ after work ‖ 课～ after class
C ▸**p. 927**〈数〉 over: 20～人 twenty-odd people ‖ 有百～人。 There are over a hundred people.
【余波】yúbō〈名〉after-effect: ～未平 there are still repercussions
【余存】yúcún〈动〉 have left over: 核对销售量和～量 check the amount of sales and stock ‖ ～的钱 the money left over
【余党】yúdǎng〈名〉 remaining confederates
【余地】 yúdì〈名〉 leeway: 留有～ leave some leeway ‖ 没有选择～ be left with no alternative ‖ 似乎还有协商的～。 There seems to be some room for negotiation.
【余毒】yúdú〈名〉 **1**（指毒素） noxious residue **2**（指祸害） harmful influence: 肃清～ remove pernicious influences ‖ 封建～ pernicious vestiges of feudalism
【余额】yú'é〈名〉 **1**（指名额） unfilled vacancies: 这个游泳班还有～吗? Are there any vacancies in the swimming class? **2**（指金额） balance: 将～全部取出 draw the balance down to nothing ‖ 我银行账上的～不多了。 My bank balance has dwindled.
【余风】yúfēng〈名〉 vestiges of a no longer prevalent custom: 先民的～ remnants of a culture of previous times
【余晖】yúhuī〈名〉 afterglow: 落日～ last rays of the setting sun
【余悸】yújì〈名〉 lingering fear: 打消～ dissipate the lingering fear ▸心有～
【余角】 yújiǎo〈名〉［数学］ complementary angle
【余烬】yújìn〈名〉 **1**（指燃烧后） embers: ～复燃 the embers caught alight again ‖ 只剩下了篝火的～。 Only the embers of the bonfire remained. **2**〈喻〉（指战争或灾难后） wreckage after a disaster
【余可类推】 yúkělèituī〈成〉 the rest may be inferred by analogy
【余款】yúkuǎn〈名〉 spare cash: 提走全部～ draw the balance down to nothing
【余力】yúlì〈名〉 surplus strength: 没有～顾及此事 have no energy left to attend to the matter ▸不遗～
【余沥】yúlì〈名〉〈书〉〈喻〉meagre share of profit: 分沾～ get a small share in the profits
【余粮】yúliáng〈名〉 surplus grain: 把～卖给国家 sell the surplus grain to the state
【余留】yúliú〈动〉 remain
【余年】yúnián〈名〉 one's remaining years: 安度～ live in peace and health for the remainder of one's life
【余孽】yúniè〈名〉 surviving supporters of an evil cause: 铲除～ wipe out remaining evil elements ‖ 封建～ dregs of feudalism
【余缺】yúquē〈名〉 surplus and shortfall: 调剂～ make up deficiencies in one place with surpluses from another
【余热】 yúrè〈名〉 **1**（指热量） surplus heat: 回收～ recoup waste heat ‖ 利用～取暖 harness surplus thermal energy for heating purposes **2**〈喻〉（指能力） efforts by senior citizens after retirement: 发挥～ do one's bit in one's old age
【余生】 yúshēng〈名〉 **1**（晚年） one's remaining years: 安度～ live out one's days

y

peacefully 2（侥幸保全的生命） survival: ▸劫后～

【余剩】 yúshèng〈名〉 surplus: 去年收成好，今年有～。 Thanks to the bumper harvest last year, we have a surplus of grain this year.

【余数】 yúshù ▸p. 691 〈名〉［数学］ remainder: 用三除十得三，～是一。 If you divide 10 by 3, the quotient is 3 with a remainder of 1.

【余威】 yúwēi〈名〉 remaining influence: 失去～ lose remaining prestige

【余味】 yúwèi〈名〉 agreeable aftertaste: ～无穷 leave a lasting and pleasant impression

【余暇】 yúxiá〈名〉 leisure time: 利用～时间读书 use one's spare time to do some reading

【余下】 yúxià〈动〉 remaining: ～的客人 remaining guests

【余弦】 yúxián〈名〉［数学］ cosine

【余兴】 yúxìng〈名〉 1（指兴致） lingering interest: ～未尽 have not enjoyed oneself to the full 2（指娱乐活动） after-party entertainment: ～节目 after-party entertainment programme

【余音】 yúyīn〈名〉 lingering sound: ～袅袅，不绝如缕。 Even when the song was finished, its reverberations did not die away but lingered like an unbroken thread.

【余音绕梁】 yúyīn-ràoliáng〈成〉 the music lingered in the air long after the performance

【余勇可贾】 yúyǒng-kěgǔ〈成〉 still having plenty of fight left in one: 体坛老将，～。 Sporting veterans still have plenty of fight left in them.

【余裕】 yúyù〈形〉 ample: ～的时间 ample time ‖ ～的资源 rich resources

【余韵】 yúyùn〈名〉 lingering charm: ～无穷 appeal lingers on

【余震】 yúzhèn〈名〉 aftershock: ～不断。 The aftershocks were continuous.

妤 yú ▸婕妤 jiéyú

盂 yú〈名〉 jar with a broad top: 漱口～ mug for mouth rinsing or teeth-brushing ▸痰～

【盂兰盆会】 Yúlánpénhuì〈名〉 Ullambana Buddhist ceremony [to redeem the souls of one's ancestors]

臾 yú ▸须臾 xūyú

鱼（魚） yú〈名〉 fish: 捕/养～ catch/raise fish ▸鳄～, 鲸～, 葬身～腹

【鱼白】 yúbái〈名〉 1（鱼的精液） fish sperm 2 = 鱼肚白 yúdùbái

【鱼鳔】 yúbiào〈名〉 air bladder of a fish

【鱼叉】 yúchā〈名〉 fish fork

【鱼场】 yúchǎng〈名〉 fish farm

【鱼池】 yúchí〈名〉 fish pond

【鱼翅】 yúchì〈名〉 shark's fin

【鱼虫】 yúchóng〈名〉 water flea [used as fish feed]: 喂～ feed fish with water fleas

【鱼船】 yúchuán〈名〉 fishing boat

【鱼唇】 yúchún〈名〉 shark's lip [used as food]

【鱼刺】 yúcì〈名〉 fish bone: 剔～ bone a fish ‖ 一根～卡在他喉咙里。 A fish bone got stuck in his throat.

【鱼雕】 yúdiāo〈名〉 fish eagle

【鱼肚】 yúdǔ〈名〉 fish maw [as food]

【鱼肚白】 yúdùbái〈名〉 grey dawn: 天边现出了～。 Day is breaking. ‖ 东方一线～，黎明已经到来。 The grey of daybreak in the east proclaims the dawn.

【鱼饵】 yú'ěr〈名〉 fish bait: 投～ cast out fishing bait ‖ 蚯蚓是最好的～。 Worms make excellent fish bait. ‖ 鱼在咬～了。 The fish is biting at the bait.

【鱼粉】 yúfěn〈名〉 fish meal

【鱼肝油】 yúgānyóu〈名〉 cod-liver oil

【鱼竿】 yúgān〈名〉 fishing rod

【鱼缸】 yúgāng〈名〉 fish tank: 金鱼～ goldfish tank

【鱼钩】 yúgōu〈名〉 fish hook

【鱼骨】 yúgǔ〈名〉 fish bone

【鱼鼓】 yúgǔ = 渔鼓 yúgǔ

【鱼贯】 yúguàn〈副〉 in single file: ～而入 enter in single file

【鱼花】 yúhuā = 鱼苗 yúmiáo

【鱼胶】 yújiāo〈名〉［材料］ fish glue

【鱼具】 yújù = 渔具 yújù

【鱼雷】 yúléi〈名〉［军事］ torpedo: 发射～ launch a torpedo

【鱼雷艇】 yúléitǐng〈名〉 torpedo boat

【鱼鳞】 yúlín〈名〉 fish scale: 刮～ scale a fish

【鱼鳞坑】 yúlínkēng〈名〉［农业］ fish-scale pits (for water conservation, tree-planting etc.)

【鱼龙混杂】 yúlóng-hùnzá〈成〉〈喻〉 a hodgepodge of good and bad people

【鱼卵】 yúluǎn〈名〉 fish roe

【鱼米之乡】 yúmǐzhīxiāng〈成〉 land of milk and honey

【鱼苗】 yúmiáo〈名〉 fish fry: 放养～ breed fish fry

【鱼目混珠】 yúmù-hùnzhū〈成〉〈喻〉 pass off sth. sham as genuine

【鱼皮】 yúpí〈名〉 fish skin

【鱼漂】 yúpiāo〈名〉 float

【鱼鳍】 yúqí〈名〉 fin

【鱼群】 yúqún〈名〉 shoal

【鱼肉】 yúròu A〈名〉 fish meat B〈动〉〈喻〉 cruelly oppress: ～百姓 victimize people

【鱼肉松】 yúròusōng〈名〉 dried fish floss

【鱼水】 yúshuǐ〈名〉 fish and water:〈喻〉军民～一家人。 The army and the people are as close as family.

【鱼水情】 yúshuǐqíng〈名〉 close relationship: 军民～。 The army and the people are as close as fish and water.

【鱼死网破】 yúsǐ-wǎngpò〈成〉〈喻〉 a life-and-death struggle between two: 拼个～ fight at the risk of mutual destruction

【鱼塘】 yútáng〈名〉 fish pond

【鱼网】 yúwǎng = 渔网 yúwǎng

【鱼尾号】 yúwěihào〈名〉 boldface square brackets

【鱼尾裙】 yúwěiqún〈名〉 fishtail skirt

【鱼尾纹】 yúwěiwén〈名〉 crow's feet

【鱼鲜】 yúxiān〈名〉 seafood: ～市场 seafood market

【鱼腥草】 yúxīngcǎo〈名〉［植物］ cordate houttuynia

【鱼汛】 yúxùn〈名〉 fishing season

【鱼雁】 yúyàn〈名〉〈书〉messengers: ～传情 convey feelings through letters ‖ 频通～ often write to each other

【鱼秧子】 yúyāngzi〈名〉 fish fry

【鱼鹰】 yúyīng〈名〉［鸟类］ 1（鹗） fish hawk 2（鸬鹚） cormorant

【鱼油】 yúyóu〈名〉 fish oil: 深海～ deep-sea fish oil

【鱼游釜中】 yúyóufǔzhōng〈成〉〈喻〉 be in imminent peril

【鱼跃】 yúyuè〈动〉 fish jump: ～救球 make a fish jump to retrieve a ball

【鱼子】 yúzǐ〈名〉 fish roe: ～酱 caviar

竽 yú〈名〉〈古〉 *yu* [36-reed wind instrument]: ▸滥～充数

舁 yú〈动〉〈书〉 carry by litter, stretcher, or pole

俞 Yú〈名〉 Yu [surname]

狳 yú ▸犰狳 qiúyú

馀（餘） yú = 余² yú

谀（諛） yú〈动〉〈书〉 toady to: ▸谄～, 阿～

【谀辞】 yúcí〈名〉 flattery

娱（娛） yú

A〈形〉 amusing: ～悦 joyous

B〈动〉 amuse: 自～自乐 enjoy oneself

【娱记】 yújì〈名〉 reporters of news of the recreational circle

【娱乐】 yúlè A〈动〉 amuse: ～场所 entertainment venue B〈名〉 amusement: 提供精神～ provide mental distraction

【娱乐片】 yúlèpiàn〈名〉entertainment film

【娱乐厅】 yúlètīng〈名〉 recreation hall

【娱乐业】 yúlèyè〈名〉 entertainment business

【娱乐中心】 yúlè zhōngxīn〈名〉recreational centre

【娱悦】 yúyuè〈动〉 make happy: ～身心 please the body and the mind

萸 yú ▸茱萸 zhūyú

雩 yú〈名〉〈古〉 sacrificial rite to pray for rain

渔（漁） yú〈动〉 1（捕鱼） fish: ▸～具 2（谋取） take sth. one is not entitled to: ▸～利

【渔霸】 yúbà〈名〉〈旧〉 fishing overlord

【渔叉】 yúchā〈名〉 harpoon

【渔产】 yúchǎn〈名〉 aquatic products: 沿海～丰富。 The coastal waters are abundant with fish.

【渔场】 yúchǎng〈名〉 fisheries: 淡水～ fresh-water fisheries ‖ 近海～ in-shore fisheries

【渔船】 yúchuán〈名〉 fishing boat: 一艘～ a fishing boat ‖ 拖网～ trawler

【渔村】 yúcūn〈名〉 fishing village

【渔夫】 yúfū〈名〉 fisherman

【渔港】 yúgǎng〈名〉 fishing port

【渔歌】 yúgē〈名〉 fisherman's song

【渔鼓】 yúgǔ〈名〉 1（指鼓） fisherman's drum 2［曲艺］ folk tales sung to the accompaniment of a fisherman's drum

【渔火】 yúhuǒ〈名〉 lights on fishing boats: 远处～点点 lights on fishing boats in the distance

【渔家】 yújiā〈名〉 1（渔夫） fisherman 2（指人家） fisherman's family: ～姑娘 fisherman's daughter

【渔具】 yújù〈名〉 fishing tackle

【渔捞】 yúlāo〈名〉 fishery

【渔利】 yúlì A〈动〉 profit at others' expense: 奸商投机倒把，从中～。 The profiteers reaped unfair gains through speculation.

B 〈名〉 profit reaped as a third party: ▸坐收～
【渔猎】 yúliè A 〈名〉 fishing and hunting: 靠～为生 fish and hunt for a living B 〈动〉〈书〉 1 (掠夺) plunder 2 (追逐) hanker after: ～女色 seek carnal pleasure
【渔轮】 yúlún 〈名〉 fishing vessel
【渔民】 yúmín 〈名〉 fisherman
【渔人之利】 yúrénzhīlì 〈成〉〈喻〉 profit reaped by a third party
【渔色】 yúsè 〈动〉〈书〉 womanize
【渔网】 yúwǎng 〈名〉 fishing net
【渔翁】 yúwēng 〈名〉 old fisherman
【渔汛】 yúxùn = 鱼汛 yúxùn
【渔业】 yúyè 〈名〉 fishery: ～资源 fishery resources ‖ 海洋～ ocean fishery
【渔舟】 yúzhōu 〈名〉〈书〉 fishing boat

隅 yú 〈名〉 1 (角落) corner: 城～ corner of a city wall ▸负～顽抗 2 〈书〉 (靠边沿处) outlying place: 海～ seaboard

揄 yú 〈动〉〈书〉 1 (赞扬) praise: ▸～扬 2 ▸揶揄 yéyú
【揄扬】 yúyáng 〈动〉〈书〉 1 (赞扬) laud 2 (宣扬) advocate

喁 yú
▸yóng
【喁喁】 yúyú 〈拟〉〈书〉 whisper: ～私语 whisper
▸yóngyóng

嵎 yú 〈名〉〈书〉 mountain recess

畲 yú 〈名〉〈书〉 land that has been cultivated for two years
▸shē

逾 yú
A 〈动〉 surpass: 年～古稀 over seventy years old ▸～期, ～越
B 〈副〉〈书〉 even more
【逾常】 yúcháng 〈动〉〈书〉 be unusual: 激动/拥挤/欣喜～ be overexcited/overcrowded/overjoyed
【逾分】 yúfèn 〈形〉〈书〉 excessive: ～的要求 exorbitant demand
【逾期】 yúqī 〈动〉 exceed the time limit: ～未还的书 overdue book ‖ 所有优惠券～作废。 All the coupons will expire after the closing date.
【逾越】 yúyuè 〈动〉 exceed: ～权限 overstep one's authority ‖ 不可～的障碍 insurmountable obstacle

腴 yú 〈形〉 1 (胖) fat: ▸丰～ 2 (肥沃) fertile: ▸膏～

渝[1] yú 〈动〉 change: 始终不～ remain forever unchanged ‖ 至死不～ be faithful to the last

渝[2] Yú ▸p. 661 〈名〉 Yu [another name for Chongqing (重庆)]

愉 yú 〈形〉 happy: 面有不～之色 wear a displeased look ▸～快, ～悦
【愉快】 yúkuài 〈形〉 happy: 心情～ be in a cheerful mood ‖ ～地接受邀请/任务 accept an invitation/a task with pleasure ‖ 祝你旅途～。 I wish you a pleasant journey.
【愉悦】 yúyuè 〈形〉 cheerful: ～的心情 cheerful mood

䱷 (鰅) yú 〈名〉 [鱼类] barracuda

瑜 yú 〈名〉 1 (美玉) fine jade 2 (优点) virtues: ▸瑕不掩～
【瑜伽】 yújiā 〈名〉 yoga: 练～ practise yoga
【瑜珈】 yújiā = 瑜伽 yújiā

榆 yú 〈名〉 elm: ▸～荚
【榆荚】 yújiá 〈名〉 elm seeds
【榆木】 yúmù 〈名〉 elmwood
【榆木疙瘩】 yúmù gēda 〈名〉〈口〉〈喻〉 stubborn person
【榆木脑袋】 yúmù nǎodai 〈名〉〈口〉 blockhead
【榆钱】 yúqián 〈名〉〈口〉 elm seeds
【榆叶梅】 yúyèméi 〈名〉 flowering plum

虞[1] **(虞)** yú 〈动〉〈书〉 1 (预料) predict: ▸不～之誉 2 (忧虑) fear: 不～匮乏 not worry about running out of supplies ‖ 无冻馁之～ be secure against hunger and cold 3 (欺骗) deceive: ▸尔～我诈

虞[2] **(虞)** Yú 〈名〉 Yu [name of a legendary dynasty founded by King Shun (舜)]
【虞美人】 yúměirén 〈名〉 [植物] corn poppy

愚 yú
A 〈形〉 foolish: ▸～笨, 大智若～
B 〈动〉 make a fool of: ▸～民政策, ～弄
C 〈代〉〈书〉〈谦〉 I: ～兄 me ‖ ～以为不然。 I beg to differ. ▸～见
【愚笨】 yúbèn 〈形〉 stupid: ～透顶 be as thick as two short planks
【愚不可及】 yúbùkějí 〈成〉 couldn't be more foolish: 他总喜欢问我一些～的问题。 He always liked to ask me the most ridiculous questions.
【愚痴】 yúchī 〈形〉 stupid
【愚蠢】 yúchǔn 〈形〉 stupid: ～的想法 stupid idea ‖ 相信他的话那就太～了。 It was so stupid to have believed him.
【愚钝】 yúdùn 〈形〉 slow-witted: 脑子～ have a thick skull
【愚公移山】 Yúgōng-yíshān 〈成〉〈喻〉 achieve the apparently impossible through dogged perseverance
【愚见】 yújiàn 〈名〉〈谦〉 my humble opinion: ～以为不可。 Humble as my opinion is, I don't think this is workable.
【愚陋】 yúlòu 〈形〉 stupid and ignorant
【愚鲁】 yúlǔ 〈形〉 stupid: 生性～ stupid and dull-witted by nature
【愚昧】 yúmèi 〈形〉 ignorant: ～无知 be stupid and ignorant ‖ 与～作斗争 combat ignorance
【愚氓】 yúméng 〈名〉〈旧〉 fool
【愚蒙】 yúméng = 愚昧 yúmèi
【愚民政策】 yúmín zhèngcè 〈名〉 policy of keeping the people in ignorance: 施行～ adopt a policy of keeping the people ignorant
【愚弄】 yúnòng 〈动〉 deceive: ～民众 fool the public ‖ 受到～ be hoodwinked
【愚懦】 yúnuò 〈形〉〈书〉 stupid and timid
【愚人节】 Yúrénjié 〈名〉 April Fool's Day
【愚顽】 yúwán 〈形〉 ignorant and stubborn
【愚妄】 yúwàng 〈形〉 stupid but conceited: ～之徒 ignorant and senseless fellow
【愚者千虑，必有一得】 yúzhě qiān lǜ, bì yǒu yī dé 〈成〉 even a fool occasionally comes up with a good idea if he thinks hard enough
【愚忠】 yúzhōng 〈名〉 blind loyalty
【愚拙】 yúzhuō 〈形〉 stupid and clumsy

覦 (覦) yú ▸觊觎 jìyú

舆[1] **(輿)** yú 〈名〉 1 〈书〉 (车) carriage: 舍～登舟 change from a carriage to a boat ‖ 舟～之便 advantages of having vessels and vehicles 2 (疆域) area: ▸～地 3 (轿子) sedan chair: 彩～ bridal sedan chair ‖ 肩～ sedan chair

舆[2] **(輿)** yú 〈形〉 public: ▸～论, ～情
【舆地】 yúdì 〈名〉〈书〉 territory
【舆论】 yúlùn 〈名〉 public opinion: 制造～ fabricate public opinion ‖ 国际～ international opinion ‖ ～导向 direction toward which people's opinion is guided ‖ 加强～监督 strengthen measures to ensure that the correct orientation is maintained in public opinion ‖ ～哗然 there is a public outcry ‖ 他们进行宣传，为他们的候选人造～。 They used publicity to prepare public opinion for their candidates.
【舆论工具】 yúlùn gōngjù 〈名〉 organs of public opinion
【舆论界】 yúlùnjiè 〈名〉 media circles
【舆情】 yúqíng 〈名〉〈书〉 popular feeling: 洞察～ know public sentiment well ‖ ～激昂。 Popular feeling is furious.
【舆图】 yútú 〈名〉〈书〉 territorial map

蝓 yú ▸蛞蝓 kuòyú

yǔ

与[1] **(與)** yǔ 〈动〉 give: ▸赠～

与[2] **(與)** yǔ
A 〈动〉〈书〉 be on good terms with: 彼此相～ be on good terms with each other ‖ ～国 allied state
B 〈介〉 with: ～本题无关 be beside the point ‖ ～事实不符 do not tally with the facts ‖ 这事～我无关。 It has nothing to do with me. ▸～众不同
C ▸p. 448 〈连〉 and: 战争～和平 war and peace ‖ 行～不行，打个招呼。 Yes or no, let me know.
▸yù
【与共】 yǔgòng 〈动〉〈书〉 stay together: 荣辱～ share weal and woe ‖ 朝夕～ be together from morning to night
【与虎谋皮】 yǔhǔ-móupí 〈成〉〈喻〉 ask an enemy to act against his interests
【与其】 yǔqí 〈连〉 rather than: ～赔钱，不如停业。 Rather than lose money, it would be better to close up the business. ‖ ～让她去干这件事，不如我自己动手干。 Rather than letting her do it, I'd prefer to do the job myself.
【与人方便，与己方便】 yǔ rén fāngbiàn, yǔ jǐ fāngbiàn 〈俗〉 he who helps others helps himself
【与人为善】 yǔrén-wéishàn 〈成〉 aim at helping others out of good will: 采取～的态度 take a sympathetic and friendly attitude
【与日俱增】 yǔrì-jùzēng 〈成〉 grow with each passing day: 要求调动工作的人～。

The number of those requesting work transfers is on the increase.

【与时俱进】yǔshí-jùjìn〈成〉keep pace with the times

【与世长辞】yǔshì-chángcí〈成〉pass away

【与世隔绝】yǔshì-géjué〈成〉be secluded from the real world: 过着～的生活 live a life far removed from reality

【与世无争】yǔshì-wúzhēng〈成〉stand aloof from worldly strife

【与众不同】yǔzhòng-bùtóng〈成〉be different from the common run: 提出～的见解 put forward a different view from the rest

予 yǔ〈动〉give: 免～处分 exempt from punishment ‖ ～人口实 give cause for gossip ▸授～
▸yú

【予以】yǔyǐ〈动〉give: ～表扬 bestow praise ‖ ～赔偿 offer compensation ‖ ～协助 lend cooperation

屿（嶼） yǔ〈名〉islet: ▸岛～

伛（傴） yǔ〈动〉bow to show respect: ～着背 bend one's back

【伛偻】yǔlǚ〈动〉〈书〉hunch one's back

宇 yǔ〈名〉**1**〈书〉(屋檐) eaves **2**(房屋) house: ▸楼～, 庙～ **3**(空间) space: ▸～宙, 寰～ **4**(气质) manner: ▸眉～, 器～轩昂 **5**(指地层单位) aeonothem [highest level division of geologic time, as corresponding to 'aeon']

【宇航】yǔháng〈动〉make a space flight: ～员 astronaut

【宇航服】yǔhángfú〈名〉spacesuit

【宇宙】yǔzhòu〈名〉**1**(天地万物) universe: 探索～奥秘 probe into the mysteries of the universe **2**［哲学］the world

【宇宙大爆炸】yǔzhòu dàbàozhà〈名〉the Big Bang

【宇宙飞船】yǔzhòu fēichuán〈名〉spaceship: 发射～ launch a spacecraft ‖ 载人～ manned spaceship

【宇宙观】yǔzhòuguān〈名〉world view

【宇宙空间】yǔzhòu kōngjiān〈名〉outer space

【宇宙年】yǔzhòunián〈名〉［天文］cosmic year

【宇宙速度】yǔzhòu sùdù〈名〉［物理］cosmic velocity: 达到～ attain cosmic speed

【宇宙站】yǔzhòuzhàn〈名〉space station

羽[1] yǔ

A〈名〉**1**(羽毛) feathers: ▸～绒 **2**(翅膀) wings: 振～ flap the wings

B〈量〉[used for birds]: 一～信鸽 a carrier pigeon

羽[2] yǔ〈名〉［音乐］note on the ancient Chinese pentatonic (五音) scale, corresponding to 6 in *jianpu* (简谱) numbered musical notation

【羽缎】yǔduàn〈名〉［纺织］sateen

【羽冠】yǔguàn〈名〉crest of a bird

【羽化】yǔhuà **A**〈动〉**1**(升天成仙) ascend to heaven and become an immortal **2** ▸**p. 772**〈敬〉［道教］(死亡) pass away: ～登仙 ascend to heaven and become an immortal **B**〈名〉［昆虫］eclosion

【羽客】yǔkè = 羽士 yǔshì

【羽量级】yǔliàngjí〈名〉［体育］featherweight

【羽林军】yǔlínjūn = 禁军 jìnjūn

【羽毛】yǔmáo〈名〉**1**(鸟的毛) feather: ▸～丰满 **2**〈喻〉(名誉) reputation: 爱惜～ cherish one's reputation

【羽毛丰满】yǔmáo-fēngmǎn〈成〉become fully fledged

【羽毛球】yǔmáoqiú〈名〉［体育］**1** ▸**p. 909**(指运动) badminton: 打～ play badminton ‖ ～场 badminton court ‖ ～球拍 badminton racket **2**(指球) shuttlecock

【羽毛扇】yǔmáoshàn〈名〉feather fan

【羽毛未丰】yǔmáo-wèifēng〈成〉not yet fully fledged

【羽绒】yǔróng〈名〉down: ～服 down coat ‖ ～被 down duvet〈英〉, down comforter〈美〉

【羽纱】yǔshā〈名〉camlet (fabric)

【羽扇】yǔshàn〈名〉feather fan

【羽士】yǔshì〈名〉Taoist priest

【羽坛】yǔtán〈名〉badminton circles

【羽翼】yǔyì〈名〉**1**(翅膀) wing **2**〈喻〉〈贬〉(辅佐的人或力量) assistant

雨 yǔ〈名〉rain: 躲～ shelter from the rain ‖ ～停了。It has stopped raining. ▸及时～, 雷阵～, 毛毛～

【雨布】yǔbù〈名〉waterproof cloth

【雨带】yǔdài〈名〉［气象］rainband

【雨滴】yǔdī〈名〉［气象］raindrop

【雨点】yǔdiǎn〈名〉raindrop: 炮弹像～般落在敌军阵地上。Shells rained on the enemy position.

【雨刮器】yǔguāqì〈名〉windscreen wiper

【雨过地皮湿】yǔ guò dìpí shī〈俗〉〈喻〉treat matters perfunctorily or superficially

【雨过天晴】yǔguò-tiānqíng〈成〉**1**〈本〉the rain stops and the sky clears **2**〈喻〉the calm after the storm

【雨后春笋】yǔhòu-chūnsǔn〈成〉〈喻〉spring up in large numbers: ～般地涌现出来 spring up like mushrooms

【雨花石】yǔhuāshí〈名〉*yuhua* pebbles [colourful fine-grained agate pebbles found in Nanjing (南京)]

【雨季】yǔjì〈名〉［气象］rainy season: 现在正值～。It's the rainy season now.

【雨脚】yǔjiǎo〈名〉lines of falling rain

【雨具】yǔjù〈名〉rain gear

【雨帘】yǔlián = 雨幕 yǔmù

【雨量】yǔliàng〈名〉rainfall: ～充足。Rainfall is plentiful.

【雨林】yǔlín〈名〉rainforest: ▸热带～

【雨露】yǔlù〈名〉**1**(雨和露) rain and dew **2**〈喻〉(恩惠) kindness

【雨幕】yǔmù〈名〉curtain of rain

【雨棚】yǔpéng〈名〉［建筑］canopy

【雨披】yǔpī〈名〉rain cape; rain poncho〈美〉

【雨期】yǔqī〈名〉［气象］rain spell

【雨前茶】yǔqiánchá〈名〉*yuqian* tea [green tea prepared from small, tender leaves picked before Grain Rain (谷雨)]

【雨情】yǔqíng〈名〉rainfall of a given area

【雨区】yǔqū〈名〉rain area

【雨伞】yǔsǎn〈名〉umbrella

【雨声】yǔshēng〈名〉sound of rain: ～滴答。The rain spattered.

【雨势】yǔshì〈名〉strength of rain: ～减弱。The rain has abated.

【雨刷】yǔshuā〈名〉= 雨刮器 yǔguāqì

【雨水】yǔshuǐ〈名〉**1**(指降雨) rainwater: 被～淹没 be deluged with rain ‖ ～不调 irregular rainfall **2** Yǔshuǐ (指节气) Rain Water [beginning of the 2nd of the 24 solar terms]

【雨丝】yǔsī〈名〉drizzle

【雨凇】yǔsōng〈名〉［水文］glazed frost

【雨蛙】yǔwā〈名〉［动物］spring peeper

【雨雾】yǔwù〈名〉misty rain

【雨鞋】yǔxié〈名〉rubber shoe

【雨靴】yǔxuē〈名〉rubber boot; wellington boot〈英〉

【雨烟】yǔyān〈名〉misty rain

【雨燕】yǔyàn〈名〉［鸟类］swift

【雨衣】yǔyī〈名〉raincoat; mackintosh〈英〉

【雨意】yǔyì〈名〉signs of approaching rain

【雨云】yǔyún〈名〉［气象］nimbus

禹 Yǔ ▸**p. 274**〈名〉Yu the Great [founder of Xia Dynasty and reputed tamer of floods]

语（語） yǔ

A〈动〉say: 低头不～ lower one's head and not say anything ▸耳～

B〈名〉**1**(话) words: ▸花言巧～, 话～ **2**(语言) language: ▸～法, 外～, 书面～ **3**(指动作或方式) [non-linguistic means of communicating ideas] sign: ▸灯～, 旗～, 哑～ **4**〈书〉(谚语) saying: ～云: "欲速则不达。" 'More haste, less speed,' as the saying goes.

【语病】yǔbìng〈名〉faulty wording

【语词】yǔcí〈名〉words and phrases

【语调】yǔdiào〈名〉［语言］intonation

【语段】yǔduàn〈名〉［语言］sentence group

【语法】yǔfǎ〈名〉grammar: 学习/研究/教～ learn/study/teach grammar ‖ ～错误 grammatical error ‖ 教学/实用～ pedagogical/practical grammar ▸～规则

【语法功能】yǔfǎ gōngnéng〈名〉grammatical function

【语法规则】yǔfǎ guīzé〈名〉grammar rules

【语法学】yǔfǎxué〈名〉grammar: ～家 grammarian

【语锋】yǔfēng〈名〉sharp points of conversation

【语感】yǔgǎn〈名〉feel for language: ～好 have a good feel for language

【语汇】yǔhuì〈名〉vocabulary: ～丰富/贫乏 have a large/small vocabulary

【语惊四座】yǔjīngsìzuò〈成〉the conversation startles all present

【语句】yǔjù〈名〉sentence: ～不通。The sentence doesn't make sense.

【语料】yǔliào〈名〉language data or material

【语料库】yǔliàokù〈名〉corpus: 建立～ create a corpus

【语录】yǔlù〈名〉quotation

【语气】yǔqì〈名〉**1**(口气) manner of speaking: 责怪的～ tone of reproach ‖ 别用那种～同我讲话。Don't talk in that tone to me. **2**［语法］mood: 祈使/陈述/虚拟～ imperative/indicative/subjunctive mood

【语气词】yǔqìcí〈名〉［语言］modal verbs

【语塞】yǔsè〈动〉be tongue-tied

【语速】yǔsù〈名〉talking speed: ～太快 talk too fast

【语素】yǔsù〈名〉［语言］morpheme: 黏着～ bound morpheme ‖ 自由～ free morpheme

【语态】yǔtài〈名〉［语言］voice: 被动/主动～ passive/active voice

【语体】yǔtǐ〈名〉register: 口语～ colloquial register ‖ 书面～ written style

【语体文】yǔtǐwén〈名〉 prose written in the vernacular
【语为心声】yǔwéixīnshēng〈成〉the words are the mirror of the mind
【语文】yǔwén〈名〉 1（语言和文字） language and writing: ～水平 language level 2（语言和文学） language and literature: ～课 language and literature class
【语文学】yǔwénxué〈名〉 philology
【语无伦次】yǔwúlúncì〈成〉 speak incoherently: 因紧张而～ mumble one's speech because of nervousness
【语系】yǔxì〈名〉 language family: 印欧～ Indo-European language family
【语序】yǔxù〈名〉［语言］ word order
【语焉不详】yǔyānbùxiáng〈成〉 it is mentioned but not in detail
【语言】yǔyán〈名〉 1（指语音系统符号） language: 精通多种～ attain proficiency in several languages 2（话语） words: ～无味 be insipid in speech ‖ 无法用～形容 have no words to describe ‖ 两人缺少共同～。 The two of them lack a common language.
【语言能力】yǔyán nénglì〈名〉 linguistic competence
【语言实验室】yǔyán shíyànshì〈名〉 language laboratory
【语言学】yǔyánxué〈名〉 linguistics: ～家 linguist ‖ 普通～ general linguistics
【语义】yǔyì〈名〉 semantic meaning: ～场 semantic field
【语义学】yǔyìxué〈名〉 semantics: 结构～ structural semantics
【语意】yǔyì〈名〉 meaning of words: ～深长 words deep in meaning
【语音】yǔyīn〈名〉 speech sound: ～清晰 clear speech
【语音合成】yǔyīn héchéng〈名〉 speech synthesis
【语音识别】yǔyīn shíbié〈名〉［计算机］ voice recognition
【语音信箱】yǔyīn xìnxiāng〈名〉［计算机］ voice mailbox
【语音学】yǔyīnxué〈名〉 phonetics: ～家 phonetician
【语用学】yǔyòngxué〈名〉 pragmatics
【语域】yǔyù〈名〉［语言］ register
【语源学】yǔyuánxué〈名〉 etymology
【语种】yǔzhǒng〈名〉 language type
【语重心长】yǔzhòng-xīncháng〈成〉 say in all sincerity: ～的劝告 weighty and earnest advice
【语助词】yǔzhùcí〈名〉［语言］ auxiliary word
【语族】yǔzú〈名〉［语言］language branch: 英语属印欧语系的日耳曼～。 English belongs to the Germanic branch of the Indo-European language family.

圄 yǔ ▸图圄 língyǔ

伛 yǔ
【伛伛】yǔyǔ〈形〉〈书〉 walking alone

庾 yǔ〈名〉〈古〉 open-air granary

瘐 yǔ
【瘐死】yǔsǐ〈动〉〈书〉 [of a prisoner] die of hunger or disease

龉（齬） yǔ ▸龃龉 jǔyǔ

窳 yǔ〈形〉〈书〉 1（质量差） inferior 2（败坏） corrupt: ▸～败
【窳败】yǔbài〈形〉〈书〉 rotten
【窳劣】yǔliè〈形〉〈书〉 inferior in quality

yù

与（與） yù〈动〉 take part in: ▸～会, 参～
▸yǔ
【与会】yùhuì〈动〉 participate in a conference: ～官员 officials attending the meeting ‖ ～者 conference participant
【与闻】yùwén〈动〉〈书〉 be let in on: 已让他们～部分事实真相。 They have already been let in on some of the facts.

玉 yù
A〈名〉 jade: 白～ white jade ‖ 碧～ jasper ‖ ～石不分 cannot tell a jewel from a stone ▸～器, ～簪, 抛砖引～
B〈形〉 1〈书〉（洁白） pure;（美丽） beautiful: ▸亭亭～立 2〈敬〉（指对方） your: ▸～体, ～音, ～照
【玉帛】yùbó〈名〉〈书〉 1（玉器和丝织品） jade objects and silk fabrics [presented as state gifts in ancient China]:〈喻〉 化干戈为～ turn hostility into friendship 2（财富） wealth
【玉成】yùchéng〈动〉〈敬〉 kindly help secure the success of sth.: 敬请～此事。 Please assist in securing the success of this matter.
【玉带】yùdài〈名〉〈古〉 jade belt (worn by high-ranking officials)
【玉帝】Yùdì = 玉皇大帝 Yùhuáng Dàdì
【玉雕】yùdiāo〈名〉 jade carving
【玉皇大帝】 Yùhuáng Dàdì〈名〉 Jade Emperor [Supreme Deity of Taoism]
【玉洁冰清】yùjié-bīngqīng〈成〉 be pure as jade and clean as ice: 她的品德～，深受人民的敬仰。 She was of such pure and noble character that she commanded deep reverence among the people.
【玉兰】yùlán〈名〉［植物］ Yulan Magnolia
【玉兰片】 yùlánpiàn〈名〉 dried slices of

ℹ 语言

■ 汉语里表示语言的词如“中文”、“英语”等都是名词，而英语的 Chinese、English 等既可做名词，也可做形容词。

■ “汉语”、“中国话”、“中文”在翻译成英语时都用 Chinese:

汉语
或 中国话
或 中文
= Chinese

同样原理:

英语
或 英文
= English

日语
或 日本语
或 日文
= Japanese

法语
或 法文
= French

■ 英语用 in 表示“用”某个语言:

用英语写
= write in English

用汉语说
= speak in Chinese

用法语写的书
= a book in French

用日语教的课
= a class in Japanese

■ 英语中表示语言的词做形容词时，可表示“该种语言的”、“用该种语言说的或写的”:

英语老师
= an English teacher

汉语习语
= a Chinese idiom

法语词条
= a French entry

德语词典
= a German dictionary

■ an English teacher 可表示教英语的老师，也可表示来自英国的老师；a Chinese book 可以是用汉语写的书，也可以是关于汉语的书。如果在汉译英时想避免这种歧义，可使用 in、from、of 等介词的帮助:

教英语的老师
= a teacher of English

英国老师
= a teacher from Britain

汉语写的书
= a book in Chinese

关于汉语的书
= a book on Chinese

法语讲的／写的故事
= a story in French

■ 其他短语:

说英语／讲英语
= speak English

用英语说这个词
= to say the word in English

李颜说流利的英语
= Li Yan speaks fluent English

王凡讲英语不带任何口音
= Wang Fan speaks English without an accent

恩里科说话时有很重的意大利口音
= Enrico speaks with a broad Italian accent

迈克有很重的英格兰口音
= Mike's got a strong English accent

吉姆说话时稍带北京腔
= Jim speaks with a slight Beijing accent

吴芳的英语写得非常好
= Wu Fang writes perfect English

她汉语写得棒极了
= Her written Chinese is excellent

tender bamboo shoots
【玉门关】Yùménguān〈名〉 Yuman Pass [at the north end of the Silk Road]
【玉米】yùmǐ〈名〉 1 (指植物) maize; corn: 爆～花 pop corn 2 (指子实) ear of corn: 甜～ sweet corn
【玉米棒子】yùmǐ bàngzi〈名〉 corn cob
【玉米秆】yùmǐgǎn〈名〉 corn stalk
【玉米面】yùmǐmiàn〈名〉 cornmeal
【玉米须】yùmǐxū〈名〉 tassels of maize
【玉米油】yùmǐyóu〈名〉 corn oil
【玉米粥】yùmǐzhōu〈名〉 maize gruel
【玉佩】yùpèi〈名〉 jade pendant
【玉器】yùqì〈名〉 jade object
【玉容】yùróng〈名〉〈书〉 beautiful face (of a woman)
【玉石】yùshí〈名〉 jade: 雕刻～ carve jade
【玉石俱焚】yùshí-jùfén〈成〉〈喻〉 be destroyed indiscriminately
【玉蜀黍】yùshǔshǔ = 玉米 yùmǐ
【玉碎】yùsuì〈动〉〈喻〉 die in glory: ▸宁为～，不为瓦全
【玉体】yùtǐ〈名〉 1〈敬〉(称别人的身体) your esteemed health 2〈书〉(指女子的身体) naked body of a beautiful woman
【玉兔】yùtù〈名〉〈书〉 moon: ～东升。The moon was rising in the east.
【玉玺】yùxǐ〈名〉 imperial jade seal
【玉液】yùyè〈名〉〈书〉 fine wine
【玉音】yùyīn〈名〉〈敬〉 your esteemed letter: 敬候～ respectfully await reply
【玉宇】yùyǔ〈名〉〈书〉 1 (指宫殿) legendary residence of the immortals 2 (宇宙) universe; (天空) sky: ～澄清。The sky is crystal-clear.
【玉殒香消】yùyǔn-xiāngxiāo〈成〉 a beautiful young lady dies
【玉簪】yùzān〈名〉 1 (指物) jade hairpin 2［植物］ fragrant plantain lily
【玉照】yùzhào〈名〉〈敬〉 your photograph
【玉镯】yùzhuó〈名〉 jade bracelet

驭（馭）yù
〈动〉 1 (驾驭) drive: ～车 drive a carriage ‖ ～马 ride a horse ▸驾～ 2 (统率) control
【驭手】yùshǒu〈名〉(驾车人) driver of a chariot; (指士兵) soldier in charge of pack animals

芋 yù
〈名〉［植物］ 1 (芋艿) taro 2 (薯类植物) potatoes and sweet potatoes
【芋艿】yùnǎi〈名〉 taro
【芋头】yùtou〈名〉［植物］ 1 = 芋艿 yùnǎi 2〈方〉(甘薯) sweet potato

吁（籲）yù
〈动〉 plead
▸xū, yū
【吁请】yùqǐng〈动〉 plead: ～社会各界支援灾区人民。We beseech people of all corners of society to help people in the disaster-stricken area.
【吁求】yùqiú〈动〉 implore

聿 yù
〈助〉〈书〉 [used at the beginning of a sentence or used in a sentence in ancient Chinese] and then

谷 yù
▸吐谷浑 Tǔyùhún
▸gǔ

饫（飫）yù
〈动〉〈书〉 have eaten one's fill: ～足 be full

妪（嫗）yù
〈名〉〈书〉 old lady: 老～ old woman

郁¹ yù
〈形〉 strongly fragrant: ▸浓～

郁²（鬱）yù
A〈形〉 lush: ▸～～葱葱, 葱～
B〈动〉 be gloomy: ▸～积, ～结, 忧～
【郁愤】yùfèn〈形〉 depressed and indignant: 满腔～ be extremely depressed and indignant
【郁积】yùjī〈动〉 be pent up: 发泄～在心中的怒火 vent one's spleen
【郁结】yùjié〈动〉 be pent-up: ～的愤懑 pent-up anger
【郁金香】yùjīnxiāng〈名〉［植物］ tulip
【郁闷】yùmèn〈形〉 depressed: 心情～ feel depressed
【郁热】yùrè〈形〉 hot and suffocating: 天气～。The weather is very muggy.
【郁悒】yùyì〈形〉〈书〉 melancholy
【郁郁】yùyù〈形〉〈书〉 1 (很有文采) refined: 文采～ displaying literary elegance 2 (香气浓) strongly fragrant: 发出～芳香 exude a strong fragrance 3 (草木茂盛) lush 4 (苦闷) gloomy: ～不乐 be depressed
【郁郁葱葱】yùyù-cōngcōng〈形〉 lush and green: ～的灌木和白色的海滩 lush green shrubs and white beaches ‖ 她一边走，一边眷恋地望着～的山丘。As she gazed longingly at the lush, green hills clothed in wild profusions of vegetation.
【郁郁寡欢】yùyù-guǎhuān〈成〉 be low in spirits: 他近来～，不知有何心事。He has been very low recently and we're not sure what's troubling him.

育 yù
A〈动〉 1 (生孩子) give birth to: 不～症 infertility ▸～龄, 生～ 2 (培育) raise: ～婴 feed and take care of babies ‖ 封山～林 seal off mountains to cultivate trees ▸～秧 3 (教育) educate: ▸～才, 教书～人
B〈名〉 education: 智/德/体～ intellectual /moral/physical education
【育才】yùcái〈动〉 cultivate talent
【育儿袋】yù'érdài〈名〉［动物］ brood pouch
【育肥】yùféi = 肥育 féiyù
【育林】yùlín〈动〉 afforest
【育龄】yùlíng〈名〉 childbearing age: ～妇女 woman of childbearing age
【育苗】yùmiáo〈动〉［农业］ grow seedlings
【育秧】yùyāng〈动〉 cultivate seedlings
【育婴堂】yùyīngtáng〈名〉〈旧〉 orphanage
【育种】yùzhǒng〈动〉 breed: 杂交～ do cross-breeding

昱 yù
〈书〉
A〈名〉 sunlight
B〈动〉 shine

狱（獄）yù
〈名〉 1 (官司) lawsuit: ▸文字～, 冤～ 2 (监狱) prison: 死在～中 die in prison ▸越～
【狱警】yùjǐng〈名〉 prison warder〈英〉; prison guard〈美〉
【狱吏】yùlì〈名〉〈旧〉 jailer
【狱卒】yùzú〈名〉〈旧〉 turnkey

彧 yù
〈形〉〈书〉 over-flowing with literary talent

峪 yù
〈名〉 valley

钰（鈺）yù
〈名〉〈书〉 treasure

浴 yù
〈动〉 take a bath: 淋～ have a shower ‖ 冷水～ cold bath ‖〈喻〉～着朝阳 be bathed in the morning sun
【浴场】yùchǎng〈名〉 outdoor bathing place: 海滨～ bathing beach
【浴池】yùchí〈名〉 1 (洗澡池) common bathing pool 2 (澡堂) public bathhouse
【浴缸】yùgāng〈名〉 bathtub; bath〈英〉
【浴巾】yùjīn〈名〉 bath towel: ～架 bath towel holder
【浴客】yùkè〈名〉 bathing guest: 女～ woman bather
【浴帘】yùlián〈名〉 shower curtain
【浴帽】yùmào〈名〉 shower cap
【浴袍】yùpáo〈名〉 bathrobe
【浴盆】yùpén〈名〉 bathtub; bath〈英〉
【浴室】yùshì〈名〉 1 (洗澡间) bathroom: 公共～ bathhouse 2 (澡堂) public bathhouse
【浴血】yùxuè〈动〉 be covered in blood: ～奋战 fight a bloody battle
【浴盐】yùyán〈名〉 bath salts
【浴液】yùyè〈名〉 shower gel
【浴衣】yùyī〈名〉 bathrobe
【浴足】yùzú〈动〉 have one's feet bathed and massaged

预（預）yù
A〈副〉 beforehand: ▸～演, ～约, ～祝, ～兆
B〈动〉 take part in: ～闻政事 participate in political and administrative matters ▸干～
【预案】yù'àn〈名〉 plan B: 制订～ work out a plan B
【预报】yùbào〈动〉 forecast: 气象台～明天下雪。The weather station predicted snow for tomorrow. ‖ 天气～ weather forecast
【预备】yùbèi〈动〉 prepare: ～功课 prepare one's lessons ‖ ～会议 preparatory meeting ‖ 我们～在这儿呆两星期。We anticipate spending two weeks here.
【预备党员】yùbèi dǎngyuán〈名〉 probationary Party member
【预备金】yùbèijīn〈名〉 reserve funds
【预备期】yùbèiqī〈名〉 probationary period
【预备役】yùbèiyì〈名〉［军事］ reserve duty: ～军官 reserve military officer ‖ ～军人 reserve military personnel
【预卜】yùbǔ〈动〉 predict: ～吉凶 predict good or bad fortune ‖ 比赛胜负难以～。The outcome of the match is hard to predict.
【预测】yùcè〈动〉 predict: ～未来 predict the future ‖ 利润～ business forecast ‖ 该公司～可销售3,000架飞机。The company has projected sales of 3,000 aircraft. ‖ 专家～股票行情将有上升趋势。Experts have forecast an upturn in stock prices.
【预产期】yùchǎnqī〈名〉 due date: ～已到。The due date has already arrived.
【预处理】yùchǔlǐ〈动〉［医学］ pretreat
【预订】yùdìng〈动〉 reserve: ～房间 reserve a room ‖ ～机票 make flight reservations ‖ ～报刊/杂志 subscribe to newspapers and periodicals/a magazine
【预定】yùdìng〈动〉 schedule: 按～计划进

行 go as planned ‖ 工程～明年完工。The project is scheduled to be finished next year.

【预定日期】yùdìng rìqī〈名〉deadline

【预断】yùduàn〈动〉predetermine

【预防】yùfáng〈动〉guard against: ～火灾 take precautions against fire ‖ ～疾病 guard against disease ‖ ～措施 precautionary measures ‖ ～事故 prevent accidents

【预防犯罪】yùfáng fànzuì〈动〉prevent crime

【预防医学】yùfáng yīxué〈名〉preventive medicine

【预防针】yùfángzhēn〈名〉1〈本〉inoculation: 护士给他注射了伤寒～。The nurse gave him an injection against typhoid. 2〈喻〉(预先警告) advance warning: 这是在给你打～，要你谨慎行事。This should serve as advance warning for you to do things more cautiously.

【预付】yùfù〈动〉pay in advance: ～租金 pay the rent in advance ‖ ～一个月的工资 give an advance of one month's pay

【预付费】yùfùfèi〈名〉prepayment: 移动电话～业务 prepaid mobile phone service

【预付款】yùfùkuǎn〈名〉advance payment

【预感】yùgǎn A〈动〉have a premonition: ～到危险/灾难临头 have a premonition of danger/disaster B〈名〉premonition: 不祥的～ ominous presentiment ‖ 她心中有一种～。She had a sort of premonition.

【预告】yùgào A〈动〉notify in advance: ～一周电视节目 announce the week's television programmes B〈名〉advance notice: 新书～ publication notice ‖ 电视节目～ programme guide

【预告片】yùgàopiàn〈名〉trailer: 电影～ trailer for a film

【预购】yùgòu〈动〉purchase in advance: ～返程火车票 pre-book a return train ticket

【预后】yùhòu〈名〉［医学］prognosis: ～不良 unfavourable prognosis

【预计】yùjì〈动〉anticipate: 经济学家们～通货膨胀率将会上升。The economists predicted an increase in the rate of inflation. ‖ 他～到3月份可以完成这一工作。He expected to finish the work by March.

【预检】yùjiǎn〈动〉check in advance: 先到门诊处进行～ go to the outpatients department for an advance check-up

【预见】yùjiàn A〈动〉predict: 未～到的情况 unforeseen circumstances ‖ 可以～，房价还会上涨。It is likely that house prices will rise. B〈名〉foresight: 科学的～ scientific prediction ‖ 英明的～ brilliant foresight

【预警】yùjǐng〈动〉give early warning: ～雷达/飞机 early-warning radar/plane

【预警机】yùjǐngjī〈名〉early warning aircraft

【预考】yùkǎo〈名〉preparatory test

【预科】yùkē〈名〉preparatory school: 上～ go to a prep school

【预亏】yùkuī〈名〉estimated loss

【预料】yùliào A〈动〉expect: 很难～ impossible to foresee ‖ 事情没有我原先～的那么糟。It's not as bad as I expected. B〈名〉expectation: 出乎～ be beyond all expectations ‖ 果然不出我的～。It turned out that things happened just as I had expected.

【预留】yùliú〈动〉reserve: ～客房 reserve a room

【预谋】yùmóu〈动〉premeditate: ～进行报复 scheme to carry out revenge ‖ 这是他们共同～的。This was what they had plotted together.

【预判】yùpàn〈动〉prejudge: 准确的～ accurate prediction

【预期】yùqī〈动〉expect: ～寿命 life expectancy ‖ 收到～的效果 get an anticipated result ‖ 达到～的目的 reach the intended objective

【预热】yùrè〈动〉preheat: ～发动机 warm up the engine

【预赛】yùsài〈名〉［体育］preliminary heat: 在～中被淘汰 get knocked out during the preliminaries

【预审】yùshěn〈名〉preliminary hearing

【预示】yùshì〈动〉forebode: 响雷～有阵雨。Thunder often heralds showers.

【预收】yùshōu〈动〉collect money in advance: ～定金 collect a deposit

【预售】yùshòu〈动〉pre-sell: ～十天内火车票 sell train tickets ten days in advance

【预算】yùsuàn A〈名〉budget: 为新项目编制～ budget for a new project ‖ 增加～ add to the budget ‖ ～内拨款 budgetary allocation ‖ 财政/广告/科研～ fiscal/advertising/research budget B〈动〉budget: 据～，工程需投资三千万。According to the budget, the project requires an investment of thirty million.

【预算赤字】yùsuàn chìzì〈名〉budget deficit

【预算平衡】yùsuàn pínghéng〈名〉balance of the budget

【预算外】yùsuànwài〈形〉off-budget: ～收入 extra-budgetary revenue

【预缩】yùsuō〈形〉［纺织］pre-shrunk

【预习】yùxí〈动〉[of students] prepare lessons before class

【预先】yùxiān〈副〉in advance: ～付款 pay in advance ‖ ～声明 state explicitly beforehand ‖ ～通知 notify in advance

【预想】yùxiǎng A〈动〉anticipate: 出这样的事是没有～到的。Nobody could have anticipated that this kind of thing could happen. B〈名〉expectation: 这比人们的～要复杂得多。It is more complicated than people thought.

【预行】yùxíng〈动〉carry out ahead of schedule: ～警报 give early warning

【预选】yùxuǎn〈名〉primary election: ～赛 qualifying round

【预言】yùyán A〈动〉foretell: 我曾～他会成功。I predicted that he would succeed. B〈名〉prediction: 证实～ verify a prediction ‖ ～应验了。The prophecy turned out to be true.

【预演】yùyǎn〈动〉preview: 最后一次～ final preview ‖ ～新电影 preview a new film ‖ 公开～ public rehearsal

【预应力】yùyìnglì〈名〉［物理］prestressing force

【预映】yùyìng〈动〉be in preview

【预约】yùyuē〈动〉make an appointment: ～看病 have an appointment with one's doctor ‖ 未经～，恕不会客。Guests will not be received without an appointment.

【预增】yùzēng〈名〉estimated profit increase

【预展】yùzhǎn〈动〉give a preview of an exhibition

【预兆】yùzhào A〈名〉omen: 感到一种不祥的～ feel an awful premonition ‖ 火山爆发的～ signs of imminent volcanic eruptions B〈动〉bode: 瑞雪～来年丰收。A timely snow promises a good harvest.

【预支】yùzhī〈动〉(指支付) pay in advance; (指支取) receive in advance: ～薪金 pay a salary in advance ‖ ～款 advanced payment

【预知】yùzhī〈动〉predict: 有些动物有～地震的本能。Some animals have an instinctive prescience of earthquakes.

【预制】yùzhì〈动〉prefabricate: ～板 precast slab

【预制房屋】yùzhì fángwū〈名〉prefabricated house

【预祝】yùzhù〈动〉wish: ～你成功。Wish you every success.

域 yù〈名〉1 (疆域) territory: ▸领～, 区～, 地～ 2 (范围) realm field: ▸音～

【域名】yùmíng〈名〉［计算机］domain name: 抢注～ cybersquatting ‖ ～抢注者 cybersquatter ‖ 注册～ register a domain name

【域外】yùwài〈形〉extraterritorial: ～庇护权 extraterritorial asylum

【域中】yùzhōng〈名〉inside the country

菀 yù〈形〉〈书〉exuberant ▸wǎn

欲[1] yù

A〈动〉1 (想要) want: ～言又止 open one's mouth only to bite one's tongue ‖ ～进不能，～退不得。Be unable either to advance or to retreat. ‖ ～知详情，请函询。For details, please inquire in writing. ▸～擒故纵，畅所～言 2〈书〉(需要) require: 胆～大而心～细 be very daring but also very meticulous

B〈副〉about to: 山雨～来风满楼。The rising wind in the mountains foretells the coming storm. ▸摇摇～坠

欲[2]（**慾**）yù〈名〉desire: 求知～ thirst for knowledge ▸禁～, 食～

【欲罢不能】yùbà-bùnéng〈成〉be unable to stop even though one wants to: 我们现在～，只有继续干了。We have passed the point of no-return.

【欲盖弥彰】yùgài-mízhāng〈成〉the harder one tries to conceal something, the more conspicuous it becomes

【欲壑难填】yùhè-nántián〈成〉avarice knows no bounds: 我们的银钱有限，他们的～。Our money is too limited to satisfy their insatiable greed.

【欲火】yùhuǒ〈名〉fire of desire: ～中烧 be burning with sexual desire

【欲加之罪，何患无辞】yù jiā zhī zuì, hé huàn wú cí〈成〉if you are out to condemn sb., you can always find a pretext

【欲念】yùniàn〈名〉desire: 世俗的～ worldly preoccupations

【欲擒故纵】yùqín-gùzòng〈成〉loosen reins the better to tighten them

【欲取姑与】yùqǔ-gūyǔ〈成〉give in order to take

【欲速则不达】yù sù zé bù dá〈成〉more haste, less speed

【欲望】yùwàng〈名〉desire: 强烈的～ strong desire ‖ 求知的～ thirst for knowledge

阈（**閾**）yù〈名〉〈书〉1 (门槛) threshold: 门～ threshold 2 (界限) limit: 视～ visual range

【阈值】yùzhí〈名〉［物理］threshold value

谕（**諭**）yù〈动〉〈书〉order: 面～ give orders personally ‖ 上～ emperor's order ▸手～

【谕旨】yùzhǐ〈名〉imperial edict

遇 yù

A〈动〉**1**（碰见） meet: ～到暴风雨 be caught in a storm ‖ 我们在车站相～。We met at the station. ▸～难，不期而～ **2**（对待） treat: ▸待～，冷～，礼～
B〈名〉 opportunity: ▸机～，际～
【遇刺】yùcì〈动〉 be attacked by an assassin: ～身亡 be assassinated
【遇到】yùdào〈动〉 run into
【遇害】yùhài〈动〉 be murdered: 不幸～ murdered
【遇见】yùjiàn〈动〉 meet: ～一位老校友 meet an old school friend
【遇救】yùjiù〈动〉 be rescued: ～脱险 be rescued from danger
【遇难】yùnàn〈动〉**1**（指死亡） die in a disaster: ～船员 shipwrecked sailors ‖ 机上110人全部～。 All 110 people aboard the plane perished. **2**（指遇到危难） face danger: ～矿工 trapped miners
【遇难呈祥】yùnàn-chéngxiáng〈成〉 change misfortune into good fortune
【遇人不淑】yùrén-bùshū〈成〉 have a scoundrel as one's husband
【遇事】yùshì〈动〉 meet with an unforeseen event: ～不慌 keep calm whatever happens ‖ ～要沉着。 Keep calm when problems arise.
【遇事生风】yùshì-shēngfēng〈成〉 stir up trouble at every opportunity
【遇险】yùxiǎn〈动〉 run into danger: 营救～船只 go to the rescue of a ship in distress ‖ ～信号 distress signal
【遇阻】yùzǔ〈动〉 encounter obstacles

喻 yù

〈动〉**1**（说明） explain: ～之以理 try to make sb. see reason ‖ 君子～于义，小人～于利。 A man of integrity cares more about justice than his own interest, only base men act solely for personal gain. ▸不可理～ **2**（明白） understand: ▸不言而～，家～户晓 **3**（打比方） draw an analogy: 人生常被～为一场戏。 Life is often compared to a drama. ▸比～
【喻世】yùshì〈动〉 admonish the masses
【喻义】yùyì〈名〉 figurative meaning

御[1] yù

A〈动〉〈书〉**1**（驱车） drive: ～者 carriage driver **2**（治理） administer: ～众以宽 rule the masses with leniency
B〈名〉 imperial: ▸～笔，～驾

御[2]（禦） yù

〈动〉 resist: ～于国门之外 fight against the enemy beyond the country's frontier ▸～寒，抵～，防～
【御笔】yùbǐ〈名〉 emperor's handwriting or painting
【御赐】yùcì〈动〉 be bestowed
【御道】yùdào〈名〉 road for the imperial carriage
【御敌】yùdí〈动〉 resist the enemy
【御夫座】Yùfūzuò〈名〉［天文］ Auriga
【御寒】yùhán〈动〉 keep out the cold: 这样单薄的上衣不能～。 Such a thin coat gives little protection against the cold.
【御花园】yùhuāyuán〈名〉 imperial garden
【御驾】yùjià〈名〉 imperial carriage: ～亲征。 The emperor led his soldiers on a military expedition in person.
【御林军】yùlínjūn〈名〉 imperial guards
【御膳】yùshàn〈名〉 food of the imperial household: ～膳房 imperial kitchen
【御手】yùshǒu = 驭手 yùshǒu
【御侮】yùwǔ〈动〉 resist foreign invasion
【御玺】yùxǐ〈名〉 imperial seal
【御医】yùyī〈名〉 court physician
【御用】yùyòng〈形〉**1**（指皇帝） for imperial use **2**（指为统治者） in the pay of: ～文人 hired hack
【御状】yùzhuàng〈名〉 suit directly filed to the emperor: 告～ file a suit directly to the emperor

鹆（鵒） yù ▸鸲鹆 qúyù

寓 yù

A〈动〉**1**（居住） inhabit: ～处 residence ▸～公，～居，寄～ **2**（寄托） imply: ～教于乐 make learning fun ▸～言，～意
B〈名〉 residence: ▸公～
【寓邸】yùdǐ〈名〉 residence of a high official
【寓公】yùgōng〈名〉〈古〉 vassal or aristocrat living in exile
【寓居】yùjū〈动〉 make one's home in: 他晚年～大连。 He made his home in Dalian in his later years.
【寓目】yùmù〈动〉〈书〉 look over: 城建规划我已～，但尚未详细研究。 I've gone through the city construction plan, but I haven't studied it in detail.
【寓所】yùsuǒ〈名〉 residence: ～地址 residential address
【寓言】yùyán〈名〉 fable: ～中的人物 allegorical character ‖《伊索～》 *Aesop's Fables*
【寓意】yùyì〈名〉 implication: 明白故事的～ see the moral of the story ‖ ～深刻 have a deep message
【寓于】yùyú〈动〉 be contained in: 矛盾～一切事物。 There are contradictions in everything.

裕[1] yù

A〈形〉 abundant: ▸富～，宽～
B〈动〉〈书〉 enrich: ～民富国 enrich one's country and people

裕[2] Yù

【裕固族】Yùgùzú〈名〉 Yugur ethnic group
【裕如】yùrú〈形〉〈书〉**1**（从容） effortless: 应付～ handle the situation with ease **2**（富足） abundant: 生活～ live a life of plenty

粥 yù

A〈动〉〈书〉（生养） bear
B = 鬻 yù
▸zhōu

蓣（蕷） yù ▸薯蓣 shǔyù

愈[1] yù

A〈动〉〈书〉 surpass: 浊富与清贫孰～? Which is better, living on ill-gotten wealth or living in honest poverty?
B〈副〉 [used reiteratively, same as 越…越… the more ... the more]: ～多～好 the more the better ‖ ～来～不得人心 be increasingly unpopular ‖ 真理～辩～明。 Truth becomes clearer through debate.

愈[2]（瘉、癒） yù

〈动〉 recover: ▸～合，病～
【愈发】yùfā〈副〉 all the more: 这～使他迷惑了。 This made him even more bewildered.
【愈合】yùhé〈动〉 heal: 伤口～了。 The wound closed up.
【愈加】yùjiā〈副〉 increasingly: 形势变得～严峻。 The situation has become increasingly grave.
【愈演愈烈】yùyǎn-yùliè〈成〉 intensify
【愈益】yùyì〈副〉 increasingly: 难民涌入致使经济负担～加重。 A flood of refugees put even more burden on the economy.

煜 yù

〈动〉〈书〉 illuminate

誉（譽） yù

A〈动〉 praise: 夏威夷被～为海岛乐园。 Hawaii is praised as an island paradise. ▸毁～，赞～
B〈名〉 reputation: ～满全球 be famed the world over ▸美～，名～，声～

蔚 Yù

〈名〉 Yu [surname]
▸wèi

蜮 yù

〈名〉〈书〉 legendary water monster: ▸鬼～

毓 yù

〈动〉〈书〉 rear: ▸钟灵～秀

熨 yù

▸yùn
【熨帖】yùtiē〈形〉**1**（恰当） apt: 用词～ use appropriate wording **2**（心情舒畅） calm: 他听了你的话，心里很～。 What you said calmed him down a lot.

豫[1] yù

〈形〉〈书〉**1**（安乐） living in ease and comfort **2**（欢快） happy and content

豫[2] Yù

▸**p. 661**〈名〉 Yu [another name for Henan Province (河南)]
【豫剧】yùjù〈名〉 Henan opera

> **豫剧**
>
> A genre of traditional Chinese opera. Also known as Henan clapper opera, it originated in the city of Kaifeng (开封) in the 18th century, and was popular in Henan, Shaanxi and Shanxi provinces. Accompanying musical instruments are clappers (梆子) and the *banhu* (板胡), a bowed stringed instrument. The repertoire includes *Hua Mulan* (《花木兰》), *Lady Marshal Mu Guiying* (《穆桂英挂帅》) and *Chaoyang Ditch* (《朝阳沟》).

燠 yù

〈形〉〈书〉 warm: ▸～热
【燠热】yùrè〈形〉 steamy

鹬（鷸） yù

〈名〉［鸟类］ sandpiper
【鹬蚌相争，渔人得利】yùbàng xiāng zhēng, yúrén dé lì〈成〉 if two parties fight, a third party will reap the advantage

鬻 yù

〈动〉〈书〉 sell: ～文为生 make a living with one's pen ‖ 卖官～爵 accept bribes in exchange for official ranks
【鬻儿卖女】yù'ér-màinǚ〈成〉 sell one's own children

yuān

鸢（鳶） yuān

〈名〉［鸟类］ hawk: 纸～ kite

Y

【鸢飞鱼跃】yuānfēi-yúyuè〈成〉everything in nature has its own proper place and is content with what it is

眢 yuān〈形〉〈书〉**1**（眼睛干枯）[of eyes] dry and sunken **2**（枯干无水） dried up: ～井 dry well

鸳（鴛） yuān ▸鸳鸯 yuānyāng

【鸳鸯】yuānyāng〈名〉**1**（指鸟） mandarin ducks: ～戏水 mandarin ducks playing in the water **2**（指人） lovebirds: ▸乱点～谱

【鸳鸯蝴蝶派】yuānyāng húdié pài〈名〉genre of romantic novel popular in China in the 1920's

冤 yuān

A〈形〉**1**（冤枉） unjust: ▸～案, ～屈, ～枉 **2**（吃亏） not worth: 那辆自行车买得真～。 I overpaid when I bought that bike. ‖ 你这钱花得真～。 You didn't get your money's worth. ▸～枉

B〈名〉**1**（冤案） injustice: 喊～ cry out against an injustice ‖ 雪～ undo a wrong ▸不白之～, 含～, 伸～ **2**（冤仇） enmity: 与某人无～无仇 have no grievance or rancour against sb. ▸～仇, ～家, ～～相报

【冤案】yuān'àn〈名〉 case of injustice: 平反～ right a wrong ‖ 制造～ bring in an unjust verdict

【冤仇】yuānchóu〈名〉 enmity: 不计较过去的～ not hold past grudges ‖ 造成世代～ breed enmity for generations

【冤大头】yuāndàtóu〈名〉 fool in money matters

【冤愤】yuānfèn〈名〉 resentment at injustice or wrongs: 满腔～ be filled with indignation at injustice

【冤魂】yuānhún〈名〉ghost of one who has suffered an injustice: ～不散 the ghost of the wronged never rests

【冤家路窄】yuānjiā-lùzhǎi〈成〉 much as one wants to one can't avoid one's enemies

【冤家宜解不宜结】yuānjiā yí jiě bùyí jié〈俗〉 better make friends than make enemies

【冤假错案】yuān-jiǎ-cuò'àn〈名〉 cases in which people were unjustly, falsely or wrongly charged or sentenced

【冤家】yuānjia〈名〉 **1**（仇人） enemy: ～对头 bitter enemy **2**（似恨实爱） [used in dramas or folk songs] person whom one can't help loving dearly in spite of all his faults: 小～ little devil

【冤孽】yuānniè〈名〉 **1**（冤仇罪孽） enmity and sin: ～深重 be steeped in enmity and sin **2**［佛教］ evil, misfortune, or trouble regarded as retribution for bad deeds done in a previous existence

【冤情】yuānqíng〈名〉 grievance: 诉说/申诉～ pour out/air one's grievances ‖ ～大白。 All the injustices have been made known.

【冤屈】yuānqū **A**〈动〉 wrong: ～某人 wrong sb. **B**〈名〉 injustice: 蒙受～ suffer wrongs ‖ 诉说～ complain of the injustices one has suffered

【冤头】yuāntóu〈名〉 enemy

【冤枉】yuānwang **A**〈形〉 **1**（不公平） unjust: 他被误判入狱，太～了。 He has been wrongly imprisoned. It's such an injustice. **2**（不值得）loss-suffering: 你这个钱花得～。 You were robbed. **B**〈动〉 treat unjustly: 别～好人。 Don't wrongfully accuse an innocent person.

【冤枉路】yuānwanglù〈名〉 unnecessarily long way: 走～ go the long way round

【冤枉气】yuānwangqì〈名〉 uncalled-for maltreatment: 受～ be treated badly for no reason

【冤枉钱】yuānwangqián〈名〉 wasted money: 花～ not get one's money's worth

【冤有头，债有主】yuān yǒu tóu, zhài yǒu zhǔ〈俗〉 reprisal for a wrong should be directed at the perpetrator

【冤狱】yuānyù〈名〉 miscarriage of justice resulting in imprisonment of an innocent person: 平反～ reverse an unjust verdict

【冤冤相报】yuānyuān-xiāngbào〈成〉 injustice begets injustice: ～，何时了？ If one wrong is avenged with another, how can there be any end to it?

渊（淵） yuān

A〈名〉 deep pool: ▸～源, 深～, 天～之别

B〈形〉 deep: ～泉 deep spring ▸～博, ～深

【渊博】yuānbó〈形〉well-informed: 知识～ be extremely knowledgeable ‖ ～的学识 profound erudition

【渊深】yuānshēn〈形〉profound: 学识～ be extremely learned

【渊薮】yuānsǒu〈名〉〈喻〉haunt: 罪恶的～ den of iniquity

【渊源】yuānyuán〈名〉 source: 探索历史/社会/思想～ enquire into the historical/social/ideological origins (of) ‖ 家学～ long tradition of family learning

箢 yuān

【箢箕】yuānjī〈名〉〈方〉 woven bamboo vessel

yuán

元[1] yuán

A〈形〉 **1**（为首） leading: ▸～首, ～勋 **2**（第一） first: ▸～旦, ～年 **3**（主要） fundamental: ▸～素, ～音 **4**（超越） meta: ▸～符号, ～规则, ～语言

B〈名〉 **1**（元素） essential factor: ▸二～论, 一～论 **2**（一部分） part: ▸～件, 单～

元[2] Yuán〈名〉 Yuan Dynasty

元[3] yuán〈名〉 **1** = 圆 yuán A2 **2**〈口〉= 圆 yuán D

【元宝】yuánbǎo〈名〉〈旧〉 gold or silver ingot [used as money]

【元旦】Yuándàn〈名〉 New Year's Day: 庆祝～ celebrate New Year's Day

【元恶】yuán'è〈名〉〈书〉principle culprit: 铲除～ eliminate a principal culprit

【元符号】yuánfúhào〈名〉 metasymbol

【元规则】yuánguīzé〈名〉［计算机］metarule

【元件】yuánjiàn〈名〉 element: 无线电～ radio elements

【元老】yuánlǎo〈名〉 founding father

【元谋人】Yuánmóurén = 元谋猿人 Yuánmóu yuánrén

【元谋猿人】Yuánmóu yuánrén〈名〉［考古］ Yuanmou Man [whose fossil remains, about 1.7 million years old, were found in Yuanmou (元谋), Yunnan Province in 1965]

【元年】yuánnián〈名〉 first year of an emperor's reign: 乾隆～ first year of the Qianlong reign

【元配】yuánpèi〈名〉= 原配 yuánpèi

【元气】yuánqì〈名〉 vitality: 大伤～ sap one's vitality ‖ 恢复～ regain one's strength

【元器件】yuánqìjiàn〈名〉 components and parts

【元曲】yuánqǔ〈名〉 Yuan drama

> 元曲
>
> ▸唐诗

【元日】yuánrì〈名〉〈书〉 lunar New Year's Day

【元首】yuánshǒu〈名〉 **1**〈书〉（君主） monarch **2**（国家最高领导人） head of state: 国家～ head of state **3**（纳粹头目） Fuehrer

【元帅】yuánshuài〈名〉 **1**（指军衔） marshal: 英陆军～ Field Marshal ‖ 皇家空军～ Marshal of the Royal Air Force **2**〈旧〉（指主帅） supreme commander

【元素】yuánsù〈名〉 **1**（要素） element **2**［数学］ element **3**［化学］ chemical element: 氢～ hydrogen ‖ 微量～ trace element

【元素符号】yuánsù fúhào〈名〉［化学］ symbol of an element

【元素周期表】yuánsù zhōuqībiǎo〈名〉［化学］ periodic table of elements

【元宵】yuánxiāo〈名〉 **1**（指时间） Lantern Festival: 闹～ celebrate Lantern Festival **2**［食品］ *yuanxiao* [dumplings made of glutinous rice flour]

【元宵节】Yuánxiāojié〈名〉Lantern Festival

> 元宵节
>
> Lantern Festival, a traditional festival celebrated on the 15th of the first month of the lunar new year, and part of the Spring Festival. The custom of hanging lanterns may have started in the Eastern Han Dynasty (AD 25-220), when the Emperor Mingdi ordered people to hang lanterns in their houses in honour of the Buddha. Dancing the *yangge* dance (扭秧歌), walking on stilts, and dragon and lion dances are all traditional activities associated with this festival. *Tangyuan* (▸汤圆) are eaten at this time to symbolize family unity and well-being.

【元凶】yuánxiōng〈名〉arch-criminal: 捉拿～归案 bring the prime culprit to justice

【元勋】yuánxūn〈名〉 founding father: 开国～ founder of a state

【元夜】yuányè〈书〉= 元宵 yuánxiāo 1

【元音】yuányīn〈名〉［语言］ vowel: 基本～ cardinal vowel

【元语言】yuányǔyán〈名〉 metalanguage

【元元本本】yuányuán-běnběn = 原原本本 yuányuán-běnběn

【元月】yuányuè〈名〉 **1**（公历一月） January **2**（农历正月） first month of the lunar year

芫 yuán
▸yán

【芫花】yuánhuā〈名〉［植物］lilac daphne

园（園） yuán〈名〉 **1**（用于种植） garden: 梅～ plum orchard ‖ 菜～ vegetable garden ‖ 葡萄～ vineyard ‖ 工业～ industrial park **2**（供人游玩） park: ▸动物～, 公～

【园地】yuándì〈名〉**1**（用于种植）garden plot: 农业～ farmland **2**〈喻〉（用于开展活动） field: 文学～ field of literature ‖ 艺术～ art field

【园丁】yuándīng〈名〉 **1** ▸**p. 966**（园艺工） gardener **2**〈喻〉（教师） teacher (usu of a primary school): 辛勤的～ hard-working teacher

【园林】yuánlín〈名〉garden: 苏州～ Suzhou garden ‖ ～建筑 landscape architecture
【园林城市】yuánlín chéngshì〈名〉garden city
【园圃】yuánpǔ〈名〉garden
【园区】yuánqū〈名〉business park: 高科技～ high-tech park
【园田】yuántián〈名〉vegetable garden: ～化 crop plantation landscaping
【园艺】yuányì〈名〉horticulture: 从事～工作 be a gardener by profession ‖ ～博览会 horticulture exposition ‖ ～师 horticulturist
【园艺学】yuányìxué〈名〉horticulture
【园囿】yuányòu〈名〉〈书〉zoological garden
【园子】yuánzi〈名〉1▶（种植处）garden: 菜～ kitchen garden, vegetable farm 2▶（戏园子）theatre

员（員）yuán

A〈名〉1▶（人员）person holding a post: 裁～ reduce personnel ▸雇～, 官～, 职～ 2▶（成员）member: 家庭的每一～ every member of the family ▸成～, 党～, 会～
B〈量〉[used to describe a brave soldier]: 一～大将 an able general
【员额】yuán'é〈名〉specified number of employees or personnel
【员工】yuángōng〈名〉staff: 熟练的～ skilled personnel ‖ 学校教职～ school personnel
【员外】yuánwài〈名〉〈古〉1▶（指官职）counsellor 2▶（指称呼）squire

垣 yuán

〈名〉1▶〈书〉（墙）low wall: 城～ city wall ▸残～断壁 2▶〈旧〉（城）city: 省～ provincial capital

爰 yuán

A〈代〉where
B〈连〉〈书〉thereupon: ～书其事以告。 Therefore I am writing to you about it.

袁 Yuán〈名〉Yuan [surname]

原[1] yuán

A〈形〉1▶（最初）basic: ▸～生, ～始 2▶（未加工）raw: ～矿石 crude ore ▸～料, ～煤, ～油 3▶（原本）original: ～作者 original author ‖ 顺着～路往回走 retrace one's steps ‖ 你引用的不是我的～话。 You misquoted what I said. ▸～意
B〈名〉origin: ▸复～, 还～

原[2] yuán〈动〉excuse: ▸～谅, 情有可～

原[3] yuán〈名〉open country: ▸～野

【原班人马】yuánbān rénmǎ〈名〉former staff
【原版】yuánbǎn〈名〉original edition: ～磁带 master tape ‖ ～书 original edition of the book ‖ ～片 original film
【原本】yuánběn A〈副〉originally: 他～是教书的，后来改行当了记者。 He started as a school teacher, but later left the profession and became a journalist. ‖ 我～不想到这里来。 I didn't want to come here in the first place. B〈名〉1▶（原稿）original manuscript 2▶（初刻本）original block-printed edition
【原材料】yuáncáiliào〈名〉raw materials: 降低～消耗 reduce the consumption of raw materials ‖ 节约～ economize on raw and processed materials
【原产地】yuánchǎndì〈名〉place of origin: ～标记 mark of origin ‖ ～证明书 certificate of origin
【原虫】yuánchóng〈名〉［动物］protozoon: 疟～ plasmodium
【原初】yuánchū〈名〉former state: 她爱说爱笑，～不是这样。 She is fond of chatting and laughing, which isn't at all how she used to be.
【原处】yuánchù〈名〉original place: 把它放回～。 Put it back where it was.
【原创】yuánchuàng〈动〉originate: ～歌曲 original song
【原创性】yuánchuàngxìng〈名〉originality: ～作品 original work ‖ 节目编排具有～和时代性。 The programming is original and timely.
【原地】yuándì〈名〉same place: ～不动 stand in place ‖ ～踏步 make no headway
【原点】yuándiǎn〈名〉［数学］origin
【原定】yuándìng〈动〉be originally decided or scheduled: ～计划 original plan
【原动力】yuándònglì〈名〉motive power: 一切人类活动的～ prime mover of all human activity
【原发】yuánfā〈形〉［医学］primary: ～性心脏病 primary heart disease
【原封】yuánfēng〈形〉intact: 把礼品～退回 return a gift to the sender unopened ‖ ～不动地把钱包归还失主 return a wallet to its owner in its original condition
【原稿】yuángǎo〈名〉original manuscript: 剧本的～ manuscript of a play ‖ ～退回 return a manuscript
【原告】yuángào〈名〉［法律］（指民事案件）plaintiff;（指刑事案件）prosecutor: 判～胜诉 rule in favour of the plaintiff
【原故】yuángù = 缘故 yuángù
【原鸡】yuánjī〈名〉［鸟类］jungle fowl
【原级】yuánjí〈名〉［语言］positive degree
【原籍】yuánjí〈名〉ancestral home: 她～西安，现居北京。 Her ancestral home was in Xi'an, but she lives in Beijing.
【原价】yuánjià〈名〉original price: 按～打八折出售 sell at a 20% discount
【原件】yuánjiàn〈名〉master copy: ～及副本 original and duplicates
【原教旨主义】yuánjiàozhǐzhǔyì〈名〉fundamentalism: ～者 fundamentalist
【原来】yuánlái A〈形〉original: 把房子恢复到～的样子 restore the house to its former state ‖ 她还住在～的地方。 She still lives in the same place. B〈副〉1▶（当初）originally: 他没有做到自己～想做的事。 He failed in what he had originally set his mind on doing. ‖ 学校～打算在这儿盖一幢物理大楼。 Our college originally planned to put up the physics building here. 2▶（表发现或醒悟）as it turns out: 我说夜里怎么这么冷，～是下雪了。 No wonder I felt rather cold during the night — it was snowing outside. ‖ 这幅画～是赝品。 The picture turned out to be a forgery.
【原来如此】yuánlái rúcǐ〈成〉(Oh,) I see
【原理】yuánlǐ〈名〉principle: 马列主义的基本～ fundamental tenets of Marxism-Leninism
【原粮】yuánliáng〈名〉unprocessed grain
【原谅】yuánliàng ▸p. 156〈动〉forgive: ～他的无知 forgive his ignorance ‖ 请求～ ask for forgiveness
【原料】yuánliào〈名〉raw materials: 供应～ provide raw materials ‖ 工业～ industrial materials ‖ ～基地 raw material site
【原路】yuánlù〈名〉original route
【原麻】yuánmá〈名〉raw hemp used as textile material
【原毛】yuánmáo〈名〉［纺织］raw wool
【原貌】yuánmào〈名〉original state: 保持～ keep sth. as it is
【原煤】yuánméi〈名〉raw coal: 开采～ mine raw coal
【原蜜】yuánmì〈名〉unprocessed honey
【原棉】yuánmián〈名〉［纺织］raw cotton: 收购～ purchase raw cotton
【原木】yuánmù〈名〉log
【原判】yuánpàn〈名〉［法律］original verdict: 维持～ uphold the original verdict
【原配】yuánpèi〈名〉first wife
【原人】yuánrén〈名〉protohuman
【原任】yuánrèn A〈动〉formerly held the post (of) B〈名〉predecessor
【原色】yuánsè〈名〉［物理］primary colour: 红、黄、兰为三～。 Red, yellow and blue are primary colours.
【原审】yuánshěn〈名〉［法律］first trial: ～判决 judgement of the lower court
【原生】yuánshēng〈形〉primordial
【原生动物】yuánshēng dòngwù〈名〉protozoan
【原生林】yuánshēnglín = 原始林 yuánshǐlín
【原生态】yuánshēngtài〈名〉primitive style: ～民歌/舞蹈 old-style folk songs/dance
【原生质】yuánshēngzhì〈名〉［生物］protoplasm
【原声】yuánshēng〈名〉original music: ～大碟 original album ‖ 电影～音乐 original movie soundtrack
【原声带】yuánshēngdài〈名〉original tape
【原始】yuánshǐ〈形〉1▶（最初）original: ～发票/单据 original invoice/receipt ▸～资料 2▶（最古老）primitive: ～的工具 primitive tools ‖ ～部落 primitive tribe ‖ ～农业 primitive agriculture ▸～积累, ～社会
【原始公社】yuánshǐ gōngshè〈名〉primitive commune
【原始股】yuánshǐgǔ〈名〉initial offerings
【原始积累】yuánshǐ jīlěi〈名〉primary accumulation: 资本的～ primary accumulation of capital
【原始林】yuánshǐlín = 原生林 yuánshēnglín
【原始群】yuánshǐqún〈名〉primitive horde
【原始人】yuánshǐrén〈名〉primitive (person)
【原始森林】yuánshǐ sēnlín〈名〉virgin forest
【原始社会】yuánshǐ shèhuì〈名〉primitive society
【原始数据】yuánshǐ shùjù〈名〉raw data
【原始资料】yuánshǐ zīliào〈名〉source material
【原诉】yuánsù〈名〉original lawsuit: 撤回～ withdraw an original lawsuit
【原索动物】yuánsuǒ dòngwù〈名〉protochordate
【原汤】yuántāng〈名〉original broth
【原糖】yuántáng〈名〉raw sugar
【原委】yuánwěi〈名〉whole story: 讲述～ tell the whole story ‖ 我倒想知道其中的～。 I should like to know the full details.
【原文】yuánwén〈名〉1▶（翻译的依据）the original: 读～ read a text in the original ‖ 译文要紧扣～。 The translation must follow the original closely. 2▶（引用对象）original text: 核对～ check the original ‖ 引用～要加引号。 Put quoted passages in quotes.
【原物】yuánwù〈名〉original thing: 归还～ return a borrowed item
【原先】yuánxiān〈名〉the original: 按～的计划去做 act according to the original plan

‖ 她～是教师，后来当了律师。She used to be a teacher, and then became a lawyer.

【原星系】yuánxīngxì〈名〉［天文］ protogalaxy

【原形】yuánxíng〈名〉 original form: 暴露～ reveal one's true nature ‖ 现～ show one's true colours

【原形毕露】yuánxíng-bìlù〈成〉 reveal one's true colours

【原型】yuánxíng〈名〉 prototype: 他就是小说主人公的～。 He is the prototype of the hero of the novel.

【原盐】yuányán〈名〉 crude salt

【原样】yuányàng〈名〉 original condition: 使房子恢复～ restore the house to its original state ‖ 她喜欢一切都保持～。 She likes everything to remain the same.

【原野】yuányě〈名〉 open country: 肥沃的～ fertile open country ‖ 辽阔的～ vast open country

【原意】yuányì〈名〉 original intention: 歪曲～ distort the meaning ‖ 有背～ go against the original intention

【原因】yuányīn〈名〉 reason: 查明～ ascertain the cause ‖ 搞清～ clear up the cause ‖ 主要～ main/leading cause ‖ 她由于健康～而辞职。 She resigned on grounds of health.

【原由】yuányóu = 缘由 yuányóu

【原油】yuányóu〈名〉 crude oil: ～价格猛涨。The price of crude oil has risen sharply.

【原宥】yuányòu〈动〉〈书〉 pardon

【原原本本】yuányuán-běnběn〈成〉 from beginning to end: 他把自己的遭遇都～跟你说了吗？ Did he give you a full description of what happened to him?

【原则】yuánzé〈名〉 **1**（法则、标准） principle: 犯～性错误 make an error of principle ‖ 坚持～ stick to one's principles ‖ 基本～ basic principles ‖ 指导～ guiding principle **2**（大体上） in general: 他们～上同意这个计划。 They agreed to the plan in principle.

【原汁】yuánzhī〈名〉 natural juice: 榨出～ squeeze out the natural juices ‖ ～鸡汤 chicken stock

【原职】yuánzhí〈名〉 former post: 官复～ be restored to one's former post

【原址】yuánzhǐ〈名〉 former address

【原纸】yuánzhǐ〈名〉 base paper

【原种】yuánzhǒng〈名〉 original breed

【原主】yuánzhǔ〈名〉 original owner: 物归～ the article was returned to its original owner

【原著】yuánzhù〈名〉 original work: 读～ read the original ‖ 莎士比亚～ Shakespeare's works in the original

【原装】yuánzhuāng〈形〉 **1**（指装配） factory-packed: 日本～彩电 colour television factory-packed in Japan **2**（指封装） original packaging: ～酒 liquor in the original packing

【原状】yuánzhuàng〈名〉 original state: 保持～ preserve the status quo ‖ 恢复～ revert to the original state

【原子】yuánzǐ〈名〉 atom: 碳/氢～ carbon/hydrogen atom

【原子弹】yuánzǐdàn〈名〉 atomic bomb: 投～ drop an atomic bomb

【原子核】yuánzǐhé〈名〉［物理］ atomic nucleus

【原子核反应堆】yuánzǐhé fǎnyìngduī〈名〉 atomic nuclear reactor

【原子量】yuánzǐliàng〈名〉［化学］atomic weight: ～单位 atomic weight unit

【原子能】yuánzǐnéng〈名〉［物理］atomic energy: ～发电站 atomic power station

【原子团】yuánzǐtuán〈名〉［化学］ atomic group

【原子武器】yuánzǐ wǔqì〈名〉 atomic weapons: 禁止～ ban atomic weapons

【原子物理学】yuánzǐ wùlǐxué〈名〉 atomic physics

【原子序数】yuánzǐ xùshù〈名〉［化学］ atomic number

【原子钟】yuánzǐzhōng〈名〉 atomic clock

【原罪】yuánzuì〈名〉［基督教］original sin

【原作】yuánzuò〈名〉 original work: 删改～ revise the original ‖ 他的译文保持了～的风格。 His translation reproduces the style of the original.

圆（圓）yuán

A〈名〉 **1**［数学］ circle: ～的面积/周长 area/circumference of a circle ▸～心，～周 **2**（硬币） coin of fixed value and weight: ▸铜～

B〈形〉 **1**（圆形） round: ～脸 round face ‖ 今晚的月亮又～又亮。 Today's moon is full and bright. ▸～括号，～桌 **2**（周全） perfect: 她这话说得不～。 What she said was not very tactful. ▸～滑，～满 **3**（婉转） melodious: ▸字正腔～

C〈动〉 perfect: ▸～谎，～梦，自～其说

D ▸**p. 328**〈量〉 *yuan* [the standard monetary unit of China, divided into 100 *fen*]: 一～人民币 a Chinese *yuan*

【圆白菜】yuánbáicài = 结球甘蓝 jiéqiú gānlán

【圆场】yuánchǎng〈动〉 **1**（调解） mediate: 打～ mediate a dispute ‖ 这事必须由你出面～。 You must personally act as a mediator in the dispute. **2** ▸跑圆场 pǎo yuánchǎng

【圆成】yuánchéng〈动〉 help sb. attain their aim

【圆唇元音】yuánchún yuányīn〈名〉［语言］ round vowel

【圆顶】yuándǐng〈名〉 **1**［建筑］ dome **2**（指形状） round top

【圆度】yuándù〈名〉 circular degree

【圆墩墩】yuándūndūn〈形〉〈口〉 podgy

【圆房】yuánfáng〈动〉〈旧〉 [of a foster daughter-in-law and her husband] consummate a marriage

【圆鼓鼓】yuángǔgǔ〈形〉 rounded and bulging: ～的肚子 rounded, bulging belly

【圆规】yuánguī〈名〉 compasses

【圆滚滚】yuángǔngǔn〈形〉 plump: ～的脸蛋儿 chubby face ‖ ～的小肥猪 podgy little pig

【圆号】yuánhào ▸**p. 929**〈名〉［音乐］ French horn

【圆乎乎】yuánhūhū〈形〉〈口〉 roundish

【圆弧】yuánhú〈名〉［数学］ arc

【圆滑】yuánhuá〈形〉 slick and sly: 说话～ have a smooth tongue ‖ 为人～ be tactful

【圆环】yuánhuán〈名〉 loop

【圆谎】yuánhuǎng〈动〉 embellish a lie

【圆浑】yuánhún〈形〉 **1**（指声音） melodious: 这段唱腔流畅而～。 This aria is soft and melodious. **2**（指诗文） natural and spontaneous

【圆寂】yuánjì〈动〉 [of Buddhist monks or nuns] die

【圆括号】yuánkuòhào〈名〉parentheses: 把…放在～内 put ... in parentheses

【圆括弧】yuánkuòhú = 圆括号 yuánkuòhào

【圆领】yuánlǐng〈名〉 round neck: ～衫 round neck shirt

【圆溜溜】yuánliūliū〈形〉 rounded

【圆颅方趾】yuánlú-fāngzhǐ〈成〉 human being

【圆满】yuánmǎn〈形〉 satisfactory: 功德～ come to a satisfactory conclusion ‖ 他把问题解决得十分～。 His solution to the problem is highly satisfactory. ‖ 试验取得～成功。 The experiment was completed successfully.

【圆梦】yuánmèng〈动〉 **1**（解梦） interpret a dream **2**（实现梦想） realize one's dream: 他最终圆了留学梦。 His dream of studying abroad came true at last.

【圆明园】Yuánmíngyuán〈名〉 the old Summer Palace [originally a large imperial Qing Dynasty garden]

【圆盘耙】yuánpánbà〈名〉［农业］disc harrow

【圆圈】yuánquān〈名〉circle: 画～ describe a circle ‖ 围成～ form a circle

【圆全】yuánquan〈形〉〈方〉 thoughtful: 想得～ be considerate

【圆润】yuánrùn〈形〉 mellow and full: ～宏亮的嗓音 sonorous voice ‖ ～的声音 rich voice

【圆实】yuánshi〈形〉 chubby

【圆熟】yuánshú〈形〉 **1**（熟练） skilful: 技术～ show consummate skill **2**（精明练达） astute

【圆通】yuántōng〈形〉 flexible: 处事干练～ handle matters with experience and flexibility

【圆舞曲】yuánwǔqǔ〈名〉［音乐］ waltz

【圆心】yuánxīn〈名〉 centre of a circle: 同心圆的～重合。 The centres of concentric circles coincide.

【圆形】yuánxíng〈形〉 circular: ～建筑 circular building ‖ ～剧场 amphitheatre

【圆凿方枘】yuánzáo-fāngruì = 方枘圆凿 fāngruì-yuánzáo

【圆周】yuánzhōu〈名〉 circumference: ～运动 circular motion

【圆周率】yuánzhōulǜ〈名〉［数学］ pi (π)

【圆珠笔】yuánzhūbǐ〈名〉 ballpoint pen

【圆柱】yuánzhù〈名〉 cylinder

【圆柱体】yuánzhùtǐ〈名〉 cylinder

【圆锥】yuánzhuī〈名〉 cone: ～花坛 pyramid flower bed

【圆桌】yuánzhuō〈名〉 round table

【圆桌会议】yuánzhuō huìyì〈名〉 round-table conference

【圆子】yuánzi〈名〉 **1**（汤圆） dumpling made of glutinous rice flour **2**〈方〉（丸子） ball: 肉～ meatball

鼋（黿）yuán

【鼋鱼】yuányú〈名〉［动物］ soft-shelled turtle

援 yuán

〈动〉 **1**（用手牵引） pull by hand: ▸攀～ **2**（引用） cite: 无先例可～ have no precedent to go by ▸～例，～引，～用 **3**（援助） aid: ～非物资 resources for African aid ▸～救，～助，支～

【援兵】yuánbīng〈名〉 reinforcements: 等待～到来 wait for reinforcements

【援建】yuánjiàn〈动〉 provide aid in construction: ～项目 assistance project

【援救】yuánjiù〈动〉 rescue: ～落水儿童 rescue a child from drowning ‖ 参加～工作 take part in the rescue

【援军】yuánjūn〈名〉 relief troops: 派～ dispatch reinforcements

【援款】yuánkuǎn〈名〉 aid fund

【援例】yuánlì〈动〉 cite a precedent

【援手】yuánshǒu **A**〈名〉 aid: 伸出～ extend a helping hand **B**〈动〉〈书〉 aid

【援外】yuánwài〈动〉 give aid to another

country: ～物资 materials in aid to a foreign country

【援引】yuányǐn〈动〉**1**（引用）cite: ～法律条文 invoke a legal provision ‖ ～最新数据 quote the latest figures **2**（引荐）recommend: ～贤能 recommend talents

【援用】yuányòng〈动〉**1**（引用）cite: ～成例 cite a precedent ‖ ～经典 quote from the classics **2**（引荐任用）recommend sb. for appointment

【援助】yuánzhù〈动〉help: 给以物质～ give material aid ‖ 伸出～之手 extend a helping hand ‖ 寻求～ seek assistance ‖ 国际～ international support ‖ 法律～ legal aid

湲 yuán ▸潺湲 chányuán

媛 yuán ▸婵媛 chányuán ▸yuàn

缘（緣）yuán

A〈介〉**1**〈书〉（沿着）along: ～江航行 sail along the river ▸～木求鱼 **2**（因为）for(reason): ▸～何

B〈连〉〈书〉because: 不识庐山真面目，只～身在此山中。 I can't tell the true shape of Mt Lushan because I am on the mountain myself.

C〈名〉**1**（原因）reason: ▸～由，～故，无～无故 **2**（缘分）destiny: 有～千里来相会。 If destiny has its way, distance is no object. ‖ 他们俩有情无～。 They have feelings for one another but are not destined to be together. ▸血～，姻～ **3**〔佛教〕karma: ▸化～，因～ **4**（边缘）edge: 沙漠的南～ southern fringe of the desert ▸边～

【缘分】yuánfèn〈名〉destiny: 婚姻是～。 Marriage relies on the hand of destiny. ‖ 咱们俩从中学到大学都是同学，真是有～。 It's our fate to be classmates from high school through to college.

【缘故】yuángù〈名〉reason: 出于健康的～ for health reasons ‖ 不知什么～，今天他没有来上班。 I don't know why, but he didn't come to work today.

【缘何】yuánhé〈副〉〈书〉why: ～出此下策？ Why do you resort to such an unwise move?

【缘木求鱼】yuánmù-qiúyú〈成〉〈喻〉bark up the wrong tree

【缘起】yuánqǐ〈名〉**1**（起因）origin: 文章～ origins of literary forms **2**（指说明文字）account of the initiation of a project or the founding of an institution

【缘石】yuánshí〈名〉kerb〈英〉; curb〈美〉

【缘由】yuányóu〈名〉cause and reason: 无～地发火 fall into a rage for no reason ‖ 说明～ explain the reason

塬 yuán〈名〉〈书〉tableland

猿 yuán〈名〉ape: 从～到人 from ape to man ▸类人～

【猿猴】yuánhóu〈名〉ape and monkey

【猿人】yuánrén〈名〉apeman: 北京～ Peking man

源 yuán〈名〉**1**（水源）fountainhead: ▸～远流长，水～ **2**（根源）source: 罪恶之～ root of all evils ‖ 理论～于实践。 All theory originates from practice. ‖ 文学作品～于生活，高于生活。 Literary works should take their inspiration from life, and yet should be greater than life itself. ▸病～，货～ **3**〔计算机〕source

【源代码】yuándàimǎ〈名〉〔计算机〕source code

【源流】yuánliú〈名〉**1**〈本〉source and course **2**〈喻〉origin and development: 汉字发展的～ the origins and evolution of Chinese writing

【源目录】yuánmùlù〈名〉〔计算机〕source directory

【源泉】yuánquán〈名〉source: 发现～ discover the source ‖ 知识的～ source of knowledge ‖〈喻〉灵感/罪恶的～ source of inspiration/evil ‖〈喻〉生活是文艺创作的～。 Life is the source of literary and artistic creation.

【源头】yuántóu〈名〉source: 河流的～ the source of the river ‖〈喻〉文学的～ origins of literature

【源语言】yuányǔyán〈名〉〔计算机〕source language

【源源】yuányuán〈形〉continuous: 前来参观的人～不断。 There is a steady stream of visitors.

【源远流长】yuányuǎn-liúcháng〈成〉〈喻〉long-standing and well-established: 中国文化的历史～。 Chinese culture goes back to time immemorial.

辕（轅）yuán〈名〉**1**（套牲口的直木）shafts of a cart or carriage: ▸驾～ **2**〈古〉（辕门）outer gate of a government office;（衙署）government office

【辕骡】yuánluó〈名〉shaft-mule

【辕马】yuánmǎ〈名〉shaft-horse

【辕门】yuánmén〈名〉〈古〉（指军营）gate of a military camp;（指官署）outer gate of a government office

【辕子】yuánzi〈名〉〈口〉shaft: 车～ shafts of a cart

橼（櫞）yuán ▸枸橼 jǔyuán

螈 yuán ▸蝾螈 róngyuán

圜 yuán〈书〉= 圆 yuán ▸huán

獂 yuán

【獂羊】yuányáng〈名〉〔动物〕ibex

yuǎn

远（遠）yuǎn

A〈形〉**1**（距离长）far away: 相隔很～ be far apart ‖ 住在离城不～的地方 live not far from town ‖ 那房子～离街道。 The house stands back from the street. ▸～方，遥～ **2**（关系不密切）distant: ▸～房，疏～ **3**（程度大）by far: 他的潜力～未发挥出来。 He isn't reaching anywhere near his potential. ‖ 这件产品～没有广告上说的那样好。 The product is not half as good as its billing indicates. ‖ 你比他差～了。 You are no way near as good as he is.

B〈动〉keep at a distance: 亲贤臣，～小人 keep able and righteous people close and bad ones at a distance ▸敬而～之

【远程】yuǎnchéng〈形〉**1**（路程远）long-distance: ～航行 long sea voyage ‖ ～导弹 long-range missile **2**〔计算机〕remote: ～用户 remote user

【远程导弹】yuǎnchéng dǎodàn〈名〉long-range missile

【远程登录】yuǎnchéng dēnglù〈名〉telnet

【远程轰炸机】yuǎnchéng hōngzhàjī〈名〉long-distance bomber

【远程教育】yuǎnchéng jiàoyù〈名〉distance learning

【远处】yuǎnchù〈名〉distant place

【远大】yuǎndà〈形〉far-reaching: 前途～ the future holds bright promise ‖ 眼光～ be far-sighted ‖ ～志向 soaring ambition

【远道】yuǎndào〈名〉long way: 走～ walk far ‖ 我专程～来拜访你。 I came from afar especially to see you.

【远地点】yuǎndìdiǎn〈名〉〔天文〕apogee

【远东】Yuǎndōng〈名〉Far East

【远东军事法庭】Yuǎndōng Jūnshì Fǎtíng〈名〉〔历史〕Far Eastern International Military Court of Justice

【远渡重洋】yuǎndù-chóngyáng〈成〉travel all the way from across oceans

【远方】yuǎnfāng〈名〉distant place: ～来客 guest from afar ‖ 有朋自～来，不亦乐乎？ Isn't it a pleasure to have a friend from afar?

【远房】yuǎnfáng〈形〉distantly related: ～亲戚 distant relative

【远隔重洋】yuǎngé-chóngyáng〈成〉be separated by vast oceans

【远古】yuǎngǔ〈名〉remote antiquity: ～时代 remote ages ‖ ～遗风 custom of remote antiquity

【远海】yuǎnhǎi〈名〉distant waters

【远航】yuǎnháng〈动〉take a long voyage

【远红外】yuǎnhóngwài〈形〉far-infrared: ～线 far-infrared ray

【远见】yuǎnjiàn〈名〉foresight: 缺乏～ lack vision ‖ 有～的政治家 statesman of vision

【远见卓识】yuǎnjiàn-zhuōshí〈成〉foresight and wisdom: 具有～的政治家 a statesman with real foresight and wisdom

【远交近攻】yuǎnjiāo-jìngōng〈成〉be friends with distant states while attacking those nearby [strategy for dealing with foreign countries adopted by the state of Qin (秦) during the Warring States Period]

【远郊】yuǎnjiāo〈名〉remoter outskirts: ～公共汽车 bus to the suburbs

【远近】yuǎnjìn **A**〈名〉distance: 这两条路～差不多。 The distance is about the same by either road. **B**〈形〉far and near: ～闻名 be known far and wide

【远景】yuǎnjǐng〈名〉**1**（远处景物）distant view: 眺望～ look into the distance **2**（前景）long-range perspective: 展示美好的～ show a favourable outlook ‖ ～规划 long-term plan

【远距离】yuǎnjùlí〈名〉long distance: ～射击 long range shooting

【远客】yuǎnkè〈名〉guest from afar

【远来的和尚好念经】yuǎn láide héshang hǎo niànjīng〈俗〉[monks from afar chant Buddhist scriptures with ease] people from afar tackle problems more easily than local people

【远虑】yuǎnlǜ〈名〉long view: 做事要有～。 It is important to plan well for the long term. ▸人无～，必有近忧

【远门】yuǎnmén **A**〈名〉journey far away from home: 出～ go on a long journey **B**〈形〉distantly related: ～兄弟 distant cousin

【远谋】yuǎnmóu〈名〉long-term plan: 胸无～ have no long-term plans

【远期】yuǎnqī〈名〉a specified future date: ～目标 long range target

【远期合同】yuǎnqī hétong〈名〉 forward contract

【远期票据】yuǎnqī piàojù〈名〉 long-dated bill

【远亲】yuǎnqīn〈名〉 distant relative: 我妻子的一个～ a distant relative of my wife's

【远亲不如近邻】yuǎnqīn bùrú jìnlín〈俗〉 a good neighbour is more helpful than a brother who is far away

【远日点】yuǎnrìdiǎn〈名〉［天文］ aphelion

【远视】yuǎnshì A〈名〉［医学］ long-sightedness〈英〉; far-sightedness〈美〉: 矫正～ correct far-sightedness B〈形〉 long-sighted〈英〉; far-sighted〈美〉

【远水解不了近渴】yuǎnshuǐ jiěbùliǎo jìnkě〈俗〉〈喻〉 if aid is too slow in coming, it isn't going to be of any help

【远水救不了近火】yuǎnshuǐ jiùbùliǎo jìnhuǒ〈俗〉〈喻〉 while the grass grows, the horse starves

【远眺】yuǎntiào〈动〉 look far into the distance from a high place

【远销】yuǎnxiāo〈动〉 sell goods to distant places: ～海外 be sold abroad

【远行】yuǎnxíng〈动〉 go on a long journey: 我们即将～，正在准备行装。 We are just setting off on a long journey and are busy making preparations for it.

【远扬】yuǎnyáng〈动〉 spread far and wide: 臭名～ be notorious ‖ 美名～ have a good reputation far and wide

【远洋】yuǎnyáng〈名〉 ocean: ～货轮 ocean-going freighter ‖ ～渔业 deep-sea fishing

【远因】yuǎnyīn〈名〉 remote cause

【远月点】yuǎnyuèdiǎn〈名〉［天文］ apocynthion

【远在天边，近在眼前】yuǎn zài tiānbiān, jìn zài yǎnqián〈俗〉 actually it's close at hand

【远征】yuǎnzhēng〈动〉 make an expedition: ～军 expeditionary force ‖ 红军不怕～难。 The Red Army did not fear the trials of the Long March.

【远志】yuǎnzhì〈名〉 noble aspiration

【远走高飞】yuǎnzǒu-gāofēi〈成〉 flee to a faraway place: 孩子大了，就让他们～吧。 The children have grown up, so you should let them flee the nest.

【远足】yuǎnzú〈动〉 go on an outing: 周末去～ go on a weekend outing

【远祖】yuǎnzǔ〈名〉 remote ancestor

yuàn

苑 yuàn〈名〉 1（皇家园林） imperial garden: 梅～ plum garden ▸林～ 2〈书〉（聚集处） centre: ▸文～, 艺～

怨 yuàn〈动〉 1（怨恨） resent: 民～ popular resentment ‖ 面有～色 wear a discontented look ▸～恨, ～声载道 2（责怪） complain: ～自己记性差 complain of a bad memory ‖ 他总是～这～那。 If he isn't complaining about one thing, he's complaining about another. ▸～天尤人, 任劳任～

【怨不得】yuànbude A〈动〉 cannot blame: 这事～任何人。 Nobody is to blame for it. B〈副〉 no wonder: 昨晚你喝了那么多酒，～你头疼。 It's no wonder that you've got a headache given how much you drank last night.

【怨仇】yuànchóu〈名〉 enmity

【怨愤】yuànfèn A〈形〉 resentful: 心中十分～ feel mad at heart B〈名〉 indignation: ～难平 can hardly restrain one's indignation

【怨恨】yuànhèn A〈动〉 resent: 从心底里～ be inwardly resentful ‖ 相互～ hate each other B〈名〉 resentment: 发泄～ take out one's resentment on sb. ‖ 对某人心怀～ bear a grudge against sb.

【怨懑】yuànmèn〈形〉〈书〉 discontented and indignant

【怨偶】yuàn'ǒu〈名〉〈书〉 unhappy couple

【怨气】yuànqì〈名〉 grievance: 一肚子～ be full of complaints

【怨声载道】yuànshēng-zàidào〈成〉 voices of discontent are heard everywhere

【怨天尤人】yuàntiān-yóurén〈成〉 blame everyone and everything but oneself: 创业失败，要总结教训，不要～。 If you fail in your career, you should draw lessons from the experience rather than look for somebody to blame.

【怨言】yuànyán〈名〉 complaint: 毫无～ have no complaints whatsoever

【怨艾】yuànyì〈动〉〈书〉 bear a grudge: 深自～ deeply blame oneself for sth.

院 yuàn〈名〉 1（院子） courtyard: 寺～ temple compound ‖ 他家屋后有个小～。 He has a small courtyard behind his house. ▸大杂～儿, 四合～ 2（机构） designation for certain government offices and public places: ▸法～, 国务～ 3（学院） college: ▸～校, 学～ 4（医院） hospital: 出～ be discharged from hospital ‖ 住～ be hospitalized

【院落】yuànluò = 院子 yuànzi

【院墙】yuànqiáng〈名〉 walls surrounding a house

【院士】yuànshì〈名〉 academician: 中国科学院～ member of the Chinese Academy of Sciences

【院体画】yuàntǐhuà〈名〉 imperial-court decorative painting

【院校】yuànxiào〈名〉 universities and colleges: ▸高等～

【院长】yuànzhǎng〈名〉 1（指医院） director 2（指学院） dean

【院子】yuànzi〈名〉 courtyard

垸 yuàn〈方〉= 垸子 yuànzi

【垸子】yuànzi〈名〉〈方〉 protective embankments [built around houses or fields in riverside and lakeside areas in Hunan and Hubei provinces]

媛 yuàn〈名〉〈书〉 beautiful woman: ▸名～
▸yuán

瑗 yuàn〈名〉〈古〉 round flat piece of jade with a big hole in its centre

愿[1] yuàn〈形〉〈书〉 honest and cautious

愿[2]（願） yuàn
A〈名〉 1（愿望） hope: ▸～望, 如～以偿, 心～ 2（愿心） vow: 还～ fulfil a vow to a deity ‖ 许～ make a vow ▸～心
B〈动〉 1（愿意） be willing: 你～上哪儿就上哪儿。 Go wherever you want to go. ‖ 他小事不～干，大事干不了。 He doesn't want to take on little jobs, yet can't handle big ones. ▸甘～, 情～ 2（祝愿） desire: ～您早日康复。 Hope you get better soon. ▸祝～

【愿景】yuànjǐng〈名〉aspiration: 和平发展是海峡两岸人民的共同～。 Peaceful development is a shared aspiration of people on both sides of the straits.

【愿望】yuànwàng〈名〉 desire: 从团结的～出发 start from the desire for unity ‖ 主观～ subjective desire ‖ 我的～实现了。 My wish has come true.

【愿心】yuànxīn〈名〉 1（许的愿） vow made to Buddha or a god 2（志向） aspiration

【愿意】yuànyì〈动〉 1（乐意） be willing: ～帮忙 be ready to help ‖ 他～为年轻人做人梯。 He is happy to help young people to make their way up the ladder of success. 2（希望） hope: 我们～你参加我们的组织。 We'd like you to join our organization.

yuē

曰 yuē〈动〉〈书〉 1（说） say: 子～: "三人行，必有我师焉。" The master said, 'Give me three men and I'll show you one who has something to teach me.' 2（叫做） call: 山上有一高塔，名～六和塔。 On the mountain there is a tall tower called the Liuhe Tower.

约（約） yuē
A〈动〉 1（限制） restrict: ▸～束, 制～ 2（约定） make an appointment: 他们和他～好在车站见面。 They arranged him to meet at the station. ‖ 我们～个日子一起吃饭吧。 Let's arrange a day to have dinner together. ▸～定, 预～ 3（邀请） invite: 我想周末～几个同事吃饭。 I'd like to invite some colleagues to dinner this weekend. 4［数学］ reduce fractions: 5/10可以～成1/2。 5/10 can be reduced to 1/2.
B〈名〉 appointment: 有～在先。 Have a previous engagement. ▸践～, 守～
C〈形〉 1（简要） brief: ～言之 in short ▸简～ 2（俭省） economical: ～减办公费 stint on office expenses ▸节～
D〈副〉 around: 我们估计距离～为500公里。 We reckon that the distance is about 500 kilometres.
▸yāo

【约旦】Yuēdàn〈名〉 Jordan: ～哈希姆王国 Hashemite Kingdom of Jordan ‖ ～人 Jordanian

【约定】yuēdìng〈动〉 arrange: 按照～的时间 at the appointed time ‖ 我们～下星期见面。 We fixed an appointment for next week.

【约定俗成】yuēdìng-súchéng〈成〉 accepted through common practice

【约法】yuēfǎ〈名〉 provisional constitution: 《中华民国临时～》 *Provisional Constitution of the Republic of China*

【约法三章】yuēfǎ-sānzhāng〈成〉 make certain rules to be observed by all concerned

【约分】yuēfēn〈动〉［数学］ reduce: 4/12可以～为1/3。 4/12 can be reduced to 1/3.

【约稿】yuēgǎo〈动〉 request contribution

【约翰内斯堡】Yuēhànnèisībǎo〈名〉 Johannesburg

【约会】yuēhuì A〈动〉 arrange a meeting: 她经常和男孩～。 She goes on a lot of dates. B〈名〉 appointment: 取消～ cancel an appointment ‖ 我4点钟有个～。 I have an appointment at four.

【约集】yuējí〈动〉invite to meet together: ～有关人士开会 gather together relevant people for a meeting

【约计】yuējì〈动〉come to about: 成本～人民币5,000元。The cost will come to about 5,000 *yuan*.

【约见】yuējiàn〈动〉make an appointment to meet: 紧急～某人 summon sb. for an urgent meeting

【约据】yuējù〈名〉general term for contract and deed

【约克郡】Yuēkèjùn〈名〉Yorkshire

【约略】yuēlüè〈副〉1 (大致) roughly: ～估计 rough estimate ‖ 我～知道一些。I know a little bit about it. 2 (依稀) faintly: 他～听见雨点拍打着窗户的声音。He could hear a faint patter of the rain against the windows.

【约莫】yuēmo A〈动〉reckon: 我～着他不会来了。I reckon he's not going to come. B〈副〉about: 等了～50分钟 wait for 50 minutes or so ‖ 她～30岁上下。She was about 30 years old.

【约摸】yuēmo = 约莫 yuēmo

【约期】yuēqī A〈动〉set a date: ～会谈 fix a date to hold talks B〈名〉1 (约定的日子) set time: 改变～ change the date ‖ 误了～ fail to keep an appointment 2 (契约期限) duration of an agreement: ～已满。The contract has expired.

【约请】yuēqǐng〈动〉invite: ～某人喝酒 invite sb. for a drink

【约束】yuēshù〈动〉restrain: 冲破旧框框的～ break through the shackles of old conventions ‖ 受合同～ be bound by a contract ‖ 用纪律～自己 keep oneself within the bounds of discipline ‖ ～机制 restraint mechanisms

【约束力】yuēshùlì〈名〉binding force: 这份协议对我们没有～。This agreement does not commit us in any way.

【约数】yuēshù〈名〉1 (大概的数目) approximate number 2 [数学] divisor

【约谈】yuētán〈动〉arrange a time for a talk

【约同】yuētóng〈动〉ask sb. to go together: ～前往 ask sb. to go together

【约言】yuēyán〈名〉pledge: 履行～ fulfil a pledge ‖ 遵守/信守～ keep one's promise

【约制】yuēzhì〈动〉keep down: ～手下人 keep one's subordinates down

yuě

哕（噦） yuě〈动〉〈口〉vomit up: 吃的药全～出来了。The medicine was thrown right up.
▸huì

yuè

月 yuè〈名〉1 (月亮) moon: 赏～ enjoy the moon ‖ ～下散步 take a walk in the moonlight ▸登～舱, 新～ 2 ▸p. 618 (月份) month: 本～ this month ‖ 下个～ the next month ‖ 她怀孕已8个～。She is 8 months pregnant. ▸～份, 腊～, 正～ 3 (每月) every month: ～收入/产量

约数

■ 用英语表达约数比用汉语简单。由于英语里不存在量词，所以表示约数的词或短语，如 about 及 a few 等，一般后面直接跟“数词 + 名词”结构；但 or so 例外，它跟在所修饰的词后面，如 a hundred pounds or so 和 a dozen or so。

约数“几”或“两”

■“几”或“两”用 several 或 a few 来表达。several 和 a few 是形容词，直接用在名词前面，表示 1–9 之间的约数：

几张邮票
= several stamps
或 a few stamps

我过两天去看你
= I'll see you in a few days

“十几”和“几十”

■ 英语里没有与“十几”完全相对应的表达法，意义比较接近的是 a dozen or so。“几十”可用 a few dozen 或 dozens of 来翻译。以上这些英语表达法都是直接用在名词前：

十几本杂志
= a dozen or so magazines

几十张桌子
= dozens of tables

几十个人
= a few dozen people

“几百”、“几千”、“几万”等

■ 英语用“a few + hundred/thousand/million 等 + 名词”：

几百册书籍
= a few hundred books

几百万棵树
= a few million trees

■ 英语里没有与“万”对应的词，所以用 tens of thousands of ... 来表达“几万”：

几万英镑
= tens of thousands of pounds

■ 其他短语：

成百上千的游客
= hundreds of tourists

成千上万的电视观众
= thousands of TV viewers

数之不尽的星星
= millions of stars

“超过”和“少于”

■ 英语里表示大于某个数字时，可以用 over、above 或 more than。这些词用在名词的前面：

9 岁多
= over 9 years old
或 above the age of 9

十多个小学生
= more than 10 pupils
或 over 10 pupils

5 吨以上
= more than 5 tons
或 over 5 tons

■ 英语里表示少于某个数字时，可以用 less than、below 或 under。这些词用在名词的前面：

不满 5 岁
= under 5 (years old)
或 below the age of 5

100 人以下
= less than 100 people
或 under 100 people

不到 3 年
= less than 3 years
或 under 3 years

“大约”、“左右”等

■ 英语用 about、around、roughly 或 or so 等来表示接近某个数量。注意 or so 的位置：

十来个生词
= about ten new words

大约二十来张票
= about 20 tickets
或 20 tickets or so

300 个儿童左右
= roughly 300 children

60 公斤上下
= about 60 kilograms

圣诞前后
= around Christmas

11 点前后
= about 11 o'clock
或 11 o'clock or so

邻近的两个数字连用

■ 英语和汉语一样，相连的两个数字连用可表示约数。不同的是，英语一般用 or 来连接这两个数字：

七八个女孩子
= seven or eight girls

五六年
= five or six years

三四千张海报
= three or four thousand posters

■ 汉语的“三五”连用时，要翻译成 three to five，因为在英语中习惯说 three or four，不说 three or five：

三五年
= three to five years

三五百英镑
= three to five hundred pounds

■ 汉语的“两三个”和“三两个”翻译成英语时都是 two or three，不能说 three or two：

两三个苹果
= two or three apples

三两天
= two or three days

monthly income/output ▸～刊, ～息, ～薪 4▸ (圆形) moon-shaped thing: ▸～饼, ～琴

【月白】yuèbái〈形〉bluish white

【月白风清】yuèbái-fēngqīng〈成〉a beautiful night

【月半】yuèbàn ▸p. 618〈名〉[of a lunar month] 15th day of a month

【月报】yuèbào〈名〉1▸ (指报刊) monthly 2▸ (指报告) monthly report

【月饼】yuèbing〈名〉moon cake [esp for the Mid-Autumn Festival]

月饼

A round pastry with a sweet or savoury filling. A symbol of reunion, moon cakes are traditionally eaten at the Mid-Autumn Festival (▸中秋节), while appreciating the moon. They are believed to have originated in the Tang Dynasty. Over the centuries, many kinds of moon cakes appeared in different parts of China. The most famous cakes come from Jiangsu and Guangdong provinces.

【月出】yuèchū〈名〉[天文] moonrise

【月初】yuèchū ▸p. 618〈名〉beginning of a month

【月底】yuèdǐ ▸p. 618〈名〉end of a month: 把截止日期延至～ extend the deadline until the end of the month

【月洞门】yuèdòngmén〈名〉[建筑] moon gate

【月度】yuèdù〈名〉monthly: ～计划 monthly plan

【月份】yuèfèn〈名〉month: 一年中最热的～ the hottest month of the year ‖ 一～有31天。January has 31 days.

【月份牌】yuèfènpái〈名〉〈口〉calendar

【月俸】yuèfèng〈名〉〈旧〉monthly pay

【月工】yuègōng〈名〉labourer hired by the month

【月供】yuègōng〈名〉monthly mortgage payment

【月宫】yuègōng〈名〉1▸ (指宫殿) Lunar Palace [legendary palace on the moon] 2▸ (月亮) moon

【月光】yuèguāng〈名〉moonbeam: 明亮的～ brilliant moonlight ‖ ～皎洁。The moon shone brightly.

【月桂】yuèguì〈名〉[植物] bay

【月黑天】yuèhēitiān〈名〉moonless night

【月黑夜】yuèhēiyè = 月黑天 yuèhēitiān

【月华】yuèhuá〈名〉1▸〈书〉(月光) moonlight: ～如水 a flood of translucent moonlight 2▸ [气象] lunar corona

【月环比】yuèhuánbǐ〈名〉comparison on a monthly basis

【月季】yuèjì〈名〉[植物] China rose

【月季花】yuèjìhuā = 月季 yuèjì

【月津贴】yuèjīntiē〈名〉monthly allowance

【月经】yuèjīng〈名〉1▸ (指生理现象) menstruation: ～不调 irregular periods 2▸ (指经血) menses

【月经初潮】yuèjīng chūcháo〈名〉[生理] menarche

【月经带】yuèjīngdài〈名〉sanitary towel

【月经失调】yuèjīng shītiáo〈名〉menstrual disorder

【月均】yuèjūn〈动〉have a monthly average of: ～销售额 monthly turnover

【月刊】yuèkān〈名〉monthly: 文学～ literary monthly

【月老】yuèlǎo〈名〉matchmaker

【月历】yuèlì〈名〉monthly calendar

【月利】yuèlì〈名〉monthly interest

【月例】yuèlì〈名〉1▸ (月钱) monthly allowance 2▸〈婉〉= 月经 yuèjīng

【月亮】yuèliang〈名〉moon: ～出来了。The moon has come out.

【月亮门儿】yuèliangménr〈名〉moon gate

【月令】yuèlìng〈名〉phenology of lunar month

❶ 月份

■ 英语里表示月份的名词是专有名词。除了五月的全称和缩写是一样之外，其他月份都分别有全称和缩写，缩写仅限于书面英语中。无论是全称还是缩写，这些名词的第一个字母都要大写：

	全称	缩写
一月	January	Jan
二月	February	Feb
三月	March	Mar
四月	April	Apr
五月	May	May
六月	June	Jun
七月	July	Jul
八月	August	Aug
九月	September	Sept
十月	October	Oct
十一月	November	Nov
十二月	December	Dec

■ 本条注释中，以 12 月为例加以说明。其他月份的用法与之相同。

哪个月?

现在是几月份? —— 12 月份
= What month is it? — It is December

你是几月份去度假的? —— 12 月
= What month did you go on holiday? — In December

表达月份用的介词

■ 英语里 January、February 等单独出现或与年一起用时要用介词 in。月、日或年、月、日一起用时，要用介词 on。表示某个月的某个上、下午或晚上时，也用介词 on:

我们可在 12 月份见面
= We could meet up in December

香港 12 月相当暖和
= Hong Kong is quite warm in December

她去年 12 月在北京
= She was in Beijing in December last year

明年 12 月她就 30 了
= She will be 30 in December next year

我 2006 年 12 月拜访过他
= I visited him in December 2006

我们 12 月 1 号要去纽约
= We are going to New York on the first of December

她 1995 年 12 月 16 日出生
= She was born on 16 December 1995

事情发生在 12 月的一个早上
= It happened on a December morning

■ 其他介词:

整个 12 月
= throughout December
或 all through December
或 for the whole of December
或 for the whole month of December

12 月初
= at the beginning of December

12 月中旬
= in the middle of December

12 月底
= at the end of December

12 月上旬
= in early December

12 月中旬
= in mid-December

12 月下旬
= in late December

■ 不用介词的情况:

今年 12 月
= this December

明年 12 月
= next December

去年 12 月
= last December

后年 12 月
= the December after next

前年 12 月
= the December before last

每年 12 月
= every December

每隔 1 年的 12 月份
= every other December

上个月
= last month

上上个月
= the month before last

下下个月
= the month after next

张山每月挣两千元
= Zhang Shan earns RMB¥2,000 a/per month

和名词、形容词连用

12 月的一个下午
= one December afternoon
或 one afternoon in December

12 月的一天
= one December day

记录中最冷的 12 月
= the coldest December on record

多雨的 12 月
= a rainy/wet December

阳光灿烂的 12 月
= a sunny December

12 月份大减价
= the December sales

12 月份航班
= December flights

农历月份
= lunar month

正月
= Lunar January

【月轮】yuèlún〈名〉full moon
【月落】yuèluò〈名〉［天文］moonset
【月末】yuèmò ▸p. 618〈名〉end of the month
【月偏食】yuèpiānshí〈名〉partial eclipse of the moon
【月票】yuèpiào〈名〉monthly ticket: 出示～ show one's monthly pass
【月钱】yuèqián〈名〉monthly allowance
【月琴】yuèqín ▸p. 929〈名〉*yueqin* [three-or-four-stringed plucked instrument with a full-moon-shaped sound box]
【月球】yuèqiú〈名〉moon: 登上～ land on the moon ‖ 环绕～飞行 orbit the moon
【月球车】yuèqiúchē〈名〉moon buggy
【月球学】yuèqiúxué〈名〉selenology
【月全食】yuèquánshí〈名〉total lunar eclipse
【月壤】yuèrǎng〈名〉lunar soil: 进行～探测 investigate lunar soil
【月入】yuèrù〈名〉monthly income
【月嫂】yuèsǎo〈名〉live-in nurse [attending to the first few months of a child's life]
【月色】yuèsè〈名〉moonlight: ～朦胧。The moon is obscure. ‖ ～明媚。The moon was shining clear and bright.
【月食】yuèshí〈名〉lunar eclipse
【月台】yuètái〈名〉1（旧）（供赏月的台子）terrace built for admiring the moon 2（前凸的平台）terrace in front of a main hall, with stairs on three of its sides 3（站台）railway platform: ～票 platform ticket
【月头儿】yuètóur ▸p. 618〈名〉〈口〉1（满一个月的时候）monthly payment time 2（月初）beginning of a month
【月尾】yuèwěi ▸p. 618〈名〉end of a month
【月息】yuèxī〈名〉monthly interest
【月下老人】yuèxià lǎorén〈名〉1（指神仙）god of marriage 2（媒人）matchmaker
【月相】yuèxiàng〈名〉［天文］phases of the moon
【月薪】yuèxīn〈名〉monthly salary: 她～5,000元。She is on a salary of 5,000 *yuan* per month.
【月牙】yuèyá〈名〉crescent moon
【月夜】yuèyè〈名〉moonlit night: ～景色 moonlit scene
【月晕】yuèyùn〈名〉lunar halo: ～而风，础润而雨 coming events cast their shadows in advance
【月震】yuèzhèn〈名〉［天文］moonquake
【月氏】Yuèzhī〈名〉Yuezhi [an ancient Central Asian people]
【月中】yuèzhōng ▸p. 618〈名〉middle of a month
【月终】yuèzhōng ▸p. 618〈名〉end of a month: ～盘点 take stock at the end of the month
【月子】yuèzi〈名〉1（指分娩后）first month of confinement after giving birth to a child: 坐～ be in confinement 2（指分娩时）time of giving birth: 她的～是下个月。She expects to give birth next month.
【月子病】yuèzibìng〈名〉puerperal fever
【月租】yuèzū〈名〉monthly rent

乐（樂）

yuè〈名〉music: 奏～ play music ▸～器，声～
▸lè
【乐池】yuèchí〈名〉orchestra pit
【乐队】yuèduì〈名〉band: 交响～ symphony orchestra ‖ 军～ military band ‖ ～指挥 conductor
【乐府】yuèfǔ〈名〉1（指官署）Music Bureau [government office set up during the Han Dynasty to collect folk songs and music for ceremonial occasions at court] 2（指作品）ballads and folk songs collected by the Music Bureau
【乐感】yuègǎn〈名〉ear for music: 培养～ cultivate an ear for music
【乐歌】yuègē〈名〉1（音乐和歌曲）music and songs 2（歌曲）song with accompaniment
【乐理】yuèlǐ〈名〉［音乐］musical theory: 学习～ study musical theory
【乐律】yuèlǜ〈名〉［音乐］temperament
【乐谱】yuèpǔ〈名〉musical score: 识～ read music ‖ 钢琴～ piano score
【乐器】yuèqì〈名〉musical instrument: 打击～ percussion instrument
【乐曲】yuèqǔ〈名〉musical composition: 谱写～ compose music ‖ 为～配词 set words to a tune
【乐师】yuèshī ▸p. 966〈名〉musician
【乐坛】yuètán〈名〉music world
【乐团】yuètuán〈名〉philharmonic orchestra: 广播～ radio philharmonic orchestra ‖ 交响～ philharmonic orchestra
【乐舞】yuèwǔ〈名〉dance accompanied by music
【乐音】yuèyīn〈名〉musical sound
【乐章】yuèzhāng〈名〉［音乐］movement: 一部交响乐一般分为四个～。A symphony is usually divided into four movements.

刖

yuè〈动〉〈古〉cut the feet [form of punishment]

玥

yuè〈名〉〈古〉legendary magic pearl

岳[1]（嶽）

yuè〈名〉high mountain: ▸五～

岳[2]

yuè〈名〉wife's parents: ▸～父，～母
【岳父】yuèfù〈名〉father-in-law [wife's father]
【岳家】yuèjiā〈名〉wife's parents' home
【岳母】yuèmǔ〈名〉mother-in-law [wife's mother]
【岳丈】yuèzhàng〈名〉father-in-law [wife's father]

钥（鑰）

yuè〈名〉key: ▸锁～
▸yào

说

yuè = 悦 yuè
▸shuì, shuō

钺（鉞）

yuè〈名〉〈古〉large battle-axe

阅（閱）

yuè〈动〉1（检阅）review: ▸～兵，检～ 2（看）read: ▸～读，～览，传～ 3（经历）experience: ～尽沧桑 go through all kinds of trials and tribulations ▸～历
【阅兵】yuèbīng〈动〉inspect troops
【阅兵式】yuèbīngshì〈名〉military review: 举行～ conduct a military review
【阅读】yuèdú〈动〉read: ～杂志/报刊 read magazines/newspapers ‖ 快速～ speed reading ‖ 他的～面很广。He reads very widely.
【阅读书目】yuèdú shūmù〈名〉reading list
【阅卷】yuèjuàn〈动〉grade examination

i 乐器

弹奏乐器

■ 英语里无论弹奏什么乐器基本上都可以用动词 play。动词与乐器之间通常要用定冠词 the:

弹钢琴
= to play the piano

拉二胡
= to play the erhu

吹长笛
= to play the flute

打鼓
= to play the drums

演奏者

■ 英语一般用 instrument（乐器）+ player 或用后缀 -ist/-er 指弹奏者、什么家或什么手:

钢琴家 / 钢琴演奏者
= a pianist
或 a piano player

音乐会大提琴演奏者
= a concert cellist

单簧管演奏者
= a clarinet player

鼓手
= a drummer

小号手
= a trumpeter

■ 表示某人乐器弹得好不好，英语有以下常见说法:

他钢琴弹得好
= He is a good pianist
或 He plays the piano well

他二胡拉得不好
= He is a bad erhu player
或 He is not a good erhu player
或 He plays the erhu badly
或 He does not play the erhu (very) well

和其他名词连用

小提琴课
= violin lessons/classes

小提琴独奏
= a violin solo

小提琴奏鸣曲
= a violin sonata

钢琴音乐会
= a piano concert

钢琴谱
= piano scores

钢琴老师
= a piano teacher

papers: 高考～ grade college entrance examination papers

【阅览】yuèlǎn〈动〉 read: ～报纸 read newspapers ‖ ～室 reading room

【阅历】yuèlì **A**〈动〉 see, hear or do for oneself: ～过很多事 have seen much of the world **B**〈名〉 experience: ～丰富/浅 have rich/little experience

【阅世】yuèshì〈动〉〈书〉 see the world: ～颇深 be well experienced in the ways of the world

悦 yuè

A〈形〉 pleased: 惹得某人不～ incur sb.'s displeasure

B〈动〉 please

【悦耳】yuè'ěr〈形〉 sweet-sounding: ～的歌声 sweet song ‖ 这乐曲～动听。 The music sounds beautiful.

【悦服】yuèfú〈动〉〈书〉 heartily admire: 令人～ arousing admiration

【悦目】yuèmù〈形〉 beautiful (to look at): 春天的景色～怡人。 Spring scenery is full of sensuous delights.

跃（躍） yuè

〈动〉 leap: ～过障碍物 leap over an obstacle ‖ ～上台阶 bound up the steps ‖ 他一～成为世界名人。 He vaulted into worldwide renown. ▸～进, ～居, 跳～

【跃层】yuècéng〈名〉 duplex: ～住宅 duplex apartment

【跃进】yuèjìn〈动〉 **1**（跳着前进） leap forward **2**〈喻〉（快速前进） increase by leaps and bounds: 生产飞速～。 Production is increasing by leaps and bounds. ▸大～

【跃居】yuèjū〈动〉 vault into: ～世界首位 vault into world leadership

【跃马】yuèmǎ〈动〉〈书〉 leap onto a horse: ～扬鞭 spring onto the horse wielding the whip

【跃然】yuèrán〈形〉〈书〉 vivid

【跃然纸上】yuèrán-zhǐshàng〈成〉 shine through in one's writing: 爱国之情～。 His patriotic feeling shows forth in his writing.

【跃升】yuèshēng〈动〉 jump: 公司排名已～至第三。 The company's ranking has leapt to the third place.

【跃跃欲试】yuèyuè-yùshì〈成〉 itch to have a go: 选手们个个～，来一个精彩的表演。 All the contestants were itching to give a good performance.

【跃增】yuèzēng〈动〉 grow by leaps and bounds: 年收入由三万元～到六万元。 The annual income leapt from 30,000 to 60,000 *yuan*.

越[1] yuè

A〈动〉 **1**（跨过） jump over: ～境逃跑 flee across the border ▸～过, 超～, 跨～ **2**（度过） go through: ▸～冬, 穿～ **3**（超出） exceed: ▸～级, ～权, ～俎代庖 **4**（昂扬） be at high pitch: ▸清～ **5**〈书〉（抢夺） plunder: 杀人～货 rob and kill

B〈形〉 superior: ▸优～, 卓～

C〈副〉 the more ... the more ...: ～多～好 the more the better ‖ 脑子～用～灵。 The more you use your brain, the keener it will become. ‖ 他～讲～起劲。 The more he talked the more confidence he gained.

越[2] Yuè

〈名〉 **1**（指国名） Yue [state in the Zhou Dynasty] **2**（浙江东部） eastern Zhejiang: ▸～剧 **3**（越南） Vietnam: ～战 Vietnam War

【越冬】yuèdōng〈动〉 survive the winter: ～作物 winter crop

【越发】yuèfā〈副〉 **1**（表程度加深） more and more: 工作～努力了 work even harder ‖ 天气～地冷了。 The weather is getting colder and colder. **2**（与前文呼应） the more ... the more ...: 越是紧张，就～容易出错。 The more nervous you are, the more likely you are to make mistakes.

【越轨】yuèguǐ〈动〉 transgress: ～行为 transgression ‖ 不要做～的事情。 Be careful not to overstep the bounds of propriety.

【越过】yuèguò〈动〉 cross: ～边境 cross over the frontier ‖ ～高山 cross high mountains

【越级】yuèjí〈动〉 skip a grade: ～上诉 bypass the immediate leadership and present one's appeals and complaints to higher levels ‖ ～提升 promote sb. more than one grade at a time

【越加】yuèjiā〈副〉 even more: 处境～糟糕 be in increasingly desperate straits

【越界】yuèjiè〈动〉 overstep a boundary

【越境】yuèjìng〈动〉 cross a border illegally: ～的恐怖分子 cross-border terrorists

【越剧】yuèjù〈名〉 Shaoxing opera

【越来越】yuèláiyuè〈副〉 more and more: ～受欢迎 become increasingly popular ‖ 天～黑。 It grows darker and darker.

【越礼】yuèlǐ〈动〉 be indecorous: ～行为 improper conduct

【越南】Yuènán〈名〉 Vietnam: ～人 Vietnamese ‖ ～社会主义共和国 Socialist Republic of Vietnam ‖ ～语 Vietnamese

【越权】yuèquán〈动〉 overstep one's authority: ～行事 overstep one's authority

【越位】yuèwèi **A**〈动〉 overstep one's position **B**〈名〉［体育］ offside: 处于～位置 be in an offside position

【越洋】yuèyáng〈动〉 cross the ocean: 打～电话 talk through transoceanic telephone ‖ ～通信光缆 transoceanic communication optical fibre cable

【越野】yuèyě〈动〉 travel cross-country: ～汽车拉力赛 cross-country rally

【越野车】yuèyěchē〈名〉 cross-country vehicle

【越野赛】yuèyěsài〈名〉 cross-country race

【越野赛跑】yuèyě sàipǎo〈名〉 cross-country running

【越狱】yuèyù〈动〉 escape from prison: ～逃跑 break out of prison ‖ ～犯 escaped prisoner

【越俎代庖】yuèzǔ-dàipáo〈成〉 take sb. else's business into one's own hands: 你不能～。 You must not overstep your position.

粤 Yuè

▸**p. 661**〈名〉 **1**（广东） Yue [another name for Guangdong Province (广东)] **2**（广东和广西） Guangdong and Guangxi: 两～ the two *Yues* [ie Guangdong and Guangxi]

【粤菜】yuècài〈名〉 Cantonese cuisine

【粤剧】yuèjù〈名〉 Cantonese opera

> **粤剧**
>
> Guangdong opera, previously known as Cantonese opera. Popular mostly in Guangdong, Guangxi, Hong Kong and Macao, and sung in Cantonese, its origins date back to the 17th century. Accompanying musical instruments are clappers (梆子), the *gaohu* (高胡), and the two-stringed instrument (二弦). The repertoire comprises more than a 1,000 pieces. Among them are *The Legend of the Purple Hairpin* (《紫钗记》) and *Butterfly and Red Pear and Blossom* (《蝶影红梨记》).

【粤语】Yuèyǔ ▸**p. 918**〈名〉 Cantonese

樾 yuè

〈名〉〈书〉 shade of a tree

龠[1]（籥） yuè

〈名〉〈古〉 short flute

龠[2] yuè

〈量〉〈古〉 unit of capacity [equal to 0.05 litre]

黦 yuè

〈形〉〈书〉 yellowish-black

瀹 yuè

〈动〉〈书〉 **1**（煮） boil: ～茗 make tea **2**（疏通） dredge

yūn

晕（暈） yūn

A〈形〉 dizzy: 头～ dizzy ▸～头转向

B〈动〉 faint: 那个年轻战士在烈日下～了过去。 The young soldier fainted in the hot sun. ‖ 他突然～倒在地。 He suddenly collapsed and passed out on the floor. ▸yùn

【晕厥】yūnjué ▸**p. 50**〈动〉［医学］ faint: 因失血过多而～ faint from excessive loss of blood

【晕头晕脑】yūntóu-yūnnǎo〈形〉 dizzy

【晕头转向】yūntóu-zhuànxiàng〈成〉 be confused and disoriented: 吓得～ be reeling with shock ‖ 生意上的事忙得我～。 Business has been so busy that I feel completely giddy.

【晕眩】yūnxuàn〈动〉 feel dizzy

【晕晕糊糊】yūnyun-hūhū〈形〉 dizzy: 两杯酒下肚他就～了。 Two drinks and he was all over the place.

氲 yūn

▸氤氲 yīnyūn

煴 yūn

〈名〉〈书〉 slow fire ▸yùn

赟（贇） yūn

〈形〉〈书〉 fine

yún

云[1] yún

〈动〉 say: 不知所～ not know what was said ▸人～亦～

云[2]（雲） yún

〈名〉 **1**（指物体） cloud: 晴转多～ fair to cloudy ‖ 朵朵白～ scattered clouds ▸～彩, 乌～ **2** ▸**p. 661** Yún（云南） Yun [another name for Yunnan Province (云南)]: ▸～贵高原

【云板】yúnbǎn〈名〉〈古〉 cloud-shaped iron plates [used as a kind of percussion instrument or in government offices or

influential families to announce the time or an event]
【云豹】yúnbào〈名〉［动物］ clouded leopard
【云鬓】yúnbìn〈名〉〈书〉 cloud-like hair (of a woman)
【云彩】yúncai〈名〉〈口〉 cloud: 天上没有一丝～ be completely cloudless ‖ 洁白的～ fleecy cloud
【云层】yúncéng〈名〉 cloud bank: 厚厚的～ heavy clouds ‖ 飞机仰头爬升穿过～。 The aeroplane climbed up through the clouds.
【云带】yúndài〈名〉［气象］ cloud band
【云端】yúnduān〈名〉 place high in the sky: 飞机从～飞来。 A plane descended through the clouds.
【云朵】yúnduǒ〈名〉 cloud mass: 北风吹散了～。 The north wind puffed away the clouds.
【云岗石窟】Yúngāng Shíkū〈名〉 Yungang caves [in Datong, Shanxi Province]
【云贵高原】Yún-Guì Gāoyuán〈名〉 Yunnan-Guizhou Plateau
【云海】yúnhǎi〈名〉 sea of clouds: ～茫茫 a mass of clouds
【云汉】yúnhàn〈名〉〈书〉 1（银河） Milky Way 2（天空） sky
【云鬟】yúnhuán〈名〉 [of woman's hair] bun
【云集】yúnjí〈动〉 gather: 球星～的足球队 star-studded football team ‖ 各地代表～北京。 Representatives from all over the country gathered in Beijing.
【云际】yúnjì〈名〉 place high in the clouds
【云锦】yúnjǐn〈名〉 cloud-pattern brocade
【云谲波诡】yúnjué-bōguǐ〈成〉 be subject to a myriad of changes
【云量】yúnliàng〈名〉［气象］ cloud cover: ～增加。 The clouds are getting heavier.
【云锣】yúnluó〈名〉 Chinese gong chimes
【云母】yúnmǔ〈名〉［矿业］ mica: ～片 isinglass
【云南】Yúnnán ▸p. 661〈名〉 Yunnan Province
【云南白药】yúnnán báiyào〈名〉 Yunnan white medicinal powder
【云泥之别】yúnnízhībié〈成〉〈喻〉 poles apart
【云霓】yúnní〈名〉 rain clouds
【云片糕】yúnpiàngāo〈名〉 rectangular sweetened rice wafers
【云气】yúnqì〈名〉 thin, floating clouds
【云雀】yúnquè〈名〉 skylark
【云散】yúnsàn〈动〉 disperse like clouds: 旧友～。 Old friends disperse like clouds. ▸烟消～
【云山雾罩】yúnshān-wùzhào〈成〉 1（指云雾） enveloped in mist 2〈喻〉（指说话） rambling: 说话～ talk aimlessly
【云杉】yúnshān〈名〉［植物］ spruce
【云梯】yúntī〈名〉 extension ladder: 架设～ erect an extension ladder ‖ 救火～ fire-fighting ladder
【云天】yúntiān〈名〉〈书〉 skies: 直插～ pierce the clouds ‖ 欢呼声响彻～。 The cheers echoed to the skies.
【云天雾地】yúntiān-wùdì〈成〉 with one's mind in a haze
【云头】yúntóu〈名〉 cloud mass
【云头儿】yúntóur〈名〉 cloud pattern
【云图】yúntú〈名〉［气象］ cloud chart: 卫星～ satellite cloud chart
【云团】yúntuán〈名〉［气象］ cloud cluster
【云吞】yúntūn〈名〉〈方〉 wonton
【云雾】yúnwù〈名〉 cloud and mist: ～缭绕的山峰 cloud-capped peaks ‖ ～笼罩山顶。 Clouds enveloped the hilltop.
【云霞】yúnxiá〈名〉 rose-tinted clouds: ～似锦。 Pink clouds are as beautiful as brocade.
【云消雾散】yúnxiāo-wùsàn〈成〉〈喻〉 vanish into thin air
【云霄】yúnxiāo〈名〉 sky: 响彻～ reverberate across the heavens ‖ 耸入～ tower into the clouds
【云兴霞蔚】yúnxīng-xiáwèi = 云蒸霞蔚 yúnzhēng-xiáwèi
【云崖】yúnyá〈名〉〈书〉 mountain peaks towering into the clouds
【云烟】yúnyān〈名〉 1（云雾和烟气） cloud and mist: ～缭绕 be enveloped in cloud and mist 2（指香烟） cigarettes produced in Yunnan Province 3〈喻〉（易消失的事物） sth. as transient as a floating cloud: 顷刻间化作～ vanish like a floating cloud
【云翳】yúnyì〈名〉 1〈书〉（阴云） dark clouds: 清澄的蓝天没有一点～。 There isn't a cloud in the blue sky. 2［中医］ corneal opacity
【云游】yúnyóu〈动〉 [of a Buddhist monk or a Taoist priest] wander about: ～四方 roam from place to place
【云雨】yúnyǔ〈动〉〈喻〉 make love
【云云】yúnyún〈助〉〈书〉 [used at the end of a quotation implying that words of the same purport are left out] and so on and so forth
【云遮雾障】yúnzhē-wùzhàng〈成〉 enveloped in mist
【云蒸霞蔚】yúnzhēng-xiáwèi〈成〉 glorious

匀 yún

A〈形〉 even: 在面包上把黄油涂～ spread butter evenly over the toast ‖ 鸡蛋的大小不～。 Eggs are not equal in size. ▸～称, 均～
B〈动〉 1（使均匀） even up: 把…～成几份 divide sth. into equal shares 2（抽出） spare: ～一些时间 spare some time ‖ 你能～一张票给我吗? Can you spare an extra ticket for me?
【匀称】yúnchèn〈形〉 well-proportioned: 身段～ be well-proportioned in stature ‖ 字写得～ write a neat hand
【匀兑】yúndui〈动〉〈口〉 spare: ～给某人一些钱 spare sb. some money
【匀和】yúnhuo〈口〉 A〈形〉 even: ～地呼吸 breathe evenly B〈动〉 even: 把苹果～了再分 divide the apples into even shares before distributing them
【匀净】yúnjing〈形〉 equal: 线纺得很～。 The threads have been woven very evenly.
【匀脸】yúnliǎn〈动〉 apply make-up evenly on one's face
【匀溜】yúnliu〈形〉〈口〉 even
【匀实】yúnshi〈形〉〈口〉 even: 麦苗出得很～。 The wheat sprouts are growing very evenly.
【匀速运动】yúnsù yùndòng〈名〉 uniform motion
【匀停】yúnting〈形〉〈方〉 of the right amount: 盐要放得～。 Add salt to taste.
【匀细】yúnxì〈形〉 even and fine: ～的鼾声 even and light snoring
【匀整】yúnzhěng〈形〉 even and orderly: ～的牙齿 even teeth ‖ 他字写得～。 He has very neat handwriting.

芸[1] yún = 芸香 yúnxiāng

芸[2]（蕓） yún ▸芸薹 yúntái

【芸豆】yúndòu〈名〉 kidney bean
【芸薹】yúntái〈名〉［植物］ rape
【芸香】yúnxiāng〈名〉［植物］ rue
【芸芸】yúnyún〈形〉〈书〉 innumerable
【芸芸众生】yúnyún-zhòngshēng〈成〉 all living things

沄[1] yún

【沄沄】yúnyún〈形〉〈书〉 flowing

沄[2]（澐） yún〈名〉〈书〉 great billowing waves

纭（紜） yún 1 ▸纷纭 fēnyún 2 ▸纭纭 yúnyún

【纭纭】yúnyún〈形〉 numerous and disorderly

昀 yún〈名〉〈书〉 sunlight

畇 yún

【畇畇】yúnyún〈形〉〈书〉 [of fields] neatly arranged

耘 yún〈动〉 weed: ～田 weed the fields ▸耕～

【耘锄】yúnchú〈名〉 hoe

筠 yún〈名〉〈书〉 1（竹子的青皮） skin of a bamboo 2（竹子） bamboo

篔（篔） yún

【篔筜】yúndāng〈名〉〈书〉 tall bamboo growing by the waterside

鋆 yún〈名〉〈书〉 gold

yǔn

允[1] yǔn〈动〉 allow: ▸～诺, ～许, 应～

允[2] yǔn〈形〉 fair: ▸公～, 平～

【允当】yǔndàng〈形〉 proper: 赏罚～ be fair in meting out rewards and punishments
【允诺】yǔnnuò〈动〉 promise: 兑现～ fulfil one's promise ‖ 欣然～ readily agree ‖ 已经～的事, 不可反悔。 Once you've promised something, you can never go back on your word.
【允许】yǔnxǔ〈动〉 allow: ～某人做某事 give sb. permission to do sth. ‖ 不得到领导的～, 你不能走。 You can't go without the permission of the leaders. ‖ 如果时间～, 我们会来看你的。 If we have enough time, we'll come and see you.
【允准】yǔnzhǔn〈动〉 approve: 我父母勉强～了这门婚事。 My parents reluctantly assented to the marriage.

陨（隕） yǔn〈动〉 fall from the sky or outer space: ▸～落, ～石

【陨落】yǔnluò〈动〉 1（从高空掉下） [of a meteorite, etc.] fall from the sky or outer space 2〈敬〉（过逝） pass away
【陨灭】yǔnmiè〈动〉 1（从高空掉下而毁灭） fall from outer space and burn up 2〈书〉（丧命） perish
【陨石】yǔnshí〈名〉［天文］ aerolite: ～雨 meteorite shower
【陨铁】yǔntiě〈名〉 meteoric iron
【陨星】yǔnxīng〈名〉 meteorite: 石～ aerolite ‖ 铁～ siderite

殒（殞） yǔn〈动〉perish: ▸～灭

【殒灭】yǔnmiè = 陨灭 yǔnmiè

【殒命】yǔnmìng〈动〉〈书〉perish: ～沙场 fall in battle

【殒没】yǔnmò〈动〉pass away

【殒身】yǔnshēn〈动〉〈书〉be killed

yùn

孕 yùn

A〈动〉be pregnant: 治疗不～不育症 cure infertility ▸～妇, ～育

B〈名〉fetus: 有～在身 be having a baby ▸避～, 怀～

【孕畜】yùnchù〈名〉pregnant domestic animal

【孕妇】yùnfù〈名〉pregnant woman: 把座位让给～ give up one's seat to a pregnant woman

【孕妇装】yùnfùzhuāng〈名〉maternity dress

【孕检】yùnjiǎn〈名〉pregnancy examination

【孕期】yùnqī〈名〉[医学] pregnancy: ～保健 antenatal care ‖ 妇女在～内不能服用这些药物。 These drugs should not be taken during pregnancy.

【孕穗】yùnsuì〈名〉[农业] booting [emergence of ear of grain]

【孕酮】yùntóng〈名〉[生化] progesterone

【孕吐】yùntù〈动〉[医学] have morning sickness

【孕育】yùnyù〈动〉**1**〈本〉give birth to: 她做过节育手术，不能再～。 She has already been sterilized and so can't have children again. **2**〈喻〉breed: ～新思想 breed new ideas ‖ 违规操作～着许多危险因素。 Doing things against the rules can give rise to danger.

贠 Yùn〈名〉Yun [surname]

运（運） yùn

A〈动〉**1**（运动）move: ▸～动, ～行, ～转 **2**（运送）carry: ～货 transport goods ‖ ～煤专线 new railway lines for the specific purpose of transporting coal ▸～输, 空～ **3**（使用）utilize: ～针 manipulate an acupuncture needle ▸～笔, ～思, ～用

B〈名〉destiny: 祝你好～。 Good luck to you. ▸～气, 命～, 时来～转

【运笔】yùnbǐ〈动〉wield one's pen: ～如飞 be quick in writing ‖ 书法之道在于～。 The art of calligraphy lies in the moving of the brush.

【运钞车】yùnchāochē〈名〉armoured bank vehicle

【运筹】yùnchóu〈动〉plan

【运筹帷幄】yùnchóu-wéiwò〈成〉devise a campaign strategy: ～之中，决胜千里之外 sit in a command tent and devise strategies that will assure victory a thousand *li* away

【运筹学】yùnchóuxué〈名〉operations research

【运单】yùndān〈名〉bill of freight

【运道】yùndao〈名〉〈方〉luck: 我～真好/不好。 My luck's in/out.

【运动】yùndòng〈名〉**1**[物理] motion: 加速～ accelerated motion ‖ 圆周～ circular motion **2**[哲学] motion: ～是物质存在的形式。 Motion is the physical manifestation of matter. **3** ▸**p. 909** [体育] sports: 爱好体育～ enjoy physical exercise ‖ 球类～ ball games ‖ 全身～ full body exercise **4**（社会政治） movement: 工人～ labour movement ‖ 群众～ mass campaign ‖ 1919年的"五四"～ the 'May 4th' Movement of 1919

【运动场】yùndòngchǎng〈名〉sports ground

【运动创伤】yùndòng chuāngshāng〈名〉sports injury

【运动定律】yùndòng dìnglǜ〈名〉[物理] laws of motion

【运动服】yùndòngfú〈名〉sportswear

【运动会】yùndònghuì〈名〉sports meet: 城市～ city sports meet ‖ 世界大学生～ World University Games ▸奥林匹克～

【运动技巧】yùndòng jìqiǎo〈名〉sporting skills

【运动健儿】yùndòng jiàn'ér〈名〉sporting hero

【运动健将】yùndòng jiànjiàng〈名〉sports master

【运动量】yùndòngliàng〈名〉[体育] workout: 大～ intense workout

【运动衫】yùndòngshān〈名〉sports/gym shirt

【运动神经】yùndòng shénjīng〈名〉motor nerve

【运动项目】yùndòng xiàngmù〈名〉sporting events

【运动鞋】yùndòngxié〈名〉sports shoes

【运动型多用途车】yùndòngxíng duōyòngtúchē〈名〉sports utility vehicle (SUV)

【运动衣】yùndòngyī〈名〉athletic suit

【运动医学】yùndòng yīxué〈名〉sports medicine

【运动饮料】yùndòng yǐnliào〈名〉sports drink

【运动员】yùndòngyuán〈名〉athlete: 为～呐喊助威 cheer players ‖ 长跑～ long-distance runner ‖ 举重～ weightlifter ‖ 田径～ track and field athletes

【运动战】yùndòngzhàn〈名〉mobile warfare

【运动】yùndong〈动〉〈贬〉pull strings to meet one's objectives: ～有关部门 canvass support from the authorities

【运费】yùnfèi〈名〉freight: 付～ pay freight ‖ 降低～ reduce the freight

【运河】yùnhé〈名〉canal: 开凿～ dig a canal

【运价】yùnjià〈名〉freight charge

【运斤成风】yùnjīn-chéngfēng〈成〉〈喻〉be extremely skilled

【运力】yùnlì〈名〉transport capacity: 安排～ arrange for transportation ‖ 提高～ improve transportation

【运气】yùnqì〈动〉direct one's energy, through concentration, to a part of the body

【运气】yùnqi **A**〈名〉luck: 碰碰～ try one's luck ‖ ～好/坏 have good/bad luck **B**〈形〉fortune: 天没下雨，真算我们～。 It was our good fortune that it did not rain.

【运球】yùnqiú〈动〉[篮球] dribble

【运输】yùnshū〈动〉transport: 安排～事宜 arrange for transportation ‖ 长距离～ long-haul transport ‖ 空中/陆路/水上～ air/land/water transportation

【运输车辆】yùnshū chēliàng〈名〉transport vehicle

【运输成本】yùnshū chéngběn〈名〉transport cost

【运输费用】yùnshū fèiyong〈名〉freight

【运输机】yùnshūjī〈名〉freight plane: 一架C-130型军用～ a C-130 military transport

【运输舰】yùnshūjiàn〈名〉[军事] naval cargo ship

【运输网】yùnshūwǎng〈名〉transport network

【运输线】yùnshūxiàn〈名〉transportation line: 开辟～ open a line ‖ 切断～ cut off the line of transportation

【运数】yùnshù〈名〉fate: ～已尽 be nearing its fated end

【运思】yùnsī〈动〉[in writing poetry] conceive an idea: ～奇巧 clever ideas

【运送】yùnsòng〈动〉transport: ～乘/旅客 carry/haul passengers ‖ ～救灾物资 transport disaster relief goods

【运算】yùnsuàn〈动〉[数学] perform calculations: 四则～ four fundamental operations of arithmetic ‖ 计算机的～速度 the computer's operating speed

【运算符号】yùnsuàn fúhào〈名〉operational symbol

【运销】yùnxiāo〈动〉be transported for sale: ～东南亚 transport for sale in South-east Asia

【运行】yùnxíng〈动〉**1**（指星球、车船等）be in motion: 绕地球轨道～ orbit round the earth ‖ 列车～时刻表 train schedule ‖ 地球围绕太阳～。 The earth moves round the sun. ‖〈喻〉建立新的～机制 set up a new operating mechanism **2**（指电脑） run: 在DOS系统下～ run in DOS mode

【运营】yùnyíng〈动〉**1**（指车船） run: 减少～成本 reduce running costs ‖ 这条铁路已开始～。 The railway line has commenced operations. **2**〈喻〉（指机构） operate effectively: 企业低效率的～状况必须改变。 The inefficient management of the enterprise must be overhauled.

【运营官】yùnyíngguān ▸**p. 966**〈名〉operating officer: 首席～ chief operating officer

【运营商】yùnyíngshāng〈名〉operator

【运用】yùnyòng〈动〉utilize: ～法律 apply the law ‖ ～技术 employ a technique ‖ 灵活～ apply in a flexible way ‖ 把理论～到实践中去 apply theory to practice

【运用自如】yùnyòng-zìrú〈成〉handle very skilfully: ～地操作电脑 operate the computer with ease

【运载】yùnzài〈动〉convey: ～货物 carry goods ‖ ～工具 means of delivery

【运载火箭】yùnzài huǒjiàn〈名〉freight rocket

【运转】yùnzhuǎn〈动〉**1**（沿轨道运行） revolve: 卫星绕着各自的行星～。 Satellites revolve around their planets. **2**（机器转动） operate: 在～中 in use ‖ 发动机～正常。 The motor runs well. **3**〈喻〉（组织机构运行） operate: 经济～水平 level of economic activity ‖ 大部分人不了解证券交易所的～情况。 The workings of the Stock Exchange are beyond most people's understanding.

【运作】yùnzuò〈动〉operate: 影响经济～ affect the performance of the economy ‖ 市场～ market operations

郓（鄆） Yùn〈名〉Yun [surname]

恽（惲） Yùn〈名〉Yun [surname]

晕（暈） yùn

A〈名〉**1**[天文] halo: ▸日～, 月～ **2**（指模糊部分） halo around colour or light: 墨～ running ink ‖ 她脸上泛起一层红～。 A blush crept over her face.

B〈动〉be dizzy: 有点头～ be giddy ‖ 她一

y

坐汽车/一喝酒就～。 Whenever she gets in a car/has a drink, she feels sick. ►～车，～针
►yūn

【晕场】yùnchǎng〈动〉 1（指在舞台上）have stage fright 2（指在考场） have a phobia about exams

【晕车】yùnchē〈动〉 be carsick

【晕车药】 yùnchēyào 〈名〉 carsickness tablet

【晕船】yùnchuán〈动〉 get seasick

【晕海宁】 yùnhǎiníng 〈名〉 ［药学］ dimenhydrinate

【晕机】yùnjī〈动〉 have airsickness

【晕针】yùnzhēn〈动〉 have a fainting spell during acupuncture or after receiving an injection

酝（醞）yùn

A〈动〉（指葡萄酒） ferment; （指啤酒） brew: ►～酿

B〈名〉 wine: 佳～ good wine

【酝酿】yùnniàng〈动〉 1（指发酵） brew 2〈喻〉（做准备工作） be in the making: ～候选人名单 mull over the list of candidates ‖ 他那本书～了20年。 His book was 20 years in the making. ‖ 我们的计划才开始～。 Our plans are very much in the embryonic stage.

愠 yùn〈动〉〈书〉 be angry

【愠怒】yùnnù〈动〉 be angry on the inside

【愠色】yùnsè〈名〉〈书〉 angry countenance: 面有～ wear an angry look

组（緼） yùn 〈名〉〈书〉 coarse hemp

韫（韞） yùn〈动〉〈书〉 hide sth. away: ～椟而藏 be hidden away in a casket

韵（韻） yùn〈名〉 1〈书〉（好听的声音） sweet music 2（韵母） final sound of a Chinese syllable: ►～脚，～律，押～ 3（情趣） appeal: ►～致，风～

【韵白】yùnbái〈名〉 1（指京剧中）spoken parts in Beijing opera where the traditional pronunciation of certain words is slightly different from that in current Beijing dialect 2（指戏曲中） rhythmical parts in Chinese traditional play

【韵调】 yùndiào 〈名〉 tone: ～优美 be sweet-toned ‖ ～悠扬 be melodious

【韵腹】yùnfù〈名〉［语言］ essential vowel in a compound vowel in Chinese

【韵脚】yùnjiǎo〈名〉［语言］rhyming word that ends a line of verse

【韵律】yùnlǜ〈名〉［语言］ rhyme scheme: 和谐的～ harmonious rhythms ‖ 诗句～严谨。 The verses have a good rhythm.

【韵律体操】 yùnlǜ tǐcāo 〈名〉 rhythmic gymnastics

【韵母】yùnmǔ〈名〉［语言］simple or compound vowel (of a Chinese syllable), consisting of an essential vowel (韵腹) with or without a head vowel (韵头) or a tail vowel (韵尾)

【韵事】yùnshì〈名〉 refined pastime: 风流～ romantic affair

【韵书】yùnshū〈名〉 rhyming dictionary

【韵头】yùntóu = 介音 jièyīn

【韵尾】yùnwěi〈名〉 tail vowel

【韵味】yùnwèi〈名〉 1（意味） quality of musical tone: 她的唱腔很有～。 Her singing has a special pleasing quality about it. 2（情趣） lingering charm: 保持其古朴的～ retain a flavour of ancient simplicity ‖ 那演员即兴插入的诙谐台词给整个演出增添了～。 The actor's witty ad-libs gave the whole performance a lasting appeal.

【韵文】yùnwén〈名〉 verse: 把～改写成散文 transpose the verse into prose

【韵语】yùnyǔ〈名〉 rhymed writing

【韵致】yùnzhì〈名〉 charm: 水仙另有一种淡雅的～。 The narcissus has a quiet beauty of its own.

煴 yùn = 熨 yùn
►yūn

蕴（藴） yùn〈书〉

A〈动〉 accumulate: ►～藏，～含，～藉

B〈名〉 profundity: ►底～

【蕴藏】yùncáng〈动〉 hold in store: 海底～着丰富的矿物。 The seabed is rich in buried minerals. ‖ 群众中～着极大的工作热情。 There is great enthusiasm for work among the masses.

【蕴藏量】yùncángliàng〈名〉 reserves

【蕴含】yùnhán = 蕴涵 yùnhán A

【蕴涵】yùnhán A〈动〉 contain: ～着深刻的哲理 contain a profound philosophy B〈名〉［逻辑］ implication

【蕴结】yùnjié〈形〉 pent-up

【蕴藉】 yùnjiè 〈形〉〈书〉 cultured and restrained: ～的微笑 bland smile

【蕴蓄】yùnxù〈动〉 be latent: 他从不向别人倾诉～在心底的感情。 He never revealed his innermost feelings to others.

熨 yùn〈动〉 iron: ～衣服 do the ironing
►yù

【熨斗】yùndǒu〈名〉 iron: 电～ electric iron ‖ 蒸汽～ steam iron

【熨烫】yùntàng〈动〉 iron and press: ～衣服 iron clothes

【熨衣板】yùnyībǎn〈名〉 ironing board

Zz

zā

扎（紮、紥） zā
A〈动〉tie: ～辫子 plait hair ‖ ～裤脚 tie up trouser legs ‖ ～领带 tie a tie ‖ ～上围裙 tie on an apron ‖ ～头发 tie up one's hair ‖ ～鞋带 do up shoelaces ‖ 把书～成捆 tie sth. up in bundles ‖ ～紧 fasten securely ‖ 他腰里～着一条皮带。 A leather belt is fastened around his waist. ▸包～，捆～
B〈量〉〈方〉bundle: 一～钞票 a bundle of bank notes ‖ 一～干草 a bundle of hay ▸zhā, zhá
【扎染】zārǎn〈动〉［纺织］tie-dye: ～布 tie-dyed cloth ‖ ～牛仔裤 tie-dyed jeans

匝 zā〈书〉
A〈量〉circle: 绕树两～ circle the tree twice
B〈形〉dense: ▸～地
【匝道】zādào〈名〉〈书〉ring road
【匝地】zādì〈动〉〈书〉be all over the ground: 绿阴～。 The trees cast their shadows over the ground.

咂 zā〈动〉**1**（用嘴吸）suck: ～口茶/酒 take a sip of tea/wine ‖ 妈妈叫儿子不要～手指。 The mother told the boy not to suck his fingers. **2**〈口〉（辨别）savour: ～～汤的味道 taste the soup ▸～摸 **3**（表赞赏）click one's tongue in admiration: ▸～舌，～嘴
【咂摸】zāmo〈动〉〈口〉savour: ～着酒 taste the wine ‖ 你再～～他这话是什么意思。 You should have a good think about what he meant by his words.
【咂舌】zāshé〈动〉click one's tongue: 开价之高令人～。 The excessiveness of the quote made people gasp.
【咂嘴】zāzuǐ〈动〉click the tongue in admiration

zá

杂（雜） zá
A〈形〉**1**（不纯）miscellaneous: ～而不乱 assorted but not confused ‖ 这里住的人很～。 A motley group of people live here. ▸～技，复～ **2**（额外）extra: ▸～费，～项
B〈动〉mix: 他～在人群中就不会被人认出来了。 No one will spot him once he blends in with the crowd. ‖ 这袋大米中～有一些稗子。 This bag of rice has a bit of barnyard millet in it. ▸掺～，混～，夹～
【杂拌儿】zábànr〈名〉**1**〈本〉mixed sweetmeats: ～糖 assorted sweets **2**〈喻〉hodgepodge: 文学～ literary miscellany
【杂草】zácǎo〈名〉weeds: 拔除～ pull up weeds ‖ ～丛生 overgrown with weeds
【杂处】záchǔ〈动〉[of people from different places] live together
【杂凑】zácòu〈动〉jumble together: 将几个场面～成一出话剧 knock a few scenes together to make a play
【杂费】záfèi〈名〉**1**（正项以外的收费）miscellaneous expenses: 减少～ cut down on miscellaneous expenses **2**（特指学校收取的杂项费用）extra expenses: 学～ tuition fees and additional expenses
【杂感】zágǎn〈名〉**1**（指感想）random thoughts **2**（指文体）literary genre recording random thoughts and impressions
【杂工】zágōng〈名〉handyman: 当～ do odd jobs
【杂烩】záhuì〈名〉**1**（指菜）mixed stew **2**〈喻〉（指事物）hodgepodge: 这台晚会是个大～。 This evening party was a real mixture of things.
【杂活儿】záhuór〈名〉odd jobs: 靠干～赚些零用钱 earn some pocket money by doing odd jobs
【杂货】záhuò〈名〉sundry goods: 日用～ various household supplies
【杂货店】záhuòdiàn〈名〉general store: 食品～ grocery store, grocer's〈英〉
【杂货铺】záhuòpù = 杂货店 záhuòdiàn
【杂货商】záhuòshāng〈名〉grocer
【杂和菜】záhuocài〈名〉mixed stew
【杂和面儿】záhuomiànr〈名〉maize flour mixed with a small quantity of soya bean flour
【杂记】zájì〈名〉**1**（指文体）miscellanies **2**（指笔记）jottings
【杂技】zájì〈名〉acrobatics: ～表演 acrobatic show/performance ‖ ～演员 acrobat

> **杂技**
> Chinese acrobatics originated about 2,500 years ago, and matured in the Western Han Dynasty. Performances include plate-spinning, juggling parasols or benches with the feet, ventriloquism, trick-cycling, tightrope walking, and sometimes magic tricks, performances on horseback, and stunts with animals.

【杂技团】zájìtuán〈名〉acrobatic troupe
【杂家】zájiā〈名〉**1**（指学派）Eclectics [school of thought flourishing at the end of China's Warring States Period and the beginning of the Han Dynasty] **2**（指人）jack of all trades
【杂交】zájiāo〈动〉［生物］cross-breed: 将马与驴～ cross a horse with a donkey ‖ ～水稻 hybrid rice ▸无性～，有性～
【杂交品种】zájiāo pǐnzhǒng〈名〉cross-breed
【杂交种】zájiāozhǒng〈名〉hybrid
【杂居】zájū〈动〉[of people of two or more ethnic groups] live together: 多个民族～地区 area inhabited by several ethnic groups
【杂剧】zájù〈名〉*zaju* [poetic drama flourishing in the Yuan Dynasty]
【杂粮】záliáng〈名〉coarse food grains [such as maize, sorghum, oat, etc.]: 五谷～ various food crops
【杂乱】záluàn〈形〉disorderly: 桌子上～地堆着书籍、报纸和文件。 Books, newspapers and documents were jumbled up on the table.
【杂乱无章】záluàn-wúzhāng〈成〉confused and disorderly: 整个工程规划得～，毫无总体布局。 The project was set up in a rather haphazard way, with no overall structure.
【杂面】zámiàn〈名〉**1**（指面粉）flour made from various coarse cereals and beans **2**（指面条）noodles made of such flour
【杂木】zámù〈名〉［林业］weed tree: ～林 weed tree forest
【杂念】zániàn〈名〉distracting thoughts: 摒除～ banish distracting thoughts from one's mind ‖ 私心～ selfish motives and personal considerations
【杂牌】zápái〈形〉inferior brand: ～货 goods of inferior brand ‖ ～军 miscellaneous troops
【杂品】zápǐn〈名〉sundry goods: 家用～ household sundries
【杂七杂八】záqī-zábā〈成〉miscellaneous: 阁楼里堆满了～的东西。 The attic was filled with all kinds of objects. ‖ 他收集了一些～的工具。 He has a collection of miscellaneous tools.
【杂糅】záróu〈动〉mix: 古今～ a mixture of the ancient and the modern
【杂色】zásè〈名〉variegation
【杂食】záshí **A**〈形〉omnivorous: ～动物 omnivore ‖ ～性 omnivory **B** = 零食 língshí
【杂史】záshǐ〈名〉unofficial history
【杂事】záshì〈名〉trivialities: ～缠身 be hassled by small things
【杂书】záshū〈名〉**1**（指与科举考试无关）books not directly related to the subjects of the imperial examination (in feudal China) **2**（指与专业无关）books not directly concerned with one's profession or speciality: 好好用功，别净看～。 Work hard. Don't read books which have no relation to your study.
【杂耍】záshuǎ〈名〉variety show: ～表演 variety show ‖ ～演员 juggler
【杂税】záshuì〈名〉sundry taxes: ▸苛捐～
【杂说】záshuō〈名〉**1**（指说法）varying accounts: 到目前为止对这场事故的起因～不一。 So far there have been different versions of the cause of the accident. **2**〈书〉（指文章）fragmentary argumentation **3**〈书〉（指学说）unorthodox doctrines
【杂碎】zásui〈名〉chopped beef or mutton entrails: 鸡～ chicken giblets ‖ 牛/猪～ chopped beef/pork entrails ‖ 羊～ mutton entrails

【杂沓】zátà〈形〉numerous and disorderly: ～的脚步声 clatter of footsteps
【杂谈】zátán〈名〉[often used in book titles] random talk
【杂文】záwén〈名〉essay: ～集 collection of essays ‖ ～作家 essayist
【杂务】záwù〈名〉odd jobs: 日常～ day-to-day chores
【杂物】záwù〈名〉odds and ends: 堆放～ stack up miscellaneous items
【杂项】záxiàng〈名〉miscellaneous items: ～开支 miscellaneous expenses
【杂役】záyì〈名〉〈旧〉1（指工作）odd jobs 2（指人）handyman
【杂音】záyīn〈名〉1（噪音）noise 2 ▸ p. 50［医学］murmur: 心脏～ heart murmur 3［电气］static
【杂院儿】záyuànr〈名〉compound shared by many different households
【杂症】zázhèng〈名〉［中医］internal diseases other than those caused by exogenous evils
【杂志】zázhì〈名〉1（期刊）magazine: 订阅～ subscribe to a magazine ‖ 科学～ scientific journal ‖ 时装/文学～ fashion/literary magazine ‖ 《生活》～ *Life* magazine 2（杂记）[often used in book titles] miscellaneous notes
【杂质】zázhì〈名〉impurity: 清除水中的～ remove impurities in the water
【杂种】zázhǒng〈名〉1［生物］crossbreed: 骡子是马和驴交配而生的～。A mule is a cross between a horse and a donkey. 2〈粗〉（用于骂人）bastard〈粗〉
【杂字】zázì〈名〉[often used in book titles] collection of daily-used characters

咱 zá
▸ zán
【咱家】zájiā〈代〉I, me

砸 zá〈动〉1（撞击）tamp: ～核桃 crack walnuts ‖ 把地基～实 tamp the foundations solid ‖ 他被山上掉下来的石头～伤了。He was injured by a rock falling from the hill. 2（打破）smash: ～玻璃 smash the glass ‖ 杯子掉在地上～了。The cup dropped onto the floor and smashed. ▸ ～饭碗 3〈口〉（失败）flop: 考～了 flunk an examination ‖ 都是我不好，把事情搞～了。I am to blame; I bungled the whole thing. ‖ 戏彻底演～了。The performance was a complete flop.
【砸饭碗】zá fànwǎn〈惯〉〈喻〉lose one's job
【砸锅】záguō〈动〉〈口〉〈喻〉bungle: 让他去办这事儿，准～。If you let him do the job, he'll certainly spoil everything.
【砸锅卖铁】záguō-màitiě〈成〉〈喻〉be ready to give away all one has: 我就是～也要帮你。I'll help you even if I have to spend my last penny.
【砸牌子】zá páizi〈惯〉〈喻〉ruin the reputation of a brand/producer

zǎ

咋 zǎ〈代〉〈方〉how, why: ～办? What's to be done? ‖ ～样? How do you like it? ‖ 你～说我～办。I'll do as you say.
▸ zé, zhā
【咋个】zǎge〈代〉〈方〉how come: 你今天～没上班? Why didn't you go to work today?

zāi

灾（災） zāi〈名〉1（灾害）disaster: 遭水～ suffer a flood ‖ ～后重建工作 disaster rehabilitation work ▸ ～区, 防～ 2（个人不幸）personal misfortune: 没病没～ suffer from neither illness nor mishap ‖ 她这一生多～多难。She suffered one misfortune after another throughout her life.
【灾变】zāibiàn〈名〉catastrophe: 提高应付各种～的能力 raise the ability of coping with all kinds of natural disasters
【灾害】zāihài〈名〉disaster: ～防治 disaster prevention ‖ 洪水造成了巨大的～。The floods created havoc. ▸ 自然～
【灾患】zāihuàn〈名〉calamity: 屡经～ suffer calamity after calamity
【灾荒】zāihuāng〈名〉famine caused by drought or flood: 死于～ die of famine ‖ 一些地区经常闹～。Some areas still suffer regularly from famine.
【灾祸】zāihuò〈名〉disaster: 一场～ a disaster ‖ 防止～ avoid catastrophe ‖ 逃避～ escape misfortune ‖ 招致～ court disaster ‖ ～临头。A great disaster is imminent.
【灾民】zāimín〈名〉disaster victims: 救济～ provide relief to disaster victims
【灾难】zāinàn〈名〉disaster:（给人民）带来～ bring suffering (to the people) ‖ 遭受～ suffer a disaster ‖ ～降临 disaster strikes ‖ ～深重 catastrophic
【灾难片】zāinànpiàn〈名〉disaster film
【灾年】zāinián〈名〉famine year
【灾情】zāiqíng〈名〉damage caused by a natural disaster: ～严重。The situation in the disaster area is serious.
【灾区】zāiqū〈名〉disaster area: 支援～ send relief to a disaster area ‖ 地震～ earthquake-stricken area ‖ 重～ severely afflicted area
【灾星】zāixīng〈名〉1〈本〉unlucky star 2〈喻〉（指运气）ill luck 3〈喻〉（指人或事物）bane
【灾殃】zāiyāng〈名〉〈书〉disaster
【灾异】zāiyì〈名〉natural calamities and unusual natural phenomena

甾 zāi〈名〉［生化］steroid

哉 zāi〈助〉〈书〉1（表感叹）[used in exclamations]: 快～此风! How refreshing the breeze is! ‖ 难矣～! It's really difficult. ▸ 呜呼哀～ 2（表疑问或反诘）[used with an interrogative word in asking a question or making a retort]: 何足道～! It's not worth mentioning. ‖ 有何难～? What's so difficult about it?

栽 zāi
A〈动〉1（种植）plant: ～花 grow flowers ‖ 沿公路～了两行树。Two rows of trees are planted along the highway. ▸ ～秧, ～种, 移～ 2（插上）stick in: 刷子的毛～得不结实。The bristles of the brush are not stuck in firmly. 3（强加）impose sth. on sb.: ～罪名 fabricate a charge against sb. ▸ ～赃 4（跌倒）fall: ～倒 fall down ‖ 他一头～进沟里。He fell head first into the ditch. ‖ 她从楼梯上～了下来。She tumbled head first down the stairs. 5〈方〉〈喻〉（失败）suffer a setback
B〈名〉seedling: 桃～ peach seedlings ▸ ～子
【栽跟头】zāi gēntou〈动〉1〈本〉fall head first: 我脚下一滑，栽了个跟头。I slipped and fell. 2〈喻〉（失败）come to grief: 他刚愎自用，不听劝告，结果栽了个大跟头。His perverse refusal to take any advice resulted in an awful blunder.
【栽培】zāipéi〈动〉1（种植）cultivate: ～花卉 grow flowers ‖ 果树～ fruit culture ‖ 温室～ hothouse cultivation 2〈喻〉（培养）foster: 感谢恩师的～ thanks to the mentoring of my beloved teacher
【栽绒】zāiróng〈名〉［纺织］tufted fabric
【栽秧】zāiyāng〈动〉transplant seedlings (as of tomatoes or eggplants)
【栽赃】zāizāng〈动〉frame sb.: ～陷害好人 frame good people
【栽植】zāizhí〈动〉plant: ～葡萄 grow grapes ‖ ～树木 plant trees
【栽种】zāizhòng〈动〉plant: ～经济作物 plant cash crops ‖ ～苹果 grow apples
【栽子】zāizi〈名〉seedling: 花～ flower seedling ‖ 树～ sapling

zǎi

仔 zǎi〈名〉1 = 崽 zǎi 2〈方〉（年轻人）young man: 打工～ young labourers ‖ 华～ young Chinese man ▸ 牛～
▸ zī, zǐ

载¹（載） zǎi〈名〉year: 三年五～ three to five years ‖ 数～ several years ▸ 千～难逢, 一年半～

载²（載） zǎi〈动〉write down: ～入史册 be written into the annals of history ▸ 登～, 转～
▸ zài

宰¹ zǎi
A〈名〉minister: 县～ county magistrate ▸ ～相
B〈动〉rule: ▸ 主～

宰² zǎi〈动〉1（杀）slaughter: 杀猪～羊 butcher and sheep ▸ ～杀, 屠～ 2〈口〉〈喻〉（索取高价）rip off: 挨～ get ripped off ‖ 那家旅馆着实把我们～了。They really ripped us off at that hotel. ▸ ～人
【宰割】zǎigē〈动〉〈喻〉invade, oppress and exploit: 我们不能任人～。We shall let no one ride roughshod over us.
【宰客】zǎikè〈动〉rip off
【宰人】zǎirén〈动〉〈喻〉rip off: 九十块钱一小杯咖啡? 真～! Ninety *yuan* for a cup of coffee? What a rip-off!
【宰杀】zǎishā〈动〉slaughter: 禁止随意～耕牛。It is forbidden to slaughter farm cattle at will.
【宰牲节】zǎishēngjié〈名〉［宗教］Korban
【宰相】zǎixiàng〈名〉〈古〉prime minister
【宰相肚里能撑船】zǎixiàng dùli néng chēng chuán〈俗〉be large-hearted

崽 zǎi〈名〉1〈方〉（儿子）son: 他两个～都还小，不能工作。Neither of his two sons are old enough to be working yet. 2（幼崽）young animal: 下～ breed
【崽子】zǎizi〈名〉〈粗〉bastard〈粗〉: ▸ 兔～

zài

再 zài

A〈副〉 **1**（两次） twice: ～拜 bow twice ▸～版，～衰三竭，一而～，～而三 **2**（又） again: ～唱一遍 sing again ‖ ～试一次 try again **3**（再继续） then: 今天就到这里，下次～接着讨论。 So much for today. We'll resume our discussion next time we meet. ▸～见 **4**（然后） only then: 把材料整理好～动笔。 Don't start writing before you have got all your materials together. ‖ 咱们看完节目～走。 Let's stay on until the programme is over. **5**（更加） more: ～多一点儿就好了。 It would be just fine if we could have a little bit more. ‖ 高点儿，～高点儿。 Higher, please. Even higher. **6**（另外） in addition: 院子里种着花，～就是树。 In the yard are planted flowers and also trees. ▸～不然，～则 **7**（引出条件） [used to indicate the continuing of a situation in conditional or suppositional clauses]: 离开车只剩半个钟头了，～不走可赶不上火车了。 There's only half an hour before the train leaves, so we'll miss it unless we get going straight away. ‖ 学习～不努力，就得留级了。 If you don't work harder, you won't make it up to the next grade. **8**（无论） [used in 再…也… followed by a negative expression] no matter how: 你～卖力，也是白搭。 No matter how hard you try, you will never succeed.
B〈动〉 recur: 良机难～。 Opportunity knocks but once. ‖ 青春不～。 One's youth never returns.

【再版】zàibǎn〈动〉 republish: 该书1998年～。 The second edition of the book came out in 1998. ‖ 这本书是～。 The book is a reissue.

【再保险】zàibǎoxiǎn〈动〉 reinsure

【再不】zàibu〈连〉〈口〉 or else: 我本打算让老吴去，～让小李也去。 I meant to send Lao Wu, but we can let Xiao Li go just as well.

【再不然】zàiburán = 再不 zàibu

【再次】zàicì〈副〉 once again: ～申明 reiterate ‖ ～感谢各位的光临。 Thank you once again for coming.

【再度】zàidù〈副〉 once again: ～当选 be re-elected ‖ 谈判～破裂。 The negotiations broke down once again.

【再犯】zàifàn **A**〈动〉 re-offend **B**〈名〉 recidivist

【再分配】zàifēnpèi〈动〉 redistribute

【再会】zàihuì〈动〉 see you again

【再婚】zàihūn〈动〉 remarry: 她～后就搬走了。 She moved to another place after she remarried.

【再加工】zàijiāgōng〈动〉 reprocess

【再嫁】zàijià〈动〉 [of a woman] remarry: 她遵循父母的意愿～了。 She remarried according to her parents' wish.

【再见】zàijiàn〈动〉〈套〉 goodbye

【再教育】zàijiàoyù〈动〉 re-educate: 接受～ be re-educated

【再醮】zàijiào〈动〉〈旧〉 [of a widow] remarry

【再接再厉】zàijiē-zàilì〈成〉 redouble one's efforts

【再就业】zàijiùyè〈动〉 find re-employment: 安置下岗工人～ arrange for the laid-off workers to be re-employed

【再三】zàisān〈副〉 again and again: ～请求 make repeated requests ‖ ～挽留 repeatedly urge sb. to stay ‖ 考虑～ ponder over

【再三再四】zàisān-zàisì〈成〉 over and over again

【再审】zàishěn〈动〉 **1**（重新审查） review **2**［法律］ retry: ～案件 reopen a case

【再生】zàishēng〈动〉 **1**（死而复生） come back to life: 人死不能～。 People who have died cannot be brought back to life. **2**［生物］ regenerate: ～林 regenerated forest ‖ 人体能～毛发。 The human body can regenerate hair. ‖ 蜥蜴的尾巴断后能～。 A lizard can grow a new tail if its tail has been cut off. **3**（循环利用） recycle: ～能源 renewable source of energy ‖ 不可～资源 non-renewable resources ‖ ～塑料 regenerated plastics ‖ ～橡胶 regenerated rubber

【再生父母】zàishēng-fùmǔ〈成〉 one's saviour

【再生纸】zàishēngzhǐ〈名〉 recycled paper

【再生产】zàishēngchǎn〈动〉［经济］ reproduce: 简单～ simple reproduction ‖ 扩大～ expanded reproduction

【再世】zàishì **A**〈名〉 afterlife **B**〈动〉 reincarnate: 华佗～ Hua Tuo reincarnated

【再衰三竭】zàishuāi-sānjié〈成〉 be weakened and demoralized

【再说】zàishuō **A**〈动〉 put off until a later time: 我现在忙得顾不上这事，过几天～。 I am too busy to attend to this matter. Let's put it aside for a couple of days. **B**〈连〉 what's more: 去约他已经来不及了，～他也不一定有工夫。 It's too late to invite him. Besides, he might be too busy to come.

【再投资】zàitóuzī〈动〉 reinvest

【再现】zàixiàn〈动〉 recur: ～辉煌 restore to former glory ‖ 在脑海里～ replay in one's mind

【再造】zàizào〈动〉 **1**（重新给予生命） give sb. a new lease of life: ▸恩同～ **2**（再现） recreate: 希望运动员们～辉煌 expect the athletes to repeat their winning performance

【再造之恩】zàizàozhī'ēn〈成〉 gratitude to sb. who has saved one's life

【再造林】zàizàolín〈动〉 reafforest

【再则】zàizé〈连〉 besides

【再者】zàizhě〈书〉= 再则 zàizé

【再植】zàizhí〈动〉 replant: 断肢～ replantation of a limb

在 zài

A〈动〉 **1**（存在） exist: 精神永～。 The spirit lives forever. ‖ 人～阵地～。 We will defend our position with our lives. ‖ 我父母都～。 Both my parents are still alive. ▸～世，存～ **2**（表位置） be at/in/on: 剩饭～冰箱里。 The leftovers are in the refrigerator. ‖ 我今晚不～家。 I won't be at home this evening. ▸～场，～座 **3**（表职位） be at one's post: ▸～位，～野，～职 **4**（在于） lie in: 贵～坚持。 Persistence is more valuable than anything else. ‖ 事情能不能办成就～你一句好话。 It all depends on whether you are willing to put in a good word for us. ▸～于，事～人为
B〈副〉 [used to indicate an action in progress]: 风～刮，雨～下。 The wind is blowing and the rain keeps falling. ‖ 姐姐～做功课而我～看电视。 My sister is doing her homework while I am watching TV.
C〈介〉 at/in: ～和平共处五项原则的基础上发展同各国的友好关系 develop friendly relations between nations on the basis of the Five Principles of Peaceful Coexistence ‖ ～此期间不得外出。 No going out allowed during this time. ‖ 事情发生～上个月。 It happened last month.

【在案】zài'àn〈动〉 be on record: 记录～ be put on record

【在编】zàibiān〈动〉 be on permanent staff: ～人员 permanent staff ‖ 他已退休，不～了。 He has retired, and so is no longer on staff.

【在册】zàicè〈动〉 be registered: 登记～ get registered ‖ ～职工 registered staff and workers

【在场】zàichǎng〈动〉 be on the scene: 当时～的人都可以作证。 All those who were present can give evidence. ‖ 事故发生时他不～。 He was not on the scene when the accident happened.

【在读】zàidú〈动〉 study at a school or research institute: ～硕士研究生 student pursuing a MA degree

【在岗】zàigǎng〈动〉 be at one's post: ～培训 on-the-job training

【在轨】zàiguǐ〈动〉［航天］ be in orbit: 神舟六号飞船的～运行 the orbiting of the Shenzhou 6 spacecraft

【在行】zàiháng〈动〉 know the ropes: 修电器他很～。 He is an expert at repairing electrical appliances. ‖ 做生意我可不～。 I'm no expert at business.

【在乎】zàihu〈动〉 **1**（在于） lie in: 用具的价值不～好看，而～实用。 The value of a utensil lies in its utility and not its appearance. **2**（介意） care about: 人家怎么说，你可以不～，我可～。 You may not mind about what people say, but I do. ▸满不～

【在即】zàijí〈动〉〈书〉 be imminent: 毕业～ be about to graduate ‖ 锦标赛～。 The tournament is around the corner.

【在家】zàijiā〈动〉 **1**（在家里） be in: ～吃饭 eat in ‖ 我打电话的时候你不～。 You were out when I called. **2**［佛教］ remain a layman

【在家靠父母，出门靠朋友】zàijiā kào fùmǔ, chūmén kào péngyou〈俗〉 when at home, one depends on one's parents, and when away from home, one needs the support of friends

【在建】zàijiàn〈动〉 be under construction: ～工程 ongoing project ‖ 现有两家宾馆～。 There are currently two hotels under construction.

【在教】zàijiào〈动〉〈口〉 **1**（信教） believe in a religion **2**（信伊斯兰教） be a Muslim

【在劫难逃】zàijié-nántáo〈成〉 there is no escaping fate: 他～。 His fate is sealed.

【在理】zàilǐ〈形〉 reasonable: 他这话说得～。 What he said is reasonable.

【在内】zàinèi〈动〉 be included: 我们大家，包括我本人～，都一直献身于教育事业。 All of us, myself included, continue to be committed to the cause of education.

【在聘】zàipìn〈动〉 be employed: ～高级员工 senior staff in employment

【在谱】zàipǔ〈动〉 be sensible: 你看我说的～不～? Do you think what I've said is sensible?

【在任】zàirèn〈动〉 be in office: ～总统 incumbent president

【在世】zàishì〈动〉 be living: 当年的老人～的不多了。 Few of the old people of that time are still alive.

【在所不辞】zàisuǒbùcí〈成〉 will not refuse under any circumstances: 尽管有些冒险，甚至流血牺牲，我也～。 It may be somewhat risky, and may even require my blood or my life, but I will not refuse under any circumstances.

【在所不惜】 zàisuǒbùxī〈成〉 will not grudge: 为了国家利益，即使牺牲生命也～。 In the interest of the country, we will baulk at no sacrifice, not even the loss of our lives.

【在所难免】 zàisuǒnánmiǎn〈成〉 be unavoidable: 错误～，改了就好。 Mistakes are inevitable. They just need to be corrected.

【在逃】zàitáo〈动〉［法律］ be at large: 该案主犯～。 The master criminal is on the run.

【在逃犯】zàitáofàn〈名〉［法律］ fugitive

【在天之灵】zàitiānzhīlíng〈成〉spirit of the deceased: 告慰～ comfort the spirits of the deceased

【在外】zàiwài〈动〉 1（不在家） be away from home: 出门～要多保重。 Take care of yourself while you are away from home. 2（不包括） be excluded: 学费每年5000元，住宿费、伙食费～。 The tuition is 5,000 *yuan* per year, not including room and board.

【在望】zàiwàng〈动〉 1（看得见） be visible: 钟楼隐隐～。 The Bell Tower is dimly visible. 2（即将到来） be in sight: 成功～。 Success is in sight. ‖ 丰收～。 The crops promise a good harvest.

【在位】zàiwèi〈动〉 1（指王位） reign: ～君主 reigning monarch 2（指职位） be in office: 他早已退休，不～了。 He retired a long time ago, and is no longer in post.

【在握】zàiwò〈动〉 be in one's hands: 大权～ with power in one's hands ‖ 成功～ success is within one's grasp

【在下】zàixià〈代〉〈旧〉〈谦〉 I, me: 先生过奖，～实不敢当。You praise is excessive. I don't deserve it at all.

【在先】zàixiān A〈副〉 1（从前） formerly: ～我年纪小，什么事也不明白。 I was very young then and could hardly understand what was happening around me. 2（事先） beforehand: 不论做什么事，～都要有个准备。 Whatever you do, be sure to be prepared in advance. B〈动〉 be in advance: 有言～ make clear in advance ‖ 犯规～，进球无效。 The foul was called in advance, so the goal didn't count.

【在线】 zàixiàn〈动〉 1［计算机］ be online: ～操作/处理 online operation/processing 2（在系统控制中） be controlled by a certain system

【在心】zàixīn〈动〉 care: 你说什么，他都不～。 He won't care, whatever you say.

【在押】zàiyā〈动〉［法律］ be in custody: ～人员 persons in custody ‖ ～犯 criminal in custody

【在野】zàiyě〈动〉 be out of office: ～党 opposition party

【在业】zàiyè〈动〉 be employed: ～工人 employed workers

【在意】zàiyì〈动〉 care about: 很～细节 care much about details ‖ 一点也不～ not mind in the slightest ‖ 这些小事他是不～的。 He won't take such trifles to heart.

【在于】zàiyú〈动〉 1（就是） lie in: 幸福～知足。 Happiness lies in contentment. 2（决定于） rest with: 去不去～你。 It's up to you to decide whether to go or not.

【在在】zàizài〈副〉〈书〉 everywhere: ～皆是 can be seen everywhere

【在职】zàizhí〈动〉 be at one's post: ～干部 cadre in active service ‖ ～研究生 on-the-job postgraduate

【在职培训】zàizhí péixùn〈名〉 on-the-job training: 接受～ receive on-the-job training

【在座】zàizuò〈动〉 be present: ～的还有几位知名学者。Among those present were a few renowned scholars.

载[1]（載） zài〈动〉 1（装载） carry: 这辆卡车可～货物三吨。 The truck can carry a load of three tons. ▸～重, 满～而归 2（充满） fill (the road): ▸怨声～道

载[2]（載） zài〈助〉〈书〉 and: ▸～歌～舞
▸zǎi

【载波】zàibō〈名〉［通信］ carrier: ～传输/通信 carrier transmission/communications

【载歌载舞】zàigē-zàiwǔ〈成〉now singing, now dancing: 人们～欢庆大丰收。 Singing and dancing, people celebrated their bumper harvest.

【载荷】zàihè = 负荷 fùhè B

【载饥载渴】 zàijī-zàikě〈成〉 suffer from hunger and thirst

【载客】zàikè〈动〉 carry passengers: 该车可～12人。 The bus carries up to 12 passengers.

【载客量】zàikèliàng〈名〉carrying capacity

【载频】 zàipín〈名〉［通信］ carrier frequency

【载人】 zàirén〈动〉 be manned: ～飞船 manned spaceship ‖ ～航天飞行 manned space flight

【载人卫星】zàirén wèixīng〈名〉 manned satellite

【载体】zàitǐ〈名〉 carrier: 催化剂～ catalyst carrier ‖ 语言文字是文化的～。Language is the purveyor of culture.

【载誉】zàiyù〈动〉 be loaded with honours: ～归来 return with great honour

【载运】zàiyùn〈动〉 carry: ～量 carrying capacity ‖ 这架飞机能～400多位乘客。 This plane can carry over 400 passengers.

【载重】zàizhòng〈动〉 have a carrying capacity: ～汽车 lorry ‖ 这辆卡车～两吨。 This truck can carry a load of 2 tons.

儎（儎） zài〈名〉 load: 过～ overload ‖ 卸～ unload

zān

糌 zān

【糌粑】zānba〈名〉 *zanba* [roasted highland barley flour, a Tibetan staple]

簪 zān

A〈名〉 hairpin: 扁～ flat hairpin ‖ 金/银/玉～ gold/silver/jade hairpin

B〈动〉 wear in one's hair: ～花 wear flowers in one's hair

【簪子】zānzi〈名〉 hairpin

zán

咱 zán〈代〉 1〈口〉（我们）（作主语） we;（作宾语） us: ～班 our class ‖ ～是从一个村儿出来的。 We're from the same village. ‖～走吧。 Let's go. 2〈方〉（我）（作主语） I;（作宾语） me: ～不懂你说什么。 I don't understand what you mean.
▸zá

【咱们】 zánmen〈代〉 1（我们）（作主语） we;（作宾语） us: ～学校 our school ‖ 客气什么，～都是一家人。Please don't be overpolite; we're all one family. 2〈方〉（你） you: ～别哭，妈妈马上就回来。 Don't cry. Mummy will be back in a minute. 3〈方〉（我）（作主语） I;（作宾语） me: 这事儿和～一点儿关系都没有，～不急。 It is none of my business; I'm not worried at all.

zǎn

拶 zǎn〈动〉 press hard: ▸～指

【拶指】zǎnzhǐ〈动〉〈古〉 squeeze a person's fingers between sticks [a torture]

【拶子】zǎnzi〈名〉〈古〉 sticks for squeezing a person's fingers [an instrument of torture]

噆 zǎn〈动〉〈书〉 1（叼） hold in the mouth 2（咬） bite

攒（攢） zǎn〈动〉 accumulate: ～钱 save money ‖ 他把～的钱都捐给了希望工程。 He donated all his savings to Project Hope. ▸积～
▸cuán

趱（趲） zǎn〈动〉 1〈旧〉（赶路） rush through: ～行 hurry on with one's journey 2（快走） urge: ～马向前 urge on a horse

zàn

暂（暫） zàn

A〈形〉 brief: ▸～时, 短～

B〈副〉 temporarily: ～不回复 put off replying ‖ 此事～不处理。 This matter has been put aside for the time being. ‖ 工作～告一段落。 The work has been brought to a temporary close. ▸～停, ～住

【暂定】zàndìng〈动〉 be provisional: 会议～开三天。 The meeting tentatively will last for three days. ‖ 讲座～下周一上午八点举行。 The lecture has been provisionally arranged for 8:00 am next Monday.

【暂缓】zànhuǎn〈动〉 postpone: ～出发 postpone one's departure ‖ 规定～执行 defer the execution of a directive

【暂且】zànqiě〈副〉 for the time being: ～如此 leave it at that ‖ 今天～告一段落吧。 That's all for today.

【暂时】zànshí〈副〉 temporarily: ～的安排 tentative arrangement ‖ 因发生事故车辆～禁止通行。 Passage of vehicles is temporarily suspended owing to an accident.

【暂停】zàntíng A〈动〉 suspend: ～施工 suspend construction ‖ 内部装修，～营业。 Business is suspended for refurbishment. B〈名〉［体育］ time out: 要求～ request a time out

【暂行】zànxíng〈形〉 provisional: ～规定 interim provisions ‖ ～条例 interim regulations

【暂住】zànzhù〈动〉 stay temporarily: ～居民 temporary resident ‖ ～证 temporary residence permit

錾（鏨） zàn

A〈名〉 chisel: ▸～刀, ～子

B〈动〉 carve: ～花 carve flowers ‖ ～字 engrave characters

【錾刀】zàndāo〈名〉 burin

【錾子】zànzi〈名〉 chisel for cutting stone

Z

赞[1]（**贊**） zàn〈动〉**1**（支持） support: ▸～成, ～助, 参～ **2**（协助） assist the master of ceremonies: ▸～礼

赞[2]（**讚**） zàn
A〈动〉 praise: ▸～美, ～扬, 盛～
B〈名〉 eulogy: 像～ inscription eulogizing the subject of a portrait

【赞比亚】Zànbǐyà〈名〉 Zambia: ～人 Zambian

【赞不绝口】zànbùjuékǒu〈成〉 be full of praise

【赞成】zànchéng〈动〉**1**（同意）approve of: 投票～ vote for ‖ ～这项提议的请举手。 Those in favour of this proposal please raise your hands. ‖ 我们大家都不～他的意见。 We all disagree with him. **2**〈书〉（促成） help accomplish: ～其行 help materialize the planned trip

【赞成票】zànchéngpiào〈名〉 affirmative vote

【赞歌】zàngē〈名〉 song of praise: 唱～ sing a song of praise ‖ 英雄～ paean of heroism

【赞礼】zànlǐ **A**〈动〉 act as master of ceremonies **B**〈名〉 master of ceremonies

【赞美】zànměi〈动〉 praise: ～之词 words of praise ‖ 他助人为乐的精神受到人们的～。 He was praised for his readiness to help.

【赞美诗】zànměishī〈名〉［基督教］psalm

【赞佩】zànpèi〈动〉〈书〉 admire: 他的英勇行为令人～。 His heroism inspires admiration.

【赞赏】zànshǎng〈动〉 appreciate: 我很～你在处理这件事情时的果断。 I admire your decisiveness in the handling of the matter.

【赞颂】zànsòng〈动〉 extol: ～祖国的大好河山 sing the praises of the beautiful land of one's country

【赞叹】zàntàn〈动〉 gasp in admiration: 杂技演员们的高超技艺令人～。 People gasped with admiration at the superb skills of the acrobats.

【赞叹不已】zàntàn-bùyǐ〈成〉 be full of praise: 这件艺术品令人～。 This work of art is beyond praise.

【赞同】zàntóng〈动〉 approve of: 大家一致～这项改革。 We endorsed the reform unanimously. ‖ 我～你的观点。 I agree with you.

【赞许】zànxǔ〈动〉 commend: 值得～ be praiseworthy

【赞扬】zànyáng〈动〉 praise: ～好人好事 commend good people and good deeds ‖ 她的诚实受到～。 She won applause for his honesty.

【赞语】zànyǔ〈名〉 words of praise: 留言簿上写满了感人的～。 The visitors' book was full of touching complimentary remarks.

【赞誉】zànyù〈动〉 praise: 该厂的产品售后服务赢得了用户的～。 The factory has been commended by consumers for the after-sale service of its products.

【赞助】zànzhù〈动〉 sponsor: ～体育赛事 sponsor sports events ‖ 拉～ solicit sponsorship ‖ ～单位 sponsor ‖ 这项救济工程是由联合国～的。 This relief project is set up under the auspices of the United Nations.

【赞助费】zànzhùfèi〈名〉 sponsorship money

【赞助人】zànzhùrén〈名〉 sponsor: 电视节目的～ sponsor of a TV programme

【赞助商】zànzhùshāng〈名〉 sponsor

zāng

赃（**贜、賍**） zāng〈名〉booty: 分～ divide up the spoils ▸贪～枉法, 追～

【赃官】zāngguān〈名〉 corrupt official

【赃款】zāngkuǎn〈名〉 embezzled funds: 退还～ return embezzled money

【赃物】zāngwù〈名〉 stolen goods: 追回～ recover stolen goods

脏（**髒**） zāng〈形〉 dirty: ～东西 dirty things ‖ ～活儿 dirty job ‖ ～衣服 dirty linen ▸～话, 肮～
▸zàng

【脏病】zāngbìng ▸**p. 50**〈名〉〈口〉 venereal disease (VD)

【脏话】zānghuà〈名〉 dirty word: 说～ use foul language

【脏钱】zāngqián〈名〉〈口〉 dirty money

【脏土】zāngtǔ〈名〉 dirt

【脏兮兮】zāngxīxī〈形〉 filthy: 把你～的手洗一下。 Wash your dirty hands.

【脏字】zāngzi〈名〉 swear word: 说话别带～。 Don't swear.

牂 zāng〈名〉〈书〉 ewe

【牂牂】zāngzāng〈形〉〈书〉 lush: 其叶～ with luxuriant foliage

臧 zāng〈书〉〈形〉 good

【臧否】zāngpǐ〈动〉〈书〉appraise: ～人物 pass judgement on a person

zǎng

驵（**駔**） zǎng〈名〉〈古〉 steed

【驵侩】zǎngkuài〈名〉〈古〉**1**（马匹交易经纪人） horse trader **2**（经纪人） broker

zàng

脏（**臟**） zàng〈名〉 internal organs of the body: ▸～腑, ～器, 内～
▸zāng

【脏腑】zàngfǔ〈名〉［中医］ viscera

【脏器】zàngqì〈名〉 viscera

奘 zàng〈形〉 **1**〈书〉（壮大） [often used in personal names] strong **2**〈方〉（粗鲁） rude
▸zhuǎng

葬 zàng〈动〉 **1**（掩埋尸体） bury: ▸安～, 埋～ **2**（以特定方式处理尸体） bury in a specified way according to local customs: ▸海～, 火～, 天～

【葬礼】zànglǐ〈名〉 funeral: 参加～ attend a funeral ‖ 举行～ hold a funeral

【葬身】zàngshēn〈动〉 be buried: ～大海 lose one's life at sea ‖ ～火海 be swallowed up in a sea of flames

【葬身鱼腹】zàngshēn-yúfù〈成〉 be drowned

【葬送】zàngsòng〈动〉 ruin: 他因卷入丑闻而～了自己的前程。 His involvement in the scandal ruined his prospects. ‖ 如此将彻底～和平进程。 This will kill the peace process completely.

藏[1] zàng〈名〉**1**（仓库） storage place: ▸宝～ **2**（指经书） Buddhist/Taoist scriptures: ▸道～

藏[2] Zàng〈名〉**1** ▸**p. 661**（指地区） Tibet: 川～公路 Sichuan-Tibet highway **2**（指人） Tibetan people: ▸～历, ～医
▸cáng

【藏獒】zàng'áo〈名〉［动物］Tibetan mastiff

【藏传佛教】Zàngchuán Fójiào = 喇嘛教 Lǎmajiào

【藏刀】zàngdāo〈名〉 clasp knife

【藏红花】zànghónghuā〈名〉 **1**［植物］ saffron crocus **2**［中药］ saffron

【藏剧】zàngjù〈名〉 Tibetan opera

【藏蓝】zànglán〈形〉 purplish blue

【藏历】Zànglì〈名〉 Tibetan lunar calendar

【藏青】zàngqīng〈形〉 dark blue

【藏青果】zàngqīngguǒ〈名〉 myrobalan

【藏区】zàngqū〈名〉Tibetan-inhabited area

【藏戏】zàngxì = 藏剧 zàngjù

【藏香】zàngxiāng〈名〉 Tibetan joss stick

【藏医】zàngyī〈名〉**1**（指医学）traditional Tibetan medicine **2**（指人） doctor specialized in traditional Tibetan medicine

【藏语】Zàngyǔ ▸**p. 918**〈名〉 Tibetan

【藏族】Zàngzú〈名〉 Tibetan ethnic group

zāo

遭[1] zāo〈动〉 meet with: ～报应 suffer a retribution ‖ ～毒手 be murdered ‖ 惨～杀害 be brutally killed ▸～难, ～殃

遭[2] zāo〈量〉 **1**（圈儿） round: 用绳子在行李箱上绕了好几～ wind a string around the suitcase several times ‖ 跑了两～之后，我超过了他。 Two laps later I overtook him. **2**（次） time: 一～生，两～熟。 Be strangers at a first meeting, but familiar at the next. ‖ 一个人出远门，我还是头一～。 This is the first time I have ever travelled alone.

【遭到】zāodào〈动〉suffer: ～反对 encounter opposition ‖ ～攻击 come under attack ‖ ～拒绝 meet with a refusal ‖ ～失败 sustain a defeat

【遭逢】zāoféng〈动〉 meet with: ～不幸 suffer misfortune ‖ ～盛世 live in prosperous times

【遭际】zāojì〈书〉 **A**〈名〉 lot: 他讲述了他个人的～。 He told of his lot. **B**〈动〉 meet with: ～不幸 meet with misfortune

【遭劫】zāojié〈动〉 meet with catastrophe

【遭难】zāonàn〈动〉 suffer misfortune

【遭受】zāoshòu〈动〉 suffer: ～挫折 suffer setbacks ‖ ～虐待/折磨 suffer ill-treatment/tortures ‖ 这场战争使人民～了重大损失。 This war inflicted great losses on the people.

【遭殃】zāoyāng〈动〉 suffer: 内战不断，百姓～。 The people suffered through the ceaseless civil war.

【遭遇】zāoyù **A**〈动〉 meet with: ～不幸 meet with misfortune ‖ ～旱灾 suffer from drought ‖ ～顽强抵抗 meet with tough resistance ‖ ～意外 meet with an accident **B**〈名〉 hard lot: 诉说～ relate one's experience ‖ 童年的不幸～ bitter experiences of one's childhood

【遭遇战】zāoyùzhàn〈名〉［军事］ encounter

【遭灾】zāozāi〈动〉 suffer disaster
【遭罪】zāozuì〈动〉 endure hardships

糟 zāo

A〈名〉 distillers' grains: ▸~糠, 酒~
B〈动〉 pickle with distillers' grains or in wine: ~鸡/肉/鱼 chicken/pork/fish pickled with distillers' grains or in wine
C〈形〉 **1**（朽烂） rotten: 木头~了。 The wood is rotten. **2**（不好） bad: 把事情搞~ make a mess of things ‖ 他身体很~。 He is in very poor health. ‖ 他在剧中的表演~透了。 He was awful in the play. ▸一团~
【糟糕】zāogāo〈形〉 terrible: ~的天气 damnable weather ‖ 更~的是，她的车中途出了故障。 To make matters worse, her car broke down halfway.
【糟践】zāojian〈动〉 **1**（浪费） waste: 别~粮食。 Don't waste grain. **2**（诋毁） insult: ~人 insult sb. ‖ 说话可别~人。 Keep from using insulting language. **3**（强奸） rape: 他~了那个姑娘。 He raped that girl.
【糟糠】zāokāng〈名〉 foodstuffs for the poor
【糟糠之妻】zāokāng zhī qī〈成〉 wife who has shared her husband's hard lot: ~不下堂 a wife who has shared her husband's hard lot must never be deserted
【糟粕】zāopò〈名〉 **1**〈本〉 waste matter **2**〈喻〉 dregs: ~电影 rubbishy film
【糟踏】zāota = 糟蹋 zāota
【糟蹋】zāota〈动〉 **1**（浪费） waste: ~粮食 waste grain ‖ 这阵大风~了不少果子。 This gust of wind has laid a lot of fruit to waste. **2**（损坏） trample on: 城镇被~得不成样子了。 The town was ravaged beyond recognition. **3**（强奸） rape: ~妇女 violate a woman
【糟心】zāoxīn〈形〉 vexed: 球队在比赛中表现不佳，教练感到~。 The coach was annoyed at the poor performance of his team in the match.

záo

凿[1]（鑿）záo

A〈名〉 **1**（凿子） chisel: 扁~ flat chisel ‖ 圆~ round chisel ▸~子 **2**〈书〉（卯眼） mortise: ▸方枘圆~
B〈动〉 **1**（打孔） chisel: ~冰 cut a hole in the ice ‖ 在墙上~个洞 knock a hole in the wall **2**（挖掘） dig: ~地道/隧道 dig a tunnel ‖ ~井 sink a well

凿[2]（鑿）záo〈形〉〈书〉 certain: ▸确~

【凿空】záokōng〈动〉〈书〉 give a far-fetched interpretation: ~之论 far-fetched argument
【凿孔机】záokǒngjī〈名〉 hole-puncher
【凿枘】záoruì **A**〈名〉〈书〉 harmony **B** = 圆凿方枘 yuánzáo-fāngruì
【凿岩机】záoyánjī〈名〉 rock drill
【凿凿】záozáo〈形〉〈书〉 true: ~有据 be supported by irrefutable evidence ▸言之~
【凿子】záozi〈名〉 chisel

zǎo

早 zǎo

A〈名〉 early morning: 从~到晚 from dawn till dusk ▸~饭, ~出晚归, 清~
B〈形〉 **1**（尽早） early: ~点儿动身 set out early ‖ ~作打算 make plans in advance ‖ 急什么，离开演还~哩。 What's the hurry? It's still quite a while before the performance starts. **2**（时间靠前） early: ▸~稻, ~期 **3** ▸p. 780（早安） morning: ~! Good morning!
C〈副〉 long ago: 他~走了。 He went away quite a while ago. ‖ 这件事我们~商量好了。 We reached an agreement on this ages ago.
【早安】zǎo'ān ▸p. 780〈名〉 good morning: 互致~ say good morning to each other
【早班】zǎobān〈名〉 morning shift: 上~ be on the morning shift
【早班车】zǎobānchē〈名〉 early morning bus
【早搏】zǎobó ▸p. 50〈名〉［医学］ premature beat
【早餐】zǎocān〈名〉 breakfast: ~吃黄油面包 have bread and butter for breakfast
【早操】zǎocāo〈名〉 morning exercises: 做~ do morning exercises
【早茶】zǎochá〈名〉 morning tea
【早产】zǎochǎn ▸p. 50〈动〉［医学］ be born prematurely
【早产儿】zǎochǎnér〈名〉 premature baby
【早场】zǎochǎng〈名〉 morning show: 看~ watch the morning show
【早朝】zǎocháo〈名〉〈旧〉 morning audience with the emperor
【早车】zǎochē〈名〉 morning train/bus
【早晨】zǎochen〈名〉 early morning
【早出晚归】zǎochū-wǎnguī〈成〉 be gone from dawn till dusk
【早春】zǎochūn ▸p. 345〈名〉 early spring: ~天气峭寒。 It is chilly in early spring.
【早祷】zǎodǎo〈名〉 morning prayer
【早稻】zǎodào〈名〉 early rice: 播种~ sow early rice
【早点】zǎodiǎn〈名〉 light breakfast
【早饭】zǎofàn〈名〉 breakfast: 吃~ have breakfast
【早慧】zǎohuì〈形〉〈书〉 precocious: ~早衰。 Soon ripe, soon rotten.
【早婚】zǎohūn〈动〉 marry before the legal age: 在一些偏远地区，~现象非常普遍。 Early marriage is very common in some remote areas.
【早就】zǎojiu〈副〉 long since
【早课】zǎokè〈名〉 chanting of sutras early in the morning
【早恋】zǎoliàn〈动〉 puppy love
【早年】zǎonián〈名〉 **1**（从前） long ago: ~这里没有自来水。 Many years ago, there was no running water here. **2**（年轻时） one's early years: 他~丧父。 His father died when he was very young.
【早期】zǎoqī ▸p. 618〈名〉 early stage: ~癌症 early stage cancer ‖ ~作品 early works
【早期白话】zǎoqī báihuà〈名〉 early vernacular [the vernacular style of written Chinese as used before the May 4th Movement of 1919]
【早起】zǎoqǐ〈动〉 get up early: 早睡~ early to bed and early to rise
【早起】zǎoqi〈名〉〈方〉 (early) morning
【早秋】zǎoqiū〈名〉 early autumn
【早日】zǎorì **A**〈副〉 soon: ~实现统一 achieve reunification as early as possible ‖ 祝您~康复。 I hope you get better soon. **B**〈名〉 the past: 他失去了~的荣耀。 He has lost his past glory.
【早上】zǎoshang ▸p. 669 ▸p. 780〈名〉 morning: ~好! Good morning!
【早市】zǎoshì〈名〉 **1**（指市场） morning market: 逛~ stroll around the morning market **2**（指营业） morning business: 本店~供应稀饭和煎饼。 We sell porridge and pancakes in the morning.
【早逝】zǎoshì ▸p. 772〈动〉〈婉〉 die young
【早熟】zǎoshú〈动〉 **1**［生理］ be precocious: ~的孩子 precocious child **2**（指农作物） mature early: ~品种 early-maturing variety
【早衰】zǎoshuāi ▸p. 50〈动〉［医学］ be prematurely senile
【早霜】zǎoshuāng〈名〉 early frost
【早岁】zǎosuì〈名〉〈书〉 one's early years
【早退】zǎotuì〈动〉 leave early: 迟到~ come late and leave early
【早晚】zǎowǎn **A**〈名〉 **1**（早和晚） morning and evening: 他每天~都散步。 He goes out for a walk every day both in the morning and in the evening. **2**（时候） time: 他昨天晚上就走了，这~多半已经到那儿了。 He left last night and should have arrived there by now. **B**〈副〉 sooner or later: ~会真相大白。 Sooner or later, the truth will out.
【早午餐】zǎowǔcān〈名〉 brunch
【早先】zǎoxiān〈名〉 the past: ~的同事/校友 former colleagues/schoolmates ‖ 你的画比~好多了。 Your painting is much better than it was.
【早泄】zǎoxiè ▸p. 50〈名〉［医学］ premature ejaculation
【早已】zǎoyǐ〈副〉 long ago: 人们~不相信他了。 People began to distrust him a long time ago. ‖ 他~离去。 He has already left.
【早育】zǎoyù〈动〉 give birth prematurely
【早早场】zǎozǎo chǎng〈名〉［影视］ early morning matinee
【早早儿】zǎozǎor〈副〉 as early as possible: 要走，就~走。 If you want to go, go as early as possible.
【早造】zǎozào〈名〉 early crops

枣（棗）zǎo〈名〉［植物］ jujube: 红~ red date ‖ ~树 jujube tree

【枣红】zǎohóng〈形〉 purplish red
【枣泥】zǎoní〈名〉 jujube paste: ~馅月饼 moon cakes with jujube paste fillings
【枣椰树】zǎoyēshù〈名〉 date palm
【枣子】zǎozi〈名〉〈方〉 jujube

蚤 zǎo〈名〉 flea: ▸跳~

澡 zǎo〈动〉 bathe: 洗个~ have a bath ▸~盆

【澡盆】zǎopén〈名〉 bathtub; bath〈英〉
【澡堂】zǎotáng〈名〉 public bathhouse
【澡堂子】zǎotángzi = 澡堂 zǎotáng
【澡塘】zǎotáng〈名〉 **1**（浴池） common bathing pool **2** = 澡堂 zǎotáng

藻 zǎo〈名〉 **1**（藻类植物） algae: ▸海~, 水~ **2**（指色彩） rich colour: ▸~井 **3**（指文辞） literary embellishment: ▸~饰, 辞~

【藻花】zǎohuā〈名〉 water bloom
【藻井】zǎojǐng〈名〉［建筑］ sunk panel
【藻类植物】zǎolèi zhíwù〈名〉 algae
【藻煤】zǎoméi〈名〉 boghead coal
【藻饰】zǎoshì〈动〉〈书〉 embellish with ornate language

zào

皂[1] zào
A〈形〉 black: ～靴/衣 black boots/coat
B〈名〉〈旧〉 runner: ～隶 *yamen* runner

皂[2] zào〈名〉 soap: ～粉 soap powder ▸肥～, 香～, 药～
【皂白】zàobái〈名〉 1〈本〉 black and white 2〈喻〉 right and wrong: ～不分 cannot tell right from wrong
【皂化】zàohuà〈动〉［化学］ saponify
【皂荚】zàojiá〈名〉［植物］ Chinese honey locust
【皂角】zàojiǎo = 皂荚 zàojiá
【皂隶】zàolì〈名〉〈旧〉 *yamen* runner
【皂片】zàopiàn〈名〉 soap flakes

灶（竈） zào〈名〉 1（指设备） kitchen range: ▸炉～, 煤气～ 2（厨房） kitchen: 学生～ students' canteen 3（灶神） kitchen god: 祭～ offer sacrifices to the kitchen god
【灶火】zàohuo〈名〉〈方〉 1（厨房） kitchen 2（指设备） kitchen range
【灶间】zàojiān〈名〉〈旧〉 kitchen
【灶具】zàojù〈名〉 cooking utensils
【灶神】Zàoshén ▸**p. 274**〈名〉 Kitchen God
【灶台】zàotái〈名〉 top of a kitchen range
【灶膛】zàotáng〈名〉 chamber of a kitchen range
【灶头】zàotou〈名〉〈方〉 stove
【灶王爷】Zàowangyé = 灶神 Zàoshén

唣 zào ▸啰唣 luózào

造[1] zào〈动〉 1〈书〉（前往） go to: ▸～访, 登峰～极 2（达到） attain: ▸～诣 3（培养） train: ▸～就, 深～, 可～之才

造[2] zào〈动〉 1（做） make: ～船 build a ship ‖ ～机器 manufacture machines ‖ ～舆论 build up public opinion ‖ ～预算 draw up a budget ▸～船, 建～, 伪～ 2（虚构） invent: ～假账 falsify accounts ▸～谣, 捏～

造[3] zào〈名〉［法律］ one of the two parties in a legal agreement or a lawsuit: 甲～ first party ‖ 乙～ second party

造[4] zào
A〈名〉〈方〉 crop: 晚/早～ late/early crop
B〈量〉 [used for crops]: 一年三～皆丰收。 All three crops of the year produced high yields.
【造币厂】zàobìchǎng〈名〉 mint
【造册】zàocè〈动〉 compile a register
【造成】zàochéng〈动〉 cause: ～既成事实 bring about a *fait accompli* ‖ ～巨大损失 incur heavy losses ‖ ～严重后果 lead to serious consequences
【造船】zàochuán〈动〉 build a ship
【造船厂】zàochuánchǎng〈名〉 shipyard
【造次】zàocì〈形〉〈书〉 1（匆忙） hurried: ～之间 in a moment of haste 2（鲁莽） imprudent: ～行事 act rashly ‖ 不可～。 Don't be impetuous.
【造反】zàofǎn〈动〉 rise up in rebellion: 起来～ rise up in revolt
【造访】zàofǎng〈动〉〈书〉 pay a visit: 登门～ call at sb.'s house
【造福】zàofú〈动〉 benefit: ～于民 benefit the populace ‖ 植树造林，～后代。 Plant trees everywhere in the interest of future generations.
【造化】zàohuà〈书〉 A〈名〉 the Creator B〈动〉 create
【造化】zàohua〈名〉 good fortune: 有～ be lucky ‖ 我没那么大的～。 I am not so lucky.
【造假】zàojiǎ〈动〉 counterfeit: ～窝点 counterfeiting den
【造价】zàojià〈名〉 cost: 降低～ lower the cost ‖ 工程～ cost of a project
【造就】zàojiù A〈动〉 train: ～人才 train qualified personnel ‖ ～一代新人 bring up a new generation B〈名〉 [usu of young people] achievements: 在技术上很有～ have a lot of technical achievements
【造句】zàojù〈动〉 construct a sentence: ～练习 sentence-making exercise
【造林】zàolín〈动〉 afforest: ～面积 afforested area
【造孽】zàoniè〈动〉［佛教］ do evil
【造市】zàoshì〈动〉 do marketing
【造势】zàoshì〈动〉 build up momentum: 利用广告为新产品～ use advertisements to promote a new product
【造物】zàowù〈名〉 divine force that created the universe
【造物主】Zàowùzhǔ〈名〉［基督教］ the Creator
【造像】zàoxiàng〈名〉［美术］ statue
【造型】zàoxíng A〈动〉 1（塑造） mould 2［机械］ mould: ～车间 moulding workshop B〈名〉 modelling: 这些玩具～简单，生动有趣。 These toys look animated and interesting even though they are simply made.
【造型师】zàoxíngshī ▸**p. 966**〈名〉 stylist
【造型艺术】zàoxíng yìshù〈名〉 plastic arts
【造血】zàoxuè〈动〉 1［医学］ form blood: ～器官 blood-forming organ 2〈喻〉（指组织、机构） tap the internal potentials of a department, organization, etc. to increase its own strength
【造谣】zàoyáo〈动〉 fabricate stories: ～生事 cause trouble by spreading false stories
【造谣惑众】zàoyáo-huòzhòng〈成〉 spread rumours to confuse people
【造诣】zàoyì〈名〉 attainments: 学术～ academic achievements ‖ 他是一位有～的作家。 He is an accomplished writer.
【造影】zàoyǐng〈名〉［医学］ radiography: 钡餐～检查 barium meal examination
【造纸】zàozhǐ〈动〉 make paper
【造纸厂】zàozhǐchǎng〈名〉 paper mill
【造纸术】zàozhǐshù〈名〉 paper-making technology
【造作】zàozuo〈形〉 affected: ▸矫揉～

噪 zào
A〈动〉 1〈书〉（鸣叫） chirp: 蝉～ chirping of cicadas ‖ 群鸦乱～。 Crows were cawing. 2（大声叫嚷） kick up a racket: 名声大～ enjoy soaring fame ▸鼓～, 名～一时
B〈形〉 clamorous: ▸～声
【噪声】zàoshēng〈名〉 noise: 降低～ reduce the noise ‖ 城市/交通～ city/traffic noise ‖ ～污染 noise pollution
【噪音】zàoyīn = 噪声 zàoshēng
【噪杂】zàozá〈形〉 noisy: 人声～ hubbub of voices

燥 zào〈形〉 dry: ▸干～, 口～唇干
【燥热】zàorè〈形〉 hot and dry: 天气～ the weather is hot and dry

躁 zào〈形〉 rash: 性子～ be quick-tempered ▸暴～, 急～, 戒骄戒～
【躁动】zàodòng〈动〉 1（骚动） move restlessly 2（跳动） keep moving up and down
【躁狂】zàokuáng ▸**p. 50**〈名〉［医学］ mania
【躁狂抑郁症】zàokuáng yìyùzhèng ▸**p. 50**〈名〉［医学］ manic-depression: ～患者 manic-depressive

zé

则[1]**（則）** zé
A〈名〉 1（规章） rule: ▸法～, 规～, 细～ 2（榜样） standard: ▸以身作～, 准～
B〈动〉〈书〉 follow an example: ～先烈之言行 follow the example of the martyrs in word and deed
C〈量〉 [used for news, writing, etc.] item: 试题三～ three examination questions ‖ 新闻一～ an item of news ‖ 寓言五～ five fables

则[2]**（則）** zé
A〈连〉 1〈书〉（表顺承） [used to indicate sequence]: 暑往～寒来。 As summer goes, so winter comes. 2（表因果） [used to indicate cause and effect, condition, etc.]: ▸穷～思变, 欲速～不达 3〈书〉（表对比） [used to indicate contrast]: 旧的制度已经腐朽，新的制度～如旭日东升。 The old system is rotten to the core while the new one is as brilliant and vigorous as the rising sun. 4（表让步） [used between two identical words to indicate concession]: 好～好，只是太贵。 It's good but it's too expensive.
B〈副〉〈书〉 [used as the copula]: 此～余之过也。 This is my fault.
C〈助〉 [used to list reasons, preceded by 一, 二 or 三]: 我不想再走了，一～力乏，二～脚痛，三～没必要这么匆忙。 I do not feel like going on any more. Firstly, I am tired; secondly, my feet hurt; thirdly, there is no need to hurry.
【则声】zéshēng〈动〉 utter a sound: 不敢～ dare not utter a word

责（責） zé
A〈动〉 1（要求） demand: ～人宽，～己严 be strict with oneself while treating others with generosity ▸～成, ～令, 求全～备 2（批评） blame: ▸～备, 自～ 3（质问） interrogate: ▸～问 4（责打） punish by beating: 笞～ flog ▸～打
B〈名〉 duty: 挽救生命是医生之～。 It is a doctor's duty to preserve life. ▸负～, 尽～, 职～
【责备】zébèi〈动〉 blame: ～不该～的人 call the wrong person to task ‖ 他只是个小孩子，～几句就算了。 He is just a little boy. A few words of reprimand will be quite sufficient. ▸求全～
【责编】zébiān〈简称〉= 责任编辑
【责成】zéchéng〈动〉 instruct: ～有关部门尽快解决问题 instruct the departments concerned to solve the problem as soon as possible
【责打】zédǎ〈动〉 punish by beating
【责罚】zéfá〈动〉 punish

【责怪】zéguài〈动〉blame: 这事我没做好，不能～他人。I didn't do it well enough. No one else should be blamed.
【责令】zélìng〈动〉instruct: ～公安部门彻底查清案情 order the public security departments to make a thorough investigation into the case
【责骂】zémà〈动〉scold: 他被狠狠～了一顿。He got a good dressing-down.
【责难】zénàn〈动〉blame: 受到～ incur/receive censure
【责任】zérèn〈名〉**1**（职责）responsibility: ～明确 have a clear responsibility ‖ 社会～ social obligation/responsibility ‖ 我不过是尽了自己的～罢了。I've done no more than what is my duty. **2**（应承担的过失）blame: 负法律/刑事～ be legally/criminally liable ‖ 追究～ ascertain where the responsibility lies
【责任编辑】zérèn biānjí〈名〉managing editor
【责任方】zérènfāng〈名〉responsible party: 对事故～进行处罚 punish those responsible for the accident
【责任感】zérèngǎn〈名〉sense of responsibility: 强烈的～ strong sense of responsibility
【责任事故】zérèn shìgù〈名〉accident due to negligence
【责任险】zérènxiǎn〈名〉liability insurance: 第三方～ third party liability insurance
【责任心】zérènxīn = 责任感 zérèngǎn
【责任制】zérènzhì〈名〉responsibility system
【责任状】zérènzhuàng〈名〉responsibility contract
【责问】zéwèn〈动〉call sb. to account: 老师～他为何无故旷课。The teacher called him to account for his unexplained absence from class.
【责无旁贷】zéwúpángdài〈成〉be duty-bound: 治病救人，～ be duty-bound to cure the sickness to save the patient
【责有攸归】zéyǒuyōuguī〈成〉blame cannot be shifted onto others

择（擇） zé〈动〉select: ～日起程 fix a departure date ▸～善而从，饥不～食，选～
▸zhái
【择吉】zéjí〈动〉choose an auspicious day: ～开张 select an auspicious day for opening a business ‖ ～迎娶 choose an auspicious day for a wedding
【择交】zéjiāo〈动〉select one's friends: 慎重～ select one's friends with care
【择偶】zé'ǒu〈动〉choose a spouse
【择期】zéqī〈动〉select a time: ～完婚 select a day for a wedding
【择善而从】zéshàn'ércóng〈成〉select what is good and follow it
【择校】zéxiào〈动〉select a school [for its academic achievements rather than geographical convenience]: ～生 students who select schools
【择业】zéyè〈动〉elect/choose a profession/job: ～指导 career guidance, vocational counsel
【择优】zéyōu〈动〉select the superior ones: ～录取 employ on the basis of competitive selection

咋 zé〈动〉〈书〉hold between the teeth
▸zǎ, zhā
【咋舌】zéshé〈动〉〈书〉be speechless with astonishment, horror, etc.

迮 zé〈形〉〈书〉narrow
【迮狭】zéxiá〈形〉〈书〉narrow

泽（澤） zé
A〈名〉**1**（聚水之处）pool: 深山大～ great mountains and vast marshes ▸湖～，沼～ **2**（恩惠）favour: ～及枯骨。Even the dead benefit from kindness. ▸恩～ **3**（光彩）lustre: ▸光～，色～
B〈动〉dampen: ▸润～
【泽国】zéguó〈名〉〈书〉**1**（指水域密布）land that abounds in rivers and lakes: 水乡～ land criss-crossed with rivers and dotted with lakes **2**（指被洪水淹没）inundated/flooded area: 全区尽成～。The whole area became submerged.
【泽兰】zélán〈名〉[植物] Japanese Eupatorium
【泽泻】zéxiè〈名〉[中药] rhizome of oriental water plantain

啧（嘖） zé〈书〉
A〈形〉chattering: ▸～有烦言
B〈拟〉（用舌头）click;（用嘴唇）smack: ▸～～
【啧有烦言】zéyǒu-fányán〈成〉full of complaints
【啧啧】zézé〈拟〉〈书〉**1**（指人）click: ～称羡 be profuse in one's praise **2**（指鸟）chirp

帻（幘） zé〈名〉〈古〉man's headdress

舴 zé
【舴艋】zéměng〈名〉〈书〉small boat

赜（賾） zé〈形〉〈书〉abstruse: 探～索隐 unravel mysteries

zè

仄[1] zè
A〈形〉〈书〉inclined
B = 仄声 zèshēng

仄[2] zè〈形〉**1**（狭窄）narrow: ▸逼～ **2**（不安）uneasy: 歉～ feel sorry
【仄声】zèshēng〈名〉[语言] oblique tones [ie the falling-rising tone (上声), the falling tone (去声) and the entering tone (入声), as distinct from the level tone (平声) in classical Chinese pronunciation]

zéi

贼（賊） zéi
A〈动〉〈书〉（伤害）harm: ▸戕～
B〈名〉**1**（指害国害民）evildoer: ▸工～，奸～，卖国～ **2**（指偷窃财物）thief: 捉～ catch a thief ‖ 盗车～ car thief ▸盗～，窃～
C〈形〉**1**（邪恶）evil: ▸～眉鼠眼，～头～脑，～心 **2**（狡猾）cunning: 狐狸真～。Foxes are sly.
D〈副〉〈方〉extremely: 今天～冷。It's terribly cold today. ‖ 他的皮鞋擦得～亮～亮的。His leather shoes were polished until they shone.
【贼船】zéichuán〈名〉pirate ship:〈喻〉上～ join a criminal gang
【贼风】zéifēng〈名〉wind that blows in through cracks in doors or windows
【贼骨头】zéigǔtou〈名〉〈方〉thief
【贼喊捉贼】zéihǎnzhuōzéi〈惯〉〈喻〉cover up one's misdemeanours by employing distraction tactics
【贼寇】zéikòu〈名〉**1**（强盗）robber **2**（入侵者）invader
【贼眉鼠眼】zéiméi-shǔyǎn〈成〉have a sneaky look
【贼去关门】zéiqù-guānmén = 贼走关门 zéizǒu-guānmén
【贼人】zéirén〈名〉**1**（小偷）thief **2**（干坏事的人）evil doer
【贼头贼脑】zéitóu-zéinǎo〈成〉behave furtively: 别～的。Don't act like a thief.
【贼心】zéixīn〈名〉evil designs: ～不死 be bent on evil doing
【贼眼】zéiyǎn〈名〉shifty eyes
【贼赃】zéizāng〈名〉booty
【贼子】zéizǐ〈名〉〈书〉traitor: ▸乱臣～
【贼走关门】zéizǒu-guānmén〈俗〉〈喻〉lock the stable door after the horse has bolted

鲗（鰂） zéi ▸乌鲗 wūzéi

zěn

怎 zěn〈代〉why, how, what: 你～不早点儿来？Why didn't you come earlier? ‖ 我～能把他丢下不管？How could I leave him alone?
【怎地】zěndi = 怎的 zěndi
【怎的】zěndi〈代〉〈方〉what, why, how: ～不见他？Why isn't he here? ‖ 看你能把我～？I'd like to see what you can do to me.
【怎么】zěnme〈代〉**1**（用于询问）how, what, why: 你～能那样对他？How could you have treated him like that? ‖ 这是～回事？What's all this about? **2**（用于任指）[used to indicate the nature, condition, manner, etc. of sth.]: 你愿意～办就～办。Do it in any way you like. ‖ 我～说，你～办。Do as I tell you. **3**（表程度）[used in the negative to indicate degree]: 他不～爱说话。He is not very talkative. ‖ 这歌我才学，还不～会唱。I have just started learning the song, and can't sing it very well yet. **4**（表惊讶）what: ～，连他们都卷进去了？What? Even they are involved? ‖ ～，她还没好？What? Hasn't she recovered yet?
【怎么样】zěnmeyàng〈代〉**1** = 怎样 zěnyàng **2**（表委婉）[used in the negative to form a mild understatement]: 他画得也并不～。He's not much of a painter either. ‖ 这本小说不～。This novel isn't up to much.
【怎么着】zěnmezhe〈代〉**1**（表询问）what: 我们都决定去了，你打算～？We've all decided to go. How about you? ‖ 我不知道～好。I'm at a loss as to what to do. **2**（表任指）whatsoever: ～想就～说 say whatever is on your mind ‖ 一个人不能想～就～。One can't just do what one wants.
【怎奈】zěnnài〈连〉〈旧〉however: 我们正想去郊游，～突然下起雨来。We were just thinking of going on an outing, when suddenly it started to rain.
【怎样】zěnyàng〈代〉**1**（表询问）how, what: 如果那是真的，会～？If that's

true, what would happen? ‖ 他们的工作进展得～了？ How are they getting on with their work? **2**（表指代）[used to indicate the nature, condition or manner of sth.]: 想想从前～，再看看现在～ think of the past and look at the present ‖ 人家～说，你就～做。 Do as you are told.

zèn

谮（譖） zèn〈动〉〈书〉 slander: ～言 calumny

zēng

曾 zēng〈形〉 related as great-grandchild to great-grandparent: ▸～孙，～祖母
▸céng

【曾母暗沙】Zēngmǔ Ànshā〈名〉 Zengmu Reef

【曾孙】zēngsūn〈名〉 great-grandson

【曾孙女】zēngsūnnǚ〈名〉 great-granddaughter

【曾祖】zēngzǔ〈名〉 (paternal) great-grandfather

【曾祖母】zēngzǔmǔ〈名〉(paternal) great-grandmother

增 zēng〈动〉 add: ～兵 reinforce an army ‖ ～派飞机 send additional planes ‖ 有～无减 keep increasing ▸～加，～强，～援

【增白剂】zēngbáijì〈名〉［化学］brightening agent

【增补】zēngbǔ〈动〉 augment: ～新委员 co-opt a new member onto the committee ‖ 在书中～新内容 supplement a book with new materials

【增补本】zēngbǔběn〈名〉enlarged edition

【增仓】zēngcāng〈动〉［金融］ increase the volume of holdings: 大幅～股票 increase one's share holdings considerably

【增产】zēngchǎn〈动〉increase production: ～措施 measures to increase production ‖ ～增收 increase both production and income ‖ ～节约 increase production and practise economy

【增持】zēngchí〈动〉［金融］ increase one's holdings: ～银行股 increase one's holdings of bank shares

【增大】zēngdà〈动〉 enlarge

【增订】zēngdìng〈动〉 revise and expand: ～本 revised and enlarged edition

【增多】zēngduō〈动〉 increase: 各类产品日益～ daily increase of various kinds of products

【增发】zēngfā〈动〉**1**（指钱物） increase in provision: ～工资 increase wages **2**（指股票） increase in issue: ～股票 release more shares

【增幅】zēngfú〈名〉 growing rate: 年～ annual increase ‖ 产量～很大。 There has been a great increase in production.

【增高】zēnggāo〈动〉**1**（变高） increase in height: 身量～ grow taller ‖ 水位～ rise in water level **2**（提高） raise: ～温度 raise the temperature

【增光】zēngguāng〈动〉 bring honour to: 为国～ bring credit to one's country

【增广】zēngguǎng〈动〉 broaden: ～见闻 widen one's knowledge

【增辉】zēnghuī〈动〉 add lustre to: ～生色 make more colourful and enjoyable

【增加】zēngjiā〈动〉 increase: ～财政收入 increase revenues ‖ ～工资 increase a salary ‖ ～难度 add to the difficulties ‖ ～体重 put on weight ‖ 大幅度～ substantial increase ‖ 旅游者的人数在不断～。 The number of tourists is on the increase.

【增进】zēngjìn〈动〉 enhance: ～健康 promote health ‖ ～友谊 enhance friendship ‖ ～相互了解 strengthen mutual understanding

【增刊】zēngkān〈名〉 supplement

【增利】zēnglì〈动〉 increase a profit: 比去年同比～三个亿。 Profits were up 300 million on the same period last year.

【增强】zēngqiáng〈动〉 strengthen: ～国力 enhance national strength ‖ ～民主法制观念 enhance people's concept of democracy and legality ‖ ～企业活力 invigorate an enterprise ‖ 发展体育运动，～人民体质。 Promote physical culture and build up people's health.

【增色】zēngsè〈动〉 add colour to

【增设】zēngshè〈动〉 establish an additional or a new organization, unit, etc.: ～机构 set up a new organization ‖ ～课程 offer a new course

【增生】zēngshēng ▸p. 50〈名〉［医学］ proliferation: 骨质～ calcium deposits

【增收】zēngshōu〈动〉 increase income: ～节支 increase income and cut expenses

【增速】zēngsù〈动〉 accelerate

【增添】zēngtiān〈动〉 add: ～麻烦 add to the trouble ‖ ～设备 get additional equipment

【增效】zēngxiào〈动〉 enhance effectiveness: 减员～ increase efficiency by downsizing staff

【增选】zēngxuǎn〈动〉 elect sb. additional member

【增压舱】zēngyācāng〈名〉 pressurized cabin

【增益】zēngyì〈动〉 increase: ～匪浅 gain a lot

【增盈】zēngyíng〈动〉 increase profits: 扭亏～ eliminate losses and increase profits

【增援】zēngyuán〈动〉［军事］ reinforce: 火速～ throw in immediate reinforcements ‖ ～部队 reinforcements

【增长】zēngzhǎng〈动〉 enhance: ～才干 develop one's abilities ‖ ～知识 enrich one's knowledge ‖ 经济～相当快。 The economy is moving ahead at a good rate.

【增长点】zēngzhǎngdiǎn〈名〉 growth engine

【增长率】zēngzhǎnglǜ〈名〉 growth rate: 人口～ rate of population growth ‖ ～有所放慢。 The rate of growth has cooled slightly.

【增长势头】zēngzhǎng shìtóu〈名〉 growing momentum

【增值】zēngzhí〈动〉［经济］ increase in value, appreciate: 这块地很快会～。 This piece of land will soon appreciate. ‖ 这种货币～了。 This currency gained in value.

【增值税】zēngzhíshuì〈名〉［经济］ value-added tax (VAT): ～发票 VAT invoice

【增殖】zēngzhí **A** = 增生 zēngshēng **B**〈动〉 breed, reproduce, multiply, propagate: ～牲畜 breed livestock

憎 zēng〈动〉 hate: ▸～恨，爱～分明

【憎称】zēngchēng〈名〉 derogatory name for sb. one hates or loathes

【憎恨】zēnghèn〈动〉 hate: ～侵略者 hate the aggressors

【憎恶】zēngwù〈动〉 loathe: ～战争 have an abhorrence of war ‖ 令人～ be detestable

缯 zēng〈名〉〈书〉 silk fabrics
▸zèng

zèng

综（綜） zèng〈名〉〈书〉［纺织］ heddle
▸zōng

锃（鋥） zèng〈形〉〈口〉 shiny

【锃亮】zèngliàng〈形〉 shiny: 皮鞋擦得～。 The leather shoes were brilliantly polished.

缯（繒） zèng〈动〉〈口〉 tie: 把袋口～起来 tie up the sack at the opening
▸zēng

赠（贈） zèng〈动〉 give as a present: 互～礼品 exchange gifts ▸～送，捐～

【赠别】zèngbié〈动〉 present a friend with gifts, poems, etc. at a parting

【赠答】zèngdá〈动〉 exchange gifts

【赠款】zèngkuǎn〈名〉 gift of money

【赠礼】zènglǐ〈名〉 gift: 接受～ accept a gift

【赠票】zèngpiào **A**〈名〉 complimentary ticket **B**〈动〉 give a complimentary ticket

【赠品】zèngpǐn〈名〉 complimentary gift

【赠券】zèngquàn〈名〉 complimentary ticket

【赠书】zèngshū **A**〈动〉 present sb. with a book **B**〈名〉 complimentary copy of a book

【赠送】zèngsòng〈动〉 present as a gift: ～礼品 present a gift

【赠言】zèngyán〈名〉 words of advice or encouragement given to a friend at parting: 临别～ parting advice

【赠与】zèngyǔ〈动〉 present to: 将200台电脑～这所大学 donate 200 computers to this university

【赠阅】zèngyuè〈动〉 be given free by the publisher

甑 zèng〈名〉**1**（指瓦制炊具） ancient earthen utensil for steaming food **2**（甑子） rice steamer **3**（指蒸馏用具） distiller: 曲颈～ U-necked distiller

【甑子】zèngzi〈名〉 rice steamer

zhā

扎[1] zhā
A〈动〉**1**（刺） pierce: 脚上～进一根钉子 run a nail into one's foot ‖ 我的车胎上～了个洞。 The tyre of my car has a puncture. **2**（钻入） get into: ～到人群里 penetrate a crowd ‖ 一头～进水里 dive into the water ‖ 这种植物的根系～得很深。 The roots of this plant go deep.
B〈名〉 draught beer

扎[2]（紮、紥） zhā〈动〉 be stationed: ▸～营，驻～
▸zā, zhá

【扎堆】zhāduī〈动〉 get together: ～聊天 get together for a chat

【扎耳朵】zhā ěrduo〈动〉〈口〉 grate on the ear: 那声尖笑让我觉得～。 That shrill laugh grated on me.

【扎根】zhāgēn〈动〉take root: 小树已经～了。The young trees have already taken root. ‖〈喻〉～基层 take root at grassroots level
【扎猛子】zhā měngzi〈动〉dive
【扎啤】zhāpí〈名〉draught beer: 一杯～ a mug of draught beer
【扎实】zhāshi〈形〉1（坚实）sturdy: 把包捆～ bundle up the package tightly 2（踏实）solid: 工作～ do a solid job ‖ 功底～ have a solid foundation
【扎手】zhāshǒu〈动〉1（刺手）prick the hand: 留神～。Take care not to prick your hands. 2（难处理）be thorny: 事情～。It's a hard nut to crack.
【扎眼】zhāyǎn〈形〉unpleasant to the eye: 她这身穿戴太～。She is dressed too garishly. ‖ 这块布的花色太～。The colour of the cloth is too loud.
【扎伊尔】Zhāyī'ěr〈名〉Zaire: ～人 Zairean
【扎营】zhāyíng〈动〉pitch a tent
【扎寨】zhāzhài〈动〉camp: 安营～ set up camp
【扎针】zhāzhēn〈动〉［中医］give acupuncture treatment

吒 zhā〈名〉〈古〉used in names of mythical beings

咋 zhā
▸zǎ, zé
【咋呼】zhāhu〈动〉〈口〉1（吆喝）cry out: 你～啥? What are you shouting about? 2（张扬）show off

查 Zhā〈名〉Zha [surname]
▸chá

哳 zhā ▸啁哳 zhāozhā

揸 zhā〈动〉1（抓取）pick up with one's fingers 2〈方〉（张开手）spread one's fingers: ～开五指 spread out one's fingers

喳 zhā
A〈叹〉〈旧〉[used by an inferior in response to instructions of a superior] yes, sir
B〈拟〉chirp: 吱～ chirp ‖ 喜鹊～～地叫。Magpies were chattering.
▸chā

渣 zhā〈名〉1（渣滓）dregs: 豆腐～ soybean residue ‖ 猪油～儿 pork scraps ▸残～, 炉～ 2（碎屑）crumbs: 饼干/点心～儿 biscuit/cake crumbs ‖ 面包～儿 bread crumbs
【渣滓】zhāzǐ〈名〉1（指物）dregs: 溶液的～ dregs of a solution 2（指人或事物）scum:〈喻〉社会～ dregs of society
【渣子】zhāzi = 渣滓 zhāzǐ

楂 zhā ▸山楂 shānzhā
▸chá

zhá

扎 zhá
▸zā, zhā
【扎挣】zházheng〈动〉〈方〉move with difficulty: 老人～着坐了起来。The old man struggled to sit up.

札 zhá〈名〉1（指小木片）thin slips of wood used for writing on in ancient China: ▸笔～ 2〈书〉（书信）letter: ▸书～, 信～
【札记】zhájì〈名〉reading notes

轧（軋） zhá〈动〉roll (steel): 把金属～成板 roll metal into plates
▸gá, yà
【轧钢】zhágāng〈动〉roll steel: ～厂 rolling mill
【轧辊】zhágǔn〈名〉［冶金］roll
【轧机】zhájī〈名〉［冶金］rolling mill: 冷～ cold rolling mill ‖ 热～ hot mill
【轧制】zházhì〈动〉［冶金］roll

闸（閘） zhá
A〈名〉1（水闸）sluice: 开～放水 sluice out the water 2（制动器）switch: 扳～ operate a switch 3（电闸）switch: 合～ turn on the electricity ‖ 拉～ turn off the power ▸～盒
B〈动〉dam: 水流得太猛，～不住。The water rushed too wildly to be dammed.
【闸盒】zháhé〈名〉fuse box
【闸口】zhákǒu〈名〉sluiceway
【闸门】zhámén〈名〉1（用于控水）sluice gate 2（用于行船）lock gate
【闸瓦】zháwǎ〈名〉［机械］brake shoe

炸 zhá〈动〉deep-fry: ～油条 deep-fry twisted dough sticks ‖ ～花生豆 deep-fried peanuts ‖ 肯德基～鸡 Kentucky Fried Chicken (KFC)
▸zhà
【炸酱面】zhájiàngmiàn〈名〉noodles served with fried bean sauce
【炸薯条】zháshǔtiáo〈名〉chips〈英〉; French fries〈美〉

铡（鍘） zhá
A〈名〉fodder chopper: ▸～刀
B〈动〉cut up with a hay cutter: ～草 chop hay with a hay cutter ‖ ～草机 hay cutter
【铡刀】zhádāo〈名〉straw cutter

劄 zhá〈名〉〈古〉official document initially submitted to one's superior and afterwards also to one's subordinates
【劄记】zhájì〈书〉= 札记 zhájì

zhǎ

苲 zhǎ
【苲草】zhǎcǎo〈名〉［植物］aquatic plants

拃 zhǎ
A〈动〉span: 用手～长度 measure sth. in spans
B〈量〉span: 三～长，两～宽 three spans long and two spans wide

眨 zhǎ〈动〉blink: ～眼睛 blink (one's eyes) ‖ 眼睛一～也不～ without batting an eyelid
【眨巴】zhǎba〈动〉〈方〉wink: ～眼睛 wink at sb.
【眨眼】zhǎyǎn A〈动〉blink: ～示意 hint with a wink ‖ 她一边笑着一边向他～。She smiled and batted her eyelids at him. B〈副〉in the twinkling of an eye: 一～的工夫就不见了 vanish in the twinkling of an eye

砟 zhǎ〈名〉tiny fragments of stone, coal, etc.: 炉灰～儿 cinder
【砟子】zhǎzi〈名〉tiny fragments of stone, coal, etc.

鲊（鮓） zhǎ〈名〉〈书〉1（指鱼类食品）salted fish 2（指拌菜）dish served with ground rice or flour and other condiments: 芸豆/茄子～ chopped kidney bean/eggplant served with ground rice and other condiments

zhà

乍 zhà
A〈副〉1（突然）suddenly: ～冷～热 suddenly cold and suddenly hot ‖ ～晴～雨 shine one moment and rain the next 2（起初）at first: ～一听 on first hearing ‖ 分别多年，～一见我都不认识你了。After so many years of separation, I could hardly recognize you when I first saw you again. ▸新来～到
B〈动〉stand on end: 吓得头发都～起来了 be so afraid that one's hair stands on end
【乍得】Zhàdé〈名〉Chad: ～人 Chadian
【乍暖还寒】zhànuǎn-huánhán〈成〉after a short warm spell, the weather has turned cold again

诈（詐） zhà〈动〉1（欺骗）swindle: ～财 get money by fraud ▸～骗, 尔虞我～, 敲～ 2（假装）feign: ～病 feign illness ‖ ～死 play dead ▸～降 3（诱使）bluff sb. into giving information: 我知道他是拿话～我。I knew he had just been bluffing me.
【诈唬】zhàhu〈动〉〈口〉bluff: 他这是～你，别害怕。Don't be scared. He's only bluffing you.
【诈骗】zhàpiàn〈动〉swindle: 蓄意～ with intent to defraud ‖ ～犯 fraud ‖ ～罪 crime of fraud
【诈取】zhàqǔ〈动〉obtain by fraud: ～钱财 swindle sb. out of his money
【诈尸】zhàshī〈动〉1（指尸体）suddenly rise before being buried 2〈粗〉（指人）scream suddenly and behave as if mad
【诈降】zhàxiáng〈动〉feign surrender

栅 zhà〈名〉railings: 木～ palisade ‖ 铁～ iron railings/bars, metal rails ▸～门
▸shān
【栅栏】zhàlan〈名〉1（围栏）railings: 铁～ iron railings ‖ 动物被～圈着。The animals are fenced in. 2［军事］boom: ～网 boom nets
【栅篱】zhàlí〈名〉hedgerow
【栅门】zhàmén〈名〉fence gate

奓 zhà = 乍 zhà B

咤 zhà ▸叱咤 chìzhà

炸 zhà〈动〉1（爆裂）explode: 这个瓶子一灌开水就～了。Hardly had the boiling water been poured in when the bottle burst. ▸爆～ 2（爆破）blow up: 狂轰滥～ wanton and indiscriminate bombing ‖ 这座楼被～塌了。The building was bombed out. ▸轰～ 3〈口〉（被激怒）

Z

fly into a rage: 气～了 explode with rage **4**〈口〉（逃散）scurry: ▸～群，～窝 ▸zhá

【炸弹】zhàdàn〈名〉 bomb: 引爆～ detonate a bomb ‖ 深水～ depth bomb

【炸锅】zhàguō〈动〉〈喻〉 get excited and angry

【炸毁】zhàhuǐ〈动〉 blow up: ～堡垒 dynamite a fort ‖ ～桥梁 blow up a bridge

【炸雷】zhàléi〈名〉 clap of thunder

【炸群】zhàqún〈动〉 [of horses, etc.] scamper

【炸市】zhàshì〈动〉 [of crowd in downtown area] flee in terror

【炸窝】zhàwō〈动〉 **1**（指鸟、蜂）flee in terror: 一声枪响，鸟儿都～了。 The birds flew off at the bang of the gun. **2**〈喻〉（指人）be thrown into chaos: 听到枪声，人群～了。 The crowd panicked at the sound of the guns.

【炸药】zhàyào〈名〉 explosive: 固体/液体～ solid/liquid explosive ‖ 烈性～ high explosive

【炸药包】zhàyàobāo〈名〉 pack of dynamite

【炸药库】zhàyàokù〈名〉 explosive magazine

痄 zhà

【痄腮】zhàsai ▸**p. 50**〈名〉［医学］ mumps

蚱 zhà

【蚱蜢】zhàměng〈名〉［昆虫］grasshopper

榨 zhà

A〈名〉 press for extracting juice, oil, etc.: 酒～ wine press ‖ 油～ oil press

B〈动〉 press: ～甘蔗 press sugar cane ‖ ～油 extract oil ‖ ～柠檬汁 squeeze juice from a lemon

【榨菜】zhàcài〈名〉 pickled mustard tuber

【榨取】zhàqǔ〈动〉 **1**（压出汁液） press: ～果汁 squeeze juice out of fruit ‖ ～棉籽油 extract oil from cotton seeds **2**（剥削） extort: ～民脂民膏 squeeze out the lifeblood of the people

【榨油水】zhà yóushui〈动〉 extort: 榨不出一点油水 not able to squeeze anything out of sb.

【榨汁机】zhàzhījī〈名〉 juicer

蜡 zhà〈名〉〈古〉 sacrifice offered at the end of a year ▸là

zha

馇（餷）zha ▸饹馇 gēzha ▸chā

zhāi

侧（側）zhāi〈动〉〈口〉 slant ▸cè

【侧棱】zhāileng〈动〉〈口〉 slant: ～着耳朵听 be all ears

【侧歪】zhāiwai〈动〉〈口〉 slant: 帽子～在一边儿 tilt one's hat to one side

斋（齋）zhāi

A〈动〉 **1**（斋戒） take a bath and abstain from meat, wine, etc. [before offering sacrifices to gods or ancestors]: ▸～戒 **2**（舍饭） give alms: ～僧 give alms to a monk

B〈名〉 **1**（房屋） building: 新～ new house ▸书～ **2**（素食） vegetarian diet adopted for religious reasons: ▸吃～

【斋饭】zhāifàn〈名〉 **1**（指化缘所得） food given to monks as alms **2**（素食） vegetarian food provided in a Buddhist temple

【斋果】zhāiguǒ〈名〉 offering

【斋醮】zhāijiào〈动〉 [of Buddhist and Taoist priests] set up an altar for prayer rites

【斋戒】zhāijiè〈动〉 **1**（禁食荤、酒） abstain from meat, wine, etc. [when offering sacrifices to gods or ancestors] **2**（封斋） fast: ～节 Ramadan

【斋戒日】zhāijièrì〈名〉 fast day

【斋堂】zhāitáng〈名〉 dining hall in a temple

【斋月】Zhāiyuè〈名〉［伊斯兰教］ Ramadan

摘 zhāi〈动〉 **1**（采下） pluck: ～春茶 pick spring tea ‖ ～棉花 pick cotton ‖ ～眼镜 take off one's glasses ▸～帽子，采～ **2**（选取） take extracts from: 从书中～选一段 select a passage from a book ▸～录，～要 **3**（斥责） rebuke: ▸指～ **4**〈口〉（借钱） borrow money when in urgent need: ▸～借

【摘编】zhāibiān **A**〈动〉 select and edit: 将资料～成书 compile the extracts from the data into a book **B**〈名〉 extracts

【摘抄】zhāichāo〈动〉 extract: ～要点 extract the main points ‖ 日记～ excerpts from a diary

【摘除】zhāichú〈动〉［医学］ excise: ～肿瘤 remove a tumour ‖ 白内障～术 cataract removal

【摘登】zhāidēng〈动〉 publish excerpts: 报纸～了他的报告。 The newspaper carried extracts from his report.

【摘发】zhāifā〈动〉 publish excerpts

【摘记】zhāijì **A**〈动〉 take notes: ～要点 jot down the main points **B**〈名〉 excerpts

【摘借】zhāijiè〈动〉 borrow money when in urgent need

【摘录】zhāilù〈动〉 make extracts: 报纸新闻～ extracts from press reports ‖ 文件～ extracts from a document

【摘帽子】zhāi màozi〈惯〉 rid oneself of a label: 摘掉落后帽子 cast off the label of 'backwardness'

【摘牌】zhāipái〈动〉 **1**（终止交易资格） cancel a security for trading on the stock market **2**（吸收运动员） draft in an athlete from another team **3**（夺取奖牌） win the prize

【摘桃子】zhāi táozi〈成〉〈喻〉 grab the fruits of other people's labour

【摘要】zhāiyào **A**〈动〉 summarize: ～发表 publish excerpts **B**〈名〉 summary: 社论～ summary of an editorial ‖ 谈话～ extracts from a conversation

【摘译】zhāiyì **A**〈动〉 translate selected passages **B**〈名〉 translation of selected passages

【摘引】zhāiyǐn〈动〉 quote: ～别人的文章要注明出处。 When you quote somebody, you must make reference to the original author and the specific work.

【摘由】zhāiyóu〈动〉 make key extracts for reference

zhái

宅 zhái〈名〉 house: 家～ home ‖ 张～ the Zhangs' residence ▸～邸

【宅邸】zháidǐ〈名〉〈书〉 mansion

【宅地】zháidì〈名〉 land used for building a house

【宅第】zháidì〈名〉〈书〉 mansion

【宅基】zháijī〈名〉 foundations of a house

【宅基地】zháijīdì〈名〉 land used for rural housing

【宅门】zháimén〈名〉 **1**（指大门） gate of a mansion **2**（指人家） family living in a mansion: 胡同里有好几个～。 There are quite a number of big families living in the lane.

【宅男】zháinán〈名〉 otaku [refers to a man]

【宅女】zháinǚ〈名〉 otaku [refers to a woman]

【宅院】zháiyuàn〈名〉 courtyard house

【宅子】zháizi〈名〉〈口〉 house: 一处/所～ a house/residence

择（擇）zhái〈动〉 choose: ～菜 trim vegetables for cooking ▸zé

【择不开】zháibukāi〈动〉 **1**（无法理清） be unable to undo: ～这团乱线 be unable to unravel the tangled threads **2**（没空闲） be unable to extricate oneself: 一点儿工夫也～ not have a moment to spare

【择席】zháixí〈动〉 be unable to sleep well in a new place: 从不～ sleep well in any place

翟 Zhái〈名〉 Zhai [surname] ▸dí

zhǎi

窄 zhǎi〈形〉 **1** ▸**p. 82**（狭小） narrow: ～道/胡同 narrow path/lane ‖ 马路太～。 The road is too narrow. ▸～小，狭～ **2**（不开朗） narrow-minded: 心胸狭～ be narrow-minded ‖ 心眼儿～ be petty **3**〈口〉（困窘） hard up: 他家的日子过得挺～。 His family was very hard up.

【窄带】zhǎidài〈名〉［通信］ narrow band

【窄轨】zhǎiguǐ〈名〉 narrow gauge

【窄小】zhǎixiǎo〈形〉 narrow and small: ～的公寓 poky flat

zhài

债（債）zhài〈名〉 debt: 还～ clear a debt ‖ 无～一身轻。 Out of debt, out of danger. ▸负～，公～

【债多不愁】zhàiduōbùchóu〈俗〉 many debts drive away worries

【债户】zhàihù〈名〉 debtor

【债款】zhàikuǎn〈名〉 loan: 偿还～ repay a loan ‖ 巨额～ huge debt

【债权】zhàiquán〈名〉［法律］ creditor's right: ～转让 cession of claim

【债权人】zhàiquánrén〈名〉 creditor: ～权益 creditor's claim

【债券】zhàiquàn〈名〉 bond: 认购～ buy bonds ‖ 发行～ issue bonds ‖ 工业/金融～ industrial/financial bonds

【债券兑换】zhàiquàn duìhuàn〈名〉 bond conversion

【债券基金】zhàiquàn jījīn〈名〉 bond fund

【债券投资】zhàiquàn tóuzī〈名〉bond investment
【债券型】zhàiquànxíng〈形〉[金融] bond-type: ～基金 bond-type fund
【债市】zhàishì〈名〉bond market
【债台高筑】zhàitái-gāozhù〈成〉be up to one's ears in debt: ～的公司 company deep in debt
【债务】zhàiwù〈名〉debt: 清偿～ pay off one's debts ‖ ～缠身 be debt-ridden
【债务顾问】zhàiwù gùwèn ▸**p. 966**〈名〉debt counsellor
【债务人】zhàiwùrén〈名〉debtor
【债主】zhàizhǔ〈名〉creditor

砦 zhài = 寨 zhài

寨 zhài〈名〉**1**（防御工事）stockade: ▸山～ **2**〈旧〉（营房）camp: ▸安营扎～, 营～ **3**〈旧〉（山寨）mountain stronghold: ▸～主 **4**（村子）stockaded village: 本村本～ this village of ours ▸村～
【寨主】zhàizhǔ〈名〉〈旧〉brigand chief
【寨子】zhàizi〈名〉**1**（防御工事）stockade **2**（村子）stockaded village

瘵 zhài〈名〉〈书〉disease: 痨～ tuberculosis (TB)

攃 zhài〈动〉〈方〉sew on: ～花边 trim with lace ‖ ～扣子 sew on a button

zhān

占 zhān〈动〉practise divination: ▸～卜, ～卦
▸zhàn
【占卜】zhānbǔ〈动〉divine
【占卜术】zhānbǔshù〈名〉augury
【占卦】zhānguà〈动〉divine by means of the Eight Trigrams (八卦): ～问卜 consult the oracle
【占课】zhānkè〈动〉divine by tossing coins
【占梦】zhānmèng〈动〉divine by interpreting dreams
【占星】zhānxīng〈动〉divine by astrology: ～术 astrology
【占星家】zhānxīngjiā ▸**p. 966**〈名〉stargazer

沾 zhān〈动〉**1**（浸湿）moisten: ～湿手帕 moisten a handkerchief ‖ 泪流～襟。Tears wet the front of the jacket. **2**（分享）gain by association: 利益均～ have an equal share of the benefit ▸～光 **3**（附着）be stained with: ～满鲜血 be gory ‖ ～上泥 be stained with mud **4**（接触）touch: 烟酒不～ touch neither tobacco nor alcohol ▸～染
【沾边】zhānbiān〈动〉**1**（挨近）touch on: 这事他没～。He has nothing to do with the matter. **2**（接近实际）be relevant: 你讲的一点也沾不上边儿。What you said is completely irrelevant.
【沾光】zhānguāng〈动〉benefit by association: 企业效益好，员工也～。When the returns of an enterprise look good, the employees benefit by association.
【沾亲带故】zhānqīn-dàigù〈成〉have ties of kinship or friendship: 他要结婚了，～的人都来道贺。Friends and relations all came to congratulate him over his marriage.
【沾染】zhānrǎn〈动〉**1**（指疾病）be infected with: 创口～了细菌。The wound was infected with germs. **2**（指坏习惯）be tainted with: ～恶习 be tainted by bad habits ‖ ～市侩作风 be stained by philistine ways
【沾手】zhānshǒu〈动〉**1**（用手接触）touch with one's hands: 雪花一～就化了。Snowflakes melt at the touch of a hand. **2**（介入）have a hand in: 这事一～就甩不掉。Once you get involved, you can't expect to get out of it.
【沾沾自喜】zhānzhān-zìxǐ〈成〉be complacent: 不要因为取得了一点成绩就～。A little success is nothing to get complacent about.

毡（氈、氊） zhān〈名〉felt: ～帽/靴 felt hat/boots ▸油～
【毡垫】zhāndiàn〈名〉felt pad
【毡房】zhānfáng〈名〉yurt
【毡帐】zhānzhàng〈名〉felt tent
【毡子】zhānzi〈名〉felt

旃 zhān〈书〉
A〈代〉[a fusion of 之 (zhī) and 焉 (yān)]: 勉～! Do it as best you can.
B = 毡 zhān

粘 zhān〈动〉**1**（相互附着）stick to: 糖～在牙上了。The sweet stuck to my teeth. ‖ 这几张邮票～在一块了。These stamps have stuck together. ▸～连 **2**（黏在一起）glue: ～信封 stick down an envelope ‖ 把两块木头～在一起 glue the two pieces of wood together ▸～贴
【粘合剂】zhānhéjì〈名〉adhesive
【粘连】zhānlián **A** ▸**p. 50**〈名〉[医学] adhesion: 肠～ intestinal adhesion **B**〈动〉have to do with: 我跟这事没什么～。I have nothing to do with it.
【粘贴】zhāntiē〈动〉stick: ～海报 stick up posters ‖ 在信封上～邮票 stick a stamp on an envelope

詹 Zhān〈名〉Zhan [surname]

谵（譫） zhān〈动〉〈书〉be delirious
【谵妄】zhānwàng ▸**p. 50**〈名〉[医学] delirium: 震颤性～ delirium tremens
【谵语】zhānyǔ〈书〉**A**〈动〉be delirious **B**〈名〉wild talk

瞻 zhān〈动〉look up: ▸高～远瞩, 观～
【瞻顾】zhāngù〈动〉look ahead and behind
【瞻礼】zhānlǐ **A**〈名〉**1**（天主教节日）religious festival **2**（工作日和周六）weekdays and Saturday **B**〈动〉〈书〉worship
【瞻前顾后】zhānqián-gùhòu〈成〉**1**（形容谨慎）weigh up the pros and cons: 做事要～。Look before you leap. **2**（形容犹豫）be overcautious and indecisive: ～, 犹豫不决 be overcautious and indecisive
【瞻望】zhānwàng〈动〉look forward: ～前途 look ahead to the future ‖ 抬头～ look up into the distance
【瞻仰】zhānyǎng〈动〉look at with reverence: ～遗容 pay one's respects to sb.'s remains ‖ ～烈士陵园 pay a visit to a martyrs' mausoleum

邅 zhān ▸迍邅 zhūnzhān

zhǎn

斩（斬） zhǎn〈动〉cut: ～断魔爪 cut off the devil's claws ▸～草除根, 抄～
【斩仓】zhǎncāng〈动〉sell out all one's securities at a price lower than the one they were bought at
【斩草除根】zhǎncǎo-chúgēn〈成〉〈喻〉eradicate the source of a trouble: ～, 不留后患 eradicate the source of a trouble and remove the cause of future problems
【斩钉截铁】zhǎndīng-jiétiě〈成〉resolute and decisive: ～地拒绝 give a categorical rebuff
【斩获】zhǎnhuò〈动〉〈喻〉score a goal: 一无～ come away with nothing
【斩尽杀绝】zhǎnjìn-shājué〈成〉wipe out: 村里的人被～。All the people in the village were killed.
【斩决】zhǎnjué〈动〉execute by decapitation
【斩客】zhǎnkè〈动〉rip off
【斩首】zhǎnshǒu〈动〉behead: ～示众 decapitate sb. and display the head to the public
【斩头去尾】zhǎntóu-qùwěi〈成〉cut off the head and tail

盏（盞） zhǎn
A〈名〉small cup: 酒～ small wine cup ▸把～
B〈量〉[used for lamps]: 一～灯 a lamp

展 zhǎn〈动〉**1**（张开）spread out: ▸～开, 伸～ **2**（扩大）expand: ▸扩～, 拓～ **3**（放宽）postpone: ▸～缓, ～期, ～限 **4**（展出）exhibit: ▸～出, ～览, 预～ **5**（施展）give free play to: ～其所长 display one's strong points ▸施～, 一筹莫～
【展板】zhǎnbǎn〈名〉exhibition board
【展播】zhǎnbō〈动〉broadcast TV/radio programmes: 电视台正举办迎春文艺节目～。The TV station is broadcasting a Spring Festival entertainment programme.
【展翅】zhǎnchì〈动〉spread the wings: ～飞翔 spread the wings for flight ‖ ～高飞 soar to the sky
【展出】zhǎnchū〈动〉exhibit: 公开～ exhibit publicly ‖ 巡回～ travelling exhibition
【展馆】zhǎnguǎn〈名〉**1**（指组成部分）showroom **2** = 展览馆 zhǎnlǎnguǎn
【展柜】zhǎnguì〈名〉display case
【展缓】zhǎnhuǎn〈动〉postpone: ～行期 postpone the date for departure ‖ 一再～ be postponed again and again
【展会】zhǎnhuì〈名〉exhibition
【展开】zhǎnkāi〈动〉**1**（张开）spread out: ～地图 spread out a map ‖ ～画卷 unfold a picture scroll **2**（大规模进行）launch: ～攻势 launch an offensive ‖ ～热烈的讨论 set off a heated discussion
【展宽】zhǎnkuān〈动〉broaden: ～街道 widen the street
【展览】zhǎnlǎn〈动〉exhibit: 绘画～ painting exhibition ‖ 摄影～ photography exhibition ‖ 图书～ book exhibition
【展览馆】zhǎnlǎnguǎn〈名〉exhibition hall: 工业～ industrial exhibition hall
【展览会】zhǎnlǎnhuì〈名〉exhibition: 工业～ industrial exhibition
【展露】zhǎnlù〈动〉display: ～才华 display one's talent
【展卖】zhǎnmài〈动〉exhibit and sell: ～活动 exhibition and sales activities

【展品】zhǎnpǐn〈名〉 exhibit: 陈列～ display exhibits ‖ 请勿触摸～。 Please do not touch the exhibits.
【展评】zhǎnpíng〈动〉 exhibit and evaluate: 家电～会 appraisal exhibition of home electrical appliances
【展期】zhǎnqī A〈动〉 postpone: 会议～举行。 The meeting has been postponed. ‖ 展览会～一周闭幕。 The exhibition will be extended for another week. B〈名〉 duration of an exhibition: ～为十天。 The exhibition will last for 10 days.
【展区】zhǎnqū〈名〉 display area
【展商】zhǎnshāng〈名〉 business person participating in an exhibition
【展示】zhǎnshì〈动〉 display: ～内心世界 reveal sb.'s inner world ‖ ～新形象 showcase a new image
【展示区】zhǎnshìqū〈名〉 exhibit area: 新型轿车～ new car exhibit
【展事】zhǎnshì〈名〉 exhibition activities
【展室】zhǎnshì〈名〉 exhibition room
【展台】zhǎntái〈名〉 stall
【展厅】zhǎntīng〈名〉 exhibition hall
【展团】zhǎntuán〈名〉 delegation participating in an exhibition
【展望】zhǎnwàng〈动〉 look ahead: ～世界局势 have a full view of the world situation ‖ ～未来 look ahead to the future ‖ 他爬上山顶，向四周～。 He climbed up to the top of the mountain and looked around.
【展位】zhǎnwèi〈名〉 display booth
【展现】zhǎnxiàn〈动〉 unfold before one's eyes: ～才华 display one's talents ‖ 一派欣欣向荣的景象～在眼前。 A picture of prosperity presented itself before our eyes.
【展限】zhǎnxiàn〈动〉 extend a time limit: 债款到期不再～。 The repayment of the loan will not be deferred any further.
【展销】zhǎnxiāo〈动〉 display and sell: ～商品 display and sell goods
【展销会】zhǎnxiāohuì〈名〉 commodities fair: 儿童用品～ children's goods fair ‖ 服装～ garment fair
【展性】zhǎnxìng〈名〉［物理］malleability: ～合金 ductile alloy ‖ ～镍 malleable nickel
【展演】zhǎnyǎn〈名〉 festival (of performances)
【展业】zhǎnyè〈动〉 promote a business [esp an insurance business]
【展映】zhǎnyìng〈名〉 festival (of films or television plays)

崭（嶄）zhǎn

A〈形〉〈书〉 towering: ▸～露头角
B〈副〉 especially: ▸～新
【崭露头角】zhǎnlù-tóujiǎo〈成〉 [of young people] come to prominence: ～的青年艺术家 up-and-coming young artist
【崭新】zhǎnxīn〈形〉 brand new: ～的机器 brand new machines ‖ ～的面貌 completely new look

搌 zhǎn〈动〉 dab to soak up liquid: 海绵可～水。 Sponges soak up water.

【搌布】zhǎnbù〈名〉 dishcloth; tea towel〈英〉

辗（輾）zhǎn

【辗转】zhǎnzhuǎn〈动〉 1（翻来覆去） toss and turn: ～不眠 toss and turn without getting a wink of sleep 2（几经转手） pass through many places: ～来到首都 pass through many places on the way to the capital ‖ ～流传 pass through many different hands
【辗转反侧】zhǎnzhuǎn-fǎncè〈成〉 have a sleepless night: ～，彻夜未眠 toss and turn all night without getting a wink of sleep

zhàn

占（佔）zhàn〈动〉 1（强占） seize: 抢～高地 vie for occupation of the highlands ▸～领，霸～，攻～ 2（拥有） constitute: ～优势 gain the upper hand ‖ 赞成的～多数。 Those in favour constitute the majority.

▸zhān
【占比】zhànbǐ〈名〉 ratio: 打算购房的～不到20%。 The proportion of people planning to buy property is under 20%.
【占道】zhàndào〈动〉 occupy the road: 小摊小贩～经营情况严重。 Stalls operating from the road are a serious problem.
【占地】zhàndì〈动〉 cover an area: 新建的博物馆～九千平方米。 The newly-built museum covers an area of 9,000 square metres.
【占据】zhànjù〈动〉 occupy: ～地盘 seize a territory ‖ ～战略要地 occupy a position of strategic importance
【占领】zhànlǐng〈动〉 1（凭武力占有） seize: ～机场 seize an airport ‖ ～要塞 capture a fort 2（占据并拥有） dominate: ～市场 dominate the market ‖ ～新的科技领域 dominate new fields in science and technology
【占领军】zhànlǐngjūn〈名〉occupying army
【占领区】zhànlǐngqū〈名〉 occupied area
【占便宜】zhàn piányi〈动〉 1（取得不应得的利益） profit at other people's expense 2〈喻〉（占优势） be in an advantageous position: 个儿高的人打篮球～。 Taller people have an advantage in playing basketball.
【占上风】zhàn shàngfēng〈惯〉〈喻〉gain the upper hand: 辩论中他始终～。 He had the upper hand throughout the debate.
【占先】zhànxiān〈动〉 take the lead
【占线】zhànxiàn〈动〉 [of telephone line] be engaged〈英〉; be busy〈美〉: 电话～，请稍候再拨。 The line is engaged. Please call back later.
【占小便宜】zhàn xiǎopiányi〈俗〉 gain petty advantages: ～吃大亏 gain petty advantages only to suffer heavy losses
【占用】zhànyòng〈动〉 occupy and use: ～耕地 occupy cultivated land and put it to other uses ‖ 很抱歉～了你的时间。 I am sorry to have taken up your time.
【占有】zhànyǒu〈动〉 1（占据） occupy 2（处于） hold: 工业在国民经济中～重要地位。 Industry holds an important place in the national economy. 3（掌握） own: ～第一手资料 possess first-hand data ‖ ～生产资料 own the means of production
【占着茅坑不拉屎】zhànzhe máokēng bù lāshǐ〈俗〉〈喻〉 be a dog in the manger

栈（棧）zhàn〈名〉 1〈书〉（棚子） pen: 马～ stable ‖ 羊～ sheep pen 2 = 栈道 zhàndào 3（用于存放货物） warehouse;（用于留宿） inn: ▸货～，客～

【栈道】zhàndào〈名〉 plank road built on wooden brackets fixed into cliffs: ▸明修～，暗度陈仓
【栈房】zhànfáng〈名〉 1（用于存放货物） warehouse 2〈方〉（用于留宿） inn
【栈桥】zhànqiáo〈名〉（在港口） landing stage;（在火车站） loading bridge

战¹（戰）zhàn

A〈动〉 fight: 为独立/自由而～ fight for independence/liberty ‖ 他们愈～愈勇。 The more involved they were in the battle, the more valiantly they fought. ▸～胜，百～百胜
B〈名〉 war: 核～ nuclear warfare ‖〈喻〉价格～ price war ▸持久～，空～，决一死～

战²（戰）zhàn〈动〉 tremble: 冷得直打～ shiver with cold ▸～抖，胆～心惊，寒～

【战败】zhànbài〈动〉 1（被打败） suffer a defeat: ～国 defeated nation ‖ 敌军～了。 The enemy troops were defeated. 2（打败） beat: 我们～了敌军。 We defeated the enemy troops.
【战报】zhànbào〈名〉 battlefield communiqué: 发表～ issue a war communiqué ‖〈喻〉 工地～ report from a construction site
【战备】zhànbèi〈名〉 combat preparedness: 加强～ step up combat readiness ‖ 进入一级～ enter into first-degree combat preparedness
【战表】zhànbiǎo〈名〉 written challenge to war: 下～ issue a written declaration of war
【战场】zhànchǎng〈名〉 battlefield: 奔赴～ march to the battlefield ‖〈喻〉 抗洪～ battlefields of flood-fighting
【战车】zhànchē〈名〉 war chariot
【战船】zhànchuán〈名〉 warship
【战刀】zhàndāo〈名〉 sabre
【战地】zhàndì〈名〉 battleground: ～指挥部 field headquarters ‖〈喻〉 参赛队已大半抵达～。 Most of the participating teams have already arrived at the venue.
【战地记者】zhàndì jìzhě ▸p. 966〈名〉 war correspondent
【战抖】zhàndǒu〈动〉 tremble: 双手～ one's hands tremble
【战斗】zhàndòu A〈名〉 battle: 投入～ go into battle ‖ 在～中牺牲 be killed in action B〈动〉 1（交战） fight: ～部队 combat forces ‖ ～任务 combat mission ‖ 并肩～ fight shoulder to shoulder ‖ ～英雄 combat hero 2（劳动或工作） take action: 投入抢险～ take quick action to meet an emergency
【战斗机】zhàndòujī〈名〉 fighter plane
【战斗舰】zhàndòujiàn〈名〉 battleship
【战斗力】zhàndòulì〈名〉 combat effectiveness: 提高～ increase combat effectiveness ‖ ～强/弱 high/low combat effectiveness
【战斗员】zhàndòuyuán〈名〉 combatant
【战端】zhànduān〈名〉〈书〉 beginning of a war: 挑起～ provoke a war
【战犯】zhànfàn〈名〉 war criminal: ～审判法庭 war crime tribunal
【战俘】zhànfú〈名〉 prisoner of war: 交换～ exchange prisoners of war ‖ 遣返～ repatriate prisoners of war
【战俘营】zhànfúyíng〈名〉 prisoner-of-war (POW) camp
【战斧式导弹】zhànfǔshì dǎodàn〈名〉 Tomahawk missile
【战歌】zhàngē〈名〉 battle song
【战功】zhàngōng〈名〉battle achievements: 立～ distinguish oneself in action ‖ ～显赫 have glorious achievements in war
【战鼓】zhàngǔ〈名〉 battle drum
【战国】Zhànguó〈名〉 Warring States

Period: ～七雄 seven states of the Warring States Period
【战果】zhànguǒ〈名〉victory: 扩大～ exploit a victory ‖〈喻〉～辉煌 splendid achievements
【战壕】zhànháo〈名〉trench: 挖掘～ dig a trench
【战后】zhànhòu〈名〉post-war period
【战火】zhànhuǒ〈名〉flames of war: ～纷飞 war-ridden
【战祸】zhànhuò〈名〉disaster of war: ～连年。The disaster of war continued for years.
【战机】zhànjī〈名〉1（指机会）opportunity for combat: 抓住～ seize the opportunity for combat ‖ 贻误～ bungle an opportunity for combat 2（指机密）war secret: 泄漏～ leak war secrets 3（指飞机）fighter plane: 出动～拦截敌机 send fighters up to intercept the enemy planes
【战绩】zhànjì〈名〉military exploits: ～辉煌 extraordinary battle achievements ‖〈喻〉在这场比赛中，我队～卓著。In this match our team won great distinction.
【战舰】zhànjiàn〈名〉battleship
【战将】zhànjiàng〈名〉able general
【战局】zhànjú〈名〉war situation: 扭转～ bring about a favourable turn in the war
【战具】zhànjù〈名〉〈书〉weapons: ～精良 be equipped with up-to-date arms
【战况】zhànkuàng〈名〉situation on the battlefield: 了解～ find out the progress of a battle ‖ ～报道 war report
【战利品】zhànlìpǐn〈名〉spoils of war
【战例】zhànlì〈名〉example of a battle: 光辉～ splendid battle example
【战栗】zhànlì〈动〉tremble: 吓得全身～ shiver with fright
【战列舰】zhànlièjiàn〈名〉battleship
【战乱】zhànluàn〈名〉chaos of war: ～的受害者 victims of war
【战略】zhànlüè〈名〉strategy: ～部署 strategic plan ‖ ～决策 strategic decision ‖ ～上藐视敌人，战术上重视敌人 despise the enemy strategically and take full account of him tactically ‖〈喻〉～眼光 strategic vision ‖〈喻〉全球～ global strategy
【战略防御】zhànlüè fángyù〈名〉strategic defence: ～计划 (US) Strategic Defence Initiative
【战略核武器】zhànlüè héwǔqì〈名〉strategic nuclear weapons
【战略轰炸机】zhànlüè hōngzhàjī〈名〉strategic bomber
【战略伙伴关系】zhànlüè huǒbàn guānxi〈名〉strategic partnership
【战略物资】zhànlüè wùzī〈名〉strategic materials: 储备～ stockpile strategic materials
【战马】zhànmǎ〈名〉warhorse
【战幕】zhànmù〈名〉war curtain:〈喻〉拉开～ kick off a match
【战袍】zhànpáo〈名〉battle dress
【战旗】zhànqí〈名〉battle colours
【战勤】zhànqín〈名〉civilian war service
【战区】zhànqū〈名〉war zone
【战胜】zhànshèng〈动〉triumph over: ～敌人 defeat the enemy ‖ ～国 victorious nation ‖ ～困难 surmount difficulties
【战时】zhànshí〈名〉wartime: ～经济 wartime economy
【战士】zhànshì〈名〉1（士兵）soldier: 解放军～ PLA soldier ‖ 新入伍的～ new recruit 2（指从事某种事业）champion: 白衣～ medical worker ‖ 国际主义～ champion of internationalism
【战事】zhànshì〈名〉war: ～频繁。Battles frequently broke out.
【战书】zhànshū〈名〉written challenge to war: 下～ issue a letter of challenge
【战术】zhànshù〈名〉tactics: ～思想 tactical thinking ‖ ～演习 tactical manoeuvres ‖ 闪电～ blitz tactics ‖〈喻〉拖延～ stalling tactics
【战天斗地】zhàntiān-dòudì〈成〉combat nature
【战无不胜】zhànwúbùshèng〈成〉be invincible
【战线】zhànxiàn〈名〉battle line: 缩短～ shorten the battle line ‖ ～拉得过长 over-extend the battle line ‖〈喻〉教育～ battlefront of education ‖〈喻〉思想～ ideological front
【战役】zhànyì〈名〉campaign: 滑铁卢～ Battle of Waterloo
【战鹰】zhànyīng〈名〉fighting eagle [pet name for a fighter plane]: 几只～直冲云霄。A few fighting eagles soared into the sky.
【战友】zhànyǒu〈名〉comrade-in-arms: 老～ old comrade-in-arms
【战云】zhànyún〈名〉〈书〉war clouds: ～密布。War clouds are gathering.
【战战兢兢】zhànzhàn-jīngjīng〈成〉1（形容恐惧）trembling with fright 2（形容谨慎）apprehensive and cautious
【战争】zhànzhēng〈名〉war: 常规～ conventional warfare ‖ 局部～ local war ‖ 医治～创伤 heal war wounds ▸解放～，鸦片～
【战争贩子】zhànzhēng fànzi〈名〉warmonger

站¹

站¹ zhàn〈动〉1（直立）stand: ～出来 step forward ‖ ～起来 stand up ‖〈喻〉～在党的立场上 uphold the Party's stand ‖〈喻〉～稳立场 take a firm stand ‖ 中国人民～起来了。The Chinese people have stood up. ▸～岗，～立 2（停下）stop: 不怕慢，只怕～。It's better to move on slowly than merely to mark time.

站²

站² zhàn〈名〉1（停车点）station: 长途汽车～ long-distance bus station ‖ 火车～ railway station ‖ 火车到～了。The train has arrived at the station. ▸终点～ 2（工作点）centre: 供应～ supply centre ‖ 雷达～ radar station ‖ 维修～ service station ▸加油～，气象～
【站队】zhànduì〈动〉line up
【站岗】zhàngǎng〈动〉stand guard: ～放哨 stand guard and assume sentry duty
【站柜台】zhàn guìtái〈动〉serve as a shop assistant
【站立】zhànlì〈动〉stand: 他默默地～在烈士纪念碑前。He stood before the war memorial without uttering a sound.
【站名】zhànmíng〈名〉name of a station: 报～ announce the name of a stop
【站牌】zhànpái〈名〉route board
【站票】zhànpiào〈名〉standing ticket: 发售～ sell standing tickets
【站台】zhàntái〈名〉platform: 列车正从四号～出站。The train is pulling out of platform four.
【站台票】zhàntáipiào〈名〉platform ticket
【站长】zhànzhǎng〈名〉head of a station
【站住】zhànzhù〈动〉1（停下）stop: 听到有人喊他，他连忙～了。He stopped when he heard someone call him. 2（站稳）stand firmly: 她大病初愈，腿软站不住。She felt weak in her legs and could hardly stand because she had just recovered from a serious illness. 3（稳固）gain a firm footing: 他在这里终于～了。He has finally consolidated his position here. 4（有说服力）hold: 你的论点站不住。Your argument doesn't hold.
【站住脚】zhànzhùjiǎo〈动〉1（停下）stop: 他跑得太快，一下子站不住脚。He was running too fast to be able to make a sudden stop. 2（歇息）stay put: 忙得站不住脚 have no time to rest 3（站稳）gain a firm footing: 这家餐馆由于经营得好，在这里～了。The restaurant has gained a firm footing thanks to good management. 4（有说服力）hold water: 这个论点能～。This argument is tenable.

绽（綻）

绽（綻）zhàn〈动〉burst: ～出笑容 crack a smile ‖ 鞋开～了。The shoe burst a seam. ▸皮开肉～
【绽放】zhànfàng〈动〉burst into full bloom: 百花～。The flowers are in full bloom.
【绽露】zhànlù〈动〉show

湛

湛 zhàn〈形〉1（深厚）profound: ▸精～ 2（清澈）crystal clear
【湛蓝】zhànlán〈形〉azure: ～的海洋 blue sea ‖ ～的天空 clear blue sky
【湛绿】zhànlǜ〈形〉dark green
【湛清】zhànqīng〈形〉crystal clear: 河水～见底。The water is so clear that the riverbed is clearly visible.

颤（顫）

颤（顫）zhàn = 战² zhàn ▸chàn
【颤栗】zhànlì = 战栗 zhànlì

蘸

蘸 zhàn〈动〉dip in: ～墨水 dip in ink ‖ ～糖吃 eat sth. dipped in sugar ‖ 大葱～酱 spring onions dipped in sauce
【蘸火】zhànhuǒ〈动〉［冶金］quench

zhāng

张（張）

张（張）zhāng
A〈动〉1（拉开）draw: ～弓射箭 draw a bow and let fly the arrow ▸剑拔弩～ 2（展开）spread: ～开翅膀 spread the wings ‖ ～网捕鱼 spread out a net to catch fish ▸～嘴 3（夸大）magnify: ▸夸～，虚～声势 4（陈设）set out: 大～宴席 lay on a feast ▸～灯结彩，～贴 5（营业）open: 新～ newly opened for business ▸开～ 6（看）look: ▸东～西望
B〈形〉wanton: ▸乖～，嚣～
C〈量〉1（用于弓）[used for bows]: 一～弓 a bow 2（用于脸、嘴）[used for human face and mouth]: 一～脸 a face ‖ 两～嘴 two mouths 3（用于纸等）[used for paper, paintings, etc.]: 一～票 a ticket ‖ 一～纸 a sheet of paper ‖ 三～照片 three photos 4（用于桌子等）[used for tables, etc.]: 一～床/桌子 a bed/table
D〈名〉one of the 28 constellations in ancient Chinese astronomy
【张榜】zhāngbǎng〈动〉put up a notice: ～招贤 advertise for talented people
【张本】zhāngběn〈名〉1（指事先准备）anticipatory action 2（指伏笔）anticipatory remark
【张大】zhāngdà〈动〉〈书〉magnify: ～其词 exaggerate
【张灯结彩】zhāngdēng-jiécǎi〈成〉be decked with lanterns and coloured streamers
【张挂】zhāngguà〈动〉hang up: ～地图 hang up a map ‖ ～蚊帐 hang up a

mosquito net
【张冠李戴】Zhāngguān-Lǐdài〈成〉confuse one thing with another
【张皇】zhānghuáng〈形〉〈书〉flustered: 神色～ look flustered
【张皇失措】zhānghuáng-shīcuò〈成〉be panic-stricken
【张家长，李家短】Zhāngjiā cháng, Lǐjiā duǎn〈俗〉gossip
【张口】zhāngkǒu = 张嘴 zhāngzuǐ
【张口结舌】zhāngkǒu-jiéshé〈成〉be at a loss for words
【张狂】zhāngkuáng〈形〉insolent: 举止～ be insolent in one's behaviour
【张力】zhānglì〈名〉［物理］tension
【张罗】zhāngluo〈动〉**1**（料理）attend to: ～后事 make arrangements for a funeral ‖ 烧伤病人太多，一个护士～不过来。There are too many burn victims for just one nurse to attend to. **2**（筹备）plan and prepare: 他们正～着开会。They are making preparations for a conference. ‖ 她正～着给儿子办婚事。She is busy making preparations for her son's wedding. **3**（接待）greet and entertain: ～客人 look after the guests
【张目】zhāngmù〈动〉**1**（睁大眼）open one's eyes wide: ～注视 watch with wide-open eyes **2**（助威）build sb. up: 为坏人～ embolden the evildoers
【张三李四】Zhāngsān-Lǐsì〈成〉any man in street
【张贴】zhāngtiē〈动〉put up: ～告示 put up an official notice ‖ ～海报 put up posters ‖ 禁止～。No bill posting.
【张望】zhāngwàng〈动〉look around: 四处～ look around in every direction ‖ 探头～ crane one's neck to look around
【张牙舞爪】zhāngyá-wǔzhǎo〈成〉make threatening gestures
【张扬】zhāngyáng〈动〉publicize: 四处～ publicize all over the place
【张嘴】zhāngzuǐ〈动〉**1**（指说话）open one's mouth to speak: 他一～，我就知道他要说什么。I knew what he was going to say as soon as he opened his mouth. **2**（指请求）ask for a favour: 向人借钱，我实在不愿～。I really don't want to have to ask anyone for money.

章 zhāng〈名〉**1**（规程）rules: ▸党～，规～，简～ **2**（条目）item: ▸约法三～ **3**（章节）chapter: 全书由36～组成。The book consists of 36 chapters. ▸～节，篇～，乐～ **4**（条理）order: ▸杂乱无～ **5**（标识）badge: ▸臂～，领～，勋～ **6**（图章）stamp: 刻～ engrave a seal ▸盖～，公～，印～ **7**〈旧〉（指文体）memorial to the emperor: ▸奏～
【章草】zhāngcǎo〈名〉［书法］memorial script
【章程】zhāngchéng〈名〉rules: 中国共产党～ the Constitution of the Chinese Communist Party ‖ 违反董事会～ violate the constitution of the board of directors
【章法】zhāngfǎ〈名〉**1**（指结构布局）organization and structure of a piece of writing: 文章～严谨。The article is well organized. **2**（指规矩、程序）procedure: 遇事要镇静，别乱了～。It's important to be calm about things, and not to mess up procedures.
【章回体】zhānghuítǐ〈名〉chapter style [type of traditional Chinese novel in which each chapter is headed by a couplet giving the gist of its content]
【章回小说】zhānghuí xiǎoshuō〈名〉chapter-by-chapter novel
【章节】zhāngjié〈名〉chapters: 全书共分十二～。The book is divided into 12 chapters.
【章句】zhāngjù〈名〉**1**（指章节、句子）chapters, sections, sentences and phrases in ancient texts **2**（指著作）syntactic and semantic analysis of ancient texts: ～之学 philological study of ancient texts
【章鱼】zhāngyú〈名〉octopus
【章则】zhāngzé〈名〉rules and regulations: 遵守～ adhere to rules and regulations
【章子】zhāngzi〈名〉〈方〉seal: 盖～ stamp sth. with a seal ‖ 刻～ engrave a seal

獐 zhāng〈名〉river deer
【獐头鼠目】zhāngtóu-shǔmù〈成〉contemptible and unsightly looking
【獐子】zhāngzi〈名〉［动物］river deer

彰 zhāng
A〈形〉evident: ▸相得益～，欲盖弥～
B〈动〉make known: ～其德威 display one's virtue and dignity ▸～善瘅恶，表～
【彰明较著】zhāngmíng-jiàozhù〈成〉conspicuous
【彰善瘅恶】zhāngshàn-dàn'è〈成〉uphold virtue and condemn vice
【彰显】zhāngxiǎn **A**〈形〉conspicuous: 名声～ be well-reputed **B**〈动〉bring out conspicuously: ～英雄本色 make a conspicuous show of the hero's character

嫜 zhāng〈名〉〈书〉father-in-law [husband's father]

璋 zhāng〈名〉〈古〉jade tablet

樟 zhāng〈名〉［植物］camphor tree
【樟木】zhāngmù〈名〉camphorwood: ～家具 camphorwood furniture
【樟脑】zhāngnǎo〈名〉camphor
【樟脑丸】zhāngnǎowán〈名〉camphor ball
【樟脑油】zhāngnǎoyóu〈名〉camphor oil
【樟树】zhāngshù〈名〉camphor tree

蟑 zhāng
【蟑螂】zhāngláng〈名〉［昆虫］cockroach

zhǎng

长（長） zhǎng
A〈动〉**1**（生长）grow: 这种树～得快。This type of tree grows very fast. ‖ 这孩子～得真壮实。This child is sturdily built. ▸～大，生～，土生土～ **2**（生出）come into being: ～胡子 grow a beard ‖ ～锈 get rusty ‖ 地上～满了杂草。The ground is overgrown with weeds. **3**（增长）increase: ～工资 get a pay rise ‖ ～见识 increase one's knowledge ‖ 这可真让我～见识了。This is a real eye-opener. ▸增～
B〈形〉**1**（年长）senior: 他～我三岁。He is three years older than me. ▸～辈，年～ **2**（年纪最大）eldest: ～女 eldest daughter ‖ ～兄 eldest brother **3**（长者）elder: ▸师～，兄～
C〈名〉（领导人）chief: 乡～ township head ▸部～，首～，校～
▸cháng
【长辈】zhǎngbèi〈名〉elder: 尊敬～ respect the elders
【长膘】zhǎngbiāo〈动〉[of domestic animal] fatten up
【长大】zhǎngdà〈动〉grow up: ～成人 become an adult
【长房】zhǎngfáng〈名〉eldest branch of a family [ie that of the eldest son]
【长个儿】zhǎnggèr〈动〉〈口〉grow taller: 他真的～了！He's really grown!
【长官】zhǎngguān〈名〉〈旧〉commanding officer
【长机】zhǎngjī〈名〉［军事］lead aircraft
【长进】zhǎngjìn〈动〉make progress: 技艺大有～ make great progress in skill
【长老】zhǎnglǎo〈名〉**1**〈书〉（年龄大的人）elder **2**［佛教］elder [respectful term of address for an elderly monk] **3**［基督教］elder
【长老会】Zhǎnglǎohuì〈名〉［基督教］Presbyterian Church
【长脸】zhǎngliǎn〈动〉〈口〉be an honour to: 这种产品获了大奖，真为咱厂～。This product has been rewarded with the highest prize, which is a great honour to our factory.
【长门】zhǎngmén = 长房 zhǎngfáng
【长女】zhǎngnǚ〈名〉eldest daughter
【长亲】zhǎngqīn〈名〉senior/elder relatives
【长上】zhǎngshàng〈名〉**1**（长辈）elder, senior **2**（上级）boss, superior
【长势】zhǎngshì〈名〉growth (of a crop): 小麦～喜人。The wheat is doing well.
【长孙】zhǎngsūn〈名〉eldest grandson
【长相】zhǎngxiàng〈名〉looks: ～好 have good looks ‖ 从他们的～上看，不像兄弟俩。They don't look like brothers.
【长兄】zhǎngxiōng〈名〉eldest brother
【长者】zhǎngzhě〈名〉**1**（指年纪、辈分高）elder **2**（指年纪、德行高）venerable elder
【长子】zhǎngzǐ〈名〉eldest son

仉 Zhǎng〈名〉Zhang [surname]

涨（漲） zhǎng〈动〉rise: 河水暴～。The river suddenly rose. ‖ 物价上～。The price is going up. ▸水～船高
▸zhàng
【涨潮】zhǎngcháo〈动〉[of tide] rise: ～了。The tide is rising
【涨风】zhǎngfēng〈名〉upward trend of prices: 煞住～ curb a price increase
【涨幅】zhǎngfú〈名〉margin of increase: ～达到3%。There was a 3% rise.
【涨幅榜】zhǎngfúbǎng〈名〉price increase table: 猪肉居～榜首。Pork is topping the table of price increases.
【涨价】zhǎngjià〈动〉raise the price: 变相～ disguised price increase
【涨落】zhǎng-luò〈动〉rise and fall: 价格的～ fluctuations of prices
【涨势】zhǎngshì〈名〉rising trend: 原材料价格～不减。The price of raw materials keeps going up.
【涨停板】zhǎngtíngbǎn〈名〉［金融］ceiling

掌 zhǎng
A〈名〉**1**（手掌）palm: ▸鼓～，手～ **2**（脚掌）pad: ▸脚～，熊～，鸭～ **3**（鞋底）shoe sole or heel: 钉～儿 have shoes soled or heeled ‖ 后～儿 heel ‖ 前～儿 sole **4**（马蹄铁）horseshoe: 这匹马该钉～了。It's time for the horse to be shod. ▸马～
B〈动〉**1**（用手掌打）slap: ▸～嘴 **2**（手持）hold: ▸～灯 **3**（掌管）control: ▸～舵，～柜，～权
【掌厨】zhǎngchú〈动〉be head chef

【掌灯】zhǎngdēng〈动〉 1 (持灯) hold a lamp in one's hand 2 (点灯) light an oil lamp: 天黑了，该～了。 It's getting dark. Let's light the lamp.
【掌舵】zhǎngduò A〈动〉 be at the helm B〈名〉 helmsman
【掌故】zhǎnggù〈名〉 anecdotes: 历史/文坛～ historical/literary anecdotes
【掌管】zhǎngguǎn〈动〉 administer: ～财政 administer finances ‖ 由专人～ be taken care of by specially assigned personnel
【掌柜】zhǎngguì〈名〉 1〈旧〉(负责人) shopkeeper: 女～ woman shopkeeper 2〈方〉(丈夫) husband: 我家～的 my husband
【掌控】zhǎngkòng〈动〉 control: ～公司的人事任免权 control the power to appoint and dismiss
【掌门人】zhǎngménrén〈名〉 1 (指武林门派) head of a martial arts school 2 (指某领域) leader of a certain field: 购物网的～ leader of a shopping network
【掌权】zhǎngquán〈动〉 hold the reins of power: 自从他～以来 since he came into power
【掌上电脑】zhǎngshàng diànnǎo〈名〉 hand-held computer, palmtop, PDA
【掌上明珠】zhǎngshàng-míngzhū〈成〉〈喻〉 beloved daughter: 女儿是他的～。 His daughter is the apple of his eye.
【掌勺儿】zhǎngsháor〈动〉 be the head chef: ～的 chef
【掌声】zhǎngshēng〈名〉 applause: 经久不息的～ prolonged applause ‖ 热烈的～ enthusiastic applause
【掌纹】zhǎngwén〈名〉 palm print
【掌握】zhǎngwò〈动〉 1 (了解并支配) grasp: ～规律 know the governing rules ‖ ～技能 master techniques ‖ 根据我所～的资料 according to the data in my possession 2 (控制) have in hand: ～政权 hold political power ‖ ～主动权 have the initiative in one's hands ‖ ～自己的命运 be the master of one's own destiny
【掌心】zhǎngxīn〈名〉 1〈本〉 hollow of the palm 2〈喻〉 control: 你怎么样也逃不出他的～。 There's no way that you can break free of his control.
【掌印】zhǎngyìn〈动〉 be in power
【掌灶】zhǎngzào〈动〉 be the chef
【掌灶儿的】zhǎngzàorde〈名〉 chef
【掌子】zhǎngzi〈名〉［矿业］ working face
【掌嘴】zhǎngzuǐ〈动〉 slap sb. in the face

zhàng

丈[1] zhàng

A〈量〉 *zhang* [unit of length, equal to 3.333 metres]
B〈动〉 survey: ▸～量，清～

丈[2] zhàng〈名〉

1 (丈夫) husband: ▸姑～，姐～ 2 (老年男子) senior: ▸岳～
【丈夫】zhàngfū〈名〉 man: ～气概 manliness
【丈夫】zhàngfu〈名〉 husband: ～的权利与义务 husbandly rights and duties
【丈量】zhàngliáng〈动〉 measure: ～地亩 measure land
【丈母娘】zhàngmuniáng〈名〉 mother-in-law [wife's mother]
【丈人】zhàngrén〈名〉〈旧〉 old gentleman [respectful form of address for an old man]
【丈人】zhàngren〈名〉 father-in-law [wife's father]

仗 zhàng

A〈名〉 1 (兵器) weapons: ▸明火执～，仪～ 2 (战斗) battle: ～打不起来。 There will be no war. ‖ 我们这一～打得真漂亮。 We did wonderfully in the battle. ▸败～，打～
B〈动〉 1 (拿着) hold (a weapon): ～剑 hold a sword 2 (倚仗) depend on: ▸～恃，狗～人势，仰～
【仗胆】zhàngdǎn〈动〉 embolden: 喝杯酒仗仗胆 drink some alcohol to get one's courage up
【仗势】zhàngshì〈动〉 take advantage of one's power or connections with influential people
【仗势欺人】zhàngshì-qīrén〈成〉 take advantage of one's power to bully people ‖ 别～。 Don't try to throw weight around.
【仗恃】zhàngshì〈动〉〈书〉 rely on: ～豪门 be patronized by a powerful family
【仗义】zhàngyì A〈动〉〈书〉 uphold justice B〈形〉 loyal: 他很～。 He is very loyal.
【仗义疏财】zhàngyì-shūcái〈成〉 spend money on a good cause
【仗义执言】zhàngyì-zhíyán〈成〉 speak out from a sense of justice

杖 zhàng〈名〉

1 (拐杖) walking stick: 扶～而行 walk with a cane ▸拐～，手～ 2 (棍棒) staff or rod used for a specific purpose: 拿刀动～ threaten with the use of force ▸擀面～，权～

帐（帳） zhàng〈名〉

curtain: ▸～篷，蚊～，营～
【帐幔】zhàngmàn〈名〉 curtain
【帐幕】zhàngmù〈名〉 tent
【帐篷】zhàngpeng〈名〉 tent: 搭～ pitch a tent ‖ 帆布/尼龙～ canvas/nylon tent
【帐子】zhàngzi〈名〉 1 (床帘) bed-curtain 2 (蚊帐) mosquito net

账（賬） zhàng〈名〉

1 (账目) account: 清～ settle the accounts ‖ 做假～ falsify accounts ▸查～，算～ 2 (账本) account book: 一本～ an account book 3 (债) debt: ▸放～，坏～，还～
【账本】zhàngběn = 账簿 zhàngbù
【账簿】zhàngbù〈名〉 accounts book
【账册】zhàngcè = 账簿 zhàngbù
【账单】zhàngdān〈名〉 bill〈英〉; check〈美〉
【账房】zhàngfáng〈名〉 1 (指处所) accountant's office, counting house/room 2 (指人) accountant
【账号】zhànghào〈名〉 account number
【账户】zhànghù〈名〉 account: (在银行)开立～ open an account (with/in a bank) ‖ 冻结～ frozen account
【账面】zhàngmiàn〈名〉 accounts: ～利润 book profit ‖ ～显示他透支了。 The accounts show that he has gone overdrawn.
【账目】zhàngmù〈名〉 accounts: 定期公布～ publish accounts regularly ‖ ～不清 the accounts are not in order

胀（脹） zhàng

A〈动〉 expand: 热～冷缩 expand when heated and contract when cooled ▸膨～
B〈形〉 bloated: 我肚子发～。 My stomach feels bloated.
【胀库】zhàngkù〈动〉 be stocked to the full
【胀闸】zhàngzhá〈名〉 hub brake

涨（漲） zhàng〈动〉

1 (膨胀) swell after absorbing water, etc.: 木耳泡～了。 The edible tree fungus swelled up after being soaked. 2 (充血) be swelled by a rush of blood to the head: 他的脸～得通红。 His face flushed scarlet. ▸头昏脑～ 3 (超出) be more than expected: 钱花～了。 The money was overspent.
▸zhǎng

障 zhàng

A〈动〉 block: ▸～碍
B〈名〉 obstacle: ▸路～，屏～
【障碍】zhàng'ài A〈动〉 hinder: ▸～物 B〈名〉 obstacle: 排除～ remove an obstacle ‖ 设置～ put up a barrier ‖ 语言～ language barrier
【障碍赛跑】zhàng'ài sàipǎo〈名〉 steeplechase: 三千米～ 3000m steeplechase
【障碍物】zhàng'àiwù〈名〉 obstruction: 清除～ remove obstructions ‖ 越过～ jump a barrier
【障蔽】zhàngbì〈动〉 obstruct: ～视线 obstruct one's view
【障眼法】zhàngyǎnfǎ〈名〉 cover-up: 玩～的把戏 throw dust in people's eyes
【障子】zhàngzi〈名〉 fence: 篱笆～ bamboo fence ‖ 树～ tree hedge

嶂 zhàng〈名〉〈书〉

screen-like precipitous mountain peak: ▸层峦叠～

幛 zhàng〈名〉

large, rectangular sheet of silk or cloth with an appropriate message inscribed on it, presented at a wedding, birthday or funeral: 挽～ funeral scroll ‖ 寿～ birthday banner
【幛子】zhàngzi = 幛 zhàng

瘴 zhàng〈名〉

miasma
【瘴疠】zhànglì〈名〉 communicable subtropical diseases
【瘴气】zhàngqì〈名〉 miasma

zhāo

钊（釗） zhāo〈动〉〈书〉

[often used in personal names] encourage

招 zhāo

A〈动〉 1 (招手) beckon: ～之即来 come immediately once beckoned ‖ 出租车扬～点 taxi stand ▸～集，～手 2 (招引) attract: ～蚊蝇 attract flies and mosquitoes ‖ ～灾 court disaster ‖ 这小男孩多～人喜欢! What a sweet little boy! ‖ 这项提案～来很多批评。 The proposal attracted a great deal of criticism. ▸树大～风 3 (招收) recruit: ～合同工/学徒 recruit contract workers/apprentices ‖ 扩～ expand enrolment numbers ▸～标，～兵，～领 4 (招惹) provoke: 这狗不认人，别～它。 This dog doesn't recognize people. Don't tease it. 5 (承认) confess: 他最后～了。 He finally confessed. ▸～供，～认，不打自～
B〈名〉 1〈旧〉(旗幡) banner: 酒～ pub flag ‖ 市～ city banner ▸～子 2 (招式) movement in *wushu*: 一～ a movement (in *wushu*) ▸～数 3 (计策) trick: 你这一～真高啊。 That was really a brilliant move

of yours. ▸高～, 绝～

【招安】zhāo'ān〈动〉[of feudal rulers] offer amnesty to rebels and promise to enlist their service: 接受～ [of former rebels] accept amnesty and pledge loyalty to the ruler

【招办】zhāobàn〈简称〉= 招生办公室

【招标】zhāobiāo〈动〉invite tenders: 采用～方式采购 purchase by way of bidding

【招兵】zhāobīng〈动〉enlist recruits

【招兵买马】zhāobīng-mǎimǎ〈成〉〈喻〉recruit personnel

【招财进宝】zhāocái-jìnbǎo〈成〉[used to wish sb. good luck in business] let riches and treasures come into the house

【招待】zhāodài **A**〈动〉attend to: ～贵宾 receive distinguished guests ‖ ～客人 entertain guests **B**〈名〉attendant: 女～ waitress

【招待费】zhāodàifèi〈名〉entertainment expenses

【招待会】zhāodàihuì〈名〉reception: 记者～ press conference ‖ 盛大的国庆～ grand National Day reception

【招待券】zhāodàiquàn〈名〉complimentary ticket

【招待所】zhāodàisuǒ〈名〉hostel

【招风】zhāofēng〈动〉attract too much attention and invite trouble: ▸树大～

【招风耳】zhāofēng'ěr〈名〉jug ears

【招抚】zhāofǔ = 招安 zhāo'ān

【招工】zhāogōng〈动〉advertise for workers

【招供】zhāogòng〈动〉confess one's crime: 拒不～ refuse to make a confession

【招股】zhāogǔ〈动〉raise capital by floating shares

【招呼】zhāohu〈动〉**1**（呼唤）call: ～工人们进来，该吃午饭了。 Call the workers in; it's time for lunch. **2**（问候）greet: 打～ greet sb. **3**（吩咐）notify: ～他做好了赶快送来。 Tell him to send it here as soon as it is finished. **4**（照料）take care of: ～病人 take care of patients ‖ 我游泳时你帮我～一下衣物，行吗？ Could you keep an eye on my clothes while I have a swim?

【招魂】zhāohún〈动〉evoke a spirit from the dead:〈喻〉他的小说实际上是在为封建制度～。 His novel was actually an attempt at reviving the feudal system.

【招集】zhāojí〈动〉call together: ～部队/人马 muster the troops ‖ 把人们～起来 call people together

【招架】zhāojià〈动〉ward off blows: 只有～之功，毫无还手之力 can hardly defend oneself, let alone go for the attack ‖ 主队实力太强，客队难以～。 The host team was such a powerful opponent that the visiting team could hardly hold their own.

【招考】zhāokǎo〈动〉admit by examination: ～飞行员 recruit pilots through examination ‖ ～公务员 recruit civil servants through a process of examination

【招徕】zhāolái〈动〉solicit (customers or business): ～顾客 solicit customers

【招揽】zhāolǎn〈动〉solicit (customers or business): ～生意 drum up business ‖ 各商行争相～顾客。 Businesses vied with each other to attract customers.

【招领】zhāolǐng〈动〉advertise in the lost-and-found column: ～失物 announce the finding of lost property ‖ 失物～处 Lost Property (Office)

【招募】zhāomù〈动〉recruit: ～新兵 enlist new recruits ‖ ～志愿者 recruit volunteers

【招纳】zhāonà〈动〉〈书〉recruit: ～贤士 recruit men of worth

【招女婿】zhāo nǚxu = 招亲 zhāoqīn 1

【招拍挂】zhāo-pāi-guà〈名〉bidding, auction, and listing: 土地实行公开～ hold the public bidding, listing, and auction of land

【招牌】zhāopai〈名〉**1**（指牌子）shop sign: 金字～ gold-lettered sign **2**（指声誉）reputation of a large business, firm or a quality product: 不良的售后服务会砸了你们企业的～。 Your poor after-service would discredit your enterprise. **3**〈喻〉〈贬〉（幌子）pretence: 打着科学的～进行残酷的动物实验 perform cruel animal experiments in the name of science

【招牌式】zhāopaishì〈形〉trademark: ～动作/笑容 trademark move/smile

【招聘】zhāopìn〈动〉invite applications for a job: ～公务员 recruit civil servants ‖ ～技术员/教师 advertise for technicians/teachers

【招亲】zhāoqīn〈动〉**1**（招女婿）take a man into the family as a son-in-law **2**（入赘）marry into and live with one's bride's family

【招惹】zhāorě〈动〉**1**（引起）invite: ～麻烦 court trouble **2**（逗引）tease: ～他可危险。 It would be dangerous to provoke him.

【招认】zhāorèn〈动〉confess one's crime: 他～偷了那辆汽车。 He confessed to having stolen the car.

【招商】zhāoshāng〈动〉solicit business: ～会 meeting to invite investments ‖ ～项目 project for investment ‖ ～引资 attract investments from overseas

【招商局】Zhāoshāngjú〈名〉China Merchants Steam Navigation Co. Ltd (China Merchants)

【招商银行】Zhāoshāng Yínháng〈名〉China Merchants Bank

【招生】zhāoshēng〈动〉recruit students: ～人数 number of students to be admitted ‖ ～简章 school prospectus

【招生办公室】zhāoshēng bàngōngshì〈名〉student admission office

【招式】zhāoshì〈名〉movement and posture in *wushu* or traditional opera

【招事】zhāoshì〈动〉invite trouble

【招收】zhāoshōu〈动〉recruit: ～新生 admit new students

【招手】zhāoshǒu〈动〉beckon: 向某人～ wave to sb. ‖ ～致意 wave in acknowledgement

【招数】zhāoshù〈名〉**1**（下棋的步子）move in chess: 最后一盘围棋他一连使出几个～，反败为胜。 In the last game of go, he made several moves which turned the tables and defeated his opponent. **2**（武术动作）movement in *wushu*: 他～狠毒，很容易伤了对手。 Every movement he made was vicious and could easily harm his opponent.

【招贴】zhāotiē〈名〉poster: ～广告 poster advertising ‖ 禁止～! No bill stickers!

【招贴画】zhāotiēhuà〈名〉pictorial poster/placard: 张贴～ stick up a poster

【招贤】zhāoxián〈动〉put a call out to recruit talent: 张榜～ put up posters to recruit qualified personnel

【招贤纳士】zhāoxián-nàshì〈成〉invite men of wisdom and virtue

【招降】zhāoxiáng〈动〉summon to surrender

【招降纳叛】zhāoxiáng-nàpàn〈成〉recruit deserters and traitors into one's service

【招眼】zhāoyǎn〈形〉conspicuous: ～的珠宝 ostentatious jewellery

【招摇】zhāoyáo〈动〉show off

【招摇过市】zhāoyáo-guòshì〈成〉swagger about

【招摇撞骗】zhāoyáo-zhuàngpiàn〈成〉swagger about deceiving people: 他冒充名医到处～。 He passed himself off as a renowned physician and cheated people left, right and centre.

【招引】zhāoyǐn〈动〉attract: ～顾客 attract customers ‖ 园里的花～来大群的蜜蜂。 The flowers in the garden have attracted swarms of bees.

【招灾】zhāozāi〈动〉invite trouble: ～惹祸 ask for trouble

【招展】zhāozhǎn〈动〉**1**（飘动）flutter: 彩旗迎风～。 Coloured flags are fluttering in the wind. ▸花枝～ **2**（招商参展）invite exhibitors

【招之则来，挥之则去】zhāo zhī zé lái, huī zhī zé qù〈成〉be at sb.'s beck and call

【招致】zhāozhì〈动〉**1**（招揽人才）scout about for: ～人才 scout about for talented people **2**（引起）bring about: ～灭亡 lead to destruction ‖ ～无谓的牺牲 cause senseless sacrifice

【招赘】zhāozhuì〈动〉have the groom move into the bride's house after marriage

【招子】zhāozi〈名〉**1**（招贴）poster **2**（店牌）shop sign **3**（计策）trick

【招租】zhāozū〈动〉be for rent: 此屋～。 Room to let.

昭 zhāo

A〈形〉clear: ▸～彰, ～著

B〈动〉〈书〉show: 以～信守 show one's good faith ▸～雪

【昭然】zhāorán〈形〉〈书〉clear: 天理～。 The heavenly principles are manifest.

【昭然若揭】zhāorán-ruòjiē〈成〉abundantly clear: 他的罪行～。 His guilt is as clear as the midday sun.

【昭示】zhāoshì〈动〉make clear to all: ～国人 make it clear to all the people ‖ ～后世 make clear to all posterity

【昭雪】zhāoxuě〈动〉exonerate: ～冤案 rehabilitate a person who has been wronged ‖ 平反～ right the wrong and exonerate the disgraced

【昭彰】zhāozhāng〈形〉manifest: 他罪恶～。 He is notorious for his crimes.

【昭昭】zhāozhāo〈书〉**A**〈形〉clear: 日月～。 Bright are the sun and the moon. **B**〈动〉be clear: 岂能以其昏昏，使人～? How can a muddle-headed person make others clear-headed?

【昭著】zhāozhù〈形〉obvious: 恶名～ be notorious ‖ 罪行～ have committed flagrant crimes ▸臭名～

啁 zhāo

▸zhōu

【啁哳】zhāozhā〈形〉〈书〉chirpy

着 zhāo

〈名〉**1**（指下棋）chess move: 高～儿 clever move ‖ 观棋不语，你可别支～儿。 Those who watch chess must not speak, so don't try to assist with any moves. ▸一～不慎，满盘皆输 **2**（计策）trick: 我没～儿了。 I'm at my wits' end. ‖ 这一～厉害。 That's a shrewd move.

▸zháo, zhe, zhuó

【着数】zhāoshù〈名〉**1**（指下棋）chess move: 使出多个～ make a number of moves **2**（指武术）movement in *wushu*: 使～ make a movement **3**（计策）trick

朝 zhāo〈名〉**1**（早晨）early morning: ▸～阳 **2**（天）day: 今～ today ‖ 一～有事 should anything happen at some point ▸cháo

【朝不保夕】zhāobùbǎoxī〈成〉hang in the balance

【朝发夕至】zhāofā-xīzhì〈成〉start out at dawn and arrive at dusk

【朝晖】zhāohuī〈名〉morning sunlight

【朝九晚五】zhāojiǔ-wǎnwǔ〈名〉nine-to-five work

【朝令夕改】zhāolìng-xīgǎi〈成〉make frequent and unpredictable changes in policy

【朝露】zhāolù〈名〉〈书〉**1**〈本〉morning dew **2**〈喻〉be short-lived: 人生如～。Life is fleeting.

【朝气】zhāoqì〈名〉dynamism: 充满～ be full of vigour

【朝气蓬勃】zhāoqì-péngbó〈成〉be full of youthful spirit: ～的青年 vigorous youth

【朝秦暮楚】zhāoQín-mùChǔ〈成〉〈喻〉be quick to switch sides: 他岂是～之辈! He is certainly not the type who frequently switches sides!

【朝日】zhāorì〈名〉morning sun

【朝三暮四】zhāosān-mùsì〈成〉blow hot and cold

【朝思暮想】zhāosī-mùxiǎng〈成〉yearn for day and night: 他终于与～的家人团聚了。Eventually he was reunited with his family whom he had yearned for day and night.

【朝夕】zhāoxī〈名〉**1**（从早到晚）all the time: ～相处 be together from morning till night, be closely associated **2**（短暂时间）very short time: 精湛的技艺非～之功所能得来。First-class skills cannot be acquired in a day's effort.

【朝霞】zhāoxiá〈名〉rosy dawn: ～满天 the morning glow filled the sky

【朝阳】zhāoyáng **A**〈名〉morning sun: 迎着～ move in the morning sunshine ‖ 一轮～从地平线上冉冉升起。The morning sun rose slowly above the horizon. **B**〈形〉promising: ～产业 nascent industry ▸cháoyáng

【朝朝暮暮】zhāozhāo-mùmù〈成〉every day

嘲 zhāo ▸cháo

【嘲哳】zhāozhā = 啁哳 zhāozhā

zháo

着 zháo〈动〉**1**〈书〉（附着）attach **2**（挨上）touch: 前不～村，后不～店 get stranded in an uninhabited area ‖ 脚疼得不能～地 one's feet cannot touch the ground because they hurt so much **3**（受到）be troubled with: ～了慌 be thrown into a panic ▸～凉, ～迷 **4**（燃烧）be ignited;（发光）be lit: 炉子～得很旺。The fire is burning briskly in the stove. ‖ 天黑了，路灯都～了。It was dark, and the street lights were lit. **5**〈方〉（睡着）fall asleep: 他一上床就～了。He fell asleep the moment he got into bed. **6**（达到目的或有了结果）succeed in doing sth.: 猜～了 have guessed right ‖ 睡～了 fall asleep ‖ 我的钱包找～了。I have found my wallet. ▸zhāo, zhe, zhuó

【着边】zháobiān〈动〉be to the point: 她的评论不～。Her comments were off the mark.

【着慌】zháohuāng〈形〉alarmed: 事故发生时，他一点儿也不～。He didn't seem at all alarmed when the accident occurred.

【着火】zháohuǒ〈动〉catch fire: 房子～了! The house is on fire!

【着急】zháojí〈形〉anxious: ～地等待救护车 wait anxiously for the ambulance ‖ 别～，你没什么大病。Don't worry. It's nothing serious.

【着凉】zháoliáng〈动〉catch cold: 外面挺冷，当心～。It's rather chilly outside. Be careful not to catch cold.

【着忙】zháománg〈口〉**A**〈动〉be in a hurry: 时间还早着呢，你着的什么忙? We've got plenty of time. What's all the hurry? ‖ 事先收拾好行李，免得临上车～。Get your luggage ready now to avoid having to rush when it's time to get on the train. **B**〈形〉worried: 听说孩子病了，她心里有点～。Hearing that her child was ill, she felt somewhat anxious.

【着迷】zháomí〈形〉fascinated: 老爷爷的故事让孩子们听得着迷了。The children were captivated by the old man's story.

【着魔】zháomó〈动〉be spellbound: 她最近看小说像着了魔似的。She's been reading novels like mad recently.

【着三不着两】zháo sān bù zháo liǎng〈惯〉scatter-brained: 说话～ speak thoughtlessly

zhǎo

爪 zhǎo〈名〉claw: 虎～ tiger's paw ‖ 鹰～ eagle's talon ▸一鳞半～, 张牙舞～ ▸zhuǎ

【爪哇】Zhǎowā〈名〉Java

【爪牙】zhǎoyá〈名〉〈喻〉underlings: 豢养一批～ keep a pack of henchmen

找 zhǎo〈动〉**1**（寻找）look for: ～地方避雨 seek shelter from the rain ‖ ～工作 look for a job ‖ 到处～孩子 search everywhere for the child ‖ 我～不到回家的路。I can't find my way home. ▸～茬儿, ～死 **2**（见面）ask for: 我想～你们总经理。I'd like to see the general manager. ‖ 刚才有人～你。Someone asked for you just now. **3**（补足）make up: ▸～补 **4**（找零）give change: 不用～了。Keep the change. ‖ 他少～了我一元钱。He short-changed me one yuan. ▸～头

【找不着北】zhǎobùzháo běi〈惯〉be at a loss: 手机品牌名目繁多，让人～。There are so many different brands of mobile phones out there. It's just dizzying.

【找补】zhǎobu〈动〉make up a deficiency: 分量不够，再～点儿。The measure is a bit short. Top it up a little. ‖ 这儿没漆好，再～两下。This part is not well painted and needs a little more paint.

【找茬儿】zhǎochár〈动〉〈口〉pick at: 看样子她是来～的。Evidently she has come to pick a quarrel. ‖ 他老想给我～。He is always trying to find fault with me.

【找刺儿】zhǎocìr〈动〉nit-pick

【找零】zhǎolíng〈动〉return change: 恕不～。No change given.

【找麻烦】zhǎo máfan〈动〉**1**（招惹麻烦）ask for trouble: 自～ look for trouble **2**（给人添麻烦）cause sb. trouble: 不好意思，给你找麻烦了。I'm sorry for causing you trouble.

【找平】zhǎopíng〈动〉make level: 那边儿还差两层砖，～了再往上砌。Two more layers of bricks are needed over there. Let's get that done before going up any higher.

【找婆家】zhǎo pójia〈动〉**1**〈本〉look for a husband **2**〈喻〉find a buyer: 这些新产品还没找到婆家呢。These new products still haven't found a buyer.

【找齐】zhǎoqí〈动〉**1**（使齐平）even up: 篱笆编成了，顶上还要～。The fence is already up. Now we just need to even up the top of it. **2**（补齐）make up a deficiency: 今儿先给你一部分，差多少明儿～。We'll pay you part of the sum today and make up the balance tomorrow.

【找事】zhǎoshì〈动〉**1**（找工作）look for a job: 赶紧～干，别老闲着。Hurry up and find yourself a job, rather than just sitting around all day. **2**（争吵）pick a quarrel: 有意～ pick a fight intentionally **3**（找麻烦）look for trouble: 你这不是没事～吗? Are you asking for trouble?

【找死】zhǎosǐ〈动〉court death: 你～啊! Do you want to get yourself killed?

【找台阶下】zhǎo táijiē xià〈惯〉find a way out of difficulty: 紧要关头他给我找了个台阶下。At the critical moment, he found an excuse to get me out of the predicament.

【找头】zhǎotou〈名〉change: 这是给你的～。Here is your change.

【找寻】zhǎoxún = 寻找 xúnzhǎo

沼 zhǎo〈名〉natural pond: ▸～气, ～泽

【沼气】zhǎoqì〈名〉methane: ～池 methane tank

【沼虾】zhǎoxiā〈名〉freshwater shrimp

【沼泽】zhǎozé ▸**p. 164**〈名〉marsh: ～地 marshland

【沼泽土】zhǎozétǔ〈名〉bog soil

zhào

召 zhào
A〈动〉convene: 他们被～到厂长办公室。They were summoned to the director's office. ▸～唤, ～开, 号～
B〈名〉monastery [often used in place names in Inner Mongolia]

【召唤】zhàohuàn〈动〉call: 响应祖国的～ answer the call of one's country

【召回】zhàohuí〈动〉call back: ～大使 recall the ambassador ‖ ～有设计问题的汽车 recall the cars with the design fault

【召集】zhàojí〈动〉assemble: ～会议 call a conference ‖ 把朋友们～起来 rally one's friends

【召集人】zhàojírén〈名〉convener

【召见】zhàojiàn〈动〉**1**（通知见面）call in officially: 我在办公室里等待主席的～。I waited in the office for an audience with the chairman. **2**［外交］summon to an interview: 明天外交部将～这位大使。The ambassador will be summoned to the Foreign Ministry tomorrow.

【召开】zhàokāi〈动〉convene: ～特别会议 call an extraordinary session ‖ 大会什么时候～? When is the conference convening?

兆 zhào
A〈名〉sign: 不祥之～ ill omen ▸～头, 征～
B〈动〉portend: 瑞雪～丰年。A timely snow promises a good harvest in the coming year.
C ▸**p. 691**〈数〉**1**（百万）million **2**〈古〉（万亿）trillion

【兆伏】zhàofú〈名〉［电气］megavolt (MV)

【兆赫】zhàohè〈名〉［物理］megahertz (MHz)

【兆头】zhàotou〈名〉omen: 好～ good omen ‖ 坏～ bad omen

【兆瓦】zhàowǎ〈名〉［电气］megawatt (MW)

诏（詔）zhào

A〈动〉〈书〉instruct

B〈名〉imperial edict: 下～ issue an imperial edict ▸～书

【诏书】zhàoshū〈名〉imperial edict: 颁布～ issue an imperial edict

赵（趙）Zhào

〈名〉**1**（指国名）Zhao [state in the Zhou Dynasty] **2**（指河北南部）Zhao [name for what is now southern Hebei Province, used in classical prose and poetry]

【赵体】Zhàotǐ〈名〉［书法］Zhao style [calligraphy of Zhao Mengfu (赵孟頫) of the Yuan Dynasty]

笊 zhào

〈名〉strainer

【笊篱】zhàoli〈名〉strainer: 用～舀 ladle with a strainer

照 zhào

A〈动〉**1**（照射）shine: 阳光～在窗户上。The sunbeams fell on the window. ‖ 用手电筒～一～。Light it with your torch. ▸～明，～耀，日～ **2**（明白）understand: ▸心～不宣 **3**（告知）notify: ▸～会，关～，知～ **4**（反射影像）reflect: ～镜子 look in the mirror **5**（查对）contrast: ▸查～，对～ **6**（看管）take care of: ▸～管，～看，～应 **7**（照相）take a photo: 这张照片～得很好。This photo is well taken. ‖ 请给我～一张。Please take a picture of me. ▸～相，拍～ **8**（按标准做）do according to a standard: ▸～发，～办

B〈名〉**1**（阳光）sunshine: ▸夕～ **2**（照片）photograph: 结婚～ wedding photograph ‖ 近～ recent photo ▸小～，玉～ **3**（执照）licence: 车～ car licence ‖ 无～驾驶/经营 drive/run without a licence ▸护～，执～

C〈介〉**1**（根据）in accordance with: ～原计划办 hold to the original plan ‖ ～这个样子做。Do it like this. ‖ 如有损坏，～价赔偿。Pay the full price in case of damage. **2**（对着）in the direction of: ～这个方向走。Go in this direction.

【照搬】zhàobān〈动〉replicate: 盲目地～外国经验 apply foreign experience blindly

【照办】zhàobàn〈动〉act in accordance with: 您吩咐的事情，都一一～了。Every one of your orders has been carried out to the letter.

【照本宣科】zhàoběn-xuānkē〈成〉regurgitate from a text: 老师上课不应当～。A teacher shouldn't just read out the textbook word for word.

【照壁】zhàobì〈名〉screen wall facing the gate of a house

【照常】zhàocháng **A**〈动〉be normal: 战争之后，生活又～了。After the war, life got back to normal. **B**〈副〉as usual: ～营业 open for business as usual ‖ 尽管天气不好，比赛～进行。Despite the bad weather, the match went ahead as scheduled.

【照抄】zhàochāo〈动〉**1**（指按原文）copy word for word: ～一份 make a copy of **2** = 照搬 zhàobān

【照登】zhàodēng〈动〉publish sth. as it is: 来函～。The letters are published unedited.

【照发】zhàofā〈动〉**1**（指照常）issue as normal: 在职学习，工资～。Those who receive in-service training are entitled to full pay. **2**（指照原样）[used for notices or circulars submitted for approval] approve for distribution

【照拂】zhàofú〈动〉〈书〉attend to

【照顾】zhàogù〈动〉**1**（考虑到）show consideration for: 对特殊情况将给以充分的～。Considerable allowances will be made for special cases. ‖ ～到检举人的安全，信件内容暂不公布。Out of consideration for the safety of the accuser, the letter is not to be revealed publicly for the time being. **2**（照料）look after: ～好孩子 take good care of the children ‖ 我去买票，你来～行李。Keep an eye on the luggage while I go and get the tickets. **3**（优待）offer preferential treatment: ～残疾人 give special care to the handicapped ‖ 老幼乘车，～座位。Give up your seats to elderly people and children. **4**（光顾）shop at: 多谢对本店的～。Thank you for your patronage.

【照管】zhàoguǎn〈动〉look after: ～店铺 tend a shop ‖ ～孩子 look after a child ‖ 委托某人～生意 give sb. charge of a business

【照葫芦画瓢】zhào húlu huà piáo〈惯〉〈喻〉copy

【照护】zhàohù〈动〉tend to: ～伤员 tend to the wounded

【照会】zhàohuì **A**〈动〉present a note to: 就这一问题～有关国家驻华使馆 present a note to the country of the embassy concerned **B**〈名〉note: 抗议～ note of protest

【照旧】zhàojiù **A**〈动〉be as before: 本书再版时，体例～，只是加了些新资料。The new edition of the book includes some latest data while its layout remains unchanged. **B**〈副〉as before: 我们休息了一下，～往前走。We continued our journey after a brief rest.

【照看】zhàokàn〈动〉watch over: ～生病的孩子 watch over a sick child ‖ ～行李 keep an eye on one's luggage

【照理】zhàolǐ〈副〉normally: ～他应该来参加这个会议。If everything is as normal, he should be attending the meeting.

【照例】zhàolì〈副〉as a rule: 春节～放假七天。People usually get seven days off for the Spring Festival.

【照料】zhàoliào〈动〉take care of: 孩子交由奶奶～。The child was left in the care of its grandmother. ‖ 病人受到护士无微不至的～。The patient received painstaking care from the nurse.

【照临】zhàolín〈动〉illuminate: 曙光～群山。The mountains were bathed in the morning sunlight.

【照猫画虎】zhàomāo-huàhǔ〈成〉〈喻〉copy sth. without catching its spirit

【照面儿】zhàomiànr〈动〉**1**（露面）[usu used in the negative] show up: 互不～ avoid each other ‖ 始终不～ never show up **2**（碰面）come across: 打个～ run into sb.

【照明】zhàomíng〈动〉illuminate: ～器材 lighting material ‖ 泛光～ flood illumination ‖ 室内～ interior illumination

【照明弹】zhàomíngdàn〈名〉［军事］flare: 发射～ fire a flare

【照排】zhàopái〈名〉phototypesetting: 激光～ laser photographing

【照片儿】zhàopiānr〈名〉〈口〉photo: 洗～ have a film developed

【照片】zhàopiàn〈名〉photograph: 彩色～ colour photo ‖ 一次成像～ instant picture

【照射】zhàoshè〈动〉illuminate: 阳光～大地 sunlight lights up the earth ‖ 用紫外线～ irradiate with ultraviolet rays

【照实】zhàoshí〈副〉according to facts: 你做了什么，～说好了。Tell me the truth about what you've done.

【照说】zhàoshuō〈副〉ordinarily: ～他不该发这么大火。Normally, he shouldn't have been in such a temper.

【照相】zhàoxiàng〈动〉take a photograph: ～器材 photographic equipment

【照相馆】zhàoxiàngguǎn〈名〉photo studio

【照相机】zhàoxiàngjī〈名〉camera: 傻瓜～ foolproof camera ‖ 数码～ digital camera

【照相纸】zhàoxiàngzhǐ〈名〉photographic paper

【照样】zhàoyàng **A**〈动〉do sth. after a pattern: 照着样儿做 do it this way **B**〈副〉as usual: 天气尽管很冷，工地上～热火朝天。Despite the bitter cold, the workers on the construction site exhibited just as much enthusiasm as ever.

【照妖镜】zhàoyāojìng〈名〉monster-revealing mirror

【照耀】zhàoyào〈动〉shine: 阳光～。The sun is shining brightly.

【照应】zhàoyìng〈动〉coordinate: 互相～ coordinate with one another ‖ 这篇文章缺乏前后～。This piece of writing lacks coherence.

【照应】zhàoying〈动〉look after: 你们俩住一间屋子相互也好有个～。You may share a room so that you can look after each other.

【照章】zhàozhāng〈动〉be in accordance with the rules: ～办事 go by the book

【照直】zhàozhí〈副〉**1**（不拐弯）straight on: ～往东，就到菜市了。Head straight east and you'll find the vegetable market. **2**（直截了当）directly: 有话就～说。If you've got anything to say then say it.

罩 zhào

A〈动〉cover: 雾～全城。The fog swallowed up the whole city. ‖ 用一块布把食物～起来。Cover the food with a cloth. ▸笼～

B〈名〉**1**（罩子）cover: 电视机～ TV cover ‖ 口～ face mask ▸灯～ **2**（外罩）overalls: ▸～袍 **3**（捕鱼器）bamboo fish trap **4**（养鸡笼）bamboo chicken coop

【罩裤】zhàokù〈名〉baggy trousers

【罩袍】zhàopáo〈名〉overall

【罩棚】zhàopéng〈名〉awning

【罩衫】zhàoshān = 罩衣 zhàoyī

【罩袖】zhàoxiù〈名〉oversleeve: 戴着～ wear oversleeves

【罩衣】zhàoyī〈名〉overall: 棉袄～ cotton-padded overalls

【罩子】zhàozi〈名〉cover: 空调～ dust cover of an air-conditioner

棹 zhào

〈名〉〈书〉**1**（桨）oar **2**（船）boat: 归～ returning boat

鲱（鮡）zhào

〈名〉［鱼类］sisorid catfish: 中华爬岩～ Glyptosternum sinensis

肇 zhào

〈动〉〈书〉**1**（开始）commence: ▸～端，～始 **2**（引发）cause: ▸～事

【肇端】zhàoduān〈名〉〈书〉inception

【肇祸】zhàohuò〈动〉 cause trouble
【肇始】zhàoshǐ〈动〉〈书〉 commence: 新时代的～ beginning of a new age
【肇事】zhàoshì〈动〉 create a disturbance: 寻衅～ find an excuse and stir up trouble ‖ ～者 troublemaker

zhē

折 zhē〈动〉〈口〉 1 (翻转) turn over: 把箱子～了个底儿朝天 turn the box upside down ▸～腾 2 (倾倒) pour back and forth between two containers: 水太热，拿两个碗～一～就凉了。 The water's too hot. Pour it back and forth from one bowl to another and it will cool down.
▸shé, zhé

【折腾】zhēteng〈动〉〈口〉 1 (翻来覆去) be restless: 凑合着睡一会儿吧，别来回～了。 You'd better stop tossing and turning and try to get some sleep. 2 (反复做) do sth. over and over again: 他把收音机装了又拆，拆了又装，～了几十回。 He took the radio apart a number of times and then fitted the parts back together again. 3 (折磨) torment: 不少人受慢性病～。 Many people are tormented by chronic diseases. 4 (做无谓的事) do pointless things

蜇 zhē〈动〉 1 (指昆虫) sting: 被马蜂～伤了 be hurt by a hornet sting 2 (指物质) sting: 切洋葱～眼睛。 Cutting onions makes the eyes sting. ‖ 这种药水擦在伤口上～得慌。 This kind of lotion smarts when it is applied to a cut.
▸zhé

遮 zhē〈动〉 1 (使看不见) hide from view: ～住视线 obstruct a view ‖ 山高～不住太阳。 No matter how tall a mountain is, it can never shut out sunlight. ▸～蔽 2 (掩盖) cover: ▸～丑, ～人耳目 3 (阻拦) block: 横～竖拦 try every means to create an obstruction

【遮蔽】zhēbì〈动〉 hide from view: ～风雨 shelter sb. from wind and rain ‖ ～视线 obstruct the view
【遮藏】zhēcáng〈动〉 hide: 他们企图～这件丑事。 They are trying to cover up the scandal.
【遮丑】zhēchǒu〈动〉 hide one's shame: 为自己～ whitewash oneself
【遮挡】zhēdǎng〈动〉 keep out: 植树造林，～风沙 plant trees to keep out wind and sand ‖ 用帘子把窗户～起来 cover the window with a curtain
【遮幅电影】zhēfú diànyǐng〈名〉 masked wide-screen film
【遮盖】zhēgài〈动〉 1 (蒙上) cover: 路给大雪～住了。 The path lay hidden under the snow. 2 (掩饰) conceal: 错误总是～不住的。 Mistakes can never be covered up.
【遮拦】zhēlán〈动〉 block: 口无～ say the first thing that comes into one's mouth ‖ 防风林可以～大风。 The windbreak can check a violent wind.
【遮人耳目】zhērén'ěrmù〈成〉 conceal the truth
【遮天蔽日】zhētiān-bìrì〈成〉 [said of a dense forest or a sandstorm] blot out the sky and the sun
【遮羞】zhēxiū〈动〉 1 (指阴部) cover up one's private parts 2〈喻〉(指丑事) cover up one's shame
【遮羞布】zhēxiūbù〈名〉 loincloth:〈喻〉"家属经商"是腐败的～。 Using a family member to do one's business is a cover-up for corrupt practices.
【遮掩】zhēyǎn〈动〉 1 (使不显露) hide: 远山被雨雾～，变得朦胧不清。 The distant hills, enveloped in rain and mist, were hazy and indistinct. 2 (掩饰) cover up: ～错误 cover up one's mistakes ‖ ～内心的不安 conceal one's anxiety
【遮眼法】zhēyǎnfǎ〈名〉 cover-up
【遮阳】zhēyáng〈动〉 hide from sunlight: ～帽 sun helmet
【遮阳篷】zhēyángpéng〈名〉 awning
【遮阳伞】zhēyángsǎn〈名〉 parasol
【遮阴】zhēyīn〈动〉 shade: ～树木 shade trees

zhé

折[1] zhé
A〈动〉 1 (使断) break: ～断树枝 snap off a twig ‖ 请勿攀～花木。 Please do not pick flowers or branches. ▸骨～ 2 (死) die: ▸夭～ 3 (挫败) defeat and frustrate: ▸挫～, 百～不挠 4 (损失) lose: ▸～寿, 损兵～将 5 (打折扣) discount: ▸不～不扣 6 (心服) have confidence: ▸～服 7 (返回) turn back: 走到大门口又～了回来 turn back at the gate ‖ 这条河～向东流。 The river bends to the east. ▸～射, 转～ 8 (抵换) substitute for: ▸将功～罪 9 (换算) convert into: 把美元～成人民币 convert US dollars into *Renminbi* ‖ 把市斤～成公斤 convert *jin* into kilograms ▸～合, ～价, ～算
B〈名〉 1 (折扣) discount: 打八～ give a 20% discount ‖ 衬衫一律九～。 All shirts are at 10% off. 2 (指笔画) [in Chinese characters] turning stroke
C〈形〉 bent: ▸曲～, 周～
D〈量〉 scene

折[2]（摺）zhé
A〈动〉 fold: ～毯子/信 fold a blanket/letter ‖ 将书的一页～个角 fold down the corner of a page ▸～尺, ～叠, ～扇
B〈名〉 booklet: ▸存～, 奏～
▸shé, zhē

【折半】zhébàn〈动〉 reduce by half: 处理品按定价～出售 on sale with 50% off
【折变】zhébiàn〈动〉〈方〉 sell off: ～家产 sell off one's family property
【折尺】zhéchǐ〈名〉 folding ruler
【折冲樽俎】zhéchōng-zūnzǔ〈成〉 1 (战胜敌人) win by superior diplomacy 2 (进行外交谈判) engage in diplomatic negotiations
【折叠】zhédié〈动〉 fold: ～衣服 fold up clothes ‖ ～床 foldaway bed ‖ ～椅 folding chair ‖ ～桌 gateleg table
【折叠伞】zhédiésǎn〈名〉 folding umbrella
【折兑】zhéduì〈动〉 convert: 把加拿大元～成人民币。 Convert Canadian dollars into *Renminbi*.
【折返】zhéfǎn〈动〉 turn back halfway: 走到半路又～回来 turn back halfway
【折返跑】zhéfǎnpǎo〈名〉[体育] shuttle run: ～训练 shuttle run training ‖〈喻〉实行一站式服务，减少～次数。 One-stop service reduces all those shuttle runs.
【折服】zhéfú〈动〉 1 (说服) subdue: 强词夺理不能～人。 Sophistry convinces no one. 2 (信服) be convinced: 令人～ turn people around
【折福】zhéfú〈动〉 compromise one's good fortune [usu because of having or getting more than one deserves]
【折光】zhéguāng〈动〉 refract light: ～镜 endoscope
【折桂】zhéguì〈动〉〈书〉 1 (科举及第) pass the imperial examination 2 (得第一) carry off first prize: 该队在联赛中两度～。 This team came out a double winner in the league.
【折合】zhéhé〈动〉 1 (指不同事物) convert into: 一英镑～成人民币是多少? How much is one pound sterling in *Renminbi*? 2 (指同一事物) amount to: 一米可以～为三尺。 One metre is equal to three *chi*.
【折回】zhéhuí〈动〉 turn back halfway: 半道～ turn back halfway
【折戟沉沙】zhéjǐ-chénshā〈成〉 reminder of a disastrous defeat
【折价】zhéjià〈动〉 evaluate in monetary terms: ～处理 be sold at reduced prices ‖ ～退赔 pay compensation at the market price
【折价率】zhéjiàlǜ〈名〉[金融] discount rate: 封闭式基金～ closed fund discount rate
【折旧】zhéjiù〈动〉 depreciate: ～费 depreciation charge ‖ 房屋～ house depreciation ‖ ～率 rate of depreciation
【折扣】zhékòu〈名〉 discount: 给予特惠～ give special rates ‖ ～价 discounted price ‖〈喻〉听他讲话要打～。 You must discount whatever he tells you.
【折扣店】zhékòudiàn〈名〉 discount store: 去～淘便宜货 shop for bargains at a discount store
【折扣率】zhékòulǜ〈名〉 discount rate: 旅游淡季，机票～为40%。 The discount rate on off-season airline tickets is 40%.
【折磨】zhémó〈动〉 torture: 受疾病的～ suffer tortuously from a disease ‖ 内疚日夜～着我的良知。 The feeling of guilt gnawed at my conscience day and night.
【折扇】zhéshàn〈名〉 folding fan
【折射】zhéshè〈动〉 refract: 光的～ refraction of light ‖〈喻〉家庭的变化～出社会的发展。 Changes in family life mirror the development of society.
【折射角】zhéshèjiǎo〈名〉 angle of refraction
【折射望远镜】zhéshè wàngyuǎnjìng〈名〉 refracting telescope
【折实】zhéshí〈动〉 1 (指折后数额) calculate the actual amount after discount 2 (指实物价格) adjust payment in accordance with the price index of certain commodities
【折寿】zhéshòu〈动〉 lessen sb.'s lifespan [usu because of having or getting more than one deserves]
【折算】zhésuàn〈动〉 convert: 把人民币～成美元 convert *Renminbi* into US dollars
【折息率】zhéxīlǜ〈名〉[金融] offer rate
【折腰】zhéyāo〈动〉〈书〉 bow in obeisance: 不为五斗米～ not give up one's dignity for material gains
【折账】zhézhàng〈动〉 pay a debt in kind: 用家产～ pay a debt with one's family property
【折纸】zhézhǐ〈名〉 paper folding
【折中】zhézhōng〈动〉 find a happy medium: 采取～方案 take the middle way ‖ 想出一个～办法 come up with a compromise
【折中主义】zhézhōng zhǔyì〈名〉 eclecticism
【折衷】zhézhōng = 折中 zhézhōng

【折皱】zhézhòu〈名〉wrinkle: 满脸～ have a wrinkled face
【折子】zhézi〈名〉concertina folder: 存款～ deposit book
【折子戏】zhézixì〈名〉opera highlights

哲（喆） zhé
A〈形〉wise: ▸～理, ～人
B〈名〉wise man: ▸先～
【哲理】zhélǐ〈名〉philosophy: ～诗 philosophical poem ‖ 他说的话挺有～。His words are quite philosophical.
【哲人】zhérén〈名〉〈书〉sage
【哲学】zhéxué〈名〉philosophy: 人生～ philosophy on life ‖ ～家 philosopher

辄（輒） zhé〈副〉〈书〉**1**（总是）always: 动～得咎 get blame for whatever one does **2**（就）then: 浅尝～止 be content with just a smattering of knowledge

蛰（蟄） zhé〈动〉〈书〉hibernate: ▸～伏, 惊～, ～居
【蛰伏】zhéfú〈动〉**1**（指动物）hibernate: ～动物 hibernating animal **2** = 蛰居 zhéjū
【蛰居】zhéjū〈动〉〈书〉live in seclusion: ～深山 live a life of solitude deep in the mountains

蜇 zhé ▸海蜇 hǎizhé
▸zhē

晢 zhé〈形〉〈书〉bright: 明星～～ bright stars are shining overhead

谪（謫） zhé〈动〉〈书〉**1**（降职远调）banish, demote: ▸～居, 贬～ **2**（责备）censure: 众口交～ be subject to public condemnation
【谪居】zhéjū〈动〉〈旧〉[of officials] live in exile: ～海南 live in exile in Hainan

磔 zhé
A〈动〉〈古〉dismember the body [a capital punishment]
B〈名〉〈书〉right-falling stroke in Chinese characters

辙（轍） zhé〈名〉**1**（车辙）rut: ▸车～, 覆～ **2**（路线）direction of traffic: 戗～行驶 drive against the direction of traffic **3**（韵）rhyme: 合～押韵 rhyme **4**〈口〉（办法）[usu used after 有 or 没] way: 我拿他真没～。There's no way I am able to carry him.

zhě

者 zhě〈助〉**1**（指性质或动作的主体）[used as a suffix after a verb or adjective, or a verbal or adjective phrase to indicate the doer of sth.]: 强～ the strong ‖ 弱～ the weak ‖ 合格～ the qualified ▸编～, 消费～, 始作俑～ **2**（指工作或信仰的主体）[used after a noun phrase to indicate a person doing the stated work or following the stated doctrine]: 教育工作～ educator ‖ 医务工作～ medical worker **3**（指上文所说事物）[used after 二, 三 or 数, etc. to refer back to sth. said earlier]: 二～必居其一。It must be either of the two. ‖ 两～缺一不可。Neither is dispensable. ▸后～, 前～ **4**〈书〉（表停顿）[used after a word, phrase, or clause to mark a pause, as in giving definitions]: 风～，空气流动而成。Wind is air in motion.

锗（鍺） zhě〈名〉［化学］germanium (Ge)

赭 zhě〈形〉reddish brown
【赭石】zhěshí〈名〉［矿业］ochre

褶 zhě〈名〉crease: 给围裙打～ pleat an apron ‖ 裤子上有一道～儿。There is a crease in the trousers. ▸百～裙
【褶皱】zhězhòu〈名〉**1**［地质］fold: ～山 folded mountain ‖ ～作用 folding **2**（皱纹）wrinkle: 满脸～ have a wrinkled face
【褶子】zhězi〈名〉**1**（衣服上的纹）pleat: 她的裙子上有～。Her skirt has pleats. **2**（折痕）crease: 用熨斗把～烙平 iron out the creases **3**（皱纹）wrinkle: 她一笑起来脸上满是～。Her face wrinkled when she smiled.

zhè

这 zhè ▸p. 968〈代〉**1**（指代近处人或事物）this [used as a determiner before a noun referring to a person or thing that is close by]: ～地方 this place ‖ ～孩子 this child ‖ ～几天 over these past few days ‖ ～一回 this time ‖ ～是魏先生。This is Mr Wei. ‖ ～你可以留着。You can keep this. **2**（表泛指）this: 问～问那 ask about this and that ‖ 怕～怕那 be afraid of this and that **3**（这时候）now, then: 他～才知道自己错了。Only then did he realize that he was wrong. ‖ 我～就去上海。I am leaving for Shanghai right now.
▸zhèi
【这般】zhèbān〈代〉so: 走～快 go this fast ‖ ～认真 so serious
【这程子】zhèchéngzi〈名〉〈口〉recently: 他～精神特别好。He has been in an extremely good mood lately.
【这次】zhècì〈代〉this time
【这个】zhège ▸p. 968〈代〉**1**（指代近处人或事物）this: ～箱子比那个沉。This box is heavier than that one. **2**〈口〉（表夸张）so: 大家～乐啊! Everybody was so blissfully happy. **3**（表特指）this: ～不是我的。This is not mine. ‖ ～东西你可以留着。You can keep this.
【这会儿】zhèhuìr〈代〉〈口〉at the moment: ～他正在休息。He is having a rest at the moment. ‖ 你～又上哪儿去呀? Where are you going now?
【这里】zhèlǐ ▸p. 968〈代〉here: ～没有姓洪的。No one here has the surname Hong. ‖ 我们～一年种两季稻子。We grow two crops of rice a year in these parts.
【这么】zhème〈代〉such: 大家都～说。That's what everybody is saying. ‖ 有～回事。There is indeed something of this kind.
【这么点儿】zhèmediǎnr〈代〉〈口〉such a little bit: 就～行李，我一个人能行。There's only this small amount of luggage. I can manage it myself. ‖ ～路几分钟就走到了。It isn't far. Just a few minutes' walk.
【这么些】zhèmexiē〈代〉〈口〉so much, so many: ～活儿,够你忙的了。You've got so much work. You must be very busy. ‖ ～问题都是他一个人解决的。He solved these problems all by himself.
【这么样】zhèmeyàng = 这样 zhèyàng
【这么着】zhèmezhe〈代〉〈口〉like this: ～好。It's better this way. ‖ 瞄准姿势要～才能打得准。Take aim like this and you'll hit your target.
【这山望着那山高】zhè shān wàngzhe nà shān gāo〈俗〉〈喻〉the grass is always greener on the other side
【这些】zhèxiē ▸p. 968〈代〉these: ～书送给你。These books are for you. ‖ ～日子老下雨。It has been raining non-stop the last few days.
【这样】zhèyàng〈代〉such: 担负～重大的责任，够难为他的。It's hard for him to shoulder such heavy responsibilities. ‖ 情况就是～。That's how it is.
【这阵子】zhèzhènzi〈代〉these days: ～你到哪里去了? Where have you been these days?

浙 Zhè ▸p. 661
【浙江】Zhèjiāng ▸p. 661〈名〉Zhejiang Province

蔗 zhè〈名〉sugar cane: ～田 sugar cane field ▸～糖, 甘～
【蔗农】zhènóng〈名〉sugar cane grower
【蔗糖】zhètáng〈名〉［化学］**1**（指有机化合物）sucrose **2**（指以甘蔗制成）cane sugar

嗻 zhè〈拟〉〈旧〉[used by servants in response to the master's command] yes

鹧（鷓） zhè
【鹧鸪】zhègū〈名〉［鸟类］Chinese partridge

zhe

着 zhe〈助〉**1**（表状态或动作持续）[used after a verb or an adjective to indicate the continuation of an action or a state]: 屋里的灯还亮～。The lights in the room are still on. ‖ 他们正谈～话呢。They are having a talk now. **2**（表动作同时发生）[used between two verbs to indicate an accompanying action or state]: 你坐～说。Please take a seat if you need to talk. ‖ 咱们走～去吧。Let's go there on foot. **3**（表命令）[used for emphasis after verbs or adjectives in imperative sentences]: 慢～! Hold it! ‖ 你听～。You just listen. ‖ 快～点儿! Hurry up!
▸zhāo, zháo, zhuó

zhèi

这（這） zhèi〈代〉〈口〉this [a variant pronunciation of 这 (zhè)]: ～个苹果 this apple ‖ ～些人 these people
▸zhè

zhēn

贞（貞） zhēn
A〈动〉〈书〉practise divination
B〈形〉**1**（坚定不移）loyal: ▸坚～, 忠～ **2**（女子守节）chaste: ～妇 woman of virtue ‖ ～女 chaste girl
【贞操】zhēncāo〈名〉**1**（坚贞的节操）loyalty: 保持～ maintain one's integrity **2**（女子的节操）chastity: 严守～ strictly maintain one's virginity

Z

【贞观】Zhēnguān〈名〉Zhenguan [reign title of Emperor Taizong, Li Shimin (李世民) of the Tang Dynasty]

【贞节】zhēnjié〈名〉1 (忠贞) loyalty: ～之士 man of integrity 2 (女子的节操) (指寡妇) chastity; (指未婚女子) virginity: 保持～ maintain one's chastity

【贞洁】zhēnjié〈形〉chaste: 处女的～ purity of a virgin

【贞烈】zhēnliè〈形〉ready to die to preserve one's chastity

针(針) zhēn

〈名〉1 (指缝衣用具) needle: 一枚绣花～ an embroidery needle ▸穿～引线 2 (针状物) needle-like object: 松～ pine needle ▸唱～, 指南～ 3 (针剂) injection: 打～ have an injection ‖ 防疫～ prophylactic inoculation ▸～剂 4 (针脚) stitch: 缝上几～ sew a couple of stitches ‖ 漏织一～ drop a stitch 5 (针灸) acupuncture: 扎～ perform acupuncture ▸～灸

【针鼻儿】zhēnbír〈名〉eye of a needle

【针砭】zhēnbiān〈动〉1 (用石针治病) perform acupuncture with a flint needle 2〈喻〉(批评) point out sb.'s errors and offer salutary advice: ～时弊 condemn social ills and demand that they be dealt with ‖ 痛下～ criticize sb.'s errors and request correction

【针插】zhēnchā〈名〉pin cushion

【针刺麻醉】zhēncì mázuì〈名〉acupuncture anaesthesia: 用～取代药物麻醉 replace drug anaesthesia with acu-anaesthesia

【针对】zhēnduì〈动〉be aimed at: 不～任何第三方/国 be not directed against any third party/country ‖ 他的话是～你的。What he said was aimed at you.

【针对性】zhēnduìxìng〈名〉aim: 工作要有～, 不能脱离实际。The work must have an objective and not lose sight of reality.

【针锋相对】zhēnfēng-xiāngduì〈成〉give tit for tat: 进行～的斗争 wage a tit-for-tat struggle

【针管】zhēnguǎn〈名〉needle tubing

【针剂】zhēnjì〈名〉injection

【针尖对麦芒】zhēnjiān duì màimáng〈俗〉tit-for-tat: 两个人你一言, 我一句, ～, 越吵越厉害。The tit-for-tat retorts between the two of them gradually escalated into a bitter quarrel.

【针脚】zhēnjiao〈名〉1 (指痕迹) line of stitches: 棉袄上的～很明显。The stitching is very obvious on the cotton-padded jacket. 2 (指距离) stitch: ～细密 short stitches ‖ ～太大了。The stitches are too long.

【针灸】zhēnjiǔ〈名〉acupuncture and moxibustion: ～疗法 acupuncture treatment

> **针灸**
>
> An aspect of traditional Chinese medicine, with ancient origins. The term combines the technique of using needles and moxibustion. In acupuncture, fine needles are inserted into acupuncture points on the patient's body to cure illnesses. Moxibustion involves placing burning moxa cones either near or on the patient's skin to cure illnesses with heat stimulus.

【针麻】zhēnmá〈简称〉= 针刺麻醉

【针式打印机】zhēnshì dǎyìnjī〈名〉matrix printer: 24针～ 24-pin dot matrix printer

【针筒】zhēntǒng = 针管 zhēnguǎn

【针头】zhēntóu〈名〉needle head

【针头线脑】zhēntóu-xiànnǎo〈成〉〈喻〉odds and ends needed for sewing: 她把～扔得到处都是。She's strewn her sewing bits and pieces all over the place.

【针线】zhēnxiàn〈名〉1 (针和线) needle and thread: ～包 sewing kit 2 (针线活儿) needlework: 学做～ learn needlework ‖ ～活儿 needlework

【针眼】zhēnyǎn〈名〉1 (针鼻儿) eye of a needle 2 (针扎后的小孔) pinhole

【针叶树】zhēnyèshù〈名〉conifer

【针织】zhēnzhī〈名〉knitting: ～背心 knitted vest ‖ ～厂 knitting mill

【针织品】zhēnzhīpǐn〈名〉knitwear

【针黹】zhēnzhǐ〈名〉〈书〉needlework: 以～谋生 do needlework for a living

侦(偵) zhēn

〈动〉investigate: ▸～察, ～缉, ～探, 刑～

【侦办】zhēnbàn〈动〉investigate and handle

【侦查】zhēnchá〈动〉investigate: 立案～ enter a case on file for investigation

【侦察】zhēnchá〈动〉reconnoitre: ～敌情 gather intelligence about the enemy ‖ 进行火力～ make a reconnaissance by firing ‖ ～兵 reconnoitre

【侦察机】zhēnchájī〈名〉reconnaissance plane: 无人驾驶～ pilotless spy plane

【侦察卫星】zhēnchá wèixīng〈名〉spy satellite

【侦察员】zhēncháyuán〈名〉scout

【侦获】zhēnhuò〈动〉investigate and crack: ～一批非法出版物 detect and seize a batch of illegal publications

【侦缉】zhēnjī〈动〉track down and arrest: ～在逃犯 track down and arrest a criminal at large ‖ ～队 tracking team

【侦结】zhēnjié〈名〉conclusion of an investigation

【侦控】zhēnkòng〈动〉do detective work: 对犯罪嫌疑人进行24小时严密～ keep the suspect under close 24-hour surveillance

【侦破】zhēnpò〈动〉investigate and uncover: 警方已经～了那起凶杀案。The police have cracked the murder case.

【侦探】zhēntàn A〈动〉do detective work: ～敌情 spy out intelligence about the enemy B〈名〉detective: 私人～ private detective

【侦探小说】zhēntàn xiǎoshuō〈名〉detective story

【侦听】zhēntīng〈动〉intercept (enemy radio communications)

珍 zhēn

A〈名〉treasure: 奇～异宝 rare valuables ▸～宝, ～珠, 如数家～

B〈形〉precious: ▸～本, ～贵, ～稀

C〈动〉treasure: ▸～爱, ～重, 敝帚自～

【珍爱】zhēn'ài〈动〉cherish: ～生命 cherish life ‖ 小女孩深受祖父的～。The little girl is her grandfather's treasure.

【珍宝】zhēnbǎo〈名〉treasure: 视同～ regard sth. as a treasure ‖ 如获～ as excited as if one had obtained a rare treasure

【珍本】zhēnběn〈名〉rare edition

【珍藏】zhēncáng A〈动〉treasure up: ～在心中的回忆 cherished memories B〈名〉collection: 捐献～ donate rare and valuable articles

【珍贵】zhēnguì〈形〉precious: ～的历史文物 precious historical artefacts ‖ ～药材 valuable ingredients in traditional Chinese medicine

【珍品】zhēnpǐn〈名〉treasure: 稀世～ rare treasures ‖ 艺术～ art treasure

【珍奇】zhēnqí〈形〉rare: ～动物 rare animals

【珍禽异兽】zhēnqín-yìshòu〈成〉rare birds and animals

【珍摄】zhēnshè〈动〉〈书〉〈套〉[used mostly in letters] take good care of yourself: 诚盼善自～! I sincerely hope you will take good care of yourself.

【珍视】zhēnshì〈动〉value: ～美好生活 prize one's happy life ‖ ～友谊 value a friendship

【珍玩】zhēnwán〈名〉rare curio

【珍闻】zhēnwén〈名〉titbits: 世界～ world news briefing

【珍惜】zhēnxī〈动〉treasure: ～人力物力 treasure human and material resources ‖ ～荣誉 cherish one's good reputation ‖ ～时间 make the best use of one's time

【珍稀】zhēnxī〈形〉rare and precious: ～动物 rare animals

【珍羞】zhēnxiū = 珍馐 zhēnxiū

【珍馐】zhēnxiū〈名〉〈书〉delicacies

【珍异】zhēnyì = 珍奇 zhēnqí

【珍重】zhēnzhòng〈动〉1 (爱惜) treasure: ～人才 value professional personnel highly 2 (保重) take care [usu said when parting]: 两人紧紧握手, 互道～。They clasped hands as they bid each other a fond farewell.

【珍珠】zhēnzhū〈名〉pearl: 养殖～ cultivate pearls ‖ ～项链 pearl necklace ‖ ～粉 pearl powder

【珍珠贝】zhēnzhūbèi〈名〉pearl oyster

【珍珠港】Zhēnzhūgǎng〈名〉Pearl Harbour

【珍珠霜】zhēnzhūshuāng〈名〉pearl cream

帧(幀) zhēn

〈量〉[of paintings or calligraphy]: 一～油画 an oil painting

胗 zhēn

〈名〉gizzard: 鸡～儿 chicken's gizzard

真 zhēn

A〈形〉1 (真实) true: 说～话 tell the truth ‖ ～假不分 not be clear what is real and what is not ‖ 梦想成～。One's dream has come true. ‖ 他说的都是～的。What he said is true. ▸～刀～枪, ～迹 2 (清楚) clear: 声音太小, 听不～。The sound is too low. I can't hear clearly. ‖ 黑板上的字你看得～么? Can you see the words on the blackboard clearly?

B〈副〉truly: ～是人见人爱 be truly lovable ‖ ～的很痛苦 be in real pain ‖ 景色～美。The view is really beautiful. ‖ 时间过得～快! How time flies!

C〈名〉1 (真书) regular script: ～草隶篆 the regular script, the cursive script, the official script and the seal script 2 (肖像) portrait; (原样) exact replica: ▸传～, 失～, 写～ 3 (本性) inherent quality: ▸返璞归～

【真才实学】zhēncái-shíxué〈成〉genuine talent: 有～的人 person of real ability and learning

【真唱】zhēnchàng〈动〉sing live [when performing]

【真诚】zhēnchéng〈形〉sincere: ～的合作 sincere cooperation ‖ ～待人 be honest with people

【真传】zhēnchuán〈名〉tricks of the trade acquired under the tutelage of the master: ～弟子 true disciples

【真刀真枪】zhēndāo-zhēnqiāng〈成〉1〈本〉real swords and spears 2〈喻〉real thing: ～地干起来 start in earnest

Z

【真谛】zhēndì〈名〉 true essence: 人生的～ true meaning of life
【真分数】zhēnfēnshù ▸p. 691 〈名〉［数学］ proper fraction
【真格的】zhēngéde〈形〉〈口〉 real: 动～ do in earnest ‖ 说～，他人不错。To tell the truth, he's a pretty good guy.
【真果】zhēnguǒ〈名〉［植物］ true fruit
【真迹】zhēnjì〈名〉 authentic work: 这幅画是齐白石的～。This is an authentic painting by Qi Baishi.
【真金不怕火炼】zhēnjīn bù pà huǒ liàn〈俗〉〈喻〉 truth fears not the flames of slander and injustice
【真菌】zhēnjūn〈名〉 fungus
【真空】zhēnkōng〈名〉 vacuum: ～包装 vacuum packaging ‖〈喻〉 权力/政治～ power/political vacuum ‖〈喻〉 ～地带 no-man's land
【真空管】zhēnkōngguǎn〈名〉 vacuum tube
【真空期】zhēnkōngqī〈名〉 vacuum: 政策/政权～ policy/political vacuum
【真空吸尘器】zhēnkōng xīchénqì〈名〉 vacuum cleaner
【真理】zhēnlǐ〈名〉 truth: 坚持～ uphold the truth ‖ 追求～ pursue the truth ‖ 实践是检验～的唯一标准。Practice is the sole criterion of truth.
【真面目】zhēnmiànmù〈名〉 true colours: 露出～ reveal one's true colours
【真名实姓】zhēnmíng-shíxìng〈成〉 real name
【真皮】zhēnpí〈名〉 1（生理） dermis 2（指兽皮） genuine leather: 这些鞋是～的。These shoes are made of real leather.
【真品】zhēnpǐn〈名〉 authentic work: 汉代青铜～ genuine Han Dynasty bronze
【真凭实据】zhēnpíng-shíjù〈成〉 concrete evidence: 拿出～ provide concrete evidence
【真枪实弹】zhēnqiāng-shídàn〈成〉 real guns and bullets
【真切】zhēnqiè〈形〉 1（清楚确实） clear: 看不～ cannot see clearly ‖ 听得～ hear distinctly 2（真挚） sincere: 情意～ genuine affection
【真情】zhēnqíng〈名〉 1（指情况） real situation: ～实况 facts ‖ 她不了解～。She doesn't know the real situation. 2（指感情） true feelings: 流露～ reveal one's true feelings ‖ ～实感 true feelings
【真人】zhēnrén〈名〉 1（得道者） true man [ie a man who has attained enlightenment or immortality; used mostly in official Taoist titles]: 太乙～ True Man of the Grand Unity 2（指非虚构） real person: 作品中所写的是～真事。The work is based on fact and on real people.
【真人秀】zhēnrénxiù〈名〉 reality TV show: ～节目 reality TV programme
【真人不露相】zhēnrén bù lòuxiàng〈俗〉 a man of true talent never shows off
【真人真事】zhēnrén-zhēnshì〈成〉 real characters and real incidents
【真善美】zhēn-shàn-měi〈名〉 the true, the good and the beautiful
【真实】zhēnshí〈形〉 true: ～身份 true identity ‖ ～感情 true feelings ‖ ～情况 real situation
【真实性】zhēnshíxìng〈名〉 truth: 怀疑某说法的～ doubt the truth of a statement
【真是】zhēnshi〈动〉 [used to express displeasure or annoyance]: 你们俩也～! Really, you two!
【真书】zhēnshū〈名〉 regular script
【真丝】zhēnsī〈名〉 pure silk: ～围巾 pure silk scarf
【真相】zhēnxiàng〈名〉 truth: 查明～ find out the truth
【真相大白】zhēnxiàng dàbái〈成〉 the whole truth has come out
【真心】zhēnxīn〈名〉 true intention: ～相爱 truly love each other ‖ 他说的是～话。He spoke sincere words.
【真心实意】zhēnxīn-shíyì〈成〉 sincerely: 我是～想帮助他。I genuinely want to help him.
【真性】zhēnxìng A ▸p. 50 〈形〉［医学］ genuine: ～霍乱 genuine cholera ‖ ～血友病 haemophilia vera B〈名〉〈书〉 nature
【真真假假】zhēnzhēn-jiǎjiǎ〈成〉 the true mingled with the false
【真正】zhēnzhèng A〈形〉 genuine: ～的中国饭菜 authentic Chinese cooking ‖ 群众是～的英雄。The masses are real heroes. ‖ 她是～的好人。She's a really good person. B〈副〉 really: ～认识到自己的错误 genuinely recognize where one has gone wrong ‖ 这东西～好吃。It really is delicious.
【真知】zhēnzhī〈名〉 real knowledge: 实践出～。Real knowledge comes from practice. ‖ 一切～都是从直接经验发源的。All real knowledge comes from direct experience.
【真知灼见】zhēnzhī-zhuójiàn〈成〉 real knowledge and profound insight
【真挚】zhēnzhì〈形〉 sincere: ～的友谊 sincere friendship
【真主】Zhēnzhǔ〈名〉［伊斯兰教］ Allah

桢（楨）

zhēn〈名〉 terminal posts used in building a wall in ancient times
【桢干】zhēngàn〈名〉〈书〉〈喻〉 pillar: 国之～ pillar of the state

砧

zhēn〈名〉 anvil: 锻～ smith anvil
【砧板】zhēnbǎn〈名〉 chopping block
【砧木】zhēnmù〈名〉［农业］ stock
【砧子】zhēnzi〈名〉 anvil

祯（禎）

zhēn〈形〉〈书〉 auspicious

蓁

zhēn
【蓁蓁】zhēnzhēn〈形〉 luxuriant

斟

zhēn〈动〉 pour: ～了满满一杯酒 pour a full cup of wine ‖ 自～自饮 pour a drink for oneself
【斟酌】zhēnzhuó〈动〉 consider: ～字句 be measured in one's speech ‖ 这件事请你～着办吧。Please think it over and handle it as you think fit.

甄

zhēn〈动〉〈书〉 discriminate: ▸～别，～选
【甄拔】zhēnbá〈动〉 select: ～人才 promote qualified personnel
【甄别】zhēnbié〈动〉 1（辨别） discriminate: ～假钞与真钞 discriminate counterfeit bills from genuine money 2（考核） examine and assess
【甄选】zhēnxuǎn〈动〉 select: ～人才 select people of talent

榛

zhēn〈名〉［植物］ hazel
【榛莽】zhēnmǎng〈名〉〈书〉 luxuriant vegetation
【榛榛】zhēnzhēn = 蓁蓁 zhēnzhēn
【榛子】zhēnzi〈名〉 1（指树） hazel 2（指果实） hazelnut

禛

zhēn〈形〉 [often used in personal names] auspicious

箴

zhēn
A〈动〉〈书〉 admonish
B〈名〉 type of didactic literary composition
【箴言】zhēnyán〈名〉〈书〉 admonition

臻

zhēn〈动〉〈书〉 attain: 渐～佳境 things turn out better and better ‖ 日～完善 slowly reach perfection

zhěn

诊（診）

zhěn〈动〉 examine: 确～ make an exact diagnosis ▸～断，～所
【诊察】zhěnchá〈动〉 examine
【诊断】zhěnduàn〈动〉 diagnose: 据医生～，我患了一种罕见的骨病。The doctor diagnosed my illness as a rare bone disease. ‖ 两位医生对我的病做出了不同的～。The two doctors gave different diagnoses of my disease.
【诊断书】zhěnduànshū〈名〉 medical certificate
【诊疗】zhěnliáo〈动〉 make a diagnosis and give treatment: ～器械 medical instruments
【诊脉】zhěnmài〈动〉 feel a pulse
【诊室】zhěnshì〈名〉 consulting room
【诊所】zhěnsuǒ〈名〉 clinic: 耳鼻喉科～ ear, nose and throat clinic ‖ 私人～ private clinic
【诊治】zhěnzhì〈动〉 make a diagnosis and give treatment: 有病应及早～。When you are ill, you should see a doctor as soon as possible.

枕

zhěn
A〈名〉 pillow: ～套 pillowcase ‖ 凉～ cool pillow ▸高～无忧
B〈动〉 rest the head on: 她把头～在他的肩上。She rested her head on his shoulder.
【枕边风】zhěnbiānfēng〈名〉 pillow talk
【枕戈待旦】zhěngē-dàidàn〈成〉 be ready for battle at all times
【枕骨】zhěngǔ〈名〉［解剖］ occipital bone
【枕藉】zhěnjiè〈动〉〈书〉 lie close together
【枕巾】zhěnjīn〈名〉 pillow towel
【枕木】zhěnmù〈名〉 sleeper (of railway)
【枕套】zhěntào〈名〉 pillowcase
【枕头】zhěntou〈名〉 pillow
【枕席】zhěnxí〈名〉 pillow mat
【枕芯】zhěnxīn〈名〉 pillow

轸（軫）

zhěn
A〈名〉 1〈古〉（车后横木） cross board at the rear of an ancient carriage 2（车） carriage 3（指星宿） one of the 28 constellations in ancient Chinese astronomy
B〈形〉〈书〉 sorrowful: ～怀 sorrowfully cherish the memory of sb.
【轸念】zhěnniàn〈动〉〈书〉 think anxiously about: 殊深～ express great solicitude

畛

zhěn〈名〉〈书〉 raised path between fields
【畛域】zhěnyù〈名〉〈书〉 boundary: 不分～ make no distinctions

疹

zhěn〈名〉 rash: ▸风～，麻～，皮～
【疹子】zhěnzi〈名〉 measles

袗 zhěn〈书〉
A〈名〉 unlined jacket
B〈形〉 resplendent: ～衣 gorgeous dress

缜（縝） zhěn〈形〉〈书〉 careful
【缜密】zhěnmì〈形〉〈书〉 meticulous: ～的计划 carefully thought-out plan ‖ 文思～。 The ideas in the article have been carefully organized.

鬒 zhěn〈名〉〈书〉 thick dark hair

zhèn

圳 zhèn〈名〉〈方〉 ditch between fields

阵[1]（陣） zhèn〈名〉 **1**（布兵方式） battle array: 摆一字长蛇～ deploy troops in a long single-file line ‖ 严～以待 be in full battle array **2**（阵地） battle: 上～杀敌 go into battle to fight the enemy ▸～亡

阵[2]（陣） zhèn〈量〉 **1**（指时间） period of time: 等了好一～子 wait quite a while ‖ 在部队呆过一～儿 have a spell in the army ‖ 这～儿 these days ‖ 这个问题我们研究了好长一～子。 We've been studying the problem for quite some time. **2**（指事情或现象） spell: 一～风 a gust of wind ‖ 一～咳嗽 a coughing fit ‖ 一～热烈的掌声 a burst of warm applause
【阵地】zhèndì〈名〉 position: 进入～ get into position ‖ 人在～在 hold one's position at all costs ‖ 前沿～ forward position ‖〈喻〉 思想～ ideological position
【阵地战】zhèndìzhàn〈名〉 positional warfare
【阵发性】zhènfāxìng ▸**p. 50**〈形〉［医学］ paroxysmal: ～气喘 clonic asthma
【阵风】zhènfēng〈名〉 gust of wind
【阵脚】zhènjiǎo〈名〉 position: 乱了～ get flustered ‖ ～大乱 be thrown into confusion
【阵容】zhènróng〈名〉 **1**（队伍面貌） battle array **2**〈喻〉（人力配备） line-up: ～强大 have a strong line-up ‖ 演员～整齐 well-balanced cast
【阵势】zhènshì〈名〉 **1**（阵容部署） battle formation: 摆开～ deploy the ranks in battle array **2**（情势） situation: 面对这种～，他惊得目瞪口呆。 He was dumbfounded by this situation.
【阵痛】zhèntòng〈名〉 **1** ▸**p. 50**［医学］ labour pains **2**〈喻〉（指困难） growing pains: 体制改革中的～ the growing pains of systems reform
【阵亡】zhènwáng〈动〉 be killed in action: ～将士名单 roll of honour
【阵线】zhènxiàn〈名〉 front: 民族统一～ national united front
【阵雪】zhènxuě〈名〉 snow shower
【阵营】zhènyíng〈名〉 camp: 社会主义～ socialist camp
【阵雨】zhènyǔ〈名〉 shower
【阵子】zhènzi〈方〉= 阵[2] zhèn

鸩（鴆） zhèn〈名〉 **1**（指鸟） legendary bird with poisonous feathers **2**（指毒） poisoned wine: 饮～止渴 quench one's thirst with poisoned wine
【鸩毒】zhèndú〈名〉〈书〉 poisoned wine

振 zhèn〈动〉 **1**（挥动） shake: ～笔疾书 write with flying strokes ‖ ～翅 flap the wings ▸～臂 **2**（振动） vibrate: ▸～幅，共～ **3**（奋发） rise with force and spirit: 士气大～。 Morale was greatly boosted. ‖ 听说比赛即将开始，观众精神一～。 The audience's spirits buoyed when they heard that the match would soon begin. ▸～奋，一蹶不～
【振臂】zhènbì〈动〉 raise one's arms: ～高呼 raise one's arms and shout
【振荡】zhèndàng〈动〉 **1**［物理］ vibrate **2**［电子］ oscillate: ～电流 oscillating current
【振动】zhèndòng〈动〉 vibrate: ～耐力 vibrational tolerance ‖ ～噪声 vibration noise
【振奋】zhènfèn **A**〈形〉 high-spirited: 人人～，个个当先。 Everyone was full of vigour as they forged. **B**〈动〉 stimulate: ～精神 elevate the soul ‖ ～人心 fill people with enthusiasm
【振幅】zhènfú〈名〉 amplitude
【振聋发聩】zhènlóng-fākuì〈成〉〈喻〉 inspire the benighted
【振兴】zhènxīng〈动〉 revitalize: ～民族工业 vigorously develop national industries ‖ ～中华 rejuvenate the Chinese nation
【振振有词】zhènzhèn-yǒucí〈成〉 speak assertively
【振作】zhènzuò **A**〈动〉 gather oneself together: ～精神 brace oneself ‖ ～起来 pull oneself together **B**〈形〉 spirited: 士气不太～。 Morale is not very high.

朕[1] zhèn〈代〉〈古〉（皇帝的自称） I

朕[2] zhèn〈名〉〈书〉 portent
【朕兆】zhènzhào〈名〉〈书〉 omen

赈（賑） zhèn〈动〉 aid: 开仓～饥 open the granaries to relieve hungry people ‖ 以工代～ provide work as a form of relief ▸～灾
【赈济】zhènjì〈动〉 aid: ～难民 provide relief for refugees
【赈灾】zhènzāi〈动〉 aid the victims of a natural calamity: ～款 disaster fund

瑱 zhèn〈名〉〈古〉 jade earring

震 zhèn
A〈名〉 **1**〈书〉（雷） thunder **2**（地震） earthquake: ▸～级，～中 **3**（指八卦） one of the Eight Trigrams, symbolizing 'thunder'
B〈动〉 **1**（震动） shake: ～塌房屋数十间。 Dozens of houses collapsed in the quake. ‖ 许多门窗玻璃在爆炸中～碎了。 A lot of glass from doors and windows was shattered in the blast. ‖ 仪表板～松了。 Vibrations shook the panel loose. ▸～耳欲聋，～撼 **2**（情绪过激） be extremely excited: ▸～惊，～怒
【震波】zhènbō〈名〉 seismic wave: ～图 seismogram
【震颤】zhènchàn〈动〉 tremble: 浑身～ tremble all over ‖ 噩耗～着人们的心。 People's hearts trembled at the grievous news.
【震旦纪】Zhèndànjì〈名〉［地质］ Sinian Period
【震荡】zhèndàng〈动〉 vibrate: 回声～，山鸣谷应。 Echoes resounded through the valley. ‖ 股市～下挫。 The stock market wobbled and then dived.
【震动】zhèndòng〈动〉 **1**（颤动） shake: 火车经过时，整座房子都在～。 The whole house shakes whenever a train passes. **2**（引起强烈反响） shock: 总统遇刺身亡的消息～了全国。 The news of the president's assassination shocked the whole country.
【震耳欲聋】zhèn'ěryùlóng〈成〉 ear-splitting: ～的雷声/鞭炮声 deafening thunder/firecrackers
【震感】zhèngǎn〈名〉 feeling of an earthquake: 离震中200公里外的地方都有～。 The earthquake was felt 200 kilometres away from the epicentre.
【震古烁今】zhèngǔ-shuòjīn〈成〉 earth-shattering
【震撼】zhènhàn〈动〉 shake: ～人心 shocking ‖ 滚滚春雷，～大地。 The rumbling spring thunder shook the earth.
【震级】zhènjí〈名〉［地质］ seismicity
【震惊】zhènjīng **A**〈形〉 shocking: 大为～ be greatly astonished ‖ 令人～的消息 shocking news **B**〈动〉 shock: ～世界 shock the world ‖ ～政界 rock the political arena
【震怒】zhènnù〈动〉 be enraged: ～之下，他用双拳重击桌面。 In a fit of fury he thumped his fists down on the desk.
【震区】zhènqū〈名〉［地质］ earthquake-affected area
【震慑】zhènshè〈动〉 frighten: ～敌人 intimidate the enemy ‖ 对罪犯起～作用 serve as a deterrent to offenders
【震悚】zhènsǒng〈动〉〈书〉 be terrified
【震天动地】zhèntiān-dòngdì〈成〉 shake heaven and earth
【震源】zhènyuán〈名〉［地质］ focus (of an earthquake)
【震中】zhènzhōng〈名〉［地质］ epicentre: ～位于… the epicentre is situated in ...

镇（鎮） zhèn
A〈动〉 **1**（压） press: ▸～尺 **2**（使安定） daunt: 他一说话，就把大家给～住了。 His words silenced everyone. ▸～静剂，～痛 **3**（用强力压服） conquer by force: ▸～压 **4**（用武力守护） guard: ▸～守，坐～ **5**（使变凉） cool: 把啤酒～一～ let the beer chill for a while ▸冰～
B〈形〉 calm: ▸～定，～静
C〈名〉 **1**（镇守的地方） garrison post: 军事重～ strategic post **2**（市镇） town: ▸城～，乡～ **3**（集市） trading centre
【镇尺】zhènchǐ〈名〉 paperweight in the shape of a ruler
【镇定】zhèndìng **A**〈形〉 composed: 神色～ be calm and collected ‖ 他接到这一消息时显得异常～。 He received the news with surprising equanimity. **B**〈动〉 collect oneself: 他心乱如麻，难以～下来。 His mind was in such a whirl that he could hardly compose his thoughts.
【镇定自若】zhèndìng-zìruò〈成〉 retain one's composure
【镇静】zhènjìng **A**〈形〉 calm: 故作～ feign composure ‖ 越是危急关头，越要～。 The more critical the situation, the more important it is to have calm. **B**〈动〉 calm down: 尽力～自己 try one's best to collect oneself
【镇静剂】zhènjìngjì〈名〉 sedative: 注射～ inject with a sedative ‖ 服用～ take tranquillizers
【镇流器】zhènliúqì〈名〉［电子］ ballast
【镇守】zhènshǒu〈动〉 guard: ～边关 defend the frontier

【镇痛】zhèntòng〈动〉［医学］ analgesia: ～剂 analgesic
【镇压】zhènyā〈动〉 suppress: ～叛乱 suppress a revolt ‖ 血腥/野蛮～ bloody/barbaric suppression
【镇长】zhènzhǎng〈名〉 town mayor
【镇纸】zhènzhǐ〈名〉 paperweight
【镇子】zhènzi〈名〉〈口〉 1（小城镇） small town 2（集镇） market town

zhēng

丁 zhēng
▸dīng
【丁丁】zhēngzhēng〈拟〉〈书〉 clang: 伐木～。 Clang, clang goes the woodman's axe.

正 zhēng〈名〉 first month of the lunar year: 新～ January of the lunar year
▸zhèng
【正旦】zhēngdàn〈名〉〈书〉 lunar New Year's Day
【正月】zhēngyuè ▸**p. 928**〈名〉 first month of the lunar year: ～初一 lunar New Year's Day

争（爭） zhēng〈动〉 1（争夺） compete: ～冠军 compete for the championship ‖ ～相购买 compete to buy ‖ 力～上游 aim high ‖ 大家～着发言。 Everyone is vying for the floor. ▸～夺, ～光, ～先恐后, 力～ 2（较量） struggle: ▸～风吃醋, ～斗 3（争吵） dispute: 意气之～ argument involving personal feelings ‖ 这两口子整天为一些小事～得没完没了。 The couple quarrelled constantly over trivial matters. ‖ 意见已经一致了，不必再～。 There is no need for further debate since consensus has already been reached. ▸～吵, ～端, ～执, 论～
【争霸】zhēngbà〈动〉 scramble for supremacy: ～世界 contend for world domination ‖ 拳王～赛 boxing championship
【争辩】zhēngbiàn〈动〉 argue: 激烈地～ argue heatedly ‖ 无休无止的～ endless debate
【争长论短】zhēngcháng-lùnduǎn〈成〉 argue over minor issues
【争吵】zhēngchǎo〈动〉 quarrel: ～不休 squabble endlessly ‖ 孩子们～到后来就打了起来。 The children's dispute ended in a fight.
【争持】zhēngchí〈动〉 refuse to give in: 他们为一件小事～了半天。 They wrangled over a small thing for quite some time.
【争宠】zhēngchǒng〈动〉 strive for sb.'s favour
【争创】zhēngchuàng〈动〉 strive for: ～最佳业绩 strive for the highest possible achievement
【争顶】zhēngdǐng〈动〉［足球］ contend for a header: 两人在～时发生碰撞。 The two players clashed heads as they fought for the header.
【争斗】zhēngdòu〈动〉 1（打架） fight 2（较量） struggle: 内部～ internal struggle
【争端】zhēngduān〈名〉 dispute: 挑起～ stir up a dispute ‖ 调解两国～ act as a mediator in a conflict between two countries ‖ 边界～ border dispute
【争夺】zhēngduó〈动〉 contend for: ～出线权 contend for qualification into the next round of contest ‖ ～冠军 compete for the championship ‖ ～市场 compete for markets
【争分夺秒】zhēngfēn-duómiǎo〈成〉 race against the clock
【争风吃醋】zhēngfēng-chīcù〈成〉 fight for sb.'s affections
【争锋】zhēngfēng〈动〉〈书〉 fight for mastery: 谁与～? Who can win the competition?
【争光】zhēngguāng〈动〉 win glory: 为国～ win glory for the homeland
【争斤论两】zhēngjīn-lùnliǎng〈成〉 haggle over every ounce
【争脸】zhēngliǎn〈动〉 try to win credit
【争论】zhēnglùn〈动〉 debate: 正在～的问题 the question under debate ‖ 我不想和你～。 I have no wish to engage in argument with you.
【争名夺利】zhēngmíng-duólì〈成〉 scramble for fame and gain
【争鸣】zhēngmíng〈动〉 contend: 百家～ let a hundred schools of thought contend
【争奇斗艳】zhēngqí-dòuyàn〈成〉［of flowers, etc.］ contend with each other to display their charm
【争气】zhēngqì〈动〉 strive for self-improvement: 孩子们真～，每次考试都名列前茅。 The children work really hard, and every time they have exams they come top.
【争抢】zhēngqiǎng〈动〉 scramble for: ～头球 scramble for the header
【争取】zhēngqǔ〈动〉 fight for: ～独立/平等/自由 fight for independence/equality/freedom ‖ ～时间 race against time ‖ ～主动 try to gain the initiative ‖ ～祖国统一 strive for China's unification ‖ 拼命～ go all out in one's struggle
【争权夺利】zhēngquán-duólì〈成〉〈贬〉 scramble for power and profit
【争胜】zhēngshèng〈动〉 try to win
【争先】zhēngxiān〈动〉 compete to be the first
【争先恐后】zhēngxiān-kǒnghòu〈成〉 rival for top spot: 听说那位知名学者要开讲座，同学们～抢占座位。 The news that the famous scholar was going to deliver a lecture made the students scramble for seats.
【争先赛】zhēngxiānsài〈名〉［体育］ bicycle sprint race
【争雄】zhēngxióng〈动〉 contend for supremacy
【争议】zhēngyì〈动〉 dispute: 引起～ spark controversy ‖ 有～的人物 controversial person
【争战】zhēngzhàn〈名〉 war: 连年～ long years of war
【争执】zhēngzhí〈动〉 argue: ～不下 each sticks to his guns ‖ 他与裁判发生了～。 He got into an argument with the referee.
【争嘴】zhēngzuǐ〈动〉〈方〉 1（争吵） quarrel 2（抢食） try to get something to eat

挣（掙） zhēng
▸zhèng
【挣扎】zhēngzhá〈动〉 struggle: ～在死亡线上 struggle for survival ‖ ～着坐起来 struggle to a sitting position

征[1] zhēng〈动〉 1（远行） go on a journey: ▸～尘, ～途, 长～ 2（出兵征讨） go on a campaign: 南～北战 fight north and south ▸～伐, ～讨, 出～

征[2]（徵） zhēng〈动〉 1（召集） conscript: 应～入伍 be conscripted into the army ‖ 这次～了三万兵员。 The levy produced an army of 30,000 men. ▸～兵 2（征收） levy: ～地 requisition a piece of land ‖ ～粮 demand grain as a tax ‖ ～烟草税 levy a tax on tobacco 3（寻求） solicit: ▸～稿, ～婚, ～文

征[3]（徵） zhēng〈名〉 1〈书〉（证明） evidence: 无～之言 unfounded assertion ‖ 有实物可～。 There is solid evidence. 2（迹象） sign, portent: ▸～兆, 特～, 象～
【征兵】zhēngbīng〈动〉 conscript〈英〉; draft〈美〉: ～工作 conscription
【征尘】zhēngchén〈名〉〈书〉 dust that settles on one during a journey: 洗去～ have a wash after a long journey
【征程】zhēngchéng〈名〉 journey: 万里～ very long journey
【征地】zhēngdì〈动〉 expropriate land for use
【征调】zhēngdiào〈动〉 requisition: ～粮食及医务人员支援灾区 requisition grain and medical workers for the disaster-stricken area
【征订】zhēngdìng〈动〉 invite subscriptions: 明年杂志的～工作从今年十月开始。 Subscriptions to next year's magazines begin this October.
【征伐】zhēngfá〈动〉 go on a punitive expedition
【征帆】zhēngfān〈名〉〈书〉 ship on a long voyage
【征服】zhēngfú〈动〉 1（指用武力） conquer: ～世界的野心 ambition to conquer the world 2（指用感染力） win over: 她的演唱～了全场观众。 Her singing took the whole theatre by storm.
【征稿】zhēnggǎo〈动〉 solicit contributions: 向某人～ solicit contributions from sb. ‖ ～启事 call for contributions
【征购】zhēnggòu〈动〉 requisition by purchase: ～土地 requisition land ‖ ～任务 state purchase quotas ‖ 粮食～ grain purchase by the state
【征管】zhēngguǎn〈动〉 levy and administer: 加强税收～工作 strengthen the work of collecting and managing taxes
【征候】zhēnghòu〈名〉 symptom: 病人已有危险～。 The patient shows critical symptoms.
【征婚】zhēnghūn〈动〉 solicit for marriage: ～广告 lonely hearts advertisement ‖ ～人 marriage-seeker
【征集】zhēngjí〈动〉 1（收集） collect: ～签名 collect signatures ‖ ～文史资料 collect accounts of historical events 2（征募） draft: ～新兵 call up raw recruits ‖ ～志愿者 recruit volunteers
【征募】zhēngmù〈动〉 recruit: ～新兵 draft recruits
【征聘】zhēngpìn〈动〉 invite applications for jobs: ～科技人员 advertise for scientific and technological personnel
【征求】zhēngqiú〈动〉 solicit: ～意见 solicit opinions
【征收】zhēngshōu〈动〉 levy: ～商业税/烟草税 levy a tax on trade/tobacco
【征讨】zhēngtǎo〈动〉 go on a punitive expedition
【征途】zhēngtú〈名〉 journey: 踏上～ embark on a journey ‖ 艰难的～ tough journey
【征文】zhēngwén A〈动〉 invite articles

on a given subject: ～启事 call for contributions **B**〈名〉commissioned articles
【征象】zhēngxiàng〈名〉sign: 日落时出现晚霞是好天气的～。A red sky at sunset is a sign of good weather to come.
【征询】zhēngxún〈动〉solicit sb.'s advice: ～律师意见 consult a lawyer
【征引】zhēngyǐn〈动〉quote
【征用】zhēngyòng〈动〉expropriate: ～房屋/土地 requisition buildings/land
【征战】zhēngzhàn〈动〉go into battle: 连年～ go on campaigns year after year
【征召】zhēngzhào〈动〉enlist: ～入伍 enlist into the army
【征兆】zhēngzhào〈名〉omen: 地震的～ signs of an impending earthquake ‖ 好的/危险的～ favourable/dangerous omen

怔 zhēng〈形〉seized with terror ▸zhèng
【怔忡】zhēngchōng〈动〉〈书〉[中医] have severe palpitations
【怔忪】zhēngzhōng〈形〉〈书〉panic-stricken

峥(崢) zhēng
【峥嵘】zhēngróng〈形〉**1**（高峻）towering: 殿宇～ towering palaces ‖ 山势～ towering mountains **2**〈喻〉（不平凡）extraordinary: ～岁月 eventful times ‖ 头角～ brilliant and promising

狰(猙) zhēng
【狰狞】zhēngníng〈形〉savage: 面目～ ferocious features

钲(鉦) zhēng ▸p. 929〈名〉〈古〉[音乐] bell-shaped percussion instrument with a long handle, used by marching troops

症(癥) zhēng〈名〉[中医] lump in the abdomen ▸zhèng
【症结】zhēngjié〈名〉**1** [中医] lump in the abdomen **2**〈喻〉（关键）nub: 这就是问题的～所在。There lies the crux of the problem.

烝 zhēng〈形〉〈书〉numerous
【烝民】zhēngmín〈名〉many people

睁(睜) zhēng〈动〉open: ～开眼睛 open one's eyes
【睁眼瞎】zhēngyǎn xiā〈俗〉〈喻〉illiterate person
【睁一只眼，闭一只眼】zhēng yī zhī yǎn, bì yī zhī yǎn〈俗〉turn a blind eye to sth.
【睁着眼睛说瞎话】zhēngzhe yǎnjing shuō xiāhuà〈俗〉tell a barefaced lie

铮(錚) zhēng
【铮铮】zhēngzhēng〈拟〉clang: ～悦耳 melodious tinkling ‖ 铁中～ be outstanding ▸zhèng

筝(箏) zhēng〈名〉**1** ▸p. 929（古筝）*zheng*, a 21-or-25-stringed plucked instrument similar to a zither **2** = 风筝 fēngzheng

蒸 zhēng〈动〉**1**（蒸发）evaporate: ▸～馏, ～气, ～腾 **2**（蒸热）steam: ～馒头 steamed buns ‖ 把剩饭～一～。Heat up leftover food. ‖ 针头要～过才能再用。The syringe needle should be steamed before use.
【蒸饼】zhēngbǐng〈名〉steamed cake
【蒸发】zhēngfā〈动〉**1**（指转化为气体）evaporate: 烈日下，雨水～快。Under the baking sun, the rainwater evaporated very quickly. **2**（消失）vanish: 一夜间该公司就从人间～了。This company disappeared overnight.
【蒸锅】zhēngguō〈名〉steamer
【蒸饺】zhēngjiǎo〈名〉steamed *jiaozi* [dumpling with meat and vegetable stuffing]
【蒸馏】zhēngliú〈动〉distil: ～器 distiller ‖ ～水 distilled water ‖ 白兰地是由果酒～制成的。Brandy is distilled from fruit wine.
【蒸笼】zhēnglóng〈名〉bamboo steamer
【蒸气】zhēngqì〈名〉vapour: 水～ steam
【蒸汽】zhēngqì〈名〉steam: ～机车/火车 steam locomotive/train ‖ ～熨斗 steam iron
【蒸汽锤】zhēngqìchuí = 汽锤 qìchuí
【蒸汽机】zhēngqìjī〈名〉steam engine
【蒸腾】zhēngténg〈动〉rise swiftly: 热气～ steaming
【蒸蒸日上】zhēngzhēng-rìshàng〈成〉become more prosperous every day: 一派～、欣欣向荣的景象 a scene of prosperity

鲭(鯖) zhēng〈名〉〈书〉dish cooked by mixing fish and other meat together ▸qīng

zhěng

拯 zhěng〈动〉rescue: ～民于水火之中 save the disaster-stricken people
【拯救】zhěngjiù〈动〉save: ～濒危物种 rescue endangered species ‖ ～生命 save sb.'s life

整 zhěng
A〈形〉**1**（整齐）tidy: 衣冠不～ be slovenly in one's dress ‖ ～然有序 be in good order ▸～洁, ～齐, 工～ **2**（完整）whole: ～机进口 import complete machines ‖ ～块土地 entire piece of land ‖ 12点～ twelve o'clock sharp ‖ 零存～取 saving by making fixed deposits by instalment ▸～个, ～套, 完～
B〈动〉**1**（整理）put in order: ～床铺 straighten out one's bed ▸～顿, ～风, 休～ **2**（修理）repair: ▸～旧如新, ～容, ～修 **3**〈方〉（搞）do: ～几个菜下酒 prepare a few dishes to go with the wine ‖ 玩具被孩子们～坏了。The toy was damaged by the children. **4**〈口〉（使吃苦头）make things difficult for sb.: 你把我～得好苦。You made me suffer a lot.
【整备】zhěngbèi〈动〉reorganize and outfit
【整编】zhěngbiān〈动〉reorganize: ～部队 reorganize troops
【整饬】zhěngchì **A**〈动〉put in order: ～军纪 strengthen army discipline **B**〈形〉tidy: 服装～ neatly dressed
【整除】zhěngchú〈动〉[数学] be divisible: 12可被2，3，4，6～。12 is divisible by 2, 3, 4 and 6.
【整党】zhěngdǎng〈动〉consolidate the Party organization
【整地】zhěngdì〈动〉[农业] prepare the soil
【整点】zhěngdiǎn ▸p. 669〈名〉the hour: ～新闻 news on the hour
【整队】zhěngduì〈动〉bring the ranks into orderly alignment: ～出发 set out in orderly formation
【整顿】zhěngdùn〈动〉rectify: ～纪律 strengthen discipline ‖ ～经济秩序 rectify the economic order ‖ ～领导班子 consolidate a leading body ‖ ～作风 rectify the style of work
【整风】zhěngfēng〈动〉rectify incorrect styles of work or thinking: ～运动 rectification movement
【整改】zhěnggǎi〈动〉rectify and reform: ～方案 programme of rectification and reform ‖ 限期～ set a deadline for rectification and reform
【整个】zhěnggè〈形〉whole: ～国家/世界 the whole nation/world ‖ ～上午 the entire morning
【整固】zhěnggù〈动〉readjust and consolidate: ～金价 readjust and consolidate the price of gold
【整合】zhěnghé〈动〉reorganize and consolidate: ～企业内部机构 reorganize the internal structure of enterprises
【整洁】zhěngjié〈形〉clean and tidy: 衣着～ be neatly dressed ‖ ～的房间 tidy room
【整旧如新】zhěngjiùrúxīn〈成〉repair sth. old and make it as good as new
【整理】zhěnglǐ〈动〉straighten out: ～房间 put a room in order ‖ ～行装 pack one's things for a journey ‖ ～资料 sort out data
【整流】zhěngliú〈名〉[电子] rectification
【整流器】zhěngliúqì〈名〉rectifier
【整齐】zhěngqí **A**〈形〉**1**（有秩序）orderly: 步伐～ march in step **2**（相差不大）regular: 阵容～ well-balanced line-up ‖ ～的牙齿 regular teeth ‖ 出苗～。The new shoots are coming out evenly. **B**〈动〉regulate: ～步调 make a group of people walk at a set pace
【整齐划一】zhěngqí-huàyī〈成〉uniform: 服装～ be dressed in uniform
【整人】zhěngrén〈动〉give sb. a hard time
【整容】zhěngróng〈动〉**1**（修饰）tidy oneself up **2**（指面部手术）facelift: ～手术 cosmetic surgery
【整容外科】zhěngróng wàikē〈名〉cosmetic surgery
【整式】zhěngshì〈名〉[数学] integral expression
【整数】zhěngshù ▸p. 691〈名〉**1** [数学] whole number **2**（指无零头）round number: 我给你个～吧，100元，零钱就甭找了。I'll round it up to 100 *yuan* and you can keep the change.
【整肃】zhěngsù〈书〉**A**〈形〉strict: 军容～ well-disciplined army **B**〈动〉consolidate: ～法纪 enforce law and discipline
【整套】zhěngtào〈名〉complete set: ～家具 complete set of furniture ‖ ～设备 complete set of equipment
【整体】zhěngtǐ〈名〉whole: 形成～ form a whole ‖ ～规划 macrocosmic layout ‖ ～利益 overall interests ‖ 不可分割/有机的～ undivided/organic whole
【整体厨房】zhěngtǐ chúfáng〈名〉integral kitchen
【整天】zhěngtiān〈名〉all day (long)
【整形】zhěngxíng〈动〉[医学] perform plastic surgery: ～手术 plastic surgery
【整形外科】zhěngxíng wàikē〈名〉plastic surgery
【整修】zhěngxiū〈动〉renovate: ～房屋 renovate a house ‖ ～水利工程 repair water conservancy projects

【整训】zhěngxùn〈动〉 train and consolidate: ～部队 train and consolidate troops

【整夜】zhěngyè〈名〉 whole night

【整整】zhěngzhěng〈副〉 fully: ～20年没有见面了 not have met for a full 20 years ‖ 干了～一个月才完工。 It took a whole month to finish it.

【整枝】zhěngzhī〈动〉［农业］ prune: 给桃树～ prune a peach tree

【整治】zhěngzhì〈动〉 ❶（整顿） repair: ～农贸市场 renovate and manage a farmers' market ‖ ～河道 dredge a river ‖ ～环境污染 remedy environmental pollution ❷（惩罚） punish: ～坏人 punish evildoers

【整装待发】zhěngzhuāng-dàifā〈成〉 be ready to set out: 士兵们～。 The soldiers were fully equipped and waiting to set out.

zhèng

正 zhèng

A〈形〉 ❶（不偏斜） straight: ～南 due south ‖ ～前方 straight ahead ‖ 把照片挂～ hang the picture straight ❷（中间） middle: ▸～房, ～门, ～中 ❸（合乎标准） regular: ▸～规, ～楷, ～式 ❹（正直） honest: 此人作风不～。 This man has no moral integrity. ‖ 此钱来路不～。 This money has not been obtained honestly. ▸～路, ～派, 义～词严 ❺（纯正） pure: ～红/黄 pure red/yellow ‖ 味儿不～ not the right flavour ‖ 颜色不～ not the right colour ❻（主要） principal: ～主任 director ‖ ～驾驶员 first pilot ‖ ～教授 full professor ▸～本, ～文, ～业 ❼（正面） obverse: 布的～面 right side of the cloth ‖ 这张纸的～反两面都很光滑。 Both sides of the paper are very smooth. ❽［数学］［物理］ positive: ～离子 positive ion ‖ 负负得～。 Two minuses make a plus. ▸～号, ～极, ～数 ❾（指时间） sharp: 10点～ at ten o'clock sharp ▸～午 ❿（指几何图形） regular: ～多面体 regular polyhedron ‖ ～六边形 regular hexagon ▸～方形 **B**〈动〉 ❶（摆正） straighten out: ～领带 adjust one's tie ‖ ～帽子 straighten out one's hat ❷（端正） rectify: ▸～人先～己 ❸（改正） correct: ▸～音, ～字 **C**〈副〉 ❶（正在进行）（指行为） just happening;（指状态） just continuing: 孩子们～在做作业。 The children are doing their homework. ‖ 外面～下着雪呢。 It's snowing outside. ❷（恰好） just: ～合我意。 It is just what I want. ‖ 援助来得～是时候。 Help came just in time. ▸～中下怀 ▸zhēng

【正版】zhèngbǎn〈名〉 official edition: ～书 official edition book

【正本】zhèngběn〈名〉 ❶（指图书） reserved copy ❷（指文书或文件） original: 合同/文件～ original of a contract/document

【正本清源】zhèngběn-qīngyuán〈成〉 carry out a radical reform: 不采取～的措施就不能解决问题。 Without adopting radical reform measures, the problem cannot be solved.

【正比】zhèngbǐ〈名〉 ❶（指变化关系） direct ratio: 成就与努力成～。 Achievement is directly proportional to effort. ❷ = 正比例 zhèngbǐlì

【正比例】zhèngbǐlì〈名〉 direct proportion: X与Y成～。 X is directly proportional to Y.

【正步】zhèngbù〈名〉［军事］ parade step: ～走! Parade step, march!

【正餐】zhèngcān〈名〉 ❶（正常饭食） regular meal ❷（晚餐） dinner

【正常】zhèngcháng〈形〉 normal: 恢复～ return to normal ‖ 运转～ be in normal working order ‖ 发育～ develop normally ‖ 他的行为极不～。 His behaviour is far from normal.

【正常化】zhèngchánghuà〈动〉 normalize: 使两国关系～ normalize relations between the two countries

【正出】zhèngchū〈动〉〈旧〉 be born to the legal wife

【正大光明】zhèngdà-guāngmíng = 光明正大 guāngmíng-zhèngdà

【正当】zhèngdāng〈动〉 be just the time for: ～春播之时 just the time for spring sowing

【正当年】zhèngdāngnián〈名〉 prime of one's life

【正当时】zhèngdāngshí〈名〉 right time: 春耕～。 Spring is the right time for ploughing.

【正当中】zhèngdāngzhōng = 正中 zhèngzhōng

【正当】zhèngdàng〈形〉 appropriate: 通过～途径 through proper channels ‖ 没有～理由 have no justifiable reason ‖ 不～关系 illicit relationship

【正当防卫】zhèngdàng fángwèi〈名〉［法律］ legitimate defence: ～行为 act of self-defence

【正道】zhèngdào〈名〉 ❶（指路） correct path: 走～ follow the correct path ❷（指道理） truth

【正点】zhèngdiǎn〈动〉 be on time: ～到达 arrive on time/punctually ‖ ～起飞 take off on time

【正电】zhèngdiàn〈名〉 positive electricity

【正电子】zhèngdiànzǐ〈名〉 positron

【正殿】zhèngdiàn〈名〉 main hall (in a royal palace or Buddhist temple)

【正多边形】zhèngduōbiānxíng〈名〉 regular polygon

【正法】zhèngfǎ〈动〉 execute: 将罪犯就地～ execute a criminal on the spot

【正犯】zhèngfàn〈名〉［法律］ principal offender

【正方】zhèngfāng **A**〈形〉 square: ～桌子 square table **B**〈名〉 positive side in a debate

【正方形】zhèngfāngxíng〈名〉 square

【正房】zhèngfáng〈名〉 ❶（指房间） principal rooms [in a quadrangle, usu facing south] ❷〈旧〉（指人） legal wife

【正负电子对撞机】zhèngfù diànzǐ duìzhuàngjī〈名〉 electron-positron collider

【正赶上】zhènggǎnshàng〈动〉 be just in time for

【正告】zhènggào〈动〉 warn sternly: ～侵略者 give the aggressors a stern warning

【正宫】zhènggōng〈名〉 ❶（指宫殿） empress's palace ❷（指人） empress: ～娘娘 queen consort

【正骨】zhènggǔ〈名〉［中医］ bone-setting: ～水 bone-setting lotion

【正规】zhèngguī〈形〉 regular: ～部队 regular troops

【正规化】zhèngguīhuà〈动〉 standardize

【正规军】zhèngguījūn〈名〉 regular army

【正轨】zhèngguǐ〈名〉 right track: 纳入～ put sth. on the right track ‖ 走上～ be on the right course

【正果】zhèngguǒ〈名〉［佛教］ proper consequence of a regulated life in this world: 修成～ attain the right fruit by practising Buddhism

【正好】zhènghǎo **A**〈形〉 just right: 你来得～。 You've come in just in time. ‖ 天气不冷不热，～出去旅行。 It's neither too hot nor too cold — just the right weather for travelling. ‖ 这笔奖金～买台电脑。 This bonus is just enough to buy a computer. **B**〈副〉 by chance: 他昏倒的时候，～有一位医生在旁。 It so happened that there was a doctor close at hand when he fainted. ‖ 这次见到他，～当面向他请教。 I take the opportunity to ask him for advice when I meet him.

【正号】zhènghào〈名〉［数学］ positive/plus sign

【正极】zhèngjí〈名〉［电气］ anode

【正教】Zhèngjiào〈名〉［宗教］ Orthodox Church: ▸东～

【正教授】zhèngjiàoshòu〈名〉 full professor

【正襟危坐】zhèngjīn-wēizuò〈成〉 straighten out one's clothes and sit bolt upright: 弟子们～，聆听大师的教诲。 The disciples straightened out their clothes and sat up straight to listen to the great master's instruction.

【正经八百】zhèngjīng-bābǎi〈成〉〈口〉 deadly serious: 你们在开玩笑，而我可是～的。 You may be joking, but I'm deadly serious.

【正经】zhèngjing〈形〉 ❶（正派） upright: ～人 decent person ▸假～ ❷（正式） serious: 谈～事 talk business ‖ 这些捐来的钱必须用在～地方。 The money donated must be put to proper use. ❸（合乎标准） standard, formal: ～货 standard goods ❹（严肃认真） earnest: 他很～地和我谈这件事。 He talked to me very seriously about the matter.

【正剧】zhèngjù〈名〉 serious drama

【正楷】zhèngkǎi〈名〉［书法］ regular script

【正课】zhèngkè〈名〉 required course

【正理】zhènglǐ〈名〉 correct principle: 合乎～ conform to reason

【正梁】zhèngliáng = 脊檩 jǐlǐn

【正路】zhènglù〈名〉 right course: 走～ follow the correct path

【正论】zhènglùn〈名〉 just argument

【正门】zhèngmén〈名〉 main entrance

【正面】zhèngmiàn **A**〈名〉 ❶（非侧面） front: ～冲突 head-on clash ‖ ～进攻 frontal attack ‖ 大楼的～有八根大理石柱子。 Eight marble pillars stand at the front of the building. ❷（非背面） right side: 钞票的～ face of a banknote ‖ 衣料的～ right side of a piece of cloth **B**〈形〉 ❶（积极） positive: ～意见 positive idea ‖ ～形象 positive image ‖ ～教育 education by positive measures or examples ❷（直接） direct: ～回答问题 answer a question directly ‖ 有问题请～提出来，别绕弯子。 If there is something you would like to ask, stop beating about the bush and come out with it.

【正面人物】zhèngmiàn rénwù〈名〉 positive character

【正面战场】zhèngmiàn zhànchǎng〈名〉 front-line battlefield

【正名】zhèngmíng〈动〉 restore one's name

【正牌】zhèngpái〈形〉 genuine: ～货 genuine goods

【正派】zhèngpài〈形〉 upright: 为人～ be honest and upright ‖ 作风～ be honest and upright in one's ways

【正片】zhèngpiàn〈名〉 ❶［摄影］ positive ❷ = 拷贝 kǎobèi A ❸［影视］ feature film

【正品】zhèngpǐn〈名〉 quality product

【正气】zhèngqì〈名〉**1**（指作风） healthy tendency: 发扬～ encourage a spirit of righteousness **2**（指气概） moral courage: ～凛然 with awe-inspiring righteousness
【正桥】zhèngqiáo〈名〉 main structure of a bridge: ～与引桥连接处 the point of connection between the approach to a bridge and the main structure itself
【正巧】zhèngqiǎo **A**〈副〉 by chance: 我身上～有100元。 It just so happens that I have 100 *yuan* on me. **B**〈形〉 timely: 你来得～。 You have come just in time.
【正切】zhèngqiē〈名〉［数学］ tangent
【正取】zhèngqǔ〈动〉 be admitted: ～生 officially enrolled candidates
【正确】zhèngquè〈形〉 correct: ～的意见 well-founded criticism ‖ 答案～。 The answer is correct. ‖ 这样做是～的。 This is the right thing to do.
【正人君子】zhèngrén-jūnzǐ〈成〉 man of integrity: 他装出一副～的样子。 He posed as a man of integrity.
【正人先正己】zhèngrén xiān zhèngjǐ〈俗〉 correct your own faults before you try to correct those of others
【正如】zhèngrú〈副〉 just as: ～你所知道的 as you know ‖ ～上文所说 as mentioned above ‖ ～所料 as might be expected
【正赛】zhèngsài〈名〉 final
【正三角形】zhèngsānjiǎoxíng〈名〉 equilateral triangle
【正色】zhèngsè **A** ▸**p. 863**〈名〉〈书〉 pure colour **B**〈动〉 adopt a stern countenance: ～拒绝 sternly refuse
【正身】zhèngshēn〈名〉 identity: 验明～ verify the identity of sb.
【正史】zhèngshǐ〈名〉 authorized history
【正式】zhèngshì〈形〉 formal: ～就职 formally take office ‖ ～党员 full Party member ‖ ～访问 official visit ‖ ～代表团的～成员 a regular member of the delegation
【正视】zhèngshì〈动〉 face up to: ～困难/危机 face up to difficulties/a crisis ‖ ～现实 face up to reality
【正事】zhèngshì〈名〉 proper business: 谈～ talk business ‖ 我们该办～了。 It is time that we got down to business.
【正室】zhèngshì〈名〉**1**〈旧〉（指妻子） legal wife **2**〈书〉（指儿子） eldest son born by one's legal wife
【正手】zhèngshǒu〈名〉［体育］ forehand: ～握拍 forehand grip
【正数】zhèngshù ▸**p. 691**〈名〉［数学］ positive number
【正态分布】zhèngtài fēnbù〈名〉［统计］ normal distribution
【正题】zhèngtí〈名〉 subject: 离开～ wander from the subject ‖ 转入～ come to the point
【正体】zhèngtǐ〈名〉**1**（指字形） standardized form of Chinese characters **2** = 楷书 kǎishū **3**（指印刷体） block letter
【正厅】zhèngtīng〈名〉**1**（中央大厅） main hall **2**（正对舞台部分） stalls
【正统】zhèngtǒng **A**〈名〉 legitimism: 王位的～继承人 legitimate heir to the throne **B**〈形〉 orthodox: ～观念/理论 orthodox idea/theory ‖ 他的思想很～。 He has a very orthodox way of thinking.
【正投影】zhèngtóuyǐng〈名〉 orthographic projection
【正文】zhèngwén〈名〉 main body: 词典～ the dictionary proper ‖ 书的～ the main text of a book
【正屋】zhèngwū〈名〉 principal room [in a quadrangle, usu facing south]
【正午】zhèngwǔ〈名〉 midday
【正误】zhèngwù〈动〉 correct errors: ～表 errata
【正弦】zhèngxián〈名〉［数学］ sine
【正项】zhèngxiàng〈名〉 regular item
【正凶】zhèngxiōng〈名〉［法律］ principal murderer: 缉拿～ apprehend the principal murderer
【正言厉色】zhèngyán-lìsè〈成〉 say gravely with a straight face
【正颜厉色】zhèngyán-lìsè〈成〉 put on a stern countenance
【正眼】zhèngyǎn〈动〉 look sb. in the eye: 他从不敢～看她。 He never dares to look her in the eye.
【正业】zhèngyè〈名〉 regular job: ▸不务～
【正义】zhèngyì **A**〈名〉**1**（指道理） justice: 伸张/主持～ uphold justice ‖ 为～而战 fight for justice **2**（指注释） orthodox interpretation [used also as part of a book title]: 《史记～》 *Correct Interpretation of the Record of History* **B**〈形〉 just: ～的战争 just war ‖ 我们的事业是～的。 Our cause is just.
【正义感】zhèngyìgǎn〈名〉 sense of justice
【正义之师】zhèngyìzhīshī〈成〉 army dedicated to a just cause
【正音】zhèngyīn **A**〈动〉［语言］ correct sb.'s pronunciation: 帮助学生～ help students to correct their pronunciation **B**〈名〉 standard pronunciation: ～辞典 dictionary of standard pronunciation
【正院儿】zhèngyuànr〈名〉 main courtyard
【正在】zhèngzài〈副〉 in the process of: ～进行磋商。 Consultations are under way. ‖ 他们～开会。 They are having a meeting.
【正直】zhèngzhí〈形〉 upright: 为人～ be an honest person ‖ ～无私 be upright and impartial
【正职】zhèngzhí〈名〉**1**（指职务） position of chief: 这些领导有的任～，有的任副职。 Some of these leaders are chiefs while the rest of them are deputies. **2**（指职业） main occupation: 她的～是作家，同时还做兼职教师。 She is a writer by profession, but she's also a part-time teacher.
【正中】zhèngzhōng〈名〉 middle: 院子～有一个花坛。 There is a raised flower bed right in the centre of the yard.
【正中下怀】zhèngzhòng-xiàhuái〈成〉 be exactly what one wants
【正中要害】zhèngzhòng-yàohài〈成〉 hit the (right) nail on the head
【正传】zhèngzhuàn〈名〉 subject under discussion: 言归～ get back to business
【正装】zhèngzhuāng〈名〉 formal wear: 主播新闻时要穿～。 News presenters must wear formal attire.
【正字】zhèngzì **A**〈动〉 correct a wrongly written character or misspelt word **B**〈名〉 standard form of Chinese characters
【正字法】zhèngzìfǎ〈名〉 orthography: ～学者 orthographer
【正宗】zhèngzōng **A**〈名〉 orthodox school **B**〈形〉 authentic: ～川菜 genuine Sichuan cuisine
【正座】zhèngzuò〈名〉 central seat directly facing the stage

证（證）zhèng

A〈动〉 prove: ▸～人, ～实, 查～, 论～
B〈名〉 evidence: 持～上岗 take a post with relevant certificates ‖ 驾驶～ driving licence ‖ 结婚～ marriage certificate ▸～书, 罪～
【证词】zhèngcí〈名〉 testimony: 提供～ give a testimony
【证婚】zhènghūn〈动〉 officiate at a wedding: ～人 chief witness at a wedding ceremony
【证件】zhèngjiàn〈名〉 credentials: 出示～ present one's credentials ‖ 检查～ examine sb.'s credentials
【证据】zhèngjù〈名〉 evidence: 搜集～ collect evidence ‖ 销毁～ destroy the evidence ‖ ～确凿 conclusive proof
【证明】zhèngmíng **A**〈动〉 prove: ～无罪/有罪 testify to sb.'s innocence/guilt ‖ ～书 certificate ‖ 产地～书 certificate of origin ‖ 出生/结婚/死亡～书 birth/marriage/death certificate ‖ 事实～这一判断是对的。 The facts bear the judgement out. ‖ 她脸红～她心中有愧。 Her blush testified to her guilt. **B**〈名〉 certificate: 开具～ write out a testimonial ‖ 出生/结婚/死亡～ birth/marriage/death certificate
【证券】zhèngquàn〈名〉 securities: 有价～ negotiable securities ‖ ～公司 securities company ‖ ～市场 stock market
【证券化】zhèngquànhuà〈动〉 engage in securitisation: 国有资产～ securitisation of state-owned assets
【证券交易所】zhèngquàn jiāoyìsuǒ〈名〉 stock exchange
【证券投资】zhèngquàn tóuzī〈名〉 portfolio investment
【证人】zhèngren〈名〉**1**（针对法庭案件） witness: 传唤～ summon a witness ‖ ～出庭作证 come to court and testify as a witness **2**（针对某件事） authenticator
【证实】zhèngshí〈动〉 bear out: 有待～ remain to be verified ‖ 未经～的报道 unconfirmed report
【证书】zhèngshū〈名〉 certificate: 颁发～ issue a certificate ‖ 毕业～ graduation certificate ‖ 学历～ school certificate ▸结婚～
【证物】zhèngwù〈名〉［法律］ evidence: 在法庭上出示～ present evidence in a court of law
【证言】zhèngyán〈名〉 testimony: 证人的～是假的。 The witness's testimony was false.
【证验】zhèngyàn **A**〈动〉 verify **B**〈名〉 real result
【证章】zhèngzhāng〈名〉 badge: 佩戴～ wear a badge
【证照】zhèngzhào〈名〉 permit: ～齐全 with all the necessary permits

郑（鄭）Zhèng

〈名〉 Zheng [state in the Zhou Dynasty]
【郑重】zhèngzhòng〈形〉 serious: ～对待 take sth. seriously ‖ ～声明 solemnly declare
【郑重其事】zhèngzhòng-qíshì〈成〉 with due care and respect: ～地宣布 solemnly declare
【郑州】Zhèngzhōu ▸**p. 661**〈名〉 Zhengzhou [capital of Henan Province (河南)]

怔 zhèng

〈动〉 be dumbfounded: 我一看诊断书，顿时～住了。 I was stunned by the diagnosis.
▸zhēng
【怔怔】zhèngzhèng〈形〉 dumbfounded: ～地站着 stand there dumbfounded

诤（諍）zhèng

〈动〉〈书〉 admonish: 力～ expostulate strongly
【诤谏】zhèngjiàn〈动〉〈书〉 criticize sb.'s faults frankly

【诤言】zhèngyán〈名〉〈书〉forthright exhortation
【诤友】zhèngyǒu〈名〉friend who will give unreserved criticism: 良师～ be both a good teacher and an outspoken friend

政 zhèng〈名〉1▸（政治）political affairs: 弃商从～ give up one's commercial interests and take up a government post ▸～策，～党，参～，议～ 2▸（政权）political power: ▸当～，执～ 3▸（指业务）administrative affairs of certain government departments: ▸财～，民～，邮～ 4▸（指事务）affairs of a family or an organization: 校～ school administration ▸家～
【政变】zhèngbiàn〈名〉coup: 发动～ stage a coup d'état ‖ 宫廷/军事～ palace/military coup
【政策】zhèngcè〈名〉policy: 落实～ implement a policy ‖ 执行～ execute a policy ‖ 制定～ formulate a policy ‖ 财政/货币/金融/经济～ fiscal/monetary/financial/economic policy ‖ 对外开放～ policy of opening up to the outside world
【政党】zhèngdǎng〈名〉political party: 组建～ organize a political party
【政敌】zhèngdí〈名〉political opponent: 战胜～ conquer a political opponent
【政法】zhèngfǎ〈名〉politics and law: ～工作 work of public security
【政府】zhèngfǔ〈名〉government: 地方/中央～ local/central government ‖ 合法～ legitimate government ‖ 流亡～ government-in-exile ‖ 省/市～ provincial/municipal government ‖ 林肯倡建一个民有、民治、民享的～。 Lincoln advocated the establishment of a government of the people, by the people, for the people. ▸临时～
【政府部门】zhèngfǔ bùmén〈名〉government department
【政府采购】zhèngfǔ cǎigòu〈名〉government procurement
【政府机构】zhèngfǔ jīgòu〈名〉government organization
【政府机关】zhèngfǔ jīguān〈名〉government body
【政府首脑】zhèngfǔ shǒunǎo〈名〉head of government
【政府要员】zhèngfǔ yàoyuán〈名〉high-ranking government official
【政改】zhènggǎi〈简称〉= 政治改革
【政纲】zhènggāng〈简称〉= 政治纲领
【政工】zhènggōng〈名〉political work: ～人员 political work personnel
【政纪】zhèngjì〈名〉government discipline
【政绩】zhèngjì〈名〉political achievement
【政见】zhèngjiàn〈名〉political view: 持不同～ hold different political views ‖ 持不同～者 political dissenter
【政教合一】zhèngjiào héyī〈名〉alliance between church and state
【政界】zhèngjiè〈名〉political circles: 退出～ withdraw from political life ‖ ～元老 senior statesman
【政局】zhèngjú〈名〉political situation: ～动荡 volatile a political situation ‖ ～稳定。 The political situation is stable.
【政客】zhèngkè〈名〉〈贬〉politician: 巧舌如簧的～ glib politician
【政令】zhènlìng〈名〉government decree
【政论】zhènglùn〈名〉political comment: 发表～ make political comments
【政派】zhèngpài〈名〉political group: 不同～ different political factions
【政权】zhèngquán〈名〉1▸（指权力）political power: 夺取～ seize power ‖ 巩固～ consolidate political power 2▸（指机关）organ of political power
【政权更迭】zhèngquán gēngdié〈名〉regime change
【政审】zhèngshěn〈简称〉= 政治审查
【政事】zhèngshì〈名〉government affairs: 处理～ attend to government affairs
【政坛】zhèngtán〈名〉political arena: 他一直活跃在～上。 He has remained active in politics.
【政体】zhèngtǐ〈名〉form of government: 议会～ parliamentary government
【政通人和】zhèngtōng-rénhé〈成〉the people are living harmoniously under the rule of an efficient government
【政委】zhèngwěi〈简称〉= 政治委员
【政务】zhèngwù〈名〉government administration: ～繁忙 be busy with government affairs
【政务院】zhèngwùyuàn〈名〉Government Administration Council (of the Central People's Government of the People's Republic of China, renamed State Council in 1954)
【政协】zhèngxié〈简称〉= 政治协商会议
【政要】zhèngyào〈名〉political heavyweights
【政治】zhèngzhì〈名〉politics: 扩大～影响 extend political influence ‖ ～策略 political strategy ‖ ～丑闻 political scandal ‖ ～思想工作 political and ideological work ‖ 他～上不成熟。 He lacks political maturity.
【政治避难】zhèngzhì bìnàn〈名〉political asylum: 提供/寻求～ grant/seek political asylum
【政治斗争】zhèngzhì dòuzhēng〈名〉political struggle
【政治犯】zhèngzhìfàn〈名〉political prisoner: 释放～ release political prisoners
【政治改革】zhèngzhì gǎigé〈名〉political reform
【政治纲领】zhèngzhì gānglǐng〈名〉political programme: 制定～ draw up a political programme
【政治家】zhèngzhìjiā ▸p. 966〈名〉statesman: 杰出的～ prominent statesman
【政治教导员】zhèngzhì jiàodǎoyuán〈名〉political instructor (of a PLA battalion)
【政治经济学】zhèngzhì jīngjìxué〈名〉political economy
【政治局】zhèngzhìjú〈名〉politburo: ～常委 member of the Standing Committee of the Political Bureau ‖ ～委员 member of the politburo
【政治立场】zhèngzhì lìchǎng〈名〉political stance
【政治面目】zhèngzhì miànmù〈名〉political affiliation: ～不清 be of dubious political background
【政治迫害】zhèngzhì pòhài〈名〉political persecution
【政治气候】zhèngzhì qìhòu〈名〉political climate
【政治权利】zhèngzhì quánlì〈名〉political right: 享有～ enjoy political rights
【政治审查】zhèngzhì shěnchá〈动〉examine sb.'s political behaviour or record: ～合格 be politically qualified ‖ 干部～ political appraisal of a cadre
【政治素质】zhèngzhì sùzhì〈名〉political calibre
【政治体制】zhèngzhì tǐzhì〈名〉political structure: ～改革 reform in political structure
【政治危机】zhèngzhì wēijī〈名〉political crisis
【政治委员】zhèngzhì wěiyuán〈名〉political commissar (of a PLA regiment and above)
【政治舞台】zhèngzhì wǔtái〈名〉political arena
【政治协商会议】zhèngzhì xiéshāng huìyì〈名〉political consultative conference: 中国人民～ the Chinese People's Political Consultative Conference (CPPCC)
【政治学】zhèngzhìxué〈名〉political science: ～家 political scientist
【政治运动】zhèngzhì yùndòng〈名〉political campaign
【政治指导员】zhèngzhì zhǐdǎoyuán〈名〉political instructor (of a PLA company)
【政治制度】zhèngzhì zhìdù〈名〉system of government

挣（掙） zhèng〈动〉1▸（摆脱束缚）struggle to get free: 他把捆绑的绳子～开。 He wriggled himself free from the rope that bound him. 2▸（努力获取）earn: ～钱 make money ‖ ～工资 earn wages ▸zhēng
【挣揣】zhèngchuài〈动〉〈书〉struggle
【挣命】zhèngmìng〈动〉struggle for survival
【挣脱】zhèngtuō〈动〉break away from: ～枷锁 shake off one's shackles

症 zhèng〈名〉disease: ▸病～，对～下药 ▸zhēng
【症候】zhènghòu〈名〉1▸（疾病）disease 2▸（症状）symptom
【症状】zhèngzhuàng〈名〉［医学］symptom: 典型～ characteristic symptoms ‖ 流感～ flu symptoms

铮（錚） zhèng〈形〉〈方〉polished: 窗玻璃擦得～亮。 The window pane was polished till it shone. ▸zhēng

zhī

之 zhī〈书〉
A〈动〉go to: 不知君之所～。 I don't know where you have been.
B〈代〉1▸（这）this;（那）that: ～子于归。 The maiden goes to her future home. 2▸（指代人或事）[used as the object of a verb to refer back to what has been mentioned previously]: ▸求～不得，取而代～
C〈助〉1▸ a（表领属或修饰关系）[used between an attribute and the word it modifies]: 百分～五十 fifty per cent ‖ 光荣～家 honourable family ‖ 千里～外 hundreds of miles away ‖ 意料～中 as was expected ▸赤子～心，缓兵～计 b（表偏正结构）[used between the subject and the predicate to turn the original structure into a nominal phrase]: 世界～大，无奇不有。 This huge world is full of extraordinary things. ‖ 他决心～大，令人佩服。 We all admired his great determination. 2▸（表虚指）[used in certain set phrases without definite designation]: 不觉手之舞～，足之蹈～ cannot help dancing with joy ▸久而久～，总～
【之后】zhīhòu〈名〉1▸（指时间）later;（指位置）afterwards: 他两天～才回来。 He didn't return until two days later. ‖ 她的名字排在我的名字～。 Her name came just after mine on the list. 2▸（指上下

文) afterwards: ～, 他就再也没有回来。Afterwards, he never came back.

【之乎者也】zhī-hū-zhě-yě〈成〉 archaism: 他这文章满篇～, 叫人似懂非懂。People can only get an obscure idea of his article, which is filled with archaisms.

【之类】zhīlèi〈名〉 the like: 他儿子数学、物理、化学～的科目学得很好。His son does well in mathematics, physics, chemistry and the like.

【之流】zhīliú〈名〉〈贬〉 ilk: 希特勒～ Hitler and the like

【之前】zhīqián〈名〉 before: 吃饭～要洗手。Wash your hands before you eat. ‖ 一个月～我还遇到过他。I met him just a month ago.

【之外】zhīwài〈名〉 besides: 除我～, 没人喜欢他。Nobody likes him except me.

【之字路】zhīzìlù〈名〉 zigzag course

支 zhī

A〈动〉 **1**(支撑) put up: ～帐篷 pitch a tent ‖ 她手～着下巴, 像是在想什么。Resting her chin in her hand, she seemed to be thinking of something. ▸～点, ～架, ～柱 **2**(维持) bear: 体力不～ be too tired to do any more ▸乐不可～ **3**(扶助) support: ▸～边, ～援 **4**(竖起) stick out: ～着耳朵听 prick up one's ears **5**(分散) separate: ▸～离破碎 **6**(调派) send away: 把人～走 send sb. away upon some pretext ▸～派, ～使 **7**(付钱) pay; (领钱) draw: 把工资～给他。Pay him his salary. ‖ 他已经～了这个月的工资。He has drawn this month's salary. ▸～出, 超～, 收～

B〈名〉 **1**(分支) branch: 邮政～局 branch post office ▸～队, ～流, ～线, 分～, 旁～ **2**(地支) Earthly Branches [used in combination with the ten Heavenly Stems to designate years, months, days and hours]

C〈量〉 **1**(用于杆状物) [used as a classifier for long, thin, inflexible objects]: 一～笔 a pen ‖ 一～箭 an arrow ‖ 一～蜡烛 a candle **2**(用于队伍) [used as a classifier for troops, fleets, etc.]: 两～队伍 two contingents of troops ‖ 一～乐队 a band **3**(用于曲子) [used as a classifier for songs or musical compositions]: 一～民歌 a folk song ‖ 一～曲子 a tune **4**(用于纱线) count: 60～纱 60-count yarn **5**(用于亮度) watt: 一个25～光的灯泡 a 25-watt bulb

【支边】zhībiān〈动〉 support border areas

【支部】zhībù〈名〉 branch of political parties or organizations: 党/团～ Party/League branch

【支部大会】zhībù dàhuì〈名〉 general membership meeting of the branch

【支部书记】zhībù shūji〈名〉 secretary of a Party or League branch

【支部委员】zhībù wěiyuán〈名〉 member of the branch committee

【支撑】zhīchēng〈动〉 **1**(承受压力) support: 这架子～得住吗? Is the stand strong enough to hold up? **2**(勉强维持) sustain: 他～着坐了起来。He propped himself up into a sitting position. ‖ 我们的储粮还能～多久? How long will our food supplies hold out?

【支持】zhīchí〈动〉 **1**(维持) hold out: 他病得～不住了。He was too sick to hold out any longer. **2**(赞成) support: 请求～ ask for support ‖ 大力～ strongly support ‖ 坚持干, 我们～你。Keep right on. We're behind you.

【支出】zhīchū **A**〈动〉 expend: 我每年在孩子的教育上～大约一万元。I spend about 10,000 *yuan* each year on my child's education. **B**〈名〉 expenditure: 财政～ fiscal expenditure ‖ 国防～ defence spending

【支绌】zhīchù〈动〉〈书〉 be insufficient: 经费～ have a want of funds

【支单】zhīdān〈名〉 certificate for withdrawing money

【支点】zhīdiǎn〈名〉 **1**[物理] fulcrum **2**(关键) keystone: 战略～ strategic strongpoint

【支队】zhīduì〈名〉 detachment: 独立～ independent detachment ‖ 游击～ guerrilla detachment

【支付】zhīfù〈动〉 pay: ～水电费 pay for electricity and water ‖ ～利息 pay interest ‖ 现金～ cash payment

【支付能力】zhīfù nénglì〈名〉 disbursement ability

【支行】zhīháng〈名〉 bank sub-branch

【支架】zhījià **A**〈名〉 support: 自行车～ bicycle stand **B**〈动〉 **1**(架起) prop up: ～屋梁 prop up the beam and rest it on the walls **2**(招架) withstand: 寡不敌众, ～不住 cannot hold out any longer because of being far outnumbered

【支离】zhīlí **A**〈动〉 be fragmented **B**〈形〉 trivial and jumbled up: ～错乱, 不成文理。The writing is full of incoherencies and confusing ideas.

【支离破碎】zhīlí-pòsuì〈成〉 be all broken up

【支流】zhīliú〈名〉 **1**(指河流) tributary: 黄河的一条～ a branch of the Yellow River **2**〈喻〉(指事物) minor aspect: 考虑问题时, 不要把～当作主流。In considering a problem, one mustn't mistake nonessentials for essentials.

【支脉】zhīmài〈名〉 offshoot of a mountain range: 秦岭的～ branch range of the Qinling Mountains

【支那】Zhīnà〈名〉China [transliteration used in translations of Buddhist scriptures, and formerly by the Japanese]: 印度～ Indo-China

【支派】zhīpài **A**〈名〉 branch **B**〈动〉 dispatch: 所有员工任你～。The whole staff is at your disposal.

【支配】zhīpèi〈动〉 **1**(安排) allocate: 合理～收入 put one's income to proper use ‖ 善于～时间 be good at planning one's time **2**(控制) control: 思想～行动。People's actions are governed by their thinking.

【支票】zhīpiào ▸**p. 328**〈名〉 cheque〈英〉; check〈美〉: 空白～ blank cheque ‖ 转账～ cheque for transfer ▸空头～

【支气管】zhīqìguǎn〈名〉 bronchial tube

【支气管炎】zhīqìguǎnyán ▸**p. 50**〈名〉[医学] bronchitis: ～患者 bronchitic

【支渠】zhīqú〈名〉 branch canal

【支取】zhīqǔ〈动〉 draw (money): ～存款 draw one's deposit (from a bank) ‖ ～工资 draw one's wages

【支使】zhīshi〈动〉 **1**(派人做) order about: 不听～ refuse to be ordered about **2**(支开) send away: 把他～走。Send him away.

【支书】zhīshū〈简称〉= 支部书记

【支吾】zhīwú〈动〉 prevaricate: ～了半天也没说清楚 hum and haw for ages and still not come out with anything clear

【支吾其词】zhīwú-qící〈成〉 speak evasively: 他～, 想回避我的问题。He was stalling, trying to dodge my question.

【支线】zhīxiàn〈名〉 feeder: ～班机 feeder liner ‖ 公路/铁路～ feeder highway/railway

【支应】zhīyìng〈动〉 **1**(应付) cope with: 一个人～不开。One person isn't going to be able to cope with it. **2**(供应) supply: ～粮草 organize supplies **3**(守候) attend to: ～门户 mind the door ‖ 我在病房～。I am keeping vigil in the sick room.

【支原体】zhīyuántǐ〈名〉[医学] mycoplasma

【支援】zhīyuán〈动〉 support: ～前线 support the front ‖ ～灾区 send relief to the disaster area ‖ 请求～ ask for assistance

【支招儿】zhīzhāor = 支着儿 zhīzhāor

【支着儿】zhīzhāor〈动〉 give advice [esp to a chess player]

【支柱】zhīzhù〈名〉 pillar: 和平事业的～ pillar of the cause of peace ‖ 农业是该国经济的～。Agriculture forms the backbone of the country's economy.

【支柱产业】zhīzhù chǎnyè〈名〉 pillar industry

【支子】zhīzi〈名〉 **1**(支架) stand: 自行车～ bicycle stand **2**(烧烤用的箅子) gridiron

【支座】zhīzuò〈名〉 support

氏 zhī ▸阏氏 yānzhī, 月氏 Yuèzhī ▸shì

只 (隻) zhī

A〈形〉 single: ▸～身, ～言片语, 独具～眼

B〈量〉 **1**(用于动物) [measure word for certain animals]: 一～鸡 a chicken ‖ 一～兔子 a rabbit **2**(用于成对事物) [measure word for one of certain paired things]: 两～手/脚 two hands/feet ‖ 一～袜子 a sock **3**(用于器物) [measure word for certain containers]: 一～箱子 a suitcase **4**(用于船) [measure word for small boats, etc.]: 一～小船 a little boat

▸zhǐ

【只身】zhīshēn〈名〉 oneself: ～前往 go by oneself ‖ ～在外 be all alone away from home

【只言片语】zhīyán-piànyǔ〈成〉 a word or two, a few isolated words and phrases: 未留下～ not leave behind even a single word

【只字不提】zhīzì-bùtí〈成〉 not say a single word about sth.

卮 zhī〈名〉 ancient wine vessel: 漏～ leaky wine vessel

汁 zhī〈名〉 juice: 牛肉～ beef extract ▸果～, 墨～, 乳～

【汁液】zhīyè〈名〉 juice

芝 zhī〈名〉〈古〉 **1** ▸灵芝 língzhī **2**(白芷) Taiwan angelica root

【芝加哥】Zhījiāgē〈名〉 Chicago

【芝兰】zhīlán〈名〉〈喻〉 **1**(指德行) noble character **2**(指友情) true friendship **3**(指环境) beautiful surroundings

【芝麻】zhīma〈名〉 **1**(指植物) sesame **2**(指种子) sesame seed: ▸捡了～, 丢了西瓜

【芝麻官】zhīmaguān〈名〉〈诙〉petty official: 小小～ petty official

【芝麻糊】zhīmahú〈名〉 sesame paste

【芝麻酱】zhīmajiàng〈名〉 sesame sauce

【芝麻开花节节高】zhīma kāihuā jiéjié gāo〈俗〉〈喻〉 [of a standard of living] rise steadily

【芝麻糖】zhīmatáng〈名〉 sesame candy

【芝麻油】zhīmayóu〈名〉 sesame oil

吱 zhī〈拟〉 sound of creaking or squeaking: 老鼠～～叫。The mice

squeaked. ‖ 门～地一声开了。 The door creaked open.
▸zī

【吱嘎】zhīgā〈拟〉 squeak: ～作响的楼梯 creaky stairs

枝 zhī

A〈名〉 twig: 柳～ willow branch ▸插～, 树～, 整～

B〈量〉 **1**（指带枝的花） [for flowers with stems intact]: 一～梅花/丁香 a spray of plum blossoms/lilacs **2**（指杆状物） [for long, thin, inflexible objects]: 两～钢笔/铅笔 two pens/pencils ‖ 一～枪 a gun

【枝杈】zhīchà〈名〉 branch: 修剪～ trim branches

【枝繁叶茂】zhīfán-yèmào〈成〉 be prosperous

【枝节】zhījié〈名〉〈喻〉 **1**（次要事情） side issue: ～问题以后再解决。 We'll come to the side issues later on. **2**（麻烦） complication: ▸横生～

【枝蔓】zhīmàn〈形〉〈喻〉complicated and confused: 此文文字～。 The writing is a jumble of words and ideas.

【枝条】zhītiáo〈名〉 branch: 长出～ branch out

【枝头】zhītóu〈名〉 top of a branch: 小鸟在～歌唱。 The birds are singing in the tree.

【枝丫】zhīyā〈名〉 branch: 多结/弯曲的～ gnarled/contorted branch

【枝桠】zhīyā = 枝丫 zhīyā

【枝叶】zhīyè〈名〉 **1**〈本〉 branches and leaves: ～繁茂 have luxuriant foliage **2**〈喻〉 minor details

【枝子】zhīzi〈名〉 branch

知 zhī

A〈名〉 **1**（知识） knowledge: ▸求～, 无～, 真～灼见 **2**（知己） bosom friend: 新～ new friend ▸～友

B〈动〉 **1**（知道） know: 据我所～ to my knowledge ‖ 要想人不～，除非己莫为。 If you don't want people to know something, the best way is not to do it. ▸～晓, 无所不～ **2**（通告） tell: ▸～会, 告～, 通～ **3**〈书〉（主管） administer: ▸～事, ～县

【知道】zhīdào〈动〉 know: 你的意思我～。 I know what you mean. ‖ 他～的事情很多。 He knows a lot.

【知底】zhīdǐ〈动〉 be in the know: 这事我也不～。 I don't know much about this matter either. ▸知根～

【知法犯法】zhīfǎ-fànfǎ〈成〉 deliberately break the law: 他是警察，怎么会～呢？ Surely, as a policeman, he couldn't have broken the law deliberately.

【知府】zhīfǔ〈名〉〈旧〉prefect, magistrate of a prefecture

【知根知底】zhīgēn-zhīdǐ〈成〉 know sb. intimately: 我们是老朋友了，彼此都～。 As old friends, we know each other very well.

【知过必改】zhīguò-bìgǎi〈成〉 correct an error whenever one becomes aware of it

【知会】zhīhui〈动〉〈方〉 give oral notification

【知己】zhījǐ **A**〈形〉 intimate: ～的朋友 close friend **B**〈名〉 bosom friend: 人生难得一～。 It is rare to find a soul mate in life.

【知彼知己，百战不殆】zhībǐ-zhījǐ, bǎizhàn-bùdài〈成〉 knowing yourself and knowing the enemy is the key to winning all battles

【知交】zhījiāo〈名〉 bosom friend: 他是我中学时代的～。 He was my great friend in our middle school days.

【知觉】zhījué〈名〉 **1**［心理］ perception **2**（感觉） consciousness: 恢复～ regain consciousness ‖ 失去～ lose consciousness

【知了】zhīliǎo〈口〉= 蝉 chán

【知名】zhīmíng〈形〉 well-known: ～作家 famous writer ‖ ～人士 celebrity

【知名度】zhīmíngdù〈名〉 popularity: 提高～ increase one's popularity ‖ 享有很高～ enjoy high popularity

【知命】zhīmìng **A**〈动〉〈书〉 understand the decree of heaven: 乐天～ accept the fate ordained to one by heaven and be optimistic about life **B**〈名〉 fifty years old: ～之年 fifty years of age

【知难而进】zhīnán'érjìn〈成〉 press ahead in the face of difficulties: ～，决不半途而废 keep going rather than giving up halfway

【知难而退】zhīnán'értuì〈成〉beat a retreat in the face of difficulties

【知其然，不知其所以然】zhī qí rán, bù zhī qí suǒyǐrán〈成〉 know the hows but not the whys

【知其一，不知其二】zhī qí yī, bù zhī qí èr〈成〉 know only one side of something

【知青】zhīqīng〈简称〉= 知识青年

【知情】zhīqíng〈动〉 **1**（感激） be grateful: 对你们的热情帮助，我很～。 I'm very grateful to you for your help. **2**（知道内情） be in the know: ～人 insider ‖ ～不报 fail to report what one knows

【知情权】zhīqíngquán〈名〉［法律］ right to know

【知趣】zhīqù〈动〉 know how to behave: 他一再纠缠她，真不～。 He is constantly pestering her, and really shows no sense of knowing how to behave.

【知人论世】zhīrén-lùnshì〈成〉 make comments on public figures and social affairs

【知人善任】zhīrén-shànrèn〈成〉 place people where they can put their abilities into full play: 做老板的要～。 A boss must know his subordinates well and make good use of them.

【知人之明】zhīrénzhīmíng〈成〉 ability to discern a person's character and capabilities: 有～ be a good judge of people

【知人知面不知心】zhī rén zhī miàn bù zhī xīn〈俗〉 a fair face may hide a foul heart

【知事】zhīshì〈名〉〈旧〉county magistrate

【知识】zhīshi〈名〉 **1**（认知） knowledge: 尊重～ respect knowledge ‖ ～渊博 be very knowledgeable **2**（学问） learning: 有～ be learned ‖ ～界 intelligentsia

【知识产权】zhīshi chǎnquán〈名〉 intellectual property right: 保护～ protect the intellectual property rights (IPR)

【知识分子】zhīshi fènzǐ〈名〉 intellectual: 尊重～ respect intellectuals

【知识经济】zhīshi jīngjì〈名〉 knowledge economy

【知识面】zhīshimiàn〈名〉 range of knowledge: ～广/窄 have a wide/narrow range of knowledge

【知识青年】zhīshi qīngnián〈名〉 educated youth [usu referring to secondary school graduates who were sent to the countryside for re-education during the Cultural Revolution]

【知书达理】zhīshū-dálǐ〈成〉 be well-educated and show a good sense of judgement

【知无不言，言无不尽】zhī wú bù yán, yán wú bù jìn〈成〉 say all you know and say it without reserve

【知悉】zhīxī〈动〉〈书〉 know: 详情～ know the details of sth.

【知县】zhīxiàn〈名〉〈旧〉 county magistrate

【知晓】zhīxiǎo〈动〉 be aware of

【知心】zhīxīn = 知己 zhījǐ A

【知性】zhīxìng〈形〉 [of a woman] intelligent and thoughtful: ～主持人 an astute anchorwoman

【知音】zhīyīn〈名〉 soul mate: 觅～ look for one's soul mate

【知友】zhīyǒu〈名〉 bosom friend

【知遇】zhīyù〈动〉〈书〉 find a patron appreciative of one's ability: 有～之恩 owe sb. a debt of gratitude for their recognition and appreciation of one's talents

【知照】zhīzhào〈动〉 notify: 你去～他一声，说我们下午到。 Please go and advise him that we will be arriving in the afternoon.

【知州】zhīzhōu〈名〉〈旧〉 prefect

【知子莫若父】zhī zǐ mòruò fù〈俗〉 no one knows a son better than his father

【知足】zhīzú〈动〉 be content with one's lot: ～常乐 happiness lies in contentment ‖ 他这人从不～。 He's never content.

肢 zhī〈名〉 limb: ▸假～, 上～, 四～

【肢解】zhījiě〈动〉 dismember: ～尸体 dismember a corpse ‖〈喻〉 ～一个国家 dismember a country

【肢体】zhītǐ〈名〉 **1**（四肢） limbs: ～发育畸形 have deformed limbs **2**（四肢和躯干） limbs and trunk

织（織） zhī〈动〉 **1**（纺织）

weave: ～地毯 weave a rug ‖ ～布 weave cloth ‖ 丝～品 silk textile ▸纺～ **2**（编织） knit: ～毛衣 knit a sweater ‖ 手/机～ knit by hand/machine ▸编～

【织补】zhībǔ〈动〉 darn

【织布机】zhībùjī〈名〉 loom

【织锦】zhījǐn〈名〉 **1**（锦缎） brocade **2**（指丝织品） picture-weaving in silk: 风景～ landscape woven in silk

【织锦缎】zhījǐnduàn〈名〉 tapestry satin

【织女】zhīnǚ〈名〉 **1**〈旧〉（指从事纺织） weaving-girl **2** Zhīnǚ（指神话人物） Weaver Girl: ▸牛郎～ **3** = 织女星 Zhīnǚxīng

【织女星】Zhīnǚxīng〈名〉［天文］ Vega

【织品】zhīpǐn〈名〉 textile: 棉/亚麻/羊毛～ cotton/linen/woollen textile

【织袜机】zhīwàjī〈名〉 hosiery machine

【织物】zhīwù〈名〉 fabric

【织造】zhīzào〈动〉 weave by machine: ～厂 weaving mill

栀 zhī

【栀子】zhīzi〈名〉［植物］ Cape jasmine

【栀子花】zhīzihuā〈名〉 gardenia

胝 zhī ▸胼胝 piánzhī

祗 zhī〈形〉〈书〉 respectful and courteous: ～候光临。 Your presence is respectfully requested.

【祗仰】zhīyǎng〈动〉〈书〉 venerate

脂 zhī〈名〉 **1**（油质） grease: 脱～奶粉 skimmed-milk powder ▸～肪, 油～ **2**（胭脂） rouge: ▸～粉, 涂～抹粉, 胭～

【脂肪】zhīfáng〈名〉 fat: 动物/植物～ animal/vegetable fat

【脂肪肝】zhīfánggān ▸p. 50〈名〉［医学］ fatty liver

【脂肪酸】zhīfángsuān〈名〉 fatty acid

【脂粉】zhīfěn〈名〉 rouge and powder: 薄施～ apply light make-up
【脂粉气】zhīfěnqì〈名〉 femininity
【脂膏】 zhīgāo 〈名〉 **1**（脂肪） fat **2**〈喻〉（劳动成果） fruits of the people's labour

跖 zhī ▸跖跗 piánzhī

稙 zhī〈形〉 [of crops] sown or ripening earlier than other varieties: ～谷子 early millet ‖ ～庄稼 crops sown early

蜘 zhī〈名〉 spider

【蜘蛛】zhīzhū〈名〉 spider: ～网 spider's web

zhí

执（執）zhí

A〈动〉 **1**（拿着） hold: 手～红旗 carry a red flag ▸～笔，明火～仗 **2**（执掌） direct: ▸～事，～政 **3**（执行） carry out: ▸～法，～行 **4**（坚持） stick to: ▸～意，各～一词
B〈名〉 **1**（凭单） written acknowledgement: ▸～照，回～ **2**〈书〉（执友） bosom friend: 父～ one's father's bosom friend ▸～友
【执棒】zhíbàng〈动〉 conduct an orchestra: 这场音乐会将由著名指挥家～。A famous conductor will take the baton at this concert.
【执笔】zhíbǐ〈动〉 write
【执鞭】zhíbiān〈动〉〈书〉 be a teacher
【执导】zhídǎo〈动〉 direct: ～电影 be a film director
【执法】zhífǎ〈动〉 administer justice: ～机关 enforcement agency ‖ 秉公～ execute justice ‖ ～如山 enforce the law strictly
【执教】zhíjiào〈动〉 work as a teacher
【执迷不悟】zhímí-bùwù〈成〉 be wilful
【执牛耳】zhí niú'ěr〈成〉 occupy a leading position: 在信息产业独～ be the leader in the IT industry
【执拗】zhíniù〈形〉 wilful: 脾气～ be stubborn
【执勤】zhíqín〈动〉 be on duty
【执事】 zhíshì 〈名〉 **1** 〈书〉（侍从） attendant **2**（对对方敬称） [in letters] you
【执事】zhíshi〈名〉〈旧〉 things to be held by a guard of honour such as flags, weapons, etc.: 打～的 guard of honour
【执行】zhíxíng〈动〉carry out: ～命令 carry out an order ‖ ～任务 perform a task ‖ 首席～官 chief executive officer (CEO)
【执行董事】zhíxíng dǒngshì〈名〉 executive director
【执行力】 zhíxínglì 〈名〉 enforcement potential: 提高政府部门的公信力和～ raise the public credibility and implementation potential of government departments
【执行主席】zhíxíng zhǔxí〈名〉 executive chairman
【执业】zhíyè〈动〉 practise one's profession: ～律师 certified lawyer
【执意】zhíyì〈副〉 insistently: 他～要去。He insisted on going there. ‖ 史密斯小姐～不肯收受佣金。 Miss Smith firmly refused to accept any commission.
【执友】zhíyǒu〈名〉〈书〉 bosom friend
【执掌】zhízhǎng〈动〉 wield: ～大权 wield great power
【执照】 zhízhào 〈名〉 licence: 驾驶～ driving licence ‖ 营业～ business licence
【执政】zhízhèng〈动〉 be in power: ～联盟 ruling coalition ‖ ～党 ruling party
【执政为民】zhízhèng wèimín〈动〉 assume power for the people: 增强～的意识和本领 strengthen awareness and skills in rule for the people
【执著】zhízhuó〈形〉 **1**（固执） stubborn **2**（坚持不懈） persistent: ～地献身于教育事业 devote oneself consistently to the cause of education

直 zhí

A〈形〉 **1**（成直线） straight: 把绳子拉～ straighten out a rope ‖ 马路又平又～。The highway is level and straight. ▸笔～ **2**（垂直） vertical: ～上～下 straight up and down ‖ 屋子很大，～里有八米，横里有六米。 The room is big, being 8 metres in length and 6 metres in width. ▸～升机 **3**（公正） just: ▸正～，理～气壮 **4**（直截） straightforward: ～呼其名 call sb. by their name ‖ ～言不讳 say readily ▸心～口快
B〈动〉 straighten: 累得～不起腰来 too tired to straighten oneself up
C〈名〉 [in Chinese characters] vertical stroke
D〈副〉 **1**（直接） directly: ～奔火车站 head straight for the railway station ‖ ～飞/达纽约 fly/run non-stop to New York **2**（一直） continuously: 他冲着我～笑。He kept smiling at me. ‖ 我冻得～哆嗦。I kept shivering with cold. **3**（简直） simply: 我胳膊痛得～像针扎一样难受。My arms hurt so much that they feel like they have been stabbed with needles.
【直白】 zhíbái 〈形〉 explicit: ～的要求 explicit request
【直报】zhíbào〈动〉 make a direct report: 疫情信息～ direct reports of epidemics
【直拨】zhíbō〈名〉［通信］ direct dial: 长途～电话 direct distance dialling (DDD)
【直播】zhíbō **A**〈名〉［农业］ direct seeding **B**〈动〉 televise live: 现场～所有比赛项目 provide live coverage of all events
【直补】zhíbǔ〈动〉 subsidize directly: 给农民的～款项已到位。 The funds for subsidizing farmers directly are already in place.
【直布罗陀】Zhíbùluótuó〈名〉 Gibraltar: ～海峡 Straits of Gibraltar
【直肠】zhícháng〈名〉 rectum
【直肠癌】zhícháng'ái ▸**p. 50**〈名〉 carcinoma of the rectum
【直肠子】zhíchángzi〈名〉〈口〉〈喻〉 straightforward person: 他是个～，有什么说什么。He's a very straightforward person who will always say what is on his mind.
【直尺】zhíchǐ〈名〉 straight edge
【直达】zhídá ▸**p. 781**〈形〉 non-stop: ～快车 express train ‖ ～航班 non-stop flight
【直待】zhídài〈动〉 be not until: ～天黑才回家 not go home until dusk
【直捣黄龙】zhídǎo-Huánglóng〈成〉 press forward to the enemy headquarters
【直到】zhídào〈动〉 be until: 这事～今天我才知道。 I did not know it until today.
【直道】zhídào〈名〉 straightaway: 跑道的～部分 the straight
【直瞪瞪】zhídēngdēng〈形〉 staring blankly: 她～地望着地面，神情木然。 She gazed at the ground with a blank expression.
【直裰】zhíduō〈名〉 loose robe worn by a Buddhist monk or a Taoist priest
【直观】zhíguān〈形〉 audio-visual: ～教具 audio-visual aids ‖ ～教学 object teaching
【直航】zhíháng〈动〉 travel direct: 两岸～包机 cross-strait direct charter flight
【直击】zhíjī〈动〉 live broadcast
【直角】zhíjiǎo〈名〉 right angle: ～三角形 right-angled triangle
【直接】zhíjiē〈形〉 direct: ～飞往东京 fly directly to Tokyo ‖ ～接触 be in direct contact with ‖ ～原因 direct cause
【直接宾语】zhíjiē bīnyǔ〈名〉 direct object
【直接经验】 zhíjiē jīngyàn 〈名〉［哲学］ direct experience
【直接推理】zhíjiē tuīlǐ〈名〉 direct reasoning
【直接选举】zhíjiē xuǎnjǔ〈名〉 direct election
【直截了当】zhíjié-liǎodàng〈成〉 straightforward: ～地告诉我! Tell it to me straight!
【直径】zhíjìng〈名〉 diameter
【直觉】zhíjué〈名〉 intuition: 凭～判断 base one's judgement on intuition
【直来直去】 zhílái-zhíqù 〈成〉 **1**（指行程） go non-stop to and from: 这次去广州是～。 This time we are travelling non-stop to and from Guangzhou. **2**（指个性） frank and outspoken: 他是个～的人，想到什么就说什么。 He's a blunt man who speaks his mind.
【直立】zhílì〈动〉 stand upright: ～行走 upright walking
【直溜溜】zhíliūliū〈形〉 straight: ～的马路 straight road
【直流电】zhíliúdiàn〈名〉 direct current
【直眉瞪眼】zhíméi-dèngyǎn〈成〉 **1**（形容发怒） glare **2**（形容发呆） be dumbfounded
【直面】zhímiàn〈动〉 face: ～人生 face up to the problems of life
【直升机】zhíshēngjī〈名〉 helicopter
【直书】zhíshū〈动〉〈书〉 give a faithful account
【直抒】zhíshū〈动〉 air one's views frankly: ～胸臆 speak one's mind
【直抒己见】 zhíshū-jǐjiàn 〈成〉 be plainspoken
【直属】zhíshǔ **A**〈动〉 be directly affiliated to: 这个机构是～文化部的。 This organization is directly affiliated to the Ministry of Culture. **B**〈形〉 directly subordinate: 国务院～机关 departments directly under the State Council
【直率】zhíshuài〈形〉 candid: 说话～ be outspoken in one's remarks
【直爽】zhíshuǎng〈形〉 candid: ～的性格 open character
【直挺挺】zhítǐngtǐng〈形〉 straight: ～地躺在床上 lie sprawled in bed ‖ ～地站着 stand straight as a ramrod
【直筒子】zhítǒngzi〈名〉〈喻〉 straightforward person
【直系亲属】zhíxì qīnshǔ〈名〉 one's immediate family
【直辖】zhíxiá〈动〉 be directly under the jurisdiction of: 文化部～机构 organization directly under the Ministry of Culture
【直辖市】zhíxiáshì〈名〉 municipality directly under the Central Government
【直线】zhíxiàn **A**〈名〉 straight line: ～运动 straight-line movement **B**〈形〉 linear: ～电话 direct-dial telephone ‖ 物价～上升了。 Prices shot up.
【直销】zhíxiāo〈动〉 direct-sale: 厂家～ factory sale
【直心眼儿】zhíxīnyǎnr〈形〉〈口〉 straightforward
【直性子】zhíxìngzi **A**〈形〉straightforward **B**〈名〉 straightforward person: 他是个～。He's a straightforward chap.

Z

【直选】zhíxuǎn〈简称〉= 直接选举
【直言】zhíyán **A**〈动〉speak bluntly: 恕我～。Excuse me for speaking bluntly. **B**〈名〉frank opinion: ～判断 frank judgement
【直言不讳】zhíyán-bùhuì〈成〉not mince one's words: ～的劝告 plain-spoken admonition
【直译】zhíyì〈名〉literal translation
【直音】zhíyīn〈名〉［语言］traditional method of indicating the pronunciation of a Chinese character by citing a simpler character with the same pronunciation
【直饮水】zhíyǐnshuǐ〈名〉drinking water: ～标准 potable water standard
【直至】zhízhì = 直到 zhídào

侄（姪）zhí〈名〉nephew [brother's son]

【侄女】zhínǚ〈名〉niece [brother's daughter]
【侄女婿】zhínǚxu〈名〉niece's husband
【侄孙】zhísūn〈名〉brother's grandson
【侄孙女】zhísūnnǚ〈名〉brother's granddaughter
【侄媳妇】zhíxífu〈名〉nephew's wife
【侄子】zhízi〈名〉nephew [brother's son]

值 zhí

A〈名〉**1**（价值）value: ▸比～，贬～，总产～ **2**［数学］value: 求X的～ find the value of X
B〈动〉**1**（相当）be worth: 这双皮鞋～八十元。This pair of leather shoes is worth 80 *yuan*. **2**（遇到）happen to: 正～国庆，老友相逢，真是分外高兴。The friends were very happy when they bumped into each other on National Day. **3**（轮到）be on duty: ～夜班 be on night shift ‖ 轮～ be on duty by turns
C〈形〉deserving: 不～一提 not worth mentioning ‖ 货真价实，买得～。Given its high quality and reasonable price, it is worth buying.
【值班】zhíbān〈动〉be on duty: 今晚我～。I'm on duty tonight.
【值得】zhídé〈动〉**1**（价钱相当）be worth: 这手表物美价廉，～买。This watch is cheap but good. It's worth buying. **2**（有意义）be worthwhile: ～研究 be worth investigating ‖ ～报道的事 newsworthy story
【值机】zhíjī〈动〉［航空］check in: ～柜台/时间 check-in counter/time
【值钱】zhíqián〈形〉valuable: 不～ worthless
【值勤】zhíqín〈动〉be on duty: ～交警 policeman on point duty ‖ ～人员 personnel on duty
【值日】zhírì〈动〉be on duty for the day: ～生 student on duty
【值守】zhíshǒu〈动〉be on duty and on guard: 车库夜间有人～。There are people on duty at the garage during night-time.
【值星】zhíxīng〈动〉[of army officers] be on duty for the week
【值夜】zhíyè〈动〉be on night duty
【值遇】zhíyù〈动〉〈书〉meet with: ～不幸 misfortune befalls on sb.

埴 zhí〈名〉〈书〉clay

职（職）zhí

A〈名〉**1**（职责）duty: 尽～ exert oneself to fulfil one's responsibilities **2**（工作）job: 求～ apply for a job **3**（职位）post: 到～ take office ▸就～，在～ **4**〈旧〉（下属对上司的自称）（用作主语）I;（用作宾语）me;（我们）we: ▸卑～
B〈动〉manage: ▸～掌
【职别】zhíbié〈名〉official rank
【职场】zhíchǎng〈名〉work arena
【职称】zhíchēng〈名〉professional title: 学术/技术～ academic/technical title
【职分】zhífèn〈名〉**1**（指本分）bounden duty **2**（官职）official post
【职高】zhígāo〈简称〉= 职业高中
【职工】zhígōng〈名〉workers and staff: ～代表大会 congress of workers and staff ‖ 铁路～ railway staff
【职级】zhíjí〈名〉rank
【职能】zhínéng〈名〉function: ～部门 functional department ‖ 转变政府～ transform government functions
【职权】zhíquán〈名〉power: 滥用～ abuse one's power ‖ 行使～ exercise one's powers ‖ ～范围 scope of one's powers
【职守】zhíshǒu〈名〉post: 恪尽～ be dutiful in one's work ‖ 玩忽～ be derelict of one's duties
【职位】zhíwèi〈名〉position: 不论～高低 regardless of how high or low one's position is
【职务】zhíwù〈名〉post: ～工资 pay according to one's post ‖ 解除～ remove sb. from their post
【职衔】zhíxián〈名〉**1**（职位和军衔）post and military rank **2**〈书〉（官衔）official title
【职业】zhíyè **A**〈名〉occupation: 从事教师～ be engaged in the teaching profession ‖ ～教育/培训 vocational education/training **B**〈形〉professional: ～军人 professional soldier ‖ ～外交官 career diplomat ‖ 他的～是医生。He is a doctor by profession.
【职业病】zhíyèbìng〈名〉occupational disease
【职业高中】zhíyè gāozhōng〈名〉vocational high school
【职业教育】zhíyè jiàoyù〈名〉vocational education
【职业介绍所】zhíyè jièshàosuǒ〈名〉job centre
【职业学校】zhíyè xuéxiào〈名〉vocational school
【职员】zhíyuán〈名〉office worker
【职责】zhízé〈名〉duty: 履行～ perform one's duty ‖ 应尽的～ bounden duty
【职掌】zhízhǎng〈动〉be in charge of: ～公司财务工作 take charge of the financial affairs of a company

絷（縶）zhí〈书〉

A〈动〉**1**（拴住）tie up **2**（拘禁）take into custody
B〈名〉horse rein

ℹ 职业

问职业

你干什么工作?
= What's your job?

你干哪一行?
或 你的职业是什么?
或 你干哪种职业?
或 你从事哪种职业?
= What's your occupation?
或 What do you do (for a living)?

你干什么工作谋生?
= What do you do for a living?

你干哪种工作?
或 你从事哪种工作?
= What sort of work do you do?

谈论职业

■ 汉语不用任何冠词，英语则用不定冠词:

她是老师
或 她当老师
= She is a teacher
或 She works as a teacher

她是职业美容师
= She is a professional beautician

她是软件专家
= She is a software specialist

她是管理顾问
= She is a management consultant

她是自由新闻记者
= She works as a freelance news journalist

■ 注意下面例句的翻译及英语介词的用法:

我做小本生意
= I run a small business

我在一家石油公司工作
= I am with an oil company

我在一家医院工作
= I work at a hospital

我在书店工作
= I work in a bookshop

我为一家出版社工作
= I work for a publisher

■ 其他短语:

我做全职
= I work full time

我做兼职
= I work part time

我做自由职业
= I work freelance
或 I am a freelancer

我干个体
= I am self-employed

她找到了一份当秘书的临时工作
= She's got a temporary job as a secretary

她有一份固定的工作
= She has a permanent job

她刚失去工作
= She has just lost her job

她向一所大学求了职
= She has applied for a job with a university

他下岗有一年了
或 他失业有一年了
或 他一年都没工作了
= He has been out of work for a year
或 He has been unemployed for a year
或 He has been jobless for a year

植 zhí
A〈动〉**1**（栽种） grow: ▸～树，移～ **2**（树立） set up: ～党营私 set up a clique for one's own selfish interests
B〈名〉 flora, plant: ▸～被
【植保】 zhíbǎo〈名〉 plant protection
【植被】 zhíbèi〈名〉 vegetation: 恢复～ restore vegetation
【植根】 zhígēn = 根植 gēnzhí
【植苗】 zhímiáo〈名〉 plant seedling
【植皮】 zhípí〈名〉 skin grafting
【植树】 zhíshù〈动〉 plant trees: ～造林 afforestation
【植树节】 Zhíshùjié〈名〉 Arbor Day [in China, March 12]
【植物】 zhíwù〈名〉 plant: 草本～ herbaceous plant ‖ ～纤维 plant fibre
【植物化石】 zhíwù huàshí〈名〉 phytolith
【植物群落】 zhíwù qúnluò〈名〉 plant community
【植物人】 zhíwùrén〈名〉 vegetable
【植物性神经】 zhíwùxìng shénjīng〈名〉［生理］ autonomic nerve
【植物学】 zhíwùxué〈名〉 botany: ～家 botanist
【植物园】 zhíwùyuán〈名〉 botanical garden
【植株】 zhízhū〈名〉 plant

殖 zhí〈动〉 breed: ▸生～
▸shi
【殖民】 zhímín〈动〉 colonize: ～统治 colonial rule ‖ ～战争 colonialist war
【殖民地】 zhímíndì〈名〉 colony: 沦为～ be reduced to a colony
【殖民主义】 zhímín zhǔyì〈名〉 colonialism

跖（蹠） zhí
A〈名〉**1**［生理］ metatarsus **2**〈书〉（脚掌） sole of the foot
B〈动〉〈书〉 tread
【跖骨】 zhígǔ〈名〉 metatarsal bone

摭 zhí〈动〉〈书〉 pick up
【摭拾】 zhíshí〈动〉〈书〉 gather: ～故事 collect stories

踯（躑） zhí
【踯躅】 zhízhú〈动〉〈书〉 walk to and fro: ～街头 wander the streets

zhǐ

止 zhǐ
A〈动〉**1**（停止） stop: 血流不～ endless flow of blood ▸适可而～，学无～境，休～ **2**（使停止） bring to an end: ～咳 relieve a cough ‖ ～痛 relieve pain ‖ ～血 stop bleeding ▸制～ **3**（截止） end: 展览从10月1日起到10月14日～。 The exhibition opens on October 1st and finishes on the 14th.
B〈副〉 only: ～此一家。 This is the only shop. ‖ 这话你说过不～一次了。 I don't think this is the first time you've said this.
【止步】 zhǐbù〈动〉 halt: ～不前 come to a halt ‖ 游人～ no visitors
【止境】 zhǐjìng〈名〉 limit: 学无～ knowledge is infinite ‖ 科学的发展是没有～的。 There is no limit to the development of science.
【止咳】 zhǐké〈动〉 relieve a cough: ～糖浆 cough syrup
【止渴】 zhǐkě〈动〉 quench one's thirst
【止损】 zhǐsǔn〈动〉 prevent losses: 市场情况尚不明朗，投资者不必忙于割肉～。 Market conditions remain uncertain, so investors shouldn't rush to cut their losses.
【止痛】 zhǐtòng〈动〉 relieve pain: ～药 painkiller
【止吐】 zhǐtù〈动〉 stop one's vomit
【止息】 zhǐxī〈动〉 stop
【止泻】 zhǐxiè〈动〉 stop diarrhoea: ～药 antidiarrheal
【止血】 zhǐxuè〈动〉 stop bleeding: 用绷带包扎伤口～ bandage a cut to staunch the bleeding
【止血带】 zhǐxuèdài〈名〉 tourniquet
【止痒】 zhǐyǎng〈动〉 relieve itching

只（衹） zhǐ〈副〉 only: ～此一家，别无分店 the only shop of this name and with no other branches [shop sign warning of sham goods] ‖ ～见树木，不见森林 cannot see the wood for the trees ‖ ～知其一，不知其二 be aware only of what is on the surface, but not know what is behind it ‖ 家里～我一个人。 I'm alone at home.
▸zhī
【只不过】 zhǐbùguò〈副〉 merely: 他～开开玩笑而已。 He was only joking.
【只得】 zhǐdé〈副〉 having no alternative but to: 我们～涉水过去。 We had no choice but to wade across.
【只读光盘】 zhǐdú guāngpán〈名〉［计算机］ compact disc read-only memory (CD-ROM)
【只顾】 zhǐgù〈副〉 single-mindedly: 他话也不答，头也不回，～专心干他的事儿。 He kept at his work without so much as a reply or a turn of his head.
【只管】 zhǐguǎn〈副〉**1**（尽管） by all means: 你有什么事，～给我写信。 If there's anything I can do for you, don't hesitate to write to me. **2**（只顾） just: 她不会使桨，小船～在湖中打转。 She couldn't use the oars so the boat just turned round and round on the lake.
【只好】 zhǐhǎo〈副〉 have to: 我等了半天，他还没回来，～留个条子就走了。 I waited a long time, but he failed to turn up. I could only leave him a note and go home.
【只可意会，不可言传】 zhǐkě yìhuì, bùkě yánchuán〈成〉 can be apprehended but not expressed
【只是】 zhǐshì **A**〈副〉**1**（仅仅是） only: 我今天进城，～去看看朋友。 I'm going to town today just to see a friend. **2**（就是） simply: 大家问他是什么事，他～笑，不回答。 When he was asked what had happened, he didn't reply but just smiled. **B**〈连〉 but: 我们本来想逛公园的，～一直下雨，没去成。 We had planned to go to the park, but the rain just wouldn't stop so we didn't go in the end.
【只消】 zhǐxiāo〈动〉 be all one has to do: 这点活儿，～几分钟就干完了。 There isn't much work. It won't take more than a few minutes to get it done.
【只许州官放火，不许百姓点灯】 zhǐ xǔ zhōuguān fànghuǒ, bùxǔ bǎixìng diǎndēng〈俗〉 people in power do whatever they desire, whilst making life difficult for ordinary people
【只要】 zhǐyào〈连〉 [usu used correlatively with 就 or 便] as long as: ～不断努力，就会事业有成。 Persistent efforts will bring you success.
【只要功夫深，铁杵磨成针】 zhǐyào gōngfu shēn, tiěchǔ móchéng zhēn〈俗〉 little strokes fell great oaks
【只有】 zhǐyǒu〈连〉 only: ～同心协力，才能把事情办好。 We can only achieve good results if we are of one mind and we coordinate our efforts.
【只争朝夕】 zhǐzhēng-zhāoxī〈成〉 seize the day, seize the hour
【只重衣衫不重人】 zhǐ zhòng yīshān bù zhòng rén〈俗〉 judge people by their clothes, and not by their qualities

旨 zhǐ
A〈形〉〈书〉 delicious: 甘～ delicacy
B〈名〉**1**（用意） purpose: 实施这一政策，～在减轻农民负担。 This policy is aimed at reducing farmers' burdens. ▸主～，要～，宗～ **2**（命令） decree: ▸圣～
【旨令】 zhǐlìng〈名〉 order
【旨趣】 zhǐqù〈名〉〈书〉 purport
【旨要】 zhǐyào〈名〉 gist
【旨意】 zhǐyì〈名〉**1**（意旨） decree: 这是谁的～? Where has this order come from? **2**（意图） purpose: ～何在? What's your purpose?

址 zhǐ〈名〉 site: 迁往新～办公 move to a new office location ▸地～，网～

抵 zhǐ〈动〉〈书〉 knock one's fist against the palm: ～掌而谈 have a happy and intimate chat

芷 zhǐ〈名〉［植物］ Taiwan angelica root

纸（紙） zhǐ
A〈名〉 paper: 一张～ a piece of paper
B〈量〉 [for letters, documents, etc.]: 一～公文 a document ‖ 一～禁令 a ban
【纸板】 zhǐbǎn〈名〉 cardboard: ～盒/箱 cardboard case/box
【纸包不住火】 zhǐ bāobuzhù huǒ〈俗〉 the truth will out
【纸币】 zhǐbì ▸**p. 328**〈名〉 paper money
【纸簿】 zhǐbù〈名〉 pad: 便条～ note pad
【纸黄金】 zhǐhuángjīn〈名〉［经济］ paper gold
【纸浆】 zhǐjiāng〈名〉 pulp
【纸巾】 zhǐjīn〈名〉 tissue: 一盒～ a box of tissues
【纸老虎】 zhǐlǎohǔ〈名〉 paper tiger: 一切反动派都是～。 All reactionaries are paper tigers.
【纸煤儿】 zhǐméir〈名〉 paper stick [used to light a pipe, etc.]
【纸捻】 zhǐniǎn〈名〉 spill of rolled paper used to light a pipe, etc.
【纸尿片】 zhǐniàopiàn〈名〉 paper nappy
【纸牌】 zhǐpái〈名〉 playing cards
【纸钱】 zhǐqián〈名〉 paper made to resemble money and burned as an offering to the dead
【纸上谈兵】 zhǐshàng-tánbīng〈成〉〈喻〉 be an armchair strategist
【纸型】 zhǐxíng〈名〉 papier mâché
【纸烟】 zhǐyān〈名〉 cigarette
【纸样】 zhǐyàng〈名〉 paper pattern
【纸张】 zhǐzhāng〈名〉 paper
【纸醉金迷】 zhǐzuì-jīnmí〈成〉 a life of luxury and dissipation

祉 zhǐ〈名〉〈书〉 blessedness: 福～ good fortune

指 zhǐ
A〈名〉 finger: ▸拇～，屈～可数

B 〈量〉 fingerwidth: 两～宽的纸条 a strip of paper two digits wide ‖ 这双鞋大了一～。This pair of shoes is a fingerwidth too big.
C 〈动〉 **1**（对着） point at: 用手一～ point one's finger at ‖ 时针正～12点。The hour hand is pointing to twelve exactly. **2**（直立） make one's hair stand on end: ▸发～ **3**（点明） indicate: ▸～出，～导，～示 **4**（针对） refer to: 我们不是～你，而是～他。We were not talking about you but about him. **5**（仰仗） rely on: 单～着一个人是不能把事情办好的。We cannot count on just one person to do a good job. ▸～望

【指标】 zhǐbiāo〈名〉 target: 生产～ production target ‖ 数量～ quota ‖ 招工～ recruitment quota ‖ 质量～ quality index

【指标股】 zhǐbiāogǔ 〈名〉［金融］ bellwether stock

【指拨】 zhǐbō〈动〉 guide

【指不胜屈】 zhǐbùshèngqū〈成〉 too many to be counted on the fingers

【指不定】 zhǐbudìng〈副〉 maybe: 你甭等他了，他～来不来呢。Don't wait for him; maybe he's not coming.

【指斥】 zhǐchì 〈动〉 denounce: ～时弊 denounce the maladies of the time

【指出】 zhǐchū〈动〉 point out

【指导】 zhǐdǎo〈动〉 guide: ～思想 guiding principle ‖ 教师正在～学生做实验。The teacher was supervising the students as they did an experiment.

【指导员】 zhǐdǎoyuán ▸**p. 966** 〈名〉 **1**（政治指导员） political instructor **2**（担任指导的人） instructor

【指点】 zhǐdiǎn〈动〉 **1**（点拨）give pointers: 老师正在～学生如何写作文。The teacher is explaining to the student how to write compositions. ‖ 他～给我看，哪是织女星，哪是牵牛星。Pointing at the stars, he told me where to find Vega and where to find Altair. **2**（指责） point to sb.'s faults: 有意见当面提，别背后指指点点。If you have something to say, say it straight and not behind anyone's back.

【指定】 zhǐdìng 〈动〉 appoint: ～律师 appoint a lawyer ‖ 在～地点见面 meet at the designated place

【指法】 zhǐfǎ〈名〉［音乐］ fingering: ～熟练 be good at fingering

【指腹为婚】 zhǐfù-wéihūn 〈成〉 prenatal betrothal

【指关节】 zhǐguānjié〈名〉 knuckle

【指画】 zhǐhuà **A**〈动〉 point to: 孩子们～着，"看，飞机!" Pointing to the sky, the children shouted, 'Look! Planes!' **B**〈名〉 finger painting

【指环】 zhǐhuán〈名〉 ring

【指挥】 zhǐhuī **A**〈动〉 direct: ～交通 direct traffic ‖ ～作战 direct operations **B**〈名〉 **1**（发令调度的人） director: 总～ general director **2**［音乐］ conductor

【指挥棒】 zhǐhuībàng 〈名〉 **1**［音乐］ baton: 指挥举起了～。The conductor raised his baton. **2**〈贬〉（导向） command: 他要大家跟着他的～转。He wants to wrap everyone around his little finger.

【指挥部】 zhǐhuībù〈名〉 command post: 防空～ air defence headquarters

【指挥刀】 zhǐhuīdāo〈名〉 officer's sword

【指挥官】 zhǐhuīguān 〈名〉 commanding officer

【指挥若定】 zhǐhuī-ruòdìng 〈成〉 direct (work, etc.) with perfect ease

【指挥所】 zhǐhuīsuǒ〈名〉 command post

【指挥塔台】 zhǐhuī tǎtái〈名〉 control tower

【指挥员】 zhǐhuīyuán ▸**p. 966**〈名〉 commander

【指鸡骂狗】 zhǐjī-màgǒu = 指桑骂槐 zhǐsāng-màhuái

【指甲】 zhǐjia〈名〉 nail: 剪～ cut one's fingernails ‖ 染～ paint one's nails

【指甲刀】 zhǐjiadāo〈名〉 nail clippers

【指甲盖儿】 zhǐjiagàir〈名〉 nail

【指甲花】 zhǐjiahuā〈名〉 garden balsam

【指甲钳】 zhǐjiaqián = 指甲刀 zhǐjiadāo

【指甲油】 zhǐjiayóu〈名〉 nail polish; nail varnish〈英〉

【指尖】 zhǐjiān〈名〉 finger tip

【指教】 zhǐjiào 〈动〉 **1**（指点教导） instruct: 在教练的～下，运动员进步很快。Guided by the coach, the sportsmen made rapid progress. **2**〈套〉（请人指

指示代词

■ "这／那"、"这些／那些"、"这里／那里"及"这儿／那儿"在汉语里都是指示代词。在英语里，this/that 和 these/those 是指示代词，here/there 是副词。

this 和 that

■ "这"与"那"做主语或宾语时，和英语的 this 和 that 对应：

这是你的
= This is yours

这不行
= This won't work

那是你的书包
= That is your schoolbag

■ "这"与"那"做定语修饰名词时后面一般要跟量词，而英语的 this/that 则直接跟名词：

这位女士是我老师
= This lady is my teacher

那个男孩是我儿子
= That boy is my son

■ 根据上下文，汉语里被修饰的名词可省略，在英语里可用 this/that one:

这个是她的
= This one is hers

我想要那个
= I want that one

these 和 those

■ these 和 those 分别是 this 和 that 的复数形式，相当于汉语的"这些"和"那些"。these/those 与"这些／那些"做主语、宾语或定语时，用法基本相同：

这些是他们的
= These are theirs

那些是我们的
= Those are ours

我要买这些
= I'll buy these

他们要把那些拿走
= They are going to take those away

这些玩具是我的
= These toys are mine

那些橡皮是她的
= Those erasers are hers

■ 当"这些"或"那些"修饰的名词需翻译成英语的不可数名词时（如 money 和 luggage），"这些"或"那些"要译成 this 或 that:

这些钱是她的
= This money is hers

那些化妆品是我姐买的
= It was my sister who got that make-up

■ 当汉语是"这／那＋数字＋量词＋名词"时，英语是"these/those＋数字＋名词"：

这 5 支笔
= these five pens

那 4 箱苹果
= those four boxes of apples

■ 汉语的"我的"、"他们的"、"小方的"、"小马的"等用在"这／那"前面时，英语用"of＋名词性物主代词（如 mine、theirs 等）或名词所有格（如 Xiao Fang's、Xiao Ma's 等）"这个结构，放在被修饰的名词后面。"这／那"指复数时，英语要用 these 或 those 来翻译：

我的这 3 双鞋
= these three pairs of shoes of mine

小李的那 5 件大衣
= those five coats of Xiao Li's

here 和 there

■ 汉语的"这里／这儿"和"那里／那儿"都是指示代词，而英语的 here 和 there 是副词，所以一般来说，它们不能像汉语的这些指示代词一样，在句中做主语或宾语。注意下面例句的翻译：

这儿不安全
= This is not a safe place
或 This place is not safe

这里很美
= This place is beautiful

我喜欢那里
= I like that place

她在那儿
= She is there

■ 汉语的"这里／这儿"和"那里／那儿"放在名词前做修饰语时，英语的 here 或 there 要置于名词后面：

这儿的人爱跳交谊舞
= People here like ball room dancing

那里的风景美如画
= The scenery there is picturesque

点）give advice: 希望多多～。Your advice and comments are appreciated.
【指靠】zhǐkào〈动〉live off: 生活有了～ have something to live off ‖ 要学会自立，不能光～别人。You should learn to be self-sufficient rather than rely on others for everything.
【指控】zhǐkòng〈动〉accuse: 提出～ indict sb. for sth. ‖ ～某人犯罪 accuse sb. of a crime
【指令】zhǐlìng **A**〈动〉order **B**〈名〉**1**（命令）order: 下达～ give instructions ‖ ～性计划 mandatory planning **2**［计算机］instruction
【指鹿为马】zhǐlùwéimǎ〈成〉〈喻〉deliberately misrepresent the facts
【指路牌】zhǐlùpái〈名〉signpost
【指名】zhǐmíng〈动〉mention by name: ～道姓 name names ‖ ～要我发言。I was designated to speak at the meeting.
【指明】zhǐmíng〈动〉point out: ～方向 show the way
【指南】zhǐnán〈名〉guide: 旅游～ guidebook ‖ 行动～ guide to action
【指南车】zhǐnánchē〈名〉〈古〉compass vehicle [fitted with a built-in compass]
【指南针】zhǐnánzhēn〈名〉compass
【指派】zhǐpài〈动〉appoint: ～代表出席会议 appoint delegates to a conference ‖ 受人～ be designated
【指认】zhǐrèn〈动〉identify: ～罪犯 identify a criminal
【指日可待】zhǐrì-kědài〈成〉be just round the corner: 工程竣工～。The end of the project is just around the corner.
【指桑骂槐】zhǐsāng-màhuái〈成〉point at one but accuse another
【指使】zhǐshǐ〈动〉instigate: 受人～ be put up to sth. ‖ 揭露幕后～者 disclose the hidden instigator
【指示】zhǐshì **A**〈动〉**1**（指给人看）indicate: ～前进的方向 indicate the direction of advance **2**（说明）instruct: ～我们把事情做好 instruct us to do a good job of sth. **B**〈名〉instructions: 奉上级～ upon the instructions of higher authorities ‖ 下达～ give instructions
【指示代词】zhǐshì dàicí〈名〉［语言］demonstrative pronoun
【指示灯】zhǐshìdēng〈名〉pilot lamp
【指示牌】zhǐshìpái〈名〉sign: 列车时刻～ train indicator
【指事】zhǐshì〈名〉［语言］self-explanatory characters [one of the six categories of Chinese characters]
【指手画脚】zhǐshǒu-huàjiǎo〈成〉**1**（说话时用手势示意）make animated gestures whilst speaking **2**（随意指责、命令）raise captious objections: 你最好不要～。You'd better stop all the unnecessary fault-finding.
【指数】zhǐshù〈名〉index: 道琼斯～ Dow Jones index ‖ 物价～ commodity price index (CPI)
【指头】zhǐtou〈名〉**1**（手指）finger **2**（脚趾）toe
【指望】zhǐwang **A**〈动〉look to: ～今年有个好收成。We're looking forward to a good harvest this year. **B**〈名〉hope: 这病还有～。There is still hope for a cure for the illness.
【指纹】zhǐwén〈名〉**1**（指纹理）loops and whorls on a finger **2**（指痕迹）fingerprint: ～鉴定 fingerprint identification
【指引】zhǐyǐn〈动〉guide: ～方向 point out the way to ‖ 猎人～他穿过了林区。A huntsman showed him the way through the forest.
【指印】zhǐyìn〈名〉fingerprint: 按～ put one's fingerprint on
【指责】zhǐzé〈动〉criticize: ～某人忘恩负义 reproach sb. for ingratitude ‖ 横加～ make unwarranted charges ‖ 互相～ trade allegations
【指摘】zhǐzhāi〈动〉find fault with: 不要过分～孩子。Don't criticize the child too harshly.
【指战员】zhǐzhànyuán ▸**p. 966**〈名〉commanders and fighters
【指针】zhǐzhēn〈名〉indicator:〈喻〉这份报告是当前一切工作的～。This report acts as a guide for all current work.
【指诊】zhǐzhěn〈名〉touch: 肛门～ rectal touch ‖ 阴道～ vaginal touch
【指正】zhǐzhèng〈动〉**1**（指出错误以便改正）point out mistakes so that they can be corrected **2**〈套〉（请人品评）make a comment or criticism: 我接受您的批评～。I stand corrected.
【指证】zhǐzhèng〈动〉identify and testify: ～凶犯 identify and testify against a criminal

枳 zhǐ〈名〉［植物］trifoliate orange

【枳椇】zhǐjǔ〈名〉raisin tree

咫 zhǐ〈量〉〈古〉measure of length, equal to eight *cun* (寸)

【咫尺】zhǐchǐ〈名〉〈书〉very short distance: 近在～ within a stone's throw
【咫尺天涯】zhǐchǐ-tiānyá〈成〉so near and yet so far

趾 zhǐ〈名〉**1**（脚趾）toe **2**（脚）foot

【趾高气扬】zhǐgāo-qìyáng〈成〉strut about and give oneself airs
【趾骨】zhǐgǔ〈名〉phalanx
【趾甲】zhǐjiǎ〈名〉toenail

黹 zhǐ〈名〉〈书〉needlework: 针～ needlework

酯 zhǐ〈名〉［化学］ester

徵 zhǐ〈名〉［音乐］note on the ancient Chinese pentatonic (五音) scale, corresponding to 5 in *jianpu* (简谱) numbered musical notation

zhì

至 zhì

A〈动〉reach: ～今 as yet ‖ ～九月底为止 up to the end of September ▸自始～终
B〈副〉extremely: 欢迎之～。You are most welcome. ‖ 三个人不够，～少需要五个。Three people is not enough at all. At least five are required.
【至爱】zhì'ài **A**〈形〉most beloved: ～之人 dearest beloved **B**〈名〉most beloved: 生命中的～ dearest person in one's life
【至宝】zhìbǎo〈名〉most valuable treasure: 如获～ as if one had found a priceless treasure
【至诚】zhìchéng〈形〉most sincere: ～待人 treat people with absolute sincerity ‖ 一片～ be completely sincere
【至迟】zhìchí〈副〉at (the) latest
【至此】zhìcǐ〈动〉**1**（到这时）be up to now: ～，问题才有了解决的希望。Only at this stage is it possible to solve the problem. **2**（到这种程度）be to such a degree: 事已～，只好就这样了。Since the matter has developed to this stage, we have to let it go at that. **3**（到这里）be up to this point: 文章～为止。The article ends at this point.
【至多】zhìduō〈副〉at most: 他～不过四十岁。He's forty at most. ‖ 这活儿～十天就干完了。The job will take no more than ten days.
【至高无上】zhìgāo-wúshàng〈成〉supreme: ～的权力 supreme power
【至关紧要】zhìguān-jǐnyào〈成〉most important
【至好】zhìhǎo〈名〉best friend
【至极】zhìjí〈副〉extremely: 可恶～ be extremely abhorrent
【至交】zhìjiāo〈名〉best friend
【至今】zhìjīn〈副〉so far: 他回家以后，～没有来信。I haven't heard from him since he returned home.
【至理名言】zhìlǐ-míngyán〈成〉famous maxim
【至亲】zhìqīn〈名〉close relative: 骨肉～ one's own flesh and blood ‖ ～好友 close relatives and good friends
【至上】zhìshàng〈形〉supreme: 顾客～。The interests of our patrons are paramount. ‖ 国家利益～。The interests of the country go above everything else.
【至少】zhìshǎo〈副〉at least: 今天参加大会的～有3,000人。At least three thousand people attended the rally today. ‖ 从这儿走到学校，～要半个小时。It takes at least half an hour to walk to school from here.
【至圣】zhìshèng〈名〉**1**（指圣人）greatest sage **2**（孔子）Confucius: ～先师 Confucius
【至死】zhìsǐ〈副〉unto death: ～不渝 remain unchanged throughout one's life
【至友】zhìyǒu〈名〉best friend
【至于】zhìyú **A**〈动〉go so far as to: 他可能晚来一会儿，但不～不来。He may be a bit late, but I don't think he will go so far as to stay away. **B**〈介〉as to: 她确实病了。～她什么时候能来，我说不准。She really is ill, so it's hard to say when she will be able to come.
【至嘱】zhìzhǔ〈动〉〈书〉[used in letters] see that you act accordingly
【至尊】zhìzūn **A**〈形〉most revered and respected **B**〈名〉the reigning emperor

志¹ zhì〈名〉will: ～坚如钢 have an iron will ▸～同道合，得～，立～

志²（誌）zhì

A〈动〉keep in mind: 永～不忘 never forget ▸～哀
B〈名〉**1**（记录）annals:《昌黎方言～》*A Survey of the Changli Dialect* ‖《三国～》*History of the Three Kingdoms* ▸县～，杂～ **2**（记号）mark: ▸标～
【志哀】zhì'āi〈动〉indicate mourning: 下半旗～ fly a flag at half-mast as a sign of mourning
【志大才疏】zhìdà-cáishū〈成〉have great ambition but little talent: 他～。His ambition outran his ability.
【志得意满】zhìdé-yìmǎn〈成〉puffed up with one's success
【志怪小说】zhìguài xiǎoshuō〈名〉tales of mystery and the supernatural
【志留纪】Zhìliújì〈名〉［地质］Silurian Period
【志气】zhìqì〈名〉aspiration: 中国人民有

Z

～。The Chinese people have high aspirations.
【志趣】zhìqù〈名〉inclination: 她与男朋友～相投。She and her boyfriend are a great match.
【志士】zhìshì〈名〉person of ideals and integrity: ～仁人 people with high ideals ‖ 爱国～ noble-minded patriot
【志同道合】zhìtóng-dàohé〈成〉share common ideas: ～的夫妻 like-minded couple
【志向】zhìxiàng〈名〉aspiration: 共同的～ shared ambition ‖ 远大的～ lofty aspiration
【志愿】zhìyuàn **A**〈名〉aspiration: 立下～ set a goal ‖ 他的～是当一名教师。His aspiration is to be a teacher. **B**〈动〉volunteer: 他～提供了一些有价值的信息。He volunteered some useful information.
【志愿兵】zhìyuànbīng〈名〉volunteer soldier: ～制 voluntary military service
【志愿军】zhìyuànjūn〈名〉volunteer forces
【志愿书】zhìyuànshū〈名〉application form: 入党～ application for Party membership
【志愿者】zhìyuànzhě〈名〉volunteer: 招募～ recruit volunteers
【志在必得】zhìzàibìdé〈成〉be determined to win
【志在四方】zhìzàisìfāng〈成〉ready to offer one's services wherever they are needed

豸 zhì〈名〉〈古〉insect without feet or legs: 虫～ worm

忮 zhì〈动〉〈书〉be jealous: ～刻 jealous and mean ‖ 不～不求 neither jealous nor greedy

识（識）zhì〈书〉
A〈动〉remember: ▸博闻强～
B〈名〉mark: ▸标～, 款～
▸shí

帜（幟）zhì〈名〉flag: ▸旗～

帙 zhì〈书〉
A〈名〉cloth slip-case (for a book or a scroll of painting): 卷～浩繁 be voluminous
B〈量〉[for books or paintings with a cloth slip-case]: 一～古书 a slip-case of ancient books

制[1]（製）zhì〈动〉**1**（裁剪）cut out: 缝～衣服 make clothes **2**（做）make: 自～教具 make teaching aids oneself ▸～版, ～图, ～造

制[2] zhì
A〈动〉**1**（规定）work out: ▸～定, 因地～宜 **2**（限定）restrict: ～敌于死命 have the enemy by the throat ▸～伏, ～空权, 管～
B〈名〉system: ▸民主集中～, 议会～
【制版】zhìbǎn〈动〉［印刷］make plates: ～车间 plate making shop
【制备】zhìbèi〈动〉［化学］prepare: ～氧气 prepare oxygen
【制币】zhìbì〈名〉standard national currency: ～厂 mint
【制表】zhìbiǎo〈动〉compile a table
【制裁】zhìcái〈动〉impose sanctions: 受到法律的～ be punished according to law ‖ 经济～ economic sanctions
【制成品】zhìchéngpǐn〈名〉finished product
【制导】zhìdǎo〈动〉control and guide: ～导弹/武器 guided missile/weapon
【制订】zhìdìng〈动〉work out: ～教学大纲 map out a teaching programme
【制定】zhìdìng〈动〉formulate: ～纲领/方针/政策 formulate a programme/principle/policy ‖ ～宪法 draw up a constitution
【制动】zhìdòng〈动〉apply the brakes: ～阀 brake valve
【制动器】zhìdòngqì〈名〉［机械］brake
【制度】zhìdù〈名〉**1**（准则）regulation: 财务～ regulations for financial work ‖ 工作～ regulations and rules for work ‖ 作息～ work schedule **2**（体系）system: 资本/社会主义～ capitalist/socialist system
【制伏】zhìfú〈动〉bring under control: ～敌人 subdue the enemy ‖ ～风沙 check wind and sand
【制服】zhìfú **A**〈名〉uniform: 军人～ military uniform ‖ 护士～ nurse's uniform **B** = 制伏 zhìfú
【制高点】zhìgāodiǎn〈名〉［军事］commanding point
【制革】zhìgé〈动〉tan: ～厂 tannery
【制海权】zhìhǎiquán〈名〉［军事］mastery of the seas
【制衡】zhìhéng〈动〉check and balance: 权力～ the checking and balancing of power
【制剂】zhìjì〈名〉［药学］preparation
【制假】zhìjiǎ〈动〉counterfeit: 捣毁～窝点 destroy counterfeiting dens
【制件】zhìjiàn〈名〉workpiece
【制空权】zhìkōngquán〈名〉［军事］control of the air
【制冷】zhìlěng〈动〉refrigerate: ～设备 refrigeration equipment
【制片】zhìpiàn〈动〉produce: 电影～厂 film studio
【制品】zhìpǐn〈名〉goods: 金属～ hardware ‖ 奶～ dairy products ‖ 音像～ video and audio products
【制钱】zhìqián〈名〉standard copper coin (made by the imperial mint during the Ming and Qing dynasties)
【制热】zhìrè〈动〉produce heat: 这台空调制冷效果很好，～不行。This air conditioner has a good cooling function, but it is no good at heating.
【制胜】zhìshèng〈动〉win victory over: 出奇～ seize victory through a surprise attack
【制式】zhìshì〈名〉standard model: ～教练 master of formation drills ‖ 两种彩电～不同。The two colour televisions have different operating systems.
【制售】zhìshòu〈动〉make and sell: ～伪劣产品 produce and sell poor quality pirated goods
【制图】zhìtú〈动〉chart, draft, make maps, chalk out: ～仪器 drafting/drawing instrument ‖ ～员 cartographer, draughtsman
【制宪】zhìxiàn〈动〉draw up a constitution: ～会议 constitutional conference
【制药厂】zhìyàochǎng〈名〉pharmaceutical factory
【制约】zhìyuē〈动〉restrict: 受历史条件的～ be inhibited by historical conditions ‖ 互相～ mutually restrict
【制造】zhìzào〈动〉**1**（变原料为成品）manufacture: 中国～ made in China **2**（人为造成）create: ～假象 put up a false front ‖ ～紧张局势 create tension ‖ ～麻烦 make trouble
【制造商】zhìzàoshāng〈名〉manufacturer
【制造业】zhìzàoyè〈名〉manufacturing industry
【制止】zhìzhǐ〈动〉curb: ～艾滋病的蔓延 check the spread of AIDS ‖ ～非法交易 stop illegal trading ‖ ～通货膨胀 check inflation
【制作】zhìzuò〈动〉manufacture: ～家具 make furniture ‖ 精心～的银器 elaborately wrought silverware

质（質）zhì
A〈名〉**1**（性质）nature: ▸本～, 变～, 实～ **2**（质量）quality: ～优价廉 high quality and low price ‖ 保～保量 guarantee both quantity and quality **3**（物质）matter: ▸流～, ～料, 物～ **4**〈书〉（抵押品）pledge: 以此为～ with this as a pledge ▸人～
B〈形〉simple: ▸～朴
C〈动〉**1**（询问）question: ▸～问, ～疑 **2**〈书〉（抵押）pawn: 以书～钱 pawn one's books
【质变】zhìbiàn〈名〉［哲学］qualitative change: 发生～ change qualitatively
【质地】zhìdì〈名〉texture: ～精美 be of fine texture ‖ ～细密 be fine-grained
【质点】zhìdiǎn〈名〉［物理］particle
【质对】zhìduì〈动〉confront in court: 警察拿出证据和他当面～。The police confronted him with evidence.
【质感】zhìgǎn〈名〉**1**（指物体）texture: 这块毛料～不错。The texture of this wool is pretty nice. **2**（指艺术品）feeling of reality: 画面山、水、树木错落有致，富有～。The picture is a patchwork of mountains, rivers and trees, and feels very real.
【质检】zhìjiǎn〈名〉quality testing
【质量】zhìliàng〈名〉**1**［物理］mass: 原子～ atomic mass **2**（优劣程度）quality: 提高产品～ improve product quality ‖ 工程～ construction quality ‖ 教学～ teaching quality
【质料】zhìliào〈名〉material: 这套衣服的～很好。This suit is made of very good fabric.
【质朴】zhìpǔ〈形〉simple and unadorned: 为人忠厚～ be simple and honest of heart ‖ 文字～ be written in a simple style
【质数】zhìshù = 素数 sùshù
【质问】zhìwèn〈动〉question: 对某人提出～ call sb. to account
【质询】zhìxún〈动〉interrogate
【质疑】zhìyí〈动〉call in question: 对某人的说法提出～ question the validity of sb.'s statement
【质疑问难】zhìyí-wènnàn〈成〉raise doubts and difficult questions for discussion
【质证】zhìzhèng〈动〉question a witness
【质子】zhìzǐ〈名〉［物理］proton

炙 zhì
A〈动〉roast: 烈日～人。The sun is scorching.
B〈名〉〈书〉roast meat: ▸脍～人口, 残羹冷～
【炙热】zhìrè〈形〉boiling hot: ～的太阳 scorching sun
【炙手可热】zhìshǒu-kěrè〈成〉〈喻〉extremely powerful and arrogant

治 zhì
A〈动〉**1**（统治）rule: ▸统～ **2**（医治）cure: ～病 treat an illness ‖ 医生～好了那孩子的病。The doctor cured the sick child. ▸根～ **3**（治理）harness **4**（消灭）exterminate: ～蝗 kill locusts ‖ ～蚜虫 kill aphids **5**（惩罚）punish: 他对我

使坏，我得～～他。 I'll pay him back for the trick he played on me. ▸～罪，惩～ 6（研究） research: 专～宋史 specialize in the history of the Song Dynasty ▸～学
B〈形〉 socially stable: ▸长～久安
C〈名〉〈旧〉 seat of a local government: 府～ prefecture seat ‖ 省～ province capital ‖ 县～ county seat
【治安】zhì'ān〈名〉 law and order: 维持～ maintain public order ‖ ～管理处罚条例 security administration punishment regulations
【治保】zhìbǎo〈动〉 maintain law and order: ～工作 security work
【治本】zhìběn〈动〉 tackle a problem at its source: 河流的～工程 river control project
【治标】zhìbiāo〈动〉 take stopgap measures: ～不如治本。 Radical treatment is better than symptomatic relief.
【治病救人】zhìbìng-jiùrén〈成〉 1〈本〉 cure the sickness to save the patient 2〈喻〉 help sb. mend his ways: 医生的天职是～。 Curing patients is a doctor's bounden duty.
【治国安民】zhìguó-ānmín〈成〉 run the country well and give the people peace and security
【治洪】zhìhóng〈动〉 check a flood
【治家】zhìjiā〈动〉 run a household
【治理】zhìlǐ〈动〉 1（统治） administer: ～国家 govern a country 2（整修） harness: ～河流 harness a river
【治疗】zhìliáo〈动〉 treat: 住院～ be hospitalized ‖ ～效果 therapeutic effect
【治丧】zhìsāng〈动〉 make funeral arrangements: ～委员会 funeral committee
【治沙】zhìshā〈动〉 control sand
【治水】zhìshuǐ〈动〉 regulate rivers and water courses: ～工程 water control project
【治丝益棼】zhìsī-yìfén〈成〉〈喻〉 try to help but only hinder
【治外法权】zhìwài fǎquán〈名〉［外交］ extraterritoriality: 大使享有～。 Ambassadors have extraterritorial rights.
【治未病】zhì wèibìng〈动〉 prevent and control disease: 开展～的宣传活动 launch activities for the promotion of disease prevention and control
【治污】zhìwū〈动〉 reduce and control pollution
【治学】zhìxué〈动〉〈书〉 do scholarly research: 严谨的～态度 rigorous scholarship
【治印】zhìyìn〈动〉 engrave a seal
【治愈】zhìyù〈动〉 work a cure: 病人已无法～。 The patient is beyond cure.
【治愈率】zhìyùlǜ〈名〉 cure rate: 提高～ improve the cure rate
【治装】zhìzhuāng〈动〉〈书〉 purchase necessary items (esp clothes) for a long journey
【治罪】zhìzuì〈动〉 punish

紩（紩）zhì〈动〉〈书〉 darn

栉（櫛）zhì〈书〉

A〈名〉 comb: 木～ wooden comb ‖ 银～ silver comb ▸鳞次～比
B〈动〉 comb: ～发 comb one's hair ▸～风沐雨
【栉比】zhìbǐ〈形〉〈书〉 placed close together
【栉比鳞次】zhìbǐ-líncì = 鳞次栉比 líncì-zhìbǐ
【栉风沐雨】zhìfēng-mùyǔ〈成〉 keep going despite wind and rain

峙 zhì〈动〉〈书〉 stand erect: ▸对～

陟 zhì〈动〉〈书〉 scale: ～山 climb a mountain

贽（贄）zhì〈名〉〈书〉 gift presented to a superior on one's first visit: ～见 present gifts to a superior when calling on him for the first time

挚（摯）zhì〈形〉〈书〉 sincere: ▸～爱，诚～

【挚爱】zhì'ài〈动〉 love with all one's heart: 深情～ deep love ‖ 对祖国的～之情 true love for one's country
【挚诚】zhìchéng〈形〉 sincere
【挚友】zhìyǒu〈名〉 confidant

桎 zhì〈名〉〈旧〉 fetters

【桎梏】zhìgù〈名〉〈书〉 1〈本〉 fetters and handcuffs 2〈喻〉 shackles: 精神～ mental shackles

轾（輊）zhì ▸轩轾 xuānzhì

致[1] zhì

A〈动〉 1（送达） send, deliver: ～欢迎词 deliver a welcome speech 2（表达） express: ～以崇高的敬意 pay high tribute (to) ▸～函，～敬，～谢 3（达到） cause: ▸～癌，～富，学以～用 4（竭尽） devote: ▸～力，专心～志
B〈名〉 engaging style: 剧情曲折有～。 The play with its many twists and turns is fascinating. ▸情～，兴～

致[2]（緻）zhì〈形〉 delicate: ▸～密，细～

【致哀】zhì'āi〈动〉 mourn a death: 向革命烈士～ pay one's respects to revolutionary martyrs
【致癌】zhì'ái〈动〉 be carcinogenic: ～物质 carcinogen
【致病】zhìbìng〈动〉 cause a disease: 高～性禽流感 highly pathogenic avian influenza
【致残】zhìcán〈动〉 cause disability: 因车祸～ become disabled in a car accident
【致词】zhìcí = 致辞 zhìcí
【致辞】zhìcí〈动〉 deliver an address: 新年～ New Year message
【致电】zhìdiàn〈动〉 send a telegraph to
【致富】zhìfù〈动〉 get rich: 劳动～ become rich through sweat and toil ‖ ～之路 road to prosperity
【致函】zhìhán〈动〉 write to: 正式～总统 write a formal letter to the president
【致敬】zhìjìng〈动〉 pay one's respects to: 向英雄们～! Salute the heroes!
【致力】zhìlì〈动〉 devote oneself to: ～于东方文化研究 devote oneself to the study of oriental cultures
【致密】zhìmì〈形〉 fine and close: 结构～ be fine and close in texture
【致敏】zhìmǐn〈动〉［医学］ sensitize
【致命】zhìmìng〈动〉 cause death: 受了～伤 be mortally wounded ‖ ～打击 deadly blow
【致歉】zhìqiàn〈动〉 apologize: 通电～ call sb. to apologize
【致使】zhìshǐ A〈动〉 result in: 山洪暴发～房屋倒塌。 Sudden mountain torrents caused houses to collapse. B〈连〉 so: 由于厂长管理不严，～事故增加。 There has been an increase in accidents as a result of the factory leader's poor supervision.
【致死】zhìsǐ〈动〉 cause death: 重伤～ die as a result of a severe injury
【致死剂量】zhìsǐ jìliàng〈名〉 lethal dose
【致谢】zhìxiè〈动〉 express one's thanks: 登门～ call on sb. to express one's thanks
【致意】zhìyì〈动〉 greet: 挥手～ wave (to sb.) in greeting ‖ 请向边防战士们～。 Please give our best to the frontier guards.

秩 zhì

A〈名〉〈书〉 1（次序） order: ▸～序 2（俸禄） official salary: 厚～ high official salary
B〈量〉 decade [usu of the age of the elderly]: 七～寿辰/华诞 seventieth birthday
【秩序】zhìxù〈名〉 order: 建立世界新～ establish a new world order ‖ 公共～ public order ‖ ～井然 be in good order

鸷（鷙）zhì〈书〉

A〈名〉 bird of prey
B〈形〉 ferocious: ～虫 ferocious bird or beast

掷（擲）zhì〈动〉 throw: ～标枪 throw a javelin ‖ ～界外球 throw-in ‖ ～铁饼/手榴弹 throw a discus/grenade ▸～地有声，孤注一～

【掷弹筒】zhìdàntǒng〈名〉 grenade launcher
【掷地有声】zhìdì-yǒushēng〈成〉 [of a speech] powerful and rousing
【掷还】zhìhuán〈动〉〈套〉 please return: 前请审阅之件，请早日～为荷。 Please return the material submitted to you for approval at your earliest convenience.

畤 zhì〈名〉〈书〉 place where heaven and earth and ancient emperors are worshipped

铚（銍）zhì〈书〉

A〈名〉 short sickle
B〈动〉 cut or reap

痔 zhì〈名〉 haemorrhoids: 内/外～ internal/external piles

【痔疮】zhìchuāng〈名〉 haemorrhoids
【痔漏】zhìlòu〈名〉 anal fistula

窒 zhì〈动〉〈书〉 obstruct: ▸～息

【窒碍】zhì'ài〈动〉〈书〉 be obstructed
【窒息】zhìxī〈动〉 suffocate: ～而死 suffocate

智 zhì

A〈名〉 wisdom: ▸～谋，～商，才～，吃一堑，长一～
B〈形〉 clever: ▸机～，明～
【智残】zhìcán〈名〉 people with cognitive disabilities: ～儿童 children with learning disabilities
【智齿】zhìchǐ〈名〉 wisdom tooth: 长～ cut one's wisdom teeth
【智多星】zhìduōxīng〈名〉 mastermind: 国家队里的～ mastermind of the national team
【智慧】zhìhuì〈名〉 wisdom: 吸取群众的～ draw on the wisdom of the masses ‖ 勤劳～的人民 industrious and ingenious people
【智库】zhìkù〈名〉 think tank: ～为企业出谋划策。 Think tanks provide advice to businesses.

【智力】zhìlì〈名〉intelligence: ～竞赛 quiz game ‖ ～超群 high intellect
【智利】Zhìlì〈名〉Chile: ～人 Chilean
【智龄】zhìlíng〈名〉mental age
【智略】zhìlüè〈名〉wisdom and resourcefulness
【智谋】zhìmóu〈名〉resourcefulness: 有～ be full of ideas ‖ 人多～高。The more people, the more ideas will emerge.
【智囊】zhìnáng〈名〉resourceful person: ～人物 good brains
【智囊团】zhìnángtuán〈名〉think tank
【智能】zhìnéng **A**〈名〉intellectual ability **B**〈形〉intelligent: ～技术 intelligent technology ‖ ～玩具 intelligent toy
【智能电话】zhìnéng diànhuà〈名〉smart phone
【智能犯罪】zhìnéng fànzuì〈名〉intelligent crime
【智能卡】zhìnéngkǎ〈名〉［金融］smart card
【智穷才尽】zhìqióng-cáijìn〈成〉be at the end of one's resources
【智取】zhìqǔ〈动〉capture by stratagem: 只可～，不能强攻。The best policy is strategy, rather than attack by force.
【智趣】zhìqù〈名〉wit and fun
【智人】zhìrén〈名〉Homo sapiens
【智商】zhìshāng〈名〉intelligence quotient (IQ): ～高/低 have a high/low IQ
【智胜】zhìshèng〈动〉outwit
【智勇双全】zhìyǒng-shuāngquán〈成〉be both intelligent and courageous
【智育】zhìyù〈名〉intellectual development: 使学生在德育、～、体育几方面都得到发展 enable the students to develop morally, intellectually and physically
【智圆行方】zhìyuán-xíngfāng〈成〉〈喻〉resourceful and upright
【智运会】zhìyùnhuì〈名〉mind sport contest: 世界首届～ The inaugural World Mind Sport Games
【智障】zhìzhàng〈形〉mentally disabled: ～者 person with mental disabilities
【智者】zhìzhě〈名〉wise man
【智者千虑，必有一失】zhìzhě qiān lǜ, bì yǒu yī shī〈成〉even the wise are not free from error

痣 zhì〈名〉mole: 脸上有一颗黑～ have a black mole on one's face ▸美人～

滞（滯） zhì〈动〉be sluggish: ▸～销，停～
【滞洪】zhìhóng〈动〉slow a flood during a flood season by means of nearby lakes, basins, etc.: ～区 detention basin ‖ ～水库 detention reservoir
【滞后】zhìhòu〈动〉lag behind: ～效应 delayed effect ‖ 体制改革～于经济改革的步伐。Structural reform is lagging behind economic reform.
【滞缓】zhìhuǎn〈形〉sluggish: 生产增长～ sluggish production growth ‖ 行动～ be slow to act
【滞留】zhìliú〈动〉be held up: ～车站的旅客 passengers delayed at the station
【滞纳金】zhìnàjīn〈名〉fine for late payment
【滞销】zhìxiāo〈动〉be unsaleable: ～商品 unsaleable products
【滞涨】zhìzhǎng〈动〉stall: 房价～甚至下跌。Property prices have stalled and even fallen.
【滞胀】zhìzhàng〈名〉［经济］stagflation

骘（騭） zhì〈动〉〈书〉arrange: 评～ evaluate ‖ 阴～ good deeds done in secret

彘 zhì〈名〉〈书〉swine

置 zhì〈动〉**1**（设立）set up: ▸设～，装～ **2**（买）buy: ～一身衣服 buy a suit ▸购～，添～ **3**（放）place: ▸～之不理，安～
【置办】zhìbàn〈动〉purchase: ～家具 buy furniture ‖ ～年货 make special purchases for the Spring Festival
【置备】zhìbèi〈动〉purchase
【置辩】zhìbiàn〈动〉〈书〉[usu used in the negative] justify: 不容～ incontestable ‖ 不屑～ disdain to argue
【置换】zhìhuàn〈动〉exchange: 房屋～ exchange houses
【置喙】zhìhuì〈动〉〈书〉[usu used in the negative] interfere: 不敢妄自～ dare not interrupt ▸不容～
【置评】zhìpíng〈动〉〈书〉[usu used in the negative] comment on: 不予～ make no comment
【置若罔闻】zhìruòwǎngwén〈成〉turn a deaf ear to: 他对我们的抱怨～。He turned a deaf ear to our complaints.
【置身】zhìshēn〈动〉place oneself: ～于群众之中 immerse oneself within the masses
【置身事外】zhìshēn-shìwài〈成〉keep oneself out sth.
【置信】zhìxìn〈动〉[usu used in the negative] believe: 令人难以～ be unbelievable
【置业】zhìyè〈动〉buy property: 在上海～ buy properties in Shanghai
【置疑】zhìyí〈动〉[usu used in the negative] doubt: ▸不容～
【置之不理】zhìzhī-bùlǐ〈成〉pay no attention to: 这等事不能～。Such matters cannot be ignored.
【置之度外】zhìzhī-dùwài〈成〉have no regard for: 把个人安危～ have no regard for one's own safety
【置之死地而后快】zhì zhī sǐdì ér hòu kuài〈成〉will be satisfied with nothing but sb.'s destruction
【置之死地而后生】zhì zhī sǐdì ér hòu shēng〈成〉confront sb. with the danger of death so that they will fight to live

锧 zhì〈名〉〈书〉**1**（铁砧）anvil **2**（铡刀座）executioner's block [on which in ancient China a criminal was cut in half at the waist]: ▸斧～

雉 zhì
A〈名〉pheasant
B〈量〉〈古〉parapet section of a city wall, 30 *chi* (尺) high and 10 *chi* (尺) long
【雉堞】zhìdié〈名〉battlement

稚 zhì〈形〉immature: ▸～嫩，幼～
【稚嫩】zhìnèn〈形〉**1**（幼小而娇嫩）young and tender: ～的童音 child's tender voice ‖ ～的心灵 innocent heart **2**（幼稚）immature: 初学写作，文笔难免～。Immaturity is unavoidable in the writing of a beginner.
【稚气】zhìqì〈名〉childishness: 一脸～ be innocent-looking
【稚子】zhìzǐ〈名〉〈书〉innocent child

疐 zhì〈动〉〈书〉**1**（遇到障碍）encounter obstacles **2**（跌倒）fall down: ▸跋前～后

踬（躓） zhì〈动〉〈书〉**1**（被绊倒）trip: ～仆 trip and fall ‖ 颠～ trip over sth. **2**（失败）suffer a setback: 屡试屡～ fail at each attempt

螲 zhì ▸蝼螲 lóuzhì

觯（觶） zhì〈名〉〈古〉drinking vessel

蛭 zhì〈名〉leech: ▸水～
【蛭石】zhìshí〈名〉［矿业］vermiculite

zhōng

中 zhōng
A〈名〉**1**（中心）centre: ▸～途，～央，～指，居～ **2**（内部）inside: 群众～ among the masses ‖ 假期～ during the vacation ‖ 跳入水～ jump into the water ▸空～ **3**（指在持续状态）[used after a verb or verbal phrase to mean in the process of]: 在设计～ being designed ‖ 在修建/讨论～ under construction/discussion ‖ 正在洽谈～ be in negotiations with sb. ▸发展～国家 **4**（两极之间）middle: ▸～等，～性 **5**（内心）heart **6** Zhōng（中国）China: ▸～文，～医，古今～外 **7**（中间人）mediator: 我来作～。I'll act as mediator. ▸～人
B〈形〉**1**（不偏不倚）halfway between two extremes: ▸～庸，适～ **2**〈方〉（可行）OK: 这办法不～! This method won't work!
C〈动〉be fit for: ▸～看，～听
▸zhòng
【中巴】zhōngbā〈名〉minibus
【中班】zhōngbān〈名〉**1**（指班次）middle shift: 上～ work the middle shift **2**（指班级）middle class in a kindergarten: 我女儿上～。My daughter is in the middle class of kindergarten.
【中饱私囊】zhōngbǎo-sīnáng〈成〉appropriate public funds for one's private use
【中表】zhōngbiǎo〈名〉〈书〉cousins
【中波】zhōngbō〈名〉medium wave
【中部】zhōngbù〈名〉central section
【中不溜儿】zhōngbuliūr〈形〉〈口〉fair to middling: 考试成绩～ get an average score ‖ 个子～ be of medium height
【中餐】zhōngcān〈名〉Chinese food
【中餐馆】zhōngcānguǎn〈名〉Chinese restaurant
【中草药】zhōngcǎoyào〈名〉Chinese herbal medicine
【中策】zhōngcè〈名〉〈书〉second best plan
【中层】zhōngcéng〈名〉middle-level: ～干部 middle-ranking cadres
【中产阶级】zhōngchǎn jiējí〈名〉middle class
【中长跑】zhōngchángpǎo〈名〉middle-distance running
【中长期】zhōngchángqī〈名〉medium-to-long term
【中常】zhōngcháng〈形〉average: ～成绩 average score ‖ ～年景 average harvest
【中场】zhōngchǎng〈名〉［体育］**1**（指球场）midfield **2**（指比赛间隙）half-time: ～休息 half-time interval

【中程导弹】zhōngchéng dǎodàn〈名〉medium-range missile
【中辍】zhōngchuò〈动〉give up halfway: ～学业 drop out of school
【中词】zhōngcí〈名〉［逻辑］middle term
【中档】zhōngdàng〈形〉of medium quality or moderate price: ～货 goods of second-class quality
【中道】zhōngdào〈名〉**1**（中途）halfway: ～而废 give up halfway **2**〈书〉（中庸之道）golden mean (of the Confucian school)
【中稻】zhōngdào〈名〉middle-season rice
【中等】zhōngděng〈形〉medium: 达到～发达国家水平 reach the level of the moderately developed countries ‖ ～城市 medium-sized city ‖ ～身材 medium height
【中等技术学校】zhōngděng jìshù xuéxiào〈名〉secondary technical school
【中等教育】zhōngděng jiàoyù〈名〉secondary school education
【中等师范学校】zhōngděng shīfàn xuéxiào〈名〉teacher-training high school
【中等职业学校】zhōngděng zhíyè xuéxiào〈名〉secondary vocational school
【中等专科学校】zhōngděng zhuānkē xuéxiào〈名〉secondary specialized school
【中低产田】zhōng-dīchǎntián〈名〉farmland with low and medium yields
【中点】zhōngdiǎn〈名〉［数学］midpoint
【中东】Zhōngdōng〈名〉Middle East: ～局势 situation in the Middle East ‖ ～战争 Middle East Wars
【中端】zhōngduān〈形〉medium-end: ～产品 medium-end product
【中断】zhōngduàn〈动〉discontinue: ～外交关系 sever diplomatic ties ‖ 铁路交通～ disruption of rail traffic ‖ 会议～了。The meeting was cut short.
【中队】zhōngduì〈名〉**1**［军事］squadron: 轰炸机/舰艇～ squadron of bombers/warships ‖ 战斗机/飞行～ fighter/air squadron **2**（指编制）detachment: 交警～ detachment of traffic police
【中耳】zhōng'ěr〈名〉［解剖］middle ear: ～炎 inflammation of the middle ear
【中幡】zhōngfān〈名〉［杂技］flagpole waving
【中饭】zhōngfàn〈名〉〈方〉lunch
【中非】Zhōng Fēi〈名〉**1** Zhōngfēi（中非共和国）Central Africa: ～共和国 Central African Republic **2**（非洲中部）central part of Africa: 阿尔及利亚不是～国家。Algeria is not in central Africa.
【中锋】zhōngfēng〈名〉**1**［篮球］centre: 高大～ power centre **2**［足球］centre forward: 他打～。He played centre forward.
【中缝】zhōngfèng〈名〉**1**（指报纸上）column on the folding line of a newspaper, usu reserved for advertisements or notices **2**（指衣服上）line sewn down the back of a jacket in the middle
【中伏】zhōngfú〈名〉**1**（指节气）middle *fu* [the second of the three ten-day periods of the hottest season] **2**（指日子）first day of the middle *fu*
【中格拉摩根郡】Zhōnggélāmógēnjùn〈名〉Mid Glamorgan
【中耕】zhōnggēng〈动〉［农业］intertill
【中共】Zhōng-Gòng〈简称〉= 中国共产党
【中共中央】Zhōng-Gòng Zhōngyāng〈简称〉= 中国共产党中央委员会
【中古】zhōnggǔ〈名〉**1**（指中国史）middle ancient times (in Chinese history, from the 3rd to the 9th century) **2**（指西方史）Middle Ages: ～史 medieval history
【中国】Zhōngguó〈名〉China: ～人 Chinese ‖ ～制造 made in China
【中国版】zhōngguóbǎn〈名〉Chinese version: 这本小说被誉为～的《教父》。This novel is hailed as the Chinese version of *The Godfather*.
【中国进出口商品交易会】Zhōngguó Jìnchūkǒu Shāngpǐn Jiāoyìhuì〈名〉Chinese Import-Export Commodities Fair
【中国共产党】Zhōngguó Gòngchǎndǎng〈名〉Communist Party of China (CPC)
【中国共产党中央委员会】Zhōngguó Gòngchǎndǎng Zhōngyāng Wěiyuánhuì〈名〉Central Committee of the Communist Party of China
【中国共产主义青年团】Zhōngguó Gòngchǎnzhǔyì Qīngniántuán〈名〉Communist Youth League of China
【中国国际旅行社】Zhōngguó Guójì Lǚxíngshè〈名〉China International Travel Service (CITS)
【中国国民党】Zhōngguó Guómíndǎng〈名〉Kuomintang
【中国国民党革命委员会】Zhōngguó Guómíndǎng Gémìng Wěiyuánhuì〈名〉Revolutionary Committee of the Chinese Kuomintang
【中国红十字会】Zhōngguó Hóngshízìhuì〈名〉Red Cross Society of China
【中国话】zhōngguóhuà ▸p. 918〈名〉Chinese: 说～ speak Chinese
【中国画】zhōngguóhuà〈名〉traditional Chinese painting
【中国结】zhōngguójié〈名〉traditional Chinese knot
【中国科学院】Zhōngguó Kēxuéyuàn〈名〉Chinese Academy of Sciences
【中国民主促进会】Zhōngguó Mínzhǔ Cùjìnhuì〈名〉China Association for Promoting Democracy
【中国民主建国会】Zhōngguó Mínzhǔ Jiànguóhuì〈名〉China Democratic National Construction Association
【中国民主同盟】Zhōngguó Mínzhǔ Tóngméng〈名〉Democratic League of China
【中国年】zhōngguónián〈名〉Chinese New Year
【中国农工民主党】Zhōngguó Nóng-Gōng Mínzhǔdǎng〈名〉Chinese Peasants' and Workers' Democratic Party
【中国人民解放军】Zhōngguó Rénmín Jiěfàngjūn〈名〉Chinese People's Liberation Army
【中国人民银行】Zhōngguó Rénmín Yínháng〈名〉People's Bank of China
【中国人民政治协商会议】Zhōngguó Rénmín Zhèngzhì Xiéshāng Huìyì〈名〉Chinese People's Political Consultative Conference (CPPCC)
【中国人民志愿军】Zhōngguó Rénmín Zhìyuànjūn〈名〉Chinese People's Volunteers
【中国日报】Zhōngguó Rìbào〈名〉China Daily
【中国通】zhōngguótōng〈名〉old China hand
【中国象棋】Zhōngguó xiàngqí〈名〉Chinese chess
【中国学】zhōngguóxué〈名〉Chinese studies
【中国银行】Zhōngguó Yínháng〈名〉Bank of China
【中国印】zhōngguóyìn〈名〉China seal
【中国字】zhōngguózì〈名〉Chinese characters
【中号】zhōnghào〈名〉medium size

> 中国文字
>
> Ideograms used for writing Chinese, also used historically in Japan, Korea, and Vietnam. A single character represents a single syllable, and has a basic meaning. *The Kangxi Dictionary*（《康熙字典》）in the Qing Dynasty recorded more than 47,000 characters. Today, *An Unbridged Chinese Dictionary on Historical Principles*（《汉语大词典》）has about 22,700 characters, although only about six or seven thousand characters are commonly used. Simplified characters were introduced in the mainland in 1956 and 1964 to increase literacy. Traditional forms are still used in Taiwan, Hong Kong, Macao and many overseas Chinese communities.

【中和】zhōnghé〈动〉［化学］neutralize: 酸能～碱，碱亦能～酸。Acids neutralize alkalis and vice versa.
【中华】Zhōnghuá〈名〉China: 振兴～ rejuvenate China
【中华民族】Zhōnghuá Mínzú〈名〉Chinese nation
【中华人民共和国】Zhōnghuá Rénmín Gònghéguó〈名〉People's Republic of China: ～国务院/外交部 State Council/Ministry of Foreign Affairs of the People's Republic of China ‖ ～主席 President of the People's Republic of China
【中华鲟】zhōnghuáxún〈名〉［鱼类］Chinese sturgeon
【中级】zhōngjí〈形〉mid-level: ～班 intermediate level class ‖ ～职称 academic title of middle rank ‖ ～人民法院 intermediate people's court
【中继线】zhōngjìxiàn〈名〉［通信］trunk line
【中继站】zhōngjìzhàn〈名〉［通信］relay point
【中坚】zhōngjiān〈名〉backbone: ～分子 backbone element ‖ 社会～ pillar of society
【中间】zhōngjiān〈名〉**1**（里面）the midst: 在人群～ in the midst of the crowd ‖ 那些人～有一个是杀人犯。Among those people is a man convicted of murder. **2**（中心）middle: 在路～画一条白线 paint a white line along the middle of the road ‖ 她坐在前排～。She sat in the middle of the front row. **3**（之间）midway: ～地带 intermediate zone ‖ 两个镇子～有一个小村庄。There's a small village midway between these two towns.
【中间价】zhōngjiānjià〈名〉middle price
【中间力量】zhōngjiān lìliàng〈名〉middle-of-the-road forces
【中间路线】zhōngjiān lùxiàn〈名〉middle course
【中间派】zhōngjiānpài〈名〉middle-of-the-roaders
【中间人】zhōngjiānrén〈名〉middleman: 两家公司谈判，他做～。He acted as a middleman in the negotiations between the two companies.
【中间商】zhōngjiānshāng〈名〉intermediary businessman: 零售～ retailing middleman
【中将】zhōngjiàng〈名〉（指英美陆军、海军陆战队或美空军）lieutenant-general;（指英美海军）vice-admiral;（指英空军）air marshal
【中介】zhōngjiè **A**〈动〉be intermediary: ～机构 intermediary institution **B**〈名〉（媒介）mediation: 房屋～ property agent
【中介子】zhōngjièzǐ〈名〉［物理］neutretto
【中景】zhōngjǐng〈名〉［影视］medium shot

【中局】zhōngjú〈名〉 [of chess] intermediate rounds
【中距离】 zhōngjùlí〈名〉[体育] middle distance: ～赛跑 middle-distance race
【中楷】 zhōngkǎi〈名〉 regular script of medium-sized Chinese characters
【中看】zhōngkàn〈动〉 be pleasant to look at：～不中用 be aesthetically attractive but of little use
【中考】 zhōngkǎo〈名〉 senior middle school entrance examination
【中馈】zhōngkuì〈名〉〈书〉 1▸(家务) housework: 主～ do housework 2▸(妻子) wife: ～犹虚 have not yet taken a wife
【中栏】zhōnglán〈名〉[体育] intermediate hurdles
【中立】zhōnglì〈动〉 be neutral: 保持～ remain neutral ‖ ～国 neutral state
【中量级】 zhōngliàngjí〈名〉[体育] middleweight: ～拳击运动员 middleweight boxer
【中流】zhōngliú〈名〉 1▸(指水流的位置) midstream: ～的水很急。 There's a fast current in midstream. 2▸(指河段) middle reaches of a river: 长江～ middle reaches of the Yangtze River 3▸(指水平) middle: ～水平 be of middling level
【中流砥柱】zhōngliú-dǐzhù〈成〉 mainstay
【中路】zhōnglù〈形〉 mediocre in quality: ～货 mediocre goods
【中洛锡安郡】Zhōngluòxī'ānjùn〈名〉 Midlothian
【中落】 zhōngluò〈动〉 decline: 家道～。 The family was at a low ebb.
【中美洲】 Zhōngměizhōu〈名〉 Central America: ～国家 Central American countries
【中脑】zhōngnǎo〈名〉[解剖] midbrain
【中年】zhōngnián ▸**p. 526**〈名〉 middle age: ～人 middle-aged person ‖ 人到～ reach one's middle age
【中农】 zhōngnóng〈名〉 middle income farmer
【中欧】Zhōng'ōu〈名〉 Central Europe: ～国家 Central European countries
【中盘】zhōngpán〈名〉 mid-game: ～告负 be defeated mid-game
【中跑】 zhōngpǎo〈名〉 middle-distance race: ～运动员 middle-distance runner
【中篇小说】 zhōngpiān xiǎoshuō〈名〉 novella
【中频】zhōngpín〈名〉[电子] intermediate frequency
【中频波】 zhōngpínbō〈名〉 intermediate wave
【中期】zhōngqī〈名〉 middle period: ～目标 medium objective ‖ 二十世纪～ mid 20th century
【中气】zhōngqì〈名〉 1▸[中医] middle-*jiao* (中焦) energy 2▸[天文] 12 of the 24 solar terms in the traditional Chinese calendar 3▸[戏曲] volume of breath: ～十足 have enough breath
【中秋节】 Zhōngqiūjié〈名〉 Mid-Autumn Festival

> **中秋节**
>
> A traditional festival celebrated on the 15th of the eighth month of the lunar calendar, in the middle of autumn at full moon. The family comes together at this time to eat moon cakes and worship Chang'e (▸嫦娥), the Goddess of the Moon. (▸月饼)

【中人】zhōngrén〈名〉 middleman
【中沙群岛】 Zhōngshā Qúndǎo〈名〉 Macclesfield Bank [called 'Zhongsha Islands' in China]
【中山狼】zhōngshānláng〈名〉〈喻〉 one who bites the hand that feeds him
【中山陵】Zhōngshānlíng〈名〉 Sun Yat-sen Mausoleum (in Nanjing)
【中山装】zhōngshānzhuāng〈名〉 Chinese tunic suit: 穿着一身～ be in Chinese tunic and trousers

> **中山装**
>
> A Chinese men's suit named after Sun Yat-sen (孙中山) and designed, it is said, by Sun himself. The Zhongshan suit is a jacket with a high collar (later turned-down), buttons down the front, and four outside pockets. Trousers are in the western style, and of the same material and colour (usually khaki-green or blue) as the jacket. The suit remained as formal dress for government officials until the late 20th century. It is also known in the West as the Mao suit.

【中生代】 zhōngshēngdài〈名〉[地质] Mesozoic Era
【中师】zhōngshī〈简称〉= 中等师范学校
【中石器时代】 zhōngshíqì shídài〈名〉 Mesolithic Period
【中士】zhōngshì〈名〉(指英美陆军、海军陆战队或英空军) sergeant;(指美海军) petty officer 2nd class;(指英海军) petty officer, first class;(指美空军) staff sergeant
【中世纪】zhōngshìjì〈名〉 Middle Ages
【中式】zhōngshì〈形〉 Chinese-style: ～服装 Chinese-style clothing
【中试】zhōngshì〈名〉 pre-production test
【中枢】 zhōngshū〈名〉 centre: 神经～ nerve centre ‖ 银行是商业的～。 Banks are the nerve centres of commerce.
【中枢神经】zhōngshū shénjīng〈名〉[解剖] nervous centralis: ～系统 central nervous system
【中水】zhōngshuǐ〈名〉 recycled water
【中堂】zhōngtáng〈名〉 1▸ = 堂屋 tángwū 2▸(指字画) central scroll of painting or calligraphy (hung in the middle of the wall of the main room) 3▸(旧时官员称号) form of address for a Grand Secretary in the Ming and Qing dynasties
【中提琴】zhōngtíqín ▸**p. 929**〈名〉[音乐] viola
【中听】zhōngtīng〈形〉 pleasant to the ear: 这些话还～。 These remarks sound quite agreeable.
【中途】zhōngtú〈名〉 halfway: ～退学 drop out of school ‖ ～下汽车 get off the car halfway
【中途岛】Zhōngtúdǎo〈名〉Midway Islands
【中外】zhōng-wài〈名〉 China and foreign countries: ～合资企业 Chinese-foreign joint venture ‖ 驰名～ be well known at home and abroad
【中卫】zhōngwèi〈名〉 [of football] centre halfback
【中尉】zhōngwèi〈名〉(指美陆军、空军和海军陆战队) first lieutenant;(指英陆军和海军陆战队) lieutenant;(指美海军) lieutenant junior grade;(指英海军) sub-lieutenant;(指英空军) flying officer
【中文】Zhōngwén〈名〉 Chinese language: 学习～ study Chinese ‖ ～书刊 Chinese books and magazines
【中午】zhōngwǔ ▸**p. 669**〈名〉 midday: 在～ at noon
【中西】zhōngxī〈名〉 China and the West: ～医结合 combine traditional Chinese medicine and Western medicine
【中线】zhōngxiàn〈名〉 1▸[体育](指篮球、排球) centre line;(指足球) halfway line 2▸[数学] median
【中校】zhōngxiào〈名〉(指美空军、英美陆军及海军陆战队) lieutenant colonel;(指英美海军) commander;(指英空军) wing commander
【中心】zhōngxīn〈名〉 centre: 市～ city centre ‖ ～工作 central task ‖ ～任务 core task ‖ 金融/文化～ financial/cultural centre ‖ 购物～ shopping centre ‖ 培训～ training centre ‖ 广场的～是一座喷泉。 In the middle of the square stands a fountain.
【中心思想】zhōngxīn sīxiǎng〈名〉 central idea: 文章的～ central theme of an essay
【中兴】zhōngxīng〈动〉 resurge
【中型】zhōngxíng〈形〉 medium-sized: ～计算机 medium-sized computer ‖ ～企业 medium-sized enterprise
【中性】zhōngxìng〈形〉 1▸[化学] neutral: ～反应 neutral reaction ‖ ～树脂 neutral resin 2▸[语言] neuter: ～名词 neuter noun 3▸(指词义) neutral
【中休】zhōngxiū〈名〉 break
【中学】 zhōngxué〈名〉 1▸(指学校) middle school: 初/高级～ junior/senior middle school 2▸Zhōngxué (指学术) traditional Chinese learning [late Qing Dynasty term]: ～为体，西学为用 Chinese learning as the base and Western learning for application
【中学生】 zhōngxuéshēng〈名〉 middle school student
【中雪】zhōngxuě〈名〉 moderate snowfall
【中旬】zhōngxún ▸**p. 618**〈名〉 middle ten days of a month: 六月～ mid-June
【中亚】Zhōng Yà〈名〉 Central Asia: ～国家 Central Asia Countries
【中央】 zhōngyāng〈名〉 1▸(指方位) centre: 舞台～ the centre of the stage ‖ 湖～有一座亭子。 In the middle of the lake, there is a pavilion. 2▸(指领导机构) centre of power: ～直属机关 department directly under the Party Central Committee of the CPC ‖ ～书记处 Secretariat of the Central Committee ▸党～
【中央处理器】 zhōngyāng chǔlǐqì〈名〉 central processing unit
【中央电视台】Zhōngyāng Diànshìtái〈名〉 China Central Television (CCTV)

> **中央电视台**
>
> China's main television broadcaster, under the State Administration of Radio, Film, and Television. It has 17 channels and one high definition channel, including four overseas channels broadcasting in Chinese, English, French and Spanish. The New Year Gala broadcast every Chinese New Year's Eve has one of the highest programme ratings in the world. CCTV first broadcast on May 1st 1958.

【中央空调】 zhōngyāng kōngtiáo〈名〉 central air-conditioning
【中央集权】zhōngyāng jíquán〈名〉 centralization (of authority): ～制 centralism
【中央气象台】 Zhōngyāng Qìxiàngtái〈名〉 Central Meteorological Observatory
【中央情报局】 Zhōngyāng Qíngbàojú〈名〉 Central Intelligence Agency (CIA)
【中央全会】 Zhōngyāng Quánhuì〈名〉 plenary session of the Central Committee (of CPC)
【中央商务区】 zhōngyāng shāngwùqū〈名〉 central business district (CBD)
【中央税】zhōngyāngshuì〈名〉national tax
【中央委员】 zhōngyāng wěiyuán〈名〉 member of the Central Committee of the CPC
【中央银行】 zhōngyāng yínháng〈名〉 central bank
【中药】zhōngyào〈名〉 traditional Chinese medicine: ～学 traditional Chinese pharmacology
【中叶】zhōngyè ▸**p. 618**〈名〉 middle

period: 20世纪～ middle of 20th century ‖ 唐朝～ middle period of the Tang Dynasty
【中衣】zhōngyī〈名〉underpants
【中医】zhōngyī〈名〉**1**（指医学）traditional Chinese medicine (TCM): ～理论 theory of traditional Chinese medicine ‖ ～学 traditional Chinese medicine **2**（指医生）doctor of traditional Chinese medicine

> **中医**
>
> The traditional science of medicine, originating in the region around the Yellow River, and said to be invented by the legendary ruler Shen Nong (神农) who tasted many herbs to discover their medicinal properties. Chinese medicine takes an holistic view of illness and the patient's condition. The human body is seen as an organic whole, with each of the organs influencing and promoting each other. Treatment includes acupuncture, moxibustion, and herbal potions aimed at restoring internal balance.

【中音】zhōngyīn〈名〉［音乐］mediant: 男/女～歌唱家 male/female middle-range singers
【中音号】zhōngyīnhào ▸**p. 929**〈名〉［音乐］althorn
【中庸】zhōngyōng **A**〈名〉golden mean of the Confucian school: ～之道 middle course **B**〈形〉〈书〉of ordinary talent: ～之才 mediocre person
【中用】zhōngyòng〈形〉useful: 我老了，不～。I'm getting old and useless.
【中游】zhōngyóu〈名〉**1**（指河段）middle reaches of a river: 黄河～ middle reaches of the Yellow River **2**（指水平）mediocrity: 甘居～ be content with mediocrity
【中雨】zhōngyǔ〈名〉moderate rain: ～转多云 moderate rain to cloudy
【中元节】Zhōngyuánjié〈名〉Zhongyuan Festival [the 15th day of the seventh lunar month when offerings are made to the dead]
【中原】Zhōngyuán〈名〉Central Plains [the middle and lower reaches of the Yellow River]: 地处～ be situated in the Central Plains
【中岳】Zhōngyuè〈名〉Central Sacred Mountain [Songshan Mountain (嵩山) in Henan Province]
【中允】zhōngyǔn〈形〉〈书〉fair: 貌似～ be seemingly impartial
【中正】zhōngzhèng〈形〉〈书〉just
【中止】zhōngzhǐ〈动〉break off: 比赛一度～。The match was suspended once.
【中指】zhōngzhǐ〈名〉middle finger
【中州】Zhōngzhōu〈名〉〈旧〉middle China [Henan Province and surrounding areas]
【中专】zhōngzhuān〈简称〉= 中等专科学校
【中转】zhōngzhuǎn〈动〉**1**（转换交通工具）transfer: ～站 transfer station ‖ ～签字 sign a transfer **2**（中间转手）transship: ～货物 goods to be shipped ‖ ～贸易 entrepôt trade
【中装】zhōngzhuāng〈名〉traditional Chinese clothing
【中资】zhōngzī〈名〉Chinese capital: ～企业 companies funded by Chinese capital
【中子】zhōngzǐ〈名〉［物理］neutron
【中子弹】zhōngzǐdàn〈名〉neutron bomb

忪 zhōng
〈形〉〈书〉terrified: ▸怔～ ▸sōng

忠 zhōng
〈形〉loyal: 尽～报国 be devoted to the service of one's country ▸效～
【忠臣】zhōngchén〈名〉loyal court official
【忠诚】zhōngchéng〈形〉loyal: ～于人民的教育事业 be devoted to the people's educational cause ‖ ～的朋友 loyal friend
【忠诚度】zhōngchéngdù〈名〉loyalty: 提高员工的～ boost staff loyalty ‖ 老年人对电视的～最高。The elderly are the most loyal to television.
【忠告】zhōnggào **A**〈动〉sincerely advise: ～某人戒赌 admonish sb. against gambling **B**〈名〉sound advice: 提出～ offer sincere advice ‖ 听从某人的～ follow sb.'s advice
【忠骨】zhōnggǔ〈名〉dead body of a martyr
【忠厚】zhōnghòu〈形〉sincere and kind-hearted: 待人/为人～ be sincere and kind to people
【忠良】zhōngliáng **A**〈形〉faithful and upright **B**〈名〉faithful and upright person: 陷害～ frame the faithful and innocent
【忠烈】zhōngliè **A**〈形〉loyal unto death **B**〈名〉martyr
【忠实】zhōngshí〈形〉**1**（忠诚可靠）loyal: ～的朋友 faithful friend ‖ ～信徒 loyal follower **2**（真实）true to fact: ～于原文 be true to the original version ‖ 现实生活～的写照 true picture of real life
【忠顺】zhōngshùn〈形〉loyal and obedient: ～的奴仆 faithful servant
【忠孝】zhōngxiào〈名〉loyalty and filial piety: ～难以两全。Loyalty and filial piety seldom go together.
【忠心】zhōngxīn〈名〉devotion: ～报国 serve one's country heart and soul ‖ 赤胆～ utter devotion
【忠心耿耿】zhōngxīn-gěnggěng〈成〉be extremely loyal and devoted: 对教育事业～ be dedicated heart and soul to the educational cause
【忠言】zhōngyán〈名〉sincere advice: 进～ give sincere advice
【忠言逆耳】zhōngyán-nì'ěr〈成〉good advice isn't easy on the ear: 良药苦口利于病，～利于行。Good medicine, though bitter to the taste, cures one's illness. Honest advice, though unpleasant on the ear, benefits one's conduct.
【忠义】zhōngyì **A**〈形〉loyal and righteous: ～之士 man of loyalty and righteousness **B**〈名〉〈旧〉loyal and righteous court official
【忠勇】zhōngyǒng〈形〉loyal and brave: ～的战士 loyal and brave fighter
【忠于】zhōngyú〈动〉be loyal to: ～职守 be devoted to one's duty ‖ ～祖国 be loyal to one's country
【忠贞】zhōngzhēn〈形〉loyal and steadfast: ～不屈 staunch and indomitable
【忠贞不渝】zhōngzhēn-bùyú〈成〉be unswervingly loyal

终（終）zhōng
A〈名〉end: ▸年～, 自始至～
B〈动〉**1**（结束）come to an end: ▸剧～, 寿～正寝 **2**（死亡）die: ▸临～
C〈形〉entire: ▸～年, ～日, ～身
D〈副〉eventually: ～非良策 not a good plan after all ‖ ～将胜利 will eventually triumph
【终裁】zhōngcái〈动〉make a final ruling: 不服～ not comply with the final ruling ‖ ～结果令人满意。The results of the final ruling were satisfying.
【终场】zhōngchǎng〈动〉come to an end: ～时，观众中响起了热烈的掌声。At the end of the performance, the audience burst into applause. ‖ ～前，主队又攻进一球。The host team scored another goal just before the final whistle.
【终场哨】zhōngchǎngshào〈名〉final whistle: 裁判吹响了～。The referee sounded the final whistle.
【终成泡影】zhōngchéng pàoyǐng〈成〉end up in smoke
【终点】zhōngdiǎn〈名〉**1**（目的地）destination: 旅行的～ destination of a journey **2**［体育］finish: 冲向～ head for the finish
【终点线】zhōngdiǎnxiàn〈名〉［体育］finishing line
【终点站】zhōngdiǎnzhàn〈名〉terminus: 公共汽车～ bus terminal
【终端】zhōngduān〈名〉terminal: 计算机～ computer terminal
【终伏】zhōngfú = 末伏 mòfú
【终古】zhōnggǔ〈名〉〈书〉forever: 这虽是一句老话，却令人感到～常新。This is an old saying, but it still sounds fresh.
【终归】zhōngguī〈副〉eventually: 要两面派～不会有好下场。Double-dealers will come to no good end.
【终极】zhōngjí〈形〉ultimate: ～目标 ultimate aim
【终结】zhōngjié **A**〈名〉end: 生命的～ end of one's life **B**〈动〉come to a close: 事情很快就～了。The matter will shortly come to a close.
【终究】zhōngjiū〈副〉**1**（毕竟）after all: 教育～不是万能的。Education is not omnipotent after all. **2**（最终）eventually: 纸包不住火，假面具～要被揭穿。One cannot wrap fire with paper just as one cannot conceal evil.
【终久】zhōngjiǔ = 终究 zhōngjiū
【终局】zhōngjú〈名〉outcome: 战争的～ outcome of a war
【终老】zhōnglǎo〈动〉live out one's years: ～故乡 spend one's remaining years in one's hometown ‖ ～山林 final years in a mountain forest
【终了】zhōngliǎo〈动〉end: 会议～ end of a conference
【终南捷径】Zhōngnán-jiéjìng〈成〉〈喻〉short cut to fame or success
【终年】zhōngnián〈名〉**1**（全年）whole year: ～抱病 be ill all year round **2**（去世时年龄）age at which one dies: ～92岁 die at the age of ninety-two
【终盘】zhōngpán〈动〉**1**（指市场行情）close for the day, make a final quotation: ～报收…点 put a final quote at, close at ... at the end of the day **2**（指棋局结果）play the final move: 白棋～以两子小胜。White won the game by two points.
【终曲】zhōngqǔ〈名〉［音乐］finale
【终日】zhōngrì〈名〉all day: ～无所事事 have nothing to do all day long
【终身】zhōngshēn〈名〉all one's life: ～残废 be permanently disabled ‖ 剥夺政治权利～ be deprived of political rights for one's whole life
【终身大事】zhōngshēn dàshì〈名〉big event in one's life [usu referring to one's marriage]
【终身监禁】zhōngshēn jiānjìn〈名〉［法律］life imprisonment
【终身教育】zhōngshēn jiàoyù〈名〉lifelong education
【终身制】zhōngshēnzhì〈名〉lifelong tenure: 废除领导干部职务～ abolish lifelong tenure for leading cadres
【终审】zhōngshěn〈动〉**1**（指审判）make a final judgement: ～法院 court of last instance ‖ ～判决 final judgement

Z

2（指审查） examine and appraise a piece of writing at the highest level: ～定稿后即可发稿。 The manuscript will be dispatched soon after it is finalized.

【终生】 zhōngshēng〈名〉 all one's life: ～难忘 will never forget

【终岁】 zhōngsuì = 终年 zhōngnián 1

【终天】 zhōngtiān **A**〈副〉 all day long: ～发愁 feel worried all day long **B**〈名〉〈书〉 all one's life: 抱恨～ have a gnawing regret all one's life

【终席】 zhōngxí〈动〉 come to a close: 没到～，很多客人便离开了。 Many guests left before the party was over.

【终于】 zhōngyú〈副〉 finally: 经过多次努力，她～获得成功。 After many attempts she eventually succeeded. ‖ 她多次想说，但～没说出口。 She had tried to speak out on several occasions but decided against it in the end.

【终止】 zhōngzhǐ〈动〉 terminate: ～合同 terminate a contract ‖ ～日期 closing date

盅 zhōng〈名〉 small handleless cup: 酒～ wine cup ‖ 我们喝了几～。 We had a few cups.

钟[1]（鐘） zhōng〈名〉 **1**（指响器） bell: 警世～ a warning bell to the world ▸～楼, 编～ **2**（指计时器） clock: ～停了。 The clock has stopped. ▸闹～, 生物～ **3**（指钟点） time [as stated in hours and minutes]: 六点～ six o'clock ‖ 从这儿到那儿只要十分～。 It only takes ten minutes to get there from here.

钟[2]（鍾） zhōng〈动〉 focus: 情有独～ affection of a particularly attentive kind ▸～爱, ～情

【钟爱】 zhōng'ài〈动〉 cherish

【钟摆】 zhōngbǎi〈名〉 pendulum (of a clock)

【钟表】 zhōngbiǎo〈名〉 timepiece

【钟表店】 zhōngbiǎodiàn〈名〉 watchmaker's shop

【钟点】 zhōngdiǎn〈名〉 **1**（时间） time specified: 到～了，快走吧! It's time for you to leave. **2**（小时） hour: 我等了一个～了，他还没来。 I've been waiting for an hour, but there is still no sign of him.

【钟点房】 zhōngdiǎnfáng〈名〉 pay-by-the-hour hotel room

【钟点工】 zhōngdiǎngōng〈名〉 worker paid by the hour

【钟鼎文】 zhōngdǐngwén = 金文 jīnwén

【钟灵毓秀】 zhōnglíng-yùxiù〈成〉 a fine natural environment nurtures great talents

【钟楼】 zhōnglóu〈名〉 **1**（指悬挂大钟） bell tower **2**（指安装时钟） clock tower

【钟鸣鼎食】 zhōngmíng-dǐngshí〈成〉 live an extravagant life

【钟情】 zhōngqíng〈动〉 be deeply in love with: ～于一位姑娘 fall in love with a girl

【钟乳石】 zhōngrǔshí〈名〉 stalactite

【钟头】 zhōngtóu〈名〉〈口〉 hour: 三个半～ three and a half hours

衷 zhōng

A〈形〉 middle: ▸折～

B〈名〉 inner feelings: ▸～心

【衷肠】 zhōngcháng〈名〉〈书〉 heartfelt remarks: 畅叙～ have a heart-to-heart talk (with sb.) ‖ 倾诉～ pour out one's heart

【衷情】 zhōngqíng〈名〉〈书〉 heartfelt emotion: 倾吐～ open one's heart

【衷曲】 zhōngqū〈名〉〈书〉 inner feelings: 倾吐～ bare one's heart

【衷心】 zhōngxīn〈形〉 heartfelt: ～拥护 give wholehearted support ‖ 表示～感谢 express one's heartfelt gratitude

螽 zhōng

【螽斯】 zhōngsī〈名〉［昆虫］ katydid

zhǒng

肿（腫） zhǒng〈动〉 be swollen: ～消了。 The swelling has gone down. ‖ 我的腿～了。 My legs are swollen. ▸浮～, 红～

【肿大】 zhǒngdà〈形〉 swollen: ▸肝～

【肿块】 zhǒngkuài ▸p. 50〈名〉 lump: 乳房有个～。 There is a lump in the breast.

【肿瘤】 zhǒngliú ▸p. 50〈名〉 tumour: 恶性～ malignant tumour ‖ 良性～ benign tumour

【肿胀】 zhǒngzhàng〈动〉 become swollen

种（種） zhǒng

A〈名〉 **1**（种子） seed: ▸播～, 稻～ **2**（物种） breed: ▸传～, 配～ **3**（人种） race: ▸～族, 人～ **4**（根源） root: ▸火～, 谬～ **5**（胆量） guts: 有～的上来比试比试。 I'm here to challenge anyone who has the guts. ▸孬～ **6**（种类） sort: 我不是那～人。 I am not that sort of person. ▸～类, 兵～, 工～ **7**［生物］ species

B〈量〉 type: 五千～进口商品 5,000 kinds of imports

▸Chóng, zhòng

【种差】 zhǒngchā〈名〉［生物］ intraspecific diversity

【种畜】 zhǒngchù〈名〉 breeding stock

【种类】 zhǒnglèi〈名〉 kind: 花的～很多。 There are many different kinds of flowers.

【种马】 zhǒngmǎ〈名〉 stud: ～场 stud farm

【种牛】 zhǒngniú〈名〉 stud bull

【种皮】 zhǒngpí〈名〉 seed coat

【种禽】 zhǒngqín〈名〉 breeding fowl

【种群】 zhǒngqún〈名〉 population

【种仁】 zhǒngrén〈名〉 kernel

【种条】 zhǒngtiáo〈名〉 branch or twig for layering

【种姓】 zhǒngxìng〈名〉 caste: ～制度 caste system

【种猪】 zhǒngzhū〈名〉 breeding hog

【种子】 zhǒngzi〈名〉 **1**［植物］ seed; pip〈英〉: ～改良 seed amelioration ‖ ～发芽了。 The seeds are sprouting. ‖〈喻〉埋下冲突的～ sow the seeds for conflict **2**［体育］ seed: ～队 seeded team ‖ 一号～选手 first seed

【种族】 zhǒngzú〈名〉 race: ～隔离 racial separation ‖ ～歧视 racial discrimination

【种族主义】 zhǒngzú zhǔyì〈名〉 racism: ～者 racist

冢（塚） zhǒng〈名〉 tomb: 古～ ancient tomb ‖ 荒～ abandoned tomb

踵 zhǒng〈书〉

A〈名〉 heel: ▸接～, 摩肩接～, 旋～

B〈动〉 **1**（亲自到） call in person: ～门道谢 call in person to express one's thanks **2**（跟随） follow: ▸～事增华

【踵事增华】 zhǒngshì-zēnghuá〈成〉 carry on a predecessor's task and make an even greater success of it

zhòng

中 zhòng〈动〉 **1**（正对上） hit: 他打了一枪，但没有～。 He fired but missed the target. ‖ 你说～了。 You've hit the nail on the head. ▸～奖, ～意, 正～下怀 **2**（受到） suffer: 腿上～了一枪 get shot in the leg ▸～毒, ～风

▸zhōng

【中标】 zhòngbiāo〈动〉 win a bid

【中彩】 zhòngcǎi〈动〉 win a prize in a lottery: 中头彩 get first prize in a lottery

【中弹】 zhòngdàn〈动〉 get shot: ～身亡 be shot dead

【中的】 zhòngdì〈动〉 **1**〈本〉 hit the target **2**〈喻〉 hit the nail on the head: 一语～ go right to the point

【中毒】 zhòngdú〈动〉 be poisoned: 食物～ food poisoning ‖〈喻〉 他迷信邪教，～很深。 He had heretic beliefs and was deeply poisoned by them.

【中风】 zhòngfēng **A**〈动〉 have a stroke: 死于～ die from a stroke **B** ▸p. 50〈名〉［医学］ stroke

【中规中矩】 zhòngguī-zhòngjù〈形〉 by-the-book: 她的表演一招一式～。 Her performance was disciplined and by-the-book .

【中计】 zhòngjì〈动〉 be taken in: 对方～了。 The opposition were taken in.

【中奖】 zhòngjiǎng〈动〉 win a prize in a lottery: 中头奖 win first prize in a lottery

【中举】 zhòngjǔ〈动〉 pass the imperial examinations at the provincial level [in the Ming and Qing dynasties]

【中肯】 zhòngkěn〈形〉 pertinent: ～的评语 pertinent remarks ‖ 她的批评很～。 Her criticisms were very pertinent.

【中魔】 zhòngmó〈动〉 be bewitched

【中签率】 zhòngqiānlǜ〈名〉［金融］ lot winning rate: 新股网上申购的～为2.75%。 Online purchase of new shares has a 2.75% lot winning rate .

【中伤】 zhòngshāng〈动〉 slander: 造谣～ spread slanderous rumours ‖ 恶意～ viciously malign

【中暑】 zhòngshǔ〈动〉 have sunstroke: ～而死 die of heatstroke

【中邪】 zhòngxié = 中魔 zhòngmó

【中选】 zhòngxuǎn〈动〉 be chosen

【中意】 zhòngyì〈动〉 be to one's liking: 颜色我不～。 I don't like the colour. ‖ 对这门亲事他很～。 He has a very favourable view of this marriage.

【中招】 zhòngzhāo〈动〉 fall into a trap: 诱使某人～ trick someone to falling into one's trap

仲 zhòng

A〈名〉 **1**（指月份） second month of a season: ▸～秋, ～夏 **2**〈书〉（指兄弟排行） second brother: ▸伯～

B〈形〉 middle: ▸～裁

【仲裁】 zhòngcái〈动〉 arbitrate: 对争端进行～ mediate in a dispute ‖ ～机构 arbitration body ‖ 法院～ judicial arbitration

【仲春】 zhòngchūn ▸p. 345〈名〉 mid-spring

【仲冬】 zhòngdōng ▸p. 345〈名〉 mid-winter

【仲秋】 zhòngqiū ▸p. 345〈名〉 mid-autumn

【仲夏】 zhòngxià ▸p. 345〈名〉 mid-summer

众（眾、衆）zhòng

A〈形〉 numerous: ▸～多, ～矢之的
B〈名〉 multitude: ▸～所周知, 大～

【众多】zhòngduō〈形〉 numerous: 中国地大物博，人口～。 China is a vast country with a large population and abundant resources.

【众寡悬殊】zhòngguǎ-xuánshū〈成〉great disparity in numerical strength: 敌我双方在人数上～。 The enemies are numerically far superior to our side.

【众口难调】zhòngkǒu-nántiáo〈成〉 tastes differ

【众口铄金】zhòngkǒu-shuòjīn〈成〉 public opinion will, over time, fail to distinguish right from wrong

【众口一词】zhòngkǒu-yīcí〈成〉speak with one voice: 他们～，说我是小偷。 They all said that I was a thief.

【众目睽睽】zhòngmù-kuíkuí〈成〉 under public gaze: 他们在～之下抢劫了一位老太太。 They robbed an old lady in broad daylight.

【众目昭彰】zhòngmù-zhāozhāng〈成〉 be clear to all

【众怒】zhòngnù〈名〉 public wrath: ～难犯 one cannot afford to incur public indignation

【众叛亲离】zhòngpàn-qīnlí〈成〉be deserted by one's supporters

【众擎易举】zhòngqíng-yìjǔ〈成〉 many hands make light work

【众人】zhòngrén〈名〉 everybody

【众人拾柴火焰高】 zhòngrén shí chái huǒyàn gāo〈俗〉〈喻〉many hands make light work

【众生】zhòngshēng〈名〉 all living beings: ▸芸芸～

【众生相】 zhòngshēngxiàng〈名〉 panorama of all kinds of people

【众矢之的】 zhòngshǐzhīdì〈成〉〈喻〉 object of public criticism

【众说纷纭】zhòngshuō-fēnyún〈成〉 opinions vary: 如何妥善处理这一问题，专家们～。 The experts disagree on the best way of dealing with the problem.

【众所周知】 zhòngsuǒzhōuzhī〈成〉 as everyone knows: 由于～的原因 for reasons known to all

【众望】 zhòngwàng〈名〉 public expectation: ▸不孚～

【众望所归】 zhòngwàng-suǒguī〈成〉 enjoy popular support: 他升任经理是～。 His promotion to manager accords with everyone's wishes.

【众星捧月】 zhòngxīng-pěngyuè〈成〉〈喻〉 enjoy the respect and support of a host of capable men

【众议院】zhòngyìyuàn〈名〉**1**（美国、澳大利亚、日本等国）House of Representatives **2**（意大利、墨西哥、智利等国）Chamber of Deputies

【众志成城】 zhòngzhì-chéngchéng〈成〉〈喻〉 unity is strength

种（種）zhòng

〈动〉 grow: ～树 plant trees ‖ ～庄稼 grow crops
▸Chóng, zhǒng

【种地】zhòngdì〈动〉 cultivate land for growing crops: 复员后他就回乡～了。 He returned to the countryside to work the land after being discharged from the military.

【种痘】 zhòngdòu〈动〉 be vaccinated against smallpox: 给小孩～ vaccinate children against smallpox

【种瓜得瓜，种豆得豆】 zhòng guā dé guā, zhòng dòu dé dòu〈俗〉〈喻〉 reap what one sows

【种花】zhònghuā〈动〉 grow flowers

【种牛痘】zhòng niúdòu = 种痘 zhòngdòu

【种田】zhòngtián〈动〉 work the land: ～人 farmer

【种植】zhòngzhí〈动〉 grow: ～玫瑰 grow roses

【种植园】 zhòngzhíyuán〈名〉 plantation: 花卉～ flower plantation

重 zhòng

A〈形〉**1**（重量大） heavy: 工作负担太～ have too heavy a work load ‖ 这箱子太～，我搬不动。 This box is too heavy for me to move. **2**（重要） important: 以国事为～ put national interest above everything else ‖ 以友谊为～ set store by friendship ▸～地, ～镇 **3**（程度深） serious: 伤势很～ be very seriously wounded ‖ 私心很～ be extremely selfish ▸恩～如山 **4**（不轻率） solemn: ▸隆～, 慎～ **5**（数量大） considerable in amount: ～金 a large sum of money
B〈名〉weight: ～达100吨 reach the weight of 100 tons ‖ 这块石头有多～? How much does this stone weigh? ▸净～, 失～
C〈动〉 attach importance to: ～调查研究 lay stress on investigation and research ▸器～
▸chóng

【重办】zhòngbàn〈动〉 punish severely

【重兵】zhòngbīng〈名〉 large number of troops: 有～把守 be heavily guarded ‖ ～压境。 A large number of forces are pressing on the border.

【重病】zhòngbìng〈名〉 serious illness

【重彩】zhòngcǎi〈名〉 rich colours: 浓墨～ elaborate and colourful descriptions

【重仓】 zhòngcāng〈动〉［金融］ hold (shares) in significant numbers: 基金～股 shares held in significant numbers by a fund

【重臣】zhòngchén〈名〉〈旧〉court minister holding a key post

【重创】 zhòngchuāng〈动〉 inflict heavy losses on: ～敌人 inflict heavy losses on the enemy ‖ 遭～ suffer heavy casualties

【重大】zhòngdà〈形〉 great: 具有～的现实意义 be of huge immediate significance ‖ 有～影响 have a big influence (on sb./sth.) ‖ ～伤亡 heavy casualties ‖ ～胜利 important victory ‖ ～损失 heavy losses ‖ ～问题 vital issue ‖ 责任～ the responsibility is great

【重担】 zhòngdàn〈名〉〈喻〉 heavy burden: 挑～ shoulder heavy burdens ‖ ～在肩 shoulder heavy responsibilities ‖ 千斤～ colossal responsibility

【重地】zhòngdì〈名〉 important place: 军事～ important military area ‖ 油库～，请勿吸烟。 Petrol station! No smoking!

【重点】zhòngdiǎn **A**〈名〉 emphasis: ～项目 key project ‖ 工作～ emphasis of the work ‖ 国家～工程 key state projects ‖ ～大学 key university **B**〈副〉 with the focus on: ～推广 make sth. the keystone of popularization ‖ 今天我们～探讨失业问题。 Today we're going to focus on the question of unemployment.

【重读】zhòngdú〈动〉 stress: 这个单词的最后一个音节应该～。 The last syllable of the word should be stressed.
▸chóngdú

【重犯】zhòngfàn〈名〉 major criminal

【重负】zhòngfù〈名〉 heavy burden: ▸如释～

【重工业】zhònggōngyè〈名〉 heavy industry: ～基地 heavy industrial base

【重话】zhònghuà〈名〉 harsh words

【重活儿】zhònghuór〈名〉heavy work: 干～ do heavy work

【重机枪】 zhòngjīqiāng〈名〉 heavy machine gun

【重价】zhòngjià〈名〉 high price: 不惜～ not baulk at exorbitant price ‖ ～购买 pay a high price

【重剑】zhòngjiàn〈名〉［体育］ épée: ～运动员 épée fencer

【重奖】 zhòngjiǎng **A**〈名〉 handsome reward **B**〈动〉 offer handsome rewards: ～有突出贡献的科技工作者 offer huge rewards to scientists and technicians who have made outstanding contributions

【重金】zhòngjīn〈名〉 huge sum of money: ～购买 pay a high price ‖ ～聘用 offer a high salary

【重金属】zhòngjīnshǔ〈名〉［化学］ heavy metal

【重力】zhònglì〈名〉 gravity

【重利】zhònglì **A**〈名〉**1**（指利息） high interest: ～盘剥 exploit people by lending money at usurious rates **2**（指利益） huge profit: 牟取～ seek excessive profits **B**〈动〉〈书〉 value material gains: ～轻义 place material gains above morality and justice

【重量】zhòngliàng ▸**p. 978**〈名〉 weight: ～相同 be equal in weight ‖ 总～ total weight

【重量级】zhòngliàngjí〈名〉［体育］heavyweight: ～举重选手 heavyweight ‖〈喻〉全国公认的～政治家 political heavyweight with national recognition

【重男轻女】zhòngnán-qīngnǚ〈成〉 regard men as superior to women

【重炮】zhòngpào〈名〉 heavy artillery

【重器】zhòngqì〈名〉〈书〉 **1**（指宝器） treasure **2**（指人才） great talent

【重任】 zhòngrèn〈名〉 important task: 身负～ be charged with important tasks ‖ 委以～ entrust sb. with important tasks

【重伤】zhòngshāng〈名〉 severe injury: 受～ be severely wounded

【重赏】 zhòngshǎng **A**〈名〉 handsome reward **B**〈动〉 offer ample rewards: ～有功人员 give handsome rewards to staff who have rendered great service

【重赏之下，必有勇夫】 zhòngshǎng zhī xià, bì yǒu yǒngfū〈成〉 when a high reward is offered, brave men are bound to come forward

【重视】zhòngshì〈动〉attach importance to: ～农业 attach great importance to agriculture ‖ ～群众的意见 set great store by the opinions of the masses ‖ 受到应有的～ receive the attention due

【重水】 zhòngshuǐ〈名〉［化学］ heavy water

【重听】zhòngtīng〈形〉 hard of hearing: 他有点～，你说话得大点声儿。 You have to raise your voice because he is a bit hard of hearing.

【重头】zhòngtóu **A**〈名〉 important part: 扫黄是我们近两个月工作的～。 We will focus on eliminating pornography in the next two months. **B**〈形〉 important: ～产品 important product ‖ ～项目 major project

【重头戏】zhòngtóuxì〈名〉**1**（指戏） traditional opera involving singing and action **2**〈喻〉（指任务或活动） important part: 节能减排是今年的～。 Saving energy and

Z

reducing emissions is this year's important task.

【重托】zhòngtuō〈名〉great trust: 不负～ live up to the great trust

【重望】zhòngwàng〈名〉**1**（指声望）good reputation: 身负～ enjoy great fame **2**（指期望）high hopes: 辜负某人的～ fall short of sb.'s great expectations

【重武器】zhòngwǔqì〈名〉heavy weaponry

【重孝】zhòngxiào〈名〉deep mourning: 戴～ be dressed in deep mourning

【重心】zhòngxīn〈名〉**1**［物理］centre of gravity **2**［数学］median point **3**（中心）heart: 把工作～转移到经济建设上来 shift the focus of one's work to economic growth

【重刑】zhòngxíng〈名〉severe punishment

【重型】zhòngxíng〈形〉heavy-duty: ～卡车 heavy-duty truck ‖ ～坦克 heavy tank

【重要】zhòngyào〈形〉important: 发挥～作用 play a vital role ‖ ～人物 important figure ‖ ～任务 vital task ‖ ～因素 key factor ‖ ～原则 cardinal principle ‖ 这件事对我们大家都很～。This matter is of great consequence to us all.

【重要性】zhòngyàoxìng〈名〉importance

【重音】zhòngyīn〈名〉**1**［语言］stress: 标～ accentuate ‖ 这个单词的～落在第一个音节上。The stress falls on the first syllable of this word. **2**［音乐］accent

【重用】zhòngyòng〈动〉put in an important position: ～有真才实学的人 put people of real ability and learning in important positions ‖ 他在公司一直受～。He has always been in key positions in his company.

【重油】zhòngyóu〈名〉heavy oil

【重于泰山】zhòngyú-Tàishān〈成〉〈喻〉be of great significance

【重元素】zhòngyuánsù〈名〉［化学］heavy element

【重灾区】zhòngzāiqū〈名〉worst-hit area

【重责】zhòngzé **A**〈名〉heavy responsibility **B**〈动〉severely criticize: 受到～ be severely criticized

【重镇】zhòngzhèn〈名〉place of strategic importance: 军事～ strategic post

【重资】zhòngzī〈名〉huge sum

【重子】zhòngzǐ〈名〉［物理］baryon

【重罪】zhòngzuì〈名〉［法律］felony

【重罪犯】zhòngzuìfàn〈名〉felon

zhōu

舟 zhōu〈名〉〈书〉boat: 泛～湖上 go boating on the lake ▸独木～, 龙～, 木已成～

【舟车】zhōuchē〈名〉〈书〉**1**（船和车）vessel and vehicle **2**（旅途）journey: ～

重量

■ 中国使用公制和市制，而英美国家使用公制及常衡。在英美国家，公制重量单位一般属官方系统；常衡的使用很广泛，可用于度量人的身高及体重、物品的重量等。

■ 常衡重量单位主要包括：

打兰	dram (dr)
盎司	ounce (oz)
磅	pound (lb)
英石	stone (st)
夸特	quarter
英担	hundredweight (cwt)
吨	ton
短吨（美吨）	short ton
长吨（英吨）	long ton

1 盎司 = 16 打兰
1 磅 = 16 盎司
1 英石 = 14 磅
1 夸特 = 2 英石
1 英担 = 8 英石
1 吨 = 20 英担
1 美吨 = 2,000 磅
1 英吨 = 2,240 磅

■ 公制重量单位主要包括：

1 公吨 tonne
= 1,000 公斤 / 千克

1 公斤 kilogram (kilo/kg)
= 1,000 克

1 克 gram (g)
= 1,000 毫克 milligrams (mg)

■ 市制重量单位主要有：

1 钱 qian
= 0.1 两
= 5 克

1 两 liang
= 10 钱
= 0.1 斤
= 50 克

1 斤 jin
= 10 两
= 500 克
= 0.5 公斤

■ 公制和常衡的换算：

1 盎司
= 28.35 克

1 磅
= 454 克

1 英石
= 6.356 公斤

1 夸特
= 12.7 公斤

1 英担
= 50.8 公斤（英国）
= 45.4 公斤（美国）

1 吨
= 1016.04 公斤

1 短吨（美吨）
= 0.907 公吨
= 907 公斤

1 长吨（英吨）
= 1.016 公吨
= 1,016 公斤

1 公吨
= 19.688 英担
= 2,204.6 磅

1 公斤
= 2.205 磅

■ 英语里，有些表示重量单位的词没有复数形式，如 hundredweight；有些表示复数时可加也可不加 s，如 stone 及 ton；有些表示复数时通常要加 s，如 pound、kilogram 及 ounce：

7 英担煤
= 7 hundredweight of coal

他体重是 6 英石
= He is six stone(s)

6 吨沙子
= 6 ton(s) of sand

3 磅红糖
= three pounds of brown sugar

5 公斤橘子
= 5 kilos of oranges

300 盎司胡椒粉
= 300 ounces of ground pepper

■ 英语的复合形容词里，表示重量单位的词不加 s：

一袋 30 公斤重的米
= a 30-kilo sack of rice

一个 20 磅重的箱子
= a 20-pound box

一个 8 盎司重的苹果
= an 8-ounce apple

■ 指人：

他体重是多少？
= What's his weight?

他有多重？
= How much does he weigh?

他重 11 英石
= He weighs 11 stone

他体重是 80 公斤
= His weight is 80 kilograms

新生儿重 6 磅 9 盎司
= The new born baby weighed 6 pounds 9 ounces

■ 指物：

这件包裹有多重？
= How heavy is the parcel?

这个箱子重多少？
= How much does the box weigh?

大约重 5 千克
= It weighs about 5 kilograms

刚好重 20 磅
= It is exactly 20 pounds

A 比 B 重
= A weighs more than B
或 A is heavier than B

A 比 B 轻
= A weighs less than B
= A is lighter than B

A 和 B 一样重
= A is as heavy as B
或 A is the same weight as B
或 A and B are the same weight

一盒两公斤重的饼干
= a box of biscuits 2 kilos in weight

苹果是按斤卖的
= Apples are sold by the jin

劳顿 be travel-worn
【舟楫】zhōují〈名〉〈书〉 vessel
【舟桥】zhōuqiáo〈名〉 pontoon bridge
【舟山群岛】 Zhōushān Qúndǎo 〈名〉 Zhoushan Archipelago [in Zhejiang Province]

州 zhōu 〈名〉 1（指古代行政区划） *zhou* [administrative division in former times] 2（在中国） autonomous prefecture: 苗族自治～ the Autonomous Prefecture of the Miao ethnic group 3（在美国） state;（在瑞士） canton: 纽约～ New York State
【州长】zhōuzhǎng〈名〉 governor

诌（謅） zhōu〈动〉make up: 胡～ make up wild tales

周[1] zhōu
A〈动〉 circle: ▸～旋
B〈形〉 1（全面） whole: ▸～身, ～游, 众所～知 2（周全） thorough: 考虑不～ not well thought through ▸～密, ～详
C〈名〉 circle: ▸～围, 四～
D〈量〉 circuit: 绕场一～ make a circuit of the arena ‖ 地球每年围绕太阳公转一～。 The earth makes one revolution round the sun each year.

周[2]**（週）** zhōu
A〈动〉 make a circuit: ▸～期, ～年
B ▸p. 836〈名〉 1（星期） week: 每～工作四十小时 work 40 hours a week ‖ 本/上/下～ this/last/next week ‖ 电影～ film week ▸～末 2（星期中某天） day of the week: ～一 Monday ‖ ～六 Saturday ‖ ～日 Sunday

周[3] zhōu〈动〉 relieve: ▸～济

周[4] Zhōu〈名〉 1（西周和东周） Zhou Dynasty 2（北周） Zhou Kingdom 3（由武则天建立） Zhou Kingdom 4（后周） Later Zhou Dynasty
【周报】zhōubào A〈名〉 weekly: 《北京～》 *Beijing Review* ‖ 《英语～》 *English Weekly* B〈动〉 report weekly: 疫情实行～制 carry out weekly reports of the epidemic
【周边】zhōubiān〈名〉 surrounding area: ～地区 neighbouring regions ‖ ～国家 neighbouring countries ‖ ～环境 neighbouring surroundings
【周长】zhōucháng〈名〉 circumference: 地球赤道的～ circumference of the earth at the equator
【周到】zhōudào〈形〉 attentive: 考虑得很～ with every detail considered ‖ 照顾得很～ take good care of sb.
【周而复始】 zhōu'érfùshǐ 〈成〉 move in cycles: 地球绕着太阳公转，～。The earth revolves around the sun periodically.
【周济】zhōujì〈动〉 relieve: ～穷人 help out the poor
【周刊】zhōukān〈名〉 weekly: 《新闻～》 *Newsweek*
【周密】zhōumì〈形〉 thorough: ～的计划 well-conceived plan ‖ ～思考 think over carefully ‖ 部署很～。 The deployment is meticulous.
【周末】zhōumò ▸p. 836〈名〉 weekend: 度～ spend a weekend ‖ ～夫妻 weekend couple
【周年】zhōunián〈名〉 anniversary: 庆祝中华人民共和国成立60～ celebrate the sixtieth anniversary of the founding of the People's Republic of China
【周期】zhōuqī〈名〉 1（重复一次） cycle: 地球自转～ period of the earth's rotation 2（重复一次的时间） period: 设备更新～ cycle for updating equipment ‖ ～性通货膨胀 cyclical inflation 3［化学］ classification of elements [as in the periodic table]: 元素～表 periodic table of elements
【周全】zhōuquán A〈形〉 comprehensive: 计划要订得～些 make your plan as comprehensive as possible B〈动〉 assist: ～好事 help bring about a good event
【周身】zhōushēn〈名〉 whole body: ～都淋湿了 be wet through ‖ ～发热 feel hot all over
【周岁】zhōusuì〈名〉 one full year of life: 今天我女儿满～。 Today is my daughter's first birthday.
【周围】 zhōuwéi 〈名〉 all-round environment: 关心～的群众 have concern for the people around ‖ ～环境 surroundings
【周详】zhōuxiáng 〈形〉 detailed: 他考虑得十分～。 He took every tiny detail into consideration.
【周恤】 zhōuxù 〈动〉〈书〉 sympathize (with) and help
【周旋】zhōuxuán 〈动〉 1（盘旋） circle round: 飞机在空中～。 The plane circled in the air. 2（应酬） mix with: 成天跟人～真烦人。 It's awfully boring to have to mix with people day in, day out. 3（较量） deal with: 和敌人～到底 manage to completely outwit the enemy
【周延】zhōuyán〈名〉［逻辑］ distribution
【周游】zhōuyóu〈动〉 travel around: ～世界 travel the world
【周缘】zhōuyuán〈名〉〈书〉 periphery
【周遭】zhōuzāo〈名〉 surrounding area: ～静悄悄的，没有一个人。 All around was soundless and there was nobody in sight.
【周章】zhōuzhāng〈书〉 A〈形〉 frightened: ～失措 be scared out of one's wits B〈名〉 trouble: 煞费～ take great pains
【周折】zhōuzhé〈名〉 twists and turns: 几经～ after many setbacks ‖ 煞费～做某事 take a lot of trouble to do sth.
【周至】zhōuzhì〈形〉〈书〉 considerate: 叮咛～ give considerate advice
【周转】 zhōuzhuǎn 〈动〉 1（指资金） turn over: 加速资金～ speed up the capital turnover 2（指开支、调度或物品） have enough to meet needs: ～不开 not be enough to go round

洲 zhōu 〈名〉 1（大洲） continent: ▸非～, 亚～ 2（小块陆地） islet in a river: 长江三角～ Yangtze River Delta ▸绿～, 沙～
【洲际】 zhōujì〈形〉 intercontinental: ～旅行 intercontinental travel ‖ 加强～合作 strengthen intercontinental cooperation
【洲际弹道导弹】 zhōujì dàndào dǎodàn〈名〉 intercontinental ballistic missile
【洲际导弹】zhōujì dǎodàn〈名〉 intercontinental missile

挏 zhōu〈动〉〈方〉 lift a heavy object from one side or one end: 把桌子～过来 turn a table upside down

啁 zhōu
▸zhāo
【啁啾】 zhōujiū〈拟〉〈书〉 twitter: 乳雀～。 Little birds chatter.

粥 zhōu〈名〉congee: 小米～ millet gruel ▸八宝～
▸yù
【粥少僧多】 zhōushǎo-sēngduō 〈成〉〈喻〉 not enough to go round

zhóu

妯 zhóu
【妯娌】zhóuli〈名〉 sisters-in-law: 她们俩是～。 They two are sisters-in-law.

轴（軸） zhóu
A〈名〉 1（指车轴） axle: 自行车～该换了。 The axles of the bike should be replaced. 2（轴状物） axle-shaped thing: ▸曲～ 3（指轴线） axis: 地～ earth's axis 4（用于绕或卷的器物） roller: ▸画～
B〈量〉 [used for rolled-up things]: 一～山水画 a scroll painting depicting landscape ‖ 一～线 a spool of thread
▸zhòu
【轴承】 zhóuchéng 〈名〉 bearing: 滚动～ rolling bearing
【轴瓦】zhóuwǎ〈名〉［机械］ axle bush
【轴线】 zhóuxiàn 〈名〉 1（指对分直线） axis: 垂直～ normal axis ‖ 圆柱体～ axis of a cylinder 2［纺织］ spool thread
【轴心】 zhóuxīn 〈名〉 1［机械］ axle centre 2〈喻〉（中心） pivot: 旅游业是本地区的～。 Tourist industry lies at the hub of this region.
【轴心国】 Zhóuxīnguó 〈名〉 Axis Powers [Germany, Italy and Japan during World War II]
【轴子】 zhóuzi 〈名〉 1（指字画下端） roller (for a scroll of calligraphy or painting) 2（指乐器上） turning peg

zhǒu

肘 zhǒu〈名〉1（指人体肘关节）elbow: 双～支撑在桌子上 rest one's elbows on the table ‖ ～关节 elbow joint ▸～窝, 捉襟见～ 2（指猪腿上部） upper part of a leg of pork: ▸～子
【肘窝】zhǒuwō〈名〉 crook of the arm
【肘腋】zhǒuyè〈名〉〈书〉1（肘关节和腋窝） elbow and armpit 2〈喻〉（极近的地方） close at hand: ～之患 trouble coming from those closest to one
【肘子】 zhǒuzi 〈名〉 1（指猪腿上部） upper part of a leg of pork 2（指人体肘关节） elbow

帚（箒） zhǒu〈名〉 broom: ▸敝～自珍, 扫～, 笤～

zhòu

纣[1]**（紂）** zhòu〈名〉crupper [strap at the back of a saddle that passes under the horse's tail to prevent the saddle from slipping forwards]: ▸～棍

纣[2]**（紂）** Zhòu〈名〉 name of the last ruler of the Shang Dynasty
【纣棍】zhòugùn〈名〉 wood crupper

㑇（㑳） zhòu〈形〉 [usu used in early vernacular] handsome

咒 zhòu
A〈动〉 curse: 你别～我。 Don't curse me. ▸～骂

Z

B〈名〉magic words: 念～ chant incantations
【咒骂】zhòumà〈动〉curse: 低声～ mutter curses
【咒语】zhòuyǔ〈名〉magic words: 念～ chant incantations

㤘（㑇） zhòu〈形〉〈方〉obstinate: ～脾气 obstinacy ‖ 这老太太脾气太～。This old woman is too stubborn.

宙 zhòu〈名〉**1**（指时间）time: ▸宇～ **2**［地质］aeon

绉（縐） zhòu〈名〉crêpe: 双～ crêpe de Chine
【绉布】zhòubù〈名〉cotton crêpe
【绉绸】zhòuchóu〈名〉crêpe
【绉纱】zhòushā〈名〉crêpe
【绉纸】zhòuzhǐ〈名〉crêpe paper

轴（軸） zhòu ▸压轴 yāzhòu ▸zhóu

葤（葤） zhòu〈方〉
A〈动〉wrap with straw
B〈量〉bundle tied with straw

胄 zhòu〈名〉〈古〉**1**（指人）descendants of feudal rulers or aristocrats: 贵～ descendant of feudal rulers or aristocrats **2**（指物）helmet: 甲～ armour and helmet

昼（晝） zhòu〈名〉daytime: ～伏夜出 hide by day and come out at night ‖ 夏天～长夜短。In summer the days are long and the nights are short. ▸～夜, 白～
【昼夜】zhòuyè〈名〉day and night: ～不停地工作 work round the clock

酎 zhòu〈名〉〈书〉double-fermented wine

皱（皺） zhòu
A〈名〉**1**（指人）wrinkle: ▸～纹 **2**（指物）crease
B〈动〉crease: 眉头一～，计上心来 knitting one's brows, come up with a good plan ‖ 这种料子不会～的。This material won't crease.
【皱巴巴】zhòubābā〈形〉creased: ～的瘦脸 thin, wrinkled face ‖ ～的衣服 crumpled dress
【皱痕】zhòuhén〈名〉fold: 熨平衣服上的～ iron out the creases in one's dress
【皱胃】zhòuwèi〈名〉［动物］abomasum
【皱纹】zhòuwén〈名〉wrinkle: 满脸～ wrinkly face ‖ 眼角～ crow's feet

骤（驟） zhòu
A〈动〉〈书〉trot: 驰～ gallop
B〈形〉speedy: ▸暴风～雨, 急～
C〈副〉suddenly: 狂风～起。A sudden gale swept past. ‖ 天气～变。The weather changed suddenly.
【骤然】zhòurán〈副〉suddenly: 温度～下降。The temperature dropped suddenly.

籀 zhòu〈书〉
A = 籀文 zhòuwén
B〈动〉read
【籀文】zhòuwén ▸**p. 918**〈名〉［书法］seal script [current in the Zhou Dynasty]

zhū

朱[1] zhū ▸**p. 863**〈形〉scarlet: ▸～笔, 近～者赤，近墨者黑

朱[2]**（硃）** zhū〈名〉vermilion
【朱笔】zhūbǐ〈名〉〈旧〉writing brush dipped in red ink [used for marking students' papers or writing comments on official documents]
【朱古力】zhūgǔlì = 巧克力 qiǎokèlì
【朱红】zhūhóng ▸**p. 863**〈形〉vermilion: ～大门 vermilion gate
【朱鹮】zhūhuán〈名〉［鸟类］red ibis
【朱槿】zhūjǐn〈名〉［植物］Chinese hibiscus
【朱门】zhūmén〈名〉wealthy family: ～酒肉臭，路有冻死骨。The portals of the rich reeked of wasted meat and wine while the skeletons of the frozen poor lay by the roadside.
【朱墨】zhūmò〈名〉**1** ▸**p. 863**（红色和黑色）red and black: ～加批 comments written in red and black ‖ ～套印 printed in red and black **2**（墨）cinnabar stick
【朱批】zhūpī〈名〉comments written in red
【朱漆】zhūqī〈名〉red paint: ～大门 vermilion gates ‖ ～家具 red-lacquered furniture
【朱雀】zhūquè〈名〉**1**（指鸟）rosefinch **2**（指星宿）Scarlet Bird [name for the seven southern mansions of the 28 constellations in ancient Chinese astronomy] **3**（指神）[of Taoism] Southern God
【朱砂】zhūshā〈名〉cinnabar
【朱文】zhūwén〈名〉characters on a seal carved in relief

侏 zhū
【侏罗纪】Zhūluójì〈名〉［地质］Jurassic Period
【侏儒】zhūrú〈名〉dwarf

诛（誅） zhū〈动〉〈书〉**1**（遣责处罚）denounce: ▸口～笔伐 **2**（杀）kill: ▸～戮
【诛戮】zhūlù〈动〉〈书〉kill: ～忠良 slaughter the loyal and upright
【诛求】zhūqiú〈动〉〈书〉extort: ～无厌 be insatiably avaricious
【诛杀】zhūshā〈动〉〈书〉kill
【诛心之论】zhūxīnzhīlùn〈成〉penetrating criticism

茱 zhū
【茱萸】zhūyú〈名〉cornel

珠 zhū〈名〉**1**（珠子）pearl: ▸～宝, ～联璧合 **2**（小球状物）bead: ▸泪～
【珠宝】zhūbǎo〈名〉jewellery: 满身～ resplendent with jewels
【珠宝店】zhūbǎodiàn〈名〉jeweller's (shop)
【珠宝商】zhūbǎoshāng〈名〉jeweller
【珠翠】zhūcuì〈名〉**1**（珍珠翠玉）pearls and jade **2**（饰品）ornaments made with pearls and jade
【珠光宝气】zhūguāng-bǎoqì〈成〉be dripping with jewels: 一身～ be decked out with jewels
【珠光漆】zhūguāngqī〈名〉pearlescent lacquer
【珠玑】zhūjī〈名〉〈书〉**1**（珍珠）jewel **2**〈喻〉（指诗文词句）exquisite or excellent wording of a piece of writing: 字字～ exquisitely worded piece of writing
【珠江】Zhūjiāng ▸**p. 294**〈名〉Pearl River: ～三角洲 Pearl River Delta [in Guangdong Province]
【珠帘】zhūlián〈名〉bead curtain
【珠联璧合】zhūlián-bìhé〈成〉an excellent combination: 你是服装设计师，她是模特，你们俩真是～。You're a clothes designer and she's a model. You'll make an excellent pair.
【珠母】zhūmǔ〈名〉mother-of-pearl
【珠穆朗玛峰】Zhūmùlǎngmǎfēng〈名〉Mount Everest [Mount Qomolangma]
【珠算】zhūsuàn〈名〉counting with an abacus
【珠圆玉润】zhūyuán-yùrùn〈成〉（指唱歌）excellent;（指写作）polished
【珠子】zhūzi〈名〉**1**（珍珠）pearl **2**（小球状物）bead: 算盘～ beads on an abacus

株 zhū
A〈名〉**1**（桩子）stump: ▸守～待兔 **2**（植株）plant: 幼～ seedling ▸～距, 植～
B〈量〉[used for plants or trees]: 两～梨树 two pear trees
【株距】zhūjù〈名〉［农业］spacing between rows
【株连】zhūlián〈动〉incriminate: ～九族 implicate all of one's close relatives
【株式会社】zhūshì huìshè〈名〉limited-liability company [in Japan]
【株守】zhūshǒu〈动〉〈书〉cling stubbornly to: ～陈规陋习 cling to old habits and customs

诸（諸） zhū〈代〉**1**（所有）all: ▸～如此类, ～子百家 **2**（每一）every: 她生活上～事顺遂。Everything in her life goes smoothly. ▸～位 **3**〈书〉（之于）[fusing of 之于 (zhīyú)]: 付～实践 put in practice
【诸多】zhūduō〈形〉〈书〉[used before abstract nouns] plenty: 造成～不便 cause quite a lot of inconvenience
【诸葛亮】Zhūgě Liàng〈名〉**1**（指三国人物）Zhuge Liang [181-234, statesman and strategist in the Three Kingdoms period, now a symbol of wisdom in Chinese folklore] **2**（指足智多谋的人）mastermind
【诸公】zhūgōng〈名〉〈书〉〈敬〉[used in addressing a group of men] gentlemen: ～以为如何？What do you gentlemen think about it?
【诸宫调】zhūgōngdiào〈名〉*zhugong* ballad [popular in the Song, Jin and Yuan dynasties]
【诸侯】zhūhóu〈名〉dukes or princes under an emperor
【诸亲好友】zhūqīn-hǎoyǒu〈成〉relatives and friends
【诸如】zhūrú〈动〉〈书〉for example: 她有很多工具书，～词典、百科全书和手册等。She has many reference books, such as dictionaries, encyclopedias and handbooks.
【诸如此类】zhūrúcǐlèi〈成〉and such like: ～的例子很多。There are numerous such cases.
【诸位】zhūwèi〈代〉[used in addressing a group of people] ladies and gentlemen: ～女士，～先生! Ladies and Gentlemen! ‖ 在座的～都是心理学专家。All of you here are experts in psychology.
【诸子百家】zhūzǐ-bǎijiā〈名〉various schools of thought and their exponents

during the period from pre-Qin times to the early Han Dynasty

铢（銖） zhū〈名〉〈古〉*zhu* [unit of weight, equal to 1/24 *liang*]: ▸锱～必较

【铢积寸累】zhūjī-cùnlěi〈成〉accumulate bit by bit

【铢两悉称】zhūliǎng-xīchèn〈成〉be exactly equal in weight or quality

猪（豬） zhū〈名〉pig: 养～专业户 household specialized in raising pigs

【猪八戒】Zhūbājiè〈名〉Pigsy [one of the main characters in the novel *Journey to the West*（《西游记》）by Wu Cheng'en]

【猪八戒倒打一耙】Zhūbājiè dào dǎ yī pá〈俗〉make a countercharge

【猪肚】zhūdǔ〈名〉pork tripe

【猪肝】zhūgān〈名〉pork liver: ～色 purplish red

【猪倌】zhūguān〈名〉〈旧〉swineherd

【猪獾】zhūhuān〈名〉［动物］hog badger

【猪圈】zhūjuàn〈名〉pigsty

【猪流感】zhūliúgǎn〈名〉swine flu

【猪笼草】zhūlóngcǎo〈名〉［植物］common nepenthes

【猪猡】zhūluó〈名〉〈方〉pig

【猪苗】zhūmiáo〈名〉piglet

【猪排】zhūpái〈名〉pork chop: 炸～ pork cutlet

【猪肉】zhūròu〈名〉pork

【猪舍】zhūshè〈名〉pigpen

【猪食】zhūshí〈名〉pigswill

【猪蹄】zhūtí〈名〉pig's trotter

【猪娃】zhūwá〈名〉〈方〉piglet

【猪瘟】zhūwēn〈名〉swine fever

【猪血】zhūxiě〈名〉coagulated pig's blood [used as food]

【猪油】zhūyóu〈名〉lard

【猪肘子】zhūzhǒuzi〈名〉pig's knuckles

【猪鬃】zhūzōng〈名〉hog bristles

蛛 zhū〈名〉spider: ▸蜘～

【蛛丝马迹】zhūsī-mǎjì〈成〉〈喻〉clues: 不露～ not disclose any traces

【蛛网】zhūwǎng〈名〉cobweb

潴（瀦） zhū〈书〉

A〈动〉[of water] collect: ～积 [of water] collect

B〈名〉puddle

【潴留】zhūliú ▸**p. 50**〈动〉［医学］retain: 尿～ urine retention

槠 zhū〈名〉〈书〉wooden stake used to tether a domestic animal

zhú

术 zhú ▸白术 báizhú, ▸苍术 cāngzhú ▸shù

竹 zhú〈名〉**1**（指植物）bamboo: ～林 bamboo forest **2**（指乐器）musical instrument made of bamboo [such as the pipe, the flute, etc.]: ▸丝～

【竹板】zhúbǎn〈名〉bamboo clappers: 打～ play bamboo clappers

【竹板书】zhúbǎnshū〈名〉ballad recited to the rhythm of bamboo clappers

【竹箅子】zhúbìzi〈名〉bamboo grid [used when steaming food]

【竹编】zhúbiān〈名〉bamboo woven articles

【竹帛】zhúbó〈名〉bamboo slips and silk [used for writing on during ancient times]: 功垂～ be recorded in history in letters of gold

【竹材】zhúcái〈名〉bamboo: 利用～代替木材。Bamboo is used instead of wood.

【竹雕】zhúdiāo〈名〉**1**（指工艺）bamboo carving **2**（指工艺品）carved bamboo article

【竹筏】zhúfá〈名〉bamboo raft

【竹竿】zhúgān〈名〉bamboo pole

【竹杠】zhúgàng〈名〉thick bamboo pole: ▸敲～

【竹黄】zhúhuáng〈名〉**1**（指工艺品）handicraft articles made from bamboo with its green skin removed **2**［中药］tabasheer

【竹简】zhújiǎn〈名〉bamboo slip [used for writing]

> **竹简**
>
> Before paper was widely used in China, texts were written on bamboo or wooden slips. A number of slips were bound together to form a volume. Such slips were widely used in the Eastern Zhou and Wei-Jin periods. The oldest slips discovered date from the Warring States period. Before use, the slips were baked in order to prevent rot and damage from insects. Moisture would seep out during this process, hence the expression '*hanqing*'（汗青, 'sweating green bamboo'), which was later used to mean 'historical records'.

【竹节虫】zhújiéchóng〈名〉stick insect

【竹刻】zhúkè〈名〉bamboo carving

【竹篮打水一场空】zhúlán dǎshuǐ yīchángkōng〈俗〉〈喻〉be all in vain

【竹笠】zhúlì〈名〉bamboo hat [with a conical crown and broad brim]

【竹帘】zhúlián〈名〉bamboo curtain

【竹林】zhúlín〈名〉bamboo forest

【竹笼】zhúlóng〈名〉bamboo cage

【竹楼】zhúlóu〈名〉bamboo house [of the Dai people in Yunnan Province]

【竹篓】zhúlǒu〈名〉bamboo basket

【竹马】zhúmǎ〈名〉bamboo horse: ▸青梅～

【竹篾】zhúmiè〈名〉thin bamboo strips [used for weaving]

【竹幕】zhúmù〈名〉bamboo curtain

【竹排】zhúpái〈名〉bamboo raft

【竹器】zhúqì〈名〉bamboo articles: ～店 shop selling bamboo articles

【竹笋】zhúsǔn〈名〉bamboo shoots

【竹筒】zhútǒng〈名〉thick bamboo tube

【竹筒倒豆子】zhútǒng dào dòuzi〈俗〉〈喻〉hold nothing back

【竹席】zhúxí〈名〉bamboo mat

【竹叶青】zhúyèqīng〈名〉**1**（指蛇）poisonous green bamboo snake **2**（指汾酒）bamboo-leaf-green liqueur [a medicinal liquor] **3**（指绍兴酒）bamboo-leaf-green wine [a light yellow *Shaoxing*（绍兴）wine]

【竹椅】zhúyǐ〈名〉bamboo chair

【竹芋】zhúyù〈名〉［植物］arrowroot

【竹枝词】zhúzhīcí〈名〉ancient folk songs of four seven-character lines

【竹子】zhúzi〈名〉bamboo

竺 Zhú ▸天竺 Tiānzhú

逐 zhú

A〈动〉**1**（追逐）pursue: ～水草而居 migrate to wherever there is water and grass ▸随波～流 **2**（驱逐）drive out: ～出门外 drive sb. out of the door ‖ 被～出境 be expelled from a country ▸～客令, 放～

B〈介〉one by one: ～条说明 explain item by item ‖ ～字～句地讲解课文 explain the text sentence by sentence ▸～步, ～个

【逐步】zhúbù〈副〉gradually: ～加以解决 settle sth. step by step ‖ ～降低生产成本 gradually bring down production costs ‖ 病人的病情～好转。There is a gradual improvement in the patient's condition.

【逐个】zhúgè〈副〉one by one: ～检查产品的质量 examine the quality of the products one by one ‖ ～介绍来宾 introduce the guests one by one

【逐户】zhúhù〈副〉house-to-house: ～调查 make door-to-door enquiries

【逐渐】zhújiàn〈副〉gradually: ～消失 gradually disappear ‖ 他的健康状况～好转。His health steadily improved.

【逐客令】zhúkèlìng〈名〉order for a guest to leave: 下～ show sb. the door

【逐鹿】zhúlù〈书〉〈喻〉**1**（争夺天下）fight for the throne **2**（争夺胜利）compete for a championship: 亚洲足球队～绿茵场，争夺亚洲杯。Asian football teams are competing for the Asian Cup.

【逐年】zhúnián〈副〉year on year: ～减少外贸逆差 reduce the deficit in foreign trade year on year ‖ 物价～上涨。Prices rose year by year.

【逐日】zhúrì〈副〉day by day: 她的病情～好转。She is getting better every day. ‖ 废品率～下降。The reject rate is going down every day.

【逐一】zhúyī〈副〉one by one: 请～回答这几个问题。Please answer these questions one by one.

【逐字】zhúzì〈副〉word by word: ～翻译 word by word translation ‖ ～研读文件 study a document sentence by sentence

烛（燭） zhú

A〈名〉**1**（蜡烛）candle: 风中之～ [candle in the wind] person too old to live long ▸～光, 洞房花～ **2**（瓦特）watt: 60～的灯泡 60-watt bulb

B〈动〉〈书〉illuminate: 洞～其奸 see through an evil intent ‖ 火光～天。The flames lit up the sky.

【烛光】zhúguāng〈名〉candlelight

【烛花】zhúhuā〈名〉snuff: 剪～ trim off the snuff of a candle

【烛泪】zhúlèi〈名〉guttering of a candle

【烛台】zhútái〈名〉candlestick

【烛照】zhúzhào〈动〉〈书〉illuminate: 阳光～万物。The sun illuminates everything on the earth.

舳 zhú〈名〉stern of a ship

【舳舻】zhúlú〈名〉〈书〉fleet of ships: ～相继。The ships sail so close to each other that the stem of one touches the stern of another.

瘃 zhú〈名〉〈书〉chilblain: 手足皲～。There are chilblains on both hands and feet.

蠋 zhú〈名〉〈书〉larva

躅 zhú ▸踯躅 zhízhú

zhǔ

主 zhǔ

A〈名〉**1**（所有者） owner: ▸车～, 物归原～ **2**（主人） master: ～仆 master and servant ▸～子, 雇～ **3**（接待客人的人） host: 宾～ guest and host ▸喧宾夺～, 东道～ **4**（当事方） person or party concerned: ▸买～, 事～ **5**［基督教］ Lord: 求～保佑! God bless (you)! **6**［伊斯兰教］ Allah **7**（牌位） memorial tablet: ▸神～
B〈动〉**1**（主持） manage: ▸～编, ～讲 **2**（主张） advocate: ～和 advocate peace ‖ ～战 advocate war **3**（有主见） hold a definite view: 心里没～ have no idea ▸～意, 六神无～ **4**（预示） indicate: 早霞～雨, 晚霞～晴。 Red sky at night is the shepherd's delight; red sky in the morning is the shepherd's warning.
C〈形〉**1**（自身） independent: ▸～动, ～观 **2**（主要） main: ▸～力, ～次

【主板】zhǔbǎn〈名〉［计算机］ motherboard

【主板市场】zhǔbǎn shìchǎng〈名〉 main board of the stock market [stock exchange market that plays a leading role in a nation's securities market system]

【主办】zhǔbàn〈动〉 host: ～奥运会 host the Olympic Games ‖ ～单位 sponsor

【主笔】zhǔbǐ **A**〈名〉 **1**（指编辑人） editor in chief **2**（指撰稿人） chief commentator **B**〈动〉 act as main writer: 这篇文章由你～。 You are to take editorial responsibility for this article.

【主币】zhǔbì〈名〉 main currency

【主编】zhǔbiān **A**〈名〉 chief editor **B**〈动〉 supervise the publication of: ～一本书 act as the chief compiler of a book

【主宾】zhǔbīn〈名〉 guest of honour

【主宾国】zhǔbīnguó〈名〉 guest-of-honour country: 以～身份参加法兰克福书展 be the guest of honour at the Frankfurt Book Fair

【主宾席】zhǔbīnxí〈名〉 head table

【主播】zhǔbō〈名〉 anchor: 财经频道～ CNBC anchor

【主产区】zhǔchǎnqū〈名〉 main production area: 小麦/棉花～ major wheat/cotton producing area

【主场】zhǔchǎng〈名〉 home ground: ～优势 home advantage

【主城】zhǔchéng〈名〉 city centre〈英〉; downtown〈美〉: ～将不再增加工业用地。 New industrial zones will no longer be located in the city centre.

【主持】zhǔchí〈动〉 **1**（负责掌管） preside over: ～日常事务 take charge of the day-to-day affairs ‖ ～会议 chair a meeting ‖ ～电视节目 host a TV programme **2**（主张） uphold: ～正义 uphold justice ‖ ～公道 uphold justice

【主持人】zhǔchírén〈名〉 **1**（指节目、活动或聚会） host; compère〈英〉; emcee〈美〉: 电视节目～ TV presenter **2**（指会议等） chairperson

【主创】zhǔchuàng〈动〉 hold the key creative role: 电视剧的～人员 the key creative role in TV dramas

【主词】zhǔcí〈名〉［逻辑］ subject

【主次】zhǔcì〈名〉 major and minor: 分清～ know what is important and what is not

【主从】zhǔcóng〈名〉 principal and subordinate: ～关系 relationship between the principal and the subordinate ‖ ～复合句 complex sentence

【主打】zhǔdǎ〈形〉 leading: ～产品 major product ‖ ～戏 leading drama

【主打歌】zhǔdǎgē〈名〉 title track: 本专辑的～ the album's title track

【主刀】zhǔdāo〈动〉 be the chief surgeon: 今天李医生亲自～。 Doctor Li is going to act as the chief surgeon today.

【主导】zhǔdǎo **A**〈形〉 leading: 起～作用 play a leading role ‖ ～思想 guiding ideology **B**〈名〉 leading factor: 工业是国民经济的～。 Industry is the leading factor in the national economy.

【主调】zhǔdiào〈名〉 keynote

【主动】zhǔdòng〈形〉 **1**（自发自觉） on one's own initiative: ～要求执行危险任务 volunteer for a dangerous mission ‖ 她～提出开车送我去机场。 She offered to drive me to the airport. **2**（有利） having the initiative: 处于～地位 be in an advantageous position ‖ 争取～ try to gain the initiative

【主动脉】zhǔdòngmài〈名〉［解剖］ aorta: ～硬化 aortosclerosis

【主动权】zhǔdòngquán〈名〉 initiative: 赢得～ win the initiative ‖ 掌握～ have the initiative

【主动语态】zhǔdòng yǔtài〈名〉［语言］ active voice

【主队】zhǔduì〈名〉［体育］ home team

【主伐】zhǔfá〈名〉［林业］ final felling

【主罚】zhǔfá〈动〉 take the penalties: 由他～点球。 He took the penalty kick.

【主犯】zhǔfàn〈名〉［法律］ principal offender: ～和从犯 principal offenders and their accomplices

【主峰】zhǔfēng〈名〉 highest peak

【主妇】zhǔfù〈名〉 housewife: 家庭～ housewife

【主干】zhǔgàn〈名〉 **1**（指植物主茎） trunk: 树的～ trunk of a tree **2**（指事物主体） mainstay: 年轻人是课题组的～。 Young people are the backbone of the research group.

【主稿】zhǔgǎo〈动〉 be the chief writer (of a joint work)

【主格】zhǔgé〈名〉［语言］ nominative case

【主根】zhǔgēn〈名〉 **1**［植物］ main root **2**［数学］ principal root

【主公】zhǔgōng〈名〉〈旧〉[used in addressing a ruler] Your Majesty

【主攻】zhǔgōng〈动〉 **1**［军事］ launch a major offensive: ～部队 main attack force ‖ ～方向 main direction of attack **2**（主要研究） specialize in: 在大学～生物化学 major in biochemistry in university

【主攻手】zhǔgōngshǒu〈名〉［排球］ ace spiker

【主顾】zhǔgù〈名〉 patron: 招徕～ solicit customers ‖ 老～ regular

【主观】zhǔguān〈形〉 subjective: ～臆断 pure conjecture ‖ ～愿望 wishful thinking

【主观能动性】zhǔguān néngdòngxìng〈名〉［哲学］ subjective initiative: 充分发挥～ bring one's initiative into full play

【主观唯心主义】zhǔguān wéixīn zhǔyì〈名〉［哲学］ subjective idealism

【主观性】zhǔguānxìng〈名〉 subjectivity

【主观主义】zhǔguān zhǔyì〈名〉［哲学］ subjectivism: ～者 subjectivist

【主管】zhǔguǎn **A**〈动〉 be responsible for: ～财务 manage the finances ‖ ～部门 department responsible for the work ‖ ～外事的副市长 vice-mayor in charge of external relations **B**〈名〉 person in charge: 她是这项工程的～。 She is the person in charge of the project.

【主婚】zhǔhūn〈动〉 officiate at a wedding: ～人 master of a wedding ceremony

【主机】zhǔjī〈名〉 **1**［机械］ main engine **2**［军事］ lead plane **3**［计算机］ host computer

【主基调】zhǔjīdiào〈名〉 key tone: 期货市场以宽幅震荡为～。 The futures market is characterized by violent fluctuations. ‖ 稳定、完善和落实政策，是今年宏观调控的～。 Stability, maturity, and policing are the keynotes of this year's macro-economic regulation.

【主祭】zhǔjì〈动〉 officiate at funeral or sacrificial rites

【主见】zhǔjiàn〈名〉 ideas of one's own: 没有～ have no definite views of one's own ‖ 有～ know one's own mind

【主讲】zhǔjiǎng〈动〉 give a lecture: ～语言学 give lectures on linguistics

【主将】zhǔjiàng〈名〉 **1**［军事］ chief commander **2**〈喻〉（主要人物） leading figure

【主叫】zhǔjiào〈名〉［通信］ caller

【主教】zhǔjiào〈名〉 bishop

【主句】zhǔjù〈名〉［语言］ main clause

【主角】zhǔjué〈名〉 **1**（指演员） main part: 男/女～ male/female lead ‖ 在影片中演～ play the lead in the film **2**〈喻〉（主要人物） leading role: 几个研究生是研究所的～。 A number of postgraduates have key roles in the research institute.

【主考】zhǔkǎo **A**〈动〉 officiate at an examination **B**〈名〉 chief examiner

【主客场】zhǔkèchǎng〈名〉 home and away matches: 比赛采用～制。 The competition involves games being played both home and away.

【主课】zhǔkè〈名〉 major course

【主力】zhǔlì〈名〉 main force: ～部队 principal force ‖ ～队员 leading player

【主力舰】zhǔlìjiàn〈名〉 battleship

【主力军】zhǔlìjūn〈名〉 principal force

【主粮】zhǔliáng〈名〉 staple food grain

【主流】zhǔliú〈名〉 **1**（指河流） trunk stream: 河流的～和支流 mainstream and tributaries of a river **2**〈喻〉（指主要趋势） main trend: ～和支流 principal and secondary trends ‖ 政治思潮的～ mainstream of political thought

【主楼】zhǔlóu〈名〉 main building: 校园的～ main building on campus

【主麻】zhǔmá〈名〉［伊斯兰教］ Jumu'ah

【主谋】zhǔmóu **A**〈动〉 mastermind **B**〈名〉［法律］ chief instigator

【主脑】zhǔnǎo〈名〉 **1**（核心部分） centre of operations **2**（首领） chief

【主拍】zhǔpāi **A**〈动〉 **1**（主持拍卖） preside over an auction: 操槌～ preside over an auction, hammer in hand **2**（主持拍摄） direct filming: 该片由年轻导演～。 This film was directed by a young director. **B**〈名〉 auctioneer: ～已经到场。 The auctioneer has arrived.

【主渠道】zhǔqúdào〈名〉〈喻〉 main channel: 民营企业成了就业的～。 Privately-run enterprises have become main channels of employment.

【主权】zhǔquán〈名〉 sovereignty: 侵犯/尊重～ violate/respect the sovereignty ‖ 行使～ exercise sovereignty

【主儿】zhǔr〈名〉〈口〉 **1**（主人） master **2**（某种类型的人） person of a specified type: 爱管闲事的～ interfering busybody **3**（婆家） husband's family: 有～了 be engaged

【主人】zhǔrén〈名〉 **1**（接待客人者） host: 女～ hostess **2**〈旧〉（雇人者） master: 女～ mistress **3**（指所有者）

owner: 房子的～ owner of the house ‖ 国家的～ masters of the country
【主人公】zhǔréngōng〈名〉 main protagonist
【主人翁】zhǔrénwēng〈名〉 1（当家作主的人） master: 人民是国家的～。 The people are the masters of the country. 2 = 主人公 zhǔréngōng
【主任】zhǔrèn〈名〉 director: 办公室～ head of an office ‖ 车间～ director of a workshop ‖ 教研室～ chief of teaching and research section
【主任医师】zhǔrèn yīshī〈名〉 chief physician
【主日】zhǔrì〈名〉 Lord's Day, Sunday: ～学校 Sunday school
【主食】zhǔshí〈名〉 staple food
【主使】zhǔshǐ〈动〉 incite: 受人～ be incited
【主事】zhǔshì〈动〉 be in charge: 他家里有老婆～。 His wife wears the trousers in the family. ‖ 家有千口，～一人。 Even though it's a big family, there is only one person who has final say.
【主帅】zhǔshuài = 主将 zhǔjiàng
【主诉】zhǔsù〈名〉 complaint: 病人～消化不良。 The patient complained of indigestion.
【主题】zhǔtí〈名〉 subject: 紧扣～ stick to the topic ‖ 时代的两大～ two major issues of the day ‖ 谈话的～ main theme of the talks
【主题词】zhǔtící〈名〉 key word
【主题歌】zhǔtígē〈名〉 theme song
【主题公园】zhǔtí gōngyuán〈名〉 theme park
【主题馆】zhǔtíguǎn〈名〉 theme pavilion
【主题曲】zhǔtíqǔ〈名〉 theme tune
【主题音乐】zhǔtí yīnyuè〈名〉theme music
【主题展】zhǔtízhǎn〈名〉 theme exhibition: 西藏今昔～ An Exhibition of Tibet Past and Present
【主体】zhǔtǐ〈名〉 1（主要部分） main body: ～工程 principal part of a project ‖ 国有企业是经济的～。 State-owned enterprises are the mainstay of the economy. 2［哲学］ subject: ～和客体 the perceiver and the world 3［法律］ subject: 国际法的～ subject of international law
【主推】zhǔtuī〈动〉 strongly recommend
【主谓句】zhǔwèijù〈名〉［语言］ subject-predicate sentence
【主席】zhǔxí〈名〉1（指主持会议） chairperson: 当会议～ chair a meeting 2（指掌管组织） president: 学生会/工会～ president of the student union/labour union ‖ 中华人民共和国～ President of the People's Republic of China
【主席台】zhǔxítái〈名〉 rostrum
【主席团】zhǔxítuán〈名〉 presidium: ～成员 members of a presidium
【主险】zhǔxiǎn〈名〉 main risks: 购买了～还可获保附加险。 When you buy a main insurance policy, you are also insured against additional risks.
【主线】zhǔxiàn〈名〉 main thread
【主心骨】zhǔxīngǔ〈名〉 1（核心力量） backbone: 母亲死后，家里没了～。 The family lost its main support after the death of the mother. 2（主见） one's own judgement: 事情来得太突然，一时间我也没了～。 Things happened too suddenly, so for a moment I didn't know what to do.
【主刑】zhǔxíng〈名〉［法律］ principal penalty
【主凶】zhǔxiōng〈名〉 chief culprit
【主修】zhǔxiū〈动〉 major in
【主旋律】zhǔxuánlǜ〈名〉 1［音乐］ main tune 2〈喻〉（主要精神） theme: 时代的～ central theme of the era
【主演】zhǔyǎn A〈动〉 play the leading role: 联袂～一部电影 co-star in a film ‖ 领衔～ head the cast B〈名〉 lead: 剧组阵容强大，无论～还是跑龙套的都很出色。 The cast is excellent, from the leading actors to the extras.
【主要】zhǔyào〈形〉 main: ～目的 major objective ‖ ～任务 primary tasks ‖ ～原因 leading cause ‖ ～责任 primary responsibility
【主业】zhǔyè〈名〉 main occupation
【主页】zhǔyè〈名〉 home page: 设计～ design a home page
【主义】zhǔyì〈名〉 1（系统理论） systematic theory: 达尔文～ Darwinism ▸唯物～ 2（思想作风） mentality: ▸本位～, 大男子～ 3（政治体系） political system;（经济体系） economical system: ▸社会～, 资本～
【主意】zhǔyi〈名〉 1（办法） idea: 出～ come up with an idea ‖ 好～ good idea ‖ 人多～多。 More people mean more ideas. 2（主见） decision: 打定～ make up one's mind ‖ 改变～ change one's mind ‖ 拿不定～ be in two minds
【主因】zhǔyīn〈名〉 major cause
【主语】zhǔyǔ〈名〉［语言］ subject: 句子的～ subject of a sentence
【主宰】zhǔzǎi A〈动〉 control: ～自己的命运 be the master of one's own fate ‖ 任何国家都不能～整个世界。 No country can dominate the whole world. B〈名〉 controller: 思想是行动的～。 Actions are controlled by thoughts. ‖ 人是万物的～。 Human beings are the controllers of all things.
【主张】zhǔzhāng A〈动〉 advocate: ～用和平的方式解决国际争端 advocate a peaceful settlement of international disputes ‖ 我们～国家无论大小一律平等。 We maintain that all nations, big or small, should be equal. B〈名〉 position: 一贯的～ consistent stand ‖ 政治～ political position
【主旨】zhǔzhǐ〈名〉 gist: 文章的～ gist of the article
【主治】zhǔzhì〈动〉 cure: 这种药～各种炎症。 This medicine is a cure for various inflammations.
【主治医师】zhǔzhì yīshī〈名〉 physician-in-charge
【主子】zhǔzi〈名〉〈贬〉 master: ～和奴才 master and servant

拄 zhǔ〈动〉 lean on: ～着拐棍走路 walk with a stick

渚 zhǔ〈名〉〈书〉 islet: 江～ islet in a river

煮 zhǔ〈动〉 boil: ～鸡蛋 boil eggs ‖ 肉没～熟。 The meat is not boiled through.
【煮豆燃萁】zhǔdòu-ránqí〈成〉〈喻〉 stir up fratricidal strife
【煮鹤焚琴】zhǔhè-fénqín〈成〉〈喻〉 destroy sth. valuable

属（屬） zhǔ〈动〉〈书〉 1（连接） join: 前后相～ join together ▸连～ 2（专注） focus on: ▸～意 ▸shǔ
【属意】zhǔyì〈动〉 fix one's mind on

褚 zhǔ〈书〉
A〈名〉 silk floss
B〈动〉 pad with silk floss
▸Chǔ

嘱（囑） zhǔ〈动〉1（吩咐）urge: ▸～咐, 叮～ 2（托付） entrust: ▸～托
【嘱咐】zhǔfù〈动〉 enjoin: ～孩子好好学习 urge the child to study hard ‖ 再三～ exhort again and again
【嘱托】zhǔtuō〈动〉 entrust: 妈妈出国前～我照看弟弟。 Before going abroad, my mother entrusted me with the care of my little brother.

瞩（矚） zhǔ〈动〉 gaze: ▸～目, ～望, 高瞻远～
【瞩目】zhǔmù〈动〉〈书〉 fix one's eyes upon: 为世界所～ attract worldwide attention ▸举世～
【瞩望】zhǔwàng〈动〉〈书〉 1（期待） look forward to: ～已久 have been looking forward to it for a long time 2（注视） gaze at: 举目～ gaze at sth.

zhù

伫（佇） zhù〈动〉〈书〉 stand for a long time: ～听风雨声 stand listening to the wind and rain for a long time
【伫候】zhùhòu〈动〉〈书〉 stand waiting: ～佳音 look forward to good news from you ‖ ～光临。 We request the pleasure of your company.
【伫立】zhùlì〈动〉〈书〉 stand still for a long time: ～窗前 stand still at the window for a long while ‖ 凝神～ stand still for a long time in deep thought

苎（苧） zhù
【苎麻】zhùmá〈名〉 ramie: ～布 ramie cloth

助 zhù〈动〉 help: ～一臂之力 lend sb. a helping hand ‖ ～消化 aid digestion ▸爱莫能～, 辅～, 资～
【助步器】zhùbùqì〈名〉 walking aid
【助残】zhùcán〈动〉 aid the disabled
【助产士】zhùchǎnshì〈名〉 midwife
【助词】zhùcí〈名〉［语言］ auxiliary word
【助动词】zhùdòngcí〈名〉［语言］ auxiliary verb
【助攻】zhùgōng〈动〉 1（指战争） make a secondary attack: ～部队 holding element 2［体育］ assist: 整场比赛中他～了六次。 He had six assists in the game.
【助教】zhùjiào〈名〉 teaching assistant: ～职务 assistantship
【助桀为虐】zhùJié-wéinüè〈成〉〈喻〉 aid and abet an evil-doer
【助理】zhùlǐ A〈形〉 assistant: ～国务卿 Assistant Secretary of State [in US] ‖ ～研究员 assistant researcher B〈名〉 assistant: 局长～ assistant director ‖ 总统～ presidential aide
【助跑】zhùpǎo〈名〉［体育］ run-up
【助燃】zhùrán〈动〉［化学］ help combust: 氧气能～。 Oxygen helps combustion.
【助人为乐】zhùrén-wéilè〈成〉 take pleasure in helping people
【助手】zhùshǒu〈名〉 assistant: 得力～ right hand man ‖ 我需要两个～帮忙。 I need two helpers.

【助听器】zhùtīngqì〈名〉hearing aid
【助推器】zhùtuīqì〈名〉［航天］launch vehicle
【助威】zhùwēi〈动〉cheer: 给中国队加油～ root for the Chinese team
【助兴】zhùxìng〈动〉liven things up: 席间有杂技表演～。The party guests were entertained with acrobatic performances.
【助学金】zhùxuéjīn〈名〉student grant
【助战】zhùzhàn〈动〉**1**（协助作战）assist in fighting **2**（助威）cheer for sb.
【助长】zhùzhǎng〈动〉〈贬〉abet: ～不正之风 encourage malpractice ‖ 什么都替孩子做会～孩子的惰性。If you always do everything for the child, it will encourage him to be lazy. ▸拔苗～
【助阵】zhùzhèn = 助威 zhùwēi
【助纣为虐】zhùZhòu-wéinüè〈成〉〈喻〉aid and abet an evildoer

住 zhù〈动〉**1**（居住）live: ～在北京 live in Beijing ‖ 跟父母～在一起 live with one's parents ‖ 你～在哪儿? Where do you live? ▸～宿, ～址, 居～ **2**（止住）stop: 不～地哆嗦 keep shivering ‖ 雨～了。The rain has stopped ▸～手, ～嘴 **3**（作补语）[used as a complement after a verb] **a**（表停顿）[indicating a stop or halt]: 被问～了 fail to find an answer ‖ 车停～了。The car came to a halt. **b**（表牢固）[indicating a steadiness or firmness]: 一把抓～不放 have a firm grip ‖ 总也记不～ have a poor memory **c**（表能力）[preceded by 得 or 不, indicating being able/unable to reach sth., meet a standard, etc.]: 禁得～ be able to stand ‖ 他的这条腿保不～了。His leg will have to be amputated. ‖ 守得～守不～? Can we keep the position safe in our hands?
【住持】zhùchí〈名〉［宗教］(Buddhist or Taoist) abbot
【住处】zhùchù〈名〉accommodation: 安排～ arrange one's accommodation
【住地】zhùdì〈名〉lodging
【住读】zhùdú〈动〉board at school: ～生 boarder
【住房】zhùfáng〈名〉housing: ～宽敞 abundantly housed ‖ ～公积金 housing reserve
【住户】zhùhù〈名〉household: 院内有三家～。There are three households in the compound.
【住家】zhùjiā **A**〈动〉live in: 他在郊区～。He lives with his family in the suburbs. **B** = 住户 zhùhù
【住居】zhùjū〈动〉inhabit: 少数民族～的地区 region inhabited by minority ethnic groups
【住口】zhùkǒu〈动〉shut up: 你给我～! Will you shut up!
【住手】zhùshǒu〈动〉stop: 快～，这东西禁不住摆弄。Leave it alone! It won't take to being messed around with. ‖ ～! 别伤害她。Stop! Don't hurt her.
【住宿】zhùsù〈动〉stay for the night: 安排～ arrange accommodation ‖ 我们今晚在哪儿～呢? Where shall we stay tonight?
【住所】zhùsuǒ〈名〉residence: 固定～ permanent residence
【住校】zhùxiào〈动〉board (at school): ～生 boarder
【住院】zhùyuàn〈动〉be hospitalized: ～治疗 be hospitalized for treatment
【住院病人】zhùyuàn bìngrén〈名〉inpatient
【住院部】zhùyuànbù〈名〉inpatients department
【住院医生】zhùyuàn yīshēng〈名〉resident physician
【住宅】zhùzhái〈名〉residence: ～电话 home telephone ‖ ～区 residential area
【住址】zhùzhǐ〈名〉address: 更换～ change one's address
【住嘴】zhùzuǐ〈动〉shut up: ～，不许你胡说! Shut up! No more of your nonsense!

杼 zhù〈名〉**1**［纺织］reed **2**〈书〉（梭）shuttle

贮（貯）zhù〈动〉lay aside: ～粮备荒 lay aside grain for a lean year ‖ 缸里～满了水。The vat is full of water.
【贮备】zhùbèi〈动〉store up: ～粮食 store up grain
【贮藏】zhùcáng〈动〉**1**（储藏）store up: ～大量御寒用的柴火 store up large quantities of firewood **2**（蕴含）contain: 该地区地下～着丰富的矿藏。The area is rich in mineral resources.
【贮存】zhùcún〈动〉save up: ～太阳能 store solar energy ‖ 地窖里～了一些白菜 have a store of cabbage in the cellar

注[1] zhù
A〈动〉**1**（灌入）pour: 把铅～在模子里 pour molten lead into a mould ‖ 大雨如～。The rain came down in buckets. ▸～射, 灌～, 倾～ **2**（集中）concentrate: ▸～视, 关～
B〈名〉stakes: ▸赌～, 下～
C〈量〉[used for deals or sums of money]: 一～交易 a deal ‖ 做了十来～生意 made a dozen transactions

注[2]（註）zhù
A〈动〉**1**（解释）annotate: 引文要～明出处。The quotation should be annotated for its source. ▸～释, 校～ **2**（登记）register: ▸～册, ～销
B〈名〉note: 这篇文章要加一点～。This article needs a few additional notes. ▸脚～, 尾～
【注册】zhùcè〈动〉register: 新生～处 registration office for new students ‖ ～设计师 registered architect ‖ ～商标 registered trademark ‖ ～资本 registered capital
【注定】zhùdìng〈动〉be destined: ～要失败 be doomed to fail ‖ 命中～ be predestined
【注脚】zhùjiǎo = 注解 zhùjiě B
【注解】zhùjiě **A**〈动〉annotate: ～语法要点 explain grammatical points with notes **B**〈名〉explanatory note: 课文～ notes to the text
【注明】zhùmíng〈动〉give clear indication (of): ～出处 give/document sources (of quotations, etc.)
【注目】zhùmù〈动〉fix one's eyes on: 引人～ attention-grabbing
【注目礼】zhùmùlǐ〈名〉greeting with the eyes: 行～ greet sth. with rapt attention
【注入】zhùrù〈动〉**1**（灌入）pour into: 给水池～两米深的水 fill the pool with two metres of water **2**（输入）inject: ～资金 inject funds ‖ ～新鲜血液 infuse with new blood **3**（流入）empty into: 这条河～大海。The river empties into the sea.
【注射】zhùshè〈动〉［医学］inject: 给病人～青霉素 give the patient an injection of penicillin
【注射剂】zhùshèjì〈名〉［医学］injection
【注射器】zhùshèqì〈名〉［医学］hypodermic syringe
【注射针头】zhùshè zhēntóu〈名〉syringe needle
【注视】zhùshì〈动〉focus one's attention on: 密切～事态发展 keep a close eye on the development of the situation
【注释】zhùshì **A**〈动〉annotate: ～古书 annotate an ancient book **B**〈名〉annotation: 正文用大字，～用小字。Use large script in the main text and small letters for the accompanying notes.
【注疏】zhùshū〈名〉commentary and sub-commentary: 《论语～》*Commentary and Sub-commentary to the Analects of Confucius*
【注水肉】zhùshuǐròu〈名〉water-injected meat
【注塑】zhùsù〈名〉［化工］injection moulding
【注文】zhùwén〈名〉explanatory notes
【注销】zhùxiāo〈动〉cancel: ～户口 cancel sb.'s household registration
【注意】zhùyì〈动〉take notice of: 引起某人的～ catch sb.'s attention ‖ ～事项 points for attention ‖ 要～卫生。Have some regard for cleanliness.
【注意力】zhùyìlì〈名〉attention: 分散～ distract sb.'s attention ‖ 他～不集中。His attention wandered.
【注音】zhùyīn〈动〉transcribe phonetically: 用拼音给汉字～ transcribe Chinese characters using *Pinyin*
【注音符号】zhùyīn fúhào = 注音字母 zhùyīn zìmǔ
【注音字母】zhùyīn zìmǔ〈名〉national phonetic alphabet
【注重】zhùzhòng〈动〉attach importance to: ～基本功的训练 focus on basic training ‖ ～经济效益 attach importance to economic results
【注资】zhùzī〈动〉put up capital: 为一项工程大量～ sink a lot of capital into a project

驻（駐）zhù〈动〉**1**〈书〉（停留）halt: ～足聆听 stop to listen **2**（设立）be based at: ～京记者 Beijing-based correspondent ‖ 中国～美大使 the Chinese ambassador to the US ‖ 那里～有军队。Troops were stationed there.
【驻跸】zhùbì〈动〉〈书〉[of a monarch on a tour] stay temporarily
【驻地】zhùdì〈名〉**1**（驻扎的地方）station: 部队～ army station ‖ 地质勘探队～ encampment of a geological prospecting team **2**（所在地）seat: 省政府～ seat of the provincial government
【驻防】zhùfáng〈动〉garrison: ～边陲 garrison the frontiers ‖ ～部队 garrison troops ‖ 该城由两个团～。The town was garrisoned with two regiments.
【驻军】zhùjūn **A**〈动〉station troops: 在岛上～ base forces on an island **B**〈名〉garrison: 岛上的～ troops on the island
【驻守】zhùshǒu〈动〉garrison: 政府将派军队～沿海城镇。The government will garrison the coastal towns.
【驻屯】zhùtún = 驻扎 zhùzhā
【驻颜】zhùyán〈动〉〈书〉preserve youthful looks: ～有术 possess the secret of preserving youthful looks
【驻在国】zhùzàiguó〈名〉［外交］country of residence
【驻扎】zhùzhā〈动〉be stationed: ～重兵 station a huge force ‖ 这支军队将～香港。The army will be stationed in Hong Kong.
【驻足】zhùzú〈动〉pause: 许多参观者～观看。Many visitors stopped to watch.

柱 zhù〈名〉 1 (柱子) post: ▸顶梁～, 石～, 偷梁换～ 2 (柱状物) column-shaped thing: ▸冰～, 水～, 中流砥～

【柱廊】zhùláng〈名〉[建筑] colonnade

【柱石】zhùshí〈名〉 1 (指基石) pillar 2〈喻〉(指人) cornerstone: 国家的～ cornerstone of the state

【柱头】zhùtóu〈名〉 1 [植物] stigma 2 [建筑] column cap

【柱子】zhùzi〈名〉 column

炷 zhù

A〈名〉〈书〉 wick of an oil lamp

B〈动〉 burn

C〈量〉 [used for sticks of incense]: 两～香 two sticks of incense

祝 zhù〈动〉 1 (祈福) pray 2 (表达美好愿望) offer good wishes: ～你旅途愉快。 Bon voyage! ‖ ～你身体健康。 I wish you good health.

【祝词】zhùcí〈名〉 congratulatory speech: 新年～ New Year's speech

【祝辞】zhùcí = 祝词 zhùcí

【祝祷】zhùdǎo〈动〉 say prayers: ～母亲康复 pray for one's mother to get better

【祝福】zhùfú ▸**p. 780** A〈动〉 bless: ～你一路平安! I wish you a safe journey. ‖ 为你～。 Bless you. B〈名〉 new year's sacrifice

【祝告】zhùgào = 祝祷 zhùdǎo

【祝贺】zhùhè ▸**p. 780**〈动〉 congratulate: 致以节日的～ extend holiday greetings ‖ ～你们演出成功! Congratulations on your successful performance!

【祝捷】zhùjié〈动〉 celebrate a victory: ～大会 victory celebration

【祝酒】zhùjiǔ〈动〉 drink a toast: 向来宾们～ toast the guests ‖ ～词 toast

【祝融】Zhùróng〈名〉 God of Fire

【祝寿】zhùshòu〈动〉 congratulate an elderly person on his/her birthday

【祝颂】zhùsòng〈动〉 express good wishes

【祝愿】zhùyuàn ▸**p. 780**〈动〉 wish: 致以良好的～ with best wishes ‖ 衷心～大家身体健康, 万事如意。 Wish you the best of health and every success.

疰 zhù

【疰夏】zhùxià〈名〉[中医] summer disease [usu contracted by children and including symptoms of fever, loss of appetite, lassitude, etc.]

著 zhù

A〈形〉 marked: ▸显～, 卓～

B〈动〉 1 (显露) show: 大～成效 prove greatly effective ▸～名 2 (写作) write: ▸～书立说, 编～

C〈名〉 1 (著作) writing: 新～ one's latest work ▸巨～, 名～ 2 (指人) aborigine: ▸土～

▸zhuó

【著称】zhùchēng〈动〉 be famous for: 以温泉胜地～ be famous for its hot spring resort

【著录】zhùlù〈动〉 put in writing

【著名】zhùmíng〈形〉 celebrated: ～作家 famous writer ‖ 吐鲁番的葡萄很～。 Turpan's grapes are very famous.

【著书立说】zhùshū-lìshuō〈成〉 write scholarly works

【著述】zhùshù A〈动〉 write: 从事～ be compiling scholarly works B〈名〉 writing: ～颇丰 be a prolific writer

【著者】zhùzhě〈名〉 writer

【著作】zhùzuò A〈名〉 writings: 古代医学～ ancient medical literature B〈动〉 write: 他一生～甚多。 He wrote many books during his lifetime.

【著作权】zhùzuòquán〈名〉 copyright: 保留～ retain the copyright (of sth.) ‖ 侵犯～ infringe on copyright ‖ ～法 copyright law

【著作人】zhùzuòrén〈名〉 writer

蛀 zhù

A〈名〉 moth: ▸～虫

B〈动〉 eat through: 这块毛毯给虫子～了。 This woollen blanket is moth-eaten.

【蛀齿】zhùchǐ〈名〉 tooth decay

【蛀虫】zhùchóng〈名〉 moth:〈喻〉 物流公司的～ vermin who are trying to undermine the logistics company

【蛀蚀】zhùshí〈动〉 eat into: 被虫子～了 be moth-eaten

【蛀牙】zhùyá〈口〉 = 龋齿 qǔchǐ

铸（鑄） zhù〈动〉 cast: 这口钟是铜～的。 This bell is cast in bronze.

【铸币】zhùbì A〈动〉 mint coins: ～厂 mint ‖ ～权 mintage B〈名〉 mintage

【铸成大错】zhùchéng-dàcuò〈成〉 make a big mistake

【铸工】zhùgōng〈名〉 1 (指工种) foundry work: ～车间 foundry 2 (指工人) foundry worker

【铸件】zhùjiàn〈名〉 casting: 金属～ metal casting

【铸铁】zhùtiě〈名〉 cast iron

【铸造】zhùzào〈动〉 cast: ～车间 foundry ‖ ～厂 foundry

【铸字】zhùzì〈动〉 cast type: ～工人 type founder

筑（築） zhù

A〈名〉 *zhu* [ancient 13-stringed instrument, played by striking with a bamboo stick]

B〈动〉 construct: ～堤 build a dyke ‖ ～路 construct a road ▸构～, 建～

【筑巢引凤】zhùcháo-yǐnfèng〈成〉〈喻〉 build the necessary facilities to attract people of talent

【筑室道谋】zhùshì-dàomóu〈成〉〈喻〉 have no ideas of one's own

翥 zhù〈形〉〈书〉 soar

箸 zhù〈名〉〈方〉 chopsticks: 举～ hold chopsticks ‖ 下～ start eating

zhuā

抓 zhuā〈动〉 1 (用手抓) grab: 两手紧紧～住车门 grab the car door with both hands ‖ ～了一把花生米 grab a handful of peanuts ▸～阄儿 2 (挠) scratch: 他的胳膊被猫～破了。 His arm has been scratched by his cat. ▸～耳挠腮 3 (不放过) grasp: ～住机会 seize an opportunity ‖ ～紧时间 make good use of one's time 4 (特别注重) pay special attention to: 一手～建设, 一手～改革。 We must promote economic development and reform simultaneously. 5 (主管) be in charge of: 他在公司里是～技术革新的。 He is in charge of technical innovation in the company. 6 (吸引) attract: 小说一开始就～住了读者。 The novel grips its readers from the very beginning. 7 (捉拿) capture: ～小偷 catch a thief

【抓辫子】zhuā biànzi = 揪辫子 jiū biànzi

【抓膘】zhuābiāo〈动〉 fatten: 放青～ graze cattle to fatten them up

【抓捕】zhuābǔ〈动〉 apprehend: ～逃犯 arrest an escaped criminal

【抓斗】zhuādǒu〈名〉[机械] grab: ～挖掘机 grab crane ‖ ～挖泥船 clamshell dredger

【抓耳挠腮】zhuā'ěr-náosāi〈成〉 1 (形容焦急) scratch one's head with anxiety 2 (形容欢喜) be beside oneself with joy

【抓饭】zhuāfàn〈名〉 rice cooked with mutton, carrots, raisins, etc. and eaten with the hands [food of the Uygur and other ethnic groups]

【抓哏】zhuāgén〈动〉[曲艺] throw in little quips

【抓工夫】zhuā gōngfu〈动〉 snatch time for: ～吃点饭 grab some food

【抓获】zhuāhuò〈动〉 capture: ～两名逃犯 seize two escaped prisoners

【抓紧】zhuājǐn〈动〉 firmly grasp: ～生产 step up production ‖ ～时机 grab an opportunity ‖ ～时间 make the best use of one's time

【抓阄儿】zhuājiūr〈动〉 draw lots

【抓举】zhuājǔ〈名〉[体育] snatch

【抓空儿】zhuā kòngr〈动〉 find time: ～休息几分钟 snatch a few minutes' rest

【抓拍】zhuāpāi〈动〉 take a snapshot

【抓破脸】zhuāpòliǎn〈口〉 = 撕破脸 sīpòliǎn

【抓手】zhuāshǒu〈名〉breakthrough point: 以医药分离为～, 解决群众看病贵的问题。 Separating hospital pharmacies from medical treatment could be the breakthrough point in solving the public's problem of high costs for medical treatment.

【抓瞎】zhuāxiā〈动〉〈口〉 get in a mess: 事先没有计划好, 到时候就～了。 You will get yourself in a mess if you don't prepare properly beforehand.

【抓药】zhuāyào〈动〉 1 (指配药) make up a prescription of Chinese herbal medicine 2 (指买药) have a prescription of Chinese herbal medicine made up

【抓周】zhuāzhōu〈动〉 give a baby a grabbing test on its first birthday [in which various articles are spread out before it and the one particular article it picks up is supposed to indicate its future interest and aspiration]

【抓壮丁】zhuā zhuàngdīng〈动〉〈旧〉 press-gang conscripts

【抓总儿】zhuāzǒngr〈动〉〈口〉 take the helm

挝（撾） zhuā〈动〉〈书〉beat: ～鼓 beat a drum

▸wō

髽 zhuā

【髽髻】zhuāji〈名〉 [of girls or women] two knots of hair worn on either side of the head: ～夫妻 husband and wife by the first marriage

zhuǎ

爪 zhuǎ〈名〉 1 (指鸟兽) claw: 猫～ cat's claw ‖ 前/后～ front/hind paw 2 (指器物) foot: 锅掉了一个～。 One of the pot's feet is missing.

▸zhǎo

【爪儿】zhuǎr〈名〉 1 (爪子) paw of a

small animal: 老鼠～ mouse paw **2**（器物的脚） foot: 三～锅 three-footed pot
【爪子】zhuǎzi〈名〉 claw: 鸡～ chicken foot ‖ 猫～ cat's claw

zhuāi

拽 zhuāi〈动〉〈口〉 hurl: 拿砖头～狗 throw a brick at a dog
▸zhuài

zhuǎi

转（轉） zhuǎi〈动〉 embellish one's speech with literary quotations: 他平时好～两句。 He often uses flowery language in his everyday speech.
▸zhuǎn, zhuàn
【转文】zhuǎiwén = 转文 zhuǎnwén

跩 zhuǎi〈动〉〈方〉 waddle: 鸭子走起路来一～一～的。 Ducks walk with a waddle.

zhuài

拽 zhuài〈动〉 drag: 生拉硬～ forcibly drag ‖ 她去买东西，硬把我给～去了。 She went shopping and dragged me along with her.
▸zhuāi

zhuān

专（專） zhuān
A〈形〉 **1**（专门） specific: 这种药片～治感冒。 The tablets are just for colds. ‖ 他～跟我作对。 He is always picking on me. ▸～长，～攻，～心 **2**（单一） special: ▸～车，～刊，～业
B〈动〉 monopolize: ▸～卖，～权
【专案】zhuān'àn〈名〉 specific case: ～材料 material connected with a case ‖ ～组 group investigating a specific case
【专版】zhuānbǎn〈名〉 special page
【专差】zhuānchāi〈名〉 **1**（指差事） special mission: 他～去了一趟上海。 He went to Shanghai on a special mission. **2**（指人） special envoy
【专长】zhuāncháng〈名〉 specialism: 发挥～ give full play to one's special skills ‖ 学有～ have specialized knowledge of a subject
【专场】zhuānchǎng〈名〉 **1**（指专项演出） special performance: 曲艺～ folk art performances **2**（指针对特定对象） show intended for a limited audience: 学生～ special show for students
【专车】zhuānchē〈名〉 **1**（指在例行车次之外） special car: 派～运送救灾物资 dispatch a special car to transport disaster relief materials **2**（指个人专用） car for a person or organization only: 局长～ car for the director only
【专诚】zhuānchéng **A**〈形〉 focused and sincere: 对爱情～不渝 be focused and sincere in love **B**〈副〉 specially: ～拜访 pay a special visit to sb.
【专程】zhuānchéng〈副〉 on a special trip: ～看望 pay a special visit to sb.
【专电】zhuāndiàn〈名〉 special dispatch
【专断】zhuānduàn **A**〈动〉 act arbitrarily: ～独行 act arbitrarily according to one's own will **B**〈形〉 peremptory: 他这个人说话很～。 He speaks in an overbearing manner.
【专访】zhuānfǎng **A**〈名〉 special article based on an interview: 写～ write up a special article after an interview **B**〈动〉 conduct a special interview: 对某人进行～ interview sb.
【专攻】zhuāngōng〈动〉 specialize in: ～儿科疾病 specialize in children's diseases
【专柜】zhuānguì〈名〉 special counter: 床上用品～ special counter for bedding
【专号】zhuānhào〈名〉 special issue: 中国历史～ special issue on Chinese history
【专横】zhuānhèng〈形〉 domineering: 态度～ have a domineering manner ‖ 他那～的口气激怒了大家。 His peremptory tone of voice irritated everybody.
【专横跋扈】zhuānhèng-báhù〈成〉 arrogant and domineering
【专机】zhuānjī〈名〉 **1**（指在班机之外） special plane **2**（私人飞机） private plane
【专集】zhuānjí〈名〉 **1**（指针对某一作者） collection **2**（指就某一内容或文体） anthology: 论文～ collection of treatises
【专辑】zhuānjí〈名〉 special album: 音乐～ music album ‖ 她已经出了两张个人～。 She has already had two albums published.
【专家】zhuānjiā〈名〉 expert: 水稻～ expert in rice-growing ‖ 爆破～ demolition expert ‖ 中国史～ specialist in Chinese history
【专刊】zhuānkān〈名〉 **1**（指报纸专栏） special column;（指期刊） special issue **2**（指单册著作） monograph
【专科】zhuānkē〈名〉 **1**（指科目） specialized subject **2**（指学校） vocational college: ～毕业 graduate from a vocational college
【专科学校】zhuānkē xuéxiào〈名〉 vocational training school
【专科医生】zhuānkē yīshēng〈名〉 (medical) specialist
【专科医院】zhuānkē yīyuàn〈名〉 special hospital
【专款】zhuānkuǎn〈名〉 special fund: 拨～ appropriate a special fund
【专栏】zhuānlán〈名〉 special column: 开辟一个～ open a column ‖ 财经～ financial column ‖ ～作家 columnist
【专力】zhuānlì〈动〉 concentrate one's efforts
【专利】zhuānlì〈名〉 patent: 申请～ apply for a patent ‖ ～许可证 patent licence ‖ 发明～ patent for invention
【专利权】zhuānlìquán〈名〉 patent: 侵犯～ infringe a patent
【专列】zhuānliè〈名〉 special train: 学生/农民工～ special train for students/migrant workers
【专卖】zhuānmài〈动〉 **1**（指由国家指定） monopolize: 在中国烟草实行政府～。 In China tobacco is monopolized by the government. **2**（指专售某一产品） specialize: 服装～店 clothing shop
【专门】zhuānmén **A**〈副〉 **1**（特地） specifically: 我是～来看你的。 I came here specifically to see you. ‖ 这件西服是～为你定做的。 The suit was made for you to order. **2**（仅限于） habitually: 他～会讲风凉话。 He is given to making sarcastic comments. **B**〈形〉 special: ～机构 specialized institution ‖ ～人才 specialized personnel ‖ ～术语 technical terms ‖ ～委员会 special committee
【专名】zhuānmíng〈名〉［语言］ proper noun
【专名号】zhuānmínghào〈名〉 proper noun mark [line under a word indicating that it is a proper noun]
【专区】zhuānqū〈名〉 prefecture
【专权】zhuānquán〈动〉 monopolize power
【专人】zhuānrén〈名〉 person responsible: 这件事有～负责。 The matter has been assigned to a specific person.
【专任】zhuānrèn〈形〉 full-time: ～教师 full-time teacher
【专擅】zhuānshàn〈动〉〈书〉 usurp authority
【专升本】zhuānshēngběn〈动〉 upgrade from technical college to university
【专史】zhuānshǐ〈名〉 history of a particular subject
【专使】zhuānshǐ〈名〉 special envoy
【专书】zhuānshū〈名〉 book on a special subject
【专属】zhuānshǔ〈形〉 exclusive: ～经济区 exclusive economic zone
【专署】zhuānshǔ〈名〉 prefectural commissioner's office
【专题】zhuāntí〈名〉 special topic: ～报告 report on a special topic ‖ ～研究 monograph ‖ 电视～节目 television special ‖ ～广告片 informercial
【专题会】zhuāntíhuì〈名〉 conference on a specialized topic: 就业～ a special conference on employment
【专文】zhuānwén〈名〉 article on a certain topic
【专席】zhuānxí〈名〉 special seat: 残疾人～ seats for the disabled
【专线】zhuānxiàn〈名〉 **1**（指铁路线） special railway line **2**（指电话线） special telephone line
【专项】zhuānxiàng〈名〉 special item: ～训练 specialized training
【专心】zhuānxīn〈动〉 be absorbed: ～读书 be absorbed in a book ‖ ～钻研历史 immerse oneself in history ‖ 她干什么事都很～。 Whatever she does, she is extremely focused.
【专心致志】zhuānxīn-zhìzhì〈成〉 be completely absorbed: ～从事研究 devote oneself to one's study
【专修】zhuānxiū〈动〉 specialize in: ～数学 specialize in mathematics ‖ ～科 special course
【专业】zhuānyè **A**〈名〉 **1**（指学业门类） special field of study: 开设新～ offer a new speciality ‖ 中文系汉语～ Chinese Language Speciality of the Chinese Department **2**（指业务门类） specialized trade: ～队伍 professional contingent ‖ ～训练 professional training ‖ ～知识 specialized knowledge **B**〈形〉 professional: ～作家/歌手 professional writer/singer
【专业户】zhuānyèhù〈名〉 specialized household: 养鸡～ household specializing in chicken farming
【专业化】zhuānyèhuà〈名〉 specialization: ～程度 level of specialization
【专业课】zhuānyèkè〈名〉 specialized course
【专一】zhuānyī〈形〉 concentrated: 爱情～ be constant in love ‖ 心思～ with concentrated attention
【专营】zhuānyíng〈动〉 monopolize
【专用】zhuānyòng〈动〉 be used for a special purpose: ～电话 special-use telephone ‖ 专款～ earmark funds for a specific use
【专有】zhuānyǒu〈动〉 have exclusively: ～权 exclusive right
【专有名词】zhuānyǒu míngcí〈名〉 proper noun

【专员】zhuānyuán〈名〉 1（指行政负责人） assistant director: 商务/文化/新闻～ commercial/cultural/press attaché 2（指专门业务人员） prefectural commissioner

【专责】zhuānzé〈名〉 specific responsibility: 对某事负～ be in sole charge of sth. ‖ 各有～。 Each is charged with specific duties.

【专政】zhuānzhèng〈名〉 dictatorship: ～工具 tools of a dictatorship ‖ ～机关 organ of dictatorship

【专职】zhuānzhí〈名〉 full time: ～干部/教师 full-time cadre/teacher

【专制】zhuānzhì **A**〈动〉 be autocratic: ～统治 despotic rule ‖ ～政府 autocratic government **B**〈形〉 dictatorial: 你不要太～了! Don't be so dictatorial!

【专制主义】zhuānzhì zhǔyì〈名〉despotism

【专注】zhuānzhù〈动〉 be concentrated: 神情～ with rapt attention

【专著】zhuānzhù〈名〉 monograph: 哲学～ monograph on philosophy

【专座】zhuānzuò〈名〉 special seat: 孕妇～ seat reserved for pregnant women

肫（膞） zhuān〈名〉〈方〉 gizzard

砖（磚） zhuān〈名〉 1（指建筑材料） brick: 砌～ lay bricks ‖ 烧～ bake bricks ‖ 耐火～ firebrick 2（砖状物） brick-shaped thing: ▸瓷～

【砖茶】zhuānchá〈名〉 brick tea

【砖厂】zhuānchǎng〈名〉 brickfield

【砖雕】zhuāndiāo〈名〉 brick carving

【砖坯】zhuānpī〈名〉 adobe

【砖头】zhuāntóu〈名〉 fragment of a brick: ～瓦块 fragments of bricks and tiles

【砖头】zhuāntou〈名〉〈方〉 brick

【砖窑】zhuānyáo〈名〉 brick-kiln

颛（顓） zhuān〈形〉〈书〉 benighted

【颛顼】Zhuānxū〈名〉 Zhuanxu [legendary monarch in ancient China]

zhuǎn

转（轉） zhuǎn〈动〉 1（变换） turn: ～败为胜 turn the tables ‖ ～危为安 get through a crisis ‖ 从计划经济～入市场经济 shift from a planned economy to a market economy ‖ 晴～多云 change from fine to cloudy ‖ 向后～ turn around ▸回心～意, 时来运～ 2（传到） transfer: 把钱从活期存款～为定期存款 transfer money from a current to a fixed savings account ‖ 把信～给某人 pass a letter on to sb. ▸～达, ～告
▸zhuǎi, zhuàn

【转氨酶】zhuǎn'ānméi〈名〉［生理］transaminase enzymes

【转按揭】zhuǎn ànjiē〈动〉 remortgage: 办理贷款～业务 handle credit remortgaging

【转包】zhuǎnbāo〈动〉 subcontract: 把一些工程～给另两个公司 subcontract some of the work to the other two firms

【转变】zhuǎnbiàn〈动〉 change: ～态度 change one's attitude ‖ 把热能～为机械能 transform heat into mechanical energy

【转播】zhuǎnbō〈动〉 rebroadcast: ～中央电视台的《新闻联播》节目 relay CCTV's 'News Broadcast' programme ‖ 实况～ live transmission

【转产】zhuǎnchǎn〈动〉 switch to the manufacture of a different product

【转车】zhuǎnchē〈动〉 change trains/buses: 在西安～去成都 change trains at Xi'an for Chengdu

【转达】zhuǎndá〈动〉 pass on: ～口信 deliver a message ‖ ～问候 give sb. one's regards

【转道】zhuǎndào〈动〉 go by way of: ～香港飞往上海 fly to Shanghai via Hong Kong

【转递】zhuǎndì〈动〉 pass on: ～邮件 forward the post

【转调】zhuǎndiào〈动〉［音乐］ modulate: 乐曲由C大调转为A小调。 The music modulates from C major to A minor.

【转动】zhuǎndòng〈动〉 turn: ～腰部 turn at the waist
▸zhuàndòng

【转发】zhuǎnfā〈动〉 1（指文件） relay: ～文件 pass the document on 2（指邮件） forward: ～电子邮件 forward an e-mail 3 = 转载 zhuǎnzǎi

【转干】zhuǎngàn〈动〉 become a cadre

【转岗】zhuǎngǎng〈动〉 be transferred to a new job

【转告】zhuǎngào〈动〉 pass on: 把我的话～他们 pass on what I said to them

【转关系】 zhuǎn guānxi〈动〉 transfer registration from one place to another

【转轨】zhuǎnguǐ〈动〉 switch to a different track: 中国经济已从计划经济向市场经济～。 China has switched from a planned economy to a market economy.

【转行】zhuǎnháng〈动〉 switch to a different profession: 他厌倦了教书, ～写小说。 He was tired of teaching and switched to writing stories.

【转化】zhuǎnhuà〈动〉 change: 将科研成果～为生产力 turn scientific research achievements into a productive force

【转圜】zhuǎnhuán〈动〉〈旧〉 1（挽回） retrieve 2（从中调停） reconcile

【转换】zhuǎnhuàn〈动〉 switch: ～话题 change the subject of conversation ‖ ～企业经营机制 transform an enterprise management mechanism

【转换器】zhuǎnhuànqì〈名〉 1［电子］ converter 2［电气］ electrometer

【转会】zhuǎnhuì〈动〉 [of sports players] transfer

【转会费】zhuǎnhuìfèi〈名〉 transfer fee

【转机】zhuǎnjī **A**〈名〉 turn for the better: 他的病情已有～。 His condition has begun to improve. ‖ 局势出现了～。 The situation took a favourable turn. **B**〈动〉 transfer: ～乘客请到机场换乘台报到。 Transfer passengers should report to the transfer desk.

【转基因】zhuǎnjīyīn〈形〉 genetically modified: ～食品 genetically modified food

【转嫁】zhuǎnjià〈动〉 shift: 把责任～给他人 put the blame on someone else ‖ 向别国～金融危机 shift a financial crisis onto other countries

【转交】zhuǎnjiāo〈动〉 pass on: 把这件包裹～给她母亲 give this parcel to her mother ‖ 来信请由李先生～。 Address my mail care of (c/o) Mr Li.

【转角】zhuǎnjiǎo〈名〉 corner

【转借】zhuǎnjiè〈动〉 lend a borrowed thing to others: 他把我的书～给他弟弟了。 He lent my book to his brother. ‖ 借书证不得～他人。 The library cards are not transferable.

【转口】zhuǎnkǒu〈动〉transit: ～贸易 transit trade

【转脸】zhuǎnliǎn〈动〉 1（掉过脸） turn one's face 2（极短时间） happen in a flash: ～就不见了 disappear in the twinkling of an eye

【转捩点】zhuǎnlièdiǎn = 转折点 zhuǎnzhédiǎn

【转录】zhuǎnlù〈动〉 make a copy of a recording: 他的原始录音已被～成激光唱盘。 His recording has been transferred to compact disc.

【转卖】zhuǎnmài〈动〉 resell: ～货物从中赚钱 resell goods at a profit

【转年】zhuǎnnián〈名〉 1（到了下一年） advent of a new year 2（下一年） following year

【转念】zhuǎnniàn〈动〉 reconsider: 她刚想叫醒丈夫, 但～一想, 又没叫。 She was on the point of waking her husband when she thought better of it.

【转配股】 zhuǎnpèigǔ〈名〉 transferred warrant: 尚未流通的～ transferred warrants that have not yet been circulated

【转让】zhuǎnràng〈动〉 transfer ownership of: ～企业经营权 cede the management rights to an enterprise ‖ 技术～ technology transfer ‖ 此票不得～。 This ticket is not transferable.

【转身】zhuǎnshēn〈动〉 1（转过身） turn around: 他～走了。 He turned and walked away. 2（极短时间） happen in a flash: 刚说好了的, 他一～就不认账了。 He suddenly denied his part in the agreement reached just a moment ago.

【转生】zhuǎnshēng = 转世 zhuǎnshì

【转世】zhuǎnshì〈动〉［佛教］ reincarnate: ～灵童 [in Tibetan Buddhism] reincarnated soul boy

> **转世**
>
> 1) The Buddhist belief that after humans or animals die, their soul is reborn to become another human being or animal. This is known as reincarnation (转生 or 转世).
>
> 2) The Tibetan Buddhist system of determining the successor of a Living Buddha (活佛). After a Living Buddha dies, divination is carried out, and religious offerings are made to find out how many infants were born at the time of the Living Buddha's death. One of these infants is chosen to be the reincarnation and successor of the Living Buddha.

【转手】zhuǎnshǒu〈动〉 resell: ～贸易 the reselling trade ‖ 那批货他一～就赚了10万元。 He resold the goods at a profit of 100,000 *yuan*.

【转述】zhuǎnshù〈动〉 retell: 我向她～了你的意见。 I told her your ideas.

【转瞬】 zhuǎnshùn〈动〉 flash: ～间我来这儿已经几天了。 The few days that have passed since I came here have gone by in a flash.

【转送】zhuǎnsòng〈动〉 1 = 转交 zhuǎnjiāo 2（转赠） make a present of sth. one has been given as a gift

【转体】zhuǎntǐ〈动〉［体育］ turn: ～一周 make a 360-degree turn

【转托】zhuǎntuō〈动〉 ask sb. to do what one has been asked to do by sb. else: 这件事我虽没法帮忙, 但是可以～给别人。 Although I myself cannot help you with this matter, I can find someone else to give you a hand.

【转弯】zhuǎnwān〈动〉 1 ▸**p. 781**（拐弯） make a turn: 来一个180度的大～ make a 180-degree turn ‖ 急/慢～ sharp/shallow turn ‖ 右～走! Right turn march! 2〈喻〉（改变想法） make an about turn: 他感到太突然, 一时转不过弯儿来。 He felt it was too sudden and so he was not ready to make a turnaround.

【转弯抹角】 zhuǎnwān-mòjiǎo 〈成〉 1 （沿曲折的道路走） proceed along a zigzag path: 汽车～地开进了村子。 The car zigzagged into the village. 2 （不直截了当） beat about the bush: 有什么就痛快说，别～的。 If you have something to say, then tell it to me straight — don't beat about the bush.

【转弯子】 zhuǎn wānzi = 转弯 zhuǎnwān 2 ▸zhuàn wānzi

【转危为安】 zhuǎnwēiwéi'ān 〈成〉 turn the corner: 他曾经病得很厉害，但现在已经～了。 He was very ill, but he has turned the corner now.

【转文】 zhuǎnwén 〈动〉 embellish one's speech with literary allusions

【转徙】 zhuǎnxǐ 〈动〉 wander about

【转向】 zhuǎnxiàng 〈动〉 1 （改变方向） change direction: 由防御～进攻 switch from the defensive to the offensive 2 （改变立场） change one's political stand: 公众舆论突然～支持民主党。 Public opinion veered suddenly toward the Democratic Party. 3 （转而向着） turn and face: 他把注意力～那个漂亮姑娘。 His attention turned towards the pretty girl. ▸zhuànxiàng

【转向灯】 zhuǎnxiàngdēng 〈名〉 indicator 〈英〉; turn signal 〈美〉

【转型】 zhuǎnxíng 〈动〉 1 （指经济结构等） be in transition: 经济～期 period of economic transition 2 （指产品） change the design or structure of a product

【转续】 zhuǎnxù 〈动〉 transfer and continue: 参保人员只需提出～书面申请，便可办理～手续。 The insured need only submit a written transfer application to process the transfer.

【转学】 zhuǎnxué 〈动〉 transfer from one school to another

【转眼】 zhuǎnyǎn 〈动〉 happen in a flash: 冬天过去了，～又到了春天。 Winter passed and in no time at all it was spring again. ‖ ～三十年过去了。 Thirty years passed in the twinkling of an eye.

【转业】 zhuǎnyè 〈动〉 be transferred to civilian work: ～军人 soldier transferred to civilian work

【转移】 zhuǎnyí 〈动〉 1 （改换位置） transfer: ～目标 shift an objective ‖ ～注意力 divert attention ‖ 战略～ strategic shift 2 （改变） change: 客观规律是不以人的意志为～的。 Objective laws are independent of man's will. 3 ▸**p. 50** ［医学］ metastasize: 癌～ metastasis of a carcinoma

【转义】 zhuǎnyì 〈名〉 transferred meaning

【转译】 zhuǎnyì 〈动〉 translate from a translated version into a third language

【转引】 zhuǎnyǐn 〈动〉 quote from a secondary source: ～自《社会语言学述评》一书 taken from a quotation in *An Introductory Survey of Sociolinguistics*

【转院】 zhuǎnyuàn 〈动〉 [of a patient] transfer from one hospital to another

【转运】 zhuǎnyùn 〈动〉 1 （指运气） have a change in fortune: 这个月我～了。 Luck has turned in my favour this month. 2 （指运输） transfer: ～业务 freight forwarding services ‖ ～中心 freight shipment agency

【转载】 zhuǎnzǎi 〈动〉 reprint: 全文～ reprint an essay in full ‖ 这篇文章是从《中国日报》上～的。 The article is reprinted from the *China Daily*.

【转载】 zhuǎnzài 〈动〉 reship

【转赠】 zhuǎnzèng 〈动〉 make a present of sth. one has been given as a gift

【转战】 zhuǎnzhàn 〈动〉 fight in one place after another: ～大江南北 fight successively north and south of the Yangtze River

【转账】 zhuǎnzhàng 〈动〉 transfer between accounts: 通过银行～结算 make a settlement by means of a transfer between accounts ‖ ～支票 transfer cheque

【转折】 zhuǎnzhé 〈动〉 1 （指发展方向） turn in the course of events: 历史性的～ historical turning point ▸～点 2 （指语意等） transition

【转折点】 zhuǎnzhédiǎn 〈名〉 turning point: 中国经济建设的～ turning point in China's economic development

【转正】 zhuǎnzhèng 〈动〉 1 （指政党成员） [of a probationary member of the Communist Party of China] become a full member after completion of the probationary period 2 （指临时工等） [of a temporary or probationary worker] be put on the regular payroll

【转制】 zhuǎnzhì 〈动〉 transform a system

【转注】 zhuǎnzhù 〈名〉 ［语言］ mutually synonymous characters

【转租】 zhuǎnzū 〈动〉 sublet: ～房屋 sublet a house

zhuàn

传（傳） zhuàn

〈名〉 1 （指注释经文） commentaries on the classics: 经～ Confucian classics and commentaries ‖ 《左～》 *The Zuo Commentary* (on *The Spring and Autumn Annals*) 2 （指人物传记） biography: 《林肯～》 *The Life of Lincoln* ‖ 名人～ biographies of famous people ▸列～, 自～ 3 （指描述人物故事） story [usu used in titles]: 《白蛇～》 *The Story of the White Snake* ‖ 《水浒～》 *The Water Margin, Outlaws of the Marsh* ▸chuán

【传记】 zhuànjì 〈名〉 biography: ～文学 biographical literature ‖ 名人～ biographies of famous people

【传略】 zhuànlüè 〈名〉 brief biography: 《孙中山～》 *A Brief Biography of Sun Yat-sen*

转（轉） zhuàn

A 〈动〉 1 （旋转） turn: 车轮飞～。 The wheel turned very fast. ‖ 地球绕着太阳～。 The earth rotates around the sun. 2 （闲逛） wander about: 到公园～一～ take a wander around in the park

B 〈量〉 revolution: 每分钟六千～ 6,000 revolutions per minute (rpm) ▸zhuǎi, zhuǎn

【转笔刀】 zhuànbǐdāo 〈名〉 pencil sharpener

【转动】 zhuàndòng 〈动〉 turn: ～门把手 turn the doorknob ‖ 车轮慢慢地～着。 The wheel turned slowly. ▸zhuǎndòng

【转筋】 zhuànjīn 〈动〉 have cramp: 腿～了 get cramp in one's leg

【转矩】 zhuànjǔ 〈名〉 ［物理］ torque: 螺旋桨～ airscrew torque

【转炉】 zhuànlú 〈名〉 ［冶金］ converter: ～炼钢法 converting process

【转门】 zhuànmén 〈名〉 revolving door

【转盘】 zhuànpán 〈名〉 1 （指圆盘） turntable 2 ［交通］ roundabout

【转圈】 zhuànquān 〈动〉 circle

【转速】 zhuànsù 〈名〉 rotation speed

【转台】 zhuàntái 〈名〉 1 （指舞台） revolving stage 2 （指桌子） revolving table

【转梯】 zhuàntī 〈名〉 spiral staircase

【转弯子】 zhuàn wānzi 〈动〉 〈喻〉 beat about the bush: 别跟我～，想要什么就说。 Don't beat about the bush. Just tell me what it is that you want. ▸zhuǎn wānzi

【转向】 zhuànxiàng 〈动〉 lose one's bearings: ▸晕头～ ▸zhuǎnxiàng

【转椅】 zhuànyǐ 〈名〉 swivel chair

【转悠】 zhuànyou 〈动〉 〈口〉 1 （转动） move from side to side: 他眼珠子直～。 He kept rolling his eyes. 2 （漫步） stroll: 在公园里～ have a wander in the park

【转子】 zhuànzǐ 〈名〉 ［机械］ rotor

啭（囀） zhuàn

〈动〉 〈书〉 twitter

赚（賺） zhuàn

A 〈动〉 1 （获利） make a profit: ～外快 go moonlighting ‖ 有～的时候，也有赔的时候。 There have been losses as well as gains. ‖ 这笔生意我们～大钱了。 This deal has brought us huge profits. 2 〈方〉 （挣） earn: 我上一天班～一百多元钱。 I make over a hundred *yuan* in a day's work.

B 〈名〉 〈口〉 profit: 照你这样做买卖还能有～儿? If you keep doing business like this, how can you expect to make any profit? ▸zuàn

【赚头】 zhuàntou 〈名〉 〈口〉 profit: ～小的生意 business operating on tight margins

撰 zhuàn

〈动〉 write: ▸～稿, 编～

【撰稿】 zhuàngǎo 〈动〉 contribute: 特约～人 special contributor

【撰述】 zhuànshù A 〈动〉 〈书〉 write B 〈名〉 writing: ～甚多 have written many pieces of writing

【撰文】 zhuànwén 〈动〉 write an essay

【撰写】 zhuànxiě 〈动〉 write [usu short articles]: ～碑文 write an epitaph ‖ ～书评 write a book review

【撰著】 zhuànzhù 〈动〉 〈书〉 write: ～中国通史 write a general history of China

篆 zhuàn

A 〈名〉 1 （指字体） seal character with curved strokes: ▸大～, 小～ 2 〈书〉 （指印章） seal

B 〈动〉 inscribe in seal characters: ～额 inscribe seal characters at the top of a tablet

【篆刻】 zhuànkè 〈名〉 seal cutting

> **篆刻**
>
> A traditional Chinese craft also known as 印章篆刻. In ancient times, seals were carved mostly in seal script (篆书). The seals were made of metal (gold, silver, copper or iron), jade, ivory or rhinoceros horn. Today, most seals are carved on stone. Seals are usually rectangular in shape, but may also be cylindrical. Characters carved in relief are known as *yangwen* (阳文) or *zhuwen* (朱文). Characters carved in intaglio are known as *yinwen* (阴文) or *baiwen* (白文). The Ming and Qing dynasties produced many famous seal-carvers and schools of carving.

【篆书】 zhuànshū 〈名〉 ［书法］ seal script

【篆字】 zhuànzì = 篆书 zhuànshū

馔（饌） zhuàn

〈名〉 〈书〉 food: 盛～ sumptuous feast

zhuāng

妆（妝） zhuāng

A 〈动〉 put on make-up: ▸化～, 浓～艳抹, 梳～

B〈名〉 1（女妆） woman's personal adornments, make-up and dress: ▸红～，卸～ 2（嫁妆） trousseau: ▸嫁～

【妆奁】zhuānglián〈名〉 1〈旧〉（镜匣） dressing case 2（嫁妆） trousseau: 置办～ prepare a dowry

【妆饰】zhuāngshì **A**〈动〉 get dressed up: ～自己 dress oneself up **B**〈名〉 outfit: ～淡雅大方 be simply but very elegantly dressed up

庄（莊）zhuāng

A〈形〉 serious: ▸～严，端～

B〈名〉 1（村子） village: ▸～户，村～ 2（大片土地） manor: ▸～园 3（商号） place of business: ▸茶～，饭～ 4（庄家） banker [in gambling game]: 是谁的～? Who's the banker? ▸坐～

【庄户】zhuānghù〈名〉 peasant household: ～人家 peasant family

【庄家】zhuāngjiā〈名〉 1（指赌博中） banker [in gambling game] 2（指股票交易中） banker

【庄稼】zhuāngjia〈名〉 crops: 种～ grow crops ‖ 长期干旱，～歉收。 The crops failed because of the long drought.

【庄稼地】zhuāngjiadì〈名〉〈口〉farmland

【庄稼汉】zhuāngjiahàn〈名〉〈口〉 male farmer

【庄稼活儿】zhuāngjiahuór〈名〉 farm work

【庄稼人】zhuāngjiarén〈名〉〈口〉 farmer

【庄稼院】zhuāngjiayuàn〈名〉〈口〉 farmer's household

【庄严】zhuāngyán〈形〉 solemn: ～地声明/宣布 solemnly declare/proclaim ‖ 场面～肃穆。 The occasion was marked with a dignified silence.

【庄园】zhuāngyuán〈名〉 estate

【庄重】zhuāngzhòng〈形〉 serious: 举止～ be dignified in manner

【庄子】Zhuāngzǐ〈名〉 1（指人） Zhuangzi [Chinese philosopher (369-286 BC)] 2（指著作） *Zhuangzi, The Book of Master Zhuang* [Taoist classic by Zhuangzi and his followers]

【庄子】zhuāngzi〈名〉〈口〉 village

桩（樁）zhuāng

A〈名〉 post: 木～ wooden post

B〈量〉 [used for events]: 一～买卖 a business transaction ‖ 一～喜事 a happy event

【桩子】zhuāngzi〈名〉 post

装 zhuāng

A〈名〉 1（包裹） luggage: ▸行～，整～待发 2（衣装） clothes: ▸军～，时～，着～ 3（装容） theatrical stage makeup and dress: ▸上～

B〈动〉 1（修饰） decorate: ▸～点，～修，～潢，化～ 2（扮演） play the part of: 她在戏里～一个老太婆。 She acted the role of an old woman in the play. ▸～神弄鬼 3（假装） pretend: ～出一副吃惊的样子 pretend to be surprised ‖ 她～作不认识我。 She pretended not to know me. ▸～疯卖傻，～腔作势 4（装载） load: ～车 load a cart ‖ ～箱 pack up a box ‖ ～有炸弹的汽车 bomb-laden car ▸瓶～，散～ 5（安装） install: ～电话 install a telephone ‖ ～门锁 fit a lock on the door

【装扮】zhuāngbàn〈动〉 1（打扮成） decorate: ～入时 be fashionably dressed ‖ 节日的广场～得分外漂亮。 The square was beautifully decorated for the festival. 2（伪装成） disguise as: 犯人～成清洁工逃跑了。 The prisoner escaped disguised as a cleaner.

【装备】zhuāngbèi **A**〈动〉 equip: ～新式武器 be equipped with modern weapons **B**〈名〉 equipment: ～精良 be well-equipped ‖ 军事～ military equipment

【装裱】zhuāngbiǎo〈动〉 mount: ～一幅画 mount a painting

【装点】zhuāngdiǎn〈动〉 decorate: 用彩灯～大楼 decorate a building with multicoloured lights

【装订】zhuāngdìng〈动〉 bind: 把散页～成书 bind loose pages into a book ‖ ～车间 bookbindery

【装疯卖傻】zhuāngfēng-màishǎ〈成〉 play the fool

【装裹】zhuāngguo **A**〈动〉 dress a corpse **B**〈名〉 shroud

【装糊涂】zhuāng hútu〈动〉 pretend not to know: 别～! 这件事你很清楚。 Don't play ignorant. You know all about it.

【装潢】zhuānghuáng **A**〈动〉 decorate: ～门面 decorate a shop front **B**〈名〉 decoration: ～讲究 be tastefully decorated

【装幌子】zhuāng huǎngzi〈动〉 maintain an outward show

【装机容量】zhuāngjī róngliàng〈名〉［电气］ installed capacity

【装甲】zhuāngjiǎ **A**〈名〉 plate armour **B**〈形〉 armoured: ～师 armoured division

【装甲兵】zhuāngjiǎbīng〈名〉（指兵种） armoured force/troops;（指士兵） soldiers of armoured force

【装甲车】zhuāngjiǎchē〈名〉 armoured car/vehicle

【装假】zhuāngjiǎ〈动〉 pretend

【装殓】zhuāngliàn〈动〉 dress and lay a corpse in a coffin

【装聋作哑】zhuānglóng-zuòyǎ〈成〉 feign ignorance: 她～，说她一点也不知道。 She pretended to know nothing about it.

【装门面】zhuāng ménmian〈动〉〈喻〉 keep up appearances: 这些规章制度只不过是为了～而已。 These regulations are just for show.

【装模作样】zhuāngmú-zuòyàng〈成〉 behave in an affected way: 她哪儿受伤了，是在～吧。 She's not really hurt. It's just pretence.

【装嫩】zhuāngnèn〈动〉 [for older people] act young

【装配】zhuāngpèi〈动〉 assemble: 把零件～成自行车 assemble bicycle parts ‖ ～车间 assembly shop

【装腔作势】zhuāngqiāng-zuòshì〈成〉 put on airs: 别～吓唬人。 Don't assume airs in order to frighten people.

【装傻】zhuāngshǎ〈动〉 play the fool

【装神弄鬼】zhuāngshén-nòngguǐ〈成〉 1（扮鬼神骗人） disguise oneself as a ghost or deity in order to fool people 2〈喻〉（故弄玄虚） be deliberately mystifying: 别～的，快把事情真相告诉我。 Stop making things confusing and tell me the truth about what is going on.

【装饰】zhuāngshì **A**〈动〉 decorate: ～橱窗 deck out store windows ‖ ～图案 decorative pattern **B**〈名〉 ornament

【装饰布】zhuāngshìbù〈名〉 upholstery fabrics

【装饰品】zhuāngshìpǐn〈名〉 decoration

【装束】zhuāngshù **A**〈名〉 attire: ～朴素/入时 be simply/fashionably dressed **B**〈动〉〈书〉 pack up

【装死】zhuāngsǐ〈动〉 play dead

【装蒜】zhuāngsuàn〈动〉〈口〉 feign ignorance: 别～了，告诉我们你的真实想法吧。 Stop pretending and tell us what you really think.

【装孙子】zhuāng sūnzi〈动〉〈口〉 pretend to be helpless and miserable

【装箱】zhuāngxiāng〈动〉 encase

【装相】zhuāngxiàng = 装模作样 zhuāngmú-zuòyàng

【装卸】zhuāngxiè〈动〉 1（装载和卸载） load and unload: ～货物 load and unload goods ‖ 野蛮～ rough handling of goods ‖ ～工 docker 2（装配和拆卸） assemble and disassemble: ～自行车 take a bicycle apart and put it back together again

【装修】zhuāngxiū〈动〉 renovate: ～门面 fit up the front of a shop ‖ 室内～ interior decorating

【装样子】zhuāng yàngzi〈动〉 do sth. for appearance's sake

【装运】zhuāngyùn〈动〉 load and transport: ～煤炭 load and ship coal ‖ ～港 port of shipment ‖ 分批～ partial shipment

【装载】zhuāngzài〈动〉 embark: ～旅客 embark passengers ‖ ～货物 load goods

【装帧】zhuāngzhēn〈名〉 binding and layout: ～精美 be beautifully designed and bound

【装置】zhuāngzhì **A**〈动〉 install: ～设备 install equipment **B**〈名〉 installation: 防护～ protective equipment ‖ 摇控～ remote-controlled device

zhuǎng

奘 zhuǎng〈形〉〈方〉 stout: 身高腰～ tall and strong ‖ 这棵树很～。 The tree is very thick.

▸zàng

zhuàng

壮（壯）zhuàng

A〈形〉 1（强健） strong: 身体很～ have a strong physique ▸～实，健～ 2（雄壮） magnificent: ▸～观，理直气～，雄～

B〈动〉 strengthen: ～声势 enhance fame and influence ‖ 你的话给他～了胆子。 Your words emboldened him.

C〈量〉［中医］ one burn of moxa in moxibustion

D Zhuàng〈名〉 Zhuang ethnic group

【壮大】zhuàngdà **A**〈动〉 grow in strength: ～海军力量 strengthen the naval forces ‖ 不断发展～ grow steadily **B**〈形〉 strong: 海军力量日益～。 Naval power is strengthening by the day.

【壮胆】zhuàngdǎn〈动〉 embolden: 出发前我喝了口酒～。 Before I went out, I took a swig of alcohol to get my courage up.

【壮丁】zhuàngdīng〈名〉〈旧〉 able-bodied man fit for army service: ▸抓～

【壮工】zhuànggōng〈名〉 unskilled labourer

【壮观】zhuàngguān **A**〈名〉 magnificent sight: 雪覆群山，蔚为～。 The snow-covered mountains make a magnificent spectacle. **B**〈形〉 spectacular: 节日的天安门广场显得格外～。 Tian'anmen Square is a particularly magnificent sight during the holidays.

【壮怀】zhuànghuái〈名〉〈书〉 lofty aspirations

【壮健】zhuàngjiàn〈形〉 healthy and strong

【壮锦】zhuàngjǐn〈名〉 Zhuang brocade

【壮举】zhuàngjǔ〈名〉magnificent feat: 史无前例的～ unprecedented feat

【壮阔】zhuàngkuò〈形〉vast: 规模～ be grand in scale ▸波澜～

【壮劳力】zhuàngláolì〈名〉able-bodied labourer

【壮丽】zhuànglì〈形〉glorious: ～的景色 magnificent scenery ‖ 山河～ the land is magnificent

【壮烈】zhuàngliè〈形〉heroic: ～牺牲 die a hero's death

【壮美】zhuàngměi〈形〉magnificent

【壮门面】zhuàng ménmian〈动〉〈喻〉lend impressiveness to an occasion: 他想邀请省长出席，以～。He wanted to make the occasion more impressive by inviting the provincial governor.

【壮年】zhuàngnián〈名〉prime: ～时期 prime of life

【壮士】zhuàngshì〈名〉warrior

【壮实】zhuàngshi〈形〉sturdy: ～的小伙子 sturdy young man

【壮戏】zhuàngxì〈名〉Zhuang opera

【壮心】zhuàngxīn = 壮志 zhuàngzhì

【壮阳】zhuàngyáng〈动〉［中医］invigorate *yang* to promote kidney function for increasing male virility and sexual potency

【壮志】zhuàngzhì〈名〉lofty ideal

【壮志凌云】zhuàngzhì-língyún〈成〉have lofty aspirations

【壮志未酬】zhuàngzhì wèichóu〈成〉with one's lofty aspirations unfulfilled

【壮族】Zhuàngzú〈名〉Zhuang ethnic group

状（狀）zhuàng

A〈名〉**1**（形态）appearance: 故作惊讶～ pretend to be surprised ▸奇形怪～, 形～ **2**（情形）state: ▸～况, 现～ **3**（叙述文字）account: 行～ brief biography of a deceased person **4**（诉状）written complaint: ▸告～, 诉～ **5**（文字凭证）certificate: ▸奖～, 军令～

B〈动〉〈书〉describe: 不可名～ be indescribable ▸摹～

【状词】zhuàngcí〈名〉［法律］written complaint

【状况】zhuàngkuàng〈名〉state of affairs: 健康～良好 be in good physical condition ‖ 财政/经济～ financial/economic situation

【状态】zhuàngtài〈名〉state: 处于昏迷～ be in a comatose state ‖ 宣布进入紧急～ declare/announce a state of emergency ‖ 固体～ solid state ‖ 心理～ mental state

【状语】zhuàngyǔ〈名〉［语法］adverbial modifier: ～从句 adverbial clause

【状元】zhuàngyuan〈名〉**1**（指科举考试）Number One Scholar [title conferred on the top-ranking candidate in the highest imperial examination] **2**（泛指考试）the very best: 她是今年的高考～。She came top in the College Entrance Examination this year. **3**〈喻〉（指某一行业）number one: 行行出～。In every profession there is a top spot to be filled.

【状纸】zhuàngzhǐ〈名〉**1**（诉状用纸）official form for filing a lawsuit **2** = 状子 zhuàngzi

【状子】zhuàngzi〈名〉〈口〉written complaint

撞 zhuàng

〈动〉**1**（猛然碰上）run into: ～钟 strike a bell ‖ 被卡车～倒 be knocked down by a truck ‖ 两架飞机在半空中相～。Two planes collided in mid-air. **2**（猛冲）rush: ▸横冲直～ **3**（偶遇）bump into: 他老躲着前妻，今天偏偏～上了。He had tried to avoid his ex-wife, but today happened to bump into her. **4**（碰运气）try one's luck: ～运气 try one's luck

【撞车】zhuàngchē〈动〉**1**（车辆相撞）

ℹ 状语

■ 英语里，状语的位置比较灵活，可置于句前、句中或句末。根据语境和文体，很多做状语的英语副词及副词短语都可用于不同的位置。

方式状语

■ 汉语里带结构助词"地"的状语通常用英语的副词来翻译。英语里没有对应的结构：

他幸福地结了婚
= He was happily married

我粗略地考虑了这个问题
= I briefly considered the problem
或 I considered the problem briefly

他怀疑地看着我
= He looked at me suspiciously
或 He looked suspiciously at me

她暗地里决定离开他
= She secretly decided to leave him

我们决定悄悄地离开学校
= We decided to leave the school secretly

我傻乎乎地忘了带电影票
= I foolishly forgot my film ticket
或 It was foolish of me to forget my film ticket

■ 汉语里做状语的形容词要翻译成英语的副词：

好好走！
= Walk properly!

快点儿跑！
= Run fast!

早点起来！
= Get up early!

地点状语

■ 英语里，表示地点的状语常放在动词后面：

她在国外居住
= She lives abroad

我在电影院看到了她
= I saw her in the cinema

■ 句中含有两个或两个以上地点状语时，英语的顺序是从小到大：

我曾在中国广州工作
= I used to work in Guangzhou, China

他在苏格兰爱丁堡附近的一个小村庄里出生
= He was born in a small village near Edinburgh, Scotland

时间状语

■ 英语里，有些时间状语既可放在句首，又可放在句末：

他最终出现了
= He appeared eventually
或 Eventually he appeared

我们昨天去电影院了
= We went to the cinema yesterday
或 Yesterday we went to the cinema

她 6 月份生了孩子
= She gave birth to a baby in June
或 In June she gave birth to a baby
（强调时间）

■ 英语里，有些时间状语（early、immediately 等）只能放在句末：

他们来晚了
= They came late

我马上要离开
= I am leaving immediately

■ 在包含助动词的英语句子里，时间状语（lately、now、recently 等）常跟在助动词后面：

我最近读完了一个硕士学位
= I have recently completed a Master's degree

火车快驶到伦敦
= The train is now approaching London

我们快将到达
= We will soon arrive

■ 汉语的"还"翻译成英语的 yet 或 still。yet 一般用于否定句中，通常放在句末。still 可用于肯定句，也可用于否定句，一般放在系动词后面，或助动词前面：

他还没完成作业
= He hasn't finished his homework yet

她还饿
= She is still hungry

他还在班上
= He is still in class

我还不懂
= I still don't understand

我还没完成论文
= I still haven't finished my essay

■ 句中含有两个或两个以上时间状语时，英语是从小单位说起：

我明天早上 6 点出发
= I will set out at 6 am tomorrow

她在 1994 年 4 月 16 日上午 9 点出生
= She was born at 9 am on 16th April 1994

复杂状语的排列次序

■ 一个句子里，状语有时包括几类词或词组，它们的排列次序在汉英里是不同的。一般情况下，英语的顺序是：方式、地点、时间；汉语是：时间、地点、方式：

我在哪儿都开开心心地工作
= I work happily anywhere

我两点钟在博物馆等你
= I will wait for you in the museum at 2 o'clock

我们以前简单地谈过这件事
= We talked about it briefly before

她每天都在公共汽车站耐心地排队等车
= She queues patiently at the bus stop every day

collide: 高速公路上两辆汽车～了。 Two cars crashed into each other on the highway. 2 〈喻〉(有冲突) clash: 安排不周，两个会～了。 Bad planning meant that the two meetings clashed.

【撞击】zhuàngjī〈动〉 strike: 波涛猛烈地～着江岸。 The waves clashed violently against the banks. ‖ 这突如其来的消息猛烈地～着她的心扉。 The unexpected news was a dagger to her heart.

【撞见】zhuàngjiàn〈动〉 1 (指遇见) meet by chance: 在街上～一位朋友 run into a friend in the street 2 (指看见) discover by chance: ～某人偷东西 catch sb. red-handed

【撞骗】zhuàngpiàn〈动〉 look for a chance to swindle: ▸招摇～

【撞墙】zhuàngqiáng〈动〉 1 (往墙上撞) bash against a wall 2 〈喻〉(遇到障碍) encounter an obstacle

【撞锁】zhuàngsuǒ A〈名〉 spring lock B〈动〉〈口〉 find sb. not in: 昨天我来过，但～了。 I came over yesterday, but you were not in.

【撞线】zhuàngxiàn〈动〉[体育] breast tape

【撞针】zhuàngzhēn〈名〉[军事] firing pin

幢 zhuàng〈量〉[used for houses or buildings]: 一～三层楼房 a three-storey building ▸chuáng

戆（戇） zhuàng〈形〉〈书〉 honest and upright ▸gàng

【戆直】zhuàngzhí〈形〉〈书〉 simple and honest

zhuī

追 zhuī〈动〉 1 (追赶) chase: 把比分～到10 : 11 close the margin to 10-11 ‖ 他走得太快，我～不上。 He walked so fast that I couldn't keep up with him. ▸～随, 你～我赶 2 (回忆) recall: ▸～思, ～忆 3 (事后补做) do sth. after the fact: ～记一等功 be posthumously awarded a first-class merit citation ▸～认 4 (力求获得) pursue: ▸～名逐利, ～寻 5 (追求异性) woo: ～女孩子 chase a girl ‖ 几个小伙子都在～她。 Several young men are after her. 6 (查究) get to the bottom of: ▸～问, ～究, ～本溯源

【追奔逐北】zhuībēn-zhúběi〈成〉 pursue a routed enemy

【追本穷源】zhuīběn-qióngyuán = 追本溯源 zhuīběn-sùyuán

【追本溯源】zhuīběn-sùyuán〈成〉 get to the bottom of a matter

【追逼】zhuībī〈动〉 1 (追赶逼近) be in hot pursuit: 乘胜～ go on the pursuit in the flush of victory 2 (强行索取或追究) press for: ～债务 press hard for the repayment of a debt

【追兵】zhuībīng〈名〉 chasing troops

【追补】zhuībǔ〈动〉 1 (追加) supplement: ～预算 make additions to a budget 2 (事后补偿) compensate retroactively: 不可～的损失 loss that can never be compensated for

【追捕】zhuībǔ〈动〉 track down: ～逃犯 go after an escaped prisoner

【追查】zhuīchá〈动〉 investigate: ～车祸的起因 investigate the cause of a car accident ‖ ～谣言的来源 trace a rumour back to its source

【追偿】zhuīcháng〈动〉 1 (逼迫使偿还) recover: ～损失 recover losses 2 (事后赔偿) compensate after the fact

【追悼】zhuīdào〈动〉 mourn a person's death: ～死者 mourn for the dead ‖ ～会 memorial meeting

【追访】zhuīfǎng〈动〉 do a follow-up interview: 记者～的对象 the subject of the reporter's follow-up interview

【追肥】zhuīféi A〈名〉[农业] top application B〈动〉 top dress

【追风】zhuīfēng〈动〉 1 (跟风) follow a trend: ～炒作 speculate with a trend 2 (追踪风源) track a wind source: 据～报告，台风正以每小时20公里的速度向偏西方向移动。 According to the wind-tracking report, the typhoon is moving in a westerly direction at 20 kilometres an hour.

【追赶】zhuīgǎn〈动〉 pursue: ～猎物 chase game ‖ ～世界先进水平 try to catch up with advanced international levels

【追根】zhuīgēn〈动〉 get to the root of sth.: ～究底 get to the bottom of sth.

【追怀】zhuīhuái〈动〉 recall: ～往事 reminisce about the old days

【追悔】zhuīhuǐ〈动〉 regret: ～不已 feel deep regret ‖ ～莫及 be too late to repent

【追击】zhuījī〈动〉 pursue and attack: 乘胜～ follow up a victory with hot pursuit

【追记】zhuījì A〈动〉 1 (指记功) award posthumously: ～特等功 be posthumously awarded a Special-Class Merit Citation 2 (指记录) record sth. after the fact: 会后，他～了几个发言的主要内容。 He noted down the main points made by some of the speakers after the meeting. B〈名〉 retrospective account

【追加】zhuījiā〈动〉 supplement: ～订单 additional order ‖ ～预算 supplementary budget

【追加成本】zhuījiā chéngběn〈名〉 additional cost

【追缴】zhuījiǎo〈动〉 1 (指应支付款项) demand payment: ～偷漏税款 demand payment of evaded taxes 2 (指非法所得) recover: ～赃款 recover the stolen money

【追究】zhuījiū〈动〉 find out: ～刑事责任 ascertain the criminal responsibility ‖ 不予～ not make enquiries

【追名逐利】zhuīmíng-zhúlì〈成〉 seek fame and wealth

【追捧】zhuīpěng〈动〉 vigorously support: 该歌星受到大批歌迷的～。The singer has a tremendous fan following.

【追求】zhuīqiú〈动〉 1 (力图获得) seek: ～更美好的生活 seek a better life ‖ ～利润 seek profits ‖ ～真理 seek truth 2 (追逐异性) woo: ～一位姑娘 chase a girl ‖ 她拒绝了他的～。 She rejected his advances.

【追认】zhuīrèn〈动〉 1 (指事后) recognize retroactively: ～一项法令 subsequently endorse a decree 2 (指死后) admit or confer posthumously: ～为中国共产党党员 be posthumously admitted as a member of the Communist Party of China

【追述】zhuīshù〈动〉 recount something that has happened: ～战争经历 recount one's wartime experiences

【追思】zhuīsī〈动〉 reminisce

【追思会】zhuīsīhuì〈名〉memorial: 迈克尔·杰克逊～ Michael Jackson's memorial

【追诉】zhuīsù〈动〉[法律] prosecute

【追溯】zhuīsù〈动〉 date back to: ～到公元前二世纪 date back to the 2nd century BC ‖ 两国人民之间的友谊可以～到宋朝。 The friendship between the two peoples dates back to the Song Dynasty.

【追随】zhuīsuí〈动〉 follow: ～一个政党 support a political party ‖ ～左右 follow sb. closely

【追随者】zhuīsuízhě〈名〉 follower

【追逃】zhuītáo〈动〉 manhunt

【追讨】zhuītǎo〈动〉 demand payment of an old debt: ～贷款/欠款 dun sb. for a loan/debt

【追亡逐北】zhuīwáng-zhúběi = 追奔逐北 zhuībēn-zhúběi

【追尾】zhuīwěi A〈动〉bump into the back of another car B〈名〉 rear-end collision

【追问】zhuīwèn〈动〉 question closely: ～事实真相 make detailed enquiries about the facts

【追星族】zhuīxīngzú〈名〉 groupies

【追叙】zhuīxù A〈动〉 recount something that has happened B〈名〉 retrospective account

【追寻】zhuīxún〈动〉 pursue: 警察一直在～死者的妹妹。 The police have been trying to track down the dead man's sister.

【追忆】zhuīyì〈动〉 recollect: ～往事，历历在目。 Looking back, I find that I can picture the past very clearly in my mind.

【追赃】zhuīzāng〈动〉 recover stolen goods

【追赠】zhuīzèng〈动〉 confer posthumous honours

【追逐】zhuīzhú〈动〉 1 (追赶) pursue: ～猎物 pursue one's prey 2 (力图获取) seek: ～高额利润 seek exorbitant profits ‖ ～名利 go after fame and profit

【追踪】zhuīzōng〈动〉pursue: ～调查 track down and question ‖ 警察在～杀人犯。 The police are on the hunt for a murderer.

骓（騅） zhuī〈名〉〈书〉 piebald

椎 zhuī〈名〉 vertebra: ▸脊～, 颈～ ▸chuí

【椎骨】zhuīgǔ〈名〉[解剖] vertebra

【椎间盘】zhuījiānpán〈名〉[解剖] intervertebral disc: ～突出 slipped disc

锥（錐） zhuī

A〈名〉 1 (锥子) awl 2 (锥形物) cone: 改～ screwdriver ‖ 圆～体 cone

B〈动〉 bore: ～个眼儿 bore a hole with an awl

【锥处囊中】zhuīchǔ-nángzhōng〈成〉〈喻〉 real talent will stand out despite temporary obscurity

【锥体】zhuītǐ〈名〉 cone

【锥子】zhuīzi〈名〉 awl

zhuì

坠（墜） zhuì

A〈动〉 1 (落下) fall: ～入大海 crash into the sea ▸～毁, ～落 2 (往下垂) droop: 她耳垂上～着一副大耳环。 Two large earrings are dangling from her earlobes. ‖ 苹果把树枝～得弯弯的。 The branches drooped with the weight of the apples.

B〈名〉 weight, hanging object, pendant: ▸耳～

【坠地】zhuìdì〈动〉〈书〉 1 (落地) fall to the ground 2 〈喻〉(出生) [of a child] be born: ▸呱呱～

【坠毁】zhuìhuǐ〈动〉 crash: 飞机起飞不久就～了。 The plane crashed shortly after take-off.

【坠机】zhuìjī〈动〉[of a plane] crash
【坠楼】zhuìlóu〈动〉1（掉下楼） fall off a building 2（跳楼自杀） commit suicide by jumping off a building
【坠落】zhuìluò〈动〉 fall: 树上的苹果在风中纷纷～。 Apples fell from the tree in the wind.
【坠琴】 zhuìqín ▸p. 929 〈名〉 *zhuiqin* [stringed musical instrument used in ballad singing in Henan Province]
【坠子】zhuìzi〈名〉 1（垂在下面的东西） pendant 2〈口〉（耳坠） pendant earrings 3 = 坠琴 zhuìqín 4 = 河南坠子 Hénán zhuìzi

缀（綴）zhuì
〈动〉1（用线缝合） sew: 能把我裤子上的洞～几针吗? Will you stitch up this hole in my trousers for me? ▸补～ 2〈书〉（联结） compose: ～字成文 write an essay ▸～合, 连～ 3（装饰） decorate: ▸点～
【缀合】zhuìhé〈动〉〈书〉 put together: ～成篇 put fragments together to make up an essay
【缀辑】zhuìjí〈动〉〈书〉 compile, edit: ～成书 compile a book
【缀文】zhuìwén〈动〉〈书〉 compose an essay
【缀玉连珠】zhuìyù-liánzhū〈成〉〈喻〉 be beautifully written

惴 zhuì
〈形〉〈书〉 anxious and fearful
【惴栗】zhuìlì〈动〉〈书〉 tremble with fear
【惴惴不安】 zhuìzhuì-bù'ān〈成〉 be anxious and fearful

缒（縋）zhuì
〈动〉 let down with a rope: 把空篮子～下来 lower the empty basket with a rope

赘（贅）zhuì
A〈形〉 superfluous: ▸～言, 累～
B〈动〉1（入赘） marry into and live with one's wife's family: ▸～婿, 入～ 2〈方〉（使受累赘） be burdensome
【赘词】zhuìcí〈名〉 superfluous words
【赘述】zhuìshù〈动〉 go into unnecessary detail: 没有必要～。 There is no need to go into details.
【赘婿】zhuìxù〈名〉 son-in-law who lives in the home of his wife's parents
【赘言】zhuìyán A〈动〉 go into unnecessary detail: 不再～。 Don't go into any more detail. B〈名〉 superfluous words
【赘疣】 zhuìyóu〈名〉 1（瘊子） wart 2〈喻〉（多余无用之物） anything superfluous or useless

zhūn

屯 zhūn
【屯邅】zhūnzhān = 迍邅 zhūnzhān
▸tún

迍 zhūn
【迍邅】zhūnzhān〈形〉〈书〉 1（行走艰难） hobbling 2（困顿） stuck

谆（諄）zhūn
【谆谆】zhūnzhūn〈形〉 earnest and sincere: ～告诫 repeatedly admonish ‖ ～教导 earnestly and tirelessly instruct

肫 zhūn
A〈形〉〈书〉 sincere: ～挚 sincere
B〈名〉 gizzard: 鸭～ duck gizzard

zhǔn

准[1]（凖）zhǔn
A〈名〉 standard: 以官方统计数字为～ take official statistics as the standard ▸～绳, 基～
B〈介〉〈书〉 in accordance with: ～此办理 handle according to instruction
C〈形〉 1（近似） partly: ～军事组织 paramilitary organization ▸～将 2（准确） accurate: 猜得～ guess right ‖ 你的表～吗? Do you have the correct time? ‖ 她什么时候到，谁也说不～。 Who can say when she'll come? ▸放之四海而皆～, 瞄～ 3（确定） definite: 心里没有～主意 have no firm ideas
D〈副〉 definitely: 他一上场～能赢。 With his participation the team will definitely come away with a win. ‖ 这件事他～干不好。 He will definitely make a poor job of it.

准[2] zhǔn
〈动〉 allow: ～假两周 grant sb. two weeks' leave ‖ 不～随地吐痰。 No spitting. ▸～许, 批～
【准保】zhǔnbǎo〈副〉 definitely: 你～三天干完吗? Do you guarantee to get it done in three days?
【准备】zhǔnbèi〈动〉 1（预先安排） prepare: 做两手～ prepare for both eventualities ‖ 为会议～文件 prepare documents for a meeting ‖ 他～得非常充分。 He is fully prepared for it. 2（计划） plan: ～看望父母 intend to visit one's parents ‖ ～去欧洲旅行 plan for a trip to Europe
【准备活动】 zhǔnbèi huódòng〈名〉［体育］ warming-up: 做～ do warming-up exercises
【准备会】 zhǔnbèihuì〈名〉 preparatory meeting: 赛前～ pre-race meeting
【准备金】zhǔnbèijīn〈名〉［经济］ reserve fund
【准点】zhǔndiǎn〈形〉 on schedule: 七点钟火车～到站。 The train arrived at seven o'clock on the dot.
【准定】 zhǔndìng〈副〉 certainly: 吃下这药你～会好。 If you take this medicine, you will definitely get better.
【准噶尔盆地】 Zhǔngá'ěr Péndì〈名〉 Dzungarian Basin [in Xinjiang]
【准话】 zhǔnhuà〈名〉〈口〉 definite answer: 你们商量好后给我个～。 Please give me a definitive answer after you've talked about it.
【准会员】 zhǔnhuìyuán〈名〉 associate member
【准将】zhǔnjiàng〈名〉（指英陆军及海军陆战队） brigadier;（指英、美海军） commodore;（指英空军） air commodore;（指美陆军、空军及海军陆战队） brigadier general
【准考证】zhǔnkǎozhèng〈名〉examination certificate
【准平原】 zhǔnpíngyuán〈名〉［地质］ peneplain
【准谱儿】zhǔnpǔr〈名〉〈口〉 definite plan: 下一步怎么个搞法儿，至今大家心里还没有个～。 So far no one is sure what to do next.
【准确】 zhǔnquè〈形〉 accurate: 发音～ pronounce accurately ‖ 他的答案～无误。 His answer is exactly right.
【准确性】zhǔnquèxìng〈名〉 accuracy: 缺乏～ lack precision
【准儿】zhǔnr〈名〉 certainty: 下一步怎么做，我心里没～。 I'm not sure what to do next.
【准入】zhǔnrù〈动〉 permit entry: 提高～门槛 increase the entry standard ‖ ～制度 door policy
【准绳】zhǔnshéng〈名〉 criterion: 以法律为～ taking the law as the standard
【准时】zhǔnshí〈形〉 punctual: ～赴约 be on time for an appointment ‖ 火车～到站。 The train arrived at the scheduled time.
【准头】zhǔntou〈名〉〈口〉 accuracy: 他说的话没～。 His words are not reliable.
【准尉】zhǔnwèi〈名〉 (chief) warrant officer
【准线】zhǔnxiàn〈名〉［数学］ directrix
【准信】zhǔnxìn〈名〉 definite answer: 你哪天能来，赶快给我个～。 Please let me know as soon as you have decided when to come.
【准星】 zhǔnxīng〈名〉 1（用于瞄准） front sight 2（用于定盘） zero point
【准许】zhǔnxǔ〈动〉 allow: 他们～他提前离开。 They granted him permission to leave earlier. ‖ 这里不～吸烟。 Smoking is not allowed here.
【准予】 zhǔnyǔ〈动〉 approve: ～入境 permit entrance to the country ‖ ～休假一周 grant a week's leave
【准则】zhǔnzé〈名〉 norm: 国际关系基本～ basic norms of international relations ‖ 行为～ code of conduct

zhuō

拙 zhuō
〈形〉 1（笨） clumsy: ～嘴笨舌 be clumsy in expressing oneself ‖ 手～ be all thumbs ▸～劣, 笨～, 弄巧成～ 2〈谦〉（我的） my: ～稿/译 my poor writing/translation
【拙笨】zhuōbèn〈形〉 clumsy: 口齿～ be awkward in speech
【拙笔】zhuōbǐ〈名〉〈谦〉 my poor writing/painting
【拙见】zhuōjiàn〈名〉〈谦〉 my humble opinion: 个人～，仅供参考。 This is my humble opinion for your reference only.
【拙荆】 zhuōjīng〈名〉〈旧〉〈谦〉 my humble wife
【拙劣】zhuōliè〈形〉clumsy and inferior: ～的文笔 poor writing ‖ 他的手法极为～。 Those tricks of his are none too clever.
【拙朴】zhuōpǔ〈形〉 simple and unadorned
【拙涩】zhuōsè〈形〉 clumsy and obscure: ～的译文 clumsy and obscure translation
【拙文】zhuōwén〈名〉〈谦〉 my poor essay
【拙著】zhuōzhù〈名〉〈谦〉 my humble writing
【拙作】zhuōzuò〈名〉〈谦〉 my poor writing, painting, etc.

捉 zhuō
〈动〉 1（握住） grasp: ～笔 hold a pen ▸～刀, ～襟见肘 2（逮住） catch: 猫～老鼠。 Cats hunt mice. ‖ 凶手被当场～住。 The murderer was caught red-handed. ‖ ～贼! Stop thief! ▸～拿, 捕～, 瓮中～鳖
【捉刀】 zhuōdāo〈动〉〈书〉 ghost-write: ～代笔 ghost-write for sb.
【捉对】zhuōduì〈副〉 in pairs: ～厮杀 fight in pairs
【捉奸】zhuōjiān〈动〉 catch adulterers in the act

Z

【捉襟见肘】zhuōjīn-jiànzhǒu〈成〉〈喻〉be desperately hard-up

【捉迷藏】zhuō mícáng **A**〈名〉hide-and-seek **B**〈动〉〈喻〉play hide-and-seek: 你就直说吧，不要跟我～了。Stop beating about the bush and get straight to the point.

【捉摸】zhuōmō〈动〉[usu used in the negative] ascertain: 难以～ be difficult to ascertain ‖ 这到底是怎么回事，令人～不透。It's hard for me to make head or tail of what has happened.

【捉拿】zhuōná〈动〉arrest: ～凶手 arrest a murderer ‖ 将罪犯～归案 arrest and bring a criminal to justice

【捉弄】zhuōnòng〈动〉tease: 你这是故意～我。You are deliberately playing the fool with me. ‖ 他被无端～了一番。He was made a fool of for no reason.

桌 zhuō

A〈名〉table: 掸掉～上的灰尘 dust down a table ▸八仙～，书～

B〈量〉[of a feast table, etc.] table: 摆一～酒席 set a table of wine and dishes ‖ 三～客人 three tables of guests

【桌布】zhuōbù〈名〉tablecloth: 铺～ spread a tablecloth

【桌面】zhuōmiàn〈名〉**1**（桌子面）tabletop: 大理石～ marble top **2**［计算机］desktop: ～背景 desktop background

【桌面儿上】zhuōmiànrshàng〈名〉the open: 把问题摆在～来谈 put the problems on the table for discussion

【桌球】zhuōqiú〈名〉billiards: 打～ play billiards

【桌子】zhuōzi〈名〉table: 抹～ wipe the table ‖ 把某物放在～上 put sth. on the table

倬 zhuō〈形〉〈书〉striking

棁 zhuō〈名〉〈书〉stud on a roof beam

焯 zhuō〈形〉〈书〉obvious
▸chāo

zhuó

灼 zhuó

A〈动〉burn: ～伤 burn ▸～热

B〈形〉bright: ～亮 bright

【灼见】zhuójiàn〈名〉penetrating view: 真知～ insightful analysis

【灼烤】zhuókǎo〈动〉bake

【灼热】zhuórè〈形〉scorching hot: ～的阳光 scorching hot sun

【灼伤】zhuóshāng〈动〉[of fire, acid, etc.] burn: X射线/化学品～ X-ray/chemical burns

【灼灼】zhuózhuó〈形〉〈书〉shining: 目光～ with bright, sparkling eyes

茁 zhuó〈形〉thriving: ▸～壮

【茁长】zhuózhǎng〈动〉〈书〉grow up strong and sturdy: 禾苗～ grain seedlings grow vigorously

【茁壮】zhuózhuàng〈形〉healthy and strong: 小麦长得很～。The wheat has grown well. ‖ 宝宝～成长。The baby grew up strong and healthy.

卓 zhuó〈形〉**1**（高而直）tall and erect: 孤峰～立。The mountain peak soars into the sky. **2**（高明）outstanding: ▸～见，～绝，～识

【卓尔不群】zhuó'ěr-bùqún〈成〉stand head and shoulders above all the others

【卓见】zhuójiàn〈名〉brilliant idea: 大家都佩服他的～。Everyone respected his excellent idea.

【卓绝】zhuójué〈形〉〈书〉extremely: 英勇～ be extremely brave

【卓荦】zhuóluò〈形〉〈书〉extraordinary

【卓然】zhuórán〈形〉outstanding: 成绩～ achieve outstanding results ‖ ～不群 stand head and shoulders above everybody else

【卓识】zhuóshí〈名〉sagacity: ▸远见～

【卓异】zhuóyì〈形〉〈书〉extraordinary: 成绩～ make remarkable achievements

【卓有成效】zhuóyǒu-chéngxiào〈成〉highly effective: 新院长上任以来，工作～。Marked progress has been made ever since the new president assumed his post.

【卓越】zhuóyuè〈形〉outstanding: 才华～ be outstandingly talented ‖ ～的贡献 outstanding contributions ‖ ～的科学家 brilliant scientist

【卓著】zhuózhù〈形〉distinguished: 成效～ have outstanding results ‖ 功勋～ have performed remarkable deeds

斫（斲）zhuó〈动〉〈书〉chop

浊（濁）zhuó〈形〉**1**（浑浊）turbid: ～酒 unstrained wine ‖ ～水 muddy water ▸浑～，污～ **2**（低沉）deep and thick: ～声～气 in a deep, raucous voice **3**（混乱）chaotic: ▸～世 **4**［语言］voiced: ▸～音

【浊世】zhuóshì〈名〉**1**〈书〉（指时代）chaotic times **2**［佛教］this mortal world

【浊音】zhuóyīn〈名〉［语言］voiced sound

酌 zhuó

A〈动〉**1**（倾倒）pour out: ～满一杯酒 pour a full glass of wine **2**（饮）drink: 独～ drink alone ‖ 对～ have a drink together **3**（考虑）think over: ～加修改 make alterations as one considers fit ▸斟～

B〈名〉〈书〉meal with wine: 聊备小～ prepare a frugal meal with some wine

【酌办】zhuóbàn〈动〉do as one considers fit: 请～。Please settle the matter as you think fit.

【酌定】zhuódìng〈动〉make a decision as one considers fit

【酌量】zhuóliáng〈动〉use one's own judgement: ～给予补助 give appropriate subsidies

【酌情】zhuóqíng〈动〉exercise discretion in light of the circumstances: ～处理 settle a matter as one sees fit ‖ ～做适当调整 make appropriate adjustments in light of the circumstances

浞 zhuó〈动〉〈方〉drench: 让雨～透了 get drenched in the rain

诼（諑）zhuó〈动〉〈书〉slander: 谣～ slander

著[1] zhuó = 着[1] zhuó

著[2] zhuó ▸执著 zhízhuó
▸zhù

啄 zhuó〈动〉peck: 小鸡～食。The chicks are pecking at the food.

【啄木鸟】zhuómùniǎo〈名〉woodpecker

着[1] zhuó

A〈动〉**1**（接触）touch: ▸～陆，不～边际，附～ **2**（使附着）apply: ▸～笔，～墨，～手，～眼 **3**（穿）wear: ～蓝色西装 wear a blue suit ‖ 吃～不尽 have as much food and clothing as one could want ▸～装

B〈名〉whereabouts: 遍寻无～ nowhere to be found ‖ 衣食无～ have neither food nor clothing ▸～落

着[2] zhuó〈动〉**1**（指派）send: ～人去请 send for sb. ‖ ～一名干部前来洽谈 assign a cadre here for talks **2**（命令）order [used in official documents, expressing peremptory tone]: ～即施行 must be enforced immediately ‖ ～即悉数上缴。Everything is to be handed in immediately.
▸zhāo, zháo, zhe

【着笔】zhuóbǐ〈动〉take up one's brush: 不知如何～ not know how to begin writing/painting

【着力】zhuólì〈动〉make efforts: 作者在小说中～描绘了农村的新面貌。In this novel, the writer spares no effort in describing the new picture of life in the countryside.

【着陆】zhuólù〈动〉land: 安全～ make a safe landing ‖ 紧急～ make an emergency landing ‖〈喻〉经济软～ an economic soft landing

【着陆舱】zhuólùcāng〈名〉landing module

【着落】zhuóluò **A**〈名〉**1**（下落）whereabouts: 遗失的文件仍没有～。The whereabouts of the missing document is still unknown. **2**（来源）assured source: 经费已有了～。We have already collected enough funds. **3**（归宿）permanent home: 女儿有个～，老太太才放心。The mother couldn't rest easy until her daughter got married. **B**〈动〉rest with sb.: 孩子们的父母去世后，抚养他们的任务就～在我身上了。The care of the children fell to me after their parents died.

【着墨】zhuómò〈动〉put pen to paper: ～不多 sketchily described/painted

【着色】zhuósè〈动〉colour

【着实】zhuóshí〈副〉**1**（确实）really: 这孩子～讨人喜欢。The child is really sweet. **2**（狠狠地）severely: ～批评某人一顿 give sb. a good talking-to ‖ ～数落一番 give sb. a good dressing-down

【着手】zhuóshǒu〈动〉set about: ～编制计划 start drawing up plans ‖ 从调查研究～ start with investigation and study

【着想】zhuóxiǎng〈动〉consider: 替别人～ consider the interests of others ‖ 为人民的利益～ consider the interests of the people

【着眼】zhuóyǎn〈动〉have in mind: ～于未来 have one's eyes on the future ‖ 从大处～ keep the bigger goal in mind

【着眼点】zhuóyǎndiǎn〈名〉starting point

【着意】zhuóyì **A**〈副〉with great care: ～经营 manage with great care ‖ ～研究实际问题 concentrate on the study of practical problems **B**〈动〉[usu in the negative] care: 别人说什么他毫不～。He doesn't care one bit what people say.

【着重】zhuózhòng〈动〉emphasize: 会上我～讲了两个问题。At the meeting I placed special stress on two particular questions. ‖ 目前政府应～于调整经济结构。At present, the government should place emphasis on restructuring the economy.

【着重号】zhuózhònghào〈名〉mark of emphasis (.)

【着装】zhuózhuāng **A**〈动〉 wear: 统一～ wear uniform clothing **B**〈名〉 clothing, headgear and footwear: 整理～ straighten one's clothing

琢 zhuó〈动〉 carve: 翡翠～成的茶壶 carved jadeite teapot ▸～磨
▸zuó

【琢磨】zhuómó〈动〉 **1**（雕琢）carve and polish: ～玉器 carve and polish jade wares **2**（精益求精） polish: 这篇文章还可以再～。This article still needs polishing.
▸zuómo

椓 zhuó〈名〉〈古〉 castration [a torture]

缴（繳） zhuó〈名〉〈书〉 silk string tied to an arrow for shooting birds
▸jiǎo

擢 zhuó〈动〉〈书〉 **1**（拔） extract: ▸～发难数 **2**（提拔） promote: ▸～升, ～用

【擢发难数】zhuófà-nánshǔ〈成〉 [of crimes] be too numerous to count

【擢升】zhuóshēng〈动〉〈书〉promote: 他由职员～为经理。He was promoted from a clerk to a manager.

【擢用】zhuóyòng〈动〉〈书〉 promote to a post: ～贤能 promote capable personnel ‖ 量才～ promote sb. to a post suited to their level of skill

濯 zhuó〈动〉〈书〉 wash: ～足 wash one's feet

【濯濯】zhuózhuó〈形〉〈书〉 [of mountains] barren: 童山～ barren hills

镯（鐲） zhuó〈名〉 bracelet: ▸手～, 玉～

【镯子】zhuózi〈名〉 bracelet: 金/银～ gold/silver bracelet

zī

仔 zī
▸zǎi, zǐ

【仔肩】zījiān〈名〉〈书〉 responsibility

吱 zī

A〈拟〉（指老鼠） squeak;（指小鸟） chirp: 老鼠在～～叫。The mouse was squeaking.

B〈动〉〈口〉 utter a sound: 叫了他半天，他一声也不～。 I called to him for ages but he did not utter a sound.
▸zhī

【吱声】zīshēng〈动〉〈口〉 make a sound: 如果你不了解情况，最好别～。 You'd better keep silent if you don't understand the facts.

孜 zī

【孜孜】zīzī〈形〉 diligent: ～以求 diligently strive after

【孜孜不倦】zīzī-bùjuàn〈成〉 diligently: ～地工作 work untiringly

咨¹（諮） zī〈动〉 consult: ▸～询

咨² zī〈名〉 official communication: ▸～文

【咨文】zīwén〈名〉 **1**〈旧〉（指公文） official communication between government offices of equal rank **2**（指政府报告） report delivered by the head of a government on affairs of state: 国情～ State of the Union Address [US] ‖ 总统～ presidential/president's message

【咨询】zīxún〈动〉 consult: 法律～ legal consultation ‖ 心理～ psychological counselling ‖ 提供～服务 provide a consulting service

【咨询公司】zīxún gōngsī〈名〉 consultancy

【咨询师】zīxúnshī ▸**p. 966**〈名〉 consultant: 心理/金融～ psychological/financial consultant

姿 zī〈名〉 **1**（形态） carriage: ▸舞～, 英～ **2**（容貌） looks: ▸～色

【姿容】zīróng〈名〉 looks: ～秀美 be good-looking

【姿色】zīsè〈名〉 [of a woman] good looks: 略有几分～ be rather good-looking

【姿势】zīshì〈名〉 pose: 保持一种～ hold a pose ‖ ～优美 have a graceful carriage

【姿态】zītài〈名〉 **1**（姿势） bearing: ～优美 have a graceful carriage ‖ 高雅的～ noble gesture **2**（态度） attitude: 故作～ pose ‖ 保持低/高～ keep a low/high profile ‖ 以一个普通劳动者的～出现 [of a senior cadre] appear among the masses as an ordinary worker

兹 zī〈书〉

A〈代〉 this: 念～在～ always remember this ‖ ～事体大。This is indeed a serious matter.

B〈名〉 **1**（现在） now: ～订于4月20日召开座谈会。The symposium is scheduled for April 20th. **2**（年） year: 今～ this year
▸cí

赀（貲） zī〈动〉〈书〉 calculate

资（資） zī

A〈名〉 **1**（钱财） money and goods: ▸～财, ～产, ～源, 物～ **2**（费用） expenses: ▸工～, 合～, 投～, 邮～ **3**（素质） aptitude: ▸～质, 天～ **4**（资格） qualifications: ▸～格, ～历, 年～ **5**（材料） material: ▸～料, 谈～

B〈动〉 **1**（帮助） support: ▸～助 **2**（提供） provide: 可～对比 provide a contrast ‖ 以～参考 for your reference ‖ 以～鼓励 as an encouragement

【资本】zīběn〈名〉 **1**（指财物） capital: 筹集～ raise capital ‖ 积累～ accumulate capital ▸官僚～, 货币～ **2**〈喻〉（指凭借） something used to one's own advantage: 捞取政治～ gain political capital

【资本家】zīběnjiā〈名〉 capitalist

【资本流通】zīběn liútōng〈名〉 circulation of capital

【资本市场】zīběn shìchǎng〈名〉 capital market

【资本主义】zīběn zhǔyì〈名〉 capitalism: ～社会 capitalist society ‖ 官僚～ bureaucrat capitalism

【资不抵债】zībùdǐzhài〈成〉 one's assets are insufficient to cover one's debts: 由于经营不善而导致～ be unable to pay off debts with one's assets as a result of poor management

【资材】zīcái〈名〉 goods, materials and equipment

【资财】zīcái〈名〉 assets: 清点～ make an inventory of the assets

【资产】zīchǎn〈名〉 **1**（财产） property: 个人～ individual property **2**（资金） capital: ～雄厚 have abundant funds **3**〔经济〕 assets: 固定～ fixed assets ‖ 国有～ state-owned assets ‖ ～重组 reorganization of assets

【资产负债表】zīchǎn fùzhàibiǎo〈名〉 balance sheet

【资产阶级】zīchǎn jiējí〈名〉 bourgeoisie: ～革命 bourgeois revolution ‖ ～个人主义 bourgeois individualism ‖ 民族～ national bourgeoisie ‖ 小～ petty bourgeoisie

【资方】zīfāng〈名〉 capitalists: ～代理人 agent of a capitalist

【资费】zīfèi〈名〉 postage: 调整电信业务～ adjust telecommunications fees

【资格】zīgé〈名〉 **1**（适合的条件） qualifications: 具备报考～ have the requisite exam qualifications ‖ 教师～证书 teacher's certificate **2**（资历） seniority: 摆老～ flaunt one's seniority

【资格赛】zīgésài〈名〉 qualifying match/tournament: 世界杯的～ World Cup qualifier

【资金】zījīn〈名〉（指国家使用） fund;（指企业使用） capital: 筹措～ raise funds ‖ ～短缺 be short of funds ‖ 流动～ current capital ‖ ～外流 capital outflow ‖ ～周转 capital turnover

【资金链】zījīnliàn〈名〉 funding chain: ～断裂 breaks in the funding chain

【资力】zīlì〈名〉 **1**（经济实力） financial strength: ～雄厚 have large capital **2**（资质和能力） talent and ability: ～有限 have limited talent and ability

【资历】zīlì〈名〉 record of service: ～浅/深 have a short/long record of service

【资料】zīliào〈名〉 **1**（需要的东西）means: 生活/生产～ means of livelihood/production **2**（信息材料） material: 收集/搜集～ gather/collect data ‖ 参考～ reference material ‖ 统计～ statistical data ‖ 学习～ material for study

【资料室】zīliàoshì〈名〉 reference room

【资深】zīshēn〈形〉 senior: ～教授 senior professor ‖ ～外交官 senior diplomat

【资送】zīsòng〈动〉〈书〉 send sb. away with some money: ～出国留学 finance sb.'s education abroad

【资望】zīwàng〈名〉〈书〉 seniority and prestige

【资信】zīxìn〈名〉 capital and credit: ～可靠 be creditworthy ‖ ～证明 certificate of financial standing

【资讯】zīxùn〈名〉 information: 交换～ exchange information

【资源】zīyuán〈名〉 resources: 矿产～ mineral resources ‖ 旅游～ tourist resources ‖ 人力～ human resources ‖ ～节约型经济 resources-saving economy

【资政】zīzhèng **A**〈动〉〈书〉 help to administer a country **B**〈名〉 senior minister [in Singapore]

【资质】zīzhì〈名〉 **1**（智力） natural endowments: ～很高 highly intelligent ‖ ～平庸 be of mediocre intelligence **2**（资格和能力） credentials and ability of a designing and engineering enterprise

【资助】zīzhù〈动〉 give financial aid: ～贫困大学生 sponsor poor students through university ‖ 该校由一慈善机构～。This school is supported by a charitable institution.

【资助人】zīzhùrén〈名〉 financial backer

菑 zī

A〈名〉〈古〉 newly cultivated land

B〈动〉〈书〉 weed

缁（緇） zī〈形〉〈书〉black: ～衣 black coat

辎（輜） zī〈名〉 ancient covered wagon

【辎重】zīzhòng〈名〉 army supplies and gear: 截获敌人～ intercept and seize equipment supplies and enemy

嗞 zī〈拟〉 1（指水） sizzle: 热烙铁往水里一蘸，发出～～的声音。 If a hot iron is dipped into water, it will sizzle. 2 = 吱 zī A

粢 zī〈名〉〈古〉 grain used as a sacrifice ►cí

孳 zī〈动〉 multiply: ►～乳, ～生

【孳乳】zīrǔ〈动〉〈书〉 1（繁殖） breed 2（派生） derive: 文字随着社会的发展～增多。 With the progress of the society, so the number of Chinese characters in use multiplies.

【孳生】zīshēng〈动〉 multiply, breed: ～蚊蝇 breed flies and mosquitoes

滋[1] zī

A〈动〉 1（生长） grow;（繁殖） multiply: ►～蔓, ～生, ～长 2（引起） cause 3（增加） increase: ►～补

B〈名〉 taste

滋[2] zī〈动〉〈口〉 spurt: 水管在～水。 Water is spurting from the pipe.

【滋补】zībǔ〈动〉 nourish: ～气血 build up vital energy and nourish the blood ‖ 鹿茸是～名药。 Pilose antler is well known for its invigorating effect.

【滋蔓】zīmàn〈动〉〈书〉 grow and spread

【滋扰】zīrǎo〈动〉 stir up trouble: ～别人工作 disturb others in their work

【滋润】zīrùn A〈形〉 1（湿润） damp: ～的皮肤 smooth skin ‖ 雨后空气～。 The air was damp after the rain. 2〈口〉（舒服） comfortable: 小日子过得挺～ live a comfortable life B〈动〉 moisten: ～皮肤 moisten one's skin ‖ 这条河～着牧场的青草。 The river provides moisture for the grass on the pasture.

【滋生】zīshēng〈动〉 1 = 孳生 zīshēng 2（引起） cause: ～事端 cause trouble ‖ ～腐败的温床 hotbed for corruption

【滋事】zīshì〈动〉 stir up trouble: 聚众～ gather a crowd to create a disturbance

【滋味】zīwèi〈名〉 1（味道） taste: 品尝～ taste the flavour ‖ 菜的～不错。 This dish tastes good. 2〈喻〉（感受） experience: 尝尝艰苦生活的～ have a taste of a hard life ‖ 心里不是～ feel bad ‖ 挨饿的～不好受。 The experience of going hungry was hard to bear.

【滋养】zīyǎng A〈动〉 nourish: ～品 nutriment ‖ 蜂蜜能～身体。 Honey is good for the health. B〈名〉 nutriment: 吸收～ take in nutriments ‖ 丰富的～ rich nourishment

【滋长】zīzhǎng〈动〉 grow: 防止～骄傲自满情绪 guard against arrogance and conceit

趑 zī

【趑趄】zījū〈形〉〈书〉 1（行走困难） hobbling 2（犹豫不决） faltering: ～不前 hesitate to advance

觜 zī〈名〉 one of the 28 constellations in ancient Chinese astronomy

訾 zī〈动〉〈书〉 calculate ►zǐ

锱（錙） zī〈名〉 *zi* [ancient unit of weight, equal to one fourth of a *liang* (两)]

【锱铢必较】zīzhū-bìjiào〈成〉 quibble over every detail: 何必～? Why quibble over these trifles?

龇（齜） zī〈动〉〈口〉 bare: ～着牙 bare one's teeth

【龇牙咧嘴】zīyá-liězuǐ〈成〉 1（面目狰狞） look fierce 2（形容疼痛） grimace with pain: 他疼得～。 His face was contorted in agony.

髭 zī〈名〉 moustache: ～须 whiskers

鲻（鯔） zī〈名〉［鱼类］ mullet

zǐ

子[1] zǐ

A〈名〉 1（儿子） son: ～承父业。 It is the son that inherits from his father. ►～女, ～孙, 母～ 2（人） person: ►君～, 男～, 女～ 3（用作称号） ancient title of respect for a learned or virtuous man: 孔～ Confucius ‖ 孟～ Mencius ‖ 荀～ Master Xun 4（指爵位） viscount: ►～爵 5〈书〉（您） your honour: ►以～之矛，攻～之盾 6（指古图书） philosophical works by important ancient scholars such as Confucius, Mencius, etc.: ►～书 7（幼崽） newborn animal;（卵） egg: ►鱼～ 8（籽实） seed: 结～儿 bear seed ‖ 无～西瓜 seedless melon ►莲～, 松～ 9（硬颗粒状物） something small and hard: ►～弹, 枪～儿, 石头～儿 10〈口〉（铜子儿） copper coin: 一个～儿不值 not worth a penny ‖ 一个～儿也没有 penniless

B〈形〉 1（幼小） young: ►不入虎穴，焉得虎～, ～鸡, ～姜, ～猪 2（附属） subsidiary: ►～公司, ～金

C〈量〉 [for something long and thin]: 一～儿挂面 a bundle of fine dried noodles ‖ 一～儿毛线 a hank of knitting wool

子[2] zǐ〈名〉 first of the twelve Earthly Branches (地支) ►zi

【子部】zǐbù〈名〉 philosophical works [third of the four traditional categories of Chinese writings]

【子城】zǐchéng〈名〉 satellite town

【子程序】zǐchéngxù〈名〉［计算机］ subprogram

【子丑寅卯】zǐ-chǒu-yín-mǎo〈成〉 1〈本〉 first four of the twelve Earthly Branches 2〈喻〉 reason: 说不出个～来 fail to come up with any convincing argument

【子畜】zǐchù〈名〉 newborn animal

【子代】zǐdài〈名〉［生物］ filial generation: 第一～ first filial generation

【子弹】zǐdàn〈名〉 bullet: 他的头部被～击中。 He was hit by a bullet in the head.

【子弹夹】zǐdànjiā〈名〉 cartridge clip

【子弹壳】zǐdànké〈名〉 cartridge case

【子弹匣】zǐdànxiá〈名〉 magazine

【子堤】zǐdī = 子埝 zǐniàn

【子弟】zǐdì〈名〉 1（子侄辈） sons and younger brothers: 高干～ children of senior cadres ‖ 职工～ children of the workers and staff 2（年轻后辈） later generations: 误人～ lead young people astray

【子弟兵】zǐdìbīng〈名〉 army made up of the sons of the people: 人民～ people's own army

【子弟学校】zǐdì xuéxiào〈名〉 school attached to a factory, etc.

【子房】zǐfáng〈名〉［植物］ ovary

【子公司】zǐgōngsī〈名〉 subsidiary company

【子宫】zǐgōng〈名〉 womb: ～肌瘤 hysteromyoma

【子宫帽】zǐgōngmào〈名〉 cervical cap

【子规】zǐguī = 杜鹃 dùjuān

【子鸡】zǐjī〈名〉 chick

【子金】zǐjīn〈名〉 interest

【子姜】zǐjiāng〈名〉 tender ginger

【子爵】zǐjué〈名〉 viscount: ～夫人 viscountess

【子粒】zǐlì = 籽粒 zǐlì

【子棉】zǐmián = 籽棉 zǐmián

【子母弹】zǐmǔdàn = 榴霰弹 liúxiàndàn

【子母扣儿】zǐmǔkòur〈名〉 press stud〈英〉; snap〈美〉

【子母钟】zǐmǔzhōng〈名〉 secondary and primary clock

【子目】zǐmù〈名〉 subtitle

【子囊】zǐnáng〈名〉［植物］ ascus

【子埝】zǐniàn〈名〉 embankment added on top of a dyke when a flood is imminent

【子女】zǐnǚ〈名〉 1（儿子和女儿） children: 他有两个～。 He has two children. 2（儿子或女儿） son or daughter: 独生～ only child

【子时】zǐshí〈名〉〈旧〉 period of the day from 11 pm to 1 am

【子实】zǐshí = 籽实 zǐshí

【子兽】zǐshòu〈名〉 cub

【子书】zǐshū〈名〉 philosophical works [one of the four traditional categories of Chinese writings]

【子嗣】zǐsì〈名〉〈书〉 male offspring

【子孙】zǐsūn〈名〉 descendants: ～后代 future generations ‖ ～满堂 be blessed with many children and grandchildren

【子午线】zǐwǔxiàn〈名〉［地理］ meridian line: 本初～ first/prime meridian

【子息】zǐxī〈名〉 1（子嗣） male offspring 2〈书〉（利息） interest

【子弦】zǐxián〈名〉 fine silk strings used for the outer strings of *sanxian* (三弦), *pipa* (琵琶) and *erhu* (二胡)

【子虚】zǐxū〈形〉〈书〉 fictitious: 事属～。 It is sheer fiction.

【子虚乌有】zǐxū-wūyǒu〈成〉 imaginary: 这些都是～的事情。 All these things are sheer fiction.

【子婿】zǐxù〈名〉〈书〉 son-in-law

【子叶】zǐyè〈名〉［植物］ cotyledon

【子夜】zǐyè〈名〉 midnight

【子音】zǐyīn〈旧〉 = 辅音 fǔyīn

【子鱼】zǐyú〈名〉 fry (of fish)

【子曰诗云】zǐyuē-shīyún〈成〉 what Confucian classics say

【子侄】zǐzhí〈名〉 sons and nephews

【子猪】zǐzhū〈名〉 piglet

仔 zǐ〈形〉 [usu of domestic animals, fowls, etc.] young: ►～鸡, ～鱼 ►zǎi, zī

【仔畜】zǐchù = 子畜 zǐchù

【仔鸡】zǐjī = 子鸡 zǐjī
【仔密】zǐmì〈形〉 close-knitted: 这块布织得很～。 This piece of cloth is close-woven.
【仔兽】zǐshòu = 子兽 zǐshòu
【仔细】zǐxì **A**〈形〉 careful: ～观察 observe carefully ‖ ～研究 study sth. in detail ‖ 做事很～ be very careful in everything one does **B**〈动〉 be careful: 路很滑，～点儿。 Watch your step! The road is very slippery.
【仔鱼】zǐyú = 子鱼 zǐyú
【仔猪】zǐzhū = 子猪 zǐzhū

姊 zǐ〈名〉 elder sister: ►～妹
【姊妹】zǐmèi〈名〉 sisters: 亲～ blood sisters
【姊妹城】zǐmèichéng〈名〉 twin cities: 这两个城市结成～。 The two cities are twinned with each other.
【姊妹篇】zǐmèipiān〈名〉 companion volume

呰 zǐ
►cí
【呰草】zǐcǎo = 紫草 zǐcǎo

籽 zǐ〈名〉 seed: ►棉～
【籽粒】zǐlì = 籽实 zǐshí
【籽棉】zǐmián〈名〉 unginned cotton
【籽实】zǐshí〈名〉 seed: ～饱满 full grains

笫 zǐ〈名〉〈书〉 mat woven of fine bamboo strips

梓 zǐ
A〈名〉 **1**［植物］ Chinese catalpa **2**〈书〉（故乡） hometown: ►～里，桑～，乡～
B〈动〉 cut blocks for printing: ►付～
【梓宫】zǐgōng〈名〉 coffin for an emperor/empress
【梓里】zǐlǐ〈名〉〈书〉 hometown: 荣归～ return to one's native place with honour

紫 zǐ〈形〉 purple: 他的嘴唇都冻～了。 His lips turned purple with cold.
【紫菜】zǐcài〈名〉［植物］ laver
【紫草】zǐcǎo〈名〉 Chinese gromwell
【紫癜】zǐdiàn ►**p. 50**〈名〉［医学］ purpura
【紫貂】zǐdiāo〈名〉 sable
【紫毫】zǐháo〈名〉 writing brush made of dark purple rabbit's hair
【紫河车】zǐhéchē〈名〉［中药］ dried human placenta
【紫红】zǐhóng〈形〉 purplish red
【紫花】zǐhuā〈名〉 pale reddish brown: ～布 nankeen
【紫禁城】Zǐjìnchéng〈名〉 Forbidden City [in Beijing]
【紫荆】zǐjīng〈名〉［植物］ Chinese redbud
【紫荆花】zǐjīnghuā〈名〉 bauhinia
【紫罗兰】zǐluólán〈名〉［植物］ violet
【紫茉莉】zǐmòlì〈名〉［植物］ four-o'clock
【紫砂】zǐshā〈名〉 boccaro ware: ～壶 boccaro teapot
【紫杉】zǐshān〈名〉［植物］(Japanese) yew
【紫苏】zǐsū〈名〉［植物］ purple perilla
【紫檀】zǐtán〈名〉 red sandalwood
【紫糖】zǐtáng〈形〉 purple brown: ～脸 purple brown face
【紫藤】zǐténg〈名〉［植物］ Chinese wisteria
【紫铜】zǐtóng〈名〉 red copper
【紫外线】zǐwàixiàn〈名〉［物理］ ultraviolet ray
【紫菀】zǐwǎn〈名〉［植物］ aster
【紫葳】zǐwēi = 凌霄花 língxiāohuā
【紫薇】zǐwēi〈名〉［植物］ crape myrtle
【紫药水】zǐyàoshuǐ〈名〉［药学］ gentian violet solution
【紫云英】zǐyúnyīng〈名〉［植物］ Chinese milk vetch
【紫竹】zǐzhú〈名〉 black bamboo

訾 zǐ〈动〉〈书〉 calumniate: ►～议
►zī
【訾议】zǐyì〈动〉〈书〉 criticize: 无可～ be above criticism

滓 zǐ〈名〉 lees: ►渣～

zì

自 zì
A〈代〉 self: 他～以为了不起。 He thinks himself very important. ►～告奋勇，～作～受
B〈副〉 naturally: ～不用说 it goes without saying ►～有公论
C〈介〉 from: ～第一天起 from the first day ‖ ～左而右 from left to right ‖ 合同～6月1日起生效。 The contract will be effective from June 1. ►～从，～古
【自爱】zì'ài〈动〉 have self-respect: 他是一个非常～的人。 He is a man of great self-respect.
【自傲】zì'ào〈形〉 arrogant: ►居功～
【自拔】zìbá〈动〉 extricate oneself: 染上毒瘾而不能～ get addicted to drugs and be unable to break the habit
【自白】zìbái〈动〉 vindicate oneself: ～书 written confession
【自暴自弃】zìbào-zìqì〈成〉 abandon oneself to despair: 不可～，破罐子破摔。 Don't give things up as hopeless and make matters worse.
【自卑】zìbēi〈形〉 self-abased: 不自满，也不～ be neither self-satisfied nor self-abased
【自卑感】zìbēigǎn〈名〉 inferiority complex: 克服～ overcome a sense of inferiority
【自备井】zìbèijǐng〈名〉 private well
【自便】zìbiàn〈动〉 do as one pleases: 请～。 Please do as you like. ‖ 听其～。 Let him do as he pleases.
【自不待言】zìbùdàiyán〈成〉 be self-evident
【自不量力】zìbùliànglì〈成〉 overestimate one's own strength
【自裁】zìcái〈动〉〈书〉take one's own life
【自残】zìcán〈动〉 **1**（残害自己） mutilate oneself **2**（相互残害） commit fratricide: 骨肉～ fight a fratricidal war
【自惭形秽】zìcán-xínghuì〈成〉feel a sense of inferiority: 使某人～ make sb. feel inferior
【自查】zìchá〈动〉 do a self-examination
【自产自销】zìchǎn-zìxiāo〈动〉 market one's own products
【自嘲】zìcháo〈动〉 laugh at oneself
【自称】zìchēng〈动〉 **1**（指称呼自己） call oneself: 项羽～西楚霸王。 Xiang Yu styled himself 'Lord of Western Chu'. **2**（声称） claim to be: ～不知情 profess ignorance ‖ ～内行 claim to be an expert
【自成一家】zìchéng-yījiā〈成〉 have a style of one's own
【自乘】zìchéng〈动〉［数学］ square: 9～得81。 Nine squared is 81.
【自持】zìchí〈动〉 exercise self-restraint: 清廉～ be incorruptible and self-restrained ‖ 他一时冲动，几乎不能～。 At that moment he became so excited that he could hardly control himself.
【自筹】zìchóu〈动〉 self-finance: ～资金 raise funds independently
【自出机杼】zìchū-jīzhù〈成〉〈喻〉 be original in conception
【自吹法螺】zìchuī-fǎluó〈成〉 blow one's own trumpet
【自吹自擂】zìchuī-zìléi〈成〉 blow one's own trumpet
【自从】zìcóng〈介〉 since: ～他来后，办公室就变得干净多了。 The office has become cleaner since he arrived.
【自大】zìdà〈形〉 self-important: 切勿骄傲～。 Guard against pride and conceit. ►夜郎～，自高～
【自得】zìdé〈形〉 contented: 安闲～ free and contented
【自得其乐】zìdé-qílè〈成〉 be content with one's lot
【自动】zìdòng〈形〉 **1**（主动） voluntary: ～参加 participate voluntarily ‖ ～交待 confess of one's own accord **2**（不用人力） self-generated: ～燃烧 spontaneous combustion ‖ 水～流到田里。 The water flowed into the fields naturally. **3**（依靠自身系统） automatic: ～充电 be self-charging ‖ ～音量控制 automatic volume control
【自动报警器】zìdòng bàojǐngqì〈名〉 automatic alarm
【自动报警系统】zìdòng bàojǐng xìtǒng〈名〉 automatic alarm system
【自动步枪】zìdòng bùqiāng〈名〉 automatic rifle
【自动挡】zìdòngdǎng〈名〉 automatic transmission: ～汽车 car with automatic transmission
【自动扶梯】zìdòng fútī〈名〉 escalator
【自动柜员机】zìdòng guìyuánjī〈名〉 automatic teller machine (ATM)
【自动化】zìdònghuà〈动〉 automate: ～生产线 automatic production line
【自动驾驶仪】zìdòng jiàshǐyí〈名〉 autopilot
【自动控制】zìdòng kòngzhì〈名〉 automatic control
【自动售货机】zìdòng shòuhuòjī〈名〉 vending machine
【自发】zìfā〈形〉 spontaneous: ～的斗争 spontaneous struggle ‖ ～地组织起来 be spontaneously organized
【自发面粉】zìfā miànfěn〈名〉 self-raising flour
【自肥】zìféi〈动〉 feather one's own nest: 损人～ enrich oneself at others' expense
【自费】zìfèi〈动〉 pay one's own expenses: ～留学 study abroad at one's own expense ‖ ～医疗 pay for one's own medical care
【自费生】zìfèishēng〈名〉 self-subsidizing student
【自焚】zìfén〈动〉 burn oneself to death: ～身亡 burn oneself to death ‖ 玩火～ those who play with fire will get burned
【自封】zìfēng〈动〉 **1**〈贬〉（自称） proclaim oneself: ～为专家 profess to be an expert **2**（自我限制） confine oneself: ►故步～
【自奉】zìfèng〈动〉〈书〉 satisfy one's own desires: ～甚俭 practise self-denial
【自负】zìfù **A**〈动〉 be responsible for one's own actions: 后果～ be responsible for the consequences of one's actions ‖ 文责～。 The author takes sole responsibility for

Z

what he writes. **B** 〈形〉 self-important: 这个人很～。 This person is rather conceited.
【自负盈亏】zìfù-yíngkuī〈成〉 assume sole responsibility for profits or losses
【自甘堕落】zìgān-duòluò〈成〉 abandon oneself to vice
【自高自大】zìgāo-zìdà〈成〉 conceited: ～的人 conceited person
【自告奋勇】zìgào-fènyǒng〈成〉 offer to undertake
【自个儿】zìgěr〈代〉〈口〉 oneself: 不要只顾～。 Don't just think about yourself.
【自供】zìgòng〈动〉 confess: ～状 confession
【自古】zìgǔ〈副〉 since ancient times: ～以来 from time immemorial ‖ 长江三角洲～是鱼米之乡。 The Yangtze Delta has been a thriving region since ancient times.
【自顾不暇】zìgù-bùxiá〈成〉 be unable even to fend for oneself (much less look after others)
【自豪】zìháo〈形〉 proud: 他以自己的家庭为～。 He is proud of his family.
【自豪感】zìháogǎn〈名〉 sense of pride: 民族～ sense of national pride
【自花授粉】zìhuā shòufěn〈名〉 self-pollination
【自画像】zìhuàxiàng〈名〉 self-portrait
【自毁】zìhuǐ〈名〉［军事］ self-destruction: ～装置 self-destructing device
【自己】zìjǐ〈代〉 **1**（用于复指） oneself: ～打～嘴巴 contradict oneself ‖ ～做主 be master of one's own affairs ‖ 他～知道该怎么做。 He himself knows what to do. **2**（指本人） one's own: ～家里 one's own family ‖ ～兄弟 one's own brothers
【自己人】zìjǐrén〈名〉 one of us: ～不必客气。 All of us here are friends, so make yourself at home. ‖ 我们一直把你看成～。 We have been treating you as one of us.
【自给】zìjǐ〈动〉 be self-sufficient: 粮食～有余 be more than self-sufficient in grain
【自给自足】zìjǐ-zìzú〈成〉 be self-supporting and self-sufficient
【自家】zìjiā〈代〉 oneself: ～的店铺 one's own shop
【自驾】zìjià〈动〉 drive one's own car: 双休日～游客较多。 There are more tourists in their own cars on the weekends.
【自驾游】zìjiàyóu〈名〉 road trip: 私家车多了，～也就多了。 As more people get cars, so road trips are becoming more common.
【自荐】zìjiàn〈动〉 put oneself forward: ▸毛遂～
【自矜】zìjīn〈动〉〈书〉 blow one's own trumpet
【自尽】zìjìn〈动〉 take one's own life: 投河～ commit suicide by drowning oneself in a river
【自刭】zìjǐng〈动〉〈书〉 commit suicide by cutting one's own throat
【自净】zìjìng〈动〉 self-purify: ～作用 self-purification
【自疚】zìjiù〈动〉 have a guilty conscience: 内心～ be stung by conscience
【自咎】zìjiù〈动〉 reproach oneself
【自救】zìjiù〈动〉 save oneself: 生产～ provide for and help oneself by engaging in production
【自居】zìjū〈动〉 pose as: 以专家～ be a self-styled expert
【自决】zìjué〈动〉 [of a nation] determine by oneself: 民族～权 right to ethnic self-determination
【自觉】zìjué **A**〈动〉be aware of: 肺结核初期时，病症并不明显，患者常常不～。 The symptoms of tuberculosis are not distinct in the early stages, so the patient is often unaware of having it. **B**〈形〉 conscious: ～地遵守纪律 conscientiously observe discipline
【自觉性】zìjuéxìng〈名〉 consciousness: 提高～ raise one's consciousness
【自觉症状】zìjué zhèngzhuàng〈名〉 subjective symptoms
【自觉自愿】zìjué-zìyuàn〈成〉 of one's own free will
【自绝】zìjué〈动〉 alienate oneself: ～于人民 alienate oneself from the people
【自掘坟墓】zìjué-fénmù〈成〉dig one's own grave
【自考】zìkǎo〈简称〉= 自学考试
【自考生】zìkǎoshēng〈名〉 candidate for the self-taught examinations
【自控】zìkòng〈名〉 **1** = 自动控制 zìdòng kòngzhì **2**（自我约束） self-control: ～能力差 not be good at controlling oneself
【自夸】zìkuā〈动〉 blow one's own trumpet: ～记性好 brag about having a good memory
【自愧不如】zìkuì-bùrú〈成〉 feel ashamed of one's inferiority
【自来】zìlái〈副〉 from the beginning: 这里～就是交通要道。 This has always been a vital communication line.
【自来水】zìláishuǐ〈名〉 tap water: ～厂 waterworks
【自来水笔】zìláishuǐbǐ〈旧〉= 钢笔 gāngbǐ
【自理】zìlǐ〈动〉 **1**（指承担） provide for oneself: 费用～ pay one's own expenses **2**（指料理） take care of oneself: 生活不能～ be unable to look after oneself
【自力更生】zìlì-gēngshēng〈成〉 self-reliance: ～，重建家园 rebuild one's home through one's own efforts
【自立】zìlì〈动〉 be self-supporting: ～于世界民族之林 stand proudly among the world nations ‖ 我的几个儿子都已经～了。 My sons are old enough to stand on their own two feet.
【自励】zìlì〈动〉 encourage oneself
【自怜】zìlián〈动〉 feel pity for oneself: ▸顾影～
【自量】zìliàng〈动〉 estimate one's own ability: 不～ overestimate oneself ‖ 你也太不～了，你哪儿是他的对手。 You think too highly of yourself. You are no match for him.
【自流】zìliú〈动〉 **1**（指液体） flow by itself: ～灌溉 gravity irrigation ‖ ～井 artesian well **2**〈喻〉（指人） do as one pleases: 听其～ let people act as they please ▸放任～
【自留地】zìliúdì〈名〉〈旧〉 private plot
【自律】zìlǜ〈动〉〈书〉 practise self-discipline: 廉洁～ be honest and self-disciplined
【自卖自夸】zìmài-zìkuā〈成〉〈喻〉 blow one's own trumpet
【自满】zìmǎn〈形〉 smug: ～情绪 self-satisfaction ‖ 我们决不能一有成绩就～。 We must not become complacent over any success. ▸骄傲～
【自勉】zìmiǎn〈动〉 encourage oneself
【自民党】Zìmíndǎng〈名〉 Liberal Democratic Party [in Japan]
【自鸣得意】zìmíng-déyì〈成〉 be puffed up with pride
【自鸣清高】zìmíng-qīnggāo〈成〉 profess to be above worldly considerations
【自鸣钟】zìmíngzhōng〈名〉 chime clock
【自命】zìmìng〈动〉 consider oneself
【自命不凡】zìmìng-bùfán〈成〉 think no end of oneself
【自谋出路】zìmóu-chūlù〈成〉 find a way out for oneself
【自谋生计】zìmóu-shēngjì〈成〉 earn one's own bread
【自馁】zìněi〈动〉 lose heart: 失败了不要～。 Don't be discouraged by the defeat.
【自虐】zìnüè〈动〉 self-torture
【自拍机】zìpāijī〈名〉［摄影］ self-timer
【自欺欺人】zìqī-qīrén〈成〉 deceive oneself as well as others: 你不要用这种伪科学～了。 Don't fool yourself and others with this kind of pseudoscience.
【自谦】zìqiān〈动〉 be self-effacing: ～之词 self-depreciating remarks made as a gesture of politeness
【自戕】zìqiāng〈动〉〈书〉 commit suicide
【自强】zìqiáng〈动〉 strive to be stronger: 自尊～的民族精神 national spirit of self-respect and self-support
【自强不息】zìqiáng-bùxī〈成〉 make unremitting efforts to improve oneself
【自取灭亡】zìqǔ-mièwáng〈成〉 court self-destruction
【自取其咎】zìqǔ-qíjiù〈成〉 bring blame on oneself: 你这是～。 You asked for it.
【自然】zìrán **A**〈名〉 nature: 回归～ return to nature ‖ ～条件 natural conditions ▸大～ **B**〈形〉 natural: ▸听其～ **C**〈副〉 naturally: 你先别问，到时候～明白。 Don't ask now. You'll understand in due course. ‖ 功到～成。 Constant efforts yield sure success.
【自然保护区】zìrán bǎohùqū〈名〉 nature reserve: 国家～ national nature reserve
【自然辩证法】zìrán biànzhèngfǎ〈名〉 dialectics of nature
【自然博物馆】zìrán bówùguǎn〈名〉 museum of natural history
【自然村】zìráncūn〈名〉 village that has come into being spontaneously and naturally
【自然地理】zìrán dìlǐ〈名〉 physical geography
【自然而然】zìrán'érrán〈成〉 naturally: 我们长期在一起工作，～地产生了友谊。 Having worked together for many years, we naturally formed a friendship.
【自然法则】zìrán fǎzé = 自然规律 zìrán guīlǜ
【自然规律】zìrán guīlǜ〈名〉 law of nature: 遵循～ follow the law of nature
【自然环境】zìrán huánjìng〈名〉 natural environment
【自然界】zìránjiè〈名〉 natural world
【自然经济】zìrán jīngjì〈名〉 natural economy
【自然科学】zìrán kēxué〈名〉 natural science
【自然力】zìránlì〈名〉 natural forces
【自然人】zìránrén〈名〉［法律］ natural person
【自然日】zìránrì〈名〉 calendar day
【自然数】zìránshù ▸**p. 691**〈名〉［数学］ natural number
【自然死亡】zìrán sǐwáng〈名〉 natural death
【自然灾害】zìrán zāihài〈名〉 natural disaster
【自然主义】zìrán zhǔyì〈名〉 naturalism
【自然资源】zìrán zīyuán〈名〉 natural resources
【自然】zìran〈形〉 natural: 神态～ look natural ‖ 他讲课态度非常～。 He looked very natural when he gave lectures.
【自燃】zìrán〈动〉 self-ignite

【自认】zìrèn〈动〉resign oneself to: ～晦气 be resigned to one's bad luck
【自如】zìrú〈形〉1（不受阻碍）easy: 行动～ move about freely ‖ 运用～ have a perfect command of sth. 2（镇定）self-possessed: 谈吐～ be calm and at ease in conversation
【自若】zìruò〈形〉〈书〉self-possessed: 神色～ appear calm and at ease ‖ 临危不惧，谈笑～ talk and laugh imperturbably in face of danger ▸泰然～
【自杀】zìshā〈动〉kill oneself: 服毒～ kill oneself by taking poison ‖ 畏罪～ commit suicide to escape punishment
【自杀性爆炸】zìshāxìng bàozhà〈名〉suicide bombing
【自杀性攻击】zìshāxìng gōngjī〈名〉suicide attack
【自伤】zìshāng〈名〉［法律］self-injury
【自上而下】zìshàng'érxià〈成〉from above to below: 把上级的指示～地传达到基层 communicate the instructions of a higher leading body to grass roots units
【自身】zìshēn〈名〉oneself: 不顾～安危 disregard one's own safety
【自身难保】zìshēn-nánbǎo〈成〉be unable even to protect oneself
【自生自灭】zìshēng-zìmiè〈成〉emerge of itself and perish of itself: 一些无名作家的作品无人理会，就这样～。Some works by unknown writers fail to get enough attention from the public and are thus left to run their own course.
【自食其果】zìshí-qíguǒ〈成〉reap what one has sown: 作恶多端，必将～。Those who are steeped in iniquity will one day be forced to face the consequences of their actions.
【自食其力】zìshí-qílì〈成〉earn one's own living: ～的劳动者 workers earning their own crusts
【自食其言】zìshí-qíyán〈成〉go back on one's word: 说到做到，我绝不～。I'll do what I say. I never go back on my word.
【自始至终】zìshǐ-zhìzhōng〈成〉from start to finish: 她在会上～一言未发。She remained silent throughout the meeting.
【自视】zìshì〈动〉consider oneself: ～甚高 think highly of oneself
【自是】zìshì A〈副〉naturally: 子女多，～个拖累。Too many children are naturally a burden. B〈形〉self-congratulatory: 他既～又顽固。He is self-willed as well as rather full of himself.
【自恃】zìshì〈书〉A〈形〉over-confident and conceited: 不可～太高 should never become too arrogant or cocky B〈动〉capitalize on: ～有功 capitalize on one's achievements
【自首】zìshǒu〈动〉give oneself up: 投案～ turn oneself in to the police
【自赎】zìshú〈动〉atone for one's crime: 立功～ perform meritorious services to atone for one's crimes
【自述】zìshù A〈动〉give an account of oneself: 序言里作者～了写书的经过。The author of the book prefaced his remarks by giving an account of how he had written the book. B〈名〉autobiography: 写一篇～ write one's autobiography
【自说自话】zìshuō-zìhuà〈成〉1（自作主张）decide for oneself 2（自言自语）talk to oneself
【自私】zìsī〈形〉selfish: 人不能太～。We must not be too selfish.
【自私自利】zìsī-zìlì〈成〉self-centred
【自诉】zìsù〈动〉［法律］take action privately
【自讨苦吃】zìtǎokǔchī〈成〉invite trouble: 这是你～，怨不得别人。Nobody is to blame for the trouble; you brought it on yourself.
【自讨没趣】zìtǎo-méiqù〈成〉ask for a snub
【自投罗网】zìtóu-luówǎng〈成〉walk right into a trap
【自卫】zìwèi〈动〉defend oneself: ～战争 war of self-defence ‖ 我打死他是出于～。I shot him dead in self-defence.
【自卫反击】zìwèi fǎnjī〈动〉strike back in self-defence
【自慰】zìwèi〈动〉1（自我安慰）console oneself: ▸聊以～ 2［生理］masturbate
【自刎】zìwěn〈动〉commit suicide by slitting one's throat: ～而死 die by slitting one's throat
【自问】zìwèn〈动〉1（问自己）ask oneself: ▸反躬～，扪心～ 2（自我衡量）reach a conclusion after weighing up a matter: 我～没有对不起他的地方。I don't remember ever having done him any wrong.
【自我】zìwǒ〈代〉oneself: 超越～ transcend oneself ‖ ～保护意识 self-protection awareness ‖ ～安慰 self-consolation ‖ ～介绍 introduce oneself ‖ ～感觉良好 feel good about oneself ‖ ～批评 self-criticism ‖ ～欣赏 self-appreciation
【自我暗示】zìwǒ ànshì〈名〉［心理］self-suggestion
【自我标榜】zìwǒ biāobǎng〈成〉sing one's own praises
【自我陶醉】zìwǒ táozuì〈成〉be carried away with a sense of one's own self-importance
【自习】zìxí〈动〉study by oneself
【自下而上】zìxià'érshàng〈成〉from bottom to top: ～地推荐 recommend sb. from below
【自相】zìxiāng〈副〉each other: ～矛盾 contradict oneself
【自相残杀】zìxiāng cánshā〈成〉kill each other
【自销】zìxiāo〈动〉sell goods through one's own channels
【自小】zìxiǎo〈副〉since childhood
【自卸卡车】zìxiè kǎchē〈名〉dump truck
【自新】zìxīn〈动〉make a fresh start: 悔过～ turn over a new leaf
【自信】zìxìn〈动〉be confident: 过于～ be over-confident ‖ ～心 self-confidence ‖ 你别太～了。Don't be overly self-confident.
【自行】zìxíng〈副〉1（自己）by oneself: ～安排 arrange by oneself ‖ ～处理 deal with on one's own 2（自动）of one's own accord: ～消亡 die out of itself
【自行车】zìxíngchē〈名〉bicycle
【自行火炮】zìxíng-huǒpào〈名〉［军事］mechanized gun
【自行其是】zìxíng-qíshì〈成〉do one's own thing: 多听听别人的意见，别～。Don't be wilful. Listen to what others have to say.
【自省】zìxǐng〈动〉〈书〉have a good look at oneself
【自修】zìxiū〈动〉1（自习）study by oneself: 在家～ study by oneself at home 2（自学）teach oneself: ～了大学的全部课程 complete on one's own all the courses offered by the university
【自许】zìxǔ〈动〉1（指称赞）take pride in 2（指声称）call oneself
【自诩】zìxǔ〈动〉〈书〉brag: 切不可～自己如何高明。Don't brag about how wise you are.
【自序】zìxù〈名〉1（指前言）preface 2（指文章）autobiographical note
【自叙】zìxù = 自序 zìxù
【自选动作】zìxuǎn dòngzuò〈名〉［体育］optional exercise
【自选商场】zìxuǎn shāngchǎng〈名〉supermarket
【自学】zìxué〈动〉teach oneself: ～成才 be self-taught ‖ ～英语专业的课程 teach oneself the courses required for English majors
【自学考试】zìxué kǎoshì〈名〉self-study examination: 参加～ sit for self-study examinations
【自寻烦恼】zìxún-fánnǎo〈成〉worry oneself needlessly
【自寻死路】zìxún-sǐlù〈成〉bring about one's own destruction
【自言自语】zìyán-zìyǔ〈成〉talk to oneself
【自贻伊戚】zìyí-yīqī〈成〉bring trouble on oneself
【自已】zìyǐ〈动〉[often used in the negative] be able to control oneself: 不能～ be unable to control oneself ‖ 思乡之情难以～ one's nostalgia is beyond control
【自以为得计】zì yǐwéi déjì〈成〉〈贬〉be pleased with one's own scheming
【自以为是】zìyǐwéishì〈成〉regard oneself as infallible
【自缢】zìyì〈动〉〈书〉hang oneself: ～而死 commit suicide by hanging
【自营】zìyíng〈动〉run by oneself
【自用】zìyòng〈动〉1〈书〉（自以为是）be self-opinionated: ▸刚愎～ 2（自己使用）keep for personal use: 留作～ keep for personal use
【自由】zìyóu A〈名〉1（指权利）freedom, liberty: 侵犯人身～ violate sb.'s freedom ‖ 集会～ freedom of assembly ‖ 言论～ freedom of speech ‖ 宗教信仰～ freedom of religious belief 2［哲学］freedom: ～和必然 freedom and necessity B〈形〉free: ～发表意见 speak one's mind freely ‖ ～行动 act of one's own free will ‖ ～选择 be free to choose
【自由港】zìyóugǎng〈名〉free port
【自由价格】zìyóu jiàgé〈名〉free price
【自由竞争】zìyóu jìngzhēng〈名〉free competition
【自由恋爱】zìyóu liàn'ài〈动〉have the freedom to choose one's own marriage partner
【自由贸易】zìyóu màoyì〈名〉free trade: ～区 free trade zone
【自由民】zìyóumín〈名〉free citizen
【自由人】zìyóurén〈名〉［足球］［排球］libero
【自由散漫】zìyóu-sǎnmàn〈成〉be slack: 我这个人～惯了。I have developed the habit of going my own way.
【自由身】zìyóushēn〈名〉free agent: 两人离婚后都成了～。Once they got divorced they were both free agents. ‖ 她已跟娱乐公司解约，是～了。Having terminated her contract with the entertainment company, she is now a free agent.
【自由诗】zìyóushī〈名〉free verse
【自由市场】zìyóu shìchǎng〈名〉free market
【自由体操】zìyóu tǐcāo〈名〉floor exercise
【自由王国】zìyóu wángguó〈名〉［哲学］realm of freedom: 人类的历史，就是一个不断地从必然王国向～发展的历史。The history of mankind is one of continuous development from the realm of necessity to the realm of freedom.
【自由行】zìyóuxíng〈名〉free individual travel: 中国内地的港澳～政策 Mainland

China's Individual Visiting Scheme to Hong Kong and Macau

【自由泳】zìyóuyǒng〈名〉［体育］freestyle

【自由职业】zìyóu zhíyè ▶p. 966〈名〉freelance profession: ～者 freelancer ‖ 她是个～者。She works freelance.

【自由主义】zìyóuzhǔyì〈名〉liberalism: ～的倾向 liberal tendencies ‖ ～者 liberal

【自由撰稿人】zìyóu zhuàngǎorén ▶p. 966〈名〉freelance writer

【自由自在】zìyóu-zìzài〈成〉leisurely and carefree: ～地玩耍 play in a free and unrestrained way

【自有公论】zìyǒu-gōnglùn〈成〉the people will make a fair judgement

【自幼】zìyòu〈副〉since childhood

【自娱】zìyú〈动〉entertain oneself

【自圆其说】zìyuán-qíshuō〈成〉justify oneself: 你的论点自相矛盾，不能～。Your argument is self-contradictory and internally inconsistent.

【自愿】zìyuàn〈动〉volunteer: ～参加开发大西北的建设 volunteer to participate in the development of north-west China ‖ 她做这件事是～的。She did it of her own free will.

【自怨自艾】zìyuàn-zìyì〈成〉be full of remorse and self-reproach: 有错误改了就好，何必～呢？Since you have already made good your errors, why are you still reproaching yourself about things?

【自在】zìzài〈形〉free: ▶逍遥～

【自在】zìzai〈形〉comfortable: 感到很不～ feel ill at ease ‖ 日子过得挺～ lead a free and easy life

【自责】zìzé〈动〉blame oneself: 这事他俩也有责任，你不要一味地～了。The two of them should also take some blame for this matter, so you should stop just blaming yourself.

【自找麻烦】zìzhǎo máfan〈成〉bring trouble upon oneself

【自斟自酌】zìzhēn-zìzhuó〈成〉enjoy a cup of wine all by oneself

【自知之明】zìzhīzhīmíng〈成〉wisdom of self-knowledge: 人贵有～。Self-knowledge is wisdom.

【自制】zìzhì〈动〉1（指制作）make by oneself: 这些设备是我们～的。We made this equipment ourselves. 2（指控制）control oneself: 他一读起小说就不能～，常常一看就是一个通宵。Whenever he starts reading a novel, he can't help himself, and often reads right through the night.

【自治】zìzhì〈动〉exercise autonomy: 享有高度～权 enjoy a high degree of autonomy ‖ 民族区域～ regional national autonomy

【自治区】zìzhìqū〈名〉autonomous region

【自治权】zìzhìquán〈名〉autonomy

【自治县】zìzhìxiàn〈名〉autonomous county

【自治州】zìzhìzhōu〈名〉autonomous prefecture

【自重】zìzhòng A〈动〉1（指尊重）conduct oneself with dignity: 不～ have no respect for oneself ‖ 请～。Please behave yourself. 2〈书〉（指自我抬高）enhance one's influence: 拥兵～ mobilize troops to extend one's influence B〈名〉deadweight: 车皮～2.5吨。The deadweight of the wagon is 2.5 tons.

【自主】zìzhǔ〈动〉be one's own master: ～经营 be one's own boss ‖ 男女婚姻～。Men and women shall choose their own spouses. ▶不由～

【自主权】zìzhǔquán〈名〉decision-making power: 扩大国有企业～ expand the decision-making powers of state-owned enterprises

【自主知识产权】zìzhǔ zhīshi chǎnquán〈名〉intellectual property rights

【自住房】zìzhùfáng〈名〉privately owned and occupied housing: 购买首套～ purchase one's first house

【自助】zìzhù〈名〉self-service: ～银行 self-service bank

【自助餐】zìzhùcān〈名〉buffet

【自助游】zìzhùyóu〈名〉independent travel: ～的实际消费往往高于旅行社团队游报价。Traveling on one's own is often more expensive than going with a group.

【自传】zìzhuàn〈名〉autobiography

【自传体小说】zìzhuàntǐ xiǎoshuō〈名〉autobiographical novel

【自转】zìzhuàn〈动〉［天文］rotate: 地球的～ rotation of the earth

【自足】zìzú A〈形〉self-satisfied: ～经济 self-sufficient economy ‖ 露出～的样子 look smug B〈动〉be self-sufficient: ▶自给～

【自尊】zìzūn〈形〉self-respecting: ～自爱 have self-respect

【自尊心】zìzūnxīn〈名〉self-respect: 伤害～ injure sb.'s pride ‖ 民族～ national self-respect ‖ ～很强的人 person of great self-respect

【自作聪明】zìzuò-cōngmíng〈成〉fancy oneself clever

【自作多情】zìzuò-duōqíng〈成〉fancy oneself as very attractive to the opposite sex

【自作孽】zìzuònìè〈动〉sow the seeds of one's own ruin

【自作主张】zìzuò-zhǔzhāng〈成〉decide things for oneself

【自作自受】zìzuò-zìshòu〈成〉suffer as a result of one's own actions

“字”和“词”

■ 汉语里“字”和“词”的区分类似于英语里 character 和 word 的区分，但 character 和 word 的概念与“字”和“词”是不同的。英语的 character 可指书写或印刷系统中的字母、数字或任何符号，甚至字与字之间的空格；word 指书面或口语中能独立表达意义的语言单位，一般翻译成“单词”。

■“字”可翻译成英语的 character、letter 或 word，但也可表示其他不同的含义，因此在具体翻译时，应根据语境选择适当的用语。“词”可翻译成英语的 word、phrase 或 expression，也跟“字”一样有各种各样的意义，因此翻译时也是灵活多样的。

“字”

■ 指用来记录语言的符号：

这个地址是用汉字写的
= The address was written in Chinese characters

这些符号是希腊字母
= These symbols are Greek characters

这篇（中文）文章不能超过两千个字
= This (Chinese) essay should be no more than two thousand characters long

■ 指文字的不同形式、书法的派别：

宋体字
= Song typeface

字帖
= copybook for calligraphy

■ 指书法作品：

字画
= calligraphy and painting

字幅
= horizontal or vertical scroll of calligraphy

■ 指合同、契约：

字据
= written pledge

立字为凭
= sign an agreement (or a contract, etc.) as proof

■ 指字迹：

我弟弟写一手好字
= My brother's handwriting is excellent

他的字很难认
= His writing is illegible

■ 指字音：

他吐字清晰
= He enunciates his words very clearly

她总是字斟句酌
= She always chooses her words with care

“词”

■ 指最小的、有意义的语言单位：

“桌子”一词在英语里叫 table
= The English word for 桌子 is 'table'

我找不到合适的词来表达我的感受
= I cannot find proper words to express my feelings

“照顾”一词在英语里是 look after
= The English phrase for 照顾 is 'look after'

英语里有不同的词表示道歉
= In English there are different ways of apologizing

■ 泛指诗歌、文章等中的词句：

歌词
= lyrics

演讲词
= speech

台词
= lines

■ 指中国古代的一种诗体（起于唐朝，盛行于宋代）：

词人
= *ci* writer

宋词
= poetry of the Song Dynasty

字 zì

A ▸**p. 999**〈名〉**1**（指文字符号）character: 认～ be able to read ‖ 常用～ characters in common use ‖ 汉～ Chinese characters **2**（指别名）name taken at the age of twenty, by which a man is sometimes called: 仲谋是孙权的～。 Zhongmou was the style of Sun Quan. ‖ 鲁迅原名周树人，～豫才。 Originally named as Zhou Shuren, Luxun styled himself Yucai. **3**（指书法字体）style of calligraphy: 黑体～ boldface type ‖ 柳～ Liu Gongquan (柳公权) style of calligraphy ‖ 篆～ seal character ‖ 他写一手漂亮的～。 He writes elegant characters. **4**（指书法）calligraphy: 一幅书法家的～ a calligrapher's script ▸～画 **5**（指用词）wording: 琢句炼～ measure one's words **6**（指字据）written pledge: 借了钱，留个～。 When borrowing money you should write an IOU. ▸立～ **7**（指发音）pronunciation: 吐～清楚 enunciate clearly ▸～正腔圆 **8**（指名字）name: 我在文件上签了～。 I put my name to the document. ▸签～
B〈动〉〈旧〉[of a girl] be engaged to: 待～闺中 remain unengaged

> 字
> ▸姓名

【字典】zìdiǎn〈名〉 dictionary: 查～ consult a dictionary ‖ 《新华字典》 *Xinhua Dictionary*
【字典纸】zìdiǎnzhǐ〈名〉 India paper
【字调】zìdiào〈名〉［语言］ tones of Chinese characters
【字符】zìfú〈名〉［计算机］ character: ～串 character string
【字幅】zìfú〈名〉 scroll of calligraphy
【字号】zìhào〈名〉 **1**（字体大小） font: 使用同一～小字体 use the small type of the same font **2**（店名） name of a shop **3**（商店） shop: 这是一家老～。 This is a shop with a long history.
【字画】zìhuà〈名〉 calligraphy and painting: 历代名家～ famous scripts and paintings through the ages
【字汇】zìhuì〈名〉〈旧〉 lexicon
【字迹】zìjì〈名〉 handwriting: ～工整/潦草/模糊 have neat/illegible/indecipherable handwriting
【字节】zìjié〈名〉［计算机］ byte
【字句】zìjù〈名〉 words and expressions: 推敲～ choose one's words with care ‖ ～通顺 coherent and smooth writing
【字据】zìjù〈名〉 written pledge: 口说无凭，须立个～。 Since verbal statements are no guarantee, a written agreement must be made.
【字库】zìkù〈名〉［计算机］ **1**（指文字库） character bank **2**（指字体库） font bank
【字里行间】zìlǐ-hángjiān〈成〉 between the lines: 她的文章～充满了乐观精神。 Reading between the lines, you'll find that her article is full of optimism.
【字谜】zìmí〈名〉 word riddle: 猜～ guess a character riddle
【字面】zìmiàn〈名〉 literal meaning: ～意思 literal meaning
【字模】zìmú〈名〉［印刷］ matrix
【字母】zìmǔ〈名〉 **1**（指书写单位） letter: 汉语拼音～ Chinese phonetic alphabet ‖ 英语～ English alphabet **2**［语言］ character representing an initial consonant (声母)
【字母表】zìmǔbiǎo〈名〉 alphabet
【字幕】zìmù〈名〉 subtitles: 中文～ Chinese subtitles
【字书】zìshū〈名〉 wordbook
【字体】zìtǐ〈名〉 **1**（指文字形体） typeface **2**（指书法派别） style of calligraphy **3**（书写） handwriting: ～工整 neat handwriting
【字条】zìtiáo〈名〉 brief note: 他走时给我留了个～。 He left me a note before leaving.
【字帖】zìtiè〈名〉 calligraphy copybook: 临摹～ practise calligraphy after a model
【字形】zìxíng〈名〉 font
【字眼】zìyǎn〈名〉 wording: 抠～儿 be fussy about wording ‖ 找不出适当的～来形容 can't find appropriate words to describe
【字样】zìyàng〈名〉 **1**（指字形规范） model of written characters **2**（指句子） printed or written words: 门上写着"卫生模范"的～。 On the door were the words 'Model Family in Hygiene Work'.
【字义】zìyì〈名〉 meaning of a (Chinese) character
【字音】zìyīn〈名〉 pronunciation of a (Chinese) character
【字斟句酌】zìzhēn-jùzhuó〈成〉 choose one's words with care: 即席讲话，顾不上～ make an impromptu speech with no time to get the words together
【字正腔圆】zìzhèng-qiāngyuán〈成〉 pronounce every word correctly and in a sweet, mellow voice
【字纸】zìzhǐ〈名〉 waste paper with characters written or printed on it: ～篓 wastepaper basket

恣 zì

A〈动〉 throw off restraint: ▸～情, ～意
B〈形〉〈方〉 comfortable
【恣情】zìqíng〈副〉〈书〉 **1**（纵情） to one's heart's content: ～欢笑 laugh heartily ‖ ～享乐 enjoy oneself as much as one pleases **2**（任意） at will
【恣肆】zìsì〈形〉〈书〉 **1**（放纵） unrestrained: 骄横～ arrogant and self-indulgent **2**（豪放挥洒） free and natural: 文笔～ write in a free and natural style
【恣睢】zìsuī〈形〉〈书〉 be unbridled: 暴戾～ be tyrannical
【恣意】zìyì〈副〉 wilfully: ～歪曲事实 wilfully distort reality ‖ ～妄为 behave wildly and wilfully

眦（眥） zì〈名〉 canthus

渍（漬） zì

A〈动〉 **1**（浸泡） steep: ～麻 ret flax, jute, etc. ‖ 汗水～黄了内衣。 The underwear has turned yellow with sweat. ▸浸～ **2**（堆积污渍） be stained: 车轴上～了很多油泥。 The axle is coated with a thick layer of greasy dirt. ‖ 烟斗里～了很多烟油。 The pipe is caked with tar.
B〈名〉 **1**（积水） floodwater on low-lying land: 防洪排～ prevention of floods and drainage of floodwater **2**（污渍） stain: 茶～ tea stain ▸污～, 油～

zi

子 zi〈后缀〉

1（用于名词后） [noun suffix]: 桌～ table ‖ 帽～ hat ‖ 鼻～ nose **2**（用于动词、形容词后） [used after a verb or an adjective]: 掸～ duster ‖ 夹～ tongs ‖ 乱～ disturbance ‖ 胖～ fatty **3**（用于量词后） [added to certain measure words]: 一下～认不出来 can't recognize at the moment ‖ 这档～事 this matter ‖ 来了一伙～人。 A group of people came.
▸zǐ

zōng

宗[1] zōng

A〈名〉 **1**（祖先） ancestor: ▸祖～ **2**（家族） clan: 同～ of the same clan ▸～亲 **3**（派别） school: ▸～派，禅～，正～ **4**（主旨） purpose: 万变不离其～ remain the same in purpose despite all apparent changes ▸～旨，开～明义 **5**（指人） great master: ▸～匠, ～师
B〈动〉 take as one's model: 他的唱工～的是哪一派? On which school does he model his singing? ▸～仰
C〈量〉 [used for things, item or sum of money]: 一～贷款 a loan ‖ 一～心事 a matter that worries one

宗[2] zōng〈名〉〈旧〉

an administrative unit in Tibet, roughly corresponding to a county
【宗祠】zōngcí〈名〉 ancestral hall
【宗法】zōngfǎ〈名〉 patriarchal clan system: ～社会 patriarchal society ‖ ～制度 patriarchal clan system
【宗匠】zōngjiàng〈名〉〈书〉 great master: 词家～ great *ci* (词) master ‖ 一代～ greatest master of one's time
【宗教】zōngjiào〈名〉 religion: ～领袖 religious leader ‖ ～活动 religious practices ‖ ～政策 religious policy
【宗教法庭】zōngjiào fǎtíng〈名〉 the Inquisition [in European history]
【宗教人士】zōngjiào rénshì〈名〉 religious personage
【宗教团体】zōngjiào tuántǐ〈名〉 religious organization
【宗教信仰】zōngjiào xìnyǎng〈名〉 religious belief
【宗庙】zōngmiào〈名〉 ancestral temple of a ruling house
【宗派】zōngpài〈名〉 **1**（指政治、学术、宗教方面） faction: ～活动 sectarian activities **2**〈书〉（指宗族内部） branch of a clan
【宗派主义】zōngpài zhǔyì〈名〉 factionalism: ～者 sectarian
【宗亲】zōngqīn〈名〉 clansmen
【宗师】zōngshī〈名〉 great master: 一代～ a great master of one's time
【宗室】zōngshì〈名〉 **1**（指宗族） imperial clan **2**（指人） imperial clansman
【宗仰】zōngyǎng〈动〉〈书〉 hold in esteem: 海内～ be esteemed both near and far
【宗旨】zōngzhǐ〈名〉 aim: 办学～ purpose of running a school ‖ 本学会的～是弘扬祖国的优秀文化传统。 The aim of this society is to publicize the fine traditions of our culture.
【宗主国】zōngzhǔguó〈名〉 suzerain
【宗主权】zōngzhǔquán〈名〉 suzerainty
【宗族】zōngzú〈名〉 **1**（指家族） patriarchal clan **2**（指成员） clansman

综（綜） zōng〈动〉

sum up: ～上所述 to sum up ▸～合, ～述
▸zèng
【综观】zōngguān〈动〉 hold a comprehensive view: ～国内外形势 take into consideration the situation at home and abroad ‖ ～全局 take a broad view of the situation

【综合】zōnghé〈动〉 1（针对同一对象）synthesize: ～群众的意见 sum up the opinions of the masses 2（针对不同事物）be comprehensive: ～研究 comprehensive study ‖ ～报道 news round-up
【综合国力】zōnghé guólì〈名〉 overall national strength
【综合利用】zōnghé lìyòng〈名〉 multipurpose use
【综合性大学】zōnghéxìng dàxué〈名〉 (comprehensive) university
【综合医院】zōnghé yīyuàn〈名〉 general hospital
【综合征】zōnghézhēng〈名〉 syndrome
【综合治理】zōnghé zhìlǐ〈动〉 tackle in a comprehensive way
【综计】zōngjì〈动〉 sum up
【综括】zōngkuò〈动〉 sum up: ～大家的意见 sum up everyone's ideas
【综述】zōngshù A〈动〉 sum up: 新闻～ summary of the latest news B〈名〉 summarization: 国际时事～ a round-up of international current affairs
【综艺】zōngyì〈名〉 variety show: ～节目 variety show

棕 zōng〈名〉 1（棕榈）palm 2（棕毛）palm fibre: ～毛 palm fibre
【棕绷】zōngbēng〈名〉 wooden bed frame strung with criss-crossed coir ropes
【棕黑】zōnghēi ▸p. 863〈名〉 dark brown
【棕红】zōnghóng ▸p. 863〈名〉 reddish brown
【棕榈】zōnglǘ〈名〉 palm: ～油 palm oil
【棕色】zōngsè ▸p. 863〈名〉 brown
【棕绳】zōngshéng〈名〉 coir rope
【棕树】zōngshù〈名〉 palm
【棕熊】zōngxióng〈名〉［动物］ brown bear
【棕衣】zōngyī〈名〉 palm-bark rain cape

腙 zōng〈名〉［化学］ hydrazone

踪（蹤） zōng〈名〉 track: ▸～迹, 跟～
【踪迹】zōngjì〈名〉 trace: 发现～ find the trail ‖ 找不到～ be off the trail
【踪影】zōngyǐng〈名〉 [usu used in the negative] trace: 一连好几天不见他的～。 We have had no sign of him for several days.

鬃 zōng〈名〉 mane: ～刷 bristle brush

zǒng

总（總） zǒng
A〈动〉 put together: 把两笔账～到一块算 settle the two accounts together ▸～结, ～括, 汇～
B〈形〉 1（全部）general: ～复习 general review ‖ ～预算 master budget ‖ 楼房～面积 total floor area ‖ ～的情况还不错。It's not bad on the whole. ▸～评 2（领导性）head: ▸～裁, ～公司, ～统
C〈副〉 1（贯）always: 他上班～是迟到。 He was always late for work. ‖ 他看起来～是这么年轻。 He always looks young. 2（毕竟）sooner or later: 个人的力量～是有限的。 The power of an individual is after all limited. ‖ 将来～会好起来的。 Things will certainly grow better in the future. ‖ 严冬～会过去的。 The severe winter will pass sooner or later. 3（大概）probably: 这房子～有十多年了。 This house is probably over ten years old.
【总编】zǒngbiān〈简称〉= 总编辑
【总编辑】zǒngbiānjí〈名〉 chief editor
【总部】zǒngbù〈名〉 general headquarters: 把～迁至北京 transfer the headquarters to Beijing ‖ 联合国～ headquarters of the United Nations
【总裁】zǒngcái〈名〉 1（指企业）company president: 微软公司～ president of the Microsoft Corporation 2（指政党）president
【总参】zǒngcān〈简称〉= 总参谋部
【总参谋部】zǒngcānmóubù〈名〉 general staff headquarters
【总参谋长】zǒngcānmóuzhǎng〈名〉 chief of general staff
【总产量】zǒngchǎnliàng〈名〉 total output
【总产值】zǒngchǎnzhí〈名〉 total output value: 工业～ total value of industrial output
【总称】zǒngchēng A〈动〉 be generally termed B〈名〉 general term
【总代理】zǒngdàilǐ〈名〉 general agency: ～人 general agent
【总得】zǒngděi〈副〉 have to: ～想个办法 have got to find a way out
【总动员】zǒngdòngyuán〈动〉 summon all forces to meet an urgency: 全国～ national mobilization
【总督】zǒngdū〈名〉 1（指中国清朝、英联邦国家）governor-general: 两广～ Governor-General of Guangdong and Guangxi ‖ 澳大利亚联邦～ Governor-General of the Commonwealth of Australia ‖ 加拿大～ Governor-General of Canada 2（指在西方历史中）ruler: 东罗马帝国的～ exarch ‖ 荷兰各省的～ stadtholder
【总队】zǒngduì〈名〉 army unit corresponding to a regiment or division: 武警～ armed division
【总额】zǒng'é〈名〉 total amount: 工资～ total wages ‖ 贸易～ total volume of trade
【总而言之】zǒng'éryánzhī〈成〉 in brief: ～，我就是不想让你去。 In short, I just don't want you to go.
【总干事】zǒnggànshì〈名〉 secretary-general
【总纲】zǒnggāng〈名〉 general principles: 中华人民共和国宪法～ General Principles of the Constitution of the People's Republic of China
【总工程师】zǒnggōngchéngshī〈名〉 chief engineer
【总工会】zǒnggōnghuì〈名〉 federation of trade unions: 中华全国～ All-China Federation of Trade Unions
【总公司】zǒnggōngsī〈名〉 head office
【总攻】zǒnggōng〈名〉［军事］ general offensive: 发起～ launch a general offensive
【总共】zǒnggòng〈副〉 altogether: 他～欠你多少钱? What is the full amount he owed you? ‖ 我们学校～90名教授。 We have a total of 90 professors in our university.
【总管】zǒngguǎn A〈动〉 be in full charge: 由厂长～全厂。 The director has full charge of the factory. B〈名〉 1（指负责人）manager: 财务～ treasurer 2〈旧〉（指仆人）chief steward
【总归】zǒngguī〈副〉 anyway: 事实～是事实。 Facts are, after all, facts.
【总行】zǒngháng〈名〉 head office of a bank
【总合】zǒnghé〈动〉 add up: 把各种力量～起来 put all forces together
【总和】zǒnghé〈名〉 sum total: 上半年产量的～ total output of the first half of the year
【总后勤部】zǒnghòuqínbù〈名〉 general logistics department
【总汇】zǒnghuì A〈动〉 come or flow together: 几条河流在这里～入海。 The confluence of several rivers flows here into the sea together. B〈名〉 1（指整体）confluence: 这个成就是人民智慧和力量的～。 The achievement is the aggregation of the strength and wisdom of the people. 2（指地方）[used as the name of the store where a wide assortment of goods are available]: 家具～ furniture store
【总机】zǒngjī〈名〉 switchboard
【总集】zǒngjí〈名〉 general collection
【总计】zǒngjì〈动〉 amount to: 费用～人民币1,500元。 The costs added up to ¥1,500.
【总监】zǒngjiān〈名〉 chief inspector: 财务～ chief financial officer (CFO)
【总检察长】zǒngjiǎncházhǎng〈名〉 attorney general
【总角】zǒngjiǎo〈名〉〈书〉 childhood: ～之交 childhood friend
【总教练】zǒngjiàoliàn〈名〉 head coach
【总结】zǒngjié A〈动〉 sum up: ～过去，展望未来 sum up the past and look into the future ‖ ～经验 sum up one's experience B〈名〉 summary: 写工作～ write a summary of one's work
【总经济师】zǒngjīngjìshī〈名〉 chief economic manager
【总经理】zǒngjīnglǐ〈名〉 general manager
【总经销】zǒngjīngxiāo〈名〉 exclusive distribution
【总会计师】zǒngkuàijìshī〈名〉 chief accountant
【总括】zǒngkuò〈动〉 sum up: ～各方面的情况 sum up all aspects of the situation
【总揽】zǒnglǎn〈动〉 assume overall responsibility: ～大权 have overall authority ‖ ～全局 take a dominant role in the overall situation
【总理】zǒnglǐ A〈动〉〈旧〉 assume overall responsibility: ～军务 have complete charge of all military affairs B〈名〉 1（指政党）[of some political parties] head 2（指国家）premier: 德国～ Chancellor of Germany ‖ 日本国～大臣 Prime Minister of Japan ‖ 中华人民共和国国务院～ Premier of the State Council of the People's Republic of China
【总量】zǒngliàng〈名〉 total capacity
【总领事】zǒnglǐngshì〈名〉 consul general: ～馆 consulate general
【总路线】zǒnglùxiàn〈名〉 general line
【总论】zǒnglùn〈名〉 introduction (at the beginning of a book)
【总目】zǒngmù〈名〉 general table of contents
【总评】zǒngpíng〈名〉 general comment
【总谱】zǒngpǔ〈名〉［音乐］ score
【总设计师】zǒngshèjìshī〈名〉 chief architect
【总是】zǒngshì〈副〉 always: 课堂上他～喜欢问问题。 He is for ever asking questions in class.
【总书记】zǒngshūjì〈名〉 general secretary
【总署】zǒngshǔ〈名〉 general administration: 海关～ customs head office
【总数】zǒngshù〈名〉 total: 人员～ total personnel
【总司令】zǒngsīlìng〈名〉 commander in chief
【总算】zǒngsuàn〈副〉 1（终于）at last: 一连下了六七天的雨～停了下来。 The

rain that had lasted for a week or so finally let up. ‖ 他昼思夜想，最后～想出了个好办法。 He hit upon a good idea after racking his brains day and night. **2**（大体过得去） all things considered: 小孩子的字能写成这样，～不错了。 The handwriting is not bad at all for a child's.

【总体】zǒngtǐ〈名〉 total: ～规划 overall plan ‖ ～上看，这一措施利大于弊。Overall, the measure did more good than harm.

【总统】zǒngtǒng〈名〉 president: ～候选人 presidential candidate

【总统府】zǒngtǒngfǔ〈名〉 presidential palace

【总务】zǒngwù〈名〉**1**（指工作）general affairs: ～处 general affairs office **2**（指人） person in charge of general affairs

【总星系】zǒngxīngxì〈名〉 metagalaxy

【总需求】zǒngxūqiú〈名〉 aggregate demand: 粮食～量 total demand for food

【总有一天】zǒngyǒuyītiān〈副〉 some day

【总则】zǒngzé〈名〉 general rules

【总站】zǒngzhàn〈名〉 main station: 长途客运～ long distance passenger transport station

【总长】zǒngzhǎng〈名〉**1**〈旧〉（中央政府部长） cabinet minister **2**（总参谋长） chief of the general staff

【总账】zǒngzhàng〈名〉 general account

【总政治部】zǒngzhèngzhìbù〈名〉 General Political Department

【总之】zǒngzhī〈连〉 in short: 政治、科学、文化、艺术，～，一切上层建筑都是跟社会的经济基础分不开的。 No branch of superstructure is separable from its social economic base whether it is politics, or science, or culture, or art, or anything else.

【总支】zǒngzhī〈名〉 general branch: 党～ CPC general branch

【总值】zǒngzhí〈名〉 gross value: 国民生产～ GNP ‖ 进口～ gross import value

【总指挥】zǒngzhǐhuī〈名〉 **1**（指战时） commander-in-chief **2**（指工作中） general director

【总装】zǒngzhuāng〈动〉assemble: ～车间 assembly workshop

【总装备部】zǒngzhuāngbèibù〈名〉 general armament department

偬（傯） zǒng ▸倥偬 kǒngzǒng

zòng

纵[1]（縱） zòng

A〈形〉**1**（垂直） vertical: 排成～队 line up in columns ‖ 京广铁路～贯南北。 The Beijing-Guangzhou railway runs from north to south. ▸～横 **2**（从前到后） from the front to the rear: ～剖面 the vertical section ▸～深 **3**（从古至今） from ancient times: 中国历史～观 a review of Chinese history from ancient times to the present day

B〈名〉 corps

纵[2]（縱） zòng〈动〉**1**（放） set free: ▸～虎归山, 欲擒故～ **2**（放任） let loose: ～声歌唱 sing at the top of one's voice ‖ 放～ indulge **3**（纵身） jump up: 他向上一～，跳过了横杆。 He jumped over the cross bar in one leap.

纵[3]（縱） zòng〈连〉 even if: ～有巧妇也难为无米之炊。 No one in this world can make something out of nothing. ‖ ～有天大的本事在这里也难以施展。 Even if you had the greatest competence, you would not be able to put your abilities to good use here.

【纵步】zòngbù **A**〈动〉 stride: ～向前走去 rapid strides **B**〈名〉 jump: 他一个～跃过了壕沟。 He crossed the entrenchment in one leap.

【纵队】zòngduì〈名〉**1**（指队伍）column: 二路～ column of twos ‖ 一路～ a single column **2**［军事］ column corps

【纵观】zòngguān〈动〉 make a general survey: ～全局 make a general survey of the situation ‖ ～科学发展的历史 give a broad overview of the history of scientific development

【纵横】zònghéng **A**〈形〉 **1**（竖和横） vertical and horizontal: ～交错 criss-cross ‖ 像蜘蛛网一样～的铁路线 web-like network of railways **2**（自如） natural: 笔意～ write with great ease **B**〈动〉 march over unhindered: 红军长征二万五千里，～11个省。 The Red Army swept over 11 provinces in its long march of 25,000 *li*.

【纵横捭阖】zònghéng-bǎihé〈成〉 artfully scheme

【纵横驰骋】zònghéng-chíchěng〈成〉 [of an army] move about freely and quickly

【纵横交错】zònghéng-jiāocuò〈成〉 criss-cross: ～的水渠 criss-cross network of irrigation channels

【纵虎归山】zònghǔ-guīshān〈成〉〈喻〉 set free a deadly enemy

【纵火】zònghuǒ〈动〉 set fire to: ～焚烧大楼 set fire to the house ‖ ～犯 arsonist

【纵酒】zòngjiǔ〈动〉 drink to excess: ～伤身。 Alcoholism is very bad for the health.

【纵览】zònglǎn〈动〉 take in a broad view: ～群书 read extensively ‖ ～四周 look around in every direction

【纵令】zònglìng〈连〉〈书〉 even if: ～有天大困难，也吓不倒我们。 We will not be cowed by any difficulties no matter how formidable.

【纵论】zònglùn〈动〉 have a wide-ranging discussion: ～天下大事 talk freely about the major events of the world

【纵目】zòngmù〈动〉〈书〉 look as far as the eye can see: ～远眺 look far into the distance

【纵剖面】zòngpōumiàn〈名〉 vertical section

【纵情】zòngqíng〈副〉 as much as one likes: ～歌唱 sing heartily ‖ ～享乐 indulge oneself in pleasures

【纵然】zòngrán〈连〉〈书〉 even if: 今天他～来，也不会带来什么鼓舞人心的消息。 Even if he comes today, I don't think he will bring us any exciting news.

【纵容】zòngróng〈动〉 tolerate: 在个别领导的～下，他的胆子越来越大。 With the nod of a few particular leaders, he became increasingly audacious.

【纵身】zòngshēn〈动〉 jump: ～上马 vault onto a horse ‖ ～一跳 jump up

【纵深】zòngshēn〈名〉 **1**［军事］ depth: ～防御 defence in depth **2**（更深层次） higher level: 向～发展 develop in depth

【纵使】zòngshǐ〈连〉〈书〉even if: ～条件再艰苦，我们也要坚持下去。 Even if things get even harder, we will not give in.

【纵谈】zòngtán〈动〉 talk freely: ～科技进步给人类带来的好处 talk freely about how advancements in science and technology have benefited human beings

【纵向】zòngxiàng〈形〉 **1**（从南到北） from south to north **2**（垂直） lengthwise: ～比较 longitudinal comparison ‖ ～联系 vertical relation

【纵欲】zòngyù〈动〉 indulge in sensual pleasures

粽 zòng

【粽子】zòngzi〈名〉 *zongzi*: 豆沙～ *zongzi* with bean paste filling ‖ 肉～ *zongzi* with meat filling

> **粽子**
>
> A food eaten at the Dragon Boat Festival (▸端午节). The story goes that the ancient Chinese poet Qu Yuan (屈原, c339-278 BC) committed suicide by drowning on the 5th day of the 5th lunar month. Ever since then, on this day people make pyramid-shaped glutinous rice dumplings which they throw into the water as an offering to Qu Yuan. The dumplings are made by first soaking glutinous rice in water, and then wrapping the rice in bamboo or reed leaves to form triangular or other-shaped packages. The packages are then tied up with string, and steamed or boiled. The filling may be jujubes, aduki beans, or fresh or smoked meat.

zōu

邹（鄒） Zōu〈名〉 state in the Zhou Dynasty [located in present-day Zouxian County in Shandong Province]

驺（騶） zōu〈名〉〈古〉 groom and carriage driver of a noble

zǒu

走 zǒu〈动〉**1**（跑） run: ▸～马观花, 奔～相告 **2**（步行） walk: ～错路 take the wrong road ‖ ～回家 walk home ‖ ～出病房 go out of the ward ‖ 我们必须～改革的道路。 We must pursue the reform road. **3**（离开） leave: 把椅子搬～。 Take the chair away. ‖ 他刚～。 He left just a moment ago. **4** ▸**p. 772**〈套〉〈婉〉（过世） pass away: 她终于撒手～了。 She finally passed away. **5**（移动） move: ～错一步棋 make a wrong move in chess ‖ 船～得很慢。 The ship moved very slowly. ‖ 钟不～了。 The clock has stopped. **6**（泄漏） let slip: ～了风声 have leaked out the secret ‖ 说～了嘴 let slip a remark ▸～漏 **7**（改变） depart from the original: ▸～板, ～样 **8**（通过） do sth. in a particular way: ～水路到大连 travel to Dalian by water **9**（来往） visit, call on: 他们两家～得很勤。 The two families visit each other frequently. ▸～亲戚

【走板】zǒubǎn〈动〉 **1**（指唱戏） be out of tune **2**〈喻〉（指说话） wander off the point: 他说着说着就～了。 He talked so much that he lost track of what he was talking about.

【走笔】zǒubǐ〈动〉〈书〉 write rapidly: ～疾书 write swiftly

【走避】zǒubì〈动〉 flee

【走步】zǒubù〈动〉 **1**［篮球］ walk with the ball **2**（学走路） learn to walk

【走村串寨】zǒucūn-chuànzhài〈成〉 go from village to village

【走道】zǒudào〈名〉 **1**（指大街两旁） pavement **2**（指室内） aisle

【走道儿】zǒudàor〈动〉〈口〉 walk: 小孩子刚会～。 The baby has just learned to toddle. ‖ 她～一扭一扭的。 She swings her hips when she walks.

【走低】zǒudī〈动〉 drop: 股价一路～。 Share prices have kept dropping.

【走调】zǒudiào〈动〉 be out of tune: 唱走了调儿 sing off-key ‖ 你～了。 You're not singing in tune.

【走动】zǒudòng〈动〉 **1**（行走） stretch one's legs: 你坐的时间长了，应该～～。 You've been sitting for a long time. You should stretch your legs a little. ‖ 他的病情已有所好转，可以下地～了。 His condition has been improving and he can move about on the floor now. **2**（来往） visit each other: 两家常常～，感情很好。 The two families often visit each other and are on very good terms.

【走读】zǒudú〈动〉 attend a day school: ～生 day student

【走访】zǒufǎng〈动〉 interview: 记者～了几位企业家。 The reporter interviewed several entrepreneurs.

【走风】zǒufēng〈动〉 leak a secret

【走钢丝】zǒu gāngsī **A**〈名〉［杂技］ tightrope walking: 表演～ perform on the tightrope **B**〈动〉〈喻〉 tread on thin ice

【走高】zǒugāo〈动〉 go up: 股价一路～。 Share prices have kept going up.

【走狗】zǒugǒu〈名〉〈喻〉〈贬〉 lackey: 充当～ act as accomplice

【走光】zǒuguāng〈动〉 accidentally expose oneself: 穿超短裙容易～。 It's easy to accidently expose oneself in a mini-skirt.

【走过场】zǒu guòchǎng〈动〉 **1**（指演戏） go from one end of the stage to the other without stopping **2**〈喻〉（指办事） go through the motions

【走红】zǒuhóng〈动〉 be a hit: ～的影片 hit movie ‖ 他是好莱坞最～的演员。 He is Hollywood's hottest property.

【走后门】zǒu hòumén〈惯〉〈喻〉 get in through the back door: 通过～进了这家公司 enter the company through the back door

【走火】zǒuhuǒ〈动〉 **1**（指武器）fire accidentally: 那杆枪～了。 The gun went off by accident. **2**〈喻〉（指说话） put sth. too strongly: 她说话好～。 When she speaks, she often goes a bit too far. **3**［电子］ spark: 电线～。 The electricity wire sent off sparks.

【走极端】zǒu jíduān〈动〉 go to extremes: 避免～ avoid extremes ‖ 从一个极端走到另一个极端 go from one extreme to the other ‖ 他凡事都～。 He takes everything to extremes.

【走江湖】zǒu jiānghú〈动〉 live the life of a wanderer

【走街串巷】zǒujiē-chuànxiàng〈成〉 walk the streets and alleyways

【走捷径】zǒu jiéjìng〈动〉 cut corners

【走廊】zǒuláng〈名〉 **1**（建筑物内的） corridor **2**（建筑物外的） veranda〈英〉; porch〈美〉 **3**〈喻〉（通道）passageway: 空中～ air passageway ‖ 河西～ the Hexi Corridor

【走露】zǒulòu = 走漏 zǒulòu 1

【走漏】zǒulòu〈动〉 **1**（泄漏） leak out: ～风声 divulge a secret ‖ ～消息 leak information **2**（走私漏税） smuggling and tax evasion: 杜绝～ put an end to smuggling and tax evasion

【走路】zǒulù〈动〉 **1**（行走） walk: 孩子已经学会～了。 The baby has learned to walk. **2**（离开） leave: 不好好儿干让她卷铺盖～。 Since she can't do things properly, let her pack her bags and leave.

【走马灯】zǒumǎdēng〈名〉 **1**（指花灯） lantern with rotating shadow figures such as horses, etc. **2**〈喻〉〈贬〉（指人员变动） constant reshuffling of personnel: 局长的更换就像～一样。 The position of bureau head changed as often as the shadow figures rotating in a revolving lantern.

> **走马灯**
> Revolving festive lantern. Riders on horseback or other figures are cut out of coloured paper and stuck onto a drum inside a lantern. A lighted candle or electric light is then placed at the base of the drum, and hot air rising causes the drum to rotate, and the figures to spin around.

【走马观花】zǒumǎ-guānhuā〈成〉〈喻〉 gain a shallow understanding through cursory observation: 日程安排得很紧，我们只能在风景区～地兜一圈。 Our itinerary is packed, so we can only get a fleeting glance at the scenic areas.

【走马上任】zǒumǎ-shàngrèn〈成〉take up one's office

【走麦城】zǒu màichéng〈惯〉 meet one's Waterloo

【走门路】zǒu ménlù〈惯〉 solicit help from potential backers

【走南闯北】zǒunán-chuǎngběi〈成〉 travel widely: 他从小就～，见多识广。 He started travelling when he was very young, so he has a lot of experience.

【走内线】zǒu nèixiàn〈惯〉 go through private channels

【走娘家】zǒu niángjia〈动〉 [of a married woman] go and visit her parents' home: 新媳妇婚礼后第二天～是当地风俗。 It's the local custom for the bride to go back to her parents' home and stay the second day after the wedding.

【走气】zǒuqì〈动〉 [of drinks, etc.] go flat

【走强】zǒuqiáng〈动〉 **1**（趋于上升） be on the rise **2**（趋于旺盛） tend to flourish

【走俏】zǒuqiào〈动〉 be in great demand: ～商品 popular goods ‖ 中国生产的丝织女衬衫在北非很～。 Silk blouses made in China are very popular in North Africa.

【走亲戚】zǒu qīnqi〈动〉 visit one's relatives: 农闲时节，多走了几家亲戚。 During the farming slack season, I paid several more visits to our relatives.

【走禽】zǒuqín〈名〉 cursorial birds

【走热】zǒurè〈动〉 become popular: 投资保险～。 Investment insurance is becoming quite popular.

【走人】zǒurén〈动〉〈口〉 leave: 已经让他～了。 He was told to pack his bags and leave.

【走软】zǒuruǎn〈动〉 **1**（趋于下降） tend to fall **2**（趋于低迷） tend to slump

【走弱】zǒuruò〈动〉 go weak

【走色】zǒushǎi〈动〉 lose colour: 这布一洗就～。 This cloth fades with washing.

【走神儿】zǒushénr〈动〉 lose concentration: 开车可不能～。 Never let your attention wander while you are driving.

【走失】zǒushī〈动〉 **1**（迷路） be lost: 孩子在庙会上～了。 The child got lost at the temple fair. ‖ 前天她家～了一只羊。 One of her sheep wandered away from the flock the day before yesterday. **2**（改变） lose: 译文～了原意。 The original meaning is lost in the translation.

【走时】zǒushí〈动〉 keep time: 手表～准确。 The watch keeps good time.

【走势】zǒushì〈名〉 **1**（趋势） trend: 市场行情～下跌。 The market shows a downward tendency. **2**（走向） direction: 勘察山谷的～ explore the valley to find where it runs

【走兽】zǒushòu〈名〉 quadruped

【走水】zǒushuǐ〈动〉 **1**（漏水） leak water: 房顶～了。 The roof is leaking. **2**（流水） flow: 渠道～很通畅。 Water flows well through the canal. **3** ▸**p. 772**〈婉〉（失火） be on fire, catch fire

【走私】zǒusī〈动〉 smuggle: ～军火 traffic arms ‖ ～团伙 smuggling ring ‖ 打击～活动 crack down on smuggling activities

【走索】zǒusuǒ〈名〉［杂技］ tightrope-walking

【走台】zǒutái〈动〉 rehearse

【走题】zǒutí〈动〉 stray from the subject: 话说～儿 go off on a tangent ‖ 作文～了。 The essay digressed from the main subject.

【走投无路】zǒutóu-wúlù〈成〉 have no way out: 逼得某人～ force sb. into a corner

【走弯路】zǒu wānlù〈惯〉 make a detour:〈喻〉 由于缺少经验，我们工作中走了一些弯路。 Owing to our lack of experience, we took a rather roundabout course in our work.

【走味儿】zǒuwèir〈动〉 **1**（指味道） lose flavour: 茶叶存放久了就会～。 If tea is kept for a long time, it loses its flavour. **2**〈喻〉（指语意） become stale: 话一从他嘴里说出来就～了。 Any words coming out of his mouth sound stale.

【走下坡路】zǒu xiàpōlù〈惯〉 **1**〈本〉 go downhill **2**〈喻〉 be on the decline: 她的健康状况日渐～了。 Her health is declining by the day.

【走险】zǒuxiǎn〈动〉 make a reckless move: ▸铤而～

【走向】zǒuxiàng〈名〉 **1**（延伸方向） course: 河流的～ the course of a river ‖ 市场～ market trend ‖ 一条南北～的路 road that runs from north to south **2**［地质］ strike: ～断层 strike fault ‖ ～节理 strike joint

【走形】zǒuxíng〈动〉 be out of shape: 这毛衣才下一次水就走了形。 The sweater lost its shape after only one wash.

【走形式】zǒu xíngshì〈惯〉 do something as a formality: 办事要讲求实效，不能图省事，～。 In our work we should strive for practical results, and not just go through the motions to save ourselves trouble.

【走秀】zǒuxiù〈动〉 perform and exhibit: ～活动 performing and exhibiting activities

【走穴】zǒuxué〈动〉〈口〉 moonlight: 不应当让演员～。 Actors and actresses should not be allowed to moonlight.

【走眼】zǒuyǎn〈动〉 see incorrectly: 拿着好货当次货，你可看～了。 In taking superior goods for inferior ones, you have made a mistake.

【走样】zǒuyàng〈动〉 lose shape: 话三传两传就～儿了。 Having been passed around several times, the message became distorted. ‖ 要保证贯彻上级的指示不～儿。 The instructions of the high level authorities must be followed.

【走一步，看一步】zǒu yī bù, kàn yī bù〈成〉 take one step and look around before taking another

【走油】zǒuyóu〈动〉 go rancid

【走运】zǒuyùn〈动〉 be in luck: 不～ be out of luck ‖ 他真～，又长了一次工资。 He's fortunate to have had another pay rise.

【走账】zǒuzhàng〈动〉 charge to an account

【走着瞧】zǒuzheqiáo〈惯〉 wait and see: 咱们～! Let's wait and see.

【走走停停】zǒuzǒu-tíngtíng〈动〉 keep starting and stopping

【走卒】zǒuzú〈名〉 lackey

【走嘴】zǒuzuǐ〈动〉 let slip an inadvertent remark: 情急之中，话说～了。The secret came out under pressure. ‖ 我本不想说，只是无意中说走了嘴。I didn't mean to say that. It just slipped out.

zòu

奏 zòu〈动〉 **1**（陈述意见） present a memorial to an emperor: ～上一本 impeach sb. in a memorial to the emperor ▸～折 **2**（取得） achieve: ▸～效 **3**（演奏） play: ～国歌 play the national anthem ▸伴～，独～，演～

【奏本】zòuběn〈动〉〈旧〉 present a memorial to the emperor/throne: 奏某人一本 impeach sb. in a memorial to the emperor/throne

【奏捷】zòujié〈动〉〈书〉 win a battle: ～归来 return in triumph

【奏凯】zòukǎi〈动〉〈书〉 be victorious

【奏鸣曲】zòumíngqǔ〈名〉［音乐］ sonata: 钢琴～ piano sonata

【奏疏】zòushū = 奏章 zòuzhāng

【奏效】zòuxiào〈动〉 prove effective: 这药吃了就能～。If you take this medicine, it will definitely work.

【奏乐】zòuyuè〈动〉 play music

【奏章】zòuzhāng〈名〉 memorial to the emperor: 上～ present a memorial to the emperor

【奏折】zòuzhé〈名〉 memorial to the throne

揍 zòu〈动〉〈口〉 strike: 挨～ get a thrashing ‖ 把他～一顿 beat him up

zū

租 zū

A〈名〉 **1**（旧）（田赋） land tax: 交～ pay land taxes ‖ ～税 land tax and other levies **2**（租金） rent: 月～ monthly rent ‖ 房～ rent

B〈动〉 **1**（租用） rent: ～三间房 rent three rooms ‖ 这辆小汽车是从另一家公司～来的。This car is on hire from another firm. **2**（出租） lease: 三楼的房子～给了学生。The second floor of the house has been let out to students.

【租户】zūhù〈名〉 leaseholder

【租界】zūjiè〈名〉 concession [territory]

【租借】zūjiè〈动〉 **1**（租用） rent: ～办公大楼 lease an office building **2**（出租） let out: 他把房子～给了我。He let out the room to me.

【租借地】zūjièdì〈名〉 leased land

【租金】zūjīn〈名〉 rent: 这套房间每月～500元。The rent for this flat is 500 *yuan* a month.

【租赁】zūlìn〈动〉 **1**（租用） rent: ～办公大楼 lease a building office **2**（出租） rent out: 她把房间～给学生。She rents out rooms to students.

【租赁期】zūlìnqī〈名〉 lease

【租赁人】zūlìnrén〈名〉 leaseholder

【租期】zūqī = 租赁期 zūlìnqī

【租用】zūyòng〈动〉 rent: ～飞机 charter a plane ‖ ～汽车 rent a car ‖ 他们～这幢大楼作仓库。They leased the building as a warehouse.

【租约】zūyuē〈名〉 lease; let〈英〉: 取消/续订～ cancel/renew a lease

【租子】zūzi〈名〉〈口〉 ground rent: 交～ pay rent ‖ 收～ collect rent

菹 zū〈书〉

A〈名〉 **1**（沼泽地） marshland **2**（酸菜） pickled Chinese cabbage

B〈动〉 mince

zú

足[1] zú〈名〉 **1**（脚） foot: 赤～行走 walk barefoot ▸～迹，手舞～蹈 **2**（腿） leg: 三～鼎 tripod ▸鼎～ **3**（足球） football: ▸～坛

足[2] zú

A〈形〉 enough: 劲头/信心～ be full of energy/confidence ‖ 证据不～ lack of evidence ▸～岁，～月

B〈副〉 **1**（足够） sufficiently: ～以胜任 be sufficiently qualified ▸不～为凭，微不～道 **2**（达到某种程度） fully: 他离开此地～有一年了。He has been away for a full year. ‖ 我们～～等了一个小时。We waited for a good hour.

【足本】zúběn〈名〉 unabridged version: ～小说 full-length novel

【足不出户】zúbùchūhù〈成〉 be confined to the house

【足赤】zúchì〈名〉 solid gold: ▸金无～，人无完人

【足够】zúgòu〈动〉 **1**（达到某种程度） be enough: ～的食物和饮用水 adequate food and drinking water ‖ 我的工资～我自己用。My wages are sufficient for my needs. **2**（满足） suffice: 我午餐有两瓶啤酒就～了。Two bottles of beer are enough for me at lunch.

【足迹】zújì〈名〉 footprint: 留下～ leave tracks ‖ 熊的～ bear prints

【足见】zújiàn〈连〉 it serves to show: 这些难题经过讨论都解决了，～走群众路线是正确的。That all these problems have been solved after consulting the people concerned shows that it is necessary to rely on the masses.

【足金】zújīn〈名〉 pure gold

【足球】zúqiú〈名〉 **1** ▸**p. 909**（指运动） football; soccer: 踢～ play football **2**（指球） football

【足球场】zúqiúchǎng〈名〉 football field

【足球队】zúqiúduì〈名〉 football team

【足球迷】zúqiúmí〈名〉 football fan

【足球赛】zúqiúsài〈名〉 game of football

【足球运动员】zúqiú yùndòngyuán〈名〉 footballer

【足色】zúsè〈形〉 [gold or silver] of standard purity

【足岁】zúsuì〈名〉 actual age: 这孩子已经七～了。The child is already seven years old.

【足坛】zútán〈名〉 football circles: ～劲旅 strong football team ‖ ～明星 football star

【足下】zúxià〈名〉〈书〉 [polite form of address between friends, used mostly in letters] you : ～以为如何? What's your opinion?

【足以】zúyǐ〈副〉 sufficiently: 不杀不～平民愤。Only execution could assuage popular indignation. ‖ 这些事实～说明问题。These facts prove my point adequately.

【足银】zúyín〈名〉 pure silver

【足浴】zúyù〈名〉 warm medicinal foot bath

【足月】zúyuè〈动〉 be born after the normal period of gestation: 不～的孩子常体弱多病。Premature children are often weak and vulnerable to disease.

【足智多谋】zúzhì-duōmóu〈成〉 wise and resourceful

【足足】zúzú〈副〉 as much as: ～50年 fully fifty years

卒[1] zú〈名〉 **1**（旧）（士兵） soldier: 一兵一～ every soldier ▸士～，小～ **2**（旧）（仆人） servant: 狱～ jailer ▸走～ **3**（指棋子） pawn: ▸～子

卒[2] zú〈书〉

A〈动〉 **1**（完成） finish: ～其事 finish the job ▸～岁，～业 **2**（亡故） die: 病～ die of an illness ‖ ～于1999年 died in 1999

B〈副〉 finally: ～底于成 finally achieve one's ends

▸cù

【卒岁】zúsuì〈动〉〈书〉 get through the year: 聊以～ just to tide over the year

【卒业】zúyè〈动〉〈书〉 finish a course of study

【卒子】zúzi〈名〉 **1**（旧）（士兵） rank-and-file soldier **2**（指棋子） pawn

族 zú

A〈名〉 **1**（家族） clan: ～兄 cousin ‖ 合～ the whole clan ▸～长，同～，宗～ **2**（民族） nationality: ▸种～，民～ **3**（某类人或事物） class or group of things with common features: 芳香～化合物 aromatic compound ‖ 水～ aquatic animals ▸追星～，上班～

B〈动〉 [in ancient China] impose a death penalty on an offender and his whole family, and even on the families of his mother and wife

【族规】zúguī〈名〉 rules and regulations of a clan

【族类】zúlèi〈名〉 same clan

【族内婚】zúnèihūn〈名〉 endogamy

【族谱】zúpǔ〈名〉 genealogical tree

【族权】zúquán〈名〉 clan authority

【族群】zúqún〈名〉 ethnic group

【族人】zúrén〈名〉 clansman

【族外婚】zúwàihūn〈名〉 exogamy

【族长】zúzhǎng〈名〉 head of a clan

镞（鏃） zú〈名〉〈书〉 arrowhead: ▸箭～

zǔ

诅（詛） zǔ〈动〉〈书〉 curse: ▸～咒

【诅咒】zǔzhòu〈动〉 curse: ～命运 curse at fate ‖ 受到～ be cursed

阻 zǔ〈动〉 obstruct: 工作受～ be hindered in one's work ‖ 通行无～ unobstructed passage ▸～止，劝～

【阻碍】zǔ'ài〈动〉 obstruct: ～和平进程 prevent the peace process from going forward ‖ ～交通 block traffic ‖ ～经济发展 hamper economic development

【阻挡】zǔdǎng〈动〉 obstruct: 不可～的历史潮流 unstoppable historical trend ‖ 他一定要去，就不要～他了。Since he insists on going, don't hinder him any further.

【阻遏】zǔ'è〈动〉 hold back

【阻隔】zǔgé〈动〉 separate: 山川～ be separated by mountains and rivers

【阻击】zǔjī〈动〉［军事］ block: ～来犯之

敌 check the invading troops ‖ ～战 blocking action
【阻截】zǔjié〈动〉 intercept: ～敌机 intercept an enemy plane ‖ ～援兵 intercept the enemy reinforcements
【阻绝】zǔjué〈动〉 block: 交通～ the traffic is blocked
【阻抗】zǔkàng〈名〉［电子］ impedance: ～匹配 impedance matching
【阻拦】zǔlán〈动〉 obstruct: 他决心要走，谁也～不住。Since he had made up his mind, no one could prevent him from leaving.
【阻力】zǔlì〈名〉 1（指妨碍发展）obstruction: 冲破各种～ break through all kinds of obstructions ‖ 遇到～ meet with resistance 2［物理］ resistance: 空气/风的～ air/wind resistance
【阻力位】zǔlìwèi〈名〉［金融］ resistance
【阻难】zǔnàn〈动〉 thwart: 无理～ create difficulties for no reason
【阻挠】zǔnáo〈动〉 thwart: ～案子的调查 put obstacles in the way of investigation of the case ‖ ～和平的实现 thwart the realization of peace
【阻塞】zǔsè〈动〉 1（无法通过） block: 交通～ traffic jam ‖ 动脉～会引起心力衰竭。The blockage of the artery may lead to heart failure. 2（使无法通过） jam up: ～言路 block channels inviting criticism and suggestions from the people
【阻止】zǔzhǐ〈动〉 prevent: ～火势蔓延 stop the spread of a fire ‖ ～某人做某事 block sb. from doing sth.
【阻滞】zǔzhì〈动〉 check

组（組）zǔ

A〈动〉 organize: 改～一个球队 reorganize a football team ▸～阁, ～装
B〈名〉 1（小组） group: 拆散一个～ separate a group ‖ 领导小～ leading group 2（系列） series: ▸～歌, ～画, ～曲, ～诗
C〈量〉 set: 几～电池 several sets of batteries ‖ 一～文章 a series of articles
【组办】zǔbàn〈动〉 organize: ～音乐会/演出 organize a concert/performance
【组成】zǔchéng〈动〉 make up: ～联合政府 assemble a coalition government ‖ 中国是一个由56个民族～的多民族国家。China is a multinational country consisting of 56 ethnic groups.
【组词】zǔcí〈动〉 form words
【组稿】zǔgǎo〈动〉 solicit contributions
【组歌】zǔgē〈名〉［音乐］ suite of songs: 《长征～》*Suite of Songs on the Long March*
【组阁】zǔgé〈动〉 1（指内阁） form a cabinet 2（指领导班子） set up a leading group
【组合】zǔhé A〈动〉 make up: 这个家庭是由没有血缘关系的三代人～而成的。This family is made up of three generations who have no blood ties. B〈名〉 1（集合） combination: 词组是词的～。Phrases are combinations of words. 2［数学］ combination
【组合家具】zǔhé jiājù〈名〉 composite furniture
【组合音响】zǔhé yīnxiǎng〈名〉 hi-fi
【组画】zǔhuà〈名〉 series of paintings
【组建】zǔjiàn〈动〉 set up: ～公司 establish a company ‖ ～新政府 form a new government
【组曲】zǔqǔ〈名〉［音乐］ suite
【组诗】zǔshī〈名〉 series of poems
【组团】zǔtuán〈动〉 form a delegation: ～参观 organize a delegation for a visit
【组委会】zǔwěihuì〈名〉 organizing committee
【组织】zǔzhī A〈动〉 organize: ～登山队 form a mountaineering team ‖ ～联欢晚会 organize an evening party B〈名〉 1（指由人组成） organization: 给予～处分 take disciplinary measures against a member of an organization ‖ 打击恐怖～ crack down a terrorist organization ‖ 工会～ trade union organizations ‖ 群众～ mass organizations 2［生理］ tissue: 肌肉～ muscular tissue ‖ 软～ parenchyma ‖ 神经～ nerve tissue
【组织部】zǔzhībù〈名〉 organization department: 中共中央～ Organization Department of the CCCPC
【组织方】zǔzhīfāng〈名〉 organiser: ～做了周密部署。The organisers carried out meticulous planning. ‖ 出了如此重大事故，～有不可推卸的责任。With a serious accident like this, there is no way that the organisers can avoid taking responsibility.
【组织关系】zǔzhī guānxi〈名〉 membership credentials
【组织生活】zǔzhī shēnghuó〈名〉 regular activities of an organization
【组织委员】zǔzhī wěiyuán〈名〉committee member in charge of organizational work
【组装】zǔzhuāng〈动〉 assemble: ～电脑/汽车 assemble a computer/car ‖ ～车间 assembly plant

俎 zǔ

〈名〉〈古〉 1（用于祭祀） sacrificial utensil: ▸越～代庖 2（用于切肉） chopping block:〈喻〉 ～上肉 helpless victim

祖 zǔ

〈名〉 1（祖先） ancestor: 远～ remote ancestors ▸～籍, ～先, ～宗 2（祖父辈） grandfather: ▸～父, ～母 3（创始人） founder: ▸～师爷, 鼻～, 佛～
【祖辈】zǔbèi〈名〉 ancestors: 我家祖祖辈辈都是农民。My family have been farmers for generation.
【祖产】zǔchǎn〈名〉 ancestral estate
【祖传】zǔchuán〈动〉 hand down from one's ancestors: 三代～ handed down from one's great grandfather
【祖传秘方】zǔchuán mìfāng〈名〉 secret prescription handed down in the family from generation to generation
【祖坟】zǔfén〈名〉 ancestral tomb
【祖父】zǔfù ▸**p. 588**〈名〉 paternal grandfather
【祖国】zǔguó〈名〉 native land: 热爱～ love one's native land
【祖籍】zǔjí〈名〉 ancestral home: ～法国 of French descent
【祖居】zǔjū A〈名〉 ancestral home B〈动〉 be a native of: ～陕西 be a native of Shaanxi
【祖鲁语】Zǔlǔyǔ ▸**p. 918**〈名〉 Zulu (language)
【祖率】zǔlǜ〈名〉［数学］ Zu's ratio [approximate ratio of the circumference of a circle to its diameter as calculated by Zu Chongzhi (祖冲之, 429-500)]
【祖母】zǔmǔ ▸**p. 588**〈名〉 paternal grandmother
【祖母绿】zǔmǔlǜ〈名〉 emerald
【祖上】zǔshàng〈名〉 forbears
【祖师】zǔshī = 祖师爷 zǔshīyé
【祖师爷】zǔshīyé〈名〉 founder
【祖孙】zǔsūn〈名〉grandparents and grandchildren: ～三代 three generations
【祖先】zǔxiān〈名〉 1（指人） ancestors 2（指其他生物） progenitor
【祖业】zǔyè〈名〉 1（指功业） ancestors' meritorious achievements 2（指产业） ancestral estate
【祖宗】zǔzong〈名〉 ancestors

zuān

钻（鑽）zuān

〈动〉 1（打眼儿） bore: ～木取火 drill wood to make fire ‖ 在木板上～一个眼 bore a hole through the board ▸～探 2（钻研） study intensively: ～书本 delve into books ‖ ～业务 be keenly focused on one's job or a subject ▸～研 3（进入） get into: ～进密林深处 go deep into a dense forest ‖ 太阳从云雾里～了出来。The sun broke through the clouds and mist. 4（钻营） secure personal gain: ▸～谋, ～营
▸zuàn
【钻空子】zuān kòngzi〈惯〉 exploit an advantage: 严防坏人～ be very careful not to allow bad people to exploit any loopholes
【钻谋】zuānmóu〈动〉 pull strings: ～肥缺 gain a plum job by fawning on the powerful and influential
【钻牛角尖】zuān niújiǎojiān〈惯〉 1（指研究问题） split hairs 2（指坚持想法） go down a dead end
【钻探】zuāntàn〈动〉 drill for exploration: 海洋～ offshore drilling ‖ ～队 drilling team ‖ ～机 drilling machine
【钻天杨】zuāntiānyáng〈名〉［植物］lombardy poplar
【钻心】zuānxīn〈动〉 be unbearable: 疼得～ feel unbearable pain ‖ 痒得～ feel so itchy that one can hardly bear it
【钻研】zuānyán〈动〉 study intensively: ～国际法 study international law intensively ‖ 努力～业务 endeavour to gain professional proficiency
【钻营】zuānyíng〈动〉 curry favour with sb. in authority in order to win personal gain: 削尖了脑袋～ try to secure personal gains by hook or by crook ‖ 四处～ seek personal gain high and low

躜（躦）zuān

〈动〉 jump up

zuǎn

缵（纘）zuǎn

〈动〉〈书〉 inherit: ～述 relate what has been handed down

纂 zuǎn

A〈动〉 compile: ▸编～
B〈名〉〈口〉 bun
【纂修】zuǎnxiū〈动〉 edit

zuàn

钻（鑽）zuàn

〈名〉 1（指工具） drill: ▸～头, 电～, 风～ 2（指钻石） diamond: 十九～的手表 watch encrusted with nineteen diamonds ▸～戒
▸zuān
【钻床】zuànchuáng〈名〉［机械］ drilling machine: 龙门～ planer drilling machine
【钻机】zuànjī〈名〉［机械］ drilling machine
【钻戒】zuànjiè〈名〉 diamond ring
【钻石】zuànshí〈名〉 1（指金刚石）

diamond: 镶嵌～ set a diamond ‖ ～项链 diamond necklace 2 (指人造宝石) jewel
【钻石婚】zuànshíhūn〈名〉 diamond wedding anniversary
【钻塔】zuàntǎ〈名〉［矿业］ boring tower
【钻台】zuàntái〈名〉 drilling platform
【钻头】zuàntóu〈名〉 drill bit

赚（賺） zuàn〈动〉〈方〉deceive: 你～我白跑了一趟。 You tricked me into making a fruitless errand. ‖ 你那点本事～不了我。 I'll not be fooled by your tricks. ▸zhuàn

攥 zuàn〈动〉〈口〉 grip: ～紧拳头 clench one's fists ‖ 手里～着一把斧子 hold an axe in one's hand

zuǐ

咀 zuǐ〈名〉〈口〉 a popular form of 嘴 [often used in geographical names] ▸jǔ

嘴 zuǐ〈名〉 1 ▸p. 614 (口) mouth: 乐得合不上～ be all smiles ‖ 张开～ open one's mouth ‖ ～上叼着烟 have a cigarette between one's lips ▸龇牙咧～, 牛头不对马～ 2 (口状物) mouth: 茶壶～ spout of a tea-pot ‖ 瓶～ mouth of a bottle ▸烟～儿 3 (食物) food: 忌～ go on a diet ▸零～, 贪～, 偷～ 4 (说的话) tongue: ～刻薄 have a bitter tongue ‖ 别多～。 Don't talk too much. ▸～甜, ～直, 插～, 贫～
【嘴巴】zuǐba〈名〉 1 (口) mouth: 张开～。 Open your mouth. 2 (用手打脸) [usu used in the following collocation]: 挨了个～ get a slap in the face
【嘴笨】zuǐbèn〈形〉 clumsy of speech: 我～，说不过你。 I'm clumsy of speech and cannot match you in articulateness.
【嘴馋】zuǐchán〈形〉 fond of good food: 见有好吃的东西就～ start drooling at the sight of good food
【嘴唇】zuǐchún〈名〉 lip: 厚/薄～ thick/thin lips ‖ 上/下～ upper/lower lip
【嘴刁】zuǐdiāo〈形〉 1 (指吃东西) particular about one's food: 她从小就～。 She's been fussy about her food since her childhood. 2 〈口〉(指说话) cunning in speech: 这小鬼～，差点儿被她骗了。 What a cunning creature she is! I almost believed her.
【嘴乖】zuǐguāi〈形〉 [of children] clever and pleasant when speaking to elders: 这女孩儿～，没人不喜欢。 Everyone likes the girl because she speaks so sweetly.
【嘴尖】zuǐjiān〈形〉 1 (指说话) sharp-tongued: 他～，爱损人。 He's sharp-tongued and what he says is liable to hurt people. 2 (指辨别味道) refined in palate: 他～,喝一口就知道是什么茶。 He has a refined sense of taste and is able to tell what tea it is with just one sip. 3 (指吃东西) fussy about one's food: 这孩子～，不合口的一点儿不吃。 This child is so fussy that he never touches food he doesn't like.
【嘴角】zuǐjiǎo〈名〉 corners of the mouth: 他～上挂着微笑。 There is a smile on his lips.
【嘴紧】zuǐjǐn〈形〉tight-lipped: 他～，你什么也别想问出来。He is very tight-lipped. Don't expect that he will tell you anything.
【嘴快】zuǐkuài〈形〉 loose-tongued: 这姑娘～，什么话也藏不住。This girl has a loose tongue and can't keep anything to herself.
【嘴脸】zuǐliǎn〈名〉〈贬〉 features: 丑恶～ ugly mug
【嘴皮子】zuǐpízi〈名〉〈贬〉 gift of the gab: ～利索 be fluent and articulate ‖ 别耍～! Don't just give it gob.
【嘴贫】zuǐpín〈形〉〈口〉 talkative
【嘴软】zuǐruǎn〈形〉 afraid to speak out: 在事实面前，他变得～了。 His voice softened in the face of the facts.
【嘴松】zuǐsōng〈形〉 loose-tongued: 性直～ have a candid nature and a loose tongue
【嘴碎】zuǐsuì〈形〉 talkative: 他平时不这么～。 He isn't normally this chatty.
【嘴损】zuǐsǔn〈形〉 acid-tongued
【嘴甜】zuǐtián〈形〉honey-tongued: 这孩子～，挺讨人喜欢。 The child always speaks sweetly, and lots of people really fell in love with him.
【嘴稳】zuǐwěn〈形〉 able to keep a secret: 这事得找个～的人商量一下。 We ought to talk it over with a man who can be discreet.
【嘴严】zuǐyán〈形〉 tight-lipped: 他～，不会把这件事向外说。 He is good at keeping secrets and certainly wouldn't let this one out.
【嘴硬】zuǐyìng〈形〉 stubborn and reluctant to admit mistakes or defeats: 做错了事还～什么? Why don't you admit your mistakes?
【嘴直】zuǐzhí〈形〉 outspoken: 他一直都心直～。 He is always straightforward and blunt.

zuì

最 zuì
A〈副〉 most: 他是我～要好的朋友。 He is my best friend. ‖ 只有妈妈～心疼我。 Of all the people around me, mum loves me most dearly.
B〈名〉 number one: 世界之～ number one in the world ‖ 中华之～ number one in China
【最爱】zuì'ài〈名〉 favourite: 小女儿是她的～。 The youngest girl is her favourite.
【最初】zuìchū〈名〉 first: 那里～还是不毛之地。 That place used to be a stretch of barren field. ‖ 我～认识他是在上中学的时候。 I first got to know him in my middle school days.
【最大公约数】zuìdà gōngyuēshù〈名〉［数学］ greatest common divisor
【最大限度】zuìdà xiàndù〈名〉 maximum: 我们必须～地满足人民需要。 We must meet the needs of the people to the maximum.
【最大值】zuìdàzhí〈名〉［数学］maximum value: 求～ find the maximum value
【最低工资】zuìdī gōngzī〈名〉 minimum wages
【最低生活保障】zuìdī shēnghuó bǎozhàng〈名〉 minimum subsistence security
【最多】zuìduō A〈形〉 most: 损失～的是经理。 The person with the most to lose is the manager. B〈副〉 at most: 那里～不过100人。 There were one hundred people there, at the very most.
【最高国务会议】zuìgāo guówù huìyì〈名〉 Supreme State Conference
【最高人民法院】Zuìgāo Rénmín Fǎyuàn〈名〉 the Supreme People's Court
【最高人民检察院】Zuìgāo Rénmín Jiǎncháyuàn〈名〉 Supreme People's Procuratorate
【最高限价】zuìgāo xiànjià〈名〉 ceiling price
【最好】zuìhǎo A〈形〉 best: ～的办法 the best way ‖ ～的例子 prime example B〈副〉 had better: 你今天～别去拜访她。 You'd better not visit her today.
【最后】zuìhòu〈名〉 the last: 站好～一班岗 [of one who is about to leave his job] continue working hard right up until the last minute ‖ 坐在～一排 sit in the back row
【最后期限】zuìhòu qīxiàn〈名〉 deadline: 确定～ set a deadline
【最后通牒】zuìhòu tōngdié〈名〉 ultimatum: 发出～ issue an ultimatum
【最坏】zuìhuài〈形〉 worst
【最惠国待遇】zuìhuìguó dàiyù〈名〉 most-favoured-nation treatment: 给予～ accord most-favoured-nation treatment
【最佳】zuìjiā〈形〉 first-rate: ～人选 first-rate candidate ‖ 提供～服务 provide top-class service
【最近】zuìjìn〈名〉 recent time: ～一期的《时代周刊》 the latest issue of *TIME* ‖ 这个戏～就要上演了。 This play will be staged soon.
【最轻量级】zuìqīngliàngjí〈名〉［体育］ bantamweight
【最为】zuìwéi〈副〉〈书〉 [used before disyllabic adjectives or verbs] most: ～可疑 most suspicious ‖ 用电话通知～省事。Sending phone messages is the most convenient way.
【最小公倍数】zuìxiǎo gōngbèishù〈名〉［数学］ least common multiple
【最新】zuìxīn〈形〉 latest: ～报道 updated report
【最终】zuìzhōng〈名〉 final: ～结果 the final outcome ‖ ～目的 ultimate aim
【最最】zuìzuì〈副〉〈口〉 extremely

罪 zuì〈名〉 1 (犯法行为) crime: 被宣判有罪 be pronounced guilty ‖ 承认自己有～ admit one's crimes ‖ 畏～潜逃 flee to escape punishment ▸～大恶极, ～人, 犯～ 2 (苦难) suffering: 活受～ suffer a living hell ‖ 他从小没爹没娘，受了不少～。 He's been an orphan since childhood and experienced a lot of misery. ▸遭～ 3 (过失) fault: 言者无～ blame not the critic ‖ 不要归～于人。 Do not shift the blame onto anyone else. ▸～过, 怪～
【罪案】zuì'àn〈名〉 criminal case: 调查/核实～ find/verify the details of a criminal case
【罪不容诛】zuìbùróngzhū〈成〉 be guilty of crimes for which even death is insufficient punishment
【罪大恶极】zuìdà-èjí〈成〉 be guilty of the most heinous crimes: ～者必须严惩。 Those guilty of the most heinous crimes must be punished severely.
【罪恶】zuì'è〈名〉 crime: ～累累 have a long record of crimes ‖ ～滔天 be guilty of monstrous crimes
【罪恶昭彰】zuì'è-zhāozhāng〈成〉 have committed heinous crimes
【罪犯】zuìfàn〈名〉 offender: 处决～ execute a criminal ‖ 被通缉的～ wanted criminal
【罪该万死】zuìgāiwànsǐ〈成〉 be guilty of a crime for which even death cannot make up for
【罪过】zuìguò〈名〉 1 (过失) fault: 他有什么～? What is his offence? 2〈套〉(不敢当) thanks, but this is really more than I deserve: 给您添了这么多麻烦，真是～。 I am really sorry to bring you so

much trouble.
【罪魁祸首】zuìkuí-huòshǒu〈成〉 chief culprit: 吸毒是导致他死亡的～。 It was his drug habit that led to his death.
【罪戾】zuìlì〈名〉〈书〉 sin
【罪名】zuìmíng〈名〉 charge: 罗织～ cook up charges ‖ 莫须有的～ trumped-up charges ‖ 她的～不成立。 Her guilt is not proved.
【罪莫大焉】zuìmòdàyān〈成〉 there is no crime greater than this
【罪孽】zuìniè〈名〉 iniquity: ～深重 be steeped in iniquity ‖ 虐待自己的母亲，～呀。 Retribution will quickly follow for your ill treatment of your mother.
【罪愆】zuìqiān〈名〉〈书〉 offence
【罪人】zuìrén〈名〉 offender: 历史的～ most infamous crook of all times ‖ 千古～ man of eternal guilt
【罪上加罪】zuìshàngjiāzuì〈成〉 be doubly guilty
【罪行】zuìxíng〈名〉 crime: 坦白交待～ confess one's crimes ‖ ～累累 have a long criminal record
【罪有应得】zuìyǒuyīngdé〈成〉 be retribution for one's sin
【罪责】zuìzé〈名〉 1（指责任） responsibility for an offence: 推卸～ shirk responsibility for a crime ‖ ～难逃 cannot get away with it 2〈书〉（指责罚） penal punishment: 免于～ be exempt from punishment
【罪证】zuìzhèng〈名〉 proof of one's guilt: 收集～ collect evidence of crimes ‖ ～确凿 one's guilt is obvious
【罪状】zuìzhuàng〈名〉 charges in an indictment: 列举～ list the charges

槜 zuì

【槜李】zuìlǐ〈名〉 1（指植物） a kind of sweet and juicy red plum 2（指果实） fruit of the plant

蕞 zuì

【蕞尔】zuì'ěr〈形〉〈书〉 [of an area] very small: ～小国 very small state

醉 zuì

〈动〉 1（饮酒过量） be drunk: ～卧街头 lie drunk in the street ‖ 她只喝了一杯啤酒就～了。 She got drunk on only one glass of beer. ▸～汉 2（沉迷） be crazy about: 看到眼前的景色我的心都～了。 I felt completely intoxicated by the scenery before me. ▸～心, 沉～, 陶～ 3（用酒泡制） be marinated in wine: ～虾 wine-soaked shrimp ‖ ～蟹 alcohol-saturated crab ‖ ～枣 alcohol-soaked dates
【醉鬼】zuìguǐ〈名〉 drunkard
【醉汉】zuìhàn〈名〉 drunk
【醉话】zuìhuà〈名〉 remarks made under the influence of alcohol
【醉拳】zuìquán〈名〉 drunken boxing
【醉人】zuìrén〈动〉 1（使人喝醉） make sb. drunk: 烈性酒容易～。 Strong drinks can easily get you drunk. 2（令人陶醉） fascinate: ～的音乐 intoxicating music
【醉生梦死】zuìshēng-mèngsǐ〈成〉 live in a fool's paradise
【醉态】zuìtài〈名〉 drunkenness
【醉翁之意不在酒】zuìwēng zhī yì bù zài jiǔ〈成〉 have ulterior motives
【醉乡】zuìxiāng〈名〉〈书〉 drunken stupor: 沉入～ fall into a drunken stupor
【醉心】zuìxīn〈动〉 be infatuated with: ～于计算机研究 be engrossed in computer research
【醉醺醺】zuìxūnxūn〈形〉 tipsy
【醉眼】zuìyǎn〈名〉〈书〉 drunk eyes: ～朦胧 drunken and bleary-eyed
【醉意】zuìyì〈名〉 feeling of getting drunk: 他已有三分～了。 He's already had a drop too much.

zūn

尊 zūn

A〈形〉 1（高贵） senior: ～卑 superiors and inferiors ▸～贵, ～长 2〈敬〉（用于指称对方） your honourable: ～夫人 your honourable wife ▸～姓大名
B〈动〉 respect: ～师重教 respect teachers and place importance on education ‖ ～老爱幼 respect the aged and love the young ▸～敬, ～重
C〈量〉 1[used for statues]: 一～佛像 a statue of Buddha 2[used for guns]: 一～大炮 one cannon
【尊称】zūnchēng A〈名〉 honorific title: "您"是"你"的～。 您 is the honorific form of 你. ‖ 先生是对成年男子的一种～。 Sir is the polite term of address for an adult man. ‖ "范老"是同事们对他的～。 'Venerable Fan' is the respectful form by which his colleagues address him. B〈动〉 address sb. respectfully
【尊崇】zūnchóng〈动〉 worship: 他受到全国人民的～。 The people of the whole country held him in great veneration.
【尊贵】zūnguì〈形〉 honourable: ～的客人 distinguished guest
【尊敬】zūnjìng A〈动〉 respect: ～老师 have respect for one's teachers ‖ ～长辈 be respectful to one's elders ‖ 博得大家的～ win respect from everyone B〈形〉 honourable: ～的张先生 the honourable Mr. Zhang
【尊老爱幼】zūnlǎo-àiyòu〈成〉 respect the aged and love the young
【尊亲】zūnqīn〈名〉 1（指亲属） one's senior relatives 2〈尊〉（用于称呼） your respectable relatives
【尊容】zūnróng〈名〉 [often used ironically] distinguished face: 瞧他那副～。 What a face he's got!
【尊尚】zūnshàng〈动〉 uphold
【尊师重道】zūnshī-zhòngdào〈成〉 respect the teacher and revere his teachings
【尊姓大名】zūnxìng-dàmíng〈名〉〈套〉 your name: 请问～? May I have your name?
【尊严】zūnyán〈名〉 dignity: 法律的～ sanctity of law ‖ 国家～ national dignity
【尊长】zūnzhǎng〈名〉 elders and betters: 目无～ with no regard for one's elders and betters
【尊重】zūnzhòng A〈动〉 1（敬重） hold in high esteem: ～父母 honour one's parents ‖ 很受～的人 highly regarded person 2（重视）value: ～他人意见 have respect for the views of others ‖ ～知识，～人才 respect for knowledge and talents B〈形〉 serious: 放～些! Behave yourself!

遵 zūn

〈动〉 observe: ～医嘱 follow the doctor's advice
【遵从】zūncóng〈动〉 defer to, comply with: ～教导 follow the advice ‖ ～上级的指示 in compliance with the directions of the leadership ‖ 我～专家的意见。 I defer to the experts' opinion.
【遵纪守法】zūnjì-shǒufǎ〈成〉 observe the law and disciplines
【遵命】zūnmìng〈动〉〈套〉 obey your command: ～办理 act in compliance with your instructions
【遵守】zūnshǒu〈动〉 comply with: ～纪律 observe discipline ‖ ～交通规则 observe traffic regulations ‖ ～诺言 stand by one's promise ‖ ～时间 be punctual
【遵行】zūnxíng〈动〉follow: ～一贯的原则 act according to one's consistent principles
【遵循】zūnxún〈动〉 follow: ～和平共处的原则 adhere to the principle of peaceful coexistence ‖ ～社会行为准则 adapt to the norms of the society ‖ 制定一个章程，使大家有所～ formulate a set of rules so that people will have something to go by
【遵照】zūnzhào〈动〉 comply with: ～政策办事 act in accordance with policy ‖ ～上级的命令 in accordance with orders from above

樽 zūn〈名〉〈古〉 wine vessel

鳟（鱒） zūn〈名〉［鱼类］ trout

zǔn

撙 zǔn〈动〉〈书〉save: ～钱 save money

zuō

作 zuō〈名〉 workshop: 石～ mason's workshop

▸zuò
【作坊】zuōfang〈名〉 workshop: 造纸～ paper mill ‖ 油漆～ painter's studio
【作女】zuōnǚ〈名〉 high-maintenance woman: ～形象 the typical image of a high-maintenance woman

嘬 zuō〈动〉〈口〉 suck: ～奶嘴儿 suck at the teat ‖ ～手指头 suck one's thumb

▸chuài

zuó

昨 zuó〈名〉 1（昨天） yesterday: ～夜 last night ▸～天 2（过去） the past: 觉今是而～非 begin to understand that what we did in the past was wrong and how what we are doing now is right

【昨日】zuórì〈名〉 yesterday
【昨天】zuótiān〈名〉 1（前一天） yesterday 2（过去） the past: ～的荒山变成了今天的果园。 The once desolate slopes have been turned into orchards.
【昨晚】zuówǎn〈名〉 last night

捽 zuó〈动〉〈方〉 seize: 一把～住小偷的衣领 hold the thief tightly by the collar ‖ 他～住绳子往上爬。 He grasped the rope and began to pull himself up.

笮 zuó〈名〉 rope made of bamboo strips

【笮桥】zuóqiáo〈名〉 bamboo suspension bridge

琢 zuó

▸zhuó
【琢磨】zuómo〈动〉 think over: ～出个办法 work out a way ‖ 这事让我再～～。

Let me have another think about this.
▸zhuómó

zuǒ

左 zuǒ

A〈名〉**1**▸**p. 781**（左边）the left: ～耳进右耳出 go in one ear and out the other ‖ ～转弯 turn left ‖ 靠～行! Keep to the left. ▸～边, ～顾右盼, ～右开弓 **2**（东边）east: 江～ east of the river ‖ 山～ areas east of the Taihang Mountains [specifically Shandong Province] **3**〈书〉（低位）inferior position: ▸～迁
B〈形〉**1**（偏、邪）unorthodox: ▸旁门～道 **2**（错误）wrong: 你想～了。Your thinking is off. ‖ 说～了。What you've said is wrong. **3**（不同）different: 意见相～ be divided in opinion **4**（进步）progressive: ▸～派, ～翼

【左膀右臂】zuǒbǎng-yòubì〈成〉right-hand man
【左边锋】zuǒbiānfēng〈名〉[体育] left wing
【左边】zuǒbian〈名〉the left: 她就坐在我的～。She just sat on my left.
【左道旁门】zuǒdào-pángmén〈成〉heterodox school: 不要搞～。Don't act in unlawful and tricky ways.
【左锋】zuǒfēng〈名〉[篮球] left forward
【左顾右盼】zuǒgù-yòupàn〈成〉look around: 不许～。No wandering eyes!
【左后卫】zuǒhòuwèi〈名〉[足球] left back
【左近】zuǒjìn〈名〉nearby area: 房子的～有一片草地。There is a lawn near the house.
【左邻右舍】zuǒlín-yòushè〈成〉neighbours: ～都在谈论这件事情。The whole neighbourhood is talking about it.
【左轮】zuǒlún〈名〉revolver
【左面】zuǒmiàn = 左边 zuǒbian
【左派】zuǒpài〈名〉**1**（指派别）the left wing: ～势力 forces of the Left **2**（指人）leftist
【左撇子】zuǒpiězi〈名〉left-handed person
【左迁】zuǒqiān〈动〉〈书〉demote
【左前卫】zuǒqiánwèi〈名〉[足球] left halfback, left half
【左倾】zuǒqīng〈形〉**1**（指倾向革命）left-leaning **2**（指急躁冒进）of left deviation: ～机会主义 'Left' opportunism ‖ ～机会主义分子 'Left' opportunist
【左券】zuǒquàn〈名〉〈书〉sure thing: 稳操～ be sure of success
【左嗓子】zuǒsǎngzi〈名〉**1**（指音调不准）out-of-tune voice: 我生就一副～，唱不了歌。I can't sing. When I do, I always sing out of tune. **2**（指人）person who sings out of tune
【左手】zuǒshǒu〈名〉**1**（左边的手）left hand **2** = 左首 zuǒshǒu
【左首】zuǒshǒu〈名〉left-hand side: ～坐着位老太太。An old lady was seated on the left side.
【左思右想】zuǒsī-yòuxiǎng〈成〉think over from different angles: 她～，总也理不出个头绪。She failed to sort things out even though she had turned the matter over and over in her mind.
【左袒】zuǒtǎn〈动〉〈书〉take sides: 对辩论双方要评判公正，不可～任一方。We should show impartiality in judging the performance of the debaters and mustn't take sides.
【左舷】zuǒxián〈名〉port (of a ship)
【左性子】zuǒxìngzi **A**〈形〉stubborn **B**〈名〉person of stubborn temperament
【左翼】zuǒyì〈名〉**1**[军事] left flank **2**（左派）left wing: ～作家联盟 League of Leftist Writers [organized in 1930]
【左右】zuǒyòu **A**〈名〉**1**（左面和右面）left and right sides: ～对称 have bilateral symmetry ‖ ～两侧 the two sides of left and right **2**（周围的人）retinue: 吩咐～退下 order one's entourage to leave **3**▸**p. 927**（表概数）[used after a number] or so: 三十岁～ around thirty years old ‖ 五点十分～ ten past five or so **B**〈动〉master: ～公众舆论 sway public opinion ‖ 他想～我，没那么容易。He wants to control me, but it isn't going to be that easy.
【左右逢源】zuǒyòu-féngyuán〈成〉**1**（指处处顺利）be able to achieve success one way or another **2**（指向各方面讨好）have one's bread buttered on both sides
【左右开弓】zuǒyòu-kāigōng〈成〉use both hands alternately in quick succession: ～打人嘴巴 slap sb. on both cheeks
【左右手】zuǒyòushǒu〈名〉right-hand man: 儿子长大成人，成了他的～。When his son grew up, he became his right-hand man.
【左右为难】zuǒyòu-wéinán〈成〉be in a dilemma: 你的话使我～，不知如何是好。What you said put me in a quandary. I really don't know what to do.
【左证】zuǒzhèng = 佐证 zuǒzhèng
【左支右绌】zuǒzhī-yòuchù〈成〉be in straitened circumstances

佐 zuǒ

A〈动〉assist: ～助 assist sb. in doing something important ▸～餐, ～理, 辅～
B〈名〉assistant: 僚～ assistant in a government office

【佐餐】zuǒcān〈动〉〈书〉go with rice or bread
【佐理】zuǒlǐ〈动〉〈书〉assist sb. with a task: ～国事 assist the emperor in handling state affairs
【佐料】zuǒliào = 作料 zuòliao
【佐证】zuǒzhèng〈名〉evidence: 缺乏～ lack evidence ‖ 提供～ offer proof
【佐治亚州】Zuǒzhìyàzhōu〈名〉Georgia

撮 zuǒ

〈量〉[used for hair] tuft: 一～黑毛 a tuft of black hair ‖ 一～山羊胡子 a goatee ▸cuō

【撮子】zuǒzi〈量〉〈口〉tuft: 一～头发 a tuft of hair

zuò

作 zuò

A〈动〉**1**（制造）make: ▸～息, 操～ **2**（兴起）rise: ▸～怪, 振～, 兴风～浪 **3**（从事）engage in an activity: ～报告 deliver a report ‖ ～斗争 wage a struggle ▸～弊, ～乱, 为非～歹 **4**（当作）regard as: ▸认贼～父 **5**（写）write: ▸～曲, ～文 **6**（假装）pretend: 故～怒容 pretend to be angry ▸装模～样
B〈名〉writings: 成功之～ successful writing ‖ 佳～ excellent work ‖ 新～ new work ▸杰～, 原～
▸zuō

【作案】zuò'àn〈动〉commit an offence: ～现场 crime scene
【作罢】zuòbà〈动〉give up: 看来也只有～了。It seems that we have to give up.
【作保】zuòbǎo〈动〉be sb.'s guarantor: 向银行借钱得有人～。If you want a loan from the bank, you will need some surety.
【作弊】zuòbì〈动〉cheat: 考试～ cheat in an examination ‖ 选举～ electoral fraud
【作壁上观】zuòbìshàngguān〈成〉〈喻〉stand by and watch: 他们吵得不可开交，你不能～。They are quarrelling fiercely. You can't just sit and watch.
【作别】zuòbié〈动〉〈书〉bid farewell: 与亲友～ take leave of one's relatives and friends
【作成】zuòchéng〈动〉help: ～俩人的婚事 help them to get married
【作词】zuòcí〈动〉write words for a song
【作答】zuòdá〈动〉respond
【作对】zuòduì〈动〉**1**（跟人为难）set oneself against: 他处处和我～。He opposes me in everything. **2**（结成配偶）pair off in marriage
【作恶】zuò'è〈动〉do evil: ～多端 commit all kinds of evil
【作伐】zuòfá〈动〉〈书〉act as matchmaker
【作法】zuòfǎ **A**〈动〉cast a spell: ～驱邪 exorcize **B**〈名〉**1**（指写作）writing technique: 文章～ art of composition **2** = 做法 zuòfǎ
【作法自毙】zuòfǎ-zìbì〈成〉be hoisted by one's own petard
【作废】zuòfèi〈动〉be nullified: 声明～ declare invalid ‖ 逾期～ become invalid upon expiration
【作风】zuòfēng〈名〉style: 保持艰苦奋斗的～ maintain the style of hard struggle and plain living ‖ 改变工作～ alter the style of work ‖ ～正派 be honest and upright in one's ways
【作复】zuòfù〈动〉〈书〉write in reply
【作梗】zuògěng〈动〉hinder: 只要你不从中～，事情就好办多了。Things will be much easier if you don't create difficulties.
【作古】zuògǔ ▸**p. 772**〈动〉〈书〉〈婉〉pass away: 老先生已于前日～。The old man passed away the day before yesterday.
【作怪】zuòguài〈动〉make trouble: 兴妖～ stir up trouble behind the scenes ‖〈喻〉重男轻女的思想至今还在一部分人的头脑里～。The concept of favouring boys over girls still lurks in the minds of some people.
【作家】zuòjiā〈名〉writer: 多产～ prolific writer
【作家协会】zuòjiā xiéhuì〈名〉writer's association
【作假】zuòjiǎ〈动〉**1**（冒充）counterfeit: 弄虚～ practise fraud **2**（耍花招）play tricks: ～骗人 play tricks to cheat people **3**（不爽快）behave affectedly: 你是海量，何必～! You have a high alcohol tolerance. Why pretend that you don't?
【作价】zuòjià〈动〉fix a price: ～赔偿 compensate sb. for sth. at the price agreed on by both parties ‖ 旧计算机～两百元 value the old computer at 200 *yuan*
【作奸犯科】zuòjiān-fànkē〈成〉commit offences against law and discipline: 若有～，严惩不贷。Whoever commits offences against law and discipline will be severely punished.
【作茧自缚】zuòjiǎn-zìfù〈成〉get caught in a web of one's own spinning: 你这样做简直是～。By doing this, you are just asking for trouble.
【作件】zuòjiàn〈名〉workpiece
【作践】zuòjian〈动〉**1**（浪费）spoil: ～粮食 waste grain **2**（侮辱）humiliate: 他

Z

这样说不是故意～人吗？ Didn't he say that just to humiliate me?

【作客】zuòkè〈动〉〈书〉 sojourn: ～他乡 sojourn in a strange land

【作困兽斗】zuò kùnshòudòu〈成〉 fight like a cornered beast

【作乐】zuòlè〈动〉 make merry: 苦中～ try to enjoy oneself in the midst of difficulties ‖ 寻欢～ indulge in merry-making ▸zuòyuè

【作料】zuòliao〈名〉 condiments

【作乱】zuòluàn〈动〉 stage an armed insurrection: 犯上～ rebel against the authorities

【作美】zuòměi〈动〉 [usu used in the negative] help: 天公不～ not helped by the foul weather

【作难】zuònán〈动〉 find oneself in a predicament: 他感到有点～，不知道该怎么办。 He found himself in a fix and didn't know what to do.

【作难】zuònàn〈动〉〈书〉 rise in revolt

【作鸟兽散】zuò niǎoshòusàn〈成〉 flee helter-skelter

【作孽】zuòniè〈动〉 commit a sin

【作弄】zuònòng〈动〉 tease: 你别～我了。 Don't make a fool of me.

【作呕】zuò'ǒu〈动〉 feel nauseous: 天天吃鸡蛋，想起来就～。 The thought of eating eggs every day makes me feel sick. ‖〈喻〉 他的行为令人～。 His conduct is disgusting.

【作陪】zuòpéi〈动〉 help entertain the guest of honour: 明天的宴会请你～。 You're to help entertain the guest at the banquet tomorrow.

【作品】zuòpǐn〈名〉 works: 文学～ literary works ‖ 音乐～ musical works ‖ 雕塑～ sculptural works

【作曲】zuòqǔ〈动〉 compose: 王洛宾～ music by Wang Luobin ‖ ～家 composer

【作如是观】zuò rúshìguān〈成〉 view the matter in this light

【作色】zuòsè〈动〉〈书〉 get worked up: 愤然～ flush with indignation

【作声】zuòshēng〈动〉 make a sound: 吓得不敢～ be intimidated into silence

【作势】zuòshì〈动〉 strike a pose: ▸装腔～

【作数】zuòshù〈动〉 count: 你说的话～不～? Is what you said still valid? ‖ 我们说话～。 We mean what we say.

【作死】zuòsǐ〈动〉 court death: 酒后开快车，这不是～吗? You must have a death wish, getting drunk and then speeding like that!

【作速】zuòsù〈动〉 lose no time: ～处理 lose no time in dealing with a matter

【作祟】zuòsuì〈动〉 **1**（指鬼怪） haunt **2**〈喻〉（指人）cause trouble: 防止有人从中～。 Measures must be taken to prevent sabotage. ‖ 虚荣心在～。The trouble is caused by vanity.

【作态】zuòtài〈动〉 pose: 忸怩～ behave coyly ‖ 惺惺～ simulate

【作痛】zuòtòng〈动〉 have a pain: 周身的筋骨隐隐～ feel a dull ache all over

【作威作福】zuòwēi-zuòfú〈成〉 act tyrannically: ～，欺压人民。 Tyrannically abuse power and ride roughshod over the people.

【作为】zuòwéi **A**〈名〉 **1**（行为） conduct: 评论一个人不仅要听其谈吐，更要观其～。 The appraisal of a person should be based not only on their words but also on their conduct. **2**（成就） accomplishment: 大有～ be able to bring one's initiative into full play **B**〈动〉 **1**（取得成绩） accomplish: 无所～ do nothing and achieve nothing in life **2**（当作） regard as: 把某人～靠山 regard sb. as a patron **C**〈介〉 as: ～公务员，必须奉公守法。 As a civil servant one must be public-spirited and respect the law.

【作伪】zuòwěi〈动〉 forge

【作文】zuòwén **A**〈动〉 write a composition **B**〈名〉 composition: 修改～ revise a composition ‖ ～竞赛 composition contest

【作物】zuòwù〈名〉 crop: ～栽培 crop culture

【作息】zuòxī〈动〉 work and rest: 按时～ work and rest according to schedule ‖ ～时间表 daily schedule

【作响】zuòxiǎng〈动〉 make a sound: 春雷在远处隆隆～。 Spring thunder rumbled in the distance.

【作协】zuòxié〈简称〉= 作家协会

【作兴】zuòxing〈动〉〈方〉 [usu used in the negative] be justifiable to: 可不～骂人。 It's not right to swear at people.

【作秀】zuòxiù〈动〉 **1**（表演） put on a show **2**（装模作样） hold exhibition and promotion activities for sales, election, etc.

【作业】zuòyè〈名〉 **1**（指学习、训练任务） school assignment: 做～ do one's homework ‖ 家庭～ homework ‖ 课堂～ assignment to be done in class **2**（指工作或活动） operation: 深海～ deep sea operation ‖ 野外～ field work ‖ 在高空～ operate high above the ground

【作揖】zuòyī〈动〉 make a slight bow with hands folded in front: 打躬～ fold one's hands and make deep bows

【作用】zuòyòng **A**〈动〉 affect: 酒精～于大脑，能令人兴奋。 Alcohol affects the brain and can make a person excited. **B**〈名〉 **1**（指活动） function: 化学～ chemical action ‖ 杠杆～ leverage ‖ 光合～ photosynthesis **2**（指效果） effect: 发挥更大～ have a greater impact ‖ 副～ side effect ‖ 带头～ leading role

【作乐】zuòyuè〈动〉〈书〉 **1**（指创作） compose music **2**（指演奏） play music ▸zuòlè

【作战】zuòzhàn〈动〉 fight a battle: ～部队 combat troops ‖ 与敌人～ battle the enemy

【作者】zuòzhě ▸**p. 966**〈名〉 author: ～不详 by an anonymous author

【作证】zuòzhèng〈动〉 **1**（作为证据） be used as evidence: 血衣可以～。 Clothes stained with blood can be used as evidence. **2**（提供证据、证言） testify: 出庭～ take the witness stand

坐 zuò

A〈动〉 **1**（指动作）sit: 请～下谈。 Please take a seat before the talk starts. ‖ 他～着一动不动。 He sat there motionless. ▸～井观天，正襟危～ **2**〈旧〉（指定罪） sentence: ～死罪 be sentenced to death ▸反～，连～ **3**（主宰） rule: ▸～江山，～庄 **4**（搭乘） travel by: ～船 travel by boat ‖ ～飞机去 go by plane ‖ ～火车/公共汽车 travel by train/bus **5**（背对） have its back towards: 大殿～北向南。 The great hall faces south. **6**（放） put on a fire: 把壶～上 put the kettle on the heat ‖ 炉子上～着一壶水。 A kettle of water is being heated on the stove. **7**（形成） have a disease: ～下了寒腿病 suffer from a cold legs condition **8**（结果实） bear, fruit: ▸～果 **9**（下陷） sink, subside: 这座塔往下～了半尺多。 This tower has sunk nearly 20 centimetres. **10**（后坐力） recoil: 无～力炮 recoilless gun **B**〈介〉〈书〉 because of: ～此解职 be sacked because of this ‖ 停车～爱枫林晚 stop the carriage to enjoy the maple trees in the evening glow

【坐班】zuòbān〈动〉 keep office hours: ～制 system of keeping office hours ‖ 大学教师不～。 University teachers do not keep office hours.

【坐班房】zuò bānfáng〈动〉〈旧〉 be put in jail

【坐标】zuòbiāo〈名〉 coordinate

【坐不住】zuòbuzhù〈动〉〈口〉 be restless: 听了这话他有些～了。 He began to fidget at the remarks.

【坐禅】zuòchán〈动〉［佛教］ sit in meditation

【坐吃山空】zuòchī-shānkōng〈成〉 sit idle and you will eat away your fortune

【坐次】zuòcì〈名〉 order of seats

【坐待】zuòdài〈动〉 sit back and wait: ～时机 sit back and wait for an opportunity

【坐得住】zuòdezhù〈动〉〈口〉 be capable of concentrating on one's work

【坐等】zuòděng〈动〉 sit back and wait: ～胜利 sit back and wait for victory

【坐地】zuòdì **A**〈动〉 stay at a fixed place: ～户 native household ‖ ～行医 practise medicine where one is registered **B**〈副〉 on the spot: ～加价 raise the price at the transaction location ‖ 货物～转手 resell the goods on the spot

【坐地分赃】zuòdì-fēnzāng〈成〉 take a share of the spoils without participating in the robbery

【坐垫】zuòdiàn〈名〉 cushion: 软～ squab

【坐而论道】zuò'érlùndào〈成〉sit back and pontificate

【坐骨】zuògǔ〈名〉［解剖］ ischium: ～神经 sciatic nerve

【坐观成败】zuòguān-chéngbài〈成〉 look on coldly

【坐果】zuòguǒ〈动〉 bear fruit: 这树明年就能～。 The tree will bear fruit next year.

【坐化】zuòhuà〈动〉 [of Buddhist monks] pass away in a sitting posture

【坐监】zuòjiān〈动〉 be in prison

【坐监狱】zuò jiānyù = 坐监 zuòjiān

【坐江山】zuò jiāngshān〈动〉 rule the country

【坐井观天】zuòjǐng-guāntiān〈成〉 have a very narrow view of the world

【坐具】zuòjù〈名〉 seat

【坐困】zuòkùn〈动〉 be confined: ～孤城 stay shut away in an isolated town

【坐牢】zuòláo〈动〉 be imprisoned: 他被判～两年。 He was sentenced to two years in prison.

【坐冷板凳】zuò lěngbǎndèng〈惯〉〈喻〉 **1**（受到冷遇） hold an unimportant post and be neglected **2**（久等） be kept waiting for an assignment or an audience with a VIP

【坐力】zuòlì〈名〉［军事］ recoil

【坐立不安】zuòlì-bù'ān〈成〉 be on tenterhooks: 都半夜了，儿子还不回家，母亲～。 By midnight her son still hadn't returned home and the mother was frantic with worry.

【坐落】zuòluò〈动〉 be situated: 我们学校～在湖边。 Our school is situated next to a lake.

【坐骑】zuòqí〈名〉 saddle horse

【坐山观虎斗】zuò shān guān hǔ dòu〈成〉 watch in safety while others fight, then reap the spoils when both sides are exhausted

【坐商】zuòshāng〈名〉 shopkeeper

【坐失】zuòshī〈动〉 give away: ～良机 let slip a golden opportunity

【坐实】zuòshí〈动〉 substantiate: ～罪名 prove a charge
【坐视】zuòshì〈动〉 sit tight and look on: ～不理 sit by idly and remain indifferent
【坐收渔利】zuòshōu-yúlì〈成〉 reap the spoils of victory without lifting a finger
【坐胎】zuòtāi〈动〉 be pregnant
【坐堂】zuòtáng〈动〉 1（旧）（指官吏）try a case in a law court 2 = 坐禅 zuòchán 3（指营业员）attend to 4（指医生）practise medicine at a pharmacy: ～医生 doctor practising at a pharmacy
【坐天下】zuò tiānxià〈动〉 rule the country
【坐卧不安】zuòwò-bù'ān〈成〉 feel restless
【坐席】zuòxí A〈动〉 attend a banquet B〈名〉 seat
【坐享其成】zuòxiǎng-qíchéng〈成〉sit idle and enjoy the fruits of others' work: 他喜欢自食其力，不喜欢～。 He prefers to earn his own living rather than reap what he has not sown.
【坐像】zuòxiàng〈名〉 statue in sitting posture
【坐夜】zuòyè〈动〉 keep vigil overnight: ～等门 keep vigil until sb. returns ‖ ～守岁 keep vigil the whole night for the coming of the new year
【坐以待毙】zuòyǐdàibì〈成〉 resign oneself to death: 我们与其～，不如先下手打他个措手不及。 It is better for us to go into action now and take the enemy by surprise rather than to wait passively for our demise.
【坐以待旦】zuòyǐdàidàn〈成〉 sit up and wait for daybreak
【坐月子】zuò yuèzi〈动〉convalesce for one month following childbirth
【坐诊】zuòzhěn〈动〉 be in situ to see patients
【坐镇】zuòzhèn〈动〉 personally attend to garrison duty:〈喻〉 总经理亲临现场～指挥。 The general manager is commanding operations himself on the spot.
【坐庄】zuòzhuāng〈动〉 1（指为采购货物） be a resident buyer of a business firm 2（指赌博时） be the banker or dealer: 轮流～ take turns to be the banker ‖ 他连坐了三庄。 He served his turn as banker three times.
【坐姿】zuòzī〈名〉 sitting posture

阼 zuò〈名〉〈旧〉 the eastern flight of stairs along which the host descends and ascends to welcome visitors or hold sacrificial ceremonies

怍 zuò〈动〉〈书〉 be ashamed: 惭～ feel ashamed ‖ 愧～ feel abashed

柞 zuò〈名〉 oak
【柞蚕】zuòcán〈名〉 tussah: ～丝 tussah silk
【柞丝绸】zuòsīchóu〈名〉 tussah silk

胙 zuò〈名〉〈古〉 sacrificial meat

祚 zuò〈名〉〈书〉 1（福）blessing: 门衰～薄 an unblessed family on the decline 2（帝位） throne: 践～ ascend to the throne ‖ 帝～ emperor's throne

唑 zuò ►噻唑 sāizuò

座 zuò
A〈名〉 1（座位） seat: 让～儿 offer one's seat to sb. ‖ 帮他找个～儿。 Please find a seat for him. ►高朋满～ 2（星座） constellation: ►大熊～，天琴～ 3（底座） stand: 雕像～儿 pedestal for a statue ‖ 花瓶～儿 vase stand 4（旧）〈敬〉（指人） [honorific salutation]: 军～ army commander
B〈量〉 [for mountains, buildings, and other similar immovable objects]: 一～宫殿 a palace ‖ 一～桥 a bridge ‖ 一～山 a mountain
【座便器】zuòbiànqì〈名〉 toilet: 一体式/分体式～ a one-piece/two-piece toilet
【座舱】zuòcāng〈名〉［航空］1（指民用飞机） passenger cabin 2（指战机） cockpit
【座舱盖】zuòcānggài〈名〉［航空］ cockpit hood
【座次】zuòcì〈名〉 order of seats: 排～ arrange the seating order
【座机】zuòjī〈名〉 1（指飞机） private plane 2（指电话） fixed-line telephone
【座落】zuòluò = 坐落 zuòluò
【座上客】zuòshàngkè〈名〉 guest of honour
【座谈】zuòtán〈动〉 have an informal discussion: ～心得体会 talk about what one has gained from one's study
【座谈会】zuòtánhuì〈名〉 symposium
【座位】zuòwèi〈名〉 seat: 安排～ arrange seats ‖ 这个大厅有一千个～。 The hall seats 1,000.
【座无虚席】zuòwúxūxí〈成〉 be packed to capacity: 礼堂里～，气氛非常热烈。 The auditorium was packed to capacity and the atmosphere was very lively.
【座右铭】zuòyòumíng〈名〉 motto
【座钟】zuòzhōng〈名〉 desk clock
【座子】zuòzi〈名〉 1（底座） stand 2（车座） saddle

做 zuò〈动〉 1（从事） do: ～功课 do one's homework ‖ ～实验 do an experiment ‖ ～针线活 do needlework ►～工，～生意 2（制造） make: ～条裙子 make a skirt ‖ 一～套家具 make a set of furniture ►～饭 3（写） write: ►～文章 4（举行） hold: ►～礼拜，～满月，～寿 5（充当） be: ～个好孩子 be a good child ‖ ～老实人 be an honest person ‖ ～秘书 be a secretary 6（联结成） be closely associated: ～夫妻 get married ‖ ～哥们儿 be buddies 7（用作） use as: 拿地～抵押 mortgage one's land ‖ 用这间房子～教室 turn this room into a classroom 8（装出） pretend: ►～样子，～作
【做爱】zuò'ài〈动〉 make love
【做伴】zuòbàn〈动〉 accompany: 母亲生病了，需要有个人～。 Mother is ill and she needs someone to keep her company.
【做操】zuòcāo〈动〉 do gymnastics: 做早操 do morning exercise
【做东】zuòdōng〈动〉 play the host: 我来～。 It is my treat.
【做法】zuòfǎ〈名〉 method of work: 按照常规～ follow conventional practice ‖ 这种～不妥当。 This way of doing things is not appropriate.
【做饭】zuòfàn〈动〉 cook
【做工】zuògōng A〈动〉 do manual work: 在纺织厂～ work in a spinning mill B〈名〉 workmanship: ～精美 be of excellent workmanship
【做功】zuògōng〈名〉 stage business
【做官】zuòguān〈动〉 be an official
【做鬼】zuòguǐ〈动〉 play tricks: 从中～ get up to mischief
【做活儿】zuòhuór〈动〉 do manual labour
【做假】zuòjiǎ〈动〉falsify: 在数字上～ falsify the numbers
【做客】zuòkè〈动〉 be a visitor
【做空】zuòkōng〈动〉［金融］ sell short
【做礼拜】zuò lǐbài〈动〉 go to church
【做买卖】zuò mǎimai〈动〉 engage in trade: ～的 trader ‖ 做成一笔买卖 make a deal
【做满月】zuò mǎnyuè〈动〉 celebrate a baby's one month birthday
【做媒】zuòméi〈动〉 be a matchmaker
【做梦】zuòmèng〈动〉 1（指睡眠时） have a dream: 做恶梦 have a nightmare 2〈喻〉（指幻想） daydream: 做白日梦 have a daydream
【做派】zuòpài〈名〉 1［戏曲］ gesture and facial expression (of an actor) 2（派头） bearing: 一副官老爷的～ the bearing of an official
【做亲】zuòqīn〈动〉 1（指两家人） become related by marriage 2（指两个人） get married
【做人】zuòrén〈动〉 1（为人处事） conduct oneself: 会～ know how to behave in society 2（做正派的人） be an honest person: 重新～ start afresh
【做生日】zuò shēngri〈动〉 celebrate a birthday
【做生意】zuò shēngyi = 做买卖 zuò mǎimai
【做声】zuòshēng = 作声 zuòshēng
【做实】zuòshí〈动〉 perform in a solid and thorough manner: 把关系人民群众根本利益的事情做细～ carefully and thoroughly act on the things that impact on the fundamental interests of the people
【做事】zuòshì〈动〉 1（办事情） get things done: 他～一向很认真。 He has been very diligent in everything he does. 2（任职） work: 他在电脑公司～。 He works in a computer company.
【做市商】zuòshìshāng〈名〉［金融］ market maker: 黄金～ gold market maker
【做手脚】zuò shǒujiǎo〈动〉use underhand methods: 她老在账目上～。 She's always fiddling the accounts.
【做寿】zuòshòu〈动〉 celebrate a birthday [usu of elderly people]
【做文章】zuò wénzhāng〈动〉 1（写文章） write a composition 2〈喻〉（借题发挥） make an issue of sth.: 有些董事想在预算上～。 Some of the board members want to make an issue of the budget.
【做戏】zuòxì〈动〉1（演戏）put on a play 2〈喻〉（故做姿态） play-act: 他这是在我面前～罢了。 He is just putting on a show in front of me.
【做学问】zuò xuéwen〈动〉 do research
【做样子】zuò yàngzi〈动〉 do sth. for the sake of appearances: 他对穷人的关心只不过是做做样子罢了。 His concern for the poor is mere posturing.
【做一天和尚撞一天钟】zuò yī tiān héshang zhuàng yī tiān zhōng〈俗〉 do the least that is expected of one
【做贼心虚】zuòzéi-xīnxū〈成〉have a guilty conscience
【做针线】zuò zhēnxian〈动〉 do some sewing
【做主】zuòzhǔ〈动〉 take the responsibility for a decision: 当家～ be the master of one's own destiny ‖ 自己的事情自己～。 Make one's own decisions about one's own affairs.
【做作】zuòzuo〈动〉 be pretentious: 他的表情太～了。 His expressions are so affected.

酢 zuò〈动〉〈书〉 propose a toast to the host: ►酬～
►cù

字 母 词
Lettered Words

（汉语中以西方语言字母开头的词语）
(words used in Chinese which start with western alphabetic letters)

【α测试】 α test [阿尔法测试]
【α粒子】 α particle [阿尔法粒子]
【α射线】 α ray [阿尔法射线]
【β测试】 β test [贝塔测试]
【β粒子】 β particle [贝塔粒子]
【β射线】 β ray [贝塔射线]
【γ刀】 gamma knife [伽马刀]
【γ射线】 γ ray [伽马射线]
【AAAA级旅游区】 AAAA tourist attraction
【AA制】 go Dutch
【ABS系统】 anti-lock brake system [防抱死制动系统]
【AB角】 AB Role [two actors or actresses who prepare for the same role in a play in case one is unable to perform]
【AB卷】 paper A/B: 出～ set paper A/B
【AB团】 Anti-Bolshevik Group [反布尔什维克组织]
【AB型血】 blood group AB
【ACE球】 ace [（网球）发球直接得分]
【AD】 Anno Domini [公元]
【ADSL】 asymmetrical digital subscriber line [非对称数字用户线路]
【AI】 artificial intelligence [人工智能]
【AIDS】 acquired immune deficiency syndrome [艾滋病，获得性免疫缺陷综合征]
【AM】 amplitude modulation [调幅]
【am】 ante meridiem [上午]
【AOD】 audio on demand [音频点播]
【APC】 aspirin, phenacetin and caffeine compound [复方阿斯匹林]
【APEC】 Asia-Pacific Economic Cooperation [亚太经济合作组织]
【API】 air pollution index [空气污染指数]
【ATB车】 all terrain bike [山地车]
【ATM】 automated teller machine [自动柜员机，自动取款机]: ～卡 ATM card
【AV】 audio-visual [音频－视频]: ～端子 AV terminal
【A股】 A-share: ～市场 A-share market
【A货】 first-class product [正品]
【A片】 adult film [成人影片]
【A型血】 blood group A
【A照】 driving licence A

【B2B电子商务】 business-to-business E-commerce [企业间电子商务]
【B2C电子商务】 business-to-customer E-commerce [网上购物]
【BA】 Bachelor of Arts [文学士]
【BB】 baby [婴儿]
【BB枪】 Ball Bullet Gun [仿真枪]
【BBS】 bulletin board system [电子布告栏]
【BC】 Before Christ [公元前]
【BEC】 Business English Certificate [商务英语证书]
【BIG5】 Big 5 Chinese characters [大5码]
【BIN】 Bank Identification Number [银行标识号]
【BIOS】 basic input/output system [基本输入/输出系统]: ～芯片 BIOS chip
【BLOG】 blog [博客]
【BMI】 body mass index [体重指数]
【BOBO族】 bourgeois-bohemia [波波族]
【BOD】 biochemical oxygen demand [生化需氧量]
【BOT模式】 build-operate-transfer mode [建设－经营－转让模式]
【BP机】 pager [寻呼机]
【BS】 Bachelor of Science [理学士]
【BYO】 bring your own [自带酒水]
【B超】 type-B ultrasonic diagnosis [B型超声诊断]: 做～ undergo ultrasonic diagnosis B
【B股】 B-share
【B货】 substandard product [次品]
【B淋巴细胞】 B lymphocyte
【B小调】 B minor
【B型血】 blood group B
【B照】 driving licence B

【C】 centigrade [摄氏度]: 水100℃开。Water boils at 100℃.
【C2C电子商务】 C2C E-commerce [客户对客户电子商务]
【C³I系统】 system of command control, communication and information [（军队）自动化指挥系统]
【CA】 certification authority [认证机构]
【CAAC】 Civil Aviation Administration of China [中国民航]
【CAD】 computer-aided design [计算机辅助设计]
【CAI】 computer-aided instruction [计算机辅助教学]
【CATV】 cable TV [有线电视]
【CBA】 China Basketball Association [中国篮球协会]: ～联赛 CBA League
【CBD】 central business district [中央商务区]
【cc】 **1** carbon copies [抄送] **2** millilitre [毫升]
【CCC认证】 China Compulsory Certification [中国强制性产品认证制度]
【CCTV】 **1** China Central Television [中国中央电视台] **2** closed-circuit television [闭路电视]
【CC系】 CC Faction [a faction of the Kuomintang, 1928-1949, headed by Chen Guofu (陈果夫) and Chen Lifu (陈立夫), with the Central Club as its venue, the initials standing for both the Chens and the Central Club]
【CD】 compact disc [光盘]: ～机 CD player ‖ ～随身听 CD Walkman
【CDM】 cash deposit machine [自动存款机]
【CDMA】 code division multiple access [码分多址]: ～手机 CDMA mobile phone
【CD-ROM】 compact disc read-only memory [只读光盘]: ～驱动器 CD-ROM drive
【CD-RW】 compact disc rewritable [可重写光盘]
【CEO】 chief executive officer [首席执行官]
【CET】 College English Test [大学英语考试]
【CE标志】 Conformité Européenne [欧洲共同市场安全标志]
【CFA】 certified financial analyst [注册金融分析师]
【CFO】 chief financial officer [首席财务官]
【CI】 **1** corporate identity [企业标识] **2** corporate image [企业形象]: ～设计 CI design
【CIA】 Central Intelligence Agency [中央情报局]
【CMOS】 complementary metal oxide semiconductor [互补金属氧化物半导体]: ～存储器 CMOS memory ‖ ～芯片 CMOS chip
【CNG】 compressed natural gas [压缩天然气]
【CNN】 Cable News Network [（美国）有线新闻网]
【CNY】 Chinese yuan [人民币]
【COD】 chemical oxygen demand [化学需氧量]
【CPA】 certified public accountant [注册会计师]
【CPI】 consumer price index [消费品价格指数]
【CPU】 central processing unit [中央处理器]
【CT】 computed tomography [计算机化断层显像]: 做～ take a CT test
【CTO】 chief technology officer [首席技术官]
【C盘】 C Drive
【C语言】 C Language
【C照】 driving licence C

【D】 dimension [维度]: 3D three dimensions
【db】 decibel [分贝]
【DDD】 domestic direct dialling [国内直拨]
【DDN网】 digital data network [数字数据网]
【DDT】 dichloro-diphenyl-trichloroethane [滴滴涕]
【DINK】 double income, no kids [双职工无子女，丁克]
【DIY】 do-it-yourself [自己动手]
【DJ】 disc jockey [流行音乐节目主持人]
【DNA】 deoxyribonucleic acid [脱氧核糖核酸]: ～指纹鉴定 DNA finger-printing
【DNS】 domain name server [域名系统]
【DOS】 disk operating system [磁盘操作系统]
【DSL】 digital subscriber line [数字用户线路]
【DTV】 digital television [数字电视]
【DV】 digital video [数字摄录]
【DVD】 **1** digital video disc [数字影碟]: ～光驱 DVD drive ‖ ～机 DVD player **2** digital versatile disc [通用数字光盘]

【ECG】 electrocardiogram [心电图]
【ED】 erectile dysfunction [男性勃起功能障碍]
【EEG】 electroencephalogram [脑电图]

【EFL】 English as a Foreign Language [作为外语的英语]
【E-mail】 electronic mail [电子邮件]: 发～ send an E-mail
【EMBA】 Executive Master of Business Administration [高级管理人员工商管理硕士]
【EMS】 express mail service [邮政特快专递]
【EPT】 English Proficiency Test [英语水平考试]
【EQ】 emotional quotient [情商]
【ERP】 enterprise resource planning [企业资源规划]
【ESL】 English as a Second Language [作为第二语言的英语]
【ESP】 English for Special Purposes [专门用途英语]
【EU】 European Union [欧盟]
【EXE】 executive file [可执行文件]
【e时代】 electronic age [电子时代]

【F】 1 Fahrenheit [华氏] 2 floor [楼层]: 2F 二楼
【F1赛车】 Formula One racing [一级方程式赛车]
【FA】 factory automation [工厂自动化]
【FAQ】 frequently asked questions [常见问题]
【FAX】 facsimile [传真]: 发/收～ send/receive a fax
【FBI】 Federal Bureau of Investigation [联邦调查局]
【flash】 flash [flash 动画]: ～播放器 flash player
【FM】 frequency modulation [调频]

【G】 generation [代]: 3G手机 3rd generation mobile phone
【G8】 Group 8 [八国集团]
【GATT】 General Agreement on Tariffs and Trade [关税及贸易总协定]
【GB】 1 China National Standard [中国国家标准] 2 gigabyte [吉字节]: 40～硬盘 a 40 GB hard disc
【GBK码】 China National Standard Extension [国家标准扩展码]
【GDP】 gross domestic product [国内生产总值]: 人均～ GDP per capita
【GMAT】 Graduate Management Admission Test [管理学研究生入学资格考试]
【GMT】 Greenwich Mean Time [格林尼治（平均）时间]
【GM食品】 genetically-modified food [转基因食品]
【GNP】 gross national product [国民生产总值]
【GPS】 Global Positioning System [全球定位系统]
【GRE】 Graduate Record Examination [研究生入学考试]
【GSM】 Global System for Mobile Communications [全球移动通信系统，全球通]: ～手机 GSM mobile phone
【G点】 G-spot [内兴奋点]

【Hb】 haemoglobin [血红蛋白]
【HB铅笔】 hard black pencil
【HDTV】 high-definition television [高清晰度电视]
【Hi-fi】 high fidelity [高保真度（音响）]
【HIV】 human immunodeficiency virus [人体免疫缺陷病毒，艾滋病病毒]
【HSK】 Chinese Proficiency Test [汉语水平考试]
【HTML】 Hypertext Markup Language [超文本标记语言]
【HTTP】 Hypertext Transport Protocol [超文本传输协议]
【H股】 H-share [港股]

【IBM】 International Business Machines [国际商用机器公司]
【ICP】 Internet content provider [因特网信息提供商]
【ICQ】 I seek you [网络寻呼（软件）]
【ICU】 intensive care unit [重症监护室]
【IC卡】 integrated circuit card [集成电路卡]
【ID】 Identity [身份]
【IDD】 international direct dialling [国际直拨]
【IELTS】 International English Language Testing System [雅思考试]
【IE浏览器】 Internet Explorer [网络浏览器]
【IMBA】 International Master of Business Administration [国际工商管理硕士]
【IMF】 International Monetary Fund [国际货币基金组织]
【I/O】 input/output [输入/输出]
【IOC】 International Olympic Committee [国际奥林匹克委员会]
【IP】 Internet Protocol [网络协议]: ～地址 IP address
【IPA】 International Phonetic Alphabet [国际音标]
【IPO】 initial public offering [首次公开发行（股票）]
【IP电话】 Internet Protocol phone [网络电话]: ～卡 IP card
【IQ】 intelligence quotient [智商]
【ISBN】 international standard book number [国际标准书号]
【ISDN】 integrated service digital network [综合业务数字网，“一线通”]
【ISO】 International Organization for Standardization [国际标准化组织]
【ISP】 Internet service provider [互联网服务提供商]
【ISSN】 international standard serial number [国际标准连续出版物编号]
【IT】 information technology [信息技术]: ～产业 IT industry

【KB】 kilobyte [千字节]
【kg】 kilogram [千克]
【KGB】 Komitet Gosudarstvennoi Bezopasnosti [克格勃]
【kHz】 kilohertz [千赫兹]
【km】 kilometre [千米]
【KTV】 karaoke television [卡拉OK包房]
【kw】 kilowatt [千瓦]
【kwh】 kilowatt hour [千瓦/小时]
【K粉】 ketamine [氯胺酮]
【K金】 carat gold: 18～ 18 carat gold

【L】 1 large size [大号] 2 litre [升]
【LAN】 local area network [局域网]
【LCD】 liquid crystal display [液晶显示屏]
【LD】 laserdisc [激光视盘]
【LED】 large electronic display [大型电子显示屏]
【logo】 logo [标识]
【LPG】 liquefied petroleum gas [液化石油气]
【LW】 long wave [长波]

【M】 medium size [中号]
【MA】 Master of Arts [文科硕士]
【MB】 megabyte [兆字节]
【MBA】 Master of Business Administration [工商管理硕士]
【MBO】 management buyout [管理层收购]
【Mbps】 megabits per second [兆比特/秒]
【MD】 MiniDisc [迷你光盘]
【MHz】 megahertz [兆赫]
【MFN】 most-favoured-nation treatment [最惠国待遇]
【MIC】 microphone [话筒，麦克风]
【MIDI】 musical instrument digital interface [乐器数字接口]
【MODEM】 modulator/demodulator [调制解调器]
【MP3】 MPEG-1 audio layer 3: ～播放器 MP3 player
【MPA】 Master of Public Administration [公共管理硕士]
【MPV】 multi-purpose vehicle [多用途车]
【MRI】 magnetic resonance imaging [磁共振成像]
【MS】 Master of Science [理科硕士]
【MS-DOS】 Microsoft disc operating system [微软磁盘操作系统]
【MTV】 music television [音乐电视]
【MVP】 most valuable player [最有价值球员]
【MW】 medium wave [中波]
【M头形态】 double top [（股票等图形的）双顶形态]

【NBA】 National Basketball Association [（美国）全国篮球协会]: ～球员 NBA player
【NG】 no good [（电影镜头）重拍]
【NGO】 non-governmental organization [非政府组织]: ～论坛 NGO forum
【NHK】 Nippon Hoso Kyokai [日本广播协会]
【NMD】 National Missile Defense System [国家导弹防御系统]
【No】 number [号码]

【OA】 office automation [办公自动化]
【OEM】 original equipment manufacturer/manufacturing [原始设备制造商/贴牌生产]
【OK镜】 Ortho Kerat [角膜塑形镜]
【OPEC】 Organization of Petroleum Exporting Countries [石油输出国组织，欧佩克]
【OTC药】 over-the-counter medicine [非处方药]
【O型血】 blood group O

【P】 1 parking lot [停车场] 2 page [页码]
【PAS手机】 PAS (Personal Access System) mobile [小灵通]
【PC】 personal computer [个人计算机]
【PDA】 personal digital assistant [个人数字助理]
【PDP】 plasma display panel [等离子显示屏]
【PE】 Polyethylene [聚乙烯]: ～保鲜膜 PE cling film
【PETS】 Public English Test System [公共英语等级考试]
【PhD】 Doctor of Philosophy [博士]
【PHS】 Personal Handy-phone System [个人手持电话系统，小灵通]
【pH计】 pH meter [酸度计]
【pH值】 power of hydrogene [氢离子浓度指数]
【PIN】 personal identification number [个人身份识别码]
【PK】 player kill, one-on-one showdown [对决]
【pm】 post meridiem [下午]
【PMP】 portable media player [便携式媒体播放器]
【PnP】 Plug and Play [即插即用]
【POS机】 point of sale terminal [销售点终端机]
【PPA】 1 pipemidic acid [吡哌酸] 2 phenylpropanolamine [苯丙醇胺]
【PPI】 Producer Price Index [工业品出厂价格指数]
【PPT】 Microsoft PowerPoint [PowerPoint 文件]
【PR】 public relations [公共关系，简称公关]
【PS】 1 Adobe Photoshop [图像处理] 2 polystyrene [聚苯乙烯]
【PSP】 PlayStation Portable [掌上游戏机]
【PT】 particular transfer [特别转让（股票）]
【PU】 polyurethane [聚氨酯]

【PVC】 polyvinyl chloride [聚氯乙烯]: ～管 PVC tube

【QA】 quality assurance [质量保证]: ～工程师 QA engineer
【QC】 quality control [质量管理]
【QFII】 qualified foreign institutional investor [合格境外投资机构]
【QQ】 ICQ [网络通讯工具]: ～号 QQ account number ‖ ～币 QQ cash
【QS】 quality specifications [质量标准体系]

【R&D】 research and development [研发]
【RAM】 random access memory [随机存储器]
【Rh血型】 Rhesus blood group: ～不合 Rh incompatibility
【RMB】 renminbi [人民币]
【RNA】 ribonucleic acid [核糖核酸]
【ROM】 read-only memory [只读存储器]
【RSVP】 Réspondez, s'il vous plaît [敬请回复]

【S】 small size [小号]
【SAR】 Special Administrative Region [特别行政区]
【SARS】 severe acute respiratory syndrome [严重急性呼吸系统综合征]: ～病人 SARS patient
【SCI】 Science Citation Index [科学引文索引]
【SIM卡】 subscriber identification module card [用户身份识别卡]
【SMS】 short message service [短信服务]
【SOHO】 small office home office [小型家居办公室]
【SOS】 save our souls [国际紧急呼救信号]
【SPA】 spa [水疗]
【SPF】 sun protection factor [防晒系数]
【ST】 special treatment [特别处理（股票）]
【SUV】 sport utility vehicle [运动型多功能车]
【SW】 short wave [短波]

【TB】 tuberculosis [结核病]
【TCFL】 Teaching Chinese as a Foreign Language [对外汉语教学]
【Tel】 telephone [电话]
【TESOL】 Teaching English to Speakers of Other Languages [对外英语教学]
【TFT显示器】 thin film transistor display [薄晶体管显示器]
【TMD】 Theater Missile Defense [战区导弹防御]
【TNT】 trinitrotoluene [梯恩梯]
【TOEFL】 Test of English as a Foreign Language [托福考试]
【TOEIC】 Test of English for International Communications [托业考试]
【TQM】 total quality management [全面质量管理]
【TV】 television [电视]
【TXT】 text file [文本文件]
【T型台】 catwalk
【T恤衫】 T-shirt

【UFO】 unidentified flying object [不明飞行物]
【UHF】 ultra-high frequency [超高频]
【UN】 United Nations [联合国]
【UPC】 universal product code [通用商品条码]
【USB】 universal serial bus [通用串行总线]: ～端口 USB port
【UV】 ultraviolet [紫外线]
【U盘】 USB memory stick

【VB】 vitamin B [维生素B]
【VC】 vitamin C [维生素C]
【VCD】 Video Compact Disk [激光视盘]: ～机 VCD player
【VCR】 video cassette recorder [录像机]
【VD】 1 vitamin D [维生素 D] 2 venereal disease [性病]
【VDR】 Video Disk Recorder [光盘录像机]
【VIP】 very important person [贵宾]: ～卡 VIP card
【VOD】 video-on-demand [视频点播]
【Vs】 versus [对]: 中国～日本 China Vs Japan

【WAN】 wide area net [广域网]
【WAP】 Wireless Application Protocol [无线应用协议]: ～手机 WAP mobile phone
【WC】 water closet [厕所]
【WHO】 World Health Organization [世界卫生组织]
【wiki】 wiki encyclopedia [维基百科]
【WPS】 word processing system [文字处理系统]
【WSK】 WSK Language Proficiency Test [外语水平考试]
【WTO】 World Trade Organization [世贸组织]: ～成员 WTO member ‖ ～总干事 WTO director-general
【WWW】 World Wide Web [万维网]
【WYSIWYG】 what you see is what you get [所见即所得]

【X】 unknown [未知数]
【XL】 extra large [特大号]
【XO】 extra old [年代久远的酒]
【XR】 ex-rights [除权]
【XXL】 extra extra large [特特大号]
【X刀】 X-knife
【X光】 X-ray
【X染色体】 X chromosome
【X射线】 X-ray

【YOYO测试】 YOYO test
【Y染色体】 Y chromosome

【ZIP】 zip file format [zip 压缩文件]

词类标签 Part of speech labels

介	介词	preposition
叹	叹词	exclamation
代	代词	pronoun
动	动词（短语）	verb (phrase)
名	名词（短语）	noun (phrase)
形	形容词	adjective
拟	拟声词	onomatopoeia
连	连词	conjunction
助	助词	auxiliary
副	副词	adverb
量	量词	measure word
数	数词	numeral
数量	数量词	numeral-classifier compound
后缀	后缀	suffix
前缀	前缀	prefix
简称	简称	abbreviation

语类标签 Idiomatic phrase labels

成	成语	idiom
俗	俗语	common saying
惯	惯用语	set phrase
歇后	歇后语	two-part allegorical saying

学科及使用领域标签 Field labels

工程	工程	engineering
天文	天文	astronomy
历史	历史	history
中医	中医	Chinese medicine
中药	中药	medicinal herbs
水文	水文	hydrology
水利	水利	hydraulic engineering
气象	气象	meteorology
化工	化工	chemical industry
化学	化学	chemistry
计算机	计算机	computing
心理	心理学	psychology
书法	书法	calligraphy
石油	石油	petroleum
电子	电子	electronics
电气	电气	electricity
生化	生化	biochemistry
生物	生物	biology
生理	生理	physiology
印刷	印刷	printing
外交	外交	diplomacy
鸟类	鸟类	ornithology
动物	动物学	zoology
考古	考古	archaeology
地质	地质	geology
地理	地理	geography
机械	机械	mechanics
曲艺	曲艺	folk vocal art forms
伊斯兰教	伊斯兰教	Muslimism
会计	会计	accountancy
杂技	杂技	acrobatics
交通	交通	transport
军事	军事	military
农业	农业	agriculture
戏曲	戏曲	drama
戏剧	戏剧	theatre
材料	材料科学	materials science
医学	医学	medical science
足球	足球	football
体育	体育	sport
佛教	佛教	Buddhism
冶金	冶金	metallurgy
陆军	陆军	army
纺织	纺织	textiles
武术	武术	martial arts
林业	林业	forestry
矿业	矿业	mining
昆虫	昆虫	insectology
物理	物理	physics
金融	金融	finance
鱼类	鱼类	ichthyology
法律	法律	law
宗教	宗教	religion
空军	空军	air force
建筑	建筑	architecture
经济	经济	economics
药学	药学	medicine
食品	食品	food
音乐	音乐	music
美术	美术	art
测绘	测绘	surveying
语言	语言学	linguistics
语法	语法	grammar